2011 Standard Catalog of

Collectibles publication partner
of Major League Baseball

BASEBALL CARDS

20th Edition

Edited by
Bob Lemke
and the editors of Sports Collectors Digest® /Tuff Stuff®

*"Perfection is not attainable, but if we chase perfection we
can catch excellence."*
—Vince Lombardi

Published by

Krause Publications, a division of F+W Media, Inc.
700 East State Street • Iola, WI 54990-0001
715-445-2214 • 888-457-2873
www.krausebooks.com

To order books or other products call toll-free 1-800-258-0929
or visit us online at www.krausebooks.com or www.Shop.Collect.com

ISSN: 1935-0546

ISBN-13: 978-1-4402-1371-7
ISBN-10: 1-4402-1371-2

Cover Design by Donna Mummery
Designed by Stacy Bloch
Edited by Joe Clemens

Printed in United States of America

ACKNOWLEDGMENTS

Hundreds of individuals have made countless valuable contributions that have been incorporated into the *Standard Catalog of Baseball Cards*. While all cannot be acknowledged, special appreciation is extended to the following principal contributors who have exhibited a special dedication by creating, revising or verifying listings and technical data, reviewing market valuations or providing cards to be illustrated.

Rob Adesso • Ken Agona • Gary Agostino • Lisa Albano • Dan Albaugh • Will Allison • Mark Anker • Ellis Anmuth • Steve Applebaum • Tom Atkins • Bill Atkinson

Rand Bailey • Bill Ballew • Andy Baran • Gary Bartolett • Judy Bartolett • Bob Bartosz • John Beisiegel • Karen Bell • Dr. Charles E. Belles • Dave Berman • Cathy Black • Jerry A. Blum • Ralph Blunt Jr. • Mike Bodner • Jeff Bossak • Bill Bossert • Bob Bostoff • Brian Boston • Jim Boushley • Mark Bowers • Mike Boyd • Roland Bracken • John Brigandi • Scott Brockelman • Lou Brown • Dan Bruner • Greg Bussineau

Billy Caldwell • Len Caprisecca • Tony Carrafiell • Brian Cataquet • Lee Champion • Dwight Chapin • Lou Chericoni • Ryan Christoff • Jim Clarke • Shane Cohen • Rich Cole • Paul Conan Jr. • Charles Conlon • Eric Cooper • Bill Cornell • Bryan Couling • Bob Crabill • Clyde Cripe • Al Cristafulli • Jim Cumpton • Robert Curtiss

Pete D'Luhosch • Tom Daniels • Stuart Dansinger • James Davis • Dick DeCourcy • Ken Degnan • Dan DeKing • Mike Del Gado • Bill Diebold • Larry Dluhy • Brett Domue • John Dorsey

Curtis Earl • Eric Eichelkraut • Mark Elliott • Jeff Emerson • Brian Engles • Shirley Eross • John B. Esch • Joe Esposito • Dan Even • Doak Ewing

Julian Fernandez • David Festberg • Robert Fisk • Jay Finglass • Nick Flaviano • Rick Fleury • Jeff Fritsch • Larry Fritsch

Gary Gagen • Richard Galasso • Tom Galic • Richard R. Gallagher • Chris Gallutia • Tony Galovich • Phillip Garrou • Gary Gatanis • Frank Giffune • Richard Gilkeson • Gerald J. Glasser • Philip Glazer • Keith David Goldfarb • Jack Goodman • Bill Goodwin • Dick Goddard • Barry Gordon • Howard Gordon •
Mike Gordon • Sean Gottlieb • Bob Gray • Wayne Grove • Gerry Guenther • Don Guilbert • Tom Guilfoile

David Hall • Joel Hall • Walter Hall • Gary Hamilton • Tom Harbin • Michael Harrington • Don Harrison • Rich Hawksley • Herbert Hecht • Bill Henderson • Mike Henderson • Kathy Henry • Pete Henrici • Steve Hershkowitz • Bob Hicks • Gregg Hitesman • John Hoffman • Dennis Hollenbeck • Jack Horkan • Jim Horne • Brent Horton • Ron Hosmer • Marvin Huck • Brad Hudecek

Bob Ivanjack

Robert Jacobsen • David Jenkins • Donn Jennings • Scott Jensen • Andrew Jerome • Jim Johnston • Stewart Jones • Larry Jordan

Judy Kay • Allan Kaye • Michael Keedy • Frank Keetz • Mark Kemmerle • Rick Keplinger • John King • John Kitleson • Terry Knouse • Bob Koehler • David Kohler • A.F. Kokol • Dan Kravitz

Steve Lacasse • Jason Lange • Mark K. Larson • Lee Lasseigne • William Lawrence • Scott Lawson • Richard Leech • Morley Leeking • Tom Leon • Don Lepore • Rod Lethbridge • Scott Letts • David Levin • Stuart Leviton • Howie Levy • Hal Lewis • Rob Lifson • Lew Lipset • Jeff Litteral • Dick Lloyd • Chuck Lobenthal • Leon Luckey

Mark Macrae • Paul Marchant • Robert Marek • Bob Marotto • Art Martineau • Bob Marquette • Richard Masson • Bill Mastro • Ralph Maya • Dan McKee • Fred McKie • Tony McLaughlin • Don McPherson • Doug McWilliams • John Mehlin • Bill Mendel • H. Dexter • Joe Merkel • Blake Meyer • Louis Middleton • Bob Miller • Jay Miller • Keith Mitchell • J.A. Monaco • Robert Montgomery • Joe Moreno • Brian Morris • Mike Mosier • Scott Mosley • Mike Mowrey • Peter Mudavin • Mark Murphy • David Musser

Frank Nagy • Steve Neimand • Roger Neufeldt • Tim Newcomb • Joe Newman • Bill Nicolls • Chuck Nobriga • Mark Nochta • Wayne Nochta

Bud Obermeyer • Jeff Obermeyer • Keith Olbermann

D.J. Panaia • Joe Pasternack • Marty Perry • Tom Pfirrman • Dan Piepenbrok • Stan Pietruska • Paul Pollard • Harvey Poris • Don "Barefoot" Post

Pat Quinn

Ed Ranson • Fred Rapaport • Jim Resseque • Steve Rice • Mike Rich • Bob Richardson • Al Richter • Gavin Riley • Mark Rios • Ron Ritzler • Tom Reid • Bob Robles • Mike Rodell • Scott Roemer • Mike Rogers • Chris Ronan • Rocky Rosato • Alan Rosen • John Rumierz • Bob Rund • Moe Ryan

Len Samworth • Jon Sands • Kevin Savage • Stephen Schauer • Allan Schoenberger • Dave Schwartz • Robert Scott • Larry Serota • 707 Sports Cards • Jim Sexton • Corey Shanus • Max Silberman • Al Simeone • Paul Sjolin • Barry Sloate • Joe Smith • Mark Soltan • John Spalding • Kevin Spears • Gene Speranza • Nigel Spill • Jerry Spillman • David Spivack • Dana Sprague • Don Steinbach • Paul Stewart • Dan Stickney • Larry Stone • Ken Stough • Al Strumpf • Doug Stultz • Jim Suckow • Rich Suen • Joe Szeremet

J.J. Teaparty • Erik Teller • Lee Temanson • K.J. Terplak • Mark Theotikos • Dick Tinsley • Gary Tkac • Bud Tompkins • Joseph Tonely • Scott Torrey • Dan Tripper

Rich Unruh • Jack Urban • Glen Van Aken • Frank Van Damme • Brian Van Horn

Geno Wager • Frank Wakefield • Pete Waldman • Eric Waller • Tony Walls • Gary Walter • Frank Ward • Adam Warshaw • Dave Weber • Ken Weimer • Jeff Weiss • Richard Weiss • Dale Weselowski • E.C. Wharton-Tigar • Charles Williamson • Jay Wolt • Frank Wozny • Bill Wright

Rhett Yeakley • Rhys Yeakley • Kit Young

Ted Zanidakis

2011 Standard Catalog of
Baseball Cards

HOW TO USE THIS CATALOG

This catalog has been uniquely designed to serve the needs of collectors and dealers at all levels from beginning to advanced. It provides a comprehensive guide to more than 140 years of baseball card issues, arranged so that even the most novice hobbyist can consult it with confidence and ease.

The following explanations summarize the general practices used in preparing this catalog's listings. However, because of specialized requirements which may vary from card set to card set, these must not be considered ironclad. Where these standards have been set aside, appropriate notations are usually incorporated.

ARRANGEMENT

The most important feature in identifying and pricing a baseball card is its set of origin. Therefore the main body of this catalog, covering cards issued from 1863-date, has been alphabetically arranged within specific eras of issue according to the name by which the set is most popularly known to collectors, or by which it can be most easily identified by a person examining a card.

Previous editions of this catalog relied heavily upon card set identification numbers originated in Jefferson Burdick's pioneering "American Card Catalog." However, since that work was last updated over 40 years ago its numbering system has become arcane and is little used by the present generation of hobbyists. Where practical, sets which were listed in previous editions by their ACC designations have been reclassified alphabetically by a more readily identifiable signpost, such as manufacturer's name. Most of those sets however continue to bear the ACC catalog number in the set heading.

Among card issuers that produced sets for more than a single year, their sets are then listed chronologically, from earliest to most recent, again within specific eras.

Within each set, the cards are listed by their designated card number, or in the absence of card numbers, alphabetically according to the last name of the player pictured. Listing numbers found in parentheses indicate the number does not appear on the card. Certain cards which fall outside the parameters of the normal card numbering for a specific set may be found at the beginning or end of the listings for that set.

Listings are generally arranged in two major sections – major league and minor league issues.

MAJOR LEAGUE ISSUES

The main body of the book details major league baseball card issues from 1863 through the first half of 2010, divided into two sections: Vintage (1863-1980) and Modern (1981-2010). In general, prior to about 1990, this will include issues that picture one or more baseball players, usually contemporary with their playing days, printed on paper or cardboard in a variety of shapes and sizes and given away as a premium with the purchase of another product or service. After 1990 or so the definition is broadened to remove the restriction of the card as an ancillary product and to include those printed on plastic, wood, metal, etc.

Included within each era's listings are related non-card collectibles featuring baseball players which do not fit under the definition previously given for baseball cards. These include many items on which players are depicted on materials other than paper or cardboard, such as pins, coins, silks, leathers, patches, felts, pennants, metallic ingots, statues, figurines, limited-edition artworks and others.

Also presented herein are foreign issues, one of the growth areas of the baseball card hobby in recent years. These encompass the various issues from countries outside of North America, particularly Latin America. Since the 1920s a variety of baseball cards, stamps and stickers have emanated from the Caribbean, South America and elsewhere chronicling the various winter baseball leagues that have flourished there, often stocked with former and future major league stars and, in the early years, providing the only contemporary cards of many U.S. and Latin Negro Leagues players.

Incorporated into the listings are some modern collectors' issues. There exists within the hobby a great body of cards known as "collectors' issues" (sometimes generically known as "broders") by virtue of their nature of having been produced solely for the hobby card market. These cards and sets are distinguished from "legitimate" issues in not having been created as a sales promotional item for another product or service – bubble gum, soda, snack cakes, dog food, cigarettes, gasoline, etc. This distinction, however, is no longer so easy to make since the early 1990s, when many baseball card issues by even the major national companies began to be sold without an accompanying product.

By their nature, and principally because the person issuing them was always free to print and distribute more of the same if they should ever attain any real value, collectors' issues were generally regarded by the hobby as having little or no premium value. Since the leagues and players' union began to enforce licensing restrictions in the early 1990s, the nature of collector's issues changed dramatically. The sets that were the work of an individual catering to the hobby market with an issue of relatively limited numbers and basic technology have given way to more sophisticated productions, often marketed to the general public, as well as the hobby.

The distinction between "collectors" and "legitimate" cards may be barely perceptible but is noted whenever possible. Generally, those collectors' emissions share some or all of these characteristics: 1) Prior to around 1990 they were not licensed by the players depicted, nor by their teams or leagues. 2) They were sold as complete sets rather than by pack or as singles. 3) The issue was marketed almost exclusively to the card collecting hobby audience through advertising in trade papers and public sporting press, and within the hobby's dealer network. 4) The cards were sold on a stand-alone basis, that is, not as a premium or adjunct to the sale of another product or service.

MINOR LEAGUE ISSUES (1867-1969)

Prior to 1970 virtually all minor league baseball cards were issued as single cards rather than as complete sets. Like contemporary major league cards they were usually intended as premiums given away with the purchase of goods and services.

The listings which follow offer individual card prices in three grades of preservation to allow accurate valuations of superstar and other special interest cards, along with cards that were short-printed or otherwise are scarce.

IDENTIFICATION

While most modern baseball cards are well identified on front, back or both, as to date and issue, such has not always been the case. In general, the back of the card is more useful in identifying the set of origin than the front. The issuer or sponsor's name will usually appear on the back since, after all, baseball cards were first produced as a promotional item to stimulate sales of other products. As often as not, that issuer's name is the name by which the set is known to collectors and under which it will be found listed in this catalog.

In some difficult cases, identifying a baseball card's general age, if not specific year of issue, can usually be accomplished by studying the biological or statistical information on the back of the card. The last year mentioned in either the biography or stats is usually the year which preceded the year of issue.

Over the years there have been many cards issued that bear no identification features at all with which to pinpoint the issuer. In such cases, they are cataloged by the names under which they are best known in the hobby. Many of the strip-card issues of the 1920s, for example, remain listed under the "W" catalog number where they were originally enumerated in the "American Card Catalog."

It is the ultimate goal, through the use of cross listings and more detailed indexes, to allow a person holding a card in his hand to find the catalog listing for that card with the greatest ease.

PHOTOGRAPHS

Wherever possible a photograph of the front and (prior to 1981) back of at least one representative card from most of the sets listed in this catalog has been incorporated into the listings to assist identification. (Persons who can provide sample cards for photography purposes for those sets which are missing photos in this volume are encouraged to contact the editor.)

Photographs have been printed in reduced size. The actual size of cards in each set is usually given in the introductory text preceding its listing, unless the card is the current standard size (2.5" by 3.5").

DATING

The dating of baseball cards by year of issue on the front or back of the card itself is a relatively new phenomenon. In most cases, to accurately determine a date of issue for an unidentified card, it must be studied for clues. As mentioned, the biography, career summary or statistics on the back of the card are the best way to pinpoint a year of issue. In most cases, the year of issue will be the year after the last season mentioned on the card.

Luckily for today's collector, earlier generations have done much of the research in determining year of issue for those cards that bear no clues. The painstaking task of matching the players' listed and/or pictured team against their career records often allowed an issue date to be determined.

In some cases, particular card sets were issued over a period of more than one calendar year, but since they are collected together as a single set, their specific year of issue is not important. Such sets will be listed with their complete known range of issue years.

There remain some early issues for which an exact year of issue cannot be reliably pinpointed. In those cases a "best guess" date or one in the middle of the possible range has been used to identify the issue; such cases are usually noted in the introductory text.

NUMBERING

While many baseball card issues as far back as the 1880s have featured card numbers assigned by the issuer to facilitate the collecting of a complete set, the practice has by no means been universal. Even today, not every set bears card numbers.

Logically, those baseball cards that were numbered by their manufacturer are presented in that numerical order within the listings of this catalog whenever possible. In a few cases, complete player checklists were obtained from earlier published sources that did not note card numbers, and so numbers have been arbitrarily assigned. Many other unnumbered issues have been assigned catalog numbers to facilitate their universal identification within the hobby, especially when buying and selling by mail. Among some issues for which the complete checklist remains unknown and for which new discoveries are still being reported, gaps have been left in the assigned numbering to facilitate future additions.

In all cases, numbers that have been assigned, or which otherwise do not appear on the card through error or by design, are shown in this catalog within parentheses. In virtually all cases, unless a more natural system suggested itself by the unique matter of a particular set, the assignment of numbers by the cataloging staff has been done by alphabetical arrangement of the players' last names or the card's principal title.

Significant collectible variations for any particular card are noted within the listings by the application of a suffix letter. In instances of variations, the suffix "a" is assigned to the variation which was created first, when it can be so identified.

NAMES

The identification of a player by full name on the front of his baseball card has been a common practice only since the 1920s. Prior to that, the player's last name and team were the usual information found on the card front.

As a general – though not universally applied – practice, the listings in this volume present the player's name exactly as it appears on the front of the card. If the player's full name only appears on the back, rather than on the front of the card, the listing may correspond to that designation.

A player's name checklisted in **bold italic** type indicates a rookie card as defined later in this introduction.

Cards that contain misspelled first or last names, or even wrong initials, will usually have included in their listings the incorrect information, with a correction accompanying in parentheses. This extends also to cases where the name on the card does not correspond to the player actually pictured.

In some cases, to facilitate efficient presentations, to maintain ease of use for the reader, or to allow for proper computer sorting of data, a player's name or card title may be listed other than as it actually appears on the card.

GRADING

It is necessary that some sort of card grading standard be used so that buyer and seller (especially when dealing through the Internet or by mail) may reach an informed agreement on the value of a card.

Pre-1981 cards are generally priced in the three grades of preservation in which those cards are most commonly encountered in the daily buying and selling in the hobby marketplace. They are listed in grades of Near Mint (NR MT), Excellent (EX) and Very Good (VG), reflecting the basic fact that few cards were able to survive for 25, 50 or even 100 years in close semblance to the condition of their issue.

The pricing of cards in these three conditions will allow readers to accurately price cards which fall in intermediate grades, such as EX-MT, or VG-EX.

Although grades below Very Good are not generally priced in this volume, close approximations of low-grade card values may be figured on the following formula: Good condition cards are valued at about 50 percent of VG price, with Fair cards about 50 percent of Good.

Cards in Poor condition have little or no market value except in the cases of the rarest and most expensive cards. In such cases, value has to be negotiated individually.

Modern (1981-date) issues, which have been preserved in top condition in considerable numbers, are listed only in the grade of Near Mint-to-Mint (NM/M). Earlier editions of this book priced such cards under the heading of Mint condition. However, the rise of independent grading services in the past decade and their use of the NM/M designation to describe the vast majority of new card specimens has influenced the marketplace to the extent that only a small percentage of cards, even fresh from the pack, can meet the strict standards for a true Mint example. The switch to a NM/M designation is part of the catalog's commitment to accurately reflect the current conditions of the card market.

As with older cards, values for lower-grade cards from 1981-date may be generally figured by using a figure of 75 percent of the NM/M price for Near Mint specimens, and 40 percent of the Mint price for Excellent cards.

For the benefit of the reader, we present herewith the grading guide which was originally formulated in 1981 by *Baseball Cards* magazine and *Sports Collectors Digest*, and has been continually refined since that time.

These grading definitions have been used in the pricing of cards in this book, but they are by no means a universally-accepted grading standard.

The potential buyer of a baseball card should keep that in mind when encountering cards of nominally the same grade, but at a price which differs widely from that quoted in this book.

Ultimately, the collector must formulate his/her own personal grading standards in deciding whether cards available for purchase meet the needs of their collection.

No collector is required to adhere to the grading standards presented herewith – nor to any other published grading standards.

Mint (MT): A perfect card. Well-centered, with parallel borders that appear equal to the naked eye. Four sharp, square corners. No creases, edge dents, surface scratches, paper flaws, loss of luster, yellowing or fading, regardless of age. No imperfectly printed card – out of register, badly cut or ink flawed – or card stained by contact with gum, wax or other substances can be considered truly Mint, even if new out of the pack. Generally, to be considered in Mint condition, a card's borders must exist in a ratio of no greater than 60/40 side to side and top to bottom.

Near Mint/Mint (NM/M): A nearly perfect card. Well-centered, with at least three sharp, square corners. No creases, edge dents, surface scratches, paper flaws, loss of luster, yellowing or fading, regardless of age. No imperfectly printed card – out of register, badly cut or ink flawed – or card stained by contact with gum, wax or other substances can be considered Near Mint/ Mint, even if new out of the pack. Generally, to be considered in NM/M condition, a card's borders must exist in a ratio of no greater than 65/35 side to side and top to bottom.

Near Mint (NR MT): At first glance, a Near Mint card appears perfect; upon closer examination, however, a minor flaw will be discovered. On well-centered cards, at least two of the four corners must be perfectly sharp; the others showing a minor imperfection upon close inspection. A slightly off-center card with one or more borders being noticeably unequal – no worse than in a ratio of 70/30 S/S or T/B – would also fit this grade.

Excellent (EX): Corners are still fairly sharp with only moderate wear. Card borders may be off-center as much as 80/20. No creases. May have very minor gum, wax or product stains, front or back. Surfaces may show slight loss of luster from rubbing across other cards.

Very Good (VG): Show obvious handling. Corners rounded and/ or perhaps showing minor creases. Other minor creases may be visible. Surfaces may exhibit loss of luster, but all printing is intact. May show major gum, wax or other packaging stains. No major creases, tape marks or extraneous markings or writing. All four borders visible, though the ratio may be as poor as 95/5. Exhibits honest wear.

Good (G): A well-worn card, but exhibits no intentional damage or abuse. May have major or multiple creases and/or corners rounded well beyond the border. A Good card will generally sell for about 50 percent the value of a card in Very Good condition.

Fair (F or Fr.): Shows excessive wear, along with damage or abuse. Will show all the wear characteristics of a Good card, along with such damage as thumb tack holes in or near margins, evidence of having been taped or pasted, perhaps small tears around the edges, or creases so heavy as to break the cardboard. Backs may show minor added pen or pencil writing, or be missing small bits of paper. Still, basically a complete card. A Fair card will generally sell for 50 percent the value of a Good specimen.

Poor (P): A card that has been tortured to death. Corners or other areas may be torn off. Card may have been trimmed, show holes from a paper punch or have been used for BB gun practice. Front may have extraneous pen or pencil writing, or other defacement. Major portions of front or back design may be missing. Not a pretty sight.

In addition to these terms, collectors may encounter intermediate grades, such as VG-EX or EX-MT. These cards usually have characteristics of both the lower and higher grades, and are generally priced midway between those two values.

With the rise in popularity of third-party authentication/grading services since the mid-1990s, it must be stressed that the grades and corresponding values presented in this book are for "raw" cards – cards which have not been independently graded. Depending on the reputation of the certification firm, cards that have been graded and encased in plastic slabs may sell for a significant premium over the values found here. This is especially true of high-grade specimens of vintage cards that in certified grades of Near Mint/Mint, Mint or Gem Mint may bring multiples of "catalog" value. Even collector-grade vintage cards can command a premium when authenticated, graded and slabbed because potential buyers may feel more secure in such cards' authenticity and freedom from tampering.

ROOKIE CARDS

While the status (and automatic premium value) that a player's rookie card carries has fluctuated in recent years, and though the hobby still has not reached a universal definition of a rookie card, many significant vintage-era rookie cards are noted in this catalog's listings by the use of *bold italic* type. Conversely, many significant modern-era rookie cards are noted in this catalog's listings by the use of **RC** or **(RC)**. Beginning with products issued in 2006, cards with an **(RC)** logo indicate the featured player has a rookie card issued prior to that year. For purposes of this catalog, a player's rookie card is considered to be any card in a nationally distributed, licensed Major League base (non-insert) set from a major manufacturer in the first year in which that player appears on a card, regardless of whether that player has yet appeared in a Major League game or is technically a rookie according to MLB definition.

VALUATIONS

Values quoted in this book represent the current retail market at the time of compilation (Summer, 2010). The quoted values are the result of a unique system of evaluation and verification created by the catalog's editors. Utilizing specialized computer analysis and drawing upon recommendations provided through their daily involvement in the publication of the hobby's leading sports collectors' periodicals, as well as the input of consultants, dealers and collectors, each listing is, in the final analysis, the interpretation of that data by one or more of the editors.

It should be stressed, however, that this book is intended to serve only as an aid in evaluating cards; actual market conditions are constantly changing. This is especially true of the cards of current players, whose on-field performance during the course of a season can greatly affect the value of their cards – upwards or downwards. Because of the extremely volatile nature of new card prices, especially high-end issues, we have chosen not to include the very latest releases from the major companies, feeling it is better to have no listings at all for those cards than to have inaccurate values in print. For the same reasons, many 21st century cards and sets are presented here without pricing. Extremely limited-production (or even unique) cards, often autographs and game-used equipment cards, may not be seen in the hobby market with enough frequency to establish realistic "book" values.

Because this volume is intended to reflect the national market, users will find regional price variances caused by demand differences. Cards of Phillies slugger Ryan Howard will, for instance, often sell at prices greater than quoted herein at shops and shows in the Philadelphia area. Conversely, his cards may be acquired at a discount from these valuations when purchased on the East or West Coast.

Publication of this book is not intended as a solicitation to buy or sell the listed cards by the editors, publisher or contributors.

Again, the values here are retail prices – what a collector can expect to pay when buying a card from a dealer. The wholesale price, that which a collector can expect to receive from a dealer when selling cards, will be significantly lower.

Many dealers operate on a 100 percent mark-up, generally paying about 50 percent of a card's retail value for cards that they are purchasing for inventory. On some high-demand cards, dealers will pay 100 percent or more of retail value, anticipating continued price increases. Conversely, for many low-demand cards, such as common (non-star) players' cards, dealers may pay as little as 10 percent or even less of retail with many base-brand cards of recent years having no resale value at all.

SET PRICES

Collectors may note that the complete set prices for newer issues quoted in these listings are usually significantly lower than the total of the value of the individual cards that comprise the set. This reflects two factors in the baseball card market. First, a seller is often willing to take a lower composite price for a complete set as a "volume discount" and to avoid carrying in inventory a large number of common-player or other lower-demand cards.

Second, to a degree, the value of common cards can be said to be inflated as a result of having a built-in overhead charge to justify the dealer's time in sorting cards, carrying them in stock and filling orders. This accounts for the fact that even brand new base-brand baseball cards, which cost the dealer around two cents each when bought in bulk, carry individual price tags of five cents or higher.

Some set prices shown, especially for vintage cards in top condition, are merely theoretical in that it is unlikely that a complete set exists in that condition. In general among older cards the range of conditions found in even the most painstakingly assembled complete set make the set values quoted useful only as a starting point for price negotiations.

ERRORS/VARIATIONS

It is often hard for the beginning collector to understand that an error on a baseball card, in and of itself, does not necessarily add premium value to that card. It is usually only when the correcting of an error in a subsequent printing creates a variation that premium value attaches to an error.

Minor errors, such as wrong stats or personal data, misspellings, inconsistencies, etc. – usually affecting the back of the card – are very common, especially in recent years. Unless a corrected variation was also printed, these errors are not noted in the listings of this book because they are not generally perceived by collectors to have premium value.

On the other hand, major effort has been expended to include the most complete listings ever for collectible variation cards. Many scarce and valuable variations are included in these listings because they are widely collected and often have significant premium value.

In the boom years of the early 1990s, some card companies produced their basic sets at more than one printing facility. This frequently resulted in numerous minor variations in photo cropping and back data presentation. Combined with a general decline in quality control from the mid-1980s through the early 1990s, which allowed unprecedented numbers of uncorrected error cards to be released, this caused a general softening of collector interest in errors and variations. Despite the fact most of these modern variations have no premium value, they are listed here as a matter of record.

COUNTERFEITS/REPRINTS

As the value of baseball cards has risen in the past 25+ years, certain cards and sets have become too expensive for the average collector to obtain. This, along with changes in the technology of color printing, has given rise to increasing numbers of counterfeit and reprint cards.

While both terms describe essentially the same thing – a modern-day copy that attempts to duplicate as closely as possible an original baseball card – there are differences that are important to the collector.

Generally a counterfeit is made with the intention of deceiving somebody into believing it is genuine, and thus paying large amounts of money for it. The counterfeiter takes every pain to try to make their fakes look as authentic as possible.

A reprint, on the other hand, while it may have been made to look as close as possible to an original card, is made with the intention of allowing collectors to buy them as substitutes for cards they may never be otherwise able to afford. The big difference is that a reprint is generally marked as such, usually on the back of the card.

In other cases, like the Topps 1952 reprint set and later Archives issues, the replicas are printed in a size markedly different from the originals, or utilizing current technology that differs from that available in the past. Collectors should be aware, however, that unscrupulous persons will sometimes cut off or otherwise obliterate the distinguishing word – "Reprint," "Copy," – or modern copyright date on the back of a reprint card in an attempt to pass it as genuine.

A collector's best defense against reprints and counterfeits is to acquire a knowledge of the look and feel of genuine baseball cards of various eras and issues.

UNLISTED CARDS

Persons encountering cards which are not listed in this reference should not immediately infer that they have something rare and/or valuable. With hundreds of thousands of baseball cards issued over the past century and thousands more being issued each year, this catalog's comprehensiveness will always remain relative. This is especially true in the area of modern cards and sets released regionally, and the vast universe of foreign and collectors' issues for which coverage has only recently begun. Readers who have cards or sets that are not covered in this edition are invited to correspond with the editor for purposes of adding to the compilation work now in progress. A photocopy or scan of the card's front and back will assist in determining its status. **For questions relating to modern-era cards, contact: Joe Clemens, *Standard Catalog of Baseball Cards*, 700 E. State St., Iola, Wis. 54990; e-mail Joseph.Clemens@fwmedia.com. For questions relating to vintage era cards, contact: Bob Lemke, P.O. Box 8, Iola, WI 54945; e-mail scbcguy@yahoo.com.** Major contributions will be acknowledged in future editions.

NEW ISSUES

Because new baseball cards are being issued all the time, the cataloging of them remains an on-going challenge. The editors will attempt to keep abreast of new issues so that they may be added to future editions of this book. Readers are invited to submit news of new issues, especially limited-edition or regionally issued cards, to the editor at the address above.

Abbreviation Key

IS: Interleague Showdown

OPS: Overprinted "Promotional Sample"

ED: Expansion Draft

AS: All-Star

HL: Hit List

RC: Rookie Class

RC or (RC): Rookie Card

UPT: Unlimited Potential/Talent

SF: Star Factor

SP: Short Print

DT: Double Team

GLS: Gold Leaf Stars

CC: Curtain Calls

GLR: Gold Leaf Rookies

TP: Top Performers

FF: Future Foundation

DK: Diamond King

RR: Rated Rookie

DP: Double Print

IA: In Action

PC: Promo Card

SR: Star Rookie

State of the Market

By any reasoned analysis, no qualified observer of the baseball card market can conclude otherwise than the period 2009-early 2010 has been one of those rare times in the hobby's recent history in which demand – and thus value – has been in retrenchment virtually across the spectrum of collectible baseball cards.

For a time after the technical beginning of the recession in December, 2007, it appeared that the card hobby was little influenced by the widespread economic downturn. Perhaps the demographics of card collectors insulated the group as a whole from the earliest effects of devastating declines in the equities and real estate markets.

The market for the newest cards, for which demand had for some years been essentially restricted to the signature cuts and uniform/equipment pieces found in chase card programs, continued to be driven by younger collectors who, by and large, were neither stockholders nor home owners and were thus not initially shocked into hobby inactivity by downturns in traditional investments. Their jobs on the lower rungs of the employment ladder were not the first to vanish so the market for autograph and relic cards of currently playing stars, invigorated each year by a fresh crop of rookie prospects, remained strong well after declines became evident in other sectors.

Similarly, within the vintage card market, the demand for collector-grade examples of all the traditionally popular issues such as Topps and Bowman cards of the 1940s-1960s, and the cigarette and candy cards of 1910s-1920s, seemed initially to be immune to outside economic influences. A commonly expressed analysis throughout 2008 and well into 2009 insisted that demand (and values) remained strong for cards selling for less than $500.

This was most frequently attributed to pent-up demand from grassroots collectors who looked upon current conditions as a buying opportunity to complete sets or whittle down want lists.

Likewise, the very top of the baseball card food chain remained strong in that period. Those who competed in the set registry realm of third-party graded Gem Mint commons and high-demand superstars of all eras were collectively assumed to be financially insulated from the recession. Either because they were retired or held high-paying positions deemed safe from declines in the labor market, those who could transact in five-figure cards remained active long after the bottom had dropped out of the rest of the card market. Many big ticket cards were sold in the last two years on the basis that they might prove to be a better investment vehicle than stock portfolios or rental units.

It became quickly evident that once middle America accepted the realities of recession in 2008, the heart of the baseball card market was going to be adversely affected. The average blue/white collar worker whose job was in jeopardy or already gone, whose retirement nest egg had been halved or who may be upside down in his home mortgage was not a buyer for baseball cards. Those whose hobby purchases might previously have stretched into the mid four figures to re-acquire a cherished reminder of their childhood or an iconic example of the great cards of earlier generations of superstars simply put their hobby purchasing on hold. In many cases, to replace lost income or take advantage of perceived market bottoms to rebuild retirement portfolios, collectors began to pour cards into the market. With increased supply and reduced demand for most cards in the $500-5,000 niches, prices predictably began to drop precipitously.

Soon the hobby's great cyber card show, eBay, was glutted with mid-range cards of all eras. It was a buyer's market, but there were fewer buyers. Worse, that venue quickly deteriorated in terms of security as chiseling, scams and fraud became rampant, eroding the trust factor necessary to maintain a market when buyer and seller were not face to face. In its heyday prior to 2007, eBay might have listings for nearly a million sportscards at any one time, today, less that half that volume comprises the category, with a significantly higher percentage going unsold.

Conversely, in 2009 there was no rush to market of the hobby's blue chip cards. Unless in the direst of fiscal straits, those who owned cards such as Cracker Jack Joe Jacksons, investment-grade Ty Cobb T-cards and Goudey Ruths, and Gem 1952 Topps Mantles chose to hold onto their cards rather than risk incurring losses. In no other year in recent history have so few T206 Honus Wagners been publicly offered. Only two low-grade examples appeared in major hobby auctions in 2009. The lone (genuine) Wagner to be offered on eBay went unsold. A better-condition example was reported sold by private treaty. Prices realized for these cards were strong, but not spectacular. These three known sales stand in contrast to the half-dozen or more that have typically changed hands in recent years.

As this is written in early 2010, it is too early to say whether the baseball card market has reached its nadir or remains in decline. The most recent spate of slick-catalog auctions from the major firms failed to show any firming of demand or prices even for cards that were once thought to be recession-proof. The result was sales prices that were well off of previous records. Declines of up to 25 percent were noted for cards that, while popular, are not truly rare, including even the biggest names in T206, American Caramels, 1930s Goudeys and 1950s Topps rookies. The recent weakness was most evident in graded cards in the ranges of VG-EX through NM in pre-war issues and EX-MT through NM-MT in 1950s and 1960s sets.

Bucking this trend have been cards that are truly rare, but not necessarily well-known, even among veteran collectors. Buyers who may have waited for a decade or more to have a chance at acquiring certain cards did not appear to be swayed by economic uncertainty when examples came up for sale. "Book" values were thrown out the window for seldom-seen cards ranging from 1911 T208 Cullivan's Firesides to 1954-55 Esskay Hot Dogs Baltimore Orioles, many of which are bringing five-figure prices even in this market.

As such bright spots – uncommon as they may be – make hobby news by defying market woes, they tend to bring similar rarities to the auction block, so it would not be unreasonable to expect to see more once-in-a-generation offerings available in the coming year. Such offerings will surely rewrite the price guides which are often forced to reflect stagnant catalog values on the greatest rarities simply because of a dearth of sales on which to base realistic pricing.

As always, the listings in this book will reflect the editors' analysis of the real-world market. That means that many cards will display pricing at levels lower than a year ago. Even so, it is not the policy of the editors to precipitously drop prices based on isolated sales or short-term market weakness. Long-time observers will have noticed that this book is quick to raise values when the market is strong, but lowers prices more cautiously, doing so only when ongoing evidence indicates sustained lowering of demand.

From the perspective of more than 30 years of daily involvement in the baseball card hobby, your editor has watched several monumental market upheavals. One lesson that seems to be repeating is that just as the card hobby lags the overall economy in turning downwards, it will follow by about a year any recovery as collectors take a cautious approach to indulging their hobby interests with such discretionary income as may become available.

This book is intended to reflect the realities of today's market, not being unduly influenced by dealers that wish to maintain an outdated illusion of value nor by collectors who seek to perpetuate a buyer's market that may have reversed itself. Whether buying or selling, in a weak market or strong, the overall interests of the hobby are best served by reference catalogs that reflect as much as possible in an annual publication, the current state of the market.

In good times and bad, demand for entire genres of baseball cards continues to be affected by cycles of popularity. The caramel cards of the 1909-1915 era that were hot for much of 2007-2008 have cooled considerably as collectors come to realization that in many cases completion of sets is unduly challenging, even impossible, especially in grades above Good.

Currently hot, as a result of increased communication between collectors on specialized internet vintage card forums, are back variations among the issue known as T206. Only now, a century after their issue and through the dedicated study by a few individuals, is the hobby coming to know which of the 525 or so T206 front designs can be found with which advertising on back, and which variations within some ad backs are rarer than others. Look for this trend to carry through to the T205 and T207 sets, as well.

Cyberspace has not been the only source for information exchange within the vintage card hobby in the past year. Several collectors have taken advantage of advances in the world of ink-on-paper to share their expertise.

The most ambitious new book of 2008-2009 is *The Photographic Baseball Cards of Goodwin & Co. (1886-1890)*. Authored by a trio of Old Judge experts – Jay Miller, Joe Gonsowski and Richard Masson, with additional contributions by other top 19th Century collectors, this book has more than 2,500 photos and nearly 500 pages. The book was quickly sold out at Amazon.com, but is occasionally offered (in the $75-125 range) on eBay or from a handful of hobby dealers including CaliforniaSportsCards.com.

A similarly comprehensive study is the 2009 book, *Sweet Recollections: The Story of the Philadelphia Caramel Company of Camden, New Jersey*. In this book, author Erik Varon extensively details the history of the candy company that gave the hobby the 1909 and 1910 baseball card sets known as E95 and E96 along with dozens of other non-sports card issues and other premiums. The book is available for $15.40 at Philadelphia Caramel.com.

Also including many issues that are routinely collected as "baseball cards," such as postcards and cabinet cards, in its coverage is *Guide to Sports Photographs*, published in 2008 by David Rudd Cycleback. That book is available on Amazon.com and similar venues with a cover price of $19.95.

While we list a few Japanese cards in this volume, the principal reference for baseball cards issued in Japan is now in its 7th edition. The book is *2008-2009 Japanese Baseball Card Checklist & Price Guide* by Gary Engel. It's over 450 pages and is available for $38.95 plus postage at PrestigeCollectibles.com.

Not ink-on-paper, but a most valuable specialty reference is Scot Reader's 2009 update to his *Inside T206*. This is an e-book and it is downloadable free (but don't be cheap, make a PayPal donation) at www.oldcardboard.com.

That enhanced sharing of information has resulted in the addition of more than a dozen previously uncataloged issues in the vintage major league and minor league sections of this edition, as well as enhancements to numerous checklists of previously published sets. In an effort to stimulate the two-way flow of information, the editor maintains a blog at www.boblemke.blogspot.com, where frequent postings present information about new discoveries and other topics relevant to the vintage card hobby. That information is also carried in "Standard Catalog Update" columns in *Sports Col-*

VINTAGE MAJOR LEAGUE CARDS (1869-1980)

The vast majority of cards and collectibles listed in this section were issued between 1869 and 1980 and feature major league players only. The term "card" is used rather loosely as in this context it is construed to include virtually any cardboard or paper product, of whatever size and/or shape, depicting baseball players and issued to stimulate the sales of another product or service.

A

1976 A & P Brewers

The Aaron and Yount cards from this regional issue support the set price. The set was issued by the A & P grocery chain. Oversize - 5-7/8" x 9" - cards (actually printed on semi-gloss paper) were given out at the stores in 1976 in s419eries of four with the purchase of select weekly grocery specials. Players are pictured in tight capless portraits. Each photo has a black facsimile autograph; backs are blank. The unnumbered cards are checklisted here in alphabetical order.

		NM	EX	VG
Complete Set (16):		35.00	17.50	10.50
Common Player:		3.00	1.50	.90
(1)	Henry Aaron	20.00	10.00	6.00
(2)	Pete Broberg	3.00	1.50	.90
(3)	Jim Colborn	3.00	1.50	.90
(4)	Mike Hegan	3.00	1.50	.90
(5)	Tim Johnson	3.00	1.50	.90
(6)	Von Joshua	3.00	1.50	.90
(7)	Sixto Lezcano	3.00	1.50	.90
(8)	Don Money	3.00	1.50	.90
(9)	Charlie Moore	3.00	1.50	.90
(10)	Darrell Porter	3.00	1.50	.90
(11)	George Scott	3.00	1.50	.90
(12)	Bill Sharp	3.00	1.50	.90
(13)	Jim Slaton	3.00	1.50	.90
(14)	Bill Travers	3.00	1.50	.90
(15)	Robin Yount	10.00	5.00	3.00
(16)	County Stadium	3.00	1.50	.90

1976 A & P Royals

Identical in format to the Brewers' set issued around Milwaukee, these 5-7/8" x 9" photos picture players without their caps in posed portraits. The cards were given away four per week with the purchase of selected grocery item specials. Cards have a Players Association logo in the upper-left corner, and a black facsimile autograph on front. Backs are blank. The unnumbered cards are checklisted here alphabetically.

	NM	EX	VG
Complete Set (16):	40.00	20.00	12.00

		NM	EX	VG
Common Player:		3.00	1.50	.90
(1)	Doug Bird	3.00	1.50	.90
(2)	George Brett	20.00	10.00	6.00
(3)	Steve Busby	3.00	1.50	.90
(4)	Al Cowens	3.00	1.50	.90
(5)	Al Fitzmorris	3.00	1.50	.90
(6)	Dennis Leonard	3.00	1.50	.90
(7)	Buck Martinez	3.00	1.50	.90
(8)	John Mayberry	3.00	1.50	.90
(9)	Hal McRae	4.50	2.25	1.25
(10)	Amos Otis	4.50	2.25	1.25
(11)	Fred Patek	3.00	1.50	.90
(12)	Tom Poquette	3.00	1.50	.90
(13)	Mel Rojas	3.00	1.50	.90
(14)	Tony Solaita	3.00	1.50	.90
(15)	Paul Splittorff	3.00	1.50	.90
(16)	Jim Wohlford	3.00	1.50	.90

1968 Aamco Roger Maris Postcard

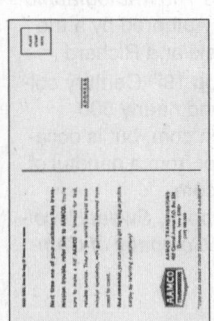

The cited date is approximate on this large-format (about 6" x 9") postcard. The borderless front has a color pose of the reigning home run king with the legend, "It's a real pennant winner!" The postcard format back is directed at auto service professionals, encouraging them to refer transmission problems to a local Aamco facility. A color Aamco logo is at bottom-left.

	NM	EX	VG
Roger Maris	150.00	75.00	45.00

1954 ABC Freight Postcard

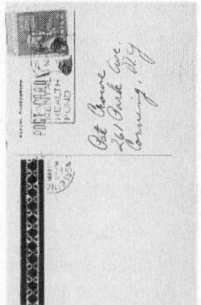

So far only one player is known in this black-and-white glossy postcard issue. The front has a posed photo with facsimile autograph. The wide white border at bottom was likely to accomodate an authentic signature. The divided back carries in its upper-left corner the two-line message "You can't miss by playing ball with / ABC Freight Forwarding Corp." However, on the sole known specimen, that message has been obliterated by being overprinted with a decorative black design. Format is 3-1/2" x 5-7/16".

		NM	EX	VG
(1)	Ted Kluszewski/Btg	150.00	75.00	45.00
(2)	Ted Kluszewski/Fldg	150.00	75.00	45.00

1932 Abdulla Tobacco

Along with several other contemporary card issues from Germany, Babe Ruth is the lone representative from American baseball in this series of 200 cards. Cards are 1-11/16" x 2-1/2" and feature sepia-tone photos on front, with the celebrity's name and nation printed in the white border at bottom. Backs are in German and include a card number.

Babe Ruth, Amerika

		NM	EX	VG
196	Babe Ruth	1,750	875.00	525.00

1949-1950 Acebo y Cia

These small (about 1-1/2" x 1-3/4") Cuban cards were issued in matchboxes, probably over more than one season, as some players are known in photo variations. Fronts have a black-and-white or duotone photo, bordered, with the player name in plain type. Backs have player information presented in one of several different styles, or are blank-backed. It is likely this checklist, which includes a significant contingent of American players, is not complete.

		NM	EX	VG
Common Player:		100.00	50.00	30.00
(1)	Bob Addis	100.00	50.00	30.00
(2)	Luis Aloma	100.00	50.00	30.00
(3)	Ferrel (Ferrell) Anderson	100.00	50.00	30.00
(4)	Bill Antonello	100.00	50.00	30.00
(5)	Mario Arencibia	100.00	50.00	30.00
(6)	Maurice Atwright	100.00	50.00	30.00
(7)	Wesley Bailey	100.00	50.00	30.00
(8)	Vic Barnhart	100.00	50.00	30.00
(9)	Carlos Blanco	100.00	50.00	30.00
(10)	Herberto Blanco	100.00	50.00	30.00
(11)	Adolfo Cabrera	100.00	50.00	30.00
(12)	Emilio Cabrera	100.00	50.00	30.00
(13)	Lorenzo "Chiquitin" Cabrera	100.00	50.00	30.00
(14)	Rafael Villa Cabrera	100.00	50.00	30.00
(15)	Samuel Calderone	100.00	50.00	30.00
(16)	Avelino Canizares	100.00	50.00	30.00
(17)	Clemente "Sungo" Carreras	100.00	50.00	30.00
(18)	Jack Cassini	100.00	50.00	30.00
(19)	Aristonico Cocorreoso	100.00	50.00	30.00
(20)	Carlos Colas	100.00	50.00	30.00
(21)	Kevin (Chuck) Connors	450.00	225.00	135.00
(22)	Sandalio "Potrellilo" Consuegra	125.00	62.00	37.00
(23)	Agustin Cordeiro	100.00	50.00	30.00
(24)	Reinaldo Cordeiro	100.00	50.00	30.00
(25)	Reinaldo Cordeiro	100.00	50.00	30.00
(26)	Alejandro Crespo	100.00	50.00	30.00
(27)	Raymond "Talua" Dandridge	500.00	250.00	150.00
(28)	Jose "Pipo" de la Noval	100.00	50.00	30.00
(29)	Carlos "Yiqui" De Souza	100.00	50.00	30.00
(30)	Mario Diaz	100.00	50.00	30.00
(31)	Lino Donoso	100.00	50.00	30.00
(32)	Claro Duany	100.00	50.00	30.00
(33)	Gumersindo Elba	100.00	50.00	30.00
(34)	Paul (Al) Epperly	100.00	50.00	30.00
(35)	Roberto "Tarzan" Estalella	125.00	65.00	35.00
(36)	Jose Ma. Fernandez	100.00	50.00	30.00
(37)	Jose Ma. Fernandez Jr.	100.00	50.00	30.00

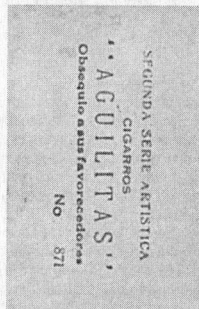

(38)	Rodolfo Fernandez	100.00	50.00	30.00
(39)	Thomas Fine	100.00	50.00	30.00
(40)	Andres Fleitas	100.00	50.00	30.00
(41)	Pedro Formental	100.00	50.00	30.00
(42)	"Sojito" Gallardo	100.00	50.00	30.00
(43)	Chicuelo Garcia	100.00	50.00	30.00
(44)	Manuel "Cocaina" Garcia	150.00	75.00	45.00
(45)	Pablo Garcia	100.00	50.00	30.00
(46)	Silvio Garcia	100.00	50.00	30.00
(47)	Lloyd Gearhart (Reverse image.)	100.00	50.00	30.00
(48)	Lloyd Gearhart (Corrected)	100.00	50.00	30.00
(49)	(Al) Gerheauser	100.00	50.00	30.00
(50)	Albert Gionfrido (Gionfriddo)	125.00	65.00	35.00
(51)	Leonardo Goicochea	100.00	50.00	30.00
(52)	Enrique Gonzalez	100.00	50.00	30.00
(53)	Hiram Gonzalez	100.00	50.00	30.00
(54)	Miguel Angel Gonzalez	125.00	65.00	35.00
(55)	Fermin Guerra	100.00	50.00	30.00
(56)	Wes Hamner	100.00	50.00	30.00
(57)	Eugene Handley	100.00	50.00	30.00
(58)	Rollie Hemsley	100.00	50.00	30.00
(59)	Salvador Hernandez	100.00	50.00	30.00
(60)	Clarence Hicks	100.00	50.00	30.00
(61)	Manuel "Chino" Hidalgo	100.00	50.00	30.00
(62)	Bob Hooper	100.00	50.00	30.00
(63)	Amado Ibanez	100.00	50.00	30.00
(64)	Don Lenhardt	100.00	50.00	30.00
(65)	Vicente Lopez	100.00	50.00	30.00
(66)	Raul Lopez	100.00	50.00	30.00
(67)	"Tony" Lorenzo	100.00	50.00	30.00
(68)	Adolfo Luque	150.00	75.00	45.00
(69)	John Bill Maldovan	100.00	50.00	30.00
(70)	Max Manning	250.00	125.00	75.00
(71)	Conrado Marrero	125.00	65.00	35.00
(72)	Rogelio "Limonar" Martinez/ Pitching	100.00	50.00	30.00
(73)	Rogelio "Limonar" Martinez/ Portrait	100.00	50.00	30.00
(74)	Agapito Mayor	100.00	50.00	30.00
(75)	Lester McCrabb	100.00	50.00	30.00
(76)	Guillermo "Willy" Miranda	125.00	65.00	35.00
(77)	Rene Monteagudo	100.00	50.00	30.00
(78)	Julio "Jiqui" Moreno	100.00	50.00	30.00
(79)	Ernesto Morrilla	100.00	50.00	30.00
(80)	Howie Moss	100.00	50.00	30.00
(81)	Rafael Sam Noble	100.00	50.00	30.00
(82)	Regino Otero	100.00	50.00	30.00
(83)	Oliverio Ortiz	100.00	50.00	30.00
(84)	Roberto Ortiz/Btg	100.00	50.00	30.00
(85)	Roberto Ortiz/Potrait	100.00	50.00	30.00
(86)	Pedro Pages	100.00	50.00	30.00
(87)	Leonard Pearson	250.00	125.00	75.00
(88)	Eddie Pellagrin (Pellagrini)	100.00	50.00	30.00
(89)	Conrado Perez	100.00	50.00	30.00
(90)	Damon Phillips	100.00	50.00	30.00
(91)	Jose "Pototo" Piloto	100.00	50.00	30.00
(92)	William Powell	100.00	50.00	30.00
(93)	Al Prendergast	100.00	50.00	30.00
(94)	Napoleon Reyes (Holding bat.)	100.00	50.00	30.00
(95)	Napoleon Reyes (No bat.)	100.00	50.00	30.00
(96)	Donald Richmond	100.00	50.00	30.00
(97)	Hector Rodriguez	100.00	50.00	30.00
(98)	Oscar Rodriguez	100.00	50.00	30.00
(99)	Julio Rojo	100.00	50.00	30.00
(100)	Octavio Rubert	100.00	50.00	30.00
(101)	Arturo Seijas	100.00	50.00	30.00
(102)	Raymond Shore (Arms crossed.)	100.00	50.00	30.00
(103)	Raymond Shore (Pose unrecorded.)	100.00	50.00	30.00
(104)	Ford Smith	100.00	50.00	30.00
(105)	Rene Solis	100.00	50.00	30.00
(106)	Roberto Fernandez Tapanes	100.00	50.00	30.00
(107)	Don Thompson	100.00	50.00	30.00
(108)	Gilberto Torres	100.00	50.00	30.00
(109)	Quincy Trouppe	150.00	75.00	45.00
(110)	Christian Van Cuyk	100.00	50.00	30.00
(111)	John Van Cuyk	100.00	50.00	30.00
(112)	Ben Wade	100.00	50.00	30.00
(113)	Archie Wilson	100.00	50.00	30.00
(114)	Edward Wright	100.00	50.00	30.00
(115)	Adrian Zabala	100.00	50.00	30.00

1970 Action Cartridge

This set of boxes with baseball players' pictures on them was issued by Action Films Inc. of Mountain View, Calif., in 1970-71. The boxes, measuring 2-5/8" x 6" x 1" deep, contained 8mm film cartridges of various professional athletes demonstrating playing tips. The movie series include 12 baseball players. (Other sports represented were football, golf, tennis, hockey and skiing, a total of 40, in all). Boxes feature color player portraits inside an oval and include a facsimile autograph. The values listed are for complete boxes or player panels, without the movie cartridge.

		NM	EX	VG
Complete Set (12):		275.00	135.00	85.00
Common Player:		7.50	3.75	2.25
Box w/Cartridge: 2X				
Viewer:		60.00	30.00	20.00
1	Tom Seaver	40.00	20.00	12.00
2	Dave McNally	7.50	3.75	2.25
3	Bill Freehan	7.50	3.75	2.25
4	Willie McCovey	25.00	12.50	7.50
5	Glenn Beckert, Don Kessinger	7.50	3.75	2.25
6	Brooks Robinson	30.00	15.00	9.00
7	Hank Aaron	60.00	30.00	18.00
8	Reggie Jackson	45.00	22.50	13.50
9	Pete Rose	50.00	25.00	15.00
10	Lou Brock	25.00	12.50	7.50
11	Willie Davis	7.50	3.75	2.25
12	Rod Carew	25.00	12.50	7.50

1933-1934 Adams Hat Stores

In the early 1930s a men's haberdasher issued a series of colorized 8" x 10" portrait photos of baseball players and other celebrities dressed in suit-and-tie and wearing a hat. Above a facsimile autograph on front is a testimonial for Adams Hats. Backs are stamped, "Property of Adams Hat Stores, Inc." The location of the issuing store or stores in unknown. Only the ballplayers are listed here.

		NM	EX	VG
Complete Set (3):		1,750	875.00	525.00
Common Player:		600.00	300.00	180.00
(1)	Carl Hubbell	600.00	300.00	180.00
(2)	Lefty Gomez	600.00	300.00	180.00
(3)	John McGraw	600.00	300.00	180.00

1910 A Fan For A Fan

These cardboard novelties were produced by the American Tobacco Co. About 7-1/4" in diameter, the bursting baseball and portrait are printed in color with a facsimile autograph. The handle is about 5" long. The back is blank. The known fans are listed here alphabetically; the checklist is likely incomplete. Modern counterfeits are known. They usually lack the baseball "stitching" on back and have a slot in the cardboard for the stick. Modern counterfeits are known. They usually lack the baseball "stitching" on back and have a slot in the cardboard for the stick.

		NM	EX	VG
Complete Set (5):		30,000	16,000	9,750
Common Player:		2,400	1,200	725.00
(1)	Frank Baker	4,500	2,250	1,350
(2)	Hal Chase	3,600	1,800	1,100
(3)	Ty Cobb	15,000	7,500	4,500
(4)	Larry Doyle	2,400	1,200	725.00
(5)	Christy Mathewson	5,500	2,750	1,650

1939 African Tobacco

The unlikely venue of the "other" U.S.A. (Union of South Africa) is the provenance of this rare Babe Ruth card. The African Tobacco Co. issued a set of 100 cards in a series titled "The World of Sport." The cards were issued in both a large (2-1/4" x 3-1/4") and small (1-3/4" x 2-1/2") format. Fronts have a black-and-white photo of Ruth, with a white border all around. Backs are printed in both English and Afrikaner.

		NM	EX	VG
34	Babe Ruth (Large)	1,250	625.00	375.00
34	Babe Ruth (Small)	1,250	625.00	375.00

1924-1925 Aguilitas Segundas

This set is known to collectors as Aguilitas Segundas for the top line of the ad on back. In reality, this second series cigarette card issue was issued several years before the Aguilitas first series counterpart. About 1-1/2" x 2-3/8", the cards have round black-and-white player portrait photos in a debossed rectangular area on glossy stock. Beneath the photo is a player name or nickname, with "BASE BALL" below. The ballplayers are a subset of a 900-card issue which included movie and stage stars, soccer players, boxers and other subjects. All baseball players are known within the numerical range of 841 through 899, though only four cards are known above #880, and none between #880-895. The known ballplayers comprise 44, many of whom were stars of the Negro Leagues, including several Hall of Famers and some who appear on no other career-contemporary cards. Cards are checklisted with the name as shown on the card, further identification, where necessary, is listed parenthetically. Many surviving specimens show evidence of having been glued into an album which largely accounts for their survival in the area's hot, humid climate. Examples are rarely seen in condition approaching Excellent.

		NM	EX	VG
Common Player:		250.00	125.00	75.00
841	(Pablo "Champion") Mesa	250.00	125.00	75.00
842	A. (Armando) Marsans	250.00	125.00	75.00
843	C. (Cristobal) Torriente	9,000	4,500	2,700
844	Merito Acosta	250.00	125.00	75.00
845	Cheo Ramos	250.00	125.00	75.00
846	Joe (John Henry "Pop") Lloyd	15,000	7,500	4,500
847	(Herman Matias) Rios	250.00	125.00	75.00
848	(Lucas) Boada	250.00	125.00	75.00
849	(Jose) Mendez	7,500	3,700	2,200
850	(Valentin) Dreke	350.00	175.00	100.00
851	(Eugenio) Morin	250.00	125.00	75.00
852	Mayari (Esteban "Mayari" Montalvo)	250.00	125.00	75.00
853	(Valentin) Dreke	350.00	175.00	105.00
854	(Julio) Rojo	250.00	125.00	75.00
855	(Rafael) Almeida	250.00	125.00	75.00
856	(Emilio) Palmero	250.00	125.00	75.00
857	(Adolfo) Luque	800.00	250.00	150.00
858	(Isidro) Fabre	250.00	125.00	75.00
859	(Manuel) Cueto	250.00	125.00	75.00
860	Dibu (Pedro Dibut)	250.00	125.00	75.00
861	Cheo Ramos	250.00	125.00	75.00
862	(Jesse) Hubbard	750.00	375.00	225.00
863	Kakin (Gonzalez)	250.00	125.00	75.00
864	(Jose Maria) Fernandez	250.00	125.00	75.00
865	(Snake) Henry	450.00	225.00	135.00
866	Cruje (Ernie Krueger)	450.00	225.00	135.00
867	(Manuel) Parrado	250.00	125.00	75.00
868	(Chuck) Dressen	250.00	125.00	75.00
869	(Oscar) Charleston	15,000	7,500	4,500
870	Sam (John Henry "Pop") Lloyd	15,000	7,500	4,500
871	Mc. Key (Raleigh "Biz" Mackey)	7,500	3,700	2,200

		NM	EX	VG
872	P. (Eusebio "Papo") Gonzalez	250.00	125.00	75.00
873	(Clint) Thomas	600.00	300.00	180.00
874	(Dobie) Moore	600.00	300.00	180.00
875	(Frank) Duncan	600.00	300.00	180.00
876	O. (Oscar) Rodriguez	250.00	125.00	75.00
877	Lopito (Jose "Lopito" Lopez)	250.00	125.00	75.00
878	E. (Eustaquio "Bombin") Pedroso	1,000	500.00	300.00
879	(Dick) Lundy	6,000	1,375	825.00
880	Sirike (Valentin "Sirique" Gonzalez)	250.00	125.00	75.00
895	(Oscar) Tuero	250.00	125.00	75.00
897	(Alejandro) Oms	1,200	600.00	360.00
898	Peter (Jesse Petty)	250.00	125.00	75.00
899	(Danny) Clark	250.00	125.00	75.00

1926-1927 Aguilitas

 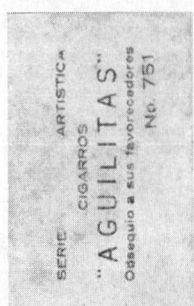

Uniforms worn by some of the players indicate this set was produced after the related series known as "Segundas," or Second Series. The baseball players - all Cuban nationals - are among 100 athletes (including soccer players and boxers) in a 900-card multi-subject set issued in packs of Aguilitas cigarettes. The cards are printed in black-and-white on glossy stock. On front is a large square portrait or action pose. In the bottom border is "BASE-BALL" with the player name and position below. Names as shown on the cards are presneted in this checklist, with further identification as necessary provided parenthetically. Several of the cards are duplicated in the series with different card numbers. Like most contemporary Latin American issues, surviving examples are seldom found in high-grade and often with evidence of having been mounted in an album.

		NM	EX	VG
Common Player:		165.00	85.00	50.00
751	Cheo Hernandez	165.00	85.00	50.00
752	(Jose Maria) Fernandez	200.00	100.00	60.00
756	R. (Ricardo) Torres	165.00	85.00	50.00
759	Jacinto Calvo	165.00	85.00	50.00
761	E. (Emilio) Palmero	165.00	85.00	50.00
763	Champion (Pablo) Mesa	250.00	125.00	75.00
769	C. (Carlos) Zarza	165.00	85.00	50.00
771	Fernando Rios	165.00	85.00	50.00
772	J. (Joseito) Rodriguez	165.00	85.00	50.00
774	(Juanelo) Mirabal (Same as #824.)	250.00	125.00	75.00
776	L. (Lalo) Rodriguez	165.00	85.00	50.00
777	A. (Adolfo) Luque	350.00	175.00	100.00
778	Alejandro Oms	3,500	1,250	750.00
779	(Armando) Marsans (Same as #829.)	375.00	185.00	110.00
782a	A. (Alfredo) Cabrera	165.00	85.00	50.00
782b	Daniel Blanco (Same as #832.)	165.00	85.00	50.00
787	B. (Bartolo) Portuando	250.00	125.00	75.00
791	A. (Agustin) Navarro	165.00	85.00	50.00
796	R. (Raphael "Busta") Quintana	165.00	85.00	50.00
797	(Roberto) Puig (Same as #847.)	165.00	85.00	50.00
817	(Oscar) Levis	165.00	85.00	50.00
819	Raul Atan	165.00	85.00	50.00
821	(Jose) Pepin Perez	165.00	85.00	50.00
822	(Isidro) Fabre	200.00	100.00	60.00
823	Bienvenido "Hooks" Jimenez	250.00	125.00	75.00
824	(Juanelo) Mirabal (Same as #774.)	250.00	125.00	75.00
825	Tomas Calvo	165.00	85.00	50.00
826	(Pelayo) Chacon	250.00	125.00	75.00
829	(Armando) Marsans (Same as #779.)	375.00	185.00	110.00
832	Daniel Blanco (Same as #782.)	165.00	85.00	50.00
836	(Valentin) Dreke	250.00	125.00	75.00
838	(Jose) Echarri	165.00	85.00	50.00
839	Miguel Angel (Gonzalez)	300.00	150.00	90.00
841	(Oscar) Estrada	300.00	150.00	90.00
846	Acostica (Jose Acosta)	300.00	150.00	90.00
847	(Roberto) Puig (Same as #797.)	165.00	85.00	50.00
849	(Cesar) Alvarez	165.00	85.00	50.00

1954 Alaga Syrup Willie Mays Postcard

The year of issue on this one-card set is approximate. In 3-1/4" x 5-1/2" format the black-and-white card has a borderless portrait on front with a facsimile autograph. Back has an ad for Alaga Syrup, along with standard postcard elements.

		NM	EX	VG
(1)	Willie Mays	600.00	450.00	390.00

1944-45 Albertype Hall of Fame Plaque Postcards - Type 1

From 1944-1952, Albertype was the official producer of the Baseball Hall of Fame's postcards available for public sale. The 3-1/2" x 5-1/2" black-and-white cards depict the bronze plaque of each inductee. Fronts have a white border. Postcard-style backs have a bit of player data and identification of the specific producer. In the first type of Albertype plaque postcards, issued 1944-45, the line of type beneath the plaque photo has an abbreviation for New York. Later Albertypes spelled out the state name. The unnumbered cards are checklisted here alphabetically.

		NM	EX	VG
Complete Set (38):		800.00	400.00	240.00
Common Player:		20.00	10.00	6.00
(1)	G.C. Alexander	25.00	12.50	7.50
(2)	Adrian Anson	20.00	10.00	6.00
(3)	Roger Bresnahan	20.00	10.00	6.00
(4)	Dan Brouthers	20.00	10.00	6.00
(5)	Morgan Bulkeley	20.00	10.00	6.00
(6)	Alexander Cartwright	20.00	10.00	6.00
(7)	Henry Chadwick	20.00	10.00	6.00
(8)	Fred Clarke	20.00	10.00	6.00
(9)	Ty Cobb	40.00	20.00	12.00
(10)	Eddie Collins	20.00	10.00	6.00
(11)	Jimmy Collins	20.00	10.00	6.00
(12)	Charles A. Comiskey	20.00	10.00	6.00
(13)	Candy Cummings	20.00	10.00	6.00
(14)	Ed Delahanty	20.00	10.00	6.00
(15)	Hugh Duffy	20.00	10.00	6.00
(16)	Buck Ewing	20.00	10.00	6.00
(17)	Lou Gehrig	50.00	25.00	15.00
(18)	Rogers Hornsby	20.00	10.00	6.00
(19)	Hughie Jennings	20.00	10.00	6.00
(20)	Ban Johnson	20.00	10.00	6.00
(21)	Walter Johnson	30.00	15.00	9.00
(22)	Willie Keeler	20.00	10.00	6.00
(23)	King Kelly	20.00	10.00	6.00
(24)	Nap Lajoie	20.00	10.00	6.00
(25)	Kenesaw Landis	20.00	10.00	6.00
(26)	Connie Mack	20.00	10.00	6.00
(27)	Christy Mathewson	30.00	15.00	9.00
(28)	John McGraw	20.00	10.00	6.00
(29)	Jim O'Rourke	20.00	10.00	6.00
(30)	Chas. Radbourn	20.00	10.00	6.00
(31)	Wilbert Robinson	20.00	10.00	6.00
(32)	Babe Ruth	65.00	32.00	19.50
(33)	George Sisler	20.00	10.00	6.00
(34)	Al Spalding	20.00	10.00	6.00
(35)	Tris Speaker	20.00	10.00	6.00
(36)	Honus Wagner	30.00	15.00	9.00
(37)	George Wright	20.00	10.00	6.00
(38)	Cy Young	30.00	15.00	9.00

1946-52 Albertype Hall of Fame Plaque Postcards - Type 2

From 1944-1952, Albertype was the official producer of the Baseball Hall of Fame's postcards available for public sale. The 3-1/2" x 5-1/2" black-and-white cards depict the bronze plaque of each inductee. Fronts have a white border. Postcard-style backs have a bit of biographical data and identification of the specific issuer. In the second series of Albertype plaque postcards, issued 1946-52, the line of type beneath the plaque photo spells out the New York state name. The unnumbered cards are checklisted here alphabetically.

Those cards found only in this series are noted with an asterisk. Because the Foxx and Ott cards were first issued in 1951, and the Paul Waner, Heilmann and 1864 Knickerboker Nine in 1952, they are scarcer than those issued earlier.

		NM	EX	VG
Complete Set (63):		1,325	675.00	425.00
Common Player:		20.00	10.00	6.00
(1)	G.C. Alexander	25.00	12.50	7.50
(2)	Adrian Anson	20.00	10.00	6.00
(3)	Roger Bresnahan	20.00	10.00	6.00
(4)	Dan Brouthers	20.00	10.00	6.00
(5)	Mordecai Brown (*)	25.00	12.50	7.50
(6)	Morgan Bulkeley	20.00	10.00	6.00
(7)	Jesse Burkett (*)	25.00	12.50	7.50
(8)	Alexander Cartwright	20.00	10.00	6.00
(9)	Henry Chadwick	20.00	10.00	6.00
(10)	Frank Chance (*)	25.00	12.50	7.50
(11)	Jack Chesbro (*)	25.00	12.50	7.50
(12)	Fred Clarke	20.00	10.00	6.00
(13)	Ty Cobb	40.00	20.00	12.00
(14)	Mickey Cochrane (*)	25.00	12.50	7.50
(15)	Eddie Collins	20.00	10.00	6.00
(16)	Jimmy Collins	20.00	10.00	6.00
(17)	Charles A. Comiskey	20.00	10.00	6.00
(18)	Candy Cummings	20.00	10.00	6.00
(19)	Ed Delahanty	20.00	10.00	6.00
(20)	Hugh Duffy	20.00	10.00	6.00
(21)	Johnny Evers (*)	25.00	12.50	7.50
(22)	Buck Ewing	20.00	10.00	6.00
(23)	James E. (Jimmy) Foxx (*)	45.00	22.00	13.50
(24)	Frankie Frisch (*)	25.00	12.50	7.50
(25)	Lou Gehrig	50.00	25.00	15.00
(26)	Charlie Gehringer (*)	25.00	12.50	7.50
(27)	Clark Griffith (*)	25.00	12.50	7.50
(28)	Lefty Grove (*)	25.00	12.50	7.50
(29)	Harry Heilmann (*)	40.00	20.00	12.00
(30)	Rogers Hornsby	20.00	10.00	6.00
(31)	Carl Hubbell (*)	25.00	12.50	7.50
(32)	Hughie Jennings	20.00	10.00	6.00
(33)	Ban Johnson	20.00	10.00	6.00
(34)	Walter Johnson	30.00	15.00	9.00
(35)	Willie Keeler	20.00	10.00	6.00
(36)	King Kelly	20.00	10.00	6.00
(37)	Nap Lajoie	20.00	10.00	6.00
(38)	Kenesaw Landis	20.00	10.00	6.00
(39)	Connie Mack	20.00	10.00	6.00
(40)	Christy Mathewson	30.00	15.00	9.00
(41)	Tommy McCarthy (*)	25.00	12.50	7.50
(62)	Joe McGinnity (*)	25.00	12.50	7.50
(43)	John McGraw	20.00	10.00	6.00
(44)	Kid Nichols (*)	25.00	12.50	7.50
(45)	Jim O'Rourke	20.00	10.00	6.00
(46)	Mel Ott (*)	35.00	17.50	10.50
(47)	Herb Pennock (*)	25.00	12.50	7.50
(48)	Ed Plank (*)	25.00	12.50	7.50
(49)	Chas. Radbourn	20.00	10.00	6.00
(50)	Wilbert Robinson	20.00	10.00	6.00
(51)	Babe Ruth	65.00	32.00	19.50
(52)	George Sisler	20.00	10.00	6.00
(53)	Al Spalding	20.00	10.00	6.00
(54)	Tris Speaker	20.00	10.00	6.00
(55)	Joe Tinker (*)	25.00	12.50	7.50
(56)	Pie Traynor (*)	25.00	12.50	7.50
(57)	Rube Waddell (*)	25.00	12.50	7.50
(58)	Honus Wagner	30.00	15.00	9.00
(59)	Ed Walsh (*)	25.00	12.50	7.50
(60)	Paul Waner (*)	35.00	17.50	10.50
(61)	George Wright	20.00	10.00	6.00
(62)	Cy Young	30.00	15.00	9.00
(63)	Knickerbocker Nine 1864	35.00	17.50	10.50

1970 Carl Aldana Orioles

Belanger

Little is known about the distribution or origin of this 12-card regional set, which was available in 1970 in the Baltimore area. Measuring 3-1/4" x 2-1/8", the unnumbered cards picture members of the Baltimore Orioles and include two poses of Brooks Robinson. The cards feature line drawings of the players surrounded by a plain border. The player's last name appears below the portrait sketch. The set was named after Carl Aldana, who supplied the artwork for the cards.

		NM	EX	VG
	Complete Set (12):	125.00	65.00	40.00
	Common Player:	12.00	6.00	3.50
(1)	Mark Belanger	12.00	6.00	3.50
(2)	Paul Blair	12.00	6.00	3.50
(3)	Mike Cuellar	12.00	6.00	3.50
(4)	Ellie Hendricks	12.00	6.00	3.50
(5)	Dave Johnson	12.00	6.00	3.50
(6)	Dave McNally	12.00	6.00	3.50
(7)	Jim Palmer	45.00	22.50	13.50
(8)	Boog Powell	25.00	12.50	7.50
(9)	Brooks Robinson (Diving - face showing.)	40.00	20.00	12.00
(10)	Brooks Robinson (Diving - back showing.)	40.00	20.00	12.00
(11)	Frank Robinson	60.00	30.00	18.00
(12)	Earl Weaver	15.00	7.50	4.50

1971 Carl Aldana

Devoid of any indication of when produced or by whom, this set of obscure players of the 1940s and 1950s was a collectors' issue from Carl Aldana circa 1971. The cards are blank-backed, about 2-1/8" x 2-3/4". Fronts have a red background with an artwork player portrait in blue. The player's last name and card number are in dark blue, his first name in white. For a few of the players, this is their only known baseball card.

		NM	EX	VG
	Complete Set (16):	125.00	60.00	37.50
	Common Player:	10.00	5.00	3.00
1	Wally Hood	10.00	5.00	3.00
2	Jim Westlake	10.00	5.00	3.00
3	Stan McWilliams	10.00	5.00	3.00
4	Les Fleming	10.00	5.00	3.00
5	John Ritchey	10.00	5.00	3.00
6	Steve Nagy	10.00	5.00	3.00
7	Ken Gables	10.00	5.00	3.00
8	Maurice Fisher	10.00	5.00	3.00
9	Don Lang	10.00	5.00	3.00
10	Harry Malmburg (Malmberg)	10.00	5.00	3.00
11	Jack Conway	10.00	5.00	3.00
12	Don White	10.00	5.00	3.00
13	Dick Lajeskie	10.00	5.00	3.00
14	Walt Judnich	10.00	5.00	3.00
15	Joe Kirrene	10.00	5.00	3.00
16	Ed Sauer	10.00	5.00	3.00

1940s Alerta Antonio Alcalde Premium Pictures

There are still gaps in the hobby's knowledge of this late-1940s/early-1950s Cuban issue. Evidently a premium used in a contest conducted by a newspaper or sports periodical, these pictures are printed on semi-gloss paper in an 8" x 11" format. Featured on front are black-and-white posed action or portrait photos. The team name and symbol are above and a portrait, presumably of Antonio, is at bottom. Pictures are highlighted by color graphics: blue for Almendares, green for Cienfuegos, red for Havana and orange for Marianao. Backs are blank, but are sometimes seen with a round rubber-stamped "Alerta" logo or red boxed "ANTONIO, ALCALDE." The unnumbered pictures are listed here alphabetically within team. The pictures include many American players and those who spent time in the major leagues.

	NM	EX	VG
Complete Set (70):	2,000	1,000	400.00

		NM	EX	VG
	Common Player:	30.00	15.00	6.00
	ALMENDARES SCORPIONS			
(1)	Bill Antonello	35.00	17.50	7.00
(2)	Francisco Campos	35.00	17.50	7.00
(3)	Avelino Canizares	30.00	15.00	6.00
(4)	Yiqui De Souza	30.00	15.00	6.00
(5)	Rodolfo Fernandez	30.00	15.00	6.00
(6)	Andres Fleitas	35.00	17.50	7.00
(7)	Al Gionfriddo	35.00	17.50	7.00
(8)	Fermin Guerra	35.00	17.50	7.00
(9)	Bob Hooper	35.00	17.50	7.00
(10)	Vincente Lopez	30.00	15.00	6.00
(11)	Conrado Marrero	35.00	17.50	7.00
(12)	Agapito Mayor	30.00	15.00	6.00
(13)	Willy Miranda	35.00	17.50	7.00
(14)	Rene Monteagudo	35.00	17.50	7.00
(15)	Roberto Ortiz	35.00	17.50	7.00
(16)	Hector Rodriguez	35.00	17.50	7.00
(17)	Octavio Rubert	30.00	15.00	6.00
(18)	Rene Solis	30.00	15.00	6.00
	CIENFUEGOS ELEPHANTS			
(1)	Bob Addis	35.00	17.50	7.00
(2)	Sam Calderone	35.00	17.50	7.00
(3)	Jack Cassini	35.00	17.50	7.00
(4)	Alejandro Crespo	35.00	17.50	7.00
(5)	Paul (Al) Epperly	35.00	17.50	7.00
(6)	Thomas Fine	35.00	17.50	7.00
(7)	Pedro Formental (Formenthal)	30.00	15.00	6.00
(8)	Francisco Gallardo	30.00	15.00	6.00
(9)	Lloyd Gearhart	35.00	17.50	7.00
(10)	Leonardo Goicochea	30.00	15.00	6.00
(11)	Salvador Hernandez	35.00	17.50	7.00
(12)	Clarence (Buddy) Hicks	35.00	17.50	7.00
(13)	Max Manning	45.00	22.00	9.00
(14)	San (Ray) Noble	35.00	17.50	7.00
(15)	Regino Otero	35.00	17.50	7.00
(16)	Pedro Pages	30.00	15.00	6.00
(17)	Napoleon Reyes	35.00	17.50	7.00
(18)	Ernie Shore	35.00	17.50	7.00
(19)	Adrian Zabala	35.00	17.50	7.00
	HAVANA LIONS			
(1)	Ferrell Anderson	35.00	17.50	7.00
(2)	Wess Bailey	30.00	15.00	6.00
(3)	Vic Barnhart	35.00	17.50	7.00
(4)	Herberto Blanco	30.00	15.00	6.00
(5)	Emilio Cabrera	30.00	15.00	6.00
(6)	Pedro Formental (Formenthal)	30.00	15.00	6.00
(7)	Al Gerheauser	35.00	17.50	7.00
(8)	Miguel Angel Gonzalez	60.00	30.00	12.00
(9)	Chino Hidalgo	30.00	15.00	6.00
(10)	Jimmy Lenhart	30.00	15.00	6.00
(11)	Adolfo Luque	60.00	30.00	12.00
(12)	Max Manning	45.00	22.50	9.00
(13)	Julio Moreno	35.00	17.50	7.00
(14)	Lenox Pearson	45.00	22.50	9.00
(15)	Don Richmond	35.00	17.50	7.00
(16)	John Ford Smith	30.00	15.00	6.00
(17)	Don Thompson	35.00	17.50	7.00
(18)	Gilberto Torres	35.00	17.50	7.00
	MARIANAO TIGERS			
(1)	Mario Arencibia	30.00	15.00	6.00
(2)	Carlos Blanco	30.00	15.00	6.00
(3)	Chiquitin Cabbera	30.00	15.00	6.00
(4)	Sandalio Consuegra	35.00	17.50	7.00
(5)	Reinaldo Cordeiro	30.00	15.00	6.00
(6)	Talua (Ray) Dandridge	350.00	175.00	75.00
(7)	Mario Diaz	30.00	15.00	6.00
(8)	Claro Duany	35.00	17.50	7.00
(9)	Roberto Estalella	35.00	17.50	7.00
(10)	Chicuelo Garcia	30.00	15.00	6.00
(11)	Wesley Hamner	35.00	17.50	7.00
(12)	Rollie Hemsley	35.00	17.50	7.00
(13)	Amado Ibanez	30.00	15.00	6.00
(14)	Limonar (Rogelio) Martinez	35.00	17.50	7.00
(15)	Don Phillips	30.00	15.00	6.00
(16)	Bartholomew (Jim) Prendergast	35.00	17.50	7.00
(17)	John Trouppe	35.00	17.50	7.00

1904 Allegheny Card Co.

By definition the rarest card issue of the early 20th Century is this baseball game set featuring only National League players. It is thought that the sole known boxed set was produced as a prototype and never actually reached distribution. The issue contains 104 player cards and a "Ball Counter" card for each team. Cards are in playing-card format, about 2-1/2" x 3-1/2" with rounded corners. Fronts are printed in blue with a circular player portrait at center. Team name is at top, with player's last name (occasionally with initials and occasionally misspelled) beneath. The unique boxed set was discovered in the late 1980s. It was sold at auction in 1991 for $26,400, and

again in 1995 for $11,000, after which it was broken up for individual card sales. The checklist is presented here in alphabetical order. All cards appear to have been hand-cut.

		NM	EX	VG
	Common Player:	1,000	500.00	300.00
(1)	Ed Abbaticchio	1,000	500.00	300.00
(2)	Harry Aubrey	1,000	500.00	300.00
(3)	Charlie Babb	1,000	500.00	300.00
(4)	George Barclay	1,000	500.00	300.00
(5)	Shad Barry	1,000	500.00	300.00
(6)	Bill Beagen (Bergen)	1,000	500.00	300.00
(7)	Ginger Beaumont	1,000	500.00	300.00
(8)	Jake Beckley	2,500	875.00	525.00
(9)	Frank Bowerman	1,000	500.00	300.00
(10)	Dave Brain	1,000	500.00	300.00
(11)	Kitty Bransfield	1,000	500.00	300.00
(12)	Roger Bresnahan	2,500	875.00	525.00
(13)	Mordecai Brown	2,500	875.00	525.00
(14)	George Browne	1,000	500.00	300.00
(15)	Al Buckenberger	1,000	500.00	300.00
(16)	Jimmy Burke	1,000	500.00	300.00
(17)	Fred Carisch	1,000	500.00	300.00
(18)	Pat Carney	1,000	500.00	300.00
(19)	Doc Casey	1,000	500.00	300.00
(20)	Frank Chance	3,500	1,750	1,050
(21)	Fred Clarke	2,500	875.00	525.00
(22)	Dick Cooley	1,000	500.00	300.00
(23)	Bill Dahlen	1,750	750.00	450.00
(24)	Tom Daly	1,000	500.00	300.00
(25)	Charlie Dexter	1,000	500.00	300.00
(26)	Johnny Dobbs	1,000	500.00	300.00
(27)	Mike Donlin	1,000	500.00	300.00
(28)	Patsy Donovan	1,000	500.00	300.00
(29)	Red Dooin	1,000	500.00	300.00
(30)	Klondike Douglas (Douglass)	1,000	500.00	300.00
(31)	Jack Doyle	1,000	500.00	300.00
(32)	Bill Duggleby	1,000	500.00	300.00
(33)	Jack Dunn	1,000	500.00	300.00
(34)	Johnny Evers	3,000	875.00	525.00
(35)	John Farrel (Farrell)	1,000	500.00	300.00
(36)	Tim Flood	1,000	500.00	300.00
(37)	Chick Fraser	1,000	500.00	300.00
(38)	Ned Garver	1,000	500.00	300.00
(39)	Doc Gessler	1,000	500.00	300.00
(40)	Billy Gilbert	1,000	500.00	300.00
(41)	Kid Gleason	2,500	750.00	450.00
(42)	Ed Greminger (Gremminger)	1,000	500.00	300.00
(43)	Jim Hackett	1,000	500.00	300.00
(44)	Noodles Hahn	1,000	500.00	300.00
(45)	Ed. Hanlon	2,500	875.00	525.00
(46)	Jack Harper	1,000	500.00	300.00
(47)	Rudy Hulswitt	1,000	500.00	300.00
(48)	Fred Jacklitsch	1,000	500.00	300.00
(49)	Davy Jones	1,000	500.00	300.00
(50)	Oscar Jones	1,000	500.00	300.00
(51)	Bill Keister	1,000	500.00	300.00
(52)	Joe Kelley	2,500	875.00	525.00
(53)	Brickyard Kennedy	1,000	500.00	300.00
(54)	Johnny Kling	1,000	500.00	300.00
(55)	Otto Kruger (Krueger)	1,000	500.00	300.00
(56)	Tommy Leach	1,000	500.00	300.00
(57)	Sam Leever	1,000	500.00	300.00
(58)	Bobby Lowe	1,750	875.00	525.00
(59)	Carl Lundgren	1,000	500.00	300.00
(60)	Christy Mathewson	8,500	4,200	2,500.
(61)	Tom McCreery	1,000	500.00	300.00
(62)	Chappie McFarland	1,000	500.00	300.00
(63)	Dan McGann	1,000	500.00	300.00
(64)	Iron Man McGinnity	2,500	875.00	525.00
(65)	John McGraw	2,500	875.00	525.00
(66)	Jock Menefee	1,000	500.00	300.00
(67)	Sam Mertes	1,000	500.00	300.00
(68)	Fred Mitchell	1,000	500.00	300.00
(69)	Pat Moran	1,000	500.00	300.00
(70)	Ed Murphy	1,000	500.00	300.00
(71)	Jack O'Neill	1,000	500.00	300.00
(72)	Mike O'Neill	1,000	500.00	300.00
(73)	Heinie Peitz	1,000	500.00	300.00
(74)	Ed Phelps	1,000	500.00	300.00
(75)	Deacon Phillippe	1,000	500.00	300.00
(76)	Togie Pittinger	1,000	500.00	300.00
(77)	Ed Poole	1,000	500.00	300.00
(78)	Tommy Raub	1,000	500.00	300.00
(79)	Bill Reidy	1,000	500.00	300.00
(80)	Claude Ritchie	1,000	500.00	300.00
(81)	Lew Ritter	1,000	500.00	300.00
(82)	Frank Roth	1,000	500.00	300.00
(83)	Jack Ryan	1,000	500.00	300.00
(84)	Jimmy Scheckard (Sheckard)	1,000	500.00	300.00
(85)	Jimmy Sebring	1,000	500.00	300.00
(86)	Frank Selee	7,500	2,000	1,200
(87)	Cy Seymour	1,000	500.00	300.00
(88)	Harry Smith	1,000	500.00	300.00
(89)	Homer Smoot	1,000	500.00	300.00
(90)	Tully Sparks	1,000	500.00	300.00
(91)	Joe Stanley	1,000	500.00	300.00
(92)	Harry Steinfeldt	1,000	500.00	300.00
(93)	Sammy Strang	1,000	500.00	300.00
(94)	Jack Suthoff (Sutthoff)	1,000	500.00	300.00
(95)	Jack Taylor	1,000	500.00	300.00
(96)	Luther Taylor	1,750	875.00	525.00
(97)	Roy Thomas	1,000	500.00	300.00
(98)	Joe Tinker	1,750	875.00	525.00
(99)	Fred Tinney (Tenney)	1,000	500.00	300.00
(100)	Honus Wagner	12,250	6,125	3,675
(101)	Jack Warner	1,000	500.00	300.00
(102)	Jake Weimer	1,000	500.00	300.00
(103)	Vic Willis	1,750	875.00	525.00
(104)	Harry Wolverton	1,000	500.00	300.00
(105)	Boston Ball Counter	165.00	80.00	50.00
(106)	Brooklyn Ball Counter	165.00	80.00	50.00
(107)	Chicago Ball Counter	165.00	80.00	50.00
(108)	Cincinnati Ball Counter	165.00	80.00	50.00
(109)	New York Ball Counter	165.00	80.00	50.00
(110)	Philadelpia Ball Counter	165.00	80.00	50.00
(111)	Pittsburgh Ball Counter	165.00	80.00	50.00
(112)	St. Louis Ball Counter	165.00	80.00	50.00

1888 Allen & Ginter World's Champions (N28)

CHARLES COMISKEY.
ALLEN & GINTER'S
RICHMOND — VIRGINIA.

This 50-card set was titled "The World Champions" and includes 10 baseball players and 40 other sports personalities such as John L. Sullivan and Buffalo Bill Cody. The approximately 1-1/2" x 2-3/4" cards were inserted in boxes of Allen & Ginter cigarettes. The card fronts are color lithographs on white card stock, and are considered among the most attractive cards ever produced. All card backs have a complete checklist for this unnumbered set, which includes six eventual Hall of Famers.

	NM	EX	VG
Complete Set (10):	16,750	8,250	5,500
Common Player:	850.00	425.00	250.00
(1) Adrian C. Anson	7,500	3,750	2,250
(2) Chas. W. Bennett	850.00	425.00	255.00
(3) R.L. Caruthers	850.00	425.00	255.00
(4) John Clarkson	2,500	925.00	550.00
(5) Charles Comiskey	2,750	1,375	825.00
(6) Capt. John Glasscock	850.00	425.00	255.00
(7) Timothy Keefe	2,500	875.00	500.00
(8) Mike Kelly	4,000	1,500	900.00
(9) Joseph Mulvey	850.00	425.00	255.00
(10) John Ward	2,500	875.00	500.00

1888 Allen & Ginter World's Champions Album (A16)

By redeeming 50 of the coupons found in boxes of A&G cigarettes, a lithographed album could be obtained in which to house the 50 cards of The World's Champions, Series 1 (N28). About 6" x 8", the album features an ornately decorated cover reproducing the cards of the day's top athletes, John L. Sullivan and Monte Ward. The back cover is blank. Inside, secured by means of string ties at three places, are 12 dual-sided color pages on which to glue the cards in the series. The album had its own designation in the American Card Catalog, A16.

	NM	EX	VG
World's Champions Album (A16)	4,000	2,000	1,200

1888 Allen & Ginter World's Champions (N29)

JAMES RYAN.
CENTRE FIELDER-CHICAGO.

Building on the success of its first series of tobacco cards, Allen & Ginter issued a second series of "World Champions" in 1888. Once again, 50 of these approximately 1-1/2" x 2-3/4" color cards were produced, in virtually the same format. Only six baseball players are included in this set. The most obvious difference from the first series cards is the absence of the Allen & Ginter name on the card fronts.

	NM	EX	VG
Complete Set (6):	9,350	4,675	2,750
Common Player:	900.00	400.00	300.00
(1) Wm. Ewing	3,000	1,100	850.00
(2) Jas. H. Fogarty	900.00	400.00	300.00
(Middle initial actually G.)			
(3) Charles H. Getzin (Getzien)	900.00	400.00	300.00
(4) Geo. F. Miller	900.00	400.00	300.00
(5) John Morrell (Morrill)	1,150	450.00	325.00
(6) James Ryan	900.00	400.00	300.00

1888 Allen & Ginter World's Champions Album (A17)

By redeeming 50 of the coupons found in boxes of A&G cigarettes, a lithographed album could be obtained in which to house the 50 cards of The World's Champions, Series 2 (N29). About 6" x 8", the album features a handsomely decorated cover of a trumpeter. The back cover is also in color with A&G's pipe-smoking man logo. Inside, secured by means of string ties at three places, are 12 dual-sided color pages on which to glue the cards in the series. The album had its own designation in the American Card Catalog, A16.

	NM	EX	VG
World's Champions Album (A17)	4,000	2,000	1,000

1888 Allen & Ginter World's Champions (N43)

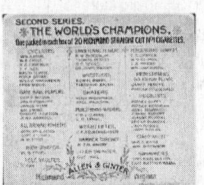

Presumably issued in a larger-than-standard cigarette package, the 50 cards designated N43 in the "American Card Catalog" are enhanced versions of the Allen & Ginter World's Champions (N29) series of 1888. As with the N29 set, six of the athletes in N43 are baseball players. The larger cards measure about 3-1/4" x 2-7/8" compared to the 1-1/2" x 2-3/4" size of the N29s. The larger format allows for the use of baseball-related color lithography to the right and left of the central player portrait. Like the N29 cards, backs of the N43 A&Gs present the entire "Series Two" checklist along with advertising of the Richmond tobacco company. Only the baseball players are cataloged here.

	NM	EX	VG
Complete Set (6):	26,400	14,000	7,700
Common Player:	3,850	1,500	1,000
(1) Wm. Ewing	8,500	3,825	2,375
(2) Jas. H. Fogarty	3,850	1,500	1,000
(Middle initial actually G.)			
(3) Charles H. Getzin (Getzien)	3,850	1,500	1,000
(4) Geo. F. Miller	3,850	1,500	1,000
(5) John Morrell (Morrill)	4,000	1,800	1,125
(6) James Ryan	3,850	1,500	1,000

1888 Allen & Ginter Girl Baseball Players (N48, N508)

At least three different brands of cigarette advertising can be found on the several different styles of photographic cards depicting women in baseball uniforms. About 1-1/2" x 2-5/8", the cards picture models, rather than real ballplayers. The sepia-toned full-length photos are usually captioned with a position and a number and have a small square or other device advertising a particular brand. Some Dixie- and Virginia Brights-brand cards are known with advertising on back but most cards are blank-backed. As many as 36 different photos are thought to exist.

	NM	EX	VG
Ad Backs: 2X			
Common Player	750.00	370.00	220.00

1946-1947 Almanaque Deportivo

Former and future Major Leaguers mix with Negro Leaguers and Caribbean stars in this issue. Apparently sold in sheets of four, well-cut examples of these cards measure a nominal 1-7/8" x 2-1/2" and are printed in color on thin paper. Player identification is on the back of the card, usually with career notes and a large advertisement from one of many different sponsors. A colorful album was issued to house the set. Like all Cuban cards of the era, specimens surviving in grades of VG or better are scarce.

	NM	EX	VG
Complete Set (160):	6,000	3,000	1,800
Common Player:	35.00	17.50	10.00
Album:	750.00	370.00	220.00
A-1 Adolfo Luque	60.00	30.00	20.00
A-2 Tomas de la Cruz	35.00	17.50	10.00
A-3 Roberto Ortiz	45.00	22.50	13.50
A-4 Evelio Martinez	35.00	17.50	10.00
A-5 Jess Jessup	90.00	45.00	27.50
A-6 Santos Amaro	35.00	17.50	10.00
A-7 Rene Gonzalez	35.00	17.50	10.00
A-8 Buck O'Neil	625.00	310.00	185.00
A-9 J. (Lefty) Gaines	90.00	45.00	27.50
A-10 Max Lanier	45.00	22.50	13.50
A-11 George Hausmann	35.00	17.50	10.00
A-12 Avelino Canizares	35.00	17.50	10.00
A-13 Calampio Leon	35.00	17.50	10.00
A-14 Conrado Marrero	50.00	25.00	15.00
A-15 Alberto Leal	35.00	17.50	10.00
A-16 Lloyd Davenport	90.00	45.00	27.50
A-17 Teodoro Oxamendi	35.00	17.50	10.00
A-18 Santiago Ulrich	35.00	17.50	10.00
A-19 Lazaro Salazar	100.00	50.00	30.00
A-20 Cheo Ramos	35.00	17.50	10.00
A-21 Jorge Comellas	35.00	17.50	10.00
A-22 Agapito Mayor	35.00	17.50	10.00
A-23 Hector Rodriguez	45.00	22.50	13.50
A-24 Joe Williams	35.00	17.50	10.00
A-25 Andres Fleitas	35.00	17.50	10.00
C-1 Martin Dihigo	500.00	250.00	150.00
C-2 Alejandro Carrasquel	35.00	17.50	10.00
C-3 Adrian Zabala	35.00	17.50	10.00
C-4 Jimmy Roy	35.00	17.50	10.00
C-5 Napoleon Reyes	80.00	40.00	25.00
C-6 Stanislas Bread	35.00	17.50	10.00
C-7 Roland Gladu	35.00	17.50	10.00
C-8 Roy Zimmerman	35.00	17.50	10.00
C-9 Max Manning	125.00	62.50	37.50
C-10 Myron Hayworth	35.00	17.50	10.00
C-11 Pedro Miro	35.00	17.50	10.00
C-12 Jose Luis Colas	35.00	17.50	10.00
C-13 Conrado Perez	35.00	17.50	10.00
C-14 Luis Tiant Sr.	45.00	22.50	13.50
C-15 Ramon Heredia	35.00	17.50	10.00
C-16 Vinicio Garcia	35.00	17.50	10.00
C-17 (Walt) Nothe	35.00	17.50	10.00
C-18 Danny Gardella	35.00	17.50	10.00
C-19 Alejandro Crespo	60.00	30.00	20.00
C-20 Ray Noble	35.00	17.50	10.00
C-21 Pedro Pages	35.00	17.50	10.00
F-1 Napoleon y C. Blanco/ Action	35.00	17.50	10.00
F-2 Chanquilon y H. Rodriguez/ Action	35.00	17.50	10.00
F-3 Estalella y Fleitas/Action	35.00	17.50	10.00
F-4 Castano y Kimbro/Action	35.00	17.50	10.00
H-1 Miguel Angel Gonzalez	55.00	27.50	16.50
H-2 Pedro (Natilla) Jimenez	35.00	17.50	10.00
H-3 Fred Martin	35.00	17.50	10.00
H-4 James Lamarque	80.00	40.00	25.00
H-5 Salvador Hernandez	35.00	17.50	10.00
H-6 S. (Hank) Thompson	50.00	25.00	15.00
H-7 Antonio Ordenana	35.00	17.50	10.00
H-8 Manuel Garcia	35.00	17.50	10.00
H-9 Alberto Hernandez	35.00	17.50	10.00
H-10 Terry McDuffie	45.00	22.50	13.50
H-11 Louis Frank Klein	35.00	17.50	10.00
H-12 Herberto Blanco	35.00	17.50	10.00
H-13 H.(Henry) Kimbro	150.00	75.00	45.00
H-14 Rene Monteagudo	35.00	17.50	10.00

H-15	Lennox Pearson	100.00	50.00	30.00
H-16	Carlos Blanco	35.00	17.50	10.00
H-17	Pedro Formental	55.00	27.50	16.50
H-18	William Bell	35.00	17.50	10.00
H-19	Raul Navarro	35.00	17.50	10.00
H-20	Lazaro Medina	35.00	17.50	10.00
L-1	Julio Moreno	35.00	17.50	10.00
L-2	Daniel Parra	35.00	17.50	10.00
L-3	Rogelio Martinez	35.00	17.50	10.00
L-4	J. Antonio Zardon	35.00	17.50	10.00
L-5	Julian Acosta	35.00	17.50	10.00
L-6	Orlando Suarez	35.00	17.50	10.00
L-7	Manuel Hidalgo	35.00	17.50	10.00
L-8	Fermin Guerra	35.00	17.50	10.00
L-9	Regino Otero	35.00	17.50	10.00
L-10	Jorge Juan Torres	35.00	17.50	10.00
L-11	Valeriano Fano	35.00	17.50	10.00
L-12	Amado Ibanez	35.00	17.50	10.00
L-13	"Atares" Garcia	35.00	17.50	10.00
L-14	Armando Gallart	35.00	17.50	10.00
L-15	Perdo Dunabeitia	35.00	17.50	10.00
L-16	Oscar del Calvo	35.00	17.50	10.00
L-17	Johnny Davis	100.00	50.00	30.00
L-18	Emilio Cabrera	35.00	17.50	10.00
L-19	Lee Holleman	35.00	17.50	10.00
L-20	Antonio Napoles	35.00	17.50	10.00
L-21	Pedro Diaz	35.00	17.50	10.00
L-22	Lazaro Bernal	35.00	17.50	10.00
L-23	Hector Arago	35.00	17.50	10.00
L-24	Oscar Garmendia	35.00	17.50	10.00
L-25	Barney Serrell	90.00	45.00	27.50
L-26	Armando Marsans	55.00	27.50	16.50
L-27	Mario Diaz	35.00	17.50	10.00
L-28	Raymond Dandridge	350.00	175.00	105.00
L-29	Leon Tredway	35.00	17.50	10.00
L-30	Orestes Perera	35.00	17.50	10.00
L-31	Armando Vazquez	35.00	17.50	10.00
L-32	Cleveland Clark	50.00	25.00	15.00
L-33	Johnny Williams	90.00	45.00	27.50
L-34	Clarence Iott	35.00	17.50	10.00
L-35	Gilberto Torres	35.00	17.50	10.00
L-36	George Brown	35.00	17.50	10.00
L-37	Wayne Johnson	35.00	17.50	10.00
L-38	Miguel Angel Carmona	35.00	17.50	10.00
L-39	Leovigildo Xiques	35.00	17.50	10.00
L-40	Rafael Rivas	35.00	17.50	10.00
L-41	Joaquin Gutierrez	35.00	17.50	10.00
L-42	Miguel Lastra	35.00	17.50	10.00
L-43	Francisco Quicutis	35.00	17.50	10.00
L-44	Silvio Garcia	90.00	45.00	27.50
L-45	Angel Fleitas	35.00	17.50	10.00
L-46	Eddy Chandler	35.00	17.50	10.00
L-47	Gilberto Castillo	35.00	17.50	10.00
L-48	Isidoro Leon	35.00	17.50	10.00
L-49	Antonio Rodriguez	35.00	17.50	10.00
L-50	Laniel Hooker	90.00	45.00	27.50
L-51	Charles Perez	35.00	17.50	10.00
L-52	Ruben Garcia	35.00	17.50	10.00
L-53	Raquel Antunez	35.00	17.50	10.00
L-54	Claro Duany	45.00	22.50	13.50
L-55	Bucker (Booker) McDaniels	90.00	45.00	27.50
L-56	Francisco Jimenez	35.00	17.50	10.00
L-57	Luis Minsal	35.00	17.50	10.00
L-58	Rogelio Linares	35.00	17.50	10.00
L-59	Isasio Gonzalez	35.00	17.50	10.00
L-60	Manolo Parrado	35.00	17.50	10.00
L-61	Jose Maria Fernandez	35.00	17.50	10.00
L-62	Rogelio Valdes	35.00	17.50	10.00
L-63	R. Franco	35.00	17.50	10.00
L-64	J. Cedan	35.00	17.50	10.00
L-65	Jacinto Roque	35.00	17.50	10.00
L-66	Pablo Garcia	35.00	17.50	10.00
M-1	Pipo de la Noval	35.00	17.50	10.00
M-2	J. Valenzuela	35.00	17.50	10.00
M-3	Oliverio Ortiz	35.00	17.50	10.00
M-4	Antonio Castanos	35.00	17.50	10.00
M-5	Sandalio Consuegra	45.00	22.50	13.50
M-6	(Jim) Lindsey	35.00	17.50	10.00
M-7	Roberto Estalella	35.00	17.50	10.00
M-8	Lino Donoso	35.00	17.50	10.00
M-9	Paul Calvert	35.00	17.50	10.00
M-10	Gilberto Valdivia	35.00	17.50	10.00
M-11	Orestes Minoso	125.00	65.00	37.50
M-12	J. Cabrera	35.00	17.50	10.00
M-13	Manuel Godinez	35.00	17.50	10.00
M-14	Frank Casanovas	35.00	17.50	10.00
M-15	Roberto Avila	60.00	30.00	20.00
M-16	Pedro Orta	35.00	17.50	10.00
M-17	Feliciano Castro	35.00	17.50	10.00
M-18	Mario Arencibia	35.00	17.50	10.00
M-19	Antonio Diaz	35.00	17.50	10.00
M-20	Aristonico Correoso	35.00	17.50	10.00
M-21	Angel Gonzalez	35.00	17.50	10.00
M-22	Murray Franklin	35.00	17.50	10.00
M-23	Francisco Campos	35.00	17.50	10.00
M-24	Angel Castro	35.00	17.50	10.00

1910 All-Star Base-Ball

This rare set was issued circa 1910 by candy maker J.H. Dockman & Son. The cards, measuring approximately 1-7/8" x 3-3/8", were printed on the front and back of boxes of candy sold as "All Star Base-Ball Package." There are two players on each box; one on front (with a thumbnail notch at top), the other on back. The cards consist of drawings that bear no resemblance to the player named. In fact, the artwork on these cards crudely reproduces the images from the T3 Turkey Red cabinet series, giving a different player's name to each of the borrowed images. Many are found which were cut from the box immediately below the "PACKAGE" line, while others were cut to the full size of the panel. Values shown here presume the latter format.

		NM	EX	VG
Complete Set (24):		50,000	25,000	12,500
Common Player:		2,000	1,200	600.00
(1)	Johnny Bates	2,000	1,200	600.00
(2)	Heinie Beckendorf	2,000	1,200	600.00
(3)	Joe Birmingham	2,000	1,200	600.00
(4)	Roger Bresnahan	4,000	2,500	1,200
(5)	Al Burch	2,000	1,200	600.00
(6)	Donie Bush	2,000	1,200	600.00
(7)	Frank Chance	4,000	2,500	1,200
(8)	Ty Cobb	10,000	5,000	3,000
(9)	Wid Conroy	2,000	1,200	600.00
(10)	Jack Coombs	2,000	1,200	600.00
(11)	George Gibson	2,000	1,200	600.00
(12)	Dick Hoblitzel	2,000	1,200	600.00
(13)	Johnny Kling	2,000	1,200	600.00
(14)	Frank LaPorte	2,000	1,200	600.00
(15)	Ed Lennox	2,000	1,200	600.00
(16)	Connie Mack	4,000	2,500	1,200
(17)	Christy Mathewson	4,500	2,750	1,500
(18)	Matty McIntyre	2,000	1,200	600.00
(19)	Al Schweitzer	2,000	1,200	600.00
(20)	Jimmy Sheckard	2,000	1,200	600.00
(21)	Bill Sweeney	2,000	1,200	600.00
(22)	Terry Turner	2,000	1,200	600.00
(23)	Hans Wagner	9,000	4,500	2,700
(24)	Harry Wolter	2,000	1,200	600.00

1950 All-Star Baseball "Pin-Ups"

This set of 10 7" diameter black-and-white player photos was issued in the form of a booklet, with the individual pictures perforated to be punched out. Each picture has a hole at the top for hanging. The front and back cover of the book are identical and picture Ted Williams, along with a list of the players inside. Backs of each player picture have how-to tips for playing a specific position, hitting, base stealing, etc. Published by Garden City Publishing Co., Inc., the book carried a cover price of 50 cents. The unnumbered pictures are checklisted here alphabetically.

		NM	EX	VG
Complete Book:		1,250	625.00	375.00
Complete Set, Singles (10):		800.00	400.00	240.00
Common Player:		25.00	12.50	7.50
(1)	Joe DiMaggio	200.00	100.00	60.00
(2)	Jim Hegan	25.00	12.50	7.50
(3)	Gil Hodges	75.00	37.50	22.50
(4)	George Kell	35.00	17.50	10.00
(5)	Ralph Kiner	45.00	22.50	13.50
(6)	Stan Musial	100.00	50.00	30.00
(7)	Mel Parnell	25.00	12.50	7.50
(8)	Phil Rizzuto	75.00	37.50	22.50
(9)	Jackie Robinson	150.00	75.00	45.00
(10)	Ted Williams	150.00	75.00	45.00

1954 All-Star Photo Pack

The complete checklist for this series of 6" x 8-3/4" blank-back, black-and-white player photos is unknown. The method of distribution is also speculative, though it is most likely they were sold in photo packs at concession stands. Photos, mostly posed action shots, are bordered in white and have the player name in a white strip near the bottom.

		NM	EX	VG
Complete Set (24):		400.00	200.00	120.00
Common Player:		10.00	5.00	3.00
(1)	Bobby Avila	10.00	5.00	3.00
(2)	Ernie Banks	25.00	12.50	7.50
(3)	Larry "Yogi" Berra	25.00	12.50	7.50
(4)	Ray Boone	10.00	5.00	3.00
(5)	Roy Campanella	25.00	12.50	7.50
(6)	Alvin Dark	10.00	5.00	3.00
(7)	Mike Garcia	10.00	5.00	3.00
(8)	Al Kaline	20.00	10.00	6.00
(9)	Ralph Kiner	15.00	7.50	4.50
(10)	Ted Kluszewski	15.00	7.50	4.50
(11)	Harvey Kuenn	10.00	5.00	3.00
(12)	Mickey Mantle	90.00	45.00	27.50
(13)	Ed Mathews	20.00	10.00	6.00
(14)	Willie Mays	50.00	25.00	15.00
(15)	Orestes Minoso	12.50	6.25	3.75
(16)	Stan Musial	35.00	17.50	10.00
(17)	Don Newcombe	12.50	6.25	3.75
(18)	Allie Reynolds	12.50	6.25	3.75
(19)	Robin Roberts	15.00	7.50	4.50
(20)	Eddie Robinson	10.00	5.00	3.00
(21)	Jackie Robinson	45.00	22.50	13.50
(22)	Al Schoendienst	15.00	7.50	4.50
(23)	Duke Snider	20.00	10.00	6.00
(24)	Ted Williams	80.00	40.00	24.00

1949 All-Stars Photo Pack

This set of "American and National League All Stars" player pictures is comprised of 6-1/4" x 9" black-and-white photos bordered in white with a simulated signature printed on front. Backs are blank. The set came in a red, black and white paper envelope with several of the pictures shown on front and red stars for decoration. The unnumbered pictures are listed here alphabetically.

		NM	EX	VG
Complete Set (20):		375.00	185.00	110.00
Common Player:		12.50	6.00	4.00
(1)	Luke Appling	17.50	9.00	5.00
(2)	Lou Boudreau	17.50	9.00	5.00
(3)	Dom DiMaggio	15.00	7.50	4.50
(4)	Joe DiMaggio	60.00	30.00	18.00
(5)	Bobby Doerr	17.50	9.00	5.00
(6)	Bob Feller	25.00	12.50	7.50
(7)	Joe Gordon	12.50	6.00	4.00
(8)	Tommy Henrich	12.50	6.00	4.00
(9)	George Kell	17.50	9.00	5.00
(10)	Ralph Kiner	17.50	9.00	5.00
(11)	Bob Lemon	17.50	9.00	5.00
(12)	Marty Marion	12.50	6.00	4.00
(13)	Stan Musial	35.00	17.50	10.00
(14)	Don Newcomb (Newcombe)	17.50	9.00	5.00
(15)	Pee Wee Reese	25.00	12.50	7.50
(16)	Phil Rizzuto	25.00	12.50	7.50
(17)	Jackie Robinson	45.00	22.50	13.50
(18)	Enos Slaughter	17.50	9.00	5.00
(19)	Vern Stephens	12.50	6.00	4.00
(20)	Ted Williams	45.00	22.50	13.50

1971 Allstate Insurance

This four-card series was distributed as part of an internal sales promotion for Allstate Insurance. Graphic artist Ray Lending, an Allstate employee, created the 2-1/2" x 3-1/4" cards in duo-tone black and green on white. Card fronts show the players in batting stance, with the player name in one of the upper corners and the "Hall of Fame Series" logo printed across the bottom of the card. The card backs carry the player's full name and position, followed by a brief career summary, biography, and Career Highlights chart listing major league totals. "1971 Charger" and "Hall of Fame Series" are printed at the bottom of the card back. 8,000 sets were distributed.

		NM	EX	VG
Complete Set (4):		400.00	200.00	120.00
Common Player:		50.00	25.00	15.00
(1)	Ty Cobb	50.00	25.00	15.00
(2)	Stan Musial	50.00	25.00	15.00
(3)	Babe Ruth	200.00	100.00	60.00
(4)	Ted Williams	150.00	75.00	45.00

1894 Alpha Photo-Engraving Baltimore Orioles

The rarest baseball card set of the 1890s (each card is known in only a single example) is the Baltimore Orioles team set issued by The Alpha Photo-Engraving Co. of that city. The round-corner 2-3/8" x 3-7/16" cards feature black-and-white photos of the National League champions in formalwear. Last-name identification is in a strip below the photo and a white border surrounds both. On the red-and-white backs a large ad for the producer is at center, while small baseball batter figures are in each corner surrounded by a leafy background. The unnumbered cards are checklisted here alphabetically, though the list may not be complete; one glaring omission is Hall of Fame outfielder Willie Keeler. In early 2006 the set was sold and broken up. Each card was authenticated and graded by SGC, with grades ranging from Fair to Very Good.

		NM	EX	VG
Common Player:				7,500
(1)	Frank Bonner			7,500
(2)	Steve Brodie			7,500
(3)	Dan Brouthers			37,500
(4)	Duke Esper			7,500
(5)	Kid Gleason			7,500
(6)	Ned Hanlon			32,500
(7)	Bill Hawke			7,500
(8)	George Hemming			7,500
(9)	Hughie Jennings			32,500
(10)	Joe Kelley			62,500
(11)	John McGraw			62,500
(12)	Sadie McMahon			7,500
(13)	Heinie Reitz			7,500
(14)	Wilbert Robinson			32,500

1916 Altoona Tribune

This Pennsylvania daily newspaper was one of several regional advertisers to use this black-and-white, 1-5/8" x 3" 200-card set for promotional purposes. The Altoona issue shares the checklist of the 1916 M101-4 Blank Backs. Type card and superstar collectors will pay a significant premium for a Tribune version of a specific card.

PREMIUM:
Common Player: 4-6X
Hall of Famer: 2-4X
    (See 1916 M101-4 Blank Backs for checklist and base card values.)

1948 American Association Babe Ruth

According to the credit line at bottom back (a version of the card is known without the credit line), this card was produced by the Midwestern AAA minor league known as the American Association. Recent discoveries also indicate that

this card was probably both produced and issued by Pacific Coast Publishing Co. about a month after Ruth's death. The black and white card measures 4" x 5-11/16".

	NM	EX	VG
Babe Ruth	200.00	100.00	60.00

1909-11 American Beauty Cigarettes

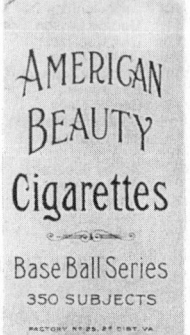

Two versions of the American Beauty Cigarettes advertising on the backs of T206 can be found; with and without a decorative border surrounding the typography, which is printed in green. All "350 Subjects" American Beauty cards originated from Factory No. 25 in Virginia. Because of the size of the original cigarette packaging in which they were a premium insert, American Beauty T206s may be a bit narrower than the standard 1-7/16". While the "350 Subjects" series is designated here as a 1910 issue, it is possible some cards were actually issued in 1909 or 1911. Among T205, AB backs may be found printed in either black or green, the latter somewhat scarcer.

PREMIUM:
T205: 2X
T206 350 Series: 1.5-2X
T206 460 Series: 2-2.5X
    (See T205, T206 for checklists and base card values. Note: Cards with American Beauty backs may be somewhat narrower than standard 1-7/16" due to smaller original cigarette packaging.)

1908 American Caramel (E91, Set A)

Issued by Philadelphia's American Caramel Co., 1908-1910, the E91 set of Base Ball Caramels has limited popularity with collectors because many of the color drawings show "generic" players rather than the named major leaguers; the same artwork was used to depict two or three different players. The player's name, position and team appear in the white border at bottom. The cards measure approximately 1-1/2" x 2-3/4" and were issued in three separate series. They can be differentiated by their backs, which checklist the cards. Set A lists the Athletics in the upper-left, the Giants at upper-right and the Cubs below. Set B lists the Cubs and Athletics on top with the Giants below, and Set C list Pittsburg and Washington on top with Boston below. A line indicating the cards were "Manufactured Only by the American Caramel Co." appears at the bottom.

	NM	EX	VG
Complete Set (33):	10,000	4,000	2,500
Common Player:	200.00	75.00	40.00

		NM	EX	VG
(1)	Charles Bender	425.00	175.00	100.00
(2)	Roger Bresnahan	600.00	300.00	180.00
(3)	Albert Bridwell	200.00	75.00	45.00
(4)	Mordecai Brown	425.00	175.00	100.00
(5)	Frank Chance	425.00	175.00	100.00
(6)	James Collins	425.00	175.00	100.00
(7)	Harry Davis	200.00	75.00	40.00
(8)	Arthur Devlin	200.00	75.00	40.00
(9)	Michael Donlin	200.00	75.00	40.00
(10)	John Evers	425.00	175.00	100.00
(11)	Frederick L. Hartsel	200.00	75.00	40.00
(12)	John Kling	200.00	75.00	40.00
(13)	Christopher Matthewson (Mathewson)	1,750	785.00	435.00
(14)	Joseph McGinnity	425.00	175.00	100.00
(15)	John J. McGraw	425.00	175.00	100.00
(16)	Daniel F. Murphy	200.00	75.00	40.00
(17)	Simon Nicholls	200.00	75.00	40.00
(18)	Reuben Oldring	200.00	75.00	40.00
(19)	Orvill Overall (Orval)	200.00	75.00	40.00
(20)	Edward S. Plank	900.00	450.00	270.00
(21)	Edward Reulbach	200.00	75.00	40.00
(22)	James Scheckard (Sheckard)	200.00	75.00	40.00
(23)	Osee Schreckengost (Ossee)	200.00	75.00	40.00
(24)	Ralph O. Seybold	200.00	75.00	40.00
(25)	J. Bentley Seymour	200.00	75.00	40.00
(26)	Daniel Shay	200.00	75.00	40.00
(27)	Frank Shulte (Schulte)	200.00	75.00	40.00
(28)	James Slagle	200.00	75.00	40.00
(29)	Harry Steinfeldt	200.00	75.00	40.00
(30)	Luther H. Taylor	400.00	160.00	100.00
(31)	Fred Tenney	200.00	75.00	40.00
(32)	Joseph B. Tinker	425.00	175.00	100.00
(33)	George Edward Waddell	425.00	175.00	100.00

1909 American Caramel (E91, Set B)

		NM	EX	VG
Complete Set (33):		9,500	4,000	2,400
Common Player:		200.00	75.00	40.00
(1)	James Archer	200.00	75.00	40.00
(2)	Frank Baker	425.00	175.00	100.00
(3)	John Barry	200.00	75.00	40.00
(4)	Charles Bender	425.00	175.00	100.00
(5)	Albert Bridwell	200.00	75.00	40.00
(6)	Mordecai Brown	425.00	175.00	100.00
(7)	Frank Chance	425.00	175.00	100.00
(8)	Edw. Collins	425.00	175.00	100.00
(9)	Harry Davis	200.00	75.00	40.00
(10)	Arthur Devlin	200.00	75.00	40.00
(11)	Michael Donlin	200.00	75.00	40.00
(12)	Larry Doyle	200.00	75.00	40.00
(13)	John Evers	425.00	175.00	100.00
(14)	Robt. Ganley	200.00	75.00	40.00
(15)	Frederick L. Hartsel	200.00	75.00	40.00
(16)	Arthur Hoffman (Hofman)	200.00	75.00	40.00
(17)	Harry Krause	200.00	75.00	40.00
(18)	Rich. W. Marquard	425.00	175.00	100.00
(19)	Christopher Matthewson (Mathewson)	1,350	675.00	405.00
(20)	John J. McGraw	425.00	175.00	100.00
(21)	J.T. Meyers	200.00	75.00	40.00
(22)	Dan Murphy	200.00	75.00	40.00
(23)	Jno. J. Murray	200.00	75.00	40.00
(24)	Orvill Overall (Orval)	200.00	75.00	40.00
(25)	Edward S. Plank	900.00	450.00	270.00
(26)	Edward Reulbach	200.00	75.00	40.00
(27)	James Scheckard (Sheckard)	200.00	75.00	40.00
(28)	J. Bentley Seymour	200.00	75.00	40.00
(29)	Harry Steinfeldt	200.00	75.00	40.00
(30)	Frank Shulte (Schulte)	200.00	75.00	40.00
(31)	Fred Tenney	200.00	75.00	40.00
(32)	Joseph B Tinker	425.00	175.00	100.00
(33)	Ira Thomas	200.00	75.00	40.00

1910 American Caramel (E91, Set C)

	NM	EX	VG
Complete Set (33):	11,000	4,400	2,850
Common Player:	200.00	75.00	40.00
(1) W.J. Barbeau	200.00	75.00	40.00
(2) Geo. Browne	200.00	75.00	40.00
(3) Robt. Chech (Charles)	200.00	75.00	40.00
(4) Fred Clarke	425.00	175.00	100.00
(5) Wid Conroy	200.00	75.00	40.00
(6) James Delehanty (Delahanty)	200.00	75.00	40.00
(7) Jon A. Donohue (Donahue)	200.00	75.00	40.00
(8) P. Donahue	200.00	75.00	40.00
(9) Geo. Gibson	200.00	75.00	40.00
(10) Robt. Groom	200.00	75.00	40.00
(11) Harry Hooper	425.00	175.00	100.00
(12) Tom Hughes	200.00	75.00	40.00
(13) Walter Johnson	1,150	575.00	345.00
(14) Edwin Karger	200.00	75.00	40.00
(15) Tommy Leach	200.00	75.00	40.00
(16) Sam'l Leever	200.00	75.00	40.00
(17) Harry Lord	200.00	75.00	40.00
(18) Geo. F. McBride	200.00	75.00	40.00
(19) Ambr. McConnell	200.00	75.00	40.00
(20) Clyde Milan	200.00	75.00	40.00
(21) J.B. Miller	200.00	75.00	40.00
(22) Harry Niles	200.00	75.00	40.00
(23) Chas. Phillipi (Phillippe)	200.00	75.00	40.00
(24) T.H. Speaker	650.00	275.00	125.00
(25) Jacob Stahl	200.00	75.00	40.00
(26) Chas. E. Street	200.00	75.00	40.00
(27) Allen Storke	200.00	75.00	40.00
(28) Robt. Unglaub	200.00	75.00	40.00
(29) C. Wagner	200.00	75.00	40.00
(30) Hans Wagner	3,500	1,750	1,050
(31) Victor Willis	425.00	175.00	100.00
(32) Owen Wilson	200.00	75.00	40.00
(33) Jos. Wood	200.00	75.00	75.00

1909-11 American Caramel (E90-1)

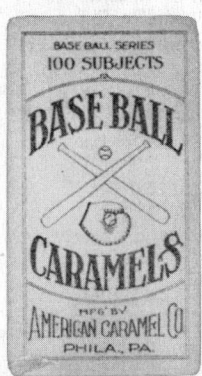

Davis, 1b Phila. Amer.

The E90-1 set was issued by the American Caramel Co. from 1909 through 1911, with the bulk of the set being produced in the first year. The cards, which nominally measure 1-1/2" x 2-3/4" (with the usual tolerances for original cutting variations), were issued with sticks of caramel candy. They are color renderings of photographs. Backs state that 100 subjects are included in the set though more actually do exist. There are several levels of scarcity in the set, those levels being mostly determined by the year the cards were issued. For the reader's convenience, the players' first names have been added in the checklist that follows. The complete set price includes all variations.

	NM	EX	VG
Complete Set (120):	225,000	112,500	67,500
Common Player:	400.00	125.00	40.00
(1) Bill Bailey	400.00	125.00	40.00
(2) Home Run Baker	1,500	350.00	125.00
(3) Jack Barry	600.00	200.00	60.00
(4) George Bell	500.00	175.00	60.00
(5) Harry Bemis	1,000	350.00	150.00
(6) Chief Bender	1,500	350.00	125.00
(7) Bob Bescher	1,000	350.00	150.00
(8) Cliff Blankenship	500.00	175.00	60.00
(9) John Bliss	500.00	175.00	60.00
(10) Bill Bradley	400.00	125.00	40.00
(11) Kitty Bransfield ("P" on shirt.)	900.00	450.00	270.00
(12) Kitty Bransfield (No "P.")	1,950	975.00	585.00
(13) Roger Bresnahan	1,500	350.00	125.00
(14) Al Bridwell	400.00	125.00	40.00
(15) Buster Brown (Boston)	2,000	500.00	200.00
(16) Mordecai Brown (Chicago)	800.00	250.00	80.00
(17) Donie Bush	400.00	125.00	40.00
(18) John Butler	500.00	175.00	60.00
(19) Howie Camnitz	500.00	175.00	60.00
(20) Frank Chance	1,500	350.00	125.00
(21) Hal Chase	1,000	200.00	90.00
(22) Fred Clarke (Philadelphia)	1,950	975.00	585.00
(23) Fred Clarke (Pittsburgh)	5,000	1,250	500.00
(24) Wally Clement	1,000	350.00	150.00
(25) "Ty" Cobb	12,500	6,250	3,750
(26) Eddie Collins	2,000	1,000	600.00
(27) Frank Corridon	400.00	125.00	40.00
(28) Sam Crawford	1,500	350.00	125.00
(29) Lou Criger	400.00	125.00	40.00
(30) George Davis	2,500	700.00	350.00
(31) Harry Davis	400.00	125.00	40.00
(32) Ray Demmitt	800.00	250.00	80.00
(33) Mike Donlin	600.00	200.00	70.00
(34) Wild Bill Donovan	500.00	175.00	60.00
(35) Red Dooin	400.00	125.00	40.00
(36) Patsy Dougherty	1,000	350.00	150.00
(37) Hugh Duffy	5,000	1,250	500.00

(38) Jimmy Dygert	400.00	125.00	40.00
(39) Rube Ellis	400.00	125.00	40.00
(40) Clyde Engle	500.00	175.00	60.00
(41) Art Fromme	800.00	250.00	80.00
(42) George Gibson (Back view.)	1,000	350.00	150.00
(43) George Gibson (Front view.)	600.00	200.00	70.00
(44) Peaches Graham	6,000	2,750	1,550
(45) Eddie Grant	600.00	200.00	70.00
(46) Dolly Gray	600.00	200.00	70.00
(47) Bob Groom	400.00	125.00	40.00
(48) Charley Hall	1,750	805.00	455.00
(49) Roy Hartzell/Fldg	400.00	125.00	40.00
(50) Roy Hartzell/Btg	600.00	200.00	70.00
(51) Heinie Heitmuller	400.00	125.00	40.00
(52) Harry Howell (Follow-through.)	400.00	125.00	40.00
(53) Harry Howell (Wind-up.)	800.00	250.00	80.00
(54) Tex Irwin (Erwin)	600.00	200.00	70.00
(55) Frank Isbell	400.00	125.00	40.00
(56) Joe Jackson	80,000	35,000	21,000
(57) Hughie Jennings	1,150	575.00	345.00
(58) Buck Jordon (Jordan)	400.00	125.00	40.00
(59) Addie Joss/Portrait	1,500	690.00	125.00
(60) Addie Joss/Pitching	6,000	2,750	1,550
(61) Ed Karger	1,500	500.00	200.00
(62) Willie Keeler/Portrait (Pink background.)	1,200	550.00	310.00
(63) Willie Keeler/Portait (Red background.)	5,000	1,250	500.00
(64) Willie Keeler/Throwing	4,000	1,000	400.00
(65) John Knight	600.00	200.00	70.00
(66) Harry Krause	400.00	125.00	40.00
(67) Nap Lajoie	2,500	700.00	300.00
(68) Tommy Leach/Throwing	1,000	350.00	150.00
(69) Tommy Leach/Btg	600.00	200.00	70.00
(70) Sam Leever	600.00	200.00	70.00
(71) Hans Lobert	1,500	500.00	200.00
(72) Harry Lumley	400.00	125.00	40.00
(73) Rube Marquard	1,500	400.00	150.00
(74) Christy Matthewson (Mathewson)	7,500	2,500	1,200
(75) Stuffy McInnes (McInnis)	400.00	125.00	40.00
(76) Harry McIntyre	400.00	125.00	40.00
(77) Larry McLean	1,000	350.00	150.00
(78) George McQuillan	400.00	125.00	40.00
(79) Dots Miller	500.00	175.00	60.00
(80) Fred Mitchell (New York)	400.00	125.00	40.00
(81) Mike Mitchell (Cincinnati)	16,500	7,600	4,300
(82) George Mullin	400.00	125.00	40.00
(83) Rebel Oakes	800.00	250.00	80.00
(84) Paddy O'Connor	800.00	250.00	80.00
(85) Charley O'Leary	400.00	125.00	40.00
(86) Orval Overall	800.00	250.00	80.00
(87) Jim Pastorius	400.00	125.00	40.00
(88) Ed Phelps	400.00	125.00	40.00
(89) Eddie Plank	2,000	920.00	520.00
(90) Lew Richie	600.00	200.00	70.00
(91) Germany Schaefer	500.00	175.00	60.00
(92) Biff Schlitzer	800.00	250.00	80.00
(93) Johnny Seigle (Siegle)	1,500	500.00	200.00
(94) Dave Shean	1,500	500.00	200.00
(95) Jimmy Sheckard	600.00	200.00	70.00
(96) Tris Speaker	10,000	2,000	800.00
(97) Jake Stahl	6,000	2,750	1,550
(98) Oscar Stanage	400.00	125.00	40.00
(99) George Stone (No hands visible.)	400.00	125.00	40.00
(100) George Stone (Left hand visible.)	600.00	200.00	70.00
(101) George Stovall	500.00	175.00	60.00
(102) Ed Summers	1,500	690.00	390.00
(103) Bill Sweeney (Boston)	5,000	1,200	700.00
(104) Jeff Sweeney (New York)	400.00	125.00	40.00
(105) Jesse Tannehill (Chicago A.L.)	400.00	125.00	40.00
(106) Lee Tannehill (Chicago N.L.)	400.00	125.00	40.00
(107) Fred Tenney	800.00	250.00	80.00
(108) Ira Thomas (Philadelphia)	400.00	125.00	40.00
(109) Roy Thomas (Boston)	400.00	125.00	40.00
(110) Joe Tinker	1,100	505.00	285.00
(111) Bob Unglaub	400.00	125.00	40.00
(112) Jerry Upp	1,500	500.00	200.00
(113) Honus Wagner/Btg	10,000	4,000	2,000
(114) Honus Wagner/Throwing	15,000	7,500	3,000
(115) Bobby Wallace	1,500	350.00	125.00
(116) Ed Walsh	10,000	2,000	800.00
(117) Vic Willis	1,500	400.00	150.00
(118) Hooks Wiltse	600.00	200.00	70.00
(119) Cy Young (Cleveland)	8,000	2,000	800.00
(120) Cy Young (Boston)	9,000	4,500	2,700

1910 American Caramel Pirates (E90-2)

WAGNER, PITTSBURG

Closely related to the E90-1 American Caramel set, the E90-2 set consists of 11 cards featuring members of the 1909 champion Pittsburgh Pirates. The cards measure a nominal 1-1/2" x 2-5/8", though tolerances must be allowed for original

cutting variations common to the era. They display a color lithograph on front set upon a solid color background of either red, green blue or pink. The player's name and "Pittsburg" appear in blue capital letters in the border beneath the portrait. The backs are identical to those in the E90-1 set, depicting a drawing of a ball, glove and crossed bats with the words "Base Ball Caramels" and a reference to "100 Subjects." The set includes Hall of Famers Honus Wagner and Fred Clarke.

	NM	EX	VG
Complete Set (11):	35,000	17,500	10,050
Common Player:	1,200	550.00	250.00
(1) Babe Adams	1,200	550.00	250.00
(2) Fred Clarke	2,750	1,350	825.00
(3) George Gibson	1,200	550.00	250.00
(4) Ham Hyatt	1,200	550.00	250.00
(5) Tommy Leach	1,200	550.00	250.00
(6) Sam Leever	1,200	550.00	250.00
(7) Nick Maddox	1,200	550.00	250.00
(8) Dots Miller	1,200	550.00	250.00
(9) Deacon Phillippe	1,200	550.00	250.00
(10) Honus Wagner	22,500	11,250	6,750
(11) Owen Wilson	1,200	550.00	250.00

1910 American Caramel White Sox/Cubs (E90-3)

Gandil, 1. b. White Sox

Similar in size (nominally 1-1/2" x 2-3/4", but with the usual tolerances for cutting variations on cards of the era) and style to the more popular E90-1 set, the E90-3 set was issued by the American Caramel Co. in 1910. The 20-card, color lithograph set includes 11 Chicago Cubs and nine White Sox. The fronts of the cards have a similar design to the E90-1 set, although different pictures were used. The backs can be differentiated by two major changes: The bottom of the card indicates the American Caramel Co. of "Chicago," rather than Philadelphia, and the top of the card contains the phrase "All The Star Players," rather than "100 Subjects."

	NM	EX	VG
Complete Set (20):	30,000	13,500	6,750
Common Player:	1,700	850.00	425.00
(1) Jimmy Archer	1,700	850.00	350.00
(2) Lena Blackburne	1,700	850.00	350.00
(3) Mordecai Brown	3,000	1,500	550.00
(4) Frank Chance	3,000	1,500	550.00
(5) King Cole	1,700	850.00	350.00
(6) Patsy Dougherty	1,700	850.00	350.00
(7) Johnny Evers	3,000	1,500	550.00
(8) Chick Gandil	4,500	2,250	900.00
(9) Ed Hahn	1,700	850.00	425.00
(10a) Solly Hofman	1,700	850.00	350.00
(10b) Solly Hofman (Broken "m" in last name gives appearance of "Hofnlan.")	3,600	1,750	900.00
(11) Orval Overall	1,700	850.00	350.00
(12) Fred Payne	1,700	850.00	425.00
(13) Billy Purtell	1,700	850.00	350.00
(14) Wildfire Schulte	1,700	850.00	350.00
(15) Jimmy Sheckard	1,700	850.00	350.00
(16) Frank Smith	1,700	850.00	350.00
(17) Harry Steinfeldt	1,700	850.00	350.00
(18a) Joe Tinker (Blue background.)	3,000	1,500	550.00
(18b) Joe Tinker (Green background.)	3,000	1,500	550.00
(19) Ed Walsh	3,000	1,500	550.00
(20) Rollie Zeider	1,700	850.00	350.00

1910 American Caramel Die-Cuts (E125)

Issued circa 1910 by the American Caramel Co., this set of die-cut cards is so rare that it wasn't even known to exist until the late 1960s. Apparently inserted in boxes of caramels, these cards, which are die-cut figures of baseball players, vary in size but are all relatively large - some measuring 7" high and 4" wide. Players from the Athletics, Red Sox, Giants and Pirates are known with a team checklist appearing on the back.

		NM	EX	VG
Common Player:		2,600	1,300	780.00
(1)	Babe Adams (Arms at sides.)	2,600	1,300	780.00
(2)	Red Ames/Throwing	2,600	1,300	780.00
(3)	Home Run Baker	5,000	2,250	1,500
(4)	Jack Barry/Fldg	2,600	1,300	780.00
(5)	Chief Bender	5,625	2,530	1,690
(6)	Al Bridwell/Fldg	2,600	1,300	780.00
(7)	Bobby Byrne/Throwing	2,600	1,300	780.00
(8)	Bill Carrigan/Catching	2,600	1,300	780.00
(9)	Ed Cicotte/Throwing	2,600	1,300	780.00
(10)	Fred Clark (Clarke)/Fldg	5,000	2,250	1,500
(11)	Eddie Collins	5,000	2,250	1,500
(12)	Harry Davis/Fldg	2,600	1,300	780.00
(13)	Art Devlin/Fldg	2,600	1,300	780.00
(14)	Josh Devore	2,600	1,300	780.00
(15)	Larry Doyle/Throwing	2,600	1,300	780.00
(16)	John Flynn/Running	2,600	1,300	780.00
(17)	George Gibson (Hands in glove.)	2,600	1,300	780.00
(18)	Topsy Hartzell (Hartsel)/Fldg	2,600	1,300	780.00
(19)	Harry Hooper/Throwing	5,000	2,250	1,500
(20)	Harry Krause	2,600	1,300	780.00
(21)	Tommy Leach/Fldg	2,600	1,300	780.00
(22)	Harry Lord/Throwing	2,600	1,300	780.00
(23)	Christy Mathewson (Wind-up.)	18,750	8,440	5,625
(24)	Amby McConnell/Fldg	2,600	1,300	780.00
(25)	Fred Merkle	2,600	1,300	780.00
(26)	Dots Miller/Throwing	2,600	1,300	780.00
(27)	Danny Murphy	2,600	1,300	780.00
(28)	Red Murray/Fldg	2,600	1,300	780.00
(29)	Harry Niles/Fldg	2,600	1,300	780.00
(30)	Rube Oldring	2,600	1,300	780.00
(31)	Eddie Plank/Throwing	18,750	8,440	5,625
(32)	Cy Seymour/Fldg	2,600	1,300	780.00
(33)	Tris Speaker/Btg	11,250	5,065	3,375
(34)	Tris Speaker/Fldg	11,250	5,065	3,375
(35)	Jake Stahl/Fldg	2,600	1,300	780.00
(36)	Ira Thomas	2,600	1,300	780.00
(37)	Heinie Wagner/Throwing	2,600	1,300	780.00
(38)	Honus Wagner/Btg	25,000	11,250	7,500
(39)	Honus Wagner/Throwing	25,000	11,250	7,500
(40)	Art Wilson	2,600	1,300	780.00
(41)	Owen Wilson/Throwing	2,600	1,300	780.00
(42)	Hooks Wiltse/Throwing	2,600	1,300	780.00

1915 American Caramel (E106)

This 48-card set, designated E106 by the American Card Catalog, was produced by the American Caramel Co., of York, Pa., in 1915 and includes players from the National, American and Federal Leagues. Cards measure 1-1/2" x 2-3/4". The set is related to the E90-1 and E92 sets, from which the artwork is taken, but this issue has a glossy coating on front, which makes the cards very susceptible to cracking.

Chase, 1b. Buffalo Feds

This card is one of a set of forty-eight leading Baseball Players in the National, American and Federal Leagues. One card is given with every piece of Baseball Caramel manufactured by the AMERICAN CARAMEL CO. YORK PA UNDER THE FAMOUS BRAND OF THE P. C. W.

		NM	EX	VG
Complete Set (48):		40,000	20,000	12,500
Common Player:		700.00	350.00	200.00
(1)	Jack Barry	700.00	350.00	200.00
(2)	Chief Bender (White hat.)	1,300	650.00	400.00
(3)	Chief Bender (Striped hat.)	1,300	650.00	400.00
(4)	Bob Bescher	700.00	350.00	200.00
(5)	Roger Bresnahan	1,300	650.00	400.00
(6)	Al Bridwell	700.00	350.00	200.00
(7)	Donie Bush	700.00	350.00	200.00
(8)	Hal Chase/Portrait	700.00	350.00	200.00
(9)	Hal Chase/Catching	700.00	350.00	200.00
(10)	Ty Cobb (W/bat, facing front.)	9,000	4,500	2,700
(11)	Ty Cobb/Btg (Facing to side.)	8,500	4,250	2,250
(12)	Eddie Collins	1,300	650.00	400.00
(13)	Sam Crawford	1,300	650.00	400.00
(14)	Ray Demmitt	700.00	350.00	200.00
(15)	Wild Bill Donovan	700.00	350.00	200.00
(16)	Red Dooin	700.00	350.00	200.00
(17)	Mickey Doolan	700.00	350.00	200.00
(18)	Larry Doyle	700.00	350.00	200.00
(19)	Clyde Engle	700.00	350.00	200.00
(20)	Johnny Evers	1,300	650.00	400.00
(21)	Art Fromme	700.00	350.00	200.00
(22)	George Gibson/Catching (Back view.)	700.00	350.00	200.00
(23)	George Gibson/Catching (Front view.)	700.00	350.00	200.00
(24)	Roy Hartzell	700.00	350.00	200.00

		NM	EX	VG
(25)	Fred Jacklitsch	700.00	350.00	200.00
(26)	Hugh Jennings	1,300	650.00	400.00
(27)	Otto Knabe	700.00	350.00	200.00
(28)	Nap Lajoie	1,300	650.00	400.00
(29)	Hans Lobert	700.00	350.00	200.00
(30)	Rube Marquard	1,300	650.00	400.00
(31)	Christy Matthewson (Mathewson)	6,000	3,000	1,800
(32)	John McGraw	1,300	650.00	400.00
(33)	George McQuillan	700.00	350.00	200.00
(34)	Dots Miller	700.00	350.00	200.00
(35)	Danny Murphy	700.00	350.00	200.00
(36)	Rebel Oakes	700.00	350.00	200.00
(37)	Eddie Plank	1,500	750.00	450.00
(38)	Germany Schaefer	700.00	350.00	200.00
(39)	Tris Speaker	3,000	1,500	900.00
(40)	Oscar Stanage	700.00	350.00	200.00
(41)	George Stovall	700.00	350.00	200.00
(42)	Jeff Sweeney	700.00	350.00	200.00
(43)	Joe Tinker/Portrait	1,300	650.00	400.00
(44)	Joe Tinker/Btg	1,300	650.00	400.00
(45)	Honus Wagner/Btg	12,500	6,250	3,750
(46)	Honus Wagner/Throwing	9,000	4,500	2,700
(47)	Hooks Wiltse	700.00	350.00	200.00
(48)	Heinie Zimmerman	700.00	350.00	200.00

1921 American Caramel Series of 80 (E121)

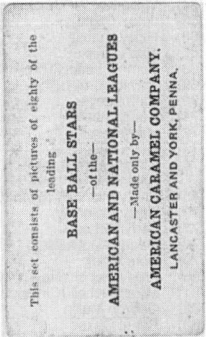

JOHN GRANEY Utl. O. F.—Cleveland Americans

This set consists of pictures of eighty of the leading BASE BALL STARS —of the— AMERICAN AND NATIONAL LEAGUES —Made only by— AMERICAN CARAMEL COMPANY. LANCASTER AND YORK, PENNA.

Issued circa 1921, the E121 Series of 80 is designated as such because of the card reverses which indicate the player pictured is just one of 80 baseball stars in the set. The figure of 80 supplied by the American Caramel Co. is incorrect as over 100 different pictures do exist. The unnumbered cards, which measure about 2" x 3-1/4", feature black and white photos. Two different backs exist for the Series of 80. The common back variation has the first line ending with the word "the," while the scarcer version ends with the word "eighty." The complete set price does not include the variations. The existence of a number of cards on this checklist is now in question.

		NM	EX	VG
Complete Set (121):		52,500	21,500	10,000
Common Player:		150.00	60.00	30.00
(1)	G.C. Alexander (Arms above head.)	Existence now questioned		
(2)	Grover Alexander (Right arm forward.)	1,500	600.00	300.00
(3)	Jim Bagby	150.00	60.00	30.00
(4a)	J. Franklin Baker	400.00	160.00	80.00
(4b)	Frank Baker	Existence now questioned		
(5)	Dave Bancroft/Btg	400.00	160.00	80.00
(6)	Dave Bancroft/Leaping	400.00	160.00	80.00
(7)	Ping Bodie	150.00	60.00	30.00
(8)	George Burns	150.00	60.00	30.00
(9)	Geo. J. Burns	150.00	60.00	30.00
(10)	Owen Bush	150.00	60.00	30.00
(11)	Max Carey/Btg	400.00	160.00	80.00
(12)	Max Carey (Hands at hips.)	400.00	160.00	80.00
(13)	Cecil Causey	150.00	60.00	30.00
(14)	Ty Cobb/Throwing (Looking front.)	Existence now questioned		
(15a)	Ty Cobb/Throwing (Looking right, Mgr. on front.)	3,250	1,600	975.00
(15b)	Ty Cobb/Throwing (Looking right, Manager on front.)	3,2500	725.00	360.00
(16)	Eddie Collins	600.00	300.00	180.00
(17)	"Rip" Collins	150.00	60.00	30.00
(18)	Jake Daubert	150.00	60.00	30.00
(19)	George Dauss	150.00	60.00	30.00
(20)	Charles Deal (Dark uniform.)	150.00	60.00	30.00
(21)	Charles Deal (White uniform.)	150.00	60.00	30.00
(22)	William Doak	150.00	60.00	30.00
(23)	Bill Donovan	150.00	60.00	30.00
(24)	"Phil" Douglas	Existence now questioned		
(25a)	Johnny Evers (Manager)	400.00	160.00	80.00
(25b)	Johnny Evers (Mgr.)	400.00	160.00	80.00
(26)	Urban Faber (Dark uniform.)	400.00	160.00	80.00
(27)	Urban Faber (White uniform.)	400.00	160.00	80.00
(28)	William Fewster (First name actually Wilson.)	150.00	60.00	
(29)	Eddie Foster	150.00	60.00	30.00
(30)	Frank Frisch	400.00	160.00	80.00
(31)	W.L. Gardner	150.00	60.00	30.00
(32a)	Alexander Gaston (No position on front.)	Existence now questioned		
(32b)	Alexander Gaston (Position on front.)	Existence now questioned		
(33)	"Kid" Gleason	150.00	60.00	30.00
(34)	"Mike" Gonzalez	150.00	60.00	30.00
(35)	Hank Gowdy	150.00	60.00	30.00
(36)	John Graney	150.00	60.00	30.00
(37)	Tom Griffith	150.00	60.00	30.00
(38)	Heinie Groh	150.00	60.00	30.00
(39)	Harry Harper	150.00	60.00	30.00

		NM	EX	VG
(40)	Harry Heilman (Heilmann)	400.00	160.00	80.00
(41)	Walter Holke/Portrait	150.00	60.00	30.00
(42)	Walter Holke/Throwing	150.00	60.00	30.00
(43)	Charles Hollacher (Hollocher)	150.00	60.00	30.00
(44)	Harry Hooper	400.00	160.00	80.00
(45)	Rogers Hornsby	1,600	800.00	475.00
(46)	Waite Hoyt	400.00	160.00	80.00
(47)	Miller Huggins	400.00	160.00	80.00
(48)	Wm. C. Jacobson	150.00	60.00	30.00
(49)	Hugh Jennings	400.00	160.00	80.00
(50)	Walter Johnson/Throwing	1,350	550.00	275.00
(51)	Walter Johnson (Hands at chest.)	1,425	575.00	285.00
(52)	James Johnston	150.00	60.00	30.00
(53)	Joe Judge	150.00	60.00	30.00
(54)	George Kelly	400.00	160.00	80.00
(55)	Dick Kerr	150.00	60.00	30.00
(56)	P.J. Kilduff	150.00	60.00	30.00
(57a)	Bill Killifer (Incorrect name.)	150.00	60.00	30.00
(57b)	Bill Killefer (Correct name.)	150.00	60.00	30.00
(58)	John Lavan	150.00	60.00	30.00
(59)	"Nemo" Leibold	150.00	60.00	30.00
(60)	Duffy Lewis	150.00	60.00	30.00
(61)	Al. Mamaux	150.00	60.00	30.00
(62)	"Rabbit" Maranville	400.00	160.00	80.00
(63a)	Carl May (Mays)	200.00	80.00	40.00
(63b)	Carl Mays (Correct name.)	200.00	80.00	40.00
(64)	John McGraw	400.00	160.00	80.00
(65)	Jack McInnis	150.00	60.00	30.00
(66)	M.J. McNally	150.00	60.00	30.00
(67)	Emil Muesel (Photo is Lou DeVormer.)	150.00	60.00	30.00
(68)	R. Meusel	150.00	60.00	30.00
(69)	Clyde Milan	150.00	60.00	30.00
(70)	Elmer Miller	150.00	60.00	30.00
(71)	Otto Miller	150.00	60.00	30.00
(72)	Guy Morton	150.00	60.00	30.00
(73)	Eddie Murphy	150.00	60.00	30.00
(74)	"Hy" Myers	150.00	60.00	30.00
(75)	Arthur Nehf	150.00	60.00	30.00
(76)	Steve O'Neill	150.00	60.00	30.00
(77a)	Roger Peckinbaugh (Incorrect name.)	150.00	60.00	30.00
(77b)	Roger Peckinpaugh (Correct name.)	150.00	60.00	30.00
(78a)	Jeff Pfeffer (Brooklyn)	150.00	60.00	30.00
(78b)	Jeff Pfeffer (St. Louis)	150.00	60.00	30.00
(79)	Walter Pipp	250.00	100.00	50.00
(80)	Jack Quinn	150.00	60.00	30.00
(81)	John Rawlings	150.00	60.00	30.00
(82)	E.C. Rice	650.00	320.00	195.00
(83)	Eppa Roush, Jr.	400.00	160.00	80.00
(84)	Robert Roth	150.00	60.00	30.00
(85a)	Ed. Roush (C.F.)	400.00	160.00	80.00
(85b)	Ed. Roush (L.F.)	400.00	160.00	80.00
(86a)	Babe Ruth	19,500	9,750	5,850
(86b)	"Babe" Ruth	17,500	7,000	3,500
(86c)	George Ruth	19,000	7,600	3,800
(87)	"Bill" Ryan	150.00	60.00	30.00
(88)	"Slim" Sallee (Glove showing.)	150.00	60.00	30.00
(89)	"Slim" Sallee (No glove showing.)	150.00	60.00	30.00
(90)	Ray Schalk	400.00	160.00	80.00
(91)	Walter Schang	150.00	60.00	30.00
(92a)	Fred Schupp (Name incorrect.)	Existence now questioned		
(92b)	Ferd Schupp (Name correct.)	150.00	60.00	30.00
(93)	Everett Scott	150.00	60.00	30.00
(94)	Hank Severeid	150.00	60.00	30.00
(95)	Robert Shawkey	150.00	60.00	30.00
(96a)	Pat Shea	Existence now questioned		
(96b)	"Pat" Shea	150.00	60.00	30.00
(97)	George Sisler/Btg	400.00	160.00	80.00
(98)	George Sisler/Throwing	400.00	160.00	80.00
(99)	Earl Smith	150.00	60.00	30.00
(100)	Frank Snyder	150.00	60.00	30.00
(101a)	Tris Speaker (Mgr.)	800.00	325.00	160.00
(101b)	Tris Speaker (Manager - large projection.)	800.00	325.00	160.00
(101c)	Tris Speaker (Manager - small projection.)	Existence now questioned		
(102)	Milton Stock	150.00	60.00	30.00
(103)	Amos Strunk	150.00	60.00	30.00
(104)	Zeb Terry	150.00	60.00	30.00
(105)	Chester Thomas	150.00	60.00	30.00
(106)	Fred Toney (Trees in background.)	150.00	60.00	30.00
(107)	Fred Toney (No trees.)	150.00	60.00	30.00
(108)	George Tyler	150.00	60.00	30.00
(109)	Jim Vaughn (Dark hat.)	150.00	60.00	30.00
(110)	Jim Vaughn (White hat.)	150.00	60.00	30.00
(111)	Bob Veach (Glove in air.)	150.00	60.00	30.00
(112)	Bob Veach (Arms crossed.)	150.00	60.00	30.00
(113)	Oscar Vitt	150.00	60.00	30.00
(114)	W. Wambsganss (Photo actually Fred Coumbe.)	150.00	60.00	30.00
(115)	Aaron Ward	150.00	60.00	30.00
(116)	Zach Wheat	400.00	160.00	80.00
(117)	George Whitted	150.00	60.00	30.00
(118)	Fred Williams	150.00	60.00	30.00
(119)	Ivy B. Wingo	150.00	60.00	30.00
(120)	Joe Wood	600.00	300.00	180.00
(121)	"Pep" Young	150.00	60.00	30.00

1922 American Caramel Series of 120 (E121)

Produced by American Caramel Co. the E121 Series of 120 has back advertising that claims that the set contained 120 subjects. Identical in design to the E121 Series of 80 set except for the card backs, the black-and-white cards measure about 2" x 3-1/4". Numerous variations are found in the set, most involving a change in the player's name, team or position. The complete set price does not include variations. A number of cards and variatins previously listed in this set have been deleted, as their existence has not been confirmed. Gaps have been left in the checklist to accommodate additions.

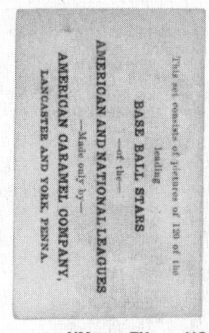

ELMER SMITH
O. F.—Boston Americans

	NM	EX	VG
Complete Set (123):	95,000	47,000	28,000
Common Player:	100.00	40.00	15.00
(1) Chas. "Babe" Adams	100.00	40.00	15.00
(2) G.C. Alexander	750.00	300.00	150.00
(3) Jim Bagby	100.00	40.00	15.00
(4) Dave Bancroft	400.00	160.00	80.00
(5) Turner Barber	100.00	40.00	15.00
(6a) Carlson L. Bigbee	100.00	40.00	15.00
(6b) L. Bigbee	100.00	40.00	15.00
(7) "Bullet Joe" Bush	100.00	40.00	15.00
(8) Max Carey	400.00	160.00	80.00
(9) Cecil Causey	100.00	40.00	15.00
(10) Ty Cobb/Btg	5,750	2,875	1,725
(11) Ty Cobb/Throwing	4,250	2,125	1,275
(12) Eddie Collins	400.00	160.00	80.00
(13) A. Wilbur Cooper	100.00	40.00	15.00
(14) Stanley Coveleskie (Coveleski)	400.00	160.00	80.00
(15) Dave Danforth	100.00	40.00	15.00
(16) Jake Daubert	100.00	40.00	15.00
(17) George Dauss	100.00	40.00	15.00
(18) Dixie Davis	100.00	40.00	15.00
(19) Lou DeVormer (Photo actually Irish Meusel.)	100.00	40.00	15.00
(20) William Doak	100.00	40.00	15.00
(22) Phil Douglas	100.00	40.00	15.00
(23) Urban Faber	400.00	160.00	80.00
(24) Bib Falk (Bibb)	100.00	40.00	15.00
(25) Wm. Fewster (First name actually Wilson.)	100.00	40.00	158.00
(26) Max Flack	100.00	40.00	15.00
(27) Ira Falgstead (Flagstead)	100.00	40.00	15.00
(28) Frank Frisch	400.00	160.00	80.00
(29) W.L. Gardner	100.00	40.00	15.00
(30) Alexander Gaston	100.00	40.00	15.00
(31) E.P. Gharrity	100.00	40.00	15.00
(32) George Gibson	100.00	40.00	15.00
(33) Chas. "Whitey" Glazner	100.00	40.00	15.00
(34) "Kid" Gleason	100.00	40.00	15.00
(35) Hank Gowdy	100.00	40.00	15.00
(36) John Graney	100.00	40.00	15.00
(37) Tom Griffith	100.00	40.00	15.00
(38) Chas. Grimm	100.00	40.00	15.00
(39) Heine Groh	100.00	40.00	15.00
(40) Jess Haines	400.00	160.00	80.00
(41) Harry Harper	100.00	40.00	15.00
(43) Harry Heilmann/Btg (Name correct.)	600.00	240.00	120.00
(44) Clarence Hodge	100.00	40.00	15.00
(45) Walter Holke/Portrait	100.00	40.00	15.00
(47) Charles Hollocher	100.00	40.00	15.00
(48) Harry Hooper	400.00	160.00	80.00
(49a) Rogers Hornsby (2B.)	1,100	450.00	225.00
(49b) Rogers Hornsby (O.F.)	1,100	450.00	225.00
(50) Waite Hoyt	400.00	160.00	80.00
(51) Miller Huggins	400.00	160.00	80.00
(52) Walter Johnson	1,350	550.00	275.00
(53) Joe Judge	100.00	40.00	15.00
(54) George Kelly	400.00	160.00	80.00
(55) Dick Kerr	100.00	40.00	15.00
(56) P.J. Kilduff	100.00	40.00	15.00
(57) Bill Killifer (Killefer)/Btg	100.00	40.00	15.00
(58) Bill Killifer (Killefer)/Throwing	100.00	40.00	15.00
(59) John Lavan	100.00	40.00	15.00
(60) Walter Mails	100.00	40.00	15.00
(61) "Rabbit" Maranville	400.00	160.00	80.00
(62) Elwood Martin	100.00	40.00	15.00
(63) Carl Mays	200.00	80.00	40.00
(64) John J. McGraw	400.00	160.00	80.00
(65) Jack McInnis	100.00	40.00	15.00
(66) M.J. McNally	100.00	40.00	15.00
(67) Emil Meusel (Photo actually Lou DeVormer.)	100.00	40.00	15.00
(68) R. Meusel	100.00	40.00	15.00
(69) Clyde Milan	100.00	40.00	15.00
(70) Elmer Miller	100.00	40.00	15.00
(71) Otto Miller	100.00	40.00	15.00
(72) Johnny Mostil	100.00	40.00	15.00
(73) Eddie Mulligan	100.00	40.00	15.00
(74a) Hy Myers	100.00	40.00	15.00
(75) Earl Neale	300.00	120.00	60.00
(76) Arthur Nehf	100.00	40.00	15.00
(77) Leslie Nunamaker	100.00	40.00	15.00
(78) Joe Oeschger	100.00	40.00	15.00
(80) Steve O'Neill	100.00	40.00	15.00
(81) D.B. Pratt	100.00	40.00	15.00
(82a) John Rawlings (2B.)	100.00	40.00	15.00
(82b) John Rawlings (Utl.)	100.00	40.00	15.00
(83) E.S. Rice (Initials actually E.C.)	400.00	160.00	80.00
(84) Eppa J. Rixey	400.00	160.00	80.00
(86) Wilbert Robinson	400.00	160.00	80.00
(87) Tom Rogers	100.00	40.00	15.00
(88a) Ed Rounnel (Rommel)	100.00	40.00	15.00
(88b) Ed. Rommel	100.00	40.00	15.00
(89) Ed Roush	400.00	160.00	80.00
(90) "Muddy" Ruel	100.00	40.00	15.00

(91) Walter Ruether	100.00	40.00	15.00
(92) "Babe" Ruth (Photo montage.)	8,000	4,000	2,400
(93) "Babe" Ruth (Holding bird.)	8,000	4,000	2,400
(94) "Babe" Ruth (Holding ball.)	8,000	4,000	2,400
(95) Bill Ryan	100.00	40.00	15.00
(96) Ray Schalk/Catching	400.00	160.00	80.00
(97) Ray Schalk/Btg	400.00	160.00	80.00
(98) Wally Schang	100.00	40.00	15.00
(100) Everett Scott	100.00	40.00	15.00
(101) Joe Sewell	400.00	160.00	80.00
(102) Robert Shawkey	100.00	40.00	15.00
(103) Pat Shea	100.00	40.00	15.00
(104) Earl Sheely	100.00	40.00	15.00
(105) Urban Schocker	100.00	40.00	15.00
(106) George Sisler/Btg	400.00	160.00	80.00
(108) Earl Smith	100.00	40.00	15.00
(109) Elmer Smith	100.00	40.00	15.00
(110) Frank Snyder	100.00	40.00	15.00
(111) Bill Southworth	400.00	200.00	120.00
(112) Tris Speaker	600.00	240.00	120.00
(113) Milton J. Stock	100.00	40.00	15.00
(114) Amos Strunk	100.00	40.00	15.00
(115) Zeb Terry	100.00	40.00	15.00
(116) Fred Toney	100.00	40.00	15.00
(117) George Topocer (Toporcer)	100.00	40.00	15.00
(118) Bob Veach	100.00	40.00	15.00
(119) Oscar Vitt	100.00	40.00	15.00
(120) Curtis Walker	100.00	40.00	15.00
(121) W. Wambsganss (Photo actually Fred Coumbe.)	100.00	40.00	15.00
(122) Aaron Ward	100.00	40.00	15.00
(123) Zach Wheat	400.00	160.00	80.00
(124) George Whitted (Pittsburgh)	100.00	40.00	15.00
(125) Fred Williams	100.00	40.00	15.00
(126) Ivy B. Wingo	100.00	40.00	15.00
(127) Ross Young (Youngs)	400.00	160.00	80.00

1922 American Caramel Series of 80 (E122)

CLAUDE HENDRIX
P-Chicago Cubs

Known as E122 in the American Card Catalog, this set is actually a parallel of the E121 American Caramel set. The cards are nearly identical to E121's "Series of 80," except the player's name, position and team are printed inside a gray rectangle at the bottom of the card, and the photos have a more coarse appearance. At 2" x 3-1/4", the E122s are slightly shorter than E121s.

	NM	EX	VG
Complete Set (81):	30,000	12,000	6,000
Common Player:	100.00	40.00	25.00
(1) Grover Alexander	1,100	550.00	330.00
(2) Jim Bagby	150.00	60.00	30.00
(3) J. Franklin Baker	400.00	160.00	80.00
(4) Dave Bancroft	400.00	160.00	80.00
(5) Ping Bodie	150.00	60.00	30.00
(6) George Burns	150.00	60.00	30.00
(7) Geo. J. Burns	150.00	60.00	30.00
(8) Owen Bush	150.00	60.00	30.00
(9) Max Carey	400.00	160.00	80.00
(10) Cecil Causey	150.00	60.00	30.00
(11) Ty Cobb	1,900	760.00	380.00
(12) Eddie Collins	400.00	160.00	80.00
(13) Jake Daubert	150.00	60.00	30.00
(14) George Dauss	150.00	60.00	30.00
(15) Charles Deal	150.00	60.00	30.00
(16) William Doak	150.00	60.00	30.00
(17) Bill Donovan	150.00	60.00	30.00
(18) Johnny Evers	400.00	160.00	80.00
(19) Urban Faber	400.00	160.00	80.00
(20) Eddie Foster	150.00	60.00	30.00
(21) W.L. Gardner	150.00	60.00	30.00
(22) "Kid" Gleason	150.00	60.00	30.00
(23) Hank Gowdy	150.00	60.00	30.00
(24) John Graney	150.00	60.00	30.00
(25) Tom Griffith	150.00	60.00	30.00
(26) Sam Harris (Stan "Bucky")	400.00	160.00	80.00
(27) Harry Heilman (Heilmann)	400.00	160.00	80.00
(28) Walter Holke	150.00	60.00	30.00
(29) Charles Hollacher (Hollocher)	150.00	60.00	30.00
(30) Harry Hooper	400.00	160.00	80.00
(31) Rogers Hornsby	600.00	240.00	120.00
(32) Wm. C. Jacobson	150.00	60.00	30.00
(33) Walter Johnson	1,100	450.00	225.00
(34) James Johnston	150.00	60.00	30.00
(35) Joe Judge	150.00	60.00	30.00
(36) George Kelly	400.00	160.00	80.00
(37) Dick Kerr	150.00	60.00	30.00
(38) P.J. Kilduff	150.00	60.00	30.00
(39) Bill Killefer	150.00	60.00	30.00
(40) John Lavan	150.00	60.00	30.00
(41) Duffy Lewis	150.00	60.00	30.00
(42) Perry Lipe	150.00	60.00	30.00
(43) Al. Mamaux	150.00	60.00	30.00
(44) "Rabbit" Maranville	400.00	160.00	80.00
(45) Carl May (Mays)	200.00	80.00	40.00

(46) John McGraw	400.00	160.00	80.00
(47) Jack McInnis	150.00	60.00	30.00
(48) Clyde Milan	150.00	60.00	30.00
(49) Otto Miller	150.00	60.00	30.00
(50) Guy Morton	150.00	60.00	30.00
(51) Eddie Murphy	150.00	60.00	30.00
(52) "Hy" Myers	150.00	60.00	30.00
(53) Steve O'Neill	150.00	60.00	30.00
(54) Roger Peckinbaugh (Peckinpaugh)	150.00	60.00	30.00
(55) Jeff Pfeffer	150.00	60.00	30.00
(56) Walter Pipp	175.00	70.00	35.00
(57) E.C. Rice	400.00	160.00	80.00
(58) Eppa Rixey, Jr.	400.00	160.00	80.00
(59) Babe Ruth	9,000	3,600	1,800
(60) "Slim" Sallee	150.00	60.00	30.00
(61) Ray Schalk	400.00	160.00	80.00
(62) Walter Schang	150.00	60.00	30.00
(63a) Fred Schupp (Name incorrect.)	150.00	60.00	30.00
(63b) Ferd Schupp (Name correct.)	150.00	60.00	30.00
(64) Everett Scott	150.00	60.00	30.00
(65) Hank Severeid	150.00	60.00	30.00
(66) George Sisler/Btg	400.00	160.00	80.00
(67) George Sisler/Throwing	400.00	160.00	80.00
(68) Tris Speaker	750.00	300.00	150.00
(69) Milton Stock	150.00	60.00	30.00
(70) Amos Strunk	150.00	60.00	30.00
(71) Chester Thomas	150.00	60.00	30.00
(72) George Tyler	150.00	60.00	30.00
(73) Jim Vaughn	150.00	60.00	30.00
(74) Bob Veach	150.00	60.00	30.00
(75) Oscar Vitt	150.00	60.00	30.00
(76) W. Wambsganss	150.00	60.00	30.00
(77) Zach Wheat	400.00	160.00	80.00
(78) Fred Williams	150.00	60.00	30.00
(79) Ivy B. Wingo	150.00	60.00	30.00
(80) Joe Wood	150.00	60.00	30.00
(81) Pep Young	150.00	60.00	30.00

1922 American Caramel Series of 240 (E120)

WALTER JOHNSON
PITCHER, WASHINGTON AMERICANS

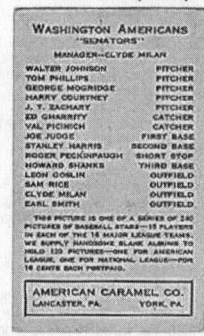

WASHINGTON AMERICANS "SENATORS"
MANAGER—CLYDE MILAN

AMERICAN CARAMEL CO.
LANCASTER, PA.   YORK, PA.

One of the most popular sets of the 1920s candy cards, the 1922 E120s were produced by the American Caramel Co. and distributed with sticks of caramel candy. The unnumbered cards measure 2" x 3-1/2". Cards depicting players from the American League are printed in brown ink on thin cream cardboard; National Leaguers are printed in green on blue-green stock. Backs carry team checklists. Many of the E120 photos were used in other sets of the era. A pair of 11-1/2" x 10-1/2" albums, holding 120 each and stamped American or National League were also issued.

	NM	EX	VG
Complete Set (240):	70,000	27,500	14,500
Common Player:	110.00	50.00	30.00
Album:	225.00	112.50	67.50
(1) Charles (Babe) Adams	175.00	70.00	35.00
(2) Eddie Ainsmith	175.00	70.00	35.00
(3) Vic Aldridge	175.00	70.00	35.00
(4) Grover C. Alexander	900.00	360.00	180.00
(5) Jim Bagby	175.00	70.00	35.00
(6) Frank (Home Run) Baker	500.00	200.00	100.00
(7) Dave (Beauty) Bancroft	500.00	200.00	100.00
(8) Walt Barbare	175.00	70.00	35.00
(9) Turner Barber	175.00	70.00	35.00
(10) Jess Barnes	175.00	70.00	35.00
(11) Clyde Barnhart	175.00	70.00	35.00
(12) John Bassler	175.00	70.00	35.00
(13) Will Bayne	175.00	70.00	35.00
(14) Walter (Huck) Betts	175.00	70.00	35.00
(15) Carson Bigbee	175.00	70.00	35.00
(16) Lu Blue	175.00	70.00	35.00
(17) Norman Boeckel	175.00	70.00	35.00
(18) Sammy Bohne	400.00	160.00	80.00
(19) George Burns	175.00	70.00	35.00
(20) George Burns	175.00	70.00	35.00
(21) "Bullet Joe" Bush	175.00	70.00	35.00
(22) Leon Cadore	175.00	70.00	35.00
(23) Marty Callaghan	175.00	70.00	35.00
(24) Frank Calloway (Callaway)	175.00	70.00	35.00
(25) Max Carey	500.00	200.00	100.00
(26) Jimmy Caveney	175.00	70.00	35.00
(27) Virgil Cheeves	175.00	70.00	35.00
(28) Vern Clemons	175.00	70.00	35.00
(29) Ty Cob (Cobb)	3,500	1,400	700.00
(30) Bert Cole	175.00	70.00	35.00
(31) Eddie Collins	500.00	200.00	100.00
(32) John (Shano) Collins	175.00	70.00	35.00
(33) T.P. (Pat) Collins	175.00	70.00	35.00
(34) Wilbur Cooper	175.00	70.00	35.00
(35) Harry Courtney	175.00	70.00	35.00
(36) Stanley Coveleski (Coveleska)	500.00	200.00	100.00
(37) Elmer Cox	175.00	70.00	35.00
(38) Sam Crane	175.00	70.00	35.00
(39) Walton Cruise	175.00	70.00	35.00

No.	Player			
(40)	Bill Cunningham	175.00	70.00	35.00
(41)	George Cutshaw	175.00	70.00	35.00
(42)	Dave Danforth	175.00	70.00	35.00
(43)	Jake Daubert	175.00	70.00	35.00
(44)	George Dauss	175.00	70.00	35.00
(45)	Frank (Dixie) Davis	175.00	70.00	35.00
(46)	Hank DeBerry	175.00	70.00	35.00
(47)	Albert Devormer (Lou DeVormer)	175.00	70.00	35.00
(48)	Bill Doak	175.00	70.00	35.00
(49)	Pete Donohue	175.00	70.00	35.00
(50)	"Shufflin" Phil Douglas	175.00	70.00	35.00
(51)	Joe Dugan	175.00	70.00	35.00
(52)	Louis (Pat) Duncan	175.00	70.00	35.00
(53)	Jimmy Dykes	175.00	70.00	35.00
(54)	Howard Ehmke	300.00	150.00	90.00
(55)	Frank Ellerbe	175.00	70.00	35.00
(56)	Urban (Red) Faber	500.00	200.00	100.00
(57)	Bib Falk (Bibb)	175.00	70.00	35.00
(58)	Dana Fillingim	175.00	70.00	35.00
(59)	Max Flack	175.00	70.00	35.00
(60)	Ira Flagstead	175.00	70.00	35.00
(61)	Art Fletcher	175.00	70.00	35.00
(62)	Horace Ford	175.00	70.00	35.00
(63)	Jack Fournier	175.00	70.00	35.00
(64)	Frank Frisch	500.00	200.00	100.00
(65)	Ollie Fuhrman	175.00	70.00	35.00
(66)	Clarence Galloway	175.00	70.00	35.00
(67)	Larry Gardner	175.00	70.00	35.00
(68)	Walter Gerber	175.00	70.00	35.00
(69)	Ed Gharrity	175.00	70.00	35.00
(70)	John Gillespie	175.00	70.00	35.00
(71)	Chas. (Whitey) Glazner	175.00	70.00	35.00
(72)	Johnny Gooch	175.00	70.00	35.00
(73)	Leon Goslin	500.00	200.00	100.00
(74)	Hank Gowdy	175.00	70.00	35.00
(75)	John Graney	175.00	70.00	35.00
(76)	Tom Griffith	175.00	70.00	35.00
(77)	Burleigh Grimes	500.00	200.00	100.00
(78)	Oscar Ray Grimes	175.00	70.00	35.00
(79)	Charlie Grimm	175.00	70.00	35.00
(80)	Heinie Groh	175.00	70.00	35.00
(81)	Jesse Haines	500.00	200.00	100.00
(82)	Earl Hamilton	175.00	70.00	35.00
(83)	Gene (Bubbles) Hargrave	175.00	70.00	35.00
(84)	Bryan Harris (Harriss)	175.00	70.00	35.00
(85)	Joe Harris	175.00	70.00	35.00
(86)	Stanley Harris	500.00	200.00	100.00
(87)	Chas. (Dowdy) Hartnett	500.00	200.00	100.00
(88)	Bob Hasty	175.00	70.00	35.00
(89)	Joe Hauser	225.00	90.00	45.00
(90)	Clif Heathcote	175.00	70.00	35.00
(91)	Harry Heilmann	500.00	200.00	100.00
(92)	Walter (Butch) Henline	175.00	70.00	35.00
(93)	Clarence (Shovel) Hodge	175.00	70.00	35.00
(94)	Walter Holke	175.00	70.00	35.00
(95)	Charles Hollocher	175.00	70.00	35.00
(96)	Harry Hooper	500.00	200.00	100.00
(97)	Rogers Hornsby	900.00	360.00	180.00
(98)	Waite Hoyt	500.00	200.00	100.00
(99)	Wilbur Hubbell (Wilbert)	175.00	70.00	35.00
(100)	Bernard (Bud) Hungling	175.00	70.00	35.00
(101)	Will Jacobson	175.00	70.00	35.00
(102)	Charlie Jamieson	175.00	70.00	35.00
(103)	Ernie Johnson	175.00	70.00	35.00
(104)	Sylvester Johnson	175.00	70.00	35.00
(105)	Walter Johnson	1,600	650.00	325.00
(106)	Jimmy Johnston	175.00	70.00	35.00
(107)	W.R. (Doc) Johnston	175.00	70.00	35.00
(108)	"Deacon" Sam Jones	175.00	70.00	35.00
(109)	Bob Jones	175.00	70.00	35.00
(110)	Percy Jones	175.00	70.00	35.00
(111)	Joe Judge	175.00	70.00	35.00
(112)	Ben Karr	175.00	70.00	35.00
(113)	Johnny Kelleher	175.00	70.00	35.00
(114)	George Kelly	500.00	200.00	100.00
(115)	Lee King	175.00	70.00	35.00
(116)	Wm (Larry) Kopff (Kopf)	175.00	70.00	35.00
(117)	Marty Krug	175.00	70.00	35.00
(118)	Johnny Lavan	175.00	70.00	35.00
(119)	Nemo Leibold	175.00	70.00	35.00
(120)	Roy Leslie	175.00	70.00	35.00
(121)	George Leverette (Leverett)	175.00	70.00	35.00
(122)	Adolfo Luque	175.00	70.00	35.00
(123)	Walter Mails	175.00	70.00	35.00
(124)	Al Mamaux	175.00	70.00	35.00
(125)	"Rabbit" Maranville	500.00	200.00	100.00
(126)	Cliff Markle	175.00	70.00	35.00
(127)	Richard (Rube) Marquard	500.00	200.00	100.00
(128)	Carl Mays	200.00	80.00	40.00
(129)	Hervey McClellan (Harvey)	175.00	70.00	35.00
(130)	Austin McHenry	175.00	70.00	35.00
(131)	"Stuffy" McInnis	175.00	70.00	35.00
(132)	Martin McManus	175.00	70.00	35.00
(133)	Mike McNally	175.00	70.00	35.00
(134)	Hugh McQuillan	175.00	70.00	35.00
(135)	Lee Meadows	175.00	70.00	35.00
(136)	Mike Menosky	175.00	70.00	35.00
(137)	Bob (Dutch) Meusel	175.00	70.00	35.00
(138)	Emil (Irish) Meusel	175.00	70.00	35.00
(139)	Clyde Milan	175.00	70.00	35.00
(140)	Edmund (Bing) Miller	175.00	70.00	35.00
(141)	Elmer Miller	175.00	70.00	35.00
(142)	Lawrence (Hack) Miller	175.00	70.00	35.00
(143)	Clarence Mitchell	175.00	70.00	35.00
(144)	George Mogridge	175.00	70.00	35.00
(145)	Roy Moore	175.00	70.00	35.00
(146)	John L. Mokan	175.00	70.00	35.00
(147)	John Morrison	175.00	70.00	35.00
(148)	Johnny Mostil	175.00	70.00	35.00
(149)	Elmer Myers	175.00	70.00	35.00
(150)	Hy Myers	175.00	70.00	35.00
(151)	Roliene Naylor (Roleine)	175.00	70.00	35.00
(152)	Earl "Greasy" Neale	175.00	70.00	35.00
(153)	Art Nehf	175.00	70.00	35.00
(154)	Les Nunamaker	175.00	70.00	35.00
(155)	Joe Oeschger	175.00	70.00	35.00
(156)	Bob O'Farrell	175.00	70.00	35.00
(157)	Ivan Olson	175.00	70.00	35.00
(158)	George O'Neil	175.00	70.00	35.00
(159)	Steve O'Neill	175.00	70.00	35.00
(160)	Frank Parkinson	175.00	70.00	35.00
(161)	Roger Peckinpaugh	175.00	70.00	35.00
(162)	Herb Pennock	500.00	200.00	100.00
(163)	Ralph (Cy) Perkins	175.00	70.00	35.00
(164)	Will Pertica	175.00	70.00	35.00
(165)	Jack Peters	175.00	70.00	35.00
(166)	Tom Phillips	175.00	70.00	35.00
(167)	Val Picinich	175.00	70.00	35.00
(168)	Herman Pillette	175.00	70.00	35.00
(169)	Ralph Pinelli	175.00	70.00	35.00
(170)	Wallie Pipp	175.00	70.00	35.00
(171)	Clark Pittenger (Clarke)	175.00	70.00	35.00
(172)	Raymond Powell	175.00	70.00	35.00
(173)	Derrill Pratt	175.00	70.00	35.00
(174)	Jack Quinn	175.00	70.00	35.00
(175)	Joe (Goldie) Rapp	175.00	70.00	35.00
(176)	John Rawlings	175.00	70.00	35.00
(177)	Walter (Dutch) Reuther (Ruether)	175.00	70.00	35.00
(178)	Sam Rice	500.00	200.00	100.00
(179)	Emory Rigney	175.00	70.00	35.00
(180)	Jimmy Ring	175.00	70.00	35.00
(181)	Eppa Rixey	500.00	200.00	100.00
(182)	Charles Robertson	175.00	70.00	35.00
(183)	Ed Rommel	175.00	70.00	35.00
(184)	Eddie Roush	500.00	200.00	100.00
(185)	Harold (Muddy) Ruel (Herold)	175.00	70.00	35.00
(186)	Babe Ruth	15,000	6,000	3,000
(187)	Ray Schalk	500.00	200.00	100.00
(188)	Wallie Schang	175.00	70.00	35.00
(189)	Ray Schmandt	175.00	70.00	35.00
(190)	Walter Schmidt	175.00	70.00	35.00
(191)	Joe Schultz	175.00	70.00	35.00
(192)	Everett Scott	175.00	70.00	35.00
(193)	Henry Severeid	175.00	70.00	35.00
(194)	Joe Sewell	500.00	200.00	100.00
(195)	Howard Shanks	175.00	70.00	35.00
(196)	Bob Shawkey	175.00	70.00	35.00
(197)	Earl Sheely	175.00	70.00	35.00
(198)	Will Sherdel	175.00	70.00	35.00
(199)	Ralph Shinners	175.00	70.00	35.00
(200)	Urban Shocker	175.00	70.00	35.00
(201)	Charles (Chick) Shorten	175.00	70.00	35.00
(202)	George Sisler	500.00	200.00	100.00
(203)	Earl Smith (N.Y. Giants)	175.00	70.00	35.00
(204)	Earl Smith (Washington)	175.00	70.00	35.00
(205)	Elmer Smith	175.00	70.00	35.00
(206)	Jack Smith	175.00	70.00	35.00
(207)	Sherrod Smith	175.00	70.00	35.00
(208)	Colonel Snover	175.00	70.00	35.00
(209)	Frank Snyder	175.00	70.00	35.00
(210)	Al Sothoron	175.00	70.00	35.00
(211)	Bill Southworth	500.00	250.00	150.00
(212)	Tris Speaker	900.00	360.00	180.00
(213)	Arnold Statz	175.00	70.00	35.00
(214)	Milton Stock	175.00	70.00	35.00
(215)	Amos Strunk	175.00	70.00	35.00
(216)	Jim Tierney	175.00	70.00	35.00
(217)	John Tobin	175.00	70.00	35.00
(218)	Fred Toney	175.00	70.00	35.00
(219)	George Toporcer	175.00	70.00	35.00
(220)	Harold (Pie) Traynor	500.00	200.00	100.00
(221)	George Uhle	175.00	70.00	35.00
(222)	Elam Vangilder	175.00	70.00	35.00
(223)	Bob Veach	175.00	70.00	35.00
(224)	Clarence (Tillie) Walker	175.00	70.00	35.00
(225)	Curtis Walker	175.00	70.00	35.00
(226)	Al Walters	175.00	70.00	35.00
(227)	Bill Wambsganss	175.00	70.00	35.00
(228)	Aaron Ward	175.00	70.00	35.00
(229)	John Watson	175.00	70.00	35.00
(230)	Frank Welch	175.00	70.00	35.00
(231)	Zach Wheat	500.00	200.00	100.00
(232)	Fred (Cy) Williams	175.00	70.00	35.00
(233)	Kenneth Williams	175.00	70.00	35.00
(234)	Ivy Wingo	175.00	70.00	35.00
(235)	Joe Wood	400.00	160.00	80.00
(236)	Lawrence Woodall	175.00	70.00	35.00
(237)	Russell Wrightstone	175.00	70.00	35.00
(238)	Everett Yaryan	175.00	70.00	35.00
(239)	Ross Young (Youngs)	500.00	200.00	100.00
(240)	J.T. Zachary	175.00	70.00	35.00

1927 American Caramel Series of 60 (E126)

This set consists of 60 of the most prominent baseball players in the country. We have made up an album which will hold the complete set. On receipt of 15 cents in stamps, we will send a handsome album to any address in the United States.

Manufactured only by the
AMERICAN CARAMEL COMPANY
Lancaster, Pa.

Issued in 1927 by the American Caramel Co., of Lancaster, Pa., this obscure 60-card set was one of the last of the caramel card issues. Measuring 2" x 3-1/4", the cards differ from most sets of the period because they are numbered. The back of each card includes an offer for an album to house the set which includes players from all 16 major league teams. The set has the American Card Catalog designation E126.

		NM	EX	VG
Complete Set (60):		36,500	14,500	7,250
Common Player:		125.00	55.00	30.00
1	John Gooch	200.00	80.00	40.00
2	Clyde L. Barnhart	200.00	80.00	40.00
3	Joe Busch (Bush)	200.00	80.00	40.00
4	Lee Meadows	200.00	80.00	40.00
5	E.T. Cox	200.00	80.00	40.00
6	"Red" Faber	750.00	370.00	220.00
7	Aaron Ward	200.00	80.00	40.00
8	Ray Schalk	750.00	370.00	220.00
9	"Specks" Toporcer ("Specs")	200.00	80.00	40.00
10	Bill Southworth	750.00	370.00	220.00
11	Allen Sothoron	200.00	80.00	40.00
12	Will Sherdel	200.00	80.00	40.00
13	Grover Alexander	1,500	750.00	450.00
14	Jack Quinn	200.00	80.00	40.00
15	C. Galloway	200.00	80.00	40.00
16	"Eddie" Collins	750.00	370.00	220.00
17	"Ty" Cobb	4,200	2,100	775.00
18	Percy Jones	200.00	80.00	40.00
19	Chas. Grimm	200.00	80.00	40.00
20	"Bennie" Karr	200.00	80.00	40.00
21	Charlie Jamieson	200.00	80.00	40.00
22	Sherrod Smith	200.00	80.00	40.00
23	Virgil Cheeves	200.00	80.00	40.00
24	James Ring	200.00	80.00	40.00
25	"Muddy" Ruel	200.00	80.00	40.00
26	Joe Judge	200.00	80.00	40.00
27	Tris Speaker	1,500	750.00	450.00
28	Walter Johnson	2,500	1,250	750.00
29	E.C. "Sam" Rice	750.00	370.00	220.00
30	Hank DeBerry	200.00	80.00	40.00
31	Walter Henline	200.00	80.00	40.00
32	Max Carey	750.00	370.00	220.00
33	Arnold J. Statz	200.00	80.00	40.00
34	Emil Meusel	200.00	80.00	40.00
35	T.P. "Pat" Collins	200.00	80.00	40.00
36	Urban Shocker	200.00	80.00	40.00
37	Bob Shawkey	200.00	80.00	40.00
38	"Babe" Ruth	16,000	8,000	4,800
39	Bob Meusel	200.00	80.00	40.00
40	Alex Ferguson	200.00	80.00	40.00
41	"Stuffy" McInnis	200.00	80.00	40.00
42	"Cy" Williams	200.00	80.00	40.00
43	Russel Wrightstone (Russell)	200.00	80.00	40.00
44	John Tobin	200.00	80.00	40.00
45	Wm. C. Jacobson	200.00	80.00	40.00
46	Bryan "Slim" Harriss	200.00	80.00	40.00
47	Elam Vangilder	200.00	80.00	40.00
48	Ken Williams	200.00	80.00	40.00
49	Geo. R. Sisler	1,500	750.00	450.00
50	Ed Brown	200.00	80.00	40.00
51	Jack Smith	200.00	80.00	40.00
52	Dave Bancroft	750.00	370.00	220.00
53	Larry Woodall	200.00	80.00	40.00
54	Lu Blue	200.00	80.00	40.00
55	Johnny Bassler	200.00	80.00	40.00
56	"Jakie" May	200.00	80.00	40.00
57	Horace Ford	200.00	80.00	40.00
58	"Curt" Walker	200.00	80.00	40.00
59	"Artie" Nehf	200.00	80.00	40.00
60	Geo. Kelly	750.00	370.00	220.00

1908 American League Pub. Co. Postcards

This set of black-and-white postcards was produced by the American League Publishing Co., Cleveland. The 3-1/2" x 5" cards have a large player posed-action photo against a white background and a smaller oval portrait photo in one of the top corners. A box at bottom contains some biographical data. The otherwise blank back has postcard indicia printed in black. As might be expected, all but two of the players in the known checklist were contemporary members of the Cleveland ballclub. A few cards have been seen with red or green overprinting on front "Collister & Sayle, Athletic Outfitters, Cleveland, O.," with a schedule printed on back.

		NM	EX	VG
Complete Set (16):		15,000	7,500	4,500
Common Player:		350.00	175.00	100.00
(1)	Harry Bay	350.00	175.00	100.00
(2)	Harry Bemis	350.00	175.00	100.00
(3)	Charles Berger	350.00	175.00	100.00
(4)	Joseph Birmingham	350.00	175.00	100.00
(5)	W. Bradley	350.00	175.00	100.00
(6)	Tyrus R. Cobb	6,000	3,000	1,800
(7)	Walter Clarkson	350.00	175.00	100.00
(8)	Elmer Flick	600.00	300.00	180.00
(9)	C.T. Hickman	350.00	175.00	100.00
(10)	William Hinchman	350.00	175.00	100.00
(11)	Addie Joss	750.00	375.00	225.00
(12)	Glen Liebhardt (Glenn)	350.00	175.00	100.00
(13)	Nap Lajoie	750.00	375.00	225.00

		NM	EX	VG
(14)	George Nill	350.00	175.00	100.00
(15)	George Perring	350.00	175.00	100.00
(16)	Honus Wagner	1,800	900.00	540.00

1950 American Nut & Chocolate Pennants (F150)

Although there is nothing on these small (1-7/8" x 4") felt pennants to identify the issuer, surviving ads show that the American Nut & Chocolate Co. of Boston sold them as a set of 22 for 50 cents. The pennants of American League players are printed in blue on white, while National Leaguers are printed in red on white. The pennants feature crude line-art drawings of the players at left, along with a facsimile autograph. A 10% variation in the size of the printing on the Elliott and Sain pennants has been noted, and may exist on others, as well. An approximately 17" x 7" version of the Ted Williams pennant is known and was available as a mail-in premium. Other players may also exist in that format. The checklist here is arranged alphabetically.

		NM	EX	VG
	Complete Set (22):	1,800	900.00	550.00
	Common Player:	65.00	32.50	20.00
(1)	Ewell Blackwell	65.00	32.50	20.00
(2)	Harry Brecheen	65.00	32.50	20.00
(3)	Phil Cavarretta	65.00	32.50	20.00
(4)	Bobby Doerr	100.00	50.00	30.00
(5)	Bob Elliott	65.00	32.50	20.00
(6)	Boo Ferriss	65.00	32.50	20.00
(7)	Joe Gordon	65.00	32.50	20.00
(8)	Tommy Holmes	65.00	32.50	20.00
(9)	Charles Keller	65.00	32.50	20.00
(10)	Ken Keltner	65.00	32.50	20.00
(11)	Ralph Kiner	100.00	50.00	30.00
(12)	Whitey Kurowski	65.00	32.50	20.00
(13)	Johnny Pesky	65.00	32.50	20.00
(14)	Pee Wee Reese	130.00	65.00	40.00
(15)	Phil Rizzuto	130.00	65.00	40.00
(16)	Johnny Sain	65.00	32.50	20.00
(17)	Enos Slaughter	100.00	50.00	30.00
(18)	Warren Spahn	100.00	50.00	30.00
(19)	Vern Stephens	65.00	32.50	20.00
(20)	Earl Torgeson	65.00	32.50	20.00
(21)	Dizzy Trout	65.00	32.50	20.00
(22)	Ted Williams	260.00	130.00	80.00
(22)	Ted Williams (17" x 7")	900.00	450.00	275.00

1968 American Oil Sweepstakes

Babe Ruth won fame as the greatest slugger in baseball history. He set many records with his 714 regular-season home runs which made him one of baseball's biggest attractions.

BABE RUTH

$1.00 ONE DOLLAR

Right side

One of several contemporary sweepstakes run by gas stations, this game required matching right- and left-side game pieces of the same athletic figure (or sporty auto) to win the stated prize. Naturally one side or the other was distributed in extremely limited quantities to avoid paying out too many prizes. Cards were given away in perforated pairs with a qualifying gasoline purchase. Uncut pairs carry a small premium over single cards. Data on which card halves were the rare part needed for redemption is incomplete and would have an effect on the collector value of surviving specimens. Individual game pieces measure 2-9/16" x 2-1/8" and are printed in color. Only the baseball players in the set are listed here.

		NM	EX	VG
(1a)	Mickey Mantle/Action (Left side, $10.)	40.00	20.00	12.00
(1b)	Mickey Mantle/Portrait (Right side, $10.)	30.00	15.00	9.00
(2a)	Willie Mays/Action (Left side, $10.)	40.00	20.00	12.00
(2b)	Willie Mays/Portrait (Right side, $10.)	25.00	12.50	7.50
(3a)	Babe Ruth/Action (Left side, $1.)	40.00	20.00	12.00
(3b)	Babe Ruth/Portrait (Right side, $1.)	25.00	12.50	7.50

1910 American Sports Candy and Jewelry

(See 1910 Orange Borders.)

1962 American Tract Society

A TIP FOR YOU

When I left the Dominican Republic to come to the states to play in organized ball, a Christian friend gave me a Bible. I packed it in my suitcase and carried it with me, but still did not take seriously the importance and necessity of a definite decision to take the Christ of that Bible as my personal Saviour.

However, early in the 1958 season (my first day in the majors) in a hotel room in San Francisco, I knew a decision HAD to be made. I opened the Bible and began to read. God did something for me that day. I was spiritually born again as I asked Jesus Christ to come into my heart. Romans 10:1 says: "Whosoever shall call upon the name of the Lord shall be saved."

The most wonderful and most important tip you could ever receive involves not the game of baseball, but the game of life. The tip is this: "Believe on the Lord Jesus Christ, and thou shalt be saved" (Acts 16:31).

"If thou shalt confess with thy mouth the Lord Jesus, and shalt believe in thine heart that God hath raised him from the dead, thou shalt be saved" (Romans 10:9).

I received this advice and did something about it. I hope you will do the same.

— FELIPE ALOU
San Francisco Giants

American Tract Society — a nonprofit organization Publishers of Christian Literature since 1825
Oradell, New Jersey

Tracard No. 52

These full-color cards, which carry religious messages on the back, were issued in 1962 by the American Tract Society, an interdenominational, non-sectarian publisher of Christian literature in the United States since 1825. Known as "Tra-cards," the cards measure 2-3/4" x 3-1/2" and feature color photographs on the fronts. The set includes religious scenes along with photos of various celebrities and sports stars, including baseball players Felipe Alou, Bobby Richardson, Jerry Kindall and Al Worthington. (There are two poses each of Alou and Kindall.) The backs carry rather lengthy, first-person religious testimonials from the players. The cards are numbered on the back in the lower right corner.

		NM	EX	VG
	Complete Set (6):	70.00	35.00	20.00
	Common Player:	10.00	5.00	3.00
43	Bobby Richardson	25.00	12.50	7.50
51a	Jerry Kindall (Cleveland)	10.00	5.00	3.00
51b	Jerry Kindall (Minnesota)	10.00	5.00	3.00
52a	Felipe Alou/Kneeling	15.00	7.50	4.50
52b	Felipe Alou/Btg	15.00	7.50	4.50
66	Al Worthington	10.00	5.00	3.00

1973 John B. Anderson Former Greats

This set of postcard-sized black-and-white cards features the artwork of John B. Anderson, a New York collector. Each card includes a facsimile autograph on front; backs are blank. The unnumbered cards are checklisted here in alphabetical order.

		NM	EX	VG
	Complete Set (12):	30.00	15.00	9.00
	Common Player:	4.00	2.00	1.25
(1)	Ty Cobb	6.00	3.00	1.75
(2)	Mickey Cochrane	4.00	2.00	1.25
(3)	Roberto Clemente	10.00	5.00	3.00
(4)	Lou Gehrig	10.00	5.00	3.00
(5)	Frank Frisch	4.00	2.00	1.25
(6)	Gil Hodges	6.00	3.00	1.75
(7)	Rogers Hornsby	4.00	2.00	1.25
(8)	Connie Mack	4.00	2.00	1.25
(9)	Christy Mathewson	6.00	3.00	1.75
(10)	Jackie Robinson	10.00	5.00	3.00
(11)	Babe Ruth	10.00	5.00	3.00
(12)	Pie Traynor	4.00	2.00	1.25

1977 John B. Anderson Aaron-Mays

This set of postcard size, black-and-white drawings is a collectors issue. Cards are blank-backed.

		NM	EX	VG
	Complete Set (4):	5.00	2.50	1.50
	Common Card:	2.00	1.00	.60
(1)	Hank Aaron (Arm in air.)	2.00	1.00	.60
(2)	Hank Aaron/Portrait	2.00	1.00	.60
(3)	Willie Mays (Giants)	2.00	1.00	.60
(4)	Willie Mays (Mets)	2.00	1.00	.60

1977 John B. Anderson New York Teams

Joe DiMaggio

Stars and local favorites of the three New York teams of the 1940s and 1950s are featured in this set of collectors cards. The 3-1/2" x 5-1/2" blank-back, black-and-white cards feature artwork by John B. Anderson. The unnumbered cards are checklisted here in alphabetical order.

		NM	EX	VG
	Complete Set (24):	45.00	27.50	13.50
	Common Player:	4.00	2.00	1.25
(1)	Yogi Berra	6.00	3.00	1.75
(2)	Ralph Branca	4.00	2.00	1.25
(3)	Dolf Camilli	4.00	2.00	1.25
(4)	Roy Campanella	6.00	3.00	1.75
(5)	Jerry Coleman	4.00	2.00	1.25
(6)	Frank Crosetti	4.00	2.00	1.25
(7)	Bill Dickey	4.00	2.00	1.25
(8)	Joe DiMaggio	15.00	7.50	4.50
(9)	Sid Gordon	4.00	2.00	1.25
(10)	Babe Herman	4.00	2.00	1.25
(11)	Carl Hubbell	4.00	2.00	1.25
(12)	Billy Johnson	4.00	2.00	1.25
(13)	Ernie Lombardi	4.00	2.00	1.25
(14)	Willard Marshall	4.00	2.00	1.25
(15)	Willie Mays	10.00	5.00	3.00
(16)	Joe McCarthy	4.00	2.00	1.25
(17)	Joe Medwick	4.00	2.00	1.25
(18)	Joe Moore	4.00	2.00	1.25
(19)	Andy Pafko	4.00	2.00	1.25
(20)	Jackie Robinson	10.00	5.00	3.00
(21)	Red Ruffing	4.00	2.00	1.25
(22)	Bill Terry	4.00	2.00	1.25
(23)	Hoyt Wilhelm	4.00	2.00	1.25
(24)	Gene Woodling	4.00	2.00	1.25

1904 Anonymous Studio Cabinets

Collins

The origins of this series of cabinet photos are unknown, as is the full entent of the issue. It is known that the portraits are the uncredited work of Boston photographer Carl Horner. Sixteen pieces were sold in the 1991 Copeland Auction, though only the players listed here have been reliably checklisted. The cabinets measure about 5-3/8" x 6-7/8" and have black or dark gray borders. Some pieces are reported to have slate-blue blank backs. The player's last name is presented in the lower-left corner in black or white outline scrip. The unnumbered cards are checklisted here in alphabetical order.

		NM	EX	VG
	Common Player:	750.00	375.00	225.00
(1)	Jake Beckley	2,000	1,000	600.00
(2)	Roger Bresnahan	2,000	1,000	600.00
(3)	Jimmy Collins	2,000	1,000	600.00
(4)	Lave Cross	750.00	370.00	220.00
(5)	Hugh Duffy	2,000	1,000	600.00
(6)	Clark Griffith	2,000	1,000	600.00
(7)	Danny Hoffman	750.00	370.00	220.00
(8)	James "Ducky" Holmes	750.00	375.00	225.00
(9)	Connie Mack	2,000	1,000	600.00
(10)	Iron Man McGinity (McGinnity)	2,000	1,000	600.00
(11)	John McGraw	750.00	375.00	225.00
(12)	Matty McIntyre	750.00	370.00	220.00

1912 Anonymous T207

While most T207s are found with one of five different cigarette brands advertised on back, there is a less commonly encountered type with no such ad. They are known as Anonymous backs. Two types are known, one originating from Factory 3 in Louisiana and one from Virginia's Factory 25. The latter is much scarcer though commands little additional premium.

(See 1912 T207 for checklist and price guide.)

1925 Anonymous Postcards

Mgr. STANLEY HARRIS
Washington Senators

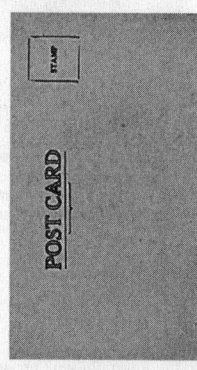

STAMP

POST CARD

The date attributed is speculative based on the limited number of known subjects. These 3-1/4" x 5-1/2" cards have a square portrait photo at center in black-and-white. With the exception of Babe Ruth, all known subjects were managers in 1925. The subject is identified by name (in either all-caps or upper- and lower-case, team, and, sometimes, title "Mgr." At least two styles of undivided backs have been found, with an ornate "POST CARD" device at top and a stamp box. The cards are printed on low-grade cardboard. Collector uncertainty as to the origins of the cards and the potential supply has kept market prices down.

	NM	EX	VG
Common Player:	300.00	150.00	90.00

	NM	EX	VG
Tyrus Cobb	400.00	200.00	120.00
Mgr. Tyrus Cobb	400.00	200.00	120.00
Stanley Harris	200.00	100.00	60.00
Walter Johnson	300.00	150.00	90.00
John McGraw	200.00	100.00	60.00
"Bill" McKechnie	200.00	100.00	60.00
Wilbert Robinson	200.00	100.00	60.00
Babe Ruth	600.00	300.00	180.00

1940s Anonymous Premium Photos

"These pictures were issued circa 1946-47. They can be found printed either on paper stock or glossy photo stock." There is no indication on these 8" x 10" black-and-white photos as to who produced them or for what purpose. The blank-backed, white-bordered pictures have the player identified with a sometimes-misspelled script signature. It is not known if this checklist is complete.

	NM	EX	VG
Complete Set (17):	300.00	150.00	90.00
Common Player:	20.00	10.00	6.00
(1) Ty Cobb	40.00	20.00	12.00
(2) Dizzy Dean	25.00	12.50	7.50
(3) Joe DiMaggio	45.00	22.00	13.50
(4) Bob Feller	25.00	12.50	7.50
(5) Lou Gehrig	40.00	20.00	12.00
(6) Harry Heilman (Heilmann)	20.00	10.00	6.00
(7) Roger (Rogers) Hornsby	25.00	12.50	7.50
(8) Carl Hubbell	20.00	10.00	6.00
(9) Walter Johnson	25.00	12.50	7.50
(10) Connie Mack	20.00	10.00	6.00
(11) Christy Mathewson	30.00	15.00	9.00
(12) Bob Meusel	20.00	10.00	6.00
(13) Irish Emil Meusel	20.00	10.00	6.00
(14) Johnny Mize	20.00	10.00	6.00
(15) Babe Ruth	50.00	25.00	15.00
(16) Babe Ruth/Lou Gehrig	40.00	20.00	12.00
(17) Zack Wheat	20.00	10.00	6.00

1949-1950 Ansco Almendares Scorpions

This set of the Cuban Professional League champions of the 1949-50 season was sponsored by Ansco Cameras and Film, whose logo appears on front. Some cards have on back a rubber-stamp with the name of an Havana photo studio, which may have distributed the cards. The cards are actual black-and-white photos on glossy photo paper, measuring about 3" x 3-7/8". The Scorpions had many former and future major leaguers on their roster. Cards are listed alphabetically here.

	NM	EX	VG
Complete Set (20):	3,250	1,625	975.00
Common Player:	150.00	60.00	40.00
(1) Bill Antonello	175.00	70.00	45.00
(2) Zungo Cabrera	150.00	60.00	40.00
(3) Tony Castanos	150.00	60.00	40.00
(4) Avelino Canizares	150.00	60.00	40.00
(5) Kevin (Chuck) Connors	450.00	180.00	110.00
(6) Andres Fleitas	150.00	60.00	40.00
(7) Al Gionfriddo	175.00	70.00	45.00
(8) Fermin Guerra	150.00	60.00	40.00
(9) Gene Handley	150.00	60.00	40.00
(10) Bob Hooper	150.00	60.00	40.00
(11) Vincente Lopez	150.00	60.00	40.00
(12) Conrado Marrero	175.00	70.00	45.00
(13) Agapito Mayor	150.00	60.00	40.00
(14) Willie Miranda	175.00	70.00	45.00
(15) Rene Monteagudo	150.00	60.00	40.00
(16) Roberto Ortiz	150.00	60.00	40.00
(17) Hector Rodriguez	150.00	60.00	40.00
(18) Octavio Rubert	150.00	60.00	40.00
(19) Rene Solis	150.00	60.00	40.00
(20) Ed Wright	150.00	60.00	40.00

1961-62 Apple Fresh Milk Minnesota Twins

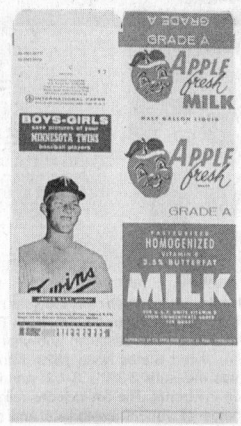

(See 1961, 1962 Cloverleaf Dairy Minnesota Twins.)

1971 Arco

In 1971, players from four major league teams in the east were featured in a set of facsimile autographed color photos in a gas station giveaway program. Following the promotion, leftover pictures were sold directly to collectors in the pages of the existing hobby media. The photos share an 8" x 10" format, with virtually all of the players being pictured without caps. Red, white and blue stars flank the player name in the bottom border. Black-and-white backs have career summary and stats, personal data, team sponsor and union logos and an ad for frames for the pictures. The unnumbered photos are listed here alphabetically within team.

	NM	EX	VG
Complete Set (49):	175.00	90.00	50.00
Common Player:	3.00	1.50	.90
RED SOX TEAM SET:	60.00	30.00	18.00
(1) Luis Aparicio	10.00	5.00	3.00
(2) Ken Brett	4.00	2.00	1.25
(3) Billy Conigliaro	4.00	2.00	1.25
(4) Ray Culp	4.00	2.00	1.25
(5) Doug Griffin	4.00	2.00	1.25
(6) Bob Montgomery	4.00	2.00	1.25
(7) Gary Peters	4.00	2.00	1.25
(8) George Scott	5.00	2.50	1.50
(9) Sonny Siebert	4.00	2.00	1.25
(10) Reggie Smith	5.00	2.50	1.50
(11) Ken Tatum	4.00	2.00	1.25
(12) Carl Yastrzemski	15.00	7.50	4.50
YANKEES TEAM SET:	65.00	32.50	20.00
(1) Jack Aker	6.00	3.00	1.75
(2) Stan Bahnsen	6.00	3.00	1.75
(3) Frank Baker	6.00	3.00	1.75
(4) Danny Cater	6.00	3.00	1.75
(5) Horace Clarke	6.00	3.00	1.75
(6) John Ellis	6.00	3.00	1.75
(7) Gene Michael	6.00	3.00	1.75
(8) Thurman Munson	12.00	6.00	3.50
(9) Bobby Murcer	7.50	3.75	2.25
(10) Fritz Peterson	6.00	3.00	1.75
(11) Mel Stottlemyre	6.00	3.00	1.75
(12) Roy White	7.50	3.75	2.25
PHILLIES TEAM SET:	40.00	20.00	12.00
(1) Larry Bowa	3.00	1.50	.90
(2) Jim Bunning	10.00	5.00	3.00
(3) Roger Freed	3.00	1.50	.90
(4) Terry Harmon	3.00	1.50	.90
(5) Larry Hisle	3.00	1.50	.90
(6) Joe Hoerner	3.00	1.50	.90
(7) Deron Johnson	3.00	1.50	.90
(8) Tim McCarver	5.00	2.50	1.50
(9) Don Money	3.00	1.50	.90
(10) Dick Selma	3.00	1.50	.90
(11) Chris Short	3.00	1.50	.90
(12) Tony Taylor	3.00	1.50	.90
(13) Rick Wise	3.00	1.50	.90
PIRATES TEAM SET:	65.00	32.50	20.00
(1) Gene Alley	3.00	1.50	.90
(2) Steve Blass	3.00	1.50	.90
(3) Roberto Clemente	30.00	15.00	9.00
(4) Dave Giusti	3.00	1.50	.90
(5) Richie Hebner	3.00	1.50	.90
(6) Bill Mazeroski	7.50	3.75	2.25
(7) Bob Moose	3.00	1.50	.90
(8) Al Oliver	4.50	2.25	1.25
(9) Bob Robertson	3.00	1.50	.90
(10) Manny Sanguillen	3.00	1.50	.90
(11) Willie Stargell	7.50	3.75	2.25
(12) Luke Walker	3.00	1.50	.90

1980-81 Argus Publishing Reggie Jackson

Some of the cars from Reggie Jackson's collection of hot rods and vintage vehicles were featured on a series of promotional cards issued by the publisher of Hot Rodding and Super Chevy magazines. The standard-size color cards have photos of Jackson with his cars on front, along with magazine and other logos. Backs have information on Jackson's cars. It was reported 10,000 of each were produced for distribution at automotive trade shows and a California drag strip.

	NM	EX	VG
Complete Set (3):	40.00	20.00	12.00
(1) 1980 SEMA Show (Reggie Jackson) (1932 Ford highboy)	20.00	10.00	6.00
2 1981 SEMA (Reggie Jackson) (1932 Ford 5-window)	10.00	5.00	3.00
3 1981 Super Chevy Sunday (Reggie Jackson) (1955 Chevrolet)	10.00	5.00	3.00

1955 Armour Coins

In 1955, Armour inserted a plastic "coin" into packages of hot dogs. A raised profile of a ballplayer is on front along with the player's name and team. On back, between a diamond diagram and crossed bats are name, team, position, birthplace and date, batting and throwing preference, and 1954 hitting or pitching record. The coins measure 1-1/2" in diameter and are unnumbered. They can be found in a variety of colors, some of which are much scarcer than others and elicit higher prices from Armour specialists who have studied their relative scarcities. Values shown are for coins in the most common colors (aqua, blue, green, orange and red). Each 1955 coin can be found in two different "bust tilts" in which the tip of the cap and back point of the bust point to distinctly different areas of the rim. These variations are too arcane for the average collector. The complete set price includes only the most common variations.

	NM	EX	VG
Complete Set (24):	800.00	400.00	240.00
Common Player:	20.00	10.00	6.00
(1a) John "Johnny" Antonelli ("New York Giants" on back.)	75.00	37.00	22.00
(1b) John "Johnny" Antonelli ("N.Y. Giants" on back.)	20.00	10.00	6.00
(2) Larry "Yogi" Berra	40.00	20.00	12.00
(3) Delmar "Del" Crandall	20.00	10.00	6.00
(4) Lawrence "Larry" Doby	30.00	15.00	9.00
(5) James "Jim" Finigan	20.00	10.00	6.00
(6) Edward "Whitey" Ford	50.00	25.00	15.00
(7a) James "Junior" Gilliam ("bats L or R,")	40.00	20.00	12.00
(7b) James "Junior" Gilliam ("bats L - R", thick lips, wide gap between "BROOKLYN" and "DODGERS")	75.00	37.00	22.00
(7c) James "Junior" Gilliam ("bats L - R", thin lips, narrow gap between "BROOKLYN" and "DODGERS")	75.00	37.00	22.00
(8) Harvey "Kitten" Haddix	20.00	10.00	6.00
(9a) Ranson "Randy" Jackson (Ransom)("nfielder" on back)	125.00	62.50	37.50
(9b) Ranson "Randy" Jackson (Ransom)("Infielder" on back.)	40.00	20.00	12.00
(10a) Jack "Jackie" Jensen ("Boston Reb Sox")	30.00	15.00	9.00
(10b) Jack "Jackie" Jensen ("Boston Red Sox")	50.00	25.00	15.00
(11) Theodore "Ted" Kluszewski	20.00	10.00	6.00
(12a) Harvey E. Kuenn (Widely spaced letters in name; last line on back is bats/throws.)	100.00	50.00	30.00
(12b) Harvey E. Kuenn (Widely spaced letters in name; last line on back is 1954 average.)	50.00	25.00	15.00

(12c)	Harvey E. Kuenn (Condensed letters in name; last line on back is 1954 average.)	50.00	25.00	15.00
(13a)	Charles "Mickey" Mantel (Incorrect spelling.)	125.00	62.50	.37.50
(13b)	Charles "Mickey" Mantle (Corrected)("bats L or R")	400.00	200.00	120.00
(13c)	Charles "Mickey" Mantle (Corrected)("bats L - R")	800.00	400.00	240.00
(14)	Donald "Don" Mueller/SP	40.00	20.00	12.00
(15)	Harold "Pee Wee" Reese	40.00	20.00	12.00
(16)	Allie P. Reynolds	20.00	10.00	6.00
(17)	Albert "Flip" Rosen	20.00	10.00	6.00
(18)	Curtis "Curt" Simmons	20.00	10.00	6.00
(19)	Edwin "Duke" Snider	50.00	25.00	15.00
(20)	Warren Spahn	40.00	20.00	12.00
(21)	Frank Thomas/SP	40.00	20.00	12.00
(22a)	Virgil "Fire" Trucks (WHITESOX)	20.00	10.00	6.00
(22b)	Virgil "Fire" Trucks (WHITE SOX)	150.00	75.00	45.00
(23)	Robert "Bob" Turley	20.00	10.00	6.00
(24)	James "Mickey" Vernon	20.00	10.00	6.00

1958 Armour S.F. Giants Tabs

In the Giants' first season on the West Coast, packages of Armour hot dogs in the Bay Area could be found with a small (about 2" x 1-5/8") lithographed tin player "tab" enclosed. In team colors of black, white and orange the tabs have black-and-white portraits at center, around which is a round, square or diamond shaped device bearing the team name and other graphic touches. At the sides are wings with baseballs or caps printed thereon. A 1/2" tab is at top with a slotted panel at bottom. The tab of one piece could be inserted into the slot of another to create a chain of these pieces, or the top tab could be folded over a shirt pocket to wear the item as a badge. The unnumbered pieces are checklisted here alphabetically. NM values quoted are for unbent pieces only.

		NM	EX	VG
Complete Set (10):		3,250	1,600	975.00
Common Player:		250.00	125.00	75.00
(1)	Johnny Antonelli	250.00	125.00	75.00
(2)	Curt Barclay	250.00	125.00	75.00
(3)	Ray Crone	250.00	125.00	75.00
(4)	Whitey Lockman	250.00	125.00	75.00
(5a)	Willie Mays (Portrait in circle.)	600.00	300.00	180.00
(5b)	Willie Mays (Portrait in diamond.)	600.00	300.00	180.00
(6)	Don Mueller	250.00	125.00	75.00
(7)	Danny O'Connell	250.00	125.00	75.00
(8)	Hank Sauer	250.00	125.00	75.00
(9)	Daryl Spencer	250.00	125.00	75.00
(10)	Bobby Thomson	250.00	125.00	75.00

1959 Armour Bacon K.C. Athletics

Not so much a baseball card set as a handful of related single-card issues used at player promotional appearances, a total of four cards are currently known of this issue. Measuring either 5-1/2" x 3-1/4" or 5-1/2" x 4", the horizontal-format cards are printed in black-and-white on paper stock and are blank-backed. A posed player photo appears at left, with an ad for Armour bacon at right. Cards were given out at player appearances at local supermarkets. To date, all known specimens have been found autographed and are priced as such.

		NM	EX	VG
Complete Set (4):		2,500	1,250	750.00
Common Player:		75.00	37.00	22.00
(1)	Harry Chiti	75.00	37.50	22.50
(2)	Whitey Herzog	90.00	45.00	27.50
(3)	Roger Maris (Photo to waist.)	1,000	500.00	300.00
(4)	Roger Maris (Hands on knees.)	1,400	700.00	425.00

1959 Armour Coins

After a three-year layoff, Armour again inserted plastic "coins" into its hot dog packages. The coins retained their 1-1/2" size but did not include as much detailed information as in 1955. Missing from the coins' backs is information such as birthplace and date, team, and batting and throwing preference. The fronts contain the player's name and, unlike 1955, only the team nickname is given. The set consists of 20 coins which come in a myriad of colors. Common colors are navy blue, royal blue, medium green, orange and red. Many other colors are known, many of them scarce and of extra value to Armour specialists. In 1959 Armour had a mail-in offer of 10 coins for $1, which accounts for half of the coins in the set being much more plentiful than the others.

		NM	EX	VG
Complete Set (20):		400.00	200.00	120.00
Common Player:		15.00	7.50	4.50
(1)	Hank Aaron	30.00	15.00	9.00
(2)	John Antonelli	15.00	7.50	4.50
(3)	Richie Ashburn	30.00	15.00	9.00
(4)	Ernie Banks	30.00	15.00	9.00
(5)	Don Blasingame	15.00	7.50	4.50
(6)	Bob Cerv	15.00	7.50	4.50
(7)	Del Crandall	15.00	7.50	4.50
(8)	Whitey Ford	25.00	12.50	7.50
(9)	Nellie Fox	20.00	10.00	6.00
(10)	Jackie Jensen	20.00	10.00	6.00
(11)	Harvey Kuenn	30.00	15.00	9.00
(12)	Frank Malzone	20.00	10.00	6.00
(13)	Johnny Podres	30.00	15.00	9.00
(14)	Frank Robinson	30.00	15.00	9.00
(15)	Roy Sievers	15.00	7.50	4.50
(16)	Bob Skinner	15.00	7.50	4.50
(17)	Frank Thomas	15.00	7.50	4.50
(18)	Gus Triandos	15.00	7.50	4.50
(19)	Bob Turley	20.00	10.00	6.00
(20)	Mickey Vernon	15.00	7.50	4.50

1960 Armour Coins

The 1960 Armour coin issue is identical in number and style to the 1959 set. The unnumbered coins, 1-1/2" in diameter, once again came in a variety of colors. Common colors for 1960 are pale blue, royal blue, red, red-orange, light green, dark green and yellow. Values shown are for common-colored pieces. Scarcer colors exist and may be of premium value to specialists. The Bud Daley coin is very scarce, although it is not known why. Theories for the scarcity center on broken molding equipment, contract disputes, or that the coin was only inserted in a test product that quickly proved to be unsuccessful. As in 1959, a mail-in offer for 10 free coins was made available by Armour. The complete set price includes only the most common variations. Many 1960 Armour coins are found with only partial rims on back (Mantle is particularly susceptible to this condition). Coins without full back rims can grade no higher than VG.

		NM	EX	VG
Complete Set (20):		1,100	550.00	325.00
Common Player:		12.50	6.25	3.75
(1a)	Hank Aaron (Braves)	25.00	12.50	7.50
(1b)	Hank Aaron (Milwaukee Braves)	40.00	20.00	12.00
(2)	Bob Allison	20.00	10.00	6.00
(3)	Ernie Banks	30.00	15.00	9.00
(4)	Ken Boyer	12.50	6.25	3.75
(5)	Rocky Colavito	35.00	17.50	10.50
(6)	Gene Conley	12.50	6.25	3.75
(7)	Del Crandall	12.50	6.25	3.75
(8)	Bud Daley	750.00	375.00	225.00
(9a)	Don Drysdale (L.A condensed.)	35.00	17.50	10.50
(9b)	Don Drysdale (Space between L. and A.)	25.00	12.50	7.50
(10)	Whitey Ford	20.00	10.00	6.00
(11)	Nellie Fox	15.00	7.50	4.50
(12)	Al Kaline	20.00	10.00	6.00
(13a)	Frank Malzone (Red Sox)	12.50	6.25	3.75
(13b)	Frank Malzone (Boston Red Sox)	20.00	10.00	6.00
(14)	Mickey Mantle	75.00	37.50	22.50
(15)	Ed Mathews	20.00	10.00	6.00
(16)	Willie Mays	50.00	25.00	15.00
(17)	Vada Pinson	12.50	6.25	3.75
(18)	Dick Stuart	12.50	6.25	3.75
(19)	Gus Triandos	12.50	6.25	3.75
(20)	Early Wynn	12.50	6.25	3.75

1908 Art Post Card Co. Our Home Team

This set of team post cards presents players from five Midwestern teams in a foldout format. The cover of the accordian-fold novelty is in orange and green. A 3-1/2" x 5-1/2" postcard depicts a ballfield and various pieces of baseball equipment. Printed on a large baseball is "Our Home Team." Folded inside are a number of 2" x 2-1/4" panels with one or two player photos printed on each side. Each player is identified, though misspelled names are common.

		NM	EX	VG
Complete Set (5):		5,500	2,750	1,650
Common Team Card:		800.00	400.00	250.00
(1)	Chicago Cubs (Three Finger Brown, Frank Chance, Johnny Evers, Chick Fraser, Solly Hofman, Johnny Kling, Carl Lundgren, Pat Moran, Jake Pfeister, Ed Reulbach, Wildfire Schulte, Jimmy Sheckard, Jimmy Slagle, Harry Steinfeldt, Joe Tinker, Heinie Zimmerman)	1,200	600.00	360.00
(2)	Chicago White Sox (Nick Altrock, John Anderson, Jake Atz, George Davis, Jiggs Donohue (Donahue), Patsy Dougherty, Eddie Hahn, Frank Isbell, Fielder Jones, Frank Owen, George Rohe, Billy Sullivan, Lee Tannehill, Ed Walsh, Doc White)	1,850	925.00	550.00
(3)	Detroit Tigers (William Caughlin (Coughlin), Ty Cobb, Sam Crawford, Wild Bill Donovan, Red Downs, Hughie Jennings, Davy Jones, Red Killefer, Ed Killian, Matty McIntyre, George Mullin, Charley O'Leary, Fred Payne, Claude Rossman, Germany Schaefer, Boss Schmidt, George Suggs, Ed Summers, Ira Thomas, George Winter, Ed Willett)	2,000	1,000	600.00
(4)	St. Louis Browns (Bob Bailey, Bert Blue, Dode Criss, Bill Dinneen, Hobe Ferris, Bill Graham, Roy Hartzell, Danny Hoffman, Harry Howell, Charlie Jones, Tom Jones, Jimmy McAleer, Jack O'Connor, Barney Pelty, Jack Powell, Al Schweitzer, Tubby Spencer, George Stone, Rube Waddell, Bobby Wallace, Jimmy Williams, Joe Yeager)	950.00	475.00	285.00
(5)	St. Louis Cardinals	800.00	400.00	240.00

1953-55 Artvue Hall of Fame Plaque Postcards - Type 1

From 1953-1963, Artvue was the official producer of the Baseball Hall of Fame's postcards available for public sale. The 3-1/2" x 5-1/2" black-and-white cards depict the bronze plaque of each inductee. Fronts have a white border. Postcard-style backs have a bit of player data and identification of the specific producer. On Type 1 Artvue cards, issued 1953-55, the bolt holes in the four corners of the plaque are open. The Type 2 Artvues have baseball bolts in each corner of the plaque. The unnumbered cards are checklisted here alphabetically.

	NM	EX	VG
Complete Set (79):	2,000	1,000	600.00
Common Player:	30.00	15.00	9.00
(1) G.C. Alexander	30.00	15.00	9.00
(2) Adrian Anson	30.00	15.00	9.00
(3) Frank Baker	30.00	15.00	9.00
(4) Ed Barrow	30.00	15.00	9.00
(5) Chief Bender	30.00	15.00	9.00
(6) Roger Bresnahan	30.00	15.00	9.00
(7) Dan Brouthers	30.00	15.00	9.00
(8) Mordecai Brown	30.00	15.00	9.00
(9) Morgan Bulkeley	30.00	15.00	9.00
(10) Jesse Burkett	30.00	15.00	9.00
(11) Alexander Cartwright	30.00	15.00	9.00
(12) Henry Chadwick	30.00	15.00	9.00
(13) Frank Chance	30.00	15.00	9.00
(14) Jack Chesbro	30.00	15.00	9.00
(15) Fred Clarke	30.00	15.00	9.00
(16) Ty Cobb	80.00	40.00	24.00
(17) Mickey Cochrane	30.00	15.00	9.00
(18) Eddie Collins	30.00	15.00	9.00
(19) Jimmy Collins	30.00	15.00	9.00
(20) Charles Comiskey	30.00	15.00	9.00
(21) Tom Connolly	30.00	15.00	9.00
(22) Candy Cummings	30.00	15.00	9.00
(23) Dizzy Dean	30.00	15.00	9.00
(24) Ed Delahanty	30.00	15.00	9.00
(25) Bill Dickey	30.00	15.00	9.00
(26) Joe DiMaggio	80.00	40.00	24.00
(27) Hugh Duffy	30.00	15.00	9.00
(28) Johnny Evers	30.00	15.00	9.00
(29) Buck Ewing	30.00	15.00	9.00
(30) Jimmie Foxx	30.00	15.00	9.00
(31) Frankie Frisch	30.00	15.00	9.00
(32) Lou Gehrig	90.00	45.00	27.50
(33) Charlie Gehringer	30.00	15.00	9.00
(34) Clark Griffith	30.00	15.00	9.00
(35) Lefty Grove	30.00	15.00	9.00
(36) Gabby Hartnett	30.00	15.00	9.00
(37) Harry Heilmann	30.00	15.00	9.00
(38) Rogers Hornsby	30.00	15.00	9.00
(39) Carl Hubbell	30.00	15.00	9.00
(40) Hughie Jennings	30.00	15.00	9.00
(41) Ban Johnson	30.00	15.00	9.00
(42) Walter Johnson	60.00	30.00	18.00
(43) Willie Keeler	30.00	15.00	9.00
(44) King Kelly	30.00	15.00	9.00
(45) Bill Klem	30.00	15.00	9.00
(46) Nap Lajoie	30.00	15.00	9.00
(47) Kenesaw Landis	30.00	15.00	9.00
(48) Ted Lyons	30.00	15.00	9.00
(49) Connie Mack	30.00	15.00	9.00
(50) Rabbit Maranville	30.00	15.00	9.00
(51) Christy Mathewson	60.00	30.00	18.00
(52) Tommy McCarthy	30.00	15.00	9.00
(53) Joe McGinnity	30.00	15.00	9.00
(54) John McGraw	30.00	15.00	9.00
(55) Kid Nichols	30.00	15.00	9.00
(56) Jim O'Rourke	30.00	15.00	9.00
(57) Mel Ott	30.00	15.00	9.00
(58) Herb Pennock	30.00	15.00	9.00
(59) Ed Plank	30.00	15.00	9.00
(60) Chas. Radbourn	30.00	15.00	9.00
(61) Wilbert Robinson	30.00	15.00	9.00
(62) Babe Ruth	120.00	60.00	35.00
(63) Ray Schalk	30.00	15.00	9.00
(64) Al Simmons	30.00	15.00	9.00
(65) George Sisler	30.00	15.00	9.00
(66) Al Spalding	30.00	15.00	9.00
(67) Tris Speaker	30.00	15.00	9.00
(68) Bill Terry	30.00	15.00	9.00
(69) Joe Tinker	30.00	15.00	9.00
(70) Pie Traynor	30.00	15.00	9.00
(71) Dazzy Vance	30.00	15.00	9.00
(72) Rube Waddell	30.00	15.00	9.00
(73) Honus Wagner	60.00	30.00	18.00
(74) Bobby Wallace	30.00	15.00	9.00
(75) Ed Walsh	30.00	15.00	9.00
(76) Paul Waner	30.00	15.00	9.00
(77) George Wright	30.00	15.00	9.00
(78) Harry Wright	30.00	15.00	9.00
(79) Cy Young	60.00	30.00	18.00

1956-63 Artvue Hall of Fame Plaque Postcards - Type 2

From 1953-1963, Artvue was the official producer of the Baseball Hall of Fame's postcards available for public sale. The 3-1/2" x 5-1/2" black-and-white cards depict the bronze plaque of each inductee. Fronts have a white border. Postcard-style backs have a bit of player data and identification of the specific producer. On Type 2 Artvue cards, issued 1956-63, there are baseball bolts in each corner of the plaque. The unnumbered cards are checklisted here alphabetically. Players unique to Type 2 are noted with an asterisk.

	NM	EX	VG
Complete Set (94):	2,000	1,000	600.00
Common Player:	25.00	12.50	7.50
(1) G.C. Alexander	25.00	12.50	7.50
(2) Adrian Anson	25.00	12.50	7.50
(3) Frank Baker	25.00	12.50	7.50
(4) Ed Barrow	25.00	12.50	7.50
(5) Chief Bender	25.00	12.50	7.50
(6) Roger Bresnahan	25.00	12.50	7.50
(7) Dan Brouthers	25.00	12.50	7.50
(8) Mordecai Brown	25.00	12.50	7.50
(9) Morgan Bulkeley	25.00	12.50	7.50
(10) Jesse Burkett	25.00	12.50	7.50
(11) Max Carey (*)	25.00	12.50	7.50
(12) Alexander Cartwright	25.00	12.50	7.50
(13) Henry Chadwick	25.00	12.50	7.50
(14) Frank Chance	25.00	12.50	7.50
(15) Jack Chesbro	25.00	12.50	7.50
(16) Fred Clarke	25.00	12.50	7.50
(17) John Clarkson (*)	25.00	12.50	7.50
(18) Ty Cobb	60.00	30.00	18.00
(19) Mickey Cochrane	25.00	12.50	7.50
(20) Eddie Collins	25.00	12.50	7.50
(21) Jimmy Collins	25.00	12.50	7.50
(22) Charles Comiskey	25.00	12.50	7.50
(23) Tom Connolly	25.00	12.50	7.50
(24) Sam Crawford (*)	25.00	12.50	7.50
(25) Joe Cronin (*)	25.00	12.50	7.50
(26) Candy Cummings	25.00	12.50	7.50
(27) Dizzy Dean	25.00	12.50	7.50
(28) Ed Delahanty	25.00	12.50	7.50
(29) Bill Dickey	25.00	12.50	7.50
(30) Joe DiMaggio	80.00	40.00	24.00
(31) Hugh Duffy	25.00	12.50	7.50
(32) Johnny Evers	25.00	12.50	7.50
(33) Buck Ewing	25.00	12.50	7.50
(34) Bob Feller (*)	25.00	12.50	7.50
(35) Elmer Flick (*)	25.00	12.50	7.50
(36) Jimmie Foxx	25.00	12.50	7.50
(37) Frank Frisch	25.00	12.50	7.50
(38) Lou Gehrig	80.00	40.00	24.00
(39) Charlie Gehringer	25.00	12.50	7.50
(40) Hank Greenberg (*)	25.00	12.50	7.50
(41) Clark Griffith	25.00	12.50	7.50
(42) Lefty Grove	25.00	12.50	7.50
(43) Billy Hamilton (*)	25.00	12.50	7.50
(44) Gabby Hartnett	25.00	12.50	7.50
(45) Harry Heilmann	25.00	12.50	7.50
(46) Rogers Hornsby	25.00	12.50	7.50
(47) Carl Hubbell	25.00	12.50	7.50
(48) Hughie Jennings	25.00	12.50	7.50
(49) Ban Johnson	25.00	12.50	7.50
(50) Walter Johnson	40.00	20.00	12.00
(51) Willie Keeler	25.00	12.50	7.50
(52) King Kelly	25.00	12.50	7.50
(53) Bill Klem	25.00	12.50	7.50
(54) Nap Lajoie	25.00	12.50	7.50
(55) Kenesaw Landis	25.00	12.50	7.50
(56) Ted Lyons	25.00	12.50	7.50
(57) Connie Mack	25.00	12.50	7.50
(58) Rabbit Maranville	25.00	12.50	7.50
(59) Christy Mathewson	40.00	20.00	12.00
(60) Joe McCarthy (*)	25.00	12.50	7.50
(61) Tommy McCarthy	25.00	12.50	7.50
(62) Joe McGinnity	25.00	12.50	7.50
(63) John McGraw	25.00	12.50	7.50
(64) Bill McKechnie (*)	25.00	12.50	7.50
(65) Kid Nichols	25.00	12.50	7.50
(66) Jim O'Rourke	25.00	12.50	7.50
(67) Mel Ott	25.00	12.50	7.50
(68) Herb Pennock	25.00	12.50	7.50
(69) Ed Plank	25.00	12.50	7.50
(70) Charles Radbourn	25.00	12.50	7.50
(71) Sam Rice (*)	25.00	12.50	7.50
(72) Eppa Rixey (*)	25.00	12.50	7.50
(73) Jackie Robinson (*)	40.00	20.00	12.00
(74) Wilbert Robinson	25.00	12.50	7.50
(75) Edd Roush (*)	25.00	12.50	7.50
(76) Babe Ruth	120.00	60.00	35.00
(77) Ray Schalk	25.00	12.50	7.50
(78) Al Simmons	25.00	12.50	7.50
(79) George Sisler	25.00	12.50	7.50
(80) Albert Spalding	25.00	12.50	7.50
(81) Tris Speaker	25.00	12.50	7.50
(82) Bill Terry	25.00	12.50	7.50
(83) Joe Tinker	25.00	12.50	7.50
(84) Pie Traynor	25.00	12.50	7.50
(85) Dazzy Vance	25.00	12.50	7.50
(86) Rube Waddell	25.00	12.50	7.50
(87) Honus Wagner	40.00	20.00	12.00
(88) Bobby Wallace	25.00	12.50	7.50
(89) Ed Walsh	25.00	12.50	7.50
(90) Paul Waner	25.00	12.50	7.50
(91) Zack Wheat (*)	25.00	12.50	7.50
(92) George Wright	25.00	12.50	7.50
(93) Harry Wright	25.00	12.50	7.50
(94) Cy Young	40.00	20.00	12.00

1967 Ashland Oil Grand Slam Baseball

These baseball player folders were issued in conjunctioon with a sweepstakes conducted at Ashland gas stations, which offered a bicycle in exchange for a completed "Baseball Player Photo Album." To avoid giving away too many bikes, the Jim Maloney card was short-printed. The cards were originally issued in the form of a sealed tri-folder. When opened to 7-1/2" x 2", a blue duotone player portrait photo is pictured at center. back of the panel offers contest rules. The unnumbered panels are listed here in alphabetical order. Prices are for complete tri-fold panels.

	NM	EX	VG
Complete Set (12):	325.00	160.00	97.50
Common Player:			
Album	150.00	75.00	45.00
(1) Jim Bunning	30.00	15.00	9.00
(2) Elston Howard	25.00	12.50	7.50
(3) Al Kaline	50.00	25.00	15.00
(4) Harmon Killebrew	30.00	15.00	9.00
(5) Ed Kranepool	20.00	10.00	6.00
(6) Jim Maloney/SP	Value Undetermined		
(7) Bill Mazeroski	30.00	15.00	9.00
(8) Frank Robinson	40.00	20.00	12.00
(9) Ron Santo	25.00	12.50	7.50
(10) Joe Torre	25.00	12.50	7.50
(11) Leon Wagner	20.00	10.00	6.00
(12) Pete Ward	20.00	10.00	6.00

1895 Ashman Studio Cabinets

The date attributed is speculative and about at the mid-point of the sole known subject's tenure with the Baltimore Orioles of the National League. In typical cabinet format, about 4-1/2" x 6-1/2", the card features a sepia-toned portrait photo attached to a blank-back, cream-colored thick cardboard mount bearing the advertising at bottom of the Baltimore photographer's studio. It is unknown whether cabinets of any of McGraw's teammates or adversaries were also produced.

	NM	EX	VG
John McGraw	10,000	5,000	3,000

1933 Astra Margarine

One of several "foreign" Babe Ruth cards issued during his prime was included in a 112-card set produced as premiums for Astra Margarine in Germany. Ruth is the only major league ballplayer in the issue. Cards are in full color, measuring 2-3/4" x 4-1/8". Backs of the unnumbered cards are printed in German. Three types of backs can be found on the Ruth card. Type 1, has the Astra name nearly centered. The Type 2 back has the brand name printed closer to the bottom of the card, with only four lines of type under it. Type 3 is a variation of Type 2 on which the appropriate page number (83) of the accompanying album is mentioned on the line immediately above "Handbuch des Sports" near the top. One card was given with the purchase of each 1/2 pound of margarine, and the album could be ordered by mail. See also Sanella Margarine.

	NM	EX	VG
Type 1 Babe Ruth (Astra centered.)	1,500	750.00	450.00
Type 2 Babe Ruth (Astra at bottom.)	1,750	875.00	525.00
Type 3 Babe Ruth	3,500	1,750	1,000
(Astra at bottom w/83.)			

1978 Atlanta Nobis Center

felipe alou

Felipe Alou
OUTFIELD
THE BRAVES

Felipe Alou
Led Braves in hits in 1966 and 1968. One of three brothers who came up through the Giants organization. A Brave from 1964 to 1969, hitting a career high .327 in 154 games for the 1966 Atlanta season.

In conjunction with a May 1978 card show to benefit the training/rehabilitation center supported by Hall of Fame linebacker Tommy Nobis, this collectors' set was issued. Most of the players on the 2-1/2" x 3-1/2" cards are former stars of the Boston, Milwaukee or Atlanta Braves, though players from a few other teams and footballer Nobis are also included; several of the players appeared at the show as autograph guests. The cards are in the style of 1959 Topps, with black-and-white player photos in a circle at center and a light green background. The career summary on back is in black-and-white. The unnumbered cards are checklisted here in alphabetical order.

		NM	EX	VG
Complete Set (24):		25.00	12.50	7.50
Common Player:		1.50	.70	.45
(1)	Hank Aaron	6.00	3.00	1.75
(2)	Joe Adcock	1.50	.70	.45
(3)	Felipe Alou	1.50	.70	.45
(4)	Frank Bolling	1.50	.70	.45
(5)	Orlando Cepeda	2.00	1.00	.60
(6)	Ty Cline	1.50	.70	.45
(7)	Tony Cloninger	1.50	.70	.45
(8)	Del Crandall	1.50	.70	.45
(9)	Fred Haney	1.50	.70	.45
(10)	Pat Jarvis	1.50	.70	.45
(11)	Ernie Johnson	1.50	.70	.45
(12)	Ken Johnson	1.50	.70	.45
(13)	Denny Lemaster	1.50	.70	.45
(14)	Eddie Mathews	2.00	1.00	.60
(15)	Lee Maye	1.50	.70	.45
(16)	Denis Menke	1.50	.70	.45
(17)	Felix Millan	1.50	.70	.45
(18)	Johnny Mize	2.00	1.00	.60
(19)	Tommy Nobis	1.50	.70	.45
(20)	Gene Oliver	1.50	.70	.45
(21)	Johnny Sain	1.75	.90	.50
(22)	Warren Spahn	2.00	1.00	.60
(23)	Joe Torre	2.00	1.00	.60
(24)	Bob Turley	1.75	.90	.50

1968 Atlantic Oil Play Ball Game Cards

Collect with American League Player numbered 7 and WIN $10

JOE PEPITONE
New York Yankees
American League

PLAYER NUMBER

Because some of the cards were redeemable either alone or in combination for cash awards, and thus were issued in lesser quantities, completion of this game issue was difficult from Day 1. Fifty different players are known in the issue, along with a number of variations. The majority of the cards can be found with card backs either explaining the game rules or picturing a pitcher throwing to a batter. The cards were issued in two-card panels, designed to be separated into a pair of 2-1/2" x 3-1/2" cards. For lack of an MLB license, the color player photos at center have the uniform logos removed. Printed at top is the face value of the particular card, while the player's name, team and league are printed in the bottom border. American Leaguers' cards are bordered in red, while the National League cards have blue borders.

		NM	EX	VG
Complete Set (Non-winners.) (40):		350.00	175.00	100.00
Common Player:		6.00	3.00	1.50
Instant Winner Card:		30.00	15.00	9.00
AMERICAN LEAGUE				
1a	Tony Oliva	6.00	3.00	1.75
1b	Brooks Robinson	15.00	7.50	4.50
1c	Pete Ward	6.00	3.00	1.75
2a	Max Alvis	6.00	3.00	1.75
2b	Campy Campaneris	6.00	3.00	1.75
2c	Jim Fregosi	6.00	3.00	1.75
2d	Al Kaline	20.00	10.00	6.00
2e	Tom Tresh	6.00	3.00	1.75
3	Bill Freehan ($2,500 winner)	300.00	150.00	90.00
4	Tommy Davis ($100 winner)	100.00	50.00	30.00
5a	Norm Cash	7.50	3.75	2.25
5b	Frank Robinson	15.00	7.50	4.50
5c	Carl Yastrzemski	25.00	12.50	7.50
6a	Joe Pepitone	7.50	3.75	2.25
6b	Boog Powell	10.00	5.00	3.00
6c	George Scott	6.00	3.00	1.75
6d	Fred Valentine	6.00	3.00	1.75
7	Tom McCraw ($10 winner)	75.00	37.00	22.00
8	Andy Etchebarren ($5 winner)	50.00	25.00	15.00
9a	Dean Chance	6.00	3.00	1.75
9b	Joel Horlen	6.00	3.00	1.75
9c	Jim Lonborg	6.00	3.00	1.75
9d	Sam McDowell	6.00	3.00	1.75
10	Earl Wilson ($1 winner)	35.00	17.50	10.50
11	Jose Santiago	6.00	3.00	1.75
NATIONAL LEAGUE				
1a	Bob Aspromonte	6.00	3.00	1.75
1b	Lou Brock	12.00	6.00	3.50
1c	Johnny Callison	6.00	3.00	1.75
1d	Pete Rose	25.00	12.50	7.50
1e	Maury Wills	7.50	3.75	2.25
2	Tommie Agee ($2,500 winner)	300.00	150.00	90.00
3a	Felipe Alou	7.50	3.75	2.25
3b	Jim Hart	6.00	3.00	1.75
3c	Vada Pinson	7.50	3.75	2.25
4a	Hank Aaron	25.00	12.50	7.50
4b	Orlando Cepeda	10.00	5.00	3.00
4c	Willie McCovey	12.00	6.00	3.50
4d	Ron Santo	9.00	4.50	2.75
5	Ernie Banks ($100 winner)	450.00	225.00	135.00
6	Ron Fairly ($10 winner)	75.00	37.50	22.50
7a	Roberto Clemente	75.00	37.50	22.50
7b	Roger Maris	25.00	12.50	7.50
7c a	Ron Swoboda	6.00	3.00	1.75
	(Collect w/ N.L. #6, win $10.)			
7c b	Ron Swoboda	45.00	22.00	13.50
	(Collect w/ N.L. #8, win $5.)			
8	Billy Williams ($5 winner)	95.00	47.00	28.00
9a	Jim Bunning	9.00	4.50	2.75
9b	Bob Gibson	12.00	6.00	3.50
9c	Jim Maloney	6.00	3.00	1.75
9d	Mike McCormick	6.00	3.00	1.75
10	Milt Pappas	6.00	3.00	1.75
11	Claude Osteen ($1 winner)	35.00	17.50	10.00

1969 Atlantic-Richfield Boston Red Sox

Mike Andrews

One of many larger-format (8" x 10") baseball premiums sponsored as gas station giveaways in the late 1960s and early 1970s was this set of Boston Red Sox player pictures by celebrity artist John Wheeldon sponsored by the Atlantic-Richfield Oil Co. Done in pastel colors, the pictures feature large portraits and smaller action pictures of the player against a bright background. A facsimile autograph is penciled in beneath the pictures, and the player's name is printed in the white bottom border. Backs are printed in black-and-white and include biographical and career data, full major and minor league stats, a self-portrait and biography of the artist and the logos of the team, players' association and sponsor. The unnumbered pictures are checklisted here alphabetically.

		NM	EX	VG
Complete Set (12):		75.00	35.00	25.00
Common Player:		6.00	3.00	1.75
(1)	Mike Andrews	6.00	3.00	1.75
(2)	Tony Conigliaro	10.00	5.00	3.00
(3)	Ray Culp	6.00	3.00	1.75
(4)	Russ Gibson	6.00	3.00	1.75
(5)	Dalton Jones	6.00	3.00	1.75
(6)	Jim Lonborg	8.00	4.00	2.50
(7)	Sparky Lyle	8.00	4.00	2.50
(8)	Syd O'Brien	6.00	3.00	1.75
(9)	George Scott	8.00	4.00	2.50
(10)	Reggie Smith	8.00	4.00	2.50
(11)	Rico Petrocelli	8.00	4.00	2.50
(12)	Carl Yastrzemski	25.00	12.50	7.50

1962 Auravision Records

Similar in design and format to the 16-record set which was issued in 1964, this test issue can be differentiated by the stats on the back. On the 1962 record, Mantle is shown in a right-handed batting pose, as compared to a follow-through on the 1964 record. Where Gentile and Colavito are shown in the

uniform of K.C. A's on the 1964 records, they are shown as a Tiger (Colavito) and Oriole (Gentile) on the earlier version. The set is checklisted here alphabetically.

		NM	EX	VG
Complete Set (8):		300.00	150.00	90.00
Common Player:		15.00	7.50	4.50
(1)	Ernie Banks	30.00	15.00	9.00
(2)	Rocky Colavito	25.00	12.50	7.50
(3)	Whitey Ford	30.00	15.00	9.00
(4)	Jim Gentile	15.00	7.50	4.50
(5)	Mickey Mantle	100.00	50.00	30.00
(6)	Roger Maris	35.00	17.50	10.50
(7)	Willie Mays	50.00	25.00	15.00
(8)	Warren Spahn	30.00	15.00	9.00

1964 Auravision Records

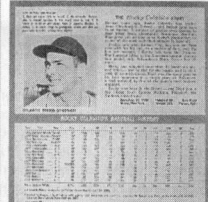

Never a candidate for the Billboard "Hot 100," this series of baseball picture records is popular with collectors due to the high-quality photos on front and back. On the grooved front side of the 6-3/4" x 6-3/4" plastic-laminated cardboard record is a color player photo with facsimile autograph, Sports Record trophy logo and 33-1/3 RPM notation. A color border surrounds the photo and is carried over to the unrecorded back side. There is another photo on back, along with a career summary and complete major and minor league stats and instructions for playing the record. In the bottom border is a copyright notice by Sports Champions Inc., and a notice that the Auravision Record is a product of Columbia Records. A hole at center of the record could be punched out for playing and the records featured a five-minute interview with the player by sportscaster Marty Glickman. The records were originally a mail-in premium available through an offer on Milk Dud candy boxes. Large quantities of the records made their way into the hobby as remainders. For early-1960s baseball items they remain reasonably priced today. The unnumbered records are checklisted here alphabetically. The Mays record is unaccountably much scarcer than the others.

		NM	EX	VG
Complete Set (16):		150.00	75.00	45.00
Common Player:		6.00	3.00	1.75
(1)	Bob Allison	6.00	3.00	1.75
(2)	Ernie Banks	9.00	4.50	2.75
(3)	Ken Boyer	6.00	3.00	1.75
(4)	Rocky Colavito	7.50	3.75	2.25
(5)	Don Drysdale	9.00	4.50	2.75
(6)	Whitey Ford	10.00	5.00	3.00
(7)	Jim Gentile	6.00	3.00	1.75
(8)	Al Kaline	10.00	5.00	3.00
(9)	Sandy Koufax	20.00	10.00	6.00
(10)	Mickey Mantle	25.00	12.50	7.50
(11)	Roger Maris	12.50	6.25	3.75
(12)	Willie Mays	75.00	37.50	22.50
(13)	Bill Mazeroski	9.00	4.50	2.75
(14)	Frank Robinson	9.00	4.50	2.75
(15)	Warren Spahn	9.00	4.50	2.75
(16)	Pete Ward	6.00	3.00	1.75

1945 Autographs Game

Politicians, movie stars and athletes are among the celebrities featured in this game from Leister Game Co. The 2-1/2" x 3-1/2" cards are printed in red and black on white and were found in pairs. The celebrity whose signature was reproduced on the card was seen in a photograph and top, while his paired partner was shown at bottom in an artist's depiction. Only two baseball players are included in the set.

	NM	EX	VG
Complete Boxed Set (55):	650.00	325.00	195.00
9A Joe DiMaggio, Babe Ruth (DiMaggio signature.)	75.00	37.50	22.50
9A Babe Ruth, Joe DiMaggio (Ruth signature.)	125.00	62.50	37.50

B

1949 Baas Cheri-Cola

 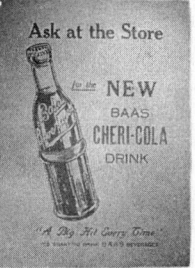

Only five of these premium issues have ever been cataloged so it's unknown how many comprise a set. The 7-5/8" x 9-1/2" pictures feature black-and-white player photos on front, with the player's name printed in white script. On back, printed in red, is an ad for Baas Cheri-Cola Drink. The unnumbered pictures are checklisted in alphabetical order.

	NM	EX	VG
Common Player:	375.00	185.00	110.00
(1) Bobby Doerr	450.00	220.00	135.00
(2) Bob Feller	750.00	370.00	220.00
(3) Ken Keltner	375.00	185.00	110.00
(4) John Sain	375.00	185.00	110.00
(5) Ted Williams	1,800	900.00	550.00

1930 Baguer Chocolate

This rare Cuban issue was apparently current between the start of the 1930 season and the redemption expiration date of Jan. 31, 1931. The set consists of 90 black-and-white player photos, about 5/8" x 7/8". The pictures have white borders and a white strip at the bottom of photo with some form of the player's name. Backs are printed in red, "Chocolate BAGUER El mas popular." An album was issued to collect the pictures and when full it could be exchanged for baseball equipment, toys or candy. The unnumbered cards are checklisted here in alphabetical order.

 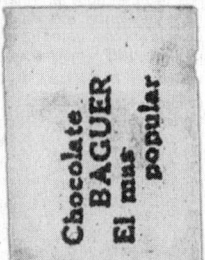

	NM	EX	VG
Complete Set (90):	5,500	3,750	2,200
Common Player:	30.00	20.00	12.00
Album:	75.00	52.00	30.00
(1) George Bancroft (Dave)	65.00	45.00	25.00
(2) Clyde Beck	30.00	20.00	12.00
(3) Larry Benton	30.00	20.00	12.00
(4) Max Bishop	30.00	20.00	12.00
(5) Clarence Blair	30.00	20.00	12.00
(6) Fred Blake	30.00	20.00	12.00
(7) Mitchell Blake/SP	80.00	55.00	30.00
(8) Joe Boley	30.00	20.00	12.00
(9) Jim Bottomley	65.00	45.00	25.00
(10) George Burns	30.00	20.00	12.00
(11) Guy Bush	30.00	20.00	12.00
(12) Mickey Cochrane	75.00	50.00	30.00
(13) Eddie Collins	75.00	50.00	30.00
(14) Kiki Cuyler	65.00	45.00	25.00
(15) Jimmy Dikes (Dykes)	30.00	20.00	12.00
(16) Leo Dixon	30.00	20.00	12.00
(17) Pete Donohue	30.00	20.00	12.00
(18) Taylor Douthit	30.00	20.00	12.00
(19) George Earnshaw	30.00	20.00	12.00
(20) R. Elliot (Jumbo Elliott)	30.00	20.00	12.00
(21) Joe (Woody) English	30.00	20.00	12.00
(22) Urban Faber	65.00	45.00	25.00
(23) Lewis Fonseca	30.00	20.00	12.00
(24) Jimmy Foxx	275.00	190.00	110.00
(25) Walter French	30.00	20.00	12.00
(26) Frankie Frisch	75.00	50.00	30.00
(27) Lou Gehrig	600.00	420.00	240.00
(28) Walter Gerber	30.00	20.00	12.00
(29) Miguel A. Gonzalez	65.00	45.00	25.00
(30) Goose Goslin	65.00	45.00	25.00

	NM	EX	VG
(31) W. Grampp (Henry)	30.00	20.00	12.00
(32) Burleigh Grimes	65.00	45.00	25.00
(33) Charlie Grimm	30.00	20.00	12.00
(34) Lefty Grove	75.00	50.00	30.00
(35) Geo. Haas	30.00	20.00	12.00
(36) (Bill) Hallahan	30.00	20.00	12.00
(37) Stanley Harris	65.00	45.00	25.00
(38) Geo. (Charles "Gabby") Hartnett	65.00	45.00	25.00
(39) Cliff Heathcote	30.00	20.00	12.00
(40) Babe Herman	30.00	20.00	12.00
(41) Andy High	30.00	20.00	12.00
(42) Rogers Hornsby	100.00	70.00	40.00
(43) Dan Howley	30.00	20.00	12.00
(44) Travis Jackson	65.00	45.00	25.00
(45) Walter Johnson	250.00	175.00	100.00
(46) Fred Lindstrom	65.00	45.00	25.00
(47) Alfonso Lopez	75.00	50.00	30.00
(48) Red Lucas	30.00	20.00	12.00
(49) (Dolf) Luque	65.00	45.00	25.00
(50) Pat Malone	30.00	20.00	12.00
(51) Harry (Heinie) Manush	65.00	45.00	25.00
(52) Fred Marberry	30.00	20.00	12.00
(53) Joe McCarthy	65.00	45.00	25.00
(54) J.J. McGraw	65.00	45.00	25.00
(55) G. Mc. Millan (Norman McMillan)	30.00	20.00	12.00
(56) Bing Miller	30.00	20.00	12.00
(57) J. (Johnny) Moore	30.00	20.00	12.00
(58) Buddy Myers (Myer)	30.00	20.00	12.00
(59) Bob O'Farrell	30.00	20.00	12.00
(60) Melvin Ott	75.00	50.00	30.00
(61) Herb Pennock	65.00	45.00	25.00
(62) Cy Perkins	30.00	20.00	12.00
(63) Jack Quinn	30.00	20.00	12.00
(64) Chas. Rhen (Rhem)	30.00	20.00	12.00
(65) Harry Rice	30.00	20.00	12.00
(66) Sam Rice	65.00	45.00	35.00
(67) Lance Richbourg	30.00	20.00	12.00
(68) W. (Wilbert) Robinson	65.00	45.00	25.00
(69) Eddie Rommell (Rommel)	30.00	20.00	12.00
(70) Charles Root	30.00	20.00	12.00
(71) Muddy Ruel	30.00	20.00	12.00
(72) Babe Ruth	900.00	630.00	360.00
(73) Wally Schang	30.00	20.00	12.00
(74) Bill Shores	30.00	20.00	12.00
(75) Al Simmons	65.00	45.00	25.00
(76) Geo. Sisler	75.00	50.00	30.00
(77) Earl Smith	30.00	20.00	12.00
(78) Riggs Stephenson	30.00	20.00	12.00
(79) Joe (Walter "Lefty") Stewart	30.00	20.00	12.00
(80) H. Summa	30.00	20.00	12.00
(81) Bill Terry	65.00	45.00	25.00
(82) Fresco Thompson	30.00	20.00	12.00
(83) Charley Tolson	30.00	20.00	12.00
(84) 'Pie' Traynor	65.00	45.00	25.00
(85) Dazzy Vance	65.00	45.00	25.00
(86) Rube Walberg	30.00	20.00	12.00
(87) 'Hack' Wilson	65.00	45.00	25.00
(88) Jimmy Wilson	30.00	20.00	12.00
(89) Glenn Wright	30.00	20.00	12.00
(90) Tom Zachary	30.00	20.00	12.00

1950s-70s Mel Bailey Player Postcards

 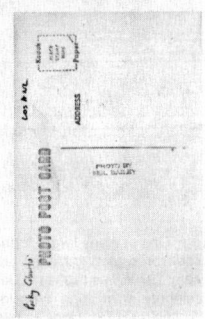

Photographer and hobbyist Mel Bailey was a prolific baseball photographer who produced many player postcards for their use in responding to fan requests for pictures and autographs. Several different formats of back design may be found. No checklist has been promulgated.

(Typical players $3-5; stars and Hall of Famers $10-30.)

1952 Bakersfield Indians Team Issue

Only one card is currently known from this set from the Globe Printing Co. line-up of minor league issues. The team is the 1952 Bakersfield Indians, the Class C farm club of the Cleveland Indians in the California League. The blank-backed, black-and-white cards are printed on thin cardboard and measure about 2-1/4" x 3-3/8". This checklist for the set was probably comprised of 8 cards when issued. An album to house the set was also issued. The card of manager Gene Lillard illustrated here was autographed after it was issued.

	NM	EX	VG
Album:	170.00	75.00	45.00
(1) Gene Lillard	75.00	40.00	25.00

1941 Ballantine Coasters

National League pitcher-catcher pairs are featured on this set of drink coasters issued by Ballantine Ale & Beer. The 4-1/2" diameter composition coasters are printed in black with orange, blue or red highlights. Fronts have line drawings of the

batterymates and a few words about the previous or coming season. Backs have a Ballantine's ad. It is unknown whether there are more than these three coasters in the series.

	NM	EX	VG
Common Coaster:	35.00	17.50	10.00
(1) Bob Klinger, Virgil Davis (Pirates)	35.00	17.50	10.00
(2a) Lon Warneke, Gus Mancuso (Cardinals)("AT THE GAME IT'S . . ." above portraits.)	35.00	17.50	10.00
(2b) Lon Warneke, Gus Mancuso (Cardinals)("At the Game it's" below portraits.)	35.00	17.50	10.00
(3) Whit Wyatt, Mickey Owen (Dodgers)	35.00	17.50	10.00

1911 Baltimore News Newsboys Series

This scarce version of E94 carries on its back the notation, "Baltimore News Newsboy Series" and offers $1 to the first 35 boys completing the full set. Unlike the Close Candy Co. cards, the newspaper version is found only with the light blue background on front. The issue was designated M131 in the American Card Catalog.

	NM	EX	VG
Complete Set (30):	85,000	42,500	25,000
Common Player:	3,000	1,500	1,000
(1) Jimmy Austin	3,000	1,500	1,000
(2) Johnny Bates	3,000	1,500	1,000
(3) Bob Bescher	3,000	1,500	1,000
(4) Bobby Byrne	3,000	1,500	1,000
(5) Frank Chance	7,500	3,750	2,250
(6) Ed Cicotte	6,000	3,000	1,800
(7) Ty Cobb	75,000	37,500	22,500
(8) Sam Crawford	7,500	3,750	2,250
(9) Harry Davis	3,000	1,500	1,000
(10) Art Devlin	3,000	1,500	1,000
(11) Josh Devore	3,000	1,500	1,000
(12) Mickey Doolan	3,000	1,500	1,000
(13) Patsy Dougherty	3,000	1,500	1,000
(14) Johnny Evers	7,500	3,750	2,250
(15) Eddie Grant	3,000	1,500	1,000
(16) Hugh Jennings	7,500	3,750	2,250
(17) Red Kleinow	3,000	1,500	1,000
(18) Joe Lake	3,000	1,500	1,000
(19) Nap Lajoie	9,000	4,500	2,700
(20) Tommy Leach	3,000	1,500	1,000
(21) Hans Lobert	3,000	1,500	1,000
(22) Harry Lord	3,000	1,500	1,000
(23) Sherry Magee	3,000	1,500	1,000
(24) John McGraw	11,250	5,625	3,375
(25) Earl Moore	3,000	1,500	1,000
(26) Red Murray	3,000	1,500	1,000
(27) Tris Speaker	13,500	6,750	4,050
(28) Terry Turner	3,000	1,500	1,000
(29) Honus Wagner	55,500	27,750	16,650
(30) "Old" Cy. Young	22,500	11,250	6,750

1914 Baltimore News Terrapins

Players from both of Baltimore's professional baseball teams are included in this set of schedule cards from the local newspaper. That season fans could support the Orioles of the International League or the Terrapins of the Federal League. The newspaper's cards are 2-5/8" x 3-5/8", monochrome printed in either red or blue with a wide border. Players are pictured in full-length posed action photos with the backgrounds erased in favor of a few artificial shadows. The player name, position and league are shown on front. Backs have a schedule of "AT HOME" and "ABROAD" of the appropriate team with an ad for the paper at top and a curious line at bottom which reads, "This Card is Given to," with space for a signature. The unnumbered cards are checklisted in alphabetical order, though it is presumed the checklist is incomplete. Only the Federal Leaguers' cards are listed here; the Orioles will be found in the minor league section of this catalog. This scarce version of E94 carries on its back the notation, "Baltimore Newsboy Series." Unlike the Close Candy Co. cards, the newspaper version is found only with the light blue background on front.

		NM	EX	VG
Common Player:		8,800	4,400	2,640
(1)	Neal Ball	8,800	4,400	2,640
(2)	Mike Doolan	8,800	4,400	2,640
(3)	Happy Finneran	8,800	4,400	2,640
(4)	Fred Jacklitch (Jacklitsch)	8,800	4,400	2,640
(5)	Otto Knabe	8,800	4,400	2,640
(6)	Benny Meyers (Meyer)	8,800	4,400	2,640
(7)	Jack Quinn	8,800	4,400	2,640
(8)	Hack Simmons	8,800	4,400	2,640
(9)	Frank Smith	8,800	4,400	2,640
(10)	George Suggs	8,800	4,400	2,640
(11)	Harry (Swats) Swacina	8,800	4,400	2,640
(12)	Ducky Yount	8,800	4,400	2,640
(13)	Guy Zinn	8,800	4,400	2,640

1954 Baltimore Orioles Picture Pack

This appears to be a team-issued photo pack in the O's first season after moving from St. Louis. The black-and-white poses are 6" x 8" in format, bordered in white and blank-backed. Pictures have a facsimile autograph on front. At least three versions of the photo pack were issued over the course of the season to reflect roster changes. It is unknown whether this checklist is complete.

		NM	EX	VG
Complete Set (33):		600.00	300.00	180.00
Common Player:		20.00	10.00	6.00
(1)	Cal Abrams	20.00	10.00	6.00
(2)	Neil Berry	20.00	10.00	6.00
(3)	Vern Bickford	20.00	10.00	6.00
(4)	Jim Brideweser	20.00	10.00	6.00
(5)	Bob Chakales	20.00	10.00	6.00
(6)	Gil Coan	20.00	10.00	6.00
(7)	Joe Coleman	20.00	10.00	6.00
(8)	Clint Courtney	20.00	10.00	6.00
(9)	Chuck Diering	20.00	10.00	6.00
(10)	Jim Dyck	20.00	10.00	6.00
(11)	Howie Fox	20.00	10.00	6.00
(12)	Jim Fridley/Btg	20.00	10.00	6.00
(13)	Jim Fridley/Portrait	20.00	10.00	6.00
(14)	Jehosie Heard	25.00	12.50	7.50
(15)	Bill Hunter	20.00	10.00	6.00
(16)	Darrell Johnson	20.00	10.00	6.00
(17)	Dick Kokos	20.00	10.00	6.00
(18)	Lou Kretlow	20.00	10.00	6.00
(19)	Dick Kryhoski	20.00	10.00	6.00
(20)	Don Larsen	40.00	20.00	12.00
(21)	Don Lenhardt	20.00	10.00	6.00
(22)	Dick Littlefield	20.00	10.00	6.00
(23)	Sam Mele	20.00	10.00	6.00
(24)	Les Moss	20.00	10.00	6.00
(25)	Ray Murray	20.00	10.00	6.00
(26)	Billy O'Dell	20.00	10.00	6.00
(27)	Duane Pillette	20.00	10.00	6.00
(28)	Vern Stephens	20.00	10.00	6.00
(29)	Marlin Stuart	20.00	10.00	6.00
(30)	Bob Turley	40.00	20.00	12.00
(31)	Eddie Waitkus	20.00	10.00	6.00
(32)	Vic Wertz	25.00	12.50	7.50
(33)	Bob Young	20.00	10.00	6.00

1958 Baltimore Orioles Team Issue

CLIFFORD CONNIE JOHNSON
(CONNIE)

These blank-backed, black-and-white cards are approximately postcard size at 3-1/4" x 5-1/2" and feature posed portraits of the players printed on semi-gloss cardboard. The unnumbered cards are checklisted here alphabetically.

		NM	EX	VG
Complete Set (16):		165.00	82.00	49.00
Common Player:		12.00	6.00	3.50
(1)	Bob Boyd	12.00	6.00	3.50
(2)	Harry Brecheen	12.00	6.00	3.50
(3)	Hal Brown	12.00	6.00	3.50
(4)	Jim Busby	12.00	6.00	3.50
(5)	Foster Castleman	12.00	6.00	3.50
(6)	Billy Gardner	12.00	6.00	3.50
(7)	Connie Johnson	12.00	6.00	3.50
(8)	Ken Lehman	12.00	6.00	3.50
(9)	Willie Miranda	12.00	6.00	3.50
(10)	Bob Nieman	12.00	6.00	3.50
(11)	Paul Richards	12.00	6.00	3.50
(12)	Brooks Robinson	36.00	18.00	11.00
(13)	Gus Triandos	12.00	6.00	3.50
(14)	Dick Williams	12.00	6.00	3.50
(15)	Gene Woodling	18.00	9.00	5.50
(16)	George Zuverink	12.00	6.00	3.50

1970 Baltimore Orioles Traffic Safety

 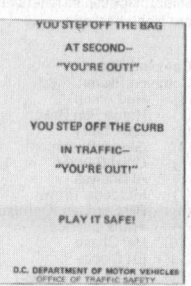

Similar in concept and design to the much more common Washington Senators safety issue of the same year, the Orioles cards are printed on yellow paper in 2-1/2" x 3-7/8" format. Fronts have player photo, name, team and position; backs have a safety message and notice of sponsorship by the D.C. Department of Motor Vehicles Office of Traffic Safety.

		NM	EX	VG
Complete Set (10):		25.00	12.50	7.50
Common Player:		2.50	1.25	.75
(1)	Mark Bellanger (Belanger)	2.50	1.25	.75
(2)	Paul Blair	2.50	1.25	.75
(3)	Don Buford	2.50	1.25	.75
(4)	Mike Cuellar (Back in Spanish.)	4.00	2.00	1.25
(5)	Dave Johnson	2.50	1.25	.75
(6)	Dave McNally	2.50	1.25	.75
(7)	Boog Powell	5.00	2.50	1.50
(8)	Merv Rettenmund	2.50	1.25	.75
(9)	Brooks Robinson	10.00	5.00	3.00
(10)	Earl Weaver	3.50	1.75	1.00

1971 Bank of Montreal Rusty Staub

This 4" x 6" color card was issued by the Bank of Montreal, probably in conjunction with an autograph appearance by the popular Expos slugger. The front has a photo of the player working on his war club. The team and sponsor's logo are at top-right. On back are the player's stats.

	NM	EX	VG
Rusty Staub	32.50	16.00	10.00

1913 Tom Barker Game (WG6)

Nearly identical in format to "The National Game" card set, this issue features a different back design of a red-and-white line art representation of a batter. Fronts of the round-cornered, 2-1/2" x 3-1/2" cards have a black-and-white player

pose, or game action photo, along with two game scenarios used when playing the card game. There are nine action photos in the set. Player cards are checklisted here alphabetically. The set originally sold for 50 cents. The set was reprinted in the 1980s.

		NM	EX	VG
Complete Set (54):		5,000	2,500	1,500
Common Player:		48.00	24.00	15.00
Game Box:		78.00	36.00	18.00
(1)	Grover Alexander	360.00	162.00	90.00
(2)	Frank Baker	120.00	54.00	30.00
(3)	Chief Bender	120.00	54.00	30.00
(4)	Bob Bescher	48.00	24.00	15.00
(5)	Joe Birmingham	48.00	24.00	15.00
(6)	Roger Bresnahan	120.00	54.00	30.00
(7)	Nixey Callahan	48.00	24.00	15.00
(8)	Bill Carrigan	48.00	24.00	15.00
(9)	Frank Chance	120.00	54.00	30.00
(10)	Hal Chase	78.00	36.00	19.00
(11)	Fred Clarke	120.00	54.00	30.00
(12)	Ty Cobb	810.00	360.00	210.00
(13)	Sam Crawford	120.00	54.00	30.00
(14)	Jake Daubert	48.00	24.00	15.00
(15)	Red Dooin	48.00	24.00	15.00
(16)	Johnny Evers	120.00	54.00	30.00
(17)	Vean Gregg	48.00	24.00	15.00
(18)	Clark Griffith	120.00	54.00	30.00
(19)	Dick Hoblitzel	48.00	24.00	15.00
(20)	Miller Huggins	120.00	54.00	30.00
(21)	Joe Jackson	1,920	870.00	480.00
(22)	Hughie Jennings	120.00	54.00	30.00
(23)	Walter Johnson	420.00	180.00	110.00
(24)	Ed Konetchy	48.00	24.00	15.00
(25)	Nap Lajoie	120.00	54.00	30.00
(26)	Connie Mack	120.00	54.00	30.00
(27)	Rube Marquard	120.00	54.00	30.00
(28)	Christy Mathewson	420.00	180.00	110.00
(29)	John McGraw	120.00	54.00	30.00
(30)	Chief Meyers	48.00	24.00	15.00
(31)	Clyde Milan	48.00	24.00	15.00
(32)	Marty O'Toole	48.00	24.00	15.00
(33)	Nap Rucker	48.00	24.00	15.00
(34)	Tris Speaker	160.00	75.00	40.00
(35)	George Stallings	48.00	24.00	15.00
(36)	Bill Sweeney	48.00	24.00	15.00
(37)	Joe Tinker	120.00	54.00	30.00
(38)	Honus Wagner	720.00	330.00	180.00
(39)	Ed Walsh	120.00	54.00	30.00
(40)	Zach Wheat	120.00	54.00	30.00
(41)	Ivy Wingo	48.00	24.00	15.00
(42)	Joe Wood	72.00	33.00	18.00
(43)	Cy Young	420.00	180.00	100.00
(---)	Rules card	48.00	24.00	15.00
(---)	Score card	48.00	24.00	15.00

ACTION PHOTO CARDS

		NM	EX	VG
(A1)	Batter swinging, looking forward.	18.00	8.10	4.50
(A2)	Batter swinging, looking back.	18.00	8.10	4.50
(A3)	Runner sliding, fielder at bag.	18.00	8.10	4.50
(A4)	Runner sliding, umpire behind.	48.00	24.00	15.00
(A5)	Runner sliding, hugging base.	18.00	8.10	4.50
(A6)	Sliding play at plate, umpire at left.	18.00	8.10	4.50
(A7)	Sliding play at plate, umpire at right.	18.00	8.10	4.50
(A8)	Play at plate, runner standing.	18.00	8.10	4.50
(A9)	Runner looking backwards.	18.00	8.10	4.50

1974-80 Bob Bartosz Postcards

 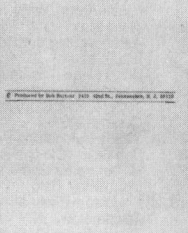

DAVEY JOHNSON

Through the last half of the 1970s, Bob Bartosz, who was a photographer covering the Phillies for a New Jersey daily newspaper, produced a series of player postcards. Most cards were produced at the request of the players for use in handling fan requests. Generally, no more than 500 cards of each player were ever produced. Most of the cards are in black-and-white with player name in a white stripe. Three cards were done in color. Size varies, but averages about 3-5/8" x 5-1/2". Back designs also vary, with most simply having Bartosz' credit line vertically at center. The unnumbered cards are checklisted here in alphabetical order.

		NM	EX	VG
Complete Set (32):				
Common Player:		3.00	1.50	.90
BLACK-AND-WHITE POSTCARDS				
(1)	Hank Aaron (16th career grand slam)	7.50	3.75	2.25
(2)	Richie Ashburn (5th Delaware Valley Show)	3.00	1.50	.90
(3)	James Cool Papa Bell	3.00	1.50	.90
(4)	Bob Boone	4.00	2.00	1.25

		NM	EX	VG
(5)	Jimmie Crutchfield	3.00	1.50	.90
(6)	Barry Foote	3.00	1.50	.90
(7)	Steve Garvey	4.00	2.00	1.25
(8)	Tommy Hutton (Phillies)	3.00	1.50	.90
(9)	Tommy Hutton (Blue Jays)	3.00	1.50	.90
(10)	Dane Iorg	3.00	1.50	.90
(11)	Davey Johnson	3.00	1.50	.90
(12)	Jay Johnstone	3.00	1.50	.90
(13)	Dave Kingman (Stadium background.)	3.00	1.50	.90
(14)	Dave Kingman (Black background.)	3.00	1.50	.90
(15)	Greg Luzinski (Both feet show.)	3.00	1.50	.90
(16)	Greg Luzinski (Only left foot shows.)	3.00	1.50	.90
(17)	Jerry Martin (Phillies)	3.00	1.50	.90
(18)	Jerry Martin (Cubs)	3.00	1.50	.90
(19)	Tim McCarver	4.00	2.00	1.25
(20)	John Montefusco	3.00	1.50	.90
(21)	Jerry Mumphrey	3.00	1.50	.90
(22)	Phil Niekro	4.00	2.00	1.25
(23)	Robin Roberts (Hall of Fame induction.)	3.00	1.50	.90
(24)	Robin Roberts (4th Delaware Valley Show)	3.00	1.50	.90
(25)	Steve Swisher	3.00	1.50	.90
(26)	Tony Taylor (Uniform number visible.)	3.00	1.50	.90
(27)	Tony Taylor (Number is covered.)	3.00	1.50	.90
(28)	Tom Underwood	3.00	1.50	.90
(29)	Billy Williams (N.L. umpire.)	3.00	1.50	.90
(30)	1974 National League All-Stars	4.00	2.00	1.25

COLOR POSTCARDS

		NM	EX	VG
(1)	Greg Luzinski	7.50	3.75	2.25
(2)	Bill Madlock	7.50	3.75	2.25
(3)	Jason Thompson	6.00	3.00	1.75

1978 Bob Bartosz Baseball Postcards

 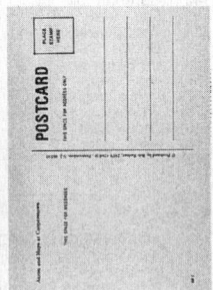

Newspaper photographer Bob Bartosz produced a book of postcards in 1978 combining player poses, action shots and stadium photos. Two dozen cards are printed in 4" x 5-1/2" black-and-white format and perforated on pages of four in the 8-1/2" x 11" book. Backs have standard postcard indicia and are numbered with a "BB" prefix and titled, all printing in black.

		NM	EX	VG
	Complete Book (24):	30.00	15.00	9.00
	Common Player:	1.50	.70	.45
1	25th anniversary of the 1950 Phillies (Group photo at old-timers game.)	1.50	.70	.45
2	Aaron and Mays at Cooperstown (Hank Aaron, Willie Mays)	4.00	2.00	1.25
3	Willie Mays	7.50	3.75	2.25
4	Aaron signing autographs (Hank Aaron)	3.00	1.50	.90
5	Dizzy Dean (Old-timers action sequence.)	2.50	1.25	.70
6	Jack Russell Stadium, Clearwater, Fla.	1.50	.70	.45
7	Paddy Livingston	1.50	.70	.45
8	Bob Feller (Old-timers game.)	2.50	1.25	.70
9	Hall of Fame Game at Doubleday Field	1.50	.70	.45
10	Doubleday Field at Cooperstown, N.Y.	1.50	.70	.45
11	Three Rivers Stadium, Pittsburgh	1.50	.70	.45
12	Hall of Fame Game at Doubleday Field	1.50	.70	.45
13	Shibe Park from the air	1.50	.70	.45
14	Olympic Stadium, Montreal	1.50	.70	.45
15	A tree grows at home plate (Shibe Park - 1974)	1.50	.70	.45
16	The Bleachers, Wrigley Field	1.50	.70	.45
17	Another Home Run (Hank Aaron)	2.50	1.25	.70
18	Home Run King (Hank Aaron)	2.25	1.25	.70
19	Autograph Time - 1950 (Phillies signing balls.)	1.50	.70	.45
20	The Champs (1976 Phillies)	1.50	.70	.45
21	Last Day - Shibe Park, 1977	1.50	.70	.45
22	Connie Mack Stadium, Philadelphia	1.50	.70	.45
23	Shibe Park	1.50	.70	.45
24	Shibe Park	1.50	.70	.45

1911 Baseball Bats

Issued circa 1911, cards in this rare 47-card issue were printed on the back panel of "Baseball Bats" penny candy. The cards themselves measure approximately 1-3/8" x 2-3/8" and feature a black-and-white player photo surrounded by an

orange or white border. Player's name and team are printed in small, black capital letters near the bottom of the photo. Cards are blank-backed.

		NM	EX	VG
	Complete Set (50):	40,000	20,000	12,000
	Common Player:	550.00	275.00	165.00
(1)	Red Ames	550.00	275.00	165.00
(2)	Home Run Baker	1,100	550.00	330.00
(3)	Jack Barry	550.00	275.00	165.00
(4)	Ginger Beaumont	550.00	275.00	165.00
(5)	Chief Bender	1,100	550.00	330.00
(6)	Al Bridwell	550.00	275.00	165.00
(7)	Mordecai Brown	1,100	550.00	330.00
(8)	Bill Corrigan (Carrigan)	550.00	275.00	165.00
(9)	Frank Chance	1,100	550.00	330.00
(10)	Hal Chase	850.00	425.00	250.00
(11)	Ed Cicotte	925.00	460.00	275.00
(12)	Fred Clark (Clarke)	1,100	550.00	330.00
(13)	Ty Cobb	6,000	4,000	2,000
(14)	King Cole	550.00	275.00	165.00
(15)	Eddie Collins	1,100	550.00	330.00
(16)	Sam Crawford	1,100	550.00	330.00
(17)	Lou Criger	550.00	275.00	165.00
(18)	Harry Davis	550.00	275.00	165.00
(19)	Jim Delehanty	550.00	275.00	165.00
(20)	Art Devlin	550.00	275.00	165.00
(21)	Josh Devore	550.00	275.00	165.00
(22)	Wild Bill Donovan	550.00	275.00	165.00
(23)	Larry Doyle	550.00	275.00	165.00
(24)	Johnny Evers	1,100	550.00	330.00
(25)	John Flynn	550.00	275.00	165.00
(26)	George Gibson	550.00	275.00	165.00
(27)	Solly Hoffman (Hofman)	550.00	275.00	165.00
(28)	Walter Johnson	2,200	1,100	660.00
(29)	Johnny Kling	550.00	275.00	165.00
(30)	Nap Lajoie	1,100	550.00	330.00
(31)	Christy Mathewson	3,000	2,000	1,000
(32)	Matty McIntyre	550.00	275.00	165.00
(33)	Fred Merkle	550.00	275.00	165.00
(34)	Danny Murphy	550.00	275.00	165.00
(35)	Tom Needham	550.00	275.00	165.00
(36)	Harry Niles	550.00	275.00	165.00
(37)	Rube Oldring	550.00	275.00	165.00
(38)	Wildfire Schulte	550.00	275.00	165.00
(39)	Cy Seymour	550.00	275.00	165.00
(40)	Jimmy Sheckard	550.00	275.00	165.00
(41)	Tris Speaker	2,400	1,600	1,000
(42)	Oscar Stanage (Batting - front view.)	550.00	275.00	165.00
(43)	Oscar Stanage (Batting - side view.)	550.00	275.00	165.00
(44)	Ira Thomas	550.00	275.00	165.00
(45)	Joe Tinker	1,100	550.00	330.00
(46)	Heinie Wagner	550.00	275.00	165.00
(47)	Honus Wagner	4,500	2,250	1,350
(48)	Ed Walsh	1,100	550.00	330.00
(49)	Art Wilson	550.00	275.00	165.00
(50)	Owen Wilson	550.00	275.00	165.00

1887-1893 Baseball Currency

Because of their similarity in size (about 7-3/4" x 3-3/8"), design and color to then-circulating U.S. paper money, this form of advertising flyer was thought to catch the attention of the general public. The notes were printed in black-and-green (some 1889 Chicago notes are printed in black-and-red) on white. Fronts have at left a large oval portrait of the team's president or manager. At right on the Chicago and Detroit notes is a full-figure rendering of an unnamed Cap Anson. On the St. Louis notes, there is a picture of the Wilman Trophy indicative of the team's 1886 World's Championship. On the 1893 note, National League President N.E. Young is pictured at left, with a grouping of baseball equipment at right. In the center is a large ornate date with either "National Base Ball League" or "National / Base Ball Association" at top in gothic typography. Backs have black-and-white woodcuts of the team's players on a decorative green (or red) background. The notes were originally printed with large open spaces on front and back so that advertising messages could be overprinted by local merchants. The value of the notes can be affected by the location of a specific advertiser and/or the content of his message. Sports collectors compete with numismatists for examples of these advertising pieces.

	NM	EX	VG
1887 Chicago White Stockings (Front: Pres. A.G. Spalding. Back: Cap Anson, Mark Baldwin, John Clarkson, Tom Daily (Daly), Dell Darling, Silver Flint, Lou Hardie, Fred Pfeffer, Jimmy Ryan, Marty Sullivan, Billy Sunday, Ed Williamson.)	2,300	1,150	750.00
1887 Detroit Wolverines (Front: Manager Bill Watkins. Back: Lady Baldwin, Charlie Bennett, Fatty Briody, Dan Brouthers, Fred Dunlap, Charlie Ganzel, Ned Hanlon, Hardy Richardson, Jack Rowe, Sam Thompson, Stump Weidman (Wiedman), Deacon White.)	2,600	1,300	775.00
1887 St. Louis Browns (Front: Pres. Chris Von Der Ahe. Back: Jack Boyle, Doc Bushong, Bob Caruthers, Charlie Comiskey, Dave Foutz, Bill Gleason, Arlie Latham, Tip O'Neil (O'Neill), Yank Robinson, Curt Welch.)	4,000	2,000	1,200
1888 Chicago White Stockings (Front: Pres. A.G. Spalding. Back: Cap Anson, Mark Baldwin, John Clarkson, Tom Daily (Daly), Dell Darling, Silver Flint, Lou Hardie, Fred Pfeffer, Jimmy Ryan, Marty Sullivan, Billy Sunday, Ed Williamson.)	2,600	1,300	750.00
1888 Detroit Wolverines (Front: Manager Bill Watkins. Back: Lady Baldwin, Charlie Bennett, Fatty Briody, Dan Brouthers, Fred Dunlap, Charlie Ganzel, Ned Hanlon, Hardy Richardson, Jack Rowe, Sam Thompson, Stump Weidman (Wiedman), Deacon White.)	2,600	1,300	775.00
1888 St. Louis Browns: Front: Pres. Chris Von Der Ahe. Back; Jack Boyle, Charles Comiskey, Silver King, Arlie Latham, Harry Lyons, Tommy McCarthy, Chippy McGarr, Jocko Milligan, Tip O'Neill, Yank Robinson.)	6,000	3,000	1,800
1889 Chicago White Stockings (Front: Pres. A.G. Spalding. Back: Cap Anson, Mark Baldwin, Tom Burns, Tom Daily (Daly), Dell Darling, Silver Flint, Bob Pettit, Fred Pfeffer, Jimmy Ryan, Marty Sullivan, George Van Haltren, Ed Williamson.)	2,600	1,300	750.00
1893 National League All-Stars (Front: Pres. N.E. Young. Back: Bob Allen, Cap Anson, Mark Baldwin, John Clarkson, Charles Comiskey, Dave Foutz, King Kelly, Billy Nash, Jim O'Rourke, Fred Pfeffer, George Van Haltren, John Ward.)	(Value Undetermined)		

1979 Baseball Favorites "1953 Bowman"

 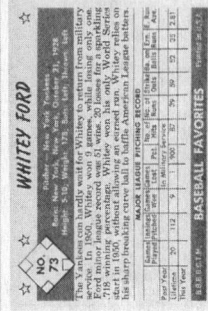

This collectors' series was designed to represent an extension of the 64-card 1953 Bowman black-and-white card issue. This series uses the same design on its 2-1/2" x 3-3/4" format. Fronts have a black-and-white player photo with no extraneous graphics. Backs are printed in red and black and offer career highlights, stats and biographical data, written as if in 1953. Many of the players in this collectors' edition originally appeared in Bowman's 1953 color series. Issue price was about $7.

		NM	EX	VG
	Complete Set (16):	25.00	12.50	7.50
	Common Player:	.75	.40	.25
65	Monte Irvin	.75	.40	.25
66	Early Wynn	.75	.40	.25
67	Robin Roberts	.75	.40	.25
68	Stan Musial	3.00	1.50	.90
69	Ernie Banks	1.50	.75	.45
70	Willie Mays	4.50	2.25	1.25
71	Yogi Berra	2.25	1.25	.70
72	Mickey Mantle	9.00	4.50	2.75
73	Whitey Ford	1.25	.60	.40
74	Bob Feller	.75	.40	.25
75	Ted Williams	4.50	2.25	1.25
76	Satchel Paige	3.00	1.50	.90
77	Jackie Robinson	3.00	1.50	.90
78	Ed Mathews	.75	.40	.25
79	Warren Spahn	.75	.40	.25
80	Ralph Kiner	.75	.40	.25

1964 Baseball Greats Postcard

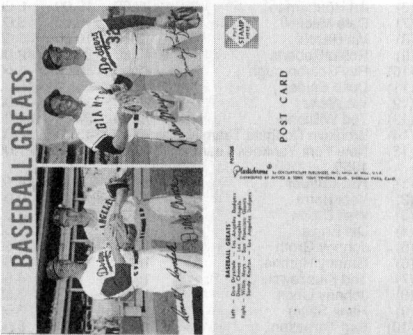

Four of California's star players are pictured on this standard-format (5-1/2" x 3-1/2") color postcard in a pair of two-player poses. Each player's facsimile autograph appears on front. Back is in typical postcard format with player identification, a stamp box and vertical center divider with publisher and distributor information. (See also Baseball Stars - Present and Future.)

	NM	EX	VG
Don Drysdale, Dean Chance, Willie Mays, Sandy Koufax	40.00	20.00	12.00

1910-57 Baseball Magazine Player Posters

Beginning shortly after its 1908 debut, Baseball Magazine produced a lengthy series of player posters which it offered as premiums to readers. Ranging in size from 9" x 12-1/4" to 9" x 20" (and a series of super-size 1957s), the posters feature poses of top players in sepia tones bordered in white. In the bottom border over the years appeared various formats of player identification, copyright information and promotion for the magazine. The unnumbered posters are listed here alphabetically by year. Some posters were reprinted over the years and there may exist pose variations as well as posters which have escaped this list. Names shown here may not coincide with the form in which they actually appear on the posters. Inaccuracies in, or incompleteness of, the checklist is the likely result of its having been compiled from ads appearing in the magazine.

		NM	EX	VG
1910				
(1)	Ty Cobb	350.00	175.00	105.00
(2)	Johnny Evers	150.00	75.00	45.00
(3)	Hughie Jennings	100.00	50.00	30.00
(4)	Honus Wagner	300.00	150.00	90.00
1912				
(1)	Babe Adams	60.00	30.00	18.00
(2)	Howie Camnitz	60.00	30.00	18.00
(3)	Frank Chance	125.00	62.00	37.00
(4)	Claude Hendrix	60.00	30.00	18.00
(5)	Marty O'Toole	60.00	30.00	18.00
(6)	Boston Red Sox Team	250.00	125.00	75.00
(7)	New York Giants Team	250.00	125.00	75.00
1913				
(1)	Jimmy Archer	60.00	30.00	18.00
(2)	Jack Barry	60.00	30.00	18.00
(3)	Joe Bush	60.00	30.00	18.00
(4)	Sam Crawford	100.00	50.00	30.00
(5)	Eddie Collins	125.00	62.00	37.00
(6)	Jake Daubert	60.00	30.00	18.00
(7)	Larry Doyle	60.00	30.00	18.00
(8)	Art Fletcher	60.00	30.00	18.00
(9)	Joe Jackson	1,000	500.00	300.00
(10)	Walter Johnson	250.00	125.00	75.00
(11)	Nap Lajoie	200.00	100.00	60.00
(12)	Connie Mack	100.00	50.00	30.00
(13)	Fritz Maisel	60.00	30.00	18.00
(14)	Rube Marquard	100.00	50.00	30.00
(15)	Christy Mathewson	250.00	125.00	75.00
(16)	John McGraw	125.00	62.00	37.00
(17)	Stuffy McInnis	60.00	30.00	18.00
(18)	"Chief" Meyers	60.00	30.00	18.00
(19)	Red Murray	60.00	30.00	18.00
(20)	Eddie Plank	125.00	62.00	37.00
(21)	"Nap" Rucker	60.00	30.00	18.00
(22)	Reb Russell	60.00	30.00	18.00
(23)	Tris Speaker	125.00	62.00	37.00
(24)	Ed Walsh	100.00	50.00	30.00
(25)	Smokey Joe Wood	75.00	37.00	22.00
(26)	Boston Braves Team	250.00	125.00	75.00
(27)	Philadelphia Athletics Team	250.00	125.00	75.00
1914				
(1)	Home Run Baker	100.00	50.00	30.00
(2)	Larry Cheney	60.00	30.00	18.00
(3)	Joe Connolly	60.00	30.00	18.00
(4)	Hank Gowdy	60.00	30.00	18.00
(5)	Bill James	60.00	30.00	18.00
(6)	Jimmy Lavender	60.00	30.00	18.00
(7)	Rabbit Maranville	100.00	50.00	30.00
(8)	Dick Rudolph	60.00	30.00	18.00
(9)	Wally Schang	60.00	30.00	18.00
(10)	Bob Shawkey	60.00	30.00	18.00
(11)	Jimmy Sheckard	60.00	30.00	18.00
(12)	Charles Schmidt	60.00	30.00	18.00
(13)	Wildfire Schulte	60.00	30.00	18.00
(14)	Lefty Tyler	60.00	30.00	18.00
(15)	Boston Braves Team	200.00	100.00	60.00
(16)	Chicago Cubs Team	200.00	100.00	60.00
(17)	Chicago Whales Team	250.00	125.00	75.00
(18)	Cincinnati Reds Team	200.00	100.00	60.00
(19)	Cleveland Indians Team	200.00	100.00	60.00
(20)	Detroit Tigers Team	200.00	100.00	60.00
(21)	New York Yankees Team	200.00	100.00	60.00
(22)	St. Louis Browns Team	200.00	100.00	60.00
(23)	Washington Senators Team	200.00	100.00	60.00
1915				
(1)	Grover Alexander	125.00	62.00	37.00
(2)	Chief Bender	100.00	50.00	30.00
(3)	Harry Hooper	100.00	50.00	30.00
(4)	Duffy Lewis	60.00	30.00	18.00
(5)	Tris Speaker	100.00	50.00	30.00
(6)	Boston Red Sox Team	200.00	100.00	60.00
(7)	Chicago White Sox Team	200.00	100.00	60.00
(8)	Philadelphia Athletics Team	200.00	100.00	60.00
(9)	Philadelphia Phillies Team	200.00	100.00	60.00
(10)	St. Louis Cardinals Team	200.00	100.00	60.00
1916				
(1)	Larry Gardner	50.00	25.00	15.00
(2)	Buck Herzog	50.00	25.00	15.00
(3)	Rogers Hornsby	75.00	37.00	22.00
(4)	Walter Johnson	160.00	80.00	48.00
(5)	Fielder Jones	50.00	25.00	15.00
(6)	Benny Kauff	50.00	25.00	15.00
(7)	Dave Robertson	50.00	25.00	15.00
(8)	Babe Ruth/Pitching	300.00	150.00	90.00
(9)	George Sisler	75.00	37.00	22.00
(10)	Zack Wheat	75.00	37.00	22.00
(11)	Boston Red Sox Team	150.00	75.00	45.00
(12)	Brooklyn Dodgers Team	100.00	50.00	30.00
(13)	Philadelphia Phillies Team	100.00	50.00	30.00
1917				
(1)	George Burns	50.00	25.00	15.00
(2)	Ed Cicotte	150.00	75.00	45.00
(3)	Art Fletcher	50.00	25.00	15.00
(4)	Red Faber	50.00	25.00	15.00
(5)	Happy Felsch	150.00	75.00	45.00
(6)	Ferd Schupp	50.00	25.00	15.00
(7)	Ray Schalk	50.00	25.00	15.00
(8)	Buck Weaver	150.00	75.00	45.00
(9)	Boston Red Sox Team	150.00	75.00	45.00
(10)	New York Giants Team	150.00	75.00	45.00
1918				
(1)	Home Run Baker	75.00	37.00	22.00
1919				
(1)	Ed Cicotte	75.00	37.00	22.00
(2)	Chicago White Sox Team	400.00	200.00	120.00
(3)	Cincinnati Reds Team	125.00	62.00	37.00
1920				
(1)	Jim Bagby	30.00	15.00	9.00
(2)	Dave Bancroft	45.00	22.00	13.50
(3)	Max Carey	45.00	22.00	13.50
(4)	Harry Coveleski	45.00	22.00	13.50
(5)	Hod Eller	30.00	15.00	9.00
(6)	Burleigh Grimes	45.00	22.00	13.50
(7)	Heinie Groh	30.00	15.00	9.00
(8)	Rogers Hornsby	45.00	22.00	13.50
(9)	Walter Johnson	75.00	37.00	22.00
(10)	Dick Kerr	30.00	15.00	9.00
(11)	Pat Moran	30.00	15.00	9.00
(12)	Duster Mails	30.00	15.00	9.00
(13)	Hy Myers	30.00	15.00	9.00
(14)	Steve O'Neill	30.00	15.00	9.00
(15)	Edd Roush	45.00	22.00	13.50
(16)	Dutch Ruether	30.00	15.00	9.00
(17)	Babe Ruth/Btg (No stands in background.)	700.00	350.00	210.00
(18)	Ray Schalk	45.00	22.00	13.50
(19)	Earl Smith	30.00	15.00	9.00
(20)	Sherrod Smith	30.00	15.00	9.00
(21)	Tris Speaker	45.00	22.00	13.50
(22)	Hippo Vaughn	30.00	15.00	9.00
(23)	Bobby Veach	30.00	15.00	9.00
(24)	Bill Wambsganss	30.00	15.00	9.00
(25)	Brooklyn Dodgers Team	125.00	62.00	37.00
(26)	Cleveland Indians Team	125.00	62.00	37.00
1921				
(1)	Dave Bancroft	45.00	22.00	13.50
(2)	Wilbur Cooper	30.00	15.00	9.00
(3)	Phil Douglas	30.00	15.00	9.00
(4)	Frank Frisch	50.00	25.00	15.00
(5)	Harry Heilmann	45.00	22.00	13.50
(6)	Waite Hoyt	45.00	22.00	13.50
(7)	George Kelly	45.00	22.00	13.50
(8)	Carl Mays	45.00	22.00	13.50
(9)	Mike McNally	30.00	15.00	9.00
(10)	Irish Meusel	30.00	15.00	9.00
(11)	Bob Meusel	30.00	15.00	9.00
(12)	Art Nehf	30.00	15.00	9.00
(13)	Wally Schang	30.00	15.00	9.00
(14)	Walter Schmidt	30.00	15.00	9.00
(15)	Frank Snyder	30.00	15.00	9.00
(16)	Aaron Ward	30.00	15.00	9.00
(17)	Ross Youngs	45.00	22.00	13.50
(18)	New York Giants Team	100.00	50.00	30.00
(19)	New York Yankees Team	300.00	150.00	90.00
(20)	Pittsburgh Pirates Team	100.00	50.00	30.00
1922 - NONE				
1923				
(1)	New York Giants Team	90.00	45.00	27.00
(2)	New York Yankees Team	200.00	100.00	60.00
1924				
(1)	Johnny Bassler	30.00	15.00	9.00
(2)	Jim Bottomley	45.00	22.00	13.50
(3)	Kiki Cuyler	45.00	22.00	13.50
(4)	Joe Dugan	30.00	15.00	9.00
(5)	Bibb Falk	30.00	15.00	9.00
(6)	Jack Fournier	30.00	15.00	9.00
(7)	Goose Goslin	45.00	22.00	13.50
(8)	Sam Harris	30.00	15.00	9.00
(9)	Gabby Hartnett	45.00	22.00	13.50
(10)	Travis Jackson	45.00	22.00	13.50
(11)	Baby Doll Jacobson	30.00	15.00	9.00
(12)	Charlie Jamieson	30.00	15.00	9.00
(13)	Herb Pennock	45.00	22.00	13.50
(14)	Sam Rice	45.00	22.00	13.50
(15)	Eppa Rixey	45.00	22.00	13.50
(16)	Muddy Ruel	30.00	15.00	9.00
(17)	Hollis Thurston	30.00	15.00	9.00
(18)	Pie Traynor	45.00	22.00	13.50
(19)	Dazzy Vance	45.00	22.00	13.50
(20)	Kenny Williams	30.00	15.00	9.00
(21)	New York Giants Team	90.00	45.00	27.00
(22)	Washington Senators Team	90.00	45.00	27.00
1925				
(1)	Vic Aldridge	30.00	15.00	9.00
(2)	Mickey Cochrane	45.00	22.00	13.50
(3)	Ted Lyons	45.00	22.00	13.50
(4)	Eddie Rommel	30.00	15.00	9.00
(5)	Al Simmons	45.00	22.00	13.50
(6)	Glenn Wright	30.00	15.00	9.00
(7)	Pittsburgh Pirates Team	90.00	45.00	27.00
(8)	Washington Senators Team	90.00	45.00	27.00
1926				
(1)	Les Bell	30.00	15.00	9.00
(2)	George H. Burns	30.00	15.00	9.00
(3)	Hughie Critz	30.00	15.00	9.00
(4)	Henry (Lou) Gehrig/Potrait	250.00	125.00	75.00
(5)	Ray Kremer	30.00	15.00	9.00
(6)	Bob O'Farrell	30.00	15.00	9.00
(7)	Tommy Thevenow	30.00	15.00	9.00
(8)	George Uhle	30.00	15.00	9.00
(9)	Hack Wilson	45.00	22.00	13.50
(10)	New York Yankees Team	250.00	125.00	75.00
(11)	St. Louis Cardinals Team	90.00	45.00	27.00
1927				
(1)	Carmen Hill	30.00	15.00	9.00
(2)	Tony Lazzeri	45.00	22.00	13.50
(3)	Fred Lindstrom	45.00	22.00	13.50
(4)	Charlie Root	30.00	15.00	9.00
(5)	Lloyd Waner	45.00	22.00	13.50
(6)	Paul Waner	45.00	22.00	13.50
(7)	New York Yankees Team	200.00	100.00	60.00
(8)	Pittsburgh Pirates Team	90.00	45.00	27.00
1928				
(1)	Jimmie Foxx	60.00	30.00	18.00
1929				
(1)	Guy Bush	30.00	15.00	9.00
(2)	Lefty Grove	45.00	22.00	13.50
(3)	Chicago Cubs Team	125.00	62.00	37.00
(4)	Philadelphia Athletics Team	90.00	45.00	27.00
1930				
(1)	George Earnshaw	30.00	15.00	9.00
(2)	Wes Ferrell	30.00	15.00	9.00
(3)	Charley Gelbert	30.00	15.00	9.00
(4)	Babe Herman	30.00	15.00	9.00
(5)	Chuck Klein	45.00	22.00	13.50
(6)	Philadelphia Athletics Team	90.00	45.00	27.00
(7)	St. Louis Cardinals Team	90.00	45.00	27.00
1931				
(1)	Earl Averill	45.00	22.00	13.50
(2)	Ed Brandt	30.00	15.00	9.00
(3)	Ben Chapman	30.00	15.00	9.00
(4)	Joe Cronin	45.00	22.00	13.50
(5)	Bill Hallahan	30.00	15.00	9.00
(6)	Pepper Martin	40.00	20.00	12.00
1932 - NONE				
1933				
(1)	Dizzy Dean	75.00	37.00	22.00
(2)	Lou Gehrig/Btg	225.00	110.00	67.00
(3)	Carl Hubbell	60.00	30.00	18.00
(4)	Heinie Manush	45.00	22.00	13.50
(5)	Mel Ott	45.00	22.00	13.50
(6)	Babe Ruth/Btg (Stands in background.)	250.00	125.00	75.00
(7)	Hal Schumacher	30.00	15.00	9.00
(8)	Lon Warneke	30.00	15.00	9.00
(9)	New York Giants Team	90.00	45.00	27.00
(10)	Washington Senators Team	90.00	45.00	27.00
1934				
(1)	Dick Bartell	30.00	15.00	9.00
(2)	Paul Dean	45.00	22.00	13.50
(3)	Lefty Gomez	45.00	22.00	13.50
(4)	Rogers Hornsby	45.00	22.00	13.50
(5)	Ducky Medwick	45.00	22.00	13.50
(6)	Van Lingle Mungo	30.00	15.00	9.00
(7)	Schoolboy Rowe	30.00	15.00	9.00
(8)	Arky Vaughan	45.00	22.00	13.50
(9)	Lloyd Waner	45.00	22.00	13.50
(10)	Paul Waner	45.00	22.00	13.50
(11)	Detroit Tigers Team	100.00	50.00	30.00
1935				
(1)	Wally Berger	30.00	15.00	9.00
(2)	Ripper Collins	30.00	15.00	9.00
(3)	Charley Gehringer	45.00	22.00	13.50
(4)	Hank Greenberg	60.00	30.00	18.00
(5)	Mel Harder	30.00	15.00	9.00
(6)	Billy Herman	45.00	22.00	13.50
(7)	Buddy Myer	30.00	15.00	9.00
(8)	Al Simmons	45.00	22.00	13.50
(9)	Bill Terry	45.00	22.00	13.50
(10)	Joe Vosmik	30.00	15.00	9.00
(11)	Chicago Cubs Team	100.00	50.00	30.00
(12)	Detroit Tigers Team	90.00	45.00	27.00
1936				
(1)	Luke Appling	45.00	22.00	13.50
(2)	Frank Demaree	30.00	15.00	9.00
(3)	Paul Derringer	30.00	15.00	9.00
(4)	Joe DiMaggio	80.00	40.00	24.00
(5)	Vern Kennedy	30.00	15.00	9.00

#	Player			
(6)	Ernie Lombardi	45.00	22.00	13.50
(7)	Joe Moore	30.00	15.00	9.00
(8)	Terry Moore	30.00	15.00	9.00
(9)	Moose Solters	30.00	15.00	9.00
(10)	Hal Trosky	30.00	15.00	9.00
(11)	Bill Werber	30.00	15.00	9.00
(12)	New York Giants Team	100.00	50.00	30.00
(13)	New York Yankees Team	200.00	100.00	60.00

1937

#	Player			
(1)	Cy Blanton	30.00	15.00	9.00
(2)	Dolph Camilli	30.00	15.00	9.00
(3)	Joe Cronin	45.00	22.00	13.50
(4)	Bill Dickey	50.00	25.00	15.00
(5)	Bob Feller	50.00	25.00	15.00
(6)	Stan Hack	30.00	15.00	9.00
(7)	Buddy Hassett	30.00	15.00	9.00
(8)	Bill Lee	30.00	15.00	9.00
(9)	Buddy Lewis	30.00	15.00	9.00
(10)	Johnny Mize	45.00	22.00	13.50
(11)	Jimmy Ripple	30.00	15.00	9.00
(12)	Charles Ruffing	45.00	22.00	13.50
(13)	Cecil Travis	30.00	15.00	9.00
(14)	Gee Walker	30.00	15.00	9.00

1938

#	Player			
(1)	Ethan Allen	30.00	15.00	9.00
(2)	Clay Bryant	30.00	15.00	9.00
(3)	Harlond Clift	30.00	15.00	9.00
(4)	Frank Crosetti	35.00	17.50	10.50
(5)	Harry Danning	30.00	15.00	9.00
(6)	Bobby Doerr	45.00	22.00	13.50
(7)	Augie Galan	30.00	15.00	9.00
(8)	Ival Goodman	30.00	15.00	9.00
(9)	Joe Gordon	30.00	15.00	9.00
(10)	Tommy Henrich	35.00	17.50	10.50
(11)	Mike Kreevich	30.00	15.00	9.00
(12)	Frank McCormick	30.00	15.00	9.00
(13)	Babe Phelps	30.00	15.00	9.00
(14)	Johnny Rizzo	30.00	15.00	9.00
(15)	Red Rolfe	30.00	15.00	9.00
(16)	Johnny Vander Meer	35.00	17.50	10.50
(17)	Rudy York	30.00	15.00	9.00

1939

#	Player			
(1)	Morrie Arnovich	30.00	15.00	9.00
(2)	Jimmie Foxx	45.00	22.00	13.50
(3)	Luke Hamlin	30.00	15.00	9.00
(4)	Bob Johnson	35.00	17.50	10.50
(5)	Charlie Keller	35.00	17.50	10.50
(6)	Ken Keltner	35.00	17.50	10.50
(7)	Emil "Dutch" Leonard	30.00	15.00	9.00
(8)	Bobo Newsom	30.00	15.00	9.00
(9)	Don Padgett	30.00	15.00	9.00
(10)	Bucky Walters	30.00	15.00	9.00
(11)	Ted Williams	120.00	60.00	36.00

1940 (9-1/2" x 12")

#	Player			
(1)	George Case	20.00	10.00	6.00
(2)	Babe Dahlgren	20.00	10.00	6.00
(3)	Elbie Fletcher	20.00	10.00	6.00
(4)	Cookie Lavagetto	20.00	10.00	6.00
(5)	Barney McCosky	20.00	10.00	6.00
(6)	Bill McGee	20.00	10.00	6.00
(7)	Ducky Medwick	40.00	20.00	12.00
(8)	Eddie Miller	20.00	10.00	6.00
(9)	Hugh Mulcahy	20.00	10.00	6.00
(10)	Claude Passeau	20.00	10.00	6.00
(11)	Rip Radcliff	20.00	10.00	6.00
(12)	Jim Tabor	20.00	10.00	6.00
(13)	Eugene "Junior" Thompson	20.00	10.00	6.00
(14)	Mike Tresh	20.00	10.00	6.00
(15)	Roy Weatherly	20.00	10.00	6.00
(16)	Norm "Babe" Young	20.00	10.00	6.00

1941 (9-1/2" x 12")

#	Player			
(1)	Sam Chapman	20.00	10.00	6.00
(2)	Ty Cobb	60.00	30.00	18.00
(3)	Mort Cooper	20.00	10.00	6.00
(4)	Dom DiMaggio	40.00	20.00	12.00
(5)	Jeff Heath	20.00	10.00	6.00
(6)	Thornton Lee	20.00	10.00	6.00
(7)	Danny Litwhiler	20.00	10.00	6.00
(8)	Al Lopez	40.00	20.00	12.00
(9)	Christy Mathewson	60.00	30.00	18.00
(10)	Joe McCarthy	40.00	20.00	12.00
(11)	Bill Nicholson	20.00	10.00	6.00
(12)	Pete Reiser	20.00	10.00	6.00
(13)	Elmer Riddle	20.00	10.00	6.00
(14)	Phil Rizzuto	60.00	30.00	18.00
(15)	Johnny Rucker	20.00	10.00	6.00
(16)	Hans Wagner	60.00	30.00	18.00

1942 (9-1/2" x 12")

#	Player			
(1)	Jim Bagby	20.00	10.00	6.00
(2)	Ernie Bonham	20.00	10.00	6.00
(3)	Lou Boudreau	40.00	20.00	12.00
(4)	Tommy Bridges	20.00	10.00	6.00
(5)	Jimmy Brown	20.00	10.00	6.00
(6)	Dolph Camilli	20.00	10.00	6.00
(7)	Walker Cooper	20.00	10.00	6.00
(8)	Bob Elliott	20.00	10.00	6.00
(9)	Lou Gehrig/Btg	100.00	50.00	30.00
(10)	Tex Hughson	20.00	10.00	6.00
(11)	Eddie Joost	20.00	10.00	6.00
(12)	Don Kolloway	20.00	10.00	6.00
(13)	Phil Marchildon	20.00	10.00	6.00
(14)	Clyde McCullough	20.00	10.00	6.00
(15)	George McQuinn	20.00	10.00	6.00
(16)	Cliff Melton	20.00	10.00	6.00
(17)	Lou Novikoff	20.00	10.00	6.00
(18)	Mickey Owen	20.00	10.00	6.00
(19)	Pee Wee Reese	50.00	25.00	15.00
(20)	Stan Spence	20.00	10.00	6.00
(21)	Vern Stephens	20.00	10.00	6.00
(22)	Virgil Trucks	20.00	10.00	6.00
(23)	Fred "Dixie" Walker	20.00	10.00	6.00
(24)	Max West	20.00	10.00	6.00

1943 (9-1/2" x 12")

#	Player			
(1)	Hiram Bithorn	20.00	10.00	6.00
(2)	Spud Chandler	20.00	10.00	6.00
(3)	Al Javery	20.00	10.00	6.00
(4)	Bill Johnson	20.00	10.00	6.00
(5)	Kenesaw Landis	40.00	20.00	12.00
(6)	Tony Lupien	20.00	10.00	6.00
(7)	Marty Marion	25.00	12.50	7.50
(8)	Stan Musial	60.00	30.00	18.00
(9)	Bobo Newsom	20.00	10.00	6.00
(10)	Babe Ruth (Portrait)	80.00	40.00	24.00
(11)	Rip Sewell	20.00	10.00	6.00
(12)	Joe Schultz	20.00	10.00	6.00
(13)	Dizzy Trout	20.00	10.00	6.00
(14)	Mickey Vernon	20.00	10.00	6.00
(15)	Dick Wakefield	20.00	10.00	6.00
(16)	Mickey Witek	20.00	10.00	6.00
(17)	Early Wynn	40.00	20.00	12.00
(18)	New York Yankees Team	90.00	45.00	27.00
(19)	St. Louis Cardinals Team	90.00	45.00	27.00

1944 (9-1/2" x 12")

#	Player			
(1)	Augie Galan	20.00	10.00	6.00
(2)	Johnny Hopp	20.00	10.00	6.00
(3)	Jack Kramer	20.00	10.00	6.00
(4)	Johnny Lindell	20.00	10.00	6.00
(5)	Ray Mueller	20.00	10.00	6.00
(6)	Hal Newhouser	40.00	20.00	12.00
(7)	Nelson Potter	20.00	10.00	6.00
(8)	Ray Sanders	20.00	10.00	6.00
(9)	"Snuffy" Stirnweiss	20.00	10.00	6.00
(10)	Jim Tobin	20.00	10.00	6.00
(11)	Thurman Tucker	20.00	10.00	6.00
(12)	Bill Voiselle	20.00	10.00	6.00
(13)	Ted Wilks	20.00	10.00	6.00
(14)	Detroit Tigers Team	90.00	45.00	27.00
(15)	St. Louis Browns Team	90.00	45.00	27.00
(16)	St. Louis Cardinals Team	90.00	45.00	27.00

1945 (9-1/2" x 12")

#	Player			
(1)	Phil Cavarretta	20.00	10.00	6.00
(2)	Russ Christopher	20.00	10.00	6.00
(3)	Tony Cuccinello	20.00	10.00	6.00
(4)	Boo Ferriss	20.00	10.00	6.00
(5)	Hal Gregg	20.00	10.00	6.00
(6)	Steve Gromek	20.00	10.00	6.00
(7)	Ducky Medwick	40.00	20.00	12.00
(8)	George Myatt	20.00	10.00	6.00
(9)	Frank Overmire	20.00	10.00	6.00
(10)	Andy Pafko	25.00	12.50	7.50
(11)	Red Schoendienst	40.00	20.00	12.00
(12)	Chicago Cubs Team	90.00	45.00	27.00
(13)	Detroit Tigers Team	75.00	37.00	22.00

1946

#	Player			
(1)	Joe Beggs	20.00	10.00	6.00
(2)	Johnny Berardino	25.00	12.50	7.50
(3)	Bill Bevens	20.00	10.00	6.00
(4)	Harry Brecheen	20.00	10.00	6.00
(5)	Mickey Harris	20.00	10.00	6.00
(6)	Kirby Higbe	20.00	10.00	6.00
(7)	Dave Koslo	20.00	10.00	6.00
(8)	Whitey Kurowski	20.00	10.00	6.00
(9)	Vic Lombardi	20.00	10.00	6.00
(10)	Phil Masi	20.00	10.00	6.00
(11)	Mike McCormick	20.00	10.00	6.00
(12)	Johnny Mize	40.00	20.00	12.00
(13)	Hal Newhouser	40.00	20.00	12.00
(14)	Johnny Pesky	20.00	10.00	6.00
(15)	Howie Pollett	20.00	10.00	6.00
(16)	Jerry Priddy	20.00	10.00	6.00
(17)	Aaron Robinson	20.00	10.00	6.00
(18)	Enos Slaughter	40.00	20.00	12.00
(19)	Eddie Stanky	20.00	10.00	6.00
(20)	Hal Wagner	20.00	10.00	6.00
(21)	Rudy York	20.00	10.00	6.00
(22)	Boston Red Sox Team	75.00	37.00	22.00
(23)	St. Louis Cardinals Team	75.00	37.00	22.00

1947

#	Player			
(1)	Ewell Blackwell	20.00	10.00	6.00
(2)	Ralph Branca	20.00	10.00	6.00
(3)	Billy Cox	20.00	10.00	6.00
(4)	Bob Dillinger	20.00	10.00	6.00
(5)	Joe Dobson	20.00	10.00	6.00
(6)	Joe Gordon	20.00	10.00	6.00
(7)	Hank Greenberg	45.00	22.00	13.50
(8)	Clint Hartung	20.00	10.00	6.00
(9)	Jim Hegan	20.00	10.00	6.00
(10)	Larry Jansen	20.00	10.00	6.00
(11)	George Kell	40.00	20.00	12.00
(12)	Ken Keltner	20.00	10.00	6.00
(13)	Ralph Kiner	40.00	20.00	12.00
(14)	Willard Marshall	20.00	10.00	6.00
(15)	Walt Masterson	20.00	10.00	6.00
(16)	"Red" Munger	20.00	10.00	6.00
(17)	Don Newcombe	25.00	12.50	7.50
(18)	Hal Newhouser	40.00	20.00	12.00
(19)	Joe Page	20.00	10.00	6.00
(20)	Babe Ruth/Portrait	100.00	50.00	30.00
(21)	Warren Spahn	40.00	20.00	12.00
(22)	Harry Taylor	20.00	10.00	6.00
(23)	Harry "The Hat" Walker	20.00	10.00	6.00
(24)	Brooklyn Dodgers Team	100.00	50.00	30.00
(25)	New York Yankees Team	150.00	75.00	45.00

1948

#	Player			
(1)	Richie Ashburn	40.00	20.00	12.00
(2)	Rex Barney	20.00	10.00	6.00
(3)	Gene Bearden	20.00	10.00	6.00
(4)	Lou Brissie	20.00	10.00	6.00
(5)	Alvin Dark	20.00	10.00	6.00
(6)	Larry Doby	40.00	20.00	12.00
(7)	Carl Furillo	25.00	12.50	7.50
(8)	Frank Gustine	20.00	10.00	6.00
(9)	Fred Hutchinson	20.00	10.00	6.00
(10)	Sheldon Jones	20.00	10.00	6.00
(11)	Bob Lemon	40.00	20.00	12.00
(12)	Hank Majeski	20.00	10.00	6.00
(13)	Barney McCosky	20.00	10.00	6.00
(14)	Mel Parnell	20.00	10.00	6.00
(15)	Carl Scheib	20.00	10.00	6.00
(16)	Al Zarilla	20.00	10.00	6.00
(17)	Boston Braves Team	75.00	37.00	22.00
(18)	Cleveland Indians Team	75.00	37.00	22.00

1949

#	Player			
(1)	Hoot Evers	20.00	10.00	6.00
(2)	Bob Feller	40.00	20.00	12.00
(3)	Billy Goodman	20.00	10.00	6.00
(4)	Sid Gordon	20.00	10.00	6.00
(5)	Gil Hodges	40.00	20.00	12.00
(6)	Art Houtteman	20.00	10.00	6.00
(7)	Dale Mitchell	20.00	10.00	6.00
(8)	Vic Raschi	20.00	10.00	6.00
(9)	Robin Roberts	40.00	20.00	12.00
(10)	Ray Scarborough	20.00	10.00	6.00
(11)	Duke Snider	50.00	25.00	15.00
(12)	Vic Wertz	20.00	10.00	6.00
(13)	Ted Williams	75.00	37.00	22.00
(14)	Brooklyn Dodgers Team	90.00	45.00	27.00
(15)	New York Yankees Team	90.00	45.00	27.00

1950

#	Player			
(1)	Hank Bauer	15.00	7.50	4.50
(2)	Yogi Berra	30.00	15.00	9.00
(3)	Walt Dropo	12.00	6.00	3.50
(4)	Del Ennis	12.00	6.00	3.50
(5)	Johnny Groth	12.00	6.00	3.50
(6)	Granny Hamner	12.00	6.00	3.50
(7)	Ted Kluszewski	15.00	7.50	4.50
(8)	Johnny Lipon	12.00	6.00	3.50
(9)	Hank Sauer	12.00	6.00	3.50
(10)	Earl Torgeson	12.00	6.00	3.50
(11)	New York Yankees Team	50.00	25.00	15.00
(12)	Philadelphia Phillies Team	35.00	17.50	10.50

1951

#	Player			
(1)	Grover Alexander	15.00	7.50	4.50
(2)	Chico Carrasquel	12.00	6.00	3.50
(3)	Bubba Church	12.00	6.00	3.50
(4)	Alvin Dark	12.00	6.00	3.50
(5)	Luke Easter	12.00	6.00	3.50
(6)	Carl Erskine	15.00	7.50	4.50
(7)	Ned Garver	12.00	6.00	3.50
(8)	Rogers Hornsby	15.00	7.50	4.50
(9)	Walter Johnson	25.00	12.50	7.50
(10)	Tony Lazzeri	15.00	7.50	4.50
(11)	Whitey Lockman	12.00	6.00	3.50
(12)	Ed Lopat	15.00	7.50	4.50
(13)	Sal Maglie	12.00	6.00	3.50
(14)	Willie Mays	150.00	75.00	45.00
(15)	Gil McDougald	20.00	10.00	6.00
(16)	Irv Noren	12.00	6.00	3.50
(17)	Eddie Robinson	12.00	6.00	3.50
(18)	Jackie Robinson	125.00	62.00	37.00
(19)	Red Rolfe	12.00	6.00	3.50
(20)	Tris Speaker	20.00	10.00	6.00
(21)	Eddie Stanky	12.00	6.00	3.50
(22)	Clyde Vollmer	12.00	6.00	3.50
(23)	Wes Westrum	12.00	6.00	3.50
(24)	Cy Young	25.00	12.50	7.50
(25)	New York Giants Team	40.00	20.00	12.00
(26)	New York Yankees Team	60.00	30.00	18.00

1952

#	Player			
(1)	Bobby Avila	12.00	6.00	3.50
(2)	Lou Boudreau	20.00	10.00	6.00
(3)	Jim Busby	12.00	6.00	3.50
(4)	Roy Campanella	30.00	15.00	9.00
(5)	Gil Coan	12.00	6.00	3.50
(6)	Walker Cooper	12.00	6.00	3.50
(7)	Al Corwin	12.00	6.00	3.50
(8)	Murry Dickson	12.00	6.00	3.50
(9)	Leo Durocher	20.00	10.00	6.00
(10)	Bob Elliott	12.00	6.00	3.50
(11)	Ferris Fain	12.00	6.00	3.50
(12)	Jimmie Foxx	20.00	10.00	6.00
(13)	Mike Garcia	12.00	6.00	3.50
(14)	Hank Greenberg	25.00	12.50	7.50
(15)	Solly Hemus	12.00	6.00	3.50
(16)	Monte Irvin	20.00	10.00	6.00
(17)	Sam Jethroe	12.00	6.00	3.50
(18)	Ellis Kinder	12.00	6.00	3.50
(19)	Dick Kryhoski	12.00	6.00	3.50
(20)	Clem Labine	15.00	7.50	4.50
(21)	Mickey Mantle	200.00	100.00	60.00
(22)	Connie Marrero	12.00	6.00	3.50
(23)	Cass Michaels	12.00	6.00	3.50
(24)	Minnie Minoso	15.00	7.50	4.50
(25)	Don Mueller	12.00	6.00	3.50
(26)	Mel Parnell	12.00	6.00	3.50
(27)	Allie Reynolds	15.00	7.50	4.50
(28)	"Preacher" Roe	15.00	7.50	4.50
(29)	Saul Rogovin	12.00	6.00	3.50
(30)	Al Rosen	15.00	7.50	4.50
(31)	Red Schoendienst	20.00	10.00	6.00
(32)	Andy Seminick	12.00	6.00	3.50
(33)	Bobby Shantz	12.00	6.00	3.50
(34)	Duke Snider	25.00	12.50	7.50
(35)	Gerry Staley	12.00	6.00	3.50
(36)	Gene Stephens	12.00	6.00	3.50
(37)	Max Surkont	12.00	6.00	3.50
(38)	Bobby Thomson	12.00	6.00	3.50
(39)	Elmer Valo	12.00	6.00	3.50
(40)	Eddie Waitkus	12.00	6.00	3.50
(41)	Gene Woodling	15.00	7.50	4.50
(42)	Eddie Yost	12.00	6.00	3.50
(43)	Gus Zernial	12.00	6.00	3.50
(44)	Brooklyn Dodgers Team	50.00	25.00	15.00
(45)	New York Yankees Team	75.00	37.00	22.00

1953

#	Player			
(1)	Joe Black	15.00	7.50	4.50
(2)	Billy Cox	12.00	6.00	3.50
(3)	Billy Loes	12.00	6.00	3.50
(4)	Billy Martin	15.00	7.50	4.50
(5)	Eddie Mathews	25.00	12.50	7.50
(6)	George Shuba	12.00	6.00	3.50
(7)	Hoyt Wilhelm	20.00	10.00	6.00

1954

#	Player			
(1)	Joe Adcock	12.00	6.00	3.50
(2)	Johnny Antonelli	12.00	6.00	3.50
(3)	Gus Bell	12.00	6.00	3.50
(4)	Jim Greengrass	12.00	6.00	3.50
(5)	Bob Grim	12.00	6.00	3.50
(6)	Frank House	12.00	6.00	3.50
(7)	Al Kaline	25.00	12.50	7.50
(8)	Jackie Jensen	12.00	6.00	3.50
(9)	Harvey Kuenn	15.00	7.50	4.50
(10)	Willie Miranda	12.00	6.00	3.50
(11)	Wally Moon	12.00	6.00	3.50

		NM	EX	VG
(12)	Ray Moore	12.00	6.00	3.50
(13)	Don Mossi	12.00	6.00	3.50
(14)	Stan Musial	30.00	15.00	9.00
(15)	Hal Naragon	12.00	6.00	3.50
(16)	Chet Nichols	12.00	6.00	3.50
(17)	Billy Pierce	12.00	6.00	3.50
(18)	Arnie Portocarrero	12.00	6.00	3.50
(19)	James "Dusty" Rhodes	12.00	6.00	3.50
(20)	Babe Ruth	50.00	25.00	15.00
(21)	Dean Stone	12.00	6.00	3.50
(22)	Bob Turley	15.00	7.50	4.50
(23)	Jim Wilson	12.00	6.00	3.50
(24)	New York Giants Team	50.00	25.00	15.00
1955				
(1)	Gene Conley	12.00	6.00	3.50
(2)	Elston Howard	15.00	7.50	4.50
(3)	Hank Sauer	12.00	6.00	3.50
1956				
(1)	Hank Bauer	15.00	7.50	4.50
(2)	Yogi Berra	25.00	12.50	7.50
(3)	Ray Boone	12.00	6.00	3.50
(4)	Ken Boyer	15.00	7.50	4.50
(5)	Tom Brewer	12.00	6.00	3.50
(6)	Bob Buhl	12.00	6.00	3.50
(7)	Nellie Fox	20.00	10.00	6.00
(8)	Bob Keegan	12.00	6.00	3.50
(9)	Don Larsen	15.00	7.50	4.50
(10)	Jim Lemon	12.00	6.00	3.50
(11)	Danny O'Connell	12.00	6.00	3.50
(12)	Jim Pendleton	12.00	6.00	3.50
(13)	Bob Rush	12.00	6.00	3.50
(14)	Roy Sievers	12.00	6.00	3.50
(15)	Gus Zernial	12.00	6.00	3.50
1957				
(1)	Hank Aaron	30.00	15.00	9.00
(2)	Joe Adcock	12.00	6.00	3.50
(3)	Luis Arroyo	12.00	6.00	3.50
(4)	Ed Bailey	12.00	6.00	3.50
(5)	Ernie Banks	25.00	12.50	7.50
(6)	Roy Campanella	20.00	10.00	6.00
(7)	Billy Cox	12.00	6.00	3.50
(8)	Del Crandall	12.00	6.00	3.50
(9)	Whitey Ford	25.00	12.50	7.50
(10)	Bob Friend	12.00	6.00	3.50
(11)	Carl Furillo	15.00	7.50	4.50
(12)	Granny Hamner	12.00	6.00	3.50
(13)	Gil Hodges	15.00	7.50	4.50
(14)	Billy Hoeft	12.00	6.00	3.50
(15)	Walter Johnson	25.00	12.50	7.50
(16)	George Kell	20.00	10.00	6.00
(17)	Ted Kluszewski	20.00	10.00	6.00
(18)	Johnny Kucks	12.00	6.00	3.50
(19)	Harvey Kuenn	12.00	6.00	3.50
(20)	Clem Labine	12.00	6.00	3.50
(21)	Vern Law	12.00	6.00	3.50
(22)	Brooks Lawrence	12.00	6.00	3.50
(23)	Bob Lemon	20.00	10.00	6.00
(24)	Sherman Lollar	12.00	6.00	3.50
(25)	Billy Martin	15.00	7.50	4.50
(25)	Eddie Mathews	20.00	10.00	6.00
(26)	Charlie Maxwell	12.00	6.00	3.50
(27)	Willie Mays	60.00	30.00	18.00
(28)	Gil McDougald	15.00	7.50	4.50
(29)	Willie Miranda	12.00	6.00	3.50
(30)	Jimmy Piersall	12.00	6.00	3.50
(31)	Pee Wee Reese	25.00	12.50	7.50
(32)	"Rip" Repulski	12.00	6.00	3.50
(33)	Robin Roberts	20.00	10.00	6.00
(34)	Frank Robinson	30.00	15.00	9.00
(35)	Al Rosen	12.00	6.00	3.50
(36)	Babe Ruth	60.00	30.00	18.00
(37)	Herb Score	15.00	7.50	4.50
(38)	Enos Slaughter	20.00	10.00	6.00
(39)	Warren Spahn	20.00	10.00	6.00
(40)	Johnny Temple	12.00	6.00	3.50
(41)	Mickey Vernon	12.00	6.00	3.50
1957 (17-1/2" x 20")				
(1)	Johnny Antonelli	30.00	15.00	9.00
(2)	Hank Bauer	45.00	22.00	13.50
(3)	Frank House	30.00	15.00	9.00
(4)	Jackie Jensen	35.00	17.50	10.00
(5)	Al Kaline	45.00	22.00	13.50
(6)	Bob Lemon	35.00	17.50	10.00
(7)	Chet Nichols	30.00	15.00	9.00
(8)	Al Rosen	30.00	15.00	9.00
(9)	Dean Stone	30.00	15.00	9.00
(10)	Bob Turley	35.00	17.50	10.00
(11)	Mickey Vernon	30.00	15.00	9.00

1915 Baseball Magazine Premiums

Two of the 1915 editions of Baseball Magazine were issued with attached premiums inside featuring color portraits of star players. The approximately 6-1/2" x 9-3/4" premiums featured artwork by frequent cover artist J.F. Kernan, printed on heavy glossy paper designed to be removed for display.

	NM	EX	VG
Honus Wagner Premium (Feb.)	1,000	500.00	300.00
Christy Mathewson Premium (April)	750.00	375.00	225.00

1913 Baseball Managers Scorecard/Fan

This novelty souvenir item was presumable made for sale or as a giveaway promotion which could be customized with sponsors' advertising on the back. The body of the fan is a heavy cardboard ovoid about 9-1/2" x 9". At center is a scorecard. Printed in color around the scoring section are colorful caricatures of each National and American League manager either in a costume representing the team nickname or holding a mascot, etc. The piece is stapled to a 6" wooden stick. Local advertising may or may not appear on the back.

	NM	EX	VG
Joe Birmingham, Nixey Callahan, Frank, Chance, Fred Clarke, Bill Dahlen, Red, Dooin, Jonny Evers, Clark Griffith,, Miller Huggins, Hughie Jennings, Connie, Mack, John McGraw, Jake Stahl, George, Stallings, George Stovall, Joe Tinker	1,150	575.00	345.00

1950 Baseball Player Charms

The date of issue for this novelty item is conjectural, based on known player selection. Packaged in plastic bubbles for sale in vending machines, these charms are found in several different shapes - rectangle, octagon, etc. - and colors of plastic. A black-and-white photo appears at center with a loop at top for hanging. Size also varies but is about 3/4" x 1-1/4". Players are not identified on the charm and there is no number. The checklist here is in alphabetical order, and likely not complete.

		NM	EX	VG
Common Player:		20.00	10.00	6.00
(1)	Yogi Berra	45.00	22.00	13.50
(2)	Ewell Blackwell	20.00	10.00	6.00
(3)	Roy Campanella	45.00	22.00	13.50
(4)	Joe DiMaggio	75.00	37.00	22.00
(5)	Carl Erskine	20.00	10.00	6.00
(6)	Bob Feller	25.00	12.50	7.50
(7)	Carl Furillo	22.50	11.00	6.75
(8)	Lou Gehrig	65.00	32.00	19.50
(9)	Hank Greenberg	45.00	22.00	13.50
(10)	Ralph Kiner	20.00	10.00	6.00
(11)	Stan Musial	55.00	27.00	16.50
(12)	Andy Pafko	20.00	10.00	6.00
(13)	Pee Wee Reese	35.00	17.50	10.50
(14)	Phil Rizzuto	30.00	15.00	9.00
(15)	Jackie Robinson	65.00	32.00	19.50
(16)	Babe Ruth	95.00	47.00	28.00
(17)	Duke Snider	35.00	17.50	10.50
(18)	Wally Westlake	20.00	10.00	6.00
(19)	Ted Williams	60.00	30.00	18.00

1952 Baseball Player Doubleheader Charms

These vending machine prizes were probably issued in the early 1950s, though pinning down a date via player selection is imprecise. About 7/8" in diameter, these novelties have black-and-white player photos on front and back, with the player's name in script beneath his portrait. A clear plastic dome covers the photos and is wrapped with a looped band for hanging. The unnumbered charms are listed here in alphabetical order.

		NM	EX	VG
Complete Set (31):		550.00	275.00	175.00
Common Player:		25.00	12.50	7.50
(1)	Richie Ashburn, Phil Masi	30.00	15.00	9.00
(2)	Hank Bauer, Johnny Pesky	25.00	12.50	7.50
(3)	Yogi Berra, Duke Snider	45.00	22.00	13.50
(4)	Ewell Blackwell, "Big" Jim Konstanty	25.00	12.50	7.50
(5)	Lou Boudreau, Allie Reynolds	27.50	13.50	8.25
(6)	Leland Brissie, Albert Schoendienst	27.50	13.50	8.25
(7)	Roy Campanella, Bob Elliott	30.00	15.00	9.00
(8)	Phil Cavarretta, Virgil Stallcup	25.00	12.50	7.50
(9)	Sam Chapman, Larry Jansen	25.00	12.50	7.50
(10)	Jerry Coleman, George Kell	27.50	13.50	8.25
(11)	Billy Cox, Junior Thompson	25.00	12.50	7.50
(12)	Walt Dropo, Myron McCormick	25.00	12.50	7.50
(13)	Al Evans, Wes Westrum	25.00	12.50	7.50
(14)	Walter Evers, Cliff Mapes	25.00	12.50	7.50
(15)	Bob Feller, Phil Rizzuto	35.00	17.50	10.50
(16)	Gordon Goldsberry, Stan Musial	30.00	15.00	9.00
(17)	Clint Hartung, Don Kolloway	25.00	12.50	7.50
(18)	Grady Hatton, Tommy Holmes	25.00	12.50	7.50
(19)	Tommy Henrich, Ted Kluszewski	27.50	13.50	8.25
(20)	Gene Hermanski, Hal Newhouser	25.00	12.50	7.50
(21)	Art Houtteman, Jackie Robinson	45.00	22.00	13.50
(22)	Sid Hudson, Andy Pafko	25.00	12.50	7.50
(23)	Ed Kazak, Bob Lemon	27.50	13.50	8.25
(24)	Ellis Kinder, Gus Zernial	25.00	12.50	7.50
(25)	Ralph Kiner, Joe Page	27.50	13.50	8.25
(26)	Ed Lopat, Paul Trout	25.00	12.50	7.50
(27)	Don Newcombe, Vic Wertz	25.00	12.50	7.50
(28)	Dave Philley, Aaron Robinson	25.00	12.50	7.50
(29)	Vic Raschi, Enos Slaughter	27.50	13.50	8.25
(30)	Pee Wee Reese, Gene Woodling	30.00	15.00	9.00
(31)	George Tebbetts, Eddie Yost	25.00	12.50	7.50

1961 Baseball Player Key Chains

The maker of these postage-stamp size (1-1/8" x 1-1/2") black-and-white, blank-back "cards" is unknown. From the inclusion of numerous journeyman Pirates players in the set, it probably has a Pittsburgh origin. Possibly intended for sale at stadium souvenir counters, they were made to be inserted into clear plastic key chain novelties, and have a semi-gloss front surface. Unnumbered, they are checklisted here alphabetically.

		NM	EX	VG
Complete Set (69):		400.00	200.00	120.00
Common Player:		5.00	2.50	1.50
(1)	Hank Aaron	15.00	7.50	4.50
(2)	Bob Allison	5.00	2.50	1.50
(3)	George Altman	5.00	2.50	1.50
(4)	Luis Aparicio	7.50	3.75	2.25
(5)	Richie Ashburn	7.50	3.75	2.25
(6)	Ernie Banks	10.00	5.00	3.00
(7)	Earl Battey	5.00	2.50	1.50
(8)	Hank Bauer	6.00	3.00	1.75
(9)	Gus Bell	5.00	2.50	1.50
(10)	Yogi Berra	10.00	5.00	3.00
(11)	Ken Boyer	6.00	3.00	1.75
(12)	Lew Burdette	5.00	2.50	1.50
(13)	Smoky Burgess	5.00	2.50	1.50
(14)	Orlando Cepeda	7.50	3.75	2.25
(15)	Gino Cimoli	5.00	2.50	1.50
(16)	Roberto Clemente	20.00	10.00	6.00
(17)	Del Crandall	5.00	2.50	1.50
(18)	Dizzy Dean	9.00	4.50	2.75
(19)	Don Drysdale	7.50	3.75	2.25

		NM	EX	VG
(20)	Sam Esposito	5.00	2.50	1.50
(21)	Roy Face	5.00	2.50	1.50
(22)	Nelson Fox	7.50	3.75	2.25
(23)	Bob Friend	5.00	2.50	1.50
(24)	Lou Gehrig	12.50	6.25	3.75
(25)	Joe Gibbon	5.00	2.50	1.50
(26)	Jim Gilliam	6.00	3.00	1.75
(27)	Fred Green	5.00	2.50	1.50
(28)	Pumpsie Green	5.00	2.50	1.50
(29)	Dick Groat	6.00	3.00	1.75
(30)	Harvey Haddix	5.00	2.50	1.50
(31)	Don Hoak	5.00	2.50	1.50
(32)	Glen Hobbie	5.00	2.50	1.50
(33)	Frank Howard	6.00	3.00	1.75
(34)	Jackie Jensen	5.00	2.50	1.50
(35)	Sam Jones	5.00	2.50	1.50
(36)	Al Kaline	9.00	4.50	2.75
(37)	Harmon Killebrew	7.50	3.75	2.25
(38)	Harvey Kuenn	5.00	2.50	1.50
(39)	Norm Larker	5.00	2.50	1.50
(40)	Vernon Law	5.00	2.50	1.50
(41)	Mickey Mantle	30.00	15.00	9.00
(42)	Roger Maris	12.00	6.00	3.50
(43)	Eddie Mathews	7.50	3.75	2.25
(44)	Willie Mays	12.00	6.00	3.50
(45)	Bill Mazeroski	7.50	3.75	2.25
(46)	Willie McCovey	7.50	3.75	2.25
(47)	Lindy McDaniel	5.00	2.50	1.50
(48)	Roy McMillan	5.00	2.50	1.50
(49)	Minnie Minoso	6.00	3.00	1.75
(50)	Danny Murtaugh	5.00	2.50	1.50
(51)	Stan Musial	12.00	6.00	3.50
(52)	Rocky Nelson	5.00	2.50	1.50
(53)	Bob Oldis	5.00	2.50	1.50
(54)	Vada Pinson	6.00	3.00	1.75
(55)	Vic Power	5.00	2.50	1.50
(56)	Robin Roberts	7.50	3.75	2.25
(57)	Pete Runnels	5.00	2.50	1.50
(58)	Babe Ruth	20.00	10.00	6.00
(59)	Ron Santo	6.00	3.00	1.75
(60)	Dick Schofield	5.00	2.50	1.50
(61)	Bob Skinner	5.00	2.50	1.50
(62)	Hal Smith	5.00	2.50	1.50
(63)	Duke Snider	9.00	4.50	2.75
(64)	Warren Spahn	7.50	3.75	2.25
(65)	Dick Stuart	5.00	2.50	1.50
(66)	Willie Tasby	5.00	2.50	1.50
(67)	Tony Taylor	5.00	2.50	1.50
(68)	Bill Virdon	5.00	2.50	1.50
(69)	Ted Williams	17.50	9.00	5.00

1978 Baseball Player Patches

These card-size (about 2-1/2" x 3-1/4") cloth patches feature embroidered player portraits on a white background with a color border. Uniform logos are not present. The patches originally sold for $2.50 apiece from the Penn Emblem Co., Philadelphia, though the company's name is not found on the patches. The unnumbered patches are listed here in alphabetical order.

		NM	EX	VG
Complete Set (103):		350.00	175.00	100.00
Common Player:		3.00	1.50	.90
(1)	Buddy Bell	3.00	1.50	.90
(2)	Johnny Bench	10.00	5.00	3.00
(3)	Vida Blue	3.00	1.50	.90
(4)	Bobby Bonds	3.00	1.50	.90
(5)	Bob Boone	3.00	1.50	.90
(6)	Larry Bowa	3.00	1.50	.90
(7)	George Brett	12.00	6.00	3.50
(8)	Lou Brock	9.00	4.50	2.75
(9)	Rick Burleson	3.00	1.50	.90
(10)	Jeff Burroughs	3.00	1.50	.90
(11)	Bert Campaneris	3.00	1.50	.90
(12)	John Candelaria	3.00	1.50	.90
(13)	Rod Carew	9.00	4.50	2.75
(14)	Steve Carlton	9.00	4.50	2.75
(15)	Gary Carter	7.50	3.75	2.25
(16)	Dave Cash	3.00	1.50	.90
(17)	Cesar Cedeno	3.00	1.50	.90
(18)	Ron Cey	3.00	1.50	.90
(19)	Chris Chambliss	3.00	1.50	.90
(20)	Jack Clark	3.00	1.50	.90
(21)	Dave Concepcion	3.00	1.50	.90
(22)	Cecil Cooper	3.00	1.50	.90
(23)	Jose Cruz	3.00	1.50	.90
(24)	Andre Dawson	3.00	1.50	.90
(25)	Dan Driessen	3.00	1.50	.90
(26)	Rawly Eastwick	3.00	1.50	.90
(27)	Dwight Evans	3.00	1.50	.90
(28)	Mark Fidrych	4.50	2.25	1.25
(29)	Rollie Fingers	7.50	3.75	2.25
(30)	Carlton Fisk	9.00	4.50	2.75
(31)	George Foster	3.00	1.50	.90
(32)	Steve Garvey	6.00	3.00	1.75
(33)	Rich Gossage	3.00	1.50	.90
(34)	Bobby Grich	3.00	1.50	.90
(35)	Ross Grimsley	3.00	1.50	.90

		NM	EX	VG
(36)	Ron Guidry	3.00	1.50	.90
(37)	Mike Hargrove	3.00	1.50	.90
(38)	Keith Hernandez	3.00	1.50	.90
(39)	Larry Hisle	3.00	1.50	.90
(40)	Bob Horner	3.00	1.50	.90
(41)	Roy Howell	3.00	1.50	.90
(42)	"Catfish" Hunter	7.50	3.75	2.25
(43)	Reggie Jackson	12.00	6.00	3.50
(44)	Tommy John	4.00	2.00	1.25
(45)	Jim Kern	3.00	1.50	.90
(46)	Chet Lemon	3.00	1.50	.90
(47)	Davey Lopes	3.00	1.50	.90
(48)	Greg Luzinski	3.00	1.50	.90
(49)	Fred Lynn	3.00	1.50	.90
(50)	Garry Maddox	3.00	1.50	.90
(51)	Bill Madlock	3.00	1.50	.90
(52)	Jon Matlack	3.00	1.50	.90
(53)	John Mayberry	3.00	1.50	.90
(54)	Lee Mazzilli	3.00	1.50	.90
(55)	Rick Monday	3.00	1.50	.90
(56)	Don Money	3.00	1.50	.90
(57)	Willie Montanez	3.00	1.50	.90
(58)	John Montefusco	3.00	1.50	.90
(59)	Joe Morgan	9.00	4.50	2.75
(60)	Thurman Munson	7.50	3.75	2.25
(61)	Bobby Murcer	3.00	1.50	.90
(62)	Graig Nettles	3.00	1.50	.90
(63)	Phil Niekro	7.50	3.75	2.25
(64)	Al Oliver	3.00	1.50	.90
(65)	Amos Otis	3.00	1.50	.90
(66)	Jim Palmer	9.00	4.50	2.75
(67)	Dave Parker	3.00	1.50	.90
(68)	Fred Patek	3.00	1.50	.90
(69)	Tony Perez	7.50	3.75	2.25
(70)	Lou Piniella	4.00	2.00	1.25
(71)	Biff Pocoroba	3.00	1.50	.90
(72)	Darrell Porter	3.00	1.50	.90
(73)	Rick Reuschel	3.00	1.50	.90
(74)	Jim Rice	6.00	3.00	1.75
(75a)	Pete Rose (Red border.)	12.00	6.00	3.50
(75b)	Pete Rose (Blue border.)	12.00	6.00	3.50
(76)	Joe Rudi	3.00	1.50	.90
(77)	Rick Reuschel	3.00	1.50	.90
(78)	Nolan Ryan	15.00	7.50	4.50
(79)	Manny Sanguillen	3.00	1.50	.90
(80)	Mike Schmidt	12.00	6.00	3.50
(81)	George Scott	3.00	1.50	.90
(82)	Tom Seaver	9.00	4.50	2.75
(83)	Ted Simmons	3.00	1.50	.90
(84)	Reggie Smith	3.00	1.50	.90
(85)	Willie Stargell	9.00	4.50	2.75
(86)	Rennie Stennett	3.00	1.50	.90
(87)	Jim Sundberg	3.00	1.50	.90
(88)	Bruce Sutter	7.50	3.75	2.25
(89)	Frank Tanana	3.00	1.50	.90
(90)	Garry Templeton	3.00	1.50	.90
(91)	Gene Tenace	3.00	1.50	.90
(92)	Jason Thompson	3.00	1.50	.90
(93)	Luis Tiant	3.00	1.50	.90
(94)	Joe Torre	4.50	2.25	1.25
(95)	Ellis Valentine	3.00	1.50	.90
(96)	Bob Watson	3.00	1.50	.90
(97)	Frank White	3.00	1.50	.90
(98)	Lou Whitaker	3.00	1.50	.90
(99)	Bump Wills	3.00	1.50	.90
(100)	Dave Winfield	9.00	4.50	2.75
(101)	Butch Wynegar	3.00	1.50	.90
(102)	Carl Yastrzemski	12.00	6.00	3.50
(103)	Richie Zisk	3.00	1.50	.90

Fantasy Baseball Player Pencil Clips

This series of modern (circa late 1990s) pencil clips features old-time baseball stars. The pieces feature enameled round buttons in various sizes attached to a steel frame designed to be slipped over a pencil, ostensibly for use with a scorecard during a ball game. These are often sold on eBay and at flea markets by persons purporting them to be old.

NO COLLECTIBLE VALUE
Ty Cobb
Christy Mathewson
Satchel Paige (St. Louis Browns)
Babe Ruth (Champions)
Honus Wagner
1959 World Series White Sox

1913 Baseball Player Stamps

The extent of this issue and the exact date and manner of its issue are not known. The large-format (about 1-13/16" x 2-1/2") stamps have color artwork of the players on a base-

ball diamond background. A solid colored frame with art deco detailing separates the picture from the white border. Backs are, of course, blank.

	NM	EX	VG
Chief Bender	200.00	100.00	60.00
Ty Cobb	1,750	875.00	525.00
Joe Jackson	2,250	1,125	675.00
Christy Mathewson	800.00	400.00	240.00
Tris Speaker	200.00	100.00	60.00

1892 Base Ball Scenes (N360)

The N360 American Card Catalog designation covers the several tobacco manufacturers who issued this type of card to advertise various brands. Obviously, the cards do not picture actual ballplayers, but rather have on their fronts color lithographs of attractive women in baseball uniforms and in game action. Approximately 2-3/16" x 3-15/16" most cards have a tiny line of type at bottom carrying a Donaldson Bros., N.Y., copyright. Those cards issued to promote the Little Rhody Cut Plus brand have a script ad message on front and a monthly schedule of the 12-team National League on back. Advertising for the various brands of tobacco companies may be printed directly on the card back, on a paper label pasted over another ad or overprinted on a previously printed ad. Cards are known with these manufacturers and brands. S.W. Venable: Cockade, Gay Head, Helmet, Ideal and Pluck; G.F. Young & Bro.: Little Rhody, and M.T. Coffey. Nine different poses are known for the card fronts.

	NM	EX	VG
Common Card:	800.00	400.00	240.00

1913 Base Ball Series Notebooks

The issue date cited is conjectural, based on writing found in a surviving specimen of this child's notebook. The 8" x 10" notebook has on its cover a baseball diamond and bleachers drawing in white on a beige background. Printed above and below the artwork are full-color reproductions of five baseball cards from the Philadelphia Caramel issues of 1909 (E95) and 1910 (E96). The cover is printed on thinner stock than the original cards and has no printing on the reverse side. This has led to cut copies of these cards being misidentified as proofs. Because similar blank-back, thin stock cards are known of other players, it is possible other notebook covers may exist.

	NM	EX	VG
Complete Notebook:			
Fred Clark (Clarke)(E96),	750.00	375.00	225.00
Nap Lajoie (E96), Jake			
Pfeister (E96), Honus			
Wagner (E95), Ed Willetts			
(Willett)(E95)			
OBSERVED SINGLES			
Harry Krause (E95)	100.00	40.00	20.00

1911 Baseball Scorecard Fan

This unusual player collectible is a combination fan and scorecard published circa 1911. The cardboard scorecard is about 10-1/2" x 9" and stapled to an approximately 11" long wooden handle. Printed in black-and-white, there are 16 player portraits at top, separated by a baseball. At center is the portrait of young lady and at bottom is a ball-in-mitt photo. The fans can be found with various local advertising overprinted on front or back: Barton's Barber Shop, Ira P. File Ice Cream and Confectionery, Maine's Bliss School of Business, Poole Pianos, Kemper pharmacy, etc. The players are identified by last name and for lack of uniform details, specific identification of a few of them is speculative.

	NM	EX	VG
Germany Schaeffer	1,500	750.00	400.00
(Schaefer), Bobby Wallace,			
Billy Sullivan, Hal Chase,			
George Moriarty, Harry Lord,			
Harry Davis, Nap Lajoie,			
Mickey Doolan, Clark			
Griffith, Bill Dahlen, Jeff			
Sweeney, Frank Chance, Art			
Devlin, Fred Clark (Clarke),			
Roger Bresnahan			

1964 Baseball Stars - Present and Future Photocard

This large-format (11" x 8-1/2") color card features three group photos of top stars of the day. In addition to the photos, there are facsimile autographs of each player on the bright yellow background. Back is blank. (See also Baseball Greats Postcard.)

	NM	EX	VG
Sheet:	25.00	12.50	7.50
Dean Chance, Don			
Drysdale, Dick Farrell, Jim			
Fregosi, Sandy Koufax,			
Willie Mays, Joe Pepitone,			
Dick Radatz			

1912 Base Ball Stars Series

This set of blank-backed, black-and-white 6" x 9" pictures features the contestants of the 1912 World Series - the Red Sox and Giants. It is possible these pictures were sold at the ballparks during the Series. The checklist here is probably incomplete. The unnumbered pictures have been listed alphabetically within team.

	NM	EX	VG
Common Player:	450.00	225.00	135.00
BOSTON RED SOX			
(1) Hugh Bedient	450.00	225.00	135.00
(2) Joe Wood	480.00	240.00	145.00
N.Y. GIANTS			
(1) Rube Marquard	525.00	260.00	150.00
(2) Christy Mathewson	1,050	525.00	315.00
(3) Jeff Tesreau	450.00	225.00	135.00

1938 Baseball Tabs

The issuer and manner of distribution for these baseball tabs is unknown. About 3/4" diameter, with bendable wings at each side, the points of which could be stuck through fabric and thus attached to a cap or jacket, the tabs have black-and-white player portraits on a baseball-style background in one of several colors. Most of the player first names have parentheses around them. The team tabs have a large nickname at center and the city and league at bottom. The inclusion of American Association teams argues for distribution in the upper Midwest. The unnumbered tabs are listed here in alphabetical order.

	NM	EX	VG
Complete Set (53):	3,000	1,500	900.00
Common Player:	50.00	25.00	15.50
Common Team:	50.00	25.00	15.00
(1) Luke Appling	75.00	37.00	22.00
(2) Earl Averill	75.00	37.00	22.00
(3) Phil Cavarretta	50.00	25.00	15.00
(4) Dizzy Dean	100.00	50.00	30.00
(5) Paul Derringer	50.00	25.00	15.00
(6) Bill Dickey	90.00	45.00	27.00
(7) Joe DiMaggio	450.00	225.00	135.00
(8) Bob Feller	75.00	37.00	22.00
(9) Lou Fette	50.00	25.00	15.00
(10) Jimmie Foxx	100.00	50.00	30.00
(11) Lou Gehrig	375.00	185.00	110.00
(12) Charley Gehringer	75.00	37.00	22.00
(13) Lefty Gomez	75.00	37.00	22.00
(14) Hank Greenberg	90.00	45.00	27.00
(15) Lefty Grove	75.00	37.00	22.00
(16) Mule Haas	50.00	25.00	15.00
(17) Gabby Hartnett	75.00	37.00	22.00
(18) Rollie Hemsley	50.00	25.00	15.00
(19) Carl Hubbell	75.00	37.00	22.00
(20) Chuck Klein	75.00	37.00	22.00
(21) Red Kress	50.00	25.00	15.00
(22) Push-Em-Up-Tony Lazzeri	75.00	37.00	22.00
(23) Ted Lyons	75.00	37.00	22.00
(24) Joe Medwick	75.00	37.00	22.00
(25) Van Lingle Mungo	50.00	25.00	15.00
(26) Rip Radcliff	50.00	25.00	15.00
(27) Schoolboy Rowe	50.00	25.00	15.00
(28) Al Simmons	75.00	37.00	22.00
(29) Little Poison Waner	75.00	37.00	22.00
(30) Athletics (Philadelphia)	50.00	25.00	15.00
(31) Bees (Boston)	50.00	25.00	15.00
(32) Blues (Kansas City)	50.00	25.00	15.00
(33) Brewers (Milwaukee)	50.00	25.00	15.00
(34) Browns (St. Louis)	50.00	25.00	15.00
(35) Cardinals (St. Louis)	50.00	25.00	15.00
(36) Colonels (Louisville)	50.00	25.00	15.00
(37) Cubs (Chicago)	50.00	25.00	15.00
(38) Dodgers (Brooklyn)	50.00	25.00	15.00
(39) Giants (New York)	50.00	25.00	15.00
(40) Indians (Cleveland)	50.00	25.00	15.00
(41) Indians (Indianapolis)	50.00	25.00	15.00
(42) Millers (Minneapolis)	50.00	25.00	15.00
(43) Mud-Hens (Toledo)	50.00	25.00	15.00
(44) Nationals (Washington)	50.00	25.00	15.00
(45) Phillies (Philadelphia)	50.00	25.00	15.00
(46) Pirates (Pittsburgh)	50.00	25.00	15.00
(47) Red Birds (Columbus)	50.00	25.00	15.00
(48) Reds (Cincinnati)	50.00	25.00	15.00
(49) Red Sox (Boston)	50.00	25.00	15.00
(50) Saints (St. Paul)	50.00	25.00	15.00
(51) Tigers (Detroit)	50.00	25.00	15.00
(52) White Sox (Chicago)	50.00	25.00	15.00
(53) Yankees (New York)	65.00	32.00	19.50

1934-36 Batter-Up (R318)

National Chicle's 192-card "Batter-Up" set was issued over a three-year period. The blank-backed cards are die-cut, enabling collectors of the era to fold the top of the card over so that it could stand upright on its own support. The cards can be found in black-and-white or a variety of color tints. Card numbers 1-80 measure 2-3/8" x 3-1/4" in size, while the high-numbered cards (#81-192) measure 2-3/8" x 3" (1/4" smaller in height). The high-numbered cards are significantly more difficult to find than the lower numbers. The set's ACC designation is R318.

	NM	EX	VG
Complete Set (192):	45,000	22,500	13,500
Common Player (1-80):	240.00	120.00	70.00
Common Player (81-192):	450.00	225.00	140.00
1 Wally Berger	420.00	210.00	125.00
2 Ed Brandt	230.00	115.00	70.00
3 Al Lopez	750.00	375.00	225.00
4 Dick Bartell	230.00	115.00	70.00
5 Carl Hubbell	800.00	400.00	240.00
6 Bill Terry	750.00	375.00	2250.00
7 Pepper Martin	230.00	115.00	70.00
8 Jim Bottomley	750.00	375.00	225.00
9 Tommy Bridges	240.00	120.00	70.00
10 Rick Ferrell	750.00	375.00	225.00
11 Ray Benge	240.00	120.00	70.00
12 Wes Ferrell	240.00	120.00	70.00
13 Bill Cissell	240.00	120.00	70.00
14 Pie Traynor	750.00	375.00	225.00
15 Roy Mahaffey	240.00	120.00	70.00
16 Chick Hafey	750.00	375.00	225.00
17 Lloyd Waner	750.00	375.00	225.00
18 Jack Burns	240.00	120.00	70.00
19 Buddy Myer	240.00	120.00	70.00
20 Bob Johnson	240.00	120.00	70.00
21 Arky Vaughn (Vaughan)	750.00	375.00	225.00
22 Red Rolfe	240.00	120.00	70.00
23 Lefty Gomez	750.00	375.00	225.00
24 Earl Averill	750.00	375.00	225.00
25 Mickey Cochrane	750.00	375.00	225.00
26 Van Mungo	240.00	120.00	70.00
27 Mel Ott	1,000	500.00	300.00
28 Jimmie Foxx	1,300	650.00	400.00
29 Jimmy Dykes	240.00	120.00	70.00
30 Bill Dickey	750.00	375.00	225.00
31 Lefty Grove	750.00	375.00	225.00
32 Joe Cronin	750.00	375.00	225.00
33 Frankie Frisch	750.00	375.00	225.00
34 Al Simmons	750.00	375.00	225.00
35 Rogers Hornsby	1,150	575.00	350.00
36 Ted Lyons	750.00	375.00	225.00
37 Rabbit Maranville	750.00	375.00	225.00
38 Jimmie Wilson	240.00	120.00	70.00
39 Willie Kamm	240.00	120.00	70.00
40 Bill Hallahan	240.00	120.00	70.00
41 Gus Suhr	240.00	120.00	70.00
42 Charlie Gehringer	750.00	375.00	225.00
43 Joe Heving	240.00	120.00	70.00
44 Adam Comorosky	240.00	120.00	70.00
45 Tony Lazzeri	750.00	375.00	225.00
46 Sam Leslie	240.00	120.00	70.00
47 Bob Smith	240.00	120.00	70.00
48 Willis Hudlin	240.00	120.00	70.00
49 Carl Reynolds	240.00	120.00	70.00
50 Fred Schulte	240.00	120.00	70.00
51 Cookie Lavagetto	240.00	120.00	70.00
52 Hal Schumacher	240.00	120.00	70.00
53 Doc Cramer	240.00	120.00	70.00
54 Si Johnson	240.00	120.00	70.00
55 Ollie Bejma	240.00	120.00	70.00
56 Sammy Byrd	240.00	120.00	70.00
57 Hank Greenberg	1,000	500.00	300.00
58 Bill Knickerbocker	240.00	120.00	70.00
59 Billy Urbanski	240.00	120.00	70.00
60 Ed Morgan	240.00	120.00	70.00
61 Eric McNair	240.00	120.00	70.00
62 Ben Chapman	240.00	120.00	70.00
63 Roy Johnson	240.00	120.00	70.00
64 "Dizzy" Dean	1,500	750.00	450.00
65 Zeke Bonura	240.00	120.00	70.00
66 Firpo Marberry	240.00	120.00	70.00
67 Gus Mancuso	240.00	120.00	70.00
68 Joe Vosmik	240.00	120.00	70.00
69 Earl Grace	240.00	120.00	70.00
70 Tony Piet	240.00	120.00	70.00
71 Rollie Hemsley	240.00	120.00	70.00
72 Fred Fitzsimmons	240.00	120.00	70.00
73 Hack Wilson	750.00	375.00	225.00
74 Chick Fullis	240.00	120.00	70.00
75 Fred Frankhouse	240.00	120.00	70.00
76 Ethan Allen	240.00	120.00	70.00
77 Heinie Manush	750.00	375.00	225.00
78 Rip Collins	240.00	120.00	70.00
79 Tony Cuccinello	240.00	120.00	70.00
80 Joe Kuhel	300.00	150.00	90.00
81 Thomas Bridges	450.00	225.00	140.00
82 Clinton Brown	450.00	225.00	140.00
83 Albert Blanche	450.00	225.00	140.00
84 "Boze" Berger	450.00	225.00	140.00
85 Goose Goslin	1,000	500.00	300.00
86 Vernon Gomez	1,100	550.00	350.00
87 Joe Glen (Glenn)	450.00	225.00	140.00
88 Cy Blanton	450.00	225.00	140.00
89 Tom Carey	450.00	225.00	140.00
90 Ralph Birkhofer	450.00	225.00	140.00
91 Frank Gabler	450.00	225.00	140.00
92 Dick Coffman	450.00	225.00	140.00
93 Ollie Bejma	450.00	225.00	140.00

		NM	EX	VG
94	Leroy Earl Parmalee	450.00	225.00	140.00
95	Carl Reynolds	450.00	225.00	140.00
96	Ben Cantwell	450.00	225.00	140.00
97	Curtis Davis	450.00	225.00	140.00
98	Wallace Moses, Billy Webb	1,000	500.00	300.00
99	Ray Benge	450.00	225.00	140.00
100	"Pie" Traynor	1,000	500.00	300.00
101	Phil. Cavarretta	450.00	225.00	140.00
102	"Pep" Young	450.00	225.00	140.00
103	Willis Hudlin	450.00	225.00	140.00
104	Mickey Haslin	450.00	225.00	140.00
105	Oswald Bluege	450.00	225.00	140.00
106	Paul Andrews	450.00	225.00	140.00
107	Edward A. Brandt	450.00	225.00	140.00
108	Dan Taylor	450.00	225.00	140.00
109	Thornton T. Lee	450.00	225.00	140.00
110	Hal Schumacher	450.00	225.00	140.00
111	Minter Hayes, Ted Lyons	1,100	550.00	350.00
112	Odell Hale	450.00	225.00	140.00
113	Earl Averill	1,000	500.00	300.00
114	Italo Chelini	450.00	225.00	140.00
115	Ivy Andrews, Jim Bottomley	1,300	650.00	400.00
116	Bill Walker	450.00	225.00	140.00
117	Bill Dickey	1,500.	750.00	450.00
118	Gerald Walker	450.00	225.00	140.00
119	Ted Lyons	1,000	500.00	300.00
120	Elden Auker (Eldon)	450.00	225.00	140.00
121	Wild Bill Hallahan	450.00	225.00	140.00
122	Freddy Lindstrom	1,000	500.00	300.00
123	Oral C. Hildebrand	450.00	225.00	140.00
124	Luke Appling	1,000	500.00	300.00
125	"Pepper" Martin	750.00	375.00	225.00
126	Rick Ferrell	1,000	500.00	300.00
127	Ival Goodman	450.00	225.00	140.00
128	Joe Kuhel	450.00	225.00	140.00
129	Ernest Lombardi	1,000	500.00	300.00
130	Charles Gehringer	1,000	500.00	300.00
131	Van L. Mungo	500.00	250.00	150.00
132	Larry French	450.00	225.00	140.00
133	"Buddy" Myer	450.00	225.00	140.00
134	Mel Harder	450.00	225.00	140.00
135	Augie Galan	450.00	225.00	140.00
136	"Gabby" Hartnett	1,000	500.00	300.00
137	Stan Hack	450.00	225.00	140.00
138	Billy Herman	1,000	500.00	300.00
139	Bill Jurges	450.00	225.00	140.00
140	Bill Lee	450.00	225.00	140.00
141	"Zeke" Bonura	450.00	225.00	140.00
142	Tony Piet	450.00	225.00	140.00
143	Paul Dean	650.00	325.00	200.00
144	Jimmy Foxx	1,700	850.00	500.00
145	Joe Medwick	1,000	500.00	300.00
146	Rip Collins	450.00	225.00	140.00
147	Melo Almada	450.00	225.00	140.00
148	Allan Cooke	450.00	225.00	140.00
149	Moe Berg	1,250	625.00	375.00
150	Adolph Camilli	450.00	225.00	140.00
151	Oscar Melillo	450.00	225.00	140.00
152	Bruce Campbell	450.00	225.00	140.00
153	Lefty Grove	1,250	625.00	375.00
154	John Murphy	450.00	225.00	140.00
155	Luke Sewell	450.00	225.00	140.00
156	Leo Durocher	1,000	500.00	300.00
157	Lloyd Waner	1,000	500.00	300.00
158	Guy Bush	450.00	225.00	140.00
159	Jimmy Dykes	450.00	225.00	140.00
160	Steve O'Neill	450.00	225.00	140.00
161	Gen. Crowder	450.00	225.00	140.00
162	Joe Cascarella	450.00	225.00	140.00
163	"Bud" Hafey	450.00	225.00	140.00
164	"Gilly" Campbell	450.00	225.00	140.00
165	Ray Hayworth	450.00	225.00	140.00
166	Frank Demaree	450.00	225.00	140.00
167	John Babich	450.00	225.00	140.00
168	Marvin Owen	450.00	225.00	140.00
169	Ralph Kress	450.00	225.00	140.00
170	"Mule" Haas	450.00	225.00	140.00
171	Frank Higgins	450.00	225.00	140.00
172	Walter Berger	450.00	225.00	140.00
173	Frank Frisch	1,000	500.00	300.00
174	Wess Ferrell (Wes)	450.00	225.00	140.00
175	Pete Fox	450.00	225.00	140.00
176	John Vergez	450.00	225.00	140.00
177	William Rogell	450.00	225.00	140.00
178	"Don" Brennan	450.00	225.00	140.00
179	James Bottomley	1,000	500.00	300.00
180	Travis Jackson	1,000	500.00	300.00
181	Robert Rolfe	450.00	225.00	140.00
182	Frank Crosetti	600.00	300.00	180.00
183	Joe Cronin	1,000	500.00	300.00
184	"Schoolboy" Rowe	500.00	250.00	150.00
185	"Chuck" Klein	1,000	500.00	300.00
186	Lon Warneke	450.00	225.00	140.00
187	Gus Suhr	450.00	225.00	140.00
188	Ben Chapman	450.00	225.00	140.00
189	Clint. Brown	500.00	250.00	150.00
190	Paul Derringer	500.00	250.00	150.00
191	John Burns	500.00	250.00	150.00
192	John Broaca	900.00	450.00	270.00

1934-36 Batter-Up Premiums

The identity of these premium pictures and their association with National Chicle Batter-Up bubblegum card set was not recognized by most collectors until the mid-2000s. These are the pictures that were mentioned on the wrappers of the high-number series of Batter-Up cards, and were apparently designed to be handed out by the retailer to the purchaser of each penny pack of gum. The 5" x 8" photos are printed in a dark red duotone on thin glossy stock. The back is blank. The pictures on the premiums are the same as on the player's Batter-Up card. The extent of the premium checklist is unknown.

	NM	EX	VG
Common Player:	1,200	725.00	350.00
Joe Vosmik	1,200	725.00	350.00
Paul Waner	2,000	1,200	600.00

1958 Bazooka "My Favorite Team" Patches

These screen-printed felt patches were available via a mail-in offer found in Topps baseball cards. Approximately 5" in diameter, they were intended to be sewn on jackets, caps, etc.

		NM	EX	VG
Complete Set (16):		450.00	225.00	135.00
Common Patch:		30.00	15.00	9.00
(1)	Baltimore Orioles	30.00	15.00	9.00
(2)	Boston Red Sox	35.00	17.50	10.50
(3)	Chicago Cubs	45.00	22.00	13.50
(4)	Chicago White Sox	30.00	15.00	9.00
(5)	Cincinnati Reds	30.00	15.00	9.00
(6)	Cleveland Indians	30.00	15.00	9.00
(7)	Detroit Tigers	30.00	15.00	9.00
(8)	Kansas City A's	30.00	15.00	9.00
(9)	Los Angeles Dodgers	40.00	20.00	12.00
(10)	Milwaukee Braves	35.00	17.50	10.50
(11)	New York Yankees	50.00	25.00	15.00
(12)	Philadelphia Phillies	30.00	15.00	9.00
(13)	Pittsburgh Pirates	30.00	15.00	9.00
(14)	San Francisco Giants	40.00	20.00	12.00
(15)	St. Louis Cardinals	30.00	15.00	9.00
(16)	Washington Senators	35.00	17.50	10.50

1959 Bazooka

The 1959 Bazooka set, consisting of 23 full-color, unnumbered cards, was printed on boxes of one-cent Topps bubble gum. The blank-backed cards measure 2-13/16" x 4-15/16", when properly cut. Nine cards were first issued, with 14 being added to the set later. The nine more plentiful cards are #'s 1, 5, 8, 9, 14, 15, 16, 17 and 22. Complete boxes would command double the price shown.

		NM	EX	VG
Complete Set (23):		9,600	4,800	2,900
Common Player:		120.00	60.00	35.00
(1a)	Hank Aaron (Name in white.)	575.00	290.00	175.00
(1b)	Hank Aaron (Name in yellow.)	550.00	275.00	165.00
(2)	Richie Ashburn/SP	500.00	250.00	150.00
(3)	Ernie Banks/SP	575.00	290.00	175.00
(4)	Ken Boyer/SP	280.00	140.00	85.00
(5)	Orlando Cepeda	225.00	110.00	65.00
(6)	Bob Cerv/SP	280.00	140.00	85.00
(7)	Rocky Colavito/SP	425.00	215.50	125.00
(8)	Del Crandall	120.00	60.00	35.00
(9)	Jim Davenport	120.00	60.00	35.00
(10)	Don Drysdale/SP	500.00	250.00	150.00
(11)	Nellie Fox/SP	500.00	250.00	150.00
(12)	Jackie Jensen/SP	280.00	140.00	85.00
(13)	Harvey Kuenn/SP	225.00	110.00	65.00
(14)	Mickey Mantle	1,350	675.00	400.00
(15)	Willie Mays	750.00	375.00	225.00
(16)	Bill Mazeroski	250.00	125.00	75.00
(17)	Roy McMillan	120.00	60.00	35.00
(18)	Billy Pierce/SP	280.00	140.00	85.00
(19)	Roy Sievers/SP	280.00	140.00	85.00
(20)	Duke Snider/SP	850.00	425.00	250.00
(21)	Gus Triandos/SP	250.00	125.00	75.00
(22)	Bob Turley	225.00	110.00	65.00
(23)	Vic Wertz/SP	280.00	140.00	85.00

1959 Bazooka Pennants

These screen-printed felt pennants were available via a mail-in offer found in Topps baseball cards. Approximately 15" long and 5" wide, they have a "COPYRIGHT BAZOOKA" bar near the wide end.

		NM	EX	VG
Complete Set (16):		600.00	300.00	180.00
Common Team:		40.00	20.00	12.00
(1)	Baltimore Orioles	40.00	20.00	12.00
(2)	Boston Red Sox	40.00	20.00	12.00
(3)	Chicago Cubs	40.00	20.00	12.00
(4)	Chicago White Sox	45.00	22.50	13.50
(5)	Cincinnati Redlegs	40.00	20.00	12.00
(6)	Cleveland Indians	40.00	20.00	12.00
(7)	Detroit Tigers	40.00	20.00	12.00
(8)	Kansas City A's	40.00	20.00	12.00
(9)	Los Angeles Dodgers	45.00	22.50	13.50
(10)	Milwaukee Braves	40.00	20.00	12.00
(11)	New York Yankees	50.00	25.00	15.00
(12)	Philadelphia Phillies	40.00	20.00	12.00
(13)	Pittsburgh Pirates	40.00	20.00	12.00
(14)	San Francisco Giants	40.00	20.00	12.00
(15)	St. Louis Cardinals	40.00	20.00	12.00
(16)	Washington Senators	40.00	20.00	12.00

1960 Bazooka

Three-card panels were printed on the bottoms of Bazooka bubble gum boxes in 1960. The blank-backed set is comprised of 36 cards with the card number located at the bottom of each full-color card. Individual cards measure 1-13/16" x 2-3/4"; the panels measure 2-3/4" x 5-1/2".

		NM	EX	VG
Complete Panel Set (12):		2,200	1,100	650.00
Complete Singles Set (36):		2,000	1,000	600.00
Common Player:		15.00	7.50	4.50
	Panel (1)	125.00	62.00	37.00
1	Ernie Banks	90.00	45.00	27.00
2	Bud Daley	15.00	7.50	4.50
3	Wally Moon	15.00	7.50	4.50
	Panel (2)	200.00	100.00	60.00
4	Hank Aaron	150.00	75.00	45.00
5	Milt Pappas	15.00	7.50	4.50
6	Dick Stuart	15.00	7.50	4.50
	Panel (3)	325.00	160.00	97.00
7	Roberto Clemente	200.00	100.00	60.00
8	Yogi Berra	90.00	45.00	27.00
9	Ken Boyer	25.00	12.50	7.50
	Panel (4)	100.00	50.00	30.00
10	Orlando Cepeda	50.00	25.00	15.00
11	Gus Triandos	15.00	7.50	4.50
12	Frank Malzone	15.00	7.50	4.50
	Panel (5)	200.00	100.00	60.00
13	Willie Mays	150.00	75.00	45.00
14	Camilo Pascual	15.00	7.50	4.50
15	Bob Cerv	15.00	7.50	4.50
	Panel (6)	125.00	62.00	37.00
16	Vic Power	15.00	7.50	4.50
17	Larry Sherry	15.00	7.50	4.50
18	Al Kaline	75.00	37.00	22.00
	Panel (7)	200.00	100.00	60.00
19	Warren Spahn	75.00	37.00	22.00
20	Harmon Killebrew	75.00	37.00	22.00
21	Jackie Jensen	25.00	12.50	7.50
	Panel (8)	175.00	87.00	52.00
22	Luis Aparicio	50.00	25.00	15.00
23	Gil Hodges	50.00	25.00	15.00
24	Richie Ashburn	50.00	25.00	15.00
	Panel (9)	125.00	62.00	37.00
25	Nellie Fox	50.00	25.00	15.00
26	Robin Roberts	50.00	25.00	15.00
27	Joe Cunningham	15.00	7.50	4.50
	Panel (10)	200.00	100.00	60.00
28	Early Wynn	50.00	25.00	15.00
29	Frank Robinson	75.00	37.00	22.00
30	Rocky Colavito	50.00	25.00	15.00
	Panel (11)	750.00	375.00	225.00
31	Mickey Mantle	500.00	250.00	150.00
32	Glen Hobbie	15.00	7.50	4.50
33	Roy McMillan	15.00	7.50	4.50

		NM	EX	VG
	Panel (12)	60.00	30.00	18.00
34	Harvey Kuenn	15.00	7.50	4.50
35	Johnny Antonelli	15.00	7.50	4.50
36	Del Crandall	15.00	7.50	4.50

1960 Bazooka Hot Iron Transfers

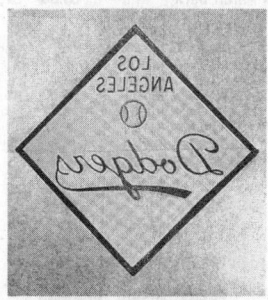

Team logo transfers were available via a mail-in offer found on cards inserted into packs of 1960 Topps. Varying in size and shape, but generally about 5" square, the transfers were packaged in a colorful envelope which provided instructions for ironing the logo to a t-shirt or other cloth surface. Unlike earlier Bazooka mail-in premiums, the gum is not named on the transfers. Values shown are for transfers without the envelope. Envelopes, which carried the name and logo of the team inside, are valued about the same as the transfer itself.

		NM	EX	VG
	Complete Set (16):	300.00	150.00	90.00
	Common Team:	20.00	10.00	6.00
	Envelope: 1X			
(1)	Baltimore Orioles	20.00	10.00	6.00
(2)	Boston Red Sox	20.00	10.00	6.00
(3)	Chicago Cubs	20.00	10.00	6.00
(4)	Chicago White Sox	20.00	10.00	6.00
(5)	Cincinnati Redlegs	20.00	10.00	6.00
(6)	Cleveland Indians	20.00	10.00	6.00
(7)	Detroit Tigers	20.00	10.00	6.00
(8)	Kansas City A's	20.00	10.00	6.00
(9)	Los Angeles Dodgers	22.50	11.00	6.75
(10)	Milwaukee Braves	20.00	10.00	6.00
(11)	New York Yankees	25.00	12.50	7.50
(12)	Philadelphia Phillies	20.00	10.00	6.00
(13)	Pittsburgh Pirates	22.50	11.00	6.75
(14)	San Francisco Giants	20.00	10.00	6.00
(15)	St. Louis Cardinals	20.00	10.00	6.00
(16)	Washington Senators	20.00	10.00	6.00

1961 Bazooka

TED KLUSZEWSKI
LOS ANGELES ANGELS 1st base
NO. 18 OF 36 CARDS

Similar in design to the 1960 Bazooka set, the 1961 edition consists of 36 cards printed in panels of three on the bottom of Bazooka bubble gum boxes. The full-color cards, which measure 1-13/16" x 2-3/4" individually and 2-3/4" x 5-1/2" as panels, are numbered 1 through 36. The backs are blank.

		NM	EX	VG
	Complete Set, Panels (12):	1,500	750.00	450.00
	Complete Set, Singles (36):	1,200	600.00	350.00
	Common Player:	12.00	6.00	3.50
	Panel (1)	750.00	375.00	225.00
1	Art Mahaffey	12.00	6.00	3.50
2	Mickey Mantle	350.00	187.50	93.75
3	Ron Santo	25.00	12.50	7.50
	Panel (2)	225.00	110.00	65.00
4	Bud Daley	12.00	6.00	3.50
5	Roger Maris	100.00	50.00	30.00
6	Eddie Yost	12.00	6.00	3.50
	Panel (3)	75.00	37.50	22.50
7	Minnie Minoso	15.00	7.50	4.50
8	Dick Groat	13.50	7.00	4.00
9	Frank Malzone	12.00	6.00	3.50
	Panel (4)	100.00	50.00	30.00
10	Dick Donovan	12.00	6.00	3.50
11	Ed Mathews	45.00	22.50	13.50
12	Jim Lemon	12.00	6.00	3.50
	Panel (5)	75.00	37.50	22.50
13	Chuck Estrada	12.00	6.00	3.50
14	Ken Boyer	15.00	7.50	4.50
15	Harvey Kuenn	12.00	6.00	3.50
	Panel (6)	100.00	50.00	30.00
16	Ernie Broglio	12.00	6.00	3.50
17	Rocky Colavito	25.00	12.50	7.50
18	Ted Kluszewski	25.00	12.50	7.50
19	Ernie Banks	100.00	50.00	30.00
20	Al Kaline	45.00	22.50	13.50
21	Ed Bailey	12.00	6.00	3.50
	Panel (7)	250.00	125.00	75.00
	Panel (8)	250.00	125.00	75.00
22	Jim Perry	12.00	6.00	3.50
23	Willie Mays	100.00	50.00	30.00
24	Bill Mazeroski	40.00	20.00	12.00
	Panel (9)	100.00	50.00	30.00
25	Gus Triandos	12.00	6.00	3.50
26	Don Drysdale	45.00	22.50	13.50
27	Frank Herrera	12.00	6.00	3.50
	Panel (10)	100.00	50.00	30.00
28	Earl Battey	12.00	6.00	3.50
29	Warren Spahn	45.00	22.50	13.50
30	Gene Woodling	12.00	6.00	3.50
	Panel (11)	100.00	50.00	30.00
31	Frank Robinson	45.00	22.50	13.50
32	Pete Runnels	12.00	6.00	3.50
33	Woodie Held	12.00	6.00	3.50
	Panel (12)	100.00	50.00	30.00
34	Norm Larker	12.00	6.00	3.50
35	Luis Aparicio	35.00	17.50	10.00
36	Bill Tuttle	12.00	6.00	3.50

1962 Bazooka

KEN BOYER
ST. LOUIS CARDINALS 3rd base

In 1962, Bazooka increased the size of its set to 45 full-color cards. The set is unnumbered and was printed in panels of three on the bottoms of bubble gum boxes. Individual cards measure 1-13/16" x 2-3/4" in size, with panels at 2-3/4" x 5-1/2". In the checklist that follows the cards have been numbered alphabetically, using the name of the player who appears on the left end of the panel. Panels (1), (11) and (15) were issued in much shorter supply and command a higher price.

		NM	EX	VG
	Complete Set, Panels (15):	4,000	2,000	1,200
	Complete Set, Singles (45)	3,750	1,850	1,100
	Common Player:	12.50	6.25	3.75
	Panel (1)	850.00	425.00	255.00
(1)	Bob Allison	160.00	80.00	45.00
(2)	Ed Mathews	400.00	200.00	120.00
(3)	Vada Pinson	200.00	100.00	60.00
	Panel (2)	100.00	50.00	30.00
(4)	Earl Battey	12.50	6.25	3.75
(5)	Warren Spahn	45.00	22.50	13.50
(6)	Lee Thomas	12.50	6.25	3.75
	Panel (3)	75.00	40.00	25.00
(7)	Orlando Cepeda	30.00	15.00	9.00
(8)	Woodie Held	12.50	6.25	3.75
(9)	Bob Aspromonte	12.50	6.25	3.75
	Panel (4)	200.00	100.00	60.00
(10)	Dick Howser	12.50	6.25	3.75
(11)	Roberto Clemente	125.00	65.00	35.00
(12)	Al Kaline	45.00	22.50	13.50
	Panel (5)	125.00	65.00	35.00
(13)	Joey Jay	12.50	6.25	3.75
(14)	Roger Maris	85.00	42.50	25.00
(15)	Frank Howard	15.00	7.50	4.50
	Panel (6)	175.00	90.00	50.00
(16)	Sandy Koufax	125.00	65.00	35.00
(17)	Jim Gentile	12.50	6.25	3.75
(18)	Johnny Callison	12.50	6.25	3.75
	Panel (7)	50.00	25.00	15.00
(19)	Jim Landis	12.50	6.25	3.75
(20)	Ken Boyer	13.00	6.50	4.00
(21)	Chuck Schilling	12.50	6.25	3.75
	Panel (8)	575.00	285.00	175.00
(22)	Art Mahaffey	12.50	6.25	3.75
(23)	Mickey Mantle	300.00	150.00	75.00
(24)	Dick Stuart	13.50	6.75	4.00
	Panel (9)	100.00	50.00	30.00
(25)	Ken McBride	12.50	6.25	3.75
(26)	Frank Robinson	45.00	22.50	13.50
(27)	Gil Hodges	30.00	15.00	9.00
	Panel (10)	175.00	85.00	50.00
(28)	Milt Pappas	12.50	6.25	3.75
(29)	Hank Aaron	125.00	65.00	35.00
(30)	Luis Aparicio	30.00	15.00	9.00
	Panel (11)	900.00	450.00	275.00
(31)	Johnny Romano	160.00	80.00	50.00
(32)	Ernie Banks	500.00	250.00	150.00
(33)	Norm Siebern	160.00	80.00	50.00
	Panel (12)	75.00	35.00	25.00
(34)	Ron Santo	20.00	10.00	6.00
(35)	Norm Cash	15.00	7.50	4.50
(36)	Jimmy Piersall	15.00	7.50	4.50
	Panel (13)	175.00	85.00	50.00
(37)	Don Schwall	12.50	6.25	3.75
(38)	Willie Mays	125.00	65.00	35.00
(39)	Norm Larker	12.50	6.25	3.75
	Panel (14)	110.00	55.00	35.00
(40)	Bill White	12.50	6.25	3.75
(41)	Whitey Ford	50.00	25.00	15.00
(42)	Rocky Colavito	30.00	15.00	9.00
	Panel (15)	750.00	375.00	225.00
(43)	Don Zimmer	200.00	100.00	60.00
(44)	Harmon Killebrew	350.00	175.00	100.00
(45)	Gene Woodling	160.00	80.00	50.00

1963 Bazooka

FRANK ROBINSON
CINN. REDS OF
NO. 31 OF 36 CARDS

The 1963 Bazooka issue reverted to a 12-panel, 36-card set, but saw a change in the size of the cards. Individual cards measure 1-9/16" x 2-1/2", while panels are 2-1/2" x 4-11/16". The card design was altered also, with the player's name, team and position situated in a white oval at the bottom of the card. The full-color, blank-backed set is numbered 1-36. The complete set was counterfeited circa 2002, with many cards sold in "FGA" certified slabs, depressing the value of cards not graded by a major certification company.

		NM	EX	VG
	Complete Set, Panels (12):	1,750	875.00	525.00
	Complete Set, Singles (36):	1,200	600.00	350.00
	Common Player:	10.00	5.00	3.00
	Panel (1)	450.00	225.00	135.00
1	Mickey Mantle (Batting righty.)	325.00	160.00	100.00
2	Bob Rodgers	10.00	5.00	3.00
3	Ernie Banks	60.00	30.00	18.00
	Panel (2)	95.00	50.00	30.00
4	Norm Siebern	10.00	5.00	3.00
5	Warren Spahn/Portrait	35.00	17.50	10.00
6	Bill Mazeroski	25.00	12.50	7.50
	Panel (3)	175.00	90.00	50.00
7	Harmon Killebrew/Btg	50.00	25.00	15.00
8	Dick Farrell/Portrait	10.00	5.00	3.00
9	Hank Aaron (Glove in front.)	90.00	45.00	27.50
	Panel (4)	150.00	75.00	45.00
10	Dick Donovan	10.00	5.00	3.00
11	Jim Gentile/Btg	10.00	5.00	3.00
12	Willie Mays (Bat in front.)	90.00	45.00	22.50
	Panel (5)	125.00	65.00	35.00
13	Camilo Pascual (Hands at waist.)	10.00	5.00	3.00
14	Roberto Clemente/Portrait	90.00	45.00	22.50
15	Johnny Callison (Pinstriped uniform.)	10.00	5.00	3.00
	Panel (6)	150.00	75.00	45.00
16	Carl Yastrzemski/ Kneeling	60.00	30.00	18.00
17	Don Drysdale	35.00	17.50	10.00
18	Johnny Romano/Portrait	10.00	5.00	3.00
	Panel (7)	45.00	22.50	13.50
19	Al Jackson	10.00	5.00	3.00
20	Ralph Terry	10.00	5.00	3.00
21	Bill Monbouquette	10.00	5.00	3.00
	Panel (8)	150.00	75.00	45.00
22	Orlando Cepeda	35.00	17.50	10.00
23	Stan Musial	75.00	40.00	25.00
24	Floyd Robinson (No pinstripes.)	10.00	5.00	3.00
	Panel (9)	45.00	22.50	13.50
25	Chuck Hinton/Btg	10.00	5.00	3.00
26	Bob Purkey	10.00	5.00	3.00
27	Ken Hubbs	12.50	6.25	3.75
	Panel (10)	75.00	40.00	25.00
28	Bill White	10.00	5.00	3.00
29	Ray Herbert	10.00	5.00	3.00
30	Brooks Robinson (Glove in front.)	40.00	20.00	12.00
	Panel (11)	100.00	50.00	30.00
31	Frank Robinson/Btg	40.00	20.00	12.00
32	Lee Thomas	10.00	5.00	3.00
33	Rocky Colavito (Detroit)	30.00	15.00	9.00
	Panel (12)	90.00	45.00	27.50
34	Al Kaline/Kneeling	45.00	22.50	13.50
35	Art Mahaffey	10.00	5.00	3.00
36	Tommy Davis (Follow-through.)	10.00	5.00	3.00

1963 Bazooka All-Time Greats

Consisting of 41 cards, the Bazooka All-Time Greats set was issued as inserts (five per box) in boxes of Bazooka bubble gum. A black-and-white portrait photo of the player is placed inside a gold plaque within a white border. Card backs contain a brief biography of the player. The numbered cards measure 1-9/16" x 2-1/2". Cards can be found with silver fronts instead of gold; the silver are worth double the values listed.

HANK GREENBERG
19 1B Detroit Tigers

BORN: JANUARY 1, 1911
HOME: NEW YORK, N. Y.

Hank became a regular on the Tigers in 1933 and immediately became one of baseball's most respected sluggers. The big rookie batted .301 in '33, but by the following year he had climbed up to .339. Hank really started to blast homers in '35 when he powdered 36 round-trippers. In 1938, the slugger blasted 58 home runs! World War II interrupted Hank's career when he was approaching his peak years, but nevertheless he finished with a .313 lifetime batting mark.

©T.C.G. PRINTED IN U.S.A.

		NM	EX	VG
	Complete Set (41):	675.00	335.00	200.00
	Common Player:	13.50	6.75	4.00
	Silver: 2.5X			
1	Joe Tinker	13.50	6.75	4.00
2	Harry Heilmann	13.50	6.75	4.00
3	Jack Chesbro	13.50	6.75	4.00
4	Christy Mathewson	30.00	15.00	9.00
5	Herb Pennock	13.50	6.75	4.00
6	Cy Young	30.00	15.00	9.00
7	Ed Walsh	13.50	6.75	4.00
8	Nap Lajoie	13.50	6.75	4.00
9	Eddie Plank	13.50	6.75	4.00
10	Honus Wagner	35.00	17.50	10.00
11	Chief Bender	13.50	6.75	4.00
12	Walter Johnson	30.00	15.00	9.00
13	Three-Fingered Brown	13.50	6.75	4.00
14	Rabbit Maranville	13.50	6.75	4.00
15	Lou Gehrig	60.00	30.00	18.00
16	Ban Johnson	13.50	6.75	4.00
17	Babe Ruth	65.00	32.50	20.00
18	Connie Mack	13.50	6.75	4.00
19	Hank Greenberg	20.00	10.00	6.00
20	John McGraw	13.50	6.75	4.00
21	Johnny Evers	13.50	6.75	4.00
22	Al Simmons	13.50	6.75	4.00
23	Jimmy Collins	13.50	6.75	4.00
24	Tris Speaker	13.50	6.75	4.00
25	Frank Chance	13.50	6.75	4.00
26	Fred Clarke	13.50	6.75	4.00
27	Wilbert Robinson	13.50	6.75	4.00
28	Dazzy Vance	13.50	6.75	4.00
29	Grover Alexander	16.00	8.00	4.75
30	Kenesaw Landis	13.50	6.75	4.00
31	Willie Keeler	13.50	6.75	4.00
32	Rogers Hornsby	16.00	8.00	4.75
33	Hugh Duffy	13.50	6.75	4.00
34	Mickey Cochrane	13.50	6.75	4.00
35	Ty Cobb	60.00	30.00	18.00
36	Mel Ott	13.50	6.75	4.00
37	Clark Griffith	13.50	6.75	4.00
38	Ted Lyons	13.50	6.75	4.00
39	Cap Anson	13.50	6.75	4.00
40	Bill Dickey	13.50	6.75	4.00
41	Eddie Collins	13.50	6.75	4.00

1964 Bazooka

The 1964 Bazooka set is identical in design and size to the previous year's effort. However, different photographs were used from year to year. The 1964 set consists of 36 full-color, blank-backed cards numbered 1 through 36. Individual cards measure 1-9/16" x 2-1/2"; three-card panels measure 2-1/2" x 4-11/16". Sheets of 10 full-color baseball stamps were inserted in each box of bubble gum.

		NM	EX	VG
	Complete Set, Panels (12):	1,400	700.00	425.00
	Complete Set, Singles (36):	950.00	475.00	275.00
	Common Player:	10.00	5.00	3.00
	Panel (1)	225.00	110.00	70.00
1	Mickey Mantle (Bat on shoulder.)	200.00	100.00	60.00
2	Dick Groat	10.00	5.00	3.00
3	Steve Barber	10.00	5.00	3.00
	Panel (2)	75.00	37.00	22.00
4	Ken McBride	10.00	5.00	3.00
5	Warren Spahn (Cap to waist.)	35.00	17.50	10.50
6	Bob Friend	10.00	5.00	3.00
	Panel (3)	150.00	75.00	45.00
7	Harmon Killebrew/Portrait	35.00	17.50	10.50
8	Dick Farrell (Hands above head.)	10.00	5.00	3.00
9	Hank Aaron (Glove to left.)	75.00	37.50	22.50
	Panel (4)	150.00	75.00	45.00
10	Rich Rollins	10.00	5.00	3.00
11	Jim Gentile/Portrait	10.00	5.00	3.00
12	Willie Mays (Looking to left.)	75.00	37.50	22.50
	Panel (5)	150.00	75.00	45.00
13	Camilo Pascual (Follow-through.)	10.00	5.00	3.00
14	Roberto Clemente/Throwing	75.00	37.50	22.50
15	Johnny Callison (Batting, screen showing.)	10.00	5.00	3.00
	Panel (6)	125.00	62.00	37.00
16	Carl Yastrzemski/Btg	40.00	20.00	12.00
17	Billy Williams/Kneeling	30.00	15.00	9.00
18	Johnny Romano/Btg	10.00	5.00	3.00
	Panel (7)	65.00	32.50	20.00
19	Jim Maloney	10.00	5.00	3.00
20	Norm Cash	12.50	6.25	3.75
21	Willie McCovey	30.00	15.00	9.00
	Panel (8)	40.00	20.00	12.00
22	Jim Fregosi/btg	10.00	5.00	3.00
23	George Altman	10.00	5.00	3.00
24	Floyd Robinson (Pinstriped uniform.)	10.00	5.00	3.00
	Panel (9)	40.00	20.00	12.00
25	Chuck Hinton/Portrait	10.00	5.00	3.00
26	Ron Hunt/Btg	10.00	5.00	3.00
27	Gary Peters/Pitching	10.00	5.00	3.00
	Panel (10)	90.00	45.00	27.00
28	Dick Ellsworth	10.00	5.00	3.00
29	Elston Howard (W/bat.)	20.00	10.00	6.00
30	Brooks Robinson (Kneeling w/ glove.)	35.00	17.50	10.50
	Panel (11)	175.00	87.00	52.00
31	Frank Robinson (Uniform number shows.)	35.00	17.50	10.50
32	Sandy Koufax (Glove in front.)	75.00	37.50	22.50
33	Rocky Colavito (Kansas City)	25.00	12.50	7.50
	Panel (12)	90.00	45.00	27.00
34	Al Kaline (Holding two bats.)	40.00	20.00	12.00
35	Ken Boyer (Cap to waist.)	10.00	5.00	3.00
36	Tommy Davis/Btg	10.00	5.00	3.00

1964 Bazooka Stamps

Occasionally mislabeled "Topps Stamps," the 1964 Bazooka stamps were produced by Topps, but found only in boxes of Bazooka bubble gum. Issued in sheets of 10, 100 color stamps make up the set. Each stamp measures 1" x 1-1/2" in size. While the stamps are not individually numbered, the sheets are numbered one through 10. The stamps are commonly found as complete sheets of 10 and are priced in that fashion in the checklist that follows.

		NM	EX	VG
	Complete Sheet Set (10x10):	750.00	375.00	225.00
	Common Sheet:	35.00	17.50	10.00
	Common Stamp:	4.00	2.00	1.25
1	Max Alvis, Ed Charles, Dick Ellsworth, Jimmie Hall, Frank Malzone, Milt Pappas, Vada Pinson, Tony Taylor, Pete Ward, Bill White	35.00	17.50	10.50
2	Bob Aspromonte, Larry Jackson, Willie Mays, Al McBean, Bill Monbouquette, Bobby Richardson, Floyd Robinson, Frank Robinson, Norm Siebern, Don Zimmer	80.00	40.00	25.00
3	Ernie Banks, Roberto Clemente, Curt Flood, Jesse Gonder, Woody Held, Don Lock, Dave Nicholson, Joe Pepitone, Brooks Robinson, Carl Yastrzemski	120.00	60.00	35.00
4	Hank Aguirre, Jim Grant, Harmon Killebrew, Jim Maloney, Juan Marichal, Bill Mazeroski, Juan Pizarro, Boog Powell, Ed Roebuck, Ron Santo	85.00	45.00	25.00
5	Jim Bouton, Norm Cash, Orlando Cepeda, Tommy Harper, Chuck Hinton, Albie Pearson, Ron Perranoski, Dick Radatz, Johnny Romano, Carl Willey	45.00	25.00	15.00
6	Steve Barber, Jim Fregosi, Tony Gonzalez, Mickey Mantle, Jim O'Toole, Gary Peters, Rich Rollins, Warren Spahn, Dick Stuart, Joe Torre	165.00	80.00	50.00
7	Felipe Alou, George Altman, Ken Boyer, Rocky Colavito, Jim Davenport, Tommy Davis, Bill Freehan, Bob Friend, Ken Johnson, Billy Moran	40.00	20.00	12.00
8	Earl Battey, Ernie Broglio, Johnny Callison, Donn Clendenon, Don Drysdale, Jim Gentile, Elston Howard, Claude Osteen, Billy Williams, Hal Woodeshick	55.00	27.50	16.50
9	Hank Aaron, Jack Baldschun, Wayne Causey, Moe Drabowsky, Dick Groat, Frank Howard, Al Jackson, Jerry Lumpe, Ken McBride, Rusty Staub	65.00	32.50	19.50
10	Vic Davalillo, Dick Farrell, Ron Hunt, Al Kaline, Sandy Koufax, Eddie Mathews, Willie McCovey, Camilo Pascual, Lee Thomas	85.00	45.00	25.00

1965 Bazooka

The 1965 Bazooka set is identical to the 1963 and 1964 sets. Different players were added each year and different photographs were used for those players being included again. Individual cards cut from the boxes measure 1-9/16" x 2-1/2". Complete three-card panels measure 2-1/2" x 4-11/16". Cards are again blank-backed.

		NM	EX	VG
	Complete Set, Panels (12):	1,300	650.00	400.00
	Complete Set, Singles (36):	900.00	450.00	275.00
	Common Player:	10.00	5.00	3.00
	Panel (1)	275.00	135.00	85.00
1	Mickey Mantle (Batting lefty.)	200.00	100.00	60.00
2	Larry Jackson	10.00	5.00	3.00
3	Chuck Hinton	10.00	5.00	3.00
	Panel (2)	40.00	20.00	12.00
4	Tony Oliva	12.50	6.25	3.75
5	Dean Chance	10.00	5.00	3.00
6	Jim O'Toole	10.00	5.00	3.00
	Panel (3)	125.00	65.00	35.00
7	Harmon Killebrew (Bat on shoulder.)	35.00	17.50	10.50
8	Pete Ward	10.00	5.00	3.00
9	Hank Aaron/Btg	75.00	37.50	22.50
	Panel (4)	125.00	62.00	37.00
10	Dick Radatz	10.00	5.00	3.00
11	Boog Powell	12.50	6.25	3.75
12	Willie Mays (Looking down.)	75.00	37.50	22.50
	Panel (5)	250.00	125.00	75.00
13	Bob Veale	10.00	5.00	3.00
14	Roberto Clemente/Btg	100.00	50.00	30.00
15	Johnny Callison/Btg (No screen in background.)	10.00	5.00	3.00
	Panel (6)	60.00	30.00	18.00
16	Joe Torre	15.00	7.50	4.50
17	Billy Williams/Btg	25.00	12.50	7.50
18	Bob Chance	10.00	5.00	3.00
	Panel (7)	50.00	25.00	15.00
19	Bob Aspromonte	10.00	5.00	3.00
20	Joe Christopher	10.00	5.00	3.00
21	Jim Bunning	25.00	12.50	7.50
	Panel (8)	75.00	37.50	22.50
22	Jim Fregosi	10.00	5.00	3.00
23	Bob Gibson	30.00	15.00	9.00
24	Juan Marichal	25.00	12.50	7.50
	Panel (9)	40.00	20.00	12.00
25	Dave Wickersham	10.00	5.00	3.00
26	Ron Hunt/Throwing	10.00	5.00	3.00
27	Gary Peters/Portrait	10.00	5.00	3.00
	Panel (10)	85.00	42.50	25.00
28	Ron Santo	15.00	7.50	4.50
29	Elston Howard (W/glove.)	12.50	6.25	3.75
30	Brooks Robinson/Portrait	35.00	17.50	10.50
	Panel (11)	200.00	100.00	60.00
31	Frank Robinson/Portrait	35.00	17.50	10.50
32	Sandy Koufax (Hands over head.)	100.00	50.00	30.00
33	Rocky Colavito (Cleveland)	20.00	10.00	6.00
	Panel (12)	75.00	37.00	22.00
34	Al Kaline/Portrait	35.00	17.50	10.50
35	Ken Boyer/Portrait	10.00	5.00	3.00
36	Tommy Davis/Fldg	10.00	5.00	3.00

1966 Bazooka

The 1966 Bazooka set was increased to 48 cards. Printed in panels of three on the bottoms of boxes of bubble gum, the full-color cards are blank-backed and numbered. Individual cards measure 1-9/16" x 2-1/2"; panels measure 2-1/2" x 4-11/16". Most of those 1966 Bazooka cards which have the same player/number combination as 1967 share the same photo and

JUAN MARICHAL
S. F. GIANTS
NO. 10 OF 48 CARDS

are indistinguishable as singles or panels; year of issue for complete boxes can be distinguished by the small photo on front of Koufax (1966) or Mantle (1967).

		NM	EX	VG
	Complete Set, Panels (16):	2,200	1,100	650.00
	Complete Set, Singles (48):	1,500	750.00	450.00
	Common Player:	10.00	5.00	3.00
	Panel (1)	175.00	85.00	50.00
1	Sandy Koufax	100.00	50.00	30.00
2	Willie Horton	13.50	6.75	4.00
3	Frank Howard	13.50	6.75	4.00
	Panel (2)	60.00	30.00	18.00
4	Richie Allen	16.50	8.25	5.00
5	Mel Stottlemyre	10.00	5.00	3.00
6	Tony Conigliaro	20.00	10.00	6.00
	Panel (3)	400.00	200.00	120.00
7	Mickey Mantle	300.00	150.00	90.00
8	Leon Wagner	10.00	5.00	3.00
9	Ed Kranepool	10.00	5.00	3.00
	Panel (4)	120.00	60.00	36.00
10	Juan Marichal	35.00	17.50	10.00
11	Harmon Killebrew	50.00	25.00	15.00
12	Johnny Callison	10.00	5.00	3.00
	Panel (5)	100.00	50.00	30.00
13	Roy McMillan	10.00	5.00	3.00
14	Willie McCovey	40.00	20.00	12.00
15	Rocky Colavito	30.00	15.00	9.00
	Panel (6)	150.00	75.00	45.00
16	Willie Mays	80.00	40.00	24.00
17	Sam McDowell	10.00	5.00	3.00
18	Vern Law	10.00	5.00	3.00
	Panel (7)	80.00	40.00	24.00
19	Jim Fregosi	10.00	5.00	3.00
20	Ron Fairly	10.00	5.00	3.00
21	Bob Gibson	40.00	20.00	12.00
	Panel (8)	110.00	55.00	35.00
22	Carl Yastrzemski	60.00	30.00	18.00
23	Bill White	10.00	5.00	3.00
24	Bob Aspromonte	10.00	5.00	3.00
	Panel (9)	150.00	75.00	45.00
25	Dean Chance (California)	10.00	5.00	3.00
26	Roberto Clemente	100.00	50.00	30.00
27	Tony Cloninger	10.00	5.00	3.00
	Panel (10)	135.00	65.00	40.00
28	Curt Blefary	10.00	5.00	3.00
29	Milt Pappas	10.00	5.00	3.00
30	Hank Aaron	80.00	40.00	24.00
	Panel (11)	130.00	65.00	40.00
31	Jim Bunning	40.00	20.00	12.00
32	Frank Robinson/Portrait	50.00	25.00	15.00
33	Bill Skowron	13.50	6.75	4.00
	Panel (12)	100.00	50.00	30.00
34	Brooks Robinson	50.00	25.00	15.00
35	Jim Wynn	10.00	5.00	3.00
36	Joe Torre	17.50	8.75	5.25
	Panel (13)	225.00	110.00	65.00
37	Jim Grant	10.00	5.00	3.00
38	Pete Rose	135.00	65.00	40.00
39	Ron Santo	20.00	10.00	6.00
	Panel (14)	90.00	45.00	27.50
40	Tom Tresh	13.50	6.75	4.00
41	Tony Oliva	13.50	6.75	4.00
42	Don Drysdale	40.00	20.00	12.00
	Panel (15)	40.00	20.00	12.00
43	Pete Richert	10.00	5.00	3.00
44	Bert Campaneris	10.00	5.00	3.00
45	Jim Maloney	10.00	5.00	3.00
	Panel (16)	130.00	65.00	40.00
46	Al Kaline	50.00	25.00	15.00
47	Eddie Fisher	10.00	5.00	3.00
48	Billy Williams	40.00	20.00	12.00

1967 Bazooka

The 1967 Bazooka set is identical in design to the sets of 1964-1966. Printed in panels of three on the bottoms of bub-

ble gum boxes, the set is made up of 48 full-color, blank-backed, numbered cards. Individual cards measure 1-9/16" x 2-1/2"; complete panels measure 2-1/2" x 4-11/16". Most of those 1967 Bazooka cards which have the same player/number combination as 1966 share the same photo and are indistinguishable as singles or panels; complete boxes can be distinguished by the small photo on front of Koufax (1966) or Mantle (1967).

		NM	EX	VG
	Complete Set, Panels (18):	3,900	1,950	1,200
	Complete Set, Singles (48):	2,400	1,200	720.00
	Common Player:	16.00	8.00	5.00
	Panel (1)	65.00	35.00	20.00
1	Rick Reichardt	16.00	8.00	5.00
2	Tommie Agee	16.00	8.00	5.00
3	Frank Howard	20.00	10.00	6.00
	Panel (2)	90.00	45.00	25.00
4	Richie Allen	30.00	15.00	10.00
5	Mel Stottlemyre	20.00	10.00	6.00
6	Tony Conigliaro	20.00	10.00	6.00
	Panel (3)	975.00	500.00	300.00
7	Mickey Mantle	650.00	325.00	200.00
8	Leon Wagner	16.00	8.00	5.00
9	Gary Peters	16.00	8.00	5.00
	Panel (4)	240.00	120.00	75.00
10	Juan Marichal	80.00	40.00	25.00
11	Harmon Killebrew	100.00	50.00	30.00
12	Johnny Callison	16.00	8.00	5.00
	Panel (5)	220.00	110.00	70.00
13	Denny McLain	35.00	20.00	12.00
14	Willie McCovey	80.00	40.00	25.00
15	Rocky Colavito	50.00	25.00	15.00
	Panel (6)	240.00	120.00	75.00
16	Willie Mays	150.00	75.00	45.00
17	Sam McDowell	16.00	8.00	5.00
18	Jim Kaat	20.00	10.00	6.00
	Panel (7)	160.00	80.00	50.00
19	Jim Fregosi	16.00	8.00	5.00
20	Ron Fairly	16.00	8.00	5.00
21	Bob Gibson	80.00	40.00	25.00
	Panel (8)	200.00	100.00	60.00
22	Carl Yastrzemski	100.00	50.00	30.00
23	Bill White	16.00	8.00	5.00
24	Bob Aspromonte	16.00	8.00	5.00
	Panel (9)	280.00	140.00	85.00
25	Dean Chance (Minnesota)	16.00	8.00	5.00
26	Roberto Clemente	160.00	80.00	50.00
27	Tony Cloninger	16.00	8.00	5.00
	Panel (10)	240.00	120.00	75.00
28	Curt Blefary	16.00	8.00	5.00
29	Phil Regan	16.00	8.00	5.00
30	Hank Aaron	150.00	75.00	45.00
	Panel (11)	280.00	140.00	85.00
31	Jim Bunning	80.00	40.00	25.00
32	Frank Robinson/Btg	100.00	50.00	30.00
33	Ken Boyer	16.00	8.00	5.00
	Panel (12)	200.00	100.00	60.00
34	Brooks Robinson	100.00	50.00	30.00
35	Jim Wynn	16.00	8.00	5.00
36	Joe Torre	30.00	15.00	10.00
	Panel (13)	450.00	225.00	135.00
37	Tommy Davis	16.00	8.00	5.00
38	Pete Rose	250.00	125.00	75.00
39	Ron Santo	35.00	20.00	12.00
	Panel (14)	160.00	80.00	50.00
40	Tom Tresh	20.00	10.00	6.00
41	Tony Oliva	20.00	10.00	6.00
42	Don Drysdale	80.00	40.00	25.00
	Panel (15)	65.00	35.00	20.00
43	Pete Richert	16.00	8.00	5.00
44	Bert Campaneris	16.00	8.00	5.00
45	Jim Maloney	16.00	8.00	5.00
	Panel (16)	280.00	140.00	85.00
46	Al Kaline	100.00	50.00	30.00
47	Matty Alou	16.00	8.00	5.00
48	Billy Williams	80.00	40.00	25.00

1968 Bazooka

The design of the 1968 Bazooka set is radically different from previous years. The player cards are situated on the sides of the boxes with the box back containing "Tipps From The Topps." Four unnumbered player cards, measuring 1-1/4" x 3-1/8", are featured on each box. The box back includes a small player photo plus illustrated tips on various aspects of the game of baseball. Boxes are numbered 1-15 on the top panels. There are 56 different player cards in the set, with four of the cards (Agee, Drysdale, Rose, Santo) being used twice to round out the set of 15 boxes.

		NM	EX	VG
	Complete Box Set (15):	4,250	2,125	1,250
	Complete Singles Set (60):	3,000	1,500	900.00
	Common Player:	10.00	5.00	3.00
	Box 1 - Bunting	275.00	135.00	80.00
1	Maury Wills	15.00	7.50	4.50
(1)	Clete Boyer	15.00	7.50	4.50
(2)	Paul Casanova	10.00	5.00	3.00
(3)	Al Kaline	65.00	32.50	20.00
(4)	Tom Seaver	80.00	40.00	25.00
	Box 2 - Batting	250.00	125.00	75.00
2	Carl Yastrzemski	80.00	40.00	25.00
(5)	Matty Alou	10.00	5.00	3.00
(6)	Bill Freehan	10.00	5.00	3.00
(7)	Jim Hunter	45.00	22.50	13.50
(8)	Jim Lefebvre	10.00	5.00	3.00
	Box 3 - Stealing Bases	175.00	85.00	50.00
3	Bert Campaneris	10.00	5.00	3.00
(9)	Bobby Knoop	10.00	5.00	3.00
(10)	Tim McCarver	15.00	7.50	4.50
(11)	Frank Robinson	65.00	32.50	20.00
(12)	Bob Veale	10.00	5.00	3.00
	Box 4 - Sliding	100.00	50.00	30.00
4	Maury Wills	15.00	7.50	4.50
(13)	Joe Azcue	10.00	5.00	3.00
(14)	Tony Conigliaro	15.00	7.50	4.50
(15)	Ken Holtzman	10.00	5.00	3.00
(16)	Bill White	10.00	5.00	3.00
	Box 5 - The Double Play	315.00	155.00	95.00
5	Julian Javier	10.00	5.00	3.00
(17)	Hank Aaron	175.00	87.00	52.00
(18)	Juan Marichal	45.00	22.50	13.50
(19)	Joe Pepitone	17.50	9.00	5.00
(20)	Rico Petrocelli	15.00	7.50	4.50
	Box 6 - Playing 1st Base	375.00	185.00	110.00
6	Orlando Cepeda	50.00	25.00	15.00
(21)	Tommie Agee	10.00	5.00	3.00
(22a)	Don Drysdale (No period after "A" in team name.)	40.00	20.00	12.00
(22b)	Don Drysdale (Period after "A.")	40.00	20.00	12.00
(23)	Pete Rose	175.00	87.00	52.00
(24)	Ron Santo	17.50	9.00	5.00
	Box 7 - Playing 2nd Base	225.00	110.00	65.00
7	Bill Mazeroski	50.00	25.00	15.00
(25)	Jim Bunning	45.00	22.50	13.50
(26)	Frank Howard	15.00	7.50	4.50
(27)	John Roseboro	10.00	5.00	3.00
(28)	George Scott	10.00	5.00	3.00
	Box 8 - Playing 3rd Base	275.00	135.00	80.00
8	Brooks Robinson	65.00	32.50	20.00
(29)	Tony Gonzalez	10.00	5.00	3.00
(30)	Willie Horton	15.00	7.50	4.50
(31)	Harmon Killebrew	65.00	32.50	20.00
(32)	Jim McGlothlin	10.00	5.00	3.00
	Box 9 - Playing Shortstop	150.00	75.00	45.00
9	Jim Fregosi	10.00	5.00	3.00
(33)	Max Alvis	10.00	5.00	3.00
(34)	Bob Gibson	45.00	22.50	13.50
(35)	Tony Oliva	15.00	7.50	4.50
(36)	Vada Pinson	15.00	7.50	4.50
	Box 10 - Catching	160.00	80.00	45.00
10	Joe Torre	17.50	9.00	5.00
(37)	Dean Chance	10.00	5.00	3.00
(38)	Tommy Davis	10.00	5.00	3.00
(39)	Ferguson Jenkins	45.00	22.00	13.50
(40)	Rick Monday	10.00	5.00	3.00
	Box 11 - Pitching	850.00	425.00	255.00
11	Jim Lonborg	15.00	7.50	4.50
(41)	Curt Flood	15.00	7.50	4.50
(42)	Joel Horlen	10.00	5.00	3.00
(43)	Mickey Mantle	650.00	325.00	195.00
(44)	Jim Wynn	10.00	5.00	3.00
	Box 12 - Fielding the Pitcher's Position	375.00	185.00	110.00
12	Mike McCormick	10.00	5.00	3.00
(45)	Roberto Clemente	200.00	100.00	60.00
(46)	Al Downing	10.00	5.00	3.00
(47)	Don Mincher	10.00	5.00	3.00
(48)	Tony Perez	45.00	22.00	13.50
	Box 13 - Coaching	225.00	110.00	65.00
13	Frank Crosetti	15.00	7.50	4.50
(49)	Rod Carew	55.00	27.50	16.50
(50)	Willie McCovey	55.00	27.50	16.50
(51)	Ron Swoboda	10.00	5.00	3.00
(52)	Earl Wilson	10.00	5.00	3.00
	Box 14 - Playing the Outfield	250.00	125.00	75.00
14	Willie Mays	175.00	87.00	52.00
(53)	Richie Allen	15.00	7.50	4.50
(54)	Gary Peters	10.00	5.00	3.00
(55)	Rusty Staub	17.50	9.00	5.00
(56)	Billy Williams	50.00	25.00	15.00
	Box 15 - Base Running	375.00	185.00	110.00
15	Lou Brock	55.00	27.50	16.50
(57)	Tommie Agee	10.00	5.00	3.00
(58)	Don Drysdale	40.00	20.00	12.00
(59)	Pete Rose	175.00	87.00	52.00
(60)	Ron Santo	17.50	9.00	5.00

1969-70 Bazooka

Issued over a two-year span, the 1969-70 Bazooka set utilized the box bottom and sides. The bottom, entitled "Baseball Extra," features an historic event in baseball; the 3" x 6-1/4" panels are numbered 1-12. Two "All-Time Great" cards were located on each side of the box. These cards are not numbered and have no distinct borders; individual cards measure 1-1/4" x 3-1/8". The prices in the checklist that follows are for complete boxes only. Cards/panels cut from the boxes have a greatly reduced value - 25 percent of the complete box prices for all cut pieces.

		NM	EX	VG
	Complete Set (12):	325.00	160.00	100.00
	Common Box:	20.00	10.00	6.00
1	No-Hit Duel By Toney & Vaughn (Mordecai Brown, Ty Cobb, Willie Keeler, Eddie Plank)	30.00	15.00	9.00
2	Alexander Conquers Yanks (Rogers Hornsby, Ban Johnson, Walter Johnson, Al Simmons)	20.00	10.00	6.00
3	Yanks' Lazzeri Sets AL Record (Grover Alexander, Chief Bender, Christy Mathewson, Cy Young)	25.00	12.50	7.50
4	HR Almost Hit Out Of Stadium (Hugh Duffy, Lou Gehrig, Tris Speaker, Joe Tinker)	20.00	10.00	6.00
5	4 Consecutive Homers By Lou (Frank Chance, Mickey Cochrane, John McGraw, Babe Ruth)	35.00	17.50	10.00
6	No-Hit Game By Walter Johnson (Johnny Evers, Walter Johnson, John McGraw, Cy Young)	20.00	10.00	6.00
7	Twelve RBIs By Bottomley (Ty Cobb, Eddie Collins, Johnny Evers, Lou Gehrig)	35.00	17.50	10.00
8	Ty Ties Record (Mickey Cochrane, Eddie Collins, Mel Ott, Honus Wagner)	20.00	10.00	6.00
9	Babe Ruth Hits 3 HRs In Game (Cap Anson, Jack Chesbro, Al Simmons, Tris Speaker)	35.00	17.50	10.00
10	Calls Shot In Series Game (Nap Lajoie, Connie Mack, Rabbit Maranville, Ed Walsh)	35.00	17.50	10.00
11	Ruth's 60th HR Sets New Record (Frank Chance, Nap Lajoie, Mel Ott, Joe Tinker)	35.00	17.50	10.00
12	Double Shutout By Ed Reulbach (Rogers Hornsby, Rabbit Maranville, Christy Mathewson, Honus Wagner)	20.00	10.00	6.00

1971 Bazooka Numbered Set

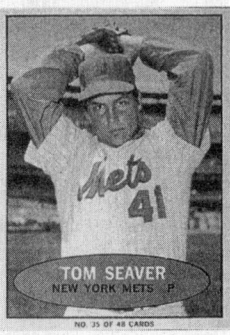

The 1971 Bazooka numbered set is a proof set produced by the company after the unnumbered set was released. The set is comprised of 48 cards as opposed to the 36 cards which make up the unnumbered set. Issued in panels of three, the 12 cards not found in the unnumbered set are #1-3, 13-15, 34-36 and 43-45. All other cards are identical to those found in the unnumbered set. The cards, which measure 2" x 2-5/8", contain full-color photos and are blank-backed.

		NM	EX	VG
	Complete Panel Set (16):	1,300	655.00	400.00
	Complete Singles Set (48):	950.00	475.00	275.00
	Common Player:	7.50	3.75	2.25
	Panel (1)	100.00	50.00	30.00
1	Tim McCarver	12.50	6.25	3.75
2	Frank Robinson	35.00	17.50	10.00
3	Bill Mazeroski	30.00	15.00	9.00
	Panel (2)	100.00	50.00	30.00
4	Willie McCovey	30.00	15.00	9.00
5	Carl Yastrzemski	40.00	20.00	12.00
6	Clyde Wright	7.50	3.75	2.25
	Panel (3)	60.00	30.00	18.00
7	Jim Merritt	7.50	3.75	2.25
8	Luis Aparicio	25.00	12.50	7.50
9	Bobby Murcer	12.50	6.25	3.75
	Panel (4)	30.00	15.00	9.00
10	Rico Petrocelli	7.50	3.75	2.25
11	Sam McDowell	7.50	3.75	2.25
12	Cito Gaston	7.50	3.75	2.25
	Panel (5)	85.00	42.50	25.00
13	Ferguson Jenkins	25.00	12.50	7.50
14	Al Kaline	35.00	17.50	10.00
15	Ken Harrelson	7.50	3.75	2.25
	Panel (6)	115.00	55.00	35.00
16	Tommie Agee	7.50	3.75	2.25
17	Harmon Killebrew	35.00	17.50	10.00

		NM	EX	VG
18	Reggie Jackson	45.00	22.50	13.50
	Panel (7)	60.00	30.00	18.00
19	Juan Marichal	25.00	12.50	7.50
20	Frank Howard	10.00	5.00	3.00
21	Bill Melton	7.50	3.75	2.25
	Panel (8)	125.00	65.00	35.00
22	Brooks Robinson	35.00	17.50	10.00
23	Hank Aaron	60.00	30.00	18.00
24	Larry Dierker	7.50	3.75	2.25
	Panel (9)	60.00	30.00	18.00
25	Jim Fregosi	7.50	3.75	2.25
26	Billy Williams	30.00	15.00	9.00
27	Dave McNally	7.50	3.75	2.25
	Panel (10)	65.00	32.50	20.00
28	Rico Carty	7.50	3.75	2.25
29	Johnny Bench	35.00	17.50	10.00
30	Tommy Harper	7.50	3.75	2.25
	Panel (11)	110.00	55.00	30.00
31	Bert Campaneris	7.50	3.75	2.25
32	Pete Rose	50.00	25.00	15.00
33	Orlando Cepeda	25.00	12.50	7.50
	Panel (12)	65.00	32.50	20.00
34	Maury Wills	7.50	3.75	2.25
35	Tom Seaver	35.00	17.50	10.00
36	Tony Oliva	10.00	5.00	3.00
	Panel (13)	120.00	60.00	35.00
37	Bill Freehan	7.50	3.75	2.25
38	Roberto Clemente	75.00	37.50	22.50
39	Claude Osteen	7.50	3.75	2.25
	Panel (14)	65.00	32.50	20.00
40	Rusty Staub	12.50	6.25	3.75
41	Bob Gibson	30.00	15.00	9.00
42	Amos Otis	7.50	3.75	2.25
	Panel (15)	55.00	27.50	16.50
43	Jim Wynn	7.50	3.75	2.25
44	Richie Allen	20.00	10.00	6.00
45	Tony Conigliaro	15.00	7.50	4.50
	Panel (16)	110.00	55.00	35.00
46	Randy Hundley	7.50	3.75	2.25
47	Willie Mays	60.00	30.00	18.00
48	Jim Hunter	25.00	12.50	7.50

1971 Bazooka Unnumbered Set

This Bazooka set was issued in 1971, consisting of 36 full-color, blank-backed, unnumbered cards. Printed in panels of three on the bottoms of bubble gum boxes, individual cards measure 2" x 2-5/8"; complete panels measure 2-5/8" x 5-5/16". In the checklist that follows, the cards have been numbered by panel using the name of the player who appears on the left end of the panel.

		NM	EX	VG
	Complete Panel Set (12):	1,050	525.00	320.00
	Complete Singles Set (36):	900.00	450.00	270.00
	Common Player:	8.00	4.00	2.50
	Panel (1)	160.00	80.00	50.00
(1)	Tommie Agee	8.00	4.00	2.50
(2)	Harmon Killebrew	55.00	30.00	20.00
(3)	Reggie Jackson	70.00	35.00	25.00
	Panel (2)	160.00	80.00	50.00
(4)	Bert Campaneris	8.00	4.00	2.50
(5)	Pete Rose	75.00	40.00	25.00
(6)	Orlando Cepeda	35.00	20.00	12.00
	Panel (3)	100.00	50.00	30.00
(7)	Rico Carty	8.00	4.00	2.50
(8)	Johnny Bench	60.00	30.00	20.00
(9)	Tommy Harper	8.00	4.00	2.50
	Panel (4)	140.00	70.00	45.00
(10)	Bill Freehan	8.00	4.00	2.50
(11)	Roberto Clemente	90.00	45.00	25.00
(12)	Claude Osteen	8.00	4.00	2.50
	Panel (5)	85.00	40.00	25.00
(13)	Jim Fregosi	8.00	4.00	2.50
(14)	Billy Williams	45.00	25.00	15.00
(15)	Dave McNally	8.00	4.00	2.50
	Panel (6)	160.00	80.00	50.00
(16)	Randy Hundley	8.00	4.00	2.50
(17)	Willie Mays	75.00	40.00	25.00
(18)	Jim Hunter	35.00	20.00	12.00
	Panel (7)	80.00	40.00	25.00
(19)	Juan Marichal	40.00	20.00	12.00
(20)	Frank Howard	12.00	6.00	4.00
(21)	Bill Melton	8.00	4.00	2.50
	Panel (8)	150.00	75.00	45.00
(22)	Willie McCovey	35.00	15.00	9.00
(23)	Carl Yastrzemski	60.00	30.00	20.00
(24)	Clyde Wright	8.00	4.00	2.50
	Panel (9)	80.00	40.00	25.00
(25)	Jim Merritt	8.00	4.00	2.50
(26)	Luis Aparicio	40.00	20.00	12.00
(27)	Bobby Murcer	15.00	8.00	5.00
	Panel (10)	40.00	20.00	12.00
(28)	Rico Petrocelli	8.00	4.00	2.50
(29)	Sam McDowell	8.00	4.00	2.50
(30)	Cito Gaston	8.00	4.00	2.50

		NM	EX	VG
	Panel (11)	175.00	90.00	50.00
(31)	Brooks Robinson	60.00	30.00	20.00
(32)	Hank Aaron	75.00	40.00	25.00
(33)	Larry Dierker	8.00	4.00	2.50
	Panel (12)	90.00	45.00	25.00
(34)	Rusty Staub	12.00	6.00	4.00
(35)	Bob Gibson	45.00	25.00	15.00
(36)	Amos Otis	12.00	6.00	4.00

1930 Becker Bros. Theatre

Only recently brought to light, the issue date attributed here is uncertain and may be clarified if and when additions to the checklist are made. About postcard size, the cards have sepia portraits of Philadelphia A's players on front, identified in the white border at bottom. Backs have advertisng for the theatre, including a list of upcoming features.

		NM	EX	VG
	Common Player:	150.00	75.00	45.00
(1)	Max Bishop	150.00	75.00	45.00
(2)	Mickey Cochrane	250.00	125.00	75.00
(3)	Sammy Hale	150.00	75.00	45.00
(4)	Jimmie Foxx	300.00	150.00	90.00
(5)	Al Simmons	250.00	125.00	75.00

1958 Bell Brand Dodgers

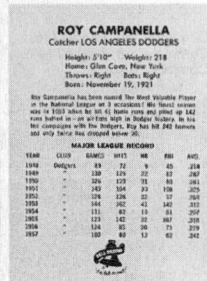

Celebrating the Dodgers first year of play in Los Angeles, Bell Brand inserted 10 different unnum- bered cards in their bags of potato chips and corn chips. The cards, which measure 3" x 4", have a sepia-colored photo inside a 1/4" green woodgrain border. The card backs feature statistical and biographical information and include the Bell Brand logo. Roy Campanella is included in the set despite a career-ending car wreck that prevented him from ever playing in Los Angeles.

		NM	EX	VG
	Complete Set (10):	6,500	3,200	1,950
	Common Player:	125.00	65.00	35.00
1	Roy Campanella	400.00	200.00	120.00
2	Gino Cimoli/SP	1,200	600.00	360.00
3	Don Drysdale	350.00	175.00	100.00
4	Junior Gilliam	125.00	65.00	35.00
5	Gil Hodges	350.00	175.00	105.00
6	Sandy Koufax	2,400.	1,200	725.00
7	Johnny Podres/SP	600.00	300.00	180.00
8	Pee Wee Reese	400.00	200.00	120.00
9	Duke Snider	900.00	450.00	270.00
10	Don Zimmer	135.00	65.00	40.00

1958 Bell Brand Dodgers Ad Posters

These point-of-purchase in-store displays were created to draw attention to the snack company's premiere baseball card offering. The posters were printed in tete-a-tete pairs designed to be hung over a string. Each single panel measures about 22" x 36", and, like the cards, is printed in green and sepia on white stock.

	NM	EX	VG
Bell Brand Dodgers Ad Poster (Don Drysdale)	4,250	2,100	1,250
Don Drysdale	2,400.	1,200.	725.00
Gil Hodges	2,000.	1,000.	600.00
Junior Gilliam	1,200.	600.00	350.00
Pee Wee Reese	2,500.	1,250.	750.00

1960 Bell Brand Dodgers

Bell Brand returned with a baseball card set in 1960 that was entirely different in style to their previous effort. The cards, which measure 2-1/2" x 3-1/2", feature beautiful, full-color photos. The backs carry a short player biography, the

1960 Dodgers home schedule, and the Bell Brand logo. Twenty different numbered cards were inserted in various size bags of potato chips and corn chips. Although sealed in cellophane, the cards were still subject to grease stains. Cards #'s 6, 12 and 18 are the scarcest in the set.

		NM	EX	VG
Complete Set (20):		1,500	750.00	450.00
Common Player:		45.00	22.50	13.50
1	Norm Larker	45.00	22.50	13.50
2	Duke Snider	150.00	75.00	45.00
3	Danny McDevitt	45.00	22.50	13.50
4	Jim Gilliam	50.00	25.00	15.00
5	Rip Repulski	45.00	22.50	13.50
6	Clem Labine/SP	90.00	45.00	27.50
7	John Roseboro	45.00	22.50	13.50
8	Carl Furillo	60.00	30.00	18.00
9	Sandy Koufax	300.00	150.00	90.00
10	Joe Pignatano	45.00	22.50	13.50
11	Chuck Essegian	45.00	22.50	13.50
12	John Klippstein/SP	150.00	75.00	45.00
13	Ed Roebuck	45.00	22.50	13.50
14	Don Demeter	45.00	22.50	13.50
15	Roger Craig	45.00	22.50	13.50
16	Stan Williams	45.00	22.50	13.50
17	Don Zimmer	60.00	30.00	18.00
18	Walter Alston/SP	100.00	50.00	30.00
19	Johnny Podres	60.00	30.00	18.00
20	Maury Wills	75.00	37.50	22.50

1961 Bell Brand Dodgers

The 1961 Bell Brand set is identical in format to the previous year, although printed on thinner stock. Cards can be distinguished from the 1960 set by the 1961 schedule on the backs. The cards, which measure 2-7/16" x 3-1/2", are numbered by the player's uniform number. Twenty different cards were inserted into various size potato chip and corn chip packages, each card being sealed in a cellophane wrapper.

		NM	EX	VG
Complete Set (20):		1,750.	875.00	525.00
Common Player:		50.00	25.00	15.00
3	Willie Davis	50.00	25.00	15.00
4	Duke Snider	175.00	85.00	50.00
5	Norm Larker	50.00	25.00	15.00
8	John Roseboro	50.00	25.00	15.00
9	Wally Moon	50.00	25.00	15.00
11	Bob Lillis	50.00	25.00	15.00
12	Tom Davis	60.00	30.00	18.00
14	Gil Hodges	150.00	75.00	45.00
16	Don Demeter	50.00	25.00	15.00
19	Jim Gilliam	60.00	30.00	18.00
22	John Podres	60.00	30.00	18.00
24	Walter Alston	75.00	37.50	22.50
30	Maury Wills	110.00	55.00	30.00
32	Sandy Koufax	425.00	210.00	125.00
34	Norm Sherry	60.00	30.00	18.00
37	Ed Roebuck	50.00	25.00	15.00
38	Roger Craig	50.00	25.00	15.00
40	Stan Williams	50.00	25.00	15.00
43	Charlie Neal	50.00	25.00	15.00
51	Larry Sherry	60.00	30.00	18.00

1962 Bell Brand Dodgers

The 1962 Bell Brand set is identical in style to the previous two years and cards can be distinguished by the 1962 Dodgers schedule on the back. Each card measures 2-7/16" x 3-1/2" and is numbered by the player's uniform number. Printed on glossy stock, the 1962 set was less susceptible to grease stains.

		NM	EX	VG
Complete Set (20):		1,700	850.00	500.00
Common Player:		50.00	25.00	15.00
3	Willie Davis	50.00	25.00	15.00
4	Duke Snider	200.00	100.00	60.00
6	Ron Fairly	50.00	25.00	15.00
8	John Roseboro	50.00	25.00	15.00
9	Wally Moon	50.00	25.00	15.00
12	Tom Davis	50.00	25.00	15.00
16	Ron Perranoski	50.00	25.00	15.00
19	Jim Gilliam	55.00	27.50	16.50
20	Daryl Spencer	50.00	25.00	15.00
22	John Podres	55.00	27.50	16.50
24	Walter Alston	75.00	37.50	22.50
25	Frank Howard	55.00	27.50	16.50
30	Maury Wills	90.00	45.00	27.50
32	Sandy Koufax	250.00	125.00	75.00
34	Norm Sherry	60.00	30.00	18.00
37	Ed Roebuck	50.00	25.00	15.00
40	Stan Williams	50.00	25.00	15.00
51	Larry Sherry	60.00	30.00	18.00
53	Don Drysdale	125.00	65.00	35.00
56	Lee Walls	50.00	25.00	15.00

1962 Bell Brand Dodgers Ad Poster

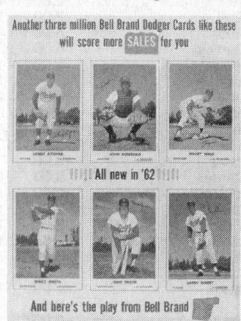

This 8-1/2" x 11-1/2" color poster was distributed to retailers to solicit sales of Bell Brand items. The sheet has actual size pictures of six of the cards from the set. On back is retailer information.

	NM	EX	VG
1962 Bell Brand Ad Poster	900.00	450.00	275.00
(Koufax, Roseboro, Wills, Moon, Snider, Sherry)			

1951 Berk Ross

 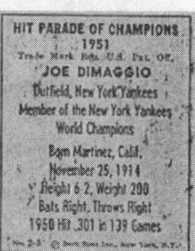

Entitled "Hit Parade of Champions," the 1951 Berk Ross set features 72 stars of various sports. The cards, which measure 2-1/16" x 2-1/2" and have tinted color photographs, were issued in four boxes containing two-card panels. The issue is divided into four subsets with the first ten players of each series being baseball players. Only the baseball players are listed in the checklist that follows. Complete panels are valued 50 percent higher than the sum of the individual cards.

		NM	EX	VG
Complete Boxed Set (72):		1,700	850.00	500.00
Complete Baseball Set (40):		1,325	660.00	395.00
Common Player:		13.50	6.75	4.00
1-1	Al Rosen	16.00	8.00	5.00
1-2	Bob Lemon	20.00	10.00	6.00
1-3	Phil Rizzuto	50.00	25.00	15.00
1-4	Hank Bauer	16.00	8.00	5.00
1-5	Billy Johnson	13.50	6.75	4.00
1-6	Jerry Coleman	13.50	6.75	4.00
1-7	Johnny Mize	25.00	12.50	7.50
1-8	Dom DiMaggio	20.00	10.00	6.00
1-9	Richie Ashburn	30.00	15.00	9.00
1-10	Del Ennis	13.50	6.75	4.00

		NM	EX	VG
2-1	Stan Musial	150.00	75.00	45.00
2-2	Warren Spahn	25.00	12.50	7.50
2-3	Tommy Henrich	16.00	8.00	5.00
2-4	Larry "Yogi" Berra	100.00	50.00	30.00
2-5	Joe DiMaggio	300.00	150.00	90.00
2-6	Bobby Brown	13.50	6.75	4.00
2-7	Granville Hamner	13.50	6.75	4.00
2-8	Willie Jones	13.50	6.75	4.00
2-9	Stanley Lopata	13.50	6.75	4.00
2-10	Mike Goliat	13.50	6.75	4.00
3-1	Ralph Kiner	20.00	10.00	6.00
3-2	Billy Goodman	13.50	6.75	4.00
3-3	Allie Reynolds	16.00	8.00	5.00
3-4	Vic Raschi	16.00	8.00	5.00
3-5	Joe Page	13.50	6.75	4.00
3-6	Eddie Lopat	13.50	6.75	4.00
3-7	Andy Seminick	13.50	6.75	4.00
3-8	Dick Sisler	13.50	6.75	4.00
3-9	Eddie Waitkus	13.50	6.75	4.00
3-10	Ken Heintzelman	13.50	6.75	4.00
4-1	Gene Woodling	16.00	8.00	5.00
4-2	Cliff Mapes	13.50	6.75	4.00
4-3	Fred Sanford	13.50	6.75	4.00
4-4	Tommy Bryne	13.50	6.75	4.00
4-5	Eddie (Whitey) Ford	180.00	90.00	55.00
4-6	Jim Konstanty	13.50	6.75	4.00
4-7	Russ Meyer	13.50	6.75	4.00
4-8	Robin Roberts	20.00	10.00	6.00
4-9	Curt Simmons	13.50	6.75	4.00
4-10	Sam Jethroe	13.50	6.75	4.00

1952 Berk Ross

Although the card size is different (2" x 3"), the style of the fronts and backs of the 1952 Berk Ross set is similar to the previous year's effort. Seventy-two unnumbered cards make up the set. Rizzuto is included twice in the set and the Blackwell and Fox cards have transposed backs. The cards were issued individually rather than as two-card panels like in 1951.

		NM	EX	VG
Complete Set (72):		5,000	2,500	1,500
Common Player:		25.00	12.50	7.50
(1)	Richie Ashburn	50.00	25.00	15.00
(2)	Hank Bauer	30.00	15.00	9.00
(3)	Larry "Yogi" Berra	175.00	85.00	50.00
(4)	Ewell Blackwell (Photo actually Nelson Fox.)	75.00	37.50	22.50
(5)	Bobby Brown	25.00	12.50	7.50
(6)	Jim Busby	25.00	12.50	7.50
(7)	Roy Campanella	140.00	70.00	40.00
(8)	Chico Carrasquel	25.00	12.50	7.50
(9)	Jerry Coleman	25.00	12.50	7.50
(10)	Joe Collins	25.00	12.50	7.50
(11)	Alvin Dark	25.00	12.50	7.50
(12)	Dom DiMaggio	35.00	17.50	10.00
(13)	Joe DiMaggio	425.00	210.00	125.00
(14)	Larry Doby	40.00	20.00	12.00
(15)	Bobby Doerr	40.00	20.00	12.00
(16)	Bob Elliot (Elliott)	25.00	12.50	7.50
(17)	Del Ennis	25.00	12.50	7.50
(18)	Ferris Fain	25.00	12.50	7.50
(19)	Bob Feller	100.00	50.00	30.00
(20)	Nelson Fox (Photo actually Ewell Blackwell.)	125.00	60.00	35.00
(21)	Ned Garver	25.00	12.50	7.50
(22)	Clint Hartung	25.00	12.50	7.50
(23)	Jim Hearn	25.00	12.50	7.50
(24)	Gil Hodges	75.00	37.50	22.50
(25)	Monte Irvin	40.00	20.00	12.00
(26)	Larry Jansen	25.00	12.50	7.50
(27)	George Kell	40.00	20.00	12.00
(28)	Sheldon Jones	25.00	12.50	7.50
(29)	Monte Kennedy	25.00	12.50	7.50
(30)	Ralph Kiner	40.00	20.00	12.00
(31)	Dave Koslo	25.00	12.50	7.50
(32)	Bob Kuzava	25.00	12.50	7.50
(33)	Bob Lemon	40.00	20.00	12.00
(34)	Whitey Lockman	25.00	12.50	7.50
(35)	Eddie Lopat	25.00	12.50	7.50
(36)	Sal Maglie	25.00	12.50	7.50
(37)	Mickey Mantle	2,000	1,000	600.00
(38)	Billy Martin	90.00	45.00	27.50
(39)	Willie Mays	500.00	250.00	150.00
(40)	Gil McDougal (McDougald)	30.00	15.00	9.00
(41)	Orestes Minoso	30.00	15.00	9.00
(42)	Johnny Mize	50.00	25.00	15.00
(43)	Tom Morgan	25.00	12.50	7.50
(44)	Don Mueller	25.00	12.50	7.50
(45)	Stan Musial	250.00	125.00	75.00
(46)	Don Newcombe	35.00	17.50	10.00
(47)	Ray Noble	25.00	12.50	7.50
(48)	Joe Ostrowski	25.00	12.50	7.50
(49)	Mel Parnell	25.00	12.50	7.50
(50)	Vic Raschi	25.00	12.50	7.50
(51)	Pee Wee Reese	125.00	65.00	35.00

		NM	EX	VG
(52)	Allie Reynolds	30.00	15.00	9.00
(53)	Bill Rigney	25.00	12.50	7.50
(54)	Phil Rizzuto/Bunting	90.00	45.00	27.00
(55)	Phil Rizzuto/Swinging	200.00	100.00	60.00
(56)	Robin Roberts	40.00	20.00	12.00
(57)	Eddie Robinson	25.00	12.50	7.50
(58)	Jackie Robinson	325.00	160.00	100.00
(59)	Elwin "Preacher" Roe	25.00	12.50	7.50
(60)	Johnny Sain	30.00	15.00	9.00
(61)	Albert "Red" Schoendienst	40.00	20.00	12.00
(62)	Duke Snider	140.00	70.00	40.00
(63)	George Spencer	25.00	12.50	7.50
(64)	Eddie Stanky	25.00	12.50	7.50
(65)	Henry Thompson	25.00	12.50	7.50
(66)	Bobby Thomson	30.00	15.00	9.00
(67)	Vic Wertz	25.00	12.50	7.50
(68)	Waldon Westlake	25.00	12.50	7.50
(69)	Wes Westrum	25.00	12.50	7.50
(70)	Ted Williams	450.00	225.00	135.00
(71)	Gene Woodling	30.00	15.00	9.00
(72)	Gus Zernial	25.00	12.50	7.50

1956 Big League Stars Statues

While the plastic statues in this set are virtually identical to the set issued in 1955 by Dairy Queen, the packaging of the Big League Stars statues on a card with all the usual elements of a baseball card makes them more collectible. The DQ versions of the statues are white, while the Big League versions are bronze colored. The statues measure about 3" tall and were sold in a 4" x 5" cardboard and plastic blister pack for about 19 cents. Complete league sets were also sold in a large package. The singles package features the player's name in a large banner near the top with his team printed below and line drawings of ballplayers in action around the statue. Backs have a player portrait photo with facsimile autograph, position, team, previous year and career stats and a career summary. A perforated tab at bottom can be pulled out to make a stand for the display. Most packages are found with the hole at top punched out to allow for hanging on a hook. Besides singles, larger packages of nine National or American league statues were also sold in a window-box. The set is checklisted alphabetically.

		NM	EX	VG
Complete Set (18):		5,200	2,600	1,500
Common Player:		60.00	30.00	18.00
	UNOPENED PACKAGED STATUES			
(1)	John Antonelli	220.00	110.00	65.00
(2)	Bob Avila	220.00	110.00	65.00
(3)	Yogi Berra	675.00	340.00	200.00
(4)	Roy Campanella	675.00	340.00	200.00
(5)	Larry Doby	300.00	150.00	100.00
(6)	Del Ennis	220.00	110.00	65.00
(7)	Jim Gilliam	250.00	125.00	75.00
(8)	Gil Hodges	675.00	340.00	200.00
(9)	Harvey Kuenn	220.00	110.00	65.00
(10)	Bob Lemon	250.00	125.00	75.00
(11)	Mickey Mantle	3,400	1,700	1,000
(12)	Ed Mathews	500.00	250.00	150.00
(13)	Minnie Minoso	220.00	110.00	65.00
(14)	Stan Musial	1,000	500.00	300.00
(15)	Pee Wee Reese	675.00	340.00	200.00
(16)	Al Rosen	220.00	110.00	65.00
(17)	Duke Snider	675.00	340.00	200.00
(18a)	Mickey Vernon (Senators)	220.00	110.00	65.00
(18b)	Mickey Vernon (Red Sox)	220.00	110.00	65.00
	STATUES			
(1)	John Antonelli	40.00	20.00	12.00
(2)	Bob Avila	40.00	20.00	12.00
(3)	Yogi Berra	150.00	75.00	45.00
(4)	Roy Campanella	150.00	75.00	45.00
(5)	Larry Doby	60.00	30.00	18.00
(6)	Del Ennis	40.00	20.00	12.00
(7)	Jim Gilliam	50.00	25.00	15.00
(8)	Gil Hodges	125.00	62.00	37.00
(9)	Harvey Kuenn	40.00	20.00	12.00
(10)	Bob Lemon	60.00	30.00	18.00
(11)	Mickey Mantle	300.00	150.00	90.00
(12)	Ed Mathews	100.00	50.00	30.00
(13)	Minnie Minoso	50.00	25.00	15.00
(14)	Stan Musial	200.00	100.00	60.00
(15)	Pee Wee Reese	150.00	75.00	45.00
(16)	Al Rosen	45.00	22.00	13.50
(17)	Duke Snider	150.00	75.00	45.00
(18a)	Mickey Vernon (Senators)	40.00	20.00	12.00
(18b)	Mickey Vernon (Red Sox)	40.00	20.00	12.00
	PACKAGE/CARD ONLY			
(1)	John Antonelli	50.00	25.00	15.00
(2)	Bob Avila	50.00	25.00	15.00
(3)	Yogi Berra	150.00	75.00	45.00
(4)	Roy Campanella	150.00	75.00	45.00
(5)	Larry Doby	75.00	37.50	22.00
(6)	Del Ennis	50.00	25.00	15.00
(7)	Jim Gilliam	65.00	32.50	20.00
(8)	Gil Hodges	100.00	50.00	30.00

		NM	EX	VG
(9)	Harvey Kuenn	50.00	25.00	15.00
(10)	Bob Lemon	75.00	37.50	22.00
(11)	Mickey Mantle	1,200	600.00	360.00
(12)	Ed Mathews	125.00	62.50	37.50
(13)	Minnie Minoso	75.00	37.50	22.00
(14)	Stan Musial	175.00	85.00	50.00
(15)	Pee Wee Reese	150.00	75.00	45.00
(16)	Al Rosen	50.00	25.00	15.00
(17)	Duke Snider	150.00	75.00	45.00
(18a)	Mickey Vernon (Senators)	50.00	25.00	15.00
(18b)	Mickey Vernon (Red Sox)	50.00	25.00	15.00

1978 Big T/Tastee Freeze Discs

One player from each major league team was selected for inclusion in this discs set distributed by Big T family restaurants and Tastee Freeze stands in North Carolina, and possibly other parts of the country. The 3-3/8" diameter discs have a sepia-toned player portrait photo at center within a white diamond and surrounded by a brightly colored border with four colored stars at top. Licensed by the Players Association through Michael Schecter Associates, the photos have had uniform logos removed. Backs are printed in red, white and blue and have the sponsor's logos and a line of 1977 stats, along with a card number.

		NM	EX	VG
Complete Set (26):		30.00	15.00	9.00
Common Player:		2.00	1.00	.60
1	Buddy Bell	2.00	1.00	.60
2	Jim Palmer	8.00	4.00	2.50
3	Steve Garvey	5.00	2.50	1.50
4	Jeff Burroughs	2.00	1.00	.60
5	Greg Luzinski	2.00	1.00	.60
6	Lou Brock	8.00	4.00	2.50
7	Thurman Munson	5.00	2.50	1.50
8	Rod Carew	8.00	4.00	2.50
9	George Brett	20.00	10.00	6.00
10	Tom Seaver	15.00	7.50	4.50
11	Willie Stargell	8.00	4.00	2.50
12	Jerry Koosman	2.00	1.00	.60
13	Bill North	2.00	1.00	.60
14	Richie Zisk	2.00	1.00	.60
15	Bill Madlock	2.00	1.00	.60
16	Carl Yastrzemski	15.00	7.50	4.50
17	Dave Cash	2.00	1.00	.60
18	Bob Watson	2.00	1.00	.60
19	Dave Kingman	2.00	1.00	.60
20	Gene Tenace	2.00	1.00	.60
21	Ralph Garr	2.00	1.00	.60
22	Mark Fidrych	4.00	2.00	1.25
23	Frank Tanana	2.00	1.00	.60
24	Larry Hisle	2.00	1.00	.60
25	Bruce Bochte	2.00	1.00	.60
26	Bob Bailor	2.00	1.00	.60

1955-60 Bill and Bob Braves Postcards

One of the most popular and scarce of the 1950s color postcard series is the run of Milwaukee Braves known as "Bill and Bobs." While some of the cards do carry a photo credit acknowledging the pair, and a few add a Bradenton, Fla., (spring training home of the Braves) address, little else is known about the issuer. The cards themselves appear to have been purchased by the players to honor photo and autograph requests. Several of the cards carry facsimile autographs preprinted on the front. The cards feature crisp full-color photos on their borderless fronts. Postcard backs have a variety of printing including card numbers, photo credits, a Kodachrome logo and player name. Some cards are found with some of those elements, some with none. There is some question whether Frank Torre's card is actually a Bill and Bob product, because it is 1/16" narrower than the standard 3-1/2" x 5-1/2" format of the other cards, features the player with a Pepsi bottle in his hand and is rubber-stamped on back with a Pepsi bottler's address. The Torre card is usually collected along with the rest of the set.

		NM	EX	VG
Complete Set (20):		4,600	2,300	1,350
Common Player:		100.00	50.00	30.00
(1)	Hank Aaron	1,200	600.00	360.00
(2)	Joe Adcock/Fldg	185.00	90.00	55.00
(3)	Joe Adcock (Bat on shoulder.)	185.00	90.00	55.00
(4)	Joe Adcock (Kneeling with two bats.)	145.00	75.00	45.00
(5)	Billy Bruton/Kneeling	185.00	90.00	55.00
(6)	Billy Bruton/Throwing	250.00	125.00	75.00
(7)	Bob Buhl	100.00	50.00	30.00
(8)	Lou Burdette	100.00	50.00	30.00
(9)	Gene Conley	100.00	50.00	30.00
(10)	Wes Covington/Kneeling (One bat.)	145.00	75.00	45.00
(11)	Wes Covington/Kneeling (Seven bats.)	145.00	75.00	45.00
(12)	Del Crandall/Kneeling (One bat.)	135.00	65.00	40.00
(13)	Del Crandall/Kneeling (Two bats.)	135.00	65.00	40.00
(14)	Chuck Dressen	145.00	75.00	45.00
(15)	Charlie Grimm	245.00	120.00	75.00
(16)	Fred Haney	235.00	115.00	70.00
(17)	Bob Keely	185.00	90.00	55.00
(18)	Eddie Mathews	400.00	200.00	120.00
(19)	Warren Spahn	500.00	250.00	150.00
(20)	Frank Torre	245.00	120.00	75.00

1923-24 Billiken

Apparently issued as a premium with its Billiken brand cigars, these cards were issued by Villaamil, Santalla y Ca. About 2" x 2-5/8", the cards have black-and-white posed photos surrounded with a white border. Below the picture the player's last name and team are presented in typewriter style. Among the scarcest and most popular of the pre-war Cuban issues, the set features many players from the Negro Leagues. Counterfeits are known.

		NM	EX	VG
Common Player:		800.00	325.00	160.00
	ALMENDARES			
(1)	Bernardo Baro	1,200	480.00	240.00
(2)	Manuel Cueto	900.00	360.00	180.00
(3)	Valentin Dreke	1,200	480.00	240.00
(4)	Isidro Fabre	900.00	360.00	180.00
(5)	Jose Maria Fernandez	900.00	360.00	180.00
(6)	Oscar Fuhr	800.00	325.00	160.00
(7)	Bienvenido "Hooks" Gimenez (Jimenez)	1,200	480.00	240.00
(8)	"Snake" Henry (Henry)	1,000	400.00	200.00
(9)	Ramon "Mike" Herrera	800.00	325.00	160.00
(10)	Jesse Hubbard	1,500	600.00	300.00
(11)	Armando Marsans	1,800	720.00	360.00
(12)	Jackie May (Jakie)	900.00	360.00	180.00
(13)	Eugenio Morin	800.00	325.00	160.00
(14)	Joseito Rodriguez	800.00	325.00	160.00
(15)	Nip Winters	2,000	800.00	400.00
	HABANA			
(16)	Eufemio Abreu	900.00	360.00	180.00
(17)	John Bischoff	800.00	325.00	160.00
(18)	Clark	800.00	325.00	160.00
(19)	Andy Cooper	5,000	2,000	1,000
(20)	Mack Eglefton (Eggleston)	1,300	520.00	260.00
(21)	Bienvenido "Hooks" Gimenez (Jimenez)	1,200	480.00	240.00
(22)	Marcelino Guerra	800.00	325.00	160.00
(23)	Oscar Levis	900.00	360.00	180.00
(24)	John Henry "Pop" Lloid (Lloyd)	19,500	9,750.	2,925
(25)	Juanelo Mirabal	900.00	360.00	180.00
(26)	Bartolo Portuando (Portuano)	1,200	480.00	240.00
(27)	Raphael "Busta" Quintana	800.00	325.00	160.00
(28)	Buster Ross	800.00	325.00	160.00
(29)	Clint Thomas	1,500	600.00	300.00
(30)	Edgar Westley (Wesley)	1,500	600.00	300.00
	MARIANAO			
(31)	Merito Acosta	800.00	325.00	160.00
(32)	Jose Acostica	800.00	325.00	160.00
(33)	D. Brown	800.00	325.00	160.00
(34)	E. Brown	800.00	325.00	160.00
(35)	Rogelio Crespo	800.00	325.00	160.00
(36)	Harry Deberry	800.00	325.00	160.00
(37)	Charlie Dressen	900.00	360.00	180.00
(38)	Freddie Fitzmann (Fitzsimmons)	800.00	325.00	160.00
(39)	Griffin	800.00	325.00	160.00
(40)	Ernie Krueger	800.00	325.00	160.00
(41)	Slim Love	800.00	325.00	160.00
(42)	Jose "Pepin" Perez	800.00	325.00	160.00
(43)	Rgal (Rigal)	800.00	325.00	160.00
(44)	Hank Sceiber (Schreiber)	800.00	325.00	160.00
(45)	Cristobal Torriente	19,500	9,750.	2,925
	SANTA CLARA			
(46)	Oscar Charleston	19,500	9,750.	2,925
(47)	Rube Currie	1,500	600.00	300.00
(48)	Pedro Dibut	900.00	360.00	180.00

(49)	Eddie Douglas (Douglass)	1,500	600.00	300.00
(50)	Frank Duncan	1,500	600.00	300.00
(51)	Oliver Marcell (Marcelle)	5,000	2,000	1,000
(52)	Mayari (Esteban Montalvo)	900.00	360.00	180.00
(53)	Jose Mendez	6,000	2,400	1,200
(54)	Augustin "Tinti" Molina	800.00	325.00	160.00
(55)	Dobie Moore	1,500	600.00	300.00
(56)	Alejandro Oms	2,000	800.00	400.00
(57)	Herman Rios	900.00	360.00	180.00
(58)	Julio Rojo	900.00	360.00	180.00
(59)	Red Ryan	1,200	480.00	240.00
(60)	Frank Wardfield (Warfield)	1,500	600.00	300.00

1916 Block and Kuhl Co.

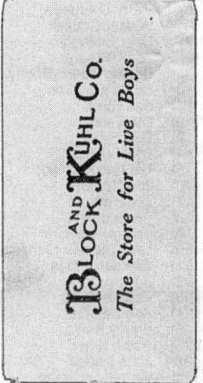

Best known for its use as a promotional medium for The Sporting News, this 200-card set can be found with ads on the back for several local and regional businesses. Among them is the Block and Kuhl department store, Peoria, Ill. Type card and superstar collectors can expect to pay a significant premium for individual cards with Block and Kuhl's advertising. The checklist is believed to generally parallel the 1916 M101-4 Blank Backs. Cards measure 1-5/8" x 3" and are printed in black-and-white.

(See 1916 M101-4 Blank Backs for checklist.)

1911 Blome's Chocolates (E94)

Advertising for Blome's Chocolates overprinted in purple on the back of these cards is one of several brands produced by George Close Candy Co. Type collectors will pay a premium of up to 5-7X for a Blome's version as opposed to the generic Close Candy version of the same player.

(See 1911 George Close Candy Co. for checklist and base card values.)

1933 Blue Bird Babe Ruth

A small hoard of the (a) cards appeared in the market in early 1994 making available a card which had previously been virtually unknown. Printed in black-and-white on thin card stock, the piece measures 3-7/8" x 5-7/8". The photo on front was used in modified form on several other early-1930s

issues. The back offers balls and gloves available for redemption with soft drink bottle caps and cash. The discovery of the (b) version came in 1999.

		NM	EX	VG
(1a)	Babe Ruth (Batting follow-through, front view.)	2,000	1,000	600.00
(1b)	Babe Ruth (Batting follow-through, side view.)	7,500	3,700	2,200

1930 Blue Ribbon Malt Chicago Cubs

These player pictures were originally printed as part of a 40" x 12" advertising piece by Blue Ribbon Malt. However, if cut from the piece, there is no identification of the issuer. Individual black-and-white pictures have facsimile autographs on front and measure 3-1/2" high by 1-7/16" to 3" wide. The backs are blank. The unnumbered pictures are checklisted here in alphabetical order, with names as they appear on the photos.

		NM	EX	VG
	Complete Uncut Sheet:	500.00	250.00	150.00
	Complete Set, Singles (28):	335.00	165.00	100.00
	Common Player:	20.00	10.00	6.00
(1)	Clyde Beck	20.00	10.00	6.00
(2)	Lester Bell	20.00	10.00	6.00
(3)	Clarence Blair	20.00	10.00	6.00
(4)	Fred Blake	20.00	10.00	6.00
(5)	Jimmie Burke	20.00	10.00	6.00
(6)	Guy Bush	20.00	10.00	6.00
(7)	Hazen "Kiki" Cuyler	40.00	20.00	12.00
(8)	Woody English	20.00	10.00	6.00
(9)	Eddie Farrell	20.00	10.00	6.00
(10)	Charlie Grimm	20.00	10.00	6.00
(11)	Leo "Gabby" Hartnett	40.00	20.00	12.00
(12)	Clift Heathcote	20.00	10.00	6.00
(13)	Rogers Hornsby	65.00	32.00	19.50
(14)	George L. Kelly	40.00	20.00	12.00
(15)	Pierce "Pat" Malone	20.00	10.00	6.00
(16)	Joe McCarthy	20.00	10.00	6.00
(17)	Lynn Nelson	20.00	10.00	6.00
(18)	Bob Osborn	20.00	10.00	6.00
(19)	Jess Petty	20.00	10.00	6.00
(20)	Charlie Root	20.00	10.00	6.00
(21)	Ray Schalk	40.00	20.00	12.00
(22)	John Schulte	20.00	10.00	6.00
(23)	Al Shealy	20.00	10.00	6.00
(24)	Riggs Stephenson	20.00	10.00	6.00
(25)	Dan Taylor	20.00	10.00	6.00
(26)	Zack Taylor	20.00	10.00	6.00
(27)	Bud Teachout	20.00	10.00	6.00
(28)	Lewis "Hack" Wilson	60.00	30.00	18.00

1930 Blue Ribbon Malt Chicago White Sox

These player pictures were originally printed as part of a 40" x 12" advertising piece by Blue Ribbon Malt. However, if cut from the piece, there is no identification of the issuer. Individual black-and-white pictures have facsimile autographs on front and measure 3-1/2" high by 1-7/16" to 2-7/8" wide. The backs are blank. The unnumbered pictures are checklisted here in alphabetical order, with names as they appear on the photos.

		NM	EX	VG
	Complete Uncut Sheet:	1,000	500.00	300.00
	Complete Set (27):	400.00	200.00	120.00
	Common Player:	20.00	10.00	6.00
(1)	"Chick" Autry	20.00	10.00	6.00
(2)	"Red" Barnes	20.00	10.00	6.00
(3)	Moe Berg	60.00	30.00	18.00
(4)	Garland Braxton	20.00	10.00	6.00
(5)	Donie Bush	20.00	10.00	6.00
(6)	Pat Caraway	20.00	10.00	6.00
(7)	Bill Cissell	20.00	10.00	6.00
(8)	"Bud" Clancy	20.00	10.00	6.00
(9)	Clyde Crouse	20.00	10.00	6.00
(10)	U.C. Faber	50.00	25.00	15.00
(11)	Bob Fothergill	20.00	10.00	6.00
(12)	Frank J. "Dutch" Henry	20.00	10.00	6.00
(13)	Smead Jolley	20.00	10.00	6.00
(14)	Bill "Willie" Kamm	20.00	10.00	6.00
(15)	Bernard "Mike" Kelly	20.00	10.00	6.00
(16)	Johnny Kerr	20.00	10.00	6.00
(17)	Ted Lyons	50.00	25.00	15.00
(18)	Harold McKain	20.00	10.00	6.00
(19)	"Jim" Moore	20.00	10.00	6.00
(20)	"Greg" Mulleavy	20.00	10.00	6.00
(21)	Carl N. Reynolds	20.00	10.00	6.00
(22)	Blondy Ryan	20.00	10.00	6.00
(23)	"Benny" Tate	20.00	10.00	6.00
(24)	Tommy Thomas	20.00	10.00	6.00
(25)	Ed Walsh, Jr.	20.00	10.00	6.00
(26)	Johnny Watwood	20.00	10.00	6.00
(27)	Bob Weiland	20.00	10.00	6.00

1930 Blue Ribbon Malt Premiums

The manner of distribution for this series is unknown. And, while the name of the sponsor does not appear, the similarity to other Blue Ribbon Malt issues pinpoints their source. The premiums are a 5" x 7" black-and-white photo (sometimes, but not

always, mounted on a heavy gray cardboard 6-1/4" x 8-3/4" backing). A facsimile autograph is on the photo. This incomplete checklist is presented alphabetically by team.

		NM	EX	VG
	Common Player:	225.00	110.00	65.00
	CHICAGO CUBS			
(1)	Clyde Beck	225.00	110.00	65.00
(2)	Lester Bell	225.00	110.00	65.00
(3)	Clarence Blair	225.00	110.00	65.00
(4)	Fred Blake	225.00	110.00	65.00
(5)	Jimmy Burke	225.00	110.00	65.00
(6)	Guy Bush	225.00	110.00	65.00
(7)	Hal Carlson	225.00	110.00	65.00
(8)	Hazen "Kiki" Cuyler	300.00	150.00	90.00
(9)	Woody English	225.00	110.00	65.00
(10)	Charlie Grimm	225.00	110.00	65.00
(11)	Leo "Gabby" Hartnett	300.00	150.00	90.00
(12)	Cliff Heathcote	225.00	110.00	65.00
(13)	Rogers Hornsby	400.00	200.00	120.00
(14)	Perce "Pat" Malone	225.00	110.00	65.00
(15)	Joe McCarthy	275.00	135.00	80.00
(16)	Malcolm Moss	225.00	110.00	65.00
(17)	Lynn Nelson	225.00	110.00	65.00
(18)	Bob Osborn	225.00	110.00	65.00
(19)	Charles Root	225.00	110.00	65.00
(20)	Ray Schalk	275.00	135.00	80.00
(21)	John Schulte	225.00	110.00	65.00
(22)	Al Shealy	225.00	110.00	65.00
(23)	Riggs Stephenson	225.00	110.00	65.00
(24)	Dan Taylor	225.00	110.00	65.00
(25)	Zack Taylor	225.00	110.00	65.00
(26)	Chas. J. Tolson	225.00	110.00	65.00
(27)	Hal Totten (Announcer)	225.00	110.00	65.00
(28)	Lewis "Hack" Wilson	350.00	175.00	105.00
	CHICAGO WHITE SOX			
(1)	Donie Bush	225.00	110.00	65.00
(2)	Bill Cissell	225.00	110.00	65.00
(4)	Red Faber	275.00	135.00	85.00
(5)	Smead Jolley	225.00	110.00	65.00
(7)	Willie Kamm	225.00	110.00	65.00
(9)	Ted Lyons	275.00	135.00	85.00
(11)	Carl Reynolds	225.00	110.00	65.00
(13)	Art Shires	225.00	110.00	65.00
(15)	Tommy Thomas	225.00	110.00	65.00
(16)	Johnny Watwood	225.00	110.00	65.00

1931 Blue Ribbon Malt

Players of the Chicago Cubs and White Sox are featured in this series of 4-7/8" x 6-7/8" black-and-white photos. Each blank-backed photo is bordered in white with "Compliments of BLUE RIBBON MALT-America's Biggest Seller" printed in the bottom border and a facsimile autograph across the photo. It is likely players other than those listed here were also issued.

		NM	EX	VG
	Common Player:	90.00	45.00	27.00
(1)	Lu Blue	90.00	45.00	27.00
(2)	Lew Fonseca	90.00	45.00	27.00
(3)	Vic Frazier	90.00	45.00	27.00
(4)	John Kerr	90.00	45.00	27.00
(5)	Bob Smith	90.00	45.00	27.00
(6)	Billy Sullivan	90.00	45.00	27.00
(7)	Lewis "Hack" Wilson	125.00	62.00	37.00

1931 Blum's Baseball Bulletin Premiums

The year of issue presented is speculative, based on biographical information on the specimens seen thus far. This series of 9-1/2" x 13-5/8" (Small) or 11-1/2" x 13-3/4" (Large) pictures was printed on premium stock with black-and-white pictures and text bordered in red or green baseballs. A credit line at bottom says the series was "Compiled by Fred J. Blum, Publisher,

Blum's Baseball Bulletin." The number of players with a connection to Rochester, N.Y., indicates Blum's firm must have been located there. The checklist here is likely incomplete.

		NM	EX	VG
Common Player:		200.00	100.00	60.00
(1)	Edward T. Collins (S)	300.00	150.00	90.00
(2)	Jacob E. Daubert (S)	200.00	100.00	60.00
(3)	William E. Donovan (L)	200.00	100.00	60.00
(4)	John J. Evers (S)	300.00	150.00	90.00
(5)	Lou Gehrig (L)	350.00	175.00	105.00
(6)	Henry K. Groh (L)	200.00	100.00	60.00
(7)	Lefty Grove (L)	400.00	200.00	120.00
(8)	Walter Johnson (S)	500.00	250.00	150.00
(9)	Napoleon Lajoie (S)	350.00	175.00	105.00
(10)	Walter J.V. Maranville (S)	300.00	150.00	90.00
(11)	James (Wicky) McAvoy (L)	200.00	100.00	60.00
(12)	Rochester 1911	200.00	100.00	60.00
	(Team composite.) (L)			
(13)	William H. Southworth (L)	300.00	150.00	90.00
(14)	Tristam Speaker (S)	400.00	200.00	120.00
(15)	George Toporcer (L)	200.00	100.00	60.00
(16)	Arthur C (Dazzy) Vance	400.00	200.00	120.00

1961-1963 Bobbin' Head Dolls

Some of the top stars of the day were caricatured in the first generation of bobbin' head dolls. Additionally, Mantle and Maris were depicted in a pair of color 5" x 7" advertising photos depicting the home run heroes of 1961 holding their dolls. The players are pictured in belt-to-cap photos wearing road uniforms and posed in a stadium setting. Backs are blank.

	NM	EX	VG
Roberto Clemente (6-1/2" doll)	2,750	1,350	825.00
Roberto Clemente	1,000	500.00	300.00
(Picture box.)			
Mickey Mantle (Ad photo.)	325.00	160.00	95.00
Mickey Mantle (6-1/2" doll,	1,000	500.00	300.00
round or square base)			
Mickey Mantle	1,200	600.00	360.00
(Mini (4-1/2") doll.)			
Mickey Mantle (Large or	750.00	375.00	225.00
small picture box.)			
Roger Maris (Ad photo.)	200.00	100.00	60.00
Roger Maris (6-1/2" doll.)	500.00	250.00	150.00
Roger Maris	650.00	325.00	195.00
(Mini (5-1/2") doll.)			
Roger Maris	900.00	450.00	275.00
(Large or small picture box.)			
Willie Mays (White base,	750.00	375.00	225.00
dark face, 6-1/2" doll.)			
Willie Mays (White base,	700.00	350.00	210.00
light face, 6-1/2" doll.)			
Willie Mays	2,250	1,125	675.00
(Gold base, 6-1/2" doll.)			

1947 Bond Bread

These cards were issued as singles by "Homogenized" Bond Bread in 1947, but had their origins in 12-card boxed sets printed by Aarco Playing Card Co., Chicago, and sold as "Collectors & Traders Sports Stars Subjects." The Bond Bread cards are in the original format of 2-1/4" x 3-3/8" black-and-white cards printed on round-cornered blank-backed stock. The borderless fronts have portraits or posed action photos with the player name in facsimile autograph or script typography. At some point after the original Bond Bread issue, half of the cards were reprinted in a square-cornered 2-1/4" x 3-1/2" size on slightly different stock, for purposes unknown. A large quantity of these 24 cards was found in a New York warehouse in the 1980s. To complicate the situation, the square-cornered cards were illegally counterfeited sometime after

2000, often sold in high-graded slabs by fraudulent grading companies. The issue was designated in the American Card Catalog as W571/D305.

Round-cornered Originals

		NM	EX	VG
Complete Set (48):		2,500	1,250	750.00
Common Player:		20.00	10.00	6.00
(1)	Rex Barney/SP	20.00	10.00	6.00
(2)	Yogi Berra/SP	150.00	75.00	45.00
(3)	Ewell Blackwell	20.00	10.00	6.00
(4)	Lou Boudreau	40.00	20.00	12.00
(5)	Ralph Branca/SP	20.00	10.00	6.00
(6)	Harry Brecheen	20.00	10.00	6.00
(7)	Dom DiMaggio/SP	50.00	25.00	15.00
(8)	Joe DiMaggio/SP	300.00	150.00	90.00
(9)	Bobbie Doerr (Bobby)	40.00	20.00	12.00
(10)	Bruce Edwards/SP	20.00	10.00	6.00
(11)	Bob Elliott	20.00	10.00	6.00
(12)	Del Ennis	20.00	10.00	6.00
(13)	Bob Feller	45.00	22.00	13.50
(14)	Carl Furillo/SP	40.00	20.00	12.00
(15)	Cid Gordon (Sid)/SP	20.00	10.00	6.00
(16)	Joe Gordon	45.00	22.00	13.50
(17)	Joe Hatten/SP	20.00	10.00	6.00
(18)	Gil Hodges/SP	75.00	37.50	22.50
(19)	Tommy Holmes	20.00	10.00	6.00
(20)	Larry Janson (Jansen)/SP	20.00	10.00	6.00
(21)	Sheldon Jones/SP	20.00	10.00	6.00
(22)	Edwin Joost/SP	20.00	10.00	6.00
(23)	Charlie Keller/SP	20.00	10.00	6.00
(24)	Ken Keltner/SP	20.00	10.00	6.00
(25)	Buddy Kerr/SP	20.00	10.00	6.00
(26)	Ralph Kiner	50.00	25.00	15.00
(27)	John Lindell/SP	20.00	10.00	6.00
(28)	Whitey Lockman/SP	20.00	10.00	6.00
(29)	Willard Marshall/SP	20.00	10.00	6.00
(30)	Johnny Mize	50.00	25.00	15.00
(31)	Stan Musial	150.00	75.00	45.00
(32)	Andy Pafko	20.00	10.00	6.00
(33)	Johnny Pesky	20.00	10.00	6.00
(34)	Pee Wee Reese/SP	125.00	65.00	35.00
(35)	Phil Rizzuto	50.00	25.00	15.00
(36)	Aaron Robinson	20.00	10.00	6.00
(37)	Jackie Robinson	250.00	125.00	75.00
(38)	John Sain	20.00	10.00	6.00
(39)	Enos Slaughter	50.00	25.00	15.00
(40)	Vern Stephens	20.00	10.00	6.00
(41)	George Tebbetts/SP	20.00	10.00	6.00
(42)	Bob Thomson/SP	40.00	20.00	12.00
(43)	Johnny Vandermeer (VanderMeer)/SP	20.00	10.00	6.00
(44)	Ted Williams	200.00	100.00	60.00
	BOXERS			
(45)	Primo Camera	20.00	10.00	6.00
(46)	Marcel Cerdan/SP	20.00	10.00	6.00
(47)	Jake LaMotta/SP	60.00	30.00	18.00
(48)	Joe Louis	40.00	20.00	12.00

Square-cornered Reprints

		NM	EX	VG
Complete Set (24):		650.00	320.00	195.00
Common Player:		15.00	7.50	4.50
(3)	Ewell Blackwell	15.00	7.50	4.50
(4)	Lou Boudreau	25.00	12.50	7.50
(6)	Harry Brecheen	15.00	7.50	4.50
(9)	Bobbie Doerr (Bobby)	25.00	12.50	7.50
(11)	Bob Elliott	15.00	7.50	4.50
(12)	Del Ennis	15.00	7.50	4.50
(13)	Bob Feller	30.00	15.00	9.00
(16)	Joe Gordon	25.00	12.50	7.50
(19)	Tommy Holmes	15.00	7.50	4.50
(24)	Ken Keltner	15.00	7.50	4.50
(26)	Ralph Kiner	25.00	12.50	7.50
(30)	Johnny Mize	25.00	12.50	7.50
(31)	Stan Musial	60.00	30.00	18.00
(32)	Andy Pafko	15.00	7.50	4.50
(33)	Johnny Pesky	15.00	7.50	4.50
(35)	Phil Rizzuto	30.00	15.00	9.00
(36)	Aaron Robinson	15.00	7.50	4.50
(37)	Jackie Robinson	90.00	45.00	27.00
(38)	John Sain	15.00	7.50	4.50
(39)	Enos Slaughter	25.00	12.50	7.50
(40)	Vern Stephens	15.00	7.50	4.50
(44)	Ted Williams	90.00	45.00	27.00
	BOXERS			
(45)	Primo Camera	15.00	7.50	4.50
(48)	Joe Louis	30.00	15.00	9.00

1947 Bond Bread Exhibits

The manner of distribution of these variants of the "Bond Bread" (W571 / D305) baseball cards is believed to have been via penny arcade dispensers. The cards can be found in two sizes, about 3-3/8" x 5-3/8" (nearly the same as contemporary Exhibit Supply Co. cards), and about 3" x 5". Over 75 percent of the baseball players known in the base Bond Bread set have been reported in this format, plus one player, Walker Coop" (nearly the same as contemporary Exhibit Supply Co. cards), and about 3" x 5". Over 75 percent of the bseball plaers known in the base Bond Bread set have been reported in this format, plus one layer, Walker Cooper, not in the base set. The four W571/D305 boxers have not yet been reported in this format.

		NM	EX	VG
Complete Set (33):		1,250	625.00	375.00
Common Player:		25.00	12.50	7.50
(1)	Rex Barney			
(2)	Yogi Berra			
(3)	Ewell Blackwell	25.00	12.50	7.50
(4)	Lou Boudreau	30.00	15.00	9.00
(5)	Ralph Branca			
(6)	Harry Brecheen	25.00	12.50	7.50
(--)	Walker Cooper	50.00	25.00	15.00
(7)	Dom DiMaggio	30.00	15.00	9.00
(8)	Joe DiMaggio	200.00	100.00	60.00
(9)	Bobbie Doerr (Bobby)	35.00	17.50	10.00
(10)	Bruce Edwards			
(11)	Bob Elliott	25.00	12.50	7.50
(12)	Del Ennis	25.00	12.50	7.50
(13)	Bob Feller	40.00	20.00	12.00
(14)	Carl Furillo	100.00	50.00	30.00
(15)	Cid Gordon (Sid)			
(16)	Joe Gordon	25.00	12.50	7.50
(17)	Joe Hatten			
(18)	Gil Hodges	90.00	45.00	27.50
(19)	Tommy Holmes	25.00	12.50	7.50
(20)	Larry Janson (Jansen)	25.00	12.50	7.50
(21)	Sheldon Jones	25.00	12.50	7.50
(22)	Edwin Joost	25.00	12.50	7.50
(23)	Charlie Keller			
(24)	Ken Keltner	25.00	12.50	7.50
(25)	Buddy Kerr	25.00	12.50	7.50
(26)	Ralph Kiner	30.00	15.00	9.00
(27)	John Lindell	25.00	12.50	7.50
(28)	Whitey Lockman	25.00	12.50	7.50
(29)	Willard Marshall			
(30)	Johnny Mize	30.00	15.00	9.00
(31)	Stan Musial	75.00	37.50	22.50
(32)	Andy Pafko	25.00	12.50	7.50
(33)	Johnny Pesky	25.00	12.50	7.50
(34)	Pee Wee Reese	100.00	50.00	30.00
(35)	Phil Rizzuto	50.00	25.00	15.00
(36)	Aaron Robinson	25.00	12.50	7.50
(37)	Jackie Robinson	175.00	90.00	55.00
(38)	John Sain	25.00	12.50	7.50
(39)	Enos Slaughter	30.00	15.00	9.00
(40)	Vern Stephens	25.00	12.50	7.50
(41)	George Tebbetts	25.00	12.50	7.50
(42)	Bob Thomson			
(43)	Johnny Vandermeer (VanderMeer)	25.00	12.50	7.50
(44)	Ted Williams	175.00	85.00	55.00

1947 Bond Bread Premiums

While there is no empirical evidence, it is believed these 6-5/8" x 9" black-and-white, blank-back player pictures are associated with the Bond Bread card issue, since they share the same photos and script names, right down to the misspellings. They were likely made available to bread buyers as some sort of premium. The checklist presented here is the same as that of the card issue. Though not all of the premium pictures have been confirmed, it is reasonable to presume their existence.

		NM	EX	VG
Common Player:		40.00	20.00	12.00
(1)	Rex Barney	40.00	20.00	12.00
(2)	Yogi Berra	150.00	75.00	45.00
(3)	Ewell Blackwell	40.00	20.00	12.00
(4)	Lou Boudreau	75.00	37.50	22.50
(5)	Ralph Branca	60.00	30.00	18.00
(6)	Harry Brecheen	40.00	20.00	12.00
(7)	Dom DiMaggio	60.00	30.00	18.00
(8)	Joe DiMaggio	600.00	300.00	180.00
(9)	Bobbie Doerr (Bobby)	60.00	30.00	18.00
(10)	Bruce Edwards	40.00	20.00	12.00
(11)	Bob Elliott	40.00	20.00	12.00
(12)	Del Ennis	50.00	25.00	15.00
(13)	Bob Feller	150.00	75.00	45.00
(14)	Carl Furillo	60.00	30.00	18.00
(15)	Cid Gordon (Sid)	40.00	20.00	12.00
(16)	Joe Gordon	40.00	20.00	12.00
(17)	Joe Hatten	40.00	20.00	12.00
(18)	Gil Hodges	100.00	50.00	30.00
(19)	Tommy Holmes	40.00	20.00	12.00
(20)	Larry Janson (Jansen)	40.00	20.00	12.00
(21)	Sheldon Jones	40.00	20.00	12.00
(22)	Edwin Joost	40.00	20.00	12.00
(23)	Charlie Keller	45.00	22.50	13.50
(24)	Ken Keltner	40.00	20.00	12.00

(25)	Buddy Kerr	40.00	20.00	12.00
(26)	Ralph Kiner	75.00	37.50	22.50
(27)	John Lindell	40.00	20.00	12.00
(28)	Whitey Lockman	40.00	20.00	12.00
(29)	Willard Marshall	40.00	20.00	12.00
(30)	Johnny Mize	75.00	37.50	22.50
(31)	Stan Musial	300.00	150.00	90.00
(32)	Andy Pafko	40.00	20.00	12.00
(33)	Johnny Pesky	40.00	20.00	12.00
(34)	Pee Wee Reese	150.00	75.00	45.00
(35)	Phil Rizzuto	150.00	75.00	45.00
(36)	Aaron Robinson	40.00	20.00	12.00
(37)	Jackie Robinson	1,000	500.00	300.00
(38)	John Sain	50.00	25.00	15.00
(39)	Enos Slaughter	75.00	37.50	22.50
(40)	Vern Stephens	40.00	20.00	12.00
(41)	George Tebbetts	40.00	20.00	12.00
(42)	Bob Thomson	60.00	30.00	18.00
(43)	Johnny Vandermeer	40.00	20.00	12.00
(44)	Ted Williams	350.00	175.00	100.00
BOXERS				
(45)	Primo Carnera	45.00	22.50	13.50
(46)	Marcel Cerdan	40.00	20.00	12.00
(47)	Jake LaMotta	60.00	30.00	18.00
(48)	Joe Louis	75.00	37.50	22.50

1947 Bond Bread Perforated, Dual-Sided

The manner of distribtion for this variant of the "Bond Bread" (W571/D305) cards is unknown, although anecdotal evidence suggests a connection with Bar Nunn show stores. About the size of the commonly seen blank-backed baseball cards (2-1/4" x 3-1/2"), these differ in that they have two, three or four sides perforated, indicating they were issued in sheet form. Also, this group has, instead of a blank back, another picture. Most of the pictures seen thus far are of Western movie stars. Only a few are named on the cards, but they include John Wayne, Hopalong Cassidy, Gene Autry and Noah Berry. The only non-Western back seen is Michigan quarterback Bob Chappius, paired with Tommy Holmes. Thus far, none of the short-printed Bond Bread cards have been seen in this format. Assigned numbers correspond to the Bond Bread set.

		NM	EX	VG
Complete Set (24):		550.00	275.00	165.00
Common Card:				
(3)	Ewell Blackwell	15.00	7.50	4.50
(4)	Lou Boudreau	22.50	11.00	6.75
(6)	Harry Brecheen	15.00	7.50	4.50
(9)	Bobbie Doerr (Bobby)	22.50	11.00	6.75
(11)	Bob Elliott	15.00	7.50	4.50
(12)	Del Ennis	15.00	7.50	4.50
(13)	Bob Feller	25.00	12.50	7.50
(16)	Joe Gordon	15.00	7.50	4.50
(19)	Tommy Holmes	15.00	7.50	4.50
(24)	Ken Keltner	15.00	7.50	4.50
(26)	Ralph Kiner	22.50	11.00	6.75
(30)	Johnny Mize	22.50	11.00	6.75
(31)	Stan Musial	60.00	30.00	18.00
(32)	Andy Pafko	15.00	7.50	4.50
(33)	Johnny Pesky	15.00	7.50	4.50
(35)	Phil Rizzuto	30.00	15.00	9.00
(36)	Aaron Robinson	15.00	7.50	4.50
(37)	Jackie Robinson	110.00	55.00	35.00
(38)	John Sain	15.00	7.50	4.50
(39)	Enos Slaughter	22.50	11.00	6.75
(40)	Vern Stephens	15.00	7.50	4.50
(44)	Ted Williams	110.00	55.00	35.00
BOXERS				
(45)	Primo Carnera	15.00	7.50	4.50
(48)	Joe Louis	30.00	15.00	9.00

1947 Bond Bread Jackie Robinson

 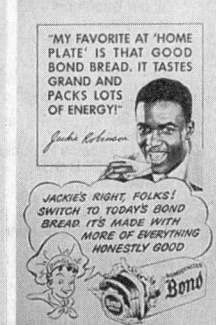

"MY FAVORITE AT 'HOME PLATE' IS THAT GOOD BOND BREAD. IT TASTES GRAND AND PACKS LOTS OF ENERGY!"

Jackie Robinson

JACKIE'S RIGHT, FOLKS! SWITCH TO TODAY'S BOND BREAD. IT'S MADE WITH MORE OF EVERYTHING HONESTLY GOOD

The modern major leagues' first black player is featured in this set issued by Bond Bread in 1947. The cards, measuring 2-1/4" x 3-1/2", are black-and-white photos of Robinson in various action and portrait poses. The unnumbered cards bear three different backs advertising Bond Bread. Four cards use a horizontal format. Card #6 was issued in greater quantities and perhaps was a promotional card; its back is the only one containing a short biography of Robinson.

		NM	EX	VG
Complete Set (13):		85,000	42,500	25,000
Common Card:		6,750	3,400	2,000
(1)	Jackie Robinson (Awaiting pitch.)	6,750	3,400	2,000
(2)	Jackie Robinson/Btg (White shirt sleeves.)	6,750	3,400	2,000
(3)	Jackie Robinson/Btg (No shirt sleeves.)	6,750	3,400	2,000
(4)	Jackie Robinson/Leaping (Scoreboard in background.)	6,750	3,400	2,000
(5)	Jackie Robinson/Leaping (No scoreboard.)	6,750	3,400	2,000
(6)	Jackie Robinson/Portrait (Facsimile autograph.)	6,750	3,400	2,000
(7)	Jackie Robinson (Portrait, holding glove in air.)	6,750	3,400	2,000
(8)	Jackie Robinson (Running down baseline.)	6,750	3,400	2,000
(9)	Jackie Robinson (Running to catch ball.)	6,750	3,400	2,000
(10)	Jackie Robinson/Sliding	6,750	3,400	2,000
(11)	Jackie Robinson (Stretching for throw, ball in glove.)	6,750	3,400	2,000
(12)	Jackie Robinson (Stretching for throw, no ball visible.)	6,750	3,400	2,000
(13)	Jackie Robinson/Throwing	6,750	3,400	2,000

1957 Borden's Dodgers Ticket Promotions

In their final season in Brooklyn, the Dodgers partnered with Borden's to offer grandstand seat tickets to those redeeming five wrappers from various Elsie-branded dairy treats. The offer was promoted on the back of what appear to be contemporary team-issued picture pack photos. On the backs of the 5" x 7" black-and-white pictures is an illustrated advertisement providing details of the offer. This checklist is very likely incomplete.

		NM	EX	VG
(1)	Gino Cimoli	150.00	75.00	45.00
(2)	Sandy Koufax	750.00	500.00	350.00
(3)	Don Newcombe	250.00	125.00	75.00

1912 Boston American Series Red Sox Postcards

 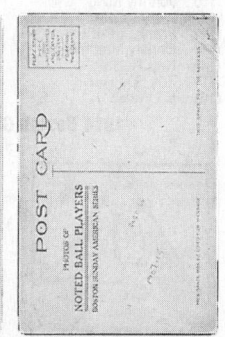

TRIS SPEAKER
STAR OUTFIELDER AND CHAMPION BATTER OF THE RED SOX
BOSTON AMERICAN SERIES

Star players from the World Champion Red Sox are featured in two sets of postcards issued by one of the city's daily newspapers. This set carries the notation "Boston American Series" at bottom right and is approximately 3-1/2" x 5-1/2". The cards are printed in sepia tones with a cream border. At bottom is the player name and position on two lines. Backs have typical postcard markings and a three-line notation, "PHOTOS OF / NOTED BALL PLAYERS / BOSTON SUNDAY AMERICAN SERIES."

		NM	EX	VG
Complete Set (6):		2,400	1,200	725.00
Common Player:		400.00	200.00	120.00
(1)	Forrest Cady	400.00	200.00	120.00
(2)	Hub Perdue	400.00	200.00	120.00
(3)	Tris Speaker	550.00	275.00	165.00
(4)	Jake Stahl	400.00	200.00	120.00
(5)	Heinie Wagner	400.00	200.00	120.00
(6)	Joe Wood	400.00	200.00	120.00

1936 Boston American Sport Stamps

BOSTON AMERICAN
SPORT STAMP
H. LAVAGETTO, 2B, PIRATES

"Harry Lavagetto — Cookie joined the Pittsburgh Pirates at their spring training camp in 1934 . . . and immediately caught on at the keystone sack . . . such associates as Arky Vaughan and Gus Suhr have helped him to hold down his job . . . bats and throws right-handed and is a very classy fielder . . . batted .290 last season . . . 23 years old . . . stands 5 feet 11½"

Similar to several contemporary issues, the Sport Stamps were printed on the pages of the daily newspaper over the course of the season. About 2" x 3-1/2", depending on the length of the biography and how well they were cut off the paper, they are printed in black-and-white. A tightly cropped player portrait is centered on a 2" x 2-5/8" stamp design with

the paper's name above and the player's name, position and team below. This checklist may not be complete. Two of the players (Castleman, R. Johnson) have the paper at top listed as "SUNDAY ADVERTISER." Many of the stamps were issued in pairs, and at least a couple of football players are known, as well as the listed baseball players.

		NM	EX	VG
Common Player:		12.00	6.00	3.50
(1)	J. (John) Allen	12.00	6.00	3.50
(2)	I. (Ivy) Andrews	12.00	6.00	3.50
(3)	E. (Elden)(Eldon) Auker	12.00	6.00	3.50
(4)	E. (Earl) Averill	20.00	10.00	6.00
(5)	R. (Richard) Bartell	12.00	6.00	3.50
(6)	R. (Roy) Bell	12.00	6.00	3.50
(7)	R. (Raymond) Benge	12.00	6.00	3.50
(8)	M. (Morris) Berg	30.00	15.00	9.00
(9)	Walter Berger	12.00	6.00	3.50
(10)	C. (Charles) Berry	12.00	6.00	3.50
(11)	(George) Blaeholder	12.00	6.00	3.50
(12)	A. (Albert) Blanche	12.00	6.00	3.50
(13)	D. (Darrell) Blanton	12.00	6.00	3.50
(14)	O. (Oswald) Bleuge (Bluege)	12.00	6.00	3.50
(15)	W. (William) Bolton	12.00	6.00	3.50
(16)	H. (Henry) Bonura	12.00	6.00	3.50
(17)	J. (James) Bottomley	20.00	10.00	6.00
(18)	J. (Joseph) Bowman	12.00	6.00	3.50
(19)	E. (Edward) Brandt	12.00	6.00	3.50
(20)	C. (Clinton) Brown	12.00	6.00	3.50
(21)	J. (John) Burnett	12.00	6.00	3.50
(22)	G. (Guy) Bush	12.00	6.00	3.50
(23)	A. (Albert) Butcher	12.00	6.00	3.50
(24)	E. (Earl) Caldwell	12.00	6.00	3.50
(25)	D. (Dolph) Camilli	12.00	6.00	3.50
(26)	B. (Bruce) Campbell	12.00	6.00	3.50
(27)	J. (Joseph) Cascarella	12.00	6.00	3.50
(28)	C. (Clyde) Castleman	12.00	6.00	3.50
(29)	P. (Philip) Cavarretta	12.00	6.00	3.50
(30)	W. (William) Chapman	12.00	6.00	3.50
(31)	L. (Louis) Chiozza	12.00	6.00	3.50
(32)	H. (Harland)(Harlond) Clift	12.00	6.00	3.50
(33)	G. (Gordon) Cochrane	25.00	12.50	7.50
(34)	J. (James) Collins	12.00	6.00	3.50
(35)	A. (Allen) Cooke	12.00	6.00	3.50
(36)	J. (Joseph) Coscarart	12.00	6.00	3.50
(37)	Roger Cramer	12.00	6.00	3.50
(38)	J. (Joseph) Cronin	20.00	10.00	6.00
(39)	F. (Frank) Crosetti	15.00	7.50	4.50
(40)	A. (Alvin) Crowder	12.00	6.00	3.50
(41)	A. (Anthony) Cuccinello	12.00	6.00	3.50
(42)	H. (Hazen) Cuyler	20.00	10.00	6.00
(43)	H. (Harry) Danning	12.00	6.00	3.50
(44)	V. (Virgil) Davis	12.00	6.00	3.50
(45)	J. (Jerome) Dean	35.00	17.50	10.50
(46)	P. (Paul) Dean	16.00	8.00	4.75
(47)	J. (Joseph) Demaree	12.00	6.00	3.50
(48)	Paul Derringer	12.00	6.00	3.50
(49)	G. (George) Dickey	12.00	6.00	3.50
(50)	W. (William) Dickey	25.00	12.50	7.50
(51)	L. (Leo) Durocher	20.00	10.00	6.00
(52)	J. (James) Dykes	12.00	6.00	3.50
(53)	G. (George) Earnshaw	12.00	6.00	3.50
(54)	E. (Elmwood)(Elwood) English	12.00	6.00	3.50
(55)	R. (Robert) Feller	25.00	12.50	7.50
(56)	R. (Richard) Ferrell	20.00	10.00	6.00
(57)	Wes Ferrell	12.00	6.00	3.50
(58)	(Louis) Finney	12.00	6.00	3.50
(59)	F. (Fred) Fitzsimmons	12.00	6.00	3.50
(60)	Jimmy Foxx	30.00	15.00	9.00
(61)	F. (Fred) Frankhouse	12.00	6.00	3.50
(62)	L. (Lawrence) French	12.00	6.00	3.50
(63)	(Frank) Frisch	20.00	10.00	6.00
(64)	A. (August) Galan	12.00	6.00	3.50
(65)	H. (Heny)(Henry) Gehrig	60.00	30.00	18.00
(66)	C. (Charles) Gehringer	20.00	10.00	6.00
(67)	(Charles) Gelbert	12.00	6.00	3.50
(68)	A. (Angelo) Giuliani	12.00	6.00	3.50
(69)	V. (Vernon) Gomez	20.00	10.00	6.00
(70)	L. (Leon) Goslin	20.00	10.00	6.00
(71)	R. (Robert) Grace	12.00	6.00	3.50
(72)	C. (Charles) Grimm	12.00	6.00	3.50
(73)	Robert Grove	25.00	12.50	7.50
(74)	G. (George) Haas	12.00	6.00	3.50
(75)	I. (Irving) Hadley	12.00	6.00	3.50
(76)	M. (Melvin) Harder	12.00	6.00	3.50
(77)	C. (Charles) Hartnett	20.00	10.00	6.00
(78)	M. (Minter) Hayes	12.00	6.00	3.50
(79)	R. (Ralston) Hemsley	12.00	6.00	3.50
(80)	F. (Floyd) Herman	12.00	6.00	3.50
(81)	(Michael) Higgins	12.00	6.00	3.50
(82)	M. (Myril) Hoag	12.00	6.00	3.50
(83)	E. (Elon) Hogsett	12.00	6.00	3.50
(84)	R. (Rogers) Hornsby	25.00	12.50	7.50
(85)	W. (Waite) Hoyt	20.00	10.00	6.00
(86)	W. (Willis) Hudlin	12.00	6.00	3.50
(87)	T. (Travis) Jackson	20.00	10.00	6.00
(88)	R. (Robert) Johnson	12.00	6.00	3.50
(89)	R. (Roy) Johnson	12.00	6.00	3.50
(90)	B. (Baxter) Jordan	12.00	6.00	3.50
(91)	W. (William) Jurgess (Jurges)	12.00	6.00	3.50
(92)	(Lloyd) Kennedy	12.00	6.00	3.50
(93)	C. (Charles) Klein	20.00	10.00	6.00
(94)	(William) Knickerbocker	12.00	6.00	3.50
(95)	J. (John) Knott	12.00	6.00	3.50
(96)	M. (Mark) Koenig	12.00	6.00	3.50
(97)	J. (Joseph) Kuhel	12.00	6.00	3.50
(98)	(Lynford) Lary	12.00	6.00	3.50
(99)	H. (Harry) Lavagetto	12.00	6.00	3.50
(100)	A. (Anthony) Lazzeri	20.00	10.00	6.00
(101)	W. (William) Lee	12.00	6.00	3.50
(102)	H. (Henry) Leiber	12.00	6.00	3.50
(103)	Wm. (William) Lewis	12.00	6.00	3.50
(104)	E. (Edward) Linke	12.00	6.00	3.50
(105)	E. (Ernest) Lombardi	20.00	10.00	6.00
(106)	Al Lopez	20.00	10.00	6.00
(107)	C. (Charles) Lucas	12.00	6.00	3.50
(108)	T. (Theodore) Lyons	20.00	10.00	6.00

(109)	Dan MacFayden	12.00	6.00	3.50
(110)	P. (Percy)(Perce) Malone	12.00	6.00	3.50
(111)	A. (Augustus) Mancuso	12.00	6.00	3.50
(112)	(John) Martin	15.00	7.50	4.50
(113)	J. (Joseph) Medwick	12.00	6.00	3.50
(114)	E. (Edmund) Miller	12.00	6.00	3.50
(115)	J. (John) Mize	20.00	10.00	6.00
(116)	Gene Moore	12.00	6.00	3.50
(117)	R. (Randolph) Moore	12.00	6.00	3.50
(118)	V. (Van Lingle) Mungo	12.00	6.00	3.50
(119)	C. (Charles) Myer	12.00	6.00	3.50
(120)	A. (Alfred) Niemiec	12.00	6.00	3.50
(121)	(Fred) Ostermueller	12.00	6.00	3.50
(122)	M. (Melvin) Ott	25.00	12.50	7.50
(123)	L. (LeRoy) Parmelee	12.00	6.00	3.50
(124)	A. (Anthony) Piet	12.00	6.00	3.50
(125)	A. (Alvin) Powell	12.00	6.00	3.50
(126)	F. (Frank) Pytlak	12.00	6.00	3.50
(127)	R. (Ray) Radcliff	12.00	6.00	3.50
(128)	R. (Robert) Reis	12.00	6.00	3.50
(129)	(Carl) Reynolds	12.00	6.00	3.50
(130)	J. (John) Rhodes	12.00	6.00	3.50
(131)	R. (Robert) Rolfe	12.00	6.00	3.50
(132)	C. (Charles) Root	12.00	6.00	3.50
(133)	L. (Lynwood) Rowe	12.00	6.00	3.50
(134)	C. (Charles) Ruffing	20.00	10.00	6.00
(135)	F. (Fred) Schulte	12.00	6.00	3.50
(136)	H. (Harold) Schumacher	12.00	6.00	3.50
(137)	J. (James) Sewell	12.00	6.00	3.50
(138)	A. (Aloysius) Simmons	20.00	10.00	6.00
(139)	J. (Julius) Soulters (Solters)	12.00	6.00	3.50
(140)	G. (George) Stainback	12.00	6.00	3.50
(141)	J. (Johnathan)(John) Stone	12.00	6.00	3.50
(142)	J. (Joseph) Stripp	12.00	6.00	3.50
(143)	W. (William) Terry	20.00	10.00	6.00
(144)	T. (Thomas) Thevenow	12.00	6.00	3.50
(145)	A. (Alphonse) Thomas	12.00	6.00	3.50
(146)	C. (Cecil) Travis	12.00	6.00	3.50
(147)	H. (Harold) Traynor	20.00	10.00	6.00
(148)	H. (Harold) Trosky	12.00	6.00	3.50
(149)	R. (Russell) Van Atta	12.00	6.00	3.50
(150)	F. (Floyd) Vaughan	20.00	10.00	6.00
(151)	J. (Joseph) Vosmik	12.00	6.00	3.50
(152)	G. (Gerald) Walker	12.00	6.00	3.50
(153)	W. (William) Walter	12.00	6.00	3.50
(154)	L. (Lloyd) Waner	20.00	10.00	6.00
(155)	P. (Paul) Waner	20.00	10.00	6.00
(156)	L. (Lonnie) Warneke	12.00	6.00	3.50
(157)	G. (George) Watkins	12.00	6.00	3.50
(158)	J. (Joyner) White	12.00	6.00	3.50
(159)	(Burgess) Whitehead	12.00	6.00	3.50
(160)	(Earl) Whitehill	12.00	6.00	3.50
(161)	A. (Arthur) Whitney	12.00	6.00	3.50
(162)	J. (Jack) Wilson	12.00	6.00	3.50
(163)	J. (James) Wilson	12.00	6.00	3.50

1912 Boston Daily American Souvenir Postcards

Boston Daily American Souvenir
HEINIE WAGNER
CAPTAIN OF RED SOX.

A second style of postcard issued by a local newspaper to honor the World Champions is labeled at bottom-left "Boston American Souvenir." The 3-1/2" x 5-1/2" cards are printed in black on a cream-colored stock. The player name and position are printed inside the photo frame. In the bottom-right border is a union logo and the number "96." The back has standard postcard markings.

		NM	EX	VG
Common Player:		450.00	225.00	135.00
(1)	Forrest Cady	450.00	225.00	135.00
(2)	Ray Collins	450.00	225.00	135.00
(3)	Rabbit Maranville	600.00	300.00	180.00
(4)	Heinie Wagner	450.00	225.00	135.00
(5)	Joe Wood	500.00	250.00	150.00

1912 Boston Garter

If it weren't for the checklist printed on the back of the few known specimens, the extent of this extremely rare issue would be unknown. Many of the cards mentioned on the back have yet to be seen. Issued by the George Frost Co. of Boston, and packed one card per box of a dozen garters, the approximately 4" x 8-1/4" cards are printed in color lithography on the front, and black-and-white on the back. Fronts have a picture of the player standing near his locker or sitting in a chair, dressing in his uniform. The issuer's Boston-brand garter is prominently shown below the player's boxer shorts. A window in the background displays a cityscape or ballpark scene. There was a card issued for one player on each of the 16 major league teams of the day. Large-format (21-1/2" x 11-1/4") cardboard window display posters which reproduce pairs of the cards are sometimes seen in the hobby.

		NM	EX	VG
Common Player:		30,000	12,000	7,250
(1)	Bob Bescher	30,000	12,000	7,250
(2)	Roger Bresnahan	40,000	13,750	8,250
(3)	Frank Chance	40,000	15,000	9,000
(4)	Hal Chase	30,000	12,500	7,500
(5)	Fred Clarke	40,000	13,750	8,250
(6)	Eddie Collins	40,000	13,750	8,250
(7)	Charles Dooin	30,000	12,000	7,250
(8)	Hugh Jennings	40,000	13,750	8,250
(9)	Walter Johnson	60,000	17,500	10,500
(10)	Johnny Kling	30,000	12,000	7,250
(11)	Larry Lajoie	45,000	15,000	9,000
(12)	Frank LaPorte	30,000	12,000	7,250
(13)	Christy Mathewson	75,000	37,500	22,500
(14)	Nap Rucker	30,000	12,000	7,250
(15)	Tris Speaker	45,000	15,000	9,000
(16)	Ed Walsh	40,000	13,750	8,250

1914 Boston Garter - Color

The second of what are presumed to have been three annual issue by the George Frost Co., Boston, contains 12 cards. The colorful lithograph fronts have a player picture in front of a ballpark diagram. A large Boston-brand garter appears at the bottom. Baseballs with the Boston Garter name appear in each upper corner. Black-and-white backs have a checklist for the set, career statistics for the player pictured and details on the cards' availability. Retailers received one card per box of dozen garters and could write to the company to complete the set. About 4" x 8-1/4", they were intended to be displayed in shop windows.

		NM	EX	VG
Common Player:		7,500	3,000	1,800
1	Tris Speaker	45,000	22,000	13,500
2	Ty Cobb	90,000	45,000	27,000
3	Burt Shotten (Shotton)	15,000	7,500	4,500
4	Joe Tinker	30,000	15,000	9,000
5	Johnny Evers	15,500	6,250	3,750
6	Joe Jackson	100,000	30,000	18,000
7	Rabbit Maranville	30,000	15,000	9,000
8	Larry Doyle	15,000	7,500	4,500
9	Frank Baker	30,000	15,000	9,000
10	Ed Konetchy	15,000	7,500	4,500
11	Walter Johnson	50,000	25,000	15,000
12	Buck Herzog	15,000	7,500	4,500

1914 Boston Garter - Sepia

The 1914 date attributed to this 10-card set may or may not be accurate. Since the company's other two known issues can be reliably dated and were produced using the color lithographic process, it is presumed that the use of photographs would have come later. Fronts of the approximately 3-3/4" x 6-1/4" cards feature a green duo-tone photo of the player. His last name appears in white script at the bottom, along with a baseball with the Boston Garter name. Backs have a checklist of the set and information on how retail store owners can send for additional cards to supplement those which were packaged one per box of a dozen garters.

		NM	EX	VG
Complete Set (10):		140,000	70,000	42,500
Common Player:		15,000	7,500	4,500
1	Christy Mathewson	35,000	20,000	12,500
2	Red Murray	7,500	3,750	2,250
3	Eddie Collins	15,000	7,500	4,500
4	Hugh Jennings	15,000	7,500	4,500
5	Hal Chase	12,000	6,000	3,600
6	Bob Bescher	7,500	3,750	2,250
7	Red Dooin	7,500	3,750	2,250
8	Larry Lajoie	15,000	7,500	4,500
9	Tris Speaker	20,000	10,000	6,000
10	Heinie Zimmerman	7,500	3,750	2,250

1909 Boston Herald Supplements

Members of the Red Sox and Braves were featured in this series of supplements in the Boston Sunday Herald. About 7-1/4" x 9-3/4", the blank-back, posed-action pictures are sepia toned. A black box at bottom has player identification, an issue date and a note to "See Story on Sporting Page." While the pictures themselves are numbered, this checklist, almost certainly incomplete, is arranged alphabetically. Some of the pictures show cross-town rivals on the same piece.

		NM	EX	VG
BOSTON BRAVES				
(1)	Chick Autry	200.00	100.00	60.00
(2)	Johnny Bates	200.00	100.00	60.00
(3)	Ginger Beaumont	200.00	100.00	60.00
(4)	Beals Becker	200.00	100.00	60.00
(5)	Frank Bowerman	200.00	100.00	60.00
(6)	Jack Coffey	200.00	100.00	60.00
(7)	Bill Dahlen	200.00	100.00	60.00
(8)	Peaches Graham	200.00	100.00	60.00
(9)	Al Mattern	200.00	100.00	60.00
(10)	Harry Smith	200.00	100.00	60.00
(11)	Bill Sweeney	200.00	100.00	60.00
(12)	("Tom") Thomas H. Tuckey	200.00	100.00	60.00
BOSTON RED SOX				
(1)	Charlie Chech	200.00	100.00	60.00
(2)	Bill Carrigan	200.00	100.00	60.00
(3)	Pat Donahue	200.00	100.00	60.00
(4)	"Doc" (Harry H.) Gessler	200.00	100.00	60.00
(5)	Harry Hooper	300.00	150.00	90.00
(6)	Harry Lord	200.00	100.00	60.00
(7)	Amby McConnell	200.00	100.00	60.00
(8)	Harry Niles	200.00	100.00	60.00
	Tris Speaker	400.00	200.00	120.00
BOSTON BRAVES/RED SOX				
(1)	Johnny Bates, Harry Hooper	150.00	75.00	45.00
(2)	Ginger Beaumont, Tris Speaker	150.00	75.00	45.00
(3)	Ed Cicotte, Tommy Tuckey	250.00	125.00	75.00
(4)	Bill Dahlen, Heinie Wagner	150.00	75.00	45.00
(5)	Doc Gessler, Frank Bowerman	150.00	75.00	45.00
(6)	Harry Lord, Unknown Brave	150.00	75.00	45.00
(7)	Amby McConnell, Jack Coffey	150.00	75.00	45.00
(8)	Harry Smith, Pat Donahue	150.00	75.00	45.00
(9)	Jake Stahl, Chick Autrey (Autry)	150.00	75.00	45.00

1908 Boston Oyster House Chicago Cubs

Located in Chicago, not Boston, this restaurant featured, according to its advertising, "The 'Cubs' Dining Room." In keeping with that theme, the business adopted as a promotion the set of Cubs/Teddy Bear postcards issued the previous

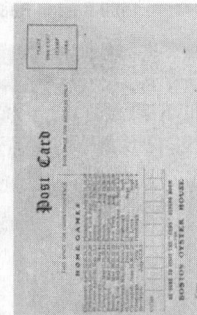

year by Grignon, a local publisher. The restaurant version has on its back a 1908 Cubs home schedule and rudimentary scorecard, along with standard postcard markings.

	NM	EX	VG
Common Player:	500.00	250.00	150.00
Stars: 1X			

(See 1907 Grignon Chicago Cubs postcards for checklist and base values.)

1908 Boston Red Sox Foldout Postcard

At first glance this standard-size (about 5-1/2" x 3-1/2") postcard reveals on its front only portrait photos of the the owners and grounds of the Boston Red Sox, with a cotter-pinned baseball at left printed in red. Hidden behind the ball, however, is an accordian-folded strip of black-and-white player photos, printed front-to-back, in a size of about 1-1/8" x 1-3/4".

	NM	EX	VG
1908 Boston Red Sox	4,500	2,250	1,350

1910 Boston Red Sox Cabinets

Details are lacking on this high-quality photographic issue depicting the 1910 Red Sox. The sepia photos picture the players in full-length poses and are glued to cardboard mattes. There is no identification on the pieces, nor on the decorative paper folders in which they were apparently originally sold.

		NM	EX	VG
Common Player:		350.00	175.00	100.00
(1)	Hugh Bradley	350.00	175.00	100.00
(2)	Bill Carrigan	350.00	175.00	100.00
(3)	Ed Cicotte	1,000	500.00	300.00
(4)	Ray Collins	350.00	175.00	100.00
(5)	Clyde Engle	350.00	175.00	100.00
(6)	Larry Gardner	350.00	175.00	100.00
(7)	Charley Hall	350.00	175.00	100.00
(8)	Harry Hooper	750.00	375.00	225.00
(9)	Ben Hunt	350.00	175.00	100.00
(10)	Duffy Lewis	500.00	250.00	150.00
(11)	Tom Madden	350.00	175.00	100.00
(12)	Doc Moskiman	350.00	175.00	100.00
(13)	Harry Smith	350.00	175.00	100.00
(14)	Tris Speaker	1,000	500.00	300.00
(15)	Jake Stahl	350.00	175.00	100.00
(16)	Heinie Wagner	350.00	175.00	100.00

1912 Boston Red Sox Tattoos

This set of tattoos is similar to a number of other issues of the era, most of which were made in Germany. This issue features members of the World Champion Boston Red Sox. Approximately 1-3/8" x 1-3/4", the tattoos are printed in mirror-image in bright colors. Images are crude line art with no resemblance to the actual players. Players are identified at bottom by at least a last name. A position is designated in the background of the picture. These items were issued on a perforated sheet. "Collins" may represent retired Red Sox Jimmy Collins or 1912 pitcher Ray Collins. The unnumbered tattoos are listed here alphabetically, though the listing may not be complete.

	NM	EX	VG
Complete Set (13):	475.00	235.00	140.00

		NM	EX	VG
Common Player:		35.00	17.50	10.00
(1)	Hugh Bedient	35.00	17.50	10.00
(2)	Hick Cady	35.00	17.50	10.00
(3)	Collins	35.00	17.50	10.00
(4)	Clyde Engle	35.00	17.50	10.00
(5)	Charley Hall	35.00	17.50	10.00
(6)	Martin Krug	35.00	17.50	10.00
(7)	Jerry McCarthy (Mascot)	35.00	17.50	10.00
(8)	Les Nunamaker	35.00	17.50	10.00
(9)	Larry Pape	35.00	17.50	10.00
(10)	Tris Speaker	125.00	65.00	35.00
(11)	Jake Stahl	35.00	17.50	10.00
(12)	Heinie Wagner	35.00	17.50	10.00
(13)	Joe Wood	50.00	25.00	15.00

1940 Boston Red Sox Photo Pack

Approximately 6" x 9", these blank-backed, black-and-white pictures depict the BoSox in (usually) neck-to-cap poses. The pictures are bordered in white and there is a facsimile autograph on each photo.

		NM	EX	VG
Complete Set (25):		300.00	150.00	75.00
Common Player:		8.00	4.00	2.50
(1)	Jim Bagby	8.00	4.00	2.50
(2)	Bill Butland	8.00	4.00	2.50
(3)	Tom Carey	8.00	4.00	2.50
(4)	Doc Cramer	8.00	4.00	2.50
(5)	Joe Cronin	15.00	7.50	4.50
(6)	Gene Desautels	8.00	4.00	2.50
(7)	Emerson Dickman	8.00	4.00	2.50
(8)	Dom DiMaggio	15.00	7.50	4.50
(9)	Bobby Doerr	15.00	7.50	4.50
(10)	Lou Finney	8.00	4.00	2.50
(11)	Jimmie Foxx	35.00	17.50	10.00
(12)	Denny Galehouse	8.00	4.00	2.50
(13)	Joe Glenn	8.00	4.00	2.50
(14)	Lefty Grove	30.00	15.00	9.00
(15)	Mickey Harris	8.00	4.00	2.50
(16)	Herbie Hash	8.00	4.00	2.50
(17)	Joe Heving	8.00	4.00	2.50
(18)	Leo Nonnenkamp	8.00	4.00	2.50
(19)	Fritz Ostermueller	8.00	4.00	2.50
(20)	Mickey Owen	8.00	4.00	2.50
(21)	John Peacock	8.00	4.00	2.50
(22)	Jim Tabor	8.00	4.00	2.50
(23)	Charles Wagner	8.00	4.00	2.50
(24)	Ted Williams	60.00	30.00	18.00
(25)	Jack Wilson	8.00	4.00	2.50

1941 Boston Red Sox Photo Pack

Approximately 6" x 9", these blank-back, black-and-white pictures depict the BoSox in informal poses, most leaning on the dugout top step. The pictures are bordered in white and there is a facsimile autograph on each photo. It is possible this checklist (arranged alphabetically) is incomplete as other players may have been added to or deleted from the set to conform to roster changes during the season.

		NM	EX	VG
Complete Set (25):		200.00	100.00	60.00
Common Player:		8.00	4.00	2.50
(1)	Paul Campbell	8.00	4.00	2.50
(2)	Tom Carey	8.00	4.00	2.50
(3)	Joe Cronin	20.00	10.00	6.00
(4)	Emerson Dickman	8.00	4.00	2.50
(5)	Dom DiMaggio	15.00	7.50	4.50
(6)	Joe Dobson	8.00	4.00	2.50
(7)	Bobby Doerr	12.00	6.00	3.50
(8)	Lou Finney	8.00	4.00	2.50
(9)	Bill Fleming	8.00	4.00	2.50
(10)	Pete Fox	8.00	4.00	2.50
(11)	Jimmie Foxx	30.00	15.00	9.00
(12)	Lefty Grove	25.00	12.50	7.50
(13)	Mickey Harris	8.00	4.00	2.50
(14)	Tex Hughson	8.00	4.00	2.50
(15)	Earl Johnson	8.00	4.00	2.50
(16)	Lefty Judd	8.00	4.00	2.50
(17)	Dick Newsome	8.00	4.00	2.50
(18)	Skeeter Newsome	8.00	4.00	2.50
(19)	John Peacock	8.00	4.00	2.50
(20)	Frank Pytlak	8.00	4.00	2.50
(21)	Mike Ryba	8.00	4.00	2.50
(22)	Stan Spence	8.00	4.00	2.50
(23)	Jim Tabor	8.00	4.00	2.50
(24)	Charlie Wagner	8.00	4.00	2.50
(25)	Ted Williams	50.00	25.00	15.00
(26)	Jack Wilson	8.00	4.00	2.50

1942 Boston Red Sox Photo Pack

In a format of approximately 6-1/2" x 9", these team-issued player portraits are blank-backed, black-and-white with a white border. Most photos are chest-to-cap presentations and all have a facsimile autograph. Some of the players in the

---

issue can be seen wearing the "HEALTH" patch which MLB adopted during World War II. This checklist may not be complete as it is possible some players were added or deleted from the set to reflect mid-season roster moves.

		NM	EX	VG
Complete Set (25):		275.00	135.00	85.00
Common Player:		10.00	5.00	3.00
(1)	Mace Brown	10.00	5.00	3.00
(2)	Bill Butland	10.00	5.00	3.00
(3)	Paul Campbell	10.00	5.00	3.00
(4)	Tom Carey	10.00	5.00	3.00
(5)	Ken Chase	10.00	5.00	3.00
(6)	Bill Conroy	10.00	5.00	3.00
(7)	Joe Cronin	20.00	10.00	6.00
(8)	Dom DiMaggio	20.00	10.00	6.00
(9)	Joe Dobson	10.00	5.00	3.00
(10)	Bobby Doerr	20.00	10.00	6.00
(11)	Lou Finney	10.00	5.00	3.00
(12)	Pete Fox	10.00	5.00	3.00
(13)	Jimmie Foxx	40.00	20.00	12.00
(14)	Tex Hughson	10.00	5.00	3.00
(15)	Oscar Judd	10.00	5.00	3.00
(16)	Tony Lupien	10.00	5.00	3.00
(17)	Dick Newsome	10.00	5.00	3.00
(18)	Skeeter Newsome	10.00	5.00	3.00
(19)	John Peacock	10.00	5.00	3.00
(20)	Johnny Pesky	10.00	5.00	3.00
(21)	Mike Ryba	10.00	5.00	3.00
(22)	Jim Tabor	10.00	5.00	3.00
(23)	Yank Terry	10.00	5.00	3.00
(24)	Charlie Wagner	10.00	5.00	3.00
(25)	Ted Williams	60.00	30.00	18.00

1943 Boston Red Sox Photo Pack

In a format of approximately 6-1/2" x 9", these team-issued player portraits are blank-backed, black-and-white with a white border. Most photos are chest-to-cap presentations and all have a facsimile autograph. Some of the players in the issue can be seen wearing the "HEALTH" patch which MLB adopted during World War II. This checklist may not be complete as it is possible some players were added or deleted from the set to reflect mid-season roster moves.

		NM	EX	VG
Complete Set (24):		125.00	65.00	40.00
Common Player:		8.00	4.00	2.50
(1)	Mace Brown	8.00	4.00	2.50
(2)	Ken Chase	8.00	4.00	2.50
(3)	Bill Conroy	8.00	4.00	2.50
(4)	Joe Cronin	15.00	7.50	4.50
(5)	Joe Dobson	8.00	4.00	2.50
(6)	Bobby Doerr	15.00	7.50	4.50
(7)	Pete Fox	8.00	4.00	2.50
(8)	Ford Garrison	8.00	4.00	2.50
(9)	Tex Hughson	8.00	4.00	2.50
(10)	Oscar Judd	8.00	4.00	2.50
(11)	Andy Karl	8.00	4.00	2.50
(12)	Eddie Lake	8.00	4.00	2.50
(13)	John Lazor	8.00	4.00	2.50
(14)	Lou Lucier	10.00	5.00	3.00
(15)	Tony Lupien	8.00	4.00	2.50
(16)	Dee Miles	8.00	4.00	2.50
(17)	Dick Newsome	8.00	4.00	2.50
(18)	Skeeter Newsome	8.00	4.00	2.50
(19)	Roy Partee	8.00	4.00	2.50
(20)	John Peacock	8.00	4.00	2.50
(21)	Mike Ryba	8.00	4.00	2.50
(22)	Al Simmons	15.00	7.50	4.50
(23)	Jim Tabor	8.00	4.00	2.50
(24)	Yank Terry	8.00	4.00	2.50

1946 Boston Red Sox Photo Pack

The American League champion Red Sox are featured in this team-issue photo pack. The player portraits are printed in black-and-white on heavy paper in 6-1/2" x 9" format. The photos have a white border and a facsimile autograph on front. Backs are blank. The unnumbered pictures are listed here in alphabetical order.

		NM	EX	VG
Complete Set (25):		225.00	110.00	65.00
Common Player:		6.00	3.00	1.75
(1)	Ernie Andres	6.00	3.00	1.75
(2)	Jim Bagby	6.00	3.00	1.75
(3)	Mace Brown	6.00	3.00	1.75
(4)	Joe Cronin	12.00	6.00	3.50
(5)	Leon Culbertston	6.00	3.00	1.75
(6)	Mel Deutsch	6.00	3.00	1.75
(7)	Dom DiMaggio	10.00	5.00	3.00
(8)	Joe Dobson	6.00	3.00	1.75
(9)	Bobby Doerr	12.00	6.00	3.50
(10)	Boo Ferriss	6.00	3.00	1.75
(11)	Mickey Harris	6.00	3.00	1.75
(12)	Randy Heflin	6.00	3.00	1.75
(13)	Tex Hughson	6.00	3.00	1.75
(14)	Earl Johnson	6.00	3.00	1.75
(15)	Ed McGah	6.00	3.00	1.75
(16)	George Metkovich	6.00	3.00	1.75
(17)	Roy Partee	6.00	3.00	1.75
(18)	Eddie Pellagrini	6.00	3.00	1.75
(19)	Johnny Pesky	7.50	3.75	2.25
(20)	Rip Russell	6.00	3.00	1.75
(21)	Mike Ryba	6.00	3.00	1.75
(22)	Charlie Wagner	6.00	3.00	1.75
(23)	Hal Wagner	6.00	3.00	1.75
(24)	Ted Williams	60.00	30.00	18.00
(25)	Rudy York	6.00	3.00	1.75

1947 Boston Red Sox Photo Pack

In the same 6-1/2" x 9" format which the team had used for its photo packs since 1942, this set of black-and-white, blank-back pictures features (usually) chest-to-cap portraits with white borders, a dark background and a facsimile autograph within the picture. Some of the photos were re-used from previous years' issues, or were re-issued in subsequent years. The unnumbered pictures are checklisted here in alphabetical order. This list may or may not be complete; it is possible other players' photos were added or deleted to reflect seasonal roster changes.

		NM	EX	VG
Complete Set (25):		200.00	100.00	60.00
Common Player:		6.00	3.00	1.75
(1)	Joe Cronin	15.00	7.50	4.50
(2)	Leon Culberson	6.00	3.00	1.75
(3)	Dom DiMaggio	12.50	6.25	3.75
(4)	Joseph Dobson	6.00	3.00	1.75
(5)	Bobby Doerr	15.00	7.50	4.50
(6)	Harry Dorish	6.00	3.00	1.75
(7)	Dave "Boo" Ferriss	6.00	3.00	1.75
(8)	Tommy Fine	6.00	3.00	1.75
(9)	Don Gutteridge	6.00	3.00	1.75
(10)	Mickey Harris	6.00	3.00	1.75
(11)	Tex Hughson	6.00	3.00	1.75
(12)	Earl Johnson	6.00	3.00	1.75
(13)	Bob Klinger	6.00	3.00	1.75
(14)	Sam Mele	6.00	3.00	1.75
(15)	Wally Moses	6.00	3.00	1.75
(16)	Johnny Murphy	6.00	3.00	1.75
(17)	Mel Parnell	6.00	3.00	1.75
(18)	Roy Partee	6.00	3.00	1.75
(19)	Eddie Pellagrini	6.00	3.00	1.75
(20)	Johnny Pesky	7.50	3.75	2.25
(21)	Rip Russell	6.00	3.00	1.75
(22)	Birdie Tebbetts	6.00	3.00	1.75
(23)	Ted Williams	60.00	30.00	18.00
(24)	Rudy York	6.00	3.00	1.75
(25)	Bill Zuber	6.00	3.00	1.75

1948 Boston Red Sox Photo Pack

In the same 6-1/2" x 9" format which the team had used for its photo packs since 1942, this set of black-and-white, blank-back pictures features (usually) chest-to-cap portraits with white borders, a dark background and a facsimile autograph within the picture. Some of the photos were re-used from previous years' issues, or were re-issued in subsequent years. The unnumbered pictures are checklisted here in alphabetical order. This list may or may not be complete; it is possible other players' photos were added or deleted to reflect seasonal roster changes.

		NM	EX	VG
Complete Set (25):		200.00	100.00	60.00
Common Player:		6.00	3.00	1.75
(1)	Matt Batts	6.00	3.00	1.75
(2)	Dom DiMaggio	15.00	7.50	4.50
(3)	Joseph Dobson	6.00	3.00	1.75
(4)	Bobby Doerr	15.00	7.50	4.50
(5)	Harry Dorish	6.00	3.00	1.75
(6)	Dave "Boo" Ferriss	6.00	3.00	1.75
(7)	Dennis Galehouse	6.00	3.00	1.75
(8)	Billy Goodman	6.00	3.00	1.75
(9)	Mickey Harris	6.00	3.00	1.75
(10)	Bill Hitchcock	6.00	3.00	1.75
(11)	Earl Johnson	6.00	3.00	1.75
(12)	Jake Jones	6.00	3.00	1.75
(13)	Ellis Kinder	6.00	3.00	1.75
(14)	Jack Kramer	6.00	3.00	1.75
(15)	Joe McCarthy	15.00	7.50	4.50
(16)	Maurice McDermott	6.00	3.00	1.75
(17)	Sam Mele	6.00	3.00	1.75
(18)	Wally Moses	6.00	3.00	1.75
(19)	Mel Parnell	6.00	3.00	1.75
(20)	Johnny Pesky	7.50	3.75	2.25
(21)	Stan Spence	6.00	3.00	1.75
(22)	Vern Stephens	6.00	3.00	1.75
(23)	Chuck Stobbs	6.00	3.00	1.75
(24)	Birdie Tebbetts	6.00	3.00	1.75
(25)	Ted Williams	60.00	30.00	18.00

1949 Boston Red Sox Photo Pack

In the same 6-1/2" x 9" format the team used for its photo packs since 1942, this set of black-and-white, blank-back pictures features (usually) chest-to-cap portraits with white borders, a dark background and a facsimile autograph within the picture. Some of the photos were re-used from previous years' issues, or were re-issued in subsequent years. The unnumbered pictures are checklisted here in alphabetical order.

		NM	EX	VG
Complete Set (25):		200.00	100.00	60.00
Common Player:		6.00	3.00	1.80
(1)	Matt Batts	6.00	3.00	1.80
(2)	Merrill Combs	6.00	3.00	1.80
(3)	Dom DiMaggio	15.00	7.50	4.50
(4)	Joe Dobson	6.00	3.00	1.80
(5)	Bobby Doerr	15.00	7.50	4.50
(6)	David "Boo" Ferris	6.00	3.00	1.80
(7)	Bill Goodman	6.00	3.00	1.80
(8)	Mickey Harris	6.00	3.00	1.80
(9)	Billy Hitchcock	6.00	3.00	1.80
(10)	Tex Hughson	6.00	3.00	1.80
(11)	Earl Johnson	6.00	3.00	1.80
(12)	Ellis Kinder	6.00	3.00	1.80
(13)	Jack Kramer	6.00	3.00	1.80
(14)	Joe McCarthy	15.00	7.50	4.50
(15)	Sam Mele	6.00	3.00	1.80
(16)	Tommy O'Brien	6.00	3.00	1.80
(17)	Mel Parnell	6.00	3.00	1.80
(18)	Johnny Pesky	6.00	3.00	1.80
(19)	Frank Quinn	6.00	3.00	1.80
(20)	Vern Stephens	6.00	3.00	1.80
(21)	Chuck Stobbs	6.00	3.00	1.80
(22)	Lou Stringer	6.00	3.00	1.80
(23)	Birdie Tebbetts	6.00	3.00	1.80
(24)	Ted Williams	60.00	30.00	18.00
(25)	Al Zarilla	6.00	3.00	1.80

1950 Boston Red Sox Photo Pack

In the same approximately 6-1/2" x 9" format which the team had used for its photo packs since the 1940s, this set of black-and-white, blank-back pictures features chest-to-cap portraits with white borders, a dark background and a facsimile autograph within the photo. Some of the photos were re-used from previous years' issues. The unnumbered pictures are checklisted here in alphabetical order. This list may or may not be complete; it is possible other players' photos were added or deleted to reflect seasonal roster changes.

		NM	EX	VG
Complete Set (25):		150.00	75.00	40.00
Common Player:		4.00	2.00	1.25
(1)	Matt Batts	4.00	2.00	1.25
(2)	Earle Combs	7.50	3.75	2.25
(3)	Dom DiMaggio	9.00	4.50	2.75
(4)	Joe Dobson	4.00	2.00	1.25
(5)	Bobby Doerr	9.00	4.50	2.75
(6)	Walt Dropo	12.00	6.00	3.50
(7)	Bill Goodman	4.00	2.00	1.25
(8)	Earl Johnson	4.00	2.00	1.25
(9)	Ken Keltner	4.00	2.00	1.25
(10)	Ellis Kinder	4.00	2.00	1.25
(11)	Walt Masterson	4.00	2.00	1.25
(12)	Joe McCarthy	9.00	4.50	2.75
(13)	Maurice McDermott	4.00	2.00	1.25
(14)	Al Papai	4.00	2.00	1.25
(15)	Mel Parnell	4.00	2.00	1.25
(16)	Johnny Pesky	4.00	2.00	1.25
(17)	Buddy Rosar	4.00	2.00	1.25
(18)	Charley Schanz	4.00	2.00	1.25
(19)	Vern Stephens	4.00	2.00	1.25
(20)	Chuck Stobbs	4.00	2.00	1.25
(21)	Lou Stringer	4.00	2.00	1.25
(22)	Birdie Tebbetts	4.00	2.00	1.25
(23)	Ted Williams	30.00	15.00	9.00
(24)	Tom Wright	4.00	2.00	1.25
(25)	Al Zarilla	4.00	2.00	1.25

1953 Boston Red Sox Photo Pack

In the same approximately 6-1/2" x 9" format which the team had used for its photo packs since the 1940s, this set of black-and-white, blank-back pictures features (usually) chest-to-cap portraits with white borders and a facsimile autograph within the photo. Some of the photos were re-used from previous years' issues. The unnumbered pictures are checklisted here in alphabetical order. This list may or may not be complete; it is possible other players' photos were added or deleted to reflect seasonal roster changes.

		NM	EX	VG
Complete Set (30):		120.00	60.00	35.00
Common Player:		4.00	2.00	1.25
(1)	Milt Bolling	4.00	2.00	1.25
(2)	Lou Boudreau	9.00	4.50	2.75
(3)	Harold Brown	4.00	2.00	1.25
(4)	Bill Consolo	4.00	2.00	1.25
(5)	Dom DiMaggio	15.00	7.50	4.50
(6)	Hoot Evers	4.00	2.00	1.25
(7)	Ben Flowers	4.00	2.00	1.25
(8)	Hershell Freeman	4.00	2.00	1.25
(9)	Dick Gernert	4.00	2.00	1.25
(10)	Bill Goodman	4.00	2.00	1.25
(11)	Marv Grissom	4.00	2.00	1.25

		NM	EX	VG
(12)	Ken Holcombe	4.00	2.00	1.25
(13)	Sid Hudson	4.00	2.00	1.25
(14)	George Kell	9.00	4.50	2.75
(15)	Bill Kennedy	4.00	2.00	1.25
(16)	Ellis Kinder	4.00	2.00	1.25
(17)	Ted Lepcio	4.00	2.00	1.25
(18)	Johnny Lipon	4.00	2.00	1.25
(19)	Maurice McDermott	4.00	2.00	1.25
(20)	John Merson	4.00	2.00	1.25
(21)	Gus Niarhos	4.00	2.00	1.25
(22)	Willard Nixon	4.00	2.00	1.25
(23)	Mel Parnell	4.00	2.00	1.25
(24)	Jim Piersall	6.00	3.00	1.75
(25)	Gene Stephens	4.00	2.00	1.25
(26)	Tommy Umphlett	4.00	2.00	1.25
(27)	Bill Werle	4.00	2.00	1.25
(28)	Sam White	4.00	2.00	1.25
(29)	Del Wilber	4.00	2.00	1.25
(30)	Al Zarilla	4.00	2.00	1.25

1954 Boston Red Sox Photo Pack

In the same approximately 6-1/2" x 9" format which the team had used for its photo packs since the 1940s, this set of black-and-white, blank-back pictures features (usually) chest-to-cap portraits with white borders and a facsimile autograph within the photo. Some of the photos were re-used from previous years' issues. The unnumbered pictures are checklisted here in alphabetical order. This list may or may not be complete; it is possible other players' photos were added or deleted to reflect seasonal roster changes. The set was sold in a red and white paper envelope.

		NM	EX	VG
Complete Set (30):		125.00	62.50	37.50
Common Player:		4.00	2.00	1.25
(1)	Harry Agganis	15.00	7.50	4.50
(2)	Milt Bolling	4.00	2.00	1.25
(3)	Lou Boudreau	9.00	4.50	2.75
(4)	Tom Brewer	4.00	2.00	1.25
(5)	Harold Brown	4.00	2.00	1.25
(6)	Truman Clevenger	4.00	2.00	1.25
(7)	Bill Consolo	4.00	2.00	1.25
(8)	Joe Dobson	4.00	2.00	1.25
(9)	Hoot Evers	4.00	2.00	1.25
(10)	Dick Gernert	4.00	2.00	1.25
(11)	Bill Goodman	4.00	2.00	1.25
(12)	Bill Henry	4.00	2.00	1.25
(13)	Tom Herrin	4.00	2.00	1.25
(14)	Sid Hudson	4.00	2.00	1.25
(15)	Jackie Jensen	6.00	3.00	1.75
(16)	George Kell	9.00	4.50	2.75
(17)	Leo Kiely	4.00	2.00	1.25
(18)	Ellis Kinder	4.00	2.00	1.25
(19)	Ted Lepcio	4.00	2.00	1.25
(20)	Charlie Maxwell	4.00	2.00	1.25
(21)	Willard Nixon	4.00	2.00	1.25
(22)	Karl Olsen	4.00	2.00	1.25
(23)	Mickey Owen	4.00	2.00	1.25
(24)	Mel Parnell	4.00	2.00	1.25
(25)	Jim Piersall	6.00	3.00	1.75
(26)	Frank Sullivan	4.00	2.00	1.25
(27)	Bill Werle	4.00	2.00	1.25
(28)	Sammy White	4.00	2.00	1.25
(29)	Ted Williams	30.00	15.00	9.00
(30)	Del Wilber	4.00	2.00	1.25

1957 Boston Red Sox Photo Pack

JIMMY PIERSALL

In approximately the same 5" x 7" black-and-white, blank-back format as the later Jay Publishing issues, this team issue is distinguished by the lack of a team name in the bottom border. Some of the photos were re-used in the following year's issue. Sets were originally sold in a manila envelope for 25 cents.

		NM	EX	VG
Complete Set (12):		45.00	22.00	13.50
Common Player:		3.00	1.50	.90
(1)	Tom Brewer	3.00	1.50	.90
(2)	Dick Gernert	3.00	1.50	.90
(3)	Mike Higgins	3.00	1.50	.90
(4)	Jackie Jensen	4.50	2.25	1.25
(5)	Frank Malzone	3.00	1.50	.90
(6)	Gene Mauch	4.50	2.25	1.25
(7)	Jimmy Piersall	4.50	2.25	1.25
(8)	Dave Sisler	3.00	1.50	.90
(9)	Frank Sullivan	3.00	1.50	.90
(10)	Mickey Vernon	3.00	1.50	.90
(11)	Sammy White	3.00	1.50	.90
(12)	Ted Williams	20.00	10.00	6.00

1958 Boston Red Sox Photo Pack

In approximately the same 5" x 7" black-and-white, blank-back format as the contemporary Jay Publishing issues, this team issue is distinguished by the lack of a team name in the bottom border. Some of the photos were re-used from the previous year's issue. Sets were originally sold in a manila envelope for 25 cents.

		NM	EX	VG
Complete Set (12):		45.00	22.00	13.50
Common Player:		3.00	1.50	.90
(1)	Ken Aspromonte	3.00	1.50	.90
(2)	Tom Brewer	3.00	1.50	.90
(3)	Mike Higgins	3.00	1.50	.90
(4)	Jack Jensen	4.50	2.25	1.25
(5)	Frank Malzone	3.00	1.50	.90
(6)	Will Nixon	3.00	1.50	.90
(7)	Jim Piersall	4.50	2.25	1.25
(8)	Pete Runnels	3.00	1.50	.90
(9)	Gene Stephens	3.00	1.50	.90
(10)	Frank Sullivan	3.00	1.50	.90
(11)	Sam White	3.00	1.50	.90
(12)	Ted Williams	20.00	10.00	6.00

1959 Boston Red Sox Photo Pack

In approximately the same 5" x 7" black-and-white, blank-back format as the contemporary Jay Publishing issues, this team issue is distinguished by the lack of a team name in the bottom border. Some of the photos were re-used from the previous years' issues. Sets were originally sold in a manila envelope for 25 cents.

		NM	EX	VG
Complete Set (12):		45.00	22.00	13.50
Common Player:		3.00	1.50	.90
(1)	Tom Brewer	3.00	1.50	.90
(2)	Don Buddin	3.00	1.50	.90
(3)	Dick Gernert	3.00	1.50	.90
(4)	Mike Higgins	3.00	1.50	.90
(5)	Jack Jensen	4.50	2.25	1.25
(6)	Frank Malzone	3.00	1.50	.90
(7)	Jim Piersall	4.50	2.25	1.25
(8)	Pete Runnels	3.00	1.50	.90
(9)	Gene Stephens	3.00	1.50	.90
(10)	Frank Sullivan	3.00	1.50	.90
(11)	Sam White	3.00	1.50	.90
(12)	Ted Williams	20.00	10.00	6.00

1960 Boston Red Sox Photo Pack

In approximately the same 5" x 7" black-and-white, blank-back format as the contemporary Jay Publishing issues, this team issue is distinguished by the lack of a team name in the bottom border. Some of the photos were re-used from the previous years' issues. Sets were originally sold in a manila envelope for 25 cents. The fact that more than 12 players are known indicates there were some changes in specific contents over the course of the season to reflect roster changes.

		NM	EX	VG
Complete Set (14):		50.00	25.00	15.00
Common Player:		3.00	1.50	.90
(1)	Tom Brewer	3.00	1.50	.90
(2)	Don Buddin	3.00	1.50	.90
(3)	Jerry Casale	3.00	1.50	.90
(4)	Ike Delock	3.00	1.50	.90
(5)	Pumpsie Green	3.00	1.50	.90
(6)	Bill Jurges	3.00	1.50	.90
(7)	Frank Malzone	3.00	1.50	.90
(8)	Pete Runnels	3.00	1.50	.90
(9)	Ed Sadowski	3.00	1.50	.90
(10)	Gene Stephens	3.00	1.50	.90
(11)	Willie Tasby	3.00	1.50	.90
(12)	Bobby Thomson	3.00	1.50	.90
(13)	Vic Wertz	3.00	1.50	.90
(14)	Ted Williams	20.00	10.00	6.00

1968 Boston Red Sox Team Issue

About 5-1/2" x 7-1/2", these black-and-white player pictures have posed photos, bordered in white, with a facsimile autograph. Backs are blank. The alphabetized checklist here is likely incomplete.

		NM	EX	VG
Complete Set (8):		15.00	7.50	4.50
Common Player:		2.00	1.00	.60
(1a)	Mike Andrews ("B" on cap.)	2.00	1.00	.60
(1b)	Mike Andrews (No "B.")	2.00	1.00	.60
(2)	Darrell Brandon	2.00	1.00	.60
(3)	Bobby Doerr	3.00	1.50	.90
(4)	Ken Harrelson	2.50	1.25	.70
(5)	Jim Lonborg	2.50	1.25	.70
(6)	Rico Petrocelli	3.00	1.50	.90
(7)	Reggie Smith	2.50	1.25	.70
(8)	Dick Williams	2.00	1.00	.60

1969 Boston Red Sox Team Issue

This team-issue photo pack features black-and-white portrait photos on a 4-1/4" x 7" blank-back format, similar to the team's 1971 issue. The player's name and team nickname are designated in the white border at top. The unnumbered cards are checklisted here in alphabetical order.

		NM	EX	VG
Complete Set (12):		60.00	30.00	15.00
Common Player:		4.00	2.00	1.25
(1)	Mike Andrews	4.00	2.00	1.25
(2)	Tony Conigliaro	9.00	4.50	2.75
(3)	Russ Gibson	4.00	2.00	1.25
(4)	Dalton Jones	4.00	2.00	1.25
(5)	Bill Landis	4.00	2.00	1.25
(6)	Jim Lonborg	5.00	2.50	1.50
(7)	Sparky Lyle	4.00	2.00	1.25
(8)	Rico Petrocelli	5.00	2.50	1.50
(9)	George Scott	5.00	2.50	1.50
(10)	Reggie Smith	4.00	2.00	1.25
(11)	Dick Williams	4.00	2.00	1.25
(12)	Carl Yastrzemski	15.00	7.50	4.50

1978 Boston Red Sox of the 1950s-1960s

The date of actual issue, the name of the issuer and even the "official" title of this collectors' edition card set is currently unknown. The 2-1/2" x 3-1/2" cards are printed in black-and-white on front and backs. Fronts have the style of the 1953 Bowmans, with only a player photo and a white border. Backs are reminiscent of the 1955 Bowman, with player identification, career highlights, stats and a Red Sox trivia question. Cards #1-64 concentrate on the 1950s, cards #65-128 feature 1960s players.

		NM	EX	VG
Complete Set (128):		100.00	50.00	30.00
Common Player:		4.00	2.00	1.25
1	Harry Agganis	12.00	6.00	3.50
2	Ken Aspromonte	4.00	2.00	1.25
3	Bobby Avila	4.00	2.00	1.25
4	Frank Baumann	4.00	2.00	1.25
5	Lou Berberet	4.00	2.00	1.25
6	Milt Bolling	4.00	2.00	1.25
7	Lou Boudreau	6.00	3.00	1.75
8	Ted Bowsfield	4.00	2.00	1.25
9	Tom Brewer	4.00	2.00	1.25
10	Don Buddin	4.00	2.00	1.25
11	Jerry Casale	4.00	2.00	1.25
12	Billy Consolo	4.00	2.00	1.25
13	Pete Daley	4.00	2.00	1.25
14	Ike Delock	4.00	2.00	1.25
15	Dom DiMaggio	9.00	4.50	2.75
16	Bobby Doerr	6.00	3.00	1.75
17	Walt Dropo	5.00	2.50	1.50
18	Arnie Earley	4.00	2.00	1.25
19	Hoot Evers	4.00	2.00	1.25
20	Mike Fornieles	4.00	2.00	1.25
21	Gary Geiger	4.00	2.00	1.25
22	Don Gile	4.00	2.00	1.25
23	Joe Ginsberg	4.00	2.00	1.25
24	Billy Goodman	4.00	2.00	1.25
25	Pumpsie Green	4.00	2.00	1.25
26	Grady Hatton	4.00	2.00	1.25
27	Billy Herman	5.00	2.50	1.50
28	Jackie Jensen	5.00	2.50	1.50
29	George Kell	6.00	3.00	1.75
30	Marty Keough	4.00	2.00	1.25
31	Leo Kiely	4.00	2.00	1.25
32	Ellis Kinder	4.00	2.00	1.25
33	Billy Klaus	4.00	2.00	1.25
34	Don Lenhardt	4.00	2.00	1.25
35	Ted Lepcio	4.00	2.00	1.25
36	Frank Malzone	4.00	2.00	1.25
37	Gene Mauch	4.00	2.00	1.25
38	Maury McDermott	4.00	2.00	1.25
39	Bill Monbouquette	4.00	2.00	1.25
40	Chet Nichols	4.00	2.00	1.25
41	Willard Nixon	4.00	2.00	1.25

42	Jim Pagliaroni	4.00	2.00	1.25
43	Mel Parnell	4.00	2.00	1.25
44	Johnny Pesky	4.00	2.00	1.25
45	Jimmy Piersall	5.00	2.50	1.50
46	Bob Porterfield	4.00	2.00	1.25
47	Pete Runnels	4.00	2.00	1.25
48	Dave Sisler	4.00	2.00	1.25
49	Riverboat Smith	4.00	2.00	1.25
50	Gene Stephens	4.00	2.00	1.25
51	Vern Stephens	4.00	2.00	1.25
52	Chuck Stobbs	4.00	2.00	1.25
53	Dean Stone	4.00	2.00	1.25
54	Frank Sullivan	4.00	2.00	1.25
55	Haywood Sullivan	4.00	2.00	1.25
56	Birdie Tebbetts	4.00	2.00	1.25
57	Mickey Vernon	4.00	2.00	1.25
58	Vic Wertz	4.00	2.00	1.25
59	Sammy White	4.00	2.00	1.25
60	Ted Williams	20.00	10.00	6.00
61	Ted Wills	4.00	2.00	1.25
62	Earl Wilson	4.00	2.00	1.25
63	Al Zarilla	4.00	2.00	1.25
64	Norm Zauchin	4.00	2.00	1.25
65	Ted Williams, Carl Yastrzemski	12.00	6.00	3.50
66	Dick Williams, Carl Yastrzemski, Jim Lonborg, George Scott	10.00	5.00	3.00
67	Tony Conigliaro, Billy Conigliaro	9.00	4.50	2.75
68	Jerry Adair	4.00	2.00	1.25
69	Mike Andrews	4.00	2.00	1.25
70	Gary Bell	4.00	2.00	1.25
71	Dennis Bennett	4.00	2.00	1.25
72	Ed Bressoud	4.00	2.00	1.25
73	Ken Brett	4.00	2.00	1.25
74	Lu Clinton	4.00	2.00	1.25
75	Billy Conigliaro	5.00	2.50	1.50
76	Tony Conigliaro	6.00	3.00	1.75
77	Gene Conley	4.00	2.00	1.25
78	Ray Culp	4.00	2.00	1.25
79	Dick Ellsworth	4.00	2.00	1.25
80	Joe Foy	4.00	2.00	1.25
81	Russ Gibson	4.00	2.00	1.25
82	Jim Gosger	4.00	2.00	1.25
83	Lennie Green	4.00	2.00	1.25
84	Ken Harrelson	4.00	2.00	1.25
85	Tony Horton	4.00	2.00	1.25
86	Elston Howard	5.00	2.50	1.50
87	Dalton Jones	4.00	2.00	1.25
88	Eddie Kasko	4.00	2.00	1.25
89	Joe Lahoud	4.00	2.00	1.25
90	Jack Lamabe	4.00	2.00	1.25
91	Jim Lonborg	5.00	2.50	1.50
92	Sparky Lyle	5.00	2.50	1.50
93	Felix Mantilla	4.00	2.00	1.25
94	Roman Mejias	4.00	2.00	1.25
95	Don McMahon	4.00	2.00	1.25
96	Dave Morehead	4.00	2.00	1.25
97	Gerry Moses	4.00	2.00	1.25
98	Mike Nagy	4.00	2.00	1.25
99	Russ Nixon	4.00	2.00	1.25
100	Gene Oliver	4.00	2.00	1.25
101	Dan Osinski	4.00	2.00	1.25
102	Rico Petrocelli	5.00	2.50	1.50
103	Juan Pizarro	4.00	2.00	1.25
104	Dick Radatz	4.00	2.00	1.25
105	Vicente Romo	4.00	2.00	1.25
106	Mike Ryan	4.00	2.00	1.25
107	Jose Santiago	4.00	2.00	1.25
108	Chuck Schilling	4.00	2.00	1.25
109	Dick Schofield	4.00	2.00	1.25
110	Don Schwall	4.00	2.00	1.25
111	George Scott	4.00	2.00	1.25
112	Norm Siebern	4.00	2.00	1.25
113	Sonny Seibert	4.00	2.00	1.25
114	Reggie Smith	4.00	2.00	1.25
115	Bill Spanswick	4.00	2.00	1.25
116	Tracy Stallard	4.00	2.00	1.25
117	Lee Stange	4.00	2.00	1.25
118	Jerry Stephenson	4.00	2.00	1.25
119	Dick Stuart	4.00	2.00	1.25
120	Tom Sturdivant	4.00	2.00	1.25
121	Jose Tartabull	4.00	2.00	1.25
122	George Thomas	4.00	2.00	1.25
123	Lee Thomas	4.00	2.00	1.25
124	Bob Tillman	4.00	2.00	1.25
125	Gary Waslewski	4.00	2.00	1.25
126	Dick Williams	4.00	2.00	1.25
127	John Wyatt	4.00	2.00	1.25
128	Carl Yastrzemski	12.00	6.00	3.50

1979 Boston Red Sox Team Issue

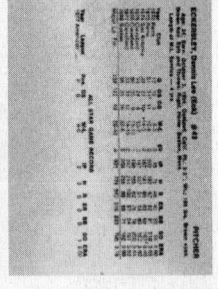

The origins of this Boston Red Sox card set are unclear. It may have been a team issue. The wide white bottom border beneath the black-and-white photo on the 2-1/2" x 3-1/2" cards

may have been intended for autographing. Backs have player personal data and complete major and minor league stats. The checklist here, listed alphabetically, may not be complete.

		NM	EX	VG
Complete Set (24):		50.00	25.00	15.00
Common Player:		3.00	1.50	.90
(1)	Gary Allenson	3.00	1.50	.90
(2)	Jack Brohamer	3.00	1.50	.90
(3)	Tom Burgmeier	3.00	1.50	.90
(4)	Rick Burleson	3.00	1.50	.90
(5)	Bill Campbell	3.00	1.50	.90
(6)	Dick Drago	3.00	1.50	.90
(7)	Dennis Eckersley	12.00	6.00	3.50
(8)	Dwight Evans	4.50	2.25	1.25
(9)	Carlton Fisk	15.00	7.50	4.50
(10)	Andy Hassler	3.00	1.50	.90
(11)	Butch Hobson	3.00	1.50	.90
(12)	Fred Lynn	7.50	3.75	2.25
(13)	Bob Montgomery	3.00	1.50	.90
(14)	Mike O'Berry	3.00	1.50	.90
(15)	Jerry Remy	3.00	1.50	.90
(16)	Steve Renko	3.00	1.50	.90
(17)	Jim Rice	7.50	3.75	2.25
(18)	George Scott	4.50	2.25	1.25
(19)	Bob Stanley	3.00	1.50	.90
(20)	Mike Torrez	3.00	1.50	.90
(21)	Larry Wolfe	3.00	1.50	.90
(22)	Jim Wright	3.00	1.50	.90
(23)	Carl Yastrzemski	20.00	10.00	6.00
(24)	Gary Hancock, Stan Papi (Two-sided.)	3.00	1.50	.90

1917 Boston Store

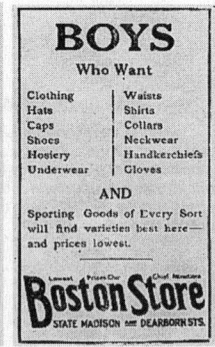

One of several regional advertisers to use this 200-card set as a promotional medium was this Chicago department store. While variations are known of cards #76, 90, 121, 146, and 190 in the Collins-McCarthy ad-back version of this set, it is unclear whether those variations also exist in the Boston Store issue. The American Card Catalog listed these 2" x 3-1/4" black-and-white cards as H801-8.

		NM	EX	VG
Complete Set (200):		80,000	40,000	24,000
Common Player:		150.00	75.00	45.00
1	Sam Agnew	150.00	75.00	45.00
2	Grover Alexander	800.00	400.00	240.00
3	W.S. Alexander (W.E.)	150.00	75.00	45.00
4	Leon Ames	150.00	75.00	45.00
5	Fred Anderson	150.00	75.00	45.00
6	Ed Appleton	150.00	75.00	45.00
7	Jimmy Archer	150.00	75.00	45.00
8	Jimmy Austin	150.00	75.00	45.00
9	Jim Bagby	150.00	75.00	45.00
10	H.D. Baird	150.00	75.00	45.00
11	J. Franklin Baker	600.00	300.00	180.00
12	Dave Bancroft	600.00	300.00	180.00
13	Jack Barry	150.00	75.00	45.00
14	Joe Benz	150.00	75.00	45.00
15	Al Betzel	150.00	75.00	45.00
16	Ping Bodie	150.00	75.00	45.00
17	Joe Boehling	150.00	75.00	45.00
18	Eddie Burns	150.00	75.00	45.00
19	George Burns	150.00	75.00	45.00
20	Geo. J. Burns	150.00	75.00	45.00
21	Joe Bush	150.00	75.00	45.00
22	Owen Bush	150.00	75.00	45.00
23	Bobby Byrne	150.00	75.00	45.00
24	Forrest Cady	150.00	75.00	45.00
25	Max Carey	600.00	300.00	180.00
26	Ray Chapman	200.00	100.00	60.00
27	Larry Cheney	150.00	75.00	45.00
28	Eddie Cicotte	900.00	450.00	275.00
29	Tom Clarke	150.00	75.00	45.00
30	Ty Cobb	6,500	3,200	1,950
31	Eddie Collins	600.00	300.00	180.00
32	"Shauno" Collins (Shano)	150.00	75.00	45.00
33	Fred Coumbe	150.00	75.00	45.00
34	Harry Coveleskie (Coveleski)	150.00	75.00	45.00
35	Gavvy Cravath	150.00	75.00	45.00
36	Sam Crawford	600.00	300.00	180.00
37	Geo. Cutshaw	150.00	75.00	45.00
38	Jake Daubert	150.00	75.00	45.00
39	Geo. Dauss	150.00	75.00	45.00
40	Charles Deal	150.00	75.00	45.00
41	"Wheezer" Dell	150.00	75.00	45.00
42	William Doak	150.00	75.00	45.00
43	Bill Donovan	150.00	75.00	45.00
44	Larry Doyle	150.00	75.00	45.00
45	Johnny Evers	600.00	300.00	180.00
46	Urban Faber	600.00	300.00	180.00
47	"Hap" Felsch	1,500	750.00	450.00
48	Bill Fischer	150.00	75.00	45.00
49	Ray Fisher	150.00	75.00	45.00

50	Art Fletcher	150.00	75.00	45.00
51	Eddie Foster	150.00	75.00	45.00
52	Jacques Fournier	150.00	75.00	45.00
53	Del Gainer (Gainor)	150.00	75.00	45.00
54	Bert Gallia	150.00	75.00	45.00
55	"Chic" Gandil (Chick)	450.00	225.00	135.00
56	Larry Gardner	150.00	75.00	45.00
57	Joe Gedeon	150.00	75.00	45.00
58	Gus Getz	150.00	75.00	45.00
59	Frank Gilhooley	150.00	75.00	45.00
60	Wm. Gleason	150.00	75.00	45.00
61	M.A. Gonzales (Gonzalez)	200.00	100.00	60.00
62	Hank Gowdy	150.00	75.00	45.00
63	John Graney	150.00	75.00	45.00
64	Tom Griffith	150.00	75.00	45.00
65	Heinie Groh	150.00	75.00	45.00
66	Bob Groom	150.00	75.00	45.00
67	Louis Guisto	150.00	75.00	45.00
68	Earl Hamilton	150.00	75.00	45.00
69	Harry Harper	150.00	75.00	45.00
70	Grover Hartley	150.00	75.00	45.00
71	Harry Heilmann	600.00	300.00	180.00
72	Claude Hendrix	150.00	75.00	45.00
73	Olaf Henriksen	150.00	75.00	45.00
74	John Henry	150.00	75.00	45.00
75	"Buck" Herzog	150.00	75.00	45.00
76a	Hugh High (White stockings, photo actually Claude Williams.)	800.00	400.00	240.00
76b	Hugh High (Black stockings, correct photo.)	200.00	100.00	60.00
77	Dick Hoblitzell	150.00	75.00	45.00
78	Walter Holke	150.00	75.00	45.00
79	Harry Hooper	600.00	300.00	180.00
80	Rogers Hornsby	750.00	375.00	225.00
81	Ivan Howard	150.00	75.00	45.00
82	Joe Jackson	30,000	15,000	9,000
83	Harold Janvrin	150.00	75.00	45.00
84	William James	150.00	75.00	45.00
85	C. Jamieson	150.00	75.00	45.00
86	Hugh Jennings	600.00	300.00	180.00
87	Walter Johnson	1,100	550.00	330.00
88	James Johnston	150.00	75.00	45.00
89	Fielder Jones	150.00	75.00	45.00
90a	Joe Judge (Bat on right shoulder, photo actually Ray Morgan.)	800.00	400.00	240.00
90b	Joe Judge (Bat on left shoulder, correct photo.)	200.00	100.00	60.00
91	Hans Lobert	150.00	75.00	45.00
92	Benny Kauff	150.00	75.00	45.00
93	Wm. Killefer Jr.	150.00	75.00	45.00
94	Ed. Konetchy	150.00	75.00	45.00
95	John Lavan	150.00	75.00	45.00
96	Jimmy Lavender	150.00	75.00	45.00
97	"Nemo" Leibold	150.00	75.00	45.00
98	H.B. Leonard	150.00	75.00	45.00
99	Duffy Lewis	150.00	75.00	45.00
100	Tom Long	150.00	75.00	45.00
101	Wm. Louden	150.00	75.00	45.00
102	Fred Luderus	150.00	75.00	45.00
103	Lee Magee	150.00	75.00	45.00
104	Sherwood Magee	150.00	75.00	45.00
105	Al Mamaux	150.00	75.00	45.00
106	Leslie Mann	150.00	75.00	45.00
107	"Rabbit" Maranville	600.00	300.00	180.00
108	Rube Marquard	600.00	300.00	180.00
109	Armando Marsans	240.00	120.00	72.00
110	J. Erskine Mayer	150.00	75.00	45.00
111	George McBride	150.00	75.00	45.00
112	Lew McCarty	150.00	75.00	45.00
113	John J. McGraw	600.00	300.00	180.00
114	Jack McInnis	150.00	75.00	45.00
115	Lee Meadows	150.00	75.00	45.00
116	Fred Merkle	150.00	75.00	45.00
117	"Chief" Meyers	150.00	75.00	45.00
118	Clyde Milan	150.00	75.00	45.00
119	Otto Miller	150.00	75.00	45.00
120	Clarence Mitchell	150.00	75.00	45.00
121a	Ray Morgan (Bat on left shoulder, photo actually Joe Judge.)	800.00	400.00	240.00
121b	Ray Morgan (Bat on right shoulder, correct photo.)	200.00	100.00	60.00
122	Guy Morton	150.00	75.00	45.00
123	"Mike" Mowrey	150.00	75.00	45.00
124	Elmer Myers	150.00	75.00	45.00
125	"Hy" Myers	150.00	75.00	45.00
126	A.E. Neale	300.00	150.00	90.00
127	Arthur Nehf	150.00	75.00	45.00
128	J.A. Niehoff	150.00	75.00	45.00
129	Steve O'Neill	150.00	75.00	45.00
130	"Dode" Paskert	150.00	75.00	45.00
131	Roger Peckinpaugh	200.00	100.00	60.00
132	"Pol" Perritt	150.00	75.00	45.00
133	"Jeff" Pfeffer	150.00	75.00	45.00
134	Walter Pipp	150.00	75.00	45.00
135	Derril Pratt (Derrill)	150.00	75.00	45.00
136	Bill Rariden	150.00	75.00	45.00
137	E.C. Rice	600.00	300.00	180.00
138	Wm. A. Ritter (Wm. H.)	150.00	75.00	45.00
139	Eppa Rixey	600.00	300.00	180.00
140	Davey Robertson	150.00	75.00	45.00
141	"Bob" Roth	150.00	75.00	45.00
142	Ed. Roush	600.00	300.00	180.00
143	Clarence Rowland	150.00	75.00	45.00
144	Dick Rudolph	150.00	75.00	45.00
145	William Rumler	150.00	75.00	45.00
146a	Reb Russell (Pitching follow-thru, photo actually Mellie Wolfgang.)	800.00	400.00	240.00
146b	Reb Russell (Hands at side, correct photo.)	200.00	100.00	60.00
147	"Babe" Ruth	25,000	12,500	7,500
148	Vic Saier	150.00	75.00	45.00
149	"Slim" Sallee	150.00	75.00	45.00
150	Ray Schalk	600.00	300.00	180.00
151	Walter Schang	150.00	75.00	45.00

#	Player	NM	EX	VG
152	Frank Schulte	150.00	75.00	45.00
153	Ferd Schupp	150.00	75.00	45.00
154	Everett Scott	150.00	75.00	45.00
155	Hank Severeid	150.00	75.00	45.00
156	Howard Shanks	150.00	75.00	45.00
157	Bob Shawkey	150.00	75.00	45.00
158	Jas. Sheckard	150.00	75.00	45.00
159	Ernie Shore	150.00	75.00	45.00
160	C.H. Shorten	150.00	75.00	45.00
161	Burt Shotton	150.00	75.00	45.00
162	Geo. Sisler	800.00	400.00	240.00
163	Elmer Smith	150.00	75.00	45.00
164	J. Carlisle Smith	150.00	75.00	45.00
165	Fred Snodgrass	150.00	75.00	45.00
166	Tris Speaker	750.00	375.00	225.00
167	Oscar Stanage	150.00	75.00	45.00
168	Charles Stengel	600.00	300.00	180.00
169	Milton Stock	150.00	75.00	45.00
170	Amos Strunk	150.00	75.00	45.00
171	"Zeb" Terry	150.00	75.00	45.00
172	"Jeff" Tesreau	150.00	75.00	45.00
173	Chester Thomas	150.00	75.00	45.00
174	Fred Toney	150.00	75.00	45.00
175	Terry Turner	150.00	75.00	45.00
176	George Tyler	150.00	75.00	45.00
177	Jim Vaughn	150.00	75.00	45.00
178	Bob Veach	150.00	75.00	45.00
179	Oscar Vitt	150.00	75.00	45.00
180	Hans Wagner	3,000	1,500	900.00
181	Clarence Walker	150.00	75.00	45.00
182	Jim Walsh	150.00	75.00	45.00
183	Al Walters	150.00	75.00	45.00
184	W. Wambsganss	150.00	75.00	45.00
185	Buck Weaver	1,200	600.00	350.00
186	Carl Weilman	150.00	75.00	45.00
187	Zack Wheat	600.00	300.00	180.00
188	Geo. Whitted	150.00	75.00	45.00
189	Joe Wilhoit	150.00	75.00	45.00
190a	Claude Williams (Black stockings, photo actually Hugh High.)	1,200	600.00	350.00
190b	Claude Williams (White stockings, correct photo.)	1,500	750.00	450.00
191	Fred Williams	150.00	75.00	45.00
192	Art Wilson	150.00	75.00	45.00
193	Lawton Witt	150.00	75.00	45.00
194	Joe Wood	200.00	100.00	60.00
195	William Wortman	150.00	75.00	45.00
196	Steve Yerkes	150.00	75.00	45.00
197	Earl Yingling	150.00	75.00	45.00
198	"Pep" Young (Photo actually Ralph Young.)	150.00	75.00	45.00
199	Rollie Zeider	150.00	75.00	45.00
200	Henry Zimmerman	150.00	75.00	45.00

1909 Boston Sunday Post Red Sox Stars

Members of the Boston American League team are presented in this series of Sunday supplements from one of the city's daily newspapers. Measuring about 8" x 10", and possibly having been issued in two-page spreads, the blank-back pieces combine artist's renderings of action photos with circular portraits about 2-3/8" in diameter, printed in sepia tones. At bottom is printed the player name, team, position and a caption for the picture, along with the newspaper's credit line. It is possible this checklist is incomplete since a few of the team's stars have yet to be reported.

		NM	EX	VG
Common Player:		150.00	75.00	45.00
(1)	Frank Arellanes	150.00	75.00	45.00
(2)	William Carrigan	150.00	75.00	45.00
(3)	Charles Chech	150.00	75.00	45.00
(4)	Edward Cicotte	250.00	125.00	75.00
(5)	Harry Hooper	250.00	125.00	75.00
(6)	Harry Lord	150.00	75.00	45.00
(7)	Ambrose McConnell	150.00	75.00	45.00
(8)	Harry Niles	150.00	75.00	45.00
(9)	Tris Speaker	300.00	150.00	90.00
(10)	Edward Spencer	150.00	75.00	45.00
(11)	Garland Stahl	150.00	75.00	45.00
(12)	Harry Wolter	150.00	75.00	45.00

1972 Bowery Bank Joe DiMaggio

These cards were issued to promote the New York City bank's relationship with spokesman Joe DiMaggio. The 2-1/2" x 3-1/2" cards have a posed color photo on front. The back has a black-and-white portrait, biographical data, career highlights and stats on a pink background.

	NM	EX	VG
Joe DiMaggio	17.50	9.00	5.00

1948 Bowman

Bowman Gum Co.'s premiere set of 1948 was one of the first major issues of the post-war period. Forty-eight black-and-white cards comprise the set, with each card measuring 2-1/16" x 2-1/2". The card backs, printed in black ink on gray stock, include the card number and the player's name, team, position, and a short biography. Twelve cards (marked with an "SP") were printed in short supply when they were removed from the 36-card printing sheet to make room for the set's high numbers (#37-48).

#	Player	NM	EX	VG
	Complete Set (48):	5,000	2,500	1,500
	Common Player (1-36):	60.00	30.00	18.00
	Common Player (37-48):	60.00	30.00	18.00
1	Bob Elliott	150.00	60.00	18.00
2	Ewell Blackwell	140.00	70.00	40.00
3	Ralph Kiner	300.00	150.00	90.00
4	Johnny Mize	170.00	84.50	50.00
5	Bob Feller	450.00	220.00	130.00
6	Yogi Berra	700.00	350.00	210.00
7	Pete Reiser/SP	300.00	150.00	90.00
8	Phil Rizzuto/SP	550.00	270.00	160.00
9	Walker Cooper	60.00	30.00	18.00
10	Buddy Rosar	60.00	30.00	18.00
11	Johnny Lindell	60.00	30.00	18.00
12	Johnny Sain	140.00	70.00	40.00
13	Willard Marshall/SP	120.00	60.00	36.00
14	Allie Reynolds	130.00	64.50	40.00
15	Eddie Joost	60.00	30.00	18.00
16	Jack Lohrke/SP	120.00	60.00	36.00
17	Enos Slaughter	210.00	100.00	60.00
18	Warren Spahn	500.00	250.00	150.00
19	Tommy Henrich	120.00	60.00	36.00
20	Buddy Kerr/SP	120.00	60.00	36.00
21	Ferris Fain	80.00	40.00	24.00
22	Floyd (Bill) Bevens/SP	120.00	60.00	36.00
23	Larry Jansen	60.00	30.00	18.00
24	Emil (Dutch) Leonard/SP	120.00	60.00	36.00
25	Barney McCoskey (McCosky)	60.00	30.00	18.00
26	Frank Shea/SP	60.00	30.00	36.00
27	Sid Gordon	60.00	30.00	18.00
28	Emil Verban/SP	120.00	60.00	36.00
29	Joe Page/SP	250.00	130.00	70.00
30	Whitey Lockman/SP	150.00	75.00	45.00
31	Bill McCahan	60.00	30.00	18.00
32	Bill Rigney	60.00	30.00	18.00
33	Billy Johnson	60.00	30.00	18.00
34	Sheldon Jones/SP	120.00	60.00	36.00
35	Snuffy Stirnweiss	60.00	30.00	18.00
36	Stan Musial	1,200	600.00	350.00
37	Clint Hartung	120.00	60.00	36.00
38	Red Schoendienst	400.00	200.00	120.00
39	Augie Galan	120.00	60.00	36.00
40	Marty Marion	200.00	100.00	60.00
41	Rex Barney	170.00	85.00	50.00
42	Ray Poat	120.00	60.00	36.00
43	Bruce Edwards	160.00	80.00	48.00
44	Johnny Wyrostek	120.00	60.00	36.00
45	Hank Sauer	120.00	60.00	36.00
46	Herman Wehmeier	120.00	60.00	36.00
47	Bobby Thomson	280.00	140.00	80.00
48	Dave Koslo	400.00	80.00	36.00

1949 Bowman

In 1949, Bowman increased the size of its issue to 240 numbered cards. The 2-1/16" x 2-1/2" cards are black-and-white photos overprinted with team uniform colors on a background of various solid pastel colors. Beginning with card #109 in the set, Bowman added the players' names on the card fronts. Twelve cards (#4, 78, 83, 85, 88, 98, 109, 124, 127, 132 and 143), which were produced in the first four series of printings, were reprinted in the seventh series with either a card front or back modification. These variations are noted in

the checklist. Cards #1-3 and 5-73 can be found with either white or gray backs. The complete set value shown here does not include the higher priced variation cards.

#	Player	NM	EX	VG
	Complete Set (240):	18,000	9,000	5,500
	Common Player (1-144):	20.00	10.00	6.00
	Common Player (145-240):	50.00	25.00	15.00
1	Vernon Bickford	200.00	15.00	9.00
2	"Whitey" Lockman	20.00	10.00	6.00
3	Bob Porterfield	20.00	10.00	6.00
4a	Jerry Priddy (No name on front.)	20.00	10.00	6.00
4b	Jerry Priddy (Name on front.)	60.00	30.00	18.00
5	Hank Sauer	20.00	10.00	6.00
6	Phil Cavarretta	20.00	10.00	6.00
7	Joe Dobson	20.00	10.00	6.00
8	Murry Dickson	20.00	10.00	6.00
9	Ferris Fain	20.00	10.00	6.00
10	Ted Gray	20.00	10.00	6.00
11	Lou Boudreau	60.00	30.00	18.00
12	Cass Michaels	20.00	10.00	6.00
13	Bob Chesnes	20.00	10.00	6.00
14	Curt Simmons	50.00	25.00	15.00
15	Ned Garver	30.00	15.00	9.00
16	Al Kozar	20.00	10.00	6.00
17	Earl Torgeson	20.00	10.00	6.00
18	Bobby Thomson	65.00	32.50	20.00
19	Bobby Brown	75.00	37.50	22.50
20	Gene Hermanski	20.00	10.00	6.00
21	Frank Baumholtz	20.00	10.00	6.00
22	Harry "P-Nuts" Lowrey	20.00	10.00	6.00
23	Bobby Doerr	60.00	30.00	18.00
24	Stan Musial	425.00	180.00	100.00
25	Carl Scheib	20.00	10.00	6.00
26	George Kell	65.00	32.50	20.00
27	Bob Feller	275.00	135.00	82.50
28	Don Kolloway	20.00	10.00	6.00
29	Ralph Kiner	95.00	47.50	27.50
30	Andy Seminick	20.00	10.00	6.00
31	Dick Kokos	20.00	10.00	6.00
32	Eddie Yost	20.00	10.00	6.00
33	Warren Spahn	250.00	125.00	62.50
34	Dave Koslo	20.00	10.00	6.00
35	Vic Raschi	100.00	50.00	30.00
36	Pee Wee Reese	225.00	112.50	56.75
37	John Wyrostek	20.00	10.00	6.00
38	Emil Verban	20.00	10.00	6.00
39	Bill Goodman	20.00	10.00	6.00
40	"Red" Munger	20.00	10.00	6.00
41	Lou Brissie	20.00	10.00	6.00
42	"Hoot" Evers	20.00	10.00	6.00
43	Dale Mitchell	20.00	10.00	6.00
44	Dave Philley	20.00	10.00	6.00
45	Wally Westlake	20.00	10.00	6.00
46	Robin Roberts	250.00	125.00	62.50
47	Johnny Sain	50.00	25.00	15.00
48	Willard Marshall	20.00	10.00	6.00
49	Frank Shea	30.00	15.00	9.00
50	Jackie Robinson	1,250	625.00	375.00
51	Herman Wehmeier	20.00	10.00	6.00
52	Johnny Schmitz	20.00	10.00	6.00
53	Jack Kramer	20.00	10.00	6.00
54	Marty Marion	35.00	17.50	10.00
55	Eddie Joost	20.00	10.00	6.00
56	Pat Mullin	20.00	10.00	6.00
57	Gene Bearden	20.00	10.00	6.00
58	Bob Elliott	20.00	10.00	6.00
59	Jack Lohrke	20.00	10.00	6.00
60	Yogi Berra	350.00	175.00	87.50
61	Rex Barney	25.00	12.50	7.50
62	Grady Hatton	20.00	10.00	6.00
63	Andy Pafko	20.00	10.00	6.00
64	Dom DiMaggio	75.00	37.50	22.50
65	Enos Slaughter	80.00	40.00	24.00
66	Elmer Valo	20.00	10.00	6.00
67	Alvin Dark	50.00	25.00	15.00
68	Sheldon Jones	20.00	10.00	6.00
69	Tommy Henrich	55.00	27.50	16.50
70	Carl Furillo	150.00	75.00	37.50
71	Vern Stephens	20.00	10.00	6.00
72	Tommy Holmes	20.00	10.00	6.00
73	Billy Cox	45.00	22.50	13.50
74	Tom McBride	20.00	10.00	6.00
75	Eddie Mayo	20.00	10.00	6.00
76	Bill Nicholson	20.00	10.00	6.00
77	Ernie Bonham	20.00	10.00	6.00
78a	Sam Zoldak (No name on front.)	20.00	10.00	6.00
78b	Sam Zoldak (Name on front.)	60.00	30.00	18.00
79	Ron Northey	20.00	10.00	6.00
80	Bill McCahan	20.00	10.00	6.00
81	Virgil "Red" Stallcup	20.00	10.00	6.00
82	Joe Page	35.00	17.50	10.00
83a	Bob Scheffing (No name on front.)	20.00	10.00	6.00
83b	Bob Scheffing (Name on front.)	60.00	30.00	18.00
84	Roy Campanella	575.00	290.00	175.00
85a	Johnny Mize (No name on front.)	85.00	42.50	25.00

		NM	EX	VG
85b	Johnny Mize (Name on front.)	120.00	60.00	36.00
86	Johnny Pesky	20.00	10.00	6.00
87	Randy Gumpert	20.00	10.00	6.00
88a	Bill Salkeld (No name on front.)	20.00	10.00	6.00
88b	Bill Salkeld (Name on front.)	60.00	30.00	18.00
89	Mizell Platt	20.00	10.00	6.00
90	Gil Coan	20.00	10.00	6.00
91	Dick Wakefield	20.00	10.00	6.00
92	Willie Jones	20.00	10.00	6.00
93	Ed Stevens	20.00	10.00	6.00
94	*Mickey Vernon*	30.00	15.00	9.00
95	Howie Pollett	20.00	10.00	6.00
96	Taft Wright	20.00	10.00	6.00
97	Danny Litwhiler	20.00	10.00	6.00
98a	Phil Rizzuto (No name on front.)	275.00	137.50	68.75
98b	Phil Rizzuto (Name on front.)	280.00	190.00	85.00
99	Frank Gustine	20.00	10.00	6.00
100	*Gil Hodges*	300.00	150.00	75.00
101	Sid Gordon	25.00	12.50	7.50
102	Stan Spence	20.00	10.00	6.00
103	Joe Tipton	20.00	10.00	6.00
104	*Ed Stanky*	35.00	17.50	10.00
105	Bill Kennedy	20.00	10.00	6.00
106	Jake Early	20.00	10.00	6.00
107	Eddie Lake	20.00	10.00	6.00
108	Ken Heintzelman	20.00	10.00	6.00
109a	Ed Fitz Gerald (Script name on back.)	20.00	10.00	6.00
109b	Ed Fitz Gerald (Printed name on back.)	60.00	30.00	18.00
110	*Early Wynn*	150.00	75.00	37.50
111	Red Schoendienst	80.00	40.00	24.00
112	Sam Chapman	20.00	10.00	6.00
113	Ray Lamanno	20.00	10.00	6.00
114	Allie Reynolds	65.00	32.50	20.00
115	Emil "Dutch" Leonard	20.00	10.00	6.00
116	Joe Hatten	20.00	10.00	6.00
117	Walker Cooper	20.00	10.00	6.00
118	Sam Mele	20.00	10.00	6.00
119	Floyd Baker	20.00	10.00	6.00
120	Cliff Fannin	20.00	10.00	6.00
121	Mark Christman	20.00	10.00	6.00
122	George Vico	20.00	10.00	6.00
123	Johnny Blatnick	20.00	10.00	6.00
124a	Danny Murtaugh (Script name on back.)	20.00	10.00	6.00
124b	Danny Murtaugh (Printed name on back.)	60.00	30.00	18.00
125	Ken Keltner	20.00	10.00	6.00
126a	Al Brazle (Script name on back.)	20.00	10.00	6.00
126b	Al Brazle (Printed name on back.)	60.00	30.00	18.00
127a	Henry Majeski (Script name on back.)	20.00	10.00	6.00
127b	Henry Majeski (Printed name on back.)	60.00	30.00	18.00
128	Johnny Vander Meer	35.00	17.50	10.00
129	Billy Johnson	30.00	15.00	9.00
130	Harry "The Hat" Walker	25.00	12.50	7.50
131	Paul Lehner	20.00	10.00	6.00
132a	Al Evans (Script name on back.)	20.00	10.00	6.00
132b	Al Evans (Printed name on back.)	60.00	30.00	18.00
133	Aaron Robinson	20.00	10.00	6.00
134	Hank Borowy	20.00	10.00	6.00
135	Stan Rojek	20.00	10.00	6.00
136	Hank Edwards	20.00	10.00	6.00
137	Ted Wilks	20.00	10.00	6.00
138	"Buddy" Rosar	20.00	10.00	6.00
139	Hank "Bow-Wow" Arft	20.00	10.00	6.00
140	Ray Scarborough	20.00	10.00	6.00
141	"Tony" Lupien	20.00	10.00	6.00
142	Eddie Waitkus	20.00	10.00	6.00
143a	Bob Dillinger (Script name on back.)	20.00	10.00	6.00
143b	Bob Dillinger (Printed name on back.)	60.00	30.00	18.00
144	Mickey Haefner	20.00	10.00	6.00
145	"Blix" Donnelly	50.00	25.00	15.00
146	Mike McCormick	55.00	27.50	16.50
147	Elmer Singleton	50.00	25.00	15.00
148	Bob Swift	50.00	25.00	15.00
149	Roy Partee	60.00	30.00	18.00
150	Allie Clark	50.00	25.00	15.00
151	Mickey Harris	50.00	25.00	15.00
152	Clarence Maddern	50.00	25.00	15.00
153	Phil Masi	50.00	25.00	15.00
154	Clint Hartung	50.00	25.00	15.00
155	Mickey Guerra	50.00	25.00	15.00
156	Al Zarilla	50.00	25.00	15.00
157	Walt Masterson	50.00	25.00	15.00
158	Harry Brecheen	50.00	25.00	15.00
159	Glen Moulder	50.00	25.00	15.00
160	Jim Blackburn	50.00	25.00	15.00
161	"Jocko" Thompson	50.00	25.00	15.00
162	*Preacher Roe*	120.00	60.00	30.00
163	Clyde McCullough	50.00	25.00	15.00
164	*Vic Wertz*	70.00	35.00	20.00
165	"Snuffy" Stirnweiss	60.00	30.00	18.00
166	Mike Tresh	50.00	25.00	15.00
167	Boris "Babe" Martin	50.00	25.00	15.00
168	Doyle Lade	50.00	25.00	15.00
169	Jeff Heath	50.00	25.00	15.00
170	Bill Rigney	50.00	25.00	15.00
171	Dick Fowler	50.00	25.00	15.00
172	Eddie Pellagrini	50.00	25.00	15.00
173	Eddie Stewart	50.00	25.00	15.00
174	*Terry Moore*	125.00	65.00	35.00
175	Luke Appling	140.00	70.00	35.00
176	Ken Raffensberger	50.00	25.00	15.00
177	Stan Lopata	50.00	25.00	15.00
178	Tommy Brown	55.00	27.50	16.50
179	Hugh Casey	55.00	27.50	16.50
180	Connie Berry	50.00	25.00	15.00
181	Gus Niarhos	50.00	25.00	15.00
182	Hal Peck	50.00	25.00	15.00
183	Lou Stringer	50.00	25.00	15.00
184	Bob Chipman	50.00	25.00	15.00
185	Pete Reiser	70.00	35.00	20.00
186	"Buddy" Kerr	50.00	25.00	15.00
187	Phil Marchildon	50.00	25.00	15.00
188	Karl Drews	50.00	25.00	15.00
189	Earl Wooten	50.00	25.00	15.00
190	*Jim Hearn*	60.00	30.00	18.00
191	Joe Haynes	50.00	25.00	15.00
192	Harry Gumbert	50.00	25.00	15.00
193	Ken Trinkle	50.00	25.00	15.00
194	Ralph Branca	95.00	47.50	27.50
195	Eddie Bockman	50.00	25.00	15.00
196	Fred Hutchinson	50.00	25.00	15.00
197	Johnny Lindell	60.00	30.00	18.00
198	Steve Gromek	50.00	25.00	15.00
199	"Tex" Hughson	50.00	25.00	15.00
200	Jess Dobernic	50.00	25.00	15.00
201	Sibby Sisti	50.00	25.00	15.00
202	Larry Jansen	50.00	25.00	15.00
203	Barney McCosky	50.00	25.00	15.00
204	Bob Savage	50.00	25.00	15.00
205	Dick Sisler	50.00	25.00	15.00
206	Bruce Edwards	55.00	27.50	16.50
207	Johnny Hopp	50.00	25.00	15.00
208	"Dizzy" Trout	50.00	25.00	15.00
209	Charlie Keller	85.00	42.50	25.00
210	Joe Gordon	50.00	25.00	15.00
211	Dave "Boo" Ferris	50.00	25.00	15.00
212	Ralph Hamner	50.00	25.00	15.00
213	Charles "Red" Barrett	50.00	25.00	15.00
214	*Richie Ashburn*	600.00	300.00	180.00
215	Kirby Higbe	50.00	25.00	15.00
216	"Schoolboy" Rowe	50.00	25.00	15.00
217	Marino Pieretti	50.00	25.00	15.00
218	Dick Kryhoski	50.00	25.00	15.00
219	*Virgil "Fire" Trucks*	60.00	30.00	18.00
220	Johnny McCarthy	50.00	25.00	15.00
221	Bob Muncrief	50.00	25.00	15.00
222	Alex Kellner	50.00	25.00	15.00
223	Bob Hofman	50.00	25.00	15.00
224	*Satchel Paige*	1,450	725.00	435.00
225	*Gerry Coleman*	100.00	50.00	30.00
226	*Duke Snider*	1,000	500.00	300.00
227	Fritz Ostermueller	50.00	25.00	15.00
228	Jackie Mayo	50.00	25.00	15.00
229	*Ed Lopat*	100.00	50.00	30.00
230	Augie Galan	50.00	25.00	15.00
231	Earl Johnson	50.00	25.00	15.00
232	George McQuinn	50.00	25.00	15.00
233	*Larry Doby*	300.00	150.00	75.00
234	"Rip" Sewell	50.00	25.00	15.00
235	Jim Russell	50.00	25.00	15.00
236	Fred Sanford	60.00	30.00	18.00
237	Monte Kennedy	50.00	25.00	15.00
238	*Bob Lemon*	200.00	100.00	50.00
239	Frank McCormick	50.00	25.00	15.00
240	Norm "Babe" Young (Photo actually Bobby Young.)	125.00	30.00	15.00

1950 Bowman

The quality of the 1950 Bowman issue showed a marked improvement over the company's previous efforts. The cards are color art reproductions of actual photographs and measure 2-1/16" x 2-1/2". Backs include the same type of information found in the previous year's issue but are designed in a horizontal format. Cards found in the first two series (#1-72) are the scarcer of the issue. The backs of the final 72 cards (#181-252) can be found with or without the copyright line at the bottom of the card, the "without" version being the less common.

		NM	EX	VG
	Complete Set (252):	12,500	6,000	3,500
	Common Player (1-72):	50.00	25.00	15.00
	Common Player (73-252):	20.00	10.00	6.00
1	Mel Parnell	700.00	87.50	43.75
2	Vern Stephens	50.00	25.00	15.00
3	Dom DiMaggio	130.00	65.00	40.00
4	*Gus Zernial*	90.00	45.00	27.50
5	Bob Kuzava	50.00	25.00	15.00
6	Bob Feller	300.00	150.00	90.00
7	Jim Hegan	50.00	25.00	15.00
8	George Kell	125.00	65.00	35.00
9	Vic Wertz	50.00	25.00	15.00
10	Tommy Henrich	75.00	37.50	22.50
11	Phil Rizzuto	325.00	162.50	81.25
12	Joe Page	65.00	32.50	20.00
13	Ferris Fain	50.00	25.00	15.00
14	Alex Kellner	50.00	25.00	15.00
15	Al Kozar	50.00	25.00	15.00
16	*Roy Sievers*	90.00	45.00	27.50
17	Sid Hudson	50.00	25.00	15.00
18	Eddie Robinson	50.00	25.00	15.00
19	Warren Spahn	300.00	150.00	75.00
20	Bob Elliott	50.00	25.00	15.00
21	Pee Wee Reese	300.00	150.00	75.00
22	Jackie Robinson	1,200	600.00	300.00
23	*Don Newcombe*	140.00	70.00	35.00
24	Johnny Schmitz	50.00	25.00	15.00
25	Hank Sauer	50.00	25.00	15.00
26	Grady Hatton	50.00	25.00	15.00
27	Herman Wehmeier	50.00	25.00	15.00
28	Bobby Thomson	100.00	50.00	30.00
29	Ed Stanky	60.00	30.00	18.00
30	Eddie Waitkus	50.00	25.00	15.00
31	*Del Ennis*	80.00	40.00	24.00
32	Robin Roberts	150.00	75.00	37.50
33	Ralph Kiner	125.00	60.00	35.00
34	Murry Dickson	50.00	25.00	15.00
35	Enos Slaughter	125.00	60.00	35.00
36	Eddie Kazak	50.00	25.00	15.00
37	Luke Appling	100.00	50.00	30.00
38	Bill Wight	50.00	25.00	15.00
39	Larry Doby	125.00	62.50	31.25
40	Bob Lemon	125.00	60.00	35.00
41	"Hoot" Evers	50.00	25.00	15.00
42	Art Houtteman	50.00	25.00	15.00
43	Bobby Doerr	100.00	50.00	30.00
44	Joe Dobson	50.00	25.00	15.00
45	Al Zarilla	50.00	25.00	15.00
46	Yogi Berra	400.00	200.00	100.00
47	Jerry Coleman	60.00	30.00	18.00
48	Lou Brissie	50.00	25.00	15.00
49	Elmer Valo	50.00	25.00	15.00
50	Dick Kokos	50.00	25.00	15.00
51	Ned Garver	50.00	25.00	15.00
52	Sam Mele	50.00	25.00	15.00
53	Clyde Vollmer	50.00	25.00	15.00
54	Gil Coan	50.00	25.00	15.00
55	"Buddy" Kerr	50.00	25.00	15.00
56	*Del Crandell* (Crandall)	55.00	27.50	16.50
57	Vernon Bickford	50.00	25.00	15.00
58	Carl Furillo	65.00	32.50	20.00
59	Ralph Branca	60.00	30.00	18.00
60	Andy Pafko	50.00	25.00	15.00
61	Bob Rush	50.00	25.00	15.00
62	Ted Kluszewski	150.00	75.00	45.00
63	Ewell Blackwell	50.00	25.00	15.00
64	Alvin Dark	50.00	25.00	15.00
65	Dave Koslo	50.00	25.00	15.00
66	Larry Jansen	50.00	25.00	15.00
67	Willie Jones	50.00	25.00	15.00
68	Curt Simmons	50.00	25.00	15.00
69	Wally Westlake	50.00	25.00	15.00
70	Bob Chesnes	50.00	25.00	15.00
71	Red Schoendienst	85.00	42.50	25.00
72	Howie Pollet	50.00	25.00	15.00
73	Willard Marshall	20.00	10.00	6.00
74	*Johnny Antonelli*	40.00	20.00	12.00
75	Roy Campanella	300.00	150.00	75.00
76	Rex Barney	25.00	12.50	7.50
77	Duke Snider	300.00	150.00	75.00
78	Mickey Owen	20.00	10.00	6.00
79	Johnny Vander Meer	25.00	12.50	7.50
80	Howard Fox	20.00	10.00	6.00
81	Ron Northey	20.00	10.00	6.00
82	"Whitey" Lockman	20.00	10.00	6.00
83	Sheldon Jones	20.00	10.00	6.00
84	Richie Ashburn	125.00	62.50	31.25
85	Ken Heintzelman	20.00	10.00	6.00
86	Stan Rojek	20.00	10.00	6.00
87	Bill Werle	20.00	10.00	6.00
88	Marty Marion	30.00	15.00	9.00
89	George Munger	20.00	10.00	6.00
90	Harry Brecheen	20.00	10.00	6.00
91	Cass Michaels	20.00	10.00	6.00
92	Hank Majeski	20.00	10.00	6.00
93	Gene Bearden	20.00	10.00	6.00
94	Lou Boudreau	70.00	35.00	20.00
95	Aaron Robinson	20.00	10.00	6.00
96	Virgil "Fire" Trucks	20.00	10.00	6.00
97	Maurice McDermott	20.00	10.00	6.00
98	Ted Williams	1,100	550.00	275.00
99	Billy Goodman	20.00	10.00	6.00
100	Vic Raschi	50.00	25.00	15.00
101	Bobby Brown	55.00	27.50	16.50
102	Billy Johnson	30.00	15.00	9.00
103	Eddie Joost	20.00	10.00	6.00
104	Sam Chapman	20.00	10.00	6.00
105	Bob Dillinger	20.00	10.00	6.00
106	Cliff Fannin	20.00	10.00	6.00
107	Sam Dente	20.00	10.00	6.00
108	Ray Scarborough	20.00	10.00	6.00
109	Sid Gordon	20.00	10.00	6.00
110	Tommy Holmes	20.00	10.00	6.00
111	Walker Cooper	20.00	10.00	6.00
112	Gil Hodges	125.00	60.00	35.00
113	Gene Hermanski	20.00	10.00	6.00
114	*Wayne Terwilliger*	25.00	12.50	7.50
115	Roy Smalley	20.00	10.00	6.00
116	Virgil "Red" Stallcup	20.00	10.00	6.00
117	Bill Rigney	20.00	10.00	6.00
118	Clint Hartung	20.00	10.00	6.00
119	Dick Sisler	20.00	10.00	6.00
120	Jocko Thompson	20.00	10.00	6.00
121	Andy Seminick	20.00	10.00	6.00
122	Johnny Hopp	20.00	10.00	6.00
123	Dino Restelli	20.00	10.00	6.00
124	Clyde McCullough	20.00	10.00	6.00
125	Del Rice	20.00	10.00	6.00
126	Al Brazle	20.00	10.00	6.00
127	Dave Philley	20.00	10.00	6.00
128	Phil Masi	20.00	10.00	6.00
129	Joe Gordon	20.00	10.00	6.00
130	Dale Mitchell	20.00	10.00	6.00
131	Steve Gromek	20.00	10.00	6.00
132	Mickey Vernon	20.00	10.00	6.00
133	Don Kolloway	20.00	10.00	6.00
134	"Dizzy" Trout	20.00	10.00	6.00
135	Pat Mullin	20.00	10.00	6.00
136	"Buddy" Rosar	20.00	10.00	6.00
137	Johnny Pesky	20.00	10.00	6.00
138	Allie Reynolds	60.00	30.00	18.00
139	Johnny Mize	65.00	32.50	20.00

140	Pete Suder	20.00	10.00	6.00
141	Joe Coleman	20.00	10.00	6.00
142	*Sherman Lollar*	25.00	12.50	7.50
143	Eddie Stewart	20.00	10.00	6.00
144	Al Evans	20.00	10.00	6.00
145	Jack Graham	20.00	10.00	6.00
146	Floyd Baker	20.00	10.00	6.00
147	*Mike Garcia*	30.00	15.00	9.00
148	Early Wynn	70.00	35.00	20.00
149	Bob Swift	20.00	10.00	6.00
150	George Vico	20.00	10.00	6.00
151	Fred Hutchinson	20.00	10.00	6.00
152	Ellis Kinder	20.00	10.00	6.00
153	Walt Masterson	20.00	10.00	6.00
154	Gus Niarhos	30.00	15.00	9.00
155	Frank "Spec" Shea	30.00	15.00	9.00
156	Fred Sanford	30.00	15.00	9.00
157	Mike Guerra	20.00	10.00	6.00
158	Paul Lehner	20.00	10.00	6.00
159	Joe Tipton	20.00	10.00	6.00
160	Mickey Harris	20.00	10.00	6.00
161	Sherry Robertson	20.00	10.00	6.00
162	Eddie Yost	20.00	10.00	6.00
163	Earl Torgeson	20.00	10.00	6.00
164	Sibby Sisti	20.00	10.00	6.00
165	Bruce Edwards	25.00	12.50	7.50
166	Joe Hatten	25.00	12.50	7.50
167	Preacher Roe	50.00	25.00	15.00
168	Bob Scheffing	20.00	10.00	6.00
169	Hank Edwards	20.00	10.00	6.00
170	Emil Leonard	20.00	10.00	6.00
171	Harry Gumbert	20.00	10.00	6.00
172	Harry Lowrey	20.00	10.00	6.00
173	Lloyd Merriman	20.00	10.00	6.00
174	*Henry Thompson*	30.00	15.00	9.00
175	Monte Kennedy	20.00	10.00	6.00
176	"Blix" Donnelly	20.00	10.00	6.00
177	Hank Borowy	20.00	10.00	6.00
178	Eddy Fitz Gerald	20.00	10.00	6.00
179	Charles Diering	20.00	10.00	6.00
180	Harry "The Hat" Walker	20.00	10.00	6.00
181	Marino Pieretti	20.00	10.00	6.00
182	Sam Zoldak	20.00	10.00	6.00
183	Mickey Haefner	20.00	10.00	6.00
184	Randy Gumpert	20.00	10.00	6.00
185	Howie Judson	20.00	10.00	6.00
186	Ken Keltner	20.00	10.00	6.00
187	Lou Stringer	20.00	10.00	6.00
188	Earl Johnson	20.00	10.00	6.00
189	Owen Friend	20.00	10.00	6.00
190	Ken Wood	20.00	10.00	6.00
191	Dick Starr	20.00	10.00	6.00
192	Bob Chipman	20.00	10.00	6.00
193	Pete Reiser	30.00	15.00	9.00
194	Billy Cox	35.00	17.50	10.00
195	Phil Cavarretta	20.00	10.00	6.00
196	Doyle Lade	20.00	10.00	6.00
197	Johnny Wyrostek	20.00	10.00	6.00
198	Danny Litwhiler	20.00	10.00	6.00
199	Jack Kramer	20.00	10.00	6.00
200	Kirby Higbe	20.00	10.00	6.00
201	Pete Castiglione	20.00	10.00	6.00
202	Cliff Chambers	20.00	10.00	6.00
203	Danny Murtaugh	20.00	10.00	6.00
204	Granny Hamner	20.00	10.00	6.00
205	Mike Goliat	20.00	10.00	6.00
206	Stan Lopata	20.00	10.00	6.00
207	Max Lanier	20.00	10.00	6.00
208	Jim Hearn	20.00	10.00	6.00
209	Johnny Lindell	20.00	10.00	6.00
210	Ted Gray	20.00	10.00	6.00
211	Charlie Keller	30.00	15.00	9.00
212	Gerry Priddy	20.00	10.00	6.00
213	Carl Scheib	20.00	10.00	6.00
214	Dick Fowler	20.00	10.00	6.00
215	Ed Lopat	50.00	25.00	15.00
216	Bob Porterfield	30.00	15.00	9.00
217	Casey Stengel	70.00	35.00	20.00
218	Cliff Mapes	30.00	15.00	9.00
219	*Hank Bauer*	70.00	35.00	20.00
220	Leo Durocher	60.00	30.00	18.00
221	Don Mueller	20.00	10.00	6.00
222	Bobby Morgan	25.00	12.50	7.50
223	Jimmy Russell	25.00	12.50	7.50
224	Jack Banta	25.00	12.50	7.50
225	Eddie Sawyer	20.00	10.00	6.00
226	*Jim Konstanty*	30.00	15.00	9.00
227	Bob Miller	20.00	10.00	6.00
228	Bill Nicholson	20.00	10.00	6.00
229	Frank Frisch	40.00	20.00	12.00
230	Bill Serena	20.00	10.00	6.00
231	Preston Ward	20.00	10.00	6.00
232	*Al Rosen*	55.00	27.50	16.50
233	Allie Clark	20.00	10.00	6.00
234	*Bobby Shantz*	45.00	22.50	13.50
235	Harold Gilbert	20.00	10.00	6.00
236	Bob Cain	20.00	10.00	6.00
237	Bill Salkeld	20.00	10.00	6.00
238	Nippy Jones	20.00	10.00	6.00
239	Bill Howerton	20.00	10.00	6.00
240	Eddie Lake	20.00	10.00	6.00
241	Neil Berry	20.00	10.00	6.00
242	Dick Kryhoski	20.00	10.00	6.00
243	Johnny Groth	20.00	10.00	6.00
244	Dale Coogan	20.00	10.00	6.00
245	Al Papai	20.00	10.00	6.00
246	*Walt Dropo*	35.00	17.50	10.00
247	*Irv Noren*	30.00	15.00	9.00
248	Sam Jethroe	40.00	20.00	12.00
249	"Snuffy" Stirnweiss	20.00	10.00	6.00
250	Ray Coleman	20.00	10.00	6.00
251	Les Moss	20.00	10.00	6.00
252	Billy DeMars	65.00	20.00	7.50

1951 Bowman

In 1951, Bowman increased the number of cards in its set for the third consecutive year when it issued 324 cards. The

cards are, like 1950, color art reproductions of actual photographs but now measure 2-1/16" x 3-1/8" in size. The player's name is in a black strip on front. Several of the pictures are enlargements of the 1950 version. The high-numbered series (#253-324), which includes the rookie cards of Mantle and Mays, are the scarcest of the issue.

		NM	EX	VG
	Complete Set (324):	20,000	9,500	5,500
	Common Player (1-252):	17.50	9.00	5.00
	Common Player (253-324):	40.00	20.00	12.00
1	*Whitey Ford*	2,000	700.00	275.00
2	Yogi Berra	400.00	200.00	100.00
3	Robin Roberts	100.00	50.00	25.00
4	Del Ennis	17.50	9.00	5.00
5	Dale Mitchell	17.50	9.00	5.00
6	Don Newcombe	50.00	25.00	12.50
7	Gil Hodges	125.00	62.50	31.25
8	Paul Lehner	17.50	9.00	5.00
9	Sam Chapman	17.50	9.00	5.00
10	Red Schoendienst	75.00	37.50	22.50
11	"Red" Munger	17.50	9.00	5.00
12	Hank Majeski	17.50	9.00	5.00
13	Ed Stanky	20.00	10.00	6.00
14	Alvin Dark	17.50	9.00	5.00
15	Johnny Pesky	17.50	9.00	5.00
16	Maurice McDermott	17.50	9.00	5.00
17	Pete Castiglione	17.50	9.00	5.00
18	Gil Coan	17.50	9.00	5.00
19	Sid Gordon	17.50	9.00	5.00
20	Del Crandall	17.50	9.00	5.00
21	"Snuffy" Stirnweiss	17.50	9.00	5.00
22	Hank Sauer	17.50	9.00	5.00
23	"Hoot" Evers	17.50	9.00	5.00
24	Ewell Blackwell	17.50	9.00	5.00
25	Vic Raschi	40.00	20.00	12.00
26	Phil Rizzuto	175.00	87.50	43.75
27	Jim Konstanty	17.50	9.00	5.00
28	Eddie Waitkus	17.50	9.00	5.00
29	Allie Clark	17.50	9.00	5.00
30	Bob Feller	125.00	62.50	31.25
31	Roy Campanella	300.00	150.00	75.00
32	Duke Snider	300.00	150.00	75.00
33	Bob Hooper	17.50	9.00	5.00
34	Marty Marion	25.00	12.50	7.50
35	Al Zarilla	17.50	9.00	5.00
36	Joe Dobson	17.50	9.00	5.00
37	Whitey Lockman	17.50	9.00	5.00
38	Al Evans	17.50	9.00	5.00
39	Ray Scarborough	17.50	9.00	5.00
40	*Gus Bell*	30.00	15.00	9.00
41	Eddie Yost	17.50	9.00	5.00
42	Vern Bickford	17.50	9.00	5.00
43	Billy DeMars	17.50	9.00	5.00
44	Roy Smalley	17.50	9.00	5.00
45	Art Houtteman	17.50	9.00	5.00
46	George Kell	50.00	25.00	15.00
47	Grady Hatton	17.50	9.00	5.00
48	Ken Raffensberger	17.50	9.00	5.00
49	Jerry Coleman	20.00	10.00	6.00
50	Johnny Mize	50.00	25.00	15.00
51	Andy Seminick	17.50	9.00	5.00
52	Dick Sisler	17.50	9.00	5.00
53	Bob Lemon	50.00	25.00	15.00
54	*Ray Boone*	35.00	17.50	10.00
55	Gene Hermanski	20.00	10.00	6.00
56	Ralph Branca	50.00	25.00	15.00
57	Alex Kellner	17.50	9.00	5.00
58	Enos Slaughter	50.00	25.00	15.00
59	Randy Gumpert	17.50	9.00	5.00
60	"Chico" Carrasquel	20.00	10.00	6.00
61	Jim Hearn	17.50	9.00	5.00
62	Lou Boudreau	45.00	22.50	13.50
63	Bob Dillinger	17.50	9.00	5.00
64	Bill Werle	17.50	9.00	5.00
65	Mickey Vernon	17.50	9.00	5.00
66	Bob Elliott	17.50	9.00	5.00
67	Roy Sievers	17.50	9.00	5.00
68	Dick Kokos	17.50	9.00	5.00
69	Johnny Schmitz	17.50	9.00	5.00
70	Ron Northey	17.50	9.00	5.00
71	Jerry Priddy	17.50	9.00	5.00
72	Lloyd Merriman	17.50	9.00	5.00
73	Tommy Byrne	20.00	10.00	6.00
74	Billy Johnson	20.00	10.00	6.00
75	Russ Meyer	17.50	9.00	5.00
76	Stan Lopata	17.50	9.00	5.00
77	Mike Goliat	17.50	9.00	5.00
78	Early Wynn	60.00	30.00	18.00
79	Jim Hegan	17.50	9.00	5.00
80	Pee Wee Reese	200.00	100.00	50.00
81	Carl Furillo	55.00	27.50	16.50
82	Joe Tipton	17.50	9.00	5.00
83	Carl Scheib	17.50	9.00	5.00
84	Barney McCosky	17.50	9.00	5.00
85	Eddie Kazak	17.50	9.00	5.00
86	Harry Brecheen	17.50	9.00	5.00

87	Floyd Baker	17.50	9.00	5.00
88	Eddie Robinson	17.50	9.00	5.00
89	Henry Thompson	17.50	9.00	5.00
90	Dave Koslo	17.50	9.00	5.00
91	Clyde Vollmer	17.50	9.00	5.00
92	Vern Stephens	17.50	9.00	5.00
93	Danny O'Connell	17.50	9.00	5.00
94	Clyde McCullough	17.50	9.00	5.00
95	Sherry Robertson	17.50	9.00	5.00
96	Sandy Consuegra	17.50	9.00	5.00
97	Bob Kuzava	17.50	9.00	5.00
98	Willard Marshall	17.50	9.00	5.00
99	Earl Torgeson	17.50	9.00	5.00
100	Sherman Lollar	17.50	9.00	5.00
101	Owen Friend	17.50	9.00	5.00
102	Emil "Dutch" Leonard	17.50	9.00	5.00
103	Andy Pafko	17.50	9.00	5.00
104	Virgil "Fire" Trucks	17.50	9.00	5.00
105	Don Kolloway	17.50	9.00	5.00
106	Pat Mullin	17.50	9.00	5.00
107	Johnny Wyrostek	17.50	9.00	5.00
108	Virgil Stallcup	17.50	9.00	5.00
109	Allie Reynolds	45.00	22.50	13.50
110	Bobby Brown	30.00	15.00	9.00
111	Curt Simmons	17.50	9.00	5.00
112	Willie Jones	17.50	9.00	5.00
113	Bill "Swish" Nicholson	17.50	9.00	5.00
114	Sam Zoldak	17.50	9.00	5.00
115	Steve Gromek	17.50	9.00	5.00
116	Bruce Edwards	20.00	10.00	6.00
117	Eddie Miksis	20.00	10.00	6.00
118	Preacher Roe	50.00	25.00	12.50
119	Eddie Joost	17.50	9.00	5.00
120	Joe Coleman	17.50	9.00	5.00
121	Gerry Staley	17.50	9.00	5.00
122	*Joe Garagiola*	100.00	50.00	25.00
123	Howie Judson	17.50	9.00	5.00
124	Gus Niarhos	17.50	9.00	5.00
125	Bill Rigney	17.50	9.00	5.00
126	*Bobby Thomson*	50.00	25.00	15.00
127	*Sal Maglie*	75.00	37.50	22.50
128	Ellis Kinder	17.50	9.00	5.00
129	Matt Batts	17.50	9.00	5.00
130	Tom Saffell	17.50	9.00	5.00
131	Cliff Chambers	17.50	9.00	5.00
132	Cass Michaels	17.50	9.00	5.00
133	Sam Dente	17.50	9.00	5.00
134	Warren Spahn	150.00	75.00	37.50
135	Walker Cooper	17.50	9.00	5.00
136	Ray Coleman	17.50	9.00	5.00
137	Dick Starr	17.50	9.00	5.00
138	Phil Cavarretta	17.50	9.00	5.00
139	Doyle Lade	17.50	9.00	5.00
140	Eddie Lake	17.50	9.00	5.00
141	Fred Hutchinson	17.50	9.00	5.00
142	Aaron Robinson	17.50	9.00	5.00
143	Ted Kluszewski	60.00	30.00	18.00
144	Herman Wehmeier	17.50	9.00	5.00
145	Fred Sanford	17.50	9.00	5.00
146	Johnny Hopp	17.50	9.00	5.00
147	Ken Heintzelman	17.50	9.00	5.00
148	Granny Hamner	17.50	9.00	5.00
149	"Bubba" Church	17.50	9.00	5.00
150	Mike Garcia	17.50	9.00	5.00
151	Larry Doby	70.00	35.00	20.00
152	Cal Abrams	20.00	10.00	6.00
153	Rex Barney	20.00	10.00	6.00
154	Pete Suder	17.50	9.00	5.00
155	Lou Brissie	17.50	9.00	5.00
156	Del Rice	17.50	9.00	5.00
157	Al Brazle	17.50	9.00	5.00
158	Chuck Diering	17.50	9.00	5.00
159	Eddie Stewart	17.50	9.00	5.00
160	Phil Masi	17.50	9.00	5.00
161	Wes Westrum	17.50	9.00	5.00
162	Larry Jansen	17.50	9.00	5.00
163	Monte Kennedy	17.50	9.00	5.00
164	Bill Wight	17.50	9.00	5.00
165	Ted Williams	800.00	400.00	200.00
166	Stan Rojek	17.50	9.00	5.00
167	Murry Dickson	17.50	9.00	5.00
168	Sam Mele	17.50	9.00	5.00
169	Sid Hudson	17.50	9.00	5.00
170	Sibby Sisti	17.50	9.00	5.00
171	Buddy Kerr	17.50	9.00	5.00
172	Ned Garver	17.50	9.00	5.00
173	Hank Arft	17.50	9.00	5.00
174	Mickey Owen	17.50	9.00	5.00
175	Wayne Terwilliger	17.50	9.00	5.00
176	Vic Wertz	17.50	9.00	5.00
177	Charlie Keller	17.50	9.00	5.00
178	Ted Gray	17.50	9.00	5.00
179	Danny Litwhiler	17.50	9.00	5.00
180	Howie Fox	17.50	9.00	5.00
181	Casey Stengel	100.00	50.00	25.00
182	Tom Ferrick	20.00	10.00	6.00
183	Hank Bauer	35.00	17.50	10.00
184	Eddie Sawyer	17.50	9.00	5.00
185	Jimmy Bloodworth	17.50	9.00	5.00
186	Richie Ashburn	100.00	50.00	30.00
187	Al Rosen	35.00	17.50	10.00
188	*Roberto Avila*	25.00	12.50	7.50
189	Erv Palica	20.00	10.00	6.00
190	Joe Hatten	20.00	10.00	6.00
191	Billy Hitchcock	17.50	9.00	5.00
192	Hank Wyse	17.50	9.00	5.00
193	Ted Wilks	17.50	9.00	5.00
194	Harry "Peanuts" Lowrey	17.50	9.00	5.00
195	Paul Richards	20.00	10.00	6.00
196	*Bill Pierce*	32.50	16.00	10.00
197	Bob Cain	17.50	9.00	5.00
198	*Monte Irvin*	120.00	60.00	30.00
199	Sheldon Jones	17.50	9.00	5.00
200	Jack Kramer	17.50	9.00	5.00
201	Steve O'Neill	17.50	9.00	5.00
202	Mike Guerra	17.50	9.00	5.00
203	*Vernon Law*	40.00	20.00	12.00
204	Vic Lombardi	17.50	9.00	5.00

205	Mickey Grasso	17.50	9.00	5.00
206	Connie Marrero	17.50	9.00	5.00
207	Billy Southworth	35.00	17.50	10.50
208	"Blix" Donnelly	17.50	9.00	5.00
209	Ken Wood	17.50	9.00	5.00
210	Les Moss	17.50	9.00	5.00
211	Hal Jeffcoat	17.50	9.00	5.00
212	Bob Rush	17.50	9.00	5.00
213	Neil Berry	17.50	9.00	5.00
214	Bob Swift	17.50	9.00	5.00
215	Kent Peterson	17.50	9.00	5.00
216	Connie Ryan	17.50	9.00	5.00
217	Joe Page	27.50	13.50	8.00
218	Ed Lopat	32.50	16.00	10.00
219	*Gene Woodling*	40.00	20.00	12.00
220	Bob Miller	17.50	9.00	5.00
221	Dick Whitman	17.50	9.00	5.00
222	Thurman Tucker	17.50	9.00	5.00
223	Johnny Vander Meer	25.00	12.50	7.50
224	Billy Cox	27.50	13.50	8.00
225	*Dan Bankhead*	30.00	15.00	9.00
226	Jimmy Dykes	17.50	9.00	5.00
227	Bobby Shantz	20.00	10.00	6.00
228	*Cloyd Boyer*	17.50	9.00	5.00
229	Bill Howerton	17.50	9.00	5.00
230	Max Lanier	17.50	9.00	5.00
231	Luis Aloma	17.50	9.00	5.00
232	*Nellie Fox*	250.00	125.00	62.50
233	Leo Durocher	40.00	20.00	12.00
234	Clint Hartung	17.50	9.00	5.00
235	Jack Lohrke	17.50	9.00	5.00
236	"Buddy" Rosar	17.50	9.00	5.00
237	Billy Goodman	17.50	9.00	5.00
238	Pete Reiser	20.00	10.00	6.00
239	Bill MacDonald	17.50	9.00	5.00
240	Joe Haynes	17.50	9.00	5.00
241	Irv Noren	17.50	9.00	5.00
242	Sam Jethroe	17.50	9.00	5.00
243	Johnny Antonelli	17.50	9.00	5.00
244	Cliff Fannin	17.50	9.00	5.00
245	John Berardino	25.00	12.50	7.50
246	Bill Serena	17.50	9.00	5.00
247	Bob Ramazotti	17.50	9.00	5.00
248	*Johnny Klippstein*	17.50	9.00	5.00
249	Johnny Groth	17.50	9.00	5.00
250	Hank Borowy	17.50	9.00	5.00
251	Willard Ramsdell	17.50	9.00	5.00
252	"Dixie" Howell	17.50	9.00	5.00
253	*Mickey Mantle*	9,500	3,100	2,000
254	*Jackie Jensen*	100.00	50.00	25.00
255	Milo Candini	40.00	20.00	12.00
256	Ken Silvestri	40.00	20.00	12.00
257	Birdie Tebbetts	40.00	20.00	12.00
258	*Luke Easter*	45.00	22.50	13.50
259	Charlie Dressen	40.00	20.00	12.00
260	*Carl Erskine*	100.00	50.00	25.00
261	Wally Moses	40.00	20.00	12.00
262	Gus Zernial	40.00	20.00	12.00
263	Howie Pollet	40.00	20.00	12.00
264	Don Richmond	40.00	20.00	12.00
265	*Steve Bilko*	40.00	20.00	12.00
266	Harry Dorish	40.00	20.00	12.00
267	Ken Holcombe	40.00	20.00	12.00
268	Don Mueller	40.00	20.00	12.00
269	Ray Noble	40.00	20.00	12.00
270	Willard Nixon	40.00	20.00	12.00
271	Tommy Wright	40.00	20.00	12.00
272	Billy Meyer	40.00	20.00	12.00
273	Danny Murtaugh	40.00	20.00	12.00
274	George Metkovich	40.00	20.00	12.00
275	Bucky Harris	50.00	25.00	15.00
276	Frank Quinn	40.00	20.00	12.00
277	Roy Hartsfield	40.00	20.00	12.00
278	Norman Roy	40.00	20.00	12.00
279	Jim Delsing	40.00	20.00	12.00
280	Frank Overmire	40.00	20.00	12.00
281	Al Widmar	40.00	20.00	12.00
282	Frank Frisch	55.00	27.50	16.50
283	Walt Dubiel	40.00	20.00	12.00
284	Gene Bearden	40.00	20.00	12.00
285	Johnny Lipon	40.00	20.00	12.00
286	Bob Usher	40.00	20.00	12.00
287	Jim Blackburn	40.00	20.00	12.00
288	Bobby Adams	40.00	20.00	12.00
289	Cliff Mapes	50.00	25.00	15.00
290	Bill Dickey	150.00	75.00	37.50
291	Tommy Henrich	55.00	27.50	16.50
292	Eddie Pellagrini	40.00	20.00	12.00
293	Ken Johnson	40.00	20.00	12.00
294	Jocko Thompson	40.00	20.00	12.00
295	Al Lopez	100.00	50.00	25.00
296	Bob Kennedy	40.00	20.00	12.00
297	Dave Philley	40.00	20.00	12.00
298	Joe Astroth	40.00	20.00	12.00
299	Clyde King	50.00	25.00	15.00
300	Hal Rice	40.00	20.00	12.00
301	Tommy Glaviano	40.00	20.00	12.00
302	Jim Busby	40.00	20.00	12.00
303	Marv Rotblatt	40.00	20.00	12.00
304	Allen Gettel	40.00	20.00	12.00
305	*Willie Mays*	3,600	1,100	575.00
306	*Jim Piersall*	120.00	60.00	30.00
307	Walt Masterson	40.00	20.00	12.00
308	Ted Beard	40.00	20.00	12.00
309	Mel Queen	40.00	20.00	12.00
310	Erv Dusak	40.00	20.00	12.00
311	Mickey Harris	40.00	20.00	12.00
312	*Gene Mauch*	50.00	25.00	15.00
313	Ray Mueller	40.00	20.00	12.00
314	Johnny Sain	45.00	22.50	13.50
315	Zack Taylor	40.00	20.00	12.00
316	Duane Pillette	40.00	20.00	12.00
317	*Smoky Burgess*	60.00	30.00	18.00
318	Warren Hacker	40.00	20.00	12.00
319	Red Rolfe	40.00	20.00	12.00
320	Hal White	40.00	20.00	12.00
321	Earl Johnson	40.00	20.00	12.00
322	Luke Sewell	40.00	20.00	12.00

323	*Joe Adcock*	100.00	50.00	25.00
324	Johnny Pramesa	125.00	62.50	31.25

1952 Bowman

Bowman reverted to a 252-card set in 1952, but retained the card size (2-1/16" x 3-1/8") employed the preceding year. The cards, which are color art reproductions of actual photographs, feature a facsimile autograph on front.

		NM	EX	VG
	Complete Set (252):	10,000	5,000	3,000
	Common Player (1-216):	20.00	10.00	6.00
	Common Player (217-252):	40.00	20.00	12.00
1	Yogi Berra	600.00	300.00	150.00
2	Bobby Thomson	60.00	30.00	15.00
3	Fred Hutchinson	20.00	10.00	6.00
4	Robin Roberts	80.00	40.00	20.00
5	*Minnie Minoso*	120.00	60.00	30.00
6	Virgil "Red" Stallcup	20.00	10.00	6.00
7	Mike Garcia	20.00	10.00	6.00
8	Pee Wee Reese	150.00	75.00	37.50
9	Vern Stephens	20.00	10.00	6.00
10	Bob Hooper	20.00	10.00	6.00
11	Ralph Kiner	50.00	25.00	12.50
12	Max Surkont	20.00	10.00	6.00
13	Cliff Mapes	20.00	10.00	6.00
14	Cliff Chambers	20.00	10.00	6.00
15	Sam Mele	20.00	10.00	6.00
16	Omar Lown	20.00	10.00	6.00
17	Ed Lopat	55.00	27.50	16.50
18	Don Mueller	20.00	10.00	6.00
19	Bob Cain	20.00	10.00	6.00
20	Willie Jones	20.00	10.00	6.00
21	Nellie Fox	100.00	50.00	25.00
22	Willard Ramsdell	20.00	10.00	6.00
23	Bob Lemon	60.00	30.00	18.00
24	Carl Furillo	50.00	25.00	15.00
25	Maurice McDermott	20.00	10.00	6.00
26	Eddie Joost	20.00	10.00	6.00
27	Joe Garagiola	30.00	15.00	9.00
28	Roy Hartsfield	20.00	10.00	6.00
29	Ned Garver	20.00	10.00	6.00
30	Red Schoendienst	45.00	22.50	13.50
31	Eddie Yost	20.00	10.00	6.00
32	Eddie Miksis	20.00	10.00	6.00
33	*Gil McDougald*	60.00	30.00	18.00
34	Al Dark	20.00	10.00	6.00
35	Granny Hamner	20.00	10.00	6.00
36	Cass Michaels	20.00	10.00	6.00
37	Vic Raschi	30.00	15.00	9.00
38	Whitey Lockman	20.00	10.00	6.00
39	Vic Wertz	20.00	10.00	6.00
40	"Bubba" Church	20.00	10.00	6.00
41	"Chico" Carrasquel	20.00	10.00	6.00
42	Johnny Wyrostek	20.00	10.00	6.00
43	Bob Feller	150.00	75.00	37.50
44	Roy Campanella	250.00	125.00	62.50
45	Johnny Pesky	20.00	10.00	6.00
46	Carl Scheib	20.00	10.00	6.00
47	Pete Castiglione	20.00	10.00	6.00
48	Vernon Bickford	20.00	10.00	6.00
49	Jim Hearn	20.00	10.00	6.00
50	Gerry Staley	20.00	10.00	6.00
51	Gil Coan	20.00	10.00	6.00
52	Phil Rizzuto	150.00	75.00	37.50
53	Richie Ashburn	120.00	60.00	30.00
54	Billy Pierce	25.00	12.50	7.50
55	Ken Raffensberger	20.00	10.00	6.00
56	Clyde King	25.00	12.50	7.50
57	Clyde Vollmer	20.00	10.00	6.00
58	Hank Majeski	20.00	10.00	6.00
59	Murry Dickson	20.00	10.00	6.00
60	Sid Gordon	20.00	10.00	6.00
61	Tommy Byrne	20.00	10.00	6.00
62	Joe Presko	20.00	10.00	6.00
63	Irv Noren	20.00	10.00	6.00
64	Roy Smalley	20.00	10.00	6.00
65	Hank Bauer	50.00	25.00	15.00
66	Sal Maglie	25.00	12.50	7.50
67	Johnny Groth	20.00	10.00	6.00
68	Jim Busby	20.00	10.00	6.00
69	Joe Adcock	20.00	10.00	6.00
70	Carl Erskine	40.00	20.00	12.00
71	Vernon Law	20.00	10.00	6.00
72	Earl Torgeson	20.00	10.00	6.00
73	Jerry Coleman	30.00	15.00	9.00
74	Wes Westrum	20.00	10.00	6.00
75	George Kell	45.00	22.50	13.50
76	Del Ennis	20.00	10.00	6.00
77	Eddie Robinson	20.00	10.00	6.00
78	Lloyd Merriman	20.00	10.00	6.00
79	Lou Brissie	20.00	10.00	6.00
80	Gil Hodges	100.00	50.00	30.00
81	Billy Goodman	20.00	10.00	6.00
82	Gus Zernial	20.00	10.00	6.00
83	Howie Pollet	20.00	10.00	6.00
84	Sam Jethroe	20.00	10.00	6.00
85	Marty Marion	25.00	12.50	7.50

86	Cal Abrams	25.00	12.50	7.50
87	Mickey Vernon	20.00	10.00	6.00
88	Bruce Edwards	20.00	10.00	6.00
89	Billy Hitchcock	20.00	10.00	6.00
90	Larry Jansen	20.00	10.00	6.00
91	Don Kolloway	20.00	10.00	6.00
92	Eddie Waitkus	20.00	10.00	6.00
93	Paul Richards	20.00	10.00	6.00
94	Luke Sewell	20.00	10.00	6.00
95	Luke Easter	20.00	10.00	6.00
96	Ralph Branca	40.00	20.00	12.00
97	Willard Marshall	20.00	10.00	6.00
98	Jimmy Dykes	20.00	10.00	6.00
99	Clyde McCullough	20.00	10.00	6.00
100	Sibby Sisti	20.00	10.00	6.00
101	Mickey Mantle	2,000	825.00	475.00
102	Peanuts Lowrey	20.00	10.00	6.00
103	Joe Haynes	20.00	10.00	6.00
104	Hal Jeffcoat	20.00	10.00	6.00
105	Bobby Brown	35.00	17.50	10.00
106	Randy Gumpert	20.00	10.00	6.00
107	Del Rice	20.00	10.00	6.00
108	George Metkovich	20.00	10.00	6.00
109	Tom Morgan	30.00	15.00	9.00
110	Max Lanier	20.00	10.00	6.00
111	"Hoot" Evers	20.00	10.00	6.00
112	"Smoky" Burgess	20.00	10.00	6.00
113	Al Zarilla	20.00	10.00	6.00
114	Frank Hiller	20.00	10.00	6.00
115	Larry Doby	60.00	30.00	18.00
116	Duke Snider	200.00	100.00	60.00
117	Bill Wight	20.00	10.00	6.00
118	Ray Murray	20.00	10.00	6.00
119	Bill Howerton	20.00	10.00	6.00
120	Chet Nichols	20.00	10.00	6.00
121	Al Corwin	20.00	10.00	6.00
122	Billy Johnson	20.00	10.00	6.00
123	Sid Hudson	20.00	10.00	6.00
124	Birdie Tebbetts	20.00	10.00	6.00
125	Howie Fox	20.00	10.00	6.00
126	Phil Cavarretta	20.00	10.00	6.00
127	Dick Sisler	20.00	10.00	6.00
128	Don Newcombe	45.00	22.50	13.50
129	Gus Niarhos	20.00	10.00	6.00
130	Allie Clark	20.00	10.00	6.00
131	Bob Swift	20.00	10.00	6.00
132	Dave Cole	20.00	10.00	6.00
133	Dick Kryhoski	20.00	10.00	6.00
134	Al Brazle	20.00	10.00	6.00
135	Mickey Harris	20.00	10.00	6.00
136	Gene Hermanski	20.00	10.00	6.00
137	Stan Rojek	20.00	10.00	6.00
138	Ted Wilks	20.00	10.00	6.00
139	Jerry Priddy	20.00	10.00	6.00
140	Ray Scarborough	20.00	10.00	6.00
141	Hank Edwards	20.00	10.00	6.00
142	Early Wynn	45.00	22.50	13.50
143	Sandy Consuegra	20.00	10.00	6.00
144	Joe Hatten	20.00	10.00	6.00
145	Johnny Mize	80.00	40.00	24.00
146	Leo Durocher	45.00	22.50	13.50
147	Marlin Stuart	20.00	10.00	6.00
148	Ken Heintzelman	20.00	10.00	6.00
149	Howie Judson	20.00	10.00	6.00
150	Herman Wehmeier	20.00	10.00	6.00
151	Al Rosen	30.00	15.00	9.00
152	Billy Cox	40.00	20.00	12.00
153	Fred Hatfield	20.00	10.00	6.00
154	Ferris Fain	20.00	10.00	6.00
155	Billy Meyer	20.00	10.00	6.00
156	Warren Spahn	120.00	60.00	30.00
157	Jim Delsing	20.00	10.00	6.00
158	Bucky Harris	30.00	15.00	9.00
159	Dutch Leonard	20.00	10.00	6.00
160	Eddie Stanky	20.00	10.00	6.00
161	Jackie Jensen	45.00	22.50	13.50
162	Monte Irvin	55.00	27.50	16.50
163	Johnny Lipon	20.00	10.00	6.00
164	Connie Ryan	20.00	10.00	6.00
165	Saul Rogovin	20.00	10.00	6.00
166	Bobby Adams	20.00	10.00	6.00
167	Bob Avila	20.00	10.00	6.00
168	Preacher Roe	35.00	17.50	10.00
169	Walt Dropo	20.00	10.00	6.00
170	Joe Astroth	20.00	10.00	6.00
171	Mel Queen	20.00	10.00	6.00
172	Ebba St. Claire	20.00	10.00	6.00
173	Gene Bearden	20.00	10.00	6.00
174	Mickey Grasso	20.00	10.00	6.00
175	Ransom Jackson	20.00	10.00	6.00
176	Harry Brecheen	20.00	10.00	6.00
177	Gene Woodling	35.00	17.50	10.00
178	Dave Williams	20.00	10.00	6.00
179	Pete Suder	20.00	10.00	6.00
180	Eddie Fitz Gerald	20.00	10.00	6.00
181	Joe Collins	30.00	15.00	9.00
182	Dave Koslo	20.00	10.00	6.00
183	Pat Mullin	20.00	10.00	6.00
184	Curt Simmons	20.00	10.00	6.00
185	Eddie Stewart	20.00	10.00	6.00
186	Frank Smith	20.00	10.00	6.00
187	Jim Hegan	20.00	10.00	6.00
188	Charlie Dressen	30.00	15.00	9.00
189	Jim Piersall	30.00	15.00	9.00
190	Dick Fowler	20.00	10.00	6.00
191	*Bob Friend*	25.00	12.50	7.50
192	John Cusick	20.00	10.00	6.00
193	Bobby Young	20.00	10.00	6.00
194	Bob Porterfield	20.00	10.00	6.00
195	Frank Baumholtz	20.00	10.00	6.00
196	Stan Musial	600.00	300.00	150.00
197	*Charlie Silvera*	35.00	17.50	10.00
198	Chuck Diering	20.00	10.00	6.00
199	Ted Gray	20.00	10.00	6.00
200	Ken Silvestri	20.00	10.00	6.00
201	Ray Coleman	20.00	10.00	6.00
202	Harry Perkowski	20.00	10.00	6.00
203	Steve Gromek	20.00	10.00	6.00

		NM	EX	VG
204	Andy Pafko	20.00	10.00	6.00
205	Walt Masterson	20.00	10.00	6.00
206	Elmer Valo	20.00	10.00	6.00
207	George Strickland	20.00	10.00	6.00
208	Walker Cooper	20.00	10.00	6.00
209	Dick Littlefield	20.00	10.00	6.00
210	Archie Wilson	20.00	10.00	6.00
211	Paul Minner	20.00	10.00	6.00
212	Solly Hemus	20.00	10.00	6.00
213	Monte Kennedy	20.00	10.00	6.00
214	Ray Boone	20.00	10.00	6.00
215	Sheldon Jones	20.00	10.00	6.00
216	Matt Batts	20.00	10.00	6.00
217	Casey Stengel	125.00	60.00	35.00
218	Willie Mays	1,500	750.00	375.00
219	Neil Berry	40.00	20.00	12.00
220	Russ Meyer	40.00	20.00	12.00
221	Lou Kretlow	40.00	20.00	12.00
222	"Dixie" Howell	40.00	20.00	12.00
223	*Harry Simpson*	45.00	22.50	13.50
224	Johnny Schmitz	40.00	20.00	12.00
225	Del Wilber	40.00	20.00	12.00
226	Alex Kellner	40.00	20.00	12.00
227	Clyde Sukeforth	40.00	20.00	12.00
228	Bob Chipman	40.00	20.00	12.00
229	Hank Arft	40.00	20.00	12.00
230	Frank Shea	40.00	20.00	12.00
231	*Dee Fondy*	40.00	20.00	12.00
232	Enos Slaughter	100.00	50.00	25.00
233	Bob Kuzava	50.00	25.00	15.00
234	Fred Fitzsimmons	40.00	20.00	12.00
235	Steve Souchock	40.00	20.00	12.00
236	Tommy Brown	40.00	20.00	12.00
237	Sherman Lollar	40.00	20.00	12.00
238	*Roy McMillan*	40.00	20.00	12.00
239	Dale Mitchell	40.00	20.00	12.00
240	*Billy Loes*	45.00	22.50	13.50
241	Mel Parnell	40.00	20.00	12.00
242	Everett Kell	40.00	20.00	12.00
243	"Red" Munger	40.00	20.00	12.00
244	*Lew Burdette*	60.00	30.00	18.00
245	George Schmees	40.00	20.00	12.00
246	Jerry Snyder	40.00	20.00	12.00
247	John Pramesa	40.00	20.00	12.00
248a	Bill Werle (. after G and most of W missing)	40.00	20.00	12.00
248b	Bill Werle (Full signature.)	40.00	20.00	12.00
249	Henry Thompson	40.00	20.00	12.00
250	Ike Delock	40.00	20.00	12.00
251	Jack Lohrke	40.00	20.00	12.00
252	Frank Crosetti	125.00	62.50	31.25

1952 Bowman Proofs

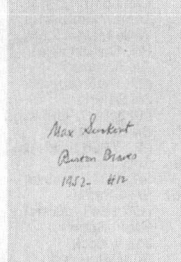

Coincident to Topps issue of its "Giant Size" baseball cards in 1952, Bowman began experimenting with up-sizing its card issues from the then-current 2-1/16" x 3-1/8". A group of proof cards was produced using 12 players from the '52 Bowman set. The proofs are 2-1/2" x 3-3/4", overall about 45% larger than the issued '52s. Each proof is found in two types, black-and-white and color. Both have blank-backs except for hand-written notes with the player's name, team and card number in the '52 set. Many of the proofs feature slight differences from the issued versions, such as uniform changes, elimination of background elements or picture cropping. The color proofs include a facsimile autograph. A small group of these proof cards entered the hobby early in the 1980s when a former Bowman executive disposed of his hobby card files. The proof cards are numbered according to their number within the 1952 Bowman set.

		NM	EX	VG
	Common Player, B/W:	1,200	600.00	360.00
	Common Player, Color:	1,800	900.00	550.00
1	Yogi Berra (B/W)	4,000	2,000	1,200
1	Yogi Berra (Color)	6,400	3,200	2,000
2	Bobby Thomson (B/W)	1,200	600.00	360.00
2	Bobby Thomson (Color)	4,000	2,000	1,200
3	Fred Hutchinson (B/W)	1,600	800.00	500.00
3	Fred Hutchinson (Color)	1,800	900.00	550.00
4	Robin Roberts (B/W)	2,900	1,450	875.00
4	Robin Roberts (Color)	4,800	2,400	1,500
10	Bob Hooper (B/W)	1,600	800.00	500.00
10	Bob Hooper (Color)	1,800	900.00	550.00
11	Ralph Kiner (B/W)	2,900	1,450	875.00
11	Ralph Kiner (Color)	4,800	2,400	1,500
12	Max Surkont (B/W)	1,600	800.00	500.00
12	Max Surkont (Color)	1,800	900.00	550.00
13	Cliff Mapes (B/W)	1,600	800.00	500.00
13	Cliff Mapes (Color)	1,800	900.00	550.00
14	Cliff Chambers (B/W)	1,600	800.00	500.00
14	Cliff Chambers (Color)	1,800	900.00	550.00
34	Alvin Dark (B/W)	1,600	800.00	500.00
34	Alvin Dark (Color)	1,800	900.00	550.00
39	Vic Wertz (B/W)	1,600	800.00	500.00
39	Vic Wertz (Color)	1,800	900.00	550.00

		NM	EX	VG
142	Early Wynn (B/W)	2,600	1,300	800.00
142	Early Wynn (Color)	4,800	2,400	1,450
176	Harry Brecheen (B/W)	1,600	800.00	500.00
176	Harry Brecheen (Color)	1,800	900.00	550.00

1953 Bowman Color

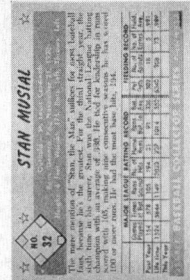

The first set of contemporary major league players featuring actual color photographs, the 160-card 1953 Bowman color set remains one of the most popular issues of the postwar era. The set is greatly appreciated for its uncluttered look; card fronts that contain no names, teams or facsimile autographs. Bowman increased the size of the cards to 2-1/2" x 3-3/4" to better compete with Topps' larger format. Bowman copied an idea from the 1952 Topps set and developed card backs that gave player career and previous-year statistics. The high-numbered cards (#113-160) are the scarcest of the set, with #113-128 being especially scarce.

		NM	EX	VG
	Complete Set (160):	18,000	9,000	5,500
	Common Player (1-112):	35.00	17.50	10.00
	Common Player (113-160):	90.00	45.00	25.00
1	Davey Williams	175.00	87.50	43.75
2	Vic Wertz	45.00	17.50	10.00
3	Sam Jethroe	35.00	17.50	10.00
4	Art Houtteman	35.00	17.50	10.00
5	Sid Gordon	35.00	17.50	10.00
6	Joe Ginsberg	35.00	17.50	10.00
7	Harry Chiti	35.00	17.50	10.00
8	Al Rosen	55.00	27.50	16.50
9	Phil Rizzuto	250.00	125.00	62.50
10	Richie Ashburn	150.00	75.00	37.50
11	Bobby Shantz	35.00	17.50	10.00
12	Carl Erskine	50.00	25.00	15.00
13	Gus Zernial	35.00	17.50	10.00
14	Billy Loes	55.00	27.50	16.50
15	Jim Busby	35.00	17.50	10.00
16	Bob Friend	35.00	17.50	10.00
17	Gerry Staley	35.00	17.50	10.00
18	Nellie Fox	150.00	75.00	37.50
19	Al Dark	35.00	17.50	10.00
20	Don Lenhardt	35.00	17.50	10.00
21	Joe Garagiola	50.00	25.00	15.00
22	Bob Porterfield	35.00	17.50	10.00
23	Herman Wehmeier	35.00	17.50	10.00
24	Jackie Jensen	45.00	22.50	13.50
25	"Hoot" Evers	35.00	17.50	10.00
26	Roy McMillan	35.00	17.50	10.00
27	Vic Raschi	70.00	35.00	20.00
28	"Smoky" Burgess	45.00	22.50	13.50
29	Roberto Avila	35.00	17.50	10.00
30	Phil Cavarretta	35.00	17.50	10.00
31	Jimmy Dykes	35.00	17.50	10.00
32	Stan Musial	600.00	300.00	150.00
33	Pee Wee Reese	750.00	370.00	220.00
34	Gil Coan	35.00	17.50	10.00
35	Maury McDermott	35.00	17.50	10.00
36	Minnie Minoso	85.00	42.50	25.00
37	Jim Wilson	35.00	17.50	10.00
38	Harry Byrd	35.00	17.50	10.00
39	Paul Richards	35.00	17.50	10.00
40	Larry Doby	100.00	50.00	25.00
41	Sammy White	35.00	17.50	10.00
42	Tommy Brown	35.00	17.50	10.00
43	Mike Garcia	35.00	17.50	10.00
44	Hank Bauer, Yogi Berra, Mickey Mantle	800.00	400.00	200.00
45	Walt Dropo	35.00	17.50	10.00
46	Roy Campanella	350.00	175.00	87.50
47	Ned Garver	35.00	17.50	10.00
48	Hank Sauer	35.00	17.50	10.00
49	Eddie Stanky	35.00	17.50	10.00
50	Lou Kretlow	35.00	17.50	10.00
51	Monte Irvin	55.00	27.50	16.50
52	Marty Marion	45.00	22.50	13.50
53	Del Rice	35.00	17.50	10.00
54	"Chico" Carrasquel	35.00	17.50	10.00
55	Leo Durocher	70.00	35.00	20.00
56	Bob Cain	35.00	17.50	10.00
57	Lou Boudreau	75.00	37.50	22.50
58	Willard Marshall	35.00	17.50	10.00
59	Mickey Mantle	1,500	750.00	450.00
60	Granny Hamner	35.00	17.50	10.00
61	George Kell	60.00	30.00	18.00
62	Ted Kluszewski	90.00	45.00	27.50
63	Gil McDougald	100.00	50.00	25.00
64	Curt Simmons	35.00	17.50	10.50
65	Robin Roberts	125.00	62.50	31.25
66	Mel Parnell	35.00	17.50	10.00
67	Mel Clark	35.00	17.50	10.00
68	Allie Reynolds	80.00	40.00	20.00
69	Charlie Grimm	35.00	17.50	10.00
70	Clint Courtney	35.00	17.50	10.00
71	Paul Minner	35.00	17.50	10.00
72	Ted Gray	35.00	17.50	10.00
73	Billy Pierce	40.00	20.00	12.00
74	Don Mueller	35.00	17.50	10.00

		NM	EX	VG
75	Saul Rogovin	35.00	17.50	10.00
76	Jim Hearn	35.00	17.50	10.00
77	Mickey Grasso	35.00	17.50	10.00
78	Carl Furillo	80.00	40.00	25.00
79	Ray Boone	35.00	17.50	10.00
80	Ralph Kiner	115.00	55.00	35.00
81	Enos Slaughter	100.00	50.00	25.00
82	Joe Astroth	35.00	17.50	10.00
83	Jack Daniels	35.00	17.50	10.00
84	Hank Bauer	80.00	40.00	25.00
85	Solly Hemus	35.00	17.50	10.00
86	Harry Simpson	35.00	17.50	10.00
87	Harry Perkowski	35.00	17.50	10.00
88	Joe Dobson	35.00	17.50	10.00
89	Sandalio Consuegra	35.00	17.50	10.00
90	Joe Nuxhall	35.00	17.50	10.00
91	Steve Souchock	35.00	17.50	10.00
92	Gil Hodges	300.00	150.00	75.00
93	Billy Martin, Phil Rizzuto	300.00	150.00	75.00
94	Bob Addis	35.00	17.50	10.00
95	Wally Moses	35.00	17.50	10.00
96	Sal Maglie	65.00	32.50	20.00
97	Eddie Mathews	350.00	175.00	87.50
98	Hector Rodriguez	35.00	17.50	10.00
99	Warren Spahn	350.00	175.00	87.50
100	Bill Wight	35.00	17.50	10.00
101	Red Schoendienst	100.00	50.00	25.00
102	Jim Hegan	35.00	17.50	10.00
103	Del Ennis	35.00	17.50	10.00
104	Luke Easter	35.00	17.50	10.00
105	Eddie Joost	35.00	17.50	10.00
106	Ken Raffensberger	35.00	17.50	10.00
107	Alex Kellner	35.00	17.50	10.00
108	Bobby Adams	35.00	17.50	10.00
109	Ken Wood	35.00	17.50	10.00
110	Bob Rush	35.00	17.50	10.00
111	Jim Dyck	35.00	17.50	10.00
112	Toby Atwell	35.00	17.50	10.00
113	Karl Drews	90.00	45.00	25.00
114	Bob Feller	500.00	250.00	125.00
115	Cloyd Boyer	90.00	45.00	25.00
116	Eddie Yost	90.00	45.00	25.00
117	Duke Snider	600.00	300.00	150.00
118	Billy Martin	400.00	200.00	100.00
119	Dale Mitchell	90.00	45.00	25.00
120	Marlin Stuart	90.00	45.00	25.00
121	Yogi Berra	800.00	400.00	200.00
122	Bill Serena	90.00	45.00	25.00
123	Johnny Lipon	90.00	45.00	25.00
124	Charlie Dressen	100.00	50.00	25.00
125	Fred Hatfield	90.00	45.00	25.00
126	Al Corwin	90.00	45.00	25.00
127	Dick Kryhoski	90.00	45.00	25.00
128	"Whitey" Lockman	90.00	45.00	25.00
129	Russ Meyer	95.00	47.50	27.50
130	Cass Michaels	90.00	45.00	25.00
131	Connie Ryan	90.00	45.00	25.00
132	Fred Hutchinson	90.00	45.00	25.00
133	Willie Jones	90.00	45.00	25.00
134	Johnny Pesky	90.00	45.00	25.00
135	Bobby Morgan	95.00	47.50	27.50
136	Jim Brideweser	100.00	50.00	30.00
137	Sam Dente	90.00	45.00	25.00
138	"Bubba" Church	90.00	45.00	25.00
139	Pete Runnels	90.00	45.00	25.00
140	Alpha Brazle	90.00	45.00	25.00
141	Frank "Spec" Shea	90.00	45.00	25.00
142	Larry Miggins	90.00	45.00	25.00
143	Al Lopez	100.00	50.00	25.00
144	Warren Hacker	90.00	45.00	25.00
145	George Shuba	125.00	60.00	35.00
146	Early Wynn	200.00	100.00	50.00
147	Clem Koshorek	90.00	45.00	25.00
148	Billy Goodman	90.00	45.00	25.00
149	Al Corwin	90.00	45.00	25.00
150	Carl Scheib	90.00	45.00	25.00
151	Joe Adcock	90.00	45.00	25.00
152	Clyde Vollmer	90.00	45.00	25.00
153	Whitey Ford	900.00	450.00	270.00
154	Omar "Turk" Lown	90.00	45.00	25.00
155	Allie Clark	90.00	45.00	25.00
156	Max Surkont	90.00	45.00	25.00
157	Sherman Lollar	90.00	45.00	25.00
158	Howard Fox	90.00	45.00	25.00
159	Mickey Vernon (Photo actually Floyd Baker.)	95.00	47.50	27.50
160	Cal Abrams	500.00	250.00	125.00

1953 Bowman Black & White

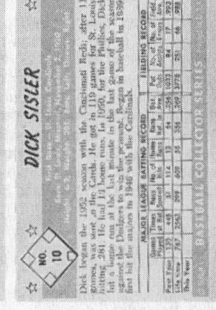

The 1953 Bowman black-and-white set is similar in all respects to the 1953 Bowman color cards, except that it lacks color. Sixty-four cards, which measure 2-1/2" x 3-3/4", comprise the set.

	NM	EX	VG
Complete Set (64):	4,500	2,125	1,275

Common Player:		55.00	25.00	15.00
1	Gus Bell	150.00	75.00	37.50
2	Willard Nixon	65.00	30.00	15.00
3	Bill Rigney	55.00	25.00	15.00
4	Pat Mullin	55.00	25.00	15.00
5	Dee Fondy	55.00	25.00	15.00
6	Ray Murray	55.00	25.00	15.00
7	Andy Seminick	55.00	25.00	15.00
8	Pete Suder	55.00	25.00	15.00
9	Walt Masterson	55.00	25.00	15.00
10	Dick Sisler	55.00	25.00	15.00
11	Dick Gernert	55.00	25.00	15.00
12	Randy Jackson	55.00	25.00	15.00
13	Joe Tipton	55.00	25.00	15.00
14	Bill Nicholson	55.00	25.00	15.00
15	Johnny Mize	125.00	62.50	31.25
16	Stu Miller	55.00	25.00	15.00
17	Virgil Trucks	55.00	25.00	15.00
18	Billy Hoeft	55.00	25.00	15.00
19	Paul LaPalme	55.00	25.00	15.00
20	Eddie Robinson	55.00	25.00	15.00
21	Clarence "Bud" Podbielan	55.00	25.00	15.00
22	Matt Batts	55.00	25.00	15.00
23	Wilmer Mizell	55.00	25.00	15.00
24	Del Wilber	55.00	25.00	15.00
25	Johnny Sain	100.00	50.00	30.00
26	Preacher Roe	90.00	45.00	25.00
27	Bob Lemon	175.00	87.50	43.75
28	Hoyt Wilhelm	125.00	62.50	31.25
29	Sid Hudson	55.00	25.00	15.00
30	Walker Cooper	55.00	25.00	15.00
31	Gene Woodling	100.00	50.00	30.00
32	Rocky Bridges	55.00	25.00	15.00
33	Bob Kuzava	55.00	25.00	15.00
34	Ebba St. Clair (St. Claire)	55.00	25.00	15.00
35	Johnny Wyrostek	55.00	25.00	15.00
36	Jim Piersall	90.00	45.00	25.00
37	Hal Jeffcoat	55.00	25.00	15.00
38	Dave Cole	55.00	25.00	15.00
39	Casey Stengel	350.00	175.00	87.50
40	Larry Jansen	55.00	25.00	15.00
41	Bob Ramazotti	55.00	25.00	15.00
42	Howie Judson	55.00	25.00	15.00
43a	Hal Bevan (Birth year 1950.)	55.00	25.00	15.00
43b	Hal Bevan (Birth year 1930.)	120.00	60.00	35.00
44	Jim Delsing	55.00	25.00	15.00
45	Irv Noren	100.00	50.00	30.00
46	Bucky Harris	100.00	50.00	35.00
47	Jack Lohrke	55.00	25.00	15.00
48	Steve Ridzik	55.00	25.00	15.00
49	Floyd Baker	55.00	25.00	15.00
50	Emil "Dutch" Leonard	55.00	25.00	15.00
51	Lew Burdette	75.00	35.00	20.00
52	Ralph Branca	100.00	50.00	30.00
53	Morris Martin	55.00	25.00	15.00
54	Bill Miller	55.00	25.00	15.00
55	Don Johnson	55.00	25.00	15.00
56	Roy Smalley	55.00	25.00	15.00
57	Andy Pafko	55.00	25.00	15.00
58	Jim Konstanty	55.00	25.00	15.00
59	Duane Pillette	55.00	25.00	15.00
60	Billy Cox	80.00	40.00	20.00
61	Tom Gorman	80.00	40.00	25.00
62	Keith Thomas	55.00	25.00	15.00
63	Steve Gromek	55.00	25.00	15.00
64	Andy Hansen	75.00	25.00	15.00

1953 Bowman Color Proofs

Four subjects are known to have survived in proof form created prior to the production of Bowman's landmark 1953 color card set. In the same 2-1/2" x 3-3/4" size as the issued cards, the proofs are blank-backed and lack the black frame line separating the picture from the white border. The Enos Slaughter card is otherwise identical to the issued version. The Spahn was changed to a different, more close-up picture for the issued card. The "Dodgers In Action" card was never issued, nor was the Ferris Fain card, probably due to Fain's trade from the A's to the White Sox prior to the 1953 season.

		NM	EX	VG
Complete Set (4):		7,200	3,600	2,150
Common Player:		1,125	560.00	325.00
(1)	Dodgers In Action	4,950	2,475	745.00
(2)	Ferris Fain	3,675	1,840	550.00
(3)	Enos Slaughter	1,690	845.00	255.00
(4)	Warren Spahn	4,050	2,025	610.00

1954 Bowman

Bowman's 1954 set consists of 224 full-color cards that measure 2-1/2" x 3-3/4". It is believed that contractual problems caused the withdrawal of card #66 (Ted Williams) from the set, creating one of the most sought-after scarcities of the

postwar era. The Williams card was replaced by Jim Piersall (who is also #210) in subsequent print runs. The set contains over 40 variations, most involving statistical errors on the card backs that were corrected. On most cards neither variation carries a premium value as both varieties appear to have been printed in equal amounts. The complete set price that follows does not include all variations or #66 Williams.

		NM	EX	VG
Complete Set (224):		5,000	2,400	1,400
Common Player (1-128):		10.00	5.00	3.00
Common Player (129-224):		12.00	6.00	3.50
1	Phil Rizzuto	200.00	100.00	50.00
2	Jack Jensen	50.00	25.00	12.50
3	Marion Fricano	10.00	5.00	3.00
4	Bob Hooper	10.00	5.00	3.00
5	Billy Hunter	10.00	5.00	3.00
6	Nellie Fox	80.00	40.00	20.00
7	Walter Dropo	10.00	5.00	3.00
8	Jim Busby	10.00	5.00	3.00
9	Dave Williams	10.00	5.00	3.00
10a	Carl Erskine (Two black loops in u-l)		Value Undetermined	
10b	Carl Erskine (No black loops)			
11	Sid Gordon	10.00	5.00	3.00
12a	Roy McMillan (551/1290 At Bat)	12.00	6.00	3.50
12b	Roy McMillan (557/1296 At Bat)	15.00	7.50	4.50
13	Paul Minner	10.00	5.00	3.00
14	Gerald Staley	10.00	5.00	3.00
15	Richie Ashburn	75.00	37.50	18.75
16	Jim Wilson	10.00	5.00	3.00
17	Tom Gorman	12.50	6.25	3.75
18	"Hoot" Evers	10.00	5.00	3.00
19	Bobby Shantz	10.00	5.00	3.00
20	Artie Houtteman	10.00	5.00	3.00
21	Vic Wertz	10.00	5.00	3.00
22a	Sam Mele (213/1661 Putouts)	12.00	6.00	3.50
22b	Sam Mele (217/1665 Putouts)	15.00	7.50	4.50
23	*Harvey Kuenn*	20.00	10.00	6.00
24	Bob Porterfield	10.00	5.00	3.00
25a	Wes Westrum (1.000/.987 Field Avg.)	12.00	6.00	3.50
25b	Wes Westrum (.982/.986 Field Avg.)	15.00	7.50	4.50
26a	Billy Cox (1.000/.960 Field Avg.)	15.00	7.50	4.50
26b	Billy Cox (.972/.960 Field Avg.)	20.00	10.00	6.00
27	Dick Cole	10.00	5.00	3.00
28a	Jim Greengrass (Birthplace Addison, N.J.)	20.00	10.00	6.00
28b	Jim Greengrass (Birthplace Addison, N.Y.)	12.00	6.00	3.50
29	Johnny Klippstein	10.00	5.00	3.00
30	Del Rice	10.00	5.00	3.00
31	"Smoky" Burgess	10.00	5.00	3.00
32	Del Crandall	10.00	5.00	3.00
33a	Vic Raschi (No trade line.)	27.50	13.50	8.25
33b	Vic Raschi (Traded line.)	50.00	25.00	15.00
34	Sammy White	10.00	5.00	3.00
35a	Eddie Joost (Quiz answer is 8.)	12.00	6.00	3.50
35b	Eddie Joost (Quiz answer is 33.)	15.00	7.50	4.50
36	George Strickland	10.00	5.00	3.00
37	Dick Kokos	10.00	5.00	3.00
38a	Minnie Minoso (.895/.961 Field Avg.)	25.00	12.50	7.50
38b	Minnie Minoso (.963/.963 Field Avg.)	30.00	15.00	9.00
39	Ned Garver	10.00	5.00	3.00
40	Gil Coan	10.00	5.00	3.00
41a	Alvin Dark (.986/.960 Field Avg.)	12.00	6.00	3.50
41b	Alvin Dark (.968/.960 Field Avg.)	15.00	7.50	4.50
42	Billy Loes	15.00	7.50	4.50
43a	Bob Friend (20 shutouts in quiz question)	12.00	6.00	3.50
43b	Bob Friend (16 shutouts in quiz question)	15.00	7.50	4.50
44	Harry Perkowski	10.00	5.00	3.00
45	Ralph Kiner	35.00	17.50	10.00
46	"Rip" Repulski	10.00	5.00	3.00
47a	Granny Hamner (.970/.953 Field Avg.)	12.00	6.00	3.50
47b	Granny Hamner (.953/.951 Field Avg.)	15.00	7.50	4.50
48	Jack Dittmer	10.00	5.00	3.00
49	Harry Byrd	12.50	6.25	3.75
50	George Kell	30.00	15.00	9.00
51	Alex Kellner	10.00	5.00	3.00
52	Joe Ginsberg	10.00	5.00	3.00
53a	Don Lenhardt (.969/.984 Field Avg.)	12.00	6.00	3.50

53b	Don Lenhardt (.966/.983 Field Avg.)	15.00	7.50	4.50
54	"Chico" Carrasquel	10.00	5.00	3.00
55	Jim Delsing	10.00	5.00	3.00
56	Maurice McDermott	10.00	5.00	3.00
57	Hoyt Wilhelm	27.50	13.50	8.25
58	Pee Wee Reese	100.00	50.00	25.00
59	Bob Schultz	10.00	5.00	3.00
60	Fred Baczewski	10.00	5.00	3.00
61a	Eddie Miksis (.954/.962 Field Avg.)	12.00	6.00	3.50
61b	Eddie Miksis (.954/.961 Field Avg.)	15.00	7.50	4.50
62	Enos Slaughter	35.00	17.50	10.00
63	Earl Torgeson	10.00	5.00	3.00
64	Eddie Mathews	80.00	40.00	20.00
65	Mickey Mantle	1,900	950.00	570.00
66a	Ted Williams	2,350	1,175	355.00
66b	Jimmy Piersall	75.00	37.50	18.75
67a	Carl Scheib (.306 Pct. with two lines under bio)	25.00	12.50	7.50
67b	Carl Scheib (.306 Pct. with one line under bio)	12.00	6.00	3.50
67c	Carl Scheib (.300 Pct.)	15.00	7.50	4.50
68	Bob Avila	10.00	5.00	3.00
69	Clinton Courtney	10.00	5.00	3.00
70	Willard Marshall	10.00	5.00	3.00
71	Ted Gray	10.00	5.00	3.00
72	Ed Yost	10.00	5.00	3.00
73	Don Mueller	10.00	5.00	3.00
74	Jim Gilliam	35.00	17.50	10.00
75	Max Surkont	10.00	5.00	3.00
76	Joe Nuxhall	10.00	5.00	3.00
77	Bob Rush	10.00	5.00	3.00
78	Sal Yvars	10.00	5.00	3.00
79	Curt Simmons	10.00	5.00	3.00
80a	Johnny Logan (106 Runs)	12.00	6.00	3.50
80b	Johnny Logan (100 Runs)	15.00	7.50	4.50
81a	Jerry Coleman (1.000/.975 Field Avg.)	15.00	7.50	4.50
81b	Jerry Coleman (.952/.975 Field Avg.)	20.00	10.00	6.00
82a	Bill Goodman (.965/.986 Field Avg.)	12.00	6.00	3.50
82b	Bill Goodman (.972/.985 Field Avg.)	15.00	7.50	4.50
83	Ray Murray	10.00	5.00	3.00
84	Larry Doby	45.00	22.50	13.50
85a	Jim Dyck (.926/.956 Field Avg.)	12.00	6.00	3.50
85b	Jim Dyck (.947/.960 Field Avg.)	15.00	7.50	4.50
86	Harry Dorish	10.00	5.00	3.00
87	Don Lund	10.00	5.00	3.00
88	Tommy Umphlett	10.00	5.00	3.00
89	Willie Mays	500.00	250.00	125.00
90	Roy Campanella	150.00	75.00	37.50
91	Cal Abrams	10.00	5.00	3.00
92	Ken Raffensberger	10.00	5.00	3.00
93a	Bill Serena (.983/.966 Field Avg.)	12.00	6.00	3.50
93b	Bill Serena (.977/.966 Field Avg.)	15.00	7.50	4.50
94a	Solly Hemus (476/1343 Assists)	12.00	6.00	3.50
94b	Solly Hemus (477/1343 Assists)	15.00	7.50	4.50
95	Robin Roberts	40.00	20.00	12.00
96	Joe Adcock	10.00	5.00	3.00
97	Gil McDougald	20.00	10.00	6.00
98	Ellis Kinder	10.00	5.00	3.00
99a	Peter Suder (.985/.974 Field Avg.)	12.00	6.00	3.50
99b	Peter Suder (.978/.974 Field Avg.)	15.00	7.50	4.50
100	Mike Garcia	10.00	5.00	3.00
101	*Don Larsen*	40.00	20.00	12.00
102	Bill Pierce	10.00	5.00	3.00
103a	Stephen Souchock (144/1192 Putouts)	12.00	6.00	3.50
103b	Stephen Souchock (147/1195 Putouts)	15.00	7.50	4.50
104	Frank Spec Shea	10.00	5.00	3.00
105a	Sal Maglie (Quiz answer is 8.)	20.00	10.00	6.00
105b	Sal Maglie (Quiz answer is 1904.)	30.00	15.00	9.00
106	Clem Labine	20.00	10.00	6.00
107	Paul LaPalme	10.00	5.00	3.00
108	Bobby Adams	10.00	5.00	3.00
109	Roy Smalley	10.00	5.00	3.00
110	Red Schoendienst	30.00	15.00	9.00
111	Murry Dickson	10.00	5.00	3.00
112	Andy Pafko	10.00	5.00	3.00
113	Allie Reynolds	20.00	10.00	6.00
114	Willard Nixon	10.00	5.00	3.00
115	Don Bollweg	10.00	5.00	3.00
116	Luke Easter	10.00	5.00	3.00
117	Dick Kryhoski	10.00	5.00	3.00
118	Bob Boyd	10.00	5.00	3.00
119	Fred Hatfield	10.00	5.00	3.00
120	Mel Hoderlein	10.00	5.00	3.00
121	Ray Katt	10.00	5.00	3.00
122	Carl Furillo	30.00	15.00	9.00
123	Toby Atwell	10.00	5.00	3.00
124a	Gus Bell (15/27 Errors)	12.00	6.00	3.50
124b	Gus Bell (11/26 Errors)	15.00	7.50	4.50
125	Warren Hacker	10.00	5.00	3.00
126	Cliff Chambers	10.00	5.00	3.00
127	Del Ennis	10.00	5.00	3.00
128	Ebba St. Claire	10.00	5.00	3.00
129	Hank Bauer	35.00	17.50	10.00
130	Milt Bolling	12.00	6.00	3.50
131	Joe Astroth	12.00	6.00	3.50
132	Bob Feller	75.00	37.50	18.75
133	Duane Pillette	12.00	6.00	3.50

No.	Player	NM	EX	VG
134	Luis Aloma	12.00	6.00	3.50
135	Johnny Pesky	12.00	6.00	3.50
136	Clyde Vollmer	12.00	6.00	3.50
137	Al Corwin	12.00	6.00	3.50
138a	Gil Hodges (.993/.991 Field Avg.)	80.00	40.00	20.00
138b	Gil Hodges (.992/.991 Field Avg.)	100.00	50.00	30.00
139a	Preston Ward (.961/.992 Field Avg.)	15.00	7.50	4.50
139b	Preston Ward (.990/.992 Field Avg.)	17.50	8.75	5.25
140a	Saul Rogovin (7-12 Won/Lost with 2 Strikeouts)	15.00	7.50	4.50
140b	Saul Rogovin (7-12 Won/Lost with 62 Strikeouts)	17.50	8.75	5.25
140c	Saul Rogovin (8-12 Won/Lost)	40.00	20.00	12.00
141	Joe Garagiola	30.00	15.00	9.00
142	Al Brazle	12.00	6.00	3.50
143	Willie Jones	12.00	6.00	3.50
144	*Ernie Johnson*	30.00	15.00	9.00
145a	Billy Martin (.985/.983 Field Avg.)	80.00	40.00	20.00
145b	Billy Martin (.983/.982 Field Avg.)	90.00	45.00	25.00
146	Dick Gernert	12.00	6.00	3.50
147	Joe DeMaestri	12.00	6.00	3.50
148	Dale Mitchell	12.00	6.00	3.50
149	Bob Young	12.00	6.00	3.50
150	Cass Michaels	12.00	6.00	3.50
151	Pat Mullin	12.00	6.00	3.50
152	Mickey Vernon	12.00	6.00	3.50
153a	"Whitey" Lockman (100/331 Assists)	15.00	7.50	4.50
153b	"Whitey" Lockman (102/333 Assists)	17.50	8.75	5.25
154	Don Newcombe	50.00	25.00	12.50
155	*Frank Thomas*	25.00	12.50	7.50
156a	Rocky Bridges (320/467 Assists)	15.00	7.50	4.50
156b	Rocky Bridges (328/475 Assists)	17.50	8.75	5.25
157	Omar Lown	12.00	6.00	3.50
158	Stu Miller	12.00	6.00	3.50
159	John Lindell	12.00	6.00	3.50
160	Danny O'Connell	12.00	6.00	3.50
161	Yogi Berra	175.00	87.50	43.75
162	Ted Lepcio	12.00	6.00	3.50
163a	Dave Philley (152 Games, no traded line)	50.00	25.00	15.00
163b	Dave Philley (152 Games, traded line)	22.50	11.00	6.75
163c	Dave Philley (157 Games, traded line)	27.50	13.50	8.25
164	Early Wynn	45.00	22.50	13.50
165	Johnny Groth	12.00	6.00	3.50
166	Sandy Consuegra	12.00	6.00	3.50
167	Bill Hoeft	12.00	6.00	3.50
168	Edward Fitz Gerald	12.00	6.00	3.50
169	Larry Jansen	12.00	6.00	3.50
170	Duke Snider	240.00	120.00	60.00
171	Carlos Bernier	12.00	6.00	3.50
172	Andy Seminick	12.00	6.00	3.50
173	Dee Fondy	12.00	6.00	3.50
174a	Pete Castiglione (.966/.959 Field Avg.)	15.00	7.50	4.50
174b	Pete Castiglione (.970/.959 Field Avg.)	17.50	8.75	5.25
175	Mel Clark	12.00	6.00	3.50
176	Vernon Bickford	12.00	6.00	3.50
177	Whitey Ford	125.00	62.50	31.25
178	Del Wilber	12.00	6.00	3.50
179a	Morris Martin (44 ERA)	15.00	7.50	4.50
179b	Morris Martin (4.44 ERA)	17.50	8.75	5.25
180	Joe Tipton	12.00	6.00	3.50
181	Les Moss	12.00	6.00	3.50
182	Sherman Lollar	12.00	6.00	3.50
183	Matt Batts	12.00	6.00	3.50
184	Mickey Grasso	12.00	6.00	3.50
185a	*Daryl Spencer* (.941/.944 Field Avg.)	15.00	7.50	4.50
185b	*Daryl Spencer* (.933/.936 Field Avg.)	17.50	8.75	5.25
186	Russ Meyer	15.00	7.50	4.50
187	Vern Law	12.00	6.00	3.50
188	Frank Smith	12.00	6.00	3.50
189	Ransom Jackson	12.00	6.00	3.50
190	Joe Presko	12.00	6.00	3.50
191	Karl Drews	12.00	6.00	3.50
192	Lew Burdette	12.00	6.00	3.50
193	Eddie Robinson	15.00	7.50	4.50
194	Sid Hudson	12.00	6.00	3.50
195	Bob Cain	12.00	6.00	3.50
196	Bob Lemon	30.00	15.00	9.00
197	Lou Kretlow	12.00	6.00	3.50
198	Virgil Trucks	12.00	6.00	3.50
199	Steve Gromek	12.00	6.00	3.50
200	Connie Marrero	12.00	6.00	3.50
201	Bob Thomson	20.00	10.00	6.00
202	George Shuba	15.00	7.50	4.50
203	Vic Janowicz	25.00	12.50	7.50
204	Jack Collum	12.00	6.00	3.50
205	Hal Jeffcoat	12.00	6.00	3.50
206	Steve Bilko	12.00	6.00	3.50
207	Stan Lopata	12.00	6.00	3.50
208	Johnny Antonelli	12.00	6.00	3.50
209	Gene Woodling (Photo reversed.)	35.00	17.50	10.00
210	Jimmy Piersall	35.00	17.50	10.00
211	Jim Robertson	12.00	6.00	3.50
212a	Owen Friend (.964/.957 Field Avg.)	15.00	7.50	4.50
212b	Owen Friend (.967/.958 Field Avg.)	17.50	8.75	5.25
213	Dick Littlefield	12.00	6.00	3.50
214	Ferris Fain	12.00	6.00	3.50
215	Johnny Bucha	12.00	6.00	3.50
216a	Jerry Snyder (.988/.988 Field Avg.)	15.00	7.50	4.50
216b	Jerry Snyder (.968/.968 Field Avg.)	17.50	8.75	5.25
217a	Henry Thompson (.956/.951 Field Avg.)	15.00	7.50	4.50
217b	Henry Thompson (.958/.952 Field Avg.)	17.50	8.75	5.25
218a	Preacher Roe (black loop at top)	35.00	17.50	10.00
(218b)	Preacher Roe (no black loop)(Value undetermined)			
219	Hal Rice	12.00	6.00	3.50
220	Hobie Landrith	12.00	6.00	3.50
221	Frank Baumholtz	12.00	6.00	3.50
222	Memo Luna	15.00	7.50	4.50
223	Steve Ridzik	12.00	6.00	3.50
224	Billy Bruton	45.00	12.00	5.00

1955 Bowman

Bowman produced its final baseball card set as an independent card maker in 1955, a popular issue that has color player photographs placed inside a television set design. The set consists of 320 cards measuring 2-1/2" x 3-3/4". High-numbered cards (#225-320) appear to have replaced certain low-numbered cards on the press sheets and are scarcer. The high series includes 31 umpire cards.

No.	Player	NM	EX	VG
	Complete Set (320):	7,000	3,500	2,000
	Common Player (1-224):	12.50	6.25	3.75
	Common Player (225-320):	25.00	12.50	7.50
1	Hoyt Wilhelm	100.00	50.00	25.00
2	Al Dark	15.00	7.50	4.50
3	Joe Coleman	12.50	6.25	3.75
4	Eddie Waitkus	12.50	6.25	3.75
5	Jim Robertson	12.50	6.25	3.75
6	Pete Suder	12.50	6.25	3.75
7	Gene Baker	12.50	6.25	3.75
8	Warren Hacker	12.50	6.25	3.75
9	Gil McDougald	25.00	12.50	7.50
10	Phil Rizzuto	125.00	62.50	31.25
11	Billy Bruton	12.50	6.25	3.75
12	Andy Pafko	12.50	6.25	3.75
13	Clyde Vollmer	12.50	6.25	3.75
14	Gus Keriazakos	12.50	6.25	3.75
15	*Frank Sullivan*	12.50	6.25	3.75
16	Jim Piersall	12.50	6.25	3.75
17	Del Ennis	12.50	6.25	3.75
18	Stan Lopata	12.50	6.25	3.75
19	Bobby Avila	12.50	6.25	3.75
20	Al Smith	12.50	6.25	3.75
21	Don Hoak	15.00	7.50	4.50
22	Roy Campanella	125.00	62.50	31.25
23	Al Kaline	150.00	75.00	37.50
24	Al Aber	12.50	6.25	3.75
25	Minnie Minoso	30.00	15.00	9.00
26	Virgil Trucks	12.50	6.25	3.75
27	Preston Ward	12.50	6.25	3.75
28	Dick Cole	12.50	6.25	3.75
29	Red Schoendienst	25.00	12.50	7.50
30	Bill Sarni	12.50	6.25	3.75
31	Johnny Temple	12.50	6.25	3.75
32	Wally Post	12.50	6.25	3.75
33	Nellie Fox	60.00	30.00	15.00
34	Clint Courtney	12.50	6.25	3.75
35	Bill Tuttle	12.50	6.25	3.75
36	Wayne Belardi	12.50	6.25	3.75
37	Pee Wee Reese	120.00	60.00	30.00
38	Early Wynn	25.00	12.50	7.50
39	Bob Darnell	15.00	7.50	4.50
40	Vic Wertz	12.50	6.25	3.75
41	Mel Clark	12.50	6.25	3.75
42	Bob Greenwood	12.50	6.25	3.75
43	Bob Buhl	12.50	6.25	3.75
44	Danny O'Connell	12.50	6.25	3.75
45	Tom Umphlett	12.50	6.25	3.75
46	Mickey Vernon	12.50	6.25	3.75
47	Sammy White	12.50	6.25	3.75
48a	Milt Bolling (Frank Bolling back.)	20.00	10.00	6.00
48b	Milt Bolling (Milt Bolling back.)	20.00	10.00	6.00
49	Jim Greengrass	12.50	6.25	3.75
50	Hobie Landrith	12.50	6.25	3.75
51	Elvin Tappe	12.50	6.25	3.75
52	Hal Rice	12.50	6.25	3.75
53	Alex Kellner	12.50	6.25	3.75
54	Don Bollweg	12.50	6.25	3.75
55	Cal Abrams	12.50	6.25	3.75
56	Billy Cox	12.50	6.25	3.75
57	Bob Friend	12.50	6.25	3.75
58	Frank Thomas	12.50	6.25	3.75
59	Whitey Ford	100.00	50.00	25.00
60	Enos Slaughter	30.00	15.00	9.00
61	Paul LaPalme	12.50	6.25	3.75
62	Royce Lint	12.50	6.25	3.75
63	Irv Noren	15.00	7.50	4.50
64	Curt Simmons	12.50	6.25	3.75
65	*Don Zimmer*	30.00	15.00	9.00
66	George Shuba	15.00	7.50	4.50
67	Don Larsen	30.00	15.00	9.00
68	**Elston Howard**	80.00	40.00	24.00
69	Bill Hunter	15.00	7.50	4.50
70	Lew Burdette	12.50	6.25	3.75
71	Dave Jolly	12.50	6.25	3.75
72	Chet Nichols	12.50	6.25	3.75
73	Eddie Yost	12.50	6.25	3.75
74	Jerry Snyder	12.50	6.25	3.75
75	Brooks Lawrence	12.50	6.25	3.75
76	Tom Poholsky	12.50	6.25	3.75
77	Jim McDonald	12.50	6.25	3.75
78	Gil Coan	12.50	6.25	3.75
79	Willie Miranda	12.50	6.25	3.75
80	Lou Limmer	12.50	6.25	3.75
81	Bob Morgan	12.50	6.25	3.75
82	Lee Walls	12.50	6.25	3.75
83	Max Surkont	12.50	6.25	3.75
84	George Freese	12.50	6.25	3.75
85	Cass Michaels	12.50	6.25	3.75
86	Ted Gray	12.50	6.25	3.75
87	Randy Jackson	12.50	6.25	3.75
88	Steve Bilko	12.50	6.25	3.75
89	Lou Boudreau	25.00	12.50	7.50
90	Art Ditmar	12.50	6.25	3.75
91	Dick Marlowe	12.50	6.25	3.75
92	George Zuverink	12.50	6.25	3.75
93	Andy Seminick	12.50	6.25	3.75
94	Hank Thompson	12.50	6.25	3.75
95	Sal Maglie	12.50	6.25	3.75
96	Ray Narleski	12.50	6.25	3.75
97	John Podres	30.00	15.00	9.00
98	Jim Gilliam	27.50	13.50	8.25
99	Jerry Coleman	15.00	7.50	4.50
100	Tom Morgan	15.00	7.50	4.50
101a	Don Johnson (Ernie Johnson (Braves) on front.)	60.00	30.00	18.00
101b	Don Johnson (Don Johnson (Orioles) on front.)	27.50	13.50	8.25
102	Bobby Thomson	17.50	8.75	5.25
103	Eddie Mathews	80.00	40.00	20.00
104	Bob Porterfield	12.50	6.25	3.75
105	Johnny Schmitz	12.50	6.25	3.75
106	Del Rice	12.50	6.25	3.75
107	Solly Hemus	12.50	6.25	3.75
108	Lou Kretlow	12.50	6.25	3.75
109	Vern Stephens	12.50	6.25	3.75
110	Bob Miller	12.50	6.25	3.75
111	Steve Ridzik	12.50	6.25	3.75
112	Granny Hamner	12.50	6.25	3.75
113	Bob Hall	12.50	6.25	3.75
114	Vic Janowicz	12.50	6.25	3.75
115	Roger Bowman	12.50	6.25	3.75
116	Sandy Consuegra	12.50	6.25	3.75
117	Johnny Groth	12.50	6.25	3.75
118	Bobby Adams	12.50	6.25	3.75
119	Joe Astroth	12.50	6.25	3.75
120	Ed Burtschy	12.50	6.25	3.75
121	Rufus Crawford	12.50	6.25	3.75
122	Al Corwin	12.50	6.25	3.75
123	Marv Grissom	12.50	6.25	3.75
124	Johnny Antonelli	12.50	6.25	3.75
125	Paul Giel	12.50	6.25	3.75
126	Billy Goodman	12.50	6.25	3.75
127	Hank Majeski	12.50	6.25	3.75
128	Mike Garcia	12.50	6.25	3.75
129	Hal Naragon	12.50	6.25	3.75
130	Richie Ashburn	50.00	25.00	15.00
131	Willard Marshall	12.50	6.25	3.75
132a	Harvey Kueen (Misspelled last name.)	25.00	12.50	7.50
132b	Harvey Kuenn (Corrected)	35.00	17.50	10.00
133	Charles King	12.50	6.25	3.75
134	Bob Feller	80.00	40.00	20.00
135	Lloyd Merriman	12.50	6.25	3.75
136	Rocky Bridges	12.50	6.25	3.75
137	Bob Talbot	12.50	6.25	3.75
138	Davey Williams	12.50	6.25	3.75
139	Billy & Bobby Shantz	15.00	7.50	4.50
140	Bobby Shantz	12.50	6.25	3.75
141	Wes Westrum	12.50	6.25	3.75
142	Rudy Regalado	12.50	6.25	3.75
143	Don Newcombe	25.00	12.50	7.50
144	Art Houtteman	12.50	6.25	3.75
145	Bob Nieman	12.50	6.25	3.75
146	Don Liddle	12.50	6.25	3.75
147	Sam Mele	12.50	6.25	3.75
148	Bob Chakales	12.50	6.25	3.75
149	Cloyd Boyer	12.50	6.25	3.75
150	Bill Klaus	12.50	6.25	3.75
151	Jim Brideweser	12.50	6.25	3.75
152	Johnny Klippstein	12.50	6.25	3.75
153	Eddie Robinson	15.00	7.50	4.50
154	*Frank Lary*	12.50	6.25	3.75
155	Gerry Staley	12.50	6.25	3.75
156	Jim Hughes	15.00	7.50	4.50
157a	Ernie Johnson (Don Johnson (Orioles) picture on front.)	15.00	7.50	4.50
157b	Ernie Johnson (Ernie Johnson (Braves) picture on front.)	30.00	15.00	9.00
158	Gil Hodges	40.00	20.00	12.00
159	Harry Byrd	12.50	6.25	3.75
160	Bill Skowron	40.00	20.00	12.00
161	Matt Batts	12.50	6.25	3.75
162	Charlie Maxwell	12.50	6.25	3.75
163	Sid Gordon	12.50	6.25	3.75
164	Toby Atwell	12.50	6.25	3.75
165	Maurice McDermott	12.50	6.25	3.75
166	Jim Busby	12.50	6.25	3.75
167	Bob Grim	15.00	7.50	4.50
168	Yogi Berra	125.00	62.50	31.25
169	Carl Furillo	27.50	13.50	8.25

		NM	EX	VG
170	Carl Erskine	25.00	12.50	7.50
171	Robin Roberts	32.50	16.00	10.00
172	Willie Jones	12.50	6.25	3.75
173	"Chico" Carrasquel	12.50	6.25	3.75
174	Sherman Lollar	12.50	6.25	3.75
175	Wilmer Shantz	12.50	6.25	3.75
176	Joe DeMaestri	12.50	6.25	3.75
177	Willard Nixon	12.50	6.25	3.75
178	Tom Brewer	12.50	6.25	3.75
179	Hank Aaron	300.00	150.00	75.00
180	Johnny Logan	12.50	6.25	3.75
181	Eddie Miksis	12.50	6.25	3.75
182	Bob Rush	12.50	6.25	3.75
183	Ray Katt	12.50	6.25	3.75
184	Willie Mays	275.00	137.50	68.75
185	Vic Raschi	12.50	6.25	3.75
186	Alex Grammas	12.50	6.25	3.75
187	Fred Hatfield	12.50	6.25	3.75
188	Ned Garver	12.50	6.25	3.75
189	Jack Collum	12.50	6.25	3.75
190	Fred Baczewski	12.50	6.25	3.75
191	Bob Lemon	30.00	15.00	9.00
192	George Strickland	12.50	6.25	3.75
193	Howie Judson	12.50	6.25	3.75
194	Joe Nuxhall	12.50	6.25	3.75
195a	Erv Palica (No traded line.)	30.00	15.00	9.00
195b	Erv Palica (Traded line.)	125.00	60.00	35.00
196	Russ Meyer	15.00	7.50	4.50
197	Ralph Kiner	35.00	17.50	10.00
198	Dave Pope	12.50	6.25	3.75
199	Vernon Law	12.50	6.25	3.75
200	Dick Littlefield	12.50	6.25	3.75
201	Allie Reynolds	25.00	12.50	7.50
202	Mickey Mantle	675.00	335.00	200.00
203	Steve Gromek	12.50	6.25	3.75
204a	Frank Bolling (Milt Bolling back.)	45.00	22.50	13.50
204b	Frank Bolling (Frank Bolling back.)	30.00	15.00	9.00
205	"Rip" Repulski	12.50	6.25	3.75
206	Ralph Beard	12.50	6.25	3.75
207	Frank Shea	12.50	6.25	3.75
208	Ed Fitz Gerald	12.50	6.25	3.75
209	"Smoky" Burgess	12.50	6.25	3.75
210	Earl Torgeson	12.50	6.25	3.75
211	John "Sonny" Dixon	12.50	6.25	3.75
212	Jack Dittmer	12.50	6.25	3.75
213	George Kell	30.00	15.00	9.00
214	Billy Pierce	12.50	6.25	3.75
215	Bob Kuzava	12.50	6.25	3.75
216	Preacher Roe	15.00	7.50	4.50
217	Del Crandall	12.50	6.25	3.75
218	Joe Adcock	12.50	6.25	3.75
219	"Whitey" Lockman	12.50	6.25	3.75
220	Jim Hearn	12.50	6.25	3.75
221	Hector "Skinny" Brown	12.50	6.25	3.75
222	Russ Kemmerer	12.50	6.25	3.75
223	Hal Jeffcoat	12.50	6.25	3.75
224	Dee Fondy	12.50	6.25	3.75
225	Paul Richards	25.00	12.50	7.50
226	W.F. McKinley (Umpire)	30.00	15.00	9.00
227	Frank Baumholtz	25.00	12.50	7.50
228	John M. Phillips	25.00	12.50	7.50
229	Jim Brosnan	25.00	12.50	7.50
230	Al Brazle	25.00	12.50	7.50
231	Jim Konstanty	25.00	12.50	7.50
232	Birdie Tebbetts	25.00	12.50	7.50
233	Cal Serena	25.00	12.50	7.50
234	Dick Bartell	25.00	12.50	7.50
235	J.A. Paparella (Umpire)	30.00	15.00	9.00
236	Murry Dickson	25.00	12.50	7.50
237	Johnny Wyrostek	25.00	12.50	7.50
238	Eddie Stanky	25.00	12.50	7.50
239	Edwin A. Rommel (Umpire)	30.00	15.00	9.00
240	Billy Loes	25.00	12.50	7.50
241	John Pesky	25.00	12.50	7.50
242	Ernie Banks	350.00	175.00	87.50
243	Gus Bell	25.00	12.50	7.50
244	Duane Pillette	25.00	12.50	7.50
245	Bill Miller	25.00	12.50	7.50
246	Hank Bauer	45.00	22.50	13.50
247	Dutch Leonard	25.00	12.50	7.50
248	Harry Dorish	25.00	12.50	7.50
249	Billy Gardner	25.00	12.50	7.50
250	Larry Napp (Umpire)	30.00	15.00	9.00
251	Stan Jok	25.00	12.50	7.50
252	Roy Smalley	25.00	12.50	7.50
253	Jim Wilson	25.00	12.50	7.50
254	Bennett Flowers	25.00	12.50	7.50
255	Pete Runnels	25.00	12.50	7.50
256	Owen Friend	25.00	12.50	7.50
257	Tom Alston	25.00	12.50	7.50
258	John W. Stevens (Umpire)	30.00	15.00	9.00
259	Don Mossi	35.00	17.50	10.00
260	Edwin H. Hurley (Umpire)	30.00	15.00	9.00
261	Walt Moryn	25.00	12.50	7.50
262	Jim Lemon	25.00	12.50	7.50
263	Eddie Joost	25.00	12.50	7.50
264	Bill Henry	25.00	12.50	7.50
265	Al Barlick (Umpire)	60.00	30.00	15.00
266	Mike Fornieles	25.00	12.50	7.50
267	George Honochick (Umpire)	50.00	25.00	15.00
268	Roy Lee Hawes	25.00	12.50	7.50
269	Joe Amalfitano	25.00	12.50	7.50
270	Chico Fernandez	25.00	12.50	7.50
271	Bob Hooper	25.00	12.50	7.50
272	John Flaherty (Umpire)	30.00	15.00	9.00
273	"Bubba" Church	25.00	12.50	7.50
274	Jim Delsing	25.00	12.50	7.50
275	William T. Grieve (Umpire)	30.00	15.00	9.00
276	Ike Delock	25.00	12.50	7.50
277	Ed Runge (Umpire)	30.00	15.00	9.00
278	Charles Neal	35.00	17.50	10.00
279	Hank Soar (Umpire)	30.00	15.00	9.00
280	Clyde McCullough	25.00	12.50	7.50
281	Charles Berry (Umpire)	30.00	15.00	9.00
282	Phil Cavarretta	30.00	15.00	9.00
283	Nestor Chylak (Umpire)	60.00	30.00	15.00
284	William A. Jackowski (Umpire)	30.00	15.00	9.00
285	Walt Dropo	25.00	12.50	7.50
286	Frank Secory (Umpire)	30.00	15.00	9.00
287	Ron Mrozinski	25.00	12.50	7.50
288	Dick Smith	25.00	12.50	7.50
289	Art Gore (Umpire)	30.00	15.00	9.00
290	Hershell Freeman	25.00	12.50	7.50
291	Frank Dascoli (Umpire)	30.00	15.00	9.00
292	Marv Blaylock	25.00	12.50	7.50
293	Thomas D. Gorman (Umpire)	30.00	15.00	9.00
294	Wally Moses	25.00	12.50	7.50
295	Lee Ballanfant (Umpire)	30.00	15.00	9.00
296	Bill Virdon	30.00	15.00	9.00
297	"Dusty" Boggess (Umpire)	30.00	15.00	9.00
298	Charlie Grimm	25.00	12.50	7.50
299	Lonnie Warneke (Umpire)	30.00	15.00	9.00
300	Tommy Byrne	30.00	15.00	9.00
301	William Engeln (Umpire)	30.00	15.00	9.00
302	Frank Malzone	30.00	15.00	9.00
303	Jocko Conlan (Umpire)	60.00	30.00	15.00
304	Harry Chiti	25.00	12.50	7.50
305	Frank Umont (Umpire)	30.00	15.00	9.00
306	Bob Cerv	30.00	15.00	9.00
307	"Babe" Pinelli (Umpire)	25.00	12.50	7.50
308	Al Lopez	35.00	17.50	10.00
309	Hal Dixon (Umpire)	30.00	15.00	9.00
310	Ken Lehman	25.00	12.50	7.50
311	Larry Goetz (Umpire)	30.00	15.00	9.00
312	Bill Wight	25.00	12.50	7.50
313	Augie Donatelli (Umpire)	30.00	15.00	9.00
314	Dale Mitchell	25.00	12.50	7.50
315	Cal Hubbard (Umpire)	60.00	30.00	18.00
316	Marion Fricano	25.00	12.50	7.50
317	Bill Summers (Umpire)	30.00	15.00	9.00
318	Sid Hudson	25.00	12.50	7.50
319	Al Schroll	25.00	12.50	7.50
320	George Susce, Jr.	60.00	30.00	15.00

1956 Bowman Prototypes

To gauge consumer demand for a 1956 baseball card set that it never issued, Bowman produced a "Baseball Card Preference Study" report. The report survives today in the form of a 24-page notebook that includes samples of the three designs apparently preferred by the pre-teen boys surveyed. All three cards are glued to one page of the report and all feature the photo of Pirates catcher Clem Koshorek used in the 1953 Bowman set. It is believed only two of the reports survive.

(Sold for $10,440 in 5/05 auction.)

1963 George Brace All Time Chicago Cubs

The year of issue attributed here is only theoretical. The set consists of a window envelope which contains 18 5-1/4" x 7" black-and-white photos of former Cubs greats by famed Chicago baseball photographer George Brace. The blank-backed unnumbered pictures have player identification in the white border at bottom. They are checklisted here alphabetically.

		NM	EX	VG
Complete Set (18):		50.00	25.00	15.00
Common Player:		7.50	3.75	2.25
(1)	Grover Cleveland Alexander	10.00	5.00	3.00
(2)	Cap Anson	10.00	5.00	3.00
(3)	Three Finger Brown	9.00	4.50	2.75
(4)	Frank Chance	9.00	4.50	2.75
(5)	Johnny Evers	9.00	4.50	2.75
(6)	Charlie Grimm	7.50	3.75	2.25
(7)	Stan Hack	7.50	3.75	2.25
(8)	Gabby Hartnett	7.50	3.75	2.25
(9)	Billy Herman	7.50	3.75	2.25
(10)	Charlie Hollocher	7.50	3.75	2.25
(11)	Billy Jurges	7.50	3.75	2.25
(12)	Johnny Kling	7.50	3.75	2.25
(13)	Joe McCarthy	7.50	3.75	2.25
(14)	Ed Reulbach	7.50	3.75	2.25
(15)	Albert Spalding	7.50	3.75	2.25

		NM	EX	VG
(16)	Joe Tinker	9.00	4.50	2.75
(17)	Hippo Vaughn	7.50	3.75	2.25
(18)	Hack Wilson	9.00	4.50	2.75

1974 Bramac 1933 National League All-Stars

This early collectors issue features black-and-white photos of the premiere N.L. All-Star team in their distinctive game uniforms. Cards are in a 2-1/2" x 3-1/4" format.

		NM	EX	VG
Complete Set (18):		30.00	15.00	9.00
Common Player:		6.00	3.00	1.75
1	Paul Waner	6.00	3.00	1.75
2	Woody English	6.00	3.00	1.75
3	Dick Bartell	6.00	3.00	1.75
4	Chuck Klein	6.00	3.00	1.75
5	Tony Cuccinello	6.00	3.00	1.75
6	Lefty O'Doul	6.00	3.00	1.75
7	Gabby Hartnett	6.00	3.00	1.75
8	Lon Warneke	6.00	3.00	1.75
9	Wally Berger	6.00	3.00	1.75
10	Chick Hafey	6.00	3.00	1.75
11	Frank Frisch	6.00	3.00	1.75
12	Carl Hubbell	6.00	3.00	1.75
13	Bill Hallahan	6.00	3.00	1.75
14	Hal Schumacher	6.00	3.00	1.75
15	Pie Traynor	6.00	3.00	1.75
16	Bill Terry	6.00	3.00	1.75
17	Pepper Martin	6.00	3.00	1.75
18	Jimmy Wilson	6.00	3.00	1.75

1951 Bread for Energy Labels
(See 1951 Fischer's Bread Labels)

1908-11 H.H. Bregstone Browns/Cardinals Post Cards (PC743)

Among the rarest of the early 20th Century baseball player postcards are those of the St. Louis Browns and Cardinals from H.H. Bregstone, also of St. Louis. The 3-1/2" x 5-1/2" cards feature sepia player photos that are borderless at top and sides. At bottom is a box with the player's name, team, position, league and the issuer's address. Backs are standard postcard format. The unnumbered cards are checklisted here alphabetically within team. With a single exception (Gregory), all of the Browns players are from 1909, while the range of Cardinals spans the era 1908-1911.

		NM	EX	VG
Complete Set, Browns (22):		9,500	4,750	2,750
Complete Set, Cardinals (34):		18,000	9,000	5,500
Common Player:		500.00	250.00	150.00
	ST. LOUIS BROWNS			
(1)	Bill Bailey	500.00	250.00	150.00
(2)	Lou Criger	500.00	250.00	150.00
(3)	Dode Criss	500.00	250.00	150.00
(4)	Bill Dineen	500.00	250.00	150.00
(5)	Hobe Ferris	500.00	250.00	150.00
(6)	Bill Graham	500.00	250.00	150.00
(7)	B Gregory	500.00	250.00	150.00
(8)	Art Griggs	500.00	250.00	150.00
(9)	Roy Hartzell	500.00	250.00	150.00
(10)	Danny Hoffman	500.00	250.00	150.00
(11)	Harry Howell	500.00	250.00	150.00
(12)	Tom Jones	500.00	250.00	150.00
(13)	Jimmy McAleer	500.00	250.00	150.00
(14)	Ham Patterson	500.00	250.00	150.00
(15)	Barney Pelty	500.00	250.00	150.00
(16)	Al Schweitzer	500.00	250.00	150.00
(17)	Wib Smith	500.00	250.00	150.00

		NM	EX	VG
(18)	Jim Stephens	500.00	250.00	150.00
(19)	George Stone	500.00	250.00	150.00
(20)	Rube Waddell	750.00	375.00	225.00
(21)	Bobby Wallace	750.00	375.00	225.00
(22)	Jimmy Williams	500.00	250.00	150.00

ST. LOUIS CARDINALS

		NM	EX	VG
(1)	Jap Barbeau	500.00	250.00	150.00
(2)	Shad Barry	500.00	250.00	150.00
(3)	Fred Beebe	500.00	250.00	150.00
(4)	Frank Betcher	500.00	250.00	150.00
(5)	Jack Bliss	500.00	250.00	150.00
(6)	Roger Bresnahan	800.00	400.00	240.00
(7)	Bobby Byrne	500.00	250.00	150.00
(8)	Chappie Charles	500.00	250.00	150.00
(9)	Frank Corridon	500.00	250.00	150.00
(10)	Joe Delahanty	700.00	350.00	210.00
(11)	Rube Ellis	500.00	250.00	150.00
(12)	Steve Evans	500.00	250.00	150.00
(13)	Art Fromme	500.00	250.00	150.00
(14)	Rube Geyer	500.00	250.00	150.00
(15)	Billy Gilbert	500.00	250.00	150.00
(16)	Bob Harmon	500.00	250.00	150.00
(17)	Irv Higginbotham	500.00	250.00	150.00
(18)	Tom Higgins	500.00	250.00	150.00
(19)	Art Hoelskoetter	500.00	250.00	150.00
(20)	Miller Huggins	750.00	375.00	225.00
(21)	Rudy Hulswitt	500.00	250.00	150.00
(22)	Adam Johnson	500.00	250.00	150.00
(23)	Ed Konetchy	500.00	250.00	150.00
(24)	Johnny Lush	500.00	250.00	150.00
(25)	Lee Magee	500.00	250.00	150.00
(26)	Stoney McGlynn	500.00	250.00	150.00
(27)	Rebel Oakes	500.00	250.00	150.00
(28)	Bill O'Hara	500.00	250.00	150.00
(29)	Patsy O'Rourke	500.00	250.00	150.00
(30)	Ed Phelps	500.00	250.00	150.00
(31)	Charlie Rhodes	500.00	250.00	150.00
(32)	Elmer Rieger	500.00	250.00	150.00
(33)	Slim Sallee	500.00	250.00	150.00
(34)	Vic Willis	750.00	375.00	225.00

1903-1904 Breisch-Williams

Many veteran collectors now believe that Breisch Williams Confectionary Co. of Oxford, Pa., was just one of several firms that used the black-and-white card issue cataloged as E107 as a premium. A relatively small percentage of E107s are found with a purple rubber-stamped "THE BREISCH- WILLIAMS CO" message diagonally on back. It is speculated the stamp may have been used to "cancel" cards there were returned in a prize redemption program. The overprinted cards currently carry a premium of 2-3X the value of blank-backed or "One of a ..." E107s. With only a single known exception, all Breisch-Williams stamped cards are of Type 1.

(See E107 Type 1 and Type 2 for checklist and base value information.)

1909-10 C.A. Briggs Co. (E97)

CY. YOUNG, BOSTON, NAT'L

This card is one of a set of 30 BALL PLAYERS Cards, as follows :—
AUSTIN, New York American
BRADLEY, Cleveland American
BIRMINGHAM, Cleveland American
BRANSFIELD, Philadelphia National
CARRIGAN, Boston American
CAMNITZ, Pittsburg National
DURHAM, New York National
DYGERT, Philadelphia American
DOOLAN, Philadelphia National
DEVORE, New York National
DAVIS, Philadelphia American
HEMPHILL, New York American
HEINCHMAN, Cleveland American
HARTSEL, Philadelphia American
KROH, Chicago National
KLINOW, New York American
KELLY, Boston National
KEELER, New York National
McINTYRE, Detroit American
McCONNELL, Boston American
MOORE, Philadelphia National
MULLIN, Detroit American
MURRAY, New York National
MEYERS, New York National
NICHOLS, Cleveland American
ROSSMAN, Detroit American
SULLIVAN, Chicago American
STEINFELDT, Cincinnati National
SCHLEI, New York National
CY. YOUNG, Cleveland American
C.A. BRIGGS CO., Lozenge Makers
Boston, Mass.

Measuring approximately 1-1/2" x 2-3/4", this set is nearly identical to several other candy issues of the same period. Designated as E97 in the American Card Catalog, the set was issued in 1909-1910 by "C.A. Briggs Co., Lozenge Makers of Boston, Mass." The front of the card shows a tinted player photo, with the player's last name, position and team printed below. Backs are printed in brown and checklist the 30 players in the set alphabetically. The C.A. Briggs Co. name appears at the bottom. Black-and-white examples of this set have also been found on a thin paper stock with blank backs and are believed to be "proof cards." They are valued about 2-3X the figures shown here. Five variations are also found in the set. The more expensive variations are not included in the complete set price.

		NM	EX	VG
Complete Set (30):		60,000	24,000	12,000
Common Player:		2,500	1,000	500
Proofs: 1.5-2X				
(1)	Jimmy Austin	2,500	1,000	500.00
(2)	Joe Birmingham	2,500	1,000	500.00
(3)	Bill Bradley	2,500	1,000	500.00
(4)	Kitty Bransfield	2,500	1,000	500.00
(5)	Howie Camnitz	2,500	1,000	500.00
(6)	Bill Carrigan	2,500	1,000	500.00
(7)	Harry Davis	2,500	1,000	500.00
(8)	Josh Devore	2,500	1,000	500.00
(9a)	Mickey Dolan (Doolan)	4,500	2,200	1,350
(9b)	Mickey Doolan	2,500	1,000	500.00
(10)	Bull Durham	2,500	1,000	500.00
(11)	Jimmy Dygert	2,500	1,000	500.00
(12a)	Topsy Hartsell (Hartsel)	4,000	1,500	750.00

		NM	EX	VG
(12b)	Topsy Hartsel	2,500	1,000	500.00
(13)	Bill Heinchman (Hinchman)	2,500	1,000	500.00
(14)	Charlie Hemphill	2,500	1,000	500.00
(15)	Wee Willie Keeler	8,000	3,200	1,600
(16)	Joe Kelly (Kelley)	8,000	3,200	1,600
(17)	Red Kleinow	2,500	1,000	500.00
(18)	Rube Kroh	2,500	1,000	500.00
(19)	Matty McIntyre	2,500	1,000	500.00
(20)	Amby McConnell	2,500	1,000	500.00
(21)	Chief Meyers	2,500	1,000	500.00
(22)	Earl Moore	2,500	1,000	500.00
(23)	George Mullin	2,500	1,000	500.00
(24)	Red Murray	2,500	1,000	500.00
(25a)	Simon Nichols (Nicholls) (Philadelphia)	10,000	5,000	2,000
(25b)	Simon Nichols (Nicholls) (Cleveland)	4,000	1,500	750.00
(26)	Claude Rossman	4,000	1,500	750.00
(27)	Admiral Schlei	2,500	1,000	500.00
(28a)	Harry Steinfeld (Name incorrect.)	4,400	1,800	900.00
(28b)	Harry Steinfeldt (Name correct.)	4,400	1,800	900.00
(29a)	Dennis Sullivan (Chicago)	2,500	1,000	500.00
(29b)	Dennis Sullivan (Boston)	10,000	5,000	3,000
(30a)	Cy. Young (Cleveland) (Picture actually Irv Young.)	7,500	3,700	2,200
(30b)	Cy. Young (Boston) (Picture actually Irv Young.)	10,000	5,000	3,000

1933 C.A. Briggs Co. Babe Ruth

Stars in a variety of sports are featured in this series of candy issues. Card #24 has a drawing on front against a red background. The player bears more than a passing resemblance to Babe Ruth and on the back of the 2-3/8" x 2-7/8" card, along with a short history of baseball, Babe Ruth and his $52,000 contract for 1933 are mentioned. At bottom are details for redeeming a set of the 31 cards for baseball equipment or a pound of chocolates.

		NM	EX	VG
24	Baseball (Babe Ruth)	3,000	1,500	900.00

1953-54 Briggs Meats

The Briggs Meat set was issued over a two-year span (1953-54) and features 28 players from the Washington Senators and 12 from the New York teams. The set was issued in two-card panels on hot dog packages sold in the Washington, D.C. vicinity. The color cards, which are blank-backed and measure 2-1/4" x 3-1/2", are printed on waxed cardboard. Pictures of the New York players can also be found on cards in the 1954 Dan-Dee Potato Chips and 1953-1955 Stahl-Meyer Franks sets. There is a slight difference in style between the Senators cards and those of the New York players. The white panel beneath the photo of the Washington players includes a facsimile autograph plus a few biographical details about the player. The New York players' cards have only the player's name and facsimile signature in that panel. Many of the Senators cards command a premium for scarcity.

		NM	EX	VG
Common Player:		900.00	450.00	180.00
(1)	Hank Bauer	1,100	550.00	330.00
(2)	James Busby	900.00	450.00	180.00
(3)	Tommy Byrne	900.00	450.00	180.00
(4)	Gil Coan/SP	6,500	3,200	1,950
(5)	John Dixon/SP	3,500	1,750	1,050
(6)	Carl Erskine	1,000	500.00	200.00
(7)	Edward Fitzgerald (Fitz Gerald)	900.00	450.00	180.00
(8)	Newton Grasso/SP	6,500	3,200	1,950
(9)	Melvin Hoderlein	900.00	450.00	180.00
(10)	Gil Hodges	3,500	1,750	1,050
(11)	Monte Irvin	1,750	875.00	525.00
(12)	Jackie Jensen	950.00	475.00	190.00
(13)	Whitey Lockman	900.00	450.00	180.00
(14)	Mickey Mantle	17,500	8,750	5,250

		NM	EX	VG
(15)	Conrado Marrero	900.00	450.00	180.00
(16)	Walter Masterson	900.00	450.00	180.00
(17)	Carmen Mauro	900.00	450.00	180.00
(18)	Willie Mays	13,500	6,750	4,050
(19)	Mickey McDermott	900.00	450.00	180.00
(20)	Gil McDougald	3,000	1,050	900.00
(21)	Julio Moreno	900.00	450.00	180.00
(22)	Don Mueller	900.00	450.00	180.00
(23)	Don Newcombe	1,000	500.00	200.00
(24)	Robert Oldis	900.00	450.00	180.00
(25)	Erwin Porterfield	900.00	450.00	180.00
(26)	Phil Rizzuto	4,250	2,100	1,250
(27)	James Runnels/SP	3,000	1,500	900.00
(28)	John Schmitz/SP	2,000	1,000	600.00
(29)	Angel Scull	900.00	450.00	180.00
(30)	Frank Shea	900.00	450.00	180.00
(31)	Albert Sima	900.00	450.00	180.00
(32)	Duke Snider	7,500	3,700	2,200
(33)	Charles Stobbs	900.00	450.00	180.00
(34)	Willard Terwilliger	2,000	1,000	600.00
(35)	Joe Tipton	900.00	450.00	180.00
(36)	Thomas Umphlett	900.00	450.00	180.00
(37)	Gene Verble	900.00	450.00	180.00
(38)	James Vernon	3,000	1,500	900.00
(39)	Clyde Vollmer	900.00	450.00	180.00
(40)	Edward Yost	900.00	450.00	180.00

1947 Brillantina Sol de Oro Managers

The approximately 6" x 8" black-and-white pictures were issued in conjunction with a contest run by an Havana shampoo company. Fronts have photos of the managers of Cuba's four professional teams, bordered in white, with a facsimile autograph and message. A sponsor's credit line is in the bottom border. Backs have further promotional copy for the shampoo and rules of the contest.

		NM	EX	VG
Complete Set (4):		600.00	300.00	180.00
Common Player:		150.00	75.00	45.00
(1)	Salvador Hernandez	150.00	75.00	45.00
(2)	Adolfo Luque	250.00	125.00	75.00
(3)	Napoleon Reyes	200.00	100.00	60.00
(4)	Lazaro Salazar	150.00	75.00	45.00

1909-12 Broad Leaf Cigarettes

Cards with the Broad Leaf brand advertising on back can be found among the three most popular cigarette card issues circa 1910: T205 Gold Border, T206 White Border and T207 Brown Background. Two types are seen in T206, one that mentions "350 Subjects" and another, much rarer, that mentions "460 Subjects." Because some of the scarcer cards in T207 are often found with Broadleaf (as it was then spelled) backs, it is not practical to quote a value multipler; premiums for such cards have already been factored into the prices under T207. In T205, Broad Leaf backs can be found printed in either black or brown-olive green.

PREMIUMS:
T205: 4-5X
T206 350 Subjects: 10-12X
T206 460 Subjects, Common: 50-60X
T206 460 Subjects, HoF: 15-25X
(See T205, T206, T207 for checklists.)

1974 Broder N.Y. Mets Tour of Japan

Veteran collector Ed Broder who was stationed with the U.S. Army in Japan, produced this collectors' issue chronicling the goodwill tour undertaken by the National League champion N.Y. Mets. Nominally measuring about 1-7/8" x 3", cards have borderless black-and-white photos on front with no player identification or other graphics. Backs have player name, team and "1974 New York Mets Tour of Japan" in type-writer font along with a team logo. The unnumbered cards are checklisted here alphabetically.

		NM	EX	VG
Complete Set (20):		60.00	30.00	18.00
Common Player:		4.00	2.00	1.25
(1)	Yogi Berra	20.00	10.00	6.00
(2)	Wayne Garrett	8.00	4.00	2.50
(3)	Ron Hodges	8.00	4.00	2.50
(4)	Tsuneo Horiuchi	8.00	4.00	2.50
(5)	Kazumasa Kono	4.00	2.00	1.25
(6)	Jerry Koosman	8.00	4.00	2.50
(7)	Ed Kranepool, John Milner, unidentified Japanese player, Joe Torre	4.00	2.00	1.25
(8)	Jon Matlack	8.00	4.00	2.50
(9)	Felix Millan	8.00	4.00	2.50
(10)	John Milner	8.00	4.00	2.50
(11)	Shigeo Nagashima	10.00	5.00	3.00
(12)	Sadaharu Oh	15.00	7.50	4.50
(13)	Tom Seaver	40.00	20.00	12.00
(14)	Yososhi Sekimoto	4.00	2.00	1.25
(15)	Tamio Suetsugu	4.00	2.00	1.25
(16)	Kazumi Takahashi	4.00	2.00	1.25
(17)	Yoshima Takahashi	4.00	2.00	1.25
(18)	George Theodore	8.00	4.00	2.50
(19)	Joe Torre, Kazuyoshi Yamamoto	15.00	7.50	4.50
(20)	Kazuyoshi Yamamoto, Tetsuhara Kawakami	10.00	5.00	3.00

1975 Broder All-Time N.Y. Mets

Veteran collector Ed Broder produced this collectors' issue. Nominally measuring about 1-7/8" x 3-1/8", cards have borderless black-and-white photos on front. Some cards have the dates of their tenure with the team on front. The unnumbered cards are checklisted here alphabetically.

		NM	EX	VG
Complete Set (12):		45.00	22.50	13.50
Common Player:		4.00	2.00	1.25
(1)	Yogi Berra	7.50	3.75	2.25
(2)	Bud Harrelson	4.00	2.00	1.25
(3)	Jim Hickman	4.00	2.00	1.25
(4)	Al Jackson	4.00	2.00	1.25
(5)	Cleon Jones	4.00	2.00	1.25
(6)	Jerry Koosman	4.00	2.00	1.25
(7)	Ed Kranepool	4.00	2.00	1.25
(8)	Tug McGraw	4.00	2.00	1.25
(9)	Nolan Ryan	15.00	7.50	4.50
(10)	Tom Seaver	9.00	4.50	2.75
(11)	Warren Spahn	6.00	3.00	1.75
(12)	Casey Stengal (Stengel)	6.00	3.00	1.75

1975 Broder 1962 "Original" N.Y. Mets

Veteran collector Ed Broder produced this collectors' issue. Nominally measuring about 2" x 3", cards have border-less black-and-white photos on front with only the player name for identification. Backs are blank. The unnumbered cards are checklisted here alphabetically.

		NM	EX	VG
Complete Set (15):		50.00	25.00	15.00
Common Player:		5.00	2.50	1.50
(1)	Richie Ashburn	10.00	5.00	3.00
(2)	Gus Bell	5.00	2.50	1.50
(3)	Roger Craig	5.00	2.50	1.50
(4)	Gil Hodges	10.00	5.00	3.00
(5)	Rogers Hornsby	7.50	3.75	2.25
(6)	Sherman Jones	5.00	2.50	1.50
(7)	Rod Kanehl	5.00	2.50	1.50
(8)	Clem Labine	5.00	2.50	1.50
(9)	Hobie Landrith	5.00	2.50	1.50
(10)	R.G. Miller	5.00	2.50	1.50
(11)	Wilmer Mizell	5.00	2.50	1.50
(12)	Charley Neal	5.00	2.50	1.50
(13)	Casey Stengal (Stengel)	7.50	3.75	2.25
(14)	Frank Thomas	5.00	2.50	1.50
(15)	Marv Throneberry	5.00	2.50	1.50

1975 Broder Major Leagues - The 1950's

Veteran collector Ed Broder produced this collectors' issue. Nominally measuring about 2" x 3", cards have borderless black-and-white photos on front with only the player name for identification. Backs are blank. The unnumbered cards are checklisted here alphabetically. The set is notable in that a number of familiar players are pictured with teams not seen on their Topps and Bowman cards. The set sold originally for $2.20.

		NM	EX	VG
Complete Set (28):		100.00	50.00	30.00
Common Player:		4.00	2.00	1.25
(1)	Bobby Adams	4.00	2.00	1.25
(2)	Richie Ashburn	6.50	3.25	2.00
(3)	Ken Aspromonte	4.00	2.00	1.25
(4)	Ray Boone	5.00	2.50	1.50
(5)	Lou Boudreau	6.50	3.25	2.00
(6)	Smoky Burgess	4.00	2.00	1.25
(7)	Phil Cavaretta (Cavarretta)	4.00	2.00	1.25
(8)	Gene Conley	4.00	2.00	1.25
(9)	Del Crandell (Crandall)	4.00	2.00	1.25
(10)	Bob Friend	4.00	2.00	1.25
(11)	Harvey Haddix	4.00	2.00	1.25
(12)	Fred Haney	4.00	2.00	1.25
(13)	Ted Kluszewski	5.00	2.50	1.50
(14)	Jim Konstanty	4.00	2.00	1.25
(15)	Sandy Koufax	7.50	3.75	2.25
(16)	Harvey Kuenn	4.00	2.00	1.25
(17)	Bob Lemon	6.00	3.00	1.75
(18)	Marty Marion	4.00	2.00	1.25
(19)	Minnie Minoso	5.00	2.50	1.50
(20)	Stan Musial	7.00	3.50	2.00
(21)	Albie Pearson	4.00	2.00	1.25
(22)	Paul Richards	4.00	2.00	1.25
(23)	Hank Sauer	4.00	2.00	1.25
(24)	Herb Score	4.00	2.00	1.25
(25)	Bob Skinner	4.00	2.00	1.25
(26)	Enos Slaughter	6.00	3.00	1.75
(27)	Gus Triandos	4.00	2.00	1.25
(28)	Gus Zernial	4.00	2.00	1.25

1975 Broder Major League Postcards

This series of 3-1/8" x 5-1/8", borderless, blank-back pictures was advertised as the first in a proposed series designed to accommodate player autographs. Only California Angels and Montreal Expos players are included. The cards are printed on thin cardboard and feature close-up portraits with the player name in black type.

		NM	EX	VG
Complete Set (9):		25.00	12.50	7.50
Common Player:		3.00	1.50	.90
(1)	Tim Foli	3.00	1.50	.90
(2)	Barry Foote	3.00	1.50	.90
(3)	Mike Jorgensen	3.00	1.50	.90
(4)	Larry Lintz	3.00	1.50	.90
(5)	Dave McNally	3.00	1.50	.90
(6)	Steve Rodgers (Rogers)	3.00	1.50	.90
(7)	Nolan Ryan	10.00	5.00	3.00
(8)	Bill Singer	3.00	1.50	.90
(9)	Dick Williams	3.00	1.50	.90

1978 Broder Photocards

This collectors' issue features late 1970s photos of some of the game's stars from the 1920s-1960s. Cards are printed in 3-1/2" x 5-1/2", blank-back, black-and-white format on thick grayback card stock. Cards were printed four to a sheet and often found on uncut sheets.

		NM	EX	VG
Complete Set (20):		40.00	20.00	12.00
Common Player:		3.00	1.50	.90
(1)	Walt Alston	3.00	1.50	.90
(2)	Luke Appling	3.00	1.50	.90
(3)	Ernie Banks	4.50	2.25	1.25
(4)	Yogi Berra	4.50	2.25	1.25
(5)	Bill Dickey	4.00	2.00	1.25
(6)	Bob Feller/Pitching	4.00	2.00	1.25
(7)	Bob Feller/Portrait	4.00	2.00	1.25
(8)	Billy Herman	3.00	1.50	.90
(9)	Bob Lemon	3.00	1.50	.90
(10)	Mickey Mantle	6.00	3.00	1.75
(11)	Willie Mays/Btg	5.00	2.50	1.50
(12)	Willie Mays/Portrait	5.00	2.50	1.50
(13)	Johnny Mize	3.00	1.50	.90
(14)	Pee Wee Reese	4.00	2.00	1.25
(15)	Allie Reynolds	3.00	1.50	.90
(16)	Brooks Robinson	4.00	2.00	1.25
(17)	Enos Slaughter	3.00	1.50	.90
(18)	Warren Spahn	3.00	1.50	.90
(19)	Lloyd Waner	3.00	1.50	.90
(20)	Ted Williams	5.00	2.50	1.50

1940 Brooklyn Dodgers Picture Pack

Rookie Pee Wee Reese appears in this team-issued set of black-and-white pictures. The 6" x 9" pictures have player portraits surrounded by a white border. A facsimile autograph appears on front. Backs are blank. The unnumbered pictures are checklisted here in alphabetical order. Because of roster changes, it is possible the specific makeup of the packs may have changed once or more over the course of the season. Some of the pictures were reused in subsequent years' offerings.

		NM	EX	VG
Complete Set (25):		150.00	75.00	45.00
Common Player:		8.00	4.00	2.50
(1)	Dolf Camilli	8.00	4.00	2.50
(2)	Tex Carleton	8.00	4.00	2.50
(3)	Hugh Casey	8.00	4.00	2.50
(4)	Pete Coscarart	8.00	4.00	2.50
(5)	Curt Davis	8.00	4.00	2.50
(6)	Leo Durocher	12.00	6.00	3.50
(7)	Fred Fitzsimmons	8.00	4.00	2.50
(8)	Herman Franks	8.00	4.00	2.50
(9)	Joe Gallagher	8.00	4.00	2.50
(10)	Charlie Gilbert	8.00	4.00	2.50
(11)	Luke Hamlin	8.00	4.00	2.50
(12)	Johnny Hudson	8.00	4.00	2.50
(13)	Newt Kimball	8.00	4.00	2.50
(14)	Cookie Lavagetto	8.00	4.00	2.50
(15)	Gus Mancuso	8.00	4.00	2.50
(16)	Joe Medwick	12.00	6.00	3.50
(17)	Van Lingle Mungo	10.00	5.00	3.00
(18)	Babe Phelps	8.00	4.00	2.50
(19)	Tot Pressnell	8.00	4.00	2.50
(20)	Pee Wee Reese	24.00	12.00	7.25
(21)	Vito Tamulis	8.00	4.00	2.50
(22)	Joe Vosmik	8.00	4.00	2.50
(23)	Dixie Walker	8.00	4.00	2.50
(24)	Jimmy Wasdell	8.00	4.00	2.50
(25)	Whitlow Wyatt	8.00	4.00	2.50

1941 Brooklyn Dodgers Picture Pack

This team-issued set of 6" x 9" black-and-white pictures has player portraits surrounded by a white border. A facsimile autograph appears on front. Backs are blank. The unnumbered pictures are checklisted here in alphabetical order. Because of roster changes, it is possible the specific makeup of the packs may have changed once or more over the course of the season and that there may have been players issued other than those listed here. Some of the pictures were reused the 1940 offering. Team-issued pictures of 1940-41 can be differentiated from later years by their ballpark backgrounds.

		NM	EX	VG
Complete Set (25):		185.00	95.00	55.00
Common Player:		10.00	5.00	3.00
(1)	Mace Brown	10.00	5.00	3.00
(2)	Dolph Camilli	10.00	5.00	3.00
(3)	Hugh Casey	10.00	5.00	3.00
(4)	Pete Coscarart	10.00	5.00	3.00
(5)	Curt Davis	10.00	5.00	3.00
(6)	Leo Durocher	15.00	7.50	4.50
(7)	Fred Fitzsimmons	10.00	5.00	3.00
(8)	Luke Hamlin	10.00	5.00	3.00
(9)	Billy Herman	15.00	7.50	4.50
(10)	Kirby Higbe	10.00	5.00	3.00
(11)	Newt Kimball	10.00	5.00	3.00
(12)	Harry "Cookie" Lavagetto	10.00	5.00	3.00
(13)	Joe Medwick	15.00	7.50	4.50
(14)	Mickey Owen	10.00	5.00	3.00
(15)	Babe Phelps	10.00	5.00	3.00
(16)	Pee Wee Reese	25.00	12.50	7.50
(17)	Pete Reiser	10.00	5.00	3.00
(18)	Lew Riggs	10.00	5.00	3.00
(19)	Bill Swift	10.00	5.00	3.00
(20)	Vito Tamulis	10.00	5.00	3.00
(21)	Joe Vosmik	10.00	5.00	3.00
(22)	Dixie Walker	10.00	5.00	3.00
(23)	Jimmy Wasdell	10.00	5.00	3.00
(24)	Kemp Wicker	10.00	5.00	3.00
(25)	Whit Wyatt	10.00	5.00	3.00

1942 Brooklyn Dodgers Picture Pack

This set of 6" x 9" black-and-white team-issued pictures features player portrait photos in a studio setting. The pictures have a white border all around, and there is a facsimile autograph on front. Backs are blank. The unnumbered pictures are checklisted here alphabetically. Pictures from the 1942 and 1943 photo packs are indistinguishable except for player selection.

		NM	EX	VG
Complete Set (25):		150.00	75.00	45.00
Common Player:		8.00	4.00	2.50
(1)	Johnny Allen	8.00	4.00	2.50
(2)	Frenchy Bordagaray	8.00	4.00	2.50
(3)	Dolf Camilli	8.00	4.00	2.50
(4)	Hugh Casey	8.00	4.00	2.50
(5)	Curt Davis	8.00	4.00	2.50
(6)	Leo Durocher	12.00	6.00	3.50
(7)	Larry French	8.00	4.00	2.50
(8)	Augie Galan	8.00	4.00	2.50
(9)	Ed Head	8.00	4.00	2.50
(10)	Billy Herman	12.00	6.00	3.50
(11)	Kirby Higbe	8.00	4.00	2.50
(12)	Alex Kampouris	8.00	4.00	2.50
(13)	Newt Kimball	8.00	4.00	2.50
(14)	Joe Medwick	12.00	6.00	3.50
(15)	Mickey Owen	8.00	4.00	2.50
(16)	Pee Wee Reese	16.00	8.00	4.75
(17)	Pete Reiser	10.00	5.00	3.00
(18)	Lew Riggs	8.00	4.00	2.50
(19)	Johnny Rizzo	8.00	4.00	2.50
(20)	Schoolboy Rowe	10.00	5.00	3.00
(21)	Billy Sullivan	8.00	4.00	2.50
(22)	Arky Vaughan	12.00	6.00	3.50
(23)	Dixie Walker	8.00	4.00	2.50
(24)	Les Webber	8.00	4.00	2.50
(25)	Whitlow Wyatt	8.00	4.00	2.50

1943 Brooklyn Dodgers Picture Pack

This set of 6" x 9" black-and-white team-issued pictures features player portrait photos in a studio setting. The pictures have a white border all around, and there is a facsimile autograph on front. Backs are blank. The unnumbered pictures are checklisted here alphabetically. Pictures from the 1942 and 1943 photo packs are indistinguishable except for player selection.

		NM	EX	VG
Complete Set (25):		150.00	75.00	45.00
Common Player:		8.00	4.00	2.50
(1)	Johnny Allen	8.00	4.00	2.50
(2)	Frenchy Bordagaray	8.00	4.00	2.50
(3)	Bob Bragan	10.00	5.00	3.00
(4)	Dolf Camilli	8.00	4.00	2.50
(5)	Johnny Cooney	8.00	4.00	2.50
(6)	John Corriden	8.00	4.00	2.50
(7)	Curt Davis	8.00	4.00	2.50
(8)	Leo Durocher	12.00	6.00	3.50
(9)	Fred Fitzsimmons	8.00	4.00	2.50
(10)	Augie Galan	8.00	4.00	2.50
(11)	Al Glossop	8.00	4.00	2.50
(12)	Ed Head	8.00	4.00	2.50
(13)	Billy Herman	12.00	6.00	3.50
(14)	Kirby Higbe	8.00	4.00	2.50
(15)	Max Macon	8.00	4.00	2.50
(16)	Joe Medwick	12.00	6.00	3.50
(17)	Rube Melton	8.00	4.00	2.50
(18)	Dee Moore	8.00	4.00	2.50
(19)	"Buck" Newsom	10.00	5.00	3.00
(20)	Mickey Owen	8.00	4.00	2.50
(21)	Arky Vaughan	12.00	6.00	3.50
(22)	Dixie Walker	8.00	4.00	2.50
(23)	Paul Waner	12.00	6.00	3.50
(24)	Les Webber	8.00	4.00	2.50
(25)	Whitlow Wyatt	8.00	4.00	2.50

1946 Brooklyn Dodgers Picture Pack

This team-issued set of player portrait pictures is in a blank-back 6-1/2" x 9" format. A facsimile autograph appears on front. Like many souvenir-stand photo packs of the era, it is possible the specific contents of this product may have changed during the course of the season as players joined and left the team.

		NM	EX	VG
Complete Set (25):		125.00	65.00	40.00
Common Player:		6.00	3.00	1.80
(1)	Andy Anderson	6.00	3.00	1.80
(2)	Henry Behrman	6.00	3.00	1.80
(3)	Ralph Branca	6.00	3.00	1.80
(4)	Hugh Casey	6.00	3.00	1.80
(5)	Leo Durocher	9.00	4.50	2.75
(6)	Carl Furillo	12.00	6.00	3.50
(7)	Augie Galan	6.00	3.00	1.80
(8)	Hal Gregg	6.00	3.00	1.80
(9)	Joe Hatten	6.00	3.00	1.80
(10)	Al Head	6.00	3.00	1.80
(11)	Art Herring	6.00	3.00	1.80
(12)	Billy Herman	9.00	4.50	2.75
(13)	Gene Hermanski	6.00	3.00	1.80
(14)	Kirby Higbe	6.00	3.00	1.80
(15)	Harry "Cookie" Lavagetto	6.00	3.00	1.80
(16)	Vic Lombardi	6.00	3.00	1.80
(17)	Pee Wee Reese	12.00	6.00	3.50
(18)	Pete Reiser	6.00	3.00	1.80
(19)	Stan Rojek	6.00	3.00	1.80
(20)	Mike Sandlock	6.00	3.00	1.80
(21)	Eddie Stanky	7.50	3.75	2.25
(22)	Ed Stevens	6.00	3.00	1.80
(23)	Dixie Walker	6.00	3.00	1.80

| (24) | Les Webber | 6.00 | 3.00 | 1.80 |
| (25) | Dick Whitman | 6.00 | 3.00 | 1.80 |

1947 Brooklyn Dodgers Picture Pack

This team-issued set of player portrait pictures is in a blank-back 6-1/2" x 9" format. A facsimile autograph appears on front. Like many souvenir-stand photo packs of the era, it is possible the specific contents of this product may have changed during the course of the season as players joined and left the team.

		NM	EX	VG
Complete Set (25):		350.00	175.00	105.00
Common Player:		9.00	4.50	2.75
(1)	Ray Blades	9.00	4.50	2.75
(2)	Bobby Bragan	9.00	4.50	2.75
(3)	Ralph Branca	9.00	4.50	2.75
(4)	Tommy Brown	9.00	4.50	2.75
(5)	Hugh Casey	9.00	4.50	2.75
(6)	Ed Chandler	9.00	4.50	2.75
(7)	Carl Furillo	20.00	10.00	6.00
(8)	Hal Gregg	9.00	4.50	2.75
(9)	Joe Hatten	9.00	4.50	2.75
(10)	Gene Hermanski	9.00	4.50	2.75
(11)	Gil Hodges	40.00	20.00	12.00
(12)	Spider Jorgensen	9.00	4.50	2.75
(13)	Clyde King	9.00	4.50	2.75
(14)	Vic Lombardi	9.00	4.50	2.75
(15)	Rube Melton	9.00	4.50	2.75
(16)	Eddie Miksis	9.00	4.50	2.75
(17)	Pee Wee Reese	30.00	15.00	9.00
(18)	Pete Reiser	9.00	4.50	2.75
(19)	Jackie Robinson	80.00	40.00	24.00
(20)	Stan Rojek	9.00	4.50	2.75
(21)	Burt Shotton	9.00	4.50	2.75
(22)	Duke Snider	40.00	20.00	12.00
(23)	Eddie Stanky	12.50	6.25	3.75
(24)	Harry Taylor	9.00	4.50	2.75
(25)	Dixie Walker	9.00	4.50	2.75

1948 Brooklyn Dodgers Picture Pack

This team-issued set of player portrait pictures is in a blank-back 6-1/2" x 9" format. A facsimile autograph appears on front. Like many souvenir-stand photo packs of the era, it is possible the specific contents of this product may have changed during the course of the season as players joined and left the team, and that pictures were re-used from year-to-year.

		NM	EX	VG
Complete Set (26):		300.00	150.00	95.00
Common Player:		8.00	4.00	2.50
(1)	Rex Barney	8.00	4.00	2.50
(2)	Ray Blades	8.00	4.00	2.50
(3)	Bobby Bragan	8.00	4.00	2.50
(4)	Ralph Branca	8.00	4.00	2.50
(5)	Tommy Brown	8.00	4.00	2.50
(6)	Hugh Casey	8.00	4.00	2.50
(7)	Billy Cox	8.00	4.00	2.50
(8)	Leo Durocher	15.00	7.50	4.50
(9)	Bruce Edwards	8.00	4.00	2.50
(10)	Carl Furillo	20.00	10.00	6.00
(11)	Joe Hatten	8.00	4.00	2.50
(12)	Gene Hermanski	8.00	4.00	2.50
(13)	Gil Hodges	30.00	15.00	9.00
(14)	Spider Jorgensen	8.00	4.00	2.50
(15)	Don Lund	8.00	4.00	2.50

		NM	EX	VG
(16)	Eddie Miksis	8.00	4.00	2.50
(17)	Jake Pitler	8.00	4.00	2.50
(18)	Pee Wee Reese	25.00	12.50	7.50
(19)	Pete Reiser	8.00	4.00	2.50
(20)	Jackie Robinson	65.00	32.00	19.50
(21)	Preacher Roe	12.00	6.00	3.50
(22)	Burt Shotton	8.00	4.00	2.50
(23)	Clyde Sukeforth	8.00	4.00	2.50
(24)	Harry Taylor	8.00	4.00	2.50
(25)	Arky Vaughan	15.00	7.50	4.50
(26)	Preston Ward	8.00	4.00	2.50

1949 Brooklyn Dodgers Picture Pack

This team-issued set of player portrait pictures is in a blank-back 6-1/2" x 9" format. A facsimile autograph appears on front. Like many souvenir-stand photo packs of the era, it is possible the specific contents of this product may have changed during the course of the season as players joined and left the team, and that pictures were re-used from year-to-year.

		NM	EX	VG
Complete Set (25):		575.00	300.00	160.00
Common Player:		8.00	5.00	3.00
(1)	Jack Banta	8.00	5.00	3.00
(2)	Rex Barney	8.00	5.00	3.00
(3)	Ralph Branca	12.50	6.25	3.75
(4)	Tommy Brown	8.00	5.00	3.00
(5)	Roy Campanella	200.00	100.00	60.00
(6)	Billy Cox	8.00	5.00	3.00
(7)	Bruce Edwards	8.00	5.00	3.00
(8)	Carl Furillo	20.00	10.00	6.00
(9)	Joe Hatten	8.00	5.00	3.00
(10)	Gene Hermanski	8.00	5.00	3.00
(11)	Gil Hodges	40.00	20.00	12.00
(12)	Johnny Hopp	8.00	5.00	3.00
(13)	Spider Jorgensen	8.00	5.00	3.00
(14)	Mike McCormick	8.00	5.00	3.00
(15)	Eddie Miksis	8.00	5.00	3.00
(16)	Don Newcombe	100.00	50.00	30.00
(17)	Erv Palica	8.00	5.00	3.00
(18)	Jake Pitler	8.00	5.00	3.00
(19)	Pee Wee Reese	50.00	25.00	15.00
(20)	Jackie Robinson	75.00	37.00	22.00
(21)	Preacher Roe	12.50	6.25	3.75
(22)	Burt Shotton	8.00	5.00	3.00
(23)	Duke Snider	50.00	25.00	15.00
(24)	Milt Stock	8.00	5.00	3.00
(25)	Clyde Sukeforth	8.00	5.00	3.00

1952 Brooklyn Dodgers Schedule Cards

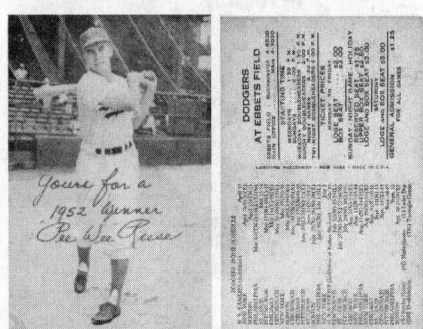

These postcard-size black-and-white cards have popular Dodgers players on front and the 1952 season's schedule printed on back. Some cards have a postcard-style back on which the right side has space for an address. Others cards have ticket price information in that space. How many different cards were issued is not known. Credit on the back is given to Lumitone Photoprint of New York.

	NM	EX	VG
Common Card:	400.00	110.00	67.00
Gil Hodges	400.00	200.00	120.00
Pee Wee Reese	400.00	200.00	120.00
Jackie Robinson	600.00	300.00	180.00
Duke Snider	400.00	200.00	120.00

1955 Brooklyn Dodgers Picture Pack

This set of approximately 5" x 7" blank-back, black-and-white pictures was a souvenir stand item at Ebbets Field. Player photos are chest-to-cap portraits surrounded by a white border with the player name at bottom in all-caps, followed by the team nickname in upper- and lower-case type.

The unnumbered pictures are listed here alphabetically. The set was sold for 25 cents in a white paper envelope with "WORLD CHAMPION Dodgers" printed in blue.

		NM	EX	VG
Complete Set (12):		100.00	50.00	30.00
Common Player:		8.00	4.00	2.50
(1)	Walter Alston	8.00	4.00	2.50
(2)	Roy Campanella	20.00	10.00	6.00
(3)	Carl Erskine	8.00	4.00	2.50
(4)	Carl Furillo	10.00	5.00	3.00
(5)	Gil Hodges	16.00	8.00	4.75
(6)	Randy Jackson	8.00	4.00	2.50
(7)	Clem Labine	8.00	4.00	2.50
(8)	Don Newcombe	8.00	4.00	2.50
(9)	Johnny Podres	8.00	4.00	2.50
(10)	Peewee Reese	13.50	6.75	4.00
(11)	Jackie Robinson	24.00	12.00	7.25
(12)	Duke Snider	16.00	8.00	4.75

1956 Brooklyn Dodgers Picture Pack

DON DRYSDALE, Dodgers

This set of 5" x 7" blank-back, black-and-white pictures was a souvenir stand item at Ebbets Field. Player photos are surrounded by a white border with the player name at bottom in all-caps, followed by the team nickname in upper- and lower-case type. The unnumbered pictures are listed here alphabetically. The same photos were offered in a 50-piece Yankees-Dodgers "World Series Picture Portfolio."

		NM	EX	VG
Complete Set (25):		250.00	125.00	75.00
Common Player:		10.00	5.00	3.00
(1)	Walter Alston	12.50	6.25	3.75
(2)	Sandy Amoros	12.50	6.25	3.75
(3)	Joe Becker	10.00	5.00	3.00
(4)	Don Bessent	10.00	5.00	3.00
(5)	Roy Campanella	30.00	15.00	9.00
(6)	Roger Craig	10.00	5.00	3.00
(7)	Don Drysdale	25.00	12.50	7.50
(8)	Carl Erskine	12.50	6.25	3.75
(9)	Chico Fernandez	10.00	5.00	3.00
(10)	Carl Furillo	15.00	7.50	4.50
(11)	Jim Gilliam	15.00	7.50	4.50
(12)	Billy Herman	12.50	6.25	3.75
(13)	Gil Hodges	25.00	12.50	7.50
(14)	Randy Jackson	10.00	5.00	3.00
(15)	Sandy Koufax	35.00	17.50	10.50
(16)	Clem Labine	12.50	6.25	3.75
(17)	Sal Maglie	10.00	5.00	3.00
(18)	Charlie Neal	10.00	5.00	3.00
(19)	Don Newcombe	12.50	6.25	3.75
(20)	Jake Pitler	10.00	5.00	3.00
(21)	Peewee Reese	20.00	10.00	6.00
(22)	Jackie Robinson	35.00	17.50	10.50
(23)	Ed Roebuck	10.00	5.00	3.00
(24)	Duke Snider	25.00	12.50	7.50
(25)	Al Walker	10.00	5.00	3.00

1957 Brooklyn Dodgers Picture Pack

In their final year in Brooklyn, the Dodgers issued this souvenir-stand picture pack, offered for 25 cents. The pictures are 5" x 7", blank-back, black-and-white. Player portraits are surrounded by a white border with the player name at bottom in all-caps and "Dodgers" in upper- and lower-case type. The unnumbered pictures are listed here alphabetically.

		NM	EX	VG
Complete Set (12):		125.00	65.00	40.00
Common Player:		10.00	5.00	3.00
(1)	Walter Alston	15.00	7.50	4.50
(2)	Roy Campanella	25.00	12.50	7.50
(3)	Carl Furillo	15.00	7.50	4.50
(4)	Jim Gilliam	15.00	7.50	4.50
(5)	Gil Hodges	20.00	10.00	6.00
(6)	Randy Jackson	10.00	5.00	3.00
(7)	Clem Labine	10.00	5.00	3.00
(8)	Sal Maglie	10.00	5.00	3.00
(9)	Don Newcombe	12.50	6.25	3.75
(10)	Johnny Podres	15.00	7.50	4.50
(11)	Peewee Reese	20.00	10.00	6.00
(12)	Duke Snider	20.00	10.00	6.00

1953-55 Brown & Bigelow

Some of baseball's biggest stars, either as they appeared in the mid-1950s or as spirit images, instruct All-American boys in the skills of baseball on this series of cards. Produced by the St. Paul firm of Brown & Bigelow, the 2-1/4" x 3-1/2", round-cornered cards can be found either as playing cards or with schedules printed on the back. The cards could be customized by local sponsors in a panel at the bottom of the artwork. The Medcalf artwork is also seen on contemporary wall and desk calendars and other printed items.

		NM	EX	VG
UNOPENED DECKS				
(1)	Ty Cobb	45.00	22.50	13.50
(2)	Lou Gehrig	50.00	25.00	15.00
(3)	Connie Mack	30.00	15.00	9.00
(4)	John McGraw	30.00	15.00	9.00
(5)	Babe Ruth	65.00	32.50	20.00
(6)	Honus Wagner	40.00	20.00	12.00
SINGLE CARDS				
(1)	Ty Cobb	6.00	3.00	1.75
(2)	Lou Gehrig	8.00	4.00	2.50
(3)	Connie Mack	4.00	2.00	1.25
(4)	John McGraw	4.00	2.00	1.25
(5)	Babe Ruth	10.00	5.00	3.00
(6)	Honus Wagner	5.00	2.50	1.50

1911-14 Brunners Bread (D304)

 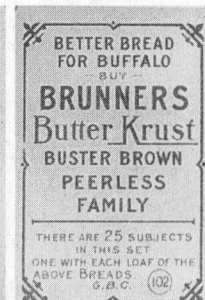

(See 1911-1914 General Baking Co. for checklist and values.)

1908-1910 Brush Detroit Tigers Postcards

 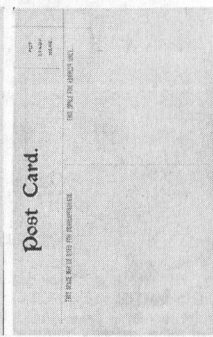

The makers of this short-lived (1907-11) automobile evidently engaged members of the hometown team to endorse their product. The 3-1/2" x 5-3/8" black-and-white postcards have a bordered photo on front showing a Tigers player (in uniform or suit) with the auto. A few lines of petry about the player complete the design. Backs have typical postcard format. It is likely the checklist here is incomplete.

		NM	EX	VG
(1)	Ty Cobb	4,000	2,000	1,200
(2)	William Coughlin	750.00	375.00	225.00
(3)	Bill Donovan	750.00	375.00	225.00
			750.00	
(4)	Hughie Jennings (Hands on steering wheel.)	1,500	750.00	450.00
(5)	Hughie Jennings (Hands in air.)	1,500	750.00	450.00
(6)	Matty McIntyre	750.00	375.00	225.00
(7)	George Mullin	750.00	375.00	225.00
(8)	Germany Schaefer, Charley O'Leary	750.00	375.00	225.00
(9)	Charlie Schmidt	750.00	375.00	225.00
(10)	Ira Thomas	750.00	375.00	225.00

1979 Bubble Yum Toronto Blue Jays

Members of the Toronto Blue Jays in the team's third season are featured in this set of 5-1/2" x 8-1/2" black-and-white player pictures. Fronts feature player portraits identified by their full name and team. In the wide bottom border are

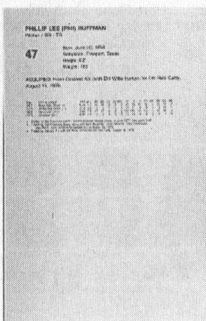

team and sponsor logos. Backs have player biographical data, major and minor league stats, acquisition information and career highlights. Cards are numbered by uniform number.

		NM	EX	VG
Complete Set (20):		65.00	32.50	20.00
Common Player:		4.00	2.00	1.25
1	Bob Bailor	4.00	2.00	1.25
4	Alfredo Griffin	4.00	2.00	1.25
7	Roy Hartsfield	4.00	2.00	1.25
9	Rick Cerone	4.00	2.00	1.25
10	John Mayberry	4.00	2.00	1.25
11	Luis Gomez	4.00	2.00	1.25
13	Roy Howell	4.00	2.00	1.25
18	Jim Clancy	4.00	2.00	1.25
19	Otto Velez	4.00	2.00	1.25
20	Al Woods	4.00	2.00	1.25
21	Rico Carty	4.00	2.00	1.25
22	Rick Bosetti	4.00	2.00	1.25
23	Dave Lemanczyk	4.00	2.00	1.25
24	Tom Underwood	4.00	2.00	1.25
31	Bobby Doerr	6.00	3.00	1.75
34	Jesse Jefferson	4.00	2.00	1.25
38	Balor Moore	4.00	2.00	1.25
44	Tom Buskey	4.00	2.00	1.25
46	Dave Freisleben	4.00	2.00	1.25
47	Phil Huffman	4.00	2.00	1.25

1976 Buckmans Discs

One of several regional sponsors of player disc sets in 1976 was Buckmans Ice Cream Village in Rochester, N.Y. The discs are 3-3/8" diameter with a black-and-white player portrait photo in the center of the baseball design. A line of red stars is above, while the left and right panels feature one of several bright colors. Produced by Michael Schecter Associates under license from the Major League Baseball Players Association, the player photos have had uniform and cap logos removed. Backs are printed in red and purple. The unnumbered checklist here is presented in alphabetical order.

		NM	EX	VG
Complete Set (70):		60.00	30.00	18.00
Common Player:		.75	.40	.25
(1)	Henry Aaron	6.00	3.00	1.75
(2)	Johnny Bench	3.50	1.75	1.00
(3)	Vida Blue	.75	.40	.25
(4)	Larry Bowa	.75	.40	.25
(5)	Lou Brock	2.50	1.25	.70
(6)	Jeff Burroughs	.75	.40	.25
(7)	John Candelaria	.75	.40	.25
(8)	Jose Cardenal	.75	.40	.25
(9)	Rod Carew	2.50	1.25	.70
(10)	Steve Carlton	2.50	1.25	.70
(11)	Dave Cash	.75	.40	.25
(12)	Cesar Cedeno	.75	.40	.25
(13)	Ron Cey	.75	.40	.25
(14)	Carlton Fisk	2.50	1.25	.70
(15)	Tito Fuentes	.75	.40	.25
(16)	Steve Garvey	2.00	1.00	.60
(17)	Ken Griffey	.75	.40	.25
(18)	Don Gullett	.75	.40	.25
(19)	Willie Horton	.75	.40	.25
(20)	Al Hrabosky	.75	.40	.25
(21)	Catfish Hunter	2.50	1.25	.70
(22)	Reggie Jackson (A's)	5.00	2.50	1.50
(23)	Randy Jones	.75	.40	.25
(24)	Jim Kaat	.75	.40	.25
(25)	Don Kessinger	.75	.40	.25
(26)	Dave Kingman	.75	.40	.25
(27)	Jerry Koosman	.75	.40	.25
(28)	Mickey Lolich	.75	.40	.25
(29)	Greg Luzinski	.75	.40	.25
(30)	Fred Lynn	.75	.40	.25
(31)	Bill Madlock	.75	.40	.25
(32)	Carlos May (White Sox)	.75	.40	.25
(33)	John Mayberry	.75	.40	.25
(34)	Bake McBride	.75	.40	.25
(35)	Doc Medich	.75	.40	.25
(36)	Andy Messersmith (Dodgers)	.75	.40	.25
(37)	Rick Monday	.75	.40	.25
(38)	John Montefusco	.75	.40	.25
(39)	Jerry Morales	.75	.40	.25
(40)	Joe Morgan	2.50	1.25	.70
(41)	Thurman Munson	2.50	1.25	.70
(42)	Bobby Murcer	.75	.40	.25
(43)	Al Oliver	.75	.40	.25
(44)	Jim Palmer	2.50	1.25	.70
(45)	Dave Parker	.75	.40	.25
(46)	Tony Perez	2.50	1.25	.70
(47)	Jerry Reuss	.75	.40	.25
(48)	Brooks Robinson	3.00	1.50	.90
(49)	Frank Robinson	3.00	1.50	.90
(50)	Steve Rogers	.75	.40	.25
(51)	Pete Rose	6.00	3.00	1.75
(52)	Nolan Ryan	20.00	10.00	6.00
(53)	Manny Sanguillen	.75	.40	.25
(54)	Mike Schmidt	5.00	2.50	1.50
(55)	Tom Seaver	3.00	1.50	.90
(56)	Ted Simmons	.75	.40	.25
(57)	Reggie Smith	.75	.40	.25
(58)	Willie Stargell	2.50	1.25	.70
(59)	Rusty Staub	.75	.40	.25
(60)	Rennie Stennett	.75	.40	.25
(61)	Don Sutton	2.50	1.25	.70
(62)	Andy Thornton (Cubs)	.75	.40	.25
(63)	Luis Tiant	.75	.40	.25
(64)	Joe Torre	1.50	.70	.45
(65)	Mike Tyson	.75	.40	.25
(66)	Bob Watson	.75	.40	.25
(67)	Wilbur Wood	.75	.40	.25
(68)	Jimmy Wynn	.75	.40	.25
(69)	Carl Yastrzemski	3.50	1.75	1.00
(70)	Richie Zisk	.75	.40	.25

1916 Bucyrus Brewing Co. (M101-4)

One of a dozen or so firms that utilized Felix Mendelsohn's baseball card issue as an advertising medium was this Ohio brewery. Unlike the other companies, however, Bucyrus did not issue individual cards, but only a 42" x 28" uncut sheet containing all 200 cards and labeled "1916 - BASEBALL'S HALL OF FAME - 1916." If cut from the sheet, the single cards would be indistinguishable from the blank-back version of M101-4.

	NM	EX	VG
Complete Uncut Sheet:	35,000	25,000	15,000

(See 1916 M101-4 Blank Backs for checklist.)

1950 Buitoni Macaroni Joe DiMaggio Pins

At least two styles of 1-1/2" diameter pinback buttons are known from the Yankee Clipper's association with a New York pasta company. One style has a black-and-white portrait photo at the center of a red-stiched baseball design. Printed in red at top is "JOE DiMAGGIO / TV CLUB." At bottom is the program sponsor's name. Another style has a photo of the player with a bat over his shoulder on a yellow background. "JOE DiMAGGIO CLUB" is at top, "BUITONI/FOODS CORP." at bottom, both in red. Each style was reproduced in 2-1/4" size early in the 21st Century; those replicas have no collectible value.

	NM	EX	VG
Joe DiMaggio (Portrait)	500.00	250.00	150.00
Joe DiMaggio (W/ bat.)	1,200	600.00	360.00

1932 Bulgaria Sport Tobacco

Despite the name of the sponsoring issuer, this set of cards is a product of Germany. Only a single major league ballplayer is pictured among the 272 cards in the set: Babe Ruth, who shares a card with boxing great Max Schmeling in a photo taken in the U.S. The black-and-white cards in the set measure 1-5/8" x 2-3/8" and have backs printed in German, including a card number.

		NM	EX	VG
256	Babe Ruth, Max Schmeling	300.00	150.00	90.00

1952-1953 Burger Beer Cincinnati Reds

Whether or not they were a promotional issue of Burger Beer (they are not marked as to issuer), advanced collectors of 1950s Reds memorabilia ascribe these 8" x 10-1/2" black-and-white photos to the long-time Reds sponsor because of their similarity to later Burger editions. The blank-back photos have portraits or posed action shots surrounded with white borders. In the wide bottom border is a C Reds logo, with the player name and (usually) position in all-capitals. The Clyde King picture, which can be reliably dated to 1953, his only season with the Reds, is a portrait drawing, rather than a photo, and has no position listed. The unnumbered pictures are listed here alphabetically and the checklist presented is likely incomplete.

		NM	EX	VG
Common Player:		30.00	15.00	9.00
(1)	Joe Adcock (Fielding)	40.00	20.00	12.00
(2)	Bob Borkowski	30.00	15.00	9.00
	(Batting follow-through.)			
(3)	Jim Greengrass	30.00	15.00	9.00
(4)	Grady Hatton (Portrait)	30.00	15.00	9.00
(5)	Niles Jordan (Portrait)	30.00	15.00	9.00
(6)	Clyde King (Portrait art.)	30.00	15.00	9.00
(7)	Willard Marshall (Batting follow-through.)	30.00	15.00	9.00
(8)	Ed Pellagrini (Portrait)	30.00	15.00	9.00
(9)	Bud Podbielan (Portrait)	30.00	15.00	9.00
(10)	Frank Smith	30.00	15.00	9.00
(11)	John Temple (Batting follow-through.)	30.00	15.00	9.00
(12)	Herm Wehmeier	30.00	15.00	9.00

1955 Burger Beer Cincinnati Reds

The evidence attributing these 8-1/2" x 11" black-and-white player pictures to one of the team's radio sponsors, Burger Beer, is apocryphal, based largely on the format, which is similar to the company's 1956-64 promotional issues. This series has player portraits or poses bordered in white. In the bottom border, flanked by team logos are three lines of capital-letter typography with the player's name, position and team. Backs are blank. This checklist is likely not complete.

		NM	EX	VG
Common Player:		30.00	15.00	9.00
(1)	Gus Bell	30.00	15.00	9.00
(2)	Rocky Bridges	30.00	15.00	9.00
(3)	Jackie Collum	30.00	15.00	9.00
(4)	Art Fowler	30.00	15.00	9.00
(5)	Ray Jablonski	30.00	15.00	9.00
(6)	Johnny Klippstein	30.00	15.00	9.00
(7)	Ted Kluszewski	45.00	22.00	13.50
(8)	Roy McMillan	30.00	15.00	9.00
(9)	Rudy Minarcin	30.00	15.00	9.00
(10)	Joe Nuxhall	45.00	22.00	13.50
(11)	Wally Post	30.00	15.00	9.00
(12)	Gerry Staley	30.00	15.00	9.00
(13)	Birdie Tebbetts	30.00	15.00	9.00

1956-1957 Burger Beer Cincinnati Reds

The 1956 and 1957 series of 8-1/2" x 11" black-and-white player photos from one of the Reds' broadcast sponsors can be distinguished from later issues by the presence of an advertising slogan at the bottom of the otherwise blank black, "COURTESY OF BURGER - A FINER BEER YEAR AFTER YEAR." Players are identified on the bottom front border in large capital letters. Because at least one player is known in both portrait and posed action photos, poses other than portraits are indicated in parentheses.

GUS BELL

		NM	EX	VG
Common Player:		30.00	15.00	9.00
(1)	Ed Bailey (Portrait to top button.)	30.00	15.00	9.00
(2)	Ed Bailey (Portrait to chest showing number.)	30.00	15.00	9.00
(3)	Gus Bell (Portrait to chest showing number.)	30.00	15.00	9.00
(4)	Joe Black	30.00	15.00	9.00
(5)	Smoky Burgess/Btg	35.00	17.50	10.50
(6)	George Crowe/Btg	30.00	15.00	9.00
(7)	Don Hoak	30.00	15.00	9.00
(8)	Waite Hoyt (Broadcaster)	30.00	15.00	9.00
(9)	Ray Jablonski/Throwing	30.00	15.00	9.00
(10)	Hal Jeffcoat (Follow-through.)	30.00	15.00	9.00
(11)	Ted Kluszewski/Btg	50.00	25.00	15.00
(12)	Ted Kluszewski (Portrait to top button.)	50.00	25.00	15.00
(13)	Brooks Lawrence (Follow-through.)	30.00	15.00	9.00
(14)	Roy McMillan/Btg	30.00	15.00	9.00
(15)	Roy McMillan/Fldg	30.00	15.00	9.00
(16)	Roy McMillan (Portrait to second button.)	30.00	15.00	9.00
(17)	Jackie Moran (Broadcaster)	30.00	15.00	9.00
(18)	Joe Nuxhall	30.00	15.00	9.00
(19)	Wally Post	30.00	15.00	9.00
(20)	Frank Robinson/Fldg	150.00	75.00	45.00
(21)	Frank Robinson (Portrait, white cap.)	125.00	62.00	37.00
(22)	Birdie Tebbetts	30.00	15.00	9.00
(23)	Johnny Temple (Portrait to second button.)	30.00	15.00	9.00
(24)	Johnny Temple (Portrait to chest showing number.)	30.00	15.00	9.00
(25)	Johnny Temple (Ready to throw.)	30.00	15.00	9.00
(26)	Bob Thurman/Btg	30.00	15.00	9.00

1958-1959 Burger Beer Cincinnati Reds

THOMAS

The 1958-1959 series of 8-1/2" x 11" black-and-white player photos can be distinguished by the presence of an advertising slogan at the bottom of the otherwise blank black, "COURTESY OF SPARKLE * BREWED BURGER BEER / HAVE FUN - HAVE A BURGER." Players are identified by first and last name, or by last name only on the bottom front border in large capital letters. The team name may or may not appear, as well.

		NM	EX	VG
Common Player:		30.00	15.00	9.00
(1)	Ed. Bailey/Portrait	30.00	15.00	9.00
(2)	Gus Bell/Portrait (Dark cap.)	30.00	15.00	9.00
(4)	Waite Hoyt (At microphone.)	30.00	15.00	9.00
(6)	Jerry Lynch/Portrait	30.00	15.00	9.00
(7)	Roy McMillan/Portait	30.00	15.00	9.00
(8)	(Don) Newcombe/Portait	30.00	15.00	9.00
(9)	Joe Nuxhall (Follow-through.)	30.00	15.00	9.00
(11)	Vada Pinson/Portait	45.00	22.00	13.50
(12)	Bob Purkey/Portait	30.00	15.00	9.00
(13)	Frank Robinson/Btg (Dark cap.)	125.00	62.00	37.00
(14)	Frank Robinson/Fldg	125.00	62.00	37.00
(15)	Frank Robinson/Portrait (White cap.)	125.00	62.00	37.00
(16)	Manager Mayo Smith (Adjusting cap.)	30.00	15.00	9.00
(17)	John Temple/Portrait	30.00	15.00	9.00
(18)	John Thomas/Btg	30.00	15.00	9.00
(19)	(Frank) Thomas/Portrait	30.00	15.00	9.00

1960-64 Burger Beer Cincinnati Reds

The sponsor is not identified (except on 1959 issues which are marked on back, "COURTESY OF SPARKLE * BREWED BURGER BEER / HAVE FUN - HAVE A BURGER)," nor the year of issue published on these 8-1/2" x 11" player photos.

VADA PINSON
CINCINNATI REDS

Uniform and cap styles can give some idea of when the photos were taken. Photos are black-and-white portraits or action poses surrounded by white borders with the player and team names at bottom. Backs are blank. The unnumbered photos are listed here in alphabetical order. Some photos were re-issued year after year with only minor changes in cropping; these are not listed separately. This checklist will likely remain incomplete for some time. Gaps have been in the assigned numbering to accommodate future additions.

		NM	EX	VG
Common Player:		15.00	7.50	4.50
(1)	Ed Bailey/Portrait	15.00	7.50	4.50
(2)	Ed. Bailey/Portrait (Dark cap)	40.00	20.00	12.00
(3)	Don Blasingame/Fldg	15.00	7.50	4.50
(4)	Gus Bell/Btg	15.00	7.50	4.50
(5)	Gus Bell (Fielding fly ball.)	15.00	7.50	4.50
(6)	Gus Bell/Portrait	15.00	7.50	4.50
(7)	Gordon Coleman (Bat behind cap.)	15.00	7.50	4.50
(8)	Gordon Coleman (Bat behind shoulder.)	15.00	7.50	4.50
(9)	Gordon Coleman/Fldg	15.00	7.50	4.50
(10)	John Edwards/Portrait (Light tower in background.)	15.00	7.50	4.50
(11)	John Edwards/Portrait (No tower.)	15.00	7.50	4.50
(12)	Gene Freese/Fldg	15.00	7.50	4.50
(13)	Don Hoak (Dark Cap)	35.00	17.50	10.50
(14)	Jay Hook (Follow-through.)	15.00	7.50	4.50
(15)	Waite Hoyt (Portrait at microphone.) (Announcer)	15.00	7.50	4.50
(16)	Waite Hoyt (Portrait w/folder.) (Announcer)	15.00	7.50	4.50
(17)	Fred Hutchinson/Portrait (C on vest.)	15.00	7.50	4.50
(18)	Fred Hutchinson/Portrait (Half of "1" and "C.")	15.00	7.50	4.50
(19)	Fred Hutchinson/Portrait (C Reds on vest.)	15.00	7.50	4.50
(20)	Fred. Hutchinson (Only top of chest emblem shows.)	15.00	7.50	4.50
(21)	Joey Jay (Follow-through.)	15.00	7.50	4.50
(22)	Joey Jay/Portrait	15.00	7.50	4.50
(23)	Hal Jeffcoat (follow thru)	15.00	7.50	4.50
(24)	Eddie Kasko/Btg	15.00	7.50	4.50
(25)	Eddie Kasko/Fldg	15.00	7.50	4.50
(26)	Gene Kelly (Announcer)	15.00	7.50	4.50
(27)	Brooks Lawrence (Follow-thru)	15.00	7.50	4.50
(28)	Jerry Lynch/Btg	15.00	7.50	4.50
(29)	Jim Maloney/Portrait	15.00	7.50	4.50
(30)	Roy McMillan/Btg	15.00	7.50	4.50
(31)	Roy McMillan/Fldg	15.00	7.50	4.50
(32)	Don Newcombe (Wind-up.)	20.00	10.00	6.00
(33)	Joe Nuxhall (Follow-through, long-sleeve undershirt.)	15.00	7.50	4.50
(34)	Joe Nuxhall (Follow-through, short-sleeve undershirt.)	15.00	7.50	4.50
(35)	Jim O'Toole/Portrait	15.00	7.50	4.50
(36)	Jim O'Toole (Wind-up.)	15.00	7.50	4.50
(37)	Jim O'Toole (Follow-through.)	15.00	7.50	4.50
(38)	Don Pavletich/Portrait	15.00	7.50	4.50
(39)	Vada Pinson/Btg (No players in background.)	20.00	10.00	6.00
(40)	Vada Pinson/Btg (Players in background.)	20.00	10.00	6.00
(41)	Vada Pinson (Catching fly ball.)	20.00	10.00	6.00
(42)	Vada Pinson (Hands on knees.)	20.00	10.00	6.00
(43)	Wally Post/Btg	15.00	7.50	4.50
(44)	Wally Post/Portrait	15.00	7.50	4.50
(45)	Bob Purkey/Pitching (Right foot visible.)	15.00	7.50	4.50
(46)	Bob Purkey/Pitching (Right foot not visible.)	15.00	7.50	4.50
(47)	Bob Purkey/Portrait (Teeth don't show.)	15.00	7.50	4.50
(48)	Bob Purkey/Portrait (Teeth show.)	15.00	7.50	4.50
(49)	Frank Robinson/Btg (Dark cap.)	45.00	22.00	13.50
(50)	Frank Robinson/Btg (White cap.)	45.00	22.00	13.50
(51)	Frank Robinson (Fielding fly ball.)	45.00	22.00	13.50
(52)	Frank Robinson/Portrait (Pinstripes, black background.)	45.00	22.00	13.50
(53)	Frank Robinson/Portrait (Pinstripes, natural sky background.)	45.00	22.00	13.50
(54)	Frankie Robinson (Head turned back to camera.)	45.00	22.00	13.50
(55)	Pete Rose (Portrait to chest.)	200.00	100.00	60.00
(56)	Johnny Temple/Portrait (Dark Cap)	25.00	12.50	7.50

1977 Burger Chef Funmeal Discs

The largest of the disc sets produced by Michael Schechter Associates is the 216-piece issue for the Burger Chef fast food restaurant chain. The discs were issued nine-per-team on a cardboard tray accompanying a 69-cent Fun-meal for kids. The 2-3/8" discs could be punched out of the tray. They share the basic design of other MSA discs of the era. A black-and-white player photo is in the center of a base-ball disc. Because the discs were licensed only by the Players Association, the player photos have had cap logos airbrushed away. The left and right side panels are in one of several bright colors. Backs feature a Burger Chef cartoon character in color. The individual discs are unnumbered.

		NM	EX	VG
Complete Set, Trays (24):		100.00	50.00	30.00
Complete Set, Singles (216):		90.00	45.00	27.00
Common Player:		.75	.35	.20
1A	Cincinnati Reds (Full tray.)	20.00	10.00	6.00
(1A1)	Johnny Bench	4.50	2.25	1.25
(1A2)	Dave Concepcion	.75	.35	.20
(1A3)	Dan Driessen	.75	.35	.20
(1A4)	George Foster	.75	.35	.20
(1A5)	Cesar Geronimo	.75	.35	.20
(1A6)	Ken Griffey	1.25	.60	.40
(1A7)	Joe Morgan	3.50	1.75	1.00
(1A8)	Gary Nolan	.75	.35	.20
(1A9)	Pete Rose	7.50	3.75	2.25
2A	St. Louis Cardinals (Full tray.)	10.00	5.00	3.00
(2A1)	Lou Brock	3.50	1.75	1.00
(2A2)	John Denny	.75	.35	.20
(2A3)	Pete Falcone	.75	.35	.20
(2A4)	Keith Hernandez	.75	.40	.25
(2A5)	Al Hrabosky	.75	.35	.20
(2A6)	Bake McBride	.75	.35	.20
(2A7)	Ken Reitz	.75	.35	.20
(2A8)	Ted Simmons	.75	.35	.20
(2A9)	Mike Tyson	.75	.35	.20
3A	Detroit Tigers (Full tray.)	8.00	4.00	2.50
(3A1)	Mark Fidrych	1.50	.70	.45
(3A2)	Bill Freehan	.75	.35	.20
(3A3)	John Hiller	.75	.35	.20
(3A4)	Willie Horton	.75	.35	.20
(3A5)	Ron LeFlore	.75	.35	.20
(3A6)	Ben Oglivie	.75	.35	.20
(3A7)	Aurelio Rodriguez	.75	.35	.20
(3A8)	Rusty Staub	1.25	.60	.40
(3A9)	Jason Thompson	.75	.35	.20
4A	Cleveland Indians (Full tray.)	8.00	4.00	2.50
(4A1)	Buddy Bell	.75	.35	.20
(4A2)	Frank Duffy	.75	.35	.20
(4A3)	Dennis Eckersley	2.75	1.50	.80
(4A4)	Ray Fosse	.75	.35	.20
(4A5)	Wayne Garland	.75	.35	.20
(4A6)	Duane Kuiper	.75	.35	.20
(4A7)	Dave LaRoche	.75	.35	.20
(4A8)	Rick Manning	.75	.35	.20
(4A9)	Rick Waits	.75	.35	.20
5A	Chicago White Sox (Full tray.)	8.00	4.00	2.50
(5A1)	Jack Brohamer	.75	.35	.20
(5A2)	Bucky Dent	1.00	.50	.30
(5A3)	Ralph Garr	.75	.35	.20
(5A4)	Bart Johnson	.75	.35	.20
(5A5)	Lamar Johnson	.75	.35	.20
(5A6)	Chet Lemon	.75	.35	.20
(5A7)	Jorge Orta	.75	.35	.20
(5A8)	Jim Spencer	.75	.35	.20
(5A9)	Richie Zisk	.75	.35	.20
6A	Chicago Cubs (Full tray.)	8.00	4.00	2.50
(6A1)	Bill Bonham	.75	.35	.20
(6A2)	Bill Buckner	1.25	.60	.40
(6A3)	Ray Burris	.75	.35	.20
(6A4)	Jose Cardenal	.75	.35	.20
(6A5)	Bill Madlock	.75	.35	.20
(6A6)	Jerry Morales	.75	.35	.20
(6A7)	Rick Reuschel	.75	.35	.20
(6A8)	Manny Trillo	.75	.35	.20
(6A9)	Joe Wallis	.75	.35	.20
7A	Minnesota Twins (Full tray.)	10.00	5.00	3.00
(7A1)	Lyman Bostock	.75	.35	.20
(7A2)	Rod Carew	3.50	1.75	1.00
(7A3)	Mike Cubbage	.75	.35	.20
(7A4)	Dan Ford	.75	.35	.20
(7A5)	Dave Goltz	.75	.35	.20
(7A6)	Larry Hisle	.75	.35	.20
(7A7)	Tom Johnson	.75	.35	.20
(7A8)	Bobby Randall	.75	.35	.20
(7A9)	Butch Wynegar	.75	.35	.20
8A	Houston Astros (Full tray.)	8.00	4.00	2.50
(8A1)	Enos Cabell	.75	.35	.20
(8A2)	Cesar Cedeno	.75	.35	.20
(8A3)	Jose Cruz	.75	.35	.20
(8A4)	Joe Ferguson	.75	.35	.20
(8A5)	Ken Forsch	.75	.35	.20
(8A6)	Roger Metzger	.75	.35	.20
(8A7)	J.R. Richard	.75	.35	.20
(8A8)	Leon Roberts	.75	.35	.20

(8A9)	Bob Watson	.75	.35	.20
1B	Baltimore Orioles (Full tray.)	15.00	7.50	4.50
(1B1)	Mark Belanger	.75	.35	.20
(1B2)	Paul Blair	.75	.35	.20
(1B3)	Al Bumbry	.75	.35	.20
(1B4)	Doug DeCinces	.75	.35	.20
(1B5)	Ross Grimsley	.75	.35	.20
(1B6)	Lee May	.75	.35	.20
(1B7)	Jim Palmer	3.50	1.75	1.00
(1B8)	Brooks Robinson	4.50	2.25	1.25
(1B9)	Ken Singleton	.75	.35	.20
2B	Boston Red Sox (Full tray.)	15.00	7.50	4.50
(2B1)	Rick Burleson	.75	.35	.20
(2B2)	Dwight Evans	.75	.40	.25
(2B3)	Carlton Fisk	3.50	1.75	1.00
(2B4)	Fergie Jenkins	2.75	1.50	.80
(2B5)	Bill Lee	.75	.35	.20
(2B6)	Fred Lynn	.75	.40	.25
(2B7)	Jim Rice	1.50	.70	.45
(2B8)	Luis Tiant	.75	.35	.20
(2B9)	Carl Yastrzemski	4.50	2.25	1.25
3B	Kansas City Royals (Full tray.)	13.50	6.75	4.00
(3B1)	Doug Bird	.75	.35	.20
(3B2)	George Brett	6.00	3.00	1.75
(3B3)	Dennis Leonard	.75	.35	.20
(3B4)	John Mayberry	.75	.35	.20
(3B5)	Hal McRae	.75	.35	.20
(3B6)	Amos Otis	.75	.35	.20
(3B7)	Fred Patek	.75	.35	.20
(3B8)	Tom Poquette	.75	.35	.20
(3B9)	Paul Splittorff	.75	.35	.20
4B	Milwaukee Brewers (Full tray.)	10.00	5.00	3.00
(4B1)	Jerry Augustine	.75	.35	.20
(4B2)	Sal Bando	.75	.35	.20
(4B3)	Von Joshua	.75	.35	.20
(4B4)	Sixto Lezcano	.75	.35	.20
(4B5)	Charlie Moore	.75	.35	.20
(4B6)	Ed Rodriguez	.75	.35	.20
(4B7)	Jim Slaton	.75	.35	.20
(4B8)	Bill Travers	.75	.35	.20
(4B9)	Robin Yount	3.50	1.75	1.00
5B	Texas Rangers (Full tray.)	10.00	5.00	3.00
(5B1)	Juan Beniquez	.75	.35	.20
(5B2)	Bert Blyleven	.75	.35	.20
(5B3)	Bert Campaneris	.75	.35	.20
(5B4)	Tom Grieve	.75	.35	.20
(5B5)	Mike Hargrove	.75	.35	.20
(5B6)	Toby Harrah	.75	.35	.20
(5B7)	Gaylord Perry	2.75	1.50	.80
(5B8)	Lenny Randle	.75	.35	.20
(5B9)	Jim Sundberg	.75	.35	.20
6B	Atlanta Braves (Full tray.)	8.00	4.00	2.50
(6B1)	Jeff Burroughs	.75	.35	.20
(6B2)	Darrel Chaney	.75	.35	.20
(6B3)	Gary Matthews	.75	.35	.20
(6B4)	Andy Messersmith	.75	.35	.20
(6B5)	Willie Montanez	.75	.35	.20
(6B6)	Phil Niekro	2.75	1.50	.80
(6B7)	Tom Paciorek	.75	.35	.20
(6B8)	Jerry Royster	.75	.35	.20
(6B9)	Dick Ruthven	.75	.35	.20
7B	Pittsburgh Pirates (Full tray.)	10.00	5.00	3.00
(7B1)	John Candelaria	.75	.35	.20
(7B2)	Duffy Dyer	.75	.35	.20
(7B3)	Al Oliver	1.25	.60	.40
(7B4)	Dave Parker	.75	.40	.25
(7B5)	Jerry Reuss	.75	.35	.20
(7B6)	Bill Robinson	.75	.35	.20
(7B7)	Willie Stargell	3.50	1.75	1.00
(7B8)	Rennie Stennett	.75	.35	.20
(7B9)	Frank Taveras	.75	.35	.20
8B	New York Yankees (Full tray.)	20.00	10.00	6.00
(8B1)	Chris Chambliss	.75	.35	.20
(8B2)	Don Gullett	.75	.35	.20
(8B3)	Catfish Hunter	2.75	1.50	.80
(8B4)	Reggie Jackson	5.00	2.50	1.50
(8B5)	Thurman Munson	4.50	2.25	1.25
(8B6)	Graig Nettles	.75	.35	.20
(8B7)	Willie Randolph	.75	.35	.20
(8B8)	Mickey Rivers	.75	.35	.20
(8B9)	Roy White	.75	.35	.20
1C	California Angels (Full tray.)	25.00	12.50	7.50
(1C1)	Bobby Bonds	.75	.35	.20
(1C2)	Dave Chalk	.75	.35	.20
(1C3)	Bobby Grich	.75	.35	.20
(1C4)	Paul Hartzell	.75	.35	.20
(1C5)	Ron Jackson	.75	.35	.20
(1C6)	Jerry Remy	.75	.35	.20
(1C7)	Joe Rudi	.75	.35	.20
(1C8)	Nolan Ryan	16.00	8.00	4.75
(1C9)	Frank Tanana	.75	.35	.20
2C	Oakland A's (Full tray.)	8.00	4.00	2.50
(2C1)	Stan Bahnsen	.75	.35	.20
(2C2)	Vida Blue	.75	.35	.20
(2C3)	Phil Garner	.75	.35	.20
(2C4)	Paul Lindblad	.75	.35	.20
(2C5)	Mike Norris	.75	.35	.20
(2C6)	Bill North	.75	.35	.20
(2C7)	Manny Sanguillen	.75	.35	.20
(2C8)	Mike Torrez	.75	.35	.20
(2C9)	Claudell Washington	.75	.35	.20
3C	Los Angeles Dodgers (Full tray.)	10.00	5.00	3.00
(3C1)	Ron Cey	.75	.35	.20
(3C2)	Steve Garvey	2.00	1.00	.60
(3C3)	Davey Lopes	.75	.35	.20
(3C4)	Rick Monday	.75	.35	.20
(3C5)	Doug Rau	.75	.35	.20
(3C6)	Rick Rhoden	.75	.35	.20
(3C7)	Reggie Smith	.75	.35	.20
(3C8)	Don Sutton	2.75	1.50	.80
(3C9)	Steve Yeager	.75	.35	.20
4C	Montreal Expos (Full tray.)	10.00	5.00	3.00
(4C1)	Gary Carter	3.00	1.50	.90
(4C2)	Dave Cash	.75	.35	.20
(4C3)	Tim Foli	.75	.35	.20
(4C4)	Barry Foote	.75	.35	.20
(4C5)	Larry Parrish	.75	.35	.20

(4C6)	Tony Perez	3.00	1.50	.90
(4C7)	Steve Rogers	.75	.35	.20
(4C8)	Del Unser	.75	.35	.20
(4C9)	Ellis Valentine	.75	.35	.20
5C	New York Mets (Full tray.)	13.50	6.75	4.00
(5C1)	Bud Harrelson	.75	.35	.20
(5C2)	Dave Kingman	1.00	.50	.30
(5C3)	Jerry Koosman	.75	.35	.20
(5C4)	Ed Kranepool	.75	.35	.20
(5C5)	Skip Lockwood	.75	.35	.20
(5C6)	Jon Matlack	.75	.35	.20
(5C7)	Felix Millan	.75	.35	.20
(5C8)	Tom Seaver	4.50	2.25	1.25
(5C9)	John Stearns	.75	.35	.20
6C	Philadelphia Phillies (Full tray.)	15.00	7.50	4.50
(6C1)	Bob Boone	1.00	.50	.30
(6C2)	Larry Bowa	.75	.35	.20
(6C3)	Steve Carlton	3.50	1.75	1.00
(6C4)	Jay Johnstone	.75	.35	.20
(6C5)	Jim Kaat	1.25	.60	.40
(6C6)	Greg Luzinski	.75	.40	.25
(6C7)	Garry Maddox	.75	.35	.20
(6C8)	Tug McGraw	1.25	.60	.40
(6C9)	Mike Schmidt	6.00	3.00	1.75
7C	San Diego Padres (Full tray.)	10.00	5.00	3.00
(7C1)	Rollie Fingers	2.75	1.50	.80
(7C2)	George Hendrick	.75	.35	.20
(7C3)	Enzo Hernandez	.75	.35	.20
(7C4)	Mike Ivie	.75	.35	.20
(7C5)	Randy Jones	.75	.35	.20
(7C6)	Butch Metzger	.75	.35	.20
(7C7)	Dave Rader	.75	.35	.20
(7C8)	Gene Tenace	.75	.35	.20
(7C9)	Dave Winfield	3.50	1.75	1.00
8C	San Francisco Giants (Full tray.)	8.00	4.00	2.50
(8C1)	Jim Barr	.75	.35	.20
(8C2)	Willie Crawford	.75	.35	.20
(8C3)	Larry Herndon	.75	.35	.20
(8C4)	Randy Moffitt	.75	.35	.20
(8C5)	John Montefusco	.75	.35	.20
(8C6)	Bobby Murcer	.75	.35	.20
(8C7)	Marty Perez	.75	.35	.20
(8C8)	Chris Speier	.75	.35	.20
(8C9)	Gary Thomasson	.75	.35	.20

1977 Burger King Tigers

This series of color 8" x 10" player portraits was given away one per week at Detroit area Burger Kings. Backs are blank and there is no player identification on the front. The photos are checklisted here alphabetically.

		NM	EX	VG
Complete Set (4):		40.00	20.00	12.00
Common Player:		10.00	5.00	3.00
(1)	Mark Fidrych (Holding glove.)	15.00	7.50	4.50
(2)	Ron LeFlore (Black guy w/bat.)	10.00	5.00	3.00
(3)	Dave Rozema (Winding up.)	10.00	5.00	3.00
(4)	Mickey Stanley (White guy w/bat.)	10.00	5.00	3.00

1977 Burger King Yankees

The first Topps-produced set for Burger King restaurants was issued in the New York area, featuring the A.L. champion Yankees. Twenty-two players plus an unnumbered checklist were issued at the beginning of the promotion with card #23 (Lou Piniella) being added to the set later. The "New York Post" reported production of the first 22 player cards at about 170,000 of each. The Piniella card was issued in limited quantities. Cards are 2-1/2" x 3-1/2" and have fronts identical to the regular 1977 Topps set except for numbers 2, 6, 7, 13, 14, 15, 17, 20 and 21. These cards feature different poses or major picture-

cropping variations. It should be noted that very minor cropping variations between the regular Topps sets and the Burger King issues exist throughout the years the sets were produced.

		NM	EX	VG
Complete Set w/Piniella (24):		20.00	10.00	6.00
Complete Set no Piniella (23):		13.50	6.75	4.00
Common Player:		.25	.13	.08
1	Yankees Team (Billy Martin)	.75	.40	.25
2	Thurman Munson	5.00	2.50	1.50
3	Fran Healy	.25	.13	.08
4	Catfish Hunter	1.50	.70	.45
5	Ed Figueroa	.25	.13	.08
6	Don Gullett	.25	.13	.08
7	Mike Torrez	.25	.13	.08
8	Ken Holtzman	.25	.13	.08
9	Dick Tidrow	.25	.13	.08
10	Sparky Lyle	.40	.20	.12
11	Ron Guidry	.45	.25	.14
12	Chris Chambliss	.25	.13	.08
13	Willie Randolph	.45	.25	.14
14	Bucky Dent	.45	.25	.14
15	Graig Nettles	.60	.30	.20
16	Fred Stanley	.25	.13	.08
17	Reggie Jackson	5.00	2.50	1.50
18	Mickey Rivers	.25	.13	.08
19	Roy White	.40	.20	.12
20	Jim Wynn	.40	.20	.12
21	Paul Blair	.25	.13	.08
22	Carlos May	.25	.13	.08
23	Lou Piniella	15.00	7.50	4.50
---	Checklist	.05	.03	.02

1978 Burger King Astros

Burger King restaurants in the Houston area distributed a Topps-produced set showcasing the Astros. Cards are standard 2-1/2" x 3-1/2" and are numbered 1-22, plus and unnumbered checklist. Fronts are identical to the regular 1978 Topps set with the exception of card numbers 21, Dave Bergman, who appeared on a Rookie Outfielders cards in the '78 Topps set; and 22, Jesus Alou, who did not have a card in the regular issue. Although not noted in the following checklist, it should be remembered that very minor picture-cropping variations between the regular Topps issues and the 1977-1980 Burger King sets do exist.

		NM	EX	VG
Complete Set (23):		15.00	7.50	4.50
Common Player:		.75	.40	.25
1	Bill Virdon	.90	.45	.25
2	Joe Ferguson	.75	.40	.25
3	Ed Herrmann	.75	.40	.25
4	J.R. Richard	1.50	.70	.45
5	Joe Niekro	1.25	.60	.40
6	Floyd Bannister	.75	.40	.25
7	Joaquin Andujar	.75	.40	.25
8	Ken Forsch	.75	.40	.25
9	Mark Lemongello	.75	.40	.25
10	Joe Sambito	.75	.40	.25
11	Gene Pentz	.75	.40	.25
12	Bob Watson	.90	.45	.25
13	Julio Gonzalez	.75	.40	.25
14	Enos Cabell	.75	.40	.25
15	Roger Metzger	.75	.40	.25
16	Art Howe	.90	.45	.25
17	Jose Cruz	1.00	.50	.30
18	Cesar Cedeno	1.00	.50	.30
19	Terry Puhl	.75	.40	.25
20	Wilbur Howard	.75	.40	.25
21	Dave Bergman	.75	.40	.25
22	Jesus Alou	1.00	.50	.30
---	Checklist	.10	.05	.03

1978 Burger King Rangers

Issued by Burger King restaurants in the Dallas-Fort Worth area, this Topps-produced set features the Texas Rangers. Cards are standard 2-1/2" x 3-1/2" and identical in style to the regular 1978 Topps set with the following exceptions: #'s 5, 8, 10, 12, 17, 21 and 22. An unnumbered checklist card was included with the set.

		NM	EX	VG
Complete Set (23):		15.00	7.50	4.50
Common Player:		.75	.40	.25
1	Billy Hunter	.75	.40	.25
2	Jim Sundberg	.75	.40	.25
3	John Ellis	.75	.40	.25
4	Doyle Alexander	.75	.40	.25
5	Jon Matlack	.75	.40	.25
6	Dock Ellis	.75	.40	.25
7	George Medich	.75	.40	.25
8	Fergie Jenkins	6.00	3.00	1.75
9	Len Barker	.75	.40	.25
10	Reggie Cleveland	.75	.40	.25
11	Mike Hargrove	1.00	.50	.30
12	Bump Wills	1.00	.50	.30
13	Toby Harrah	1.00	.50	.30
14	Bert Campaneris	1.00	.50	.30
15	Sandy Alomar	1.00	.50	.30
16	Kurt Bevacqua	.75	.40	.25
17	Al Oliver	1.50	.70	.45
18	Juan Beniquez	.75	.40	.25
19	Claudell Washington	.75	.40	.25
20	Richie Zisk	.75	.40	.25
21	John Lowenstein	.75	.40	.25
22	Bobby Thompson	.75	.40	.25
---	Checklist	.10	.05	.03

1978 Burger King Tigers

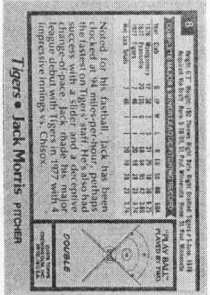

JACK MORRIS

Rookie cards of Morris, Trammell and Whitaker make the Topps-produced 1978 Burger King Detroit Tigers issue the most popular of the BK sets. Twenty-two player cards and an unnumbered checklist card make up the Detroit area issue. Cards measure 2-1/2" x 3-1/2", and are identical to the regular 1978 Topps issue with the following exceptions: #'s 6, 7, 8, 13, 15 and 16. Numerous minor picture-cropping variations between the regular Topps issues and the Burger King sets appear from 1977-1980; these minor variations are not noted in the following checklist.

		NM	EX	VG
Complete Set (23):		25.00	12.50	7.50
Common Player:		.75	.40	.25
1	Ralph Houk	.90	.45	.25
2	Milt May	.75	.40	.25
3	John Wockenfuss	.75	.40	.25
4	Mark Fidrych	2.50	1.25	.70
5	Dave Rozema	.75	.40	.25
6	Jack Billingham	.75	.40	.25
7	Jim Slaton	.75	.40	.25
8	Jack Morris	3.00	1.50	.90
9	John Hiller	.75	.40	.25
10	Steve Foucault	.75	.40	.25
11	Milt Wilcox	.75	.40	.25
12	Jason Thompson	.75	.40	.25
13	Lou Whitaker	6.00	3.00	1.75
14	Aurelio Rodriguez	.75	.40	.25
15	Alan Trammell	10.00	5.00	3.00
16	Steve Dillard	.75	.40	.25
17	Phil Mankowski	.75	.40	.25
18	Steve Kemp	.75	.40	.25
19	Ron LeFlore	.90	.45	.25
20	Tim Corcoran	.75	.40	.25
21	Mickey Stanley	.75	.40	.25
22	Rusty Staub	.90	.45	.25
---	Checklist	.10	.05	.03

1978 Burger King Yankees

RICH GOSSAGE

Produced by Topps for Burger King outlets in the New York area for the second year in a row, the 1978 Yankees set contains 22 cards plus an unnumbered checklist. The cards are numbered 1 through 22 and are the standard size of 2-1/2" x 3-1/2". The cards feature the same pictures found in the regular 1978

Topps set except for numbers 10, 11 and 16. Only those variations containing different poses or major picture-cropping differences are noted. Numerous minor picture-cropping variations, that are very insignificant in nature, exist between the regular Topps sets and the Burger King issues of 1977-1980.

		NM	EX	VG
Complete Set (23):		15.00	7.50	4.50
Common Player:		.50	.25	.15
1	Billy Martin	1.50	.70	.45
2	Thurman Munson	5.00	2.50	1.50
3	Cliff Johnson	.50	.25	.15
4	Ron Guidry	1.00	.50	.30
5	Ed Figueroa	.50	.25	.15
6	Dick Tidrow	.50	.25	.15
7	Catfish Hunter	2.00	1.00	.60
8	Don Gullett	.50	.25	.15
9	Sparky Lyle	1.00	.50	.30
10	Rich Gossage	1.50	.70	.45
11	Rawly Eastwick	.50	.25	.15
12	Chris Chambliss	.50	.25	.15
13	Willie Randolph	1.00	.50	.30
14	Graig Nettles	1.00	.50	.30
15	Bucky Dent	1.00	.50	.30
16	Jim Spencer	.50	.25	.15
17	Fred Stanley	.50	.25	.15
18	Lou Piniella	1.25	.60	.40
19	Roy White	1.00	.50	.30
20	Mickey Rivers	.50	.25	.15
21	Reggie Jackson	6.00	3.00	1.75
22	Paul Blair	.50	.25	.15
---	Checklist	.10	.05	.03

1979 Burger King Phillies

PETE ROSE

Twenty-two Phillies players are featured in the 1979 Burger King issue given out in the Philadelphia area. The Topps-produced set, measuring 2-1/2" x 3-1/2", also includes an unnumbered checklist. Cards are identical to the regular 1979 Topps set except #1, 11, 12, 13, 14, 17 and 22, which have different poses. Very minor picture-cropping variations between the regular Topps issues and the Burger King sets can be found throughout the four years the cards were produced, but only those variations featuring major changes are noted in the checklists.

		NM	EX	VG
Complete Set (23):		7.50	3.75	2.25
Common Player:		.25	.13	.08
1	Danny Ozark	.25	.13	.08
2	Bob Boone	.45	.25	.14
3	Tim McCarver	.50	.25	.15
4	Steve Carlton	1.50	.70	.45
5	Larry Christenson	.25	.13	.08
6	Dick Ruthven	.25	.13	.08
7	Ron Reed	.25	.13	.08
8	Randy Lerch	.25	.13	.08
9	Warren Brusstar	.25	.13	.08
10	Tug McGraw	.40	.20	.12
11	Nino Espinosa	.25	.13	.08
12	Doug Bird	.25	.13	.08
13	Pete Rose	3.00	1.50	.90
14	Manny Trillo	.25	.13	.08
15	Larry Bowa	.40	.20	.12
16	Mike Schmidt	3.00	1.50	.90
17	Pete Mackanin	.25	.13	.08
18	Jose Cardenal	.25	.13	.08
19	Greg Luzinski	.25	.13	.08
20	Garry Maddox	.25	.13	.08
21	Bake McBride	.25	.13	.08
22	Greg Gross	.25	.13	.08
---	Checklist	.08	.04	.02

1979 Burger King Yankees

LUIS TIANT

The New York Yankees were featured in a Topps-produced Burger King set for the third consecutive year in 1979. Once again, 22 numbered player cards and an unnumbered

checklist made up the set. Cards measure 2-1/2" x 3-1/2", and are identical to the 1979 Topps regular set except for #4, 8, 9 and 22 which included new poses. Numerous minor picture cropping variations between the regular Topps issue and the Burger King sets of 1977-1980 exist.

		NM	EX	VG
Complete Set (23):		7.50	3.75	2.25
Common Player:		.25	.13	.08
1	Yankees Team (Bob Lemon)	.75	.40	.25
2	Thurman Munson	2.50	1.25	.70
3	Cliff Johnson	.25	.13	.08
4	Ron Guidry	.60	.30	.20
5	Jay Johnstone	.40	.20	.12
6	Catfish Hunter	1.25	.60	.40
7	Jim Beattie	.25	.13	.08
8	Luis Tiant	.40	.20	.12
9	Tommy John	.75	.40	.25
10	Rich Gossage	.60	.30	.20
11	Ed Figueroa	.25	.13	.08
12	Chris Chambliss	.25	.13	.08
13	Willie Randolph	.40	.20	.12
14	Bucky Dent	.40	.20	.12
15	Graig Nettles	.40	.20	.12
16	Fred Stanley	.25	.13	.08
17	Jim Spencer	.25	.13	.08
18	Lou Piniella	.60	.30	.20
19	Roy White	.40	.20	.12
20	Mickey Rivers	.25	.13	.08
21	Reggie Jackson	4.00	2.00	1.25
22	Juan Beniquez	.25	.13	.08
---	Checklist	.06	.03	.02

1980 Burger King Phillies

LONNIE SMITH

Philadelphia-area Burger King outlets issued a 23-card set featuring the Phillies for the second in a row in 1980. The Topps-produced set, measuring 2-1/2" x 3-1/2", contains 22 player cards and an unnumbered checklist. Fronts are identical in design to the regular 1980 Topps sets with the following exceptions: #1, 3, 8, 14 and 22 feature new poses. Very minor picture-cropping variations between the regular Topps issues and the Burger King sets exist in all years. Those minor differences are not noted in the checklists. The 1980 Burger King sets were the first to include the Burger King logo on the card backs.

		NM	EX	VG
Complete Set (23):		6.00	3.00	1.75
Common Player:		.10	.05	.03
1	Dallas Green	.15	.08	.05
2	Bob Boone	.50	.25	.15
3	Keith Moreland	.25	.13	.08
4	Pete Rose	2.50	1.25	.70
5	Manny Trillo	.10	.05	.03
6	Mike Schmidt	2.50	1.25	.70
7	Larry Bowa	.20	.10	.06
8	John Vukovich	.10	.05	.03
9	Bake McBride	.10	.05	.03
10	Garry Maddox	.10	.05	.03
11	Greg Luzinski	.25	.13	.08
12	Greg Gross	.10	.05	.03
13	Del Unser	.10	.05	.03
14	Lonnie Smith	.40	.20	.12
15	Steve Carlton	1.00	.50	.30
16	Larry Christenson	.10	.05	.03
17	Nino Espinosa	.10	.05	.03
18	Randy Lerch	.10	.05	.03
19	Dick Ruthven	.10	.05	.03
20	Tug McGraw	.15	.08	.05
21	Ron Reed	.10	.05	.03
22	Kevin Saucier	.10	.05	.03
---	Checklist	.05	.03	.02

1980 Burger King Pitch, Hit & Run

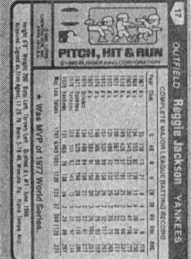

REGGIE JACKSON

In 1980, Burger King issued, in conjunction with its "Pitch, Hit & Run" promotion, a Topps-produced set featuring pitchers (card #s 1-11), hitters (#s 12-22), and base stealers (#s 23-

33). Fronts, which carry the Burger King logo, are identical in design to the regular 1980 Topps set except for numbers 1, 4, 5, 7, 9, 10, 16, 17, 18, 22, 23, 27, 28, 29 and 30, which feature different poses. Cards measure 2-1/2" x 3-1/2" in size. An unnumbered checklist was included with the set.

		NM	EX	VG
Complete Set (34):		10.00	5.00	3.00
Common Player:		.10	.05	.03
1	Vida Blue	.10	.05	.03
2	Steve Carlton	1.00	.50	.30
3	Rollie Fingers	.65	.35	.20
4	Ron Guidry	.25	.13	.08
5	Jerry Koosman	.10	.05	.03
6	Phil Niekro	.65	.35	.20
7	Jim Palmer	1.00	.50	.30
8	J.R. Richard	.10	.05	.03
9	Nolan Ryan	4.00	2.00	1.25
10	Tom Seaver	1.00	.50	.30
11	Bruce Sutter	1.00	.50	.30
12	Don Baylor	.10	.05	.03
13	George Brett	2.00	1.00	.60
14	Rod Carew	1.00	.50	.30
15	George Foster	.10	.05	.03
16	Keith Hernandez	.10	.05	.03
17	Reggie Jackson	1.50	.70	.45
18	Fred Lynn	.10	.05	.03
19	Dave Parker	.10	.05	.03
20	Jim Rice	.30	.15	.09
21	Pete Rose	3.00	1.50	.90
22	Dave Winfield	1.00	.50	.30
23	Bobby Bonds	.10	.05	.03
24	Enos Cabell	.10	.05	.03
25	Cesar Cedeno	.10	.05	.03
26	Julio Cruz	.10	.05	.03
27	Ron LeFlore	.10	.05	.03
28	Dave Lopes	.10	.05	.03
29	Omar Moreno	.10	.05	.03
30	Joe Morgan	1.00	.50	.30
31	Bill North	.10	.05	.03
32	Frank Taveras	.10	.05	.03
33	Willie Wilson	.10	.05	.03
---	Checklist	.05	.03	.02

1916 Burgess-Nash Clothiers

GAVVY CRAVATH
Rt. F.—Philadelphia Nat'ls

This 200-card set can be found with ads on the back for several local and regional businesses. Among them is Burgess-Nash clothiers, from Omaha, Neb. Type and superstar collectors can expect to pay a significant premium for cards with the Burgess-Nash advertising, compared to the generic M101-4 Blank Backs values. Cards measure about 1-5/8" x 3" and are printed in black-and-white.

PREMIUM: 12-15X
(See 1916 M101-4 Blank Backs for checklist.)

1935 George Burke Detroit Tigers Photo Stamps

RALPH PERKINS
COACH - DETROIT

This team set of black-and-white, 1-1/16" x 1-1/4" photo stamps was produced by baseball photographer George Burke. The set was printed on two sheets of 12 players each. Each stamp has the player's name, position abbreviation and city in black or white typography. The blank-backed ungummed stamps of the 1935 World's Champs are checklisted here in alphabetical order.

		NM	EX	VG
Complete Set (24):		325.00	160.00	95.00
Common Player:		10.00	5.00	3.00
(1)	Elden Auker	10.00	5.00	3.00
(2)	Del Baker	10.00	5.00	3.00
(3)	Tom Bridges	10.00	5.00	3.00
(4)	Herman Clifton	10.00	5.00	3.00
(5)	Mickey Cochrane	30.00	15.00	9.00
(6)	Alvin Crowder	10.00	5.00	3.00
(7)	Ervin Fox	10.00	5.00	3.00
(8)	Charles Gehringer	30.00	15.00	9.00
(9)	Leon Goslin	30.00	15.00	9.00
(10)	Henry Greenberg	45.00	22.50	13.50
(11)	Raymond Hayworth	10.00	5.00	3.00
(12)	Elon Hogsett	10.00	5.00	3.00
(13)	Roxie Lawson	10.00	5.00	3.00
(14)	Marvin Owen	10.00	5.00	3.00
(15)	Ralph Perkins	10.00	5.00	3.00
(16)	Frank Reiber	10.00	5.00	3.00
(17)	Wm. Rogell	10.00	5.00	3.00
(18)	Lynwood Rowe	12.50	6.25	3.75
(19)	Henry Schuble	10.00	5.00	3.00
(20)	Hugh Shelley	10.00	5.00	3.00
(21)	Victor Sorrell	10.00	5.00	3.00
(22)	Joseph Sullivan	10.00	5.00	3.00
(23)	Gerald Walker	10.00	5.00	3.00
(24)	Joyner White	10.00	5.00	3.00

1935-37 George Burke Postage Stamp Photos

These small (3/4" x 1") black-and-white stamps were produced by Chicago baseball portraitist George Burke for sale to individual players for use in answering fan mail. The stamps were not a big seller, though the checklist presented alphabetically here is surely incomplete. The unnumbered stamps, which are blank-backed, were not self-adhesive and were printed in sheets of at least six of the same player. Some of the photo-stamps have facsimile autographs, others do not.

	NM	EX	VG
Common Player:	10.00	5.00	3.00
Luke Appling	20.00	10.00	6.00
Jimmy Austin	10.00	5.00	3.00
Dick Bartell	10.00	5.00	3.00
Huck Betts	10.00	5.00	3.00
George Blaeholder	10.00	5.00	3.00
Jim Bottomley	20.00	10.00	6.00
Earl Browne	10.00	5.00	3.00
Irving Burns	10.00	5.00	3.00
Sam Byrd	10.00	5.00	3.00
Gilly Campbell	10.00	5.00	3.00
James (Tex) Carleton	10.00	5.00	3.00
Hugh Casey	10.00	5.00	3.00
James "Rip" Collins	10.00	5.00	3.00
Earle Combs	20.00	10.00	6.00
Adam Comorosky	10.00	5.00	3.00
Jocko Conlan	20.00	10.00	6.00
Kiki Cuyler	20.00	10.00	6.00
Paul Derringer	10.00	5.00	3.00
Jim DeShong	10.00	5.00	3.00
Bill Dickey	20.00	10.00	6.00
Bill Dietrich	10.00	5.00	3.00
Carl Doyle	10.00	5.00	3.00
Chuck Dressen	10.00	5.00	3.00
Jimmy Dykes	10.00	5.00	3.00
Hank Erickson	10.00	5.00	3.00
Wes Ferrell	10.00	5.00	3.00
Arthur Fletcher	10.00	5.00	3.00
Jimmie Foxx (Facsimile autograph.)	40.00	20.00	12.00
Jimmie Foxx (No autograph.)	40.00	20.00	12.00
Larry French	10.00	5.00	3.00
Benny Frey	10.00	5.00	3.00
Tony Freitas	10.00	5.00	3.00
Frankie Frisch	20.00	10.00	6.00
Ed Gharrity	10.00	5.00	3.00
Lefty Gomez	20.00	10.00	6.00
Charlie Grimm	10.00	5.00	3.00
Stan Hack	10.00	5.00	3.00
Chick Hafey	20.00	10.00	6.00
Mel Harder	10.00	5.00	3.00
Bucky Harris	20.00	10.00	6.00
Gabby Hartnett	20.00	10.00	6.00
Roy Henshaw	10.00	5.00	3.00
Babe Herman	15.00	7.50	4.50
Billy Herman	20.00	10.00	6.00
Leroy Herrmann	10.00	5.00	3.00
Myril Hoag	10.00	5.00	3.00
Al Hollingsworth	10.00	5.00	3.00
Carl Hubbell	30.00	15.00	9.00
Bob Johnson	10.00	5.00	3.00
Douglas Johnson	10.00	5.00	3.00
Si Johnson	10.00	5.00	3.00
George L. Kelly	20.00	10.00	6.00
Chuck Klein	20.00	10.00	6.00
Mark Koenig	10.00	5.00	3.00
Tony Lazzeri	30.00	15.00	9.00
Bill Lee	10.00	5.00	3.00
Dutch Leonard	10.00	5.00	3.00
Ernie Lombardi	20.00	10.00	6.00
Al Lopez	20.00	10.00	6.00
Adolfo Luque	15.00	7.50	4.50
Earle Mack	10.00	5.00	3.00
Roy Mahaffey	10.00	5.00	3.00
Gus Mancuso	10.00	5.00	3.00
Rabbit Maranville	20.00	10.00	6.00
Johnny Marcum	10.00	5.00	3.00
Joe McCarthy	20.00	10.00	6.00
Eric McNair	10.00	5.00	3.00
Van Lingle Mungo	10.00	5.00	3.00
Skeeter Newsome	10.00	5.00	3.00
Mel Ott	40.00	20.00	12.00
Claude Passeau	10.00	5.00	3.00
Monte Pearson	10.00	5.00	3.00
Raymond Pepper	10.00	5.00	3.00
Charlie Root	10.00	6.00	3.00
Red Ruffing	20.00	10.00	6.00
George Selkirk	10.00	5.00	3.00
Joe Sewell	20.00	10.00	6.00
Luke Sewell	10.00	5.00	3.00
Al Simmons	20.00	10.00	6.00
Casey Stengel	20.00	10.00	6.00
Riggs Stephenson	10.00	5.00	3.00
Alan Strange	10.00	5.00	3.00
Gus Suhr	10.00	5.00	3.00
Billy Sullivan	10.00	5.00	3.00
Dan Taylor	10.00	5.00	3.00
Fay Thomas	10.00	5.00	3.00
Hal Trosky	10.00	5.00	3.00
Honus Wagner	40.00	20.00	12.00
Rube Walberg	10.00	5.00	3.00
Paul Waner	20.00	10.00	6.00
Lon Warneke	10.00	5.00	3.00
Harold Warstler	10.00	5.00	3.00
Billy Webb	10.00	5.00	3.00
Whitlow Wyatt	10.00	5.00	3.00

1933 Butter Cream (R306)

 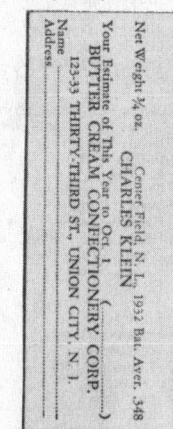

The 1933 Butter Cream set consists of unnumbered, black-and-white cards which measure 1-1/4" x 3-1/2". Backs feature a contest in which the collector was to estimate players' statistics by a specific date. Two different backs are known: 1) Estimate through Sept. 1 and no company address, and 2) Estimate through Oct. 1 with the Butter Cream address. The ACC designation for the set is R306.

		NM	EX	VG
Complete Set w/o Ruth:		25,000	12,500	6,000
Common Player:		750.00	375.00	165.00
(1)	Earl Averill	1,000	500.00	225.00
(2)	Ed. Brandt	750.00	375.00	165.00
(3)	Guy T. Bush	750.00	375.00	165.00
(4)	Gordon Cochrane	1,000	500.00	225.00
(5)	Joe Cronin	1,000	500.00	225.00
(6)	George Earnshaw	750.00	375.00	165.00
(7)	Wesley Ferrell	750.00	375.00	165.00
(8)	"Jimmy" E. Foxx	4,500	2,200	1,350
(9)	Frank C. Frisch	1,000	500.00	225.00
(10)	Charles M. Gelbert	750.00	375.00	165.00
(11)	"Lefty" Robert M. Grove	1,200	600.00	265.00
(12)	Leo Charles Hartnett	1,000	500.00	225.00
(13)	"Babe" Herman	750.00	375.00	165.00
(14)	Charles Klein	1,000	500.00	220.00
(15)	Ray Kremer	750.00	375.00	165.00
(16)	Fred C. Linstrom (Lindstrom)	1,000	500.00	225.00
(17)	Ted A. Lyons	1,000	500.00	225.00
(18)	"Pepper" John L. Martin	900.00	450.00	200.00
(19)	Robert O'Farrell	750.00	375.00	165.00
(20)	Ed. A. Rommel	750.00	375.00	165.00
(21)	Charles Root	750.00	375.00	165.00
(22)	Harold "Muddy" Ruel (Herold)	750.00	375.00	165.00
(23)	Babe Ruth	45,000	22,000	13,500
(24)	"Al" Simmons	1,000	500.00	225.00
(25)	"Bill" Terry	1,000	500.00	225.00
(26)	George E. Uhle	750.00	375.00	165.00
(27)	Lloyd J. Waner	1,000	500.00	225.00
(28)	Paul G. Waner	1,000	500.00	225.00
(29)	Hack Wilson	1,000	500.00	225.00
(30)	Glen. Wright	750.00	375.00	165.00

1934 Butterfinger (R310)

Cards in this set were available as a premium with Butterfinger and other candy products. The unnumbered cards measure approximately 7-3/4" x 9-1/2". The black-and-white cards feature a player photo with facsimile autograph. Similar cards in a 6-1/2" x 8-1/2" format are a companion Canadian issue.

		NM	EX	VG
	Complete Set (65):	6,500	3,250	2,000
	Common Player:	60.00	30.00	18.00
	Cardboard Ad Variety: 4X	.00	.00	.00
(1)	Earl Averill	110.00	55.00	35.00
(2)	Richard Bartell	60.00	30.00	18.00
(3)	Larry Benton	60.00	30.00	18.00
(4)	Walter Berger	60.00	30.00	18.00
(5)	Jim Bottomly (Bottomley)	110.00	55.00	35.00
(6)	Ralph Boyle	60.00	30.00	18.00
(7)	Tex Carleton	60.00	30.00	18.00
(8)	Owen T. Carroll	60.00	30.00	18.00
(9)	Ben Chapman	60.00	30.00	18.00
(10)	Gordon (Mickey) Cochrane	110.00	55.00	35.00
(11)	James Collins	60.00	30.00	18.00
(12)	Joe Cronin	110.00	55.00	35.00
(13)	Alvin Crowder	60.00	30.00	18.00
(14)	"Dizzy" Dean	240.00	120.00	75.00
(15)	Paul Derringer	60.00	30.00	18.00
(16)	William Dickey	125.00	62.00	37.00
(17)	Leo Durocher	110.00	55.00	35.00
(18)	George Earnshaw	60.00	30.00	18.00
(19)	Richard Ferrell	110.00	55.00	35.00
(20)	Lew Fonseca	60.00	30.00	18.00
(21a)	Jimmy Fox (Name incorrect.)	225.00	110.00	70.00
(21b)	Jimmy Foxx (Name correct.)	185.00	95.00	55.00
(22)	Benny Frey	60.00	30.00	18.00
(23)	Frankie Frisch	110.00	55.00	35.00
(24)	Lou Gehrig	750.00	375.00	225.00
(25)	Charles Gehringer	110.00	55.00	35.00
(26)	Vernon Gomez	110.00	55.00	35.00
(27)	Ray Grabowski	60.00	30.00	18.00
(28)	Robert (Lefty) Grove	150.00	75.00	45.00
(29)	George (Mule) Haas	60.00	30.00	18.00
(30)	"Chick" Hafey	110.00	55.00	35.00
(31)	Stanley Harris	110.00	55.00	35.00
(32)	J. Francis Hogan	60.00	30.00	18.00
(33)	Ed Holley	60.00	30.00	18.00
(34)	Rogers Hornsby	150.00	75.00	45.00
(35)	Waite Hoyt	110.00	55.00	35.00
(36)	Walter Johnson	250.00	125.00	75.00
(37)	Jim Jordan	60.00	30.00	18.00
(38)	Joe Kuhel	60.00	30.00	18.00
(39)	Hal Lee	60.00	30.00	18.00
(40)	Gus Mancuso	60.00	30.00	18.00
(41)	Henry Manush	110.00	55.00	35.00
(42)	Fred Marberry	60.00	30.00	18.00
(43)	Pepper Martin	85.00	45.00	25.00
(44)	Oscar Melillo	60.00	30.00	18.00
(45)	Johnny Moore	60.00	30.00	18.00
(46)	Joe Morrissey	60.00	30.00	18.00
(47)	Joe Mowrey	60.00	30.00	18.00
(48)	Bob O'Farrell	60.00	30.00	18.00
(49)	Melvin Ott	125.00	65.00	35.00
(50)	Monte Pearson	60.00	30.00	18.00
(51)	Carl Reynolds	60.00	30.00	18.00
(52)	Charles Ruffing	110.00	55.00	35.00
(53)	Babe Ruth	750.00	375.00	225.00
(54)	John "Blondy" Ryan	60.00	30.00	18.00
(55)	Al Simmons	110.00	55.00	35.00
(56)	Al Spohrer	60.00	30.00	18.00
(57)	Gus Suhr	60.00	30.00	18.00
(58)	Steve Swetonic	60.00	30.00	18.00
(59)	Dazzy Vance	110.00	55.00	35.00
(60)	Joe Vosmik	60.00	30.00	18.00
(61)	Lloyd Waner	110.00	55.00	35.00
(62)	Paul Waner	110.00	55.00	35.00
(63)	Sam West	60.00	30.00	18.00
(64)	Earl Whitehill	60.00	30.00	18.00
(65)	Jimmy Wilson	60.00	30.00	18.00

1934 Butterfinger - Canadian (V94)

Similar to the U.S. issue, though smaller in size at 6-1/2" x 8-1/2", these black-and-white paper cards include a number of players not found in the U.S. issue. Like the "regular" Butterfinger cards, each of the Canadian pieces includes a facsimile autograph on the front; backs are blank. The existence of Canadian versions of Lou Gehrig and Babe Ruth are now questionable.

		NM	EX	VG
	Complete Set (58):	3,500	1,750	1,100
	Common Player:	50.00	25.00	15.00
(1)	Earl Averill	100.00	50.00	30.00
(2)	Larry Benton	50.00	25.00	15.00
(3)	Jim Bottomly (Bottomley)	100.00	50.00	30.00
(4)	Tom Bridges	50.00	25.00	15.00
(5)	Bob Brown	50.00	25.00	15.00
(6)	Owen T. Carroll	50.00	25.00	15.00
(7)	Gordon (Mickey) Cochrane	100.00	50.00	30.00
(8)	Roger Cramer	50.00	25.00	15.00
(9)	Joe Cronin	100.00	50.00	30.00
(10)	Alvin Crowder	50.00	25.00	15.00
(11)	"Dizzy" Dean	185.00	95.00	55.00
(12)	Edward Delker	50.00	25.00	15.00
(13)	William Dickey	125.00	62.00	37.00
(14)	Richard Ferrell	100.00	50.00	30.00
(15)	Lew Fonseca	50.00	25.00	15.00
(16a)	Jimmy Fox (Name incorrect.)	145.00	75.00	45.00

		NM	EX	VG
(16b)	Jimmy Foxx (Name correct.)	145.00	75.00	45.00
(17)	Chick Fullis	50.00	25.00	15.00
(19)	Charles Gehringer	100.00	50.00	30.00
(20)	Vernon Gomez	100.00	50.00	30.00
(21)	Robert (Lefty) Grove	125.00	62.00	37.00
(22)	George (Mule) Haas	50.00	25.00	15.00
(23)	"Chick" Hafey	100.00	50.00	30.00
(24)	Stanley Harris	100.00	50.00	30.00
(25)	Frank Higgins	50.00	25.00	15.00
(26)	J. Francis Hogan	50.00	25.00	15.00
(27)	Ed Holley	50.00	25.00	15.00
(28)	Waite Hoyt	100.00	50.00	30.00
(29)	Jim Jordan	50.00	25.00	15.00
(30)	Hal Lee	50.00	25.00	15.00
(31)	Gus Mancuso	50.00	25.00	15.00
(32)	Oscar Melillo	50.00	25.00	15.00
(33)	Austin Moore	50.00	25.00	15.00
(34)	Randy Moore	50.00	25.00	15.00
(35)	Joe Morrissey	50.00	25.00	15.00
(36)	Joe Mowrey	50.00	25.00	15.00
(37)	Bobo Newsom	50.00	25.00	15.00
(38)	Ernie Orsatti	50.00	25.00	15.00
(39)	Carl Reynolds	50.00	25.00	15.00
(40)	Walter Roettger	50.00	25.00	15.00
(41)	John "Blondy" Ryan	50.00	25.00	15.00
(43)	John Salveson	50.00	25.00	15.00
(44)	Al Simmons	100.00	50.00	30.00
(45)	Al Smith	50.00	25.00	15.00
(46)	Harold Smith	50.00	25.00	15.00
(47)	Allyn Stout	50.00	25.00	15.00
(48)	Fresco Thompson	50.00	25.00	15.00
(49)	Art Veltman	50.00	25.00	15.00
(50)	Johnny Vergez	50.00	25.00	15.00
(51)	Gerald Walker	50.00	25.00	15.00
(52)	Paul Waner	100.00	50.00	30.00
(53)	Burgess Whitehead	50.00	25.00	15.00
(54)	Earl Whitehill	50.00	25.00	15.00
(55)	Robert Weiland	50.00	25.00	15.00
(56)	Jimmy Wilson	50.00	25.00	15.00
(57)	Bob Worthington	50.00	25.00	15.00
(58)	Tom Zachary	50.00	25.00	15.00

1934 Butterfingers Display Cards

An unknown subset of the 64 players that comprise the 1934 Butterfingers set were also issued in a red-overprinted cardboard stock format to be displayed standing up in the box of candy bars to advertise the availability of the standard paper-stock "cards". The display versions measure about the same as the give-aways, 7-3/4" x 9-1/2". This checklist, probably incomplete, of the display cards is numbered to coincide with those assigned to the regular version.

		NM	EX	VG
	Common Player:	350.00	175.00	100.00
(2)	Richard Bartell	350.00	175.00	100.00
(4)	Walter Berger	350.00	175.00	100.00
(6)	Ralph Boyle	350.00	175.00	100.00
(7)	Tex Carleton	350.00	175.00	100.00
(9)	Ben Chapman	350.00	175.00	100.00
(11)	James Collins	350.00	175.00	100.00
(15)	Paul Derringer	350.00	175.00	100.00
(18)	George Earnshaw	350.00	175.00	100.00
(22)	Benny Frey	350.00	175.00	100.00
(24)	Lou Gehrig	4,000	2,000	1,200
(27)	Ray Grabowski	350.00	175.00	100.00
(45)	Johnny Moore	350.00	175.00	100.00
(48)	Bob O'Farrell	350.00	175.00	100.00
(49)	Mel Ott	900.00	450.00	250.00
(56)	Al Spohrer	350.00	1750.00	100.00
(58)	Steve Swetonic	350.00	175.00	100.00

1911-14 Butter Krust Bread (D304)

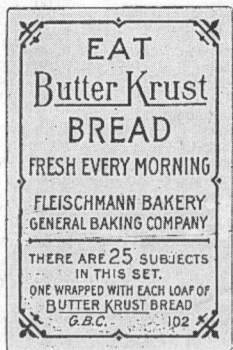

(See 1911-14 General Baking Co. for checklist and values.)

1933 Button Gum

(See 1933 Cracker Jack.)

1914 B18 Blankets

These 5-1/4"-square flannels were issued in 1914 wrapped around several popular brands of tobacco. The flannels, whose American Card Catalog designation is B18, picked up the nickname blankets because many of them were sewn together to form bed covers or throws. Different color combinations on the flannels exist for all 10 teams included in the set. The complete set price includes only the lowest-priced variation for each of the 90 players.

		NM	EX	VG
	Complete Set (90):	7,000	3,500	2,000
	Complete Set W/Variations (201):	55,000	27,500	16,500
	Common Player:	40.00	20.00	12.00
(1a)	Babe Adams (Purple pennants.)	80.00	40.00	25.00
(1b)	Babe Adams (Red pennants.)	130.00	65.00	40.00
(2a)	Sam Agnew (Purple basepaths.)	80.00	40.00	25.00
(2b)	Sam Agnew (Red basepaths.)	125.00	65.00	35.00
(3a)	Eddie Ainsmith (Green pennants.)	40.00	20.00	12.00
(3b)	Eddie Ainsmith (Brown pennants.)	40.00	20.00	12.00
(4a)	Jimmy Austin (Purple basepaths.)	80.00	40.00	25.00
(4b)	Jimmy Austin (Red basepaths.)	90.00	45.00	27.00
(5a)	Del Baker (White infield.)	40.00	20.00	12.00
(5b)	Del Baker (Brown infield.)	150.00	75.00	45.00
(5c)	Del Baker (Red infield.)	1,650	825.00	495.00
(6a)	Johnny Bassler (Purple pennants.)	90.00	45.00	27.00
(6b)	Johnny Bassler (Yellow pennants.)	125.00	65.00	35.00
(7a)	Paddy Bauman (Baumann) (White infield.)	40.00	20.00	12.00
(7b)	Paddy Bauman (Baumann) (Brown infield.)	150.00	75.00	45.00
(7c)	Paddy Bauman (Baumann) (Red infield.)	1,650	825.00	495.00
(8a)	Luke Boone (Blue infield.)	40.00	20.00	12.00
(8b)	Luke Boone (Green infield.)	40.00	20.00	12.00
(9a)	George Burns (Brown basepaths.)	40.00	20.00	12.00
(9b)	George Burns (Green basepaths.)	40.00	20.00	12.00
(10a)	Tioga George Burns (White infield.)	40.00	20.00	12.00
(10b)	Tioga George Burns (Brown infield.)	150.00	75.00	45.00
(10c)	Tioga George Burns (Red infield.)	1,650	825.00	495.00
(11a)	Max Carey (Purple pennants.)	150.00	75.00	45.00
(11b)	Max Carey (Red pennants.)	175.00	85.00	55.00
(12a)	Marty Cavanaugh (Kavanaugh) (White infield.)	40.00	20.00	12.00
(12b)	Marty Cavanaugh (Kavanaugh) (Brown infield.)	150.00	75.00	45.00
(12c)	Marty Cavanaugh (Kavanaugh) (Red infield.)	1,650	825.00	495.00
(12d)	Marty Kavanaugh (Kavanaugh)	200.00	100.00	60.00
(13a)	Frank Chance (Green infield.)	100.00	50.00	30.00
(13b)	Frank Chance (Brown pennants, blue infield.)	100.00	50.00	30.00
(13c)	Frank Chance (Yellow pennants, blue infield.)	450.00	225.00	135.00
(14a)	Ray Chapman (Purple pennants.)	125.00	65.00	35.00
(14b)	Ray Chapman (Yellow pennants.)	200.00	100.00	60.00
(15a)	Ty Cobb (White infield.)	500.00	250.00	150.00
(15b)	Ty Cobb (Brown infield.)	700.00	350.00	210.00
(15c)	Ty Cobb (Red infield.)	15,000	7,500	4,500
(16a)	King Cole (Blue infield.)	40.00	20.00	12.00
(16b)	King Cole (Green infield.)	40.00	20.00	12.00
(17a)	Joe Connolly (White infield.)	40.00	20.00	12.00
(17b)	Joe Connolly (Brown infield.)	150.00	75.00	45.00
(17c)	Joe Connolly (Red infield.)	1,650	825.00	495.00
(18a)	Harry Coveleski (White infield.)	40.00	20.00	12.00
(18b)	Harry Coveleski (Brown infield.)	150.00	75.00	45.00
(18c)	Harry Coveleski (Red infield.)	1,650	825.00	495.00
(19a)	George Cutshaw (Blue infield.)	40.00	20.00	12.00
(19b)	George Cutshaw (Green infield.)	40.00	20.00	12.00
(20a)	Jake Daubert (Blue infield.)	45.00	22.50	13.50
(20b)	Jake Daubert (Green infield.)	45.00	22.50	13.50
(21a)	Ray Demmitt (White infield.)	40.00	20.00	12.00
(21b)	Ray Demmitt (Brown infield.)	150.00	75.00	45.00
(21c)	Ray Demmitt (Red infield.)	1,650	825.00	495.00
(22a)	Bill Doak (Purple pennants.)	80.00	40.00	24.00
(22b)	Bill Doak (Yellow pennants.)	125.00	65.00	35.00
(23a)	Cozy Dolan (Purple pennants.)	80.00	40.00	25.00
(23b)	Cozy Dolan (Yellow pennants.)	150.00	75.00	45.00

#	Player	NM	EX	VG
(24a)	Larry Doyle (Brown basepaths.)	45.00	22.50	13.50
(24b)	Larry Doyle (Green basepaths.)	45.00	22.50	13.50
(25a)	Art Fletcher (Brown basepaths.)	40.00	20.00	12.00
(25b)	Art Fletcher (Green basepaths.)	40.00	20.00	12.00
(26a)	Eddie Foster (Brown pennants.)	40.00	20.00	12.00
(26b)	Eddie Foster (Green pennants.)	40.00	20.00	12.00
(27a)	Del Gainor (White infield.)	50.00	25.00	15.00
(27b)	Del Gainor (Brown infield.)	150.00	75.00	45.00
(28a)	Chick Gandil (Brown pennants.)	100.00	50.00	30.00
(28b)	Chick Gandil (Green pennants.)	125.00	65.00	35.00
(29a)	George Gibson (Purple pennants.)	80.00	40.00	25.00
(29b)	George Gibson (Red pennants.)	90.00	45.00	27.00
(30a)	Hank Gowdy (White infield.)	40.00	20.00	12.00
(30b)	Hank Gowdy (Brown infield.)	150.00	75.00	45.00
(30c)	Hank Gowdy (Red infield.)	1,650	825.00	495.00
(31a)	Jack Graney (Purple pennants.)	90.00	45.00	27.00
(31b)	Jack Graney (Yellow pennants.)	125.00	65.00	35.00
(32a)	Eddie Grant (Brown basepaths.)	40.00	20.00	12.00
(32b)	Eddie Grant (Green basepaths.)	40.00	20.00	12.00
(33a)	Tommy Griffith (White infield, green pennants.)	40.00	20.00	12.00
(33b)	Tommy Griffith (White infield, red pennants.)	1,500	750.00	450.00
(33c)	Tommy Griffith (Brown infield.)	125.00	65.00	35.00
(33d)	Tommy Griffith (Red infield.)	1,650	825.00	495.00
(34a)	Earl Hamilton (Purple pennants.)	80.00	40.00	25.00
(34b)	Earl Hamilton (Red pennants.)	90.00	45.00	27.00
(35a)	Roy Hartzell (Blue infield.)	40.00	20.00	12.00
(35b)	Roy Hartzell (Green infield.)	40.00	20.00	12.00
(36a)	Miller Huggins (Purple pennants.)	160.00	80.00	45.00
(36b)	Miller Huggins (Yellow pennants.)	245.00	120.00	75.00
(37a)	John Hummel (Blue infield.)	40.00	20.00	12.00
(37b)	John Hummel (Green infield.)	40.00	20.00	12.00
(38a)	Ham Hyatt (Purple pennants.)	80.00	40.00	24.00
(38b)	Ham Hyatt (Red pennants.)	90.00	45.00	27.00
(39a)	Joe Jackson (Purple pennants.)	1,350	675.00	400.00
(39b)	Joe Jackson (Yellow pennants.)	1,100	550.00	330.00
(40a)	Bill James (White infield.)	40.00	20.00	12.00
(40b)	Bill James (Brown infield.)	160.00	80.00	50.00
(40c)	Bill James (Red infield.)	1,650	825.00	495.00
(41a)	Walter Johnson (Brown pennants.)	300.00	150.00	90.00
(41b)	Walter Johnson (Green pennants.)	275.00	135.00	80.00
(42a)	Ray Keating (Blue infield.)	40.00	20.00	12.00
(42b)	Ray Keating (Green infield.)	40.00	20.00	12.00
(43a)	Joe Kelley (Kelly) (Purple pennants.)	90.00	45.00	27.00
(43b)	Joe Kelley (Kelly) (Red pennants.)	90.00	45.00	27.00
(44a)	Ed Konetchy (Purple pennants.)	60.00	30.00	18.00
(44b)	Ed Konetchy (Red pennants.)	90.00	45.00	27.00
(45a)	Nemo Leibold (Purple pennants.)	75.00	37.50	22.00
(45b)	Nemo Leibold (Yellow pennants.)	150.00	75.00	45.00
(46a)	Fritz Maisel (Blue infield.)	40.00	20.00	12.00
(46b)	Fritz Maisel (Green infield.)	40.00	20.00	12.00
(47a)	Les Mann (White infield.)	40.00	20.00	12.00
(47b)	Les Mann (Brown infield.)	150.00	75.00	45.00
(47c)	Les Mann (Red infield.)	1,650	825.00	495.00
(48a)	Rabbit Maranville (White infield.)	130.00	65.00	39.00
(48b)	Rabbit Maranville (Brown infield.)	250.00	125.00	75.00
(48c)	Rabbit Maranville (Red infield.)	3,000	1,500	900.00
(49a)	Bill McAllister (McAllester) (Purple basepaths.)	80.00	40.00	25.00
(49b)	Bill McAllister (McAllester) (Red basepaths.)	100.00	50.00	30.00
(50a)	George McBride (Brown pennants.)	40.00	20.00	12.00
(50b)	George McBride (Green pennants.)	40.00	20.00	12.00
(51a)	Chief Meyers (Brown basepaths.)	40.00	20.00	12.00
(51b)	Chief Meyers (Green basepaths.)	40.00	20.00	12.00
(52a)	Clyde Milan (Brown pennants.)	40.00	20.00	12.00
(52b)	Clyde Milan (Green pennants.)	40.00	20.00	12.00
(53a)	J. Miller (Purple pennants.)	80.00	40.00	25.00
(53b)	J. Miller (Yellow pennants.)	125.00	65.00	35.00
(54a)	Otto Miller (Blue infield.)	40.00	20.00	12.00
(54b)	Otto Miller (Green infield.)	40.00	20.00	12.00
(55a)	Willie Mitchell (Purple pennants.)	80.00	40.00	25.00
(55b)	Willie Mitchell (Yellow pennants.)	150.00	75.00	45.00
(56a)	Danny Moeller (Brown pennants.)	40.00	20.00	12.00
(56b)	Danny Moeller (Green pennants.)	40.00	20.00	12.00
(57a)	Ray Morgan (Brown pennants.)	40.00	20.00	12.00

#	Player	NM	EX	VG
(57b)	Ray Morgan (Green pennants.)	40.00	20.00	12.00
(58a)	George Moriarty (White infield.)	40.00	20.00	12.00
(58b)	George Moriarty (Brown infield.)	150.00	75.00	45.00
(58c)	George Moriarty (Red infield.)	1,650	825.00	495.00
(59a)	Mike Mowrey (Purple pennants.)	80.00	40.00	25.00
(59b)	Mike Mowrey (Red pennants.)	90.00	45.00	27.00
(60a)	Red Murray (Brown basepaths.)	40.00	20.00	12.00
(60b)	Red Murray (Green basepaths.)	40.00	20.00	12.00
(61a)	Ivy Olson (Purple pennants.)	80.00	40.00	25.00
(61b)	Ivy Olson (Yellow pennants.)	160.00	80.00	50.00
(62a)	Steve O'Neill (Purple pennants.)	75.00	37.50	22.00
(62b)	Steve O'Neill (Red pennants.)	150.00	75.00	45.00
(62c)	Steve O'Neill (Yellow pennants.)	150.00	75.00	45.00
(63a)	Marty O'Toole (Purple pennants.)	80.00	40.00	25.00
(63b)	Marty O'Toole (Red pennants.)	90.00	45.00	27.00
(64a)	Roger Peckinpaugh (Blue infield.)	45.00	22.50	13.50
(64b)	Roger Peckinpaugh (Green infield.)	45.00	22.50	13.50
(65a)	Hub Perdue (White infield.)	40.00	20.00	12.00
(65b)	Hub Perdue (Brown infield.)	150.00	75.00	45.00
(65c)	Hub Purdue (Red infield.)	1,650	825.00	495.00
(66a)	Del Pratt (Purple basepaths.)	80.00	40.00	25.00
(66b)	Del Pratt (Red basepaths.)	90.00	45.00	27.00
(67a)	Hank Robinson (Purple pennants.)	80.00	40.00	25.00
(67b)	Hank Robinson (Yellow pennants.)	130.00	65.00	40.00
(68a)	Nap Rucker (Blue infield.)	40.00	20.00	12.00
(68b)	Nap Rucker (Green infield.)	40.00	20.00	12.00
(69a)	Slim Sallee (Purple pennants.)	100.00	50.00	30.00
(69b)	Slim Sallee (Yellow pennants.)	150.00	75.00	45.00
(70a)	Howard Shanks (Brown pennants.)	40.00	20.00	12.00
(70b)	Howard Shanks (Green pennants.)	40.00	20.00	12.00
(71a)	Burt Shotton (Purple basepaths.)	80.00	40.00	25.00
(71b)	Burt Shotton (Red basepaths.)	75.00	37.50	22.00
(72a)	Red Smith (Blue infield.)	40.00	20.00	12.00
(72b)	Red Smith (Green infield.)	40.00	20.00	12.00
(73a)	Fred Snodgrass (Brown basepaths.)	40.00	20.00	12.00
(73b)	Fred Snodgrass (Green basepaths.)	40.00	20.00	12.00
(74a)	Bill Steele (Purple pennants.)	80.00	40.00	24.00
(74b)	Bill Steele (Yellow pennants.)	150.00	75.00	45.00
(75a)	Casey Stengel (Blue infield.)	100.00	50.00	30.00
(75b)	Casey Stengel (Green infield.)	100.00	50.00	30.00
(76a)	Jeff Sweeney (Blue infield.)	40.00	20.00	12.00
(76b)	Jeff Sweeney (Green infield.)	40.00	20.00	12.00
(77a)	Jeff Tesreau (Brown basepaths.)	40.00	20.00	12.00
(77b)	Jeff Tesreau (Green basepaths.)	40.00	20.00	12.00
(78a)	Terry Turner (Purple pennants.)	80.00	40.00	25.00
(78b)	Terry Turner (Yellow pennants.)	150.00	75.00	45.00
(79a)	Lefty Tyler (White infield.)	40.00	20.00	12.00
(79b)	Lefty Tyler (Brown infield.)	150.00	75.00	45.00
(79c)	Lefty Tyler (Red infield.)	1,650	825.00	495.00
(80a)	Jim Viox (Purple pennants.)	80.00	40.00	25.00
(80b)	Jim Viox (Red pennants.)	90.00	45.00	27.00
(81a)	Bull Wagner (Blue infield.)	40.00	20.00	12.00
(81b)	Bull Wagner (Green infield.)	40.00	20.00	12.00
(82a)	Bobby Wallace (Purple basepaths.)	150.00	75.00	45.00
(82b)	Bobby Wallace (Red basepaths.)	150.00	75.00	45.00
(83a)	Dee Walsh (Purple basepaths.)	80.00	40.00	25.00
(83b)	Dee Walsh (Red basepaths.)	90.00	45.00	27.00
(84a)	Jimmy Walsh (Blue infield.)	40.00	20.00	12.00
(84b)	Jimmy Walsh (Green infield.)	40.00	20.00	12.00
(85a)	Bert Whaling (White infield.)	40.00	20.00	12.00
(85b)	Bert Whaling (Brown infield.)	150.00	75.00	45.00
(85c)	Bert Whaling (Red infield.)	1,650	825.00	495.00
(86a)	Zach Wheat (Blue infield.)	125.00	65.00	35.00
(86b)	Zach Wheat (Green infield.)	100.00	50.00	30.00
(87a)	Possum Whitted (Purple pennants.)	80.00	40.00	25.00
(87b)	Possum Whitted (Yellow pennants.)	125.00	65.00	35.00
(88a)	Gus Williams (Purple pennants.)	80.00	40.00	25.00
(88b)	Gus Williams (Red basepaths.)	90.00	45.00	27.00
(89a)	Owen Wilson (Purple pennants.)	80.00	40.00	25.00
(89b)	Owen Wilson (Yellow pennants.)	150.00	75.00	45.00
(90a)	Hooks Wiltse (Brown basepaths.)	40.00	20.00	12.00
(90b)	Hooks Wiltse (Green basepaths.)	40.00	20.00	12.00

1937 BF-UNC Felt Pennants

Based on the known player-team combinations in this probably incomplete checklist, 1937 seems the most likely date of issue. The pennants measure about 2-1/4" across the top and taper to a point at the end of their 5" length. About halfway down is a blue-and-white trapezoid with a player photo within a

circle on a pinstriped background. The team name is printed in two lines at top. It is believed each player can be found with more than one base pennant color and team-name printing.

		NM	EX	VG
	Common Player:	150.00	75.00	45.00
(1)	Dizzy Dean	650.00	325.00	195.00
(2)	Bobby Feller	500.00	250.00	150.00
(3)	Hank Greenberg	500.00	250.00	150.00
(4)	Lefty Grove	450.00	225.00	135.00
(5)	Carl Hubbell	450.00	220.00	135.00
(6)	Joe Moore	150.00	75.00	45.00
(7)	Wallace Moses	150.00	75.00	45.00
(8)	Van Lingle Mungo	150.00	75.00	45.00
(9)	Lynwood Rowe	150.00	75.00	45.00
(10)	Joe Stripp	150.00	75.00	45.00
(11)	Floyd Vaughan	400.00	200.00	120.00

1916 BF2 Felt Pennants

Issued circa 1916, this unnumbered set consists of 97 felt pennants with a small black-and-white player photo glued to each. The triangular pennants measure approximately 2-7/8" across the top and taper to a length of about 5-3/4" long, while the photos are 1-3/4" x 1-1/4" and appear to be identical to photos used for M101-4/M101-5 issues of the same period. The pennants list the player's name and team. The pennants were given away as premiums with the purchase of five-cent loaves of Ferguson Bakery bread in the Roxbury, Mass., area.

(See 1916 Ferguson Bakery Felt Pennants for checklist and values.)

1936-37 BF3 Felt Player/Team Pennants

The checklists for these series of felt pennants issued circa 1936-1938 are not complete, and new examples are still being reported. The pennants do not carry any manufacturer's name although packages found with various pieces attribute the issues to Red Ball Sales, a gum company in Chicago, and Grandpa Brands Co., Cincinnati, another gum company. One pennant was given away with the purchase of a stick of gum, and at least one wrapper indicates large format (28" x 12") versions of the Red Ball pennants could be had in a redemption program. The pennants vary in size slightly but generally measure approximately 2-1/2" x 4-1/2" and were issued in various styles and colors. Most of the printing is white, although some pennants have been found with other colors of printing, and the same pennant is often found in more than one color combination. The pennants feature both individual players and teams, including some minor league clubs. The pennants were grouped together in the American Card Catalog under the designation of BF3. Advanced collectors have categorized the pennants into a number of basic design types, depending on what elements are included on the pennant. The unnumbered felts are listed alphabetically within type. Gaps have been left in the assigned numbers to accommodate future discoveries.

	NM	EX	VG
Common Pennant:	25.00	12.50	7.50

1936-37 Type 1 - Player Name and Silhouette

Generic silhouette figures in action poses are featured at the left end of this series of pennants. Player names at right can be found in a number of different typographic styles. Gaps have been left in the assigned numbering for future additions.

		NM	EX	VG
	Common Pennant:	60.00	30.00	18.00
(1)	Luke Appling/Btg	80.00	40.00	25.00
(2)	Earl Averill/Btg	80.00	40.00	25.00
(3)	Wally Berger/Fldg	60.00	30.00	18.00
(4)	Zeke Bonura/Fldg	60.00	30.00	18.00
(5)	Dolph Camilli/Fldg	60.00	30.00	18.00
(6)	Ben Chapman/Btg	60.00	30.00	18.00
(7)	Mickey Cochrane/Catching	90.00	45.00	27.00
(8)	Rip Collins/Btg	60.00	30.00	18.00
(9)	Joe Cronin/Btg	80.00	40.00	25.00
(10)	Kiki Cuyler/Running	80.00	40.00	25.00
(11)	Dizzy Dean/Pitching	135.00	65.00	40.00
(12)	Frank Demaree/Btg	60.00	30.00	18.00
(13)	Paul Derringer/Pitching	60.00	30.00	18.00
(14)	Bill Dickey/Catching	90.00	45.00	27.00
(15)	Joe DiMaggio/Btg	300.00	150.00	90.00
(16)	Jimmy Dykes/Fldg	60.00	30.00	18.00
(17)	Bob Feller/Pitching	110.00	55.00	35.00
(18)	Wes Ferrell/Btg	60.00	30.00	18.00
(19)	Jimmy Foxx	100.00	50.00	30.00
(20)	Larry French/Btg	60.00	30.00	18.00
(21)	Franky Frisch/Running	90.00	45.00	27.00
(22)	Lou Gehrig/Throwing	300.00	150.00	90.00
(23)	Charlie Gehringer/Running	90.00	45.00	27.00
(24)	Lefty Gomez/Pitching	80.00	40.00	25.00
(25)	Goose Goslin/Btg	80.00	40.00	25.00
(26)	Hank Greenberg/Fldg	110.00	55.00	35.00
(27)	Charley Grimm/Fldg	60.00	30.00	18.00
(28)	Lefty Grove/Throwing	90.00	45.00	27.00
(29)	Gabby Hartnett/Catching	80.00	40.00	25.00
(30)	Rollie Hemsley/Catching	60.00	30.00	18.00
(31)	Billy Herman/Fldg	80.00	40.00	25.00
(32)	Frank Higgins/Fldg	60.00	30.00	18.00
(33)	Rogers Hornsby/Btg	100.00	50.00	30.00
(34)	Carl Hubbell (Pitching)	90.00	45.00	27.00
(35)	Chuck Klein/Throwing	80.00	40.00	25.00
(36)	Tony Lazzeri/Btg	80.00	40.00	25.00
(37)	Hank Leiber/Fldg	60.00	30.00	18.00
(38)	Ernie Lombardi/Catching	80.00	40.00	25.00
(39)	Al Lopez/Throwing	80.00	40.00	25.00
(40)	Gus Mancuso/Running	60.00	30.00	18.00
(41)	Heinie Manush/Btg	80.00	40.00	25.00
(42)	Pepper Martin/Btg	70.00	35.00	20.00
(43)	Joe McCarthy/Kneeling	80.00	40.00	25.00
(44)	Wally Moses/Running	60.00	30.00	18.00
(45)	Van Mungo/Standing	60.00	30.00	18.00
(46)	Mel Ott (Throwing)	90.00	45.00	27.00
(47)	Schoolboy Rowe/Pitching	60.00	30.00	18.00
(48)	Babe Ruth/Btg	450.00	225.00	135.00
(49)	George Selkirk/Btg	60.00	30.00	18.00
(50)	Luke Sewell/Sliding	60.00	30.00	18.00
(51)	Joe Stripp/Btg	60.00	30.00	18.00
(52)	Pie Traynor/Btg	80.00	40.00	25.00
(53)	Hal Trosky/Fldg	60.00	30.00	18.00
(54)	Floyd Vaughan/Running (Script name.)	80.00	40.00	25.00
(55)	Floyd Vaughan/Running (Block name.)	80.00	40.00	25.00
(56)	Joe Vosmik/Running	60.00	30.00	18.00
(57)	Paul Waner/Btg	80.00	40.00	25.00
(58)	Lon Warneke/Pitching	60.00	30.00	18.00
(59)	Jimmy Wilson/Fldg	60.00	30.00	18.00

1936-37 Type 2 - Player's Name, Team Nickname, Figure

Team nicknames have been added at the spine of this style of pennant. As with Type 1, some players can be found in more than one pose and/or typography. Gaps have been left in the assigned numbering to accomodate future additions.

		NM	EX	VG
	Common Pennant:	60.00	30.00	18.00
(1)	Luke Appling/Btg (Block name.)	80.00	40.00	25.00

		NM	EX	VG
(2)	Luke Appling/Btg (Script name.)	80.00	40.00	25.00
(3)	Earl Averill/Fldg	80.00	40.00	25.00
(4)	Earl Averill/Running	80.00	40.00	24.00
(5)	Wally Berger/Throwing	60.00	30.00	18.00
(6)	Zeke Bonura/Btg	60.00	30.00	18.00
(7)	Dolph Camilli/Btg	60.00	30.00	18.00
(8)	Ben Chapman/Throwing	60.00	30.00	18.00
(9)	Mickey Cochrane/Throwing	90.00	45.00	27.00
(10)	Rip Collins/Btg	60.00	30.00	18.00
(11)	Joe Cronin/Throwing	80.00	40.00	25.00
(12)	Kiki Cuyler/Throwing	80.00	40.00	25.00
(13)	Dizzy Dean/Btg	110.00	55.00	35.00
(14)	Dizzy Dean/Throwing	110.00	55.00	35.00
(15)	Frank Demaree/Btg	60.00	30.00	18.00
(16)	Paul Derringer/Throwing	60.00	30.00	18.00
(17)	Bill Dickey/Throwing	110.00	55.00	35.00
(18)	Joe DiMaggio (Block letters through figure.)	260.00	130.00	80.00
(19)	Joe DiMaggio (Script)	260.00	130.00	80.00
(20)	Jimmy Dykes/Throwing	60.00	30.00	18.00
(21)	Bob Feller (Block letters.)	110.00	55.00	35.00
(22)	Bob Feller (Script)	110.00	55.00	35.00
(23)	Wes Ferrell/Throwing	60.00	30.00	18.00
(24)	Larry French/Btg	60.00	30.00	18.00
(25)	Frank Frisch/Fldg	90.00	45.00	27.00
(27)	Lou Gehrig/Btg (Block letters.)	300.00	150.00	90.00
(28)	Lou Gehrig/Btg (Script)	300.00	150.00	90.00
(29)	Lou Gehrig/Fldg	300.00	150.00	90.00
(31)	Lefty Gomez/Pitching	90.00	45.00	27.00
(32)	Goose Goslin/Throwing	90.00	45.00	27.00
(33)	Hank Greenberg/Btg	110.00	55.00	35.00
(34)	Hank Greenberg/Throwing	110.00	55.00	35.00
(35)	Charlie Grimm/Fldg	60.00	30.00	18.00
(36)	Lefty Grove/Btg	90.00	45.00	27.00
(37)	Lefty Grove/Pitching	90.00	45.00	27.00
(38)	Gabby Hartnett/Btg	80.00	40.00	25.00
(39)	Gabby Hartnett/Catching	80.00	40.00	25.00
(40)	Billy Herman/Btg (Facing right, name over figure.)	80.00	40.00	25.00
(41)	Billy Herman/Btg (Facing right, name through body.)	80.00	40.00	25.00
(42)	Billy Herman/Btg (Facing left.)	80.00	40.00	25.00
(44)	Roger (Rogers) Hornsby/Btg	100.00	50.00	30.00
(45)	Carl Hubbell/Pitching	90.00	45.00	27.00
(49)	Tony Lazzeri/Throwing	80.00	40.00	25.00
(50)	Hank Leiber/Btg	60.00	30.00	18.00
(52)	Ernie Lombardi/Btg	80.00	40.00	25.00
(54)	Gus Mancuso/Btg	60.00	30.00	18.00
(55)	Heinie Manush/Btg	80.00	40.00	25.00
(56)	Pepper Martin/Btg	75.00	37.50	22.00
(57)	Joe McCarthy/Btg	80.00	40.00	25.00
(58)	Joe Medwick/Btg	80.00	40.00	25.00
(59)	Van Lingle Mungo/Btg	60.00	30.00	18.00
(60)	Van Lingo Mungo/Btg (Lingle)	60.00	30.00	18.00
(64)	Schoolboy Rowe/Btg	60.00	30.00	18.00
(65)	Babe Ruth/Btg	450.00	225.00	135.00
(67)	George Selkirk/Btg	60.00	30.00	18.00
(68)	Luke Sewell/Btg	60.00	30.00	18.00
(69)	Joe Stripp/Btg	60.00	30.00	18.00
(70)	Bill Terry/Btg	80.00	40.00	25.00
(71)	Bill Terry/Fldg	80.00	40.00	25.00
(73)	Pie Traynor/Throwing	80.00	40.00	25.00
(74)	Hal Trosky/Btg	60.00	30.00	18.00
(75)	Floyd Vaughan/Btg	80.00	40.00	25.00
(76)	Joe Vosmik/Throwing	60.00	30.00	18.00
(77)	Paul Waner/Btg	80.00	40.00	25.00
(80)	Lon Warneke/Btg	60.00	30.00	18.00
(81)	Lon Warneke (Wind-up.)	60.00	30.00	18.00
(83)	Jimmy Wilson/Pitching	60.00	30.00	18.00

1936-37 Type 3 - Player's Name, Team Nickname

No player silhouettes are found on this series of pennants. The player name is at right, with his team's nickname at the spine. Despite the fact he left the team in 1934, Babe Ruth's pennant shows him with the Yankees. Gaps have been left in the assigned numbering to accomodate future additions.

		NM	EX	VG
	Common Pennant:	60.00	30.00	18.00
(1)	Luke Appling (Block letters.)	80.00	40.00	25.00
(2)	Luke Appling (Script)	80.00	40.00	25.00
(4)	Wally Berger	60.00	30.00	18.00
(6)	Zeke Bonura	60.00	30.00	18.00
(7)	Dolph Camilli	60.00	30.00	18.00
(9)	Ben Chapman	60.00	30.00	18.00
(10)	Mickey Cochrane	80.00	40.00	25.00
(11)	Rip Collins	60.00	30.00	18.00
(12)	Joe Cronin	80.00	40.00	25.00
(13)	Kiki Cuyler	80.00	40.00	25.00
(14)	Dizzy Dean	135.00	65.00	40.00
(15)	Frank Demaree	60.00	30.00	18.00
(16)	Paul Derringer	60.00	30.00	18.00
(17)	Bill Dickey	110.00	55.00	35.00
(18)	Joe DiMaggio (Script name.)	300.00	150.00	90.00
(19)	Jimmy Dykes	60.00	30.00	18.00
(20)	Bob Feller (Script name.)	110.00	55.00	35.00
(21)	Wes Ferrell	60.00	30.00	18.00

		NM	EX	VG
(22)	Jimmie Foxx	90.00	45.00	27.00
(23)	Larry French	60.00	30.00	18.00
(24)	Franky Frisch	80.00	40.00	25.00
(25)	Lou Gehrig (Script name.)	300.00	150.00	90.00
(26)	Charlie Gehringer	80.00	40.00	25.00
(28)	Lefty Gomez	80.00	40.00	25.00
(29)	Goose Goslin	80.00	40.00	24.00
(30)	Hank Greenberg	90.00	45.00	27.00
(31)	Charley Grimm	60.00	30.00	18.00
(32)	Lefty Grove	90.00	45.00	27.00
(33)	Gabby Hartnett	80.00	40.00	25.00
(35)	Rollie Hemsley	60.00	30.00	18.00
(36)	Billy Herman (Block letters.)	80.00	40.00	25.00
(37)	Billy Herman (Script)	80.00	40.00	25.00
(38)	Frank Higgins	60.00	30.00	18.00
(39)	Roger Hornsby (Rogers)	90.00	45.00	27.00
(40)	Carl Hubbell	80.00	40.00	25.00
(42)	Chuck Klein	80.00	40.00	25.00
(43)	Tony Lazzeri	80.00	40.00	25.00
(44)	Hank Leiber	60.00	30.00	18.00
(45)	Ernie Lombardi	80.00	40.00	25.00
(46)	Al Lopez	80.00	40.00	25.00
(48)	Gus Mancuso	60.00	30.00	18.00
(49)	Heinie Manush	80.00	40.00	25.00
(50)	Pepper Martin	70.00	35.00	20.00
(51)	Joe McCarthy	80.00	40.00	25.00
(52)	Joe Medwick	80.00	40.00	25.00
(53)	Wally Moses	60.00	30.00	18.00
(54)	Van Mungo	60.00	30.00	18.00
(55)	Mel Ott	80.00	40.00	25.00
(56)	Schoolboy Rowe	60.00	30.00	18.00
(57)	Babe Ruth	400.00	200.00	120.00
(58)	George Selkirk	60.00	30.00	18.00
(59)	Luke Sewell	60.00	30.00	18.00
(60)	Al Simmons	80.00	40.00	25.00
(61)	Joe Stripp	60.00	30.00	18.00
(62)	Bill Terry	80.00	40.00	25.00
(63)	Pie Traynor	80.00	40.00	25.00
(64)	Hal Trosky	60.00	30.00	18.00
(65)	Joe Vosmik	60.00	30.00	18.00
(66)	Floyd Vaughan	80.00	40.00	25.00
(67)	Paul Waner	80.00	40.00	25.00
(68)	Lon Warneke	60.00	30.00	18.00
(71)	Jimmy Wilson	60.00	30.00	18.00

1936-37 Type 4 - Team Nickname and Silhouette Player

One of two closely related series of these collectible pennants, this type has a team nickname in combination with a silhouette figure of one or more baseball figures. Collectors should be aware that similar pennants, perhaps even sharing the same designs, were issued circa 1950 in boxes of candy from American Nut & Chocolate of Boston. The AN&C pennants should be distinguishable by their smaller size of approximately 4" x 1-7/8". Gaps in the assigned numbering have been left to accomodate future additions.

		NM	EX	VG
	Common Pennant:	40.00	20.00	12.00
(1)	Athletics/Fielder	40.00	20.00	12.00
(2)	Browns/Catcher	40.00	20.00	12.00
(3)	Cubs/Batter	40.00	20.00	12.00
(4)	Dodgers/Batter	40.00	20.00	12.00
(5)	Dodgers/Fielder	40.00	20.00	12.00
(7)	Giants (Sliding into base.)	40.00	20.00	12.00
(8)	Giants (Standing at base.)	40.00	20.00	12.00
(9)	Giants (Two players.)	40.00	20.00	12.00
(10)	Phillies/Pitcher	40.00	20.00	12.00
(12)	Reds/Batter	40.00	20.00	12.00
(13)	Reds/Catcher	40.00	20.00	12.00
(14)	Reds/Pitcher	40.00	20.00	12.00
(15)	Red Sox/Batter and Catcher	40.00	20.00	12.00
(16)	White Sox (Batter left of team name.)	40.00	20.00	12.00
(17)	White Sox (Batter inside "W.")	40.00	20.00	12.00
(18)	White Sox/Catcher	40.00	20.00	12.00
(19)	White Sox (Profile)	40.00	20.00	12.00
(20)	White Sox/Pitcher	40.00	20.00	12.00
(21)	Yankees/Batter	40.00	20.00	12.00
(22)	Yankees/Fielder	40.00	20.00	12.00

1936-37 Type 5 - Team Nickname with Emblem

Closely related to the Type 4 style, these pennants combine a team nickname with a symbolic figure or depictions of baseball equipment. Collectors should be aware that similar pennants, perhaps even sharing the same designs, were issued circa 1950 in boxes of candy from American Nut & Chocolate of Boston. The AN&C pennants should be distinguishable by their smaller size of approximately 4" x 1-7/8". Gaps have been left in the numbering to accomodate future additions.

		NM	EX	VG
Common Pennant:		40.00	20.00	12.00
(1)	Athletics (Elephant, no tusks.)	40.00	20.00	12.00
(2)	Athletics (Elephant, w/tusks.)	40.00	20.00	12.00
(3)	Athletics (Gothic script, w/bat, ball.)	40.00	20.00	12.00
(5)	Bees (Bee is crossbar of "B.")	40.00	20.00	12.00
(6)	Bees (Bee is loops of "B.")	40.00	20.00	12.00
(7)	Brooklyn (Crossed bats over "B.")	40.00	20.00	12.00
(9)	Browns (Ball)	40.00	20.00	12.00
(10)	Browns (Bat)	40.00	20.00	12.00
(11)	Browns (Bat is spine of "B," balls in loops.)	40.00	20.00	12.00
(12)	Cardinals (Bat)	40.00	20.00	12.00
(13)	Cardinals (Cardinal inside "C," profile.)	40.00	20.00	12.00
(14)	Cardinals (Cardinal inside "C" front view.)	40.00	20.00	12.00
(15)	Cardinals (Four birds on "C.")	40.00	20.00	12.00
(16)	Cubs (Cub w/bat.)	40.00	20.00	12.00
(17)	Cubs (Cub's head.)	40.00	20.00	12.00
(18)	Cubs (Cub sitting in "C.")	40.00	20.00	12.00
19	Cubs (Full-body profile.)	40.00	20.00	12.00
(20)	Dodgers (Ball)	40.00	20.00	12.00
(21)	Dodgers (Ball, bat and glove.)	40.00	20.00	12.00
(22)	Dodgers (Trolley car.)	40.00	20.00	12.00
(23)	Giants (Crossed bats and ball.)	40.00	20.00	12.00
(25)	Indians (Indians)	40.00	20.00	12.00
(26)	Indians (Indian profile, nine feathers.)	40.00	20.00	12.00
(27)	Indians (Indian profile, headdress.)	40.00	20.00	12.00
(30)	Phillies (Liberty Bell.)	40.00	20.00	12.00
(32)	Pirates (Pirate, no knife.)	40.00	20.00	12.00
(33)	Pirates (Pirate w/knife.)	40.00	20.00	12.00
(34)	Pirates (Peg-legged pirate w/sword.)	40.00	20.00	12.00
(35)	Pirates (Skull and crossed bones.)	40.00	20.00	12.00
(36)	Reds (Man with stein.)	40.00	20.00	12.00
(37)	Reds (W/ball.)	40.00	20.00	12.00
(39)	Red Sox (Ball)	40.00	20.00	12.00
(40)	Red Sox (Bat)	40.00	20.00	12.00
(41)	Red Sox (Ball and bat.)	40.00	20.00	12.00
(42)	Red Sox (Stocking)	40.00	20.00	12.00
(44)	Senators (Bat)	40.00	20.00	12.00
(45)	Senators (Cap. Dome, "S" superimposed.)	40.00	20.00	12.00
(46)	Senators (Capital Dome, "S" to right.)	40.00	20.00	12.00
(47)	Senators (Man's profile in top hat.)	40.00	20.00	12.00
(48)	Sox (W/bat and ball.)	40.00	20.00	12.00
(49)	Tigers (Bat left, ball right.)	40.00	20.00	12.00
(50)	Tigers (Cap)	40.00	20.00	12.00
(51)	Tigers (Prowling tiger.)	40.00	20.00	12.00
(52)	Tigers (Tiger head in circle.)	40.00	20.00	12.00
(53)	Tigers (Tiger head, no circle.)	40.00	20.00	12.00

1936-37 Type 6 - Team Name Only

		NM	EX	VG
Common Pennant:		40.00	20.00	12.00
(1)	ATHLETICS	40.00	20.00	12.00
(2)	ATHLETICS (PHILA. on spine.)	40.00	20.00	12.00
(3)	BEES	40.00	20.00	12.00
(4)	BEES (BOSTON on spine.)	40.00	20.00	12.00
(5)	CARDINALS	40.00	20.00	12.00
(6)	CUBS	40.00	20.00	12.00
(7)	CUBS (CHICAGO on spine.)	40.00	20.00	12.00
(8)	DODGERS	40.00	20.00	12.00
(9)	DODGERS (BROOKLYN on spine.)	40.00	20.00	12.00
(10)	GIANTS	40.00	20.00	12.00
(11)	GIANTS (NEW YORK on spine.)	40.00	20.00	12.00
(12)	INDIANS	40.00	20.00	12.00
(13)	PHILLIES	40.00	20.00	12.00
(14)	PHILLIES (PHILLIES on spine.)	40.00	20.00	12.00
(15)	PIRATES	40.00	20.00	12.00
(16)	PIRATES (PITTSBURGH on spine.)	40.00	20.00	12.00
(17)	REDS	40.00	20.00	12.00
(18)	REDS (CINCINNATI on spine.)	40.00	20.00	12.00
(19)	SENATORS	40.00	20.00	12.00
(20)	WASH. SENATORS	40.00	20.00	12.00
(21)	SOX	40.00	20.00	12.00
(22)	TIGERS	40.00	20.00	12.00
(23)	WHITE SOX	40.00	20.00	12.00
(24)	YANKEES	40.00	20.00	12.00
(25)	YANKEES (NEW YORK on spine.)	40.00	20.00	12.00

1936 Type 7 - Player, Team W/pennant, Cap, Ball, etc.

This group of pennants is slightly longer, at about 5-1/4", than the majority of BF 3 pennants. It is believed that two players from each team will eventually be accounted for.

		NM	EX	VG
Common Pennant:		40.00	20.00	12.00
(1)	Luke Appling	55.00	27.00	16.50
(2)	Wally Berger	40.00	20.00	12.00
(3)	Dolph Camilli	40.00	20.00	12.00
(4)	Dizzy Dean	90.00	45.00	27.00
(5)	Frank Demaree	40.00	20.00	12.00
(6)	Joe DiMaggio	200.00	100.00	60.00
(7)	Jimmie Foxx	75.00	37.00	22.00
(8)	Lou Gehrig	200.00	100.00	60.00
(9)	Earl Grace	40.00	20.00	12.00
(10)	Hank Greenberg	75.00	37.00	22.00
(11)	Gabby Hartnett	55.00	27.00	16.50
(12)	Rollie Hemsley	40.00	20.00	12.00
(13)	Carl Hubbell	55.00	27.00	16.50
(14)	Bob Johnson	40.00	20.00	12.00
(15)	Ernie Lombardi	55.00	27.00	16.50
(16)	Al Lopez	55.00	27.00	16.50
(17)	Joe Medwick	55.00	27.00	16.50
(18)	Van Lingle Mungo	45.00	22.00	13.50
(19)	Billy Myers	40.00	20.00	12.00
(20)	Mel Ott	55.00	27.00	16.50
(21)	Frank Pytlak	40.00	20.00	12.00
(23)	Schoolboy Rowe	40.00	20.00	12.00
(25)	Hal Trosky	40.00	20.00	12.00
(28)	Arky Vaughan	55.00	27.00	16.50
(29)	Paul Waner	55.00	27.00	16.50
(30)	Earl Whitehill	40.00	20.00	12.00

1936-37 Type 8 - Misc. Designs

Pennants in this series are generally unique in their style and do not fit into any of the other categories.

		NM	EX	VG
Common Pennant:		60.00	30.00	18.00
(1)	Wes Ferrell ("RED SOX" reversed out of bat on spine.)	60.00	30.00	18.00
(2)	Larry French (Name, team, year on ball.)	60.00	30.00	18.00
(3)	Goose Goslin (Name above and below bat, "TIGERS" on bat.)	75.00	37.50	22.00
(4)	Charley Root (Name above and below bat, "CUBS" on bat.)	60.00	30.00	18.00
(5)	Billy Sullivan ("INDIANS" reversed out of bat on spine.)	60.00	30.00	18.00
(6)	CHAMPIONS/YANKEES/1936 (Team name in red triangle at center.)	100.00	50.00	30.00

1937 Type 9 - Player Name, 1937 on Ball, Team Name

Players from only four teams - Bees, Cardinals, Cubs and White Sox - are known in this style. The pennants have a large baseball at left with three panels containing the player's first name, last name and "1937." At right is the team nickname.

		NM	EX	VG
Common Pennant:		60.00	30.00	18.00
(1)	Luke Appling	80.00	40.00	25.00
(2)	Wally Berger	60.00	30.00	18.00
(3)	Zeke Bonura	60.00	30.00	18.00
(4)	Frenchy Bordagaray	60.00	30.00	18.00
(5)	Clint Brown	60.00	30.00	18.00
(6)	Clay Bryant	60.00	30.00	18.00
(7)	Guy Bush	60.00	30.00	18.00
(8)	Sugar Cain	60.00	30.00	18.00
(9)	Tex Carleton	60.00	30.00	18.00
(10)	Phil Cavaretta (Cavarretta)	60.00	30.00	18.00
(11)	Phil Cavarretta	60.00	30.00	18.00
(12)	Irving Cherry	60.00	30.00	18.00
(13)	Ripper Collins	60.00	30.00	18.00
(14)	Tony Cuccinello	60.00	30.00	18.00
(15)	Curt Davis	60.00	30.00	18.00
(16)	Dizzy Dean	135.00	65.00	40.00
(17)	Paul Dean	75.00	37.50	22.00
(18)	Frank Demaree	60.00	30.00	18.00
(19)	Bill Dietrich	60.00	30.00	18.00
(21)	Vinc DiMaggio (Vince)	75.00	37.50	22.00
(22)	Leo Durocher	80.00	40.00	25.00
(23)	Jimmy Dykes	60.00	30.00	18.00
(24)	Burt Fletcher	60.00	30.00	18.00
(25)	Wes Flowers	60.00	30.00	18.00
(26)	Vic Frasier	60.00	30.00	18.00
(27)	Larry French	60.00	30.00	18.00
(28)	Linus Frey	60.00	30.00	18.00
(29)	Frank Frisch	80.00	40.00	25.00
(30)	Augie Galan	60.00	30.00	18.00
(31)	Charlie Grimm	60.00	30.00	18.00
(32)	Geo. Haas	60.00	30.00	18.00
(33)	Stan Hack	70.00	35.00	21.00
(34)	Jessie Haines	80.00	40.00	25.00
(35)	Gabby Hartnett	80.00	40.00	25.00
(36)	Minter Hayes	60.00	30.00	18.00
(37)	Billy Herman	80.00	40.00	25.00
(38)	Walter Highbee (Kirby Higbe)	60.00	30.00	18.00
(39)	Roy Johnson	60.00	30.00	18.00
(41)	Baxter Jordan	60.00	30.00	18.00
(42)	Billy Jurges	60.00	30.00	18.00
(43)	Vernon Kennedy	60.00	30.00	18.00
(44)	Mike Kreevich	60.00	30.00	18.00
(45)	Bill Lee	60.00	30.00	18.00
(46)	Thorn Lee	60.00	30.00	18.00
(47)	Al Lopez	80.00	40.00	25.00
(48)	Andy Lotshaw	60.00	30.00	18.00
(49)	Ted Lyons	80.00	40.00	25.00
(50)	Dan MacFayden	60.00	30.00	18.00
(51)	Henry Majeski	60.00	30.00	18.00
(52)	Pepper Martin	70.00	35.00	20.00
(53)	Stuart Martin	60.00	30.00	18.00
(54)	Joe Marty	60.00	30.00	18.00
(55)	Tommy McBride	60.00	30.00	18.00
(56)	Bill McKechnie	80.00	40.00	25.00
(57)	Joe Medwick	80.00	40.00	25.00
(58)	Steve Mesner	60.00	30.00	18.00
(59)	Hank Meyer	60.00	30.00	18.00
(61)	Johnny Mize	80.00	40.00	25.00
(62)	Gene Moore	60.00	30.00	18.00
(63)	Terry Moore	60.00	30.00	18.00
(64)	Ken O'Dea	60.00	30.00	18.00
(65)	Brusie Ogrodowski	60.00	30.00	18.00
(66)	Tony Piet	60.00	30.00	18.00
(67)	Ray Radcliff	60.00	30.00	18.00
(68)	Bob Reis	60.00	30.00	18.00
(69)	Dunc Rigney	60.00	30.00	18.00
(70)	Les Rock	60.00	30.00	18.00
(71)	Chas. Root	60.00	30.00	18.00
(72)	Larry Rosenthal	60.00	30.00	18.00
(73)	Luke Sewell	60.00	30.00	18.00
(74)	Merv Shea	60.00	30.00	18.00
(75)	Tuck Stainback	60.00	30.00	18.00
(76)	Hank Steinbacher	60.00	30.00	18.00
(77)	Monty Stratton	70.00	35.00	20.00
(78)	Ken Sylvestri	60.00	30.00	18.00
(79)	Billie Urbanski	60.00	30.00	18.00
(81)	Fred Walker	60.00	30.00	18.00
(82)	Lon Warneke	60.00	30.00	18.00
(83)	Johnnie Whitehead	60.00	30.00	18.00

1938 Type 10 - Player Name, 1938 on Ball, Team Name

Identical in format to the 1937 version, these pennants feature only members of the Detroit Tigers. The player's first name, last name and "1938" are stacked on the panels of a large baseball design at left, while "TIGERS" is at right.

		NM	EX	VG
Common Pennant:		60.00	30.00	18.00
(1)	Harry Eisenstat	60.00	30.00	18.00
(2)	Pete Fox	60.00	30.00	18.00
(3)	Vern Kennedy	60.00	30.00	18.00
(4)	Roxie Lawson	60.00	30.00	18.00
(5)	Tony Piet	60.00	30.00	18.00
(6)	Rudy York	60.00	30.00	18.00

1936-37 Type 11 - Minor League and Team

Minor league team nicknames and a league designation are combined with a player figure or symbol in this series. The checklist is believed complete with eight teams each from the Southern Association, International League and American Association.

		NM	EX	VG
Complete Set (24):		950.00	475.00	275.00
Common Pennant:		40.00	20.00	12.00
(1)	Barons - Southern	40.00	20.00	12.00
(2)	Bears - International	40.00	20.00	12.00
(3)	Bisons - International	40.00	20.00	12.00
(4)	Blues - Amer. Assn.	40.00	20.00	12.00
(5)	Brewers - Amer. Assn.	40.00	20.00	12.00
(6)	Chicks - Southern	40.00	20.00	12.00
(7)	Chiefs - International	40.00	20.00	12.00
(8)	Colonels - Amer. Assn.	40.00	20.00	12.00
(9)	Crackers - Sou'n. Ass'n.	40.00	20.00	12.00
(10)	Giants - International	40.00	20.00	12.00
(11)	Indians - Amer. Assn.	40.00	20.00	12.00
(12)	Lookouts - Sou'n. Ass'n.	40.00	20.00	12.00
(13)	Maple Leafs - International	40.00	20.00	12.00
(14)	Millers - Amer. Assn.	40.00	20.00	12.00
(15)	Mud Hens - Amer. Assn.	40.00	20.00	12.00
(16)	Orioles - International	40.00	20.00	12.00
(17)	Pelicans - Sou'n. Ass'n.	40.00	20.00	12.00
(18)	Red Birds - Amer. Assn.	40.00	20.00	12.00
(19)	Red Wings - Int'l	40.00	20.00	12.00
(20)	Royals - Int'l	40.00	20.00	12.00
(21)	Saints - Amer. Assn.	40.00	20.00	12.00
(22)	Smokies - Southern	40.00	20.00	12.00
(23)	Travelers - Sou'n. Ass'n.	40.00	20.00	12.00
(24)	Vols - Sou'n Ass'n.	40.00	20.00	12.00

1936-37 Type 12 - Jumbo Teams

According to advertising on the Red Ball Gum packaging with which most types of the Bf3 felt pennants were sold, jumbo size - about 28-1/2" x 11" - versions of 16 team pennants could be had by redeeming 25 wrappers and 15 cents for each desired pennant. The large-format pennants are identical in design to some of the smaller pieces from Types 4, 5 and 8.

		NM	EX	VG
Complete Set (16):		300.00	150.00	90.00
Common Pennant:		300.00	150.00	90.00
(1)	Boston Bees	300.00	150.00	90.00
(2)	Boston Red Sox	300.00	150.00	90.00
(3)	Brooklyn Dodgers	300.00	150.00	90.00
(4)	Chicago Cubs	300.00	150.00	90.00
(5)	Chicago White Sox	300.00	150.00	90.00
(6)	Cincinnati Reds	300.00	150.00	90.00
(7)	Cleveland Indians	300.00	150.00	90.00
(8)	Detroit Tigers	300.00	150.00	90.00
(9)	New York Giants	300.00	150.00	90.00
(10)	New York Yankees	400.00	200.00	120.00
(11)	Philadelphia Athletics	300.00	150.00	90.00
(12)	Philadelphia Phillies	300.00	150.00	90.00
(13)	Pittsburgh Pirates	300.00	150.00	90.00
(14)	St. Louis Browns	300.00	150.00	90.00
(15)	St. Louis Cardinals	300.00	150.00	90.00
(16)	Washington Senators	300.00	150.00	90.00

1937 BF104 Blankets

A throwback to the 1914 B18 blankets, little is known about these 3-1/2"-square felts. They were designated as BF104 in the American Card Catalog. The issuer and manner of distribution remain a mystery. Subjects are depicted in either portrait or action artwork. This checklist likely is not complete.

		NM	EX	VG
Common Player:		300.00	150.00	90.00
(1)	Moe Berg	500.00	250.00	150.00
(2)	Cy Blanton	300.00	150.00	90.00
(3)	Earle Brucker	300.00	150.00	90.00
(4)	Mickey Cochrane	600.00	300.00	180.00
(5)	Joe Cronin	600.00	300.00	180.00
(6)	Tony Cuccinello	300.00	150.00	90.00
(7)	Dizzy Dean	1,200	600.00	360.00
(8)	Frank Demaree	300.00	150.00	90.00
(9)	Jimmie Foxx	900.00	450.00	275.00
(10)	Larry French	300.00	150.00	90.00
(11)	Frankie Frisch	600.00	300.00	180.00
(12)	Hank Greenberg	1,000	500.00	300.00
(13)	Stan Hack	300.00	150.00	90.00
(14)	Gabby Hartnett	600.00	300.00	180.00
(15)	Billy Herman	600.00	300.00	180.00
(16)	Woody Jensen	300.00	150.00	90.00
(17)	Billy Jurges	300.00	150.00	90.00
(18)	Harry Kelly (Kelley)	300.00	150.00	90.00
(19)	Thornton Lee	300.00	150.00	90.00
(20)	Danny MacFayden	300.00	150.00	90.00
(21)	Connie Mack	600.00	300.00	180.00
(22)	Stu Martin	300.00	150.00	90.00
(23)	Joe Medwick	600.00	300.00	180.00
(24)	Ray Mueller	300.00	150.00	90.00
(25)	L. Newsome	300.00	150.00	90.00
(26)	Charlie Root	300.00	150.00	90.00
(27)	Monty Stratton	405.00	200.00	120.00
(28)	Pie Traynor	600.00	300.00	180.00
(29)	Jim Turner	300.00	150.00	90.00
(30)	Bill Werber	300.00	150.00	90.00
(31)	Jack Wilson	300.00	150.00	90.00
(32)	Rudy York	300.00	150.00	90.00

C

1909 Cabanas

In conjunction with a post-season visit by the A.L. Champion Detroit Tigers (who without Hall of Famer Ty Cobb and Sam Crawford won only four of 12 games from the locals), Cabanas brand cigarettes issued this set. About 1-1/2" x 2-1/4" the cards feature black-and-white portrait photos. Players from the Almendares team have a blue frame and some colorized blue details on their uniforms, Havana players are in red, the Tigers are in gray. Printed on backs of the cards is (roughly translated) "The best way to form a valuable collection of baseball players of the Cuban clubs and the foreign visitors is to smoke Cabanas." It is unknown whether the checklists presented here alphabetically are complete.

		NM	EX	VG
Common Cuban Player:		600.00	300.00	175.00
Common Tigers Player:		900.00	450.00	275.00
ALMENDARES B.B.C.				
(1)	Rafael Almeida	700.00	350.00	210.00
(2)	Armando Cabanas	700.00	350.00	210.00
(3)	Alfredo Cabrera	600.00	300.00	175.00
(4)	Regino "Mamelo" Garcia	1,150	575.00	345.00
(5a)	Heliodoro Hidalgo (C.F.)	1,150	575.00	345.00
(5b)	Heliodoro Hidalgo (C.F. Jabuco)	1,150	575.00	345.00
(6)	Armando Marsans	700.00	350.00	210.00
(7)	Esteban Prats	600.00	300.00	175.00
(8)	Carlos "Bebe" Royer	700.00	350.00	210.00
HABANA B.B.C.				
(1)	Luis Bustamante	2,250	1,125	675.00
(2)	Luis "Chico" Gonzalez	600.00	300.00	175.00
(3)	Valentin "Sirique" Gonzalez	600.00	300.00	175.00
(4)	Ricardo Hernandez	600.00	300.00	175.00
(5)	Preston "Pete" Hill (Value Undetermined)			
(6)	Angel D. Mesa	600.00	300.00	175.00
(7)	Augustin "Tinti" Molina	700.00	350.00	210.00
(8)	Carlos "Chino" Moran	600.00	300.00	175.00
(9)	Luis "Mulo" Padron	3,500	1,750	1,050
(10)	Elilio Palomino	600.00	300.00	175.00
(11)	Pastor H. Pareda	600.00	300.00	180.00
(12)	Agustin Parpetti	2,000	1,000	600.00
(13)	Inocencio Perez	600.00	300.00	175.00
(14)	Bruce Petway	7,500	3,750	2,250
(15)	Gonzalo Sanchez	600.00	300.00	175.00

DETROIT TIGERS
(1)	C. Beckendorff (Beckendorf)	900.00	450.00	275.00
(2)	Owen (Donie) Bush	900.00	450.00	275.00
(3)	Hopke	900.00	450.00	275.00
(4)	David Jones	900.00	450.00	275.00
(5)	William Lelivelt	900.00	450.00	275.00
(6)	Matty Mc. Intyre	900.00	450.00	275.00
(7)	George Moriarty	900.00	450.00	275.00
(8)	George Mullin	900.00	450.00	275.00
(9)	Frank O'Laughlin (O'Loughlin)/Umpire	1,200	600.00	360.00
(10)	Charles O'Leary	900.00	450.00	275.00
(11)	Charles Schmidt	900.00	450.00	275.00
(12)	Edgar Willetts (Willett)	900.00	450.00	275.00

1955 Cain's Jimmy Piersall

The date of issue is speculative for these promotional postcards. The borderless black-and-white photo on the front of the 3-1/2" x 5-1/2" cards shows the popular BoSox star in a fielding pose. A blue facsimile autograph is printed at top. The postcard-format back has a drawing of the product beneath an advertising message bearing Piersall's signature. Similar cards advertising Colonial Meats are also known.

	NM	EX	VG
Autographed:	300.00	150.00	90.00
Jimmy Piersall (Mayonnaise)	125.00	62.50	37.50
Jimmy Piersall (Potato chips.)	125.00	62.50	37.50
Jimmy Piersall (Riviera dressing.)	125.00	62.50	37.50

1965 California Angels Matchbook Covers

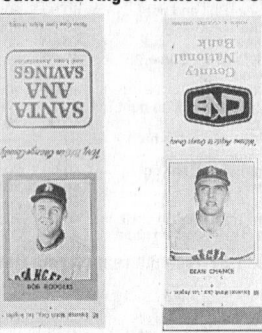

These 1-1/2" x 4-1/2" matchbooks can be found with the advertising of two different banks printed on them; both are products of the local Universal Match Corp., and are printed in black and gold on front, with the inside surface in black-and-white. The County National Bank version has the player portrait photo within a plain black frame. Inside, the CNB matchbooks have player identification and personal data and 1964 stats. There is also an offer to redeem 15 different players' matchbooks for two free game tickets. The Santa Ana Savings matchbooks have the same player information and ads for the bank and the Angels' radio station. The player photos on front of the Santa Ana matchbooks have a gold frame. Values shown are for complete but empty covers, with the striker surface intact. Complete matchbooks with matches bring about 2X the values quoted.

		NM	EX	VG
Complete Set (15):		120.00	60.00	35.00
Common Player:		10.00	5.00	3.00
(1)	Dean Chance	12.50	6.25	3.75
(2)	Lu Clinton	10.00	5.00	3.00
(3)	Jim Fregosi	10.00	5.00	3.00
(4)	Ed Kirkpatrick	10.00	5.00	3.00
(5)	Bobby Knoop	10.00	5.00	3.00
(6)	Barry Latman	10.00	5.00	3.00
(7)	Bob Lee	10.00	5.00	3.00
(8)	Ken McBride	10.00	5.00	3.00
(9)	Fred Newman	10.00	5.00	3.00
(10)	Jimmy Piersall	20.00	10.00	6.00
(11)	Rick Reichardt	10.00	5.00	3.00
(12)	Bill Rigney	10.00	5.00	3.00
(13)	Bob Rodgers	10.00	5.00	3.00
(14)	Tom Satriano	10.00	5.00	3.00
(15)	Willie Smith	10.00	5.00	3.00

1976 California Pacific Bank

Whether these are a legitimate promotional issue or a made-for-collectors set is unknown. The cards may have been created for use at autograph appearances at a Fullerton,

"I get Big League Service at California Pacific Bank, Fullerton, Calif."

Calif., bank. About 3-5/8" x 5", though the size varies, the black-and-white blank-back cards have player photos on front (some of which are reproductions of team-issued photos) and a promotional message describing the bank's "Big League Service." Two poses of Steve Carlton are known.

		NM	EX	VG
	Complete Set (7):	60.00	30.00	18.00
	Common Player:	5.00	2.50	1.50
(1)	Steve Busby	5.00	2.50	1.50
(2)	Steve Carlton	15.00	7.50	4.50
(3)	Steve Carlton	15.00	7.50	4.50
(4)	Bill Russell	5.00	2.50	1.50
(5)	Mike Schmidt	20.00	10.00	6.00
(6)	Ted Simmons	5.00	2.50	1.50
(7)	Don Sutton	10.00	5.00	3.00

1950 Callahan Hall of Fame

These cards, which feature artist Mario DeMarco's drawings of Hall of Famers, were produced from 1950 through 1956 and sold by the Baseball Hall of Fame in Cooperstown and at major league ballparks. The cards measure 1-3/4" x 2-1/2" and include a detailed player biography on the back. When introduced in 1950 the set included all members of the Hall of Fame up to that time, and then new cards were added each year as more players were elected. Therefore, cards of players appearing in all previous editions are more common than those players who appeared in just one or two years. When the set was discontinued in 1956 it consisted of 82 cards, which is now considered a complete set. The cards are not numbered and are listed here alphabetically. B.E. Callahan of Chicago, the publisher of "Who's Who in Baseball," produced the card set.

		NM	EX	VG
	Original 1950 Boxed Set (62):	750.00	370.00	220.00
	Complete Set (82):	1,900	950.00	575.00
	Common Player:	6.00	3.00	1.75
(1)	Grover Alexander	25.00	12.50	7.50
(2)	"Cap" Anson	15.00	7.50	4.50
(3)	J. Franklin "Home Run" Baker	150.00	75.00	45.00
(4)	Edward G. Barrow	35.00	17.50	10.00
(5a)	Charles "Chief" Bender (Bio ends ". . . immortal name for him.")	25.00	12.50	7.50
(5b)	Charles "Chief" Bender (Bio ends ". . . died in 1954.")	35.00	17.50	10.00
(6)	Roger Bresnahan	10.00	5.00	3.00
(7)	Dan Brouthers	15.00	7.50	4.50
(8)	Mordecai Brown	10.00	5.00	3.00
(9)	Morgan G. Bulkeley	10.00	5.00	3.00
(10)	Jesse Burkett	16.00	8.00	4.75
(11)	Alexander Cartwright	12.50	6.25	3.75
(12)	Henry Chadwick	12.00	6.00	3.50
(13)	Frank Chance	16.00	8.00	4.75
(14)	Albert B. Chandler	225.00	110.00	67.50
(15)	Jack Chesbro	7.50	3.75	2.25
(16)	Fred Clarke	10.00	5.00	3.00
(17)	Ty Cobb	50.00	25.00	15.00
(18a)	Mickey Cochran (Name incorrect.)	10.00	5.00	3.00
(18b)	Mickey Cochrane (Name correct.)	12.00	6.00	3.50
(19a)	Eddie Collins (Second paragraph of bio begins "Eddie had every . . .")	9.00	4.50	2.75
(19b)	Eddie Collins (Second paragraph of bio begins "He was brilliant . . .")	13.50	6.75	4.00
(20)	Jimmie Collins	12.50	6.25	3.75
(21)	Charles A. Comiskey	12.50	6.25	3.75
(22)	Tom Connolly	50.00	25.00	15.00
(23)	Candy Cummings	9.00	4.50	2.75

(24)	Dizzy Dean	45.00	22.50	13.50
(25)	Ed Delahanty	6.00	3.00	1.75
(26a)	Bill Dickey (First paragraph of bio ends ". . . He was right-handed all the way.")	75.00	37.00	22.00
(26b)	Bill Dickey (First paragraph of bio ends ". . . during his final year.")	35.00	17.50	10.50
(27)	Joe DiMaggio	180.00	90.00	54.00
(28)	Hugh Duffy	7.50	3.75	2.25
(29)	Johnny Evers	13.50	6.75	4.00
(30)	Buck Ewing	10.00	5.00	3.00
(31)	Jimmie Foxx	20.00	10.00	6.00
(32)	Frank Frisch	6.00	3.00	1.75
(33)	Lou Gehrig	85.00	42.50	25.00
(34a)	Charles Gehringer (White cap.)	9.00	4.50	2.75
(34b)	Charlie Gehringer (Dark cap.)	11.00	5.50	3.25
(35)	Clark Griffith	6.00	3.00	1.75
(36)	Lefty Grove	10.00	5.00	3.00
(37)	Leo "Gabby" Hartnett	40.00	20.00	12.00
(38)	Harry Heilmann	25.00	12.50	7.50
(39)	Rogers Hornsby	16.00	8.00	4.75
(40)	Carl Hubbell	12.00	6.00	3.50
(41)	Hughey Jennings	6.00	3.00	1.75
(42)	Ban Johnson	7.50	3.75	2.25
(43)	Walter Johnson	10.00	5.00	3.00
(44)	Willie Keeler	7.50	3.75	2.25
(45)	Mike Kelly	10.00	5.00	3.00
(46)	Bill Klem	50.00	25.00	15.00
(47)	Napoleon Lajoie	11.00	5.50	3.25
(48)	Kenesaw M. Landis	6.00	3.00	1.75
(49)	Ted Lyons	100.00	50.00	30.00
(50)	Connie Mack	12.00	6.00	3.50
(51)	Walter Maranville	20.00	10.00	6.00
(52)	Christy Mathewson	25.00	12.50	7.50
(53)	Tommy McCarthy	12.50	6.25	3.75
(54)	Joe McGinnity	6.00	3.00	1.75
(55)	John McGraw	10.00	5.00	3.00
(56)	Charles Nichols	16.00	8.00	4.75
(57)	Jim O'Rourke	9.00	4.50	2.75
(58)	Mel Ott	16.00	8.00	4.75
(59)	Herb Pennock	9.00	4.50	2.75
(60)	Eddie Plank	10.00	5.00	3.00
(61)	Charles Radbourne	10.00	5.00	3.00
(62)	Wilbert Robinson	6.00	3.00	1.75
(63)	Babe Ruth	100.00	50.00	30.00
(64)	Ray "Cracker" Schalk	30.00	15.00	9.00
(65)	Al Simmons	60.00	30.00	18.00
(66a)	George Sisler (Bio ends "Sisler today is . . .")	13.50	6.75	4.00
(66b)	George Sisler (Bio ends "Sisler was chosen as . . .")	9.00	4.50	2.75
(67)	A. G. Spalding	10.00	5.00	3.00
(68)	Tris Speaker	16.00	8.00	4.75
(69)	Bill Terry	30.00	15.00	9.00
(70)	Joe Tinker	10.00	5.00	3.00
(71)	"Pie" Traynor	10.00	5.00	3.00
(72)	Clarence A. "Dazzy" Vance	30.00	15.00	9.00
(73)	Rube Waddell	9.00	4.50	2.75
(74)	Hans Wagner	30.00	15.00	9.00
(75)	Bobby Wallace	13.50	6.75	4.00
(76)	Ed Walsh	10.00	5.00	3.00
(77a)	Paul Waner (Complete black frame line around picture.)	9.00	4.50	2.75
(77b)	Paul Waner (Bottom missing on black frame line around picture.)	40.00	20.00	12.00
(78)	George Wright	15.00	7.50	4.50
(79)	Harry Wright	40.00	20.00	12.00
(80)	Cy Young	12.50	6.25	3.75
(---)	Museum Exterior View (No date at top of list on back.)	35.00	17.50	10.00
(---)	Museum Exterior View (Date "1954" on top of list on back.)	60.00	30.00	18.00
(---)	Museum Interior View (Back copy ends, ". . . to all baseball men.")	30.00	15.00	9.00
(---)	Museum Interior View (Back copy ends ". . . playing days are concluded.")	13.50	6.75	4.00

1898 Cameo Pepsin Gum Pins

The first large set of baseball player pins is this issue from Whitehead & Hoag, advertising Cameo Pepsin Gum. The 1-1/4" pins have a sepia player portrait photo at center, with name and team at top left and right. It is very difficult to find pins with clear pictures as they tend to darken or fade with time. Pins were issued with a paper inset in back advertising the gum, but are often found with the paper missing. It is likely that there will be future additions to this checklist. The unnumbered pins are presented here in alphabetical order.

		NM	EX	VG
	Common Player:	1,300	650.00	400.00
(1)	John Anderson	1,300	650.00	400.00
(2)	Cap Anson	3,300	1,300	800.00
(3)	Jimmy Bannon	1,300	650.00	400.00
(4)	Billy Barnie	1,300	650.00	400.00
(5)	Marty Bergen	1,300	650.00	400.00

(6)	Beville (Indianapolis)	1,300	650.00	400.00
(7)	Louis Bierbauer	1,300	650.00	400.00
(8)	Frank Bowerman	1,300	650.00	400.00
(9)	Ted Breitenstein	1,300	650.00	400.00
(10)	Herbert "Buttons" Briggs	1,300	650.00	400.00
(11)	Richard Brown	1,300	650.00	400.00
(12)	Eddie Burk (Burke)	1,300	650.00	400.00
(13)	Jesse Burkett	4,000	2,000	1,200
(14)	Frank "Buster" Burrell	1,300	650.00	400.00
(15)	Jimmy Canavan	1,300	650.00	400.00
(16)	Cupid Childs	1,300	650.00	400.00
(17)	William (Dad) Clark (Clarke)	1,300	650.00	400.00
(18)	Boileyard Clark (Clarke) (Balt.)	1,300	650.00	400.00
(19)	Jack Clements	1,300	650.00	400.00
(20)	Archibald B. Cole (Cedar Rapids)	1,300	650.00	400.00
(21)	Jimmy Collins	2,850	1,300	800.00
(22)	Tommy Corcoran	1,300	650.00	400.00
(23)	James Corkman (Cockman) (Indianapolis)	1,300	650.00	400.00
(24)	Lave Cross	1,300	650.00	400.00
(25)	Nig Cuppy	1,300	650.00	400.00
(26)	Bill Dahlen	1,300	650.00	400.00
(27)	Bill Dammon (Dammann)	1,300	650.00	400.00
(28)	Dan Daub	1,300	650.00	400.00
(29)	George Decker	1,300	650.00	400.00
(30)	Ed Delahanty	1,300	650.00	400.00
(31)	Cozy Dolan	1,300	650.00	400.00
(32)	Tim Donahue	1,300	650.00	400.00
(33)	Patsy Donovan	1,300	650.00	400.00
(34)	Frank Donnelly (Cedar Rapids) (Cedar Rapids)	1,300	650.00	400.00
(35)	Hugh Duffy	2,850	1,300	800.00
(36)	Jack Dunn	1,300	650.00	400.00
(37)	Frank Dwyer	1,300	650.00	400.00
(38)	Bones Ely	1,300	650.00	400.00
(39)	Bill Everett (Everitt)	1,300	650.00	400.00
(40)	Buck Ewing	5,000	2,500	1,500
(41)	James Fields (Buffalo)	1,300	650.00	400.00
(42)	Al Fisher (Cedar Rapids)	1,300	650.00	400.00
(43)	Chauncey Fisher (Brooklyn)	1,300	650.00	400.00
(44)	Tim Flood	1,300	650.00	400.00
(45)	Frank Foreman (Indianapolis)	1,300	650.00	400.00
(46)	James Franklin (Owner - Buffalo)	1,300	650.00	400.00
(47)	William Fuller (Cedar Rapids)	1,300	650.00	400.00
(48)	Charlie Ganzel	1,300	650.00	400.00
(49)	Jot Goar (Pittsburgh)	1,300	650.00	400.00
(50)	Jot Goar (Indianapolis)	1,300	650.00	400.00
(51)	Bill Gray (Indianapolis)	1,300	650.00	400.00
(52)	Mike Griffin	1,300	650.00	400.00
(53)	Clark Griffith	2,650	1,300	800.00
(54)	John Grim	1,300	650.00	400.00
(55)	Billy Hamilton	2,750	1,375	825.00
(56)	Bill Hart	1,300	650.00	400.00
(57)	Charles Hastings	1,300	650.00	400.00
(58)	Pink Hawley	1,300	650.00	400.00
(59)	Belden Hill (Cedar Rapids)	1,300	650.00	400.00
(60)	Bill Hoffer	1,300	650.00	400.00
(61)	George Hogriever (Indianapolis)	1,300	650.00	400.00
(62)	Bug Holliday	1,300	650.00	400.00
(63)	Elmer Horton (Baltimore)	1,300	650.00	400.00
(64)	Dummy Hoy	2,450	1,550	900.00
(65)	Jim Hughey	1,300	650.00	400.00
(66)	Edwin Hutchinson (Cedar Rapids)	1,300	650.00	400.00
(67)	Charlie Irwin	1,300	650.00	400.00
(68)	Hughie Jennings	2,650	1,300	800.00
(69)	Willie Keeler	2,650	1,300	800.00
(70)	A.F. Kennedy (Cedar Rapids)	1,300	650.00	400.00
(71)	Frank Killen	1,300	650.00	400.00
(72)	Malachi Kittredge	1,300	650.00	400.00
(73)	Candy LaChance	1,300	650.00	400.00
(74)	Bill Lange	1,300	650.00	400.00
(75)	Herman Long	1,300	650.00	400.00
(76)	Bobby Lowe	1,300	650.00	400.00
(77)	Denny Lyons	1,300	650.00	400.00
(78)	Connie Mack	3,300	1,300	800.00
(79)	Louis Mahaffy (Mahaffey) (Cedar Rapids)	1,300	650.00	400.00
(80)	Willard Mains	1,300	650.00	400.00
	Jimmy McAleer (Cleveland)	1,300	650.00	400.00
(81)	Barry McCormick	1,300	650.00	400.00
(82)	McDougal (Cedar Rapids)	1,300	650.00	400.00
(83)	Chippy McGarr	1,300	650.00	400.00
(84)	John McGraw	1,750	1,100	650.00
(85)	Ed McKean (Cleveland)	1,300	650.00	400.00
(86)	Sadie McMann (McMahon)	1,300	650.00	400.00
(87)	Bid McPhee	4,200	2,450	1,100
(88)	Bill Merritt	1,300	650.00	400.00
(89)	Dusty Miller	1,300	650.00	400.00
(90)	Frank Motz (Indianapolis)	1,300	650.00	400.00
(91)	Kid Nichols	2,750	1,375	825.00
(92)	Tom O'Brien (Balt.)	1,300	650.00	400.00
(93)	Jack O'Connor	1,300	650.00	400.00
(94)	John Pappaulan (Pappalau) (Pitcher, not R.F.)	1,300	650.00	400.00
(95)	Harley Payne	1,300	650.00	400.00
(96)	Heinie Peitz	1,300	650.00	400.00
(97)	Silver Bill Phillips (Indianapolis)	1,300	650.00	400.00
(98)	Arlie Pond	1,300	650.00	400.00
(99)	Jack Powell	1,300	650.00	400.00
(100)	Joe Quinn (Balt.)	1,300	650.00	400.00
(101)	Bill Reidy	1,300	650.00	400.00
(102)	Heinie Reitz	1,300	650.00	400.00
(103)	Billy Rhines	1,300	650.00	400.00
(104)	Claude Richie (Ritchey)	1,300	650.00	400.00
(105)	Jack Rowe (Buffalo)	1,300	650.00	400.00
(106)	Jimmy Ryan (Chicago)	1,300	650.00	400.00
(107)	Jack (John) Ryan (Boston)	1,300	650.00	400.00
(108)	Pop Schreiber (Schriver)	1,300	650.00	400.00
(109)	Cy Seymour	1,300	650.00	400.00
(110)	Billy Shindle	1,300	650.00	400.00
(111)	"Broadway" Aleck Smith	1,300	650.00	400.00
(112)	Elmer Smith (Pittsburg)	1,300	650.00	400.00

(113)	Germany Smith	1,300	650.00	400.00
(114)	Harry T. Smith (Buffalo)	1,300	650.00	400.00
(115)	Louis Sockalexis	2,000	1,300	650.00
(116)	George Speer (Milwaukee)	1,300	650.00	400.00
(117)	Jake Stentzel (Stenzel)	1,300	650.00	400.00
(118)	Jack Stivetts	1,300	650.00	400.00
(119)	Joe Sugden	1,300	650.00	400.00
(120)	Jim "Suter" Sullivan	1,300	650.00	400.00
(121)	Patsy Tebeau	1,300	650.00	400.00
(122)	Fred Tenney	1,300	650.00	400.00
(123)	Adonis Terry	1,300	650.00	400.00
(124)	Tommy Tucker (Boston)	1,300	650.00	400.00
(125)	William Urquhart (Buffalo)	1,300	650.00	400.00
(126)	Edward Van Buren (Cedar Rapids)	1,300	650.00	400.00
(127)	Farmer Vaughn	1,300	650.00	400.00
(128)	Bobby Wallace	2,650	1,300	800.00
(129)	Bill Watkins (Indianapolis)	1,300	650.00	400.00
(130)	William Weaver (Milwaukee)	1,300	650.00	400.00
(131)	Robert Wood (Indianapolis)	1,300	650.00	400.00
(132)	Cy Young	6,000	3,000	1,800
(133)	Chief Zimmer	1,300	625.00	400.00
(134)	1897 Brooklyn Team	1,400	700.00	400.00
(135)	1897 Buffalo Team	1,400	700.00	400.00
(136)	1897 Indianapolis Team	1,400	700.00	400.00
(137)	1897 Pittsburg Team	1,600	800.00	475.00
(138)	1897 Toronto Team	1,400	700.00	400.00
(139)	1897 New Castle Baseball Club 1897	1,400	700.00	400.00

1958 Roy Campanella Career Summary Card

This card was probably produced to allow Campy to respond to fan mail following his career-ending auto wreck in 1957. The 3-1/8" x 5" card is printed in black-and-white on thin semi-gloss cardboard. Front has a portrait photo and facsimile autograph, with a white stripe at top and bottom. The back has a career statistical summary, apparently taken from a contemporary Baseball Register.

	NM	EX	VG
Roy Campanella	20.00	10.00	6.00

1974 Capital Publishing Co.

 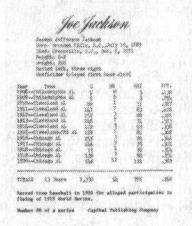

This ambitious collectors issue offered more than 100 cards of "old-timers" in an attractive 4-1/8" x 5-1/4" format. Card fronts have black-and-white photos with white borders all-around. Backs have player identification, biographical data and major league stats.

		NM	EX	VG
	Complete Set (104):	200.00	100.00	60.00
	Common Player:	6.00	3.00	1.75
1	Babe Ruth	15.00	7.50	4.50
2	Lou Gehrig	10.00	5.00	3.00
3	Ty Cobb	9.00	4.50	2.75
4	Jackie Robinson	7.50	3.75	2.25
5	Roger Connor	6.00	3.00	1.75
6	Harry Heilmann	6.00	3.00	1.75
7	Clark Griffith	6.00	3.00	1.75
8	Ed Walsh	6.00	3.00	1.75
9	Hugh Duffy	6.00	3.00	1.75
10	Russ Christopher	6.00	3.00	1.75
11	Snuffy Stirnweiss	6.00	3.00	1.75
12	Willie Keeler	6.00	3.00	1.75
13	Buck Ewing	6.00	3.00	1.75
14	Tony Lazzeri	6.00	3.00	1.75
15	King Kelly	6.00	3.00	1.75
16	Jimmy McAleer	6.00	3.00	1.75
17	Frank Chance	6.00	3.00	1.75
18	Sam Zoldak	6.00	3.00	1.75
19	Christy Mathewson	7.50	3.75	2.25
20	Eddie Collins	6.00	3.00	1.75
21	Cap Anson	6.00	3.00	1.75
22	Steve Evans	6.00	3.00	1.75
23	Mordecai Brown	6.00	3.00	1.75
24	Don Black	6.00	3.00	1.75
25	Home Run Baker	6.00	3.00	1.75

26	Jack Chesbro	6.00	3.00	1.75
27	Gil Hodges	6.00	3.00	1.75
28	Dan Brouthers	6.00	3.00	1.75
29	Don Hoak	6.00	3.00	1.75
30	Herb Pennock	6.00	3.00	1.75
31	Vern Stephens	6.00	3.00	1.75
32	Cy Young	7.50	3.75	2.25
33	Ed Cicotte	7.50	3.75	2.25
34	Sam Jones	6.00	3.00	1.75
35	Ed Waitkus	6.00	3.00	1.75
36	Roger Bresnahan	6.00	3.00	1.75
37	Fred Merkle	6.00	3.00	1.75
38	Ed Delehanty (Delahanty)	6.00	3.00	1.75
39	Tris Speaker	6.00	3.00	1.75
40	Fred Clarke	6.00	3.00	1.75
41	Johnny Evers	6.00	3.00	1.75
42	Mickey Cochrane	6.00	3.00	1.75
43	Nap Lajoie	6.00	3.00	1.75
44	Charles Comiskey	6.00	3.00	1.75
45	Sam Crawford	6.00	3.00	1.75
46	Ban Johnson	6.00	3.00	1.75
47	Ray Schalk	6.00	3.00	1.75
48	Pat Moran	6.00	3.00	1.75
49	Walt Judnich	6.00	3.00	1.75
50	Bill Killefer	6.00	3.00	1.75
51	Jimmie Foxx	6.00	3.00	1.75
52	Red Rolfe	6.00	3.00	1.75
53	Howie Pollett	6.00	3.00	1.75
54	Wally Pipp	6.00	3.00	1.75
55	Chief Bender	6.00	3.00	1.75
56	Connie Mack	6.00	3.00	1.75
57	Bump Hadley	6.00	3.00	1.75
58	Al Simmons	6.00	3.00	1.75
59	Hughie Jennings	6.00	3.00	1.75
60	Johnny Allen	6.00	3.00	1.75
61	Fred Snodgrass	6.00	3.00	1.75
62	Heinie Manush	6.00	3.00	1.75
63	Dazzy Vance	6.00	3.00	1.75
64	George Sisler	6.00	3.00	1.75
65	Jim Bottomley	6.00	3.00	1.75
66	Ray Chapman	6.00	3.00	1.75
67	Hal Chase	6.00	3.00	1.75
68	Jack Barry	6.00	3.00	1.75
69	George Burns	6.00	3.00	1.75
70	Jim Barrett	6.00	3.00	1.75
71	Grover Alexander	6.00	3.00	1.75
72	Elmer Flick	6.00	3.00	1.75
73	Jake Flowers	6.00	3.00	1.75
74	Al Orth	6.00	3.00	1.75
75	Cliff Aberson	6.00	3.00	1.75
76	Moe Berg	7.50	3.75	2.25
77	Bill Bradley	6.00	3.00	1.75
78	Max Bishop	6.00	3.00	1.75
79	Jimmy Austin	6.00	3.00	1.75
80	Beals Becker	6.00	3.00	1.75
81	Jack Clements	6.00	3.00	1.75
82	Cy Blanton	6.00	3.00	1.75
83	Garland Braxton	6.00	3.00	1.75
84	Red Ames	6.00	3.00	1.75
85	Hippo Vaughn	6.00	3.00	1.75
86	Ray Caldwell	6.00	3.00	1.75
87	Clint Brown	6.00	3.00	1.75
88	Joe Jackson	15.00	7.50	4.50
89	Pete Appleton	6.00	3.00	1.75
90	Ed Brandt	6.00	3.00	1.75
91	Walter Johnson	7.50	3.75	2.25
92	Dizzy Dean	6.00	3.00	1.75
93	Nick Altrock	6.00	3.00	1.75
94	Buck Weaver	7.50	3.75	2.25
95	George Blaeholder	6.00	3.00	1.75
96	Jim Bagby	6.00	3.00	1.75
97	Ted Blankenship	6.00	3.00	1.75
98	Babe Adams	6.00	3.00	1.75
99	Lefty Williams	7.50	3.75	2.25
100	Tommy Bridges	6.00	3.00	1.75
101	Rube Benton	6.00	3.00	1.75
102	Unknown	6.00	3.00	1.75
103	Max Butcher	6.00	3.00	1.75
104	Chick Gandil	7.50	3.75	2.25

1945-46 Caramelo Deportivo Cuban League

One of the better-known of Cuba's baseball card issues is the 100-card set issued by Caramelo Deportivo (Sporting Caramels) covering the 1945-46 Cuban winter league season. Printed in black-and-white on very thin 1-7/8" x 2-5/8" paper, the cards were intended to be pasted into an album issued for the purpose. Fronts have a card number, but no player identification; backs have the player's name, a few biographical and career details and an ad for the issuer, in as many as three different configurations. Many former and future Major Leaguers and stars of the U.S. Negro Leagues will be found on this checklist; sometimes providing the only cards issued contemporary with their playing careers.

	NM	EX	VG
Complete Set, No Reyes (99):	6,500	3,250	1,950
Common Player:	25.00	12.50	7.50

	Album:	200.00	100.00	60.00
1	Caramelo Deportivo Title Card	7.50	3.75	2.25
2	Action Scene	12.50	6.25	3.75
3	Amado Maestri/Umpire	25.00	12.50	7.50
4	Bernardino Rodriguez/ Umpire	25.00	12.50	7.50
5	Quico Magrinat/Umpire	25.00	12.50	7.50
6	Cuco Conder/Announcer	25.00	12.50	7.50
7	Marianao Team Banner	10.00	5.00	3.00
8	Armando Marsans	75.00	37.50	22.00
9	Jose Fernandez	25.00	12.50	7.50
10	Jose Luis Colas	25.00	12.50	7.50
11	"Charlotio" Orta (Charolito)	25.00	12.50	7.50
12	Barney Serrell	50.00	25.00	15.00
13	Claro Duany	30.00	15.00	9.00
14	Antonio Castanos	25.00	12.50	7.50
15	Virgilio Arteaga	25.00	12.50	7.50
16	Gilberto Valdivia	25.00	12.50	7.50
17	Jugo Cabrera	25.00	12.50	7.50
18	Lazaro Salazar	75.00	37.50	22.00
19	Julio Moreno	25.00	12.50	7.50
20	Oliverio Ortiz	25.00	12.50	7.50
21	Lou Knerr	25.00	12.50	7.50
22	Francisco Campos	25.00	12.50	7.50
23	Red Adams	25.00	12.50	7.50
24	Sandalio Consuegra	25.00	12.50	7.50
25	Ray Dandridge	1,500	750.00	450.00
26	Booker McDaniels	40.00	20.00	12.00
27	Orestes Minoso	675.00	335.00	200.00
28	Daniel Parra	25.00	12.50	7.50
29	Roberto Estalella	25.00	12.50	7.50
30	Raymond Brown	2,150	1,100	650.00
31	Havana Team Banner	10.00	5.00	3.00
32	Miguel Gonzalez	40.00	20.00	12.00
33	Julio Rojo	25.00	12.50	7.50
34	Herberto Blanco	25.00	12.50	7.50
35	Pedro Formenthal	30.00	15.00	9.00
36	Rene Monteagudo	25.00	12.50	7.50
37	Carlos Blanco	25.00	12.50	7.50
38	Salvador Hernandez	25.00	12.50	7.50
39	Rogelio Linares	25.00	12.50	7.50
40	Antionio Ordenana	25.00	12.50	7.50
41	Pedro Jiminez	25.00	12.50	7.50
42	Charley Kaiser	25.00	12.50	7.50
43	Manuel "Cocaina" Garcia	80.00	40.00	24.00
44	Sagua Hernandez	25.00	12.50	7.50
45	Lou Klein	25.00	12.50	7.50
46	Manuel Hidalgo	25.00	12.50	7.50
47	Dick Sisler	35.00	17.50	10.00
48	Jim Rebel	25.00	12.50	7.50
49	Raul Navarro	25.00	12.50	7.50
50	Pedero Medina	25.00	12.50	7.50
51	Charlie (Terries) McDuffie	75.00	37.50	22.00
52	Fred Martin	25.00	12.50	7.50
53	Julian Acosta	25.00	12.50	7.50
54	Cienfuegos Team Banner	10.00	5.00	3.00
55	Adolfo Luque	125.00	62.00	37.00
56	Jose Ramos	25.00	12.50	7.50
57	Conrado Perez	25.00	12.50	7.50
58	Antonio Rodriguez	25.00	12.50	7.50
59	Alejandro Crespo	30.00	15.00	9.00
60	Roland Gladu	25.00	12.50	7.50
61	Pedro Pages	25.00	12.50	7.50
62	Silvio Garcia	80.00	40.00	24.00
63	Carlos Colas	25.00	12.50	7.50
64	Salvatore Maglie	125.00	60.00	35.00
65	Martin Dihigo	4,500	2,200	1,350
66	Luis Tiant Sr.	185.00	90.00	55.00
67	Jim Roy	25.00	12.50	7.50
68	Ramon Roger	25.00	12.50	7.50
69	Adrian Zabala	25.00	12.50	7.50
70	Armando Gallart	25.00	12.50	7.50
71	Jose Zardon	25.00	12.50	7.50
72	Ray Berres	25.00	12.50	7.50
73	Napoleon Reyes/SP	2,400	1,200	725.00
74	Jose Gomez	25.00	12.50	7.50
75	Loevigildo Xiques	25.00	12.50	7.50
76	Almendares Team Banner	10.00	5.00	3.00
77	Reinaldo Coreiro	25.00	12.50	7.50
78	Bartalo Portaundo (Bartalo Portuondo)	25.00	12.50	7.50
79	Jacinto Roque	25.00	12.50	7.50
80	Hector Arago	25.00	12.50	7.50
81	Gilberto Torres	30.00	15.00	9.00
82	Roberto Ortiz	30.00	15.00	9.00
83	Hector Rodriguez	25.00	12.50	7.50
84	Chifian Clark	40.00	20.00	12.00
85	Fermin Guerra	30.00	15.00	9.00
86	Jorge Comellas	25.00	12.50	7.50
87	Regino Otero	25.00	12.50	7.50
88	Tomas de la Cruz	30.00	15.00	9.00
89	Mario Diaz	25.00	12.50	7.50
90	Luis Aloma	25.00	12.50	7.50
91	Lloyd Davenport	40.00	20.00	12.00
92	Agapito Mayor	25.00	12.50	7.50
93	Ramon Bragana	100.00	50.00	30.00
94	Avelino Canizares	25.00	12.50	7.50
95	Santiago Ulrich	25.00	12.50	7.50
96	Beto Avila	50.00	25.00	15.00
97	Santos Amaro	30.00	15.00	9.00
98	Andres Fleitas	25.00	12.50	7.50
99	Limonar Martinez	25.00	12.50	7.50
100	Juan Montero	25.00	12.50	7.50

1946-47 Caramelo Deportivo Cuban League

Following its 100-card issue of the previous Cuban winter league season, this candy company issued a 185-card set for 1946-47. Besides more players, extra cards included banners, stadiums, managers, umpires and sportscasters. Printed on paper stock and intended to be pasted into an accompanying album, the cards measure about 1-7/8" x 2-1/2", though inconsistent cutting creates both over- and under-sized cards. Fronts have black-and-white player photos and a circle with a card number. Photos are often fuzzy or dark, indicative of their having been picked up from another source, such as a newspaper.

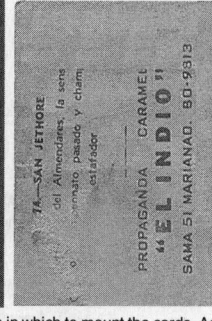

Backs repeat the card number and have the player name at top, along with his Cuban League and, frequently, U.S. professional affiliation. Some 60 of the players in the set played in the segregated Negro Leagues of the era. A large ad for the candy and its sellers appear at bottom of the back. Because of the thin stock and placement in albums, these cards are usually found creased and/or with back damage.

		NM	EX	VG
Complete Set (185):		12,000	6,000	3,600
Common Player:		50.00	25.00	15.00
Album:		250.00	125.00	75.00
1	Introduction Card	25.00	12.50	7.50
2	New El Cerro Stadium	25.00	12.50	7.50
3	Stadium La Tropical	25.00	12.50	7.50
4	Maestri, Bernardino and Magrinat (El Cerro umpires.)	50.00	25.00	15.00
5	La Tropical umpires (Atan, Lopez, Vidal and Morales)	50.00	25.00	15.00
6	Cuco Conde/Announcer	25.00	12.50	7.50
7	Cienfuegos Team Banner	25.00	12.50	7.50
8	Martin Dihigo	750.00	375.00	225.00
9a	Napoleon Reyes	60.00	30.00	18.00
9b	Napoleon Reyes	60.00	30.00	18.00
10	Adrian Zabala	50.00	25.00	15.00
11	Roland Gladu	50.00	25.00	15.00
12	Alejandro Crespo	100.00	50.00	30.00
13	Alejandro Carrasquel	50.00	25.00	15.00
14	Napoleon Heredia	50.00	25.00	15.00
15	Andres Mesa	50.00	25.00	15.00
16	Pedro Pages	50.00	25.00	15.00
17	Danny Gardella	50.00	25.00	15.00
18	Conrado Perez	50.00	25.00	15.00
19	Myron Hayworth	50.00	25.00	15.00
20	Pedro Miro	50.00	25.00	15.00
21	Guillermo Vargas	50.00	25.00	15.00
22	Hoot Gibson	50.00	25.00	15.00
23	Rafael Noble	55.00	27.50	16.50
24	Ramon Roger	50.00	25.00	15.00
25	Luis Arango	50.00	25.00	15.00
26	Roy Zimmerman	50.00	25.00	15.00
27	Luis Tiant Sr.	125.00	65.00	35.00
28	Jean Roy	55.00	27.50	16.50
29	Stanislov Bread	50.00	25.00	15.00
30	Walter Nothe	50.00	25.00	15.00
31	Vinicio Garcia	50.00	25.00	15.00
32	Dan (Max) Manning	200.00	100.00	60.00
33	Habana Lions Team Banner	25.00	12.50	7.50
34	Miguel A. Gonzalez	80.00	40.00	24.00
35	Pedro Formental	100.00	50.00	30.00
36	Ray Navarro	50.00	25.00	15.00
37	Pedro Jiminez	50.00	25.00	15.00
38	Rene Monteagudo	50.00	25.00	15.00
39	Salvador Hernandez	50.00	25.00	15.00
40	Hugh (Terris) Mc. Duffie	70.00	35.00	20.00
41	Herberto Blanco	50.00	25.00	15.00
42	Harry (Henry) Kimbro	130.00	65.00	40.00
43	Lloyd (Lennie) Pearson	180.00	90.00	55.00
44	W. Bell	55.00	27.50	16.50
45	Carlos Blanco	50.00	25.00	15.00
46	Hank Thompson	70.00	35.00	20.00
47	Manuel ("Cocaina") Garcia	150.00	75.00	45.00
48	Alberto Hernandez	50.00	25.00	15.00
49	Tony Ordenana	50.00	25.00	15.00
50	Lazaro Medina	50.00	25.00	15.00
51	Fred Martin	50.00	25.00	15.00
52	Eddie (Jim) Lamarque	150.00	75.00	45.00
53	Juan Montero	50.00	25.00	15.00
54	Lou Klein	50.00	25.00	15.00
55	Pablo Garcia	50.00	25.00	15.00
56	Julio Rojo	50.00	25.00	15.00
57	Almendares Team Banner	25.00	12.50	7.50
58	Adolfo Luque	90.00	45.00	27.50
59	Cheo Ramos	50.00	25.00	15.00
60	Avelino Canizares	50.00	25.00	15.00
61	George Hausmann	50.00	25.00	15.00
62	Homero Ariosa	50.00	25.00	15.00
63	Santos Amaro	50.00	25.00	15.00
64	Hank Robinson	60.00	30.00	18.00
65	Lazaro Salazar	200.00	100.00	60.00
66	Andres Fleitas	50.00	25.00	15.00
67	Hector Rodriguez	80.00	40.00	24.00
68	Jorge Comellas	50.00	25.00	15.00
69	Lloyd Davenport	130.00	65.00	40.00
70	Tomas de la Cruz	50.00	25.00	15.00
71a	Roberto Ortiz	80.00	40.00	24.00
71b	Roberto Ortiz	50.00	25.00	15.00
72	Jess (Gentry) Jessup	130.00	65.00	40.00
73	Agapito Mayor	50.00	25.00	15.00
74	William	50.00	25.00	15.00
75	Santiago Ullrich	50.00	25.00	15.00
76	Coty Leal	50.00	25.00	15.00
77	Max Lanier	55.00	27.50	16.50
78	Buck O'Neill	800.00	400.00	240.00
79	Mario Ariosa	50.00	25.00	15.00
80	Lefty Gaines	130.00	65.00	40.00
81	Marianao Team Banner	25.00	12.50	7.50
82	Armando Marsans	80.00	40.00	24.00
83	Antonio Castanos	50.00	25.00	15.00

84	Orestes Minoso	200.00	100.00	60.00
85	Murray Franklin	50.00	25.00	15.00
86	Roberto Estalella	50.00	25.00	15.00
87	A. Castro	50.00	25.00	15.00
88	Gilberto Valdivia	50.00	25.00	15.00
89	Baffeth (Lloyd "Pepper" Bassett)	130.00	65.00	40.00
90	Oliverio Ortiz	50.00	25.00	15.00
91	Francisco Campos	50.00	25.00	15.00
92	Sandalio Consuegra	65.00	32.50	20.00
93	Lorenzo Cabrera	50.00	25.00	15.00
94	Roberto Avila	80.00	40.00	24.00
95	Chanquilon Diaz	50.00	25.00	15.00
96	Pedro Orta	50.00	25.00	15.00
97	Cochihuila Valenzuela	50.00	25.00	15.00
98	Ramon Carneado	50.00	25.00	15.00
99	Aristonico Correoso	50.00	25.00	15.00
100	Daniel Doy	50.00	25.00	15.00
101	Joe Lindsay	50.00	25.00	15.00
102	Habana Reds Team Banner	25.00	12.50	7.50
103	Gilberto Torres	50.00	25.00	15.00
104	Oscar Rodriguez	50.00	25.00	15.00
105	Isidoro Leon	50.00	25.00	15.00
106	Julio Moreno	50.00	25.00	15.00
107	Chulungo del Monte	50.00	25.00	15.00
108	Len Hooker	100.00	50.00	30.00
109	Antonio Napoles	50.00	25.00	15.00
110	Orlando Suarez	50.00	25.00	15.00
111	Guillermo Monje	50.00	25.00	15.00
112	Isasio Gonzalez	50.00	25.00	15.00
113	Regino Otero	50.00	25.00	15.00
114	Angel Fleitas	50.00	25.00	15.00
115	Jorge Torres	50.00	25.00	15.00
116	Claro Duany	100.00	50.00	30.00
117	Charles Perez	50.00	25.00	15.00
118	Francisco Quicutis	50.00	25.00	15.00
119	Lazaro Bernal	50.00	25.00	15.00
120	Tommy Warren	50.00	25.00	15.00
121	Clarence Iott	55.00	27.00	16.50
122	P. Newcomb (Don Newcombe)	600.00	300.00	180.00
123	Gilberto Castillo	50.00	25.00	15.00
124	Matanzas Team Banner	25.00	12.50	7.50
125	Silvio Garcia	200.00	100.00	60.00
126	Bartolo Portuondo	50.00	25.00	15.00
127	Pedro Arango	50.00	25.00	15.00
128	Yuyo Acosta	50.00	25.00	15.00
129	Jose Cendan	50.00	25.00	15.00
130	Eddie Chandler	50.00	25.00	15.00
131	Rogelio Martinez	50.00	25.00	15.00
132	Atares Garcia	50.00	25.00	15.00
133	Manuel Godinez	50.00	25.00	15.00
134	John Williams	130.00	65.00	40.00
135	Emilio Cabrera	50.00	25.00	15.00
136	Barney Serrell	130.00	65.00	40.00
137	Armando Gallart	50.00	25.00	15.00
138	Ruben Garcia	50.00	25.00	15.00
139	Loevigildo Xiques	50.00	25.00	15.00
140	Chifian (Chiflan) Clark	130.00	65.00	40.00
141	Jacinto Roque	50.00	25.00	15.00
142	John (Johnny) Davis	150.00	75.00	45.00
143	Norman Wilson	50.00	25.00	15.00
144	Camaguey Team Banner	25.00	12.50	7.50
145	Antonio Rodriguez	50.00	25.00	15.00
146	Manuel Parrado	50.00	25.00	15.00
147	Leon Treadway	50.00	25.00	15.00
148	Amado Ibanez	50.00	25.00	15.00
149	Teodoro Oxamendi	50.00	25.00	15.00
150	Adolfo Cabrera	50.00	25.00	15.00
151	Oscar Garmendia	50.00	25.00	15.00
152	Hector Arago	50.00	25.00	15.00
153	Evelio Martinez	50.00	25.00	15.00
154	Raquel Antunez	50.00	25.00	15.00
155	Lino Donoso	50.00	25.00	15.00
156	Eliecer Alvarez	50.00	25.00	15.00
157	George Brown	50.00	25.00	15.00
158	Roberto Johnson	50.00	25.00	15.00
159	Rafael Franco	50.00	25.00	15.00
160	Miguel A. Carmona	50.00	25.00	15.00
161	Lilo Fano	50.00	25.00	15.00
162	Orestes Pereda	50.00	25.00	15.00
163	Pedro Diaz	50.00	25.00	15.00
164	Oriente Team Banner	25.00	12.50	7.50
165	Fermin Guerra	50.00	25.00	15.00
166	Jose M. Fernandez	50.00	25.00	15.00
167	Cando Lopez	50.00	25.00	15.00
168	Conrado Marrero	60.00	30.00	18.00
169	Oscar del Calvo	50.00	25.00	15.00
170	Booker McDaniels	150.00	75.00	45.00
171	Rafael Rivas	50.00	25.00	15.00
172	Daniel Parra	50.00	25.00	15.00
173	L. Holleman	50.00	25.00	15.00
174	Rogelio Valdes	50.00	25.00	15.00
175	Raymond Dandridge	950.00	475.00	285.00
176	Manuel Hidalgo	50.00	25.00	15.00
177	Miguel Lastra	50.00	25.00	15.00
178	Luis Minsal	50.00	25.00	15.00
179	Andres Vazquez	50.00	25.00	15.00
180	Jose A. Zardon	50.00	25.00	15.00
181	Jose Luis Colas	50.00	25.00	15.00
182	Rogelio Linares	50.00	25.00	15.00
183	Mario Diaz	50.00	25.00	15.00
184	R. Verdes	50.00	25.00	15.00
185	Indio Jiminez	50.00	25.00	15.00

1948-1949 Caramelos El Indio

Perhaps the rarest of the late-1940s Cuban caramel cards is this issue picturing members of the island's four-team professional winter league. Measuring 1-5/8" x 2-7/16", the cards are printed in black-and-white on thick paper stock. Front photos are bordered in black with no player identification. On back at top is a card number and player name, along with a few words about the player. At bottom is an ad for the sponsor. Many American players, including Negro Leaguers, are included in the issue. The set is arranged alphabetically by

team. An album was available in which to mount the cards. As with most contemporary Cuban issues, low-grade survivors are the norm, with Good condition being about the best seen, making the pricing here somewhat hypothetical.

		NM	EX	VG
Common Player:		200.00	100.00	60.00
Album:		300.00	150.00	90.00
1	Fermin Guerra	275.00	135.00	80.00
2	Rodolfo Fernandez	200.00	100.00	60.00
3	Reinaldo Cordeiro	200.00	100.00	60.00
4	Andres Fleitas	200.00	100.00	60.00
5	Tango Suarez	200.00	100.00	60.00
6	Ken Connors (Kevin "Chuck")	600.00	300.00	180.00
7	Rene Gonzalez	200.00	100.00	60.00
8	Jinny Bloodwrth (Jimmy Bloodworth)	275.00	135.00	80.00
9	Sojito Gallardo	200.00	100.00	60.00
10	Hector Rodriguez	275.00	135.00	80.00
11	Avelino Canizares	200.00	100.00	60.00
12	Gilberto Torres	200.00	100.00	60.00
13	Monte Yrving (Monte Irvin)	1,600	800.00	475.00
14	San Jethore (Sam Jethroe)	325.00	160.00	100.00
15	Al Gionfrido (Gionfriddo)	275.00	135.00	80.00
16	Santos Amaro	275.00	135.00	80.00
17	Hiram Gonzalez	200.00	100.00	60.00
18	Conrado Marrero	275.00	135.00	80.00
19	Jorge Comellas	200.00	100.00	60.00
20	Agapito Mayor	200.00	100.00	60.00
21	Octavio Rubert	200.00	100.00	60.00
22	Tata Solis	200.00	100.00	60.00
23	Morris Martin	275.00	135.00	80.00
24	Cyde (Clyde) King	275.00	135.00	80.00
25	Miguel Angel Gonzalez	325.00	160.00	100.00
26	Joseito Rodriguez	200.00	100.00	60.00
27	Sungo Carreras	200.00	100.00	60.00
28	Hank Anderson	275.00	135.00	80.00
29	Emilio Cabrera	200.00	100.00	60.00
30	Lennox Pearson	325.00	160.00	100.00
31	Herberto Blanco	200.00	100.00	60.00
32	Pablo Garcia	200.00	100.00	60.00
33	Chino Hidalgo	200.00	100.00	60.00
34	Amado Ibanez	200.00	100.00	60.00
35	Carlos Blanco	200.00	100.00	60.00
36	Henry Thompson	275.00	135.00	80.00
37	Henry Kimbro	275.00	135.00	80.00
38	Pedro Formental	275.00	135.00	80.00
39	Saguita Hernandez	200.00	100.00	60.00
40	Francisco Quicutis	200.00	100.00	60.00
41	George Stancer (Stanceu)	275.00	135.00	80.00
42	Jim Yockin (Yochim)	275.00	135.00	80.00
43	Tony Lorenzo	200.00	100.00	60.00
44	Rafael Rivas	200.00	100.00	60.00
45	Jose Cerdan	200.00	100.00	60.00
46	Cocaina Garcia	325.00	160.00	100.00
47	Bill Schuster	275.00	135.00	80.00
48	Oliverio Ortiz	200.00	100.00	60.00
49	Salvador Hernandez	200.00	100.00	60.00
50	Oscar Rodriguez	200.00	100.00	60.00
51	Julio Rojo	200.00	100.00	60.00
52	Ray Noble	250.00	125.00	75.00
53	Regino Otero	200.00	100.00	60.00
54	Peter Coscarat (Coscarart)	275.00	135.00	80.00
55	Jimmy Redmond	275.00	135.00	80.00
56	Mc. Quillan (Glenn McQuillen)	275.00	135.00	80.00
57	Stan Bread	275.00	135.00	80.00
58	Armando Gallart	200.00	100.00	60.00
59	Angel Fleitas	200.00	100.00	60.00
60	Pedro Pages	200.00	100.00	60.00
61	Alejandro Crespo	275.00	135.00	80.00
62	Jose Luis Colas	200.00	100.00	60.00
63	Conrado Perez	200.00	100.00	60.00
64	Coaker Triplett (Triplett)	275.00	135.00	80.00
65	Pedro Dunabeitia	200.00	100.00	60.00
66	Maik Sukont (Max Surkont)	275.00	135.00	80.00
67	Max Mamming (Manning)	525.00	260.00	150.00
68	Jom Mikan	275.00	135.00	80.00
69	Herman Bess (Besse)	275.00	135.00	80.00
70	Wito (Luis) Aloma	275.00	135.00	80.00
71	Raul Lopez	200.00	100.00	60.00
72	Silvio Garcia	300.00	150.00	90.00
73	Gilberto Torres	200.00	100.00	60.00
74	Pipo de la Noval	200.00	100.00	60.00
75	Jose Maria Fernandez	200.00	100.00	60.00
76	Vitico Munoz	200.00	100.00	60.00
77	Luis Suarez	200.00	100.00	60.00
78	Wilfredo Salas	200.00	100.00	60.00
79	Julio Moreno	200.00	100.00	60.00
80	Bill Harrington	275.00	135.00	80.00
81	Oreste (Minnie) Minoso	525.00	260.00	150.00
82	Clarence Hicks	275.00	135.00	80.00
83	Pedro Ballester	200.00	100.00	60.00
84	Jose Hawerton	200.00	100.00	60.00
85	Ramon Roger	200.00	100.00	60.00
86	M Arenciba	200.00	100.00	60.00
87	Louis Kahn	275.00	135.00	80.00
88	Mario Diaz	200.00	100.00	60.00

		NM	EX	VG
89	Chiquitin Cabrera	200.00	100.00	60.00
90	Beto Avila	200.00	100.00	60.00
91	Cisco Campos	200.00	100.00	60.00
92	Johnny Simmons	275.00	135.00	80.00
93	Claro Duany	275.00	135.00	80.00
94	Clyde (Dave) Barnhill	800.00	400.00	240.00
95	Clarence Beer	275.00	135.00	80.00
96	Joaquin Gutierrez	200.00	100.00	60.00

1955 Carling Beer Cleveland Indians

Apparently the first of a line of premium photos which extended into the early 1960s. Measuring 8-1/2" x 12" and printed in black-and-white on semi-gloss thin card stock, these photocards are blank-backed. The 1955 Carling photos are identifiable from the 1956 issue, with which they share a "DBL" prefix to the card number in the lower-right corner, by the phrase "Great Champions" appearing just under the player photo.

		NM	EX	VG
Complete Set (11):		750.00	375.00	225.00
Common Player:		60.00	30.00	18.00
96A	Ralph Kiner	110.00	55.00	35.00
96Ba	Larry Doby	100.00	50.00	30.00
96Bb	Herb Score	75.00	37.50	22.50
96C	Al Rosen	75.00	37.50	22.50
96D	Mike Garcia	60.00	30.00	18.00
96E	Early Wynn	90.00	45.00	27.50
96F	Bob Feller	150.00	75.00	45.00
96G	Jim Hegan	60.00	30.00	18.00
96H	George Strickland	60.00	30.00	18.00
96K	Bob Lemon	90.00	45.00	27.50
96L	Art Houtteman	60.00	30.00	18.00

1956 Carling Beer Cleveland Indians

This set was sponsored by Carling Black Label Beer. The oversized (8-1/2" x 12") cards feature black-and-white posed photos with the player's name in a white strip and a Carling ad at the bottom of the card front. Backs are blank. Like the cards issued in 1955, the 1956 set carries a DBL 96 series indication in the lower-right corner and lists brewery locations as Cleveland, St. Louis and Belleville, Ill. Unlike the '55 photocards, however, the first line under the player photo on the 1956 issue is "Premium Quality." Cards numbered DBL 96I and DBL 96J are unknown.

		NM	EX	VG
Complete Set (10):		900.00	450.00	275.00
Common Player:		60.00	30.00	18.00
96A	Al Smith	60.00	30.00	18.00
96B	Herb Score	120.00	60.00	35.00
96C	Al Rosen	90.00	45.00	27.50
96D	Mike Garcia	60.00	30.00	18.00
96E	Early Wynn	120.00	60.00	35.00
96F	Bob Feller	200.00	100.00	60.00
96G	Jim Hegan	60.00	30.00	18.00
96H	George Strickland	60.00	30.00	18.00
96K	Bob Lemon	120.00	60.00	35.00
96L	Art Houtteman	60.00	30.00	18.00

1957 Carling Beer Cleveland Indians

The fact that Kerby Farrell managed the Indians only in 1957 pinpoints the year of issue for those Carling Beer photocards which carry a DBL 179 series number in the lower-right corner. Following the black-and-white, blank-backed 8-1/2" x 12" format of earlier issues, the 1957 Carlings list on the bottom line breweries at Cleveland; Frankenmuth, Mich.; Natick, Mass.; and, Belleville, Ill. Cards numbered DBL 179I and DBL 179J are currently unknown.

		NM	EX	VG
Complete Set (10):		900.00	450.00	275.00
Common Player:		60.00	30.00	18.00
179A	Vic Wertz	60.00	30.00	18.00
179B	Early Wynn	100.00	50.00	30.00
179C	Herb Score	90.00	45.00	27.50
179D	Bob Lemon	100.00	50.00	30.00
179E	Ray Narleski	60.00	30.00	18.00
179F	Jim Hegan	60.00	30.00	18.00
179G	Bob Avila	60.00	30.00	18.00
179H	Al Smith	60.00	30.00	18.00
179K	Kerby Farrell	60.00	30.00	18.00
179L	Rocky Colavito	300.00	150.00	90.00

1958 Carling Beer Cleveland Indians

Identical in format to earlier issues, the 1958 premium photos can be distinguished by the card number printed in the lower-right corner. Cards in the 1958 series have numbers which begin with a DBL 2 or DBL 217 prefix.

		NM	EX	VG
Complete Set (10):		725.00	360.00	215.00
Common Player:		60.00	30.00	18.00
2	Vic Wertz	60.00	30.00	18.00
217	Minnie Minoso	100.00	50.00	30.00
217B	Gene Woodling	60.00	30.00	18.00
217C	Russ Nixon	60.00	30.00	18.00
217D	Bob Lemon	120.00	60.00	35.00
217E	Bobby Bragan	60.00	30.00	18.00
217F	Cal McLish	60.00	30.00	18.00
217G	Rocky Colavito	150.00	75.00	45.00
217H	Herb Score	100.00	50.00	30.00
217J	Chico Carrasquel	60.00	30.00	18.00

1959 Carling Beer Cleveland Indians

The appearance of Billy Martin among Carling photocards labeled with a DBL 266 prefix fixes the year of issue to 1959, the fiery second baseman's only year with the Tribe. Once again the 8-1/2" x 12" black-and-white, blank-backed cards follow the format of previous issues. Breweries listed on the bottom of the 1959 Carlings are Cleveland; Atlanta; Frankenmuth, Mich.; Natick, Mass.; Belleville, Ill.; and, Tacoma, Wash.

		NM	EX	VG
Complete Set (6):		600.00	300.00	180.00
Common Player:		75.00	37.50	22.50
266A	Vic Power	75.00	37.50	22.50
266B	Minnie Minoso	100.00	50.00	30.00
266C	Herb Score	100.00	50.00	30.00
266D	Rocky Colavito	150.00	75.00	45.00
266E	Jimmy Piersall	100.00	50.00	30.00
266F	Billy Martin	150.00	75.00	45.00

1960 Carling Beer

Because of the numbering and the fact that manager Joe Gordon was at the helm in 1960, these are believed to be from that year. Like the others, these are 8-1/2" x 12-1/2", black and white, and blank-backed.

		NM	EX	VG
Checklist is likely incomplete				
DBL347D	Joe Gordon	100.00	50.00	30.00
DBL347E	Bubba Phillips	60.00	30.00	18.00
DBL347K	Tito Francona	60.00	30.00	18.00

1960 Carling Beer Cleveland Indians

Only a single premium photo of the presumed 10 issued in the brewery's series of Cleveland Indians pictures has thus far been cataloged for 1960. Like the other years' issues, the picture is black-and-white, blank-back and measures 8-1/2" x

12". Unlike earlier issues, which had a lengthier list of brewery locations, the 1960 premium lists only Cleveland. That format was continued in 1961. The 1960 picture has a DBL prefix to the number at lower-right.

		NM	EX	VG
Common Player:		75.00	37.50	22.50
247E	Bubba Phillips	75.00	37.50	22.50

1961 Carling Beer Cleveland Indians

Totally different player selection and the use of an LB prefix to the number in the lower-right corner define the 1961 issue from Carling Beer. Otherwise the photocards share the same 8-1/2" x 12" black-and-white format with earlier issues. The blank-backed cards of the 1961 issue list only a single brewery, Cleveland, at the bottom of the ad portion of the issues. The checklist here is arranged alphabetically. Cards numbered LB 420I and LB420J are unknown.

		NM	EX	VG
Complete Set (10):		600.00	300.00	180.00
Common Player:		60.00	.30.00	18.00
420A	Jimmy Piersall	100.00	50.00	30.00
420B	Willie Kirkland	60.00	30.00	18.00
420C	Johnny Antonelli	60.00	30.00	18.00
420D	John Romano	60.00	30.00	18.00
420E	Woodie Held	60.00	30.00	18.00
420F	Tito Francona	60.00	30.00	18.00
420G	Jim Perry	90.00	45.00	27.50
420H	Bubba Phillips	60.00	30.00	18.00
420K	John Temple	60.00	30.00	18.00
420L	Vic Power	60.00	30.00	18.00

1909-11 Carolina Brights

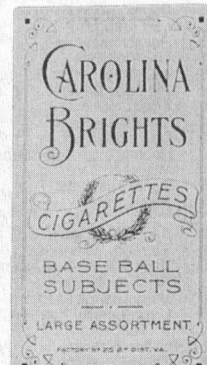

Among the last of the T206 cards printed, those with Carolina Brights advertising on back are scarce and command a significant premium. The advertising on back is printed in black.

PREMIUMS:
Common Player: 6-8X
Typical Hall of Famer: 3-4X
(See T206 for checklist and base card values.)

1976 Carousel Discs

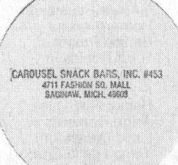

One of several regional sponsors of player disc sets in 1976 was the Michigan snack bar chain, Carousel. The sponsor's discs are unique in that they do not have pre-printed backs, but rather have a black rubber-stamp on the otherwise blank back. To date more than 20 such stamps have been seen, reportedly from New Jersey to Alaska. The discs are 3-3/8" diameter with a black-and-white player portrait photo in the center of the baseball design. A line of red stars is above, while the left and right panels feature one of several bright colors. Produced by Michael Schecter Associates under license from the Major League Baseball Players Association, the player photos have had uniform and cap logos removed. The unnumbered checklist here is presented in alphabetical order.

		NM	EX	VG
Complete Set (70):		35.00	17.50	10.00
Common Player:		2.00	1.00	.60
(1)	Henry Aaron	12.50	6.25	3.75
(2)	Johnny Bench	7.50	3.75	2.25
(3)	Vida Blue	2.00	1.00	.60
(4)	Larry Bowa	2.00	1.00	.60
(5)	Lou Brock	5.00	2.50	1.50
(6)	Jeff Burroughs	2.00	1.00	.60
(7)	John Candelaria	2.00	1.00	.60
(8)	Jose Cardenal	2.00	1.00	.60
(9)	Rod Carew	5.00	2.50	1.50
(10)	Steve Carlton	5.00	2.50	1.50
(11)	Dave Cash	2.00	1.00	.60
(12)	Cesar Cedeno	2.00	1.00	.60
(13)	Ron Cey	2.00	1.00	.60
(14)	Carlton Fisk	5.00	2.50	1.50
(15)	Tito Fuentes	2.00	1.00	.60
(16)	Steve Garvey	3.50	1.75	1.00
(17)	Ken Griffey	2.00	1.00	.60
(18)	Don Gullett	2.00	1.00	.60
(19)	Willie Horton	2.00	1.00	.60
(20)	Al Hrabosky	2.00	1.00	.60
(21)	Catfish Hunter	5.00	2.50	1.50
(22a)	Reggie Jackson (A's)	7.50	3.75	2.25
(22b)	Reggie Jackson (Orioles)	10.00	5.00	3.00
(23)	Randy Jones	2.00	1.00	.60
(24)	Jim Kaat	2.00	1.00	.60
(25)	Don Kessinger	2.00	1.00	.60
(26)	Dave Kingman	1.75	.90	.50
(27)	Jerry Koosman	2.00	1.00	.60
(28)	Mickey Lolich	2.00	1.00	.60
(29)	Greg Luzinski	2.00	1.00	.60
(30)	Fred Lynn	2.00	1.00	.60
(31)	Bill Madlock	2.00	1.00	.60
(32a)	Carlos May (White Sox)	3.00	1.50	.90
(32b)	Carlos May (Yankees)	2.00	1.00	.60
(33)	John Mayberry	2.00	1.00	.60
(34)	Bake McBride	2.00	1.00	.60
(35)	Doc Medich	2.00	1.00	.60
(36a)	Andy Messersmith (Dodgers)	3.00	1.50	.90
(36b)	Andy Messersmith (Braves)	2.00	1.00	.60
(37)	Rick Monday	2.00	1.00	.60
(38)	John Montefusco	2.00	1.00	.60
(39)	Jerry Morales	2.00	1.00	.60
(40)	Joe Morgan	5.00	2.50	1.50
(41)	Thurman Munson	4.50	2.25	1.25
(42)	Bobby Murcer	2.00	1.00	.60
(43)	Al Oliver	2.00	1.00	.60
(44)	Jim Palmer	5.00	2.50	1.50
(45)	Dave Parker	2.00	1.00	.60
(46)	Tony Perez	5.00	2.50	1.50
(47)	Jerry Reuss	2.00	1.00	.60
(48)	Brooks Robinson	6.00	3.00	1.75
(49)	Frank Robinson	6.00	3.00	1.75
(50)	Steve Rogers	2.00	1.00	.60
(51)	Pete Rose	12.50	6.25	3.75
(52)	Nolan Ryan	15.00	7.50	4.50
(53)	Manny Sanguillen	2.00	1.00	.60
(54)	Mike Schmidt	12.00	6.00	3.50
(55)	Tom Seaver	5.00	2.50	1.50
(56)	Ted Simmons	2.00	1.00	.60
(57)	Reggie Smith	2.00	1.00	.60
(58)	Willie Stargell	5.00	2.50	1.50
(59)	Rusty Staub	1.75	.90	.50
(60)	Rennie Stennett	2.00	1.00	.60
(61)	Don Sutton	5.00	2.50	1.50
(62a)	Andy Thornton (Cubs)	3.00	1.50	.90
(62b)	Andy Thornton (Expos)	2.00	1.00	.60
(63)	Luis Tiant	2.00	1.00	.60
(64)	Joe Torre	3.00	1.50	.90
(65)	Mike Tyson	2.00	1.00	.60
(66)	Bob Watson	2.00	1.00	.60
(67)	Wilbur Wood	2.00	1.00	.60
(68)	Jimmy Wynn	2.00	1.00	.60
(69)	Carl Yastrzemski	6.00	3.00	1.75
(70)	Richie Zisk	2.00	1.00	.60

1973 Norm Cash Day Card

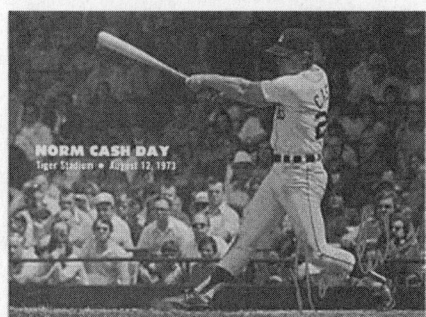

As part of the Tiger Stadium festivities on August 12, this 7" x 5" color card was given to fans. Besides an action photo of the feared slugger, his facsimile autograph appears.

	NM	EX	VG
Norm Cash	12.50	6.25	3.75

1939 Centennial of Baseball Stamps

Part of the pagentry surrounding the 1939 centennial of the fabled beginnings of baseball was this set of player and history stamps and an accompanying 36-page album. The single stamps measure about 1-5/8" x 2-1/8" and are blank-backed.

Stamps #1-13 deal with the game's history; most feature artwork by famed baseball artist and former major league pitcher Al Demaree. Stamps #14-25 feature photos of the game's greats in tombstone frames surrounded by colorful borders.

		NM	EX	VG
Complete Set, w/Album (25):		1,000	500.00	300.00
Common Player:		50.00	25.00	15.00
Common Historical:		20.00	10.00	6.00
Uncut Stamp Sheet (25):		1,000	500.00	300.00
Album:		80.00	40.00	25.00
1	Abner Doubleday	50.00	25.00	15.00
2	1849 Knickerbockers	50.00	25.00	15.00
3	Ball/bat Standards	20.00	10.00	6.00
4	1858 Brooklyn vs. New York Series	50.00	25.00	15.00
5	1859 Amherst vs. Williams Series	20.00	10.00	6.00
6	Curve Ball (Arthur Cummings)	50.00	25.00	15.00
7	First Admission Fee	20.00	10.00	6.00
8	First Professional Players	50.00	25.00	15.00
9	First No-Hitter (George Bradley)	50.00	25.00	15.00
10	Morgan G. Bulkeley	50.00	25.00	15.00
11	First World's Champions	50.00	25.00	15.00
12	Byron Bancroft (Ban) Johnson	50.00	25.00	15.00
13	First Night Game	20.00	10.00	6.00
14	Grover Cleveland Alexander	60.00	30.00	18.00
15	Tyrus Raymond Cobb	150.00	75.00	45.00
16	Eddie Collins	50.00	25.00	15.00
17	Wee Willie Keeler	50.00	25.00	15.00
18	Walter Perry Johnson	75.00	37.50	22.50
19	Napoleon (Larry) Lajoie	50.00	25.00	15.00
20	Christy Mathewson	75.00	37.50	22.50
21	George Herman (Babe) Ruth	300.00	150.00	90.00
22	George Sisler	50.00	25.00	15.00
23	Tristam E. (Tris) Speaker	60.00	30.00	18.00
24	Honus Wagner	100.00	50.00	30.00
25	Denton T. (Cy) Young	75.00	37.50	22.50

1952 Central National Bank of Cleveland

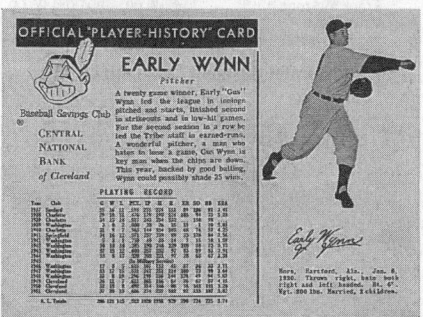

The scope of this issue is undetermined. It is possible a player card was given as a premium for deposits in the bank's "Baseball Savings Club." The cards are about 6-3/4" x 4-3/4", printed in dark blue on cream-colored stock with a blank back. Titled "OFFICIAL "PLAYER-HISTORY" CARD," it features an action pose, facsimile signature, personal data, career summary and complete stats.

	NM	EX	VG
Common Player:	100.00	50.00	30.00
Early Wynn	200.00	100.00	60.00

1929 Certified's Ice Cream Pins

Unless or until further players are seen in this series, the date of issue will have to remain uncertain. Apparently given away by Wrigley Field's ice cream concessionaire, these 1" diameter pin-backs feature player portraits and typography in sepia tones lithographed on a white background.

		NM	EX	VG
Complete Set (5):		2,600	1,300	775.00
Common Player:		450.00	225.00	135.00
(1)	Joe Bush	450.00	225.00	135.00
(2)	Kiki Cuyler	600.00	300.00	180.00
(3)	Rogers Hornsby	725.00	360.00	215.00
(4)	Riggs Stephenson	450.00	225.00	135.00
(5)	Hack Wilson	600.00	300.00	180.00

1964 Challenge the Yankees Game

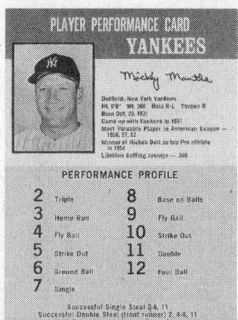

The 50 player cards in this set were part of a boxed dice baseball game produced by Hassenfeld Bros. of Pawtucket, R.I. Cards are approximately 4" x 5-1/2" and blank-backed, featuring a small black-and-white photo, a facsimile autograph and a few biographical details and stats. Player selection is virtually the same for the games issued in 1964 and 1965, and the only way to distinguish cards from each year is to study the stats. Cards are unnumbered and are checklisted below in alphabetical order.

		NM	EX	VG
Complete Boxed Set:		1,200	600.00	350.00
Complete Card Set (50):		850.00	425.00	250.00
Common Player:		9.00	4.50	2.75
(1)	Hank Aaron	150.00	75.00	45.00
(2)	Yogi Berra	45.00	22.50	13.50
(3)	Johnny Blanchard	9.00	4.50	2.75
(4)	Jim Bouton	20.00	10.00	6.00
(5)	Clete Boyer	15.00	7.50	4.50
(6)	Marshall Bridges	9.00	4.50	2.75
(7)	Harry Bright	9.00	4.50	2.75
(8)	Tom Cheney	9.00	4.50	2.75
(9)	Del Crandall	9.00	4.50	2.75
(10)	Al Downing	9.00	4.50	2.75
(11)	Whitey Ford	40.00	20.00	12.00
(12)	Tito Francona	9.00	4.50	2.75
(13)	Lee Gibbs	9.00	4.50	2.75
(14)	Pedro Gonzalez	9.00	4.50	2.75
(15)	Dick Groat	9.00	4.50	2.75
(16)	Steve Hamilton	9.00	4.50	2.75
(17)	Elston Howard	20.00	10.00	6.00
(18)	Al Kaline	45.00	22.50	13.50
(19)	Tony Kubek	30.00	15.00	9.00
(20)	Phil Linz	9.00	4.50	2.75
(21)	Hector Lopez	9.00	4.50	2.75
(22)	Art Mahaffey	9.00	4.50	2.75
(23)	Frank Malzone	9.00	4.50	2.75
(24)	Mickey Mantle	250.00	125.00	75.00
(25)	Juan Marichal	30.00	15.00	9.00
(26)	Roger Maris	75.00	37.50	22.50
(27)	Eddie Mathews	30.00	15.00	9.00
(28)	Bill Mazeroski	30.00	15.00	9.00
(29)	Ken McBride	9.00	4.50	2.75
(30)	Willie McCovey	30.00	15.00	9.00
(31)	Tom Metcalf	9.00	4.50	2.75
(32)	Jim O'Toole	9.00	4.50	2.75
(33)	Milt Pappas	9.00	4.50	2.75
(34)	Joe Pepitone	15.00	7.50	4.50
(35)	Ron Perranoski	9.00	4.50	2.75
(36)	Johnny Podres	9.00	4.50	2.75
(37)	Dick Radatz	9.00	4.50	2.75
(38)	Hal Reniff	9.00	4.50	2.75
(39)	Bobby Richardson	30.00	15.00	9.00
(40)	Rich Rollins	9.00	4.50	2.75
(41)	Ron Santo	20.00	10.00	6.00
(42)	Moose Skowron	20.00	10.00	6.00
(43)	Duke Snider	30.00	15.00	9.00
(44)	Bill Stafford	9.00	4.50	2.75
(45)	Ralph Terry	9.00	4.50	2.75
(46)	Tom Tresh	15.00	7.50	4.50
(47)	Pete Ward	9.00	4.50	2.75
(48)	Carl Warwick	9.00	4.50	2.75
(49)	Stan Williams	9.00	4.50	2.75
(50)	Carl Yastrzemski	75.00	37.50	22.50

1965 Challenge the Yankees Game

The player cards in this set were part of a boxed dice baseball game produced by Hassenfeld Bros. of Pawtucket, R.I. Cards are approximately 4" x 5-1/2" and blank-backed, featuring a small black-and-white photo, a facsimile autograph and a few biographical details and stats. Player selection is virtually the same for the games issued in 1964 and 1965, and the only way to distinguish cards from each year is to study the stats. Cards are unnumbered and are checklisted below in alphabetical order. The card of Yankee pitcher Rollie Sheldon was apparently withdrawn following his May 3 trade to Kansas City and is scarcer than the rest of the set.

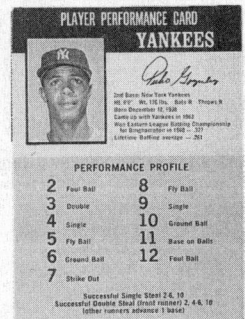

	NM	EX	VG
Complete Boxed Set:	1,500	750.00	450.00
Complete Card Set (50):	1,000	500.00	300.00
Common Player:	10.00	5.00	3.00
(1) Henry Aaron	125.00	62.00	37.00
(2) Johnny Blanchard	10.00	5.00	3.00
(3) Jim Bouton	12.50	6.25	3.75
(4) Clete Boyer	12.50	6.25	3.75
(5) Leon Carmel	10.00	5.00	3.00
(6) Joe Christopher	10.00	5.00	3.00
(7) Vic Davalillo	10.00	5.00	3.00
(8) Al Downing	10.00	5.00	3.00
(9) Whitey Ford	50.00	25.00	15.00
(10) Bill Freehan	10.00	5.00	3.00
(11) Jim Gentile	10.00	5.00	3.00
(12) Jake Gibbs	10.00	5.00	3.00
(13) Pedro Gonzalez	10.00	5.00	3.00
(14) Dick Groat	10.00	5.00	3.00
(15) Steve Hamilton	10.00	5.00	3.00
(16) Elston Howard	20.00	10.00	6.00
(17) Al Kaline	50.00	25.00	15.00
(18) Tony Kubek	25.00	12.50	7.50
(19) Phil Linz	10.00	5.00	3.00
(20) Don Lock	10.00	5.00	3.00
(21) Hector Lopez	10.00	5.00	3.00
(22) Art Mahaffey	10.00	5.00	3.00
(23) Frank Malzone	10.00	5.00	3.00
(24) Mickey Mantle	350.00	175.00	100.00
(25) Juan Marichal	40.00	20.00	12.00
(26) Roger Maris	90.00	45.00	27.00
(27) Eddie Mathews	50.00	25.00	15.00
(28) Bill Mazeroski	40.00	20.00	12.00
(29) Ken McBride	10.00	5.00	3.00
(30) Tim McCarver	15.00	7.50	4.50
(31) Willie McCovey	40.00	20.00	12.00
(32) Tom Metcalf	10.00	5.00	3.00
(33) Pete Mikkelsen	10.00	5.00	3.00
(34) Jim O'Toole	10.00	5.00	3.00
(35) Milt Pappas	10.00	5.00	3.00
(36) Joe Pepitone	12.50	6.25	3.75
(37) Ron Perranoski	10.00	5.00	3.00
(38) Johnny Podres	12.50	6.25	3.75
(39) Dick Radatz	10.00	5.00	3.00
(40) Pedro Ramos	10.00	5.00	3.00
(41) Hal Reniff	10.00	5.00	3.00
(42) Bobby Richardson	25.00	12.50	7.50
(43) Rich Rollins	10.00	5.00	3.00
(44) Ron Santo	20.00	10.00	6.00
(45) Rollie Sheldon/SP	75.00	37.00	22.00
(46) Bill Stafford	10.00	5.00	3.00
(47) Mel Stottlemyre	12.50	6.25	3.75
(48) Tom Tresh	12.50	6.25	3.75
(49) Pete Ward	10.00	5.00	3.00
(50) Carl Yaztrzemski	75.00	37.00	22.00

1947 Champ Hats Premiums

The attributed date is speculative, based on the limited known player selection. These 8" x 10" sepia photo cards have player pictures in uniform. In the wide bottom border is: "(Player Name) says:" and an ad message. Backs are blank.

	NM	EX	VG
Common Player:	250.00	125.00	75.00
(1) Mickey Vernon	250.00	125.00	75.00
(2) Dixie Walker	250.00	125.00	75.00

1957-1962 Charcoal Steak House Ted Kluszewski

The true scope of this issue combined with the related Ted Kluszewski Steak House cards (see also) is not known. Based on cards showing Klu in Reds and Angels uniforms, it is possible examples may yet be seen in Pirates and White Sox uniforms. About 4" x 6", the black-and-white cards have a

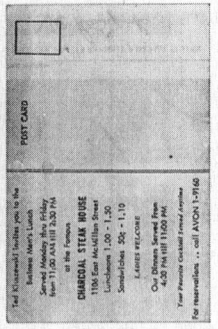

facsimile signature of Kluszewski on front. The back is in post-card style and advertises the Cincinnati restaurant he operated with Jack Stayin.

	NM	EX	VG
Ted Kluszewski (Angels)	75.00	40.00	25.00

1961 Chemstrand Iron-On Patches

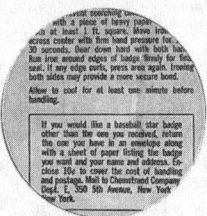

These colorful 2-1/2" diameter cloth patches were included with the purchase of a boy's sport shirt for a short period in 1961. The patches were issued in a cello package with instructions for ironing it onto the shirt. The package also offered the opportunity to trade the player patch for a different star.

	NM	EX	VG
Complete Set (9):	825.00	400.00	225.00
Common Player:	60.00	30.00	20.00
(1) Ernie Banks	125.00	60.00	35.00
(2) Yogi Berra	125.00	60.00	35.00
(3) Nelson Fox	90.00	45.00	25.00
(4) Dick Groat	60.00	30.00	20.00
(5) Al Kaline	90.00	45.00	25.00
(6) Harmon Killebrew	90.00	45.00	25.00
(7) Frank Malzone	60.00	30.00	20.00
(8) Willie Mays	180.00	90.00	50.00
(9) Warren Spahn	90.00	45.00	25.00

1976 Chevrolet Baseball Centennial Prints

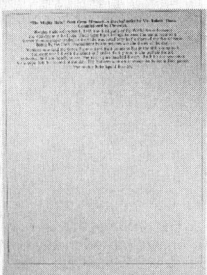

In conjunction with the centennial of organized baseball, Chevrolet commissioned a set of paintings by artist Robert Thom which were reproduced in an 8-1/2" x 11" format and distributed by local auto dealers. Fronts carry the picture's title in the white border at bottom. Backs have a description of the picture on front.

	NM	EX	VG
Complete Set (4):	40.00	20.00	12.00
Common Print:	8.00	4.00	2.50
(1) The First Game (1876)	8.00	4.00	2.50
(2) The Gashouse Gang (Pepper Martin, Bill Werber)	8.00	4.00	2.50
(3) The Mighty Babe (Babe Ruth)	15.00	7.50	4.50
(4) The Record Breaker (Hank Aaron)	12.50	6.25	3.75

1908 Chicago Cubs/White Sox Postcards

The issuer of this postcard set is unknown. The only identification on the card is a dollar sign within a shield which appears near the center on back, along with standard postcard indicia. Fronts of the 3-7/16" x 5-3/8" cards have black-and-white player photos on a gray background. A plain strip at bottom has the player's name on a top line; his position and team on a second line. The checklist presented here is probably not complete.

	NM	EX	VG
Complete Set, Cubs (11):	3,000	1,500	900.00
Complete Set, White Sox (9):	3,500	1,750	1,000
Common Player:	200.00	100.00	60.00
CUBS			
(1) Mordecai Brown	400.00	200.00	120.00
(2) Frank Chance	400.00	200.00	120.00
(3) Johnny Evers	400.00	200.00	120.00
(4) Solly Hoffman (Hofman)	200.00	100.00	60.00
(5) John Kling	200.00	100.00	60.00
(6) "Jack" Pfiester	200.00	100.00	60.00
(7) Edw. Reulbach	200.00	100.00	60.00
(8) James Sheckard	200.00	100.00	60.00
(9) Harry Steinfeldt	200.00	100.00	60.00
(10) Joe Tinker	400.00	200.00	120.00
(11) Chicago National League, Cubs. (Team photo.)	500.00	250.00	150.00
WHITE SOX			
(1) "Nic" Altrock	400.00	200.00	120.00
(2) "Jakey" Atz	500.00	250.00	150.00
(3) Geo. Davis	600.00	300.00	180.00
(4) "Jiggs" Donahue	300.00	150.00	90.00
(5) "Pat" Dougherty	300.00	150.00	90.00
(6) "Eddie" Hahn	300.00	150.00	90.00
(7) Frank Isbell	300.00	150.00	90.00
(8) Fielder Jones	300.00	150.00	90.00
(9) "Ed" Walsh	650.00	325.00	195.00

1972 Chicago Cubs & Chicago White Sox Color Caricatures

Produced by Chi-Foursome, Inc., these color caricatures were intended for sale at gas stations and supermarkets, but were never released at these locations. Apparently, only a small quantity was sold at Wrigley Field, and it is believed only about 3,000 of each player was produced. The caricatures were produced on 11" x 14" textured cardboard stock, with a facsimile autograph next to each player on front. Backs are blank.

	NM	EX	VG
	10.00	5.00	3.00
CUBS			
Complete Set (15):	100.00	50.00	30.00
Common Player:	10.00	5.00	3.00
Ernie Banks	20.00	10.00	6.00
Glenn Beckert	10.00	5.00	3.00
Fergie Jenkins	14.00	7.00	4.50
Don Kessinger	10.00	5.00	3.00
Milt Pappas	10.00	5.00	3.00
Joe Pepitone	10.00	5.00	3.00
Ron Santo	20.00	10.00	6.00
Billy Williams	10.00	5.00	3.00
WHITE SOX			
Mike Andrews	10.00	5.00	3.00
Ed Herrmann	10.00	5.00	3.00
Pat Kelly	10.00	5.00	3.00
Carlos May	10.00	5.00	3.00
Bill Melton	14.00	7.00	4.50
Chuck Tanner	10.00	5.00	3.00
Wilbur Wood	14.00	7.00	4.50

1931 Chicago Cubs Picture Pack

In the second-year of team-issued photo packs during the 1930s-1940s was this set of 1931 Cubs. The 6-1/8" x 9-1/2" sepia-toned pictures have facsimile autographs across the front and a white border around. Backs are blank. Like all the team's other photo packs, it is possible the specific make-up of the 30 pictures in each set changed as personnel came and went during the season. A number of non-playing team personnel are also in the set.

	NM	EX	VG
Complete Set (35):	450.00	225.00	135.00
Common Player:	12.50	6.25	3.75
(1) Ed Baecht	12.50	6.25	3.75
(2) Clyde Beck	12.50	6.25	3.75
(3) Les Bell	12.50	6.25	3.75
(4) Clarence Blair	12.50	6.25	3.75
(5) John F. Blake	12.50	6.25	3.75
(6) Guy Bush	12.50	6.25	3.75
(7) Kiki Cuyler	30.00	15.00	9.00
(8) Woody English	12.50	6.25	3.75
(9) Earl Grace	12.50	6.25	3.75
(10) Charlie Grimm	15.00	7.50	4.50
(11) Gabby Hartnett	30.00	15.00	9.00
(12) Rollie Hemsley	12.50	6.25	3.75
(13) Rogers Hornsby	60.00	30.00	18.00
(14) Bill Jurges	12.50	6.25	3.75
(15) Pat Malone	12.50	6.25	3.75
(16) Jakie May	12.50	6.25	3.75
(17) John Moore	12.50	6.25	3.75
(18) Charley O'Leary	12.50	6.25	3.75
(19) Charlie Root	15.00	7.50	4.50
(20) Ray Schalk	30.00	15.00	9.00
(21) Bob Smith	12.50	6.25	3.75
(22) Riggs Stephenson	15.00	7.50	4.50
(23) Les Sweetland	12.50	6.25	3.75
(24) Dan Taylor	12.50	6.25	3.75
(25) Zack Taylor	12.50	6.25	3.75
(26) Bud Teachout	12.50	6.25	3.75
(27) Lon Warneke	12.50	6.25	3.75
(28) Hack Wilson	45.00	22.00	13.50
Non-Playing Personnel			
(29) Margaret Donahue	12.50	6.25	3.75
(30) Bob Lewis	12.50	6.25	3.75
(Traveling secretary.)			
(31) Andy Lotshaw/Trainer	12.50	6.25	3.75
(32) John Seys	12.50	6.25	3.75
(33) William Veeck/President	45.00	22.00	13.50
(34) W.M. Walker/VP	12.50	6.25	3.75
(35) P.K. Wrigley	12.50	6.25	3.75
(36) William Wrigley/Owner	17.50	8.75	5.25

1932 Chicago Cubs Picture Pack

This is one of many Cubs team issues of player pictures in the 1930s-1940s. The large format (6-1/8" x 9-1/4"), set features action poses of the players in black-and-white on a black background. A bit of the ground at the players' feet is also included in the photo portion. A white facsimile autograph in the black background identifies the player. Backs are blank. The unnumbered pictures are checklisted here in alphabetical order. Some pictures of non-playing personnel were also issued.

	NM	EX	VG
Complete Set (35):	325.00	165.00	100.00
Common Player:	12.50	6.25	3.75
(1) Guy Bush	12.50	6.25	3.75
(2) Gilly Campbell	12.50	6.25	3.75
(3) Red Corriden	12.50	6.25	3.75
(4) Kiki Cuyler	25.00	12.50	7.50
(5) Frank Demaree	12.50	6.25	3.75
(6) Woody English	12.50	6.25	3.75
(7) Burleigh Grimes	25.00	12.50	7.50
(8) Charlie Grimm	12.50	6.25	3.75
(9) Marv Gudat	12.50	6.25	3.75
(10) Stan Hack	15.00	7.50	4.50
(11) Gabby Hartnett	25.00	12.50	7.50
(12) Rollie Hemsley	12.50	6.25	3.75
(13) Billy Herman	25.00	12.50	7.50
(14) LeRoy Herrmann	12.50	6.25	3.75
(15) Billy Jurges	12.50	6.25	3.75
(16) Mark Koenig	12.50	6.25	3.75
(17) Pat Malone	12.50	6.25	3.75
(18) Jake May	12.50	6.25	3.75
(19) Johnny Moore	12.50	6.25	3.75
(20) Charley O'Leary	12.50	6.25	3.75
(21) Lance Richbourg	12.50	6.25	3.75
(22) Charlie Root	15.00	7.50	4.50
(23) Bob Smith	12.50	6.25	3.75
(24) Riggs Stephenson	15.00	7.50	4.50
(25) Harry Taylor	12.50	6.25	3.75
(26) Zack Taylor	12.50	6.25	3.75
(27) Bud Tinning	12.50	6.25	3.75
(28) Lon Warneke	12.50	6.25	3.75
Non-Playing Personnel			
(29) Marge Donahue	12.50	6.25	3.75
(30) Bob Lewis	12.50	6.25	3.75
(Traveling secretary.)			
(31) John Seys	12.50	6.25	3.75
(32) Bill Veeck (President)	25.00	12.50	7.50
(33) W.M. Walker	12.50	6.25	3.75
(34) Phil Wrigley	12.50	6.25	3.75
(35) William Wrigley	12.50	6.25	3.75

1932 Chicago Cubs Team Issue

Because of its similarity in format to the team's picture pack issue of 1932, it is presumed this card set was also a team production. The blank-back cards are about 2-1/4" x 2-1/2" with player poses and a bit of ground underfoot set against a white background which has a facsimile autograph. This checklist is incomplete and arranged alphabetically.

	NM	EX	VG
Common Player:	300.00	150.00	90.00
Charlie Grimm	300.00	150.00	90.00
Marv Gudat	300.00	150.00	90.00
Stanley C. Hack	350.00	175.00	100.00
Rolly Hemsley	300.00	150.00	90.00
Jakie May	300.00	150.00	90.00
Bud Tinning	300.00	150.00	90.00

1933 Chicago Cubs Picture Pack

Likely a concession stand souvenir item, this large format (5-7/8" x 8-7/8"), set features action poses of the players in black-and-white on a black background. A bit of the ground at the players' feet is also included in the photo portion. A white facsimile autograph in the black background identifies the player. Backs are blank. The unnumbered pictures are checklisted here in alphabetical order. Some pictures of non-playing personnel were included.

	NM	EX	VG
Complete Set (30):	275.00	135.00	85.00
Common Player:	12.50	6.25	3.75
(1) Guy Bush	12.50	6.25	3.75
(2) Gilly Campbell	12.50	6.25	3.75
(3) John M. Corriden	12.50	6.25	3.75
(4) Kiki Cuyler	25.00	12.50	7.50
(5) J. Frank Demaree	12.50	6.25	3.75
(6) Woody English	12.50	6.25	3.75
(7) Burleigh A. Grimes	25.00	12.50	7.50
(8) Charlie Grimm	12.50	6.25	3.75
(9) Leo "Gabby" Hartnett	25.00	12.50	7.50
(10) Harvey Hendrick	12.50	6.25	3.75
(11) Roy Henshaw	12.50	6.25	3.75
(12) Babe Herman	15.00	7.50	4.50
(13) William Herman	25.00	12.50	7.50
(14) William Jurges	12.50	6.25	3.75
(15) Mark Koenig	12.50	6.25	3.75
(16) Perce "Pat" Malone	12.50	6.25	3.75
(17) Lynn Nelson	12.50	6.25	3.75
(18) Charlie Root	15.00	7.50	4.50
(19) John Schulte	12.50	6.25	3.75
(20) Riggs Stephenson	15.00	7.50	4.50
(21) Zack Taylor	12.50	6.25	3.75
(22) Bud Tinning	12.50	6.25	3.75
(23) L. Warneke	12.50	6.25	3.75
Non-Playing Personnel			
(24) Margaret Donahue	12.50	6.25	3.75
(25) Robert C. Lewis	12.50	6.25	3.75
(Traveling secretary.)			
(26) John O. Seys	12.50	6.25	3.75
(27) William L. Veeck/President	25.00	12.50	7.50
(28) W.M. Walker	12.50	6.25	3.75
(29) Philip K. Wrigley	12.50	6.25	3.75
(30) Wm. Wrigley	12.50	6.25	3.75

1936 Chicago Cubs Picture Pack

Nearly identical in format to the 1933 issue, these 5-7/8" x 8-7/8" pictures are printed in black-and-white on a black background with (usually) a white facsimile autograph. Backs are blank. The specific make-up of photo packs sold at Wrigley Field may have changed over the course of the season as players came and went. The unnumbered pictures are checklisted here in alphabetical order.

	NM	EX	VG
Complete Set (34):	240.00	120.00	72.00

	NM	EX	VG
Common Player:	9.00	4.50	2.75
(1) Ethan Allen	9.00	4.50	2.75
(2) Clay Bryant	9.00	4.50	2.75
(3) Tex Carleton	9.00	4.50	2.75
(4) Phil Cavarretta	12.00	6.00	3.50
(5) John Corriden	9.00	4.50	2.75
(6) Frank Demaree	9.00	4.50	2.75
(7) Curt Davis	9.00	4.50	2.75
(8) Woody English	9.00	4.50	2.75
(9) Larry French	9.00	4.50	2.75
(10) Augie Galan	9.00	4.50	2.75
(11) Johnny Gill	9.00	4.50	2.75
(12) Charlie Grimm	12.00	6.00	3.50
(13) Stan Hack	12.00	6.00	3.50
(14) Gabby Hartnett	18.00	9.00	5.50
(15) Roy Henshaw	9.00	4.50	2.75
(16) Billy Herman	18.00	9.00	5.50
(17) Roy Johnson	9.00	4.50	2.75
(18) Bill Jurges	9.00	4.50	2.75
(19) Chuck Klein	18.00	9.00	5.50
(20) Fabian Kowalik	9.00	4.50	2.75
(21) Bill Lee	9.00	4.50	2.75
(22) Gene Lillard	9.00	4.50	2.75
(23) Ken O'Dea	9.00	4.50	2.75
(24) Charlie Root	12.00	6.00	3.50
(25) Clyde Shoun	9.00	4.50	2.75
(26) Tuck Stainback	9.00	4.50	2.75
(27) Walter Stephenson	9.00	4.50	2.75
(28) Lon Warneke	9.00	4.50	2.75
Non-Playing personnel			
(29) Margaret Donahue	9.00	4.50	2.75
(30) Bob Lewis	9.00	4.50	2.75
(Traveling secretary.)			
(31) Andy Lotshaw/Trainer	9.00	4.50	2.75
(32) John O. Seys	9.00	4.50	2.75
(33) Charles Weber	9.00	4.50	2.75
(34) Wrigley Field	18.00	9.00	5.50

1939 Chicago Cubs Picture Pack

The use of a textured paper stock for these 6-1/2" x 9" pictures helps identify the 1939 team issue. The pictures once again feature sepia portrait photos with a white border. A facsimile autograph is at bottom. Backs are blank. The specific make-up of photo packs sold at Wrigley Field may have changed over the course of the season as players came and went. The unnumbered pictures are checklisted here in alphabetical order.

	NM	EX	VG
Complete Set (25):	225.00	115.00	65.00
Common Player:	9.00	4.50	2.75
(1) Dick Bartell	9.00	4.50	2.75
(2) Clay Bryant	9.00	4.50	2.75
(3) Phil Cavarretta	12.00	6.00	3.50
(4) John Corriden	9.00	4.50	2.75
(5) Dizzy Dean	40.00	20.00	12.00
(6) Larry French	9.00	4.50	2.75
(7) Augie Galan	9.00	4.50	2.75
(8) Bob Garbark	9.00	4.50	2.75
(9) Jim Gleeson	9.00	4.50	2.75
(10) Stan Hack	12.00	6.00	3.50
(11) Gabby Hartnett	20.00	10.00	6.00
(12) Billy Herman	20.00	10.00	6.00
(13) Roy Johnson	9.00	4.50	2.75
(14) Bill Lee	9.00	4.50	2.75
(15) Hank Leiber	9.00	4.50	2.75
(16) Gene Lillard	9.00	4.50	2.75
(17) Gus Mancuso	9.00	4.50	2.75
(18) Bobby Mattick	9.00	4.50	2.75
(19) Vance Page	9.00	4.50	2.75
(20) Claude Passeau	9.00	4.50	2.75
(21) Carl Reynolds	9.00	4.50	2.75
(22) Charlie Root	12.00	6.00	3.50
(23) Glenn "Rip" Russell	9.00	4.50	2.75
(24) Jack Russell	9.00	4.50	2.75
(25) Earl Whitehill	9.00	4.50	2.75

1940 Chicago Cubs Picture Pack

The 1940 team-issue is identical in format to the 1939s: 6-1/2" x 9", printed on rough-surfaced paper stock with black-and-white portraits surrounded by a wide border and a facsimile autograph on front. Study of the uniforms, however, may help differentiate the issue from 1939, as the 1940 uniforms have no stripe on the shoulders. It is possible that 1939 pictures continued to be issued in the 1940 photo packs and that specific make-up of the packs changed with the team's roster. The blank-back pictures are unnumbered and checklisted here in alphabetical order.

	NM	EX	VG
Complete Set (25):	80.00	40.00	24.00
Common Player:	9.00	4.50	2.75
(1) Dick Bartell	9.00	4.50	2.75
(2) Clay Bryant	9.00	4.50	2.75
(3) Phil Cavarretta	12.00	6.00	3.50

		NM	EX	VG
(4)	John Corriden	9.00	4.50	2.75
(5)	Bob Collins	9.00	4.50	2.75
(6)	"Del" Dallessandro	9.00	4.50	2.75
(7)	Larry French	9.00	4.50	2.75
(8)	Augie Galan	9.00	4.50	2.75
(9)	Jim Gleeson	9.00	4.50	2.75
(10)	Stan Hack	12.00	6.00	3.50
(11)	Gabby Hartnett	20.00	10.00	6.00
(12)	Billy Herman	20.00	10.00	6.00
(13)	Roy Johnson	9.00	4.50	2.75
(14)	Bill Lee	9.00	4.50	2.75
(15)	Hank Leiber	9.00	4.50	2.75
(16)	Bobby Mattick	9.00	4.50	2.75
(17)	Jake Mooty	9.00	4.50	2.75
(18)	Bill Nicholson	9.00	4.50	2.75
(19)	Vance Page	9.00	4.50	2.75
(20)	Claude Passeau	9.00	4.50	2.75
(21)	Ken Raffensberger	9.00	4.50	2.75
(22)	Bill Rogell	9.00	4.50	2.75
(23)	Charlie Root	9.00	4.50	2.75
(24)	Rip Russell	9.00	4.50	2.75
(25)	Al Todd	9.00	4.50	2.75

1941 Chicago Cubs Picture Pack

A change of paper stock to a smooth finish helps differentiate the 1941 team-issue from previous years' offerings. Size remains at 6-1/2" x 9" with sepia player portraits surrounded by a white border and overprinted with a facsimile autograph. Backs are blank on these unnumbered photos. The pictures are listed here in alphabetical order.

		NM	EX	VG
Complete Set (25):		190.00	95.00	57.00
Common Player:		9.00	4.50	2.75
(1)	Phil Cavarretta	12.00	6.00	3.50
(2)	Dom Dallessandro	9.00	4.50	2.75
(3)	Paul Erickson	9.00	4.50	2.75
(4)	Larry French	9.00	4.50	2.75
(5)	Augie Galan	9.00	4.50	2.75
(6)	Greek George	9.00	4.50	2.75
(7)	Charlie Gilbert	9.00	4.50	2.75
(8)	Stan Hack	12.00	6.00	3.50
(9)	Johnny Hudson	9.00	4.50	2.75
(10)	Bill Lee	9.00	4.50	2.75
(11)	Hank Leiber	9.00	4.50	2.75
(12)	Clyde McCullough	9.00	4.50	2.75
(13)	Jake Mooty	9.00	4.50	2.75
(14)	Bill Myers	9.00	4.50	2.75
(15)	Bill Nicholson	9.00	4.50	2.75
(16)	Lou Novikoff	9.00	4.50	2.75
(17)	Vern Olsen	9.00	4.50	2.75
(18)	Vance Page	9.00	4.50	2.75
(19)	Claude Passeau	9.00	4.50	2.75
(20)	Tot Pressnell	9.00	4.50	2.75
(21)	Charlie Root	12.00	6.00	3.50
(22)	Bob Scheffing	9.00	4.50	2.75
(23)	Lou Stringer	9.00	4.50	2.75
(24)	Bob Sturgeon	9.00	4.50	2.75
(25)	Cubs Staff (Dizzy Dean, Charlie Grimm, Dick Spalding, Jimmie Wilson)	12.00	6.00	3.50

1942 Chicago Cubs Picture Pack

The relatively small number of photos in this team-issued set indicates it may have been issued as a supplement to update earlier photo packs with players who were new to the Cubs. In the same 6-1/2" x 9" format as previous issues, the 1942s are printed in sepia on a smooth-surfaced paper. A facsimile autograph graces the front and the portrait photo is surrounded by a border. Backs are blank and the pictures are not numbered. The checklist here is in alphabetical order.

		NM	EX	VG
Complete Set (26):		175.00	90.00	55.00
Common Player:		9.00	4.50	2.75
(1)	Hiram Bithorn	12.00	6.00	3.50
(2)	Phil Cavarretta	9.00	4.50	2.75
(3)	"Del" Dallasandro	9.00	4.50	2.75
(4)	Paul Erickson	9.00	4.50	2.75
(5)	Bill Fleming	9.00	4.50	2.75
(6)	Charlie Gilbert	9.00	4.50	2.75
(7)	Stan Hack	15.00	7.50	4.50
(8)	Ed Hanyzewski	9.00	4.50	2.75
(9)	Chico Hernandez	9.00	4.50	2.75
(10)	Bill Lee	9.00	4.50	2.75
(11)	Harry Lowrey	9.00	4.50	2.75
(12)	Clyde McCullough	9.00	4.50	2.75
(13)	Lennie Merullo	9.00	4.50	2.75
(14)	Jake Mooty	9.00	4.50	2.75
(15)	Bill Nicholson	9.00	4.50	2.75
(16)	Lou Novikoff	9.00	4.50	2.75
(17)	Vern Olsen	9.00	4.50	2.75
(18)	Claude Passeau	9.00	4.50	2.75
(19)	Tot Pressnell	9.00	4.50	2.75
(20)	Glen "Rip" Russell	9.00	4.50	2.75
(21)	Bob Scheffing	9.00	4.50	2.75
(22)	Johnny Schmitz	9.00	4.50	2.75
(23)	Lou Stringer	9.00	4.50	2.75
(24)	Bob Sturgeon	9.00	4.50	2.75
(25)	Kiki Cuyler, Dick Spalding, Jimmie Wilson	9.00	4.50	2.75
(26)	Jimmie Wilson, Dick Spalding, Charlie Grimm, Dizzy Dean	15.00	7.50	4.50

1943 Chicago Cubs Picture Pack

It is impossible to differentiate pictures from the 1943 issue from those of early years and of 1944, since many pictures were reused and the format is identical: 6-1/2" x 9", black-and-white portrait photos with facsimile autograph and white borders. Backs are blank and the photos are not numbered. They are checklisted here alphabetically.

		NM	EX	VG
Complete Set (25):		215.00	105.00	65.00
Common Player:		9.00	4.50	2.75
(1)	Dick Barrett	9.00	4.50	2.75
(2)	Heinz Becker	9.00	4.50	2.75
(3)	Hiram Bithorn	12.00	6.00	3.50
(4)	Phil Cavarretta	9.00	4.50	2.75
(5)	"Del" Dallassandro	9.00	4.50	2.75
(6)	Paul Derringer	9.00	4.50	2.75
(7)	Paul Erickson	9.00	4.50	2.75
(8)	Bill Fleming	9.00	4.50	2.75
(9)	Stan Hack	12.00	6.00	3.50
(10)	Ed Hanyzewski	9.00	4.50	2.75
(11)	Chico Hernandez	9.00	4.50	2.75
(12)	Bill Lee	9.00	4.50	2.75
(13)	Peanuts Lowrey	9.00	4.50	2.75
(14)	Stu Martin	9.00	4.50	2.75
(15)	Clyde McCullough	9.00	4.50	2.75
(16)	Len Merullo	9.00	4.50	2.75
(17)	Bill Nicholson	9.00	4.50	2.75
(18)	Lou Novikoff	9.00	4.50	2.75
(19)	Claude Passeau	9.00	4.50	2.75
(20)	Ray Prim	9.00	4.50	2.75
(21)	Eddie Stanky	12.00	6.00	3.50
(22)	Al Todd	9.00	4.50	2.75
(23)	Lon Warneke	9.00	4.50	2.75
(24)	Hank Wyse	9.00	4.50	2.75
(25)	Cubs Coaches (Kiki Cuyler, Dick Spalding, Jimmie Wilson)	9.00	4.50	2.75

1944 Chicago Cubs Picture Pack

A slight size reduction, to 6" x 8-1/2", helps identify the team's 1944 photo pack. The pictures feature black-and-white portrait photos with a white border. A facsimile autograph is at bottom. Backs are blank. The specific make-up of photo packs sold at Wrigley Field may have changed over the course of the season as players came and went. The unnumbered pictures are checklisted here in alphabetical order.

		NM	EX	VG
Complete Set (25):		215.00	105.00	65.00
Common Player:		9.00	4.50	2.75
(1)	Heinz Becker	9.00	4.50	2.75
(2)	John Burrows	9.00	4.50	2.75
(3)	Phil Cavarretta	12.00	6.00	3.50
(4)	"Del" Dallessandro	9.00	4.50	2.75
(5)	Paul Derringer	9.00	4.50	2.75
(6)	Roy Easterwood	9.00	4.50	2.75
(7)	Paul Erickson	9.00	4.50	2.75
(8)	Bill Fleming	9.00	4.50	2.75
(9)	Jimmie Foxx	30.00	15.00	9.00
(10)	Ival Goodman	9.00	4.50	2.75
(11)	Ed Hanyzewski	9.00	4.50	2.75
(12)	Billy Holm	9.00	4.50	2.75
(13)	Don Johnson	9.00	4.50	2.75
(14)	Garth Mann	9.00	4.50	2.75
(15)	Len Merullo	9.00	4.50	2.75
(16)	John Miklos	9.00	4.50	2.75
(17)	Bill Nicholson	9.00	4.50	2.75
(18)	Lou Novikoff	9.00	4.50	2.75
(19)	Andy Pafko	12.00	6.00	3.50
(20)	Ed Sauer	9.00	4.50	2.75
(21)	Bill Schuster	9.00	4.50	2.75
(22)	Eddie Stanky	12.00	6.00	3.50
(23)	Hy Vandenberg	9.00	4.50	2.75
(24)	Hank Wyse	9.00	4.50	2.75
(25)	Tony York	9.00	4.50	2.75

1924 Chicago Evening American Cubs/White Sox Pins

These 1-3/8" diameter pins were issued by the Chicago Evening American newspaper to promote its peach-colored sports section. Rather crude blue-and-white line drawings of the players are at center, within an orange peach with the player's name at bottom. Borders are either white or dark blue. The pins were produced by Greenduck Metal Stamping of Chicago.

		NM	EX	VG
Complete Set (12):		3,500	1,750	1,000
Common Player:		200.00	100.00	65.00
(1)	Grover Alexander	750.00	375.00	225.00
(2)	Eddie Collins	450.00	225.00	135.00
(3)	"Red" Faber	350.00	175.00	105.00
(4)	Ray Grimes	200.00	100.00	65.00
(5)	Charlie Hollocher	200.00	100.00	65.00
(6)	Harry Hooper	350.00	175.00	105.00
(7)	Willie Kamm	200.00	100.00	65.00
(8)	Bill Killefer	200.00	100.00	65.00
(9)	Bob O'Farrell	200.00	100.00	65.00
(10)	Charlie Robertson	200.00	100.00	65.00
(11)	Ray Schalk	350.00	175.00	100.00
(12)	Jigger Statz	200.00	100.00	65.00

1930 Chicago Evening American Pins

Members of the Cubs and White Sox are featured on this series of pins issued by one of the local daily newspapers. Player portraits are featured in black-and-white on a white background on these 1-1/4" celluloid pins. Above the picture are the player's position, last name and team; below is the sponsor's name. The unnumbered pins are listed here in alphabetical order within team.

		NM	EX	VG
Complete Set (20):		6,500	3,250	1,950
Common Player:		250.00	125.00	75.00
	Chicago Cubs Team Set (11):	3,500	1,750	1,000
(1)	Les Bell	250.00	125.00	75.00
(2)	Guy Bush	250.00	125.00	75.00
(3)	Kiki Cuyler	350.00	175.00	100.00
(4)	Woody English	250.00	125.00	75.00
(5)	Charlie Grimm	250.00	125.00	75.00
(6)	Gabby Hartnett	350.00	175.00	100.00

		NM	EX	VG
(7)	Rogers Hornsby	750.00	375.00	225.00
(8)	Joe McCarthy	350.00	175.00	100.00
(9)	Charlie Root	250.00	125.00	75.00
(10)	Riggs Stephenson	250.00	125.00	75.00
(11)	Hack Wilson	400.00	200.00	120.00
	Chicago White Sox Team Set (9):	3,000	1,500	900.00
(1)	Moe Berg	1,000	500.00	300.00
(2)	Bill Cissel (Cissell)	250.00	125.00	75.00
(3)	Red Faber	350.00	175.00	105.00
(4)	Bill Hunnefield	250.00	125.00	75.00
(5)	Smead Jolley	250.00	125.00	75.00
(6)	Willie Kamm	250.00	125.00	75.00
(7)	Jimmy Moore	250.00	125.00	75.00
(8)	Carl Reynolds	250.00	125.00	75.00
(9)	Art Shires	250.00	125.00	75.00

1930 Chicago Herald and Examiner Babe Ruth Premium

This premium picture with a black-and-white batting pose of Ruth was issued by a Chicago newspaper. Two sizes are known, approximately 8-1/2" x 11-1/2" and 5" x 7". The pictures are blank-back. The year attributed is speculative.

	NM	EX	VG
Babe Ruth (Large)	1,350	625.00	400.00
Babe Ruth (Small)	1,350	625.00	400.00

1976 Chicagoland Collectors Association Chicago Greats

Former stars of the Cubs and White Sox are featured in this collectors issue produced in conjunction with an early sports card and memorabilia show in Chicago. The 2-1/2" x 3-1/2" cards feature black-and-white action photos at center of most cards, with a portrait photo inset at top. Graphics around the front are in red. Backs have detailed career summaries. A starting team, manager and president for each of the Chicago teams is represented in the set. Complete sets were originally sold for about $2 with uncut sheets sold for $6.

		NM	EX	VG
	Complete Set (25):	15.00	7.50	4.50
	Common Player:	2.00	1.00	.60
(1)	Luke Appling	2.00	1.00	.60
(2)	Ernie Banks	6.00	3.00	1.75
(3)	Zeke Bonura	2.00	1.00	.60
(4)	Phil Cavarretta	2.00	1.00	.60
(5)	Jimmy Dykes	2.00	1.00	.60
(6)	Red Faber, Ted Lyons	2.00	1.00	.60
(7)	Nellie Fox	4.00	2.00	1.25
(8)	Larry French	2.00	1.00	.60
(9)	Charlie Grimm	2.00	1.00	.60
(10)	Gabby Hartnett	2.00	1.00	.60
(11)	Billy Herman	2.00	1.00	.60
(12)	Mike Kreevich	2.00	1.00	.60
(13)	Sherman Lollar	2.00	1.00	.60
(14)	Al Lopez	2.00	1.00	.60
(15)	Minnie Minoso	3.00	1.50	.90
(16)	Wally Moses	2.00	1.00	.60
(17)	Bill Nicholson	2.00	1.00	.60
(18)	Claude Passeau	2.00	1.00	.60
(19)	Billy Pierce	2.00	1.00	.60
(20)	Ron Santo	2.00	1.00	.60
(21)	Hank Sauer	2.00	1.00	.60
(22)	Riggs Stephenson	2.00	1.00	.60
(23)	Bill Veeck	2.00	1.00	.60
(24)	P.K. Wrigley	2.00	1.00	.60
(25)	Checklist	2.00	1.00	.60

1915 Chicago Tribune Supplements

As the 1915 baseball season opened, the Chicago Sunday Tribune ran supplements in its April 4 and April 11 editions featuring pictures of Chicago players. The black-and-white pictures are 8" x 11". Saier is pictured in uniform, the others are in street clothes. Printed in the white border beneath each photo is "Supplement to The Chicago Sunday Tribune, April 4 (or) 11, 1915." Each picture bears a facsimile autograph of the player and is blank-backed.

		NM	EX	VG
	Complete Set (4):	400.00	200.00	120.00
	Common Player:	50.00	25.00	15.00
(1)	Roger Bresnahan (April 11)	100.00	50.00	30.00
(2)	Eddie Collins (April 11)	100.00	50.00	30.00
(3)	Vic Saier (April 11)	50.00	25.00	15.00
(4)	Joe Tinker (April 4)	150.00	75.00	45.00

1917 Chicago White Sox Team Issue

This set of the World Champion White Sox (including several of the notorious Black Sox) was produced by Davis Printing Works in Chicago and apparently sold as a complete boxed set by the team. Individual cards measure about 1-11/16" x 2-3/4". Fronts feature full-length black-and-white photos of the players on a light background with a white border. Player name and position are in black beneath the picture. Backs are blank. To date, only one set is known to exist. It sold at auction in 1991 for $45,100, again in 1997 for $46,000 and in 2001 for $50,330. The unnumbered cards are checklisted here alphabetically.

Complete Set (25):
Value Undetermined

(1)	Joe Benz
(2)	Eddie Cicotte
(3)	Eddie Collins
(4)	Shano Collins
(5)	Charles Comiskey
(6)	Dave Danforth
(7)	Red Faber
(8)	Happy Felsch
(9)	Chick Gandil
(10)	Kid Gleason
(11)	Joe Jackson
(12)	Joe Jenkins
(13)	Ted Jourdan
(14)	Nemo Leibold
(15)	Byrd Lynn
(16)	Fred McMullin
(17)	Eddie Murphy
(18)	Swede Risberg
(19)	Pants Rowland
(20)	Reb Russell
(21)	Ray Schalk
(22)	James Scott
(23)	Buck Weaver
(24)	Lefty Williams
(25)	Mellie Wolfgang

1940 Chicago White Sox Photo Pack

This set of souvenir photos was produced by Andy Lotshaw, who was a Cubs trainer. The 5-1/2" x 6-3/4" pictures have a sepia pose bordered in white, with a facsimile autograph. Backs are blank. The unnumbered pictures are checklisted here in alphabetical order.

		NM	EX	VG
	Complete Set (25):	300.00	150.00	90.00
	Common Player:	15.00	7.50	4.50
(1)	Pete Appleton	15.00	7.50	4.50
(2)	Luke Appling	30.00	15.00	9.00
(3)	Clint Brown	15.00	7.50	4.50
(4)	Bill Dietrich	15.00	7.50	4.50
(5)	Jimmy Dykes	15.00	7.50	4.50
(6)	Mule Haas	15.00	7.50	4.50
(7)	Jack Hayes	15.00	7.50	4.50
(8)	Bob Kennedy	15.00	7.50	4.50
(9)	Jack Knott	15.00	7.50	4.50
(10)	Mike Kreevich	15.00	7.50	4.50
(11)	Joe Kuhel	15.00	7.50	4.50
(12)	Thornton Lee	15.00	7.50	4.50
(13)	Ted Lyons	25.00	12.50	7.50
(14)	Eric McNair	15.00	7.50	4.50
(15)	John Rigney	15.00	7.50	4.50
(16)	Larry Rosenthal	15.00	7.50	4.50
(17)	Ken Silvestri	15.00	7.50	4.50
(18)	Eddie Smith	15.00	7.50	4.50
(19)	J. Solters	15.00	7.50	4.50
(20)	Monty Stratton	20.00	10.00	6.00
(21)	Mike Tresh	15.00	7.50	4.50
(22)	Tom Turner	15.00	7.50	4.50
(23)	Skeeter Webb	20.00	10.00	6.00
(24)	Ed Weiland	15.00	7.50	4.50
(25)	Taft Wright	15.00	7.50	4.50

1948 Chicago White Sox Photo Pack

The last-place White Sox of 1948 are immortalized in this team-issued set of player photos. Individual players are pictured in a 6-1/2" x 9" portrait photo with a thin white border around. A facsimile autograph also appears on front. Backs are blank. A team photo was also included in the set. The photo pack was sold in a large white envelope with a red and blue team logo. The unnumbered pictures are checklisted here in alphabetical order.

		NM	EX	VG
	Complete Set (30):	180.00	90.00	54.00
	Common Player:	7.50	3.75	2.25
(1)	Luke Appling	18.00	9.00	5.50
(2)	Floyd Baker	7.50	3.75	2.25
(3)	Fred Bradley	7.50	3.75	2.25
(4)	Earl Caldwell	7.50	3.75	2.25
(5)	Red Faber	15.00	7.50	4.50
(6)	Bob Gillespie	7.50	3.75	2.25
(7)	Jim Goodwin	12.00	6.00	3.50
(8)	Orval Grove	7.50	3.75	2.25
(9)	Earl Harrist	7.50	3.75	2.25
(10)	Joe Haynes	7.50	3.75	2.25
(11)	Ralph Hodgin	7.50	3.75	2.25
(12)	Howie Judson	7.50	3.75	2.25
(13)	Bob Kennedy	7.50	3.75	2.25
(14)	Don Kolloway	7.50	3.75	2.25
(15)	Tony Lupien	7.50	3.75	2.25
(16)	Ted Lyons	15.00	7.50	4.50
(17)	Cass Michaels	7.50	3.75	2.25
(18)	Bing Miller	7.50	3.75	2.25
(19)	Buster Mills	7.50	3.75	2.25
(20)	Glen Moulder	7.50	3.75	2.25
(21)	Frank Papish	7.50	3.75	2.25
(22)	Ike Pearson	7.50	3.75	2.25
(23)	Dave Philley	7.50	3.75	2.25
(24)	Aaron Robinson	7.50	3.75	2.25
(25)	Mike Tresh	7.50	3.75	2.25
(26)	Jack Wallaesa	7.50	3.75	2.25
(27)	Ralph Weigel	7.50	3.75	2.25
(28)	Bill Wight	7.50	3.75	2.25
(29)	Taft Wright	7.50	3.75	2.25
(30)	Team Picture	18.00	9.00	5.50

1960-64 Chicago White Sox Ticket Stubs

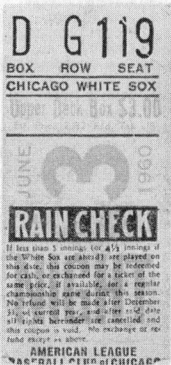

From 1960-64 tickets to White Sox home games at Comiskey Park were issued bearing player photos. Along with the photos on the backs of the 1-5/16" x 2-5/8" ticket stubs are career information and facsimile autographs. Photos were generally re-used from year to year and color variations, depending on the type of ticket, are known. Players from each year are listed here alphabetically.

		NM	EX	VG
Complete Set (113):		2,250	1,125	675.00
Common Player:		30.00	15.00	9.00
60-1	Luis Aparicio	75.00	37.00	22.00
60-2	Earl Battey	30.00	15.00	9.00
60-3	Frank Baumann	30.00	15.00	9.00
60-4	Dick Donovan	30.00	15.00	9.00
60-5	Nelson Fox	75.00	37.00	22.00
60-6	Gene Freese	30.00	15.00	9.00
60-7	Ted Kluszewski	60.00	30.00	18.00
60-8	Jim Landis	30.00	15.00	9.00
60-9	Barry Latman	30.00	15.00	9.00
60-10	Sherm Lollar	30.00	15.00	9.00
60-11	Al Lopez	45.00	22.00	13.50
60-12	Turk Lown	30.00	15.00	9.00
60-13	Orestes Minoso	50.00	25.00	15.00
60-14	Bill Pierce	30.00	15.00	9.00
60-15	Jim Rivera	30.00	15.00	9.00
60-16	Bob Shaw	30.00	15.00	9.00
60-17	Roy Sievers	30.00	15.00	9.00
60-18	Al Smith	30.00	15.00	9.00
60-19	Gerry Staley	30.00	15.00	9.00
60-20	Early Wynn	45.00	22.00	13.50
61-1	Luis Aparicio	75.00	37.00	22.00
61-2	Frank Baumann	30.00	15.00	9.00
61-3	Camilo Carreon	30.00	15.00	9.00
61-4	Sam Esposito	30.00	15.00	9.00
61-5	Nelson Fox	75.00	37.00	22.00
61-6	Billy Goodman	30.00	15.00	9.00
61-7	Jim Landis	30.00	15.00	9.00
61-8	Sherman Lollar	30.00	15.00	9.00
61-9	Al Lopez	45.00	22.00	13.50
61-10	J.C. Martin	30.00	15.00	9.00
61-11	Cal McLish	30.00	15.00	9.00
61-12	Orestes Minoso	50.00	25.00	15.00
61-13	Bill Pierce	30.00	15.00	9.00
61-14	Juan Pizarro	30.00	15.00	9.00
61-15	Bob Roselli	30.00	15.00	9.00
61-16	Herb Score	35.00	17.50	10.50
61-17	Bob Shaw	30.00	15.00	9.00
61-18	Roy Sievers	30.00	15.00	9.00
61-19	Al Smith	30.00	15.00	9.00
61-20	Gerry Staley	30.00	15.00	9.00
61-21	Early Wynn	45.00	22.00	13.50
62-1	Luis Aparicio	75.00	37.00	22.00
62-2	Frank Baumann	30.00	15.00	9.00
62-3	John Buzhardt	30.00	15.00	9.00
62-4	Camilo Carreon	30.00	15.00	9.00
62-5	Joe Cunningham	30.00	15.00	9.00
62-6	Bob Farley	30.00	15.00	9.00
62-7	Eddie Fisher	30.00	15.00	9.00
62-8	Nelson Fox	75.00	37.00	22.00
62-9	Jim Landis	30.00	15.00	9.00
62-10	Sherm Lollar	30.00	15.00	9.00
62-11	Al Lopez	45.00	22.00	13.50
62-12	Turk Lown	30.00	15.00	9.00
62-13	J.C. Martin	30.00	15.00	9.00
62-14	Cal McLish	30.00	15.00	9.00
62-15	Gary Peters	30.00	15.00	9.00
62-16	Juan Pizarro	30.00	15.00	9.00
62-17	Floyd Robinson	30.00	15.00	9.00
62-18	Bob Roselli	30.00	15.00	9.00
62-19	Herb Score	35.00	17.50	10.50
62-20	Al Smith	30.00	15.00	9.00
62-21	Charles Smith	30.00	15.00	9.00
62-22	Early Wynn	45.00	22.00	13.50
63-1	Frank Baumann	30.00	15.00	9.00
63-2	John Buzhardt	30.00	15.00	9.00
63-3	Camilo Carreon	30.00	15.00	9.00
63-4	Joe Cunningham	30.00	15.00	9.00
63-5	Dave DeBusschere	40.00	20.00	12.00
63-6	Eddie Fisher	30.00	15.00	9.00
63-7	Nelson Fox	75.00	37.00	22.00
63-8	Ron Hansen	30.00	15.00	9.00
63-9	Ray Herbert	30.00	15.00	9.00
63-10	Mike Hershberger	30.00	15.00	9.00
63-11	Joe Horlen	30.00	15.00	9.00
63-12	Grover Jones	30.00	15.00	9.00
63-13	Mike Joyce	30.00	15.00	9.00
63-14	Frank Kreutzer	30.00	15.00	9.00
63-15	Jim Landis	30.00	15.00	9.00
63-16	Sherman Lollar	30.00	15.00	9.00
63-17	Al Lopez	45.00	22.00	13.50
63-18	J.C. Martin	30.00	15.00	9.00
63-19	Charlie Maxwell	30.00	15.00	9.00
63-20	Dave Nicholson	30.00	15.00	9.00
63-21	Juan Pizarro	30.00	15.00	9.00
63-22	Floyd Robinson	30.00	15.00	9.00
63-23	Charley Smith	30.00	15.00	9.00
63-24	Pete Ward	30.00	15.00	9.00
63-25	Al Weis	30.00	15.00	9.00
63-26	Hoyt Wilhelm	45.00	22.00	13.50
63-27	Dom Zanni	30.00	15.00	9.00
64-1	Fritz Ackley	30.00	15.00	9.00
64-2	Frank Baumann	30.00	15.00	9.00
64-3	Don Buford	30.00	15.00	9.00
64-4	John Buzhardt	30.00	15.00	9.00
64-5	Camilo Carreon	30.00	15.00	9.00
64-6	Joe Cunningham	30.00	15.00	9.00
64-7	Dave DeBusschere	40.00	20.00	12.00
64-8	Eddie Fisher	30.00	15.00	9.00
64-9	Jim Golden	30.00	15.00	9.00
64-10	Ron Hansen	30.00	15.00	9.00
64-11	Ray Herbert	30.00	15.00	9.00
64-12	Mike Hershberger	30.00	15.00	9.00
64-13	Joe Horlen	30.00	15.00	9.00
64-14	Jim Landis	30.00	15.00	9.00
64-15	Al Lopez	45.00	22.00	13.50
64-16	J.C. Martin	30.00	15.00	9.00
64-17	Dave Nicholson	30.00	15.00	9.00
64-18	Gary Peters	30.00	15.00	9.00
64-19	Juan Pizarro	30.00	15.00	9.00
64-20	Floyd Robinson	30.00	15.00	9.00
64-21	Gene Stephens	30.00	15.00	9.00
64-22	Pete Ward	30.00	15.00	9.00
64-23	Al Weis	30.00	15.00	9.00
64-24	Hoyt Wilhelm	45.00	22.00	13.50

1899 Chickering Studio Boston Beaneaters Cabinets

These oversize (8-7/8" x 9-7/8") cabinet cards feature virtually every regular on the 1899 National League runners-up and this checklist may not be complete. The cards feature chest-up, capless sepia portraits of the players, glued to either black or gray cardboard mounts with the advertising of Boston's Elmer Chickering Studio in silver or gold leaf at bottom. Players are identified by first and last name in fancy black script at the bottom of the photo. Backs are blank.

		NM	EX	VG
Common Player:		3,000	650.00	425.00
(1)	Harvey Bailey	3,000	650.00	425.00
(2)	Martin Bergen	3,000	650.00	425.00
(3)	William Clarke	3,000	650.00	425.00
(4)	Jimmy Collins	7,500	2,700	1,725
(5)	Hugh Duffy	9,000	3,200	1,900
(6)	Billy Hamilton	7,500	3,000	1,800
(7)	Frank Killen	3,000	650.00	425.00
(8)	Ted Lewis	3,000	650.00	425.00
(9)	Herman Long	7,500	2,425	1,450
(10)	Bobby Lowe	3,000	1,125	675.00
(11)	Jouett Meekin	7,500	1,500	900.00
(12)	Charles Nichols	9,000	3,200	1,875
(13)	Fred Tenney	3,000	650.00	425.00

1956-1957 Chicle Peloteros

75.—Napoleón Reyes, Manager

One of the few gumcard issues from Cuba, this set took a cue from American companies by skip-numbering the set to keep youngsters buying gum in search of cards that did not exist. The cards measure about 2" x 3". Fronts feature color portrait photos bordered in white with the player name and card number in a colored strip below. Backs are in black-and-white with a few biographical notes and career highlights. The cards are printed on thick gray stock. A colorful album to house the cards was also produced.

		NM	EX	VG
Complete Set (40):		2,750	1,375	850.00
Common Player:		60.00	30.00	18.00
Album:		100.00	50.00	30.00
2	Emilio Cabrera	60.00	30.00	18.00
4	Conrado Marrero	100.00	50.00	30.00
5	Silvio Garcia	250.00	125.00	75.00
6	Russel (Russell) Nixon	75.00	37.50	22.50
7	Enrique Izquierdo	60.00	30.00	18.00
8	Lou Skinner	60.00	30.00	18.00
9	Robert Mc Kee	60.00	30.00	18.00
10	Gonzalo Naranjo	60.00	30.00	18.00
11	Trompoloco Rodriguez	60.00	30.00	18.00
12	Evelio Hernandez	60.00	30.00	18.00
26	Oscar Rodriguez	60.00	30.00	18.00
27	Jose (Cheo) Ramos	60.00	30.00	18.00
28	Napoleon Heredia	60.00	30.00	18.00
29	Camilo Pascual	150.00	75.00	45.00
30	Pedro Ramos	90.00	45.00	27.50
31	Rene Gutierrez	60.00	30.00	18.00
32	Julio (Jiqui) Moreno	65.00	32.50	20.00
33	Bud Daley	65.00	32.50	20.00
34	Dick Tomaneck (Tomanek)	60.00	30.00	18.00
35	Rafael Noble	65.00	32.50	20.00
50	Gilberto Torres	60.00	30.00	18.00
51	Salvador Hernandez	60.00	30.00	18.00
52	Pipo de la Noval	60.00	30.00	18.00
53	Juan Soler	60.00	30.00	18.00
54	Oscar Sierra	60.00	30.00	18.00
55	Billy Muffet (Muffett)	60.00	30.00	18.00
56	Robert Bluaylock (Blaylock)	60.00	30.00	18.00
57	Edwin Mayers	60.00	30.00	18.00
58	Vicente Amor	60.00	30.00	18.00
59	Raul Sanchez	60.00	30.00	18.00
75	Napoleon Reyes	90.00	45.00	27.50
76	Jose Maria Fernandez	90.00	45.00	27.50
77	Juan Izaguirre	60.00	30.00	18.00
79	Rene Friol	60.00	30.00	18.00
80	Asdrubal Baro	60.00	30.00	18.00
82	Juan Delis	60.00	30.00	18.00
83	Julio Becquer	60.00	30.00	18.00
84	Rodolfo Arias	60.00	30.00	18.00
86	Patricio Quintana	60.00	30.00	18.00
87	Aldo Salvent	60.00	30.00	18.00

1900 Chickering Studio Cabinets

The extent of this issue of standard-format (about 4-1/4" x 6-1/2") cabinets is unknown. Fronts have a studio pose with a decorative studio logo in the bottom border. Backs have a large ad for the renowned Boston photographer.

		NM	EX	VG
Common Player:				
(1)	Win Mercer	1,500	750.00	450.00
(2)	Kid Nichols	9,000	4,500	2,750

1977 Chilly Willee Discs

Virtually identical in format to the several locally sponsored disc sets of the previous year, these 3-3/8" diameter player discs were given away at participating frozen drink stands. Discs once again feature black-and-white player portrait photos in the center of a baseball design. The left and right panels are in one of several bright colors. Licensed by the Players Association through Mike Schechter Associates, the player photos carry no uniform logos. Backs are printed in blue and red. The unnumbered discs are checklisted here alphabetically.

		NM	EX	VG
Complete Set (70):		65.00	32.50	20.00
Common Player:		1.00	.50	.30
(1)	Sal Bando	1.00	.50	.30
(2)	Buddy Bell	1.00	.50	.30
(3)	Johnny Bench	5.00	2.50	1.50
(4)	Larry Bowa	1.00	.50	.30
(5)	Steve Braun	1.00	.50	.30
(6)	George Brett	12.00	6.00	3.50
(7)	Lou Brock	5.00	2.50	1.50
(8)	Jeff Burroughs	1.00	.50	.30
(9)	Bert Campaneris	1.00	.50	.30
(10)	John Candelaria	1.00	.50	.30
(11)	Jose Cardenal	1.00	.50	.30
(12)	Rod Carew	5.00	2.50	1.50
(13)	Steve Carlton	5.00	2.50	1.50
(14)	Dave Cash	1.00	.50	.30
(15)	Cesar Cedeno	1.00	.50	.30
(16)	Ron Cey	1.00	.50	.30
(17)	Dave Concepcion	1.00	.50	.30
(18)	Dennis Eckersley	5.00	2.50	1.50
(19)	Mark Fidrych	2.50	1.25	.70
(20)	Rollie Fingers	4.00	2.00	1.25
(21)	Carlton Fisk	5.00	2.50	1.50
(22)	George Foster	1.00	.50	.30
(23)	Wayne Garland	1.00	.50	.30
(24)	Ralph Garr	1.00	.50	.30
(25)	Steve Garvey	2.00	1.00	.60
(26)	Cesar Geronimo	1.00	.50	.30
(27)	Bobby Grich	1.00	.50	.30
(28)	Ken Griffey Sr.	1.00	.50	.30
(29)	Don Gullett	1.00	.50	.30
(30)	Mike Hargrove	1.00	.50	.30
(31)	Al Hrabosky	1.00	.50	.30
(32)	Catfish Hunter	4.00	2.00	1.25
(33)	Reggie Jackson	10.00	5.00	3.00

		NM	EX	VG
(34)	Randy Jones	1.00	.50	.30
(35)	Dave Kingman	1.00	.50	.30
(36)	Jerry Koosman	1.00	.50	.30
(37)	Dave LaRoche	1.00	.50	.30
(38)	Greg Luzinski	1.00	.50	.30
(39)	Fred Lynn	1.00	.50	.30
(40)	Bill Madlock	1.00	.50	.30
(41)	Rick Manning	1.00	.50	.30
(42)	Jon Matlock	1.00	.50	.30
(43)	John Mayberry	1.00	.50	.30
(44)	Hal McRae	1.00	.50	.30
(45)	Andy Messersmith	1.00	.50	.30
(46)	Rick Monday	1.00	.50	.30
(47)	John Montefusco	1.00	.50	.30
(48)	Joe Morgan	5.00	2.50	1.50
(49)	Thurman Munson	4.00	2.00	1.25
(50)	Bobby Murcer	1.00	.50	.30
(51)	Bill North	1.00	.50	.30
(52)	Jim Palmer	5.00	2.50	1.50
(53)	Tony Perez	5.00	2.50	1.50
(54)	Jerry Reuss	1.00	.50	.30
(55)	Brooks Robinson	5.00	2.50	1.50
(56)	Pete Rose	10.00	5.00	3.00
(57)	Joe Rudi	1.00	.50	.30
(58)	Nolan Ryan	20.00	10.00	6.00
(59)	Manny Sanguillen	1.00	.50	.30
(60)	Mike Schmidt	12.00	6.00	3.50
(61)	Tom Seaver	5.00	2.50	1.50
(62)	Bill Singer	1.00	.50	.30
(63)	Willie Stargell	5.00	2.50	1.50
(64)	Rusty Staub	1.50	.70	.45
(65)	Luis Tiant	1.00	.50	.30
(66)	Bob Watson	1.00	.50	.30
(67)	Butch Wynegar	1.00	.50	.30
(68)	Carl Yastrzemski	5.00	2.50	1.50
(69)	Robin Yount	5.00	2.50	1.50
(70)	Richie Zisk	1.00	.50	.30

1929 Churchman's Cigarettes

Though he is identified nowhere on this English cigarette card, the home run swing of Babe Ruth on the front is unmistakable. The last of a set of 25 "Sports & Games in Many Lands" series, the approximately 2-5/8" x 1-3/8" cards have color artwork on the front and green-and-white backs. The back of the baseball card provides a short history of "The great national sport of the U.S.A."

		NM	EX	VG
25	Baseball, U.S.A. (Babe Ruth)	350.00	175.00	100.00

1963 Cincinnati Enquirer Reds' Scrapbook

One of the city's newspapers carried this series that could be out of the newspaper and saved. The black-and-white clippings feature a player photo, stats, career notes and biographical data.

		NM	EX	VG
	Complete Set (33):	150.00	75.00	45.00
	Common Player:	3.00	1.50	.90
(1)	Don Blasingame	3.00	1.50	.90
(2)	Harry Bright	3.00	1.50	.90
(3)	Jim Brosnan	3.00	1.50	.90
(4)	Leo Cardenas	3.00	1.50	.90
(5)	Gerry Coleman	3.00	1.50	.90
(6)	John Edwards	3.00	1.50	.90
(7)	Sam Ellis	3.00	1.50	.90
(8)	Hank Foiles	3.00	1.50	.90
(9)	Gene Freese	3.00	1.50	.90
(10)	Jesse Gonder	3.00	1.50	.90
(11)	Tommy Harper	3.00	1.50	.90

		NM	EX	VG
(12)	Bill Henry	3.00	1.50	.90
(13)	Ken Hunt	3.00	1.50	.90
(14)	Fred Hutchinson	3.00	1.50	.90
(15)	Joey Jay	3.00	1.50	.90
(16)	Eddie Kasko	3.00	1.50	.90
(17)	Marty Keough	3.00	1.50	.90
(18)	Johnny Klippstein	3.00	1.50	.90
(19)	Jerry Lynch	3.00	1.50	.90
(20)	Jim Maloney	3.00	1.50	.90
(21)	Joe Nuxhall	4.50	2.25	1.25
(22)	Jim O'Toole	3.00	1.50	.90
(23)	Jim Owens	3.00	1.50	.90
(24)	Don Pavletich	3.00	1.50	.90
(25)	Vada Pinson	6.00	3.00	1.75
(26)	Wally Post	3.00	1.50	.90
(27)	Bob Purkey	3.00	1.50	.90
(28)	Frank Robinson	20.00	10.00	6.00
(29)	Pete Rose	90.00	45.00	27.00
(30)	Dave Sisler	3.00	1.50	.90
(31)	John Tsitouris	3.00	1.50	.90
(32)	Ken Walters	3.00	1.50	.90
(33)	Al Worthington	3.00	1.50	.90

1980 Cincinnati Enquirer Cincinnati Reds

This set of paper "cards" was printed within the pages of the Cincinnati Enquirer newspaper. The 2-1/4" x 3" cards are printed in black-and-white (both front and back) on newsprint. Dotted lines show where the cards were to be cut. Fronts have a player photo and a drawing of Riverfront Stadium. The team logo is in an upper corner and player identification in a black band towards the bottom. Backs have biographical and career details along with stats. Cards are checklisted here according to the uniform numbers printed on front.

		NM	EX	VG
	Complete Set (32):	100.00	50.00	30.00
	Common Player:	3.00	1.50	.90
2	Russ Nixon	3.00	1.50	.90
3	John McNamara	3.00	1.50	.90
4	Harry Dunlop	3.00	1.50	.90
5	Johnny Bench	9.00	4.50	2.75
6	Bill Fischer	3.00	1.50	.90
7	Hector Cruz	3.00	1.50	.90
9	Vic Correll	3.00	1.50	.90
11	Ron Plaza	3.00	1.50	.90
12	Harry Spilman	3.00	1.50	.90
13	Dave Concepcion	3.00	1.50	.90
15	George Foster	3.00	1.50	.90
16	Ron Oester	3.00	1.50	.90
19	Don Werner	3.00	1.50	.90
20	Cesar Geronimo	3.00	1.50	.90
22	Dan Driessen	3.00	1.50	.90
23	Rick Auerbach	3.00	1.50	.90
25	Ray Knight	3.00	1.50	.90
26	Junior Kennedy	3.00	1.50	.90
28	Sam Mejias	3.00	1.50	.90
29	Dave Collins	3.00	1.50	.90
30	Ken Griffey	3.00	1.50	.90
31	Paul Moskau	3.00	1.50	.90
34	Sheldon Burnside	3.00	1.50	.90
35	Frank Pastore	3.00	1.50	.90
36	Mario Soto	3.00	1.50	.90
37	Dave Tomlin	3.00	1.50	.90
40	Doug Bair	3.00	1.50	.90
41	Tom Seaver	7.50	3.75	2.25
42	Bill Bonham	3.00	1.50	.90
44	Charlie Leibrandt	3.00	1.50	.90
47	Tom Hume	3.00	1.50	.90
51	Mike LaCoss	3.00	1.50	.90

1938 Cincinnati Post Reds

Over the course of several weeks during the summer of 1938, daily editions of the Cincinnati Post sports section carried a set of player portraits designed to be cut out and saved. The pieces measure 6" x 11" and feature a large photo with facsimile autograph, topped by a headline and carrying a short biography below. Everything is in black-and-white. The unnumbered series is checklisted here in alphabetical order.

		NM	EX	VG
	Complete Set (25):	450.00	225.00	135.00
	Common Player:	20.00	10.00	6.00
(1)	Wally Berger	30.00	15.00	9.00
(2)	Joe Cascarella	20.00	10.00	6.00
(3)	Harry Craft	20.00	10.00	6.00
(4)	Dusty Cooke	20.00	10.00	6.00
(5)	Peaches Davis	20.00	10.00	6.00
(6)	Paul Derringer	25.00	12.50	7.50
(7)	Linus (Junior) Frey	20.00	10.00	6.00
(8)	Lee Gamble	20.00	10.00	6.00
(9)	Ival Goodman	20.00	10.00	6.00
(10)	Hank Gowdy	20.00	10.00	6.00
(11)	Lee Grissom	20.00	10.00	6.00
(12)	Willard Hershberger	25.00	12.50	7.50
(13)	Don Lang	20.00	10.00	6.00
(14)	Ernie Lombardi	35.00	17.50	10.50

		NM	EX	VG
(15)	Buck McCormick	20.00	10.00	6.00
(16)	Bill McKechnie	35.00	17.50	10.50
(17)	Whitey Moore	20.00	10.00	6.00
(18)	Billy Myers	20.00	10.00	6.00
(19)	Clifford Richardson	20.00	10.00	6.00
(20)	Lewis Riggs	20.00	10.00	6.00
(21)	Edd Roush	35.00	17.50	10.50
(22)	Gene Schott	20.00	10.00	6.00
(23)	Johnny Vander Meer	30.00	15.00	9.00
(24)	Bucky Walter	20.00	10.00	6.00
(25)	James Weaver	20.00	10.00	6.00

1919-20 Cincinnati Reds Postcards

Two versions of each of the cards in this issue are known. Picturing members of the 1919 World Champions, the foils of the Black Sox scandal, these 3-1/2" x 5-1/2" cards have black-and-white player poses on front. In the white border at bottom (or occasionally, at top) are two lines of type. The top line has the player name and position. The second line can be found in two versions. One reads, "Cincinnati 'Reds' - Champions of National League 1919," the other, presumably a second printing following the World Series, reads, "Cincinnati 'Reds' World's Champions 1919." Backs are printed with standard postcard indicia. Some cards have been found with the advertising of Mt. Union Dairy on the back. The unnumbered cards are checklisted here in alphabetical order.

		NM	EX	VG
	Complete Set (24):	3,000	1,500	900.00
	Common Player:	150.00	75.00	45.00
(1)	Nick Allen	150.00	75.00	45.00
(2)	Rube Bressler	150.00	75.00	45.00
(3)	Jake Daubert	150.00	75.00	45.00
(4)	Pat Duncan	150.00	75.00	45.00
(5)	Hod Eller	150.00	75.00	45.00
(6)	Ray Fisher	150.00	75.00	45.00
(7)	Eddie Gerner	150.00	75.00	45.00
(8)	Heinie Groh	150.00	75.00	45.00
(9)	Larry Kopf	150.00	75.00	45.00
(10)	Adolfo Luque	175.00	85.00	50.00
(11)	Sherwood Magee	150.00	75.00	45.00
(12)	Roy Mitchell	150.00	75.00	45.00
(13)	Pat Moran	150.00	75.00	45.00
(14)	Greasy Neale	200.00	100.00	60.00
(15)	Bill Rariden	150.00	75.00	45.00
(16)	Morris Rath	150.00	75.00	45.00
(17)	Walter Reuther (Ruether)	150.00	75.00	45.00
(18)	Jimmy Ring	150.00	75.00	45.00
(19)	Eddie Roush	400.00	200.00	120.00
(20)	Harry Sallee	150.00	75.00	45.00
(21)	Hank Schreiber	150.00	75.00	45.00
(22)	Charles See	150.00	75.00	45.00
(23)	Jimmy Smith	150.00	75.00	45.00
(24)	Ivy Wingo	150.00	75.00	45.00

1938 Cincinnati Reds Team Issue

This set of 2" x 3" cards were sold as a boxed set at the ballpark. Fronts feature a black-and-white photo of the player with his name and position in a red strip beneath the picture. Backs have the player's name, position and a generally flattering description of the player's talents. The cards are not numbered. In the American Card Catalog, this issue was designated W711-1.

		NM	EX	VG
	Complete Set (23):	1,000	500.00	300.00
	Common Player:	40.00	20.00	12.00
(1)	Wally Berger ("... in a trade with the Giants in June.")	40.00	20.00	12.00
(2)	Joe Cascarella	40.00	20.00	12.00
(3)	Allen "Dusty" Cooke	40.00	20.00	12.00
(4)	Harry Craft	40.00	20.00	12.00
(5)	Ray "Peaches" Davis	40.00	20.00	12.00
(6)	Paul Derringer ("Won 22 games...this season.")	40.00	20.00	12.00
(7)	Linus Frey ("... only 25 now.")	40.00	20.00	12.00
(8)	Lee Gamble ("... Syracuse last year.")	40.00	20.00	12.00
(9)	Ival Goodman (No mention of 30 homers.)	40.00	20.00	12.00
(10)	Harry "Hank" Gowdy	40.00	20.00	12.00
(11)	Lee Grissom (No mention of 1938.)	40.00	20.00	12.00
(12)	Willard Hershberger	100.00	50.00	30.00
(13)	Ernie Lombardi (No mention of 1938 MVP.)	225.00	110.00	67.00
(14)	Frank McCormick	40.00	20.00	12.00
(15)	Bill McKechnie ("Last year he led ...")	200.00	100.00	60.00
(16)	Lloyd "Whitey" Moore ("... last year with Syracuse.")	40.00	20.00	12.00
(17)	Billy Myers ("... in his fourth year.")	40.00	20.00	12.00

		NM	EX	VG
(18)	Lee Riggs ("... in his fourth season ...")	40.00	20.00	12.00
(19)	Eddie Roush	200.00	100.00	60.00
(20)	Gene Schott	40.00	20.00	12.00
(21)	Johnny Vander Meer (Portrait)	75.00	37.00	22.00
(22)	Wm. "Bucky" Walter ("... won 14 games ...")	40.00	20.00	12.00
(23)	Jim Weaver	40.00	20.00	12.00

1939 Cincinnati Reds Team Issue

PAUL DERRINGER
Pitcher

This big Kentuckian has been one of the National League's greatest hurlers since he came up with the St. Louis Cardinals in 1931. He was the league's leading hurler as a rookie and started the first game of the 1931 World Series. Came to the Reds in 1933. Won 22 games for the Reds in 1935 and 21 last year.

An updating by one season of the team-issued 1938 W711-1 set, most of the players and poses on the 2" x 3" cards remained the same. A close study of the career summary on the card's back is necessary to determine which year of issue is at hand. The Livengood card is believed to have been withdrawn from distribution early and is scarce.

		NM	EX	VG
	Complete Set (27):	1,250	625.00	375.00
	Common Player:	40.00	20.00	12.00
(1)	Wally Berger ("... in a trade with the Giants in June, 1938.")	40.00	20.00	12.00
(2)	Nino Bongiovanni	40.00	20.00	12.00
(3)	Stanley "Frenchy" Bordagaray	40.00	20.00	12.00
(4)	Harry Craft	40.00	20.00	12.00
(5)	Ray "Peaches" Davis	40.00	20.00	12.00
(6)	Paul Derringer ("Won 21 games ... last year.")	45.00	22.00	13.50
(7)	Linus Frey ("... only 26 now.")	40.00	20.00	12.00
(8)	Lee Gamble ("... Syracuse in 1937.")	40.00	20.00	12.00
(9)	Ival Goodman (Mentions hitting 30 homers.)	40.00	20.00	12.00
(10)	Harry "Hank" Gowdy	40.00	20.00	12.00
(11)	Lee Grissom (Mentions 1938.)	40.00	20.00	12.00
(12)	Willard Hershberger	100.00	50.00	30.00
(13)	Eddie Joost	40.00	20.00	12.00
(14)	Wes Livengood	250.00	125.00	75.00
(15)	Ernie Lombardi (Mentions MVP of 1938.)	225.00	110.00	67.00
(16)	Frank McCormick	40.00	20.00	12.00
(17)	Bill McKechnie ("In 1937 he led ...")	200.00	100.00	60.00
(18)	Lloyd "Whitey" Moore ("... in 1937 with Syracuse.")	40.00	20.00	12.00
(19)	Billy Myers ("... in his fifth year ...")	40.00	20.00	12.00
(20)	Lee Riggs ("... in his fifth season...")	40.00	20.00	12.00
(21)	Les Scarsella	40.00	20.00	12.00
(22)	Eugene "Junior" Thompson	40.00	20.00	12.00
(23)	Johnny Vander Meer/Pitching	50.00	25.00	15.00
(24)	Wm. "Bucky" Walters ("Won 15 games ...")	40.00	20.00	12.00
(25)	Jim Weaver	40.00	20.00	12.00
(26)	Bill Werber	40.00	20.00	12.00
(27)	Jimmy Wilson	40.00	20.00	12.00

1940 Cincinnati Reds Team Issue

JOHN HUTCHINGS
Pitcher

Born: April 14, 1916, Sherman, Texas.
Height: 6 feet 2 inches.
Weight: 200 lbs.
Bats: Both right and lefthanded.
Throws: Righthanded.
Professional Start: With Peoria in 1935, winning 13 and losing 17 games for a percentage of .433.

FIVE YEAR RECORD

Year	Team	Won	Lost	Pct.
1935	Peoria	13	17	.433
1936	Portsmouth	13	9	.591
1937	Birmingham	6	5	.546
1938	Pensacola	18	6	.750
1939	Pensacola	22	10	.688

Another early Reds team issue, this set of black-and-white 2-1/8" x 2-5/8" cards is unnumbered and features player portrait photos on the front. Name, position, biographical information and five years' worth of stats are on the back. The Reds were World Champions in 1940 (defeating Detroit), and the set features several special World Series cards, making it one of the first to feature events as well as individuals. The set was listed in the American Card Catalog as W711-2. The existence of card #35 is now questioned."

		NM	EX	VG
	Complete Set (32):	900.00	450.00	275.00
	Common Player:	25.00	12.50	7.50
(1)	Morris Arnovich	25.00	12.50	7.50
(2)	William (Bill) Baker	25.00	12.50	7.50
(3)	Joseph Beggs	25.00	12.50	7.50
(4)	Harry Craft	25.00	12.50	7.50
(5)	Paul Derringer	25.00	12.50	7.50
(6)	Linus Frey	25.00	12.50	7.50
(7)	Ival Goodman	25.00	12.50	7.50
(8)	Harry (Hank) Gowdy	25.00	12.50	7.50
(9)	Witt Guise	25.00	12.50	7.50
(10)	Harry (Socko) Hartman	25.00	12.50	7.50
(11)	Willard Hershberger	35.00	17.50	10.50
(12)	John Hutchings	25.00	12.50	7.50
(13)	Edwin Joost	25.00	12.50	7.50
(14)	Ernie Lombardi	60.00	30.00	18.00
(15)	Frank McCormick	25.00	12.50	7.50
(16)	Myron McCormick	25.00	12.50	7.50
(17)	William Boyd McKechnie	60.00	30.00	18.00
(18)	Lloyd (Whitey) Moore	25.00	12.50	7.50
(19)	William (Bill) Myers	25.00	12.50	7.50
(20)	Lewis Riggs	25.00	12.50	7.50
(21)	Elmer Riddle	25.00	12.50	7.50
(22)	James A. Ripple	25.00	12.50	7.50
(23)	Milburn Shoffner	25.00	12.50	7.50
(24)	Eugene Thompson	25.00	12.50	7.50
(25)	James Turner	25.00	12.50	7.50
(26)	John Vander Meer	30.00	15.00	9.00
(27)	Wm. (Bucky) Walters	25.00	12.50	7.50
(28)	William (Bill) Werber	25.00	12.50	7.50
(29)	James Wilson	25.00	12.50	7.50
(30a)	The Cincinnati Reds	25.00	12.50	7.50
(30b)	The Cincinnati Reds/World's Champions	25.00	12.50	7.50
(31a)	Tell the World About the Cincinnati Reds	25.00	12.50	7.50
(31b)	Tell the World About the Cincinnati Reds/World's Champions	25.00	12.50	7.50
(32)	Results 1940 World's Series	25.00	12.50	7.50

1954-1955 Cincinnati Reds Postcards

The first team-issued Redlegs postcards of the modern era were produced during the 1954 and 1955 seasons for use by players in answering fan requests for pictures and autographs. The cards are 3-1/2" x 5-5/8", printed in black-and-white on non-glossy cardboard stock. Fronts have poses which are borderless at top and sides. At bottom is a 3/4" white strip which is either blank or which has the player and team name printed. Many cards are found with stamped facsimile autographs, and/or authentically signed. Backs have a vertical line at center. At top-left is: "Cincinnati Baseball Club / Crosley Field / Cincinnati, Ohio." While there is no stamp box on the back, many of the cards have been postally used. The issue was listed in the "American Card Catalog" as PC746.

		NM	EX	VG
	Common Player:	15.00	7.50	4.50
(1)	Bobby Adams/Fldg	15.00	7.50	4.50
(2)	Bobby Adams (Portrait to neck.)	15.00	7.50	4.50
(3)	Dr. Wayne Anderson/Trainer (Chest-up.)	30.00	15.00	9.00
(4)	Fred Baczewski (Ready to pitch.)	15.00	7.50	4.50
(5)	Ed Bailey (Batting to waist.)	15.00	7.50	4.50
(6)	Dick Bartell (Portrait to neck.)	15.00	7.50	4.50
(7)	Dick Bartell (Portrait to shoulders.)	15.00	7.50	4.50
(8)	Matt Batts (Batting follow-through.)	15.00	7.50	4.50
(9)	Gus Bell (Portrait to neck.)	15.00	7.50	4.50
(10)	Gus Bell (Waist up, ready to hit.)	15.00	7.50	4.50
(11)	Joe Black (Standing in dugout.)	15.00	7.50	4.50
(12)	Bob Borkowski (Batting follow-through.)	15.00	7.50	4.50
(13)	Buzz Boyle (Scout) (Chest-up in suit.)	40.00	20.00	12.00
(14)	Rocky Bridges (Portrait to neck.)	15.00	7.50	4.50
(15)	Smoky Burgess (Portrait to neck.)	15.00	7.50	4.50
(16)	Jackie Collum (Pitching follow-through.)	15.00	7.50	4.50
(17)	Jackie Collum (Portrait to neck.)	15.00	7.50	4.50
(18)	Powell Crosley, Jr. (Portrait)(President)	15.00	7.50	4.50
(19)	Jimmy Dykes (Standing in dugout.)	15.00	7.50	4.50
(20)	Nino Escalera (Portrait to neck.)	15.00	7.50	4.50
(21)	Tom Ferrick (Portrait to neck.)	15.00	7.50	4.50
(22)	Art Fowler (Hands over head.)	15.00	7.50	4.50
(23)	Art Fowler (Portrait to neck.)	15.00	7.50	4.50
(24)	Hershell Freeman (Portrait to shoulders.)	15.00	7.50	4.50
(26)	Jim Greengrass/Btg (Waist-up.)	15.00	7.50	4.50
(27)	Don Gross (Portrait to neck.)	15.00	7.50	4.50
(28)	Charley Harmon (Batting to belt.)	15.00	7.50	4.50
(29)	Ray Jablonski (Batting to belt.)	15.00	7.50	4.50
(30)	Howie Judson (Portrait to neck.)	15.00	7.50	4.50
(31)	Johnny Klippstein (Pitching follow-through.)	15.00	7.50	4.50
(32)	Ted Kluszewski (Batting, cut out sleeves.)	30.00	15.00	9.00
(33)	Ted Kluszewski (Batting to belt.)	30.00	15.00	9.00
(34)	Ted Kluszewski (Batting follow-through, full length.)	30.00	15.00	9.00
(35)	Ted Kluszewski (Batting follow-through to waist.)	30.00	15.00	9.00
(36)	Ted Kluszewski (Batting follow-through, #18 on back.)	30.00	15.00	9.00
(37)	Ted Kluszewski (Stretching at 1B.)	30.00	15.00	9.00
(38)	Ted Kluszewski (Standing w/ four bats.)	30.00	15.00	9.00
(39)	Ted Kluszewski (Portrait to neck, looking right.)	30.00	15.00	9.00
(40)	Ted Kluszewski (Portrait to shoulders, leaning right.)	30.00	15.00	9.00
(41)	Hobie Landrith/Catching	15.00	7.50	4.50
(42)	Hobie Landrith (Pose to neck.)	15.00	7.50	4.50
(43)	William McKechnie, Jr./Portrait (Farm club supervisor.)	15.00	7.50	4.50
(44)	Roy McMillan (Portrait to neck.)	15.00	7.50	4.50
(45)	Roy McMillan (Ready to hit.)	15.00	7.50	4.50
(46)	Lloyd Merriman (Ready to hit.)	15.00	7.50	4.50
(47)	Rudy Minarcin (Portrait to neck.)	15.00	7.50	4.50
(48)	Rudy Minarcin (Portrait to shoulders, chain.)	15.00	7.50	4.50
(49)	Joe Nuxhall (Portrait to neck.)	15.00	7.50	4.50
(51)	Joe Nuxhall (Pitching follow-through.)	15.00	7.50	4.50
(52)	Stan Palys (Batting follow-through.)	15.00	7.50	4.50
(53)	Harry Perkowski (Portrait to neck.)	15.00	7.50	4.50
(54)	Bud Podbielan (Ready to pitch, belt visible.)	15.00	7.50	4.50
(55)	Bud Podbielan (Ready to pitch, no belt.)	15.00	7.50	4.50
(56)	Wally Post (Ready to hit to belt, fans in back.)	22.50	11.00	6.75
(57)	Wally Post (Ready to hit to hips.)	22.50	11.00	6.75
(58)	Wally Post (Batting follow-through, pole on left.)	22.50	11.00	6.75
(59)	Wally Post (Batting follow-through, no pole.)	22.50	11.00	6.75
(60)	Wally Post (Portrait to neck.)	22.50	11.00	6.75
(61)	Ken Raffensberger (Pitching wind-up.)	15.00	7.50	4.50
(62)	Steve Ridzik (Portrait to neck.)	15.00	7.50	4.50
(63)	Connie Ryan (Portrait to neck.)	15.00	7.50	4.50
(64)	Moe Savransky (Portrait to neck.)	15.00	7.50	4.50
(65)	Andy Seminick (Batting follow-through.)	15.00	7.50	4.50
(66)	Al Silvera (Portrait to shoulders.)	15.00	7.50	4.50
(67)	Frank Smith (Ready to pitch.)	15.00	7.50	4.50
(68)	Milt Smith (Portrait to shoulders.)	15.00	7.50	4.50
(69)	Gerry Staley (Ready to pitch.)	15.00	7.50	4.50
(70)	Birdie Tebbetts (Portrait to neck.)	15.00	7.50	4.50
(71)	Birdie Tebbetts (Portrait to shoulders.)	15.00	7.50	4.50
(72)	Johnny Temple (Portrait to neck, mouth closed.)	15.00	7.50	4.50
(73)	Johnny Temple (Portrait to neck, mouth open.)	15.00	7.50	4.50
(74)	Bob Thurman (Batting follow-through.)	15.00	7.50	4.50
(76)	Corky Valentine (Pitching follow-through.)	15.00	7.50	4.50
(77)	Herm Wehmeier (Portrait to neck.)	15.00	7.50	4.50
(78)	George Zuverink (Portrait to neck.)	15.00	7.50	4.50
(79)	Crosley Field	15.00	7.50	4.50

1956 Cincinnati Reds Postcards

TOM ACKER
Cincinnati Redlegs

After a number of years issuing printed postcards for players to answer fan mail, the team began a three-year run of glossy black-and-white photographic card sets in 1956.

About 3-1/2" x 5-3/4", the cards usually feature portrait photos, though some action poses are also seen. The pictures are bordered in white with a 1" or so border at bottom with the player and team names. Differentiating the 1956s from similarly formatted issues in 1957-1958 is best done on back. The 1956 cards are divided-back with "Post Card" at top. At right, in the stamp box, is "Place Postage Stamp Here" and, at bottom, "This space for address." Cards are numbered here alphabetically, with gaps left in the assigned numbering for future additions.

		NM	EX	VG
Complete Set (31):		350.00	175.00	105.00
Common Player:		10.00	5.00	3.00
(1)	Tom Acker	10.00	5.00	3.00
(2)	Ed Bailey	10.00	5.00	3.00
(3)	Gus Bell	10.00	5.00	3.00
(4)	Joe Black	10.00	5.00	3.00
(5)	"Rocky" Bridges	10.00	5.00	3.00
(6)	"Smoky" Burgess	12.50	6.25	3.75
(7)	George Crowe	10.00	5.00	3.00
(8)	Jim Dyck	10.00	5.00	3.00
(9)	Jimmy Dykes	10.00	5.00	3.00
(11)	Bruce Edwards (Non-'56 back.)	10.00	5.00	3.00
(12)	Tom Ferrick	10.00	5.00	3.00
(13)	Joe Frazier	10.00	5.00	3.00
(14)	Hersh Freeman	10.00	5.00	3.00
(15)	Alex Grammas	10.00	5.00	3.00
(16)	Don Gross	10.00	5.00	3.00
(17)	Ray Jablonski	10.00	5.00	3.00
(18)	Larry Jansen	10.00	5.00	3.00
(19)	Hal Jeffcoat	10.00	5.00	3.00
(21)	Johnny Klippstein	10.00	5.00	3.00
(22)	Ted Kluszewski	20.00	10.00	6.00
(23)	Brooks Lawrence	10.00	5.00	3.00
(24)	Frank McCormick	10.00	5.00	3.00
(25)	Roy McMillan	10.00	5.00	3.00
(26)	Joe Nuxhall	12.50	6.25	3.75
(27)	Stan Palys ('56 back)	10.00	5.00	3.00
(28)	Stan Palys (Non-'56 back.)	10.00	5.00	3.00
(29)	Wally Post	10.00	5.00	3.00
(31)	Frank Robinson	75.00	37.00	22.00
(32)	"Birdie" Tebbetts	10.00	5.00	3.00
(33)	Johnny Temple	10.00	5.00	3.00
(34)	Bob Thurman	10.00	5.00	3.00

1957 Cincinnati Reds Picture Pack

FRANK ROBINSON, Redlegs

Similar in format to the Jay Publishing photo packs, this appears to be a team-issued souvenir item, with many of the pictures having been seen in other team-related contexts. The black-and-white, blank-backed pictures measure 5" x 7". They can be differentiated from contemporary Jay packs by the fact that only the team nickname, "Redlegs," appears, rather than city and team. Player names are in all-caps.

		NM	EX	VG
Complete Set (12):		45.00	22.50	13.50
Common Player:		4.00	2.00	1.25
(1)	Ed Bailey	4.00	2.00	1.25
(2)	Gus Bell	4.00	2.00	1.25
(3)	Smoky Burgess	4.00	2.00	1.25
(4)	Hersh Freeman	4.00	2.00	1.25
(5)	Ted Kluszewski	7.50	3.75	2.25
(6)	Brooks Lawrence	4.00	2.00	1.25
(7)	Roy McMillan	4.00	2.00	1.25
(8)	Joe Nuxhall	4.00	2.00	1.25
(9)	Wally Post	4.00	2.00	1.25
(10)	Frank Robinson	15.00	7.50	4.50
(11)	Birdie Tebbetts	4.00	2.00	1.25
(12)	Johnny Temple	4.00	2.00	1.25

1957 Cincinnati Reds Postcards

JOHNNY KLIPPSTEIN
Cincinnati Redlegs

The second in a long run of glossy-front, black-and-white annual postcard issues, the 1957 can be distinguished from the 1956 and 1958 cards by the appearance of players in sleeveless uniforms with dark undershirts. Even more distinguishing is that the 1957s, on back, have "PHOTO POST CARD" across the top, and lack the notice "This Space for Address" which appeared on the 1956 cards. The '57s can also be identified by "Divolite Peerless" which appears in the postage-stamp box. The 3-1/2" x 5-3/4" cards have white borders. At bottom is 1" white space with the player name and "Cincinnati Redlegs" and space for an autograph. The unnumbered cards are checklisted here in alphabetical order.

		NM	EX	VG
Complete Set (34):		300.00	150.00	90.00
Common Player:		9.00	4.50	2.75
(1)	Tom Acker	9.00	4.50	2.75
(2)	Ed Bailey	9.00	4.50	2.75
(3)	Gus Bell	9.00	4.50	2.75
(4)	"Rocky" Bridges	9.00	4.50	2.75
(5)	"Smoky" Burgess	11.00	5.50	3.25
(6)	George Crowe	9.00	4.50	2.75
(7)	Bobby Durnbaugh	9.00	4.50	2.75
(8)	Jimmy Dykes	9.00	4.50	2.75
(9)	Tom Ferrick	9.00	4.50	2.75
(10)	Art Fowler	9.00	4.50	2.75
(11)	Hersh Freeman	9.00	4.50	2.75
(12)	Alex Grammas	9.00	4.50	2.75
(13)	Don Gross	9.00	4.50	2.75
(14)	Warren Hacker	9.00	4.50	2.75
(15)	Bobby Henrich	9.00	4.50	2.75
(16)	Don Hoak	11.00	5.50	3.25
(17)	Hal Jeffcoat	9.00	4.50	2.75
(18)	Johnny Klippstein	9.00	4.50	2.75
(19)	Ted Kluszewski/Btg	18.00	9.00	5.50
(20)	Ted Kluszewski/Portrait	18.00	9.00	5.50
(21)	Brooks Lawrence	9.00	4.50	2.75
(22)	Jerry Lynch	9.00	4.50	2.75
(23)	Frank McCormick	9.00	4.50	2.75
(24)	Roy McMillan	9.00	4.50	2.75
(25)	Joe Nuxhall	9.00	4.50	2.75
(26)	Wally Post	9.00	4.50	2.75
(27)	Frank Robinson	45.00	22.00	13.50
(28)	Raul Sanchez	9.00	4.50	2.75
(29)	Art Schult	9.00	4.50	2.75
(30)	"Birdie" Tebbetts	9.00	4.50	2.75
(31)	Johnny Temple	9.00	4.50	2.75
(32)	Bob Thurman	9.00	4.50	2.75
(33)	Pete Whisenant/Btg	9.00	4.50	2.75
(34)	Pete Whisenant/Portrait	9.00	4.50	2.75

1958 Cincinnati Reds Postcards

WALT DROPO
Cincinnati Redlegs

Cards from the third of a long run of glossy-front, black-and-white annual postcard issues can be most often distinguished from similarly formatted 1956-57 cards by the appearance of players in white uniforms with white caps. Two back styles are known. One, like the 1957 issue, has a postage box with "Divolite Peerless" inside and one without the box, but with "Post Card" and "Actual Photograph." Both have a vertical dividing line. The 3-1/2" x 5-3/4" cards have white borders. At bottom is 1" white space with the player name and "Cincinnati Redlegs" and space for an autograph. The unnumbered cards are checklisted here in alphabetical order, though this list may not be complete as several stars are unknown in this style.

		NM	EX	VG
Complete Set (30):		300.00	150.00	90.00
Common Player:		9.00	4.50	2.75
(1)	Tom Acker	9.00	4.50	2.75
(2)	Dr. Wayne Anderson/Trainer	9.00	4.50	2.75
(3)	Ed Bailey	9.00	4.50	2.75
(4)	Steve Bilko	9.00	4.50	2.75
(5)	"Smoky" Burgess	11.00	5.50	3.25
(6)	George Crowe	9.00	4.50	2.75
(7)	Walt Dropo	9.00	4.50	2.75
(8)	Jimmie Dykes	9.00	4.50	2.75
(9)	Tom Ferrick	9.00	4.50	2.75
(10)	Dee Fondy	9.00	4.50	2.75
(11)	Alex Grammas	9.00	4.50	2.75
(12)	Harvey Haddix	9.00	4.50	2.75
(13)	Hal Jeffcoat	9.00	4.50	2.75
(14)	Alex Kellner	9.00	4.50	2.75
(15)	Johnny Klippstein	9.00	4.50	2.75
(16)	Turk Lown	9.00	4.50	2.75
(17)	Jerry Lynch	9.00	4.50	2.75
(18)	Roy McMillan	9.00	4.50	2.75
(19)	Ed Miksis (Pinstripes)	9.00	4.50	2.75
(20)	Joe Nuxhall	10.00	5.00	3.00
(21)	Vada Pinson	15.00	7.50	4.50
(22)	Bob Purkey	9.00	4.50	2.75
(23)	Charley Rabe	9.00	4.50	2.75
(24)	John Riddle	9.00	4.50	2.75
(25)	Willard Schmidt	9.00	4.50	2.75

		NM	EX	VG
(26)	Manager "Birdie" Tebbetts (Portrait to neck.)	9.00	4.50	2.75
(27)	Manager "Birdie" Tebbetts (Portrait, white background, #1 shows.)	9.00	4.50	2.75
(28)	Johnny Temple	9.00	4.50	2.75
(29)	Bob Thurman	9.00	4.50	2.75
(30)	Pete Whisenant	9.00	4.50	2.75

1964 Cincinnati Enquirer Reds Scrapbook

Designed to look like a 5" x 7" pages torn from a notebook, this series was printed in the pages of one of Cincinnati's daily newspapers between March 12-April 10. The black-and-white pieces have a player photo, personal data, lifetime stats and a career summary. The scrapbook features are listed here in alphabetical order.

		NM	EX	VG
Complete Set (30):		200.00	100.00	60.00
Common Player:		6.00	3.00	1.80
(1)	Steve Boros	6.00	3.00	1.80
(2)	Leo Cardenas	6.00	3.00	1.80
(3)	Gordy Coleman	6.00	3.00	1.80
(4)	Lincoln Curtis	6.00	3.00	1.80
(5)	Jim Dickson	6.00	3.00	1.80
(6)	John Edwards	6.00	3.00	1.80
(7)	Sam Ellis	6.00	3.00	1.80
(8)	Tom Harper	6.00	3.00	1.80
(9)	Bill Henry	6.00	3.00	1.80
(10)	Fred Hutchinson	6.00	3.00	1.80
(11)	Joey Jay	6.00	3.00	1.80
(12)	Deron Johnson	6.00	3.00	1.80
(13)	Marty Keough	6.00	3.00	1.80
(14)	Bobby Klaus	6.00	3.00	1.80
(15)	Jim Maloney	6.00	3.00	1.80
(16)	Bill McCool	6.00	3.00	1.80
(17)	Charley Neal	6.00	3.00	1.80
(18)	Chet Nichols	6.00	3.00	1.80
(19)	Joe Nuxhall	6.00	3.00	1.80
(20)	Jim O'Toole	6.00	3.00	1.80
(21)	Vada Pinson	15.00	7.50	4.50
(22)	Bob Purkey	6.00	3.00	1.80
(23)	Mel Queen	6.00	3.00	1.80
(24)	Frank Robinson	30.00	15.00	9.00
(25)	Pete Rose	50.00	25.00	15.00
(26)	Chico Ruiz	6.00	3.00	1.80
(27)	Bob Skinner	6.00	3.00	1.80
(28)	Hal Smith	6.00	3.00	1.80
(29)	John Tsitouris	6.00	3.00	1.80
(30)	Al Worthington	6.00	3.00	1.80

1966 Cincinnati Enquirer Reds Scrapbook

This series of 5" x 7" cut-out features was printed in the pages of one of Cincinnati's daily newspapers between March 6-April 4. The black-and-white pieces have a player photo, personal data, lifetime stats and a career summary. The scrapbook features are listed here in alphabetical order.

		NM	EX	VG
Complete Set (29):		200.00	100.00	60.00
Common Player:		6.00	3.00	1.80
(1)	Jack Baldshun	6.00	3.00	1.80
(2)	Leo Cardenas	6.00	3.00	1.80
(3)	Gordy Coleman	6.00	3.00	1.80
(4)	Jim Coker	6.00	3.00	1.80
(5)	Roger Craig	6.00	3.00	1.80
(6)	Teddy Davidson	6.00	3.00	1.80
(7)	John Edwards	6.00	3.00	1.80
(8)	Sam Ellis	6.00	3.00	1.80
(9)	Tom Harper	6.00	3.00	1.80
(10)	Don Heffner	6.00	3.00	1.80
(11)	Tommy Helms	6.00	3.00	1.80
(12)	Joey Jay	6.00	3.00	1.80
(13)	Deron Johnson	6.00	3.00	1.80
(14)	Marty Keough	6.00	3.00	1.80
(15)	Jim Maloney	6.00	3.00	1.80
(16)	Lee May	6.00	3.00	1.80
(17)	Bill McCool	6.00	3.00	1.80
(18)	Joe Nuxhall	6.00	3.00	1.80
(19)	Jim O'Toole	6.00	3.00	1.80
(20)	Milt Pappas	6.00	3.00	1.80
(21)	Don Pavletich	6.00	3.00	1.80
(22)	Tony Perez	20.00	10.00	6.00
(23)	Vada Pinson	15.00	7.50	4.50
(24)	Mel Queen	6.00	3.00	1.80
(25)	Pete Rose	50.00	25.00	15.00
(26)	Chico Ruiz	6.00	3.00	1.80
(27)	Art Shamsky	6.00	3.00	1.80
(28)	Richard Simpson	6.00	3.00	1.80
(29)	John Tsitouris	6.00	3.00	1.80

1966 Cincinnati Reds Postcards

This set of black-and-white postcards is in the standard 3-1/2" x 5-1/2" size with glossy fronts and typical postcard indicia on the back. Player photos are mostly posed action shots with white border around. The player name is printed in all caps in the wide white bottom border, with "Cincinnati Reds" below the name. The set was issued in a manila envelope with Reds logo and the team address. The unnumbered postcards are listed here in alphabetical order.

		NM	EX	VG
Complete Set (30):		375.00	190.00	115.00
Common Player:		12.00	6.00	3.50
(1)	Jack Baldshun	12.00	6.00	3.50
(2)	Dave Bristol	12.00	6.00	3.50
(3)	Leo Cardenas	12.00	6.00	3.50
(4)	Jim Coker	12.00	6.00	3.50
(5)	Ted Davidson	12.00	6.00	3.50
(6)	John Edwards	12.00	6.00	3.50
(7)	Sam Ellis	12.00	6.00	3.50
(8)	Mel Harder	12.00	6.00	3.50
(9)	Tommy Harper	12.00	6.00	3.50
(10)	Don Heffner	12.00	6.00	3.50
(11)	Tommy Helms	12.00	6.00	3.50

		NM	EX	VG
(12)	Joey Jay	12.00	6.00	3.50
(13)	Deron Johnson	12.00	6.00	3.50
(14)	Jim Maloney	12.00	6.00	3.50
(15)	Billy McCool	12.00	6.00	3.50
(16)	Don Nottebart	12.00	6.00	3.50
(17)	Joe Nuxhall	12.00	6.00	3.50
(18)	Jim O'Toole	12.00	6.00	3.50
(19)	Milt Pappas	12.00	6.00	3.50
(20)	Don Pavletich	12.00	6.00	3.50
(21)	Tony Perez	25.00	12.50	7.50
(22)	Vada Pinson	18.00	9.00	6.00
(23)	Mel Queen	12.00	6.00	3.50
(24)	Pete Rose	60.00	30.00	18.00
(25)	Chico Ruiz	12.00	6.00	3.50
(26)	Art Shamsky	12.00	6.00	3.50
(27)	Ray Shore	12.00	6.00	3.50
(28)	Roy Sievers	12.00	6.00	3.50
(29)	Dick Simpson	12.00	6.00	3.50
(30)	Whitey Wietelman	12.00	6.00	3.50

1969 Citgo Coins

This 20-player set of small (about 1" in diameter) metal coins was issued by Citgo in 1969 to commemorate professional baseball's 100th anniversary. The brass-coated coins, susceptible to oxidation, display the player in a crude portrait with his name across the top. The backs honor the 100th anniversary of pro ball. The coins are unnumbered but are generally checklisted according to numbers that appear on a red, white and blue paper display folder that was available from Citgo by mail.

		NM	EX	VG
	Complete Set (20):	80.00	40.00	25.00
	Common Player:	2.00	1.00	.60
	Cardboard Display Folder:	30.00	15.00	9.00
	Unopened Pack:	12.00	.00	.00
1	Denny McLain	2.50	1.25	.70
2	Dave McNally	2.00	1.00	.60
3	Jim Lonborg	2.00	1.00	.60
4	Harmon Killebrew	6.50	3.25	2.00
5	Mel Stottlemyre	2.00	1.00	.60
6	Willie Horton	2.00	1.00	.60
7	Jim Fregosi	2.00	1.00	.60
8	Rico Petrocelli	2.00	1.00	.60
9	Stan Bahnsen	2.00	1.00	.60
10	Frank Howard	2.50	1.25	.70
11	Joe Torre	2.50	1.25	.70
12	Jerry Koosman	2.00	1.00	.60
13	Ron Santo	3.50	1.75	1.00
14	Pete Rose	20.00	10.00	6.00
15	Rusty Staub	2.00	1.00	.60
16	Henry Aaron	20.00	10.00	6.00
17	Richie Allen	3.50	1.75	1.00
18	Ron Swoboda	2.00	1.00	.60
19	Willie McCovey	6.50	3.25	2.00
20	Jim Bunning	5.00	2.50	1.50

1969 Citgo New York Mets

One of several regional issues in the Mets World Championship season of 1969, this set of 8" x 10" player portraits was sponsored by Citgo, whose gas stations distributed the pictures with fuel purchases. Fronts feature large portraits and smaller action pictures of the player, done in pastels, set against a bright pastel background. The paintings are the work of noted celebrity artist John Wheeldon. Beneath the pictures is a facsimile autograph. The player's name is printed in the bottom border. Backs are printed in black-and-white and include biography and career details, full major and minor league stats and a self-portrait and biography of the artist. Logos of the Mets, the Players Association and the sponsor complete the back design. The unnumbered player pictures are checklisted here in alphabetical order.

		NM	EX	VG
	Complete Set (8):	65.00	32.00	19.50
	Common Player:	6.50	3.25	2.00
(1)	Tommie Agee	8.00	4.00	2.50
(2)	Ken Boswell	6.50	3.25	2.00
(3)	Gary Gentry	6.50	3.25	2.00
(4)	Jerry Grote	6.50	3.25	2.00
(5)	Cleon Jones	6.50	3.25	2.00
(6)	Jerry Koosman	8.00	4.00	2.50
(7)	Ed Kranepool	6.50	3.25	2.00
(8)	Tom Seaver	25.00	12.50	7.50

1975 Clark & Sons Baseball Favorites

To commemorate the firm's 10 years in business and the Boston Red Sox first pennant since 1967, Clark & Sons Locksmiths of Rhode Island issued this set of Red Sox greats. Two versions were issued. The first has a "324 Waterman Avenue, Providence" address on back. A second printing corrected the errors to "324A Waterman Avenue, East Providence" and added a wavy line around the photo and name on front. Cards measure 2-1/2" x 3-5/8" and are printed in black-and-white.

		NM	EX	VG
	Complete Set (4):	12.50	6.25	3.75
	Common Player:	1.25	.60	.40
1	Bobby Doerr	2.00	1.00	.60
2	Ted Williams	10.00	5.00	3.00
3	Dom DiMaggio	2.50	1.25	.70
4	Johnny Pesky	1.25	.60	.40

1921 Clark's Bread

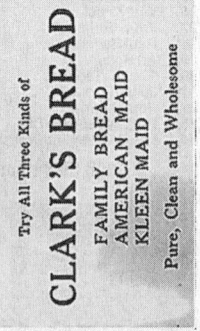

It is not known to what extent this set's checklist of base cards and possible variations parallels the contemporary blank-back 1921-1922 W575-1 strip cards. The cards measure about 2" x 3-1/4" and are printed in black-and-white. It is unknown into which region the bread cards might have been issued. Collectors have been known to pay a premium of 10X for this version.

	NM	EX	VG
Common Player:	1,200	600.00	350.00
Hall of Famers: 4-6X			

(See 1921 American Caramel Series of 80 or 1922 W575-1 for checklists and base card values.)

1972 Classic Cards

The set depicts players from 1900-1909 in sepiatone photos printed on thin, cream-colored card stock by the Flint, MI company not related to the 1990s card maker of the same name. The first series features sequentially numbered cards, the remainder marked only with a series number. Card size is 2-3/4" x 4-1/2" for the first series and 2-3/4" x 4-1/4" for the last three 30-card series.

		NM	EX	VG
	Complete Set (120):	50.00	25.00	10.00
	Common Player:	2.00	1.00	.60
1	Griffith, Cincinnati	2.00	1.00	.60
2	Johnson, Washington	2.00	1.00	.60
3	Ganley, Washington	2.00	1.00	.60
4	Tinker, Chicago	2.00	1.00	.60
5	Chance, Chicago	2.00	1.00	.60
6	Conroy, Washington	2.00	1.00	.60
7	Bresnahan, N.Y.	2.00	1.00	.60
8	Powell, Pittsburgh	2.00	1.00	.60
9	Pfeister, Chicago	2.00	1.00	.60
10	McCarthy, Boston	2.00	1.00	.60
11	McConnell, Boston	2.00	1.00	.60
12	Jennings, Detroit	2.00	1.00	.60
13	Lennox, Brooklyn	2.00	1.00	.60
14	McCormick, N.Y.	2.00	1.00	.60
15	Merkle, N.Y.	2.00	1.00	.60
16	Hoblitzell, Cincinnati	2.00	1.00	.60
17	Dahlen, Boston	2.00	1.00	.60
18	Chance, Chicago	2.00	1.00	.60
19	Ferguson, Boston	2.00	1.00	.60
20	Camnitz, Pittsburgh	2.00	1.00	.60
21	N.Y. (Neal Ball)	2.00	1.00	.60
22	Hemphill, N.Y.	2.00	1.00	.60
23	Baker, Philadelphia	2.00	1.00	.60
24	Mathewson, N.Y.	5.00	2.50	1.50
25	Burch, Brooklyn	2.00	1.00	.60
26	Grant, Philadelphia	2.00	1.00	.60
27	Ames, N.Y.	2.00	1.00	.60
28	Newton, N.Y.	2.00	1.00	.60
29	Moran, Chicago	2.00	1.00	.60
30	Lajoie, Cleveland	2.00	1.00	.60
(31)	Abstein, Pittsburgh	2.00	1.00	.60
(32)	Brown, Chicago	2.00	1.00	.60
(33)	Campbell, Cincinnati	2.00	1.00	.60
(34)	Cobb, Detroit	5.00	2.50	1.50
(35)	Crawford, Detroit	2.00	1.00	.60
(36)	Devlin, N.Y.	2.00	1.00	.60
(37)	Dooin, Philadelphia	2.00	1.00	.60
(38)	Dougherty, Chicago	2.00	1.00	.60
(39)	Downey, Cincinnati	2.00	1.00	.60
(40)	Doyle, New York	2.00	1.00	.60
(41)	Dunn, Brooklyn	2.00	1.00	.60
(42)	Durham, N.Y.	2.00	1.00	.60
(43)	Gibson, Pittsburgh	2.00	1.00	.60
(44)	Hartzel, Philadelphia	2.00	1.00	.60
(45)	Higginbotham, Chicago	2.00	1.00	.60
(46)	Hinchman	2.00	1.00	.60
(47)	Lajoie	2.00	1.00	.60
(48)	Mowery, Cincinnati	2.00	1.00	.60
(49)	Mullin, Detroit	2.00	1.00	.60
(50)	O'Hara, New York	2.00	1.00	.60
(51)	Overall, Chicago	2.00	1.00	.60
(52)	Perring, Cleveland	2.00	1.00	.60
(53)	Rossman, Detroit	2.00	1.00	.60
(54)	Schmidt, Detroit	2.00	1.00	.60
(55)	Steinfeldt, Chicago	2.00	1.00	.60
(56)	Stone, St. Louis	2.00	1.00	.60
(57)	Titus, Philadelphia	2.00	1.00	.60
(58)	Wagner, Pittsburgh	2.00	1.00	.60
(59)	Wamhow, N.Y.	2.00	1.00	.60
(60)	Wiltse, New York	2.00	1.00	.60
(61)	Barger, Brooklyn	2.00	1.00	.60
(62)	Bergen, Brooklyn	2.00	1.00	.60
(63)	Bowerman, Boston	2.00	1.00	.60
(64)	Bransfeld, Philadelphia	2.00	1.00	.60
(65)	Bresnahan, St. Louis	2.00	1.00	.60
(66)	Coakley, Chicago	2.00	1.00	.60
(67)	Donovan, Detroit	2.00	1.00	.60
(68)	Elberfeld, New York	2.00	1.00	.60
(69)	Evers, Chicago	2.00	1.00	.60
(70)	Fromme, Cincinnati	2.00	1.00	.60
(71)	Herzog, N.Y.	2.00	1.00	.60
(72)	Hummell, Cincinnati	2.00	1.00	.60
(73)	Jordan, Brooklyn	2.00	1.00	.60
(74)	Keeler, New York	2.00	1.00	.60
(75)	Lumley, Brooklyn	2.00	1.00	.60
(76)	Maddox, Pittsburgh	2.00	1.00	.60
(77)	McGinnity, New York	2.00	1.00	.60
(78)	McGraw, New York	2.00	1.00	.60
(79)	McIntyre, Brooklyn	2.00	1.00	.60
(80)	Moriarity, New York	2.00	1.00	.60
(81)	Pastorius, Brooklyn	2.00	1.00	.60
(82)	Purtell, Chicago	2.00	1.00	.60
(83)	Schulte, Chicago	2.00	1.00	.60
(84)	Sebring, Brooklyn	2.00	1.00	.60
(85)	Smith, Washington	2.00	1.00	.60
(86)	Speaker, Boston	5.00	2.50	1.50
(87)	Spencer, Boston	2.00	1.00	.60
(88)	Tuckey, Boston	2.00	1.00	.60
(89)	Vaughn, New York	2.00	1.00	.60
(90)	Wheat, Brooklyn	2.00	1.00	.60
(91)	Altzier, Chicago	2.00	1.00	.60
(92)	Bender, Philadelphia	2.00	1.00	.60
(93)	Cincinnati (Bob Ewing)	2.00	1.00	.60
(94)	Bresnahan, St. Louis	2.00	1.00	.60
(95)	Chappelle, Boston	2.00	1.00	.60
(96)	Chase, New York	2.00	1.00	.60
(97)	Daley, Cincinnati	2.00	1.00	.60
(98)	Davis, Chicago	2.00	1.00	.60
(99)	Delahanty, St. Louis	2.00	1.00	.60
(100)	Donohue, Washington	2.00	1.00	.60
(101)	Doyle, New York	2.00	1.00	.60
(102)	Ellis, St. Louis	2.00	1.00	.60
(103)	Graham, St. Louis	2.00	1.00	.60
(104)	Herzog, New York	2.00	1.00	.60
(105)	Hyatt, Pittsburgh	2.00	1.00	.60
(106)	Konetchy, St. Louis	2.00	1.00	.60
(107)	Lake, New York	2.00	1.00	.60
(108)	Lord, Boston	2.00	1.00	.60
(109)	New York (Luther Taylor)	2.00	1.00	.60
(110)	McLean, Cincinnati	2.00	1.00	.60
(111)	Needham, Chicago	2.00	1.00	.60
(112)	Pearce, Cincinnati	2.00	1.00	.60
(113)	Powell, Pittsburgh	2.00	1.00	.60
(114)	Purtell, Chicago	2.00	1.00	.60
(115)	Schreck, Philadelphia	2.00	1.00	.60
(116)	Storke, Pittsburgh	2.00	1.00	.60
(117)	Strunk, Philadelphia	2.00	1.00	.60
(118)	Summers, Detroit	2.00	1.00	.60
(119)	Thomas, Philadelphia	2.00	1.00	.60
(120)	Wagner, Boston	2.00	1.00	.60

1973 Roberto Clemente Memorial Postcard

This collectors' issue postcard was isused as a memorial. In standard 3-1/2" x 5-1/2" format with a postcard-style back, the black-and-white card has printed in the wide bottom border, the player's name, dates of his birth and death and, "In Memory OF A COURAGEOUS HUMAN BEING." On back is a credit line to Allied Printing.

	NM	EX	VG
Roberto Clemente	25.00	12.50	7.50

1913 Cleveland Indians Schedule Postcards

The extent to which the team may have used this type of postcard to announce forthcoming home series is unknown. It can be assumed other cards with other players featured were used during the course of the season. About 7" x 3-1/2", the card has a portrait photo on the left end of its black-and-white front. On back, in red and black, are details of upcoming series and ticket outlet information.

	NM	EX	VG
Joe Birmingham	900.00	450.00	275.00
Ray Chapman	1,350	675.00	400.00
Jack Graney	900.00	450.00	275.00
Joe Jackson, Fred Clarke (Pirates exhibition game.)	2,500	1,250	750.00
Doc Johnston	900.00	450.00	275.00
Willie Mitchell	900.00	450.00	275.00

1947 Cleveland Indians Picture Pack

The first of several annual issues of player photo packs, the 1947 version offered "autographed photos" of all players on the team's roster as of July 1. All players were presented in studio quality portraits in 6" x 8-1/2" format, lithographed on heavy paper with a facsimile autograph. A thin white border surrounds the photo. Backs are blank. The photos were sold in sets for 50 cents. The unnumbered pictures are checklisted here alphabetically.

		NM	EX	VG
Complete Set (25):		100.00	50.00	30.00
Common Player:		3.00	1.50	.90
(1)	Don Black	4.00	2.00	1.25
(2)	Eddie Bockman	3.00	1.50	.90
(3)	Lou Boudreau	9.00	4.50	2.75
(4)	Jack Conway	3.00	1.50	.90
(5)	Larry Doby	25.00	12.50	7.50
(6)	Hank Edwards	3.00	1.50	.90
(7)	"Red" Embree	3.00	1.50	.90
(8)	Bob Feller	25.00	12.50	7.50
(9)	Les Fleming	3.00	1.50	.90
(10)	Allen Gettel	3.00	1.50	.90
(11)	Joe Gordon	9.00	4.50	2.75
(12)	Steve Gromek	3.00	1.50	.90
(13)	Mel Harder	4.50	2.25	1.25
(14)	Jim Hegan	3.00	1.50	.90
(15)	Ken Keltner	4.50	2.25	1.25
(16)	Ed Klieman	3.00	1.50	.90
(17)	Bob Lemon	9.00	4.50	2.75
(18)	Al Lopez	9.00	4.50	2.75
(19)	George Metkovich	3.00	1.50	.90
(20)	Dale Mitchell	4.00	2.00	1.25
(21)	Hal Peck	3.00	1.50	.90
(22)	Eddie Robinson	3.00	1.50	.90
(23)	Hank Ruszkowski	3.00	1.50	.90
(24)	Pat Seerey	3.00	1.50	.90
(25)	Bryan Stephens	3.00	1.50	.90
(26)	Les Willis	3.00	1.50	.90

1947 Van Patrick Cleveland Indians Postcards

Fans could obtain these black-and-white postcard-size (3-1/2" x 5-1/2") photos of their favorite Indians players by writing to radio broadcaster Van Patrick. Backs do not have postcard markings, and carry a message from Patrick. The unnumbered cards are checklisted here alphabetically, though the listing may not be complete.

		NM	EX	VG
Common Player:		100.00	50.00	30.00
(1)	Don Black	100.00	50.00	30.00
(2)	Eddie Bockman	100.00	50.00	30.00
(3)	Lou Boudreau	200.00	100.00	60.00
(4)	Jack Conway	100.00	50.00	30.00
(5)	Hank Edwards	100.00	50.00	30.00
(6)	Red Embree	100.00	50.00	30.00
(7)	Bob Feller/Pitching	300.00	150.00	90.00
(8)	Bob Feller (Pitching, leg in air.)	300.00	150.00	90.00
(9)	Les Fleming	100.00	50.00	30.00
(10)	Allen Gettel	100.00	50.00	30.00
(11)	Joe Gordon	200.00	100.00	60.00
(12)	Steve Gromek	100.00	50.00	30.00
(13)	Mel Harder	125.00	62.00	37.00
(14)	Jim Hegan	110.00	55.00	33.00
(15)	Ken Keltner	110.00	55.00	33.00
(16)	Ed Klieman	100.00	50.00	30.00
(17)	Bob Lemon	200.00	100.00	60.00
(18)	Al Lopez	200.00	100.00	60.00
(19)	George Metkovich	100.00	50.00	30.00
(20)	Dale Mitchell	100.00	50.00	30.00
(21)	Hal Peck	100.00	50.00	30.00
(22)	Eddie Robinson	100.00	50.00	30.00
(23)	Hank Ruszkowski	100.00	50.00	30.00
(24)	Pat Seerey	100.00	50.00	30.00
(25)	Bryan Stephens	100.00	50.00	30.00
(26)	Les Willis	100.00	50.00	30.00

1948-52 Cleveland Indians Pencil Clips

These celluloid and steel pencil clips were sold at the ballpark to be used on pencils given away with scorecards, The round button portion of the clip is about 3/4" in diameter, while the clip itself is a little over 1-1/2". Black-and-white player portraits are centered in a colored border with the team name at top and player name at bottom. While many of the same players and photos were used year after year, issue date of the clips can be determined by the border color. In 1951-1952, when blue borders were used, the year is distinguished by the presence (1951) or absence (1952) of a white union logo on back.

		NM	EX	VG
Common Player:		35.00	17.50	10.50
1948 (Black)				
(1)	Gene Bearden	35.00	17.50	10.50
(2)	John Berardino	40.00	20.00	12.00
(3)	Don Black	35.00	17.50	10.50
(4)	Lou Boudreau	45.00	22.00	13.50
(5)	Russ Christopher	35.00	17.50	10.50
(6)	Allie Clark	35.00	17.50	10.50
(7)	Larry Doby	60.00	30.00	18.00
(8)	Hank Edwards	35.00	17.50	10.50
(9)	Bob Feller	50.00	25.00	15.00
(10)	Al Gettel	35.00	17.50	10.50

		NM	EX	VG
(11)	Joe Gordon	45.00	22.00	13.50
(12)	Walt Judnich	35.00	17.50	10.50
(13)	Ken Keltner	35.00	17.50	10.50
(14)	Bob Lemon	45.00	22.00	13.50
(15)	Dale Mitchell	35.00	17.50	10.50
(16)	Bob Muncrief	35.00	17.50	10.50
(17)	Eddie Robinson	35.00	17.50	10.50
(18)	Pat Seerey	35.00	17.50	10.50
(19)	Joe Tipton	35.00	17.50	10.50
(20)	Thurman Tucker	35.00	17.50	10.50
1949 (Brown)				
(1)	Gene Bearden	35.00	17.50	10.50
(2)	Ray Boone	35.00	17.50	10.50
(3)	Lou Boudreau	45.00	22.00	13.50
(4)	Allie Clark	35.00	17.50	10.50
(5)	Larry Doby	55.00	27.00	16.50
(6)	Bob Feller	50.00	25.00	15.00
(7)	Mike Garcia	35.00	17.50	10.50
(8)	Joe Gordon	45.00	22.00	13.50
(9)	Steve Gromek	35.00	17.50	10.50
(10)	Jim Hegan	35.00	17.50	10.50
(11)	Ken Keltner	35.00	17.50	10.50
(12)	Bob Kennedy	35.00	17.50	10.50
(13)	Bob Lemon	45.00	22.00	13.50
(14)	Dale Mitchell	35.00	17.50	10.50
(15)	Satchel Paige	125.00	62.00	37.00
(16)	Mike Tresh	35.00	17.50	10.50
(17)	Bill Veeck	45.00	22.00	13.50
(18)	Mickey Vernon	35.00	17.50	10.50
(19)	Early Wynn	45.00	22.00	13.50
(20)	Sam Zoldak	35.00	17.50	10.50
1950 (White)				
(1)	Bobby Avila	35.00	17.50	10.50
(2)	Al Benton	35.00	17.50	10.50
(3)	Ray Boone	35.00	17.50	10.50
(4)	Lou Boudreau	45.00	22.00	13.50
(5)	Larry Doby	55.00	27.00	16.50
(6)	Luke Easter	40.00	20.00	12.00
(7)	Bob Feller	50.00	25.00	15.00
(8)	Mike Garcia	40.00	20.00	12.00
(9)	Steve Gromek	35.00	17.50	10.50
(10)	Jim Hegan	35.00	17.50	10.50
(11)	Bob Kennedy	35.00	17.50	10.50
(12)	Bob Lemon	45.00	22.00	13.50
(13)	Dale Mitchell	35.00	17.50	10.50
(14)	Ray Murray	35.00	17.50	10.50
(15)	Al Rosen	40.00	20.00	12.00
(16)	Thurman Tucker	35.00	17.50	10.50
(17)	Dick Weik	35.00	17.50	10.50
(18)	Early Wynn	45.00	22.00	13.50
1950 (Blue w/union logo.)				
(1)	Bobby Avila	35.00	17.50	10.50
(2)	Ray Boone	35.00	17.50	10.50
(3)	Larry Doby	55.00	27.00	16.50
(4)	Luke Easter	40.00	20.00	12.00
(5)	Bob Feller	50.00	25.00	15.00
(6)	Jim Hegan	35.00	17.50	10.50
(7)	Bob Kennedy	35.00	17.50	10.50
(8)	Bob Lemon	45.00	22.00	13.50
(9)	Al Lopez	45.00	22.00	13.50
(10)	Dale Mitchell	35.00	17.50	10.50
(11)	Al Rosen	40.00	20.00	12.00
(12)	Early Wynn	45.00	22.00	13.50
1952 (Blue, no logo.)				
(1)	Bobby Avila	35.00	17.50	10.50
(2)	Lou Brissie	35.00	17.50	10.50
(3)	Bob Chakales	35.00	17.50	10.50
(4)	Merrill Combs	35.00	17.50	10.50
(5)	Larry Doby	55.00	27.00	16.50
(6)	Luke Easter	40.00	20.00	12.00
(7)	Bob Feller	50.00	25.00	15.00
(8)	Mike Garcia	40.00	20.00	12.00
(9)	Steve Gromek	35.00	17.50	10.50
(10)	Jim Hegan	35.00	17.50	10.50
(11)	Sam Jones	35.00	17.50	10.50
(12)	Bob Lemon	45.00	22.00	13.50
(13)	Barney McCosky	35.00	17.50	10.50
(14)	Dale Mitchell	35.00	17.50	10.50
(15)	Pete Reiser	35.00	17.50	10.50
(16)	Al Rosen	45.00	22.50	13.50
(17)	Harry Simpson	35.00	17.50	10.50
(18)	Birdie Tebbetts	35.00	17.50	10.50
(19)	Early Wynn	45.00	22.00	13.50

1949 Cleveland Indians Sun Picture Camera

These novelty cards are self-developing photoprints sold by the team in packages of four that included negatives and pieces of photo-sensative paper which were used to make the 1-7/8" x 2" black-and-white blank-back pictures. Because existing negatives could be used to make many new prints, values for the prints themselves are low. Prices quoted here are for negative/print combinations.

		NM	EX	VG
Complete Set Negatives/Prints (20):		3,000	1,500	900.00
Common Negative/Print:		125.00	65.00	35.00
(1)	Gene Bearden	125.00	65.00	35.00
(2)	Al Benton	125.00	65.00	35.00
(3)	Ray Boone	125.00	65.00	35.00

		NM	EX	VG
(4)	Lou Boudreau	200.00	100.00	60.00
(5)	Allie Clark	125.00	65.00	35.50
(6)	Larry Doby	250.00	125.00	75.00
(7)	Bob Feller	250.00	125.00	75.00
(8)	Mike Garcia	135.00	70.00	40.00
(9)	Joe Gordon	200.00	100.00	60.00
(10)	Steve Gromek	125.00	65.00	35.00
(11)	Jim Hegan	125.00	65.00	35.00
(12)	Ken Keltner	135.00	70.00	40.00
(13)	Bob Kennedy	125.00	65.00	35.00
(14)	Bob Lemon	200.00	100.00	60.00
(15)	Dale Mitchell	125.00	65.00	35.00
(16)	Hal Peck	125.00	65.00	35.00
(17)	Satchel Paige	400.00	200.00	120.00
(18)	Thurman Tucker	125.00	65.00	35.00
(19)	Mickey Vernon	125.00	65.00	35.00
(20)	Early Wynn	200.00	100.00	60.00

1948 Cleveland Indians Four-on-One Pack

One of the team-issued souvenirs issued to commemorate the Indians 1948 World Series win over the Boston Braves was this photo pack. Printed in black-and-white on 5" x 7" heavy matte paper stock, the set was sold in a manila envelope imprinted with the team logo and "WORLD CHAMPS." The Four-on-One set uses the same facsimile-autographed portraits found in the large format photo pack. The only differences in players represented is the absence of Al Lopez and subsequent double printing of Bob Feller. The pictures are listed here alphabetically by the player in the upper-left.

		NM	EX	VG
Complete Set (8):		250.00	150.00	75.00
Common Card:		12.00	7.50	3.75
(1)	Gene Bearden , Larry Doby, Ken Keltner, Satchell Paige	100.00	60.00	30.00
(2)	Don Black, Russ Christopher, Joe Tipton, Bob Kennedy	12.00	7.50	3.75
(3)	Jim Hegan, Bob Lemon, Lou Boudreau, Bob Feller	30.00	18.00	9.00
(4)	Dale Mitchell, Johnny Berardino, Joe Gordon, Steve Gromek	25.00	15.00	7.50
(5)	Hal Peckn, Thurman Tucker, Walter Judnick, Herold Ruel	12.00	7.50	3.75
(6)	Eddie Robinson, Ed Klieman, Allie Clark, Hank Edwards	12.00	7.50	3.75
(7)	Bill Veeck, Cleveland Stadium, Hank Greenberg (uniform), Bob Feller	50.00	30.00	15.00
(8)	Sam Zoldak, Bill McKechnie, Mel Harder, Bob Muncrief	20.00	12.00	6.00

1949 Cleveland Indians Display Photos

BOB FELLER • P, CLEVELAND INDIANS

Members of the Tribe are pictured (in the same poses found on their photo-pack issues) on these large-format (11" x 14") display photos, said to have been used for in-stadium promotions. It is possible there are others besides those checklisted here.

		NM	EX	VG
Complete Set (11):		650.00	325.00	200.00
Common Player:		40.00	20.00	12.00
(1)	Ray Boone	45.00	22.00	13.50
(2)	Larry Doby	100.00	50.00	30.00
(3)	Luke Easter	50.00	25.00	15.00
(4)	Bob Feller	125.00	62.00	37.00
(5)	Jim Hegan	40.00	20.00	12.00
(6)	Bob Kennedy	40.00	20.00	12.00
(7)	Bob Lemon	75.00	37.00	22.00
(8)	Al Lopez	75.00	37.00	22.00
(9)	Dale Mitchell	40.00	20.00	12.00
(10)	Al Rosen	50.00	25.00	15.00
(11)	Early Wynn	75.00	37.00	22.00

1949 Cleveland Indians Picture Pack - Action

Posed action photos are the focus of this team-issued picture pack. The black-and-white 6-1/2" x 9" photos feature white borders all around and a facsimile autograph on front. Backs are blank. The set was sold in a red and white paper envelope labeled "World Champion Cleveland Indians Autographed Action Photos." Backs are blank. The unnumbered pictures are checklisted here alphabetically. Unmarked reprints of this team-issue, complete with mailing envelope, were made in the late 1980s.

		NM	EX	VG
Complete Set (30):		175.00	90.00	55.00
Common Player:		4.00	2.00	1.25
(1)	Bob Avila	6.00	3.00	1.75
(2)	Gene Bearden	4.00	2.00	1.25
(3)	Al Benton	4.00	2.00	1.25
(4)	John Berardino	12.00	6.00	3.50
(5)	Ray Boone	6.00	3.00	1.75
(6)	Lou Boudreau	16.00	8.00	4.75
(7)	Allie Clark	4.00	2.00	1.25
(8)	Larry Doby	17.50	8.75	5.25
(9)	Bob Feller	20.00	10.00	6.00
(10)	Mike Garcia	6.00	3.00	1.75
(11)	Joe Gordon	16.00	8.00	4.75
(12)	Hank Greenberg (GM)	12.00	6.00	3.50
(13)	Steve Gromek	4.00	2.00	1.25
(14)	Jim Hegan	4.00	2.00	1.25
(15)	Ken Keltner	4.00	2.00	1.25
(16)	Bob Kennedy	4.00	2.00	1.25
(17)	Bob Lemon	12.00	6.00	3.50
(18)	Dale Mitchell	4.00	2.00	1.25
(19)	Satchel Paige	40.00	20.00	12.00
(20)	Frank Papish	4.00	2.00	1.25
(21)	Hal Peck	4.00	2.00	1.25
(22)	Al Rosen	8.00	4.00	2.50
(23)	Mike Tresh	4.00	2.00	1.25
(24)	Thurman Tucker	4.00	2.00	1.25
(25)	Bill Veeck (Owner)	12.00	6.00	3.50
(26)	Mickey Vernon	6.00	3.00	1.75
(27)	Early Wynn	12.00	6.00	3.50
(28)	Sam Zoldak	4.00	2.00	1.25
(29)	Indians coaches (Mel Harder, Steve O'Neill, Bill McKechnie, Muddy Ruel, George Susce)	4.00	2.00	1.25
(30)	Municipal Stadium	6.00	3.00	1.75

1949 Cleveland Indians Picture Pack - Portraits

This set of player photos was produced by Big League Novelty Co., Cleveland, as credited on the paper envelope in which they were sold. The envelope has a crowned, big-nosed Indian caricature and mini-pictures of three of the players. The pictures are in a 6-1/2" x 9" blank-back format. They are black-and-white and virtually all depict the players in chest-to-cap portraits (many the same as previous and later years' issues) with a facsimile autograph. The unnumbered pictures are checklisted here alphabetically.

		NM	EX	VG
Complete Set (20):		75.00	40.00	25.00
Common Player:		3.00	1.50	.90
(1)	Bob Avila	4.50	2.25	1.25
(2)	Gene Bearden	3.00	1.50	.90
(3)	John Berardino	4.50	2.25	1.25
(4)	Lou Boudreau	7.50	3.75	2.25
(5)	Larry Doby	10.00	5.00	3.00
(6)	Bob Feller	12.50	6.25	3.75
(7)	Mike Garcia	4.50	2.25	1.25
(8)	Joe Gordon	7.50	3.75	2.25
(9)	Steve Gromek	3.00	1.50	.90
(10)	Jim Hegan	3.00	1.50	.90
(11)	Ken Keltner	3.00	1.50	.90
(12)	Bob Kennedy	3.00	1.50	.90
(13)	Bob Lemon	5.00	2.50	1.50
(14)	Dale Mitchell	3.00	1.50	.90
(15)	Satchel Paige	30.00	15.00	9.00
(16)	Hal Peck	3.00	1.50	.90
(17)	Thurman Tucker	3.00	1.50	.90
(18)	Mickey Vernon	4.00	2.00	1.25
(19)	Early Wynn	5.00	2.50	1.50
(20)	Sam Zoldak	3.00	1.50	.90

1949 Cleveland Indians Sun Picture Camera

Lou Boudreau

These novelty cards are self-developing photoprints sold by the team in packages of four that included negatives and pieces of photo-sensative paper which were used to make the 1-7/8" x 2" black-and-white blank-back pictures. Because existing negatives could be used to make many new prints, values for the prints themselves are low. Prices quoted here are for negative/print combinations.

		NM	EX	VG
Complete Set Negatives/Prints (20):		3,000	1,500	900.00
Common Negative/Print:		125.00	65.00	35.00
(1)	Gene Bearden	125.00	65.00	35.00
(2)	Al Benton	125.00	65.00	35.00
(3)	Ray Boone	125.00	65.00	35.00
(4)	Lou Boudreau	200.00	100.00	60.00
(5)	Allie Clark	125.00	65.00	35.50
(6)	Larry Doby	250.00	125.00	75.00
(7)	Bob Feller	250.00	125.00	75.00
(8)	Mike Garcia	135.00	70.00	40.00
(9)	Joe Gordon	200.00	100.00	60.00
(10)	Steve Gromek	125.00	65.00	35.00
(11)	Jim Hegan	125.00	65.00	35.00
(12)	Ken Keltner	135.00	70.00	40.00
(13)	Bob Kennedy	125.00	65.00	35.00
(14)	Bob Lemon	200.00	100.00	60.00
(15)	Dale Mitchell	125.00	65.00	35.00
(16)	Hal Peck	125.00	65.00	35.00
(17)	Satchel Paige	400.00	200.00	120.00
(18)	Thurman Tucker	125.00	65.00	35.00
(19)	Mickey Vernon	125.00	65.00	35.00
(20)	Early Wynn	200.00	100.00	60.00

1950 Cleveland Indians Picture Pack

Similar in format to previous years' issues, these 6-1/2" x 9" black-and-white player poses have a white border and facsimile autograph on front. Backs are blank. The unnumbered photos are checklisted here alphabetically. It is possible the contents of specific picture packs changed over the course of the season to reflect roster moves.

		NM	EX	VG
Complete Set (27):		160.00	80.00	50.00
Common Player:		4.00	2.00	1.20
(1)	Bobby Avila	5.00	2.50	1.50
(2)	Gene Bearden	4.00	2.00	1.20
(3)	Al Benton	4.00	2.00	1.20
(4)	Ray Boone	5.00	2.50	1.50
(5)	Lou Boudreau	12.00	6.00	3.50
(6)	Allie Clark	4.00	2.00	1.20
(7)	Larry Doby	17.50	8.75	5.25
(8)	Luke Easter	6.00	3.00	1.75
(9)	Bob Feller	20.00	10.00	6.00
(10)	Jess Flores	4.00	2.00	1.20
(11)	Mike Garcia	5.00	2.50	1.50
(12)	Joe Gordon	12.00	6.00	3.50
(13)	Hank Greenberg/GM	12.00	6.00	3.50
(14)	Steve Gromek	4.00	2.00	1.20
(15)	Jim Hegan	4.00	2.00	1.20
(16)	Bob Kennedy	4.00	2.00	1.20
(17)	Bob Lemon	12.00	6.00	3.50
(18)	Dale Mitchell	4.00	2.00	1.20
(19)	Ray Murray	4.00	2.00	1.20
(20)	Chick Pieretti	4.00	2.00	1.20
(21)	Al Rosen	6.00	3.00	1.75
(22)	Dick Rozek	4.00	2.00	1.20
(23)	Ellis Ryan/Owner	4.00	2.00	1.20
(24)	Thurman Tucker	4.00	2.00	1.20
(25)	Early Wynn	12.00	6.00	3.50
(26)	Sam Zoldak	4.00	2.00	1.20
(27)	Cleveland Municipal Stadium	8.00	4.00	2.50

1951 Cleveland Indians Picture Pack

While this set of Indians pictures shares the 6-1/2" x 9" format of the Tribe's other team issues of the era, it is unique in its use of a much glossier front surface. Pictures are, with the exception of the manager, game-action or posed-action in black-and-white, bordered in white and with a facsimile autograph. Backs are blank. It is unknown whether this checklist is complete or whether players were added or removed to reflect in-season roster changes.

		NM	EX	VG
Complete Set (26):		150.00	75.00	45.00
Common Player:		4.00	2.00	1.25
(1)	Bob Avila	4.00	2.00	1.25
(2)	Gene Bearden	4.00	2.00	1.25
(3)	Ray Boone	6.00	3.00	1.75
(4)	Lou Brissie	4.00	2.00	1.25
(5)	Bob Chakales	4.00	2.00	1.25
(6)	Sam Chapman	4.00	2.00	1.25
(7)	Merrill Combs	4.00	2.00	1.25
(8)	Larry Doby	15.00	7.50	4.50
(9)	Luke Easter	6.00	3.00	1.75
(10)	Red Fahr	4.00	2.00	1.25
(11)	Bob Feller	20.00	10.00	6.00
(12)	Mike Garcia	6.00	3.00	1.75
(13)	Steve Gromek	4.00	2.00	1.25
(14)	Jim Hegan	4.00	2.00	1.25
(15)	Bob Kennedy	4.00	2.00	1.25
(16)	Bob Lemon	12.50	6.25	3.75
(17)	Al Lopez	12.50	6.25	3.75
(18)	Milt Neilsen	4.00	2.00	1.25
(19)	Al Rosen	8.00	4.00	2.50
(20)	Dick Rozek	4.00	2.00	1.25
(21)	Harry Simpson	4.00	2.00	1.25
(22)	Snuffy Stirnweiss	4.00	2.00	1.25
(23)	Birdie Tebbetts	4.00	2.00	1.25
(24)	Johnny Vander Meer	6.00	3.00	1.75
(25)	Early Wynn	12.50	6.25	3.75
(26)	George Zuverink	4.00	2.00	1.25

1952 Cleveland Indians Picture Pack

Like the 1951 Picture Pack, these pictures contain action poses, but are slightly smaller at 6" x 8-3/4". Unnumbered prints here are checklisted alphabetically.

		NM	EX	VG
Complete Set (25):		150.00	75.00	45.00
Common Player:		6.00	3.00	2.00
(1)	Bobby Avila	6.00	3.00	2.00
(2)	Johnny Bernardino	6.00	3.00	2.00
(3)	Ray Boone	6.00	3.00	2.00
(4)	Lou Brissie	6.00	3.00	2.00
(5)	Merrill Combs	6.00	3.00	2.00
(6)	Larry Doby	12.00	6.00	4.00
(7)	Luke Easter	6.00	3.00	2.00
(8)	Bob Feller	20.00	10.00	6.00
(9)	Jim Fridley	6.00	3.00	2.00
(10)	Mike Garcia	6.00	3.00	2.00
(11)	Steve Gromek	6.00	3.00	2.00
(12)	Mickey Harris	6.00	3.00	2.00
(13)	Jim Hegan	6.00	3.00	2.00
(14)	Sam Jones	6.00	3.00	2.00
(15)	Bob Lemon	12.00	6.00	4.00
(16)	Al Lopez	12.00	6.00	4.00
(17)	Dale Mitchell	6.00	3.00	2.00
(18)	Barney McCosky	6.00	3.00	2.00
(19)	Pete Reiser	6.00	3.00	2.00
(20)	Al Rosen	6.00	3.00	2.00
(21)	Dick Rozek	6.00	3.00	2.00
(22)	Harry Simpson	6.00	3.00	2.00
(23)	Birdie Tebbetts	6.00	3.00	2.00
(24)	Joe Tipton	6.00	3.00	2.00
(25)	Early Wynn	12.00	6.00	4.00

1954 Cleveland Indians Picture Pack

Because many of the pictures found in the championship season picture pack are the same poses found in earlier issues, size can be used to differentiate the years of issue. For 1954, the pictures were down-sized slightly in height, to a 6" x 8-3/4" format, and printed on heavier paper than in previous years. Each of the portraits, poses and action photos are bordered in white and include a facsimile autograph. The unnumbered pictures are checklisted here alphabetically.

		NM	EX	VG
Complete Set (27):		125.00	65.00	40.00
Common Player:		4.00	2.00	1.25
(1)	Bobby Avila	4.00	2.00	1.25
(2)	Sam Dente	4.00	2.00	1.25
(3)	Larry Doby	10.00	5.00	3.00
(4)	Bob Feller	15.00	7.50	4.50
(5)	Mike Garcia	4.00	2.00	1.25
(6)	Bill Glynn	4.00	2.00	1.25
(7)	Mike Hegan	4.00	2.00	1.25
(8)	Bob Hooper	4.00	2.00	1.25
(9)	Dave Hoskins	4.00	2.00	1.25
(10)	Art Houtteman	4.00	2.00	1.25
(11)	Bob Lemon	7.50	3.75	2.25
(12)	Al Lopez	7.50	3.75	2.25
(13)	Hank Majeski	4.00	2.00	1.25
(14)	Dale Mitchell	4.00	2.00	1.25
(15)	Don Mossi	6.00	3.00	1.75
(16)	Hal Naragon	4.00	2.00	1.25
(17)	Ray Narleski	4.00	2.00	1.25
(18)	Hal Newhouser	7.50	3.75	2.25
(19)	Dave Philley	4.00	2.00	1.25
(20)	Dave Pope	4.00	2.00	1.25
(21)	Rudy Regalado	4.00	2.00	1.25
(22)	Al Rosen	6.00	3.00	1.75
(23)	Al Smith	4.00	2.00	1.25
(24)	George Strickland	4.00	2.00	1.25
(25)	Vic Wertz	4.00	2.00	1.25
(26)	Wally Westlake	4.00	2.00	1.25
(27)	Early Wynn	7.50	3.75	2.25

1955 Cleveland Indians Postcards

These team-issued black-and-white player postcards can be distinguished from earlier and later issues by the uniformity of the photos. All pictures are head-and-shoulder portraits against a white background. Players are wearing caps with Chief Wahoo inside a "C." Some cards are found with a notation on back, "Pub. by Ed Wood, Forestville, Calif." Cards were sent out to fans by the team and/or player and are usually found with an autograph on front.

		NM	EX	VG
Complete Set (29):		400.00	200.00	120.00
Common Player:		12.00	6.00	3.50
(1)	Bob Avila	15.00	7.50	4.50
(2)	Tony Cuccinello	12.00	6.00	3.50
(3)	Bud Daley	12.00	6.00	3.50
(4)	Sam Dente	12.00	6.00	3.50
(5)	Larry Doby	18.00	9.00	5.50
(6)	Bob Feller	30.00	15.00	9.00
(7)	Hank Foiles	12.00	6.00	3.50
(8)	Mike Garcia	12.00	6.00	3.50
(9)	Mel Harder	12.00	6.00	3.50
(10)	Jim Hegan	12.00	6.00	3.50
(11)	Art Houtteman	12.00	6.00	3.50
(12)	Ralph Kiner	20.00	10.00	6.00
(13)	Red Kress	12.00	6.00	3.50
(14)	Ken Kuhn	12.00	6.00	3.50
(15)	Bob Lemon	18.00	9.00	5.50
(16)	Bill Lobe	12.00	6.00	3.50
(17)	Dale Mitchell	12.00	6.00	3.50
(18)	Don Mossi	12.00	6.00	3.50
(19)	Hal Naragon	12.00	6.00	3.50
(20)	Ray Narleski	12.00	6.00	3.50
(21)	Dave Philley	12.00	6.00	3.50
(22)	Al Rosen	15.00	7.50	4.50
(23)	Herb Score	24.00	12.00	7.25
(24)	Al Smith	12.00	6.00	3.50
(25)	George Strickland	12.00	6.00	3.50
(26)	Vic Wertz	12.00	6.00	3.50
(27)	Wally Westlake	12.00	6.00	3.50
(28)	Bill Wright	12.00	6.00	3.50
(29)	Early Wynn	18.00	9.00	5.50

1956 Cleveland Indians Picture Pack

The Indians used a mix of styles in its souvenir picture pack for 1956. About 6-1/8" x 8-7/8", with white borders and blank backs, the pictures have a mix of portraits and posed action photos. Some pictures have a facsimile autograph while others have the players name in a white strip.

		NM	EX	VG
Complete Set (22):		90.00	45.00	27.50
Common Player:		4.00	2.00	1.25
(1)	Earl Averill	4.00	2.00	1.25
(2)	Bob Avila	4.00	2.00	1.25
(3)	Jim Busby	4.00	2.00	1.25
(4)	Chico Carrasquel	4.00	2.00	1.25
(5)	Rocky Colavito	20.00	10.00	6.00
(6)	Bob Feller	15.00	7.50	4.50
(7)	Mike Garcia	4.00	2.00	1.25
(8)	Jim Hegan	4.00	2.00	1.25
(9)	Art Houtteman	4.00	2.00	1.25
(10)	Bob Lemon	7.50	3.75	2.25
(11)	Al Lopez	7.50	3.75	2.25
(12)	Sam Mele	4.00	2.00	1.25
(13)	Dale Mitchell	4.00	2.00	1.25
(14)	Don Mossi	4.00	2.00	1.25
(15)	Hal Naragon	4.00	2.00	1.25
(16)	Ray Narleski	4.00	2.00	1.25
(17)	Al Rosen	5.00	2.50	1.50
(18)	Herb Score	7.50	3.75	2.25
(19)	Al Smith	4.00	2.00	1.25
(20)	George Strickland	4.00	2.00	1.25
(21)	Gene Woodling	4.00	2.00	1.25
(22)	Early Wynn	7.50	3.75	2.25

1937 Cleveland Press Indians Album

These newspaper cut-outs from the 1937 Cleveland Press depict Cleveland Indians players and coaches staff. Published at the start of their new season. Each cut-out has a paragraph at the bottom highlighting the player's performance in the 1936 season. The cut-outs measure 3-1/2 wide but measure between 7-9 inches long depending on the length of text and photo.

		NM	EX	VG
Complete Set (29):		300.00	150.00	75.00
Common player:		10.00	5.00	2.50
1	Frank Pytlak	10.00	5.00	2.50
2	Roy Weatherly	10.00	5.00	2.50
3	Roy Hughes	10.00	5.00	2.50
4	Bruce Campbell	10.00	5.00	2.50
5	Lyn Lary	10.00	5.00	2.50
6	Julius Solters	15.00	7.50	4.50
7	Earl Averill	15.00	7.50	4.50
8	Mel Harder	10.00	5.00	2.50
9	Tom Drake	10.00	5.00	2.50
10	Billy Sullivan	10.00	5.00	2.50
11	Whitlow Wyatt	10.00	5.00	2.50
12	Denny Galehouse	10.00	5.00	2.50
13	Earl Whitehill	10.00	5.00	2.50
14	Willis Hudlin	10.00	5.00	2.50
15	Odell Hale	10.00	5.00	2.50
16	Carl Fischer	10.00	5.00	2.50
17	Joe Becker	10.00	5.00	2.50
18	Bob Feller	30.00	15.00	9.00
19	Hal Trosky	15.00	7.50	4.50
20	Jeff Heath	10.00	5.00	2.50
21	Ivy Paul Andrews	10.00	5.00	2.50
22	Lloyd Brown	10.00	5.00	2.50
23	Johnny Allen	10.00	5.00	2.50
24	Joe Heving	10.00	5.00	2.50
25	John Kroner	10.00	5.00	2.50
26	George Uhle	10.00	5.00	2.50
27	Wally Schang	10.00	5.00	2.50
28	Max Weisman	10.00	5.00	2.50
29	Steve O'Neill	10.00	5.00	2.50

1884 Climax Poster

"Representatives of Professional Baseball in America" is the title of this sepia-toned lithograph produced by Lorillard tobacco as a premium for its Climax Red Tin Tag Plug chew. About 26" x 20", the poster depicts 16 top stars, managers and executives in street-clothed portraits on a background of ballplayers, equipment and ballparks.

	NM	EX	VG
1884 Climax	25,000	12,500	7,500
Representatives of Baseball			

1911 George Close Candy Co. (E94)

This 1911 issue is nearly identical to several contemporary candy and caramel sets. Issued by The George Close Co. of Cambridge, Mass., the approximately 1-1/2" x 2-3/4" cards feature color-tinted black-and-white player photos. Each card can be found with any of seven different background colors (blue, gold, green, olive, red, violet and yellow). Backs carry a set checklist. Eleven different back variations are known to exist. One variation contains just the checklist without any advertising, while 10 other variations include overprinted backs advertising various candy products manufactured by Close. The set carries the ACC designation E94.

	NM	EX	VG
Complete Set (30):	103,500	52,000	31,000

		NM	EX	VG
Common Player:		1,800	900.00	350.00
Advertising Backs: 3-5X				
(1)	Jimmy Austin	1,800	900.00	350.00
(2)	Johnny Bates	1,800	900.00	350.00
(3)	Bob Bescher	1,800	900.00	350.00
(4)	Bobby Byrne	1,800	900.00	350.00
(5)	Frank Chance	3,000	1,500	900.00
(6)	Ed Cicotte	3,000	1,500	650.00
(7)	Ty Cobb	40,000	20,000	12,000
(8)	Sam Crawford	3,000	1,500	900.00
(9)	Harry Davis	1,800	900.00	350.00
(10)	Art Devlin	1,800	900.00	350.00
(11)	Josh Devore	1,800	900.00	350.00
(12)	Mickey Doolan	1,800	900.00	350.00
(13)	Patsy Dougherty	1,800	900.00	350.00
(14)	Johnny Evers	3,000	1,500	900.00
(15)	Eddie Grant	1,800	900.00	350.00
(16)	Hugh Jennings	3,000	1,500	900.00
(17)	Red Kleinow	1,800	900.00	350.00
(18)	Joe Lake	1,800	900.00	350.00
(19)	Nap Lajoie	3,000	1,500	750.00
(20)	Tommy Leach	1,800	900.00	350.00
(21)	Hans Lobert	1,800	900.00	350.00
(22)	Harry Lord	1,800	900.00	350.00
(23)	Sherry Magee	1,800	900.00	350.00
(24)	John McGraw	3,000	1,500	900.00
(25)	Earl Moore	1,800	900.00	350.00
(26)	Red Murray	1,800	900.00	350.00
(27)	Tris Speaker	4,000	2,000	1,000
(28)	Terry Turner	1,800	900.00	350.00
(29)	Honus Wagner	20,000	10,000	3,600
(30)	"Old" Cy Young	15,000	7,500	2,500

1961 Cloverleaf Dairy Minnesota Twins

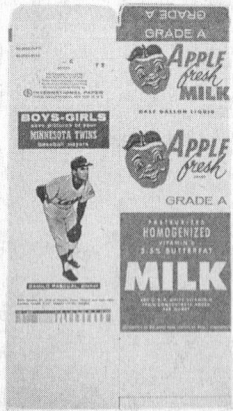

These unnumbered cards picture members of the debut Minnesota Twins team. Measuring approximately 3-3/4" x 7-3/4", the cards were actually side panels from Cloverleaf (and Apple Fresh brand) Milk cartons. Complete cartons are valued at about twice the prices listed. The card includes a black-and-white player photo with name, position, personal data and year-by-year statistics appearing below. Green graphics highlight the panels. Some pictures were reissued in 1962 but can be differentiated from the 1961 set by the stats at bottom.

		NM	EX	VG
Complete Set (17):		1,125	550.00	335.00
Common Player:		75.00	37.00	22.00
(1)	Earl Battey	75.00	37.00	22.00
(2)	Reno Bertoia	75.00	37.00	22.00
(3)	Billy Gardner	75.00	37.00	22.00
(4)	Paul Giel	75.00	37.00	22.00
(5)	Lenny Green	75.00	37.00	22.00
(6)	Jim Kaat	80.00	40.00	24.00
(7)	Jack Kralick	75.00	37.00	22.00
(8)	Don Lee	75.00	37.00	22.00
(9)	Jim Lemon	75.00	37.00	22.00
(10)	Billy Martin	90.00	45.00	27.00
(11)	Don Mincher	75.00	37.00	22.00
(12)	Camilo Pascual	80.00	40.00	24.00
(13)	Pedro Ramos	75.00	37.00	22.00
(14)	Chuck Stobbs	75.00	37.00	22.00
(15)	Bill Tuttle	75.00	37.00	22.00
(16)	Jose Valdivielso	75.00	37.00	22.00
(17)	Zoilo Versalles	80.00	40.00	24.00

1962 Cloverleaf Dairy Minnesota Twins

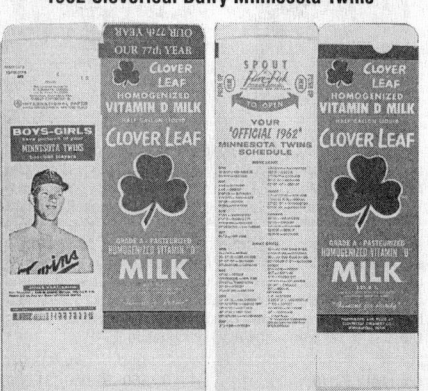

These unnumbered cards picture members of the Minnesota Twins. Measuring approximately 3-3/4" x 7-3/4", the cards were actually side panels from Cloverleaf (and Apple Fresh brand) Milk cartons. Complete cartons are valued at about twice the prices listed. The card includes a black-and-white player photo with name, position, personal data and year-by-year statistics appearing below. Green graphics highlight the panels. Some pictures were reissued in 1962 but can be differentiated from the 1961 set by the stats at bottom.

		NM	EX	VG
Complete Set (24):		1,400	700.00	425.00
Common Player:		75.00	37.00	22.00
(1)	Bernie Allen	75.00	37.00	22.00
(2)	George Banks	75.00	37.00	22.00
(3)	Earl Battey	75.00	37.00	22.00
(4)	Joe Bonikowski	75.00	37.00	22.00
(5)	John Goryl	75.00	37.00	22.00
(6)	Lenny Green	75.00	37.00	22.00
(7)	Jim Kaat	80.00	40.00	24.00
(8)	Jack Kralick	75.00	37.00	22.00
(9)	Jim Lemon	75.00	37.00	22.00
(10)	Georges Maranda	75.00	37.00	22.00
(11)	Orlando Martinez	75.00	37.00	22.00
(12)	Don Mincher	75.00	37.00	22.00
(13)	Ray Moore	75.00	37.00	22.00
(14)	Hal Naragon	75.00	37.00	22.00
(15)	Camilo Pascual	80.00	40.00	24.00
(16)	Vic Power	80.00	40.00	24.00
(17)	Rich Rollins	75.00	37.00	22.00
(18)	Theodore Sadowski	75.00	37.00	22.00
(19)	Albert Stange	75.00	37.00	22.00
(20)	Dick Stigman	75.00	37.00	22.00
(21)	Bill Tuttle	75.00	37.00	22.00
(22)	Zoilo Versalles	80.00	40.00	24.00
(23)	Gerald Zimmerman	75.00	37.00	22.00
(24)	Manager and Coaches (Floyd Baker, Edward Fitz Gerald, Gordon Maltzberger, Sam Mele, George Strickland)	75.00	37.00	22.00

1912 Ty Cobb Postcard

There is no indication of a publisher on this card, nor that it is part of a multi-player series. In standard postcard format of 5-1/2" x 3-1/2", the card has a black-and-white photograph of a smiling Cobb and a caption in the bottom border, "TY COBB WORLDS'S GREATEST BALL PLAYER AND HIS FAVORITE BAT." The divided back has standard postcard markings.

	NM	EX	VG
Ty Cobb	3,500	1,750	1,000

1947 Coca-Cola All Time Sports Favorite

In 1947 Coke produced a series of 10 All Time Sports Favorite cardboard signs. On heavy cardboard with a framed look, the 13" x 15" signs have color artwork at center. In the bottom border are a few words about the athlete, along with a Coke bottle and round red logo. Only one baseball player appears in the series.

	NM	EX	VG
Ty Cobb	2,000	1,000	600.00

1952 Coca-Cola Playing Tips Test Cards

Apparently a regional issue to test the concept of baseball playing tips cards inserted into cartons of soda bottles, these test cards have a number of differences to the version which was more widely issued. The test cards feature a colorful drawing of the player with a bottle of Coke, along with his name in script and his team. Backs are printed in red on gray cardboard. Rizzuto's card has been seen with three different playing tips. Mays' card has a biography instead of a playing tip. The cards are irregularly shaped, measuring about 3-1/2" at their widest point, and about 7-1/2" in length.

		NM	EX	VG
Complete Set (4):		16,000	8,000	4,800
(1)	Willie Mays	6,500	3,200	1,950
(2)	Phil Rizzuto (Bunting tips.)	4,500	2,200	1,350
(3)	Phil Rizzuto (Pitching tips.)	4,500	2,200	1,350
(4)	Phil Rizzuto (SS fielding tips.)	4,500	2,200	1,350

1952 Coca-Cola Playing Tips

While more widely distributed than the three test cards, the 10-card set of playing tips cards is still scarce today. Issued in the metropolitan New York region, the cards include only players from the Yankees, Giants and Dodgers. Fronts feature color paintings of players in action, though the artwork bears little actual resemblance to the players named. The phrase "Coke is a natural" is in the background on pennants, panels, etc. The player's name, team and position are included in the picture. In the portion of the card meant to be inserted into the soda-bottle carton, the home schedule of the player's team for 1952 is presented. Printed in red on back are tips for playing the position of the pictured player. Cards are irregularly shaped, measuring about 3-1/2" at their widest point, and 7-1/2" in length. The unnumbered cards are checklisted here in alphabetical order.

		NM	EX	VG
Complete Set (10):		2,100	1,050	625.00
Common Player:		160.00	80.00	50.00
(1)	Hank Bauer	275.00	135.00	82.00
(2)	Carl Furillo	350.00	175.00	105.00
(3)	Gil Hodges	450.00	225.00	135.00
(4)	Ed Lopat	190.00	95.00	57.00
(5)	Gil McDougald	250.00	125.00	75.00
(6)	Don Mueller	150.00	75.00	45.00
(7)	Pee Wee Reese	450.00	225.00	135.00
(8)	Bobby Thomson (3B)	250.00	125.00	75.00
(9)	Bobby Thomson (Hitting)	350.00	175.00	105.00
(10)	Wes Westrum	150.00	75.00	45.00

1953 Coca-Cola Signs

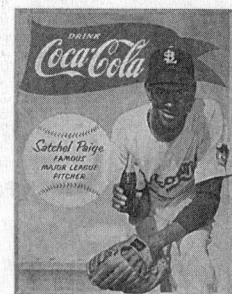

The attributed date is approximate, based on the uniforms in which the players are pictured. It is possible the series was issued over more than one year. The signs vary in size from about 10" x 12" to 12" x 15" and are made of cardboard. Some are die-cut to produce an irregular shape. Players are pictured in color artwork holding a bottle of Coke with one of several styles of Coca-Cola logo in the background.

		NM	EX	VG
Common Player:		750.00	375.00	225.00
(1)	Bill Bruton	1,600	800.00	480.00
(2)	Roy Campanella	5,000	2,500	1,500
(3)	Larry Doby	3,000	1,500	900.00
(4)	Monte Irvin	3,000	1,500	900.00

		NM	EX	VG
(5)	Satchel Paige	8,000	4,000	2,400
(6)	Phil Rizzuto	3,000	1,500	900.00

1967-68 Coca-Cola Bottle Caps

Over two seasons, bottles of Coke products (Coca-Cola, Fresca, Tab, Sprite and Fanta) were sealed with caps bearing the pictures of major league ballplayers. The 1" diameter caps have a small baseball symbol on the top of the cap. Inside, protected by a clear plastic liner, is a black-and-white portrait photo of a player. (Most photos have cap insignia blacked out.) His team nickname is printed at top, his name at bottom and his position at right (1967 only in team issues, 1967-68 in All-Stars). To the left of the picture is an identification number, usually with a letter prefix. In areas with major league baseball teams, regional issues of the caps featured local players with a letter prefix to the number. Also released in those areas were American League or National League All-Star sets, with cap number preceded by an "A" or "N." In areas not served by major league teams, a 35-cap All-Star series with no prefix letter was issued. While most caps were identical in both years of issue, some player team changes, etc., are reflected in updated caps in 1968. Severe bending by bottle openers and rust are specific detriments to condition often found on these caps. Collectors usually save these caps without regard to which specific brand of soda appears on top, though obviously the Coca-Cola pieces are much more common. Cap-saver sheets are available which, when filled, could be exchanged for a team set of photocards (see 1967 Dexter Press Premiums) or other prizes.

	NM	EX	VG
Complete Set (580):	4,000	2,000	1,200
Common Player:	5.00	2.50	1.50
Playing Tips (16):	3.00	1.50	.90
Sprite, Fresca, Tab + 10 Percent			

MAJOR LEAGUE ALL-STARS

		NM	EX	VG
1	Richie Allen	7.50	3.75	2.25
2	Pete Rose	32.50	16.00	9.75
3	Brooks Robinson	25.00	12.50	7.50
4	Marcelino Lopez	5.00	2.50	1.50
5	Rusty Staub	5.00	2.50	1.50
6	Ron Santo	7.50	3.75	2.25
7	Jim Nash	5.00	2.50	1.50
8	Jim Fregosi	5.00	2.50	1.50
9	Paul Casanova	5.00	2.50	1.50
10	Willie Mays	45.00	22.50	13.50
11	Willie Stargell	15.00	7.50	4.50
12	Tony Oliva	7.50	3.75	2.25
13	Joe Pepitone	7.50	3.75	2.25
14	Juan Marichal	12.00	6.00	3.50
15	Jim Bunning	12.00	6.00	3.50
16	Claude Osteen	5.00	2.50	1.50
17	Carl Yastrzemski	25.00	12.50	7.50
18	Harmon Killebrew	25.00	12.50	7.50
19	Hank Aaron	45.00	22.50	13.50
20	Joe Torre	7.50	3.75	2.25
21	Ernie Banks	25.00	12.50	7.50
22	Al Kaline	25.00	12.50	7.50
23	Frank Robinson	25.00	12.50	7.50
24	Max Alvis	5.00	2.50	1.50
25	Elston Howard	7.50	3.75	2.25
26	Gaylord Perry	12.00	6.00	3.50
27	Bill Mazeroski	12.00	6.00	3.50
28	Ron Swoboda	5.00	2.50	1.50
29	Vada Pinson	7.50	3.75	2.25
30	Joe Morgan	25.00	12.50	7.50
31	Cleon Jones	5.00	2.50	1.50
32	Willie Horton	5.00	2.50	1.50
33	Leon Wagner	5.00	2.50	1.50
34	George Scott	5.00	2.50	1.50
35	Ed Charles	5.00	2.50	1.50

NATIONAL LEAGUE ALL-STARS

		NM	EX	VG
N7	Tom Seaver	15.00	7.00	4.50
N19	Hank Aaron	40.00	20.00	12.00
N20	Jim Bunning	10.00	5.00	3.00
N21	Joe Torre	6.00	3.00	1.75
N22	Claude Osteen	5.00	2.50	1.50
N23	Ron Santo	6.00	3.00	1.75
N24	Joe Morgan	20.00	10.00	6.00
N25	Richie Allen	6.00	3.00	1.75
N26	Ron Swoboda	5.00	2.50	1.50
N27	Ernie Banks	20.00	10.00	6.00
N28	Bill Mazeroski	12.00	6.00	3.50
N29	Willie Stargell	12.00	6.00	3.50
N30	Pete Rose	25.00	12.50	7.50
N31	Gaylord Perry	10.00	5.00	3.00
N32	Rusty Staub	5.00	2.50	1.50
N33	Vada Pinson	6.00	3.00	1.75
N34	Juan Marichal	10.00	5.00	3.00
N35	Cleon Jones	5.00	2.50	1.50

AMERICAN LEAGUE ALL-STARS

		NM	EX	VG
A19	Al Kaline	20.00	10.00	6.00
A20	Frank Howard	5.00	2.50	1.50
A21	Brooks Robinson	20.00	10.00	6.00
A22	George Scott	5.00	2.50	1.50
A23	Willie Horton	5.00	2.50	1.50
A24	Jim Fregosi	5.00	2.50	1.50
A25	Ed Charles	5.00	2.50	1.50
A26	Harmon Killebrew	20.00	10.00	6.00
A27	Tony Oliva	6.00	3.00	1.75
A28	Joe Pepitone	6.00	3.00	1.75
A29	Elston Howard	6.00	3.00	1.75
A30	Jim Nash	5.00	2.50	1.50

		NM	EX	VG
A31	Marcelino Lopez	5.00	2.50	1.50
A32	Frank Robinson	20.00	10.00	6.00
A33	Leon Wagner	5.00	2.50	1.50
A34	Max Alvis	5.00	2.50	1.50
A35	Paul Casanova	5.00	2.50	1.50

PLAYING TIPS

		NM	EX	VG
19	SS fields ball . . .	3.00	1.50	.90
20	2b relays . . .	3.00	1.50	.90
21	1b completes DP	3.00	1.50	.90
22	Pitcher fields bunt . . .	3.00	1.50	.90
23	2b relays . . .	3.00	1.50	.90
24	1b complete DP	3.00	1.50	.90
25	CF makes catch . . .	3.00	1.50	.90
26	Catcher tags runner	3.00	1.50	.90

1967 ATLANTA BRAVES

		NM	EX	VG
B1	Gary Geiger	5.00	2.50	1.50
B2	Ty Cline	5.00	2.50	1.50
B3	Hank Aaron	45.00	22.50	13.50
B4	Gene Oliver	5.00	2.50	1.50
B5	Tony Cloninger	5.00	2.50	1.50
B6	Denis Menke	5.00	2.50	1.50
B7	Denny Lemaster	5.00	2.50	1.50
B8	Woody Woodward	5.00	2.50	1.50
B9	Joe Torre	7.50	3.75	2.25
B10	Ken Johnson	5.00	2.50	1.50
B11	Bob Bruce	5.00	2.50	1.50
B12	Felipe Alou	7.50	3.75	2.25
B13	Clete Boyer	5.00	2.50	1.50
B14	Wade Blasingame	5.00	2.50	1.50
B15	Don Schwall	5.00	2.50	1.50
B16	Dick Kelley	5.00	2.50	1.50
B17	Rico Carty	6.00	3.00	1.75
B18	Mack Jones	5.00	2.50	1.50

1968 ATLANTA BRAVES

		NM	EX	VG
B1	Cecil Upshaw	5.00	2.50	1.50
B2	Tito Francona	5.00	2.50	1.50
B3	Hank Aaron	40.00	20.00	12.00
B4	Pat Jarvis	5.00	2.50	1.50
B5	Tony Cloninger	5.00	2.50	1.50
B6	Phil Niekro	15.00	7.50	4.50
B7	Felix Millan	5.00	2.50	1.50
B8	Woody Woodward	5.00	2.50	1.50
B9	Joe Torre	7.50	3.75	2.25
B10	Ken Johnson	5.00	2.50	1.50
B11	Marty Martinez	5.00	2.50	1.50
B12	Felipe Alou	7.50	3.75	2.25
B13	Clete Boyer	5.00	2.50	1.50
B14	Sonny Jackson	5.00	2.50	1.50
B15	Deron Johnson	5.00	2.50	1.50
B16	Claude Raymond	5.00	2.50	1.50
B17	Rico Carty	6.00	3.00	1.75
B18	Mack Jones	5.00	2.50	1.50

1967 BALTIMORE ORIOLES

		NM	EX	VG
O1	Dave McNally	5.00	2.50	1.50
O2	Luis Aparicio	20.00	10.00	6.00
O3	Paul Blair	5.00	2.50	1.50
O4	Frank Robinson	25.00	12.50	7.50
O5	Jim Palmer	30.00	15.00	9.00
O6	Russ Snyder	5.00	2.50	1.50
O7	Stu Miller	5.00	2.50	1.50
O8	Dave Johnson	5.00	2.50	1.50
O9	Andy Etchebarren	5.00	2.50	1.50
O10	Brooks Robinson	25.00	12.50	7.50
O11	John Powell	12.00	6.00	3.50
O12	Sam Bowens	5.00	2.50	1.50
O13	Curt Blefary	5.00	2.50	1.50
O14	Ed Fisher	5.00	2.50	1.50
O15	Wally Bunker	5.00	2.50	1.50
O16	Moe Drabowsky	5.00	2.50	1.50
O17	Larry Haney	5.00	2.50	1.50
O18	Tom Phoebus	5.00	2.50	1.50

1968 BALTIMORE ORIOLES

		NM	EX	VG
O1	Dave McNally	5.00	2.50	1.50
O2	Jim Hardin	5.00	2.50	1.50
O3	Paul Blair	5.00	2.50	1.50
O4	Frank Robinson	25.00	12.50	7.50
O5	Bruce Howard	5.00	2.50	1.50
O6	John O'Donoghue	5.00	2.50	1.50
O7	Dave May	5.00	2.50	1.50
O8	Dave Johnson	5.00	2.50	1.50
O9	Andy Etchebarren	5.00	2.50	1.50
O10	Brooks Robinson	25.00	12.50	7.50
O11	John Powell	8.00	4.00	2.50
O12	Pete Richert	5.00	2.50	1.50
O13	Curt Blefary	5.00	2.50	1.50
O14	Mark Belanger	6.00	3.00	1.75
O15	Wally Bunker	5.00	2.50	1.50
O16	Don Buford	5.00	2.50	1.50
O17	Larry Haney	5.00	2.50	1.50
O18	Tom Phoebus	5.00	2.50	1.50

1967 BOSTON RED SOX

		NM	EX	VG
R1	Lee Stange	5.00	2.50	1.50
R2	Carl Yastrzemski	30.00	15.00	9.00
R3	Don Demeter	5.00	2.50	1.50
R4	Jose Santiago	5.00	2.50	1.50
R5	Darrell Brandon	5.00	2.50	1.50
R6	Joe Foy	5.00	2.50	1.50
R7	Don McMahon	5.00	2.50	1.50
R8	Dalton Jones	5.00	2.50	1.50
R9	Mike Ryan	5.00	2.50	1.50
R10	Bob Tillman	5.00	2.50	1.50
R11	Rico Petrocelli	6.00	3.00	1.75
R12	George Scott	5.00	2.50	1.50
R13	George Smith	5.00	2.50	1.50
R14	Dennis Bennett	5.00	2.50	1.50
R15	Hank Fischer	5.00	2.50	1.50
R16	Jim Lonborg	6.00	3.00	1.75
R17	Jose Tartabull	5.00	2.50	1.50
R18	George Thomas	5.00	2.50	1.50

1968 BOSTON RED SOX

		NM	EX	VG
R1	Lee Stange	5.00	2.50	1.50
R2	Gary Waslewski	5.00	2.50	1.50
R3	Gary Bell	5.00	2.50	1.50
R4	John Wyatt	5.00	2.50	1.50
R5	Darrell Brandon	5.00	2.50	1.50
R6	Joe Foy	5.00	2.50	1.50
R7	Ray Culp	5.00	2.50	1.50
R8	Dalton Jones	5.00	2.50	1.50

1967 CALIFORNIA ANGELS

		NM	EX	VG
R9	Gene Oliver	5.00	2.50	1.50
R10	Jose Santiago	5.00	2.50	1.50
R11	Rico Petrocelli	6.00	3.00	1.75
R12	George Scott	5.00	2.50	1.50
R13	Mike Andrews	5.00	2.50	1.50
R14	Dick Ellsworth	5.00	2.50	1.50
R15	Norm Siebern	5.00	2.50	1.50
R16	Jim Lonborg	6.00	3.00	1.75
R17	Jerry Adair	5.00	2.50	1.50
R18	Elston Howard	5.00	2.50	1.50

1967 CALIFORNIA ANGELS

		NM	EX	VG
L19	Len Gabrielson	5.00	2.50	1.50
L20	Jackie Hernandez	5.00	2.50	1.50
L21	Paul Schaal	5.00	2.50	1.50
L22	Lew Burdette	5.00	2.50	1.50
L23	Jimmie Hall	5.00	2.50	1.50
L24	Fred Newman	5.00	2.50	1.50
L25	Don Mincher	5.00	2.50	1.50
L26	Bob Rodgers	5.00	2.50	1.50
L27	Jack Sanford	5.00	2.50	1.50
L28	Bobby Knoop	5.00	2.50	1.50
L29	Jose Cardenal	5.00	2.50	1.50
L30	Jim Fregosi	5.00	2.50	1.50
L31	George Brunet	5.00	2.50	1.50
L32	Marcelino Lopez	5.00	2.50	1.50
L33	Minnie Rojas	5.00	2.50	1.50
L34	Jay Johnstone	5.00	2.50	1.50
L35	Ed Kirkpatrick	5.00	2.50	1.50

1967 CHICAGO CUBS

		NM	EX	VG
C1	Ferguson Jenkins	15.00	7.50	4.50
C2	Ernie Banks	30.00	15.00	9.00
C3	Glenn Beckert	5.00	2.50	1.50
C4	Bob Hendley	5.00	2.50	1.50
C5	John Boccabella	5.00	2.50	1.50
C6	Ron Campbell	5.00	2.50	1.50
C7	Ray Culp	5.00	2.50	1.50
C8	Adolfo Phillips	5.00	2.50	1.50
C9	Don Bryant	5.00	2.50	1.50
C10	Randy Hundley	5.00	2.50	1.50
C11	Ron Santo	6.00	3.00	1.75
C12	Lee Thomas	5.00	2.50	1.50
C13	Billy Williams	25.00	12.50	7.50
C14	Ken Holtzman	5.00	2.50	1.50
C15	Cal Koonce	5.00	2.50	1.50
C16	Curt Simmons	5.00	2.50	1.50
C17	George Altman	5.00	2.50	1.50
C18	Bryon Browne	5.00	2.50	1.50

CHICAGO WHITE SOX

		NM	EX	VG
L1	Gary Peters	5.00	2.50	1.50
L2	Jerry Adair	5.00	2.50	1.50
L3	Al Weis	5.00	2.50	1.50
L4	Pete Ward	5.00	2.50	1.50
L5	Hoyt Wilhelm	15.00	7.50	4.50
L6	Don Buford	5.00	2.50	1.50
L7	John Buzhardt	5.00	2.50	1.50
L8	Wayne Causey	5.00	2.50	1.50
L9	Jerry McNertney	5.00	2.50	1.50
L10	Ron Hansen	5.00	2.50	1.50
L11	Tom McCraw	5.00	2.50	1.50
L12	Jim O'Toole	5.00	2.50	1.50
L13	Bill Skowron	6.00	3.00	1.75
L14	Joel Horlen	5.00	2.50	1.50
L15	Tommy John	12.00	6.00	3.50
L16	Bob Locker	5.00	2.50	1.50
L17	Ken Berry	5.00	2.50	1.50
L18	Tommie Agee	5.00	2.50	1.50

1967 CINCINNATI REDS

		NM	EX	VG
F1	Floyd Robinson	5.00	2.50	1.50
F2	Leo Cardenas	5.00	2.50	1.50
F3	Gordy Coleman	5.00	2.50	1.50
F4	Tommy Harper	5.00	2.50	1.50
F5	Tommy Helms	5.00	2.50	1.50
F6	Deron Johnson	5.00	2.50	1.50
F7	Jim Maloney	5.00	2.50	1.50
F8	Tony Perez	25.00	12.50	7.50
F9	Don Pavletich	5.00	2.50	1.50
F10	John Edwards	5.00	2.50	1.50
F11	Vada Pinson	7.50	3.75	2.25
F12	Chico Ruiz	5.00	2.50	1.50
F13	Pete Rose	40.00	20.00	12.00
F14	Bill McCool	5.00	2.50	1.50
F15	Joe Nuxhall	5.00	2.50	1.50
F16	Milt Pappas	5.00	2.50	1.50
F17	Art Shamsky	5.00	2.50	1.50
F18	Dick Simpson	5.00	2.50	1.50

1967 CLEVELAND INDIANS

		NM	EX	VG
I1	Luis Tiant	6.00	3.00	1.75
I2	Max Alvis	5.00	2.50	1.50
I3	Larry Brown	5.00	2.50	1.50
I4	Rocky Colavito	10.00	5.00	3.00
I5	John O'Donoghue	5.00	2.50	1.50
I6	Pedro Gonzalez	5.00	2.50	1.50
I7	Gary Bell	5.00	2.50	1.50
I8	Sonny Siebert	5.00	2.50	1.50
I9	Joe Azcue	5.00	2.50	1.50
I10	Lee Maye	5.00	2.50	1.50
I11	Chico Salmon	5.00	2.50	1.50
I12	Leon Wagner	5.00	2.50	1.50
I13	Fred Whitfield	5.00	2.50	1.50
I14	Jack Kralick	5.00	2.50	1.50
I15	Sam McDowell	6.00	3.00	1.75
I16	Dick Radatz	5.00	2.50	1.50
I17	Vic Davalillo	5.00	2.50	1.50
I18	Chuck Hinton	5.00	2.50	1.50

1968 CLEVELAND INDIANS

		NM	EX	VG
I1	Luis Tiant	6.00	3.00	1.75
I2	Max Alvis	5.00	2.50	1.50
I3	Larry Brown	5.00	2.50	1.50
I4	Tommy Harper	5.00	2.50	1.50
I5	Vern Fuller	5.00	2.50	1.50
I6	Jose Cardenal	5.00	2.50	1.50
I7	Dave Nelson	5.00	2.50	1.50
I8	Sonny Siebert	5.00	2.50	1.50
I9	Joe Azcue	5.00	2.50	1.50
I10	Lee Maye	5.00	2.50	1.50
I11	Chico Salmon	5.00	2.50	1.50
I12	Leon Wagner	5.00	2.50	1.50
I13	Eddie Fisher	5.00	2.50	1.50

I14	Stan Williams	5.00	2.50	1.50
I15	Sam McDowell	6.00	3.00	1.75
I16	Steve Hargan	5.00	2.50	1.50
I17	Vic Davalillo	5.00	2.50	1.50
I18	Duke Sims	5.00	2.50	1.50

1967 DETROIT TIGERS

T1	Larry Sherry	5.00	2.50	1.50
T2	Norm Cash	7.50	3.75	2.25
T3	Jerry Lumpe	5.00	2.50	1.50
T4	Dave Wickersham	5.00	2.50	1.50
T5	Joe Sparma	5.00	2.50	1.50
T6	Dick McAuliffe	5.00	2.50	1.50
T7	Fred Gladding	5.00	2.50	1.50
T8	Jim Northrup	5.00	2.50	1.50
T9	Bill Freehan	5.00	2.50	1.50
T10	Earl Wilson	5.00	2.50	1.50
T11	Dick Tracewski	5.00	2.50	1.50
T12	Don Wert	5.00	2.50	1.50
T13	Jake Wood	5.00	2.50	1.50
T14	Mickey Lolich	6.00	3.00	1.75
T15	Johnny Podres	5.00	2.50	1.50
T16	Bill Monbouquette	5.00	2.50	1.50
T17	Al Kaline	30.00	15.00	9.00
T18	Willie Horton	5.00	2.50	1.50

1968 DETROIT TIGERS

T1	Ray Oyler	5.00	2.50	1.50
T2	Norm Cash	7.50	3.75	2.25
T3	Mike Marshall	5.00	2.50	1.50
T4	Mickey Stanley	5.00	2.50	1.50
T5	Joe Sparma	5.00	2.50	1.50
T6	Dick McAuliffe	5.00	2.50	1.50
T7	Gates Brown	5.00	2.50	1.50
T8	Jim Northrup	5.00	2.50	1.50
T9	Bill Freehan	5.00	2.50	1.50
T10	Earl Wilson	5.00	2.50	1.50
T11	Dick Tracewski	5.00	2.50	1.50
T12	Don Wert	5.00	2.50	1.50
T13	Dennis Ribant	5.00	2.50	1.50
T14	Mickey Lolich	6.00	3.00	1.75
T15	Denny McLain	12.00	6.00	3.50
T16	Ed Mathews	25.00	12.50	7.50
T17	Al Kaline	30.00	15.00	9.00
T18	Willie Horton	5.00	2.50	1.50

1967 HOUSTON ASTROS

H1	Dave Giusti	5.00	2.50	1.50
H2	Bob Aspromonte	5.00	2.50	1.50
H3	Ron Davis	5.00	2.50	1.50
H4	Claude Raymond	5.00	2.50	1.50
H5	Barry Latman	5.00	2.50	1.50
H6	Chuck Harrison	5.00	2.50	1.50
H7	Bill Heath	5.00	2.50	1.50
H8	Sonny Jackson	5.00	2.50	1.50
H9	John Bateman	5.00	2.50	1.50
H10	Ron Brand	5.00	2.50	1.50
H11	Aaron Pointer	5.00	2.50	1.50
H12	Joe Morgan	25.00	12.50	7.50
H13	Rusty Staub	6.00	3.00	1.75
H14	Mike Cuellar	5.00	2.50	1.50
H15	Larry Dierker	5.00	2.50	1.50
H16	Dick Farrell	5.00	2.50	1.50
H17	Jim Landis	5.00	2.50	1.50
H18	Ed Mathews	25.00	12.50	7.50

1968 HOUSTON ASTROS

H1	Dave Giusti	5.00	2.50	1.50
H2	Bob Aspromonte	5.00	2.50	1.50
H3	Ron Davis	5.00	2.50	1.50
H4	Julio Gotay	5.00	2.50	1.50
H5	Fred Gladding	5.00	2.50	1.50
H6	Lee Thomas	5.00	2.50	1.50
H7	Wade Blasingame	5.00	2.50	1.50
H8	Denis Menke	5.00	2.50	1.50
H9	John Bateman	5.00	2.50	1.50
H10	Ron Brand	5.00	2.50	1.50
H11	Doug Rader	5.00	2.50	1.50
H12	Joe Morgan	25.00	12.50	7.50
H13	Rusty Staub	6.00	3.00	1.75
H14	Mike Cuellar	5.00	2.50	1.50
H15	Larry Dierker	5.00	2.50	1.50
H16	Denny Lemaster	5.00	2.50	1.50
H17	Jim Wynn	5.00	2.50	1.50
H18	Don Wilson	5.00	2.50	1.50

1967 KANSAS CTIY ATHLETICS

K1	Jim Nash	5.00	2.50	1.50
K2	Bert Campaneris	5.00	2.50	1.50
K3	Ed Charles	5.00	2.50	1.50
K4	Wes Stock	5.00	2.50	1.50
K5	John Odom	5.00	2.50	1.50
K6	Ossie Chavarria	5.00	2.50	1.50
K7	Jack Aker	5.00	2.50	1.50
K8	Dick Green	5.00	2.50	1.50
K9	Phil Roof	5.00	2.50	1.50
K10	Rene Lacheman	5.00	2.50	1.50
K11	Mike Hershberger	5.00	2.50	1.50
K12	Joe Nossek	5.00	2.50	1.50
K13	Roger Repoz	5.00	2.50	1.50
K14	Chuck Dobson	5.00	2.50	1.50
K15	Jim Hunter	15.00	7.50	4.50
K16	Lew Krausse	5.00	2.50	1.50
K17	Danny Cater	5.00	2.50	1.50
K18	Jim Gosger	5.00	2.50	1.50

1967 LOS ANGELES DODGERS

L1	Phil Regan	5.00	2.50	1.50
L2	Bob Bailey	5.00	2.50	1.50
L3	Ron Fairly	5.00	2.50	1.50
L4	Joe Moeller	5.00	2.50	1.50
L5	Don Sutton	15.00	7.50	4.50
L6	Ron Hunt	5.00	2.50	1.50
L7	Jim Brewer	5.00	2.50	1.50
L8	Lou Johnson	5.00	2.50	1.50
L9	John Roseboro	5.00	2.50	1.50
L10	Jeff Torborg	5.00	2.50	1.50
L11	Jim Kennedy	5.00	2.50	1.50
L12	Jim Lefebvre	5.00	2.50	1.50
L13	Wes Parker	5.00	2.50	1.50
L14	Bob Miller	5.00	2.50	1.50
L15	Claude Osteen	5.00	2.50	1.50
L16	Ron Perranoski	5.00	2.50	1.50
L17	Willie Davis	5.00	2.50	1.50

L18	Al Ferrera	5.00	2.50	1.50

1968 LOS ANGELES DODGERS

L1	Phil Regan	5.00	2.50	1.50
L2	Bob Bailey	5.00	2.50	1.50
L3	Ron Fairly	5.00	2.50	1.50
L4	Jim Brewer	5.00	2.50	1.50
L5	Don Sutton	15.00	7.50	4.50
L6	Tom Haller	5.00	2.50	1.50
L7	Rocky Colavito	12.00	6.00	3.50
L8	Jim Grant	5.00	2.50	1.50
L9	Jim Campanis	5.00	2.50	1.50
L10	Jeff Torborg	5.00	2.50	1.50
L11	Zoilo Versalles	6.00	3.00	1.75
L12	Jim Lefebvre	5.00	2.50	1.50
L13	Wes Parker	5.00	2.50	1.50
L14	Bill Singer	5.00	2.50	1.50
L15	Claude Osteen	5.00	2.50	1.50
L16	Len Gabrielson	5.00	2.50	1.50
L17	Willie Davis	5.00	2.50	1.50
L18	Al Ferrera	5.00	2.50	1.50

1967 MINNESOTA TWINS

M1	Ron Kline	5.00	2.50	1.50
M2	Bob Allison	6.00	3.00	1.75
M3	Earl Battey	5.00	2.50	1.50
M4	Jim Merritt	5.00	2.50	1.50
M5	Jim Perry	6.00	3.00	1.75
M6	Harmon Killebrew	25.00	12.50	7.50
M7	Dave Boswell	5.00	2.50	1.50
M8	Rich Rollins	5.00	2.50	1.50
M9	Jerry Zimmerman	5.00	2.50	1.50
M10	Al Worthington	5.00	2.50	1.50
M11	Cesar Tovar	5.00	2.50	1.50
M12	Sandy Valdespino	5.00	2.50	1.50
M13	Zoilo Versalles	6.00	3.00	1.75
M14	Dean Chance	6.00	3.00	1.75
M15	Jim Grant	5.00	2.50	1.50
M16	Jim Kaat	9.00	4.50	2.75
M17	Tony Oliva	10.00	5.00	3.00
M18	Andy Kosco	5.00	2.50	1.50

1968 MINNESOTA TWINS

M1	Rich Reese	5.00	2.50	1.50
M2	Bob Allison	6.00	3.00	1.75
M3	Ron Perranoski	5.00	2.50	1.50
M4	John Roseboro	5.00	2.50	1.50
M5	Jim Perry	6.00	3.00	1.75
M6	Harmon Killebrew	25.00	12.50	7.50
M7	Dave Boswell	5.00	2.50	1.50
M8	Rich Rollins	5.00	2.50	1.50
M9	Jerry Zimmerman	5.00	2.50	1.50
M10	Al Worthington	5.00	2.50	1.50
M11	Cesar Tovar	5.00	2.50	1.50
M12	Jim Merritt	5.00	2.50	1.50
M13	Bob Miller	5.00	2.50	1.50
M14	Dean Chance	6.00	3.00	1.75
M15	Ted Uhlaender	5.00	2.50	1.50
M16	Jim Kaat	9.00	4.50	2.75
M17	Tony Oliva	10.00	5.00	3.00
M18	Rod Carew	40.00	20.00	12.00

1967 NEW YORK METS

V19	Chuck Hiller	5.00	2.50	1.50
V20	Johnny Lewis	5.00	2.50	1.50
V21	Ed Kranepool	5.00	2.50	1.50
V22	Al Luplow	5.00	2.50	1.50
V23	Don Cardwell	5.00	2.50	1.50
V24	Cleon Jones	5.00	2.50	1.50
V25	Bob Shaw	5.00	2.50	1.50
V26	John Stephenson	5.00	2.50	1.50
V27	Ron Swoboda	5.00	2.50	1.50
V28	Ken Boyer	6.00	3.00	1.75
V29	Ed Bressoud	5.00	2.50	1.50
V30	Tommy Davis	5.00	2.50	1.50
V31	Roy McMillan	5.00	2.50	1.50
V32	Jack Fisher	5.00	2.50	1.50
V33	Tug McGraw	6.00	3.00	1.75
V34	Jerry Grote	5.00	2.50	1.50
V35	Jack Hamilton	5.00	2.50	1.50

1967 NEW YORK YANKEES

V1	Mel Stottlemyre	5.00	2.50	1.50
V2	Ruben Amaro	5.00	2.50	1.50
V3	Jake Gibbs	5.00	2.50	1.50
V4	Dooley Womack	5.00	2.50	1.50
V5	Fred Talbot	5.00	2.50	1.50
V6	Horace Clarke	5.00	2.50	1.50
V7	Jim Bouton	6.00	3.00	1.75
V8	Mickey Mantle	125.00	60.00	35.00
V9	Elston Howard	7.50	3.75	2.25
V10	Hal Reniff	5.00	2.50	1.50
V11	Charley Smith	5.00	2.50	1.50
V12	Bobby Murcer	6.00	3.00	1.75
V13	Joe Pepitone	6.00	3.00	1.75
V14	Al Downing	5.00	2.50	1.50
V15	Steve Hamilton	5.00	2.50	1.50
V16	Fritz Peterson	5.00	2.50	1.50
V17	Tom Tresh	6.00	3.00	1.75
V18	Roy White	6.00	3.00	1.75

1967 PHILADELPHIA PHILLIES

P1	Richie Allen	7.50	3.75	2.25
P2	Bob Wine	5.00	2.50	1.50
P3	Johnny Briggs	5.00	2.50	1.50
P4	John Callison	5.00	2.50	1.50
P5	Doug Clemens	5.00	2.50	1.50
P6	Dick Groat	5.00	2.50	1.50
P7	Dick Ellsworth	5.00	2.50	1.50
P8	Phil Linz	5.00	2.50	1.50
P9	Clay Dalrymple	5.00	2.50	1.50
P10	Bob Uecker	10.00	5.00	3.00
P11	Cookie Rojas	5.00	2.50	1.50
P12	Tony Taylor	5.00	2.50	1.50
P13	Bill White	5.00	2.50	1.50
P14	Larry Jackson	5.00	2.50	1.50
P15	Chris Short	5.00	2.50	1.50
P16	Jim Bunning	15.00	7.50	4.50
P17	Tony Gonzalez	5.00	2.50	1.50
P18	Don Lock	5.00	2.50	1.50

1967 PITTSBURGH PIRATES

E1	Al McBean	5.00	2.50	1.50
E2	Gene Alley	5.00	2.50	1.50
E3	Donn Clendenon	5.00	2.50	1.50
E4	Bob Veale	5.00	2.50	1.50
E5	Pete Mikkelsen	5.00	2.50	1.50
E6	Bill Mazeroski	20.00	10.00	6.00
E7	Steve Blass	5.00	2.50	1.50
E8	Manny Mota	5.00	2.50	1.50
E9	Jim Pagliaroni	5.00	2.50	1.50
E10	Jesse Gonder	5.00	2.50	1.50
E11	Jose Pagan	5.00	2.50	1.50
E12	Willie Stargell	25.00	12.50	7.50
E13	Maury Wills	9.00	4.50	2.75
E14	Elroy Face	5.00	2.50	1.50
E15	Woodie Fryman	5.00	2.50	1.50
E16	Vern Law	5.00	2.50	1.50
E17	Matty Alou	5.00	2.50	1.50
E18	Roberto Clemente	60.00	30.00	18.00

1967 SAN FRANCISCO GIANTS

G1	Bob Bolin	5.00	2.50	1.50
G2	Ollie Brown	5.00	2.50	1.50
G3	Jim Davenport	5.00	2.50	1.50
G4	Tito Fuentes	5.00	2.50	1.50
G5	Norm Siebern	5.00	2.50	1.50
G6	Jim Hart	5.00	2.50	1.50
G7	Juan Marichal	15.00	7.50	4.50
G8	Hal Lanier	5.00	2.50	1.50
G9	Tom Haller	5.00	2.50	1.50
G10	Bob Barton	5.00	2.50	1.50
G11	Willie McCovey	20.00	10.00	6.00
G12	Mike McCormick	5.00	2.50	1.50
G13	Frank Linzy	5.00	2.50	1.50
G14	Ray Sadecki	5.00	2.50	1.50
G15	Gaylord Perry	15.00	7.50	4.50
G16	Lindy McDaniel	5.00	2.50	1.50
G17	Willie Mays	60.00	30.00	18.00
G18	Jesus Alou	5.00	2.50	1.50

1968 SAN FRANCISCO GIANTS

G1	Bob Bolin	5.00	2.50	1.50
G2	Ollie Brown	5.00	2.50	1.50
G3	Jim Davenport	5.00	2.50	1.50
G4	Bob Barton	5.00	2.50	1.50
G5	Jack Hiatt	5.00	2.50	1.50
G6	Jim Hart	5.00	2.50	1.50
G7	Juan Marichal	15.00	7.50	4.50
G8	Hal Lanier	5.00	2.50	1.50
G9	Ron Hunt	5.00	2.50	1.50
G10	Ron Herbel	5.00	2.50	1.50
G11	Willie McCovey	20.00	10.00	6.00
G12	Mike McCormick	5.00	2.50	1.50
G13	Frank Linzy	5.00	2.50	1.50
G14	Ray Sadecki	5.00	2.50	1.50
G15	Gaylord Perry	15.00	7.50	4.50
G16	Lindy McDaniel	5.00	2.50	1.50
G17	Willie Mays	60.00	30.00	18.00
G18	Jesus Alou	5.00	2.50	1.50

1967 WASHINGTON SENATORS

S1	Bob Humphreys	5.00	2.50	1.50
S2	Bernie Allen	5.00	2.50	1.50
S3	Ed Brinkman	5.00	2.50	1.50
S4	Pete Richert	5.00	2.50	1.50
S5	Camilo Pascual	5.00	2.50	1.50
S6	Frank Howard	7.50	3.75	2.25
S7	Casey Cox	5.00	2.50	1.50
S8	Jim King	5.00	2.50	1.50
S9	Paul Casanova	5.00	2.50	1.50
S10	Dick Lines	5.00	2.50	1.50
S11	Dick Nen	5.00	2.50	1.50
S12	Ken McMullen	5.00	2.50	1.50
S13	Bob Saverine	5.00	2.50	1.50
S14	Jim Hannan	5.00	2.50	1.50
S15	Darold Knowles	5.00	2.50	1.50
S16	Phil Ortega	5.00	2.50	1.50
S17	Ken Harrelson	5.00	2.50	1.50
S18	Fred Valentine	5.00	2.50	1.50

1971 Coca-Cola Houston Astros

 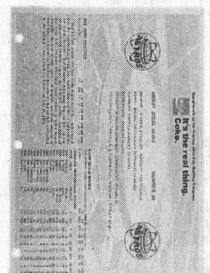

The constitution and distribution of these Coke premium pictures is unknown. Players are pictured in pastel drawings on the semi-gloss fronts of these 8" x 11" sheets. (The punch holes on the photographed card are not original.) A black facsimile autograph appears in the lower portion of the drawing and the player's name is printed in black in the white bottom border. Backs are printed in blue and red with a background photo of the Astrodome. Data on back includes biographical information, complete pro record and career summary. The unnumbered cards are checklisted here in alphabetical order; but this list is probably not complete.

	NM	EX	VG
Complete Set (12):	50.00	25.00	15.00
Common Player:	5.00	2.50	1.50
(1) Jesus Alou	5.00	2.50	1.50
(2) Wade Blasingame/SP	9.00	4.50	2.75
(3) Cesar Cedeno	7.50	3.75	2.25
(4) Larry Dierker	7.50	3.75	2.25
(5) John Edwards	5.00	2.50	1.50
(6) Denis Menke	5.00	2.50	1.50
(7) Roger Metzger	5.00	2.50	1.50
(8) Joe Morgan	15.00	7.50	4.50

		NM	EX	VG
(9)	Doug Rader	5.00	2.50	1.50
(10)	Bob Watson	5.00	2.50	1.50
(11)	Don Wilson	5.00	2.50	1.50
(12)	Jim Wynn/SP	12.00	6.00	3.50

1978 Coca-Cola/WPLO Atlanta Braves

BOB HORNER
Infield

James Robert Horner. Born August 6, 1957 at Junction City, Kansas. Bats and throws right. Graduated from Apollo High School, Glendale, Arizona, 1975. Attended Arizona State University, Tempe, Arizona. Single. Lives in Glendale, Arizona. Acquired— Signed after selection in the first round of the 1978 free agent draft, June 14, 1978. Bob Horner, baseball's No. 1 pick in the '78 draft, set a National Collegiate Athletic Association records for home runs in a season with 25 and set a record with 56 in the 1976-78 seasons. He broke the single-season RBI record for a college player by driving in 100 runs in 60 games for Arizona State. Bob earned All-America honors each of the last two seasons, was named the Outstanding Player in the College World Series and earned all-tournament honors at the Series in '77. He led the nation in hits, home runs, runs batted in and total bases.

Co-sponsored by Coke and a local radio station, this set of Braves cards is rendered in blue-and-white line art portraits in a 3" x 4-1/4" format. A soda discount coupon was distributed with the set.

		NM	EX	VG
Complete Set (14):		30.00	15.00	9.00
Common Player:		3.00	1.50	.90
(1)	Barry Bonnell	3.00	1.50	.90
(2)	Jeff Burroughs	3.00	1.50	.90
(3)	Rick Camp	3.00	1.50	.90
(4)	Gene Garber	3.00	1.50	.90
(5)	Rod Gilbreath	3.00	1.50	.90
(6)	Bob Horner	4.50	2.25	1.25
(7)	Glenn Hubbard	3.00	1.50	.90
(8)	Gary Matthews	3.00	1.50	.90
(9)	Larry McWilliams	3.00	1.50	.90
(10)	Dale Murphy	9.00	4.50	2.75
(11)	Phil Niekro	5.00	2.50	1.50
(12)	Rowland Office	3.00	1.50	.90
(13)	Biff Pocoroba	3.00	1.50	.90
(14)	Jerry Royster	3.00	1.50	.90

1979 Coca-Cola/7-Eleven MVPs

The co-MVPs of the National League for 1979 are pictured on this 5" x 7" blank-back photo card. A red band at top identifies the player and the award. At bottom are Coke and 7-Eleven logos.

	NM	EX	VG
Keith Hernandez, Willie Stargell	6.00	3.00	1.80

1955 Coffee-Time Syrup Jimmy Piersall

 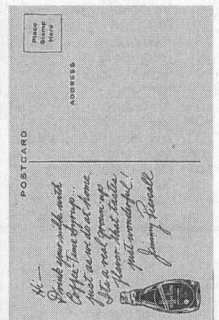

The date of issue is speculative for this promotional postcard. The borderless black-and-white photo on the front on this 3-1/2" x 5-1/2" card shows the popular BoSox star in a relaxed pose with right arm on knee. A blue or brown facsimile autograph is printed at center. The postcard-format back has at left a product picture and an advertising message bearing Piersall's signature. Similar cards advertising Colonial Meats, Cain's and other products are also known, valued similarly.

	NM	EX	VG
Autographed:	300.00	150.00	90.00
Jimmy Piersall	125.00	62.50	37.50

1909-1911 Colgan's Chips Stars of the Diamond (E254)

This unusual set of 1-7/16"-diameter round cards was issued over a three-year period by the Colgan Gum Co., Louisville, Ky. The cards were inserted in five-cent tins of Colgan's Mint Chips and Violet Chips brands of gum. The borderless cards feature a black-and-white player portrait on the front along with the player's last name, team and league. On more than a dozen cards, variations are known in the size of the photo and/or lettering on front. Since they cannot be identified without another card to compare with, they are noted here only with an asterisk. The card back identifies the set as "Stars of the Diamond" and carries advertising for Colgan's Gum. Some backs are seen with a line of type at the bottom stating, "208 IN PRESENT SERIES." Over 225 different players were pictured over the three-year period, but because of team changes and other notable variations, at least 289 different cards exist. This issue was catalogued as E254 in the American Card Catalog. A number of cards and variations which had been listed in earlier editions of this catalog have been eliminated for lack of proof of their existence. Gaps have been left in the assigned numbering to accommodate future additions. Persons with "Stars of the Diamond" players or variations that do no appear on this list should contact the editor. Recent hobby finds suggest a rare variation with violet- printed backs exist, perhaps packaged with "Violet Chips." Further confirmation is required before pricing data will be established.

		NM	EX	VG
Common Player:		75.00	35.00	20.00
Round Tin Package:		30.00	15.00	9.00
(1)	Ed Abbaticchio	75.00	35.00	20.00
(2)	Fred Abbott	75.00	35.00	20.00
(3a)	Bill Abstein (Pittsburg)	75.00	35.00	20.00
(3b)	Bill Abstein (Jersey City)	75.00	35.00	20.00
(4)	Babe Adams	75.00	35.00	20.00
(5)	Doc Adkins	75.00	35.00	20.00
(6a)	Dave Altizer (Cincinnati)	75.00	35.00	20.00
(6b)	Dave Altizer (Minneapolis)	75.00	35.00	20.00
(7)	Nick Altrock	95.00	50.00	30.00
(8)	Red Ames	75.00	35.00	20.00
(9a)	Jimmy Austin (New York)	75.00	35.00	20.00
(9b)	Jimmy Austin (St. Louis)	75.00	35.00	20.00
(10a)	Charlie Babb (Memphis)	75.00	35.00	20.00
(10b)	Charlie Babb (Norfolk)	75.00	35.00	20.00
(11)	Baerwald	75.00	35.00	20.00
(12)	Bill Bailey	75.00	35.00	20.00
(13)	Home Run Baker (*)	215.00	110.00	65.00
(14)	Jack Barry (*)	75.00	35.00	20.00
(15a)	Bill Bartley (Curved letters.)	75.00	35.00	20.00
(15b)	Bill Bartley (Horizontal letters.)	75.00	35.00	20.00
(16a)	Johnny Bates (Cincinnati)	75.00	35.00	20.00
(16b)	Johnny Bates (Philadelphia, black letters.)	75.00	35.00	20.00
(16c)	Johnny Bates (Philadelphia, white letters.)	75.00	35.00	20.00
(17)	Dick Bayless	75.00	35.00	20.00
(18a)	Ginger Beaumont (Boston)	75.00	35.00	20.00
(18b)	Ginger Beaumont (Chicago)	75.00	35.00	20.00
(18c)	Ginger Beaumont (St. Paul)	75.00	35.00	20.00
(19)	Beals Becker	75.00	35.00	20.00
(20)	George Bell	75.00	35.00	20.00
(21a)	Harry Bemis (Cleveland)	75.00	35.00	20.00
(21b)	Harry Bemis (Columbus)	75.00	35.00	20.00
(22a)	Heinie Berger (Cleveland)	75.00	35.00	20.00
(22b)	Heinie Berger (Columbus)	75.00	35.00	20.00
(23)	Beumiller	75.00	35.00	20.00
(24)	Joe Birmingham	75.00	35.00	20.00
(25)	Kitty Bransfield	75.00	35.00	20.00
(26)	Roger Bresnahan	215.00	110.00	65.00
(27)	Al Bridwell	75.00	35.00	20.00
(28)	Lew Brockett	75.00	35.00	20.00
(29)	Al Burch (*)	75.00	35.00	20.00
(30)	Burke	75.00	35.00	20.00
(31)	Donie Bush	75.00	35.00	20.00
(32)	Bill Byers	75.00	35.00	20.00
(33)	Howie Cammitz (Camnitz)	75.00	35.00	20.00
(34a)	Charlie Carr (Indianapolis)	75.00	35.00	20.00
(34b)	Charlie Carr (Utica)	75.00	35.00	20.00
(35)	Frank Chance	215.00	110.00	65.00
(36)	Hal Chase	150.00	80.00	40.00
(37)	Bill Clancy (Clancey)	75.00	35.00	20.00
(38a)	Fred Clarke (Pittsburg)	215.00	110.00	65.00
(38b)	Fred Clarke (Pittsburgh)	215.00	110.00	65.00
(39)	Tommy Clarke (Cincinnati)	75.00	35.00	20.00
(40)	Bill Clymer	75.00	35.00	20.00
(41)	Ty Cobb (*)	1,750	875.00	525.00
(42)	Eddie Collins	215.00	110.00	65.00
(43)	Bunk Congalton	75.00	35.00	20.00
(44)	Wid Conroy	75.00	35.00	20.00
(45)	Ernie Courtney	75.00	35.00	20.00
(46a)	Harry Coveleski (Cincinnati)	75.00	35.00	20.00
(46b)	Harry Coveleski (Chattanooga)	75.00	35.00	20.00
(47)	Doc Crandall	75.00	35.00	20.00
(48)	Gavvy Cravath	75.00	35.00	20.00
(49)	Dode Criss	75.00	35.00	20.00

		NM	EX	VG
(50a)	Jake Daubert (Memphis)	75.00	35.00	20.00
(50b)	Jake Daubert (Brooklyn)	75.00	35.00	20.00
(51)	Harry Davis (Philadelphia)	75.00	35.00	20.00
(52)	Davis (St. Paul)	75.00	35.00	20.00
(53)	Frank Delahanty	75.00	35.00	20.00
(54a)	Ray Demmett (Demmitt) (New York)	75.00	35.00	20.00
(54b)	Ray Demmett (Demmitt) (Montreal)	75.00	35.00	20.00
(55)	Art Devlin	75.00	35.00	20.00
(56)	Wild Bill Donovan	75.00	35.00	20.00
(57)	Mickey Doolin (Doolan)	75.00	35.00	20.00
(58)	Patsy Dougherty	75.00	35.00	20.00
(59)	Tom Downey	75.00	35.00	20.00
(60)	Larry Doyle	75.00	35.00	20.00
(61)	Jack Dunn	95.00	50.00	30.00
(62)	Dick Eagan (Egan)	75.00	35.00	20.00
(63a)	Kid Elberfield (Elberfeld) (Washington)	75.00	35.00	20.00
(63b)	Kid Elberfield (Elberfeld) (New York)	75.00	35.00	20.00
(64)	Rube Ellis	75.00	35.00	20.00
(65)	Clyde Engle (Boston)	75.00	35.00	20.00
(66)	Steve Evans (Horizontal letters.)	75.00	35.00	20.00
(67)	Johnny Evers	215.00	110.00	65.00
(68)	Cecil Ferguson	75.00	35.00	20.00
(69)	Hobe Ferris	75.00	35.00	20.00
(70)	Field (Montreal) (Photo actually Michael Joyce)	75.00	35.00	20.00
(71)	Fitzgerald	75.00	35.00	20.00
(72a)	Patsy Flaherty (Kansas City)	75.00	35.00	20.00
(72b)	Patsy Flaherty (Atlanta)	75.00	35.00	20.00
(73)	Jack Flater	75.00	35.00	20.00
(74a)	Elmer Flick (Cleveland)	215.00	110.00	65.00
(74b)	Elmer Flick (Toledo)	215.00	110.00	65.00
(75a)	James Freck (Frick, Baltimore)	90.00	45.00	30.00
(75b)	James Freck (Frick, Toronto)	75.00	35.00	20.00
(76)	Jerry Freeman (Photo actually Buck Freeman.)	75.00	35.00	20.00
(77)	Art Fromme (*)	75.00	35.00	20.00
(78a)	Larry Gardner (Boston)	75.00	35.00	20.00
(78b)	Larry Gardner (New York)	75.00	35.00	20.00
(79)	Harry Gaspar	75.00	35.00	20.00
(80a)	Gus Getz (Boston)	75.00	35.00	20.00
(80b)	Gus Getz (Indianapolis)	75.00	35.00	20.00
(81)	George Gibson	75.00	35.00	20.00
(82a)	Moose Grimshaw (Toronto)	75.00	35.00	20.00
(82b)	Moose Grimshaw (Louisville)	75.00	35.00	20.00
(83)	Ed Hahn	75.00	35.00	20.00
(84)	John Halla (*)	75.00	35.00	20.00
(85)	Ed Hally (Holly)	75.00	35.00	20.00
(86)	Charlie Hanford	75.00	35.00	20.00
(87)	Topsy Hartsel	75.00	35.00	20.00
(88a)	Roy Hartzell (St. Louis)	75.00	35.00	20.00
(88b)	Roy Hartzell (New York)	75.00	35.00	20.00
(89)	Weldon Henley	75.00	35.00	20.00
(91)	Harry Hinchman	75.00	35.00	20.00
(92)	Solly Hofman	75.00	35.00	20.00
(93a)	Harry Hooper (Boston Na'l)	215.00	110.00	65.00
(93b)	Harry Hooper (Boston Am. L.)	240.00	120.00	75.00
(94)	Howard (*)	75.00	35.00	20.00
(95a)	Hughes (No name in uniform.)	75.00	35.00	20.00
(95b)	Hughes (Name and team name in uniform.)	75.00	35.00	20.00
(96b)	Rudy Hulswitt (St. Louis)	75.00	35.00	20.00
(96c)	Rudy Hulswitt (Chattanooga)	75.00	35.00	20.00
(97)	John Hummel	75.00	35.00	20.00
(98)	George Hunter	75.00	35.00	20.00
(99)	Hugh Jennings	215.00	110.00	65.00
(100)	Davy Jones	75.00	35.00	20.00
(101)	Tom Jones	75.00	35.00	20.00
(102a)	Tim Jordon (Jordan, Brooklyn)	75.00	35.00	20.00
(102b)	Tim Jordon (Jordan, Atlanta)	75.00	35.00	20.00
(102c)	Tim Jordon (Jordan, Louisville)	75.00	35.00	20.00
(103)	Addie Joss	240.00	120.00	75.00
(104)	Al Kaiser	75.00	35.00	20.00
(105)	Joe Kelly (Kelley)	215.00	110.00	65.00
(106)	Bill Killefer (*)	75.00	35.00	20.00
(107a)	Ed Killian (Detroit)	75.00	35.00	20.00
(107b)	Ed Killian (Toronto)	75.00	35.00	20.00
(108)	Otto Knabe	75.00	35.00	20.00
(109)	Jack Knight	75.00	35.00	20.00
(111)	Ed Konetchy	75.00	35.00	20.00
(112)	Rube Kroh	75.00	35.00	20.00
(113)	James Lafitte	75.00	35.00	20.00
(114)	Lakoff	75.00	35.00	20.00
(115)	Frank Lange	75.00	35.00	20.00
(116a)	Frank LaPorte (St. Louis)	75.00	35.00	20.00
(116b)	Frank LaPorte (New York)	75.00	35.00	20.00
(117)	Tommy Leach	75.00	35.00	20.00
(118)	Bill Lelivelt	75.00	35.00	20.00
(119a)	Jack Lewis (Milwaukee)	75.00	35.00	20.00
(119b)	Jack Lewis (Indianapolis)	75.00	35.00	20.00
(120a)	Vive Lindaman (Boston)	75.00	35.00	20.00
(120b)	Vive Lindaman (Louisville)	75.00	35.00	20.00
(120c)	Vive Lindaman (Indianapolis)	75.00	35.00	20.00
(121)	Bris Lord	75.00	35.00	20.00
(122a)	Harry Lord (Boston)	75.00	35.00	20.00
(122b)	Harry Lord (Chicago)	75.00	35.00	20.00
(123)	Bill Ludwig (Milwaukee)	75.00	35.00	20.00
(124)	Nick Maddox	75.00	35.00	20.00
(125a)	Manser (Jersey City)	75.00	35.00	20.00
(125b)	Manser (Rochester)	75.00	35.00	20.00
(126)	Al Mattern	75.00	35.00	20.00
(127)	Bill Matthews	75.00	35.00	20.00
(128)	George McBride	75.00	35.00	20.00
(129)	Joe McCarthy (Toledo)	215.00	110.00	65.00
(130)	McConnell	75.00	35.00	20.00
(131)	Moose McCormick	75.00	35.00	20.00
(132)	Dan McGann	75.00	35.00	20.00
(133)	Jim McGinley	75.00	35.00	20.00
(134)	Iron Man McGinnity	215.00	110.00	65.00
(135a)	Matty McIntyre (Detroit)	75.00	35.00	20.00
(135b)	Matty McIntyre (Chicago)	75.00	35.00	20.00
(136)	Larry McLean (*)(Three photo size variations known.)	75.00	35.00	20.00
(137)	Fred Merkle	75.00	35.00	20.00

No.	Player			
(138a)	Merritt (Buffalo)	75.00	35.00	20.00
(138b)	Merritt (Jersey City)	75.00	35.00	20.00
(139)	Meyer (Newark)	75.00	35.00	20.00
(140)	Chief Meyers (New York)	75.00	35.00	20.00
(141)	Clyde Milan	75.00	35.00	20.00
(142)	Dots Miller	75.00	35.00	20.00
(143)	Mike Mitchell	75.00	35.00	20.00
(144)	Moran	75.00	35.00	20.00
(145a)	Bill Moriarty (Louisville)	75.00	35.00	20.00
(145b)	Bill Moriarty (Omaha)	75.00	35.00	20.00
(146)	George Moriarty	75.00	35.00	20.00
(147a)	George Mullen (Name incorrect.)	75.00	35.00	20.00
(147b)	George Mullin (Name correct.)	75.00	35.00	20.00
(148a)	Simmy Murch (Chattanooga)	75.00	35.00	20.00
(148b)	Simmy Murch (Indianapolis)	75.00	35.00	20.00
(149)	Danny Murphy	75.00	35.00	20.00
(150a)	Red Murray (New York, white letters.)	75.00	35.00	12.00
(150b)	Red Murray (St. Paul)	75.00	35.00	20.00
(151)	Billy Nattress (*)	75.00	35.00	20.00
(152a)	Red Nelson (St. Louis)	75.00	35.00	20.00
(152b)	Red Nelson (Toledo)	75.00	35.00	20.00
(153)	Rebel Oakes	75.00	35.00	20.00
(154)	Fred Odwell	75.00	35.00	20.00
(155a)	Al Orth (New York)	75.00	35.00	20.00
(155b)	Al Orth (Indianapolis)	75.00	35.00	20.00
(156)	Fred Osborn	75.00	35.00	20.00
(157)	Orval Overall	75.00	35.00	20.00
(158)	Owens	75.00	35.00	20.00
(159)	Fred Parent	75.00	35.00	20.00
(161a)	Dode Paskert (Cincinnati)	75.00	35.00	20.00
(161b)	Dode Paskert (Philadelphia)	75.00	35.00	20.00
(162)	Heinie Peitz	75.00	35.00	20.00
(163)	Bob Peterson	75.00	35.00	20.00
(164)	Jake Pfeister	75.00	35.00	20.00
(165)	Deacon Phillipe (Phillippe)	75.00	35.00	20.00
(166a)	Ollie Pickering (Louisville)	75.00	35.00	20.00
(166b)	Ollie Pickering (Minneapolis)	75.00	35.00	20.00
(166c)	Ollie Pickering (Omaha)	75.00	35.00	20.00
(167a)	Billy Purtell (Chicago)	75.00	35.00	20.00
(167b)	Billy Purtell (Boston)	75.00	35.00	20.00
(168)	Bugs Raymond	75.00	35.00	20.00
(169)	Pat Regan (Ragan)	75.00	35.00	20.00
(170)	Barney Reilly	75.00	35.00	20.00
(171)	Duke Reilly (Reilley)	75.00	35.00	20.00
(172)	Ed Reulbach	75.00	35.00	20.00
(173)	Claude Ritchey	75.00	35.00	20.00
(174)	Lou Ritter	75.00	35.00	20.00
(175)	William "Rabbit" Robinson (Louisville)	75.00	35.00	20.00
(176)	Rock	75.00	35.00	20.00
(177a)	Jack Rowan (Cincinnati)	75.00	35.00	20.00
(177b)	Jack Rowan (Philadelphia)	75.00	35.00	20.00
(178)	Nap Rucker	75.00	35.00	20.00
(179a)	Dick Rudolph (New York)	75.00	35.00	20.00
(179b)	Dick Rudolph (Toronto)	75.00	35.00	20.00
(180)	Jack Ryan (St. Paul)(Photo actually Jimmy Ryan.)	75.00	35.00	20.00
(181)	Slim Sallee	75.00	35.00	20.00
(182a)	Bill Schardt (Birmingham)	75.00	35.00	20.00
(182b)	Bill Schardt (Milwaukee)	75.00	35.00	20.00
(183)	Jimmy Scheckard (Sheckard)	75.00	35.00	20.00
(184a)	George Schirm (Birmingham)	75.00	35.00	20.00
(184b)	George Schirm (Buffalo)	75.00	35.00	20.00
(185)	Larry Schlafly	75.00	35.00	20.00
(186)	Wildfire Schulte	75.00	35.00	20.00
(187a)	James Seabaugh (Looking to left, photo actually Julius Weisman.)	75.00	35.00	20.00
(187b)	James Seabaugh (Looking straight ahead, correct photo.)	75.00	35.00	20.00
(188)	Selby (*)	75.00	35.00	20.00
(189a)	Cy Seymour (New York)	75.00	35.00	20.00
(189b)	Cy Seymour (Baltimore)	75.00	35.00	20.00
(190)	Hosea Siner	75.00	35.00	20.00
(191)	G. Smith	75.00	35.00	20.00
(192a)	Sid Smith (Atlanta)	75.00	35.00	20.00
(192b)	Sid Smith (Buffalo)	75.00	35.00	20.00
(193)	Fred Snodgrass	75.00	35.00	20.00
(194a)	Bob Spade (Cincinnati)	75.00	35.00	20.00
(194b)	Bob Spade (Newark)	75.00	35.00	20.00
(195a)	Tully Sparks (Philadelphia)	75.00	35.00	20.00
(195b)	Tully Sparks (Richmond)	75.00	35.00	20.00
(196)	Tris Speaker (Boston Am.)	260.00	120.00	80.00
(197)	Tubby Spencer	75.00	35.00	20.00
(198)	Jake Stahl	75.00	35.00	20.00
(199)	John Stansberry (Stansbury)	75.00	35.00	20.00
(200)	Harry Steinfeldt (*)	75.00	35.00	20.00
(201)	George Stone	75.00	35.00	20.00
(202)	George Stovall	75.00	35.00	20.00
(203)	Gabby Street	75.00	35.00	20.00
(204a)	Sullivan (Louisville)	75.00	35.00	20.00
(204b)	Sullivan (Omaha)	75.00	35.00	20.00
(205a)	Ed Summers (No white in uniform.)	75.00	35.00	20.00
(205b)	Ed Summers (White in uniform.)	75.00	35.00	20.00
(206)	Suter	75.00	35.00	20.00
(207)	Lee Tannehill	75.00	35.00	20.00
(208)	Taylor	75.00	35.00	20.00
(209)	Joe Tinker	215.00	110.00	65.00
(210)	John Titus	75.00	35.00	20.00
(211)	Terry Turner	75.00	35.00	20.00
(212a)	Bob Unglaub (Washington)	75.00	35.00	20.00
(212b)	Bob Unglaub (Lincoln)	75.00	35.00	20.00
(213a)	Rube Waddell (St. Louis)	215.00	110.00	65.00
(213b)	Rube Waddell (Minneapolis)	300.00	150.00	90.00
(213c)	Rube Waddell (Newark)	300.00	150.00	90.00
(214)	Honus Wagner (*)	1,650	825.00	495.00
(215)	Walker	75.00	35.00	20.00
(216)	Waller	75.00	35.00	20.00
(217)	Clarence Wauner (Wanner)	75.00	35.00	20.00
(218)	Julius Weisman (Name correct.)	75.00	35.00	20.00
(219)	Jack White (Buffalo)	75.00	35.00	20.00
(220)	Kirby White (Boston)	75.00	35.00	20.00
(221)	Julius Wiesman (Weisman)	75.00	35.00	20.00
(222)	Ed Willett	75.00	35.00	20.00
(223)	Otto Williams	75.00	35.00	20.00
(224)	Owen Wilson	75.00	35.00	20.00
(225)	Hooks Wiltse	75.00	35.00	20.00
(226a)	Orville Woodruff (Indianapolis)	75.00	35.00	20.00
(226b)	Orville Woodruff (Louisville)	75.00	35.00	20.00
(227)	Woods	75.00	35.00	20.00
(228)	Cy Young	570.00	280.00	170.00
(229)	Bill Zimmerman	75.00	35.00	20.00
(230)	Heinie Zimmerman	75.00	35.00	20.00

1969 Citgo New York Mets

One of several regional issues in the Mets World Championship season of 1969, this set of 8" x 10" player portraits was sponsored by Citgo, whose gas stations distributed the pictures with fuel purchases. Fronts feature large portraits and smaller action pictures of the player, done in pastels, set against a bright pastel background. The paintings are the work of noted celebrity artist John Wheeldon. Beneath the pictures is a facsimile autograph. The player's name is printed in the bottom border. Backs are printed in black-and-white and include biography and career details, full major and minor league stats and a self-portrait and biography of the artist. Logos of the Mets, the Players Association and the sponsor complete the back design. The unnumbered player pictures are checklisted here in alphabetical order.

		NM	EX	VG
Complete Set (8):		65.00	32.00	19.50
Common Player:		6.50	3.25	2.00
(1)	Tommie Agee	8.00	4.00	2.50
(2)	Ken Boswell	6.50	3.25	2.00
(3)	Gary Gentry	6.50	3.25	2.00
(4)	Jerry Grote	6.50	3.25	2.00
(5)	Cleon Jones	6.50	3.25	2.00
(6)	Jerry Koosman	8.00	4.00	2.50
(7)	Ed Kranepool	6.50	3.25	2.00
(8)	Tom Seaver	25.00	12.50	7.50

1912 Colgan's Chips Premium

Backs of the 1912 and 1913 Colgan's Chips cards offered a photograph of the "World's Pennant Winning Team," to those sending in 25 proofs of purchase. This blank-back, paper stock 18" x 10" team photo of the 1912 New York Giants is that premium. The black-and-white picture has an embossed border and a line of advertising at lower-left for Adams' Pepsin Tutti-Frutti Gum, a successor brand to Colgan's.

	NM	EX	VG
1912 N.Y. Giants Premium	4,000	2,000	1,200

1912 Colgan's Chips Red Borders (E270)

This set, issued in 1912 by Colgan Gum Co., Louisville, Ky., is very similar to the 1909-11 Colgan's release. Measuring about 1-3/8" in diameter, the black-and-white player pictures were inserted in tins of Colgan's Mint and Violet Chips gum. They are differentiated from the earlier issues by their distinctive red borders and by the back of the cards, which advises collectors to "Send 25 Box Tops" for a photo of the "World's Pennant Winning Team." The issue is designated as the E270 Red Border set in the American Card Catalog. A Red Border card of Gavvy Cravath previous cataloged is now believed not to exist.

		NM	EX	VG
Complete Set (184):		50,000	25,000	14,400
Common Player:		375.00	190.00	110.00
(1)	Ed Abbaticchio	375.00	190.00	110.00
(2)	Fred Abbott	375.00	190.00	110.00
(3)	Babe Adams	375.00	190.00	110.00
(4)	Doc Adkins	375.00	190.00	110.00
(5)	Red Ames	375.00	190.00	110.00
(6)	Charlie Babb	375.00	190.00	110.00
(7)	Bill Bailey	375.00	190.00	110.00
(8)	Home Run Baker	600.00	300.00	180.00
(9)	Jack Barry	375.00	190.00	110.00
(10)	Johnny Bates	375.00	190.00	110.00
(11)	Dick Bayless	375.00	190.00	110.00
(12)	Ginger Beaumont	375.00	190.00	110.00
(13)	Beals Becker	375.00	190.00	110.00
(14)	George Bell	375.00	190.00	110.00
(15)	Harry Bemis	375.00	190.00	110.00
(16)	Heinie Berger	375.00	190.00	110.00
(17)	Beumiller	375.00	190.00	110.00
(18)	Joe Birmingham	375.00	190.00	110.00
(19)	Kitty Bransfield	375.00	190.00	110.00
(20)	Roger Bresnahan	750.00	370.00	220.00
(21)	Lew Brockett	375.00	190.00	110.00
(22)	Al Burch	375.00	190.00	110.00
(23)	Donie Bush	375.00	190.00	110.00
(24)	Bill Byers	375.00	190.00	110.00
(25)	Howie Cammitz (Camnitz)	375.00	190.00	110.00
(26)	Charlie Carr	375.00	190.00	110.00
(27)	Frank Chance	750.00	370.00	220.00
(28)	Hal Chase	460.00	230.00	140.00
(29)	Fred Clarke (Pittsburg)	750.00	370.00	220.00
(30)	Tommy Clarke (Cincinnati)	375.00	190.00	110.00
(31)	Bill Clymer	375.00	190.00	110.00
(32)	Ty Cobb	6,500	3,200	1,950
(33)	Eddie Collins	750.00	370.00	220.00
(34)	Wid Conroy	375.00	190.00	110.00
(35)	Harry Coveleski	375.00	190.00	110.00
(36)	Dode Criss	375.00	190.00	110.00
(37)	Jake Daubert	375.00	190.00	110.00
(38)	Harry Davis (Philadelphia)	375.00	190.00	110.00
(39)	Davis (St. Paul)	375.00	190.00	110.00
(40)	Frank Delahanty	375.00	190.00	110.00
(41)	Ray Demmett (Demmitt)	375.00	190.00	110.00
(42)	Art Devlin	375.00	190.00	110.00
(43)	Wild Bill Donovan	375.00	190.00	110.00
(44)	Mickey Doolin (Doolan)	375.00	190.00	110.00
(45)	Patsy Dougherty	375.00	190.00	110.00
(46)	Tom Downey	375.00	190.00	110.00
(47)	Larry Doyle	375.00	190.00	110.00
(48)	Jack Dunn	375.00	190.00	110.00
(49)	Dick Eagan (Egan)	375.00	190.00	110.00
(50)	Kid Elberfield (Elberfeld)	375.00	190.00	110.00
(51)	Rube Ellis	375.00	190.00	110.00
(52)	Steve Evans	375.00	190.00	110.00
(53)	Johnny Evers	750.00	370.00	220.00
(54)	Cecil Ferguson	375.00	190.00	110.00
(55)	Hobe Ferris	375.00	190.00	110.00
(56)	Fisher	375.00	190.00	110.00
(57)	Fitzgerald	375.00	190.00	110.00
(58)	Elmer Flick	1,125	560.00	340.00
(59)	James Freck (Frick)	375.00	190.00	110.00
(60)	Art Fromme	375.00	190.00	110.00
(61)	Larry Gardner	375.00	190.00	110.00
(62)	Harry Gaspar	375.00	190.00	110.00
(63)	George Gibson	375.00	190.00	110.00
(64)	Moose Grimshaw	375.00	190.00	110.00
(65)	John Halla	375.00	190.00	110.00
(66)	Ed Hally (Holly)	375.00	190.00	110.00
(67)	Charlie Hanford	375.00	190.00	110.00
(68)	Topsy Hartsel	375.00	190.00	110.00
(69)	Roy Hartzell	375.00	190.00	110.00
(70)	Weldon Henley (Two sizes photo variations noted.)	375.00	190.00	110.00
(71)	Harry Hinchman	375.00	190.00	110.00
(72)	Solly Hofman	375.00	190.00	110.00
(73)	Harry Hooper	750.00	370.00	220.00
(74)	Howard	375.00	190.00	110.00
(75)	Hughes	375.00	190.00	110.00
(76)	Rudy Hulswitt	375.00	190.00	110.00
(77)	John Hummel	375.00	190.00	110.00
(78)	George Hunter	375.00	190.00	110.00
(79)	Hugh Jennings	750.00	370.00	220.00
(80)	Davy Jones	375.00	190.00	110.00
(81)	Tom Jones	375.00	190.00	110.00
(82)	Tim Jordon (Jordan)	375.00	190.00	110.00
(83)	Joe Kelly (Kelley)	750.00	370.00	220.00
(84)	Bill Killefer	375.00	190.00	110.00
(85)	Ed Killian	375.00	190.00	110.00
(86)	Otto Knabe	375.00	190.00	110.00
(87)	Jack Knight	375.00	190.00	110.00
(88)	Ed Konetchy	375.00	190.00	110.00
(89)	Rube Kroh	375.00	190.00	110.00
(90)	LaCrosse (Photo actually Bill Schardt.)	375.00	190.00	110.00
(91)	Frank LaPorte	375.00	190.00	110.00
(92)	Tommy Leach	375.00	190.00	110.00
(93)	Jack Lelivelt	375.00	190.00	110.00
(94)	Jack Lewis	375.00	190.00	110.00
(95)	Vive Lindaman	375.00	190.00	110.00
(96)	Bris Lord	375.00	190.00	110.00
(97)	Harry Lord	375.00	190.00	110.00
(98)	Bill Ludwig	375.00	190.00	110.00
(99)	Nick Maddox	375.00	190.00	110.00
(100)	Manser	375.00	190.00	110.00
(101)	Al Mattern	375.00	190.00	110.00
(102)	George McBride	375.00	190.00	110.00
(103)	Joe McCarthy (Toledo)	750.00	370.00	220.00
(104)	McConnell	375.00	190.00	110.00
(105)	Moose McCormick	375.00	190.00	110.00
(106)	Dan McGann	375.00	190.00	110.00
(107)	Jim McGinley	375.00	190.00	110.00
(108)	Iron Man McGinnity	750.00	370.00	220.00
(109)	Matty McIntyre	375.00	190.00	110.00
(110)	Larry McLean	375.00	190.00	110.00
(111)	Fred Merkle	375.00	190.00	110.00
(112)	Merritt	375.00	190.00	110.00
(113)	Meyer (Newark)	375.00	190.00	110.00
(114)	Chief Meyers	375.00	190.00	110.00
(115)	Clyde Milan	375.00	190.00	110.00
(116)	Dots Miller	375.00	190.00	110.00
(117)	Mike Mitchell	375.00	190.00	110.00
(118)	Bill Moriarty (Omaha)	375.00	190.00	110.00
(119)	George Moriarty (Detroit)	375.00	190.00	110.00
(120)	George Mullen (Mullin)	375.00	190.00	110.00
(121)	Simmy Murch (Chattanooga)	375.00	190.00	110.00
(122)	Simmy Murch (Indianapolis)	375.00	190.00	110.00
(123)	Danny Murphy	375.00	190.00	110.00
(124)	Red Murray	375.00	190.00	110.00
(125)	Red Nelson	375.00	190.00	110.00
(126)	Rebel Oakes	375.00	190.00	110.00
(127)	Fred Odwell (Columbus)	375.00	190.00	110.00
(128)	Al Orth (Indianapolis)	375.00	190.00	110.00

		NM	EX	VG
(129)	Orval Overall	375.00	190.00	110.00
(130)	Owens	375.00	190.00	110.00
(131)	Fred Parent	375.00	190.00	110.00
(132)	Dode Paskert	375.00	190.00	110.00
(133)	Bob Peterson	375.00	190.00	110.00
(134)	Jake Pfeister (Pfiester)	375.00	190.00	110.00
(135)	Deacon Phillipe (Phillippe)	375.00	190.00	110.00
(136)	Ollie Pickering	375.00	190.00	110.00
(137)	Heinie Pietz (Peitz)	375.00	190.00	110.00
(138)	Bugs Raymond	375.00	190.00	110.00
(139)	Pat Regan (Ragan)	375.00	190.00	110.00
(140)	Ed Reulbach	375.00	190.00	110.00
(141)	Robinson	375.00	190.00	110.00
(142)	Rock	375.00	190.00	110.00
(143)	Jack Rowan	375.00	190.00	110.00
(144)	Nap Rucker	375.00	190.00	110.00
(145)	Dick Rudolph	375.00	190.00	110.00
(146)	Slim Sallee	375.00	190.00	110.00
(147)	Jimmy Scheckard (Sheckard)	375.00	190.00	110.00
(148)	George Schirm	375.00	190.00	110.00
(149)	Wildfire Schulte	375.00	190.00	110.00
(150)	James Seabaugh	375.00	190.00	110.00
(151)	Selby	375.00	190.00	110.00
(152)	Cy Seymour	375.00	190.00	110.00
(153)	Hosea Siner	375.00	190.00	110.00
(154)	Sid Smith	375.00	190.00	110.00
(155)	Fred Snodgrass	375.00	190.00	110.00
(156)	Bob Spade	375.00	190.00	110.00
(157)	Tully Sparks	375.00	190.00	110.00
(158)	Tris Speaker	1,125	560.00	340.00
(159)	Tubby Spencer	375.00	190.00	110.00
(160)	John Stausberry (Stansbury)	375.00	190.00	110.00
(161)	Harry Steinfeldt	375.00	190.00	110.00
(162)	George Stone	375.00	190.00	110.00
(163)	George Stovall	375.00	190.00	110.00
(164)	Gabby Street	375.00	190.00	110.00
(165)	Sullivan (Omaha)	375.00	190.00	110.00
(166)	John Sullivan (Louisville)	375.00	190.00	110.00
(167)	Ed Summers	375.00	190.00	110.00
(168)	Joe Tinker	750.00	370.00	220.00
(169)	John Titus	375.00	190.00	110.00
(170)	Terry Turner	375.00	190.00	110.00
(171)	Bob Unglaub	375.00	190.00	110.00
(172)	Rube Waddell	750.00	370.00	220.00
(173)	Walker	375.00	190.00	110.00
(174)	Waller	375.00	190.00	110.00
(175)	Kirby White (Boston)	375.00	190.00	110.00
(176)	Jack White (Buffalo)	375.00	190.00	110.00
(177)	Julius Wiesman (Weisman)	375.00	190.00	110.00
(178)	Otto Williams	375.00	190.00	110.00
(179)	Hooks Wiltse	375.00	190.00	110.00
(180)	Orville Woodruff	375.00	190.00	110.00
(181)	Woods	375.00	190.00	110.00
(182)	Cy Young	2,340	1,170	700.00
(183)	Bill Zimmerman	375.00	190.00	110.00
(184)	Heinie Zimmerman	375.00	190.00	110.00

1913 Colgan's Chips Tin Tops

Except for the backs, these round black-and-white cards (about 1-7/16" in diameter) are identical to the 1909-11 Colgan's Chips issue, and were inserted in tin cannisters of Colgan's Mint Chips and Violet Chips. The front features a portrait photo along with the player's last name, team and, where necessary, league. The back advises collectors to "Send 25 Tin Tops" and a two-cent stamp to receive a photo of the "World's Pennant Winning Team." The set carries the designation E270 in the American Card Catalog.

		NM	EX	VG
Complete Set (227):		60,000	30,000	18,000
Common Player:		180.00	90.00	54.00
(1)	Ed Abbaticchio	180.00	90.00	54.00
(2)	Doc Adkins	180.00	90.00	54.00
(3)	Joe Agler	180.00	90.00	54.00
(4)	Eddie Ainsmith	180.00	90.00	54.00
(5)	Whitey Alperman	180.00	90.00	54.00
(6)	Red Ames (New York)	180.00	90.00	54.00
(7)	Red Ames (Cincinnati)	180.00	90.00	54.00
(8)	Jimmy Archer	180.00	90.00	54.00
(9)	Tommy Atkins (Atlanta)	180.00	90.00	54.00
(10)	Tommy Atkins (Ft. Wayne)	180.00	90.00	54.00
(11)	Jake Atz (New Orleans)	180.00	90.00	54.00
(12)	Jake Atz (Providence)	180.00	90.00	54.00
(13)	Jimmy Austin	180.00	90.00	54.00
(14)	Home Run Baker	360.00	180.00	110.00
(15)	Jack Barry	180.00	90.00	54.00
(16)	Johnny Bates	180.00	90.00	54.00
(17)	Beck (Buffalo)	180.00	90.00	54.00
(18)	Beebe	180.00	90.00	54.00
(19)	Harry Bemis	180.00	90.00	54.00
(20)	Bob Bescher	180.00	90.00	54.00
(21)	Beumiller (Louisville)	180.00	90.00	54.00
(22)	Joe Birmingham	180.00	90.00	54.00
(23)	Bliss	180.00	90.00	54.00
(24)	Roger Bresnahan	360.00	180.00	110.00
(25)	Al Bridwell	180.00	90.00	54.00
(26)	George Brown (Browne)	180.00	90.00	54.00
(27)	Al Burch	180.00	90.00	54.00
(28)	Burns	180.00	90.00	54.00
(29)	Donie Bush	180.00	90.00	54.00
(30)	Bobby Byrne	180.00	90.00	54.00

		NM	EX	VG
(31)	Nixey Callahan	180.00	90.00	54.00
(32)	Howie Camnitz	180.00	90.00	54.00
(33)	Billy Campbell	180.00	90.00	54.00
(34)	Charlie Carr	180.00	90.00	54.00
(35)	Jay Cashion	180.00	90.00	54.00
(36)	Frank Chance	360.00	180.00	110.00
(37)	Hal Chase	220.00	110.00	65.00
(38)	Ed Cicotte	270.00	135.00	80.00
(39)	Clarke (Indianapolis)	180.00	90.00	54.00
(40)	Fred Clarke (Pittsburg)	360.00	180.00	110.00
(41)	Tommy Clarke (Cincinnati)	180.00	90.00	54.00
(42)	Clemons	180.00	90.00	54.00
(43)	Bill Clymer	180.00	90.00	54.00
(44)	Ty Cobb	2,400	1,200	720.00
(45)	Eddie Collins	360.00	180.00	110.00
(46)	Bunk Congalton (Omaha)	180.00	90.00	54.00
(47)	Bunk Congalton (Toledo)	180.00	90.00	54.00
(48)	Cook	180.00	90.00	54.00
(49)	Jack Coombs	180.00	90.00	54.00
(50)	Corcoran	180.00	90.00	54.00
(51)	Karl Crandell (Memphis)	180.00	90.00	54.00
(52)	Gavvy Cravath	180.00	90.00	54.00
(53)	Sam Crawford	360.00	180.00	110.00
(54)	Bill Dahlen	180.00	90.00	54.00
(55)	Bert Daniels	180.00	90.00	54.00
(56a)	Jake Daubert	180.00	90.00	54.00
(56b)	Jake Daubert (White cap.)	180.00	90.00	54.00
(57)	Josh Devore (Cincinnati)	180.00	90.00	54.00
(58)	Josh Devore (New York)	180.00	90.00	54.00
(59)	Mike Donlin	180.00	90.00	54.00
(60)	Wild Bill Donovan	180.00	90.00	54.00
(61)	Red Dooin	180.00	90.00	54.00
(62)	Mickey Doolan	180.00	90.00	54.00
(63)	Larry Doyle	180.00	90.00	54.00
(64)	Delos Drake	180.00	90.00	54.00
(65)	Dick Egan	180.00	90.00	54.00
(66)	Kid Elberfield (Elberfeld)	180.00	90.00	54.00
(67)	Roy Ellam	180.00	90.00	54.00
(68)	Elliott	180.00	90.00	54.00
(69)	Rube Ellis	180.00	90.00	54.00
(70)	Elwert	180.00	90.00	54.00
(71)	Clyde Engle	180.00	90.00	54.00
(72)	Jimmy Esmond	180.00	90.00	54.00
(73)	Steve Evans	180.00	90.00	54.00
(74)	Johnny Evers	360.00	180.00	110.00
(75)	Hobe Ferris	180.00	90.00	54.00
(76)	Russ Ford	180.00	90.00	54.00
(77)	Ed Foster	180.00	90.00	54.00
(78)	Friel	180.00	90.00	54.00
(79)	John Frill	180.00	90.00	54.00
(80)	Art Fromme	180.00	90.00	54.00
(81)	Gus Getz (Newark)	180.00	90.00	54.00
(82)	George Gibson	180.00	90.00	54.00
(83)	Graham	180.00	90.00	54.00
(84)	Eddie Grant (Cincinnati)	180.00	90.00	54.00
(85)	Eddie Grant (New York)	180.00	90.00	54.00
(86)	Gravath	180.00	90.00	54.00
(87)	Grief	180.00	90.00	54.00
(88)	Bob Groom	180.00	90.00	54.00
(89)	Topsy Hartsel	180.00	90.00	54.00
(90)	Roy Hartzell	180.00	90.00	54.00
(91)	Harry Hinchman	180.00	90.00	54.00
(92)	Dick Hoblitzell	180.00	90.00	54.00
(93)	Happy Hogan (St. Louis)	180.00	90.00	54.00
(94)	Happy Hogan (San Francisco)	180.00	90.00	54.00
(95)	Harry Hooper	360.00	180.00	110.00
(96)	Miller Huggins	360.00	180.00	110.00
(97)	Hughes (Milwaukee)	180.00	90.00	54.00
(98)	Hughes (Rochester)	180.00	90.00	54.00
(99)	Rudy Hulswitt	180.00	90.00	54.00
(100)	John Hummel	180.00	90.00	54.00
(101)	George Hunter	180.00	90.00	54.00
(102)	Shoeless Joe Jackson	20,000	4,800	2,880
(103)	Jameson (Buffalo)	180.00	90.00	54.00
(104)	Hugh Jennings	360.00	180.00	110.00
(105)	Pete Johns	180.00	90.00	54.00
(106)	Walter Johnson	780.00	390.00	235.00
(107)	Davy Jones (Toledo)	180.00	90.00	54.00
(108)	Tim Jordan	180.00	90.00	54.00
(109)	Bob Keefe	180.00	90.00	54.00
(110)	Wee Willie Keeler	360.00	180.00	110.00
(111)	Joe Kelly (Kelley)	360.00	180.00	110.00
(112)	Ed Killian	180.00	90.00	54.00
(113)	Bill Killifer (Killefer)	180.00	90.00	54.00
(114)	Johnny Kling (Boston)	180.00	90.00	54.00
(115)	Klipfer	180.00	90.00	54.00
(116)	Otto Knabe	180.00	90.00	54.00
(117)	Jack Knight	180.00	90.00	54.00
(118)	Ed Konetchy	180.00	90.00	54.00
(119)	Paul Krichell	180.00	90.00	54.00
(120)	James Lafitte	180.00	90.00	54.00
(121)	Nap Lajoie	360.00	180.00	110.00
(122)	Frank Lange	180.00	90.00	54.00
(123)	Lee	180.00	90.00	54.00
(124)	Jack Lewis	180.00	90.00	54.00
(125)	Harry Lord	180.00	90.00	54.00
(126)	Johnny Lush	180.00	90.00	54.00
(127)	Madden	180.00	90.00	54.00
(128)	Nick Maddox	180.00	90.00	54.00
(129)	Sherry Magee	180.00	90.00	54.00
(130)	Manser	180.00	90.00	54.00
(131)	Frank Manusch (Manush) (New Orleans)	180.00	90.00	54.00
(132)	Frank Manush (Toledo)	180.00	90.00	54.00
(133)	Rube Marquard	360.00	180.00	110.00
(134)	McAllister	180.00	90.00	54.00
(135)	George McBride	180.00	90.00	54.00
(136)	McCarthy (Newark)	180.00	90.00	54.00
(137)	Joe McCarthy (Toledo)	360.00	180.00	110.00
(138)	McConnell	180.00	90.00	54.00
(139)	Moose McCormick	180.00	90.00	54.00
(140)	Larry McLean	180.00	90.00	54.00
(141)	Fred Merkle	180.00	90.00	54.00
(142)	Chief Meyers	180.00	90.00	54.00
(143)	Clyde Milan	180.00	90.00	54.00
(144)	Miller (Columbus)	180.00	90.00	54.00
(145)	Dots Miller (Pittsburg)	180.00	90.00	54.00
(146)	Clarence Mitchell	180.00	90.00	54.00

		NM	EX	VG
(147)	Mike Mitchell	180.00	90.00	54.00
(148)	Roy Mitchell	180.00	90.00	54.00
(149)	Carlton Molesworth	180.00	90.00	54.00
(150)	Herbie Moran	180.00	90.00	54.00
(151)	George Moriarty	180.00	90.00	54.00
(152)	George Mullen (Mullin)	180.00	90.00	54.00
(153)	Danny Murphy	180.00	90.00	54.00
(154)	Murray (Buffalo)	180.00	90.00	54.00
(155)	Jim Murray	180.00	90.00	54.00
(156)	Niles (Indianapolis)	180.00	90.00	54.00
(157)	Jake Northrop	180.00	90.00	54.00
(158)	Rebel Oakes	180.00	90.00	54.00
(159)	Rube Oldring	180.00	90.00	54.00
(160)	Steve O'Neil (O'Neill)	180.00	90.00	54.00
(161)	O'Rourke	180.00	90.00	54.00
(162)	Owens (Minneapolis)	180.00	90.00	54.00
(163)	Larry Pape	180.00	90.00	54.00
(164)	Fred Parent	180.00	90.00	54.00
(165)	Dode Paskert	180.00	90.00	54.00
(166)	Heinie Peitz	180.00	90.00	54.00
(167)	Perry	180.00	90.00	54.00
(168)	Billy Purtell	180.00	90.00	54.00
(169)	Bill Rariden	180.00	90.00	54.00
(170)	Morrie Rath	180.00	90.00	54.00
(171)	Bugs Raymond	180.00	90.00	54.00
(172)	Ed Reulbach	180.00	90.00	54.00
(173)	Nap Rucker	180.00	90.00	54.00
(174)	Dick Rudolph	180.00	90.00	54.00
(175)	Bud Ryan	180.00	90.00	54.00
(176)	Slim Sallee	180.00	90.00	54.00
(177)	Ray Schalk	180.00	90.00	54.00
(178)	Schardt (Indianapolis)	180.00	90.00	54.00
(179)	Jimmy Scheckard (Sheckard)	180.00	90.00	54.00
(180)	Wildfire Schulte	180.00	90.00	54.00
(181)	Cy Seymour (Baltimore)	180.00	90.00	54.00
(182)	Bob Shawkey	180.00	90.00	54.00
(183)	Skeeter Shelton	180.00	90.00	54.00
(184)	Burt Shotten (Shotton)	180.00	90.00	54.00
(185)	Sisson (Atlanta)	180.00	90.00	54.00
(186)	Smith (Montreal)	180.00	90.00	54.00
(187)	Sid Smith (Atlanta)	180.00	90.00	54.00
(188)	Sid Smith (Newark)	180.00	90.00	54.00
(189)	Fred Snodgrass	180.00	90.00	54.00
(190)	Tris Speaker	540.00	270.00	160.00
(191)	Jake Stahl	180.00	90.00	54.00
(192)	John Stansberry (Stansbury)	180.00	90.00	54.00
(193)	George Stovall	180.00	90.00	54.00
(194)	Amos Strunk	180.00	90.00	54.00
(195)	Sullivan	180.00	90.00	54.00
(196)	Suter	180.00	90.00	54.00
(197)	Harry Swacina	180.00	90.00	54.00
(198)	Bill Sweeney	180.00	90.00	54.00
(199)	Jeff Sweeney	180.00	90.00	54.00
(200)	Lee Tannehill	180.00	90.00	54.00
(201)	Dummy Taylor (Topeka)	300.00	150.00	90.00
(202)	Jim Thorpe	12,000	3,900	2,340
(203)	Joe Tinker	360.00	180.00	110.00
(204)	John Titus (Boston)	180.00	90.00	54.00
(205)	John Titus (Philadelphia)	180.00	90.00	54.00
(206)	Terry Turner	180.00	90.00	54.00
(207)	Bob Unglaub	180.00	90.00	54.00
(208)	Viebahn	180.00	90.00	54.00
(209)	Rube Waddell	360.00	180.00	110.00
(210)	Honus Wagner	2,500	750.00	450.00
(211)	Bobby Wallace	360.00	180.00	110.00
(212)	Ed Walsh	360.00	180.00	110.00
(213)	Jack Warhop	180.00	90.00	54.00
(214)	Harry Welchouce (Welchonce)(Nashville)	180.00	90.00	54.00
(215)	Harry Welchouce (Welchonce) (Atlanta)	180.00	90.00	54.00
(216)	Zach Wheat	360.00	180.00	110.00
(217)	Kirb. White	180.00	90.00	54.00
(218)	Kaiser Wilhelm	180.00	90.00	54.00
(219a)	Ed Willett	180.00	90.00	54.00
(219b)	Ed Willett (White cap.)	180.00	90.00	54.00
(220)	Otto Williams	180.00	90.00	54.00
(221)	Owen Wilson	180.00	90.00	54.00
(222)	Hooks Wiltse	180.00	90.00	54.00
(223)	Joe Wood	180.00	90.00	54.00
(224)	Orville Woodruff	180.00	90.00	54.00
(225)	Joe Yeager	180.00	90.00	54.00
(226)	Bill Zimmerman	180.00	90.00	54.00
(227)	Heinie Zimmerman	180.00	90.00	54.00

1909 "Colgan's Chips" Square Proofs

COLLINS
Phila. Am. L.

Though widely identified as being connected to the Colgan's Chips disc issues of 1909-1912, there is nothing to tie these square cards to the gum company except for the shared use of player photos. The squares measure about 1-3/8" x 1-3/4" and are blank-backed. Black-and-white player portrait photos have a last name and team identification beneath. Many, but not all, of the surviving specimens have paper and/or glue residue on back, leading to speculation they may have been part of an advertising piece. The extent of the checklist is unknown, with verified examples listed here.

		NM	EX	VG
Common Player:		250.00	120.00	80.00
(1)	Red Ames	250.00	120.00	80.00
(2)	Charlie Babb (Memphis)	250.00	120.00	80.00
(3)	Baerwald (Memphis)	250.00	124.00	74.00
(4)	Home Run Baker	600.00	300.00	180.00
(5)	Johnny Bates	250.00	120.00	80.00
(6)	Ginger Beaumont (Boston)	250.00	120.00	80.00
(7)	Beals Becker	250.00	120.00	80.00
(8)	Roger Bresnahan	600.00	300.00	180.00
(9)	Al Bridwell	250.00	120.00	80.00
(10)	Lew Brockett	250.00	124.00	74.00
(11)	Al Burch	250.00	120.00	80.00
(12)	Donie Bush	250.00	120.00	80.00
(13)	Howie Camnitz	250.00	120.00	80.00
(14)	Frank Chance	600.00	300.00	180.00
(15)	Fred Clarke (Pittsburg)	600.00	300.00	180.00
(16)	Ty Cobb	4,000	2,000	1,200
(17)	Eddie Collins	600.00	300.00	180.00
(18)	Dode Criss	250.00	120.00	80.00
(19)	Jake Daubert (Memphis)	250.00	120.00	80.00
(20)	Harry Davis (Philadelphia)	250.00	120.00	80.00
(21)	Ray Demmett (Demmitt) (New York)	250.00	120.00	80.00
(22)	Clyde Engle (New York)	250.00	120.00	80.00
(23)	Steve Evans	250.00	120.00	80.00
(24)	Johnny Evers	600.00	300.00	180.00
(25)	Harry Gaspar	250.00	120.00	80.00
(26)	Gus Getz (Boston)	250.00	120.00	80.00
(27)	George Gibson	250.00	120.00	80.00
(28)	Weldon Henley (Rochester)	250.00	120.00	180.00
(29)	Harry Hooper (Boston A.L.)	600.00	300.00	180.00
(30)	Hugh Jennings	600.00	300.00	180.00
(31)	Addie Joss	600.00	300.00	180.00
(32)	Otto Knabe	250.00	120.00	80.00
(33)	James Lafitte	250.00	120.00	80.00
(34)	Bill Lelivelt	250.00	120.00	80.00
(35)	Bill Ludwig (Milwaukee)	250.00	120.00	80.00
(36)	Nick Maddox	250.00	120.00	80.00
(37)	Dots Miller	250.00	120.00	80.00
(38)	Mike Mitchell	250.00	120.00	80.00
(39)	Danny Murphy	250.00	120.00	80.00
(40)	Heinie Peitz	250.00	120.00	80.00
(41)	Bill Schardt (Milwaukee)	250.00	120.00	80.00
(42)	Cy Seymour (New York)	250.00	124.00	74.00
(43)	Fred Snodgrass	250.00	120.00	80.00
(44)	Bob Spade (Cincinnati)	250.00	120.00	80.00
(45)	Bob Unglaub	250.00	120.00	80.00
(46)	Rube Waddell (St. Louis)	600.00	300.00	180.00
(47)	Honus Wagner (Pittsburg)	1,500	750.00	450.00
(48)	Owen Wilson	250.00	120.00	80.00
(49)	Hooks Wiltse	250.00	120.00	80.00
(50)	Woods (Buffalo)	250.00	120.00	80.00

1947 Collectors & Traders Sport Star Subjects

This set was the origination point for the Bond Bread insert cards and related other issues. The cards were produced by Aarco Playing Card Co., Chicago. They were originally sold in window-boxed series of 12 cards each comprising 11 baseball players and a boxer. The individual cards are printed in black-and-white on 3-3/8" x 2-1/4" blank-back cardboard with rounded corners..

	NM	EX	VG
Complete Boxed Set (48):	4,500	2,250	1,350

(See 1947 Bond Bread for checklist and single card values.)

1917 Collins-McCarthy (E135)

This is one of the 200 pictures representing
BASEBALL'S HALL of FAME
There are 199 others
Distributed by
Collins-McCarthy Candy Co.
SAN FRANCISCO · CAL.
"Just a little better"
Zee Nut and Candy Makers

CLAUDE HENDRIX
P.—Chicago Cubs
72

Produced by the Collins-McCarthy Candy Co. of San Francisco, the 200-card, black-and-white set represents the company's only venture into issuing non-Pacific Coast League players. The cards, numbered alphabetically, measure 2" x 3-1/4" and are printed on thin stock. Though the set is entitled "Baseball's Hall of Fame," many nondescript players appear in the issue. The complete set price does not include the more expensive variations. The same cards can be found with the advertising of other regional issuers on back, or blank-backed. Blank backs are much more scarce.

		NM	EX	VG
Complete Set (200):		100,000	50,000	30,000
Common Player:		150.00	75.00	45.00
1	Sam Agnew	150.00	75.00	45.00
2	Grover Alexander	4,000	2,000	1,200
3	W.S. Alexander (W.E.)	150.00	75.00	45.00
4	Leon Ames	150.00	75.00	45.00
5	Fred Anderson	150.00	75.00	45.00
6	Ed Appleton	150.00	75.00	45.00
7	Jimmy Archer	150.00	75.00	45.00
8	Jimmy Austin	150.00	75.00	45.00
9	Jim Bagby	150.00	75.00	45.00
10	H.D. Baird	150.00	75.00	45.00

11	J. Franklin Baker	1,400	700.00	425.00
12	Dave Bancroft	1,400	700.00	425.00
13	Jack Barry	150.00	75.00	45.00
14	Joe Benz	150.00	75.00	45.00
15	Al Betzel	150.00	75.00	45.00
16	Ping Bodie	150.00	75.00	45.00
17	Joe Boehling	150.00	75.00	45.00
18	Eddie Burns	150.00	75.00	45.00
19	George Burns	150.00	75.00	45.00
20	Geo. J. Burns	150.00	75.00	45.00
21	Joe Bush	150.00	75.00	45.00
22	Owen Bush	150.00	75.00	45.00
23	Bobby Byrne	150.00	75.00	45.00
24	Forrest Cady	150.00	75.00	45.00
25	Max Carey	4,000	2,000	1,200
26	Ray Chapman	700.00	350.00	210.00
27	Larry Cheney	150.00	75.00	45.00
28	Eddie Cicotte	4,000	2,000	1,200
29	Tom Clarke	150.00	75.00	45.00
30	Ty Cobb	10,000	5,000	3,000
31	Eddie Collins	2,000	1,000	600.00
32	"Shauno" Collins (Shano)	150.00	75.00	45.00
33	Fred Coumbe	150.00	75.00	45.00
34	Harry Coveleskie (Coveleski)	150.00	75.00	45.00
35	Gavvy Cravath	150.00	75.00	45.00
36	Sam Crawford	2,000	1,000	600.00
37	Geo. Cutshaw	150.00	75.00	45.00
38	Jake Daubert	150.00	75.00	45.00
39	Geo. Dauss	150.00	75.00	45.00
40	Charles Deal	150.00	75.00	45.00
41	"Wheezer" Dell	150.00	75.00	45.00
42	William Doak	150.00	75.00	45.00
43	Bill Donovan	150.00	75.00	45.00
44	Larry Doyle	150.00	75.00	45.00
45	Johnny Evers	4,000	2,000	1,200
46	Urban Faber	4,000	2,000	1,200
47	"Hap" Felsch	4,000	2,000	1,200
48	Bill Fischer	150.00	75.00	45.00
49	Ray Fisher	150.00	75.00	45.00
50	Art Fletcher	150.00	75.00	45.00
51	Eddie Foster	150.00	75.00	45.00
52	Jacques Fournier	150.00	75.00	45.00
53	Del Gainer (Gainor)	150.00	75.00	45.00
54	Bert Gallia	150.00	75.00	45.00
55	"Chic" Gandil (Chick)	4,000	2,000	1,200
56	Larry Gardner	150.00	75.00	45.00
57	Joe Gedeon	150.00	75.00	45.00
58	Gus Getz	150.00	75.00	45.00
59	Frank Gilhooley	150.00	75.00	45.00
60	Wm. Gleason	150.00	75.00	45.00
61	M.A. Gonzales (Gonzalez)	660.00	330.00	200.00
62	Hank Gowdy	150.00	75.00	45.00
63	John Graney	150.00	75.00	45.00
64	Tom Griffith	150.00	75.00	45.00
65	Heinie Groh	150.00	75.00	45.00
66	Bob Groom	150.00	75.00	45.00
67	Louis Guisto	150.00	75.00	45.00
68	Earl Hamilton	150.00	75.00	45.00
69	Harry Harper	150.00	75.00	45.00
70	Grover Hartley	150.00	75.00	45.00
71	Harry Heilmann	20,000	10,000	6,000
72	Claude Hendrix	150.00	75.00	45.00
73	Olaf Henriksen	150.00	75.00	45.00
74	John Henry	150.00	75.00	45.00
75	"Buck" Herzog	150.00	75.00	45.00
76a	Hugh High (White stockings, photo actually Claude Williams.)	800.00	400.00	240.00
76b	Hugh High (Black stockings, correct photo.)	700.00	350.00	210.00
77	Dick Hoblitzell	150.00	75.00	45.00
78	Walter Holke	150.00	75.00	45.00
79	Harry Hooper	4,000	2,000	1,200
80	Rogers Hornsby	6,000	3,000	1,800
81	Ivan Howard	150.00	75.00	45.00
82	Joe Jackson	66,000	33,000	20,000
83	Harold Janvrin	150.00	75.00	45.00
84	William James	150.00	75.00	45.00
85	C. Jamieson	150.00	75.00	45.00
86	Hugh Jennings	4,000	2,000	1,200
87	Walter Johnson	12,000	6,000	3,600
88	James Johnston	150.00	75.00	45.00
89	Fielder Jones	150.00	75.00	45.00
90a	Joe Judge (Bat on right shoulder, photo actually Ray Morgan.)	800.00	400.00	240.00
90b	Joe Judge (Bat on left shoulder, correct photo.)	700.00	350.00	210.00
91	Hans Lobert	150.00	75.00	45.00
92	Benny Kauff	150.00	75.00	45.00
93	Wm. Killefer Jr.	150.00	75.00	45.00
94	Ed. Konetchy	150.00	75.00	45.00
95	John Lavan	150.00	75.00	45.00
96	Jimmy Lavender	150.00	75.00	45.00
97	"Nemo" Leibold	150.00	75.00	45.00
98	H.B. Leonard	150.00	75.00	45.00
99	Duffy Lewis	150.00	75.00	45.00
100	Tom Long	150.00	75.00	45.00
101	Wm. Louden	150.00	75.00	45.00
102	Fred Luderus	150.00	75.00	45.00
103	Lee Magee	150.00	75.00	45.00
104	Sherwood Magee	150.00	75.00	45.00
105	Al Mamaux	150.00	75.00	45.00
106	Leslie Mann	150.00	75.00	45.00
107	"Rabbit" Maranville	8,000	4,000	2,400
108	Rube Marquard	8,000	4,000	2,400
109	Armando Marsans	1,320	660.00	400.00
110	J. Erskine Mayer	150.00	75.00	45.00
111	George McBride	150.00	75.00	45.00
112	Lew McCarty	150.00	75.00	45.00
113	John J. McGraw	4,000	2,000	1,200
114	Jack McInnis	150.00	75.00	45.00
115	Lee Meadows	150.00	75.00	45.00
116	Fred Merkle	150.00	75.00	45.00
117	"Chief" Meyers	150.00	75.00	45.00
118	Clyde Milan	150.00	75.00	45.00
119	Otto Miller	150.00	75.00	45.00
120	Clarence Mitchell	150.00	75.00	45.00

121a	Ray Morgan (Bat on left shoulder, photo actually Joe Judge)	800.00	400.00	240.00
121b	Ray Morgan (Bat on right shoulder, correct photo.)	700.00	350.00	210.00
122	Guy Morton	150.00	75.00	45.00
123	"Mike" Mowrey	150.00	75.00	45.00
124	Elmer Myers	150.00	75.00	45.00
125	"Hy" Myers	150.00	75.00	45.00
126	A.E. Neale	660.00	330.00	200.00
127	Arthur Nehf	150.00	75.00	45.00
128	J.A. Niehoff	150.00	75.00	45.00
129	Steve O'Neill	150.00	75.00	45.00
130	"Dode" Paskert	150.00	75.00	45.00
131	Roger Peckinpaugh	150.00	75.00	45.00
132	"Pol" Perritt	150.00	75.00	45.00
133	"Jeff" Pfeffer	150.00	75.00	45.00
134	Walter Pipp	150.00	75.00	45.00
135	Derril Pratt (Derrill)	150.00	75.00	45.00
136	Bill Rariden	150.00	75.00	45.00
137	E.C. Rice	1,400	700.00	425.00
138	Wm. A. Ritter (Wm. H.)	150.00	75.00	45.00
139	Eppa Rixey	4,000	2,000	1,200
140	Davey Robertson	150.00	75.00	45.00
141	"Bob" Roth	150.00	75.00	45.00
142	Ed. Roush	4,000	2,000	1,200
143	Clarence Rowland	150.00	75.00	45.00
144	Dick Rudolph	150.00	75.00	45.00
145	William Rumler	150.00	75.00	45.00
146a	Reb Russell (Pitching follow-thru, photo actually Mellie Wolfgang.)	800.00	400.00	240.00
146b	Reb Russell (Hands at side, correct photo.)	700.00	350.00	210.00
147	"Babe" Ruth	50,000	25,000	15,000
148	Vic Saier	150.00	75.00	45.00
149	"Slim" Sallee	150.00	75.00	45.00
150	Ray Schalk	4,000	2,000	1,200
151	Walter Schang	150.00	75.00	45.00
152	Frank Schulte	150.00	75.00	45.00
153	Ferd Schupp	150.00	75.00	45.00
154	Everett Scott	150.00	75.00	45.00
155	Hank Severeid	150.00	75.00	45.00
156	Howard Shanks	150.00	75.00	45.00
157	Bob Shawkey	150.00	75.00	45.00
158	Jas. Sheckard	150.00	75.00	45.00
159	Ernie Shore	150.00	75.00	45.00
160	C.H. Shorten	150.00	75.00	45.00
161	Burt Shotton	150.00	75.00	45.00
162	Geo. Sisler	1,600	800.00	475.00
163	Elmer Smith	150.00	75.00	45.00
164	J. Carlisle Smith	150.00	75.00	45.00
165	Fred Snodgrass	150.00	75.00	45.00
166	Tris Speaker	8,000	4,000	2,400
167	Oscar Stanage	150.00	75.00	45.00
168	Charles Stengel	4,000	2,000	1,200
169	Milton Stock	150.00	75.00	45.00
170	Amos Strunk	150.00	75.00	45.00
171	"Zeb" Terry	150.00	75.00	45.00
172	"Jeff" Tesreau	150.00	75.00	45.00
173	Chester Thomas	150.00	75.00	45.00
174	Fred Toney	150.00	75.00	45.00
175	Terry Turner	150.00	75.00	45.00
176	George Tyler	150.00	75.00	45.00
177	Jim Vaughn	150.00	75.00	45.00
178	Bob Veach	150.00	75.00	45.00
179	Oscar Vitt	150.00	75.00	45.00
180	Hans Wagner	14,000	7,000	4,250
181	Clarence Walker	150.00	75.00	45.00
182	Jim Walsh	150.00	75.00	45.00
183	Al Walters	150.00	75.00	45.00
184	W. Wambsganss	150.00	75.00	45.00
185	Buck Weaver	4,000	2,000	1,200
186	Carl Weilman	150.00	75.00	45.00
187	Zack Wheat	8,000	4,000	2,400
188	Geo. Whitted	150.00	75.00	45.00
189	Joe Wilhoit	150.00	75.00	45.00
190a	Claude Williams (Black stockings, photo actually Hugh High.)	2,400	1,200	725.00
190b	Claude Williams (White stockings, correct photo.)	3,000	1,500	900.00
191	Fred Williams	150.00	75.00	45.00
192	Art Wilson	150.00	75.00	45.00
193	Lawton Witt	150.00	75.00	45.00
194	Joe Wood	150.00	75.00	45.00
195	William Wortman	150.00	75.00	45.00
196	Steve Yerkes	150.00	75.00	45.00
197	Earl Yingling	150.00	75.00	45.00
198	"Pep" (Ralph) Young	150.00	75.00	45.00
199	Rollie Zeider	150.00	75.00	45.00
200	Henry Zimmerman	150.00	75.00	45.00

1954 Colonial Meats Jimmy Piersall

These promotional postcards are known in at least two varieties. Each of the 3-1/2" x 5-1/2" cards shows the popular

BoSox star in a portrait pose with facsimile autograph. The postcard-format back has at left a cartoon butcher and an advertising message bearing Piersall's signature. Similar cards advertising Cain's grocery products are also known.

	NM	EX	VG
Autographed: 2-3X	300.00	150.00	90.00
(1) Jimmy Piersall (Chest-to-cap, back printed in black.)	125.00	62.50	37.50
(2) Jimmy Piersall (Waist-to-cap, back printed in black and blue.)	125.00	62.50	37.50

1888 Conly Cabinets

Contemporary, but much less numerous than, the Old Judge cabinet cards is this issue from a Boston photo studio. Carrying an April, 1888, copyright date, the 4-1/4" x 6-1/2" have sepia photos of the players in action poses. Backs have decorative advertising for the studio. The extent of the checklist is unknown.

	NM	EX	VG
John Clarkson (Ball in hands at chest.)	3,000	1,200	725.00
John Clarkson (Ball in hands at chest.)	3,000	1,200	725.00
John Clarkson (Right arm at back.)	3,000	1,200	725.00
John Clarkson (Right arm extended.)	3,000	1,200	725.00

1891 Conly Studio Cabinets

The extent of this issue from a Boston photo studio is unknown. The checklist begins here with three players from the Boston Reds American Associations champions. The 4-1/4" x 6-1/2" cards have a sepia portrait photo of the player in street clothes. Back has decorative advertising for the studio.

	NM	EX	VG
Common Player:	1,000	500.00	300.00
(1) Duke Farrell	1,200	500.00	300.00
(2) George Haddock	1,200	500.00	300.00
(3) Cub Stricker	1,200	500.00	300.00

1950s-70s L.L. Cook Milwaukee Braves/Brewers Postcards

From a period of (roughly) 1956 through 1972 the L.L. Cook Co. of Milwaukee undertook the production of black-and-white photo postcards for various members of the local teams. Apparently printed to order to allow players and staff to respond to fan requests for pictures and autographs, the 3-1/2" x 5-1/2" cards have (usually) borderless poses on front. Postcard-style divided backs may or may not have a credit line vertically at center, and various versions of the standard postcard markings are seen. This checklist is likely incomplete.

	NM	EX	VG
Common Player:	30.00	15.00	9.00
(1) Hank Aaron	150.00	75.00	45.00
(2) Tommie Aaron	30.00	15.00	9.00
(3) Joe Adcock	40.00	20.00	12.00
(4) Ed Bailey	30.00	15.00	9.00
(5) Frank Bolling	30.00	15.00	9.00
(6) Bobby Bragan	30.00	15.00	9.00
(7) Ty Cline	30.00	15.00	9.00
(8) Wes Covington	30.00	15.00	9.00
(9) Ray Crone (White name on front.)	30.00	15.00	9.00
(10) Ray Crone (No name.)	30.00	15.00	9.00
(11) Fred Haney	30.00	15.00	9.00
(12) Ernie Johnson	30.00	15.00	9.00
(13) Ernie Johnson (Part of light tower shows.)	30.00	15.00	9.00
(14) Charlie Lau	30.00	15.00	9.00
(15) Mike Krsnich	30.00	15.00	9.00
(16) Roy McMillan	30.00	15.00	9.00
(17) Jerry McNertney (Brewers)	30.00	15.00	9.00
(18) Don Nottebart	30.00	15.00	9.00
(19) Phil Paine	30.00	15.00	9.00
(20) Ron Piche	30.00	15.00	9.00
(21) Juan Pizarro	30.00	15.00	9.00
(22) Bob Sadowski	30.00	15.00	9.00
(13) Red Schoendienst	50.00	25.00	15.00
(14) George Scott (Brewers)	30.00	15.00	9.00
(15) Bob Shaw	30.00	15.00	9.00
(16) Warren Spahn (Artwork portrait, white background.)	40.00	20.00	12.00
(17) Warren Spahn (Artwork portrait, yellow in background.)	40.00	20.00	12.00
(18) Warren Spahn (Eating with son.)	30.00	15.00	9.00
(19) Warren Spahn (Showing son new car.)	30.00	15.00	9.00
(20) Warren Spahn (In car, waving to family.)	30.00	15.00	9.00
(21) Al Spangler	30.00	15.00	9.00
(22) Frank Torre (Holding Pepsi.)	30.00	15.00	9.00
(23) Frank Torre (Holding Pepsi, facsimile autograph.)	30.00	15.00	9.00
(24) Frank Torre (Holding Pepsi, Brave patch shows.)	30.00	15.00	9.00
(25) Joe Torre Kneeling	40.00	20.00	12.00
(26) Joe Torre/Portrait	40.00	20.00	12.00

1910 Coupon Cigarettes Type 1 (T213)

Though they feature the same pictures used in the contemporary T206 tobacco issue, Coupon Cigarette cards make up three distinct sets, produced between 1910 and 1919. Type 1 Coupon cards feature a mix of players from the National and American Leagues, and the Southern League. Nominally the traditional 1-7/16" x 2-1/8" cigarette-card size, fronts of the Coupons are identical to the more popular T206 series. Backs, however, clearly identify the cards as being a product of Coupon Cigarettes and allow the collector to easily differentiate among the three types. Type 1 cards, produced in 1910, carry a general advertisement for Coupon "Mild" Cigarettes, with no mention of price. Distribution of the Coupons was limited to the Louisiana area, making the set very difficult to checklist and even moreso to collect. Numerous variations further complicate the situation. It is quite possible the checklists here are incomplete and additions will surface in the future. Type 1 cards are considered the rarest of the Coupon issues, and, because they were printed on a thinner stock, they are especially difficult to find in top condition.

	NM	EX	VG
Complete Set (68):	30,000	15,000	8,500
Common Player:	450.00	170.00	85.00
(1) Harry Bay	450.00	170.00	85.00
(2) Beals Becker	450.00	170.00	85.00
(3) Chief Bender	1,275	500.00	250.00
(4) Bernhard	450.00	170.00	85.00
(5) Ted Breitenstein	450.00	170.00	85.00
(6) Bobby Byrne	450.00	170.00	85.00
(7) Billy Campbell	450.00	170.00	85.00
(8) Scoops Carey	1,275	500.00	250.00
(9) Frank Chance	1,275	500.00	250.00
(10) Chappy Charles	450.00	170.00	85.00
(11) Hal Chase/Portrait	625.00	250.00	125.00
(12) Hal Chase/Throwing	625.00	250.00	125.00
(13) Ty Cobb	11,625	4,650	2,325
(14) Bill Cranston	450.00	170.00	85.00
(15) Birdie Cree	450.00	170.00	85.00
(16) Wild Bill Donovan	450.00	170.00	85.00
(17) Mickey Doolan	450.00	170.00	85.00
(18) Jean Dubuc	450.00	170.00	85.00
(19) Joe Dunn	450.00	170.00	85.00
(20) Roy Ellam	450.00	170.00	85.00
(21) Clyde Engle	450.00	170.00	85.00
(22) Johnny Evers	1,275	500.00	250.00
(23) Art Fletcher	450.00	170.00	85.00
(24) Charlie Fritz	450.00	170.00	85.00
(25) Ed Greminger	450.00	170.00	85.00
(26) Bill Hart (Little Rock)	450.00	170.00	85.00
(27) Jimmy Hart (Montgomery)	450.00	170.00	85.00
(28) Topsy Hartsel	450.00	170.00	85.00
(29) Gordon Hickman	450.00	170.00	85.00
(30) Danny Hoffman	450.00	170.00	85.00
(31) Harry Howell	450.00	170.00	85.00
(32) Miller Huggins (Hands at mouth.)	1,275	500.00	250.00
(33) Miller Huggins/Portrait	1,275	500.00	250.00
(34) George Hunter	450.00	170.00	85.00
(35) A.O. "Dutch" Jordan	450.00	170.00	85.00
(36) Ed Killian	450.00	170.00	85.00
(37) Otto Knabe	450.00	170.00	85.00
(38) Frank LaPorte	450.00	170.00	85.00
(39) Ed Lennox	450.00	170.00	85.00
(40) Harry Lentz (Sentz)	450.00	170.00	85.00
(41) Rube Marquard	1,275	500.00	250.00
(42) Doc Marshall	450.00	170.00	85.00
(43) Christy Mathewson	3,225	1,300	650.00
(44) George McBride	450.00	170.00	85.00
(45) Pryor McElveen	450.00	170.00	85.00
(46) Matty McIntyre	450.00	170.00	85.00
(47) Mike Mitchell	450.00	170.00	85.00
(48) Carlton Molesworth	450.00	170.00	85.00
(49) Mike Mowrey	450.00	170.00	85.00
(50) Chief Myers (Meyers)/Btg	450.00	170.00	85.00
(51) Chief Myers (Meyers)/Fldg	450.00	170.00	85.00
(52) Dode Paskert	450.00	170.00	85.00
(53) Hub Perdue	450.00	170.00	85.00
(54) Arch Persons	450.00	170.00	85.00
(55) Ed Reagan	450.00	170.00	85.00
(56) Bob Rhoades (Rhoads)	450.00	170.00	85.00
(57) Ike Rockenfeld	450.00	170.00	85.00
(58) Claude Rossman	450.00	170.00	85.00
(59) Boss Schmidt	450.00	170.00	85.00
(60) Sid Smith	450.00	170.00	85.00
(61) Charlie Starr	450.00	170.00	85.00
(62) Gabby Street	450.00	170.00	85.00
(63) Ed Summers	450.00	170.00	85.00
(64) Jeff Sweeney	450.00	170.00	85.00
(65) Ira Thomas	450.00	170.00	85.00
(66) Woodie Thornton	450.00	170.00	85.00
(67) Ed Willett	450.00	170.00	85.00
(68) Owen Wilson	450.00	170.00	85.00

1914-16 Coupon Cigarettes Type 2 (T213)

Though they feature the same photos used in the contemporary T206 tobacco issue, Coupon Cigarette cards make up three distinct sets, produced between 1910 and 1919. Type 2 Coupons feature a mix of players from the three major leagues (National, American and Federal), and several minor leagues. The 1-7/16" x 2-5/8" Coupon fronts are virtually identical, except for the use of blue typography, to the more popular T206 series. Backs, however, clearly identify the cards as being a product of Coupon Cigarettes and allow the collector to easily differentiate among the three types. Type 2 cards, issued from 1914 to 1916, contain the words "MILD and SWEET" and "20 for 5 cents." Distribution of the Coupon cards was limited to the Louisiana area, making the set difficult to checklist and even moreso to collect. Numerous variations further complicate the situation. It is quite possible the checklists here are incomplete and additions will surface in the future. Although Type 2 cards are the most common, they were printed with a "glossy" coating, making them susceptible to cracking and creasing.

	NM	EX	VG
Complete Set (188):	80,000	36,000	17,500
Common Player:	275.00	125.00	60.00
(1) Red Ames (Cincinnati)	275.00	125.00	60.00
(2) Red Ames (St. Louis)	275.00	125.00	60.00

#	Player	NM	EX	VG
(3)	Home Run Baker (Phila. Amer.)	550.00	245.00	120.00
(4)	Home Run Baker (Philadelphia Amer.)	600.00	275.00	130.00
(5)	Home Run Baker (New York)	550.00	245.00	120.00
(6)	Cy Barger	275.00	125.00	60.00
(7)	Chief Bender (Trees in background, Philadelphia Amer.)	550.00	245.00	120.00
(8)	Chief Bender (Trees in background, Baltimore.)	550.00	245.00	120.00
(9)	Chief Bender (Trees in background, Philadelphia Nat.)	550.00	245.00	120.00
(10)	Chief Bender (No trees, Philadelphia Amer.)	550.00	245.00	120.00
(11)	Chief Bender (No trees, Baltimore.)	550.00	245.00	120.00
(12)	Chief Bender (No trees, Philadelphia Natl.)	550.00	240.00	120.00
(13)	Bill Bradley	275.00	125.00	60.00
(14)	Roger Bresnahan (Chicago)	550.00	245.00	120.00
(15)	Roger Bresnahan (Toledo)	550.00	245.00	120.00
(16)	Al Bridwell (St. Louis)	275.00	125.00	60.00
(17)	Al Bridwell (Nashville)	275.00	125.00	60.00
(18)	Mordecai Brown (Chicago)	550.00	245.00	120.00
(19)	Mordecai Brown (St. Louis)	550.00	245.00	120.00
(20)	Bobby Byrne	275.00	125.00	60.00
(21)	Howie Camnitz (Arm at side.)	275.00	125.00	60.00
(22)	Howie Camnitz (Pittsburgh, hands above head.)	275.00	125.00	60.00
(23)	Howie Camnitz (Savannah, hands above head.)	275.00	125.00	60.00
(24)	Billy Campbell	275.00	125.00	60.00
(25)	Frank Chance/Btg (New York)	550.00	245.00	120.00
(26)	Frank Chance/Btg (Los Angeles)	600.00	270.00	130.00
(27)	Frank Chance/Portrait (New York)	550.00	245.00	120.00
(28)	Frank Chance/Portrait (Los Angeles)	600.00	270.00	130.00
(29)	Bill Chapelle (Brooklyn, "R" on shirt.)	275.00	125.00	60.00
(30)	Larry Chapelle (Chappel) (Cleveland, no "R" on shirt, photo actually Bill Chapelle.)	275.00	125.00	60.00
(31)	Hal Chase (Chicago, holding trophy.)	365.00	165.00	80.00
(32)	Hal Chase (Buffalo, holding trophy.)	365.00	165.00	80.00
(33)	Hal Chase/Portrait (Chicago, blue background.)	365.00	165.00	80.00
(34)	Hal Chase/Portrait (Buffalo, blue background.)	365.00	165.00	80.00
(35)	Hal Chase/Throwing (Chicago)	365.00	165.00	80.00
(36)	Hal Chase/Throwing (Buffalo)	365.00	165.00	80.00
(37)	Ty Cobb/Portrait	7,250	3,250	1,600
(38)	Ty Cobb (Bat off shoulder.)	6,000	2,700	1,325
(39)	Eddie Collins (Philadelphia, "A" on shirt.)	600.00	270.00	130.00
(40)	Eddie Collins (Chicago, "A" on shirt.)	600.00	270.00	130.00
(41)	Eddie Collins (Chicago, no "A" on shirt.)	600.00	270.00	130.00
(42)	Doc Crandall (St. Louis Fed.)	275.00	125.00	60.00
(43)	Doc Crandall (St. Louis Amer.)	275.00	125.00	60.00
(44)	Sam Crawford	550.00	245.00	120.00
(45)	Birdie Cree	275.00	125.00	60.00
(46)	Harry Davis (Phila. Amer.)	275.00	125.00	60.00
(47)	Harry Davis (Philadelphia Amer.)	275.00	125.00	60.00
(48)	Ray Demmitt (Chicago Amer. (New York uniform.))	275.00	125.00	60.00
(49)	Ray Demmitt (Chicago Amer. (St. Louis uniform.))	275.00	125.00	60.00
(50)	Josh Devore (Philadelphia)	275.00	125.00	60.00
(51)	Josh Devore (Chillicothe)	275.00	125.00	60.00
(52)	Mike Donlin (New York)	275.00	125.00	60.00
(53)	Mike Donlin (.300 batter 7 years)	275.00	125.00	60.00
(54)	Wild Bill Donovan	275.00	125.00	60.00
(55)	Mickey Doolan/Btg (Baltimore)	275.00	125.00	60.00
(56)	Mickey Doolan/Btg (Chicago)	275.00	125.00	60.00
(57)	Mickey Doolan/Fldg (Baltimore)	275.00	125.00	60.00
(58)	Mickey Doolan/Fldg (Chicago)	275.00	125.00	60.00
(59)	Tom Downey	275.00	125.00	60.00
(60)	Larry Doyle/Btg	275.00	125.00	60.00
(61)	Larry Doyle/Portrait	275.00	125.00	60.00
(62)	Jean Dubuc	275.00	125.00	60.00
(63)	Jack Dunn (Picture is Joe Dunn.)	275.00	125.00	60.00
(64)	Kid Elberfield (Elberfeld) (Brooklyn)	275.00	125.00	60.00
(65)	Kid Elberfield (Elberfeld) (Chatanooga)	275.00	125.00	60.00
(66)	Steve Evans	275.00	125.00	60.00
(67)	Johnny Evers	550.00	245.00	120.00
(68)	Russ Ford	275.00	125.00	60.00
(69)	Art Fromme	275.00	125.00	60.00
(70)	Chick Gandil (Washington)	1,000	450.00	220.00
(71)	Chick Gandil (Cleveland)	550.00	245.00	120.00
(72)	Rube Geyer	275.00	125.00	60.00
(73)	Clark Griffith	550.00	245.00	120.00
(74)	Bob Groom	275.00	125.00	60.00
(75)	Buck Herzog ("B" on shirt.)	300.00	135.00	66.00
(76)	Buck Herzog (No "B" on shirt.)	400.00	180.00	88.00
(77)	Dick Hoblitzell (Cincinnati)	275.00	125.00	60.00
(78)	Dick Hoblitzell (Boston Nat.)	275.00	125.00	60.00
(79)	Dick Hoblitzell (Boston Amer.)	275.00	125.00	60.00
(80)	Solly Hofman	275.00	125.00	60.00
(81)	Solly Hofmann (Hofman)	275.00	125.00	60.00
(82)	Miller Huggins (Hands at mouth.)	550.00	245.00	120.00
(83)	Miller Huggins/Portrait	550.00	245.00	120.00
(84)	John Hummel (Brooklyn Nat.)	275.00	125.00	60.00
(85)	John Hummel (Brooklyn)	275.00	125.00	60.00
(86)	Hughie Jennings (Both hands showing.)	550.00	245.00	120.00
(87)	Hughie Jennings (One hand showing.)	550.00	245.00	120.00
(88)	Walter Johnson	2,500	1,125	550.00
(89)	Tim Jordan (Toronto)	275.00	125.00	60.00
(90)	Tim Jordan (Ft. Worth)	275.00	125.00	60.00
(91)	Joe Kelley (New York)	550.00	245.00	120.00
(92)	Joe Kelley (Toronto)	550.00	245.00	120.00
(93)	Otto Knabe	275.00	125.00	60.00
(94)	Ed Konetchy (Pittsburgh Nat.)	275.00	125.00	60.00
(95)	Ed Konetchy (Pittsburgh Fed.)	275.00	125.00	60.00
(96)	Ed Konetchy (Boston)	275.00	125.00	60.00
(97)	Harry Krause	275.00	125.00	60.00
(98)	Nap Lajoie (Phila. Amer.)	550.00	245.00	120.00
(99)	Nap Lajoie (Philadelphia Amer.)	550.00	245.00	120.00
(100)	Nap Lajoie (Cleveland)	2,000	1,000	600.00
(101)	Tommy Leach (Chicago)	275.00	125.00	60.00
(102)	Tommy Leach (Cincinnati)	275.00	125.00	60.00
(103)	Tommy Leach (Rochester)	275.00	125.00	60.00
(104)	Ed Lennox	275.00	125.00	60.00
(105)	Sherry Magee (Phila. Nat.)	275.00	125.00	60.00
(106)	Sherry Magee (Philadelphia Nat.)	275.00	125.00	60.00
(107)	Sherry Magee (Boston)	275.00	125.00	60.00
(108)	Rube Marquard/Pitching (New York, "NY" on shirt.)	600.00	270.00	130.00
(109)	Rube Marquard/Pitching (Brooklyn, no "NY" on shirt.)	550.00	245.00	120.00
(110)	Rube Marquard/Portrait (New York, "NY" on shirt.)	2,000	1,000	600.00
(111)	Rube Marquard/Portrait (Brooklyn, no "NY" on shirt.)	550.00	245.00	120.00
(112)	Christy Mathewson	3,000	1,350	660.00
(113)	John McGraw (Glove at side.)	550.00	245.00	120.00
(114)	John McGraw/Portrait	550.00	245.00	120.00
(115)	Larry McLean	275.00	125.00	60.00
(116)	George McQuillan (Pittsburgh)	275.00	125.00	60.00
(117)	George McQuillan (Phila. Nat.)	275.00	125.00	60.00
(118)	George McQuillan (Philadelphia Nat.)	275.00	125.00	60.00
(119)	Fred Merkle	275.00	125.00	60.00
(120)	Chief Meyers (New York, fielding.)	275.00	125.00	60.00
(121)	Chief Meyers (Brooklyn, fielding.)	275.00	125.00	60.00
(122)	Chief Meyers (New York, portrait.)	275.00	125.00	60.00
(123)	Chief Meyers (Brooklyn, portrait.)	275.00	125.00	60.00
(124)	Dots Miller	275.00	125.00	60.00
(125)	Mike Mitchell	275.00	125.00	60.00
(126)	Mike Mowrey (Pittsburgh Nat.)	275.00	125.00	60.00
(127)	Mike Mowrey (Pittsburgh Fed.)	275.00	125.00	60.00
(128)	Mike Mowrey (Brooklyn)	275.00	125.00	60.00
(129)	George Mullin (Indianapolis)	275.00	125.00	60.00
(130)	George Mullin (Newark)	275.00	125.00	60.00
(131)	Danny Murphy	275.00	125.00	60.00
(132)	Red Murray (New York)	275.00	125.00	60.00
(133)	Red Murray (Chicago)	275.00	125.00	60.00
(134)	Red Murray (Kansas City)	275.00	125.00	60.00
(135)	Tom Needham	275.00	125.00	60.00
(136)	Rebel Oakes	275.00	125.00	60.00
(137)	Rube Oldring (Phila. Amer.)	275.00	125.00	60.00
(138)	Rube Oldring (Philadelphia Amer.)	275.00	125.00	60.00
(139)	Dode Paskert (Phila. Nat.)	275.00	125.00	60.00
(140)	Dode Paskert (Philadelphia Nat.)	275.00	125.00	60.00
(141)	Billy Purtell	275.00	125.00	60.00
(142)	Jack Quinn (Baltimore)	275.00	125.00	60.00
(143)	Jack Quinn (Vernon)	275.00	125.00	60.00
(144)	Ed Reulbach (Brooklyn Nat.)	275.00	125.00	60.00
(145)	Ed Reulbach (Brooklyn Fed.)	275.00	125.00	60.00
(146)	Ed Reulbach (Pittsburgh)	275.00	125.00	60.00
(147)	Nap Rucker (Brooklyn)	275.00	125.00	60.00
(148)	Nap Rucker (Brooklyn Nat.)	275.00	125.00	60.00
(149)	Dick Rudolph	275.00	125.00	60.00
(150)	Germany Schaefer (Washington, "W" on shirt.)	275.00	125.00	60.00
(151)	Germany Schaefer (K.C. Fed., "W" on shirt.)	275.00	125.00	60.00
(152)	Germany Schaefer (New York, no "W" on shirt.)	275.00	125.00	60.00
(153)	Admiral Schlei/Btg	275.00	125.00	60.00
(154)	Admiral Schlei/Portrait	275.00	125.00	60.00
(155)	Boss Schmidt	275.00	125.00	60.00
(156)	Wildfire Schulte	275.00	125.00	60.00
(157)	Frank Smith	275.00	125.00	60.00
(158)	Tris Speaker	2,400	1,200	725.00
(159)	George Stovall	275.00	125.00	60.00
(160)	Gabby Street/Catching	275.00	125.00	60.00
(161)	Gabby Street/Portrait	275.00	125.00	60.00
(162)	Ed Summers	275.00	125.00	60.00
(163)	Bill Sweeney (Boston)	275.00	125.00	60.00
(164)	Bill Sweeney (Chicago)	275.00	125.00	60.00
(165)	Jeff Sweeney (New York)	275.00	125.00	60.00
(166)	Jeff Sweeney (Richmond)	275.00	125.00	60.00
(167)	Ira Thomas (Phila. Amer.)	275.00	125.00	60.00
(168)	Ira Thomas (Philadelphia Amer.)	275.00	125.00	60.00
(169)	Joe Tinker (Chicago Fed., bat off shoulder.)	550.00	245.00	120.00
(170)	Joe Tinker (Chicago Nat., bat off shoulder.)	550.00	245.00	120.00
(171)	Joe Tinker (Chicago Fed., bat off shoulder.)	550.00	245.00	120.00
(172)	Joe Tinker (Chicago Nat., bat off shoulder.)	550.00	245.00	120.00
(173)	Heinie Wagner	275.00	125.00	60.00
(174)	Jack Warhop (New York, "NY" on shirt.)	275.00	125.00	60.00
(175)	Jack Warhop (St. Louis, no "NY" on shirt.)	275.00	125.00	60.00
(176)	Zach Wheat (Brooklyn)	550.00	245.00	120.00
(177)	Zach Wheat (Brooklyn Nat.)	550.00	245.00	120.00
(178)	Kaiser Wilhelm	275.00	125.00	60.00
(179)	Ed Willett (St. Louis)	275.00	125.00	60.00
(180)	Ed Willett (Memphis)	275.00	125.00	60.00
(181)	Owen Wilson	275.00	125.00	60.00
(182)	Hooks Wiltse/Pitching (New York)	275.00	125.00	60.00
(183)	Hooks Wiltse/Pitching (Brooklyn)	275.00	125.00	60.00
(184)	Hooks Wiltse/Pitching (Jersey City)	275.00	125.00	60.00
(185)	Hooks Wiltse/Portrait (New York)	275.00	125.00	60.00
(186)	Hooks Wiltse/Portrait (Brooklyn)	275.00	125.00	60.00
(187)	Hooks Wiltse/Portrait (Jersey City)	275.00	125.00	60.00
(188)	Heinie Zimmerman	275.00	125.00	60.00

1919 Coupon Cigarettes Type 3 (T213)

Though using the same photos seen in the contemporary T206 tobacco issue, Coupon Cigarette cards comprise three distinct sets produced between 1910 and 1919. Coupon cards feature a mix of players from the National and American Leagues, and several minor leagues. Slightly smaller than the usual cigarette-card format, Type 3 Coupons nominally measure 1-3/8" x 2-9/16", but are more prone to original size deviations than Type 1 or Type 2 Coupons. Except for the blue ink used in the player identification line, the fronts of the Coupon cards are virtually identical to the more popular T206 series. Backs, however, clearly identify the cards as being a product of Coupon Cigarettes and allow the collector to easily differentiate among the three types. Type 3 cards, issued in 1919, advertise "16 for 10 cts." and mention "70 leading players." Distribution of the Coupon cards was limited to the Louisiana area, making the set difficult to checklist and even more difficult to collect. Numerous variations further complicate the situation. It is quite possible the checklists here are incomplete and additions will surface in the future. While most Type 3 Coupons mention on their backs, "FACTORY No. 3, DIST OF LA," some have been seen with that designation blacked out and an overprint applied citing "FACTORY No. 8, DIST OF LA."

#	Player	NM	EX	VG
	Complete Set (70):	30,000	13,500	6,750
	Common Player:	300.00	135.00	65.00
(1)	Red Ames	300.00	135.00	65.00
(2)	Home Run Baker	600.00	275.00	130.00
(3)	Chief Bender (No trees in background.)	600.00	275.00	130.00
(4)	Chief Bender (Trees in background.)	600.00	275.00	130.00
(5)	Roger Bresnahan	600.00	275.00	130.00
(6)	Al Bridwell	300.00	135.00	65.00
(7)	Miner Brown	600.00	275.00	130.00
(8)	Bobby Byrne	300.00	135.00	65.00
(9)	Frank Chance/Btg	600.00	275.00	130.00
(10)	Frank Chance/Portrait	600.00	275.00	130.00
(11)	Hal Chase (Holding trophy.)	450.00	200.00	100.00
(12)	Hal Chase/Portrait	450.00	200.00	100.00
(13)	Hal Chase/Throwing	450.00	200.00	100.00
(14)	Ty Cobb/Btg	3,750	1,675	825.00
(15)	Ty Cobb/Portrait	3,750	1,675	825.00
(16)	Eddie Collins	600.00	275.00	130.00
(17)	Sam Crawford	600.00	275.00	130.00
(18)	Harry Davis	300.00	135.00	65.00
(19)	Mike Donlin	300.00	135.00	65.00
(20)	Wild Bill Donovan	300.00	135.00	65.00
(21)	Mickey Doolan/Btg	300.00	135.00	65.00
(22)	Mickey Doolan/Fldg	300.00	135.00	65.00
(23)	Larry Doyle/Btg	300.00	135.00	65.00
(24)	Larry Doyle/Portrait	300.00	135.00	65.00
(25)	Jean Dubuc	300.00	135.00	65.00
(26)	Jack Dunn	300.00	135.00	65.00
(27)	Kid Elberfeld	300.00	135.00	65.00
(28)	Johnny Evers	600.00	275.00	130.00
(29)	Chick Gandil	550.00	250.00	125.00
(30)	Clark Griffith	600.00	275.00	130.00
(31)	Buck Herzog	300.00	135.00	65.00
(32)	Dick Hoblitzell	300.00	135.00	65.00
(33)	Miller Huggins (Hands at mouth.)	600.00	275.00	130.00
(34)	Miller Huggins/Portrait	600.00	275.00	130.00
(35)	John Hummel	300.00	135.00	65.00

ɔm	300.00	110.00	65.00
vore	300.00	110.00	65.00
Neill	300.00	110.00	65.00
er	300.00	110.00	65.00
mmell (Hummel)	300.00	110.00	65.00
ker	300.00	110.00	65.00
eat	1,750	875.00	525.00
er	300.00	110.00	65.00
Toole	300.00	110.00	65.00
litzel (Hoblitzell)	300.00	110.00	65.00
lan	300.00	110.00	65.00
hnson	6,000	3,000	1,800
hang	300.00	110.00	65.00
sler	300.00	110.00	65.00
ugey	300.00	110.00	65.00
alk	1,100	450.00	225.00
tchell	300.00	110.00	65.00
ams	300.00	110.00	65.00
rcher	300.00	110.00	65.00
aker	1,700	680.00	340.00
ie	2,000	1,000	600.00
ndall	300.00	110.00	65.00
agner	11,000	5,500	3,250
Graw	1,100	450.00	225.00
rke	1,100	450.00	225.00
yers	300.00	110.00	65.00
nling	300.00	110.00	65.00
ey	1,100	450.00	225.00
vens	300.00	110.00	65.00
ggins	1,100	450.00	225.00
endrix	300.00	110.00	65.00
ennings	1,100	450.00	225.00
rkle	300.00	110.00	65.00
lie	300.00	110.00	65.00
each	300.00	110.00	65.00
hanty (Delahanty)	300.00	110.00	65.00
ravath	300.00	110.00	65.00
rd	300.00	110.00	65.00
etzer	300.00	110.00	65.00
rzog	300.00	110.00	65.00
tten	300.00	110.00	65.00
ily	300.00	110.00	65.00
Mathewson	6,600	2,650	1,325
eney	300.00	110.00	65.00
nith	300.00	110.00	65.00
ckinpaugh	350.00	140.00	70.00
ree	300.00	110.00	65.00
	300.00	110.00	65.00
cotte	1,000	400.00	200.00
ring	300.00	110.00	65.00
cker	300.00	110.00	65.00
nton	300.00	110.00	65.00
porte (LaPorte)	600.00	240.00	120.00
se	300.00	110.00	65.00
ton	300.00	110.00	65.00
Schulte	300.00	110.00	65.00
er	300.00	110.00	65.00
son	30,000	15,000	9,000
	300.00	110.00	65.00
avender	300.00	110.00	65.00
ingham	300.00	110.00	65.00
vney	300.00	110.00	65.00
agee	300.00	110.00	65.00
nding	300.00	110.00	65.00
cher	300.00	110.00	65.00
oran	300.00	110.00	65.00
ney	300.00	110.00	65.00
uggs	300.00	110.00	65.00
Moriarity (Moriarty)	300.00	110.00	65.00
ian	300.00	110.00	65.00
ider	300.00	110.00	65.00
erly	300.00	110.00	65.00
tchy	300.00	110.00	65.00
Perring	300.00	110.00	65.00
oolan	300.00	110.00	65.00
due	300.00	110.00	65.00
ush	300.00	110.00	65.00
ee	300.00	110.00	65.00
ore (Earl)	300.00	110.00	65.00
off	300.00	110.00	65.00
air	300.00	110.00	65.00
hmidt	300.00	110.00	65.00
ans	300.00	110.00	65.00
well	300.00	110.00	65.00
o	300.00	110.00	65.00
Baumgardner	300.00	110.00	65.00
amaker	300.00	110.00	65.00
ickey	1,100	450.00	225.00
Marsans	425.00	175.00	85.00
r (Killefer)	300.00	110.00	65.00
aranville	1,100	450.00	225.00
en	300.00	110.00	65.00
wdy	300.00	110.00	65.00
akes	300.00	110.00	65.00
urphy	300.00	110.00	65.00
er	300.00	110.00	65.00
ckard	300.00	110.00	65.00
ubert	300.00	110.00	65.00
alsh	300.00	110.00	65.00
er	325.00	130.00	65.00
er	325.00	130.00	65.00
ee	325.00	130.00	65.00
ilson	325.00	130.00	65.00
rin	325.00	130.00	65.00
nston	325.00	130.00	65.00
Whitted	325.00	130.00	65.00
IcQuillen (McQuillan)	325.00	130.00	65.00
s	325.00	130.00	65.00
olph	325.00	130.00	65.00
nolly	325.00	130.00	65.00
uc	325.00	130.00	65.00
Kaiserling	325.00	130.00	65.00
sel	325.00	130.00	65.00
roh	325.00	130.00	65.00
auff	325.00	130.00	65.00
sch (Roush)	1,250	500.00	250.00
Stallings	325.00	130.00	65.00
sling	325.00	130.00	65.00

164	Bob Shawkey	325.00	130.00	65.00
165	Eddie Murphy	325.00	130.00	65.00
166	Bullet Joe Bush	325.00	130.00	65.00
167	Clark Griffith	1,250	500.00	250.00
168	Vin Campbell	325.00	130.00	65.00
169	Ray Collins	325.00	130.00	65.00
170	Hans Lobert	325.00	130.00	65.00
171	Earl Hamilton	325.00	130.00	65.00
172	Erskine Mayer	450.00	180.00	90.00
173	Tilly Walker	325.00	130.00	65.00
174	Bobby Veach	325.00	130.00	65.00
175	Joe Benz	325.00	130.00	65.00
176	Hippo Vaughn	1,100	200.00	75.00

1933 Cracker Jack Pins (PR4)

Although no manufacturer is indicated on the pins themselves, the manufacturer has been identified as Button Gum Co., Chicago, but there is still some indication that Cracker Jack inserted this 25-player set in their products circa 1933. Each pin measures 13/16" in diameter and features a line drawing of a player portrait. The unnumbered pins are printed in blue and gray with backgrounds found in either yellow or gray.

		NM	EX	VG
	Complete Set (25):	1,600	800.00	475.00
	Common Player:	35.00	17.50	10.00
(1)	Charles Berry	35.00	17.50	10.00
(2)	Bill Cissell	35.00	17.50	10.00
(3)	KiKi Cuyler	60.00	30.00	18.00
(4)	Dizzy Dean	100.00	50.00	30.00
(5)	Wesley Ferrell	35.00	17.50	10.00
(6)	Frank Frisch	60.00	30.00	18.00
(7)	Lou Gehrig	250.00	125.00	75.00
(8)	Vernon Gomez	60.00	30.00	18.00
(9)	Goose Goslin	60.00	30.00	18.00
(10)	George Grantham	35.00	17.50	10.00
(11)	Charley Grimm	35.00	17.50	10.00
(12)	Lefty Grove	75.00	37.00	22.00
(13)	Gabby Hartnett	60.00	30.00	18.00
(14)	Travis Jackson	60.00	30.00	18.00
(15)	Tony Lazzeri	60.00	30.00	18.00
(16)	Ted Lyons	60.00	30.00	18.00
(17)	Rabbit Maranville	60.00	30.00	18.00
(18)	Carl Reynolds	35.00	17.50	10.00
(19)	Charles Ruffing	60.00	30.00	18.00
(20)	Al Simmons	60.00	30.00	18.00
(21)	Gus Suhr	35.00	17.50	10.00
(22)	Bill Terry	60.00	30.00	18.00
(23)	Dazzy Vance	60.00	30.00	18.00
(24)	Paul Waner	60.00	30.00	18.00
(25)	Lon Warneke	35.00	17.50	10.00

1979 Larry Crain Prints

"Baseball's Greatest Team," as voted during baseball's centennial, was featured on a set of 8-1/2" x 11" black-and-white prints by artist Larry Crain. Each print is signed and numbered by the artist. The set of 11 was originally sold for $25.

		NM	EX	VG
	Complete Set (11):	25.00	12.50	7.50
	Common Player:	3.00	1.50	.90
(1)	Yogi Berra	3.00	1.50	.90
(2)	Joe DiMaggio	5.00	2.50	1.50
(3)	Lou Gehrig	4.00	2.00	1.25
(4)	Rogers Hornsby	3.00	1.50	.90
(5)	Walter Johnson	3.00	1.50	.90
(6)	Willie Mays	4.00	2.00	1.25
(7)	Brooks Robinson	3.00	1.50	.90
(8)	Babe Ruth	5.00	2.50	1.50
(9)	Warren Spahn	3.00	1.50	.90
(10)	Casey Stengel	3.00	1.50	.90
(11)	Honus Wagner	3.00	1.50	.90

1976 Crane Potato Chips Discs

This unnumbered 70-card set of player discs was issued with Crane Potato Chips in 1976. The front of the discs are designed to look like a baseball with the player's black-and-white portrait in the center and vital data in side panels containing one of several bright colors. Discs measure 3-3/8" in diameter. This is the most common among several regionally issued sets sharing the same card fronts with different ads on back. The discs were produced by Michael Schechter Associates under license from the players' union. All uniform and cap logos have been deleted from the discs' photos. The unnumbered discs are checklisted here in alphabetical order. Several of the discs have team variations reflecting player moves. These are known only among the Crane discs and have not been verified in the issues of other advertisers.

		NM	EX	VG
	Complete Set (70):	25.00	12.50	7.50
	Common Player:	1.00	.50	.30
(1)	Henry Aaron	9.00	4.50	2.75
(2)	Johnny Bench	4.00	2.00	1.25
(3)	Vida Blue	1.00	.50	.30
(4)	Larry Bowa	1.00	.50	.30
(5)	Lou Brock	3.00	1.50	.90
(6)	Jeff Burroughs	1.00	.50	.30
(7)	John Candelaria	1.00	.50	.30
(8)	Jose Cardenal	1.00	.50	.30

(9)	Rod Carew	3.00	1.50	.90
(10)	Steve Carlton	3.00	1.50	.90
(11)	Dave Cash	1.00	.50	.30
(12)	Cesar Cedeno	1.00	.50	.30
(13)	Ron Cey	1.00	.50	.30
(14)	Carlton Fisk	3.00	1.50	.90
(15)	Tito Fuentes	1.00	.50	.30
(16)	Steve Garvey	2.00	1.00	.60
(17)	Ken Griffey	1.00	.50	.30
(18)	Don Gullett	1.00	.50	.30
(19)	Willie Horton	1.00	.50	.30
(20)	Al Hrabosky	1.00	.50	.30
(21)	Catfish Hunter	3.00	1.50	.90
(22a)	Reggie Jackson (A's)	6.00	3.00	1.75
(22b)	Reggie Jackson (Orioles)	15.00	7.50	4.50
(23)	Randy Jones	1.00	.50	.30
(24)	Jim Kaat	1.00	.50	.30
(25)	Don Kessinger	1.00	.50	.30
(26)	Dave Kingman	1.00	.50	.30
(27)	Jerry Koosman	1.00	.50	.30
(28)	Mickey Lolich	1.00	.50	.30
(29)	Greg Luzinski	1.00	.50	.30
(30)	Fred Lynn	1.00	.50	.30
(31)	Bill Madlock	1.00	.50	.30
(32a)	Carlos May (White Sox)	1.00	.50	.30
(32b)	Carlos May (Yankees)	1.00	.50	.30
(33)	John Mayberry	1.00	.50	.30
(34)	Bake McBride	1.00	.50	.30
(35)	Doc Medich	1.00	.50	.30
(36a)	Andy Messersmith (Dodgers)	1.00	.50	.30
(36b)	Andy Messersmith (Braves)	1.00	.50	.30
(37)	Rick Monday	1.00	.50	.30
(38)	John Montefusco	1.00	.50	.30
(39)	Jerry Morales	1.00	.50	.30
(40)	Joe Morgan	3.00	1.50	.90
(41)	Thurman Munson	3.00	1.50	.90
(42)	Bobby Murcer	1.00	.50	.30
(43)	Al Oliver	1.00	.50	.30
(44)	Jim Palmer	3.00	1.50	.90
(45)	Dave Parker	1.00	.50	.30
(46)	Tony Perez	1.00	.50	.30
(47)	Jerry Reuss	1.00	.50	.30
(48)	Brooks Robinson	3.50	1.75	1.00
(49)	Frank Robinson	3.50	1.75	1.00
(50)	Steve Rogers	1.00	.50	.30
(51)	Pete Rose	8.00	4.00	2.50
(52)	Nolan Ryan	15.00	7.50	4.50
(53)	Manny Sanguillen	1.00	.50	.30
(54)	Mike Schmidt	6.00	3.00	1.75
(55)	Tom Seaver	4.00	2.00	1.25
(56)	Ted Simmons	1.00	.50	.30
(57)	Reggie Smith	1.00	.50	.30
(58)	Willie Stargell	3.00	1.50	.90
(59)	Rusty Staub	1.00	.50	.30
(60)	Rennie Stennett	1.00	.50	.30
(61)	Don Sutton	3.00	1.50	.90
(62a)	Andy Thornton (Cubs)	1.00	.50	.30
(62b)	Andy Thornton (Expos)	1.00	.50	.30
(63)	Luis Tiant	1.00	.50	.30
(64)	Joe Torre	2.00	1.00	.60
(65)	Mike Tyson	1.00	.50	.30
(66)	Bob Watson	1.00	.50	.30
(67)	Wilbur Wood	1.00	.50	.30
(68)	Jimmy Wynn	1.00	.50	.30
(69)	Carl Yastrzemski	4.00	2.00	1.25
(70)	Richie Zisk	1.00	.50	.30

1913 Cravats Felt Pennants

Little is known about this felt pennant issue, including the complete checklist. The name "Cravats" in the baseball above the player picture may represent the issuer, or describe the issue; the word "cravat" is an arcane term for a triangular piece of cloth. The pennants measure 4-1/8" across the top and are 9" long. Background colors are dark, with all printing in white. At center is a line reprsentation of the player, with his name horizontally beneath and his team nickname vertically at bottom. At top is a bat and ball logo with the "Cravats" name. Most specimens are seen with a metal ring reinforcing the hole punched at top center. The known checklist points to 1913 as the most probable year of issue.

	NM	EX	VG
Common Player:	250.00	125.00	75.00

		NM	EX	VG
(36)	Hughie Jennings (Both hands showing.)	600.00	275.00	130.00
(37)	Hughie Jennings (One hand showing.)	600.00	275.00	130.00
(38)	Walter Johnson	900.00	400.00	200.00
(39)	Tim Jordan	300.00	135.00	65.00
(40)	Joe Kelley	600.00	275.00	130.00
(41)	Ed Konetchy	300.00	135.00	65.00
(42)	Larry Lajoie	600.00	275.00	130.00
(43)	Sherry Magee	300.00	135.00	65.00
(44)	Rube Marquard	600.00	275.00	130.00
(45)	Christy Mathewson	2,100	1,050	625.00
(47)	John McGraw (Glove at side.)	600.00	275.00	130.00
(48)	John McGraw/Portrait	600.00	275.00	130.00
(49)	George McQuillan	300.00	135.00	65.00
(50)	Fred Merkle	300.00	135.00	65.00
(51)	Dots Miller	300.00	135.00	65.00
(52)	Mike Mowrey	300.00	135.00	65.00
(53)	Chief Myers (Meyers) (Brooklyn)	300.00	135.00	65.00
(54)	Chief Myers (Meyers) (New Haven)	300.00	135.00	65.00
(55)	Dode Paskert	300.00	135.00	65.00
(56)	Jack Quinn	300.00	135.00	65.00
(57)	Ed Reulbach	300.00	135.00	65.00
(58)	Nap Rucker	300.00	135.00	65.00
(59)	Dick Rudolph	300.00	135.00	65.00
(60)	Herman Schaeffer (Schaefer)	300.00	135.00	65.00
(61)	Wildfire Schulte	300.00	135.00	65.00
(62)	Tris Speaker	1,600	800.00	475.00
(63)	Gabby Street/Catching	300.00	135.00	65.00
(64)	Gabby Street/Portrait	300.00	135.00	65.00
(65)	Jeff Sweeney	300.00	135.00	65.00
(66)	Ira Thomas	300.00	135.00	65.00
(67)	Joe Tinker	600.00	275.00	130.00
(68)	Zach Wheat	600.00	275.00	130.00
(69)	Geo. Wiltse	300.00	135.00	65.00
(70)	Heinie Zimmerman	300.00	135.00	65.00

1919 Coupon Cigarettes Type 3, Factory 8 Overprint

Of interest to specialty collectors is a variation of Type 3 Coupon cards on which the normal "FACTORY No. 3 . . ." line at bottom has been blacked out and a "FACTORY No. 8 . . ." designation overprinted. The extent of the overprint checklist is unknown and at least one card (Cobb, bat off shoulder) is found as a Factory 8, but not yet verified to exist as a Factory 3 version.

	NM	EX	VG
Common Player:	600.00	300.00	180.00
Hall of Famers: 5-7X			

Chief Bender (No trees.)
Ty Cobb (Bat off shoulder.)
Eddie Collins
Jean Dubuc
Hughie Jennings (Both hands showing.)
Rube Marquard
John McGraw/Portrait

1914 Cracker Jack (E145)

DOYLE, New York • National

Lawrence J. Doyle, second baseman of the New York National League team, was born in Caseyville, Ill., July 31, 1886. He was an amateur ball player until 1905, when he joined the Mattoon Club of the "Kitty" League. At the close of the season of 1906 he was bought by the Giants for $4500. He has been the regular second baseman of the team since 1908.

This is one of a series of colored pictures of famous Ball Players and Managers given Free with Cracker Jack, "The Famous Popcorn Confection," one card in each package. Our first issue is 10,000,000 pictures. Complete set has 144 pictures of Stars in the American, National and Federal Leagues. RUECKHEIM BROS. & ECKSTEIN Brooklyn, N.Y. Chicago, Ill.

The 1914 Cracker Jack set, whose ACC designation is E145-1, is one of the most popular of the "E" card sets and features baseball stars from the American, National and Federal leagues. The 2-1/4" x 3" cards, are printed on thin stock and were inserted in boxes of Cracker Jack. The 1914 issue consists of 144 cards with tinted color photographs on a red background. Numbered backs feature a short biography plus

an advertisement. The advertising on the low-numbered cards in the set indicates that 10 million cards were issued, while the high-numbered cards boast that 15 million were printed.

		NM	EX	VG
Complete Set (144):		375,000	115,000	45,000
Common Player:		850.00	260.00	100.00
1	Otto Knabe	2,000	325.00	125.00
2	Home Run Baker	2,350	775.00	350.00
3	Joe Tinker	2,350	775.00	350.00
4	Larry Doyle	850.00	260.00	100.00
5	Ward Miller	850.00	260.00	100.00
6	Eddie Plank	2,500	825.00	375.00
7	Eddie Collins	2,300	760.00	345.00
8	Rube Oldring	850.00	260.00	100.00
9	Artie Hoffman (Hofman)	850.00	260.00	100.00
10	Stuffy McInnis	850.00	260.00	100.00
11	George Stovall	850.00	260.00	100.00
12	Connie Mack	3,600	1,200	540.00
13	Art Wilson	850.00	260.00	100.00
14	Sam Crawford	2,300	760.00	345.00
15	Reb Russell	850.00	260.00	100.00
16	Howie Camnitz	850.00	260.00	100.00
17a	Roger Bresnahan (No number on back.)	7,500	2,475	1,125
17b	Roger Bresnahan (Number on back.)	2,300	760.00	345.00
18	Johnny Evers	2,300	760.00	345.00
19	Chief Bender	2,300	760.00	345.00
20	Cy Falkenberg	850.00	260.00	100.00
21	Heinie Zimmerman	850.00	260.00	100.00
22	Smokey Joe Wood	1,500	495.00	225.00
23	Charles Comiskey	2,300	760.00	345.00
24	George Mullen (Mullin)	850.00	260.00	100.00
25	Mike Simon	850.00	260.00	100.00
26	Jim Scott	850.00	260.00	100.00
27	Bill Carrigan	850.00	260.00	100.00
28	Jack Barry	850.00	260.00	100.00
29	Vean Gregg	850.00	260.00	100.00
30	Ty Cobb	30,000	10,000	4,500
31	Heinie Wagner	850.00	260.00	100.00
32	Mordecai Brown	2,300	760.00	345.00
33	Amos Strunk	850.00	260.00	100.00
34	Ira Thomas	850.00	260.00	100.00
35	Harry Hooper	2,300	760.00	345.00
36	Ed Walsh	2,300	760.00	345.00
37	Grover C. Alexander	9,000	2,975	1,350
38	Red Dooin	850.00	260.00	100.00
39	Chick Gandil	1,625	535.00	245.00
40	Jimmy Austin	850.00	260.00	100.00
41	Tommy Leach	850.00	260.00	100.00
42	Al Bridwell	850.00	260.00	100.00
43	Rube Marquard	3,900	1,300	585.00
44	Jeff Tesreau	850.00	260.00	100.00
45	Fred Luderus	850.00	260.00	100.00
46	Bob Groom	850.00	260.00	100.00
47	Josh Devore	850.00	260.00	100.00
48	Harry Lord	850.00	260.00	100.00
49	Dots Miller	850.00	260.00	100.00
50	John Hummell (Hummel)	850.00	260.00	100.00
51	Nap Rucker	850.00	260.00	100.00
52	Zach Wheat	2,300	760.00	345.00
53	Otto Miller	850.00	260.00	100.00
54	Marty O'Toole	850.00	260.00	100.00
55	Dick Hoblitzel (Hoblitzell)	850.00	260.00	100.00
56	Clyde Milan	850.00	260.00	100.00
57	Walter Johnson	8,500	2,800	1,275
58	Wally Schang	850.00	260.00	100.00
59	Doc Gessler	850.00	260.00	100.00
60	Rollie Zeider	850.00	260.00	100.00
61	Ray Schalk	2,300	760.00	345.00
62	Jay Cashion	850.00	260.00	100.00
63	Babe Adams	850.00	260.00	100.00
64	Jimmy Archer	850.00	260.00	100.00
65	Tris Speaker	7,200	2,400	1,080
66	Nap Lajoie	7,200	2,400	1,080
67	Doc Crandall	850.00	260.00	100.00
68	Honus Wagner	16,500	5,450	2,475
69	John McGraw	2,300	760.00	345.00
70	Fred Clarke	2,300	760.00	345.00
71	Chief Meyers	850.00	260.00	100.00
72	Joe Boehling	850.00	260.00	100.00
73	Max Carey	2,300	760.00	345.00
74	Frank Owens	850.00	260.00	100.00
75	Miller Huggins	2,300	760.00	345.00
76	Claude Hendrix	850.00	260.00	100.00
77	Hughie Jennings	2,300	760.00	345.00
78	Fred Merkle	850.00	260.00	100.00
79	Ping Bodie	850.00	260.00	100.00
80	Ed Reulbach	850.00	260.00	100.00
81	Jim Delehanty (Delahanty)	850.00	260.00	100.00
82	Gavvy Cravath	850.00	260.00	100.00
83	Russ Ford	850.00	260.00	100.00
84	Elmer Knetzer	850.00	260.00	100.00
85	Buck Herzog	850.00	260.00	100.00
86	Burt Shotten	850.00	260.00	100.00
87	Hick Cady	850.00	260.00	100.00
88	Christy Mathewson	120,000	40,000	18,000
89	Larry Cheney	850.00	260.00	100.00
90	Frank Smith	850.00	260.00	100.00
91	Roger Peckinpaugh	900.00	295.00	135.00
92	Al Demaree	850.00	260.00	100.00
93	Del Pratt	850.00	260.00	100.00
94	Eddie Cicotte	2,200	725.00	330.00
95	Ray Keating	850.00	260.00	100.00
96	Beals Becker	850.00	260.00	100.00
97	Rube Benton	850.00	260.00	100.00
98	Frank Laporte (LaPorte)	850.00	260.00	100.00
99	Frank Chance	9,000	3,000	1,350
100	Tom Seaton	850.00	260.00	100.00
101	Wildfire Schulte	850.00	260.00	100.00
102	Ray Fisher	850.00	260.00	100.00
103	Joe Jackson	65,000	21,450	9,750
104	Vic Saier	850.00	260.00	100.00
105	Jimmy Lavender	850.00	260.00	100.00
106	Joe Birmingham	850.00	260.00	100.00
107	Tom Downey	850.00	260.00	100.00
108	Sherry Magee	850.00	260.00	100.00

109	Fred Blanding
110	Bob Bescher
111	Nixey Callahan
112	Jeff Sweeney
113	George Suggs
114	George Moriarity
115	Ad Brennan
116	Rollie Zeider
117	Ted Easterly
118	Ed Konetchy
119	George Perring
120	Mickey Doolan
121	Hub Perdue
122	Donie Bush
123	Slim Sallee
124	Earle Moore (Ea...
125	Bert Niehoff
126	Walter Blair
127	Butch Schmidt
128	Steve Evans
129	Ray Caldwell
130	Ivy Wingo
131	George Baumga...
132	Les Nunamaker
133	Branch Rickey
134	Armando Marsar...
135	Bill Killifer (Killefe...
136	Rabbit Maranvill...
137	Bill Rariden
138	Hank Gowdy
139	Rebel Oakes
140	Danny Murphy
141	Cy Barger
142	Gene Packard
143	Jake Daubert
144	Jimmy Walsh

1915 C...

JOHNSON, Washington • Americ...

The 1915 Cracker ... 1914 edition with some ... designation changes, a ... comprise the set. Cards ... or 1915 by the advertisi... the set complete at 144 ... pictures. Backs of 191... upside-down in relation ... album were available fr...

Complete Set (176):	
Common Player (1-144):	
Common Player (145-17...	
Album:	
1	Otto Knabe
2	Home Run Baker
3	Joe Tinker
4	Larry Doyle
5	Ward Miller
6	Eddie Plank
7	Eddie Collins
8	Rube Oldring
9	Artie Hoffman (Ho...
10	Stuffy McInnis
11	George Stovall
12	Connie Mack
13	Art Wilson
14	Sam Crawford
15	Reb Russell
16	Howie Camnitz
17	Roger Bresnahan
18	Johnny Evers
19	Chief Bender
20	Cy Falkenberg
21	Heinie Zimmerma...
22	Smokey Joe Woo...
23	Charles Comiskey
24	George Mullen (M...
25	Mike Simon
26	Jim Scott
27	Bill Carrigan
28	Jack Barry
29	Vean Gregg
30	Ty Cobb
31	Heinie Wagner
32	Mordecai Brown
33	Amos Strunk
34	Ira Thomas
35	Harry Hooper
36	Ed Walsh
37	Grover C. Alexand...
38	Red Dooin
39	Chick Gandil
40	Jimmy Austin
41	Tommy Leach
42	Al Bridwell
43	Rube Marquard
44	Jeff Tesreau
45	Fred Luderus

46	Bob
47	Josh
48	Steve
49	Dots
50	Johr
51	Nap
52	Zach
53	Otto
54	Mart
55	Dick
56	Clyd
57	Walt
58	Wall
59	Doc
60	Osca
61	Ray
62	Willie
63	Babe
64	Jimm
65	Tris
66	Nap
67	Doc
68	Hone
69	Johr
70	Fred
71	Chie
72	Joe E
73	Max
74	Fran
75	Mille
76	Clau
77	Hugl
78	Fred
79	Ping
80	Ed F
81	Jim
82	Gav
83	Russ
84	Elme
85	Buck
86	Burt
87	Hick
88	Chris
89	Larry
90	Fran
91	Roge
92	Al D
93	Del
94	Eddi
95	Ray
96	Beal
97	Rube
98	Fran
99	Hal
100	Tom
101	Wild
102	Ray
103	Joe
104	Vic S
105	Jimn
106	Joe
107	Tom
108	She
109	Fred
110	Bob
111	Hert
112	Ed S
113	Geo
114	Geo
115	Ad E
116	Rolli
117	Ted
118	Ed K
119	Geo
120	Mick
121	Hub
122	Don
123	Slim
124	Earl
125	Bert
126	Walt
127	Butc
128	Stev
129	Ray
130	Ivy V
131	Geo
132	Les
133	Brar
134	Arm
135	Bill
136	Rab
137	Bill
138	Han
139	Reb
140	Dan
141	Cy E
142	Gen
143	Jake
144	Jimr
145	Ted
146	Leff
147	Lee
148	Owe
149	Hal
150	Doc
151	Pos
152	Geo
153	Bill
154	Dick
155	Joe
156	Jea
157	Gec
158	Fritz
159	Heir
160	Ben
161	Edd
162	
163	Ber...

		NM	EX	VG
(1)	Eddie Ainsmith	250.00	125.00	75.00
(2)	"Home Run" Baker	450.00	225.00	135.00
(3)	Hugh Bedient	250.00	125.00	75.00
(4)	C.A. Bender	450.00	225.00	135.00
(5)	Ray Caldwell	250.00	125.00	75.00
(6)	Jack Coombs	250.00	125.00	75.00
(7)	C.S. Dooin	250.00	125.00	75.00
(8)	Lawrence Doyle	250.00	125.00	75.00
(9)	Ed Konethy (Konetchy)	250.00	125.00	75.00
(10)	James Lavender	250.00	125.00	75.00
(11)	John J. McGraw	450.00	225.00	135.00
(12)	Stuffy McInnes (McInnis)	250.00	125.00	75.00
(13)	Christy Mathewson	1,150	575.00	345.00
(14)	J.T. (Chief) Meyer (Meyers)	250.00	125.00	75.00
(15)	Nap Rucker	250.00	125.00	75.00
(16)	Tris Speaker	600.00	300.00	180.00
(17)	Ed Sweeney	250.00	125.00	75.00
(18)	Jeff Tesreau	250.00	125.00	75.00
(19)	Ira Thomas	250.00	125.00	75.00
(20)	Joe Tinker	450.00	225.00	135.00
(21)	Ed Walsh	450.00	225.00	135.00

1922 Cream Nut/Goodie Bread

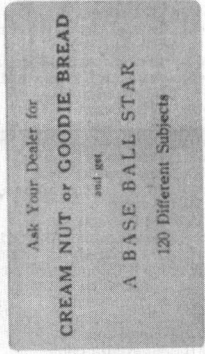

According to the advertising on back this set should comprise half of the known players from the generic W573 strip card issue. The black-and-white cards, about 2-1/16" x 3-3/8", share their format and player selection not only with W573, but also E120 American Caramel. Printed horizontally on the backs is: "Ask Your Dealer for / CREAM NUT or GOODIE BREAD / and get / A BASE BALL STAR / 120 Different Subjects." The location of the issuing entity, the specific manner of distribution and the checklist are unknown as only a handful of this particular ad-back series have survived. Collectors will pay a premium for this version above the normal W573 blank-back.

(See 1922 W573.)

	NM	EX	VG
Common Player:	800.00	400.00	240.00
Hall of Famers: 8-10X			

1909 Croft's Candy (E92)

Because they share the format and pictures with several related issues (Croft's Cocoa, Dockman Gum, Nadja Caramels, etc.) this set shared the E92 designation in the American Card Catalog. It is more logical to present these sets as separate issues, based on the advertising which appears on back. Fronts of the 1-1/2" x 2-3/4" cards feature a color lithograph of the player. His last name, position and team are printed in black in the border below. Backs feature a shield-shaped logo for Croft's Candy, a product of Croft & Allen Co., Philadelphia. Backs can be found printed in black, in blue (scarcer) or in red (extremely rare). Cards are unnumbered and the checklist is presented here alphabetically.

		NM	EX	VG
Complete Set (50):		125,000	50,000	25,000
Common Player:		1,065	425.00	220.00
Blue Back: 1.5-2.5X				
Red Back: 12-15X				
(1)	Jack Barry	1,565	625.00	315.00
(2)	Harry Bemis	1,065	425.00	220.00
(3)	Chief Bender (Striped cap.)	4,065	1,625	815.00
(4)	Chief Bender (White cap.)	3,440	1,375	690.00
(5)	Bill Bergen	1,065	425.00	220.00
(6)	Bob Bescher	1,065	425.00	220.00
(7)	Al Bridwell	1,065	425.00	220.00
(8)	Doc Casey	1,065	425.00	220.00
(9)	Frank Chance	3,440	1,375	690.00
(10)	Hal Chase	2,000	815.00	405.00
(11)	Ty Cobb	18,750	7,500	3,750
(12)	Eddie Collins	3,750	1,500	750.00
(13)	Sam Crawford	2,815	1,125	565.00
(14)	Harry Davis	1,065	425.00	220.00
(15)	Art Devlin	1,065	425.00	220.00
(16)	Wild Bill Donovan	1,065	425.00	220.00
(17)	Red Dooin	1,500	600.00	300.00
(18)	Mickey Doolan	1,065	425.00	220.00
(19)	Patsy Dougherty	1,065	425.00	220.00
(20)	Larry Doyle/Throwing	1,065	425.00	220.00
(21)	Larry Doyle (With bat.)	1,065	425.00	220.00
(22)	Johnny Evers	3,440	1,375	690.00
(23)	George Gibson	1,065	425.00	220.00
(24)	Topsy Hartsel	1,065	425.00	220.00
(25)	Fred Jacklitsch	1,500	600.00	300.00
(26)	Hugh Jennings	2,815	1,125	565.00
(27)	Red Kleinow	1,065	425.00	220.00
(28)	Otto Knabe	1,250	500.00	250.00
(29)	Jack Knight	1,500	600.00	300.00
(30)	Nap Lajoie	4,065	1,625	815.00
(31)	Hans Lobert	1,065	425.00	220.00
(32)	Sherry Magee	1,065	425.00	220.00
(33)	Christy Matthewson (Mathewson)	9,690	3,875	1,940
(34)	John McGraw	2,815	1,125	565.00
(35)	Larry McLean	1,065	425.00	220.00
(36)	Dots Miller/Btg	1,065	425.00	220.00
(37)	Dots Miller/Fldg	1,500	600.00	300.00
(38)	Danny Murphy	1,065	425.00	220.00
(39)	Bill O'Hara	4,065	425.00	220.00
(40)	Germany Schaefer	1,065	425.00	220.00
(41)	Admiral Schlei	1,065	425.00	220.00
(42)	Boss Schmidt	1,065	425.00	220.00
(43)	Johnny Seigle (Siegle)	1,065	425.00	220.00
(44)	Dave Shean	1,065	425.00	220.00
(45)	Boss Smith (Schmidt)	1,065	425.00	220.00
(46)	Joe Tinker	2,815	1,125	565.00
(47)	Honus Wagner/Btg	15,000	6,000	3,000
(48)	Honus Wagner (Throwing)	15,000	6,000	3,000
(49)	Cy Young	8,125	3,250	1,625
(50)	Heinie Zimmerman	1,065	425.00	220.00

1909 Croft's Cocoa (E92)

Like related issues once cataloged together as E92 (Croft's Candy, Dockman Gum, Nadja Caramels, etc.), these 1-1/2" x 2-3/4" cards feature a color player lithograph on front, which his name, position and team printed in the white border below. Backs have an ad for Crofts Swiss Milk Cocoa of Philadelphia. The checklist, presented here alphabetically, is identical to that of Croft's Candy.

		NM	EX	VG
Complete Set (50):		100,000	50,000	30,000
Common Player:		790.00	315.00	150.00
(1)	Jack Barry	1,200	490.00	240.00
(2)	Harry Bemis	790.00	315.00	150.00
(3)	Chief Bender (Striped hat.)	3,000	1,200	600.00
(4)	Chief Bender (White hat.)	1,800	720.00	360.00
(5)	Bill Bergen	790.00	315.00	150.00
(6)	Bob Bescher	790.00	315.00	150.00
(7)	Al Bridwell	790.00	315.00	150.00
(8)	Doc Casey	790.00	315.00	150.00
(9)	Frank Chance	1,650	660.00	330.00
(10)	Hal Chase	1,240	495.00	250.00
(11)	Ty Cobb	22,500	9,000	5,000
(12)	Eddie Collins	1,650	675.00	340.00
(13)	Sam Crawford	1,650	675.00	340.00
(14)	Harry Davis	790.00	315.00	150.00
(15)	Art Devlin	790.00	315.00	150.00
(16)	Wild Bill Donovan	790.00	315.00	150.00
(17)	Red Dooin	1,240	495.00	250.00
(18)	Mickey Doolan	790.00	315.00	150.00
(19)	Patsy Dougherty	790.00	315.00	150.00
(20)	Larry Doyle/Throwing	790.00	315.00	150.00
(21)	Larry Doyle (With bat.)	790.00	315.00	150.00
(22)	Johnny Evers	3,150	1,260	640.00
(23)	George Gibson	790.00	315.00	150.00
(24)	Topsy Hartsel	790.00	315.00	150.00
(25)	Fred Jacklitsch	1,240	495.00	250.00
(26)	Hugh Jennings	1,650	675.00	340.00
(27)	Red Kleinow	790.00	315.00	150.00
(28)	Otto Knabe	1,240	495.00	250.00
(29)	Jack Knight	1,240	495.00	250.00
(30)	Nap Lajoie	2,025	825.00	415.00
(31)	Hans Lobert	790.00	315.00	150.00
(32)	Sherry Magee	790.00	315.00	150.00
(33)	Christy Matthewson (Mathewson)	10,125	4,050	2,500
(34)	John McGraw	1,650	675.00	340.00
(35)	Larry McLean	790.00	315.00	150.00
(36)	Dots Miller/Btg	790.00	315.00	150.00
(37)	Dots Miller/Fldg	1,240	495.00	250.00
(38)	Danny Murphy	790.00	315.00	150.00
(39)	Bill O'Hara	790.00	315.00	150.00
(40)	Germany Schaefer	790.00	315.00	150.00
(41)	Admiral Schlei	790.00	315.00	150.00
(42)	Boss Schmidt	790.00	315.00	150.00
(43)	Johnny Seigle (Siegle)	1,015	405.00	205.00
(44)	Dave Shean	790.00	315.00	150.00
(45)	Boss Smith (Schmidt)	790.00	315.00	150.00
(46)	Joe Tinker	1,650	675.00	340.00
(47)	Honus Wagner/Btg	11,000	5,500	3,250
(48)	Honus Wagner/Throwing	11,000	5,500	3,250
(49)	Cy Young	7,000	3,500	2,100
(50)	Heinie Zimmerman	790.00	315.00	150.00

1969 Crown Brooks Robinson

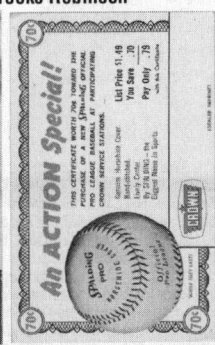

The attributed date is speculative. This 3-9/16" x 5-11/16" card features a black-and-white portrait photo on front with the player name in blue scrip. A blue panel at bottom has the gas company's logo and an ad slogan. On back is a black, red and white coupon offering a discount on a baseball. A blank panel at bottom was intended for use by individual service stations to print their name and address.

	NM	EX	VG
Brooks Robinson	150.00	75.00	45.00

1977-78 Cubic Corp. Sports Deck Playing Cards

Playing cards featuring pencil drawings of stars in various sports were produced on a limited basis in the late 1970s by Cubic Corp. of San Diego. The cards are standard bridge size (2-1/4" x 3-1/2") with rounded corners and feature the artwork of Al Landsman along with a facsimile autograph within a colored frame. Each deck has the same athlete on the back and sold for $1.60. There is no indication of the manufacturer on individual cards, it is only found on the box. It is believed most of the decks were only produced in limited sample quantities. Similar cards were produced for Pepsi and are listed thereunder. Only the baseball players are checklisted here, in alphabetical order.

		NM	EX	VG
(1)	Johnny Bench (Boxed deck.)	17.50	8.75	5.25
(1)	Johnny Bench (Single card.)	.50	.25	.15
(2)	Lou Gehrig (Boxed deck.)	25.00	12.50	7.50
(2)	Lou Gehrig (Single card.)	1.50	.70	.45
(3)	Catfish Hunter (Boxed deck.)	15.00	7.50	4.50
(3)	Catfish Hunter (Single card.)	.50	.25	.15
(4)	Randy Jones (Boxed deck.)	10.00	5.00	3.00
(4)	Randy Jones (Single card.)	.50	.25	.15
(5)	Mickey Mantle (Boxed deck.)	40.00	20.00	12.00
(5)	Mickey Mantle (Single card.)	4.00	2.00	1.25
(6)	Butch Metzger (Boxed deck.)	10.00	5.00	3.00
(6)	Butch Metzger (Single card.)	.50	.25	.15
(7)	Joe Morgan (Boxed deck.)	12.50	6.25	3.75
(7)	Joe Morgan (Single card.)	.50	.25	.15
(8)	Stan Musial (Boxed deck.)	25.00	12.50	7.50
(8)	Stan Musial (Single card.)	1.50	.70	.45
(9)	Jackie Robinson (Boxed deck.)	25.00	12.50	7.50
(9)	Jackie Robinson (Single card.)	1.50	.70	.45
(10)	Pete Rose (Boxed deck.)	35.00	17.50	10.00
(10)	Pete Rose (Single card.)	1.00	.50	.30
(11)	Babe Ruth (Boxed deck.)	30.00	15.00	9.00
(11)	Babe Ruth (Single card.)	3.00	1.50	.90
(12)	Tom Seaver (Boxed deck.)	30.00	15.00	9.00
(12)	Tom Seaver (Single card.)	1.00	.50	.30

(13)	Frank Tanana (Boxed deck.)	10.00	5.00	3.00
(13)	Frank Tanana (Single card.)	.50	.25	.15
(14)	Phillies logo/autographs (Boxed deck.)	10.00	5.00	3.00
(14)	Phillies logo/autographs (Single card.)	1.00	.50	.30

1911 Cullivan's Fireside Philadelphia A's (T208)

The 1911 T208 Firesides, an 18-card Philadelphia Athletics set issued by the Thomas Cullivan Tobacco Company of Syracuse, N.Y., is among the rarest of all 20th Century tobacco issues. Cullivan issued the set to commemorate the Athletics' 1910 Championship season, and, except for pitcher Jack Coombs, the checklist includes nearly all key members of the club, including manager Connie Mack. The cards are the standard size for tobacco issues, about 1-1/2" x 2-5/8". The front of each card features a player portrait set against a colored background. The player's name and the word "Athletics" appear at the bottom, while "World's Champions 1910" is printed along the top. Backs advertise the set as the "Athletics Series" and advise that one card is included in each package of "Cullivan's Fireside Plain Scrap" tobacco. The same checklist was used for a similar Athletics set issued by Rochester Baking/Williams Baking (D359). Blank-backed versions are also known to exist.

		NM	EX	VG
	Common Player:	9,000	5,650	
(1)	Home Run Baker	16,000	10,000	
(2)	Jack Barry	9,000	5,650	
(3)	Chief Bender	16,000	10,000	
(4)	Eddie Collins	30,000	18,000	
(5)	Harry Davis	9,000	5,650	
(6)	Jimmy Dygert	40,000	24,000	
(7)	Topsy Hartsel	9,000	5,650	
(8)	Harry Krause	9,000	5,650	
(9)	Jack Lapp	9,000	5,650	
(10)	Paddy Livingston	9,000	5,650	
(11)	Bris Lord	9,000	5,650	
(12)	Connie Mack	16,000	10,000	
(13)	Cy Morgan	9,000	5,650	
(14)	Danny Murphy	9,000	5,650	
(15)	Rube Oldring	18,000	11,500	
(16)	Eddie Plank	25,000	16,500	
(17)	Amos Strunk	9,000	5,650	
(18)	Ira Thomas	9,000	5,650	

1964+ Curteichcolor Hall of Fame Plaque Postcards

 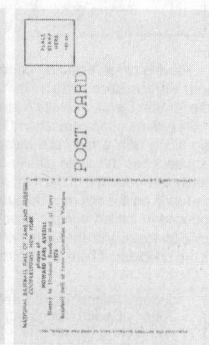

(See Hall of Fame Yellow Plaque Postcards for checklist, price data.)

1960(?) CVC Baseball Hi-Lites

The attributed year of issue is speculative, based on the issue date of the Nu-Card Baseball Hi-Lites set, of which the CVC issue parallels the first 18 cards. The CVC Hi-Lites cards are 3-1/4" x 5-3/8". While the Nu-Card Hi-Lites are printed with black-and-red on front and green-and-red on back, the CVC cards are printed only in black on front and blank-backed. This issue has a CVC copyright notice in the "dateline" of the newspaper front; the Nu-Card set carries and NCI copyright. The manner of distribution of the CVC cards is unknown, possibly having been available in arcade-type vending machines. Another difference between the two issues is that while the Nu-Card version has a photographic illustration on card #1, the CVC card has a line drawing. While the CVC cards are much scarcer than the Nu-Cards, their value is not appreciably greater due to lower demand for the smaller, cruder set.

		NM	EX	VG
	Complete Set (18):	150.00	75.00	50.00
	Common Player:	7.50	3.75	2.00
(1)	Babe Hits 3 Homers in a Series Game	40.00	20.00	12.00
(2)	Podres Pitching Wins Series	7.50	3.75	2.00
(3)	Bevans Pitches No Hitter, Almost	7.50	3.75	2.00
(4)	Box Score Devised by Reporter	7.50	3.75	2.00
(5)	VanderMeer Pitches 2 No Hitters	7.50	3.75	2.00
(6)	Indians Take Burns	7.50	3.75	2.00
(7)	DiMag Comes Thru	25.00	12.50	7.50
(8)	Mathewson Pitches 3 W.S. Shutouts	10.00	5.00	3.00
(9)	Haddix Pitches 12 Perfect Innings	7.50	3.75	2.00
(10)	Thomson's Homer Sinks Dodgers	10.00	5.00	3.00
(11)	Hubbell Strikes Out 5 A.L. Stars	9.00	4.50	2.50
(12)	Pickoff Ends Series (Marty Marion)	7.50	3.75	2.00
(13)	Cards Take Series from Yanks	9.00	4.50	2.50
(14)	Dizzy and Daffy Win Series	10.00	5.00	3.00
(15)	Owens Drops Third Strike	7.50	3.75	2.00
(16)	Ruth Calls His Shot	40.00	20.00	12.00
(17)	Merkle Pulls Boner	7.50	3.75	2.00
(18)	Larsen Hurls Perfect World Series Game	9.00	4.50	2.50

1909-12 Cycle Cigarettes

Cycle brand advertising found on the backs of T205, T206 and T207 cards generally indicates a slightly greater degree of scarcity than the most common back variations from those sets. While a value multiplier can generate a ballpark approximation of value for most cards from T205 and T206, it is not practical for T207s because all Cycle cards from that set are scarce and much of that scarcity has already been factored into the individual player prices quoted in the base T207 listings.

PREMIUMS:
T205: 1.5-2X
T206 350 Series: 2-3X
T206 460 Series: 2-3X
(See T205, T206, T207 for checklists and base card values.)

D

1959 Dad's Cookies Exhibits

A Vancouver bakery that issued several type of hockey cards in later years created this set of baseball cards by overprinting the usually blank backs of the 64 cards in Exhibit Supply Co.'s 1959 issue. Cards measure 3-3/8" x 5-3/8" and are printed in reddish-gray-brown. The back indicates an album was available to house the set.

		NM	EX	VG
	Complete Set (64):	3,000	1,500	900.00
	Common Player:	35.00	17.50	10.00
(1)	Hank Aaron	200.00	100.00	60.00
(2)	Joe Adcock (Script name.)	35.00	17.50	10.00
(3)	Johnny Antonelli (Giants)	35.00	17.50	10.00
(4)	Luis Aparicio/Portrait	80.00	40.00	24.00
(5)	Richie Ashburn (Phillies)	100.00	50.00	30.00
(6)	Ed Bailey (With cap.)	35.00	17.50	10.00
(7)	Ernie Banks (Bat on shoulder, script name.)	150.00	75.00	45.00
(8)	Hank Bauer (N.Y. cap.)	50.00	25.00	15.00
(9)	Yogi Berra	150.00	75.00	45.00
(10)	Don Blasingame	35.00	17.50	10.00
(11)	Bill Bruton	35.00	17.50	10.00
(12)	Lew Burdette (Pitching, side view.)	35.00	17.50	10.00
(13)	Chico Carrasquel/Portrait	35.00	17.50	10.00
(14)	Orlando Cepeda (To chest.)	80.00	40.00	24.00
(15)	Bob Cerv (A's cap.)	35.00	17.50	10.00
(16)	Delmar Crandall	35.00	17.50	10.00
(17)	Alvin Dark (Cubs)	35.00	17.50	10.00
(18)	Larry Doby	80.00	40.00	24.00
(19)	Dick Donovan (Sox cap.)	35.00	17.50	10.00
(20)	Don Drysdale/Portrait	90.00	45.00	27.00
(21)	Del Ennis	35.00	17.50	10.00
(22)	Whitey Ford/Pitching	125.00	62.00	37.00
(23)	Nelson Fox	80.00	40.00	24.00
(24)	Bob Friend	35.00	17.50	10.00
(25)	Billy Goodman/Btg	35.00	17.50	10.00
(26)	Whitey Herzog	35.00	17.50	10.00
(27)	Gil Hodges (LA on cap.)	75.00	37.50	22.00
(28)	Elston Howard	50.00	25.00	15.00
(29)	Jackie Jensen	50.00	25.00	15.00
(30)	Al Kaline (Portrait w/ two bats.)	100.00	50.00	30.00
(31)	Harmon Killebrew/Btg	100.00	50.00	30.00
(32)	Billy Klaus	35.00	17.50	10.00
(33)	Ted Kluzewski (Kluszewski) (Pirates uniform.)	60.00	30.00	18.00
(34)	Tony Kubek (Light background.)	60.00	30.00	18.00
(35)	Harvey Kuenn (D on cap.)	35.00	17.50	10.00
(36)	Don Larsen	35.00	17.50	10.00
(37)	Johnny Logan	35.00	17.50	10.00
(38)	Dale Long (C on cap.)	35.00	17.50	10.00
(39)	Mickey Mantle/Btg (No pinstripes, "c k" of "Mickey" separated.)	350.00	175.00	100.00
(40)	Eddie Mathews	100.00	50.00	30.00
(41)	Willie Mays/Portrait	200.00	100.00	60.00
(42)	Bill Mazeroski/Portrait	80.00	40.00	24.00
(43)	Lindy McDaniel	35.00	17.50	10.00
(44)	Gil McDougald	45.00	22.50	13.50
(45)	Orestes Minoso (C on cap.)	45.00	22.50	13.50
(46)	Stan Musial	175.00	87.00	52.00
(47)	Don Newcombe (Plain jacket.)	45.00	22.50	13.50
(48)	Andy Pafko (Yours truly.) (Plain uniform.)	35.00	17.50	10.00
(49)	Billy Pierce	35.00	17.50	10.00
(50)	Robin Roberts (Script name.)	80.00	40.00	24.00
(51)	Carl Sawatski (P on cap.)	35.00	17.50	10.00
(52)	Herb Score (C on cap.)	35.00	17.50	10.00
(53)	Roy Sievers/Portrait (W on cap, light background.)	35.00	17.50	10.00
(54)	Curt Simmons	35.00	17.50	10.00
(55)	Bill Skowron	50.00	25.00	15.00
(56)	Duke Snider (LA on cap.)	100.00	50.00	30.00
(57)	Warren Spahn (M on cap.)	100.00	50.00	30.00
(58)	Frankie Thomas (Photo actually Bob Skinner.)	50.00	25.00	15.00
(59)	Earl Torgeson (Plain uniform.)	35.00	17.50	10.00
(60)	Gus Triandos	35.00	17.50	10.00
(61)	Vic Wertz/Portrait	35.00	17.50	10.00
(62)	Ted Williams (Sincerely yours.) (#9 not showing.)	200.00	100.00	60.00
(63)	Gene Woodling (Script name.)	35.00	17.50	10.00
(64)	Gus Zernial (Script name.)	35.00	17.50	10.00

1972 Daily Juice Co.

This one-card "set" was regionally issued to Roberto Clemente Fan Club members. Large numbers of the cards found their way into the hobby, including in uncut sheet form. The cards feature a full-color front black-and-white back. The card measures the standard 2-1/2 in. width but is somewhat longer, at 3-3/4". This unnumbered card remains about the least expensive baseball card that was issued during Clemente's lifetime.

		NM	EX	VG
	Uncut Sheet (30):	200.00	100.00	60.00
1	Roberto Clemente	15.00	7.50	4.50

1950s Dairy Council Curt Simmons Postcard

Issued by "The Dairy Council," probably locally, this black-and-white postcard features an action-pose photo of the star Phillies pitcher. There is a white facsimile autograph on front. Back of the 3-3/4" x 5-3/4" card has another facsimile autograph and the legend, "Dairy Council and the Philadelphia Phillies join me in wishing you good luck and good health."

		NM	EX	VG
	Curt Simmons	60.00	30.00	18.00

1976 Dairy Isle Discs

One of several regional sponsors of player disc sets in 1976 was the upstate New York area chain, Dairy Isle. The discs are 3-3/8" diameter with a black-and-white player portrait photo in the center of the baseball design. A line of red stars is above, while the left and right panels feature one of several bright colors. Produced by Michael Schecter Associates under license from the Major League Baseball Players Association, the player photos have had uniform and cap logos removed. Backs are printed in red and purple. The unnumbered checklist here is presented in alphabetical order.

		NM	EX	VG
Complete Set (70):		45.00	22.50	13.50
Common Player:		1.00	.50	.30
(1)	Henry Aaron	10.00	5.00	3.00
(2)	Johnny Bench	4.50	2.25	1.25
(3)	Vida Blue	1.00	.50	.30
(4)	Larry Bowa	1.00	.50	.30
(5)	Lou Brock	4.00	2.00	1.25
(6)	Jeff Burroughs	1.00	.50	.30
(7)	John Candelaria	1.00	.50	.30
(8)	Jose Cardenal	1.00	.50	.30
(9)	Rod Carew	4.00	2.00	1.25
(10)	Steve Carlton	4.00	2.00	1.25
(11)	Dave Cash	1.00	.50	.30
(12)	Cesar Cedeno	1.00	.50	.30
(13)	Ron Cey	1.00	.50	.30
(14)	Carlton Fisk	4.00	2.00	1.25
(15)	Tito Fuentes	1.00	.50	.30
(16)	Steve Garvey	3.00	1.50	.90
(17)	Ken Griffey	1.00	.50	.30
(18)	Don Gullett	1.00	.50	.30
(19)	Willie Horton	1.00	.50	.30
(20)	Al Hrabosky	1.00	.50	.30
(21)	Catfish Hunter	4.00	2.00	1.25
(22)	Reggie Jackson (A's)	6.00	3.00	1.75
(23)	Randy Jones	1.00	.50	.30
(24)	Jim Kaat	1.00	.50	.30
(25)	Don Kessinger	1.00	.50	.30
(26)	Dave Kingman	1.00	.50	.30
(27)	Jerry Koosman	1.00	.50	.30
(28)	Mickey Lolich	1.00	.50	.30
(29)	Greg Luzinski	1.00	.50	.30
(30)	Fred Lynn	1.00	.50	.30
(31)	Bill Madlock	1.00	.50	.30
(32)	Carlos May (White Sox)	1.00	.50	.30
(33)	John Mayberry	1.00	.50	.30
(34)	Bake McBride	1.00	.50	.30
(35)	Doc Medich	1.00	.50	.30
(36)	Andy Messersmith	1.00	.50	.30
(37)	Rick Monday	1.00	.50	.30
(38)	John Montefusco	1.00	.50	.30
(39)	Jerry Morales	1.00	.50	.30
(40)	Joe Morgan	4.00	2.00	1.25
(41)	Thurman Munson	3.00	1.50	.90
(42)	Bobby Murcer	1.00	.50	.30
(43)	Al Oliver	1.00	.50	.30
(44)	Jim Palmer	4.00	2.00	1.25
(45)	Dave Parker	1.00	.50	.30
(46)	Tony Perez	4.00	2.00	1.25
(47)	Jerry Reuss	1.00	.50	.30
(48)	Brooks Robinson	4.50	2.25	1.25
(49)	Frank Robinson	4.50	2.25	1.25
(50)	Steve Rogers	1.00	.50	.30
(51)	Pete Rose	10.00	5.00	3.00
(52)	Nolan Ryan	20.00	10.00	6.00
(53)	Manny Sanguillen	1.00	.50	.30
(54)	Mike Schmidt	6.00	3.00	1.75
(55)	Tom Seaver	4.50	2.25	1.25
(56)	Ted Simmons	1.00	.50	.30
(57)	Reggie Smith	1.00	.50	.30
(58)	Willie Stargell	4.00	2.00	1.25
(59)	Rusty Staub	1.25	.60	.40
(60)	Rennie Stennett	1.00	.50	.30
(61)	Don Sutton	4.00	2.00	1.25
(62)	Andy Thornton (Cubs)	1.00	.50	.30
(63)	Luis Tiant	1.00	.50	.30
(64)	Joe Torre	3.00	1.50	.90
(65)	Mike Tyson	1.00	.50	.30
(66)	Bob Watson	1.00	.50	.30
(67)	Wilbur Wood	1.00	.50	.30
(68)	Jimmy Wynn	1.00	.50	.30
(69)	Carl Yastrzemski	4.50	2.25	1.25
(70)	Richie Zisk	1.00	.50	.30

1977 Dairy Isle Discs

Virtually identical in format to the 1976 issue (substituting red and blue for the back ad in 1977, instead of the previous year's red and purple), these 3-3/8" diameter player discs were given away at Dairy Isle outlets. Discs once again feature black-and-white player portrait photos in the center of a baseball design. The left and right panels are in one of several bright colors. Licensed by the players' association through Mike Schechter Associates, the player photos carry no uniform logos. The unnumbered discs are checklisted here alphabetically.

		NM	EX	VG
Complete Set (70):		30.00	15.00	9.00
Common Player:		1.00	.50	.30
(1)	Sal Bando	1.00	.50	.30
(2)	Buddy Bell	1.00	.50	.30
(3)	Johnny Bench	4.50	2.25	1.25
(4)	Larry Bowa	1.00	.50	.30
(5)	Steve Braun	1.00	.50	.30
(6)	George Brett	10.00	5.00	3.00
(7)	Lou Brock	3.50	1.75	1.00
(8)	Jeff Burroughs	1.00	.50	.30
(9)	Bert Campaneris	1.00	.50	.30
(10)	John Candelaria	1.00	.50	.30
(11)	Jose Cardenal	1.00	.50	.30
(12)	Rod Carew	3.50	1.75	1.00
(13)	Steve Carlton	3.50	1.75	1.00
(14)	Dave Cash	1.00	.50	.30
(15)	Cesar Cedeno	1.00	.50	.30
(16)	Ron Cey	1.00	.50	.30
(17)	Dave Concepcion	1.00	.50	.30
(18)	Dennis Eckersley	3.50	1.75	1.00
(19)	Mark Fidrych	2.00	1.00	.60
(20)	Rollie Fingers	3.50	1.75	1.00
(21)	Carlton Fisk	3.50	1.75	1.00
(22)	George Foster	1.00	.50	.30
(23)	Wayne Garland	1.00	.50	.30
(24)	Ralph Garr	1.00	.50	.30
(25)	Steve Garvey	3.50	1.75	1.00
(26)	Cesar Geronimo	1.00	.50	.30
(27)	Bobby Grich	1.00	.50	.30
(28)	Ken Griffey	1.00	.50	.30
(29)	Don Gullett	1.00	.50	.30
(30)	Mike Hargrove	1.00	.50	.30
(31)	Al Hrabosky	1.00	.50	.30
(32)	Jim Hunter	3.50	1.75	1.00
(33)	Reggie Jackson	6.00	3.00	1.75
(34)	Randy Jones	1.00	.50	.30
(35)	Dave Kingman	1.00	.50	.30
(36)	Jerry Koosman	1.00	.50	.30
(37)	Dave LaRoche	1.00	.50	.30
(38)	Greg Luzinski	1.00	.50	.30
(39)	Fred Lynn	1.00	.50	.30
(40)	Bill Madlock	1.00	.50	.30
(41)	Rick Manning	1.00	.50	.30
(42)	Jon Matlack	1.00	.50	.30
(43)	John Mayberry	1.00	.50	.30
(44)	Hal McRae	1.00	.50	.30
(45)	Andy Messersmith	1.00	.50	.30
(46)	Rick Monday	1.00	.50	.30
(47)	John Montefusco	1.00	.50	.30
(48)	Joe Morgan	3.50	1.75	1.00
(49)	Thurman Munson	2.50	1.25	.70
(50)	Bobby Murcer	1.00	.50	.30
(51)	Bill North	1.00	.50	.30
(52)	Jim Palmer	3.50	1.75	1.00
(53)	Tony Perez	3.50	1.75	1.00
(54)	Jerry Reuss	1.00	.50	.30
(55)	Brooks Robinson	4.50	2.25	1.25
(56)	Pete Rose	10.00	5.00	3.00
(57)	Joe Rudi	1.00	.50	.30
(58)	Nolan Ryan	15.00	7.50	4.50
(59)	Manny Sanguillen	1.00	.50	.30
(60)	Mike Schmidt	6.00	3.00	1.75
(61)	Tom Seaver	4.50	2.25	1.25
(62)	Bill Singer	1.00	.50	.30
(63)	Willie Stargell	3.50	1.75	1.00
(64)	Rusty Staub	1.25	.60	.40
(65)	Luis Tiant	1.00	.50	.30
(66)	Bob Watson	1.00	.50	.30
(67)	Butch Wynegar	1.00	.50	.30
(68)	Carl Yastrzemski	4.50	2.25	1.25
(69)	Robin Yount	3.50	1.75	1.00
(70)	Richie Zisk	1.00	.50	.30

1956 Dairy Queen Stars Statues

This set is identical in composition and manufacture to the carded figures sold as Big League Stars (see listing). The DQ versions of the statues are white, while the Big League versions are bronze colored. The statues measure about 3" tall and were evidently sold or given away with a purchase at the chain of ice cream shops.

		NM	EX	VG
Complete Set (18):		1,100	550.00	350.00
Common Player:		40.00	20.00	12.00
(1)	John Antonelli	40.00	20.00	12.00
(2)	Bob Avila	40.00	20.00	12.00
(3)	Yogi Berra	100.00	50.00	30.00
(4)	Roy Campanella	100.00	50.00	30.00
(5)	Larry Doby	65.00	32.50	20.00
(6)	Del Ennis	40.00	20.00	12.00
(7)	Jim Gilliam	40.00	20.00	12.00
(8)	Gil Hodges	75.00	37.50	22.50
(9)	Harvey Kuenn	40.00	20.00	12.00
(10)	Bob Lemon	50.00	25.00	15.00
(11)	Mickey Mantle	325.00	160.00	100.00
(12)	Ed Mathews	75.00	37.50	22.50
(13)	Minnie Minoso	40.00	20.00	12.00
(14)	Stan Musial	160.00	80.00	50.00
(15)	Pee Wee Reese	100.00	50.00	30.00
(16)	Al Rosen	40.00	20.00	12.00
(17)	Duke Snider	100.00	50.00	30.00
(18)	Mickey Vernon	40.00	20.00	12.00

1950s Dairylea Mickey Mantle Decal

There is currently no way to specify the year of release for this decal, though a release date in the late 1950s seems like a reasonable assumption. About 2-1/4" square, these decals feature glow-in-the-dark ink in red and green on front. The back is printed in blue on an orange background. There seems to have been a small hoard of these decals discovered circa 2009. Dairylea was a milk producers' cooperative in Orange County, just north and west of New York City.

	NM	EX	VG
Mickey Mantle	150.00	90.00	45.00

1954 Dan-Dee Potato Chips

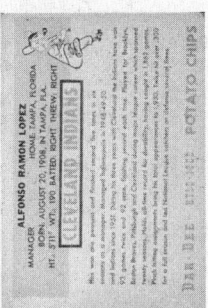

Issued in bags of potato chips, the cards in this 29-card set are commonly found with grease stains despite their waxed surface. The unnumbered cards, which measure 2-1/2" x 3-5/8", feature color pictures. Backs have player statistical and biographical information. The set consists mostly of players from the Indians and Pirates. Photos of the Yankees players were also used for the Briggs Meats and Stahl-Meyer Franks sets.

		NM	EX	VG
Complete Set (29):		8,750	4,400	2,600
Common Player:		140.00	70.00	40.00
(1)	Bob Avila	140.00	70.00	40.00
(2)	Hank Bauer	170.00	85.00	50.00
(3)	Walker Cooper/SP	475.00	250.00	150.00
(4)	Larry Doby	175.00	90.00	50.00
(5)	Luke Easter	160.00	80.00	50.00
(6)	Bob Feller	450.00	225.00	140.00
(7)	Bob Friend	140.00	70.00	40.00
(8)	Mike Garcia	140.00	70.00	40.00
(9)	Sid Gordon	140.00	70.00	40.00
(10)	Jim Hegan	140.00	70.00	40.00
(11)	Gil Hodges	575.00	300.00	175.00
(12)	Art Houtteman	140.00	70.00	40.00
(13)	Monte Irvin	175.00	90.00	50.00
(14)	Paul LaPalm (LaPalme)	140.00	70.00	40.00
(15)	Bob Lemon	175.00	90.00	50.00
(16)	Al Lopez	175.00	90.00	50.00
(17)	Mickey Mantle	3,000	1,500	900.00
(18)	Dale Mitchell	140.00	70.00	40.00
(19)	Phil Rizzuto	320.00	160.00	100.00
(20)	Curtis Roberts	140.00	70.00	40.00
(21)	Al Rosen	160.00	80.00	50.00
(22)	Red Schoendienst	175.00	90.00	50.00
(23)	Paul Smith/SP	500.00	250.00	150.00
(24)	Duke Snider	375.00	190.00	120.00
(25)	George Strickland	140.00	70.00	40.00
(26)	Max Surkont	140.00	70.00	40.00
(27)	Frank Thomas/SP	250.00	125.00	75.00
(28)	Wally Westlake	140.00	70.00	40.00
(29)	Early Wynn	175.00	90.00	50.00

1977 Tom Daniels Burleigh Grimes

"OLD STUBBLEBEARD"

An era came to pass when "Old Stubblebeard" tossed his last spitball in 1934. Only 17 pitchers were allowed to continue throwing the spitball when it was banned in 1920. Burleigh not only won more games than any of the other "legal" spitballers but also outlasted all others.

Perhaps it was a quirk of fate that allowed Burleigh to rise to fame while his brother Shurleigh was destined to never advance beyond the Texas League. Burleigh stated, "Shurleigh was seven years younger than me and still was in the minors when the spitball was banned. Had he been allowed to continue to throw the spitter I believe he would also have had a chance to pitch big league ball."

© Copyright 1977, Tom Daniels and Burleigh Grimes

"OLD STUBBLEBEARD"

The career of Hall of Fame spitballer Burleigh Grimes is traced in this collectors' issue. The 2-1/2" x 3-1/2" cards have black-and-white photos from Grimes' collection, bordered in bright blue. A card title is in black in the bottom border. Backs are printed in black and blue on white and have a description of the front photo. One card in each set is authentically autographed by Grimes. Price at issue was $3.50; uncut sheets were also available.

	NM	EX	VG
Complete Set (16):	10.00	5.00	3.00
Common Card:	1.00	.50	.30
1 Dodger Manager 1937-38	1.00	.50	.30
2 "Lord Burleigh"	1.00	.50	.30
3 Last Spitballers	1.00	.50	.30
4 Grimes, Hornsby, McGraw, Roush	1.00	.50	.30
5 Winning Combination	1.00	.50	.30
6 World Champion	1.00	.50	.30
7 "Old Stubblebeard"	1.00	.50	.30
8 Grimes Meets McCarthy	1.00	.50	.30
9 Dodger Greats	1.00	.50	.30
10 "The Babe"	2.00	1.00	.60
11 Dodger Strategists	1.00	.50	.30
12 Bender and Grimes	1.00	.50	.30
13 Number '270'	1.00	.50	.30
14 The Origin	1.00	.50	.30
15 1964 HoF Inductees	1.00	.50	.30
16 "Lord Burleigh" 1977	1.00	.50	.30

1910 Darby Chocolates (E271)

The 1910 Darby Chocolates cards are among the rarest of all candy cards. The cards were printed on boxes of "Pennant" Chocolates, two players per box - one each on front and back. The cards feature black-and-white player action photos outlined with a thick dark shadow. The boxes are accented with orange or green graphics. Most of the known examples of this set were not found until 1982 when a group in fire-damaged condition was inadvisedly subjected to restoration. Values shown here are for cards in untampered-with state of preservation. Values for restored cards must be adjusted significantly downward. This checklist may or may not be complete.

		NM	EX	VG
Common Player:		12,000	6,000	3,500
(1)	Jimmy Archer	12,000	6,000	3,500
(2)	Chief Bender	16,000	8,000	4,800
(3)	Bob Bescher	12,000	6,000	3,600
(4)	Roger Bresnahan	16,000	8,000	4,800
(5)	Al Bridwell	12,000	6,000	3,600
(6)	Mordicai Brown (Mordecai)	16,000	8,000	4,800
(7)	"Eddie" Cicotte	13,500	6,750	4,000
(8)	Fred Clark (Clarke)	12,000	6,000	3,600
(9)	Ty. Cobb (Batting)	30,000	15,000	9,000
(10)	"Ty" Cobb (Fielding)	30,000	15,000	9,000
(11)	King Cole	12,000	6,000	3,600
(12)	E. Collins	16,000	8,000	4,800
(13)	Wid Conroy	12,000	6,000	3,600
(14)	"Sam" Crawford	16,000	8,000	4,800
(15)	Bill Dahlin (Dahlen)	12,000	6,000	3,600
(16)	Bill Donovan	12,000	6,000	3,600
(17)	"Pat" Dougherty	12,000	6,000	3,600
(18)	Kid Elberfeld	12,000	6,000	3,600
(19)	"Johnny" Evers	16,000	8,000	4,800
(20)	Charlie Herzog	12,000	6,000	3,600
(21)	Hughie Jennings	16,000	8,000	4,800
(22)	Walter Johnson	20,000	10,000	6,000
(23)	Ed Konetchy	12,000	6,000	3,600
(24)	Tommy Leach	12,000	6,000	3,600
(25)	Fred Luderous (Luderus)	12,000	6,000	3,600
(26)	"Mugsy" McGraw	16,000	8,000	4,800
(27)	"Mike" Mowery (Mowrey)	12,000	6,000	3,600
(28)	Jack Powell	12,000	6,000	3,600
(29)	Slim Sallee	12,000	6,000	3,600
(30)	James Scheckard (Sheckard)	12,000	6,000	3,600
(31)	Walter Snodgrass	12,000	6,000	3,600
(32)	"Tris" Speaker	17,500	8,750	5,250
(33)	Charlie Suggs	12,000	6,000	3,600
(34)	Fred Tenney	12,000	6,000	3,600
(35)	"Jim" Vaughn	12,000	6,000	3,600
(36)	"Hans" Wagner	40,000	13,750	8,250

1911 Harry Davis Day Postcard

In his final season with the Philadelphia Athletics, the star first baseman of the famed $100,000 Infield was honored with a "day" at Shibe Park. This standard-size black-and-white postcard was created to remind fans to attend the event. A pre-printed message on back over the facsimile signature of Connie Mack urges fans to "show our appreciation of what Captain Davis has done for baseball and the city of his birth."

HARRY DAVIS DAY
SHIBE PARK
WEDNESDAY, MAY 31st

Harry Davis

	NM	EX	VG
	750.00	375.00	225.00

1970 Dayton Daily News Bubble-Gumless Cards

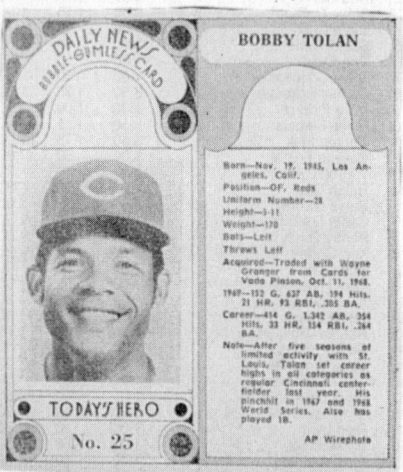

These "cards" are actually newspaper clippings which were issued on a daily basis during the baseball season by the Ohio newspaper. Labeled "Today's Hero," the clippings measure approximately 3-1/2" x 4" and are printed in black-and-white. At left is a portrait photo of the player, at right are personal data, stats and career highlights. At least two All-Star versions of these paper cards were issued. They differ from the regular format in their use of red background printing and an "All-Star" designation in place of a card number.

		NM	EX	VG
Complete Set (160):		2,000	1,000	600.00
Common Player:		9.00	4.50	2.75
1	Pete Rose	40.00	20.00	12.00
2	Johnny Bench	20.00	10.00	6.00
3	Maury Wills	12.00	6.00	3.50
4	Harmon Killebrew	20.00	10.00	6.00
5	Frank Robinson	20.00	10.00	6.00
6	Willie Mays	60.00	30.00	18.00
7	Hank Aaron	60.00	30.00	18.00
8	Tom Seaver	20.00	10.00	6.00
9	Sam McDowell	9.00	4.50	2.75
10	Rico Petrocelli	9.00	4.50	2.75
11a	Tony Perez (Dark cap.)	20.00	10.00	6.00
11b	Tony Perez (Light cap.)	20.00	10.00	6.00
12	Hoyt Wilhelm	15.00	7.50	4.50
13	Alex Johnson	9.00	4.50	2.75
14	Gary Nolan	9.00	4.50	2.75
15	Al Kaline	25.00	12.50	7.50
16	Bob Gibson	15.00	7.50	4.50
17	Larry Dierker	9.00	4.50	2.75
18	Ernie Banks	30.00	15.00	9.00
19	Lee May	9.00	4.50	2.75
20	Claude Osteen	9.00	4.50	2.75
21	Tony Horton	9.00	4.50	2.75
22	Mack Jones	9.00	4.50	2.75
23	Wally Bunker	9.00	4.50	2.75
24	Bill Hands	9.00	4.50	2.75
25	Bobby Tolan	9.00	4.50	2.75
26	Jim Wynn	9.00	4.50	2.75
27	Tom Haller	9.00	4.50	2.75
28	Carl Yastrzemski	25.00	12.50	7.50
29	Jim Merritt	9.00	4.50	2.75
30	Tony Oliva	12.00	6.00	3.50
31	Reggie Jackson	40.00	20.00	12.00
32	Bob Clemente	90.00	45.00	27.00
33	Tommy Helms	9.00	4.50	2.75
34	Boog Powell	12.00	6.00	3.50
35	Mickey Lolich	12.00	6.00	3.50
36	Frank Howard	12.00	6.00	3.50
37	Jim McGlothlin	9.00	4.50	2.75
38	Rusty Staub	12.00	6.00	3.50
39	Mel Stottlemyre	9.00	4.50	2.75
40	Rico Carty	9.00	4.50	2.75
41	Nate Colbert	9.00	4.50	2.75
42	Wayne Granger	9.00	4.50	2.75
43	Mike Hegan	9.00	4.50	2.75
44	Jerry Koosman	9.00	4.50	2.75
45	Jim Perry	9.00	4.50	2.75
46	Pat Corrales	9.00	4.50	2.75
47	Dick Bosman	9.00	4.50	2.75
48	Bert Campaneris	9.00	4.50	2.75
49	Larry Hisle	9.00	4.50	2.75
50	Bernie Carbo	9.00	4.50	2.75
51	Wilbur Wood	9.00	4.50	2.75
52	Dave McNally	9.00	4.50	2.75
53	Andy Messersmith	9.00	4.50	2.75
54	Jimmy Stewart	9.00	4.50	2.75
55	Luis Aparicio	15.00	7.50	4.50
56	Mike Cuellar	9.00	4.50	2.75
57	Bill Grabarkewitz	9.00	4.50	2.75
58	Dick Dietz	9.00	4.50	2.75
59	Dave Concepcion	9.00	4.50	2.75
60	Gary Gentry	9.00	4.50	2.75
61	Don Money	9.00	4.50	2.75
62	Rod Carew	20.00	10.00	6.00
63	Denis Menke	9.00	4.50	2.75
64	Hal McRae	9.00	4.50	2.75
65	Felipe Alou	9.00	4.50	2.75
66	Richie Hebner	9.00	4.50	2.75
67	Don Sutton	15.00	7.50	4.50
68	Wayne Simpson	9.00	4.50	2.75
69	Art Shamsky	9.00	4.50	2.75
70	Luis Tiant	9.00	4.50	2.75
71	Clay Carroll	9.00	4.50	2.75
72	Jim Hickman	9.00	4.50	2.75
73	Clarence Gaston	9.00	4.50	2.75
74	Angel Bravo	9.00	4.50	2.75
75	Jim Hunter	15.00	7.50	4.50
76	Lou Piniella	10.00	5.00	3.00
77	Jim Bunning	15.00	7.50	4.50
78	Don Gullett	9.00	4.50	2.75
79	Dan Cater	9.00	4.50	2.75
80	Richie Allen	13.50	6.75	4.00
81	Jim Bouton	10.00	5.00	3.00
82	Jim Palmer	15.00	7.50	4.50
83	Woody Woodward	9.00	4.50	2.75
84	Tom Agee	9.00	4.50	2.75
85	Carlos May	9.00	4.50	2.75
86	Ray Washburn	9.00	4.50	2.75
87	Denny McLain	10.00	5.00	3.00
88	Lou Brock	15.00	7.50	4.50
89	Ken Henderson	9.00	4.50	2.75
90	Roy White	9.00	4.50	2.75
91	Chris Cannizzaro	9.00	4.50	2.75
92	Willie Horton	9.00	4.50	2.75
93	Jose Cardenal	9.00	4.50	2.75
94	Jim Fregosi	9.00	4.50	2.75
95	Richie Hebner	9.00	4.50	2.75
96	Tony Conigliaro	10.00	5.00	3.00
97	Tony Cloninger	9.00	4.50	2.75
98	Mike Epstein	9.00	4.50	2.75
99	Ty Cline	9.00	4.50	2.75
100	Tommy Harper	9.00	4.50	2.75
101	Jose Azcue	9.00	4.50	2.75
102a	Glenn Beckert	9.00	4.50	2.75
102b	Ray Fosse	9.00	4.50	2.75
103	Not Issued			
104	Gerry Moses	9.00	4.50	2.75
105	Bud Harrelson	9.00	4.50	2.75
106	Joe Torre	13.50	6.75	4.00
107	Dave Johnson	9.00	4.50	2.75
108	Don Kessinger	9.00	4.50	2.75
109	Bill Freehan	9.00	4.50	2.75
110	Sandy Alomar	9.00	4.50	2.75
111	Matty Alou	9.00	4.50	2.75
112	Joe Morgan	15.00	7.50	4.50
113	John Odom	9.00	4.50	2.75
114	Amos Otis	9.00	4.50	2.75
115	Jay Johnstone	9.00	4.50	2.75
116	Ron Perranoski	9.00	4.50	2.75
117	Manny Mota	9.00	4.50	2.75
118	Billy Conigliaro	9.00	4.50	2.75
119	Leo Cardenas	9.00	4.50	2.75
120	Rich Reese	9.00	4.50	2.75
121	Ron Santo	12.00	6.00	3.50
122	Gene Michael	9.00	4.50	2.75
123	Milt Pappas	9.00	4.50	2.75
124	Joe Pepitone	10.00	5.00	3.00
125	Jose Cardenal	9.00	4.50	2.75
126	Jim Northrup	9.00	4.50	2.75
127	Wes Parker	9.00	4.50	2.75
128	Fritz Peterson	9.00	4.50	2.75
129	Phil Regan	9.00	4.50	2.75
130	John Callison	9.00	4.50	2.75
131	Cookie Rojas	9.00	4.50	2.75
132	Claude Raymond	9.00	4.50	2.75
133	Darrel Chaney	9.00	4.50	2.75
134	Gary Peters	9.00	4.50	2.75
135	Del Unser	9.00	4.50	2.75
136	Joey Foy	9.00	4.50	2.75
137	Luke Walker	9.00	4.50	2.75
138	Bill Mazeroski	15.00	7.50	4.50
139	Tony Taylor	9.00	4.50	2.75
140	Leron Lee	9.00	4.50	2.75
141	Jesus Alou	9.00	4.50	2.75
142	Donn Clendenon	9.00	4.50	2.75
143	Merv Rettenmund	9.00	4.50	2.75
144	Bob Moose	9.00	4.50	2.75
145	Jim Kaat	10.00	5.00	3.00
146	Randy Hundley	9.00	4.50	2.75
147	Jim McAndrew	9.00	4.50	2.75
148	Manny Sanguillen	9.00	4.50	2.75
149	Bob Allison	9.00	4.50	2.75
150	Jim Maloney	9.00	4.50	2.75
151	Don Buford	9.00	4.50	2.75
152	Gene Alley	9.00	4.50	2.75
153	Cesar Tovar	9.00	4.50	2.75
154	Brooks Robinson	20.00	10.00	6.00
155	Milt Wilcox	9.00	4.50	2.75
156	Willie Stargell	20.00	10.00	6.00
157	Paul Blair	9.00	4.50	2.75
158	Andy Etchebarren	9.00	4.50	2.75
159	Mark Belanger	9.00	4.50	2.75
160	Elrod Hendricks	9.00	4.50	2.75
All-Star	Johnny Bench	30.00	15.00	9.00
All-Star	Tony Perez	25.00	12.50	7.50

1973 Dean's Photo Service San Diego Padres

DAVE MARSHALL
OUTFIELDER

DEAN'S

A true rookie-year issue for Dave Winfield is included in this set of 5-1/2" x 8-1/2" black-and-white, blank-backed player photos sponsored by Dean's Photo Service and given away by the team in five six-card series at various home games. Pictures have posed player portraits surrounded by a white border. Beneath are the name and position, with team and sponsor logos at bottom. The set is checklisted here alphabetically.

		NM	EX	VG
Complete Set (31):		80.00	40.00	24.00
Common Player:		4.00	2.00	1.25
(1)	Steve Arlin	4.00	2.00	1.25
(2)	Mike Caldwell	4.00	2.00	1.25
(3)	Dave Campbell	4.00	2.00	1.25
(4)	Nate Colbert	4.00	2.00	1.25
(5)	Mike Corkins	4.00	2.00	1.25
(6)	Pat Corrales	4.00	2.00	1.25
(7)	Jim Davenport	4.00	2.00	1.25
(8)	Dave Garcia	4.00	2.00	1.25
(9)	Clarence Gaston	4.00	2.00	1.25
(10)	Bill Greif	4.00	2.00	1.25
(11)	John Grubb	4.00	2.00	1.25
(12)	Enzo Hernandez	4.00	2.00	1.25
(13)	Randy Jones	4.00	2.00	1.25
(14)	Fred Kendall	4.00	2.00	1.25
(15)	Clay Kirby	4.00	2.00	1.25
(16)	Leron Lee	4.00	2.00	1.25
(17)	Dave Marshall	4.00	2.00	1.25
(18)	Don Mason	4.00	2.00	1.25
(19)	Jerry Morales	4.00	2.00	1.25
(20)	Ivan Murrell	4.00	2.00	1.25
(21)	Fred Norman	4.00	2.00	1.25
(22)	Johnny Podres	4.00	2.00	1.25
(23)	Dave Roberts	4.00	2.00	1.25
(24)	Vicente Romo	4.00	2.00	1.25
(25)	Gary Ross	4.00	2.00	1.25
(26)	Bob Skinner	4.00	2.00	1.25
(27)	Derrel Thomas	4.00	2.00	1.25
(28)	Rich Troedson	4.00	2.00	1.25
(29)	Whitey Wietelmann	4.00	2.00	1.25
(30)	Dave Winfield	25.00	12.50	7.50
(31)	Don Zimmer	5.00	2.50	1.50

1974 Dean's Photo Service San Diego Padres

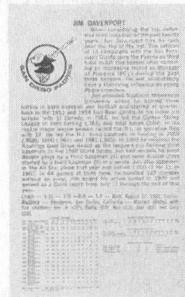

Padres

padres   DEAN'S

This issue shares the same basic format as the years which preceded it and succeeded it. Fronts of the 5-1/2" x 8-1/2" cards have a large player portrait or pose at top, with the player's name and position below. In the wide white border at bottom are the team and sponsor's logos. Backs, for the first time, have a lengthy career summary, personal data and full professional stats. All printing is in black-and-white. The unnumbered cards are checklisted here alphabetically.

		NM	EX	VG
Complete Set (30):		70.00	35.00	21.00
Common Player:		4.00	2.00	1.25
(1)	Matty Alou	4.00	2.00	1.25
(2)	Bob Barton	4.00	2.00	1.25
(3)	Glenn Beckert	4.00	2.00	1.25
(4)	Jack Bloomfield	4.00	2.00	1.25
(5)	Nate Colbert	4.00	2.00	1.25
(6)	Mike Corkins	4.00	2.00	1.25
(7)	Jim Davenport	4.00	2.00	1.25
(8)	Dave Freisleben	4.00	2.00	1.25
(9)	Cito Gaston	4.00	2.00	1.25
(10)	Bill Greif	4.00	2.00	1.25
(11)	Johnny Grubb	4.00	2.00	1.25
(12)	Larry Hardy	4.00	2.00	1.25
(13)	Enzo Hernandez	4.00	2.00	1.25
(14)	Dave Hilton	4.00	2.00	1.25
(15)	Randy Jones	4.00	2.00	1.25
(16)	Fred Kendall	4.00	2.00	1.25

(17)	Gene Locklear	4.00	2.00	1.25
(18)	Willie McCovey	10.00	5.00	3.00
(19)	John McNamara	4.00	2.00	1.25
(20)	Rich Morales	4.00	2.00	1.25
(21)	Bill Posedel	4.00	2.00	1.25
(22)	Dave Roberts	4.00	2.00	1.25
(23)	Vicente Romo	4.00	2.00	1.25
(24)	Dan Spillner	4.00	2.00	1.25
(25)	Bob Tolan	4.00	2.00	1.25
(26)	Derrel Thomas	4.00	2.00	1.25
(27)	Rich Troedson	4.00	2.00	1.25
(28)	Whitey Wietelmann	4.00	2.00	1.25
(29)	Bernie Williams	4.00	2.00	1.25
(30)	Dave Winfield	15.00	7.50	4.50

1975 Dean's Photo Service San Diego Padres

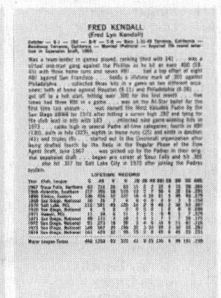

FRED KENDALL
(Fred Lyn Kendall)

padres   DEAN'S

Player biographical data and stats continued on the backs of the cards in the 1975 series sponsored by Dean's. Once again the black-and-white pictures were in 5-1/2" x 8-1/2" format. Fronts have the player photo at top, with his name and position beneath. At bottom are the team and sponsor logos. The Padres logo consists of a cartoon character robed monk in various baseball poses. The pictures were given away at autograph nights during the season. The unnumbered photos are checklisted here in alphabetical order.

		NM	EX	VG
Complete Set (30):		60.00	30.00	18.00
Common Player:		4.00	2.00	1.25
(1)	Jim Davenport	4.00	2.00	1.25
(2)	Bob Davis	4.00	2.00	1.25
(3)	Rich Folkers	4.00	2.00	1.25
(4)	Alan Foster	4.00	2.00	1.25
(5)	Dave Freisleben	4.00	2.00	1.25
(6)	Danny Frisella	4.00	2.00	1.25
(7)	Tito Fuentes	4.00	2.00	1.25
(8)	Bill Greif	4.00	2.00	1.25
(9)	Johnny Grubb	4.00	2.00	1.25
(10)	Enzo Hernandez	4.00	2.00	1.25
(11)	Randy Hundley (Blank back.)	4.00	2.00	1.25
(12)	Mike Ivie	4.00	2.00	1.25
(13)	Jerry Johnson	4.00	2.00	1.25
(14)	Randy Jones	4.00	2.00	1.25
(15)	Fred Kendall	4.00	2.00	1.25
(16)	Ted Kubiak	4.00	2.00	1.25
(17)	Gene Locklear	4.00	2.00	1.25
(18)	Willie McCovey	10.00	5.00	3.00
(19)	Joe McIntosh	4.00	2.00	1.25
(20)	John McNamara	4.00	2.00	1.25
(21)	Tom Morgan	4.00	2.00	1.25
(22)	Dick Sharon	4.00	2.00	1.25
(23)	Dick Sisler	4.00	2.00	1.25
(24)	Dan Spillner	4.00	2.00	1.25
(25)	Brent Strom	4.00	2.00	1.25
(26)	Bobby Tolan	4.00	2.00	1.25
(27)	Dave Tomlin	4.00	2.00	1.25
(28)	Hector Torres (Blank back.)	4.00	2.00	1.25
(29)	Whitey Wietelmann	4.00	2.00	1.25
(30)	Dave Winfield	15.00	7.50	4.50

1976 Dean's Photo Service San Diego Padres

TED KUBIAK
Theodore Rodger Kubiak

padres   DEAN'S

The last of four black-and-white team sets which were sponsored by Dean's was issued in 1976. The format was little different than previous years. Cards are 5-1/2" x 8-1/2" black-and-white. Fronts have a player portrait or pose surrounded by a white border. At bottom front are team and sponsor logos. Backs have personal data, a career summary and complete professional stats. The unnumbered cards are checklisted here in alphabetical order.

	NM	EX	VG
Complete Set (30):	60.00	30.00	18.00

Common Player:		4.00	2.00	1.25
(1)	Joe Amalfitano	4.00	2.00	1.25
(2)	Roger Craig	4.00	2.00	1.25
(3)	Bob Davis	4.00	2.00	1.25
(4)	Willie Davis	4.00	2.00	1.25
(5)	Rich Folkers	4.00	2.00	1.25
(6)	Alan Foster	4.00	2.00	1.25
(7)	Dave Freisleben	4.00	2.00	1.25
(8)	Tito Fuentes	4.00	2.00	1.25
(9)	John Grubb	4.00	2.00	1.25
(10)	Enzo Hernandez	4.00	2.00	1.25
(11)	Mike Ivie	4.00	2.00	1.25
(12)	Jerry Johnson	4.00	2.00	1.25
(13)	Randy Jones	4.00	2.00	1.25
(14)	Fred Kendall	4.00	2.00	1.25
(15)	Ted Kubiak	4.00	2.00	1.25
(16)	Willie McCovey	10.00	5.00	3.00
(17)	John McNamara	4.00	2.00	1.25
(18)	Luis Melendez	4.00	2.00	1.25
(19)	Butch Metzger	4.00	2.00	1.25
(20)	Doug Rader	4.00	2.00	1.25
(21)	Merv Rettenmund	4.00	2.00	1.25
(22)	Ken Reynolds	4.00	2.00	1.25
(23)	Dick Sisler	4.00	2.00	1.25
(24)	Dan Spillner	4.00	2.00	1.25
(25)	Brent Strom	4.00	2.00	1.25
(26)	Dave Tomlin	4.00	2.00	1.25
(27)	Hector Torres	4.00	2.00	1.25
(28)	Jerry Turner	4.00	2.00	1.25
(29)	Whitey Wietelmann	4.00	2.00	1.25
(30)	Dave Winfield	15.00	7.50	4.50

1938 Dizzy Dean's Service Station

DIZZY DEAN'S
SERVICE STATION

ON TAMIAMI TRAIL
TWO BLOCKS FROM
FOOT OF MILLION
DOLLAR GREEN BRIDGE
IN DOWN TOWN
BRADENTON

SPECIALIZED LUBRICATION
COMPLETE SERVICE
•
STANDARD OIL PRODUCTS

The date of issue of this one-card set is only a guess. The 4" x 6" black-and-white card advertises Dean's service station in Florida.

	NM	EX	VG
Dizzy Dean	350.00	175.00	100.00

1978 Dearborn Show

DEARBORN BASEBALL CARD
& SPORTS MEMORABILIA SHOW

#13 NORM CASH

Former members of the Detroit Tigers, some of whom were scheduled to appear as autograph guests, are featured in this collectors' issue produced in conjunction with the 1978 Dearborn Baseball Card & Sports Memorabilia Show. The 2-5/8" x 3-5/8" cards have black-and-white player photos on front with the player name and card number in the white border at bottom. Backs, also in black-and-white, advertise the fall, 1978, and spring, 1979 shows.

		NM	EX	VG
Complete Set (18):		60.00	30.00	18.00
Common Player:		4.00	2.00	1.25
1	Rocky Colavito	15.00	7.50	4.50
2	Ervin Fox	4.00	2.00	1.25
3	Lynwood Rowe	4.00	2.00	1.25
4	Gerald Walker	4.00	2.00	1.25
5	Leon Goslin	4.00	2.00	1.25
6	Harvey Kuenn	6.00	3.00	1.75
7	Frank Howard	6.00	3.00	1.75
8	Woodie Fryman	4.00	2.00	1.25
9	Don Wert	4.00	2.00	1.25
10	Jim Perry	4.00	2.00	1.25
11	Mayo Smith	4.00	2.00	1.25
12	Al Kaline	20.00	10.00	6.00
13	Norm Cash	12.00	6.00	3.50
14	Mickey Cochrane	9.00	4.50	2.75
15	Fred Marberry	4.00	2.00	1.25
16	Bill Freehan	6.00	3.00	1.75
17	Charlie Gehringer	9.00	4.50	2.75
18	Jim Northrup	4.00	2.00	1.25

1980 Delacorte Press

As a promotion for its book, "Number 1," written by Billy Martin, Delacorte Press issued this card picturing Martin some-

Writer
5'11"/165 lbs.
Born: 5/16/28
Berkeley, Ca.
BILLY MARTIN
Plays: Hard   Writes: Tough

A brilliant rookie author, Billy brings to Number 1 the same brash, fiery style that has made him the scourge of club owners and umpires for the past 30 years. Adored by fans for his combative spirit, considered by many experts to be the best baseball strategist since Casey Stengel, Billy's aggressive attitude has made him the most controversial figure in baseball today. Every team he's coached has been a winner and he's been fired by them all. Number 1 is the book fans have been waiting for: Billy's side of the story. A candid, no-holds barred look at baseball from the inside, Number 1 makes Billy the runaway favorite for publishing's rookie of the year.

NUMBER 1   DELACORTE PRESS

what in the style of a 1978 Topps manager card. The 3-1/2" x 2-1/2" card has a black-and-white photo of Martin as a Yankees manager, and a color photo as the A's manager. The front is bordered in red. Backs are printed in black, white and red with biographical details and promotional copy for the book.

		NM	EX	VG
1	Billy Martin	6.00	3.00	1.75

1971 Dell Today's Team Stamps

JACK DILAURO

Pitcher — Bats right and left, throws right. Born 1943. Height 6-2. Weight 185. Relieved 42 times in 1970. Has good breaking ball and control. Good fielding pitcher who demonstrated ability to win three straight years in Triple-A ball. Originally signed by Tigers.

This issue was produced as a series of individual team (plus one All-Star) albums. The 8-1/2" x 10-7/8" booklets offer team and league histories and stats, photos of all-time team stars and two pages of 12 player stamps each. Each stamp is 1-7/8" x 2-15/16" and has a posed color photo and black facsimile autograph on front. Backs have the player name, biographical details and a few career highlights, along with an underprint of the team logo. The stamps are perforated for easy seperation, though there are no spaces in the 12-page album for their housing once removed from the sheet. The team albums were sold individually (39 cents) as well as in six-team divisional sets ($2). The checklist is arranged alphabetically by team within league; individual stamps are unnumbered.

	NM	EX	VG
Complete Set, Albums (25):	225.00	110.00	65.00
Complete Set, Stamps (600):	175.00	90.00	50.00
Common Player:	1.00	.50	.30

Complete All-Star Album: 20.00 / 10.00 / 6.00

(#)	Player	NM	EX	VG
(1)	Hank Aaron	7.50	3.75	2.25
(2)	Luis Aparicio	2.50	1.25	.70
(3)	Ernie Banks	5.00	2.50	1.50
(4)	Johnny Bench	3.00	1.50	.90
(5)	Rico Carty	1.00	.50	.30
(6)	Roberto Clemente	10.00	5.00	3.00
(7)	Bob Gibson	2.50	1.25	.70
(8)	Willie Horton	1.00	.50	.30
(9)	Frank Howard	1.50	.70	.45
(10)	Reggie Jackson	6.00	3.00	1.75
(11)	Fergie Jenkins	1.50	.70	.45
(12)	Alex Johnson	1.00	.50	.30
(13)	Al Kaline	3.00	1.50	.90
(14)	Harmon Killebrew	3.00	1.50	.90
(15)	Willie Mays	7.50	3.75	2.25
(16)	Sam McDowell	1.00	.50	.30
(17)	Denny McLain	1.50	.70	.45
(18)	Boog Powell	1.50	.70	.45
(19)	Brooks Robinson	3.00	1.50	.90
(20)	Frank Robinson	3.00	1.50	.90
(21)	Pete Rose	7.50	3.75	2.25
(22)	Tom Seaver	3.00	1.50	.90
(23)	Rusty Staub	1.50	.70	.45
(24)	Carl Yastrzemski	3.00	1.50	.90

Complete Atlanta Braves Album: 15.00 / 7.50 / 4.50

(#)	Player	NM	EX	VG
(1)	Hank Aaron	7.50	3.75	2.25
(2)	Tommie Aaron	1.00	.50	.30
(3)	Hank Allen	1.00	.50	.30
(4)	Clete Boyer	1.50	.70	.45
(5)	Oscar Brown	1.00	.50	.30
(6)	Rico Carty	1.00	.50	.30
(7)	Orlando Cepeda	2.50	1.25	.70
(8)	Bob Didier	1.00	.50	.30
(9)	Ralph Garr	1.00	.50	.30
(10)	Gil Garrido	1.00	.50	.30
(11)	Ron Herbel	1.00	.50	.30
(12)	Sonny Jackson	1.00	.50	.30
(13)	Pat Jarvis	1.00	.50	.30
(14)	Larry Jaster	1.00	.50	.30
(15)	Hal King	1.00	.50	.30
(16)	Mike Lum	1.00	.50	.30
(17)	Felix Millan	1.00	.50	.30
(18)	Jim Nash	1.00	.50	.30
(19)	Phil Niekro	2.00	1.00	.60
(20)	Bob Priddy	1.00	.50	.30
(21)	Ron Reed	1.00	.50	.30
(22)	George Stone	1.00	.50	.30
(23)	Cecil Upshaw	1.00	.50	.30
(24)	Hoyt Wilhelm	2.00	1.00	.60

Complete Chicago Cubs Album: 15.00 / 7.50 / 4.50

(#)	Player	NM	EX	VG
(1)	Ernie Banks	5.00	2.50	1.50
(2)	Glenn Beckert	1.00	.50	.30
(3)	Danny Breeden	1.00	.50	.30
(4)	Johnny Callison	1.00	.50	.30
(5)	Jim Colborn	1.00	.50	.30
(6)	Joe Decker	1.00	.50	.30
(7)	Bill Hands	1.00	.50	.30
(8)	Jim Hickman	1.00	.50	.30
(9)	Ken Holtzman	1.00	.50	.30
(10)	Randy Hundley	1.00	.50	.30
(11)	Fergie Jenkins	2.00	1.00	.60
(12)	Don Kessinger	1.00	.50	.30
(13)	J.C. Martin	1.00	.50	.30
(14)	Bob Miller	1.00	.50	.30
(15)	Milt Pappas	1.00	.50	.30
(16)	Joe Pepitone	1.00	.50	.30
(17)	Juan Pizarro	1.00	.50	.30
(18)	Paul Popovich	1.00	.50	.30
(19)	Phil Regan	1.00	.50	.30
(20)	Roberto Rodriguez	1.00	.50	.30
(21)	Ken Rudolph	1.00	.50	.30
(22)	Ron Santo	1.50	.70	.45
(23)	Hector Torres	1.00	.50	.30
(24)	Billy Williams	2.50	1.25	.70

Complete Cincinnati Reds Album: 20.00 / 10.00 / 6.00

(#)	Player	NM	EX	VG
(1)	Johnny Bench	3.00	1.50	.90
(2)	Angel Bravo	1.00	.50	.30
(3)	Bernie Carbo	1.00	.50	.30
(4)	Clay Carroll	1.00	.50	.30
(5)	Darrel Chaney	1.00	.50	.30
(6)	Ty Cline	1.00	.50	.30
(7)	Tony Cloninger	1.00	.50	.30
(8)	Dave Concepcion	1.00	.50	.30
(9)	Pat Corrales	1.00	.50	.30
(10)	Greg Garrett	1.00	.50	.30
(11)	Wayne Granger	1.00	.50	.30
(12)	Don Gullett	1.00	.50	.30
(13)	Tommy Helms	1.00	.50	.30
(14)	Lee May	1.00	.50	.30
(15)	Jim McGlothlin	1.00	.50	.30
(16)	Hal McRae	1.00	.50	.30
(17)	Jim Merritt	1.00	.50	.30
(18)	Gary Nolan	1.00	.50	.30
(19)	Tony Perez	2.50	1.25	.70
(20)	Pete Rose	7.50	3.75	2.25
(21)	Wayne Simpson	1.00	.50	.30
(22)	Jimmy Stewart	1.00	.50	.30
(23)	Bobby Tolan	1.00	.50	.30
(24)	Woody Woodward	1.00	.50	.30

Complete Houston Astros Album: 10.00 / 5.00 / 3.00

(#)	Player	NM	EX	VG
(1)	Jesus Alou	1.00	.50	.30
(2)	Jack Billingham	1.00	.50	.30
(3)	Ron Cook	1.00	.50	.30
(4)	George Culver	1.00	.50	.30
(5)	Larry Dierker	1.00	.50	.30
(6)	Jack DiLauro	1.00	.50	.30
(7)	Johnny Edwards	1.00	.50	.30
(8)	Fred Gladding	1.00	.50	.30
(9)	Tom Griffin	1.00	.50	.30
(10)	Skip Guinn	1.00	.50	.30
(11)	Jack Hiatt	1.00	.50	.30
(12)	Denny Lemaster	1.00	.50	.30
(13)	Marty Martinez	1.00	.50	.30
(14)	John Mayberry	1.00	.50	.30
(15)	Denis Menke	1.00	.50	.30
(16)	Norm Miller	1.00	.50	.30
(17)	Joe Morgan	2.50	1.25	.70
(18)	Doug Rader	1.00	.50	.30
(19)	Jim Ray	1.00	.50	.30
(20)	Scipio Spinks	1.00	.50	.30
(21)	Bob Watkins	1.00	.50	.30
(22)	Bob Watson	1.00	.50	.30
(23)	Don Wilson	1.00	.50	.30
(24)	Jim Wynn	1.00	.50	.30

Complete Los Angeles Dodgers Album: 12.50 / 6.25 / 3.75

(#)	Player	NM	EX	VG
(1)	Rich Allen	1.50	.70	.45
(2)	Jim Brewer	1.00	.50	.30
(3)	Bill Buckner	1.00	.50	.30
(4)	Willie Crawford	1.00	.50	.30
(5)	Willie Davis	1.00	.50	.30
(6)	Al Downing	1.00	.50	.30
(7)	Steve Garvey	6.00	3.00	1.75
(8)	Billy Grabarkewitz	1.00	.50	.30
(9)	Tom Haller	1.00	.50	.30
(10)	Jim Lefebvre	1.00	.50	.30
(11)	Pete Mikkelsen	1.00	.50	.30
(12)	Joe Moeller	1.00	.50	.30
(13)	Manny Mota	1.00	.50	.30
(14)	Claude Osteen	1.00	.50	.30
(15)	Wes Parker	1.00	.50	.30
(16)	Jose Pena	1.00	.50	.30
(17)	Bill Russell	1.00	.50	.30
(18)	Duke Sims	1.00	.50	.30
(19)	Bill Singer	1.00	.50	.30
(20)	Mike Strahler	1.00	.50	.30
(21)	Bill Sudakis	1.00	.50	.30
(22)	Don Sutton	2.00	1.00	.60
(23)	Jeff Torborg	1.00	.50	.30
(24)	Maury Wills	1.00	.50	.30

Complete Montreal Expos Album: 10.00 / 5.00 / 3.00

(#)	Player	NM	EX	VG
(1)	Bob Bailey	1.00	.50	.30
(2)	John Bateman	1.00	.50	.30
(3)	John Boccabella	1.00	.50	.30
(4)	Ron Brand	1.00	.50	.30
(5)	Boots Day	1.00	.50	.30
(6)	Jim Fairey	1.00	.50	.30
(7)	Ron Fairly	1.00	.50	.30
(8)	Jim Gosger	1.00	.50	.30
(9)	Don Hahn	1.00	.50	.30
(10)	Ron Hunt	1.00	.50	.30
(11)	Mack Jones	1.00	.50	.30
(12)	Jose Laboy	1.00	.50	.30
(13)	Mike Marshall	1.00	.50	.30
(14)	Dan McGinn	1.00	.50	.30
(15)	Carl Morton	1.00	.50	.30
(16)	John O'Donoghue	1.00	.50	.30
(17)	Adolfo Phillips	1.00	.50	.30
(18)	Claude Raymond	1.00	.50	.30
(19)	Steve Renko	1.00	.50	.30
(20)	Marv Staehle	1.00	.50	.30
(21)	Rusty Staub	1.25	.60	.40
(22)	Bill Stoneman	1.00	.50	.30
(23)	Gary Sutherland	1.00	.50	.30
(24)	Bobby Wine	1.00	.50	.30

Complete New York Mets Album: 25.00 / 12.50 / 7.50

(#)	Player	NM	EX	VG
(1)	Tommie Agee	1.00	.50	.30
(2)	Bob Aspromonte	1.00	.50	.30
(3)	Ken Boswell	1.00	.50	.30
(4)	Dean Chance	1.00	.50	.30
(5)	Donn Clendenon	1.00	.50	.30
(6)	Duffy Dyer	1.00	.50	.30
(7)	Dan Frisella	1.00	.50	.30
(8)	Wayne Garrett	1.00	.50	.30
(9)	Gary Gentry	1.00	.50	.30
(10)	Jerry Grote	1.00	.50	.30
(11)	Bud Harrelson	1.00	.50	.30
(12)	Cleon Jones	1.00	.50	.30
(13)	Jerry Koosman	1.00	.50	.30
(14)	Ed Kranepool	1.00	.50	.30
(15)	Dave Marshall	1.00	.50	.30
(16)	Jim McAndrew	1.00	.50	.30
(17)	Tug McGraw	1.00	.50	.30
(18)	Nolan Ryan	20.00	10.00	6.00
(19)	Ray Sadecki	1.00	.50	.30
(20)	Tom Seaver	3.00	1.50	.90
(21)	Art Shamsky	1.00	.50	.30
(22)	Ron Swoboda	1.00	.50	.30
(23)	Ron Taylor	1.00	.50	.30
(24)	Al Weis	1.00	.50	.30

Complete Philadelphia Phillies Album: 10.00 / 5.00 / 3.00

(#)	Player	NM	EX	VG
(1)	Larry Bowa	1.00	.50	.30
(2)	Johnny Briggs	1.00	.50	.30
(3)	Bryon Browne	1.00	.50	.30
(4)	Jim Bunning	2.00	1.00	.60
(5)	Billy Champion	1.00	.50	.30
(6)	Mike Compton	1.00	.50	.30
(7)	Denny Doyle	1.00	.50	.30
(8)	Roger Freed	1.00	.50	.30
(9)	Woody Fryman	1.00	.50	.30
(10)	Oscar Gamble	1.00	.50	.30
(11)	Terry Harmon	1.00	.50	.30
(12)	Larry Hisle	1.00	.50	.30
(13)	Joe Hoerner	1.00	.50	.30
(14)	Deron Johnson	1.00	.50	.30
(15)	Barry Lersch	1.00	.50	.30
(16)	Tim McCarver	1.50	.70	.45
(17)	Don Money	1.00	.50	.30
(18)	Mike Ryan	1.00	.50	.30
(19)	Dick Selma	1.00	.50	.30
(20)	Chris Short	1.00	.50	.30
(21)	Ron Stone	1.00	.50	.30
(22)	Tony Taylor	1.00	.50	.30
(23)	Rick Wise	1.00	.50	.30
(24)	Billy Wilson	1.00	.50	.30

Complete Pittsburgh Pirates Album: 30.00 / 15.00 / 9.00

(#)	Player	NM	EX	VG
(1)	Gene Alley	1.00	.50	.30
(2)	Steve Blass	1.00	.50	.30
(3)	Nelson Briles	1.00	.50	.30
(4)	Jim Campanis	1.00	.50	.30
(5)	Dave Cash	1.00	.50	.30
(6)	Roberto Clemente	10.00	5.00	3.00
(7)	Vic Davalillo	1.00	.50	.30
(8)	Dock Ellis	1.00	.50	.30
(9)	Jim Grant	1.00	.50	.30
(10)	Dave Giusti	1.00	.50	.30
(11)	Richie Hebner	1.00	.50	.30
(12)	Jackie Hernandez	1.00	.50	.30
(13)	Johnny Jeter	1.00	.50	.30
(14)	Lou Marone	1.00	.50	.30
(15)	Jose Martinez	1.00	.50	.30
(16)	Bill Mazeroski	2.50	1.25	.70
(17)	Bob Moose	1.00	.50	.30
(18)	Al Oliver	1.25	.60	.40
(19)	Jose Pagan	1.00	.50	.30
(20)	Bob Robertson	1.00	.50	.30
(21)	Manny Sanguillen	1.00	.50	.30
(22)	Willie Stargell	2.50	1.25	.70
(23)	Bob Veale	1.00	.50	.30
(24)	Luke Walker	1.00	.50	.30

Complete San Diego Padres Album: 10.00 / 5.00 / 3.00

(#)	Player	NM	EX	VG
(1)	Jose Arcia	1.00	.50	.30
(2)	Bob Barton	1.00	.50	.30
(3)	Fred Beene	1.00	.50	.30
(4)	Ollie Brown	1.00	.50	.30
(5)	Dave Campbell	1.00	.50	.30
(6)	Chris Cannizzaro	1.00	.50	.30
(7)	Nate Colbert	1.00	.50	.30
(8)	Mike Corkins	1.00	.50	.30
(9)	Tommy Dean	1.00	.50	.30
(10)	Al Ferrara	1.00	.50	.30
(11)	Rod Gaspar	1.00	.50	.30
(12)	Cito Gaston	1.00	.50	.30
(13)	Enzo Hernandez	1.00	.50	.30
(14)	Clay Kirby	1.00	.50	.30
(15)	Don Mason	1.00	.50	.30
(16)	Ivan Murrell	1.00	.50	.30
(17)	Gerry Nyman	1.00	.50	.30
(18)	Tom Phoebus	1.00	.50	.30
(19)	Dave Roberts	1.00	.50	.30
(20)	Gary Ross	1.00	.50	.30
(21)	Al Santorini	1.00	.50	.30

(22)	Al Severinsen	1.00	.50	.30
(23)	Ron Slocum	1.00	.50	.30
(24)	Ed Spiezio	1.00	.50	.30
	Complete San Francisco Giants Album:	12.50	6.25	3.75
(1)	Bobby Bonds	1.25	.60	.40
(2)	Ron Bryant	1.00	.50	.30
(3)	Don Carrithers	1.00	.50	.30
(4)	John Cumberland	1.00	.50	.30
(5)	Mike Davison	1.00	.50	.30
(6)	Dick Dietz	1.00	.50	.30
(7)	Tito Fuentes	1.00	.50	.30
(8)	Russ Gibson	1.00	.50	.30
(9)	Jim Ray Hart	1.00	.50	.30
(10)	Bob Heise	1.00	.50	.30
(11)	Ken Henderson	1.00	.50	.30
(12)	Steve Huntz	1.00	.50	.30
(13)	Frank Johnson	1.00	.50	.30
(14)	Jerry Johnson	1.00	.50	.30
(15)	Hal Lanier	1.00	.50	.30
(16)	Juan Marichal	2.00	1.00	.60
(17)	Willie Mays	7.50	3.75	2.25
(18)	Willie McCovey	2.50	1.25	.70
(19)	Don McMahon	1.00	.50	.30
(20)	Jim Moyer	1.00	.50	.30
(21)	Gaylord Perry	2.00	1.00	.60
(22)	Frank Reberger	1.00	.50	.30
(23)	Rich Robertson	1.00	.50	.30
(24)	Bernie Williams	1.00	.50	.30
	Complete St. Louis Cardinals Album:	10.00	5.00	3.00
(1)	Matty Alou	1.00	.50	.30
(2)	Jim Beauchamp	1.00	.50	.30
(3)	Frank Bertaina	1.00	.50	.30
(4)	Lou Brock	2.50	1.25	.70
(5)	George Brunet	1.00	.50	.30
(6)	Jose Cardenal	1.00	.50	.30
(7)	Steve Carlton	2.50	1.25	.70
(8)	Moe Drabowsky	1.00	.50	.30
(9)	Bob Gibson	2.50	1.25	.70
(10)	Joe Hague	1.00	.50	.30
(11)	Julian Javier	1.00	.50	.30
(12)	Leron Lee	1.00	.50	.30
(13)	Frank Linzy	1.00	.50	.30
(14)	Dal Maxvill	1.00	.50	.30
(15)	Jerry McNertney	1.00	.50	.30
(16)	Fred Norman	1.00	.50	.30
(17)	Milt Ramirez	1.00	.50	.30
(18)	Dick Schofield	1.00	.50	.30
(19)	Mike Shannon	1.00	.50	.30
(20)	Ted Sizemore	1.00	.50	.30
(21)	Bob Stinson	1.00	.50	.30
(22)	Carl Taylor	1.00	.50	.30
(23)	Joe Torre	1.50	.70	.45
(24)	Mike Torrez	1.00	.50	.30
	Complete Baltimore Orioles Album:	15.00	7.50	4.50
(1)	Mark Belanger	1.00	.50	.30
(2)	Paul Blair	1.00	.50	.30
(3)	Don Buford	1.00	.50	.30
(4)	Terry Crowley	1.00	.50	.30
(5)	Mike Cuellar	1.00	.50	.30
(6)	Clay Dalrymple	1.00	.50	.30
(7)	Pat Dobson	1.00	.50	.30
(8)	Andy Etchebarren	1.00	.50	.30
(9)	Dick Hall	1.00	.50	.30
(10)	Jim Hardin	1.00	.50	.30
(11)	Elrod Hendricks	1.00	.50	.30
(12)	Grant Jackson	1.00	.50	.30
(13)	Dave Johnson	1.00	.50	.30
(14)	Dave Leonhard	1.00	.50	.30
(15)	Marcelino Lopez	1.00	.50	.30
(16)	Dave McNally	1.00	.50	.30
(17)	Curt Motton	1.00	.50	.30
(18)	Jim Palmer	2.00	1.00	.60
(19)	Boog Powell	1.00	.50	.30
(20)	Merv Rettenmund	1.00	.50	.30
(21)	Brooks Robinson	3.00	1.50	.90
(22)	Frank Robinson	3.00	1.50	.90
(23)	Pete Richert	1.00	.50	.30
(24)	Chico Salmon	1.00	.50	.30
	Complete Boston Red Sox Album:	15.00	7.50	4.50
(1)	Luis Aparicio	2.50	1.25	.70
(2)	Bobby Bolin	1.00	.50	.30
(3)	Ken Brett	1.00	.50	.30
(4)	Billy Conigliaro	1.00	.50	.30
(5)	Ray Culp	1.00	.50	.30
(6)	Mike Fiore	1.00	.50	.30
(7)	John Kennedy	1.00	.50	.30
(8)	Cal Koonce	1.00	.50	.30
(9)	Joe Lahoud	1.00	.50	.30
(10)	Bill Lee	1.00	.50	.30
(11)	Jim Lonborg	1.00	.50	.30
(12)	Sparky Lyle	1.00	.50	.30
(13)	Mike Nagy	1.00	.50	.30
(14)	Don Pavletich	1.00	.50	.30
(15)	Gary Peters	1.00	.50	.30
(16)	Rico Petrocelli	1.00	.50	.30
(17)	Vicente Romo	1.00	.50	.30
(18)	Tom Satriano	1.00	.50	.30
(19)	George Scott	1.00	.50	.30
(20)	Sonny Siebert	1.00	.50	.30
(21)	Reggie Smith	1.00	.50	.30
(22)	Jarvis Tatum	1.00	.50	.30
(23)	Ken Tatum	1.00	.50	.30
(24)	Carl Yastrzemski	3.00	1.50	.90
	Complete California Angels Album:	10.00	5.00	3.00
(1)	Sandy Alomar	1.00	.50	.30
(2)	Joe Azcue	1.00	.50	.30
(3)	Ken Berry	1.00	.50	.30
(4)	Gene Brabender	1.00	.50	.30
(5)	Billy Cowan	1.00	.50	.30
(6)	Tony Conigliaro	1.50	.70	.45
(7)	Eddie Fisher	1.00	.50	.30
(8)	Jim Fregosi	1.00	.50	.30
(9)	Tony Gonzales (Gonzalez)	1.00	.50	.30

(10)	Alex Johnson	1.00	.50	.30
(11)	Fred Lasher	1.00	.50	.30
(12)	Jim Maloney	1.00	.50	.30
(13)	Rudy May	1.00	.50	.30
(14)	Ken McMullen	1.00	.50	.30
(15)	Andy Messersmith	1.00	.50	.30
(16)	Gerry Moses	1.00	.50	.30
(17)	Syd O'Brien	1.00	.50	.30
(18)	Mel Queen	1.00	.50	.30
(19)	Roger Repoz	1.00	.50	.30
(20)	Archie Reynolds	1.00	.50	.30
(21)	Chico Ruiz	1.00	.50	.30
(22)	Jim Spencer	1.00	.50	.30
(23)	Clyde Wright	1.00	.50	.30
(24)	Billy Wynne	1.00	.50	.30
	Complete Chicago White Sox Album:	10.00	5.00	3.00
(1)	Luis Alvarado	1.00	.50	.30
(2)	Mike Andrews	1.00	.50	.30
(3)	Tom Egan	1.00	.50	.30
(4)	Steve Hamilton	1.00	.50	.30
(5)	Ed Hermann	1.00	.50	.30
(6)	Joel Horlen	1.00	.50	.30
(7)	Tommy John	1.25	.60	.40
(8)	Bart Johnson	1.00	.50	.30
(9)	Jay Johnstone	1.00	.50	.30
(10)	Duane Josephson	1.00	.50	.30
(11)	Pat Kelly	1.00	.50	.30
(12)	Bobby Knoop	1.00	.50	.30
(13)	Carlos May	1.00	.50	.30
(14)	Lee Maye	1.00	.50	.30
(15)	Tom McGraw	1.00	.50	.30
(16)	Bill Melton	1.00	.50	.30
(17)	Rich Morales	1.00	.50	.30
(18)	Tom Murphy	1.00	.50	.30
(19)	Don O'Riley	1.00	.50	.30
(20)	Rick Reichardt	1.00	.50	.30
(21)	Bill Robinson	1.00	.50	.30
(22)	Bob Spence	1.00	.50	.30
(23)	Walt Williams	1.00	.50	.30
(24)	Wilbur Wood	1.00	.50	.30
	Complete Cleveland Indians Album:	10.00	5.00	3.00
(1)	Rick Austin	1.00	.50	.30
(2)	Buddy Bradford	1.00	.50	.30
(3)	Larry Brown	1.00	.50	.30
(4)	Lou Camilli	1.00	.50	.30
(5)	Vince Colbert	1.00	.50	.30
(6)	Ray Fosse	1.00	.50	.30
(7)	Alan Foster	1.00	.50	.30
(8)	Roy Foster	1.00	.50	.30
(9)	Rich Hand	1.00	.50	.30
(10)	Steve Hargan	1.00	.50	.30
(11)	Ken Harrelson	1.00	.50	.30
(12)	Jack Heidemann	1.00	.50	.30
(13)	Phil Hennigan	1.00	.50	.30
(14)	Dennis Higgins	1.00	.50	.30
(15)	Chuck Hinton	1.00	.50	.30
(16)	Tony Horton	1.00	.50	.30
(17)	Ray Lamb	1.00	.50	.30
(18)	Eddie Leon	1.00	.50	.30
(19)	Sam McDowell	1.00	.50	.30
(20)	Graig Nettles	1.25	.60	.40
(21)	Mike Paul	1.00	.50	.30
(22)	Vada Pinson	1.25	.60	.40
(23)	Ken Suarez	1.00	.50	.30
(24)	Ted Uhlaender	1.00	.50	.30
	Complete Detroit Tigers Album:	10.00	5.00	3.00
(1)	Ed Brinkman	1.00	.50	.30
(2)	Gates Brown	1.00	.50	.30
(3)	Ike Brown	1.00	.50	.30
(4)	Les Cain	1.00	.50	.30
(5)	Norm Cash	1.50	.70	.45
(6)	Joe Coleman	1.00	.50	.30
(7)	Bill Freehan	1.00	.50	.30
(8)	Cesar Gutierrez	1.00	.50	.30
(9)	John Hiller	1.00	.50	.30
(10)	Willie Horton	1.00	.50	.30
(11)	Dalton Jones	1.00	.50	.30
(12)	Al Kaline	3.00	1.50	.90
(13)	Mike Kilkenny	1.00	.50	.30
(14)	Mickey Lolich	1.00	.50	.30
(15)	Dick McAuliffe	1.00	.50	.30
(16)	Joe Niekro	1.00	.50	.30
(17)	Jim Northrup	1.00	.50	.30
(18)	Daryl Patterson	1.00	.50	.30
(19)	Jimmie Price	1.00	.50	.30
(20)	Bob Reed	1.00	.50	.30
(21)	Aurelio Rodriguez	1.00	.50	.30
(22)	Fred Scherman	1.00	.50	.30
(23)	Mickey Stanley	1.00	.50	.30
(24)	Tom Timmermann	1.00	.50	.30
	Complete Kansas City Royals Album:	10.00	5.00	3.00
(1)	Ted Abernathy	1.00	.50	.30
(2)	Wally Bunker	1.00	.50	.30
(3)	Tom Burgmeier	1.00	.50	.30
(4)	Bill Butler	1.00	.50	.30
(5)	Bruce Dal Canton	1.00	.50	.30
(6)	Dick Drago	1.00	.50	.30
(7)	Bobby Floyd	1.00	.50	.30
(8)	Gail Hopkins	1.00	.50	.30
(9)	Joe Keough	1.00	.50	.30
(10)	Ed Kirkpatrick	1.00	.50	.30
(11)	Tom Matchick	1.00	.50	.30
(12)	Jerry May	1.00	.50	.30
(13)	Aurelio Monteagudo	1.00	.50	.30
(14)	Dave Morehead	1.00	.50	.30
(15)	Bob Oliver	1.00	.50	.30
(16)	Amos Otis	1.00	.50	.30
(17)	Fred Patek	1.00	.50	.30
(18)	Lou Piniella	1.25	.60	.40
(19)	Cookie Rojas	1.00	.50	.30
(20)	Jim Rooker	1.00	.50	.30
(21)	Paul Schaal	1.00	.50	.30
(22)	Rich Severson	1.00	.50	.30
(23)	George Spriggs	1.00	.50	.30

(24)	Carl Taylor	1.00	.50	.30
	Complete Milwaukee Brewers Album:	10.00	5.00	3.00
(1)	Dave Baldwin	1.00	.50	.30
(2)	Dick Ellsworth	1.00	.50	.30
(3)	John Gelnar	1.00	.50	.30
(4)	Tommy Harper	1.00	.50	.30
(5)	Mike Hegan	1.00	.50	.30
(6)	Bob Humphreys	1.00	.50	.30
(7)	Andy Kosco	1.00	.50	.30
(8)	Lew Krausse	1.00	.50	.30
(9)	Ted Kubiak	1.00	.50	.30
(10)	Skip Lockwood	1.00	.50	.30
(11)	Dave May	1.00	.50	.30
(12)	Bob Meyer	1.00	.50	.30
(13)	John Morris	1.00	.50	.30
(14)	Marty Pattin	1.00	.50	.30
(15)	Roberto Pena	1.00	.50	.30
(16)	Eduardo Rodriguez	1.00	.50	.30
(17)	Phil Roof	1.00	.50	.30
(18)	Ken Sanders	1.00	.50	.30
(19)	Ted Savage	1.00	.50	.30
(20)	Russ Snyder	1.00	.50	.30
(21)	Bob Tillman	1.00	.50	.30
(22)	Bill Voss	1.00	.50	.30
(23)	Danny Walton	1.00	.50	.30
(24)	Floyd Wicker	1.00	.50	.30
	Complete Minnesota Twins Album:	15.00	7.50	4.50
(1)	Brant Alyea	1.00	.50	.30
(2)	Bert Blyleven	1.00	.50	.30
(3)	Dave Boswell	1.00	.50	.30
(4)	Leo Cardenas	1.00	.50	.30
(5)	Rod Carew	2.50	1.25	.70
(6)	Tom Hall	1.00	.50	.30
(7)	Jim Holt	1.00	.50	.30
(8)	Jim Kaat	1.00	.50	.30
(9)	Harmon Killebrew	2.50	1.25	.70
(10)	Charlie Manuel	1.00	.50	.30
(11)	George Mitterwald	1.00	.50	.30
(12)	Tony Oliva	1.25	.60	.40
(13)	Ron Perranoski	1.00	.50	.30
(14)	Jim Perry	1.00	.50	.30
(15)	Frank Quilici	1.00	.50	.30
(16)	Rich Reese	1.00	.50	.30
(17)	Rick Renick	1.00	.50	.30
(18)	Danny Thompson	1.00	.50	.30
(19)	Luis Tiant	1.00	.50	.30
(20)	Tom Tischinski	1.00	.50	.30
(21)	Cesar Tovar	1.00	.50	.30
(22)	Stan Williams	1.00	.50	.30
(23)	Dick Woodson	1.00	.50	.30
(24)	Bill Zepp	1.00	.50	.30
	Complete New York Yankees Album:	15.00	7.50	4.50
(1)	Jack Aker	1.00	.50	.30
(2)	Stan Bahnsen	1.00	.50	.30
(3)	Curt Blefary	1.00	.50	.30
(4)	Bill Burbach	1.00	.50	.30
(5)	Danny Cater	1.00	.50	.30
(6)	Horace Clarke	1.00	.50	.30
(7)	John Ellis	1.00	.50	.30
(8)	Jake Gibbs	1.00	.50	.30
(9)	Ron Hansen	1.00	.50	.30
(10)	Mike Kekich	1.00	.50	.30
(11)	Jerry Kenney	1.00	.50	.30
(12)	Ron Klimkowski	1.00	.50	.30
(13)	Steve Kline	1.00	.50	.30
(14)	Mike McCormick	1.00	.50	.30
(15)	Lindy McDaniel	1.00	.50	.30
(16)	Gene Michael	1.00	.50	.30
(17)	Thurman Munson	1.50	.70	.45
(18)	Bobby Murcer	1.25	.60	.40
(19)	Fritz Peterson	1.00	.50	.30
(20)	Mel Stottlemyre	1.00	.50	.30
(21)	Pete Ward	1.00	.50	.30
(22)	Gary Waslewski	1.00	.50	.30
(23)	Roy White	1.00	.50	.30
(24)	Ron Woods	1.00	.50	.30
	Complete Oakland A's Album:	15.00	7.50	4.50
(1)	Felipe Alou	1.00	.50	.30
(2)	Sal Bando	1.00	.50	.30
(3)	Vida Blue	1.00	.50	.30
(4)	Bert Campaneris	1.00	.50	.30
(5)	Ron Clark	1.00	.50	.30
(6)	Chuck Dobson	1.00	.50	.30
(7)	Dave Duncan	1.00	.50	.30
(8)	Frank Fernandez	1.00	.50	.30
(9)	Rollie Fingers	2.00	1.00	.60
(10)	Dick Green	1.00	.50	.30
(11)	Steve Hovley	1.00	.50	.30
(12)	Catfish Hunter	2.00	1.00	.60
(13)	Reggie Jackson	6.00	3.00	1.75
(14)	Marcel Lacheman	1.00	.50	.30
(15)	Paul Lindblad	1.00	.50	.30
(16)	Bob Locker	1.00	.50	.30
(17)	Don Mincher	1.00	.50	.30
(18)	Rick Monday	1.00	.50	.30
(19)	John Odom	1.00	.50	.30
(20)	Jim Roland	1.00	.50	.30
(21)	Joe Rudi	1.00	.50	.30
(22)	Diego Segui	1.00	.50	.30
(23)	Bob Stickels	1.00	.50	.30
(24)	Gene Tenace	1.00	.50	.30
	Complete Washington Senators Album:	12.50	6.25	3.75
(1)	Bernie Allen	1.00	.50	.30
(2)	Dick Bosman	1.00	.50	.30
(3)	Jackie Brown	1.00	.50	.30
(4)	Paul Casanova	1.00	.50	.30
(5)	Casey Cox	1.00	.50	.30
(6)	Tim Cullen	1.00	.50	.30
(7)	Mike Epstein	1.00	.50	.30
(8)	Curt Flood	1.25	.60	.40
(9)	Joe Foy	1.00	.50	.30
(10)	Jim French	1.00	.50	.30
(11)	Bill Gogolewski	1.00	.50	.30

(12)	Tom Grieve	1.00	.50	.30
(13)	Joe Grzenda	1.00	.50	.30
(14)	Frank Howard	1.25	.60	.40
(15)	Joe Janeski	1.00	.50	.30
(16)	Darold Knowles	1.00	.50	.30
(17)	Elliott Maddox	1.00	.50	.30
(18)	Denny McLain	1.25	.60	.40
(19)	Dave Nelson	1.00	.50	.30
(20)	Horacio Pina	1.00	.50	.30
(21)	Jim Shellenback	1.00	.50	.30
(22)	Ed Stroud	1.00	.50	.30
(23)	Del Unser	1.00	.50	.30
(24)	Don Wert	1.00	.50	.30

1933 DeLong (R333)

The DeLong Co. of Boston was among the first to sell baseball cards with gum, issuing a set of 24 cards in 1933. DeLong cards measure about 1-15/16" x 2-15/16", with black-and-white player photos on a color background. The photos show the players in various action poses and positions them in the middle of a miniature stadium setting so that they appear to be giants. Most of the cards are vertically designed, but a few are horizontal. Backs were by Austen Lake, editor of the Boston Transcript, and contain tips to help youngsters become better ballplayers. The ACC designation for this set is R333.

		NM	EX	VG
Complete Set (24):		30,000	8,000	4,000
Common Player:		700.00	280.00	140.00
1	"Marty" McManus	1,260	280.00	140.00
2	Al Simmons	945.00	385.00	190.00
3	Oscar Melillo	700.00	280.00	140.00
4	William (Bill) Terry	945.00	385.00	190.00
5	Charlie Gehringer	945.00	385.00	190.00
6	Gordon (Mickey) Cochrane	945.00	385.00	190.00
7	Lou Gehrig	7,700	3,080	1,260
8	Hazen S. (Kiki) Cuyler	945.00	385.00	190.00
9	Bill Urbanski	700.00	280.00	140.00
10	Frank J. (Lefty) O'Doul	980.00	395.00	195.00
11	Freddie Lindstrom	945.00	385.00	190.00
12	Harold (Pie) Traynor	945.00	385.00	190.00
13	"Rabbit" Maranville	945.00	385.00	190.00
14	Vernon "Lefty" Gomez	945.00	385.00	190.00
15	Riggs Stephenson	700.00	280.00	140.00
16	Lon Warneke	700.00	280.00	140.00
17	Pepper Martin	700.00	280.00	140.00
18	Jimmy Dykes	700.00	280.00	140.00
19	Chick Hafey	945.00	385.00	190.00
20	Joe Vosmik	700.00	280.00	140.00
21	Jimmy Foxx (Jimmie)	1,600	800.00	475.00
22	Charles (Chuck) Klein	945.00	385.00	190.00
23	Robert (Lefty) Grove	1,540	595.00	300.00
24	"Goose" Goslin	945.00	385.00	190.00

1934 Al Demaree Die-Cuts (R304)

Among the rarest 1930s gum cards are those issued by Dietz Gum Co., a Chicago confectioner, in packages of "Ball Players in Action Chewing Gum." The cards are so rare that the complete checklist may never be known. The set was cataloged as R304 in the American Card Catalog. The cards feature photographic portraits of players set upon cartoon bodies drawn by former major league pitcher Demaree. The photo and artwork are generally in black-and-white, while the players on some teams have blue or red uniform details printed on. The cards can be folded to create a stand-up figure, but did not have a background to be cut or torn away, as is common with most die-cut baseball cards. Unfolded, the cards measure 6-1/2" long and from 1-5/8" to 1-3/4" wide, depending on pose.

		NM	EX	VG
Common Player:		500.00	250.00	150.00
1	Lyn Lary	1,000	500.00	300.00
3	Earle Combs	1,650	825.00	495.00
4	Babe Ruth	12,500	6,250	3,750
5	Sam Byrd	1,200	600.00	350.00
6	Tony Lazzeri	1,650	825.00	495.00
7	Frank Crosetti	1,500	750.00	450.00
9	Lou Gehrig	12,000	6,000	3,600
10	Lefty Gomez	1,650	825.00	495.00
11	Mule Haas	1,000	500.00	300.00
12	Evar Swenson	1,000	500.00	300.00
13	Marv Shea	1,000	500.00	300.00
14	Al Simmons/Throwing	1,650	825.00	495.00
15	Jack Hayes	1,000	500.00	300.00
16	Al Simmons/Btg	1,650	825.00	495.00
17	Jimmy Dykes	1,000	500.00	300.00
18	Luke Appling	1,650	825.00	495.00
19	Ted Lyons	1,650	825.00	495.00
20	Red Kress	1,000	500.00	300.00
21	Gee Walker	1,000	500.00	300.00
22	Charlie Gehringer	1,650	825.00	495.00
23	Mickey Cochrane/Catching	1,650	825.00	495.00
24	Mickey Cochrane/Btg	1,650	825.00	495.00
25	Pete Fox	1,000	500.00	300.00
26	Firpo Marberry	1,000	500.00	300.00
28	Mickey Owen	1,000	500.00	300.00
29	Hank Greenberg	2,500	1,250	750.00
30	Goose Goslin	1,650	825.00	495.00
31	Earl Averill	1,650	825.00	495.00
32	Frankie Pytlak	1,000	500.00	300.00
33	Willie Kamm	1,000	500.00	300.00
34	Johnny Burnett	1,000	500.00	300.00
35	Joe Vosmik	1,000	500.00	300.00
36	Dick Porter	1,000	500.00	300.00
38	Harley Boss	1,000	500.00	300.00
39	Joe Vismik	1,000	500.00	300.00
40	Orel Hildebrand	1,000	500.00	300.00
41	Jack Burns	1,000	500.00	300.00
42	Frank Grube	1,000	500.00	300.00
43	Oscar Melillo	1,000	500.00	300.00
44	Sam West	1,000	500.00	300.00
45	Ray Pepper	1,000	500.00	300.00
46	Bruce Campbell	1,000	500.00	300.00
47	Sam West	1,000	500.00	300.00
48	Art Scharein	1,000	500.00	300.00
49	George Blaeholder	1,000	500.00	300.00
50	Rogers Hornsby	2,200	1,100	660.00
51	Eric McNair	1,000	500.00	300.00
52	Bob Johnson	1,000	500.00	300.00
53	Pinky Higgins	1,000	500.00	300.00
54	Jimmie Foxx	2,500	1,250	750.00
56	Dib Williams	1,000	500.00	300.00
57	Lou Finney	1,000	500.00	300.00
60	Ray Mahaffey	1,000	500.00	300.00
61	Ossie Bluege	1,000	500.00	300.00
62	Luke Sewell	1,000	500.00	300.00
63	John Stone	1,000	500.00	300.00
64	Joe Cronin	1,650	825.00	495.00
65	Joe Cronin	1,650	825.00	495.00
66	Buddy Myer	1,000	500.00	300.00
67	Earl Whitehill	1,000	500.00	300.00
68	Fred Schulte	1,000	500.00	300.00
70	Joe Kuhel	1,000	500.00	300.00
71	Ed Morgan	1,000	500.00	300.00
73	Rick Ferrell	1,650	825.00	495.00
74	Carl Reynolds	1,000	500.00	300.00
76	Bill Cissell	1,000	500.00	300.00
77	Johnny Hodapp	1,000	500.00	300.00
78	Dusty Cooke	1,000	500.00	300.00
79	Lefty Grove	1,650	825.00	495.00
80	Max Bishop	1,000	500.00	300.00
81	Hughie Critz	1,000	500.00	300.00
82	Gus Mancuso	1,000	500.00	300.00
83	Kiddo Davis	1,000	500.00	300.00
84	Blondy Ryan	1,000	500.00	300.00
86	Travis Jackson	1,650	825.00	495.00
87	Mel Ott	2,200	1,100	650.00
89	Bill Terry	1,650	825.00	495.00
90	Carl Hubbell	2,200	1,100	650.00
91	Tony Cuccinello	1,000	500.00	300.00
92	Al Lopez	1,650	825.00	495.00
94	Johnny Frederick	1,000	500.00	300.00
95	Glenn Wright	1,000	500.00	300.00
96	Hack Wilson	1,650	825.00	495.00
97	Danny Taylor	1,000	500.00	300.00
98	Van Mungo	1,000	500.00	300.00
99	John Frederick	1,000	500.00	300.00
100	Sam Leslie	1,000	500.00	300.00
101	Sparky Adams	1,000	500.00	300.00
102a	Mark Koenig	1,000	500.00	300.00
102b	Ernie Lombardi	1,650	825.00	495.00
104	Tony Piet	1,000	500.00	300.00
105	Chick Hafey	1,650	825.00	495.00
107	Syl Johnson	1,000	500.00	300.00
108	Jim Bottomley	1,650	825.00	495.00
109	Chick Hafey	1,650	825.00	495.00
110	Adam Comorosky	1,000	500.00	300.00
111	Dick Bartell	1,000	500.00	300.00
112	Harvey Hendrick	1,000	500.00	300.00
114	Fritz Knothe	1,000	500.00	300.00
115	Don Hurst/Btg	1,000	500.00	300.00
117	Prince Oana	1,800	900.00	550.00
118	Ed Holley	1,000	500.00	300.00
120	Don Hurst/Throwing	1,000	500.00	300.00
121	Spud Davis	1,000	500.00	300.00
122	George Watkins	1,000	500.00	300.00
123	Frankie Frisch	1,650	825.00	495.00
124	Pepper Martin/Btg	1,000	500.00	300.00
125	Ripper Collins	1,000	500.00	300.00
126	Dizzy Dean	2,500	1,250	750.00
127	Pepper Martin/Fldg	1,000	500.00	300.00
128	Joe Medwick	1,650	825.00	495.00
129	Leo Durocher	1,650	825.00	495.00
130	Ernie Orsatti	1,000	500.00	300.00
131	Buck Jordan	1,000	500.00	300.00
132	Shanty Hogan	1,000	500.00	300.00
133a	Wes Shulmerich (Schulmerich)	1,000	500.00	300.00
133b	Randy Moore	1,000	500.00	300.00
134	Billy Urbanski	1,000	500.00	300.00
135	Wally Berger	1,000	500.00	300.00
136	Pinky Whitney	1,000	500.00	300.00
137	Wally Berger	1,000	500.00	300.00
139	Rabbit Maranville	1,650	825.00	495.00
140	Ben Cantwell	1,000	500.00	300.00
141	Gus Suhr	1,000	500.00	300.00
142	Earl Grace	1,000	500.00	300.00
143	Fred Lindstrom	2,200	1,100	660.00
144	Arky Vaughan	1,650	825.00	495.00
145	Pie Traynor/Hitting	1,650	825.00	495.00
146	Tommy Thevenow	1,000	500.00	300.00
147	Lloyd Waner	1,650	825.00	495.00
148	Paul Waner	1,650	825.00	495.00
149	Pie Traynor/Throwing	1,650	825.00	495.00
150	Larry French	1,000	500.00	300.00
151	Kiki Cuyler	1,650	825.00	495.00
152	Gabby Hartnett	1,650	825.00	495.00
153	Chuck Klein/Throwing	1,650	825.00	495.00
154	Chuck Klein	1,650	825.00	495.00
155a	Bill Jurges	1,000	500.00	300.00
155b	Jimmy Foxx	2,500	1,250	750.00
156	Woody English	1,000	500.00	300.00
157	Lonnie Warnecke	1,000	500.00	300.00
158	Billy Herman	1,650	825.00	495.00
159	Babe Herman	1,200	600.00	350.00
160	Charlie Grimm	1,000	500.00	300.00
161	Cy Rigler/Umpire	1,800	900.00	550.00
162	Bill Klem/Umpire	2,500	1,250	750.00
163	Cy Pfirman	1,000	500.00	300.00
165	Bill Dineen (Dinneen)	1,200	600.00	350.00
166	Charlie Moran	1,000	500.00	300.00
167	George Hildebrand/Umpire	1,000	500.00	300.00

1950-51 Denia Puerto Rican League

JIM DAVIS

This issue was produced in conjunction with the 1950-51 Puerto Rican League winter season. Measurements vary slightly from a norm of about 1-3/4" x 2-1/8". Cards have colorized portrait photos with blank backs, probably intended to be glued into an album. Cards are unnumbered. This checklist is alphabetized, with gaps left for what is believed to be 57 uncataloged cards. Some of the players are veterans of the Negro Leagues and American major and minor leagues. Black-and-white reprints of the cards are known. A few cards have been found with a prize-redemption stamp on back.

		NM	EX	VG
Common Player:		125.00	65.00	40.00
(1)	Alberto Alberdeston	125.00	65.00	40.00
(2)	Jaime Almendro	125.00	65.00	40.00
(3)	Yiyo Alonso	125.00	65.00	40.00
(4)	Luis (Tite) Arroyo	150.00	75.00	45.00
(5)	Pedro J. Arroyo	125.00	65.00	40.00
(6)	Joe Atkins	150.00	75.00	45.00
(7)	Eugene Baker	200.00	100.00	60.00
(8)	Dan Bankhead	200.00	100.00	60.00
(9)	Sammy Bankhead	1,200	600.00	360.00
(10)	Ramon Bayron	125.00	65.00	40.00
(11)	Hiram Bithorn	200.00	100.00	60.00
(12)	Rafael Blasini	125.00	65.00	40.00
(13)	Bob Boyd	150.00	75.00	45.00
(14)	Roger Breard	125.00	65.00	40.00
(15)	Stan Breard	125.00	65.00	40.00
(16)	Barney Brown	1,000	500.00	300.00
(17)	Raymond Brown	2,000	1,000	600.00
(18)	Willard Brown	2,000	1,000	600.00
(19)	Jose A. Burgos	125.00	65.00	40.00
(20)	Joe Buzas	125.00	65.00	40.00
(21)	Luis R. Cabrera	125.00	65.00	40.00
(22)	Rafael Casanovas	125.00	65.00	40.00
(23)	N. Zurdo Castro	125.00	65.00	40.00
(24)	Perucho Cepeda	800.00	400.00	240.00
(25)	T. Gomez Checo	125.00	65.00	40.00
(26)	Al Cihoki (Cihocki)	125.00	65.00	40.00
(27)	Buster Clarkson	250.00	125.00	75.00
(28)	Francisco Coimbre	800.00	400.00	240.00
(29)	Eugene Collins	350.00	175.00	105.00
(30)	Monchile Concepcion	150.00	75.00	45.00
(31)	Charlie Corin	125.00	65.00	40.00
(32)	Herminio Cortfu	125.00	65.00	40.00
(33)	Johnny Cox	125.00	65.00	40.00
(34)	George Crowe	200.00	100.00	60.00

(35)	Jim Davis	125.00	65.00	40.00
(36)	Johnny Davis	450.00	225.00	135.00
(37)	Piper Davis	450.00	225.00	135.00
(38)	Leon Day	6,000	3,000	1,800
(39)	Ellis "Cot" Deal	150.00	75.00	45.00
(40)	Jack Dittmer	125.00	65.00	40.00
(41)	Verdes Drake	150.00	75.00	45.00
(42)	Saturnino Escalera	125.00	65.00	40.00
(43)	C. Guillaro Estrella	125.00	65.00	40.00
(44)	S. Federico	125.00	65.00	40.00
(45)	Dumbo Fernandez	125.00	65.00	40.00
(46)	Elias Frias	125.00	65.00	40.00
(47)	Les Fusselmann (Fusselman)	125.00	65.00	40.00
(48)	Felipe Garcia	125.00	65.00	40.00
(49)	(Carden) Gillenwater	125.00	65.00	40.00
(50)	Jim Gilliam	250.00	125.00	75.00
(51)	Ruben Gomez	200.00	100.00	60.00
(52)	Faelo Gonzalez	125.00	65.00	40.00
(53)	Gely Goyco	125.00	65.00	40.00
(54)	Jack Harshmann (Harshman)	125.00	65.00	40.00
(55)	Rudy Hernandez	125.00	65.00	40.00
(56)	Roy Hughes	125.00	65.00	40.00
(57)	Pachy Irizarry	125.00	65.00	40.00
(58)	Indian (Indio) Jiminez	125.00	65.00	40.00
(59)	Sam Jones	125.00	65.00	40.00
(60)	Walt Judnich	125.00	65.00	40.00
(61)	Russ Kearns	125.00	65.00	40.00
(62)	Billy Klaus	150.00	75.00	45.00
(63)	Jim Lamarque	350.00	175.00	105.00
(64)	Red Lynn	125.00	65.00	40.00
(65)	Bob Malloy	125.00	65.00	40.00
(66)	Clifford Mapes	125.00	65.00	40.00
(67)	Canena Marquez	450.00	225.00	135.00
(68)	Achin Matos	125.00	65.00	40.00
(69)	Benny Meyers	125.00	65.00	40.00
(70)	Henry Miller	150.00	75.00	45.00
(71)	Oscar Mir Flores	125.00	65.00	40.00
(72)	Jose E. Montalvo	125.00	65.00	40.00
(73)	Willie Morales	125.00	65.00	40.00
(74)	Gallego Munoz	125.00	65.00	40.00
(75)	Earl Naylor	125.00	65.00	40.00
(76)	Ernest Nevel	125.00	65.00	40.00
(77)	Don Nicholas	125.00	65.00	40.00
(78)	John O'Donnell	125.00	65.00	40.00
(79)	Guayuvin Olivo	150.00	75.00	45.00
(80)	Miguel Payano	125.00	65.00	40.00
(81)	Les Peden	125.00	65.00	40.00
(82)	Juan Perez	125.00	65.00	40.00
(83)	Palomo Perez	125.00	65.00	40.00
(84)	German Pizarro	125.00	65.00	40.00
(85)	Dave Pope	150.00	75.00	45.00
(86)	Milton Ralat	125.00	65.00	40.00
(87)	Enrique Reinoso	125.00	65.00	40.00
(88)	Roberto Rivera	125.00	65.00	40.00
(89)	Julio Rodriguez	125.00	65.00	40.00
(90)	Pedro Rodriguez	125.00	65.00	40.00
(91)	Domingo Rosello	125.00	65.00	40.00
(92)	Joe Rossi	125.00	65.00	40.00
(93)	Miguel Rueda	125.00	65.00	40.00
(94)	Ramon Salgado	125.00	65.00	40.00
(95)	Juan Sanchez	125.00	65.00	40.00
(96)	Carlos M. Santiago	125.00	65.00	40.00
(97)	Jose G. Santiago	125.00	65.00	40.00
(98)	V. Scarpatte	125.00	65.00	40.00
(99)	Jose Seda	125.00	65.00	40.00
(100)	Barney Serrell	350.00	175.00	105.00
(101)	Al Smith	200.00	100.00	60.00
(102)	Jose St. Clair	125.00	65.00	40.00
(103)	Tetelo Sterling	125.00	65.00	40.00
(104)	Russ Sullivan	125.00	65.00	40.00
(105)	Lonnie Summers	150.00	75.00	45.00
(106)	Jim Tabor	125.00	65.00	40.00
(107)	Bert Thiel	125.00	65.00	40.00
(108)	Valmy Thomas	125.00	65.00	40.00
(109)	Bob Thurman	350.00	175.00	105.00
(110)	Tiant Tineo	125.00	65.00	40.00
(111)	Gilberto Torres	125.00	65.00	40.00
(112)	Manuel Traboux	125.00	65.00	40.00
(113)	Joe Tuminelli	125.00	65.00	40.00
(114)	Jose L. Velazquez	125.00	65.00	40.00
(115)	Ben Wade	150.00	75.00	45.00
(116)	Johnny Williams	250.00	125.00	75.00
(117)	Marvin Williams	150.00	75.00	45.00
(118)	Artie Wilson	450.00	225.00	135.00
(119)	Pedrin Zorrilla	125.00	65.00	40.00
(120)	Pito entrevista a Hornsby	300.00	150.00	90.00
(121)	El galardon del triunfo	125.00	65.00	40.00
(122)	Fanaticos de alta posicion	125.00	65.00	40.00
(123)	VOLO LA VERJA	125.00	65.00	40.00

1950-51 Denia Puerto Rican League - Action

115- Gilliam dió out a Casanovas

These 2-1/2" x 3-1/2" cards are part of a set of about 150 covering many different sports. The pictures are colorized photographs and the cards are blank-backed, intended to be glued into an album. The number of baseball subjects is not known. Confirmed subjects are listed here, with identified players listed parenthetically.

		NM	EX	VG
Common Card:		50.00	25.00	15.00
1	Tetelo tambien joronea. (Tetelo Vargas)	85.00	40.00	25.00
2	Taborn saca en home. (Earl Taborn)	50.00	25.00	15.00
3	Se la aguo la blanqueada.	50.00	25.00	15.00
4	R. Blasini se lesiona. (Rafael Blasini)	50.00	25.00	15.00
5	Atkins mofa, Polaco safe. (Joe Atkins)	50.00	25.00	15.00
6	CERCADO-	50.00	25.00	15.00
7	Pitcher se desliza - safe.	50.00	25.00	15.00
8	Fdo. Ramos tras homer (Fernando Ramos)	50.00	25.00	15.00
9	Wilson safe en terecera. (Artie Wilson)	110.00	55.00	32.50
10	Tiro malo - SAFE.	50.00	25.00	15.00
11	VILLODAS LO ESPERA - OUT. (Luis Villodas)	50.00	25.00	15.00
12	Perry da out a Gilliam - (Alonso Perry, Jim Gilliam)	85.00	40.00	25.00
13	Safe en primera -	50.00	25.00	15.00
14	Medina obsequia a Brown. (Medina Chapman, Willard Brown)	200.00	100.00	60.00
15	Tiro malo, Almendaro anota. (Jaime Almendro)	50.00	25.00	15.00
16	Ramos toco primero - OUT. (Fernando Ramos)	50.00	25.00	15.00
17	Brazo contra brazo -	50.00	25.00	15.00
18	Pedroso felicitado tras homer - (Fernando Pedroso)	50.00	25.00	15.00
19	QUE PASA, CEFO? (Cefo Conde)	50.00	25.00	15.00
20	Canena estafa home - (Canena Marquez)	65.00	30.00	20.00
21	Buen slide - SAFE.	50.00	25.00	15.00
22	Mucha vista, Powell. (Bill Powell)	50.00	25.00	15.00
23	OUT FORZADO.	50.00	25.00	15.00
24	Alomar out en home. (Guinea Alomar)	50.00	25.00	15.00
25	Regreso a base - SAFE.	50.00	25.00	15.00
26	Pitcher trata sorprender - SAFE.	50.00	25.00	15.00
27	LOS RECUERDA USTED?	50.00	25.00	15.00
28	Leo Thomas sale de juego. (Leo Thomas)	50.00	25.00	15.00
29	Atkins es felicitado por tribu. (Joe Atkins)	50.00	25.00	15.00
30	Trio campeonil cagueno (Manuel Hernandez, Quincy Trouppe, Chet Brewer)	135.00	65.00	40.00
31	Llegando y llegando -	50.00	25.00	15.00
32	El fotografoen accion -	50.00	25.00	15.00
33	El fotografo en accion	50.00	25.00	15.00
34	No me toques Arroyito - OUT. (Luis "Tite" Arroyo)	50.00	25.00	15.00
35	Taborn propina out. (Earl Taborn)	50.00	25.00	15.00
36	El Mucaro conecta homer - (Bob Thurman)	65.00	30.00	20.00
37	PANTALONES Y FALDAS. (Jose G. Santiago)	50.00	25.00	15.00
38	Buzas en la derrota. (Joe Buzas)	50.00	25.00	15.00
39	El Gran Jurado se reune. (Raymond Brown)	135.00	65.00	40.00
40	Canena se desliza - (Canena Marquez)	65.00	30.00	20.00
41	Que dijo el umpire?	50.00	25.00	15.00
42	Bernier sabe escurrirse - (Carlos Bernier)	50.00	25.00	15.00
43	Se la escapo, la bola - SAFE.	50.00	25.00	15.00
44	Squeeze play perfecto.	50.00	25.00	15.00
45	Cuidado, que la lleva!	50.00	25.00	15.00
46	Que el umpire diga -	50.00	25.00	15.00
47	Pepe Lucas boto la bola. (Pepe Lucas)	50.00	25.00	15.00
48	Gachito se apunta hit.	50.00	25.00	15.00
49	Peloteros o Luchadores?	50.00	25.00	15.00
50	Otoniel lo toca - OUT. (Otoniel Ortiz)	50.00	25.00	15.00
51	Premian a Jorge Rosas. (Jorge Rosas)	50.00	25.00	15.00
52	Markland dio homerun - (Jim Markland)	50.00	25.00	15.00
53	Blasini safe en primera. (Rafael Blasini)	50.00	25.00	15.00
54	Graham conecto homer - (Jack Graham)	50.00	25.00	15.00
55	Penalver se prepara - SAFE.	50.00	25.00	15.00
56	No quiere riesgos	50.00	25.00	15.00
57	Bin Torres esquiva - SAFE. (Bin Torres)	50.00	25.00	15.00
58	Mutua embestida- SAFE.	50.00	25.00	15.00
59	Lo sacaron a media base.	50.00	25.00	15.00
60	Llego transqueando.	50.00	25.00	15.00
61	Quedate quieto - dice el coach.	50.00	25.00	15.00
62	Buscando en vano su presa -	50.00	25.00	15.00
63	Besando la base?	50.00	25.00	15.00
64	Pescaron al Jueyito. (Jueyito Andrade)	50.00	25.00	15.00
65	Greco da tremendo toletazo.	50.00	25.00	15.00
66	Thomas catcher, Wallaesa al bate. (Valmy Thomas, Jack Wallaesa)	50.00	25.00	15.00
67	Trofeos de TRIPLE CAMPEON.	50.00	25.00	15.00
74	H. Reyes lanza, Sanchez Batea. (Herminio Reyes, Juan Sanchez)	50.00	25.00	15.00
77	Wilson apacigua a Bernier . . . (Artie Wilson, Carlos Bernier)	85.00	40.00	25.00
78	Cogida de cuatro estrellas . . .	50.00	25.00	15.00

80	Davis out de Gachito - Wallaesa . . . (Johnny Davis, Jack Wallaesa)	50.00	25.00	15.00
81	Arroyo busca double-play. (Pedro J. Arroyo)	50.00	25.00	15.00
82	Ruben sale por lesion. (Ruben Gomez)	50.00	25.00	15.00
83	SAFE EN EL PLATO.	50.00	25.00	15.00
84	Buen esfuerzo, pero en vano	50.00	25.00	15.00
85	ESTAS TRISTE, JONES? (Sam Jones)	50.00	25.00	15.00
87	Equipo ESTRELLAS NATIVAS	50.00	25.00	15.00
88	Arroyo batea, Scarpatte recibe (Pedro J. Arroyo, V. Scarpatte)	50.00	25.00	15.00
93	Cihoki recoge . . . out (Al Cihocki)	50.00	25.00	15.00
95	El arbitro pensativo . . . out.	50.00	25.00	15.00
97	Buena atrapada . . . del fotografo.	50.00	25.00	15.00
103	Villodas da hit. . . (Luis Villodas)	50.00	25.00	15.00
106	HIT EL BATAZO . . .	50.00	25.00	15.00
110	LO COGIERON LLEGANDO . . .	50.00	25.00	15.00
115	Gilliam dio out a Casanovas (Jim Gilliam, Rafael Casanovas)	85.00	40.00	15.00
124	Canena pone fuera a Bernier . . . (Canena Marquez, Carlos Bernier)	50.00	25.00	15.00
137	Terminado el swing . . .	50.00	25.00	15.00

1932 Charles Denby Cigars Cubs

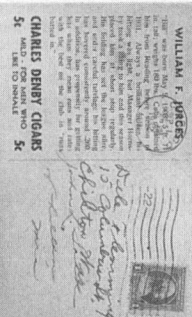

This series of Chicago Cubs postcards was issued by the Fendrich Cigar Co., Evansville, Ind., to promote its Charles Denby brand in 1932. It is the last major tobacco-card issue produced before World War II. The cards are a standard post-card size (5-1/4" x 3-3/8") and feature a glossy black-and-white player photo with a facsimile autograph. In typical post-card style, the back of the card is divided in half, with a printed player profile on the left and room for the mailing address on the right. The back also includes an advertisement for Charles Denby Cigars, the mild five-cent cigar "for men who like to inhale." Eight players are known but more may exist.

		NM	EX	VG
Complete Set (8):		3,750	1,850	1,100
Common Player:		500.00	200.00	100.00
(1)	Hazen Cuyler	625.00	250.00	125.00
(2)	Elwood English	500.00	200.00	100.00
(3)	Charles J. Grimm	500.00	200.00	100.00
(4)	William Herman	750.00	300.00	150.00
(5)	Rogers Hornsby	1,000	400.00	200.00
(6)	William F. Jurges	500.00	200.00	100.00
(7)	Riggs Stephenson	500.00	200.00	100.00
(8)	Lonnie Warneke	500.00	200.00	100.00

1909 Derby Cigars N.Y. Giants

Although there is no advertising on these cards to indicate their origin, it is believed that this set was issued by Derby Cigars, a product of American Tobacco Co. A dozen subjects, all New York Giants, have been found. The cards, many of which appear to be hand-cut measure about 1-3/4" x 2-3/4". The cards feature an oval black-and-white player portrait on a red background. The player's name and position are in a white strip at bottom.

		NM	EX	VG
Complete Set (12):		45,000	22,500	13,500
Common Player:		3,700	1,850	1,100
(1)	Josh Devore	3,700	1,850	1,100
(2)	Larry Doyle	3,700	1,850	1,100
(3)	Art Fletcher	3,700	1,850	1,100
(4)	Buck Herzog	3,700	1,850	1,100
(5)	Rube Marquard	4,250	2,100	1,275
(6)	Christy Mathewson	8,500	4,250	2,500
(7)	Fred Merkle	3,700	1,850	1,100
(8)	Chief Meyers	3,700	1,850	1,100
(9)	Red Murray	3,700	1,850	1,100
(10)	John McGraw	3,700	1,850	1,100
(11)	Fred Snodgrass	3,700	1,850	1,100
(12)	Hooks Wiltse	3,700	1,850	1,100

1977 Detroit Caesars Discs

Virtually identical in format to the several locally sponsored disc sets of the previous year, these 3-3/8" diameter player discs were sponsored by a professional slow-pitch softball team. Discs once again feature black-and-white player portrait photos in the center of a baseball design. The left and right panels are in one of several bright colors. Licensed by the Players Association through Mike Schechter Associates, the player photos carry no uniform logos. Backs are printed in green. The unnumbered discs are checklisted here alphabetically.

		NM	EX	VG
Complete Set (70):		125.00	65.00	35.00
Common Player:		2.50	1.25	.75
(1)	Sal Bando	2.50	1.25	.75
(2)	Buddy Bell	2.50	1.25	.75
(3)	Johnny Bench	6.00	3.00	1.75
(4)	Larry Bowa	2.50	1.25	.75
(5)	Steve Braun	2.50	1.25	.75
(6)	George Brett	15.00	7.50	4.50
(7)	Lou Brock	6.00	3.00	1.75
(8)	Jeff Burroughs	2.50	1.25	.75
(9)	Bert Campaneris	2.50	1.25	.75
(10)	John Candelaria	2.50	1.25	.75
(11)	Jose Cardenal	2.50	1.25	.75
(12)	Rod Carew	4.50	2.25	1.25
(13)	Steve Carlton	4.50	2.25	1.25
(14)	Dave Cash	2.50	1.25	.75
(15)	Cesar Cedeno	2.50	1.25	.75
(16)	Ron Cey	2.50	1.25	.75
(17)	Dave Concepcion	2.50	1.25	.75
(18)	Dennis Eckersley	3.00	1.50	.90
(19)	Mark Fidrych	5.00	2.50	1.50
(20)	Rollie Fingers	5.00	2.50	1.50
(21)	Carlton Fisk	6.00	3.00	1.75
(22)	George Foster	2.50	1.25	.75
(23)	Wayne Garland	2.50	1.25	.75
(24)	Ralph Garr	2.50	1.25	.75
(25)	Steve Garvey	4.00	2.00	1.25
(26)	Cesar Geronimo	2.50	1.25	.75
(27)	Bobby Grich	2.50	1.25	.75
(28)	Ken Griffey Sr.	2.50	1.25	.75
(29)	Don Gullett	2.50	1.25	.75
(30)	Mike Hargrove	2.50	1.25	.75
(31)	Al Hrabosky	2.50	1.25	.75
(32)	Jim Hunter	5.00	2.50	1.50
(33)	Reggie Jackson	9.00	4.50	2.75
(34)	Randy Jones	2.50	1.25	.75
(35)	Dave Kingman	3.50	1.75	1.00
(36)	Jerry Koosman	2.50	1.25	.75
(37)	Dave LaRoche	2.50	1.25	.75
(38)	Greg Luzinski	2.50	1.25	.75
(39)	Fred Lynn	2.50	1.25	.75
(40)	Bill Madlock	2.50	1.25	.75
(41)	Rick Manning	2.50	1.25	.75
(42)	Jon Matlock	2.50	1.25	.75
(43)	John Mayberry	2.50	1.25	.75
(44)	Hal McRae	2.50	1.25	.75
(45)	Andy Messersmith	2.50	1.25	.75
(46)	Rick Monday	2.50	1.25	.75
(47)	John Montefusco	2.50	1.25	.75
(48)	Joe Morgan	6.00	3.00	1.75
(49)	Thurman Munson	5.00	2.50	1.50
(50)	Bobby Murcer	2.50	1.25	.75
(51)	Bill North	2.50	1.25	.75
(52)	Jim Palmer	6.00	3.00	1.75
(53)	Tony Perez	5.00	2.50	1.50
(54)	Jerry Reuss	2.50	1.25	.75
(55)	Brooks Robinson	5.00	2.50	1.50
(56)	Pete Rose	15.00	7.50	4.50
(57)	Joe Rudi	2.50	1.25	.75
(58)	Nolan Ryan	30.00	15.00	9.00
(59)	Manny Sanguillen	2.50	1.25	.75
(60)	Mike Schmidt	15.00	7.50	4.50
(61)	Tom Seaver	7.50	3.75	2.25
(62)	Bill Singer	2.50	1.25	.75
(63)	Willie Stargell	6.00	3.00	1.75
(64)	Rusty Staub	3.50	1.75	1.00
(65)	Luis Tiant	2.50	1.25	.75
(66)	Bob Watson	2.50	1.25	.75
(67)	Butch Wynegar	2.50	1.25	.75
(68)	Carl Yastrzemski	7.50	3.75	2.25
(69)	Robin Yount	6.00	3.00	1.75
(70)	Richie Zisk	2.50	1.25	.75

1908 Detroit Free Press Tigers Postcards

Most of the stars of the 1907-09 American League Champion Detroit Tigers are found in this set of postcards issued by a local newspaper and reportedly sold at the stadium for $1 a set. The cards are 3-1/2" x 5-1/4", printed in black-and-white. Fronts have a border around the photo with the line, "Copyright by the Detroit Free Press, 1908" beneath the photo. At bottom is the player's last name in capital letters with his position in parentheses. Backs have standard postcard indicia. The unnumbered cards are checklisted here alphabetically. It is possible this list is not complete.

		NM	EX	VG
Complete Set (11):		12,500	6,250	3,750
Common Player:		400.00	200.00	120.00
(1)	Ty Cobb	8,000	4,000	2,400
(2)	Sam Crawford	1,500	750.00	450.00
(3)	Wild Bill Donovan	400.00	200.00	120.00
(4)	Hughie Jennings	1,500	750.00	450.00
(5)	Ed Killian	400.00	200.00	120.00
(6)	Matty McIntyre	400.00	200.00	120.00
(7)	George Mullen (Mullin)	400.00	200.00	120.00
(8)	Charley O'Leary	400.00	200.00	120.00
(9)	Boss Schmidt	400.00	200.00	120.00
(10)	Ed Summer (Summers)	400.00	200.00	120.00
(11)	Ed Willett	400.00	200.00	120.00

1934 Detroit Tigers Team Issue

This set of blank-back, postcard-sized black-and-white player photo cards is presumed to have been a team issue. A recently-discovered poster associates them with Detroit retailer Newton Annis Furs. Photos have white borders with the wider top border having three stipes. Player name and position are printed within the picture. The unnumbered cards are checklisted here alphabetically. Envelopes in which some of the cards were sold specify 10 "Tiger Photos" for 10 cents.

		NM	EX	VG
Complete Set (23):		1,200	600.00	350.00
Common Player:		60.00	30.00	18.00
(1)	Eldon Auker	120.00	60.00	35.00
(2)	Del Baker	120.00	60.00	35.00
(3)	Tommy Bridges	120.00	60.00	35.00
(4)	Mickey Cochrane	300.00	150.00	90.00
(5)	General Crowder	120.00	60.00	35.00
(6)	Frank Doljack	120.00	60.00	35.00
(7)	Carl Fischer	120.00	60.00	35.00
(8)	Pete Fox	120.00	60.00	35.00
(9)	Charlie Gehringer	300.00	150.00	90.00
(10)	Goose Goslin	300.00	150.00	90.00
(11)	"Hank" Greenberg	500.00	250.00	150.00
(12)	Luke Hamlin	120.00	60.00	35.00
(13)	Ray Hayworth	120.00	60.00	35.00
(14)	Elon Hogsett	120.00	60.00	35.00
(15)	Firpo Marberry	120.00	60.00	35.00
(16)	Marvin Owen	120.00	60.00	35.00
(17)	Cy Perkins	120.00	60.00	35.00
(18)	Billy Rogell	120.00	60.00	35.00
(19)	Schoolboy Rowe	120.00	60.00	35.00
(20)	Heinie Schuble	120.00	60.00	35.00
(21)	Vic Sorrell	120.00	60.00	35.00
(22)	Gee Walker	120.00	60.00	35.00
(23)	Jo-Jo White	120.00	60.00	35.00

1935 Detroit Free Press Tigers

Colorized photos with brightly colored backgrounds and borders are featured in this series of newspaper pictures featuring the World Champion Detroit Tigers. About 9" x 11", the pictures are blank-backed. These premiums pictures were issued

every Sunday between April 28-Aug. 25.". The unnumbered pictures are checklisted here alphabetically. In the American Card Catalog, the set carried the designation M120.

		NM	EX	VG
Complete Set (18):		750.00	370.00	220.00
Common Player:		40.00	20.00	12.00
(1)	Eldon Auker	40.00	20.00	12.00
(2)	Tommy Bridges	40.00	20.00	12.00
(3)	Flea Clifton	40.00	20.00	12.00
(4)	Gordon Stanley (Mickey) Cochrane	100.00	50.00	30.00
(5)	Alvin Crowder	40.00	20.00	12.00
(6)	Pete Fox	40.00	20.00	12.00
(7)	Charles Gehringer	75.00	37.50	22.50
(8)	Goose Goslin	75.00	37.50	22.50
(9)	Henry Greenberg	125.00	65.00	35.00
(10)	Ray Hayworth	40.00	20.00	12.00
(11)	Elon Hogsett	40.00	20.00	12.00
(12)	Marvin Owen	40.00	20.00	12.00
(13)	Billy Rogell	40.00	20.00	12.00
(14)	Lynwood (Schoolboy) Rowe	45.00	22.50	13.50
(15)	Victor "Vic" Sorrell	40.00	20.00	12.00
(16)	Joe Sullivan	40.00	20.00	12.00
(17)	Jerry Walker	40.00	20.00	12.00
(18)	Jo-Jo White	40.00	20.00	12.00

1968 Detroit Free Press Bubblegumless Tiger Cards

The World Champion Tigers are featured in this series of newspaper inserts published in August, 1968, by the "Detroit Magazine" rotogravure section of the Sunday "Detroit Free Press." The full-color fronts and the backs were printed on separate pages to allow them to be cut out and pasted on cardboard to make a baseball card. Backs are horizontally formatted and include a drawing of the player at left; biographical data and recent stats at right. Card elements measure 2-1/2" x 3-1/2". Values quoted are for front/back pairs. Unmatched fronts are priced at 45 percent of the prices shown; backs should be priced at 30 percent.

		NM	EX	VG
Complete Set, Uncut Pages:		250.00	125.00	75.00
Complete Set, Singles (28):		200.00	100.00	60.00
Common Player:		10.00	5.00	3.00
(1)	Gates Brown	10.00	5.00	3.00
(2)	Norm Cash	15.00	7.50	4.50
(3)	Tony Cuccinello	10.00	5.00	3.00
(4)	Pat Dobson	10.00	5.00	3.00
(5)	Bill Freehan	12.50	6.25	3.75
(6)	John Hiller	10.00	5.00	3.00
(7)	Willie Horton	10.00	5.00	3.00
(8)	Al Kaline	35.00	17.50	10.50
(9)	Fred Lasher	10.00	5.00	3.00
(10)	Mickey Lolich	15.00	7.50	4.50
(11)	Tom Matchick	10.00	5.00	3.00
(12)	Dick McAuliffe	10.00	5.00	3.00
(13)	Denny McLain	12.50	6.25	3.75
(14)	Don McMahon	10.00	5.00	3.00
(15)	Wally Moses	10.00	5.00	3.00
(16)	Jim Northrup	10.00	5.00	3.00
(17)	Ray Oyler	10.00	5.00	3.00
(18)	Daryl Patterson	10.00	5.00	3.00
(19)	Jim Price	10.00	5.00	3.00
(20)	Johnny Sain	10.00	5.00	3.00
(21)	Mayo Smith	10.00	5.00	3.00
(22)	Joe Sparma	10.00	5.00	3.00
(23)	Mickey Stanley	10.00	5.00	3.00
(24)	Dick Tracewski	10.00	5.00	3.00
(25)	Jon Warden	10.00	5.00	3.00
(26)	Don Wert	10.00	5.00	3.00
(27)	Earl Wilson	10.00	5.00	3.00
(28)	Jon Wyatt (John)	10.00	5.00	3.00

1978 Detroit Free Press Tigers

In its Sunday color magazine of April 16, 1978, the newspaper printed presumably authorized reproductions of all 1978 Topps cards which featured members of the Detroit Tigers. The magazine has a cover photo of Mark Fidrych. In the centerspread, reproduced in color, are pictures of the fronts of 20 Tigers cards. Two pages later the cards of three departed Tigers, five multi-player rookie cards and the team card are printed, also in full color. Three more pages have the backs of the cards, printed in black-and-white, rather than the orange-and-blue of genuine Topps cards. Instructions with the article invited readers to cut out the fronts and backs and paste them onto pieces of cardboard to make their own cards. Values shown are for complete front/back pairs.

		NM	EX	VG
Complete Magazine:		60.00	30.00	20.00
Complete Set, Singles (28):		30.00	15.00	9.00
Common Player:		3.00	1.50	.90
21	Steve Kemp	3.00	1.50	.90
45	Mark Fidrych	6.00	3.00	1.75
68	Steve Foucault	3.00	1.50	.90
94	Chuck Scrivener	3.00	1.50	.90
124	Dave Rozema	3.00	1.50	.90
151	Milt Wilcox	3.00	1.50	.90
176	Milt May	3.00	1.50	.90
232	Mickey Stanley	3.00	1.50	.90
258	John Hiller	3.00	1.50	.90
286	Ben Oglivie	3.00	1.50	.90
342	Aurelio Rodriguez	3.00	1.50	.90
370	Rusty Staub	6.00	3.00	1.75
385	Tito Fuentes	3.00	1.50	.90
404	Tigers team card (Color checklist back.)	6.00	3.00	1.75
456	Vern Ruhle	3.00	1.50	.90
480	Ron LeFlore	3.50	1.75	1.00
515	Tim Corcoran	3.00	1.50	.90
536	Roric Harrison	3.00	1.50	.90
559	Phil Mankowski	3.00	1.50	.90
607	Fernando Arroyo	3.00	1.50	.90
633	Tom Veryzer	3.00	1.50	.90
660	Jason Thompson	3.00	1.50	.90
684	Ralph Houk	3.50	1.75	1.00
701	Tom Hume, Larry Landreth, Steve McCatty, Bruce Taylor (Rookie Pitchers)	3.00	1.50	.90
703	Larry Andersen, Tim Jones, Mickey Mahler, Jack Morris (Rookie Pitchers)	7.50	3.75	2.25
704	Garth Iorg, Dave Oliver, Sam Perlozzo, Lou Whitaker (Rookie 2nd Basemen)	9.00	4.50	2.75
707	Mickey Klutts, Paul Molitor, Alan Trammell, U.L. Washington (Rookie Shortstops)	20.00	10.00	6.00
708	Bo Diaz, Dale Murphy, Lance Parrish, Ernie Whitt (Rookie Catchers)	10.00	5.00	3.00
723	Johnny Wockenfuss	3.00	1.50	.90

1964 Detroit Tigers Milk Bottle Caps

These small (1-5/16" diameter) cardboard milk bottle caps feature line drawings of the 1964 Tigers. The caps are printed in dark blue and orange on front and blank on back. The unnumbered caps are checklisted here in alphabetical order. A wire staple is found in most caps. The caps were reportedly produced for Twin Pines Dairy for use on bottles of chocolate milk.

		NM	EX	VG
Complete Set (14):		400.00	200.00	120.00
Common Player:		25.00	12.50	7.50
(1)	Hank Aguirre	25.00	12.50	7.50
(2)	Billy Bruton	25.00	12.50	7.50
(3)	Norman Cash	50.00	25.00	15.00
(4)	Don Demeter	25.00	12.50	7.50
(5)	Chuck Dressen	25.00	12.50	7.50
(6)	Bill Freehan	35.00	17.50	10.50
(7)	Al Kaline	150.00	75.00	45.00
(8)	Frank Lary	25.00	12.50	7.50
(9)	Jerry Lumpe	25.00	12.50	7.50
(10)	Dick McAuliffe	25.00	12.50	7.50
(11)	Bubba Phillips	25.00	12.50	7.50
(12)	Ed Rakow	25.00	12.50	7.50
(13)	Phil Regan	25.00	12.50	7.50
(14)	Dave Wickersham	25.00	12.50	7.50

1936 Detroit Times Sports Stamps

Printed as part of the regular newspaper page, these feature items have a stamp-design photo element of about 2" x 2-1/2" atop a biographical and career summary. These stamps were printed between June and August and include stars of other sports such as boxing, football, hockey, golf, etc."

		NM	EX	VG
Common Player:		15.00	7.50	4.50
(1)	Eldon Auker	15.00	7.50	4.50
(2)	Del Baker	15.00	7.50	4.50
(3)	Tommy Bridges	15.00	7.50	4.50
(4)	Jack Burns	15.00	7.50	4.50
(5)	Ty Cobb	40.00	20.00	12.00
(6)	Mickey Cochrane (Dark cap.)	20.00	10.00	6.00
(7)	Mickey Cochrane (White cap.)	20.00	10.00	6.00
(8)	Joe Cronin	20.00	10.00	6.00
(9)	Alvin Crowder	15.00	7.50	4.50
(10a)	Dizzy Dean (Bio first line "Star pitcher of.")	30.00	15.00	9.00
(10b)	Dizzy Dean (Bio "of" on second line.)	30.00	15.00	9.00
(11)	Paul Dean	15.00	7.50	4.50
(12)	Wes Ferrell	15.00	7.50	4.50
(13)	Pete Fox	15.00	7.50	4.50
(14)	Jimmy Foxx	30.00	15.00	9.00
(15)	Frank Frisch	20.00	10.00	6.00
(16a)	Lou Gehrig (Bio first line "...slugging first.")	40.00	20.00	12.00
(16b)	Lou Gehrig (Bio first line "slugging.")	40.00	20.00	12.00
(17)	Charles Gehringer	20.00	10.00	6.00
(18)	Chas. Gehringer	20.00	10.00	6.00
(19)	Lefty Gomez	20.00	10.00	6.00
(20a)	Goose Goslin (White cap.)	20.00	10.00	6.00
(20b)	Goose Goslin (Dark cap.)	20.00	10.00	6.00
(21)	Hank Greenberg	20.00	10.00	6.00
(22)	Charley Grimm	15.00	7.50	4.50
(23)	Ray Hayworth	15.00	7.50	4.50
(24)	Elon Hogsett	15.00	7.50	4.50
(25)	Walter Johnson	30.00	15.00	9.00
(26)	Chuck Klein	20.00	10.00	6.00
(27)	Connie Mack	20.00	10.00	6.00
(28)	Heinie Manush	20.00	10.00	6.00
(29)	Van Lingle Mungo	15.00	7.50	4.50
(30)	Glenn Myatt	15.00	7.50	4.50
(31)	Steve O'Neill	15.00	7.50	4.50
(32)	Billy Rogell	15.00	7.50	4.50
(33a)	Schoolboy Rowe (White cap.)	15.00	7.50	4.50
(33b)	Schoolboy Rowe (Dark cap.)	15.00	7.50	4.50
(34)	Babe Ruth	40.00	20.00	12.00
(35)	Al Simmons	30.00	15.00	9.00
(36)	Vic Sorrell	15.00	7.50	4.50
(37)	Tris Speaker	30.00	15.00	9.00
(38)	Casey Stengel	20.00	10.00	6.00
(39)	Joe Sullivan	15.00	7.50	4.50
(40)	Bill Terry	15.00	7.50	4.50
(41)	Joe Vosmik	15.00	7.50	4.50
(42)	Gerry Walker	15.00	7.50	4.50
(43)	Lon Warneke	15.00	7.50	4.50
(44)	Jo Jo White	15.00	7.50	4.50
(45)	Earl Whitehill	15.00	7.50	4.50
(46)	Jimmy Wilson	15.00	7.50	4.50

1966 Dexter Press California Angels

Less well-known than the New York firm's premium issues for Coca-Cola are Dexter Press' team issues. Sold for 50 cents in a cellophane bag with a colorful cardboard header the team issues are in the same basic design as the premium cards of 1967, but measure only 4" x 5-7/8". Though they were sold in sets of eight, more individual cards exist for the known teams, so it is evident there was some exchange of cards within the sets over the course of the sales period. Cards have color player poses with a black facsimile autograph at top and with or without

 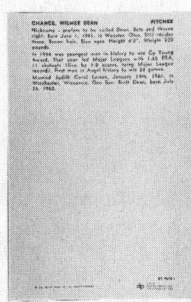

a white border around. Backs are printed in blue with personal data and career highlights at top and copyright information at bottom. The cards are checklisted here alphabetically.

		NM	EX	VG
Complete Set (17):		100.00	50.00	30.00
Common Player:		10.00	5.00	3.00
(1)	Jose Cardenal	10.00	5.00	3.00
(2)	George Brunet	10.00	5.00	3.00
(3)	Dean Chance	12.00	6.00	3.50
(4)	Jim Fregosi	10.00	5.00	3.00
(5)	Ed Kirkpatrick	10.00	5.00	3.00
(6)	Bob Knoop	10.00	5.00	3.00
(7)	Bob Lee	10.00	5.00	3.00
(8)	Marcelino Lopez	10.00	5.00	3.00
(9)	Fred Newman	10.00	5.00	3.00
(10)	Albie Pearson	10.00	5.00	3.00
(11)	Jim Piersall	13.50	6.75	4.00
(12)	Rick Reichardt	10.00	5.00	3.00
(13)	Bob Rodgers	10.00	5.00	3.00
(14)	Paul Schaal	10.00	5.00	3.00
(15)	Norm Siebern	10.00	5.00	3.00
(16)	Willie Smith	10.00	5.00	3.00
(17)	Anaheim Stadium	10.00	5.00	3.00

1966 Dexter Press California Angels 8x10

The extent to which this larger format premium parallels the smaller set is currently unknown.

		NM	EX	VG
Common Player:		10.00	5.00	3.00
(1)	Dean Chance	15.00	7.50	4.50
(2)	Willie Smith	10.00	5.00	3.00

1966 Dexter Press California Angels Booklet

This souvenir-stand bound booklet offered pictures of the 1966 California Angels in two different sizes. Each 8-1/8" x 3-1/2" page features a pair of identical color photo cards. A postcard-size (3-1/2" x 5-1/2") portrait has a facsimile autograph of the player at top, attached by perforations to a 2-1/4" x 3-1/2" card, which in turn is perforated into the bound end of the book. Booklets originally sold for 50 cents. The unnumbered cards are checklisted here in alphabetical order.

		NM	EX	VG
Complete Booklet:		150.00	75.00	45.00
Complete Set, Large (10):		60.00	30.00	18.00
Complete Set, Small (10):		40.00	20.00	12.00
Common Player, Large:		8.00	4.00	2.40
Common Player, Small:		6.00	3.00	1.80
Large Format (3-1/2" x 5-1/2")				
(1)	Jose Cardenal	8.00	4.00	2.50
(2)	Dean Chance	8.00	4.00	2.50
(3)	Jim Fregosi	8.00	4.00	2.50
(4)	Bob Knoop	8.00	4.00	2.50
(5)	Albie Pearson	8.00	4.00	2.50
(6)	Rick Reichardt	8.00	4.00	2.50
(7)	Bob Rodgers	8.00	4.00	2.50
(8)	Paul Schaal	8.00	4.00	2.50
(9)	Willie Smith	8.00	4.00	2.50
(10)	Anaheim Stadium	8.00	4.00	2.50
Small Format (2-1/4" x 3-1/2")				
(1)	Jose Cardenal	6.00	3.00	1.80
(2)	Dean Chance	6.00	3.00	1.80
(3)	Jim Fregosi	6.00	3.00	1.80
(4)	Bob Knoop	6.00	3.00	1.80
(5)	Albie Pearson	6.00	3.00	1.80
(6)	Rick Reichardt	6.00	3.00	1.80
(7)	Bob Rodgers	6.00	3.00	1.80
(8)	Paul Schaal	6.00	3.00	1.80
(9)	Willie Smith	6.00	3.00	1.80
(10)	Anaheim Stadium	6.00	3.00	1.80

1966-67 Dexter Press N.Y. Yankees

Less commonly encountered than the later Dexter Press/Coca-Cola premium issues are the team-set photocards produced by the New York firm. Cards were sold in bagged sets with a colorful cardboard header. Virtually identical in design to the 5-1/2" x 7" premium cards of 1967, the team-set pictures measure 4" x 5-7/8" with a white border around, and a black facsimile autograph at the top of, color

player poses. Backs are printed in blue with a few biographical details at top and copyright information at bottom. The unnumbered cards are checklisted here in alphabetical order.

		NM	EX	VG
	Complete Set (12):	200.00	100.00	60.00
	Common Player:	15.00	7.50	4.50
(1)	Jim Bouton	17.50	8.75	5.25
(2)	Horace Clarke	15.00	7.50	4.50
(3)	Al Downing	15.00	7.50	4.50
(4)	Whitey Ford	20.00	10.00	6.00
(5)	Steve Hamilton	15.00	7.50	4.50
(6)	Elston Howard	17.50	8.75	5.25
(7)	Mickey Mantle	60.00	30.00	18.00
(8)	Joe Pepitone	17.50	8.75	5.25
(9)	Bill Robinson	15.00	7.50	4.50
(10)	Mel Stottlemyre	15.00	7.50	4.50
(11)	Tom Tresh	17.50	8.75	5.25
(12)	Steve Whitaker	15.00	7.50	4.50

1967 Dexter Press Premiums

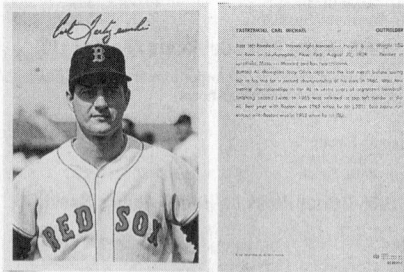

Among the most attractive baseball collectibles issued during the 1960s were the cards produced by Dexter Press and issued in team sets as a premium by Coca-Cola. Eighteen of the 20 Major League teams participated in the promotion (only one California Angels player and no St. Louis Cardinals). The cards are in 5-1/2" x 7" glossy format. All of the color photos are waist-to-cap poses shot during spring training, and all cards feature a black facsimile autograph at the top of the photo. The cards have a 1/4" white border around the picture. Backs are printed in blue on white and include a few biographical details and career highlights. Nine of the 12 players in the All-Star issue can be differentiated from the same players' cards in the team sets by the lengthier biographies on back. The bios on the cards of Bunning, Mays and Santo are the same in both versions. While each of the cards has a number printed on back in the lower-right, they are checklisted here alphabetically within team. Sixteen of the Dexter Press premiums were issued in a smaller, borderless sticker set in 1983; it is an unauthorized collector issue.

		NM	EX	VG
	Complete Set (229):	1,500	750.00	450.00
	Common Player:	5.00	2.50	1.50
ALL-STARS				
(1)	Jim Bunning	7.50	3.75	2.25
(2)	Roberto Clemente	15.00	7.50	4.50
(3)	Willie Davis	5.00	2.50	1.50
(4)	Al Kaline	10.00	5.00	3.00
(5)	Harmon Killebrew	10.00	5.00	3.00
(6)	Willie Mays	12.50	6.25	3.75
(7)	Joe Pepitone	6.00	3.00	1.75
(8)	Brooks Robinson	10.00	5.00	3.00
(9)	Frank Robinson	10.00	5.00	3.00
(10)	Ron Santo	6.00	3.00	1.75
(11)	Joe Torre	6.00	3.00	1.75
(12)	Carl Yastrzemski	12.00	6.00	3.50
CALIFORNIA ANGELS				
(13)	Paul Schall	125.00	62.00	37.00
HOUSTON ASTROS				
(14)	Bob Aspromonte	5.00	2.50	1.50
(15)	John Bateman	5.00	2.50	1.50
(16)	Ron Davis	5.00	2.50	1.50
(17)	Larry Dierker	5.00	2.50	1.50
(18)	Dick Farrell	5.00	2.50	1.50
(19)	Dave Giusti	5.00	2.50	1.50
(20)	Chuck Harrison	5.00	2.50	1.50
(21)	Sonny Jackson	5.00	2.50	1.50
(22)	Jim Landis	5.00	2.50	1.50
(23)	Eddie Mathews	10.00	5.00	3.00
(24)	Joe Morgan	12.00	6.00	3.50
(25)	Rusty Staub	7.50	3.75	2.25
KANSAS CITY ATHLETICS				
(26)	Jack Aker	5.00	2.50	1.50
(27)	Campy Campaneris	5.00	2.50	1.50
(28)	Danny Cater	5.00	2.50	1.50

(29)	Ed Charles	5.00	2.50	1.50
(30)	Ossie Chavarria	5.00	2.50	1.50
(31)	Dick Green	5.00	2.50	1.50
(32)	Mike Hershberger	5.00	2.50	1.50
(33)	Lew Krausse	5.00	2.50	1.50
(34)	Jim Nash	5.00	2.50	1.50
(35)	Joe Nossek	5.00	2.50	1.50
(36)	Roger Repoz	5.00	2.50	1.50
(37)	Phil Roof	5.00	2.50	1.50
ATLANTA BRAVES				
(38)	Hank Aaron	25.00	12.50	7.50
(39)	Felipe Alou	6.00	3.00	1.75
(40)	Wade Blasingame	5.00	2.50	1.50
(41)	Clete Boyer	5.00	2.50	1.50
(42)	Bob Bruce	5.00	2.50	1.50
(43)	Ty Cline	5.00	2.50	1.50
(44)	Tony Cloninger	5.00	2.50	1.50
(45)	Ken Johnson	5.00	2.50	1.50
(46)	Dennis Menke	5.00	2.50	1.50
(47)	Gene Oliver	5.00	2.50	1.50
(48)	Joe Torre	7.50	3.75	2.25
(49)	Woody Woodward	5.00	2.50	1.50
CHICAGO CUBS				
(50)	George Altman	5.00	2.50	1.50
(51)	Ernie Banks	18.00	9.00	5.50
(52)	Glen Beckert (Glenn)	5.00	2.50	1.50
(53)	John Boccabella	5.00	2.50	1.50
(54)	Ray Culp	5.00	2.50	1.50
(55)	Ken Holtzman	5.00	2.50	1.50
(56)	Randy Hundley	5.00	2.50	1.50
(57)	Cal Koonce	5.00	2.50	1.50
(58)	Adolfo Phillips	5.00	2.50	1.50
(59)	Ron Santo	6.00	3.00	1.75
(60)	Lee Thomas	5.00	2.50	1.50
(61)	Billy Williams	10.00	5.00	3.00
LOS ANGELES DODGERS				
(62)	Bob Bailey	5.00	2.50	1.50
(63)	Willie Davis	5.00	2.50	1.50
(64)	Ron Fairly	5.00	2.50	1.50
(65)	Ron Hunt	5.00	2.50	1.50
(66)	Lou Johnson	5.00	2.50	1.50
(67)	John Kennedy	5.00	2.50	1.50
(68)	Jim Lefebvre	5.00	2.50	1.50
(69)	Claude Osteen	5.00	2.50	1.50
(70)	Wes Parker	5.00	2.50	1.50
(71)	Ron Perranoski	5.00	2.50	1.50
(72)	Phil Regan	5.00	2.50	1.50
(73)	Don Sutton	7.50	3.75	2.25
SAN FRANCISCO GIANTS				
(74)	Jesus Alou	5.00	2.50	1.50
(75)	Ollie Brown	5.00	2.50	1.50
(76)	Jim Davenport	5.00	2.50	1.50
(77)	Tito Fuentes	5.00	2.50	1.50
(78)	Tom Haller	5.00	2.50	1.50
(79)	Jim Hart	5.00	2.50	1.50
(80)	Hal Lanier	5.00	2.50	1.50
(81)	Willie Mays	15.00	7.50	4.50
(82)	Mike McCormick	5.00	2.50	1.50
(83)	Willie McCovey	12.00	6.00	3.50
(84)	Gaylord Perry	8.00	4.00	2.50
(85)	Norman Siebern	5.00	2.50	1.50
CLEVELAND INDIANS				
(86)	Max Alvis	5.00	2.50	1.50
(87)	Joe Azcue	5.00	2.50	1.50
(88)	Gary Bell	5.00	2.50	1.50
(89)	Larry Brown	5.00	2.50	1.50
(90)	Rocky Colavito	7.50	3.75	2.25
(91)	Vic Davalillo	5.00	2.50	1.50
(92)	Pedro Gonzalez	5.00	2.50	1.50
(93)	Chuck Hinton	5.00	2.50	1.50
(94)	Sam McDowell	6.00	3.00	1.75
(95)	Luis Tiant	6.00	3.00	1.75
(96)	Leon Wagner	5.00	2.50	1.50
(97)	Fred Whitfield	5.00	2.50	1.50
NEW YORK METS				
(98)	Ed Bressoud	5.00	2.50	1.50
(99)	Ken Boyer	7.00	3.50	2.00
(100)	Tommy Davis	6.00	3.00	1.75
(101)	Jack Fisher	5.00	2.50	1.50
(102)	Jerry Grote	5.00	2.50	1.50
(103)	Jack Hamilton	5.00	2.50	1.50
(104)	Cleon Jones	6.00	3.00	1.75
(105)	Ed Kranepool	5.00	2.50	1.50
(106)	Johnny Lewis	5.00	2.50	1.50
(107)	Bob Shaw	5.00	2.50	1.50
(108)	John Stephenson	5.00	2.50	1.50
(109)	Ron Swoboda	5.00	2.50	1.50
BALTIMORE ORIOLES				
(110)	Luis Aparicio	10.00	5.00	3.00
(111)	Curt Blefary	5.00	2.50	1.50
(112)	Wally Bunker	5.00	2.50	1.50
(113)	Andy Etchebarren	5.00	2.50	1.50
(114)	Eddie Fisher	5.00	2.50	1.50
(115)	Dave Johnson	5.00	2.50	1.50
(116)	Dave McNally	5.00	2.50	1.50
(117)	Jim Palmer	10.00	5.00	3.00
(118)	John "Boog" Powell	8.00	4.00	2.50
(119)	Brooks Robinson	15.00	7.50	4.50
(120)	Frank Robinson	15.00	7.50	4.50
(121)	Russ Snyder	5.00	2.50	1.50
PHILADELPHIA PHILLIES				
(122)	Rich Allen	7.50	3.75	2.25
(123)	John Briggs	5.00	2.50	1.50
(124)	Jim Bunning	7.50	3.75	2.25
(125)	Johnny Callison	5.00	2.50	1.50
(126)	Clay Dalrymple	5.00	2.50	1.50
(127)	Dick Groat	5.00	2.50	1.50
(128)	Larry Jackson	5.00	2.50	1.50
(129)	Don Lock	5.00	2.50	1.50
(130)	Cookie Rojas	5.00	2.50	1.50
(131)	Chris Short	5.00	2.50	1.50
(132)	Tony Taylor	5.00	2.50	1.50
(133)	Bill White	5.00	2.50	1.50
PITTSBURGH PIRATES				
(134)	Gene Alley	5.00	2.50	1.50
(135)	Matty Alou	5.00	2.50	1.50
(136)	Roberto Clemente	45.00	22.00	13.50

(137)	Donn Clendenon	5.00	2.50	1.50
(138)	Woodie Fryman	5.00	2.50	1.50
(139)	Vern Law	5.00	2.50	1.50
(140)	Bill Mazeroski	10.00	5.00	3.00
(141)	Manny Mota	5.00	2.50	1.50
(142)	Jim Pagliaroni	5.00	2.50	1.50
(143)	Wilver Stargell	12.00	6.00	3.50
(144)	Bob Veale	5.00	2.50	1.50
(145)	Maury Wills	6.00	3.00	1.75
CINCINNATI REDS				
(146)	Leo Cardenas	5.00	2.50	1.50
(147)	Gordy Coleman	5.00	2.50	1.50
(148)	Johnny Edwards	5.00	2.50	1.50
(149)	Tommy Harper	5.00	2.50	1.50
(150)	Tommy Helms	5.00	2.50	1.50
(151)	Deron Johnson	5.00	2.50	1.50
(152)	Jim Maloney	5.00	2.50	1.50
(153)	Bill McCool	5.00	2.50	1.50
(154)	Milt Pappas	5.00	2.50	1.50
(155)	Vada Pinson	6.00	3.00	1.75
(156)	Pete Rose	30.00	15.00	9.00
(157)	Art Shamsky	5.00	2.50	1.50
BOSTON RED SOX				
(158)	Don Demeter	5.00	2.50	1.50
(159)	Bill Fischer	5.00	2.50	1.50
(160)	Joe Foy	5.00	2.50	1.50
(161)	Dalton Jones	5.00	2.50	1.50
(162)	Jim Lonborg	5.00	2.50	1.50
(163)	Rico Petrocelli	5.00	2.50	1.50
(164)	Jose Santiago	5.00	2.50	1.50
(165)	George Scott	5.00	2.50	1.50
(166)	George Smith	5.00	2.50	1.50
(167)	Jose Tartabull	5.00	2.50	1.50
(168)	Bob Tillman	5.00	2.50	1.50
(169)	Carl Yastrzemski	15.00	7.50	4.50
WASHINGTON SENATORS				
(170)	Bernie Allen	5.00	2.50	1.50
(171)	Ed Brinkman	5.00	2.50	1.50
(172)	Paul Casanova	5.00	2.50	1.50
(173)	Ken Harrelson	5.00	2.50	1.50
(174)	Frank Howard	6.00	3.00	1.75
(175)	Jim King	5.00	2.50	1.50
(176)	Ken McMullen	5.00	2.50	1.50
(177)	Dick Nen	5.00	2.50	1.50
(178)	Phil Ortega	5.00	2.50	1.50
(179)	Pete Richert	5.00	2.50	1.50
(180)	Bob Saverine	5.00	2.50	1.50
(181)	Fred Valentine	5.00	2.50	1.50
DETROIT TIGERS				
(182)	Norm Cash	6.00	3.00	1.75
(183)	Bill Freehan	5.00	2.50	1.50
(184)	Willie Horton	5.00	2.50	1.50
(185)	Al Kaline	12.00	6.00	3.50
(186)	Mickey Lolich	5.00	2.50	1.50
(187)	Jerry Lumpe	5.00	2.50	1.50
(188)	Dick McAuliffe	5.00	2.50	1.50
(189)	Johnny Podres	5.00	2.50	1.50
(190)	Joe Sparma	5.00	2.50	1.50
(191)	Dave Wickersham	5.00	2.50	1.50
(192)	Earl Wilson	5.00	2.50	1.50
(193)	Don Wert	5.00	2.50	1.50
MINNESOTA TWINS				
(194)	Bob Allison	5.00	2.50	1.50
(195)	Earl Battey	5.00	2.50	1.50
(196)	Dave Boswell	5.00	2.50	1.50
(197)	Dean Chance	5.00	2.50	1.50
(198)	Mudcat Grant	5.00	2.50	1.50
(199)	Harmon Killebrew	12.00	6.00	3.50
(200)	Jim Merritt	5.00	2.50	1.50
(201)	Tony Oliva	8.00	4.00	2.50
(202)	Rich Rollins	5.00	2.50	1.50
(203)	Ted Uhlaender	5.00	2.50	1.50
(204)	Sandy Valdespino	5.00	2.50	1.50
(205)	Zoilo Versalles	5.00	2.50	1.50
CHICAGO WHITE SOX				
(206)	Tommie Agee	5.00	2.50	1.50
(207)	Ken Berry	5.00	2.50	1.50
(208)	Don Buford	5.00	2.50	1.50
(209)	Ron Hansen	5.00	2.50	1.50
(210)	Joel Horlen	5.00	2.50	1.50
(211)	Tommy John	6.00	3.00	1.75
(212)	Bob Locker	5.00	2.50	1.50
(213)	Tommy McCraw	5.00	2.50	1.50
(214)	Jerry McNertney	5.00	2.50	1.50
(215)	Jim O'Toole	5.00	2.50	1.50
(216)	Bill "Moose" Skowron	7.00	3.50	2.00
(217)	Pete Ward	5.00	2.50	1.50
NEW YORK YANKEES				
(218)	Jim Bouton	6.00	3.00	1.75
(219)	Horace Clarke	5.00	2.50	1.50
(220)	Al Downing	5.00	2.50	1.50
(221)	Steve Hamilton	5.00	2.50	1.50
(222)	Elston Howard	7.50	3.75	2.25
(223)	Mickey Mantle	40.00	20.00	12.00
(224)	Joe Pepitone	6.00	3.00	1.75
(225)	Fritz Peterson	5.00	2.50	1.50
(226)	Charley Smith	5.00	2.50	1.50
(227)	Mel Stottlemyre	6.00	3.00	1.75
(228)	Tom Tresh	6.00	3.00	1.75
(229)	Roy White	6.00	3.00	1.75

1967 Dexter Press Team Posters

These 17" x 11" color posters reproduce the 12 cards (or on the Cubs sheet, three additional players) found in the 1967 Dexter Press premium team sets, in images about 2" x 3". The cards are pictured on a solid color background with color team logos. Printed on back are player identification and biographical information. Dexter Press copyright and credit lines are at bottom. It is not known whether other teams involved in the premium program can also be found in poster format.

	NM	EX	VG
California Angels	270.00	135.00	80.00
Chicago Cubs	360.00	180.00	110.00
Chicago White Sox	270.00	135.00	80.00
N.Y. Mets	360.00	180.00	110.00
N.Y. Yankees	600.00	300.00	180.00
Washington Senators	360.00	180.00	110.00

1968 Dexter Press Postcards

In its second year of printing premium cards for Coca-Cola, Dexter Press changed format and greatly reduced the number of participating teams and players. Only six teams were represented by 12-card sets, while an additional four teams had one or two players included. For 1968, Dexter Press produced its premiums in postcard (3-1/2" x 5-1/2") size. The cards featured borderless color player poses on front. Backs were printed in blue on white and included a facsimile autograph, biographical details and career highlights. Cards carry a Dexter Press serial number on back, but are checklisted here alphabetically within team.

		NM	EX	VG
Complete Set (77):		500.00	250.00	150.00
Common Player:		4.00	2.00	1.25
CALIFORNIA ANGELS				
(1)	Jim Fregosi	6.00	3.00	1.75
HOUSTON ASTROS				
(2)	Bob Aspromonte	4.00	2.00	1.25
(3)	John Bateman	4.00	2.00	1.25
(4)	Ron Brand	4.00	2.00	1.25
(5)	Mike Cuellar	4.00	2.00	1.25
(6)	Ron Davis	4.00	2.00	1.25
(7)	Dave Giusti	4.00	2.00	1.25
(8)	Julio Gotay	4.00	2.00	1.25
(9)	Denny Lemaster	4.00	2.00	1.25
(10)	Denis Menke	4.00	2.00	1.25
(11)	Joe Morgan	10.00	5.00	3.00
(12)	Rusty Staub	5.00	2.50	1.50
(13)	Jim Wynn	4.00	2.00	1.25
ATLANTA BRAVES				
(14)	Hank Aaron	15.00	7.50	4.50
(15)	Felipe Alou	5.00	2.50	1.50
(16)	Clete Boyer	4.00	2.00	1.25
(17)	Clay Carroll	4.00	2.00	1.25
(18)	Rico Carty	4.00	2.00	1.25
(19)	Tony Cloninger	4.00	2.00	1.25
(20)	Sonny Jackson	4.00	2.00	1.25
(21)	Ray Jarvis	4.00	2.00	1.25
(22)	Ken Johnson	4.00	2.00	1.25
(23)	Phil Niekro	8.00	4.00	2.50
(24)	Joe Torre	7.50	3.75	2.25
(25)	Woody Woodward	4.00	2.00	1.25
SAN FRANCISCO GIANTS				
(26)	Jesus Alou	4.00	2.00	1.25
(27)	Bob Bolin	4.00	2.00	1.25
(28)	Jim Davenport	4.00	2.00	1.25
(29)	Jim Hart	4.00	2.00	1.25
(30)	Jack Hiatt	4.00	2.00	1.25
(31)	Ron Hunt	4.00	2.00	1.25
(32)	Frank Linzy	4.00	2.00	1.25
(33)	Juan Marichal	9.00	4.50	2.75
(34)	Willie Mays	15.00	7.50	4.50
(35)	Mike McCormick	4.00	2.00	1.25
(36)	Gaylord Perry	8.00	4.00	2.50
(37)	Ray Sadecki	4.00	2.00	1.25
BALTIMORE ORIOLES				
(38)	Mark Belanger	4.00	2.00	1.25
(39)	Paul Blair	4.00	2.00	1.25
(40)	Curt Blefary	4.00	2.00	1.25
(41)	Don Buford	4.00	2.00	1.25
(42)	Moe Drabowsky	4.00	2.00	1.25
(43)	Andy Etchebarren	4.00	2.00	1.25

(44)	Dave Johnson	4.00	2.00	1.25
(45)	Dave McNally	4.00	2.00	1.25
(46)	Tom Phoebus	4.00	2.00	1.25
(47)	Boog Powell	5.00	2.50	1.50
(48)	Brooks Robinson	12.00	6.00	3.50
(49)	Frank Robinson	12.00	6.00	3.50
PHILADELPHIA PHILLIES				
(50)	Dick Allen	9.00	4.50	2.75
PITTSBURGH PIRATES		.00	.00	.00
(51)	Roberto Clemente	25.00	12.50	7.50
(52)	Bill Mazeroski	10.00	5.00	3.00
BOSTON RED SOX				
(53)	Jerry Adair	4.00	2.00	1.25
(54)	Mike Andrews	4.00	2.00	1.25
(55)	Gary Bell	4.00	2.00	1.25
(56)	Darrell Brandon	4.00	2.00	1.25
(57)	Dick Ellsworth	4.00	2.00	1.25
(58)	Joe Foy	4.00	2.00	1.25
(59)	Dalton Jones	4.00	2.00	1.25
(60)	Jim Lonborg	5.00	2.50	1.50
(61)	Dave Morehead	4.00	2.00	1.25
(62)	Rico Petrocelli	4.00	2.00	1.25
(63)	George Scott	4.00	2.00	1.25
(64)	John Wyatt	4.00	2.00	1.25
DETROIT TIGERS				
(65)	Bill Freehan	6.00	3.00	1.75
MINNESOTA TWINS				
(66)	Bob Allison	4.00	2.00	1.25
(67)	Dave Boswell	4.00	2.00	1.25
(68)	Rod Carew	10.00	5.00	3.00
(69)	Dean Chance	4.00	2.00	1.25
(70)	Jim Kaat	4.00	2.00	1.25
(71)	Harmon Killebrew	10.00	5.00	3.00
(72)	Russ Nixon	4.00	2.00	1.25
(73)	Tony Oliva	6.00	3.00	1.75
(74)	Rich Rollins	4.00	2.00	1.25
(75)	John Roseboro	4.00	2.00	1.25
(76)	Cesar Tovar	4.00	2.00	1.25
(77)	Ted Uhlaender	4.00	2.00	1.25

1979 Dexter Press Hall of Fame Plaque Postcards

(See Hall of Fame (Dexter Press) for checklist, value data.)

1960 Diamond Associates Postcards

 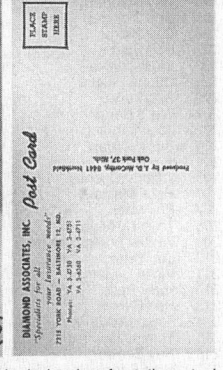

Based on the uniform style depicted on front, the actual year of issue for this card could be anywhere between 1958-1962. Produced by photographer J.D. McCarthy, apparently for the star catcher's off-season business, the 3-1/4" x 5-1/2" black-and-white card has a facsimile autograph on front. The postcard-style back has the address and phone numbers of the insurance company.

	NM	EX	VG
Gus Triandos	30.00	15.00	9.00

1940 Diamond Dust Punchboard Cards

These paper cards are the consolation prizes from a popular gambling device of the Depression era, the punchboard. For five cents a customer could choose one of 624 holes on the punchboard and push a wood or metal punch through the paper on front, driving out the back a 1" x about 1-3/4" picture of a baseball player. Fifteen of the players were $1 winners and were produced in much shorter supply than the others; any which were redeemed would probably have been destroyed. The pictures are printed on ribbed paper to assist in fitting them into the board. They are pictures taken from the photos on contemporary "Salutation" Exhibit cards, though without uniform logos. They are printed in bright colors with the player name in a color bar at bottom. Backs are blank. The

unnumbered cards are listed here in alphabetical order, with an asterisk indicating winners. The punchboard itself is highly collectible, with colorful baseball graphics and player pictures and names. Earlier and later versions of Diamond Dust punchboards are also known, but have not been checklisted.

		NM	EX	VG
Complete Set (33):		850.00	425.00	250.00
Common Player:		15.00	7.50	4.50
Complete Unused Punchboard:		1,200	600.00	350.00
(1)	Luke Appling (*)	45.00	22.00	13.50
(2)	Earl Averill (*)	45.00	22.00	13.50
(3)	Adolf Camilli	15.00	7.50	4.50
(4)	Harland Clift (Harlond)	15.00	7.50	4.50
(5)	Joe Cronin (*)(Unconfirmed)	45.00	22.00	13.50
(6)	Tony Cuccinello	15.00	7.50	4.50
(7)	Dizzy Dean	35.00	17.50	10.50
(8)	Bill Dickey (*)	50.00	25.00	15.00
(9)	Joe DiMaggio (*)	125.00	62.00	37.00
(10)	Bob Feller	30.00	15.00	9.00
(11)	Jimmie Foxx (*)	45.00	22.00	13.50
(12)	Charlie Gehringer (*)	45.00	22.00	13.50
(13)	Lefty Gomez	25.00	12.50	7.50
(14)	Hank Greenberg	30.00	15.00	9.00
(15)	Lefty Grove	25.00	12.50	7.50
(16)	Gabby Hartnett	15.00	7.50	4.50
(17)	Carl Hubbell	25.00	12.50	7.50
(18)	Bob Johnson	15.00	7.50	4.50
(19)	Chuck Klein	25.00	12.50	7.50
(20)	Bill Lee	15.00	7.50	4.50
(21)	Ernie Lombardi (*)	45.00	22.00	13.50
(22)	Frank McCormick (*)	25.00	12.50	7.50
(23)	Joe Medwick	25.00	12.50	7.50
(24)	Johnny Mize (*)	45.00	22.00	13.50
(25)	Buck Newson (Newsom)	15.00	7.50	4.50
(26)	Mel Ott (*)	45.00	22.00	13.50
(27)	Johnny Rizzo (*)	25.00	12.50	7.50
(28)	Red Ruffing (*)(Unconfirmed)	45.00	22.00	13.50
(29)	Cecil Travis	15.00	7.50	4.50
(30)	Johnny Vander Meer	15.00	7.50	4.50
(31)	Arky Vaughan (*)	45.00	22.00	13.50
(32)	Lon Warneke	15.00	7.50	4.50
(33)	Rudy York (*)(Unconfirmed)	25.00	12.50	7.50

1979 Diamond Greats

Card collector, dealer and later Donruss photographer Jack Wallin produced this collectors' issue. Cards are in the 2-1/2" x 3-1/2" format, printed in black-and-white and blank-backed. Besides the player photo on front, there is identification and a line of career stats. Four 100-card series were issued. Series 1 concentrates on Yankees, Giants, Senators and Dodgers. Series 2 comprises the Cubs, White Sox, Cardinals and Browns. The third series features Braves, Red Sox, Reds and Indians. Series 4 concentrates on the Phillies, A's, Pirates and Tigers.

		NM	EX	VG
Complete Set (400):		275.00	135.00	85.00
Series 1 (1-100):		60.00	30.00	18.00
Series 2 (101-200):		50.00	25.00	15.00
Series 3 (201-300):		50.00	25.00	15.00
Series 4 (301-400):		50.00	25.00	15.00
Common Player:		2.00	1.00	.60
1	Joe DiMaggio	12.00	6.00	3.50
2	Ben Chapman	2.00	1.00	.60
3	Joe Dugan	2.00	1.00	.60
4	Bobby Shawkey	2.00	1.00	.60
5	Joe Sewell	2.00	1.00	.60
6	George Pipgras	2.00	1.00	.60
7	George Selkirk	2.00	1.00	.60
8	Babe Dahlgren	2.00	1.00	.60
9	Spud Chandler	2.00	1.00	.60
10	Duffy Lewis	2.00	1.00	.60
11	Lefty Gomez	3.00	1.50	.90
12	Atley Donald	2.00	1.00	.60
13	Whitey Witt	2.00	1.00	.60
14	Marius Russo	2.00	1.00	.60
15	Buddy Rosar	2.00	1.00	.60
16	Russ Van Atta	2.00	1.00	.60
17	Johnny Lindell	2.00	1.00	.60
18	Bobby Brown	2.00	1.00	.60
19	Tony Kubek	2.50	1.25	.70
20	Joe Beggs	2.00	1.00	.60
21	Don Larsen	2.50	1.25	.70
22	Andy Carey	2.00	1.00	.60
23	Johnny Kucks	2.00	1.00	.60
24	Elston Howard	2.50	1.25	.70
25	Roger Maris	4.00	2.00	1.25
26	Rube Marquard	2.50	1.25	.70
27	Sam Leslie	2.00	1.00	.60
28	Freddy Leach	2.00	1.00	.60
29	Fred Fitzsimmons	2.00	1.00	.60

No.	Name			
30	Bill Terry	2.50	1.25	.70
31	Joe Moore	2.00	1.00	.60
32	Waite Hoyt	2.00	1.00	.60
33	Travis Jackson	2.00	1.00	.60
34	Gus Mancuso	2.00	1.00	.60
35	Carl Hubbell	3.00	1.50	.90
36	Bill Voiselle	2.00	1.00	.60
37	Hank Leiber	2.00	1.00	.60
38	Burgess Whitehead	2.00	1.00	.60
39	Johnny Mize	3.00	1.50	.90
40	Bill Lohrman	2.00	1.00	.60
41	Bill Rigney	2.00	1.00	.60
42	Cliff Melton	2.00	1.00	.60
43	Willard Marshall	2.00	1.00	.60
44	Wes Westrum	2.00	1.00	.60
45	Monte Irvin	3.00	1.50	.90
46	Marv Grissom	2.00	1.00	.60
47	Clyde Castleman	2.00	1.00	.60
48	Harry Gumbert	2.00	1.00	.60
49	Daryl Spencer	2.00	1.00	.60
50	Willie Mays	9.00	4.50	2.75
51	Sam West	2.00	1.00	.60
52	Fred Schulte	2.00	1.00	.60
53	Cecil Travis	2.00	1.00	.60
54	Tommy Thomas	2.00	1.00	.60
55	Dutch Leonard	2.00	1.00	.60
56	Jimmy Wasdell	2.00	1.00	.60
57	Doc Cramer	2.00	1.00	.60
58	Harland Clift (Harlond)	2.00	1.00	.60
59	Ken Chase	2.00	1.00	.60
60	Buddy Lewis	2.00	1.00	.60
61	Ossie Bluege	2.00	1.00	.60
62	Chuck Stobbs	2.00	1.00	.60
63	Jimmy DeShong	2.00	1.00	.60
64	Roger Wolff	2.00	1.00	.60
65	Luke Sewell	2.00	1.00	.60
66	Sid Hudson	2.00	1.00	.60
67	Jack Russell	2.00	1.00	.60
68	Walt Masterson	2.00	1.00	.60
69	George Myatt	2.00	1.00	.60
70	Monte Weaver	2.00	1.00	.60
71	Cliff Bolton	2.00	1.00	.60
72	Ray Scarborough	2.00	1.00	.60
73	Albie Pearson	2.00	1.00	.60
74	Gil Coan	2.00	1.00	.60
75	Roy Sievers	2.00	1.00	.60
76	Burleigh Grimes	2.00	1.00	.60
77	Charlie Hargreaves	2.00	1.00	.60
78	Babe Herman	2.00	1.00	.60
79	Fred Frankhouse	2.00	1.00	.60
80	Al Lopez	2.00	1.00	.60
81	Lonny Frey	2.00	1.00	.60
82	Dixie Walker	2.00	1.00	.60
83	Kirby Higbe	2.00	1.00	.60
84	Bobby Bragan	2.00	1.00	.60
85	Leo Durocher	2.00	1.00	.60
86	Woody English	2.00	1.00	.60
87	Preacher Roe	2.00	1.00	.60
88	Vic Lombardi	2.00	1.00	.60
89	Clyde Sukeforth	2.00	1.00	.60
90	Pee Wee Reese	5.00	2.50	1.50
91	Joe Hatten	2.00	1.00	.60
92	Gene Hermanski	2.00	1.00	.60
93	Ray Benge	2.00	1.00	.60
94	Duke Snider	5.00	2.50	1.50
95	Walter Alston	2.00	1.00	.60
96	Don Drysdale	3.00	1.50	.90
97	Andy Pafko	2.00	1.00	.60
98	Don Zimmer	2.00	1.00	.60
99	Carl Erskine	2.00	1.00	.60
100	Dick Williams	2.00	1.00	.60
101	Charlie Grimm	2.00	1.00	.60
102	Clarence Blair	2.00	1.00	.60
103	Johnny Moore	2.00	1.00	.60
104	Clay Bryant	2.00	1.00	.60
105	Billy Herman	2.00	1.00	.60
106	Hy Vandenberg	2.00	1.00	.60
107	Lennie Merullo	2.00	1.00	.60
108	Hank Wyse	2.00	1.00	.60
109	Dom Dallessandro	2.00	1.00	.60
110	Al Epperly	2.00	1.00	.60
111	Bill Nicholson	2.00	1.00	.60
112	Vern Olsen	2.00	1.00	.60
113	Johnny Schmitz	2.00	1.00	.60
114	Bob Scheffing	2.00	1.00	.60
115	Bob Rush	2.00	1.00	.60
116	Roy Smalley	2.00	1.00	.60
117	Ransom Jackson	2.00	1.00	.60
118	Cliff Chambers	2.00	1.00	.60
119	Harry Chiti	2.00	1.00	.60
120	Johnny Klippstein	2.00	1.00	.60
121	Gene Baker	2.00	1.00	.60
122	Walt Moryn	2.00	1.00	.60
123	Dick Littlefield	2.00	1.00	.60
124	Bob Speake	2.00	1.00	.60
125	Hank Sauer	2.00	1.00	.60
126	Monty Stratton	2.50	1.25	.70
127	Johnny Kerr	2.00	1.00	.60
128	Milt Gaston	2.00	1.00	.60
129	Eddie Smith	2.00	1.00	.60
130	Larry Rosenthal	2.00	1.00	.60
131	Orval Grove	2.00	1.00	.60
132	Johnny Hodapp	2.00	1.00	.60
133	Johnny Rigney	2.00	1.00	.60
134	Willie Kamm	2.00	1.00	.60
135	Ed Lopat	2.00	1.00	.60
136	Smead Jolley	2.00	1.00	.60
137	Ralph Hodgin	2.00	1.00	.60
138	Ollie Bejma	2.00	1.00	.60
139	Zeke Bonura	2.00	1.00	.60
140	Al Hollingsworth	2.00	1.00	.60
141	Thurman Tucker	2.00	1.00	.60
142	Cass Michaels	2.00	1.00	.60
143	Bill Wight	2.00	1.00	.60
144	Don Lenhardt	2.00	1.00	.60
145	Sammy Esposito	2.00	1.00	.60
146	Jack Harshman	2.00	1.00	.60
147	Turk Lown	2.00	1.00	.60
148	Jim Landis	2.00	1.00	.60
149	Bob Shaw	2.00	1.00	.60
150	Minnie Minoso	2.50	1.25	.70
151	Les Bell	2.00	1.00	.60
152	Taylor Douthit	2.00	1.00	.60
153	Jack Rothrock	2.00	1.00	.60
154	Terry Moore	2.00	1.00	.60
155	Max Lanier	2.00	1.00	.60
156	Don Gutteridge	2.00	1.00	.60
157	Stu Martin	2.00	1.00	.60
158	Stan Musial	5.00	2.50	1.50
159	Frank Crespi	2.00	1.00	.60
160	Johnny Hopp	2.00	1.00	.60
161	Ernie Koy	2.00	1.00	.60
162	Joe Garagiola	3.00	1.50	.90
163	Ed Kazak	2.00	1.00	.60
164	Joe Orengo	2.00	1.00	.60
165	Howie Krist	2.00	1.00	.60
166	Enos Slaughter	3.00	1.50	.90
167	Ray Sanders	2.00	1.00	.60
168	Walker Cooper	2.00	1.00	.60
169	Nippy Jones	2.00	1.00	.60
170	Dick Sisler	2.00	1.00	.60
171	Harvey Haddix	2.00	1.00	.60
172	Solly Hemus	2.00	1.00	.60
173	Ray Jablonski	2.00	1.00	.60
174	Alex Grammas	2.00	1.00	.60
175	Joe Cunningham	2.00	1.00	.60
176	Debs Garms	2.00	1.00	.60
177	Chief Hogsett	2.00	1.00	.60
178	Alan Strange	2.00	1.00	.60
179	Rick Ferrell	2.00	1.00	.60
180	Jack Kramer	2.00	1.00	.60
181	Jack Knott	2.00	1.00	.60
182	Bob Harris	2.00	1.00	.60
183	Billy Hitchcock	2.00	1.00	.60
184	Jim Walkup	2.00	1.00	.60
185	Roy Cullenbine	2.00	1.00	.60
186	Bob Muncrief	2.00	1.00	.60
187	Chet Laabs	2.00	1.00	.60
188	Vern Kennedy	2.00	1.00	.60
189	Bill Trotter	2.00	1.00	.60
190	Denny Galehouse	2.00	1.00	.60
191	Al Zarilla	2.00	1.00	.60
192	Hank Arft	2.00	1.00	.60
193	Nelson Potter	2.00	1.00	.60
194	Ray Coleman	2.00	1.00	.60
195	Bob Dillinger	2.00	1.00	.60
196	Dick Kokos	2.00	1.00	.60
197	Bob Cain	2.00	1.00	.60
198	Virgil Trucks	2.00	1.00	.60
199	Duane Pillette	2.00	1.00	.60
200	Bob Turley	2.00	1.00	.60
201	Wally Berger	2.00	1.00	.60
202	John Lanning	2.00	1.00	.60
203	Buck Jordan	2.00	1.00	.60
204	Jim Turner	2.00	1.00	.60
205	Johnny Cooney	2.00	1.00	.60
206	Hank Majeski	2.00	1.00	.60
207	Phil Masi	2.00	1.00	.60
208	Tony Cuccinello	2.00	1.00	.60
209	Whitey Wietelmann	2.00	1.00	.60
210	Lou Fette	2.00	1.00	.60
211	Vince DiMaggio	2.50	1.25	.70
212	Huck Betts	2.00	1.00	.60
213	Red Barrett	2.00	1.00	.60
214	Pinky Whitney	2.00	1.00	.60
215	Tommy Holmes	2.00	1.00	.60
216	Ray Berres	2.00	1.00	.60
217	Mike Sandlock	2.00	1.00	.60
218	Max Macon	2.00	1.00	.60
219	Sibby Sisti	2.00	1.00	.60
220	Johnny Beazley	2.00	1.00	.60
221	Bill Posedel	2.00	1.00	.60
222	Connie Ryan	2.00	1.00	.60
223	Del Crandall	2.00	1.00	.60
224	Bob Addis	2.00	1.00	.60
225	Warren Spahn	3.00	1.50	.90
226	Johnny Pesky	2.00	1.00	.60
227	Dom DiMaggio	2.50	1.25	.70
228	Emerson Dickman	2.00	1.00	.60
229	Bobby Doerr	2.00	1.00	.60
230	Tony Lupien	2.00	1.00	.60
231	Roy Partee	2.00	1.00	.60
232	Stan Spence	2.00	1.00	.60
233	Jim Bagby	2.00	1.00	.60
234	Buster Mills	2.00	1.00	.60
235	Fabian Gaffke	2.00	1.00	.60
236	George Metkovich	2.00	1.00	.60
237	Tom McBride	2.00	1.00	.60
238	Charlie Wagner	2.00	1.00	.60
239	Eddie Pellagrini	2.00	1.00	.60
240	Harry Dorish	2.00	1.00	.60
241	Ike Delock	2.00	1.00	.60
242	Mel Parnell	2.00	1.00	.60
243	Matt Batts	2.00	1.00	.60
244	Gene Stephens	2.00	1.00	.60
245	Milt Bolling	2.00	1.00	.60
246	Charlie Maxwell	2.00	1.00	.60
247	Willard Nixon	2.00	1.00	.60
248	Sammy White	2.00	1.00	.60
249	Dick Gernert	2.00	1.00	.60
250	Rico Petrocelli	2.00	1.00	.60
251	Edd Roush	2.00	1.00	.60
252	Mark Koenig	2.00	1.00	.60
253	Jimmy Outlaw	2.00	1.00	.60
254	Ethan Allen	2.00	1.00	.60
255	Tony Freitas	2.00	1.00	.60
256	Frank McCormick	2.00	1.00	.60
257	Bucky Walters	2.00	1.00	.60
258	Harry Craft	2.00	1.00	.60
259	Nate Andrews	2.00	1.00	.60
260	Ed Lukon	2.00	1.00	.60
261	Elmer Riddle	2.00	1.00	.60
262	Lee Grissom	2.00	1.00	.60
263	Johnny Vander Meer	2.00	1.00	.60
264	Eddie Joost	2.00	1.00	.60
265	Kermit Wahl	2.00	1.00	.60
266	Ival Goodman	2.00	1.00	.60
267	Clyde Vollmer	2.00	1.00	.60
268	Grady Hatton	2.00	1.00	.60
269	Ted Kluszewski	3.00	1.50	.90
270	Johnny Pramesa	2.00	1.00	.60
271	Joe Black	2.50	1.25	.70
272	Roy McMillan	2.00	1.00	.60
273	Wally Post	2.00	1.00	.60
274	Joe Nuxhall	2.00	1.00	.60
275	Jerry Lynch	2.00	1.00	.60
276	Stan Coveleski	2.00	1.00	.60
277	Bill Wambsganss	2.00	1.00	.60
278	Bruce Campbell	2.00	1.00	.60
279	George Uhle	2.00	1.00	.60
280	Earl Averill	2.00	1.00	.60
281	Whit Wyatt	2.00	1.00	.60
282	Oscar Grimes	2.00	1.00	.60
283	Roy Weatherly	2.00	1.00	.60
284	Joe Dobson	2.00	1.00	.60
285	Bob Feller	3.00	1.50	.90
286	Jim Hegan	2.00	1.00	.60
287	Mel Harder	2.00	1.00	.60
288	Ken Keltner	2.00	1.00	.60
289	Red Embree	2.00	1.00	.60
290	Al Milnar	2.00	1.00	.60
291	Lou Boudreau	2.00	1.00	.60
292	Ed Klieman	2.00	1.00	.60
293	Steve Gromek	2.00	1.00	.60
294	George Strickland	2.00	1.00	.60
295	Gene Woodling	2.00	1.00	.60
296	Hank Edwards	2.00	1.00	.60
297	Don Mossi	2.00	1.00	.60
298	Eddie Robinson	2.00	1.00	.60
299	Sam Dente	2.00	1.00	.60
300	Herb Score	2.00	1.00	.60
301	Dolf Camilli	2.00	1.00	.60
302	Jack Warner	2.00	1.00	.60
303	Ike Pearson	2.00	1.00	.60
304	Johnny Peacock	2.00	1.00	.60
305	Gene Corbett	2.00	1.00	.60
306	Walt Millies	2.00	1.00	.60
307	Vance Dinges	2.00	1.00	.60
308	Joe Marty	2.00	1.00	.60
309	Hugh Mulcahey	2.00	1.00	.60
310	Boom Boom Beck	2.00	1.00	.60
311	Charley Schanz	2.00	1.00	.60
312	John Bolling	2.00	1.00	.60
313	Danny Litwhiler	2.00	1.00	.60
314	Emil Verban	2.00	1.00	.60
315	Andy Semenick	2.00	1.00	.60
316	John Antonelli	2.00	1.00	.60
317	Robin Roberts	3.00	1.50	.90
318	Richie Ashburn	3.00	1.50	.90
319	Curt Simmons	2.00	1.00	.60
320	Murry Dickson	2.00	1.00	.60
321	Jim Greengrass	2.00	1.00	.60
322	Gene Freese	2.00	1.00	.60
323	Bobby Morgan	2.00	1.00	.60
324	Don Demeter	2.00	1.00	.60
325	Eddie Sawyer	2.00	1.00	.60
326	Bob Johnson	2.00	1.00	.60
327	Ace Parker	3.00	1.50	.90
328	Joe Hauser	2.00	1.00	.60
329	Walt French	2.00	1.00	.60
330	Tom Ferrick	2.00	1.00	.60
331	Bill Werber	2.00	1.00	.60
332	Walt Masters	2.00	1.00	.60
333	Les McCrabb	2.00	1.00	.60
334	Ben McCoy	2.00	1.00	.60
335	Eric Tipton	2.00	1.00	.60
336	Al Rubeling	2.00	1.00	.60
337	Nick Etten	2.00	1.00	.60
338	Carl Scheib	2.00	1.00	.60
339	Dario Lodigiani	2.00	1.00	.60
340	Earle Brucker	2.00	1.00	.60
341	Al Brancato	2.00	1.00	.60
342	Lou Limmer	2.00	1.00	.60
343	Elmer Valo	2.00	1.00	.60
344	Bob Hooper	2.00	1.00	.60
345	Joe Astroth	2.00	1.00	.60
346	Pete Suder	2.00	1.00	.60
347	Dave Philley	2.00	1.00	.60
348	Gus Zernial	2.00	1.00	.60
349	Bobby Shantz	2.00	1.00	.60
350	Joe DeMaestri	2.00	1.00	.60
351	Fred Lindstrom	2.00	1.00	.60
352	Red Lucas	2.00	1.00	.60
353	Clyde Barnhart	2.00	1.00	.60
354	Nick Strincevich	2.00	1.00	.60
355	Lloyd Waner	2.00	1.00	.60
356	Guy Bush	2.00	1.00	.60
357	Joe Bowman	2.00	1.00	.60
358	Al Todd	2.00	1.00	.60
359	Mace Brown	2.00	1.00	.60
360	Larry French	2.00	1.00	.60
361	Elbie Fletcher	2.00	1.00	.60
362	Woody Jensen	2.00	1.00	.60
363	Rip Sewell	2.00	1.00	.60
364	Johnny Dickshot	2.00	1.00	.60
365	Pete Coscarart	2.00	1.00	.60
366	Bud Hafey	2.00	1.00	.60
367	Ken Heintzelman	2.00	1.00	.60
368	Wally Westlake	2.00	1.00	.60
369	Frank Gustine	2.00	1.00	.60
370	Smoky Burgess	2.00	1.00	.60
371	Dick Groat	2.00	1.00	.60
372	Vern Law	2.00	1.00	.60
373	Bob Skinner	2.00	1.00	.60
374	Don Cardwell	2.00	1.00	.60
375	Bob Friend	2.00	1.00	.60
376	Frank O'Rourke	2.00	1.00	.60
377	Birdie Tebbetts	2.00	1.00	.60
378	Charlie Gehringer	3.00	1.50	.90
379	Eldon Auker	2.00	1.00	.60
380	Tuck Stainback	2.00	1.00	.60
381	Chet Morgan	2.00	1.00	.60
382	Johnny Lipon	2.00	1.00	.60
383	Paul Richards	2.00	1.00	.60

384	Johnny Gorsica	2.00	1.00	.60
385	Ray Hayworth	2.00	1.00	.60
386	Jimmy Bloodworth	2.00	1.00	.60
387	Gene Desautels	2.00	1.00	.60
388	Jo Jo White	2.00	1.00	.60
389	Boots Poffenberger	2.00	1.00	.60
390	Barney McCosky	2.00	1.00	.60
391	Dick Wakefield	2.00	1.00	.60
392	Johnny Groth	2.00	1.00	.60
393	Steve Souchock	2.00	1.00	.60
394	George Vico	2.00	1.00	.60
395	Hal Newhouser	2.00	1.00	.60
396	Ray Herbert	2.00	1.00	.60
397	Jim Bunning	2.00	1.00	.60
398	Frank Lary	2.00	1.00	.60
399	Harvey Kuenn	2.00	1.00	.60
400	Eddie Mathews	3.00	1.50	.90

1911 Diamond Gum Pins (PE2)

The World's Champion Philadelphia A's are well represented and specially marked in this series of small 1" diameter pins. The sepia-toned center portion of the pin has a player portrait photo with his last name, team and league in white at left and right. Around that is a metallic blue border with a white inscription; either "World's Champions" on the A's players, or "Free with Diamond Gum" on the other players.

		NM	EX	VG
	Complete Set (31):	30,000	15,000	9,000
	Common Player:	500.00	250.00	150.00
(1)	Babe Adams	500.00	250.00	150.00
(2)	Home Run Baker	1,600	800.00	475.00
(3)	Chief Bender	1,600	800.00	475.00
(4)	Mordecai Brown	1,600	800.00	475.00
(5)	Donie Bush	500.00	250.00	150.00
(6)	Bill Carrigan	500.00	250.00	150.00
(7)	Frank Chance	1,600	800.00	475.00
(8)	Hal Chase	800.00	400.00	240.00
(9)	Ty Cobb	3,250	1,600	975.00
(10)	Eddie Collins	1,600	800.00	475.00
(11)	George Davis	500.00	250.00	150.00
(12)	Red Dooin	500.00	250.00	150.00
(13)	Larry Doyle	500.00	250.00	150.00
(14)	Johnny Evers	1,600	800.00	475.00
(15)	Miller Huggins	1,600	800.00	475.00
(16)	Hughie Jennings	1,600	800.00	475.00
(17)	Nap Lajoie	1,600	800.00	475.00
(18)	Harry Lord	500.00	250.00	150.00
(19)	Christy Mathewson	2,000	1,000	600.00
(20)	Dots Miller	500.00	250.00	150.00
	Herbie Moran, Chet Spencer (Rochester)	500.00	250.00	150.00
(21)	George Mullen (Mullin)	500.00	250.00	150.00
(22)	Danny Murphy	500.00	250.00	150.00
(23)	Orval Overall	500.00	250.00	150.00
(24)	Eddie Plank	1,600	800.00	475.00
(25)	Ryan (Rochester)	500.00	250.00	150.00
(26)	Ralph Savidge (Rochester)	500.00	250.00	150.00
(27)	Hack Simmons	500.00	250.00	150.00
(28)	Ira Thomas	500.00	250.00	150.00
(29)	Joe Tinker	1,600	800.00	475.00
(30)	Honus Wagner	3,000	1,500	900.00
(31)	Cy Young	2,000	1,000	600.00

1934 Diamond Matchbooks - Silver Border

During much of the Great Depression, the hobby of matchbook collecting swept the country. Generally selling at two for a penny, the matchbooks began to feature photos and artwork to attract buyers. In the late 1930s, several series of sports subjects were issued by Diamond Match Co., of New York City. The first issue was a set of 200 baseball players known to collectors as "silver border" for the color of the photo frame on of the approximately 1-1/2" x 4-1/8" (open) matchbooks. Player portrait or posed photos are printed in sepia on front, and can be found bordered in either red, green, blue or orange (though

it is unclear whether all players can actually be found in the red version), theoretically creating an 800-piece color variation set. The player's name and team are printed on the "saddle" and there is a career summary on back, along with a design of glove, ball and bats. Matchbooks are commonly collected with the matches removed and the striker at back-bottom intact. Pieces without the striker are valued at 50 percent of these listed prices. Complete covers with matches bring a premium of 2-3X. The players are listed here alphabetically.

		NM	EX	VG
	Complete Set (200):	4,500	2,250	1,350
	Common Player:	20.00	10.00	6.00
(1)	Earl Adams	20.00	10.00	6.00
(2)	Ethan Allen	20.00	10.00	6.00
(3)	Eldon L. Auker	20.00	10.00	6.00
(4)	Delmar David Baker	20.00	10.00	6.00
(5)	Richard "Dick" Bartell	20.00	10.00	6.00
(6)	Walter Beck	20.00	10.00	6.00
(7)	Herman Bell	20.00	10.00	6.00
(8)	Ray Benge	20.00	10.00	6.00
(9)	Larry J. Benton	20.00	10.00	6.00
(10)	Louis W. Berger	20.00	10.00	6.00
(11)	Walter "Wally" Berger	20.00	10.00	6.00
(12)	Ray Berres	20.00	10.00	6.00
(13)	Charlie Berry	20.00	10.00	6.00
(14)	Walter M. "Huck" Betts	20.00	10.00	6.00
(15)	Ralph Birkofer	20.00	10.00	6.00
(16)	George F. Blaeholder	20.00	10.00	6.00
(17)	Jim Bottomley	40.00	20.00	12.00
(18a)	Ralph Boyle (Photo actually Virgil Davis, white cap.)	20.00	10.00	6.00
(18b)	Ralph Boyle (Correct photo, cark cap.)	20.00	10.00	6.00
(19)	Ed Brandt	20.00	10.00	6.00
(20)	Don Brennan	20.00	10.00	6.00
(21)	Irving (Jack) Burns	20.00	10.00	6.00
(22)	Guy "Joe" Bush	20.00	10.00	6.00
(23)	Adolph Camilli	20.00	10.00	6.00
(24)	Ben Cantwell	20.00	10.00	6.00
(25)	Tex Carleton	20.00	10.00	6.00
(26)	Owen Carroll	20.00	10.00	6.00
(27)	Louis Chiozza	20.00	10.00	6.00
(28)	Watson Clark	20.00	10.00	6.00
(29)	James A. Collins	20.00	10.00	6.00
(30)	Phil Collins	20.00	10.00	6.00
(31)	Edward J. Connolly	20.00	10.00	6.00
(32)	Raymond F. Coombs	20.00	10.00	6.00
(33)	Roger Cramer	20.00	10.00	6.00
(34)	Clifford Crawford	20.00	10.00	6.00
(35)	Hugh M. Critz	20.00	10.00	6.00
(36)	Alvin Crowder	20.00	10.00	6.00
(37)	Tony Cuccinello	20.00	10.00	6.00
(38)	Hazen "Kiki" Cuyler	40.00	20.00	12.00
(39)	Virgil Davis	20.00	10.00	6.00
(40)	Jerome "Dizzy" Dean	80.00	40.00	24.00
(41)	Paul Dean	35.00	17.50	10.50
(42)	Edward Delker	20.00	10.00	6.00
(43)	Paul Derringer	20.00	10.00	6.00
(44)	Eugene DeSautel	20.00	10.00	6.00
(45)	William J. Dietrich	20.00	10.00	6.00
(46)	Frank F. Doljack	20.00	10.00	6.00
(47)	Edward F. Durham	20.00	10.00	6.00
(48)	Leo Durocher	40.00	20.00	12.00
(49)	Jim Elliott	20.00	10.00	6.00
(50)	Charles D. English	20.00	10.00	6.00
(51)	Elwood G. English	20.00	10.00	6.00
(52)	Richard Ferrell	40.00	20.00	12.00
(53)	Wesley Ferrell (EXISTENCE DOUBTED)			
(54)	Charles W. Fischer	20.00	10.00	6.00
(55)	Freddy Fitzsimmons	20.00	10.00	6.00
(56)	Lew Fonseca	20.00	10.00	6.00
(57)	Fred Frankhouse	20.00	10.00	6.00
(58)	John Frederick	20.00	10.00	6.00
(59)	Benny Frey (Reds)	20.00	10.00	6.00
(60)	Linus Frey (Dodgers)	20.00	10.00	6.00
(61)	Frankie Frisch	45.00	22.00	13.50
(62)	Chick Fullis	20.00	10.00	6.00
(63)	August Galan	20.00	10.00	6.00
(64)	Milton Galatzer	120.00	60.00	36.00
(65)	Dennis W. Galehouse	20.00	10.00	6.00
(66)	Milton Gaston	20.00	10.00	6.00
(67)	Chas. Gehringer	45.00	22.00	13.50
(68)	Edward P. Gharrity	20.00	10.00	6.00
(69)	George Gibson	20.00	10.00	6.00
(70)	Isidore Goldstein	250.00	125.00	75.00
(71)	"Hank" Gowdy	20.00	10.00	6.00
(72)	Earl Grace	20.00	10.00	6.00
(73)	Chas. Grimm (Fielding)	20.00	10.00	6.00
(74)	Chas. Grimm (Portrait)	20.00	10.00	6.00
(75)	Frank T. Grube	20.00	10.00	6.00
(76)	Richard Gyselman	20.00	10.00	6.00
(77)	Stanley C. Hack	25.00	12.50	7.50
(78)	Irving Hadley	20.00	10.00	6.00
(79)	Charles "Chick" Hafey	40.00	20.00	12.00
(80)	Harold A. Haid	20.00	10.00	6.00
(81)	Jesse Haines	40.00	20.00	12.00
(82)	Odell A. Hale	20.00	10.00	6.00
(83)	Bill Hallahan	20.00	10.00	6.00
(84)	Luke D. Hamlin	20.00	10.00	6.00
(85)	Roy Hansen	20.00	10.00	6.00
(86)	Melvin Harder	20.00	10.00	6.00
(87)	William M. Harris	20.00	10.00	6.00
(88)	Gabby Hartnett	40.00	20.00	12.00
(89)	Harvey Hendrick	20.00	10.00	6.00
(90)	Floyd "Babe" Herman	25.00	12.50	7.50
(91)	William Herman	40.00	20.00	12.00
(92)	J. Francis Hogan	20.00	10.00	6.00
(93)	Elon Hogsett	20.00	10.00	6.00
(94)	Waite Hoyt	40.00	20.00	12.00
(95)	Carl Hubbell	50.00	25.00	15.00
(96)	Silas K. Johnson	20.00	10.00	6.00
(97)	Sylvester Johnson	20.00	10.00	6.00
(98)	Roy M. Joiner	20.00	10.00	6.00
(99)	Baxter Jordan	20.00	10.00	6.00
(100)	Arndt Jorgens	20.00	10.00	6.00

		NM	EX	VG
(101)	William F. Jurges	20.00	10.00	6.00
(102)	Vernon Kennedy	20.00	10.00	6.00
(103)	John F. Kerr	20.00	10.00	6.00
(104)	Charles "Chuck" Klein	40.00	20.00	12.00
(105)	Theodore Kleinhans	20.00	10.00	6.00
(106)	Bill Klem (Umpire)	125.00	65.00	35.00
(107)	Robert G. Kline	20.00	10.00	6.00
(108)	William Knickerbocker	20.00	10.00	6.00
(109)	Jack H. Knott	20.00	10.00	6.00
(110)	Mark Koenig	20.00	10.00	6.00
(111)	William Lawrence	20.00	10.00	6.00
(112)	Thornton S. Lee	20.00	10.00	6.00
(113)	Wm. C. "Bill" Lee	20.00	10.00	6.00
(114)	Emil Leonard	20.00	10.00	6.00
(115)	Ernest Lombardi	40.00	20.00	12.00
(116)	Alfonso Lopez	40.00	20.00	12.00
(117)	Red Lucas	20.00	10.00	6.00
(118)	Ted Lyons	40.00	20.00	12.00
(119)	Daniel MacFayden	20.00	10.00	6.00
(120)	Ed. Majeski	20.00	10.00	6.00
(121)	Leroy Mahaffey	20.00	10.00	6.00
(122)	Pat Malone	20.00	10.00	6.00
(123)	Leo Mangum	20.00	10.00	6.00
(124)	Rabbit Maranville	40.00	20.00	12.00
(125)	Charles K. Marrow	20.00	10.00	6.00
(126)	William McKechnie	40.00	20.00	12.00
(127)	Justin McLaughlin	20.00	10.00	6.00
(128)	Marty McManus	20.00	10.00	6.00
(129)	Eric McNair	20.00	10.00	6.00
(130)	Joe Medwick	40.00	20.00	12.00
(131)	Jim Mooney	20.00	10.00	6.00
(132)	Joe Moore	20.00	10.00	6.00
(133)	John Moore	20.00	10.00	6.00
(134)	Randy Moore	20.00	10.00	6.00
(135)	Joe Morrissey	20.00	10.00	6.00
(136)	Joseph Mowrey	20.00	10.00	6.00
(137)	Fred W. Muller	20.00	10.00	6.00
(138)	Van Mungo	25.00	12.50	7.50
(139)	Glenn Myatt	20.00	10.00	6.00
(140a)	Lynn Nelson (Photo actually Eugene DeSautel, no "C" on cap.)	20.00	10.00	6.00
(140b)	Lynn Nelson (Correct photo, "C" on cap.)	20.00	10.00	6.00
(141)	Henry Oana	60.00	30.00	18.00
(142)	Lefty O'Doul	35.00	17.50	10.50
(143)	Robert O'Farrell	20.00	10.00	6.00
(144)	Ernest Orsatti	20.00	10.00	6.00
(145)	Fritz R. Ostermueller	20.00	10.00	6.00
(146)	Melvin Ott	45.00	22.00	13.50
(147)	Roy Parmelee	20.00	10.00	6.00
(148)	Ralph Perkins	20.00	10.00	6.00
(149)	Frank Pytlak	20.00	10.00	6.00
(150)	Ernest C. Quigley (Umpire)	45.00	22.00	13.50
(151)	George Rensa	20.00	10.00	6.00
(152)	Harry Rice	20.00	10.00	6.00
(153)	Walter Roettger	20.00	10.00	6.00
(154)	William G. Rogell	20.00	10.00	6.00
(155)	Edwin A. Rommel	20.00	10.00	6.00
(156)	Charlie Root	20.00	10.00	6.00
(157)	John Rothrock	20.00	10.00	6.00
(158)	Jack Russell	20.00	10.00	6.00
(159)	Blondy Ryan	20.00	10.00	6.00
(160)	Alexander (Al) Schacht	35.00	17.50	10.50
(161)	Wesley Schultmerick	20.00	10.00	6.00
(162)	Truett B. Sewell	20.00	10.00	6.00
(163)	Gordon Slade	20.00	10.00	6.00
(164)	Bob Smith	20.00	10.00	6.00
(165)	Julius J. Solters	20.00	10.00	6.00
(166)	Glenn Spencer	20.00	10.00	6.00
(167)	Al Spohrer	20.00	10.00	6.00
(168)	George Stainback	20.00	10.00	6.00
(169)	Albert "Dolly" Stark (Umpire)	40.00	20.00	12.00
(170)	Casey Stengel	50.00	25.00	15.00
(171)	Riggs Stephenson	20.00	10.00	6.00
(172)	Walter C. Stewart	20.00	10.00	6.00
(173)	Lin Storti	20.00	10.00	6.00
(174)	Allyn (Fish Hook) Stout	20.00	10.00	6.00
(175)	Joe Stripp	20.00	10.00	6.00
(176)	Gus Suhr	20.00	10.00	6.00
(177)	Billy Sullivan, Jr.	20.00	10.00	6.00
(178)	Benny Tate	20.00	10.00	6.00
(179)	Danny Taylor	20.00	10.00	6.00
(180)	Tommy Thevenow	20.00	10.00	6.00
(181)	Bud Tinning	20.00	10.00	6.00
(182)	Cecil Travis	20.00	10.00	6.00
(183)	Forest F. Twogood	20.00	10.00	6.00
(184)	Bill Urbanski	20.00	10.00	6.00
(185)	Dazzy Vance	40.00	20.00	12.00
(186)	Arthur Veltman (SP)	100.00	50.00	30.00
(187)	John L. Vergez	20.00	10.00	6.00
(188)	Gerald (Jerry) Walker	20.00	10.00	6.00
(189)	William H. Walker	20.00	10.00	6.00
(190)	Lloyd Waner	40.00	20.00	12.00
(191)	Paul Waner	40.00	20.00	12.00
(192)	Lon Warnecke	20.00	10.00	6.00
(193)	Harold B. Warstler	20.00	10.00	6.00
(194)	Bill Werber	20.00	10.00	6.00
(195)	Joyner White	20.00	10.00	6.00
(196)	Arthur Whitney	20.00	10.00	6.00
(197)	James Wilson	20.00	10.00	6.00
(198)	Lewis (Hack) Wilson	40.00	20.00	12.00
(199)	Ralph L. Winegarner	20.00	10.00	6.00
(200)	Thomas Zachary	20.00	10.00	6.00

1935 Diamond Matchbooks - Black Border

Only 24 players were issued in the 1935 Diamond Matchbook baseball series. Similar in design to the 1934 issue, these 1-1/2" x 4-1/8" matchbooks have sepia player portrait photos on front, framed in either red, green or blue. The overall borders of the cover are black. Backs of the 1935 issue feature a career summary overprinted on a silhouetted batting figure. The "saddle" has the player name and team superimposed on a baseball. These matchbooks are commonly collected with the matches removed and the striker at back-bottom intact. Pieces without the striker are valued at 50 percent of these listed prices. Complete covers with matches bring a premium of 2-3X. The players are listed here alphabetically.

		NM	EX	VG
Complete Set (24):		850.00	425.00	250.00
Common Player:		25.00	12.50	7.50
(1)	Ethan Allen (Red)	25.00	12.50	7.50
(2)	Walter Berger (Red)	25.00	12.50	7.50
(3)	Tommy Carey (Blue)	25.00	12.50	7.50
(4)	Louis Chiozza (Blue)	25.00	12.50	7.50
(5)	Jerome (Dizzy) Dean (Green)	65.00	32.50	20.00
(6)	Frankie Frisch (Red)	50.00	25.00	15.00
(7)	Charles Grimm (Blue)	25.00	12.50	7.50
(8)	Charles Hafey (Red)	40.00	20.00	12.00
(9)	J. Francis Hogan (Red)	25.00	12.50	7.50
(10)	Carl Hubbell (Green)	50.00	25.00	15.00
(11)	Charles Klein (Green)	40.00	20.00	12.00
(12)	Ernest Lombardi (Blue)	40.00	20.00	12.00
(13)	Alfonso Lopez (Blue)	40.00	20.00	12.00
(14)	Rabbit Maranville (Green)	40.00	20.00	12.00
(15)	Joe Moore (Red)	25.00	12.50	7.50
(16)	Van Mungo (Green)	25.00	12.50	7.50
(17)	Melvin (Mel) Ott (Blue)	50.00	25.00	15.00
(18)	Gordon Slade (Green)	25.00	12.50	7.50
(19)	Casey Stengel (Green)	50.00	25.00	15.00
(20)	Tommy Thevenow (Red)	25.00	12.50	7.50
(21)	Lloyd Waner (Red)	40.00	20.00	12.00
(22)	Paul Waner (Green)	50.00	25.00	15.00
(23)	Lon Warnecke (Blue)	25.00	12.50	7.50
(24)	James Wilson (Blue)	25.00	12.50	7.50

1935-36 Diamond Matchbooks

By the career summaries on back of these covers it is evident this series was issued over a two-year period. Measuring about 1-1/2" x 4-1/8", the fronts have posed player photos printed in sepia. Borders can be found in red, green or blue, and it is believed that most, if not all, players can be found in those three color varieties. Matchbooks in this series do not have the team name on back beneath the player name, as is the case on later series. Collectors generally prefer matchbooks to be complete with striker surface on bottom-back, though with matches removed. Values shown should be halved for covers without strikers. Complete with matches, covers will sell for a 2-3X premium over the values shown.

		NM	EX	VG
Complete Set (156):		3,500	1,750	1,000
Common Player:		20.00	10.00	6.00
(1)	Ethan Allen	20.00	10.00	6.00
(2)	Melo Almada	30.00	15.00	9.00
(3)	Eldon Auker	20.00	10.00	6.00
(4)	Dick Bartell	20.00	10.00	6.00
(5)	Aloysius Bejma	20.00	10.00	6.00
(6)	Ollie Bejma	20.00	10.00	6.00
(7)	Roy Chester Bell	20.00	10.00	6.00
(8)	Louis Berger	20.00	10.00	6.00
(9)	Walter Berger	20.00	10.00	6.00
(10)	Ralph Birkofer	20.00	10.00	6.00
(11)	Max Bishop	20.00	10.00	6.00
(12)	George Blaeholder	20.00	10.00	6.00
(13)	Henry (Zeke) Bonura	20.00	10.00	6.00
(14)	Jim Bottomley	35.00	17.50	10.50
(15)	Ed Brandt	20.00	10.00	6.00
(16)	Don Brennan	20.00	10.00	6.00
(17)	Lloyd Brown	20.00	10.00	6.00
(18)	Walter G. Brown	20.00	10.00	6.00
(19)	Claiborne Bryant	20.00	10.00	6.00
(20)	Jim Bucher	20.00	10.00	6.00
(21)	John Burnett	20.00	10.00	6.00
(22)	Irving Burns	20.00	10.00	6.00
(23)	Merritt Cain	20.00	10.00	6.00
(24)	Ben Cantwell	20.00	10.00	6.00
(25)	Tommy Carey	20.00	10.00	6.00
(26)	Tex Carleton	20.00	10.00	6.00
(27)	Joseph Cascarella	20.00	10.00	6.00
(28)	Thomas H. Casey	20.00	10.00	6.00
(29)	George Caster	20.00	10.00	6.00
(30)	Phil Cavarretta	20.00	10.00	6.00
(31)	Louis Chiozza	20.00	10.00	6.00
(32)	Edward Cihocki	20.00	10.00	6.00
(33)	Herman E. Clifton	20.00	10.00	6.00
(34)	Richard Coffman	20.00	10.00	6.00
(35)	Edward P. Coleman	20.00	10.00	6.00
(36)	James A. Collins	20.00	10.00	6.00
(37)	John Conlan	40.00	20.00	12.00
(38)	Roger Cramer	20.00	10.00	6.00
(39)	Hugh M. Critz	20.00	10.00	6.00
(40)	Alvin Crowder	20.00	10.00	6.00
(41)	Tony Cuccinello	20.00	10.00	6.00
(42)	Hazen "Kiki" Cuyler	35.00	17.50	10.50
(43)	Virgil Davis	20.00	10.00	6.00
(44)	Jerome Dean	75.00	37.00	22.00
(45)	Paul Derringer	20.00	10.00	6.00
(46)	James DeShong	20.00	10.00	6.00
(47)	William Dietrich	20.00	10.00	6.00
(48)	Leo Durocher	35.00	17.50	10.50
(49)	George Earnshaw	20.00	10.00	6.00
(50)	Elwood English	20.00	10.00	6.00
(51)	Louis Finney	20.00	10.00	6.00
(52)	Charles Fischer	20.00	10.00	6.00
(53)	Freddy Fitzsimmons	20.00	10.00	6.00
(54)	Benny Frey	20.00	10.00	6.00
(55)	Linus B. Frey	20.00	10.00	6.00
(56)	Frankie Frisch	40.00	20.00	12.00
(57)	August Galan	20.00	10.00	6.00
(58)	Milton Galatzer	20.00	10.00	6.00
(59)	Dennis Galehouse	20.00	10.00	6.00
(60)	Debs Garms	20.00	10.00	6.00
(61)	Angelo J. Giuliani	20.00	10.00	6.00
(62)	Earl Grace	20.00	10.00	6.00
(63)	Charles Grimm	20.00	10.00	6.00
(64)	Frank Grube	20.00	10.00	6.00
(65)	Stanley Hack	25.00	12.50	7.50
(66)	Irving "Bump" Hadley	20.00	10.00	6.00
(67)	Odell Hale	20.00	10.00	6.00
(68)	Bill Hallahan	20.00	10.00	6.00
(69)	Roy Hansen	20.00	10.00	6.00
(70)	Melvin Harder	20.00	10.00	6.00
(71)	Charles Hartnett	35.00	17.50	10.50
(72)	"Gabby" Hartnett	35.00	17.50	10.50
(73)	Clyde Hatter	20.00	10.00	6.00
(74)	Raymond Hayworth	20.00	10.00	6.00
(75)	Raymond Hayworth (W/chest protector.)	20.00	10.00	6.00
(76)	William Herman	35.00	17.50	10.50
(77)	Gordon Hinkle	20.00	10.00	6.00
(78)	George Hockette	20.00	10.00	6.00
(79)	James Holbrook	20.00	10.00	6.00
(80)	Alex Hooks	20.00	10.00	6.00
(81)	Waite Hoyt	35.00	17.50	10.50
(82)	Carl Hubbell	40.00	20.00	12.00
(83)	Roy M. Joiner	20.00	10.00	6.00
(84)	Sam Jones	20.00	10.00	6.00
(85)	Baxter Jordan	20.00	10.00	6.00
(86)	Arndt Jorgens	20.00	10.00	6.00
(87)	William F. Jurges	20.00	10.00	6.00
(88)	William Kamm	20.00	10.00	6.00
(89)	Vernon Kennedy	20.00	10.00	6.00
(90)	John Kerr	20.00	10.00	6.00
(91)	Charles Klein	40.00	20.00	12.00
(92)	Ted Kleinhans	20.00	10.00	6.00
(93)	Wm. Knickerbocker (Thighs-up.)	20.00	10.00	6.00
(94)	Wm. Knickerbocker (Waist-up.)	20.00	10.00	6.00
(95)	Jack Knott	20.00	10.00	6.00
(96)	Mark Koenig	20.00	10.00	6.00
(97)	Fabian L. Kowalik	20.00	10.00	6.00
(98)	Ralph Kress	20.00	10.00	6.00
(99)	Wm. C. "Bill" Lee	20.00	10.00	6.00
(100)	Louis Legett	20.00	10.00	6.00
(101)	Emil "Dutch" Leonard	20.00	10.00	6.00
(102)	Fred Lindstrom	35.00	17.50	10.50
(103)	Edward Linke (Pole in background.)	20.00	10.00	6.00
(104)	Edward Linke (No pole.)	20.00	10.00	6.00
(105)	Ernest Lombardi	35.00	17.50	10.50
(106)	Al Lopez	35.00	17.50	10.50
(107)	John Marcum	20.00	10.00	6.00
(108)	William McKechnie	35.00	17.50	10.50
(109)	Eric McNair	20.00	10.00	6.00
(110)	Joe Medwick	35.00	17.50	10.50
(111)	Oscar Melillo	20.00	10.00	6.00
(112)	John Michaels	20.00	10.00	6.00
(113)	Joe Moore	20.00	10.00	6.00
(114)	John Moore	20.00	10.00	6.00
(115)	Wallace Moses	20.00	10.00	6.00
(116)	Joseph Milligan	20.00	10.00	6.00
(117)	Van Mungo	25.00	12.50	7.50
(118)	Glenn Myatt	20.00	10.00	6.00
(119)	James O'Dea	20.00	10.00	6.00
(120)	Ernest Orsatti	20.00	10.00	6.00
(121)	Fred Ostermueller	20.00	10.00	6.00
(122)	Melvin "Mel" Ott	40.00	20.00	12.00
(123)	LeRoy Parmelee	20.00	10.00	6.00
(124)	Monte Pearson	20.00	10.00	6.00
(125)	Raymond Pepper	20.00	10.00	6.00
(126)	Raymond Phelps	20.00	10.00	6.00
(127)	George Pipgras	20.00	10.00	6.00
(128)	Frank Pytlak	20.00	10.00	6.00
(129)	Gordon Rhodes	20.00	10.00	6.00
(130)	Charlie Root	20.00	10.00	6.00
(131)	John Rothrock	20.00	10.00	6.00
(132)	Herold "Muddy" Ruel	20.00	10.00	6.00
(133)	Jack Saltzgaver	20.00	10.00	6.00
(134)	Fred Schulte	20.00	10.00	6.00
(135)	George Selkirk	20.00	10.00	6.00
(136)	Mervyn Shea	20.00	10.00	6.00
(137)	Al Spohrer	20.00	10.00	6.00
(138)	George Stainback	20.00	10.00	6.00
(139)	Casey Stengel	40.00	20.00	12.00
(140)	Walter Stephenson	20.00	10.00	6.00
(141)	Lee Stine	20.00	10.00	6.00
(142)	John Stone	20.00	10.00	6.00
(143)	Gus Suhr	20.00	10.00	6.00
(144)	Tommy Thevenow	20.00	10.00	6.00
(145)	Fay Thomas	20.00	10.00	6.00
(146)	Leslie Tietje	20.00	10.00	6.00
(147)	Bill Urbanski	20.00	10.00	6.00
(148)	William H. Walker	20.00	10.00	6.00
(149)	Lloyd Waner	40.00	20.00	12.00
(150)	Paul Waner	40.00	20.00	12.00
(151)	Lon Warnecke	20.00	10.00	6.00
(152)	Harold Warstler	20.00	10.00	6.00
(153)	Bill Werber	20.00	10.00	6.00
(154)	Vernon Wiltshere	20.00	10.00	6.00
(155)	James Wilson	20.00	10.00	6.00
(156)	Ralph Winegarner	20.00	10.00	6.00

1936 Diamond Matchbooks - Team on Back

This is the smallest series of baseball player matchbooks, with only 13 subjects, each found with borders of red, green or blue. Player poses on front are printed in sepia (except one variation of Grimm that is in black-and-white). This series can be differentiated from contemporary series by the appearance of the player's team name on back, beneath his name. Backs have a career summary. About 1-1/2" x 4-1/8", these matchbooks are commonly collected with the matches removed and the striker at back bottom intact. Pieces without the striker are valued at 50 percent of these listed prices. Complete covers with matches bring a premium of 2-3X. The players are listed here alphabetically.

		NM	EX	VG
Complete Set (13):		350.00	175.00	100.00
Common Player:		20.00	10.00	6.00
(1)	Tommy Carey	20.00	10.00	6.00
(2)	Tony Cuccinello	20.00	10.00	6.00
(3)	Freddy Fitzsimmons	20.00	10.00	6.00
(4)	Frank Frisch	45.00	22.00	13.50
(5a)	Charles Grimm (Home uniform, b/w.)	20.00	10.00	6.00
(5b)	Charlie Grimm (Home uniform, sepia.)	20.00	10.00	6.00
(6)	Charlie Grimm (Road uniform.)	20.00	10.00	6.00
(7)	Carl Hubbell	45.00	22.00	13.50
(8)	Baxter Jordan	20.00	10.00	6.00
(9)	Chuck Klein	45.00	22.00	13.50
(10)	Al Lopez	35.00	17.50	10.50
(11)	Joe Medwick	35.00	17.50	10.50
(12)	Van Lingle Mungo	25.00	12.50	7.50
(13)	Mel Ott	45.00	22.00	13.50

1936 Diamond Matchbooks - Chicago Cubs

This short series of baseball player matchbooks can each be found with borders of red, green or blue. Except for Dean, all photos are portraits, printed in sepia or black-and-white. Dean and Paul Waner are the only subjects in the set who were not members of the Chicago Cubs. This series can be differentiated from 1935-36 Diamond Matchbooks only by studying the career summary and stats on back. About 1-1/2" x 4-1/8", these matchbooks are commonly collected with the matches removed and the striker at back-bottom intact. Pieces without the striker are valued at 50 percent of these listed prices. Complete covers with matches bring a premium of 2-3X. The players are listed here alphabetically.

		NM	EX	VG
	Complete Set (23):	350.00	175.00	100.00
	Common Player:	12.50	6.25	3.75
(1)	Claiborne Bryant	12.50	6.25	3.75
(2)	Tex Carleton	12.50	6.25	3.75
(3)	Phil Cavarretta	12.50	6.25	3.75
(4)	James A. Collins	12.50	6.25	3.75
(5)	Curt Davis	12.50	6.25	3.75
(6)	Jerome "Dizzy" Dean	50.00	25.00	15.00
(7)	Frank Demaree	12.50	6.25	3.75
(8)	Larry French	12.50	6.25	3.75
(9)	Linus R. Frey	12.50	6.25	3.75
(10)	August Galan	12.50	6.25	3.75
(11)	Bob Garbark	12.50	6.25	3.75
(12)	Stanley Hack	15.00	7.50	4.50
(13)	Charles Hartnett	30.00	15.00	9.00
(14)	William Herman	30.00	15.00	9.00
(15)	William F. Jurges	12.50	6.25	3.75
(16)	William C. "Bill" Lee	12.50	6.25	3.75
(17)	Joe Marty	12.50	6.25	3.75
(18)	James K. O'Dea	12.50	6.25	3.75
(19)	LeRoy Parmelee	12.50	6.25	3.75
(20)	Charlie Root	12.50	6.25	3.75
(21)	Clyde Shoun	12.50	6.25	3.75
(22)	George Stainback	12.50	6.25	3.75
(23)	Paul Waner	40.00	20.00	12.00

1889 Diamond S Cigars Boston N.L.

(See 1889 Number 7 Cigars for checklist and value information.)

1934-36 Diamond Stars (R327)

Issued from 1934-36, the Diamond Stars set (ACC designation R327) consists of 108 cards. Produced by National Chicle, the cards measure 2-3/8" x 2-7/8" and are color art renderings of actual photographs on art deco backgrounds. The year of issue can usually be determined by the player's statistics found on the reverse of the card. Backs also feature either a player biography or a playing tip. Some cards can be found with either green or blue printing on the backs. The complete set price does not include the higher priced variations which make up the 170-card "master" set.

		NM	EX	VG
	Complete Set (108):	22,500	9,000	4,000
	Complete Set (170):	35,000	14,000	6,250
	Common Player (1-84):	100.00	35.00	20.00
	Common Player (85-96):	200.00	85.00	45.00
	Common Player (97-108):	500.00	245.00	120.00
1a	"Lefty" Grove (1934 green back)	5,040	770.00	245.00
1b	"Lefty" Grove (1935 green back)	5,040	770.00	245.00
2a	Al Simmons (1934 green back)	840.00	225.00	155.00
2b	Al Simmons (1935 green back)	840.00	225.00	155.00
2c	Al Simmons (1936 blue back)	910.00	365.00	180.00
3a	"Rabbit" Maranville (1934 green back)	455.00	180.00	90.00
3b	"Rabbit" Maranville (1935 green back)	455.00	180.00	90.00
4a	"Buddy" Myer (1934 green back)	100.00	35.00	20.00
4b	"Buddy" Myer (1935 green back)	100.00	35.00	20.00
4c	"Buddy" Myer (1936 blue back)	105.00	45.00	20.00
5a	Tom Bridges (1934 green back)	100.00	35.00	20.00
5b	Tom Bridges (1935 green back)	100.00	35.00	20.00
5c	Tom Bridges (1936 blue back)	105.00	45.00	20.00
6a	Max Bishop (1934 green back)	100.00	35.00	20.00
6b	Max Bishop (1935 green back)	100.00	35.00	20.00
7a	Lew Fonseca (1934 green back)	100.00	35.00	20.00
7b	Lew Fonseca (1935 green back)	100.00	35.00	20.00
8a	Joe Vosmik (1934 green back)	100.00	35.00	20.00
8b	Joe Vosmik (1935 green back)	100.00	35.00	20.00
8c	Joe Vosmik (1936 blue back)	105.00	45.00	20.00
9a	"Mickey" Cochrane (1934 green back)	455.00	180.00	90.00
9b	"Mickey" Cochrane (1935 green back)	455.00	180.00	90.00
9c	"Mickey" Cochrane (1936 blue back)	525.00	210.00	105.00
10a	Roy Mahaffey (1934 green back)	100.00	35.00	20.00
10b	Roy Mahaffey (1935 green back)	100.00	35.00	20.00
10c	Roy Mahaffey (1936 blue back)	105.00	45.00	20.00
11a	Bill Dickey (1934 green back)	525.00	210.00	105.00
11b	Bill Dickey (1935 green back)	525.00	210.00	105.00
12a	Dixie Walker (1934 green back)	100.00	35.00	20.00
12b	Dixie Walker (1935 green back)	100.00	35.00	20.00
12c	Dixie Walker (1936 blue back)	105.00	45.00	20.00
13a	George Blaeholder (1934 green back)	100.00	35.00	20.00
13b	George Blaeholder (1935 green back)	100.00	35.00	20.00
14a	Bill Terry (1934 green back)	455.00	180.00	90.00
14b	Bill Terry (1935 green back)	455.00	180.00	90.00
15a	Dick Bartell (1934 green back)	100.00	35.00	20.00
15b	Dick Bartell (1935 green back)	100.00	35.00	20.00
16a	Lloyd Waner (1934 green back)	455.00	180.00	90.00
16b	Lloyd Waner (1935 green back)	455.00	180.00	90.00
16c	Lloyd Waner (1936 blue back)	560.00	225.00	115.00
17a	Frankie Frisch (1934 green back)	455.00	180.00	90.00
17b	Frankie Frisch (1935 green back)	455.00	180.00	90.00
18a	"Chick" Hafey (1934 green back)	455.00	180.00	90.00
18b	"Chick" Hafey (1935 green back)	455.00	180.00	90.00
19a	Van Mungo (1934 green back)	315.00	125.00	65.00
19b	Van Mungo (1935 green back)	315.00	125.00	65.00
20a	"Shanty" Hogan (1934 green back)	100.00	35.00	20.00
20b	"Shanty" Hogan (1935 green back)	100.00	35.00	20.00
21a	Johnny Vergez (1934 green back)	100.00	35.00	20.00
21b	Johnny Vergez (1935 green back)	100.00	35.00	20.00
22a	Jimmy Wilson (1934 green back)	100.00	35.00	20.00
22b	Jimmy Wilson (1935 green back)	100.00	35.00	20.00
22c	Jimmy Wilson (1936 blue back)	105.00	45.00	20.00
23a	Bill Hallahan (1934 green back)	100.00	35.00	20.00
23b	Bill Hallahan (1935 green back)	100.00	35.00	20.00
24a	"Sparky" Adams (1934 green back)	100.00	35.00	20.00
24b	"Sparky" Adams (1935 green back)	100.00	35.00	20.00
25	Walter Berger	100.00	35.00	20.00
26a	"Pepper" Martin	160.00	65.00	30.00
26b	"Pepper" Martin (1936 blue back)	175.00	70.00	35.00
27	"Pie" Traynor	200.00	85.00	45.00
28	"Al" Lopez	200.00	85.00	45.00
29	Robert Rolfe	100.00	35.00	20.00
30a	"Heinie" Manush (1935 green back)	200.00	85.00	45.00
30b	"Heinie" Manush (1936 blue back)	245.00	100.00	50.00
31a	"Kiki" Cuyler (1935 green back)	200.00	85.00	45.00
31b	"Kiki" Cuyler (1936 blue back)	245.00	100.00	50.00
32	Sam Rice	200.00	85.00	45.00
33	"Schoolboy" Rowe	125.00	50.00	20.00
34	Stanley Hack	125.00	50.00	20.00
35	Earle Averill	200.00	85.00	45.00
36a	Earnie Lombardi	560.00	225.00	115.00
36b	Ernie Lombardi	245.00	100.00	50.00
37	"Billie" Urbanski	100.00	35.00	20.00
38	Ben Chapman	100.00	35.00	20.00
39	Carl Hubbell	295.00	120.00	55.00
40	"Blondy" Ryan	100.00	35.00	20.00
41	Harvey Hendrick	100.00	35.00	20.00
42	Jimmy Dykes	100.00	35.00	20.00
43	Ted Lyons	200.00	85.00	45.00
44	Rogers Hornsby	525.00	210.00	105.00
45	"Jo Jo" White	100.00	35.00	20.00
46	"Red" Lucas	100.00	35.00	20.00
47	Cliff Bolton	100.00	35.00	20.00
48	"Rick" Ferrell	200.00	85.00	45.00
49	"Buck" Jordan	100.00	35.00	20.00
50	"Mel" Ott	310.00	120.00	55.00
51	John Whitehead	100.00	35.00	20.00
52	George Stainback	100.00	35.00	20.00
53	Oscar Melillo	100.00	35.00	20.00
54a	"Hank" Greenburg (Greenberg)	1,600	800.00	475.00
54b	"Hank" Greenberg	805.00	325.00	160.00
55	Tony Cuccinello	100.00	35.00	20.00
56	"Gus" Suhr	100.00	35.00	20.00
57	Cy Blanton	100.00	35.00	20.00
58	Glenn Myatt	100.00	35.00	20.00
59	Jim Bottomley	200.00	85.00	45.00
60	Charley "Red" Ruffing	200.00	85.00	45.00
61	"Billie" Werber	100.00	35.00	20.00
62	Fred M. Frankhouse	100.00	35.00	20.00
63	"Stonewall" Jackson	200.00	85.00	45.00
64	Jimmie Foxx	560.00	225.00	115.00
65	"Zeke" Bonura	100.00	35.00	20.00
66	"Ducky" Medwick	200.00	85.00	45.00
67	Marvin Owen	100.00	35.00	20.00
68	"Sam" Leslie	100.00	35.00	20.00
69	Earl Grace	100.00	35.00	20.00
70	"Hal" Trosky	100.00	35.00	20.00
71	"Ossie" Bluege	100.00	35.00	20.00
72	"Tony" Piet	100.00	35.00	20.00
73a	"Fritz" Ostermueller (1935 green back)	100.00	35.00	20.00
73b	"Fritz" Ostermueller (1935 blue back)	100.00	35.00	20.00
73c	"Fritz" Ostermueller (1936 blue back)	105.00	45.00	20.00
74a	Tony Lazzeri (1935 green back)	365.00	140.00	70.00
74b	Tony Lazzeri (1935 blue back)	365.00	140.00	70.00
74c	Tony Lazzeri (1936 blue back)	385.00	155.00	77.00
75a	Irving Burns (1935 green back)	100.00	35.00	20.00
75b	Irving Burns (1935 blue back)	100.00	35.00	20.00
75c	Irving Burns (1936 blue back)	105.00	45.00	20.00
76a	Bill Rogell (1935 green back)	100.00	35.00	20.00
76b	Bill Rogell (1935 blue back)	105.00	45.00	20.00
76c	Bill Rogell (1936 blue back)	105.00	45.00	20.00
77a	Charlie Gehringer (1935 green back)	350.00	140.00	70.00
77b	Charlie Gehringer (1935 blue back)	350.00	140.00	70.00
77c	Charlie Gehringer (1936 blue back)	370.00	140.00	70.00
78a	Joe Kuhel (1935 green back)	100.00	35.00	20.00
78b	Joe Kuhel (1935 blue back)	100.00	35.00	20.00
78c	Joe Kuhel (1936 blue back)	105.00	45.00	20.00
79a	Willis Hudlin (1935 green back)	100.00	35.00	20.00
79b	Willis Hudlin (1935 blue back)	100.00	35.00	20.00
79c	Willis Hudlin (1936 blue back)	105.00	45.00	20.00
80a	Louis Chiozza (1935 green back)	100.00	35.00	20.00
80b	Louis Chiozza (1935 green back)	100.00	35.00	20.00
80c	Louis Chiozza (1936 blue back)	105.00	45.00	20.00
81a	Bill DeLancey (1935 green back)	100.00	35.00	20.00
81b	Bill DeLancey (1935 blue back)	100.00	35.00	20.00
81c	Bill DeLancey (1936 blue back)	105.00	45.00	20.00
82a	John Babich (1935 green back)	100.00	35.00	20.00
82b	John Babich (1935 blue back)	100.00	35.00	20.00
82c	John Babich (1936 blue back)	105.00	45.00	20.00
83a	Paul Waner (1935 green back)	200.00	85.00	45.00
83b	Paul Waner (1935 blue back)	200.00	85.00	45.00
83c	Paul Waner (1936 blue back)	225.00	85.00	45.00
84a	Sam Byrd (1935 green back)	100.00	35.00	20.00
84b	Sam Byrd (1935 blue back)	100.00	35.00	20.00
84c	Sam Byrd (1936 blue back)	105.00	45.00	20.00
85	Julius Solters	200.00	85.00	45.00
86	Frank Crosetti	350.00	140.00	70.00
87	Steve O'Neil (O'Neill)	200.00	85.00	45.00
88	Geo. Selkirk	200.00	85.00	45.00
89	Joe Stripp	200.00	85.00	45.00
90	Ray Hayworth	200.00	85.00	45.00
91	Bucky Harris	455.00	185.00	90.00
92	Ethan Allen	200.00	85.00	45.00
93	Alvin Crowder	200.00	85.00	45.00
94	Wes Ferrell	200.00	85.00	45.00
95	Luke Appling	455.00	185.00	90.00
96	Lew Riggs	200.00	85.00	45.00
97	"Al" Lopez	840.00	335.00	170.00
98	"Schoolboy" Rowe	500.00	245.00	120.00
99	"Pie" Traynor	805.00	325.00	160.00
100	Earle Averill (Earl)	805.00	325.00	160.00
101	Dick Bartell	500.00	245.00	120.00
102	Van Mungo	665.00	265.00	135.00
103	Bill Dickey	1,085	435.00	215.00
104	Robert Rolfe	500.00	245.00	120.00
105	"Ernie" Lombardi	840.00	335.00	170.00
106	"Red" Lucas	500.00	245.00	120.00
107	Stanley Hack	630.00	250.00	125.00
108	Walter Berger	1,120	280.00	135.00

1924 Diaz Cigarettes

Because they were printed in Cuba and feature only pitchers, the 1924 Diaz Cigarette cards are among the rarest and most intriguing of all tobacco issues. Produced in Havana for the Diaz brand, the black-and-white cards measure 1-3/4" x 2-1/2" and were printed on a semi-gloss stock. The player's name and position are listed at the bottom of the card, while his team and league appear at the top. According to the card backs, printed in Spanish, the set consists of 136 cards - all major league pitchers. But to date only the cards checklisted here have been discovered, and several of them never played in the major leagues.

		NM	EX	VG
Common Player:		900.00	360.00	180.00
1	Walter P. Johnson	5,250	2,200	1,100
2	Waite C. Hoyt	1,500	600.00	300.00
3	Grover C. Alexander	2,250	900.00	450.00
4	Thomas Sheehan	900.00	360.00	180.00
5	Pete Donohue	900.00	360.00	180.00
6	Herbert J. Pennock	1,350	550.00	275.00
7				
8	Carl Mays	1,100	450.00	225.00
9				
10	Allan S. Sothoron (Allen)	900.00	360.00	180.00
11	Wm. Piercy	900.00	360.00	180.00
12	Curtis Fullerton	900.00	360.00	180.00
13	Hollis Thurston	900.00	360.00	180.00
14	George Walberg	900.00	360.00	180.00
15	Fred Heimach	900.00	360.00	180.00
16	Sherrod M. Smith	900.00	360.00	180.00
17	Warren H. Ogden	900.00	360.00	180.00
18	Ernest P. Osborne (Earnest)	900.00	360.00	180.00
19	Walter H. Ruether	900.00	360.00	180.00
20	Burleigh A. Grimes	1,350	550.00	275.00
21	Joseph Genewich	900.00	360.00	180.00
22	Victor Aldridge	900.00	360.00	180.00
23	Arnold E. Stone	900.00	360.00	180.00
24	Lester C. Howe	900.00	360.00	180.00
25	George K. Murry (Murray)	900.00	360.00	180.00
26	Herman Pillette	900.00	360.00	180.00
27	John D. Couch	900.00	360.00	180.00
28	Tony C. Kaufmann	900.00	360.00	180.00
29	Frank (Jake) May	900.00	360.00	180.00
30	Howard J. Ehmke	900.00	360.00	180.00
31				
32				
33	Gorham V. Leverett	900.00	360.00	180.00
34	Bryan Harris	900.00	360.00	180.00
35	Paul F. Schreiber	900.00	360.00	180.00
36	Dewey Hinkle	900.00	360.00	180.00
37	Arthur C. Vance	1,350	550.00	275.00
38	Jesse J. Haines	1,350	550.00	275.00
39	Earl Hamilton	900.00	360.00	180.00
40	A. Wilbur Cooper	900.00	360.00	180.00
41	Thomas F. Long	900.00	360.00	180.00
42	Alex Ferguson	900.00	360.00	180.00
43	Chester Ross	900.00	360.00	180.00
44	John J. Quinn (Middle initial actually P.)	900.00	360.00	180.00
45	Ray C. Kolp	900.00	360.00	180.00
46	Arthur N. Nehf	900.00	360.00	180.00
47				
48				
49	Edwin A. Rommel	900.00	360.00	180.00
50	Theodore A. Lyons	1,350	550.00	275.00
51	Roy Meeker	900.00	360.00	180.00
52	John D. Stuart	900.00	360.00	180.00
53	Joseph Oeschger	900.00	360.00	180.00
54	Wayland Dean	900.00	360.00	180.00
55	Guy Morton	900.00	360.00	180.00
56	William L. Doak	900.00	360.00	180.00
57	Edward J. Pfeffer	900.00	360.00	180.00
58	Sam Gray	900.00	360.00	180.00
59				
60	Godfrey Brogan	900.00	360.00	180.00
61				
62	Howard E. Baldwin	900.00	360.00	180.00
63	Bert Lewis	900.00	360.00	180.00
64				
65	Dennis Burns	900.00	360.00	180.00
66	Roline C. Naylor (Roleine)	900.00	360.00	180.00
67	Walter H. Huntzinger	900.00	360.00	180.00
68	S. F. Baumgartner	900.00	360.00	180.00
69				
70	Clarence E. Mitchell	900.00	360.00	180.00
71				
72	Charles F. Clazner (Glazner)	900.00	360.00	180.00
73				
74				
75	Dennis J. Gearin	900.00	360.00	180.00
76	Jonathan T. Zachary	900.00	360.00	180.00
77				
78	Jess F. Winter (Jesse Winters)	900.00	360.00	180.00
79	Charles Ruffing	1,350	550.00	275.00
80	John W. Cooney	900.00	360.00	180.00
81	Leslie J. Bush (Middle initial A.)	900.00	360.00	180.00
82	William Harris	900.00	360.00	180.00
83	Joseph B. Shaute	900.00	360.00	180.00
84				
85	Eppa J. Rixey	1,350	550.00	275.00
86	William L. Sherdel	900.00	360.00	180.00
87	John C. Benton	900.00	360.00	180.00
88	Arthur R. Decatur	900.00	360.00	180.00
89	Harry G. Shriver	900.00	360.00	180.00
90	John D. Morrison	900.00	360.00	180.00
91	Walter M. Betts	900.00	360.00	180.00
92	Oscar Roettger	900.00	360.00	180.00
93				
94	Mike Cvengros	900.00	360.00	180.00
95	Leo L. Dickerman	900.00	360.00	180.00
96	Philip B. Weinart	2,400	960.00	480.00
97	Nicholas Dumovich	900.00	360.00	180.00
98				
99	Timothy A. McNamara	900.00	360.00	180.00
100	Allan Russell	900.00	360.00	180.00
101	Ted Blankenship	900.00	360.00	180.00
102	Howard E. Baldwin	900.00	360.00	180.00
103	Frank T. Davis	900.00	360.00	180.00
104	James C. Edwards	900.00	360.00	180.00
105	Hubert F. Pruett	900.00	360.00	180.00
106	Richard Rudolph	900.00	360.00	180.00
107				
108	Claude Jonnard	900.00	360.00	180.00
109				
110				
111	John M. Bentley (Initial actually N.)	900.00	360.00	180.00
112	Wilfred D. Ryan	900.00	360.00	180.00
113	George D. Metivier	900.00	360.00	180.00

		NM	EX	VG
114				
115	Sylvester Johnson	900.00	360.00	180.00
116	O.L. Fuhr	900.00	360.00	180.00
117				
118	Stanley Coveleski	1,350	550.00	275.00
119	Dave C. Danforth	900.00	360.00	180.00
120	Elam Van Gilder	900.00	360.00	180.00
121	Bert Cole	900.00	360.00	180.00
122	Kenneth E. Holoway (Holloway)	900.00	360.00	180.00
123	Charles Robertson	900.00	360.00	180.00
124				
125	George Dauss	900.00	360.00	180.00
126				
127				
128				
129	Phillip Bedgood	900.00	360.00	180.00
130	Fred Wingfield	900.00	360.00	180.00
131	George Mogridge	900.00	360.00	180.00
132	J. Martina	900.00	360.00	180.00
133	B.F. Speece	900.00	360.00	180.00
134	Harold Carlson	900.00	360.00	180.00
135	Wilbert W. Hubbell	900.00	360.00	180.00
136	Milton Gaston	900.00	360.00	180.00

(The following pitchers are known to have been included in the set, though their card numbers are unknown. They are listed here alphabetically, though the names may be different on the cards.)

		NM	EX	VG
---	Jess L. Barnes	900.00	360.00	180.00
---	Virgil E. Barnes	900.00	360.00	180.00
---	William Bayne	900.00	360.00	180.00
---	Lawrence J. Benton	900.00	360.00	180.00
---	Warren Collins (Rip)	900.00	360.00	180.00
---	Joubert Davenport (Lum)	900.00	360.00	180.00
---	Urban C. Faber	900.00	360.00	180.00
---	Robert K. Hasty	900.00	360.00	180.00
---	Frank J. Henry	900.00	360.00	180.00
---	Samuel P. Jones	900.00	360.00	180.00
---	Adolfo Luque	1,200	600.00	350.00
---	Fred Marberry	900.00	360.00	180.00
---	Richard W. Marquard	900.00	360.00	180.00
---	Walter H. McGrew (Slim)	900.00	360.00	180.00
---	Herbert McQuaid	900.00	360.00	180.00
---	Hugh A. McQuillan	900.00	360.00	180.00
---	Lee Meadows	900.00	360.00	180.00
---	Louis A. North	900.00	360.00	180.00
---	George W. Pipgras	900.00	360.00	180.00
---	James J. Ring	900.00	360.00	180.00
---	Robert Shawkey	900.00	360.00	180.00
---	Urban J. Shocker	900.00	360.00	180.00
---	George Uhle	900.00	360.00	180.00
---	John R. Watson	900.00	360.00	180.00
---	Ed L. Wells	900.00	360.00	180.00
---	Byron W. Yarrison	900.00	360.00	180.00
---	Paul V. Zahniser	900.00	360.00	180.00

1962 Dickson Orde & Co.

One of several English tobacco cards to include baseball among a series of world's sports, this card is of marginal interest to U.S. collectors because its color front pictures (from the back) a batter who could be Babe Ruth as part of a baseball scene on the front of the 2-5/8" x 1-3/8" card. The short description of baseball on the card's black-and-white back does mention Ruth. The "Sports of the Countries" series comprises 25 cards.

		NM	EX	VG
11	America (Babe Ruth)	25.00	12.50	7.50

1980 Did You Know . . . ?

This collectors' edition was produced by artist Mel (?) Anderson. The blank-backed 3-1/4" x 6-3/8" cards have black-and-white drawings of ballplayers and a "Did You Know" trivia fact. The unnumbered cards are checklisted here alphabetically.

		NM	EX	VG
Complete Set (30):		25.00	12.50	7.50
Common Player:		2.00	1.00	.60
(1)	Richie Ashburn	4.00	2.00	1.25
(2)	Hank Bauer	2.50	1.25	.70
(3)	Ewell "The Whip" Blackwell	2.50	1.25	.70
(4)	Johnny Callison	2.00	1.00	.60
(5)	Roger "Doc" Cramer	2.00	1.00	.60
(6)	Harry Danning	2.00	1.00	.60
(7)	Ferris Fain	2.00	1.00	.60
(8)	Ned Garver	2.00	1.00	.60
(9)	Harvey Haddix	2.00	1.00	.60
(10)	Clint Hartung	2.00	1.00	.60
(11)	"Bobo" Holloman	2.00	1.00	.60
(12)	Ron Hunt	2.00	1.00	.60
(13)	Howard "Spud" Krist	2.00	1.00	.60
(14)	Emil "Dutch" Leonard	2.00	1.00	.60
(15)	Buddy Lewis	2.00	1.00	.60
(16)	Jerry Lynch	2.00	1.00	.60
(17)	Roy McMillan	2.00	1.00	.60
(18)	Johnny Mize	3.00	1.50	.90
(19)	Hugh Mulcahy	2.00	1.00	.60
(20)	Hal Newhouser	2.00	1.00	.60
(21)	Jim Perry	2.00	1.00	.60
(22)	Phil Rizzuto	4.00	2.00	1.25
(23)	Bobby Shantz	2.00	1.00	.60
(24)	Roy Sievers	2.00	1.00	.60
(25)	Nick Testa	3.00	1.50	.90
(26)	Cecil Travis	2.00	1.00	.60
(27)	Elmer "Valient" Valo	2.00	1.00	.60
(28)	Bill Werber	2.00	1.00	.60
(29)	Mickey Witek	2.00	1.00	.60
(30)	Hal Woodeshick	2.00	1.00	.60

1907-09 Dietsche Detroit Tigers Postcards (PC765-1)

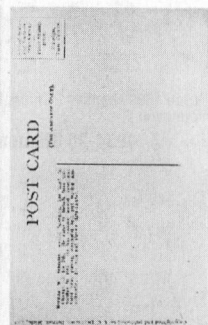

Three apparent annual issues (1907-09) of the home team by Detroit postcard publisher A.C. Dietsche, these 3-1/2" x 5-1/2" black-and-white postcards have most of the photographic background on front blackened out. The player's last name usually appears on the front. On back, along with the postcard legalities are a short player biography and a dated copyright line. The postcards were sold in sets of 15 cards for 25 cents.

		NM	EX	VG
Common Player:		150.00	60.00	30.00
Series 1 - 1907				
	Complete Set (16):	7,000	2,800	1,400
(1)	Tyrus R. Cobb/Btg	2,000	800.00	400.00
(2)	Tyrus R. Cobb/Fldg	3,000	1,200	600.00
(3)	William Coughlin	150.00	60.00	30.00
(4)	Samuel S. Crawford	325.00	130.00	65.00
(5)	William E. Donovan	150.00	60.00	30.00
(6)	Jerome W. Downs	150.00	60.00	30.00
(7)	Hughie A. Jennings	325.00	130.00	65.00
(8)	David Jones	150.00	60.00	30.00
(9)	Edward H. Killian	150.00	60.00	30.00
(10)	George J. Mullin	150.00	60.00	30.00
(11)	Charles O'Leary	150.00	60.00	30.00
(12)	Fred T. Payne	150.00	60.00	30.00
(13)	Claude Rossman	150.00	60.00	30.00
(14)	Herman W. Schaefer	150.00	60.00	30.00
(15)	Charles Schmidt	150.00	60.00	30.00
(16)	Edward Siever	150.00	60.00	30.00
Series 2 - 1908				
	Complete Set (22):	6,000	2,400	1,200
(1)	Henry Beckendorf	180.00	70.00	35.00
(2)	Owen Bush	180.00	70.00	35.00
(3)	Tyrus R. Cobb	2,500	1,000	500.00
(4)	William Coughlin	180.00	70.00	35.00
(5)	Sam Crawford	350.00	140.00	70.00
(6)	William E. Donovan	180.00	70.00	35.00
(7)	Jerome W. Downs	180.00	70.00	35.00
(8)	Hughie A. Jennings	350.00	140.00	70.00
(9)	Tom Jones	180.00	70.00	35.00
(10)	Edward H. Killian	180.00	70.00	35.00
(11)	Matthew McIntyre	180.00	70.00	35.00
(12)	George J. Moriarty	180.00	70.00	35.00
(13)	George J. Mullin	180.00	70.00	35.00
(14)	Charles O'Leary	180.00	70.00	35.00
(15)	Fred T. Payne	180.00	70.00	35.00
(16)	Germany Schaefer	180.00	70.00	35.00
(17)	Charles Schmidt	180.00	70.00	35.00
(18)	Oscar Stanage	180.00	70.00	35.00
(19)	Oren Edgar Summers	180.00	70.00	35.00
(20)	Ira Thomas	180.00	70.00	35.00
(21)	Edgar Willett	180.00	70.00	35.00
(22)	George Winter	180.00	70.00	35.00

Series 3 - 1909

		NM	EX	VG
	Complete Set (4):	750.00	300.00	150.00
(1)	James Delehanty	200.00	80.00	40.00
(2)	Tom Jones	180.00	70.00	35.00
(3)	Ralph Works	180.00	70.00	35.00
(4)	Detroit Tigers Team	300.00	125.00	60.00

1907 Dietsche Chicago Cubs Postcards (PC765-2)

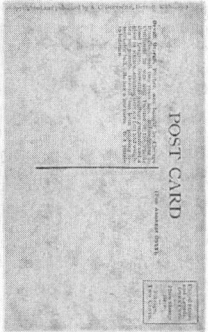

This series of early Cubs postcards was published by the same Detroit printer who issued Tigers postcard series from 1907-09. The Dietsche Cubs postcards are scarcer than the Tigers issues because they were only offered for sale in Detroit in conjunction with the 1907 World Series between the Tigers and Cubs, and few people bought the visiting team's cards. The 3-1/2" x 5-1/2" black-and-white cards have most of the photographic background blacked out on front. The player's last name may or may not appear on the front. Postcard style backs include a short career summary and a dated copyright line. The 15-card sets originally sold for 25 cents.

		NM	EX	VG
	Complete Set (15):	5,500	2,200	1,100
	Common Player:	340.00	135.00	65.00
(1)	Mordecai Brown	500.00	200.00	100.00
(2)	Frank L. Chance	500.00	200.00	100.00
(3)	John Evers	500.00	200.00	100.00
(4)	Arthur F. Hoffman (Hofman)	340.00	135.00	65.00
(5)	John Kling	340.00	135.00	65.00
(6)	Carl Lundgren	340.00	135.00	65.00
(7)	Patrick J. Moran	340.00	135.00	65.00
(8)	Orval Overall	340.00	135.00	65.00
(9)	John A. Pfeister	340.00	135.00	65.00
(10)	Edw. M. Ruelbach	340.00	135.00	65.00
(11)	Frank M. Schulte	340.00	135.00	65.00
(12)	James T. Sheckard	340.00	135.00	65.00
(13)	James Slagle	340.00	135.00	65.00
(14)	Harry Steinfeldt	340.00	135.00	65.00
(15)	Joseph B. Tinker	500.00	200.00	100.00

1907 Dietsche Posters

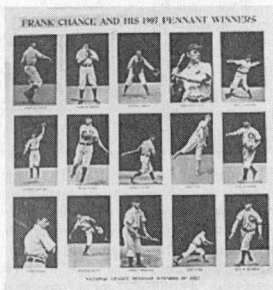

The images found on the Dietsche postcards were conglomerated on a pair of black-and-white cardboard posters. About 22" square, the posters are headlined: "FRANK CHANCE AND HIS 1907 PENNANT WINNERS" and "HUGHIE JENNINGS AND HIS GREA 1970 TIGERS."

	NM	EX	VG
1907 Chicago Cubs	1,000	500.00	300.00
1907 Detroit Tigers	1,000	500.00	300.00

1934 Dietz Gum Ball Players in Action

See 1934 Al Demaree Die-cuts (R304).

1942 Joe DiMaggio Candy Box Card

With no maker's name visible, this crudely executed war-era card is believed to have been printed on a candy box. In a format of 2-7/16" x 3-3/16" it is printed in blue and orange on white, is perforated on the sides and blank-backed.

	NM	EX	VG
Joe DiMaggio	150.00	75.00	45.00

1950 Joe DiMaggio Oriental Tour Postcard

In the post-season of 1950, during the Korean War, Joe DiMaggio led a goodwill tour of the Orient, including stops to visit the troops and to baseball-related destinations in Japan. This Italian postcard shows DiMaggio and Lefty O'Doul in a colorized photo surrounded by Japanese schoolboy ballplayers. The postcard-style back describes the scene. The card measures about 6" x 4".

	NM	EX	VG
Joe DiMaggio	125.00	65.00	40.00

1951 Joe DiMaggio Baseball Shoes

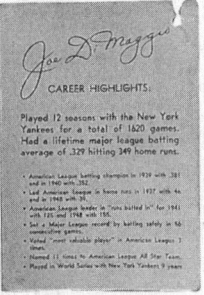

This 2-1/2" x 3-1/2" card was included with DiMaggio brand baseball shoes. A hole punched in the upper-left corner allowed the card to be attached to the shoe strings. Front has an action pose of DiMaggio printed in black-and-white on a dark green background. A facsimile autograph is at center. At bottom is printed: "THE YANKEE CLIPPER." The back has another facsimile signature and the player's career highlights through the 1950 season.

	NM	EX	VG
Joe DiMaggio (Hang-tag card.)	140.00	70.00	40.00
Joe DiMaggio (Complete box, shoes, tag.)	650.00	325.00	200.00

1972-83 Dimanche/Derniere Heure Photos

From 1972-74, and 1977-83, the Montreal magazine Dimanche / Derniere Heure (loosely translated, "Sunday / Latest Hour," issued color photos of Expos (and a few other) players. The 8-1/2" x 11" photos are printed on semi-gloss paper stock that is punched for a three-ring binder. Fronts have a large color photo with player data, stats and career highlights printed in black beneath - all in French. At left or top is usually the issue date in which the photo was included in the magazine. Backs are blank.

	NM	EX	VG
Common Player:	5.00	2.50	1.50
(Stars are valued up to $50.)			

1972 Dimanche/Derniere Heure Expos

		NM	EX	VG
	Complete Set (27):	155.00	78.00	47.00
	Common Player:	5.00	2.50	1.50
(1)	Bill Stoneman (April 9)	5.00	2.50	1.50
(2)	John Boccabella (April 16)	5.00	2.50	1.50
(3)	Gene Mauch (April 23)	5.00	2.50	1.50
(4)	Ron Hunt (April 30)	5.00	2.50	1.50
(5)	Steve Renko (May 7)	5.00	2.50	1.50
(6)	Boots Day (May 14)	5.00	2.50	1.50
(7)	Bob Bailey (May 21)	5.00	2.50	1.50
(8)	Ernie McAnally (May 28)	5.00	2.50	1.50
(9)	Ken Singleton (June 4)	5.00	2.50	1.50
(10)	Ron Fairly (June 11)	5.00	2.50	1.50
(11)	Ron Woods (June 18)	5.00	2.50	1.50
(12)	Mike Jorgensen (June 25)	5.00	2.50	1.50
(13)	Bobby Wine (July 2)	5.00	2.50	1.50
(14)	Mike Torrez (July 9)	5.00	2.50	1.50
(15)	Terry Humphrey (July 16)	5.00	2.50	1.50
(16)	Jim Fairey (July 23)	5.00	2.50	1.50
(17)	Tim Foli (July 30)	5.00	2.50	1.50
(18)	Clyde Mashore (Aug. 6)	5.00	2.50	1.50
(19)	Tim McCarver (Aug. 13)	9.00	4.50	2.75
(20)	Hector Torres (Aug. 20)	5.00	2.50	1.50
(21)	Tom Walker (Aug. 27)	5.00	2.50	1.50
(22)	Cal McLish (Sept. 3)	5.00	2.50	1.50
(23)	Balor Moore (Sept. 10)	5.00	2.50	1.50
(24)	John Strohmayer (Sept. 17)	5.00	2.50	1.50
(25)	Larry Doby (Sept. 24)	12.00	6.00	3.50
(26)	Hal Breeden (Oct. 1)	5.00	2.50	1.50
(27)	Mike Marshall (Oct. 8)	5.00	2.50	1.50

1973 Dimanche/Derniere Heure National Leaguers

		NM	EX	VG
	Complete Set (16):	185.00	90.00	55.00
	Common Player:	6.00	3.00	1.75
(1)	Roberto Clemente (April 15)	25.00	12.50	7.50
(2)	Coco Laboy (April 22)	6.00	3.00	1.75
(3)	Rusty Staub (April 29)	8.00	4.00	2.50
(4)	Johnny Bench (May 6)	12.50	6.25	3.75
(5)	Ferguson Jenkins (May 13)	9.00	4.50	2.75
(6)	Bob Gibson (May 20)	10.00	5.00	3.00
(7)	Hank Aaron (May 27)	20.00	10.00	6.00
(8)	Willie Montanez (June 3)	6.00	3.00	1.75
(9)	Willie McCovey (June 10)	10.00	5.00	3.00
(10)	Willie Davis (June 17)	6.00	3.00	1.75
(11)	Steve Carlton (June 24)	10.00	5.00	3.00
(12)	Willie Stargell (July 1)	10.00	5.00	3.00
(13)	Dave Bristol (July 8)	6.00	3.00	1.75
(14)	Larry Bowa (July 15)	6.00	3.00	1.75
(15)	Pete Rose (July 22)	20.00	10.00	6.00
(16)	Pepe Frias (July 29)	6.00	3.00	1.75

1974 Dimanche/Derniere Heure Expos

		NM	EX	VG
	Complete Set (10):	40.00	20.00	12.00
	Common Player:	5.00	2.50	1.50
(1)	Dennis Blair	5.00	2.50	1.50
(2)	Don Carrithers	5.00	2.50	1.50
(3)	Jim Cox	5.00	2.50	1.50
(4)	Willie Davis	5.00	2.50	1.50
(5)	Don Demola	5.00	2.50	1.50
(6)	Barry Foote	5.00	2.50	1.50
(7)	Larry Lintz	5.00	2.50	1.50
(8)	John Montague	5.00	2.50	1.50
(9)	Steve Rogers	5.00	2.50	1.50
(10)	Chuck Taylor	5.00	2.50	1.50

1977 Dimanche/Derniere Heure Expos

		NM	EX	VG
Complete Set (26):		125.00	62.00	37.00
Common Player:		5.00	2.50	1.50
(1)	Steve Rogers (April 24)	5.00	2.50	1.50
(2)	Tim Foli (May 1)	5.00	2.50	1.50
(3)	Dick Williams (May 8)	5.00	2.50	1.50
(4)	Larry Parrish (May 15)	5.00	2.50	1.50
(5)	Jose Morales (May 22)	5.00	2.50	1.50
(6)	Don Stanhouse (May 29)	5.00	2.50	1.50
(7)	Gary Carter (June 5)	10.00	5.00	3.00
(8)	Ellis Valentine (June 12)	5.00	2.50	1.50
(9)	Dave Cash (June 19)	5.00	2.50	1.50
(10)	Jackie Brown (June 26)	5.00	2.50	1.50
(11)	Barry Foote (July 3)	5.00	2.50	1.50
(12)	Dan Warthen (July 10)	5.00	2.50	1.50
(13)	Tony Perez (July 17)	10.00	5.00	3.00
(14)	Wayne Garrett (July 24)	5.00	2.50	1.50
(15)	Bill Atkinson (July 31)	5.00	2.50	1.50
(16)	Joe Kerrigan (Aug. 7)	5.00	2.50	1.50
(17)	Mickey Vernon (Aug. 14)	5.00	2.50	1.50
(18)	Jeff Terpko (Aug. 21)	5.00	2.50	1.50
(19)	Andre Dawson (Aug. 28)	10.00	5.00	3.00
(20)	Del Unser (Sept. 4)	5.00	2.50	1.50
(21)	Stan Bahnsen (Sept. 11)	5.00	2.50	1.50
(22)	Warren Cromartie (Sept. 18)	5.00	2.50	1.50
(23)	Santo Alcala (Sept. 25)	5.00	2.50	1.50
(24)	Wayne Twitchell (Oct. 2)	5.00	2.50	1.50
(25)	Pepe Frias (Oct. 9)	5.00	2.50	1.50
(26)	Sam Mejias (Oct. 16)	5.00	2.50	1.50

1978 Dimanche/Derniere Heure Expos

		NM	EX	VG
Complete Set (13):		62.00	31.00	18.50
Common Player:		5.00	2.50	1.50
(1)	Ross Grimsley (May 7)	5.00	2.50	1.50
(2)	Chris Speier (May 14)	5.00	2.50	1.50
(3)	Norm Sherry (May 21)	5.00	2.50	1.50
(4)	Hal Dues (May 28)	5.00	2.50	1.50
(5)	Rudy May (June 4)	5.00	2.50	1.50
(6)	Stan Papi (June 11)	5.00	2.50	1.50
(7)	Darold Knowles (June 18)	5.00	2.50	1.50
(8)	Bob Reece (June 25)	5.00	2.50	1.50
(9)	Dan Schatzeder (July 2)	5.00	2.50	1.50
(10)	Jim Brewer (July 9)	5.00	2.50	1.50
(11)	Mike Garman (July 16)	5.00	2.50	1.50
(12)	Woodie Fryman (July 23)	5.00	2.50	1.50
(13)	Ed Hermann	5.00	2.50	1.50

1979 Dimanche/Derniere Heure Expos

	NM	EX	VG
Complete Set (8):	35.00	17.50	10.50

		NM	EX	VG
Common Player:		5.00	2.50	1.50
(1)	Bill Lee (May 6)	5.00	2.50	1.50
(2)	Elias Sosa (May 13)	5.00	2.50	1.50
(3)	Tommy Hutton (May 20)	5.00	2.50	1.50
(4)	Tony Solaita (May 27)	5.00	2.50	1.50
(5)	Rodney Scott (June 3)	5.00	2.50	1.50
(6)	Duffy Dyer (June 10)	5.00	2.50	1.50
(7)	Jim Mason (June 17)	5.00	2.50	1.50
(8)	Ken Macha (June 24)	5.00	2.50	1.50

1980 Dimanche/Derniere Heure Expos

		NM	EX	VG
Complete Set (23):		125.00	62.00	37.00
Common Player:		5.00	2.50	1.50
(1)	Steve Rogers (April 20)	5.00	2.50	1.50
(2)	Dick Williams (April 27)	5.00	2.50	1.50
(3)	Bill Lee (May 4)	5.00	2.50	1.50
(4)	Jerry White (May 11)	5.00	2.50	1.50
(5)	Scott Sanderson (May 18)	5.00	2.50	1.50
(6)	Ron LeFlore (May 25)	5.00	2.50	1.50
(7)	Elias Sosa (June 1)	5.00	2.50	1.50
(8)	Ellis Valentine (June 8)	5.00	2.50	1.50
(9)	Rodney Scott (June 22)	5.00	2.50	1.50
(10)	Woodie Fryman (June 29)	5.00	2.50	1.50
(11)	Chris Speier (July 6)	5.00	2.50	1.50
(12)	Warren Cromartie (July 13)	5.00	2.50	1.50
(13)	Stan Bahnsen (July 20)	5.00	2.50	1.50
(14)	Tommy Hutton (July 27)	5.00	2.50	1.50
(15)	Bill Almon (Aug. 3)	5.00	2.50	1.50
(16)	Fred Norman (Aug. 10)	5.00	2.50	1.50
(17)	Andre Dawson (Aug. 17)	10.00	5.00	3.00
(18)	John Tamargo (Aug. 24)	5.00	2.50	1.50
(19)	Larry Parrish (Aug. 31)	5.00	2.50	1.50
(20)	David Palmer (Sept. 7)	5.00	2.50	1.50
(21)	Tony Bernazard (Sept. 14)	5.00	2.50	1.50
(22)	Gary Carter (Sept. 21)	10.00	5.00	3.00
(23)	Ken Macha (Sept. 28)	5.00	2.50	1.50

1888 Dixie Cigarettes Girl Baseball Players (N48)

(See 1888 Allen & Ginter Girl Baseball Players.)

1937 Dixie Lids

This unnumbered set of Dixie cup ice cream tops was issued in 1937 and consists of 24 different lids, although only six picture sports stars; four of whom are baseball players. The lids are found in two different sizes, either 2-11/16" in diameter or 2-5/16" in diameter. The 1937 Dixie lids have their "picture" side printed in black or dark red. The reverse carries the advertising of one of many local dairies which packaged the ice cream treats. The lids must have the small tab still intact to command top value.

		NM	EX	VG
Complete Set (4):		700.00	350.00	210.00
Common Player:		180.00	90.00	55.00
(1)	Charles Gehringer	180.00	90.00	55.00
(2)	Charles ("Gabby") Hartnett	180.00	90.00	55.00
(3)	Carl Hubbell (Mouth closed.)	195.00	95.00	55.00
(4)	Joe Medwick	180.00	90.00	55.00

1937 Dixie Lids Premiums

Issued as a premium offer in conjunction with the 1937 Dixie lids, this unnumbered set of color 8" x 10" pictures was printed on heavy paper and features the same subjects as the Dixie lids set. The 1937 Dixie premiums have a distinctive dark green band along the left margin containing the player's name. The back has smaller photos of the player in action with a large star at the top and a player write-up. The 1937 premiums are easily distinguished from the 1938 issue by the use of yellow ink for the names in the left border. A "My Scrapbook of Stars" album was issued in which to house the 24 sports and movie stars issued in the series.

		NM	EX	VG
Complete Set (4):		500.00	250.00	150.00
Common Player:		150.00	75.00	45.00
Album:		300.00	150.00	90.00
(2)	Charles Gehringer	150.00	75.00	45.00
(3)	Charles (Gabby) Hartnett	150.00	75.00	45.00
(4)	Carl Hubbell	175.00	87.00	52.00
(5)	Joe (Ducky) Medwick	150.00	75.00	45.00

1938 Dixie Lids

Similar to its set of the previous year, the 1938 Dixie lids set is a 24-subject set that includes six sports stars - four of whom are baseball players. The lids are found in two sizes, either 2-11/16" in diameter or 2-5/16" in diameter. The 1938 Dixie Lids have their "picture" side printed in blue ink. The reverse carries advertising from one of many local dairies which packaged the ice cream cups. Dixie lids must have the small tab still intact to command top value.

		NM	EX	VG
Complete Set (4):		600.00	300.00	180.00
Common Player:		80.00	40.00	25.00
(1)	Bob Feller	200.00	100.00	60.00
(2)	Jimmie Foxx	200.00	100.00	60.00
(3)	Carl Hubbell (Mouth open.)	175.00	85.00	50.00
(4)	Wally Moses	80.00	40.00	25.00

1938 Dixie Lids Premiums

Issued in conjunction with the 1938 Dixie cup lids, this unnumbered set of 8" x 10" pictures contains the same subjects. A colored border surrounds the entire picture with the player's name in black at left. The back contains smaller photos of the player in action with his name in script at the top and a short write-up. A "My Scrapbook of Stars" album was issued in which to house the 24 sports and movie stars that comprise the complete series.

		NM	EX	VG
Complete Set (4):		425.00	210.00	125.00
Common Player:		62.00	31.00	18.50
Album:		300.00	150.00	90.00
(1)	Bob Feller	125.00	62.00	37.00
(2)	Jimmy Foxx	125.00	62.00	37.00
(3)	Carl Hubbell	125.00	62.00	37.00
(4)	Wally Moses	60.00	30.00	18.00

1952 Dixie Lids

After a 14-year break, another Dixie lid set, featuring 24 baseball players, appeared in 1952. The unnumbered lids are found in three sizes, the most common being 2-11/16" in diameter. Somewhat scarcer, and carrying a modest premium over the values listed, are lids in sizes of 2-1/4" or 3-3/16". All are printed with a blue tint on their "picture" side. The backs carry advertising from one of the many local or regional dairies which packaged the ice cream treats. The Dixie lids of the 1950s can be distinguished from earlier issues because the bottom of the photo is squared off to accomodate the player's name. Dixie lids must contain the small tab to command top value.

		NM	EX	VG
Complete Set (24):		5,500	2,750	1,650
Common Player:		200.00	100.00	60.00
(1)	Richie Ashburn	325.00	160.00	95.00
(2)	Tommy Byrne	200.00	100.00	60.00
(3)	Chico Carrasquel	200.00	100.00	60.00
(4)	Pete Castiglione	200.00	100.00	60.00
(5)	Walker Cooper	200.00	100.00	60.00
(6)	Billy Cox	225.00	110.00	65.00
(7)	Ferris Fain	200.00	100.00	60.00
(8)	Bobby Feller	350.00	175.00	100.00
(9)	Nelson Fox	325.00	160.00	95.00
(10)	Monte Irvin	275.00	135.00	80.00
(11)	Ralph Kiner	275.00	135.00	80.00
(12)	Cass Michaels	200.00	100.00	60.00
(13)	Don Mueller	200.00	100.00	60.00
(14)	Mel Parnell	200.00	100.00	60.00
(15)	Allie Reynolds	225.00	110.00	65.00
(16)	Preacher Roe	225.00	110.00	65.00
(17)	Connie Ryan	200.00	100.00	60.00
(18)	Hank Sauer	200.00	100.00	60.00
(19)	Al Schoendienst	275.00	135.00	80.00
(20)	Andy Seminick	200.00	100.00	60.00
(21)	Bobby Shantz	200.00	100.00	60.00
(22)	Enos Slaughter	275.00	135.00	80.00
(23)	Virgil Trucks	200.00	100.00	60.00
(24)	Gene Woodling	250.00	125.00	75.00

1952 Dixie Lids Premiums

This unnumbered set of 24 player photos was issued as a premium in conjunction with the 1952 Dixie cup lids and features the same subjects. The player's team and facsimile autograph appear along the bottom of the 8" x 10" blank-backed photo, which was printed on heavy paper. The 1952 Dixie premiums show the player's 1951 season statistics in the lower right corner.

		NM	EX	VG
Complete Set (24):		2,250	1,125	675.00
Common Player:		90.00	45.00	25.00
(1)	Richie Ashburn	225.00	110.00	65.00
(2)	Tommy Byrne	90.00	45.00	25.00
(3)	Chico Carrasquel	90.00	45.00	25.00
(4)	Pete Castiglione	90.00	45.00	25.00
(5)	Walker Cooper	90.00	45.00	25.00
(6)	Billy Cox	100.00	50.00	30.00
(7)	Ferris Fain	90.00	45.00	25.00
(8)	Bob Feller	225.00	110.00	65.00
(9)	Nelson Fox	200.00	100.00	60.00
(10)	Monte Irvin	125.00	60.00	35.00
(11)	Ralph Kiner	125.00	60.00	35.00
(12)	Cass Michaels	90.00	45.00	25.00
(13)	Don Mueller	90.00	45.00	25.00
(14)	Mel Parnell	90.00	45.00	25.00
(15)	Allie Reynolds	100.00	50.00	30.00
(16)	Preacher Roe	100.00	50.00	30.00
(17)	Connie Ryan	90.00	45.00	25.00
(18)	Hank Sauer	90.00	45.00	25.00
(19)	Al Schoendienst	125.00	60.00	35.00
(20)	Andy Seminick	90.00	45.00	25.00
(21)	Bobby Shantz	90.00	45.00	25.00
(22)	Enos Slaughter	125.00	60.00	35.00
(23)	Virgil Trucks	90.00	45.00	25.00
(24)	Gene Woodling	100.00	50.00	30.00

1953 Dixie Lids

The 1953 Dixie lids set again consists of 24 unnumbered players and is identical in design to the 1952 set. Lids are either 2-1/4" or 2-11/16" in diameter and must include the small tab to command top value. Backs of the lids may be found with advertising of many local or regional dairies which packaged the ice cream cups.

	NM	EX	VG
Complete Set (24):	4,000	2,000	1,200

		NM	EX	VG
Common Player:		120.00	60.00	35.00
(1)	Richie Ashburn	250.00	125.00	75.00
(2)	Chico Carrasquel	120.00	60.00	35.00
(3)	Billy Cox	130.00	65.00	40.00
(4)	Ferris Fain	120.00	60.00	35.00
(5)	Nelson Fox	200.00	100.00	60.00
(6a)	Sid Gordon (Boston)	240.00	120.00	70.00
(6b)	Sid Gordon (Milwaukee)	120.00	60.00	35.00
(7)	Warren Hacker	120.00	60.00	35.00
(8)	Monte Irvin	200.00	100.00	60.00
(9)	Jackie Jensen	180.00	90.00	55.00
(10a)	Ralph Kiner (Pittsburgh)	350.00	175.00	100.00
(10b)	Ralph Kiner (Chicago)	200.00	100.00	60.00
(11)	Ted Kluszewski	200.00	100.00	60.00
(12)	Bob Lemon	200.00	100.00	60.00
(13)	Don Mueller	120.00	60.00	35.00
(14)	Mel Parnell	120.00	60.00	35.00
(15)	Jerry Priddy	120.00	60.00	35.00
(16)	Allie Reynolds	130.00	65.00	40.00
(17)	Preacher Roe	130.00	65.00	40.00
(18)	Hank Sauer	120.00	60.00	35.00
(19)	Al Schoendienst	200.00	100.00	60.00
(20)	Bobby Shantz	120.00	60.00	35.00
(21)	Enos Slaughter	200.00	100.00	60.00
(22a)	Warren Spahn (Boston)	550.00	275.00	165.00
(22b)	Warren Spahn (Milwaukee)	500.00	250.00	150.00
(23a)	Virgil Trucks (Chicago)	250.00	125.00	75.00
(23b)	Virgil Trucks (St. Louis)	150.00	75.00	45.00
(24)	Gene Woodling	130.00	65.00	40.00

1953 Dixie Lids Premiums

This set of 8" x 10" photos was issued as a premium in conjunction with the 1953 Dixie lids set and includes the same subjects. A premium picture could be obtained in exchange for 12 lids. The player's team and facsimile autograph are at the bottom of the unnumbered, blank-backed photos. His 1952 season stats are shown in the lower right corner.

		NM	EX	VG
Complete Set (24):		3,000	1,500	900.00
Common Player:		100.00	50.00	30.00
(1)	Richie Ashburn	250.00	125.00	75.00
(2)	Chico Carrasquel	100.00	50.00	30.00
(3)	Billy Cox	120.00	60.00	35.00
(4)	Ferris Fain	100.00	50.00	30.00
(5)	Nelson Fox	200.00	100.00	60.00
(6)	Sid Gordon	100.00	50.00	30.00
(7)	Warren Hacker	100.00	50.00	30.00
(8)	Monte Irvin	180.00	90.00	55.00
(9)	Jack Jensen	120.00	60.00	35.00
(10)	Ralph Kiner	180.00	90.00	55.00
(11)	Ted Kluszewski	180.00	90.00	55.00
(12)	Bob Lemon	180.00	90.00	55.00
(13)	Don Mueller	100.00	50.00	30.00
(14)	Mel Parnell	100.00	50.00	30.00
(15)	Jerry Priddy	100.00	50.00	30.00
(16)	Allie Reynolds	120.00	60.00	35.00
(17)	Preacher Roe	120.00	60.00	35.00
(18)	Hank Sauer	100.00	50.00	30.00
(19)	Al Schoendienst	180.00	90.00	55.00
(20)	Bobby Shantz	120.00	60.00	35.00
(21)	Enos Slaughter	180.00	90.00	55.00
(22)	Warren Spahn	260.00	130.00	75.00
(23)	Virgil Trucks	100.00	50.00	30.00
(24)	Gene Woodling	120.00	60.00	35.00

1954 Dixie Lids

The 1954 Dixie lids set consists of 18 players. Each player is foind in both a "left" and "right" version. The picture side features a black-and-white photo. The lids usually measure 2-11/16" in diameter, although two other sizes (2-1/4" and 3-3/16") also exist and are valued at a significant premium above the prices listed. The 1954 Dixie lids are similar to earlier issues, except they carry an offer for a "3-D Starviewer" around the outside edge. The small tabs must be attached to command top value. The lids are unnumbered. Backs can be found with advertising from many local or regional dairies which packaged the ice cream cups.

	NM	EX	VG
Complete Set (18):	2,000	1,000	600.00
Common Player:	120.00	60.00	35.00

		NM	EX	VG
2-1/4" or 3-3/16": 2-3X				
(1)	Richie Ashburn	250.00	125.00	75.00
(2)	Clint Courtney	120.00	60.00	35.00
(3)	Sid Gordon	120.00	60.00	35.00
(4)	Billy Hoeft	120.00	60.00	35.00
(5)	Monte Irvin	200.00	100.00	60.00
(6)	Jackie Jensen	130.00	65.00	40.00
(7)	Ralph Kiner	200.00	100.00	60.00
(8)	Ted Kluszewski	200.00	100.00	60.00
(9)	Gil McDougald	130.00	65.00	40.00
(10)	Minny Minoso	130.00	65.00	40.00
(11)	Danny O'Connell	120.00	60.00	35.00
(12)	Mel Parnell	120.00	60.00	35.00
(13)	Preacher Roe	130.00	65.00	40.00
(14)	Al Rosen	130.00	65.00	40.00
(15)	Al Schoendienst	200.00	100.00	60.00
(16)	Enos Slaughter	200.00	100.00	60.00
(17)	Gene Woodling	130.00	65.00	40.00
(18)	Gus Zernial	120.00	60.00	35.00

1909 Dockman & Sons Gum (E92)

Once cataloged as a part of the E92 compendium, the John Dockman & Sons Gum card issue differs from the Croft's Candy/Cocoa sets in that it has 10 fewer cards. Otherwise the format (1-1/2" x 2-3/4") and color litho player pictures are identical. Beneath the player picture on front is his last name, position and team. Backs, which describe the set as having 50 cards, are an ad for the gum company. Cards are checklisted here alphabetically.

		NM	EX	VG
Complete Set (40):		50,000	20,000	10,000
Common Player:		910.00	365.00	180.00
(1)	Harry Bemis	910.00	365.00	180.00
(2)	Chief Bender	1,620	660.00	330.00
(3)	Bill Bergen	910.00	365.00	180.00
(4)	Bob Bescher	910.00	365.00	180.00
(5)	Al Bridwell	910.00	365.00	180.00
(6)	Doc Casey	910.00	365.00	180.00
(7)	Frank Chance	1,800	720.00	360.00
(8)	Hal Chase	1,110	450.00	220.00
(9)	Sam Crawford	1,620	660.00	330.00
(10)	Harry Davis	910.00	365.00	180.00
(11)	Art Devlin	910.00	365.00	180.00
(12)	Wild Bill Donovan	910.00	365.00	180.00
(13)	Mickey Doolan	910.00	365.00	180.00
(14)	Patsy Dougherty	910.00	365.00	180.00
(15)	Larry Doyle/Throwing	910.00	365.00	180.00
(16)	Larry Doyle (With bat.)	910.00	365.00	180.00
(17)	George Gibson	910.00	365.00	180.00
(18)	Topsy Hartsel	910.00	365.00	180.00
(19)	Hugh Jennings	1,620	660.00	330.00
(20)	Red Kleinow	910.00	365.00	180.00
(21)	Nap Lajoie	1,800	720.00	360.00
(22)	Hans Lobert	910.00	365.00	180.00
(23)	Sherry Magee	910.00	365.00	180.00
(24)	Christy Matthewson (Mathewson)	5,400	2,160	1,080
(25)	John McGraw	1,620	660.00	330.00
(26)	Larry McLean	910.00	365.00	180.00
(27)	Dots Miller	910.00	365.00	180.00
(28)	Danny Murphy	910.00	365.00	180.00
(29)	Bill O'Hara	910.00	365.00	180.00
(30)	Germany Schaefer	910.00	365.00	180.00
(31)	Admiral Schlei	910.00	365.00	180.00
(32)	Boss Schmidt	910.00	365.00	180.00
(33)	Johnny Seigle	910.00	365.00	180.00
(34)	Dave Shean	910.00	365.00	180.00
(35)	Boss Smith (Schmidt)	910.00	365.00	180.00
(36)	Joe Tinker	1,620	660.00	330.00
(37)	Honus Wagner/Btg	10,000	2,880	1,440
(38)	Honus Wagner/Throwing	10,000	2,880	1,440
(39)	Cy Young	4,200	1,680	840.00
(40)	Heinie Zimmerman	910.00	365.00	180.00

1969-1972 Dodge Postcards

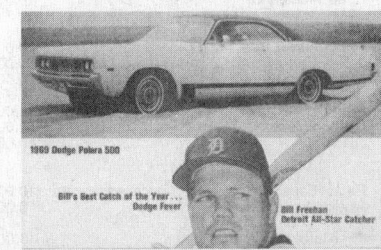

Between 1969-1972 Dodge issued a series of black-and-white promotional postcards featuring sports figures endorsing the car company's line-up. Player portrait photos on front are combined with a photo of one of the cars and some extraneous sales copy. Divided backs of the 5-1/2" x 3-1/2" cards have a couple sentences of career summary or highlights and a sales pitch. Only the baseball players are listed here, though stars from football, basketball, golf, hockey and racing were also included in the series.

	NM	EX	VG
Common Player:	15.00	7.50	4.50
(1) Lou Brock (1970)	40.00	20.00	12.00
(2) Lou Brock (1971)	40.00	20.00	12.00
(3) Bill Freehan (1969)	30.00	15.00	9.00
(4) Bill Freehan (1970)	15.00	7.50	4.50
(5) Bill Freehan (1971)	15.00	7.50	4.50
(6) Bill Freehan (1972)	15.00	7.50	4.50
(7) Bill Freehan (1973)	15.00	7.50	4.50
(8) Joe Garagiola (1970)	20.00	10.00	6.00
(9) Mickey Lolich (1969)	15.00	7.50	4.50

1888-1889 Dogs Head Cabinets (N173)

(See 1888-1889 Old Judge Cabinets.)

1950 Dominican Republic

151 Phil Rizzuto

Selection of known Major League players makes 1950 the best guess for year of issue of this Caribbean card set. Like many contemporary Latin issues, these were probably produced to be collected in an accompanying album. Printed on fragile paper in blue, red or green duo-tones, the cards measure about 1-5/8" x 2-3/8" and are blank-backed. The set may or may not be complete at 292, the highest number currently known. Players featured in the issue are drawn from the Dominican and Cuban winter leagues (including Negro Leagues and minor league players) as well as the majors. In the bottom border beneath the player photo is a card number and name. Names are frequently misspelled and this list may not have succeeded in correcting all of them, particularly the Latino players. It is hoped that gaps in the checklist will eventually be filled with confirmed specimens. Many of the photos on these cards appear to have been lifted - some even with the typography intact - from Bowman baseball cards of the era. Some, perhaps all, of the cards were printed in more than one color.

	NM	EX	VG
Common Player:			
1 Guillermo Estrella			10.00
2 Benitez Redondo			10.00
3 Vidal Lopez			10.00
4 R. del Monte y C.			10.00
5			
6			
7 Juan Delfin Garcia			10.00
8 J. Raf. Carretero			10.00
9 J. Benjamin (Papo)			10.00
10			
11 Rufo E. Felix			10.00
12 Gallego Munoz			10.00
13 Julio A. Lara			10.00
14			
15			
16 Rafael Espada			10.00
17 Aladino Paez			10.00
18			
19 Pepe Lucas			10.00

20	Manolete Caceres	10.00
21	E.A. Lantigua	10.00
22	Olmedo Suarez	10.00
23	Chucho Ramos	10.00
24	Gullabin Olivo	10.00
25	Jose Luis Velazquez	10.00
26		
27	Felle Delgado	10.00
28		
29		
30	Alcibades Colon	10.00
31	Horacio Martinez	10.00
32	Ramon Burgos	10.00
33	Carlos A. Piallo	10.00
34	W.E. Springfield	10.00
35	Fiquito Suarez	10.00
36		
37		
38	Rafael Ortiz	10.00
39		
40		
41	Tetelo Vargas	10.00
42	Miguel Rueda	10.00
43	Hector Salazar	10.00
44		
45	Rafael Vargas	10.00
46		
47		
48		
49		
50	Gerard Thorne	10.00
51	Bienvenido Arias	10.00
52	Son Howell	15.00
53		
54		
55		
56		
57	P. Mateo (Richard)	10.00
58		
59		
60	Martin Dihigo	150.00
61		
62		
63		
64		
65	Octavio Blanco	10.00
66	Daniel Rodriguez	10.00
67		
68	Luis Villodas	10.00
69	Miguel Aracena	10.00
70	Amor Diaz	10.00
71	Juan B. Perdomo	10.00
72	Julio Martinez	10.00
73	Fernando Bueno	10.00
74	Rene Gutierrez	10.00
75	Israel Hernandez	10.00
76	Tomas Gomez Checo	10.00
77		
78	Miguel Tian Tineo	10.00
79	Rafael Valdez	10.00
80	Calampio Leon	10.00
81	Leonardo Coicochea	10.00
82	Herberto Blanco	10.00
83		
84	Rogelio Martinez	10.00
85		
86		
87	Silvio Garcia	10.00
88		
89	Napoleon Reyes	15.00
90		
91		
92		
93	Claro Duane (Duany)	10.00
94		
95		
96	Regino Otero	10.00
97	Avelino Canizares	10.00
98	Sandalio Consuegra	25.00
99	Roberto R. Topane	10.00
100	Jaok Cassin (Jack Cassini)	20.00
101	Jaime B. Prendesgart (Jim Prendergast)	20.00
102	Pablo Garcia	10.00
103		
104		
105		
106	Alejandro Crespo	20.00
107	Hiran Gonzalez	10.00
108	Rafael Noble	20.00
109		
110	Jose R. Lopez	10.00
111		
112		
113	Gilberto Torres	10.00
114		
115	Patato Pascual	10.00
116		
117		
118		
119	Gilberto Valdivia	10.00
120	Svdor. Hernandez	10.00
121		
122		
123		
124	Pedro Formental (Formenthal)	10.00
125		
126		
127		
128		
129		
130		
131		
132		
133		
134		
135	H. Wilson	25.00
136		

137		
138		
139	Carl Hubbell	35.00
140		
141		
142	Cocaina Garcia	10.00
143		
144		
145		
146		
147		
148		
149		
150		
151	Phill Rizzuto (Phil)	75.00
152	Bill Mc Cahan	20.00
153		
154	Allie Reynolds	55.00
155	Gill Coan (Gil)	20.00
156		
157	Mizell Platt	20.00
158		
159	Al S. "Red" (Schoendienst)	50.00
160	Jack Lorke (Lohrke)	20.00
161		
162		
163	Bill Nicholson	20.00
164	Sam Mele	20.00
165	Bob Schiffino (Scheffing)	20.00
166		
167		
168		
169	Harri Gumbert (Harry)	20.00
170		
171	Johnny Wyrostek	20.00
172		
173		
174		
175		
176		
177	Ken Keltner	25.00
178		
179	Harry Walker	25.00
180		
181		
182		
183		
184		
185	Sibby Sisti	20.00
186		
187	Eddie Waiticus (Waitkus)	25.00
188	Eddie Lake	20.00
189		
190	Hank Arft	20.00
191		
192		
193		
194	Walker Cooper	20.00
195	Al Brazle	20.00
196	Sam Champmann (Chapman)	20.00
197		
198	Doyle Lade	20.00
199		
200	Henry Eduards (Edwards)	20.00
201		
202		
203	N.Y. "Baby" (Norman "Babe" Young)	20.00
204		
205		
206	Bob Feller	75.00
207	Ralph Branca	35.00
208		
209		
210		
211	Larry (Yogi) Berra	75.00
212	Eddie Joost	20.00
213		
214		
215		
216		
217		
218		
219	Gil Hodges	55.00
220		
221		
222		
223	James, Vernon (Mickey)	25.00
224		
225		
226		
227		
228		
229		
230		
231		
232		
233		
234	Pete Raiser (Reiser)	30.00
235		
236	Bob Elliot	20.00
237		
238	Lou Boudreau	45.00
239	Danny Murtany (Photo is Joe Gordon.)	25.00
240	Jakie Robinson (Jackie)	125.00
241		
242		
243	Tommy Henrick (Henrich)	25.00
244	Pee Wee Reese	55.00
245	Bobby Brower (Brown)	25.00
246		
247		
248	Enos Slaughter	35.00
249		
250		
251	Tommy Henrich	25.00
252	George Koslo (Dave)	20.00

253	Frank Gustino (Gustine)	20.00
254		
255		
256		
257	Bill Rigney	20.00
258		
259	Rex Barney	25.00
260		
261	Mark Christman	20.00
262	Whetey Lockman (Whitey)	20.00
263		
264	Ralph Kiner	55.00
265		
266	Cliff Fannin	20.00
267	Joe Page	25.00
268		
269		
270		
271	Johnny Sain	30.00
272		
273		
274		
275		
276		
277		
278		
279	Joe Dobson	20.00
280		
281	Carrol Lockman (Whitey)	20.00
282		
283	Monte Kennedy	20.00
284		
285		
286	Carlos Bernier	20.00
287		
288		
289	Buster Clarkson	20.00
290	Williard Brown (Willard)	25.00
291	Jim Rivera	25.00
292	Saturnino Escalera	20.00

1958 Dominican Republic

Felipe R. Alou.

The date of issue is speculative, based on the known winter ball career of the sole card known. The identity of the issuer and manner of distribution is unknown, though from their wide borders it is possible these were printed on some type of box or package and intended to be cut out and possibly placed into an album, as is customary with many Latin American baseball card issues. The cards are nominally about 2" x 2-1/2" and are printed in sepia on thin, blank-back cardboard. As with many issues of the era and area, when these cards are found they are usually in wretched condition.

	NM	EX	VG
Felipe R. Alou			35.00

1959 Dominican Republic

WALTER JAMES

The date of issue is speculative. The identity of the issuer and manner of distribution is unknown, though they appear to have been sold in strips or panels and intended to be separated and possibly placed into an album, as is customary with many Latin American baseball cards. The cards are nominally about 2-1/8" x 3-1/4" and printed in black or blue on thin, blank-back cardboard. As with many issues of the era and area, when these cards are found they are usually in wretched condition. These players certainly represent only a portion of the checklist.

	NM	EX	VG
Walter James			15.00
Osvaldo Virgil			25.00

1966 Dominican Republic

WILLY McCOVY

The date of issue is speculative, based on the fact these cards "borrowed" their images from 1965 Topps cards. The identity of the issuer and manner of distribution is unknown, though from their wide borders it is possible these were printed on some type of box or package and intended to be cut out and possibly placed into an album, as is customary with many Latin American baseball card issues. The cards are nominally about 1-3/4" x 2-1/2" and are printed in red on thin, blank-back cardboard. As with many issues of the era and area, when these cards are found they are usually in wretched condition. These players probably represent only a portion of the checklist which may or may not comprise only Major League players.

		NM	EX	VG
(1)	Sandy Koufax			200.00
(2)	Juan Marichal			100.00
(3)	Willy Mays (Willie)			200.00
(4)	Willy McCovy (Willie McCovey)			45.00

1937 Donut Co. of American Thrilling Moments

The official title of this multi-subject card set is "Thrilling Moments in the Lives of Famous Americans." The cards, about 1-7/8" x 2-7/8", were printed in groups of 18 on donut boxes. Each card is printed in black-and-white on a single background color. The cards themselves do not name the famous American depicted, but his biography is found in the album which was issued to house the set. Cards are blank-backed. There is only a single baseball playered in the 72-card set.

	NM	EX	VG
Beloved Baseball Idol of All Boys (Babe Ruth)	4,000	1,600	800.00

1952-55 Dormand Postcards

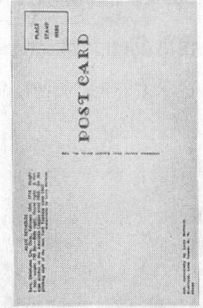

This mid-1950s issue features only selected players from the Yankees, Brooklyn Dodgers, White Sox and Philadelphia A's. Apparently produced on order by the players by Louis Dormand, a Long Island, N.Y., photographer, the cards were used to honor fan requests for photos and autographs. All cards have a facsimile autograph printed in front. Otherwise the fronts of these 3-1/2" x 5-1/2" postcards feature only sharp color photos with no border. Backs, printed in blue or green, feature a few player biographical and career details, one or

two lines identifying the producer and usually product and series numbers. Most have a Kodachrome logo. Some cards do not have all of these elements and several are found blank-backed. The Gil Hodges card is considerably scarcer than the others in the set, with those of Jim Konstanty, Elston Howard, and Casey Stengel also seldom seen. Besides the standard-sized cards listed below, there are oversize versions of Rizzuto's and Mantle's cards. A variation of Johnny Sain's card shows his Arkansas Chevrolet dealership in a photo above the player's picture. The complete set price includes only the standard-size cards.

		NM	EX	VG
	Common Player:	25.00	12.50	7.50
101a	Phil Rizzuto (Large autograph parallel to top.)	40.00	20.00	12.00
101b	Phil Rizzuto (Small autograph parallel to top.)	45.00	22.50	13.50
101c	Phil Rizzuto (Autograph angles downward.)	50.0019 41	25.00	15.00
101d	Phil Rizzuto (9" x 12")	55.00	27.50	16.50
102	Yogi Berra	65.00	32.50	20.00
103	Ed Lopat	30.00	15.00	9.00
104	Hank Bauer (Small autograph.)	30.00	15.00	9.00
104	Hank Bauer (Large autograph.)	60.00	30.00	18.00
105	Joe Collins (Patch on sleeve, autograph at top.)	60.00	30.00	18.00
105	Joe Collins (Patch on sleeve, autograph at bottom.)	60.00	30.00	18.00
105	Joe Collins (No patch on sleeve.)	40.00	20.00	12.00
106	Ralph Houk	30.00	15.00	9.00
107	Bill Miller	27.50	13.50	8.25
108	Ray Scarborough	35.00	17.50	10.00
109	Allie Reynolds	25.00	12.50	7.50
110	Gil McDougald (Small autograph.)	25.00	12.50	7.50
110	Gil McDougald (Large autograph.)	25.00	12.50	7.50
111	Mickey Mantle (Bat on shoulder.)	100.00	50.00	30.00
111	Mickey Mantle (Batting stance, 3-1/2" x 5-1/2".)	235.00	120.00	70.00
111	Mickey Mantle (Bat on shoulder, 6" x 9".)	550.00	275.00	165.00
111	Mickey Mantle (Bat on shoulder, 9" x 12".)	1,200	600.00	360.00
112	Johnny Mize	90.00	45.00	27.50
113	Casey Stengel (Autograph at top.)	165.00	80.00	50.00
113	Casey Stengel (Autograph at bottom.)	165.00	80.00	50.00
114	Bobby Shantz (Autograph parallel to top.)	40.00	20.00	12.00
114	Bobby Shantz (Autograph angles downward.)	75.00	37.00	22.00
115	Whitey Ford	60.00	30.00	18.00
116	Johnny Sain (Beginning windup.)	35.00	17.50	10.00
116	Johnny Sain (Leg kick.)	25.00	12.50	7.50
116	Johnny Sain (With auto dealership ad.)	150.00	75.00	45.00
117	Jim McDonald	25.00	12.50	7.50
118	Gene Woodling	25.00	12.50	7.50
119	Charlie Silvera	30.00	15.00	9.00
120	Don Bollweg	25.00	12.50	7.50
121	Billy Pierce	30.00	15.00	9.00
122	Chico Carrasquel	25.00	12.50	7.50
123	Willie Miranda	25.00	12.50	7.50
124	Carl Erskine	65.00	32.50	20.00
125	Roy Campanella	150.00	75.00	45.00
126	Jerry Coleman	25.00	12.50	7.50
127	Pee Wee Reese	50.00	25.00	15.00
128	Carl Furillo	50.00	25.00	15.00
129	Gil Hodges	75.00	37.50	22.50
130	Billy Martin	30.00	15.00	9.00
131	Not Issued			
132	Irv Noren	35.00	17.50	10.50
133	Enos Slaughter	175.00	87.50	52.50
134	Tom Gorman	25.00	12.50	7.50
135	Ed Robinson	35.00	17.50	10.00
136	Frank Crosetti	150.00	75.00	45.00
137	Not Issued			
138	Jim Konstanty	150.00	75.00	45.00
139	Elston Howard	150.00	75.00	45.00
140	Bill Skowron	400.00	200.00	120.00

1941 Double Play (R330)

JOE DI MAGGIO — NEW YORK YANKEES. Center fielder. Born Nov. 25, 1914. Bats right. Throws right. Height 6 ft. Weight 195 lbs. Batted .352. No. 63 Double Play

CHARLEY KELLER — NEW YORK YANKEES. Left fielder. Born Sept. 12, 1916. Bats left. Throws right. Height 5 ft. 10 in. Wt. 190 lbs. Batted .286. No. 64 Double Play

Issued by Gum Products Inc., Cambridge, Mass., this set comprises 75 numbered cards with two consecutive numbers per card featuring 150 (130 different) players. The blank-backed cards measure about 3-1/8" x 2-1/2". Most feature sepia-toned portrait photos. Cards 81-82 through 99-100 have vertical "in action" photos of 40 of the players who also appear in portraits. The last 50 cards in the series are scarcer than the early numbers. Cards which have been cut in half to form single cards have little collector value.

		NM	EX	VG
Complete Set (75):		10,000	4,000	2,000
Common Player (1/2-99/100):		70.00	25.00	12.50
Common Player (101/102-149/150):		90.00	35.00	15.00
1-2	Larry French, Vance Page	90.00	30.00	15.00
3-4	Billy Herman, Stanley Hack	125.00	50.00	25.00
5-6	Linus Frey, John Vander Meer	75.00	30.00	15.00
7-8	Paul Derringer, Bucky Walters	70.00	25.00	12.50
9-10	Frank McCormick, Bill Werber	70.00	25.00	12.50
11-12	Jimmy Ripple, Ernie Lombardi	85.00	35.00	15.00
13-14	Alex Kampouris, John Wyatt	70.00	25.00	12.50
15-16	Mickey Owen, Paul Waner	110.00	45.00	20.00
17-18	Cookie Lavagetto, Harold Reiser	75.00	30.00	15.00
19-20	Jimmy Wasdell, Dolph Camilli	70.00	25.00	12.50
21-22	Dixie Walker, Ducky Medwick	110.00	45.00	20.00
23-24	Harold Reese, Kirby Higbe	600.00	240.00	120.00
25-26	Harry Danning, Cliff Melton	70.00	25.00	12.50
27-28	Harry Gumbert, Burgess Whitehead	70.00	25.00	12.50
29-30	Joe Orengo, Joe Moore	70.00	25.00	12.50
31-32	Mel Ott, Babe Young	200.00	80.00	40.00
33-34	Lee Handley, Arky Vaughan	110.00	45.00	20.00
35-36	Bob Klinger, Stanley Brown	70.00	25.00	12.50
37-38	Terry Moore, Gus Mancuso	70.00	25.00	12.50
39-40	Johnny Mize, Enos Slaughter	700.00	280.00	140.00
41-42	John Cooney, Sibby Sisti	70.00	25.00	12.50
43-44	Max West, Carvel Rowell	70.00	25.00	12.50
45-46	Danny Litwhiler, Merrill May	70.00	25.00	12.50
47-48	Frank Hayes, Al Brancato	70.00	25.00	12.50
49-50	Bob Johnson, Bill Nagel	70.00	25.00	12.50
51-52	Buck Newsom, Hank Greenberg	200.00	80.00	40.00
53-54	Barney McCosky, Charley Gehringer	140.00	55.00	25.00
55-56	Pinky Higgins, Dick Bartell	70.00	25.00	12.50
57-58	Ted Williams, Jim Tabor	650.00	260.00	130.00
59-60	Joe Cronin, Jimmy Foxx	275.00	110.00	55.00
61-62	Lefty Gomez, Phil Rizzuto	675.00	275.00	135.00
63-64	Joe DiMaggio, Charley Keller	750.00	300.00	150.00
65-66	Red Rolfe, Bill Dickey	125.00	50.00	25.00
67-68	Joe Gordon, Red Ruffing	125.00	62.50	37.50
69-70	Mike Tresh, Luke Appling	110.00	45.00	20.00
71-72	Moose Solters, John Rigney	70.00	25.00	12.50
73-74	Buddy Meyer, Ben Chapman (Myer)	70.00	25.00	12.50
75-76	Cecil Travis, George Case	70.00	25.00	12.50
77-78	Joe Krakauskas, Bob Feller	200.00	80.00	40.00
79-80	Ken Keltner, Hal Trosky	70.00	25.00	12.50
81-82	Ted Williams, Joe Cronin/IA	550.00	220.00	110.00
83-84	Joe Gordon, Charley Keller/IA	90.00	35.00	15.00
85-86	Hank Greenberg, Red Ruffing/IA	225.00	90.00	45.00
87-88	Hal Trosky, George Case/IA	70.00	25.00	12.50
89-90	Mel Ott, Burgess Whitehead/IA	210.00	85.00	40.00
91-92	Harry Danning, Harry Gumbert/IA	70.00	25.00	12.50
93-94	Babe Young, Cliff Melton/IA	70.00	25.00	12.50
95-96	Jimmy Ripple, Bucky Walters/IA	70.00	25.00	12.50
97-98	Stanley Hack, Bob Klinger/IA	70.00	25.00	12.50
99-100	Johnny Mize, Dan Litwhiler/IA	135.00	55.00	25.00
101-102	Dom Dallessandro, Augie Galan	70.00	25.00	12.50
103-104	Bill Lee, Phil Cavarretta	90.00	35.00	15.00
105-106	Lefty Grove, Bobby Doerr	210.00	85.00	40.00
107-108	Frank Pytlak, Dom DiMaggio	115.00	45.00	20.00
109-110	Gerald Priddy, John Murphy	90.00	35.00	15.00
111-112	Tommy Henrich, Marius Russo	100.00	40.00	20.00
113-114	Frank Crosetti, John Sturm	100.00	40.00	20.00
115-116	Ival Goodman, Myron McCormick	90.00	35.00	15.00
117-118	Eddie Joost, Ernie Koy	90.00	35.00	15.00
119-120	Lloyd Waner, Hank Majeski	125.00	50.00	25.00
121-122	Buddy Hassett, Eugene Moore	90.00	35.00	15.00
123-124	Nick Etten, John Rizzo	90.00	35.00	15.00
125-126	Sam Chapman, Wally Moses	90.00	35.00	15.00
127-128	John Babich, Richard Siebert	90.00	35.00	15.00
129-130	Nelson Potter, Benny McCoy	90.00	35.00	15.00
131-132	Clarence Campbell, Louis Boudreau	125.00	50.00	25.00
133-134	Rolly Hemsley, Mel Harder	90.00	35.00	15.00
135-136	Gerald Walker, Joe Heving	90.00	35.00	15.00
137-138	John Rucker, Ace Adams	90.00	35.00	15.00
139-140	Morris Amovich, Carl Hubbell	225.00	90.00	45.00
141-142	Lew Riggs, Leo Durocher	135.00	55.00	30.00
143-144	Fred Fitzsimmons, Joe Vosmik	90.00	35.00	15.00
145-146	Frank Crespi, Jim Brown	90.00	35.00	15.00
147-148	Don Heffner, Harland Clift (Harlond)	90.00	35.00	15.00
149-150	Debs Garms, Elbie Fletcher	90.00	35.00	15.00

1976 Douglas Cool Papa Bell

This collectors' issue was produced following the 1974 induction of James "Cool Papa" Bell into the Hall of Fame. Collector John Douglas collaborated with Bell to produce the set chronicling Bell's career (1922-46) in the Negro and Latin American pro leagues. Fronts have vintage sepia-toned photos of Bell surrounded by a yellow, green or orange woodgrain frame with a title plaque at bottom. Backs are in brown-and-white with a drawing of Bell at top and autobiographical material at center. A description of the photo and copyright data are at bottom. The unnumbered cards are checklisted here alphabetically by their titles.

		NM	EX	VG
Complete Set (13):		10.00	5.00	3.00
Common Card:		1.00	.50	.30
(1)	Amazing Speed	1.00	.50	.30
(2)	Brock Sets SB Record	1.00	.50	.30
(3)	Cool Papa	1.00	.50	.30
(4)	Cuba, 1928	1.00	.50	.30
(5)	Great Fielder, Too	1.00	.50	.30
(6)	HOF, Cooperstown	1.00	.50	.30
(7)	HOF Favorite	1.00	.50	.30
(8)	Induction Day, 1974	1.00	.50	.30
(9)	Monarchs' Manager	1.00	.50	.30
(10)	On Deck in Cuba	1.00	.50	.30
(11)	The Mexican Leagues	1.00	.50	.30
(12)	Touring Havana	1.00	.50	.30
(13)	With Josh Gibson	1.00	.50	.30

1977 Douglas Johnny Mize

In an effort to promote Johnny Mize for induction to the Hall of Fame, John Douglas created this collectors' issue. The Big Cat's career is traced on a series of 3-1/4" x 3-7/8" cards with black-and-white photos on a greenish-brown background. Black-and-white backs have a drawing of Mize at top with lengthy narrative below. The unnumbered cards are checklisted here by the title which appears on the front. Mize was selected for the Hall of Fame in 1981.

		NM	EX	VG
Complete Set (20):		9.00	4.50	2.75
Common Card:		1.00	.50	.30
(1)	Blattner, Gordon, Lombardi, Mize, Marshall	1.00	.50	.30
(2)	Call for Phillip Morris	1.00	.50	.30
(3)	Cardinal Slugger	1.00	.50	.30
(4)	Card's Big Stick	1.00	.50	.30
(5)	Early Photo - 1913	1.00	.50	.30
(6)	51 Homers, 1947	1.00	.50	.30
(7)	Home Run, 1952 Series	1.00	.50	.30
(8)	June 16, 1953	1.00	.50	.30
(9)	Louisville Poster - 1947	1.00	.50	.30
(10)	Mize, Happy Chandler, Bucky Harris	1.00	.50	.30
(11)	Mize, Reynolds, Johnson	1.00	.50	.30
(12)	N.L. Homer Champ 1948	1.00	.50	.30
(13)	Series MVP - 1952	1.00	.50	.30
(14)	St. Louis Star	1.00	.50	.30
(15)	The Navy - 1943	1.00	.50	.30
(16)	Vu-Master Slide	1.00	.50	.30
(17)	With Enos Slaughter	1.00	.50	.30
(18)	With Roy Rogers	1.00	.50	.30
(19)	With Terry Moore	1.00	.50	.30
(20)	Woodling, Raschi, Mize - 1952	1.00	.50	.30

1978 Dover Publications Great Players Postcards

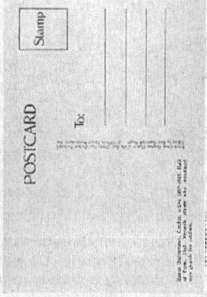

This set of 32 collectors' issue postcards was originally issued in the form of an 8" x 11" booklet from which individual cards could be separated. The 3-7/8" x 5-1/2" cards are perforated on two sides, depending on their placement on a four-card page. Fronts have borderless sepia photos. Black-and-white backs have standard postcard indicia, copyright data, player identification and a brief career summary. The unnumbered cards are checklisted here alphabetically.

		NM	EX	VG
Complete Set, Booklet:		7.50	3.75	2.25
Complete Set, Singles (32):		7.50	3.75	2.25
Common Player:		.50	.25	.15
(1)	Grover Cleveland Alexander	.60	.30	.20
(2)	Chief Bender	.50	.25	.15
(3)	Roger Bresnahan	.50	.25	.15
(4)	Bullet Joe Bush	.50	.25	.15
(5)	Frank Chance	.50	.25	.15
(6)	Ty Cobb	1.25	.60	.40
(7)	Eddie Collins	.50	.25	.15
(8)	Stan Coveleski	.50	.25	.15
(9)	Sam Crawford	.50	.25	.15
(10)	Frankie Frisch	.50	.25	.15
(11)	Goose Goslin	.50	.25	.15
(12)	Harry Heilmann	.50	.25	.15
(13)	Rogers Hornsby	.75	.40	.25
(14)	Joe Jackson	4.00	2.00	1.25
(15)	Hughie Jennings	.50	.25	.15
(16)	Walter Johnson	1.00	.50	.30
(17)	Sad Sam Jones	.50	.25	.15
(18)	Rabbit Maranville	.50	.25	.15
(19)	Rube Marquard	.50	.25	.15
(20)	Christy Mathewson	1.00	.50	.30
(21)	John McGraw	.50	.25	.15
(22)	Herb Pennock	.50	.25	.15
(23)	Eddie Plank	.50	.25	.15
(24)	Edd Roush	.50	.25	.15
(25)	Babe Ruth	4.00	2.00	1.25
(26)	George Sisler	.50	.25	.15
(27)	Tris Speaker	.75	.40	.25
(28)	Casey Stengel	.50	.25	.15
(29)	Joe Tinker	.50	.25	.15
(30)	Pie Traynor	.50	.25	.15
(31)	Dazzy Vance	.50	.25	.15
(32)	Cy Young	.75	.40	.25

1925 Drake's

Among a series of 64 movie stars packaged with Drake's Cake in the mid-1920s was a card of Babe Ruth, who did some movie work for Universal Pictures at the time. The 2-7/16" x 4-3/16" black-and-white card has a portrait of Ruth on front, with his name, studio and card number in the bottom border. Backs have been seen with at least two styles of advertising, one for Drake's Cake and one for Yankee Cake.

		NM	EX	VG
61	Babe Ruth	3,750	1,875	1,125

1950 Drake's

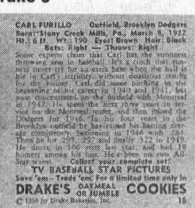

Entitled "TV Baseball Series," the 1950 Drake's Bakeries set pictures 36 different players on a television screen format. The cards, 2-1/2" x 2-1/2", contain black-and-white photos surrounded by a black border. Backs carry a player biography plus an advertisement advising collectors to look for the cards in packages of Oatmeal or Jumble cookies.

		NM	EX	VG
Complete Set (36):		9,975	5,000	3,000
Common Player:		200.00	100.00	60.00
1	Elwin "Preacher" Roe	340.00	170.00	100.00
2	Clint Hartung	200.00	100.00	60.00
3	Earl Torgeson	200.00	100.00	60.00
4	Leland "Lou" Brissie	200.00	100.00	60.00
5	Edwin "Duke" Snider	675.00	340.00	200.00
6	Roy Campanella	675.00	340.00	200.00
7	Sheldon "Available" Jones	200.00	100.00	60.00
8	Carroll "Whitey" Lockman	200.00	100.00	60.00
9	Bobby Thomson	240.00	120.00	75.00
10	Dick Sisler	200.00	100.00	60.00
11	Gil Hodges	400.00	200.00	120.00
12	Eddie Waitkus	200.00	100.00	60.00
13	Bobby Doerr	350.00	175.00	100.00
14	Warren Spahn	400.00	200.00	120.00
15	John "Buddy" Kerr	200.00	100.00	60.00
16	Sid Gordon	200.00	100.00	60.00
17	Willard Marshall	200.00	100.00	60.00

		NM	EX	VG
18	Carl Furillo	400.00	200.00	120.00
19	Harold "Pee Wee" Reese	540.00	270.00	160.00
20	Alvin Dark	200.00	100.00	60.00
21	Del Ennis	200.00	100.00	60.00
22	Ed Stanky	200.00	100.00	60.00
23	Tommy "Old Reliable" Henrich	240.00	120.00	75.00
24	Larry "Yogi" Berra	675.00	350.00	200.00
25	Phil "Scooter" Rizzuto	675.00	350.00	200.00
26	Jerry Coleman	200.00	100.00	60.00
27	Joe Page	200.00	100.00	60.00
28	Allie Reynolds	240.00	120.00	75.00
29	Ray Scarborough	200.00	100.00	60.00
30	George "Birdie" Tebbetts	200.00	100.00	60.00
31	Maurice "Lefty" McDermott	200.00	100.00	60.00
32	Johnny Pesky	200.00	100.00	60.00
33	Dom "Little Professor" DiMaggio	250.00	125.00	75.00
34	Vern "Junior" Stephens	200.00	100.00	60.00
35	Bob Elliott	200.00	100.00	60.00
36	Enos "Country" Slaughter	440.00	220.00	130.00

1909-11 Drum Cigarettes

Other than Ty Cobb brand, Drum is the rarest of the various cigarette advertisements to be found on the backs of T206. Typography on the back is printed in a plum color. Multipliers shown are for "common" players; Hall of Fame players and other high-demand cards command a lesser premium relative to common-brand backs. Among T205 backs, Drum, printed in brown, ranks as the scarcest of the brands.

PREMIUMS
T205 Common Players: 50X
T205 Hall of Famers: 25X
T206 Common Players: 75X
T206 Hall of Famers: 35X
(See T205, T206 for checklists and base card values.)

1972 Don Drysdale's Restaurant Postcards

 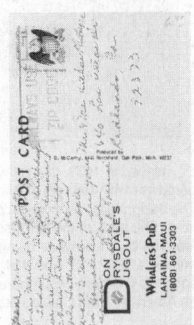

The date cited is taken from the postmark of an observed example. The actual span during which the cards were current is unknown. These versions of J.D. McCarthy postcards have on their 3-1/4" x 5-1/2" fronts a borderless black-and-white pose. The salutation and facsimile autograph are incuse printed in blue ink. Postcard style backs are known in three styles. One advertises Don Drysdale's Dugout in Santa Ana, Calif., another advertises his Club 53 in Kona, Hawaii, while a third advertizes Don Drysdale's Dugout and the Whaler's Pub on Maui.

	NM	EX	VG
Don Drysdale	16.00	8.00	4.75

1965 Dugan Bros. Casey Stengel

In celebration of the Ol' Perfesser's 75th birthday, the N.Y. Mets held a birthday party for him at Shea Stadium on July 25. This approximately 2-1/2" x 3-1/2" card was given to each of the 40,000+ fans in attendance, sponsored by Dugan Bros., a local bakery which also provided a birthday cake for the occasion. Unfortunately, Stengel was unable to attend the fete; early that morning he broke his hip leaving a nightclub, ending his managerial career. The card is printed in blue on white. The back provides career highlights.

CASEY STENGEL

	NM	EX	VG
Casey Stengel	25.00	12.50	7.50

1888 Duke Talk of the Diamond (N135)

One of the more obscure 19th Century tobacco issues is a 25-card set issued by Honest Long Cut Tobacco in the late 1880's. Titled "Talk of the Diamond," the set features full-color cards measuring 4-1/8" x 2-1/2". Each card features a cartoon-like drawing illustrating a popular baseball term or expression. The left portion of the card pictures an unspecified player in a fielding position, and some of the artwork for that part of the set was borrowed from the more popular Buchner Gold Coin set (N284) issued about the same time. Because the "Talk of the Diamond" set does not feature individual players, it has never really captured the attention of baseball card collectors. It does, however, hold interest as a novelty item of the period. It carries an N135 American Card Catalog designation.

		NM	EX	VG
Complete Set (25):		9,350	3,850	1,925
Common Card:		400.00	155.00	75.00
(1)	A Base Tender	400.00	155.00	75.00
(2)	A Big Hit	400.00	155.00	75.00
(3)	A Chronic Kicker	400.00	155.00	75.00
(4)	A Foul Balk	400.00	155.00	75.00
(5)	A Foul Catch	400.00	155.00	75.00
(6)	A Good Catch	400.00	155.00	75.00
(7)	A Good Throw	400.00	155.00	75.00
(8)	A Heavy Batter	400.00	155.00	75.00
(9)	A Home Run	400.00	155.00	75.00
(10)	A Hot Ball	400.00	155.00	75.00
(11)	A Low Ball	400.00	155.00	75.00
(12)	A Pitcher in the Box	400.00	155.00	75.00
(13)	A Regular Ball	400.00	155.00	75.00
(14)	A Rounder	400.00	155.00	75.00
(15)	A Short Stop	400.00	155.00	75.00
(16)	After the Ball	400.00	155.00	75.00
(17)	Going for Third Base	400.00	155.00	75.00
(18)	He Serves the Ball	400.00	155.00	75.00
(19)	Left Field	400.00	155.00	75.00
(20)	Left on Base	400.00	155.00	75.00
(21)	Lively Game	400.00	155.00	75.00
(22)	No Game	400.00	155.00	75.00
(23)	Out	400.00	155.00	75.00
(24)	Stealing a Base	400.00	155.00	75.00
(25)	Three out-All out	400.00	155.00	75.00

1889 Duke's Terrors of America

 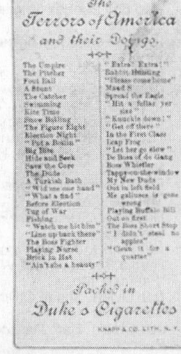

Officially titled "The Terrors of America and their Doings," this set of tobacco inserts features color artwork of boys in all manners of activities, some mischievous. Several of the cards picture the lads playing sports, including baseball. The cards were issued in three sizes. The smallest measure 1-7/16" x 2-3/4" and have an ad on the checklist back for Duke's Cigarettes. A slightly larger 1-3/4" x 3-1/8" version advertises Duke's Mixture. The largest features the card design on an ornate background and measures 2-1/2" x 4-3/16", advertising Honest Long Cut on back.

	NM	EX	VG
Duke's Cigarettes	80.00	40.00	24.00
Duke's Mixture	100.00	50.00	30.00
Honest Long Cut	200.00	100.00	60.00

1969 Dunkin' Donuts Chicago Cubs Bumper Stickers

This series of Cubs novelty collectibles was the first of two annual presentations. The stickers measure about 8" x 4" and have at their left end a photographic portrait of a player at one end of an artwork bat on a black background. At right is a baseball design with the sponsor's logo. A second version exists with "Cub Power" in place of the DD advertising. The unnumbered stickers are checklisted here alphabetically.

		NM	EX	VG
Complete Set (6):		350.00	175.00	100.00
Common Player:		30.00	15.00	9.00
(1)	Ernie Banks	125.00	65.00	35.00
(2)	Glenn Beckert	30.00	15.00	9.00
(3)	Randy Hundley	30.00	15.00	9.00
(4)	Don Kessinger	30.00	15.00	9.00
(5)	Ron Santo	60.00	30.00	18.00
(6)	Billy Williams	75.00	37.00	22.00

1970 Dunkin' Donuts Chicago Cubs Bumper Stickers

This series of Cubs novelty collectibles was the second of two annual presentations. The stickers measure about 8" x 4" and have at their left end a photographic portrait (without cap) of a player in a vaguely baseball-like design. In upper-left is a blue facsimile autograph. At right is "Cubs are no. 1," at bottom is a DD credit line. Basic color scheme of the graphics is red, white and blue. The unnumbered stickers are checklisted here alphabetically.

		NM	EX	VG
Complete Set (6):		350.00	175.00	100.00
Common Player:		30.00	15.00	9.00
(1)	Ernie Banks	125.00	62.00	37.00
(2)	Glenn Beckert	30.00	15.00	9.00
(3)	Randy Hundley	30.00	15.00	9.00
(4)	Don Kessinger	30.00	15.00	9.00
(5)	Ron Santo	60.00	30.00	18.00
(6)	Billy Williams	75.00	37.00	22.00

1947 DuPont Cavalcade of America Premium

This 6" x 9" black-and-white card was distributed by NBC radio in conjunction with one of its weekly programs, which featured Babe Ruth on Sept. 29, 1947. The front has a bordered photo of Ruth in his classic batting follow-through. The back has information about the broadcast and details "The Babe's 54 Major League Records."

	NM	EX	VG
Babe Ruth	500.00	250.00	150.00

1972 Durochrome Chicago White Sox Decals

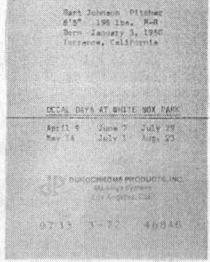

While they are technically stickers rather than decals, this set of six White Sox was given away during the course of half a dozen "Decal Days" at Comiskey Park, as listed on the peel-off back. The stickers measure 3-9/16" x 4-9/16" and feature posed action photos of the players in their vintage red-trimmed uniforms. Fronts have a facsimile autograph and, in the bottom border, the team name. Backs are printed in green and have a few vital statistics, an ad by the manufacturer and an enigmatic row of numbers at the bottom. The unnumbered stickers are checklisted here in alphabetical order.

		NM	EX	VG
Complete Set (6):		60.00	30.00	18.00
Common Player:		9.00	4.50	2.75
(1)	Richard Allen	25.00	12.50	7.50
(2)	Ed Hermann	9.00	4.50	2.75
(3)	Bart Johnson	9.00	4.50	2.75
(4)	Carlos May	9.00	4.50	2.75
(5)	Bill Melton	9.00	4.50	2.75
(6)	Wilbur Wood	9.00	4.50	2.75

1914 E. & S. Publishing Co.

Currently, a dozen players have been reported from this issue. Front of the 5-1/2" x 3-3/4" postcards has a large portrait or action picture of the player at center, with a number of cartoons around. The printing is in blue ink. The back is done in ornate typography with copyright line, stamp box, etc. Other players may yet be discovered.

		NM	EX	VG
(1)	"Jimmie" Archer	300.00	150.00	90.00
(2)	Joe Benz	300.00	150.00	90.00
(3)	Frank Chance	300.00	150.00	90.00
(4)	Ty Cobb	4,500	2,250	1,350
(5)	Miller Huggins	600.00	300.00	180.00
(6)	Joe Jackson	6,000	3,000	1,800
(7)	James Lavender	300.00	150.00	90.00
(8)	Christy Mathewson	2,500	1,250	750.00
(9)	"Tex" Russell	300.00	150.00	90.00
(10)	Frank Schulte	300.00	150.00	90.00
(11)	Jim Scott	300.00	150.00	90.00
(12)	Art Wilson	300.00	150.00	90.00

1940s Eagle Hall of Fame

The date of this issue can only be approximated, probably in the late 1940s. The 9-1/4" x 11-1/4" cards have high-gloss sepia photos on thick cardboard. A wood-look frame and identification plaques are pictured around the central photo. Backs are blank. The pictures were issued by the Carnegie (Pa.) Aerie of the Eagles, lodge #1134, according to the bottom "plaque." At top is "Eagle Hall of Fame." Presumably the four ballplayers and two boxers known were all members of that fraternal order. The unnumbered pieces are checklisted alphabetically.

		NM	EX	VG
Complete Set (7):		700.00	350.00	210.00
Common Player:		40.00	20.00	12.00
(1)	Bob Fitzsimmons/Boxer	40.00	20.00	12.00
(2)	Lefty Grove	150.00	75.00	45.00
(3)	Connie Mack	150.00	75.00	45.00
(4)	Stan Musial	200.00	100.00	60.00
(5)	John Sullivan/Boxer	75.00	37.00	22.00
(6)	Honus Wagner	175.00	87.00	52.00
(7)	Cy Young	175.00	87.00	52.00

1979 Early Red Sox Favorites

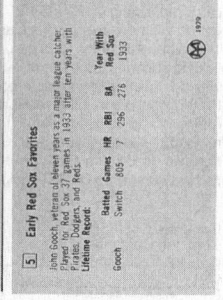

This collectors' issue from Maine features players of the 1920s-1930s Red Sox. Cards are printed in black-and-white in a 2-5/8" x 3-3/4" format. Front photos are bordered in white and have identification of the players overprinted in black. Backs have a few stats, highlights or an explanation of the photo on front. Many cards feature more than one player.

		NM	EX	VG
Complete Set (24):		40.00	20.00	12.00
Common Player:		4.00	2.00	1.25
1	New Fenway Park	4.00	2.00	1.25
2	Mrs. Tom Yawkey and Mrs. Eddie Collins	4.00	2.00	1.25
3	Red Sox Outfielders - 1932 (Tom Oliver, Earl Webb, Jack Rothrock)	4.00	2.00	1.25
4	Red Sox Ace Pitchers (John Marcum, Wes Ferrell, Lefty Grove, Fritz Ostermueller)	4.00	2.00	1.25
5	John Gooch	4.00	2.00	1.25
6	Red Sox Recruits at Sarasota, Fla. (Joe Cronin)	4.00	2.00	1.25
7	Danny MacFayden	4.00	2.00	1.25
8	Dale Alexander	4.00	2.00	1.25
9	Robert (Fatsy) Fothergill	4.00	2.00	1.25
10	Red Sox Sunday Morning Workout	4.00	2.00	1.25
11	Jimmie Foxx (Signing ball for Mrs. Yawkey.)	6.00	3.00	1.75
12	Lefty Grove (Presented keys to new car.)	6.00	3.00	1.75
13	"Fireball" Lefty Grove	6.00	3.00	1.75
14	Praciticng Base Stealing (Jack Rothrock, Urban Pickering)	4.00	2.00	1.25
15	Tom Daly, Al Schacht, Herb Pennock	4.00	2.00	1.25
16	Eddie Collins, Heinie Manush	6.00	3.00	1.75
17	Tris Speaker	6.00	3.00	1.75
18	Home Run Star (Jimmie Foxx)	6.00	3.00	1.75
19	Smead Jolley	4.00	2.00	1.25
20	Hal Trosky, Jimmie Foxx	6.00	3.00	1.75
21	Herold "Muddy" Ruel, Wilcy "Fireman" Moore	4.00	2.00	1.25
22	Bob Quinn, Shano Collins	4.00	2.00	1.25
23	Tom Oliver	4.00	2.00	1.25
24	Joe Cronin, Herb Pennock, Buetter	4.00	2.00	1.25

1966 East Hills Pirates

Stores in the East Hills Shopping Center, a large mall located in suburban Pittsburgh, distributed cards from this 25-card full-color set in 1966. The cards, which measure 3-1/4" x 4-1/4", are blank-backed and are numbered by the players' uniform numbers. The numbers appear in the lower right corners of the cards.

		NM	EX	VG
Complete Set (25):		50.00	25.00	15.00
Common Player:		2.50	1.25	.70
3	Harry Walker	2.50	1.25	.70
7	Bob Bailey	2.50	1.25	.70
8	Willie Stargell	10.00	5.00	3.00
9	Bill Mazeroski	10.00	5.00	3.00
10	Jim Pagliaroni	2.50	1.25	.70
11	Jose Pagan	2.50	1.25	.70
12	Jerry May	2.50	1.25	.70
14	Gene Alley	2.50	1.25	.70
15	Manny Mota	2.50	1.25	.70
16	Andy Rodgers	2.50	1.25	.70
17	Donn Clendenon	2.50	1.25	.70
18	Matty Alou	2.50	1.25	.70
19	Pete Mikkelsen	2.50	1.25	.70
20	Jesse Gonder	2.50	1.25	.70
21	Bob Clemente	30.00	15.00	9.00
22	Woody Fryman	2.50	1.25	.70
24	Jerry Lynch	2.50	1.25	.70
25	Tommie Sisk	2.50	1.25	.70
26	Roy Face	2.50	1.25	.70
28	Steve Blass	2.50	1.25	.70
32	Vernon Law	3.50	1.75	1.00
34	Al McBean	2.50	1.25	.70
39	Bob Veale	2.50	1.25	.70
43	Don Cardwell	2.50	1.25	.70
45	Gene Michael	2.50	1.25	.70

1933 Eclipse Import

Issued in 1933, this set was sold in eight-card strips. Numbered from 401 through 424, the cards measure 2-7/16" x 2-7/8". The design features a crude colored drawing of the player on the front. The back of the card displays the card number at the top followed by the player's name, team and a brief write-up. Card numbers 403, 413, and 414 are missing and probably correspond to the three unnumbered cards in the set. The set carries an American Card Catalog designation of R337.

		NM	EX	VG
Complete Set (24):		10,000	5,000	3,000
Common Player:		165.00	65.00	30.00
401	Johnny Vergez	165.00	65.00	30.00
402	Babe Ruth	3,200	1,600	960.00
403	Not Issued			
404	George Pipgras	165.00	65.00	30.00
405	Bill Terry	425.00	170.00	85.00
406	George Connally	165.00	65.00	30.00
407	Watson Clark	165.00	65.00	30.00
408	"Lefty" Grove	500.00	200.00	100.00
409	Henry Johnson	165.00	65.00	30.00
410	Jimmy Dykes	165.00	65.00	30.00
411	Henry Hine Schuble	165.00	65.00	30.00
412	Bucky Harris	425.00	170.00	85.00
413	Not Issued			
414	Not Issued			
415	Al Simmons	425.00	170.00	85.00
416	Henry "Heinie" Manush	425.00	170.00	85.00
417	Glen Myatt (Glenn)	165.00	65.00	30.00
418	Babe Herman	175.00	70.00	35.00
419	Frank Frisch	425.00	170.00	85.00
420	Tony Lazzeri	425.00	170.00	85.00
421	Paul Waner	425.00	170.00	85.00
422	Jimmy Wilson	165.00	65.00	30.00
423	Charles Grimm	165.00	65.00	30.00
424	Dick Bartell	165.00	65.00	30.00
----	Jimmy Fox (Jimmie Foxx)	600.00	240.00	120.00
----	Roy Johnson	165.00	65.00	30.00
----	Pie Traynor	425.00	170.00	85.00

1942 Editorial Bruguera Babe Ruth

The Babe is the only baseball player appearing is this 12-card series of "Figuras deportivas de fama mundial" (World famous sports figures) issued in Spain. The cards are blank-backed, about 4-3/4" x 3-1/2", with color artwork on front.

	NM	EX	VG
Babe Ruth	175.00	90.00	50.00

1930s Edwards, Ringer & Bigg Cigarettes

Though he is identified nowhere on this English cigarette card, the home run swing of Babe Ruth on the front is unmistakable. The last card in a set of 25 "Sports & Games in Many Lands" series, the approximately 2-5/8" x 1-3/8" cards have color artwork on the front and green-and-white backs. The back of the baseball card provides a short history of "The great national sport of the U.S.A." The card is nearly identical to the much more common 1929 Churchman's brand, except for the ads on back and the lack on the later card of the Churchman's name on top-right front.

		NM	EX	VG
25	Baseball, U.S.A. (Babe Ruth)	400.00	200.00	120.00

1909-11 El Principe de Gales Cigarettes

PREMIUMS:
Commons: 1-2X
Hall of Famers: 1-2X
(See T206 for checklist and base card values.)

1976 English's Chicken Baltimore Orioles Lids

It is uncertain whether the checklist presented here is complete. These 8-3/8" diameter fried chicken bucket lids are printed on heavy waxed cardboard in black-and-white. Cap logos have been airbrushed off. A few previous seasons' stats are printed to the left and right of the player photo.

		NM	EX	VG
Complete Set (5):		400.00	200.00	125.00
Common Player:		20.00	10.00	6.00
(1)	Mike Cuellar	20.00	10.00	6.00
(2)	Ken Holtzman	20.00	10.00	6.00
(3)	Lee May	20.00	10.00	6.00
(4)	Jim Palmer	100.00	50.00	30.00
(5)	Brooks Robinson	300.00	150.00	90.00

1963-1973 Equitable Sports Hall of Fame

This series of black-and-white art prints was produced over more than a decade. About 8" x 11", the prints feature the artwork of Robert Riger or George Loh, reproduced from ads for the life insurance company. Nearly 95 pieces honoring athletes from many sports were produced. Only the baseball players are listed here.

		NM	EX	VG
Common Player:		6.00	3.00	1.80
(1)	Ernie Banks	7.50	3.75	2.25
(2)	Roy Campanella	7.50	3.75	2.25
(3)	Johnny Evers	6.00	3.00	1.80
(4)	Bob Feller	6.00	3.00	1.80
(5)	Lou Gehrig	10.00	5.00	3.00
(6)	Lefty Grove	6.00	3.00	1.80
(7)	Tommy Henrich	6.00	3.00	1.80
(8)	Carl Hubbell	6.00	3.00	1.80
(9)	Al Kaline	6.00	3.00	1.80
(10)	Jerry Koosman	6.00	3.00	1.80
(11)	Mickey Mantle	15.00	7.50	4.50
(12)	Eddie Mathews	6.00	3.00	1.80
(13)	Willie Mays	9.00	4.50	2.75
(14)	Stan Musial	9.00	4.50	2.75
(15)	Pee Wee Reese	6.00	3.00	1.80
(16)	Allie Reynolds	6.00	3.00	1.80
(17)	Robin Roberts	6.00	3.00	1.80
(18)	Brooks Robinson	6.00	3.00	1.80
(19)	Red Ruffing	6.00	3.00	1.80
(20)	Babe Ruth	12.50	6.25	3.75
(21)	Warren Spahn	6.00	3.00	1.80

1954 Esskay Hot Dogs Orioles

Measuring 2-1/4" x 3-1/2", the 1954 Esskay Hot Dogs set features the Baltimore Orioles. The unnumbered color cards were issued in panels of two on packages of hot dogs and are usually found with grease stains. The cards have waxed fronts with blank backs on a white stock. Complete boxes of Esskay Hot Dogs are scarce and command a price of 2-3 times greater than the single card values.

		NM	EX	VG
Complete Set (34):		112,500	56,000	34,000
Common Player:		3,750	1,875	1,125
(1)	Neil Berry	3,750	1,875	1,125
(2)	Michael Blyzka	3,750	1,875	1,125
(3)	Harry Brecheen	3,750	1,875	1,125
(4)	Gil Coan	3,750	1,875	1,125
(5)	Joe Coleman	3,750	1,875	1,125
(6)	Clinton Courtney	3,750	1,875	1,125
(7)	Charles E. Diering	3,750	1,875	1,125
(8)	Jimmie Dykes	3,750	1,875	1,125
(9)	Frank J. Fanovich	3,750	1,875	1,125
(10)	Howard Fox	3,750	1,875	1,125
(11)	Jim Fridley	3,750	1,875	1,125
(12)	Vinicio "Chico" Garcia	3,750	1,875	1,125
(13)	Jehosie Heard	5,000	2,500	1,500
(14)	Darrell Johnson	3,750	1,875	1,125
(15)	Bob Kennedy	3,750	1,875	1,125
(16)	Dick Kokos	3,750	1,875	1,125
(17)	Dave Koslo	3,750	1,875	1,125
(18)	Lou Kretlow	3,750	1,875	1,125
(19)	Richard D. Kryhoski	3,750	1,875	1,125
(20)	Don Larsen	6,250	3,100	1,875
(21)	Donald E. Lenhardt	3,750	1,875	1,125
(22)	Richard Littlefield	3,750	1,875	1,125
(23)	Sam Mele	3,750	1,875	1,125
(24)	Les Moss	3,750	1,875	1,125
(25)	Ray L. Murray	3,750	1,875	1,125
(26a)	"Bobo" Newsom (No stadium lights in background.)	4,400	2,200	1,300
(26b)	"Bobo" Newson (Stadium lights in background.)	4,400	2,200	1,300
(27)	Tom Oliver	3,750	1,875	1,125
(28)	Duane Pillette	3,750	1,875	1,125
(29)	Francis M. Skaff	3,750	1,875	1,125
(30)	Marlin Stuart	3,750	1,875	1,125
(31)	Robert L. Turley	5,600	2,800	1,700
(32)	Eddie Waitkus	3,750	1,875	1,125
(33)	Vic Wertz	3,750	1,875	1,125
(34)	Robert G. Young	3,750	1,875	1,125

1955 Esskay Hot Dogs Orioles

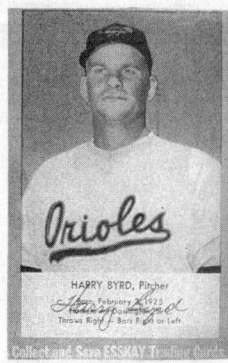

For the second consecutive year, Esskay Meats placed baseball cards of Orioles players on their boxes of hot dogs. The unnumbered, color cards measure 2-1/4" x 3-1/2" and can be distinguished from the previous year by their unwaxed fronts and blank gray backs. Many of the same photos from 1954 were used with only minor picture-cropping differences. For 1955, only one player card per box was printed. The space which was occupied by the second player card in 1954 carried a prize redemption coupon on 1955 boxes.

		NM	EX	VG
Complete Set (26):		94,000	47,000	28,500
Common Player:		3,750	1,875	1,125
(1)	Cal Abrams	3,750	1,875	1,125
(2)	Robert S. Alexander	3,750	1,875	1,125
(3)	Harry Byrd	3,750	1,875	1,125
(4)	Gil Coan	3,750	1,875	1,125
(5)	Joseph P. Coleman	3,750	1,875	1,125
(6)	William R. Cox	3,750	1,875	1,125
(7)	Charles E. Diering	3,750	1,875	1,125
(8)	Walter A. Evers	3,750	1,875	1,125
(9)	Don Johnson	3,750	1,875	1,125
(10)	Robert D. Kennedy	3,750	1,875	1,125
(11)	Lou Kretlow	3,750	1,875	1,125
(12)	Robert L. Kuzava	3,750	1,875	1,125
(13)	Fred Marsh	3,750	1,875	1,125
(14)	Charles Maxwell	3,750	1,875	1,125
(15)	Jimmie McDonald	3,750	1,875	1,125
(16)	Bill Miller	3,750	1,875	1,125
(17)	Willy Miranda	3,750	1,875	1,125
(18)	Raymond L. Moore	3,750	1,875	1,125
(19)	John Lester Moss	3,750	1,875	1,125
(20)	"Bobo" Newsom	3,750	1,875	1,125
(21)	Duane Pillette	3,750	1,875	1,125
(22)	Edward S. Waitkus	3,750	1,875	1,125
(23)	Harold W. Smith	3,750	1,875	1,125
(24)	Gus Triandos	3,750	1,875	1,125
(25)	Eugene R. Woodling	4,400	2,200	1,300
(26)	Robert G. Young	3,750	1,875	1,125

1972 Esso Hispanic Coins

Little is known of these coins, except that they were distributed in Puerto Rico. Even the sponsor, Esso Oil Co., is not mentioned anywhere on the pieces. Made of aluminum and 1-1/4" in diameter, coin fronts have a portrait of the player with his name above. Backs are in Spanish and have the player's position, team, height, weight, date and place of birth. The coins of

Tony Perez and, to a lesser extent, Rod Carew are scarcer than the others. A person receiving a Perez coin was able to exchange it for a full tank of gas. In 2006, a brass-finish Roberto Clemente coin was first reported, probably also a short-printed exchange coin.

		NM	EX	VG
Complete Set (13):		325.00	160.00	95.00
Common Player:		9.00	4.50	2.75
(1)	Luis Aparicio	15.00	7.50	4.50
(2)	Rod Carew	50.00	25.00	15.00
(3)	Rico Carty	9.00	4.50	2.75
(4)	Cesar Cedeno	9.00	4.50	2.75
(5)	Orlando Cepeda	15.00	7.50	4.50
(6)	Roberto Clemente	110.00	55.00	35.00
(7)	Mike Cuellar	9.00	4.50	2.75
(8)	Juan Marichal	15.00	7.50	4.50
(9)	Felix Millan	9.00	4.50	2.75
(10)	Guillermo Montanez	9.00	4.50	2.75
(11)	Tony Oliva	12.00	6.00	3.50
(12a)	Tany Perez (Tony)	75.00	37.50	22.50
(12b)	Tony Perez	75.00	37.50	22.50
(13)	Manny Sanguillen	9.00	4.50	2.75

1909 E-NUC Candy

The attributed date is speculative, based on the only season in which all of the known players on this surely incomplete checklist played with the teams listed on their cards. It is also speculative to list these as a candy or caramel card issue because nothing is currently known of their maker or issuer, if indeed they were actually issued and are not just prototypes for one or more of the E-card sets that followed in the 1910s. All known examples also appear to be hand-cut in approximately 1-1/2" x 2-3/4" size that was to become that standard for many caramel issues. Cards have blank backs and blue captions giving the player name, team and league, where necessary.

		NM	EX	VG
(1)	Moose McCormick			350.00
(2)	Bill O'Hara			350.00
(3)	Hans Wagner			4,500

1949 Eureka Sportstamps

The commissioner of baseball, president of the National League and 198 N.L. players are included in this issue. The stamps were issued on team sheets measuring 7-1/2" x 10", with individual stamps measuring 1-1/2" x 2". An album issued with the set provided short player biographies. The stamps feature colorized posed player action photos. At bottom is a yellow strip with the player's name, stamp number and copyright line. Stamps are numbered alphabetically within teams.

		NM	EX	VG
Complete Set (200):		900.00	450.00	275.00
Common Player:		5.00	2.50	1.50
Album w/mounted stamps:		400.00	200.00	120.00
Album:		75.00	37.50	22.00
1	Albert B. (Happy) Chandler	15.00	7.50	4.50
2	Ford Frick	5.00	2.50	1.50
3	Billy Southworth	5.00	2.50	1.50
4	Johnny Antonelli	5.00	2.50	1.50
5	Red Barrett	5.00	2.50	1.50
6	Clint Conatser	5.00	2.50	1.50
7	Alvin Dark	5.00	2.50	1.50
8	Bob Elliott	5.00	2.50	1.50
9	Glenn Elliott	5.00	2.50	1.50
10	Elbie Fletcher	5.00	2.50	1.50
11	Bob Hall	5.00	2.50	1.50
12	Jeff Heath	5.00	2.50	1.50
13	Bobby Hogue	5.00	2.50	1.50
14	Tommy Holmes	5.00	2.50	1.50
15	Al Lakeman	5.00	2.50	1.50
16	Phil Masi	5.00	2.50	1.50
17	Nelson Potter	5.00	2.50	1.50
18	Pete Reiser	10.00	5.00	3.00
19	Rick Rickert	5.00	2.50	1.50
20	Connie Ryan	5.00	2.50	1.50
21	Jim Russell	5.00	2.50	1.50
22	Johnny Sain	10.00	5.00	3.00
23	Bill Salkeld	5.00	2.50	1.50
24	Sibby Sisti	5.00	2.50	1.50
25	Warren Spahn	25.00	12.50	7.50
26	Eddie Stanky	5.00	2.50	1.50
27	Bill Voiselle	5.00	2.50	1.50
28	Bert Shotton	5.00	2.50	1.50
29	Jack Banta	5.00	2.50	1.50
30	Rex Barney	7.50	3.75	2.25
31	Ralph Branca	15.00	7.50	4.50
32	Tommy Brown	5.00	2.50	1.50
33	Roy Campanella	40.00	20.00	12.00
34	Billy Cox	7.50	3.75	2.25
35	Bruce Edwards	5.00	2.50	1.50
36	Carl Furillo	20.00	10.00	6.00

37	Joe Hatten	5.00	2.50	1.50
38	Gene Hermanski	5.00	2.50	1.50
39	Gil Hodges	25.00	12.50	7.50
40	Johnny Jorgensen	5.00	2.50	1.50
41	Lefty Martin	5.00	2.50	1.50
42	Mike McCormick	5.00	2.50	1.50
43	Eddie Miksis	5.00	2.50	1.50
44	Paul Minner	5.00	2.50	1.50
45	Sam Narron	10.00	5.00	3.00
46	Don Newcombe	20.00	10.00	6.00
47	Jake Pitler	5.00	2.50	1.50
48	Pee Wee Reese	35.00	17.50	10.50
49	Jackie Robinson	50.00	25.00	15.00
50	Duke Snider	40.00	20.00	12.00
51	Dick Whitman	5.00	2.50	1.50
52	Forrest Burgess	10.00	5.00	3.00
53	Phil Cavaretta	5.00	2.50	1.50
54	Bob Chipman	5.00	2.50	1.50
55	Walter Dubiel	5.00	2.50	1.50
56	Hank Edwards	5.00	2.50	1.50
57	Frankie Gustine	5.00	2.50	1.50
58	Hal Jeffcoat	5.00	2.50	1.50
59	Emil Kush	5.00	2.50	1.50
60	Doyle Lade	5.00	2.50	1.50
61	Dutch Leonard	5.00	2.50	1.50
62	Peanuts Lowrey	5.00	2.50	1.50
63	Gene Mauch	7.50	3.75	2.25
64	Cal McLish	5.00	2.50	1.50
65	Rube Novotney	5.00	2.50	1.50
66	Andy Pafko	5.00	2.50	1.50
67	Bob Ramozzotti	5.00	2.50	1.50
68	Herman Reich	5.00	2.50	1.50
69	Bob Rush	5.00	2.50	1.50
70	Johnny Schmitz	5.00	2.50	1.50
71	Bob Scheffing	5.00	2.50	1.50
72	Roy Smalley	5.00	2.50	1.50
73	Emil Verban	5.00	2.50	1.50
74	Al Walker	5.00	2.50	1.50
75	Harry Walker	5.00	2.50	1.50
76	Bucky Walters	5.00	2.50	1.50
77	Bob Adams	5.00	2.50	1.50
78	Ewell Blackwell	5.00	2.50	1.50
79	Jimmy Bloodworth	5.00	2.50	1.50
80	Walker Cooper	5.00	2.50	1.50
81	Tony Cuccinello	5.00	2.50	1.50
82	Jess Dobernic	5.00	2.50	1.50
83	Eddie Erautt	5.00	2.50	1.50
84	Frank Fanovich	5.00	2.50	1.50
85	Howie Fox	5.00	2.50	1.50
86	Grady Hatton	5.00	2.50	1.50
87	Homer Howell	5.00	2.50	1.50
88	Ted Kluszewski	20.00	10.00	6.00
89	Danny Litwhiler	5.00	2.50	1.50
90	Everett Lively	5.00	2.50	1.50
91	Lloyd Merriman	5.00	2.50	1.50
92	Phil Page	5.00	2.50	1.50
93	Kent Peterson	5.00	2.50	1.50
94	Ken Raffensberger	5.00	2.50	1.50
95	Luke Sewell	5.00	2.50	1.50
96	Virgil Stallcup	5.00	2.50	1.50
97	Johnny Vander Meer	10.00	5.00	3.00
98	Herman Wehmeier	5.00	2.50	1.50
99	Johnny Wyrostek	5.00	2.50	1.50
100	Benny Zientara	5.00	2.50	1.50
101	Leo Durocher	12.50	6.25	3.75
102	Hank Behrman	5.00	2.50	1.50
103	Augie Galan	5.00	2.50	1.50
104	Sid Gordon	5.00	2.50	1.50
105	Bert Haas	5.00	2.50	1.50
106	Andy Hansen	5.00	2.50	1.50
107	Clint Hartung	5.00	2.50	1.50
108	Kirby Higbe	5.00	2.50	1.50
109	George Hausman	5.00	2.50	1.50
110	Larry Jansen	5.00	2.50	1.50
111	Sheldon Jones	5.00	2.50	1.50
112	Monte Kennedy	5.00	2.50	1.50
113	Buddy Kerr	5.00	2.50	1.50
114	Dave Koslo	5.00	2.50	1.50
115	Joe Lafata	5.00	2.50	1.50
116	Whitey Lockman	5.00	2.50	1.50
117	Jack Lohrke	5.00	2.50	1.50
118	Willard Marshall	5.00	2.50	1.50
119	Bill Milne	5.00	2.50	1.50
120	Johnny Mize	15.00	7.50	4.50
121	Don Mueller	5.00	2.50	1.50
122	Ray Mueller	5.00	2.50	1.50
123	Bill Rigney	5.00	2.50	1.50
124	Bobby Thomson	7.50	3.75	2.25
125	Sam Webb	5.00	2.50	1.50
126	Wesley Westrum	5.00	2.50	1.50
127	Eddie Sawyer	5.00	2.50	1.50
128	Richie Ashburn	30.00	15.00	9.00
129	Benny Bengough	5.00	2.50	1.50
130	Charlie Bicknell	5.00	2.50	1.50
131	Buddy Blattner	5.00	2.50	1.50
132	Hank Borowy	5.00	2.50	1.50
133	Ralph Caballero	5.00	2.50	1.50
134	Blix Donnelly	5.00	2.50	1.50
135	Del Ennis	5.00	2.50	1.50
136	Granville Hamner	5.00	2.50	1.50
137	Ken Heintzelman	5.00	2.50	1.50
138	Stan Hollmig	5.00	2.50	1.50
139	Willie Jones	5.00	2.50	1.50
140	Jim Konstanty	5.00	2.50	1.50
141	Stan Lopata	5.00	2.50	1.50
142	Jackie Mayo	5.00	2.50	1.50
143	Bill Nicholson	5.00	2.50	1.50
144	Robin Roberts	60.00	30.00	18.00
145	Schoolboy Rowe	5.00	2.50	1.50
146	Andy Seminick	5.00	2.50	1.50
147	Ken Silvestri	5.00	2.50	1.50
148	Curt Simmons	5.00	2.50	1.50
149	Dick Sisler	5.00	2.50	1.50
150	Ken Trinkle	5.00	2.50	1.50
151	Eddie Waitkus	5.00	2.50	1.50
152	Bill Meyer	5.00	2.50	1.50
153	Monte Basgall	5.00	2.50	1.50
154	Eddie Bockman	5.00	2.50	1.50

155	Ernie Bonham	5.00	2.50	1.50
156	Hugh Casey	5.00	2.50	1.50
157	Pete Castiglione	5.00	2.50	1.50
158	Cliff Chambers	5.00	2.50	1.50
159	Murry Dickson	5.00	2.50	1.50
160	Ed Fitz Gerald	5.00	2.50	1.50
161	Les Fleming	5.00	2.50	1.50
162	Hal Gregg	5.00	2.50	1.50
163	Goldie Holt	5.00	2.50	1.50
164	Johnny Hopp	5.00	2.50	1.50
165	Ralph Kiner	20.00	10.00	6.00
166	Vic Lombardi	5.00	2.50	1.50
167	Clyde McCullough	5.00	2.50	1.50
168	Danny Murtaugh	5.00	2.50	1.50
169	Bill Posedel	5.00	2.50	1.50
170	Elmer Riddle	5.00	2.50	1.50
171	Stan Rojek	5.00	2.50	1.50
172	Rip Sewell	5.00	2.50	1.50
173	Eddie Stevens	5.00	2.50	1.50
174	Dixie Walker	5.00	2.50	1.50
175	Bill Werle	5.00	2.50	1.50
176	Wally Westlake	5.00	2.50	1.50
177	Eddie Dyer	5.00	2.50	1.50
178	Bill Baker	5.00	2.50	1.50
179	Al Brazle	5.00	2.50	1.50
180	Harry Brecheen	5.00	2.50	1.50
181	Chuck Diering	5.00	2.50	1.50
182	Joe Garagiola	13.50	6.75	4.00
183	Tom Galviano	5.00	2.50	1.50
184	Jim Hearn	5.00	2.50	1.50
185	Ken Johnson	5.00	2.50	1.50
186	Nippy Jones	5.00	2.50	1.50
187	Ed Kazak	5.00	2.50	1.50
188	Lou Klein	5.00	2.50	1.50
189	Marty Marion	5.00	2.50	1.50
190	George Munger	5.00	2.50	1.50
191	Stan Musial	45.00	22.00	13.50
192	Spike Nelson	5.00	2.50	1.50
193	Howie Pollet	5.00	2.50	1.50
194	Bill Reeder	5.00	2.50	1.50
195	Del Rice	5.00	2.50	1.50
196	Ed Sauer	5.00	2.50	1.50
197	Red Schoendienst	20.00	10.00	6.00
198	Enos Slaughter	20.00	10.00	6.00
199	Ted Wilks	5.00	2.50	1.50
200	Ray Yochim	5.00	2.50	1.50

1914 Evening Sun N.Y. Giants

The World's Champion 1913 N.Y. Giants are featured in this set of newspaper supplements titled, "Evening Sun's Gallery of Famous Baseball Players." It is believed the paper was published in Norwich, N.Y. Slightly larger than 9" x 12", the supplements feature black-and-white portraits by Lawrence Semon, who also produced a contemporary series of baseball postcards.

		NM	EX	VG
Complete Set (21):		7,000	3,500	2,100
Common Player:		200.00	100.00	60.00
(1)	George Burns	200.00	100.00	60.00
(2)	Doc Crandall	200.00	100.00	60.00
(3)	Al Demaree	200.00	100.00	60.00
(4)	Art Fletcher	200.00	100.00	60.00
(5)	Art Fromme	200.00	100.00	60.00
(6)	Grover Hartley	200.00	100.00	60.00
(7)	Buck Herzog	200.00	100.00	60.00
(8)	Rube Marquard	400.00	200.00	120.00
(9)	Christy Mathewson	1,200	600.00	360.00
(10)	Moose McCormick	200.00	100.00	60.00
(11)	John McGraw	400.00	200.00	120.00
(12)	Fred Merkle	200.00	100.00	60.00
(13)	Chief Meyers	200.00	100.00	60.00
(14)	Red Murray	200.00	100.00	60.00
(15)	Wilbert Robinson	400.00	200.00	120.00
(16)	Arthur Shafer	200.00	100.00	60.00
(17)	Fred Snodgrass	200.00	100.00	60.00
(18)	Jeff Tesreau	200.00	100.00	60.00
(19)	Jim Thorpe	1,750	875.00	525.00
(20)	Art Wilson	200.00	100.00	60.00
(21)	Hooks Wiltse	200.00	100.00	60.00

1916 Everybody's

Where "Everybody's" department store was located is unknown, but in 1916 they chose to use baseball cards to promote their boy's wear department. The approximately 1-5/8" x 3" black-and-white cards share the format and checklist with the much more common M101-4 blank-back version and several other regional advertisers. Everybody's is one of the scarcest advertising backs to be found in this issue and the cards command a premium from type-card and superstar collectors. There are four styles of typography on back.

DICK RUDOLPH
P.—Boston Braves
149

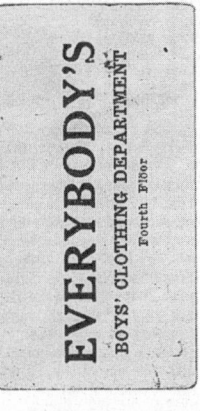

EVERYBODY'S
BOYS' CLOTHING DEPARTMENT
Fourth Floor

Premium: 15-25X
(See 1916 M101-4 Blank Backs for checklist and base card values.)

1921 Exhibits

Geo.H.Babe Ruth
OUTFIELDER, NEW YORK, A.M.L.

Ty.R.Cobb
OUTFIELDER, DETROIT, A.M.L.

The Exhibit Supply Company of Chicago issued the first in a long series of postcard-size (3-3/8" x 5-3/8") baseball cards in 1921. The Exhibit cards were commonly sold in "penny arcade" vending machines. The 1921 series consists of 64 cards and includes four players from each of the 16 major league teams. The cards feature black-and-white photos with the player's name printed in a fancy script. The player's position and team appear below the name in small, hand-lettered capital letters. American League is designated as "AM.L.," which can help differentiate the 1921 series from future years. Some of the cards contain white borders while others do not. All have blank backs. There are various spelling errors in the picture legends.

		NM	EX	VG
Complete Set (64):		15,000	7,500	4,500
Common Player:		75.00	35.00	20.00
(1)	Chas. B. Adams	75.00	35.00	20.00
(2)	Grover C. Alexander	275.00	135.00	80.00
(3)	David Bancroft	175.00	85.00	50.00
(4)	Geo. J. Burns	75.00	35.00	20.00
(5)	Owen Bush	75.00	35.00	20.00
(6)	Max J. Carey	175.00	85.00	50.00
(7)	Ty R. Cobb	1,600	800.00	480.00
(8)	Eddie T. Collins	175.00	85.00	50.00
(9)	John Collins	75.00	35.00	20.00
(10)	Stanley Coveleskie (Coveleski)	200.00	100.00	60.00
(11)	Walton E. Cruise	75.00	35.00	20.00
(12)	Jacob E. Daubert	75.00	35.00	20.00
(13)	George Dauss	75.00	35.00	20.00
(14)	Charles A. Deal	75.00	35.00	20.00
(15)	Joe A. Dugan	75.00	35.00	20.00
(16)	James Dykes	75.00	35.00	20.00
(17)	U.C. "Red" Faber	175.00	85.00	50.00
(18)	J.F. Fournier	75.00	35.00	20.00
(19)	Frank F. Frisch	175.00	85.00	50.00
(20)	W.L. Gardner	75.00	35.00	20.00
(21)	H.M. "Hank" Gowdy	75.00	35.00	20.00
(22)	Burleigh A. Grimes	200.00	100.00	60.00
(23)	Heinie Groh	75.00	35.00	20.00
(24)	Jesse Haines	200.00	100.00	60.00
(25)	Sam Harris (Stanley)	200.00	100.00	60.00
(26)	Walter L. Holke	75.00	35.00	20.00
(27)	Charles J. Hollicher (Hollocher)	75.00	35.00	20.00
(28)	Rogers Hornsby	325.00	160.00	95.00
(29)	James H. Johnson (Johnston)	75.00	35.00	20.00
(30)	Walter P. Johnson	750.00	375.00	225.00
(31)	Sam P. Jones	75.00	35.00	20.00
(32)	Geo. L. Kelly	200.00	100.00	60.00
(33)	Dick Kerr	75.00	35.00	20.00
(34)	William L. Killifer (Killefer)	75.00	35.00	20.00
(35)	Ed Konetchy	75.00	35.00	20.00
(36)	John "Doc" Lavan	75.00	35.00	20.00
(37)	Walter J. Maranville	500.00	250.00	150.00
(38)	Carl W. Mays	75.00	35.00	20.00
(39)	J. "Stuffy" McInnis	75.00	35.00	20.00
(40)	Rollie C. Naylor	75.00	35.00	20.00
(41)	A. Earl Neale (Earle)	125.00	60.00	35.00
(42)	Ivan M. Olsen	75.00	35.00	20.00
(43)	S.F. "Steve" O'Neil (O'Neill)	75.00	35.00	20.00
(44)	Robert (Roger) Peckinpaugh	300.00	150.00	90.00
(45)	Ralph "Cy" Perkins	75.00	35.00	20.00
(46)	Raymond R. Powell	75.00	35.00	20.00
(47)	Joe "Goldie" Rapp	75.00	35.00	20.00
(48)	Edgar S. Rice	450.00	220.00	135.00
(49)	Jimmy Ring	75.00	35.00	20.00
(50)	Geo. H. "Babe" Ruth	5,000	2,500	1,500
(51)	Ray W. Schalk	450.00	220.00	135.00
(52)	Wallie Schang	75.00	35.00	20.00
(53)	Everett Scott	75.00	35.00	20.00
(54)	H.S. Shanks (Photo actually Wally Schang.)	75.00	35.00	20.00
(55)	Urban Shocker	75.00	35.00	20.00
(56)	Geo. H. Sisler	175.00	85.00	50.00
(57)	Tris Speaker	900.00	450.00	270.00
(58)	John Tobin	75.00	35.00	20.00
(59)	Robt. Veach	75.00	35.00	20.00
(60)	Zack D. Wheat	175.00	85.00	50.00
(61)	Geo. B. Whitted	75.00	35.00	20.00
(62)	Cy Williams	75.00	35.00	20.00
(63)	Kenneth R. Williams	75.00	35.00	20.00
(64)	Ivy B. Wingo	75.00	35.00	20.00

1922 Exhibits

Moses Yellowhorse
PITTSBURGH, N.L.

The Exhibit Supply Co. continued the 3-3/8" x 5-3/8" format in 1922 but doubled the number of cards in the series to 128, including eight players from each team. All but nine of the players who appeared in the 1921 series are pictured in the 1922 set, along with 74 new players. The cards again display black-and-white photos with blank backs. Some photos have white borders. The player's name appears in script with the postition and team below in small block capital letters. American League is designated as "A.L." Again, there are several spelling errors and incorrect player identifications. Only the 74 new additions are included in this checklist.

		NM	EX	VG
Complete Set (74):		7,500	3,750	2,250
Common Player:		85.00	40.00	25.00
(1)	Jim Bagby	85.00	40.00	25.00
(2)	J. Frank Baker	150.00	75.00	45.00
(3)	Walter Barbare	85.00	40.00	25.00
(4)	Turner Barber	85.00	40.00	25.00
(5)	John Bassler	85.00	40.00	25.00
(6)	Carlson L. Bigbee (Carson)	85.00	40.00	25.00
(7)	Sam Bohne	125.00	62.50	37.50
(8)	Geo. Burns	85.00	40.00	25.00
(9)	George Burns	85.00	40.00	25.00
(10)	Jeo Bush (Joe)	85.00	40.00	25.00
(11)	Leon Cadore	85.00	40.00	25.00
(12)	Jim Caveney	85.00	40.00	25.00
(13)	Wilbur Cooper	85.00	40.00	25.00
(14)	George Cutshaw	85.00	40.00	25.00
(15)	Dave Danforth	85.00	40.00	25.00
(16)	Bill Doak	85.00	40.00	25.00
(17)	Joe Dugan	85.00	40.00	25.00
(18)	Pat Duncan	85.00	40.00	25.00
(19)	Howard Emke (Ehmke)	85.00	40.00	25.00
(20)	Wm. Evans/Umpire	375.00	185.00	110.00
(21)	Bib Falk (Bibb)	85.00	40.00	25.00
(22)	Dana Fillingin (Fillingim)	85.00	40.00	25.00
(23)	Ira Flagstead	85.00	40.00	25.00
(24)	(Art) Fletcher	85.00	40.00	25.00
(25)	(Wally) Gerber	85.00	40.00	25.00
(26)	Ray Grimes	85.00	40.00	25.00
(27)	Harry Heilman (Heilmann)	150.00	75.00	45.00
(28)	George Hildebrand/Umpire	200.00	100.00	60.00
(29)	Wibur Hubbell (Wilbert)	85.00	40.00	25.00
(30)	Bill Jacobson	85.00	40.00	25.00
(31)	E.R. Johnson	85.00	40.00	25.00
(32)	Joe Judge	85.00	40.00	25.00
(33)	Bill Klem/Umpire	375.00	185.00	110.00
(34)	Harry Liebold (Leibold)	85.00	40.00	25.00
(35)	Walter Mails	85.00	40.00	25.00
(36)	Geo. Maisel	85.00	40.00	25.00
(37)	Lee Meadows	85.00	40.00	25.00
(38)	Clyde Milam (Milan)	85.00	40.00	25.00
(39)	Ed (Bing) Miller	85.00	40.00	25.00
(40)	Hack Miller	85.00	40.00	25.00
(41)	George Moriarty/Umpire	500.00	250.00	150.00
(42)	Robert Muesel (Meusel)	85.00	40.00	25.00
(43)	Harry Myers	85.00	40.00	25.00
(44)	Arthur Nehf	85.00	40.00	25.00
(45)	Joe Oeschger	85.00	40.00	25.00
(46)	Geo. O'Neil	85.00	40.00	25.00
(47)	Roger Peckinpaugh	85.00	40.00	25.00
(48)	Val Picinich	85.00	40.00	25.00
(49)	Bill Piercy	85.00	40.00	25.00
(50)	Derrill Pratt	85.00	40.00	25.00
(51)	Jack Quinn	85.00	40.00	25.00
(52)	Walter Reuther (Ruether)	85.00	40.00	25.00
(53)	Charles Rigler/Umpire	200.00	100.00	60.00
(54)	Eppa Rixey	150.00	75.00	45.00
(55)	Chas. Robertson	85.00	40.00	25.00
(56)	Everett Scott	85.00	40.00	25.00
(57)	Earl Sheely	85.00	40.00	25.00
(58)	Earl Smith (portrait)	85.00	40.00	25.00
(59)	Earl Smith (Standing) (Photo actually Brad Kocher.)	85.00	40.00	25.00
(60)	Elmer Smith	85.00	40.00	25.00
(61)	Jack Smith (Photo actually Jimmy Smith.)	85.00	40.00	25.00
(62)	Sherrod Smith	85.00	40.00	25.00
(63)	Frank Snyder	85.00	40.00	25.00
(64)	Allan Sothoron (Allen)	85.00	40.00	25.00
(65)	Arnold Statz	85.00	40.00	25.00
(66)	Milton Stock	85.00	40.00	25.00
(67)	James Tierney	85.00	40.00	25.00
(68)	George Toporcer	85.00	40.00	25.00
(69)	Clarence (Tilly) Walker	85.00	40.00	25.00
(70)	Curtis Walker	85.00	40.00	25.00
(71)	Aaron Ward	85.00	40.00	25.00
(72)	Joe Wood	100.00	50.00	30.00
(73)	Moses Yellowhorse	400.00	300.00	200.00
(74)	Ross Young (Youngs)	150.00	75.00	45.00

1922 Eastern Exhibit Supply Co.

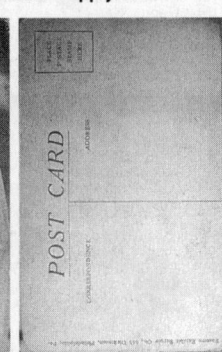

POST CARD

Postcard-style backs differentiate these cards from the more common Exhibit Supply Co., cards from Chicago. This 20-card series was produced by a Philadelphia company, although on some cards, the Eastern Exhibit copyright line on back has been blacked out and that of the Chicago company printed beneath it. The sepia tone, or more rarely black-and-white, cards measure 3-3/8" x 5-5/8".

		NM	EX	VG
Complete Set (20):		7,500	3,700	2,200
Common Player:		80.00	40.00	20.00
(1)	Grover Alexander	200.00	100.00	60.00
(2)	Dave Bancroft	125.00	65.00	35.00
(3)	Jesse Barnes	80.00	40.00	20.00
(4)	Joe Bush	80.00	40.00	20.00
(5)	Ty Cobb	750.00	375.00	225.00
(6)	Eddie Collins	125.00	65.00	35.00
(7)	Urban Faber	125.00	65.00	35.00
(8)	Clarence Galloway	80.00	40.00	20.00
(9)	Heinie Groh	80.00	40.00	20.00
(10)	Harry Heilmann	350.00	175.00	105.00
(11)	Charlie Hollocher	80.00	40.00	20.00
(12)	Rogers Hornsby	200.00	100.00	60.00
(13)	Walter Johnson	600.00	300.00	180.00
(14)	Eddie Rommel	80.00	40.00	20.00
(15)	Babe Ruth	2,500	1,250	750.00
(16)	Ray Schalk	125.00	65.00	35.00
(17)	Wallie Schang	80.00	40.00	20.00
(18)	Tris Speaker	200.00	100.00	60.00
(19)	Zach Wheat	125.00	65.00	35.00
(20)	Kenneth Williams	80.00	40.00	20.00

1923-24 Exhibits

Raymond R.Powell

John J. McGraw
MANAGER, NEW YORK, N.L.

The Exhibit cards for 1923 and 1924 are generally collected as a single 128-card series. The format remained basically the same as the previous year, 3-3/8" x 5-3/8", with black-and-white photos (some surrounded by a white border) and blank backs. The player's name is again shown in script with the position and team printed below in a small, square block-type style. Many of the same photos were used from previous years, although some are cropped differently, and some players have new team designations, background changes, team emblems removed, borders added or taken away, and other minor changes. Fifty-eight new cards are featured, including 38 players pictured for the first time in an Exhibit set. Only the 58 new cards are included in this checklist. The Babe Ruth card, which differs from the 1921 issue in the addition of a white border, is very rare with only a handful known."

		NM	EX	VG
Complete Set (59):		25,000	12,500	7,500
Common Player:		225.00	110.00	65.00
(1)	Clyde Barnhart	225.00	110.00	65.00
(2)	Ray Blades	225.00	110.00	65.00
(3)	James Bottomley	400.00	200.00	120.00
(4)	George Burns	225.00	110.00	65.00
(5)	Dan Clark	225.00	110.00	65.00
(6)	Bill Doak	225.00	110.00	65.00
(7)	Joe Dugan	225.00	110.00	65.00
(8)	Howard J. Ehmke	225.00	110.00	65.00
(9)	Ira Flagstead	225.00	110.00	65.00
(10)	J.F. Fournier	225.00	110.00	65.00
(11)	Howard Freigan (Freigau)	225.00	110.00	65.00
(12)	C.E. Galloway	225.00	110.00	65.00
(13)	Joe Genewich	225.00	110.00	65.00
(14)	Mike Gonzales (Gonzalez)	275.00	135.00	82.00
(15)	H.M. "Hank" Gowdy	225.00	110.00	65.00
(16)	Charles Grimm	225.00	110.00	65.00
(17)	Heinie Groh	225.00	110.00	65.00
(18)	Chas. L. Harnett (Hartnett)	400.00	200.00	120.00
(19)	George Harper	225.00	110.00	65.00
(20)	Slim Harris (Harriss)	225.00	110.00	65.00
(21)	Clifton Heathcote	225.00	110.00	65.00
(22)	Andy High	225.00	110.00	65.00
(23)	Walter L. Holke	225.00	110.00	65.00
(24)	Charles D. Jamieson	225.00	110.00	65.00
(25)	Willie Kamm	225.00	110.00	65.00
(26)	Tony Kaufmann	225.00	110.00	65.00
(27)	Dudley Lee	225.00	110.00	65.00
(28)	Harry Liebold (Leibold)	225.00	110.00	65.00
(29)	Aldofo Luque	225.00	110.00	65.00
(30)	W.C. (Wid) Matthews	225.00	110.00	65.00
(31)	John J. McGraw	400.00	200.00	120.00
(32)	J. "Stuffy" McInnis	225.00	110.00	65.00
(33)	Johnny Morrison	225.00	110.00	65.00
(34)	John A. Mostil	225.00	110.00	65.00
(35)	J.F. O'Neill (Should be S.F.)	225.00	110.00	65.00
(36)	Ernest Padgett	225.00	110.00	65.00
(37)	Val Picinich	225.00	110.00	65.00
(38)	Bill Piercy	225.00	110.00	65.00
(39)	Herman Pillette	225.00	110.00	65.00
(40)	Wallie Pipp	275.00	135.00	82.00
(41)	Raymond R. Powell (Black background.)	225.00	110.00	65.00
(43)	Del. Pratt	225.00	110.00	65.00
(44)	E.E. Rigney	225.00	110.00	65.00
(45)	Eddie Rommel	225.00	110.00	65.00
(46)	Geo. H. "Babe" Ruth	12,000	6,500	5,000
(47)	Muddy Ruel	225.00	110.00	65.00
(48)	J.H. Sand	225.00	110.00	65.00
(49)	Henry Severeid	225.00	110.00	65.00
(50)	Joseph Sewell	400.00	200.00	120.00
(51)	Al. Simmons	1,000	500.00	300.00
(52)	R.E. Smith	225.00	110.00	65.00
(53)	Sherrod Smith	225.00	110.00	65.00
(54)	Casey Stengel	500.00	400.00	300.00
(55)	J.R. Stevenson (Stephenson)	225.00	110.00	65.00
(56)	James Tierney	225.00	110.00	65.00
(57)	Robt. Veach	225.00	110.00	65.00
(58)	L. Woodall	225.00	110.00	65.00
(59)	Russell G. Wrighstone	225.00	110.00	65.00

1925 Exhibits

The 1925 series of Exhibits contains 128 unnumbered cards, each measuring 3-3/8" x 5-3/8". The player's name (in all capital letters), position and team (along with a line reading "Made in U.S.A.") are printed in a small white box in a lower corner of the card. Most of the photos are vertical, however a few are horizontal. There are several misspellings in the set. Lou Gehrig's first baseball card appears in this issue. The cards are listed here in alphabetical order.

		NM	EX	VG
Complete Set (128):		60,000	30,000	18,000
Common Player:		125.00	65.00	35.00
(1)	Sparky Adams	125.00	65.00	35.00
(2)	Grover C. Alexander	300.00	150.00	90.00
(3)	David Bancroft	200.00	100.00	60.00
(4)	Jesse Barnes	125.00	65.00	35.00
(5)	John Bassler	125.00	65.00	35.00
(6)	Lester Bell	125.00	65.00	35.00
(7)	Lawrence Benton	125.00	65.00	35.00
(8)	Carson Bigbee	125.00	65.00	35.00
(9)	Max Bishop	125.00	65.00	35.00

		NM	EX	VG
(10)	Raymond Blates (Blades)	125.00	65.00	35.00
(11)	Oswald Bluege	125.00	65.00	35.00
(12)	James Bottomly (Bottomley)	200.00	100.00	60.00
(13)	Raymond Bressler	125.00	65.00	35.00
(14)	John Brooks	125.00	65.00	35.00
(15)	Maurice Burrus	125.00	65.00	35.00
(16)	Max Carey	200.00	100.00	60.00
(17)	Tyrus Cobb	4,000	2,000	1,200
(18)	Eddie Collins	200.00	100.00	60.00
(19)	Stanley Coveleski	200.00	100.00	60.00
(20)	Hugh M. Critz	125.00	65.00	35.00
(21)	Hazen Cuyler	225.00	110.00	65.00
(22)	George Dauss	125.00	65.00	35.00
(23)	I.M. Davis	125.00	65.00	35.00
(24)	John H. DeBerry	125.00	65.00	35.00
(25)	Art Decatur	125.00	65.00	35.00
(26)	Peter Donohue	125.00	65.00	35.00
(27)	Charles Dressen	125.00	65.00	35.00
(28)	James J. Dykes	125.00	65.00	35.00
(29)	Howard Ehmke	125.00	65.00	35.00
(30)	Bib Falk (Bibb)	125.00	65.00	35.00
(31)	Wilson Fewster	125.00	65.00	35.00
(32)	Max Flack	125.00	65.00	35.00
(33)	Ira Flagstead	125.00	65.00	35.00
(34)	Jacques F. Fournier	125.00	65.00	35.00
(35)	Howard Freigan	125.00	65.00	35.00
(36)	Frank Frisch	200.00	100.00	60.00
(37)	Henry L. Gehrig	17,500	8,750	5,250
(38)	Joseph Genewich	125.00	65.00	35.00
(39)	Walter Gerber	125.00	65.00	35.00
(40)	Frank Gibson	125.00	65.00	35.00
(41)	Leon Goslin	200.00	100.00	60.00
(42)	George Grantham	125.00	65.00	35.00
(43)	Samuel Gray	125.00	65.00	35.00
(44)	Burleigh A. Grimes	200.00	100.00	60.00
(45)	Charles Grimm	125.00	65.00	35.00
(46)	Heine Groh (Heinie)	125.00	65.00	35.00
(47)	Samuel Hale	125.00	65.00	35.00
(48)	George Harper	125.00	65.00	35.00
(49)	David Harris	125.00	65.00	35.00
(50)	Stanley Harris	200.00	100.00	60.00
(51)	Leo Hartnett	200.00	100.00	60.00
(52)	Nelson Hawks	125.00	65.00	35.00
(53)	Harry Heilmann	200.00	100.00	60.00
(54)	Walter Henline	125.00	65.00	35.00
(55)	Walter Holke	125.00	65.00	35.00
(56)	Harry Hooper	200.00	100.00	60.00
(57)	Rogers Hornsby	1,500	750.00	450.00
(58)	Wilbur Hubbell	125.00	65.00	35.00
(59)	Travis C. Jackson	200.00	100.00	60.00
(60)	William Jacobson	125.00	65.00	35.00
(61)	Charles Jamieson	125.00	65.00	35.00
(62)	James H. Johnson (Johnston)	125.00	65.00	35.00
(63)	Walter Johnson	2,500	1,250	750.00
(64)	Joseph Judge	125.00	65.00	35.00
(65)	Willie Kamm	125.00	65.00	35.00
(66)	Ray Kremer	125.00	65.00	35.00
(67)	Walter Lutzke	125.00	65.00	35.00
(68)	Walter Maranville	200.00	100.00	60.00
(69)	John ("Stuffy") McInnes (McInnis)	125.00	65.00	35.00
(70)	Martin McManus	125.00	65.00	35.00
(71)	Earl McNeely	125.00	65.00	35.00
(72)	Emil Meusel	125.00	65.00	35.00
(73)	Edmund (Bing) Miller	125.00	65.00	35.00
(74)	John Mokan	125.00	65.00	35.00
(75)	Clarence Mueller	125.00	65.00	35.00
(76)	Robert W. Muesel (Meusel)	125.00	65.00	35.00
(77)	Glenn Myatt	125.00	65.00	35.00
(78)	Arthur Nehf	125.00	65.00	35.00
(79)	George O'Neil	125.00	65.00	35.00
(80)	Frank O'Rourke	125.00	65.00	35.00
(81)	Ralph Perkins	125.00	65.00	35.00
(82)	Valentine Picinich	125.00	65.00	35.00
(83)	Walter C. Pipp	125.00	65.00	35.00
(84)	John Quinn	125.00	65.00	35.00
(85)	Emory Rigney	125.00	65.00	35.00
(86)	Eppa Rixey	200.00	100.00	60.00
(87)	Edwin Rommel	125.00	65.00	35.00
(88)	Ed (Edd) Roush	200.00	100.00	60.00
(89)	Harold Ruel (Herold)	125.00	65.00	35.00
(90)	Charles Ruffing	200.00	100.00	60.00
(91)	George H. "Babe" Ruth	7,500	3,700	2,200
(92)	John Sand	125.00	65.00	35.00
(93)	Henry Severid (Severeid)	125.00	65.00	35.00
(94)	Joseph Sewell	200.00	100.00	60.00
(95)	Ray Shalk (Schalk)	200.00	100.00	60.00
(96)	Walter H. Shang (Schang)	125.00	65.00	35.00
(97)	J.R. Shawkey	125.00	65.00	35.00
(98)	Earl Sheely	125.00	65.00	35.00
(99)	William Sherdell (Sherdel)	125.00	65.00	35.00
(100)	Urban J. Shocker	125.00	65.00	35.00
(101)	George Sissler (Sisler)	1,350	675.00	405.00
(102)	Earl Smith	125.00	65.00	35.00
(103)	Sherrod Smith	125.00	65.00	35.00
(104)	Frank Snyder	125.00	65.00	35.00
(105)	Wm. H. Southworth	125.00	65.00	35.00
(106)	Tristram Speaker	3,500	1,750	1,050
(107)	Milton J. Stock	125.00	65.00	35.00
(108)	Homer Summa	125.00	65.00	35.00
(109)	William Terry	225.00	110.00	65.00
(110)	Hollis Thurston	125.00	65.00	35.00
(111)	John Tobin	125.00	65.00	35.00
(112)	Philip Todt	125.00	65.00	35.00
(113)	George Torporcer (Toporcer)	125.00	65.00	35.00
(114)	Harold Traynor	200.00	100.00	60.00
(115)	A.C. "Dazzy" Vance	200.00	100.00	60.00
(116)	Robert Veach (Photo actually Ernest Vache.)	125.00	65.00	35.00
(117)	William Wambsganss	125.00	65.00	35.00
(118)	Aaron Ward	125.00	65.00	35.00
(119)	A.J. Weis	125.00	65.00	35.00
(120)	Frank Welch	125.00	65.00	35.00
(121)	Zack Wheat	200.00	100.00	60.00
(122)	Fred Williams	125.00	65.00	35.00
(123)	Kenneth Williams	125.00	65.00	35.00
(124)	Ernest Wingard	125.00	65.00	35.00
(125)	Ivy Wingo	125.00	65.00	35.00
(126)	Al Wings (Wingo)	125.00	65.00	35.00
(127)	Larry Woodall	125.00	65.00	35.00
(128)	Glen Wright (Glenn)	125.00	65.00	35.00

1925-31 Postcard-Back Four-on-One Exhibits

The Exhibit Supply Company experimented with a four-on-one format in the late 1920s, ultimately adopting the format for several years from 1929-1938 for its main issues. This group of cards contains seven known cards in two distinct formats; a mixed subjects group containing two baseball players and two boxers or two entertainers; and a group containing four baseball players. The mixed subjects group was issued first, very likely circa 1926-1928 and is the rarer of the two. The all-baseball group certainly was issued as late as 1931 based on the team designations of certain players. Examples have been found with blank backs, postcard backs, and a postcard back with coupon (1 known), and in a variety of colors. Some cards have been found with two contrasting colors used, primarily blue and orange.

		NM	EX	VG
(1)	Lou Gehrig, Lefty Grove, Pete Donahue, Gordon Cochrane	2,200	1,100	650.00
(2)	Lefty O'Doul, Dazzy Vance, Hughey Critz, Art Shires	650.00	325.00	195.00
(3)	Eugene Criqui/Boxer, Dave Shade/Boxer, Joe Judge, Ty Cobb	3,000	1,500	900.00
(4)	Joe Judge, Ty Cobb, Charlie Chaplin/Actor, Marie Prevost/Actress)	2,500	1,250	750.00
(5)	Joe Judge, Paul Waner, Willie Kamm, Travis Jackson	750.00	375.00	225.00
(6)	Bucky Harris, Heinie Groh, Jack Dempsey/Boxer, Rocky Kansas/Boxer	750.00	375.00	225.00
(7)	Walter Johnson, Al Simmons, Gene Tunney/Boxer, Benny Leonard/Boxer	1,250	750.00	225.00
(8)	Babe Ruth, Rogers Hornsby, Mickey Walker/Boxer, Georges Carpentier/Boxer	3,500	1,750	1,000

1925-31 Postcard-Back Exhibits

These cards can be found with plain backs; postcard backs including the legend: "This Side for Correspondence"; and postcard backs including the legend "Not to be used in Exhibit machines." Some printings also have the legend "Made in U.S.A." added to the backs. Cards will rarely be found with a coupon on the back corner. The fronts are borderless photos that generally have the player's name, team, and league designation handwritten across the fronts. Over the years of issue, players were added to and removed from the set and corrections were made to account for team changes, resulting in significant short-prints and variations. Cards can be found in a variety of colors. The "plain background" cards designated below are "cut-outs" of previous images reused against plain backgrounds.

		NM	EX	VG
Common Player:		90.00	45.00	25.00
(1)	Virgie Barnes	90.00	45.00	25.00
(2)	Johnny Bassler	90.00	45.00	25.00
(3)	Sammy Bohne	200.00	100.00	60.00
(4)	Jim Bottomley	250.00	125.00	75.00
(5)	Ty Cobb (Detroit)	900.00	450.00	270.00
(6)	Ty Cobb (Athletics)	900.00	450.00	270.00
(7)	Mickey Cochrane	250.00	125.00	75.00
(8)	Urban Faber (Photo background.)	250.00	125.00	75.00
(9)	Urban Faber (Plain background.)	500.00	250.00	150.00
(10)	Jack Fournier	90.00	45.00	25.00
(11)	Jimmy Foxx	600.00	300.00	180.00
(12)	Frank Frisch (New York)	250.00	125.00	75.00
(13)	Frank Frisch (St. Louis)	450.00	225.00	135.00
(14)	Lou Gehrig/Btg (Photo background.)	2,000	1,000	600.00
(15)	Lou Gehrig/Btg (Plain background.)	4,000	2,000	1,200
(16)	Lou Gehrig/Portrait	2,000	1,000	600.00
(17)	Tom Griffith	90.00	45.00	25.00
(18)	Heinie Groh	90.00	45.00	25.00
(19)	Lefty Grove	500.00	250.00	150.00
(20)	George Haas	90.00	45.00	25.00
(21)	Stanley Harris	250.00	125.00	75.00
(22)	Charlie Hartnett (Photo background.)	250.00	125.00	75.00
(23)	Charlie Hartnett (Plain background.)	500.00	250.00	150.00
(24)	Harry Heilmann	250.00	125.00	75.00
(25)	Rogers Hornsby (St. Louis)	600.00	300.00	180.00
(26)	Rogers Hornsby (Boston)	600.00	300.00	180.00
(27)	Rogers Hornsby (Chicago)	600.00	300.00	180.00
(28)	Walter Johnson	600.00	300.00	180.00
(29)	Jimmy Johnston	90.00	45.00	25.00
(30)	Joe Judge	90.00	45.00	25.00
(31)	George Kelly	250.00	125.00	75.00
(32)	Chuck Klein	250.00	125.00	75.00
(33)	Hugh McQuillan	180.00	90.00	54.00
(34)	"Bob" Meusel	90.00	45.00	25.00
(35)	Bing Miller	90.00	45.00	25.00
(36)	Lefty O'Doul	150.00	75.00	45.00
(37)	Roger Peckinpaugh (Washington)	200.00	100.00	60.00
(38)	Roger Peckinpaugh (Cleveland)	500.00	300.00	200.00
(39)	Ralph Pinelli	90.00	45.00	25.00
(40)	Walter Pipp	125.00	60.00	35.00
(41)	Jimmy Ring	90.00	45.00	25.00
(42)	Eppa Rixey	250.00	125.00	75.00

		NM	EX	VG
(43)	Ed Rouch (Edd Roush) (Cincinnati)	250.00	125.00	75.00
(44)	Ed Rouch (Edd Roush) (New York)	375.00	185.00	110.00
(45)	Babe Ruth (Pose)	2,200	1,100	660.00
(46)	Babe Ruth (Batting follow-through.)	2,200	1,100	660.00
(47)	John Sand	90.00	45.00	25.00
(48)	Everett Scott	180.00	90.00	54.00
(49)	Al Simmons (View from side, "AM.L.")	500.00	250.00	150.00
(50)	Al Simmons (View from front, "A.L.")	250.00	125.00	75.00
(51)	George Sisler (Photo background.)	250.00	125.00	75.00
(52)	George Sisler (Plain background.)	500.00	250.00	150.00
(53)	Jack Smith	90.00	45.00	25.00
(54)	Tris Speaker (Photo background.)	350.00	175.00	100.00
(55)	Tris Speaker (Plain background.)	700.00	350.00	210.00
(56)	Phil Todt (Photo background.)	90.00	45.00	25.00
(57)	Phil Todt (Plain background.)	180.00	90.00	54.00
(58)	Specs Toporcer	180.00	90.00	54.00
(59)	Pie Traynor	250.00	125.00	75.00
(60)	Dazzy Vance	250.00	125.00	75.00
(61)	Rube Walberg	90.00	45.00	25.00
(62)	Paul Waner/Btg (Photo background.)	250.00	125.00	75.00
(63)	Paul Waner/Btg (Plain background.)	500.00	250.00	150.00
(64)	Paul Waner /Portrait	250.00	125.00	75.00
(65)	Zack Wheat	250.00	125.00	75.00
(66)	Cy Williams	90.00	45.00	25.00
(67)	Hack Wilson	250.00	125.00	75.00
(68)	Jimmy Wilson (Photo background.)	90.00	45.00	25.00
(69)	Jimmy Wilson (Plain background.)	180.00	90.00	54.00

1925 Champions Babe Ruth Exhibit

This is part of a (presumably) 32-card multi-sport "World's Champions" issue and the only baseball player in the set. The 3-3/8" x 5-3/8" card is printed in black-and-white and has a blank back.

	NM	EX	VG
Babe Ruth	3,500	2,500	1,000

1926 Exhibits

The 1926 Exhibit cards are the same size (3-3/8" x 5-3/8") as previous Exhibit issues but are easily distinguished because of their blue-gray color. The set consists of 128 cards, 91 of which are identical to the photos in the 1925 series. The 37 new photos do not include the boxed caption used in 1925. The cards are unnumbered and are listed here alphabetically.

		NM	EX	VG
Complete Set (128):		30,000	15,000	9,000
Common Player:		160.00	80.00	50.00
(1)	Sparky Adams	160.00	80.00	50.00
(2)	David Bancroft	500.00	250.00	150.00
(3)	John Bassler	160.00	80.00	50.00
(4)	Lester Bell	160.00	80.00	50.00
(5)	John M. Bentley	160.00	80.00	50.00

		NM	EX	VG
(6)	Lawrence Benton	160.00	80.00	50.00
(7)	Carson Bigbee	160.00	80.00	50.00
(8)	George Bischoff (Team actually Boston A.L.)	160.00	80.00	50.00
(9)	Max Bishop	160.00	80.00	50.00
(10)	J. Fred Blake	160.00	80.00	50.00
(11)	Ted Blankenship	160.00	80.00	50.00
(12)	Raymond Blates (Blades)	160.00	80.00	50.00
(13)	Lucerne A. Blue (Luzerne)	160.00	80.00	50.00
(14)	Oswald Bluege	160.00	80.00	50.00
(15)	James Bottomly (Bottomley)	500.00	250.00	150.00
(16)	Raymond Bressler	160.00	80.00	50.00
(17)	Geo. H. Burns	160.00	80.00	50.00
(18)	Maurice Burrus	160.00	80.00	50.00
(19)	John Butler	160.00	80.00	50.00
(20)	Max Carey	500.00	250.00	150.00
(21)	Tyrus Cobb	1,750	875.00	525.00
(22)	Eddie Collins	500.00	250.00	150.00
(23)	Patrick T. Collins	160.00	80.00	50.00
(24)	Earl B. Combs (Earle)	280.00	140.00	85.00
(25)	James E. Cooney	160.00	80.00	50.00
(26)	Stanley Coveleski	500.00	250.00	150.00
(27)	Hugh M. Critz	160.00	80.00	50.00
(28)	Hazen Cuyler	500.00	250.00	150.00
(29)	George Dauss	160.00	80.00	50.00
(30)	Peter Donohue	160.00	80.00	50.00
(31)	Charles Dressen	160.00	80.00	50.00
(32)	James J. Dykes	160.00	80.00	50.00
(33)	Bib Falk (Bibb)	160.00	80.00	50.00
(34)	Edward S. Farrell	160.00	80.00	50.00
(35)	Wilson Fewster	160.00	80.00	50.00
(36)	Ira Flagstead	160.00	80.00	50.00
(37)	Howard Freigau	160.00	80.00	50.00
(38)	Bernard Friberg	160.00	80.00	50.00
(39)	Frank Frisch	500.00	250.00	150.00
(40)	Jacques F. Furnier (Fournier)	160.00	80.00	50.00
(41)	Joseph Galloway (Clarence)(Photo reversed.)	160.00	80.00	50.00
(42)	Henry L. Gehrig	3,000	1,500	900.00
(43)	Charles Gehringer	625.00	320.00	190.00
(44)	Joseph Genewich	160.00	80.00	50.00
(45)	Walter Gerber	160.00	80.00	50.00
(46)	Leon Goslin	500.00	250.00	150.00
(47)	George Grantham	160.00	80.00	50.00
(48)	Burleigh A. Grimes	250.00	125.00	75.00
(49)	Charles Grimm	160.00	80.00	50.00
(50)	Fred Haney	160.00	80.00	50.00
(51)	Wm. Hargrave	160.00	80.00	50.00
(52)	George Harper	160.00	80.00	50.00
(53)	Stanley Harris	250.00	125.00	75.00
(54)	Leo Hartnett	250.00	125.00	75.00
(55)	Joseph Hauser	160.00	80.00	50.00
(56)	C.E. Heathcote	160.00	80.00	50.00
(57)	Harry Heilmann	500.00	250.00	150.00
(58)	Walter Henline	160.00	80.00	50.00
(59)	Ramon Herrera	160.00	80.00	50.00
(60)	Andrew A. High	160.00	80.00	50.00
(61)	Rogers Hornsby	575.00	300.00	175.00
(62)	Clarence Huber	160.00	80.00	50.00
(63)	Wm. Hunnefield (Photo actually Tommy Thomas.)	160.00	80.00	50.00
(64)	William Jacobson	160.00	80.00	50.00
(65)	Walter Johnson	750.00	375.00	225.00
(66)	Joseph Judge	160.00	80.00	50.00
(67)	Willie Kamm	160.00	80.00	50.00
(68)	Ray Kremer	160.00	80.00	50.00
(69)	Anthony Lazzeri	625.00	320.00	190.00
(70)	Frederick Lindstrom	575.00	300.00	175.00
(71)	Walter Lutzke	160.00	80.00	50.00
(72)	John Makan (Mokan)	160.00	80.00	50.00
(73)	Walter Maranville	500.00	250.00	150.00
(74)	Martin McManus	160.00	80.00	50.00
(75)	Earl McNeely	160.00	80.00	50.00
(76)	Hugh A. McQuillan	160.00	80.00	50.00
(77)	Douglas McWeeny	160.00	80.00	50.00
(78)	Oscar Melillo	160.00	80.00	50.00
(79)	Edmund (Bind)(Bing) Miller	160.00	80.00	50.00
(80)	Clarence Mueller	160.00	80.00	50.00
(81)	Robert W. Muesel (Meusel)	160.00	80.00	50.00
(82)	Joseph W. Munson	160.00	80.00	50.00
(83)	Emil Musel (Meusel)	160.00	80.00	50.00
(84)	Glenn Myatt	160.00	80.00	50.00
(85)	Bernie F. Neis	160.00	80.00	50.00
(86)	Robert O'Farrell	160.00	80.00	50.00
(87)	George O'Neil	160.00	80.00	50.00
(88)	Frank O'Rourke	160.00	80.00	50.00
(89)	Ralph Perkins	160.00	80.00	50.00
(90)	Walter C. Pipp	160.00	80.00	50.00
(91)	Emory Rigney	160.00	80.00	50.00
(92)	James J. Ring	160.00	80.00	50.00
(93)	Eppa Rixey	250.00	125.00	75.00
(94)	Edwin Rommel	160.00	80.00	50.00
(95)	Ed. Roush	250.00	125.00	75.00
(96)	Harold Ruel (Herold)	160.00	80.00	50.00
(97)	Charles Ruffing	500.00	250.00	150.00
(98)	Geo. H. "Babe" Ruth	2,400	1,200	720.00
(99)	John Sand	160.00	80.00	50.00
(100)	Joseph Sewell	250.00	125.00	75.00
(101)	Ray Shalk (Schalk)	500.00	250.00	150.00
(102)	J.R. Shawkey	160.00	80.00	50.00
(103)	Earl Sheely	160.00	80.00	50.00
(104)	William Sherdell (Sherdel)	160.00	80.00	50.00
(105)	Urban J. Shocker	160.00	80.00	50.00
(106)	George Sissler (Sisler)	500.00	250.00	150.00
(107)	Earl Smith	160.00	80.00	50.00
(108)	Sherrod Smith	160.00	80.00	50.00
(109)	Frank Snyder	160.00	80.00	50.00
(110)	Tristram Speaker	540.00	270.00	165.00
(111)	Fred Spurgeon	160.00	80.00	50.00
(112)	Homer Summa	160.00	80.00	50.00
(113)	Edward Taylor	160.00	80.00	50.00
(114)	J. Taylor	160.00	80.00	50.00
(115)	William Terry	500.00	250.00	150.00
(116)	Hollis Thurston	160.00	80.00	50.00
(117)	Philip Todt	160.00	80.00	50.00
(118)	George Torporcer (Toporcer)	160.00	80.00	50.00
(119)	Harold Traynor	500.00	250.00	150.00

		NM	EX	VG
(120)	Wm. Wambsganss	160.00	80.00	50.00
(121)	John Warner	160.00	80.00	50.00
(122)	Zach Wheat	500.00	250.00	150.00
(123)	Kenneth Williams	160.00	80.00	50.00
(124)	Ernest Wingard	160.00	80.00	50.00
(125)	Fred Wingfield	160.00	80.00	50.00
(126)	Ivy Wingo	160.00	80.00	50.00
(127)	Glen Wright (Glenn)	160.00	80.00	50.00
(128)	Russell Wrightstone	160.00	80.00	50.00

1927 Exhibits

The Exhibit Supply Co. issued a set of 64 cards in 1927, each measuring 3-3/8" x 5-3/8". The set can be identified from earlier issues by its light green tint. The player's name and team appear in capital letters in one lower corner, while "Ex. Sup. Co., Chgo." and "Made in U.S.A." appear in the other. All 64 photos used in the 1927 set were borrowed from previous issues, but 13 players are listed with new teams. There are several misspellings and other labeling errors in the set. The unnumbered cards are listed here in alphabetical order. Cards will rarely be found with a corner coupon in purple printed or stamped on the back of the card.

		NM	EX	VG
Complete Set (64):		25,000	12,500	7,500
Common Player:		100.00	50.00	30.00
(1)	Sparky Adams	100.00	50.00	30.00
(2)	Grover C. Alexander	320.00	160.00	100.00
(3)	David Bancroft	200.00	100.00	60.00
(4)	John Bassler	100.00	50.00	30.00
(5)	John M. Bentley (Middle initial actually N.)	100.00	50.00	30.00
(6)	Fred Blankenship (Ted)	100.00	50.00	30.00
(7)	James Bottomly (Bottomley)	200.00	100.00	60.00
(8)	Raymond Bressler	100.00	50.00	30.00
(9)	Geo. H. Burns	100.00	50.00	30.00
(10)	John Buttler (Butler)	100.00	50.00	30.00
(11)	Tyrus Cobb	4,000	2,000	1,200
(12)	Eddie Collins	200.00	100.00	60.00
(13)	Hazen Cuyler	200.00	100.00	60.00
(14)	George Daus (Dauss)	100.00	50.00	30.00
(15)	A.R. Decatur	100.00	50.00	30.00
(16)	Wilson Fewster	100.00	50.00	30.00
(17)	Ira Flagstead	100.00	50.00	30.00
(18)	Henry L. Gehrig	6,500	3,200	1,950
(19)	Charles Gehringer	200.00	100.00	60.00
(20)	Joseph Genewich	100.00	50.00	30.00
(21)	Leon Goslin	200.00	100.00	60.00
(22)	Burleigh A. Grimes	200.00	100.00	60.00
(23)	Charles Grimm	100.00	50.00	30.00
(24)	Fred Haney	100.00	50.00	30.00
(25)	Wm. Hargrave	100.00	50.00	30.00
(26)	George Harper	100.00	50.00	30.00
(27)	Leo Hartnett	200.00	100.00	60.00
(28)	Clifton Heathcote	100.00	50.00	30.00
(29)	Harry Heilman (Heillmann)	200.00	100.00	60.00
(30)	Walter Henline	100.00	50.00	30.00
(31)	Andrew High	100.00	50.00	30.00
(32)	Rogers Hornsby	320.00	160.00	100.00
(33)	Wm. Hunnefield (Photo actually Tommy Thomas.)	100.00	50.00	30.00
(34)	Walter Johnson	820.00	410.00	250.00
(35)	Willie Kamm	100.00	50.00	30.00
(36)	Ray Kremer	100.00	50.00	30.00
(37)	Anthony Lazzeri	200.00	100.00	60.00
(38)	Fredrick Lindstrom (Frederick)	200.00	100.00	60.00
(39)	Walter Lutzke	100.00	50.00	30.00
(40)	John "Stuffy" McInnes (McInnis)	100.00	50.00	30.00
(41)	John Mokan	100.00	50.00	30.00
(42)	Robert W. Muesel (Meusel)	100.00	50.00	30.00
(43)	Glenn Myatt	100.00	50.00	30.00
(44)	Bernie Neis	100.00	50.00	30.00
(45)	Robert O'Farrell	100.00	50.00	30.00
(46)	Walter C. Pipp	125.00	65.00	40.00
(47)	Eppa Rixey	200.00	100.00	60.00
(48)	Harold Ruel (Herold)	100.00	50.00	30.00
(49)	Geo. H. "Babe" Ruth	8,000	4,000	2,400
(50)	Ray Schalk	200.00	100.00	60.00
(51)	George Sissler (Sisler)	200.00	100.00	60.00
(52)	Earl Smith	100.00	50.00	30.00
(53)	Wm. H. Southworth	100.00	50.00	30.00
(54)	Tristam Speaker (Tristram)	320.00	160.00	100.00
(55)	J. Taylor	100.00	50.00	30.00
(56)	Philip Todt	100.00	50.00	30.00
(57)	Harold Traynor	200.00	100.00	60.00
(58)	William Wambsganns (Wambsganss)	100.00	50.00	30.00
(59)	Zach Wheat	200.00	100.00	60.00

(60)	Kenneth Williams	100.00	50.00	30.00
(61)	Ernest Wingard	100.00	50.00	30.00
(62)	Fred Wingfield	100.00	50.00	30.00
(63)	Ivy Wingo	100.00	50.00	30.00
(64)	Russell Wrightstone	100.00	50.00	30.00

1928 Exhibits

FREDERICK LINDSTROM

The Exhibit Supply Co. switched to a blue tint for the photos in its 64-card set in 1928. There are 36 new photos in the set, including 24 new players. Four players from the previous year are shown with new teams and 24 of the cards are identical to the 1927 series, except for the color of the card. They are blank backed, or found with a purple printed or stamped corner coupon on the back. The photos are captioned in the same style as the 1927 set. The set again includes some misspelling and incorrect labels. The cards are unnumbered and are listed here in alphabetical order.

		NM	EX	VG
	Complete Set (64):	12,000	6,000	3,600
	Common Player:	100.00	50.00	30.00
(1)	Grover C. Alexander	500.00	250.00	150.00
(2)	David Bancroft	250.00	125.00	75.00
(3)	Virgil Barnes	100.00	50.00	30.00
(4)	Francis R. Blades	100.00	50.00	30.00
(5)	L.A. Blue	100.00	50.00	30.00
(6)	Edward W. Brown	100.00	50.00	30.00
(7)	Max G. Carey	250.00	125.00	75.00
(8)	Chalmer W. Cissell	100.00	50.00	30.00
(9)	Gordon S. Cochrane	250.00	125.00	75.00
(10)	Pat Collins	100.00	50.00	30.00
(11)	Hugh M. Critz	100.00	50.00	30.00
(12)	Howard Ehmke	100.00	50.00	30.00
(13)	E. English	100.00	50.00	30.00
(14)	Bib Falk (Bibb)	100.00	50.00	30.00
(15)	Ira Flagstead	100.00	50.00	30.00
(16)	Robert Fothergill	100.00	50.00	30.00
(17)	Frank Frisch	250.00	125.00	75.00
(18)	Lou Gehrig	1,500	750.00	450.00
(19)	Leon Goslin	250.00	125.00	75.00
(20)	Eugene Hargrave	100.00	50.00	30.00
(21)	Charles R. Hargraves (Hargreaves)	100.00	50.00	30.00
(22)	Stanley Harris	250.00	125.00	75.00
(23)	Bryan "Slim" Harriss	100.00	50.00	30.00
(24)	Leo Hartnett	250.00	125.00	75.00
(25)	Joseph Hauser	100.00	50.00	30.00
(26)	Fred Hoffman (Hofmann)	100.00	50.00	30.00
(27)	J. Francis Hogan	100.00	50.00	30.00
(28)	Rogers Hornsby	360.00	180.00	120.00
(29)	Chas. Jamieson	100.00	50.00	30.00
(30)	Sam Jones	100.00	50.00	30.00
(31)	Ray Kremer	100.00	50.00	30.00
(32)	Fred Leach	100.00	50.00	30.00
(33)	Fredrick Lindstrom (Frederick)	250.00	125.00	75.00
(34)	Adolph Luque (Adolfo)	120.00	60.00	40.00
(35)	Theodore Lyons	250.00	125.00	75.00
(36)	Harry McCurdy	100.00	50.00	30.00
(37)	Glenn Myatt	100.00	50.00	30.00
(38)	John Ogden (Photo actually Warren Ogden.)	100.00	50.00	30.00
(39)	James Ring	100.00	50.00	30.00
(40)	A.C. Root (Should be C.H.)	100.00	50.00	30.00
(41)	Edd. Roush	250.00	125.00	75.00
(42)	Harold Ruel (Herold)	100.00	50.00	30.00
(43)	Geo. H. "Babe" Ruth	1,700	850.00	500.00
(44)	Henry Sand	100.00	50.00	30.00
(45)	Fred Schulte	100.00	50.00	30.00
(46)	Joseph Sewell	250.00	125.00	75.00
(47)	Walter Shang (Schang)	100.00	50.00	30.00
(48)	Urban J. Shocker	100.00	50.00	30.00
(49)	Al. Simmons	250.00	125.00	75.00
(50)	Earl Smith	100.00	50.00	30.00
(51)	Robert Smith	100.00	50.00	30.00
(52)	Jack Tavener	100.00	50.00	30.00
(53)	J. Taylor	100.00	50.00	30.00
(54)	Philip Todt	100.00	50.00	30.00
(55)	Geo. Uhle	100.00	50.00	30.00
(56)	Arthur "Dazzy" Vance	250.00	125.00	75.00
(57)	Paul Waner	250.00	125.00	75.00
(58)	Earl G. Whitehill (Middle initial actually O.)	100.00	50.00	30.00
(59)	Fred Williams	100.00	50.00	30.00
(60)	James Wilson	100.00	50.00	30.00
(61)	L.R. (Hack) Wilson	250.00	125.00	75.00
(62)	Lawrence Woodall	100.00	50.00	30.00
(63)	Glen Wright (Glenn)	100.00	50.00	30.00
(64)	William A. Zitzman (Zitzmann)	100.00	50.00	30.00

1929-30 Four-on-One Exhibits

Although the size of the card remained the same, the Exhibit Supply Co. of Chicago began putting four players' pictures on each card in 1929 - a practice that would continue for the next decade. Known as "four-on-one" cards, the players are identified by name and team at the bottom of the photos, which are separated by borders. The 32 cards in the 1929-30 series have postcard backs and were printed in a wide range of color combinations of black, brown and blue ink on blue, orange, green, red, white, and yellow backgrounds. Most of the backs are uncolored, however, cards with a black on red front have been seen with red backs, and cards with blue on yellow fronts have been seen with yellow backs. There are numerous spelling and caption errors in the set, and the player identified as Babe Herman is actually Jesse Petty.

		NM	EX	VG
	Complete Set (32):	5,500	2,750	1,600
	Common Player:	65.00	32.00	20.00
(1)	Earl J. Adams, R. Bartell, Earl Sheely, Harold Traynor	150.00	75.00	45.00
(2)	Dale Alexander, C. Gehringer, G.F. McManus (Should be M.J.), H.F. Rice	150.00	75.00	45.00
(3)	Grover C. Alexander, James Bottomly (Bottomley), Frank Frisch, James Wilson	250.00	125.00	75.00
(4)	Martin G. Autrey (Autry), Alex Metzler, Carl Reynolds, Alphonse Thomas	65.00	32.50	20.00
(5)	Earl Averill, B.A. Falk, K. Holloway, L. Sewell	150.00	75.00	45.00
(6)	David Bancroft, Del L. Bisonette (Bissonette), John H. DeBerry, Floyd C. Herman (Photo actually Jesse Petty.)	150.00	75.00	45.00
(7)	C.E. Beck, Leo Hartnett, Rogers Hornsby, L.R. (Hack) Wilson	200.00	100.00	60.00
(8)	Ray Benge, Lester L. Sweetland, A.C. Whitney, Cy. Williams	65.00	32.50	20.00
(9)	Benny Bengough, Earl B. Coombs (Combs), Waite Hoyt, Anthony Lazzeri	200.00	100.00	60.00
(10)	L. Benton, Melvin Ott, Andrew Reese, William Terry	150.00	75.00	45.00
(11)	Max Bishop, James Dykes, Samuel Hale, Homer Summa	65.00	32.50	20.00
(12)	L.A. Blue, O. Melillo, F.O. Rourke (Frank O'Rourke), F. Schulte	65.00	32.50	20.00
(13)	Oswald Bluege, Leon Goslin, Joseph Judge, Harold Ruel (Herold)	150.00	75.00	45.00
(14)	Chalmer W. Cissell, John W. Clancy, Willie Kamm, John L. Kerr (Kerr's middle initial actually "F.")	65.00	32.50	20.00
(15)	Gordon S. Cochrane, Jimmy Foxx, Robert M. Grove, George Haas	250.00	125.00	75.00
(16)	Pat Collins, Joe Dugan, Edward Farrel (Farrell), George Sisler	150.00	75.00	45.00
(17)	H.M. Critz, G.L. Kelly, V.J. Picinich, W.C. Walker	150.00	75.00	45.00
(18)	Nick Cullop, D'Arcy Flowers, Harvey Hendrick, Arthur "Dazzy" Vance	150.00	75.00	45.00
(19)	Hazen Cuyler, E. English, C.J. Grimm, C.H. Root	150.00	75.00	45.00
(20)	Taylor Douthit, Chas. M. Gilbert (Gelbert), Chas. J. Hafey, Fred G. Haney	150.00	75.00	45.00
(21)	Leo Durocher, Henry L. Gehrig, Mark Koenig, Geo. H. "Babe" Ruth	1,400	700.00	400.00
(22)	L.A. Fonseca, Carl Lind, J. Sewell, J. Tavener	150.00	75.00	45.00
(23)	H.E. Ford, C.F. Lucas, C.A. Pittenger, E.V. Purdy	65.00	32.50	20.00
(24)	Bernard Friberg, Donald Hurst, Frank O'Doul, Fresco Thompson	65.00	32.50	20.00
(25)	S. Gray, R. Kress, H. Manush, W.H. Shang (Schang)	150.00	75.00	45.00
(26)	Charles R. Hargreaves, Ray Kremer, Lloyd Waner, Paul Waner	150.00	75.00	45.00
(27)	George Harper, Fred Maguire, Lance Richbourg, Robert Smith	65.00	32.50	20.00
(28)	Jack Hayes, Sam P. Jones, Chas. M. Myer, Sam Rice	150.00	75.00	45.00
(29)	Harry E. Heilman (Heilmann), C.N. Richardson, M.J. Shea, G.E. Uhle	150.00	75.00	45.00
(30)	J.A. Heving, R.R. Reeves (Should be R.E.), J. Rothrock, C.H. Ruffing	150.00	75.00	45.00
(31)	J.F. Hogan, T.C. Jackson, Fred Lindstrom, J.D. Welsh	150.00	75.00	45.00
(32)	W.W. Regan, H. Rhyne, D. Taitt, P.J. Todt	65.00	32.50	20.00

1929 Exhibit "Star Picture Stamps"

This series of movie star Exhibit cards includes pictures of other celebrities who were featured in contemporary movies. Produced by Exhibit Supply Co. of Chicago, whose advertising appears on the postcard-style back, the 5-3/8" x 3-3/8" card has a variety of colors on the front which pictures the stars in the format of eight "Star Pictures Stamps." On this card, Ruth is pictured in the uniform he wore in the 1927 film "The Babe Comes Home."

	NM	EX	VG
Babe Ruth (W/Tom Mix, Charles Lindbergh, Charlie Chaplin, Jack Dempsey, Harold Lloyd, Douglas Fairbanks and Al Jolson.)	750.00	375.00	225.00

1931-32 Four-on-One Exhibits

The 1931-1932 series issued by the Exhibit Co. again consisted of 32 cards, each picturing four players. The series can be differentiated from the previous year by the coupon backs, which list various premiums available (including kazoos, toy pistols and other prizes). The cards again were printed in various color combinations, including; black on green, blue on green, black on orange, black on red, blue on white and black on yellow. There are numerous spelling and caption errors in the series. The Babe Herman/Jesse Petty error of the previous year was still not corrected, and the card of Rick Ferell not only misspells his name ("Farrel"), but also pictures the wrong player (Edward Farrell).

		NM	EX	VG
	Complete Set (32):	5,500	2,750	1,600
	Common Card:	90.00	45.00	27.00
(1)	Earl J. Adams, James Bottomly (Bottomley), Frank Frisch, James Wilson	150.00	75.00	45.00
(2)	Dale Alexander, C. Gehringer, G.F. McManus (Should be M.J.), G.E. Uhle	150.00	75.00	45.00
(3)	L.L. Appling (Should be L.B.), Chalmer W. Cissell, Willie Kamm, Ted Lyons	150.00	75.00	45.00
(4)	Buzz Arlett, Ray Benge, Chuck Klein, A.C. Whitney	150.00	75.00	45.00
(5)	Earl Averill, B.A. Falk, L.A. Fonseca, L. Sewell	150.00	75.00	45.00
(6)	Richard Bartell, Bernard Friberg, Donald Hurst, Harry McCurdy	90.00	45.00	27.00
(7)	Walter Berger, Fred Maguire, Lance Richbourg, Earl Sheely	90.00	45.00	27.00
(8)	Chas. Berry, Robt. Reeves, R.R. Reeves (Should be R.E.), J. Rothrock	90.00	45.00	27.00

		NM	EX	VG
(9)	Del L. Bisonette (Bissonette), Floyd C. Herman (Photo - J. Petty, Jack Quinn, Glenn Wright	90.00	45.00	27.00
(10)	L.A. Blue, Smead Jolley, Carl Reynolds, Henry Tate	90.00	45.00	27.00
(11)	O. Bluege, Joe Judge, Chas. M. Myer, Sam Rice	150.00	75.00	45.00
(12)	John Boley, James Dykes, E.J. Miller, Al. Simmons	150.00	75.00	45.00
(13)	Gordon S. Cochrane, Jimmy Foxx, Robert M. Grove, George Haas	325.00	160.00	95.00
(14)	Adam Comorosky, Gus Suhr, T.J. Thevenow, Harold Traynor	150.00	75.00	45.00
(15)	Earl B. Coombs (Combs), W. Dickey, Anthony Lazzeri, H. Pennock	225.00	110.00	65.00
(16)	H.M. Critz, J.F. Hogan, T.C. Jackson, Fred Lindstrom	150.00	75.00	45.00
(17)	Joe Cronin, H. Manush, F. Marberry, Roy Spencer	150.00	75.00	45.00
(18)	Nick Cullop, Les Durocher (Leo), Harry Heilmann, W.C. Walker	150.00	75.00	45.00
(19)	Hazen Cuyler, E. English, C.J. Grimm, C.H. Root	150.00	75.00	45.00
(20)	Taylor Douthit, Chas. M. Gilbert (Gelbert), Chas. J. Hafey, Bill Hallahan	90.00	45.00	27.00
(21)	Richard Farrel (Ferrell), S. Gray, R. Kress, W. Stewart (Photo actually Ed Farrell.)	90.00	45.00	27.00
(22)	W. Ferrell, J. Goldman, Hunnefield, Ed Morgan	125.00	62.50	37.50
(23)	Fred Fitzsimmons, Robert O'Farrell, Melvin Ott, William Terry	150.00	75.00	45.00
(24)	D'Arcy Flowers, Frank O'Doul, Fresco Thompson, Arthur "Dazzy" Vance	150.00	75.00	45.00
(25)	H.E. Ford (Should be H.H.), Gooch, C.F. Lucas, W. Roettger	90.00	45.00	27.00
(26)	E. Funk, W. Hoyt, Mark Koenig, Wallie Schang	90.00	45.00	27.00
(27)	Henry L. Gehrig, Lyn Lary, James Reese (Photo actually Andy Reese.), Geo. H. "Babe" Ruth	1,150	575.00	345.00
(28)	George Grantham, Ray Kremer, Lloyd Waner, Paul Waner	150.00	75.00	45.00
(29)	Leon Goslin, O. Melillo, F.O. Rourke (Frank O'Rourke), F. Schulte	150.00	75.00	45.00
(30)	Leo Hartnett, Rogers Hornsby, J.R. Stevenson (Stephenson), L.R. (Hack) Wilson	200.00	100.00	60.00
(31)	D. MacFayden, H. Rhyne, Bill Sweeney, E.W. Webb	90.00	45.00	27.00
(32)	Walter Maranville, Randolph Moore, Alfred Spohrer, J.T. Zachary	150.00	75.00	45.00

1931-32 Babe Ruth Exhibit

 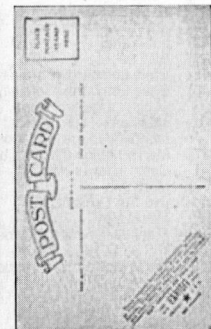

The rarest Exhibit card to feature Babe Ruth, this circa 1931 issue has a photographic portrait of him in dress clothes, and is part of a 32-card movie stars series. Found in black-and-white or various color tints, this approximately 3-1/2" x 5-1/2" card has a facsimile autograph in white on front. It can be found with either a postcard-style back or a back offering premium merchandise.

	NM	EX	VG
Babe Ruth	3,500	1,750	1,050

1933 Four-on-One Exhibits

The 1933 series of four-on-one Exhibits consists of 16 cards with blank backs. Color combinations include: blue on green, black on orange, black on red, blue on white and black on yellow. Most have a plain, white back, although the black on yellow cards are also found with a yellow back. Most of the pictures used are reprinted from previous series, and there are some spelling and caption errors, including the Richard Ferrell/Edward Farrel mixup from the previous year. Al Lopez is shown as "Vincent" Lopez.

	NM	EX	VG
Complete Set (16):	4,000	2,000	1,200
Common Card:	85.00	40.00	25.00

		NM	EX	VG
(1)	Earl J. Adams, Frank Frisch, Chas. Gilbert (Gelbert), Bill Hallahan	150.00	75.00	45.00
(2)	Earl Averill, W. Ferrell, Ed Morgan, L. Sewell	150.00	75.00	45.00
(3)	Richard Bartell, Ray Benge, Donald Hurst, Chuck Klein	150.00	75.00	45.00
(4)	Walter Berger, Walter Maranville, Alfred Spohrer, J.T. Zachary	150.00	75.00	45.00
(5)	Charles Berry, L.A. Blue, Ted Lyons, Bob Seeds	150.00	75.00	45.00
(6)	Chas. Berry, D. MacFayden, H. Rhyne, E.W. Webb	85.00	40.00	25.00
(7)	Mickey Cochrane, Jimmy Foxx, Robert M. Grove, Al. Simmons	450.00	225.00	135.00
(8)	H.M. Critz, Fred Fitzsimmons, Fred Lindstrom, Robert O'Farrell	150.00	75.00	45.00
(9)	W. Dickey, Anthony Lazzeri, H. Pennock, George H. "Babe" Ruth	2,000	1,000	600.00
(10)	Taylor Douthit, George Grantham, Chas. J. Hafey, C.F. Lucas	150.00	75.00	45.00
(11)	E. English, C.J. Grimm, C.H. Root, J.R. Stevenson (Stephenson)	85.00	40.00	25.00
(12)	Richard Farrel (Farrell), Leon Goslin, S. Gray, O. Melillo (photo actually Ed Farrell)	150.00	75.00	45.00
(13)	C. Gehringer, "Muddy" Ruel, Jonathan Stone (first name - John, G.E. Uhle	150.00	75.00	45.00
(14)	Joseph Judge, H. Manush, F. Marberry, Roy Spencer	150.00	75.00	45.00
(15)	Vincent Lopez (Al), Frank O'Doul, Arthur "Dazzy" Vance, Glenn Wright	150.00	75.00	45.00
(16)	Gus Suhr, Tom J. Thevenow, Lloyd Waner, Paul Waner	150.00	75.00	45.00

1934 Four-on-One Exhibits

This 16-card series issued by the Exhibit Co. in 1934 is again blank-backed and continues the four-on-one format in a 3-3/8" x 5-3/8" size. The 1934 series can be differentiated from previous years by the more subdued colors of the cards, which include lighter shades of blue, brown, green and violet - all printed on white card stock. Many new photos were also used in the 1934 series. Of the 64 players included, 25 appear for the first time and another 16 were given new poses. Spelling was improved, but Al Lopez is still identified as "Vincent."

	NM	EX	VG
Complete Set (16):	3,300	1,650	1,000
Common Card:	100.00	50.00	30.00

		NM	EX	VG
(1)	Luke Appling, George Earnshaw, Al Simmons, Evar Swanson	150.00	75.00	45.00
(2)	Earl Averill, W. Ferrell, Willie Kamm, Frank Pytlak	150.00	75.00	45.00
(3)	Richard Bartell, Donald Hurst, Wesley Schulmerich, Jimmy Wilson	100.00	50.00	30.00
(4)	Walter Berger, Ed Brandt, Frank Hogan, Bill Urbanski	100.00	50.00	30.00
(5)	Jim Bottomley, Chas. J. Hafey, Botchi Lombardi, Tony Piet	150.00	75.00	45.00
(6)	Irving Burns, Irving Hadley, Rollie Hemsley, O. Melillo	100.00	50.00	30.00
(7)	Bill Cissell, Rick Ferrell, Lefty Grove, Roy Johnson	150.00	75.00	45.00
(8)	Mickey Cochrane, C. Gehringer, Goose Goslin, Fred Marberry	150.00	75.00	45.00
(9)	George Cramer (Roger), Jimmy Foxx, Frank Higgins, Slug Mahaffey	180.00	90.00	55.00
(10)	Joe Cronin, Alvin Crowder, Joe Kuhel, H. Manush	150.00	75.00	45.00
(11)	W. Dickey, Lou Gehrig, Vernon Gomez, Geo. H. "Babe" Ruth	1,700	850.00	500.00
(12)	E. English, C.J. Grimm, Chas. Klein, Lon Warneke	150.00	75.00	45.00
(13)	Frank Frisch, Bill Hallahan, Pepper Martin, John Rothrock	150.00	75.00	45.00

		NM	EX	VG
(14)	Carl Hubbell, Mel Ott, Blondy Ryan, Bill Terry	180.00	90.00	55.00
(15)	Leonard Koenecke, Sam Leslie, Vincent Lopez (Al), Glenn Wright	150.00	75.00	45.00
(16)	T.J. Thevenow, Pie Traynor, Lloyd Waner, Paul Waner	150.00	75.00	45.00

1935 Four-on-One Exhibits

Continuing with the same four-on-one format, the Exhibit Supply Co. issued another 16-card series in 1935. All cards were printed in a slate-blue color with a blank back. Seventeen of the players included in the 1935 series appear for the first time. While another 11 are shown with new poses. There are several spelling and caption errors. Babe Ruth appears in a regular Exhibit issue for the last time.

		NM	EX	VG
Complete Set (16):		4,000	2,000	1,200
Common Card:		75.00	35.00	20.00
(1)	Earl Averill, Mel Harder, Willie Kamm, Hal Trosky	125.00	60.00	35.00
(2)	Walter Berger, Ed Brandt, Frank Hogan, "Babe" Ruth	2,000	1,000	600.00
(3)	Henry Bonura, Jimmy Dykes, Ted Lyons, Al Simmons	125.00	60.00	35.00
(4)	Jimmy Bottomley, Paul Derringer, Chas. J. Hafey, Botchi Lombardi	125.00	60.00	35.00
(5)	Irving Burns, Rollie Hemsley, O. Melillo, L.N. Newson	75.00	35.00	20.00
(6)	Guy Bush, Pie Traynor, Floyd Vaughn (Vaughan), Paul Waner	125.00	60.00	35.00
(7)	Mickey Cochrane, C. Gehringer, Goose Goslin, Linwood Rowe (Lynwood)	125.00	60.00	35.00
(8)	Phil Collins, John "Blondy" Ryan, Geo. Watkins, Jimmy Wilson	75.00	35.00	20.00
(9)	George Cramer (Roger), Jimmy Foxx, Bob Johnson, Slug Mahaffey	150.00	75.00	45.00
(10)	Hughie Critz, Carl Hubbell, Mel Ott, Bill Terry	150.00	75.00	45.00
(11)	Joe Cronin, Rick Ferrell, Lefty Grove, Billy Werber	145.00	70.00	40.00
(12)	Tony Cuccinello, Vincent Lopez (Al), Van Mungo, Dan Taylor (photo actually George Puccinelli)	125.00	60.00	35.00
(13)	Jerome "Dizzy" Dean, Paul Dean, Frank Frisch, Pepper Martin	325.00	160.00	95.00
(14)	W. Dickey, Lou Gehrig, Vernon Gomez, Tony Lazzeri	900.00	450.00	275.00
(15)	C.J. Grimm, Gabby Hartnett, Chas. Klein, Lon Warneke	125.00	60.00	35.00
(16)	H. Manush, Buddy Meyer (Myer), Fred Schulte, Earl Whitehill	125.00	60.00	35.00

1936 Four-on-One Exhibits

The 1936 series of four-on-one cards again consisted of 16 cards in either green or slate blue with plain, blank backs.

The series can be differentiated from the previous year's Exhibit cards by the line "PTD. IN U.S.A." at the bottom. Of the 64 players pictured, 16 appear for the first time and another nine are shown in new poses. The series is again marred by several spelling and caption errors.

		NM	EX	VG
Complete Set (16):		3,000	1,500	900.00
Common Card:		80.00	40.00	25.00
(1)	Paul Andrews, Harland Clift (Harland), Rollie Hemsley, Sammy West	80.00	40.00	25.00
(2)	Luke Appling, Henry Bonura, Jimmy Dykes, Ted Lyons	100.00	50.00	30.00
(3)	Earl Averill, Mel Harder, Hal Trosky, Joe Vosmik	100.00	50.00	30.00
(4)	Walter Berger, Danny MacFayden, Bill Urbanski, Pinky Whitney	80.00	40.00	25.00
(5)	Charles Berry, Frank Higgins, Bob Johnson, Puccinelli	80.00	40.00	25.00
(6)	Ossie Bluege, Buddy Meyer (Myer), L.N. Newsom, Earl Whitehill	80.00	40.00	25.00
(7)	Stan. Bordagaray, Dutch Brandt, Fred Lindstrom, Van Mungo	100.00	50.00	30.00
(8)	Guy Bush, Pie Traynor, Floyd Vaughn (Vaughan), Paul Waner	100.00	50.00	30.00
(9)	Dolph Camilli, Curt Davis, Johnny Moore, Jimmy Wilson	80.00	40.00	25.00
(10)	Mickey Cochrane, C. Gehringer, Goose Goslin, Linwood Rowe (Lynwood)	100.00	50.00	30.00
(11)	Joe Cronin, Rick Ferrell, Jimmy Foxx, Lefty Grove	175.00	85.00	50.00
(12)	Jerome "Dizzy" Dean, Paul Dean, Frank Frisch, Joe "Ducky" Medwick	300.00	150.00	90.00
(13)	Paul Derringer, Babe Herman, Alex Kampouris, Botchi Lombardi	100.00	50.00	30.00
(14)	Augie Galan, Gabby Hartnett, Billy Herman, Lon Warneke	100.00	50.00	30.00
(15)	Lou Gehrig, Vernon Gomez, Tony Lazzeri, Red Ruffing	1,300	650.00	390.00
(16)	Carl Hubbell, Gus Mancuso, Mel Ott, Bill Terry	125.00	60.00	35.00

1937 Four-on-One Exhibits

The 1937 four-on-one Exhibit cards were printed in either green or bright blue. The backs are again blank. The 1937 cards are difficult to distinguish from the 1936 series, because both contain the "PTD. IN U.S.A." line along the bottom. Of the 64 photos, 47 are re-issues from previous series.

		NM	EX	VG
Complete Set (16):		2,750	1,350	825.00
Common Card:		125.00	65.00	40.00
(1)	Earl Averill, Bob Feller, Frank Pytlak, Hal Trosky	300.00	150.00	90.00
(2)	Luke Appling, Henry Bonura, Jimmy Dykes, Vernon Kennedy	250.00	125.00	75.00
(3)	Walter Berger, Alfonso Lopez, Danny MacFayden, Bill Urbanski	250.00	125.00	75.00
(4)	Cy Blanton, Gus Suhr, Floyd Vaughn (Vaughan), Paul Waner	250.00	125.00	75.00
(5)	Dolph Camilli, Johnny Moore, Wm. Walters, Pinky Whitney	125.00	65.00	40.00
(6)	Harland Clift (Harland), Rollie Hemsley, Orval Hildebrand (Oral), Sammy West	125.00	65.00	40.00
(7)	Mickey Cochrane, C. Gehringer, Goose Goslin, Linwood Rowe (Lynwood)	250.00	125.00	75.00
(8)	Joe Cronin, Rick Ferrell, Jimmy Foxx, Lefty Grove	300.00	150.00	90.00
(9)	Jerome "Dizzy" Dean, Stuart Martin, Joe "Ducky" Medwick, Lon Warneke	350.00	175.00	100.00
(10)	Paul Derringer, Botchi Lombardi, Lew Riggs, Phil Weintraub	250.00	125.00	75.00
(11)	Joe DiMaggio, Lou Gehrig, Vernon Gomez, Tony Lazzeri	2,700	1,350	800.00

(12)	E. English, Johnny Moore, Van Mungo, Gordon Phelps	125.00	65.00	40.00
(13)	Augie Galan, Gabby Hartnett, Billy Herman, Bill Lee	250.00	125.00	75.00
(14)	Carl Hubbell, Sam Leslie, Gus. Mancuso, Mel Ott	250.00	125.00	75.00
(15)	Bob Johnson, Harry Kelly (Kelley), Wallace Moses, Billy Weber (Werber)	125.00	65.00	40.00
(16)	Joe Kuhel, Buddy Meyer (Myer), L.N. Newsom, Jonathan Stone (First name actually John.)	125.00	65.00	40.00

1938 Four-on-One Exhibits

The Exhibit Co. used its four-on-one format for the final time in 1938, issuing another 16-card series. The cards feature brown printing on white stock with the line "MADE IN U.S.A." appearing along the bottom. The backs are blank. Twelve players appeared for the first time and three others are shown in new poses. Again, there are several spelling and caption mistakes.

		NM	EX	VG
Complete Set (16):		5,000	2,500	1,500
Common Card:		125.00	65.00	40.00
(1)	Luke Appling, Mike Kreevich, Ted Lyons, L. Sewell	200.00	100.00	60.00
(2)	Morris Arnovich, Chas. Klein, Wm. Walters, Pinky Whitney	125.00	65.00	40.00
(3)	Earl Averill, Bob Feller, Odell Hale, Hal Trosky	250.00	125.00	75.00
(4)	Beau Bell, Harland Clift (Harland), L.N. Newsom, Sammy West	125.00	65.00	40.00
(5)	Cy Blanton, Gus Suhr, Floyd Vaughn (Vaughan), Paul Waner	200.00	100.00	60.00
(6)	Tom Bridges, C. Gehringer, Hank Greenberg, Rudy York	200.00	100.00	60.00
(7)	Dolph Camilli, Leo Durocher, Van Mungo, Gordon Phelps	200.00	100.00	60.00
(8)	Joe Cronin, Jimmy Foxx, Lefty Grove, Joe Vosmik	250.00	125.00	75.00
(9)	Tony Cuccinello, Vince DiMaggio, Roy Johnson, Danny MacFayden (Photo actually George Puccinelli.)	140.00	70.00	40.00
(10)	Jerome "Dizzy" Dean, Augie Galan, Gabby Hartnett, Billy Herman	300.00	150.00	90.00
(11)	Paul Derringer, Ival Goodman, Botchi Lombardi, Lew Riggs	200.00	100.00	60.00
(12)	W. Dickey, Joe DiMaggio, Lou Gehrig, Vernon Gomez	2,000	1,000	600.00
(13)	Rick Ferrell, W. Ferrell, Buddy Meyer (Myer), Jonathan Stone (First name actually John.)	200.00	100.00	60.00
(14)	Carl Hubbell, Hank Leiber, Mel Ott, Jim Ripple	200.00	100.00	60.00
(15)	Bob Johnson, Harry Kelly (Kelley), Wallace Moses, Billy Weber (Werber)	125.00	65.00	40.00
(16)	Stuart Martin, Joe "Ducky" Medwick, Johnny Mize, Lon Warneke	200.00	100.00	60.00

1939-46 Salutation Exhibits

Referred to as "Exhibits" because they were issued by the Exhibit Supply Co. of Chicago, Ill., the bulk of this group was produced over an eight-year span, though production and sale of some players' cards continued well into the period of the 1947-66 Exhibits. These cards are frequently called "Salutations" because of the personalized greeting found on the card. The black-and-white cards, which measure 3-3/8" x 5-3/8", are unnumbered and blank-backed. Most Exhibits were sold through vending machines for a penny. The complete set price includes all variations.

		NM	EX	VG
Complete Set (83):		6,500	3,250	1,950
Common Player:		15.00	7.50	4.50
(1)	Luke Appling ("Made In U.S.A." in left corner.)	20.00	10.00	6.00
(2)	Luke Appling ("Made In U.S.A." in right corner.)	45.00	22.50	13.50
(3)	Earl Averill	400.00	200.00	120.00
(4)	Charles "Red" Barrett	20.00	10.00	6.00
(5)	Henry "Hank" Borowy	15.00	7.50	4.50
(6)	Lou Boudreau (Large projection, small projection. Look at the feet and bat top.)	25.00	12.50	7.50
(7)	Adolf Camilli	30.00	15.00	9.00
(8)	Phil Cavarretta	15.00	7.50	4.50
(9)	Harland Clift (Harland)	20.00	10.00	6.00
(10)	Tony Cuccinello	50.00	30.00	20.00
(11)	Dizzy Dean	140.00	70.00	45.00
(12)	Paul Derringer	20.00	10.00	6.00
(13)	Bill Dickey ("Made In U.S.A." in left corner.)	35.00	17.50	10.00
(14)	Bill Dickey ("Made In U.S.A." in right corner.)	55.00	27.50	16.50
(15)	Joe DiMaggio (Issued into the 1950s.)	150.00	75.00	45.00
(16)	Bob Elliott	15.00	7.50	4.50
(17)	Bob Feller (Portrait)	120.00	60.00	35.00
(18)	Bob Feller (Pitching)	50.00	25.00	15.00
(19)	Dave Ferriss	45.00	22.50	13.50
(20)	Jimmy Foxx	75.00	37.50	22.50
(21)	Lou Gehrig	1,750	875.00	525.00
(22)	Charlie Gehringer	150.00	100.00	50.00
(23)	Vernon Gomez	300.00	150.00	100.00
(24)	Joe Gordon (Cleveland)	40.00	20.00	12.00
(25)	Joe Gordon (New York)	25.00	12.50	7.50
(26)	Hank Greenberg (Truly yours.)	35.00	17.50	10.00
(27)	Hank Greenberg (Very truly yours.)	160.00	80.00	50.00
(28)	Robert Grove	50.00	25.00	15.00
(29)	Gabby Hartnett	350.00	225.00	150.00
(30)	Buddy Hassett	20.00	10.00	6.00
(31)	Jeff Heath (Large projection.)	25.00	12.50	7.50
(32)	Jeff Heath (Small projection.)	25.00	12.50	7.50
(33)	Kirby Higbe	20.00	10.00	6.00
(34)	Tommy Holmes (Yours truly: with and without "An Exhibit Card.")	15.00	7.50	4.50
(35)	Tommy Holmes (Sincerely yours.)	130.00	65.00	40.00
(36)	Carl Hubbell	40.00	20.00	12.00
(37)	Bob Johnson	40.00	20.00	12.00
(38)	Charles Keller ("MADE IN U.S.A." left corner.)	25.00	12.50	7.50
(39)	Charles Keller ("MADE IN U.S.A." right corner.)	15.00	7.50	4.50
(40)	Ken Keltner	25.00	12.50	7.50
(41)	Chuck Klein	350.00	225.00	150.00
(42)	Mike Kreevich	300.00	200.00	100.00
(43)	Joe Kuhel	20.00	10.00	6.00
(44)	Bill Lee	20.00	10.00	6.00
(45)	Ernie Lombardi (Cordially)	325.00	160.00	95.00
(46)	Ernie Lombardi (Cordially yours: Large projection, small projection. Look at the cropping on the lead foot.)	20.00	10.00	6.00
(47)	Martin Marion ("An Exhibit Card" in lower-left.)	20.00	10.00	6.00
(48)	Marty Marion (No "An Exhibit Card.")	20.00	10.00	6.00
(49)	Merrill May	25.00	12.50	7.50
(50)	Frank McCormick ("Made in U.S.A." in left corner.)	30.00	15.00	9.00
(51)	Frank McCormick ("Made in U.S.A." in right corner.)	15.00	7.50	4.50
(52)	George McQuinn ("Made in U.S.A." in left corner.)	20.00	10.00	6.00
(53)	George McQuinn ("Made in U.S.A." in right corner.)	15.00	7.50	4.50
(54)	Joe Medwick	55.00	27.50	16.50
(55)	Johnny Mize ("Made in U.S.A." in left corner.)	35.00	17.50	10.00
(56)	Johnny Mize ("Made in U.S.A." in right corner.)	20.00	10.00	6.00
(57)	Hugh Mulcahy	150.00	75.00	45.00
(58)	Hal Newhouser	30.00	15.00	9.00
(59)	Buck Newson (Newsom)	275.00	135.00	80.00
(60)	Louis (Buck) Newsom	15.00	7.50	4.50
(61)	Mel Ott ("Made in U.S.A." in left corner.)	40.00	20.00	12.00
(62)	Mel Ott ("Made in U.S.A." in right corner.)	25.00	12.50	7.50
(63)	Andy Pafko ("C" on cap.)	20.00	10.00	6.00
(64)	Andy Pafko (Plain cap.)	15.00	7.50	4.50
(65)	Claude Passeau	15.00	7.50	4.50
(66)	Howard Pollet ("Made In U.S.A." in left corner.)	20.00	10.00	6.00
(67)	Howard Pollet ("Made In U.S.A." in right corner.)	15.00	7.50	4.50
(68)	Pete Reiser ("Made In U.S.A." in left corner.)	45.00	22.50	13.50
(69)	Pete Reiser ("Made In U.S.A." in right corner.)	20.00	10.00	6.00
(70)	Johnny Rizzo	300.00	200.00	100.00
(71)	Glenn Russell	75.00	37.50	22.00
(72)	George Stirnweiss	20.00	10.00	6.00

		NM	EX	VG
(73)	Cecil Travis	45.00	20.00	12.50
(74)	Paul Trout	15.00	7.50	4.50
(75)	Johnny Vander Meer	65.00	32.50	20.00
(76)	Arky Vaughn (Vaughan)	50.00	25.00	15.00
(77)	Fred "Dixie" Walker ("D" on cap.)	20.00	10.00	6.00
(78)	Fred "Dixie" Walker ("D" blanked out.)	60.00	30.00	18.00
(79)	"Bucky" Walters	15.00	7.50	4.50
(80)	Lon Warneke	20.00	10.00	6.00
(81)	Ted Williams (#9 shows)	750.00	370.00	220.00
(82)	Ted Williams (#9 not showing: large projection, small projection. Look at the space from the bottom of the foot at the right side to the card bottom.)	45.00	22.50	13.50
(83)	Rudy York (large projection, small projection.)	20.00	10.00	6.00

1947-66 Exhibits

Jackie Robinson

Produced by the Exhibit Supply Co. of Chicago, these issues cover a span of 20 years. Each unnumbered, black-and-white card is printed on heavy cardboard measuring 3-3/8" x 5-3/8" and is blank-backed. The company issued new sets each year, with many players being repeated year after year. Other players appeared in only one or two years, thereby creating levels of scarcity. Many cards can be found with minor variations in the wording and placement of the credit line at bottom. Some pieces have been found printed on a semi-gloss paper stock, perhaps as proofs. Their value is 50 percent or less than the issued version.

		NM	EX	VG
	Common Player:	9.00	4.50	2.75
(1)	Hank Aaron	80.00	40.00	24.00
(2)	Joe Adcock (White signature.)	9.00	4.50	2.75
(3)	Joe Adcock (Black signature.)	10.00	5.00	3.00
(4)	Max Alvis	30.00	15.00	9.00
(5)	Johnny Antonelli (Braves)	9.00	4.50	2.75
(6)	Johnny Antonelli (Giants)	10.00	5.00	3.00
(7)	Luis Aparicio/Portrait	12.00	6.00	3.50
(8)	Luis Aparicio/Btg	17.50	8.75	5.25
(9)	Luke Appling (With and without "An Exhibit Card.")	20.00	10.00	6.00
(10)	Ritchie Ashburn (Phillies, first name incorrect. With and without "An Exhibit Card.")	12.00	6.00	3.50
(11)	Richie Ashburn (Phillies, first name correct.)	12.00	6.00	3.50
(12)	Richie Ashburn (Cubs)	17.50	8.75	5.25
(13)	Bob Aspromonte	9.00	4.50	2.75
(14)	Toby Atwell	9.00	4.50	2.75
(15)	Ed Bailey (With cap.)	10.00	5.00	3.00
(16)	Ed Bailey (No cap.)	9.00	4.50	2.75
(17)	Gene Baker	9.00	4.50	2.75
(18)	Ernie Banks (Bat on shoulder, script signature.)	55.00	27.50	16.50
(19)	Ernie Banks (Bat on shoulder, plain signature.)	17.50	8.75	5.25
(20)	Ernie Banks/Portrait	30.00	15.00	9.00
(21)	Steve Barber	9.00	4.50	2.75
(22)	Earl Battey	10.00	5.00	3.00
(23)	Matt Batts	9.00	4.50	2.75
(24)	Hank Bauer (N.Y. cap.)	10.00	5.00	3.00
(25)	Hank Bauer (Plain cap.)	12.00	6.00	3.50
(26)	Frank Baumholtz	9.00	4.50	2.75
(27)	Gene Bearden (With and without "An Exhibit Card.")	9.00	4.50	2.75
(28)	Joe Beggs	15.00	7.50	4.50
(29)	Larry "Yogi" Berra	60.00	30.00	18.00
(30a)	Yogi Berra ("MADE IN U.S.A." lower-right.)	35.00	17.50	10.00
(30b)	Yogi Berra ("PRINTED IN U.S.A." lower-right. With and without "An Exhibit Card.")	35.00	17.50	10.00
(31)	Steve Bilko	10.00	5.00	3.00
(32)	Ewell Blackwell/Pitching	10.00	5.00	3.00
(33)	Ewell Blackwell/Portrait	9.00	4.50	2.75
(34)	Don Blasingame (St. Louis cap.)	9.00	4.50	2.75
(35)	Don Blasingame (Plain cap.)	17.50	8.75	5.25
(36)	Ken Boyer	12.00	6.00	3.50
(37)	Ralph Branca (With and without "An Exhibit Card.")	12.00	6.00	3.50
(38)	Jackie Brandt	40.00	20.00	12.00
(39)	Harry Brecheen	9.00	4.50	2.75
(40)	Tom Brewer	13.50	6.75	4.00
(41)	Lou Brissie	10.00	5.00	3.00
(42)	Bill Bruton	9.00	4.50	2.75

		NM	EX	VG
(43)	Lew Burdette/Pitching (Side view.)	9.00	4.50	2.75
(44)	Lew Burdette/Pitching (Front view.)	10.00	5.00	3.00
(45)	Johnny Callison	12.50	6.25	3.75
(46)	Roy Campanella	25.00	12.50	7.50
(47)	Chico Carrasquel/Portrait	15.00	7.50	4.50
(48)	Chico Carrasquel/Leaping	9.00	4.50	2.75
(49)	George Case	13.50	6.75	4.00
(50)	Hugh Casey	40.00	30.00	20.00
(51)	Norm Cash	12.00	6.00	3.50
(52)	Orlando Cepeda/Portrait	15.00	7.50	4.50
(53)	Orlando Cepeda/Btg	15.00	7.50	4.50
(54)	Bob Cerv (A's cap.)	12.00	6.00	3.50
(55)	Bob Cerv (Plain cap.)	20.00	10.00	6.00
(56)	Dean Chance	9.00	4.50	2.75
(57)	Spud Chandler	40.00	30.00	20.00
(58)	Tom Cheney	9.00	4.50	2.75
(59)	Bubba Church	10.00	5.00	3.00
(60)	Roberto Clemente	40.00	20.00	12.00
(61)	Rocky Colavito/Portrait	35.00	17.50	10.00
(62)	Rocky Colavito/Btg	25.00	12.50	7.50
(63)	Choo Choo Coleman	12.00	6.00	3.50
(64)	Gordy Coleman	30.00	15.00	9.00
(65)	Jerry Coleman	10.00	5.00	3.00
(66)	Mort Cooper	35.00	17.50	10.00
(67)	Walker Cooper (With and without "Made in USA")	9.00	4.50	2.75
(68)	Roger Craig	12.00	6.00	3.50
(69)	Delmar Crandall	9.00	4.50	2.75
(70)	Joe Cunningham/btg	40.00	20.00	12.00
(71)	Joe Cunningham/Portrait	65.00	32.00	19.50
(72)	Guy Curtwright (Curtright)	10.00	5.00	3.00
(73)	Bud Daley	35.00	17.50	10.00
(74)	Alvin Dark (Braves)	12.00	6.00	3.50
(75)	Alvin Dark (Giants)	10.00	5.00	3.00
(76)	Alvin Dark (Cubs)	12.00	6.00	3.50
(77)	Murray Dickson (Murry)	25.00	12.50	7.50
(78)	Bob Dillinger (With and without "An Exhibit Card.")	12.00	6.00	3.50
(79)	Dom DiMaggio	25.00	12.50	7.50
(80)	Joe Dobson	25.00	15.00	10.00
(81a)	Larry Doby (Three forms: Without "An Exhibit Card," with "An Exhibit Card," and with "An Exhibit Card" scratched out.)	40.00	20.00	12.00
(81b)	Larry Doby (Bat well off right border.)	25.00	12.50	7.50
(82a)	Bobby Doerr ("AN EXHIBIT CARD" lower-left.)	15.00	7.50	4.50
(82b)	Bobby Doerr (No "AN EXHIBIT CARD.")	15.00	7.50	4.50
(83)	Dick Donovan (Plain cap.)	12.00	6.00	3.50
(84)	Dick Donovan (Sox cap.)	9.00	4.50	2.75
(85)	Walter Dropo	9.00	4.50	2.75
(86)	Don Drysdale (Glove at waist.)	20.00	10.00	6.00
(87)	Don Drysdale/Portrait	35.00	17.50	10.00
(88)	Luke Easter	15.00	7.50	4.50
(89)	Bruce Edwards	15.00	7.50	4.50
(90)	Del Ennis	15.00	7.50	4.50
(91)	Al Evans	10.00	5.00	3.00
(92)	Walter Evers	9.00	4.50	2.75
(93)	Ferris Fain/Fldg	12.00	6.00	3.50
(94)	Ferris Fain/Portrait	15.00	7.50	4.50
(95)	Dick Farrell	9.00	4.50	2.75
(96)	Ed "Whitey" Ford	30.00	15.00	9.00
(97)	Whitey Ford/Pitching	30.00	15.00	9.00
(98)	Whitey Ford/Portrait	175.00	85.00	50.00
(99)	Dick Fowler	12.50	6.25	3.75
(100)	Nelson Fox	25.00	12.50	7.50
(101)	Tito Francona	9.00	4.50	2.75
(102)	Bob Friend	9.00	4.50	2.75
(103)	Carl Furillo	25.00	12.50	7.50
(104)	Augie Galan	30.00	15.00	9.00
(105)	Jim Gentile	9.00	4.50	2.75
(106)	Tony Gonzalez	9.00	4.50	2.75
(107)	Billy Goodman/Leaping	17.50	8.75	5.25
(108)	Billy Goodman/btg	12.00	6.00	3.50
(109)	Ted Greengrass (Jim)	9.00	4.50	2.75
(110)	Dick Groat	10.00	5.00	3.00
(111)	Steve Gromek	9.00	4.50	2.75
(112)	Johnny Groth	9.00	4.50	2.75
(113)	Orval Grove	15.00	7.50	4.50
(114)	Frank Gustine (Pirates uniform.)	20.00	10.00	6.00
(115)	Frank Gustine (Plain uniform.)	10.00	5.00	3.00
(116)	Berthold Haas	20.00	10.00	6.00
(117)	Grady Hatton	10.00	5.00	3.00
(118)	Jim Hegan	9.00	4.50	2.75
(119)	Tom Henrich	12.00	6.00	3.50
(120)	Ray Herbert	15.00	7.50	4.50
(121)	Gene Hermanski	10.00	5.00	3.00
(122)	Whitey Herzog	12.00	6.00	3.50
(123)	Kirby Higbe	30.00	15.00	9.00
(124)	Chuck Hinton	9.00	4.50	2.75
(125)	Don Hoak	15.00	7.50	4.50
(126)	Gil Hodges ("B" on cap.)	12.50	6.25	3.75
(127)	Gil Hodges ("LA" on cap.)	25.00	12.50	7.50
(128)	Johnny Hopp	25.00	15.00	8.00
(129)	Elston Howard	12.00	6.00	3.50
(130)	Frank Howard	15.00	7.50	4.50
(131)	Ken Hubbs	30.00	15.00	9.00
(132)	Tex Hughson	25.00	15.00	8.00
(133)	Fred Hutchinson	60.00	30.00	18.00
(134)	Monty Irvin (Monte)	12.00	6.00	3.50
(135)	Joey Jay	9.00	4.50	2.75
(136)	Jackie Jensen	45.00	22.50	13.50
(137)	Sam Jethroe	10.00	5.00	3.00
(138)	Bill Johnson	30.00	15.00	9.00
(139)	Walter Judnich	13.50	6.75	4.00
(140)	Al Kaline/Kneeling	25.00	12.50	7.50
(141)	Al Kaline (Portrait w/ two bats.)	17.50	8.75	5.25
(142)	George Kell	20.00	10.00	6.00
(143)	Charley Keller (With and without "An Exhibit Card.")	12.50	6.25	3.75
(144)	Alex Kellner	9.00	4.50	2.75
(145)	Kenn (Ken) Keltner	10.00	5.00	3.00

		NM	EX	VG
(146)	Harmon Killebrew (With bat.)	50.00	25.00	15.00
(147)	Harmon Killebrew/Throwing	40.00	20.00	12.00
(148)	Harmon Killibrew (Killebrew)/Portrait	50.00	25.00	15.00
(149)	Ellis Kinder	9.00	4.50	2.75
(150)	Ralph Kiner	25.00	12.50	7.50
(151)	Billy Klaus	30.00	15.00	9.00
(152)	Ted Kluzewski (Kluszewski)/Btg	17.50	8.75	5.25
(153)	Ted Kluzewski (Kluszewski) (Pirates uniform.)	12.00	6.00	3.50
(154)	Ted Kluzewski (Kluszewski) (Plain uniform.)	17.50	8.75	5.25
(155)	Don Kolloway	20.00	10.00	6.00
(156)	Jim Konstanty	10.00	5.00	3.00
(157)	Sandy Koufax	40.00	20.00	12.00
(158)	Ed Kranepool	55.00	27.50	16.50
(159)	Tony Kubek (Light background.)	16.00	8.00	4.75
(160)	Tony Kubek (Dark background.)	45.00	22.50	13.50
(161)	Harvey Kuenn ("D" on cap.)	30.00	15.00	9.00
(162)	Harvey Kuenn (Plain cap.)	16.00	8.00	4.75
(163)	Harvey Kuenn ("SF" on cap.)	15.00	7.50	4.50
(164)	Whitey Kurowski	30.00	15.00	9.00
(165)	Eddie Lake	25.00	15.00	8.00
(166)	Jim Landis	9.00	4.50	2.75
(167)	Don Larsen	10.00	5.00	3.00
(168)	Bob Lemon (Glove not visible.)	15.00	7.50	4.50
(169)	Bob Lemon (Glove partially visible.)	25.00	12.50	7.50
(170)	Buddy Lewis	25.00	12.50	7.50
(171)	Johnny Lindell	35.00	17.50	10.00
(172)	Phil Linz	25.00	12.50	7.50
(173)	Don Lock	25.00	12.50	7.50
(174)	Whitey Lockman	9.00	4.50	2.75
(175)	Johnny Logan	9.00	4.50	2.75
(176)	Dale Long ("P" on cap.)	9.00	4.50	2.75
(177)	Dale Long ("C" on cap.)	20.00	10.00	6.00
(178)	Ed Lopat	10.00	5.00	3.00
(179)	Harry Lowery (Name misspelled.)	10.00	5.00	3.00
(180)	Harry Lowrey (Name correct.)	10.00	5.00	3.00
(181)	Sal Maglie	9.00	4.50	2.75
(182)	Art Mahaffey	10.00	5.00	3.00
(183)	Hank Majeski	9.00	4.50	2.75
(184)	Frank Malzone	16.00	8.00	4.75
(185)	Mickey Mantle (Batting, full-length.)	140.00	70.00	40.00
(186)	Mickey Mantle/Btg (Waist-up, "ck" in "Mickey" connected.)	120.00	60.00	35.00
(187)	Mickey Mantle/Btg (Waist-up, "c k" in "Mickey" connected.)	175.00	85.00	50.00
(188)	Mickey Mantle/Portrait	600.00	300.00	180.00
(189)	Martin Marion	20.00	10.00	6.00
(190)	Roger Maris	25.00	12.50	7.50
(191)	Willard Marshall (With and without "An Exhibit Card.")	10.00	5.00	3.00
(192)	Eddie Matthews (Name incorrect.)	16.00	8.00	4.75
(193)	Eddie Mathews (Name correct.)	30.00	15.00	9.00
(194)	Ed Mayo	10.00	5.00	3.00
(195)	Willie Mays/Btg	45.00	22.50	13.50
(196)	Willie Mays/Portait	60.00	30.00	18.00
(197)	Bill Mazeroski/Portrait	16.00	8.00	4.75
(198)	Bill Mazeroski/Btg	16.00	8.00	4.75
(199)	Ken McBride	15.00	7.50	4.50
(200)	Bamey McCaskey (McCosky)	13.50	6.75	4.00
(201)	Bamey McCoskey (McCosky)	200.00	100.00	50.00
(202)	Lindy McDaniel	9.00	4.50	2.75
(203a)	Gil McDougald ("MADE IN U.S.A." lower-right.)	15.00	7.50	4.50
(203b)	Gil McDougald ("PRINTED IN U.S.A." lower-right.)	15.00	7.50	4.50
(204)	Albert Mele	30.00	15.00	9.00
(205)	Sam Mele	20.00	10.00	6.00
(206)	Orestes Minoso ("C" on cap.)	12.50	6.25	3.75
(207)	Orestes Minoso (Sox on cap.)	9.00	4.50	2.75
(208)	Dale Mitchell	9.00	4.50	2.75
(209)	Wally Moon	12.00	6.00	3.50
(210)	Don Mueller	10.00	5.00	3.00
(211)	Stan Musial ("Made in USA" and "Printed in USA")	60.00	30.00	18.00
(212)	Stan Musial/Btg	70.00	35.00	20.00
(213)	Charley Neal	15.00	7.50	4.50
(214)	Don Newcombe (Shaking hands.)	25.00	12.50	7.50
(215)	Don Newcombe (Dodgers on jacket.)	9.00	4.50	2.75
(216)	Don Newcombe (Plain jacket.)	10.00	5.00	3.00
(217)	Hal Newhouser	35.00	17.50	10.00
(218)	Ron Northey	20.00	10.00	6.00
(219)	Bill O'Dell	9.00	4.50	2.75
(220)	Joe Page	20.00	10.00	6.00
(221)	Satchel Paige	90.00	45.00	25.00
(222)	Milt Pappas	9.00	4.50	2.75
(223)	Camilo Pascual	9.00	4.50	2.75
(224)	Albie Pearson	25.00	12.50	7.50
(225)	Johnny Pesky	9.00	4.50	2.75
(226)	Gary Peters	25.00	12.50	7.50
(227)	Dave Philley	9.00	4.50	2.75
(228)	Billy Pierce	9.00	4.50	2.75
(229)	Jimmy Piersall	15.00	7.50	4.50
(230)	Vada Pinson	12.50	6.25	3.75
(231)	Bob Porterfield	9.00	4.50	2.75
(232)	John "Boog" Powell	45.00	22.50	13.50
(233)	Vic Raschi	15.00	7.50	4.50
(234)	Harold "Peewee" Reese/Fldg (Ball partially visible.)	35.00	17.50	10.00
(235)	Harold "Peewee" Reese/Fldg (Ball not visible.)	25.00	12.50	7.50
(236)	Del Rice	12.50	6.25	3.75
(237)	Bobby Richardson	125.00	60.00	35.00

		NM	EX	VG
(238)	Phil Rizzuto (Has a small and large projection. The large projection is known in two forms: with "An Exhibit Card," and with "An Exhibit Card" scratched out.)	25.00	12.50	7.50
(239)	Robin Roberts (White signature.)	14.50	7.25	4.25
(240)	Robin Roberts (Black signature.)	25.00	12.50	7.50
(241)	Brooks Robinson	17.50	8.75	5.25
(242)	Eddie Robinson	9.00	4.50	2.75
(243)	Floyd Robinson	17.50	8.75	5.25
(244)	Frankie Robinson	60.00	30.00	18.00
(245)	Jackie Robinson	50.00	25.00	15.00
(246)	Preacher Roe	35.00	17.50	10.00
(247)	Bob Rogers (Rodgers)	30.00	15.00	9.00
(248)	Richard Rollins	25.00	12.50	7.50
(249)	Pete Runnels	13.50	6.75	4.00
(250)	John Sain	12.50	6.25	3.75
(251)	Ron Santo	25.00	12.50	7.50
(252)	Henry Sauer	10.00	5.00	3.00
(253)	Carl Sawatski ("M" on cap.)	9.00	4.50	2.75
(254)	Carl Sawatski ("P" on cap.)	9.00	4.50	2.75
(255)	Carl Sawatski (Plain cap.)	17.50	8.75	5.25
(256)	Johnny Schmitz	10.00	5.00	3.00
(257)	Red Schoendeinst (Schoendienst)/Fldg (Name in white.)	25.00	12.50	7.50
(258)	Red Schoendeinst (Schoendienst)/Fldg (Name in red-brown.)	30.00	15.00	9.00
(259)	Red Schoendinst (Schoendienst)/Btg	12.50	6.25	3.75
(260)	Herb Score ("C" on cap.)	15.00	7.50	4.50
(261)	Herb Score (Plain cap.)	17.50	8.75	5.25
(262)	Andy Seminick	9.00	4.50	2.75
(263)	Rip Sewell	20.00	10.00	6.00
(264)	Norm Siebern	9.00	4.50	2.75
(265)	Roy Sievers/Btg	15.00	7.50	4.50
(266)	Roy Sievers/Portrait ("W" on cap, light background.)	12.00	6.00	3.50
(267)	Roy Sievers/Portrait ("W" on cap, dark background.)	10.00	5.00	3.00
(268)	Roy Sievers/Portrait (Plain cap.)	20.00	10.00	6.00
(269)	Curt Simmons	10.00	5.00	3.00
(270)	Dick Sisler	10.00	5.00	3.00
(271)	Bill Skowron	12.50	6.25	3.75
(272)	Bill "Moose" Skowron	65.00	32.50	20.00
(273)	Enos Slaughter	20.00	10.00	6.00
(274)	Duke Snider ("B" on cap.)	22.50	11.00	6.75
(275)	Duke Snider ("LA" on cap.)	20.00	10.00	6.00
(276)	Warren Spahn ("B" on cap.)	20.00	10.00	6.00
(277)	Warren Spahn ("M" on cap.)	20.00	10.00	6.00
(278)	Stanley Spence	16.00	8.00	4.75
(279)	Ed Stanky (Plain uniform. With and without "An Exhibit Card")	17.50	8.75	5.25
(280)	Ed Stanky (Giants uniform.)	10.00	5.00	3.00
(281)	Vern Stephens/Btg	10.00	5.00	3.00
(282)	Vern Stephens/Portrait	10.00	5.00	3.00
(283)	Ed Stewart	10.00	5.00	3.00
(284)	Snuffy Stirnweiss	12.50	6.25	3.75
(285)	George "Birdie" Tebbetts	17.50	8.75	5.25
(286)	Frankie Thomas (Photo actually Bob Skinner.)	35.00	17.50	10.00
(287)	Frank Thomas/Portrait ("Best Wishes.")	16.00	8.00	4.75
(288)	Lee Thomas	9.00	4.50	2.75
(289)	Bobby Thomson (With and without "An Exhibit Card")	25.00	12.50	7.50
(290)	Earl Torgeson (Braves uniform.)	9.00	4.50	2.75
(291)	Earl Torgeson (Plain uniform.)	10.00	5.00	3.00
(292)	Gus Triandos	12.00	6.00	3.50
(293)	Virgil Trucks	9.00	4.50	2.75
(294)	Johnny Vandermeer (VanderMeer)	25.00	12.50	7.50
(295)	Emil Verban	12.00	6.00	3.50
(296)	Mickey Vernon/Throwing	15.00	7.50	4.50
(297)	Mickey Vernon/Btg	9.00	4.50	2.75
(298)	Bill Voiselle	30.00	15.00	9.00
(299)	Leon Wagner	6.50	3.25	1.75
(300)	Eddie Waitkus/Throwing (Chicago uniform.)	40.00	20.00	12.00
(301)	Eddie Waitkus/Throwing (Plain uniform.)	10.00	5.00	3.00
(302)	Eddie Waitkus/Portrait	15.00	7.50	4.50
(303)	Dick Wakefield	10.00	5.00	3.00
(304)	Harry Walker	40.00	20.00	12.00
(305)	Bucky Walters	20.00	10.00	6.00
(306)	Pete Ward	75.00	37.50	22.50
(307)	Herman Wehmeier	10.00	5.00	3.00
(308)	Vic Wertz/Btg	9.00	4.50	2.75
(309)	Vic Wertz/Portrait	9.00	4.50	2.75
(310)	Wally Westlake	10.00	5.00	3.00
(311)	Wes Westrum	17.50	8.75	5.25
(312)	Billy Williams	20.00	10.00	6.00
(313)	Maurice Wills	15.00	7.50	4.50
(314)	Gene Woodling (White signature.)	9.00	4.50	2.75
(315)	Gene Woodling (Black signature.)	12.00	6.00	3.50
(316)	Taffy Wright	10.00	5.00	3.00
(317)	Carl Yastrazemski (Yastrzemski)	200.00	100.00	60.00
(318)	Al Zarilla	12.50	6.25	3.75
(319)	Gus Zernial (White signature.)	9.00	4.50	2.75
(320)	Gus Zernial (Black signature.)	12.00	6.00	3.50
(321)	Braves Team - 1948	50.00	25.00	15.00
(322)	Dodgers Team - 1949	75.00	37.50	22.50
(323)	Dodgers Team - 1952	65.00	32.50	20.00
(324)	Dodgers Team - 1955	125.00	60.00	35.00
(325)	Dodgers Team - 1956	60.00	30.00	18.00
(326)	Giants Team - 1951	60.00	30.00	18.00
(327a)	Giants Team - 1954 (Plain back.)	50.00	25.00	15.00
(328)	Indians Team - 1948	55.00	27.50	16.50
(329)	Indians Team - 1954	50.00	25.00	15.00
(330)	Phillies Team - 1950	40.00	20.00	12.00
(331)	Yankees Team - 1949	60.00	30.00	18.00
(332)	Yankees Team - 1950	65.00	32.50	20.00
(333)	Yankees Team - 1951	65.00	32.50	20.00
(334)	Yankees Team - 1952	70.00	35.00	20.00
(335)	Yankees Team - 1955	70.00	35.00	20.00
(336)	Yankees Team - 1956	70.00	35.00	20.00

1948 Baseball's Great Hall of Fame Exhibits

Titled "Baseball's Great Hall of Fame," this 32-player set features black and white player photos against a gray background. The photos are accented by Greek columns on either side with brief player information printed at the bottom. The blank-backed cards are unnumbered and are listed here alphabetically. The cards measure 3-3/8" x 3-3/8". Collectors should be aware that 24 cards from this set were reprinted on whiter stock in 1974.

		NM	EX	VG
	Complete Set (33):	500.00	250.00	150.00
	Common Player:	7.50	3.75	2.25
(1)	Grover Cleveland Alexander	15.00	7.50	4.50
(2)	Roger Bresnahan	7.50	3.75	2.25
(3)	Frank Chance	7.50	3.75	2.25
(4)	Jack Chesbro	7.50	3.75	2.25
(5)	Fred Clarke	7.50	3.75	2.25
(6)	Ty Cobb	55.00	27.50	16.50
(7)	Mickey Cochrane	7.50	3.75	2.25
(8)	Eddie Collins	7.50	3.75	2.25
(9)	Hugh Duffy	7.50	3.75	2.25
(10)	Johnny Evers	7.50	3.75	2.25
(11)	Frankie Frisch	7.50	3.75	2.25
(12)	Lou Gehrig	35.00	17.50	10.00
(13)	Clark Griffith	7.50	3.75	2.25
(14)	Robert "Lefty" Grove	7.50	3.75	2.25
(15)	Rogers Hornsby	10.00	5.00	3.00
(16)	Carl Hubbell	7.50	3.75	2.25
(17)	Hughie Jennings	7.50	3.75	2.25
(18)	Walter Johnson	15.00	7.50	4.50
(19)	Willie Keeler	7.50	3.75	2.25
(20)	Napolean Lajoie	7.50	3.75	2.25
(21)	Connie Mack	7.50	3.75	2.25
(22)	Christy Matthewson (Mathewson)	20.00	10.00	6.00
(23)	John J. McGraw	7.50	3.75	2.25
(24)	Eddie Plank	7.50	3.75	2.25
(25)	Babe Ruth/Btg	60.00	30.00	18.00
(26)	Babe Ruth (Standing with bats.)	250.00	125.00	75.00
(27)	George Sisler	7.50	3.75	2.25
(28)	Tris Speaker	10.00	5.00	3.00
(29)	Joe Tinker	7.50	3.75	2.25
(30)	Rube Waddell	7.50	3.75	2.25
(31)	Honus Wagner	25.00	12.50	7.50
(32)	Ed Walsh	7.50	3.75	2.25
(33)	Cy Young	15.00	7.50	4.50

1953 Canadian Exhibits

This Canadian-issued set consists of 64 cards and includes both major leaguers and players from the Montreal Royals of the International League. The cards are slightly smaller than the U.S. exhibit cards, measuring 3-1/4" x 5-1/4",

and are numbered. The blank-backed cards were printed on gray stock. Card numbers 1-32 have a green or red tint, while card numbers 33-64 have a blue or reddish-brown tint.

		NM	EX	VG
	Complete Set (64):	1,750	875.00	525.00
	Common Player (1-32):	30.00	15.00	9.00
	Common Player (33-64):	18.00	9.00	5.50
1	Preacher Roe	40.00	20.00	12.00
2	Luke Easter	40.00	20.00	12.00
3	Gene Bearden	30.00	15.00	9.00
4	Chico Carrasquel	40.00	20.00	12.00
5	Vic Raschi	40.00	20.00	12.00
6	Monty (Monte) Irvin	60.00	30.00	18.00
7	Henry Sauer	30.00	15.00	9.00
8	Ralph Branca	40.00	20.00	12.00
9	Ed Stanky	40.00	20.00	12.00
10	Sam Jethroe	30.00	15.00	9.00
11	Larry Doby	60.00	30.00	18.00
12	Hal Newhouser	60.00	30.00	18.00
13	Gil Hodges	100.00	50.00	30.00
14	Harry Brecheen	30.00	15.00	9.00
15	Ed Lopat	40.00	20.00	12.00
16	Don Newcombe	50.00	25.00	15.00
17	Bob Feller	120.00	60.00	36.00
18	Tommy Holmes	30.00	15.00	9.00
19	Jackie Robinson	130.00	65.00	40.00
20	Roy Campanella	110.00	55.00	33.00
21	Harold "Peewee" Reese	100.00	50.00	30.00
22	Ralph Kiner	120.00	60.00	36.00
23	Dom DiMaggio	50.00	25.00	15.00
24	Bobby Doerr	60.00	30.00	18.00
25	Phil Rizzuto	60.00	30.00	18.00
26	Bob Elliott	30.00	15.00	9.00
27	Tom Henrich	40.00	20.00	12.00
28	Joe DiMaggio	400.00	200.00	120.00
29	Harry Lowery (Lowrey)	30.00	15.00	9.00
30	Ted Williams	150.00	75.00	45.00
31	Bob Lemon	80.00	40.00	24.00
32	Warren Spahn	100.00	50.00	30.00
33	Don Hoak	50.00	25.00	15.00
34	Bob Alexander	30.00	15.00	9.00
35	John Simmons	30.00	15.00	9.00
36	Steve Lembo	30.00	15.00	9.00
37	Norman Larker	40.00	20.00	12.00
38	Bob Ludwick	30.00	15.00	9.00
39	Walter Moryn	40.00	20.00	12.00
40	Charlie Thompson	30.00	15.00	9.00
41	Ed Roebuck	40.00	20.00	12.00
42	Russell Rose	30.00	15.00	9.00
43	Edmundo (Sandy) Amoros	50.00	25.00	15.00
44	Bob Milliken	30.00	15.00	9.00
45	Art Fabbro	30.00	15.00	9.00
46	Spook Jacobs	30.00	15.00	9.00
47	Carmen Mauro	30.00	15.00	9.00
48	Walter Fiala	30.00	15.00	9.00
49	Rocky Nelson	30.00	15.00	9.00
50	Tom La Sorda (Lasorda)	120.00	60.00	35.00
51	Ronnie Lee	30.00	15.00	9.00
52	Hampton Coleman	30.00	15.00	9.00
53	Frank Marchio	30.00	15.00	9.00
54	William Sampson	30.00	15.00	9.00
55	Gil Mills	30.00	15.00	9.00
56	Al Ronning	30.00	15.00	9.00
57	Stan Musial	150.00	75.00	45.00
58	Walker Cooper	18.00	9.00	5.50
59	Mickey Vernon	18.00	9.00	5.50
60	Del Ennis	18.00	9.00	5.50
61	Walter Alston	80.00	40.00	24.00
62	Dick Sisler	18.00	9.00	5.50
63	Billy Goodman	18.00	9.00	5.50
64	Alex Kellner	18.00	9.00	5.50

1955 Exhibits - Post Card Backs

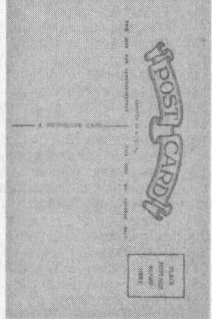

For an unknkown purpose, the 64 Exhibit cards issued in 1955 (including many re-issued from earlier years) were produced in a very limited edition with a post card back, as opposed to the blank-back format usually found on the 3-3/8" x 5-3/8" cards. The postcard back can be found with or without the words "A Mutoscope Card."

		NM	EX	VG
	Complete Set (64):	6,000	3,000	1,800
	Common Player:	50.00	30.00	20.00
(1)	Joe Adcock	50.00	25.00	15.00
(2)	Ritchie (Richie) Ashburn	90.00	45.00	27.00
(3)	Toby Atwell	50.00	25.00	15.00
(4)	Gene Baker	50.00	25.00	15.00
(5)	Ernie Banks (Bat on shoulder, printed name.)	150.00	75.00	45.00
(6)	Matt Batts	50.00	25.00	15.00
(7)	Frank Baumholtz	50.00	25.00	15.00
(8)	Yogi Berra	150.00	75.00	45.00
(9)	Steve Bilko	50.00	25.00	15.00
(10)	Roy Campanella	125.00	62.00	37.00

		NM	EX	VG
(11)	Chico Carrasquel/Leaping	50.00	25.00	15.00
(12)	Alvin Dark (Giants)	50.00	25.00	15.00
(13)	Larry Doby	90.00	45.00	27.00
(14)	Walter Dropo	50.00	25.00	15.00
(15)	Del Ennis	50.00	25.00	15.00
(16)	Ferris Fain/Portrait	90.00	45.00	27.00
(17)	Bob Feller (Yours truly.)	200.00	100.00	60.00
(18)	Billy Goodman (Leaping)	90.00	45.00	27.00
(19)	Ted (Jim) Greengrass	50.00	25.00	15.00
(20)	Steve Gromek	50.00	25.00	15.00
(21)	Johnny Groth	50.00	25.00	15.00
(22)	Jim Hegan	50.00	25.00	15.00
(23)	Gene Hermanski	50.00	25.00	15.00
(24)	Gil Hodges (B on cap.)	100.00	50.00	30.00
(25)	Monty (Monte) Irvin	90.00	45.00	27.00
(26)	Al Kaline/Kneeling	150.00	75.00	45.00
(27)	George Kell	90.00	45.00	27.00
(28)	Alex Kellner	50.00	25.00	15.00
(29)	Ted Kluzewski (Kluszewski)/Btg	125.00	62.00	37.00
(30)	Bob Lemon (Glove not showing.)	90.00	45.00	27.00
(31)	Whitey Lockman	50.00	25.00	15.00
(32)	Ed Lopat	60.00	30.00	18.00
(33)	Sal Maglie	50.00	25.00	15.00
(34)	Mickey Mantle (Batting, waist-up.)	800.00	400.00	240.00
(35)	Ed Matthews (Mathews)	125.00	62.00	37.00
(36)	Willie Mays (Batting)	400.00	200.00	120.00
(37)	Gil McDougald	60.00	30.00	18.00
(38)	Sam Mele	50.00	25.00	15.00
(39)	Orestes Minoso (C on cap.)	90.00	45.00	27.00
(40)	Dale Mitchell	50.00	25.00	15.00
(41)	Stan Musial (Kneeling)	200.00	100.00	60.00
(42)	Andy Pafko (Yours truly.) (C on cap.)	50.00	25.00	15.00
(43)	Bob Porterfield	50.00	25.00	15.00
(44)	Vic Raschi	50.00	25.00	15.00
(45)	Harold "Peewee" Reese	125.00	62.00	37.00
(46)	Phil Rizzuto	125.00	62.00	37.00
(47)	Robin Roberts	90.00	45.00	27.00
(48)	Jackie Robinson	300.00	150.00	90.00
(49)	Henry Sauer	50.00	25.00	15.00
(50)	Johnny Schmitz	50.00	25.00	15.00
(51)	Red Schoendinst (Schoendienst)	90.00	45.00	27.00
(52)	Andy Seminick	50.00	25.00	15.00
(53)	Duke Snider (B on cap.)	125.00	62.00	37.00
(54)	Warren Spahn (B on cap.)	125.00	62.00	37.00
(55)	Vern Stephens/Portrait	50.00	25.00	15.00
(56)	Earl Torgeson (Braves uniform.)	50.00	25.00	15.00
(57)	Virgil Trucks	50.00	25.00	15.00
(58)	Mickey Vernon/Btg	50.00	25.00	15.00
(59)	Eddie Waitkus	50.00	25.00	15.00
(60)	Vic Wertz (Batting)	50.00	25.00	15.00
(61)	Gene Woodling	50.00	25.00	15.00
(62)	Gus Zernial	50.00	25.00	15.00
(63)	Cleveland Indians 1954 American League Champions	300.00	150.00	90.00
(64)	New York Giants 1954 National League Champions	300.00	150.00	90.00

1959 Exhibits - Dad's Cookies

(See 1959 Dad's Cookies.)

1961 Exhibits - Wrigley Field

JOHN JOSEPH EVERS

Distributed at Chicago's Wrigley Field circa 1961, this 24-card set features members of the Baseball Hall of Fame. The cards measure 3-3/8" x 5-3/8" and include the player's full name along the bottom. They were printed on gray stock and have a postcard back or blank back. The set is unnumbered.

		NM	EX	VG
Complete Set (24):		750.00	375.00	225.00
Common Player:		10.00	5.00	3.00
(1)	Grover Cleveland Alexander	15.00	7.50	4.50
(2)	Adrian Constantine Anson	12.50	6.25	3.75
(3)	John Franklin Baker	10.00	5.00	3.00
(4)	Roger Phillip Bresnahan	10.00	5.00	3.00
(5)	Mordecai Peter Brown	10.00	5.00	3.00
(6)	Frank Leroy Chance	10.00	5.00	3.00
(7)	Tyrus Raymond Cobb	145.00	75.00	45.00
(8)	Edward Trowbridge Collins	10.00	5.00	3.00
(9)	James J. Collins	10.00	5.00	3.00
(10)	John Joseph Evers	10.00	5.00	3.00
(11)	Henry Louis Gehrig	145.00	75.00	45.00
(12)	Clark C. Griffith	10.00	5.00	3.00
(13)	Walter Perry Johnson	25.00	12.50	7.50
(14)	Anthony Michael Lazzeri	10.00	5.00	3.00
(15)	James Walter Vincent Maranville	10.00	5.00	3.00
(16)	Christopher Mathewson	30.00	15.00	9.00
(17)	John Joseph McGraw	10.00	5.00	3.00
(18)	Melvin Thomas Ott	10.00	5.00	3.00
(19)	Herbert Jeffries Pennock	10.00	5.00	3.00
(20)	George Herman Ruth	180.00	90.00	55.00
(21)	Aloysius Harry Simmons	10.00	5.00	3.00
(22)	Tristram Speaker	25.00	12.50	7.50
(23)	Joseph B. Tinker	10.00	5.00	3.00
(24)	John Peter Wagner	40.00	20.00	12.00

1962 Pittsburgh Exhibits

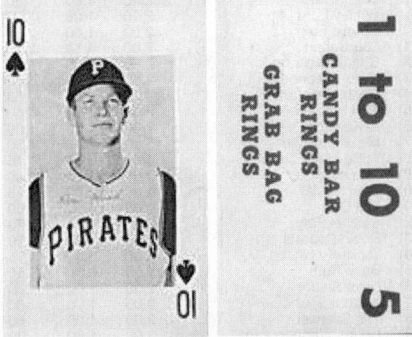

The attributed date is approximate since none is shown on the cards; nor is a credit line to the manufacturer. Player content suggests Pittsburgh was the center of distribution and veteran collectors report having received the cards in penny arcade vending machines at Kennywood Amusement Park near there. It has also been reported that the cards were given over the counter as prizes for getting a winning gumball from a machine. The 3-1/4" x 5-1/4" cards are printed in black-and-white, or red, black and white. They are usually blank-backed, but examples have been seen with apprarent prize references printed on back. Most of the card "denominations" can be found with more than one subject. Besides the ballplayers listed here, the set contained TV and movie cowboys, rock-and-roll stars, boxers, wrestlers and cartoon characters.

		NM	EX	VG
Complete Set (81):		2,500	1,250	750.00
Common Player:		5.00	2.50	1.50
AC	Bill Mazeroski	25.00	12.50	7.50
2C	Whitey Ford	30.00	15.00	9.00
2C	Al Kaline	20.00	10.00	6.00
2C	Pirates logo cartoon	5.00	2.50	1.50
4C	Frank Robinson	20.00	10.00	6.00
4C	Babe Ruth	125.00	65.00	35.00
5C	Wilmer Mizell	5.00	2.50	1.50
5C	Mickey Mantle	175.00	85.00	50.00
5C	Honus Wagner	35.00	17.50	10.00
6C	Eddie Mathews	20.00	10.00	6.00
6C	Willie Mays	90.00	45.00	27.00
7C	Dodgers' "Bum" cartoon logo	5.00	2.50	1.50
7C	Eddie Mathews	20.00	10.00	6.00
7C	Willie Mays	90.00	45.00	27.00
8C	Walter Johnson	20.00	10.00	6.00
8C	Mickey Mantle	175.00	85.00	50.00
8C	Wilmer Mizell	5.00	2.50	1.50
9C	Hank Aaron	90.00	45.00	27.00
9C	Frank Robinson	20.00	10.00	6.00
10C	Lew Burdette	5.00	2.50	1.50
JC	Harvey Haddix	5.00	2.50	1.50
JC	Bill Mazeroski	25.00	12.50	7.50
JC	Al McBean	5.00	2.50	1.50
QC	Ty Cobb	60.00	30.00	18.00
QC	Whitey Ford	30.00	15.00	9.00
QC	Don Leppert	5.00	2.50	1.50
KC	Al Kaline	20.00	10.00	6.00
KC	Honus Wagner	35.00	17.50	10.00
AS	Lew Burdette	5.00	2.50	1.50
AS	Ty Cobb	60.00	30.00	18.00
2S	Smoky Burgess	5.00	2.50	1.50
3S	Don Hoak	5.00	2.50	1.50
4S	Roy Face	5.00	2.50	1.50
5S	Roberto Clemente	125.00	65.00	35.00
5S	Danny Murtaugh	5.00	2.50	1.50
6S	Christy Mathewson	25.00	12.50	7.50
6S	Dick Stuart	5.00	2.50	1.50
7S	Christy Mathewson	25.00	12.50	7.50
7S	Dick Stuart	5.00	2.50	1.50
8S	Danny Murtaugh	5.00	2.50	1.50
9S	Roy Face	5.00	2.50	1.50

		NM	EX	VG
10S	Don Hoak	5.00	2.50	1.50
JS	Smoky Burgess	5.00	2.50	1.50
QS	Walter Johnson	20.00	10.00	6.00
QS	Babe Ruth	125.00	65.00	35.00
KS	Hank Aaron	90.00	45.00	27.00
KS	Harvey Haddix	5.00	2.50	1.50
AH	Don Drysdale	20.00	10.00	6.00
AH	Ken Boyer	5.00	2.50	1.50
2H	Satchel Paige	60.00	30.00	18.00
3H	Rocky Colavito	20.00	10.00	6.00
4H	Stan Musial	50.00	25.00	15.00
4H	Bobby Richardson	15.00	7.50	4.50
5H	Ken Boyer	5.00	2.50	1.50
5H	Harmon Killebrew	20.00	10.00	6.00
6H	Luis Aparicio	20.00	10.00	6.00
6H	Ralph Kiner	20.00	10.00	6.00
7H	Sandy Koufax	75.00	37.50	22.00
8H	Warren Spahn	20.00	10.00	6.00
9H	Jimmy Piersall	5.00	2.50	1.50
10H	Yogi Berra	30.00	15.00	9.00
10H	Ralph Kiner	20.00	10.00	6.00
JH	Orlando Cepeda	20.00	10.00	6.00
JH	Ken Boyer	5.00	2.50	1.50
QH	Roger Maris	75.00	37.50	22.00
QH	Stan Musial	50.00	25.00	15.00
KH	Bob Purkey	5.00	2.50	1.50
AD	Don Drysdale	20.00	10.00	6.00
AD	Don Hoak	5.00	2.50	1.50
2D	Satchel Paige	60.00	30.00	18.00
6D	Luis Aparicio	20.00	10.00	6.00
6D	Ernie Banks	25.00	12.50	7.50
7D	Bill Virdon	5.00	2.50	1.50
7D	Sandy Koufax	75.00	37.50	22.00
8D	Bob Skinner	5.00	2.50	1.50
9D	Dick Groat	5.00	2.50	1.50
10D	Vernon Law	5.00	2.50	1.50
JD	Joe Adcock	5.00	2.50	1.50
JD	Orlando Cepeda	20.00	10.00	6.00
QD	Roger Maris	75.00	37.50	22.00
KD	Bob Friend	5.00	2.50	1.50

1962 Statistic Back Exhibits

In 1962, the Exhibit Supply Co. added career statistics to the yearly set they produced. The black-and-white, unnumbered cards measure 3-3/8" x 5-3/8". The statistics found on the back are printed in black or red.

		NM	EX	VG
Complete Set (32):		500.00	250.00	150.00
Common Player:		6.00	3.00	1.75
Red Backs: 1.5X				
(1)	Hank Aaron	35.00	17.50	10.00
(2)	Luis Aparicio	15.00	7.50	4.50
(3)	Ernie Banks	25.00	12.50	7.50
(4)	Larry "Yogi" Berra	25.00	12.50	7.50
(5)	Ken Boyer	7.50	3.75	2.25
(6)	Lew Burdette	6.00	3.00	1.75
(7)	Norm Cash	7.50	3.75	2.25
(8)	Orlando Cepeda	15.00	7.50	4.50
(9)	Roberto Clemente	50.00	25.00	15.00
(10)	Rocky Colavito	15.00	7.50	4.50
(11)	Ed "Whitey" Ford	17.50	8.75	5.25
(12)	Nelson Fox	15.00	7.50	4.50
(13)	Tito Francona	6.00	3.00	1.75
(14)	Jim Gentile	6.00	3.00	1.75
(15)	Dick Groat	6.00	3.00	1.75
(16)	Don Hoak	6.00	3.00	1.75
(17)	Al Kaline	17.50	8.75	5.25
(18)	Harmon Killebrew	17.50	8.75	5.25
(19)	Sandy Koufax	30.00	15.00	9.00
(20)	Jim Landis	6.00	3.00	1.75
(21)	Art Mahaffey	6.00	3.00	1.75
(22)	Frank Malzone	6.00	3.00	1.75
(23)	Mickey Mantle	100.00	50.00	30.00
(24)	Roger Maris	17.50	8.75	5.25
(25)	Eddie Mathews	17.50	8.75	5.25
(26)	Willie Mays	35.00	17.50	10.00
(27)	Wally Moon	6.00	3.00	1.75
(28)	Stan Musial	30.00	15.00	9.00
(29)	Milt Pappas	6.00	3.00	1.75
(30)	Vada Pinson	7.50	3.75	2.25
(31)	Norm Siebern	6.00	3.00	1.75
(32)	Warren Spahn	17.50	8.75	5.25

1963 Statistic Back Exhibits

The Exhibit Supply Co. issued a 64-card set with career statistics on the backs of the cards in 1963. The unnumbered, black-and-white cards are printed on thick cardboard and measure 3-3/8" x 5-3/8" in size. The statistics on the back are only found printed in red.

		NM	EX	VG
	Complete Set (64):	900.00	450.00	275.00
	Common Player:	7.50	3.75	2.25
(1)	Hank Aaron	35.00	17.50	10.00
(2)	Luis Aparicio	15.00	7.50	4.50
(3)	Bob Aspromonte	7.50	3.75	2.25
(4)	Ernie Banks	25.00	12.50	7.50
(5)	Steve Barber	7.50	3.75	2.25
(6)	Earl Battey	7.50	3.75	2.25
(7)	Larry "Yogi" Berra	25.00	12.50	7.50
(8)	Ken Boyer	9.00	4.50	2.75
(9)	Lew Burdette	7.50	3.75	2.25
(10)	Johnny Callison	7.50	3.75	2.25
(11)	Norm Cash	9.00	4.50	2.75
(12)	Orlando Cepeda	15.00	7.50	4.50
(13)	Dean Chance	7.50	3.75	2.25
(14)	Tom Cheney	7.50	3.75	2.25
(15)	Roberto Clemente	40.00	20.00	12.00
(16)	Rocky Colavito	15.00	7.50	4.50
(17)	Choo Choo Coleman	7.50	3.75	2.25
(18)	Roger Craig	7.50	3.75	2.25
(19)	Joe Cunningham	7.50	3.75	2.25
(20)	Don Drysdale	15.00	7.50	4.50
(21)	Dick Farrell	7.50	3.75	2.25
(22)	Ed "Whitey" Ford	20.00	10.00	6.00
(23)	Nelson Fox	15.00	7.50	4.50
(24)	Tito Francona	7.50	3.75	2.25
(25)	Jim Gentile	7.50	3.75	2.25
(26)	Tony Gonzalez	7.50	3.75	2.25
(27)	Dick Groat	7.50	3.75	2.25
(28)	Ray Herbert	7.50	3.75	2.25
(29)	Chuck Hinton	7.50	3.75	2.25
(30)	Don Hoak	7.50	3.75	2.25
(31)	Frank Howard	9.00	4.50	2.75
(32)	Ken Hubbs	12.00	6.00	3.50
(33)	Joey Jay	7.50	3.75	2.25
(34)	Al Kaline	15.00	7.50	4.50
(35)	Harmon Killebrew	15.00	7.50	4.50
(36)	Sandy Koufax	30.00	15.00	9.00
(37)	Harvey Kuenn	7.50	3.75	2.25
(38)	Jim Landis	7.50	3.75	2.25
(39)	Art Mahaffey	7.50	3.75	2.25
(40)	Frank Malzone	7.50	3.75	2.25
(41)	Mickey Mantle	150.00	75.00	45.00
(42)	Roger Maris	15.00	7.50	4.50
(43)	Eddie Mathews	15.00	7.50	4.50
(44)	Willie Mays	35.00	17.50	10.00
(45)	Bill Mazeroski	15.00	7.50	4.50
(46)	Ken McBride	7.50	3.75	2.25
(47)	Wally Moon	7.50	3.75	2.25
(48)	Stan Musial	30.00	15.00	9.00
(49)	Charlie Neal	7.50	3.75	2.25
(50)	Bill O'Dell	7.50	3.75	2.25
(51)	Milt Pappas	7.50	3.75	2.25
(52)	Camilo Pascual	7.50	3.75	2.25
(53)	Jimmy Piersall	9.00	4.50	2.75
(54)	Vada Pinson	9.00	4.50	2.75
(55)	Brooks Robinson	20.00	10.00	6.00
(56)	Frankie Robinson	20.00	10.00	6.00
(57)	Pete Runnels	7.50	3.75	2.25
(58)	Ron Santo	9.00	4.50	2.75
(59)	Norm Siebern	7.50	3.75	2.25
(60)	Warren Spahn	20.00	10.00	6.00
(61)	Lee Thomas	7.50	3.75	2.25
(62)	Leon Wagner	7.50	3.75	2.25
(63)	Billy Williams	15.00	7.50	4.50
(64)	Maurice Wills	13.50	6.75	4.00

1974 Baseball's Great Hall of Fame Exhibits

Two dozen of the cards from the 1948 issue were reprinted in 1974 by the original publisher, Exhibit Supply Co., Chicago. The 1974 reissues are in the same 3-3/8" x 5-3/8" format as the originals, and in the same design. They are blank-backed and printed on a thinner, slicker cardboard stock than the 1948 cards. The reprints can be found printed in black, blue or brown. The unnumbered cards are checklisted here alphabetically.

		NM	EX	VG
	Complete Set (24):	20.00	10.00	6.00
	Common Player:	3.00	1.50	.90
(1)	Grover Cleveland Alexander	3.50	1.75	1.00
(2)	Roger Bresnahan	3.00	1.50	.90
(3)	Frank Chance	3.00	1.50	.90
(4)	Jack Chesbro	3.00	1.50	.90
(5)	Fred Clarke	3.00	1.50	.90
(6)	Ty Cobb	10.00	5.00	3.00
(7)	Mickey Cochrane	3.00	1.50	.90
(8)	Eddie Collins	3.00	1.50	.90
(9)	Johnny Evers	3.00	1.50	.90
(10)	Frankie Frisch	3.00	1.50	.90
(11)	Clark Griffith	3.00	1.50	.90
(12)	Robert "Lefty" Grove	3.00	1.50	.90
(13)	Rogers Hornsby	4.00	2.00	1.25

(14)	Hughie Jennings	3.00	1.50	.90
(15)	Walter Johnson	5.00	2.50	1.50
(16)	Connie Mack	3.00	1.50	.90
(17)	Christy Mathewson	5.00	2.50	1.50
(18)	John McGraw	3.00	1.50	.90
(19)	George Sisler	3.00	1.50	.90
(20)	Joe Tinker	3.00	1.50	.90
(21)	Rube Waddell	3.00	1.50	.90
(22)	Honus Wagner	6.00	3.00	1.75
(23)	Ed Walsh	3.00	1.50	.90
(24)	Cy Young	5.00	2.50	1.50

1977 Baseball's Great Hall of Fame Exhibits

A second set of "Baseball's Great Hall of Fame" exhibit cards was produced in 1977, most cards featuring more recent players than the 1948 issue. The cards were produced in the same 3-3/8" x 5-3/8" blank-back, black-and-white design as the 1948 cards, and are a genuine product of Exhibit Supply Co., Chicago. The new cards were printed on an extremely high grade of semi-gloss cardboard, in contrast to the earlier versions. Production was announced at 500,000 cards. The unnumbered cards are checklisted here alphabetically.

		NM	EX	VG
	Complete Set (32):	35.00	17.50	10.00
	Common Player:	2.00	1.00	.60
(1)	Luke Appling	2.00	1.00	.60
(2)	Ernie Banks	3.00	1.50	.90
(3)	Yogi Berra	3.00	1.50	.90
(4)	Roy Campanella	3.00	1.50	.90
(5)	Roberto Clemente	9.00	4.50	2.75
(6)	Alvin Dark	2.00	1.00	.60
(7)	Joe DiMaggio	9.00	4.50	2.75
(8)	Bob Feller	2.00	1.00	.60
(9)	Whitey Ford	2.00	1.00	.60
(10)	Jimmie Foxx	2.00	1.00	.60
(11)	Lou Gehrig	9.00	4.50	2.75
(12)	Charlie Gehringer	2.00	1.00	.60
(13)	Hank Greenberg	2.50	1.25	.70
(14)	Gabby Hartnett	2.00	1.00	.60
(15)	Carl Hubbell	2.00	1.00	.60
(16)	Al Kaline	2.00	1.00	.60
(17)	Mickey Mantle	15.00	7.50	4.50
(18)	Willie Mays	6.00	3.00	1.75
(19)	Johnny Mize	2.00	1.00	.60
(20)	Stan Musial	4.00	2.00	1.25
(21)	Mel Ott	2.00	1.00	.60
(22)	Satchel Paige	2.50	1.25	.70
(23)	Robin Roberts	2.00	1.00	.60
(24)	Jackie Robinson	6.00	3.00	1.75
(25)	Babe Ruth	12.00	6.00	3.50
(26)	Duke Snider	2.00	1.00	.60
(27)	Warren Spahn	2.00	1.00	.60
(28)	Tris Speaker	2.00	1.00	.60
(29)	Honus Wagner	3.00	1.50	.90
(30)	Ted Williams	6.00	3.00	1.75
(31)	Rudy York	2.00	1.00	.60
(32)	Cy Young	2.00	1.00	.60

1980 Exhibits

Following the purchase of the "remains" of the Exhibit Supply Co., by a collector in the late 1970s, this set of Exhibits was issued in 1980. The set utilized photos from earlier issues in the same 3-3/8" x 5-3/8" size. Each card carries a notation in white at the bottom, "An Exhibit Card 1980," to distinguish them from the older version. Sets could be purchased printed in sepia, red or blue, at $4.50 per set. A total of 5,000 sets were reported printed. The unnumbered cards are checklisted here alphabetically.

		NM	EX	VG
	Complete Set (32):	40.00	20.00	12.00
	Common Player:	2.00	1.00	.60
(1)	Johnny Antonelli	2.00	1.00	.60
(2)	Richie Ashburn	2.00	1.00	.60
(3)	Earl Averill	2.00	1.00	.60
(4)	Ernie Banks	4.00	2.00	1.25
(5)	Ewell Blackwell	2.00	1.00	.60
(6)	Lou Brock	2.00	1.00	.60
(7)	Dean Chance	2.00	1.00	.60
(8)	Roger Craig	2.00	1.00	.60
(9)	Lou Gehrig	20.00	10.00	6.00
(10)	Gil Hodges	2.00	1.00	.60
(11)	Jack Jensen	2.00	1.00	.60
(12)	Willie Keeler	2.00	1.00	.60
(13)	George Kell	2.00	1.00	.60
(14)	Alex Kellner	2.00	1.00	.60
(15)	Harmon Killebrew	2.00	1.00	.60
(16)	Dale Long	2.00	1.00	.60
(17)	Sal Maglie	2.00	1.00	.60

(18)	Roger Maris	4.00	2.00	1.25
(19)	Willie Mays	13.50	6.75	4.00
(20)	Minnie Minoso	2.00	1.00	.60
(21)	Stan Musial	10.00	5.00	3.00
(22)	Billy Pierce	2.00	1.00	.60
(23)	Jimmy Piersall	2.00	1.00	.60
(24)	Eddie Plank	2.00	1.00	.60
(25)	Pete Reiser	2.00	1.00	.60
(26)	Brooks Robinson	2.00	1.00	.60
(27)	Pete Runnels	2.00	1.00	.60
(28)	Herb Score	2.00	1.00	.60
(29)	Warren Spahn	2.00	1.00	.60
(30)	Billy Williams	2.00	1.00	.60
(31)	1948 Boston Braves Team	3.00	1.50	.90
(32)	1948 Cleveland Indians Team	3.00	1.50	.90

1980 Hall of Fame Exhibits

Following the purchase of the "remains" of the Exhibit Supply Co., by a collector in the late 1970s, this set of Exhibits was issued in 1980. The set utilizes photos from earlier issues in the same 3-3/8" x 5-3/8" size. Each card has a notation in white at the bottom, "An Exhibit Card 1980 Hall Of Fame," to distinguish them from the older issues. Sets could be purchased printed in sepia, red or blue for $5. The unnumbered cards are checklisted here alphabetically.

		NM	EX	VG
	Complete Set (32):	25.00	12.50	7.50
	Common Player:	2.00	1.00	.60
(1)	Grover Cleveland Alexander	2.50	1.25	.70
(2)	Lou Boudreau	2.00	1.00	.60
(3)	Roger Bresnahan	2.00	1.00	.60
(4)	Roy Campanella	2.00	1.00	.60
(5)	Frank Chance	2.00	1.00	.60
(6)	Ty Cobb	5.00	2.50	1.50
(7)	Mickey Cochrane	2.00	1.00	.60
(8)	Dizzy Dean	2.50	1.25	.70
(9)	Joe DiMaggio	6.00	3.00	1.75
(10)	Bill Dickey	2.00	1.00	.60
(11)	Johnny Evers	2.00	1.00	.60
(12)	Jimmy Foxx	2.50	1.25	.70
(13)	Vernon Gomez	2.00	1.00	.60
(14)	Robert "Lefty" Grove	2.00	1.00	.60
(15)	Hank Greenberg	2.50	1.25	.70
(16)	Rogers Hornsby	2.00	1.00	.60
(17)	Carl Hubbell	2.00	1.00	.60
(18)	Hughie Jennings	2.00	1.00	.60
(19)	Walter Johnson	2.50	1.25	.70
(20)	Napoleon Lajoie	2.00	1.00	.60
(21)	Bob Lemon	2.00	1.00	.60
(22)	Mickey Mantle	12.00	6.00	3.50
(23)	Christy Mathewson	2.00	1.00	.60
(24)	Mel Ott	2.00	1.00	.60
(25)	Satchel Paige	2.50	1.25	.70
(26)	Jackie Robinson	4.00	2.00	1.25
(27)	Babe Ruth	9.00	4.50	2.75
(28)	Tris Speaker	2.00	1.00	.60
(29)	Joe Tinker	2.00	1.00	.60
(30)	Honus Wagner	3.00	1.50	.90
(31)	Ted Williams	4.00	2.00	1.25
(32)	Cy Young	2.50	1.25	.70

1990s Exhibit Card Unauthorized Reprints

Sometime during the 1990s (and possibly continuing today), unauthorized reprints of 16 popular Exhibit cards from the 1940s and 1950s were made. Besides printing anomalies on front resulting from re-screening genuine cards, the reprints are on the wrong weight (too thin) and color (too white on back) of cardboard. Collectors should use caution when purchasing any of the cards found in this group. Because the reprints are unauthorized, they have no collector value.

Complete Set (16):
(1)   Hank Aaron
(2)   Yogi Berra
(3)   Roy Campanella
(4)   Whitey Ford/Pitching
(5)   Nelson Fox
(6)   Gil Hodges ("B"on cap.)
(7)   Mickey Mantle/Btg
        (Waist-up, "ck" in "Mickey"
        connected.)
(8)   Willie Mays/Btg
(9)   Stan Musial/Kneling
(10) Don Newcombe
        ("Dodgers" on jacket.)
(11) Harold "Peewee" Reese
        (Ball partially visible.)
(12) Duke Snider ("B" on cap.)
(13) Warren Spahn ("B" on cap.)
(14) Ted Williams (#9 not showing)
(15) 1956 Brooklyn Dodgers
(16) 1956 N.Y. Yankees

1910 E-UNC Candy

Little is known about these 1910-era cards except that they appear to have been cut from a candy box. Printed in blue or red duo-tone and blank-backed, the cards measure about 2-3/4" per side. A 1-3/8" x 2-1/2" central image has a player photo with a diamond design around. Player identification is in a white strip at bottom.

	NM	EX	VG
Common Player:	1,000	500.00	300.00
(1) "Ty" Cobb	6,000	3,000	1,800
(2) Eddie Collins	1,000	500.00	300.00
(3) Johnny Evers	1,000	500.00	300.00
(4) "Christy" Mathewson	2,000	1,000	600.00
(5) "Honus" Wagner	3,500	1,750	1,050
(6) "Cy" Young (Photo actually Irv Young)	750.00	370.00	220.00

1936 E-UNC Candy

These cards appear to be a secondary use of the center portions of the 1936 S and S Game cards, having the same player photos and data in a size which varies from about 1-3/4" to 1-7/8" wide and between 2-3/8" and 2-1/2" tall. These differ in that instead of the green backs found on most of the game cards, these have plain backs which are sometimes found with a rubber-stamped message to present the card for a free gift or candy bar. These stamps indicate the cards were used as a prize premium in an as yet unidentified candy company's promotion. With more than half of the S and S players known in this candy company version, it is not unreasonable to assume the checklists for both sets are the same.

	NM	EX	VG
Complete Set (52):	3,000	1,500	900.00
Common Player:	45.00	22.50	13.50
(1) Luke Appling	90.00	45.00	25.00
(2) Earl Averill	90.00	45.00	25.00
(3) Zeke Bonura	45.00	22.50	13.50
(4) Dolph Camilli	45.00	22.50	13.50
(5) Ben Cantwell	45.00	22.50	13.50
(6) Phil Cavaretta (Cavarretta)	45.00	22.50	13.50
(7) Rip Collins	45.00	22.50	13.50
(8) Joe Cronin	90.00	45.00	25.00
(9) Frank Crosetti	60.00	30.00	18.00
(10) Kiki Cuyler	90.00	45.00	25.00

(11) Virgil Davis	45.00	22.50	13.50
(12) Frank Demaree	45.00	22.50	13.50
(13) Paul Derringer	45.00	22.50	13.50
(14) Bill Dickey	120.00	60.00	35.00
(15) Woody English	45.00	22.50	13.50
(16) Fred Fitzsimmons	45.00	22.50	13.50
(17) Richard Ferrell	90.00	45.00	25.00
(18) Pete Fox	45.00	22.50	13.50
(19) Jimmy Foxx	150.00	75.00	45.00
(20) Larry French	45.00	22.50	13.50
(21) Frank Frisch	100.00	50.00	30.00
(22) August Galan	45.00	22.50	13.50
(23) Chas. Gehringer	100.00	50.00	30.00
(24) John Gill	45.00	22.50	13.50
(25) Charles Grimm	45.00	22.50	13.50
(26) Mule Haas	45.00	22.50	13.50
(27) Stanley Hack	45.00	22.50	13.50
(28) Bill Hallahan	45.00	22.50	13.50
(29) Melvin Harder	45.00	22.50	13.50
(30) Gabby Hartnett	90.00	45.00	25.00
(31) Ray Hayworth	45.00	22.50	13.50
(32) Ralston Hemsley	45.00	22.50	13.50
(33) Bill Herman	90.00	45.00	25.00
(34) Frank Higgins	45.00	22.50	13.50
(35) Carl Hubbell	120.00	60.00	35.00
(36) Bill Jurges	45.00	22.50	13.50
(37) Vernon Kennedy	45.00	22.50	13.50
(38) Chuck Klein	90.00	45.00	25.00
(39) Mike Kreevich	45.00	22.50	13.50
(40) Bill Lee	45.00	22.50	13.50
(41) Jos. Medwick	90.00	45.00	25.00
(42) Van Mungo	45.00	22.50	13.50
(43) James O'Dea	45.00	22.50	13.50
(44) Mel Ott	120.00	60.00	35.00
(45) Rip Radcliff	45.00	22.50	13.50
(46) Pie Traynor	90.00	45.00	25.00
(47) Arky Vaughan (Vaughn)	90.00	45.00	25.00
(48) Joe Vosmik	45.00	22.50	13.50
(49) Lloyd Waner	90.00	45.00	25.00
(50) Paul Waner	90.00	45.00	25.00
(51) Lon Warneke	45.00	22.50	13.50
(52) Floyd Young	45.00	22.50	13.50

1909-11 E90-1, E90-2, E90-3 American Caramel

(See 1909-11 American Caramel Co. for checklists, values.)

1908-09 E91 American Caramel Co.

(See 1908-09 American Caramel Co. for checklists, values.)

1909 E92 Nadja Caramels

(See 1909 Nadja Caramels.)

1910 E93 Standard Caramel Co.

(See 1910 Standard Caramel Co. for checklist, values.)

1911 E94

(See 1911 George Close Candy Co. for checklist and value data.)

1909 E95 Philadelphia Caramel

(See 1909 Philadelphia Caramel for checklist, price guide.)

1910 E96 Philadelphia Caramel

(See 1910 Philadelphia Caramel for checklist, values.)

1910 E98 "Set of 30"

This set of 30 subjects was issued in 1910 and is closely related to several other early candy issues that are nearly identical. The cards measure 1-1/2" x 2-3/4" and feature color lithograph player pictures. The backs, printed in brown, contain a checklist of the set but no advertising or other information indicating the manufacturer. The set was designated E98 by the "American Card Catalog." While the cards are unnumbered, they are listed here according to the numbers on the back checklist. Some or all of the cards may be found with different colored backgrounds. Mathewsons' card is only one in the set with the caption set in serif type.

	NM	EX	VG
Complete Set (30):	125,000	62,500	37,500
Common Player:	1,500	480.00	180.00
(1) Christy Matthewson (Mathewson)	12,000	6,000	3,500
(2) John McGraw	4,000	2,000	1,200
(3) Johnny Kling	1,500	480.00	200.00
(4) Frank Chance	4,000	2,000	1,200
(5) "Hans" Wagner	17,500	8,750	5,250

(6) Fred Clarke	4,000	2,000	1,200
(7) Roger Bresnahan	4,000	2,000	1,200
(8) Hal Chase	2,000	800.00	350.00
(9) Russ Ford	1,200	480.00	180.00
(10) "Ty" Cobb	18,000	9,000	5,500
(11) Hughey Jennings	4,000	2,000	1,200
(12) Chief Bender	4,000	2,000	1,200
(13) Ed Walsh	2,750	1,500	400.00
(14) "Cy" Young (Picture actually Irv Young.)	9,000	3,000	1,500
(15) Al Bridwell	1,500	480.00	180.00
(16) Miner Brown	4,000	2,000	1,200
(17) George Mullin	1,500	480.00	180.00
(18) Chief Meyers	1,500	480.00	180.00
(19) Hippo Vaughn	3,500	1,750	400.00
(20) Red Dooin	1,500	480.00	180.00
(21) Fred Tenny (Tenney)	3,000	1,500	400.00
(22) Larry McLean	1,500	480.00	180.00
(23) Nap Lajoie	5,000	2,500	1,000
(24) Joe Tinker	4,000	2,000	1,200
(25) Johnny Evers	4,000	2,000	1,200
(26) Harry Davis	1,500	480.00	180.00
(27) Eddie Collins	4,000	2,000	1,200
(28) Bill Dahlen	3,000	1,500	500.00
(29) "Connie" Mack	5,000	2,500	1,000
(30) Jack Coombs	3,500	1,750	400.00

1909 E101 "Set of 50"

This 50-card set is closely related to the E92 issues by Nadja, Croft's, Dockman, etc. The fronts of the 1-1/2" x 2-3/4" E101 cards are identical to the E92 set, but the back is "anonymous," containing no advertising or other information regarding the set's sponsor. The backs read simply "This card is one of a set of 50 Base Ball Players Prominent Members of National and American Leagues."

	NM	EX	VG
Complete Set (50):	60,000	30,000	15,000
Common Player:	750.00	375.00	220.00
(1) Jack Barry	750.00	375.00	220.00
(2) Harry Bemis	750.00	375.00	220.00
(3) Chief Bender (White hat.)	2,800	1,400	700.00
(4) Chief Bender (Striped hat.)	3,200	1,600	950.00
(5) Bill Bergen	750.00	375.00	220.00
(6) Bob Bescher	750.00	375.00	220.00
(7) Al Bridwell	1,200	600.00	300.00
(8) Doc Casey	750.00	375.00	220.00
(9) Frank Chance	3,200	1,600	950.00
(10) Hal Chase	2,400	1,200	650.00
(11) Ty Cobb	15,000	7,500	4,000
(12) Eddie Collins	3,200	1,600	950.00
(13) Sam Crawford	3,200	1,600	950.00
(14) Harry Davis	1,200	600.00	375.00
(15) Art Devlin	750.00	375.00	220.00
(16) Wild Bill Donovan	750.00	375.00	220.00
(17) Red Dooin	750.00	375.00	220.00
(18) Mickey Doolan	750.00	375.00	220.00
(19) Patsy Dougherty	750.00	375.00	220.00
(20) Larry Doyle (With bat.)	750.00	375.00	220.00
(21) Larry Doyle/Throwing	750.00	375.00	220.00
(22) Johnny Evers	3,200	1,600	950.00
(23) George Gibson	750.00	375.00	220.00
(24) Topsy Hartsel	750.00	375.00	220.00
(25) Fred Jacklitsch	750.00	375.00	220.00
(26) Hugh Jennings	3,200	1,600	950.00
(27) Red Kleinow	750.00	375.00	220.00
(28) Otto Knabe	750.00	375.00	220.00
(29) Jack Knight	750.00	375.00	220.00
(30) Nap Lajoie	3,200	1,600	950.00
(31) Hans Lobert	750.00	375.00	220.00
(32) Sherry Magee	750.00	375.00	220.00
(33) Christy Matthewson (Mathewson)	10,500	5,200	3,000
(34) John McGraw	3,200	1,600	950.00
(35) Larry McLean	750.00	375.00	220.00
(36) Dots Miller/Btg	750.00	375.00	220.00
(37) Dots Miller/Fldg	750.00	375.00	220.00
(38) Danny Murphy	750.00	375.00	220.00
(39) Bill O'Hara	750.00	375.00	220.00
(40) Germany Schaefer	1,200	600.00	400.00
(41) Admiral Schlei	750.00	375.00	220.00
(42) Boss Schmidt	750.00	375.00	220.00
(43) Johnny Seigle	1,200	600.00	400.00
(44) Dave Shean	750.00	375.00	220.00
(45) Boss Smith (Schmidt)	750.00	375.00	220.00
(46) Joe Tinker	3,200	1,600	950.00
(47) Honus Wagner/Btg	13,500	7,000	4,000
(48) Honus Wagner/Throwing	13,500	7,000	4,000
(49) Cy Young	9,500	5,000	2,800
(50) Heinie Zimmerman	750.00	375.00	220.00

1909 E102 "Set of 25"

 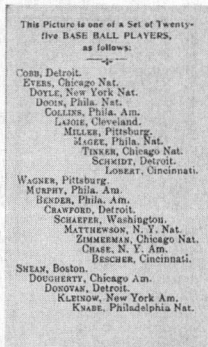

This Picture is one of a Set of Twenty-five Base Ball Players, as follows:

Cobb, Detroit.
Evers, Chicago Nat.
Doyle, New York Nat.
Dooin, Phila. Nat.
Collins, Cleveland.
Lajoie, Cleveland.
Miller, Pittsburg.
Magee, Phila. Nat.
Tinker, Chicago Nat.
Schmidt, Detroit.
Loseat, Cincinnati.
Wagner, Pittsburg.
Murphy, Phila. Am.
Bender, Phila. Am.
Crawford, Detroit.
Schaefer, Washington.
Matthewson, N. Y. Nat.
Zimmerman, Chicago Nat.
Chase, N. Y. Am.
Bescher, Cincinnati.
Shean, Boston.
Dougherty, Chicago Am.
Donovan, Detroit.
Kleinow, New York Am.
Knabe, Philadelphia Nat.

Wagner, s.s. Pittsburg Nat'l

One of many similar early candy card sets, this set - designated as E102 in the American Card Catalog - was published no earlier than mid-1909. The producer of the set is unknown. Measuring approximately 1-1/2" x 2-3/4", the set is almost identical in design to the E101 set and other closely related issues. The set consists of 25 players, which are checklisted on the back of the card. Four of the players have been found in two variations, resulting in 29 different cards. Because there is no advertising on the cards, the set can best be identified by the words - "This Picture is one of a Set of Twenty-five Base Ball Players, as follows" - which appears on the back of each card.

	NM	EX	VG
Complete Set (29):	55,000	22,000	11,000
Common Player:	850.00	350.00	175.00
(1) Chief Bender	1,450	575.00	290.00
(2) Bob Bescher	850.00	350.00	175.00
(3) Hal Chase	900.00	360.00	180.00
(4) Ty Cobb	15,000	6,000	3,000
(5) Eddie Collins	1,450	575.00	290.00
(6) Sam Crawford	1,450	575.00	290.00
(7) Wild Bill Donovan	850.00	350.00	175.00
(8) Red Dooin	850.00	350.00	175.00
(9) Patsy Dougherty	850.00	350.00	175.00
(10) Larry Doyle/Btg	850.00	350.00	175.00
(11) Larry Doyle/Throwing	850.00	350.00	175.00
(12) Johnny Evers	1,450	575.00	290.00
(13) Red Kleinow	850.00	350.00	175.00
(14) Otto Knabe	850.00	350.00	175.00
(15) Nap Lajoie	1,825	725.00	365.00
(16) Hans Lobert	850.00	350.00	175.00
(17) Sherry Magee	850.00	350.00	175.00
(18) Christy Matthewson (Mathewson)	5,000	2,000	1,000
(19) Dots Miller/Btg	850.00	350.00	175.00
(20) Dots Miller/Fldg	1,650	650.00	325.00
(21) Danny Murphy	850.00	350.00	175.00
(22) Germany Schaefer	850.00	350.00	175.00
(23) Boss Schmidt	850.00	350.00	175.00
(24) Dave Shean	850.00	350.00	175.00
(25) Boss Smith (Schmidt)	850.00	350.00	175.00
(26) Joe Tinker	1,450	575.00	290.00
(27) Honus Wagner/Btg	10,000	2,600	1,300
(28) Honus Wagner/Throwing	10,000	2,600	1,300
(29) Heinie Zimmerman	850.00	350.00	175.00

1910 E104 Nadja Caramels

(See 1910 Nadja Caramels.)

1915 E106 American Caramel Co.

(See 1915 American Caramel Co.)

1903-1904 E107 Type 1

 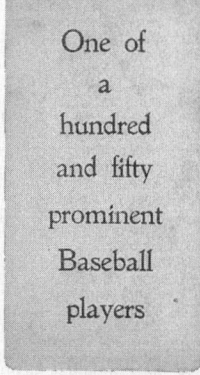

One of
a
hundred
and fifty
prominent
Baseball
players

W. Gleason, 2 B, Phila., N

Identified by the American Card Catalog as E107, this set is significant because it was one of the first major baseball card sets since the 1880s. It established the pattern for most of the tobacco and candy cards that followed over the next two decades. Measuring approximately 1-3/8" x 2-5/8", cards feature black-and-white player photos with the name, position and team in the bottom border. Most are found either with black

back printing reading, "One of a hundred and fifty prominent Baseball players," or blank-backed, in about equal numbers. Also found are cards with a purple diagonal overprint stating "THE BREISCH-WILLIAMS CO." Type 1 consists of 147 known different players, plus 11 additional variations. The Type 2 cards are thicker than those of Type 1 and some (Keeler and Delehanty) cards have captions different from those found in Type 1. Values shown for EX and NM grades are mostly theoretical, as few cards are known in better than VG condition.

	NM	EX	VG
Common Player:	9,000	4,500	2,700
Breisch-Williams Overprint: 2-3X			
(1a) John Anderson (St. Louis)	9,000	4,500	2,700
(1b) John Anderson (New York)	9,000	4,500	2,700
(2) Jimmy Barret (Barrett)	9,000	4,500	2,700
(3) Ginger Beaumont	9,000	4,500	2,700
(4) Fred Beck	9,000	4,500	2,700
(5) Jake Beckley	30,000	15,000	9,000
(6) Harry Bemis	9,000	4,500	2,700
(7) Chief Bender	30,000	15,000	9,000
(8) Bill Bernhard	9,000	4,500	2,700
(9) Harry Bey (Bay)	9,000	4,500	2,700
(10) Bill Bradley	9,000	4,500	2,700
(11) Fritz Buelow	9,000	4,500	2,700
(12) Nixey Callahan	9,000	4,500	2,700
(13) Scoops Carey	9,000	4,500	2,700
(14) Charley Carr	9,000	4,500	2,700
(15) Bill Carrick	9,000	4,500	2,700
(16) Doc Casey	10,500	4,080	2,040
(17) Frank Chance	30,000	15,000	9,000
(18) Jack Chesbro	30,000	15,000	9,000
(19) Boileryard Clark (Clarke)	9,000	4,500	2,700
(20) Fred Clarke	30,000	15,000	9,000
(21) Jimmy Collins	30,000	15,000	9,000
(22) Duff Cooley	9,000	4,500	2,700
(23) Tommy Corcoran	9,000	4,500	2,700
(24) Bill Coughlan (Coughlin)	9,000	4,500	2,700
(25) Lou Criger	9,000	4,500	2,700
(26) Lave Cross	9,000	4,500	2,700
(27) Monte Cross	9,000	4,500	2,700
(28a) Bill Dahlen (Brooklyn)	9,000	4,500	2,700
(28b) Bill Dahlen (New York)	17,000	4,080	2,040
(29) Tom Daly	9,000	4,500	2,700
(30) George Davis	30,000	15,000	9,000
(31) Harry Davis	9,000	4,500	2,700
(32) Ed Delehanty (Delahanty)	30,000	15,000	9,000
(33) Gene DeMont (DeMontreville)	9,000	4,500	2,700
(34a) Pop Dillon (Detroit)	9,000	4,500	2,700
(34b) Pop Dillon (Brooklyn)	16,200	8,100	4,800
(35) Bill Dineen (Dinneen)	9,000	4,500	2,700
(36) Red Donahue	9,000	4,500	2,700
(37) Mike Donlin	9,000	4,500	2,700
(38) Patsy Donovan	9,000	4,500	2,700
(39) Patsy Dougherty (Photo actually Tom Hughes.)	9,000	4,500	2,700
(40) Klondike Douglass	9,000	4,500	2,700
(41a) Jack Doyle (Brooklyn)	9,000	4,500	2,700
(41b) Jack Doyle (Philadelphia)	9,000	4,500	2,700
(42) Lew Drill	9,000	4,500	2,700
(43) Jack Dunn	9,000	4,500	2,700
(44a) Kid Elberfield (Elberfeld) (Detroit)	9,000	4,500	2,700
(44b) Kid Elberfield (Elberfeld) (No team designation.)	9,000	4,500	2,700
(45) Duke Farrell	9,000	4,500	2,700
(46) Hobe Ferris	9,000	4,500	2,700
(47) Elmer Flick	30,000	15,000	9,000
(48) Buck Freeman	9,000	4,500	2,700
(49) Bill Freil (Friel)	9,000	4,500	2,700
(50) Dave Fultz	9,000	4,500	2,700
(51) Ned Garvin	9,000	4,500	2,700
(52) Billy Gilbert	9,000	4,500	2,700
(53) Harry Gleason	9,000	4,500	2,700
(54a) Kid Gleason (New York)	9,000	4,500	2,700
(54b) Kid Gleason (Philadelphia)	9,000	4,500	2,700
(55) John Gochnauer (Gochnaur)	9,000	4,500	2,700
(56) Danny Green	9,000	4,500	2,700
(57) Noodles Hahn	9,000	4,500	2,700
(58) Bill Hallman	9,000	4,500	2,700
(59) Ned Hanlon	30,000	15,000	9,000
(60) Dick Harley	9,000	4,500	2,700
(61) Jack Harper	9,000	4,500	2,700
(62) Topsy Hartsell (Hartsel)	9,000	4,500	2,700
(63) Emmet Heidrick	9,000	4,500	2,700
(64) Charlie Hemphill	9,000	4,500	2,700
(65) Weldon Henley	9,000	4,500	2,700
(66) Piano Legs Hickman	9,000	4,500	2,700
(67) Harry Howell	9,000	4,500	2,700
(68) Frank Iasbel (Isbell)	9,000	4,500	2,700
(69) Fred Jacklitzch (Jacklitsch)	9,000	4,500	2,700
(70) Fielder Jones (Chicago)	9,000	4,500	2,700
(71) Charlie Jones (Boston)	9,000	4,500	2,700
(72) Addie Joss	30,000	15,000	9,000
(73) Mike Kahoe	9,000	4,500	2,700
(74) Wee Willie Keeler	30,000	15,000	9,000
(75) Joe Kelley	30,000	15,000	9,000
(76) Brickyard Kennedy	9,000	4,500	2,700
(77) Frank Kitson	9,000	4,500	2,700
(78a) Malachi Kittredge (Boston)	9,000	4,500	2,700
(78b) Malachi Kittredge (Washington)	9,000	4,500	2,700
(79) Candy LaChance	9,000	4,500	2,700
(80) Nap Lajoie	30,000	15,000	9,000
(81) Tommy Leach	9,000	4,500	2,700
(82a) Watty Lee (Washington)	9,000	4,500	2,700
(82b) Watty Lee (Pittsburg)	9,000	4,500	2,700
(83) Sam Leever	9,000	4,500	2,700
(84) Herman Long	9,000	4,500	2,700
(85a) Billy Lush (Detroit)	9,000	4,500	2,700
(85b) Billy Lush (Cleveland)	9,000	4,500	2,700
(86) Christy Mathewson	125,000	62,500	37,500
(87) Sport McAllister	9,000	4,500	2,700
(88) Jack McCarthy	9,000	4,500	2,700
(89) Barry McCormick	9,000	4,500	2,700
(90) Ed McFarland (Chicago)	9,000	4,500	2,700
(91) Herm McFarland (New York)	9,000	4,500	2,700
(92) Joe McGinnity	30,000	15,000	9,000
(93) John McGraw	30,000	15,000	9,000
(94a) Deacon McGuire (Brooklyn)	9,000	4,500	2,700
(94b) Deacon McGuire (New York)	17,000	4,080	2,040
(95) Jock Menefee	9,000	4,500	2,700
(96) Sam Mertes	9,000	4,500	2,700
(97) Roscoe Miller (Picture actually George Mullin.)	9,000	4,500	2,700
(98) Fred Mitchell	9,000	4,500	2,700
(99) Earl Moore	9,000	4,500	2,700
(100) Danny Murphy	9,000	4,500	2,700
(101) Jack O'Connor	9,000	4,500	2,700
(102) Al Orth	9,000	4,500	2,700
(103) Dick Padden	9,000	4,500	2,700
(104) Freddy Parent	9,000	4,500	2,700
(105) Roy Patterson	9,000	4,500	2,700
(106) Heinie Peitz	9,000	4,500	2,700
(107) Deacon Phillipi (Phillippe)	9,000	4,500	2,700
(108) Wiley Piatt	9,000	4,500	2,700
(109) Ollie Pickering	9,000	4,500	2,700
(110) Eddie Plank	78,000	39,000	24,000
(111a) Ed Poole (Cincinnati)	9,000	4,500	2,700
(111b) Ed Poole (Brooklyn)	9,000	4,500	2,700
(112a) Jack Powell (St. Louis)	9,000	4,500	2,700
(112b) Jack Powell (New York)	9,000	4,500	2,700
(113) Mike Powers	9,000	4,500	2,700
(114) Claude Ritchie (Ritchey)	9,000	4,500	2,700
(115) Jimmy Ryan	9,000	4,500	2,700
(116) Ossee Schreckengost	9,000	4,500	2,700
(117) Kip Selbach	9,000	4,500	2,700
(118) Socks Seybold	9,000	4,500	2,700
(119) Jimmy Sheckard	9,000	4,500	2,700
(120) Ed Siever	9,000	4,500	2,700
(121) Harry Smith	9,000	4,500	2,700
(122) Tully Sparks	9,000	4,500	2,700
(123) Jake Stahl	9,000	4,500	2,700
(124) Harry Steinfeldt	9,000	4,500	2,700
(125) Sammy Strang	9,000	4,500	2,700
(126) Willie Sudhoff	9,000	4,500	2,700
(127) Joe Sugden	9,000	4,500	2,700
(128) Billy Sullivan	9,000	4,500	2,700
(129) Jack Taylor	9,000	4,500	2,700
(130) Fred Tenney	9,000	4,500	2,700
(131) Roy Thomas	9,000	4,500	2,700
(132a) Jack Thoney (Cleveland)	9,000	4,500	2,700
(132b) Jack Thoney (New York)	9,000	4,500	2,700
(133) Jack Townsend	9,000	4,500	2,700
(134) George Van Haltren	9,000	4,500	2,700
(135) Rube Waddell	30,000	15,000	9,000
(136) Honus Wagner	360,000	180,000	108,000
(137) Bobby Wallace	30,000	15,000	9,000
(138) Jack Warner	9,000	4,500	2,700
(139) Jimmy Wiggs	9,000	4,500	2,700
(140) Jimmy Williams	9,000	4,500	2,700
(141) Vic Willis	30,000	15,000	9,000
(142) Hooks Wiltse	9,000	4,500	2,700
(143) George Winters (Winter)	9,000	4,500	2,700
(144) Bob Wood	9,000	4,500	2,700
(145) Joe Yeager	9,600	4,800	2,880
(146) Cy Young	125,000	62,500	37,500
(147) Chief Zimmer	9,000	4,500	2,700

1903-1904 E107 Type 2

Delahanty, Fielder, Wash.

Many of the Type 2 E107 cards seen to date do not measure the nominal 1-3/8" x 2-5/8" of the Type 1 cards, often having been cut more narrowly. Once thought to have been cut from an advertising piece, it now appears these were a regular production issue, as at least one specimen has been found with the purple diagonal overprint stating "THE BREISCH-WILLIAMS CO." Type 2 cards are printed on a thicker and more gray card stock than Type 1 and at least a few (Keeler and Delehanty) cards have captions different from those found in Type 1. NM values are principally theoretical as few cards in known in conditions better than EX.

	NM	EX	VG
Common Player:	6,000	3,000	1,800
(1) Ed Delehanty (Delahanty)	33,500	17,000	10,000
(2) Jack Doyle	6,000	3,000	1,800
(3) Wee Willie Keeler	33,500	17,000	10,000
(4) Nap Lajoie	33,500	17,000	10,000
(5) Tommy Leach	6,000	3,000	1,800
(6) Socks Seybold	6,000	3,000	1,800
(7) Fred Tenney	6,000	3,000	1,800
(8) Rube Waddell	33,500	17,000	10,000

1922 E120 American Caramel Series of 240

(See 1922 American Caramel Series of 240.)

1921-22 E121 American Caramel Series of 80/120

(See 1921 American Caramel Series of 80, Series of 120.)

1922 E122 American Caramel Series of 80

(See 1922 American Caramel Series of 80 for checklist, values.)

1910 E125 American Caramel Die-Cuts

(See 1910 American Caramel Die-Cuts for checklist, values.)

1927 E126 American Caramel Series of 60

(See 1927 American Caramel Series of 60.)

1927 E210 York Caramels

(See York Caramels.)

1921 E253 Oxford Confectionery

(See 1921 Oxford Confectionery.)

F

1961 F & M Bank Minnesota Twins Matchbook Covers

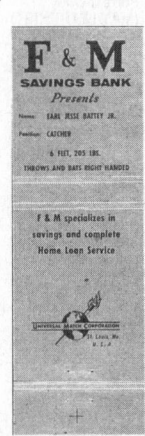

The star players on the inaugural Twins team are featured in this series of matchbook covers. The 1-1/2" x 4-7/16" matchbooks are printed in black, red and blue on white, and include a player portrait (players are shown wearing Washington Senators caps) and team logo on front. The sponsoring bank's picture and logo are on back. Inside the front cover are a few details about the player. Values shown are for complete but empty covers, with the striker surface intact. Complete matchbooks with matches bring about 2X the values quoted.

		NM	EX	VG
Complete Set (10):		140.00	70.00	42.50
Common Player:		24.00	12.00	7.50
(1)	Bob Allison	24.00	12.00	7.50
(2)	Earl Battey	18.00	9.00	5.50
(3)	Reno Bertoia	15.00	7.50	4.50
(4)	Billy Gardner	15.00	7.50	4.50
(5)	Lenny Green	15.00	7.50	4.50
(6)	Harmon Killebrew	40.00	20.00	12.00
(7)	Cookie Lavagetto	15.00	7.50	4.50
(8)	Jim Lemon	24.00	12.00	7.50
(9)	Camilo Pascual	24.00	12.00	7.50
(10)	Pedro Ramos	15.00	7.50	4.50

1962 F & M Bank Minnesota Twins Matchbook Covers

The '62 Twins are featured in this series of matchbook covers. The 1-1/2" x 4-7/16" matchbooks are printed in black, red and blue on white, and include a player portrait (new players who did not appear in the 1961 set are shown in Twins caps) and team logo on front. The sponsoring bank's picture and logo are on back. Inside the front cover are a few details about the player. Values shown are for complete but empty covers, with the striker surface intact. Complete matchbooks with matches bring about 2X the values quoted.

		NM	EX	VG
Complete Set (10):		150.00	75.00	45.00
Common Player:		15.00	7.50	4.50
(1)	Bob Allison	24.00	12.00	7.25
(2)	Earl Battey	18.00	9.00	5.50
(3)	Lenny Green	15.00	7.50	4.50
(4)	Jim Kaat	24.00	12.00	7.25
(5)	Harmon Killebrew	40.00	20.00	12.00
(6)	Jack Kralick	15.00	7.50	4.50
(7)	Jim Lemon	24.00	12.00	7.25
(8)	Camilo Pascual	24.00	12.00	7.25
(9)	Pedro Ramos	15.00	7.50	4.50
(10)	Zoilo Versalles	24.00	12.00	7.25

1966 Fairway Minnesota Twins

Color portraits of Twins favorites comprise this regional issue from a local grocery chain. The 8" x 10" glossy pictures have blue facsimile autographs on front and a white border. Black-and-white backs have a lengthy career summary, biographical data and full major and minor league stats. The unnumbered pictures are checklisted here in alphabetical order. There are no markings on the picture to identify the Fairway store.

		NM	EX	VG
Complete Set (17):		175.00	85.00	55.00
Common Player:		7.50	3.75	2.25
(1)	Bernie Allen	7.50	3.75	2.25
(2)	Bob Allison	13.50	6.75	4.00
(3)	Earl Battey	10.00	5.00	3.00
(4)	Jim Grant	7.50	3.75	2.25
(5)	Jimmie Hall	7.50	3.75	2.25
(6)	Jim Kaat	15.00	7.50	4.50
(7)	Harmon Killebrew	30.00	15.00	9.00
(8)	Jim Merritt	7.50	3.75	2.25
(9)	Don Mincher	7.50	3.75	2.25
(10)	Tony Oliva	15.00	7.50	4.50
(11)	Camilo Pascual	10.00	5.00	3.00
(12)	Jim Perry	10.00	5.00	3.00
(13)	Frank Quilici	7.50	3.75	2.25
(14)	Rich Rollins	7.50	3.75	2.25
(15)	Sandy Valdespino	7.50	3.75	2.25
(16)	Zoilo Versalles	13.50	6.75	4.00
(17)	Al Worthington	7.50	3.75	2.25

1964 Falstaff Beer

This 6" x 4" black-and-white postcard pictures the principal radio announcers for the CBS "Game of the Week" sponsored by the brewing company and was probably used to respond to fan requests for autographs. Facsimile signatures of the Hall of Famers are featured on front.

	NM	EX	VG
"Dizzy" Dean, "Pee Wee" Reese	20.00	10.00	6.00

1977 Family Fun Centers Padres

For 1977, Family Fun Centers, a chain of mini theme parks, took over sponsorship of the Padres annual issue of black-and-white player photos. The 5-1/2" x 8-1/2" photos have a large player pose at top-center, with his name and position below. In the bottom corners are team and sponsor logos. Backs have biographical data, complete stats and career highlights. Players are checklisted here alphabetically.

	NM	EX	VG
Complete Set (33):	90.00	45.00	27.50
Common Player:	4.50	2.25	1.25

(1)	Billy Almon	4.50	2.25	1.25
(2)	Joey Amalfitano	4.50	2.25	1.25
(3)	Tucker Ashford	4.50	2.25	1.25
(4)	Mike Champion	4.50	2.25	1.25
(5)	Roger Craig	4.50	2.25	1.25
(6)	Alvin Dark	4.50	2.25	1.25
(7)	Bob Davis	4.50	2.25	1.25
(8)	Rollie Fingers	12.50	6.25	3.75
(9)	Dave Freisleben	4.50	2.25	1.25
(10)	Tom Griffin	4.50	2.25	1.25
(11)	George Hendrick	4.50	2.25	1.25
(12)	Mike Ivie	4.50	2.25	1.25
(13)	Randy Jones	4.50	2.25	1.25
(14)	John McNamara	4.50	2.25	1.25
(15)	Bob Owchinko	4.50	2.25	1.25
(16)	Merv Rettenmund	4.50	2.25	1.25
(17)	Gene Richards	4.50	2.25	1.25
(18)	Dave Roberts	4.50	2.25	1.25
(19)	Jackie Robinson (Blank back.)	25.00	12.50	7.50
(20)	Rick Sawyer	4.50	2.25	1.25
(21)	Pat Scanlon	4.50	2.25	1.25
(22)	Bob Shirley	4.50	2.25	1.25
(23)	Bob Skinner	4.50	2.25	1.25
(24)	Dan Spillner	4.50	2.25	1.25
(25)	Gary Sutherland	4.50	2.25	1.25
(26)	Gene Tenace	4.50	2.25	1.25
(27)	Dave Tomlin	4.50	2.25	1.25
(28)	Jerry Turner	4.50	2.25	1.25
(29)	Bobby Valentine	4.50	2.25	1.25
(30)	Dave Wehrmeister	4.50	2.25	1.25
(31)	Whitey Wietelmann	4.50	2.25	1.25
(32)	Don Williams	4.50	2.25	1.25
(33)	Dave Winfield	15.00	7.50	4.50

1978 Family Fun Centers Angels

NOLAN RYAN

The players, manager and coaches of the '78 Angels are featured in this set of 3-1/2" x 5-1/2" sepia-tone cards. The unnumbered cards are checklisted here alphabetically.

		NM	EX	VG
Complete Set (38):		90.00	45.00	25.00
Common Player:		2.50	1.25	.70
(1)	Don Aase	2.50	1.25	.70
(2)	Mike Barlow	2.50	1.25	.70
(3)	Don Baylor	3.50	1.75	1.00
(4)	Lyman Bostock	2.50	1.25	.70
(5)	Ken Brett	2.50	1.25	.70
(6)	Dave Chalk	2.50	1.25	.70
(7)	Bob Clear	2.50	1.25	.70
(8)	Brian Downing	2.50	1.25	.70
(9)	Ron Fairly	2.50	1.25	.70
(10)	Gil Flores	2.50	1.25	.70
(11)	Dave Frost	2.50	1.25	.70
(12)	Dave Garcia	2.50	1.25	.70
(13)	Bobby Grich	2.50	1.25	.70
(14)	Tom Griffin	2.50	1.25	.70
(15)	Marv Grissom	2.50	1.25	.70
(16)	Ike Hampton	2.50	1.25	.70
(17)	Paul Hartzell	2.50	1.25	.70
(18)	Terry Humphrey	2.50	1.25	.70
(19)	Ron Jackson	2.50	1.25	.70
(20)	Chris Knapp	2.50	1.25	.70
(21)	Ken Landreaux	2.50	1.25	.70
(22)	Carney Lansford	2.50	1.25	.70
(23)	Dave LaRoche	2.50	1.25	.70
(24)	John McNamara	2.50	1.25	.70
(25)	Dyar Miller	2.50	1.25	.70
(26)	Rick Miller	2.50	1.25	.70
(27)	Balor Moore	2.50	1.25	.70
(28)	Rance Mulliniks	2.50	1.25	.70
(29)	Floyd Rayford	2.50	1.25	.70
(30)	Jimmie Reese	4.00	2.00	1.25
(31)	Merv Rettenmund	2.50	1.25	.70
(32)	Joe Rudi	2.50	1.25	.70
(33)	Nolan Ryan	45.00	22.50	13.50
(34)	Bob Skinner	2.50	1.25	.70
(35)	Tony Solaita	2.50	1.25	.70
(36)	Frank Tanana	2.50	1.25	.70
(37)	Dickie Thon	2.50	1.25	.70
---	Header Card	.70	.35	.20

1978 Family Fun Centers Padres

In conjunction with the Padres' hosting of the 1978 All-Star Game, Family Fun Centers issued this set of cards covering the players, coaches, announcers and even the owner. The 3-1/2" x 5-1/2" cards have a plaque look with a 3" x 3-1/4" posed color photo set on a wood background. The player's name is in a gold box at bottom, with the team and sponsor's logos in between. Backs are in black-and-white with a player portrait photo and facsimile autograph at bottom, a few biographical details and career stats at top and an essay in the middle titled, "My Greatest Thrill in Baseball." A uniform number appears at top-left. The set is checklisted here in alphabetical order.

	NM	EX	VG
Complete Set (39):	75.00	37.50	22.50
Common Player:	3.00	1.50	.90
(1) Bill Almon	3.00	1.50	.90
(2) Tucker Ashford	3.00	1.50	.90
(3) Chuck Baker	3.00	1.50	.90
(4) Dave Campbell/Announcer	3.00	1.50	.90
(5) Mike Champion	3.00	1.50	.90
(6) Jerry Coleman/Announcer	3.00	1.50	.90
(7) Roger Craig	3.00	1.50	.90
(8) John D'Acquisto	3.00	1.50	.90
(9) Bob Davis	3.00	1.50	.90
(10) Chuck Estrada	3.00	1.50	.90
(11) Rollie Fingers	9.00	4.50	2.75
(12) Dave Freisleben	3.00	1.50	.90
(13) Oscar Gamble	3.00	1.50	.90
(14) Fernando Gonzalez	3.00	1.50	.90
(15) Billy Herman	4.00	2.00	1.25
(16) Randy Jones	3.00	1.50	.90
(17) Ray Kroc (owner)	5.00	2.50	1.50
(18) Mark Lee	3.00	1.50	.90
(19) Mickey Lolich	3.00	1.50	.90
(20) Bob Owchinko	3.00	1.50	.90
(21) Broderick Perkins	3.00	1.50	.90
(22) Gaylord Perry	9.00	4.50	2.75
(23) Eric Rasmussen	3.00	1.50	.90
(24) Don Reynolds	3.00	1.50	.90
(25) Gene Richards	3.00	1.50	.90
(26) Dave Roberts	3.00	1.50	.90
(27) Phil Roof	3.00	1.50	.90
(28) Bob Shirley	3.00	1.50	.90
(29) Ozzie Smith	60.00	30.00	18.00
(30) Dan Spillner	3.00	1.50	.90
(31) Rick Sweet	3.00	1.50	.90
(32) Gene Tenace	3.00	1.50	.90
(33) Derrel Thomas	3.00	1.50	.90
(34) Jerry Turner	3.00	1.50	.90
(35) Dave Wehrmeister	3.00	1.50	.90
(36) Whitey Wietelmann	3.00	1.50	.90
(37) Don Williams	3.00	1.50	.90
(38) Dave Winfield	15.00	7.50	4.50
(39) All-Star Game	3.00	1.50	.90

1979 Family Fun Centers Padres

Each card features a posed color photo against a woodgrain border. Fronts have player identification, the Padres mascot and the logo of one of the sponsors - Family Fun Centers or Dean's Photo Service. Black-and-white backs have player personal data, major and minor league stats, a notation to "COLLECT ALL 36 CARDS" and a list of distribution dates. The 3-1/4" x 4-3/4" cards were issued in 12-1/2" x 9-1/2" perforated panels of six cards plus a coupon from each sponsor. Panels were given out one per month May through September at promotional games, making the set difficult to complete. Cards #25-30 have not been confirmed as issued.

	NM	EX	VG
Complete Set (30):	60.00	30.00	18.00
Common Player:	3.00	1.50	.90
1 Roger Craig	3.00	1.50	.90
2 John D'Acquisto	3.00	1.50	.90
3 Ozzie Smith	25.00	12.50	7.50
4 KGB Chicken	4.00	2.00	1.25
5 Gene Richards	3.00	1.50	.90
6 Jerry Turner	3.00	1.50	.90
7 Bob Owchinko	3.00	1.50	.90
8 Gene Tenace	3.00	1.50	.90
9 Whitey Wietelmann	3.00	1.50	.90
10 Bill Almon	3.00	1.50	.90
11 Dave Winfield	15.00	7.50	4.50

		NM	EX	VG
12	Mike Hargrove	3.00	1.50	.90
13	Fernando Gonzalez	3.00	1.50	.90
14	Barry Evans	3.00	1.50	.90
15	Steve Mura	3.00	1.50	.90
16	Chuck Estrada	3.00	1.50	.90
17	Bill Fahey	3.00	1.50	.90
18	Gaylord Perry	6.00	3.00	1.75
19	Dan Briggs	3.00	1.50	.90
20	Billy Herman	4.00	2.00	1.25
21	Mickey Lolich	3.00	1.50	.90
22	Broderick Perkins	3.00	1.50	.90
23	Fred Kendall	3.00	1.50	.90
24	Rollie Fingers	6.00	3.00	1.75
31	Bobby Tolan	3.00	1.50	.90
32	Doug Rader	3.00	1.50	.90
33	Dave Campbell	3.00	1.50	.90
34	Jay Johnstone	3.00	1.50	.90
35	Mark Lee	3.00	1.50	.90
36	Bob Shirley	3.00	1.50	.90

1980 Family Fun Centers Padres

Six Padres players or staff are featured on these 13" x 10" or 12-1/2" x 9-1/2" coupon sheets. At the right end of each glossy paper sheet is a group of coupons and advertising for the recreation centers, printed in black, yellow and green. At left are six photos. Each of the 3" x 4" photos has a color player pose. At either top or bottom, depending on placement on the sheet, is the player name in black, "FAMILY FUN CENTER" in green and a red building logo. Backs are blank and the sheets are not perforated.

		NM	EX	VG
Complete Set (7):		80.00	40.00	24.00
Common Sheet:		7.00	3.50	2.00
(1)	Kurt Bevacqua, Dave Cash, Paul Dade, Rollie Fingers, Don Williams, Dave Winfield	20.00	10.00	6.00
(2)	Ed Brinkman, Dave Edwards, Jack Krol, Luis Salazar, Craig Stimac, John Urrea	7.00	3.50	2.00
(3)	Jerry Coleman, John D'Acquisto, Bill Fahey, Randy Jones, Gene Richards, Ozzie Smith	30.00	15.00	9.00
(4)	Dave Campbell, Juan Eichelberger, Barry Evans, Bobby Tolan, Jerry Turner, Rick Wise	7.00	3.50	2.00
(5)	John Curtis, Al Heist, Gary Lucas, Willie Montanez, Aurelio Rodriguez, Gene Tenace	7.00	3.50	2.00
(6)	Eddie Doucette, Chuck Estrada, Tim Flannery, Eric Rasmussen, Bob Shirley, San Diego Chicken	10.00	5.00	3.00
(7)	Von Joshua, Fred Kendall, Dennis Kinney, Jerry Mumphrey, Steve Mura, Dick Phillips	7.00	3.50	2.00

1916 Famous and Barr Clothiers

GAVVY CRAVATH
R.F.—Philadelphia Nat'ls

This is among the most complex of the regional advertising-backed card sets that utilized the fronts generated by Felix Mendelsohn because players have been found that parallel both the M101-5 and M101-4 issues. Additionally the advertis-

ing for the St. Louis clothing store on the backs can be found reading both top-to-bottom and bottom-to-top in relation to the front, the latter usually found on a card stock that is whiter than the former. Like the related issues, the Famous and Barr cards are printed in black-and-white in a size of approximately 1-5/8" x 3". Because of the mixing of M101-5 and M101-4 fronts, the exact composition of the Famous and Barr set is unknown and checklist additions can be expected."

		NM	EX	VG
Common Player:		125.00	50.00	25.00
1	Babe Adams	190.00	65.00	25.00
2	Sam Agnew	125.00	50.00	25.00
3	Eddie Ainsmith	125.00	50.00	25.00
4	Grover Alexander	2,065	825.00	415.00
5	Leon Ames	125.00	50.00	25.00
6	Jimmy Archer	125.00	50.00	25.00
7	Jimmy Austin	125.00	50.00	25.00
8a	J. Franklin Baker	800.00	400.00	240.00
8b	H.D. Baird (3rd B.)	125.00	50.00	25.00
8c	H.D. Baird (C.F.)	125.00	50.00	25.00
9	Dave Bancroft	800.00	400.00	240.00
10	Jack Barry	125.00	50.00	25.00
11	Zinn Beck	125.00	50.00	25.00
12	Lute Boone	125.00	50.00	25.00
13	Joe Benz	125.00	50.00	25.00
14	Bob Bescher	125.00	50.00	25.00
15	Al Betzel	125.00	50.00	25.00
16	Roger Bresnahan	800.00	400.00	240.00
17	Eddie Burns	125.00	50.00	25.00
18	Geo. J. Burns	125.00	50.00	25.00
19	Joe Bush	125.00	50.00	25.00
20	Owen Bush	125.00	50.00	25.00
21	Art Butler	125.00	50.00	25.00
22	Bobbie Byrne	125.00	50.00	25.00
23a	Forrest Cady (MAY NOT EXIST)			
23b	Mordecai Brown	800.00	400.00	240.00
24	Jimmy Callahan	125.00	50.00	25.00
25	Ray Caldwell	125.00	50.00	25.00
26	Max Carey	800.00	400.00	240.00
27	George Chalmers	125.00	50.00	25.00
28	Frank Chance	800.00	400.00	240.00
29	Ray Chapman	155.00	65.00	30.00
30	Larry Cheney	125.00	50.00	25.00
31	Eddie Cicotte	800.00	400.00	240.00
32	Tom Clarke	125.00	50.00	25.00
33	Eddie Collins	800.00	400.00	240.00
34	"Shauno" Collins	125.00	50.00	25.00
35	Charles Comisky (Comiskey)	800.00	400.00	240.00
36	Joe Connolly	125.00	50.00	25.00
37	Luther Cook	125.00	50.00	25.00
38	Jack Coombs	125.00	50.00	25.00
39	Dan Costello	125.00	50.00	25.00
40	Harry Coveleskie (Coveleski)	125.00	50.00	25.00
41	Gavvy Cravath	125.00	50.00	25.00
42	Sam Crawford	800.00	400.00	240.00
43	Jean Dale	125.00	50.00	25.00
44	Jake Daubert	125.00	50.00	25.00
45	Geo. A. Davis Jr.	125.00	50.00	25.00
46	Charles Deal	125.00	50.00	25.00
47	Al Demaree	125.00	50.00	25.00
48	William Doak	125.00	50.00	25.00
49	Bill Donovan	125.00	50.00	25.00
50	Charles Dooin	125.00	50.00	25.00
51	Mike Doolan	125.00	50.00	25.00
52	Larry Doyle	125.00	50.00	25.00
53	Jean Dubuc	125.00	50.00	25.00
54	Oscar Dugey	125.00	50.00	25.00
55	Johnny Evers	800.00	400.00	240.00
56	Urban Faber	800.00	400.00	240.00
57	"Hap" Felsch	1,000	400.00	200.00
58	Bill Fischer	125.00	50.00	25.00
59	Ray Fisher	125.00	50.00	25.00
60	Max Flack	125.00	50.00	25.00
61	Art Fletcher	125.00	50.00	25.00
62	Eddie Foster	125.00	50.00	25.00
63	Jacques Fournier	125.00	50.00	25.00
64	Del Gainer (Gainor)	125.00	50.00	25.00
65	Larry Gardner	125.00	50.00	25.00
66	Joe Gedeon	125.00	50.00	25.00
67	Gus Getz	125.00	50.00	25.00
68	Geo. Gibson	125.00	50.00	25.00
69	Wilbur Good	125.00	50.00	25.00
70	Hank Gowdy	125.00	50.00	25.00
71	John Graney	125.00	50.00	25.00
72	Tom Griffith	125.00	50.00	25.00
73	Heinie Groh	125.00	50.00	25.00
74	Earl Hamilton	125.00	50.00	25.00
75	Bob Harmon	125.00	50.00	25.00
76	Roy Hartzell	125.00	50.00	25.00
77	Claude Hendrix	125.00	50.00	25.00
78	Olaf Henriksen	125.00	50.00	25.00
79	John Henry	125.00	50.00	25.00
80	"Buck" Herzog	125.00	50.00	25.00
81	Hugh High	125.00	50.00	25.00
82	Dick Hoblitzell	125.00	50.00	25.00
83	Harry Hooper	800.00	400.00	240.00
84	Ivan Howard	125.00	50.00	25.00
85	Miller Huggins	800.00	400.00	240.00
86	Joe Jackson	25,000	10,000	5,000
87	William James	125.00	50.00	25.00
88	Harold Janvrin	125.00	50.00	25.00
89	Hugh Jennings	800.00	400.00	240.00
90	Walter Johnson	2,500	1,250	750.00
91	Fielder Jones	125.00	50.00	25.00
92	Bennie Kauff	125.00	50.00	25.00
93	Wm. Killefer Jr.	125.00	50.00	25.00
94	Ed. Konetchy	125.00	50.00	25.00
95	Napoleon Lajoie	800.00	400.00	240.00
96	Jack Lapp	125.00	50.00	25.00
97a	John Lavan (Correct spelling.)	125.00	50.00	25.00
97b	John Lavin (Incorret spelling.) (MAY NOT EXIST)			
98	Jimmy Lavender	125.00	50.00	25.00
99	"Nemo" Leibold	125.00	50.00	25.00
100	H.B. Leonard	125.00	50.00	25.00

		NM	EX	VG
101	Duffy Lewis	125.00	50.00	25.00
102	Hans Lobert	125.00	50.00	25.00
103	Tom Long	125.00	50.00	25.00
104	Fred Luderus	125.00	50.00	25.00
105	Connie Mack	800.00	400.00	240.00
106	Lee Magee	125.00	50.00	25.00
107	Al. Mamaux	125.00	50.00	25.00
108	Leslie Mann	125.00	50.00	25.00
109	"Rabbit" Maranville	800.00	400.00	240.00
110	Rube Marquard	800.00	400.00	240.00
111	Armando Marsans	155.00	65.00	30.00
112	J. Erskine Mayer	155.00	65.00	30.00
113	George McBride	125.00	50.00	25.00
114	John J. McGraw	800.00	400.00	240.00
115	Jack McInnis	125.00	50.00	25.00
116	Fred Merkle	125.00	50.00	25.00
117	Chief Meyers	125.00	50.00	25.00
118	Clyde Milan	125.00	50.00	25.00
119	Otto Miller	125.00	50.00	25.00
120	Willie Mitchel (Mitchell)	125.00	50.00	25.00
121	Fred Mollwitz	125.00	50.00	25.00
122	J. Herbert Moran	125.00	50.00	25.00
123	Pat Moran	125.00	50.00	25.00
124	Ray Morgan	125.00	50.00	25.00
125	Geo. Moriarty	125.00	50.00	25.00
126	Guy Morton	125.00	50.00	25.00
127	Ed. Murphy (Photo actually Danny Murphy.)	125.00	50.00	25.00
128	John Murray	125.00	50.00	25.00
129	"Hy" Myers	125.00	50.00	25.00
130	J.A. Niehoff	125.00	50.00	25.00
131	Leslie Nunamaker	125.00	50.00	25.00
132	Rube Oldring	125.00	50.00	25.00
133	Oliver O'Mara	125.00	50.00	25.00
134	Steve O'Neill	125.00	50.00	25.00
135	"Dode" Paskert	125.00	50.00	25.00
136	Roger Peckinpaugh (Photo actually Gavvy Cravath.)	125.00	50.00	25.00
137	E.J. Pfeffer (Photo actually Jeff Pfeffer.)	125.00	50.00	25.00
138	Geo. Pierce (Pearce)	125.00	50.00	25.00
139	Walter Pipp	125.00	50.00	25.00
140	Derril Pratt (Derrill)	125.00	50.00	25.00
141	Bill Rariden	125.00	50.00	25.00
142	Eppa Rixey	800.00	400.00	240.00
143	Davey Robertson	125.00	50.00	25.00
144	Wilbert Robinson	800.00	400.00	240.00
145	Bob Roth	125.00	50.00	25.00
146	Ed. Roush	800.00	400.00	240.00
147	Clarence Rowland	125.00	50.00	25.00
148	"Nap" Rucker	125.00	50.00	25.00
149	Dick Rudolph	125.00	50.00	25.00
150	Reb Russell	125.00	50.00	25.00
151	Babe Ruth	68,750	27,500	13,750
152	Vic Saier	125.00	50.00	25.00
153	"Slim" Sallee	125.00	50.00	25.00
154	"Germany" Schaefer	125.00	50.00	25.00
155	Ray Schalk	800.00	400.00	240.00
156	Walter Schang	125.00	50.00	25.00
157	Chas. Schmidt	125.00	50.00	25.00
158	Frank Schulte	125.00	50.00	25.00
159	Jim Scott	125.00	50.00	25.00
160	Everett Scott	125.00	50.00	25.00
161	Tom Seaton	125.00	50.00	25.00
162	Howard Shanks	125.00	50.00	25.00
163	Bob Shawkey (Photo actually Jack McInnis.)	125.00	50.00	25.00
164	Ernie Shore	125.00	50.00	25.00
165	Burt Shotton	125.00	50.00	25.00
166	George Sisler	800.00	400.00	240.00
167	J. Carlisle Smith	125.00	50.00	25.00
168	Fred Snodgrass	125.00	50.00	25.00
169	Geo. Stallings	125.00	50.00	25.00
170	Oscar Stanage (Photo actually Chas. Schmidt.)	125.00	50.00	25.00
171	Charles Stengel	815.00	325.00	165.00
172	Milton Stock	125.00	50.00	25.00
173	Amos Strunk (Photo actually Olaf Henriksen.)	125.00	50.00	25.00
174	Billy Sullivan	125.00	50.00	25.00
175	Chas. Tesreau	125.00	50.00	25.00
176	Jim Thorpe	13,750	5,500	2,750
177	Joe Tinker	800.00	400.00	240.00
178a	Fred Toney	125.00	50.00	25.00
178b				
179	Terry Turner	125.00	50.00	25.00
180	Jim Vaughn	125.00	50.00	25.00
181	Bob Veach	125.00	50.00	25.00
182a	James Voix	125.00	50.00	25.00
182b	Hans Wagner	6,500	3,200	1,950
183	Oscar Vitt	125.00	50.00	25.00
184	Hans Wagner	6,500	3,200	1,950
185	Clarence Walker (Photo not Walker.)	125.00	50.00	25.00
186	Zach Wheat	800.00	400.00	240.00
187	Ed. Walsh	800.00	400.00	240.00
188	Buck Weaver	800.00	400.00	240.00
189	Carl Weilman	125.00	50.00	25.00
190	Geo. Whitted	125.00	50.00	25.00
191	Fred Williams	125.00	50.00	25.00
192	Art Wilson	125.00	50.00	25.00
193	J. Owen Wilson	125.00	50.00	25.00
194	Ivy Wingo	125.00	50.00	25.00
195	"Mel" Wolfgang	125.00	50.00	25.00
196	Joe Wood	600.00	300.00	180.00
197	Steve Yerkes	125.00	50.00	25.00
198	Rollie Zeider	125.00	50.00	25.00
199	Heiny Zimmerman	125.00	50.00	25.00
200	Ed. Zwilling	125.00	50.00	25.00

1906 Fan Craze - American League

One of the earliest 20th Century baseball card sets, this issue from the Fan Craze Co. of Cincinnati was designed as a deck of playing cards and was intended to be used as a baseball table game. Separate sets were issued for the National League, with backs printed in red, and the American League,

which are blue-backed. Both sets feature black-and-white player portraits in an oval vignette with the player's name and team below. The top of the card indicates one of many various baseball plays, such as "Single," "Out at First," "Strike," "Stolen Base," etc. The unnumbered cards measure 2-1/2" x 3-1/2". An ad card identifies the set as "An Artistic Constellation of Great Stars." Sears sold the set for 48 cents, postpaid.

		NM	EX	VG
	Complete Set (51):	8,250	4,125	2,475
	Complete Boxed Set:	9,350	4,675	2,750
	Common Player:	90.00	45.00	25.00
(1)	Nick Altrock	110.00	55.00	35.00
(2)	Jim Barrett	90.00	45.00	25.00
(3)	Harry Bay	90.00	45.00	25.00
(4)	Albert Bender	330.00	165.00	100.00
(5)	Bill Bernhardt	90.00	45.00	25.00
(6)	W. Bradley	90.00	45.00	25.00
(7)	Jack Chesbro	330.00	165.00	100.00
(8)	Jimmy Collins	330.00	165.00	100.00
(9)	Sam Crawford	330.00	165.00	100.00
(10)	Lou Criger	90.00	45.00	25.00
(11)	Lave Cross	90.00	45.00	25.00
(12)	Monte Cross	90.00	45.00	25.00
(13)	Harry Davis	90.00	45.00	25.00
(14)	Bill Dinneen	90.00	45.00	25.00
(15)	Pat (Bill) Donovan	90.00	45.00	25.00
(16)	Pat Dougherty	90.00	45.00	25.00
(17)	Norman Elberfield (Elberfeld)	90.00	45.00	25.00
(18)	Hoke Ferris (Hobe)	90.00	45.00	25.00
(19)	Elmer Flick	330.00	165.00	100.00
(20)	Buck Freeman	90.00	45.00	25.00
(21)	Fred Glade	90.00	45.00	25.00
(22)	Clark Griffith	330.00	165.00	100.00
(23)	Charley Hickman	90.00	45.00	25.00
(24)	Wm. Holmes	90.00	45.00	25.00
(25)	Harry Howell	90.00	45.00	25.00
(26)	Frank Isbel (Isbell)	90.00	45.00	25.00
(27)	Albert Jacobson	90.00	45.00	25.00
(28)	Ban Johnson	330.00	165.00	100.00
(29)	Fielder Jones	90.00	45.00	25.00
(30)	Adrian Joss	330.00	165.00	100.00
(31)	Billy Keeler	330.00	165.00	100.00
(32)	Napolean Lajoie	330.00	165.00	100.00
(33)	Connie Mack	330.00	165.00	100.00
(34)	Jimmy McAleer	90.00	45.00	25.00
(35)	Jim McGuire	90.00	45.00	25.00
(36)	Earl Moore	90.00	45.00	25.00
(37)	George Mullen (Mullin)	90.00	45.00	25.00
(38)	Billy Owen (Frank Owens)	90.00	45.00	25.00
(39)	Fred Parent	90.00	45.00	25.00
(40)	Case Patten	90.00	45.00	25.00
(41)	Ed Plank	550.00	275.00	165.00
(42)	Ossie Schreckengost	90.00	45.00	25.00
(43)	Jake Stahl	90.00	45.00	25.00
(44)	Fred (George) Stone	90.00	45.00	25.00
(45)	Wm. Sudhoff	90.00	45.00	25.00
(46)	Roy (Terry) Turner	90.00	45.00	25.00
(47)	G.E. Waddell	330.00	165.00	100.00
(48)	Bob Wallace	330.00	165.00	100.00
(49)	G. Harris White	90.00	45.00	25.00
(50)	Geo. Winters (Winter)	90.00	45.00	25.00
(51)	Cy Young	1,320	660.00	395.00

1906 Fan Craze - National League

Identical in size and format to the American League set of two years previous, this set of unnumbered cards was issued by the Fan Craze Co. of Cincinnati in 1906 and was designed like a deck of playing cards. The cards were intended to be used in playing a baseball table game. The National League cards are printed with red backs and black-and-white player photos on front. Sears sold the set for 48 cents postpaid.

		NM	EX	VG
	Complete Set (54):	11,000	5,500	3,300
	Complete Boxed Set:	17,600	8,800	5,225
	Common Player:	65.00	35.00	20.00
(1)	Leon Ames	65.00	35.00	20.00
(2)	Clarence Beaumont	65.00	35.00	20.00
(3)	Jake Beckley	330.00	165.00	100.00
(4)	Billy Bergen	65.00	35.00	20.00
(5)	Roger Bresnahan	330.00	165.00	100.00
(6)	George Brown (Browne)	65.00	35.00	20.00
(7)	Mordacai Brown	330.00	165.00	100.00
(8)	Jas. Casey	65.00	35.00	20.00
(9)	Frank Chance	330.00	165.00	100.00
(10)	Fred Clarke	330.00	165.00	100.00
(11)	Thos. Corcoran	65.00	35.00	20.00
(12)	Bill Dahlen	65.00	35.00	20.00
(13)	Mike Donlin	65.00	35.00	20.00
(14)	Charley Dooin	65.00	35.00	20.00
(15)	Mickey Doolin (Doolan)	65.00	35.00	20.00
(16)	Hugh Duffy	330.00	165.00	100.00
(17)	John E. Dunleavy	65.00	35.00	20.00
(18)	Bob Ewing	65.00	35.00	20.00
(19)	"Chick" Fraser	65.00	35.00	20.00
(20)	J. Edward (Edward H.) Hanlon	330.00	165.00	100.00
(21)	G.E. Howard	65.00	35.00	20.00
(22)	Miller Huggins	330.00	165.00	100.00
(23)	Joseph Kelley	330.00	165.00	100.00
(24)	John Kling	65.00	35.00	20.00
(25)	Tommy Leach	65.00	35.00	20.00
(26)	Harry Lumley	65.00	35.00	20.00
(27)	Carl Lundgren	65.00	35.00	20.00
(28)	Bill Maloney	65.00	35.00	20.00
(29)	Dan McGann	65.00	35.00	20.00
(30)	Joe McGinnity	330.00	165.00	100.00
(31)	John J. McGraw	330.00	165.00	100.00
(32)	Harry McIntire (McIntyre)	65.00	35.00	20.00
(33)	Charley Nichols	550.00	275.00	165.00
(34)	Mike O'Neil (O'Neill)	65.00	35.00	20.00
(35)	Orville (Orval) Overall	65.00	35.00	20.00
(36)	Frank Pfeffer	65.00	35.00	20.00
(37)	Deacon Phillippe	65.00	35.00	20.00
(38)	Charley Pittinger	65.00	35.00	20.00
(39)	Harry C. Pulliam	65.00	35.00	20.00
(40)	Claude Ritchey	65.00	35.00	20.00
(41)	Ed Ruelbach (Reulbach)	65.00	35.00	20.00
(42)	J. Bentley Seymour	65.00	35.00	20.00
(43)	Jim Sheckard	65.00	35.00	20.00
(44)	Jack Taylor	65.00	35.00	20.00
(45)	Luther H. Taylor	220.00	110.00	65.00
(46)	Fred Tenny (Tenney)	65.00	35.00	20.00
(47)	Harry Theilman (Jake Thielman)	65.00	35.00	20.00
(48)	Roy Thomas	65.00	35.00	20.00
(49)	Hans Wagner	5,000	2,065	1,240
(50)	Jake Weimer	65.00	35.00	20.00
(51)	Bob Wicker	65.00	35.00	20.00
(52)	Victor Willis	330.00	165.00	100.00
(53)	Lew (George "Hooks") Wiltsie	65.00	35.00	20.00
(54)	Irving Young	65.00	35.00	20.00

1922 Fans Cigarettes (T231)

More mystery surrounds this obscure set than any other tobacco issue. In fact, the only evidence of its existence until 1992 was a photocopy of a single card of Pittsburgh Pirates out-fielder Carson Bigbee. Even the owner of the card is unknown. Cards measure approximately 2-1/2" x 1-1/2" and are black-and-white. Adding to the mystery is the number "85" which appears in the lower right corner on the front of the card, apparently indicating there were at least that many cards in the set. In 1992 card "61" was reported. Card backs displays the player's batting averages for each season from 1918 through 1921 and includes the line: "I select (name) leading batter of all (position), packed with FANS cigarettes." The statement is followed by blanks for a person to fill in his name and address, as if the card were some sort of "ballot." With only one specimen known of each, these are among the rarest baseball cards in the hobby. Their American Card Catalog designation is T231.

Values Undetermined
61   Frank Baker
85   Carson Bigbee

1939 Father & Son Shoes

Chuck Klein, outfielder, Phillies
Compliments Father and Son

This set features Phillies and A's players and was distributed in the Philadelphia area in 1939 by Father & Son Shoes stores. The unnumbered black and white cards measure 3" x 4". The player's name, position and team appear below the photo, along with the line "Compliments of Fathers & Son Shoes." The backs are blank. The checklist, arranged here alphabetically, may be incomplete.

		NM	EX	VG
Complete Set (17):		5,000	2,500	1,500
Common Player:		450.00	220.00	135.00
(1)	Morrie Arnovich	450.00	220.00	135.00
(2)	Earl Brucker	450.00	220.00	135.00
(3)	George Caster	450.00	220.00	135.00
(4)	Sam Chapman	450.00	220.00	135.00
(5)	Spud Davis	450.00	220.00	135.00
(6)	Joe Gantenbein	450.00	220.00	135.00
(7)	Bob Johnson	450.00	220.00	135.00
(8)	Chuck Klein	1,125	565.00	340.00
(9)	Herschel Martin	450.00	220.00	135.00
(10)	Merrill May	450.00	220.00	135.00
(11)	Wally Moses	450.00	220.00	135.00
(12)	Emmett Mueller	450.00	220.00	135.00
(13)	Hugh Mulcahy	450.00	220.00	135.00
(14)	Skeeter Newsome	450.00	220.00	135.00
(15)	Claude Passeau	450.00	220.00	135.00
(16)	George Scharien (Scharein)	450.00	220.00	135.00
(17)	Dick Siebert	450.00	220.00	135.00

1913 Fatima Team Cards (T200)

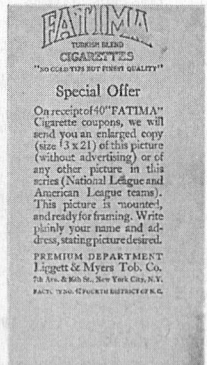

Issued by the Ligget & Myers Tobacco Co. in 1913 with Fatima brand cigarettes, the T200 set consists of eight National and eight American League team cards. The cards measure 2-5/8" x 4-3/4" and are glossy photographs on paper stock. Although it is unknown why, several of the cards are more difficult to obtain than others. The team cards feature 369 different players, managers and mascots. The card backs contain an offer for an enlarged copy (13" x 21") of a team card, minus the advertising on front, in exchange for 40 Fatima cigarette coupons.

		NM	EX	VG
Complete Set (16):		40,000	12,000	6,000
Common Card:		1,200	375.00	180.00
(1)	Boston Nationals	4,000	1,200	600.00
(2)	Brooklyn Nationals	2,000	600.00	300.00
(3)	Chicago Nationals	1,200	375.00	180.00
(4)	Cincinnati Nationals	1,400	420.00	220.00
(5)	New York Nationals	2,200	660.00	330.00
(6)	Philadelphia Nationals	1,200	375.00	180.00
(7)	Pittsburg Nationals	1,500	450.00	225.00
(8)	St. Louis Nationals	3,500	1,000	525.00
(9)	Boston Americans	3,300	1,000	500.00
(10)	Chicago Americans	2,000	600.00	300.00
(11)	Cleveland Americans	4,000	1,200	600.00
(12)	Detroit Americans	7,500	2,250	1,125
(13)	New York Americans	4,500	1,350	675.00
(14)	Philadelphia Americans	1,400	420.00	220.00
(15)	St. Louis Americans	3,200	1,000	500.00
(16)	Washington Americans	4,200	1,300	650.00

1913 Fatima Premiums

Among the rarest of the tobacco cards are the large-format (21" x 13") versions of the T200 Fatima team photos which could be obtained by redeeming 40 coupons from cigarette packs. The premium-size team photos are virtually identical to the smaller ones, except they do not carry the Fatima advertising on the front. Because of their large size, the premiums are seldom seen in top grade. The complete set price is quoted as a hypothetical proposition only; none is known.

	NM	EX	VG
Common Card:	15,000	4,500	2,200

(1)	Boston Nationals	16,000	5,000	2,500
(2)	Brooklyn Nationals	16,000	5,000	2,500
(3)	Chicago Nationals	20,000	6,000	3,000
(4)	Cincinnati Nationals	15,000	4,500	2,200
(5)	New York Nationals	16,000	5,000	2,500
(6)	Philadelphia Nationals	15,000	4,500	2,200
(7)	Pittsburg Nationals	20,000	6,000	3,000
(8)	St. Louis Nationals	15,000	4,500	2,200
(9)	Boston Americans	25,000	7,500	3,750
(10)	Chicago Americans	16,000	5,000	2,500
(11)	Cleveland Americans	30,000	9,000	4,500
(12)	Detroit Americans	30,000	9,000	4,500
(13)	New York Americans	25,000	7,500	3,750
(14)	Philadelphia Americans	20,000	6,000	3,000
(15)	St. Louis Americans	20,000	6,000	3,000
(16)	Washington Americans	15,000	4,500	2,200

1913-1915 Fatima Posters

These blank-back, black-and-white (1913) or b/w with a color picture of a cigarette pack (1914-15) window posters were produced by Pictorial News Co. of New York for distribution by Fatima Cigarettes, whose advertising appears in the lower-right corner of the 12-1/2" x 19" pictures. To the left of the advertising are a couple of sentences about the player(s) pictured (usually in an action pose). The pictures are numbered, but there is currently no idea as to the extent of the issue.

		NM	EX	VG
6	Frank Chance's New York Americans in Bermuda	1,200	600.00	360.00
15	Christy Mathewson	6,000	3,000	2,000
22	Ty Cobb	7,500	3,500	2,500
31	Pittsburgh Pirates Only Hope of West in National Race	1,000	500.00	300.00
33	Joe Jackson	4,500	2,250	1,350
35	Athletics' Star Pitchers the Giants Will Have to Beat (Chief Bender, Jack Coombs, Eddie Plank)	450.00	225.00	135.00
36	Cleveland Strong Second in the American League Race	650.00	325.00	200.00
43	Chicago Cubs team	1,200	600.00	360.00
45	Plays that Made Baseball History (Various action photos.)	250.00	125.00	75.00
51	Walter Johnson	5,500	2,750	1,650
56	Opposing Pitchers in the Coming World's Series Battles (Christy Mathewson, Rube Marquard, Jeff Tesreau, Al Demaree, Chief Bender, Boardwalk Brown, Byron Houck, Eddie Plank)	650.00	325.00	195.00
105	Giants 'Clearing the Deck for Action' Down in Marlin (Mathewson, Snodgrass, Fletcher, etc.)	325.00	160.00	95.00
153	American League Pennant Winners Ready For the World's Series (1914 Philadelphia A's)	1,500	750.00	450.00
226	Ty Cobb, The Most Talked About Man in Big League Baseball	7,500	3,750	2,250
259	(1915 Philadelphia Phillies)	2,500	1,250	750.00
260	Red Sox Ready to do Battle for World's Championship (1915 Red Sox)	3,500	1,750	1,050

1914 Fatima (T222)

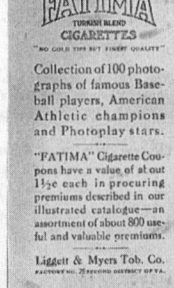

Unlike the typical 20th Century tobacco card issues, the T222 Fatima cards are glossy photographs on a thin paper stock and measure a larger 2-1/2" x 4-1/2". According to the back of the card, the set includes "100 photographs of famous Baseball Players, American Athletic Champions and Photoplay stars." The baseball portion of the set appears to be complete at 52. The set includes players from 13 of the 16 major league teams (no Red Sox, White Sox or Pirates). Most cards are seen with a small black number from 2-9 or 12-15 beneath the player's name. The same number can be found on up to seven cards. Cards with numbers 12-15 are considered short-prints and so designated in this alphabetical checklist.

		NM	EX	VG
Complete Set (52):		137,500	56,250	28,125
Common Player:		1,440	565.00	280.00
(1)	Grover Alexander	20,000	4,500	2,250
(2)	Jimmy Archer	1,440	565.00	280.00
(3)	Jimmy Austin/SP	3,440	1,375	690.00
(4)	Jack Barry	1,440	565.00	280.00
(5)	George Baumgardner/SP	3,440	1,375	690.00
(6)	Rube Benton	1,440	565.00	280.00
(7)	Roger Bresnahan	4,500	1,815	905.00
(8)	Boardwalk Brown	1,440	565.00	280.00
(9)	George Burns	1,440	565.00	280.00
(10)	Bullet Joe Bush	1,440	565.00	280.00
(11)	George Chalmers	1,440	565.00	280.00
(12)	Frank Chance	4,500	1,815	905.00
(13)	Al Demaree	1,440	565.00	280.00
(14)	Art Fletcher	1,440	565.00	280.00
(15)	Earl Hamilton/SP	3,440	1,375	690.00
(16)	John Henry/SP	3,440	1,375	690.00
(17)	Byron Houck	1,440	565.00	280.00
(18)	Miller Huggins	4,500	1,815	905.00
(19)	Hughie Jennings	4,500	1,815	905.00
(20)	Walter Johnson/SP	15,625	6,250	3,125
(21)	Ray Keating/SP	3,440	1,375	690.00
(22)	Jack Lapp	1,440	565.00	280.00
(23)	Tommy Leach	1,440	565.00	280.00
(24)	Nemo Leibold/SP	3,440	1,375	690.00
(25)	Jack Lelivelt/SP	3,440	1,375	690.00
(26)	Hans Lobert/SP	3,440	1,375	690.00
(27)	Lee Magee/SP	3,440	1,375	690.00
(28)	Sherry Magee/SP	3,440	1,375	690.00
(29)	Fritz Maisel	1,440	565.00	280.00
(30)	Rube Marquard	4,500	1,815	905.00
(31)	George McBride/SP	3,440	1,375	690.00
(32)	Stuffy McInnis	1,440	565.00	280.00
(33)	Larry McLean	1,440	565.00	280.00
(34)	Ray Morgan/SP	3,440	1,375	690.00
(35)	Eddie Murphy	1,440	565.00	280.00
(36)	Red Murray	1,440	565.00	280.00
(37)	Rube Oldring	1,440	565.00	280.00
(38)	Bill Orr	1,440	565.00	280.00
(39)	Hub Perdue	1,440	565.00	280.00
(40)	Art Phelan	1,440	565.00	280.00
(41)	Ed Reulbach	1,440	565.00	280.00
(42)	Vic Saier	1,140	565.00	280.00
(43)	Slim Sallee	1,440	565.00	280.00
(44)	Wally Schang	1,440	565.00	280.00
(45)	Wildfire Schulte/SP	3,440	1,375	690.00
(46)	J.C. "Red" Smith/SP	3,440	1,375	690.00
(47)	Amos Strunk	1,440	565.00	280.00
(48)	Bill Sweeney	1,440	565.00	280.00
(49)	Lefty Tyler	1,440	565.00	280.00
(50)	Ossie Vitt	1,440	565.00	280.00
(51)	Ivy Wingo	1,440	565.00	280.00
(52)	Heinie Zimmerman	1,440	565.00	280.00

1955 Felin's Franks

Because of the relatively few specimens in collectors' hands, it is believed this hot dog issue was never actually released. The 4" x 3-5/8" round-cornered panels have a red border front and back with a color player photo on the left side of the front. At right-front are the 1954 stats of a player different than that pictured. Each half of the front shares a large black number. According to the card back, hot dog buyers were supposed to match the pictures and stats of 30 different players to have a chance to win prizes.

		NM	EX	VG
Common Player:		1,250	625.00	375.00
1	Mayo Smith	1,250	625.00	375.00
2	Unknown (Probably coach Benny Bengough.)			
3	Wally Moses	1,250	625.00	375.00
4	Whit Wyatt	1,250	625.00	375.00
5	Maje McDonnell	1,250	625.00	375.00
6	Wiechec/Trainer	750.00	375.00	225.00
7	Murry Dickson	1,250	625.00	375.00
8	Earl Torgeson	1,250	625.00	375.00
9	Bobby Morgan	1,250	625.00	375.00
10	John Meyer	1,250	625.00	375.00
11	Bob Miller	1,250	625.00	375.00
12	Jim Owens	1,250	625.00	375.00
13	Steve Ridzik	1,250	625.00	375.00
14	Robin Roberts	2,000	1,000	600.00

15	Unknown			
	(Probably Curt Simmons.)			
16	Herm Wehmeier	1,250	625.00	375.00
17	Smoky Burgess	1,250	625.00	375.00
18	Stan Lopata	1,250	625.00	375.00
19	Gus Niarhos	1,250	625.00	375.00
20	Floyd Baker	1,250	625.00	375.00
21	Marv Blaylock	1,250	625.00	375.00
22	Granny Hamner	1,250	625.00	375.00
23	Willie Jones	1,250	625.00	375.00
24	Unknown			
25	Unknown			
26	Richie Ashburn	2,250	1,125	675.00
27	Joe Lonnett	1,250	625.00	375.00
28	Mel Clark	1,250	625.00	375.00
29	Bob Greenwood	1,250	625.00	375.00
30	Unknown			

1913 Fenway Breweries/Tom Barker Game

Presumably distributed as a promotion for its Fenway brand of beer, a specially labeled boxed set of the Tom Barker baseball game cards was issued. Only the box, the Score Card and the card of Frank "Home Run" Baker are found bearing the red advertising overprint.

	NM	EX	VG
Complete Set (54):	6,000	3,000	1,800
Frank Baker	350.00	175.00	105.00
Score Card	40.00	20.00	12.00

1916 Ferguson Bakery Felt Pennants (BF2)

Issued circa 1916, this unnumbered set consists of 97 felt pennants with a small black-and-white player photo glued to each. The triangular pennants measure approximately 2-7/8" across the wide top and taper to a length of about 6". The photos are about 1-1/4" x 1-3/4" and appear to be identical to photos used for The Sporting News issues of the same period. The pennants list the player's name and team. The pennants were given away as premiums with the purchase of five-cent loaves of Ferguson Bakery Bread in the Roxbury, Mass. area. It is believed that each player can be found on several different colors of background felt.

		NM	EX	VG
Complete Set (97):		27,500	13,500	8,250
Common Player:		175.00	85.00	50.00
(1)	Grover Alexander	600.00	300.00	180.00
(2)	Jimmy Archer	175.00	85.00	50.00
(3)	J. Franklin Baker	450.00	225.00	135.00
(4)	Dave Bancroft	450.00	225.00	135.00
(5)	Jack Barry	175.00	85.00	50.00
(6)	"Chief" Bender	450.00	225.00	135.00
(7)	Joe Benz	175.00	85.00	50.00
(8)	Mordecai Brown	450.00	225.00	135.00
(9)	Geo. J. Burns	175.00	85.00	50.00
(10)	"Donie" Bush	175.00	85.00	50.00
(11)	Forrest Cady	175.00	85.00	50.00
(12)	Max Carey	450.00	225.00	135.00
(13)	Ray Chapman	300.00	150.00	90.00
(14)	Ty Cobb	1,800	900.00	550.00
(15)	Eddie Collins	450.00	225.00	135.00
(16)	"Shauno" Collins	175.00	85.00	50.00
(17)	Charles Comiskey	450.00	225.00	135.00
(18)	Harry Coveleskie (Coveleski)	175.00	85.00	50.00
(19)	Gavvy Cravath	175.00	85.00	50.00

(20)	Sam Crawford	450.00	225.00	135.00
(21)	Jake Daubert	175.00	85.00	50.00
(22)	Josh Devore	175.00	85.00	50.00
(23)	Charles Dooin	175.00	85.00	50.00
(24)	Larry Doyle	175.00	85.00	50.00
(25)	Jean Dubuc	175.00	85.00	50.00
(26)	Johnny Evers	450.00	225.00	135.00
(27)	Urban Faber	450.00	225.00	135.00
(28)	Eddie Foster	175.00	85.00	50.00
(29)	Del Gainer (Gainor)	175.00	85.00	50.00
(30)	"Chic" Gandil	375.00	185.00	110.00
(31)	Joe Gedeon	175.00	85.00	50.00
(32)	Hank Gowdy	175.00	85.00	50.00
(33)	Earl Hamilton	175.00	85.00	50.00
(34)	Claude Hendrix	175.00	85.00	50.00
(35)	Buck Herzog	175.00	85.00	50.00
(36)	Harry Hooper	450.00	225.00	135.00
(37)	Miller Huggins	450.00	225.00	135.00
(38)	Joe Jackson	3,500	1,750	1,000
(39)	William James	175.00	85.00	50.00
(40)	Hugh Jennings	450.00	225.00	135.00
(41)	Walter Johnson	900.00	450.00	275.00
(42)	Fielder Jones	175.00	85.00	50.00
(43)	Joe Judge	175.00	85.00	50.00
(44)	Benny Kauff	175.00	85.00	50.00
(45)	Wm. Killefer	175.00	85.00	50.00
(46)	Napoleon Lajoie	450.00	225.00	135.00
(47)	Jack Lapp	175.00	85.00	50.00
(48)	John Lavan	175.00	85.00	50.00
(49)	Jimmy Lavender	175.00	85.00	50.00
(50)	"Dutch" Leonard	175.00	85.00	50.00
(51)	Duffy Lewis	175.00	85.00	50.00
(52)	Hans Lobert	175.00	85.00	50.00
(53)	Fred Luderus	175.00	85.00	50.00
(54)	Connie Mack	450.00	225.00	135.00
(55)	Sherwood Magee	175.00	85.00	50.00
(56)	Al Mamaux	175.00	85.00	50.00
(57)	"Rabbit" Maranville	450.00	225.00	135.00
(58)	Rube Marquard	450.00	225.00	135.00
(59)	George McBride	175.00	85.00	50.00
(60)	John J. McGraw	450.00	225.00	135.00
(61)	Jack McInnis	175.00	85.00	50.00
(62)	Fred Merkle	175.00	85.00	50.00
(63)	Chief Meyers	175.00	85.00	50.00
(64)	Clyde Milan	175.00	85.00	50.00
(65)	Otto Miller	175.00	85.00	50.00
(66)	Pat Moran	175.00	85.00	50.00
(67)	Ray Morgan	175.00	85.00	50.00
(68)	Guy Morton	175.00	85.00	50.00
(69)	Ed. Murphy	175.00	85.00	50.00
(70)	Rube Oldring	175.00	85.00	50.00
(71)	"Dode" Paskert	175.00	85.00	50.00
(72)	Walter Pipp	175.00	85.00	50.00
(73)	Clarence Rowland	175.00	85.00	50.00
(74)	"Nap" Rucker	175.00	85.00	50.00
(75)	Dick Rudolph	175.00	85.00	50.00
(76)	Reb Russell	175.00	85.00	50.00
(77)	Vic Saier	175.00	85.00	50.00
(78)	"Slim" Sallee	175.00	85.00	50.00
(79)	Ray Schalk	450.00	225.00	135.00
(80)	Walter Schang	175.00	85.00	50.00
(81)	Frank Schulte	175.00	85.00	50.00
(82)	Jim Scott	175.00	85.00	50.00
(83)	George Sisler	450.00	225.00	135.00
(84)	Geo. Stallings	175.00	85.00	50.00
(85)	Oscar Stanage	175.00	85.00	50.00
(86)	"Jeff" Tesreau	175.00	85.00	50.00
(87)	Joe Tinker	450.00	225.00	135.00
(88)	Geo. Tyler	175.00	85.00	50.00
(89)	Jim Vaughn	175.00	85.00	50.00
(90)	Bobby Veach	175.00	85.00	50.00
(91)	Hans Wagner	1,350	675.00	400.00
(92)	Ed. Walsh	450.00	225.00	135.00
(93)	Buck Weaver	750.00	375.00	225.00
(94)	Ivy Wingo	175.00	85.00	50.00
(95)	Joe Wood	350.00	175.00	100.00
(96)	"Pep" Young	175.00	85.00	50.00
(97)	Heiny Zimmerman	175.00	85.00	50.00

1916 Ferguson Bakery Photo Prize Pennants

As part of its baseball insert and premium program, the Roxbury, Mass., bakery issued this series of large (9" x 24") felt pennants bearing a black-and-white player photo (3" x 5"). The colorful pennants are decorated with baseball graphics

and have player and team identification. The pennants were a premium for redeeming 50 tickets from five-cent loaves of bread. Examples of the large-format pennants are so scarce only a handful of players are checklisted thus far.

		NM	EX	VG
Common Player:		9,000	4,500	2,750
(1)	Grover Alexander	15,000	7,500	4,500
(2)	Jack Barry	9,000	4,500	2,750
(3)	Ty Cobb	20,000	10,000	6,000
(4)	Eddie Collins	9,000	4,500	2,750
(5)	Bill Donovan	9,000	4,500	2,750
(6)	Miller Huggins	12,500	6,250	3,750
(7)	John McGraw	12,500	6,250	3,750
(8)	Joe Tinker	9,000	4,500	2,750

1957 Fine Arts Studio

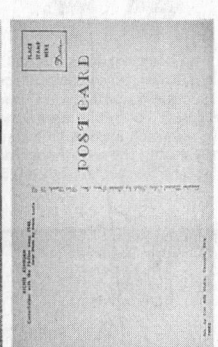

The date of issue on this card is theoretical with no real evidence present on the piece. Published by Fine Arts Studio of Cleveland, the 3-1/2" x 5-1/2" card has a borderless color photo on front. Player identification is on back with standard postcard markings and credit lines to the publisher and printer (Dexter Press of New York).

		NM	EX	VG
75062	Richie Ashburn	100.00	50.00	30.00

1959 First Federal Savings Famous Senators Matchbooks

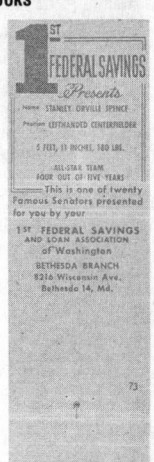

Star Senators of the 20th Century are featured in this series of matchbook covers. The 1-1/2" x 4-1/2" matchbooks include a black-and-white player portrait photo and team logo on front. The sponsoring bank's advertising is on back. Player identification and information are printed inside. Values shown are for complete but empty covers, with the striker surface intact. Complete matchbooks with matches bring about 2X the values quoted.

		NM	EX	VG
Complete Set (20):		325.00	160.00	95.00
Common Player:		15.00	7.50	4.50
(1)	Nick Altrock	15.00	7.50	4.50
(2)	Ossie Bluege	15.00	7.50	4.50
(3)	Joe Cronin	20.00	10.00	6.00
(4)	Alvin Crowder	15.00	7.50	4.50
(5)	Goose Goslin	20.00	10.00	6.00
(6)	Clark Griffith	20.00	10.00	6.00
(7)	Bucky Harris	20.00	10.00	6.00
(8)	Walter Johnson	45.00	22.00	13.50
(9)	Joe Judge	15.00	7.50	4.50
(10)	Harmon Killebrew	25.00	12.50	7.50
(11)	Joe Kuhel	15.00	7.50	4.50
(12)	Buddy Lewis	15.00	7.50	4.50
(13)	Clyde Milan	15.00	7.50	4.50
(14)	Buddy Myer	15.00	7.50	4.50
(15)	Roger Peckinpaugh	15.00	7.50	4.50
(16)	Sam Rice	20.00	10.00	6.00
(17)	Roy Sievers	15.00	7.50	4.50
(18)	Stanley Spence	15.00	7.50	4.50
(19)	Mickey Vernon	15.00	7.50	4.50
(20)	Samuel West	15.00	7.50	4.50

1953 First National Super Market Boston Red Sox

Four of the early 1950s Red Sox appear in this series issued by a Boston grocery chain. The cards may have been distributed in conjunction with players' in-store appearances. The cards measure 3-3/4" x 5" and are printed in black-and-white. A facsimile autograph appears on the front. Backs have the sponsor's advertising. The unnumbered cards are checklisted here alphabetically. See also 1953 Stop & Shop Boston Red Sox.

	NM	EX	VG
Complete Set (4):	2,500	1,250	750.00
Common Player:	750.00	375.00	225.00
(1) Billy Goodman	750.00	375.00	225.00
(2) Ellis Kinder	750.00	375.00	225.00
(3) Mel Parnell	750.00	375.00	225.00
(4) Sammy White	750.00	375.00	225.00

1951 Fischer's Bread Labels

This set of end-labels from loaves of bread consists of 32 player photos, each measuring approximately 2-3/4" square. The labels include the player's name, team and position, along with a few words about him. The bakery's slogan "Bread For Energy" appears in a dark band along the bottom. The set, which is unnumbered, was distributed in the Northeast.

	NM	EX	VG
Complete Set (32):	25,000	10,000	5,000
Common Player:	750.00	375.00	225.00
(1) Vern Bickford	750.00	300.00	150.00
(2) Ralph Branca	825.00	325.00	175.00
(3) Harry Brecheen	750.00	300.00	150.00
(4) "Chico" Carrasquel	750.00	300.00	150.00
(5) Cliff Chambers	750.00	300.00	150.00
(6) "Hoot" Evers	750.00	300.00	150.00
(7) Ned Garver	750.00	300.00	150.00
(8) Billy Goodman	750.00	300.00	150.00
(9) Gil Hodges	1,350	550.00	275.00
(10) Larry Jansen	750.00	300.00	150.00
(11) Willie Jones	750.00	300.00	150.00
(12) Eddie Joost	750.00	300.00	150.00
(13) George Kell	1,250	500.00	250.00
(14) Alex Kellner	750.00	300.00	150.00
(15) Ted Kluszewski	1,200	480.00	240.00
(16) Jim Konstanty	750.00	300.00	150.00
(17) Bob Lemon	1,250	500.00	250.00
(18) Cass Michaels	750.00	300.00	150.00
(19) Johnny Mize	1,250	500.00	250.00
(20) Irv Noren	750.00	300.00	150.00
(21) Andy Pafko	750.00	300.00	150.00
(22) Joe Page	750.00	300.00	150.00
(23) Mel Parnell	750.00	300.00	150.00
(24) Johnny Sain	825.00	330.00	165.00
(25) "Red" Schoendienst	1,250	500.00	250.00
(26) Roy Sievers	750.00	300.00	150.00
(27) Roy Smalley	750.00	300.00	150.00
(28) Herman Wehmeier	750.00	300.00	150.00
(29) Bill Werle	750.00	300.00	150.00
(30) Wes Westrum	750.00	300.00	150.00
(31) Early Wynn	1,250	500.00	250.00
(32) Gus Zernial	750.00	300.00	150.00

1970 Flavor-est Milk Milwaukee Brewers

While purporting to be a dairy issue, this is actually a collectors' set produced by Illinois hobbyist Bob Solon. The cards picture members of the 1970 Brewers in their first year in Milwaukee. Posed action photos and portraits are printed in blue-and-white on a 2-3/8" x 4-1/4" format. The pictures are borderless at top and sides. At bottom is a white strip with the player name. Backs have a dairy ad. The unnumbered cards are checklisted here alphabetically. Ironically, this set was later reissued in a marked reprint.

Mike Hershberger

	NM	EX	VG
Complete Set (24):	25.00	12.50	7.50
Common Player:	2.50	1.25	.70
(1) Gene Brabender	2.50	1.25	.70
(2) Dave Bristol	2.50	1.25	.70
(3) Wayne Comer	2.50	1.25	.70
(4) Cal Ermer	2.50	1.25	.70
(5) Greg Goossen	2.50	1.25	.70
(6) Tom Harper	3.50	1.75	1.00
(7) Mike Hegan	3.50	1.75	1.00
(8) Mike Hershberger	2.50	1.25	.70
(9) Steve Hovley	2.50	1.25	.70
(10) John Kennedy	2.50	1.25	.70
(11) Lew Krausse	2.50	1.25	.70
(12) Ted Kubiak	2.50	1.25	.70
(13) Bob Locker	2.50	1.25	.70
(14) Roy McMillan	2.50	1.25	.70
(15) Jerry McNertney	2.50	1.25	.70
(16) Bob Meyer	2.50	1.25	.70
(17) John Morris	2.50	1.25	.70
(18) John O'Donoghue	2.50	1.25	.70
(19) Marty Pattin	2.50	1.25	.70
(20) Rich Rollins	2.50	1.25	.70
(21) Phil Roof	2.50	1.25	.70
(22) Ted Savage	2.50	1.25	.70
(23) Russ Snyder	2.50	1.25	.70
(24) Dan Walton	3.50	1.75	1.00

1923 Fleer

While only a few specimens are known to date, from the print on the back it can be presumed that all 60 of the baseball players from the blank-back strip card set cataloged as W515 were also issued with Fleer advertising on the verso. Several cards are also known with boxers, indicating another 60 cards of non-baseball athletes and other famous people were also produced. The 1-5/8" x 2-3/8" cards feature crude color line art of the player on front, with a black-and-white ad on back. The cards pre-date by more than a decade Fleer's "Cops and Robbers" set of 1935, and are some 35 years in advance of Fleer's first modern baseball issue.

	NM	EX	VG
Complete Set (60):	15,000	7,500	4,500
Common Player:	175.00	85.00	50.00
1 Bill Cunningham	175.00	85.00	50.00
2 Al Mamaux	175.00	85.00	50.00
3 "Babe" Ruth	1,325	660.00	400.00
4 Dave Bancroft	350.00	175.00	105.00
5 Ed Rommel	175.00	85.00	50.00
6 "Babe" Adams	175.00	85.00	50.00
7 Clarence Walker	175.00	85.00	50.00
8 Waite Hoyt	350.00	175.00	105.00
9 Bob Shawkey	175.00	85.00	50.00
10 "Ty" Cobb	1,000	500.00	300.00
11 George Sisler	350.00	175.00	105.00
12 Jack Bentley	175.00	85.00	50.00
13 Jim O'Connell	175.00	85.00	50.00
14 Frank Frisch	350.00	175.00	105.00
15 Frank Baker	350.00	175.00	105.00
16 Burleigh Grimes	350.00	175.00	105.00
17 Wally Schang	175.00	85.00	50.00
18 Harry Heilman (Heilmann)	350.00	175.00	105.00
19 Aaron Ward	175.00	85.00	50.00
20 Carl Mays	200.00	100.00	60.00
21 The Meusel Bros. (Bob Meusel, Irish Meusel)	225.00	110.00	67.00
22 Arthur Nehf	175.00	85.00	50.00
23 Lee Meadows	175.00	85.00	50.00
24 "Casey" Stengel	375.00	185.00	110.00
25 Jack Scott	175.00	85.00	50.00

26 Kenneth Williams	175.00	85.00	50.00
27 Joe Bush	175.00	85.00	50.00
28 Tris Speaker	400.00	200.00	120.00
29 Ross Young (Youngs)	350.00	175.00	105.00
30 Joe Dugan	175.00	85.00	50.00
31 The Barnes Bros. (Jesse Barnes, Virgil Barnes)	200.00	100.00	60.00
32 George Kelly	350.00	175.00	105.00
33 Hugh McQuillen (McQuillan)	175.00	85.00	50.00
34 Hugh Jennings	350.00	175.00	105.00
35 Tom Griffith	175.00	85.00	50.00
36 Miller Huggins	350.00	175.00	105.00
37 "Whitey" Witt	175.00	85.00	50.00
38 Walter Johnson	500.00	250.00	150.00
39 "Wally" Pipp	200.00	100.00	60.00
40 "Dutch" Reuther (Ruether)	175.00	85.00	50.00
41 Jim Johnston	175.00	85.00	50.00
42 Willie Kamm	175.00	85.00	50.00
43 Sam Jones	175.00	85.00	50.00
44 Frank Snyder	175.00	85.00	50.00
45 John McGraw	350.00	175.00	105.00
46 Everett Scott	175.00	85.00	50.00
47 "Babe" Ruth	1,325	660.00	400.00
48 Urban Shocker	175.00	85.00	50.00
49 Grover Alexander	400.00	200.00	120.00
50 "Rabbit" Maranville	350.00	175.00	105.00
51 Ray Schalk	350.00	175.00	105.00
52 "Heinie" Groh	175.00	85.00	50.00
53 Wilbert Robinson	350.00	175.00	105.00
54 George Burns	175.00	85.00	50.00
55 Rogers Hornsby	400.00	200.00	120.00
56 Zack Wheat	350.00	175.00	105.00
57 Eddie Roush	350.00	175.00	105.00
58 Eddie Collins	350.00	175.00	105.00
59 Charlie Hollocher	175.00	85.00	50.00
60 Red Faber	350.00	175.00	105.00

1959 Fleer Ted Williams

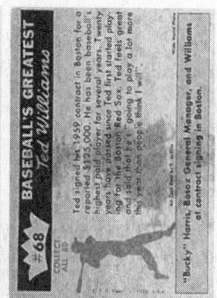

This 80-card 1959 Fleer set tells of the life of baseball great Ted Williams, from his childhood years up to 1958. The full-color cards measure 2-1/2" x 3-1/2" in size and make use of both horizontal and vertical formats. The card backs, all designed horizontally, contain a continuing biography of Williams. Card #68 was withdrawn from the set early in production and is scarce. Counterfeit cards of #68 have been produced and can be distinguished by a cross-hatch pattern which appears over the photo on the card fronts.

	NM	EX	VG
Complete Set (80):	1,250	625.00	312.50
Common Card:	15.00	7.50	3.75
Wax Pack (6):	400.00	.00	.00
1 The Early Years	100.00	50.00	25.00
2 Ted's Idol (Babe Ruth)	120.00	60.00	30.00
3 Practice Makes Perfect	15.00	7.50	3.75
4 1934 - Ted Learns The Fine Points	15.00	7.50	3.75
5 Ted's Fame Spreads - 1935-36	15.00	7.50	3.75
6 Ted Turns Professional	20.00	10.00	6.00
7 1936 - From Mound To Plate	15.00	7.50	3.75
8 1937 - First Full Season	15.00	7.50	3.75
9 1937 - First Step To The Majors (With Eddie Collins.)	15.00	7.50	3.75
10 1938 - Gunning As A Pastime	15.00	7.50	3.75
11 1938 - First Spring Training (With Jimmie Foxx.)	30.00	15.00	9.00
12 1939 - Burning Up The Minors	20.00	10.00	6.00
13 1939 - Ted Shows He Will Stay	15.00	7.50	3.75
14 Outstanding Rookie of 1939	20.00	10.00	6.00
15 1940 - Williams Licks Sophomore Jinx	20.00	10.00	6.00
16 1941 - Williams' Greatest Year	15.00	7.50	3.75
17 1941 - How Ted Hit .400	30.00	15.00	9.00
18 1941 - All-Star Hero	15.00	7.50	3.75
19 1942 - Ted Wins Triple Crown	15.00	7.50	3.75
20 1942 - On To Naval Training	15.00	7.50	3.75
21 1943 - Honors For Williams	15.00	7.50	3.75
22 1944 - Ted Solos	15.00	7.50	3.75
23 1944 - Williams Wins His Wings	15.00	7.50	3.75
24 1945 - Sharpshooter	15.00	7.50	3.75
25 1945 - Ted Is Discharged	15.00	7.50	3.75
26 1946 - Off To A Flying Start	15.00	7.50	3.75
27 July 9, 1946 - One Man Show	15.00	7.50	3.75
28 July 14, 1946 - The Williams Shift	15.00	7.50	3.75
29 July 21, 1946, Ted Hits For The Cycle	20.00	10.00	6.00
30 1946 - Beating The Williams Shift	15.00	7.50	3.75
31 Oct. 1946 - Sox Lose The Series	15.00	7.50	3.75
32 1946 - Most Valuable Player	15.00	7.50	3.75

		NM	EX	VG
33	1947 - Another Triple Crown For Ted	15.00	7.50	3.75
34	1947 - Ted Sets Runs-Scored Record	15.00	7.50	3.75
35	1948 - The Sox Miss The Pennant	15.00	7.50	3.75
36	1948 - Banner Year For Ted	15.00	7.50	3.75
37	1949 - Sox Miss Out Again	15.00	7.50	3.75
38	1949 - Power Rampage	15.00	7.50	3.75
39	1950 - Great Start (With Joe Cronin and Eddie Collins.)	15.00	7.50	3.75
40	July 11, 1950 - Ted Crashes Into Wall	15.00	7.50	3.75
41	1950 - Ted Recovers	15.00	7.50	3.75
42	1951 - Williams Slowed By Injury	15.00	7.50	3.75
43	1951 - Leads Outfielders In Double Play	15.00	7.50	3.75
44	1952 - Back To The Marines	15.00	7.50	3.75
45	1952 - Farewell To Baseball?	15.00	7.50	3.75
46	1952 - Ready For Combat	15.00	7.50	3.75
47	1953 - Ted Crash Lands Jet	15.00	7.50	3.75
48	July 14, 1953 - Ted Returns	15.00	7.50	3.75
49	1953 - Smash Return	15.00	7.50	3.75
50	March 1954 - Spring Injury	15.00	7.50	3.75
51	May 16, 1954 - Ted Is Patched Up	15.00	7.50	3.75
52	1954 - Ted's Comeback	15.00	7.50	3.75
53	1954 - Ted's Comeback Is A Sucess	15.00	7.50	3.75
54	Dec. 1954, Fisherman Ted Hooks a Big On	15.00	7.50	3.75
55	1955 - Ted Decides Retirement Is "No Go (With Joe Cronin.)	15.00	7.50	3.75
56	1955 - 2,000th Major League Hit	15.00	7.50	3.75
57	1956 - Ted Reaches 400th Homer	15.00	7.50	3.75
58	1957 - Williams Hits .388	15.00	7.50	3.75
59	1957 - Hot September For Ted	15.00	7.50	3.75
60	1957 - More Records For Ted	15.00	7.50	3.75
61	1957 - Outfielder Ted	15.00	7.50	3.75
62	1958 - 6th Batting Title For Ted	15.00	7.50	3.75
63	Ted's All-Star Record	35.00	17.50	10.00
64	1958 - Daughter And Famous Daddy	15.00	7.50	3.75
65	August 30, 1958	15.00	7.50	3.75
66	1958 - Powerhouse	15.00	7.50	3.75
67	Two Famous Fishermen (With Sam Snead.)	20.00	10.00	6.00
68	Jan. 23, 1959 - Ted Signs For 1959	650.00	325.00	162.50
69	A Future Ted Williams?	15.00	7.50	3.75
70	Ted Williams & Jim Thorpe	30.00	15.00	9.00
71	Ted's Hitting Fundamentals #1	15.00	7.50	3.75
72	Ted's Hitting Fundamentals #2	15.00	7.50	3.75
73	Ted's Hitting Fundamentals #3	15.00	7.50	3.75
74	Here's How!	15.00	7.50	3.75
75	Williams' Value To Red Sox (With Babe Ruth, Eddie Collins.)	30.00	15.00	9.00
76	Ted's Remarkable "On Base" Record	15.00	7.50	3.75
77	Ted Relaxes	15.00	7.50	3.75
78	Honors For Williams	15.00	7.50	3.75
79	Where Ted Stands	25.00	12.50	7.50
80	Ted's Goals For 1959	40.00	15.00	9.00

1960 Fleer Baseball Greats

The 1960 Fleer Baseball Greats set consists of 78 cards of the game's top players from the past, plus a card of Ted Williams, who was in his final major league season. The cards are standard size (2-1/2" x 3-1/2") and feature color photos inside blue, green, red or yellow borders. The card backs carry a short player biography plus career hitting or pitching statistics. Unissued cards with a Pepper Martin back (#80), but with another player pictured on the front, exist. All have been either cancelled with a slit cut out of the bottom, or show evidence of having been hand-cut from a sheet.

		NM	EX	VG
	Complete Set (79):	500.00	250.00	125.00
	Common Player:	6.00	3.00	1.50
	Wax Pack:	300.00	.00	.00
1	Nap Lajoie	22.50	7.50	4.00
2	Christy Mathewson	16.00	8.00	5.00
3	Babe Ruth	100.00	50.00	25.00
4	Carl Hubbell	6.00	3.00	1.50
5	Grover Cleveland Alexander	15.00	7.50	4.50
6	Walter Johnson	20.00	10.00	6.00
7	Chief Bender	6.00	3.00	1.50
8	Roger Bresnahan	6.00	3.00	1.50
9	Mordecai Brown	6.00	3.00	1.50
10	Tris Speaker	6.00	3.00	1.50

		NM	EX	VG
11	Arky Vaughan	6.00	3.00	1.50
12	Zack Wheat	6.00	3.00	1.50
13	George Sisler	6.00	3.00	1.50
14	Connie Mack	6.00	3.00	1.50
15	Clark Griffith	6.00	3.00	1.50
16	Lou Boudreau	6.00	3.00	1.50
17	Ernie Lombardi	6.00	3.00	1.50
18	Heinie Manush	6.00	3.00	1.50
19	Marty Marion	6.00	3.00	1.50
20	Eddie Collins	6.00	3.00	1.50
21	Rabbit Maranville	6.00	3.00	1.50
22	Joe Medwick	6.00	3.00	1.50
23	Ed Barrow	6.00	3.00	1.50
24	Mickey Cochrane	6.00	3.00	1.50
25	Jimmy Collins	6.00	3.00	1.50
26	Bob Feller	13.50	6.75	4.00
27	Luke Appling	6.00	3.00	1.50
28	Lou Gehrig	100.00	50.00	25.00
29	Gabby Hartnett	6.00	3.00	1.50
30	Chuck Klein	6.00	3.00	1.50
31	Tony Lazzeri	6.00	3.00	1.50
32	Al Simmons	6.00	3.00	1.50
33	Wilbert Robinson	6.00	3.00	1.50
34	Sam Rice	6.00	3.00	1.50
35	Herb Pennock	6.00	3.00	1.50
36	Mel Ott	6.00	3.00	1.50
37	Lefty O'Doul	6.00	3.00	1.50
38	Johnny Mize	6.00	3.00	1.50
39	Bing Miller	6.00	3.00	1.50
40	Joe Tinker	6.00	3.00	1.50
41	Frank Baker	6.00	3.00	1.50
42	Ty Cobb	50.00	25.00	12.50
43	Paul Derringer	6.00	3.00	1.50
44	Cap Anson	6.00	3.00	1.50
45	Jim Bottomley	6.00	3.00	1.50
46	Eddie Plank	6.00	3.00	1.50
47	Cy Young	16.00	8.00	5.00
48	Hack Wilson	6.00	3.00	1.50
49	Ed Walsh	6.00	3.00	1.50
50	Frank Chance	6.00	3.00	1.50
51	Dazzy Vance	6.00	3.00	1.50
52	Bill Terry	6.00	3.00	1.50
53	Jimmy Foxx	15.00	7.50	4.50
54	Lefty Gomez	6.00	3.00	1.50
55	Branch Rickey	6.00	3.00	1.50
56	Ray Schalk	6.00	3.00	1.50
57	Johnny Evers	6.00	3.00	1.50
58	Charlie Gehringer	6.00	3.00	1.50
59	Burleigh Grimes	6.00	3.00	1.50
60	Lefty Grove	6.00	3.00	1.50
61	Rube Waddell	6.00	3.00	1.50
62	Honus Wagner	15.00	7.50	4.50
63	Red Ruffing	6.00	3.00	1.50
64	Judge Landis	6.00	3.00	1.50
65	Harry Heilmann	6.00	3.00	1.50
66	John McGraw	6.00	3.00	1.50
67	Hughie Jennings	6.00	3.00	1.50
68	Hal Newhouser	6.00	3.00	1.50
69	Waite Hoyt	6.00	3.00	1.50
70	Bobo Newsom	6.00	3.00	1.50
71	Earl Averill	6.00	3.00	1.50
72	Ted Williams	80.00	40.00	20.00
73	Warren Giles	6.00	3.00	1.50
74	Ford Frick	6.00	3.00	1.50
75	Ki Ki Cuyler	6.00	3.00	1.50
76	Paul Waner	6.00	3.00	1.50
77	Pie Traynor	6.00	3.00	1.50
78	Lloyd Waner	6.00	3.00	1.50
79	Ralph Kiner	6.00	3.00	1.50
80	Pepper Martin (Unissued, slit-cancelled proof, Lefty Grove, Joe Tinker or Eddie Collins on front.)	2,000	800.00	400.00
80	Pepper Martin (Unissued hand-cut proof. Lefty Grove, Eddie Collins or Joe Tinker on front.)	2,750	1,350	825.00

1960-62 Fleer Team Logo Decals

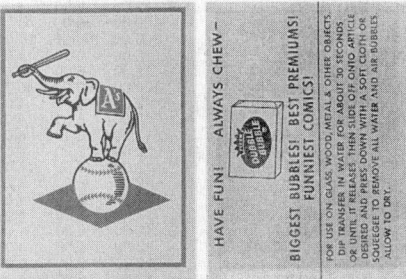

These colorful team logo decals were pack inserts in Fleer's 1960-62 baseball card issues. The decals measure 2-1/4" x 3". Those issued in 1960 have a blue background on front. The 1961-62 decals have a white background on front. Backs have advertising for Fleer bubblegum and instructions on applying the decals. The 1961 decals have back printing in blue; the 1962s are in red.

	NM	EX	VG
Complete Set, 1960 (16):	100.00	50.00	30.00
Complete Set, 1961 (18):	100.00	50.00	30.00
Complete Set, 1962 (20):	250.00	125.00	75.00
1960 team decal, blue background	9.00	4.50	2.75
1961 decal, white background, blue back	4.50	2.25	1.25
1962 decal, white background, red back	9.00	4.50	2.75

1961 Fleer Baseball Greats

In 1961, Fleer issued another set utilizing the Baseball Greats theme. The 154-card set was issued in two series and features a color (or colorized) player portrait against a colored background. The player's name is located in a pennant at bottom. Card backs feature orange and black on white stock and contain player biographical and statistical information. The cards measure 2-1/2" x 3-1/2" in size. Five-cent wax packs included five cards plus a team logo decal and sticker.

		NM	EX	VG
	Complete Set (154):	1,400	700.00	425.00
	Common Player:	10.00	5.00	3.00
	Wax Pack (5+1+1):	265.00		
1	Checklist (Frank Baker, Ty Cobb, Zach Wheat)	65.00	35.00	20.00
2	G.C. Alexander	12.00	6.00	3.00
3	Nick Altrock	10.00	5.00	3.00
4	Cap Anson	10.00	5.00	3.00
5	Earl Averill	10.00	5.00	3.00
6	Home Run Baker	10.00	5.00	3.00
7	Dave Bancroft	10.00	5.00	3.00
8	Chief Bender	10.00	5.00	3.00
9	Jim Bottomley	10.00	5.00	3.00
10	Roger Bresnahan	10.00	5.00	3.00
11	Mordecai Brown	10.00	5.00	3.00
12	Max Carey	10.00	5.00	3.00
13	Jack Chesbro	10.00	5.00	3.00
14	Ty Cobb	65.00	35.00	20.00
15	Mickey Cochrane	10.00	5.00	3.00
16	Eddie Collins	10.00	5.00	3.00
17	Earle Combs	10.00	5.00	3.00
18	Charles Comiskey	10.00	5.00	3.00
19	Ki Ki Cuyler	10.00	5.00	3.00
20	Paul Derringer	10.00	5.00	3.00
21	Howard Ehmke	10.00	5.00	3.00
22	Billy Evans	10.00	5.00	3.00
23	Johnny Evers	10.00	5.00	3.00
24	Red Faber	10.00	5.00	3.00
25	Bob Feller	12.00	6.00	4.00
26	Wes Ferrell	10.00	5.00	3.00
27	Lew Fonseca	10.00	5.00	3.00
28	Jimmy Foxx	10.00	5.00	3.00
29	Ford Frick	10.00	5.00	3.00
30	Frankie Frisch	10.00	5.00	3.00
31	Lou Gehrig	125.00	60.00	40.00
32	Charlie Gehringer	10.00	5.00	3.00
33	Warren Giles	10.00	5.00	3.00
34	Lefty Gomez	10.00	5.00	3.00
35	Goose Goslin	10.00	5.00	3.00
36	Clark Griffith	10.00	5.00	3.00
37	Burleigh Grimes	10.00	5.00	3.00
38	Lefty Grove	10.00	5.00	3.00
39	Chick Hafey	10.00	5.00	3.00
40	Jesse Haines	10.00	5.00	3.00
41	Gabby Hartnett	10.00	5.00	3.00
42	Harry Heilmann	10.00	5.00	3.00
43	Rogers Hornsby	10.00	5.00	3.00
44	Waite Hoyt	10.00	5.00	3.00
45	Carl Hubbell	10.00	5.00	3.00
46	Miller Huggins	10.00	5.00	3.00
47	Hughie Jennings	10.00	5.00	3.00
48	Ban Johnson	10.00	5.00	3.00
49	Walter Johnson	15.00	8.00	5.00
50	Ralph Kiner	10.00	5.00	3.00
51	Chuck Klein	10.00	5.00	3.00
52	Johnny Kling	10.00	5.00	3.00
53	Judge Landis	10.00	5.00	3.00
54	Tony Lazzeri	10.00	5.00	3.00
55	Ernie Lombardi	10.00	5.00	3.00
56	Dolf Luque	10.00	5.00	3.00
57	Heinie Manush	10.00	5.00	3.00
58	Marty Marion	10.00	5.00	3.00
59	Christy Mathewson	15.00	8.00	5.00
60	John McGraw	10.00	5.00	3.00
61	Joe Medwick	10.00	5.00	3.00
62	Bing Miller	10.00	5.00	3.00
63	Johnny Mize	10.00	5.00	3.00
64	Johnny Mostil	10.00	5.00	3.00
65	Art Nehf	10.00	5.00	3.00
66	Hal Newhouser	10.00	5.00	3.00
67	Bobo Newsom	10.00	5.00	3.00
68	Mel Ott	10.00	5.00	3.00
69	Allie Reynolds	10.00	5.00	3.00
70	Sam Rice	10.00	5.00	3.00
71	Eppa Rixey	10.00	5.00	3.00
72	Edd Roush	10.00	5.00	3.00
73	Schoolboy Rowe	10.00	5.00	3.00
74	Red Ruffing	10.00	5.00	3.00
75	Babe Ruth	150.00	75.00	40.00
76	Joe Sewell	10.00	5.00	3.00
77	Al Simmons	10.00	5.00	3.00
78	George Sisler	10.00	5.00	3.00
79	Tris Speaker	10.00	5.00	3.00
80	Fred Toney	10.00	5.00	3.00
81	Dazzy Vance	10.00	5.00	3.00

		NM	EX	VG
82	Jim Vaughn	10.00	5.00	3.00
83	Big Ed Walsh	10.00	5.00	3.00
84	Lloyd Waner	10.00	5.00	3.00
85	Paul Waner	10.00	5.00	3.00
86	Zach Wheat	10.00	5.00	3.00
87	Hack Wilson	10.00	5.00	3.00
88	Jimmy Wilson	10.00	5.00	3.00
89	Checklist	75.00	40.00	25.00
	(George Sisler, Pie Traynor)			
90	Babe Adams	10.00	5.00	3.00
91	Dale Alexander	10.00	5.00	3.00
92	Jim Bagby	10.00	5.00	3.00
93	Ossie Bluege	10.00	5.00	3.00
94	Lou Boudreau	10.00	5.00	3.00
95	Tommy Bridges	10.00	5.00	3.00
96	Donnie Bush (Donie)	10.00	5.00	3.00
97	Dolph Camilli	10.00	5.00	3.00
98	Frank Chance	10.00	5.00	3.00
99	Jimmy Collins	10.00	5.00	3.00
100	Stanley Coveleskie	10.00	5.00	3.00
	(Coveleski)			
101	Hughie Critz	10.00	5.00	3.00
102	General Crowder	10.00	5.00	3.00
103	Joe Dugan	10.00	5.00	3.00
104	Bibb Falk	10.00	5.00	3.00
105	Rick Ferrell	10.00	5.00	3.00
106	Art Fletcher	10.00	5.00	3.00
107	Dennis Galehouse	10.00	5.00	3.00
108	Chick Galloway	10.00	5.00	3.00
109	Mule Haas	10.00	5.00	3.00
110	Stan Hack	10.00	5.00	3.00
111	Bump Hadley	10.00	5.00	3.00
112	Billy Hamilton	10.00	5.00	3.00
113	Joe Hauser	10.00	5.00	3.00
114	Babe Herman	10.00	5.00	3.00
115	Travis Jackson	10.00	5.00	3.00
116	Eddie Joost	10.00	5.00	3.00
117	Addie Joss	10.00	5.00	3.00
118	Joe Judge	10.00	5.00	3.00
119	Joe Kuhel	10.00	5.00	3.00
120	Nap Lajoie	10.00	5.00	3.00
121	Dutch Leonard	10.00	5.00	3.00
122	Ted Lyons	10.00	5.00	3.00
123	Connie Mack	10.00	5.00	3.00
124	Rabbit Maranville	10.00	5.00	3.00
125	Fred Marberry	10.00	5.00	3.00
126	Iron Man McGinnity	10.00	5.00	3.00
127	Oscar Melillo	10.00	5.00	3.00
128	Ray Mueller	10.00	5.00	3.00
129	Kid Nichols	10.00	5.00	3.00
130	Lefty O'Doul	10.00	5.00	3.00
131	Bob O'Farrell	10.00	5.00	3.00
132	Roger Peckinpaugh	10.00	5.00	3.00
133	Herb Pennock	10.00	5.00	3.00
134	George Pipgras	10.00	5.00	3.00
135	Eddie Plank	10.00	5.00	3.00
136	Ray Schalk	10.00	5.00	3.00
137	Hal Schumacher	10.00	5.00	3.00
138	Luke Sewell	10.00	5.00	3.00
139	Bob Shawkey	10.00	5.00	3.00
140	Riggs Stephenson	10.00	5.00	3.00
141	Billy Sullivan	10.00	5.00	3.00
142	Bill Terry	10.00	5.00	3.00
143	Joe Tinker	10.00	5.00	3.00
144	Pie Traynor	10.00	5.00	3.00
145	George Uhle	10.00	5.00	3.00
146	Hal Troskey (Trosky)	10.00	5.00	3.00
147	Arky Vaughan	10.00	5.00	3.00
148	Johnny Vander Meer	10.00	5.00	3.00
149	Rube Waddell	10.00	5.00	3.00
150	Honus Wagner	65.00	35.00	20.00
151	Dixie Walker	10.00	5.00	3.00
152	Ted Williams	150.00	75.00	40.00
153	Cy Young	15.00	8.00	5.00
154	Ross Young (Youngs)	10.00	5.00	3.00

1961 Fleer World Champions Pennant Decals

The winner of each World Series from 1913-1960 is honored in this pack insert. The 3" x 1-1/4" decals have a large red or blue pennant at center, with a team name or logo and the "WORLD CHAMPIONS" notation. The year of the Series win is at left on the pennant. The number of games won by each team is at top and bottom on right. Backs offer instructions for applying the decals.

		NM	EX	VG
Complete Set (48):		300.00	150.00	90.00
Common Decal:		6.00	3.00	1.75
(1)	1913 - A's	6.00	3.00	1.75
(2)	1914 - Braves	6.00	3.00	1.75
(3)	1915 - Red Sox	6.00	3.00	1.75
(4)	1916 - Red Sox	6.00	3.00	1.75
(5)	1917 - White Sox	6.00	3.00	1.75
(6)	1918 - Red Sox	6.00	3.00	1.75
(7)	1919 - Reds	9.00	4.50	2.75
(8)	1920 - Indians	6.00	3.00	1.75
(9)	1921 - Giants	6.00	3.00	1.75
(10)	1922 - Giants	6.00	3.00	1.75
(11)	1923 - Yankees	7.50	3.75	2.25
(12)	1924 - Senators	6.00	3.00	1.75
(13)	1925 - Yankees	7.50	3.75	2.25
(14)	1926 - Cardinals	6.00	3.00	1.75
(15)	1927 - Yankees	7.50	3.75	2.25
(14)	1928 - Yankees	7.50	3.75	2.25
(15)	1929 - A's	6.00	3.00	1.75
(16)	1930 - A's	6.00	3.00	1.75
(17)	1931 - Cardinals	6.00	3.00	1.75
(18)	1932 - Yankees	7.50	3.75	2.25
(19)	1933 - Giants	6.00	3.00	1.75
(20)	1934 - Cardinals	6.00	3.00	1.75
(21)	1935 - Tigers	6.00	3.00	1.75
(22)	1936 - Yankees	7.50	3.75	2.25
(23)	1937 - Yankees	7.50	3.75	2.25
(24)	1938 - Yankees	7.50	3.75	2.25
(25)	1939 - Yankees	7.50	3.75	2.25
(26)	1940 - Reds	6.00	3.00	1.75
(27)	1941 - Yankees	7.50	3.75	2.25
(28)	1942 - Cardinals	6.00	3.00	1.75
(29)	1943 - Yankees	7.50	3.75	2.25
(30)	1944 - Cardinals	6.00	3.00	1.75
(31)	1945 - Tigers	6.00	3.00	1.75
(32)	1946 - Cardinals	6.00	3.00	1.75
(33)	1947 - Yankees	7.50	3.75	2.25
(34)	1948 - Indians	6.00	3.00	1.75
(35)	1949 - Yankees	7.50	3.75	2.25
(36)	1950 - Yankees	7.50	3.75	2.25
(37)	1951 - Yankees	7.50	3.75	2.25
(38)	1952 - Yankees	7.50	3.75	2.25
(41)	1953 - Yankees	7.50	3.75	2.25
(42)	1954 - Giants	6.00	3.00	1.75
(43)	1955 - Dodgers	9.00	4.50	2.75
(44)	1956 - Yankees	7.50	3.75	2.25
(45)	1957 - Braves	7.50	3.75	2.25
(46)	1958 - Yankees	7.50	3.75	2.25
(47)	1959 - Dodgers	9.00	4.50	2.75
(48)	1960 - Pirates	9.00	4.50	2.75

1963 Fleer

A lawsuit by Topps stopped Fleer's 1963 set at one series of 66 cards. Issued with a cookie rather than gum, the set features color photos of current players. The card backs include statistical information for 1962 and career plus a brief player biography. The cards, which measure 2-1/2" x 3-1/2", are numbered 1-66. An unnumbered checklist was issued with the set and is included in the complete set price in the checklist that follows. The checklist and #46 Adcock are scarce.

		NM	EX	VG
Complete Set (67):		1,800	900.00	550.00
Common Player:		12.00	6.00	4.00
Wax Pack:		1,000		
1	Steve Barber	50.00	25.00	15.00
2	Ron Hansen	12.00	6.00	4.00
3	Milt Pappas	12.00	6.00	4.00
4	Brooks Robinson	120.00	60.00	40.00
5	Willie Mays	200.00	100.00	60.00
6	Lou Clinton	12.00	6.00	4.00
7	Bill Monbouquette	12.00	6.00	4.00
8	Carl Yastrzemski	120.00	60.00	40.00
9	Ray Herbert	12.00	6.00	4.00
10	Jim Landis	12.00	6.00	4.00
11	Dick Donovan	12.00	6.00	4.00
12	Tito Francona	12.00	6.00	4.00
13	Jerry Kindall	12.00	6.00	4.00
14	Frank Lary	12.00	6.00	4.00
15	Dick Howser	12.00	6.00	4.00
16	Jerry Lumpe	12.00	6.00	4.00
17	Norm Siebern	12.00	6.00	4.00
18	Don Lee	12.00	6.00	4.00
19	Albie Pearson	12.00	6.00	4.00
20	Bob Rodgers	12.00	6.00	4.00
21	Leon Wagner	12.00	6.00	4.00
22	Jim Kaat	20.00	10.00	6.00
23	Vic Power	12.00	6.00	4.00
24	Rich Rollins	12.00	6.00	4.00
25	Bobby Richardson	20.00	10.00	6.00
26	Ralph Terry	12.00	6.00	4.00
27	Tom Cheney	12.00	6.00	4.00
28	Chuck Cottier	12.00	6.00	4.00
29	Jimmy Piersall	15.00	8.00	5.00
30	Dave Stenhouse	12.00	6.00	4.00
31	Glen Hobbie	12.00	6.00	4.00
32	Ron Santo	30.00	15.00	9.00
33	Gene Freese	12.00	6.00	4.00
34	Vada Pinson	15.00	8.00	5.00
35	Bob Purkey	12.00	6.00	4.00
36	Joe Amalfitano	12.00	6.00	4.00
37	Bob Aspromonte	12.00	6.00	4.00
38	Dick Farrell	12.00	6.00	4.00
39	Al Spangler	12.00	6.00	4.00

FRANK BOLLING
Milwaukee Braves—2nd Base

		NM	EX	VG
40	Tommy Davis	12.00	6.00	4.00
41	Don Drysdale	90.00	45.00	30.00
42	Sandy Koufax	240.00	120.00	70.00
43	*Maury Wills*	120.00	60.00	40.00
44	Frank Bolling	12.00	6.00	4.00
45	Warren Spahn	90.00	45.00	30.00
46	Joe Adcock/SP	180.00	90.00	50.00
47	Roger Craig	12.00	6.00	4.00
48	Al Jackson	12.00	6.00	4.00
49	Rod Kanehl	12.00	6.00	4.00
50	Ruben Amaro	12.00	6.00	4.00
51	John Callison	12.00	6.00	4.00
52	Clay Dalrymple	12.00	6.00	4.00
53	Don Demeter	12.00	6.00	4.00
54	Art Mahaffey	12.00	6.00	4.00
55	"Smoky" Burgess	12.00	6.00	4.00
56	Roberto Clemente	220.00	110.00	60.00
57	Elroy Face	12.00	6.00	4.00
58	Vernon Law	12.00	6.00	4.00
59	Bill Mazeroski	25.00	12.00	7.00
60	Ken Boyer	15.00	7.50	4.00
61	Bob Gibson	90.00	45.00	30.00
62	Gene Oliver	12.00	6.00	4.00
63	Bill White	15.00	8.00	5.00
64	Orlando Cepeda	30.00	15.00	9.00
65	Jimmy Davenport	12.00	6.00	4.00
66	Billy O'Dell	25.00	12.00	8.00
---	Checklist/SP	550.00	275.00	160.00

1966 Fleer All Star Match Baseball

This seldom-seen issue was produced in the years when Fleer was locked out of the "regular" baseball card market. Standard 2-1/2" x 3-1/2" format cards are designed for playing a baseball match game. Backs have a portion of a black-and-white photo of Dodger pitcher Don Drysdale, which can be assembled in jigsaw puzzle fashion. Fronts are printed in red, blue, yellow and black, and numbered F1-F66. Because single cards have little collector appeal, the value of a set is considerably higher than the sum of the parts.

	NM	EX	VG
Complete Set (66):	400.00	200.00	120.00
Common Card:	6.00	3.00	1.75
Wax Pack:	200.00		
Don Drysdale			

1968-70 Fleer Major League Baseball Patches

 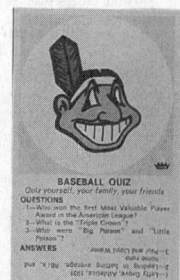

From 1968-70, Fleer sold bubblegum in wax packs which also included four team logo/quiz cards and half a dozen cloth patches, all for a dime. The 2-9/16" x 4-1/16" cards are blank-back and have on front a color team logo at top and three baseball trivia questions at bottom. The cloth patches are about 2-1/2" x 3-5/16" and are die-cut to allow the team logos and nameplates to be removed from the paper backing and stuck on jackets, etc.

	NM	EX	VG
Complete Set Logo Cards (24):	18.00	9.00	5.50
Common Logo Card:	1.50		.45
Complete Set Cloth Patches (29):	35.00	17.50	10.00
Common Cloth Patch:	1.50	.75	.45
Wax Pack:	2.00		
Wax Box (24):	30.00		

LOGO/QUIZ CARDS

		NM	EX	VG
(1)	Atlanta Braves	1.50	.70	.45
(2)	Baltimore Orioles	1.50	.70	.45
(3)	Boston Red Sox	1.50	.70	.45
(4)	California Angels	1.50	.70	.45
(5)	Chicago Cubs	1.50	.70	.45
(6)	Chicago White Sox	1.50	.70	.45
(7)	Cincinnati Reds	1.50	.70	.45
(8)	Cleveland Indians	1.50	.70	.45
(9)	Detroit Tigers	1.50	.70	.45
(10)	Houston Astros	1.50	.70	.45
(11)	Kansas City Royals	1.50	.70	.45
(12)	Los Angeles Dodgers	1.50	.70	.45
(13)	Minnesota Twins	1.50	.70	.45

		NM	EX	VG
(14)	Montreal Expos	2.50	1.25	.70
(15)	New York Mets	3.00	1.50	.90
(16)	New York Yankees	4.00	2.00	1.25
(17)	Oakland A's	2.50	1.25	.70
(18)	Philadelphia Phillies	1.50	.70	.45
(19)	Pittsburgh Pirates	1.50	.70	.45
(20)	San Diego Padres	2.50	1.25	.70
(21)	San Francisco Giants	1.50	.70	.45
(22)	Seattle Pilots	6.00	3.00	1.75
(23)	St. Louis Cardinals	1.50	.70	.45
(24)	Washington Senators	1.50	.70	.45

TEAM LOGO CLOTH PATCHES

(1)	Atlanta Braves	1.50	.70	.45
(2)	Baltimore Orioles	1.50	.70	.45
(3)	Boston Red Sox	1.50	.70	.45
(4)	California Angels	1.50	.70	.45
(5)	Chicago Cubs	1.50	.70	.45
(6)	Chicago White Sox	1.50	.70	.45
(7)	Cincinnati Reds	1.50	.70	.45
(8)	Cleveland Indians (Indian head)	1.50	.70	.45
(9)	Cleveland Indians (Btg Indian.)	1.50	.70	.45
(10)	Detroit Tigers	1.50	.70	.45
(11)	Houston Astros	1.50	.70	.45
(12)	Kansas City Royals	1.50	.70	.45
(13)	Los Angeles Dodgers	1.50	.70	.45
(14)	Milwaukee Brewers (M)	1.50	.70	.45
(15)	Milwaukee Brewers (Batting keg.)	1.50	.70	.45
(16)	Minnesota Twins	1.50	.70	.45
(17)	Montreal Expos	2.00	1.00	.60
(18)	New York Mets	2.00	1.00	.60
(19)	New York Yankees	3.00	1.50	.90
(20)	Oakland A's (Plain ball.)	2.00	1.00	.60
(21)	Oakland A's ("The SWINGIN,'" white shoes, on ball.)	1.50	.70	.45
(22)	Philadelphia Phillies	1.50	.70	.45
(23)	Pittsburgh Pirates	1.50	.70	.45
(24)	San Diego Padres	2.00	1.00	.60
(25)	San Francisco Giants	1.50	.70	.45
(26)	Seattle Pilots	3.00	1.50	.90
(27)	St. Louis Cardinals	1.50	.70	.45
(28)	Washington Senators	1.50	.70	.45
(29)	Major League Baseball	1.50	.70	.45

1969 Fleer Cap Plaques

This set of novelty plaques features 3D impressions of each team's cap on thin plastic stock in a 3" x 4" format. Each cap plaque was sold in a wrapper with an easel backing board, surviving specimens of which are quite scarce.

		NM	EX	VG
Complete Set (24):		1,200	600.00	350.00
Common Plaque:		45.00	22.50	13.50
Easel Backing Board:		22.00	11.00	6.50
Unopened Pack:		45.00		
(1)	Atlanta Braves	50.00	25.00	15.00
(2)	Baltimore Orioles	60.00	30.00	18.00
(3)	Boston Red Sox	50.00	25.00	15.00
(4)	California Angels	45.00	22.50	13.50
(5)	Chicago Cubs	60.00	30.00	18.00
(6)	Chicago White Sox	45.00	22.50	13.50
(7)	Cincinnati Reds	45.00	22.50	13.50
(8)	Cleveland Indians	45.00	22.50	13.50
(9)	Detroit Tigers	45.00	22.50	13.50
(10)	Houston Astros	45.00	22.50	13.50
(11)	Kansas City Royals	45.00	22.50	13.50
(12)	Los Angeles Dodgers	50.00	25.00	15.00
(13)	Minnesota Twins	45.00	22.50	13.50
(14)	Montreal Expos	45.00	22.50	13.50
(15)	New York Mets	75.00	37.50	22.50
(16)	New York Yankees	115.00	55.00	35.00
(17)	Oakland A's	60.00	30.00	18.00
(18)	Philadelphia Phillies	45.00	22.50	13.50
(19)	Pittsburgh Pirates	50.00	25.00	15.00
(20)	San Diego Padres	45.00	22.50	13.50
(21)	San Francisco Giants	45.00	22.50	13.50
(22)	Seattle Pilots	125.00	62.50	37.00
(23)	St. Louis Cardinals	50.00	25.00	15.00
(24)	Washington Senators	50.00	25.00	15.00

1970 Fleer Team Logo Decals

These colorful team logo decals were pack inserts in Fleer's 1970 World Series issue. The decals measure 2-7/16" x 2-3/4". Backs have instructions for applying the decals.

		NM	EX	VG
Complete Set (24):		90.00	45.00	27.50
Common Team:		7.50	3.75	2.25
(1)	Atlanta Braves	7.50	3.75	2.25
(2)	Baltimore Orioles	9.00	4.50	2.75
(3)	Boston Red Sox	7.50	3.75	2.25
(4)	California Angels	7.50	3.75	2.25
(5)	Chicago Cubs	7.50	3.75	2.25
(6)	Chicago White Sox	7.50	3.75	2.25
(7)	Cincinnati Reds	7.50	3.75	2.25
(8)	Cleveland Indians	7.50	3.75	2.25
(9)	Detroit Tigers	7.50	3.75	2.25
(10)	Houston Astros	7.50	3.75	2.25
(11)	Kansas City Royals	7.50	3.75	2.25
(12)	Los Angeles Dodgers	7.50	3.75	2.25
(13)	Milwaukee Brewers	7.50	3.75	2.25
(14)	Minnesota Twins	7.50	3.75	2.25
(15)	Montreal Expos	7.50	3.75	2.25
(16)	New York Mets	7.50	3.75	2.25
(17)	New York Yankees	9.00	4.50	2.75
(18)	Oakland A's	7.50	3.75	2.25
(19)	Philadelphia Phillies	7.50	3.75	2.25
(20)	Pittsburgh Pirates	9.00	4.50	2.75
(21)	San Diego Padres	7.50	3.75	2.25
(22)	San Francisco Giants	7.50	3.75	2.25
(23)	St. Louis Cardinals	7.50	3.75	2.25
(24)	Washington Senators	10.00	5.00	3.00

1970 Fleer World Series

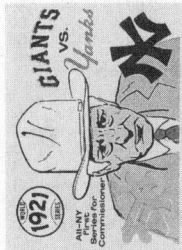

Utilizing the artwork done by Robert Laughlin a few years earlier for a privately marketed set, Fleer offered the first of two World Series highlights sets in 1970. Cards have color front with light blue backs. No card was issued for the 1904 World Series because no Series was played. Cards are checklisted in chronological order.

		NM	EX	VG
Complete Set (66):		150.00	75.00	45.00
Common Card:		1.50	.70	.45
Wax Pack:		35.00		
1	1903 Red Sox/Pirates	2.50	1.25	.70
2	1905 Giants/A's (Christy Mathewson)	2.50	1.25	.70
3	1906 White Sox/Cubs	1.50	.70	.45
4	1907 Cubs/Tigers	1.50	.70	.45
5	1908 Cubs/Tigers (Tinker/Evers/Chance)	3.00	1.50	.90
6	1909 Pirates/Tigers (Honus Wagner/Ty Cobb)	7.50	3.75	2.25
7	1910 A's/Cubs (Chief Bender/Jack Coombs)	2.00	1.00	.60
8	1911 A's/Giants (John McGraw)	2.00	1.00	.60
9	1912 Red Sox/Giants	2.00	1.00	.60
10	1913 A's/Giants	1.50	.70	.45
11	1914 Braves/A's	2.00	1.00	.60
12	1915 Red Sox/Phillies (Babe Ruth)	5.00	2.50	1.50
13	1916 Red Sox/Dodgers (Babe Ruth)	5.00	2.50	1.50
14	1917 White Sox/Giants	1.50	.70	.45
15	1918 Red Sox/Cubs	1.50	.70	.45
16	1919 Reds/White Sox	3.00	1.50	.90
17	1920 Indians/Dodgers (Stan Coveleski)	2.00	1.00	.60
18	1921 Giants/Yankees (Kenesaw Landis)	2.00	1.00	.60
19	1922 Giants/Yankees (Heinie Groh)	2.00	1.00	.60
20	1923 Yankees/Giants (Babe Ruth)	7.50	3.75	2.25
21	1924 Senators/Giants (John McGraw)	2.50	1.25	.70
22	1925 Pirates/Senators (Walter Johnson)	3.00	1.50	.90
23	1926 Cardinals/Yankees (Grover Cleveland Alexander/Tony Lazzeri)	3.00	1.50	.90
24	1927 Yankees/Pirates	2.50	1.25	.70
25	1928 Yankees/Cardinals (Babe Ruth/Lou Gehrig)	7.50	3.75	2.25
26	1929 A's/Cubs	1.50	.70	.45
27	1930 A's/Cardinals	1.50	.70	.45
28	1931 Cardinals/A's (Pepper Martin)	2.00	1.00	.60
29	1932 Yankees/Cubs (Babe Ruth/Lou Gehrig)	7.50	3.75	2.25
30	1933 Giants/Senators (Mel Ott)	2.50	1.25	.70
31	1934 Cardinals/Tigers	1.50	.70	.45
32	1935 Tigers/Cubs (Charlie Gehringer/Tommy Bridges)	2.00	1.00	.60
33	1936 Yankees/Giants	2.00	1.00	.60
34	1937 Yankees/Giants (Carl Hubbell)	2.50	1.25	.70

35	1938 Yankees/Cubs (Lou Gehrig)	4.00	2.00	1.25
36	1939 Yankees/Reds	1.50	.70	.45
37	1940 Reds/Tigers (Mike McCormick)	1.50	.70	.45
38	1941 Yankees/Dodgers	2.00	1.00	.60
39	1942 Cardinals/Yankees	1.50	.70	.45
40	1943 Yankees/Cardinals	1.50	.70	.45
41	1944 Cardinals/Browns	2.00	1.00	.60
42	1945 Tigers/Cubs (Hank Greenberg)	2.50	1.25	.70
43	1946 Cardinals/Red Sox (Enos Slaughter)	2.00	1.00	.60
44	1947 Yankees/Dodgers (Al Gionfriddo)	2.00	1.00	.60
45	1948 Indians/Braves	1.50	.70	.45
46	1949 Yankees/Dodgers (Allie Reynolds/Preacher Roe)	2.00	1.00	.60
47	1950 Yankees/Phillies	2.00	1.00	.60
48	1951 Yankees/Giants	1.50	.70	.45
49	1952 Yankees/Dodgers (Johnny Mize/Duke Snider)	2.50	1.25	.70
50	1953 Yankees/Dodgers (Carl Erskine)	2.00	1.00	.60
51	1954 Giants/Indians (Johnny Antonelli)	1.50	.70	.45
52	1955 Dodgers/Yankees	2.00	1.00	.60
53	1956 Yankees/Dodgers	2.00	1.00	.60
54	1957 Braves/Yankees (Lew Burdette)	3.00	1.50	.90
55	1958 Yankees/Braves (Bob Turley)	1.50	.70	.45
56	1959 Dodgers/White Sox (Chuck Essegian)	2.00	1.00	.60
57	1960 Pirates/Yankees	2.00	1.00	.60
58	1961 Yankees/Reds (Whitey Ford)	2.00	1.00	.60
59	1962 Yankees/Giants	1.50	.70	.45
60	1963 Dodgers/Yankees (Bill Skowron)	1.50	.70	.45
61	1964 Cardinals/Yankees (Bobby Richardson)	2.00	1.00	.60
62	1965 Dodgers/Twins	2.00	1.00	.60
63	1966 Orioles/Dodgers	1.50	.70	.45
64	1967 Cardinals/Red Sox	1.50	.70	.45
65	1968 Tigers/Cardinals	2.00	1.00	.60
66	1969 Mets/Orioles	4.50	2.25	1.25

1971-80 Fleer World Series

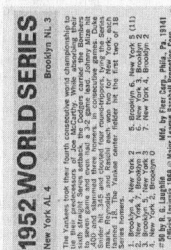

New artwork by Robert Laughlin is featured in the second of Fleer's World Series highlights sets. Fronts feature color art with backs printed in black. It appears as if the original set issued in 1971 was updated intermittently.

		NM	EX	VG
Complete Set (68):		135.00	65.00	40.00
Complete Set (75):		350.00	175.00	100.00
Common Card:		2.00	1.00	.60
Wax Pack:		30.00		
1	1903 Red Sox/Pirates (Cy Young)	6.00	3.00	1.75
2	1904 No World Series (John McGraw)	5.00	2.50	1.50
3	1905 Giants/A's (Christy Mathewson/Chief Bender)	5.00	2.50	1.50
4	1906 White Sox/Cubs	2.00	1.00	.60
5	1907 Cubs/Tigers	2.00	1.00	.60
6	1908 Cubs/Tigers (Ty Cobb)	5.00	2.50	1.50
7	1909 Pirates/Tigers	2.50	1.25	.70
8	1910 A's/Cubs (Eddie Collins)	2.50	1.25	.70
9	1911 A's/Giants (Home Run Baker)	2.50	1.25	.70
10	1912 Red Sox/Giants	2.00	1.00	.60
11	1913 A's/Giants (Christy Mathewson)	3.00	1.50	.90
12	1914 Braves/A's	2.00	1.00	.60
13	1915 Red Sox/Phillies (Grover Cleveland Alexander)	3.00	1.50	.90
14	1916 Red Sox/Dodgers (Jack Coombs)	2.00	1.00	.60
15	1917 White Sox/Giants (Red Faber)	2.50	1.25	.70
16	1918 Red Sox/Cubs (Babe Ruth)	6.00	3.00	1.75
17	1919 Reds/White Sox	4.00	2.00	1.25
18	1920 Indians/Dodgers (Elmer Smith)	2.50	1.25	.70
19	1921 Giants/Yankees (Waite Hoyt)	4.00	2.00	1.25
20	1922 Giants/Yankees (Art Nehf)	2.50	1.25	.70
21	1923 Yankees/Giants (Herb Pennock)	2.50	1.25	.70
22	1924 Senators/Giants (Walter Johnson)	4.00	2.00	1.25
23	1925 Pirates/Senators (Walter Johnson/Ki Ki Cuyler)	4.00	2.00	1.25
24	1926 Cardinals/Yankees (Rogers Hornsby)	4.00	2.00	1.25

25	1927 Yankees/Pirates	2.50	1.25	.70
26	1928 Yankees/Cardinals (Lou Gehrig)	5.00	2.50	1.50
27	1929 A's/Cubs (Howard Ehmke)	2.00	1.00	.60
28	1930 A's/Cardinals (Jimmie Foxx)	3.00	1.50	.90
29	1931 Cardinals/A's (Pepper Martin)	2.50	1.25	.70
30	1932 Yankees/Cubs (Babe Ruth)	6.00	3.00	1.75
31	1933 Giants/Senators (Carl Hubbell)	3.00	1.50	.90
32	1934 Cardinals/Tigers	2.00	1.00	.60
33	1935 Tigers/Cubs (Mickey Cochrane)	2.50	1.25	.70
34	1936 Yankees/Giants (Red Rolfe)	2.50	1.25	.70
35	1937 Yankees/Giants (Tony Lazerri)	4.00	2.00	1.25
36	1938 Yankees/Cubs	3.00	1.50	.90
37	1939 Yankees/Reds	3.00	1.50	.90
38	1940 Reds/Tigers (Mike McCormick)	2.00	1.00	.60
39	1941 Yankees/Dodgers (Charlie Keller)	2.50	1.25	.70
40	1942 Cardinals/Yankees (Whitey Kurowski/Johnny Beazley)	2.00	1.00	.60
41	1943 Yankees/Cardinals (Spud Chandler)	2.00	1.00	.60
42	1944 Cardinals/Browns (Mort Cooper)	2.50	1.25	.70
43	1945 Tigers/Cubs (Hank Greenberg)	3.00	1.50	.90
44	1946 Cardinals/Red Sox (Enos Slaughter)	2.50	1.25	.70
45	1947 Yankees/Dodgers (Johnny Lindell/Hugh Casey)	2.50	1.25	.70
46	1948 Indians/Braves	2.00	1.00	.60
47	1949 Yankees/Dodgers (Preacher Roe)	2.00	1.00	.60
48	1950 Yankees/Phillies (Allie Reynolds)	2.50	1.25	.70
49	1951 Yankees/Giants (Ed Lopat)	2.50	1.25	.70
50	1952 Yankees/Dodgers (Johnny Mize)	2.50	1.25	.70
51	1953 Yankees/Dodgers	2.50	1.25	.70
52	1954 Giants/Indians	2.00	1.00	.60
53	1955 Dodgers/Yankees (Duke Snider)	4.00	2.00	1.25
54	1956 Yankees/Dodgers	2.50	1.25	.70
55	1957 Braves/Yankees	2.50	1.25	.70
56	1958 Yankees/Braves (Hank Bauer)	2.50	1.25	.70
57	1959 Dodgers/White Sox (Duke Snider)	3.00	1.50	.90
58	1960 Pirates/Yankees (Bill Skowron/Bobby Richardson)	2.50	1.25	.70
59	1961 Yankees/Reds (Whitey Ford)	2.50	1.25	.70
60	1962 Yankees/Giants	2.00	1.00	.60
61	1963 Dodgers/Yankees	2.00	1.00	.60
62	1964 Cardinals/Yankees	2.50	1.25	.70
63	1965 Dodgers/Twins	2.50	1.25	.70
64	1966 Orioles/Dodgers	2.00	1.00	.60
65	1967 Cardinals/Red Sox	2.00	1.00	.60
66	1968 Tigers/Cardinals	2.50	1.25	.70
67	1969 Mets/Orioles	6.00	3.00	1.75
68	1970 Orioles/Reds	5.00	2.50	1.50
69	1971 Pirates/Orioles (Roberto Clemente)	35.00	17.50	10.00
70	1972 A's/Reds	15.00	7.50	4.50
71	1973 A's/Mets	15.00	7.50	4.50
(72)	1974 A's/Dodgers	50.00	25.00	15.00
(73)	1975 Reds/Red Sox	50.00	25.00	15.00
(74)	1976 Reds/Yankees	50.00	25.00	15.00
(75)	1977 Yankees/Dodgers	50.00	25.00	15.00

1972 Fleer Famous Feats

This 40-card set by sports artist R.G. Laughlin is over-sized, 2-1/2" x 4". It features the pen and ink work of the artist, with several colors added to the front. The backs are printed in blue on white card stock. The Major League Baseball logo appears on the front of the card, one of the few Laughlin issues to do so. Selling price at issue was about $3.

		NM	EX	VG
Complete Set (40):		40.00	20.00	12.00
Common Player:		1.50	.75	.45
1	Joe McGinnity	2.00	1.00	.60
2	Rogers Hornsby	3.50	1.75	1.00
3	Christy Mathewson	4.00	2.00	1.25

4	Dazzy Vance	2.00	1.00	.60
5	Lou Gehrig	7.50	3.75	2.25
6	Jim Bottomley	2.00	1.00	.60
7	Johnny Evers	2.00	1.00	.60
8	Walter Johnson	4.00	2.00	1.25
9	Hack Wilson	2.00	1.00	.60
10	Wilbert Robinson	2.00	1.00	.60
11	Cy Young	3.50	1.75	1.00
12	Rudy York	1.50	.75	.45
13	Grover C. Alexander	2.00	1.00	.60
14	Fred Toney, Hippo Vaughn	1.50	.75	.45
15	Ty Cobb	7.50	3.75	2.25
16	Jimmie Foxx	3.50	1.75	1.00
17	Hub Leonard	1.50	.75	.45
18	Eddie Collins	2.00	1.00	.60
19	Joe Oeschger, Leon Cadore	1.50	.75	.45
20	Babe Ruth	9.00	4.50	2.75
21	Honus Wagner	4.00	2.00	1.25
22	Red Rolfe	1.50	.75	.45
23	Ed Walsh	2.00	1.00	.60
24	Paul Waner	2.00	1.00	.60
25	Mel Ott	2.50	1.25	.70
26	Eddie Plank	2.00	1.00	.60
27	Sam Crawford	2.00	1.00	.60
28	Napoleon Lajoie	2.00	1.00	.60
29	Ed Reulbach	1.50	.75	.45
30	Pinky Higgins	1.50	.75	.45
31	Bill Klem	2.00	1.00	.60
32	Tris Speaker	3.00	1.50	.90
33	Hank Gowdy	1.50	.75	.45
34	Lefty O'Doul	1.50	.75	.45
35	Lloyd Waner	2.00	1.00	.60
36	Chuck Klein	2.00	1.00	.60
37	Deacon Phillippe	1.50	.75	.45
38	Ed Delahanty	2.00	1.00	.60
39	Jack Chesbro	2.00	1.00	.60
40	Willie Keeler	2.00	1.00	.60

1973 Fleer Team Logo Decals

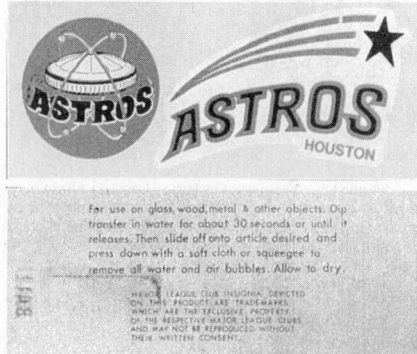

These colorful team logo decals were pack inserts in Fleer's "Wildest Days and Plays." The decals measure 4" x 2-11/16". Backs have instructions for applying the decals.

		NM	EX	VG
Complete Set (24):		110.00	55.00	33.00
Common Team:		9.00	4.50	2.75
(1)	Atlanta Braves	9.00	4.50	2.75
(2)	Baltimore Orioles	9.00	4.50	2.75
(3)	Boston Red Sox	9.00	4.50	2.75
(4)	California Angels	9.00	4.50	2.75
(5)	Chicago Cubs	9.00	4.50	2.75
(6)	Chicago White Sox	9.00	4.50	2.75
(7)	Cincinnati Reds	9.00	4.50	2.75
(8)	Cleveland Indians	9.00	4.50	2.75
(9)	Detroit Tigers	9.00	4.50	2.75
(10)	Houston Astros	9.00	4.50	2.75
(11)	Kansas City Royals	9.00	4.50	2.75
(12)	Los Angeles Dodgers	9.00	4.50	2.75
(13)	Milwaukee Brewers	9.00	4.50	2.75
(14)	Minnesota Twins	9.00	4.50	2.75
(15)	Montreal Expos	9.00	4.50	2.75
(16)	New York Mets	12.00	6.00	3.50
(17)	New York Yankees	10.00	5.00	3.00
(18)	Oakland A's	10.00	5.00	3.00
(19)	Philadelphia Phillies	9.00	4.50	2.75
(20)	Pittsburgh Pirates	11.00	5.50	3.25
(21)	San Diego Padres	9.00	4.50	2.75
(22)	San Francisco Giants	9.00	4.50	2.75
(23)	St. Louis Cardinals	9.00	4.50	2.75
(24)	Texas Rangers	12.00	6.00	3.50

1973 Fleer Team Signs

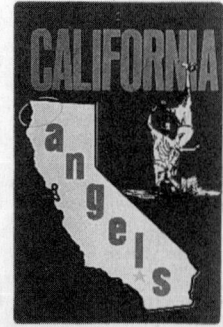

Each of the major league teams was represented in this issue of thick oversized (7-3/4" x 11-1/2") team logo signs. The blank-back signs have rounded corners and a grommeted hole at top-center for hanging. The unnumbered signs are checklisted here alphabetically.

		NM	EX	VG
Complete Set (24):		35.00	17.50	10.00
Common Team:		4.00	2.00	1.25
(1)	Atlanta Braves	4.00	2.00	1.25
(2)	Baltimore Orioles	4.00	2.00	1.25
(3)	Boston Red Sox	4.00	2.00	1.25
(4)	California Angels	4.00	2.00	1.25
(5)	Chicago Cubs	4.00	2.00	1.25
(6)	Chicago White Sox	4.00	2.00	1.25
(7)	Cincinnati Reds	5.00	2.50	1.50
(8)	Cleveland Indians	4.00	2.00	1.25
(9)	Detroit Tigers	4.00	2.00	1.25
(10)	Houston Astros	4.00	2.00	1.25
(11)	Kansas City Royals	4.00	2.00	1.25
(12)	Los Angeles Dodgers	4.00	2.00	1.25
(13)	Milwaukee Brewers	4.00	2.00	1.25
(14)	Minnesota Twins	4.00	2.00	1.25
(15)	Montreal Expos	4.00	2.00	1.25
(16)	New York Mets	5.00	2.50	1.50
(17)	New York Yankees	5.00	2.50	1.50
(18)	Oakland A's	5.00	2.50	1.50
(19)	Philadelphia Phillies	4.00	2.00	1.25
(20)	Pittsburgh Pirates	4.00	2.00	1.25
(21)	St. Louis Cardinals	4.00	2.00	1.25
(22)	San Francisco Giants	4.00	2.00	1.25
(23)	San Diego Padres	4.00	2.00	1.25
(24)	Texas Rangers	4.00	2.00	1.25

1973 Fleer Wildest Days and Plays

This 42-card set highlights unusual plays and happenings in baseball history, with the fronts featuring artwork by R.G. Laughlin. The cards are 2-1/2" x 4" and printed with color on the front and in red on the back. Original retail price was about $3.25.

		NM	EX	VG
Complete Set (42):		35.00	17.50	10.00
Common Player:		1.50	.70	.45
1	Cubs and Phillies Score 49 Runs in Game	1.50	.70	.45
2	Frank Chance Five HBP's in One Day	2.00	1.00	.60
3	Jim Thorpe Homered Into Three States	2.00	1.00	.60
4	Eddie Gaedel Midget in Majors	2.00	1.00	.60
5	Most Tied Game Ever	1.50	.70	.45
6	Seven Errors in One Inning	1.50	.70	.45
7	Four 20-Game Winners But No Pennant	1.50	.70	.45
8	Dummy Hoy Umpire Signals Strikes	2.00	1.00	.60
9	Fourteen Hits in One Inning	1.50	.70	.45
10	Yankees Not Shut Out for Two Years	1.50	.70	.45
11	Buck Weaver 17 Straight Fouls	2.00	1.00	.60
12	George Sisler Greatest Thrill	1.50	.70	.45
13	Wrong-Way Baserunner	1.50	.70	.45
14	Kiki Cuyler Sits Out Series	1.50	.70	.45
15	Grounder Climbed Wall	1.50	.70	.45
16	Gabby Street Washington Monument	1.50	.70	.45
17	Mel Ott Ejected Twice	2.00	1.00	.60
18	Shortest Pitching Career	1.50	.70	.45
19	Three Homers in One Inning	1.50	.70	.45
20	Bill Byron Singing Umpire	1.50	.70	.45
21	Fred Clarke Walking Steal of Home	1.50	.70	.45
22	Christy Mathewson 373rd Win Discovered	2.00	1.00	.60
23	Hitting Through the Unglaub Arc	1.50	.70	.45
24	Jim O'Rourke Catching at 52	1.50	.70	.45
25	Fired for Striking Out in Series	1.50	.70	.45
26	Eleven Run Inning on One Hit	1.50	.70	.45
27	58 Innings in 3 Days	1.50	.70	.45
28	Homer on Warm-up Pitch	1.50	.70	.45
29	Giants Win 26 Straight But Finish Fourth	1.50	.70	.45
30	Player Who Stole First Base	1.50	.70	.45
31	Ernie Shore Perfect Game in Relief	1.50	.70	.45
32	Greatest Comeback	1.50	.70	.45
33	All-Time Flash-in-the-Pan	1.50	.70	.45
34	Pruett Fanned Ruth 19 Out of 31	2.00	1.00	.60

		NM	EX	VG
35	Fixed Batting Race (Ty Cobb, Nap Lajoie)	2.00	1.00	.60
36	Wild Pitch Rebound Play	1.50	.70	.45
37	17 Straight Scoring Innings	1.50	.70	.45
38	Wildest Opening Day	1.50	.70	.45
39	Baseball's Strike One	1.50	.70	.45
40	Opening Day No-Hitter That Didn't Count	1.50	.70	.45
41	Jimmie Foxx 6 Straight Walks in One Game	2.00	1.00	.60
42	Entire Team Hit and Scored in Inning	1.50	.70	.45

1974 Fleer Baseball Firsts

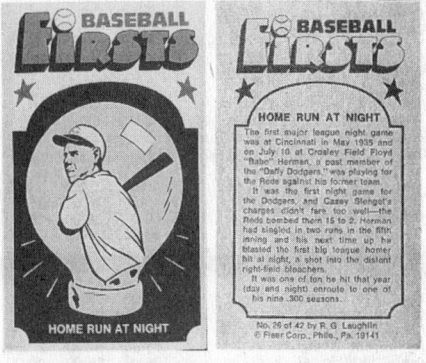

HOME RUN AT NIGHT

This 42-card set from Fleer is titled "Baseball Firsts" and features several historical moments in baseball, as captured through the artwork of sports artist R.G. Laughlin. The cards are 2-1/2" x 4" and are numbered on the back, which is gray card stock with black printing. The set is not licensed by Major League Baseball.

		NM	EX	VG
Complete Set (42):		80.00	40.00	25.00
Common Player:		2.00	1.00	.60
1	Slide	2.00	1.00	.60
2	Spring Training	2.00	1.00	.60
3	Bunt	2.00	1.00	.60
4	Catcher's Mask	2.00	1.00	.60
5	Four Straight Homers (Lou Gehrig)	10.00	5.00	3.00
6	Radio Broadcast	2.00	1.00	.60
7	Numbered Uniforms	2.00	1.00	.60
8	Shin Guards	2.00	1.00	.60
9	Players Association	2.00	1.00	.60
10	Knuckleball	2.00	1.00	.60
11	Player With Glasses	2.00	1.00	.60
12	Baseball Cards	12.00	6.00	3.50
13	Standardized Rules	2.00	1.00	.60
14	Grand Slam	2.00	1.00	.60
15	Player Fined	2.00	1.00	.60
16	Presidential Opener	2.00	1.00	.60
17	Player Transaction	2.00	1.00	.60
18	All-Star Game	2.00	1.00	.60
19	Scoreboard	2.00	1.00	.60
20	Cork-center Ball	2.00	1.00	.60
21	Scorekeeping	2.00	1.00	.60
22	Domed Stadium	2.00	1.00	.60
23	Batting Helmet	2.00	1.00	.60
24	Fatality	4.00	2.00	1.25
25	Unassisted Triple Play	2.00	1.00	.60
26	Home Run at Night	2.00	1.00	.60
27	Black Major Leaguer	4.00	2.00	1.25
28	Pinch Hitter	2.00	1.00	.60
29	Million Dollar World Series	2.00	1.00	.60
30	Tarpaulin	2.00	1.00	.60
31	Team Initials	2.00	1.00	.60
32	Pennant Playoff	2.00	1.00	.60
33	Glove	2.00	1.00	.60
34	Curve Ball	2.00	1.00	.60
35	Night Game	2.00	1.00	.60
36	Admission Charge	2.00	1.00	.60
37	Farm System	2.00	1.00	.60
38	Telecast	2.00	1.00	.60
39	Commissioner	2.00	1.00	.60
40	.400 Hitter	2.00	1.00	.60
41	World Series	2.00	1.00	.60
42	Player Into Service	2.00	1.00	.60

1975 Fleer Pioneers of Baseball

This 28-card set did not draw a great deal of interest in the hobby. The cards are slightly oversized (2-1/2" x 4") and feature sepia-toned photographs of old baseball players. The backs feature information about the player and the card number. A "Pioneers of Baseball" banner appears at the top of the card back. Each 10-cent pack included one card and one each cloth team pennant and patch, plus a stick of gum.

		NM	EX	VG
Complete Set (28):		20.00	10.00	6.00
Common Player:		1.50	.75	.45
Wax Pack:		6.00		
Wax Box (24):		65.00		
1	Cap Anson	1.50	.75	.45
2	Harry Wright	1.50	.75	.45
3	Buck Ewing	1.50	.75	.45
4	A.G. Spalding	1.50	.75	.45
5	Old Hoss Radbourn	1.50	.75	.45
6	Dan Brouthers	1.50	.75	.45
7	Roger Bresnahan	1.50	.75	.45
8	Mike Kelly	1.50	.75	.45
9	Ned Hanlon	1.50	.75	.45
10	Ed Delahanty	1.50	.75	.45
11	Pud Galvin	1.50	.75	.45
12	Amos Rusie	1.50	.75	.45
13	Tommy McCarthy	1.50	.75	.45
14	Ty Cobb	6.00	3.00	1.75
15	John McGraw	1.50	.75	.45
16	Home Run Baker	1.50	.75	.45
17	Johnny Evers	1.50	.75	.45
18	Nap Lajoie	1.50	.75	.45
19	Cy Young	2.50	1.25	.70
20	Eddie Collins	1.50	.75	.45
21	John Glasscock	1.50	.75	.45
22	Hal Chase	1.50	.75	.45
23	Mordecai Brown	1.50	.75	.45
24	Jake Daubert	1.50	.75	.45
25	Mike Donlin	1.50	.75	.45
26	John Clarkson	1.50	.75	.45
27	Buck Herzog	1.50	.75	.45
28	Art Nehf	1.50	.75	.45

1980 Fleer Baseball's Famous Feats

Yet another incarnation of Robert Laughlin's "Baseball's Famous Feats" cartoon artwork is this 22-card issue, in standard 2-1/2" x 3-1/2" format. The player art is backed with team logo and pennant stickers, creating a huge variety of possible front/back combinations. The cards are licensed by Major League Baseball and numbered on the front.

		NM	EX	VG
Complete Set (22):		6.00	3.00	1.75
Common Player:		.75	.40	.25
1	Grover Cleveland Alexander	.75	.40	.25
2	Jimmy (Jimmie) Foxx	1.00	.50	.30
3	Ty Cobb	1.50	.70	.45
4	Walter Johnson	1.00	.50	.30
5	Hack Wilson	.75	.40	.25
6	Tris Speaker	1.00	.50	.30
7	Hank Gowdy	.75	.40	.25
8	Bill Klem	.75	.40	.25
9	Ed Reulbach	.75	.40	.25
10	Fred Toney, Hippo Vaughn	.75	.40	.25
11	Joe Oeschger, Leon Cadore	.75	.40	.25
12	Lloyd Waner	.75	.40	.25
13	Eddie Plank	.75	.40	.25
14	Deacon Phillippe	.75	.40	.25
15	Ed Dalahanty (Delahanty)	.75	.40	.25
16	Eddie Collins	.75	.40	.25
17	Jack Chesbro	.75	.40	.25
18	Red Rolfe	.75	.40	.25
19	Ed Walsh	.75	.40	.25
20	Honus Wagner	1.25	.60	.40
21	Nap Lajoie	.75	.40	.25
22	Cy Young	1.00	.50	.30

1980 Fleer World Series/Team Logo Stickers

World Series cards similar to previous Fleer issues of the 1970s were issued in a new version in 1980. Wax packs containing five stickercards and a piece of bubblegum were offered for a nickel. Each card/sticker combination carried a World Series cartoon card from one of the Autumn Classics from 1940-1979. Unlike the earlier Fleer-Laughlin W.S. cards, these are backed with a team-logo sticker, some of which bear the team's 1979 record, and some of which do not.

		NM	EX	VG
Complete Set (40):		50.00	25.00	15.00
Common Card:		1.50	.75	.45
Wax Pack (5):		4.00		
Wax Box (36):		80.00		
(1)	1940 Reds/Tigers (Mike McCormick)	1.50	.75	.45
(2)	1941 Yankees/Dodgers (Charlie Keller)	2.25	1.25	.75
(3)	1942 Cardinals/Yankees (Whitey Kurowski/Johnny Beazley)	2.25	1.25	.75
(4)	1943 Yankees/Cardinals (Spud Chandler)	2.25	1.25	.75
(5)	1944 Cardinals/Browns (Mort Cooper)	2.25	1.25	.75
(6)	1945 Tigers/Cubs (Hank Greenberg)	3.00	1.50	.90
(7)	1946 Cardinals/Red Sox (Enos Slaughter)	1.50	.75	.45
(8)	1947 Yankees/Dodgers (Johnny Lindell/Hugh Casey)	3.00	1.50	.90
(9)	1948 Indians/Braves	1.50	.75	.45
(10)	1949 Yankees/Dodgers (Preacher Roe)	3.00	1.50	.90
(11)	1950 Yankees/Phillies (Allie Reynolds)	3.00	1.50	.90
(12)	1951 Yankees/Giants (Ed Lopat)	3.00	1.50	.90
(13)	1952 Yankees/Dodgers (Johnny Mize)	4.00	2.00	1.25
(14)	1953 Yankees/Dodgers	4.00	2.00	1.25
(15)	1954 Giants/Indians	3.00	1.50	.90
(16)	1955 Dodgers/Yankees (Duke Snider)	4.50	2.25	1.25
(17)	1956 Yankees/Dodgers	4.00	2.00	1.25
(18)	1957 Braves/Yankees	4.00	2.00	1.25
(19)	1958 Yankees/Braves (Hank Bauer)	3.00	1.50	.90
(20)	1959 Dodgers/White Sox (Duke Snider)	3.00	1.50	.90
(21)	1960 Pirates/Yankees (Bill Skowron/Bobby Richardson)	4.50	2.25	1.25
(22)	1961 Yankees/Reds (Whitey Ford)	3.00	1.50	.90
(23)	1962 Yankees/Giants	3.00	1.50	.90
(24)	1963 Dodgers/Yankees	3.00	1.50	.90
(25)	1964 Cardinals/Yankees	3.00	1.50	.90
(26)	1965 Dodgers/Twins	1.50	.75	.45
(27)	1966 Orioles/Dodgers	1.50	.75	.45
(28)	1967 Cardinals/Red Sox	1.50	.75	.45
(29)	1968 Tigers/Cardinals	1.50	.75	.45
(30)	1969 Mets/Orioles	4.00	2.00	1.25
(31)	1970 Orioles/Reds	1.50	.75	.45
(32)	1971 Pirates/Orioles	1.50	.75	.45
(33)	1972 A's/Reds	1.50	.75	.45
(34)	1973 A's/Mets	1.50	.75	.45
(35)	1974 A's/Dodgers	1.50	.75	.45
(36)	1975 Reds/Red Sox	2.25	1.25	.75
(37)	1976 Reds/Yankees	1.50	.75	.45
(38)	1977 Yankees/Dodgers	2.25	1.25	.75
(39)	1978 Yankees/Dodgers	2.25	1.25	.75
(40)	1979 Pirates/Orioles	2.25	1.25	.75

1916 Fleischmann Bakery (D381)

B. W. Kocher, Catcher
New York National

These cards were issued by a New York City bakery, presumably given away with the purchase of bread or other goods. The blank-back cards are printed in black-and-white in a 2-3/4" x 5-3/8" format. Fronts have player photos with the name, team and position in two lines beneath. Most cards have an Underwood & Underwood copyright notice on the picture. At bottom is a coupon that could be redeemed for an album to house the cards. Prices shown here are for cards without the coupon. Cards with coupon are valued at about the premium shown below. Cards are checklisted here in alphabetical order. Some cards can be found with differing sizes of the player's photo and/or with wrong and corrected photos. A nearly identical issue was produced contemporarily by Ferguson Bread. The two can be distinguished by the two-line identification on front of the Fleischmann cards, and one-line identification on Fergusons.

		NM	EX	VG
Common Player:		400.00	200.00	100.00
With Coupon: 8-10X				
(1)	Babe Adams	400.00	200.00	100.00
(2)	Grover Alexander	700.00	300.00	150.00
(3)	Walt E. Alexander	400.00	200.00	100.00
(4)	Frank Allen	400.00	200.00	100.00
(5)	Fred Anderson	400.00	200.00	100.00
(6)	Dave Bancroft	550.00	225.00	110.00
(7)	Jack Barry	400.00	200.00	100.00
(8a)	Beals Becker (No uniform logo.)	400.00	200.00	100.00
(8b)	Beals Becker (Partial uniform logo.)	400.00	200.00	100.00
(9)	Eddie Burns	400.00	200.00	100.00
(10)	George J. Burns	400.00	200.00	100.00
(11)	Bobby Byrne	400.00	200.00	100.00
(12)	Ray Caldwell	400.00	200.00	100.00
(13)	James Callahan	400.00	200.00	100.00
(14)	William Carrigan	400.00	200.00	100.00
(15)	Larry Cheney	400.00	200.00	100.00
(16a)	Tom Clark (No hand/glove.)	400.00	200.00	100.00
(16b)	Tom Clark (Hand and glove show.)	400.00	200.00	100.00
(17)	Ty Cobb	2,900	1,450	725.00
(18a)	Ray W. Collins (Partial top button.)	400.00	200.00	100.00
(18b)	Ray W. Collins (Full top button.)	400.00	200.00	100.00
(19)	Jack Coombs	400.00	200.00	100.00
(20)	A. Wilbur Cooper	400.00	200.00	100.00
(21)	George Cutshaw	400.00	200.00	100.00
(22)	Jake Daubert	400.00	200.00	100.00
(23)	Wheezer Dell	400.00	200.00	100.00
(24)	Bill Donovan	400.00	200.00	100.00
(25)	Larry Doyle	400.00	200.00	100.00
(26)	R.J. Egan	400.00	200.00	100.00
(27)	Johnny Evers	550.00	225.00	110.00
(28)	Ray Fisher	400.00	200.00	100.00
(29)	Harry Gardner (Larry)	400.00	200.00	100.00
(30)	Joe Gedeon	400.00	200.00	100.00
(31)	Larry Gilbert	400.00	200.00	100.00
(32)	Frank Gilhooley	400.00	200.00	100.00
(33)	Hank Gowdy	400.00	200.00	100.00
(34)	Sylvanus Gregg	400.00	200.00	100.00
(35)	Tom Griffith	400.00	200.00	100.00
(36)	Heinie Groh	400.00	200.00	100.00
(37)	Bob Harmon	400.00	200.00	100.00
(38)	Roy A. Hartzell	400.00	200.00	100.00
(39)	Claude Hendrix	400.00	200.00	100.00
(40)	Olaf Henriksen	400.00	200.00	100.00
(41)	Buck Herzog	400.00	200.00	100.00
(42)	Hugh High	400.00	200.00	100.00
(43)	Dick Hoblitzell	400.00	200.00	100.00
(44)	Herb Hunter	400.00	200.00	100.00
(45)	Harold Janvrin	400.00	200.00	100.00
(46)	Hugh Jennings	550.00	225.00	110.00
(47)	John Johnston	400.00	200.00	100.00
(48)	Erving Kantlehner	400.00	200.00	100.00
(49)	Benny Kauff	400.00	200.00	100.00
(50a)	Ray Keating (Error, striped cap, photo is Kocher.)	400.00	200.00	100.00
(50b)	Ray Keating (Correct, "NY" on cap.)	400.00	200.00	100.00
(51)	Wade Killefer	400.00	200.00	100.00
(52a)	Elmer Knetzer (Error, no "B" on cap, photo is Konetchy.)	400.00	200.00	100.00
(52b)	Elmer Knetzer (Correct, "B" on cap.)	400.00	200.00	100.00
(53a)	B.W. Kocher (Error, "NY" on cap, photo is Keating.)	400.00	200.00	100.00
(53b)	B.W. Kocher (Correct, striped cap.)	400.00	200.00	100.00
(54a)	Ed. Konetchy (Error, "B" on cap, photo is Knetzer.)	400.00	200.00	100.00
(54b)	Ed. Konetchy (Correct, no "B" on cap.)	400.00	200.00	100.00
(55)	Fred Lauderous (Luderous)	400.00	200.00	100.00
(56)	Dutch Leonard	400.00	200.00	100.00
(57)	Duffy Lewis	400.00	200.00	100.00
(58)	Slim Love	400.00	200.00	100.00
(59)	Albert L. Mamaux	400.00	200.00	100.00
(60)	Rabbit Maranville	550.00	225.00	110.00
(61)	Rube Marquard	540.00	215.00	110.00
(62)	Christy Mathewson	1,900	950.00	475.00
(63)	Bill McKechnie	550.00	225.00	110.00
(64)	Chief Meyer (Meyers)	400.00	200.00	100.00
(65)	Otto Miller	400.00	200.00	100.00
(66)	Fred Mollwitz	400.00	200.00	100.00
(67)	Herbie Moran	400.00	200.00	100.00
(68)	Mike Mowrey	400.00	200.00	100.00
(69)	Dan Murphy	400.00	200.00	100.00
(70)	Art Nehf	400.00	200.00	100.00
(71)	Rube Oldring	400.00	200.00	100.00
(72)	Oliver O'Mara	400.00	200.00	100.00
(73)	Dode Paskert	400.00	200.00	100.00
(74)	D.C. Pat Ragan	400.00	200.00	100.00
(75)	William A. Rariden	400.00	200.00	100.00
(76)	Davis Robertson	400.00	200.00	100.00
(77)	Wm. Rodgers	400.00	200.00	100.00
(78)	Edw. F. Rousch (Roush)	550.00	225.00	110.00
(79)	Nap Rucker	400.00	200.00	100.00
(80)	Dick Rudolph	400.00	200.00	100.00
(81)	Wally Schang	400.00	200.00	100.00
(82)	Rube Schauer	400.00	200.00	100.00
(83)	Pete Schneider	400.00	200.00	100.00
(84)	Ferd Schupp	400.00	200.00	100.00
(85)	Ernie Shore	400.00	200.00	100.00
(86)	Red Smith	400.00	200.00	100.00
(87)	Fred Snodgrass	400.00	200.00	100.00
(88)	Tris Speaker	700.00	350.00	175.00
(89)	George Stallings	400.00	200.00	100.00
(90)	C.D. Stengel (Casey Stengel)	600.00	300.00	150.00
(91)	Sailor Stroud	400.00	200.00	100.00
(92)	Amos Strunk	400.00	200.00	100.00
(93)	Chas. (Jeff) Tesreau	400.00	200.00	100.00
(94a)	Chester D. Thomas (One button shows.)	400.00	200.00	100.00
(94b)	Chester D. Thomas (Two buttons.)	400.00	200.00	100.00
(95)	Fred Toney	400.00	200.00	100.00
(96)	Walt Tragesser	400.00	200.00	100.00
(97)	Honus Wagner	5,000	1,000	500.00
(98)	Carl Weilman	400.00	200.00	100.00
(99)	Zack Wheat	550.00	225.00	110.00
(100)	George Whitted	400.00	200.00	100.00
(101)	Arthur Wilson	400.00	200.00	100.00
(102)	Ivy Wingo	400.00	200.00	100.00
(103)	Joe Wood	500.00	250.00	125.00

1940s Ford Babe Ruth Premium

The exact date of this premium photo's issue is unknown. The approximately 5" x 6-1/2" blank-back, black-and-white photo features Ruth in an oft-seen batting pose. In the wide white border at bottom is printed, "CONSULTANT / FORD MOTOR COMPANY / AMERICAN LEGION JUNIOR BASEBALL."

	NM	EX	VG
Babe Ruth	300.00	150.00	90.00

1961 Ford Pittsburgh Pirates Prints

The year after the team's dramatic World Series win over the Yankees, Pittsburgh area Ford dealers distributed a set of six player prints. The blank-back, 11-7/8" x 14-3/4" prints feature action drawings of the players by artist Robert Riger. Some of the prints are horizontal in format, some are vertical. A Ford Motor Co. copyright line appears in the lower-left corner and a line at bottom center identifies the player in the form of a title for the picture. The unnumbered prints are listed here in alphabetical order. The pictures were reprinted by an unauthorized party circa 1998.

		NM	EX	VG
Complete Set (6):		125.00	65.00	35.00
Common Player:		15.00	7.50	4.50
(1)	BOB FRIEND COMES IN WITH THE FAST ONE (Bob Friend)	15.00	7.50	4.50
(2)	CLEMENTE LINES ONE OVER SECOND (Roberto Clemente)	75.00	37.50	22.00
(3)	GROAT CUTS DOWN A BRAVE STEAL (Dick Groat)	15.00	7.50	4.50
(4)	HOAK HANDLES A HOT SHOT AT THIRD (Don Hoak)	15.00	7.50	4.50
(5)	MAZ GETS THE BIG HIT (Bill Mazeroski)	30.00	15.00	9.00
(6)	THE LAW (Vern Law)	15.00	7.50	4.50

1962 Ford Detroit Tigers Postcards

Because baseball card collectors have to compete with auto memorabilia hobbyists for these scarce cards, they are among the most valuable postcard issues of the early 1960s. In 3-1/4" x 5-1/2" postcard format, the full-color cards feature photos taken on a golf course of players posed in front of various new Fords. White backs have a name, position and team, with a box for a stamp. Probably given out in conjunction with autograph appearances at car dealers (they are frequently found autographed), the set lacks some of the team's biggest stars (Al Kaline, Norm Cash), and includes coaches and even

trainer Jack Homel. Probably because of lack of demand, the coaches' and trainer's cards are the scarcest to find today. The unnumbered cards are checklisted here alphabetically.

		NM	EX	VG
Complete Set (16):		1,425	710.00	425.00
Common Player:		60.00	30.00	18.00
(1)	Hank Aguirre	90.00	45.00	27.50
(2)	Steve Boros	120.00	60.00	35.00
(3)	Dick Brown	90.00	45.00	27.50
(4)	Jim Bunning	150.00	75.00	45.00
(5)	Phil Cavaretta	135.00	65.00	40.00
(6)	Rocky Colavito	185.00	90.00	55.00
(7)	Terry Fox	60.00	30.00	18.00
(8)	Purn Goldy	75.00	37.50	22.50
(9)	Jack Homel	135.00	65.00	40.00
(10)	Ron Kline	90.00	45.00	27.50
(11)	Don Mossi	60.00	30.00	18.00
(12)	George Myatt	120.00	60.00	35.00
(13)	Ron Nischwitz	90.00	45.00	27.50
(14)	Larry Osborne	60.00	30.00	18.00
(15)	Phil Regan	90.00	45.00	27.50
(16)	Mike Roarke	135.00	65.00	40.00

1938 Foto Fun

Sponsored by Poll-Parrott Shoes, this set was an early attempt at a self-developing player photocard (a technology that Topps used in the 1940s-50s) used a black-and-white negative and a piece of photo paper to create a blue-tint photo that could be placed in a gold cardboard frame. The back of the 2-3/4" x 3-5/8" frame is printed in brown and gives instructions for developing the photo. The checklist of the unnumbered cards, presented here alphabetically, may or may not be complete at 93.

		NM	EX	VG
Common Player:		160.00	80.00	45.00
(1)	Luke Appling	375.00	185.00	110.00
(2)	Morris Arnovich	160.00	80.00	45.00
(3)	Eldon Auker	160.00	80.00	45.00
(4)	Jim Bagby	160.00	80.00	45.00
(5)	Red Barrett	160.00	80.00	45.00
(6)	Roy Bell	160.00	80.00	45.00
(7)	Wally Berger	160.00	80.00	45.00
(8)	Oswald Bluege	160.00	80.00	45.00
(9)	Frenchy Bordagaray	160.00	80.00	45.00
(10)	Tom Bridges	160.00	80.00	45.00
(11)	Dolf Camilli	160.00	80.00	45.00
(12)	Ben Chapman	160.00	80.00	45.00
(13)	Harland Clift (Harland)	160.00	80.00	45.00
(14)	Harry Craft	160.00	80.00	45.00
(15)	Roger Cramer	160.00	80.00	45.00
(16)	Joe Cronin	375.00	185.00	110.00
(17)	Tony Cuccinello	160.00	80.00	45.00
(18)	Kiki Cuyler	375.00	185.00	110.00
(19)	Ellsworth Dahlgren	160.00	80.00	45.00
(20)	Harry Danning	160.00	80.00	45.00
(21)	Frank Demaree	160.00	80.00	45.00
(22)	Gene Desautels	160.00	80.00	45.00
(23)	Jim Deshong	160.00	80.00	45.00
(24)	Bill Dickey	450.00	225.00	135.00
(25)	Lou Fette	160.00	80.00	45.00
(26)	Lou Finney	160.00	80.00	45.00
(27)	Larry French	160.00	80.00	45.00
(28)	Linus Frey	160.00	80.00	45.00
(29)	Augie Galan	160.00	80.00	45.00
(30)	Debs Garms	160.00	80.00	45.00
(31)	Charles Gehringer	450.00	225.00	135.00
(32)	Lefty Gomez	450.00	225.00	135.00
(33)	Ival Goodman	160.00	80.00	45.00
(34)	Lee Grissom	160.00	80.00	45.00
(35)	Stan Hack	180.00	90.00	55.00
(36)	Irving Hadley	160.00	80.00	45.00
(37)	Rollie Hemsley	160.00	80.00	45.00
(38)	Tommy Henrich	160.00	80.00	45.00

(39)	Billy Herman	375.00	185.00	110.00
(40)	Willard Hershberger	160.00	80.00	45.00
(41)	Michael Higgins	160.00	80.00	45.00
(42)	Oral Hildebrand	160.00	80.00	45.00
(43)	Carl Hubbell	450.00	225.00	135.00
(44)	Willis Hudlin	160.00	80.00	45.00
(45)	Mike Kreevich	160.00	80.00	45.00
(46)	Ralph Kress	160.00	80.00	45.00
(47)	John Lanning	160.00	80.00	45.00
(48)	Lyn Lary	160.00	80.00	45.00
(49)	Cookie Lavagetto	160.00	80.00	45.00
(50)	Thornton Lee	160.00	80.00	45.00
(51)	Ernie Lombardi	375.00	185.00	110.00
(52)	Al Lopez	375.00	185.00	110.00
(53)	Ted Lyons	375.00	185.00	110.00
(54)	Danny MacFayden	160.00	80.00	45.00
(55)	Max Macon	160.00	80.00	45.00
(56)	Pepper Martin	250.00	125.00	75.00
(57)	Joe Marty	160.00	80.00	45.00
(58)	Frank McCormick	160.00	80.00	45.00
(59)	Bill McKechnie	375.00	185.00	110.00
(60)	Joe Medwick	375.00	185.00	110.00
(61)	Cliff Melton	160.00	80.00	45.00
(62)	Charley Meyer (Myer)	160.00	80.00	45.00
(63)	John Mize	450.00	225.00	135.00
(64)	Terry Moore	180.00	90.00	55.00
(65)	Whitey Moore	160.00	80.00	45.00
(66)	Emmett Mueller	160.00	80.00	45.00
(67)	Hugh Mulcahy	160.00	80.00	45.00
(68)	Van L. Mungo	160.00	80.00	45.00
(69)	Johnny Murphy	160.00	80.00	45.00
(70)	Lynn Nelson	160.00	80.00	45.00
(71)	Mel Ott	450.00	225.00	135.00
(72)	Monte Pearson	160.00	80.00	45.00
(73)	Bill Rogell	160.00	80.00	45.00
(74)	George Selkirk	160.00	80.00	45.00
(75)	Milt Shofner	160.00	80.00	45.00
(76)	Al Simmons	375.00	185.00	110.00
(77)	Clyde Shoun	160.00	80.00	45.00
(78)	Gus Suhr	160.00	80.00	45.00
(79)	Billy Sullivan	160.00	80.00	45.00
(80)	Cecil Travis	160.00	80.00	45.00
(81)	Pie Traynor	375.00	185.00	110.00
(82)	Hal Trosky	160.00	80.00	45.00
(83)	Jim Turner	160.00	80.00	45.00
(84)	Johnny Vander Meer	160.00	80.00	45.00
(85)	Oscar Vitt	160.00	80.00	45.00
(86)	Gerald Walker	160.00	80.00	45.00
(87)	Paul Waner	375.00	185.00	110.00
(88)	Rabbit Warstler	160.00	80.00	45.00
(89)	Bob Weiland	160.00	80.00	45.00
(90)	Burgess Whitehead	160.00	80.00	45.00
(91)	Earl Whitehill	160.00	80.00	45.00
(92)	Rudy York	160.00	80.00	45.00
(93)	Del Young	160.00	80.00	45.00

1887 Four Base Hits

Although the exact origin of this set is still in doubt, the Four Base Hits cards are among the rarest and most sought after of all 19th century tobacco issues. There is some speculation that the cards, measuring 2-1/4" x 3-7/8", were produced by Charles Gross & Co. because of their similarity to the Kalamazoo Bats issues, but there is also some evidence to support the theory that they were issued by August Beck & Co., producer of the Yum Yum set. The Four Base Hits cards feature sepia-toned photos with the player's name and position below the picture, and the words "Smoke Four Base Hits. Four For 10 Cents." along the bottom. The card labeled "Daily" is a double error. The name should have been spelled "Daly," but the card actually pictures Billy Sunday. Many of the cards on this surely incomplete checklist are known to survive in only a single example; few in grades above VG.

		NM EX	VG
Common Player:		35,000	15,000
(1)	John Clarkson	150,000	80,000
(2)	Tido Daily (Daly)	60,000	24,000
	(Photo is Billy Sunday.)		
(3)	Pat Deasley	35,000	15,000
(4)	Mike Dorgan	35,000	15,000
(5)	Buck Ewing	175,000	80,000
(6)	Pete Gillespie	35,000	15,000
(7)	Frank Hankinson	35,000	15,000
(8)	King Kelly	250,000	120,000
(9)	Al Mays	35,000	15,000
(10)	Jim Mutrie	35,000	15,000
(11)	Chief Roseman	35,000	15,000
(12)	Marty Sullivan	35,000	15,000
(13)	Rip Van Haltren	35,000	15,000

(14)	John Ward	150,000	80,000
(15)	Mickey Welch	150,000	80,000

1960s Nellie Fox Bowl Postcard

 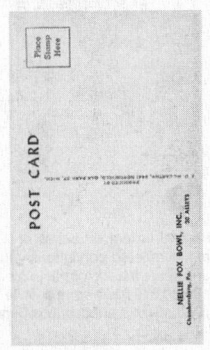

This specially marked version of a typical J.D. McCarthy postcard advertises on back the White Sox second baseman's bowling enterprise in Chambersburg, Pa. The card is black-and-white with a facsimile autograph on front.

	NM	EX	VG
Nellie Fox	35.00	17.50	10.50

1980 Franchise Babe Ruth

The first in a series of collectors' issues relative to Maryland baseball, this 80-card set chronicles the life - on and off the field - of Babe Ruth. Fronts of the 2-1/2" x 3-1/2" cards have black-and-white photos surrounded by wide white borders. Backs are printed in red and black and include a caption and description of the front photo. At the time of issue, the set sold for about $8.

	NM	EX	VG
Complete Set (80):	35.00	17.50	10.00
Common Card:	1.00	.50	.30
1-80 Babe Ruth			

1961 Franklin Milk

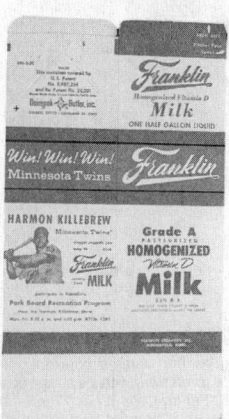

While it is not part of the contemporary Cloverleaf Dairy milk carton Minnesota Twins issues, this carton is often collected alongside the others. Printed in red and blue, the portion of the milk carton advertising Harmon Killebrew's radio show measures about 4" x 4-1/2".

		NM	EX	VG
(1)	Harmon Killebrew	1,600	800.00	480.00
	(Complete carton.)			
(1)	Harmon Killebrew (Cut panel.)	250.00	125.00	75.00

1964 Freihofer's Philadelphia Phillies

The attributed date is speculative, based on the players checklisted from this issue. These 8" x 10" pictures feature studio poses and are printed on heavy, non-glossy paper. A white border surrounds the photo, with the player name in typewriter-style all-caps at bottom. Backs are blank. Two styles of advertising have been seen imprinted on the pic-

tures. Type 1 pictures have a bakery logo as part of the legend "ANOTHER FAVORITE / FROM FREIHOFER'S / that's who!" Type 2 pictures have a script inscription: "Best WISHES to a / Fellow Freihofer's Booster."

	NM	EX	VG
TYPE 1 (Logo)			
Ruben Amaro	50.00	25.00	15.00
Wes Covington	50.00	25.00	15.00
TYPE 2 (No logo.)			
Wes Covington	30.00	15.00	9.00

1963 French Bauer Reds Milk Caps

This regional set of cardboard milk bottle caps was issued in the Cincinnati area in 1963 and features 30 members of the Cincinnati Reds. The unnumbered, blank-backed discs are approximately 1-1/4" in diameter and feature rather crude drawings of the players with their names in script alongside the artwork and the words "Visit Beautiful Crosley Field/See The Reds in Action" along the outside. An album was issued to house the set. Some caps have been seen with incorrect picture/name combinations.

		NM	EX	VG
Complete Set (30):		1,300	650.00	400.00
Common Player:		25.00	12.50	7.50
Album:		100.00	50.00	30.00
(1)	Don Blasingame	25.00	12.50	7.50
(2)	Leo Cardenas	25.00	12.50	7.50
(3)	Gordon Coleman	25.00	12.50	7.50
(4)	Wm. O. DeWitt	25.00	12.50	7.50
(5)	John Edwards	25.00	12.50	7.50
(6)	Jesse Gonder	25.00	12.50	7.50
(7)	Tommy Harper	25.00	12.50	7.50
(8)	Bill Henry	25.00	12.50	7.50
(9)	Fred Hutchinson	25.00	12.50	7.50
(10)	Joey Jay	25.00	12.50	7.50
(11)	Eddie Kasko	25.00	12.50	7.50
(12)	Marty Keough	25.00	12.50	7.50
(13)	Jim Maloney	25.00	12.50	7.50
(14)	Joe Nuxhall	30.00	15.00	9.00
(15)	Reggie Otero	25.00	12.50	7.50
(16)	Jim O'Toole	25.00	12.50	7.50
(17)	Jim Owens	25.00	12.50	7.50
(18)	Vada Pinson	30.00	15.00	9.00
(19)	Bob Purkey	25.00	12.50	7.50
(20)	Frank Robinson	125.00	60.00	35.00
(21)	Dr. Richard Rohde	25.00	12.50	7.50
(22)	Pete Rose	500.00	250.00	150.00
(23)	Ray Shore	25.00	12.50	7.50
(24)	Dick Sisler	25.00	12.50	7.50
(25)	Bob Skinner	25.00	12.50	7.50
(26)	John Tsitorius	25.00	12.50	7.50
(27)	Jim Turner	25.00	12.50	7.50
(28)	Ken Walters	25.00	12.50	7.50
(29)	Al Worthington	25.00	12.50	7.50
(30)	Dom Zanni	25.00	12.50	7.50

1946 Friedman's Dodger Aces Postcard

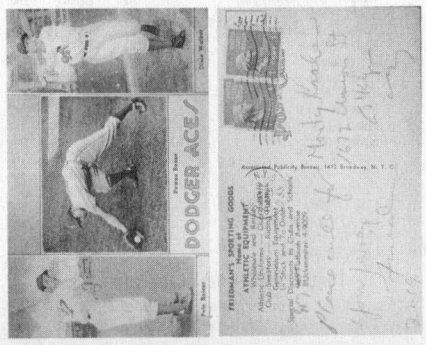

The date of issue is conjectural and could actually have been anytime in the 1940s until 1947, though the cards continued to be used at least into 1953 according to postally used examples. The 5-1/2" x 3-1/2" postcard has a linen finish on front and features color posed action photos of three Dodgers stars. Backs have information about the sporting goods store, a postage stamp box and a credit line to Associated Publicity Bureau.

	NM	EX	VG
Dodger Aces (Pete Reiser, Pewee (Pee Wee) Reese, Dixie Walker)	35.00	17.50	10.50

1960-61 Fritos Ticket Folders

Only a few players are known in this issue of folders which includes a "Jr. Guest Ticket" to selected Dodgers games. About 5-5/8" x 3", the folder has a black-and-white player portrait on front and is highlighted in red and yellow. When opened, the folder has advertising for Fritos corn chips (or other Firtos-Lay brands) and a Dodgers home schedule. Others may exist.

		NM	EX	VG
Common Player:		90.00	45.00	25.00
(1)	Don Drysdale (1960) (Crispies advertising.)	250.00	125.00	75.00
(1)	Don Drysdale (1961)	200.00	100.00	60.00
(2)	Gil Hodges (1960)	200.00	100.00	60.00
(3)	Frank Howard (1961)	90.00	45.00	25.00
(4)	Wally Moon (1960)	150.00	75.00	45.00
(5)	Charley Neal (1960)	150.00	75.00	45.00

1977 Fritsch One-Year Winners

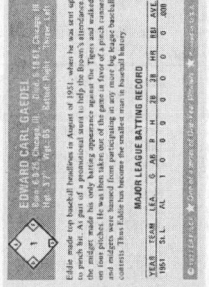

First printed in 1977, this collector's issue features players with brief, but often well-known, major league baseball careers. Because of the timing or duration of their playing days, few ever appeared on a major baseball card issue. The 2-1/2" x 3-1/2" cards have black-and-white photos on front, bordered in green, with the player name in white within a green strip at bottom. Backs are printed in black, red and white in similitude of the 1953 Bowman backs and contain personal data, stats and career highlights.

		NM	EX	VG
Complete Set (18):		12.00	6.00	3.50
Common Player:		1.00	.50	.30
1	Eddie Gaedel	5.00	2.50	1.50
2	Chuck Connors	3.00	1.50	.90
3	Joe Brovia	1.00	.50	.30
4	Ross Grimsley	1.00	.50	.30
5	Bob Thorpe	1.00	.50	.30
6	Pete Gray	5.00	2.50	1.50
7	Cy Buker	1.00	.50	.30
8	Ted Fritsch	2.00	1.00	.60
9	Ron Necciai	1.00	.50	.30
10	Nino Escalera	1.00	.50	.30
11	Bobo Holloman	1.00	.50	.30
12	Tony Roig	1.00	.50	.30
13	Paul Pettit	1.00	.50	.30
14	Paul Schramka	1.00	.50	.30
15	Hal Trosky	1.00	.50	.30
16	Floyd Wooldridge	1.00	.50	.30
17	Jim Westlake	1.00	.50	.30
18	Leon Brinkopf	1.00	.50	.30

1979 Fritsch One-Year Winners

Players with short major-league careers, few of whom appeared on contemporary baseball cards, are featured in the

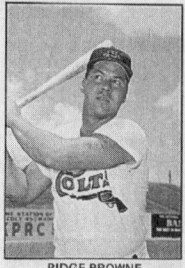

PIDGE BROWNE

second collectors' series of "One-Year Winners." The cards are numbered contiguously from the end of the 1977 issue and share a back format printed in red, white and black. Fronts of the 1979 issue have a white border and feature color player photos with a shadow box beneath carrying the name.

		NM	EX	VG
Complete Set (36):		40.00	20.00	12.00
Common Player:		3.00	1.50	.90
19	Daryl Robertson	3.00	1.50	.90
20	Gerry Schoen	3.00	1.50	.90
21	Jim Brenneman	3.00	1.50	.90
22	Pat House	3.00	1.50	.90
23	Ken Poulsen	3.00	1.50	.90
24	Arlo Brunsberg	3.00	1.50	.90
25	Jay Hankins	3.00	1.50	.90
26	Chuck Nieson	3.00	1.50	.90
27	Dick Joyce	3.00	1.50	.90
28	Jim Ellis	3.00	1.50	.90
29	John Duffie	3.00	1.50	.90
30	Vern Holtgrave	3.00	1.50	.90
31	Bill Bethea	3.00	1.50	.90
32	Joe Moock	3.00	1.50	.90
33	John Hoffman	3.00	1.50	.90
34	Jorge Rubio	3.00	1.50	.90
35	Fred Rath	3.00	1.50	.90
36	Jess Hickman	3.00	1.50	.90
37	Tom Fisher	3.00	1.50	.90
38	Dick Scott	3.00	1.50	.90
39	Jim Hibbs	3.00	1.50	.90
40	Paul Gilliford	3.00	1.50	.90
41	Bob Botz	3.00	1.50	.90
42	Jack Kubiszyn	3.00	1.50	.90
43	Rich Rusteck	3.00	1.50	.90
44	Roy Gleason	3.00	1.50	.90
45	Glenn Vaughn	3.00	1.50	.90
46	Bill Graham	3.00	1.50	.90
47	Dennis Musgraves	3.00	1.50	.90
48	Ron Henry	3.00	1.50	.90
49	Mike Jurewicz	3.00	1.50	.90
50	Pidge Browne	3.00	1.50	.90
51	Ron Keller	3.00	1.50	.90
52	Doug Gallagher	3.00	1.50	.90
53	Dave Thies	3.00	1.50	.90
54	Don Eaddy	3.00	1.50	.90

1928 Fro-joy (F52)

George Herman ("Babe") Ruth

"The Sultan of Swat," who holds the world's record for home-run hits in a single season with all circuit clouts during the regular playing season of 1927, topped by 2 more against Pittsburgh during the World's Series games last year.

Boys—Girls:
Fro-joy Ice Cream, in Fro-joy Cones, builds bone and strength. Eat one every day.

Chock-full of "YOUTH UNITS"

PICTURE NO. 1
This is the first in a series of six pictures of "Babe" Ruth being given with Fro-joy Cones during Fro-joy Cone Week, August 6th-11th, 1928. The complete set can be exchanged for a large reproduction of "Babe" Ruth's autographed photo. Ask your dealer for a FREE circular giving full details.

Capitalizing on the extreme popularity of Babe Ruth, these cards were given away with ice cream cones during the Aug. 6-11, 1928, "Fro-joy Cone Week." The 2-1/16" x 4" cards have black-and-white photos on front with a title and a few sentences explaining the photo. Backs contain advertising for Fro-joy Ice Cream and Cones. An uncut sheet along with a large-format action photo of Ruth was available in a mail-in redemption offer. Virtually all uncut sheets offered in the market today, and all color Fro-joy cards are modern counterfeits. Purchase of an uncut sheet without the original mailing envelope and/or premium picture is not advised. Cards graded by a major authentication firm carry a significant premium due to the prevalence of single-card counterfeits in the market.

		NM	EX	VG
Complete Set (6):		3,250	1,625	975.00
Uncut Sheet:		2,575	1,275	775.00
1	George Herman ("Babe") Ruth	750.00	375.00	225.00
2	Look Out, Mr. Pitcher!	500.00	250.00	150.00
3	Bang! The Babe Lines One Out!	500.00	250.00	150.00
4	When the "Babe" Comes Home	500.00	250.00	150.00
5	"Babe" Ruth's Grip!	200.00	100.00	60.00
6	Ruth is a Crack Fielder	500.00	250.00	150.00

1928 Fro-Joy Premium Photo

This 8-1/2" x 10" photo of Babe Ruth was given away when a complete set of individual Fro-joy Babe Ruth cards was sent in for redemption. It is extremely scarce in its own right and is vital for verification of the authenticity of uncut Fro-joy card sheets. The premium photo is printed in blue in the debossed center area of a cream-colored card. A facsimile autograph of Ruth adorns the image.

	NM	EX	VG
Babe Ruth	1,200	600.00	360.00

1969 Fud's Photography Montreal Expos

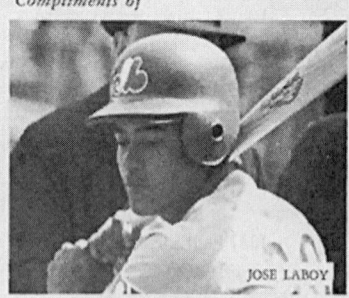

JOSE LABOY
FUD'S PHOTOGRAPHY

This collectors' issue was produced by Bob Solon sometime after 1969. The 3-1/2" x 3" black-and-white horizontal cards have action photos of the players with a white strip in the lower-right corner bearing the name. In the white border at top is "Compliments of," while the purported photo studio name is centered at bottom. Backs are blank. The unnumbered cards are checklisted here alphabetically.

		NM	EX	VG
Complete Set (14):		40.00	20.00	12.00
Common Player:		4.00	2.00	1.25
(1)	Bob Bailey	4.00	2.00	1.25
(2)	John Bateman	4.00	2.00	1.25
(3)	Don Bosch	4.00	2.00	1.25
(4)	Jim Grant	4.00	2.00	1.25
(5)	Mack Jones	4.00	2.00	1.25
(6)	Jose Laboy	4.00	2.00	1.25
(7)	Dan McGinn	4.00	2.00	1.25
(8)	Cal McLish	4.00	2.00	1.25
(9)	Carl Morton	4.00	2.00	1.25
(10)	Manny Mota	6.00	3.00	1.75
(11)	Rusty Staub	9.00	4.50	2.75
(12)	Gary Sutherland	4.00	2.00	1.25
(13)	Mike Wegener	4.00	2.00	1.25
(14)	Floyd Wicker	4.00	2.00	1.25

G

1888 G & B Chewing Gum (E223)

NEW YORK'S
NATIONAL LEAGUE CHEWING GUM.

This set, issued with G&B Chewing Gum, produced in New York City by Green & Blackwell, is the first baseball card issued with candy or gum and the only 19th Century candy issue. The cards in the G&B set are small, measuring approximately 1-1/16" x 2-1/8", and nearly identical in format to the August Beck Yum Yum tobacco issue (N403). Many of the photos and pictures were shared between the sets. The player's name and position appear in thin capital letters below the photo, followed by either "National League" or "American League" (actually referring to the American Association). At the very bottom of the card, the manufacturer, "G & B N.Y." is indicated. Some of the "National League" cards also include the words "Chewing Gum" under the league designation. The set was assigned the ACC number E223. All of the action poses and some of the portraits are line drawings rather than photographs. Gaps have been left in the assigned numbering to accommodate future additions.

	Common Player:	NM	EX	VG
(3)	Cap Anson/Btg	10,000	4,000	2,500
(4)	Cap Anson (Photo portrait.)	37,500	15,000	9,375
(7)	Lady Baldwin (Detroit) (Left arm extended.)	10,000	4,000	2,500
(9)	Mark Baldwin (Chicago) (Bat at side.)	10,000	4,000	2,500
(10)	Mark Baldwin (Chicago) (Photo portrait.)	31,250	12,500	7,815
(13)	Sam Barkley (Line portrait.)	10,000	4,000	2,500
(15)	Steve Brady (Photo portrait.)	31,250	12,500	7,815
(17)	Dan Brouthers (Pose unrecorded.)	31,250	12,500	7,815
(19)	Willard (California) Brown (Photo portrait.)	31,250	12,500	7,815
(20)	Willard (California) Brown (Line art.)	10,000	4,000	2,500
(23)	Charles Buffington (Buffinton) (Photo portrait.)	31,250	12,500	7,815
(25)	Tom Burns (Photo portrait.)	31,250	12,500	7,815
(27)	Doc Bushong (Line portrait.)	10,000	4,000	2,500
(29)	Bob Caruthers (Line portrait.)	10,000	4,000	2,500
(33)	John Clarkson (Photo portrait.)	37,500	15,000	9,375
(35)	John Coleman (Photo portrait.)	31,250	12,500	7,815
(37)	Charlie Comiskey (Line portrait.)	18,750	7,500	4,690
(39)	Roger Connor/Btg	18,750	7,500	4,690
(40)	Roger Connor (Photo portrait.)	37,500	15,000	9,375
(43)	Con Daily (Photo portrait.)	31,250	12,500	7,815
(45)	Tom Deasley (Photo portrait.)	31,250	12,500	7,815
(47)	Jim Donahue (Photo portrait.)	31,250	12,500	7,815
(49)	Mike Dorgan (Photo portrait.)	31,250	12,500	7,815
(51)	Dude Esterbrook (Photo portrait.)	31,250	12,500	7,815
(53)	Buck Ewing (Photo portrait.)	37,500	15,000	9,375
(54)	Buck Ewing (With bat.)	18,750	7,500	4,690
(57)	Charlie Ferguson (Right arm head-high.)	10,000	4,000	2,500
(59)	Silver Flint (Line portrait.)	15,625	6,250	3,905
(61)	Pud Galvin (Ball in hands at front.)	18,750	7,500	4,690
(63)	Charlie Getzein/Throwing (Getzien)	10,000	4,000	2,500
(65)	Jack Glasscock (Line art.)	10,000	4,000	2,500
(67)	Will Gleason/Btg	10,000	4,000	2,500
(69)	Ed Greer (Photo portrait.)	31,250	12,500	7,815
(71)	Frank Hankinson (Photo portrait.)	31,250	12,500	7,815
(73)	Ned Hanlon/Btg	18,750	7,500	4,690
(75)	Fred Hotaling/Btg	15,625	6,250	3,905
(77)	Spud Johnson/Btg	10,000	4,000	2,500
(79)	Tim Keefe (Ball in hands above waist.)	18,750	7,500	4,690
(80)	Tim Keefe/Btg	18,750	7,500	4,690
(81)	Tim Keefe (Photo portrait.)	37,500	15,000	9,375
(83)	King Kelly/Btg	25,000	10,000	6,250
(84)	King Kelly (Photo, standing by urn.)	100,000	20,000	12,500
(87)	Gus Krock (Photo portrait.)	31,250	12,500	7,815
(89)	Arlie Latham (Line portrait.)	10,000	4,000	2,500
(91)	Connie Mack/Throwing	37,500	15,000	9,375
(93)	Kid Madden/Pitching	10,000	4,000	2,500
(95)	Al Mays (Photo portrait.)	31,250	12,500	7,815
(97)	Jumbo McGinnis (Line portrait.)	10,000	4,000	2,500
(99)	Doggie Miller (Leaning on bat.)	10,000	4,000	2,500
(101)	John Morrill (Bat at side.)	10,000	4,000	2,500
(103)	James Mutrie (Photo portrait.)	31,250	12,500	7,815
(105)	Hugh Nicoll (Nicol) (Line portrait.)	10,000	4,000	2,500
(107)	Tip O'Neill (Line portrait.)	10,000	4,000	2,500
(109)	Jim O'Rourke (Photo portrait.)	37,500	15,000	9,375
(111)	Dave Orr/Btg	10,000	4,000	2,500
(112)	Dave Orr (Photo portrait.)	31,250	12,500	7,815
(115)	Fred Pfeffer (Bat on shoulder.)	10,000	4,000	2,500
(117)	Henry Porter/Pitching	10,000	4,000	2,500
(119)	Al Reache (Reach) (Line portrait.) (Possibly unique; value undetermined.)	.00	.00	.00
(121)	Danny Richardson/Btg	10,000	4,000	2,500
(122)	Danny Richardson (Photo portrait.)	31,250	12,500	7,815
(125)	Yank Robinson (Btg)	10,000	4,000	2,500
(127)	Chief Roseman (Photo portrait.)	31,250	12,500	7,815
(129)	Jimmy Ryan (Photo portrait.)	31,250	12,500	7,815
(130)	Jimmy Ryan/Throwing	10,000	4,000	2,500
(133)	Pop Smith (Photo portrait.)	31,250	12,500	7,815
(137)	Bill Sowders (Ball in hands at chest.)	10,000	4,000	2,500
(138)	Bill Sowders/Throwing	10,000	4,000	2,500
(139)	Albert Spaulding (Spalding) (Line portrait.) (Possibly unique; value undetermined.)	.00	.00	.00
(141)	Marty Sullivan (Line portrait.)	10,000	4,000	2,500
(143)	Billy Sunday/Fldg	15,620	6,250	3,905
(144)	Billy Sunday (Photo portrait.)	34,375	13,750	8,595
(145)	Ezra Sutton/Btg	10,000	4,000	2,500
(149)	Sam Thompson/Btg	18,750	7,500	4,690
(153)	Mike Tiernan/Btg	10,000	4,000	2,500
(154)	Mike Tieman (Photo portrait.)	31,250	12,500	7,815
(157)	Larry Twitchell (Photo portrait.)	31,250	12,500	7,815
(159)	Rip Van Haltren (Photo portrait.)	31,250	12,500	7,815
(161)	Chris Von Der Ahe (Line portrait.)	10,000	4,000	2,500
(165)	John Ward (Photo portrait.)	37,500	15,000	9,375
(169)	Mickey Welch (Ball in hands above waist.)	18,750	7,500	4,690
(170)	Mickey Welch (Right arm extended forward.)	18,750	7,500	4,690
(171)	Mickey Welch (Photo portrait.)	37,500	15,000	9,375
(173)	Curt Welsh (Welch)	10,000	4,000	2,500
(177)	Jim Whitney	10,000	4,000	2,500
(181)	Pete Wood/Throwing	10,000	4,000	2,500

1966 H.F. Gardner Postcards

Baseball players (and track legend Jesse Owens) who were born in Alabama are featured in this issue credited on some of the cards' backs to a Bessemer, Ala., firm, Scenic South Card Co. Fronts feature borderless color photos attributed to H.F. Gardner. The date given is somewhat arbitrary based on the mention of the Atlanta Braves on the back of a card. Cards are in standard 3-1/2" x 5-1/2" postcard size and format. A brief biography of the athletes appears on the back, along with the credits. A quantity of the Aarons and Williams cards were found in a warehouse in 1999, driving down their prices.

		NM	EX	VG
	Complete Set (5):	20.00	10.00	6.00
	Common Player:	3.00	1.50	.90
(1)	Hank Aaron, Tommie Aaron	15.00	7.50	4.50
(2)	Bill Bruton	3.50	1.75	1.00
(3)	Lee Maye	3.50	1.75	1.00
(4)	Jesse Owens	4.50	2.25	1.25
(5)	Billy Williams	3.00	1.50	.90

1922 Gassler's American Maid Bread

These 2" x 3-1/4" black-and-white cards are one of several versions of the W575-1 strip cards with custom-printed advertising on the backs. It is unknown whether each card in the W575-1 checklist can be found with the Gassler's back.

	NM	EX	VG
Common Player:	150.00	75.00	45.00
Stars: 4-6X			

(See W575-1 for checklist; Gassler values 3X-4X.)

1962 Gehl's Ice Cream

Issued only in the Milwaukee area to promote sales of Gold-Mine brand ice cream, the six cards in this black-and-white set all feature Roger Maris, who the previous year had broken Babe Ruth's season home run record. The 4" x 5" cards are blank backed and each has a facsimile autograph on front reading "To My / Gold Mine Pal / Roger Maris." The cards are unnumbered; a description of each is provided in the checklist.

		NM	EX	VG
	Complete Set (6):	1,600	800.00	480.00
	Common Card:	400.00	200.00	120.00
(1)	Roger Maris (Bat on shoulder, close-up.)	400.00	200.00	120.00
(2)	Roger Maris (Bat on shoulder, photo to waist.)	400.00	200.00	120.00
(3)	Roger Maris (Batting stance.)	400.00	200.00	120.00
(4)	Roger Maris ("Hitting My 61st," ballpark photo.)	325.00	160.00	100.00
(5)	Roger Maris (Holding bat in hands.)	400.00	200.00	120.00
(6)	Roger Maris (Portrait in warm-up jacket.)	400.00	200.00	120.00

1941 Lou Gehrig Memorial Ticket

On July 4, 1941, just a month after his death, the N.Y. Yankees scheduled special memorial ceremonies for the Iron Horse. Tickets for the event picture Gehrig and were issued in several colors and price ranges based on seat location. Most often found in stub form of about 3-3/8" x 2-1/2", full tickets are also occasionally seen, probably because a rainout on July 4 forced the ceremonies to the following Sunday.

	NM	EX	VG
Lou Gehrig (Ticket stub.)	1,300	650.00	390.00
Lou Gehrig (Full ticket.)	3,250	1,625	975.00

1911-14 General Baking Co. (D304)

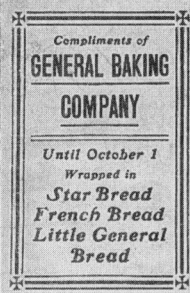

This issue by a bakery based in Buffalo, N.Y., is similar in design to contemporary tobacco and candy cards, but is larger in size, at 1-3/4" x 2-1/2". Fronts feature a color lithograph with the player's name and team below in capital letters. Some players who changed teams in 1913-14 are found with the team name obliterated at bottom by a black line. Five different back styles are known, listed here by the principal brand name: 1) Brunners, 2) Butter Krust, 3) General Baking Co., 4) Weber Bakery, 5) Martens Bakery. The complete set price does not include "no-team" variations. Modern counterfeits of the issue are widely seen in the hobby market.

		NM	EX	VG
	Complete Set (25):	135,000	67,500	40,500
	Common Player:	1,600	800.00	475.00
(1)	J. Frank Baker	5,500	2,750	1,650
(2)	Jack Barry	1,500	750.00	450.00
(3)	George Bell	1,600	800.00	480.00
(4)	Charles Bender	5,250	2,625	1,575
(5a)	Frank Chance (Chicago)	5,250	2,625	1,575
(5b)	Frank Chance (No team.)	7,000	3,500	2,100
(6a)	Hal Chase (N.Y.)	2,000	1,000	600.00
(6b)	Hal Chase (No team.)	2,500	1,250	750.00
(7)	Ty Cobb	62,500	31,250	18,750
(8)	Eddie Collins	5,250	2,625	1,575
(9a)	Otis Crandall (N.Y.)	1,600	800.00	480.00
(9b)	Otis Crandall (No team.)	2,400	1,200	725.00
(10)	Sam Crawford	5,250	2,625	1,575
(11a)	John Evers (Chicago)	5,250	2,625	1,575
(11b)	John Evers (No team.)	7,000	3,500	2,100
(12)	Arthur Fletcher	1,600	800.00	480.00
(13a)	Charles Herzog (N.Y.)	1,600	800.00	480.00
(13b)	Charles Herzog (No team.)	2,400	1,200	725.00
(14)	M. (Billy) Kelly	1,600	800.00	475.00
(15)	Napoleon Lajoie	7,000	3,500	2,100
(16)	Rube Marquard	5,250	2,625	1,575
(17)	Christy Mathewson	20,000	10,000	6,000
(18)	Fred Merkle	1,600	800.00	480.00
(19)	"Chief" Meyers	1,600	800.00	480.00
(20)	Marty O'Toole	1,600	800.00	480.00
(21)	Nap. Rucker	1,600	800.00	480.00
(22)	Arthur Shafer	1,600	800.00	480.00
(23)	Fred Tenny (Tenney)	4,000	2,000	1,200
(24)	Honus Wagner	30,000	15,000	9,000
(25)	Cy Young	17,500	8,750	5,250

1915 General Baking Co. (D303)

COMPLIMENTS OF

GENERAL BAKING CO.

UNTIL SEPTEMBER 1ST
WRAPPED IN

STAR BREAD
FRENCH BREAD
LITTLE GENERAL
BREAD

Cobb, c. f. Detroit Americans

Issued in 1915 by the General Baking Co., these unnumbered cards measure 1-1/2" x 2-3/4". The player pictures and format of the cards are identical to the E106 set, but the D303 cards are easily identified by the advertisement for General Baking on the back.

		NM	EX	VG
Complete Set (51):		80,000	32,000	16,000
Common Player:		1,600	800.00	300.00
(1)	Jack Barry	1,600	800.00	300.00
(2)	Chief Bender	3,000	1,700	800.00
	(Blue background.)			
(3)	Chief Bender	3,000	1,750	800.00
	(Green background.)			
(4)	Bob Bescher (New York)	1,600	800.00	300.00
(5)	Bob Bescher (St. Louis)	1,600	800.00	300.00
(6)	Roger Bresnahan	3,000	1,750	800.00
(7)	Al Bridwell	1,600	800.00	300.00
(8)	Donie Bush	1,600	800.00	300.00
(9)	Hal Chase/Catching	1,800	800.00	360.00
(10)	Hal Chase/Portrait	1,800	900.00	360.00
(11)	Ty Cobb/Btg	20,000	10,000	4,000
(12)	Ty Cobb (Leaning on bat.)	30,000	15,000	6,000
(13)	Eddie Collins	3,000	1,700	800.00
(14)	Sam Crawford	3,000	1,700	800.00
(15)	Ray Demmitt	1,600	800.00	300.00
(16)	Wild Bill Donovan	1,600	800.00	300.00
(17)	Red Dooin	1,600	800.00	300.00
(18)	Mickey Doolan	1,600	800.00	300.00
(19)	Larry Doyle	1,600	800.00	300.00
(20)	Clyde Engle	1,600	800.00	300.00
(21)	Johnny Evers	3,000	1,700	800.00
(22)	Art Fromme	1,600	800.00	300.00
(23)	George Gibson/Catching	1,600	800.00	300.00
	(back view.)			
(24)	George Gibson/Catching	1,600	800.00	300.00
	(Front view.)			
(25)	Roy Hartzell	1,600	800.00	300.00
(26)	Fred Jacklitsch	1,600	800.00	300.00
(27)	Hugh Jennings	3,000	1,750	800.00
(28)	Otto Knabe	1,600	800.00	300.00
(29)	Nap Lajoie	4,000	2,000	1,000
(30)	Hans Lobert	1,600	800.00	300.00
(31)	Rube Marquard	1,500	850.00	400.00
(32)	Christy Mathewson	10,000	7,000	3,000
(33)	John McGraw	1,500	850.00	400.00
(34)	George McQuillan	1,600	800.00	300.00
(35)	Dots Miller	1,600	800.00	300.00
(36)	Danny Murphy	1,600	800.00	300.00
(37)	Rebel Oakes	1,600	800.00	300.00
(38)	Eddie Plank	3,000	1,700	750.00
	(No position on front.)			
(39)	Eddie Plank	6,000	3,000	1,500
	(Position on front.)			
(40)	Germany Schaefer	1,600	800.00	300.00
(41)	Boss Smith (Schmidt)	1,600	800.00	300.00
(42)	Tris Speaker	8,000	3,500	1,500
(43)	Oscar Stanage	1,600	800.00	300.00
(44)	George Stovall	1,600	800.00	300.00
(45)	Jeff Sweeney	1,600	800.00	300.00
(46)	Joe Tinker/Btg	2,000	1,200	600.00
(47)	Joe Tinker/Portrait	2,000	1,200	600.00
(48)	Honus Wagner/Btg	20,000	10,000	4,000
(49)	Honus Wagner/Throwing	30,000	15,000	6,000
(50)	Hooks Wiltse	1,600	800.00	300.00
(51)	Heinie Zimmerman	1,600	800.00	300.00

1908 General Photo Co. St. Louis Browns Postcards

The extent of this postcard issue by a hometown printer is unknown. It is likely other single-player postcards were issued. Approximately 3-1/2" x 5-1/2", the cards are black-and-white with a credit line on bottom: "Photo by General Photo Co., 610 Granite Bldg., St. Louis." On the team photo card, players are identified below the group photo.

		NM	EX	VG
(1)	"Rube" Waddell	500.00	250.00	150.00
(2)	St. Louis Browns - 1908	750.00	375.00	225.00

1948 Gentle's Bread Boston Braves

These 3" x 9" waxed-paper end labels were found on loaves of Gentle's bread. Printed in blue and red, the labels depict action poses of the National League Champion '48 Braves. A facsimile autograph appears with the photo. Backs are blank. The unnumbered labels are checklisted here alphabetically.

		NM	EX	VG
Complete Set (9):		3,000	1,500	900.00
Common Player:		400.00	200.00	120.00
(1)	Alvin Dark	450.00	225.00	135.00
(2)	Bob Elliott	400.00	200.00	120.00
(3)	Tommy Heath	400.00	200.00	120.00
(4)	Tommy Holmes	400.00	200.00	120.00
(5)	Phil Masi	400.00	200.00	120.00
(6)	John Sain	450.00	225.00	135.00
(7)	Warren Spahn	600.00	300.00	180.00
(8)	Eddie Stanky	450.00	225.00	135.00
(9)	Earl Torgeson	400.00	200.00	120.00

1956 Gentry Magazine Ty Cobb

In issue #20 of Gentry magazine, dated Fall, 1956, a feature article on card collecting was enhanced with the inclusion of an original Ty Cobb card tipped onto an interior page. Measuring about 4" x 2-1/4" and blank-backed, the color card is similar in design to the T205 tobacco card issue.

	NM	EX	VG
Complete Magazine:	125.00	65.00	40.00
Ty Cobb	90.00	45.00	27.00

1909-10 German Baseball Stamps

A marginal notation "Made in Germany" on one of the stamps in this series identifies its origins. Little else in known of them. The stamps measure about 1-3/8" to 1-1/2" by 1-3/4" to 1-7/8". They are printed in bright colors on a pink background with name and team in blue. Because of their European origins, there are many mistakes in player and team names. The crude pictures are not representative of the player named. Unnumbered stamps are listed here in alphabetical order. It is evident several different configurations of 35-stamp sheets must have been issued.

		NM	EX	VG
Complete Sheet (35):		1,150	575.00	345.00
Complete Set (41):		1,300	650.00	400.00
Common Player:		65.00	32.50	20.00
(1)	Ginger Beaumont	65.00	32.50	20.00
(2)	Frank Bowerman	65.00	32.50	20.00
(3)	Kitty Bransfield	65.00	32.50	20.00
(4)	Al Bridwell	65.00	32.50	20.00
(5a)	Roger Bresnahan (Light shirt.)	100.00	50.00	30.00
(5b)	Roger Bresnahan (Dark shirt.)	100.00	50.00	30.00
(6)	Bill Carrigan	65.00	32.50	20.00
(7)	Hal Chase	80.00	40.00	24.00
(8)	Eddie Collins	100.00	50.00	30.00
(9)	Harry Davis	65.00	32.50	20.00
(10)	Wild Bill Donovan	65.00	32.50	20.00
(11)	Larry Doyle	65.00	32.50	20.00
(12)	Jean Dubuc	65.00	32.50	20.00
(13)	Kid Elberfeld (Elberfield)	65.00	32.50	20.00
(14)	Dick Hoblitzell	65.00	32.50	20.00
(15)	Solly Hoffman (Hofman)	65.00	32.50	20.00
(16)	Tim Jordan	65.00	32.50	20.00
(17)	Willie Keeler	100.00	50.00	30.00
(18)	Nap Lajoie	100.00	50.00	30.00
(19)	Tommy Leach	65.00	32.50	20.00
(20)	Christy Mathewson	325.00	160.00	100.00
(21)	Dots Miller	65.00	32.50	20.00
(22)	John McGraw	100.00	50.00	30.00
(23)	Eddie Plank	100.00	50.00	30.00
(24)	Jack Rowan	65.00	32.50	20.00
(25)	Nap Rucker	65.00	32.50	20.00
(26)	Shannon (Boston)	65.00	32.50	20.00
(27)	Frank Smith	65.00	32.50	20.00
(28)	Tris Speaker	120.00	60.00	35.00
(29)	Jake Stahl	65.00	32.50	20.00
(30)	Lee Tannehill	65.00	32.50	20.00
(31)	Fred Tenney	65.00	32.50	20.00
(32)	Ira Thomas	65.00	32.50	20.00
(33)	Joe Tinker	100.00	50.00	30.00
(34)	Honus Wagner	285.00	140.00	85.00
(35)	Jimmy Williams	65.00	32.50	20.00
(36)	Cy Young	165.00	85.00	50.00
(37)	Baseball	15.00	7.50	4.50
(38)	Bat	15.00	7.50	4.50
(39)	Body Protector	15.00	7.50	4.50
(40)	Catcher's Mask	15.00	7.50	4.50
(41)	Crossed Bats	15.00	7.50	4.50
(42)	Glove	15.00	7.50	4.50

1923 German Baseball Transfers

With crude artwork lifted from the W515 strip card set, this issue of baseball player (and boxer) transfers was produced in Germany. Approximately 1-3/16" x 1-1/2", the stamps are printed in red on a green background. All of the design, except for the "MADE IN GERMANY" notation in the white bottom margin, is in mirror-image, befitting their use as tattoos or transfers. Two of the baseball players are double-prints. The unnumbered stamps (baseball only) are checklisted here alphabetically.

		NM	EX	VG
Complete Baseball Set (13):		350.00	175.00	105.00
Complete Sheet (25):		400.00	200.00	120.00
Common Player:		40.00	20.00	12.00
(1)	Grover Alexander	45.00	22.00	13.50
(2)	Dave Bancroft	40.00	20.00	12.00
(3)	George (J.) Burns	30.00	15.00	9.00
(4)	"Ty" Cobb	100.00	50.00	30.00
(5)	Red Faber (DP)	25.00	12.50	7.50
(6)	Arthur Nehf	30.00	15.00	9.00
(7)	"Babe" Ruth	200.00	100.00	60.00
(8)	Ray Schalk	40.00	20.00	12.00
(9)	Everett Scott	30.00	15.00	9.00
(10)	Bob Shawkey	30.00	15.00	9.00
(11)	Tris Speaker	45.00	22.00	13.50
(12)	"Casey" Stengel	45.00	22.00	13.50
(13)	Zack Wheat (DP)	30.00	15.00	9.00

1922 Lou Gertenrich

One of the most attractive advertising backs of the 1920s is found on this version of the 1922 issue which is most often found with American Caramel ads on back. Gertenrich had a three-game major league career between 1901-1903, supporting his advertising claim of "The Baseball Player Candy Manufacturer." Probably originating in Chicago, these cards are 2" x 3-1/2" black-and-white. The set shares the checklist with the American

Caramel Co. (E121) set of 120. Because of the scarcity and appeal of this regional issue, the Gertenrich versions carry a substantial premium for type-card and superstar collectors.

	NM	EX	VG
Common Player:	600.00	300.00	175.00

Stars: 2-3X

(See 1922 American Caramel Series of 120 for checklist.)

1888 Gilbert & Bacon Cabinets

The known range of this cabinet card issue comprises mostly members of the 1888 Philadelphia Athletics and Phillies. The posed action photos on the approximately 4-1/4" x 6-1/2" cards are the same pictures seen on many of the players' Old Judge and Old Judge cabinet cards. The G&B cabinets have an embossed Goodwin & Co. copyright seal. An elaborate typescript Gilbert & Bacon studio logo is found in the bottom-left border, with the city named at right. Backs have an ornate studio logo.

		NM	EX	VG
Common Player:		3,000	1,200	700.00
(1)	Louis Bierbauer	3,000	1,200	700.00
(2)	Bill Blair	3,000	1,200	700.00
(3)	Charlie Ferguson	3,000	1,200	700.00
	(Ball in hands at chest.)			
(4)	Charlie Ferguson/Btg	3,000	1,200	700.00
(5)	Charlie Ferguson/Throwing	3,000	1,200	700.00
(6)	Kid Gleason	3,000	1,200	700.00
(7)	John Henry	3,000	1,200	700.00
(8)	Henry Larkin	3,000	1,200	700.00
(9)	Denny Lyons	3,000	1,200	700.00
(11)	Deacon McGuire	3,000	1,200	700.00
	(Bat behind head.)			
(12)	Deacon McGuire	3,000	1,200	700.00
	(Bat on shoulder.)			
(13)	Deacon McGuire	3,000	1,200	700.00
	(Fielding, hands at waist.)			
(14)	Deacon McGuire/Fldg	3,000	1,200	700.00
	(Hands head-high.)			
(15)	Deacon McGuire/Throwing	3,000	1,200	700.00
(16)	George Pinkney	3,000	1,200	700.00
	(Bat at 45-degree angle.)			
(17)	George Pinkney	3,000	1,200	700.00
	(Bat at 60-degree angle.)			
(18)	George Pinkney	3,000	1,200	700.00
	(Bat nearly horizontal.)			
(19)	George Pinkney	3,000	1,200	700.00
	(Fielding fly ball.)			
(21)	George Pinkney	3,000	1,200	700.00
	(Fielding line drive.)			
(22)	George Pinkney/Throwing	3,000	1,200	700.00
(23)	Ben Sanders	3,000	1,200	700.00
	(Ball in hands at chest.)			
(24)	Ben Sanders/Btg	3,000	1,200	700.00
(25)	Ben Sanders (Fielding fly ball.)	3,000	1,200	700.00
(26)	Ben Sanders/Throwing	3,000	1,200	700.00
(27)	Harry Stovey	3,000	1,200	700.00
(28)	Michael Sullivan	3,000	1,200	700.00
(29)	Gus Weyhing	3,000	1,200	700.00
(31)	John Weyhing	3,000	1,200	700.00
(32)	Harry Wright	7,500	3,700	2,200

1916 Gimbels

This version of the 1916 M101-5 and M101-4 Blank Backs can be found with three slightly different styles of typography on back.

	NM	EX	VG
Common Player:	225.00	112.50	67.50

Stars: 2-3X

(See 1916 M101-5 and M101-4 Blank Backs for checklists and base pricing.)

(An SGC-graded Good #151 Babe Ruth sold at auction for $17,834 in 7/09.)

1953 Glendale Hot Dogs Tigers

Glendale Meats issued these unnumbered, full- color cards (2-5/8" x 3-3/4") in packages of hot dogs Featuring only Detroit Tigers players, the card fronts contain a player picture with his name, a facsimile autograph, and the Tigers logo. Backs carry player statistical and biographical information plus an offer for a trip for two to the World Series. Collectors were advised to mail all the cards they had saved to Glendale Meats. The World Series trip plus 150 other prizes were to be given to the individuals sending in the most cards. As with most cards issued with food products, high-grade cards are tough to find because of the cards' susceptibilty to stains. The Houtteman card is extremely scarce.

		NM	EX	VG
Complete Set (28):		55,000	27,500	16,500
Common Player:		1,800	900.00	550.00
Ad Booklet:		80,000	40,000	25,000
(1)	Matt Batts	1,800	900.00	550.00
(2)	Johnny Bucha	1,800	900.00	550.00
(3)	Frank Carswell	1,800	900.00	550.00
(4)	Jim Delsing	1,800	900.00	550.00
(5)	Walt Dropo	1,800	900.00	550.00
(6)	Hal Erickson	1,800	900.00	550.00
(7)	Paul Foytack	1,800	900.00	550.00
(8)	Owen Friend	1,800	900.00	550.00
(9)	Ned Garver	1,800	900.00	550.00
(10)	Joe Ginsberg	1,800	900.00	550.00
(11)	Ted Gray	1,800	900.00	550.00
(12)	Fred Hatfield	1,800	900.00	550.00
(13)	Ray Herbert	1,800	900.00	550.00
(14)	Bill Hitchcock	1,800	900.00	550.00
(15)	Bill Hoeft	1,800	900.00	550.00
(16)	Art Houtteman	10,000	5,000	3,000
(17)	Milt Jordan	1,800	900.00	550.00
(18)	Harvey Kuenn	2,500	1,250	750.00
(19)	Don Lund	1,800	900.00	550.00
(20)	Dave Madison	1,800	900.00	550.00
(21)	Dick Marlowe	1,800	900.00	550.00
(22)	Pat Mullin	1,800	900.00	550.00
(23)	Bob Nieman	1,800	900.00	550.00
(24)	Johnny Pesky	1,800	900.00	550.00
(25)	Jerry Priddy	1,800	900.00	550.00
(26)	Steve Souchock	1,800	900.00	550.00
(27)	Russ Sullivan	1,800	900.00	550.00
(28)	Bill Wight	2,200	1,100	600.00

1916 Globe Clothing Store (H801-9)

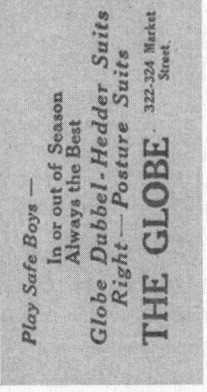

This 200-card set can be found with ads on the back for several local and regional businesses. Among them is the Globe clothing store in St. Louis. Type card, team- and single-player card collectors may pay a modest premium for individual cards with the Globe store's advertising over the parallel 1916 M101-4 Blank Backs values. This version carries an "American Card Catalog" designation of H801-9. Cards measure 1-5/8" x 3" and are printed in black-and-white.

	NM	EX	VG
Common Player:	400.00	200.00	120.00

Stars: 3-5X

(See 1916 M101-4 Blank Backs for checklist and base values.)

1969 Globe Imports Playing Cards

Largely ignored by collectors for more than 35 years, this issue has little to offer any but the most avid superstar collector. Printed in black-and-white on very thin white cardboard, either with blank backs, or with red-and-white checkerboard patterned backs, the cards measure 1-5/8" x 2-1/4". Muddy player action photos are at center of each card, with the player's name reversed out of a black strip at the bottom. It is likely this set was issued over a period of more than one year. The plain-back version was probably issued first, and has photos which include cap and jersey logos. The checked-back version seems to have been a later issue with many of the cards showing uniform logos airbrushed away. The photo quality of the checked-back cards is also much poorer than the plain-backs. A few players were substituted between the issues, and there may be more yet to be reported. The Babe Ruth AD card listed here is actually part of a multi-topic deck in similar format issued contemprarily with the baseball decks.

		NM	EX	VG
Complete Set (52+Joker):		20.00	10.00	6.00
Common Player:		.25	.15	.10
PLAIN BACK HEARTS				
2	Chris Short	.25	.15	.10
3	Tony Conigliaro	.75	.40	.25
4	Bill Freehan	.25	.15	.10
5	Willie McCovey	2.00	1.00	.60
6	Joel Horlen	.25	.15	.10
7	Ernie Banks	2.00	1.00	.60
8	Jim Wynn	.25	.15	.10
9	Brooks Robinson	2.00	1.00	.60
10	Orlando Cepeda	1.00	.50	.30
J	Al Kaline	2.00	1.00	.60
Q	Gene Alley	.25	.15	.10
K	Rusty Staub	.75	.40	.25
A	Willie Mays	4.00	2.00	1.25
CLUBS				
2	Reggie Smith	.25	.15	.10
3	Mike McCormick	.25	.15	.10
4	Tony Oliva	.50	.25	.15
5	Bud Harrelson	.25	.15	.10
6	Rick Reichardt	.25	.15	.10
7	Billy Williams	1.00	.50	.30
8	Pete Rose	6.00	3.00	1.75
9	Jim Maloney	.25	.15	.10
10	Tim McCarver	.75	.40	.25
J	Max Alvis	.25	.15	.10
Q	Ron Swoboda	.25	.15	.10
K	Johnny Callison	.25	.15	.10
A	Richie Allen	.75	.40	.25
DIAMONDS				
2	Paul Casanova	.25	.15	.10
3	Juan Marichal	1.00	.50	.30
4	Jim Fregosi	.25	.15	.10
5	Earl Wilson	.25	.15	.10
6	Tony Horton	.25	.15	.10
7	Harmon Killebrew	2.00	1.00	.60
8	Tom Seaver	3.00	1.50	.90
9	Curt Flood	.75	.40	.25
10	Frank Robinson	2.00	1.00	.60
J	Bob Aspromonte	.25	.15	.10
Q	Lou Brock	2.00	1.00	.60
K	Jim Lonborg	.25	.15	.10
A(a)	Bob Gibson	2.00	1.00	.60
A(b)	Babe Ruth	12.00	6.00	3.60
SPADES		.00	.00	.00
2	Cesar Tovar	.25	.15	.10
3	Rick Monday	.25	.15	.10
4	Richie Allen	.75	.40	.25
5	Mel Stottlemyre	.50	.25	.15
6	Tommy John	.75	.40	.25
7	Don Mincher	.25	.15	.10
8	Chico Cardenas	.25	.15	.10
9	Willie Davis	.25	.15	.10
10	Bert Campaneris	.25	.15	.10
J	Ron Santo	.75	.40	.25
Q	Al Ferrera	.25	.15	.10
K	Clete Boyer	.50	.25	.15
A(a)	Don Drysdale	3.00	1.50	.90
A(b)	Mickey Mantle	40.00	20.00	12.00
CHECKERBOARD BACK HEARTS				
2	Chris Short	.25	.15	.10
3	Tony Conigliaro	.75	.40	.25
4	Bill Freehan	.25	.15	.10
5	Willie McCovey	2.00	1.00	.60
6	Joel Horlen	.25	.15	.10
7	Ernie Banks	2.00	1.00	.60
8	Jim Wynn	.25	.15	.10
9	Brooks Robinson	2.00	1.00	.60
10	Orlando Cepeda	1.00	.50	.30
J	Al Kaline	2.00	1.00	.60
Q	Gene Alley	.25	.15	.10
K	Rusty Staub	.75	.40	.25
A	Willie Mays	6.00	3.00	1.75

CLUBS

2	Reggie Smith	.25	.15	.10
3	Jerry Koosman	.25	.15	.10
4	Tony Oliva	.50	.25	.15
5	Bud Harrelson	.25	.15	.10
6	Rick Reichardt	.25	.15	.10
7	Billy Williams	1.00	.50	.30
8	Pete Rose	6.00	3.00	1.75
9	Jim Maloney	.25	.15	.10
10	Tim McCarver	.75	.40	.25
J	Max Alvis	.25	.15	.10
Q	Ron Swoboda	.25	.15	.10
K	Johnny Callison	.25	.15	.10
A	Richie Allen	.75	.40	.25

DIAMONDS

2	Paul Casanova	.25	.15	.10
3	Juan Marichal	1.00	.50	.30
4	Jim Fregosi	.25	.15	.10
5	Earl Wilson	.25	.15	.10
6	Tony Horton	.25	.15	.10
7	Harmon Killebrew	2.00	1.00	.60
8	Tom Seaver	3.00	1.50	.90
9	Curt Flood	.75	.40	.25
10	Frank Robinson	2.00	1.00	.60
J	Bob Aspromonte	.25	.15	.10
Q	Lou Brock	2.00	1.00	.60
K	Jim Lonborg	.25	.15	.10
A	Bob Gibson	2.00	1.00	.60

SPADES

2	Denny McLain	.50	.25	.15
3	Rick Monday	.25	.15	.10
4	Richie Allen	.75	.40	.25
5	Mel Stottlemyre	.50	.25	.15
6	Tommy John	.75	.40	.25
7	Don Mincher	.25	.15	.10
8	Chico Cardenas	.25	.15	.10
9	Willie Davis	.25	.15	.10
10	Bert Campaneris	.25	.15	.10
J	Ron Santo	.75	.40	.25
Q	Al Ferrera	.25	.15	.10
K	Clete Boyer	.50	.25	.15
A	Ken Harrelson	.25	.15	.10

1887 Gold Coin (Buchner) (N284)

Issued circa 1887, the N284 issue was produced by D. Buchner & Co.for its Gold Coin brand of chewing tobacco. Actually, the series was not comprised only of baseball players - actors, jockeys, firemen and policemen were also included. The cards, which measure 1-3/4" x 3", are color drawings. The set is not a popular one among collectors as the drawings do not in all cases represent the players designated on the cards. In most instances, players at a given position share the same drawing depicted on the card front. Three different card backs are found, all advising collectors to save the valuable chewing tobacco wrappers. Wrappers could be redeemed for various prizes.

		NM	EX	VG
	Complete Set (143):	200,000	60,000	30,000
	Common Player:	1,200	360.00	180.00
(1)	Ed Andrews (Hands at neck.)	1,200	360.00	180.00
(2)	Ed Andrews (Hands waist high.)	1,200	360.00	180.00
(3)	Cap Anson (Hands outstretched.)	6,000	1,800	900.00
(4)	Cap Anson (Left hand on hip.)	8,000	2,400	1,200
(5)	Tug Arundel	1,200	360.00	180.00
(6)	Sam Barkley (Pittsburg)	1,200	360.00	180.00
(7)	Sam Barkley (St. Louis)	1,200	360.00	180.00
(8)	Charley Bassett	1,200	360.00	180.00
(9)	Charlie Bastian	1,200	360.00	180.00
(10)	Ed Beecher	1,200	360.00	180.00
(11)	Charlie Bennett	1,200	360.00	180.00
(12)	Henry Boyle	1,200	360.00	180.00
(13)	Dan Brouthers (Hands outstretched.)	4,700	1,400	700.00
(14)	Dan Brouthers (With bat.)	4,700	1,400	700.00
(15)	Tom Brown	1,200	360.00	180.00
(16)	Jack Burdock	1,200	360.00	180.00
(17)	Oyster Burns (Baltimore)	1,200	360.00	180.00
(18)	Tom Burns (Chicago)	1,200	360.00	180.00
(19)	Doc Bushong	1,200	360.00	180.00
(20)	John Cahill	1,200	360.00	180.00
(21)	Cliff Carroll (Washington)	1,200	360.00	180.00
(22)	Fred Carroll (Pittsburg)	1,200	360.00	180.00
(23)	Bob Carruthers (Caruthers)	1,200	360.00	180.00
(24)	Dan Casey	1,200	360.00	180.00
(25)	John Clarkson (Ball at chest.)	4,200	1,250	625.00
(26)	John Clarkson (Arm oustretched.)	4,700	1,400	700.00
(27)	Jack Clements	1,200	360.00	180.00
(28)	John Coleman	1,200	360.00	180.00
(29)	Charles Comiskey	5,200	1,600	800.00

(30)	Roger Connor (Hands outstretched chest-level, "New York.")	4,250	1,250	625.00
(31)	Roger Connor (Hands oustretched face-level, "N.Y.")	4,700	1,400	700.00
(32)	John Corbett	1,200	360.00	180.00
(33)	Sam Craig (Crane)	1,200	360.00	180.00
(34)	Sam Crane	1,200	360.00	180.00
(35)	John Crowley	1,200	360.00	180.00
(36)	Ed Cushmann (Cushman)	1,200	360.00	180.00
(37)	Ed Dailey (Daily)	1,200	360.00	180.00
(38)	Con Daley (Daily)	1,200	360.00	180.00
(39)	Pat Deasley	1,200	360.00	180.00
(40)	Jerry Denny (Hands on knees.)	1,200	360.00	180.00
(41)	Jerry Denny (Hands on thighs.)	1,200	360.00	180.00
(42)	Jim Donnelly	1,200	360.00	180.00
(43)	Jim Donohue (Donahue)	1,200	360.00	180.00
(44)	Mike Dorgan (Right field.)	1,200	360.00	180.00
(45)	Mike Dorgan/Batter	1,200	360.00	180.00
(46)	Fred Dunlap	1,200	360.00	180.00
(47)	Dude Esterbrook	1,200	360.00	180.00
(48)	Buck Ewing (Ready to tag.)	4,250	1,250	625.00
(49)	Buck Ewing (Hands at neck.)	4,700	1,400	700.00
(50)	Sid Farrar	1,200	360.00	180.00
(51)	Jack Farrell (Ready to tag.)	1,200	360.00	180.00
(52)	Jack Farrell (Hands at knees.)	1,200	360.00	180.00
(53)	Charlie Ferguson	1,200	360.00	180.00
(54)	Silver Flint	1,200	360.00	180.00
(55)	Jim Fogerty (Fogarty)	1,200	360.00	180.00
(56)	Tom Forster	1,200	360.00	180.00
(57)	Dave Foutz	1,200	360.00	180.00
(58)	Chris Fulmer	1,200	360.00	180.00
(59)	Joe Gerhardt	1,200	360.00	180.00
(60)	Charlie Getzein (Getzien)	1,200	360.00	180.00
(61)	Pete Gillespie (Left field.)	1,200	360.00	180.00
(62)	Pete Gillespie/Batter	1,200	360.00	180.00
(63)	Barney Gilligan	1,200	360.00	180.00
(64)	Jack Glasscock (Fielding grounder.)	1,200	360.00	180.00
(65)	Jack Glasscock (Hands on knees.)	1,200	360.00	180.00
(66)	Will Gleason	1,200	360.00	180.00
(67)	George Gore	1,200	360.00	180.00
(68)	Frank Hankinson	1,200	360.00	180.00
(69)	Ned Hanlon	4,250	1,250	625.00
(70)	Jim Hart	1,200	360.00	180.00
(71)	Egyptian Healy	1,200	360.00	180.00
(72)	Paul Hines (Centre field.)	1,200	360.00	180.00
(73)	Paul Hines (Batter)	1,200	360.00	180.00
(74)	Joe Hornung	1,200	360.00	180.00
(75)	Arthur Irwin	1,200	360.00	180.00
(76)	Dick Johnston	1,200	360.00	180.00
(77)	Tim Keefe (Ball in hand.)	4,250	1,250	625.00
(78)	Tim Keefe (Ball out of hand.)	4,700	1,400	700.00
(79)	King Kelly (Right field.)	5,200	1,500	750.00
(80)	King Kelly/Catcher	5,200	1,500	750.00
(81)	Ted Kennedy	1,200	360.00	180.00
(82)	Matt Kilroy	1,200	360.00	180.00
(83)	Arlie Latham	1,200	360.00	180.00
(84)	Jimmy Manning	1,200	360.00	180.00
(85)	Bill McClellan	1,200	360.00	180.00
(86)	Jim McCormick	1,200	360.00	180.00
(87)	Jack McGeachy	1,200	360.00	180.00
(88)	Jumbo McGinnis	1,200	360.00	180.00
(89)	George Meyers (Myers)	1,200	360.00	180.00
(90)	Doggie Miller	1,200	360.00	180.00
(91)	John Morrill (Hands outstretched.)	1,200	360.00	180.00
(92)	John Morrill (Hands at neck.)	1,200	360.00	180.00
(93)	Tom Morrissy (Morrissey)	1,200	360.00	180.00
(94)	Joe Mulvey (Hands on knees.)	1,200	360.00	180.00
(95)	Joe Mulvey (Hands above head.)	1,200	360.00	180.00
(96)	Al Myers	1,200	360.00	180.00
(97)	Candy Nelson	1,200	360.00	180.00
(98)	Hugh Nichol	1,200	360.00	180.00
(99)	Billy O'Brien	1,200	360.00	180.00
(100)	Tip O'Neil (O'Neill)	1,200	360.00	180.00
(101)	Orator Jim O'Rourke (Hands cupped.)	4,700	1,400	700.00
(102)	Orator Jim O'Rourke (Hands on thighs.)	4,700	1,400	700.00
(103)	Dave Orr	1,200	360.00	180.00
(104)	Jimmy Peoples	1,200	360.00	180.00
(105)	Fred Pfeffer	1,200	360.00	180.00
(106)	Bill Phillips	1,200	360.00	180.00
(107)	Mark Polhemus	1,200	360.00	180.00
(108)	Henry Porter	1,200	360.00	180.00
(109)	Blondie Purcell	1,200	360.00	180.00
(110)	Old Hoss Radbourn (Hands at chest.)	4,250	1,250	625.00
(111)	Old Hoss Radbourn (Hands above waist.)	4,700	1,400	700.00
(112)	Danny Richardson (New York, hands at knees.)	1,200	360.00	180.00
(113)	Danny Richardson (New York, foot on base.)	1,200	360.00	180.00
(114)	Hardy Richardson (Detroit, hands at right shoulder.)	1,200	360.00	180.00
(115)	Hardy Richardson (Detroit, right hand above head.)	1,200	360.00	180.00
(116)	Yank Robinson	1,200	360.00	180.00
(117)	George Rooks	1,200	360.00	180.00
(118)	Chief Roseman (Roseman)	1,200	360.00	180.00
(119)	Jimmy Ryan	1,200	360.00	180.00
(120)	Emmett Seery (Hands at right shoulder.)	1,200	360.00	180.00
(121)	Emmett Seery (Hands outstretched.)	1,200	360.00	180.00
(122)	Otto Shomberg (Schomberg)	1,200	360.00	180.00
(123)	Pap Smith	1,200	360.00	180.00
(124)	Joe Strauss	1,200	360.00	180.00
(125)	Danny Sullivan (St. Louis)	1,200	360.00	180.00
(126)	Marty Sullivan (Chicago)	1,200	360.00	180.00
(127)	Billy Sunday	2,400	700.00	350.00

(128)	Ezra Sutton	1,200	360.00	180.00
(129)	Sam Thompson (Hand at belt.)	4,250	1,250	625.00
(130)	Sam Thompson (Hands chest high.)	4,700	1,400	700.00
(131)	Chris Von Der Ahe	4,250	1,250	625.00
(132)	John Ward (Fielding grounder.)	4,250	1,250	625.00
(133)	John Ward (Hands by knee.)	4,700	1,400	700.00
(134)	John Ward (Hands on knees.)	4,700	1,400	700.00
(135)	Curt Welch	1,200	360.00	180.00
(136)	Deacon White	1,200	360.00	180.00
(137)	Art Whitney (Pittsburgh)	1,200	360.00	180.00
(138)	Jim Whitney (Washington)	1,200	360.00	180.00
(139)	Ned Williamson (Fielding grounder.)	1,200	360.00	180.00
(140)	Ned Williamson (Hands at chest.)	1,200	360.00	180.00
(141)	Medoc Wise	1,200	360.00	180.00
(142)	George Wood (Hands at right shoulder.)	1,200	360.00	180.00
(143)	George Wood (Stealing base.)	1,200	360.00	180.00

1961 Golden Press

The 1961 Golden Press set features 33 players, all enshrined in the Baseball Hall of Fame. The full color cards measure 2-1/2" x 3-1/2" and came in a booklet with perforations so that they could be easily removed. Full books with the cards intact would command 50 percent over the set price in the checklist that follows. Card numbers 1-3 and 28-33 are slightly higher in price as they were located on the book's front and back covers, making them more susceptible to scuffing and wear. Cards in a larger (2-3/4" x 3-5/8"), apparently unperforated format are also known, though their method of distribution is unclear.

		NM	EX	VG
	Complete Set (33):	100.00	50.00	30.00
	Complete Set in Book:	175.00	85.00	50.00
	Common Player:	3.00	1.50	.90
1	Mel Ott	3.00	1.50	.90
2	Grover Cleveland Alexander	5.00	2.50	1.50
3	Babe Ruth	40.00	20.00	12.00
4	Hank Greenberg	5.00	2.50	1.50
5	Bill Terry	3.00	1.50	.90
6	Carl Hubbell	3.00	1.50	.90
7	Rogers Hornsby	4.00	2.00	1.25
8	Dizzy Dean	5.00	2.50	1.50
9	Joe DiMaggio	20.00	10.00	6.00
10	Charlie Gehringer	3.00	1.50	.90
11	Gabby Hartnett	3.00	1.50	.90
12	Mickey Cochrane	3.00	1.50	.90
13	George Sisler	3.00	1.50	.90
14	Joe Cronin	3.00	1.50	.90
15	Pie Traynor	3.00	1.50	.90
16	Lou Gehrig	20.00	10.00	6.00
17	Lefty Grove	3.00	1.50	.90
18	Chief Bender	3.00	1.50	.90
19	Frankie Frisch	3.00	1.50	.90
20	Al Simmons	3.00	1.50	.90
21	Home Run Baker	3.00	1.50	.90
22	Jimmy Foxx	4.00	2.00	1.25
23	John McGraw	3.00	1.50	.90
24	Christy Mathewson	10.00	5.00	3.00
25	Ty Cobb	20.00	10.00	6.00
26	Dazzy Vance	3.00	1.50	.90
27	Bill Dickey	3.00	1.50	.90
28	Eddie Collins	3.00	1.50	.90
29	Walter Johnson	9.00	4.50	2.75
30	Tris Speaker	4.00	2.00	1.25
31	Nap Lajoie	3.00	1.50	.90
32	Honus Wagner	12.00	6.00	3.50
33	Cy Young	9.00	4.50	2.75

1955 Golden Stamp Books

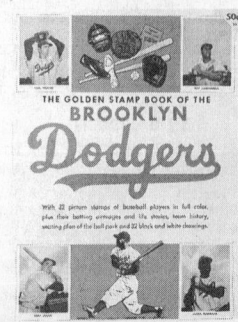

The 1954 World Series contestants, Cleveland and the Giants, along with the popular Dodgers and Braves are featured in this set of stamp books. The 32-page albums measure about 8-1/2" x 11" and include drawings and write-ups for each of the 32 players and managers featured. Other pages of the album include team histories, stats, etc. Sheets of 16 color stamps each are bound into the front and back of the album. Individual stamps measure about 2" x 2-5/8" and are unnumbered. Values shown are for complete albums with the stamps not pasted in; albums with stamps affixed to the pages are worth about 50 percent. The players for each team are listed in the order in which they appear in the album.

		NM	EX	VG
Complete Set (4):		500.00	250.00	150.00
Common Stamp:		5.00	2.50	1.50
S-1	**NEW YORK GIANTS ALBUM**	125.00	65.00	35.00
(1)	1954 Team Photo	5.00	2.50	1.50
(2)	Leo Durocher	6.00	3.00	1.75
(3)	Johnny Antonelli	5.00	2.50	1.50
(4)	Sal Maglie	5.00	2.50	1.50
(5)	Ruben Gomez	5.00	2.50	1.50
(6)	Hoyt Wilhelm	6.00	3.00	1.75
(7)	Marv Grissom	5.00	2.50	1.50
(8)	Jim Hearn	5.00	2.50	1.50
(9)	Paul Giel	5.00	2.50	1.50
(10)	Al Corwin	5.00	2.50	1.50
(11)	George Spencer	5.00	2.50	1.50
(12)	Don Liddle	5.00	2.50	1.50
(13)	Windy McCall	5.00	2.50	1.50
(14)	Al Worthington	5.00	2.50	1.50
(15)	Wes Westrum	5.00	2.50	1.50
(16)	Whitey Lockman	5.00	2.50	1.50
(17)	Dave Williams	5.00	2.50	1.50
(18)	Hank Thompson	5.00	2.50	1.50
(19)	Alvin Dark	5.00	2.50	1.50
(20)	Monte Irvin	7.50	3.75	2.25
(21)	Willie Mays	50.00	25.00	15.00
(22)	Don Mueller	5.00	2.50	1.50
(23)	Dusty Rhodes	5.00	2.50	1.50
(24)	Ray Katt	5.00	2.50	1.50
(25)	Joe Amalfitano	5.00	2.50	1.50
(26)	Bill Gardner	5.00	2.50	1.50
(27)	Foster Castleman	5.00	2.50	1.50
(28)	Bobby Hofman	5.00	2.50	1.50
(29)	Bill Taylor	5.00	2.50	1.50
(30)	Manager and Coaches	5.00	2.50	1.50
(31)	Bobby Weinstein (Batboy)	5.00	2.50	1.50
(32)	Polo Grounds	5.00	2.50	1.50
S-2	**MILWAUKEE BRAVES ALBUM**	125.00	65.00	35.00
(1)	1954 Team Photo	5.00	2.50	1.50
(2)	Charlie Grimm	5.00	2.50	1.50
(3)	Warren Spahn	7.50	3.75	2.25
(4)	Lew Burdette	5.00	2.50	1.50
(5)	Chet Nichols	5.00	2.50	1.50
(6)	Gene Conley	5.00	2.50	1.50
(7)	Bob Buhl	5.00	2.50	1.50
(8)	Jim Wilson	5.00	2.50	1.50
(9)	Dave Jolly	5.00	2.50	1.50
(10)	Ernie Johnson	5.00	2.50	1.50
(11)	Joey Jay	5.00	2.50	1.50
(12)	Dave Koslo	5.00	2.50	1.50
(13)	Charlie Gorin	5.00	2.50	1.50
(14)	Ray Crone	5.00	2.50	1.50
(15)	Del Crandall	5.00	2.50	1.50
(16)	Joe Adcock	5.00	2.50	1.50
(17)	Jack Dittmer	5.00	2.50	1.50
(18)	Eddie Mathews	15.00	7.50	4.50
(19)	Johnny Logan	5.00	2.50	1.50
(20)	Andy Pafko	5.00	2.50	1.50
(21)	Bill Bruton	5.00	2.50	1.50
(22)	Bobby Thomson	5.00	2.50	1.50
(23)	Charlie White	5.00	2.50	1.50
(24)	Danny O'Connell	5.00	2.50	1.50
(25)	Hank Aaron	50.00	25.00	15.00
(26)	Jim Pendleton	5.00	2.50	1.50
(27)	George Metkovich	5.00	2.50	1.50
(28)	Mel Roach	5.00	2.50	1.50
(29)	John Cooney	5.00	2.50	1.50
(30)	Bucky Walters	5.00	2.50	1.50
(31)	Charles Lacks (Trainer)	5.00	2.50	1.50
(32)	Milwaukee County Stadium	5.00	2.50	1.50
S-3	**BROOKLYN DODGERS ALBUM**	200.00	100.00	60.00
(1)	Walter Alston	6.00	3.00	1.75
(2)	Don Newcombe	6.00	3.00	1.75
(3)	Carl Erskine	5.00	2.50	1.50
(4)	Johnny Podres	5.00	2.50	1.50
(5)	Billy Loes	5.00	2.50	1.50
(6)	Russ Meyer	5.00	2.50	1.50
(7)	Jim Hughes	5.00	2.50	1.50
(8)	Sandy Koufax	100.00	50.00	30.00
(9)	Joe Black	5.00	2.50	1.50
(10)	Karl Spooner	5.00	2.50	1.50
(11)	Clem Labine	5.00	2.50	1.50
(12)	Roy Campanella	15.00	7.50	4.50
(13)	Gil Hodges	12.00	6.00	3.50
(14)	Jim Gilliam	6.00	3.00	1.75
(15)	Jackie Robinson	50.00	25.00	15.00
(16)	Pee Wee Reese	15.00	7.50	4.50
(17)	Duke Snider	15.00	7.50	4.50
(18)	Carl Furillo	6.00	3.00	1.75
(19)	Sandy Amoros	5.00	2.50	1.50
(20)	Frank Kellert	5.00	2.50	1.50
(21)	Don Zimmer	6.00	3.00	1.75
(22)	Al Walker	5.00	2.50	1.50
(23)	Tommy Lasorda	7.50	3.75	2.25
(24)	Ed Roebuck	5.00	2.50	1.50
(25)	Don Hoak	5.00	2.50	1.50
(26)	George Shuba	5.00	2.50	1.50
(27)	Billy Herman	6.00	3.00	1.75
(28)	Jake Pitler	5.00	2.50	1.50
(29)	Joe Becker	5.00	2.50	1.50
(30)	Doc Wendler (Trainer) Carl Furillo	5.00	2.50	1.50

		NM	EX	VG
(31)	Charlie Di Giovanna (Batboy)	5.00	2.50	1.50
(32)	Ebbets Field	5.00	2.50	1.50
S-4	**CLEVELAND INDIANS ALBUM**	100.00	50.00	30.00
(1)	Al Lopez	6.00	3.00	1.75
(2)	Bob Lemon	6.00	3.00	1.75
(3)	Early Wynn	6.00	3.00	1.75
(4)	Mike Garcia	5.00	2.50	1.50
(5)	Bob Feller	12.00	6.00	3.50
(6)	Art Houtteman	5.00	2.50	1.50
(7)	Herb Score	7.50	3.75	2.25
(8)	Don Mossi	7.50	3.75	2.25
(9)	Ray Narleski	5.00	2.50	1.50
(10)	Jim Hegan	5.00	2.50	1.50
(11)	Vic Wertz	5.00	2.50	1.50
(12)	Bobby Avila	5.00	2.50	1.50
(13)	George Strickland	5.00	2.50	1.50
(14)	Al Smith	5.00	2.50	1.50
(15)	Larry Doby	6.00	3.00	1.75
(16)	Ralph Kiner	7.50	3.75	2.25
(17)	Al Smith	5.00	2.50	1.50
(18)	Wally Westlake	5.00	2.50	1.50
(19)	Hal Naragon	5.00	2.50	1.50
(20)	Hank Foiles	5.00	2.50	1.50
(21)	Hank Majeski	5.00	2.50	1.50
(22)	Bill Wight	5.00	2.50	1.50
(23)	Sam Dente	5.00	2.50	1.50
(24)	Dave Pope	5.00	2.50	1.50
(25)	Dave Philley	5.00	2.50	1.50
(26)	Dale Mitchell	5.00	2.50	1.50
(27)	Hank Greenberg/GM	10.00	5.00	3.00
(28)	Mel Harder	5.00	2.50	1.50
(29)	Ralph Kress	5.00	2.50	1.50
(30)	Tony Cuccinello	5.00	2.50	1.50
(31)	Bill Lobe	5.00	2.50	1.50
(32)	Cleveland Municipal Stadium	5.00	2.50	1.50

1934 Gold Medal Foods (R313A)

This set of unnumbered, blank-backed cards was issued by Gold Medal Foods (the Minneapolis parent company of Wheaties) to commemorate the 1934 World Series. The black-and-white cards measure 3-1/4" x 5-3/8". The checklist comprises six members each of the Detroit Tigers and St. Louis Cardinals, who were participants in the '34 World Series.

		NM	EX	VG
Complete Set (12):		1,000	500.00	300.00
Common Player:		60.00	30.00	18.00
(1)	Tommy Bridges	60.00	30.00	18.00
(2)	Mickey Cochrane	90.00	45.00	27.50
(3)	Dizzy Dean	350.00	175.00	100.00
(4)	Paul Dean	75.00	37.50	22.50
(5)	Frank Frisch	90.00	45.00	27.50
(6)	"Goose" Goslin	90.00	45.00	27.50
(7)	William Hallahan	60.00	30.00	18.00
(8)	Fred Marberry	60.00	30.00	18.00
(9)	Johnny "Pepper" Martin	60.00	30.00	18.00
(10)	Joe Medwick	90.00	45.00	27.50
(11)	William Rogell	60.00	30.00	18.00
(12)	"Jo Jo" White	60.00	30.00	18.00

1930s Goodrich Tire Mickey Cochrane

Without postmarked examples for verification, the issue date of this promotional postcard can only be estimated. Front of the 5-1/4" x 3-1/4" postcard has line art of Cochrane and his endorsement for the company's tires. The card is printed in yellow, orange and black. The lower-right quadrant was likely left blank to allow local tire retailers to place their advertisement. Back of the card has a pre-printed one-cent stamp.

	NM	EX	VG
Mickey Cochrane	100.00	50.00	30.00

1888 Goodwin Champions (N162)

Issued in 1888 by New York's Goodwin & Co., the 50-card "Champions" set includes eight baseball players - seven from the National League and one from the American Association. The full-color cards, which measure 1-1/2" x 2-5/8", were inserted in packages of Old Judge and Gypsy Queen Cigarettes. A small ad for the cards lists all 50 subjects of the "Champions" set, which also included popular billiards players, bicyclists, marksmen, pugilists, runners, wrestlers, college football stars, weightlifters, and Wild West star Buffalo Bill Cody. Four of the eight baseball players in the set (Anson, Kelly, Keefe and Brouthers) are Hall of Famers. The cards feature very attractive player portraits, making the "Champions" set among the most beautiful of all the 19th Century tobacco inserts. All cards can be found with or without a tiny line of type at the bottom of the back which reads, "Geo. S. Harris & Sons, Lith, Phila." Trademarked cards are 3-5X scarcer, but currently carry little or no premium value."

		NM	EX	VG
Complete Set (8):		50,000	25,000	15,000
Common Player:		3,850	1,600	725.00
Album:		17,500	8,750	5,250
(1)	Ed Andrews	3,850	1,600	725.00
(2)	Cap Anson	19,000	9,500	5,750
(3)	Dan Brouthers	6,250	3,125	1,875
(4)	Bob Caruthers	3,850	1,600	725.00
(5)	Fred Dunlap	3,850	1,600	725.00
(6)	Jack Glasscock	3,850	1,600	725.00
(7)	Tim Keefe	6,250	3,125	1,875
(8)	King Kelly	9,000	4,500	2,700

1889 Goodwin & Co. Baseball Album (A35)

As a mail-in redemption premium for 75 coupons from its Old Judge and Dog's Head cigarette brands, Goodwin offered this 12-page lithographed album. In an unusual 8-1/4" diameter format, the pages have a single hole punched at the side and are attached by a fancy tasseled cord allowing them to be fanned out for viewing. Front and back covers of the album depict a baseball, with the inside covers advertising the cigarettes, as does the sixth page of the album. The nine other pages depict in vivid color either single stars of the game or groups of four players, with an emphasis on the N.Y. Giants champions of 1888. Backs of the pages offer player stats for the previous season and schedules for various leagues for 1889. Because these albums are sometimes offered as single pages, they are priced as such here.

		NM	EX	VG
Complete Album:		20,000	10,000	6,000
(1)	Front Cover	225.00	110.00	65.00
(2)	Mickey Welch, John Ward, Buck Ewing, Tim Keefe	1,100	550.00	330.00
(3)	Cap Anson	4,000	1,500	900.00
(4)	Jim O'Rourke, Danny Richardson, Roger Connor, George Gore	1,200	460.00	275.00
(5)	Mike "King" Kelly	3,000	1,500	900.00
(6)	Advertising	350.00	100.00	60.00
(7)	John Ward	2,125	1,050	635.00
(8)	Mike Slattery, Pat Murphy, Gil Hatfield, Ed Crane	750.00	375.00	225.00
(9)	Charles Comiskey	2,125	1,050	635.00
(10)	Willard Brown, Bill George, Elmer Foster, Michael Tiernan	850.00	425.00	255.00
(11)	Jim Mutrie, Lidell Titcomb, Art Whitney, Willie Breslin - Mascot	875.00	435.00	260.00
(12)	Back Cover	200.00	100.00	60.00

1933 Goudey (R319)

Goudey Gum Co.'s first baseball card issue was a 239-card effort in 1933. The cards are color art reproductions of either portrait or action photos. The numbered cards measure 2-3/8" x 2-7/8" and carry a short player biography on the reverse. Card #106 (Napoleon Lajoie) is listed in the set though it was not actually issued until 1934. The card is very scarce and is unique in that it carries a 1934 design front and a 1933 back. The Lajoie card is not included in the complete set prices quoted here. The ACC designation for the set is R319. Grading companies and auction houses have found a few examples of these cards with blue printing on the backs instead of the customary green.

		NM	EX	VG
	Complete Set (239):	110,000	37,500	19,500
	Common Player (1-40):	250.00	85.00	45.00
	Common Player (41-44):	175.00	87.50	52.50
	Common Player (45-52):	200.00	70.00	35.00
	Common Player (53-240):	175.00	87.50	52.50
1	Benny Bengough	5,500	900.00	200.00
2	Arthur (Dazzy) Vance	1,000	500.00	300.00
3	Hugh Critz	500.00	250.00	150.00
4	Henry "Heinie" Schuble	500.00	250.00	150.00
5	Floyd (Babe) Herman	600.00	300.00	180.00
6a	Jimmy Dykes (Age is 26 in bio.)	335.00	167.50	100.00
6b	Jimmy Dykes (Age is 36 in bio.)	335.00	167.50	100.00
7	Ted Lyons	1,250	435.00	225.00
8	Roy Johnson	250.00	85.00	45.00
9	Dave Harris	250.00	85.00	45.00
10	Glenn Myatt	250.00	85.00	45.00
11	Billy Rogell	250.00	85.00	45.00
12	George Pipgras	250.00	87.00	45.00
13	Lafayette Thompson	250.00	85.00	45.00
14	Henry Johnson	250.00	85.00	45.00
15	Victor Sorrell	250.00	85.00	45.00
16	George Blaeholder	250.00	85.00	45.00
17	Watson Clark	250.00	85.00	45.00
18	Herold (Muddy) Ruel	250.00	85.00	45.00
19	Bill Dickey	900.00	315.00	160.00
20	Bill Terry	1,250	435.00	225.00
21	Phil Collins	250.00	85.00	45.00
22	Harold (Pie) Traynor	1,250	435.00	225.00
23	Hazen (Ki-Ki) Cuyler	1,250	435.00	225.00
24	Horace Ford	250.00	85.00	45.00
25	Paul Waner	1,750	610.00	315.00
26	Chalmer Cissell	250.00	85.00	45.00
27	George Connally	250.00	85.00	45.00
28	Dick Bartell	250.00	85.00	45.00
29	Jimmy Foxx	2,350	1,175	705.00
30	Frank Hogan	250.00	85.00	45.00
31	Tony Lazzeri	1,250	435.00	225.00
32	John (Bud) Clancy	250.00	85.00	45.00
33	Ralph Kress	250.00	85.00	45.00
34	Bob O'Farrell	250.00	85.00	45.00
35	Al Simmons	1,250	435.00	225.00
36	Tommy Thevenow	250.00	85.00	45.00
37	Jimmy Wilson	250.00	85.00	45.00
38	Fred Brickell	250.00	85.00	45.00
39	Mark Koenig	250.00	87.00	45.00
40	Taylor Douthit	250.00	85.00	45.00
41	Gus Mancuso	175.00	87.50	52.50
42	Eddie Collins	475.00	165.00	85.00
43	Lew Fonseca	175.00	87.50	52.50
44	Jim Bottomley	425.00	150.00	75.00
45	Larry Benton	200.00	70.00	35.00
46	Ethan Allen	200.00	70.00	35.00
47a	Henry "Heinie" Manush (Chain-link fence at top left.)	600.00	210.00	110.00
47b	Henry "Heinie" Manush (No fence.)	600.00	210.00	110.00
48	Marty McManus	200.00	70.00	35.00
49	Frank Frisch	800.00	280.00	145.00
50	Ed Brandt	200.00	70.00	35.00
51	Charlie Grimm	200.00	70.00	35.00
52	Andy Cohen	225.00	80.00	40.00
53	George Herman (Babe) Ruth	13,500	4,900	2,100
54	Ray Kremer	175.00	87.50	52.50
55	Perce (Pat) Malone	175.00	87.50	52.50
56	Charlie Ruffing	425.00	150.00	80.00
57	Earl Clark	175.00	87.50	52.50
58	Frank (Lefty) O'Doul	350.00	120.00	65.00
59	Edmund (Bing) Miller	175.00	87.50	52.50
60	Waite Hoyt	600.00	300.00	180.00
61	Max Bishop	175.00	87.50	52.50
62	"Pepper" Martin	275.00	90.00	50.00
63	Joe Cronin	425.00	150.00	75.00
64	Burleigh Grimes	425.00	150.00	75.00
65	Milton Gaston	175.00	87.50	52.50
66	George Grantham	175.00	87.50	52.50
67	Guy Bush	175.00	87.50	52.50
68	Horace Lisenbee	175.00	87.50	52.50
69	Randy Moore	175.00	87.50	52.50
70	Floyd (Pete) Scott	175.00	87.50	52.50
71	Robert J. Burke	175.00	87.50	52.50
72	Owen Carroll	175.00	87.50	52.50

73	Jesse Haines	425.00	150.00	75.00
74	Eppa Rixey	425.00	150.00	75.00
75	Willie Kamm	175.00	87.50	52.50
76	Gordon (Mickey) Cochrane	475.00	165.00	85.00
77	Adam Comorosky	175.00	87.50	52.50
78	Jack Quinn	175.00	87.50	52.50
79	Urban (Red) Faber	425.00	150.00	75.00
80	Clyde Manion	175.00	87.50	52.50
81	Sam Jones	175.00	87.50	52.50
82	Dibrell Williams	175.00	87.50	52.50
83	Pete Jablonowski	175.00	87.50	52.50
84	Glenn Spencer	175.00	87.50	52.50
85	John Henry "Heinie" Sand	175.00	87.50	52.50
86	Phil Todt	175.00	87.50	52.50
87	Frank O'Rourke	175.00	87.50	52.50
88	Russell Rollings	175.00	87.50	52.50
89	Tris Speaker	825.00	415.00	250.00
90	Jess Petty	175.00	87.50	52.50
91	Tom Zachary	175.00	87.50	52.50
92	Lou Gehrig	3,750	1,750	800.00
93	John Welch	175.00	87.50	52.50
94	Bill Walker	175.00	87.50	52.50
95	Alvin Crowder	175.00	87.50	52.50
96	Willis Hudlin	175.00	87.50	52.50
97	Joe Morrissey	175.00	87.50	52.50
98	Walter Berger	175.00	87.50	52.50
99	Tony Cuccinello	175.00	87.50	52.50
100	George Uhle	175.00	87.50	52.50
101	Richard Coffman	175.00	87.50	52.50
102	Travis C. Jackson	425.00	150.00	75.00
103	Earl Combs (Earle)	600.00	300.00	180.00
104	Fred Marberry	175.00	87.50	52.50
105	Bernie Friberg	175.00	87.50	52.50
106	Napoleon (Larry) Lajoie	37,500	24,000	8,500
106p	Leo Durocher (Unique proof card.)			8,000
107	Henry (Heinie) Manush	425.00	150.00	75.00
108	Joe Kuhel	165.00	55.00	30.00
109	Joe Cronin	425.00	150.00	75.00
110	Leon (Goose) Goslin/Portrait	600.00	300.00	180.00
110p	Leon (Goose) Goslin (Proof card, batting - same as #168 - name in two lines on front.)	1,200	420.00	215.00
111	Monte Weaver	175.00	87.50	52.50
112	Fred Schulte	175.00	87.50	52.50
113	Oswald Bluege	175.00	87.50	52.50
114	Luke Sewell	175.00	87.50	52.50
115	Cliff Heathcote	175.00	87.50	52.50
116	Eddie Morgan	175.00	87.50	52.50
117	Walter (Rabbit) Maranville	425.00	150.00	75.00
118	Valentine J. (Val) Picinich	175.00	87.50	52.50
119	Rogers Hornsby	1,250	435.00	225.00
120	Carl Reynolds	175.00	87.50	52.50
121	Walter Stewart	175.00	87.50	52.50
122	Alvin Crowder	175.00	87.50	52.50
123	Jack Russell (Orange background, white cap.)	175.00	87.50	52.50
123(p a)	Jack Russell (Proof card, red background, dark cap - same as #167 - name in one line on front.)	600.00	210.00	110.00
123(p b)	Luke Sewell (Proof card, otherwise identical to #163.)	8,000	2,800	1,450
124	Earl Whitehill	175.00	87.50	52.50
125	Bill Terry	425.00	150.00	75.00
126	Joe Moore	175.00	87.50	52.50
127	Melvin Ott	725.00	250.00	125.00
128	Charles (Chuck) Klein	450.00	155.00	80.00
128(p)	George Walberg (Unique proof card.)			8,000
129	Harold Schumacher	175.00	87.50	52.50
130	Fred Fitzsimmons	175.00	87.50	52.50
131	Fred Frankhouse	175.00	87.50	52.50
132	Jim Elliott	175.00	87.50	52.50
133	Fred Lindstrom	425.00	150.00	75.00
134	Edgar (Sam) Rice	425.00	150.00	75.00
135	Elwood (Woody) English	175.00	87.50	52.50
136	Flint Rhem	175.00	87.50	52.50
137	Fred (Red) Lucas	175.00	87.50	52.50
138	Herb Pennock	415.00	145.00	75.00
139	Ben Cantwell	175.00	87.50	52.50
140	Irving (Bump) Hadley	175.00	87.50	52.50
141	Ray Benge	175.00	87.50	52.50
142	Paul Richards	175.00	87.50	52.50
143	Glenn Wright	175.00	87.50	52.50
144	George Herman (Babe) Ruth (Double-print; replaced card #106 on press sheet.)	9,000	3,250	1,650
145	George Walberg	175.00	87.50	52.50
146	Walter Stewart	175.00	87.50	52.50
147	Leo Durocher	425.00	150.00	75.00
148	Eddie Farrell	175.00	87.50	52.50
149	George Herman (Babe) Ruth	9,500	3,600	2,000
150	Ray Kolp	175.00	87.50	52.50
151	D'Arcy (Jake) Flowers	175.00	87.50	52.50
152	James (Zack) Taylor	175.00	87.50	52.50
153	Charles (Buddy) Myer	175.00	87.50	52.50
154	Jimmy Foxx	1,600	500.00	200.00
155	Joe Judge	175.00	87.50	52.50
156	Danny Macfayden (MacFayden)	175.00	87.50	52.50
157	Sam Byrd	175.00	87.50	52.50
158	Morris (Moe) Berg	600.00	300.00	180.00
159	Oswald Bluege	175.00	87.50	52.50
160	Lou Gehrig	5,750	2,000	900.00
161	Al Spohrer	175.00	87.50	52.50
162	Leo Mangum	175.00	87.50	52.50
163	Luke Sewell	175.00	87.50	52.50
164	Lloyd Waner	450.00	155.00	75.00
165	Joe Sewell	450.00	155.00	75.00
166	Sam West	175.00	87.50	52.50
167	Jack Russell (Name on two lines, see also #123p.)	175.00	87.50	52.50
168	Leon (Goose) Goslin (Name on one line, see also #110p.)	600.00	210.00	110.00
169	Al Thomas	175.00	87.50	52.50
170	Harry McCurdy	175.00	87.50	52.50
171	Charley Jamieson	175.00	87.50	52.50

172	Billy Hargrave	175.00	87.50	52.50
173	Roscoe Holm	175.00	87.50	52.50
174	Warren (Curley) Ogden	175.00	87.50	52.50
175	Dan Howley	175.00	87.50	52.50
176	John Ogden	175.00	87.50	52.50
177	Walter French	175.00	87.50	52.50
178	Jackie Warner	175.00	87.50	52.50
179	Fred Leach	175.00	87.50	52.50
180	Eddie Moore	175.00	87.50	52.50
181	George Herman (Babe) Ruth	7,500	3,700	2,200
182	Andy High	175.00	87.50	52.50
183	George Walberg	175.00	87.50	52.50
184	Charley Berry	175.00	87.50	52.50
185	Bob Smith	175.00	87.50	52.50
186	John Schulte	175.00	87.50	52.50
187	Henry (Heinie) Manush	425.00	150.00	75.00
188	Rogers Hornsby	1,200	425.00	215.00
189	Joe Cronin	425.00	150.00	75.00
190	Fred Schulte	175.00	87.50	52.50
191	Ben Chapman	175.00	87.50	52.50
192	Walter Brown	175.00	87.50	52.50
193	Lynford Lary	175.00	87.50	52.50
194	Earl Averill	425.00	150.00	75.00
195	Evar Swanson	175.00	87.50	52.50
196	Leroy Mahaffey	175.00	87.50	52.50
197	Richard (Rick) Ferrell	425.00	150.00	75.00
198	Irving (Jack) Burns	175.00	87.50	52.50
199	Tom Bridges	175.00	87.50	52.50
200	Bill Hallahan	175.00	87.50	52.50
201	Ernie Orsatti	175.00	87.50	52.50
202	Charles Leo (Gabby) Hartnett	425.00	150.00	75.00
203	Lonnie Warneke	175.00	87.50	52.50
204	Jackson Riggs Stephenson	175.00	87.50	52.50
205	Henry (Heinie) Meine	175.00	87.50	52.50
206	Gus Suhr	175.00	87.50	52.50
207	Melvin Ott	1,300	400.00	200.00
208	Byrne (Bernie) James	175.00	87.50	52.50
209	Adolfo Luque	200.00	70.00	36.00
210	Virgil Davis	175.00	87.50	52.50
211	Lewis (Hack) Wilson	700.00	250.00	140.00
212	Billy Urbanski	175.00	87.50	52.50
213	Earl Adams	175.00	87.50	52.50
214	John Kerr	175.00	87.50	52.50
215	Russell Van Atta	175.00	87.50	52.50
216	Vernon Gomez	425.00	150.00	75.00
217	Frank Crosetti	275.00	96.00	49.00
218	Wesley Ferrell	175.00	87.50	52.50
219	George (Mule) Haas	175.00	87.50	52.50
220	Robert (Lefty) Grove	775.00	275.00	140.00
221	Dale Alexander	175.00	87.50	52.50
222	Charley Gehringer	600.00	210.00	110.00
223	Jerome (Dizzy) Dean	1,500	500.00	275.00
224	Frank Demaree	175.00	87.50	52.50
225	Bill Jurges	175.00	87.50	52.50
226	Charley Root	175.00	87.50	52.50
227	Bill Herman	425.00	150.00	75.00
228	Tony Piet	175.00	87.50	52.50
229	Floyd Vaughan	425.00	150.00	75.00
230	Carl Hubbell	725.00	255.00	130.00
231	Joe Moore	175.00	87.50	52.50
232	Frank (Lefty) O'Doul	300.00	150.00	90.00
233	Johnny Vergez	175.00	87.50	52.50
234	Carl Hubbell	725.00	255.00	130.00
235	Fred Fitzsimmons	175.00	87.50	52.50
236	George Davis	175.00	87.50	52.50
237	Gus Mancuso	175.00	87.50	52.50
238	Hugh Critz	175.00	87.50	52.50
239	Leroy Parmelee	175.00	87.50	52.50
240	Harold Schumacher	350.00	75.00	35.00

1933 Goudey Blue Backs

The reason for production of the two known (each currently unique) 1933 Goudey cards with blue, rather than the standard green, printing on back is unknown, as is the manner of their distribution. The cards otherwise conform precisely to the regularly issued versions in size (2-3/8" x 2-7/8") and composition.

		NM	EX	VG
47	Henry "Heinie" Manush (Value undetermined)			
53	George Herman (Babe) Ruth (SGC-Authentic auctioned for $7,638 5/09)			

1934 Goudey (R320)

The 1934 Goudey set contains 96 cards (2-3/8" x 2-7/8") that feature color art reproductions of player photographs. Card fronts have two different designs; one featuring a small portrait photo of Lou Gehrig with the words "Lou Gehrig says..." inside a blue strip at the bottom, while the other design carries a red "Chuck Klein says..." strip and also has his photo. The card backs contain a short player biography that purports to have been written by Gehrig or Klein. The ACC designation for the set is R320. Albums, blue for N.L., and magenta for A.L., were given away to the person who bought the last penny pack in each box of high-numbers or who mailed 50 wrappers to the gum company.

	NM	EX	VG
Complete Set (96):	30,000	11,000	5,250
Common Player (1-48):	120.00	45.00	20.00
Common Player (49-72):	160.00	55.00	25.00
Common Player (73-96):	250.00	100.00	50.00
Album:	500.00	250.00	150.00
1 Jimmy Foxx	4,500	600.00	210.00
2 Gordon (Mickey) Cochrane	550.00	220.00	110.00
3 Charlie Grimm	120.00	45.00	20.00
4 Elwood (Woody) English	120.00	45.00	20.00
5 Ed Brandt	120.00	45.00	20.00
6 Jerome (Dizzy) Dean	1,700	400.00	190.00
7 Leo Durocher	350.00	140.00	70.00
8 Tony Piet	120.00	45.00	20.00
9 Ben Chapman	120.00	45.00	20.00
10 Charles (Chuck) Klein	350.00	140.00	70.00
11 Paul Waner	350.00	140.00	70.00
12 Carl Hubbell	350.00	140.00	70.00
13 Frank Frisch	350.00	140.00	70.00
14 Willie Kamm	120.00	45.00	20.00
15 Alvin Crowder	120.00	45.00	20.00
16 Joe Kuhel	120.00	45.00	20.00
17 Hugh Critz	120.00	45.00	20.00
18 Henry (Heinie) Manush	350.00	140.00	70.00
19 Robert (Lefty) Grove	675.00	225.00	110.00
20 Frank Hogan	120.00	45.00	20.00
21 Bill Terry	350.00	140.00	70.00
22 Floyd Vaughan	350.00	140.00	70.00
23 Charley Gehringer	475.00	190.00	95.00
24 Ray Benge	120.00	45.00	20.00
25 Roger Cramer	120.00	45.00	20.00
26 Gerald Walker	120.00	45.00	20.00
27 Luke Appling	350.00	140.00	70.00
28 Ed. Coleman	120.00	45.00	20.00
29 Larry French	120.00	45.00	20.00
30 Julius Solters	120.00	45.00	20.00
31 Baxter Jordan	120.00	45.00	20.00
32 John (Blondy) Ryan	120.00	45.00	20.00
33 Frank (Don) Hurst	120.00	45.00	20.00
34 Charles (Chick) Hafey	350.00	140.00	70.00
35 Ernie Lombardi	350.00	140.00	70.00
36 Walter (Huck) Betts	120.00	45.00	20.00
37 Lou Gehrig	4,750	1,800	850.00
38 Oral Hildebrand	120.00	45.00	20.00
39 Fred Walker	120.00	45.00	20.00
40 John Stone	120.00	45.00	20.00
41 George Earnshaw	120.00	45.00	20.00
42 John Allen	120.00	45.00	20.00
43 Dick Porter	120.00	45.00	20.00
44 Tom Bridges	120.00	45.00	20.00
45 Oscar Melillo	120.00	45.00	20.00
46 Joe Stripp	120.00	45.00	20.00
47 John Frederick	120.00	45.00	20.00
48 James (Tex) Carleton	120.00	45.00	20.00
49 Sam Leslie	160.00	55.00	25.00
50 Walter Beck	160.00	55.00	25.00
51 Jim (Rip) Collins	160.00	55.00	25.00
52 Herman Bell	160.00	55.00	25.00
53 George Watkins	160.00	55.00	25.00
54 Wesley Schulmerich	160.00	55.00	25.00
55 Ed Holley	160.00	55.00	25.00
56 Mark Koenig	160.00	55.00	25.00
57 Bill Swift	160.00	55.00	25.00
58 Earl Grace	160.00	55.00	25.00
59 Joe Mowry	160.00	55.00	25.00
60 Lynn Nelson	160.00	55.00	25.00
61 Lou Gehrig	1,950	975.00	585.00
62 Henry Greenberg	1,350	550.00	275.00
63 Minter Hayes	160.00	55.00	25.00
64 Frank Grube	160.00	55.00	25.00
65 Cliff Bolton	160.00	55.00	25.00
66 Mel Harder	160.00	55.00	25.00
67 Bob Weiland	160.00	55.00	25.00
68 Bob Johnson	160.00	55.00	25.00
69 John Marcum	160.00	55.00	25.00
70 Ervin (Pete) Fox	160.00	55.00	25.00
71 Lyle Tinning	160.00	55.00	25.00
72 Arndt Jorgens	160.00	55.00	25.00
73 Ed Wells	250.00	100.00	50.00
74 Bob Boken	250.00	100.00	50.00
75 Bill Werber	250.00	100.00	50.00
76 Hal Trosky	250.00	100.00	50.00
77 Joe Vosmik	250.00	100.00	50.00
78 Frank (Pinkey) Higgins	250.00	100.00	50.00
79 Eddie Durham	250.00	100.00	50.00
80 Marty McManus	250.00	100.00	50.00
81 Bob Brown	250.00	100.00	50.00
82 Bill Hallahan	250.00	100.00	50.00
83 Jim Mooney	250.00	100.00	50.00
84 Paul Derringer	250.00	100.00	50.00
85 Adam Comorosky	250.00	100.00	50.00
86 Lloyd Johnson	250.00	100.00	50.00
87 George Darrow	250.00	100.00	50.00
88 Homer Peel	250.00	100.00	50.00
89 Linus Frey	250.00	100.00	50.00
90 Hazen (Ki-Ki) Cuyler	250.00	100.00	50.00
91 Dolph Camilli	250.00	100.00	50.00
92 Steve Larkin	250.00	100.00	50.00
93 Fred Ostermueller	250.00	100.00	50.00
94 Robert A. (Red) Rolfe	400.00	160.00	80.00
95 Myril Hoag	250.00	100.00	50.00
96 Jim DeShong	525.00	160.00	60.00

1933-34 Goudey Premiums (R309-1)

Consisting of just four unnumbered cards, this set of black-and-white photos was printed on heavy cardboard and issued as a premium by the Goudey Gum Co. in 1933. Cards (1), (2), and (4) were issued in 1933 and card (3) was issued in 1934. The cards measure 5-1/2" x 8-13/16" and are accented with a gold, picture-frame border and an easel on the back. Besides the game's greatest player, the set has team photos of the 1933 All-Star squads from each league and the World's Champion 1933 N.Y. Giants.

	NM	EX	VG
Complete Set (4):	3,250	1,625	975.00
Common Card:	600.00	300.00	180.00
(1) American League All Stars	650.00	325.00	195.00
(2) National League All Stars	600.00	300.00	180.00
(3) "Worlds Champions 1933" (New York Giants)	750.00	375.00	225.00
(4) George Herman (Babe) Ruth	1,350	675.00	405.00

1935 Goudey 4-in-1 (R321)

PICTURE 3. CARD F

The 1935 Goudey set features color portraits of four players (usually) from the same team on each card. Thirty-six card fronts make up the set with 114 front/back combinations existing. The card backs form nine different puzzles: 1) Tigers Team, 2) Chuck Klein, 3) Frankie Frisch, 4) Mickey Cochrane, 5) Joe Cronin, 6) Jimmy Foxx, 7) Al Simmons, 8) Indians Team, and 9) Senators Team. The cards, which measure 2-3/8" x 2-7/8", have an ACC designation of R321. The numbering has been assigned for this checklist on the basis of alphabetical order of the players found on each card front.

	NM	EX	VG
Complete Set (36):	11,000	4,400	2,200
Complete Set (114):	62,500	25,000	12,500
Common Card:	125.00	50.00	25.00
(1) Sparky Adams, Jim Bottomley, Adam Comorosky, Tony Piet	300.00	120.00	60.00
(2) Ethan Allen, Fred Brickell, Bubber Jonnard, Jimmie Wilson	125.00	30.00	15.00
(3) Johnny Allen, Jimmie Deshong, Red Rolfe, Dixie Walker (DeShong)	125.00	30.00	15.00
(4) Luke Appling, Jimmie Dykes, George Earnshaw, Luke Sewell	300.00	120.00	60.00
(5) Earl Averill, Oral Hildebrand, Willie Kamm, Hal Trosky	300.00	120.00	60.00
(6) Dick Bartell, Hughie Critz, Gus Mancuso, Mel Ott	300.00	120.00	60.00
(7) Ray Benge, Fred Fitzsimmons, Mark Koenig, Tom Zachary	125.00	30.00	15.00
(8) Larry Benton, Ben Cantwell, Flint Rhem, Al Spohrer	125.00	30.00	15.00
(9) Charlie Berry, Bobby Burke, Red Kress, Dazzy Vance	300.00	120.00	60.00
(10) Max Bishop, Bill Cissell, Joe Cronin, Carl Reynolds	300.00	120.00	60.00
(11) George Blaeholder, Dick Coffman, Oscar Melillo, Sammy West	125.00	30.00	15.00
(12) Cy Blanton, Babe Herman, Tom Padden, Gus Suhr	125.00	30.00	15.00
(13) Zeke Bonura, Mule Haas, Jackie Hayes, Ted Lyons	300.00	120.00	60.00
(14) Jim Bottomley, Adam Comorosky, Willis Hudlin, Glenn Myatt	300.00	120.00	60.00
(15) Ed Brandt, Fred Frankhouse, Shanty Hogan, Gene Moore	125.00	50.00	25.00
(16) Ed Brandt, Rabbit Maranville, Marty McManus, Babe Ruth	3,250	1,000	450.00
(17) Tommy Bridges, Mickey Cochrane, Charlie Gehringer, Billy Rogell	350.00	140.00	70.00
(18) Jack Burns, Frank Grube, Rollie Hemsley, Bob Weiland	125.00	30.00	15.00
(19) Guy Bush, Waite Hoyt, Lloyd Waner, Paul Waner	350.00	140.00	70.00
(20) Sammy Byrd, Danny MacFayden, Pepper Martin, Bob O'Farrell	125.00	30.00	15.00
(21a) Gilly Campbell, Ival Goodman, Alex Kampouris, Billy Meyers (Myers) (no "Meyers")	200.00	80.00	40.00
(21b) Gilly Campbell, Ival Goodman, Alex Kampouris, Billy Meyers (Myers)	150.00	60.00	30.00
(22) Tex Carleton, Dizzy Dean, Frankie Frisch, Ernie Orsatti	650.00	260.00	130.00
(23) Watty Clark, Lonny Frey, Sam Leslie, Joe Stripp	125.00	30.00	15.00
(24) Mickey Cochrane, Willie Kamm, Muddy Ruel, Al Simmons	350.00	140.00	70.00
(25) Ed Coleman, Doc Cramer, Bob Johnson, Johnny Marcum	125.00	30.00	15.00
(26) General Crowder, Goose Goslin, Firpo Marberry, Heinie Schuble	300.00	120.00	60.00
(27) Kiki Cuyler, Woody English, Burleigh Grimes, Chuck Klein	350.00	140.00	70.00
(28) Bill Dickey, Tony Lazzeri, Pat Malone, Red Ruffing	400.00	160.00	80.00
(29) Rick Ferrell, Wes Ferrell, Fritz Ostermueller, Bill Werber	300.00	120.00	60.00
(30) Pete Fox, Hank Greenberg, Schoolboy Rowe, Gee Walker	350.00	140.00	70.00
(31) Jimmie Foxx, Pinky Higgins, Roy Mahaffey, Dib Williams	400.00	160.00	80.00
(32) Bump Hadley, Lyn Lary, Heinie Manush, Monte Weaver	300.00	120.00	60.00
(33) Mel Harder, Bill Knickerbocker, Lefty Stewart, Joe Vosmik	125.00	30.00	15.00
(34) Travis Jackson, Gus Mancuso, Hal Schumacher, Bill Terry	300.00	120.00	60.00
(35) Joe Kuhel, Buddy Meyer, John Stone, Earl Whitehill (Myer)	125.00	30.00	15.00
(36) Red Lucas, Tommy Thevenow, Pie Traynor, Glenn Wright	300.00	120.00	60.00

1935 Goudey Puzzle-Backs

JIMMY FOXX

Each of the 36 card fronts in 1935 Goudey can be found with from two to four different backs that could be used to assemble a six-piece (single player) or 12-piece (team photo or composite) puzzle. This listing checklists the different backs found with each card front as well as the cards that comprise each of the nine puzzles. The numbers given for each puzzle piece correspond to the assigned numbers of the card fronts.

Sparky Adams, Jim Bottomley, Adam Comorosky, Tony Piet
1H Tigers, H
3F Frisch, F
4F Cochrane, F
5F Cronin, F
Ethan Allen, Fred Brickell, Bubber Jonnard, Jimmie Wilson
1E Tigers, E
3C Frisch, C
5C Cronin, C
6C Foxx, C
Johnny Allen, Jimmie Deshong, Red Rolfe, Dixie Walker (DeShong)
8E Indians, E
9E Senators, E
Luke Appling, Jimmie Dykes, George Earnshaw, Luke Sewell
1I Tigers, I
2F Klein, F
6F Foxx, F
7F Simmons, F
Earl Averill, Oral Hildebrand, Willie Kamm, Hal Trosky
1L Tigers, L
2E Klein, E
6E Foxx, E
7E Simmons, E
Dick Bartell, Hughie Critz, Gus Mancuso, Mel Ott
2A Klein, A
4A Cochrane, A
7A Simmons, A
Ray Benge, Fred Fitzsimmons, Mark Koenig, Tom Zachary
8A Indians, A
9A Senators, A
Larry Benton, Ben Cantwell, Flint Rhem, Al Spohrer
8L Indians, L
9L Senators, L
Charlie Berry, Bobby Burke, Red Kress, Dazzy Vance
2C Klein, C
4C Cochrane, C
7C Simmons, C
Max Bishop, Bill Cissell, Joe Cronin, Carl Reynolds
1G Tigers, G
3E Frisch, E
5E Cronin, E
6E Foxx, E
George Blaeholder, Dick Coffman, Oscar Melillo, Sammy West
1F Tigers, F
3D Frisch, D
5D Cronin, D
6D Foxx, D
Cy Blanton, Babe Herman, Tom Padden, Gus Suhr
8K Indians, K
9K Senators, K
Zeke Bonura, Mule Haas, Jackie Hayes, Ted Lyons
8B Indians, B
9B Senators, B
Jim Bottomley, Adam Comorosky, Willis Hudlin, Glenn Myatt
1K Tigers, K
3B Frisch, B
5B Cronin, B
6B Foxx, B
Ed Brandt, Fred Frankhouse, Shanty Hogan, Gene Moore
2E Klein, E

4E Cochrane, E
7E Simmons, E
   Ed Brandt, Rabbit Maranville, Marty McManus, Babe Ruth
1J Tigers, J
3A Frisch, A
4A Cochrane, A
5A Cronin, A
   Tommy Bridges, Mickey Cochrane, Charlie Gehringer, Billy Rogell
1D Tigers, D
2D Klein, D
6D Foxx, D
7D Simmons, D
   Jack Burns, Frank Grube, Rollie Hemsley, Bob Weiland
8C Indians, C
9C Senators, C
   Guy Bush, Waite Hoyt, Lloyd Waner, Paul Waner
1E Tigers, E
3C Frisch, C
4C Cochrane, C
5C Cronin, C
   Sammy Byrd, Danny MacFayden, Pepper Martin, Bob O'Farrell
2F Klein, F
4F Cochrane, F
7F Simmons, F
   Gilly Campbell, Ival Goodman, Alex Kampouris, Billy Meyers (Myers)
8D Indians, D
9D Senators, D
   Tex Carleton, Dizzy Dean, Frankie Frisch, Ernie Orsatti
1A Tigers, A
2A Klein, A
6A Foxx, A
7A Simmons, A
   Watty Clark, Lonny Frey, Sam Leslie, Joe Stripp
1G Tigers, G
3E Frisch, E
4E Cochrane, E
5E Cronin, E
   Mickey Cochrane, Willie Kamm, Muddy Ruel, Al Simmons
1J Tigers, J
3A Frisch, A
5A Cronin, A
6A Foxx, A
   Ed Coleman, Doc Cramer, Bob Johnson, Johnny Marcum
8J Indians, J
9J Senators, J
   General Crowder, Goose Goslin, Firpo Marberry, Heinie Schuble
1H Tigers, H
3F Frisch, F
5F Cronin, F
6F Foxx, F
   Kiki Cuyler, Woody English, Burleigh Grimes, Chuck Klein
1F Tigers, F
3D Frisch, D
4D Cochrane, D
5D Cronin, D
   Bill Dickey, Tony Lazzeri, Pat Malone, Red Ruffing
2D Klein, D
4D Cochrane, D
7D Simmons, D
   Rick Ferrell, Wes Ferrell, Fritz Ostermueller, Bill Werber
8G Indians, G
9G Senators, G
   Pete Fox, Hank Greenberg, Schoolboy Rowe, Gee Walker
8F Indians, F
9F Senators, F
   Jimmie Foxx, Pinky Higgins, Roy Mahaffey, Dib Williams
1B Tigers, B
2B Klein, B
6B Foxx, B
7B Simmons, B
   Bump Hadley, Lyn Lary, Heinie Manush, Monte Weaver
1C Tigers, C
2C Klein, C
6C Foxx, C
7C Simmons, C
   Mel Harder, Bill Knickerbocker, Lefty Stewart, Joe Vosmik
8I Indians, I
9I Senators, I
   Travis Jackson, Gus Mancuso, Hal Schumacher, Bill Terry
1K Tigers, K
3B Frisch, B
4B Cochrane, B
5B Cronin, B
   Joe Kuhel, Buddy Meyer, John Stone, Earl Whitehill (Myer)
8H Indians, H
9H Senators, H
   Red Lucas, Tommy Thevenow, Pie Traynor, Glenn Wright
2B Klein, B
4B Cochrane, B
7B Simmons, B

Picture 1, Detroit Tigers Team Photo
A (22)
B (31)
C (32)
D (17)
E (2)
E (19)
F (11)
F (27)
G (10)
G (23)
H (1)
H (26)
I (4)
J (16)
J (24)
K (14)
K (34)
L (5)

Picture 2, Chuck Klein
A (6)
A (22)

B (31)
B (36)
C (9)
D (17)
D (28)
E (5)
E (15)
F (4)
F (20)

Picture 3, Frankie Frisch
A (16)
A (24)
B (14))
B (34)
C (2)
C (19)
D (11)
D (27)
E (10)
E (23)
F (1)
F (26)

Picture 4, Gordon (Mickey) Cochrane
A (6)
A (16)
B (34)
B (36)
C (9)
C (19)
D (27)
D (28)
E (15)
E (23)
F (1)
F (20)

Picture 5, Joe Cronin
A (16)
A (24)
B (14)
B (34)
C (2)
C (19)
D (11)
D (27)
E (10)
E (23)
F (1)
F (26)

Picture 6, Jimmy (Jimmie) Foxx
A (22)
A (24)
B (14)
B (31)
C (2)
C (32)
D (11)
D (17)
E (5)
E (10)
F (4)
F (26)

Picture 7, Al Simmons
A (6)
A (22)
B (31)
B (36)
C (9)
C (32)
D (17)
D (28)
E (5)
E (15)
F (4)
F (20)

Picture 8, Cleve. Indians Composite
A (7)
B (13)
C (18)
D (21)
E (3)
F (30)
G (34)
H (35)
I (32)
J (25)
K (12)
L (8)

Picture 9, Wash. Senators Composite
A (7)
B (13)
C (18)
D (21)
E (3)
F (30)
G (29)
H (35)
I (33)
J (25)
K (12)
L (8)

1935 Goudey Premiums (R309-2)

The black-and-white photos in this set were issued as a premium by retailers in exchange for coupons from 10 Goudey wrappers in 1935. The pictures measure 5-1/2" x 9" (or a bit longer), and are printed on thin, glossy paper. The unnumbered set includes three team collages and players, whose names are written in script in the "wide pen" style.

	NM	EX	VG
Complete Set (16):	5,000	2,500	1,500
Common Player:	275.00	135.00	82.00
(1) Elden Auker	275.00	135.00	82.00
(2) Johnny Babich	275.00	135.00	82.00
(3) Dick Bartell	275.00	135.00	82.00
(4) Lester R. Bell	275.00	135.00	82.00
(5) Wally Berger	275.00	135.00	82.00
(6) Mickey Cochrane	400.00	200.00	120.00
(7) Ervin Fox, Leon "Goose" Goslin, Gerald Walker	325.00	160.00	97.00
(8) Vernon Gomez	400.00	200.00	120.00
(9) Hank Greenberg	500.00	250.00	150.00
(10) Oscar Melillo	275.00	135.00	82.00
(11) Mel Ott	400.00	200.00	120.00
(12) Schoolboy Rowe	275.00	135.00	82.00
(13) Vito Tamulis	275.00	135.00	82.00
(14) Boston Red Sox	300.00	150.00	90.00
(15) Cleveland Indians	300.00	150.00	90.00
(16) Washington Senators	300.00	150.00	90.00

1936 Goudey (R322)

The 1936 Goudey set consists of black-and-white cards measuring 2-3/8" x 2-7/8". A facsimile autograph is positioned on the card fronts. Backs contain a brief player biography and were designed to be used to play a baseball game. Different game situations (out, single, double, etc.) are given on each card. Numerous front/back combinations exist in the set. The ACC designation for the set is R322.

	NM	EX	VG
Complete Set (25):	2,625	1,300	785.00
Common Player:	80.00	40.00	25.00
(1) Walter Berger	80.00	40.00	25.00
(2) Henry Bonura	80.00	40.00	25.00
(3) Stan Bordagaray	80.00	40.00	25.00
(4) Bill Brubaker	80.00	40.00	25.00
(5) Dolf Camilli	80.00	40.00	25.00
(6) Clydell Castleman	80.00	40.00	25.00
(7) "Mickey" Cochrane	175.00	85.00	50.00
(8) Joe Coscarart	80.00	40.00	25.00
(9) Frank Crosetti	110.00	55.00	30.00
(10) "Kiki" Cuyler	140.00	70.00	40.00
(11) Paul Derringer	80.00	40.00	25.00
(12) Jimmy Dykes	80.00	40.00	25.00
(13) "Rick" Ferrell	140.00	70.00	40.00
(14) "Lefty" Gomez	175.00	85.00	50.00
(15) Hank Greenberg	275.00	135.00	80.00
(16) "Bucky" Harris	140.00	70.00	40.00
(17) "Rolly" Hemsley	80.00	40.00	25.00
(18) Frank Higgins	80.00	40.00	25.00
(19) Oral Hildebrand	80.00	40.00	25.00
(20) "Chuck" Klein	140.00	70.00	40.00
(21) "Pepper" Martin	110.00	55.00	30.00
(22) "Buck" Newsom	80.00	40.00	25.00
(23) Joe Vosmik	80.00	40.00	25.00
(24) Paul Waner	140.00	70.00	40.00
(25) Bill Werber	80.00	40.00	25.00

1936 Goudey "Wide Pen" Premiums (R314)

The premium cards originally listed in the American Card Catalog as R314 are known to generations of collectors as "Wide Pens" because of the distinctive, thick style of cursive printing used for the facsimile autographs. Current thinking is that the issue is actually comprised of several distinct types issued over the course of at least two years and sharing a basic 3-1/4" x 5-1/2" black-and-white unnumbered format. Dates attributed are speculative.

1936 Goudey "Wide Pen" Premiums - Type 1

Al Simmons

These in-store premiums are known to collectors as "Wide Pens" because of the distinctive, thick style of cursive printing used for the facsimile autographs. Cards have a 3-1/4" x 5-1/2" black-and-white, unnumbered format. Type 1 cards have bordered photos with "LITHO IN U.S.A." in the bottom border.

		NM	EX	VG
Complete Set (120):		9,000	3,750	1,250
Common Player:		60.00	25.00	15.00
(1)	Ethan Allen/Kneeling	60.00	25.00	15.00
(2)	Earl Averill/Portrait	90.00	38.00	23.00
(3)	Dick Bartell/Portrait	60.00	25.00	15.00
(4)	Dick Bartell (Sliding)	60.00	25.00	15.00
(5)	Walter Berger/Portrait	60.00	25.00	15.00
(6)	Geo. Blaeholder/Portrait	60.00	25.00	15.00
(7)	"Cy" Blanton/Portrait	60.00	25.00	15.00
(8)	"Cliff" Bolton/Portrait	60.00	25.00	15.00
(9)	Stan Bordagaray/Portrait	60.00	25.00	15.00
(10)	Tommy Bridges/Portrait	60.00	25.00	15.00
(11)	Bill Brubaker/Portrait	60.00	25.00	15.00
(12)	Sam Byrd/Portrait	60.00	25.00	15.00
(13)	Dolph Camilli/Portrait	60.00	25.00	15.00
(14)	Clydell Castleman/Pitching	60.00	25.00	15.00
(15)	Clydell Castleman/Portrait	60.00	25.00	15.00
(16)	"Phil" Cavaretta (Cavarretta)/Fldg	60.00	25.00	15.00
(17)	Ben Chapman, Bill Werber	75.00	31.00	19.50
(18)	"Mickey" Cochrane/Portrait	100.00	42.00	26.00
(19)	Earl Coombs (Earle Combs)/Btg	90.00	38.00	23.00
(20)	Joe Coscarart/Portrait	60.00	25.00	15.00
(21)	Joe Cronin/Kneeling	90.00	38.00	23.00
(22)	Frank Crosetti/Btg	65.00	27.00	17.00
(23)	Tony Cuccinello/Portrait	60.00	25.00	15.00
(24)	"Kiki" Cuyler/Portrait	90.00	38.00	23.00
(25)	Curt Davis/Pitching	60.00	25.00	15.00
(26)	Virgil Davis/Catching	60.00	25.00	15.00
(27)	Paul Derringer/Portrait	60.00	25.00	15.00
(28)	"Bill" Dickey/Catching	100.00	42.00	26.00
(29)	Joe DiMaggio, Joe McCarthy	850.00	355.00	220.00
(30)	Jimmy Dykes/Kneeling	60.00	25.00	15.00
(31)	"Rick" Ferrell/Catching	90.00	38.00	23.00
(32)	"Wes" Ferrell/Portrait	60.00	25.00	15.00
(33)	Rick Ferrell, Wes Ferrell	100.00	42.00	26.00
(34)	Lou Finney/Portrait	60.00	25.00	15.00
(35)	Ervin "Pete" Fox/Portrait	60.00	25.00	15.00
(36)	Tony Freitas/Portrait	60.00	25.00	15.00
(37)	Lonnie Frey/Btg	60.00	25.00	15.00
(38)	Frankie Frisch/Portrait	90.00	38.00	23.00
(39)	"Augie" Galan/Portrait	60.00	25.00	15.00
(40)	Charles Gehringer/Portrait	100.00	42.00	26.00
(41)	Charlie Gelbert/Portrait	60.00	25.00	15.00
(42)	"Lefty" Gomez/Portrait	100.00	42.00	26.00
(43)	"Goose" Goslin/Portrait	90.00	38.00	23.00
(44)	Earl Grace/Catching	60.00	25.00	15.00
(45)	Hank Greenberg/Portrait	260.00	110.00	68.00
(46)	"Mule" Haas/Btg	60.00	25.00	15.00
(47)	Odell Hale/Portrait	60.00	25.00	15.00
(48)	Bill Hallahan/Portrait	60.00	25.00	15.00
(49)	"Mel" Harder/Portrait	60.00	25.00	15.00
(50)	"Bucky" Harris/Portrait	90.00	38.00	23.00
(51)	"Gabby" Hartnett/Catching	90.00	38.00	23.00
(52)	Ray Hayworth/Catching	60.00	25.00	15.00
(53)	"Rolly" Hemsley/Catching	60.00	25.00	15.00
(54)	Babe Herman/Portrait	75.00	31.00	19.50
(55)	Frank Higgins/Portrait	60.00	25.00	15.00
(56)	Oral Hildebrand/Portrait	60.00	25.00	15.00
(57)	Myril Hoag/Portrait	60.00	25.00	15.00
(58)	Waite Hoyt/Pitching	90.00	38.00	23.00
(59)	Woody Jensen/Btg	60.00	25.00	15.00
(60)	Bob Johnson/Btg	60.00	25.00	15.00
(61)	"Buck" Jordan/Portrait	60.00	25.00	15.00
(62)	Alex Kampouris/Portrait	60.00	25.00	15.00
(63)	"Chuck" Klein/Portrait	90.00	38.00	23.00
(64)	Joe Kuhel/Portrait	60.00	25.00	15.00
(65)	Lyn Lary/Portrait	60.00	25.00	15.00
(66)	Harry Lavagetto/Portrait	60.00	25.00	15.00
(67)	Sam Leslie/Portrait	60.00	25.00	15.00
(68)	Freddie Lindstrom/Portrait	90.00	38.00	23.00
(69)	Ernie Lombardi/Throwing	90.00	38.00	23.00
(70)	"Al" Lopez/Throwing	90.00	38.00	23.00
(71)	Dan MacFayden/Portrait	60.00	25.00	15.00
(72)	John Marcum/Pitching	60.00	25.00	15.00
(73)	"Pepper" Martin/Portrait	75.00	31.00	19.50
(74)	Eric McNair/Portrait	60.00	25.00	15.50
(75)	"Ducky" Medwick/Kneeling	90.00	38.00	23.00
(76)	Gene Moore/Portrait	60.00	25.00	15.00
(77)	Randy Moore/Portrait	60.00	25.00	15.00
(78)	Terry Moore/Portrait	60.00	25.00	15.00

		NM	EX	VG
(79)	Edw. Moriarty/Portrait	60.00	25.00	15.00
(80)	"Wally" Moses/Portrait	60.00	25.00	15.00
(81)	"Buddy" Myer/Btg	60.00	25.00	15.00
(82)	"Buck" Newsom/Portrait	60.00	25.00	15.00
(83)	Steve O'Neill, Frank Pytlak	60.00	25.00	15.00
(84)	Fred Ostermueller/Portrait	60.00	25.00	15.00
(85)	Marvin Owen/Portrait	60.00	25.00	15.00
(86)	Tommy Padden/Portrait	60.00	25.00	15.00
(87)	Ray Pepper/Btg	60.00	25.00	15.00
(88)	Tony Piet/Portrait	60.00	25.00	15.00
(89)	"Rabbit" Pytlak/Throwing	60.00	25.00	15.00
(90)	"Rip" Radcliff/Portrait	60.00	25.00	15.00
(91)	Bobby Reis/Portrait	60.00	25.00	15.00
(92)	"Lew" Riggs/Fldg	60.00	25.00	15.00
(93)	Bill Rogell/Portrait	60.00	25.00	15.00
(94)	"Red" Rolfe/Portrait	60.00	25.00	15.00
(95)	"Schoolboy" Rowe/Portrait	65.00	27.00	17.00
(96)	Al Schacht/Portrait	75.00	31.00	19.50
(97)	"Luke" Sewell/Catching	60.00	25.00	15.00
(98)	Al Simmons/Portrait	90.00	38.00	23.00
(99)	John Stone/Portrait	60.00	25.00	15.00
(100)	Gus Suhr/Fldg	60.00	25.00	15.00
(101)	Joe Sullivan/Portrait	60.00	25.00	15.00
(102)	Bill Swift/Portrait	60.00	25.00	15.00
(103)	Vito Tamulis/Portrait	60.00	25.00	15.00
(104)	Dan Taylor/Portrait	60.00	25.00	15.00
(105)	Cecil Travis/Portrait	60.00	25.00	15.00
(106)	Hal Trosky/Portrait	60.00	25.00	15.00
(107)	"Bill" Urbanski/Portrait	60.00	25.00	15.00
(108)	Russ Van Atta/Portrait	60.00	25.00	15.00
(109)	"Arky" Vaughan/Portrait	90.00	38.00	23.00
(110)	Gerald Walker/Portrait	60.00	25.00	15.00
(111)	"Buck" Walter (Walters)/Portrait	60.00	25.00	15.00
(112a)	Lloyd Waner/Portrait (No "LITHO IN U.S.A.)	90.00	38.00	23.00
(112b)	Lloyd Waner/Portrait ("LITHO IN U.S.A.)	90.00	38.00	23.00
(113)	Paul Waner/Portrait	90.00	38.00	23.00
(114)	"Lon" Warneke/Portrait	60.00	25.00	15.00
(115)	"Rabbit" Warstler/Btg	60.00	25.00	15.00
(116)	Bill Werber/Portrait	60.00	25.00	15.00
(117)	"Jo Jo" White/Portrait	60.00	25.00	15.00
(118)	Burgess Whitehead/Portrait	60.00	25.00	15.00
(119)	John Whitehead/Portrait	60.00	25.00	15.00
(120)	Whitlow Wyatt/Portrait	60.00	25.00	15.00

1936 Goudey "Wide Pen" Premiums - Type 2

These 3-1/4" x 5-1/2" black-and-white, unnumbered cards are known as "Wide Pens" because of the distinctive cursive printing of the facsimile autographs. Type 2 and Type 3 cards share their photos. Type 2 cards have borders, but no "LITHO IN U.S.A." line. Some Type 2 cards also share their photos with Type 1, but have a different projection (size). Those are indicated parenthetically with an asterisk.

		NM	EX	VG
Complete Set (24):		2,700	1,250	750.00
Common Player:		90.00	40.00	25.00
(1)	Mel Almada/Kneeling	110.00	49.00	27.00
(2)	Lucius Appling/Portrait	135.00	61.00	34.00
(3)	Henry Bonura/Portrait	90.00	40.00	25.00
(4)	Ben Chapman, Bill Werber	120.00	54.00	30.00
(5)	Herman Clifton/Btg	90.00	40.00	25.00
(6)	Roger "Doc" Cramer/Portrait	90.00	40.00	25.00
(7)	Joe Cronin/Kneeling*	135.00	61.00	34.00
(8)	Jimmy Dykes/Kneeling*	90.00	40.00	25.00
(9)	Erwin "Pete" Fox (Ervin)/Portrait*	90.00	40.00	25.00
(10)	Jimmy Foxx/Portrait	260.00	115.00	65.00
(11)	Hank Greenberg/Portrait*	350.00	155.00	87.00
(12)	Oral Hildebrand/Portrait	90.00	40.00	25.00
(13)	Alex Hooks/Fldg	90.00	40.00	25.00
(14)	Willis Hudlin/Throwing	90.00	40.00	25.00
(15)	Bill Knickerbocker/Portrait	90.00	40.00	25.00
(16)	Heine (Heinie) Manush/Portrait*	135.00	61.00	34.00
(17)	Steve O'Neill/Portrait	90.00	40.00	25.00
(18)	Marvin Owen/Portrait*	90.00	40.00	25.00
(19)	Al Simmons (Bats on shoulder.)	135.00	61.00	34.00
(20)	Lem "Moose" Solters/Btg (First name actually Julius.)	90.00	40.00	25.00
(21)	Hal Trosky/Btg	90.00	40.00	25.00
(22)	Joe Vosmik/Btg	90.00	40.00	25.00
(23)	Joe Vosmik/Portrait	90.00	40.00	25.00
(24)	Earl Whitehill/Throwing	90.00	40.00	25.00

1936 Goudey "Wide Pen" Premiums - Type 3

Al Simmons

These 3-1/4" x 5-1/2" black-and-white, unnumbered cards are known as "Wide Pens" because of the distinctive cursive printing of the facsimile autographs. Type 2 and Type 3 cards share their photos. Type 3 cards are borderless and some also share their photos with Type 1, but have a different projection (size). Those are indicated parenthetically with an asterisk.

		NM	EX	VG
Complete Set (24):		2,700	1,250	750.00
Common Player:		90.00	40.00	25.00
(1)	Mel Almada/Kneeling	120.00	54.00	30.00
(2)	Lucius Appling/Portrait	135.00	61.00	34.00
(3)	Henry Bonura/Portrait	90.00	40.00	25.00
(4)	Ben Chapman, Bill Werber	120.00	54.00	30.00
(5)	Herman Clifton/Btg	90.00	40.00	25.00
(6)	Roger "Doc" Cramer/Portrait	90.00	40.00	25.00
(7)	Joe Cronin/Kneeling*	135.00	61.00	34.00
(8)	Jimmy Dykes/Kneeling*	90.00	40.00	25.00
(9)	Erwin "Pete" Fox (Ervin)/Portrait*	90.00	40.00	25.00
(10)	Jimmy Foxx/Portrait	260.00	115.00	65.00
(11)	Hank Greenberg/Portrait*	350.00	155.00	87.00
(12)	Oral Hildebrand/Portrait*	90.00	40.00	25.00
(13)	Alex Hooks/Fldg	90.00	40.00	25.00
(14)	Willis Hudlin/Throwing	90.00	40.00	25.00
(15)	Bill Knickerbocker/Portrait	90.00	40.00	25.00
(16)	Heine (Heinie) Manush/Portrait	135.00	61.00	34.00
(17)	Steve O'Neill/Portrait	90.00	40.00	25.00
(18)	Marvin Owen/Portrait*	90.00	40.00	25.00
(19)	Al Simmons (Bats on shoulder.)	135.00	61.00	34.00
(20)	Lem "Moose" Solters/Btg (First name actually Julius.)	90.00	40.00	25.00
(21)	Hal Trosky/Btg	90.00	40.00	25.00
(22)	Joe Vosmik/Btg	90.00	40.00	25.00
(23)	Joe Vosmik/Portrait	90.00	40.00	25.00
(24)	Earl Whitehill/Throwing	90.00	40.00	25.00

1937 Goudey "Wide Pen" Premiums - Type 4

Bobby Doerr

These premium cards are known to generations of collectors as "Wide Pens" because of the distinctive, thick style of cursive typography used for the facsimile autographs. They have a 3-1/4" x 5-1/2" black-and-white, unnumbered format. Type 4 cards are printed on a paper stock usually described as "creamy." They are bordered, but do not have a "LITHO IN U.S.A." line. Type 5 cards share the creamy paper stock of Type 4, and may have been part of the same issue, which would indicate Canadian origins. An asterisk after the pose indicates a photo shared with Type 1, though possibly of a larger or smaller projection.

		NM	EX	VG
Complete Set (36):		6,750	3,000	1,800
Common Player:		90.00	40.00	25.00
(1)	"Luke" Appling/Btg	135.00	61.00	34.00
(2)	Earl Averill/Portrait*	135.00	61.00	34.00
(3)	"Cy" Blanton/Pitching	90.00	40.00	25.00
(4)	"Zeke" Bonura/Btg	90.00	40.00	25.00
(5)	Tom Bridges/Throwing	90.00	40.00	25.00
(6)	Tommy Bridges/Portrait*	90.00	40.00	25.00
(7)	Mickey Cochrane/Portrait*	135.00	61.00	34.00
(8)	Joe Cronin/Kneeling*	135.00	61.00	34.00
(9)	"Joe" DiMaggio/Kneeling*	3,000	1,350	750.00
(10)	"Bobby" Doeer (Doerr)/Btg	135.00	61.00	34.00
(11)	Jimmy Dykes/Fldg	90.00	40.00	25.00
(12)	"Bob" Feller/Pitching	300.00	135.00	75.00
(13)	"Elbie" Fletcher/Fldg	90.00	40.00	25.00
(14)	Erwin "Pete" Fox (Ervin)/Portrait*	90.00	40.00	25.00
(15)	Pete Fox/Btg	90.00	40.00	25.00
(16)	"Gus" Galan/Btg	90.00	40.00	25.00
(17)	Charles Gehringer/Portrait*	135.00	61.00	34.00
(18)	Hank Greenberg/Portrait*	225.00	100.00	56.00
(19)	"Goose" Goslin/Portrait	135.00	61.00	34.00
(20)	Mel Harder/Portrait	90.00	40.00	25.00
(21)	"Gabby" Hartnett/Catching*	135.00	61.00	34.00
(22)	Ray Hayworth/Catching*	90.00	40.00	25.00
(23)	"Pinky" Higgins/Btg	90.00	40.00	25.00
(24)	Carl Hubbell/Pitching	135.00	61.00	34.00
(25)	"Wally" Moses/Btg	90.00	40.00	25.00
(26)	Lou Newsom/Portrait	90.00	40.00	25.00
(27)	Marvin Owen/Portrait*	90.00	40.00	25.00
(28)	Bill Rogell/Portrait*	90.00	40.00	25.00
(29)	"Schoolboy" Rowe/Pitching	90.00	40.00	25.00
(30)	"Schoolboy" Rowe/Portrait	90.00	40.00	25.00
(31)	Al Simmons/Portrait*	135.00	61.00	34.00
(32)	Julius Solters/Btg	90.00	40.00	25.00
(33)	"Hal" Trosky/Btg	90.00	40.00	25.00

		NM	EX	VG
(34)	Joe Vosmik/Kneeling	90.00	40.00	25.00
(35)	"Jo Jo" White/Portrait*	90.00	40.00	25.00
(36)	Johnnie Whitehead/Pitching	90.00	40.00	25.00

1937 Goudey "Wide Pen" Premiums - Type 5

These premium cards are known as "Wide Pens" because of the distinctive, thick style of cursive printing used for the facsimile autographs. they have a 3-1/4" x 5-1/2" black-and-white, unnumbered format. The photos are bordered, but do not have a "LITHO IN U.S.A." line. Type 5 cards are printed on a paper stock usually described as "creamy" and may have been part of the same issue as Type 4. Type 5 is comprised only of Toronto and Montreal (International League) players.

		NM	EX	VG
Complete Set (39):		4,750	2,400	1,350
Common Player:		135.00	65.00	35.00
(1)	Buddy Bates	135.00	65.00	35.00
(2)	Del Bisonette/Portrait	135.00	65.00	35.00
(3)	Lincoln Blakely	135.00	65.00	35.00
(4)	Isaac J. Boone	135.00	65.00	35.00
(5)	John H. Burnett/Btg	135.00	65.00	35.00
(6)	Leon Chagon	135.00	65.00	35.00
(7)	Gus Dugas/Portrait	135.00	65.00	35.00
(8)	Henry N. Erickson/Catching	135.00	65.00	35.00
(9)	Art Funk/Portrait	135.00	65.00	35.00
(10)	George Granger/Portrait	135.00	65.00	35.00
(11)	Thomas G. Heath	135.00	65.00	35.00
(12)	Phil Hensiek/Portrait	135.00	65.00	35.00
(13)	Leroy Herrmann/Throwing	135.00	65.00	35.00
(14)	Henry Johnson	135.00	65.00	35.00
(15)	Hal King/Portrait	135.00	65.00	35.00
(16)	Charles F. Lucas/Portrait	135.00	65.00	35.00
(17)	Edward S. Miller/Btg (Middle initial actually R.)	135.00	65.00	35.00
(18)	Jake F. Mooty/Pitching	135.00	65.00	35.00
(19)	Guy Moreau/Portrait (Street clothes.)	135.00	65.00	35.00
(20)	George Murray/Portrait	135.00	65.00	35.00
(21)	Glenn Myatt	135.00	65.00	35.00
(22)	Lauri Myllykangas	135.00	65.00	35.00
(23)	Francis J. Nicholas/Pitching	135.00	65.00	35.00
(24)	Bill O'Brien (Montreal trainer)	135.00	65.00	35.00
(25)	Thomas Oliver/Btg	135.00	65.00	35.00
(26)	James Pattison	135.00	65.00	35.00
(27)	Crip Polli/Portrait	135.00	65.00	35.00
(28)	Harlan Pool (Bats)	135.00	65.00	35.00
(29)	Walter Purcey/Pitching	135.00	65.00	35.00
(30)	Bill Rhiel	135.00	65.00	35.00
(31)	Ben Sankey	135.00	65.00	35.00
(32)	Les Scarcella (Scarsella)/Kneeling	135.00	65.00	35.00
(33)	Bob Seeds/Portrait	135.00	65.00	35.00
(34)	Frank Shaugnessy/Portrait	135.00	65.00	35.00
(35)	Harry Smythe/Portrait	135.00	65.00	35.00
(36)	Ben Tate/Portrait	135.00	65.00	35.00
(37)	Fresco Thompson/Portrait	135.00	65.00	35.00
(38)	Charles Wilson/Portrait	135.00	65.00	35.00
(39)	Francis Wistert/Pitching	135.00	65.00	35.00

1937 Goudey Knot Hole League

Though they do not picture or name any players, the fact these game cards were issued by Goudey makes them collectible for many hobbyists. While they carry a copyright date of 1935, the cards were not issued until 1937. About 2-3/8" x 2-7/8", and printed in red, white and blue, the cards were intended to be used to play a baseball game using the situations printed on the fronts. Despite advertising a series of 100 cards, only 24 were actually issued. The cards were designated R325 in the American Card Catalog.

		NM	EX	VG
Complete Set (24):		450.00	180.00	90.00
Common Card:		25.00	10.00	5.00
1	Double/Foul	25.00	10.00	5.00
2	Steals Home!!/Strike	25.00	10.00	5.00
3	Ball/Out	25.00	10.00	5.00
4	Strike/Ball	25.00	10.00	5.00
5	Strike/Wild Pitch	25.00	10.00	5.00
6	Ball/Out	25.00	10.00	5.00
7	Bunt - Scratch Hit!!/ Stolen Base !!	25.00	10.00	5.00
8	Hit by Pitched Ball/Out	25.00	10.00	5.00
9	Foul/Ball	25.00	10.00	5.00
10	Foul/Double!	25.00	10.00	5.00
11	Out/Ball	25.00	10.00	5.00
12	Foul/Force Out	25.00	10.00	5.00
13	Out/Single	25.00	10.00	5.00
14	Strike/Ball	25.00	10.00	5.00
15	Foul Tip/Strike!	25.00	10.00	5.00
16	Three Bagger/Out	25.00	10.00	5.00
17	Ball/Out	25.00	10.00	5.00
18	Out!!/Error!!!	25.00	10.00	5.00
19	Strike/Foul	25.00	10.00	5.00
20	Out/Double Play	25.00	10.00	5.00
21	!!Home Run!!/Ball	25.00	10.00	5.00
22	Out/Strike	25.00	10.00	5.00
23	Ball/Out	25.00	10.00	5.00
24	Lout!!/Error!!!	25.00	10.00	5.00

1937 Goudey Thum Movies

These 2" x 3" baseball novelty booklets create the illusion of baseball action in motion when the pages are rapidly flipped. The booklets are numbered on the top of the back page. Thum Movies were listed in the American Card Catalog as R342.

		NM	EX	VG
Complete Set (13):		1,750	875.00	525.00
Common Player:		70.00	35.00	20.00
1	John Irving Burns	70.00	35.00	20.00
2	Joe Vosmik	70.00	35.00	20.00
3	Mel Ott	225.00	110.00	65.00
4	Joe DiMaggio	525.00	260.00	155.00
5	Wally Moses	70.00	35.00	20.00
6	Van Lingle Mungo	70.00	35.00	20.00
7	Luke Appling	100.00	50.00	30.00
8	Bob Feller	225.00	110.00	65.00
9	Paul Derringer	70.00	35.00	20.00
10	Paul Waner	100.00	50.00	30.00
11	Joe Medwick	100.00	50.00	30.00
12	James Emory Foxx	225.00	110.00	65.00
13	Wally Berger	70.00	35.00	20.00

1938 Goudey (R323)

Sometimes referred to as the Goudey Heads-Up set, this issue begins numbering (#241) where the 1933 Goudey set left off. On the card fronts, a photo is used for the player's head with the body being a cartoon drawing. Twenty-four different players are pictured twice in the set. Cards #241-264 feature plain backgrounds on the fronts. Cards #265-288 contain the same basic design and photo but include small drawings and comments within the background. Backs have player statistical and biographical information. The ACC designation for the issue is R323.

		NM	EX	VG
Complete Set (48):		29,000	11,500	5,750
Common Player (241-264):		200.00	85.00	30.00
Common Player (265-288):		225.00	100.00	35.00
241	Charlie Gehringer	600.00	250.00	100.00
242	Ervin Fox	300.00	100.00	40.00
243	Joe Kuhel	200.00	85.00	30.00
244	Frank DeMaree	200.00	85.00	30.00
245	Frank Pytlak	200.00	85.00	30.00
246a	Ernie Lombardi (Red Sox)	800.00	320.00	160.00
246b	Ernie Lombardi (Reds followed by black baseball.)	450.00	180.00	90.00
246c	Ernie Lombardi (Reds)	350.00	140.00	70.00
247	Joe Vosmik	200.00	85.00	30.00
248	Dick Bartell	200.00	85.00	30.00
249	Jimmy Foxx	900.00	350.00	150.00
250	Joe DiMaggio	5,000	2,000	1,100
251	Bump Hadley	200.00	85.00	30.00
252	Zeke Bonura	200.00	85.00	30.00
253	Hank Greenberg	1,100	450.00	225.00
254	Van Lingle Mungo	300.00	120.00	40.00
255	Julius Solters	200.00	85.00	30.00
256	Vernon Kennedy	200.00	85.00	30.00
257	Al Lopez	425.00	200.00	85.00
258	Bobby Doerr	500.00	200.00	85.00
259	Bill Werber	200.00	85.00	30.00
260	Rudy York	200.00	85.00	30.00
261	Rip Radcliff	200.00	85.00	30.00
262	Joe Ducky Medwick	425.00	200.00	85.00
263	Marvin Owen	200.00	85.00	30.00
264	Bob Feller	2,000	700.00	300.00
265	Charlie Gehringer	600.00	200.00	85.00
266	Ervin Fox	225.00	100.00	35.00
267	Joe Kuhel	225.00	100.00	35.00
268	Frank DeMaree	225.00	100.00	35.00
269	Frank Pytlak	225.00	100.00	35.00
270	Ernie Lombardi	500.00	225.00	100.00
271	Joe Vosmik	225.00	100.00	35.00
272	Dick Bartell	225.00	100.00	35.00
273	Jimmy Foxx	1,200	500.00	200.00
274	Joe DiMaggio	5,250	2,000	1,100
275	Bump Hadley	225.00	100.00	35.00

		NM	EX	VG
276	Zeke Bonura	225.00	100.00	35.00
277	Hank Greenberg	1,300	600.00	300.00
278	Van Lingle Mungo	225.00	100.00	35.00
279	Julius Solters	225.00	100.00	35.00
280	Vernon Kennedy	225.00	100.00	35.00
281	Al Lopez	500.00	225.00	90.00
282	Bobby Doerr	550.00	250.00	100.00
283	Bill Werber	225.00	100.00	35.00
284	Rudy York	225.00	100.00	35.00
285	Rip Radcliff	225.00	100.00	35.00
286	Joe Ducky Medwick	600.00	250.00	100.00
287	Marvin Owen	225.00	100.00	35.00
288	Bob Feller	2,250	900.00	450.00

1938 Goudey Big League Baseball Movies

Probably issued in both 1937-38, according to the biographies on back, this set of "flip movies" was comprised of small (2" x 3") booklets whose pages produced a movie effect when flipped rapidly, similar to a penny arcade novelty popular at the time. There are 13 players in the set; each movie having two cleary labeled parts. The cover of the booklets identify the set as "Big League Baseball Movies." They carry the American Card Catalog designation R326.

		NM	EX	VG
Complete Set (26):		3,750	1,875	1,125
Common Player:		75.00	37.50	22.50
1a	John Irving Burns (Part 1)	75.00	37.50	22.50
1b	John Irving Burns (Part 2)	75.00	37.50	22.50
2a	Joe Vosmik (Part 1)	75.00	37.50	22.50
2b	Joe Vosmik (Part 2)	75.00	37.50	22.50
3a	Mel Ott (Part 1)	185.00	95.00	55.00
3b	Mel Ott (Part 2)	185.00	95.00	55.00
4a	Joe DiMaggio (Part 1, Joe DiMaggio cover photo.)	475.00	235.00	140.00
4aa	Joe DiMaggio (Part 1, Vince DiMaggio cover photo.)	375.00	185.00	110.00
4b	Joe DiMaggio (Part 2, Joe DiMaggio cover photo.)	475.00	235.00	140.00
4ba	Joe DiMaggio (Part 2, Vince DiMaggio cover photo.)	375.00	185.00	110.00
5a	Wally Moses (Part 1)	75.00	37.50	22.50
5b	Wally Moses (Part 2)	75.00	37.50	22.50
6a	Van Lingle Mungo (Part 1)	75.00	37.50	22.50
6b	Van Lingle Mungo (Part 2)	75.00	37.50	22.50
7a	Luke Appling (Part 1)	110.00	55.00	35.00
7b	Luke Appling (Part 2)	110.00	55.00	35.00
8a	Bob Feller (Part 1)	225.00	110.00	65.00
8b	Bob Feller (Part 2)	225.00	110.00	65.00
9a	Paul Derringer (Part 1)	75.00	37.50	22.50
9b	Paul Derringer (Part 2)	75.00	37.50	22.50
10a	Paul Waner (Part 1)	110.00	55.00	35.00
10b	Paul Waner (Part 2)	110.00	55.00	35.00
11a	Joe Medwick (Part 1)	110.00	55.00	35.00
11b	Joe Medwick (Part 2)	110.00	55.00	35.00
12a	James Emory Foxx (Part 1)	260.00	130.00	75.00
12b	James Emory Foxx (Part 2)	260.00	130.00	75.00
13a	Wally Berger (Part 1)	75.00	37.50	22.50
13b	Wally Berger (Part 2)	75.00	37.50	22.50

1939 Goudey Premiums (R303-A)

Although this unnumbered set of paper premiums has the name "Diamond Stars Gum" on the back, it is not related to National Chicle's Diamond Stars card sets. Rather, this 48-player set was a premium issued by the Goudey Gum Co. Each premium photo measures 4" x 6-3/16" and is printed in a brown-toned sepia. The front of the photo includes a facsimile autograph, while the back contains drawings that illustrate various baseball tips. These pictures are soemtimes found with top and bottom border trimmed to a depth of 5-3/4" for distribution in Canada.

		NM	EX	VG
Complete Set (48):		6,000	2,400	1,200
Common Player:		75.00	30.00	15.00
(1)	Luke Appling	135.00	55.00	25.00
(2)	Earl Averill	135.00	55.00	25.00
(3)	Wally Berger	75.00	30.00	15.00
(4)	Darrell Blanton	75.00	30.00	15.00
(5)	Zeke Bonura	75.00	30.00	15.00
(6)	Mace Brown	75.00	30.00	15.00
(7)	George Case	75.00	30.00	15.00
(8)	Ben Chapman	75.00	30.00	15.00
(9)	Joe Cronin	135.00	55.00	25.00
(10)	Frank Crosetti	90.00	36.00	18.00
(11)	Paul Derringer	75.00	30.00	15.00
(12)	Bill Dickey	150.00	60.00	30.00
(13)	Joe DiMaggio	650.00	260.00	130.00
(14)	Bob Feller	225.00	90.00	45.00
(15)	Jimmy (Jimmie) Foxx	235.00	95.00	45.00
(16)	Charles Gehringer	135.00	55.00	25.00
(17)	Lefty Gomez	135.00	55.00	25.00
(18)	Ival Goodman	75.00	30.00	15.00
(19)	Joe Gordon	135.00	55.00	25.00
(20)	Hank Greenberg	175.00	70.00	35.00
(21)	Buddy Hassett	75.00	30.00	15.00
(22)	Jeff Heath	75.00	30.00	15.00
(23)	Tom Henrich	75.00	30.00	15.00
(24)	Billy Herman	135.00	54.00	27.00
(25)	Frank Higgins	75.00	30.00	15.00
(26)	Fred Hutchinson	75.00	30.00	15.00
(27)	Bob Johnson	75.00	30.00	15.00
(28)	Ken Keltner	75.00	30.00	15.00
(29)	Mike Kreevich	75.00	30.00	15.00
(30)	Ernie Lombardi	135.00	55.00	25.00
(31)	Gus Mancuso	75.00	30.00	15.00
(32)	Eric McNair	75.00	30.00	15.00
(33)	Van Mungo	75.00	30.00	15.00
(34)	Buck Newsom	75.00	30.00	15.00
(35)	Mel Ott	150.00	55.00	25.00
(36)	Marvin Owen	75.00	30.00	15.00
(37)	Frank Pytlak	75.00	30.00	15.00
(38)	Woodrow Rich	75.00	30.00	15.00
(39)	Charley Root	75.00	30.00	15.00
(40)	Al Simmons	135.00	55.00	25.00
(41)	James Tabor	75.00	30.00	15.00
(42)	Cecil Travis	75.00	30.00	15.00
(43)	Hal Trosky	75.00	30.00	15.00
(44)	Arky Vaughan	135.00	55.00	25.00
(45)	Joe Vosmik	75.00	30.00	15.00
(46)	Lon Warneke	75.00	30.00	15.00
(47)	Ted Williams	2,000	1,000	600.00
(48)	Rudy York	75.00	30.00	15.00

1939 Goudey Premiums (R303-B)

Although larger (4-3/4" x 7-1/4" to 7-3/8"), the photos in this 24-player set are identical to those in the R303-A issue of the same year, and the format of the set is unchanged. The set, designated as R303-B in the American Card Catalog, can be found in both black-and-white and sepia-toned, with backs printed in brown.

		NM	EX	VG
Complete Set (24):		2,500	1,000	500.00
Common Player:		60.00	24.00	12.00
(1)	Luke Appling	90.00	35.00	15.00
(2)	George Case	60.00	25.00	12.00
(3)	Ben Chapman	60.00	25.00	12.00
(4)	Joe Cronin	90.00	35.00	15.00
(5)	Bill Dickey	110.00	45.00	20.00
(6)	Joe DiMaggio	850.00	425.00	250.00
(7)	Bob Feller	150.00	60.00	30.00
(8)	Jimmy (Jimmie) Foxx	175.00	70.00	35.00
(9)	Lefty Gomez	90.00	35.00	15.00
(10)	Ival Goodman	60.00	25.00	12.00
(11)	Joe Gordon	90.00	45.00	27.00
(12)	Hank Greenberg	125.00	50.00	25.00
(13)	Jeff Heath	60.00	25.00	12.00
(14)	Billy Herman	90.00	35.00	15.00
(15)	Frank Higgins	60.00	25.00	12.00
(16)	Ken Keltner	60.00	25.00	12.00
(17)	Mike Kreevich	60.00	25.00	12.00
(18)	Ernie Lombardi	90.00	35.00	15.00
(19)	Gus Mancuso	60.00	25.00	12.00
(20)	Mel Ott	110.00	45.00	20.00
(21)	Al Simmons	90.00	35.00	15.00
(22)	Arky Vaughan	90.00	35.00	15.00
(23)	Joe Vosmik	60.00	25.00	12.00
(24)	Rudy York	60.00	25.00	12.00

1941 Goudey (R324)

Goudey Gum's last set was issued in 1941. The 2-3/8" x 2-7/8" (size approximate due to imprecise cutting) cards feature black-and-white photos set against blue, green, red or yellow backgrounds. The player's name, team and position plus the card number are supposed to be situated in a box at

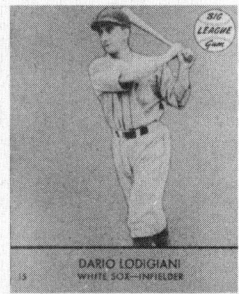

the bottom of the card. However, due to vagaries of cutting, some or all of the bottom printing might appear at the top of the card, greatly reducing its value. The card backs are blank. The ACC designation for the set is R324.

		NM	EX	VG
Complete Set (33):		8,500	3,400	1,700
Common Player:		250.00	100.00	50.00
1	Hugh Mulcahy	250.00	100.00	50.00
2	Harland Clift	250.00	100.00	50.00
3	Louis Chiozza	250.00	100.00	50.00
4	Warren (Buddy) Rosar	250.00	100.00	50.00
5	George McQuinn	250.00	100.00	50.00
6	Emerson Dickman	250.00	100.00	50.00
7	Wayne Ambler	250.00	100.00	50.00
8	Bob Muncrief	250.00	100.00	50.00
9	Bill Dietrich	250.00	100.00	50.00
10	Taft Wright	250.00	100.00	50.00
11	Don Heffner	250.00	100.00	50.00
12	Fritz Ostermueller	250.00	100.00	50.00
13	Frank Hayes	250.00	100.00	50.00
14	John (Jack) Kramer	250.00	100.00	50.00
15	Dario Lodigiani	275.00	110.00	55.00
16	George Case	250.00	100.00	50.00
17	Vito Tamulis	250.00	100.00	50.00
18	Whitlow Wyatt	250.00	100.00	50.00
19	Bill Posedel	250.00	100.00	50.00
20	Carl Hubbell	675.00	275.00	125.00
21	Harold Warstler/SP	400.00	175.00	85.00
22	Joe Sullivan/SP	400.00	175.00	85.00
23	Norman (Babe) Young/SP	400.00	175.00	85.00
24	Stanley Andrews/SP	400.00	175.00	85.00
25	Morris Arnovich/SP	700.00	260.00	90.00
26	Elburt Fletcher	250.00	100.00	50.00
27	Bill Crouch	275.00	110.00	55.00
28	Al Todd	250.00	100.00	50.00
29	Debs Garms	250.00	100.00	50.00
30	Jim Tobin	250.00	100.00	50.00
31	Chester Ross	250.00	100.00	50.00
32	George Coffman	250.00	100.00	50.00
33	Mel Ott	600.00	240.00	120.00

1955 Robert Gould All Stars Cards

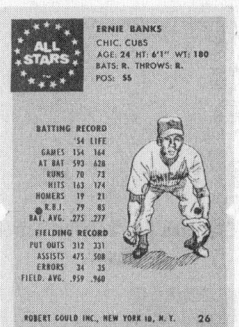

One of three issues of miniature plastic player statues issued in the mid-Fifties was the All Stars series by Robert Gould Inc. of New York. The white plastic statues, which sold for about a quarter, came rubber-banded to a baseball card. The card measures 2-1/2" x 3-1/2" with a white border. A rather crude black-and-white line drawing of the player is set against a green background. There are a few biographical details and 1954 and lifetime stats. An "All Stars" logo is in an upper corner, while the card number is at lower-right. The cards are blank-backed. All cards have a pair of notches at the sides and two punch holes to hold the rubber band. Prices shown here are for the cards alone. A 2-5/8" x 3-5/8" album reproducing all 28 player cards was also issued.

		NM	EX	VG
Complete Set, Cards (28):		17,000	8,500	5,000
Common Player:		500.00	250.00	150.00
Album:		400.00	200.00	120.00
1	Willie Mays	2,200	1,100	660.00
2	Gus Zernial	500.00	250.00	150.00
3	Red Schoendienst	650.00	325.00	200.00
4	Chico Carrasquel	500.00	250.00	150.00
5	Jim Hegan	500.00	250.00	150.00
6	Curt Simmons	500.00	250.00	150.00
7	Bob Porterfield	500.00	250.00	150.00
8	Jim Busby	500.00	250.00	150.00
9	Don Mueller	500.00	250.00	150.00
10	Ted Kluszewski	600.00	300.00	200.00
11	Ray Boone	500.00	250.00	150.00
12	Smoky Burgess	500.00	250.00	150.00
13	Bob Rush	500.00	250.00	150.00
14	Early Wynn	600.00	300.00	180.00

		NM	EX	VG
15	Bill Bruton	500.00	250.00	150.00
16	Gus Bell	500.00	250.00	150.00
17	Jim Finigan	500.00	250.00	150.00
18	Granny Hamner	500.00	250.00	150.00
19	Hank Thompson	500.00	250.00	150.00
20	Joe Coleman	500.00	250.00	150.00
21	Don Newcombe	550.00	275.00	160.00
22	Richie Ashburn	650.00	325.00	20.00
23	Bobby Thomson	500.00	250.00	150.00
24	Sid Gordon	500.00	250.00	150.00
25	Gerry Coleman	500.00	250.00	150.00
26	Ernie Banks	1,700	850.00	500.00
27	Billy Pierce	500.00	250.00	150.00
28	Mel Parnell	500.00	250.00	150.00

1955 Robert Gould All Stars Statues

One of three issues of miniature plastic player statues issued in the mid-Fifties was the All Stars series by Robert Gould Inc. of New York. The white plastic statues, which sold for about a quarter, came rubber-banded to a baseball card. Depending on pose, they vary in size from around 2" to 2-1/2". The figures have a round base with the player's name. Prices shown here are for the statues alone. The statues were also sold in seven-player boxed sets labeled "A" through "D."

		NM	EX	VG
Complete Set, Statues (28):		3,000	1,500	900.00
Common Player:		80.00	40.00	25.00
1	Willie Mays	600.00	300.00	180.00
2	Gus Zernial	80.00	40.00	25.00
3	Red Schoendienst	150.00	75.00	40.00
4	Chico Carrasquel	80.00	40.00	25.00
5	Jim Hegan	80.00	40.00	25.00
6	Curt Simmons	80.00	40.00	25.00
7	Bob Porterfield	80.00	40.00	25.00
8	Jim Busby	80.00	40.00	25.00
9	Don Mueller	80.00	40.00	25.00
10	Ted Kluszewski	100.00	50.00	30.00
11	Ray Boone	80.00	40.00	25.00
12	Smoky Burgess	80.00	40.00	25.00
13	Bob Rush	80.00	40.00	25.00
14	Early Wynn	120.00	60.00	40.00
15	Bill Bruton	80.00	40.00	25.00
16	Gus Bell	80.00	40.00	25.00
17	Jim Finigan	80.00	40.00	25.00
18	Granny Hamner	80.00	40.00	25.00
19	Hank Thompson	80.00	40.00	25.00
20	Joe Coleman	80.00	40.00	25.00
21	Don Newcombe	90.00	45.00	30.00
22	Richie Ashburn	150.00	75.00	45.00
23	Bobby Thomson	90.00	45.00	30.00
24	Sid Gordon	80.00	40.00	25.00
25	Gerry Coleman	80.00	40.00	25.00
26	Ernie Banks	480.00	240.00	150.00
27	Billy Pierce	80.00	40.00	25.00
28	Mel Parnell	80.00	40.00	25.00

1978 Grand Slam

This collectors' edition card set was produced by Jack Wallin. The black-and-white 2-1/4" x 3-1/4" cards have player poses or action photos on front, with the name in the white border at bottom. Backs have a career summary.

		NM	EX	VG
Complete Set (200):		120.00	60.00	35.00
Common Player:		2.00	1.00	.60
1	Leo Durocher	2.00	1.00	.60
2	Bob Lemon	2.00	1.00	.60
3	Earl Averill	2.00	1.00	.60
4	Dale Alexander	2.00	1.00	.60
5	Hank Greenberg	12.00	6.00	3.50
6	Waite Hoyt	2.00	1.00	.60
7	Al Lopez	2.00	1.00	.60

8	Lloyd Waner	2.00	1.00	.60
9	Bob Feller	2.00	1.00	.60
10	Guy Bush	2.00	1.00	.60
11	Stan Hack	2.00	1.00	.60
12	Zeke Bonura	2.00	1.00	.60
13	Wally Moses	2.00	1.00	.60
14	Fred Fitzsimmons	2.00	1.00	.60
15	Johnny Vander Meer	2.00	1.00	.60
16	Riggs Stephenson	2.00	1.00	.60
17	Bucky Walters	2.00	1.00	.60
18	Charlie Grimm	2.00	1.00	.60
19	Phil Cavarretta	2.00	1.00	.60
20	Wally Berger	2.00	1.00	.60
21	Joe Sewell	2.00	1.00	.60
22	Edd Roush	2.00	1.00	.60
23	Johnny Mize	2.00	1.00	.60
24	Bill Dickey	2.00	1.00	.60
25	Lou Boudreau	2.00	1.00	.60
26	Bill Terry	2.00	1.00	.60
27	Willie Kamm	2.00	1.00	.60
28	Charlie Gehringer	2.00	1.00	.60
29	Stan Coveleski	2.00	1.00	.60
30	Larry French	2.00	1.00	.60
31	George Kelly	2.00	1.00	.60
32	Terry Moore	2.00	1.00	.60
33	Billy Herman	2.00	1.00	.60
34	Babe Herman	2.00	1.00	.60
35	Carl Hubbell	2.00	1.00	.60
36	Buck Leonard	2.00	1.00	.60
37	Gus Suhr	2.00	1.00	.60
38	Burleigh Grimes	2.00	1.00	.60
39	Al Fonseca	2.00	1.00	.60
40	Travis Jackson	2.00	1.00	.60
41	Enos Slaughter	2.00	1.00	.60
42	Fred Lindstrom	2.00	1.00	.60
43	Rick Ferrell	2.00	1.00	.60
44	Cookie Lavagetto	2.00	1.00	.60
45	Stan Musial	12.00	6.00	3.50
46	Hal Trosky	2.00	1.00	.60
47	Hal Newhouser	2.00	1.00	.60
48	Paul Dean	2.00	1.00	.60
49	George Halas	6.00	3.00	1.75
50	Jocko Conlan	2.00	1.00	.60
51	Joe DiMaggio	30.00	15.00	9.00
52	Bobby Doerr	2.00	1.00	.60
53	Carl Reynolds	2.00	1.00	.60
54	Pete Reiser	2.00	1.00	.60
55	Frank McCormick	2.00	1.00	.60
56	Mel Harder	2.00	1.00	.60
57	George Uhle	2.00	1.00	.60
58	Doc Cramer	2.00	1.00	.60
59	Taylor Douthit	2.00	1.00	.60
60	Cecil Travis	2.00	1.00	.60
61	James Bell	2.00	1.00	.60
62	Charlie Keller	2.00	1.00	.60
63	Bill Hallahan	2.00	1.00	.60
64	Debs Garms	2.00	1.00	.60
65	Rube Marquard	2.00	1.00	.60
66	Rube Walberg	2.00	1.00	.60
67	Augie Galan	2.00	1.00	.60
68	George Pipgras	2.00	1.00	.60
69	Hal Schumacher	2.00	1.00	.60
70	Dolf Camilli	2.00	1.00	.60
71	Paul Richards	2.00	1.00	.60
72	Judy Johnson	2.00	1.00	.60
73	Frank Crosetti	2.00	1.00	.60
74	Harry Lowery	2.00	1.00	.60
75	Walter Alston	2.00	1.00	.60
76	Dutch Leonard	2.00	1.00	.60
77	Barney McCosky	2.00	1.00	.60
78	Joe Dobson	2.00	1.00	.60
79	George Kell	2.00	1.00	.60
80	Ted Lyons	2.00	1.00	.60
81	Johnny Pesky	2.00	1.00	.60
82	Hank Borowy	2.00	1.00	.60
83	Ewell Blackwell	2.00	1.00	.60
84	Pee Wee Reese	12.00	6.00	3.50
85	Monte Irvin	2.00	1.00	.60
86	Joe Moore	2.00	1.00	.60
87	Joe Wood	2.00	1.00	.60
88	Babe Dahlgren	2.00	1.00	.60
89	Bibb Falk	2.00	1.00	.60
90	Ed Lopat	2.00	1.00	.60
91	Rip Sewell	2.00	1.00	.60
92	Marty Marion	2.00	1.00	.60
93	Taft Wright	2.00	1.00	.60
94	Allie Reynolds	2.00	1.00	.60
95	Harry Walker	2.00	1.00	.60
96	Tex Hughson	2.00	1.00	.60
97	George Selkirk	2.00	1.00	.60
98	Dom DiMaggio	10.00	5.00	3.00
99	Walker Cooper	2.00	1.00	.60
100	Phil Rizzuto	10.00	5.00	3.00
101	Robin Roberts	2.00	1.00	.60
102	Joe Adcock	2.00	1.00	.60
103	Hank Bauer	2.00	1.00	.60
104	Frank Baumholtz	2.00	1.00	.60
105	Ray Boone	2.00	1.00	.60
106	Smoky Burgess	2.00	1.00	.60
107	Walt Dropo	2.00	1.00	.60
108	Alvin Dark	2.00	1.00	.60
109	Carl Erskine	2.00	1.00	.60
110	Dick Donovan	2.00	1.00	.60
111	Dee Fondy	2.00	1.00	.60
112	Mike Garcia	2.00	1.00	.60
113	Bob Friend	2.00	1.00	.60
114	Ned Garver	2.00	1.00	.60
115	Billy Goodman	2.00	1.00	.60
116	Larry Jansen	2.00	1.00	.60
117	Jackie Jensen	2.00	1.00	.60
118	John Antonelli	2.00	1.00	.60
119	Ted Kluszewski	2.00	1.00	.60
120	Harvey Kuenn	2.00	1.00	.60
121	Clem Labine	2.00	1.00	.60
122	Red Schoendienst	2.00	1.00	.60
123	Don Larsen	2.00	1.00	.60
124	Vern Law	2.00	1.00	.60
125	Charlie Maxwell	2.00	1.00	.60

126	Wally Moon	2.00	1.00	.60
127	Bob Nieman	2.00	1.00	.60
128	Don Newcombe	2.00	1.00	.60
129	Wally Post	2.00	1.00	.60
130	Johnny Podres	2.00	1.00	.60
131	Vic Raschi	2.00	1.00	.60
132	Dusty Rhodes	2.00	1.00	.60
133	Jim Rivera	2.00	1.00	.60
134	Pete Runnels	2.00	1.00	.60
135	Hank Sauer	2.00	1.00	.60
136	Roy Sievers	2.00	1.00	.60
137	Bobby Shantz	2.00	1.00	.60
138	Curt Simmons	2.00	1.00	.60
139	Bob Skinner	2.00	1.00	.60
140	Bill Skowron	2.00	1.00	.60
141	Warren Spahn	2.00	1.00	.60
142	Gerry Staley	2.00	1.00	.60
143	Frank Thomas	2.00	1.00	.60
144	Bobby Thomson	2.00	1.00	.60
145	Bob Turley	2.00	1.00	.60
146	Vic Wertz	2.00	1.00	.60
147	Bill Virdon	2.00	1.00	.60
148	Gene Woodling	2.00	1.00	.60
149	Eddie Yost	2.00	1.00	.60
150	Sandy Koufax	25.00	12.50	7.50
151	Lefty Gomez	2.00	1.00	.60
152	Al Rosen	2.00	1.00	.60
153	Vince DiMaggio	2.00	1.00	.60
154	Bill Nicholson	2.00	1.00	.60
155	Mark Koenig	2.00	1.00	.60
156	Max Lanier	2.00	1.00	.60
157	Ken Keltner	2.00	1.00	.60
158	Whit Wyatt	2.00	1.00	.60
159	Marv Owen	2.00	1.00	.60
160	Red Lucas	2.00	1.00	.60
161	Babe Phelps	2.00	1.00	.60
162	Pete Donohue	2.00	1.00	.60
163	Johnny Cooney	2.00	1.00	.60
164	Glenn Wright	2.00	1.00	.60
165	Willis Hudlin	2.00	1.00	.60
166	Tony Cuccinello	2.00	1.00	.60
167	Bill Bevens	2.00	1.00	.60
168	Dave Ferris	2.00	1.00	.60
169	Whitey Kurowski	2.00	1.00	.60
170	Buddy Hassett	2.00	1.00	.60
171	Ossie Bluege	2.00	1.00	.60
172	Hoot Evers	2.00	1.00	.60
173	Thornton Lee	2.00	1.00	.60
174	Virgil Davis	2.00	1.00	.60
175	Bob Shawkey	2.00	1.00	.60
176	Smead Jolley	2.00	1.00	.60
177	Andy High	2.00	1.00	.60
178	George McQuinn	2.00	1.00	.60
179	Mickey Vernon	2.00	1.00	.60
180	Birdie Tebbetts	2.00	1.00	.60
181	Jack Kramer	2.00	1.00	.60
182	Don Kolloway	2.00	1.00	.60
183	Claude Passeau	2.00	1.00	.60
184	Frank Shea	2.00	1.00	.60
185	Bob O'Farrell	2.00	1.00	.60
186	Bob Johnson	2.00	1.00	.60
187	Ival Goodman	2.00	1.00	.60
188	Mike Kreevich	2.00	1.00	.60
189	Joe Stripp	2.00	1.00	.60
190	Mickey Owen	2.00	1.00	.60
191	Hughie Critz	2.00	1.00	.60
192	Ethan Allen	2.00	1.00	.60
193	Billy Rogell	2.00	1.00	.60
194	Joe Kuhel	2.00	1.00	.60
195	Dale Mitchell	2.00	1.00	.60
196	Eldon Auker	2.00	1.00	.60
197	Johnny Beazley	2.00	1.00	.60
198	Spud Chandler	2.00	1.00	.60
199	Ralph Branca	2.00	1.00	.60
200	Joe Cronin	2.00	1.00	.60

1957-58 Graphics Arts Service Detroit Tigers Postcards

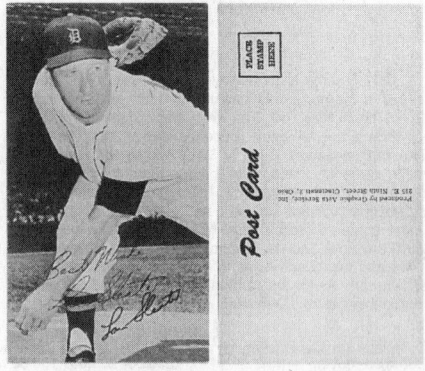

This series of Tigers postcards was issued over a two-year span by a Cincinnati printer. The 3-3/16" x 5-7/16" cards have a black-and-white borderless player photo on front with or without a facsimile autograph. Backs have standard postcard indicia, including the producer's name and address.

		NM	EX	VG
Complete Set (22):		1,500	750.00	450.00
Common Player:		60.00	30.00	18.00
(1)	Al Aber	60.00	30.00	18.00
(2)	Hank Aguirre	60.00	30.00	18.00
(3)	Reno Bertoia/Fldg	60.00	30.00	18.00
(4)	Reno Bertoia/Portrait	60.00	30.00	18.00
(5)	Frank Bolling	60.00	30.00	18.00

(6)	Jim Bunning	120.00	60.00	35.00
(7)	Jack Dittmer	60.00	30.00	18.00
(8)	Paul Foytack	60.00	30.00	18.00
(9)	Jim Hegan	60.00	30.00	18.00
(10)	Tommy Henrich	80.00	40.00	24.00
(11)	Billy Hoeft	60.00	30.00	18.00
(12)	Frank House	60.00	30.00	18.00
(13)	Al Kaline	180.00	90.00	55.00
(14)	Harvey Kuenn	80.00	40.00	24.00
(15)	Don Lee	60.00	30.00	18.00
(16)	Billy Martin	90.00	45.00	25.00
(17)	Tom Morgan	60.00	30.00	18.00
(18)	J.W. Porter	60.00	30.00	18.00
(19)	Ron Samford	60.00	30.00	18.00
(20)	Bob Shaw	60.00	30.00	18.00
(21)	Lou Sleater	60.00	30.00	18.00
(22)	Tim Thompson	60.00	30.00	18.00

1888 Gray Studio Cabinets

The posed action photos on the approximately 4-1/4" x 6-1/2" cards are the same pictures seen on many of the players' Old Judge and Old Judge cabinet cards. Gray cabinets are found with two fancy logotypes at lower-left. On one, the tail of the "y" underscores the "Gra," while on the other, fancy decorations bookend the studio name. The Boston address of the studio is at lower-right. Players are not identified on the cards, and the backs are blank.

		NM	EX	VG
Common Player:		1,500	700.00	450.00
(1)	Charlie Buffinton/Btg	1,500	700.00	450.00
(2)	Charlie Buffinton (Right arm forward.)	1,500	700.00	450.00
(3)	Dan Casey (Arms at sides.)	1,500	700.00	450.00
(4)	Dan Casey (Ball in hands at chest.)	1,500	700.00	450.00
(5)	Dan Casey (Left arm outstretched.)	1,500	700.00	450.00
(6)	Jack Clements/Btg	1,500	700.00	450.00
(7)	Jack Clements/Fldg (Hands chest-high.)	1,500	700.00	450.00
(8)	Jack Clements (Hands on knees.)	1,500	700.00	450.00
(12)	Ed Daily/Btg	1,500	700.00	450.00
(13)	Ed Daily (Holding ball in front of face.)	1,500	700.00	450.00
(14)	Ed Daily/Throwing	1,500	700.00	450.00
(16)	Sid Farrar (Arms crossed.)	1,500	700.00	450.00
(17)	Sid Farrar (Fielding grounder.)	1,500	700.00	450.00
(18)	Sid Farrar (Fielding fly ball.)	1,500	700.00	450.00
(19)	Sid Farrar (Right hand on belt buckle.)	1,500	700.00	450.00
(21)	Charlie Ferguson (Ball in hands at chest.)	1,500	700.00	450.00
(22)	Charlie Ferguson/btg	1,500	700.00	450.00
(23)	Charlie Ferguson (Tagging Tommy McCarthy.)	1,800	900.00	550.00
(24)	Charlie Ferguson/Throwing (Right arm back.)	1,500	700.00	450.00
(26)	Jim Fogarty/Btg	1,500	700.00	450.00
(27)	Jim Fogarty (Fielding grounder.)	1,500	700.00	450.00
(28)	Jim Fogarty (Fielding, hands at neck.)	1,500	700.00	450.00
(29)	Jim Fogarty (Fielding on the run.)	1,500	700.00	450.00
(32)	Tom Gunning/Fldg (Hands at knees.)	1,500	700.00	450.00
(33)	Arthur Irwin/Btg	1,500	700.00	450.00
(34)	Arthur Irwin/Fldg (Hands chest-high.)	1,500	700.00	450.00
(35)	Arthur Irwin/Throwing	1,500	700.00	450.00
(39)	Tommy McCarthy/Btg	3,000	1,500	900.00
(40)	Tommy McCarthy/Fldg (Hands chest-high.)	3,000	1,500	900.00
(41)	Tommy McCarthy (Tagging baserunner.)	3,000	1,500	900.00
(42)	Tommy McCarthy/Throwing	3,000	1,500	900.00
(44)	Deacon McGuire/Btg	1,500	700.00	450.00
(45)	Deacon McGuire/Fldg (Hands chest-high.)	1,500	700.00	450.00
(48)	Joe Mulvey/Btg	1,500	700.00	450.00
(49)	Joe Mulvey/Fldg (Hands at waist.)	1,500	700.00	450.00
(50)	Joe Mulvey (Watching ball.)	1,500	700.00	450.00
(60)	George Wood/Btg	1,500	700.00	450.00
(61)	George Wood (Fielding fly ball.)	1,500	700.00	450.00
(62)	George Wood (Fielding grounder.)	1,500	700.00	450.00
(63)	George Wood/Throwing	1,500	700.00	450.00

1975-76 Great Plains Greats

This collectors' issue was issued in two series in conjunction with shows conducted by the Great Plains Sports Collectors Association. Cards are about 2-5/8" x 3-3/4". Fronts have black-and-white photos with heavy colored frames and white borders. Player name is overprinted on a diamond at bottom. Backs have a career summary and stats, and a sponsor's ad. The 1975 issue (#1-24) was sponsored by Sheraton Inns; the 1976 cards (#25-42) were sponsored by Nu-Sash Corp.

		NM	EX	VG
Complete Set (43):		20.00	10.00	6.00
Common Player:		1.00	.50	.30
1	Bob Feller	2.00	1.00	.60
2	Carl Hubbell	1.00	.50	.30
3	Jocko Conlan	1.00	.50	.30
4	Hal Trosky	1.00	.50	.30
5	Allie Reynolds	1.00	.50	.30
6	Burleigh Grimes	1.00	.50	.30
7	Jake Beckley	1.00	.50	.30
8	Al Simmons	1.00	.50	.30
9	Paul Waner	1.00	.50	.30
10	Chief Bender	1.00	.50	.30
11	Fred Clarke	1.00	.50	.30
12	Jim Bottomley	1.00	.50	.30
13	Dave Bancroft	1.00	.50	.30
14	Bing Miller	1.00	.50	.30
15	Walter Johnson	2.50	1.25	.70
16	Grover Alexander	2.50	1.25	.70
17	Bob Johnson	1.00	.50	.30
18	Roger Maris	2.50	1.25	.70
19	Ken Keltner	1.00	.50	.30
20	Red Faber	1.00	.50	.30
21	"Cool Papa" Bell	1.00	.50	.30
22	Yogi Berra	2.50	1.25	.70
23	Fred Lindstrom	1.00	.50	.30
24	Ray Schalk	1.00	.50	.30
---	Checklist	.10	.05	.03
25	Lloyd Waner	1.00	.50	.30
26	Johnny Hopp	1.00	.50	.30
27	Mel Harder	1.00	.50	.30
28	Dutch Leonard	1.00	.50	.30
29	Bob O'Farrell	1.00	.50	.30
30	Cap Anson	1.00	.50	.30
31	Dazzy Vance	1.00	.50	.30
32	Red Schoendienst	1.00	.50	.30
33	George Pipgras	1.00	.50	.30
34	Harvey Kuenn	1.00	.50	.30
35	Red Ruffing	1.00	.50	.30
36	Roy Sievers	1.00	.50	.30
37	Ken Boyer	1.00	.50	.30
38	Al Smith	1.00	.50	.30
39	Casey Stengel	1.00	.50	.30
40	Bob Gibson	1.50	.70	.45
41	Mickey Mantle	10.00	5.00	3.00
42	Denny McLain	1.00	.50	.30

1908-1909 Greenfield's Chocolates Postcards

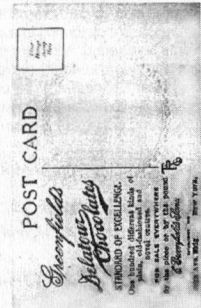

These special advertising versions of the Rose Co. postcards were produced circa 1908-09. The 3-1/2" x 5-1/2" cards feature a black-and-white player portrait photo at center, surrounded by an embossed round gold frame. The player's surname and (usually) team are in a white panel under the photo. The background is green and includes crossed bats and a baseball, a diamond diagram and pictures of a fielder and batter. The postcard-format back is printed in black-and-white with a TRC logo at bottom-center. Printed at left in ornate typography is advertising for the New York confectioner. Two back styles are known apparently the result of the candy company's move from Fifth Ave. to Barclay St. (or vice versa) during the issuing period. It is unknown how many of the player postcards in the Rose Co. series can be found with this advertising on back.

(See 1908-1909 Rose Company Postcards for checklist and base values.)
PREMIUM: 3-5X

1916 Green-Joyce

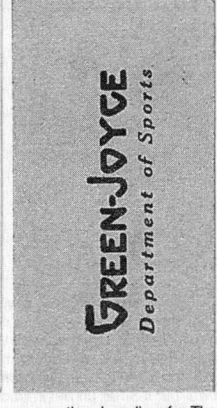

BOB BESCHER
L.F.—St. Louis Cardinals
15

Best known for its use as a promotional medium for The Sporting News, this 200-card set can be found with blank backs or with ads on the back for several local and regional businesses. Among them is Green-Joyce "Department of Sports," location Columbus, OH. Type-card and superstar collectors can expect to pay a premiu, for individual cards with Green- Joyce advertising as opposed to the more common M101-4 blank-back values. Cards measure 1-5/8" x 3" and are printed in black-and-white.

	NM	EX	VG
Common Player:	900.00	450.00	275.00
Stars: 12-20X			

(See 1916 M101-4 Blank Backs for checklist and base values.)

1969 Greiner Tires Pittsburgh Pirates

Good Luck to Roberto Clemente and Pittsburgh Pirates
from
GREINER TIRE SERVICE
Route 30 West   Phone 527-2841   Jeanette, Pa.

One of the scarcer of the many Pirates regionals of the late 1960s is this eight-card issue. Printed on heavy paper in black-and-white, the 5-1/2" x 8-1/2" cards are blank-backed and unnumbered. They are checklisted here alphabetically. Some sources say the Matty Alou card is scarcer than the rest of the set.

		NM	EX	VG
Complete Set (8):		80.00	40.00	24.00
Common Player:		4.50	2.25	1.25
(1)	Gene Alley	4.50	2.25	1.25
(2)	Matty Alou	30.00	15.00	9.00
(3)	Steve Blass	4.50	2.25	1.25
(4)	Roberto Clemente	30.00	15.00	9.00
(5)	Jerry May	4.50	2.25	1.25
(6)	Bill Mazeroski	12.50	6.25	3.75
(7)	Larry Shepard	4.50	2.25	1.25
(8)	Willie Stargell	12.50	6.25	3.75

1928 Greiners Bread

This set of about 1-3/8" x 2-1/2" black-and-white cards is believed to parallel the W502 strip card set. Only a few examples are known, and they are too scarce to price.

		NM	EX	VG
Complete Set (60):				
Common Player:				
1	Burleigh Grimes			
2	Walter Reuther (Ruether)			
3	Joe Dugan			
4	Red Faber			
5	Gabby Hartnett			
6	Babe Ruth			
7	Bob Meusel			
8	Herb Pennock			
9	George Burns			
10	Joe Sewell			
11	George Uhle			
12	Bob O'Farrell			
13	Rogers Hornsby			
14	"Pie" Traynor			
15	Clarence Mitchell			
16	Eppa Jepha Rixey			
17	Carl Mays			
18	Adolfo Luque			
19	Dave Bancroft			
20	George Kelly			
21	Earl (Earle) Combs			
22	Harry Heilmann			
23	Ray W. Schalk			
24	Johnny Mostil			
25	Hack Wilson			
26	Lou Gehrig			
27	Ty Cobb			
28	Tris Speaker			
29	Tony Lazzeri			
30	Waite Hoyt			
31	Sherwood Smith			
32	Max Carey			
33	Eugene Hargrave			
34	Miguel L. Gonzales (Miguel A. Gonzalez)			
35	Joe Judge			
36	E.C. (Sam) Rice			
37	Earl Sheely			
38	Sam Jones			
39	Bib (Bibb) A. Falk			
40	Willie Kamm			
41	Stanley Harris			
42	John J. McGraw			
43	Artie Nehf			
44	Grover Alexander			
45	Paul Waner			
46	William H. Terry			
47	Glenn Wright			
48	Earl Smith			
49	Leon (Goose) Goslin			
50	Frank Frisch			
51	Joe Harris			
52	Fred (Cy) Williams			
53	Eddie Roush			
54	George Sisler			
55	Ed. Rommel			
56	Rogers Peckinpaugh (Roger)			
57	Stanley Coveleskie (Coveleski)			
58	Lester Bell			
59	L. Waner			
60	John P. McInnis			

1974 Greyhound Heroes on the Base Paths

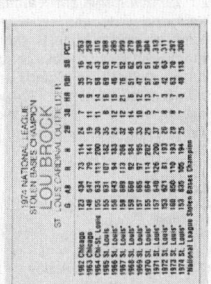

The first of three annual baseball card folders honoring the stolen base leaders and runners-up in each league, this 20" x 9" five-panel sheet features six 4" x 3" cards printed in black-and-white with sepia graphics. Backs are printed in black, brown and white. Besides the cards, the folder contains information about the bus company's award, as well as major league stolen base records and base-stealing tips. Besides individual cards of the 1974 winner and runner-up in each league, the folder has cards picturing all winners and runners-up since 1965.

		NM	EX	VG
Complete Set, Folder:		10.00	5.00	3.00
Complete Set, Singles:		8.00	4.00	2.50
Common Player:		2.00	1.00	.60
(1)	Lou Brock	4.00	2.00	1.25
(2)	Rod Carew	4.00	2.00	1.25
(3)	Davey Lopes	2.00	1.00	.60
(4)	Bill North	2.00	1.00	.60
(5)	A.L. Winners/Runners-Up (Don Buford, Bert Campaneris, Rod Carew, Tommy Harper, Dave Nelson, Bill North, Amos Otis, Fred Patek)	2.00	1.00	.60
(6)	N.L. Winners/Runners-Up (Lou Brock, Jose Cardenal, Sonny Jackson, Davey Lopes, Joe Morgan, Bobby Tolan, Maury Wills)	2.00	1.00	.60

1975 Greyhound Heroes on the Base Paths

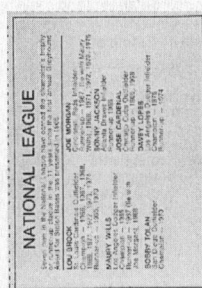

Six perforated 3-7/8" x 3" cards are featured on this folded five-panel 20" x 9" sheet honoring top base stealers in both leagues for the 1975 season. Four of the cards have each league's SB leader and runner-up in a black-and-white portrait photo with blue background. Backs are printed in black, blue and white and include major league stats. There are also two action photo cards with lists on the back of each year's winner and runner-up for the Greyhound Stolen Base Awards since 1965.

	NM	EX	VG
Complete Set, Folder:	7.00	3.50	2.00
Complete Set, Singles:	4.00	2.00	1.25
Common Player:	1.50	.70	.45
(1) Davey Lopes	1.50	.70	.45
(2) Davey Lopes/Action	1.50	.70	.45
(3) Joe Morgan	2.50	1.25	.70
(4) Bill North/Action	1.50	.70	.45
(5) Mickey Rivers	1.50	.70	.45
(6) Claudell Washington	1.50	.70	.45

1976 Greyhound Heroes on the Base Paths

 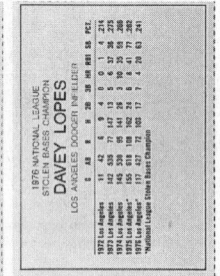

The last of three annual baseball card folders honoring the stolen base leaders and runners-up in each league, this 20" x 9" five-panel sheet features six 4" x 3" cards printed in black-and-white with sepia graphics. Backs are printed in black, brown and white. Besides the cards, the folder contains information about the bus company's award, as well as major league stolen base records and base-stealing tips. Besides individual cards of the 1974 winner and runner-up in each league, the folder includes two action-photo cards listing all winners and runners-up since 1965.

	NM	EX	VG
Complete Set, Folder:	6.00	3.00	1.75
Complete Set, Singles:	5.00	2.50	1.50
Common Player:	1.50	.70	.45
(1) Ronald Le Flore	1.50	.70	.45
(2) Davey Lopes	1.50	.70	.45
(3) Davey Lopes/Action	1.50	.70	.45
(4) Joe Morgan	3.00	1.50	.90
(5) Bill North	1.50	.70	.45
(6) Bill North/Action	1.50	.70	.45

1907 Grignon Chicago Cubs Postcards

The eventual 1907 World Champion Cubs are featured in this set of novelty postcards. Fronts of the 3-1/2" x 5-1/2" horizontal cards have a green background with white border. The central figure on each is a teddy bear in a baseball pose. In an upper corner is a black-and-white circular portrait of one of the Cubs, with identification below. A line of infield chatter - i.e., "This is a Cinch" - completes the design. Backs have standard postcard markings and some have been seen with advertising for local businesses. The unnumbered cards are checklisted here alphabetically.

	NM	EX	VG
Complete Set (16):	12,000	6,000	3,500
Common Player:	475.00	235.00	140.00
(1) Mordecai Brown	1,600	800.00	480.00
(2) Frank Chance	1,600	800.00	480.00
(3) John Evers	1,600	800.00	480.00
(4) Arthur Hofman	475.00	235.00	140.00
(5) John Kling	475.00	235.00	140.00
(6) Carl Lundgren	475.00	235.00	140.00
(7) Pat Moran	475.00	235.00	140.00
(8) Orvie Overall	475.00	235.00	140.00
(9) Jack Pfeister	475.00	235.00	140.00
(10) Ed Reulbach	475.00	235.00	140.00
(11) Frank Schulte	475.00	235.00	140.00
(12) James Sheckard	475.00	235.00	140.00
(13) James Slagle	475.00	235.00	140.00
(14) Harry Steinfeldt	475.00	235.00	140.00
(15) Jack Taylor	475.00	235.00	140.00
(16) Joe Tinker	1,600	800.00	480.00

"1959-60" Gulf Oil Corporation

These fantasy/fraud cards were first reported in the hobby in 1999, though the copyright line on back purports to date them from 1959-1960. Two types of cards were produced, one series of eight featuring line-art portraits, the other featuring re-screened photos taken from team photo packs and similar sources. Cards are 2-1/2" x 3-1/2" printed in black-and-white. The unnumbered cards are checklisted here alphabetically within series. Because the cards were illegally produced in violation of player rights and team copyrights, no collector value is attributed.

Complete Set (16):
Artwork Series
(1) Ty Cobb
(2) Bill Dickey
(3) Joe DiMaggio
(4) Lou Gehrig
(5) Rogers Hornsby
(6) Walter Johnson
(7) Babe Ruth
(8) Pie Traynor
Photo Series
(1) Don Drysdale
(2) Bob Gibson
(3) Sandy Koufax
(4) Mickey Mantle
(5) Roger Maris
(6) Willie Mays
(7) Willie McCovey
(8) Stan Musial

1956 Gum Products Adventure

 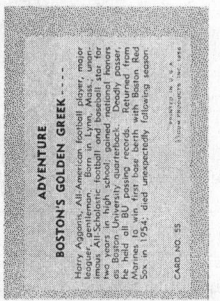

This series of 100 cards depicts all manner of action and adventure scenes, including several sports subjects, one of which is a baseball player. The card depicts Boston U. quarterback and Boston Red Sox prospect Harry Agganis, who died unexpectedly in 1955. The 3-1/2" x 2-1/2" horizontal card has a central portrait artwork of Agganis as a Red Sox, surrounded by other scenes from his personal and sporting life. The black-and-white back has a short biography.

		NM	EX	VG
55	Harry Agganis (Boston's Golden Greek)	25.00	12.50	7.50

1948 Gunther Beer Washington Senators Postcards

These postcards were apparently made available by writing to the radio voice of the Senators, Arch McDonald. A preprinted message on the left side of the back urges the fan to keep listening to McDonald's program, sponsored by "Gunther's, the dry, beery beer." The black-and-white cards

measure 3-1/2" x 5-1/2" and feature portrait photos of the Washington players. Most cards have two players side-by-side while manager Joe Kuhel has his own card. Player names are in heavy black letters across their chests. The cards are unnumbered and it is possible others will surface.

	NM	EX	VG
Complete Set (11):	3,000	1,500	900.00
Common Card:	285.00	140.00	85.00
(1) Joe Kuhel	285.00	140.00	85.00
(2) Gil Coan, Mickey Vernon	285.00	140.00	85.00
(3) Al Evans, Scott Cary	285.00	140.00	85.00
(4) Tom Ferrick, Harold Keller	285.00	140.00	85.00
(5) Mickey Haefner, Forrest Thompson	285.00	140.00	85.00
(6) Sid Hudson, Al Kozar	285.00	140.00	85.00
(7) Walter Masterson, Rick Ferrell	325.00	160.00	95.00
(8) Tom McBride, Milo Candini	285.00	140.00	85.00
(9) Marino Pieretti, Leon Culberson	285.00	140.00	85.00
(10) Sherrard Robertson, Eddie Lyons	285.00	140.00	85.00
(11) Ray Scarborough, Kenneth McCreight	285.00	140.00	85.00
(12) Early Wynn, Eddie Yost	400.00	200.00	120.00

1888 Gutenkunst Philadelphia Athletics Cabinets

The issue date for this series of cabinet cards is speculative and cannot be more definitely pinpointed unless or until other players are found; all five known subjects played together 1887-1889. The cards were produced by the studio of Frederick Gutenkunst and are in the standard 4-1/4" x 6-1/2" format with sepia toned player photos. This checklist is likely incomplete and gaps in the assigned numbering have been left for future additions.

	NM	EX	VG
Common Card:	3,500	1,750	1,050
(1) Lou Bierbauer	3,500	1,750	1,050
(4) Henry Larkin	3,500	1,750	1,050
(5) Denny Lyons	3,500	1,750	1,050
(8) Wilbert Robinson	7,500	3,750	2,250
(10) Ed Seward	3,500	1,750	1,050

1923-1924 Tomas Gutierrez

The largest of the Cuban baseball card issues of the 1920s, this is also one of the scarcest and most popular. Printed in dark brown (some backs are in black) on sepia paper, the 1-5/8" x 2-3/8" cards were inserted into packs of Diaz cigarettes. Cards have portrait photos on front with team name at top and the player name (sometimes misspelled and sometimes a nickname) and position below. Backs, which can be found in three styles, have the card number and an offer for an album. It is the album offer which accounts for much of this issue's scarcity. The album was a hardcover, ornate book with pictures of each card pre-printed. It is believed that the album was available by turning in a complete set of the cards, which were not returned. Adding to the set's popularity is its inclusion of many Negro Leagues players including future Hall of Famers Oscar Charleston and Pop Lloyd. Following the checklist are the names of cards known to exist from their presence in the album, but whose number is unknkown.

		NM	EX	VG
Complete Set (85): Value Undetermined				
Common Player:		350.00	140.00	70.00
Album:		4,500	2,250	1,350
SANTA CLARA				
1	(Agustin) "Tinti" Molina	350.00	140.00	70.00
2	Julio Rojo	450.00	180.00	90.00
3	Frank Duncan	1,750	700.00	350.00
4	Eustaquio "Bombin" Pedroso	2,250	900.00	450.00
5	Dave Brown	2,250	900.00	450.00
6	Pedro Dibut	450.00	180.00	90.00
7	Rube Currie	1,750	700.00	350.00
8	Jose Mendez	6,000	2,400	1,200
9	Esteban "Mayari" Montalvo	850.00	340.00	170.00
10	Frank Warfield	1,750	700.00	350.00
11	Oliver Marcelle	2,250	900.00	450.00
12	Dobie Moore	1,750	700.00	350.00
13	Herman Matias Rios	350.00	140.00	70.00
14	Oscar Charleston	30,000	15,000	9,000
15	Alejandro Oms	2,250	900.00	450.00
16	Pablo "Champion" Mesa	850.00	340.00	170.00
17	Bill Holland	2,250	900.00	450.00
18	Oscar "Heavy" Johnson	2,250	900.00	450.00
ALMENDARES				
19	Eugenio Morin	350.00	140.00	70.00
20	Snake Henry	350.00	140.00	70.00
21	Manuel Cueto	350.00	140.00	70.00
22	Jesse Hubbard	850.00	340.00	170.00
23	Kakin Gonzalez	350.00	140.00	70.00

		NM	EX	VG
24	Jose Maria Fernandez	350.00	140.00	70.00
25	Oscar Rodriguez	350.00	140.00	70.00
26	Lucas Boada	350.00	140.00	70.00
27	Eusebio "Papo" Gonzalez	350.00	140.00	70.00
28	Ramon "Paito" Herrera	350.00	140.00	70.00
29	Bernardo Baro	850.00	340.00	170.00
30	Armando Marsans	1,200	480.00	240.00
31	Isidro Fabre	850.00	340.00	170.00
32	Oscar Fuhr	350.00	140.00	70.00
33	Valentin Dreke	850.00	340.00	170.00
34	Joseito Rodriguez	350.00	140.00	70.00
35	Jose "Cheo" Ramos	350.00	140.00	70.00
36	Willis "Pud" Flournoy	1,200	480.00	240.00
37	Oscar Tuero	350.00	140.00	70.00
38	Rafael Almeida	850.00	340.00	170.00
39	Almendares Pennant	350.00	140.00	70.00

MARIANAO

		NM	EX	VG
40	Chuck Dressen	600.00	300.00	180.00
41	Don Brown	350.00	140.00	70.00
42	Merito Acosta	350.00	140.00	70.00
43	(Ed) Morris	350.00	140.00	70.00
44	Ernie Krueger	350.00	140.00	70.00
45	Pepin Perez	350.00	140.00	70.00
46	(Harry) McCurdy	350.00	140.00	70.00
47	Jose "Acostica" Acosta	350.00	140.00	70.00
48	Jacinto Calvo	350.00	140.00	70.00
49	(Eddie) Brown	350.00	140.00	70.00
50	(Rosy) Ryan	350.00	140.00	70.00
51	Rogelio Crespo	350.00	140.00	70.00
52	Hank Deberry	350.00	140.00	70.00
53	(Art) Phelan	350.00	140.00	70.00
54	Jess Petty	500.00	250.00	150.00
55	(Jimmy) Cooney	350.00	140.00	70.00
56a	H. Scheiber	350.00	140.00	70.00
	(Hank Schreiber)/Infielder			
56b	H. Scheiber	350.00	140.00	70.00
	(Hank Schreiber)/Infielder			
57				
58	Maianaro Pennant	350.00	140.00	70.00
59	Bienvenido Jimenez	350.00	140.00	70.00
---	Otis Brannan	350.00	140.00	70.00
---	Emilio Palmero	350.00	140.00	70.00

HAVANA

		NM	EX	VG
60	Buste Ross	350.00	140.00	70.00
61	Juanelo Mirabal	350.00	140.00	70.00
62	Cristobal Torriente	17,500	7,000	3,500
63	John Henry "Pop" Lloyd	30,000	15,000	9,000
64	Oscar Levis	700.00	280.00	140.00
65	Pelayo Chacon	850.00	340.00	170.00
66	Eufemio Abreu	350.00	140.00	70.00
67	Mack Eggleston	850.00	340.00	170.00
68	(Tauca "Manzanillo") Campos	350.00	140.00	70.00
69	Raphael "Busta" Quintana	350.00	140.00	70.00
70	Merven "Red" Ryan	850.00	340.00	170.00
71	(Danny) Clark	350.00	140.00	70.00
72	Clint Thomas	1,000	400.00	200.00
73	Adolfo Luque	1,200	480.00	240.00
74	Marcelino Guerra	350.00	140.00	70.00
75	Bartolo Portuondo	850.00	340.00	170.00
76	Andy Cooper	6,000	2,400	1,200
77	(John) Bischoff	350.00	140.00	70.00
78	Edgar Wesley	1,750	700.00	350.00
79	Havana Pennant	350.00	140.00	70.00
---	Jacinto Calvo	300.00	120.00	60.00

MISCELLANEOUS

		NM	EX	VG
80	Hector Magrinat/Umpire	350.00	140.00	70.00
81	Valentin "Sirique" Gonzalez/Umpire	350.00	140.00	70.00
82	Slim Love (Marianao)	350.00	140.00	70.00
83	Cristobal Torriente (Marianao)	22,500	11,250	6,750
84				
85	Jakie May (Almendares)	450.00	180.00	90.00

1887 Gypsy Queen (N175)

The 1887 Gypsy Queen set is very closely related to the N172 Old Judge set and employs the same photos. Gypsy Queens are easily identified by the advertising along the top. A line near the bottom lists the player's name, position and team, followed by an 1887 copyright line and words "Cigarettes" and "Goodwin & Co. N.Y." Although the checklist is still considered incomplete, some 140 different poses have been discovered so far. Gypsy Queens were issued in two distinct sizes, the more common version measuring 1-1/2" x 2-1/2" (same as Old Judge) and a larger size measuring 2" x 3-1/2" which are considered extremely rare. The large Gypsy Queens are identical in format to the smaller size; the nine known examples are designated here.

		NM	EX	VG
	Common Player:	3,300	1,650	1,200
(13 1)	J. (Tug) Arundel/Fldg	3,300	1,650	1,200
(13 2)	J. (Tug) Arundel/Btg	3,300	1,650	1,200
(17)	Mark Baldwin	3,300	1,650	1,200
(19 1)	Sam Barkley/Fldg	3,300	1,650	1,200
(19 2)	Sam Barkley (Tagging player.)	3,300	1,650	1,200
(19 3)	Sam Barkley/Throwing	3,300	1,650	1,200
(35)	Henry Boyle	3,300	1,650	1,200
	(Right arm outstretched.)			
(43 1)	Dan Brouthers	8,250	4,125	2,475
	(Looking at ball.)			
(43 2)	Dan Brouthers	8,250	4,125	2,475
	(Looking to right.)			
(44 1)	Tom Brown	3,300	1,650	1,200
	(Pittsburgh, bat at side.)			
(44 2)	Tom Brown/Catching	3,300	1,650	1,200
	(Pittsburgh)			
(45L)	Willard /Throwing (California)	20,625	10,300	6,200
	Brown (N.Y., large)			
(45 1)	Willard/Throwing (California)	3,300	1,650	1,200
	Brown (N.Y.)			
(45 2)	Willard (California) Brown	3,800	1,900	1,125
	(N.Y., wearing mask.)			
(50)	Charlie Buffington (Buffinton)	3,300	1,650	1,200
	(Bat at 45 degrees.)			
(51)	Ernie Burch/Fldg (Hands	4,000	1,650	1,200
	above head, outdoors.)			
(53)	Jack Burdock	4,000	1,650	1,200
	(Fielding grounder.)			
(55)	Watch Burnham	3,300	1,650	1,200
(59)	Tom Burns	3,300	1,650	1,200
(60)	Doc Bushong	5,850	2,925	1,750
	(Brown's Champions)			
(61)	John (Patsy) Cahill	3,300	1,650	1,200
(68)	Fred Carroll (Bat at side.)	3,300	1,650	1,200
(71)	Bob Caruthers	3,300	1,650	1,200
(72 1)	Dan Casey (Hands at chest.)	3,800	1,900	1,125
(72 2)	Dan Casey	3,300	1,650	1,200
	(Left arm extended.)			
(79 1)	Jack Clements	3,300	1,650	1,200
	(Hands on knees.)			
(79 2)	Jack Clements (With bat.)	3,300	1,650	1,200
(83)	John Coleman (Bat at side.)	3,300	1,650	1,200
(86)	Charlie Comiskey	8,250	4,125	2,475
(88 1)	Roger Connor	29,150	15,450	9,300
	(Hands on knees.)			
(88 2)	Roger Connor	8,250	4,125	2,475
	(Bat at 45 degrees.)			
(89)	Dick Conway	3,300	1,650	1,200
(94)	Larry Corcoran	3,300	1,650	1,200
(97 1)	Sam Crane	3,300	1,650	1,200
	(Fielding grounder.)			
(97 2)	Sam Crane (With bat.)	3,300	1,650	1,200
(109)	Ed Dailey	3,300	1,650	1,200
(113)	Abner Dalrymple	3,300	1,650	1,200
	(Right arm cap-high.)			
(117)	Dell Darling	3,300	1,650	1,200
(121 1)	Pat Dealey (Bat at side.)	3,300	1,650	1,200
(121 2)	Pat Dealey (Bat on shoulder.)	3,300	1,650	1,200
(125L)	Jerry Denny (Large, with bat.)	20,625	10,300	6,200
(125 1)	Jerry Denny/Catching	3,300	1,650	1,200
(125 2)	Jerry Denny (With bat.)	3,300	1,650	1,200
(130)	Jim Donnelly	3,300	1,650	1,200
	(Bat at 45 degrees.)			
(133)	Mike Dorgan (Arms crossed.)	3,300	1,650	1,200
(149L)	Buck Ewing	32,000	15,450	9,300
	(Large, catching fly ball.)			
(149 1)	Buck Ewing	8,250	4,125	2,475
	(Bat at 45 degrees.)			
(149 2)	Buck Ewing (Fielding fly ball.)	8,250	4,125	2,475
(149 3)	Buck Ewing	8,250	4,125	2,475
	(Fielding ground ball.)			
(156 1)	Jack Farrell (Bat at side.)	3,300	1,650	1,200
(156 2)	Jack Farrell (Bat in air.)	3,300	1,650	1,200
(156 3)	Jack Farrell/Fldg	3,300	1,650	1,200
(156 4)	Jack Farrell (Hands on thighs.)	3,300	1,650	1,200
(158 1)	Charlie Ferguson	4,000	1,650	1,200
	(Hands at chest.)			
(158 2)	Charlie Ferguson	6,500	3,200	1,950
	(Right arm extended back.)			
(158 3)	Charlie Ferguson	3,300	1,650	1,200
	(Tagging player.)			
(158 4)	Charlie Ferguson (With bat.)	3,300	1,650	1,200
(161 1)	Jocko Fields/Catching	3,300	1,650	1,200
(161 2)	Jocko Fields (Tagging player.)	3,800	1,900	1,125
(161 3)	Jocko Fields/Throwing	3,300	1,650	1,200
(167 1)	Jim Fogarty (Bat on shoulder.)	3,300	1,650	1,200
(167 2)	Jim Fogarty (Fielding fly ball.)	3,300	1,650	1,200
(171)	Dave Foutz	5,850	2,925	1,750
	(Brown's Champions)			
(178)	John Gaffney	3,300	1,650	1,200
	(Bending to right.)			
(171 1)	Pud Galvin (Leaning on bat.)	11,000	5,500	3,250
(171 2)	Pud Galvin (Without bat.)	11,000	5,500	3,250
(184 1)	Emil Geiss	3,300	1,650	1,200
	(Hands above waist.)			
(184 2)	Emil Geiss	3,300	1,650	1,200
	(Right hand extended.)			
(191 1)	Pete Gillespie (Fielding)	3,300	1,650	1,200
(191 2)	Pete Gillespie (With bat.)	3,300	1,650	1,200
(192)	Barney Gilligan	3,300	1,650	1,200
(194 1)	Jack Glasscock	4,750	2,400	1,400
	(Hands on knees.)			
(194 2)	Jack Glasscock/Throwing	4,750	2,400	1,400
(194 3)	Jack Glasscock (With bat.)	4,750	2,400	1,400
(195)	Bill Gleason	5,850	2,925	1,700
	(Brown's Champions)			
(199 1)	George Gore/Fldg	3,300	1,650	1,200
(199 2)	George Gore	3,300	1,650	1,200
	(Hand at head level.)			
(202)	Ed Greer (Batting, outdoors.)	5,150	2,600	1,550
(207 1)	Tom Gunning (Stooping to	3,300	1,650	1,200
	catch low ball on left.)			
(207 2)	Tom Gunning/Bending	3,300	1,650	1,200
	(Hands by right knee.)			
(215 1)	Ned Hanlon/Catching	8,250	4,125	2,475

		NM	EX	VG
(215 2)	Ned Hanlon	8,250	4,125	2,475
	(Bat at 45 degrees.)			
(218 1)	John Harkins (Hands above	4,000	1,650	1,200
	waist, outdoors.)			
(218 2)	John Harkins	5,150	2,600	1,550
	(Throwing, outdoors.)			
(223)	Egyptian Healey/Btg	3,300	1,650	1,200
	(Healy)			
(232)	Paul Hines (Hands at sides.)	3,300	1,650	1,200
(241)	Joe Horning (Hornung)	3,300	1,650	1,200
	(Bat at 45 degrees.)			
(244)	Nat Hudson	5,850	2,925	1,700
	(Brown's Champions)			
(248 1)	Arthur Irwin/Btg	3,300	1,650	1,200
(248 2)	Arthur Irwin/Fldg	3,300	1,650	1,200
	(Hands below knees.)			
(253 1)	Dick Johnston/Catching	3,300	1,650	1,200
(253 2)	Dick Johnston (With bat.)	3,300	1,650	1,200
(256L)	Tim Keefe (Large, ball in	33,000	16,500	10,000
	hands at chest.)			
(256 1)	Tim Keefe	8,250	4,125	2,475
	(Ball in hands at chest.)			
(256 2)	Tim Keefe (Hands above	8,250	4,125	2,475
	waist, facing front.)			
(256 3)	Tim Keefe (Right hand	8,250	4,125	2,475
	extended at head level.)			
(256 4)	Tim Keefe (With bat.)	8,250	4,125	2,475
(DP 13)	Fielding Ball, Danny	12,000	6,000	3,600
	Richardson Sliding. ("Keefe			
	and Richardson Stealing 2d,			
	N.Y.'s)			
(261L)	King Kelly	55,000	27,000	16,500
	(Large, bat horizontal.)			
(261 1)	King Kelly/Fldg	12,375	6,200	3,700
	(Hands chest-high.)			
(261 2)	King Kelly/Portrait	12,375	6,200	3,700
(261 4)	King Kelly (With bat.)	11,700	5,850	3,500
(262)	Rudy Kemmler	3,300	1,650	1,200
(273 1)	Bill Krieg	3,300	1,650	1,200
	(Fielding thigh-high ball.)			
(273 2)	Bill Krieg (With bat.)	3,300	1,650	1,200
(278)	Arlie Latham	3,300	1,650	1,200
(302 1)	Mike Mattimore	3,300	1,650	1,200
	(Hands above head.)			
(302 2)	Mike Mattimore	3,300	1,650	1,200
	(Hands at neck.)			
(302 3)	Mike Mattimore/Sliding	3,300	1,650	1,200
(307 1)	Tommy McCarthy/Catching	8,250	4,125	2,475
(307 2)	Tommy McCarthy/Sliding	8,250	4,125	2,475
(307 3)	Tommy McCarthy (With bat.)	8,250	4,125	2,475
(309)	Bill McClellan	3,300	1,650	1,200
(311 1)	Jim McCormick	3,300	1,650	1,200
	(Ball in hands at chest.)			
(311 2)	Jim McCormick	3,300	1,650	1,200
	(Bat at 45 degrees.)			
(316 1)	Jack McGeachy	4,000	1,650	1,125
	(Bat at 45 degrees.)			
(316 2)	Jack McGeachy	5,150	2,600	1,550
	(Fielding ball over head.)			
(318 1)	Deacon McGuire/Btg	3,300	1,650	1,200
(318 2)	Deacon McGuire/Catching	3,300	1,650	1,200
(321)	Alex McKinnon/Fldg	3,300	1,650	1,200
	(Hands waist-high.)			
(326 1)	Jim McTamany	4,000	1,650	1,125
	(Bat on shoulder, outdoors.)			
(326 2)	Jim McTamany/Fldg	4,000	1,650	1,125
	(Outdoors)			
(330)	Doggie Miller	3,300	1,650	1,200
(336)	John Morrell (Morrill)	3,800	1,900	1,125
	(Hands on hips.)			
(339)	Joe Mulvey	3,300	1,650	1,200
	(Fiedling ball at waist.)			
(344 1)	Al Myers	3,300	1,650	1,200
	(Washington, bat vertical.)			
(344 2)	Al Myers (Washington,	3,300	1,650	1,200
	hands on knees.)			
(344 3)	Al Myers/Portrait	3,300	1,650	1,200
	(With arms folded.)			
(345 1)	George Myers/Stooping	3,300	1,650	1,200
	(Indianapolis)			
(345 2)	George Myers	3,300	1,650	1,200
	(Indianapolis, with bat.)			
(347)	Billy Nash/Portrait	3,300	1,650	1,200
(353)	Hugh Nicol	9,000	4,500	2,700
	(Brown's Champions)			
(358)	Jack O'Brien (Bat over	3,300	1,650	1,200
	shoulder, outdoors.)			
(362 1)	Hank O'Day (Ball in hand.)	3,300	1,650	1,200
(362 2)	Hank O'Day (With bat.)	3,300	1,650	1,200
(365)	Tip O'Neill	6,425	3,200	1,900
	(Brown's Champions)			
(366)	Orator Jim O'Rourke/Fldg	6,200	3,100	1,850
(367)	Tom O'Rourke	3,300	1,650	1,200
	(Bat at 45 degrees.)			
(371)	Jimmy Peeples	3,300	1,650	1,200
	(Catching, outdoors.)			
(374)	Fred Pfeffer/Throwing	3,300	1,650	1,200
(378)	George Pinkney (Pinckney)	3,300	1,650	1,200
(380)	Henry Porter/Throwing	4,000	1,650	1,125
	(Right hand cap-high,			
	outdoors.)			
(386)	Old Hoss Radbourn (With bat.)	8,250	4,125	2,475
(393L)	Danny Richardson N.Y.,	24,200	12,000	7,200
	large, bat at 45 degrees.)			
(393 1)	Danny Richardson	3,300	1,650	1,200
	(N.Y., bat at 45 degrees.)			
(393 2)	Danny Richardson (N.Y.,	3,300	1,650	1,200
	moving to left, arms at sides.)			
(394)	Hardy Richardson (Detroit)	3,300	1,650	1,200
(396)	John Roach/Btg	3,300	1,650	1,200
(399)	Yank Robinson	6,000	3,000	1,800
	(Brown's Champions)			
(403)	Jack Rowe (Bat at side.)	3,300	1,650	1,200
(405)	Jimmy Ryan (Ball in hands at	3,300	1,650	1,200
	chest.)			
(415 1)	Emmett Seery (Arms folded.)	3,300	1,650	1,200
(415 2)	Emmett Seery (Ball in hands.)	3,300	1,650	1,200
(415 3)	Emmett Seery/Catching	3,300	1,650	1,200

		NM	EX	VG
(425 1)	George Shoch/Btg (W/umpire)	3,300	1,650	1,200
(425 2)	George Schoch (Shoch)/Fldg (Hands head high.)	3,300	1,650	1,200
(426)	Otto Shomberg (Schomberg) (Ball in hands at shoulder.)	3,300	1,650	1,200
(435)	Pop Smith	3,300	1,650	1,200
(446 1)	Bill Stemmyer (Stemmeyer) (Ball in hands at chest.)	3,300	1,650	1,200
(446 2)	Bill Stemmyer (Stemmeyer) (With bat.)	3,300	1,650	1,200
(459 1)	Ezra Sutton/Fldg	3,300	1,650	1,200
(459 2)	Ezra Sutton/Throwing	3,300	1,650	1,200
(459 3)	Ezra Sutton (With bat.)	3,300	1,650	1,200
(460)	Ed Swartwood (Kneeling to field, outdoors.)	5,150	2,600	1,550
(464)	Pop Tate/Fldg	3,300	1,650	1,200
(467)	William "Adonis" Terry (Batting outdoors.)	3,300	1,650	1,200
(468 1)	Sam Thompson (Arms folded.)	8,250	4,125	2,475
(468 2)	Sam Thompson (Bat at side.)	8,250	4,125	2,475
(468 3)	Sam Thompson (Swinging at ball.)	8,250	4,125	2,475
(469L)	Mike Tiernan (Large, fielding fly ball.)	20,625	10,300	6,200
(469)	Mike Tiernan (Fielding grounder.)	3,300	1,650	1,200
(472)	Steve Toole (With bat, outdoors.)	5,150	2,600	1,550
(480 1)	Larry Twitchell (Hands by chest.)	3,300	1,650	1,200
(480 2)	Larry Twitchell (Right hand extended.)	3,300	1,650	1,200
(489)	Chris Von Der Ahe	4,800	2,400	1,375
(491L)	John Ward/Throwing (Large)	32,000	15,450	9,300
(491)	John Ward	14,500	7,250	4,350
(493)	Bill Watkins/Portrait	3,300	1,650	1,200
(498)	Curt Welch	3,300	1,650	1,200
(511 1)	Art Whitney/Bending (Pittsburgh)	3,300	1,650	1,200
(511 2)	Art Whitney (Pittsburgh, with bat.)	3,300	1,650	1,200
(513)	Jim Whitney (Washington, throwing, r. hand waist-high.)	3,300	1,650	1,200
(515)	Ned Williamson/Throwing	4,000	1,650	1,125
(519)	Sam Wise	3,300	1,650	1,200
(521 1)	George Wood/Btg	3,300	1,650	1,200
(521 2)	George Wood/Throwing	3,300	1,650	1,200

H

1953 H-O Instant Oatmeal Records

Baseball playing tips from several star New York players are featured in this set of box-top premium records. For 25 cents and two oatmeal box tops, a set of three of the four records could be ordered by mail. The records are 4-3/4" in diameter and have a color player portrait with facsimile autograph on the back side, while the grooved recording side has an action pose in black-and-white.

		NM	EX	VG
Complete Set (4):		1,050	525.00	315.00
Common Player:		160.00	80.00	48.00
(1)	Roy Campanella	350.00	175.00	105.00
(2)	"Whitey" Lockman	175.00	87.00	52.00
(3)	Allie Reynolds	225.00	110.00	67.00
(4)	Duke Snider	350.00	175.00	105.00

1922 Haffner's Big-Tayto-Loaf Bread

The bakery ad on the back is all that sets this issue apart from the blank-back W575-1 and several other versions with different sponsors named on back. The cards are 2" x 3-1/4" black-and-white. It is unknown whether each of the cards in the W575-1 checklist can be found in the Haffner's version.

PREMIUMS:
Common Players: 5-6X
Hall of Famers: 3-4X
(See W575-1 for checklist and card values.)

1951 Hage's Ice Cream Cleveland Indians

Similar in format to the Pacific Coast League cards produced by the dairy from 1949-51, these cards feature former members of the San Diego Padres, then a farm club of the Indians. Cards measure 2-5/8" x 3-1/8" and are printed in tones of sepia and green. Fronts have posed action photos similar to those found on contemporary Num Num and team photo pack pictures. A small white box on front has the player name and "CLEVELAND." There is a white border around the front photo. Backs are blank and unnumbered; the cards are presented here in alphabetical order.

		NM	EX	VG
Complete Set (10):		5,000	2,500	1,500
Common Player:		850.00	425.00	250.00
(1)	Ray Boone	850.00	425.00	250.00
(2)	Allie Clark	850.00	425.00	250.00
(3)	Luke Easter	900.00	450.00	270.00
(4)	Jesse Flores	850.00	425.00	250.00
(5)	Johnny Gorsica	400.00	200.00	100.00
(6)	Dennis Luby/Fldg	375.00	185.00	110.00
(7)	Al Olsen	850.00	425.00	250.00
(8)	Al Rosen	900.00	450.00	270.00
(9)	Harry Simpson	850.00	425.00	250.00
(10)	George Zuverink	850.00	425.00	250.00

1888 Joseph Hall Cabinets

These cabinet-sized (6-1/2" x 4-1/2") cards feature team photos taken by Joseph Hall, a well-known photographer of the day. Extremely rare, all have Hall's name beneath the photo and some include his Brooklyn address. The team is identified in large capital letters with the individual players identified in smaller type on both sides. Fourteen teams are known to date, but others may also exist, and Hall may have produced similar team cabinets in other years as well.

		NM	EX	VG
Common Team:		12,000	6,000	3,600
(1)	Athletic Ball Club, 1888	12,000	6,000	3,600
(2)	Baltimore Ball Club, 1888	16,800	8,400	5,000
(3)	Boston Ball Club, 1888	18,000	9,000	5,400
(4)	Brooklyn Ball Club, 1888	21,000	10,500	6,300
(5)	Chicago Ball Club, 1888	42,000	21,000	12,000
(6)	Cincinnati Ball Club, 1888	18,000	9,000	5,400
(7)	Cleveland Ball Club, 1888	15,000	7,500	4,500
(8)	Detroit Ball Club, 1888	19,200	9,600	5,800
(9)	Indianapolis Ball Club, 1888	18,000	9,000	5,400
(10)	Kansas City Ball Club, 1888	21,000	10,500	6,300
(11)	Louisville Ball Club, 1888	15,000	7,500	4,500
(12)	New York Ball Club, League Champions - 1889 (Wearing baseball uniforms.)	27,000	13,500	8,100
(13)	New York Ball Club, 1888 (Wearing tuxedos.)	22,000	11,000	6,660
(14)	St. Louis Baseball Club, 1888	15,000	7,500	4,500
(15)	Washington Baseball Club, 1888	48,000	24,000	14,400

1888 Joseph Hall Imperial Cabinets

Besides the standard-sized team-photo cabinet cards, super-sized versions of some (possibly all) teams were also available in a format known to collectors as an imperial cabinet. The large pictures use the same photos as the regular cabinets, enlarged to sizes as diverse as approximately 13" x 10" and 24" x 19" and mounted on heavy black or white backing boards. Printed on the mount in gold are the team name, date, player names and the Joseph Hall studio identification. Only those teams which have actually been observed in this format are listed here, with values generally set by their infrequent appearances in hobby auctions.

		NM	EX	VG
Cincinnati Ball Club, 1888 (13" x 10")		13,750	6,350	3,750
New York Ball Club/1888 (13" x 10")		20,625	9,525	5,625
St. Louis Ball Club - 1888 (24" x 19")		13,750	6,350	3,750

1908 Hall's Studio N.Y. Giants Cabinets

Members of the N.Y. Giants are pictured in this series of approximately 4-1/2" x 6-1/2" cabinet photos from New York City photographer, Hall's Studio. The players are all identically posed bare-headed in white shirts buttoned at the collar. It is unknown whether this checklist is complete.

		NM	EX	VG
Common Player:		600.00	300.00	180.00
(1)	Al Bridwell	600.00	300.00	180.00
(2)	Doc Crandall	600.00	300.00	180.00
(3)	Larry Doyle	600.00	300.00	180.00
(4)	Buck Herzog	600.00	300.00	180.00
(5)	Rube Marquard	800.00	400.00	240.00
(6)	John McGraw	800.00	400.00	240.00
(7)	Fred Merkle	600.00	300.00	180.00

1939-43 Hall of Fame Sepia Postcards

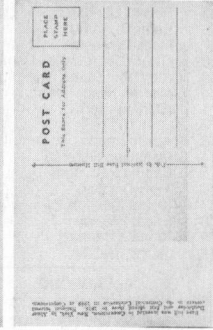

The first Hall of Fame postcards were issued in two types between 1939-1943. They share an identical format and are differentiated by the typography on back, one set having been issued prior to the Hall of Fame's opening in June, 1939, and a later version issued after the opening. The 3-1/2" x 5-1/2" cards are similar in format to the later series printed in black-and-white and various colors, but this initial effort is printed in sepia on a cream-colored background. Most fronts picture the plaque of one of the 25 first inductees, with a wide bottom border to accomodate an autograph. Designated Type 1, this issue has a back caption which ends with, "National interest centers in the Centennial Celebration in 1939 at Cooperstown." The later version, Type 2, ends its description, "The National Base Ball Museum and Hall of Fame and Doubleday Field are maintained here as a Shrine to the national game." On both types, vertically at centers is a credit line "Pub. by National Base Ball Museum." At right are a stamp box and line for the mailing address. The unnumbered cards are listed here in alphabetical order within type.

		NM	EX	VG
Complete Set, Type 1 (35):		3,750	1,850	1,100
Complete Set, Type 2 (37):		3,250	1,625	975.00
Common Card:		50.00	25.00	15.00
	TYPE 1			
(1)	G.C. Alexander	100.00	50.00	30.00
(2)	Adrian Anson	100.00	50.00	30.00
(3)	Morgan Bulkeley	100.00	50.00	30.00
(4)	Alexander Cartwright	100.00	50.00	30.00
(5)	Henry Chadwick	100.00	50.00	30.00
(6)	Ty Cobb	225.00	110.00	65.00
(7)	Eddie Collins	100.00	50.00	30.00
(8)	Chas. Comiskey	100.00	50.00	30.00
(9)	Candy Cummings	100.00	50.00	30.00
(10)	Buck Ewing	100.00	50.00	30.00
(11)	Ban Johnson	100.00	50.00	30.00
(12)	Walter Johnson	175.00	85.00	50.00
(13)	Willie Keeler	100.00	50.00	30.00
(14)	Napoleon Lajoie	100.00	50.00	30.00
(15)	Connie Mack	100.00	50.00	30.00
(16)	Christy Mathewson	175.00	85.00	50.00
(17)	John McGraw	100.00	50.00	30.00
(18)	Chas. Radbourne	100.00	50.00	30.00
(19)	Babe Ruth	450.00	225.00	135.00

(20)	George Sisler	100.00	50.00	30.00
(21)	Al Spalding	100.00	50.00	30.00
(22)	Tris Speaker	100.00	50.00	30.00
(23)	Honus Wagner	200.00	100.00	60.00
(24)	George Wright	100.00	50.00	30.00
(25)	Cy Young	150.00	75.00	45.00
(26)	The Abner Doubleday Baseball	50.00	25.00	15.00
(27)	Abner Doubleday, Major Gen'l	50.00	25.00	15.00
(28)	Doubleday Field in its Original State	50.00	25.00	15.00
(29)	Doubleday Field in 1938	50.00	25.00	15.00
(30)	Exhibition Game on Doubleday Field	50.00	25.00	15.00
(31)	Exterior - Ntl. Baseball Hall of Fame (no title on front)	50.00	25.00	15.00
(32)	Interior - Ntl. Baseball Museum	50.00	25.00	15.00
(33)	The Bust of Christy Mathewson	50.00	25.00	15.00
(34)	Entrance of the Hall of Fame	50.00	25.00	15.00
(35)	Ntl. Baseball Museum "Immortals"	50.00	25.00	15.00

TYPE 2

(1)	G.C. Alexander	100.00	50.00	30.00
(2)	Adrian Anson	100.00	50.00	30.00
(3)	Morgan Bulkeley	100.00	50.00	30.00
(4)	Alexander Cartwright	100.00	50.00	30.00
(5)	Henry Chadwick	100.00	50.00	30.00
(6)	Ty Cobb	225.00	110.00	65.00
(7)	Eddie Collins	100.00	50.00	30.00
(8)	Charles Comiskey	100.00	50.00	30.00
(9)	Candy Cummings	100.00	50.00	30.00
(10)	Buck Ewing	100.00	50.00	30.00
(11)	Lou Gehrig	300.00	150.00	90.00
(12)	Rogers Hornsby	125.00	65.00	35.00
(13)	Ban Johnson	100.00	50.00	30.00
(14)	Walter Johnson	175.00	85.00	50.00
(15)	Willie Keeler	100.00	50.00	30.00
(16)	Napoleon Lajoie	100.00	50.00	30.00
(17)	Connie Mack	100.00	50.00	30.00
(18)	Christy Mathewson	175.00	85.00	50.00
(19)	John McGraw	100.00	50.00	30.00
(20)	Chas. Radbourne	100.00	50.00	30.00
(21)	Babe Ruth	450.00	225.00	135.00
(22)	George Sisler	100.00	50.00	30.00
(23)	Al Spalding	100.00	50.00	30.00
(24)	Tris Speaker	100.00	50.00	30.00
(25)	Honus Wagner	200.00	100.00	60.00
(26)	George Wright	100.00	50.00	30.00
(27)	Cy Young	150.00	75.00	45.00
(28)	The Abner Doubleday Baseball	50.00	25.00	15.00
(29)	Abner Doubleday, Major Gen'l	50.00	25.00	15.00
(30)	Doubleday Field in its Original State	50.00	25.00	15.00
(31)	Doubleday Field in 1938	50.00	25.00	15.00
(32)	Exhibition Game on Doubleday Field	50.00	25.00	15.00
(33)	Exterior - Ntl. Baseball Hall of Fame	50.00	25.00	15.00
(34)	Interior - Ntl. Baseball Hall of Fame	50.00	25.00	15.00
(35)	The Bust of Christy Mathewson	50.00	25.00	15.00
(36)	Entrance of the Hall of Fame	50.00	25.00	15.00
(37)	Ntl. Baseball Museum - "Immortals"	50.00	25.00	15.00

1944-63 Hall of Fame Black-and-White Plaque Postcards

(See listings cataloged under Albertype and Artvue.)

1939-63 Hall of Fame B/W Plaque Postcards - Autographed

Collecting Hall of Fame plaque postcards autographed by inductees has long been popular in the hobby. Obviously, completion of a set is impossible because many Hall of Famers have been inducted posthumously. Generally, the value of a genuinely autographed HoF plaque postcard is not so much dependent on star status of the player, but on the perception of how many such cards could have been autographed in his remaining lifetime. Players who died within months of their induction or who were un-cooperative with autograph requests have cards that are far more valuable than many players of greater renown. While the majority of the players checklisted here could have signed both Albertye and Artvue

cards, some players are possible only on the latter brand because their induction or death happened after 1952. Values quoted are for cards signed on the front. Cards signed on back can be worth 50 percent less .

	NM	EX	VG
Complete Set (55): Value Undetermined			
G.C. Alexander	1,250	1,125	935.00
Frank Baker	1,600	1,450	1,200
Ed Barrow	1,500	1,350	1,125
Chief Bender	550.00	500.00	410.00
Jesse Burkett	1,100	990.00	825.00
Max Carey	100.00	90.00	75.00
Fred Clarke	1,700	1,525	1,275
Ty Cobb	2,500	2,250	1,875
Mickey Cochrane	1,500	1,350	1,125
Eddie Collins	8,000	7,200	6,000
Tom Connolly	3,000	2,700	2,250
Sam Crawford	400.00	200.00	120.00
Joe Cronin	250.00	125.00	75.00
Dizzy Dean	325.00	290.00	245.00
Bill Dickey	150.00	135.00	110.00
Joe DiMaggio	400.00	200.00	120.00
Hugh Duffy	1,500	1,350	1,125
Johnny Evers	450.00	400.00	335.00
Bob Feller	35.00	30.00	25.00
Elmer Flick	500.00	450.00	375.00
Jimmie Foxx	3,500	1,750	1,050
Frankie Frisch	350.00	175.00	105.00
Lou Gehrig (Sepia only.)	2,000	1,800	1,500
Charlie Gehringer	75.00	37.00	22.00
Hank Greenberg	325.00	290.00	245.00
Clark Griffith	2,750	2,475	2,050
Lefty Grove	250.00	225.00	185.00
Gabby Hartnett	475.00	425.00	355.00
Rogers Hornsby	1,600	1,450	1,200
Carl Hubbell (Deduct 33 percent for post-stroke signature.)	65.00	58.00	49.00
Walter Johnson	1,400	1,250	1,050
Nap Lajoie	2,500	2,250	1,875
Ted Lyons	300.00	275.00	225.00
Connie Mack	2,000	1,000	600.00
Joe McCarthy	200.00	180.00	150.00
Bill McKechnie	900.00	810.00	675.00
Kid Nichols	3,500	3,150	2,625
Mel Ott	2,000	1,000	600.00
Sam Rice	175.00	155.00	130.00
Eppa Rixey (Possible but unlikely.)			
Jackie Robinson	1,450	725.00	435.00
Edd Roush	75.00	65.00	55.00
Babe Ruth (Value Undetermined)			
Ray Schalk	500.00	450.00	375.00
Al Simmons	1,750	1,575	1,300
George Sisler	400.00	200.00	120.00
Tris Speaker	1,500	1,350	1,125
Bill Terry	60.00	55.00	45.00
Joe Tinker	550.00	500.00	410.00
Pie Traynor	850.00	765.00	635.00
Dazzy Vance	1,700	1,525	1,275
Honus Wagner	2,800	2,525	2,100
Bobby Wallace	1,800	900.00	550.00
Ed Walsh	1,250	1,125	935.00
Paul Waner	1,550	1,400	1,150
Zack Wheat	550.00	270.00	165.00
Cy Young	2,000	1,000	600.00

1963 Hall of Fame Picture Pack

The attributed date is only approximate for this set of 5" x 7" black-and-white, blank-back pictures sold by the Hall of Fame. In the wide border beneath the player photo are identification, teams and years played, a few stats and induction year along with an HoF logo. Some of the same pictures were repeated in the later version of the issue.

		NM	EX	VG
Complete Set (24):		40.00	20.00	12.00
Common Player:		3.00	1.50	.90
(1)	Grover Alexander	4.00	2.00	1.25
(2)	Ty Cobb	6.00	3.00	1.75
(3)	Mickey Cochrane	3.00	1.50	.90
(4)	Eddie Collins	3.00	1.50	.90
(5)	Joe Cronin	3.00	1.50	.90
(6)	Bill Dickey	3.00	1.50	.90
(7)	Joe DiMaggio	7.50	3.75	2.25
(8)	Bob Feller	4.00	2.00	1.25
(9)	Frank Frisch	3.00	1.50	.90
(10)	Lou Gehrig	7.50	3.75	2.25
(11)	Rogers Hornsby	3.00	1.50	.90
(12)	Walter Johnson	4.00	2.00	1.25
(13)	Connie Mack	3.00	1.50	.90
(14)	Christy Mathewson	4.00	2.00	1.25
(15)	John McGraw	3.00	1.50	.90
(16)	Jackie Robinson	5.00	2.50	1.50
(17)	Babe Ruth	10.00	5.00	3.00
(18)	George Sisler	3.00	1.50	.90
(19)	Tris Speaker	3.00	1.50	.90
(20)	Bill Terry	3.00	1.50	.90
(21)	Pie Traynor	3.00	1.50	.90
(22)	Honus Wagner	4.00	2.00	1.25
(23)	Paul Waner	3.00	1.50	.90
(24)	Cy Young	4.00	2.00	1.25

1973 Hall of Fame Picture Pack

This set of 5" x 6-3/4" black-and-white player photos picture "Baseball's Greats Enshrined at Cooperstown, N.Y." Player career data is printed in the wide white border at bottom and there is a Hall of Fame logo at lower-left. The unnumbered pictures are listed here in alphabetical order.

		NM	EX	VG
Complete Set (20):		20.00	10.00	6.00
Common Player:		2.00	1.00	.60
(1)	Yogi Berra	3.00	1.50	.90
(2)	Roy Campanella	3.00	1.50	.90
(3)	Ty Cobb	4.00	2.00	1.25
(4)	Joe Cronin	2.50	1.25	.70
(5)	Dizzy Dean	3.00	1.50	.90
(6)	Joe DiMaggio	7.50	3.75	2.25
(7)	Bob Feller	3.00	1.50	.90
(8)	Lou Gehrig	7.50	3.75	2.25
(9)	Rogers Hornsby	3.00	1.50	.90
(10)	Sandy Koufax	5.00	2.50	1.50
(11)	Christy Mathewson	3.00	1.50	.90
(12)	Stan Musial	3.00	1.50	.90
(13)	Satchel Paige	3.00	1.50	.90
(14)	Jackie Robinson	5.00	2.50	1.50
(15)	Babe Ruth	10.00	5.00	3.00
(16)	Warren Spahn	2.50	1.25	.70
(17)	Casey Stengel	3.00	1.50	.90
(18)	Honus Wagner	3.00	1.50	.90
(19)	Ted Williams	5.00	2.50	1.50
(20)	Cy Young	3.00	1.50	.90

1979 Hall of Fame (Dexter Press) Plaque Postcards

This short-lived series, begun no later than 1979, features the Hall of Fame inductees' plaques on bright backgrounds of red, orange, blue and green. Because of the cards' color and finish, they are difficult to autograph.

		NM	EX	VG
Complete Set (53):		350.00	175.00	105.00
Common Player:		6.00	3.00	1.75
(1)	Grover Alexander	6.00	3.00	1.75
(2)	Lou Boudreau	6.00	3.00	1.75
(3)	Roy Campanella	10.00	5.00	3.00
(4)	Roberto Clemente	20.00	10.00	6.00
(5)	Ty Cobb	15.00	7.50	4.50
(6)	Stan Coveleski	6.00	3.00	1.75
(7)	Sam Crawford	6.00	3.00	1.75
(8)	Martin Dihigo	6.00	3.00	1.75
(9)	Joe DiMaggio	22.50	11.00	6.75
(10)	Billy Evans	6.00	3.00	1.75
(11)	Johnny Evers	6.00	3.00	1.75
(12)	Red Faber	6.00	3.00	1.75
(13)	Elmer Flick	6.00	3.00	1.75
(14)	Ford Frick	6.00	3.00	1.75
(15)	Frank Frisch	6.00	3.00	1.75
(16)	Pud Galvin	6.00	3.00	1.75
(17)	Lou Gehrig	20.00	10.00	6.00
(18)	Warren Giles	6.00	3.00	1.75
(19)	Will Harridge	6.00	3.00	1.75
(20)	Harry Heilmann	6.00	3.00	1.75
(21)	Harry Hooper	6.00	3.00	1.75
(22)	Waite Hoyt	6.00	3.00	1.75
(23)	Miller Huggins	6.00	3.00	1.75
(24)	Judy Johnson	6.00	3.00	1.75
(25)	Addie Joss	6.00	3.00	1.75
(26)	Tim Keefe	6.00	3.00	1.75
(27)	Willie Keeler	6.00	3.00	1.75
(28)	George Kelly	6.00	3.00	1.75
(29)	Sandy Koufax	15.00	7.50	4.50
(30)	Nap Lajoie	6.00	3.00	1.75
(31)	Pop Lloyd	6.00	3.00	1.75
(32)	Connie Mack	6.00	3.00	1.75
(33)	Larry MacPhail	6.00	3.00	1.75
(34)	Mickey Mantle	25.00	12.50	7.50
(35)	Heinie Manush	6.00	3.00	1.75
(36)	Eddie Mathews	6.00	3.00	1.75
(37)	Willie Mays	15.00	7.50	4.50
(38)	Ducky Medwick	6.00	3.00	1.75
(39)	Stan Musial	12.00	6.00	3.50
(40)	Herb Pennock	6.00	3.00	1.75
(41)	Edd Roush	6.00	3.00	1.75
(42)	Babe Ruth	25.00	12.50	7.50
(43)	Amos Rusie	6.00	3.00	1.75
(44)	Ray Schalk	6.00	3.00	1.75
(45)	Al Simmons	6.00	3.00	1.75
(46)	Albert Spalding	6.00	3.00	1.75
(47)	Joe Tinker	6.00	3.00	1.75

		NM	EX	VG
(48)	Pie Traynor	6.00	3.00	1.75
(49)	Dazzy Vance	6.00	3.00	1.75
(50)	Lloyd Waner	6.00	3.00	1.75
(51)	Ted Williams	20.00	10.00	6.00
(52)	Hack Wilson	6.00	3.00	1.75
(53)	Ross Youngs	6.00	3.00	1.75

1979 HoF (Dexter Press) Plaque Postcards - Autographed

		NM	EX	VG
(2)	Lou Boudreau	30.00	27.00	22.00
(3)	Roy Campanella (Value Undetermined)			
(6)	Stan Coveleski	50.00	45.00	37.00
(9)	Joe DiMaggio	350.00	315.00	260.00
(22)	Waite Hoyt	100.00	90.00	75.00
(24)	Judy Johnson	65.00	60.00	50.00
(28)	George Kelly	75.00	65.00	55.00
(29)	Sandy Koufax	150.00	135.00	110.00
(34)	Mickey Mantle	400.00	360.00	300.00
(36)	Eddie Mathews	50.00	45.00	37.00
(37)	Willie Mays	50.00	45.00	37.00
(39)	Stan Musial	25.00	22.00	18.50
(41)	Edd Roush	50.00	45.00	37.00
(50)	Lloyd Waner	50.00	45.00	37.00
(51)	Ted Williams	300.00	270.00	225.00

1964-Date Hall of Fame Yellow Plaque Postcards

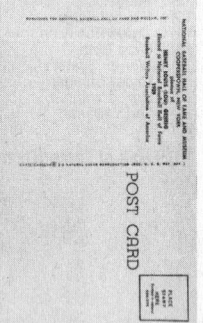

Since 1964 a number of related series of Hall of Fame Plaque Postcards have been produced by a pair of printers. The 3-1/2" x 5-1/2" postcards were first produced by Curteich-color and, later, by Mike Roberts Color Productions. Like earlier HoF postcards, these series feature a color photo of an inductee's plaque on a yellow background. Black-and-white backs have a variety of player information, postcard indicia, copyright data and credit lines. Few hobbyists attmept to collect these by issuer, rather trying to assemble a complete set of each player regardless of who did the printing and when. Prior to 1977, single postcards sold for five cents at the HoF gift shop; in 1977 the price doubled to a dime, with complete sets (about 150) selling for $6. Today a complete set is available from the Hall of Fame for about $45, with singles at 25 cents apiece.

	NM	EX	VG
Complete Set (281)	45.00	22.00	13.50
Common Player:	.50	.25	.15
Hank Aaron	.50	.25	.15
Grover Alexander	.50	.25	.15
Walter Alston	.50	.25	.15
Sparky Anderson	.50	.25	.15
Cap Anson	.50	.25	.15
Luis Aparicio	.50	.25	.15
Luke Appling	.50	.25	.15
Richie Ashburn	.50	.25	.15
Earl Averill	.50	.25	.15
Frank Baker	.50	.25	.15
Dave Bancroft	.50	.25	.15
Ernie Banks	.50	.25	.15
Al Barlick	.50	.25	.15
Ed Barrow	.50	.25	.15
Jake Beckley	.50	.25	.15
Cool Papa Bell	.50	.25	.15
Johnny Bench	.50	.25	.15
Chief Bender	.50	.25	.15
Yogi Berra	.50	.25	.15
Wade Boggs	.50	.25	.15
Jim Bottomley	.50	.25	.15
Lou Boudreau	.50	.25	.15
Roger Bresnahan	.50	.25	.15
George Brett	.50	.25	.15
Lou Brock	.50	.25	.15
Dan Brouthers	.50	.25	.15
Mordecai Brown	.50	.25	.15
Ray Brown	.50	.25	.15
Willard Brown	.50	.25	.15
Morgan Bulkeley	.50	.25	.15
Jim Bunning	.50	.25	.15
Jesse Burkett	.50	.25	.15
Roy Campanella	.50	.25	.15
Rod Carew	.50	.25	.15
Max Carey	.50	.25	.15
Steve Carlton	.50	.25	.15
Gary Carter	.50	.25	.15
Alexander Cartwright	.50	.25	.15
Orlando Cepeda	.50	.25	.15
Henry Chadwick	.50	.25	.15
Frank Chance	.50	.25	.15
A.B. (Happy) Chandler	.50	.25	.15
Oscar Charleston	.50	.25	.15
Jack Chesbro	.50	.25	.15
Nestor Chylak	.50	.25	.15

	NM	EX	VG
Fred Clarke	.50	.25	.15
John Clarkson	.50	.25	.15
Roberto Clemente	.50	.25	.15
Ty Cobb	.50	.25	.15
Mickey Cochrane	.50	.25	.15
Eddie Collins	.50	.25	.15
Jimmy Collins	.50	.25	.15
Earle Combs	.50	.25	.15
Charles Comiskey	.50	.25	.15
Jocko Conlan	.50	.25	.15
Tom Connolly	.50	.25	.15
Roger Connor	.50	.25	.15
Andy Cooper	.50	.25	.15
Stan Coveleski	.50	.25	.15
Sam Crawford	.50	.25	.15
Joe Cronin	.50	.25	.15
Candy Cummings	.50	.25	.15
Kiki Cuyler	.50	.25	.15
Ray Dandridge	.50	.25	.15
George Davis	.50	.25	.15
Leon Day	.50	.25	.15
Dizzy Dean	.50	.25	.15
Ed Delahanty	.50	.25	.15
Bill Dickey	.50	.25	.15
Martin Dihigo	.50	.25	.15
Joe DiMaggio	.50	.25	.15
Larry Doby	.50	.25	.15
Bobby Doerr	.50	.25	.15
Barney Dreyfuss	.50	.25	.15
Don Drysdale	.50	.25	.15
Hugh Duffy	.50	.25	.15
Leo Durocher	.50	.25	.15
Dennis Eckersley	.50	.25	.15
Billy Evans	.50	.25	.15
Johnny Evers	.50	.25	.15
Buck Ewing	.50	.25	.15
Red Faber	.50	.25	.15
Bob Feller	.50	.25	.15
Rick Ferrell	.50	.25	.15
Rollie Fingers	.50	.25	.15
Carlton Fisk	.50	.25	.15
Elmer Flick	.50	.25	.15
Whitey Ford	.50	.25	.15
Bill Foster	.50	.25	.15
Rube Foster	.50	.25	.15
Nellie Fox	.50	.25	.15
Jimmie Foxx	.50	.25	.15
Ford Frick	.50	.25	.15
Frank Frisch	.50	.25	.15
Pud Galvin	.50	.25	.15
Lou Gehrig	.50	.25	.15
Charlie Gehringer	.50	.25	.15
Bob Gibson	.50	.25	.15
Josh Gibson	.50	.25	.15
Warren Giles	.50	.25	.15
Lefty Gomez	.50	.25	.15
Goose Goslin	.50	.25	.15
Rich "Goose" Gossage	.50	.25	.15
Frank Grant	.50	.25	.15
Hank Greenberg	.50	.25	.15
Clark Griffith	.50	.25	.15
Burleigh Grimes	.50	.25	.15
Lefty Grove	.50	.25	.15
Tony Gwynn	.50	.25	.15
Chick Hafey	.50	.25	.15
Jesse Haines	.50	.25	.15
Billy Hamilton	.50	.25	.15
Ned Hanlon	.50	.25	.15
Will Harridge	.50	.25	.15
Bucky Harris	.50	.25	.15
Gabby Hartnett	.50	.25	.15
Harry Heilmann	.50	.25	.15
Billy Herman	.50	.25	.15
Pete Hill	.50	.25	.15
Harry Hooper	.50	.25	.15
Rogers Hornsby	.50	.25	.15
Waite Hoyt	.50	.25	.15
Cal Hubbard	.50	.25	.15
Carl Hubbell	.50	.25	.15
Miller Huggins	.50	.25	.15
William Hulbert	.50	.25	.15
Catfish Hunter	.50	.25	.15
Monte Irvin	.50	.25	.15
Reggie Jackson	.50	.25	.15
Travis Jackson	.50	.25	.15
Fergie Jenkins	.50	.25	.15
Hughie Jennings	.50	.25	.15
Ban Johnson	.50	.25	.15
Judy Johnson	.50	.25	.15
Walter Johnson	.50	.25	.15
Addie Joss	.50	.25	.15
Al Kaline	.50	.25	.15
Tim Keefe	.50	.25	.15
Willie Keeler	.50	.25	.15
George Kell	.50	.25	.15
Joe Kelley	.50	.25	.15
George Kelly	.50	.25	.15
Mike "King" Kelly	.50	.25	.15
Harmon Killebrew	.50	.25	.15
Ralph Kiner	.50	.25	.15
Chuck Klein	.50	.25	.15
Bill Klem	.50	.25	.15
Sandy Koufax	.50	.25	.15
Bowie Kuhn	.50	.25	.15
Nap Lajoie	.50	.25	.15
Kenesaw M. Landis	.50	.25	.15
Tommy Lasorda	.50	.25	.15
Tony Lazzeri	.50	.25	.15
Bob Lemon	.50	.25	.15
Buck Leonard	.50	.25	.15
Freddie Lindstrom	.50	.25	.15
Pop Lloyd	.50	.25	.15
Ernie Lombardi	.50	.25	.15
Al Lopez	.50	.25	.15
Ted Lyons	.50	.25	.15
Connie Mack	.50	.25	.15
Biz Mackey	.50	.25	.15
Larry MacPhail	.50	.25	.15

	NM	EX	VG
Effa "Effie" Manley	.50	.25	.15
Mickey Mantle	.50	.25	.15
Heinie Manush	.50	.25	.15
Rabbit Maranville	.50	.25	.15
Juan Marichal	.50	.25	.15
Rube Marquard	.50	.25	.15
Eddie Mathews	.50	.25	.15
Christy Mathewson	.50	.25	.15
Willie Mays	.50	.25	.15
Bill Mazeroski	.50	.25	.15
Joe McCarthy	.50	.25	.15
Tommy McCarthy	.50	.25	.15
Willie McCovey	.50	.25	.15
Joe McGinnity	.50	.25	.15
Bill McGowan	.50	.25	.15
John McGraw	.50	.25	.15
Bill McKechnie	.50	.25	.15
Lee MacPhail	.50	.25	.15
Bid McPhee	.50	.25	.15
Ducky Medwick	.50	.25	.15
Jose Mendez	.50	.25	.15
Johnny Mize	.50	.25	.15
Paul Molitor	.50	.25	.15
Joe Morgan	.50	.25	.15
Eddie Murray	.50	.25	.15
Stan Musial	.50	.25	.15
Hal Newhouser	.50	.25	.15
Kid Nichols	.50	.25	.15
Phil Niekro	.50	.25	.15
Walter O'Malley	.50	.25	.15
Jim O'Rourke	.50	.25	.15
Mel Ott	.50	.25	.15
Satchel Paige	.50	.25	.15
Jim Palmer	.50	.25	.15
Herb Pennock	.50	.25	.15
Tony Perez	.50	.25	.15
Gaylord Perry	.50	.25	.15
Ed Plank	.50	.25	.15
Alex Pompez	.50	.25	.15
Cum Posey	.50	.25	.15
Kirby Puckett	.50	.25	.15
Charles Radbourne	.50	.25	.15
Pee Wee Reese	.50	.25	.15
Sam Rice	.50	.25	.15
Cal Ripken Jr.	.50	.25	.15
Branch Rickey	.50	.25	.15
Eppa Rixey	.50	.25	.15
Phil Rizzuto	.50	.25	.15
Robin Roberts	.50	.25	.15
Brooks Robinson	.50	.25	.15
Frank Robinson	.50	.25	.15
Jackie Robinson	.50	.25	.15
Wilbert Robinson	.50	.25	.15
Bullet Rogan	.50	.25	.15
Edd Roush	.50	.25	.15
Red Ruffing	.50	.25	.15
Amos Rusie	.50	.25	.15
Babe Ruth	.50	.25	.15
Nolan Ryan	.50	.25	.15
Ryne Sandberg	.50	.25	.15
Louis Santop	.50	.25	.15
Ray Schalk	.50	.25	.15
Mike Schmidt	.50	.25	.15
Red Schoendienst	.50	.25	.15
Tom Seaver	.50	.25	.15
Frank Selee	.50	.25	.15
Joe Sewell	.50	.25	.15
Al Simmons	.50	.25	.15
George Sisler	.50	.25	.15
Enos Slaughter	.50	.25	.15
Hilton Smith	.50	.25	.15
Ozzie Smith	.50	.25	.15
Duke Snider	.50	.25	.15
Billy Southworth	.50	.25	.15
Warren Spahn	.50	.25	.15
Albert Spalding	.50	.25	.15
Tris Speaker	.50	.25	.15
Willie Stargell	.50	.25	.15
Turkey Stearnes	.50	.25	.15
Casey Stengel	.50	.25	.15
Mule Suttles	.50	.25	.15
Don Sutton	.50	.25	.15
Ben Taylor	.50	.25	.15
Bill Terry	.50	.25	.15
Sam Thompson	.50	.25	.15
Joe Tinker	.50	.25	.15
Cristobal Torriente	.50	.25	.15
Paul Traynor	.50	.25	.15
Dazzy Vance	.50	.25	.15
Arky Vaughan	.50	.25	.15
Bill Veeck	.50	.25	.15
Rube Waddell	.50	.25	.15
Honus Wagner	.50	.25	.15
Bobby Wallace	.50	.25	.15
Ed Walsh	.50	.25	.15
Lloyd Waner	.50	.25	.15
Paul Waner	.50	.25	.15
Monte Ward	.50	.25	.15
Earl Weaver	.50	.25	.15
George Weiss	.50	.25	.15
Mickey Welch	.50	.25	.15
Willie Wells	.50	.25	.15
Zack Wheat	.50	.25	.15
Sol White	.50	.25	.15
Hoyt Wilhelm	.50	.25	.15
J.L. Wilkinson	.50	.25	.15
Billy Williams	.50	.25	.15
Dick Williams	.50	.25	.15
Joe Williams	.50	.25	.15
Ted Williams	.50	.25	.15
Vic Willis	.50	.25	.15
Hack Wilson	.50	.25	.15
Jud Wilson	.50	.25	.15
Dave Winfield	.50	.25	.15
George Wright	.50	.25	.15
Harry Wright	.50	.25	.15
Early Wynn	.50	.25	.15
Carl Yastrzemski	.50	.25	.15

	NM	EX	VG
Tom Yawkey	.50	.25	.15
Cy Young	.50	.25	.15
Ross Youngs	.50	.25	.15
Robin Yount	.50	.25	.15

1964-Date Hall of Fame Yellow Plaque Postcards - Autographed

This listing represents the Curteichcolor and Mike Roberts yellow Hall of Fame plaque postcards which are known to exist, or in a few cases are theoretically possible. Value of genuinely autographed HoF plaque postcards is not so much dependent on star status of the player, but on perception of how many such cards could exist given the time the player remained alive and in good health following his selection at Cooperstown. Players who died or were incapacitated shortly after induction may have more valuable autographed cards than currently living players of greater renown. Values quoted are for cards autographed on front; cards signed on the back can be worth 50 percent less.

	NM	EX	VG
Hank Aaron	55.00	45.00	35.00
Walter Alston	150.00	120.00	90.00
Sparky Anderson	55.00	45.00	35.00
Luis Aparicio	15.00	12.00	9.00
Luke Appling	20.00	16.00	12.00
Richie Ashburn	55.00	45.00	35.00
Earl Averill	50.00	40.00	30.00
Dave Bancroft	2,250	1,800	1,350
Ernie Banks	45.00	35.00	25.00
Al Barlick	15.00	12.00	9.00
Cool Papa Bell	50.00	40.00	30.00
Johnny Bench	45.00	36.00	27.00
Yogi Berra	25.00	20.00	15.00
Wade Boggs	50.00	40.00	30.00
Lou Boudreau	15.00	12.00	9.00
George Brett	125.00	100.00	75.00
Lou Brock	30.00	24.00	18.00
Jim Bunning	40.00	32.00	24.00
Roy Campanella (Value Undetermined)			
Rod Carew	50.00	40.00	30.00
Max Carey	60.00	50.00	35.00
Steve Carlton	35.00	30.00	20.00
Gary Carter	100.00	80.00	60.00
Orlando Cepeda	35.00	30.00	20.00
A.B. (Happy) Chandler	20.00	16.00	12.00
Earle Combs	300.00	240.00	180.00
Jocko Conlan	25.00	20.00	15.00
Stan Coveleski	30.00	24.00	18.00
"Stanislaus Kowalewski"	150.00	120.00	90.00
Sam Crawford	600.00	480.00	360.00
Joe Cronin	50.00	40.00	30.00
Ray Dandridge	15.00	12.00	9.00
Dizzy Dean	300.00	240.00	180.00
Bill Dickey	50.00	40.00	30.00
Joe DiMaggio	225.00	180.00	135.00
Larry Doby	90.00	70.00	55.00
Bobby Doerr	7.50	6.00	4.50
Don Drysdale	45.00	35.00	25.00
Dennis Eckersley	75.00	60.00	45.00
Red Faber	165.00	130.00	100.00
Bob Feller	7.50	6.00	4.50
Rick Ferrell	15.00	12.00	9.00
Rollie Fingers	20.00	16.00	12.00
Carlton Fisk	80.00	65.00	45.00
Elmer Flick	600.00	480.00	360.00
Whitey Ford	35.00	30.00	20.00
Jimmie Foxx (Usually signed on back.)	1,750	1,400	1,050
Ford Frick	225.00	180.00	135.00
Frank Frisch	300.00	240.00	180.00
Charlie Gehringer	30.00	24.00	18.00
Bob Gibson	30.00	24.00	18.00
Lefty Gomez	35.00	30.00	20.00
Goose Goslin (Usually signed on back; value of such $750-1,000.)	2,250	1,800	1,350
Hank Greenberg	175.00	140.00	100.00
Burleigh Grimes	35.00	30.00	20.00
Lefty Grove	160.00	130.00	95.00
Tony Gwynn	150.00	120.00	90.00
Chick Hafey	725.00	580.00	435.00
Jesse Haines	125.00	100.00	75.00
Bucky Harris	325.00	260.00	195.00
Gabby Hartnett	725.00	580.00	435.00
Billy Herman	12.00	9.50	7.25
Harry Hooper	235.00	190.00	140.00
Waite Hoyt	40.00	32.00	24.00
Cal Hubbard	1,250	1,000	750.00

	NM	EX	VG
Carl Hubbell (Pre-stroke.)	40.00	32.00	24.00
Carl Hubbell (Post-stroke.)	25.00	20.00	15.00
Catfish Hunter	30.00	24.00	18.00
Monte Irvin	10.00	8.00	6.00
Reggie Jackson	75.00	60.00	45.00
Travis Jackson	30.00	24.00	18.00
Fergie Jenkins	15.00	12.00	9.00
Judy Johnson	30.00	24.00	18.00
Al Kaline	20.00	16.00	12.00
George Kell	7.50	6.00	4.50
George Kelly	40.00	32.00	24.00
Harmon Killebrew	25.00	20.00	15.00
Ralph Kiner	15.00	12.00	9.00
Sandy Koufax	125.00	100.00	75.00
Tommy Lasorda	100.00	80.00	60.00
Bob Lemon	12.00	9.50	7.25
Buck Leonard (Post-stroke autographed cards worth 50 percent.)	15.00	12.00	9.00
Freddie Lindstrom	75.00	60.00	45.00
Al Lopez	40.00	32.00	24.00
Ted Lyons	45.00	35.00	25.00
Lee MacPhail	35.00	28.00	21.00
Mickey Mantle	235.00	190.00	140.00
Heinie Manush	325.00	260.00	195.00
Juan Marichal	15.00	12.00	9.00
Rube Marquard	40.00	32.00	24.00
Eddie Mathews	25.00	20.00	15.00
Willie Mays	50.00	40.00	30.00
Bill Mazeroski	50.00	40.00	30.00
Joe McCarthy	80.00	65.00	45.00
Willie McCovey	35.00	28.00	21.00
Bill McKechnie (Possible, not likely.)	185.00	150.00	110.00
Ducky Medwick	185.00	150.00	110.00
Johnny Mize	15.00	12.00	9.00
Paul Molitor	90.00	75.00	55.00
Joe Morgan	30.00	24.00	18.00
Eddie Murray	125.00	100.00	75.00
Stan Musial	25.00	20.00	15.00
Hal Newhouser	15.00	12.00	9.00
Phil Niekro	35.00	30.00	20.00
Satchel Paige	235.00	190.00	140.00
Jim Palmer	20.00	16.00	12.00
Tony Perez	50.00	40.00	30.00
Gaylord Perry	25.00	20.00	15.00
Kirby Puckett	125.00	100.00	75.00
Pee Wee Reese	45.00	35.00	25.00
Sam Rice	185.00	150.00	110.00
Cal Ripken Jr.	100.00	80.00	60.00
Phil Rizzuto	30.00	24.00	18.00
Robin Roberts	12.50	10.00	7.50
Brooks Robinson	12.50	10.00	7.50
Frank Robinson	25.00	20.00	15.00
Jackie Robinson (Often signed on back; value of such $550.)	1,600	1,275	960.00
Edd Roush	30.00	24.00	18.00
Red Ruffing	200.00	160.00	120.00
Nolan Ryan	65.00	50.00	40.00
Ryne Sandberg	60.00	45.00	35.00
Ray Schalk	450.00	360.00	270.00
Mike Schmidt	80.00	65.00	50.00
Red Schoendienst	30.00	24.00	18.00
Tom Seaver	40.00	32.00	24.00
Joe Sewell	15.00	12.00	9.00
George Sisler	200.00	160.00	120.00
Enos Slaughter	10.00	8.00	6.00
Ozzie Smith	95.00	75.00	55.00
Duke Snider	20.00	16.00	12.00
Warren Spahn	20.00	16.00	12.00
Willie Stargell	50.00	40.00	30.00
Casey Stengel	225.00	180.00	135.00
Bruce Sutter	60.00	45.00	35.00
Don Sutton	40.00	32.00	24.00
Bill Terry	25.00	20.00	15.00
Pie Traynor	850.00	680.00	510.00
Lloyd Waner	30.00	24.00	18.00
Paul Waner (Possible, not likely.)			
Earl Weaver	35.00	30.00	20.00
George Weiss (Possible, not likely.)			
Zack Wheat	450.00	360.00	270.00
Hoyt Wilhelm	15.00	12.00	9.00
Billy Williams	15.00	12.00	9.00
Ted Williams	200.00	160.00	120.00
Dave Winfield	100.00	80.00	60.00
Early Wynn	25.00	20.00	15.00
Carl Yastrzemski	55.00	45.00	35.00
Robin Yount	150.00	120.00	90.00

1973 Jack Hamilton's "The Pzazz" Postcard

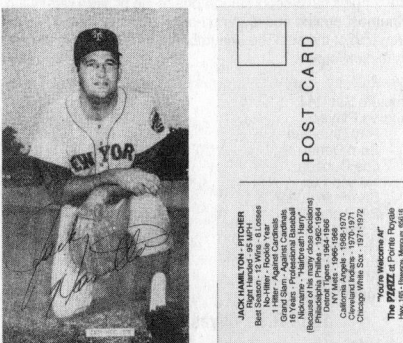

The date attributed is speculative, based on the not totally honest major league career summary printed on the back of this standard-size, black-and-white postcard. The front reproduces a J.D. McCarthy postcard of the pitcher in a New York Mets uniform. There is a white border all around and a facsimile autograph in blue. The back has a few career highlights and advertisement for Hamilton's "The Pzazz" restaurant in Branson, Mo.

	NM	EX	VG
Jack Hamilton	6.00	3.00	1.75

1961 Harmony Milk Pittsburgh Pirates

The attributed year of issue is approximate and subject to change if and when further players are added to the checklist. These premium photos are 8" x 10" in format, round-cornered with blank backs.

		NM	EX	VG
Common Player:		175.00	90.00	50.00
(1)	Roberto Clemente	600.00	300.00	180.00
(2)	Dick Groat	175.00	90.00	50.00
(3)	Don Hoak	175.00	90.00	50.00
(4)	Vern Law	175.00	90.00	50.00
(5)	Danny Murtaugh	175.00	90.00	50.00

1928 Harrington's Ice Cream

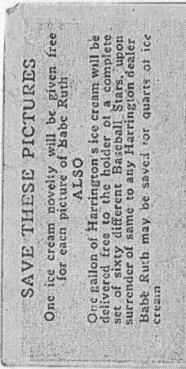

Sharing the same format and checklist with several other (Tharp's, Yeungling's, Sweetman, etc.) contemporary ice cream sets this 60-card set from a Dushore, Pa., dairy includes all of the top stars of the day. Cards are printed in black-and-white on a 1-3/8" x 2-1/2" format. The player's name and a card number appear either in a strip within the frame of the photo, or printed in the border beneath the photo. Card backs have a redemption offer that includes an ice cream bar in exchange for a Babe Ruth card, or a gallon of ice cream for a complete set of 60.

		NM	EX	VG
Complete Set (no #48 Smith) (59):		20,000	8,000	4,000
Common Player:		90.00	35.00	20.00
1	Burleigh Grimes	350.00	140.00	70.00
2	Walter Reuther (Ruether)	90.00	35.00	20.00
3	Joe Dugan	90.00	35.00	20.00
4	Red Faber	350.00	140.00	70.00
5	Gabby Hartnett	350.00	140.00	70.00
6	Babe Ruth	7,000	3,500	2,100
7	Bob Meusel	90.00	35.00	20.00
8	Herb Pennock	350.00	140.00	70.00
9	George Burns	90.00	35.00	20.00
10	Joe Sewell	350.00	140.00	70.00
11	George Uhle	90.00	35.00	20.00
12	Bob O'Farrell	90.00	35.00	20.00
13	Rogers Hornsby	450.00	180.00	90.00
14	"Pie" Traynor	350.00	140.00	70.00
15	Clarence Mitchell	90.00	35.00	20.00
16	Eppa Jepha Rixey	350.00	140.00	70.00
17	Carl Mays	125.00	50.00	25.00
18	Adolfo Luque	100.00	40.00	20.00
19	Dave Bancroft	350.00	140.00	70.00
20	George Kelly	350.00	140.00	70.00
21	Earl (Earle) Combs	350.00	140.00	70.00
22	Harry Heilmann	350.00	140.00	70.00
23	Ray W. Schalk	350.00	140.00	70.00
24	Johnny Mostil	90.00	35.00	20.00
25	Hack Wilson	350.00	140.00	70.00
26	Lou Gehrig	6,000	1,400	700.00
27	Ty Cobb	5,000	2,500	1,500
28	Tris Speaker	450.00	180.00	90.00
29	Tony Lazzeri	350.00	140.00	70.00

30	Waite Hoyt	350.00	140.00	70.00
31	Sherwood Smith	90.00	35.00	20.00
32	Max Carey	350.00	140.00	70.00
33	Eugene Hargrave	90.00	35.00	20.00
34	Miguel L. Gonzalez (Middle initial A.)	100.00	40.00	20.00
35	Joe Judge	90.00	35.00	20.00
36	E.C. (Sam) Rice	350.00	140.00	70.00
37	Earl Sheely	90.00	35.00	20.00
38	Sam Jones	90.00	35.00	20.00
39	Bib (Bibb) A. Falk	90.00	35.00	20.00
40	Willie Kamm	90.00	35.00	20.00
41	Stanley Harris	350.00	140.00	70.00
42	John J. McGraw	350.00	140.00	70.00
43	Artie Nehf	90.00	35.00	20.00
44	Grover Alexander	450.00	180.00	90.00
45	Paul Waner	350.00	140.00	70.00
46	William H. Terry	350.00	140.00	70.00
47	Glenn Wright	90.00	35.00	20.00
48	Earl Smith (Printed in green only) (Value Undetermined)			
49	Leon (Goose) Goslin	350.00	140.00	70.00
50	Frank Frisch	350.00	140.00	70.00
51	Joe Harris	90.00	35.00	20.00
52	Fred (Cy) Williams	90.00	35.00	20.00
53	Eddie Roush	350.00	140.00	70.00
54	George Sisler	350.00	140.00	70.00
55	Ed. Rommel	90.00	35.00	20.00
56	Rogers Peckinpaugh (Roger)	90.00	35.00	20.00
57	Stanley Coveleskie (Coveleski)	350.00	140.00	70.00
58	Lester Bell	90.00	35.00	20.00
59	L. Waner	350.00	140.00	70.00
60	John P. McInnis	90.00	35.00	20.00

1930-1931 Harrison Studio Homestead Grays Postcards

Whether the famed Negro League powerhouse team, the Homestead Grays, were in Little Rock, Ark., for spring training or on a barnstorming tour, they became the subjects of a series of postcards from the local photographer, Harrison Studio. The cards are in standard postcard format, featuring borderless black-and-white photographic poses. It is likely the checklist here is incomplete.

(1) Josh Gibson (Front/back autographed card sold at auction 4/06 for $81,200.)
(2) Ted Page
(3) Ambrose Reed
(4) Homestead Grays 1930 Team Photo
(5) Homestead Grays 1931 Team Photo

1951 Hartford Chiefs Team Issue

This set pictures on 4-1/4" x 5-1/4" blank-back cardstock posed black-and-white action photos of members of the Boston Braves' Class A Eastern League farm club. Whether the checklist here is complete is not known.

		NM	EX	VG
Complete Set (17):		800.00	400.00	240.00
Common Player:		60.00	30.00	18.00
(1)	Earl Bass	60.00	30.00	18.00
(2)	Gene Conley	75.00	37.50	22.50
(3)	Jack Daniels	60.00	30.00	18.00
(4)	Pete Fox	60.00	30.00	18.00
(5)	Harry Hanebrink	60.00	30.00	18.00
(6)	Tommy Holmes	75.00	37.50	22.50
(7)	Travis Jackson	90.00	45.00	27.50
(8)	Ford Jordan	60.00	30.00	18.00
(9)	Tom Keenan	60.00	30.00	18.00
(10)	Dick Kelly	60.00	30.00	18.00
(11)	Ed Lenthe	60.00	30.00	18.00
(12)	Jack Mulcahy	60.00	30.00	18.00
(13)	Len Pearson	75.00	37.50	22.50
(14)	Don Schmidt	60.00	30.00	18.00
(15)	Harry Sullivan	60.00	30.00	18.00
(16)	Elmer Toth	60.00	30.00	18.00
(17)	Bob Verrier	60.00	30.00	18.00

1911-12 Hassan Cigarettes

Prior to its sole sponsorship of the T202 Triplefolders set of 1912, Hassan was one of 10 American Tobacco Co. brands advertising on the backs of 1911 T205 Gold Borders. Two different factories are noted on these backs, No. 30 and No. 649, the former being slightly scarcer, though currently no more valuable. Hassan backs in T205 are printed in green and do not command any significant premium in the market.

(See T202, T205.)

1887 Hastings Cabinets

From the Boston studio of G.H. Hastings, this standard-format (about 3-3/4" x 5-3/4") cabinet card depicts the 19th Century's most popular star in stylish street clothers. Printed beneath the portrait is a copyright line, player and team identification and the logo and address of the studio. Back is blank. It is unknown whether other ballplayers' portraits were produced, though it is likely.

	NM	EX	VG
M.J. Kelly	12,500	5,000	2,500

1952 Hawthorn-Mellody Chicago White Sox Pins

This issue was sponsored by a local dairy. The 1-3/8" diameter pins have sepia lithographs of the players with "Club of Champs" printed above. A non-pictorial membership button is also part of the set. The unnumbered pins are listed here in alphabetical order.

		NM	EX	VG
Complete Set (11):		400.00	200.00	120.00
Common Player:		35.00	17.50	10.50
(1)	Ray Coleman	35.00	17.50	10.50
(2)	Sam Dente	35.00	17.50	10.50
(3)	Joe Dobson	35.00	17.50	10.50
(4)	Nelson Fox	80.00	40.00	24.00
(5)	Sherman Lollar	45.00	22.00	13.50
(6)	Bill Pierce	45.00	22.00	13.50
(7)	Eddie Robinson	35.00	17.50	10.50
(8)	Hector Rodriguez	35.00	17.50	10.50
(9)	Eddie Stewart	35.00	17.50	10.50
(10)	Al Zarilla	35.00	17.50	10.50
(11)	Member's pin	15.00	7.50	4.50

1959 R.H. Hayes Postcards

Whether there are any other player postcards distributed by R.H. Hayes of Kansas is unknown. Produced for Hayes by Dexter Press, which issued cards for Coke in later years, the 3-1/2" x

5-1/2" postcard has a borderless color photo on front with a facsimile autograph at bottom. The postcard back has credit lines for Hayes and Dexter and a short biography of the player.

		NM	EX	VG
(1)	Hank Bauer	45.00	22.50	13.50

1911 Helmar Stamps (T332)

A collectible departure from the traditional tobacco cards of the period, Helmar Cigarettes in 1911 issued a series of small major league baseball player "stamps." The stamps, each measuring approximately 1-1/8" x 1-3/8", feature a black and white player portrait surrounded by a colorful, ornate frame. The stamps were originally issued in a 2" x 2-1/2" glassine envelope which advertised the Helmar brand and promoted "Philately - the Popular European Rage." To date, 181 different player stamps have been found. The set includes as many as 50 different frame designs. The Helmar stamp set has been assigned a T332 designation by the American Card Catalog.

		NM	EX	VG
Complete Set (180):		8,000	4,000	2,400
Common Player:		50.00	25.00	15.00
(1)	Babe Adams	50.00	25.00	15.00
(2)	Red Ames	50.00	25.00	15.00
(3)	Jimmy Archer	50.00	25.00	15.00
(4)	Jimmy Austin	50.00	25.00	15.00
(5)	Home Run Baker	100.00	50.00	30.00
(6)	Neal Ball	50.00	25.00	15.00
(7)	Cy Barger	50.00	25.00	15.00
(8)	Jack Barry	50.00	25.00	15.00
(9)	Johnny Bates	50.00	25.00	15.00
(10)	Fred Beck	50.00	25.00	15.00
(11)	Beals Becker	50.00	25.00	15.00
(12)	George Bell	50.00	25.00	15.00
(13)	Chief Bender	100.00	50.00	30.00
(14)	Bob Bescher	50.00	25.00	15.00
(15)	Joe Birmingham	50.00	25.00	15.00
(16)	John Bliss	50.00	25.00	15.00
(17)	Bruno Block	50.00	25.00	15.00
(18)	Ping Bodie	50.00	25.00	15.00
(19)	Roger Bresnahan	100.00	50.00	30.00
(20)	Al Bridwell	50.00	25.00	15.00
(21)	Lew Brockett	50.00	25.00	15.00
(22)	Mordecai Brown	100.00	50.00	30.00
(23)	Bill Burns	50.00	25.00	15.00
(24)	Donie Bush	50.00	25.00	15.00
(25)	Bobby Byrne	50.00	25.00	15.00
(26)	Nixey Callahan	50.00	25.00	15.00
(27)	Howie Camnitz	50.00	25.00	15.00
(28)	Max Carey	100.00	50.00	30.00
(29)	Bill Carrigan	50.00	25.00	15.00
(30)	Frank Chance	100.00	50.00	30.00
(31)	Hal Chase	50.00	25.00	15.00
(32)	Ed Cicotte	80.00	40.00	24.00
(33)	Fred Clarke	100.00	50.00	30.00
(34)	Tommy Clarke	50.00	25.00	15.00
(35)	Ty Cobb	750.00	375.00	225.00
(36)	King Cole	50.00	25.00	15.00
(37)	Eddie Collins (Philadelphia)	100.00	50.00	30.00
(38)	Shano Collins (Chicago)	50.00	25.00	15.00
(39)	Wid Conroy	50.00	25.00	15.00
(40)	Doc Crandall	50.00	25.00	15.00
(41)	Sam Crawford	100.00	50.00	30.00
(42)	Birdie Cree	50.00	25.00	15.00
(43)	Bill Dahlen	50.00	25.00	15.00
(44)	Jake Daubert	50.00	25.00	15.00
(45)	Harry Davis	50.00	25.00	15.00
(46)	Jim Delahanty	50.00	25.00	15.00
(47)	Art Devlin	50.00	25.00	15.00
(48)	Josh Devore	50.00	25.00	15.00
(49)	Mike Donlin	50.00	25.00	15.00
(50)	Wild Bill Donovan	50.00	25.00	15.00

		NM	EX	VG
(51)	Red Dooin	50.00	25.00	15.00
(52)	Mickey Doolan	50.00	25.00	15.00
(53)	Patsy Dougherty	50.00	25.00	15.00
(54)	Tom Downey	50.00	25.00	15.00
(55)	Larry Doyle	50.00	25.00	15.00
(56)	Louis Drucke	50.00	25.00	15.00
(57)	Clyde Engle	50.00	25.00	15.00
(58)	Tex Erwin	50.00	25.00	15.00
(59)	Steve Evans	50.00	25.00	15.00
(60)	Johnny Evers	100.00	50.00	30.00
(61)	Jack Ferry	50.00	25.00	15.00
(62)	Ray Fisher	50.00	25.00	15.00
(63)	Art Fletcher	50.00	25.00	15.00
(64)	Russ Ford	50.00	25.00	15.00
(65)	Art Fromme	50.00	25.00	15.00
(66)	Earl Gardner	50.00	25.00	15.00
(67)	Harry Gaspar	50.00	25.00	15.00
(68)	George Gibson	50.00	25.00	15.00
(69)	Roy Golden	50.00	25.00	15.00
(70)	Hank Gowdy	50.00	25.00	15.00
(71)	Peaches Graham	50.00	25.00	15.00
(72)	Eddie Grant	50.00	25.00	15.00
(73)	Dolly Gray	50.00	25.00	15.00
(74)	Clark Griffith	100.00	50.00	30.00
(75)	Bob Groom	50.00	25.00	15.00
(76)	Bob Harmon	50.00	25.00	15.00
(77)	Grover Hartley	50.00	25.00	15.00
(78)	Arnold Hauser	50.00	25.00	15.00
(79)	Buck Herzog	50.00	25.00	15.00
(80)	Dick Hoblitzell	50.00	25.00	15.00
(81)	Solly Hoffman (Hofman)	50.00	25.00	15.00
(82)	Miller Huggins	100.00	50.00	30.00
(83)	Long Tom Hughes	50.00	25.00	15.00
(84)	John Hummel	50.00	25.00	15.00
(85)	Hughie Jennings	100.00	50.00	30.00
(86)	Walter Johnson	275.00	135.00	82.00
(87)	Davy Jones	50.00	25.00	15.00
(88)	Johnny Kling	50.00	25.00	15.00
(89)	Otto Knabe	50.00	25.00	15.00
(90)	Jack Knight	50.00	25.00	15.00
(91)	Ed Konetchy	50.00	25.00	15.00
(92)	Harry Krause	50.00	25.00	15.00
(93)	Nap Lajoie	100.00	50.00	30.00
(94)	Joe Lake	50.00	25.00	15.00
(95)	Frank LaPorte	50.00	25.00	15.00
(96)	Tommy Leach	50.00	25.00	15.00
(97)	Lefty Leifield	50.00	25.00	15.00
(98)	Ed Lennox	50.00	25.00	15.00
(99)	Paddy Livingston	50.00	25.00	15.00
(100)	Hans Lobert	50.00	25.00	15.00
(101)	Harry Lord	50.00	25.00	15.00
(102)	Fred Luderus	50.00	25.00	15.00
(103)	Sherry Magee	50.00	25.00	15.00
(104)	Rube Marquard	100.00	50.00	30.00
(105)	Christy Mathewson	300.00	150.00	90.00
(106)	Al Mattern	50.00	25.00	15.00
(107)	George McBride	50.00	25.00	15.00
(108)	Amby McConnell	50.00	25.00	15.00
(109)	John McGraw	100.00	50.00	30.00
(110)	Harry McIntire (McIntyre)	50.00	25.00	15.00
(111)	Matty McIntyre	50.00	25.00	15.00
(112)	Larry McLean	50.00	25.00	15.00
(113)	Fred Merkle	50.00	25.00	15.00
(114)	Chief Meyers	50.00	25.00	15.00
(115)	Clyde Milan	50.00	25.00	15.00
(116)	Dots Miller	50.00	25.00	15.00
(117)	Mike Mitchell	50.00	25.00	15.00
(118)	Earl Moore	50.00	25.00	15.00
(119)	Pat Moran	50.00	25.00	15.00
(120)	George Moriarty	50.00	25.00	15.00
(121)	Mike Mowrey	50.00	25.00	15.00
(122)	George Mullin	50.00	25.00	15.00
(123)	Danny Murphy	50.00	25.00	15.00
(124)	Red Murray	50.00	25.00	15.00
(125)	Tom Needham	50.00	25.00	15.00
(126)	Rebel Oakes	50.00	25.00	15.00
(127)	Rube Oldring	50.00	25.00	15.00
(128)	Marty O'Toole	50.00	25.00	15.00
(129)	Fred Parent	50.00	25.00	15.00
(130)	Dode Paskert	50.00	25.00	15.00
(131)	Barney Pelty	50.00	25.00	15.00
(132)	Eddie Phelps	50.00	25.00	15.00
(133)	Jack Powell	50.00	25.00	15.00
(134)	Jack Quinn	50.00	25.00	15.00
(135)	Ed Reulbach	50.00	25.00	15.00
(136)	Lew Richie	50.00	25.00	15.00
(137)	Reggie Richter	50.00	25.00	15.00
(138)	Jack Rowan	50.00	25.00	15.00
(139)	Nap Rucker	50.00	25.00	15.00
(140)	Slim Sallee	50.00	25.00	15.00
(141)	Doc Scanlan	50.00	25.00	15.00
(142)	Germany Schaefer	50.00	25.00	15.00
(143)	Boss Schmidt	50.00	25.00	15.00
(144)	Wildfire Schulte	50.00	25.00	15.00
(145)	Jim Scott	50.00	25.00	15.00
(146)	Tillie Shafer	50.00	25.00	15.00
(147)	Dave Shean	50.00	25.00	15.00
(148)	Jimmy Sheckard	50.00	25.00	15.00
(149)	Mike Simon	50.00	25.00	15.00
(150)	Fred Snodgrass	50.00	25.00	15.00
(151)	Tris Speaker	125.00	62.00	37.00
(152)	Oscar Stanage	50.00	25.00	15.00
(153)	Bill Steele	50.00	25.00	15.00
(154)	Harry Stovall	50.00	25.00	15.00
(155)	Gabby Street	50.00	25.00	15.00
(156)	George Suggs	50.00	25.00	15.00
(157)	Billy Sullivan	50.00	25.00	15.00
(158)	Bill Sweeney	50.00	25.00	15.00
(159)	Jeff Sweeney	50.00	25.00	15.00
(160)	Lee Tannehill	50.00	25.00	15.00
(161)	Ira Thomas	50.00	25.00	15.00
(162)	Joe Tinker	100.00	50.00	30.00
(163)	John Titus	50.00	25.00	15.00
(164)	Fred Toney	50.00	25.00	15.00
(165)	Terry Turner	50.00	25.00	15.00
(166)	Hippo Vaughn	50.00	25.00	15.00
(167)	Heinie Wagner	50.00	25.00	15.00
(168)	Bobby Wallace	100.00	50.00	30.00

(169)	Ed Walsh	100.00	50.00	30.00
(170)	Jack Warhop	50.00	25.00	15.00
(171)	Zach Wheat	100.00	50.00	30.00
(172)	Doc White	50.00	25.00	15.00
(173)	Ed Willett	50.00	25.00	15.00
(174)	Art Wilson (New York)	50.00	25.00	15.00
(175)	Owen Wilson (Pittsburgh)	50.00	25.00	15.00
(176)	Hooks Wiltse	50.00	25.00	15.00
(177)	Harry Wolter	50.00	25.00	15.00
(178)	Harry Wolverton	50.00	25.00	15.00
(179)	Cy Young	400.00	200.00	120.00
(180)	Irv Young	50.00	25.00	15.00

1920-21 Hendlers Ice Cream

This Baltimore-area regional issue is a parallel to the 120-card strip card set known as W514, though it is not known whether all or only some of the W514 cards can be found with the ice cream company's advertising printed in blue on the backs. The cards were originally issued in strips of 10, cut horizontally from larger sheets. Well-cut cards should measure about 1-3/8" x 2-1/2". The back printing on each card has the same two top lines: HENDLERS ICE CREAM/"The Velvet Kind," with the third line being one of five currently known ad slogans. See W514 for checklist and base price information.

Common Player: 500.00 200.00 100.00
Stars: 4-6X corresponding W514

1910 Hermes Ice Cream Pirates Pins

The World's Champion Pittsburgh Pirates are featured on this colorful set of 1-1/4" pins. Sepia player portraits at center have a yellow border around with a blue banner at bottom and a skull and crossbones. The players are not identified on the buttons, making them difficult to collect.

		NM	EX	VG
Complete Set (12):		11,000	5,500	3,250
Common Player:		450.00	225.00	135.00
(1)	Bill Abstein	450.00	225.00	135.00
(2)	Red Adams	450.00	225.00	135.00
(3)	Bobby Byrne	450.00	225.00	135.00
(4)	Howie Camnitz	450.00	225.00	135.00
(5)	Fred Clarke	450.00	225.00	135.00
(6)	George Gibson	450.00	225.00	135.00
(7)	Tommy Leach	450.00	225.00	135.00
(8)	Sam Leever	450.00	225.00	135.00
(9)	Dots Miller	450.00	225.00	135.00
(10)	Mike Simon	450.00	225.00	135.00
(11)	Honus Wagner	6,500	3,250	2,000
(12)	Owen Wilson	450.00	225.00	135.00

1916 Herpolsheimer Co.

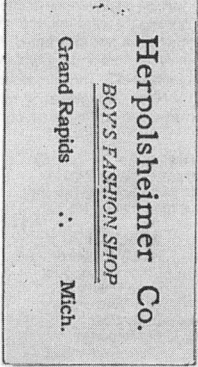

HOWARD SHANKS
L. F.—Washington Am.
160

Grand Rapids :: Mich.

Herpolsheimer Co.
BOY'S FASHION SHOP

Advertising for a Michigan clothier is all that differentiates these cards from the more common Sporting News or blankback M101-4 and M101-5 versions and those of other regional advertisers. The cards are black-and-white in 1-5/8" x 3" format. The Herpolsheimer cards command a significant premium from type-card and superstar collectors.

PREMIUMS:
Common Players: 3-4X
Hall of Famers: 2-3X
(See 1916 M101-4 and M101-5 Blank Backs for checklists and price guides.)

1921 Herpolsheimer's

Evidently prepared for, but never actually issued by, a Grand Rapids, Mich., department store, this issue shares a basic format with the blank-backed strip card set designated W575-1 and the American Caramel Co. E121 Series of 80, though the known checklist for the Herpolsheimers includes cards that have not been verified in either or both of those

CHARLES STENGEL
R. F.—Philadelphia Nationals

HERPOLSHEIMER'S
Boys Fashion Shop
THE HOME OF
BOY'S FASHIONABLE CLOTHING
SECOND FLOOR

sets. It is also not known to what extent the variations in W575-1/E121 are found among the Michigan store's version. The 2-1/16" x 3-3/8" black-and-white cards are each currently known in only one copy each. The checklist here is likely incomplete; gaps have been left in the assigned numbering to accommodate future additions. All known examples originated from a series of eBay auctions in late 2004, with each card having a dollar sign and numeral penciled on back."

		NM	EX	VG
Common Player:				450.00
(3)	Grover Alexander			1,100
(5)	Jim Bagby			450.00
(11)	J. Franklin Baker			750.00
(13)	Ping Bodie			450.00
(15)	George Burns			450.00
(16)	Geo. J. Burns			450.00
(18)	Owen Bush			450.00
(21)	Ty Cobb			4,000
(22)	Eddie Collins			750.00
(28)	George Dauss			450.00
(29)	Dave Davenport			450.00
(30)	Charles Deal			450.00
(33)	William Doak			450.00
(34)	Bill Donovan/Pitching			450.00
(39)	Urban Faber (Dark uniform.)			750.00
(45)	Art Fletcher			450.00
(47)	Jacques Fournier			450.00
(49)	W.L. Gardner			450.00
(52)	"Kid" Gleason			450.00
(54)	Hank Gowdy			450.00
(55)	John Graney (L.F.)			450.00
(57)	Tom Griffith			450.00
(67)	John Henry			450.00
(74)	Rogers Hornsby (2nd B.)			2,000
(79)	Hugh Jennings			500.00
(80)	Walter Johnson			4,500
(82)	James Johnston			450.00
(84)	Joe Judge/Btg			450.00
(89)	P.J. Kilduff			450.00
(93)	"Nemo" Leibold			450.00
(94)	Duffy Lewis			450.00
(95)	Al Mamaux			450.00
(96)	"Rabbit" Maranville			750.00
(101)	John McGraw/Manager			750.00
(102)	Jack McInnis			450.00
(107)	Clyde Milan			450.00
(109)	Otto Miller			450.00
(112)	Guy Morton			450.00
(115)	Eddie Murphy			450.00
(116)	"Hy" Myers (C.F.)			450.00
(123)	Steve O'Neill			450.00
(124)	Roger Peckinbaugh (Peckinpaugh)			450.00
(125)	Jeff Pfeffer (Brooklyn)			450.00
(133)	E.C. Rice			750.00
(134)	Eppa Rixey, Jr.			750.00
(145)	Babe Ruth (R.F.)			10,000
(149)	"Slim" Sallee (Glove showing.)			450.00
(151)	Ray Schalk/Bunting			750.00
(153)	Walter Schang			450.00
(155)	Everett Scott (Boston)			450.00
(173)	Tris Speaker/Manager			1,625
(175)	Charles Stengel/Btg			750.00
(177)	Milton Stock			450.00
(178)	Amos Strunk (R.F.)			450.00
(181)	Zeb Terry (White uniform.)			450.00
(182)	Chester Thomas			450.00
(183)	Fred Toney (Both feet on ground.)			450.00
(186)	George Tyler			450.00
(187)	Jim Vaughn (Dark cap.)			450.00
(190)	Bob Veach (Arms folded.)			450.00
(191)	Oscar Vitt (3rd B.)			450.00
(193)	W. Wambsganss			450.00
(194)	Carl Weilman			450.00
(195)	Zach Wheat			750.00
(196)	George Whitted			450.00
(198)	Ivy B. Wingo			450.00
(200)	Joe Wood			675.00
(202)	"Pep" (Ralph) Young			450.00

1888 S.F. Hess (N338-2)

The most popular of the S.F. Hess & Co. issues, this 21-card set was issued in 1889 and pictures 16 players from the New York Giants, two New York Mets players, two from St. Louis and one from Detroit. The cards measure 2-3/4" x 1-1/2" and feature sepia-toned photographs, most of which are enclosed in ovals with a dark background. The player's name is printed in capital letters just beneath the photo, and the S.F. Hess & Co. logo appears at the bottom (without using the Creole Cigarette brand name).

S. F. HESS & CO.'S CIGARETTES.

		NM	EX	VG
Common Player:		7,900	3,950	2,500
(1)	Bill Brown	7,900	3,950	2,500
(2)	Roger Conner (Connor)	20,000	10,000	6,000
(3)	Ed Crane	7,900	3,950	2,500
(4)	Buck Ewing	21,000	10,500	6,200
(5)	Elmer Foster	7,900	3,950	2,500
(6)	Wm. George	7,900	3,950	2,500
(7)	Joe Gerhardt	7,900	3,950	2,500
(8)	Chas. Getzein (Getzien)	7,900	3,950	2,500
(9)	Geo. Gore	7,900	3,950	2,500
(10)	Gil Hatfield	7,900	3,950	2,500
(11)	Tim Keefe	20,000	10,000	6,000
(12)	Arlie Latham	7,900	3,950	2,500
(13)	Pat Murphy	7,900	3,950	2,500
(14)	Jim Mutrie	7,900	3,950	2,500
(15)	Dave Orr	7,900	3,950	2,500
(16)	Danny Richardson	7,900	3,950	2,500
(17)	Mike Slattery	7,900	3,950	2,500
(18)	Silent Mike Tiernan	7,900	3,950	2,500
(19)	Lidell Titcomb	7,900	3,950	2,500
(20)	Johnny Ward	20,000	10,000	6,000
(21)	Curt Welch	7,900	3,950	2,500
(22)	Mickey Welch	20,000	10,000	6,000
(23)	Arthur Whitney	7,900	3,950	2,500

1909-11 Hindu Cigarettes

Hindu backs are among the more difficult to find among the various cigarette-brand ads seen on T205 and T206 cards. T206s are usually found with the ad printed in brown ink. Much scarcer are those with the ad in red. Fewer than 50 T205s have ever been seen with the Hindu ad on back, printed in brown. Multipliers shown are for "common" player cards. It is noteworthy that more than a few T206 Hindus are found with the cryptic notation "7C" or "FC" in crayon or grease pencil on the back.

PREMIUMS
T205: 15-20X
T206 Brown Commons: 6-8X
T206 Brown Hall of Famers: 4-6X
T206 Brown Southern Leaguers: 2.5-3.5X
T206 Red Commons: 16-20X
T206 Red Hall of Famers: 7-9X
(See T205, T206 for checklists and base card values.)

1958 Hires Root Beer Test Set

Johnny Antonelli

PITCHER—SAN FRANCISCO GIANTS

Johnny Antonelli

San Francisco Giants

Among the scarcest of the regional issues of the late 1950s is the eight-card test issue which preceded the Hires Root Beer set of 66 cards. The test cards differ from the regular issue in that they have sepia-toned, rather than color pictures, which are set against plain yellow or orange backgrounds (much like the 1958 Topps), instead of viewed through a knothole. Like the regular Hires cards, the 2-5/16" x 3-1/2" cards were issued with an attached wedge-shaped tab of like size. The tab offered membership in Hires' baseball fan club, and served to hold the card into the carton of bottled root beer with which it was given away.

	NM	EX	VG
Complete Set, W/Tab (8):	10,000	4,000	2,000
Common Player, W/Tab:	725.00	290.00	145.00
Complete Set, No Tab (8):	3,000	1,200	600.00
Common Player, No Tab:	250.00	100.00	50.00

WITH TAB

		NM	EX	VG
(1)	Johnny Antonelli	725.00	290.00	145.00
(2)	Jim Busby	725.00	290.00	145.00
(3)	Chico Fernandez	725.00	290.00	145.00
(4)	Bob Friend	725.00	290.00	145.00
(5)	Vern Law	725.00	290.00	145.00
(6)	Stan Lopata	725.00	290.00	145.00
(7)	Willie Mays	5,000	2,000	1,000
(8)	Al Pilarcik	725.00	290.00	145.00

NO TAB

		NM	EX	VG
(1)	Johnny Antonelli	250.00	100.00	50.00
(2)	Jim Busby	250.00	100.00	50.00
(3)	Chico Fernandez	250.00	100.00	50.00
(4)	Bob Friend	250.00	100.00	50.00
(5)	Vern Law	250.00	100.00	50.00
(6)	Stan Lopata	250.00	100.00	50.00
(7)	Willie Mays	2,150	1,075	645.00
(8)	Al Pilarcik	250.00	100.00	50.00

1958 Hires Root Beer

PEE WEE REESE
INFIELD—LOS ANGELES DODGERS

JOIN THE HIRES BASEBALL CLUB TODAY!

Like most baseball cards issued with a tab in the 1950s, the Hires cards are extremely scarce today in their original form. The basic card was attached to a wedge-shaped tab that served the dual purpose of offering a fan club membership and of holding the card into the cardboard carton of soda bottles with which it was distributed. Measurements of the card vary somewhat, from about 2-3/8" to 2-5/8" wide and 3-3/8" to 3-5/8" tall (without tab). The tab extends for another 3-1/2". Numbering of the Hires set begins at 10 and goes through 76, with card #69 never issued, making a set complete at 66 cards.

	NM	EX	VG
Complete Set, W/Tab (66):	5,250	2,650	1,550
Common Player, W/Tab:	60.00	30.00	18.00
Complete Set, No Tab (66):	3,250	1,600	975.00
Common Player, No Tab:	35.00	17.50	10.00

WITH TAB

		NM	EX	VG
10	Richie Ashburn	165.00	80.00	50.00
11	Chico Carrasquel	60.00	30.00	18.00
12	Dave Philley	60.00	30.00	18.00
13	Don Newcombe	110.00	55.00	35.00
14	Wally Post	60.00	30.00	18.00
15	Rip Repulski	60.00	30.00	18.00
16	Chico Fernandez	60.00	30.00	18.00
17	Larry Doby	95.00	50.00	25.00
18	Hector Brown	60.00	30.00	18.00
19	Danny O'Connell	60.00	30.00	18.00
20	Granny Hamner	60.00	30.00	18.00
21	Dick Groat	60.00	30.00	18.00
22	Ray Narleski	60.00	30.00	18.00
23	Pee Wee Reese	165.00	85.00	50.00
24	Bob Friend	60.00	30.00	18.00
25	Willie Mays	500.00	250.00	150.00
26	Bob Nieman	60.00	30.00	18.00
27	Frank Thomas	60.00	30.00	18.00
28	Curt Simmons	60.00	30.00	18.00
29	Stan Lopata	60.00	30.00	18.00
30	Bob Skinner	60.00	30.00	18.00
31	Ron Kline	60.00	30.00	18.00
32	Willie Miranda	60.00	30.00	18.00
33	Bob Avila	60.00	30.00	18.00
34	Clem Labine	90.00	45.00	27.50
35	Ray Jablonski	60.00	30.00	18.00
36	Bill Mazeroski	110.00	55.00	35.00
37	Billy Gardner	60.00	30.00	18.00
38	Pete Runnels	60.00	30.00	18.00
39	Jack Sanford	60.00	30.00	18.00

40	Dave Sisler	60.00	30.00	18.00
41	Don Zimmer	90.00	45.00	27.00
42	Johnny Podres	90.00	45.00	27.50
43	Dick Farrell	60.00	30.00	18.00
44	Hank Aaron	425.00	210.00	125.00
45	Bill Virdon	60.00	30.00	18.00
46	Bobby Thomson	75.00	37.50	22.50
47	Willard Nixon	60.00	30.00	18.00
48	Billy Loes	60.00	30.00	18.00
49	Hank Sauer	60.00	30.00	18.00
50	Johnny Antonelli	60.00	30.00	18.00
51	Daryl Spencer	60.00	30.00	18.00
52	Ken Lehman	75.00	37.50	22.50
53	Sammy White	60.00	30.00	18.00
54	Charley Neal	75.00	37.50	22.50
55	Don Drysdale	165.00	80.00	50.00
56	Jack Jensen	65.00	32.50	20.00
57	Ray Katt	60.00	30.00	18.00
58	Franklin Sullivan	60.00	30.00	18.00
59	Roy Face	60.00	30.00	18.00
60	Willie Jones	60.00	30.00	18.00
61	Duke Snider/SP	250.00	125.00	75.00
62	Whitey Lockman	60.00	30.00	18.00
63	Gino Cimoli	75.00	37.00	22.50
64	Marv Grissom	60.00	30.00	18.00
65	Gene Baker	60.00	30.00	18.00
66	George Zuverink	60.00	30.00	18.00
67	Ted Kluszewski	135.00	70.00	40.00
68	Jim Busby	60.00	30.00	18.00
69	Not Issued			
70	Curt Barclay	60.00	30.00	18.00
71	Hank Foiles	60.00	30.00	18.00
72	Gene Stephens	60.00	30.00	18.00
73	Al Worthington	60.00	30.00	18.00
74	Al Walker	60.00	30.00	18.00
75	Bob Boyd	60.00	30.00	18.00
76	Al Pilarcik	60.00	30.00	18.00

NO TAB

10	Richie Ashburn	110.00	55.00	35.00
11	Chico Carrasquel	35.00	17.50	10.00
12	Dave Philley	35.00	17.50	10.00
13	Don Newcombe	65.00	32.50	20.00
14	Wally Post	35.00	17.50	10.00
15	Rip Repulski	35.00	17.50	10.00
16	Chico Fernandez	35.00	17.50	10.00
17	Larry Doby	75.00	37.50	22.50
18	Hector Brown	35.00	17.50	10.00
19	Danny O'Connell	35.00	17.50	10.00
20	Granny Hamner	35.00	17.50	10.00
21	Dick Groat	35.00	17.50	10.00
22	Ray Narleski	35.00	17.50	10.00
23	Pee Wee Reese	100.00	50.00	30.00
24	Bob Friend	35.00	17.50	10.00
25	Willie Mays	200.00	100.00	60.00
26	Bob Nieman	35.00	17.50	10.00
27	Frank Thomas	35.00	17.50	10.00
28	Curt Simmons	35.00	17.50	10.00
29	Stan Lopata	35.00	17.50	10.00
30	Bob Skinner	35.00	17.50	10.00
31	Ron Kline	35.00	17.50	10.00
32	Willie Miranda	35.00	17.50	10.00
33	Bob Avila	35.00	17.50	10.00
34	Clem Labine	45.00	22.50	13.50
35	Ray Jablonski	35.00	17.50	10.00
36	Bill Mazeroski	75.00	37.50	22.50
37	Billy Gardner	35.00	17.50	10.00
38	Pete Runnels	35.00	17.50	10.00
39	Jack Sanford	35.00	17.50	10.00
40	Dave Sisler	35.00	17.50	10.00
41	Don Zimmer	45.00	22.50	13.50
42	Johnny Podres	45.00	22.50	13.50
43	Dick Farrell	35.00	17.50	10.00
44	Hank Aaron	200.00	100.00	60.00
45	Bill Virdon	35.00	17.50	10.00
46	Bobby Thomson	45.00	22.50	13.50
47	Willard Nixon	35.00	17.50	10.00
48	Billy Loes	35.00	17.50	10.00
49	Hank Sauer	35.00	17.50	10.00
50	Johnny Antonelli	35.00	17.50	10.00
51	Daryl Spencer	35.00	17.50	10.00
52	Ken Lehman	40.00	20.00	12.00
53	Sammy White	35.00	17.50	10.00
54	Charley Neal	40.00	20.00	12.00
55	Don Drysdale	75.00	37.50	22.50
56	Jack Jensen	40.00	20.00	12.00
57	Ray Katt	35.00	17.50	10.00
58	Franklin Sullivan	35.00	17.50	10.00
59	Roy Face	35.00	17.50	10.00
60	Willie Jones	35.00	17.50	10.00
61	Duke Snider/SP	180.00	90.00	55.00
62	Whitey Lockman	35.00	17.50	10.00
63	Gino Cimoli	40.00	20.00	10.00
64	Marv Grissom	35.00	17.50	10.00
65	Gene Baker	35.00	17.50	10.00
66	George Zuverink	35.00	17.50	10.00
67	Ted Kluszewski	75.00	37.50	22.50
68	Jim Busby	35.00	17.50	10.00
69	Not Issued			
70	Curt Barclay	35.00	17.50	10.00
71	Hank Foiles	35.00	17.50	10.00
72	Gene Stephens	35.00	17.50	10.00
73	Al Worthington	35.00	17.50	10.00
74	Al Walker	35.00	17.50	10.00
75	Bob Boyd	35.00	17.50	10.00
76	Al Pilarcik	35.00	17.50	10.00

1951-52 Hit Parade of Champions

(See 1951-52 Berk Ross.)

1977 Holiday Inn Discs

Virtually identical in format to the several locally sponsored disc sets of the previous year, these 3-3/8" diameter player discs were given away five at a time with the purchase of a children's dinner at some 72 participating Holiday Inns in the Midwest. Discs once again feature black-and-white player portrait photos in the center of a baseball design. The left and right panels are in one of several bright colors. Licensed by the Players Association through Mike Schechter Associates, the player photos carry no uniform logos. Backs are printed in green. The unnumbered discs are checklisted here alphabetically.

		NM	EX	VG
Complete Set (70):		160.00	80.00	45.00
Common Player:		2.00	1.00	.60
(1)	Sal Bando	2.00	1.00	.60
(2)	Buddy Bell	2.00	1.00	.60
(3)	Johnny Bench	6.00	3.00	1.75
(4)	Larry Bowa	2.00	1.00	.60
(5)	Steve Braun	2.00	1.00	.60
(6)	George Brett	20.00	10.00	6.00
(7)	Lou Brock	6.00	3.00	1.75
(8)	Jeff Burroughs	2.00	1.00	.60
(9)	Bert Campaneris	2.00	1.00	.60
(10)	John Candelaria	2.00	1.00	.60
(11)	Jose Cardenal	2.00	1.00	.60
(12)	Rod Carew	6.00	3.00	1.75
(13)	Steve Carlton	6.00	3.00	1.75
(14)	Dave Cash	2.00	1.00	.60
(15)	Cesar Cedeno	2.00	1.00	.60
(16)	Ron Cey	2.00	1.00	.60
(17)	Dave Concepcion	2.00	1.00	.60
(18)	Dennis Eckersley	5.00	2.50	1.50
(19)	Mark Fidrych	3.00	1.50	.90
(20)	Rollie Fingers	5.00	2.50	1.50
(21)	Carlton Fisk	6.00	3.00	1.75
(22)	George Foster	2.00	1.00	.60
(23)	Wayne Garland	2.00	1.00	.60
(24)	Ralph Garr	2.00	1.00	.60
(25)	Steve Garvey	4.00	2.00	1.25
(26)	Cesar Geronimo	2.00	1.00	.60
(27)	Bobby Grich	2.00	1.00	.60
(28)	Ken Griffey Sr.	2.50	1.25	.70
(29)	Don Gullett	2.00	1.00	.60
(30)	Mike Hargrove	2.00	1.00	.60
(31)	Al Hrabosky	2.00	1.00	.60
(32)	Jim Hunter	5.00	2.50	1.50
(33)	Reggie Jackson	10.00	5.00	3.00
(34)	Randy Jones	2.00	1.00	.60
(35a)	Dave Kingman (Mets)	2.50	1.25	.70
(35b)	Dave Kingman (Padres)	4.00	2.00	1.25
(36)	Jerry Koosman	2.00	1.00	.60
(37)	Dave LaRoche	2.00	1.00	.60
(38)	Greg Luzinski	2.00	1.00	.60
(39)	Fred Lynn	2.00	1.00	.60
(40)	Bill Madlock	2.00	1.00	.60
(41)	Rick Manning	2.00	1.00	.60
(42)	Jon Matlock	2.00	1.00	.60
(43)	John Mayberry	2.00	1.00	.60
(44)	Hal McRae	2.00	1.00	.60
(45)	Andy Messersmith	2.00	1.00	.60
(46)	Rick Monday	2.00	1.00	.60
(47)	John Montefusco	2.00	1.00	.60
(48)	Joe Morgan	6.00	3.00	1.75
(49)	Thurman Munson	4.00	2.00	1.25
(50)	Bobby Murcer	2.00	1.00	.60
(51)	Bill North	2.00	1.00	.60
(52)	Jim Palmer	6.00	3.00	1.75
(53)	Tony Perez	5.00	2.50	1.50
(54)	Jerry Reuss	2.00	1.00	.60
(55)	Brooks Robinson	6.00	3.00	1.75
(56)	Pete Rose	15.00	7.50	4.50
(57)	Joe Rudi	2.00	1.00	.60
(58)	Nolan Ryan	40.00	20.00	12.00
(59)	Manny Sanguillen	2.00	1.00	.60
(60)	Mike Schmidt	15.00	7.50	4.50
(61)	Tom Seaver	6.00	3.00	1.75
(62)	Bill Singer	2.00	1.00	.60
(63)	Willie Stargell	6.00	3.00	1.75
(64)	Rusty Staub	3.00	1.50	.90
(65)	Luis Tiant	2.00	1.00	.60
(66)	Bob Watson	2.00	1.00	.60
(67)	Butch Wynegar	2.00	1.00	.60
(68)	Carl Yastrzemski	7.50	3.75	2.25
(69)	Robin Yount	6.00	3.00	1.75
(70)	Richie Zisk	2.00	1.00	.60

1925 Holland World's Champions Washington Senators

The World's Champion Washington Senators were featured on a set issued in Winnipeg, Manitoba, of all places. The 1-1/2" x 3" cards have player portrait photos printed in blue on front. The black-printed back has a card number and details of a redemption offer of cards for ice cream. Like many such offers it appears as if card #16 was intentionally withheld or minimally distributed, making it very scarce today.

		NM	EX	VG
Complete Set, No #16 (17):		35,000	17,500	10,250
Common Player:		1,600	800.00	475.00
1	Ralph Miller	1,600	800.00	475.00
2	Earl McNeely	1,600	800.00	475.00
3	Allan Russell	1,600	800.00	475.00
4	Ernest Shirley	1,600	800.00	475.00
5	Sam Rice	2,400	1,200	725.0
6	Muddy Ruel	1,600	800.00	475.00
7	Ossie Bluege	1,600	800.00	475.00
8	Nemo Leibold	1,600	800.00	475.00
9	Paul Zahniser	1,600	800.00	475.00
10	Firpo Marberry	1,600	800.00	475.00
11	Warren Ogden	1,600	800.00	475.00
12	George Mogridge	1,600	800.00	475.00
13	Tom Zachary	1,600	800.00	475.00
14	Goose Goslin	2,400	1,200	725.00
15	Joe Judge	1,600	800.00	475.00
16	Roger Peckinpaugh	5,000	2,500	1,500
17	Bucky Harris	2,40	1,200	725.00
18	Walter Johnson	7,000	3,500	2,100

1916 Holmes to Homes Bread

Most often found with blank backs, this 200-card set can also be found with ads on the back for several local and regional businesses. Among them is Holmes to Homes Milk-Made Bread, location unknown. Type card collectors and superstar collectors can expect to pay a significant premium for individual cards with Holmes to Homes advertising. Cards measure 1-5/8" x 3" and are printed in black-and-white.

(See 1916 M101-5 Blank Backs for checklist and base value information.)
PREMIUM: 15-25X

1920 Holsum Bread

Issued by the Weil Baking Co., New Orleans, which produced several sets in the 1910s, this issue shares a format, but not the checklist of the 1921 American Caramel Co. set known as E121, Series of 80, and the contemporary W575-1 blank-back strip cards. To what extent the base cards and known variations in those set are found among the Holsum version is unknown. The Holsum cards differ from E121 primarily in the advertising on the back and sometimes in photo and/or caption details. The approximately 2" x 3-1/4" black-and-white cards are much scarcer than the caramel version. The trial checklist presented here is incomplete.

		NM	EX	VG
Common Player:		350.00	175.00	100.00
(2)	Grover Alexander	1,000	500.00	300.00
(4)	Jimmy Austin	350.00	175.00	100.00
(7)	Dave Bancroft	600.00	300.00	180.00
(13)	Jack Barry	350.00	175.00	100.00
(16)	Ping Bodie	350.00	175.00	100.00
(19)	George Burns	350.00	175.00	100.00

(20)	Geo. S. Burns	350.00	175.00	100.00
(23)	Max Carey	600.00	300.00	180.00
(26)	Ray Chapman	425.00	210.00	125.00
(28)	Eddie Cicotte	600.00	300.00	180.00
(30)	Eddie Collins	750.00	370.00	220.00
(32)	Harry Coveleskie	350.00	175.00	100.00
(37)	Geo. Cutshaw	350.00	175.00	100.00
(39)	George Dauss	350.00	175.00	100.00
(40)	Dave Davenport	350.00	175.00	100.00
(42)	Charles Deal (Dark uniform.)	350.00	175.00	100.00
(44)	Williams Doak	350.00	175.00	100.00
(45)	Johnny Evers	600.00	300.00	180.00
(46)	Urban Faber (Dark uniform.)	600.00	300.00	180.00
(50)	Art Fletcher	350.00	175.00	100.00
(51)	Eddie Foster	350.00	175.00	100.00
(52)	Jacques Fournier	350.00	175.00	100.00
(56)	W.L. Gardner	350.00	175.00	100.00
(64)	Hank Gowdy	350.00	175.00	100.00
(66)	John Graney	350.00	175.00	100.00
(69)	John Henry	350.00	175.00	100.00
(70)	Tom Griffith	350.00	175.00	100.00
(71)	Harry Hooper	600.00	300.00	180.00
(80)	Rogers Hornsby	1,250	625.00	375.00
(85)	Joe Jackson (Value Undetermined)			
(88)	Walter Johnson (Hands at chest.)	2,000	1,000	600.00
(89)	James Johnston	350.00	175.00	100.00
(91)	Joe Judge	350.00	175.00	100.00
(92)	P.J. Kilduff	350.00	175.00	100.00
(93)	Wm. Killefer Jr.	350.00	175.00	100.00
(95)	John Lavan	350.00	175.00	100.00
(97)	H.B. Leonard	350.00	175.00	100.00
(99)	Duffy Lewis	350.00	175.00	100.00
(105)	Al Mamaux	350.00	175.00	100.00
(107)	"Rabbit" Maranville	600.00	300.00	180.00
(110)	John McGraw	600.00	300.00	180.00
(115)	Clyde Milan	350.00	175.00	100.00
(116)	Otto Miller	350.00	175.00	100.00
(120)	Ray Morgan	350.00	175.00	100.00
(122)	Guy Morton	350.00	175.00	100.00
(124)	"Hy" Myers	350.00	175.00	100.00
(127)	Arthur Nehf	350.00	175.00	100.00
(129)	Steve O'Neill	350.00	175.00	100.00
(132)	Roger Peckinpaugh	400.00	200.00	120.00
(133)	Jeff Pfeffer	350.00	175.00	100.00
(136)	Bill Rariden	350.00	175.00	100.00
(138)	Davey Robertson	350.00	175.00	100.00
(140)	"Bob" Roth	350.00	175.00	100.00
(142)	Edd Roush	600.00	300.00	180.00
(150)	Slim Sallee	350.00	175.00	100.00
(153)	Walter Schang	350.00	175.00	100.00
(155)	Everett Scott	350.00	175.00	100.00
(159)	Hank Severied	350.00	175.00	100.00
(162)	Geo. Sisler	600.00	300.00	180.00
(164)	J. Carlisle Smith	350.00	175.00	100.00
(166)	Tris Speaker	1,250	625.00	375.00
(168)	Charles Stengel	600.00	300.00	180.00
(170)	Amos Strunk/Btg (Chicago Americans.)	350.00	175.00	100.00
(171)	Amos Strunk (Arms at side, Chicago White Sox.)	350.00	175.00	100.00
(173)	Chester Thomas	350.00	175.00	100.00
(174)	Fred Toney	350.00	175.00	100.00
(175)	Jim Vaughn (Plain uniform)	350.00	175.00	100.00
(178)	Bob Veach	350.00	175.00	100.00
(184)	W. Wambsganss	350.00	175.00	100.00
(186)	Carl Weilman	350.00	175.00	100.00
(187)	Zack Wheat	600.00	300.00	180.00
(190)	Claude Williams (White stockings, correct photo.)	2,500	1,250	750.00
(192)	Ivy Wingo	350.00	175.00	100.00
(202)	Pep Young	350.00	175.00	100.00

1959 Home Run Derby

GIL HODGES
LOS ANGELES DODGERS

This 20-card unnumbered set was produced by American Motors to publicize the Home Run Derby television program. The cards measure approximately 3-1/4" x 5-1/4" and feature black-and-white player photos on blank-backed white stock. The player name and team are printed beneath the photo. This set was reprinted (marked as such) in 1988 by Card Collectors' Co. of New York. An advertising poster is sometimes seen which is essentially an uncut sheet of the cards with a promotional message at bottom.

		NM	EX	VG
Complete Set (20):		17,500	8,750	5,000
Common Player:		300.00	150.00	90.00
Advertising Poster:		6,200	3,100	1,900
(1)	Hank Aaron	1,600	800.00	500.00
(2)	Bob Allison	300.00	150.00	90.00

		NM	EX	VG
(3)	Ernie Banks	1,250	650.00	400.00
(4)	Ken Boyer	350.00	175.00	100.00
(5)	Bob Cerv	300.00	150.00	90.00
(6)	Rocky Colavito	600.00	300.00	180.00
(7)	Gil Hodges	600.00	300.00	180.00
(8)	Jackie Jensen	300.00	150.00	90.00
(9)	Al Kaline	1,100	650.00	325.00
(10)	Harmon Killebrew	1,100	650.00	325.00
(11)	Jim Lemon	300.00	150.00	90.00
(12)	Mickey Mantle	4,000	2,000	1,200
(13)	Ed Mathews	1,000	500.00	300.00
(14)	Willie Mays	1,600	800.00	500.00
(15)	Wally Post	300.00	150.00	90.00
(16)	Frank Robinson	1,000	500.00	300.00
(17)	Mark Scott (host)	600.00	300.00	180.00
(18)	Duke Snider	1,200	600.00	375.00
(19)	Dick Stuart	300.00	150.00	90.00
(20)	Gus Triandos	300.00	150.00	90.00

1894 Honest (Duke) Cabinets (N142)

These color cabinet cards, which measure 6" x 9-1/2", were produced by W.H. Duke for its Honest tobacco brand. The player name is centered at the bottom of the card front. The brand name "Honest" is located in the lower-left corner with the words "New York" in the lower-right corner. Three bicyclists are also part of the set.

		NM	EX	VG
Complete Set (4):		49,500	24,750	14,850
Common Player:		18,700	9,350	5,610
(1)	G.S. Davis	24,200	12,100	7,260
(2)	E.J. Delahanty	35,200	17,600	10,560
(3)	W.M. Nash	18,700	9,350	5,610
(4)	W. Robinson	36,850	18,425	11,055

1911-12 Honest Long Cut Tobacco

Advertising, printed in black, for Honest Long Cut tobacco is among the more commonly found on the backs of T205 Gold Border cards of 1911. The brand also advertised on the multi-sport T227 Series of Champions in 1912.

(See T205, T227 for checklists and values.)

1927 Honey Boy

The date of issue for this rare Canadian issue is conjectural. These black-and-white 1-5/8" x 2-3/8" cards were issued by the Purity Ice Cream Company in Winnipeg, Canada, and were redeemable as a set of 21 for a brick of "Delicious Honey Boy Ice Cream." Besides the major leaguers in the set, there

---

are also cards of local amateurs and semi-pros, including hockey Hall of Famer Steamer Maxwell and Chicago Blackhawks star Cecil Browne. The major leaguers are not identified by team, nor do their photos have team insignias present. When redeemed, cards were punch-cancelled. Values shown are for uncancelled cards; cards exhibiting the punch-holes would be worth about 50 percent of the indicated figures.

		NM	EX	VG
Complete Set (21):		24,000	12,000	7,500
Common (Major League) Player:		900.00	450.00	275.00
1	"Steamer" Maxwell (Arenas)	2,000	1,000	600.00
2	Cecil Browne (Dominion Express)	400.00	200.00	120.00
3	Carson McVey (Transcona)	400.00	200.00	120.00
4	Sam Perlman (Tigers)	400.00	200.00	120.00
5	"Snake" Siddle (Arenas)	400.00	200.00	120.00
6	Eddie Cass (Columbus)	400.00	200.00	120.00
7	Jimmy Bradley (Columbus)	400.00	200.00	120.00
8	Gordon Caslake (Dominion Express)	400.00	200.00	120.00
9	Ward McVey (Tigers)	400.00	200.00	120.00
10	"Tris" Speaker	2,750	1,350	825.00
11	George Sisler	2,000	1,000	600.00
12	E. Meusel	900.00	450.00	275.00
13	Ed. Roush	2,000	1,000	600.00
14	"Babe" Ruth	22,500	11,250	6,750
15	Harry Heilmann	2,000	1,000	600.00
16	Heinie Groh	900.00	450.00	275.00
17	Eddie Collins	2,000	1,000	600.00
18	Grover Alexander	3,250	1,600	975.00
19	Dave Bancroft	2,000	1,000	600.00
20	Frank Frisch	2,000	1,000	600.00
21	George Burns	900.00	450.00	275.00

1905-1909 Carl Horner Cabinets

Carl Horner was the premier baseball portraitist of the early 20th Century. From his Boston studio came the images of the day's stars and journeymen which live on today on some of the most popular baseball cards of the era - including the famed T206 Honus Wagner. Highly collectible in their own right are the cabinet photos produced by the studio. Because of rarity, values can be determined only on those rare occasions when an example comes onto the market. Because the body of his work was accomplished over a number of years, mounting style and other technical details of the generally 5-1/2" x 7" cabinets may vary. Because the players are not identified on the cabinet, identification can be a problem, though quite often a contemporary notation of the player's name can be found written on back.

	NM	EX	VG
Common Player:	1,200	600.00	350.00
Hall of Famer:	3,000	1,500	900.00
Walter Johnson	15,000	6,000	3,600
Honus Wagner	20,000	8,000	4,800

1959 Hostess Bob Turley

The date attributed to this card is speculative. The 3-1/2" x 4-3/8" black-and-white card has an action pose of the Yankees pitcher on front surrounded by a white border. On back is a list of Hostess Cakes products.

	NM	EX	VG
Bob Turley	125.00	60.00	40.00

1975 Hostess

The first of what would become five annual issues, the 1975 Hostess set consists of 50 three-card panels which formed the bottom of boxes of family-size snack cake products. Unlike many similar issues, the Hostess cards do not share common borders, so it was possible to cut them neatly and evenly from the box. Well-cut single cards measure 2-1/4" x 3-1/4", while a three-card panel measures 7-1/4" x 3-1/4".

Because some of the panels were issued on packages of less popular snack cakes, they are somewhat scarcer today. Since the hobby was quite well-developed when the Hostess cards were first issued, there is no lack of complete panels. Even unused complete boxes are available today. Some of the photos in this issue also appear on Topps cards of the era.

		NM	EX	VG
Complete Panel Set (50):		350.00	175.00	100.00
Complete Set, Singles (150):		165.00	80.00	50.00
Common Panel:		5.00	2.50	1.50
Common Player:		1.00	.50	.30
	Panel (1)	5.00	2.50	1.50
1	Bobby Tolan	1.00	.50	.30
2	Cookie Rojas	1.00	.50	.30
3	Darrell Evans	1.25	.60	.40
	Panel (2)	10.00	5.00	3.00
4	Sal Bando	1.00	.50	.30
5	Joe Morgan	5.00	2.50	1.50
6	Mickey Lolich	1.25	.60	.40
	Panel (3)	10.00	5.00	3.00
7	Don Sutton	4.50	2.25	1.25
8	Bill Melton	1.00	.50	.30
9	Tim Foli	1.00	.50	.30
	Panel (4)	5.00	2.50	1.50
10	Joe Lahoud	1.00	.50	.30
11a	Bert Hooten (Incorrect spelling.)	1.50	.70	.45
11b	Burt Hooton (Corrected)	1.00	.50	.30
12	Paul Blair	1.00	.50	.30
	Panel (5)	5.00	2.50	1.50
13	Jim Barr	1.00	.50	.30
14	Toby Harrah	1.00	.50	.30
15	John Milner	1.00	.50	.30
	Panel (6)	5.00	2.50	1.50
16	Ken Holtzman	1.00	.50	.30
17	Cesar Cedeno	1.00	.50	.30
18	Dwight Evans	1.00	.50	.30
	Panel (7)	10.00	5.00	3.00
19	Willie McCovey	5.00	2.50	1.50
20	Tony Oliva	1.25	.60	.40
21	Manny Sanguillen	1.00	.50	.30
	Panel (8)	10.00	5.00	3.00
22	Mickey Rivers	1.00	.50	.30
23	Lou Brock	5.00	2.50	1.50
24	Graig Nettles	1.50	.70	.45
	Panel (9)	5.00	2.50	1.50
25	Jim Wynn	1.00	.50	.30
26	George Scott	1.00	.50	.30
27	Greg Luzinski	1.00	.50	.30
	Panel (10)	15.00	7.50	4.50
28	Bert Campaneris	1.00	.50	.30
29	Pete Rose	12.50	6.25	3.75
30	Buddy Bell	1.00	.50	.30
	Panel (11)	5.00	2.50	1.50
31	Gary Matthews	1.00	.50	.30
32	Fred Patek	1.00	.50	.30
33	Mike Lum	1.00	.50	.30
	Panel (12)	5.00	2.50	1.50
34	Ellie Rodriguez	1.00	.50	.30
35	Milt May	1.00	.50	.30
36	Willie Horton	1.00	.50	.30
	Panel (13)	10.00	5.00	3.00
37	Dave Winfield	5.00	2.50	1.50
38	Tom Grieve	1.00	.50	.30
39	Barry Foote	1.00	.50	.30
	Panel (14)	5.00	2.50	1.50
40	Joe Rudi	1.00	.50	.30
41	Bake McBride	1.00	.50	.30
42	Mike Cuellar	1.00	.50	.30
	Panel (15)	5.00	2.50	1.50
43	Garry Maddox	1.00	.50	.30
44	Carlos May	1.00	.50	.30
45	Bud Harrelson	1.00	.50	.30
	Panel (16)	10.00	5.00	3.00
46	Dave Chalk	1.00	.50	.30
47	Dave Concepcion	1.00	.50	.30
48	Carl Yastrzemski	7.50	3.75	2.25
	Panel (17)	10.00	5.00	3.00
49	Steve Garvey	3.00	1.50	.90
50	Amos Otis	1.00	.50	.30
51	Ricky Reuschel	1.00	.50	.30
	Panel (18)	10.00	5.00	3.00
52	Rollie Fingers	4.50	2.25	1.25
53	Bob Watson	1.00	.50	.30
54	John Ellis	1.00	.50	.30
	Panel (19)	10.00	5.00	3.00
55	Bob Bailey	1.00	.50	.30
56	Rod Carew	6.00	3.00	1.75
57	Richie Hebner	1.00	.50	.30

		NM	EX	VG
	Panel (20)	20.00	10.00	6.00
58	Nolan Ryan	15.00	7.50	4.50
59	Reggie Smith	1.00	.50	.30
60	Joe Coleman	1.00	.50	.30
	Panel (21)	10.00	5.00	3.00
61	Ron Cey	1.00	.50	.30
62	Darrell Porter	1.00	.50	.30
63	Steve Carlton	5.00	2.50	1.50
	Panel (22)	5.00	2.50	1.50
64	Gene Tenace	1.00	.50	.30
65	Jose Cardenal	1.00	.50	.30
66	Bill Lee	1.00	.50	.30
	Panel (23)	5.00	2.50	1.50
67	Davey Lopes	1.00	.50	.30
68	Wilbur Wood	1.00	.50	.30
69	Steve Renko	1.00	.50	.30
	Panel (24)	10.00	5.00	3.00
70	Joe Torre	3.00	1.50	.90
71	Ted Sizemore	1.00	.50	.30
72	Bobby Grich	1.00	.50	.30
	Panel (25)	12.50	6.25	3.75
73	Chris Speier	1.00	.50	.30
74	Bert Blyleven	1.25	.60	.40
75	Tom Seaver	6.00	3.00	1.75
	Panel (26)	5.00	2.50	1.50
76	Nate Colbert	1.00	.50	.30
77	Don Kessinger	1.00	.50	.30
78	George Medich	1.00	.50	.30
	Panel (27)	20.00	10.00	6.00
79	Andy Messersmith	1.00	.50	.30
80	Robin Yount	12.50	6.25	3.75
81	Al Oliver	1.25	.60	.40
	Panel (28)	15.00	7.50	4.50
82	Bill Singer	1.00	.50	.30
83	Johnny Bench	6.00	3.00	1.75
84	Gaylord Perry	4.50	2.25	1.25
	Panel (29)	5.00	2.50	1.50
85	Dave Kingman	1.00	.50	.30
86	Ed Herrmann	1.00	.50	.30
87	Ralph Garr	1.00	.50	.30
	Panel (30)	12.50	6.25	3.75
88	Reggie Jackson	7.50	3.75	2.25
89a	Doug Radar	1.50	.70	.45
	(Incorrect spelling.)			
89b	Doug Rader (Corrected)	1.00	.50	.30
90	Elliott Maddox	1.00	.50	.30
	Panel (31)	5.00	2.50	1.50
91	Bill Russell	1.00	.50	.30
92	John Mayberry	1.00	.50	.30
93	Dave Cash	1.00	.50	.30
	Panel (32)	5.00	2.50	1.50
94	Jeff Burroughs	1.00	.50	.30
95	Ted Simmons	1.00	.50	.30
96	Joe Decker	1.00	.50	.30
	Panel (33)	10.00	5.00	3.00
97	Bill Buckner	1.25	.60	.40
98	Bobby Darwin	1.00	.50	.30
99	Phil Niekro	4.50	2.25	1.25
	Panel (34)	5.00	2.50	1.50
100	Mike Sundberg (Jim)	1.00	.50	.30
101	Greg Gross	1.00	.50	.30
102	Luis Tiant	1.00	.50	.30
	Panel (35)	5.00	2.50	1.50
103	Glenn Beckert	1.00	.50	.30
104	Hal McRae	1.00	.50	.30
105	Mike Jorgensen	1.00	.50	.30
	Panel (36)	5.00	2.50	1.50
106	Mike Hargrove	1.00	.50	.30
107	Don Gullett	1.00	.50	.30
108	Tito Fuentes	1.00	.50	.30
	Panel (37)	5.00	2.50	1.50
109	Johnny Grubb	1.00	.50	.30
110	Jim Kaat	1.25	.60	.40
111	Felix Millan	1.00	.50	.30
	Panel (38)	5.00	2.50	1.50
112	Don Money	1.00	.50	.30
113	Rick Monday	1.00	.50	.30
114	Dick Bosman	1.00	.50	.30
	Panel (39)	10.00	5.00	3.00
115	Roger Metzger	1.00	.50	.30
116	Fergie Jenkins	4.50	2.25	1.25
117	Dusty Baker	1.25	.60	.40
	Panel (40)	10.00	5.00	3.00
118	Billy Champion	1.00	.50	.30
119	Bob Gibson	5.00	2.50	1.50
120	Bill Freehan	1.00	.50	.30
	Panel (41)	5.00	2.50	1.50
121	Cesar Geronimo	1.00	.50	.30
122	Jorge Orta	1.00	.50	.30
123	Cleon Jones	1.00	.50	.30
	Panel (42)	10.00	5.00	3.00
124	Steve Busby	1.00	.50	.30
125a	Bill Madlock/Pitcher	1.50	.70	.45
125b	Bill Madlock/Infield	1.00	.50	.30
126	Jim Palmer	5.00	2.50	1.50
	Panel (43)	10.00	5.00	3.00
127	Tony Perez	5.00	2.50	1.50
128	Larry Hisle	1.00	.50	.30
129	Rusty Staub	1.25	.60	.40
	Panel (44)	20.00	10.00	6.00
130	Hank Aaron	13.50	6.75	4.00
131	Rennie Stennett	1.00	.50	.30
132	Rico Petrocelli	1.00	.50	.30
	Panel (45)	15.00	7.50	4.50
133	Mike Schmidt	12.50	6.25	3.75
134	Sparky Lyle	1.00	.50	.30
135	Willie Stargell	5.00	2.50	1.50
	Panel (46)	10.00	5.00	3.00
136	Ken Henderson	1.00	.50	.30
137	Willie Montanez	1.00	.50	.30
138	Thurman Munson	5.00	2.50	1.50
	Panel (47)	5.00	2.50	1.50
139	Richie Zisk	1.00	.50	.30
140	George Hendricks (Hendrick)	1.00	.50	.30
141	Bobby Murcer	1.50	.70	.45
	Panel (48)	15.00	7.50	4.50
142	Lee May	1.00	.50	.30
143	Carlton Fisk	5.00	2.50	1.50

		NM	EX	VG
144	Brooks Robinson	6.00	3.00	1.75
	Panel (49)	5.00	2.50	1.50
145	Bobby Bonds	1.25	.60	.40
146	Gary Sutherland	1.00	.50	.30
147	Oscar Gamble	1.00	.50	.30
	Panel (50)	10.00	5.00	3.00
148	Jim Hunter	4.50	2.25	1.25
149	Tug McGraw	1.25	.60	.40
150	Dave McNally	1.00	.50	.30

1975 Hostess Twinkies

Believed to have been issued only in selected markets, and on a limited basis at that, the 1975 Hostess Twinkie set features 60 of the cards from the "regular" Hostess set of that year. The cards were issued one per pack with the popular snack cake. Cards #1-36 are a direct pick-up from the Hostess set, while the remaining 24 cards in the set were selected from the more popular names in the remainder of the Hostess issue - with an emphasis on West Coast players. Thus, after card #36, the '75 Twinkie cards are skip-numbered from 40-136. In identical 2-1/4" x 3-1/4" size, the Twinkie cards differ from the Hostess issue only in the presence of small black bars at top and bottom center of the back of the card. While cards actually issued with snack cakes are virtually always found with brown stains, enough unissued cards were leaked into the hobby to provide clean examples for those willing to search them out and pay the price.

		NM	EX	VG
	Complete Set (60):	800.00	325.00	80.00
	Common Player:	4.00	1.50	.40
1	Bobby Tolan	4.00	1.50	.40
2	Cookie Rojas	4.00	1.50	.40
3	Darrell Evans	4.00	1.50	.40
4	Sal Bando	4.00	1.50	.40
5	Joe Morgan	24.00	9.50	2.50
6	Mickey Lolich	6.00	2.50	.60
7	Don Sutton	20.00	8.00	2.00
8	Bill Melton	4.00	1.50	.40
9	Tim Foli	4.00	1.50	.40
10	Joe Lahoud	4.00	1.50	.40
11	Bert Hooten (Burt Hooton)	4.00	1.50	.40
12	Paul Blair	4.00	1.50	.40
13	Jim Barr	4.00	1.50	.40
14	Toby Harrah	4.00	1.50	.40
15	John Milner	4.00	1.50	.40
16	Ken Holtzman	4.00	1.50	.40
17	Cesar Cedeno	4.00	1.50	.40
18	Dwight Evans	4.00	1.50	.40
19	Willie McCovey	24.00	9.50	2.50
20	Tony Oliva	8.00	3.25	.80
21	Manny Sanguillen	4.00	1.50	.40
22	Mickey Rivers	4.00	1.50	.40
23	Lou Brock	24.00	9.50	2.50
24	Graig Nettles	6.00	2.50	.60
25	Jim Wynn	4.00	1.50	.40
26	George Scott	4.00	1.50	.40
27	Greg Luzinski	4.00	1.50	.40
28	Bert Campaneris	4.00	1.50	.40
29	Pete Rose	80.00	32.00	8.00
30	Buddy Bell	4.00	1.50	.40
31	Gary Matthews	4.00	1.50	.40
32	Fred Patek	4.00	1.50	.40
33	Mike Lum	4.00	1.50	.40
34	Ellie Rodriguez	4.00	1.50	.40
35	Milt May	4.00	1.50	.40
	(Photo actually Lee May.)			
36	Willie Horton	4.00	1.50	.40
40	Joe Rudi	4.00	1.50	.40
43	Garry Maddox	4.00	1.50	.40
46	Dave Chalk	4.00	1.50	.40
49	Steve Garvey	15.00	6.00	1.50
52	Rollie Fingers	20.00	8.00	2.00
58	Nolan Ryan	100.00	40.00	10.00
61	Ron Cey	4.00	1.50	.40
64	Gene Tenace	4.00	1.50	.40
65	Jose Cardenal	4.00	1.50	.40
67	Dave Lopes	4.00	1.50	.40
68	Wilbur Wood	4.00	1.50	.40
73	Chris Speier	4.00	1.50	.40
77	Don Kessinger	4.00	1.50	.40
79	Andy Messersmith	4.00	1.50	.40
80	Robin Yount	40.00	16.00	4.00
82	Bill Singer	4.00	1.50	.40
103	Glenn Beckert	4.00	1.50	.40
110	Jim Kaat	6.00	2.50	.60
112	Don Money	4.00	1.50	.40
113	Rick Monday	4.00	1.50	.40
122	Jorge Orta	4.00	1.50	.40
125	Bill Madlock	4.00	1.50	.40
130	Hank Aaron	75.00	30.00	7.50
136	Ken Henderson	4.00	1.50	.40

1976 Hostess

The second of five annual Hostess issues, the 1976 cards carried a "Bicentennial" color theme, with red, white and blue

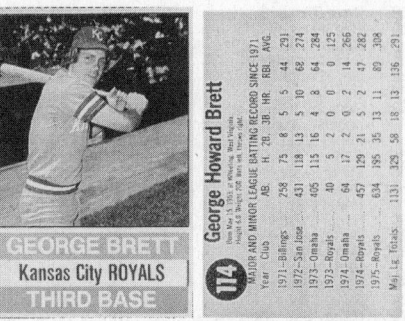

stripes at the bottom of the 2-1/4" x 3-1/4" cards. Like other Hostess issues, the cards were printed in panels of three as the bottom of family-size boxes of snack cake products. This leads to a degree of scarcity for some of the 150 cards in the set; those which were found on less-popular brands. A well-trimmed three-card panel measures 7-1/4" x 3-1/4". Some of the photos used in the 1976 Hostess set can also be found on Topps issues of the era. A "Hostess All-Star Team" album with spaces for 18 cards was available. Card backs can be found printed in black or brown, though it is not known if all cards can be found in both colors.

		NM	EX	VG
	Complete Panel Set (50):	300.00	150.00	90.00
	Complete Set, Singles (150):	250.00	125.00	75.00
	Common Panel:	5.00	2.50	1.50
	Common Player:	.75	.40	.25
	Album:	20.00	10.00	6.00
	Panel (1)	20.00	10.00	6.00
1	Fred Lynn	1.00	.50	.30
2	Joe Morgan	5.00	2.50	1.50
3	Phil Niekro	4.00	2.00	1.25
	Panel (2)	10.00	5.00	3.00
4	Gaylord Perry	4.00	2.00	1.25
5	Bob Watson	.75	.40	.25
6	Bill Freehan	.75	.40	.25
	Panel (3)	10.00	5.00	3.00
7	Lou Brock	5.00	2.50	1.50
8	Al Fitzmorris	.75	.40	.25
9	Rennie Stennett	.75	.40	.25
	Panel (4)	10.00	5.00	3.00
10	Tony Oliva	1.00	.50	.30
11	Robin Yount	5.00	2.50	1.50
12	Rick Manning	.75	.40	.25
	Panel (5)	7.00	3.50	2.00
13	Bobby Grich	.75	.40	.25
14	Terry Forster	.75	.40	.25
15	Dave Kingman	1.00	.50	.30
	Panel (6)	10.00	5.00	3.00
16	Thurman Munson	4.50	2.25	1.25
17	Rick Reuschel	.75	.40	.25
18	Bobby Bonds	1.00	.50	.30
	Panel (7)	10.00	5.00	3.00
19	Steve Garvey	3.50	1.75	1.00
20	Vida Blue	.75	.40	.25
21	Dave Rader	.75	.40	.25
	Panel (8)	10.00	5.00	3.00
22	Johnny Bench	5.00	2.50	1.50
23	Luis Tiant	.75	.40	.25
24	Darrell Evans	.75	.40	.25
	Panel (9)	7.00	3.50	2.00
25	Larry Dierker	.75	.40	.25
26	Willie Horton	.75	.40	.25
27	John Ellis	.75	.40	.25
	Panel (10)	7.00	3.50	2.00
28	Al Cowens	.75	.40	.25
29	Jerry Reuss	.75	.40	.25
30	Reggie Smith	.75	.40	.25
	Panel (11)	10.00	5.00	3.00
31	Bobby Darwin	.75	.40	.25
32	Fritz Peterson	.75	.40	.25
33	Rod Carew	5.00	2.50	1.50
	Panel (12)	20.00	10.00	6.00
34	Carlos May	.75	.40	.25
35	Tom Seaver	6.00	3.00	1.75
36	Brooks Robinson	6.00	3.00	1.75
	Panel (13)	7.00	3.50	2.00
37	Jose Cardenal	.75	.40	.25
38	Ron Blomberg	.75	.40	.25
39	Lee Stanton	.75	.40	.25
	Panel (14)	7.00	3.50	2.00
40	Dave Cash	.75	.40	.25
41	John Montefusco	.75	.40	.25
42	Bob Tolan	.75	.40	.25
	Panel (15)	7.00	3.50	2.00
43	Carl Morton	.75	.40	.25
44	Rick Burleson	.75	.40	.25
45	Don Gullett	.75	.40	.25
	Panel (16)	7.00	3.50	2.00
46	Vern Ruhle	.75	.40	.25
47	Cesar Cedeno	.75	.40	.25
48	Toby Harrah	.75	.40	.25
	Panel (17)	10.00	5.00	3.00
49	Willie Stargell	5.00	2.50	1.50
50	Al Hrabosky	.75	.40	.25
51	Amos Otis	.75	.40	.25
	Panel (18)	7.00	3.50	2.00
52	Bud Harrelson	.75	.40	.25
53	Jim Hughes	.75	.40	.25
54	George Scott	.75	.40	.25
	Panel (19)	10.00	5.00	3.00
55	Mike Vail	.75	.40	.25
56	Jim Palmer	5.00	2.50	1.50
57	Jorge Orta	.75	.40	.25
	Panel (20)	7.00	3.50	2.00
58	Chris Chambliss	.75	.40	.25

		NM	EX	VG
59	Dave Chalk	.75	.40	.25
60	Ray Burris	.75	.40	.25
	Panel (21)	10.00	5.00	3.00
61	Bert Campaneris	.75	.40	.25
62	Gary Carter	5.00	2.50	1.50
63a	Ron Cey	.75	.40	.25
63b	Ron Cey (Reversed negatives, unissued proof.)	35.00	17.50	10.50
	Panel (22)	27.50	13.50	8.25
64	Carlton Fisk	5.00	2.50	1.50
65	Marty Perez	.75	.40	.25
66	Pete Rose	12.00	6.00	3.50
	Panel (23)	7.00	3.50	2.00
67	Roger Metzger	.75	.40	.25
68	Jim Sundberg	.75	.40	.25
69	Ron LeFlore	.75	.40	.25
	Panel (24)	7.00	3.50	2.00
70	Ted Sizemore	.75	.40	.25
71	Steve Busby	.75	.40	.25
72	Manny Sanguillen	.75	.40	.25
	Panel (25)	10.00	5.00	3.00
73	Larry Hisle	.75	.40	.25
74	Pete Broberg	.75	.40	.25
75	Boog Powell	3.00	1.50	.90
	Panel (26)	8.00	4.00	2.50
76	Ken Singleton	.75	.40	.25
77	Rich Gossage	1.25	.60	.40
78	Jerry Grote	.75	.40	.25
	Panel (27)	35.00	17.50	10.50
79	Nolan Ryan	16.00	8.00	4.75
80	Rick Monday	.75	.40	.25
81	Graig Nettles	1.25	.60	.40
	Panel (28)	27.50	13.50	8.25
82	Chris Speier	.75	.40	.25
83	Dave Winfield	5.00	2.50	1.50
84	Mike Schmidt	7.50	3.75	2.25
	Panel (29)	10.00	5.00	3.00
85	Buzz Capra	.75	.40	.25
86	Tony Perez	5.00	2.50	1.50
87	Dwight Evans	.75	.40	.25
	Panel (30)	7.00	3.50	2.00
88	Mike Hargrove	.75	.40	.25
89	Joe Coleman	.75	.40	.25
90	Greg Gross	.75	.40	.25
	Panel (31)	7.00	3.50	2.00
91	John Mayberry	.75	.40	.25
92	John Candelaria	.75	.40	.25
93	Bake McBride	.75	.40	.25
	Panel (32)	20.00	10.00	6.00
94	Hank Aaron	12.00	6.00	3.50
95	Buddy Bell	.75	.40	.25
96	Steve Braun	.75	.40	.25
	Panel (33)	7.00	3.50	2.00
97	Jon Matlack	.75	.40	.25
98	Lee May	.75	.40	.25
99	Wilbur Wood	.75	.40	.25
	Panel (34)	7.00	3.50	2.00
100	Bill Madlock	.75	.40	.25
101	Frank Tanana	.75	.40	.25
102	Mickey Rivers	.75	.40	.25
	Panel (35)	10.00	5.00	3.00
103	Mike Ivie	.75	.40	.25
104	Rollie Fingers	4.00	2.00	1.25
105	Davey Lopes	.75	.40	.25
	Panel (36)	7.00	3.50	2.00
106	George Foster	.75	.40	.25
107	Denny Doyle	.75	.40	.25
108	Earl Williams	.75	.40	.25
	Panel (37)	7.00	3.50	2.00
109	Tom Veryzer	.75	.40	.25
110	J.R. Richard	.75	.40	.25
111	Jeff Burroughs	.75	.40	.25
	Panel (38)	17.50	8.75	5.25
112	Al Oliver	1.00	.50	.30
113	Ted Simmons	.75	.40	.25
114	George Brett	7.50	3.75	2.25
	Panel (39)	7.00	3.50	2.00
115	Frank Duffy	.75	.40	.25
116	Bert Blyleven	.75	.40	.25
117	Darrell Porter	.75	.40	.25
	Panel (40)	8.00	4.00	2.50
118	Don Baylor	1.00	.50	.30
119	Bucky Dent	.75	.40	.25
120	Felix Millan	.75	.40	.25
	Panel (41)	8.00	4.00	2.50
121a	Mike Cuellar	.75	.40	.25
121b	Andy Messersmith (Unissued proof.)	25.00	12.50	7.50
122	Gene Tenace	.75	.40	.25
123	Bobby Murcer	1.25	.60	.40
	Panel (42)	10.00	5.00	3.00
124	Willie McCovey	5.00	2.50	1.50
125	Greg Luzinski	.75	.40	.25
126	Larry Parrish	.75	.40	.25
	Panel (43)	8.00	4.00	2.50
127	Jim Rice	2.00	1.00	.60
128	Dave Concepcion	.75	.40	.25
129	Jim Wynn	.75	.40	.25
	Panel (44)	7.00	3.50	2.00
130	Tom Grieve	.75	.40	.25
131	Mike Cosgrove	.75	.40	.25
132	Dan Meyer	.75	.40	.25
	Panel (45)	7.00	3.50	2.00
133	Dave Parker	1.00	.50	.30
134	Don Kessinger	.75	.40	.25
135	Hal McRae	.75	.40	.25
	Panel (46)	13.50	6.75	4.00
136	Don Money	.75	.40	.25
137	Dennis Eckersley	5.00	2.50	1.50
138a	Fergie Jenkins	4.00	2.00	1.25
138b	Johnny Briggs (Unissued proof.)	25.00	12.50	7.50
	Panel (47)	10.00	5.00	3.00
139	Mike Torrez	.75	.40	.25
140	Jerry Morales	.75	.40	.25
141	Jim Hunter	4.00	2.00	1.25
	Panel (48)	7.00	3.50	2.00
142	Gary Matthews	.75	.40	.25

		NM	EX	VG
143	Randy Jones	.75	.40	.25
144	Mike Jorgensen	.75	.40	.25
	Panel (49)	17.50	8.75	5.25
145	Larry Bowa	.75	.40	.25
146	Reggie Jackson	7.50	3.75	2.25
147	Steve Yeager	.75	.40	.25
	Panel (50)	13.50	6.75	4.00
148	Dave May	.75	.40	.25
149	Carl Yastrzemski	6.00	3.00	1.75
150	Cesar Geronimo	.75	.40	.25

1976 Hostess Twinkies

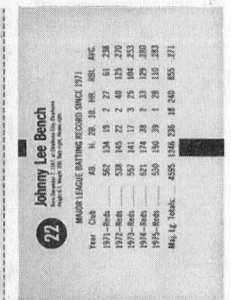

The 60 cards in this regionally issued (test markets only) set closely parallel the first 60 cards in the numerical sequence of the "regular" 1976 Hostess issue. The singular difference is the appearance on the back of the card at a black band toward the center of the card at top and bottom. Also unlike the three-card panels of the regular Hostess issue, the 2-1/4" x 3-1/4" Twinkie cards were issued singly, as the cardboard stiffener for the cellophane-wrapped snack cakes. While cards actually issued with snack cakes are virtually always found with brown stains, enough unissued cards were leaked into the hobby to provide clean examples for those willing to search them out and pay the price.

		NM	EX	VG
	Complete Set (60):	500.00	200.00	50.00
	Common Player:	4.00	1.50	.40
1	Fred Lynn	4.00	1.50	.40
2	Joe Morgan	24.00	9.50	2.50
3	Phil Niekro	20.00	8.00	2.00
4	Gaylord Perry	20.00	8.00	2.00
5	Bob Watson	4.00	1.50	.40
6	Bill Freehan	4.00	1.50	.40
7	Lou Brock	24.00	9.50	2.50
8	Al Fitzmorris	4.00	1.50	.40
9	Rennie Stennett	4.00	1.50	.40
10	Tony Oliva	6.00	2.50	.60
11	Robin Yount	24.00	9.50	2.50
12	Rick Manning	4.00	1.50	.40
13	Bobby Grich	4.00	1.50	.40
14	Terry Forster	4.00	1.50	.40
15	Dave Kingman	5.00	2.00	.50
16	Thurman Munson	15.00	6.00	1.50
17	Rick Reuschel	4.00	1.50	.40
18	Bobby Bonds	4.00	1.50	.40
19	Steve Garvey	12.00	4.75	1.25
20	Vida Blue	4.00	1.50	.40
21	Dave Rader	4.00	1.50	.40
22	Johnny Bench	24.00	9.50	2.50
23	Luis Tiant	4.00	1.50	.40
24	Darrell Evans	4.00	1.50	.40
25	Larry Dierker	4.00	1.50	.40
26	Willie Horton	4.00	1.50	.40
27	John Ellis	4.00	1.50	.40
28	Al Cowens	4.00	1.50	.40
29	Jerry Reuss	4.00	1.50	.40
30	Reggie Smith	4.00	1.50	.40
31	Bobby Darwin	4.00	1.50	.40
32	Fritz Peterson	4.00	1.50	.40
33	Rod Carew	24.00	9.50	2.50
34	Carlos May	4.00	1.50	.40
35	Tom Seaver	30.00	12.00	3.00
36	Brooks Robinson	24.00	9.50	2.50
37	Jose Cardenal	4.00	1.50	.40
38	Ron Blomberg	4.00	1.50	.40
39	Lee Stanton	4.00	1.50	.40
40	Dave Cash	4.00	1.50	.40
41	John Montefusco	4.00	1.50	.40
42	Bob Tolan	4.00	1.50	.40
43	Carl Morton	4.00	1.50	.40
44	Rick Burleson	4.00	1.50	.40
45	Don Gullett	4.00	1.50	.40
46	Vern Ruhle	4.00	1.50	.40
47	Cesar Cedeno	4.00	1.50	.40
48	Toby Harrah	4.00	1.50	.40
49	Willie Stargell	24.00	9.50	2.50
50	Al Hrabosky	4.00	1.50	.40
51	Amos Otis	4.00	1.50	.40
52	Bud Harrelson	4.00	1.50	.40
53	Jim Hughes	4.00	1.50	.40
54	George Scott	4.00	1.50	.40
55	Mike Vail	4.00	1.50	.40
56	Jim Palmer	20.00	8.00	2.00
57	Jorge Orta	4.00	1.50	.40
58	Chris Chambliss	4.00	1.50	.40
59	Dave Chalk	4.00	1.50	.40
60	Ray Burris	4.00	1.50	.40

1976 Hostess Unissued Proofs

To help prevent a recurrence of the errors which plagued Hostess' debut set in 1975, the company prepared proof sheets of the cards before they were printed onto the bottoms of snack cake boxes. Probably to have ready substitutes in case problems were found, or a card had to be withdrawn at

the last minute, there were seven players printed in proof version that were never issued on boxes. In addition, changes to cards #61, 121 and 138 were made between the proof stage and issued versions (they are detailed in the 1976 Hostess listings). The proofs share the format and 2-1/4" x 3-1/4" size of the issued cards.

		NM	EX	VG
	Complete Set (9):	400.00	200.00	120.00
	Common Player:	40.00	20.00	12.00
151	Fergie Jenkins (Issued as #138.)	75.00	37.50	22.50
152	Mike Cuellar (Issued as #121.)	40.00	20.00	12.00
153	Tom Murphy	40.00	20.00	12.00
154	Dusty Baker	40.00	20.00	12.00
155	Barry Foote	40.00	20.00	12.00
156	Steve Carlton	100.00	50.00	30.00
157	Richie Zisk	40.00	20.00	12.00
158	Ken Holtzman	40.00	20.00	12.00
159	Cliff Johnson	40.00	20.00	12.00

1977 Hostess

The third of five consecutive annual issues, the 1977 Hostess cards retained the same card size - 2-1/4" x 3-1/4", set size - 150 cards, and mode of issue - three cards on a 7-1/4" x 3-1/4" panel, as the previous two efforts. Because they were issued as the bottom panel of snack cake boxes, and because some brands of Hostess products were more popular than others, certain cards in the set are scarcer than others. A fold-out (to 8-1/2" x 22") All-Star Team album was available.

		NM	EX	VG
	Complete Panel Set (50):	250.00	125.00	75.00
	Complete Set, Singles (150):	200.00	100.00	60.00
	Common Panel:	4.00	2.00	1.25
	Common Player:	.75	.40	.25
	Album:	20.00	10.00	6.00
	Panel (1)	20.00	10.00	6.00
1	Jim Palmer	3.00	1.50	.90
2	Joe Morgan	3.00	1.50	.90
3a	Reggie Jackson	5.00	2.50	1.50
3b	Rod Carew (Unissued proof.)	20.00	10.00	6.00
	Panel (2)	25.00	12.50	7.50
4	Carl Yastrzemski	3.50	1.75	1.00
5	Thurman Munson	2.50	1.25	.70
6	Johnny Bench	3.50	1.75	1.00
	Panel (3)	30.00	15.00	9.00
7	Tom Seaver	3.00	1.50	.90
8	Pete Rose	7.50	3.75	2.25
9a	Rod Carew	3.00	1.50	.90
9b	Reggie Jackson (Unissued proof.)	75.00	37.00	22.00
	Panel (4)	4.00	2.00	1.25
10	Luis Tiant	.75	.40	.25
11	Phil Garner	.75	.40	.25
12	Sixto Lezcano	.75	.40	.25
	Panel (5)	4.00	2.00	1.25
13	Mike Torrez	.75	.40	.25
14	Davey Lopes	.75	.40	.25
15	Doug DeCinces	.75	.40	.25
	Panel (6)	4.00	2.00	1.25
16	Jim Spencer	.75	.40	.25
17	Hal McRae	.75	.40	.25
18	Mike Hargrove	.75	.40	.25

		NM	EX	VG
Panel (7)		4.00	2.00	1.25
19	Willie Montanez	.75	.40	.25
20	Roger Metzger	.75	.40	.25
21	Dwight Evans	.75	.40	.25
Panel (8)		5.00	2.50	1.50
22	Steve Rogers	.75	.40	.25
23	Jim Rice	1.25	.60	.40
24	Pete Falcone	.75	.40	.25
Panel (9)		6.00	3.00	1.75
25	Greg Luzinski	.75	.40	.25
26	Randy Jones	.75	.40	.25
27	Willie Stargell	3.00	1.50	.90
Panel (10)		5.00	2.50	1.50
28	John Hiller	.75	.40	.25
29	Bobby Murcer	.75	.40	.25
30	Rick Monday	.75	.40	.25
Panel (11)		6.00	3.00	1.75
31	John Montefusco	.75	.40	.25
32	Lou Brock	3.00	1.50	.90
33	Bill North	.75	.40	.25
Panel (12)		15.00	7.50	4.50
34	Robin Yount	3.00	1.50	.90
35	Steve Garvey	1.00	.50	.30
36	George Brett	5.00	2.50	1.50
Panel (13)		4.00	2.00	1.25
37	Toby Harrah	.75	.40	.25
38	Jerry Royster	.75	.40	.25
39	Bob Watson	.75	.40	.25
Panel (14)		5.00	2.50	1.50
40	George Foster	.75	.40	.25
41	Gary Carter	3.00	1.50	.90
42	John Denny	.75	.40	.25
Panel (15)		20.00	10.00	6.00
43	Mike Schmidt	5.00	2.50	1.50
44	Dave Winfield	3.00	1.50	.90
45	Al Oliver	.90	.45	.25
Panel (16)		4.00	2.00	1.25
46	Mark Fidrych	.75	.40	.25
47	Larry Herndon	.75	.40	.25
48	Dave Goltz	.75	.40	.25
Panel (17)		4.00	2.00	1.25
49	Jerry Morales	.75	.40	.25
50	Ron LeFlore	.75	.40	.25
51	Fred Lynn	.75	.40	.25
Panel (18)		4.00	2.00	1.25
52	Vida Blue	.75	.40	.25
53	Rick Manning	.75	.40	.25
54	Bill Buckner	.75	.40	.25
Panel (19)		4.00	2.00	1.25
55	Lee May	.75	.40	.25
56	John Mayberry	.75	.40	.25
57	Darrel Chaney	.75	.40	.25
Panel (20)		4.00	2.00	1.25
58	Cesar Cedeno	.75	.40	.25
59	Ken Griffey	.75	.40	.25
60	Dave Kingman	.75	.40	.25
Panel (21)		4.00	2.00	1.25
61	Ted Simmons	.75	.40	.25
62	Larry Bowa	.75	.40	.25
63	Frank Tanana	.75	.40	.25
Panel (22)		4.00	2.00	1.25
64	Jason Thompson	.75	.40	.25
65	Ken Brett	.75	.40	.25
66	Roy Smalley	.75	.40	.25
Panel (23)		4.00	2.00	1.25
67	Ray Burris	.75	.40	.25
68	Rick Burleson	.75	.40	.25
69	Buddy Bell	.75	.40	.25
Panel (24)		5.00	2.50	1.50
70	Don Sutton	2.50	1.25	.70
71	Mark Belanger	.75	.40	.25
72	Dennis Leonard	.75	.40	.25
Panel (25)		5.00	2.50	1.50
73	Gaylord Perry	2.50	1.25	.70
74	Dick Ruthven	.75	.40	.25
75	Jose Cruz	.75	.40	.25
Panel (26)		4.00	2.00	1.25
76	Cesar Geronimo	.75	.40	.25
77	Jerry Koosman	.75	.40	.25
78	Garry Templeton	.75	.40	.25
Panel (27)		25.00	12.50	7.50
79	Jim Hunter	2.50	1.25	.70
80	John Candelaria	.75	.40	.25
81	Nolan Ryan	10.00	5.00	3.00
Panel (28)		4.00	2.00	1.25
82	Rusty Staub	.90	.45	.25
83	Jim Barr	.75	.40	.25
84	Butch Wynegar	.75	.40	.25
Panel (29)		4.00	2.00	1.25
85	Jose Cardenal	.75	.40	.25
86	Claudell Washington	.75	.40	.25
87	Bill Travers	.75	.40	.25
Panel (30)		4.00	2.00	1.25
88	Rick Waits	.75	.40	.25
89	Ron Cey	.75	.40	.25
90	Al Bumbry	.75	.40	.25
Panel (31)		4.00	2.00	1.25
91	Bucky Dent	.90	.45	.25
92	Amos Otis	.75	.40	.25
93	Tom Grieve	.75	.40	.25
Panel (32)		4.00	2.00	1.25
94	Enos Cabell	.75	.40	.25
95	Dave Concepcion	.75	.40	.25
96	Felix Millan	.75	.40	.25
Panel (33)		4.00	2.00	1.25
97	Bake McBride	.75	.40	.25
98	Chris Chambliss	.75	.40	.25
99	Butch Metzger	.75	.40	.25
Panel (34)		4.00	2.00	1.25
100	Rennie Stennett	.75	.40	.25
101	Dave Roberts	.75	.40	.25
102	Lyman Bostock	.75	.40	.25
Panel (35)		6.00	3.00	1.75
103	Rick Reuschel	.75	.40	.25
104	Carlton Fisk	3.00	1.50	.90
105	Jim Slaton	.75	.40	.25
Panel (36)		5.00	2.50	1.50
106	Dennis Eckersley	2.50	1.25	.70
107	Ken Singleton	.75	.40	.25
108	Ralph Garr	.75	.40	.25
Panel (37)		5.00	2.50	1.50
109	Freddie Patek	.75	.40	.25
110	Jim Sundberg	.75	.40	.25
111	Phil Niekro	2.50	1.25	.70
Panel (38)		4.00	2.00	1.25
112	J.R. Richard	.75	.40	.25
113	Gary Nolan	.75	.40	.25
114	Jon Matlack	.75	.40	.25
Panel (39)		7.50	3.75	2.25
115	Keith Hernandez	.75	.40	.25
116	Graig Nettles	.90	.45	.25
117	Steve Carlton	3.00	1.50	.90
Panel (40)		4.00	2.00	1.25
118	Bill Madlock	.75	.40	.25
119	Jerry Reuss	.75	.40	.25
120	Aurelio Rodriguez	.75	.40	.25
Panel (41)		4.00	2.00	1.25
121	Dan Ford	.75	.40	.25
122	Ray Fosse	.75	.40	.25
123	George Hendrick	.75	.40	.25
Panel (42)		4.00	2.00	1.25
124	Alan Ashby	.75	.40	.25
125	Joe Lis	.75	.40	.25
126	Sal Bando	.75	.40	.25
Panel (43)		5.00	2.50	1.50
127	Richie Zisk	.75	.40	.25
128	Rich Gossage	.75	.40	.25
129	Don Baylor	.75	.40	.25
Panel (44)		4.00	2.00	1.25
130	Dave McKay	.75	.40	.25
131	Bobby Grich	.75	.40	.25
132	Dave Pagan	.75	.40	.25
Panel (45)		4.00	2.00	1.25
133	Dave Cash	.75	.40	.25
134	Steve Braun	.75	.40	.25
135	Dan Meyer	.75	.40	.25
Panel (46)		5.00	2.50	1.50
136	Bill Stein	.75	.40	.25
137	Rollie Fingers	2.50	1.25	.70
138	Brian Downing	.75	.40	.25
Panel (47)		4.00	2.00	1.25
139	Bill Singer	.75	.40	.25
140	Doyle Alexander	.75	.40	.25
141	Gene Tenace	.75	.40	.25
Panel (48)		4.00	2.00	1.25
142	Gary Matthews	.75	.40	.25
143	Don Gullett	.75	.40	.25
144	Wayne Garland	.75	.40	.25
Panel (49)		4.00	2.00	1.25
145	Pete Broberg	.75	.40	.25
146	Joe Rudi	.75	.40	.25
147	Glenn Abbott	.75	.40	.25
Panel (50)		4.00	2.00	1.25
148	George Scott	.75	.40	.25
149	Bert Campaneris	.75	.40	.25
150	Andy Messersmith	.75	.40	.25

1977 Hostess Twinkies

The 1977 Hostess Twinkie issue, at 150 different cards, is the largest of the single-panel Twinkie sets. It is also the most obscure. The cards, which measure 2-1/4" x 3-1/4" but are part of a larger panel, were found not only with Twinkies, but with Hostess Cupcakes as well. Cards #1-30 and 111-150 are Twinkies panels and #31-135 are Cupcakes panels. Complete Cupcakes panels are approximately 2-1/4" x 4-1/2" in size, while complete Twinkies panels measure 3-1/8" x 4-1/4". The photos used in the set are identical to those in the 1977 Hostess three-card panel set. The main difference is the appearance of a black band at the center of the card back. While cards actually issued with snack cakes are virtually always found with brown stains, enough unissued cards were leaked into the hobby to provide clean examples for those willing to search them out and pay the price.

		NM	EX	VG
Complete Set (150):		725.00	300.00	75.00
Common Player:		4.00	1.50	.40
1	Jim Palmer	25.00	10.00	2.50
2	Joe Morgan	25.00	10.00	2.50
3	Reggie Jackson	40.00	16.00	4.00
4	Carl Yastrzemski	32.50	13.00	3.25
5	Thurman Munson	15.00	6.00	1.50
6	Johnny Bench	25.00	10.00	2.50
7	Tom Seaver	25.00	10.00	2.50
8	Pete Rose	65.00	26.00	6.50
9	Rod Carew	25.00	10.00	2.50
10	Luis Tiant	4.00	1.50	.40
11	Phil Garner	4.00	1.50	.40
12	Sixto Lezcano	4.00	1.50	.40
13	Mike Torrez	4.00	1.50	.40
14	Dave Lopes	4.00	1.50	.40
15	Doug DeCinces	4.00	1.50	.40
16	Jim Spencer	4.00	1.50	.40
17	Hal McRae	4.00	1.50	.40
18	Mike Hargrove	4.00	1.50	.40
19	Willie Montanez	4.00	1.50	.40
20	Roger Metzger	4.00	1.50	.40
21	Dwight Evans	4.00	1.50	.40
22	Steve Rogers	4.00	1.50	.40
23	Jim Rice	12.50	5.00	1.25
24	Pete Falcone	4.00	1.50	.40
25	Greg Luzinski	4.00	1.50	.40
26	Randy Jones	4.00	1.50	.40
27	Willie Stargell	25.00	10.00	2.50
28	John Hiller	4.00	1.50	.40
29	Bobby Murcer	4.00	1.50	.40
30	Rick Monday	4.00	1.50	.40
31	John Montefusco	4.00	1.50	.40
32	Lou Brock	25.00	10.00	2.50
33	Bill North	4.00	1.50	.40
34	Robin Yount	25.00	10.00	2.50
35	Steve Garvey	12.50	5.00	1.25
36	George Brett	40.00	16.00	4.00
37	Toby Harrah	4.00	1.50	.40
38	Jerry Royster	4.00	1.50	.40
39	Bob Watson	4.00	1.50	.40
40	George Foster	4.00	1.50	.40
41	Gary Carter	25.00	10.00	2.50
42	John Denny	4.00	1.50	.40
43	Mike Schmidt	40.00	16.00	4.00
44	Dave Winfield	25.00	10.00	2.50
45	Al Oliver	4.00	1.50	.40
46	Mark Fidrych	6.50	2.50	.60
47	Larry Herndon	4.00	1.50	.40
48	Dave Goltz	4.00	1.50	.40
49	Jerry Morales	4.00	1.50	.40
50	Ron LeFlore	4.00	1.50	.40
51	Fred Lynn	4.00	1.50	.40
52	Vida Blue	4.00	1.50	.40
53	Rick Manning	4.00	1.50	.40
54	Bill Buckner	4.00	1.50	.40
55	Lee May	4.00	1.50	.40
56	John Mayberry	4.00	1.50	.40
57	Darrel Chaney	4.00	1.50	.40
58	Cesar Cedeno	4.00	1.50	.40
59	Ken Griffey	4.00	1.50	.40
60	Dave Kingman	6.50	2.50	.60
61	Ted Simmons	4.00	1.50	.40
62	Larry Bowa	4.00	1.50	.40
63	Frank Tanana	4.00	1.50	.40
64	Jason Thompson	4.00	1.50	.40
65	Ken Brett	4.00	1.50	.40
66	Roy Smalley	4.00	1.50	.40
67	Ray Burris	4.00	1.50	.40
68	Rick Burleson	4.00	1.50	.40
69	Buddy Bell	4.00	1.50	.40
70	Don Sutton	20.00	8.00	2.00
71	Mark Belanger	4.00	1.50	.40
72	Dennis Leonard	4.00	1.50	.40
73	Gaylord Perry	20.00	8.00	2.00
74	Dick Ruthven	4.00	1.50	.40
75	Jose Cruz	4.00	1.50	.40
76	Cesar Geronimo	4.00	1.50	.40
77	Jerry Koosman	4.00	1.50	.40
78	Garry Templeton	4.00	1.50	.40
79	Catfish Hunter	20.00	8.00	2.00
80	John Candelaria	4.00	1.50	.40
81	Nolan Ryan	100.00	40.00	10.00
82	Rusty Staub	6.50	2.50	.60
83	Jim Barr	4.00	1.50	.40
84	Butch Wynegar	4.00	1.50	.40
85	Jose Cardenal	4.00	1.50	.40
86	Claudell Washington	4.00	1.50	.40
87	Bill Travers	4.00	1.50	.40
88	Rick Waits	4.00	1.50	.40
89	Ron Cey	4.00	1.50	.40
90	Al Bumbry	4.00	1.50	.40
91	Bucky Dent	4.00	1.50	.40
92	Amos Otis	4.00	1.50	.40
93	Tom Grieve	4.00	1.50	.40
94	Enos Cabell	4.00	1.50	.40
95	Dave Concepcion	4.00	1.50	.40
96	Felix Millan	4.00	1.50	.40
97	Bake McBride	4.00	1.50	.40
98	Chris Chambliss	4.00	1.50	.40
99	Butch Metzger	4.00	1.50	.40
100	Rennie Stennett	4.00	1.50	.40
101	Dave Roberts	4.00	1.50	.40
102	Lyman Bostock	4.00	1.50	.40
103	Rick Reuschel	4.00	1.50	.40
104	Carlton Fisk	25.00	10.00	2.50
105	Jim Slaton	4.00	1.50	.40
106	Dennis Eckersley	20.00	8.00	2.00
107	Ken Singleton	4.00	1.50	.40
108	Ralph Garr	4.00	1.50	.40
109	Freddie Patek	4.00	1.50	.40
110	Jim Sundberg	4.00	1.50	.40
111	Phil Niekro	20.00	8.00	2.00
112	J. R. Richard	4.00	1.50	.40
113	Gary Nolan	4.00	1.50	.40
114	Jon Matlack	4.00	1.50	.40
115	Keith Hernandez	4.00	1.50	.40
116	Graig Nettles	4.00	1.50	.40
117	Steve Carlton	25.00	10.00	2.50
118	Bill Madlock	4.00	1.50	.40
119	Jerry Reuss	4.00	1.50	.40
120	Aurelio Rodriguez	4.00	1.50	.40
121	Dan Ford	4.00	1.50	.40
122	Ray Fosse	4.00	1.50	.40
123	George Hendrick	4.00	1.50	.40
124	Alan Ashby	4.00	1.50	.40
125	Joe Lis	4.00	1.50	.40
126	Sal Bando	4.00	1.50	.40
127	Richie Zisk	4.00	1.50	.40
128	Rich Gossage	4.00	1.50	.40
129	Don Baylor	6.50	2.50	.60
130	Dave McKay	4.00	1.50	.40
131	Bob Grich	4.00	1.50	.40
132	Dave Pagan	4.00	1.50	.40
133	Dave Cash	4.00	1.50	.40
134	Steve Braun	4.00	1.50	.40
135	Dan Meyer	4.00	1.50	.40

136	Bill Stein	4.00	1.50	.40
137	Rollie Fingers	20.00	8.00	2.00
138	Brian Downing	4.00	1.50	.40
139	Bill Singer	4.00	1.50	.40
140	Doyle Alexander	4.00	1.50	.40
141	Gene Tenace	4.00	1.50	.40
142	Gary Matthews	4.00	1.50	.40
143	Don Gullett	4.00	1.50	.40
144	Wayne Garland	4.00	1.50	.40
145	Pete Broberg	4.00	1.50	.40
146	Joe Rudi	4.00	1.50	.40
147	Glenn Abbott	4.00	1.50	.40
148	George Scott	4.00	1.50	.40
149	Bert Campaneris	4.00	1.50	.40
150	Andy Messersmith	4.00	1.50	.40

1977 Hostess Unissued Proofs

The reason for the existence of these rare Hostess proofs is unknown, but there seems little doubt that they were never actually circulated; perhaps being held in reserve in case the cards actually printed on product boxes had to be replaced. The 10 cards were printed on a sheet in three-card panels, like the issued Hostess cards, plus a single of Briles. The proofs share the format of the issued cards, and the 2-1/4" x 3-1/4" size. Besides these "high number" proofs, there also exist numbering-variation proofs of cards #3, 9, 65 and 119 (see 1977 Hostess listings).

		NM	EX	VG
Complete Set (10):		400.00	200.00	120.00
Common Single:		40.00	20.00	12.00
151	Ed Kranepool	40.00	20.00	12.00
152	Ross Grimsley	40.00	20.00	12.00
153	Ken Brett	40.00	20.00	12.00
	(#65 in regular-issue set)			
154	Rowland Office	40.00	20.00	12.00
155	Rick Wise	40.00	20.00	12.00
156	Paul Splittorff	40.00	20.00	12.00
157	Jerry Augustine	40.00	20.00	12.00
158	Ken Forsch	40.00	20.00	12.00
159	Jerry Reuss	40.00	20.00	12.00
160	Nelson Briles	40.00	20.00	12.00

1978 Hostess

JOE FERGUSON HOUSTON ASTROS — MICKEY RIVERS NEW YORK YANKEES — PAUL SPLITTORFF KANSAS CITY ROYALS

Other than the design on the front of the card, there was little different about the 1978 Hostess cards from the three years' issues which had preceded it, or the one which followed. The 2-1/4" x 3-1/4" cards were printed in panels of three (7-1/4" x 3-1/4") as the bottom of family-sized boxes of snack cakes. The 1978 set was again complete at 150 cards. Like other years of Hostess issues, there are scarcities within the 1978 set that are the result of those panels having been issued with less-popular brands of snack cakes.

		NM	EX	VG
Complete Panel Set (50):		275.00	135.00	80.00
Complete Set, Singles (150):		225.00	110.00	65.00
Common Panel:		6.00	3.00	1.75
Common Player:		.75	.40	.25
Album:		25.00	12.50	7.50
	Panel (1)	6.00	3.00	1.75
1	Butch Hobson	.75	.40	.25
2	George Foster	.75	.40	.25
3	Bob Forsch	.75	.40	.25
	Panel (2)	13.50	6.75	4.00
4	Tony Perez	4.00	2.00	1.25
5	Bruce Sutter	1.25	.40	.25
6	Hal McRae	.75	.40	.25
	Panel (3)	7.50	3.75	2.25
7	Tommy John	1.25	.60	.40
8	Greg Luzinski	.75	.40	.25
9	Enos Cabell	.75	.40	.25
	Panel (4)	10.00	5.00	3.00
10	Doug DeCinces	.75	.40	.25
11	Willie Stargell	4.50	2.25	1.25
12	Ed Halicki	.75	.40	.25
	Panel (5)	6.00	3.00	1.75
13	Larry Hisle	.75	.40	.25
14	Jim Slaton	.75	.40	.25
15	Buddy Bell	.75	.40	.25
	Panel (6)	6.00	3.00	1.75
16	Earl Williams	.75	.40	.25
17	Glenn Abbott	.75	.40	.25
18	Dan Ford	.75	.40	.25
	Panel (7)	6.00	3.00	1.75
19	Gary Matthews	.75	.40	.25
20	Eric Soderholm	.75	.40	.25
21	Bump Wills	.75	.40	.25
	Panel (8)	6.00	3.00	1.75
22	Keith Hernandez	.75	.40	.25
23	Dave Cash	.75	.40	.25
24	George Scott	.75	.40	.25
	Panel (9)	20.00	10.00	6.00
25	Ron Guidry	1.25	.60	.40
26	Dave Kingman	.75	.40	.25
27	George Brett	9.00	4.50	2.75
	Panel (10)	6.00	3.00	1.75
28	Bob Watson	.75	.40	.25
29	Bob Boone	.90	.45	.25
30	Reggie Smith	.75	.40	.25
	Panel (11)	45.00	22.00	13.50
31	Eddie Murray	18.50	9.25	5.50
32	Gary Lavelle	.75	.40	.25
33	Rennie Stennett	.75	.40	.25
	Panel (12)	6.00	3.00	1.75
34	Duane Kuiper	.75	.40	.25
35	Sixto Lezcano	.75	.40	.25
36	Dave Rozema	.75	.40	.25
	Panel (13)	6.00	3.00	1.75
37	Butch Wynegar	.75	.40	.25
38	Mitchell Page	.75	.40	.25
39	Bill Stein	.75	.40	.25
	Panel (14)	6.00	3.00	1.75
40	Elliott Maddox	.75	.40	.25
41	Mike Hargrove	.75	.40	.25
42	Bobby Bonds	.75	.40	.25
	Panel (15)	20.00	10.00	6.00
43	Garry Templeton	.75	.40	.25
44	Johnny Bench	4.50	2.25	1.25
45	Jim Rice	1.50	.70	.45
	Panel (16)	17.50	8.75	5.25
46	Bill Buckner	.75	.40	.25
47	Reggie Jackson	9.00	4.50	2.75
48	Freddie Patek	.75	.40	.25
	Panel (17)	10.00	5.00	3.00
49	Steve Carlton	4.50	2.25	1.25
50	Cesar Cedeno	.75	.40	.25
51	Steve Yeager	.75	.40	.25
	Panel (18)	6.00	3.00	1.75
52	Phil Garner	.75	.40	.25
53	Lee May	.75	.40	.25
54	Darrell Evans	.75	.40	.25
	Panel (19)	6.00	3.00	1.75
55	Steve Kemp	.75	.40	.25
56a	Dusty Baker	.90	.45	.25
56b	Andre Thornton (Unissued proof.)	18.00	9.00	5.50
57	Ray Fosse	.75	.40	.25
	Panel (20)	6.00	3.00	1.75
58	Manny Sanguillen	.75	.40	.25
59	Tom Johnson	.75	.40	.25
60	Lee Stanton	.75	.40	.25
	Panel (21)	10.00	5.00	3.00
61	Jeff Burroughs	.75	.40	.25
62	Bobby Grich	.75	.40	.25
63	Dave Winfield	4.50	2.25	1.25
	Panel (22)	6.00	3.00	1.75
64	Dan Driessen	.75	.40	.25
65	Ted Simmons	.75	.40	.25
66	Jerry Remy	.75	.40	.25
	Panel (23)	6.00	3.00	1.75
67	Al Cowens	.75	.40	.25
68	Sparky Lyle	.75	.40	.25
69	Manny Trillo	.75	.40	.25
	Panel (24)	9.00	4.50	2.75
70	Don Sutton	4.00	2.00	1.25
71	Larry Bowa	.75	.40	.25
72	Jose Cruz	.75	.40	.25
	Panel (25)	10.00	5.00	3.00
73	Willie McCovey	4.50	2.25	1.25
74	Bert Blyleven	.75	.40	.25
75	Ken Singleton	.75	.40	.25
	Panel (26)	6.00	3.00	1.75
76	Bill North	.75	.40	.25
77	Jason Thompson	.75	.40	.25
78	Dennis Eckersley	4.00	2.00	1.25
	Panel (27)	6.00	3.00	1.75
79	Jim Sundberg	.75	.40	.25
80	Jerry Koosman	.75	.40	.25
81	Bruce Bochte	.75	.40	.25
	Panel (28)	45.00	22.00	13.50
82	George Hendrick	.75	.40	.25
83	Nolan Ryan	20.00	10.00	6.00
84	Roy Howell	.75	.40	.25
	Panel (29)	10.00	5.00	3.00
85	Butch Metzger	.75	.40	.25
86	George Medich	.75	.40	.25
87	Joe Morgan	4.50	2.25	1.25
	Panel (30)	6.00	3.00	1.75
88	Dennis Leonard	.75	.40	.25
89	Willie Randolph	.90	.45	.25
90	Bobby Murcer	.90	.45	.25
	Panel (31)	6.00	3.00	1.75
91	Rick Manning	.75	.40	.25
92	J.R. Richard	.75	.40	.25
93	Ron Cey	.75	.40	.25
	Panel (32)	6.00	3.00	1.75
94	Sal Bando	.75	.40	.25
95	Ron LeFlore	.75	.40	.25
96	Dave Goltz	.75	.40	.25
	Panel (33)	6.00	3.00	1.75
97	Dan Meyer	.75	.40	.25
98	Chris Chambliss	.75	.40	.25
99	Biff Pocoroba	.75	.40	.25
	Panel (34)	6.00	3.00	1.75
100	Oscar Gamble	.75	.40	.25
101	Frank Tanana	.75	.40	.25
102	Lenny Randle	.75	.40	.25
	Panel (35)	6.00	3.00	1.75
103	Tommy Hutton	.75	.40	.25
104	John Candelaria	.75	.40	.25
105	Jorge Orta	.75	.40	.25
	Panel (36)	6.00	3.00	1.75
106	Ken Reitz	.75	.40	.25
107	Bill Campbell	.75	.40	.25
108	Dave Concepcion	.75	.40	.25
	Panel (37)	6.00	3.00	1.75
109	Joe Ferguson	.75	.40	.25
110	Mickey Rivers	.75	.40	.25
111	Paul Splittorff	.75	.40	.25
	Panel (38)	20.00	10.00	6.00
112	Davey Lopes	.75	.40	.25
113	Mike Schmidt	9.00	4.50	2.75
114	Joe Rudi	.75	.40	.25
	Panel (39)	10.00	5.00	3.00
115	Milt May	.75	.40	.25
116	Jim Palmer	4.50	2.25	1.25
117	Bill Madlock	.75	.40	.25
	Panel (40)	6.00	3.00	1.75
118	Roy Smalley	.75	.40	.25
119	Cecil Cooper	.75	.40	.25
120	Rick Langford	.75	.40	.25
	Panel (41)	9.00	4.50	2.75
121	Ruppert Jones	.75	.40	.25
122	Phil Niekro	4.00	2.00	1.25
123	Toby Harrah	.75	.40	.25
	Panel (42)	6.00	3.00	1.75
124	Chet Lemon	.75	.40	.25
125	Gene Tenace	.75	.40	.25
126	Steve Henderson	.75	.40	.25
	Panel (43)	35.00	17.50	10.50
127	Mike Torrez	.75	.40	.25
128	Pete Rose	10.00	5.00	3.00
129	John Denny	.75	.40	.25
	Panel (44)	6.00	3.00	1.75
130	Darrell Porter	.75	.40	.25
131	Rick Reuschel	.75	.40	.25
132	Graig Nettles	.90	.45	.25
	Panel (45)	6.00	3.00	1.75
133	Garry Maddox	.75	.40	.25
134	Mike Flanagan	.75	.40	.25
135	Dave Parker	.75	.40	.25
	Panel (46)	10.00	5.00	3.00
136	Terry Whitfield	.75	.40	.25
137	Wayne Garland	.75	.40	.25
138	Robin Yount	4.50	2.25	1.25
	Panel (47)	20.00	10.00	6.00
139a	Gaylord Perry (San Diego)	4.00	2.00	1.25
139b	Gaylord Perry (Texas, unissued proof.)	30.00	15.00	9.00
140	Rod Carew	4.50	2.25	1.25
141	Wayne Gross	.75	.40	.25
	Panel (48)	9.00	4.50	2.75
142	Barry Bonnell	.75	.40	.25
143	Willie Montanez	.75	.40	.25
144	Rollie Fingers	4.00	2.00	1.25
	Panel (49)	35.00	17.50	10.50
145	Lyman Bostock	.75	.40	.25
146	Gary Carter	4.50	2.25	1.25
147	Ron Blomberg	.75	.40	.25
	Panel (50)	30.00	15.00	9.00
148	Bob Bailor	.75	.40	.25
149	Tom Seaver	5.00	2.50	1.50
150	Thurman Munson	4.00	2.00	1.25

1978 Hostess Unissued Proofs

Different versions of two of the issued cards (see 1978 Hostess #56, 139) plus 10 players who do not appear on the snack cake boxes constitute the proof set for '78 Hostess. The unissued proofs are identical in format to the cards actually issued and measure 2-1/4" x 3-1/4" at the dotted lines.

		NM	EX	VG
Complete Set (10):		450.00	225.00	135.00
Common Player:		50.00	25.00	15.00
151	Bill Robinson	50.00	25.00	15.00
152	Lou Piniella	75.00	37.50	22.50
153	Lamar Johnson	50.00	25.00	15.00
154	Mark Belanger	50.00	25.00	15.00
155	Ken Griffey	75.00	37.50	22.50
156	Ken Forsch	50.00	25.00	15.00
157	Ted Sizemore	50.00	25.00	15.00
158	Don Baylor	50.00	25.00	15.00
159	Dusty Baker	60.00	30.00	18.00
160	Al Oliver	75.00	37.50	22.50

1979 Hostess

The last of five consecutive annual issues, the 1979 Hostess set retained the 150-card set size, 2-1/4" x 3-1/4" single-card size and 7-1/4" x 3-1/4" three-card panel format from the previous years. The cards were printed as the bottom panel on family-size boxes of Hostess snack cakes. Some panels, which were printed on less-popular brands, are somewhat scarcer today than the rest of the set. Like all Hostess issues, because the hobby was in a well-developed state at the time of issue, the 1979s survive today in complete panels and complete unused boxes for collectors who like original packaging.

		NM	EX	VG
	Complete Panel Set (50):	250.00	125.00	75.00
	Complete Singles Set (150):	175.00	85.00	50.00
	Common Panel:	4.50	2.25	1.25
	Common Single Player:	.75	.40	.25
	Panel (1)	7.50	3.75	2.25
1	John Denny	.75	.40	.25
2a	Jim Rice ("d-of", unissued proof)	15.00	7.50	4.50
2b	Jim Rice ("dh-of")	1.50	.70	.45
3	Doug Bair	.75	.40	.25
	Panel (2)	6.00	3.00	1.75
4	Darrell Porter	.75	.40	.25
5	Ross Grimsley	.75	.40	.25
6	Bobby Murcer	1.00	.50	.30
	Panel (3)	25.00	12.50	7.50
7	Lee Mazzilli	.75	.40	.25
8	Steve Garvey	1.50	.70	.45
9	Mike Schmidt	6.00	3.00	1.75
	Panel (4)	12.00	6.00	3.50
10	Terry Whitfield	.75	.40	.25
11	Jim Palmer	2.50	1.25	.70
12	Omar Moreno	.75	.40	.25
	Panel (5)	5.00	2.50	1.50
13	Duane Kuiper	.75	.40	.25
14	Mike Caldwell	.75	.40	.25
15	Steve Kemp	.75	.40	.25
	Panel (6)	5.00	2.50	1.50
16	Dave Goltz	.75	.40	.25
17	Mitchell Page	.75	.40	.25
18	Bill Stein	.75	.40	.25
	Panel (7)	5.00	2.50	1.50
19	Gene Tenace	.75	.40	.25
20	Jeff Burroughs	.75	.40	.25
21	Francisco Barrios	.75	.40	.25
	Panel (8)	7.50	3.75	2.25
22	Mike Torrez	.75	.40	.25
23	Ken Reitz	.75	.40	.25
24	Gary Carter	2.50	1.25	.70
	Panel (9)	9.00	4.50	2.75
25	Al Hrabosky	.75	.40	.25
26	Thurman Munson	1.50	.70	.45
27	Bill Buckner	.75	.40	.25
	Panel (10)	6.00	3.00	1.75
28	Ron Cey	.75	.40	.25
29	J.R. Richard	.75	.40	.25
30	Greg Luzinski	.75	.40	.25
	Panel (11)	5.00	2.50	1.50
31	Ed Ott	.75	.40	.25
32	Denny Martinez	.75	.40	.25
33	Darrell Evans	.75	.40	.25
	Panel (12)	5.00	2.50	1.50
34	Ron LeFlore	.75	.40	.25
35	Rick Waits	.75	.40	.25
36	Cecil Cooper	.75	.40	.25
	Panel (13)	15.00	7.50	4.50
37	Leon Roberts	.75	.40	.25
38a	Rod Carew (Large head.) (Botton of collar trim does not show.)	3.00	1.50	.90
38b	Rod Carew (Small head.) (Bottom of collar trim shows.)	3.00	1.50	.90
39	John Henry Johnson	.75	.40	.25
	Panel (14)	5.00	2.50	1.50
40	Chet Lemon	.75	.40	.25
41	Craig Swan	.75	.40	.25
42	Gary Matthews	.75	.40	.25
	Panel (15)	5.00	2.50	1.50
43	Lamar Johnson	.75	.40	.25
44	Ted Simmons	.75	.40	.25
45	Ken Griffey	.75	.40	.25
	Panel (16)	6.00	3.00	1.75
46	Freddie Patek	.75	.40	.25
47	Frank Tanana	.75	.40	.25
48	Rich Gossage	1.00	.50	.30
	Panel (17)	5.00	2.50	1.50
49	Burt Hooton	.75	.40	.25
50	Ellis Valentine	.75	.40	.25
51	Ken Forsch	.75	.40	.25
	Panel (18)	6.00	3.00	1.75
52	Bob Knepper	.75	.40	.25
53	Dave Parker	.75	.40	.25
54	Doug DeCinces	.75	.40	.25
	Panel (19)	20.00	10.00	6.00
55	Robin Yount	3.00	1.50	.90
56	Rusty Staub	1.00	.50	.30
57	Gary Alexander	.75	.40	.25
	Panel (20)	5.00	2.50	1.50
58	Julio Cruz	.75	.40	.25
59	Matt Keough	.75	.40	.25
60	Roy Smalley	.75	.40	.25
	Panel (21)	15.00	7.50	4.50
61	Joe Morgan	3.00	1.50	.90
62	Phil Niekro	2.00	1.00	.60
63	Don Baylor	.75	.40	.25
	Panel (22)	20.00	10.00	6.00
64	Dwight Evans	.75	.40	.25

65	Tom Seaver	3.00	1.50	.90
66	George Hendrick	.75	.40	.25
	Panel (23)	25.00	12.50	7.50
67	Rick Reuschel	.75	.40	.25
68	George Brett	6.00	3.00	1.75
69	Lou Piniella	1.00	.50	.30
	Panel (24)	12.00	6.00	3.50
70	Enos Cabell	.75	.40	.25
71	Steve Carlton	2.50	1.25	.70
72	Reggie Smith	.75	.40	.25
	Panel (25)	5.00	2.50	1.50
73	Rick Dempsey	.75	.40	.25
74	Vida Blue	.75	.40	.25
75	Phil Garner	.75	.40	.25
	Panel (26)	5.00	2.50	1.50
76	Rick Manning	.75	.40	.25
77	Mark Fidrych	1.00	.50	.30
78	Mario Guerrero	.75	.40	.25
	Panel (27)	5.00	2.50	1.50
79	Bob Stinson	.75	.40	.25
80	Al Oliver	.75	.40	.25
81	Doug Flynn	.75	.40	.25
	Panel (28)	7.50	3.75	2.25
82	John Mayberry	.75	.40	.25
83	Gaylord Perry	2.00	1.00	.60
84	Joe Rudi	.75	.40	.25
	Panel (29)	5.00	2.50	1.50
85	Dave Concepcion	.75	.40	.25
86	John Candelaria	.75	.40	.25
87	Pete Vuckovich	.75	.40	.25
	Panel (30)	5.00	2.50	1.50
88	Ivan DeJesus	.75	.40	.25
89	Ron Guidry	.75	.40	.25
90	Hal McRae	.75	.40	.25
	Panel (31)	6.00	3.00	1.75
91	Cesar Cedeno	.75	.40	.25
92	Don Sutton	2.00	1.00	.60
93	Andre Thornton	.75	.40	.25
	Panel (32)	5.00	2.50	1.50
94	Roger Erickson	.75	.40	.25
95	Larry Hisle	.75	.40	.25
96	Jason Thompson	.75	.40	.25
	Panel (33)	5.00	2.50	1.50
97	Jim Sundberg	.75	.40	.25
98	Bob Horner	.75	.40	.25
99	Ruppert Jones	.75	.40	.25
	Panel (34)	60.00	30.00	18.00
100	Willie Montanez	.75	.40	.25
101	Nolan Ryan	12.00	6.00	3.50
102	Ozzie Smith	15.00	7.50	4.50
	Panel (35)	12.00	6.00	3.50
103	Eric Soderholm	.75	.40	.25
104	Willie Stargell	2.50	1.25	.70
105a	Bob Bailor (Photo reversed, unissued proof.)			
105b	Bob Bailor (Photo corrected.)	.75	.40	.25
	Panel (36)	12.50	6.25	3.75
106	Carlton Fisk	2.50	1.25	.70
107	George Foster	.75	.40	.25
108	Keith Hernandez	.75	.40	.25
	Panel (37)	5.00	2.50	1.50
109	Dennis Leonard	.75	.40	.25
110	Graig Nettles	1.00	.50	.30
111	Jose Cruz	.75	.40	.25
	Panel (38)	5.00	2.50	1.50
112	Bobby Grich	.75	.40	.25
113	Bob Boone	.75	.40	.25
114	Davey Lopes	.75	.40	.25
	Panel (39)	15.00	7.50	4.50
115	Eddie Murray	3.00	1.50	.90
116	Jack Clark	.75	.40	.25
117	Lou Whitaker	.75	.40	.25
	Panel (40)	20.00	10.00	6.00
118	Miguel Dilone	.75	.40	.25
119	Sal Bando	.75	.40	.25
120	Reggie Jackson	6.00	3.00	1.75
	Panel (41)	15.00	7.50	4.50
121	Dale Murphy	2.00	1.00	.60
122	Jon Matlack	.75	.40	.25
123	Bruce Bochte	.75	.40	.25
	Panel (42)	12.50	6.25	3.75
124	John Stearns	.75	.40	.25
125	Dave Winfield	3.00	1.50	.90
126	Jorge Orta	.75	.40	.25
	Panel (43)	25.00	12.50	7.50
127	Garry Templeton	.75	.40	.25
128	Johnny Bench	3.00	1.50	.90
129	Butch Hobson	.75	.40	.25
	Panel (44)	6.00	3.00	1.75
130	Bruce Sutter	2.50	1.25	.70
131	Bucky Dent	.75	.40	.25
132	Amos Otis	.75	.40	.25
	Panel (45)	5.00	2.50	1.50
133	Bert Blyleven	.75	.40	.25
134	Larry Bowa	.75	.40	.25
135	Ken Singleton	.75	.40	.25
	Panel (46)	5.00	2.50	1.50
136	Sixto Lezcano	.75	.40	.25
137	Roy Howell	.75	.40	.25
138	Bill Madlock	.75	.40	.25
	Panel (47)	5.00	2.50	1.50
139	Dave Revering	.75	.40	.25
140	Richie Zisk	.75	.40	.25
141	Butch Wynegar	.75	.40	.25
	Panel (48)	25.00	12.50	7.50
142	Alan Ashby	.75	.40	.25
143	Sparky Lyle	.75	.40	.25
144	Pete Rose	7.50	3.75	2.25
	Panel (49)	6.00	3.00	1.75
145	Dennis Eckersley	2.50	1.25	.70
146	Dave Kingman	.75	.40	.25
147	Buddy Bell	.75	.40	.25
	Panel (50)	5.00	2.50	1.50
148	Mike Hargrove	.75	.40	.25
149	Jerry Koosman	.75	.40	.25
150	Toby Harrah	.75	.40	.25

1979 Hostess Unissued Proofs

Identical in format to the 150 cards which were issued on boxes of Hostess snack cakes, these cards were possibly prepared in the event trades of players in the issued set required quick replacement. The reason these cards were never released is unknown. Cards measure 2-1/4" x 3-1/4" at the dotted-line borders. While some of the proofs are numbered on back, others have no card number.

		NM	EX	VG
	Complete Set (17):	1,100	550.00	330.00
	Common Player:	50.00	25.00	15.00
151	Dusty Baker	60.00	30.00	18.00
152	Mark Belanger	60.00	30.00	18.00
154	Al Cowens	50.00	25.00	15.00
155	Dan Driessen	50.00	25.00	15.00
157	Steve Henderson	50.00	25.00	15.00
159	Tommy John	75.00	37.50	22.50
160	Garry Maddox	50.00	25.00	15.00
(161)	Willie McCovey	250.00	125.00	75.00
(162)	Scott McGregor	50.00	25.00	15.00
(163)	Bill Nahorodny	50.00	25.00	15.00
(164)	Terry Puhl	50.00	25.00	15.00
(165)	Willie Randolph	50.00	25.00	15.00
(166)	Jim Slaton	50.00	25.00	15.00
(167)	Paul Splittorff	50.00	25.00	15.00
(168)	Frank Taveras	50.00	25.00	15.00
(169)	Alan Trammell	125.00	65.00	35.00
(170)	Bump Wills	50.00	25.00	15.00

1971 House of Jazz

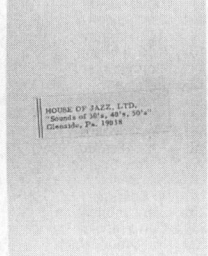

Controversy has dogged this card set since the first reports of its existence in the early 1970s. The legitimacy of the issue has been questioned though certain hobby journalists traced the cards to a record store which supposedly gave them away with music purchases, along with similar cards depicting musicians. The 2-3/8" x 3-1/2" cards are printed in black-and-white with round corners. Backs of some, but not all, cards have a blue-and-white address sticker for "HOUSE OF JAZZ, LTD." The unnumbered cards are checklisted here in alphabetical order.

		NM	EX	VG
	Complete Set (35):	200.00	100.00	60.00
	Common Player:	5.00	2.50	1.50
(1)	John Antonelli	5.00	2.50	1.50
(2)	Richie Ashburn	6.00	3.00	1.75
(3)	Ernie Banks	6.50	3.25	2.00
(4)	Hank Bauer	5.00	2.50	1.50
(5)	Joe DiMaggio	15.00	7.50	4.50
(6)	Bobby Doerr	5.00	2.50	1.50
(7)	Herman Franks	5.00	2.50	1.50
(8)	Lou Gehrig	15.00	7.50	4.50
(9)	Granny Hamner	5.00	2.50	1.50
(10)	Al Kaline	6.50	3.25	2.00
(11)	Harmon Killebrew	6.00	3.00	1.75
(12)	Jim Konstanty	5.00	2.50	1.50
(13)	Bob Lemon	5.00	2.50	1.50
(14)	Ed Lopat	5.00	2.50	1.50
(15)	Stan Lopata	5.00	2.50	1.50
(16)	Peanuts Lowrey	5.00	2.50	1.50
(17)	Mickey Mantle	35.00	17.50	10.00
(18)	Phil Marchildon	5.00	2.50	1.50
(19)	Walt Masterson	5.00	2.50	1.50
(20)	Ed Mathews	6.00	3.00	1.75
(21)	Willie Mays	10.00	5.00	3.00
(22)	Don Newcombe	5.00	2.50	1.50
(23)	Joe Nuxhall	5.00	2.50	1.50
(24)	Satchel Paige	7.50	3.75	2.25
(25)	Roy Partee	5.00	2.50	1.50
(26)	Jackie Robinson	7.50	3.75	2.25
(27)	Babe Ruth	20.00	10.00	6.00
(28)	Carl Scheib	5.00	2.50	1.50
(29)	Bobby Shantz	5.00	2.50	1.50
(30)	Burt Shotton	5.00	2.50	1.50

		NM	EX	VG
(31)	Duke Snider	6.50	3.25	2.00
(32)	Warren Spahn	6.00	3.00	1.75
(33)	Johnny Temple	5.00	2.50	1.50
(34)	Ted Williams	10.00	5.00	3.00
(35)	Early Wynn	5.00	2.50	1.50

1962 Houston Colt .45s Booklets

 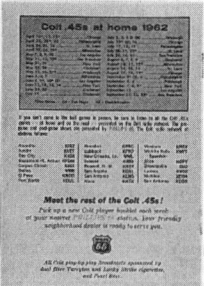

To introduce the members of the new Houston National League team, Phillips 66 gasoline sponsored (along with the team's cigarette and beer broadcast sponsors) this set of 24 player profile booklets given away one per week during the season. Fronts of the 16-page 5-3/8" x 7-7/16" booklets feature a blue and white action photo of the player on a bright orange background. Black and white graphics complete the design. The player's name appears in a Texas map outline. Backs have the 1962 Houston Colt .45s home-game schedule and details of the team's statewide radio network. Inside the booklet are a complete biography, stats and both posed and action photos of the players, along with families, teammates, etc. Because of player trades during the season, and lessened demand for some of the non-player booklets, some of the series are quite scarce. Each of the booklets can be found with different sponsors logos on front.

		NM	EX	VG
Complete Set (24):		240.00	120.00	72.00
Common Booklet:		15.00	7.50	4.50
(1)	Joe Amalfitano	15.00	7.50	4.50
(2)	Bob Aspromonte	15.00	7.50	4.50
(3)	Bob Bruce	15.00	7.50	4.50
(4)	Jim Campbell	18.00	9.00	5.50
(5)	Harry Craft	15.00	7.50	4.50
(6)	Dick Farrell	15.00	7.50	4.50
(7)	Dave Giusti	15.00	7.50	4.50
(8)	Jim Golden	15.00	7.50	4.50
(9)	J.C. Hartman	18.00	9.00	5.50
(10)	Ken Johnson	15.00	7.50	4.50
(11)	Norm Larker	15.00	7.50	4.50
(12)	Bob Lillis	15.00	7.50	4.50
(13)	Don McMahon	15.00	7.50	4.50
(14)	Roman Mejias	15.00	7.50	4.50
(15)	Jim Pendleton	18.00	9.00	5.50
(16)	Paul Richards (GM)	15.00	7.50	4.50
(17)	Bobby Shantz	30.00	15.00	9.00
(18)	Hal Smith	15.00	7.50	4.50
(19)	Al Spangler	15.00	7.50	4.50
(20)	Jim Umbricht	15.00	7.50	4.50
(21)	Carl Warwick	15.00	7.50	4.50
(22)	Hal Woodeshick	15.00	7.50	4.50
(23)	Coaches (James Adair, Bobby Bragan, Cot Deal, Luman Harris)	25.00	12.50	7.50
(24)	Announcers (Rene Cardenas, Orlando Diego, Gene Elston, Al Helfer, Lowell Passe, Guy Savage)	19.00	9.50	5.75

1967 Houston Astros Team Issue

 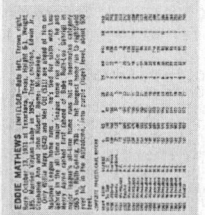

This set of 12 player cards was issued by the Houston Astros, though the exact nature of the promotion is not known. Individual cards of 2-5/8" x 3-1/8" were printed on a perforated sheet about 9" x 10-1/2". Fronts have a posed color photo with a black facsimile autograph. Backs are printed in black on white with a yellow color block behind the player data and career notes. Full major and minor league stats are at bottom. The unnumbered cards are checklisted here in alphabetical order.

		NM	EX	VG
Complete Set, Sheet:		65.00	32.50	20.00
Complete Set, Singles (12):		65.00	32.50	20.00
Common Player:		8.00	4.00	2.50
(1)	Bob Aspromonte	8.00	4.00	2.50
(2)	John Bateman	8.00	4.00	2.50
(3)	Mike Cuellar	8.00	4.00	2.50
(4)	Larry Dierker	8.00	4.00	2.50
(5)	Dave Giusti	8.00	4.00	2.50
(6)	Grady Hatton	8.00	4.00	2.50
(7)	Bill Heath	8.00	4.00	2.50

		NM	EX	VG
(8)	Sonny Jackson	8.00	4.00	2.50
(9)	Ed Mathews	20.00	10.00	6.00
(10)	Joe Morgan	20.00	10.00	6.00
(11)	Rusty Staub	12.50	6.25	3.75
(12)	Jim Wynn	8.00	4.00	2.50

1953-1955 Howard Photo Service Postcards

Little is known about these postcards. Player and team combinations on the known pieces suggest a range of issue dates between 1953 and 1955. The 3-1/2" x 5-5/8" cards have a glossy black-and-white front photo. A rubber-stamp on the back attributes the card to "Howard Photo Service, N.Y.C." The specific pose on the second Turley card is not known. It is possible other cards may yet be discovered.

		NM	EX	VG
Common Player:		20.00	10.00	6.00
(1)	Ned Garver	20.00	10.00	6.00
(2)	Billy Hitchcock	20.00	10.00	6.00
(3)	Dave Madison	20.00	10.00	6.00
(4)	Willie Mays	165.00	85.00	50.00
(5)	Willie Mays (Seven-Up ad on back.)	750.00	370.00	220.00
(6)	Bob Turley (Follow-through.)	30.00	15.00	9.00
(7)	Bob Turley (Wind-up.)	30.00	15.00	9.00

1976 HRT/RES 1942 Play Ball

TED WILLIAMS — Of Boston Red Sox

This "phantom" continuation of the Play Ball series of 1939-41 was the creation of Ted Taylor and Bob Schmierer, whose initials appear in the copyright line on back. The 2-1/2" x 3-1/8" cards feature black-and-white photos on front and were printed on gray clay-content cardboard in a near replication of the stock found on the vintage Play Ball series. Backs were also done in style reminiscent of 1940s issues. Besides player data and career summaries, backs have a "1942 PLAY BALL - U.S.A." title line and either a "Buy War Bonds" or "'Keep Baseball Going' - FDR" slogan above the 1976 copyright line. The pair produced a number of other original and reprint issues in the 1970s. All of the others carry advertisements for their "Philly" card shows.

		NM	EX	VG
Complete Set (36):		30.00	15.00	9.00
Common Card:		1.00	.50	.30
1	Lou Gehrig	7.50	3.75	2.25
2	Joe DiMaggio	7.50	3.75	2.25
3	Phil Rizzuto	3.00	1.50	.90
4	Ted Williams	6.00	3.00	1.75
5	Charles Wagner	1.00	.50	.30
6	Thornton Lee	1.00	.50	.30
7	Taft Wright	1.00	.50	.30
8	Jeff Heath	1.00	.50	.30
9	Roy Mack	1.00	.50	.30
10	Pat Mullin	1.00	.50	.30
11	Al Benton	1.00	.50	.30
12	Bob Harris	1.00	.50	.30
13	Roy Cullenbine	1.00	.50	.30
14	Cecil Travis	1.00	.50	.30
15	Buck Newsom	1.00	.50	.30
16	Eddie Collins Jr.	1.00	.50	.30
17	Dick Siebert	1.00	.50	.30
18	Dee Miles	1.00	.50	.30
19	Pete Reiser	1.00	.50	.30
20	Dolph Camilli	1.00	.50	.30
21	Curt Davis	1.00	.50	.30
22	Spud Krist	1.00	.50	.30
23	Frank Crespi	1.00	.50	.30
24	Elmer Riddle	1.00	.50	.30
25	Bucky Walters	1.00	.50	.30
26	Vince DiMaggio	1.50	.70	.45
27	Max Butcher	1.00	.50	.30
28	Mel Ott	3.00	1.50	.90
29	Bob Carpenter	1.00	.50	.30
30	Claude Passeau	1.00	.50	.30
31	Dom Dallessandro	1.00	.50	.30
32	Casey Stengel	3.00	1.50	.90

1976-77 HRT/RES 1947 Bowman

 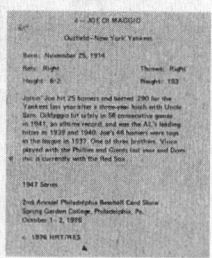

Advertised as "The Set That Never Was," this collectors' issue from Ted Taylor and Bob Schmierer used a 2-1/8" x 2-1/2" black-and-white format and gray cardboard stock to replicate the feel of the first post-WWII baseball cards. The set was issued in three series with advertising on back promoting the second (1976) and third (1977) annual EPSCC "Philly" shows. Series one (#1-49) was issued in 1976; series two (#50-81) and three (#82-113) were 1977 issues.

		NM	EX	VG
Complete Set (113):		90.00	45.00	27.50
Common Player:		1.00	.50	.30
1	Bobby Doerr	1.00	.50	.30
2	Stan Musial	3.00	1.50	.90
3	Babe Ruth	7.50	3.75	2.25
4	Joe DiMaggio	6.00	3.00	1.75
5	Andy Pafko	1.00	.50	.30
6	Johnny Pesky	1.00	.50	.30
7	Gil Hodges	1.50	.70	.45
8	Tommy Holmes	1.00	.50	.30
9	Ralph Kiner	1.00	.50	.30
10	Yogi Berra	2.00	1.00	.60
11	Bob Feller	1.50	.70	.45
12	Joe Gordon	1.00	.50	.30
13	Eddie Joost	1.00	.50	.30
14	Del Ennis	1.00	.50	.30
15	Johnny Mize	1.00	.50	.30
16	Pee Wee Reese	1.25	.60	.40
17	Jackie Robinson	4.00	2.00	1.25
18	Enos Slaughter	1.00	.50	.30
19	Vern Stephens	1.00	.50	.30
20	Bobby Thomson	1.00	.50	.30
21	Ted Williams	6.00	3.00	1.75
22	Bob Elliott	1.00	.50	.30
23	Mickey Vernon	1.00	.50	.30
24	Ewell Blackwell	1.00	.50	.30
25	Lou Boudreau	1.00	.50	.30
26	Ralph Branca	1.00	.50	.30
27	Harry Breechen (Brecheen)	1.00	.50	.30
28	Dom DiMaggio	1.00	.50	.30
29	Bruce Edwards	1.00	.50	.30
30	Sam Chapman	1.00	.50	.30
31	George Kell	1.00	.50	.30
32	Jack Kramer	1.00	.50	.30
33	Hal Newhouser	1.00	.50	.30
34	Charlie Keller	1.00	.50	.30
35	Ken Keltner	1.00	.50	.30
36	Hank Greenberg	1.25	.60	.40
37	Howie Pollet	1.00	.50	.30
38	Luke Appling	1.00	.50	.30
39	Pete Suder	1.00	.50	.30
40	Johnny Sain	1.00	.50	.30
41	Phil Cavaretta (Cavarretta)	1.00	.50	.30
42	Johnny Vander Meer	1.00	.50	.30
43	Mel Ott	1.00	.50	.30
44	Walker Cooper	1.00	.50	.30
45	Birdie Tebbetts	1.00	.50	.30
46	George Stirnweiss	1.00	.50	.30
47	Connie Mack	1.00	.50	.30
48	Jimmie Foxx	1.00	.50	.30
49	Checklist (Joe DiMaggio, Babe Ruth)	1.50	.70	.45
(50)	Honus Wagner T206 Card (First series.)	1.00	.50	.30
51	Ted Taylor (First series.)	1.00	.50	.30
52	Bob Schmierer (First series.)	1.00	.50	.30
50	Schoolboy Rowe (Second series.)	1.00	.50	.30
51	Andy Seminick (Second series.)	1.00	.50	.30
52	Fred Walker (Second series.)	1.00	.50	.30
53	Virgil Trucks	1.00	.50	.30
54	Dizzy Trout	1.00	.50	.30
55	Walter Evers	1.00	.50	.30
56	Thurman Tucker	1.00	.50	.30
57	Fritz Ostermueller	1.00	.50	.30
58	Augie Galan	1.00	.50	.30
59	Norman Young	1.00	.50	.30
60	Skeeter Newsome	1.00	.50	.30
61	Jack Lohrke	1.00	.50	.30
62	Rudy York	1.00	.50	.30
63	Tex Hughson	1.00	.50	.30
64	Sam Mele	1.00	.50	.30
65	Fred Hutchinson	1.00	.50	.30
66	Don Black	1.00	.50	.30
67	Les Fleming	1.00	.50	.30
68	George McQuinn	1.00	.50	.30
69	Mike McCormick	1.00	.50	.30
70	Mickey Witek	1.00	.50	.30
71	Blix Donnely	1.00	.50	.30
72	Elbie Fletcher	1.00	.50	.30
73	Hal Gregg	1.00	.50	.30

		NM	EX	VG
74	Dick Whitman	1.00	.50	.30
75	Johnny Neun	1.00	.50	.30
76	Doyle Lade	1.00	.50	.30
77	Ron Northey	1.00	.50	.30
78	Walker Cooper	1.00	.50	.30
79	Warren Spahn	1.00	.50	.30
80	Happy Chandler	1.00	.50	.30
81	Checklist (Connie Mack, Roy Mack, Connie Mack III)	1.00	.50	.30
82	Earle Mack	1.00	.50	.30
83	Buddy Rosar	1.00	.50	.30
84	Walt Judnich	1.00	.50	.30
85	Bob Kennedy	1.00	.50	.30
86	Mike Tresh	1.00	.50	.30
87	Sid Hudson	1.00	.50	.30
88	Eugene Thompson	1.00	.50	.30
89	Bill Nicholson	1.00	.50	.30
90	Stan Hack	1.00	.50	.30
91	Terry Moore	1.00	.50	.30
92	Ted Lyons	1.00	.50	.30
93	Barney McCosky	1.00	.50	.30
94	Stan Spence	1.00	.50	.30
95	Larry Jansen	1.00	.50	.30
96	Whitey Kurowski	1.00	.50	.30
97	Honus Wagner	1.50	.70	.45
98	Billy Herman	1.00	.50	.30
99	Jim Tabor	1.00	.50	.30
100	Phil Marchildon	1.00	.50	.30
101	Dave Ferriss	1.00	.50	.30
102	Al Zarilla	1.00	.50	.30
103	Bob Dillinger	1.00	.50	.30
104	Bob Lemon	1.00	.50	.30
105	Jim Hegan	1.00	.50	.30
106	Johnny Lindell	1.00	.50	.30
107	Willard Marshall	1.00	.50	.30
108	Walt Masterson	1.00	.50	.30
109	Carl Scheib	1.00	.50	.30
110	Bobby Brown	1.00	.50	.30
111	Cy Block	1.00	.50	.30
112	Sid Gordon	1.00	.50	.30
113	Checklist (Ty Cobb, Babe Ruth, Tris Speaker)	1.50	.70	.45

1977 HRT/RES Philadelphia 'Favorites'

This collectors' issue was produced by promoters Ted Taylor and Bob Schmierer to promote their third annual "Philly Show" in 1977. Printed in black-and-white on front and back, the 2-3/8" x 3-5/8" cards feature former Philadelphia A's and Phillies player photos on front, and an ad for the show on back. Cards were given away at area malls and sporting events to promote the show. Complete sets were originally sold for $2.75.

		NM	EX	VG
	Complete Set (25):	30.00	15.00	9.00
	Common Player:	2.00	1.00	.60
1	Connie Mack	2.00	1.00	.60
2	Larry Lajoie	2.50	1.25	.70
3	Eddie Collins	2.00	1.00	.60
4	Lefty Grove	2.50	1.25	.70
5	Al Simmons	2.00	1.00	.60
6	Jimmie Foxx	3.00	1.50	.90
7	Frank Baker	2.00	1.00	.60
8	Ferris Fain	2.00	1.00	.60
9	Jimmy Dykes	2.00	1.00	.60
10	Willie Jones	2.00	1.00	.60
11	Del Ennis	2.00	1.00	.60
12	Granny Hamner	2.00	1.00	.60
13	Andy Seminick	2.00	1.00	.60
14	Robin Roberts	4.00	2.00	1.25
15	Ed Delahanty	2.00	1.00	.60
16	Gavvy Cravath	2.00	1.00	.60
17	Cy Williams	2.00	1.00	.60
18	Chuck Klein	2.00	1.00	.60
19	Rich Ashburn	4.00	2.00	1.25
20	Bobby Shantz	2.00	1.00	.60
21	Gus Zernial	2.00	1.00	.60
22	Eddie Sawyer	2.00	1.00	.60
23	Grover Alexander	2.00	1.00	.60
24	Wally Moses	2.00	1.00	.60
25	Connie Mack Stadium	2.00	1.00	.60

1978 HRT/RES 1939 Father and Son Reprints

Reprints of scarce 1939 Father and Son Shoes stores cards of local ballplayers (minus the original advertising on front) were created by Ted Taylor and Bob Schmierer to promote their fourth "Philly Show" in March, 1978. The 3" x 4" cards have black-and-white player photos on front. Backs carry an ad for the show and information about the reprints.

Wally Moses, outfielder, Phila. Athletics

		NM	EX	VG
	Complete Set (8):	7.50	3.75	2.25
	Common Player:	1.00	.50	.30
(1)	Sam Chapman	1.00	.50	.30
(2)	Chuck Klein	1.50	.70	.45
(3)	Herschel Martin	1.00	.50	.30
(4)	Wally Moses	1.00	.50	.30
(5)	Hugh Mulcahy	1.00	.50	.30
(6)	Skeeter Newsome	1.00	.50	.30
(7)	George Scharien (Scharein)	1.00	.50	.30
(8)	Dick Siebert	1.00	.50	.30

1979 HRT/RES 1950 Phillies/A's "Doubleheaders"

Stan Lopata, Catcher   Eddie Waitkus, Infield

Though their names or initials do not appear on the cards, this collectors' set was issued by Ted Taylor and Bob Schmierer to promote the March and September 1979, "Philly Shows," the sixth and seventh in the show's history. Borrowing from the format of the 1941 "Doubleheaders" bubblegum card issue, these 2-1/2" x 2-1/8" cards depict members of the 1950 Phillies "Whiz Kids" and the 1950 A's, the last team managed by Connie Mack. Fronts are printed in blue and white, backs in maroon and white. The dual-player cards feature various ads on back, while the managers' cards have a team narrative. The unnumbered cards are checklisted here alphabetically within team, by the last name of the player on the left.

		NM	EX	VG
	Complete Set (30):	25.00	12.50	7.50
	Common Card:	1.50	.70	.45
(1)	Joe Astroth, Dick Fowler	1.50	.70	.45
(2)	Sam Chapman, Lou Brissie	1.50	.70	.45
(3)	Bob Dillinger, Billy Hitchcock	1.50	.70	.45
(4)	Ben Guintini, Joe Tipton	1.50	.70	.45
(5)	Bob Hooper, Barney McCosky	1.50	.70	.45
(6)	Eddie Joost, Kermit Wahl	1.50	.70	.45
(7)	Ed Klieman, Mike Guerra	1.50	.70	.45
(8)	Paul Lehner, Ferris Fain	1.50	.70	.45
(9)	Connie Mack	1.50	.70	.45
(10)	Earle Mack, Mickey Cochrane	1.50	.70	.45
(11)	Wally Moses, Carl Scheib	1.50	.70	.45
(12)	Pete Suder, Alex Kellner	1.50	.70	.45
(13)	Elmer Valo, Bobby Shantz	1.50	.70	.45
(14)	Bob Wellman, Joe Coleman	1.50	.70	.45
(15)	Hank Wyse, Gene Markland	1.50	.70	.45
(16)	Johnny Blatnik, Ed Wright	1.50	.70	.45
(17)	Ralph Caballero, Bubba Church	1.50	.70	.45
(18)	Milo Candini, Hank Borowy	1.50	.70	.45
(19)	Blix Donnelly, Bill Nicholson	1.50	.70	.45
(20)	Del Ennis, Ken Heintzelman	1.50	.70	.45
(21)	Mike Goliat, Dick Whitman	1.50	.70	.45
(22)	Granny Hamner, Rich Ashburn	3.50	1.75	1.00
(23)	Willie Jones, Russ Meyer	1.50	.70	.45
(24)	Jim Konstanty, Ken Silvestri	1.50	.70	.45
(25)	Stan Lopata, Eddie Waitkus	1.50	.70	.45
(26)	Ed Sanicki, Robin Roberts	3.50	1.75	1.00
(27)	Eddie Sawyer	1.50	.70	.45
(28)	Andy Seminick, Ken Trinkle	1.50	.70	.45
(29)	Dick Sisler, Stan Hollmig (DP)	1.50	.70	.45
(30)	Jocko Thompson, Curt Simmons	1.50	.70	.45

1957-1959 Hudepohl Beer Cincinnati Reds

These 8" x 10" black-and-white photos were distributed by Hudepohl Beer, although the brewery or brand is not mentioned on the pictures. They are identical in format to the team-issued publicity photos. The Hudepohl pictures differ from the team-issue in that the beer pictures have a semi-gloss finish and no printing on the back, while the team pictures have a glossy surface and a four-line warning on back not to use them for advertising purposes. The pictures have portrait or posed action photos, sometimes with the background removed. They are bordered in white with the player and team name at bottom. The type style is sans-serif for 1957 pictures, and serifed in 1959. Years of issue have been attributed according to corresponding team-issue photos and uniforms pictured. Because so many of the Hudepohl pictures are found autographed, it is possible they were distributed in conjunction with player promotional appearances. This checklist may well not be complete.

	NM	EX	VG
Common Player:	20.00	10.00	6.00
1957 (Redlegs, sans-serif.)			
Ed. Bailey/Btg	20.00	10.00	6.00
George Crowe/Btg	20.00	10.00	6.00
Ted Kluszewski/Btg	35.00	17.50	10.50
Brooks Lawrence (Follow-through.)	20.00	10.00	6.00
Roy McMillan/Btg	20.00	10.00	6.00
Joe Nuxhall (Follow-through.)	25.00	12.50	7.50
Manager "Birdie" Tebbetts/Portrait	20.00	10.00	6.00
1959 (Reds, serif.)			
Brooks Lawrence/Portrait	20.00	10.00	6.00

1960 Hudepohl Beer Cincinnati Reds

These 8" x 10" black-and-white photos were distributed by Hudepohl Beer, although the brewery or brand is not mentioned on the pictures. Similar in format to the team-issued publicity photos, the Hudepohl pictures differ in that they have a semi-gloss finish and no printing on the back, while the team pictures have a glossy surface and a four-line warning on back not to use them for advertising purposes. The pictures have portrait or posed action photos, sometimes with the background removed. They are bordered in white with the player and team name at bottom in a light sans-serif type. Years of issue have been attributed according to corresponding team-issue photos and uniforms pictured. Because so many of the Hudepohl pictures are found autographed, it is possible they were distributed in conjunction with player promotional appearances. This checklist may not be complete.

		NM	EX	VG
	Common Player:	20.00	10.00	6.00
(1)	Ed. Bailey	20.00	10.00	6.00
(2)	Gus Bell	20.00	10.00	6.00
(3)	Jerry Lynch	20.00	10.00	6.00
(4)	Roy McMillan	20.00	10.00	6.00
(5)	Don Newcombe	20.00	10.00	6.00
(6)	Joe Nuxhall	25.00	12.50	7.50
(7)	Vada Pinson	30.00	15.00	9.00
(8)	Frank Robinson	85.00	42.50	25.00

1907 Geo. W. Hull Chicago White Sox Postcards

 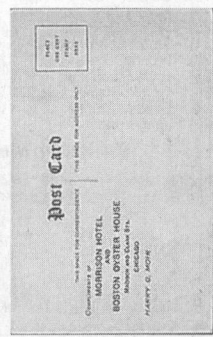

Members of the World Champion White Sox are featured on this single-team issue. Horizontal in format, the black-and-white cards measure about 5-1/2" x 3-1/2". All of the cards share a basic design of a player action posed photo at right, with his name, position, and "White Sox, World's Champions" in a white box beneath. The main part of the card pictures a clothesline full of white socks, each of which has a small round portrait photo of one of the players - 15 in all. In a larger portrait at lower-left is team owner Charles Comiskey. In the white border at top, each card has a witty statement such as "String of World-Beaters" and "Not Worn By Ladies, But Admired By Them." In the bottom border is, "Copyright 1907, Geo. W. Hull." Backs have been seen with a schedule of home games and with an ad from the Morrison Hotel and Boston Oyster House of Chicago.

		NM	EX	VG
	Complete Set (16):	10,000	5,000	3,000
	Common Player:	600.00	300.00	180.00
(1)	Nick Altrock	600.00	300.00	180.00
(2)	George Davis	950.00	475.00	285.00
(3)	Jiggs Donahue	600.00	300.00	180.00
(4)	Pat Dougherty	600.00	300.00	180.00
(5)	Eddie Hahn	600.00	300.00	180.00
(6)	Frank Isbell	600.00	300.00	180.00
(7)	Fielder Jones	600.00	300.00	180.00
(8)	Ed McFarland	600.00	300.00	180.00

		NM	EX	VG
(9)	Frank Owens	600.00	300.00	180.00
(10)	Roy Patterson	600.00	300.00	180.00
(11)	George Rohe	600.00	300.00	180.00
(12)	Frank Smith	600.00	300.00	180.00
(13)	Billy Sullivan	600.00	300.00	180.00
(14)	Lee Tannehill	600.00	300.00	180.00
(15)	Eddie Walsh	950.00	475.00	285.00
(16)	Doc White	600.00	300.00	180.00

1953 Hunter Wieners Cardinals

From the great era of the regionally issued hot dog cards in the mid-1950s, the 1953 Hunter wieners set of St. Louis Cardinals is among the rarest today. Originally issued in two-card panels, the cards are most often found as 2-1/4" x 3-1/4" singles today when they can be found at all. The cards feature a light blue facsimile autograph printed over the stat box at the bottom. They are blank-backed.

		NM	EX	VG
Complete Set (26):		20,000	10,000	6,000
Common Player:		600.00	300.00	180.00
(1)	Steve Bilko	600.00	300.00	180.00
(2)	Cloyd Boyer	600.00	300.00	180.00
(3)	Al Brazle	600.00	300.00	180.00
(4)	Cliff Chambers	600.00	300.00	180.00
(5)	Michael Clark	600.00	300.00	180.00
(6)	Jack Crimian	600.00	300.00	180.00
(7)	Lester Fusselman	600.00	300.00	180.00
(8)	Harvey Haddix	650.00	320.00	195.00
(9)	Solly Hemus	600.00	300.00	180.00
(10)	Ray Jablonski	600.00	300.00	180.00
(11)	William Johnson	600.00	300.00	180.00
(12)	Harry Lowrey	600.00	300.00	180.00
(13)	Lawrence Miggins	600.00	300.00	180.00
(14)	Stuart Miller	600.00	300.00	180.00
(15)	Wilmer Mizell	600.00	300.00	180.00
(16)	Stanley Musial	6,000	3,000	1,800
(17)	Joseph Presko	600.00	300.00	180.00
(18)	Delbert Rice	600.00	300.00	180.00
(19)	Harold Rice	600.00	300.00	180.00
(20)	Willard Schmidt	600.00	300.00	180.00
(21)	Albert Schoendienst	1,300	650.00	400.00
(22)	Richard Sisler	600.00	300.00	180.00
(23)	Enos Slaughter	1,300	650.00	400.00
(24)	Gerald Staley	600.00	300.00	180.00
(25)	Edward Stanky	650.00	320.00	195.00
(26)	John Yuhas	600.00	300.00	180.00

1954 Hunter Wieners Cardinals

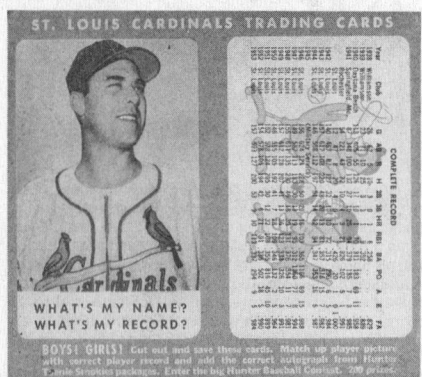

A nearly impossible set to complete today by virtue of the method of its issue, the 1954 Hunter hot dog set features what would traditionally be the front and back of a normal baseball card on two different cards. The "front," has a color photo with a box at bottom challenging the collector to name the player and quote his stats. The "back" features cartoon Cardinals in action, and contains the answers. However, because both parts were printed on a single panel. Because most of the back (non-picture) portions of the panels were thrown away years ago, it is a formidable challenge to complete a '54 Hunter set today. There is no back printing on the 2-1/4" x 3-1/2" cards.

	NM	EX	VG
Complete Set (30):	18,000	9,000	5,500

		NM	EX	VG
Common Player:		500.00	250.00	150.00
(1)	Tom Alston	500.00	250.00	150.00
(2)	Steve Bilko	500.00	250.00	150.00
(3)	Al Brazle	500.00	250.00	150.00
(4)	Tom Burgess	500.00	250.00	150.00
(5)	Cot Deal	500.00	250.00	150.00
(6)	Alex Grammas	500.00	250.00	150.00
(7)	Harvey Haddix	500.00	250.00	150.00
(8)	Solly Hemus	500.00	250.00	150.00
(9)	Ray Jablonski	500.00	250.00	150.00
(10)	Royce Lint	500.00	250.00	150.00
(11)	Peanuts Lowrey	500.00	250.00	150.00
(12)	Memo Luna	500.00	250.00	150.00
(13)	Stu Miller	500.00	250.00	150.00
(14)	Stan Musial	4,000	2,000	1,200
(15)	Tom Poholsky	500.00	250.00	150.00
(16)	Bill Posedel	500.00	250.00	150.00
(17)	Joe Presko	500.00	250.00	150.00
(18)	Dick Rand	500.00	250.00	150.00
(19)	Vic Raschi	500.00	250.00	150.00
(20)	Rip Repulski	500.00	250.00	150.00
(21)	Del Rice	500.00	250.00	150.00
(22)	John Riddle	500.00	250.00	150.00
(23)	Mike Ryba	500.00	250.00	150.00
(24)	Red Schoendienst	1,000	500.00	300.00
(25)	Dick Schofield	550.00	270.00	165.00
(26)	Enos Slaughter	1,000	500.00	300.00
(27)	Gerry Staley	500.00	250.00	150.00
(28)	Ed Stanky	500.00	250.00	150.00
(29)	Ed Yuhas	500.00	250.00	150.00
(30)	Sal Yvars	500.00	250.00	150.00

1955 Hunter Wieners Cardinals

The 1955 team set of St. Louis Cardinals, included with packages of Hunter hot dogs, features the third format change in three years of issue. For 1955, the cards were printed in a tall, narrow (2" wide with the height tapering from 4-3/4" at left to 4-1/2" at right) format, two to a panel. The cards feature both a posed action photo and a portrait photo, along with a facsimile autograph and brief biographical data on the front. There is no back printing, as the cards were part of the wrapping for packages of hot dogs.

		NM	EX	VG
Complete Set (30):		22,000	11,000	6,500
Common Player:		500.00	250.00	150.00
(1)	Thomas Edison Alston	500.00	250.00	150.00
(2)	Kenton Lloyd Boyer	1,350	675.00	405.00
(3)	Harry Lewis Elliott	500.00	250.00	150.00
(4)	John Edward Faszholz	500.00	250.00	150.00
(5)	Joseph Filmore Frazier	500.00	250.00	150.00
(6)	Alexander Pete Grammas	500.00	250.00	150.00
(7)	Harvey Haddix	500.00	250.00	150.00
(8)	Solly Joseph Hemus	500.00	250.00	150.00
(9)	Lawrence Curtis Jackson	500.00	250.00	150.00
(10)	Tony R. Jacobs	500.00	250.00	150.00
(11)	Gordon Bassett Jones	500.00	250.00	150.00
(12)	Paul Edmore LaPalme	500.00	250.00	150.00
(13)	Brooks Ulysses Lawrence	500.00	250.00	150.00
(14)	Wallace Wade Moon	800.00	400.00	240.00
(15)	Stanley Frank Musial	5,400	2,700	1,620
(16)	Thomas George Poholsky	500.00	250.00	150.00
(17)	William John Posedel	500.00	250.00	150.00
(18)	Victor Angelo John Raschi	500.00	250.00	150.00
(19)	Eldon John Repulski	500.00	250.00	150.00
(20)	Delbert Rice	500.00	250.00	150.00
(21)	John Ludy Riddle	500.00	250.00	150.00
(22)	William F. Sarni	500.00	250.00	150.00
(23)	Albert Fred Schoendienst	1,100	550.00	325.00
(24)	Richard John Schofield (Actually John Richard.)	500.00	250.00	150.00
(25)	Frank Thomas Smith	500.00	250.00	150.00
(26)	Edward R. Stanky	550.00	275.00	165.00
(27)	Bobby Gene Tiefenauer	500.00	250.00	150.00
(28)	William Charles Virdon	800.00	400.00	240.00
(29)	Frederick E. Walker	500.00	250.00	150.00
(30)	Floyd Lewis Woolridge	500.00	250.00	150.00

1941 Huskies

This advertising card was issued by Huskies Whole Wheat Flakes cereal. In black-and-white, the card measures about 5-1/2" x 3-1/2". Facsimile autographs appear on the borderless front photo.

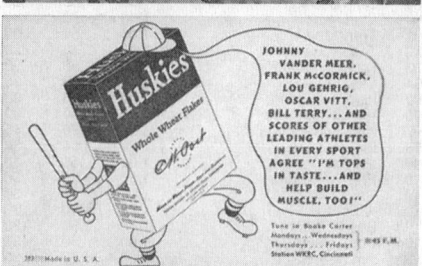

	NM	EX	VG
John Vander Meer, Frank McCormick	125.00	65.00	40.00

1976 Icee Drinks Reds

Issued in 1976 in the Cincinnati area by Icee Drinks, this 12-card set of semi-circular cards features members of the Reds. The cards measure approximately 2" in diameter with the bottom of the disc squared off. The cards were originally issued as soft drink lids. Fronts have a portrait photo in black-and-white, with uniform logos removed. Backs are blank. The cards are unnumbered. A 7" x 12" cap saver sheet was also available; it does not picture the players.

		NM	EX	VG
Complete Set (12):		60.00	30.00	18.00
Common Player:		2.00	1.00	.60
Saver Sheet:		27.00	13.50	8.00
(1)	Johnny Bench	10.00	5.00	3.00
(2)	Dave Concepcion	2.25	1.25	.70
(3)	Rawly Eastwick	2.00	1.00	.60
(4)	George Foster	2.25	1.25	.70
(5)	Cesar Geronimo	2.00	1.00	.60
(6)	Ken Griffey	2.50	1.25	.70
(7)	Don Gullett	2.00	1.00	.60
(8)	Will McEnaney	2.00	1.00	.60
(9)	Joe Morgan	6.00	3.00	1.75
(10)	Gary Nolan	2.00	1.00	.60
(11)	Tony Perez	4.00	2.00	1.25
(12)	Pete Rose	27.50	13.50	8.25

1963 I.D.L. Drug Store Pittsburgh Pirates

This set of 26 black-and-white cards was regionally distributed. The 4" x 5" semi-gloss cards are blank-backed and unnumbered. The checklist is arranged alphabetically. Johnny Logan's card is considered scarce and may have been pulled from distribution early.

		NM	EX	VG
Complete Set (27):		450.00	220.00	135.00
Common Player:		15.00	7.50	4.50
(1)	Bob Bailey	15.00	7.50	4.50

(2)	Forrest "Smoky" Burgess	15.00	7.50	4.50
(3)	Don Cardwell	15.00	7.50	4.50
(4)	Roberto Clemente	150.00	75.00	45.00
(5)	Donn Clendenon	20.00	10.00	6.00
(6)	Roy Face	15.00	7.50	4.50
(7)	Earl Francis	15.00	7.50	4.50
(8)	Bob Friend	15.00	7.50	4.50
(9)	Joe Gibbon	15.00	7.50	4.50
(10)	Julio Gotay	15.00	7.50	4.50
(11)	Harvey Haddix	15.00	7.50	4.50
(12)	Johnny Logan/SP	15.00	7.50	4.50
(13)	Bill Mazeroski	50.00	25.00	15.00
(14)	Al McBean	15.00	7.50	4.50
(15)	Danny Murtaugh	15.00	7.50	4.50
(16)	Sam Narron	15.00	7.50	4.50
(17)	Ron Northey	15.00	7.50	4.50
(18)	Frank Oceak	15.00	7.50	4.50
(19)	Jim Pagliaroni	15.00	7.50	4.50
(20)	Ted Savage	15.00	7.50	4.50
(21)	Dick Schofield	15.00	7.50	4.50
(22)	Bob Skinner/SP	30.00	15.00	9.00
(23)	Willie Stargell	50.00	25.00	15.00
(24)	Tom Sturdivant	15.00	7.50	4.50
(25)	Virgil "Fire" Trucks	15.00	7.50	4.50
(26)	Bob Veale	15.00	7.50	4.50
(27)	Bill Virdon	15.00	7.50	4.50

1952 Independence Browns Team Issue

Only one card is currently known from this set from the Globe Printing Co. line-up of minor league issues. The team is the 1952 Independence (Kans.) Browns, the Class D farm club of the St. Louis Browns in the Kansas-Oklahoma-Missouri League's final season. The blank-backed, black-and-white cards are printed on thin cardboard and measure about 2-1/4" x 3-3/8". This checklist for the set was probably comprised of about 18 cards when issued.

		NM	EX	VG
(1)	Fred "Rip" Collins	75.00	40.00	25.00

1916 Indianapolis Brewing Co.

THIS is one of a series of 200 pictures of Major League Baseball Players — all action pictures.

Complete set will be sent to you upon receipt of 25 cents.

INDIANAPOLIS BREWING CO.
INDIANAPOLIS, INDIANA

LIEBER'S GOLD MEDAL
PROGRESS BEER
LIEBER'S SPECIAL BREW

World's Standard of Perfection

HOWARD SHANKS
L. F.—Washington Am.
160

Best known in blank-back form or with ads on back for The Sporting News, this 200-card set can be found with the imprint of several other local and regional businesses. Among them is the Indianapolis Brewing Co. Type-card and superstar collectors can expect to pay a significant premium for individual cards with Indianapolis Brewing advertising. The checklist parallels that of the 1916 M101-4 Blank Backs. Cards measure 1-5/8" x 3" and are printed in black-and-white. The brewery originally advertised the set on its "Facts for Fans" booklet, at a cost of 25 cents.

		NM	EX	VG
	Complete Set (200):	96,000	48,000	28,800
	Common Player:	275.00	135.00	82.50
1	Babe Adams	360.00	120.00	75.00
2	Sam Agnew	275.00	135.00	82.50
3	Eddie Ainsmith	275.00	135.00	82.50
4	Grover Alexander	900.00	450.00	270.00
5	Leon Ames	275.00	135.00	82.50
6	Jimmy Archer	275.00	135.00	82.50
7	Jimmy Austin	275.00	135.00	82.50
8	H.D. Baird	275.00	135.00	82.50
9	J. Franklin Baker	650.00	320.00	195.00
10	Dave Bancroft	650.00	320.00	195.00
11	Jack Barry	275.00	135.00	82.50
12	Zinn Beck	275.00	135.00	82.50
13	"Chief" Bender	650.00	320.00	195.00
14	Joe Benz	275.00	135.00	82.50
15	Bob Bescher	275.00	135.00	82.50
16	Al Betzel	275.00	135.00	82.50
17	Mordecai Brown	650.00	320.00	195.00
18	Eddie Burns	275.00	135.00	82.50
19	George Burns	275.00	135.00	82.50
20	Geo. J. Burns	275.00	135.00	82.50
21	Joe Bush	275.00	135.00	82.50
22	"Donie" Bush	275.00	135.00	82.50
23	Art Butler	275.00	135.00	82.50
24	Bobbie Byrne	275.00	135.00	82.50
25	Forrest Cady	275.00	135.00	82.50
26	Jimmy Callahan	275.00	135.00	82.50
27	Ray Caldwell	275.00	135.00	82.50
28	Max Carey	650.00	320.00	195.00
29	George Chalmers	275.00	135.00	82.50
30	Ray Chapman	300.00	150.00	90.00
31	Larry Cheney	275.00	135.00	82.50
32	Eddie Cicotte	650.00	320.00	195.00
33	Tom Clarke	275.00	135.00	82.50
34	Eddie Collins	650.00	320.00	195.00

35	"Shauno" Collins	275.00	135.00	82.50
36	Charles Comiskey	650.00	320.00	195.00
37	Joe Connolly	275.00	135.00	82.50
38	Ty Cobb	6,500	3,200	1,950
39	Harry Coveleskie (Coveleski)	275.00	135.00	82.50
40	Gavvy Cravath	275.00	135.00	82.50
41	Sam Crawford	650.00	320.00	195.00
42	Jean Dale	275.00	135.00	82.50
43	Jake Daubert	275.00	135.00	82.50
44	Charles Deal	275.00	135.00	82.50
45	Al Demaree	275.00	135.00	82.50
46	Josh Devore	275.00	135.00	82.50
47	William Doak	275.00	135.00	82.50
48	Bill Donovan	275.00	135.00	82.50
49	Charles Dooin	275.00	135.00	82.50
50	Mike Doolan	275.00	135.00	82.50
51	Larry Doyle	275.00	135.00	82.50
52	Jean Dubuc	275.00	135.00	82.50
53	Oscar Dugey	275.00	135.00	82.50
54	Johnny Evers	650.00	320.00	195.00
55	Urban Faber	650.00	320.00	195.00
56	"Hap" Felsch	800.00	400.00	240.00
57	Bill Fischer	275.00	135.00	82.50
58	Ray Fisher	275.00	135.00	82.50
59	Max Flack	275.00	135.00	82.50
60	Art Fletcher	275.00	135.00	82.50
61	Eddie Foster	275.00	135.00	82.50
62	Jacques Fournier	275.00	135.00	82.50
63	Del Gainer (Gainor)	275.00	135.00	82.50
64	"Chic" Gandil	650.00	320.00	195.00
65	Larry Gardner	275.00	135.00	82.50
66	Joe Gedeon	275.00	135.00	82.50
67	Gus Getz	275.00	135.00	82.50
68	Geo. Gibson	275.00	135.00	82.50
69	Wilbur Good	275.00	135.00	82.50
70	Hank Gowdy	275.00	135.00	82.50
71	John Graney	275.00	135.00	82.50
72	Clark Griffith	650.00	320.00	195.00
73	Tom Griffith	275.00	135.00	82.50
74	Heinie Groh	275.00	135.00	82.50
75	Earl Hamilton	275.00	135.00	82.50
76	Bob Harmon	275.00	135.00	82.50
77	Roy Hartzell	275.00	135.00	82.50
78	Claude Hendrix	275.00	135.00	82.50
79	Olaf Henriksen	275.00	135.00	82.50
80	John Henry	275.00	135.00	82.50
81	"Buck" Herzog	275.00	135.00	82.50
82	Hugh High	275.00	135.00	82.50
83	Dick Hoblitzell	275.00	135.00	82.50
84	Harry Hooper	650.00	320.00	195.00
85	Ivan Howard	275.00	135.00	82.50
86	Miller Huggins	650.00	320.00	195.00
87	Joe Jackson	20,000	7,500	4,500
88	William James	275.00	135.00	82.50
89	Harold Janvrin	275.00	135.00	82.50
90	Hugh Jennings	650.00	320.00	195.00
91	Walter Johnson	2,500	1,250	750.00
92	Fielder Jones	275.00	135.00	82.50
93	Joe Judge	275.00	135.00	82.50
94	Bennie Kauff	275.00	135.00	82.50
95	Wm. Killefer Jr.	275.00	135.00	82.50
96	Ed. Konetchy	275.00	135.00	82.50
97	Napoleon Lajoie	750.00	370.00	220.00
98	Jack Lapp	275.00	135.00	82.50
99	John Lavan	275.00	135.00	82.50
100	Jimmy Lavender	275.00	135.00	82.50
101	"Nemo" Leibold	275.00	135.00	82.50
102	H.B. Leonard	275.00	135.00	82.50
103	Duffy Lewis	275.00	135.00	82.50
104	Hans Lobert	275.00	135.00	82.50
105	Tom Long	275.00	135.00	82.50
106	Fred Luderus	275.00	135.00	82.50
107	Connie Mack	650.00	320.00	195.00
108	Lee Magee	275.00	135.00	82.50
109	Sherwood Magee	275.00	135.00	82.50
110	Al. Mamaux	275.00	135.00	82.50
111	Leslie Mann	275.00	135.00	82.50
112	"Rabbit" Maranville	650.00	320.00	195.00
113	Rube Marquard	650.00	320.00	195.00
114	J. Erskine Mayer	360.00	180.00	110.00
115	George McBride	275.00	135.00	82.50
116	John J. McGraw	650.00	320.00	195.00
117	Jack McInnis	275.00	135.00	82.50
118	Fred Merkle	275.00	135.00	82.50
119	Chief Meyers	275.00	135.00	82.50
120	Clyde Milan	275.00	135.00	82.50
121	John Miller	275.00	135.00	82.50
122	Otto Miller	275.00	135.00	82.50
123	Willie Mitchell	275.00	135.00	82.50
124	Fred Mollwitz	275.00	135.00	82.50
125	Pat Moran	275.00	135.00	82.50
126	Ray Morgan	275.00	135.00	82.50
127	Geo. Moriarty	275.00	135.00	82.50
128	Guy Morton	275.00	135.00	82.50
129	Mike Mowrey	275.00	135.00	82.50
130	Ed. Murphy	275.00	135.00	82.50
131	"Hy" Myers	275.00	135.00	82.50
132	J.A. Niehoff	275.00	135.00	82.50
133	Rube Oldring	275.00	135.00	82.50
134	Oliver O'Mara	275.00	135.00	82.50
135	Steve O'Neill	275.00	135.00	82.50
136	"Dode" Paskert	275.00	135.00	82.50
137	Roger Peckinpaugh	275.00	135.00	82.50
138	Walter Pipp	275.00	135.00	82.50
139	Derril Pratt (Derrill)	275.00	135.00	82.50
140	Pat Ragan	275.00	135.00	82.50
141	Bill Rariden	275.00	135.00	82.50
142	Eppa Rixey	650.00	320.00	195.00
143	Davey Robertson	275.00	135.00	82.50
144	Wilbert Robinson	650.00	320.00	195.00
145	Bob Roth	275.00	135.00	82.50
146	Ed. Roush	650.00	320.00	195.00
147	Clarence Rowland	275.00	135.00	82.50
148	"Nap" Rucker	275.00	135.00	82.50
149	Dick Rudolph	275.00	135.00	82.50
150	Reb Russell	275.00	135.00	82.50
151	Babe Ruth	24,000	12,000	7,200
152	Vic Saier	275.00	135.00	82.50

153	"Slim" Sallee	275.00	135.00	82.50
154	Ray Schalk	650.00	320.00	195.00
155	Walter Schang	275.00	135.00	82.50
156	Frank Schulte	275.00	135.00	82.50
157	Everett Scott	275.00	135.00	82.50
158	Jim Scott	275.00	135.00	82.50
159	Tom Seaton	275.00	135.00	82.50
160	Howard Shanks	275.00	135.00	82.50
161	Bob Shawkey	275.00	135.00	82.50
162	Ernie Shore	275.00	135.00	82.50
163	Burt Shotton	275.00	135.00	82.50
164	Geo. Sisler	650.00	320.00	195.00
165	J. Carlisle Smith	275.00	135.00	82.50
166	Fred Snodgrass	275.00	135.00	82.50
167	Geo. Stallings	275.00	135.00	82.50
168	Oscar Stanage	275.00	135.00	82.50
169	Charles Stengel	650.00	320.00	195.00
170	Milton Stock	275.00	135.00	82.50
171	Amos Strunk	275.00	135.00	82.50
172	Billy Sullivan	275.00	135.00	82.50
173	"Jeff" Tesreau	275.00	135.00	82.50
174	Joe Tinker	650.00	320.00	195.00
175	Fred Toney	275.00	135.00	82.50
176	Terry Turner	275.00	135.00	82.50
177	George Tyler	275.00	135.00	82.50
178	Jim Vaughn	275.00	135.00	82.50
179	Bob Veach	275.00	135.00	82.50
180	James Viox	275.00	135.00	82.50
181	Oscar Vitt	275.00	135.00	82.50
182	Hans Wagner	5,500	2,700	1,650
183	Clarence Walker	275.00	135.00	82.50
184	Ed. Walsh	650.00	320.00	195.00
185	W. Wambsganss (Photo actually Fritz Coumbe.)	275.00	135.00	82.50
186	Buck Weaver	2,400	1,200	725.00
187	Carl Weilman	275.00	135.00	82.50
188	Zach Wheat	650.00	320.00	195.00
189	Geo. Whitted	275.00	135.00	82.50
190	Fred Williams	275.00	135.00	82.50
191	Art Wilson	275.00	135.00	82.50
192	J. Owen Wilson	275.00	135.00	82.50
193	Ivy Wingo	275.00	135.00	82.50
194	"Mel" Wolfgang	275.00	135.00	82.50
195	Joe Wood	450.00	220.00	135.00
196	Steve Yerkes	275.00	135.00	82.50
197	"Pep" Young	275.00	135.00	82.50
198	Rollie Zeider	275.00	135.00	82.50
199	Heiny Zimmerman	275.00	135.00	82.50
200	Ed. Zwilling	275.00	135.00	82.50

1923 Curtis Ireland Candy (E123)

This set, identified in the ACC as E123, was issued in 1923 by the Curtis Ireland Candy Corp. of St. Louis and was distributed with Ireland's "All Star Bars." Except for the backs, the Ireland set is identical to the Willard Chocolate V100 set of the same year. Measuring 3-1/4" x 2-1/16", the cards feature sepia-toned photos with the player's name in script on the front. The backs advertise a contest which required the collector to mail in the cards in exchange for prizes, which probably explains their relative scarcity today.

		NM	EX	VG
	Complete Set (180):	250,000	50,000	30,000
	Common Player:	1,200	360.00	180.00
(1)	Chas. B Adams	1,200	360.00	180.00
(2)	Grover C. Alexander	2,000	600.00	300.00
(3)	J.P. Austin	1,200	360.00	180.00
(4)	J.C. Bagby	1,200	360.00	180.00
(5)	J. Franklin Baker	1,800	550.00	275.00
(6)	David J. Bancroft	1,800	550.00	275.00
(7)	Turner Barber	1,200	360.00	180.00
(8)	Jesse L. Barnes	1,200	360.00	180.00
(9)	J.C. Bassler	1,200	360.00	180.00
(10)	L.A. Blue	1,200	360.00	180.00
(11)	Norman D. Boeckel	1,200	360.00	180.00
(12)	F.L. Brazill (Brazill)	1,200	360.00	180.00
(13)	G.H. Burns	1,200	360.00	180.00
(14)	Geo. J. Burns	1,200	360.00	180.00
(15)	Leon Cadore	1,200	360.00	180.00
(16)	Max G. Carey	1,800	550.00	275.00
(17)	Harold G. Carlson	1,200	360.00	180.00
(18)	Lloyd R. Christenberry (Christenbury)	1,200	360.00	180.00
(19)	Vernon J. Clemons	1,200	360.00	180.00
(20)	T.R. Cobb	17,000	5,200	2,600
(21)	Bert Cole	1,200	360.00	180.00
(22)	John F. Collins	1,200	360.00	180.00
(23)	S. Coveleskie (Coveleski)	1,800	550.00	275.00
(24)	Walton E. Cruise	1,200	360.00	180.00
(25)	G.W. Cutshaw	1,200	360.00	180.00
(26)	Jacob E. Daubert	1,200	360.00	180.00
(27)	Geo. Dauss	1,200	360.00	180.00
(28)	F.T. Davis	1,200	360.00	180.00
(29)	Chas. A. Deal	1,200	360.00	180.00

(30) William L. Doak	1,200	360.00	180.00
(31) William E. Donovan	1,800	550.00	275.00
(32) Hugh Duffy	1,200	360.00	180.00
(33) J.A. Dugan	1,200	360.00	180.00
(34) Louis B. Duncan	1,200	360.00	180.00
(35) James Dykes	1,200	360.00	180.00
(36) H.J. Ehmke	1,200	360.00	180.00
(37) F.R. Ellerbe	1,200	360.00	180.00
(38) E.G. Erickson	1,200	360.00	180.00
(39) John J. Evers	1,800	550.00	275.00
(40) U.C. Faber	1,800	550.00	275.00
(41) B.A. Falk	1,200	360.00	180.00
(42) Max Flack	1,200	360.00	180.00
(43) Lee Fohl	1,200	360.00	180.00
(44) Jacques F. Fournier	1,200	360.00	180.00
(45) Frank F. Frisch	1,800	550.00	275.00
(46) C.E. Galloway	1,200	360.00	180.00
(47) W.C. Gardner	1,200	360.00	180.00
(48) E.P. Gharrity	1,200	360.00	180.00
(49) Geo. Gibson	1,200	360.00	180.00
(50) Wm. Gleason	1,200	360.00	180.00
(51) William Gleason	1,200	360.00	180.00
(52) Henry M. Gowdy	1,200	360.00	180.00
(53) I.M. Griffin	1,200	360.00	180.00
(54) Thomas Griffith	1,200	360.00	180.00
(55) Burleigh A. Grimes	1,800	550.00	275.00
(56) Charles J. Grimm	1,200	360.00	180.00
(57) Jesse J. Haines	1,800	550.00	275.00
(58) S.R. Harris	1,800	550.00	275.00
(59) W.B. Harris	1,200	360.00	180.00
(60) R.K. Hasty	1,200	360.00	180.00
(61) H.E. Heilman (Heilmann)	1,800	550.00	275.00
(62) Walter J. Henline	1,200	360.00	180.00
(63) Walter L. Holke	1,200	360.00	180.00
(64) Charles J. Hollocher	1,200	360.00	180.00
(65) H.B. Hooper	1,800	550.00	275.00
(66) Rogers Hornsby	2,500	750.00	375.00
(67) W.C. Hoyt	1,800	550.00	275.00
(68) Miller Huggins	1,800	550.00	275.00
(69) W.C. Jacobsen (Jacobson)	1,200	360.00	180.00
(70) C.D. Jamieson	1,200	360.00	180.00
(71) Ernest Johnson	1,200	360.00	180.00
(72) W.P. Johnson	4,500	1,350	700.00
(73) James H. Johnston	1,200	360.00	180.00
(74) R.W. Jones	1,200	360.00	180.00
(75) Samuel Pond Jones	1,200	360.00	180.00
(76) J.I. Judge	1,200	360.00	180.00
(77) James W. Keenan	1,200	360.00	180.00
(78) Geo. L. Kelly	1,800	550.00	275.00
(79) Peter J. Kilduff	1,200	360.00	180.00
(80) William Killefer	1,200	360.00	180.00
(81) Lee King	1,200	360.00	180.00
(82) Ray Kolp	1,200	360.00	180.00
(83) John Lavan	1,200	360.00	180.00
(84) H.L. Leibold	1,200	360.00	180.00
(85) Connie Mack	1,800	550.00	275.00
(86) J.W. Mails	1,200	360.00	180.00
(87) Walter J. Maranville	1,800	550.00	275.00
(88) Richard W. Marquard	1,800	550.00	275.00
(89) C.W. Mays	1,200	360.00	180.00
(90) Geo. F. McBride	1,200	360.00	180.00
(91) H.M. McClellan	1,200	360.00	180.00
(92) John J. McGraw	1,800	550.00	275.00
(93) Austin B. McHenry	1,200	360.00	180.00
(94) J. McInnis	1,200	360.00	180.00
(95) Douglas McWeeney (McWeeny)	1,200	360.00	180.00
(96) M. Menosky	1,200	360.00	180.00
(97) Emil F. Meusel	1,200	360.00	180.00
(98) R. Meusel	1,200	360.00	180.00
(99) Henry W. Meyers	1,200	360.00	180.00
(100) J.C. Milan	1,200	360.00	180.00
(101) John K. Miljus	1,200	360.00	180.00
(102) Edmund J. Miller	1,200	360.00	180.00
(103) Elmer Miller	1,200	360.00	180.00
(104) Otto L. Miller	1,200	360.00	180.00
(105) Fred Mitchell	1,200	360.00	180.00
(106) Geo. Mogridge	1,200	360.00	180.00
(107) Patrick J. Moran	1,200	360.00	180.00
(108) John D. Morrison	1,200	360.00	180.00
(109) J.A. Mostil	1,200	360.00	180.00
(110) Clarence F. Mueller	1,200	360.00	180.00
(111) A. Earle Neale	1,200	360.00	180.00
(112) Joseph Oeschger	1,200	360.00	180.00
(113) Robert J. O'Farrell	1,200	360.00	180.00
(114) J.C. Oldham	1,200	360.00	180.00
(115) I.M. Olson	1,200	360.00	180.00
(116) Geo. M. O'Neil	1,200	360.00	180.00
(117) S.F. O'Neill	1,200	360.00	180.00
(118) Frank J. Parkinson	1,200	360.00	180.00
(119) Geo. H. Paskert	1,200	360.00	180.00
(120) R.T. Peckinpaugh	1,200	360.00	180.00
(121) H.J. Pennock	1,800	550.00	275.00
(122) Ralph Perkins	1,200	360.00	180.00
(123) Edw. J. Pfeffer	1,200	360.00	180.00
(124) W.C. Pipp	1,200	360.00	180.00
(125) Charles Elmer Ponder	1,200	360.00	180.00
(126) Raymond R. Powell	1,200	360.00	180.00
(127) D.B. Pratt	1,200	360.00	180.00
(128) Joseph Rapp	1,200	360.00	180.00
(129) John H. Rawlings	1,200	360.00	180.00
(130) E.S. Rice (Should be E.C.)	1,800	550.00	275.00
(131) Branch Rickey	2,000	600.00	300.00
(132) James J. Ring	1,200	360.00	180.00
(133) Eppa J. Rixey	1,800	550.00	275.00
(134) Davis A. Robertson	1,200	360.00	180.00
(135) Edwin Rommel	1,200	360.00	180.00
(136) Edd J. Roush	1,800	550.00	275.00
(137) Harold Ruel (Herold)	1,200	360.00	180.00
(138) Allen Russell	1,200	360.00	180.00
(139) G.H. Ruth	25,000	7,500	3,800
(140) Wilfred D. Ryan	1,200	360.00	180.00
(141) Henry F. Sallee	1,200	360.00	180.00
(142) W.H. Schang	1,200	360.00	180.00
(143) Raymond H. Schmandt	1,200	360.00	180.00
(144) Everett Scott	1,200	360.00	180.00
(145) Henry Severeid	1,200	360.00	180.00
(146) Jos. W. Sewell	1,800	550.00	275.00
(147) Howard S. Shanks	1,200	360.00	180.00
(148) E.H. Sheely	1,200	360.00	180.00
(149) Ralph Shinners	1,200	360.00	180.00
(150) U.J. Shocker	1,200	360.00	180.00
(151) G.H. Sisler	1,800	550.00	275.00
(152) Earl L. Smith	1,200	360.00	180.00
(153) Earl S. Smith	1,200	360.00	180.00
(154) Geo. A. Smith	1,200	360.00	180.00
(155) J.W. Smith	1,200	360.00	180.00
(156) Tris E. Speaker	2,700	800.00	400.00
(157) Arnold Staatz	1,200	360.00	180.00
(158) J.R. Stephenson	1,200	360.00	180.00
(159) Milton J. Stock	1,200	360.00	180.00
(160) John L. Sullivan	1,200	360.00	180.00
(161) H.F. Tormahlen	1,200	360.00	180.00
(162) Jas. A. Tierney	1,200	360.00	180.00
(163) J.T. Tobin	1,200	360.00	180.00
(164) Jas. L. Vaughn	1,200	360.00	180.00
(165) R.H. Veach	1,200	360.00	180.00
(166) C.W. Walker	1,200	360.00	180.00
(167) A.L. Ward	1,200	360.00	180.00
(168) Zack D. Wheat	1,800	550.00	275.00
(169) George B. Whitted	1,200	360.00	180.00
(170) Irvin K. Wilhelm	1,200	360.00	180.00
(171) Roy H. Wilkinson	1,200	360.00	180.00
(172) Fred C. Williams	1,200	360.00	180.00
(173) K.R. Williams	1,200	360.00	180.00
(174) Sam'l W. Wilson	1,200	360.00	180.00
(175) Ivy B. Wingo	1,200	360.00	180.00
(176) L.W. Witt	1,200	360.00	180.00
(177) Joseph Wood	1,200	360.00	180.00
(178) E. Yaryan	1,200	360.00	180.00
(179) R.S. Young	1,200	360.00	180.00
(180) Ross Young (Youngs)	1,800	550.00	275.00

1967 Irvindale Dairy Atlana Braves

the milk of Athletes!

This quartet of Braves was printed in shades of deep red on the white background of a milk carton panel. Well-cut individual pieces measure 1-3/4" x 2-5/8" and are blank-backed.

	NM	EX	VG
Complete Set, Panel:	250.00	125.00	75.00
Complete Set, Singles:	175.00	85.00	45.00
Common Player:	40.00	20.00	12.00
(1) Clete Boyer	40.00	20.00	12.00
(2) Mack Jones	40.00	20.00	12.00
(3) Denis Menke	40.00	20.00	12.00
(4) Joe Torre	60.00	30.00	18.00

1976 Isaly's/Sweet William discs

 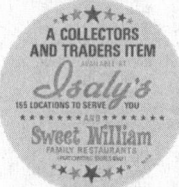

One of several regional sponsors of player disc sets in 1976 was the Pittsburgh area dairy store chain, Isaly's, and the Sweet William restaurants. The discs are 3-3/8" diameter with a black-and-white player portrait photo in the center of the baseball design. A line of red stars is above, while the left and right panels feature one of several bright colors. Produced by Michael Schecter Associates under license from the Major League Baseball Players Association, the player photos have had uniform and cap logos removed. Backs are printed in red and purple. The unnumbered checklist here is presented in alphabetical order.

	NM	EX	VG
Complete Set (70):	15.00	7.50	4.50
Common Player:	.50	.25	.15
(1) Henry Aaron	4.00	2.00	1.25
(2) Johnny Bench	2.00	1.00	.60
(3) Vida Blue	.50	.25	.15
(4) Larry Bowa	.50	.25	.15
(5) Lou Brock	2.00	1.00	.60
(6) Jeff Burroughs	.50	.25	.15
(7) John Candelaria	.50	.25	.15
(8) Jose Cardenal	.50	.25	.15
(9) Rod Carew	2.00	1.00	.60
(10) Steve Carlton	2.00	1.00	.60
(11) Dave Cash	.50	.25	.15
(12) Cesar Cedeno	.50	.25	.15
(13) Ron Cey	.50	.25	.15
(14) Carlton Fisk	2.00	1.00	.60
(15) Tito Fuentes	.50	.25	.15
(16) Steve Garvey	1.50	.70	.45
(17) Ken Griffey	.50	.25	.15
(18) Don Gullett	.50	.25	.15
(19) Willie Horton	.50	.25	.15
(20) Al Hrabosky	.50	.25	.15
(21) Catfish Hunter	2.00	1.00	.60
(22) Reggie Jackson (A's)	3.00	1.50	.90
(23) Randy Jones	.50	.25	.15
(24) Jim Kaat	.50	.25	.15
(25) Don Kessinger	.50	.25	.15
(26) Dave Kingman	.50	.25	.15
(27) Jerry Koosman	.50	.25	.15
(28) Mickey Lolich	.50	.25	.15
(29) Greg Luzinski	.50	.25	.15
(30) Fred Lynn	.50	.25	.15
(31) Bill Madlock	.50	.25	.15
(32) Carlos May (White Sox)	.50	.25	.15
(33) John Mayberry	.50	.25	.15
(34) Bake McBride	.50	.25	.15
(35) Doc Medich	.50	.25	.15
(36) Andy Messersmith (Dodgers)	.50	.25	.15
(37) Rick Monday	.50	.25	.15
(38) John Montefusco	.50	.25	.15
(39) Jerry Morales	.50	.25	.15
(40) Joe Morgan	2.00	1.00	.60
(41) Thurman Munson	2.00	1.00	.60
(42) Bobby Murcer	.50	.25	.15
(43) Al Oliver	.50	.25	.15
(44) Jim Palmer	2.00	1.00	.60
(45) Dave Parker	.50	.25	.15
(46) Tony Perez	2.00	1.00	.60
(47) Jerry Reuss	.50	.25	.15
(48) Brooks Robinson	2.00	1.00	.60
(49) Frank Robinson	2.00	1.00	.60
(50) Steve Rogers	.50	.25	.15
(51) Pete Rose	6.00	3.00	1.75
(52) Nolan Ryan	12.00	6.00	3.50
(53) Manny Sanguillen	.50	.25	.15
(54) Mike Schmidt	3.00	1.50	.90
(55) Tom Seaver	2.00	1.00	.60
(56) Ted Simmons	.50	.25	.15
(57) Reggie Smith	.50	.25	.15
(58) Willie Stargell	2.00	1.00	.60
(59) Rusty Staub	.75	.40	.25
(60) Rennie Stennett	.50	.25	.15
(61) Don Sutton	2.00	1.00	.60
(62) Andy Thornton (Cubs)	.50	.25	.15
(63) Luis Tiant	.50	.25	.15
(64) Joe Torre	1.50	.70	.45
(65) Mike Tyson	.50	.25	.15
(66) Bob Watson	.50	.25	.15
(67) Wilbur Wood	.50	.25	.15
(68) Jimmy Wynn	.50	.25	.15
(69) Carl Yastrzemski	2.50	1.25	.70
(70) Richie Zisk	.50	.25	.15

1976 ISCA Hoosier Hot-Stove All-Stars

Famous native Hoosier ballplayers are featured in this collectors' issue from the Indiana Sports Collectors Assn. The 2-5/8" x 3-5/8" cards have black-and-white player photos on front framed in the state's outline. Red and blue graphics on a white background complete the design. Backs are in black and blue on white and include a career summary. A star on the state map at bottom indicates where the player was born.

	NM	EX	VG
Complete Set (26):	15.00	7.50	4.50
Common Player:	2.00	1.00	.60
1 Edd Roush	2.00	1.00	.60
2 Sam Thompson	2.00	1.00	.60
3 Chuck Klein	2.00	1.00	.60
4 Lou Criger	2.00	1.00	.60
5 Amos Rusie	2.00	1.00	.60
6 Billy Herman	2.00	1.00	.60
7 George Dauss	2.00	1.00	.60
8 Tom Thevenow	2.00	1.00	.60
9 Mordecai Brown	2.00	1.00	.60
10 Freddie Fitzsimmons	2.00	1.00	.60
11 Art Nehf	2.00	1.00	.60
12 Carl Erskine	3.00	1.50	.90
13 Don Larsen	3.00	1.50	.90
14 Gil Hodges	6.00	3.00	1.75
15 Pete Fox	2.00	1.00	.60
16 Butch Henline	2.00	1.00	.60
17 Doc Crandall	2.00	1.00	.60
18 Dizzy Trout	2.00	1.00	.60
19 Donie Bush	2.00	1.00	.60
20 Max Carey	2.00	1.00	.60
21 Eugene Hargrave, William Hargrave	2.00	1.00	.60
22 Sam Rice	2.00	1.00	.60
23 Babe Adams	2.00	1.00	.60
24 Cy Williams	2.00	1.00	.60

		NM	EX	VG
25	1913 Indianapolis Federal League Team	2.00	1.00	.60
26	Paul Frisz	2.00	1.00	.60

J

1912 J=K Candy

Originally printed on the front and back of candy boxes which advertised "100 Principal League Players," the extent of this series is currently unknown and the checklist presented here is almost certainly incomplete. The blank-back, black-and-white (some have a bit of color tinting) cards can be found in two sizes, 1-7/8" x 3-1/2" if printed on the box front, or 1-7/8" x 2-7/8" if printed on back. Player photos are framed with an ornate-cornered border. In a plaque at bottom, all in capital letters, are the player's name, position, team and league; the latter three designations are abbreviated. Gaps have been left in the assigned numbering to accommodate future discoveries.

		NM	EX	VG
	Type I Common:	2,000	1,200	750.00
	Type II Common:	3,000	1,500	1,000
(1)	Hugh Bedient	2,000	1,200	750.00
(2)	Hick Cady	2,000	1,200	750.00
(3)	Bill Carrigan (Type II)	3,000	1,500	1,000
(4)	Hal Chase	2,500	1,250	800.00
(5)	Eddie Collins	3,000	1,500	900.00
(6)	Doc Crandall	2,000	1,200	750.00
(7)	Lou Criger	2,000	1,200	750.00
(8)	Harry Davis	2,000	1,200	750.00
(9)	Jim Delahanty	2,000	1,200	750.00
(10)	Art Devlin	2,000	1,200	750.00
(11)	Josh Devore (Type II)	3,000	1,500	1,000
(12)	Larry Doyle	2,000	1,200	750.00
(13)	Larry Gardner	2,000	1,200	750.00
(14)	George Gibson	2,000	1,200	750.00
(15)	Charley Hall	2,000	1,200	750.00
(16)	Topsy Hartsel	2,000	1,200	750.00
(17)	Buck Herzog (Type II)	3,000	1,500	1,000
(18)	Solly Hofman	2,000	1,200	750.00
(19)	Johnny Kling	3,000	1,500	1,000
(20)	Marty Krug	2,000	1,200	750.00
(21)	Napoleon Lajoie	6,500	3,200	1,950
(22)	Duffy Lewis	2,000	1,200	750.00
(23)	Rube Marquard	8,500	4,200	2,500
(24)	Christy Mathewson	6,000	3,000	1,800
(25)	John McGraw	3,000	1,500	900.00
(26)	Red Murray	2,000	1,200	750.00
(27)	Harry Niles	2,000	1,200	750.00
(28)	Orval Overall	2,000	1,200	750.00
(29)	Larry Pape	2,000	1,200	750.00
(30)	Ed Reulbach	2,000	1,200	750.00
(31)	Cy Seymour	2,000	1,200	750.00
(32)	Jimmy Sheckard	2,000	1,200	750.00
(33)	Hack Simmons	2,000	1,200	750.00
(34)	Tris Speaker (Type II)	6,500	3,200	1,950
(35)	Jake Stahl	2,000	1,200	750.00
(36)	Oscar Stanage	2,000	1,200	750.00
(37)	Harry Steinfeldt	2,000	1,200	750.00
(38)	Jeff Tesreau (Type II)	3,000	1,500	1,000
(39)	Ira Thomas	2,000	1,200	750.00
(40)	Joe Tinker	3,000	1,500	1,000
(41)	Honus Wagner (Type II)	15,000	7,500	4,500
(42)	Ed Walsh	3,000	1,500	1,000
(43)	Owen Wilson	2,000	1,200	750.00

1969 Jack In The Box California Angels

HOYT WILHELM
Pitcher
Career Record, 2.47 ERA

This regional issue was distributed a few cards per week at the chain's fast food restaurants. Blank-back cards are printed in black-and-white on thin white stock in a 1-15/16" x 3-1/2" format. The checklist for the unnumbered cards is presented here alphabetically.

		NM	EX	VG
	Complete Set (13):	30.00	15.00	9.00
	Common Player:	3.00	1.50	.90
(1)	Sandy Alomar	3.00	1.50	.90
(2)	Joe Azcue	3.00	1.50	.90
(3)	Jim Fregosi	3.50	1.75	1.00
(4)	Lou Johnson	3.00	1.50	.90
(5)	Jay Johnstone	6.00	3.00	1.75
(6)	Rudy May	3.00	1.50	.90
(7)	Jim McGlothlin	3.00	1.50	.90
(8)	Andy Messersmith	3.00	1.50	.90
(9)	Tom Murphy	3.00	1.50	.90
(10)	Rick Reichardt	3.00	1.50	.90
(11)	Aurelio Rodriguez	3.00	1.50	.90
(12)	Jim Spencer	3.00	1.50	.90
(13)	Hoyt Wilhelm	10.00	5.00	3.00

1971 Jack In The Box California Angels

Rudy May
CALIFORNIA ANGELS
P

Unlike the legitimate issue of 1969, this is an unauthorized collectors issue with no official connection to either the team or the fast food restaurant chain. The cards are printed in horizontal format on 4" x 2-1/2" manila paper in black ink. Fronts have a player portrait photo at left. Stacked at right are the player's name, team, position and Jack in the Box logo. Backs are blank. The set is checklisted here in alphabetical order.

		NM	EX	VG
	Complete Set (10):	25.00	12.50	7.50
	Common Player:	3.00	1.50	.90
(1)	Sandy Alomar	3.00	1.50	.90
(2)	Ken Berry	3.00	1.50	.90
(3)	Tony Conigliaro	15.00	7.50	4.50
(4)	Jim Fregosi	3.00	1.50	.90
(5)	Alex Johnson	3.00	1.50	.90
(6)	Rudy May	3.00	1.50	.90
(7)	Andy Messersmith	3.00	1.50	.90
(8)	"Lefty" Phillips	3.00	1.50	.90
(9)	Jim Spencer	3.00	1.50	.90
(10)	Clyde Wright	3.00	1.50	.90

1970 Jack in the Box Pittsburgh Pirates

DAVE GIUSTI
Pittsburgh Pirates P
1969: 22g. 3-7 3.60

Though this set is known within the hobby as the "Jack in the Box" Pirates, it bears no such advertising and has no actual connection to the restaurant chain; they are a collector's issue. The black-and-white cards measure 2" x 3-1/2" and are blank-backed. Beneath the photo on front is the player identification and a few stats from the 1969 season.

		NM	EX	VG
	Complete Set (12):	35.00	17.50	10.00
	Common Player:	3.00	1.50	.90
(1)	Gene Alley	3.00	1.50	.90
(2)	Dave Cash	3.00	1.50	.90
(3)	Dock Ellis	3.00	1.50	.90
(4)	Dave Giusti	3.00	1.50	.90
(5)	Jerry May	3.00	1.50	.90
(6)	Bill Mazeroski	12.50	6.25	3.75
(7)	Al Oliver	6.00	3.00	1.75
(8)	Jose Pagan	3.00	1.50	.90
(9)	Fred Patek	3.00	1.50	.90
(10)	Bob Robertson	3.00	1.50	.90
(11)	Manny Sanguillen	4.50	2.25	1.25
(12)	Willie Stargell	12.50	6.25	3.75

1954 Bill Jacobellis N.Y. Giants

James (Dusty) Rhodes

In the Giants' championship season, New York photographer Bill Jacobellis produced this set of player/team pictures, probably to be sold at the Polo Grounds souvenir stands. The black-and-white pictures are blank-backed and measure about 8-1/4" x 10-1/2", printed on semi-gloss paper. The player name is centered in bold type in the white bottom border; at right is "Bill Jacobellis Photo." The unnumbred pictures are listed here in alphabetical order.

		NM	EX	VG
	Complete Set (8):	110.00	55.00	32.50
	Common Player:	12.50	6.25	3.75
(1)	John Antonelli	12.50	6.25	3.75
(2)	Alvin Dark	12.50	6.25	3.75
(3)	Ruben Gomez	12.50	6.25	3.75
(4)	Whitey Lockman	12.50	6.25	3.75
(5)	Willie Mays	60.00	30.00	18.00
(6)	Don Mueller	12.50	6.25	3.75
(7)	James (Dusty) Rhodes	12.50	6.25	3.75
(8)	N.Y. Giants of 1954	20.00	10.00	6.00

1933 Jamaica Theatre

Cards that were originally issued as a black-backed set by Kashin Publications in 1929 were repurposed by a Queens, N.Y., movie theater in 1933 to serve as promotion to draw "kiddies" into the Saturday matinee. A number printed on the back of each card was used in prize drawings, while most of the rest of the space was occupied with the movie offerings for the coming week. Cards measure about 3-1/2" x 4-1/2". It is unknown how many of the 101 player cards originally issued in 1929 were used in this manner in 1933..

	NM	EX	VG
Common Player:	150.00	75.00	45.00
Stars: 2-3X			

(See 1929 Kashin Publications for checklist and base card values.)

1968-1970 Jamesway Trucking Co.

PETE ROSE
CINCINNATI REDS

Jamesway was a southern Ohio trucking company reportedly a division of Partridge Meats. Over the course of several years they issued a number of these 4" x 5-1/4" black-and-white, blank-backed cards with the company logo printed in red. The cards were reported stadium give-aways.

		NM	EX	VG
(1)	Johnny Bench	400.00	200.00	120.00
(2)	Pete Rose	550.00	275.00	125.00
(3)	Willie Stargell	150.00	75.00	45.00

1958-1965 Jay Publishing Picture Packs

JOHN CALLISON, Philadelphia Phillies

JOHN CALLISON, Philadelphia Phillies

The name "Picture Packs" has been used to describe this massive series of 5" x 7" black-and-white player photos issued by Jay Publishing's Big League Books division over the eight-year period from 1958-1965. The company also produced yearbooks for various major league teams during that period; many of the photos used in the yearbooks also appear in the Picture Packs. Picture Pack sets consist of 12 player/manager photos with name, city and team nickname in the bottom border. They were available by mail, at the ballparks and in stores. They were sold in either plain brown or white envelopes, or in clear plastic. Most were printed on a glossy, slick paper stock, although the quality of the paper may vary from team to team and year to year. The photos were issued anonymously, with no indication of the producer or year of issue. Two different types were issued, differentiated by the typeface used in the captions. Type 1 photos, issued from 1958 through 1961, were printed with a sans-serif style typeface, while Type 2 photos, issued from 1962 through 1965, used a serif typeface. Besides team sets there were a few special picture packs such as All-Stars, old-timers and World Series participants. Some years' team-set packs were updated (sometimes more than once) to reflect roster changes. Many pictures were reused from year to year.

	NM	EX	VG
Typical Team Set:	40.00	20.00	12.00
Common Player:	3.00	1.50	.90
Typical Hall of Famer:	10.00	5.00	3.00
Superstars:	20.00	10.00	6.00

1962 Jell-O

Virtually identical in content to the 1962 Post cereal cards, the '62 Jell-O set of 197 was only issued in the Midwest. Players and card numbers are identical in the two sets, except Brooks Robinson (#29), Ted Kluszewski (#82) and Smoky Burgess (#176) were not issued in the Jell-O version. The Jell-O cards are easy to distinguish from the Post of that year by the absence of the red oval Post logo and red or blue border around the stat box. Cards which have been neatly trimmed from the box on which they were printed will measure 3-3/8" by just under 2-1/2". Cards of some non-star players can be very scarce because they originally appeared on a limited number of boxes, or unpopular flavors or sizes.

		NM	EX	VG
Complete Set (197):		4,250	2,125	1,065
Common Player:		5.00	2.50	1.25
1	Bill Skowron	30.00	12.00	7.50
2	Bobby Richardson	500.00	200.00	125.00
3	Cletis Boyer	30.00	12.00	7.50
4	Tony Kubek	35.00	14.00	9.00
5	Mickey Mantle	300.00	150.00	75.00
6	Roger Maris	125.00	50.00	30.00
7	Yogi Berra	60.00	30.00	15.00
8	Elston Howard	30.00	12.00	7.50
9	Whitey Ford	60.00	25.00	15.00
10	Ralph Terry	25.00	10.00	6.25
11	John Blanchard	30.00	12.00	7.50
12	Luis Arroyo	15.00	6.00	3.75
13	Bill Stafford	30.00	12.00	7.50
14	Norm Cash	20.00	8.00	5.00
15	Jake Wood	5.00	2.50	1.25
16	Steve Boros	5.00	2.50	1.25
17	Chico Fernandez	5.00	2.50	1.25
18	Billy Bruton	5.00	2.50	1.25
19	Ken Aspromonte	5.00	2.50	1.25
20	Al Kaline	75.00	30.00	17.50
21	Dick Brown	5.00	2.50	1.25
22	Frank Lary	5.00	2.50	1.25
23	Don Mossi	5.00	2.50	1.25
24	Phil Regan	5.00	2.50	1.25
25	Charley Maxwell	5.00	2.50	1.25
26	Jim Bunning	30.00	12.00	7.50
27	Jim Gentile	5.00	2.50	1.25
28	Marv Breeding	5.00	2.50	1.25
29	Not Issued			
30	Ron Hansen	5.00	2.50	1.25
31	Jackie Brandt	50.00	20.00	12.50
32	Dick Williams	5.00	2.50	1.25
33	Gus Triandos	5.00	2.50	1.25
34	Milt Pappas	5.00	2.50	1.25
35	Hoyt Wilhelm	30.00	12.00	7.50
36	Chuck Estrada	5.00	2.50	1.25
37	Vic Power	5.00	2.50	1.25
38	Johnny Temple	5.00	2.50	1.25
39	Bubba Phillips	30.00	12.00	7.50
40	Tito Francona	5.00	2.50	1.25
41	Willie Kirkland	5.00	2.50	1.25
42	John Romano	5.00	2.50	1.25
43	Jim Perry	15.00	6.00	3.75
44	Woodie Held	5.00	2.50	1.25
45	Chuck Essegian	5.00	2.50	1.25
46	Roy Sievers	15.00	6.00	3.75
47	Nellie Fox	40.00	16.00	10.00
48	Al Smith	15.00	6.00	3.75
49	Luis Aparicio	40.00	16.00	10.00
50	Jim Landis	5.00	2.50	1.25
51	Minnie Minoso	25.00	10.00	6.25
52	Andy Carey	30.00	12.00	7.50
53	Sherman Lollar	5.00	2.50	1.25
54	Bill Pierce	5.00	2.50	1.25
55	Early Wynn	50.00	20.00	12.50
56	Chuck Schilling	60.00	30.00	15.00
57	Pete Runnels	5.00	2.50	1.25
58	Frank Malzone	20.00	8.00	5.00
59	Don Buddin	15.00	6.00	3.75
60	Gary Geiger	5.00	2.50	1.25
61	Carl Yastrzemski	200.00	100.00	50.00
62	Jackie Jensen	60.00	24.00	15.00
63	Jim Pagliaroni	30.00	12.00	7.50
64	Don Schwall	5.00	2.50	1.25
65	Dale Long	5.00	2.50	1.25
66	Chuck Cottier	20.00	8.00	5.00
67	Billy Klaus	30.00	12.00	7.50
68	Coot Veal	5.00	2.50	1.25
69	Marty Keough	60.00	25.00	15.00
70	Willie Tasby	60.00	25.00	15.00
71	Gene Woodling	5.00	2.50	1.25
72	Gene Green	60.00	25.00	15.00
73	Dick Donovan	15.00	6.00	3.75
74	Steve Bilko	25.00	10.00	6.25
75	Rocky Bridges	30.00	12.00	7.50
76	Eddie Yost	15.00	6.00	3.75
77	Leon Wagner	15.00	6.00	3.75
78	Albie Pearson	15.00	6.00	3.75
79	Ken Hunt	20.00	8.00	5.00
80	Earl Averill	75.00	30.00	17.50
81	Ryne Duren	15.00	6.00	3.75
82	Not Issued			
83	Bob Allison	15.00	6.00	3.75
84	Billy Martin	20.00	8.00	5.00
85	Harmon Killebrew	75.00	30.00	17.50
86	Zoilo Versalles	15.00	6.00	3.75
87	Lennie Green	50.00	25.00	12.50
88	Bill Tuttle	60.00	25.00	15.00
89	Jim Lemon	90.00	45.00	22.50
90	Earl Battey	30.00	12.00	7.50
91	Camilo Pascual	25.00	10.00	6.25
92	Norm Siebern	5.00	2.50	1.25
93	Jerry Lumpe	5.00	2.50	1.25
94	Dick Howser	15.00	6.00	3.75
95	Gene Stephens	60.00	25.00	15.00
96	Leo Posada	15.00	6.00	3.75
97	Joe Pignatano	15.00	6.00	3.75
98	Jim Archer	15.00	6.00	3.75
99	Haywood Sullivan	30.00	12.00	7.50
100	Art Ditmar	5.00	2.50	1.25
101	Gil Hodges	80.00	40.00	20.00
102	Charlie Neal	15.00	6.00	3.75
103	Daryl Spencer	15.00	6.00	3.75
104	Maury Wills	30.00	12.00	7.50
105	Tommy Davis	30.00	12.00	7.50
106	Willie Davis	15.00	6.00	3.75
107	John Roseboro	60.00	25.00	15.00
108	John Podres	30.00	12.00	7.50
109	Sandy Koufax	80.00	40.00	20.00
110	Don Drysdale	50.00	25.00	12.50
111	Larry Sherry	75.00	37.50	18.75
112	Jim Gilliam	30.00	12.00	7.50
113	Norm Larker	60.00	25.00	15.00
114	Duke Snider	70.00	35.00	17.50
115	Stan Williams	60.00	25.00	15.00
116	Gordon Coleman	70.00	35.00	17.50
117	Don Blasingame	30.00	12.00	7.50
118	Gene Freese	50.00	20.00	12.50
119	Ed Kasko	60.00	25.00	15.00
120	Gus Bell	30.00	12.00	7.50
121	Vada Pinson	15.00	6.00	3.75
122	Frank Robinson	40.00	15.00	10.00
123	Bob Purkey	15.00	6.00	3.75
124	Joey Jay	15.00	6.00	3.75
125	Jim Brosnan	15.00	6.00	3.75
126	Jim O'Toole	15.00	6.00	3.75
127	Jerry Lynch	15.00	6.00	3.75
128	Wally Post	15.00	6.00	3.75
129	Ken Hunt	15.00	6.00	3.75
130	Jerry Zimmerman	15.00	6.00	3.75
131	Willie McCovey	60.00	25.00	15.00
132	Jose Pagan	30.00	12.00	7.50
133	Felipe Alou	15.00	6.00	3.75
134	Jim Davenport	15.00	6.00	3.75
135	Harvey Kuenn	15.00	6.00	3.75
136	Orlando Cepeda	50.00	20.00	12.50
137	Ed Bailey	15.00	6.00	3.75
138	Sam Jones	15.00	6.00	3.75
139	Mike McCormick	15.00	6.00	3.75
140	Juan Marichal	60.00	25.00	15.00
141	Jack Sanford	15.00	6.00	3.75
142	Willie Mays	80.00	40.00	20.00
143	Stu Miller	70.00	35.00	17.50
144	Joe Amalfitano	15.00	6.00	3.75
145	Joe Adcock	15.00	6.00	3.75
146	Frank Bolling	30.00	12.00	7.50
147	Ed Mathews	75.00	37.50	18.75
148	Roy McMillan	5.00	2.50	1.25
149	Hank Aaron	75.00	37.50	18.75
150	Gino Cimoli	30.00	12.00	7.50
151	Frank J. Thomas	5.00	2.50	1.25
152	Joe Torre	60.00	25.00	15.00
153	Lou Burdette	15.00	6.00	3.75
154	Bob Buhl	5.00	2.50	1.25
155	Carlton Willey	5.00	2.50	1.25
156	Lee Maye	50.00	20.00	12.50
157	Al Spangler	60.00	25.00	15.00
158	Bill White	80.00	40.00	20.00
159	Ken Boyer	55.00	27.50	13.75
160	Joe Cunningham	15.00	6.00	3.75
161	Carl Warwick	15.00	6.00	3.75
162	Carl Sawatski	65.00	32.50	16.25
163	Lindy McDaniel	5.00	2.50	1.25
164	Ernie Broglio	15.00	6.00	3.75
165	Larry Jackson	5.00	2.50	1.25
166	Curt Flood	25.00	10.00	6.25
167	Curt Simmons	60.00	25.00	15.00
168	Alex Grammas	30.00	12.00	7.50
169	Dick Stuart	15.00	6.00	3.75
170	Bill Mazeroski	60.00	25.00	15.00
171	Don Hoak	15.00	6.00	3.75
172	Dick Groat	15.00	6.00	3.75
173	Roberto Clemente	180.00	70.00	45.00
174	Bob Skinner	30.00	12.00	7.50
175	Bill Virdon	60.00	25.00	15.00
176	Not Issued			
177	Elroy Face	15.00	6.00	3.75
178	Bob Friend	15.00	6.00	3.75
179	Vernon Law	30.00	12.00	7.50
180	Harvey Haddix	60.00	25.00	15.00
181	Hal Smith	30.00	12.00	7.50
182	Ed Bouchee	50.00	20.00	12.50
183	Don Zimmer	60.00	25.00	15.00
184	Ron Santo	35.00	15.00	9.00
185	Andre Rodgers	5.00	2.50	1.25
186	Richie Ashburn	50.00	20.00	12.50
187	George Altman	5.00	2.50	1.25
188	Ernie Banks	50.00	20.00	12.50
189	Sam Taylor	5.00	2.50	1.25
190	Don Elston	5.00	2.50	1.25
191	Jerry Kindall	50.00	20.00	12.50
192	Pancho Herrera	5.00	2.50	1.25
193	Tony Taylor	5.00	2.50	1.25
194	Ruben Amaro	30.00	12.00	7.50
195	Don Demeter	5.00	2.50	1.25
196	Bobby Gene Smith	60.00	25.00	15.00
197	Clay Dalrymple	5.00	2.50	1.25
198	Robin Roberts	60.00	25.00	15.00
199	Art Mahaffey	5.00	2.50	1.25
200	John Buzhardt	5.00	2.50	1.25

1963 Jell-O

Like the other Post and Jell-O issues of the era, the '63 Jell-O set includes many scarce cards; primarily those which were printed as the backs of less popular brands and sizes of the gelatin dessert. Slightly smaller than the virtually identical Post cereal cards of the same year, the 200 cards in the Jell-O issue measure 3-3/8" x 2-1/2". The easiest way to distinguish 1963 Jell-O cards from Post cards is by the red line that separates the 1962 stats from the lifetime stats. On Post cards, the line extends almost all the way to the side borders, on the Jell-O cards, the line begins and ends much closer to the stats. The high value of some non-star players' cards can be attributed to scarcity caused by the cards having originally been printed on unpopular flavors or sizes.

		NM	EX	VG
Complete Set (200):		5,500	2,200	1,325
Common Player:		7.50	3.00	2.00
1	Vic Power	15.00	6.00	3.50
2	Bernie Allen	65.00	25.00	15.00
3	Zoilo Versalles	65.00	25.00	15.00
4	Rich Rollins	7.50	3.00	2.00
5	Harmon Killebrew	50.00	20.00	12.50
6	Lenny Green	35.00	15.00	10.00
7	Bob Allison	15.00	6.00	3.50
8	Earl Battey	55.00	22.50	13.50
9	Camilo Pascual	10.00	4.00	2.50
10	Jim Kaat	60.00	25.00	15.00
11	Jack Kralick	7.50	3.00	2.00
12	Bill Skowron	65.00	25.00	15.00
13	Bobby Richardson	10.00	4.00	2.50
14	Cletis Boyer	7.50	3.00	2.00
15	Mickey Mantle	125.00	62.50	31.25
16	Roger Maris	40.00	15.00	10.00
17	Yogi Berra	30.00	12.00	7.50
18	Elston Howard	35.00	15.00	10.00
19	Whitey Ford	20.00	8.00	5.00
20	Ralph Terry	7.50	3.00	2.00
21	John Blanchard	30.00	12.00	7.50
22	Bill Stafford	25.00	10.00	6.00
23	Tom Tresh	7.50	3.00	2.00
24	Steve Bilko	7.50	3.00	2.00
25	Bill Moran	7.50	3.00	2.00
26	Joe Koppe	7.50	3.00	2.00
27	Felix Torres	7.50	3.00	2.00
28	Leon Wagner	10.00	4.00	2.50
29	Albie Pearson	7.50	3.00	2.00
30	Lee Thomas	7.50	3.00	2.00
31	Bob Rodgers	65.00	25.00	15.00
32	Dean Chance	7.50	3.00	2.00
33	Ken McBride	35.00	15.00	10.00
34	George Thomas	35.00	15.00	10.00
35	Joe Cunningham	60.00	25.00	15.00
36	Nelson Fox	12.50	5.00	3.00
37	Luis Aparicio	12.50	5.00	3.00
38	Al Smith	7.50	3.00	2.00
39	Floyd Robinson	7.50	3.00	2.00
40	Jim Landis	7.50	3.00	2.00

		NM	EX	VG
41	Charlie Maxwell	7.50	3.00	2.00
42	Sherman Lollar	15.00	6.00	3.50
43	Early Wynn	20.00	8.00	5.00
44	Juan Pizarro	75.00	30.00	17.50
45	Ray Herbert	50.00	20.00	12.50
46	Norm Cash	17.50	7.00	4.50
47	Steve Boros	35.00	15.00	10.00
48	Dick McAuliffe	7.50	3.00	2.00
49	Bill Bruton	15.00	6.00	3.75
50	Rocky Colavito	25.00	10.00	6.00
51	Al Kaline	30.00	12.00	7.50
52	Dick Brown	35.00	15.00	10.00
53	Jim Bunning	15.00	6.00	3.50
54	Hank Aguirre	7.50	3.00	2.00
55	Frank Lary	40.00	15.00	10.00
56	Don Mossi	40.00	15.00	10.00
57	Jim Gentile	7.50	3.00	2.00
58	Jackie Brandt	7.50	3.00	2.00
59	Brooks Robinson	30.00	12.00	7.50
60	Ron Hansen	7.50	3.00	2.00
61	Jerry Adair	100.00	50.00	25.00
62	John Powell	9.00	3.50	2.25
63	Russ Snyder	35.00	15.00	10.00
64	Steve Barber	7.50	3.00	2.00
65	Milt Pappas	40.00	15.00	10.00
66	Robin Roberts	10.00	4.00	2.50
67	Tito Francona	7.50	3.00	2.00
68	Jerry Kindall	35.00	15.00	10.00
69	Woodie Held	7.50	3.00	2.00
70	Bubba Phillips	7.50	3.00	2.00
71	Chuck Essegian	7.50	3.00	2.00
72	Willie Kirkland	35.00	15.00	10.00
73	Al Luplow	35.00	15.00	10.00
74	Ty Cline	55.00	27.50	13.75
75	Dick Donovan	7.50	3.00	2.00
76	John Romano	7.50	3.00	2.00
77	Pete Runnels	12.50	5.00	3.00
78	Ed Bressoud	100.00	40.00	25.00
79	Frank Malzone	7.50	3.00	2.00
80	Carl Yastrzemski	100.00	40.00	25.00
81	Gary Geiger	7.50	3.00	2.00
82	Lou Clinton	40.00	15.00	10.00
83	Earl Wilson	7.50	3.00	2.00
84	Bill Monbouquette	7.50	3.00	2.00
85	Norm Siebern	7.50	3.00	2.00
86	Jerry Lumpe	9.00	3.50	2.00
87	Manny Jimenez	9.00	3.50	2.25
88	Gino Cimoli	12.50	5.00	3.00
89	Ed Charles	70.00	35.00	17.50
90	Ed Rakow	7.50	3.00	2.00
91	Bob Del Greco	125.00	62.50	31.25
92	Haywood Sullivan	40.00	15.00	10.00
93	Chuck Hinton	7.50	3.00	2.00
94	Ken Retzer	35.00	15.00	10.00
95	Harry Bright	30.00	12.00	7.50
96	Bob Johnson	10.00	4.00	2.50
97	Dave Stenhouse	35.00	15.00	10.00
98	Chuck Cottier	7.50	3.00	2.00
99	Tom Cheney	9.00	3.50	2.00
100	Claude Osteen	75.00	30.00	17.50
101	Orlando Cepeda	15.00	6.00	3.50
102	Charley Hiller	35.00	15.00	10.00
103	Jose Pagan	35.00	15.00	10.00
104	Jim Davenport	7.50	3.00	2.00
105	Harvey Kuenn	7.50	3.00	2.00
106	Willie Mays	60.00	30.00	15.00
107	Felipe Alou	7.50	3.00	2.00
108	Tom Haller	35.00	15.00	10.00
109	Juan Marichal	25.00	10.00	6.00
110	Jack Sanford	12.50	5.00	3.00
111	Bill O'Dell	7.50	3.00	2.00
112	Willie McCovey	100.00	40.00	25.00
113	Lee Walls	35.00	15.00	10.00
114	Jim Gilliam	60.00	25.00	15.00
115	Maury Wills	10.00	4.00	2.50
116	Ron Fairly	7.50	3.00	2.00
117	Tommy Davis	7.50	3.00	2.00
118	Duke Snider	20.00	8.00	5.00
119	Willie Davis	20.00	8.00	5.00
120	John Roseboro	7.50	3.00	2.00
121	Sandy Koufax	50.00	20.00	12.50
122	Stan Williams	50.00	25.00	12.50
123	Don Drysdale	12.50	5.00	3.00
124	Daryl Spencer	7.50	3.00	2.00
125	Gordy Coleman	7.50	3.00	2.00
126	Don Blasingame	50.00	20.00	12.50
127	Leo Cardenas	7.50	3.00	2.00
128	Eddie Kasko	80.00	35.00	20.00
129	Jerry Lynch	7.50	3.00	2.00
130	Vada Pinson	7.50	3.00	2.00
131	Frank Robinson	20.00	8.00	5.00
132	John Edwards	40.00	15.00	10.00
133	Joey Jay	7.50	3.00	2.00
134	Bob Purkey	7.50	3.00	2.00
135	Marty Keough	95.00	47.50	23.75
136	Jim O'Toole	40.00	15.00	10.00
137	Dick Stuart	7.50	3.00	2.00
138	Bill Mazeroski	12.50	5.00	3.00
139	Dick Groat	7.50	3.00	2.00
140	Don Hoak	7.50	3.00	2.00
141	Bob Skinner	12.50	5.00	3.00
142	Bill Virdon	7.50	3.00	2.00
143	Roberto Clemente	100.00	40.00	25.00
144	Smoky Burgess	7.50	3.00	2.00
145	Bob Friend	7.50	3.00	2.00
146	Al McBean	50.00	20.00	12.50
147	ElRoy Face	7.50	3.00	2.00
148	Joe Adcock	7.50	3.00	2.00
149	Frank Bolling	7.50	3.00	2.00
150	Roy McMillan	7.50	3.00	2.00
151	Eddie Mathews	12.50	5.00	3.00
152	Hank Aaron	50.00	20.00	12.50
153	Del Crandall	35.00	15.00	10.00
154	Bob Shaw	7.50	3.00	2.00
155	Lew Burdette	7.50	3.00	2.00
156	Joe Torre	50.00	20.00	12.50
157	Tony Cloninger	100.00	50.00	25.00
158	Bill White	7.50	3.00	2.00

		NM	EX	VG
159	Julian Javier	60.00	25.00	15.00
160	Ken Boyer	9.00	3.50	2.00
161	Julio Gotay	75.00	30.00	17.50
162	Curt Flood	25.00	10.00	6.00
163	Charlie James	65.00	25.00	15.00
164	Gene Oliver	50.00	20.00	12.50
165	Ernie Broglio	15.00	6.00	3.50
166	Bob Gibson	135.00	67.50	33.75
167	Lindy McDaniel	35.00	15.00	10.00
168	Ray Washburn	7.50	3.00	2.00
169	Ernie Banks	40.00	15.00	10.00
170	Ron Santo	15.00	6.00	3.50
171	George Altman	7.50	3.00	2.00
172	Billy Williams	100.00	40.00	25.00
173	Andre Rodgers	75.00	30.00	17.50
174	Ken Hubbs	15.00	6.00	3.75
175	Don Landrum	60.00	25.00	15.00
176	Dick Bertell	65.00	25.00	15.00
177	Roy Sievers	7.50	3.00	2.00
178	Tony Taylor	35.00	15.00	10.00
179	John Callison	7.50	3.00	2.00
180	Don Demeter	7.50	3.00	2.00
181	Tony Gonzalez	80.00	40.00	20.00
182	Wes Covington	50.00	20.00	12.50
183	Art Mahaffey	7.50	3.00	2.00
184	Clay Dalrymple	7.50	3.00	2.00
185	Al Spangler	7.50	3.00	2.00
186	Roman Mejias	7.50	3.00	2.00
187	Bob Aspromonte	200.00	100.00	50.00
188	Norm Larker	7.50	3.00	2.00
189	Johnny Temple	7.50	3.00	2.00
190	Carl Warwick	35.00	15.00	10.00
191	Bob Lillis	35.00	15.00	10.00
192	Dick Farrell	90.00	45.00	22.50
193	Gil Hodges	15.00	6.00	3.50
194	Marv Throneberry	7.50	3.00	2.00
195	Charlie Neal	75.00	30.00	17.50
196	Frank Thomas	25.00	10.00	6.00
197	Richie Ashburn	15.00	6.00	3.50
198	Felix Mantilla	60.00	25.00	15.00
199	Rod Kanehl	35.00	15.00	10.00
200	Roger Craig	75.00	30.00	17.50

1969 Jewel Food Chicago Cubs

This set of premium pictures was issued by the midwest regional home-delivery food service. The pictures are 6" x 9" color poses with white borders and blank backs. A facsimile autograph appears on front.

		NM	EX	VG
	Complete Set (20):	125.00	65.00	35.00
	Common Player:	6.00	3.00	1.80
(1)	Ted Abernathy	6.00	3.00	1.80
(2)	Hank Aguirre	6.00	3.00	1.80
(3)	Ernie Banks	30.00	15.00	9.00
(4)	Glenn Beckert	7.50	3.75	2.25
(5)	Bill Hands	6.00	3.00	1.80
(6)	Jim Hickman	6.00	3.00	1.80
(7)	Kenny Holtzman	6.00	3.00	1.75
(8)	Randy Hundley	7.50	3.75	2.25
(9)	Fergie Jenkins	12.50	6.25	3.75
(10)	Don Kessinger	7.50	3.75	2.25
(11)	Rich Nye	6.00	3.00	1.80
(12)	Paul Popovich	6.00	3.00	1.80
(13)	Jim Qualls	6.00	3.00	1.80
(14)	Phil Regan	6.00	3.00	1.80
(15)	Ron Santo	15.00	7.50	4.50
(16)	Dick Selma	6.00	3.00	1.80
(17)	Willie Smith	6.00	3.00	1.80
(18)	Al Spangler	6.00	3.00	1.80
(19)	Billy Williams	15.00	7.50	4.50
(20)	Don Young	6.00	3.00	1.80

1973 Jewel Food Baseball Photos

Jewel Food Stores, a midwestern grocery chain, issued three team sets of large-format baseball player photos in 1973. The 5-7/8" x 9" blank-back photos are full color and feature a facsimile autograph. Photos were sold in groups of four or five per week at five or ten cents per picture. There are 24 Milwaukee Brewers in the issue, and 16 each Chicago Cubs and Chicago White Sox. The unnumbered cards are alphabetized by team in the checklist below.

		NM	EX	VG
CHICAGO CUBS				
	Complete Set (16):	40.00	20.00	12.00
	Common Player:	4.00	2.00	1.25
(1)	Jack Aker	4.00	2.00	1.25
(2)	Glenn Beckert	5.00	2.50	1.50
(3)	Jose Cardenal	4.00	2.00	1.25
(4)	Carmen Fanzone	4.00	2.00	1.25
(5)	Burt Hooton	4.00	2.00	1.25
(6)	Fergie Jenkins	10.00	5.00	3.00
(7)	Don Kessinger	5.00	2.50	1.50
(8)	Jim Hickman	4.00	2.00	1.25
(9)	Randy Hundley	5.00	2.50	1.50
(10)	Bob Locker	4.00	2.00	1.25
(11)	Rick Monday	4.00	2.00	1.25
(12)	Milt Pappas	4.00	2.00	1.25
(13)	Rick Reuschel	4.00	2.00	1.25
(14)	Ken Rudolph	4.00	2.00	1.25
(15)	Ron Santo	10.00	5.00	3.00
(16)	Billy Williams	15.00	7.50	4.50
CHICAGO WHITE SOX				
	Complete Set (16):	30.00	15.00	9.00
	Common Player:	4.00	2.00	1.25
(17)	Dick Allen	7.50	3.75	2.25
(18)	Mike Andrews	4.00	2.00	1.25
(19)	Stan Bahnsen	4.00	2.00	1.25
(20)	Eddie Fisher	4.00	2.00	1.25
(21)	Terry Forster	4.00	2.00	1.25
(22)	Ken Henderson	4.00	2.00	1.25
(23)	Ed Hermann	4.00	2.00	1.25
(24)	John Jeter	4.00	2.00	1.25
(25)	Pat Kelly	4.00	2.00	1.25
(26)	Eddie Leon	4.00	2.00	1.25
(27)	Carlos May	4.00	2.00	1.25
(28)	Bill Melton	4.00	2.00	1.25
(29)	Tony Muser	4.00	2.00	1.25
(30)	Jorge Orta	4.00	2.00	1.25
(31)	Rick Reichardt	4.00	2.00	1.25
(32)	Wilbur Wood	4.00	2.00	1.25
MILWAUKEE BREWERS				
	Complete Set (25):	35.00	17.50	10.00
	Common Player:	4.00	2.00	1.25
(33)	Jerry Bell	4.00	2.00	1.25
(34)	John Briggs	4.00	2.00	1.25
(35)	Ollie Brown	4.00	2.00	1.25
(36)	Billy Champion	4.00	2.00	1.25
(37)	Jim Colborn	4.00	2.00	1.25
(38)	Bob Coluccio	4.00	2.00	1.25
(39)	John Felske	4.00	2.00	1.25
(40)	Pedro Garcia	4.00	2.00	1.25
(41)	Rob Gardner	4.00	2.00	1.25
(42)	Bob Heise	4.00	2.00	1.25
(43)	Tim Johnson	4.00	2.00	1.25
(44)	Joe Lahoud	4.00	2.00	1.25
(45)	Frank Linzy	4.00	2.00	1.25
(46)	Skip Lockwood	4.00	2.00	1.25
(47)	Dave May	4.00	2.00	1.25
(48)	Bob Mitchell	4.00	2.00	1.25
(49)	Don Money	4.00	2.00	1.25
(50)	Bill Parsons	4.00	2.00	1.25
(51)	Darrell Porter	4.00	2.00	1.25
(52)	Eduardo Rodriguez	4.00	2.00	1.25
(53)	Ellie Rodriguez	4.00	2.00	1.25
(54)	George Scott	5.00	2.50	1.50
(55)	Chris Short	4.00	2.00	1.25
(56)	Jim Slaton	4.00	2.00	1.25
(57)	John Vukovich	4.00	2.00	1.25

1977 Jewel Food Chicago Cubs/White Sox

Once again in 1977, Jewel grocery stores in the Chicago area offered photos of local players with specific product purchases over a four-week period. The 5-7/8" x 9" color photos are printed on heavy paper. Fronts have player poses, a facsimile signature and the MLB Players Association logo in the upper-left corner. Backs are blank. The pictures are not numbered and are checklisted here alphabetically within team. It was reported 12,000 of each picture were produced.

	NM	EX	VG
Complete Set, Cubs (16):	12.00	6.00	3.50
Complete Set, White Sox (16):	12.00	6.00	3.50
Common Player:	1.50	.70	.45

CHICAGO CUBS

(1)	Larry Biittner	1.50	.70	.45
(2)	Bill Bonham	1.50	.70	.45
(3)	Bill Buckner	2.50	1.25	.70
(4)	Ray Burris	1.50	.70	.45
(5)	Jose Cardenal	1.50	.70	.45
(6)	Gene Clines	1.50	.70	.45
(7)	Ivan DeJesus	1.50	.70	.45
(8)	Willie Hernandez	1.50	.70	.45
(9)	Mike Krukow	1.50	.70	.45
(10)	George Mitterwald	1.50	.70	.45
(11)	Jerry Morales	1.50	.70	.45
(12)	Bobby Murcer	2.50	1.25	.70
(13)	Steve Ontiveros	1.50	.70	.45
(14)	Rick Reuschel	1.50	.70	.45
(15)	Bruce Sutter	3.50	1.75	1.00
(16)	Manny Trillo	1.50	.70	.45

CHICAGO WHITE SOX

(1)	Alan Bannister	1.50	.70	.45
(2)	Francisco Barrios	1.50	.70	.45
(3)	Jim Essian	1.50	.70	.45
(4)	Oscar Gamble	1.50	.70	.45
(5)	Ralph Garr	1.50	.70	.45
(6)	Lamar Johnson	1.50	.70	.45
(7)	Chris Knapp	1.50	.70	.45
(8)	Ken Kravec	1.50	.70	.45
(9)	Lerrin LaGrow	1.50	.70	.45
(10)	Chet Lemon	1.50	.70	.45
(11)	Jorge Orta	1.50	.70	.45
(12)	Eric Soderholm	1.50	.70	.45
(13)	Jim Spencer	1.50	.70	.45
(14)	Steve Stone	2.50	1.25	.70
(15)	Wilbur Wood	1.50	.70	.45
(16)	Richie Zisk	1.50	.70	.45

1949 Jimmy Fund Boston Braves Die-cuts

The reigning National League champions undertook the support of the Jimmy Fund, a Boston charity for children's cancer research, with a set of die-cut counter cards accompanying contributions boxes. Between about 6" and 8" at the base, and up to a foot tall, these heavy cardboard pieces feature sepia-toned player action photos in front of a large baseball on which is written, "THANK YOU! in behalf of 'JIMMY'." with a facsimile signature below. Backs have a fold-out easel to stand the card up, and a notation that following the fund drive, the card should be given to the largest contributor at that location.

		NM	EX	VG
Complete Set (21):		15,000	7,500	4,500
Common Player:		750.00	375.00	225.00
(1)	Johnny Antonelli	750.00	375.00	225.00
(2)	Red Barrett	750.00	375.00	225.00
(3)	Vern Bickford	750.00	375.00	225.00
(4)	Jimmy Bronw	750.00	375.00	225.00
(5)	Clint Conatser	750.00	375.00	225.00
(6)	Al Dark	750.00	375.00	225.00
(7)	Bob Elliott	750.00	375.00	225.00
(8)	Glenn Elliott	750.00	375.00	225.00
(9)	Bobby Hogue	750.00	375.00	225.00
(10)	Tommy Holmes	750.00	375.00	225.00
(11)	Pete Reiser	750.00	375.00	225.00
(12)	Marv Rickert	750.00	375.00	225.00
(13)	Jim Russell	750.00	375.00	225.00
(14)	Connie Ryan	750.00	375.00	225.00
(15)	Johnny Sain	850.00	425.00	255.00
(16)	Bill Salkeld	750.00	375.00	225.00
(17)	Sibby Sisti	750.00	375.00	225.00
(18)	Warren Spahn	1,200	600.00	360.00
(19)	Don Thompson	750.00	375.00	225.00
(20)	Earl Torgeson	750.00	375.00	225.00
(21)	Bill Voiselle	750.00	375.00	225.00

1978 JJH Reading Remembers

This collectors' issue was created to honor baseball players (and a few others) who were born, lived in or played in Berks County, Pa., particularly in Reading. The cards are 3" x 4" featuring borderless sepia photos on front. Most of the photos picture players in big league uniforms. Backs are in black-and-white and have career stats and summaries. A number of major leaguers who did not have cards contemporary with their careers are found in this set. Cards are numbered by uniform number. Production was reported as 1,000 sets.

		NM	EX	VG
Complete Set (23):		25.00	12.50	7.50
Common Player:		2.00	1.00	.60
1	Whitey Kurowski	2.00	1.00	.60
6	Carl Furillo	5.00	2.50	1.50
9	Roger Maris	10.00	5.00	3.00
12	Stan Wetzel	2.00	1.00	.60
17	Doug Clemens	2.00	1.00	.60
18	Randy Gumpert	2.00	1.00	.60
18	Ty Stofflet (Softball)	2.00	1.00	.60
21	George Eyrich	2.00	1.00	.60
23	Vic Wertz	2.00	1.00	.60
24	Lenny Moore (Football)	2.00	1.00	.60
25	Dick Gernert	2.00	1.00	.60
27	Herb Score	2.00	1.00	.60
27	Charlie Wagner	2.00	1.00	.60
28	Carl Mathias	2.00	1.00	.60
32	Jesse Levan	2.00	1.00	.60
34	Betz Klopp	2.00	1.00	.60
36	Robin Roberts	9.00	4.50	2.75
39	Bob Katz	2.00	1.00	.60
39	Harry Schaeffer	2.00	1.00	.60
40	Tommy Brown (Baseball/Football)	1.50	.70	.45
46	Dom Dallessandro	2.00	1.00	.60
---	Lauer's Park	2.00	1.00	.60
---	John Updike (Author)	2.00	1.00	.60

1950s J.J.K. Copyart Postcards

Issued from about 1950 through at least 1956, this series of glossy black-and-white player postcards appears to have been produced on order of the individual players to respond to fan requests for pictures and/or autographs. Fronts have player poses bordered in white in about 3-1/2" x 5-1/2" format; most have facsimile autographs. Backs have typical postcard layout with a credit line to J.J.K. Copyart Photographers of New York City. Some players are known in more than one pose.

		NM	EX	VG
Common Player:		15.00	7.50	4.50
BOSTON/MILWAUKEE BRAVES				
(1)	Del Crandall	15.00	7.50	4.50
(2)	Tommy Holmes	15.00	7.50	4.50
(3)	Willard Marshall	15.00	7.50	4.50
(4)	Eddie Mathews	60.00	30.00	18.00
(5)	Eddie Mathews	60.00	30.00	18.00
(6)	Danny O'Connell	15.00	7.50	4.50
(7)	Sibby Sisti	15.00	7.50	4.50
(8)	Eddie Stanky	25.00	12.50	7.50
BROOKLYN DODGERS				
(1)	Jackie Robinson	200.00	100.00	60.00
NEW YORK GIANTS				
(1)	Johnny Antonelli	15.00	7.50	4.50
(2)	Johnny Antonelli	15.00	7.50	4.50
(3)	Sam Calderone	15.00	7.50	4.50
(4)	Jim Hearn	15.00	7.50	4.50
(5)	Jim Hearn	15.00	7.50	4.50
(6)	Larry Jansen	15.00	7.50	4.50
(7)	Whitey Lockman	15.00	7.50	4.50
(8)	Whitey Lockman	15.00	7.50	4.50
(9)	Don Mueller	15.00	7.50	4.50
(10)	Bill Rigney	15.00	7.50	4.50
(11)	Bill Rigney	15.00	7.50	4.50
(12)	Hank Sauer	15.00	7.50	4.50
(13)	Red Schoendienst	30.00	15.00	9.00
(14)	Daryl Spencer	15.00	7.50	4.50
(15)	Eddie Stanky	25.00	12.50	7.50
(16)	Wes Westrum	15.00	7.50	4.50
(17)	Wes Westrum	15.00	7.50	4.50
(18)	Hoyt Wilhelm	30.00	15.00	9.00
(19)	Al Worthington	15.00	7.50	4.50
PHILADELPHIA PHILLIES				
(1)	Del Ennis	15.00	7.50	4.50
(2)	Robin Roberts	30.00	15.00	9.00
(3)	Curt Simmons	15.00	7.50	4.50

1973 Johnny Pro Orioles

This regional set of large (4-1/4" x 7-1/4") die-cut cards was issued by Johnny Pro Enterprises Inc. of Baltimore and features only Orioles. The cards were designed to be punched out and folded to make baseball player figures that can stand up. The full-color die-cut figures appear against a green background. The cards are numbered according to the player's uniform number, which appears in a white box along with his name and position. The backs are blank. Three players (Robinson, Grich, and Palmer) appear in two poses each, and cards of Orlando Pena were not die-cut. Values listed are for complete cards not punched out. Cards originally sold for 15 cents apiece.

		NM	EX	VG
Complete Set (28):		135.00	65.00	40.00
Common Player:		3.00	1.50	.90
1	Al Bumbry	3.00	1.50	.90
2	Rich Coggins	3.00	1.50	.90
3a	Bobby Grich (Batting)	5.00	2.50	1.50
3b	Bobby Grich (Fielding)	5.00	2.50	1.50
4	Earl Weaver	6.00	3.00	1.75
5a	Brooks Robinson (Batting)	25.00	12.50	7.50
5b	Brooks Robinson (Fielding)	25.00	12.50	7.50
6	Paul Blair	4.00	2.00	1.25
7	Mark Belanger	4.00	2.00	1.25
8	Andy Etchebarren	3.00	1.50	.90
10	Elrod Hendricks	3.00	1.50	.90
11	Terry Crowley	3.00	1.50	.90
12	Tommy Davis	4.00	2.00	1.25
13	Doyle Alexander	3.00	1.50	.90
14	Merv Rettenmund	3.00	1.50	.90
15	Frank Baker	3.00	1.50	.90
19	Dave McNally	4.00	2.00	1.25
21	Larry Brown	3.00	1.50	.90
22a	Jim Palmer (Follow-through.)	15.00	7.50	4.50
22b	Jim Palmer (Wind-up)	15.00	7.50	4.50
23	Grant Jackson	3.00	1.50	.90
25	Don Baylor	6.00	3.00	1.75
26	Boog Powell	7.00	3.50	2.00
27	Orlando Pena	8.00	4.00	2.50
32	Earl Williams	3.00	1.50	.90
34	Bob Reynolds	3.00	1.50	.90
35	Mike Cuellar	5.00	2.50	1.50
39	Eddie Watt	3.00	1.50	.90

1974 Johnny Pro Phillies

Although slightly smaller (3-3/4" x 7-1/8") and featuring members of the Phillies, this set is very similar to the 1973 Johnny Pro Orioles set. The full-color die-cut player figures are set against a white background. Again, the set is numbered according to the player's uniform number. The values listed are for complete cards.

		NM	EX	VG
Complete Set (12):		100.00	50.00	30.00
Common Player:		3.00	1.50	.90
8	Bob Boone	7.50	3.75	2.25
10	Larry Bowa	7.50	3.75	2.25
16	Dave Cash	3.00	1.50	.90
19	Greg Luzinski	5.00	2.50	1.50
20	Mike Schmidt	50.00	25.00	15.00
22	Mike Anderson	3.00	1.50	.90
24	Bill Robinson	3.00	1.50	.90
25	Del Unser	3.00	1.50	.90
27	Willie Montanez	3.00	1.50	.90
32	Steve Carlton	25.00	12.50	7.50
37	Ron Schueler	3.00	1.50	.90
41	Jim Lonborg	3.00	1.50	.90

1922 Henry A. Johnson Wholesale Confectioner

To compete with other candy issues featuring baseball cards as premiums, Alameda, Calif., confectioner Henry A. Johnson purchased uncut sheets of the blank-back strip cards known as W575-1, overprinted their backs and packaged them with his Likem brand candy bars. The advertising on back gives the firm's name, address and telephone number. Collectors can expect to pay a premium of about 3X for this version. Only the type style shown here can definitely be traced to the 1920s. Other styles of typography are known to have been applied in the 1980s and later.

	NM	EX	VG
Common Player:	85.00	42.50	25.00
Stars: 6-8X			

(See W575-1 for checklist and base card values.)

1953 Johnston Cookies Braves

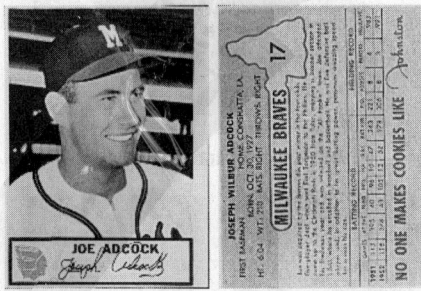

The first and most common of three annual issues, the '53 Johnstons were inserted into boxes of cookies on a regional basis. Complete sets were also available via a mail-in offer from the company, whose factory sits in the shadow of Milwaukee County Stadium. While at first glance appearing to be color photos, the pictures on the 25 cards in the set are actually well-done colorizations of black-and-white photos. Cards measure 2-9/16" x 3-5/8". Write-ups on the backs were "borrowed" from the Braves' 1953 yearbook.

		NM	EX	VG
Complete Set (25):		500.00	250.00	150.00
Common Player:		15.00	7.50	4.50
1	Charlie Grimm	15.00	7.50	4.50
2	John Antonelli	15.00	7.50	4.50
3	Vern Bickford	15.00	7.50	4.50
4	Bob Buhl	15.00	7.50	4.50
5	Lew Burdette	15.00	7.50	4.50
6	Dave Cole	15.00	7.50	4.50
7	Ernie Johnson	15.00	7.50	4.50
8	Dave Jolly	15.00	7.50	4.50
9	Don Liddle	15.00	7.50	4.50
10	Warren Spahn	150.00	75.00	45.00
11	Max Surkont	15.00	7.50	4.50
12	Jim Wilson	15.00	7.50	4.50
13	Sibby Sisti	15.00	7.50	4.50
14	Walker Cooper	15.00	7.50	4.50
15	Del Crandall	15.00	7.50	4.50
16	Ebba St. Claire	15.00	7.50	4.50
17	Joe Adcock	15.00	7.50	4.50
18	George Crowe	15.00	7.50	4.50
19	Jack Dittmer	15.00	7.50	4.50
20	Johnny Logan	15.00	7.50	4.50
21	Ed Mathews	150.00	75.00	45.00
22	Bill Bruton	15.00	7.50	4.50
23	Sid Gordon	15.00	7.50	4.50
24	Andy Pafko	15.00	7.50	4.50
25	Jim Pendleton	15.00	7.50	4.50

1954 Johnston Cookies Braves

In its second of three annual issues, Johnston's increased the number of cards in its 1954 Braves issue to 35, and switched to an unusual size, a narrow format, 2" x 3-7/8". Cards are listed here by uniform number. After his early-season injury (which gave Hank Aaron a chance to play regularly), Bobby Thomson's card was withdrawn, accounting for its scarcity and high value. Uncut sheets of 42 cards (including seven double-prints) in a size of about 12-1/2" x 27-3/4" are not uncommon. A 21-1/2" x 31" wall-hanging display poster with die-cuts into which cards could be inserted was available as a premium offer.

BOB THOMSON

		NM	EX	VG
Complete Set (35):		1,500	750.00	450.00
Common Player:		20.00	10.00	6.00
Uncut Sheet:		3,450	1,725	1,035
Display Poster:		500.00	250.00	150.00
1	Del Crandall	20.00	10.00	6.00
3	Jim Pendleton	20.00	10.00	6.00
4	Danny O'Connell	20.00	10.00	6.00
5	Henry Aaron	750.00	375.00	225.00
6	Jack Dittmer	20.00	10.00	6.00
9	Joe Adcock	20.00	10.00	6.00
10	Robert Buhl	20.00	10.00	6.00
11	Phillip Paine (Phillips)(DP)	20.00	10.00	6.00
12	Ben Johnson	20.00	10.00	6.00
13	Sibby Sisti	20.00	10.00	6.00
15	Charles Gorin	20.00	10.00	6.00
16	Chet Nichols	20.00	10.00	6.00
17	Dave Jolly (DP)	20.00	10.00	6.00
19	Jim Wilson (DP)	20.00	10.00	6.00
20	Ray Crone	20.00	10.00	6.00
21	Warren Spahn (DP)	100.00	50.00	30.00
22	Gene Conley	20.00	10.00	6.00
23	Johnny Logan (DP)	20.00	10.00	6.00
24	Charlie White	20.00	10.00	6.00
27	George Metkovich	20.00	10.00	6.00
28	John Cooney	20.00	10.00	6.00
29	Paul Burris	20.00	10.00	6.00
31	Wm. Walters (DP)	20.00	10.00	6.00
32	Ernest T. Johnson	20.00	10.00	6.00
33	Lew Burdette	20.00	10.00	6.00
34	Bob Thomson (SP)	165.00	80.00	50.00
35	Robert Keely	20.00	10.00	6.00
38	Billy Bruton	20.00	10.00	6.00
40	Charles Grimm	20.00	10.00	6.00
41	Ed Mathews	100.00	50.00	30.00
42	Sam Calderone (DP)	20.00	10.00	6.00
47	Joey Jay	20.00	10.00	6.00
48	Andy Pafko	20.00	10.00	6.00
----	Dr. Charles Lacks (Asst. trainer.)	20.00	10.00	6.00
----	Joseph F. Taylor (Asst. trainer.)	20.00	10.00	6.00

1955 Johnston Cookies Braves

GEORGE CROWE

A third change in size and format was undertaken in the final year of Braves sets produced by Johnston's. The 35 cards in the 1955 set were issued in six fold-out panels of six cards each (Andy Pafko was double-printed). As in 1954, cards are numbered by uniform number, except those of the team equipment manager, trainer and road secretary (former Boston star Duffy Lewis). Single cards measure 2-7/8" x 4". Besides including panels in boxes of cookies, the '55 Johnstons could be ordered for five cents per panel by mail. The scarcest of the Johnston's issues, the 1955 set can be found today still in complete panels, or as single cards.

		NM	EX	VG
Complete Folder Set (6):		1,250	625.00	375.00
Complete Singles Set (35):		1,500	750.00	450.00
Common Player:		30.00	20.00	12.00
Common Folder:		200.00	100.00	60.00
1	Del Crandall	30.00	20.00	12.00
3	Jim Pendleton	30.00	20.00	12.00
4	Danny O'Connell	30.00	20.00	12.00
6	Jack Dittmer	30.00	20.00	12.00
9	Joe Adcock	30.00	20.00	12.00
10	Bob Buhl	30.00	20.00	12.00
11	Phil Paine	30.00	20.00	12.00
12	Ray Crone	30.00	20.00	12.00
15	Charlie Gorin	30.00	20.00	12.00

		NM	EX	VG
16	Dave Jolly	30.00	20.00	12.00
17	Chet Nichols	30.00	20.00	12.00
18	Chuck Tanner	30.00	20.00	12.00
19	Jim Wilson	30.00	20.00	12.00
20	Dave Koslo	30.00	20.00	12.00
21	Warren Spahn	100.00	50.00	30.00
22	Gene Conley	30.00	20.00	12.00
23	John Logan	30.00	20.00	12.00
24	Charlie White	30.00	20.00	12.00
28	Johnny Cooney	30.00	20.00	12.00
30	Roy Smalley	30.00	20.00	12.00
31	Bucky Walters	30.00	20.00	12.00
32	Ernie Johnson	30.00	20.00	12.00
33	Lew Burdette	30.00	20.00	12.00
34	Bobby Thomson	35.00	17.50	10.50
35	Bob Keely	30.00	20.00	12.00
38	Billy Bruton	30.00	20.00	12.00
39	George Crowe	30.00	20.00	12.00
40	Charlie Grimm	30.00	20.00	12.00
41	Eddie Mathews	100.00	50.00	30.00
44	Hank Aaron	450.00	225.00	135.00
47	Joe Jay	30.00	20.00	12.00
48	Andy Pafko	30.00	20.00	12.00
----	Dr. Charles K. Lacks	30.00	20.00	12.00
---	Duffy Lewis	30.00	20.00	12.00
---	Joe Taylor	30.00	20.00	12.00
Series 1 Folder		475.00	240.00	140.00
	Hank Aaron, Lew Burdette, Del Crandall, Charlie Gorin, Bob Keely, Danny O'Connell			
Series 2 Folder		160.00	80.00	45.00
	Joe Adcock, Joe Jay, Dr. Charles K. Lacks, Chet Nichols, Andy Pafko, Charlie White			
Series 3 Folder		175.00	90.00	50.00
	Gene Conley, George Crowe, Jim Pendleton, Roy Smalley, Warren Spahn, Joe Taylor			
Series 4 Folder		160.00	80.00	45.00
	Billy Bruton, John Cooney, Dave Jolly, Dave Koslo, Johnny Logan, Andy Pafko			
Series 5 Folder		190.00	95.00	55.00
	Ray Crone, Ernie Johnson, Duffy Lewis, Eddie Mathews, Phil Paine, Chuck Tanner			
Series 6 Folder		160.00	80.00	45.00
	Bob Buhl, Jack Dittmer, Charlie Grimm, Bobby Thomson, Bucky Walters, Jim Wilson			

1976 Jerry Jonas Productions All Time Greats

This card set was produced only in prototype form with an estimated 50 of each printed. The cards were designed to introduce a baseball card promotion to team executives at their annual World Series meeting. The 2-3/4" x 3-3/4" cards have black-and-white player photos at center with colored borders reminiscent of the 1975 Topps cards. Backs are printed in black on blue and feature biographical data, career highlights and stats along with a credit line to Jerry Jones Productions. The proposed promotion was never adopted. The unnumbered cards are checklisted here in alphabetical order.

		NM	EX	VG
Complete Set, Uncut Sheet:		225.00	110.00	70.00
Complete Set, Singles (8):		225.00	110.00	70.00
Common Player:		15.00	7.50	4.50
(1)	Grover Alexander	15.00	7.50	4.50
(2)	Rogers Hornsby	15.00	7.50	4.50
(3)	Sandy Koufax	75.00	37.00	22.00
(4)	Willie Mays	50.00	25.00	15.00
(5)	Stan Musial	25.00	12.50	7.50
(6)	Mel Ott	15.00	7.50	4.50
(7)	Robin Roberts	15.00	7.50	4.50
(8)	Honus Wagner	15.00	7.50	4.50

1911 Jones, Keyser & Arras Cabinets

Contemporary with the better-known Sporting Life, Turkey Red and Pinkerton cabinet photos, this series of baseball player cabinets was issued by the New York City studio of Jones, Keyser & Arras, whose address appears on the back of the card. The 4-1/2" x 7-1/4" cabinets have photos glued to stiff gray cardboard mounts. Both photo and mount are numbered within the known range of 301-349, making it likely there are 50 baseball players in the series. Most known subjects are from the three New York teams of the era. Photos carry at bottom a stylized J, K & A logo, a 1911 copyright and a number. That number is repeated in the bottom border of the mount, along with the player's last name and the team/league. Several photos are known which have been removed from the mount, making identification difficult.

		NM	EX	VG
Common Player:		2,400	1,200	720.00
301	Russ Ford	2,400	1,200	720.00
303	John Warhop	2,400	1,200	720.00
304	Bill Dahlen	2,400	1,200	720.00
306	Zack Wheat	4,000	2,000	1,200
307	Al Bridwell	2,400	1,200	720.00
308	Red Murray	2,400	1,200	720.00
310	Fred Snodgrass	2,400	1,200	720.00
311	Red Ames	2,400	1,200	720.00
312	Fred Merkle	2,400	1,200	720.00
313	Art Devlin	2,400	1,200	720.00
314	Hooks Wiltse	2,400	1,200	720.00
315	Josh Devore	2,400	120.00	720.00
316	Eddie Collins	4,000	2,000	1,200
317	Ed Reulbach	2,400	1,200	720.00
318	Jimmy Scheckard (Sheckard)	2,400	120.00	720.00
320	Frank Schulte	2,400	1,200	720.00
321	Solly Hofman	2,400	1,200	720.00
322	Bill Bergen	2,400	1,200	720.00
323	George Bell	2,400	1,200	720.00
324	Nap Rucker	2,400	120.00	720.00
325	Fred Clarke	4,000	2,000	1,200
326	Clark Griffith, Mgr.	4,000	2,000	1,200
327	Roger Bresnahan	4,000	2,000	1,200
328	Fred Tenney	2,400	1,200	720.00
329	Harry Lord	2,400	1,200	720.00
331	Walter Johnson	12,000	6,000	3,600
332	Nap Lajoie	4,000	2,000	1,200
333	Joe Tinker	4,000	2,000	1,200
334	Mordecai Brown	4,000	2,000	1,200
336	Jimmy Archer	2,400	1,200	720.00
338	Nixey Callahan	2,400	1,200	720.00
340	Hal Chase	3,500	1,750	1,050
341	Larry Doyle	2,400	1,200	720.00
342	Chief Meyers	2,400	1,200	720.00
343	Christy Mathewson	12,000	6,000	3,600
344	Bugs Raymond	2,400	1,200	720.00
345	John J. McGraw, Mgr.	4,000	2,000	1,200
346	Honus Wagner	15,000	7,500	4,500
347	Ty Cobb	25,000	12,500	7,500
348	Johnny Evers	4,000	2,000	1,200
349	Frank Chance	4,000	2,000	1,200

1863 Jordan & Co.

Because this card pictures a ballplayer on front with advertising on back, it has been described as the world's first baseball card. The 2-7/16" x 4-1/16" card doubled as a ticket to a benefit (to the players!) series of matches between New York and Brooklyn teams and all-stars at Hoboken, N.J., in Sept., 1863. The ticket cards were sold for 50 cents apiece, twice the cost of regular admission. According to surviving records, photos of four different players were used on the tickets.

(1) William Crossley (1/08 auction, $7,100)
(2) William Hammond (12/04 auction, $19,364)
(3) Sam Wright (Unknown)
(4) Harry Wright (Clipped-corners, 7/00 auction, $83,545.)

1931 Josetti Tobacco

This is one of several early 1930s German cigarette cards to picture Babe Ruth. In this case he is pictured on the 1-5/8" x 2-3/8" black-and-white card with American comedic actor Harold Lloyd. The card is part of a numbered set of 272 movie star cards. Backs are printed in German. The card can be found with Ruth's first name printed as George or as Babe.

		NM	EX	VG
151a	George Ruth, Harold Lloyd	450.00	225.00	135.00
151b	Babe Ruth, Harold Lloyd	450.00	225.00	135.00

1910 Ju-Ju Drums (E286)

Issued in 1910 with Ju Ju Drum Candy, this extremely rare set of circular baseball cards is very similar in design to the more common Colgan's Chips cards. About the size of a silver dollar (1-7/16" in diameter) the cards display a player photo on the front with the player's name and team printed below in a semi-circle design. The backs carry advertising for Ju-Ju Drums. The checklist contains 45 different players to date, but the issue - known as E286 in the American Card Catalog - is so rare that others are likely to exist.

		NM	EX	VG
Complete Set (45):		80,000	40,000	24,000
Common Player:		1,500	750.00	450.00
(1)	Eddie Ainsmith	1,500	750.00	450.00
(2)	Jimmy Austin	1,500	750.00	450.00
(3)	Chief Bender	3,000	1,500	900.00
(4)	Bob Bescher	1,500	750.00	450.00
(5)	Bruno Bloch (Block)	1,500	750.00	450.00
(6)	Frank Burke	1,500	750.00	450.00
(7)	Donie Bush	1,500	750.00	450.00
(8)	Frank Chance	3,000	1,500	900.00
(9)	Harry Cheek	1,500	750.00	450.00
(10)	Ed Cicotte	3,000	1,500	900.00
(11)	Ty Cobb	13,000	6,500	4,000
(12)	King Cole	1,500	750.00	450.00
(13)	Jack Coombs	1,500	750.00	450.00
(14)	Bill Dahlen	1,500	750.00	450.00
(15)	Bert Daniels	1,500	750.00	450.00
(16)	Harry Davis	1,500	750.00	450.00
(17)	Larry Doyle	1,500	750.00	450.00
(18)	Rube Ellis	1,500	750.00	450.00
(19)	Cecil Ferguson	1,500	750.00	450.00
(20)	Russ Ford	1,500	750.00	450.00
(21)	Bob Harnion (Harmon)	1,500	750.00	450.00
(22)	Ham Hyatt	1,500	750.00	450.00
(23)	Red Kellifer (Killifer)	1,500	750.00	450.00
(24)	Art Kruger (Krueger)	1,500	750.00	450.00
(25)	Tommy Leach	1,500	750.00	450.00
(26)	Harry Lumley	1,500	750.00	450.00
(27)	Christy Mathewson	7,000	3,500	2,100
(28)	John McGraw	3,000	1,500	900.00
(29)	Deacon McGuire	1,500	750.00	450.00
(30)	Chief Meyers	1,500	750.00	450.00
(31)	Otto Miller	1,500	750.00	450.00
(32)	Charlie Mullen	1,500	750.00	450.00
(33)	Tom Needham	1,500	750.00	450.00
(34)	Rube Oldring	1,500	750.00	450.00
(35)	Barney Pelty	1,500	750.00	450.00
(36)	Ed Reulbach	1,500	750.00	450.00
(37)	Jack Rowan	1,500	750.00	450.00
(38)	Dave Shean	1,500	750.00	450.00
(39)	Tris Speaker	4,000	2,000	1,200
(40)	Ed Sweeney	1,500	750.00	450.00
(41)	Honus Wagner	9,000	4,500	2,700
(42)	Jimmy Walsh	1,500	750.00	450.00
(43)	Kirby White	1,500	750.00	450.00
(44)	Ralph Works	1,500	750.00	450.00
(45)	Elmer Zacher	1,500	750.00	450.00

1893 Just So Tobacco

This set is so rare that only a dozen or so examples are known, although it is possible others remain to be reported. The set features only members of the Cleveland club, known then as the "Spiders." Measuring 2-1/2" x 3-7/8", these sepia-colored cards were printed on heavy paper. The player appears in a portrait photo with his name beneath and an ad for Just So Tobacco at bottom. The existence of this set wasn't even established until the 1960s, and for 15 years only two subjects were known. In 1981 and 1989 several more cards were discovered. To date only one or two copies of each of the known cards have turned up in collectors' hands, making it among the rarest of all baseball card issues.

		NM	EX	VG
Common Player:		30,000	19,000	
(1)	F.W. Boyd	30,000	19,000	
(2)	Burkette (Jesse Burkett) (Unique. Trimmed and restored. Value undetermined.)			
(3)	C.L. Childs ("Cupid")	30,000	19,000	
(4)	John Clarkson (Unique. Value undetermined.)			
(5)	J.O. Connor (John O'Connor)	30,000	19,000	
(6)	G. Cuppy	30,000	19,000	
(7)	G.W. Davies	30,000	19,000	
(8)	W. Ewing (Unique. Value undetermined.)			
(9)	C.M. Hastings	30,000	19,000	
(10)	E.J. McKean	30,000	19,000	
(11)	CAPt Tebeau ("Patsy")	30,000	19,000	
(12)	J.K. Virtue	30,000	19,000	
(13)	T.C. Williams	30,000	19,000	
(14)	D.T. Young (Cy)(Unique. Value undetermined.)			
(15)	C.L. Zimmer ("Chief")	30,000	19,000	

K

1950s Kabaya Caramel Babe Ruth

This card was part of a series produced by an Okayama, Japan candy company. The card measures about 1-1/2" x 2-1/8" with color artwork of Ruth on front. On back is Japanese script within the design of an open book.

	NM	EX	VG
Babe Ruth	1,200	600.00	350.00

1955 Kahn's Wieners Reds

The first of what would become 15 successive years of baseball card issues by the Kahn's meat company of Cincinnati is also the rarest. The set consists of six Cincinnati Redlegs player cards, 3-1/4" x 4". Printed in black and white, with blank backs, the '55 Kahn's cards were distributed at a one-day promotional event at a Cincinnati amusement park, where the featured players were on hand to sign autographs. Like the other Kahn's issues through 1963, the '55 cards have a 1/2" white panel containing an advertising message below the player photo. These cards are sometimes found with this portion cut off, greatly reducing the value of the card.

	NM	EX	VG
Complete Set (6):	13,000	6,500	4,000

Common Player:	2,000	1,000	600.00
(1) Gus Bell	2,500	1,250	750.00
(2) Ted Kluszewski	2,900	1,450	870.00
(3) Roy McMillan	2,000	1,000	600.00
(4) Joe Nuxhall	2,000	1,000	600.00
(5) Wally Post	2,000	1,000	600.00
(6) Johnny Temple	2,000	1,000	600.00

1956 Kahn's Wieners Reds

Compliments of Kahn's Wieners
"THE WIENER THE WORLD AWAITED"

In 1956, Kahn's expanded its baseball card program to include 15 Redlegs players, and began issuing the cards one per pack in packages of hot dogs. Because the cards were packaged in direct contact with the meat, they are often found today in stained condition. In 3-1/4" x 4" format, black and white with blank backs, the '56 Kahn's cards can be distinguished from later issues by the presence of full stadium photographic backgrounds behind the player photos. Like all Kahn's issues, the 1956 set is unnumbered; the checklists are arranged alphabetically for convenience. The set features the first-ever baseball card of Hall of Famer Frank Robinson.

	NM	EX	VG
Complete Set (15):	3,250	1,625	1,000
Common Player:	150.00	75.00	45.00
(1) Ed Bailey	150.00	75.00	45.00
(2) Gus Bell	175.00	90.00	55.00
(3) Joe Black	225.00	110.00	65.00
(4) "Smoky" Burgess	200.00	100.00	60.00
(5) Art Fowler	150.00	75.00	45.00
(6) Hershell Freeman	150.00	75.00	45.00
(7) Ray Jablonski	150.00	75.00	45.00
(8) John Klippstein	150.00	75.00	45.00
(9) Ted Kluszewski	365.00	180.00	110.00
(10) Brooks Lawrence	150.00	75.00	45.00
(11) Roy McMillan	150.00	75.00	45.00
(12) Joe Nuxhall	150.00	75.00	45.00
(13) Wally Post	150.00	75.00	45.00
(14) Frank Robinson	1,000	500.00	300.00
(15) Johnny Temple	150.00	75.00	45.00

1957 Kahn's Wieners

Compliments of Kahn's Wieners
"THE WIENER THE WORLD AWAITED"

In its third season of baseball card issue, Kahn's kept the basic 3-1/4" x 4" format, with black-and-white photos and blank backs. The issue was expanded to 28 players, all Pirates or Reds. The last of the blank-backed Kahn's sets until 1966, the 1957 Reds players can be distinguished from the 1956 issue by the general lack of background photo detail, in favor of a neutral light gray background. The Dick Groat card appears with two name variations, a facsimile autograph, "Richard Groat," and a printed "Dick Groat." Both Groat varieties are included in the complete set price.

	NM	EX	VG
Complete Set (29):	4,000	2,000	1,200
Common Player:	80.00	40.00	24.00
(1) Tom Acker	80.00	40.00	24.00
(2) Ed Bailey	80.00	40.00	24.00
(3) Gus Bell	100.00	50.00	30.00
(4) Smoky Burgess	100.00	50.00	30.00
(5) Roberto Clemente	1,250	625.00	375.00
(6) George Crowe	80.00	40.00	24.00
(7) Elroy Face	80.00	40.00	24.00
(8) Hershell Freeman	80.00	40.00	24.00
(9) Robert Friend	80.00	40.00	24.00
(10a) Dick Groat	190.00	95.00	55.00
(10b) Richard Groat	190.00	95.00	55.00
(11) Don Gross	80.00	40.00	24.00
(12) Warren Hacker	80.00	40.00	24.00
(13) Don Hoak	80.00	40.00	24.00
(14) Hal Jeffcoat	80.00	40.00	24.00
(15) Ron Kline	80.00	40.00	24.00
(16) John Klippstein	80.00	40.00	24.00
(17) Ted Kluszewski	225.00	110.00	65.00
(18) Brooks Lawrence	80.00	40.00	24.00
(19) Dale Long	80.00	40.00	24.00
(20) Bill Mazeroski	325.00	160.00	95.00

(21) Roy McMillan	80.00	40.00	24.00
(22) Joe Nuxhall	80.00	40.00	24.00
(23) Wally Post	80.00	40.00	24.00
(24) Frank Robinson	300.00	150.00	90.00
(25) Johnny Temple	80.00	40.00	24.00
(26) Frank Thomas	80.00	40.00	24.00
(27) Bob Thurman	80.00	40.00	24.00
(28) Lee Walls	80.00	40.00	24.00

1958 Kahn's Wieners

Compliments of Kahn's Wieners
"THE WIENER THE WORLD AWAITED"

MY GREATEST THRILL IN BASEBALL
By GEORGE CROWE

I've had lots of big and little thrills in my baseball career, both in the minors and when I was playing with Milwaukee. Looking back, I think my biggest moment was really a whole season long. It was the 1957 season when I was playing first base for the Cincinnati Redlegs.

I played in 133 games that year, managed to hit 31 home runs and drive in 92 runs, leading the Redlegs in both departments that year. No doubt about it—1957 was my top thrill in baseball.

Long-time Cincinnati favorite Wally Post became the only Philadelphia Phillies ballplayer to appear in the 15-year run of Kahn's issues when he was traded in 1958, but included as part of the otherwise exclusively Pirates-Reds set. Like previous years, the '58 Kahn's were 3-1/4" x 4", with black and white player photos. Unlike previous years, however, the cards had printing on the back, a story by the pictured player, titled "My Greatest Thrill in Baseball." Quite similar to the 1959 issue, the '58 Kahn's can be distinguished by the fact that the top line of the advertising panel at bottom has the word "Wieners" in 1958, but not in 1959. Several of cards in the set appear to have been short-printed.

	NM	EX	VG
Complete Set (29):	4,500	2,250	1,350
Common Player:	100.00	50.00	30.00
(1) Ed Bailey	100.00	50.00	30.00
(2) Gene Baker	100.00	50.00	30.00
(3) Gus Bell	110.00	55.00	35.00
(4) Smoky Burgess	110.00	55.00	35.00
(5) Roberto Clemente	900.00	450.00	275.00
(6) George Crowe	100.00	50.00	30.00
(7) Elroy Face	100.00	50.00	30.00
(8) Henry Foiles	100.00	50.00	30.00
(9) Dee Fondy	100.00	50.00	30.00
(10) Robert Friend	100.00	50.00	30.00
(11) Richard Groat	110.00	55.00	35.00
(12) Harvey Haddix	100.00	50.00	30.00
(13) Don Hoak	110.00	55.00	35.00
(14) Hal Jeffcoat	110.00	55.00	35.00
(15) Ronald L. Law	110.00	55.00	35.00
(16) Ted Kluszewski	200.00	100.00	60.00
(17) Vernon Law	100.00	50.00	30.00
(18) Brooks Lawrence	100.00	50.00	30.00
(19) Bill Mazeroski	300.00	150.00	90.00
(20) Roy McMillan	100.00	50.00	30.00
(21) Joe Nuxhall	100.00	50.00	30.00
(22) Wally Post	300.00	150.00	90.00
(23) John Powers	100.00	50.00	30.00
(24) Robert T. Purkey	100.00	50.00	30.00
(25) Charles Rabe	300.00	150.00	90.00
(26) Frank Robinson	600.00	300.00	180.00
(27) Robert Skinner	100.00	50.00	30.00
(28) Johnny Temple	100.00	50.00	30.00
(29) Frank Thomas	300.00	150.00	90.00

1959 Kahn's Wieners

Compliments of Kahn's
"THE WIENER THE WORLD AWAITED"

THE TOUGHEST PLAY I HAVE TO MAKE
by VADA PINSON

The most difficult play I've ever had to make in baseball was a game with Cincinnati against the Giants. It was a diving catch in the outfield with a man on second base. I think that's a difficult play in anyone's book. If the ball gets through, the runner scores and there's another man in scoring position.

"You are how I handled it. Well, it was a 'do-or-die' trick, but with a bit of luck, I was able to come up with the ball and stop a run from scoring."

A third team was added to the Kahn's lineup in 1959, the Cleveland Indians joining the Pirates and Reds. Again printed in black-and-white in the 3-1/4" x 4" size, the 1959 Kahn's cards can be differentiated from the previous issue by the lack of the word "Wieners" on the top line of the advertising panel at bottom. Backs again featured a story written by the pictured player, such as "The Toughest Play I Had to Make," "My Most Difficult Moment in Baseball," etc. A number of the cards were short-printed.

	NM	EX	VG
Complete Set (38):	6,000	3,000	1,800
Common Player:	75.00	37.50	22.50
(1) Ed Bailey	75.00	37.50	22.50
(2) Gary Bell	75.00	37.50	22.50
(3) Gus Bell	75.00	37.50	22.50
(4) Richard Brodowski	500.00	250.00	150.00
(5) Forrest Burgess	75.00	37.50	22.50
(6) Roberto Clemente	850.00	425.00	255.00
(7) Rocky Colavito	325.00	160.00	100.00
(8) ElRoy Face	75.00	37.50	22.50
(9) Robert Friend	75.00	37.50	22.50
(10) Joe Gordon	75.00	37.50	22.50
(11) Jim Grant	75.00	37.50	22.50

(12) Richard M. Groat	90.00	45.00	27.00
(13) Harvey Haddix	450.00	225.00	135.00
(14) Woodie Held	450.00	225.00	135.00
(15) Don Hoak	75.00	37.50	22.50
(16) Ronald Kline	75.00	37.50	22.50
(17) Ted Kluszewski	200.00	100.00	60.00
(18) Vernon Law	75.00	37.50	22.50
(19) Jerry Lynch	75.00	37.50	22.50
(20) Billy Martin	115.00	55.00	35.00
(21) Bill Mazeroski	250.00	125.00	75.00
(22) Cal McLish	450.00	225.00	135.00
(23) Roy McMillan	75.00	37.50	22.50
(24) Minnie Minoso	80.00	40.00	24.00
(25) Russell Nixon	75.00	37.50	22.50
(26) Joe Nuxhall	75.00	37.50	22.50
(27) Jim Perry	75.00	37.50	22.50
(28) Vada Pinson	200.00	100.00	60.00
(29) Vic Power	75.00	37.50	22.50
(30) Robert Purkey	75.00	37.50	22.50
(31) Frank Robinson	235.00	120.00	75.00
(32) Herb Score	75.00	37.50	22.50
(33) Robert Skinner	75.00	37.50	22.50
(34) George Strickland	275.00	135.00	85.00
(35) Richard L. Stuart	75.00	37.50	22.50
(36) John Temple	75.00	37.50	22.50
(37) Frank Thomas	75.00	37.50	22.50
(38) George A. Witt	75.00	37.50	22.50

1960 Kahn's Wieners

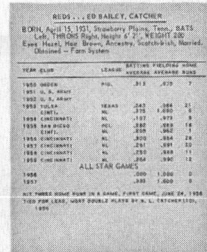

Compliments of Kahn's
"THE WIENER THE WORLD AWAITED"

Three more teams joined the Kahn's roster in 1960, the Chicago Cubs, Chicago White Sox and St. Louis Cardinals. Again 3-1/4" x 4" with black-and-white photos, the 1960 Kahn's cards featured for the first time player stats and personal data on the back, except Harvey Kuenn, which was issued with blank back, probably because of the lateness of his trade to the Indians.

	NM	EX	VG
Complete Set (42):	3,000	1,500	900.00
Common Player:	40.00	20.00	12.00
(1) Ed Bailey	40.00	20.00	12.00
(2) Gary Bell	40.00	20.00	12.00
(3) Gus Bell	45.00	22.50	13.50
(4) Forrest Burgess	45.00	22.50	13.50
(5) Gino N. Cimoli	40.00	20.00	12.00
(6) Roberto Clemente	725.00	360.00	215.00
(7) ElRoy Face	40.00	20.00	12.00
(8) Tito Francona	40.00	20.00	12.00
(9) Robert Friend	40.00	20.00	12.00
(10) Jim Grant	40.00	20.00	12.00
(11) Richard Groat	40.00	20.00	12.00
(12) Harvey Haddix	40.00	20.00	12.00
(13) Woodie Held	40.00	20.00	12.00
(14) Bill Henry	40.00	20.00	12.00
(15) Don Hoak	40.00	20.00	12.00
(16) Jay Hook	40.00	20.00	12.00
(17) Eddie Kasko	40.00	20.00	12.00
(18) Ronnie Kline	50.00	25.00	15.00
(19) Ted Kluszewski	300.00	150.00	90.00
(20) Harvey Kuenn	200.00	100.00	60.00
(21) Vernon S. Law	45.00	22.50	13.50
(22) Brooks Lawrence	40.00	20.00	12.00
(23) Jerry Lynch	40.00	20.00	12.00
(24) Billy Martin	90.00	45.00	27.00
(25) Bill Mazeroski	150.00	75.00	45.00
(26) Cal McLish	40.00	20.00	12.00
(27) Roy McMillan	40.00	20.00	12.00
(28) Don Newcombe	45.00	22.50	13.50
(29) Russ Nixon	40.00	20.00	12.00
(30) Joe Nuxhall	40.00	20.00	12.00
(31) James J. O'Toole	40.00	20.00	12.00
(32) Jim Perry	45.00	22.00	13.50
(33) Vada Pinson	65.00	32.50	20.00
(34) Vic Power	40.00	20.00	12.00
(35) Robert T. Purkey	40.00	20.00	12.00
(36) Frank Robinson	200.00	100.00	60.00
(37) Herb Score	45.00	22.50	13.50
(38) Robert R. Skinner	40.00	20.00	12.00
(39) Richard L. Stuart	40.00	20.00	12.00
(40) John Temple	40.00	20.00	12.00
(41) Frank Thomas	50.00	25.00	15.00
(42) Lee Walls	40.00	20.00	12.00

1961 Kahn's Wieners

Compliments of Kahn's
"THE WIENER THE WORLD AWAITED"

After a single season, the Chicago and St. Louis teams dropped out of the Kahn's program, but the 1961 set was larger than ever, at 43 cards. The same basic format - 3-1/4" x 4" size, black-and-white photos and statistical information on the back - was retained. For the first time in '61, the meat company made complete sets of the Kahn's cards available to collectors via a mail-in offer. This makes the 1961 and later Kahn's cards considerably easier to obtain than the earlier issues.

		NM	EX	VG
Complete Set (43):		2,650	1,300	800.00
Common Player:		40.00	20.00	12.00
(1)	John A. Antonelli	40.00	20.00	12.00
(2)	Ed Bailey	40.00	20.00	12.00
(3)	Gary Bell	40.00	20.00	12.00
(4)	Gus Bell	45.00	22.00	13.50
(5)	James P. Brosnan	40.00	20.00	12.00
(6)	Forrest Burgess	45.00	22.00	13.50
(7)	Gino Cimoli	40.00	20.00	12.00
(8)	Roberto Clemente	825.00	410.00	245.00
(9)	Gordon Coleman	40.00	20.00	12.00
(10)	Jimmie Dykes	40.00	20.00	12.00
(11)	ElRoy Face	40.00	20.00	12.00
(12)	Tito Francona	40.00	20.00	12.00
(13)	Gene L. Freese	40.00	20.00	12.00
(14)	Robert Friend	40.00	20.00	12.00
(15)	Jim Grant	40.00	20.00	12.00
(16)	Richard M. Groat	40.00	20.00	12.00
(17)	Harvey Haddix	40.00	20.00	12.00
(18)	Woodie Held	40.00	20.00	12.00
(19)	Don Hoak	40.00	20.00	12.00
(20)	Jay Hook	40.00	20.00	12.00
(21)	Joe Jay	40.00	20.00	12.00
(22)	Eddie Kasko	40.00	20.00	12.00
(23)	Willie Kirkland	40.00	20.00	12.00
(24)	Vernon S. Law	40.00	20.00	12.00
(25)	Jerry Lynch	40.00	20.00	12.00
(26)	Jim Maloney	40.00	20.00	12.00
(27)	Bill Mazeroski	150.00	75.00	45.00
(28)	Wilmer D. Mizell	40.00	20.00	12.00
(29)	Glenn R. Nelson	40.00	20.00	12.00
(30)	James J. O'Toole	40.00	20.00	12.00
(31)	Jim Perry	40.00	20.00	12.00
(32)	John M. Phillips	40.00	20.00	12.00
(33)	Vada E. Pinson Jr.	55.00	27.00	16.50
(34)	Wally Post	40.00	20.00	12.00
(35)	Vic Power	40.00	20.00	12.00
(36)	Robert T. Purkey	40.00	20.00	12.00
(37)	Frank Robinson	250.00	125.00	75.00
(38)	John A. Romano Jr.	40.00	20.00	12.00
(39)	Dick Schofield	40.00	20.00	12.00
(40)	Robert Skinner	40.00	20.00	12.00
(41)	Hal Smith	40.00	20.00	12.00
(42)	Richard Stuart	40.00	20.00	12.00
(43)	John E. Temple	40.00	20.00	12.00

1962 Kahn's Wieners

Compliments of Kahn's
"THE WIENER THE WORLD AWAITED"

Besides the familiar Reds, Pirates and Indians players in the 1962 Kahn's set, a fourth team was added, the Minnesota Twins, though the overall size of the set was decreased from the previous year, to 38 players in 1962. The cards retained the 3-1/4" x 4" black-and-white format of previous years. The '62 Kahn's set is awash in variations. Besides the photo and front design variations on the Bell, Purkey and Power cards, each Cleveland player can be found with two back variations, listing the team either as "Cleveland" or "Cleveland Indians." The complete set values listed below include all variations.

		NM	EX	VG
Complete Set (51):		2,250	1,125	675.00
Common Player:		15.00	7.50	4.50
(1a)	Gary Bell (Cleveland Indians back.)	100.00	50.00	30.00
(1b)	Gary Bell (Cleveland back.)	35.00	17.50	10.00
(2)	James P. Brosnan	15.00	7.50	4.50
(3)	Forrest Burgess	30.00	15.00	9.00
(4)	Leonardo Cardenas	15.00	7.50	4.50
(5)	Roberto Clemente	250.00	125.00	75.00
(6a)	Ty Cline (Cleveland Indians back.)	70.00	35.00	20.00
(6b)	Ty Cline (Cleveland back.)	30.00	15.00	9.00
(7)	Gordon Coleman	15.00	7.50	4.50
(8)	Dick Donovan	30.00	15.00	9.00
(9)	John Edwards	15.00	7.50	4.50
(10a)	Tito Francona (Cleveland Indians back.)	70.00	35.00	20.00
(10b)	Tito Francona (Cleveland back.)	30.00	15.00	9.00
(11)	Gene Freese	15.00	7.50	4.50
(12)	Robert B. Friend	20.00	10.00	6.00
(13)	Joe Gibbon	75.00	37.50	22.50
(14a)	Jim Grant (Cleveland Indians back.)	70.00	35.00	20.00
(14b)	Jim Grant (Cleveland back.)	30.00	15.00	9.00
(15)	Richard M. Groat	40.00	20.00	12.00
(16)	Harvey Haddix	15.00	7.50	4.50

		NM	EX	VG
(17a)	Woodie Held (Cleveland Indians back.)	70.00	35.00	20.00
(17b)	Woodie Held (Cleveland back.)	30.00	15.00	9.00
(18)	Bill Henry	15.00	7.50	4.50
(19)	Don Hoak	15.00	7.50	4.50
(20)	Ken Hunt	15.00	7.50	4.50
(21)	Joseph R. Jay	15.00	7.50	4.50
(22)	Eddie Kasko	15.00	7.50	4.50
(23a)	Willie Kirkland (Cleveland Indians back.)	70.00	35.00	20.00
(23b)	Willie Kirkland (Cleveland back.)	30.00	15.00	9.00
(24a)	Barry Latman (Cleveland Indians back.)	70.00	35.00	20.00
(24b)	Barry Latman (Cleveland back.)	30.00	15.00	9.00
(25)	Jerry Lynch	15.00	7.50	4.50
(26)	Jim Maloney	20.00	10.00	6.00
(27)	Bill Mazeroski	100.00	50.00	30.00
(28)	Jim O'Toole	15.00	7.50	4.50
(29a)	Jim Perry (Cleveland Indians back.)	70.00	35.00	20.00
(29b)	Jim Perry (Cleveland back.)	30.00	15.00	9.00
(30a)	John M. Phillips (Cleveland Indians back.)	70.00	35.00	20.00
(30b)	John M. Phillips (Cleveland back.)	30.00	15.00	9.00
(31)	Vada E. Pinson	30.00	15.00	9.00
(32)	Wally Post	15.00	7.50	4.50
(33a)	Vic Power (Cleveland Indians back.)	70.00	35.00	20.00
(33b)	Vic Power (Cleveland back.)	30.00	15.00	9.00
(33c)	Vic Power (Minnesota Twins back.)	150.00	75.00	45.00
(34a)	Robert T. Purkey (No autograph.)	150.00	75.00	45.00
(34b)	Robert T. Purkey (With autograph.)	35.00	17.50	10.00
(35)	Frank Robinson	100.00	50.00	30.00
(36a)	John Romano (Cleveland Indians back.)	70.00	35.00	20.00
(36b)	John Romano (Cleveland back.)	30.00	15.00	9.00
(37)	Dick Stuart	15.00	7.50	4.50
(38)	Bill Virdon	15.00	7.50	4.50

1963 Kahn's Wieners

Compliments of Kahn's
"THE WIENER THE WORLD AWAITED"

In 1963, for the first time since Kahn's began issuing baseball cards in 1955, the design underwent a significant change, white borders were added to the top and sides of player photo. Also, the card size was changed to 3-3/16" x 4-1/4". Statistical and personal data continued to be printed on the card backs. Joining traditional Reds, Pirates and Indians personnel in the 1963 set were a handful of New York Yankees and Dick Groat, in his new identity as a St. Louis Cardinal.

		NM	EX	VG
Complete Set (30):		2,400	1,200	750.00
Common Player:		60.00	30.00	20.00
(1)	Robert Bailey	60.00	30.00	20.00
(2)	Don Blasingame	60.00	30.00	20.00
(3)	Clete Boyer	120.00	60.00	40.00
(4)	Forrest Burgess	75.00	40.00	25.00
(5)	Leonardo Cardenas	60.00	30.00	20.00
(6)	Roberto Clemente	420.00	220.00	125.00
(7)	Don Clendennon (Don Clendenon)	60.00	30.00	20.00
(8)	Gordon Coleman	60.00	30.00	20.00
(9)	John A. Edwards	60.00	30.00	20.00
(10)	Gene Freese	60.00	30.00	20.00
(11)	Robert B. Friend	60.00	30.00	20.00
(12)	Joe Gibbon	60.00	30.00	20.00
(13)	Dick Groat	120.00	60.00	40.00
(14)	Harvey Haddix	60.00	30.00	20.00
(15)	Elston Howard	120.00	60.00	40.00
(16)	Joey Jay	60.00	30.00	20.00
(17)	Eddie Kasko	60.00	30.00	20.00
(18)	Tony Kubek	120.00	60.00	40.00
(19)	Jerry Lynch	60.00	30.00	20.00
(20)	Jim Maloney	75.00	40.00	25.00
(21)	Bill Mazeroski	180.00	90.00	50.00
(22)	Joe Nuxhall	75.00	40.00	25.00
(23)	Jim O'Toole	60.00	30.00	20.00
(24)	Vada E. Pinson	120.00	60.00	40.00
(25)	Robert T. Purkey	60.00	30.00	20.00
(26)	Bob Richardson	120.00	60.00	40.00
(27)	Frank Robinson	250.00	125.00	75.00
(28)	Bill Stafford	75.00	40.00	25.00
(29)	Ralph W. Terry	75.00	40.00	25.00
(30)	Bill Virdon	75.00	40.00	25.00

1964 Kahn's Wieners

After nearly a decade of virtually identical card issues, the 1964 Kahn's issue was an abrupt change. In a new size, 3" x 3-1/2", the nearly square cards featured a borderless color photo. The only other design element on the front of the card

JOHN "HONEY" ROMANO (Catcher)

Compliments of Kahn's
"THE WIENER THE WORLD AWAITED"

was a facsimile autograph. The advertising slogan which had traditionally appeared on the front of the card was moved to the back, where it joined the player's stats and personal data. The teams in the 1964 issue once again reverted to the Reds, Pirates and Indians.

		NM	EX	VG
Complete Set (31):		1,150	600.00	350.00
Common Player:		20.00	10.00	6.00
(1)	Max Alvis	20.00	10.00	6.00
(2)	Bob Bailey	20.00	10.00	6.00
(3)	Leonardo Cardenas	20.00	10.00	6.00
(4)	Roberto Clemente	300.00	150.00	90.00
(5)	Donn A. Clendenon	20.00	10.00	6.00
(6)	Victor Davalillo	20.00	10.00	6.00
(7)	Dick Donovan	20.00	10.00	6.00
(8)	John A. Edwards	20.00	10.00	6.00
(9)	Robert Friend	20.00	10.00	6.00
(10)	Jim Grant	20.00	10.00	6.00
(11)	Tommy Harper	20.00	10.00	6.00
(12)	Woodie Held	20.00	10.00	6.00
(13)	Joey Jay	20.00	10.00	6.00
(14)	Jack Kralick	20.00	10.00	6.00
(15)	Jerry Lynch	20.00	10.00	6.00
(16)	Jim Maloney	20.00	10.00	6.00
(17)	Bill Mazeroski	75.00	37.50	22.00
(18)	Alvin McBean	20.00	10.00	6.00
(19)	Joe Nuxhall	20.00	10.00	6.00
(20)	Jim Pagliaroni	20.00	10.00	6.00
(21)	Vada E. Pinson Jr.	35.00	17.50	10.00
(22)	Robert T. Purkey	20.00	10.00	6.00
(23)	Pedro Ramos	20.00	10.00	6.00
(24)	Frank Robinson	75.00	37.50	22.50
(25)	John Romano	20.00	10.00	6.00
(26)	Pete Rose	250.00	125.00	75.00
(27)	John Tsitouris	20.00	10.00	6.00
(28)	Robert A. Veale Jr.	20.00	10.00	6.00
(29)	Bill Virdon	20.00	10.00	6.00
(30)	Leon Wagner	20.00	10.00	6.00
(31)	Fred Whitfield	20.00	10.00	6.00

1965 Kahn's Wieners

Compliments of Kahn's
"THE WIENER THE WORLD AWAITED"

There was little change for the Kahn's issue in 1965 beyond the addition of Milwaukee Braves players to the Reds, Pirates and Indians traditionally included in the set. At 45 players, the 1965 issue was the largest of the Kahn's sets. Once again in 3" x 3-1/2" size, the 1965s retained the borderless color photo design of the previous season. A look at the stats on the back will confirm the year of issue, allowing differentiation between the 1964 and 1965 cards.

		NM	EX	VG
Complete Set (45):		1,750	875.00	520.00
Common Player:		20.00	10.00	6.00
(1)	Hank Aaron	180.00	90.00	50.00
(2)	Max Alvis	20.00	10.00	6.00
(3)	Jose Azcue	20.00	10.00	6.00
(4)	Bob Bailey	20.00	10.00	6.00
(5)	Frank Bolling	20.00	10.00	6.00
(6)	Leonardo Cardenas	20.00	10.00	6.00
(7)	Rico Ricardo Carty	20.00	10.00	6.00
(8)	Donn A. Clendenon	20.00	10.00	6.00
(9)	Tony Cloninger	20.00	10.00	6.00
(10)	Gordon Coleman	20.00	10.00	6.00
(11)	Victor Davalillo	20.00	10.00	6.00
(12)	John A. Edwards	20.00	10.00	6.00
(13)	Sam Ellis	20.00	10.00	6.00
(14)	Robert Friend	20.00	10.00	6.00
(15)	Tommy Harper	20.00	10.00	6.00
(16)	Chuck Hinton	20.00	10.00	6.00
(17)	Dick Howser	20.00	10.00	6.00
(18)	Joey Jay	20.00	10.00	6.00
(19)	Deron Johnson	20.00	10.00	6.00
(20)	Jack Kralick	20.00	10.00	6.00
(21)	Denny Lemaster	20.00	10.00	6.00
(22)	Jerry Lynch	20.00	10.00	6.00
(23)	Jim Maloney	20.00	10.00	6.00
(24)	Lee Maye	20.00	10.00	6.00
(25)	Bill Mazeroski	80.00	40.00	25.00
(26)	Alvin McBean	20.00	10.00	6.00
(27)	Bill McCool	20.00	10.00	6.00
(28)	Sam McDowell	30.00	15.00	9.00
(29)	Donald McMahon	20.00	10.00	6.00

		NM	EX	VG
(30)	Denis Menke	20.00	10.00	6.00
(31)	Joe Nuxhall	20.00	10.00	6.00
(32)	Gene Oliver	20.00	10.00	6.00
(33)	Jim O'Toole	20.00	10.00	6.00
(34)	Jim Pagliaroni	20.00	10.00	6.00
(35)	Vada E. Pinson Jr.	35.00	20.00	12.00
(36)	Frank Robinson	140.00	70.00	40.00
(37)	Pete Rose	400.00	200.00	120.00
(38)	Willie Stargell	80.00	40.00	25.00
(39)	Ralph W. Terry	20.00	10.00	6.00
(40)	Luis Tiant	30.00	15.00	9.00
(41)	Joe Torre	35.00	20.00	12.00
(42)	John Tsitouris	20.00	10.00	6.00
(43)	Robert A. Veale Jr.	20.00	10.00	6.00
(44)	Bill Virdon	20.00	10.00	6.00
(45)	Leon Wagner	20.00	10.00	6.00

1966 Kahn's Wieners

The fourth new format in five years greeted collectors with the introduction of Kahn's 1966 issue. The design consists of a color photo bordered by white and yellow vertical stripes. The player's name is printed above the photo, and a facsimile autograph appears across the photo. As printed, the cards are 2-13/16" x 4-9/16" in size. The player photo area is about 2-13/16" x x 2-11/16", separated at top by a dotted line from an advertising panel with a red rose logo and the word "Kahn's" and by a dotted line at bottom from an irregularly shaped piece marked "CUT ALONG DOTTED LINES." Naturally, many of the cards are found today with the top and/or bottom portion cut off. Values listed here are for complete uncut cards; those without the ad portion and bottom panel are valued at 50 percent or less. Players from the Cincinnati Reds, Pittsburgh Pirates, Cleveland Indians and Atlanta Braves were included in the set. Since the cards are blank-backed, collectors must learn to differentiate player poses to determine year of issue for some cards.

		NM	EX	VG
Complete Set (32):		1,250	625.00	375.00
Common Player:		15.00	7.50	4.50
(1)	Henry Aaron	200.00	100.00	60.00
(2)	Felipe Alou	20.00	10.00	6.00
(3)	Max Alvis	15.00	7.50	4.50
(4)	Robert Bailey	15.00	7.50	4.50
(5)	Wade Blasingame	15.00	7.50	4.50
(6)	Frank Bolling	15.00	7.50	4.50
(7)	Leo Cardenas	15.00	7.50	4.50
(8)	Roberto Clemente	400.00	200.00	120.00
(9)	Tony Cloninger	15.00	7.50	4.50
(10)	Vic Davalillo	15.00	7.50	4.50
(11)	John Edwards	15.00	7.50	4.50
(12)	Sam Ellis (White cap.)	15.00	7.50	4.50
(13)	Pedro Gonzalez	15.00	7.50	4.50
(14)	Tommy Harper	15.00	7.50	4.50
(15)	Deron Johnson	15.00	7.50	4.50
(16)	Mack Jones	15.00	7.50	4.50
(17)	Denny Lemaster	15.00	7.50	4.50
(18)	Jim Maloney (White cap.)	15.00	7.50	4.50
(19)	Bill Mazeroski	90.00	45.00	27.00
(20)	Bill McCool	15.00	7.50	4.50
(21)	Sam McDowell	25.00	12.50	7.50
(22)	Denis Menke	15.00	7.50	4.50
(23)	Joe Nuxhall	15.00	7.50	4.50
(24)	Jim Pagliaroni	15.00	7.50	4.50
(25)	Milt Pappas	15.00	7.50	4.50
(26)	Vada Pinson	25.00	12.50	7.50
(27)	Pete Rose (Right hand in glove.)	250.00	125.00	75.00
(28)	Sonny Siebert	15.00	7.50	4.50
(29)	Willie Stargell	90.00	45.00	27.00
(30)	Joe Torre	25.00	12.50	7.50
(31)	Bob Veale	15.00	7.50	4.50
(32)	Fred Whitfield	15.00	7.50	4.50

1967 Kahn's Wieners

Retaining the 1966 format, the '67 Kahn's set was expanded to 41 players by adding several New York Mets to the previous season's lineup of Reds, Pirates, Indians and Braves. Making this set especially challenging for collectors is the fact that some cards are found in a smaller size and/or with different colored stripes bordering the color player photo. On the majority of cards, the size remained about 2-13/16" x 4-9/16" (with ad at top and bottom panel; about 2-13/16" x 2-1/8" when cut on dotted lines). However, because of packing in different products, some cards can be found in 2-13/16" x 3-1/4" size (with ad and bottom panel; 2-13/16" x 2-1/8" without ad). The border stripe variations are listed below. Values quoted are for complete uncut cards; values drop by 50 percent or more for cards without the ad and/or bottom panels. All variation cards are included in the valuations given for the complete set.

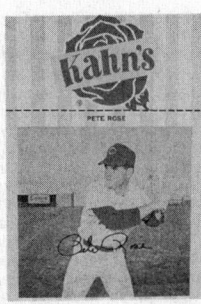

		NM	EX	VG
Complete Set (51):		1,800	900.00	550.00
Common Player:		20.00	10.00	6.00
(1a)	Henry Aaron (Large size.)	125.00	65.00	35.00
(1b)	Henry Aaron (Small size.)	125.00	65.00	35.00
(2)	Gene Alley	20.00	10.00	6.00
(3a)	Felipe Alou (Large size.)	25.00	12.50	7.50
(3b)	Felipe Alou (Small size.)	25.00	12.50	7.50
(4a)	Matty Alou (Yellow & white striped border.)	25.00	12.50	7.50
(4b)	Matty Alou (Red & white striped border.)	30.00	15.00	9.00
(5)	Max Alvis	20.00	10.00	6.00
(6a)	Ken Boyer (Yellow & white striped border.)	30.00	15.00	9.00
(6b)	Ken Boyer (Red, white & green striped border.)	35.00	17.50	10.00
(7)	Leo Cardenas	20.00	10.00	6.00
(8)	Rico Carty	20.00	10.00	6.00
(9)	Tony Cloninger	20.00	10.00	6.00
(10)	Tommy Davis	20.00	10.00	6.00
(11)	John Edwards	20.00	10.00	6.00
(12a)	Sam Ellis (Large size.) (Red cap.)	20.00	10.00	6.00
(12b)	Sam Ellis (Small size.) (Red cap.)	30.00	15.00	9.00
(13)	Jack Fisher	20.00	10.00	6.00
(14)	Steve Hargan	20.00	10.00	6.00
(15)	Tom Harper	20.00	10.00	6.00
(16a)	Tom Helms (Large size.)	20.00	10.00	6.00
(16b)	Tom Helms (Small size.)	35.00	17.50	10.00
(17)	Deron Johnson	20.00	10.00	6.00
(18)	Ken Johnson	20.00	10.00	6.00
(19)	Cleon Jones	20.00	10.00	6.00
(20a)	Ed Kranepool (Yellow & white striped border.)	20.00	10.00	6.00
(20b)	Ed Kranepool (Red & white striped border.)	30.00	15.00	9.00
(21a)	James Maloney (Yellow & white striped border.)	25.00	12.50	7.50
(21b)	James Maloney (Red & white striped border.)	30.00	15.00	9.00
(22)	Lee May	20.00	10.00	6.00
(23a)	Wm. Mazeroski (Large size.)	75.00	37.50	22.50
(23b)	Wm. Mazeroski (Small size.)	75.00	37.50	22.50
(24)	Wm. McCool	20.00	10.00	6.00
(25)	Sam McDowell (Blue sleeves.)	25.00	12.50	7.50
(26)	Dennis Menke (Denis)	20.00	10.00	6.00
(27)	Jim Pagliaroni	20.00	10.00	6.00
(28)	Don Pavletich	20.00	10.00	6.00
(29)	Tony Perez	60.00	30.00	18.00
(30)	Vada Pinson	30.00	15.00	9.00
(31)	Dennis Ribant	20.00	10.00	6.00
(32)	Pete Rose (Batting)	275.00	135.00	85.00
(33)	Art Shamsky	20.00	10.00	6.00
(34)	Bob Shaw	20.00	10.00	6.00
(35)	Sonny Siebert	20.00	10.00	6.00
(36)	Wm. Stargell (First name actually Wilver.)	80.00	40.00	24.00
(37a)	Joe Torre (Large size.)	35.00	17.50	10.00
(37b)	Joe Torre (Small size.)	35.00	17.50	10.00
(38)	Bob Veale	20.00	10.00	6.00
(39)	Leon Wagner	20.00	10.00	6.00
(40a)	Fred Whitfield (Large size.)	20.00	10.00	6.00
(40b)	Fred Whitfield (Small size.)	20.00	10.00	6.00
(41)	Woody Woodward	20.00	10.00	6.00

1968 Kahn's Wieners

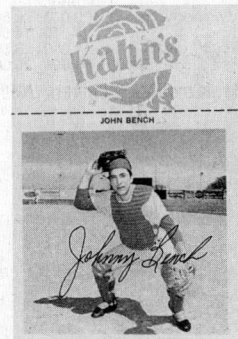

The number of card size and stripe color variations increased with the 1968 Kahn's issue, though the basic card format was retained. Basic size is about 2-13/16" x 4-9/16" with top ad panel and bottom panel intact; 2-13/16" x 2-11/16" with ad and bottom panels cut off. Color photos are bordered by yellow and white vertical stripes. In addition to the basic issue, a number of the cards appear in a smaller, 2-13/16" x

3-1/4", size, while some appear with variations in the color of border stripes. One card, Maloney, can be found with a top portion advertising Blue Mountain brand meats, as well as Kahn's. The 1968 set features the largest number of teams represented in any Kahn's issue: Braves, Cubs, White Sox, Reds, Indians, Tigers, Mets and Pirates. Values quoted are for complete uncut cards, those without the ad and/or bottom panel are worth 50 percent or less. Complete set prices include all variations.

		NM	EX	VG
Complete Set (56):		4,500	2,200	1,350
Common Player:		40.00	20.00	12.00
(1a)	Hank Aaron (Large size.)	200.00	100.00	60.00
(1b)	Hank Aaron (Small size.)	250.00	125.00	75.00
(2)	Tommy Agee	40.00	20.00	12.00
(3a)	Gene Alley (Large size.)	40.00	20.00	12.00
(3b)	Gene Alley (Small size.)	60.00	30.00	18.00
(4)	Felipe Alou	50.00	25.00	15.00
(5a)	Matty Alou (Yellow striped border.)	50.00	25.00	15.00
(5b)	Matty Alou (Red striped border.)	50.00	25.00	15.00
(6a)	Max Alvis (Large size.)	40.00	20.00	12.00
(6b)	Max Alvis (Small size.)	60.00	30.00	18.00
(7)	Gerry Arrigo	40.00	20.00	12.00
(8)	John Bench	650.00	320.00	195.00
(9a)	Clete Boyer (Large size.)	40.00	20.00	12.00
(9b)	Clete Boyer (Small size.)	60.00	30.00	18.00
(10)	Larry Brown	40.00	20.00	12.00
(11a)	Leo Cardenas (Large size.)	40.00	20.00	12.00
(11b)	Leo Cardenas (Small size.)	60.00	30.00	18.00
(12a)	Bill Freehan (Large size.)	60.00	30.00	18.00
(12b)	Bill Freehan (Small size.)	60.00	30.00	18.00
(13)	Steve Hargan	40.00	20.00	12.00
(14)	Joel Horlen	40.00	20.00	12.00
(15)	Tony Horton	60.00	30.00	18.00
(16)	Willie Horton	50.00	25.00	15.00
(17)	Ferguson Jenkins	150.00	75.00	45.00
(18)	Deron Johnson	40.00	20.00	12.00
(19)	Mack Jones	40.00	20.00	12.00
(20)	Bob Lee	40.00	20.00	12.00
(21a)	Jim Maloney (Large size, rose ad.)	50.00	25.00	15.00
(21b)	Jim Maloney (Large size, Blue Mountain logo.)	120.00	60.00	35.00
(21c)	Jim Maloney (Small size, yellow & white striped border.)	60.00	30.00	18.00
(21d)	Jim Maloney (Small size, yellow, white & green striped border.)	60.00	30.00	18.00
(22a)	Lee May (Large size.)	50.00	25.00	15.00
(22b)	Lee May (Small size.)	60.00	30.00	18.00
(23a)	Wm. Mazeroski (Large size.)	100.00	50.00	30.00
(23b)	Wm. Mazeroski (Small size.)	130.00	65.00	40.00
(24)	Dick McAuliffe	40.00	20.00	12.00
(25)	Bill McCool	40.00	20.00	12.00
(26a)	Sam McDowell (Yellow striped border.)	40.00	20.00	12.00
(26b)	Sam McDowell (Red striped border.)	60.00	30.00	18.00
(27a)	Tony Perez (Yellow striped border.)	90.00	45.00	27.00
(27b)	Tony Perez (Red striped border.)	100.00	50.00	30.00
(28)	Gary Peters	40.00	20.00	12.00
(29a)	Vada Pinson (Large size.)	60.00	30.00	18.00
(29b)	Vada Pinson (Small size.)	60.00	30.00	18.00
(30)	Chico Ruiz	40.00	20.00	12.00
(31a)	Ron Santo (Yellow striped border.)	60.00	30.00	18.00
(31b)	Ron Santo (Red striped border.)	80.00	40.00	24.00
(32)	Art Shamsky	40.00	20.00	12.00
(33)	Luis Tiant (Arms above head.)	40.00	20.00	12.00
(34a)	Joe Torre (Large size.)	60.00	30.00	18.00
(34b)	Joe Torre (Small size.)	70.00	35.00	21.00
(35a)	Bob Veale (Large size.)	40.00	20.00	12.00
(35b)	Bob Veale (Small size.)	60.00	30.00	18.00
(36)	Leon Wagner	40.00	20.00	12.00
(37)	Billy Williams	150.00	75.00	45.00
(38)	Earl Wilson	40.00	20.00	12.00

1969 Kahn's Wieners

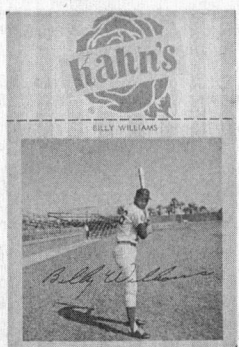

In its 15th consecutive year of baseball card issue, Kahn's continued the format adopted in 1966. The basic 22 players' cards were printed in about 2-13/16" x 4-9/16" size (with ad panel at top and bottom panel; 2-13/16" x 2-11/16" without panels) and are blanked-backed. Teams represented in the set are the Braves, Cubs, White Sox, Reds, Cardinals, Indians and Pirates. Cards feature a color photo and facsimile autograph bordered by yellow and white vertical stripes. At top is an ad panel consisting of the Kahn's red rose logo. However, because some cards were produced for inclusion in packages other than the standard hot dogs, a number of variations in card size and stripe color were created, as noted in the listings. The smaller size cards, 2-13/16" x 3-1/4" with top and bottom panels; 3/16" x 2-1/8" without panels, were created by more closely cropping the player photo at top and bottom. Values quoted are for complete uncut cards with both panels intact; deduct a minimum 50 percent for cards without the ad and/or bottom panel. Complete set values include all variations. For years an (18b) (red-striped border) Ron Santo had been documented. Recent evidence now suggests that such a variations does not exist.

	NM	EX	VG
Complete Set (29):	1,200	600.00	375.00
Common Player:	25.00	12.50	7.50
(1a) Hank Aaron (Large size.)	125.00	62.00	37.00
(1b) Hank Aaron (Small size.)	140.00	70.00	42.00
(2) Matty Alou	25.00	12.50	7.50
(3) Max Alvis	25.00	12.50	7.50
(4) Gerry Arrigo	25.00	12.50	7.50
(5) Steve Blass	25.00	12.50	7.50
(6) Clay Carroll (Follow-through.)	25.00	12.50	7.50
(7) Tony Cloninger	25.00	12.50	7.50
(8) George Culver	25.00	12.50	7.50
(9) Joel Horlen (Follow-through.)	25.00	12.50	7.50
(10) Tony Horton/Btg	35.00	17.50	10.50
(11) Alex Johnson	25.00	12.50	7.50
(12a) Jim Maloney (Large size.) (Arms at sides.)	30.00	15.00	9.00
(12b) Jim Maloney (Small size.) (Arms at sides.)	35.00	17.50	10.50
(13a) Lee May (Yellow striped border.) (Foot on bag.)	30.00	15.00	9.00
(13b) Lee May (Red striped border.) (Foot on bag.)	35.00	17.50	10.50
(14a) Bill Mazeroski (Yellow striped border.)	50.00	25.00	15.00
(14b) Bill Mazeroski (Red striped border.)	55.00	27.00	16.50
(15a) Sam McDowell (Yellow striped border.) (Right leg raised.)	30.00	15.00	9.00
(15b) Sam McDowell (Red striped border.) (Right leg raised.)	35.00	17.50	10.50
(16a) Tony Perez (Large size.) (Glove on base.)	60.00	30.00	18.00
(16b) Tony Perez (Small size.) (Glove on base.)	75.00	37.50	22.50
(17) Gary Peters (Follow-through.)	25.00	12.50	7.50
(18a) Ron Santo (Yellow striped border.)	50.00	25.00	15.00
(18b) Ron Santo (Red striped border. Now believed not to exist.)			
(19) Luis Tiant (Arms at knees.)	25.00	12.50	7.50
(20) Joe Torre	35.00	17.50	10.50
(21) Bob Veale	25.00	12.50	7.50
(22) Billy Williams (Bat behind head.)	80.00	40.00	24.00

1970s Kahn's Kielbasa Singles Carl Yastrzemski

The exact year or years of this label's issue are not known. The 4-7/8" x 3-1/8" cardboard package insert has a color portrait photo of baseball's most famous Polish player endorsing the polish sausage product.

	NM	EX	VG
Carl Yastrzemski	15.00	7.50	4.50

1887 Kalamazoo Bats (N690)

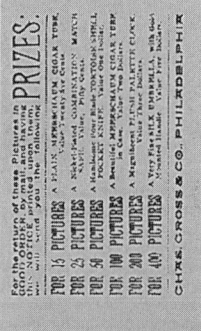

This set, issued circa 1887 by Charles Gross & Co. Phila., is one of the most difficult of all 19th Century tobacco issues. The cards measure a rather large 2-1/4" x 4" and feature a sepia-toned photograph on heavy cardboard. The player's name and team appear inside a white strip at the bottom of the photo, while a small ad for Kalamazoo Bats cigarettes is printed at the very bottom of the card. Some cards carry an 1887 copyright line, but there are indications that some of the cards date from 1886 or 1888. The unnumbered set pictures players from four teams - two from New York (Giants and Mets) and two from Philadelphia (Athletics and Phillies). A few of the cards picture more than one player, and some Philadelphia cards have been found with an ad on the back offering various prizes in exchange for saving the cards. The set has been assigned the American Card Catalog number N690. This checklist is likely not complete. Players from the New York teams are significantly rarer than those of the Philadelphia teams.

	NM	EX	VG
Common Player:	11,000	5,500	3,250
Advertising-back: 1.5X			
(1) Ed Andrews	11,000	5,500	3,250
(2) Charles Bastian, Lyons	11,000	5,500	3,250
(3) Lou Bierbauer	11,000	5,500	3,250
(4) Lou Bierbauer, Gallagher	11,000	5,500	3,250
(5) Charles Buffington (Buffinton)	11,000	5,500	3,250
(6) Dan Casey	11,000	5,500	3,250
(7) Jack Clements	11,000	5,500	3,250
(8) Roger Connor (Three known.)	65,000	24,000	16,000
(9) Larry Corcoran	24,000	12,000	7,250
(10) Ed Cushman	24,000	12,000	7,250
(11) Pat Deasley	24,000	12,000	7,250
(12) Jim Devlin	11,000	5,500	3,250
(13) Jim Donahue	24,000	12,000	7,250
(14) Mike Dorgan	24,000	12,000	7,250
(15) Dude Esterbrooke (Esterbrook)	24,000	12,000	7,250
(16) Buck Ewing (Possibly unique.)	85,000	27,000	18,000
(17) Sid Farrar	11,000	5,500	3,250
(18) Charlie Ferguson	11,000	5,500	3,250
(19) Jim Fogarty	11,000	5,500	3,250
(20) Jim Fogarty, Deacon McGuire	11,000	5,500	3,250
(21) Elmer Foster	24,000	12,000	7,250
(22) Whitey Gibson	11,000	5,500	3,250
(23) Pete Gillespie	24,000	12,000	7,250
(24) Tom Gunning	11,000	5,500	3,250
(25) Arthur Irwin	11,000	5,500	3,250
(26) Arthur Irwin, Al Maul	11,000	5,500	3,250
(27) Tim Keefe	65,000	21,000	14,000
(28) Henry Larkin	11,000	5,500	3,250
(29) Henry Larkins (Larkin), Jocko Milligan	11,000	5,500	3,250
(30) Jack Lynch	24,000	12,000	7,250
(31) Denny Lyons (Athletics)	11,000	5,500	3,250
(32) Harry Lyons (Phila.)	7,000	4,200	2,800
(33) Harry Lyons (Phila.), Billy Taylor	7,000	4,200	2,800
(34) Fred Mann	7,000	4,200	2,800
(35) Charlie Mason	7,000	4,200	2,800
(36) Bobby Mathews	7,000	4,200	2,800
(37) Al Maul	11,000	5,500	3,250
(38) Al Mays	24,000	12,000	7,250
(39) Chippy McGan (McGarr)	11,000	5,500	3,250
(40) Deacon McGuire (Catching)	11,000	5,500	3,250
(41) Deacon McGuire (Throwing)	11,000	5,500	3,250
(42) Tom McLaughlin	24,000	12,000	7,250
(43) Jocko Milligan, Harry Stowe (Stovey)	11,000	5,500	3,250
(44) Joseph Mulvey	11,000	5,500	3,250
(45) Candy Nelson	24,000	12,000	7,250
(46) Orator Jim O'Rourke (Possibly unique.)	75,000	21,000	14,000
(47) Dave Orr	24,000	12,000	7,250
(48) Tom Poorman	11,000	5,500	3,250
(49) Danny Richardson	24,000	12,000	7,250
(50) Wilbert Robinson	15,000	7,500	4,500
(51) Wilbert Robinson, Fred Mann	15,000	7,500	4,500
(52) Chief Roseman	24,000	12,000	7,250
(53) Ed Seward (Possibly unique.)	20,000	10,000	6,000
(54) Harry Stowe (Stovey) (Hands on hips.)	75,000	21,000	14,000
(55) Harry Stowe (Stovey) (Hands outstretched.)	11,000	5,500	3,250
(56) George Townsend	11,000	5,500	3,250
(57) Jocko Milligan, George Townsend	12,500	6,250	3,750
(58) John Ward (Possibly unique.)	100,000	28,500	19,000
(59) Gus Weyhing	24,000	14,500	9,500
(60) George Wood	11,000	5,500	3,250
(61) Harry Wright	40,000	25,000	15,000

1887 Kalamazoo Bats Cabinets (N690-1)

This extremely rare issue of cabinet cards was issued as a premium by Charles Gross & Co. of Philadelphia, makers of the Kalamazoo Bats brand of cigarettes. Two distinct types have been found, both measuring 4-1/4" x 6-1/2". One variety displays the photo on a black mount with the words "Smoke Kalamazoo Bats" embossed in gold to the left. The other contains no advertising, although there is an oval embossment on the card, along with the words "Chas. Gross & Co." and an 1887 copyright line. These cards also have a distinctive pink color on the back of the cardboard mount. Because of the rarity of Kalamazoo Bats cabinets, and uncertainty as to completeness of this checklist, gaps have been left in the assigned numbering.

	NM	EX	VG
Common Player:	15,000	7,500	4,500
(1) Ed Andrews	15,000	7,500	4,500
(2) Charles Bastian, Daniel Casey, Billy Taylor	15,000	7,500	4,500
(3) Charles Bastian, Denny Lyons	15,000	7,500	4,500
(4) Louis Bierbauer, Gallagher	15,000	7,500	4,500
(5) Charles Buffington (Buffinton)	15,000	7,500	4,500
(6) Daniel Casey	15,000	7,500	4,500
(7) Jack Clements	15,000	7,500	4,500
(8) Jim Devlin	15,000	7,500	4,500
(9) Sid Farrar	15,000	7,500	4,500
(10) Charlie Ferguson	15,000	7,500	4,500
(11) Jim Fogarty	15,000	7,500	4,500
(12) Whitey Gibson	15,000	7,500	4,500
(13) Tom Gunning	15,000	7,500	4,500
(14) Arthur Irwin	15,000	7,500	4,500
(15) Arthur Irwin, Al Maul	15,000	7,500	4,500
(16) Henry Larkins (Larkin), Jocko Milligan	15,000	7,500	4,500
(17) Harry Lyons	15,000	7,500	4,500
(18) Harry Lyons, Billy Taylor	15,000	7,500	4,500
(19) Fred Mann	15,000	7,500	4,500
(20) Fred Mann, Wilbert Robinson	25,000	12,500	7,500
(21) Bobby Mathews	15,000	7,500	4,500
(22) Al Maul	15,000	7,500	4,500
(23) Chippy McCan (McGarr)	15,000	7,500	4,500
(24) Deacon McGuire/Fldg	15,000	7,500	4,500
(25) Deacon McGuire/Throwing	15,000	7,500	4,500
(26) Jocko Milligan, Harry Stowe (Stovey)	15,000	7,500	4,500
(27) Joseph Mulvey	15,000	7,500	4,500
(28) Tom Townsend	15,000	7,500	4,500
(29) Ed Seward	15,000	7,500	4,500
(30) Harry Stowe (Stovey)	15,000	7,500	4,500
(31) George Townsend	15,000	7,500	4,500
(32) George Wood	15,000	7,500	4,500
(33) Harry Wright	62,500	31,250	18,750
(35) Athletic Club (Three known, $9,031 paid in 12/04 auction for Good example.)			
(36) Boston B.B.C. (Believed unique, mount restored, brought $14,434 in 5/05 auction.)			
(37) Detroit B.B.C. (Believed unique)			
(38) Philadelphia B.B.C. (Believed unique, VG, brought $9,935 in 12/04 auction.)			
(39) Pittsburg B.B.C. (Believed unique, sold for $62,299 in Excellent in 12/05 auction.)			

1887 Kalamazoo Bats Team Cards (N693)

The team photos in this set were issued by Charles Gross & Co. of Philadelphia as a promotion for its Kalamazoo Bats brand of cigarettes. The cards, which are similar in design and size (about 4" x 2-1/4") to the related N690 series, are extremely rare. They feature a team photo with the caption in a white box at the bottom of the photo and an ad for Kalamazoo Bats to the left.

	NM	EX	VG
Common Team:	12,000	6,000	3,600
(1) Athletic Club	12,000	6,000	3,600
(2) Baltimore B.B.C.	38,000	19,000	12,000
(3) Boston B.B.C.	30,000	15,000	9,000
(4) Detroit B.B.C.	32,000	16,000	9,500
(5) Philadelphia B.B.C.	15,000	7,500	4,500
(6) Pittsburg B.B.C.	38,000	19,000	12,000

1955 Kansas City Athletics Photo Pack

In the first year following the team's move from Philadelphia to K.C., this set of player pictures was issued, probably sold as a souvenir stand item. The black-and-white photos are in an 8" x 10" format on heavy cardboard. Player poses or portraits are bordered in white with the player name in all-caps at bottom. Backs are blank. This checklist may be incomplete.

VIC POWER

		NM	EX	VG
Complete Set (29):		200.00	100.00	60.00
Common Player:		9.00	4.50	2.75
(1)	Joe Astroth	9.00	4.50	2.75
(2)	Lou Boudreau	25.00	12.50	7.50
(3)	Cloyd Boyer	9.00	4.50	2.75
(4)	Art Ceccarelli	9.00	4.50	2.75
(5)	Harry Craft	9.00	4.50	2.75
(6)	Joe DeMaestri	9.00	4.50	2.75
(7)	Art Ditmar	9.00	4.50	2.75
(8)	Jim Finigan	9.00	4.50	2.75
(9)	Tom Gorman	9.00	4.50	2.75
(10)	Ray Herbert	9.00	4.50	2.75
(11)	Alex Kellner	9.00	4.50	2.75
(12)	Dick Kryhoski	9.00	4.50	2.75
(13)	Jack Littrell	9.00	4.50	2.75
(14)	Hector Lopez	9.00	4.50	2.75
(15)	Oscar Melillo	9.00	4.50	2.75
(16)	Arnie Portocarrero	9.00	4.50	2.75
(17)	Vic Power	15.00	7.50	4.50
(18)	Vic Raschi	12.00	6.00	3.50
(19)	Bill Renna	9.00	4.50	2.75
(20)	Johnny Sain	12.00	6.00	3.50
(21)	Bobby Shantz	12.00	6.00	3.50
(22)	Wilmer Shantz	9.00	4.50	2.75
(23)	Harry Simpson	15.00	7.50	4.50
(24)	Enos Slaughter	30.00	15.00	9.00
(25)	Lou Sleator	9.00	4.50	2.75
(26)	George Susce	9.00	4.50	2.75
(27)	Elmer Valo	9.00	4.50	2.75
(28)	Bill Wilson	9.00	4.50	2.75
(29)	Gus Zernial	15.00	7.50	4.50

1956-61 Kansas City Athletics Photocards

Issued over a period of several years these black-and-white photocards share an identical format. The cards are 3-1/4" x 5-1/2" with borderless poses and facsimile autographs on front. Backs are blank. The unnumbered cards are checklisted here in alphabetical order, though the list is surely not complete. Gaps have been left in the assigned numbering for future additions.

		NM	EX	VG
Common Player:		15.00	7.50	4.50
(1)	Jim Archer	15.00	7.50	4.50
(2)	Mike Baxes	15.00	7.50	4.50
(3)	Zeke Bella	15.00	7.50	4.50
(4)	Lou Boudreau	30.00	15.00	9.00
(5)	Cletis Boyer	20.00	10.00	6.00
(6)	Wally Burnette	15.00	7.50	4.50
(7)	Chico Carrasquel	17.50	8.75	5.25
(8)	Bob Cerv	15.00	7.50	4.50
(9)	Harry Chiti	15.00	7.50	4.50
(10)	Harry Craft	15.00	7.50	4.50
(11)	Jack Crimian	15.00	7.50	4.50
(12)	Bud Daley	15.00	7.50	4.50
(13)	Bob Davis	15.00	7.50	4.50
(14)	Joe DeMaestri	15.00	7.50	4.50
(15)	Art Ditmar	15.00	7.50	4.50
(16)	Jim Ewell/Trainer	15.00	7.50	4.50
(17)	Jim Finigan	15.00	7.50	4.50
(18)	Hank Foiles	15.00	7.50	4.50
(19)	Ned Garver	17.50	8.75	5.25
(20)	Joe Ginsberg	15.00	7.50	4.50
(21)	Tom Gorman (Cap-to-knees.)	15.00	7.50	4.50
(22)	Tom Gorman/Pitching	15.00	7.50	4.50
(23)	Bob Grim	15.00	7.50	4.50
(24)	Johnny Groth	15.00	7.50	4.50
(25)	Kent Hadley	15.00	7.50	4.50
(26)	Ray Herbert	15.00	7.50	4.50
(27)	Troy Herriage	15.00	7.50	4.50

(28)	Whitey Herzog	20.00	10.00	6.00
(29)	Frank House	15.00	7.50	4.50
(32)	Alex Kellner	15.00	7.50	4.50
(33)	Lou Kretlow	15.00	7.50	4.50
(34)	Hec Lopez	15.00	7.50	4.50
(35)	Roger Maris	125.00	62.00	37.00
(36)	Oscar Melillo	15.00	7.50	4.50
(37)	Rance Pless	15.00	7.50	4.50
(38)	Vic Power	20.00	10.00	6.00
(39)	Jose Santiago	15.00	7.50	4.50
(40)	Bobby Shantz	25.00	12.50	7.50
(41)	Harry Simpson	17.50	8.75	5.25
(42)	Lou Skizas	15.00	7.50	4.50
(43)	Enos Slaughter	45.00	22.00	13.50
(44)	Hal Smith	15.00	7.50	4.50
(45)	George Susce	15.00	7.50	4.50
(46)	Wayne Terwilliger	15.00	7.50	4.50
(47)	Charles Thompson	15.00	7.50	4.50
(48)	Dick Tomanek	15.00	7.50	4.50
(49)	Bill Tuttle	15.00	7.50	4.50
(52)	Jack Urban	15.00	7.50	4.50
(53)	Preston Ward	15.00	7.50	4.50
(54)	Dick Williams	17.50	8.75	5.25
(55)	Gus Zernial/Btg	17.50	8.75	5.25
(56)	Gus Zernial/Fldg	17.50	8.75	5.25

1929 Kashin Publications (R316)

This set of 101 unnumbered cards was issued in 25-card boxed series, with cards measuring 3-1/2" x 4-1/2". The cards feature black-and-white photos with the player's name printed in script near the bottom of the photo. Team and league are designated at bottom in printed letters. The backs of the cards are blank. Four of the cards (Hadley, Haines, Siebold and Todt) are considered to be scarcer than the rest of the set. Some cards have been seen with "MADE IN U.S.A." in one of the picture's lower corners; their significance and value are undetermined.

		NM	EX	VG
Complete Set (101):		9,500	4,750	2,750
Common Player:		40.00	20.00	12.00
(1)	Dale Alexander	40.00	20.00	12.00
(2)	Ethan N. Allen	40.00	20.00	12.00
(3)	Larry Benton	40.00	20.00	12.00
(4)	Moe Berg	250.00	125.00	75.00
(5)	Max Bishop	40.00	20.00	12.00
(6)	Del Bissonette	40.00	20.00	12.00
(7)	Lucerne A. Blue	40.00	20.00	12.00
(8)	James Bottomley	100.00	50.00	30.00
(9)	Guy T. Bush	40.00	20.00	12.00
(10)	Harold G. Carlson	40.00	20.00	12.00
(11)	Owen Carroll	40.00	20.00	12.00
(12)	Chalmers W. Cissell (Chalmer)	40.00	20.00	12.00
(13)	Earl Combs	100.00	50.00	30.00
(14)	Hugh M. Critz	40.00	20.00	12.00
(15)	H.J. DeBerry	40.00	20.00	12.00
(16)	Pete Donohue	40.00	20.00	12.00
(17)	Taylor Douthit	40.00	20.00	12.00
(18)	Chas. W. Dressen	40.00	20.00	12.00
(19)	Jimmy Dykes	40.00	20.00	12.00
(20)	Howard Ehmke	40.00	20.00	12.00
(21)	Elwood English	40.00	20.00	12.00
(22)	Urban Faber	100.00	50.00	30.00
(23)	Fred Fitzsimmons	40.00	20.00	12.00
(24)	Lewis A. Fonseca	40.00	20.00	12.00
(25)	Horace H. Ford	40.00	20.00	12.00
(26)	Jimmy Foxx	235.00	115.00	70.00
(27)	Frank Frisch	100.00	50.00	30.00
(28)	Lou Gehrig	1,125	560.00	335.00
(29)	Charles Gehringer	100.00	50.00	30.00
(30)	Leon Goslin	100.00	50.00	30.00
(31)	George Grantham	40.00	20.00	12.00
(32)	Burleigh Grimes	100.00	50.00	30.00
(33)	Robert Grove	200.00	100.00	60.00
(34)	Bump Hadley	150.00	75.00	45.00
(35)	Charlie Hafey	100.00	50.00	30.00
(36)	Jesse J. Haines	250.00	125.00	75.00
(37)	Harvey Hendrick	40.00	20.00	12.00
(38)	Floyd C. Herman	40.00	20.00	12.00
(39)	Andy High	40.00	20.00	12.00
(40)	Urban J. Hodapp	40.00	20.00	12.00
(41)	Frank Hogan	40.00	20.00	12.00
(42)	Rogers Hornsby	175.00	85.00	50.00
(43)	Waite Hoyt	100.00	50.00	30.00
(44)	Willis Hudlin	40.00	20.00	12.00
(45)	Frank O. Hurst	40.00	20.00	12.00
(46)	Charlie Jamieson	40.00	20.00	12.00
(47)	Roy C. Johnson	40.00	20.00	12.00
(48)	Percy Jones	40.00	20.00	12.00
(49)	Sam Jones	40.00	20.00	12.00
(50)	Joseph Judge	40.00	20.00	12.00
(51)	Willie Kamm	40.00	20.00	12.00
(52)	Charles Klein	100.00	50.00	30.00

(53)	Mark Koenig	40.00	20.00	12.00
(54)	Ralph Kress	40.00	20.00	12.00
(55)	Fred M. Leach	40.00	20.00	12.00
(56)	Fred Lindstrom	100.00	50.00	30.00
(57)	Ad Liska	40.00	20.00	12.00
(58)	Fred Lucas (Red)	40.00	20.00	12.00
(59)	Fred Maguire	40.00	20.00	12.00
(60)	Perce L. Malone	40.00	20.00	12.00
(61)	Harry Manush (Henry)	100.00	50.00	30.00
(62)	Walter Maranville	100.00	50.00	30.00
(63)	Douglas McWeeney (McWeeny)	40.00	20.00	12.00
(64)	Oscar Melillo	40.00	20.00	12.00
(65)	Ed "Bing" Miller	40.00	20.00	12.00
(66)	Frank O'Doul	80.00	40.00	24.00
(67)	Melvin Ott	200.00	100.00	60.00
(68)	Herbert Pennock	100.00	50.00	30.00
(69)	William W. Regan	40.00	20.00	12.00
(70)	Harry F. Rice	40.00	20.00	12.00
(71)	Sam Rice	100.00	50.00	30.00
(72)	Lance Richbourgh (Richbourg)	40.00	20.00	12.00
(73)	Eddie Rommel	40.00	20.00	12.00
(74)	Chas. H. Root	40.00	20.00	12.00
(75)	Ed (Edd) Roush	100.00	50.00	30.00
(76)	Harold Ruel (Herold)	40.00	20.00	12.00
(77)	Charles Ruffing	125.00	65.00	35.00
(78)	Jack Russell	40.00	20.00	12.00
(79)	Babe Ruth	1,650	825.00	500.00
(80)	Fred Schulte	40.00	20.00	12.00
(81)	Harry Seibold	150.00	75.00	45.00
(82)	Joe Sewell	100.00	50.00	30.00
(83)	Luke Sewell	40.00	20.00	12.00
(84)	Art Shires	40.00	20.00	12.00
(85)	Al Simmons	100.00	50.00	30.00
(86)	Bob Smith	40.00	20.00	12.00
(87)	Riggs Stephenson	40.00	20.00	12.00
(88)	Wm. H. Terry	100.00	50.00	30.00
(89)	Alphonse Thomas	40.00	20.00	12.00
(90)	Lafayette F. Thompson	40.00	20.00	12.00
(91)	Phil Todt	150.00	75.00	45.00
(92)	Harold J. Traynor	100.00	50.00	30.00
(93)	Dazzy Vance	100.00	50.00	30.00
(94)	Lloyd Waner	100.00	50.00	30.00
(95)	Paul Waner	100.00	50.00	30.00
(96)	Jimmy Welsh	40.00	20.00	12.00
(97)	Earl Whitehill	40.00	20.00	12.00
(98)	A.C. Whitney	40.00	20.00	12.00
(99)	Claude Willoughby	40.00	20.00	12.00
(100)	Hack Wilson	200.00	100.00	60.00
(101)	Tom Zachary	40.00	20.00	12.00

1964 KDKA Pittsburgh Pirates Portraits

Issued prior to the radio/TV stations' much more common color player cards of 1968, this seldom-seen regional issue presents the 1964 Pittsburgh Pirates in a set of 28 large-format (8" x 11-7/8") schedule cards. The cards are printed in sepia tones on blank-backed cardboard. Fronts present a player pose and a '64 Pirates schedule. A redemption offer states that a pair of Bucs' tickets will be given in exchange for a complete set of the portraits, and the pictures will be returned, presumably cancelled in some fashion. The unnumbered cards are checklisted here alphabetically. While the cards advertise the Pirates' broadcasting partners, they were actually issued by Sweet Clean laundry as stiffeners for men's shirts that had been washed. The laundry's name is not mentioned anywhere on the cards.

		NM	EX	VG
Complete Set (28):		3,500	1,750	1,000
Common Player:		100.00	50.00	30.00
(1)	Gene Alley	100.00	50.00	30.00
(2)	Bob Bailey	100.00	50.00	30.00
(3)	Frank Bork	100.00	50.00	30.00
(4)	Smoky Burgess	100.00	50.00	30.00
(5)	Tom Butters	100.00	50.00	30.00
(6)	Don Cardwell	100.00	50.00	30.00
(7)	Roberto Clemente	600.00	300.00	180.00
(8)	Donn Clendenon	100.00	50.00	30.00
(9)	Elroy Face	100.00	50.00	30.00
(10)	Gene Freese	100.00	50.00	30.00
(11)	Bob Friend	100.00	50.00	30.00
(12)	Joe Gibbon	100.00	50.00	30.00
(13)	Julio Gotay	100.00	50.00	30.00
(14)	Rex Johnston	100.00	50.00	30.00
(15)	Vernon Law	100.00	50.00	30.00
(16)	Jerry Lynch	100.00	50.00	30.00
(17)	Bill Mazeroski	250.00	125.00	75.00
(18)	Al McBean	100.00	50.00	30.00
(19)	Orlando McFarlane	100.00	50.00	30.00
(20)	Manny Mota	100.00	50.00	30.00
(21)	Danny Murtaugh	100.00	50.00	30.00

(22)	Jim Pagliaroni	100.00	50.00	30.00
(23)	Dick Schofield	100.00	50.00	30.00
(24)	Don Schwall	100.00	50.00	30.00
(25)	Tommie Sisk	100.00	50.00	30.00
(26)	Willie Stargell	250.00	125.00	75.00
(27)	Bob Veale	100.00	50.00	30.00
(28)	Bill Virdon	100.00	50.00	30.00

1968 KDKA Pittsburgh Pirates

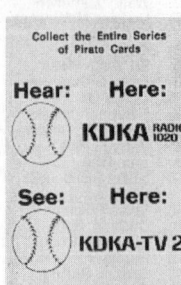

The most common of the many Pirates regional issues of the late 1960s, this 23-card set was sponsored by the Pirates' TV and radio flagship stations, KDKA in Pittsburgh. Cards measure 2-1/2" x 4" and feature at top front a color posed photo of the player, with no top or side borders. In the white panel beneath the photo are a facsimile autograph, the player's name, position and uniform number and the broadcasters' logo. Backs are printed in black on white and feature advertising for the radio and TV station. The checklist is presented here by uniform number.

		NM	EX	VG
Complete Set (23):		125.00	65.00	35.00
Common Player:		5.00	2.50	1.50
7	Larry Shepard	5.00	2.50	1.50
8	Willie Stargell	15.00	7.50	4.50
9	Bill Mazeroski	15.00	7.50	4.50
10	Gary Kolb	5.00	2.50	1.50
11	Jose Pagan	5.00	2.50	1.50
12	Gerry May (Jerry)	5.00	2.50	1.50
14	Jim Bunning	10.00	5.00	3.00
15	Manny Mota	5.00	2.50	1.50
17	Donn Clendenon	5.00	2.50	1.50
18	Matty Alou	5.00	2.50	1.50
21	Roberto Clemente	40.00	20.00	12.00
22	Gene Alley	5.00	2.50	1.50
25	Tommy Sisk	5.00	2.50	1.50
26	Roy Face	5.00	2.50	1.50
27	Ron Kline	5.00	2.50	1.50
28	Steve Blass	5.00	2.50	1.50
29	Juan Pizarro	5.00	2.50	1.50
30	Maury Wills	6.50	3.25	2.00
34	Al McBean	5.00	2.50	1.50
35	Manny Sanguillen	5.00	2.50	1.50
38	Bob Moose	5.00	2.50	1.50
39	Bob Veale	5.00	2.50	1.50
40	Dave Wickersham	5.00	2.50	1.50

1922 Keating Candy Co.

To compete with other candy issues featuring baseball cards as premiums, Sacramento, Calif., wholesale candy merchant James P. Keating appears to have purchased uncut sheets of the blank-back strip cards known as W575-1, overprinted their backs and packaged them with his product. The advertising on back is rubber-stamped. The fact that examples are known that have been cancelled with a hole punch probably indicates there was some sort of prize redemption program attached to the issue. Collectors can expect to pay a premium of about 3X for this version.

	NM	EX	VG
Common Player:	85.00	45.00	25.00
Stars: 3X			

(See 1922 W575-1 for checklist and base card values.)

1971 Keds Kedcards

These (usually) 2-1/4" x 2-1/8" cards were printed on the side of Keds athletic shoe boxes. The cards have colorful drawings of various athletes, with dotted lines for cutting. Backs are blank.

		NM	EX	VG
Complete Panel Set (3):		150.00	75.00	45.00
Complete Set (10):		120.00	60.00	35.00
Common Player:		8.00	4.00	2.50
	PANEL 1	40.00	20.00	12.00
(1)	Dave Bing (Basketball)	8.00	4.00	2.50
(2)	Clark Graebner (Tennis)	8.00	4.00	2.50
(3)	Jim Maloney	10.00	5.00	3.00
(4)	Bubba Smith (Football)	10.00	5.00	3.00
	PANEL 2	65.00	32.00	19.50
(5)	Johnny Bench	30.00	15.00	9.00
(6)	Willis Reed (Basketball)	10.00	5.00	3.00
(7)	Bubba Smith (Football)	10.00	5.00	3.00
(8)	Stan Smith (Tennis)	8.00	4.00	2.50
	PANEL 3	50.00	25.00	15.00
(9)	Willis Reed (Basketball) (5-1/4" x 3-1/2")	15.00	7.50	4.50
(10)	Johnny Bench (5-1/4" x 3-1/2")	30.00	15.00	9.00

1937 Kellogg's Pep Sports Stamps

Kellogg's packaged a four-stamp panel of "Sports Stamps" in boxes of Pep cereal. While 24 panels comprise a complete set, six of the stamps were double-printed, creating a set of 90. Backs of the stamp panels gave details for ordering an album and game boards for playing with the stamps. The color-tinted stamps measure 1-1/8" x 2-3/4" individually, and 2-1/4" x 4-1/4" as a panel. Besides the ballplayers checklisted here, the Kellogg's/Pep stamps included football, tennis and golf players, swimmers, boxers, aviaators and race horses. Baseball player stamps are listed here according to the number of the four-stamp panel on which they appeared. Prices for complete panels would be considerably higher, factoring in the other stamps on the sheet.

		NM	EX	VG
Complete Set (18):		900.00	450.00	275.00
Common Player:		60.00	30.00	18.00
Album:		300.00	150.00	100.00
1	Joe Medwick	60.00	30.00	18.00
3	Leo Durocher	60.00	30.00	18.00
5	Gabby Hartnett	60.00	30.00	18.00
6	Billy Herman	60.00	30.00	18.00
7	Luke Appling	60.00	30.00	18.00
8	Floyd Vaughan	60.00	30.00	18.00
9	Paul Waner	60.00	30.00	18.00
11	Bill Terry	60.00	30.00	18.00
12	George Selkirk	60.00	30.00	18.00
13	Walter Johnson	120.00	60.00	36.00
15	Lew Fonseca	60.00	30.00	18.00
16	Richard Ferrell	60.00	30.00	18.00
17	Johnny Evers	60.00	30.00	18.00
18	Sam West	60.00	30.00	18.00
19	Buddy Myer	60.00	30.00	18.00
20	Tris Speaker (Double print, also on Panel 23.)	60.00	30.00	18.00
21	Joe Tinker	60.00	30.00	18.00
22	Mordecai Brown	60.00	30.00	18.00
23	Tris Speaker (Double-print, also on Panel 20.)	60.00	30.00	18.00

1948 Kellogg's Corn Flakes Cuban Postcards

These advertising postcards were issued in Cuba. The approximately 3-1/2" x 5-3/8" black-and-white cards have a portrait photo on front. A small logo for the cereal appears in the lower-left corner, while a facsimile autograph is at lower-right. The back is in traditional postcard format, printed in English. This checklist is likely incomplete.

		NM	EX	VG
(1)	Tomas de la Cruz	400.00	200.00	120.00
(2)	Salvador Hernandez	400.00	200.00	120.00
(3)	Adolfo Luque	600.00	300.00	180.00
(4)	Roberto Ortiz	400.00	200.00	120.00
(5)	Napoleon Reyes	400.00	200.00	120.00
(6)	Lazaro Salazar	400.00	200.00	120.00

1948 Kellogg's Pep Celebrities

Five baseball players are included among the 18 athletes in this set of 1-3/8" x 1-5/8" cards. Fronts have player photos bordered in white. Backs have player name at top, a short career summary and a Kellogg's ad. The baseball players from the unnumbered set are listed here alphabetically.

		NM	EX	VG
Complete Set (5):		175.00	90.00	55.00
Common Player:		40.00	20.00	12.00
(1)	Phil Cavaretta	40.00	20.00	12.00
(2)	Orval Grove	40.00	20.00	12.00
(3)	Mike Tresh	40.00	20.00	12.00
(4)	Paul "Dizzy" Trout	40.00	20.00	12.00
(5)	Dick Wakefield	40.00	20.00	12.00

1970 Kellogg's

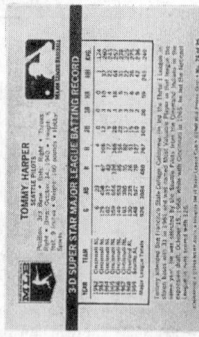

For 14 years in the 1970s and early 1980s, the Kellogg's cereal company provided Topps with virtually the only meaningful national competition in the baseball card market. Kellogg's kicked off its baseball card program in 1970 with a 75-player set of simulated 3-D cards. Single cards were available in selected brands of the company's cereal, while a mail-in program offered complete sets. The 3-D effect was achieved by the sandwiching of a clear color player photo between a purposely blurred stadium background scene and a layer of ribbed plastic. The relatively narrow dimension of the card, 2-1/4" x 3-1/2", and the nature of the plastic overlay seem to conspire to cause the cards to curl, often cracking the plastic layer, if not stored properly. Cards with major cracks in the plastic can be considered in Fair condition, at best.

		NM	EX	VG
Complete Set (75):		300.00	150.00	90.00
Common Player:		3.50	1.75	1.00
1	Ed Kranepool	3.50	1.75	1.00
2	Pete Rose	20.00	10.00	6.00
3	Cleon Jones	3.50	1.75	1.00
4	Willie McCovey	10.00	5.00	3.00
5	Mel Stottlemyre	3.50	1.75	1.00
6	Frank Howard	3.50	1.75	1.00
7	Tom Seaver	15.00	7.50	4.50
8	Don Sutton	10.00	5.00	3.00
9	Jim Wynn	3.50	1.75	1.00
10	Jim Maloney	3.50	1.75	1.00
11	Tommie Agee	3.50	1.75	1.00
12	Willie Mays	25.00	12.50	7.50

#	Player	NM	EX	VG
13	Juan Marichal	10.00	5.00	3.00
14	Dave McNally	3.50	1.75	1.00
15	Frank Robinson	15.00	7.50	4.50
16	Carlos May	3.50	1.75	1.00
17	Bill Singer	3.50	1.75	1.00
18	Rick Reichardt	3.50	1.75	1.00
19	Boog Powell	4.50	2.25	1.25
20	Gaylord Perry	10.00	5.00	3.00
21	Brooks Robinson	15.00	7.50	4.50
22	Luis Aparicio	10.00	5.00	3.00
23	Joel Horlen	3.50	1.75	1.00
24	Mike Epstein	3.50	1.75	1.00
25	Tom Haller	3.50	1.75	1.00
26	Willie Crawford	3.50	1.75	1.00
27	Roberto Clemente	35.00	17.50	10.00
28	Matty Alou	3.50	1.75	1.00
29	Willie Stargell	12.50	6.25	3.75
30	Tim Cullen	3.50	1.75	1.00
31	Randy Hundley	3.50	1.75	1.00
32	Reggie Jackson	20.00	10.00	6.00
33	Rich Allen	4.25	2.25	1.25
34	Tim McCarver	3.50	1.75	1.00
35	Ray Culp	3.50	1.75	1.00
36	Jim Fregosi	3.50	1.75	1.00
37	Billy Williams	12.50	6.25	3.75
38	Johnny Odom	3.50	1.75	1.00
39	Bert Campaneris	3.50	1.75	1.00
40	Ernie Banks	20.00	10.00	6.00
41	Chris Short	3.50	1.75	1.00
42	Ron Santo	6.00	3.00	1.75
43	Glenn Beckert	3.50	1.75	1.00
44	Lou Brock	12.50	6.25	3.75
45	Larry Hisle	3.50	1.75	1.00
46	Reggie Smith	3.50	1.75	1.00
47	Rod Carew	15.00	7.50	4.50
48	Curt Flood	3.50	1.75	1.00
49	Jim Lonborg	3.50	1.75	1.00
50	Sam McDowell	3.50	1.75	1.00
51	Sal Bando	3.50	1.75	1.00
52	Al Kaline	15.00	7.50	4.50
53	Gary Nolan	3.50	1.75	1.00
54	Rico Petrocelli	3.50	1.75	1.00
55	Ollie Brown	3.50	1.75	1.00
56	Luis Tiant	3.50	1.75	1.00
57	Bill Freehan	3.50	1.75	1.00
58	Johnny Bench	15.00	7.50	4.50
59	Joe Pepitone	3.50	1.75	1.00
60	Bobby Murcer	3.50	1.75	1.00
61	Harmon Killebrew	15.00	7.50	4.50
62	Don Wilson	3.50	1.75	1.00
63	Tony Oliva	3.50	1.75	1.00
64	Jim Perry	3.50	1.75	1.00
65	Mickey Lolich	3.50	1.75	1.00
66	Coco Laboy	3.50	1.75	1.00
67	Dean Chance	3.50	1.75	1.00
68	Ken Harrelson	3.50	1.75	1.00
69	Willie Horton	3.50	1.75	1.00
70	Wally Bunker	3.50	1.75	1.00
71a	Bob Gibson (1959 IP blank)	12.50	6.25	3.75
71b	Bob Gibson (1959 IP 76)	12.50	6.25	3.75
72	Joe Morgan	12.50	6.25	3.75
73	Denny McLain	3.50	1.75	1.00
74	Tommy Harper	3.50	1.75	1.00
75	Don Mincher	3.50	1.75	1.00

1971 Kellogg's

The scarcest and most valuable of the Kellogg's editions, the 75-card 1971 set was the only one not offered by the company on a mail-in basis. The only way to complete it was to buy ... and buy and buy ... boxes of cereal. Kellogg's again used the simulated 3-D effect in the cards' design, with the same result being many of the 2-1/4" x 3-1/2" cards are found today with cracks resulting from the cards' curling. A number of scarcer back variations are checklisted below. Most, but not all of the base cards and variations can be found both with and without a 1970 date before the Xograph copyright on back."

		NM	EX	VG
Complete Set (75):		1,000	500.00	300.00
Common Player:		13.50	6.75	4.00
1a	Wayne Simpson (SO 120)	13.50	6.75	4.00
1b	Wayne Simpson (SO 119)	20.00	10.00	6.00
2a	Tom Seaver (IP 1092)	30.00	15.00	9.00
2b	Tom Seaver (IP 1093)	45.00	22.00	13.50
3a	Jim Perry (IP 2238)	13.50	6.75	4.00
3b	Jim Perry (IP 2239)	20.00	10.00	6.00
4a	Bob Robertson (RBI 94)	13.50	6.75	4.00
4b	Bob Robertson (RBI 95)	20.00	10.00	6.00
5	Roberto Clemente	70.00	35.00	20.00
6a	Gaylord Perry (IP 2014)	25.00	12.50	7.50
6b	Gaylord Perry (IP 2015)	30.00	15.00	9.00
7a	Felipe Alou (1970 Oakland NL)	20.00	10.00	6.00

#	Player	NM	EX	VG
7b	Felipe Alou (1970 Oakland AL)	25.00	12.50	7.50
8	Denis Menke	13.50	6.75	4.00
9a	Don Kessinger (Hits 849)	13.50	6.75	4.00
9b	Don Kessinger (Hits 850)	20.00	10.00	6.00
10	Willie Mays	45.00	22.00	13.50
11	Jim Hickman	13.50	6.75	4.00
12	Tony Oliva	17.50	8.75	5.25
13	Manny Sanguillen	13.50	6.75	4.00
14a	Frank Howard (1968 Washington NL)	30.00	15.00	9.00
14b	Frank Howard (1968 Washington AL)	20.00	10.00	6.00
15	Frank Robinson	30.00	15.00	9.00
16	Willie Davis	13.50	6.75	4.00
17	Lou Brock	25.00	12.50	7.50
18	Cesar Tovar	13.50	6.75	4.00
19	Luis Aparicio	25.00	12.50	7.50
20	Boog Powell	17.50	8.75	5.25
21a	Dick Selma (SO 584)	13.50	6.75	4.00
21b	Dick Selma (SO 587)	20.00	10.00	6.00
22	Danny Walton	13.50	6.75	4.00
23	Carl Morton	13.50	6.75	4.00
24a	Sonny Siebert (SO 1054)	13.50	6.75	4.00
24b	Sonny Siebert (SO 1055)	20.00	10.00	6.00
25	Jim Merritt	13.50	6.75	4.00
26a	Jose Cardenal (Hits 828)	13.50	6.75	4.00
26b	Jose Cardenal (Hits 829)	20.00	10.00	6.00
27	Don Mincher	13.50	6.75	4.00
28a	Clyde Wright (California state logo.)	13.50	6.75	4.00
28b	Clyde Wright (Angels crest logo.)	20.00	10.00	6.00
29	Les Cain	13.50	6.75	4.00
30	Danny Cater	13.50	6.75	4.00
31	Don Sutton	25.00	12.50	7.50
32	Chuck Dobson	13.50	6.75	4.00
33	Willie McCovey	25.00	12.50	7.50
34	Mike Epstein	13.50	6.75	4.00
35a	Paul Blair (Runs 386)	13.50	6.75	4.00
35b	Paul Blair (Runs 385)	20.00	10.00	6.00
36a	Gary Nolan (SO 577)	13.50	6.75	4.00
36b	Gary Nolan (SO 581)	20.00	10.00	6.00
37	Sam McDowell	13.50	6.75	4.00
38	Amos Otis	13.50	6.75	4.00
39a	Ray Fosse (RBI 69)	13.50	6.75	4.00
39b	Ray Fosse (RBI 70)	20.00	10.00	6.00
40	Mel Stottlemyre	13.50	6.75	4.00
41a	Cito Gaston (Runs 112)	13.50	6.75	4.00
41b	Cito Gaston (Runs 113)	20.00	10.00	6.00
42	Dick Dietz	13.50	6.75	4.00
43	Roy White	13.50	6.75	4.00
44	Al Kaline	30.00	15.00	9.00
45	Carlos May	13.50	6.75	4.00
46a	Tommie Agee (RBI 313)	13.50	6.75	4.00
46b	Tommie Agee (RBI 314)	20.00	10.00	6.00
47	Tommy Harper	13.50	6.75	4.00
48	Larry Dierker	13.50	6.75	4.00
49	Mike Cuellar	13.50	6.75	4.00
50	Ernie Banks	30.00	15.00	9.00
51	Bob Gibson	25.00	12.50	7.50
52	Reggie Smith	13.50	6.75	4.00
53a	Matty Alou (RBI 273)	13.50	6.75	4.00
53b	Matty Alou (RBI 274)	20.00	10.00	6.00
54a	Alex Johnson (California state logo.)	13.50	6.75	4.00
54b	Alex Johnson (Angels crest logo.)	20.00	10.00	6.00
55	Harmon Killebrew	30.00	15.00	9.00
56	Billy Grabarkewitz	13.50	6.75	4.00
57	Rich Allen	17.50	8.75	5.25
58	Tony Perez	25.00	12.50	7.50
59a	Dave McNally (SO 1065)	13.50	6.75	4.00
59b	Dave McNally (SO 1067)	20.00	10.00	6.00
60a	Jim Palmer (SO 564)	25.00	12.50	7.50
60b	Jim Palmer (SO 567)	30.00	15.00	9.00
61	Billy Williams	25.00	12.50	7.50
62	Joe Torre	20.00	10.00	6.00
63a	Jim Northrup (AB 2773)	13.50	6.75	4.00
63b	Jim Northrup (AB 2772)	20.00	10.00	6.00
64a	Jim Fregosi (Calif. state logo - Hits 1326)	13.50	6.75	4.00
64b	Jim Fregosi (Calif. state logo - Hits 1327)	20.00	10.00	6.00
64c	Jim Fregosi (Angels crest logo.)	20.00	10.00	6.00
65	Pete Rose	60.00	30.00	18.00
66a	Bud Harrelson (RBI 112)	13.50	6.75	4.00
66b	Bud Harrelson (RBI 113)	20.00	10.00	6.00
67	Tony Taylor	13.50	6.75	4.00
68	Willie Stargell	25.00	12.50	7.50
69	Tony Horton	25.00	12.50	7.50
70a	Claude Osteen (No number.)	25.00	12.50	7.50
70b	Claude Osteen (#70 on back)	13.50	6.75	4.00
71	Glenn Beckert	13.50	6.75	4.00
72	Nate Colbert	13.50	6.75	4.00
73a	Rick Monday (AB 1705)	13.50	6.75	4.00
73b	Rick Monday (AB 1704)	20.00	10.00	6.00
74a	Tommy John (BB 444)	20.00	10.00	6.00
74b	Tommy John (BB 443)	25.00	12.50	7.50
75	Chris Short	13.50	6.75	4.00

1972 Kellogg's

For 1972, Kellogg's reduced both the number of cards in its set and the dimensions of each card, moving to a 2-1/8" x 3-1/4" size and fixing the set at 54 cards. Once again, the cards were produced to simulate a 3-D effect (see description for 1970 Kellogg's). The set was available via a mail-in offer. The checklist includes variations which resulted from the correction of erroneous statistics on the backs of some cards. The complete set values quoted do not include the scarcer variations.

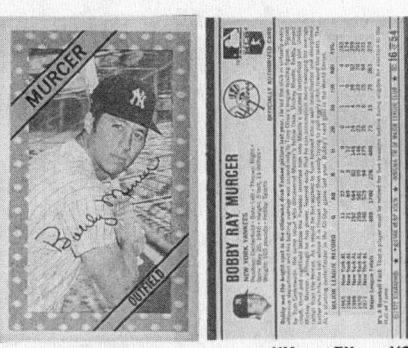

		NM	EX	VG
Complete Set (54):		125.00	65.00	35.00
Common Player:		1.00	.50	.30
1a	Tom Seaver (1970 ERA 2.85)	10.00	5.00	3.00
1b	Tom Seaver (1970 ERA 2.81)	7.50	3.75	2.25
2	Amos Otis	1.00	.50	.30
3a	Willie Davis (Runs 842)	2.00	1.00	.60
3b	Willie Davis (Runs 841)	1.25	.60	.40
4	Wilbur Wood	1.00	.50	.30
5	Bill Parsons	1.00	.50	.30
6	Pete Rose	15.00	7.50	4.50
7a	Willie McCovey (HR 360)	6.00	3.00	1.75
7b	Willie McCovey (HR 370)	5.00	2.50	1.50
8	Fergie Jenkins	3.50	1.75	1.00
9a	Vida Blue (ERA 2.35)	2.00	1.00	.60
9b	Vida Blue (ERA 2.31)	1.25	.60	.40
10	Joe Torre	2.50	1.25	.70
11	Merv Rettenmund	1.00	.50	.30
12	Bill Melton	1.00	.50	.30
13a	Jim Palmer (Games 170)	6.00	3.00	1.75
13b	Jim Palmer (Games 168)	4.50	2.25	1.25
14	Doug Rader	1.00	.50	.30
15a	Dave Roberts (...Seaver, the NL leader...)	2.00	1.00	.60
15b	Dave Roberts (...Seaver, the league leader...)	1.25	.60	.40
16	Bobby Murcer	1.25	.60	.40
17	Wes Parker	1.00	.50	.30
18a	Joe Coleman (BB 394)	2.00	1.00	.60
18b	Joe Coleman (BB 393)	1.25	.60	.40
19	Manny Sanguillen	1.00	.50	.30
20	Reggie Jackson	10.00	5.00	3.00
21	Ralph Garr	1.00	.50	.30
22	Jim "Catfish" Hunter	3.50	1.75	1.00
23	Rick Wise	1.00	.50	.30
24	Glenn Beckert	1.00	.50	.30
25	Tony Oliva	1.00	.50	.30
26a	Bob Gibson (SO 2577)	6.00	3.00	1.75
26b	Bob Gibson (SO 2578)	4.50	2.25	1.25
27a	Mike Cuellar (1971 ERA 3.80)	2.00	1.00	.60
27b	Mike Cuellar (1971 ERA 3.08)	1.25	.60	.40
28	Chris Speier	1.00	.50	.30
29a	Dave McNally (ERA 3.18)	2.00	1.00	.60
29b	Dave McNally (ERA 3.15)	1.25	.60	.40
30	Chico Cardenas	1.00	.50	.30
31a	Bill Freehan (AVG. .263)	2.00	1.00	.60
31b	Bill Freehan (AVG. .262)	1.25	.60	.40
32a	Bud Harrelson (Hits 634)	2.00	1.00	.60
32b	Bud Harrelson (Hits 624)	1.25	.60	.40
33a	Sam McDowell (...less than 200 innings...)	2.00	1.00	.60
33b	Sam McDowell (...less than 225 innings...)	1.25	.60	.40
34a	Claude Osteen (1971 ERA 3.25)	2.00	1.00	.60
34b	Claude Osteen (1971 ERA 3.51)	1.25	.60	.40
35	Reggie Smith	1.00	.50	.30
36	Sonny Siebert	1.00	.50	.30
37	Lee May	1.00	.50	.30
38	Mickey Lolich	1.00	.50	.30
39a	Cookie Rojas (2B 149)	2.00	1.00	.60
39b	Cookie Rojas (2B 150)	1.25	.60	.40
40	Dick Drago	1.00	.50	.30
41	Nate Colbert	1.00	.50	.30
42	Andy Messersmith	1.00	.50	.30
43a	Dave Johnson (AVG. .262)	2.00	1.00	.60
43b	Dave Johnson (AVG. .264)	1.25	.60	.40
44	Steve Blass	1.00	.50	.30
45	Bob Robertson	1.00	.50	.30
46a	Billy Williams (...missed only one last season...)	6.00	3.00	1.75
46b	Billy Williams (Phrase omitted.)	4.50	2.25	1.25
47	Juan Marichal	4.00	2.00	1.25
48	Lou Brock	4.00	2.00	1.25
49	Roberto Clemente	17.50	8.75	5.25
50	Mel Stottlemyre	1.00	.50	.30
51	Don Wilson	1.00	.50	.30
52a	Sal Bando (RBI 355)	2.00	1.00	.60
52b	Sal Bando (RBI 356)	1.25	.60	.40
53a	Willie Stargell (2B 197)	6.00	3.00	1.75
53b	Willie Stargell (2B 196)	4.50	2.25	1.25
54a	Willie Mays (RBI 1855)	15.00	7.50	4.50
54b	Willie Mays (RBI 1856)	12.00	6.00	3.50

1972 Kellogg's All-Time Baseball Greats

Kellogg's issued a second baseball card set in 1972, inserted into packages of breakfast rolls. The 2-1/4" x 3-1/2" cards also featured a simulated 3-D effect, but the 15 players in the set were "All-Time Baseball Greats," rather than current players. The set is virtually identical to a Rold Gold pretzel issue of 1970; the only difference being the 1972 copyright date on the back of the Kellog's cards, while the pretzel issue bears a 1970 date. The pretzel cards are considerably scarcer than the Kellogg's.

	NM	EX	VG
Complete Set (15):	45.00	22.50	13.50
Common Player:	2.50	1.25	.70
1 Walter Johnson	3.50	1.75	1.00
2 Rogers Hornsby	2.50	1.25	.70
3 John McGraw	2.50	1.25	.70
4 Mickey Cochrane	2.50	1.25	.70
5 George Sisler	2.50	1.25	.70
6 Babe Ruth	15.00	7.50	4.50
(Portrait photo on back.)			
7 Robert "Lefty" Grove	2.50	1.25	.70
8 Harold "Pie" Traynor	2.50	1.25	.70
9 Honus Wagner	5.00	2.50	1.50
10 Eddie Collins	2.50	1.25	.70
11 Tris Speaker	2.50	1.25	.70
12 Cy Young	3.50	1.75	1.00
13 Lou Gehrig	10.00	5.00	3.00
14 Babe Ruth	15.00	7.50	4.50
(Action photo on back.)			
15 Ty Cobb	10.00	5.00	3.00

1973 Kellogg's

The lone exception to Kellogg's long run of simulated 3-D effect cards came in 1973, when the cereal company's 54-card set was produced by "normal" printing methods. In 2-1/4" x 3-1/2" size, the design was otherwise quite compatible with the issues which preceded and succeeded it. Because it was available via a mail-in offer ($1.25 and two Raisin Bran box-tops), it is not as scarce as the earlier Kellogg's issues.

	NM	EX	VG
Complete Set (54):	65.00	32.50	20.00
Common Player:	.90	.45	.25
1 Amos Otis	.90	.45	.25
2 Ellie Rodriguez	.90	.45	.25
3 Mickey Lolich	.90	.45	.25
4 Tony Oliva	1.25	.60	.40
5 Don Sutton	3.50	1.75	1.00
6 Pete Rose	12.00	6.00	3.50
7 Steve Carlton	4.50	2.25	1.25
8 Bobby Bonds	.90	.45	.25
9 Wilbur Wood	.90	.45	.25
10 Billy Williams	4.50	2.25	1.25
11 Steve Blass	.90	.45	.25
12 Jon Matlack	.90	.45	.25
13 Cesar Cedeno	.90	.45	.25
14 Bob Gibson	4.50	2.25	1.25
15 Sparky Lyle	.90	.45	.25
16 Nolan Ryan	17.50	8.75	5.25
17 Jim Palmer	4.50	2.25	1.25
18 Ray Fosse	.90	.45	.25
19 Bobby Murcer	.90	.45	.25
20 Jim "Catfish" Hunter	3.50	1.75	1.00
21 Tug McGraw	.90	.45	.25
22 Reggie Jackson	9.00	4.50	2.75
23 Bill Stoneman	.90	.45	.25
24 Lou Piniella	.90	.45	.25
25 Willie Stargell	4.50	2.25	1.25
26 Dick Allen	2.50	1.25	.70
27 Carlton Fisk	4.50	2.25	1.25
28 Fergie Jenkins	3.50	1.75	1.00
29 Phil Niekro	3.50	1.75	1.00
30 Gary Nolan	.90	.45	.25
31 Joe Torre	2.50	1.25	.70
32 Bobby Tolan	.90	.45	.25
33 Nate Colbert	.90	.45	.25
34 Joe Morgan	4.50	2.25	1.25
35 Bert Blyleven	.90	.45	.25
36 Joe Rudi	.90	.45	.25
37 Ralph Garr	.90	.45	.25
38 Gaylord Perry	3.50	1.75	1.00
39 Bobby Grich	.90	.45	.25
40 Lou Brock	4.00	2.00	1.25
41 Pete Broberg	.90	.45	.25

42 Manny Sanguillen	.90	.45	.25
43 Willie Davis	.90	.45	.25
44 Dave Kingman	.90	.45	.25
45 Carlos May	.90	.45	.25
46 Tom Seaver	6.00	3.00	1.75
47 Mike Cuellar	.90	.45	.25
48 Joe Coleman	.90	.45	.25
49 Claude Osteen	.90	.45	.25
50 Steve Kline	.90	.45	.25
51 Rod Carew	4.50	2.25	1.25
52 Al Kaline	6.00	3.00	1.75
53 Larry Dierker	.90	.45	.25
54 Ron Santo	2.50	1.25	.70

1974 Kellogg's

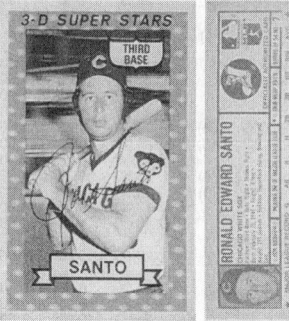

For 1974, Kellogg's returned to the use of simulated 3-D for its 54-player baseball card issue (see 1970 Kellogg's listing for description). In 2-1/8" x 3-1/4" size, the cards were available as a complete set via a mail-in offer. The complete set price listed here does not include the more expensive variations.

	NM	EX	VG
Complete Set (54):	65.00	32.50	20.00
Common Player:	.90	.45	.25
1 Bob Gibson	3.50	1.75	1.00
2 Rick Monday	.90	.45	.25
3 Joe Coleman	.90	.45	.25
4 Bert Campaneris	.90	.45	.25
5 Carlton Fisk	4.00	2.00	1.25
6 Jim Palmer	3.50	1.75	1.00
7a Ron Santo (Chicago Cubs)	2.25	1.25	.70
7b Ron Santo (Chicago White Sox)	1.25	.60	.40
8 Nolan Ryan	16.00	8.00	4.75
9 Greg Luzinski	.90	.45	.25
10a Buddy Bell (Runs 134)	2.25	1.25	.70
10b Buddy Bell (Runs 135)	1.00	.50	.30
11 Bob Watson	.90	.45	.25
12 Bill Singer	.90	.45	.25
13 Dave May	.90	.45	.25
14 Jim Brewer	.90	.45	.25
15 Manny Sanguillen	.90	.45	.25
16 Jeff Burroughs	.90	.45	.25
17 Amos Otis	.90	.45	.25
18 Ed Goodson	.90	.45	.25
19 Nate Colbert	.90	.45	.25
20 Reggie Jackson	6.50	3.25	2.00
21 Ted Simmons	.90	.45	.25
22 Bobby Murcer	1.00	.50	.30
23 Willie Horton	1.00	.50	.30
24 Orlando Cepeda	3.50	1.75	1.00
25 Ron Hunt	.90	.45	.25
26 Wayne Twitchell	.90	.45	.25
27 Ron Fairly	.90	.45	.25
28 Johnny Bench	4.50	2.25	1.25
29 John Mayberry	.90	.45	.25
30 Rod Carew	4.00	2.00	1.25
31 Ken Holtzman	.90	.45	.25
32 Billy Williams	3.50	1.75	1.00
33 Dick Allen	1.50	.70	.45
34a Wilbur Wood (SO 959)	1.50	.70	.45
34b Wilbur Wood (SO 960)	1.00	.50	.30
35 Danny Thompson	.90	.45	.25
36 Joe Morgan	3.50	1.75	1.00
37 Willie Stargell	3.50	1.75	1.00
38 Pete Rose	10.00	5.00	3.00
39 Bobby Bonds	.90	.45	.25
40 Chris Speier	.90	.45	.25
41 Sparky Lyle	.90	.45	.25
42 Cookie Rojas	.90	.45	.25
43 Tommy Davis	.90	.45	.25
44 Jim "Catfish" Hunter	3.50	1.75	1.00
45 Willie Davis	.90	.45	.25
46 Bert Blyleven	.90	.45	.25
47 Pat Kelly	.90	.45	.25
48 Ken Singleton	.90	.45	.25
49 Manny Mota	.90	.45	.25
50 Dave Johnson	.90	.45	.25
51 Sal Bando	.90	.45	.25
52 Tom Seaver	4.50	2.25	1.25
53 Felix Millan	.90	.45	.25
54 Ron Blomberg	.90	.45	.25

1975 Kellogg's

While the card size remained the same at 2-1/8" x 3-1/4", the size of the 1975 Kellogg's "3-D" set was increased by three, to 57 cards. Despite the fact cards could be obtained by a mail-in offer, as well as in cereal boxes, the '75 Kellogg's are noticeably scarcer than the company's other issues, with the exception of the 1971 set. Also helping to raise the value of the cards is the presence of an unusually large number of current and future Hall of Famers.

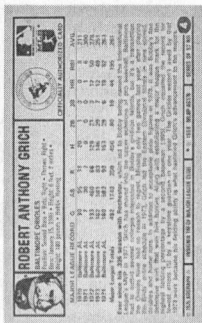

	NM	EX	VG
Complete Set (57):	175.00	90.00	55.00
Common Player:	2.00	1.00	.60
1 Roy White	2.00	1.00	.60
2 Ross Grimsley	2.00	1.00	.60
3 Reggie Smith	2.00	1.00	.60
4a Bob Grich ("...1973 work..." in last line)	3.00	1.50	.90
4b Bob Grich (no "...1973 work...")	2.00	1.00	.60
5 Greg Gross	2.00	1.00	.60
6 Bob Watson	2.00	1.00	.60
7 Johnny Bench	10.00	5.00	3.00
8 Jeff Burroughs	2.00	1.00	.60
9 Elliott Maddox	2.00	1.00	.60
10 Jon Matlack	2.00	1.00	.60
11 Pete Rose	25.00	12.50	7.50
12 Leroy Stanton	2.00	1.00	.60
13 Bake McBride	2.00	1.00	.60
14 Jorge Orta	2.00	1.00	.60
15 Al Oliver	2.50	1.25	.70
16 John Briggs	2.00	1.00	.60
17 Steve Garvey	4.50	2.25	1.25
18 Brooks Robinson	10.00	5.00	3.00
19 John Hiller	2.00	1.00	.60
20 Lynn McGlothen	2.00	1.00	.60
21 Cleon Jones	2.00	1.00	.60
22 Fergie Jenkins	6.00	3.00	1.75
23 Bill North	2.00	1.00	.60
24 Steve Busby	2.00	1.00	.60
25 Richie Zisk	2.00	1.00	.60
26 Nolan Ryan	35.00	17.50	10.50
27 Joe Morgan	7.50	3.75	2.25
28 Joe Rudi	2.00	1.00	.60
29 Jose Cardenal	2.00	1.00	.60
30 Andy Messersmith	2.00	1.00	.60
31 Willie Montanez	2.00	1.00	.60
32 Bill Buckner	2.00	1.00	.60
33 Rod Carew	7.50	3.75	2.25
34 Lou Piniella	2.50	1.25	.70
35 Ralph Garr	2.00	1.00	.60
36 Mike Marshall	2.00	1.00	.60
37 Garry Maddox	2.00	1.00	.60
38 Dwight Evans	2.00	1.00	.60
39 Lou Brock	7.50	3.75	2.25
40 Ken Singleton	2.00	1.00	.60
41 Steve Braun	2.00	1.00	.60
42 Dick Allen	3.50	1.75	1.00
43 Johnny Grubb	2.00	1.00	.60
44a Jim Hunter (Oakland)	9.00	4.50	2.75
44b Jim Hunter (New York)	7.50	3.75	2.25
45 Gaylord Perry	6.00	3.00	1.75
46 George Hendrick	2.00	1.00	.60
47 Sparky Lyle	2.00	1.00	.60
48 Dave Cash	2.00	1.00	.60
49 Luis Tiant	2.00	1.00	.60
50 Cesar Geronimo	2.00	1.00	.60
51 Carl Yastrzemski	12.00	6.00	3.50
52 Ken Brett	2.00	1.00	.60
53 Hal McRae	2.00	1.00	.60
54 Reggie Jackson	15.00	7.50	4.50
55 Rollie Fingers	6.00	3.00	1.75
56 Mike Schmidt	15.00	7.50	4.50
57 Richie Hebner	2.00	1.00	.60

1976 Kellogg's

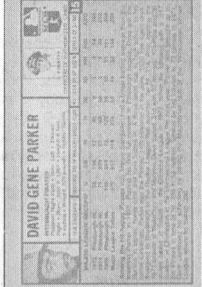

A sizeable list of corrected errors and other variation cards dots the checklist for the 57-card 1976 Kellogg's 3-D set. Again containing 57 cards, the first three cards in the set are found far less often than cards #4-57, indicating they were short-printed in relation to the rest of the set. The complete set values quoted below do not include the scarcer variation cards. Card size remained at 2-1/8" x 3-1/4". Cards #1-3 were significantly short-printed.

	NM	EX	VG
Complete Set (57):	70.00	35.00	20.00

	Common Player:	1.25	.60	.40
1	Steve Hargan	10.00	5.00	3.00
2	Claudell Washington	10.00	5.00	3.00
3	Don Gullett	10.00	5.00	3.00
4	Randy Jones	1.25	.60	.40
5	Jim "Catfish" Hunter	3.50	1.75	1.00
6a	Clay Carroll (Cincinnati)	2.25	1.25	.70
6b	Clay Carroll (Chicago)	1.25	.60	.40
7	Joe Rudi	1.25	.60	.40
8	Reggie Jackson	9.00	4.50	2.75
9	Felix Millan	1.25	.60	.40
10	Jim Rice	2.00	1.00	.60
11	Bert Blyleven	1.25	.60	.40
12	Ken Singleton	1.25	.60	.40
13	Don Sutton	3.50	1.75	1.00
14	Joe Morgan	4.00	2.00	1.25
15	Dave Parker	1.50	.70	.45
16	Dave Cash	1.25	.60	.40
17	Ron LeFlore	1.25	.60	.40
18	Greg Luzinski	1.25	.60	.40
19	Dennis Eckersley	6.00	3.00	1.75
20	Bill Madlock	1.25	.60	.40
21	George Scott	1.25	.60	.40
22	Willie Stargell	4.00	2.00	1.25
23	Al Hrabosky	1.25	.60	.40
24	Carl Yastrzemski	7.50	3.75	2.25
25a	Jim Kaat (White Sox logo on back.)	3.00	1.50	.90
25b	Jim Kaat (Phillies logo on back.)	1.50	.70	.45
26	Marty Perez	1.25	.60	.40
27	Bob Watson	1.25	.60	.40
28	Eric Soderholm	1.25	.60	.40
29	Bill Lee	1.25	.60	.40
30a	Frank Tanana (1975 ERA 2.63)	2.00	1.00	.60
30b	Frank Tanana (1975 ERA 2.62)	1.25	.60	.40
31	Fred Lynn	1.50	.70	.45
32a	Tom Seaver (1967 PCT. 552)	7.50	3.75	2.25
32b	Tom Seaver (1967 Pct. .552)	6.00	3.00	1.75
33	Steve Busby	1.25	.60	.40
34	Gary Carter	4.00	2.00	1.25
35	Rick Wise	1.25	.60	.40
36	Johnny Bench	5.00	2.50	1.50
37	Jim Palmer	4.00	2.00	1.25
38	Bobby Murcer	1.50	.70	.45
39	Von Joshua	1.25	.60	.40
40	Lou Brock	4.00	2.00	1.25
41a	Mickey Rivers (last line begins "In three...")	2.00	1.00	.60
41b	Mickey Rivers (last line begins "The Yankees...")	1.25	.60	.40
42	Manny Sanguillen	1.25	.60	.40
43	Jerry Reuss	1.25	.60	.40
44	Ken Griffey	1.25	.60	.40
45a	Jorge Orta (AB 1616)	1.75	.90	.50
45b	Jorge Orta (AB 1615)	1.25	.60	.40
46	John Mayberry	1.25	.60	.40
47a	Vida Blue (2nd line reads "...pitched more innings ...")	2.25	1.25	.70
47b	Vida Blue (2nd line reads "...struck out more...")	1.25	.60	.40
48	Rod Carew	4.00	2.00	1.25
49a	Jon Matlack (1975 ER 87)	1.75	.90	.50
49b	Jon Matlack (1975 ER 86)	1.25	.60	.40
50	Boog Powell	2.25	1.25	.70
51a	Mike Hargrove (AB 935)	1.75	.90	.50
51b	Mike Hargrove (AB 934)	1.25	.60	.40
52a	Paul Lindblad (1975 ERA 2.72)	1.75		.50
52b	Paul Lindblad (1975 ERA 2.73)	1.25		.40
53	Thurman Munson	4.00	2.00	1.25
54	Steve Garvey	2.50	1.25	.70
55	Pete Rose	12.50	6.25	3.75
56a	Greg Gross (Games 302)	1.75	.90	.50
56b	Greg Gross (Games 334)	1.25	.60	.40
57	Ted Simmons	1.25	.60	.40

1977 Kellogg's

Other than another innovative card design to complement the simulated 3-D effect, there was little change in the 1977 Kellogg's issue. Set size remained at 57 cards, the set remained in the 2-1/8" x 3-1/4" format, and the cards were available either individually in boxes of cereal, or as a complete set via a mail-in box top offer. The 1977 set is the last in which Kellogg's used a player portrait photo on the back of the card.

		NM	EX	VG
	Complete Set (57):	60.00	30.00	18.00
	Common Player:	.75	.40	.25
1	George Foster	.75	.40	.25
2	Bert Campaneris	.75	.40	.25
3	Fergie Jenkins	2.50	1.25	.70

4	Dock Ellis	.75	.40	.25
5	John Montefusco	.75	.40	.25
6	George Brett	12.50	6.25	3.75
7	John Candelaria	.75	.40	.25
8	Fred Norman	.75	.40	.25
9	Bill Travers	.75	.40	.25
10	Hal McRae	.75	.40	.25
11	Doug Rau	.75	.40	.25
12	Greg Luzinski	.75	.40	.25
13	Ralph Garr	.75	.40	.25
14	Steve Garvey	1.50	.70	.45
15	Rick Manning	.75	.40	.25
16a	Lyman Bostock (Back photo is N.Y. Yankee Dock Ellis.)	7.50	3.75	2.25
16b	Lyman Bostock (Correct back photo.)	.75	.40	.25
17	Randy Jones	.75	.40	.25
18a	Ron Cey (58 homers in first sentence)	1.00	.50	.30
18b	Ron Cey (48 homers in first sentence)	.75	.40	.25
19	Dave Parker	.75	.40	.25
20	Pete Rose	15.00	7.50	4.50
21a	Wayne Garland (Last line begins "Prior to...")	1.00	.50	.30
21b	Wayne Garland (Last line begins "There he...")	.75	.40	.25
22	Bill North	.75	.40	.25
23	Thurman Munson	4.50	2.25	1.25
24	Tom Poquette	.75	.40	.25
25	Ron LeFlore	.75	.40	.25
26	Mark Fidrych	1.00	.50	.30
27	Sixto Lezcano	.75	.40	.25
28	Dave Winfield	7.50	3.75	2.25
29	Jerry Koosman	.75	.40	.25
30	Mike Hargrove	.75	.40	.25
31	Willie Montanez	.75	.40	.25
32	Don Stanhouse	.75	.40	.25
33	Jay Johnstone	.75	.40	.25
34	Bake McBride	.75	.40	.25
35	Dave Kingman	.75	.40	.25
36	Freddie Patek	.75	.40	.25
37	Garry Maddox	.75	.40	.25
38a	Ken Reitz (Last line begins "The previous...")	1.00	.50	.30
38b	Ken Reitz (Last line begins "In late...")	.75	.40	.25
39	Bobby Grich	.75	.40	.25
40	Cesar Geronimo	.75	.40	.25
41	Jim Lonborg	.75	.40	.25
42	Ed Figueroa	.75	.40	.25
43	Bill Madlock	.75	.40	.25
44	Jerry Remy	.75	.40	.25
45	Frank Tanana	.75	.40	.25
46	Al Oliver	1.00	.50	.30
47	Charlie Hough	.75	.40	.25
48	Lou Piniella	1.00	.50	.30
49	Ken Griffey	.75	.40	.25
50	Jose Cruz	.75	.40	.25
51	Rollie Fingers	2.50	1.25	.70
52	Chris Chambliss	.75	.40	.25
53	Rod Carew	4.50	2.25	1.25
54	Andy Messersmith	.75	.40	.25
55	Mickey Rivers	.75	.40	.25
56	Butch Wynegar	.75	.40	.25
57	Steve Carlton	3.50	1.75	1.00

1978 Kellogg's

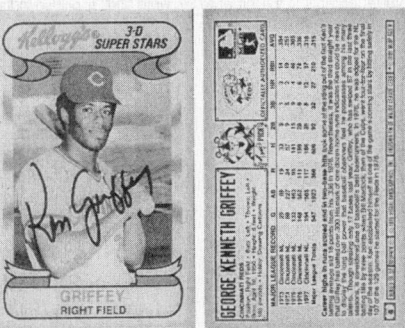

Besides the substitution of a Tony the Tiger drawing for a player portrait photo on the back of the card, the 1978 Kellogg's set offered no major changes from the previous few years issues. Cards were once again in the 2-1/8" x 3-1/4" format, with 57 cards comprising a complete set. Single cards were available in selected brands of the company's cereal, while complete sets could be obtained by a mail-in offer.

		NM	EX	VG
	Complete Set (57):	60.00	30.00	18.00
	Common Player:	.90	.45	.25
1	Steve Carlton	4.50	2.25	1.25
2	Bucky Dent	1.25	.60	.40
3	Mike Schmidt	13.50	6.75	4.00
4	Ken Griffey	.90	.45	.25
5	Al Cowens	.90	.45	.25
6	George Brett	13.50	6.75	4.00
7	Lou Brock	4.50	2.25	1.25
8	Rich Gossage	1.25	.60	.40
9	Tom Johnson	.90	.45	.25
10	George Foster	.90	.45	.25
11	Dave Winfield	4.50	2.25	1.25
12	Dan Meyer	.90	.45	.25
13	Chris Chambliss	.90	.45	.25
14	Paul Dade	.90	.45	.25
15	Jeff Burroughs	.90	.45	.25
16	Jose Cruz	.90	.45	.25

17	Mickey Rivers	.90	.45	.25
18	John Candelaria	.90	.45	.25
19	Ellis Valentine	.90	.45	.25
20	Hal McRae	.90	.45	.25
21	Dave Rozema	.90	.45	.25
22	Lenny Randle	.90	.45	.25
23	Willie McCovey	4.50	2.25	1.25
24	Ron Cey	.90	.45	.25
25	Eddie Murray	17.50	8.75	5.25
26	Larry Bowa	.90	.45	.25
27	Tom Seaver	5.00	2.50	1.50
28	Garry Maddox	.90	.45	.25
29	Rod Carew	4.50	2.25	1.25
30	Thurman Munson	4.50	2.25	1.25
31	Garry Templeton	.90	.45	.25
32	Eric Soderholm	.90	.45	.25
33	Greg Luzinski	.90	.45	.25
34	Reggie Smith	.90	.45	.25
35	Dave Goltz	.90	.45	.25
36	Tommy John	1.25	.60	.40
37	Ralph Garr	.90	.45	.25
38	Alan Bannister	.90	.45	.25
39	Bob Bailor	.90	.45	.25
40	Reggie Jackson	12.00	6.00	3.50
41	Cecil Cooper	.90	.45	.25
42	Burt Hooton	.90	.45	.25
43	Sparky Lyle	.90	.45	.25
44	Steve Ontiveros	.90	.45	.25
45	Rick Reuschel	.90	.45	.25
46	Lyman Bostock	.90	.45	.25
47	Mitchell Page	.90	.45	.25
48	Bruce Sutter	3.50	1.75	1.00
49	Jim Rice	2.50	1.25	.70
50	Bob Forsch	.90	.45	.25
51	Nolan Ryan	17.50	8.75	5.25
52	Dave Parker	.90	.45	.25
53	Bert Blyleven	.90	.45	.25
54	Frank Tanana	.90	.45	.25
55	Ken Singleton	.90	.45	.25
56	Mike Hargrove	.90	.45	.25
57	Don Sutton	3.50	1.75	1.00

1979 Kellogg's

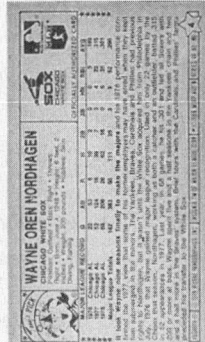

For its 1979 3-D issue, Kellogg's increased the size of the set to 60 cards, but reduced the width of the cards to 1-15/16". Depth stayed the same as in previous years, 3-1/4". The narrower card format seems to have compounded the problem of curling and subsequent cracking of the ribbed plastic surface which helps give the card a 3-D effect. Cards with major cracks can be graded no higher than VG. The complete set price in the checklist that follows does not include the scarcer variations. Numerous minor variations featuring copyright and trademark logos can be found in the set.

		NM	EX	VG
	Complete Set (60):	30.00	15.00	9.00
	Common Player:	.60	.30	.20
1	Bruce Sutter	2.50	1.25	.70
2	Ted Simmons	.60	.30	.20
3	Ross Grimsley	.60	.30	.20
4	Wayne Nordhagen	.60	.30	.20
5a	Jim Palmer (PCT. .649)	3.00	1.50	.90
5b	Jim Palmer (PCT. .650)	3.00	1.50	.90
6	John Henry Johnson	.60	.30	.20
7	Jason Thompson	.60	.30	.20
8	Pat Zachry	.60	.30	.20
9	Dennis Eckersley	3.00	1.50	.90
10a	Paul Splittorff (IP 1665)	.60	.30	.20
10b	Paul Splittorff (IP 1666)	.60	.30	.20
11a	Ron Guidry (Hits 397)	.60	.30	.20
11b	Ron Guidry (Hits 396)	.60	.30	.20
12	Jeff Burroughs	.60	.30	.20
13	Rod Carew	3.00	1.50	.90
14a	Buddy Bell (No trade line in bio.)	1.00	.50	.30
14b	Buddy Bell (Trade line in bio.)	.60	.30	.20
15	Jim Rice	1.00	.50	.30
16	Garry Maddox	.60	.30	.20
17	Willie McCovey	3.00	1.50	.90
18	Steve Carlton	3.00	1.50	.90
19a	J. R. Richard (Stats begin with 1972.)	.60	.30	.20
19b	J. R. Richard (Stats begin with 1971.)	.60	.30	.20
20	Paul Molitor	3.00	1.50	.90
21a	Dave Parker (AVG. .281)	.60	.30	.20
21b	Dave Parker (AVG. .318)	.60	.30	.20
22a	Pete Rose (1978 3B 3)	7.50	3.75	2.25
22b	Pete Rose (1978 3B 33)	7.50	3.75	2.25
23a	Vida Blue (Runs 819)	.60	.30	.20
23b	Vida Blue (Runs 818)	.60	.30	.20
24	Richie Zisk	.60	.30	.20

25a	Darrell Porter (2B 101)	.60	.30	.20
25b	Darrell Porter (2B 111)	.60	.30	.20
26a	Dan Driessen (Games 642)	.60	.30	.20
26b	Dan Driessen (Games 742)	.60	.30	.20
27a	Geoff Zahn (1978 Minnesota)	.60	.30	.20
27b	Geoff Zahn (1978 Minnesota)	.60	.30	.20
28	Phil Niekro	2.50	1.25	.70
29	Tom Seaver	3.00	1.50	.90
30	Fred Lynn	.60	.30	.20
31	Bill Bonham	.60	.30	.20
32	George Foster	.60	.30	.20
33a	Terry Puhl (Last line of bio begins "Terry...")	.60	.30	.20
33b	Terry Puhl (Last line of bio begins "His...")	.60	.30	.20
34a	John Candelaria (Age is 24.)	.60	.30	.20
34b	John Candelaria (Age is 25.)	.60	.30	.20
35	Bob Knepper	.60	.30	.20
36	Freddie Patek	.60	.30	.20
37	Chris Chambliss	.60	.30	.20
38a	Bob Forsch (1977 Games 86)	.60	.30	.20
38b	Bob Forsch (1977 Games 35)	.60	.30	.20
39a	Ken Griffey (1978 AB 674)	.60	.30	.20
39b	Ken Griffey (1978 AB 614)	.60	.30	.20
40	Jack Clark	.60	.30	.20
41a	Dwight Evans (1978 Hits 13)	.60	.30	.20
41b	Dwight Evans (1978 Hits 123)	.60	.30	.20
42	Lee Mazzilli	.60	.30	.20
43	Mario Guerrero	.60	.30	.20
44	Larry Bowa	.60	.30	.20
45a	Carl Yastrzemski (Games 9930)	4.00	2.00	1.25
45b	Carl Yastrzemski (Games 9929)	4.00	2.00	1.25
46a	Reggie Jackson (1978 Games 162)	6.00	3.00	1.75
46b	Reggie Jackson (1978 Games 139)	6.00	3.00	1.75
47	Rick Reuschel	.60	.30	.20
48a	Mike Flanagan (1976 SO 57)	.60	.30	.20
48b	Mike Flanagan (1976 SO 56)	.60	.30	.20
49a	Gaylord Perry (1973 Hits 325)	2.50	1.25	.70
49b	Gaylord Perry (1973 Hits 315)	2.50	1.25	.70
50	George Brett	6.00	3.00	1.75
51a	Craig Reynolds (Last line of bio begins "He spent...")	.60	.30	.20
51b	Craig Reynolds (Last line of bio begins "In those...")	.60	.30	.20
52	Davey Lopes	.60	.30	.20
53a	Bill Almon (2B 31)	.60	.30	.20
53b	Bill Almon (2B 41)	.60	.30	.20
54	Roy Howell	.60	.30	.20
55	Frank Tanana	.60	.30	.20
56a	Doug Rau (1978 PCT. .577)	.60	.30	.20
56b	Doug Rau (1978 PCT. .625)	.60	.30	.20
57a	Rick Monday (1976 Runs 197)	.60	.30	.20
57b	Rick Monday (1976 Runs 107)	.60	.30	.20
58	Jon Matlack	.60	.30	.20
59a	Ron Jackson (Last line of bio begins "His best...")	.60	.30	.20
59b	Ron Jackson (Last line of bio begins "The Twins...")	.60	.30	.20
60	Jim Sundberg	.60	.30	.20

1980 Kellogg's

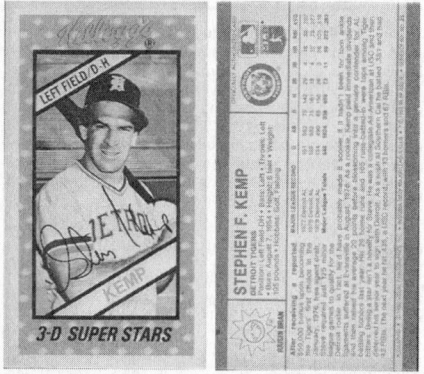

3-D SUPER STARS

The 1980 cereal company issue featured the narrowest format of any Kellogg's card, 1-7/8" x 3-1/4". For the second straight year, set size remained at 60 cards, available either singly in boxes of cereal, or as complete sets by a mail-in offer.

		NM	EX	VG
Complete Set (60):		25.00	12.50	7.50
Common Player:		.60	.30	.20
1	Ross Grimsley	.60	.30	.20
2	Mike Schmidt	4.00	2.00	1.25
3	Mike Flanagan	.60	.30	.20
4	Ron Guidry	.60	.30	.20
5	Bert Blyleven	.60	.30	.20
6	Dave Kingman	.60	.30	.20
7	Jeff Newman	.60	.30	.20
8	Steve Rogers	.60	.30	.20
9	George Brett	4.00	2.00	1.25
10	Bruce Sutter	2.00	1.00	.60
11	Gorman Thomas	.60	.30	.20
12	Darrell Porter	.60	.30	.20
13	Roy Smalley	.60	.30	.20
14	Steve Carlton	2.00	1.00	.60
15	Jim Palmer	2.00	1.00	.60
16	Bob Bailor	.60	.30	.20
17	Jason Thompson	.60	.30	.20
18	Graig Nettles	.60	.30	.20
19	Ron Cey	.60	.30	.20
20	Nolan Ryan	7.50	3.75	2.25

21	Ellis Valentine	.60	.30	.20
22	Larry Hisle	.60	.30	.20
23	Dave Parker	.60	.30	.20
24	Eddie Murray	2.00	1.00	.60
25	Willie Stargell	2.00	1.00	.60
26	Reggie Jackson	4.00	2.00	1.25
27	Carl Yastrzemski	2.50	1.25	.70
28	Andre Thornton	.60	.30	.20
29	Davey Lopes	.60	.30	.20
30	Ken Singleton	.60	.30	.20
31	Steve Garvey	1.00	.50	.30
32	Dave Winfield	2.00	1.00	.60
33	Steve Kemp	.60	.30	.20
34	Claudell Washington	.60	.30	.20
35	Pete Rose	6.00	3.00	1.75
36	Cesar Cedeno	.60	.30	.20
37	John Stearns	.60	.30	.20
38	Lee Mazzilli	.60	.30	.20
39	Larry Bowa	.60	.30	.20
40	Fred Lynn	.60	.30	.20
41	Carlton Fisk	2.00	1.00	.60
42	Vida Blue	.60	.30	.20
43	Keith Hernandez	.60	.30	.20
44	Jim Rice	1.00	.50	.30
45	Ted Simmons	.60	.30	.20
46	Chet Lemon	.60	.30	.20
47	Fergie Jenkins	2.00	1.00	.60
48	Gary Matthews	.60	.30	.20
49	Tom Seaver	2.50	1.25	.70
50	George Foster	.60	.30	.20
51	Phil Niekro	2.00	1.00	.60
52	Johnny Bench	2.50	1.25	.70
53	Buddy Bell	.60	.30	.20
54	Lance Parrish	.60	.30	.20
55	Joaquin Andujar	.60	.30	.20
56	Don Baylor	.60	.30	.20
57	Jack Clark	.60	.30	.20
58	J.R. Richard	.60	.30	.20
59	Bruce Bochte	.60	.30	.20
60	Rod Carew	2.00	1.00	.60

1969 Kelly's Potato Chips Pins

Consisting of 20 pins, each measuring approximately 1-3/16" in diameter, this set was issued by Kelly's Potato Chips in 1969 and has a heavy emphasis on St. Louis Cardinals. The pin has a black-and-white player photo in the center surrounded by either a red border (for A.L. players) or a blue border (for N.L. players) that displays the player's team and name at the top and bottom. "Kelly's" appears to the left while the word "Zip!" is printed to the right. The pins are unnumbered.

		NM	EX	VG
Complete Set (20):		350.00	175.00	100.00
Common Player:		5.00	2.50	1.50
(1)	Luis Aparicio	25.00	12.50	7.50
(2)	Ernie Banks	45.00	22.00	13.50
(3)	Glenn Beckert	5.00	2.50	1.50
(4)	Lou Brock	25.00	12.50	7.50
(5)	Curt Flood	5.00	2.50	1.50
(6)	Bob Gibson	25.00	12.50	7.50
(7)	Joel Horlen	5.00	2.50	1.50
(8)	Al Kaline	45.00	22.00	13.50
(9)	Don Kessinger	5.00	2.50	1.50
(10)	Mickey Lolich	5.00	2.50	1.50
(11)	Juan Marichal	25.00	12.50	7.50
(12)	Willie Mays	75.00	37.00	22.00
(13)	Tim McCarver	7.50	3.75	2.25
(14)	Denny McLain	6.00	3.00	1.75
(15)	Pete Rose	65.00	32.00	19.50
(16)	Ron Santo	7.50	3.75	2.25
(17)	Joe Torre	15.00	7.50	4.50
(18)	Pete Ward	5.00	2.50	1.50
(19)	Billy Williams	25.00	12.50	7.50
(20)	Carl Yastrzemski	60.00	30.00	18.00

1887 W.S. Kimball Champions (N184)

Similar to sets issued by Allen & Ginter and Goodwin, the Kimball tobacco company of Rochester, N.Y., issued its own 50-card set of "Champions of Games and Sport" in 1887, and included four baseball players among the "billiardists, girl riders, tight-rope walkers" and other popular celebrities featured in the series. Measuring 1-1/2" x 2-3/4", the color lithographed artwork on the card features a posed portrait, which occupies the top three-fourths, and a drawing of the player in action at the bottom. The back of the card contains an ad for Kimball Cigarettes along with a list of the various sports and activities depicted in the set. The Kimball promotion also included an album to house the card set.

	NM	EX	VG
Complete Set (4):	9,500	4,700	2,800
Common Player:	2,400	1,200	725.00
Album:	4,125	1,650	1,000
(1) E.A. Burch	2,400	1,200	725.00
(2) Dell Darling	2,400	1,200	725.00
(3) Hardie Henderson	2,400	1,200	725.00
(4) James O'Neil (O'Neill)	2,400	1,200	725.00

1957-1959 Kiwanis Orioles Clinic

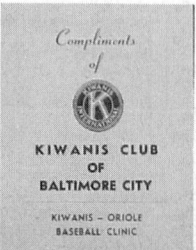

Details are lacking on this card which may or may not have been part of a series. Unless or until further players are check-listed, it is impossible to date the issue any more precisely. The front of the 2-7/8" x 3-1/4" card has a sepia photo that appears to have been copied from a team-issued postcard or picture. On back is the Kiwanis International logo with "Compliments / of" above and "KIWANIS CLUB / OF / BALTIMORE CITY / KIWANIS - ORIOLE / BASEBALL CLINIC" below.

	NM	EX	VG
Bob Nieman	40.00	20.00	12.00

1955-1957 Ted Kluszewski Steak House

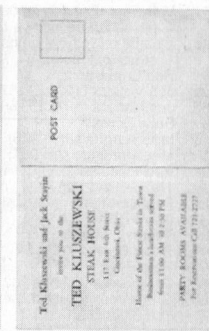

The true scope of this issue combined with the related Charcoal Steak House card (see also) is not known. Based on cards showing Klu in Reds and Angels uniforms, it is possible examples may yet be seen in Pirates and White Sox uniforms. Measuring about 3-1/2" x 5-1/2", the black-and-white cards have a facsimile signature of Kluszewski on front. The back is postcard style and advertises the Cincinnati restaurant he operated with Jack Stayin.

	NM	EX	VG
Ted Kluszewski (Reds, fielding, white cap.)	75.00	37.50	22.50
Ted Kluszewski (Reds, portrait, dark cap.)	100.00	50.00	30.00

1930s Knickerbocker Beer Yankees Premium

Jacob Ruppert, who owned both the Yankees and the Knickerbocker Brewing Co., is pictured on this 10" x 8" black-and-white, blank-backed premium photo with a trio of his Italian stars. Facsimile autographs of all are printed on front.

	NM	EX	VG
Tony Lazzeri, Jacob Ruppert, Joe DiMaggio, Frank Crosetti	150.00	75.00	45.00

1921 Koester Bread N.Y. Giants/Yankees

CHAS. STENGEL
Outf.—New York Nationals

The 1921 World Series was the first of many for the N.Y. Yankees, and it was the first "subway series," as their opponents were the Giants. This special card issue, a blank-backed version of the 1921-22 American Caramel Series of 90/120 (E121), featured the players, managers and coaches of each team. The 2" x about 3-1/4" cards feature black-and-white photos on front. They were distributed in October 1921, by E.H. Koester, a New York bakery. The unnumbered cards are checklisted here alphabetically within team. Several of the players in this issue do not appear in the contemporary American Caramel sets. A rarely seen album was issued to house the cards.

		NM	EX	VG
Complete Set (52):		45,000	22,500	13,500
Common Player:		400.00	200.00	120.00
Album:		800.00	400.00	240.00
N.Y. Giants Team Set:		19,000	9,500	5,700
(1)	Dave Bancroft	1,200	600.00	350.00
(2)	Jesse Barnes	400.00	200.00	120.00
(3)	Howard Berry	400.00	200.00	120.00
(4)	"Ed." Brown	400.00	200.00	120.00
(5)	Jesse Burkett	3,500	1,750	1,050
(6)	Geo. J. Burns	400.00	200.00	120.00
(7)	Cecil Causey	400.00	200.00	120.00
(8)	"Bill" Cunningham	400.00	200.00	120.00
(9)	"Phil" Douglas	400.00	200.00	120.00
(10)	Frank Frisch	1,200	600.00	350.00
(11)	Alexander Gaston	400.00	200.00	120.00
(12)	"Mike" Gonzalez	600.00	300.00	180.00
(13)	Hugh Jennings	1,200	600.00	350.00
(14)	George Kelly	1,200	600.00	350.00
(15)	John McGraw	1,200	600.00	350.00
(16)	Emil Meusel	400.00	200.00	120.00
(17)	Arthur Nehf	400.00	200.00	120.00
(18)	John Rawlings	400.00	200.00	120.00
(19)	"Bill" Ryan	400.00	200.00	120.00
(20)	"Slim" Sallee	400.00	200.00	120.00
(21)	"Pat" Shea	400.00	200.00	120.00
(22)	Earl Smith	400.00	200.00	120.00
(23)	Frank Snyder	17,500	8,750	5,250
(24)	Chas. Stengel	1,200	600.00	350.00
(25)	Fred Toney	400.00	200.00	120.00
(26)	Ross Young (Youngs)	1,200	600.00	350.00
N.Y. Yankees Team Set:		26,000	13,000	7,800
(1)	Frank Baker	1,200	600.00	350.00
(2)	"Rip" Collins	400.00	200.00	120.00
(3)	Lou De Vormer	400.00	200.00	120.00
(4)	Alex Ferguson	400.00	200.00	120.00
(5)	William Fewster	400.00	200.00	120.00
(6)	Harry Harper	400.00	200.00	120.00
(7)	"Chicken" Hawks	400.00	200.00	120.00
(8)	Fred Hoffmann (Hofmann)	400.00	200.00	120.00
(9)	Waite Hoyt	1,200	600.00	350.00
(10)	Miller Huggins	1,200	600.00	350.00
(11)	Carl Mays	400.00	200.00	120.00
(12)	M.J. McNally	400.00	200.00	120.00
(13)	R. Meusel	400.00	200.00	120.00
(14)	Elmer Miller	400.00	200.00	120.00
(15)	John Mitchell	400.00	200.00	120.00
(16)	Chas. O'Leary	400.00	200.00	120.00
(17)	Roger Peckinpaugh	400.00	200.00	120.00
(18)	William Piercy	400.00	200.00	120.00
(19)	Walter Pipp	400.00	200.00	120.00
(20)	Jack Quinn	400.00	200.00	120.00
(21)	Tom Rogers	400.00	200.00	120.00
(22)	Robert Roth	400.00	200.00	120.00
(23)	George Ruth	15,000	7,500	4,500
(24)	Walter Schang	400.00	200.00	120.00
(25)	Robert Shawkey	400.00	200.00	120.00
(26)	Aaron Ward	400.00	200.00	120.00

1911-16 Kotton Tobacco

The T216 baseball card set, issued with several brands by the People's Tobacco Co., is the last of the Louisiana cigarette sets and the most confusing. Issued over a period of several years between 1911 and 1916, the set uses the same pictures as several contemporary caramel and bakery sets. Cards measure a nominal 1-1/2" x 2-5/8", though reasonable allowance must be made for original cutting vari-

Cobb, c.f. Detroit Am.

KOTTON CIGARETTES
NEVER GO OUT.
MADE BY
Peoples Tobacco Co. Ltd.
NEW ORLEANS, LA.

ances. Positive identification can be made by the back of the cards. The Peoples Tobacco cards carry advertising for one of three brands of cigarettes: Kotton, Mino or Virginia Extra. The Kotton brand is the most common, with cards found in two types; one has a glossy front finish, while a second scarcer type is printed on a thin paper. The thin paper cards command an additional 15 percent premium. The glossy-front cards can be found with either of two ad styles on back: "KOTTON / TOBACCO" (Factory No. 11) or "KOTTON / CIGARETTES" (Factory No. 4). The cards include players from the American, National and Federal Leagues. The complete set price includes only the least expensive of each variation.

		NM	EX	VG
Common Player:		1,000	500.00	300.00
(1)	Jack Barry/Btg	1,000	500.00	300.00
(2)	Jack Barry/Fldg	1,000	500.00	300.00
(3)	Harry Bemis	1,000	500.00	300.00
(4a)	Chief Bender (Philadelphia, striped cap.)	2,400	1,200	725.00
(4b)	Chief Bender (Baltimore, striped cap.)	2,400	1,200	725.00
(5a)	Chief Bender (Philadelphia, white cap.)	2,400	1,200	725.00
(5b)	Chief Bender (Baltimore, white cap.)	2,400	1,200	725.00
(6)	Bill Bergen	1,000	500.00	300.00
(7a)	Bob Bescher (Cincinnati)	1,000	500.00	300.00
(7b)	Bob Bescher (St. Louis)	1,000	500.00	300.00
(8)	Roger Bresnahan	2,400	1,200	725.00
(9)	Al Bridwell/Btg	1,000	500.00	300.00
(10a)	Al Bridwell/Sliding (New York)	1,000	500.00	300.00
(10b)	Al Bridwell/Sliding (St. Louis)	1,000	500.00	300.00
(11)	Donie Bush	1,000	500.00	300.00
(12)	Doc Casey	1,000	500.00	300.00
(13)	Frank Chance	2,400	1,200	725.00
(14a)	Hal Chase/Fldg (New York)	1,000	500.00	300.00
(14b)	Hal Chase/Fldg (Buffalo)	2,400	1,200	725.00
(15)	Hal Chase/Portrait	1,600	800.00	475.00
(16a)	Ty Cobb/Standing (Detroit Am.)	24,000	12,000	7,200
(16b)	Ty Cobb/Standing (Detroit Americans)	24,000	12,000	7,250
(17)	Ty Cobb/Btg (Detroit Americans)	20,000	10,000	6,000
(18a)	Eddie Collins (Phila. Am.)	2,400	1,200	725.00
(18b)	Eddie Collins (Phila. Amer.)	2,400	1,200	725.00
(19)	Eddie Collins (Chicago)	2,400	1,200	725.00
(20a)	Sam Crawford (Small print.)	2,400	1,200	725.00
(20b)	Sam Crawford (Large print.)	2,400	1,200	725.00
(21)	Harry Davis	1,000	500.00	300.00
(22)	Ray Demmitt	1,000	500.00	300.00
(23)	Art Devlin	1,000	500.00	300.00
(24a)	Wild Bill Donovan (Detroit)	1,000	500.00	300.00
(24b)	Wild Bill Donovan (New York)	1,000	500.00	300.00
(25a)	Red Dooin (Philadelphia)	1,000	500.00	300.00
(25b)	Red Dooin (Cincinnati)	1,000	500.00	300.00
(26a)	Mickey Doolan (Philadelphia)	1,000	500.00	300.00
(26b)	Mickey Doolan (Baltimore)	1,000	500.00	300.00
(27)	Patsy Dougherty	1,000	500.00	300.00
(28a)	Larry Doyle, Larry Doyle/Btg (N.Y. Nat'l)	1,000	500.00	300.00
(28b)	Larry Doyle/Btg (New York Nat'l)	1,000	500.00	300.00
(29)	Larry Doyle/Throwing	1,000	500.00	300.00
(30)	Clyde Engle	1,000	500.00	300.00
(31a)	Johnny Evers (Chicago)	2,400	1,200	725.00
(31b)	Johnny Evers (Boston)	2,400	1,200	725.00
(32)	Art Fromme	1,000	500.00	300.00
(33a)	George Gibson (Pittsburg Nat'l., back view.)	1,000	500.00	300.00
(33b)	George Gibson (Pittsburgh Nat'l., back view.)	1,000	500.00	300.00
(34a)	George Gibson (Pittsburg Nat'l., front view.)	1,000	500.00	300.00
(34b)	George Gibson (Pittsburgh Nat'l., front view.)	1,000	500.00	300.00
(35a)	Topsy Hartsel (Phila. Am.)	1,000	500.00	300.00
(35b)	Topsy Hartsel (Phila. Amer.)	1,000	500.00	300.00
(36)	Roy Hartzell/Btg	1,000	500.00	300.00
(37)	Roy Hartzell/Catching	1,000	500.00	300.00
(38a)	Fred Jacklitsch (Philadelphia)	1,000	500.00	300.00
(38b)	Fred Jacklitsch (Baltimore)	1,000	500.00	300.00
(39a)	Hughie Jennings (Orange background.)	2,400	1,200	725.00
(39b)	Hughie Jennings (Red background.)	2,400	1,200	725.00
(40)	Red Kleinow	1,000	500.00	300.00
(41a)	Otto Knabe (Philadelphia)	1,000	500.00	300.00
(41b)	Otto Knabe (Baltimore)	1,000	500.00	300.00
(42)	Jack Knight	1,000	500.00	300.00
(43a)	Nap Lajoie/Fldg (Philadelphia)	2,400	1,200	725.00
(43b)	Nap Lajoie/Fldg (Cleveland)	2,400	1,200	725.00
(44)	Nap Lajoie/Portrait	2,400	1,200	725.00
(45a)	Hans Lobert (Cincinnati)	1,000	500.00	300.00
(45b)	Hans Lobert (New York)	1,000	500.00	300.00
(46)	Sherry Magee	1,000	500.00	300.00
(47)	Rube Marquard	2,400	1,200	725.00
(48a)	Christy Matthewson (Mathewson) (Large print.)	8,000	4,000	2,500
(48b)	Christy Matthewson (Mathewson) (Small print.)	8,000	4,000	2,500
(49a)	John McGraw (Large print.)	2,400	1,200	725.00
(49b)	John McGraw (Small print.)	2,400	1,200	725.00
(50)	Larry McLean	1,000	500.00	300.00
(51)	George McQuillan	1,000	500.00	300.00
(52)	Dots Miller/Btg	1,000	500.00	300.00
(53a)	Dots Miller/Fldg (Pittsburg)	1,000	500.00	300.00
(53b)	Dots Miller/Fldg (St. Louis)	2,000	1,000	600.00
(54a)	Danny Murphy (Philadelphia)	1,000	500.00	300.00
(54b)	Danny Murphy (Brooklyn)	1,000	500.00	300.00
(55)	Rebel Oakes	1,000	500.00	300.00
(56)	Bill O'Hara	1,000	500.00	300.00
(57)	Eddie Plank	4,000	2,000	1,200
(58a)	Germany Schaefer (Washington)	1,000	500.00	300.00
(58b)	Germany Schaefer (Newark)	1,000	500.00	300.00
(59)	Admiral Schlei	1,000	500.00	300.00
(60)	Boss Schmidt	1,000	500.00	300.00
(61)	Johnny Seigle	1,000	500.00	300.00
(62)	Dave Shean	1,000	500.00	300.00
(63)	Boss Smith (Schmidt)	1,000	500.00	300.00
(64)	Tris Speaker	4,000	2,000	1,200
(65)	Oscar Stanage	1,000	500.00	300.00
(66)	George Stovall	1,000	500.00	300.00
(67)	Jeff Sweeney	1,000	500.00	300.00
(68a)	Joe Tinker/Btg (Chicago Nat'l)	2,400	1,200	725.00
(68b)	Joe Tinker/Btg (Chicago Feds)	2,400	1,200	725.00
(69)	Joe Tinker/Portrait	2,400	1,200	725.00
(70a)	Honus Wagner/Btg (S.S.)	18,000	9,000	5,400
(70b)	Honus Wagner/Btg (2b.)	18,000	9,000	5,400
(71a)	Honus Wagner/Throwing (S.S.)	18,000	9,000	5,400
(71b)	Honus Wagner /Throwing (2b.)	18,000	9,000	5,400
(72)	Hooks Wiltse	6,500	3,200	1,950
(73)	Cy Young	4,200	2,100	1,260
(74a)	Heinie Zimmerman (2b.)	1,000	500.00	300.00
(74b)	Heinie Zimmerman (3b.)	1,000	500.00	300.00

1964 Sandy Koufax's Tropicana Postcard

In the early 1960s, Dodgers pitcher Sandy Koufax owned the Tropicana Motor Hotel in Hollywood. Among the collectible souvenirs of that venture are these color postcards picturing the player overlooking the pool. The original version pictures Koufax in civilian clothes. A later version uses the same photo, but has a Dodgers uniform crudely drawn on Koufax' photo.

	NM	EX	VG
Sandy Koufax (Civilian)	175.00	90.00	50.00
Sandy Koufax (Uniform)	150.00	75.00	45.00
Sandy Koufax (Uniform) 4" x 5-1/2"	800.00	400.00	240.00

1907 Krieg & Co. Chicago Cubs Base Ball Mail Card

Distributed by a shoe retailers' supply firm, this foldout black-and-white postcard features the World Champion Cubs. About 5-1/4" x 3-1/2" closed, the foldout opens to reveal portrait photos of 16 of the players, two per post-card size panel. Manager Frank Chance and the team president each have their own panel. The back cover of the mailer has a composite photo of the team, with a 1907 National League schedule on its flip side.

	NM	EX	VG
1907 Chicago Cubs Foldout	2,000	1,000	600.00

1976 Kroger Cincinnati Reds

Blank-backed and unnumbered, they are checklisted here alphabetically. Because the photos were licensed only by the players' union, and not Major League Baseball, photos do not show uniform logos. The grocery store chain gave away these 6 x 9 color photos, four per week, during a span in September and October.

		NM	EX	VG
Complete Set (16):		50.00	25.00	15.00
Common Player:		3.00	1.50	.90
Week 1				
(1)	Dan Driessen	3.00	1.50	.90
(2)	Ken Griffey Sr.	4.00	2.00	1.25
(3)	Fred Norman	3.00	1.50	.90
(4)	Pete Rose	25.00	12.50	7.50
Week 2				
(1)	Ed Armbrister	3.00	1.50	.90
(2)	Johnny Bench	15.00	7.50	4.50
(3)	Jack Billingham	3.00	1.50	.90
(4)	Tony Perez	8.00	4.00	2.50
Week 3				
(1)	Rawly Eastwick	3.00	1.50	.90
(2)	George Foster	4.00	2.00	1.25
(3)	Cesar Geronimo	3.00	1.50	.90
(4)	Don Gullett	3.00	1.50	.90
Week 4				
(1)	Bob Bailey	3.00	1.50	.90
(2)	Dave Concepcion	3.00	1.50	.90
(3)	Joe Morgan	12.50	6.75	4.00
(4)	Gary Nolan	3.00	1.50	.90

1977 Kurland Tom Seaver

These large-format (4-3/16" x 5-1/2") black-and-white cards appear to have been produced in conjunction with promotional appearances by Seaver for Kurland Cadillac-Oldsmobile, a metropolitan New York auto dealer. Most of the cards seen are autographed by Seaver. The back is blank.

		NM	EX	VG
Complete Set (2):		150.00	75.00	45.00
Common Card:		75.00	37.00	22.00
(1)	Tom Seaver (N.Y. Mets)	75.00	37.00	22.00
(2)	Tom Seaver (Cincinnati Reds)	75.00	37.00	22.00

1926 Kut Outs Giants/Yankees Die-Cuts

These black-and-white, blank-back, die-cut cards were sold as complete sets for 10 cents per team. The size varies with the pose depicted, but the cards are generally about 2" wide and 4-1/2" tall. The player's name is printed at the bottom of his photo. The unnumbered cards are checklisted here in alphabetical order by team. The issue is very similar to the Middy Bread Cardinals/Browns cards of 1927.

		NM	EX	VG
Complete Set (20):		14,500	5,800	2,900
Common Player:		350.00	140.00	70.00
	N.Y. Giants Team Set:	4,500	1,800	900.00
(1)	Ed Farrell	350.00	140.00	70.00
(2)	Frank Frisch	1,200	600.00	350.00
(3)	George Kelly	1,200	600.00	350.00
(4)	Freddie Lindstrom	1,200	600.00	350.00
(5)	John McGraw	1,200	600.00	350.00
(6)	Emil Meusel	350.00	140.00	70.00
(7)	John Scott	350.00	140.00	70.00
(8)	Frank Snyder	350.00	140.00	70.00
(9)	Billy Southworth	350.00	140.00	70.00
(10)	Ross Young (Youngs)	1,200	600.00	350.00
	N.Y. Yankees Team Set:	10,000	4,000	2,000
(11)	Pat Collins	350.00	140.00	70.00
(12)	Earle Combs	1,200	600.00	350.00
(13)	Joe Dugan	350.00	140.00	70.00
(14)	Lou Gehrig	2,500	1,000	500.00
(15)	Miller Huggins	1,200	600.00	350.00
(16)	Mark Koenig	350.00	140.00	70.00
(17)	Tony Lazzeri	1,200	600.00	350.00
(18)	Bob Meusel	350.00	140.00	70.00
(19)	Herb Pennock	1,200	600.00	350.00
(20)	Babe Ruth	5,000	2,000	1,000

L

1912 La Azora Cigars

These postcard-size (about 3-3/8" x 5-3/8") ad cards were issued by a Detroit cigar maker. Both cards feature of their front a borderless sepia photo of Ty Cobb, though he is not named. The backs differ somewhat in format and content, but basically provide the Tigers' home and road schedules for the season.

		NM	EX	VG
Complete Set (2):		5,000	2,500	1,500
(1)	Ty Cobb/Fldg (Home schedule.)	3,000	1,500	900.00
(2)	Ty Cobb/Sliding (Road schedule.)	3,000	1,500	900.00

1958-60 L.A. Dodgers Premium Pictures

Apparently issued over a period of years from 1958 through at least 1960, these black-and-white, 8-1/2" x 11" premium pictures were sold as a set through Dodgers souvenir outlets, though the make-up of a set changed with the comings and goings of players. The blank-backed pictures feature on front a pencil portrait of the player, with his name printed towards the bottom. The signature of sports artist Nicholas Volpe also appears on front. The unnumbered pictures are checklisted here alphabetically.

		NM	EX	VG
Complete Set (16):		300.00	150.00	90.00
Common Player:		15.00	7.50	4.50
(1)	Walter Alston	17.50	8.75	5.25
(2)	Roy Campanella	30.00	15.00	9.00
(3)	Gino Cimoli	15.00	7.50	4.50
(4)	Don Drysdale	30.00	15.00	9.00
(5)	Carl Erskine	15.00	7.50	4.50
(6)	Carl Furillo	20.00	10.00	6.00
(7)	Jim Gilliam	17.50	8.75	5.25
(8)	Gil Hodges	30.00	15.00	9.00
(9)	Clem Labine	15.00	7.50	4.50
(10)	Wally Moon	15.00	7.50	4.50
(11)	Don Newcombe	17.50	8.75	5.25
(12)	Johnny Podres	17.50	8.75	5.25
(13)	Pee Wee Reese	30.00	15.00	9.00
(14)	Rip Repulski	15.00	7.50	4.50
(15)	Vin Scully, Jerry Doggett (Announcers)	15.00	7.50	4.50
(16)	Duke Snider	30.00	15.00	9.00

1959 L.A. Dodgers Postcards

In the team's second year in California, the Dodgers began production of an on-going set of color player postcards. Cards were usually sold in 10-card packs in stadium souvenir stands. The makeup of the packs sold varied as players came and went and cards were issued or withdrawn. When supplies of any player's cards were exhausted, he would be included in the current printing. Various photographers and printers were responsible for the issue over the years, but all utilized a sim-

ilar format of 3-1/2" x 5-1/2" glossy borderless fronts and postcard style backs. The initial effort in 1959 has no player identification on the front. Backs are printed in brown, including player ID, birthdate and place, copyright date and credits to Mirro Krome and Crocker Co. Cards are numbered as shown here, but with an "LA-D-" prefix. The set was also available in the form of an accordian-foldout.

		NM	EX	VG
Complete Set (12):		400.00	200.00	125.00
Common Player:		30.00	15.00	9.00
901	Duke Snider	40.00	20.00	12.00
902	Gil Hodges	35.00	17.50	10.00
903	Johnny Podres	30.00	15.00	9.00
904	Carl Furillo	30.00	15.00	9.00
905	Don Drysdale	40.00	20.00	12.00
906	Sandy Koufax	75.00	37.50	22.50
907	Jim Gilliam	30.00	15.00	9.00
908	Don Zimmer	30.00	15.00	9.00
909	Charlie Neal	30.00	15.00	9.00
910	Norm Larker (Photo actually Joe Pignatano.)	30.00	15.00	9.00
911	Clem Labine (Photo actually Stan Williams.)	30.00	15.00	9.00
912	John Roseboro	30.00	15.00	9.00

1960 L.A. Dodgers Postcards

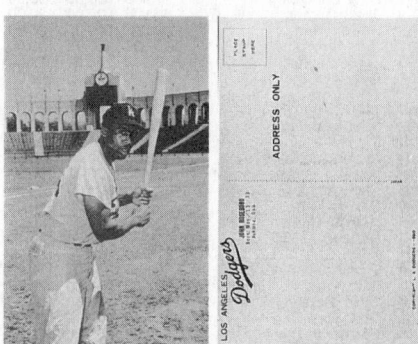

Like many baseball souvenirs, this set of team-issued postcards was "Made in Japan." The 3-1/2" x 5-1/2" cards share the basic format of the 1959 premiere issue with borderless color poses on front and postcard-style back. Backs are printed in blue with player ID and copyright date, but the cards are unnumbered. They are checklisted here alphabetically. The Carl Furillo card is scarce because it was withdrawn when he retired after playing only eight games in 1960.

		NM	EX	VG
Complete Set (12):		250.00	125.00	75.00
Common Player:		12.50	6.25	3.75
(1)	Walt Alston	12.50	6.25	3.75
(2)	Roger Craig	12.50	6.25	3.75
(3)	Don Drysdale	15.00	7.50	4.50
(4)	Carl Furillo	75.00	37.00	22.00
(5)	Gil Hodges	15.00	7.50	4.50
(6)	Sandy Koufax	60.00	30.00	18.00
(7)	Wally Moon	12.50	6.25	3.75
(8)	Charlie Neal	12.50	6.25	3.75
(9)	Johnny Podres	12.50	6.25	3.75
(10)	John Roseboro	12.50	6.25	3.75
(11)	Larry Sherry	12.50	6.25	3.75
(12)	Duke Snider	15.00	7.50	4.50

1962 L.A. Dodgers Pins

The attributed date is speculative based on available checklist information. This series of, presumably, stadium souvenir pinback buttons is in an unusually large 3-1/2" format. The pins have black-and-white photos on a white or light blue background. Two styles of name presentation are known, those with names in a white strip at the bottom of the pin and those with the names overprinted on the photo and more towards the bottom.

	NM	EX	VG
Common Player:	75.00	37.50	22.00
NAME IN STRIP			
Don Drysdale	60.00	30.00	18.00
Duke Snider	125.00	62.00	37.00
NAME OVERPRINTED			
Gil Hodges	95.00	47.00	28.00
Sandy Koufax	500.00	250.00	150.00
Maury Wills	75.00	37.50	22.00

1963 L.A. Dodgers Pin-Ups

Borrowing on the concept of the 1938 Goudey Heads-up cards, this set was sold, probably at the stadium souvenir stands, in a white envelope labeled "Los Angeles Dodgers Pin-Ups." The cards feature large full-color head-and-cap photos set atop cartoon ballplayers' bodies. Cards are printed on 7-1/4" x 8-1/2" semi-gloss cardboard with blank backs. The player's name appears in black on the front, along with the instructions, "Push out character carefully. Take scissors and trim white around player's head." Each figure was die-cut to allow its easy removal from the background.

	NM	EX	VG
Complete Set (10):	75.00	35.00	25.00
Common Player:	6.00	3.00	1.75
(1) Tommy Davis	7.50	3.75	2.25
(2) Willie Davis	7.50	3.75	2.25
(3) Don Drysdale	10.00	5.00	3.00
(4) Ron Fairly	6.00	3.00	1.75
(5) Frank Howard	7.50	3.75	2.25
(6) Sandy Koufax	25.00	12.50	7.50
(7) Joe Moeller	6.00	3.00	1.75
(8) Ron Perranoski	6.00	3.00	1.75
(9) John Roseboro	6.00	3.00	1.75
(10) Maury Wills	7.50	3.75	2.25

1965 L.A. Dodgers Motion Pins

These "flasher" pins were issued in conjunction with the Dodgers' World Series appearance and ultimate victory in 1965. The 2-1/2" diameter pins feature player portraits on a seamed blue background resembling a baseball. When the angle of view is changed, the player's name and team logo and the starbursts pop in and out of sight.

	NM	EX	VG
Don Drysdale	15.00	7.50	4.50
Sandy Koufax	25.00	12.50	7.50
Dodgers Logo - "Our Champs"	15.00	7.50	4.50

1979 L.A. Dodgers

Presumed to be a collectors' issue due to lack of sponsors or licensors logos, this set features the top players of the '79 Dodgers. Fronts of the 2-1/2" x 3-3/8" cards are borderless color photos. Backs are printed in blue and white with career highlights and personal data. Cards are checklisted here in alphabetical order.

 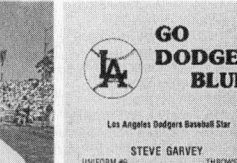

	NM	EX	VG
Complete Set (15):	15.00	7.50	4.50
Common Player:	2.00	1.00	.60
(1) Dusty Baker	3.00	1.50	.90
(2) Ron Cey	2.00	1.00	.60
(3) Terry Forster	2.00	1.00	.60
(4) Steve Garvey	4.00	2.00	1.25
(5) Burt Hooton	2.00	1.00	.60
(6) Charlie Hough	2.00	1.00	.60
(7) Tommy Lasorda	3.00	1.50	.90
(8) Dave Lopes	2.00	1.00	.60
(9) Rick Monday	2.00	1.00	.60
(10) Manny Mota	2.00	1.00	.60
(11) Doug Rau	2.00	1.00	.60
(12) Bill Russell	2.00	1.00	.60
(13) Reggie Smith	2.00	1.00	.60
(14) Don Sutton	4.00	2.00	1.25
(15) Steve Yeager	2.00	1.00	.60

1980 L.A. Dodgers Police

 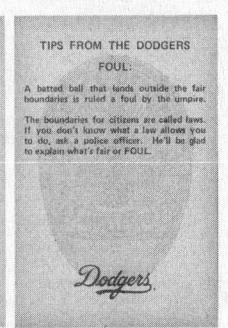

Producers of one of the most popular police and safety sets in the hobby, the Dodgers began this successful promotion in 1980. The 2-13/16" x 4-1/8" cards feature full-color photos on front, along with brief personal statistics. Backs include "Tips from the Dodgers" along with the team and LAPD logos. Cards are numbered by player uniform number, with an unnumbered team card also included in the set.

	NM	EX	VG
Complete Set (30):	6.00	3.00	1.75
Common Player:	.50	.25	.15
5 Johnny Oates	.50	.25	.15
6 Steve Garvey	2.00	1.00	.60
7 Steve Yeager	.50	.25	.15
8 Reggie Smith	.50	.25	.15
9 Gary Thomasson	.50	.25	.15
10 Ron Cey	.60	.30	.20
12 Dusty Baker	.60	.30	.20
13 Joe Ferguson	.50	.25	.15
15 Davey Lopes	.50	.25	.15
16 Rick Monday	.50	.25	.15
18 Bill Russell	.50	.25	.15
20 Don Sutton	2.00	1.00	.60
21 Jay Johnstone	.50	.25	.15
23 Teddy Martinez	.50	.25	.15
27 Joe Beckwith	.50	.25	.15
28 Pedro Guerrero	.50	.25	.15
29 Don Stanhouse	.50	.25	.15
30 Derrel Thomas	.50	.25	.15
31 Doug Rau	.50	.25	.15
34 Ken Brett	.50	.25	.15
35 Bob Welch	.50	.25	.15
37 Robert Castillo	.50	.25	.15
38 Dave Goltz	.50	.25	.15
41 Jerry Reuss	.50	.25	.15
43 Rick Sutcliffe	.60	.30	.20
44 Mickey Hatcher	.50	.25	.15
46 Burt Hooton	.50	.25	.15
49 Charlie Hough	.50	.25	.15
51 Terry Forster	.50	.25	.15
--- Team Photo	.50	.25	.15

1913 Napoleon Lajoie Game

Although individual cards are not marked, these cards were produced as part of a Parker Bros. baseball board game called "The National American Baseball Game." Each of the approximately 2-3/8" x 3-1/4", round-cornered cards has a borderless photo on front picturing the Hall of Famer at bat. Backs have a chart of various baseball plays used in the game. Cards can be found with the Lajoie photo tinted either blue or red, the latter being somewhat scarcer.

	NM	EX	VG
Complete Game Set:	1,500	750.00	450.00
SINGLE CARD			
Napoleon Lajoie (Blue)	25.00	12.50	7.50
Napoleon Lajoie (Red)	45.00	22.50	13.50

1960 Lake To Lake Dairy Braves

 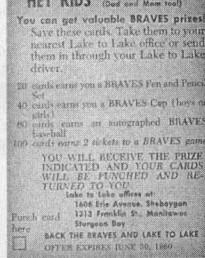

This 28-card set of unnumbered 2-1/2" x 3-1/4" cards offers a special challenge for the condition- conscious collector. Originally issued by being stapled to milk cartons, the cards were redeemable for prizes ranging from pen and pencil sets to Braves tickets. When sent in for redemption, the cards had a hole punched in the corner. Naturally, collectors most desire cards without the staple or punch holes. Cards are printed in blue ink on front, red ink on back. Because he was traded in May, and his card withdrawn, the Ray Boone card is scarce; the Billy Bruton card is unaccountably scarcer still.

	NM	EX	VG
Complete Set (28):	2,250	1,125	650.00
Common Player:	35.00	17.50	10.00
(1) Henry Aaron	500.00	250.00	150.00
(2) Joe Adcock	35.00	17.50	10.00
(3) Ray Boone	250.00	125.00	75.00
(4) Bill Bruton	500.00	250.00	150.00
(5) Bob Buhl	35.00	17.50	10.00
(6) Lou Burdette	35.00	17.50	10.00
(7) Chuck Cottier	35.00	17.50	10.00
(8) Wes Covington	35.00	17.50	10.00
(9) Del Crandall	35.00	17.50	10.00
(10) Charlie Dressen	35.00	17.50	10.00
(11) Bob Giggie	35.00	17.50	10.00
(12) Joey Jay	35.00	17.50	10.00
(13) Johnny Logan	35.00	17.50	10.00
(14) Felix Mantilla	35.00	17.50	10.00
(15) Lee Maye	35.00	17.50	10.00
(16) Don McMahon	35.00	17.50	10.00
(17) George Myatt	35.00	17.50	10.00
(18) Andy Pafko	35.00	17.50	10.00
(19) Juan Pizarro	35.00	17.50	10.00
(20) Mel Roach	35.00	17.50	10.00
(21) Bob Rush	35.00	17.50	10.00
(22) Bob Scheffing	35.00	17.50	10.00
(23) Red Schoendienst	75.00	37.50	22.50
(24) Warren Spahn	150.00	75.00	45.00
(25) Al Spangler	35.00	17.50	10.00
(26) Frank Torre	35.00	17.50	10.00
(27) Carl Willey	35.00	17.50	10.00
(28) Whitlow Wyatt	35.00	17.50	10.00

1923-24 La Moda

This is appears to be a parallel to the more frequently encountered Cuban cigar cards advertising the Billiken brand. Specialists feel that the La Moda ("The Fashion") branded cards survive at a rate about one per 10 Billikens, though demand is not such that prices follow such a ratio.

	NM	EX	VG
Common Player:	1,000	400.00	200.00
Stars: 2X			

(See 1923-24 Billiken for checklist and base card values.)

1970 La Pizza Royale Expos

La Pizza Royale

RUSTY STAUB
Voltigeur

This colorful collectors' issue features only Montreal Expos. Each of the 2-1/2" x 5" cards can be found printed in red, yellow, blue of green duo-tones. "La Pizza Royale" is printed in white above the player photo. Below the photo is the player's name and, in French, his position. Backs are blank and the cards are unnumbered. The checklist is presented here alphabetically. The La Pizza Royale cards are a fantasy issue produced by a collector for sale within the hobby.

		NM	EX	VG
Complete Set (14):		20.00	10.00	6.00
Common Player:		2.00	1.00	.60
(1)	Bob Bailey	2.00	1.00	.60
(2)	John Boccabella	2.00	1.00	.60
(3)	Ron Fairly	3.00	1.50	.90
(4)	Jim Gosger	2.00	1.00	.60
(5)	Coco Laboy	2.00	1.00	.60
(6)	Gene Mauch	3.00	1.50	.90
(7)	Rich Nye	2.00	1.00	.60
(8)	John O'Donoghue	2.00	1.00	.60
(9)	Adolfo Phillips	2.00	1.00	.60
(10)	Howie Reed	2.00	1.00	.60
(11)	Marv Staehle	2.00	1.00	.60
(12)	Rusty Staub	4.50	2.25	1.25
(13)	Gary Sutherland	2.00	1.00	.60
(14)	Bobby Wine	2.00	1.00	.60

1967 Laughlin World Series

Apparently a prototype set for subsequent offerings by the sports artist R.G. Laughlin that were produced by Fleer, this set of 64 cards was printed in black-and-white with the cartoon line drawings for which Laughlin was noted. The cards are an odd size, 2-3/4" x 3-1/2", like so many of the Laughlin/Fleer issues of the period. The text on the back is printed in red and offer details of the World Series from that year.

		NM	EX	VG
Complete Set (64):		450.00	225.00	135.00
Common Card:		9.00	4.50	2.75
1	1903 Red Sox/Pirates	9.00	4.50	2.75
2	1905 Giants/A's (Christy Mathewson)	20.00	10.00	6.00
3	1906 White Sox/Cubs	9.00	4.50	2.75
4	1907 Cubs/Tigers	9.00	4.50	2.75
5	1908 Cubs/Tigers (Joe Tinker, Evers, Frank Chance)	20.00	10.00	6.00
6	1909 Pirates/Tigers (Honus Wagner, Ty Cobb)	30.00	15.00	9.00
7	1910 A's/Cubs	9.00	4.50	2.75
8	1911 A's/Giants (John McGraw)	9.00	4.50	2.75
9	1912 Red Sox/Giants	9.00	4.50	2.75
10	1913 A's/Giants	9.00	4.50	2.75
11	1914 Braves/A's	9.00	4.50	2.75
12	1915 Red Sox/Phillies (Babe Ruth)	35.00	17.50	10.00
13	1916 White Sox/Dodgers (Babe Ruth)	35.00	17.50	10.00
14	1917 White Sox/Giants	9.00	4.50	2.75
15	1918 Red Sox/Cubs	9.00	4.50	2.75
16	1919 Reds/White Sox	35.00	17.50	10.00
17	1920 Indians/Dodgers (Bill Wambsganss)	9.00	4.50	2.75
18	1921 Giants/Yankees (Waite Hoyt)	9.00	4.50	2.75
19	1922 Giants/Yankees (Frank Frisch, Heinie Groh)	9.00	4.50	2.75
20	1923 Yankees/Giants (Babe Ruth)	35.00	17.50	10.00

21	1924 Senators/Giants (Walter Johnson)	15.00	7.50	4.50
22	1925 Pirates/Senators (Walter Johnson)	15.00	7.50	4.50
23	1926 Cardinals/Yankees (Grover Alexander, Anthony Lazzeri)	15.00	7.50	4.50
24	1927 Yankees/Pirates	9.00	4.50	2.75
25	1928 Yankees/Cardinals (Babe Ruth, Lou Gehrig)	35.00	17.50	10.00
26	1929 A's/Cubs	9.00	4.50	2.75
27	1930 A's/Cardinals	9.00	4.50	2.75
28	1931 Cardinals/A's (Pepper Martin)	9.00	4.50	2.75
29	1932 Yankees/Cubs (Babe Ruth)	35.00	17.50	10.00
30	1933 Giants/Senators (Mel Ott)	12.50	6.25	3.75
31	1934 Cardinals/Tigers (Dizzy Dean, Paul Dean)	20.00	10.00	6.00
32	1935 Tigers/Cubs	9.00	4.50	2.75
33	1936 Yankees/Giants	9.00	4.50	2.75
34a	1937 Yankees/Giants (Carl Hubbell) (#11 on uniform)	12.50	6.25	3.75
34b	1937 Yankees/Giants (Carl Hubbell) (#14 on uniform)	12.50	6.25	3.75
35	1938 Yankees/Cubs	9.00	4.50	2.75
36	1939 Yankees/Reds (Joe DiMaggio)	30.00	15.00	9.00
37	1940 Reds/Tigers	9.00	4.50	2.75
38	1941 Yankees/Dodgers (Mickey Owen)	9.00	4.50	2.75
39	1942 Cardinals/Yankees	9.00	4.50	2.75
40	1943 Yankees/Cardinals (Joe McCarthy)	9.00	4.50	2.75
41	1944 Cardinals/Browns	9.00	4.50	2.75
42	1945 Tigers/Cubs (Hank Greenberg)	15.00	7.50	4.50
43	1946 Cardinals/Red Sox (Enos Slaughter)	9.00	4.50	2.75
44	1947 Yankees/Dodgers (Al Gionfriddo)	9.00	4.50	2.75
45	1948 Indians/Braves (Bob Feller)	12.50	6.25	3.75
46	1949 Yankees/Dodgers (Allie Reynolds, Preacher Roe)	20.00	10.00	6.00
47	1950 Yankees/Phillies	9.00	4.50	2.75
48	1951 Yankees/Giants	9.00	4.50	2.75
49	1952 Yankees/Dodgers (Johnny Mize, Duke Snider)	20.00	10.00	6.00
50	1953 Yankees/Dodgers (Casey Stengel)	20.00	10.00	6.00
51	1954 Giants/Indians (Dusty Rhodes)	9.00	4.50	2.75
52	1955 Dodgers/Yankees (Johnny Podres)	20.00	10.00	6.00
53	1956 Yankees/Dodgers (Don Larsen)	25.00	12.50	7.50
54	1957 Braves/Yankees (Lew Burdette)	9.00	4.50	2.75
55	1958 Yankees/Braves (Hank Bauer)	9.00	4.50	2.75
56	1959 Dodgers/White Sox (Larry Sherry)	9.00	4.50	2.75
57	1960 Pirates/Yankees	25.00	12.50	7.50
58	1961 Yankees/Reds (Whitey Ford)	20.00	10.00	6.00
59	1962 Yankees/Giants	9.00	4.50	2.75
60	1963 Dodgers/Yankees (Sandy Koufax)	20.00	10.00	6.00
61	1964 Cardinals/Yankees (Mickey Mantle)	35.00	17.50	10.00
62	1965 Dodgers/Twins (Sandy Koufax)	9.00	4.50	2.75
63	1966 Orioles/Dodgers	9.00	4.50	2.75
64	1967 Cardinals/Red Sox (Bob Gibson)	9.00	4.50	2.75

1972 Laughlin Great Feats

Great Feats 5

George Sisler made 257 hits in 1920

Sports artist R.G. Laughlin created this set of 50 numbered cards and one unnumbered title card highlighting top performances by stars over the years. The cards depict the player in pen and ink, with one variation of the set adding flesh tones to the players. One variation of the set has red borders, the other (with the flesh tones) blue. The cards are blank backed and numbered on the front with a brief caption. Cards measure about 2-9/16" x 3-9/16". Sets originally sold for about $3.

		NM	EX	VG
Complete Set, Red (51):		45.00	22.50	13.50
Complete Set, Blue (51):		60.00	30.00	18.00
Common Player (Red):		1.50	.70	.45
Common Player (Blue): 1.5-2X				
1	Joe DiMaggio	12.00	6.00	3.50

2	Walter Johnson	4.50	2.25	1.25
3	Rudy York	1.50	.70	.45
4	Sandy Koufax	9.00	4.50	2.75
5	George Sisler	1.50	.70	.45
6	Iron Man McGinnity	1.50	.70	.45
7	Johnny VanderMeer	1.50	.70	.45
8	Lou Gehrig	12.00	6.00	3.50
9	Max Carey	1.50	.70	.45
10	Ed Delahanty	1.50	.70	.45
11	Pinky Higgins	1.50	.70	.45
12	Jack Chesbro	1.50	.70	.45
13	Jim Bottomley	1.50	.70	.45
14	Rube Marquard	1.50	.70	.45
15	Rogers Hornsby	1.50	.70	.45
16	Lefty Grove	1.50	.70	.45
17	Johnny Mize	1.50	.70	.45
18	Lefty Gomez	1.50	.70	.45
19	Jimmie Fox (Foxx)	1.50	.70	.45
20	Casey Stengel	1.50	.70	.45
21	Dazzy Vance	1.50	.70	.45
22	Jerry Lynch	1.50	.70	.45
23	Hughie Jennings	1.50	.70	.45
24	Stan Musial	4.50	2.25	1.25
25	Christy Mathewson	4.50	2.25	1.25
26	Elroy Face	1.50	.70	.45
27	Hack Wilson	1.50	.70	.45
28	Smoky Burgess	1.50	.70	.45
29	Cy Young	3.00	1.50	.90
30	Wilbert Robinson	1.50	.70	.45
31	Wee Willie Keeler	1.50	.70	.45
32	Babe Ruth	15.00	7.50	4.50
33	Mickey Mantle	15.00	7.50	4.50
34	Hub Leonard	1.50	.70	.45
35	Ty Cobb	7.50	3.75	2.25
36	Carl Hubbell	1.50	.70	.45
37	Joe Oeschger, Leon Cadore	1.50	.70	.45
38	Don Drysdale	1.50	.70	.45
39	Fred Toney, Hippo Vaughn	1.50	.70	.45
40	Joe Sewell	1.50	.70	.45
41	Grover Cleveland Alexander	1.50	.70	.45
42	Joe Adcock	1.50	.70	.45
43	Eddie Collins	1.50	.70	.45
44	Bob Feller	2.00	1.00	.60
45	Don Larsen	2.00	1.00	.60
46	Dave Philley	1.50	.70	.45
47	Bill Fischer	1.50	.70	.45
48	Dale Long	1.50	.70	.45
49	Bill Wambsganss	1.50	.70	.45
50	Roger Maris	4.50	2.25	1.25
---	Title Card	1.50	.70	.45

1973 Laughlin Super Stand-Ups

Babe

A dozen Hall of Famers are featured in this collectors' issue of stand-up figures. Printed in color on heavy cardboard, each is die-cut around the player action picture with typical measurements being 7" x 11". The stand-ups are much scarcer than most of the artist's other baseball issues. They are listed here alphabetically. The stand-ups originally retailed for $3.50 apiece.

		NM	EX	VG
Complete Set (13):		7,500	3,750	2,250
Common Player:		450.00	225.00	135.00
(1)	Hank Aaron	650.00	325.00	195.00
(2)	Johnny Bench	450.00	225.00	135.00
(3)	Roberto Clemente	750.00	375.00	225.00
(4)	Joe DiMaggio	750.00	375.00	225.00
(5)	Lou Gehrig	750.00	375.00	225.00
(6)	Gil Hodges	450.00	225.00	135.00
(7)	Sandy Koufax	750.00	375.00	225.00
(8)	Mickey Mantle	1,500	750.00	450.00
(9)	Willie Mays	650.00	325.00	195.00
(10)	Stan Musial	500.00	250.00	150.00
(11)	Babe Ruth	1,200	600.00	360.00
(12)	Tom Seaver	450.00	225.00	135.00
(13)	Ted Williams	650.00	325.00	195.00

1974 Laughlin All-Star Games

With pen and ink drawings by R.G. Laughlin on the fronts, this set (40 cards) features one card from each year of the game from 1933 to 1973. The 2-3/4" x 3-3/8" cards show a player in black ink in front of a light blue background with a glossy finish, with red printing for the title of the set and the year. The backs are printed in blue, with the year of the All-Star Game serving as the card number. Issue price was $3.50.

1963 Game

Municipal Stadium, Cleve. After four years, the All-Star game returned to one meeting. Mays drove in 2, walked, stole two bases, scored 2 and contributed a great catch. Bunning had his 4th hitless AS stint. AL reliever Radatz K'd 5.

NL-0 1 2 0 1 0 0 1 0—5
AL-0 1 2 0 0 0 0 0 0—3
WP:Jackson LP:Bunning
© 1974 R.G. Laughlin

		NM	EX	VG
	Complete Set (40):	60.00	30.00	18.00
	Common Player:	3.00	1.50	.90
33	Babe's Homer (Babe Ruth)	25.00	12.50	7.50
34a	Hub Fans Five (Carl Hubbell) (Uniform #11.)	4.50	2.25	1.25
34b	Hub Fans Five (Carl Hubbell) (Uniform #14.)	4.50	2.25	1.25
35	Foxx Smashes HR (Jimmie Foxx)	4.50	2.25	1.25
36	Ol' Diz Fogs 'Em (Dizzy Dean)	4.50	2.25	1.25
37	Four Hits for Ducky (Ducky Medwick)	3.00	1.50	.90
38	No-Hit Vandy (John VanderMeer)	3.00	1.50	.90
39	DiMaggio Homers (Joe DiMaggio)	20.00	10.00	6.00
40	West's 3-Run Shot (Max West)	3.00	1.50	.90
41	Vaughan Busts Two (Arky Vaughan)	3.00	1.50	.90
42	York's 2-Run Smash (Rudy York)	3.00	1.50	.90
43	Doerr's 3-Run Blast (Bobby Doerr)	3.00	1.50	.90
44	Cavarretta Reaches (Phil Cavarretta)	3.00	1.50	.90
46	Field Day for Ted (Ted Williams)	15.00	7.50	4.50
47	Big Cat Plants One (Johnny Mize)	3.00	1.50	.90
48	Raschi Pitches (Vic Raschi)	3.00	1.50	.90
49	Jackie Scores (Jackie Robinson)	12.00	6.00	3.50
50	Schoendienst Breaks (Red Schoendienst)	3.00	1.50	.90
51	Kiner Homers (Ralph Kiner)	3.00	1.50	.90
52	Sauer's Shot (Hank Sauer)	3.00	1.50	.90
53	Slaughter Hustles (Enos Slaughter)	3.00	1.50	.90
54	Rosen Hits (Al Rosen)	3.00	1.50	.90
55	Stan the Man's HR (Stan Musial)	7.50	3.75	2.25
56	Boyer Super (Ken Boyer)	3.00	1.50	.90
57	Kaline's Hits (Al Kaline)	4.50	2.25	1.25
58	Nellie Gets Two (Nellie Fox)	3.00	1.50	.90
59	Robbie Perfect (Frank Robinson)	4.50	2.25	1.25
60	Willie 3-for-4 (Willie Mays)	12.00	6.00	3.50
61	Bunning Hitless (Jim Bunning)	3.00	1.50	.90
62	Roberto Perfect (Roberto Clemente)	15.00	7.50	4.50
63	Monster Strikeouts (Dick Radatz)	3.00	1.50	.90
64	Callison's Homer (Johnny Callison)	3.00	1.50	.90
65	Stargell's Big Day (Willie Stargell)	3.00	1.50	.90
66	Brooks Gets Triple (Brooks Robinson)	4.50	2.25	1.25
67	Fergie Fans Six (Fergie Jenkins)	3.00	1.50	.90
68	Tom Terrific (Tom Seaver)	5.00	2.50	1.50
69	Stretch Belts Two (Willie McCovey)	3.00	1.50	.90
70	Yaz' Four Hits (Carl Yastrzemski)	4.50	2.25	1.25
71	Reggie Unloads (Reggie Jackson)	6.00	3.00	1.75
72	Henry Hammers (Hank Aaron)	12.00	6.00	3.50
73	Bonds Perfect (Bobby Bonds)	3.00	1.50	.90

1974 Laughlin Old-Time Black Stars

This set of slightly oversized cards (2-5/8" x 3-1/2") features drawings by R.G. Laughlin. The artwork is printed in brown and a light tan; backs are printed in brown on white stock. The set features many of the greatest players from the Negro Leagues. The cards carry no copyright date and no

mention of the prolific Laughlin, but the simple line drawings are obviously his work, and a subsequent issue four years later by Laughlin removes any doubt. Original retail price at time of issue was about $3.25.

		NM	EX	VG
	Complete Set (36):	60.00	30.00	18.00
	Common Player:	2.00	1.00	.60
1	Smokey Joe Williams	5.00	2.50	1.50
2	Rap Dixon	2.00	1.00	.60
3	Oliver Marcelle	2.00	1.00	.60
4	Bingo DeMoss	4.00	2.00	1.25
5	Willie Foster	2.50	1.25	.70
6	John Beckwith	2.00	1.00	.60
7	Floyd (Jelly) Gardner	2.00	1.00	.60
8	Josh Gibson	10.00	5.00	3.00
9	Jose Mendez	5.00	2.50	1.50
10	Pete Hill	5.00	2.50	1.50
11	Buck Leonard	5.00	2.50	1.50
12	Jud Wilson	5.00	2.50	1.50
13	Willie Wells	5.00	2.50	1.50
14	Jimmie Lyons	2.00	1.00	.60
15	Satchel Paige	10.00	5.00	3.00
16	Louis Santop	5.00	2.50	1.50
17	Frank Grant	7.50	3.75	2.25
18	Christobel Torrienti	5.00	2.50	1.50
19	Bullet Rogan	4.00	2.00	1.25
20	Dave Malarcher	2.50	1.25	.70
21	Spot Poles	2.00	1.00	.60
22	Home Run Johnson	2.50	1.25	.70
23	Charlie Grant	4.00	2.00	1.25
24	Cool Papa Bell	5.00	2.50	1.50
25	Cannonball Dick Redding	2.00	1.00	.60
26	Ray Dandridge	5.00	2.50	1.50
27	Biz Mackey	7.50	3.75	2.25
28	Fats Jenkins	2.00	1.00	.60
29	Martin Dihigo	5.00	2.50	1.50
30	Mule Suttles	5.00	2.50	1.50
31	Bill Monroe	2.00	1.00	.60
32	Dan McClellan	2.00	1.00	.60
33	Pop Lloyd	5.00	2.50	1.50
34	Oscar Charleston	5.00	2.50	1.50
35	Andrew "Rube" Foster	5.00	2.50	1.50
36	William (Judy) Johnson	5.00	2.50	1.50

1974 Laughlin Sportslang

Featuring the cartoon artwork of R.G. Laughlin, this 41-card set features 40 cards (plus one unnumbered title card) detailing the history and derivation of slang terms from several sports. The cards are 2-3/4" x 3-1/4", with red and blue printing on the front and red on the back. The cards are numbered on the back.

		NM	EX	VG
	Complete Set (41):	80.00	40.00	24.00
	Common Card:	3.00	1.50	.80
1	Bull Pen	3.00	1.50	.80
2	Charley Horse	3.00	1.50	.80
3	Derby	3.00	1.50	.80
4	Anchor Man	3.00	1.50	.80
5	Mascot	3.00	1.50	.80
6	Annie Oakley	3.00	1.50	.80
7	Taxi Squad	3.00	1.50	.80
8	Dukes	3.00	1.50	.80
9	Rookie	3.00	1.50	.80
10	Jinx	3.00	1.50	.80
11	Dark Horse	3.00	1.50	.80
12	Hat Trick	3.00	1.50	.80
13	Bell Wether	3.00	1.50	.80
14	Love	3.00	1.50	.80
15	Red Dog	3.00	1.50	.80
16	Barnstorm	3.00	1.50	.80
17	Bull's Eye	3.00	1.50	.80
18	Rabbit Punch	3.00	1.50	.80
19	The Upper Hand	3.00	1.50	.80
20	Handi Cap	3.00	1.50	.80
21	Marathon	3.00	1.50	.80
22	Southpaw	3.00	1.50	.80
23	Boner	3.00	1.50	.80
24	Gridiron	3.00	1.50	.80
25	Fan	3.00	1.50	.80
26	Moxie	3.00	1.50	.80
27	Birdie	3.00	1.50	.80
28	Sulky	3.00	1.50	.80
29	Dribble	3.00	1.50	.80
30	Donnybrook	3.00	1.50	.80
31	The Real McCoy	3.00	1.50	.80
32	Even Stephen	3.00	1.50	.80
33	Chinese Homer	3.00	1.50	.80
34	English	3.00	1.50	.80
35	Garrison Finish	3.00	1.50	.80
36	Foot in the Bucket	3.00	1.50	.80
37	Steeple Chase	3.00	1.50	.80
38	Long Shot	3.00	1.50	.80
39	Nip and Tuck	3.00	1.50	.80
40	Battery	3.00	1.50	.80
----	Header Card	3.00	1.50	.80

1975 Laughlin Batty Baseball

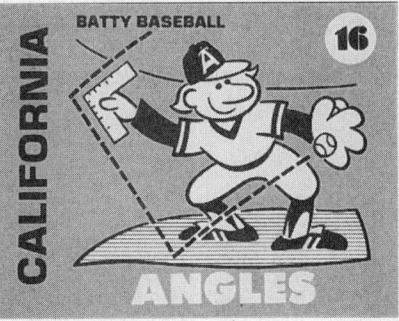

This 25-card set depicts one humorous nickname for each of 24 Major League teams, plus one unnumbered title card. The cards are approximately standard size at 2-1/2" x 3-1/2", with simple black and white cartoon drawings on the front with orange back-grounds. The backs are blank and the cards are numbered on front.

		NM	EX	VG
	Complete Set (25):	60.00	30.00	18.00
	Common Card:	3.00	1.50	.90
1	Oakland Daze	3.00	1.50	.90
2	Boston Wet Sox	3.00	1.50	.90
3	Cincinnati Dreads	3.00	1.50	.90
4	Chicago Wide Sox	3.00	1.50	.90
5	Milwaukee Boozers	3.00	1.50	.90
6	Philadelphia Fillies	3.00	1.50	.90
7	Cleveland Engines	3.00	1.50	.90
8	New York Mitts	3.00	1.50	.90
9	Texas Ranchers	3.00	1.50	.90
10	San Francisco Gents	3.00	1.50	.90
11	Houston Disastros	3.00	1.50	.90
12	Chicago Clubs	3.00	1.50	.90
13	Minnesota Wins	3.00	1.50	.90
14	St. Louis Gardeners	3.00	1.50	.90
15	New York Yankees	3.00	1.50	.90
16	California Angles	3.00	1.50	.90
17	Pittsburgh Irates	3.00	1.50	.90
18	Los Angeles Smoggers	3.00	1.50	.90
19	Baltimore Oreos	3.00	1.50	.90
20	Montreal Expose	3.00	1.50	.90
21	San Diego Parties	3.00	1.50	.90
22	Detroit Taggers	3.00	1.50	.90
23	Kansas City Broils	3.00	1.50	.90
24	Atlanta Briefs	3.00	1.50	.90
----	Header Card	3.00	1.50	.90

1976 Laughlin Diamond Jubilee

Busby hurls his first no-hitter

Detroit, April 27, 1973 — Steve Busby recorded the first of his two no-hitters in a night game, stopping the Tigers, 3-0. There were 7 routine fly balls and one nice stop by shortstop Patek. In the ninth first baseman Mayberry turned a line drive into a double play. The next season, young Busby pitched his second no-hitter, against the Milwaukee club.

• Based on the MOST MEMORABLE MOMENTS voted by the media and fans in each major league city.

This set of 32 oversized cards (2-3/4" x 4") features Laughlin's drawings of baseball stars highlighting specific events or records. The fronts are printed in black and blue over a red background; the backs are numbered and printed in blue with information about the specific event. Sets originally sold for $3.50.

		NM	EX	VG
	Complete Set (32):	90.00	45.00	25.00
	Common Player:	2.00	1.00	.60
1	Nolan Ryan	30.00	15.00	9.00
2	Ernie Banks	4.50	2.25	1.25
3	Mickey Lolich	2.00	1.00	.60
4	Sandy Koufax	9.00	4.50	2.75
5	Frank Robinson	3.00	1.50	.90
6	Bill Mazeroski	3.00	1.50	.90
7	Catfish Hunter	2.00	1.00	.60
8	Hank Aaron	9.00	4.50	2.75
9	Carl Yastrzemski	3.00	1.50	.90
10	Jim Bunning	2.00	1.00	.60
11	Brooks Robinson	3.00	1.50	.90
12	John VanderMeer	2.00	1.00	.60
13	Harmon Killebrew	3.00	1.50	.90
14	Lou Brock	2.50	1.25	.70
15	Steve Busby	2.00	1.00	.60
16	Nate Colbert	2.00	1.00	.60
17	Don Larsen	2.50	1.25	.70
18	Willie Mays	9.00	4.50	2.75
19	David Clyde	2.00	1.00	.60
20	Mack Jones	2.00	1.00	.60
21	Mike Hegan	2.00	1.00	.60
22	Jerry Koosman	2.00	1.00	.60
23	Early Wynn	2.50	1.25	.70
24	Nellie Fox	2.50	1.25	.70
25	Joe DiMaggio	15.00	7.50	4.50
26	Jackie Robinson	12.00	6.00	3.50
27	Ted Williams	12.00	6.00	3.50

		NM	EX	VG
28	Lou Gehrig	12.00	6.00	3.50
29	Bobby Thomson	2.50	1.25	.70
30	Roger Maris	7.50	3.75	2.25
31	Harvey Haddix	2.00	1.00	.60
32	Babe Ruth	20.00	10.00	6.00

1976 Laughlin Indianapolis Clowns

Founder Syd Pollock

Syd Pollock organized the Miami Ethiopian Clowns in 1929. His concept was to create a black club that not only could play pro ball but add laughs and showmanship to the game. The Clowns preceded the Harlem Globetrotters by a year. The national semi-pro champions turned pro in 1942, becoming the Cincinnati Clowns and later the Indianapolis Clowns, as they won numerous Negro AL titles. Also a Braves scout, Pollock retired from traveling baseball in 1964, turning the team over to Ed Hamman. Syd passed away in 1968.

Founder Syd Pollock

In a departure from the style of most Laughlin issues, this 42-card set does not use his artwork but rather black and white photos framed by a light blue border. The cards are oversized at 2-5/8" x 4-1/4", with red printing on front and back. The cards are numberd on the front.

		NM	EX	VG
Complete Set (42):		30.00	15.00	9.00
Common Player:		.60	.30	.20
1	Ed Hamman (Ed the Clown)	1.00	.50	.30
2	Dero Austin	.60	.30	.20
3	James Williams (Natureboy)	.60	.30	.20
4	Sam Brison (Birmingham)	.60	.30	.20
5	Richard King (King Tut)	.60	.30	.20
6	Syd Pollock (Founder)	.60	.30	.20
7	Nataniel (Lefty) Small	.60	.30	.20
8	Grant Greene (Double Duty)	.60	.30	.20
9	Nancy Miller (Lady Umpire)	.60	.30	.20
10	Billy Vaughn	.60	.30	.20
11	Sam Brison (Putout for Sam)	.60	.30	.20
12	Ed Hamman	.60	.30	.20
13	Dero Austin (Home Delivery)	.60	.30	.20
14	Steve (Nub) Anderson	.60	.30	.20
15	Joe Cherry	.60	.30	.20
16	Reece (Goose) Tatum	3.00	1.50	.90
17	James Williams (Natureboy)	.60	.30	.20
18	Byron Purnell	.60	.30	.20
19	Bat Boy	.60	.30	.20
20	Spec BeBop	.60	.30	.20
21	Satchel Paige	5.00	2.50	1.50
22	Prince Jo Henry	.60	.30	.20
23	Ed Hamman, Syd Pollock	.60	.30	.20
24	Paul Casanova	.60	.30	.20
25	Steve (Nub) Anderson (Nub Singles)	.60	.30	.20
26	Comiskey Park	.60	.30	.20
27	Toni Stone (Second Basewoman)	1.50	.70	.45
28	Dero Austin (Small Target)	.60	.30	.20
29	Calling Dr. Kildare (Sam Brison, Natureboy Williams)	.60	.30	.20
30	Oscar Charleston	2.00	1.00	.60
31	Richard King (King Tut)	.60	.30	.20
32	Ed and Prospects (Ed Hamman, Joe Cherry, Hal King)	.60	.30	.20
33	Team Bus	.60	.30	.20
34	Hank Aaron	6.00	3.00	1.75
35	The Greta Yogi	1.50	.70	.45
36	W.H. (Chauff) Wilson	.60	.30	.20
37	Doin' Their Thing (Sam Brison, Sonny Jackson)	.60	.30	.20
38	Billy Vaughn (The Hard Way)	.60	.30	.20
39	James Williams (18 the easy way)	.60	.30	.20
40	Casey & Ed (Ed Hamman, Casey Stengel)	1.25	.60	.40
---	Header Card	.60	.30	.20
---	Baseball Laff Book	.60	.30	.20

1978 Laughlin Long Ago Black Stars

2 .... LARRY BROWN C

This sparkplug came from Birmingham to join the Pitt Keystones in 1921, and became one of the great defensive catchers of black baseball. He caught for the two Chicago teams of '26 and '27 that won the black World Series. After he threw out Ty Cobb five successive times in a '26 game in Havana, Ty asked the light-skinned Brown to join the Tigers—as a Cuban—but Larry declined. In '30 "Iron Man" Brown caught 234 games! He never pulled off his mask on a foul. A .300 hitter, Larry played longest for the Memphis Red Sox and also managed. He was voted catcher on many All-Star teams. Died in '72.
©1978 R.G. Laughlin

In what appears very much like a second series save for slight title alteration, sports artist R.G. Laughlin produced this 36-card set in a format very similar to his 1974 issue highlighting Negro League stars. This set is printed in dark and light

green on a non-glossy front, with printing on the back in black. Most of the more widely known Negro League stars appeared in the 1974 issue.

		NM	EX	VG
Complete Set (36):		60.00	30.00	18.00
Common Player:		1.50	.70	.45
1	Ted Trent	1.50	.70	.45
2	Larry Brown	1.50	.70	.45
3	Newt Allen	3.00	1.50	.90
4	Norman Stearns	4.50	2.25	1.25
5	Leon Day	6.00	3.00	1.75
6	Dick Lundy	1.50	.70	.45
7	Bruce Petway	1.50	.70	.45
8	Bill Drake	1.50	.70	.45
9	Chaney White	1.50	.70	.45
10	Webster McDonald	2.50	1.25	.70
11	Tommy Butts	1.50	.70	.45
12	Ben Taylor	4.50	2.25	1.25
13	James (Joe) Greene	1.50	.70	.45
14	Dick Seay	1.50	.70	.45
15	Sammy Hughes	1.50	.70	.45
16	Ted Page	3.00	1.50	.90
17	Willie Cornelius	1.50	.70	.45
18	Pat Patterson	1.50	.70	.45
19	Frank Wickware	1.50	.70	.45
20	Albert Haywood	1.50	.70	.45
21	Bill Holland	1.50	.70	.45
22	Sol White	4.50	2.25	1.25
23	Chet Brewer	3.00	1.50	.90
24	Crush Holloway	1.50	.70	.45
25	George Johnson	1.50	.70	.45
26	George Scales	1.50	.70	.45
27	Dave Brown	1.50	.70	.45
28	John Donaldson	1.50	.70	.45
29	William Johnson	3.00	1.50	.90
30	Bill Yancey	3.00	1.50	.90
31	Sam Bankhead	4.00	2.00	1.25
32	Leroy Matlock	1.50	.70	.45
33	Quincy Troupe	2.50	1.25	.70
34	Hilton Smith	3.00	1.50	.90
35	Jim Crutchfield	3.00	1.50	.90
36	Ted Radcliffe	4.00	2.00	1.25

1980 Laughlin Famous Feats

A set of 40 cards, this Famous Feats set by sports artist R.G. Laughlin carries a subtitle as the Second Series, apparently a reference to a 1972 issue of the same name by Laughlin that was produced by Fleer. Unlike many of the odd sized Laughlin issues, this one is the standard 2-1/2" x 3-1/2", with full color used with the artist's pen and ink drawings on the front. The cards are numbered on the front and the backs are blank. This set has been reprinted; the reprints have lighter faces and blurry text.

		NM	EX	VG
Complete Set (40):		30.00	15.00	9.00
Common Player:		1.50	.75	.40
1	Honus Wagner	5.00	2.50	1.50
2	Herb Pennock	1.50	.75	.40
3	Al Simmons	1.50	.75	.40
4	Hack Wilson	1.50	.75	.40
5	Dizzy Dean	3.00	1.50	.90
6	Chuck Klein	1.50	.75	.40
7	Nellie Fox	1.50	.75	.40
8	Lefty Grove	1.50	.75	.40
9	George Sisler	1.50	.75	.40
10	Lou Gehrig	7.00	3.50	2.00
11	Rube Waddell	1.50	.75	.40
12	Max Carey	1.50	.75	.40
13	Thurman Munson	4.00	2.00	1.25
14	Mel Ott	1.50	.75	.40
15	Doc White	1.50	.75	.40
16	Babe Ruth	12.00	6.00	3.50
17	Schoolboy Rowe	1.50	.75	.40
18	Jackie Robinson	7.00	3.50	2.00
19	Joe Medwick	1.50	.75	.40
20	Casey Stengel	1.50	.75	.40
21	Roberto Clemente	9.00	4.50	3.00
22	Christy Mathewson	3.00	1.50	.90
23	Jimmie Foxx	2.50	1.25	.75
24	Joe Jackson	12.00	6.00	3.50
25	Walter Johnson	3.00	1.50	.90
26	Tony Lazzeri	1.50	.75	.40
27	Hugh Casey	1.50	.75	.40
28	Ty Cobb	7.00	3.50	2.00
29	Stuffy McInnis	1.50	.75	.40
30	Cy Young	2.50	1.25	.75
31	Lefty O'Doul	1.50	.75	.40
32	Eddie Collins	1.50	.75	.40
33	Joe McCarty	1.50	.75	.40
34	Ed Walsh	1.50	.75	.40
35	George Burns	1.50	.75	.40
36	Walt Dropo	1.50	.75	.40

		NM	EX	VG
37	Connie Mack	1.50	.75	.40
38	Babe Adams	1.50	.75	.40
39	Rogers Hornsby	2.00	1.00	.60
40	Grover C. Alexander	1.50	.75	.40

1980 Laughlin 300/400/500

This unusual set features a combination of the line drawings of R.G. Laughlin and a photo head shot of the player depicted. The cards are actually square, 3-1/4" x 3-1/4", with a background in color depicting a baseball diamond. The set is based on 300 wins, batting .400 or better and 500 homers, with a total of 30 cards in the blank backed set. The cards are numbered on the front. This set has been reprinted; the reprints have lighter faces and blurry text.

		NM	EX	VG
Complete Set (30):		50.00	25.00	15.00
Common Player:		3.00	1.50	.90
1	Header Card	3.00	1.50	.90
2	Babe Ruth	20.00	10.00	6.00
3	Walter Johnson	6.00	3.00	1.75
4	Ty Cobb	12.00	6.00	3.50
5	Christy Mathewson	6.00	3.00	1.75
6	Ted Williams	8.00	4.00	2.50
7	Bill Terry	3.00	1.50	.90
8	Grover C. Alexander	3.00	1.50	.90
9	Napoleon Lajoie	3.00	1.50	.90
10	Willie Mays	8.00	4.00	2.50
11	Cy Young	6.00	3.00	1.75
12	Mel Ott	3.00	1.50	.90
13	Joe Jackson	20.00	10.00	6.00
14	Harmon Killebrew	3.00	1.50	.90
15	Warren Spahn	3.00	1.50	.90
16	Hank Aaron	8.00	4.00	2.50
17	Rogers Hornsby	3.00	1.50	.90
18	Mickey Mantle	20.00	10.00	6.00
19	Lefty Grove	3.00	1.50	.90
20	Ted Williams	8.00	4.00	2.50
21	Jimmie Fox	3.00	1.50	.90
22	Eddie Plank	3.00	1.50	.90
23	Frank Robinson	3.00	1.50	.90
24	George Sisler	3.00	1.50	.90
25	Eddie Mathews	3.00	1.50	.90
26	Early Wynn	3.00	1.50	.90
27	Ernie Banks	3.00	1.50	.90
28	Harry Heilmann	3.00	1.50	.90
29	Lou Gehrig	15.00	7.50	4.50
30	Willie McCovey	3.00	1.50	.90

1929 Leader Novelty Candy Co.

Though unmarked as such, these cards are believed to have been an insert in boxes of Leader Novelty Candy, or at least were so advertised in the famous Copeland Collection auction of 1991. They are one of two "mini" versions of the R316 Kashin Publications cards (see also W553), though it is not known whether the entire 101-card Kashin set was so paralleled. While sizes seem to vary significantly, nominal measurements for this version are about 1-3/4" x 2-5/8". Cards have been seen in duotones of red, sepia, purple and green. They are unnumbered and blank-backed. This checklist is known to be incomplete. Gaps have been left in the assigned numbering to accommodate additions.

		NM	EX	VG
Common Player:		225.00	110.00	70.00
(7)	Lucerne A. Blue	225.00	110.00	70.00
(8)	James Bottomley	450.00	220.00	135.00
(13)	Earl (Earle) Combs	450.00	220.00	135.00
(26)	Jimmy Foxx	750.00	370.00	220.00
(27)	Frank Frisch	450.00	220.00	135.00
(33)	Robert Grove	525.00	265.00	160.00
(42)	Rogers Hornsby	600.00	300.00	180.00

(45)	Sam Jones	225.00	110.00	70.00
(50)	Joseph Judge	225.00	110.00	70.00
(52)	Charles Klein	450.00	220.00	135.00
(62)	Walter Maranville	450.00	220.00	135.00
(65)	Ed "Bing" Miller	225.00	110.00	70.00
(66)	Frank O'Doul	300.00	150.00	90.00
(67)	Melvin Ott	525.00	265.00	160.00
(74)	Eddie Rommel	225.00	110.00	70.00
(85)	Al Simmons	450.00	220.00	135.00
(92)	Pie J. Traynor	450.00	220.00	135.00
(93)	Dazzy Vance	450.00	220.00	135.00
(95)	Paul Waner	450.00	220.00	135.00
(100)	Hack Wilson	525.00	265.00	160.00

1922 Leader Theatre

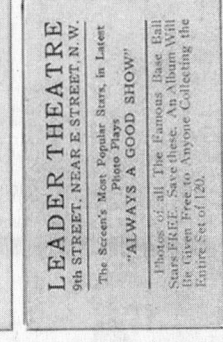

This issue by a Washington, D.C. moviehouse is a version of the W573 and W575-1 strip card sets on which at least two forms of customized advertising were printed on the card backs. The ads state that 120 cards (paralleling W573 and/or W575-1) were originally issued in this version. An album was also offered.

	NM	EX	VG
Common Player:	500.00	250.00	150.00

(See 1922 W573 and W575-1 for checklists and base card values. Add 5X premium for non-commons.)

1949 Leaf

The first color baseball cards of the post-World War II era were the 98-card, 2-3/8" x 2-7/8", set produced by Chicago's Leaf Gum Co. for issue in 1949. One of the toughest postwar sets to complete, exactly half of the issue - 49 cards - are significantly harder to find than the others. Probably intended to confound bubblegum buyers of the day, the set is skip-numbered between 1-168. Card backs contain offers of felt pennants, an album for the cards or 5-1/2" x 7-1/2" premium photos of Hall of Famers. While some cards carry a 1948 copyright date on back, it is now believed the issue was not released until 1949. The complete set price does not include the higher value in the variation pairs.

	NM	EX	VG
Complete Set (98):	85,000	35,000	17,500
Common Player:	125.00	45.00	22.50
Common Short-print:	900.00	360.00	180.00
Album:	900.00	450.00	275.00
1 Joe DiMaggio	3,250	1,600	975.00
3 Babe Ruth	2,500	1,250	750.00
4 Stan Musial	1,700	850.00	510.00
5 Virgil Trucks/SP	1,150	460.00	230.00
8 Satchel Paige/SP	17,000	8,500	5,000
10 Paul Trout	125.00	45.00	22.50
11 Phil Rizzuto	325.00	130.00	65.00
13 Casimer Michaels/SP	900.00	360.00	180.00
14 Billy Johnson	125.00	45.00	22.50
17 Frank Overmire	125.00	45.00	22.50
19 John Wyrostek/SP	900.00	360.00	180.00
22 Hank Sauer/SP	1,000	400.00	200.00
22 Al Evans	125.00	45.00	22.50
26 Sam Chapman	125.00	45.00	22.50
27 Mickey Harris	125.00	45.00	22.50
28 Jim Hegan	125.00	45.00	22.50
29 Elmer Valo	125.00	45.00	22.50
30 Bill Goodman/SP	900.00	360.00	180.00
31 Lou Brissie	125.00	45.00	22.50
32 Warren Spahn	450.00	180.00	90.00
33 Harry Lowrey/SP	900.00	360.00	180.00
36 Al Zarilla/SP	900.00	360.00	180.00
38 Ted Kluszewski	300.00	120.00	60.00
39 Ewell Blackwell	130.00	50.00	25.00
42a Kent Peterson (Red cap.)	2,500	1,250	750.00
42b Kent Peterson (Black cap.)	125.00	45.00	22.50
43 Eddie Stevens/SP	900.00	360.00	180.00
45 Ken Keltner/SP	900.00	360.00	180.00
46 Johnny Mize	300.00	120.00	60.00
47 George Vico	125.00	45.00	22.50

48	Johnny Schmitz/SP	900.00	360.00	180.00
49	Del Ennis	130.00	50.00	25.00
50	Dick Wakefield	125.00	45.00	22.50
51	Alvin Dark/SP	1,750	700.00	350.00
53	John Vandermeer (Vander Meer)	225.00	90.00	45.00
54	Bobby Adams/SP	900.00	360.00	180.00
55	Tommy Henrich/SP	1,800	900.00	550.00
56	Larry Jensen	130.00	50.00	25.00
57	Bob McCall	125.00	45.00	22.50
59	Luke Appling	200.00	80.00	40.00
61	Jake Early	125.00	45.00	22.50
62	Eddie Joost/SP	900.00	360.00	180.00
63	Barney McCosky/SP	900.00	360.00	180.00
65	Bob Elliot (Elliott)	125.00	45.00	22.50
66	Orval Grove/SP	900.00	360.00	180.00
68	Ed Miller/SP	900.00	360.00	180.00
70	Honus Wagner	500.00	200.00	100.00
72	Hank Edwards	125.00	45.00	22.50
73	Pat Seerey	125.00	45.00	22.50
75	Dom DiMaggio/SP	1,400	560.00	280.00
76	Ted Williams	1,850	925.00	555.00
77	Roy Smalley	125.00	45.00	22.50
78	Walter Evers/SP	900.00	360.00	180.00
79	Jackie Robinson	2,150	1,075	645.00
81	George Kurowski/SP	900.00	360.00	180.00
82	Johnny Lindell	125.00	45.00	22.50
83	Bobby Doerr	225.00	90.00	45.00
84	Sid Hudson	125.00	45.00	22.50
85	Dave Philley/SP	900.00	360.00	180.00
86	Ralph Weigel	125.00	45.00	22.50
88	Frank Gustine/SP	900.00	360.00	180.00
91	Ralph Kiner	175.00	70.00	35.00
93	Bob Feller/SP	3,250	1,300	650.00
95	George Stirnweiss	125.00	45.00	22.50
97	Martin Marion	150.00	60.00	30.00
98a	Hal Newhouser/SP	1,800	725.00	360.00
98b	Hal Newhouser (Unique prototype, blue/yellow background). Sold in 2/09 auction for $84,000.			
102a	Gene Hermansk (Incorrect spelling.)	2,750	1,100	550.00
102b	Gene Hermanski (Correct spelling.)	135.00	55.00	25.00
104	Edward Stewart/SP	900.00	360.00	180.00
106	Lou Boudreau	200.00	80.00	40.00
108	Matthew Batts/SP	900.00	360.00	180.00
111	Gerald Priddy	125.00	45.00	22.50
113	Emil Leonard/SP	900.00	360.00	180.00
117	Joe Gordon	125.00	45.00	22.50
120	George Kell/SP	1,100	440.00	220.00
121	John Pesky/SP	1,000	400.00	200.00
123	Clifford Fannin/SP	900.00	360.00	180.00
125	Andy Pafko	160.00	65.00	30.00
127	Enos Slaughter/SP	1,750	700.00	350.00
128	Warren Rosar	125.00	45.00	22.50
129	Kirby Higbe/SP	900.00	360.00	180.00
131	Sid Gordon/SP	900.00	360.00	180.00
133	Tommy Holmes/SP	1,000	400.00	200.00
136a	Cliff Aberson (Full sleeve.)	125.00	50.00	25.00
136b	Cliff Aberson (Short sleeve.)	175.00	70.00	35.00
137	Harry Walker/SP	900.00	360.00	180.00
138	Larry Doby/SP	4,500	2,200	1,350
139	Johnny Hopp	125.00	45.00	22.50
142	Danny Murtaugh/SP	1,500	750.00	450.00
143	Dick Sisler/SP	900.00	360.00	180.00
144	Bob Dillinger/SP	900.00	360.00	180.00
146	Harold Reiser/SP	1,000	400.00	200.00
149	Henry Majeski/SP	900.00	360.00	180.00
153	Floyd Baker/SP	900.00	360.00	180.00
158	Harry Brecheen/SP	900.00	360.00	180.00
159	Mizell Platt	125.00	45.00	22.50
160	Bob Scheffing/SP	900.00	360.00	180.00
161	Vernon Stephens/SP	1,000	400.00	200.00
163	Freddy Hutchinson/SP	1,000	400.00	200.00
165	Dale Mitchell/SP	1,000	400.00	200.00
168	Phil Cavaretta/SP	1,650	825.00	495.00

1949 Leaf Premiums

These blank-back, sepia photos were available with the purchase of 1948 Leaf baseball cards. Measuring 5-5/8" x 7-1/4", the pictures have a facsimile autograph and a black box labeled "BASEBALL'S IMMORTALS" at bottom containing a short biography. The unnumbered pictures are checklisted alphabetically.

	NM	EX	VG
Complete Set (9):	6,000	3,000	1,800
Common Player:	400.00	200.00	120.00
(1) Grover Alexander	450.00	225.00	135.00
(2) Mickey Cochrane	400.00	200.00	120.00
(3) Lou Gehrig	1,200	600.00	360.00
(4) Walter Johnson	450.00	225.00	135.00
(5) Christy Mathewson	525.00	260.00	155.00
(6) John McGraw	400.00	200.00	120.00
(7) Babe Ruth (Dark background, text boxes.)	1,200	600.00	360.00
(8) Babe Ruth (Light background, no text.)	1,200	600.00	360.00
(9) Ed Walsh	400.00	200.00	120.00

1949 Leaf Prototype

This currently unique card is believed to have been prepared for issue with the first series of 1949 Leaf but for unknown reasons was withdrawn. A Newhouser card with a completely different front and changes to the back was issued with the set's short-printed second series. Graded SGC-Poor, this discovery card was auctioned for $84,000 in 2/09.

	NM	EX	VG
98 Hal Newhouser			

1960 Leaf Pre-Production

Evidently produced prior to final approval for the design of the 1960 Leaf set, these cards all feature much larger player photos than the issued versions. Generally the issued cards have cap-to-waist photos while the pre-production cards have to cap-to-chin shots. Backs of the pre-production cards are virtually identical to the regular cards. The pre-production cards were never publically issued and show evidence of having been hand-cut. The cards of Donovan and Jay appear to be more common than the others.

	NM	EX	VG
Complete Set (8):	15,000	7,500	4,500
Common Player:	1,500	750.00	450.00
1 Luis Aparicio	4,500	2,250	1,350
12 Ken Boyer	2,150	1,075	645.00
17 Walt Moryn	1,250	625.00	375.00
23 Joey Jay	1,250	625.00	375.00
35 Jim Coates	2,250	1,125	675.00
58 Hal Smith	1,950	975.00	585.00
61 Vic Rehm	1,500	750.00	450.00
72 Dick Donovan	1,250	625.00	375.00

1960 Leaf

While known to the hobby as "Leaf" cards, this set of 144 carries the copyright of Sports Novelties Inc., Chicago. The 2-1/2" x 3-1/2" cards feature black-and-white player portrait photos, with plain background. Cards were sold in nickel wax packs with a marble, rather than a piece of bubble gum. The second half of the set, #73-144, are quite scarce. Card #25, Jim Grant, is found in two versions, with his own picture (black cap) and with a photo of Brooks Lawrence (white cap). Three back variations of Hal Smith card #58 are also known. Complete set prices do not include variations. In the late 1990s, a large group of high-number (Series 2) boxes - in excess of 4,000 cards - was added to the surviving supply.

	NM	EX	VG
Complete Set (144):	2,000	1,000	500.00
Common Player (1-72):	9.00	4.50	2.75
Common Player (73-144):	12.00	6.00	3.50
Wax Pack, Series 1 (5):	120.00		
Wax Box, Series 1 (24):	2,400		
Wax Pack, Series 2 (5):	190.00		
Wax Box, Series 2 (24):	3,250		
1 Luis Aparicio	55.00	15.00	9.00
2 Woody Held	9.00	4.50	2.75
3 Frank Lary	9.00	4.50	2.75
4 Camilo Pascual	9.00	4.50	2.75
5 Frank Herrera	9.00	4.50	2.75
6 Felipe Alou	8.00	4.00	2.50
7 Bennie Daniels	9.00	4.50	2.75
8 Roger Craig	9.00	4.50	2.75
9 Eddie Kasko	9.00	4.50	2.75
10 Bob Grim	9.00	4.50	2.75

11	Jim Busby	9.00	4.50	2.75
12	Ken Boyer	17.50	8.75	5.25
13	Bob Boyd	9.00	4.50	2.75
14	Sam Jones	9.00	4.50	2.75
15	Larry Jackson	9.00	4.50	2.75
16	Roy Face	9.00	4.50	2.75
17	Walt Moryn	9.00	4.50	2.75
18	Jim Gilliam	8.00	4.00	2.50
19	Don Newcombe	8.00	4.00	2.50
20	Glen Hobbie	9.00	4.50	2.75
21	Pedro Ramos	9.00	4.50	2.75
22	Ryne Duren	8.00	4.00	2.50
23	Joe Jay	9.00	4.50	2.75
24	Lou Berberet	9.00	4.50	2.75
25a	Jim Grant (White cap, photo actually Brooks Lawrence.)	15.00	7.50	4.50
25b	Jim Grant (Dark cap, correct photo.)	22.50	11.00	6.75
26	Tom Borland	9.00	4.50	2.75
27	Brooks Robinson	25.00	12.50	7.50
28	Jerry Adair	9.00	4.50	2.75
29	Ron Jackson	9.00	4.50	2.75
30	George Strickland	9.00	4.50	2.75
31	Rocky Bridges	9.00	4.50	2.75
32	Bill Tuttle	9.00	4.50	2.75
33	Ken Hunt	9.00	4.50	2.75
34	Hal Griggs	9.00	4.50	2.75
35	Jim Coates	9.00	4.50	2.75
36	Brooks Lawrence	9.00	4.50	2.75
37	Duke Snider	30.00	15.00	9.00
38	Al Spangler	9.00	4.50	2.75
39	Jim Owens	9.00	4.50	2.75
40	Bill Virdon	9.00	4.50	2.75
41	Ernie Broglio	9.00	4.50	2.75
42	Andre Rodgers	9.00	4.50	2.75
43	Julio Becquer	9.00	4.50	2.75
44	Tony Taylor	9.00	4.50	2.75
45	Jerry Lynch	9.00	4.50	2.75
46	Clete Boyer	8.00	4.00	2.50
47	Jerry Lumpe	9.00	4.50	2.75
48	Charlie Maxwell	9.00	4.50	2.75
49	Jim Perry	9.00	4.50	2.75
50	Danny McDevitt	9.00	4.50	2.75
51	Juan Pizarro	9.00	4.50	2.75
52	*Dallas Green*	20.00	10.00	6.00
53	Bob Friend	9.00	4.50	2.75
54	Jack Sanford	9.00	4.50	2.75
55	Jim Rivera	9.00	4.50	2.75
56	Ted Wills	9.00	4.50	2.75
57	Milt Pappas	9.00	4.50	2.75
58a	Hal Smith (Team & position on back.)	9.00	4.50	2.75
58b	Hal Smith (Team blackened out on back.)	750.00	375.00	225.00
58c	Hal Smith (Team missing on back.)	75.00	37.50	22.50
59	Bob Avila	9.00	4.50	2.75
60	Clem Labine	9.00	4.50	2.75
61	Vic Rehm	9.00	4.50	2.75
62	John Gabler	9.00	4.50	2.75
63	John Tsitouris	9.00	4.50	2.75
64	Dave Sisler	9.00	4.50	2.75
65	Vic Power	9.00	4.50	2.75
66	Earl Battey	9.00	4.50	2.75
67	Bob Purkey	9.00	4.50	2.75
68	Moe Drabowsky	9.00	4.50	2.75
69	Hoyt Wilhelm	15.00	7.50	4.50
70	Humberto Robinson	9.00	4.50	2.75
71	Whitey Herzog	12.50	6.25	3.75
72	Dick Donovan	9.00	4.50	2.75
73	Gordon Jones	12.00	6.00	3.50
74	Joe Hicks	12.00	6.00	3.50
75	*Ray Culp*	12.00	6.00	3.50
76	Dick Drott	12.00	6.00	3.50
77	Bob Duliba	12.00	6.00	3.50
78	Art Ditmar	12.00	6.00	3.50
79	Steve Korcheck	12.00	6.00	3.50
80	Henry Mason	12.00	6.00	3.50
81	Harry Simpson	12.00	6.00	3.50
82	Gene Green	12.00	6.00	3.50
83	Bob Shaw	12.00	6.00	3.50
84	Howard Reed	12.00	6.00	3.50
85	Dick Stigman	12.00	6.00	3.50
86	Rip Repulski	12.00	6.00	3.50
87	Seth Morehead	12.00	6.00	3.50
88	Camilo Carreon	12.00	6.00	3.50
89	John Blanchard	17.50	8.75	5.25
90	Billy Hoeft	12.00	6.00	3.50
91	Fred Hopke	12.00	6.00	3.50
92	Joe Martin	12.00	6.00	3.50
93	Wally Shannon	12.00	6.00	3.50
94	Baseball's Two Hal Smiths	50.00	25.00	15.00
95	Al Schroll	12.00	6.00	3.50
96	John Kucks	12.00	6.00	3.50
97	Tom Morgan	12.00	6.00	3.50
98	Willie Jones	12.00	6.00	3.50
99	Marshall Renfroe	12.00	6.00	3.50
100	Willie Tasby	12.00	6.00	3.50
101	Irv Noren	12.00	6.00	3.50
102	Russ Snyder	12.00	6.00	3.50
103	Bob Turley	17.50	8.75	5.25
104	Jim Woods	12.00	6.00	3.50
105	Ronnie Kline	12.00	6.00	3.50
106	Steve Bilko	12.00	6.00	3.50
107	Elmer Valo	12.00	6.00	3.50
108	Tom McAvoy	12.00	6.00	3.50
109	Stan Williams	12.00	6.00	3.50
110	Earl Averill	12.00	6.00	3.50
111	Lee Walls	12.00	6.00	3.50
112	Paul Richards	12.00	6.00	3.50
113	Ed Sadowski	12.00	6.00	3.50
114	Stover McIlwain (Photo actually Jim McAnany.)	17.50	8.75	5.25
115	Chuck Tanner (Photo actually Ken Kuhn.)	17.50	8.75	5.25
116	Lou Klimchock	12.00	6.00	3.50
117	Neil Chrisley	12.00	6.00	3.50
118	Johnny Callison	12.00	6.00	3.50

119	Hal Smith	12.00	6.00	3.50
120	Carl Sawatski	12.00	6.00	3.50
121	Frank Leja	12.00	6.00	3.50
122	Earl Torgeson	12.00	6.00	3.50
123	Art Schult	12.00	6.00	3.50
124	Jim Brosnan	12.00	6.00	3.50
125	Sparky Anderson	60.00	30.00	18.00
126	Joe Pignatano	12.00	6.00	3.50
127	Rocky Nelson	12.00	6.00	3.50
128	Orlando Cepeda	45.00	22.50	13.50
129	Daryl Spencer	12.00	6.00	3.50
130	Ralph Lumenti	12.00	6.00	3.50
131	Sam Taylor	12.00	6.00	3.50
132	Harry Brecheen	12.00	6.00	3.50
133	Johnny Groth	12.00	6.00	3.50
134	Wayne Terwilliger	12.00	6.00	3.50
135	Kent Hadley	12.00	6.00	3.50
136	Faye Throneberry	12.00	6.00	3.50
137	Jack Meyer	12.00	6.00	3.50
138	*Chuck Cottier*	12.00	6.00	3.50
139	Joe DeMaestri	12.00	6.00	3.50
140	Gene Freese	12.00	6.00	3.50
141	Curt Flood	30.00	15.00	9.00
142	Gino Cimoli	12.00	6.00	3.50
143	Clay Dalrymple	12.00	6.00	3.50
144	Jim Bunning	50.00	25.00	15.00

1923 Lections

EMIL MEUSEL
New York Giants

This series of cards was virtually unknown in the hobby until 1997 when 28 cards turned up in Albany, N.Y. The cards measure about 4" x 2-1/2" with rounded corners and are printed on very thick cardboard. At left front is an oval black-and-white player photo with name and team below. At right is green or orange art of a baseball game with the issuer's logo and trademark information. It is unknown with what, if any, product these cards were issued; a candy premium seems the most likely source. Most of the cards seen so far are in grades from Fair-Good, though a few are known in Ex-Mt.

	NM	EX	VG
Complete Set (10):	30,000	15,000	9,000
Common Player:	2,000	1,000	600.00
(1) Frank Chance	3,500	1,750	1,050
(2) Howard Ehmke	2,000	1,000	600.00
(3) Frank Frisch	3,500	1,750	1,050
(4) Roger (Rogers) Hornsby	5,000	2,500	1,500
(5) Charles Jamieson	2,000	1,000	600.00
(6) "Bob" Meusel	2,000	1,000	600.00
(7) Emil Meusel	2,000	1,000	600.00
(8) "Babe" Ruth	9,000	4,500	2,700
(9) Charles Schmidt	2,000	1,000	600.00
(10) "Bob" Shawkey	2,000	1,000	600.00

1975 Lee's Sweets

Professing to be an issue of 68 cards of "Baseball Greats," this collectors' issue first appeared about 1975. Only four players are known. Fronts of the 2-1/2" x 3-3/16" cards have crudely printed black-and-white player photos. Backs describe the series and give the Lee's Sweets address as Camp Hill, Ala.

	NM	EX	VG
Complete Set (4):	25.00	12.50	7.50
Common Player:	6.00	3.00	1.75
(1) Ty Cobb	6.00	3.00	1.75
(2) Joe DiMaggio	6.00	3.00	1.75
(3) Lou Gehrig	6.00	3.00	1.75
(4) Babe Ruth	6.00	3.00	3.50

1909-11 Lenox Cigarettes

Many collectors rank the Lenox back as the third rarest among T206, behind only Ty Cobb and Drum. Lenox cards can be found with the back printing in either black or brown.

PREMIUMS
Black, Common Players: 16-24X
Black, Hall of Famers: 15-20X
Brown, Common Players: 75-100X
Brown, Hall of Famers: 40-60X
(See T206 for checklist and base card values.)

1969 Lincoln-Mercury Sports Panel Postcards

Various celebrity spokesmen on the Lincoln-Mercury Sports Panel can be found on a series of color postcards. In standard 5-1/2" x 3-1/2" format, cards have borderless color photos on front of the spokesman standing with one of the company's new cars; a facsimile autograph also appears. Divided backs identify the player and the automobile.

	NM	EX	VG
Al Kaline	80.00	40.00	25.00

1906 Lincoln Publishing Philadelphia A's

Members of the American League Champions (says so right at the top) Philadelphia A's, decked out in their Sunday-best, are featured in this set of black-and-white postcards. The portraits are framed in fancy graphics which include a baseball, the dates 1905 and 1906 and the player's name in a banner beneath the photo. At bottom is a box with "ATHLETIC BASE BALL TEAM." Back of the approximately 3-1/2" x 5-1/2" cards has a box at upper-left enclosing "POST CARD." The unnumbered cards are listed here alphabetically.

		NM	EX	VG
Complete Set (20):		10,000	5,000	3,000
Common Player:		300.00	150.00	90.00
(1)	Chief Bender	1,500	750.00	450.00
(2)	Andy Coakley	300.00	150.00	90.00
(3)	Lave Cross	300.00	150.00	90.00
(4)	Monte Cross	300.00	150.00	90.00
(5)	Harry Davis	300.00	150.00	90.00
(6)	Jimmy Dygert	300.00	150.00	90.00
(7)	Topsy Hartsel	300.00	150.00	90.00
(8)	Weldon Henley	300.00	150.00	90.00
(9)	Danny Hoffman	300.00	150.00	90.00
(10)	John Knight	300.00	150.00	90.00

(11)	Bris Lord	300.00	150.00	90.00
(12)	Connie Mack	1,500	750.00	450.00
(13)	Danny Murphy	300.00	150.00	90.00
(14)	Joe Myers	300.00	150.00	90.00
(15)	Rube Oldring	300.00	150.00	90.00
(16)	Eddie Plank	2,000	1,000	600.00
(17)	Mike Powers	300.00	150.00	90.00
(18)	Ossee Schreckengost	300.00	150.00	90.00
(19)	Ralph Seybold	300.00	150.00	90.00
(20)	Rube Waddell	1,500	750.00	450.00

1975 Linnett MLB All-Stars

This series of pencil-portrait prints was done by sports artist Charles Linnett of Walpole, Mass. The black-and-white prints are on 8-1/2" x 11" textured paper, featuring a facsimile autograph of the player. Because the portraits are licensed only by the Players Association, the players are pictured capless with no uniform logos visible. Backs are blank. The 1975 pictures differ from the 1976 issue in that they include a printed player name, besides the facsimile autograph. At least some of the portraits were given away in a ballpark "Portrait Day" promotion at Fenway Park, sponsored by Grant City (W.T. Grant Co.) department stores. A coupon accompanying the SGA portraits offered a discount on a package of three pictures, apparently the standard retail offering that carried a $1.19 price tag. This rudimentary checklist is certainly incomplete.

		NM	EX	VG
Common Player:		6.00	3.00	1.75
(25)	Fred Lynn	9.00	4.50	2.75
(50)	Tom Seaver	9.00	4.50	2.75
(75)	Carl Yastrzemski	12.00	6.00	3.50

1976 Linnett Portraits

This series of pencil-portrait prints was done by sports artist Charles Linnett of Walpole, Mass., and includes baseball, football, hockey, NBA and Harlem Globetrotters players (only baseball listed here). The black-and-white prints are on 8-1/2" x 11" textured paper, featuring a facsimile autograph of the player. Because the portraits are licensed only by the Players Association, the players are pictured capless with no uniform logos visible. Backs are blank. The portraits originally sold for 50 cents apiece by mail.

		NM	EX	VG
Complete Baseball Set (176):		300.00	150.00	90.00
Common Player:		2.50	1.25	.75
(1)	Hank Aaron	10.00	5.00	3.00
(2)	Dick Allen	4.00	2.00	1.25
(3)	Matty Alou	2.50	1.25	.75
(4)	Mike Anderson	2.50	1.25	.75
(5)	Luis Aparicio	5.00	2.50	1.50
(6)	Sal Bando	2.50	1.25	.75
(7)	Mark Belanger	2.50	1.25	.70
(8)	Buddy Bell	2.50	1.25	.75
(9)	Johnny Bench	6.00	3.00	1.75
(10)	Jim Bibby	2.50	1.25	.75
(11)	Paul Blair	2.50	1.25	.75
(12)	Bert Blyleven	3.00	1.50	.90
(13)	Ron Blomberg	2.50	1.25	.75
(14)	Bob Bolin	2.50	1.25	.75
(15)	Bill Bonham	2.50	1.25	.75
(16)	Pedro Borbon	2.50	1.25	.75
(17)	Bob Boone	3.00	1.50	.90
(18)	Larry Bowa	2.50	1.25	.75
(19)	Steve Braun	2.50	1.25	.75
(20)	Ken Brett	2.50	1.25	.75
(21)	John Briggs	2.50	1.25	.75
(22)	Lou Brock	5.00	2.50	1.50
(23)	Jack Brohamer	2.50	1.25	.75
(24)	Steve Brye	2.50	1.25	.75
(25)	Bill Buckner	2.50	1.25	.70
(26)	Jeff Burroughs	2.50	1.25	.75
(27)	Steve Busby	2.50	1.25	.75
(28)	Bert Campaneris	2.50	1.25	.75
(29)	Bernie Carbo	2.50	1.25	.75
(30)	Jose Cardenal	2.50	1.25	.75
(31)	Steve Carlton	5.00	2.50	1.50
(32)	Rod Carew	5.00	2.50	1.50
(33)	Dave Cash	2.50	1.25	.75
(34)	Norm Cash	3.00	1.50	.90
(35)	Danny Cater	2.50	1.25	.75
(36)	Cesar Cedeno	2.50	1.25	.75
(37)	Orlando Cepeda	5.00	2.50	1.50
(38)	Ron Cey	2.50	1.25	.70
(39)	Chris Chambliss	2.50	1.25	.75
(40)	David Clyde	2.50	1.25	.75
(41)	Rich Coggins	2.50	1.25	.75
(42)	Jim Colborn	2.50	1.25	.75
(43)	Dave Concepcion	3.00	1.50	.90
(44)	Willie Crawford	2.50	1.25	.75
(45)	John Curtis	2.50	1.25	.75
(46)	Bobby Darwin	2.50	1.25	.75
(47)	Dan Driessen	2.50	1.25	.75
(48)	Duffy Dyer	2.50	1.25	.75
(49)	John Ellis	2.50	1.25	.75
(50)	Darrell Evans	2.50	1.25	.70
(51)	Dwight Evans	2.50	1.25	.70
(52)	Joe Ferguson	2.50	1.25	.75
(53)	Rollie Fingers	4.00	2.00	1.25
(54)	Carlton Fisk	5.00	2.50	1.50
(55)	Bill Freehan	2.50	1.25	.70
(56)	Jim Fregosi	2.50	1.25	.75
(57)	Oscar Gamble	2.50	1.25	.75
(58)	Pedro Garcia	2.50	1.25	.75
(59)	Ralph Garr	2.50	1.25	.75
(60)	Wayne Garrett	2.50	1.25	.70
(61)	Steve Garvey	2.50	1.25	.75
(62)	Cesar Geronimo	2.50	1.25	.75
(63)	Bob Gibson	5.00	2.50	1.50
(64)	Dave Giusti	2.50	1.25	.75
(65)	Bobby Grich	2.50	1.25	.75
(66)	Doug Griffin	2.50	1.25	.75
(67)	Mario Guerrero	2.50	1.25	.75
(68)	Don Gullett	2.50	1.25	.75
(69)	Tommy Harper	2.50	1.25	.75
(70)	Toby Harrah	2.50	1.25	.75
(71)	Bud Harrelson	2.50	1.25	.75
(72)	Vic Harris	2.50	1.25	.75
(73)	Richie Hebner	2.50	1.25	.75
(74)	George Hendrick	2.50	1.25	.75
(75)	Ed Hermann	2.50	1.25	.75
(76)	John Hiller	2.50	1.25	.75
(77)	Willie Horton	2.50	1.25	.75
(78)	Jim Hunter	4.00	2.00	1.25
(79)	Tommy Hutton	2.50	1.25	.75
(80)	Reggie Jackson	7.50	3.75	2.25
(81)	Fergie Jenkins	4.00	2.00	1.25
(82)	Dave Johnson	2.50	1.25	.75
(83)	Cleon Jones	2.50	1.25	.75
(84)	Al Kaline	6.00	3.00	1.75
(85)	John Kennedy	2.50	1.25	.75
(86)	Steve Kline	2.50	1.25	.75
(87)	Jerry Koosman	2.50	1.25	.75
(88)	Bill Lee	2.50	1.25	.75
(89)	Eddie Leon	2.50	1.25	.75
(90)	Bob Locker	2.50	1.25	.75
(91)	Mickey Lolich	3.00	1.50	.90
(92)	Jim Lonborg	2.50	1.25	.75
(93)	Davey Lopes	2.50	1.25	.75
(94)	Mike Lum	2.50	1.25	.75
(95)	Greg Luzinski	2.50	1.25	.75
(96)	Sparky Lyle	2.50	1.25	.75
(97)	Teddy Martinez	2.50	1.25	.75
(98)	Jon Matlack	2.50	1.25	.75
(99)	Dave May	2.50	1.25	.75
(100)	John Mayberry	2.50	1.25	.75
(101)	Willie Mays	10.00	5.00	3.00
(102)	Jim McAndrew	2.50	1.25	.75
(103)	Dick McAuliffe	2.50	1.25	.75
(104)	Sam McDowell	2.50	1.25	.70
(105)	Lynn McGlothen	2.50	1.25	.75
(106)	Tug McGraw	2.50	1.25	.70
(107)	Hal McRae	2.50	1.25	.75
(108)	Bill Melton	2.50	1.25	.75
(109)	Andy Messersmith	2.50	1.25	.75
(110)	Gene Michael	2.50	1.25	.75
(111)	Felix Millan	2.50	1.25	.75
(112)	Rick Miller	2.50	1.25	.75
(113)	John Milner	2.50	1.25	.75
(114)	Rick Monday	2.50	1.25	.75
(115)	Don Money	2.50	1.25	.75
(116)	Bob Montgomery	2.50	1.25	.75
(117)	Joe Morgan	5.00	2.50	1.50
(118)	Carl Morton	2.50	1.25	.75
(119)	Thurman Munson	4.00	2.00	1.25
(120)	Bobby Murcer	2.50	1.25	.75
(121)	Graig Nettles	3.00	1.50	.90
(122)	Jim Northrup	2.50	1.25	.75
(123)	Ben Oglivie	2.50	1.25	.75
(124)	Al Oliver	3.00	1.50	.90
(125)	Bob Oliver	2.50	1.25	.75
(126)	Jorge Orta	2.50	1.25	.75
(127)	Amos Otis	2.50	1.25	.75
(128)	Jim Palmer	5.00	2.50	1.50
(129)	Harry Parker	2.50	1.25	.75
(130)	Fred Patek	2.50	1.25	.75
(131)	Marty Pattin	2.50	1.25	.75
(132)	Tony Perez	4.00	2.00	1.25
(133)	Gaylord Perry	4.00	2.00	1.25
(134)	Jim Perry	2.50	1.25	.75
(135)	Rico Petrocelli	2.50	1.25	.75
(136)	Rick Reichardt	2.50	1.25	.75
(137)	Ken Reitz	2.50	1.25	.75
(138)	Jerry Reuss	2.50	1.25	.75
(139)	Bill Robinson	2.50	1.25	.75
(140)	Brooks Robinson	5.00	2.50	1.50
(141)	Frank Robinson	5.00	2.50	1.50
(142)	Cookie Rojas	2.50	1.25	.75
(143)	Pete Rose	9.00	4.50	2.75
(144)	Bill Russell	2.50	1.25	.75
(145)	Nolan Ryan	15.00	7.50	4.50
(146)	Manny Sanguillen	2.50	1.25	.75
(147)	George Scott	2.50	1.25	.75
(148)	Mike Schmidt	7.50	3.75	2.25
(149)	Tom Seaver	6.00	3.00	1.75
(150)	Sonny Siebert	2.50	1.25	.75
(151)	Ted Simmons	2.50	1.25	.75
(152)	Bill Singer	2.50	1.25	.75
(153)	Reggie Smith	2.50	1.25	.75
(154)	Chris Speier	2.50	1.25	.75
(155)	Charlie Spikes	2.50	1.25	.75
(156)	Paul Splittorff	2.50	1.25	.75
(157)	Mickey Stanley	2.50	1.25	.75
(158)	Lee Stanton	2.50	1.25	.75
(159)	Willie Stargell	5.00	2.50	1.50
(160)	Rusty Staub	3.00	1.50	.90
(161)	Rennie Stennett	2.50	1.25	.75
(162)	Steve Stone	3.00	1.50	.90
(163)	Mel Stottlemyre	2.50	1.25	.75
(164)	Don Sutton	4.00	2.00	1.25
(165)	George Theodore	2.50	1.25	.75
(166)	Danny Thompson	2.50	1.25	.75
(167)	Luis Tiant	3.00	1.50	.90
(168)	Joe Torre	3.50	1.75	1.00
(169)	Bobby Valentine	2.50	1.25	.75
(170)	Bob Veale	2.50	1.25	.75
(171)	Billy Williams	5.00	2.50	1.50
(172)	Wilbur Wood	2.50	1.25	.75
(173)	Jim Wynn	2.50	1.25	.75
(174)	Carl Yastrzemski	6.00	3.00	1.75
(175)	Robin Yount	5.00	2.50	1.50
(175)	Richie Zisk	2.50	1.25	.75

1976 Linnett Superstars

This frequently encountered set of 36 cards has enjoyed little collector interest since its issue in 1976. Officially known as "Pee-Wee Superstars," the cards measure 4" x 5-5/8". Player portraits by artist Charles Linnett are rendered in black-and-white pencil and set against a pale yellow background. Players are shown without caps or uniforms (most appear to be wearing white T-shirts). According to the logos at top the set was fully licensed by both the Players Association and Major League Baseball, and team logos do appear in the lower-left corner. A facsimile autograph in red or purple appears on each card. Front borders are bright purple, red, green, dark brown, or white. Card backs feature either a photo of an antique auto or a drawing of an historic sailing ship. Each of the 12 different back designs appears on one card from each team set. The Linnetts were sold in panels of six perforated cards. An offer on the back of each card makes 8" x 10" premium portraits of each player available for 95 cents. The premium pictures have about the same value as the cards. Inexplicably, the cards are numbered from 90-125. Only the World's Champion Cincinnati Reds, A.L. Champion Boston Red Sox and N.L. runner-up Dodgers are represented in the issue.

		NM	EX	VG
Complete Panel Set (6):		15.00	7.50	4.50
Complete Singles Set (36):		15.00	7.50	4.50
Common Player:		.60	.30	.20
Panel 1		7.50	3.75	2.25
90	Don Gullett	.60	.30	.20
91	Johnny Bench	2.50	1.25	.70
92	Tony Perez	1.25	.60	.40
93	Mike Lum	.60	.30	.20
94	Ken Griffey	.60	.30	.20
95	George Foster	.60	.30	.20
Panel 2		9.00	4.50	2.75
96	Joe Morgan	2.50	1.25	.70
97	Pete Rose	6.00	3.00	1.75
98	Dave Concepcion	.60	.30	.20
99	Cesar Geronimo	.60	.30	.20
100	Dan Driessen	.60	.30	.20
101	Pedro Borbon	.60	.30	.20
Panel 3		7.50	3.75	2.25
102	Carl Yastrzemski	2.50	1.25	.70
103	Fred Lynn	.60	.30	.20
104	Dwight Evans	.60	.30	.20
105	Ferguson Jenkins	1.25	.60	.40
106	Rico Petrocelli	.60	.30	.20
107	Denny Doyle	.60	.30	.20
Panel 4		6.00	3.00	1.75
108	Luis Tiant	.60	.30	.20
109	Carlton Fisk	2.50	1.25	.70
110	Rick Burleson	.60	.30	.20
111	Bill Lee	.60	.30	.20
112	Rick Wise	.60	.30	.20
113	Jim Rice	1.00	.50	.30
Panel 5		6.00	3.00	1.75
114	Davey Lopes	.60	.30	.20
115	Steve Garvey	1.25	.60	.40
116	Bill Russell	.60	.30	.20
117	Ron Cey	.60	.30	.20

		NM	EX	VG
118	Steve Yaeger	.60	.30	.20
119	Doug Rau	.60	.30	.20
Panel 6		6.00	3.00	1.75
120	Don Sutton	1.75	.90	.50
121	Joe Ferguson	.60	.30	.20
122	Mike Marshall	.60	.30	.20
123	Bill Buckner	.60	.30	.20
124	Rick Rhoden	.60	.30	.20
125	Ted Sizemore	.60	.30	.20

1923 Little Wonder Picture Series

Some versions of the W515-2 strip cards are found with part of a line of type in the top border that reads "THE LITTLE WONDER PICTURE SERIES" and includes a Underwood (U&U) logo.

(See W515-2.)

1887 Lone Jack St. Louis Browns (N370)

The Lone Jack set is among the rarest of all 19th Century tobacco issues. Issued by the Lone Jack Cigarette Co. of Lynchburg, Va., the set consists of 13 subjects, all members of the American Association champion St. Louis Browns. Photos for the set are enlarged versions of those used in the more popular N172 Old Judge series. Cards in the set measure 2-1/2" x 1-1/2" and carry an ad for Lone Jack Cigarettes along the bottom of the front. The set features the Browns' starting lineup for 1886 along with their two top pitchers, backup catcher and owner, Chris Von Der Ahe.

		NM	EX	VG
Common Player:		12,000	7,150	4,950
(1)	Doc Bushong	12,000	7,150	4,950
(2)	Parisian Bob Caruthers	12,000	7,150	4,950
(3)	Charles Commiskey (Comiskey)	75,000	12,000	8,000
(4)	Dave Foutz	12,000	7,150	4,950
(5)	Will Gleason	12,000	7,150	4,950
(6)	Nat Hudson	12,000	7,150	4,950
(7)	Rudy Kimler (Kemmler)	12,000	7,150	4,950
(8)	Arlie Latham	12,000	7,150	4,950
(9)	Little Nick Nicol	12,000	7,150	4,950
(10)	Tip O'Neil (O'Neill)	12,000	7,150	4,950
(11)	Yank Robinson	11,000	6,500	4,500
(12)	Chris Von Der Ahe	18,000	10,800	7,200
(13)	Curt Welsh (Welch)	12,000	7,150	4,950

1886 Lorillard Team Cards

Issued in 1886 by Lorillard Tobacco Co., these 4" x 5-1/2" cards were issued for the Chicago, Detroit and New York baseball clubs. Each card carries the team's schedule (start-

ing with June) on one side and features 11 player portraits enclosed in circles on the other. Each side has advertising for one of Lorillard's tobacco brands - Climax, Rebecca, etc.

		NM	EX	VG
Complete Set (4):		45,000	22,500	13,500
Common Team:		10,000	5,000	3,000
(1)	Chicago League Base Ball Club	13,500	7,200	6,000
(2)	Detroit League Base Ball Club	12,000	6,000	3,600
(3)	New York League Base Ball Club	10,000	5,000	3,250
(4)	Philadelphia League Base Ball Club	7,500	3,750	3,000

1949 Lummis Peanut Butter Phillies

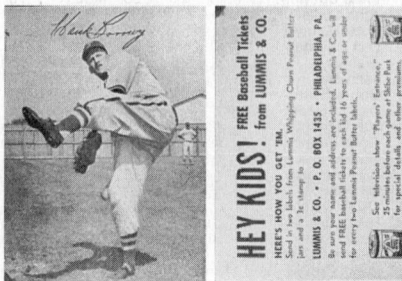

This 12-card regional set featuring the Phillies was issued in the Philadelphia area by Lummis Peanut Butter in 1949. The cards measure 3-1/4" x 4-1/4" and are unnumbered. The fronts feature an action photo with a facsimile autograph, while the backs advertise a game ticket promotion by Lummis Peanut Butter. The same photos and checklist were also used for a regional sticker set issued by Sealtest Dairy the same year.

		NM	EX	VG
Complete Set (12):		22,500	11,250	6,750
Common Player:		1,350	675.00	400.00
(1)	Rich Ashburn	4,500	2,250	1,350
(2)	Hank Borowy	1,350	675.00	400.00
(3)	Del Ennis	1,500	750.00	450.00
(4)	Granny Hamner	1,350	675.00	400.00
(5)	Puddinhead Jones	1,350	675.00	400.00
(6)	Russ Meyer	1,350	675.00	400.00
(7)	Bill Nicholson	1,350	675.00	400.00
(8)	Robin Roberts	4,500	2,250	1,350
(9)	"Schoolboy" Rowe	1,350	675.00	400.00
(10)	Andy Seminick	1,350	675.00	400.00
(11)	Curt Simmons	1,500	750.00	450.00
(12)	Eddie Waitkus	1,350	675.00	400.00

1910 Luxello Cigars A's/Phillies Pins (P13)

Players from the two Philadelphia teams are pictured in this series of 7/8" black-and-white pins. The player's last name, team and position are printed below the photo; the Luxello Cigar name at top. On left and right are a horseshoe with monogram inside.

		NM	EX	VG
Complete Set (21):		21,000	11,000	6,500
Common Player:		900.00	450.00	300.00
	Philadelphia Athletics			
(1)	Franklin Baker	1,800	900.00	500.00
(2)	Jack Barry	900.00	450.00	300.00
(3)	Eddie Collins	1,800	900.00	550.00
(4)	John W. Coombs	900.00	450.00	300.00
(5)	Harry Davis	900.00	450.00	300.00
(6)	James Dygert	900.00	450.00	300.00
(7)	Heinie Heitmuller	900.00	450.00	300.00
(8)	Harry Krause	900.00	450.00	300.00
(9)	Paddy Livingston	900.00	450.00	300.00
(10)	Danny Murphy	900.00	450.00	300.00
(11)	Ed Plank	1,800	900.00	550.00
	Philadelphia Phillies			
(12)	John W. Bates	900.00	450.00	300.00
(13)	Chas. S. Dooin	900.00	450.00	300.00
(14)	Mike Doolan	900.00	450.00	300.00
(15)	Eddie Grant	900.00	450.00	300.00
(16)	Otto Knabe	900.00	450.00	300.00
(17)	Geo. McQuillan	900.00	450.00	300.00
(18)	Earl Moore	900.00	450.00	300.00
(19)	Lew Moren	900.00	450.00	300.00
(20)	Louis Schettler	900.00	450.00	300.00
(21)	Tully Sparks	900.00	450.00	300.00
(22)	John Titus	900.00	450.00	300.00

1912 L1 Leathers

One of the more unusual baseball collectibles of the tobacco era, the L1 "Leathers" were issued by Helmar Tobacco Co. in 1912 as a premium with its "Turkish Trophies" brand of cigarettes. The set featured 25 of the top baseball

players and shared a checklist with the closely-related S81 "Silks," which were another part of the same promotion. The "Leathers," advertised as being 10" x 12", featured drawings of baseball players on horsehide-shaped pieces of leather. The drawings were based on the pictures used for the popular T3 Turkey Red series issued a year earlier. Twenty of the 25 players in the "Leathers" set are from the T3 set. Five pitchers (Rube Marquard, Rube Benton, Marty O'Toole, Grover Alexander and Russ Ford) not pictured in T3 were added to the "Leathers" set, and the Frank Baker error was corrected. According to the promotion, each "Leather" was available in exchange for 50 Helmar coupons. In addition to the 25 baseball stars, the "Leathers" set also included more than 100 other subjects, including female athletes and bathing beauties, famous generals, Indian chiefs, actresses, national flags, college mascots, and others.

		NM	EX	VG
Common Player:		2,250	1,150	700.00
86	Rube Marquard	5,750	2,900	1,700
87	Marty O'Toole	2,250	1,150	700.00
88	Rube Benton	2,250	1,150	700.00
89	Grover Alexander	6,400	3,200	2,000
90	Russ Ford	2,250	1,150	700.00
91	John McGraw	5,750	2,900	1,700
92	Nap Rucker	2,250	1,150	700.00
93	Mike Mitchell	2,250	1,150	700.00
94	Chief Bender	5,750	2,900	1,700
95	Home Run Baker	5,750	2,900	1,700
96	Nap Lajoie	5,750	2,900	1,700
97	Joe Tinker	5,750	2,900	1,700
98	Sherry Magee	2,250	1,150	700.00
99	Howie Camnitz	2,250	1,150	700.00
100	Eddie Collins	5,750	2,900	1,700
101	Red Dooin	2,250	1,150	700.00
102	Ty Cobb	45,000	22,500	13,500
103	Hugh Jennings	5,750	2,900	1,700
104	Roger Bresnahan	5,750	2,900	1,700
105	Jake Stahl	2,250	1,150	700.00
106	Tris Speaker	6,400	3,200	2,000
107	Ed Walsh	5,750	2,900	1,700
108	Christy Mathewson	12,000	6,000	3,600
109	Johnny Evers	5,750	2,900	1,700
110	Walter Johnson	12,000	6,000	3,600

M

1947 Mabley & Carew Cincinnati Reds

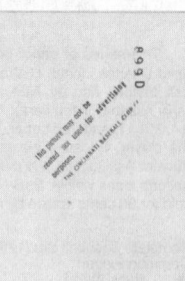

Pictures of Reds players and staff were given away and sold by the boys' shop of the Cincinnati department store. The black-and-white glossy photos measure 3-5/8" x 5-1/16" and have a white border. Backs have a rubber-stamped alphanumeric identifier and the notice: "This picture may not be rented nor used for advertising purposes. The Cincinnati Baseball Club." The players are not named on the pictures. Small groups of pictures were apparently given away in a tan-and-orange paper folder measuring about 3-7/8" x 5-1/4". The folder pictures the store, has a team roster and schedule and a coupon for purchasing addtional photos at a relatively hefty 10 cents apiece. The pictures are listed here alphabetically.

		NM	EX	VG
Complete Set (28):		850.00	425.00	250.00
Common Player:		30.00	15.00	9.00
Folder:		30.00	15.00	9.00
(1)	Bob Adams	30.00	15.00	9.00
(2)	Frank Baumholtz	30.00	15.00	9.00
(3)	Ewell Blackwell	40.00	20.00	12.00
(4)	Ed Erautt	30.00	15.00	9.00
(5)	Augie Galan	30.00	15.00	9.00
(6)	Harry Gumbert	30.00	15.00	9.00

		NM	EX	VG
(7)	Bert Haas	30.00	15.00	9.00
(8)	Grady Hatton	30.00	15.00	9.00
(9)	John Hetki	30.00	15.00	9.00
(10)	George Kelly	30.00	15.00	9.00
(11)	Ray Lamanno	30.00	15.00	9.00
(12)	Everett Lively	30.00	15.00	9.00
(13)	Ed Lukon	30.00	15.00	9.00
(14)	Eddie Miller	30.00	15.00	9.00
(15)	Ray Mueller	30.00	15.00	9.00
(16)	John Neun	30.00	15.00	9.00
(17)	Phil Page	30.00	15.00	9.00
(18)	Kent Peterson	30.00	15.00	9.00
(19)	Hugh Poland	30.00	15.00	9.00
(20)	Ken Raffensberger	30.00	15.00	9.00
(21)	Elmer Riddle	30.00	15.00	9.00
(22)	Tom Tatum	30.00	15.00	9.00
(23)	Johnny Vander Meer	40.00	20.00	12.00
(24)	Clyde Vollmer	30.00	15.00	9.00
(25)	Kermit Wahl	30.00	15.00	9.00
(26)	Bucky Walters	30.00	15.00	9.00
(27)	Babe Young	30.00	15.00	9.00
(28)	Ben Zientara	30.00	15.00	9.00

1951 Mabley & Carew Cincinnati Reds

This set is similar to the 1947 issue, with numbered player cards that were given away with a folder and schedule.

The checklist is incomplete.

		NM	EX	VG
		.00	.00	.00
19	Lloyd Merriman	30.00	15.00	9.00
35	Ken Raffensberger	30.00	15.00	9.00

1950s-70s MacGregor Advisory Staff Photos

Advisory staff photos were a promotional item which debuted in the early 1950s, flourished in the Sixties and died in the early 1970s. Generally 8" x 10" (sometimes a little larger), these black-and-white (a few later were color) glossy photos picture players who had contracted with a major baseball equipment company to endorse and use their product. Usually the product - most often a glove - was prominently displayed in the photo. The pictures were often displayed in the windows of sporting goods stores or the walls of sports departments and were sometimes made available to customers. Because the companies tended to stick with players over the years, some photos were reissued, sometimes with and sometimes without a change of team, pose or typography. All MacGregor staff photos of the era are checklisted here in alphabetical order. Team designation and pose description is given for each known picture. The photos are checklisted here in alphabetical order. It is unlikely this list is complete. Several arrangements of typography in the bottom border are seen and some photos have a facsimile autograph.

	NM	EX	VG
Common Player:	15.00	7.50	4.50
Hank Aaron/Btg (Atlanta, color.)	25.00	12.50	7.50
Richie Ashburn (Cubs, full-length, hands on knees.)	25.00	12.50	7.50
Richie Ashburn (Phillies, full-length, hands on knees.)	40.00	20.00	12.00
Gus Bell/Kneeling (Reds)	15.00	7.50	4.50
Ed Bouchee (Phillies, upper body.)	15.00	7.50	4.50
Ed Brinkman (Senators, upper body.)	15.00	7.50	4.50
Roberto Clemente (Full-length.)	125.00	65.00	35.00
Del Crandall (Braves, catching crouch in gear, large.)	15.00	7.50	4.50
Del Crandall (Braves, catching crouch in gear, small.)	15.00	7.50	4.50
Del Crandall (Braves, catching crouch, no gear.)	15.00	7.50	4.50
Del Crandall/Kneeling (Braves, glove on knee.)	15.00	7.50	4.50
Al Downing (Dodgers, glove at waist.)	15.00	7.50	4.50
Al Downing (Yankees, upper body.)	15.00	7.50	4.50
Ron Hansen/Fldg (White Sox)	15.00	7.50	4.50
Tommy Helms (Reds, full-length.)	15.00	7.50	4.50
Randy Hundley (Cubs, upper body.)	15.00	7.50	4.50
Jackie Jensen (Red Sox, chest-up.)	15.00	7.50	4.50
Jack Jensen/Btg (Red Sox, full-length)	15.00	7.50	4.50
Jack Jensen (Red Sox, full-length, hands on knees.)	15.00	7.50	4.50
Ralph Kiner (Cubs, hands on knees.)	30.00	15.00	9.00
Ralph Kiner (Pirates, full-length.)	25.00	12.50	7.50
Ted Kluszewski/Btg (Reds)	25.00	12.50	7.50
Ted Kluszewski/Fldg (White Sox)	25.00	12.50	7.50
Ted Kluszewski/Portrait (Reds)	35.00	17.50	10.00
Johnny Kucks/Pitching (Yankees.)	15.00	7.50	4.50
Willie Mays (Giants, full-length.)	90.00	45.00	27.00
Bill Mazeroski/Btg (Pirates)	30.00	15.00	9.00
Mike McCormick (Giants, follow-through.)	15.00	7.50	4.50
Gil McDougald/Throwing (Yankees)	15.00	7.50	4.50
Gil McDougald (Yankees, upper-body portrait.)	15.00	7.50	4.50
Tony Oliva/Btg (Twins)	15.00	7.50	4.50
Tony Oliva (Twins, upper body.)	15.00	7.50	4.50
Claude Osteen/Pitching (Dodgers)	15.00	7.50	4.50
Claude Osteen/Portrait (Dodgers)	15.00	7.50	4.50
Juan Pizzaro (White Sox, follow-through.)	15.00	7.50	4.50
Robin Roberts (Phillies, portrait.)	25.00	12.50	7.50
Robin Roberts (Phillies, follow-through.)	25.00	12.50	7.50
Frank Robinson/Portrait (Orioles)	25.00	12.50	7.50
Pete Rose/Kneeling (Reds)	35.00	17.50	10.00
Pete Rose (Reds, leading off, color.)	65.00	32.50	20.00
Pete Rose (Reds, chest-to-cap portrait.)	35.00	17.50	10.00
Al Schoendienst/Kneeling (Cardinals)	25.00	12.50	7.50
Warren Spahn (Boston Braves, follow-through.)	25.00	12.50	7.50
Daryl Spencer (Cardinals, fielding grounder.)	15.00	7.50	4.50
Don Sutton (Dodgers, color, ready to pitch.)	20.00	10.00	6.00
Frank Torre (Braves, ready to throw.)	15.00	7.50	4.50

1960 MacGregor

The MacGregor Sporting Goods Co. was one of the pioneers in celebrity marketing, creating an advisory staff in 1960 to promote its products. The 25-card set features black-and-white photography of several stars and lesser lights, and even a couple of managers. The cards are 3-3/4" x 5" with a white border and the words "MacGregor Baseball Advisory Staff of Champions" on the bottom panel. The cards are not numbered and are blank-backed, and include a facsimile autograph in white on the front photo. The checklist is arranged here alphabetically.

		NM	EX	VG
Complete Set (25):		700.00	350.00	210.00
Common Player:		15.00	7.50	4.50
1	Hank Aaron	110.00	55.00	35.00
2	Richie Ashburn	35.00	17.50	10.00
3	Gus Bell	15.00	7.50	4.50
4	Lou Berberet	15.00	7.50	4.50
5	Jerry Casale	15.00	7.50	4.50
6	Del Crandall	15.00	7.50	4.50
7	Art Ditmar	15.00	7.50	4.50
8	Gene Freese	15.00	7.50	4.50
9	James Gilliam	17.50	8.75	5.25
10	Ted Kluszewski	35.00	17.50	10.00
11	Jim Landis	15.00	7.50	4.50
12	Al Lopez	30.00	15.00	9.00
13	Willie Mays	110.00	55.00	35.00
14	Bill Mazeroski	35.00	17.50	10.00
15	Mike McCormick	15.00	7.50	4.50
16	Gil McDougald	15.00	7.50	4.50
17	Russ Nixon	15.00	7.50	4.50
18	Bill Rigney	15.00	7.50	4.50
19	Robin Roberts	35.00	17.50	10.00
20	Frank Robinson	45.00	22.50	13.50
21	John Roseboro	15.00	7.50	4.50
22	Red Schoendienst	35.00	17.50	10.00
23	Bill Skowron	20.00	10.00	6.00
24	Daryl Spencer	15.00	7.50	4.50
25	Johnny Temple	15.00	7.50	4.50

1960-70s MacGregor Pete Rose

Besides the several series of card issues and Advisory Staff photos issued over the years, MacGregor produced a number of special Pete Rose cards to promote its relationship with one of

baseball's top stars of the 1960s and 1970s. All cards in this listing are in black-and-white with blank backs. The 1965-66 cards are 3-1/2" x 5". The later cards are 5" x 7-1/4" to 7-1/2".

		NM	EX	VG
1965	Pete Rose (Full-length photo, crouching w/glove.)	200.00	100.00	60.00
1966	Pete Rose (Half-length photo, crouching w/glove.)	200.00	100.00	60.00
1969	Pete Rose (Portrait to chest.)	100.00	50.00	30.00
1970	Pete Rose/Fldg (White background.)	75.00	37.50	22.00
1973	Pete Rose/Portrait	75.00	37.50	22.00
1974	Pete Rose (Portrait to waist, w/glove.)	75.00	37.50	22.00

1965 MacGregor

The 1965 MacGregor set is similar to earlier issues, with only a slight change in dimension to 3-1/2" x 5-1/8" and reduced in size to only 10 players. The cards are blank-backed and unnumbered and have a glossy finish. They are checklisted here alphabetically.

		NM	EX	VG
Complete Set (10):		375.00	185.00	110.00
Common Player:		10.00	5.00	3.00
(1)	Roberto Clemente	150.00	75.00	45.00
(2)	Al Downing	10.00	5.00	3.00
(3)	Johnny Edwards	10.00	5.00	3.00
(4)	Ron Hansen	10.00	5.00	3.00
(5)	Deron Johnson	10.00	5.00	3.00
(6)	Willie Mays	135.00	65.00	40.00
(7)	Tony Oliva	15.00	7.50	4.50
(8)	Claude Osteen	10.00	5.00	3.00
(9)	Bobby Richardson	15.00	7.50	4.50
(10)	Zoilo Versalles	10.00	5.00	3.00

1970s MacGregor Advisory Staff Photos

This advisory staff photo series was among the last in a line of promotional items which debuted in the early 1950s, flourished in the Sixties and died in the 1970s. While earlier advisory staff photos were generally 8" x 10", this later series of black-and-white glossy photos is in a 5" x 7" format. They picture players who had contracted with MacGregor to endorse and use its product. The pictures were often displayed in the windows of sporting goods stores or the walls of sports departments and were sometimes made available to customers. Because the companies tended to stick with players over the years, some photos were reissued, sometimes with a change of team, pose or typography. Known MacGregor staff photos of the era are checklisted here in alphabetical order. Team designation and pose description is given for each picture. It is unlikely this list is complete. Gaps have been left in the assigned numbering to accommodate future additions.

		NM	EX	VG
Common Player:		15.00	7.50	4.50
(1)	Hank Aaron	40.00	20.00	12.00
	(Braves, chest-to-cap.)			
(2)	Rod Carew	25.00	12.50	7.50
	(Twins, chest-to-cap.)			
(3)	Rod Carew	25.00	12.50	7.50
	(Twins, chin-to-cap.)			
(5)	George Foster	15.00	7.50	4.50
	(Reds, chest-to-cap.)			
(8)	Lee May	15.00	7.50	4.50
	(Orioles, chest-to-cap.)			
(10)	Joe Morgan	25.00	12.50	7.50
	(Reds, neck-to-cap.)			
(11)	Joe Morgan	25.00	12.50	7.50
	(Reds, waist-to-cap.)			
(12)	Thurman Munson	27.50	13.50	8.25
	(Yankees, neck-to-cap.)			
(15)	Tony Perez	25.00	12.50	7.50
	(Reds, neck-to-cap.)			
(16)	Tony Perez	25.00	12.50	7.50
	(Expos, chest-to-cap.)			
(20)	Don Sutton	20.00	10.00	6.00
	(Dodgers, chest-to-cap.)			
(21)	Don Sutton	20.00	10.00	6.00
	(Dodgers, neck-to-cap.)			

1974-1975 MacGregor Advisory Staff Posters

The 19-1/2" x 26" color posters feature game-action photos. Two lines of type, "Winners Play MacGregor" and "The Greatest Name in Sports," are above the picture. Back is blank.

	NM	EX	VG
Hank Aaron	50.00	25.00	15.00
Pete Rose	50.00	25.00	15.00

1886 MacIntire Studio Cabinets

The number of baseball players who found themselves in front of the lens at the MacIntire photography studio in Philadelphia is unknown, but all those thus far seen were members of the 1886 Philadelphia National League team. In standard cabinet-card format of about 3-3/4" x 5-3/4", the pieces feature a cream-colored mount with a sepia photo.

		NM	EX	VG
Common Player:		4,500	3,000	2,000
(1)	Tony Cusick	4,500	3,000	2,000
(2)	Edward Dailey	4,500	3,000	2,000
(3)	Jack Farrell	4,500	3,000	2,000
(4)	Charlie Ganzel	4,500	3,000	2,000
(5)	Deacon McGuire	4,500	3,000	2,000
(6)	Cannonball Titcomb	4,500	3,000	2,000
(7)	Harry Wright (Facing his right.)	10,000	4,500	2,800
(8)	Harry Wright (Pose unrecorded.)	10,000	4,500	2,800
(9)	Team Photo	6,500	4,500	2,800

1951 Connie Mack Book

In conjunction with the publication of Connie Mack's book "My 66 Years in the Big Leagues," a folder of cards titled, "Four Mighty Heroes" was also issued. The folder contained a quartet of black-and-white player cards. Fronts feature a

player photo against a white background. Backs have a bit of player career data and an ad for Mack's book. Cards measure 2-1/4" x 3-1/2".

		NM	EX	VG
Complete Set (4):		2,400	1,200	725.00
Common Player:		275.00	135.00	80.00
Book:		60.00	30.00	18.00
(1)	Connie Mack	275.00	135.00	80.00
(2)	Christy Mathewson	400.00	200.00	120.00
(3)	Babe Ruth	1,500	750.00	450.00
(4)	Rube Waddell	275.00	135.00	80.00

1924 Walter Mails Card Game (WG7)

This set of playing cards features 56 subjects. Card backs are printed in either red or blue, featuring player and umpire figures in each corner. At center is the picture of a pitcher with the name of the game's creator beneath. Walter Mails was a major league pitcher between 1915-26. Fronts feature a black-and-white player photo with a facsimile autograph. Printed beneath are the player's name, position and team. At bottom is the designation of a play used in the card game. Both major and minor league players are included in the set. Cards are round-cornered and measure 2-5/16" x 3-1/2". The unnumbered cards are checklisted here alphabetically. It appears as if the blue-back set was issued first and in lesser quantities than those with red backs. Many variations of player personal data between the two colors of backs are reported.

		NM	EX	VG
Complete Set (56):		12,000	6,000	3,500
Common Player, Major Leaguer:		250.00	100.00	60.00
Common Player, Minor Leaguer:		200.00	80.00	50.00
Rules Card:		50.00	20.00	10.00
(1)	Russell "Buzz" Arlett	200.00	80.00	50.00
(2)	J.C. "Jim" Bagby	200.00	80.00	50.00
(3)	Dave "Beauty" Bancroft	500.00	200.00	125.00
(4)	Johnny Basseler (Bassler)	250.00	100.00	60.00
(5)	Jack Bentley	250.00	100.00	60.00
(6)	J.C. "Rube" Benton	250.00	100.00	60.00
(7)	Geo. Burns	250.00	100.00	60.00
(8)	"Bullet Joe" Bush	250.00	100.00	60.00
(9)	Harold P. Chavezo	200.00	80.00	50.00
(10)	Hugh Critz	200.00	80.00	50.00
(11)	"Jake" E. Daubert	250.00	100.00	60.00
(12)	Wheezer Dell	200.00	80.00	50.00
(13)	Joe Dugan	250.00	100.00	60.00
(14)	Pat Duncan	250.00	100.00	60.00
(15)	Howard J. Ehmke	250.00	100.00	60.00
(16)	Lewis Fonseca	250.00	100.00	60.00
(17)	Ray French	250.00	100.00	60.00
(18)	Ed Gharity (Gharrity)	250.00	100.00	60.00
(19)	Heinie Groh	250.00	100.00	60.00
(20)	George N. Groves	250.00	100.00	60.00
(21)	E.F. "Red" Hargrave	250.00	100.00	60.00
(22)	Elmer Jacobs	250.00	100.00	60.00
(23)	Walter Johnson	1,200	480.00	300.00
(24)	WM. "Duke" Kenworthy	250.00	100.00	60.00
(25)	Harry Krause	200.00	80.00	50.00
(26)	Ray Kremer	250.00	100.00	60.00
(27)	Walter Mails	250.00	100.00	60.00
(28)	Walter "Rabbitt" Maranville	500.00	200.00	125.00
(29)	John "Stuffy" McInnis	250.00	100.00	60.00
(30)	Marty McManus	250.00	100.00	60.00
(31)	Bob Meusel	250.00	100.00	60.00
(32)	Hack Miller	250.00	100.00	60.00
(33)	Pat J. Moran	250.00	100.00	60.00
(34)	Guy Morton	250.00	100.00	60.00
(35)	Johnny Mostil	250.00	100.00	60.00
(36)	Rod Murphy	200.00	80.00	50.00
(37)	Jimmy O'Connell	250.00	100.00	60.00
(38)	Steve O'Neil	250.00	100.00	60.00
(39)	Joe Oeschger	250.00	100.00	60.00
(40)	Roger Peckinpaugh	250.00	100.00	60.00
(41)	Ralph "Babe" Pinelli	250.00	100.00	60.00
(42)	Wally Pipp	250.00	100.00	60.00
(43)	Elmer Ponder	200.00	80.00	50.00
(44)	Sam Rice	500.00	200.00	125.00
(45)	Edwin Rommell (Rommel)	250.00	100.00	60.00
(46)	Walter Schmidt	250.00	100.00	60.00
(47)	Wilford Shupes	200.00	80.00	50.00
(48)	Joe Sewell	500.00	200.00	125.00
(49)	Pat Shea	200.00	80.00	50.00
(50)	W. "Paddy" Siglin	200.00	80.00	50.00
(51)	Geo. H. Sisler	500.00	200.00	125.00
(52)	William "Bill" Skiff	200.00	80.00	50.00
(53)	J. Smith	250.00	100.00	60.00
(54)	Harry "Suds" Sutherland	200.00	80.00	50.00
(55)	James A. Tierney	250.00	100.00	60.00
(56)	Geo. Uhle	250.00	100.00	60.00

1921-1930 Major League Ball Die-Cuts

These die-cut, blank-back player cards were issued over the period 1921-30 for use with a board game called, "Major League Ball - The Indoor Baseball Game Supreme," from The National Game Makers of Washington, D.C. Measuring about

2-1/2" to 2-3/4" tall x 1" to 1-1/4" wide, the cards were originally printed on a sheet of 14 from which they were punched out to play the game. The cards were issued in team sets with on-field roster changes reflected in the player cards over the years. Individual cards are generic, liberally sharing the same poses and portraits with identification possible only by changes to the uniform and the player ID printed in the box below the figure. That player data changed from year to year and the only way to determine exact year of issue is when the player card is found with a complete team set, often in a small pre-printed manila envelope. It is unknown whether all teams were issued in all years. According to information found with the game, stickers could be purchased each year to update the game's figures with new player identification. Beginning in at least 1925 player cards were numbered at bottom within team set.

	NM	EX	VG
Typical Team Set:	300.00	150.00	90.00
Common Player:	50.00	25.00	15.00
Typical Hall of Famer:	75.00	37.50	22.50
Ty Cobb	150.00	75.00	45.00
Lou Gehrig	200.00	100.00	60.00
Walter Johnson	125.00	65.00	40.00
Babe Ruth	350.00	175.00	100.00

1969 Major League Baseball Photostamps

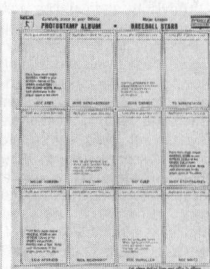

This set of 216 player stamps, sponsored by the Major League Baseball Players Association (not authorized by MLB, thus the lack of team uniform insignia) was issued in professional baseball's centennial year of 1969 and was sold in 18 different uncut sheets, with 12 stamps on each sheet. Each individual stamp measured 2" x 3-1/4". There were nine sheets picturing National League players and nine picturing American Leaguers. The full-color stamps display facsimilie autographs on the fronts. The backs carry instructions to moisten the stamps and place them in a special album that was also available. Many sheets of these stamps were uncovered by a dealer in the early 1980s and they were available at inexpensive prices.

		NM	EX	VG
Complete Sheet Set (18):		60.00	30.00	18.00
Complete Singles Set (216):		60.00	30.00	18.00
A.L. Album and Sheets:		25.00	12.50	7.50
N.L. Album and Sheets:		35.00	17.50	10.00
Common Sheet:		3.50	1.75	1.00
Common Player:		.50	.25	.15
Sheet A.L. 1		3.75	2.00	1.00
(1)	Don Buford	.50	.25	.15
(2)	Mike Andrews	.50	.25	.15
(3)	Max Alvis	.50	.25	.15
(4)	Bill Freehan	.50	.25	.15
(5)	Horace Clarke	.50	.25	.15
(6)	Bernie Allen	.50	.25	.15
(7)	Jim Fregosi	.50	.25	.15
(8)	Joe Horlen	.50	.25	.15
(9)	Jerry Adair	.50	.25	.15
(10)	Harmon Killebrew	3.00	1.50	.90
(11)	Johnny Odom	.50	.25	.15
(12)	Steve Barber	.50	.25	.15
Sheet A.L. 2		2.50	1.25	.75
(13)	Tom Harper	.50	.25	.15
(14)	Boog Powell	1.00	.50	.30
(15)	Jose Santiago	.50	.25	.15
(16)	Sonny Siebert	.50	.25	.15
(17)	Mickey Lolich	.75	.40	.25
(18)	Tom Tresh	.75	.40	.25
(19)	Camilo Pascual	.50	.25	.15
(20)	Bob Rodgers	.50	.25	.15
(21)	Pete Ward	.50	.25	.15

(22)	Dave Morehead	.50	.25	.15
(23)	John Roseboro	.50	.25	.15
(24)	Bert Campaneris	.50	.25	.15
Sheet A.L. 3		**3.75**	**2.00**	**1.00**
(25)	Danny Cater	.50	.25	.15
(26)	Rich Rollins	.50	.25	.15
(27)	Brooks Robinson	3.00	1.50	.90
(28)	Rico Petrocelli	.50	.25	.15
(29)	Larry Brown	.50	.25	.15
(30)	Norm Cash	.75	.40	.25
(31)	Jake Gibbs	.50	.25	.15
(32)	Mike Epstein	.50	.25	.15
(33)	George Brunet	.50	.25	.15
(34)	Tom McCraw	.50	.25	.15
(35)	Steve Whitaker	.50	.25	.15
(36)	Bob Allison	.50	.25	.15
Sheet A.L. 4		**2.50**	**1.25**	**.75**
(37)	Jim Kaat	.65	.35	.20
(38)	Sal Bando	.50	.25	.15
(39)	Ray Oyler	.50	.25	.15
(40)	Dave McNally	.50	.25	.15
(41)	George Scott	.50	.25	.15
(42)	Joe Azcue	.50	.25	.15
(43)	Jim Northrup	.50	.25	.15
(44)	Fritz Peterson	.50	.25	.15
(45)	Paul Casanova	.50	.25	.15
(46)	Roger Repoz	.50	.25	.15
(47)	Tommy John	.75	.40	.25
(48)	Moe Drabowsky	.50	.25	.15
Sheet A.L. 5		**2.50**	**1.25**	**.75**
(49)	Ed Kirkpatrick	.50	.25	.15
(50)	Dean Chance	.50	.25	.15
(51)	Mike Hershberger	.50	.25	.15
(52)	Jack Aker	.50	.25	.15
(53)	Andy Etchebarren	.50	.25	.15
(54)	Ray Culp	.50	.25	.15
(55)	Luis Tiant	.65	.35	.20
(56)	Willie Horton	.50	.25	.15
(57)	Roy White	.50	.25	.15
(58)	Ken McMullen	.50	.25	.15
(59)	Rick Reichardt	.50	.25	.15
(60)	Luis Aparicio	3.00	1.50	.90
Sheet A.L. 6		**2.50**	**1.25**	**.75**
(61)	Ken Berry	.50	.25	.15
(62)	Wally Bunker	.50	.25	.15
(63)	Tony Oliva	1.00	.50	.30
(64)	Rick Monday	.50	.25	.15
(65)	Chico Salmon	.50	.25	.15
(66)	Paul Blair	.50	.25	.15
(67)	Jim Lonborg	.50	.25	.15
(68)	Zoilo Versalles	.50	.25	.15
(69)	Denny McLain	.75	.40	.25
(70)	Mel Stottlemyre	.50	.25	.15
(71)	Joe Coleman	.50	.25	.15
(72)	Bob Knoop	.50	.25	.15
Sheet A.L. 7		**2.50**	**1.25**	**.75**
(73)	Chuck Hinton	.50	.25	.15
(74)	Duane Josephson	.50	.25	.15
(75)	Roger Nelson	.50	.25	.15
(76)	Ted Uhlaender	.50	.25	.15
(77)	John Donaldson	.50	.25	.15
(78)	Tommy Davis	.50	.25	.15
(79)	Frank Robinson	3.00	1.50	.90
(80)	Dick Ellsworth	.50	.25	.15
(81)	Sam McDowell	.50	.25	.15
(82)	Dick McAuliffe	.50	.25	.15
(83)	Bill Robinson	.50	.25	.15
(84)	Frank Howard	.75	.40	.25
Sheet A.L. 8		**5.00**	**2.50**	**1.50**
(85)	Ed Brinkman	.50	.25	.15
(86)	Vic Davalillo	.50	.25	.15
(87)	Gary Peters	.50	.25	.15
(88)	Joe Foy	.50	.25	.15
(89)	Rod Carew	3.00	1.50	.90
(90)	Jim "Catfish" Hunter	2.00	1.00	.60
(91)	Gary Bell	.50	.25	.15
(92)	Dave Johnson	.50	.25	.15
(93)	Ken Harrelson	.50	.25	.15
(94)	Tony Horton	.50	.25	.15
(95)	Al Kaline	3.00	1.50	.90
(96)	Steve Hamilton	.50	.25	.15
Sheet A.L. 9		**2.50**	**1.25**	**.75**
(97)	Joseph Pepitone	.75	.40	.25
(98)	Ed Stroud	.50	.25	.15
(99)	Jim McGlothlin	.50	.25	.15
(100)	Wilbur Wood	.50	.25	.15
(101)	Paul Schaal	.50	.25	.15
(102)	Cesar Tovar	.50	.25	.15
(103)	Jim Nash	.50	.25	.15
(104)	Don Mincher	.50	.25	.15
(105)	Thomas Phoebus	.50	.25	.15
(106)	Reggie Smith	.50	.25	.15
(107)	Jose Cardenal	.50	.25	.15
(108)	Mickey Stanley	.50	.25	.15
Sheet N.L. 1		**5.00**	**2.50**	**1.50**
(109)	Billy Williams	2.00	1.00	.60
(110)	Mack Jones	.50	.25	.15
(111)	Tom Seaver	3.00	1.50	.90
(112)	Rich Allen	1.50	.70	.45
(113)	Bob Veale	.50	.25	.15
(114)	Curt Flood	.65	.35	.20
(115)	Pat Jarvis	.50	.25	.15
(116)	Jim Merritt	.50	.25	.15
(117)	Joe Morgan	2.50	1.25	.70
(118)	Tom Haller	.50	.25	.15
(119)	Larry Stahl	.50	.25	.15
(120)	Willie McCovey	2.50	1.25	.70
Sheet N.L. 2		**6.00**	**3.00**	**1.75**
(121)	Ron Hunt	.50	.25	.15
(122)	Ernie Banks	3.00	1.50	.90
(123)	Jim Fairey	.50	.25	.15
(124)	Tommy Agee	.50	.25	.15
(125)	Cookie Rojas	.50	.25	.15
(126)	Mateo Alou	.50	.25	.15
(127)	Mike Shannon	.50	.25	.15
(128)	Milt Pappas	.50	.25	.15
(129)	Johnny Bench	3.00	1.50	.90

(130)	Larry Dierker	.50	.25	.15
(131)	Willie Davis	.50	.25	.15
(132)	Tony Gonzalez	.50	.25	.15
Sheet N.L. 3		**3.75**	**2.00**	**1.00**
(133)	Dick Selma	.50	.25	.15
(134)	Jim Ray Hart	.50	.25	.15
(135)	Phil Regan	.50	.25	.15
(136)	Manny Mota	.50	.25	.15
(137)	Cleon Jones	.50	.25	.15
(138)	Rick Wise	.50	.25	.15
(139)	Willie Stargell	2.50	1.25	.70
(140)	Robert Gibson	2.50	1.25	.70
(141)	Rico Carty	.50	.25	.15
(142)	Gary Nolan	.50	.25	.15
(143)	Doug Rader	.50	.25	.15
(144)	Wes Parker	.50	.25	.15
Sheet N.L. 4		**2.50**	**1.25**	**.75**
(145)	Bill Singer	.50	.25	.15
(146)	Bill McCool	.50	.25	.15
(147)	Juan Marichal	2.00	1.00	.60
(148)	Randy Hundley	.50	.25	.15
(149)	"Mudcat" Grant	.50	.25	.15
(150)	Ed Kranepool	.50	.25	.15
(151)	Tony Taylor	.50	.25	.15
(152)	Gene Alley	.50	.25	.15
(153)	Dal Maxvill	.50	.25	.15
(154)	Felipe Alou	.65	.35	.20
(155)	Jim Maloney	.50	.25	.15
(156)	Jesus Alou	.50	.25	.15
Sheet N.L. 5		**8.00**	**4.00**	**2.50**
(157)	Curt Blefary	.50	.25	.15
(158)	Ron Fairly	.50	.25	.15
(159)	Dick Kelley	.50	.25	.15
(160)	Frank Linzy	.50	.25	.15
(161)	Fergie Jenkins	2.00	1.00	.60
(162)	Maury Wills	.75	.40	.25
(163)	Jerry Grote	.50	.25	.15
(164)	Chris Short	.50	.25	.15
(165)	Jim Bunning	2.00	1.00	.60
(166)	Nelson Briles	.50	.25	.15
(167)	Orlando Cepeda	2.50	1.25	.70
(168)	Pete Rose	8.00	4.00	2.50
Sheet N.L. 6		**3.00**	**1.50**	**.90**
(169)	Tony Cloninger	.50	.25	.15
(170)	Jim Wynn	.50	.25	.15
(171)	Jim Lefebvre	.50	.25	.15
(172)	Ron Davis	.50	.25	.15
(173)	Mike McCormick	.50	.25	.15
(174)	Ron Santo	.75	.40	.25
(175)	Ty Cline	.50	.25	.15
(176)	Jerry Koosman	.50	.25	.15
(177)	Mike Ryan	.50	.25	.15
(178)	Jerry May	.50	.25	.15
(179)	Tim McCarver	.75	.40	.25
(180)	Phil Niekro	2.00	1.00	.60
Sheet N.L. 7		**15.00**	**7.50**	**4.50**
(181)	Hank Aaron	5.00	2.50	1.50
(182)	Tommy Helms	.50	.25	.15
(183)	Denis Menke	.50	.25	.15
(184)	Don Sutton	2.00	1.00	.60
(185)	Al Ferrera	.50	.25	.15
(186)	Willie Mays	5.00	2.50	1.50
(187)	Bill Hands	.50	.25	.15
(188)	Rusty Staub	.70	.35	.20
(189)	Bud Harrelson	.50	.25	.15
(190)	Johnny Callison	.50	.25	.15
(191)	Roberto Clemente	8.00	4.00	2.50
(192)	Julian Javier	.50	.25	.15
Sheet N.L. 8		**2.50**	**1.25**	**.75**
(193)	Joe Torre	1.25	.60	.40
(194)	Bob Aspromonte	.50	.25	.15
(195)	Lee May	.50	.25	.15
(196)	Don Wilson	.50	.25	.15
(197)	Claude Osteen	.50	.25	.15
(198)	Ed Spiezio	.50	.25	.15
(199)	Hal Lanier	.50	.25	.15
(200)	Glenn Beckert	.50	.25	.15
(201)	Bob Bailey	.50	.25	.15
(202)	Ron Swoboda	.50	.25	.15
(203)	John Briggs	.50	.25	.15
(204)	Bill Mazeroski	2.50	1.25	.70
Sheet N.L. 9		**3.75**	**2.00**	**1.00**
(205)	Tommie Sisk	.50	.25	.15
(206)	Lou Brock	2.50	1.25	.70
(207)	Felix Millan	.50	.25	.15
(208)	Tony Perez	2.00	1.00	.60
(209)	John Edwards	.50	.25	.15
(210)	Len Gabrielson	.50	.25	.15
(211)	Ollie Brown	.50	.25	.15
(212)	Gaylord Perry	2.00	1.00	.60
(213)	Don Kessinger	.50	.25	.15
(214)	John Bateman	.50	.25	.15
(215)	Ed Charles	.50	.25	.15
(216)	Woodie Fryman	.50	.25	.15

1969 Major League Baseball Player Pins

ROBERTO CLEMENTE
PITTSBURGH PIRATES

Black-and-white or color player portraits (noted parenthetically) are featured in the center of a red, white and blue design on these 3-1/2" diameter pins. The existing checklist, which may be incomplete, shows a mix of contemporary and retired players. The celluloid pinback buttons were sold at concession stands around the Major Leagues. Production continued at least into 1970, based on some observed player/team combinations.

		NM	EX	VG
	Common Player:	20.00	12.00	6.00
(1)	Hank Aaron (B/W)	60.00	30.00	18.00
(2)	Tommie Agee (B/W)	20.00	10.00	6.00
(3)	Mike Andrews (B/W)	20.00	10.00	6.00
(4)	Mike Andrews (Color)	20.00	10.00	6.00
(5)	Luis Aparicio (B/W)	25.00	12.50	7.50
(6)	Ernie Banks (B/W)	60.00	30.00	18.00
(7)	Ernie Banks (B/W, 2-1/2")	60.00	30.00	18.00
(8)	Ernie Banks (Color)	60.00	30.00	18.00
(9)	Glenn Beckert (B/W)	20.00	10.00	6.00
(10)	Curt Blefary (B/W)	20.00	10.00	6.00
(11)	Ken Boswell (B/W)	20.00	10.00	6.00
(12)	Lou Brock (B/W)	30.00	15.00	9.00
(13)	John Callison (B/W)	20.00	10.00	6.00
(14)	Orlando Cepeda (B/W)	25.00	12.50	7.50
(15)	Ed Charles (B/W)	20.00	10.00	6.00
(16)	Horace Clarke (B/W)	20.00	10.00	6.00
(17)	Roberto Clemente (B/W)	75.00	37.00	22.00
(18)	Donn Clendenon (B/W)	20.00	10.00	6.00
(19)	Billy Conigliaro (B/W)	20.00	10.00	6.00
(20)	Tony Conigliaro (B/W)	25.00	12.50	7.50
(21)	Tony Conigliaro (Color)	25.00	12.50	7.50
(22)	Ray Culp (Color)	20.00	10.00	6.00
(23)	Joe DiMaggio (B/W)	50.00	25.00	15.00
(24)	Don Drysdale (B/W)	30.00	15.00	9.00
(25)	Frank Fernandez (Color)	20.00	10.00	6.00
(26)	Curt Flood (B/W)	20.00	10.00	6.00
(27)	Lou Gehrig (B/W)	50.00	25.00	15.00
(28)	Bob Gibson (B/W)	30.00	15.00	9.00
(29)	Jerry Grote (B/W)	20.00	10.00	6.00
(30)	Jim Hickman (B/W)	20.00	10.00	6.00
(31)	Ken Holtzman (B/W)	20.00	10.00	6.00
(32)	Frank Howard (B/W)	22.50	11.00	6.75
(33)	Randy Hundley (B/W)	20.00	10.00	6.00
(34)	Reggie Jackson (Color)	60.00	30.00	18.00
(35)	Ferguson Jenkins (B/W)	30.00	15.00	9.00
(36)	Dalton Jones (B/W)	20.00	10.00	6.00
(37)	Al Kaline (B/W)	60.00	30.00	18.00
(38)	Don Kessinger (B/W)	20.00	10.00	6.00
(39)	Harmon Killebrew (B/W)	30.00	15.00	9.00
(40)	Jerry Koosman (Color)	20.00	10.00	6.00
(41)	Jim Lonborg (B/W)	20.00	10.00	6.00
(42)	Mickey Mantle (B/W)	100.00	50.00	30.00
(43)	Carlos May (B/W)	20.00	10.00	6.00
(44)	Willie Mays (B/W)	75.00	37.00	22.00
(45)	Willie McCovey (B/W)	25.00	12.50	7.50
(46)	Denny McLain (B/W)	22.50	11.00	6.75
(47)	Gene Michael (B/W)	20.00	10.00	6.00
(48)	Gene Michael (Color)	20.00	10.00	6.00
(49)	Bobby Murcer (Color)	22.50	11.00	6.75
(50)	Joe Pepitone (B/W)	25.00	12.50	7.50
(51)	Rico Petrocelli (B/W)	20.00	10.00	6.00
(52)	Rico Petrocelli (Color)	20.00	10.00	6.00
(53)	Pete Rose (B/W)	75.00	37.00	22.00
(54)	Babe Ruth (B/W)	50.00	25.00	15.00
(55)	Ron Santo (B/W)	22.50	11.00	6.75
(56)	Ron Santo (Color)	22.50	11.00	6.75
(57)	Ron Santo (B/W, 2-1/2")	60.00	30.00	18.00
(58)	George Scott (B/W)	20.00	10.00	6.00
(59)	Tom Seaver (B/W)	45.00	22.00	13.50
(60)	Tom Seaver (Color)	45.00	22.00	13.50
(61)	Reggie Smith (B/W)	20.00	10.00	6.00
(62)	Reggie Smith (Color)	20.00	10.00	6.00
(63)	Mel Stottlemyre (Color)	20.00	10.00	6.00
(64)	Tony Taylor (B/W, 2-1/2")	20.00	10.00	6.00
(65)	Joe Torre (B/W)	22.50	11.00	6.75
(66)	Tom Tresh (Color)	20.00	10.00	6.00
(67)	Pete Ward (B/W)	20.00	10.00	6.00
(68)	Roy White (B/W)	20.00	10.00	6.00
(69)	Billy Williams (B/W)	25.00	12.50	7.50
(70)	Carl Yastrzemski (B/W)	60.00	30.00	18.00
(71)	Carl Yastrzemski (Color)	60.00	30.00	18.00

1969 Major League Baseball Players Ass'n Pins

CINCINNATI REDS
PETE ROSE

Issued by the Major League Baseball Players Association in 1969, this unnumbered set consists of 60 pins - 30 players from the N.L. and 30 from the A.L. Each pin measures approximately 7/8" in diameter and features a black-and-white player photo. A.L. players are surrounded by a red border, while N.L. players are framed in blue. The player's name and team appear at the top and bottom. Also along the bottom is a line reading "1969 MLBPA MFG. R.R. Winona, Minn."

	NM	EX	VG
Complete Set (60):	250.00	125.00	75.00

		NM	EX	VG
Common Player:		6.00	3.00	1.75
(1)	Hank Aaron	30.00	15.00	9.00
(2)	Richie Allen	10.00	5.00	3.00
(3)	Felipe Alou	7.50	3.75	2.25
(4)	Max Alvis	6.00	3.00	1.75
(5)	Luis Aparicio	12.50	6.25	3.75
(6)	Ernie Banks	15.00	7.50	4.50
(7)	Johnny Bench	15.00	7.50	4.50
(8)	Lou Brock	15.00	7.50	4.50
(9)	George Brunet	6.00	3.00	1.75
(10)	Johnny Callison	6.00	3.00	1.75
(11)	Rod Carew	15.00	7.50	4.50
(12)	Orlando Cepeda	12.50	6.25	3.75
(13)	Dean Chance	6.00	3.00	1.75
(14)	Roberto Clemente	40.00	20.00	12.00
(15)	Willie Davis	6.00	3.00	1.75
(16)	Don Drysdale	15.00	7.50	4.50
(17)	Ron Fairly	6.00	3.00	1.75
(18)	Curt Flood	6.00	3.00	1.75
(19)	Bill Freehan	6.00	3.00	1.75
(20)	Jim Fregosi	6.00	3.00	1.75
(21)	Bob Gibson	15.00	7.50	4.50
(22)	Ken Harrelson	6.00	3.00	1.75
(23)	Bud Harrelson	6.00	3.00	1.75
(24)	Jim Ray Hart	6.00	3.00	1.75
(25)	Tommy Helms	6.00	3.00	1.75
(26)	Joe Horlen	6.00	3.00	1.75
(27)	Tony Horton	7.50	3.75	2.25
(28)	Willie Horton	6.00	3.00	1.75
(29)	Frank Howard	7.50	3.75	2.25
(30)	Al Kaline	15.00	7.50	4.50
(31)	Don Kessinger	6.00	3.00	1.75
(32)	Harmon Killebrew	15.00	7.50	4.50
(33)	Jerry Koosman	6.00	3.00	1.75
(34)	Mickey Lolich	6.00	3.00	1.75
(35)	Jim Lonborg	6.00	3.00	1.75
(36)	Jim Maloney	6.00	3.00	1.75
(37)	Juan Marichal	12.50	6.25	3.75
(38)	Willie Mays	30.00	15.00	9.00
(39)	Tim McCarver	7.50	3.75	2.25
(40)	Willie McCovey	15.00	7.50	4.50
(41)	Sam McDowell	6.00	3.00	1.75
(42)	Denny McLain	7.50	3.75	2.25
(43)	Rick Monday	6.00	3.00	1.75
(44)	Tony Oliva	7.50	3.75	2.25
(45)	Joe Pepitone	7.50	3.75	2.25
(46)	Boog Powell	7.50	3.75	2.25
(47)	Rick Reichardt	6.00	3.00	1.75
(48)	Pete Richert	6.00	3.00	1.75
(49)	Brooks Robinson	15.00	7.50	4.50
(50)	Frank Robinson	15.00	7.50	4.50
(51)	Pete Rose	25.00	12.50	7.50
(52)	Ron Santo	9.00	4.50	2.75
(53)	Mel Stottlemyre	6.00	3.00	1.75
(54)	Ron Swoboda	6.00	3.00	1.75
(55)	Luis Tiant	6.00	3.00	1.75
(56)	Joe Torre	9.00	4.50	2.75
(57)	Pete Ward	6.00	3.00	1.75
(58)	Billy Williams	12.50	6.25	3.75
(59)	Jim Wynn	6.00	3.00	1.75
(60)	Carl Yastrzemski	15.00	7.50	4.50

1889 Margeau & Power Indianapolis Hoosier Cabinets

This series of cabinet cards is in the standard 4-1/4" x 6-1/2" format with sepia toned player photos of the Indianapolis National League team of 1889. Unlike most contemporary baseball cabinets, this series includes the player last name and position printed on the mount. This checklist is likely incomplete and gaps in the assigned numbering have been left for future additions.

		NM	EX	VG
Common Player:		3,500	1,750	1,050
(1)	Henry Boyle	3,500	1,750	1,050
(2)	Bill Burdick	3,500	1,750	1,050
(4)	Jerry Denny	3,500	1,750	1,050
(6)	Jack Glasscock	3,500	1,750	1,050
(7)	Paul Hines	3,500	1,750	1,050
(11)	Emmett Seery	3,500	1,750	1,050
(13)	Jim Whitney	3,500	1,750	1,050

1983 "1969" MLBPA Pins

Virtually identical in format to the 60-pin 1969 MLBPA issue, these pins were probably not issued prior to 1983 and despite what is printed thereon, are not a licensed issue of the Players Association. The 7/8" diameter pins have a black-and-white player portrait photo on a white background at center. The photo is bordered in red or blue with the player name at top and team at bottom in white. A copyright line on back reads, "1969 MLBPA MFG IN U.S.A." Latter-day pins can be distinguished from the 1969s by the absence of mention of Winona, Minn., on the replicas.

Complete Set (36):

(1)	Hank Aaron
(2)	Bob Allison
(3)	Yogi Berra
(4)	Roy Campanella
(5)	Norm Cash
(6)	Orlando Cepeda
(7)	Roberto Clemente
(8)	Joe DiMaggio
(9)	Bobby Doerr
(10)	Don Drysdale
(11)	Bob Feller
(12)	Whitey Ford
(13)	Nellie Fox
(14)	Frank Howard
(15)	Jim "Catfish" Hunter
(16)	Al Kaline
(17)	Sandy Koufax
(18)	Mickey Mantle
(19)	Juan Marichal
(20)	Eddie Mathews
(21)	Willie Mays
(22)	Willie McCovey
(23)	Stan Musial
(24)	Tony Oliva
(25)	Satchel Paige
(26)	Phil Rizzuto
(27)	Robin Roberts
(28)	Brooks Robinson
(29)	Jackie Robinson
(30)	Ron Santo
(31)	Duke Snider
(32)	Warren Spahn
(33)	Bill Skowron
(34)	Billy Williams
(35)	Ted Williams
(36)	Maury Wills

1970 Major League Baseball Photostamps

BILL MELTON

For a second year, ballplayer "stamps" were sold in conjunction with team albums. Approximately 1-7/8" x 3", the pieces are printed on glossy paper in full color with a white border and facsimile autograph. Backs, which are not gummed, have gluing instructions and the players name at bottom. The 1970 issue can be differentiated from the 1969 issue in that they have uniform insignia present on the photos whereas the 1969 stamps do not. The unnumbered stamps are checklisted here alphabetically within team.

		NM	EX	VG
Complete Set (288):		200.00	100.00	60.00
Common Player:		1.00	.50	.30
ATLANTA BRAVES				
(1)	Hank Aaron	15.00	7.50	4.50
(2)	Bob Aspromonte	1.00	.50	.30
(3)	Rico Carty	1.00	.50	.30
(4)	Orlando Cepeda	6.00	3.00	1.75
(5)	Bob Didier	1.00	.50	.30
(6)	Tony Gonzalez	1.00	.50	.30
(7)	Pat Jarvis	1.00	.50	.30
(8)	Felix Millan	1.00	.50	.30
(9)	Jim Nash	1.00	.50	.30
(10)	Phil Niekro	4.00	2.00	1.25
(11)	Milt Pappas	1.00	.50	.30
(12)	Ron Reed	1.00	.50	.30
BALTIMORE ORIOLES				
(1)	Mark Belanger	1.00	.50	.30
(2)	Paul Blair	1.00	.50	.30
(3)	Don Buford	1.00	.50	.30
(4)	Mike Cuellar	1.00	.50	.30
(5)	Andy Etchebarren	1.00	.50	.30
(6)	Dave Johnson	1.00	.50	.30
(7)	Dave McNally	1.00	.50	.30
(8)	Tom Phoebus	1.00	.50	.30
(9)	Boog Powell	2.00	1.00	.60
(10)	Brooks Robinson	6.00	3.00	1.75
(11)	Frank Robinson	6.00	3.00	1.75
(12)	Chico Salmon	1.00	.50	.30
BOSTON RED SOX				
(1)	Mike Andrews	1.00	.50	.30
(2)	Ray Culp	1.00	.50	.30
(3)	Jim Lonborg	1.00	.50	.30
(4)	Sparky Lyle	1.00	.50	.30
(5)	Gary Peters	1.00	.50	.30
(6)	Rico Petrocelli	1.00	.50	.30
(7)	Vicente Romo	1.00	.50	.30
(8)	Tom Satriano	1.00	.50	.30
(9)	George Scott	1.00	.50	.30
(10)	Sonny Siebert	1.00	.50	.30
(11)	Reggie Smith	1.00	.50	.30
(12)	Carl Yastrzemski	6.00	3.00	1.75
CALIFORNIA ANGELS				
(1)	Sandy Alomar	1.00	.50	.30
(2)	Jose Azcue	1.00	.50	.30
(3)	Tom Egan	1.00	.50	.30

		NM	EX	VG
(4)	Jim Fregosi	1.00	.50	.30
(5)	Alex Johnson	1.00	.50	.30
(6)	Jay Johnstone	1.00	.50	.30
(7)	Rudy May	1.00	.50	.30
(8)	Andy Messersmith	1.00	.50	.30
(9)	Rick Reichardt	1.00	.50	.30
(10)	Roger Repoz	1.00	.50	.30
(11)	Aurelio Rodriguez	1.00	.50	.30
(12)	Ken Tatum	1.00	.50	.30
CHICAGO CUBS				
(1)	Ernie Banks	7.50	3.75	2.25
(2)	Glenn Beckert	1.00	.50	.30
(3)	Johnny Callison	1.00	.50	.30
(4)	Bill Hands	1.00	.50	.30
(5)	Randy Hundley	1.00	.50	.30
(6)	Ken Holtzman	1.00	.50	.30
(7)	Fergie Jenkins	4.00	2.00	1.25
(8)	Don Kessinger	1.00	.50	.30
(9)	Phil Regan	1.00	.50	.30
(10)	Ron Santo	2.00	1.00	.60
(11)	Dick Selma	1.00	.50	.30
(12)	Billy Williams	5.00	2.50	1.50
CHICAGO WHITE SOX				
(1)	Luis Aparicio	5.00	2.50	1.50
(2)	Ken Berry	1.00	.50	.30
(3)	Buddy Bradford	1.00	.50	.30
(4)	Ron Hansen	1.00	.50	.30
(5)	Joel Horlen	1.00	.50	.30
(6)	Tommy John	1.50	.70	.45
(7)	Duane Josephson	1.00	.50	.30
(8)	Bobby Knoop	1.00	.50	.30
(9)	Tom McCraw	1.00	.50	.30
(10)	Bill Melton	1.00	.50	.30
(11)	Walt Williams	1.00	.50	.30
(12)	Wilbur Wood	1.00	.50	.30
CINCINNATI REDS				
(1)	Johnny Bench	7.50	3.75	2.25
(2)	Tony Cloninger	1.00	.50	.30
(3)	Wayne Granger	1.00	.50	.30
(4)	Tommy Helms	1.00	.50	.30
(5)	Jim Maloney	1.00	.50	.30
(6)	Lee May	1.00	.50	.30
(7)	Jim McGlothlin	1.00	.50	.30
(8)	Jim Merritt	1.00	.50	.30
(9)	Gary Nolan	1.00	.50	.30
(10)	Tony Perez	5.00	2.50	1.50
(11)	Pete Rose	12.50	6.25	3.75
(12)	Bobby Tolan	1.00	.50	.30
CLEVELAND INDIANS				
(1)	Max Alvis	1.00	.50	.30
(2)	Larry Brown	1.00	.50	.30
(3)	Dean Chance	1.00	.50	.30
(4)	Dick Ellsworth	1.00	.50	.30
(5)	Vern Fuller	1.00	.50	.30
(6)	Ken Harrelson	1.00	.50	.30
(7)	Chuck Hinton	1.00	.50	.30
(8)	Tony Horton	1.00	.50	.30
(9)	Sam McDowell	1.00	.50	.30
(10)	Vada Pinson	1.50	.70	.45
(11)	Duke Sims	1.00	.50	.30
(12)	Ted Uhlaender	1.00	.50	.30
DETROIT TIGERS				
(1)	Norm Cash	1.50	.70	.45
(2)	Bill Freehan	1.00	.50	.30
(3)	Willie Horton	1.00	.50	.30
(4)	Al Kaline	7.50	3.75	2.25
(5)	Mike Kilkenny	1.00	.50	.30
(6)	Mickey Lolich	1.00	.50	.30
(7)	Dick McAuliffe	1.00	.50	.30
(8)	Denny McLain	1.50	.70	.45
(9)	Jim Northrup	1.00	.50	.30
(10)	Mickey Stanley	1.00	.50	.30
(11)	Tom Tresh	1.00	.50	.30
(12)	Earl Wilson	1.00	.50	.30
HOUSTON ASTROS				
(1)	Jesus Alou	1.00	.50	.30
(2)	Tommy Davis	1.00	.50	.30
(3)	Larry Dierker	1.00	.50	.30
(4)	Johnny Edwards	1.00	.50	.30
(5)	Fred Gladding	1.00	.50	.30
(6)	Denver Lemaster	1.00	.50	.30
(7)	Denis Menke	1.00	.50	.30
(8)	Joe Morgan	6.00	3.00	1.75
(9)	Joe Pepitone	1.50	.70	.45
(10)	Doug Rader	1.00	.50	.30
(11)	Don Wilson	1.00	.50	.30
(12)	Jim Wynn	1.00	.50	.30
KANSAS CITY ROYALS				
(1)	Jerry Adair	1.00	.50	.30
(2)	Wally Bunker	1.00	.50	.30
(3)	Bill Butler	1.00	.50	.30
(4)	Moe Drabowsky	1.00	.50	.30
(5)	Jackie Hernandez	1.00	.50	.30
(6)	Pat Kelly	1.00	.50	.30
(7)	Ed Kirkpatrick	1.00	.50	.30
(8)	Dave Morehead	1.00	.50	.30
(9)	Roger Nelson	1.00	.50	.30
(10)	Bob Oliver	1.00	.50	.30
(11)	Lou Piniella	1.50	.70	.45
(12)	Paul Schaal	1.00	.50	.30
LOS ANGELES DODGERS				
(1)	Willie Davis	1.00	.50	.30
(2)	Len Gabrielson	1.00	.50	.30
(3)	Tom Haller	1.00	.50	.30
(4)	Jim Lefebvre	1.00	.50	.30
(5)	Manny Mota	1.00	.50	.30
(6)	Claude Osteen	1.00	.50	.30
(7)	Wes Parker	1.00	.50	.30
(8)	Bill Russell	1.00	.50	.30
(9)	Bill Singer	1.00	.50	.30
(10)	Ted Sizemore	1.00	.50	.30
(11)	Don Sutton	4.00	2.00	1.25
(12)	Maury Wills	1.00	.50	.30
MINNESOTA TWINS				
(1)	Bob Allison	1.00	.50	.30
(2)	Dave Boswell	1.00	.50	.30
(3)	Leo Cardenas	1.00	.50	.30
(4)	Rod Carew	6.00	3.00	1.75

(5)	Jim Kaat	1.50	.70	.45
(6)	Harmon Killebrew	6.00	3.00	1.75
(7)	Tony Oliva	1.50	.70	.45
(8)	Jim Perry	1.00	.50	.30
(9)	Ron Perranoski	1.00	.50	.30
(10)	Rich Reese	1.00	.50	.30
(11)	Luis Tiant	1.00	.50	.30
(12)	Cesar Tovar	1.00	.50	.30

MONTREAL EXPOS

(1)	John Bateman	1.00	.50	.30
(2)	Bob Bailey	1.00	.50	.30
(3)	Ron Brand	1.00	.50	.30
(4)	Ty Cline	1.00	.50	.30
(5)	Ron Fairly	1.00	.50	.30
(6)	Mack Jones	1.00	.50	.30
(7)	Jose Laboy	1.00	.50	.30
(8)	Claude Raymond	1.00	.50	.30
(9)	Joe Sparma	1.00	.50	.30
(10)	Rusty Staub	1.50	.70	.45
(11)	Bill Stoneman	1.00	.50	.30
(12)	Bobby Wine	1.00	.50	.30

NEW YORK METS

(1)	Tommie Agee	1.00	.50	.30
(2)	Donn Clendenon	1.00	.50	.30
(3)	Joe Foy	1.00	.50	.30
(4)	Jerry Grote	1.00	.50	.30
(5)	Bud Harrelson	1.00	.50	.30
(6)	Cleon Jones	1.00	.50	.30
(7)	Jerry Koosman	1.00	.50	.30
(8)	Ed Kranepool	1.00	.50	.30
(9)	Nolan Ryan	25.00	12.50	7.50
(10)	Tom Seaver	6.00	3.00	1.75
(11)	Ron Swoboda	1.00	.50	.30
(12)	Al Weis	1.00	.50	.30

NEW YORK YANKEES

(1)	Jack Aker	1.00	.50	.30
(2)	Curt Blefary	1.00	.50	.30
(3)	Danny Cater	1.00	.50	.30
(4)	Horace Clarke	1.00	.50	.30
(5)	Jake Gibbs	1.00	.50	.30
(6)	Steve Hamilton	1.00	.50	.30
(7)	Bobby Murcer	1.50	.70	.45
(8)	Fritz Peterson	1.00	.50	.30
(9)	Bill Robinson	1.00	.50	.30
(10)	Mel Stottlemyre	1.00	.50	.30
(11)	Pete Ward	1.00	.50	.30
(12)	Roy White	1.50	.70	.45

OAKLAND A's

(1)	Felipe Alou	1.50	.70	.45
(2)	Sal Bando	1.00	.50	.30
(3)	Bert Campaneris	1.00	.50	.30
(4)	Chuck Dobson	1.00	.50	.30
(5)	Tito Francona	1.00	.50	.30
(6)	Dick Green	1.00	.50	.30
(7)	Catfish Hunter	4.00	2.00	1.25
(8)	Reggie Jackson	10.00	5.00	3.00
(9)	Don Mincher	1.00	.50	.30
(10)	Rick Monday	1.00	.50	.30
(11)	John Odom	1.00	.50	.30
(12)	Ray Oyler	1.00	.50	.30

PHILADELPHIA PHILLIES

(1)	Johnny Briggs	1.00	.50	.30
(2)	Jim Bunning	4.00	2.00	1.25
(3)	Curt Flood	1.50	.70	.45
(4)	Woodie Fryman	1.00	.50	.30
(5)	Larry Hisle	1.00	.50	.30
(6)	Joe Hoerner	1.00	.50	.30
(7)	Grant Jackson	1.00	.50	.30
(8)	Tim McCarver	1.50	.70	.45
(9)	Mike Ryan	1.00	.50	.30
(10)	Chris Short	1.00	.50	.30
(11)	Tony Taylor	1.00	.50	.30
(12)	Rick Wise	1.00	.50	.30

PITTSBURGH PIRATES

(1)	Gene Alley	1.00	.50	.30
(2)	Matty Alou	1.00	.50	.30
(3)	Roberto Clemente	20.00	10.00	6.00
(4)	Ron Davis	1.00	.50	.30
(5)	Richie Hebner	1.00	.50	.30
(6)	Jerry May	1.00	.50	.30
(7)	Bill Mazeroski	6.00	3.00	1.75
(8)	Bob Moose	1.00	.50	.30
(9)	Al Oliver	1.50	.70	.45
(10)	Manny Sanguillen	1.00	.50	.30
(11)	Willie Stargell	5.00	2.50	1.50
(12)	Bob Veale	1.00	.50	.30

SAN DIEGO PADRES

(1)	Ollie Brown	1.00	.50	.30
(2)	Dave Campbell	1.00	.50	.30
(3)	Nate Colbert	1.00	.50	.30
(4)	Pat Dobson	1.00	.50	.30
(5)	Al Ferrara	1.00	.50	.30
(6)	Dick Kelley	1.00	.50	.30
(7)	Clay Kirby	1.00	.50	.30
(8)	Bill McCool	1.00	.50	.30
(9)	Frank Reberger	1.00	.50	.30
(10)	Tommie Sisk	1.00	.50	.30
(11)	Ed Spiezio	1.00	.50	.30
(12)	Larry Stahl	1.00	.50	.30

SAN FRANCISCO GIANTS

(1)	Bobby Bonds	1.50	.70	.45
(2)	Jim Davenport	1.00	.50	.30
(3)	Dick Dietz	1.00	.50	.30
(4)	Jim Ray Hart	1.00	.50	.30
(5)	Ron Hunt	1.00	.50	.30
(6)	Hal Lanier	1.00	.50	.30
(7)	Frank Linzy	1.00	.50	.30
(8)	Juan Marichal	5.00	2.50	1.50
(9)	Willie Mays	15.00	7.50	4.50
(10)	Mike McCormick	1.00	.50	.30
(11)	Willie McCovey	6.00	3.00	1.75
(12)	Gaylord Perry	4.00	2.00	1.25

SEATTLE PILOTS

(1)	Steve Barber	1.00	.50	.30
(2)	Bobby Bolin	1.00	.50	.30
(3)	George Brunet	1.00	.50	.30
(4)	Wayne Comer	1.00	.50	.30
(5)	John Donaldson	1.00	.50	.30

(6)	Tommy Harper	1.00	.50	.30
(7)	Mike Hegan	1.00	.50	.30
(8)	Mike Hershberger	1.00	.50	.30
(9)	Steve Hovley	1.00	.50	.30
(10)	Bob Locker	1.00	.50	.30
(11)	Gerry McNertney	1.00	.50	.30
(12)	Rich Rollins	1.00	.50	.30

ST. LOUIS CARDINALS

(1)	Richie Allen	2.50	1.25	.70
(2)	Nelson Briles	1.00	.50	.30
(3)	Lou Brock	6.00	3.00	1.75
(4)	Jose Cardenal	1.00	.50	.30
(5)	Steve Carlton	6.00	3.00	1.75
(6)	Vic Davalillo	1.00	.50	.30
(7)	Bob Gibson	6.00	3.00	1.75
(8)	Julian Javier	1.00	.50	.30
(9)	Dal Maxvill	1.00	.50	.30
(10)	Cookie Rojas	1.00	.50	.30
(11)	Mike Shannon	1.00	.50	.30
(12)	Joe Torre	3.00	1.50	.90

WASHINGTON SENATORS

(1)	Bernie Allen	1.00	.50	.30
(2)	Dick Bosman	1.00	.50	.30
(3)	Ed Brinkman	1.00	.50	.30
(4)	Paul Casanova	1.00	.50	.30
(5)	Joe Coleman	1.00	.50	.30
(6)	Mike Epstein	1.00	.50	.30
(7)	Frank Howard	1.50	.70	.45
(8)	Ken McMullen	1.00	.50	.30
(9)	John Roseboro	1.00	.50	.30
(10)	Ed Stroud	1.00	.50	.30
(11)	Del Unser	1.00	.50	.30
(12)	Zoilo Versalles	1.00	.50	.30

1910 Makaroff Cigarettes World Series Postcard

The text on this postcard indicates it may have been given out at World Series games in Philadelphia and Chicago. Two versions are known, one with Connie Mack's portrait at left and the Athletics score listed first, and one with Frank Chance's portrait at left and the Cubs score listed first. On the black-and-white address side are photographic portraits of the A's and Cubs managers with appropriate team pennants. Below is scripted, "Saw the world's championship game to-day." Beneath that are lines to record the score. The front of the card is printed in black, white and red and has a picture of a smoking cigarette and a two-headed Russian eagle logo. At center is this "Dictum. / Think big, talk little, love much, laugh easily, / work hard, give freely, pay cash and be kind - / it is enough! Do these and you may smoke without / danger to your immortal soul."

	NM	EX	VG
Frank Chance, Connie Mack	350.00	175.00	100.00
Connie Mack, Frank Chance	350.00	175.00	100.00

1916 Mall Theatre

Best known for its use as a promotional medium for The Sporting News, this 200-card set can be found with ads on the back for several local and regional businesses. Among them is the Mall Theatre, location unknown. Type-card and superstar collectors can expect to pay a significant premium for individual cards with this advertising over generic 1916 M101-4 Blank Backs values. Cards measure 1-5/8" x 3" and are printed in black-and-white.

PREMIUM: 3-5X
(See 1916 M101-4 Blank Backs for checklist and base card values.)

1926-1927 Mallorquina Caramels

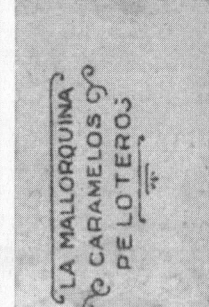

These tiny (about 3/4" x 1-1/8") cards were distributed with Mallorquina brand caramels in Cuba. The black-and-white images are printed on hard photographic paper stock. The bordered portrait photos on front have a box at bottom with player identification and card number. Backs are printed in dark blue with the wording "LA MALLORQUINA / CARAMELOS / PELOTEROS" and a few graphic flourishes. The set's first 17 cards feature professional players, including a number of Negro Leagues stars. The last 83 cards in the set are Cuban amateurs. While there was probably some sort of album issued to house the set, none has been reported to date. Because the card of Hall of Famer Willie Foster is his only known career-contemporary issue, and that of Martin Dihigo is his earliest known, "book" values have not been assigned.

		NM	EX	VG
	Common Player:	200.00	100.00	60.00
1	Adolfo Luque	750.00	375.00	225.00
2	Alfredo Cabrera	250.00	125.00	75.00
3	George Scales	350.00	175.00	105.00
4	Jose Maria Fernandez	250.00	125.00	75.00
5	Oliver Marcelle	3,000	1,500	900.00
6	Oscar Rodriguez	200.00	100.00	60.00
7	Martin Dihigo (Value Undetermined)			
8	Cheo Ramos	250.00	125.00	75.00
9	Pop Lloyd	4,500	2,250	1,350
10	Joe Olivares	200.00	100.00	60.00
11	Brujo Rosell	200.00	100.00	60.00
12	Willie Foster (Value Undetermined)			
13	Cho Cho Correa	250.00	125.00	75.00
14	Larry Brown	350.00	175.00	105.00
15	Oscar Levis	250.00	125.00	75.00
16	Raul Alvarez	250.00	125.00	75.00
17	Juan Eckelson	250.00	125.00	75.00
18	Quesada	200.00	100.00	60.00
19	J. Rosado	200.00	100.00	60.00
20	A. Unanuo	200.00	100.00	60.00
21	A. Echavarria	200.00	100.00	60.00
22	C. Beltran	200.00	100.00	60.00
23	J. Beltran	200.00	100.00	60.00
24	G. Orama	200.00	100.00	60.00
25	E. Carrillo	200.00	100.00	60.00
26	A. Casuso	200.00	100.00	60.00
27	A. Consuegra	200.00	100.00	60.00
28	R. Gallardo	200.00	100.00	60.00
29	M. Sotolongo	200.00	100.00	60.00
30	M. Llano	200.00	100.00	60.00
31	H. Rocamora	200.00	100.00	60.00
32	Calvo	200.00	100.00	60.00
33	R. Inclan	200.00	100.00	60.00
34	Mendizabal	200.00	100.00	60.00
35	H. Alonso	200.00	100.00	60.00
36	C. Leonard	200.00	100.00	60.00
37	Cap Cordova	200.00	100.00	60.00
38	Cordova	200.00	100.00	60.00
39	Sarasua	200.00	100.00	60.00
40	E. Cubillas	200.00	100.00	60.00
41	B. Wilryc	200.00	100.00	60.00
42	Morera	200.00	100.00	60.00
43	C. Fernandez	200.00	100.00	60.00
44	Milian	200.00	100.00	60.00
45	P. Espinosa	200.00	100.00	60.00
46	Macia	200.00	100.00	60.00
47	J. Lagueruela	200.00	100.00	60.00
48	Bernal	200.00	100.00	60.00
49	J.A. Ruiz	200.00	100.00	60.00
50	Unknown			
51	J. Gayoso	200.00	100.00	60.00
52	Castro	200.00	100.00	60.00
53	C. Hernandez	200.00	100.00	60.00
54	Reynolds	200.00	100.00	60.00
55	M. Rodriguez	200.00	100.00	60.00
56	P. Flores	200.00	100.00	60.00
57	A. Collazo	200.00	100.00	60.00
58	R. Gonzalez	200.00	100.00	60.00
59	A. Casas	200.00	100.00	60.00
60	Barcena	200.00	100.00	60.00

61	Quesada	200.00	100.00	60.00
62	Riquerin	200.00	100.00	60.00
63	Carbonere	200.00	100.00	60.00
64	Vega	200.00	100.00	60.00
65	Rodriguez	200.00	100.00	60.00
66	A. Castillo	200.00	100.00	60.00
67	Y. Balleste	200.00	100.00	60.00
68	Fernandez	200.00	100.00	60.00
69	Garros	200.00	100.00	60.00
70	Cabada	200.00	100.00	60.00
71	R.P. Fernandez	200.00	100.00	60.00
72	R. Cejas	200.00	100.00	60.00
73	Gros	200.00	100.00	60.00
74	Mendez	200.00	100.00	60.00
75	M. Sotolongo	200.00	100.00	60.00
76	E. Vela	200.00	100.00	60.00
77	A. Vela	200.00	100.00	60.00
78	F. Pinera	200.00	100.00	60.00
79	M. Valdes	200.00	100.00	60.00
80	L. Romero	200.00	100.00	60.00
81	A. Febles	200.00	100.00	60.00
82	Lugo	200.00	100.00	60.00
83	Polo Calvo	200.00	100.00	60.00
84	Silvio O. Farrill	200.00	100.00	60.00
85	Zalazar	200.00	100.00	60.00
86	Tapia	200.00	100.00	60.00
87	Hernandez	200.00	100.00	60.00
88	Manrrara	200.00	100.00	60.00
89	J. Deschapelle	200.00	100.00	60.00
90	Arguelles	200.00	100.00	60.00
91	E. Arechaede	200.00	100.00	60.00
92	E. Quintanal	200.00	100.00	60.00
93	M. Valdes	200.00	100.00	60.00
94	J. Martinez	200.00	100.00	60.00
95	R. Martinez	200.00	100.00	60.00
96	F. Gali	200.00	100.00	60.00
97	A. Martinez	200.00	100.00	60.00
98	G. Hernandez	200.00	100.00	60.00
99	A. Fernandez	200.00	100.00	60.00
100	Armando Figarola	200.00	100.00	60.00

1961 Manny's Baseball Land 8x10s

In 1961, Manny's Baseball Land issued 18 10-piece 8" x 10" printed black-and-white photo packs, arranged by team. Manny's was a next-door neighbor of Yankee Stadium and the nation's largest purveyor of baseball souvenirs. These photo sets were sold for $1.50 per team. The blank-back photos were printed on semi-gloss paper. Portraits or posed action photos were surrounded by a white border which contains the player's name in all caps at bottom. The unnumbered pictures are checklisted here alphabetically by and within team.

		NM	EX	VG
Complete Set (180):		2,500	1,250	750.00
Common Player:		10.00	5.00	3.00
BALTIMORE ORIOLES				
(1)	Jackie Brandt	10.00	5.00	3.00
(2)	Marv Breeding	10.00	5.00	3.00
(3)	Chuck Estrada	10.00	5.00	3.00
(4)	Jack Fisher	10.00	5.00	3.00
(5)	Jim Gentile	10.00	5.00	3.00
(6)	Ron Hansen	10.00	5.00	3.00
(7)	Milt Pappas	10.00	5.00	3.00
(8)	Brooks Robinson	30.00	15.00	9.00
(9)	Gus Triandos	10.00	5.00	3.00
(10)	Jerry Walker	10.00	5.00	3.00
BOSTON RED SOX				
(11)	Tom Brewer	10.00	5.00	3.00
(12)	Don Buddin	10.00	5.00	3.00
(13)	Gene Conley	10.00	5.00	3.00
(14)	Mike Fornieles	10.00	5.00	3.00
(15)	Gary Geiger	10.00	5.00	3.00
(16)	Pumpsie Green	10.00	5.00	3.00
(17)	Jackie Jensen	15.00	7.50	4.50
(18)	Frank Malzone	10.00	5.00	3.00
(19)	Pete Runnels	10.00	5.00	3.00
(20)	Vic Wertz	10.00	5.00	3.00
CHICAGO CUBS				
(21)	George Altman	10.00	5.00	3.00
(22)	Bob Anderson	10.00	5.00	3.00
(23)	Richie Ashburn	30.00	15.00	9.00
(24)	Ernie Banks	35.00	17.50	10.00
(25)	Don Cardwell	10.00	5.00	3.00
(26)	Moe Drabowsky	10.00	5.00	3.00
(27)	Don Elston	10.00	5.00	3.00
(28)	Jerry Kindall	10.00	5.00	3.00
(29)	Ron Santo	15.00	7.50	4.50
(30)	Bob Will	10.00	5.00	3.00
CHICAGO WHITE SOX				
(31)	Luis Aparicio	25.00	12.50	7.50
(32)	Frank Baumann	10.00	5.00	3.00
(33)	Sam Esposito	10.00	5.00	3.00
(34)	Nellie Fox	30.00	15.00	9.00
(35)	Jim Landis	10.00	5.00	3.00
(36)	Sherman Lollar	10.00	5.00	3.00
(37)	Minnie Minoso	20.00	10.00	6.00

(38)	Billy Pierce	10.00	5.00	3.00
(39)	Bob Shaw	10.00	5.00	3.00
(40)	Early Wynn	25.00	12.50	7.50
CINCINNATI REDLEGS				
(41)	Ed Bailey	10.00	5.00	3.00
(42)	Gus Bell	10.00	5.00	3.00
(43)	Gordon Coleman	10.00	5.00	3.00
(44)	Bill Henry	10.00	5.00	3.00
(45)	Jerry Lynch	10.00	5.00	3.00
(46)	Claude Osteen	10.00	5.00	3.00
(47)	Vada Pinson	12.50	6.25	3.75
(48)	Wally Post	10.00	5.00	3.00
(49)	Bob Purkey	10.00	5.00	3.00
(50)	Frank Robinson	35.00	17.50	10.00
CLEVELAND INDIANS				
(51)	Mike de la Hoz	10.00	5.00	3.00
(52)	Tito Francona	10.00	5.00	3.00
(53)	Woody Held	10.00	5.00	3.00
(54)	Barry Latman	10.00	5.00	3.00
(55)	Jim Perry	10.00	5.00	3.00
(56)	Bubba Phillips	10.00	5.00	3.00
(57)	Jim Piersall	12.50	6.25	3.75
(58)	Vic Power	10.00	5.00	3.00
(59)	John Romano	10.00	5.00	3.00
(60)	Johnny Temple	10.00	5.00	3.00
DETROIT TIGERS				
(61)	Hank Aguirre	10.00	5.00	3.00
(62)	Billy Bruton	10.00	5.00	3.00
(63)	Jim Bunning	25.00	12.50	7.50
(64)	Norm Cash	20.00	10.00	6.00
(65)	Rocky Colavito	25.00	12.50	7.50
(66)	Chico Fernandez	10.00	5.00	3.00
(67)	Paul Foytack	10.00	5.00	3.00
(68)	Al Kaline	35.00	17.50	10.00
(69)	Frank Lary	10.00	5.00	3.00
(70)	Don Mossi	10.00	5.00	3.00
KANSAS CITY ATHLETICS				
(71)	Hank Bauer	10.00	5.00	3.00
(72)	Andy Carey	10.00	5.00	3.00
(73)	Leo "Bud" Daley	10.00	5.00	3.00
(74)	Ray Herbert	10.00	5.00	3.00
(75)	John Kucks	10.00	5.00	3.00
(76)	Jerry Lumpe	10.00	5.00	3.00
(77)	Norm Siebern	10.00	5.00	3.00
(78)	Haywood Sullivan	10.00	5.00	3.00
(79)	Marv Throneberry	10.00	5.00	3.00
(80)	Dick Williams	10.00	5.00	3.00
LOS ANGELES ANGELS				
(81)	Ken Aspromonte	10.00	5.00	3.00
(82)	Steve Bilko	10.00	5.00	3.00
(83)	Bob Cerv	10.00	5.00	3.00
(84)	Ned Garver	10.00	5.00	3.00
(85)	Ken Hunt	10.00	5.00	3.00
(86)	Ted Kluszewski	25.00	12.50	7.50
(87)	Jim McAnany	10.00	5.00	3.00
(88)	Duke Maas	10.00	5.00	3.00
(89)	Albie Pearson	10.00	5.00	3.00
(90)	Eddie Yost	10.00	5.00	3.00
LOS ANGELES DODGERS				
(91)	Don Drysdale	30.00	15.00	9.00
(92)	Jim Gilliam	12.50	6.25	3.75
(93)	Frank Howard	12.50	6.25	3.75
(94)	Sandy Koufax	50.00	25.00	15.00
(95)	Norm Larker	10.00	5.00	3.00
(96)	Wally Moon	10.00	5.00	3.00
(97)	Charles Neal	10.00	5.00	3.00
(98)	Johnny Podres	12.50	6.25	3.75
(99)	Larry Sherry	10.00	5.00	3.00
(100)	Maury Wills	12.50	6.25	3.75
MILWAUKEE BRAVES				
(101)	Hank Aaron	50.00	25.00	15.00
(102)	Joe Adcock	10.00	5.00	3.00
(103)	Frank Bolling	10.00	5.00	3.00
(104)	Bob Buhl	10.00	5.00	3.00
(105)	Lew Burdette	10.00	5.00	3.00
(106)	Del Crandall	10.00	5.00	3.00
(107)	Ed Mathews	35.00	17.50	10.00
(108)	Roy McMillan	10.00	5.00	3.00
(109)	Warren Spahn	35.00	17.50	10.00
(110)	Al Spangler	10.00	5.00	3.00
MINNESOTA TWINS				
(111)	Bob Allison	10.00	5.00	3.00
(112)	Earl Battey	10.00	5.00	3.00
(113)	Reno Bertola (Bertoia)	10.00	5.00	3.00
(114)	Billy Consolo	10.00	5.00	3.00
(115)	Billy Gardner	10.00	5.00	3.00
(116)	Harmon Killebrew	35.00	17.50	10.00
(117)	Jim Lemon	10.00	5.00	3.00
(118)	Camilo Pascual	10.00	5.00	3.00
(119)	Pedro Ramos	10.00	5.00	3.00
(120)	Chuck Stobbs	10.00	5.00	3.00
NEW YORK YANKEES				
(121)	Larry "Yogi" Berra	35.00	17.50	10.00
(122)	John Blanchard	10.00	5.00	3.00
(123)	Ed "Whitey" Ford	35.00	17.50	10.00
(124)	Elston Howard	15.00	7.50	4.50
(125)	Tony Kubek	15.00	7.50	4.50
(126)	Mickey Mantle	65.00	32.50	20.00
(127)	Roger Maris	40.00	20.00	12.00
(128)	Bobby Richardson	15.00	7.50	4.50
(129)	Bill Skowron	15.00	7.50	4.50
(130)	Bob Turley	10.00	5.00	3.00
PHILADELPHIA PHILLIES				
(131)	John Callison	10.00	5.00	3.00
(132)	Dick Farrell	10.00	5.00	3.00
(133)	Pancho Herrera	10.00	5.00	3.00
(134)	Joe Koppe	10.00	5.00	3.00
(135)	Art Mahaffey	10.00	5.00	3.00
(136)	Gene Mauch	10.00	5.00	3.00
(137)	Jim Owens	10.00	5.00	3.00
(138)	Robin Roberts	30.00	15.00	9.00
(139)	Frank Sullivan	10.00	5.00	3.00
(140)	Tony Taylor	10.00	5.00	3.00
PITTSBURGH PIRATES				
(141)	Roberto Clemente	60.00	30.00	18.00
(142)	Roy Face	10.00	5.00	3.00
(143)	Bob Friend	10.00	5.00	3.00
(144)	Dick Groat	10.00	5.00	3.00

(145)	Harvey Haddix	10.00	5.00	3.00
(146)	Don Hoak	10.00	5.00	3.00
(147)	Vern Law	10.00	5.00	3.00
(148)	Bill Mazeroski	30.00	15.00	9.00
(149)	Wilmer Mizell	10.00	5.00	3.00
(150)	Bill Virdon	10.00	5.00	3.00
SAN FRANCISCO GIANTS				
(151)	Felipe Alou	12.50	6.25	3.75
(152)	Orlando Cepeda	30.00	15.00	9.00
(153)	Sam Jones	10.00	5.00	3.00
(154)	Harvey Kuenn	10.00	5.00	3.00
(155)	Willie Mays	50.00	25.00	15.00
(156)	Mike McCormick	10.00	5.00	3.00
(157)	Willie McCovey	30.00	15.00	9.00
(158)	Stu Miller	10.00	5.00	3.00
(159)	Billy O'Dell	10.00	5.00	3.00
(160)	Jack Sanford	10.00	5.00	3.00
ST. LOUIS CARDINALS				
(161)	Ernie Broglio	10.00	5.00	3.00
(162)	Ken Boyer	12.50	6.25	3.75
(163)	Joe Cunningham	10.00	5.00	3.00
(164)	Alex Grammas	10.00	5.00	3.00
(165)	Larry Jackson	10.00	5.00	3.00
(166)	Julian Javier	10.00	5.00	3.00
(167)	Lindy McDaniel	10.00	5.00	3.00
(168)	Stan Musial	45.00	22.50	13.50
(169)	Hal Smith	10.00	5.00	3.00
(170)	Daryl Spencer	10.00	5.00	3.00
WASHINGTON SENATORS				
(171)	Pete Daley	10.00	5.00	3.00
(172)	Dick Donovan	10.00	5.00	3.00
(173)	Bob Johnson	10.00	5.00	3.00
(174)	Marty Keough	10.00	5.00	3.00
(175)	Billy Klaus	10.00	5.00	3.00
(176)	Dale Long	10.00	5.00	3.00
(177)	Carl Mathias	10.00	5.00	3.00
(178)	Willie Tasby	10.00	5.00	3.00
(179)	Mickey Vernon	10.00	5.00	3.00
(180)	Gene Woodling	10.00	5.00	3.00

1959 Mickey Mantle's Holiday Inn Postcard

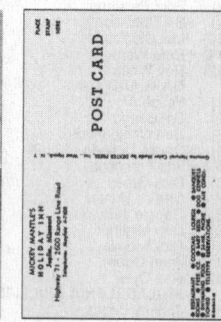

The attributed date is speculative. Much rarer than the more common pose of Mantle in civvies in his Joplin, Mo. motel's lounge, this approximately 3-1/2" x 5-1/2" card features two color poses of the Mick in Yankees uniform on its front. The postcard-style back is printed in blue and gives motel information and features.

	NM	EX	VG
Mickey Mantle	100.00	50.00	30.00

1962 Mickey Mantle's Holiday Inn Postcard

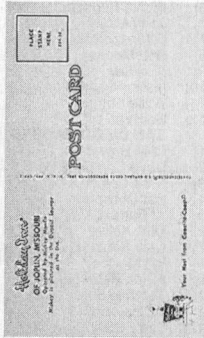

This color postcard pictures Mantle in civilian clothes. On the back of the standard-size (about 3-1/2" x 5-1/2") card it says the Mick is "pictured in the Dugout Lounge at the Inn." The "Inn" is the Joplin, Mo., Holiday Inn which Mantle owned. This was one of the more popular, and thus more common, of the souvenirs issued in conjunction with Mantle's motel.

	NM	EX	VG
Mickey Mantle	30.00	15.00	9.00

1962 Mickey Mantle's Holiday Inn Premium Photo

Probably issued in 1962, though not dated, this 8" x 10" photo pictures the M&M Boys in the lounge of Mantle's motel. Back is blank.

	NM	EX	VG
Mickey Mantle, Roger Maris	600.00	300.00	180.00

1963 Mickey Mantle Hospital Postcard

 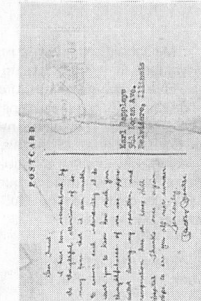

With a broken foot in 1963 following hard on a knee injury the previous season, Mantle spent considerable time in the hospital. To assist in answering a mountain of goodwill messages from fans, he had these postcards created. On front of the 3-1/2" x 5-1/2" card is a glossy black-and-white batting-pose photo. The back is printed in blue with a "Dear Friend" message thanking the fan for "the thoughtful attention" and ending optimistically, "Hope to see you all next season," above his facsimile autograph.

	NM	EX	VG
Mickey Mantle	450.00	225.00	135.00

1923 Maple Crispette (V117)

Issued by a Montreal candy company, these small (1-3/8" x 2-1/4") black-and-white cards were redeemable for baseball equipment, accounting for their scarcity today. Card #15, Stengel, was only discovered in 1992 and was obviously short-printed by the issuer to avoid giving away many bats, balls and gloves. Only a single specimen of the Stengel card is currently known; it is not included in the complete set prices. The existence of the card checklisted as 14a Wingo is now in doubt.

		NM	EX	VG
Complete Set, no Stengel (29):		40,000	20,000	12,000
Common Player:		450.00	220.00	135.00
1	Jesse Barnes	450.00	220.00	135.00
2	Harold Traynor	1,100	550.00	325.00
3	Ray Schalk	1,100	550.00	325.00
4	Eddie Collins	1,100	550.00	325.00
5	Lee Fohl	450.00	220.00	135.00
6	Howard Summa	450.00	220.00	135.00
7	Waite Hoyt	1,100	550.00	325.00
8	Babe Ruth	10,000	5,000	3,000
9	Cozy Dolan	450.00	220.00	135.00
10	Johnny Bassler	450.00	220.00	135.00
11	George Dauss	450.00	220.00	135.00
12	Joe Sewell	1,100	550.00	325.00
13	Syl Johnson	450.00	220.00	135.00
14a	Wingo (Existence questioned)	450.00	220.00	135.00
14b	Ivy Wingo	450.00	220.00	135.00
15	Casey Stengel	18,000	9,000	4,500
16	Arnold Statz	450.00	220.00	135.00
17	Emil Meusel	450.00	220.00	135.00
18	Bill Jacobson	450.00	220.00	110.00
19	Jim Bottomley	5,000	2,500	1,500
20	Sam Bohne	650.00	395.00	195.00
21	(Bucky) Harris	1,100	550.00	325.00

22	(Ty) Cobb	7,000	3,500	2,100
23	Roger Peckinpaugh	450.00	220.00	135.00
24	Muddy Ruel	450.00	220.00	135.00
25	(Bill) McKechnie	1,100	550.00	325.00
26	Riggs Stephenson	450.00	220.00	135.00
27	(Herby) Pennock	1,100	550.00	325.00
28	Ed (Edd) Roush	1,100	550.00	325.00
29	Bill Wambsganss	450.00	220.00	135.00
30	Walter Johnson	2,400	960.00	600.00

1962 Roger Maris Action Baseball Game

 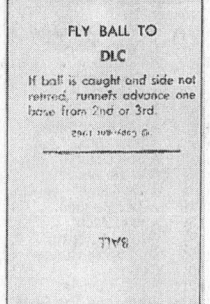

Baseball's new home run king was featured in this board game by Pressman Toy Co. Besides the colorful metal game board and other pieces, the set contains 88 playing cards. Each 2-1/4" x 3-1/2" card has a black-and-white photo on front of Maris in a batting pose, along with a white facsimile autograph. Backs have two possible game action plays printed, along with a copyright line.

	NM	EX	VG
Complete Game:	425.00	210.00	125.00
Single Card:	45.00	22.00	13.50
Roger Maris			

1913-14 Martens Bakery

 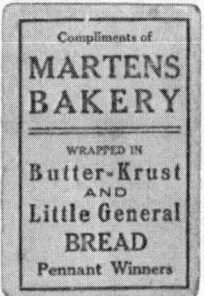

(See 1911-14 General Baking Co. (D304).)

1955 Mascot Dog Food

The date of issue shown is approximate. It is likely other players' cards exist, since the back mentions eight stars printed on the label, presumably of the dog food can. In black-and-white, the 3-1/2" x 5-1/2" card has on front a glossy action pose with a facsimile autograph personalized, "To My Mascot" and the player name and position printed in black in the bottom border. The back has an ad for a fan club offering an autographed 8" x 10" membership card and and set of eight postcards for a quarter and a label. label.

		NM	EX	VG
(1)	Robin Roberts (Value undetermined)			

1971 Mattel Instant Replay Records

These 2-3/8" diameter plastic records were produced in conjunction with a hand-held, battery-operated record player. Paper inserts featured illustrations of players in baseball, football and basketball, as well as various racing vehicles and airplanes. The audio recounts career highlights of the depicted player. Additional records were sold in sets of four.

	NM	EX	VG
Complete Set (12):	250.00	125.00	75.00
Common Player:	10.00	5.00	3.00
(1) Hank Aaron	30.00	15.00	9.00
(2) Ernie Banks	15.00	7.50	4.50
(3) Roberto Clemente	50.00	25.00	15.00
(4) Al Kaline	15.00	7.50	4.50
(5) Sandy Koufax	40.00	20.00	12.00
(6) Roger Maris	15.00	7.50	4.50
(7) Willie Mays (Plays one side only; came with record player purchase.)	12.00	6.00	3.50
(8) Willie McCovey	12.00	6.00	3.50
(9) Tony Oliva	10.00	5.00	3.00
(10) Frank Robinson	13.50	6.75	4.00
(11) Tom Seaver	15.00	7.50	4.50
(12) Willie Stargell	12.00	6.00	3.50

1895 Mayo's Cut Plug (N300)

These 1-5/8" x 2-7/8" cards were issued by the Mayo Tobacco Works of Richmond, Va. There are 48 cards in the set, with 40 different players pictured. Twenty-eight of the players are pictured in uniform and 12 are shown in street clothes. Eight players appear both ways. Eight of the uniformed players also appear in two variations, creating the 48-card total. Card fronts are black-and-white or sepia portraits on black cardboard, with a Mayo's Cut Plug ad at the bottom of each card. Cards have a blank black back and are unnumbered.

		NM	EX	VG
Complete Set (48):		200,000	100,000	60,000
Common Player:		2,000	1,000	600.00
(1)	Charlie Abbey	2,000	1,000	600.00
(2)	Cap Anson	18,000	9,000	5,500
(3)	Jimmy Bannon	2,000	1,000	600.00
(4a)	Dan Brouthers (Baltimore on shirt.)	11,500	5,750	3,450
(4b)	Dan Brouthers (Louisville on shirt.)	13,000	6,500	4,000
(5)	Ed Cartwright	2,000	1,000	600.00
(6)	John Clarkson	7,500	3,700	2,100
(7)	Tommy Corcoran	2,000	1,000	600.00
(8)	Lave Cross	2,000	1,000	600.00
(9)	Bill Dahlen	3,000	1,200	600.00
(10)	Tom Daly	2,000	1,000	600.00
(11)	E.J. Delehanty (Delahanty)	14,500	7,250	4,350
(12)	Hugh Duffy	7,500	3,700	2,100
(13a)	Buck Ewing (Cleveland on shirt.)	13,000	6,500	4,000
(13b)	Buck Ewing (Cincinnati on shirt.)	10,000	4,000	2,000
(14)	Dave Foutz	2,000	1,000	600.00
(15)	Charlie Ganzel	2,000	1,000	600.00
(16a)	Jack Glasscock (Pittsburg on shirt.)	3,000	1,200	600.00
(16b)	Jack Glasscock (Louisville on shirt.)	2,000	1,000	600.00
(17)	Mike Griffin	2,000	1,000	600.00
(18a)	George Haddock (No team on shirt.)	3,300	1,300	650.00
(18b)	George Haddock (Philadelphia on shirt.)	2,000	1,000	600.00
(19)	Bill Hallman	2,000	1,000	600.00
(20)	Billy Hamilton	7,500	3,700	2,100
(21)	Bill Joyce	2,000	1,000	600.00
(22)	Brickyard Kennedy	2,000	1,000	600.00
(23a)	Tom Kinslow (No team on shirt.)	3,300	1,300	650.00
(23b)	Tom Kinslow (Pittsburg on shirt.)	2,000	1,000	600.00
(24)	Arlie Latham	2,000	1,000	600.00
(25)	Herman Long	2,000	1,000	600.00
(26)	Tom Lovett	2,000	1,000	600.00
(27)	Bobby Lowe	2,000	1,000	600.00
(28)	Tommy McCarthy	7,500	3,700	2,100

		NM	EX	VG
(29)	Yale Murphy	2,000	1,000	600.00
(30)	Billy Nash	2,000	1,000	600.00
(31)	Kid Nichols	13,000	6,500	4,000
(32a)	Fred Pfeffer (2nd Base)	2,000	1,000	600.00
(32b)	Fred Pfeffer (Retired)	2,000	1,000	600.00
(33)	Wilbert Robinson	7,500	3,700	2,100
(34a)	Amos Russie (Incorrect spelling.)	16,500	6,600	3,300
(34b)	Amos Rusie (Correct)	11,500	5,750	3,450
(35)	Jimmy Ryan	2,000	1,000	600.00
(36)	Bill Shindle	2,000	1,000	600.00
(37)	Germany Smith	2,000	1,000	600.00
(38)	Otis Stocksdale (Stockdale)	2,000	1,000	600.00
(39)	Tommy Tucker	2,000	1,000	600.00
(40a)	Monte Ward (2nd Base)	10,000	5,000	3,000
(40b)	Monte Ward (Retired)	8,000	4	2,400

1896 Mayo's Die-Cut Game Cards (N301)

Mayo Tobacco Works of Richmond, Va., issued an innovative, if not very popular, series of die-cut baseball player figures in 1896. These tiny (1-1/2" long by just 3/16" wide) cardboard figures were inserted in packages of Mayo's Cut Plug Tobacco and were designed to be used as part of a baseball board game. A "grandstand, base and teetotum" were available free by mail to complete the game pieces. Twenty-eight different die-cut figures were available, representing 26 unspecified New York and Boston players along with two umpires. The players are shown in various action poses - either running, batting, pitching or fielding. The backs carry an ad for Mayo's Tobacco. The players shown do not relate to any actual members of the New York or Boston clubs, diminishing the popularity of this issue, which has an American Card Catalog designation of N301.

		NM	EX	VG
Complete Set (28):		4,000	1,600	800.00
Common Player:		150.00	60.00	30.00
(1a)	Pitcher (Boston)	150.00	60.00	30.00
(1b)	Pitcher (New York)	150.00	60.00	30.00
(2a)	1st Baseman (Boston)	150.00	60.00	30.00
(2b)	1st Baseman (New York)	150.00	60.00	30.00
(3a)	2nd Baseman (Boston)	150.00	60.00	30.00
(3b)	2nd Baseman (New York)	150.00	60.00	30.00
(4a)	3rd Baseman (Boston)	150.00	60.00	30.00
(4b)	3rd Baseman (New York)	150.00	60.00	30.00
(5a)	Right Fielder (Boston)	150.00	60.00	30.00
(5b)	Right Fielder (New York)	150.00	60.00	30.00
(6a)	Center Fielder (Boston)	150.00	60.00	30.00
(6b)	Center Fielder (New York)	150.00	60.00	30.00
(7a)	Left Fielder (Boston)	150.00	60.00	30.00
(7b)	Left Fielder (New York)	150.00	60.00	30.00
(8a)	Short Stop (Boston)	150.00	60.00	30.00
(8b)	Short Stop (New York)	150.00	60.00	30.00
(9a)	Catcher (Boston)	150.00	60.00	30.00
(9b)	Catcher (New York)	150.00	60.00	30.00
(10a)	Batman (Boston)	150.00	60.00	30.00
(10b)	Batman (New York)	150.00	60.00	30.00
(11a)	Runner (Boston, standing upright.)	150.00	60.00	30.00
(11b)	Runner (New York, standing upright.)	150.00	60.00	30.00
(12a)	Runner (Boston, bent slightly forward)	150.00	60.00	30.00
(12b)	Runner (New York, bent slightly forward)	150.00	60.00	30.00
(13a)	Runner (Boston, bent well forward.)	150.00	60.00	30.00
(13b)	Runner (New York, bent well forward.)	150.00	60.00	30.00
(14)	Umpire (Facing front.)	150.00	60.00	30.00
(15)	Field Umpire (Rear view.)	150.00	60.00	30.00

1900 Mayo's Baseball Comics (T203)

"A Star Catcher"

As their name implies, the T203 Baseball Comics feature cartoon-like drawings that illustrate various baseball phrases and terminology. Issued with Winner Cut Plug and Mayo Cut Plug tobacco products, the complete set consists of 25 different comics, each measuring approximately 2-1/16" x 3-1/8". Because they do not picture individual players, these cards have never attracted much of a following among serious baseball card collectors. They do, however, hold some interest as a novelty item of the period.

		NM	EX	VG
Complete Set (25):		3,000	1,500	650.00
Common Card:		150.00	75.00	30.00
(1)	"A Crack Outfielder"	150.00	75.00	30.00
(2)	"A Fancy Twirler"	150.00	75.00	30.00
(3)	"A Fine Slide"	150.00	75.00	30.00
(4)	"A Fowl Bawl"	150.00	75.00	30.00
(5)	"A Great Game"	150.00	75.00	30.00
(6)	"A Home Run"	150.00	75.00	30.00
(7)	"An All Star Battery"	150.00	75.00	30.00
(8)	"A Short Stop"	150.00	75.00	30.00
(9)	"A Star Catcher"	150.00	75.00	30.00
(10)	"A White Wash"	150.00	75.00	30.00
(11)	"A Tie Game"	150.00	75.00	30.00
(12)	"A Two Bagger"	150.00	75.00	30.00
(13)	"A Wild Pitch"	150.00	75.00	30.00
(14)	"Caught Napping"	150.00	75.00	30.00
(15)	"On To The Curves"	150.00	75.00	30.00
(16)	"Out"	150.00	75.00	30.00
(17)	"Put Out On 1st"	150.00	75.00	30.00
(18)	"Right Over The Plate"	150.00	75.00	30.00
(19)	"Rooting For The Home Team"	150.00	75.00	30.00
(20)	"Stealing A Base"	150.00	75.00	30.00
(21)	"Stealing Home"	150.00	75.00	30.00
(22)	"Strike One"	150.00	75.00	30.00
(23)	"The Bleacher"	150.00	75.00	30.00
(24)	"The Naps"	150.00	75.00	30.00
(25)	"The Red Sox"	150.00	75.00	30.00

1948 Thom McAn Bob Feller Premium

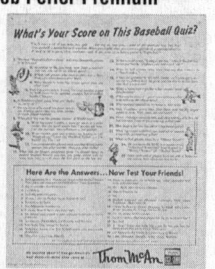

This black-and-white 8" x 10" premium picture has on front a posed action photo and facsimile autograph. On back is a 25-question baseball quiz and advertising for the shoe store chain, along with a copyright for Melville Shoe Co.

	NM	EX	VG
Bob Feller	150.00	75.00	45.00

1950s-80s J.D. McCarthy Player Postcards

From the 1950s into the 1980s, Detroit area photographer J.D. McCarthy produced black-and-white postcards to order for hundreds of ballplayers to use in answering fan mail requests for pictures and autographs. Sizes and formats differed through the years, but most are about standard postcard size (3-1/2" x 5-1/2") with borderless poses on front. Some cards have a white strip with printed name on front, others have a facsimile autograph, while others have no identification at all. Some card fronts carry his stylized JcMD monogram. Backs, likewise, differ in the style and manner of their markings. Printing was generally done on thin, semi-gloss cardboard. Many players are found in more than one pose, or in cropping variations of a pose. Many players continued to re-order postcards long after their careers were over. Following McCarthy's death, archives of his negatives were sold into the hobby, making it theoretically possible for many cards to be reproduced in perpetuity. That mitigates against many of these cards attaining any great degree of collectible value, though they are popular with team and single-player collectors. Postally-used cards which carry a dated postmark are of the greatest value. Many cards, as the one pictured here, are autographed.

	NM	EX	VG
Common Player:	3.00	1.50	.90

1970 McDonald's Brewers

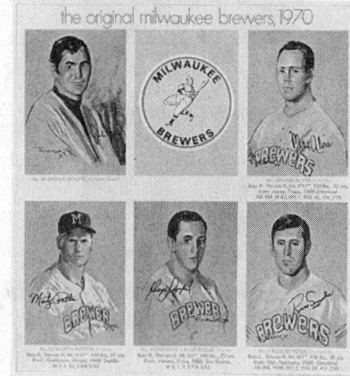

the original milwaukee brewers, 1970

McDonald's welcomed the American League Brewers to Milwaukee in 1970 by issuing a set of six baseball card panels. Five of the panels picture five players and a team logo, while the sixth panel contains six players, resulting in 31 different players. The panels measure 9" x 9-1/2" and feature full-color paintings of the players. Each sheet displays the heading, "the original milwaukee brewers, 1970." The cards are numbered by uniform number and the backs are blank. Although distributed by McDonald's, their name does not appear on the cards.

		NM	EX	VG
Complete Sheet Set (6):		15.00	7.50	4.50
Complete Singles Set (32):		15.00	7.50	4.50
Common Player:		.50	.25	.15
1	Ted Kubiak	.50	.25	.15
2	Ted Savage	.50	.25	.15
4	Dave Bristol	.50	.25	.15
5	Phil Roof	.50	.25	.15
6	Mike Hershberger	.50	.25	.15
7	Russ Snyder	.50	.25	.15
8	Mike Hegan	.50	.25	.15
9	Rich Rollins	.50	.25	.15
10	Max Alvis	.50	.25	.15
11	John Kennedy	.50	.25	.15
12	Dan Walton	.50	.25	.15
15	Jerry McNertney	.50	.25	.15
18	Wes Stock	.50	.25	.15
20	Wayne Comer	.50	.25	.15
21	Tommy Harper	.50	.25	.15
23	Bob Locker	.50	.25	.15
24	Lew Krausse	.50	.25	.15
25	John Gelnar	.50	.25	.15
26	Roy McMillan	.50	.25	.15
27	Cal Ermer	.50	.25	.15
28	Sandy Valdespino	.50	.25	.15
30	Jackie Moore	.50	.25	.15
32	Gene Brabender	.50	.25	.15
33	Marty Pattin	.50	.25	.15
34	Greg Goossen	.50	.25	.15
35	John Morris	.50	.25	.15
36	Steve Hovley	.50	.25	.15
38	Bob Meyer	.50	.25	.15
39	Bob Bolin	.50	.25	.15
43	John O'Donoghue	.50	.25	.15
49	George Lauzerique	.50	.25	.15
---	Logo Card	.50	.25	.15

1974 McDonald's Gene Michael

GENE "THE STICK" MICHAEL

Though there is no advertising or logo on this one-card "set," this black-and-white card of "The Stick" in his last year as a Yankee was distributed by a Staten Island McDonald's restaurant during an autograph appearance. The card measures 2-5/8" x 4-3/8" and is blank-backed.

	NM	EX	VG
Gene "The Stick" Michael	25.00	12.50	7.50

1974 McDonald's Padres Discs

Envisioned as part of a line of sports promotional sets, this concept died following the test with San Diego area McDonalds. At the July 30, 1974, game, Padres fans were given a hinged plastic baseball containing five Padres player photo discs plus a disc with the team's schedule and a Ronald McDonald disc which listed the dates on which the remaining eight player cards would be distributed at area McDonalds. Only 60,000 of the "starter set" discs were made, while 180,000 of each of the other player discs were printed. The 2-3/8" diameter discs feature a color photo on front and player stats on back. The promotion was the work of Photo Sports, Inc., of Los Angeles.

		NM	EX	VG
Complete Set (15):		25.00	12.50	7.50
Common Player:		1.00	.50	.30
(1)	Matty Alou	1.00	.50	.30
(2)	Glenn Beckert	3.00	1.50	.90
(3)	Nate Colbert	1.00	.50	.30
(4)	Bill Grief	1.00	.50	.30
(5)	John Grubb	1.00	.50	.30
(6)	Enzo Hernandez	3.00	1.50	.90
(7)	Randy Jones	3.00	1.50	.90
(8)	Fred Kendall	3.00	1.50	.90
(9)	Willie McCovey	6.00	3.00	1.75
(10)	John McNamara	3.00	1.50	.90
(11)	Dave Roberts	1.00	.50	.30
(12)	Bobby Tolan	1.00	.50	.30
(13)	Dave Winfield	15.00	7.50	4.50
(14)	Padres home game schedule	1.50	.70	.45
(15)	Ronald McDonald	1.50	.70	.45

1978 McDonald's Boston Red Sox

Reportedly because of a production problem, distribtution of these cards was limited to a few Boston-area McDonald's restaurants for a very limited time. The blank-back, approximately 3-1/2" x 6" color cards have borderless portraits on front with the player's facsimile autograph. The cards were reportedly distributed in Treasure Chest meals for kids under 12.

		NM	EX	VG
Complete Set (6):		450.00	225.00	135.00
Common Player:		35.00	17.50	10.00
(1)	Rick Burleson	35.00	17.50	10.00
(2)	Carlton Fisk	125.00	60.00	35.00
(3)	Fred Lynn	75.00	37.50	22.50
(4)	Jim Rice	100.00	50.00	30.00
(5)	Luis Tiant	50.00	25.00	15.00
(6)	Carl Yastrzemski	150.00	75.00	45.00

1950-1952 Bill McGowan's School for Umpires

Over a period of at least three years in the early 1950s, Hall of Fame American League umpire Bill McGowan issued a series of black-and-white postcards to promote his umpires' school in Florida. The 3-1/2" x 5-1/2" cards have bordered or borderless photos on front, some of which bear the imprint of Grogan Photo, Danville, Ill.

		NM	EX	VG
(1)	Bill McGowan's Umpire School Cocoa - 1950 - Florida (Students on bleachers.)	60.00	30.00	20.00
(2)	Bill McGowman's Umpire School - 1950 - Florida (Students standing on field.)	60.00	30.00	20.00
(3)	Bill McGowan (1951)	500.00	250.00	150.00
(4)	Donatelli Instructs (Augie Donatelli) (1952)	65.00	32.50	20.00
(5)	Guglielmo Instructs (Augie Guglielmo) (1952)	65.00	32.50	20.00

1970s-80s Doug McWilliams Postcards

 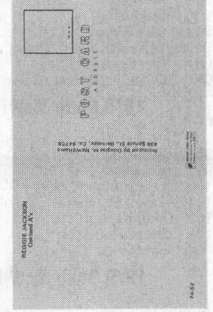

For more than two decades, California photographer Doug McWilliams (who also worked for Topps for 23 years) produced a series of black-and-white and color postcards for individual use by ballplayers, mostly members of the Oakland A's. Almost uniformly, the 3-1/2" x 5-1/2" cards have no graphics on front (a few have facsimile autographs), just a player pose or portrait. Backs have standard postcard markings, player identification, and McWilliams' credit lines. Backs carry a two-digit year of issue prefix to the card number. Postcards are printed in black-and-white unless noted.

	NM	EX	VG
Common Player:	3.00	1.50	.90

(See individual years for checklists and values.)

1970 Doug McWilliams Postcards

		NM	EX	VG
1	Jim Roland	1.00	.50	.30
2a	Mudcat Grant, Mudcat Grant	1.50	.75	.45
2b	Mudcat Grant	1.50	.75	.45
3	Reggie Jackson (Color - only 50 produced.)	150.00	75.00	45.00
4	Darrell Osteen	1.00	.50	.30
5a	Tom Hafey (First printing.)	1.00	.50	.30
5b	Tom Hafey (Second printing.)	1.00	.50	.30
6	Chick Hafey	1.50	.75	.45

1970 Doug McWilliams Collectors' Issue Postcards

This set of black-and-white player postcards was produced by San Fransisco art photographer Doug McWilliams as a custom order for an Eastern collector. Fewer than 50 sets were reportedly produced. The 3-1/2" x 5-1/2" cards have glossy photographic fronts and standard postcard backs with player identification. The unnumbered cards are checklisted here in alphabetical order.

		NM	EX	VG
Complete Set (22):		400.00	200.00	125.00
Common Player:		20.00	10.00	6.00
(1)	Jerry Adair	20.00	10.00	6.00
(2)	Brant Alyea	20.00	10.00	6.00
(3)	Brant Alyea	20.00	10.00	6.00
(4)	Dwain Anderson	20.00	10.00	6.00
(5)	Curt Blefary	20.00	10.00	6.00
(6)	Bill Daniels	20.00	10.00	6.00
(7)	Mike Epstein	22.50	11.00	6.75
(8)	Adrian Garrett	20.00	10.00	6.00
(9)	Frank Fernandez	20.00	10.00	6.00
(10)	Mike Hegan	20.00	10.00	6.00
(11)	George Hendrick	20.00	10.00	6.00
(12)	Reggie Jackson	125.00	62.00	37.00
(13)	Reggie Jackson	125.00	62.00	37.00
(14)	Ron Klimkowski	20.00	10.00	6.00
(15)	Darold Knowles	20.00	10.00	6.00
(16)	Jerry Lumpe	20.00	10.00	6.00
(17)	Angel Mangual	20.00	10.00	6.00
(18)	Denny McLain	30.00	15.00	9.00
(19)	Denny McLain	30.00	15.00	9.00
(20)	Irv Noren	20.00	10.00	6.00
(21)	Ramon Webster	20.00	10.00	6.00
(22)	Dick Williams	20.00	10.00	6.00

1970 Doug McWilliams Oakland A's Postcards

These 3-1/2" x 5-1/2" black-and-white player postcards were produced by San Francisco photographer Doug McWilliams for sale by Sports Cards for Collectors, a forerunner of TCMA. Each card can be found either with or without borders on front, the latter having a slightly enlarged image. Player identification is on back. The unnumbered cards are checklisted here alphabetically. Fewer than 50 sets were reported produced.

		NM	EX	VG
19	Larry Brown	3.00	1.50	.90
20a	Dick Green (First printing - glossy.)	3.00	1.50	.90
20b	Dick Green (Second printing - glossy, more contrast.)	3.00	1.50	.90
20c	Dick Green (Third printing - matte.)	3.00	1.50	.90
21	Vida Blue (Color)	6.00	3.00	1.75
22a	Joe Horlen (First printing - bright.)	3.00	1.50	.90
22b	Joe Horlen (Second printing - dark.)	3.00	1.50	.90
23	Gene Tenace (Color)	6.00	3.00	1.75
24a	Ted Kubiak (Glossy)	3.00	1.50	.90
24b	Ted Kubiak (Matte)	3.00	1.50	.90
A	Emeryville Ball Park	3.00	1.50	.90
B	Oakland Coliseum	3.00	1.50	.90

1973 Doug McWilliams Postcards

		NM	EX	VG
25	Rene Lachemann	3.00	1.50	.90
26	Tom Greive	3.00	1.50	.90
27	John Odom (Color)	6.00	3.00	1.75
28a	Rollie Fingers (First printing.)	9.00	4.50	2.75
28b	Rollie Fingers (Second printing - thinner stock.)	9.00	4.50	2.75
29	Jim Hunter (Color)	9.00	4.50	2.75
30	Ray Fosse (Color)	6.00	3.00	1.75
31	Charley Pride (Color)	15.00	7.50	4.50
32	Charley Pride (Color)	15.00	7.50	4.50
33	Bill North	3.00	1.50	.90
34	Damasco Blanco	3.00	1.50	.90
35	Paul Lindblad	3.00	1.50	.90
36	Rollie Fingers (Color)	9.00	4.50	2.75
37	Horacio Pina	3.00	1.50	.90
38	Bert Campaneris (Color)	7.50	3.75	2.25
39	Jim Holt (Color)	6.00	3.00	1.75
40	Sal Bando (Color)	6.00	3.00	1.75
41	Joe Rudi (Color)	6.00	3.00	1.75
42	Dick Williams (Color)	6.00	3.00	1.75
43	Jesus Alou	3.00	1.50	.90
44	Joe Niekro	3.75	2.00	1.25
45	Johnny Oates	3.00	1.50	.90

1974 Doug McWilliams Postcards

		NM	EX	VG
46a	Ray Fosse (Color - first printing - w/signature.)	6.00	3.00	1.75
46b	Ray Fosse (Color - second printing - no signature.)	6.00	3.00	1.75
46c	Ray Fosse (Color - third printing - no sig., very green grass.)	6.00	3.00	1.75
47	Jesus Alou	3.00	1.50	.90
48	John Summers	3.00	1.50	.90
49	Dal Maxvill	3.00	1.50	.90
50	Joe Rudi (Color)	6.00	3.00	1.75
51	Sal Bando (Color)	6.00	3.00	1.75
52	Reggie Jackson (Color)	20.00	10.00	6.00
53	Ted Kubiak (Color)	6.00	3.00	1.75
54	Dave Hamilton	3.00	1.50	.90
55	Gene Tenace (Color)	6.00	3.00	1.75
56a	Bob Locker (First printing - back foot near edge.)	3.00	1.50	.90
56b	Bob Locker (Second printing - foot 3/4" from edge.)	3.00	1.50	.90
57	Manny Trillo	3.00	1.50	.90

1975 Doug McWilliams Postcards

		NM	EX	VG
58a	Dan Godby (First printing.)	3.00	1.50	.90
58b	Dan Godby (Second printing - blank back.)	3.00	1.50	.90
58c	Dan Godby (Third printing - flat contrast.)	3.00	1.50	.90
59	Bob Locker	3.00	1.50	.90
60	Rollie Fingers (Color)	9.00	4.50	2.75
61	Glenn Abbott	3.00	1.50	.90
62	Jim Todd	3.00	1.50	.90
63	Phil Garner	3.00	1.50	.90
64	Paul Lindblad	3.00	1.50	.90
65	Bill North (Color)	6.00	3.00	1.75
66	Dick Sisler	3.00	1.50	.90
67	Angel Mangual	3.00	1.50	.90
68	Claudell Washington	3.00	1.50	.90

1976 Doug McWilliams Postcards

		NM	EX	VG
69	Oakland Coliseum (Color)	6.00	3.00	1.75
70	Sal Bando (Color)	6.00	3.00	1.75
71	Mike Torrez (Color)	6.00	3.00	1.75
72	Joe Lonnett	3.00	1.50	.90
73	Chuck Tanner	3.00	1.50	.90

		NM	EX	VG
74	Tommy Sandt	3.00	1.50	.90
75	Dick Bosman (Color)	6.00	3.00	1.75
76	Bert Campaneris (Color)	6.00	3.00	1.75
77	Ken Brett	6.00	3.00	1.75
78	Jim Todd (Color)	6.00	3.00	1.75
79	Jeff Newman	3.00	1.50	.90
80	John McCall	3.00	1.50	.90

1977 Doug McWilliams Postcards

		NM	EX	VG
81	Don Baylor (Color)	9.00	4.50	2.75
82	Lee Stange	3.00	1.50	.90
83	Rob Picciolo	3.00	1.50	.90
84	Jack Mc Keon (Color)	6.00	3.00	1.75
85	Rollie Fingers (Color)	9.00	4.50	2.75
86	Manny Sanguillen	3.00	1.50	.90
87	Tony Armas	3.00	1.50	.90
88	Jim Tyrone	3.00	1.50	.90
89	Wayne Gross	3.00	1.50	.90
90	Rick Langford	3.00	1.50	.90
91	Rich Gossage	3.00	1.50	.90
92	Phil Garner (Color)	6.00	3.00	1.75
93	Del Alston	3.00	1.50	.90
94	Bert Blyleven (Color)	7.50	3.75	2.25
95	Willie McCovey (Color)	9.00	4.50	2.75
96	Ken Brett (Color)	6.00	3.00	1.75
97	Doyle Alexander (Color)	6.00	3.00	1.75

1978 Doug McWilliams Postcards

		NM	EX	VG
98	Rene Lacheman	3.00	1.50	.90
99	Del Alston	3.00	1.50	.90
100	Lee Stange (Color)	6.00	3.00	1.75
101	Taylor Duncan	3.00	1.50	.90
102	Matt Keough	3.00	1.50	.90
103	Bruce Robinson	3.00	1.50	.90
104	Sal Bando (Color)	6.00	3.00	1.75

1979 Doug McWilliams Postcards

		NM	EX	VG
105	Alan Wirth	3.00	1.50	.90
106	Mike Edwards	3.00	1.50	.90
107	Craig Minetto	3.00	1.50	.90
108	Mike Morgan	3.00	1.50	.90
109	Brian Kingman	3.00	1.50	.90

1980 Doug McWilliams Postcards

		NM	EX	VG
110	Jim Essian	3.00	1.50	.90
111a	Willie McCovey (Color - first printing - no signature.)	9.00	4.50	2.75
111b	Willie McCovey (Color - second printing - w/signature, stamp at top.)	9.00	4.50	2.75
111c	Willie McCovey (Color - third printing - w/sig., stamp at bottom.)	9.00	4.50	2.75
112a	Willie McCovey (Color - first printing - no signature.)	9.00	4.50	2.75
112b	Willie McCovey (Color - second printing - w/signature.)	9.00	4.50	2.75

1964 Meadowgold Dairy

Four of the mid-60s' biggest stars appear as a panel on this milk carton issue. The four-player portion measures about 3-3/4" x 4-1/4" and is printed in shades of blue or green on the white background. Individual cards measure about 1-1/8" x 2-1/16" and are, of course, blank-backed. In 1998, a complete milk carton was sold at auction for $2,475.

		NM	EX	VG
Complete Set, Panel:		4,250	2,100	1,250
Complete Set, Singles (4):		4,000	2,000	1,200
Common Player:		600.00	300.00	180.00
(1)	Sandy Koufax	1,350	675.00	405.00
(2)	Mickey Mantle	2,000	1,000	600.00
(3)	Willie Mays	1,000	500.00	300.00
(4)	Bill Mazeroski	600.00	300.00	180.00

1911 Mecca Cigarettes

(See 1911 T201 Double Folders.)

1937 Joe "Ducky" Medwick

Little is known about these cards featuring the perennial All-Star of the Gashouse Gang. Both styles are in a round-cornered playing card format, about 2-1/4" x 3-1/2". Fronts have black-and-white artwork of Medwick swinging a bat against a large baseball. The background is black-and-orange with a facsimile autograph at bottom. Most cards are found with some sort of card-game baseball scenario on back, while another type has a black-and-white photo of Medwick signing

autographs amid a gaggle of children. His name and the date appear at bottom. It is not known whether the two types of cards were distributed together.

	NM	EX	VG
Joe "Ducky" Medwick (Game card.)	45.00	22.50	13.50
Joe "Ducky" Medwick (Photo back.)	90.00	45.00	25.00

1910 Mello-Mint (E105)

Issued circa 1910 by Smith's Mello-Mint, "The Texas Gum," this set of 50 cards shares the same checklist and artwork as the better known E101 set. Mello-Mint cards are slightly smaller, measuring approximately 1-3/8" x 2-5/8", and are printed on thin paper, making them difficult to find in top condition. Also contributing to condition problems is the fact that many cards were folded vertically to fit the packaging. The backs contain advertising, printed in green, for Mello-Mint Gum. The set carries an ACC designation of E105. Two finds of multiple examples of about eight cards in the 1980s can mislead collectors into thinking the rest of the cards in the set are more common than is actually the case. The cards most heavily overrepresented in those finds are indicated with an asterisk.

		NM	EX	VG
Complete Set (50):		195,000	75,000	35,000
Common Player:		1,000	500.00	300.00
(1)	Jack Barry	3,200	1,300	650.00
(2)	Harry Bemis	3,200	1,300	650.00
(3)	Chief Bender (White hat.)	6,400	2,600	1,300
(4)	Chief Bender (Striped hat.)	6,400	2,600	1,300
(5)	Bill Bergen	3,200	1,300	650.00
(6)	Bob Bescher (*)	1,000	500.00	300.00
(7)	Al Bridwell	3,200	1,300	650.00
(8)	Doc Casey (*)	1,000	500.00	300.00
(9)	Frank Chance	7,200	2,900	1,450
(10)	Hal Chase	4,600	1,850	925.00
(11)	Ty Cobb	25,000	12,500	7,500
(12)	Eddie Collins	7,200	2,900	1,450
(13)	Sam Crawford	7,200	2,900	1,450
(14)	Harry Davis	3,200	1,300	650.00
(15)	Art Devlin	3,200	1,300	650.00
(16)	Wild Bill Donovan	3,200	1,300	650.00
(17)	Red Dooin	3,200	1,300	650.00
(18)	Mickey Doolan	3,200	1,300	650.00
(19)	Patsy Dougherty	3,200	1,300	650.00
(20)	Larry Doyle (With bat.)	3,200	1,300	650.00
(21)	Larry Doyle/Throwing	3,200	1,300	650.00
(22)	Johnny Evers	7,200	2,900	1,450
(23)	George Gibson	3,200	1,300	650.00
(24)	Topsy Hartsel (*)	1,000	500.00	300.00
(25)	Fred Jacklitsch	3,200	1,300	650.00
(26)	Hugh Jennings	7,200	2,900	1,450
(27)	Red Kleinow	3,200	1,300	650.00
(28)	Otto Knabe	3,200	1,300	650.00
(29)	Jack Knight (*)	1,000	500.00	300.00
(30)	Nap Lajoie (*)	5,000	2,500	1,500
(31)	Hans Lobert	3,200	1,300	650.00
(32)	Sherry Magee	3,200	1,300	650.00
(33)	Christy Matthewson (Mathewson)	21,000	10,500	6,250
(34)	John McGraw	7,200	2,900	1,450
(35)	Larry McLean	3,200	1,300	650.00
(36)	Dots Miller/Btg	3,200	1,300	650.00
(37)	Dots Miller/Fldg	3,200	1,300	650.00
(38)	Danny Murphy (*)	1,000	500.00	300.00
(39)	Bill O'Hara	3,200	1,300	650.00
(40)	Germany Schaefer	3,200	1,300	650.00
(41)	Admiral Schlei	3,200	1,300	650.00
(42)	Boss Schmidt	3,200	1,300	650.00
(43)	Johnny Seigle	3,200	1,300	650.00

		NM	EX	VG
(44)	Dave Shean (*)	1,000	500.00	300.00
(45)	Boss Smith (Schmidt)	3,200	1,300	650.00
(46)	Joe Tinker	7,200	2,900	1,450
(47)	Honus Wagner/Btg	22,500	11,250	6,750
(48)	Honus Wagner/Throwing	20,000	10,000	6,000
(49)	Cy Young (*)	7,500	3,700	2,200
(50)	Heinie Zimmerman	3,200	1,300	650.00

1916 Felix Mendelsohn

JIM THORPE
R. F.—New York Giants
176

This Chicago printing and publishing firm was the originator of the card set often found bearing the advertising of The Sporting News on back, or less frequently with ads from other concerns. Mendelsohn is not mentioned on the cards, which are blank-backed. Fronts of the 1-5/8" x 3" black-and-white cards have a player photo, name, position abbreviation, team and card number. The first version of the set, designated M101-5 in the ACC, was prepared in advance of the 1916 season and offered in ads in The Sporting News for $1, or a framed uncut sheet for $2.50. An updated version, designated M101-4 in the American Card Catalog, was released later in the summer.

(See 1916 M101-4 and M101-5 Blank Backs and 1917 M-UNC.)

1917 Felix Mendelsohn (M101-UNC)

RAY SCHALK
CATCHER—CHICAGO WHITE SOX

These 2-1/4" x 4" blank-back, black-and-white cards may have been prototypes for a "Hall of Fame" card set advertised early in 1917 by Felix Mendelsohn in The Sporting News. A set of 200 was offered for $1, but may not have actually been produced. Each example of this set is believed to be unique.

(1) Walter Johnson (Value Undetermined)
(2) Christy Mathewson (Value Undetermined)
(3) Ray Schalk (Brought $1,464 in 4/05 auction, in Excellent condition.)

1917-1920 Felix Mendelsohn

Gandil
1st B. Chicago White Sox.

This set of glossy black-and-white player photos was produced by Chicago publisher Felix Mendelsohn, whose initials appear beneath the copyright logo. The photos measure about 4-3/8" x 6-3/8" and feature action poses of the player whose name, position and team appear at the bottom of the borderless pictures. Four of the players in the checklist appear with two different teams, indicating the photos were issued over a period of several seasons. The set was offered in ads in The Sporting News at $5 for 100 pictures. This checklist may not be complete. Gaps have been left in the assigned numbering to accommodate future additions.

		NM	EX	VG
Complete Set (119):		56,000	28,000	17,000
Common Player:		175.00	90.00	50.00
(1)	Grover C. Alexander (Philadelphia)	850.00	425.00	275.00
(2)	Grover C. Alexander (Chicago)	850.00	425.00	275.00
(3)	Jim Bagby	175.00	90.00	50.00
(4)	Doug Baird	175.00	90.00	50.00
(5)	Franklin Baker	425.00	220.00	125.00
(6)	Dave Bancroft	425.00	220.00	125.00
(7)	Jack Barry	175.00	90.00	50.00
(8)	Johnny Bates	175.00	90.00	50.00
(9)	Carson Bigbee	175.00	90.00	50.00
(10)	"Ping" Bodie	175.00	90.00	50.00
(11)	George Burns	175.00	90.00	50.00
(12)	Joe Bush	175.00	90.00	50.00
(13)	Owen Bush	175.00	90.00	50.00
(14)	Ray Caldwell	175.00	90.00	50.00
(15)	Max Carey	425.00	220.00	125.00
(16)	Ray Chapman	220.00	120.00	75.00
(17)	Hal Chase	350.00	175.00	100.00
(18)	Eddie Cicotte	420.00	220.00	125.00
(19)	Ty Cobb	5,000	2,500	1,500
(20)	Eddie Collins	420.00	220.00	125.00
(21)	Harry Coveleskie (Coveleskie)	175.00	90.00	50.00
(22)	"Gavvy" Cravath	175.00	90.00	50.00
(23)	Sam Crawford	420.00	220.00	125.00
(24)	Walton Cruise	175.00	90.00	50.00
(26)	George Cutshaw	175.00	90.00	50.00
(27)	Jake Daubert	175.00	90.00	50.00
(28)	George Dauss	175.00	90.00	50.00
(29)	Dave Davenport	175.00	90.00	50.00
(30)	Bill Doak	175.00	90.00	50.00
(31)	Larry Doyle	175.00	90.00	50.00
(32)	George Dumont	175.00	90.00	50.00
(33)	Howard Ehmke	175.00	90.00	50.00
(34)	Urban Faber	420.00	220.00	125.00
(35)	Happy Felsch	850.00	425.00	250.00
(36)	Art Fletcher	175.00	90.00	50.00
(37)	Del Gainer (Gainor)	175.00	90.00	50.00
(38)	Chick Gandil	420.00	220.00	125.00
(39)	Larry Gardner	175.00	90.00	50.00
(40)	Mike Gonzales (Gonzalez)	175.00	90.00	50.00
(41)	Jack Graney	175.00	90.00	50.00
(42)	Heinie Groh	175.00	90.00	50.00
(43)	Earl Hamilton	175.00	90.00	50.00
(44)	Harry Heilmann	420.00	220.00	125.00
(45)	Buck Herzog	175.00	90.00	50.00
(46)	Hugh High (New York, photo actually Bob Shawkey.)	175.00	90.00	50.00
(47)	Hugh High (Detroit, correct photo.)	175.00	90.00	50.00
(48)	Bill Hinchman	175.00	90.00	50.00
(49)	Dick Hoblitzell	175.00	90.00	50.00
(51)	Walter Holke (New York)	175.00	90.00	50.00
(52)	Walter Holke (Boston)	175.00	90.00	50.00
(53)	Harry Hooper	420.00	220.00	125.00
(54)	Rogers Hornsby	600.00	300.00	180.00
(55)	Joe Jackson	7,000	3,500	2,200
(56)	Bill Jacobson	175.00	90.00	50.00
(57)	Walter Johnson	1,300	650.00	400.00
(58)	Sam Jones	175.00	90.00	50.00
(59)	Joe Judge	175.00	90.00	50.00
(60)	Benny Kauff	175.00	90.00	50.00
(61)	Bill Killefer	175.00	90.00	50.00
(62)	Ed Konetchy (Boston)	175.00	90.00	50.00
(63)	Ed Konetchy (Brooklyn)	175.00	90.00	50.00
(64)	Nemo Leibold	175.00	90.00	50.00
(65)	Duffy Lewis	175.00	90.00	50.00
(66)	Fred Luderas (Luderus)	175.00	90.00	50.00
(67)	Fred Luderus	175.00	90.00	50.00
(68)	Al Mamaux	175.00	90.00	50.00
(69)	Les Mann	175.00	90.00	50.00
(70)	"Rabbit" Maranville	420.00	220.00	125.00
(71)	Armando Marsans	175.00	90.00	50.00
(72)	John McGraw	420.00	220.00	125.00
(73)	Stuffy McInnis	175.00	90.00	50.00
(74)	Lee Meadows	175.00	90.00	50.00
(76)	Fred Merkle	175.00	90.00	50.00
(77)	Clyde Milan	175.00	90.00	50.00
(78)	Otto Miller	175.00	90.00	50.00
(79)	Guy Morton	175.00	90.00	50.00
(80)	Hy Myers	175.00	90.00	50.00
(81)	Greasy Neale	200.00	100.00	60.00
(82)	Dode Paskert	175.00	90.00	50.00
(83)	Roger Peckinpaugh	175.00	90.00	50.00
(84)	Jeff Pfeffer	175.00	90.00	50.00
(85)	Walter Pipp	175.00	90.00	50.00
(86)	Bill Rariden	175.00	90.00	50.00
(87)	Johnny Rawlings	175.00	90.00	50.00
(88)	Sam Rice	420.00	220.00	125.00
(89)	Dave Robertson	175.00	90.00	50.00
(90)	Bob Roth	175.00	90.00	50.00
(91)	Ed Roush	420.00	220.00	125.00
(92)	Dick Rudolph	175.00	90.00	50.00
(93)	Babe Ruth (Red Sox)	6,500	3,250	2,000
(94)	Babe Ruth (New York)	7,000	3,500	2,200
(95)	Vic Saier	175.00	90.00	50.00
(96)	Ray Schalk	420.00	220.00	125.00
(97)	Hank Severeid	175.00	90.00	50.00
(98)	Ernie Shore	175.00	90.00	50.00
(99)	Burt Shotton	175.00	90.00	50.00
(101)	George Sisler	420.00	220.00	125.00
(102)	Jack Smith	175.00	90.00	50.00
(103)	Frank Snyder	175.00	90.00	50.00
(104)	Tris Speaker	600.00	300.00	180.00
(105)	Oscar Stanage	175.00	90.00	50.00

		NM	EX	VG
(106)	Casey Stengel	420.00	220.00	125.00
(107)	Amos Strunk	175.00	90.00	50.00
(108)	Jeff Tesreau	175.00	90.00	50.00
(109)	Fred Toney	175.00	90.00	50.00
(110)	Terry Turner	175.00	90.00	50.00
(111)	Jim Vaughn	175.00	90.00	50.00
(112)	Bobby Veach	175.00	90.00	50.00
(113)	Oscar Vitt	175.00	90.00	50.00
(114)	"Honus" Wagner	4,200	2,100	1,300
(115)	Tilly Walker	175.00	90.00	50.00
(116)	Bill Wambsganss	175.00	90.00	50.00
(117)	"Buck" Weaver	850.00	425.00	250.00
(118)	Zack Wheat	420.00	220.00	125.00
(119)	George Whitted	175.00	90.00	50.00
(120)	Cy Williams	175.00	90.00	50.00
(121)	Ivy Wingo	175.00	90.00	50.00
(122)	Pep ("Pep" Young)	175.00	90.00	50.00
(123)	Heinie Zimmerman	175.00	90.00	50.00

1975 Clarence Mengler Baseball's Best

Hank Aaron

This collectors' issue art set holds the distinction of being one of the first whose distribition was halted by the Major League Baseball Players Association for lack of a license to depict current players. Produced as an autograph medium by Illinois collector Clarence Mengler, the 5" x 3" blank-back cards have portraits drawn by Keith Peterson. Of the original production of 200 sets, fewer than half were sold before the union intervened with threatened legal action. Because of a spelling error, the Ralph Garr card was withdrawn early. Hal McRae's card, also misspelled, was not withdrawn. Originally sold in five series, the unnumbered cards are checklisted alphabetically within series.

		NM	EX	VG
Complete Set (125):		150.00	75.00	45.00
Common Player:		1.00	.50	.30
SERIES A				
(1)	Sal Bando	1.00	.50	.30
(2)	Johnny Bench	4.00	2.00	1.25
(3)	Jack Billingham	1.00	.50	.30
(4)	Paul Blair	1.00	.50	.30
(5)	Bert Blyleven	1.50	.70	.45
(6)	Lou Brock	2.50	1.25	.70
(7)	Jeff Burroughs	1.00	.50	.30
(8)	Nate Colbert	1.00	.50	.30
(9)	Carlton Fisk	2.50	1.25	.70
(10)	Bob Gibson	2.50	1.25	.70
(11)	Ferguson Jenkins	2.00	1.00	.60
(12)	Bob Johnson	1.00	.50	.30
(13)	Dave McNally	1.00	.50	.30
(14)	Bobby Murcer	1.50	.70	.45
(15)	Tony Muser	1.00	.50	.30
(16)	Phil Niekro	2.00	1.00	.60
(17)	Brooks Robinson	3.00	1.50	.90
(18)	Frank Robinson	3.00	1.50	.90
(19)	Nolan Ryan	12.00	6.00	3.50
(20)	Mike Schmidt	6.00	3.00	1.75
(21)	Willie Stargell	2.50	1.25	.70
(22)	Andre Thornton	1.00	.50	.30
(23)	Bobby Tolan	1.00	.50	.30
(24)	Jim Wynn	1.00	.50	.30
(25)	Richie Zisk	1.00	.50	.30
SERIES B				
(26)	Hank Aaron	9.00	4.50	2.75
(27)	Larry Bowa	1.00	.50	.30
(28)	Steve Carlton	2.50	1.25	.70
(29)	Cesar Cedeno	1.00	.50	.30
(30)	Jim Colborn	1.00	.50	.30
(31)	Tim Foli	1.00	.50	.30
(32)	Steve Garvey	1.50	.70	.45
(33)	Bud Harrelson	1.00	.50	.30
(34)	Willie Horton	1.00	.50	.30
(35)	Jim Hunter	2.00	1.00	.60
(36)	Reggie Jackson	6.00	3.00	1.75
(37)	Billy Martin	1.50	.70	.45
(38)	Bake McBride	1.00	.50	.30
(39)	Andy Messersmith	1.00	.50	.30
(40)	Rick Monday	1.00	.50	.30
(41)	Joe Morgan	2.50	1.25	.70
(42)	Tony Oliva	1.50	.70	.45
(43)	Amos Otis	1.00	.50	.30
(44)	Gaylord Perry	2.00	1.00	.60
(45)	Tom Seaver	5.00	2.50	1.50
(46)	Ken Singleton	1.00	.50	.30
(47)	Chris Speier	1.00	.50	.30
(48)	Gene Tenace	1.00	.50	.30
(49)	Del Unser	1.00	.50	.30
(50)	Carl Yastrzemski	5.00	2.50	1.50
SERIES C				
(51)	Steve Busby	1.00	.50	.30
(52)	Jose Cardenal	1.00	.50	.30
(53)	Rod Carew	2.50	1.25	.70
(54)	Ron Cey	1.00	.50	.30
(55)	Willie Davis	1.00	.50	.30
(56)	Barry Foote	1.00	.50	.30
(57)	Ken Holtzman	1.00	.50	.30
(58)	Davey Lopes	1.00	.50	.30
(59)	Greg Luzinski	1.00	.50	.30

		NM	EX	VG
(60)	Sparky Lyle	1.00	.50	.30
(61)	Dave May	1.00	.50	.30
(62)	Lee May	1.00	.50	.30
(63)	Doc Medich	1.00	.50	.30
(64)	Bill Melton	1.00	.50	.30
(65)	Randy Moffitt	1.00	.50	.30
(66)	Don Money	1.00	.50	.30
(67)	Al Oliver	1.50	.70	.45
(68)	George Scott	1.00	.50	.30
(69)	Ted Simmons	1.00	.50	.30
(70)	Charlie Spikes	1.00	.50	.30
(71)	Rusty Staub	1.25	.60	.40
(72)	Jim Sundberg	1.00	.50	.30
(73)	Bob Watson	1.00	.50	.30
(74)	Dick Williams	1.00	.50	.30
(75)	Dave Winfield	2.50	1.25	.70
	SERIES D			
(76)	Vida Blue	1.00	.50	.30
(77)	Bobby Bonds	1.00	.50	.30
(78)	Jerry Coleman	1.00	.50	.30
(79)	Bob Coluccio	1.00	.50	.30
(80)	Joe Decker	1.00	.50	.30
(81)	Darrell Evans	1.00	.50	.30
(82)	Ralph Gaar (Garr)/SP	4.00	2.00	1.25
(83)	Richie Hebner	1.00	.50	.30
(84)	Ken Henderson	1.00	.50	.30
(85)	Bill Madlock	1.00	.50	.30
(86)	Jon Matlack	1.00	.50	.30
(87)	Carlos May	1.00	.50	.30
(88)	John Mayberry	1.00	.50	.30
(89)	Willie McCovey	2.50	1.25	.70
(90)	Lynn McGlothen	1.00	.50	.30
(91)	Tug McGraw	1.00	.50	.30
(92)	Roger Metzger	1.00	.50	.30
(93)	Jim Palmer	2.00	1.00	.60
(94)	Rico Petrocelli	1.00	.50	.30
(95)	Ellie Rodriguez	1.00	.50	.30
(96)	Steve Rogers	1.00	.50	.30
(97)	Pete Rose	9.00	4.50	2.75
(98)	Bill Singer	1.00	.50	.30
(99)	Don Sutton	2.00	1.00	.60
(100)	Billy Williams	2.50	1.25	.70
	SERIES E			
(101)	Mark Belanger	1.00	.50	.30
(102)	Buddy Bell	1.00	.50	.30
(103)	Jim Bibby	1.00	.50	.30
(104)	Bob Boone	1.00	.50	.30
(105)	Ken Brett	1.00	.50	.30
(106)	Ron Bryant	1.00	.50	.30
(107)	Bill Buckner	1.00	.50	.30
(108)	Buzz Capra	1.00	.50	.30
(109)	Dave Concepcion	1.00	.50	.30
(110)	Rollie Fingers	2.00	1.00	.60
(111)	Bill Freehan	1.00	.50	.30
(112)	Bobby Grich	1.00	.50	.30
(113)	Fred Kendall	1.00	.50	.30
(114)	Don Kessinger	1.00	.50	.30
(115)	Hal McCrae (McRae)	1.00	.50	.30
(116)	Thurman Munson	2.50	1.25	.70
(117)	Fred Patek	1.00	.50	.30
(118)	Doug Rader	1.00	.50	.30
(119)	A. (Aurelio) Rodriguez	1.00	.50	.30
(120)	Manny Sanguillen	1.00	.50	.30
(121)	Reggie Smith	1.00	.50	.30
(122)	Danny Thompson	1.00	.50	.30
(123)	Luis Tiant	1.00	.50	.30
(124)	Joe Torre	1.50	.70	.45
(125)	Wilbur Wood	1.00	.50	.30

1953-54 Marshall Merrell Milwaukee Braves Portfolio

One of several portfolios of Milwaukee Braves artwork produced during the team's first few years, this issue of 8" x 10" black-and-white lithographs was sold at County Stadium for 25 cents apiece. The player checklist here is believed to be complete, but it is possible other poses may yet be reported. The cards are blank-backed and unnumbered; the checklist here has been arranged alphabetically.

		NM	EX	VG
	Complete Set (25):	900.00	450.00	275.00
	Common Player:	25.00	12.50	7.50
(1)	Henry Aaron	200.00	100.00	60.00
(2)	Joe Adcock	25.00	12.50	7.50
(3)	Johnny Antonelli	25.00	12.50	7.50
(4)	Billy Bruton	25.00	12.50	7.50
(5)	Bob Buhl	25.00	12.50	7.50
(6)	Lou Burdette (Follow-through.)	25.00	12.50	7.50
(7)	Lew Burdette (Wind-up.)	25.00	12.50	7.50
(8)	Gene Conley	25.00	12.50	7.50
(9)	Del Crandall	25.00	12.50	7.50
(10)	Jack Dittmer	25.00	12.50	7.50
(11)	Sid Gordon/Btg	25.00	12.50	7.50
(12)	Sid Gordon/Standing	25.00	12.50	7.50
(13)	Charlie Grimm (Tomahawk on jersey.)	25.00	12.50	7.50
(14)	Charlie Grimm (No tomahawk.)	25.00	12.50	7.50
(15)	Don Liddle	25.00	12.50	7.50
(16)	Johnny Logan	25.00	12.50	7.50

		NM	EX	VG
(17)	Ed Mathews/Btg	75.00	37.50	22.50
(18)	Ed Mathews/Standing	75.00	37.50	22.50
(19)	Danny O'Connell	25.00	12.50	7.50
(20)	Andy Pafko	25.00	12.50	7.50
(21)	Jim Pendleton	25.00	12.50	7.50
(22)	Warren Spahn	75.00	37.50	22.50
(23)	Max Surkont	25.00	12.50	7.50
(24)	Bobby Thomson	45.00	22.50	13.50
(25)	Jim Wilson	25.00	12.50	7.50

1979 Metallic Creations Signature Miniatures

This collectors' issue was created by combining an approximately 3-1/2" tall pewter statue with a 3-5/8" x 5" baseball card. The statues were released in pewter at about $10 apiece and silver-plate at $20. The black-bordered cards feature color portraits in front of a pair of sepia action pictures. The artwork was by J. Payette. Fronts also feature a facsimile autograph. Backs have basic player personal data and career stats. It was reported that 5,000 of each card were printed, though most were never issued due to failure of the venture. The remaining cards and statues were sold into the hobby as remainders. It is unclear whether a Munson card exists, although the Munson status and the Rose and Ryan cards have been confirmed.

		NM	EX	VG
	Complete Set, Cards (22):	240.00	120.00	70.00
	Common Card:	7.50	3.75	2.25
	Complete Set, Pewter Statues (22):	200.00	100.00	60.00
	Common Statue:	7.50	3.75	2.25
	Silver-Plate Statues: 2X			
(1)	Hank Aaron (Card)	12.50	6.25	3.75
(1)	Hank Aaron (Statue)	12.50	6.25	3.75
(2)	Rod Carew (Card)	7.50	3.75	2.25
(2)	Rod Carew (Statue)	7.50	3.75	2.25
(3)	Cesar Cedeno (Card)	7.50	3.75	2.25
(4)	Ty Cobb (Card)	15.00	7.50	4.50
(4)	Ty Cobb (Statue)	12.50	6.25	3.75
(5)	Steve Garvey (Card)	15.00	7.50	4.50
(5)	Steve Garvey (Statue)	15.00	7.50	4.50
(6)	Lou Gehrig (Card)	15.00	7.50	4.50
(6)	Lou Gehrig (Statue)	15.00	7.50	4.50
(7)	Ron Guidry (Card)	7.50	3.75	2.25
(7)	Ron Guidry (Statue)	7.50	3.75	2.25
(8)	Rogers Hornsby (Card)	7.50	3.75	2.25
(8)	Rogers Hornsby (Statue)	7.50	3.75	2.25
(9)	Walter Johnson (Card)	10.00	5.00	3.00
(9)	Walter Johnson (Statue)	10.00	5.00	3.00
(10)	Ralph Kiner (Card)	7.50	3.75	2.25
(10)	Ralph Kiner (Statue)	7.50	3.75	2.25
(11)	Sandy Koufax (Card)	20.00	10.00	6.00
(11)	Sandy Koufax (Statue)	20.00	10.00	6.00
(12)	Davey Lopes (Card)	7.50	3.75	2.25
(12)	Davey Lopes (Statue)	7.50	3.75	2.25
(13)	Christy Mathewson (Card)	10.00	5.00	3.00
(13)	Christy Mathewson (Statue)	10.00	5.00	3.00
(14)	Willie Mays (Card)	15.00	7.50	4.50
(14)	Willie Mays (Statue)	15.00	7.50	4.50
(15)	Willie McCovey (Card)	10.00	5.00	3.00
(15)	Willie McCovey (Statue)	10.00	5.00	3.00
(16)	Thurman Munson (Statue)	10.00	5.00	3.00
(17)	Mel Ott (Card)	7.50	3.75	2.25
(17)	Mel Ott (Statue)	7.50	3.75	2.25
(18)	Pete Rose (Card)	30.00	15.00	9.00
(19)	Babe Ruth (Card)	12.50	6.25	3.75
(19)	Babe Ruth (Statue)	12.50	6.25	3.75
(20)	Nolan Ryan (Card)	30.00	15.00	9.00
(21)	Tris Speaker (Card)	7.50	3.75	2.25
(21)	Tris Speaker (Statue)	7.50	3.75	2.25
(22)	Honus Wagner (Card)	10.00	5.00	3.00
(22)	Honus Wagner (Statue)	10.00	5.00	3.00

1938-39 Metropolitan Clothing Cincinnati Reds Postcards

(See 1937-39 Orcajo Cincinnati Reds postcards for checklist, values.)

1968 Metropolitan Museum of Art Burdick Collection

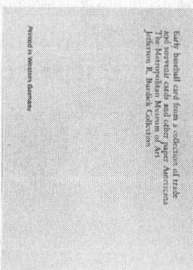

The date of issue is approximate for this set promoting New York's Metropolitan Museum of Art as the repository for the Jefferson Burdick collection, once the world's premier accumulation of trading cards. Burdick, author of the once-standard "American Card Catalog" donated his collection to the Met. The 2-3/4" x 3-5/8" black-and-white glossy card fronts reproduce 1928 R315 cards of major leaguers and earlier Zeenuts cards of minor leaguers. Backs have a few words about the museum and a "Printed in Western Germany" line. The unnumbered cards are checklisted here in alphabetical order.

		NM	EX	VG
	Complete Set (8):	125.00	65.00	35.00
	Common Player:	10.00	5.00	3.00
(1)	Max Bishop	10.00	5.00	3.00
(2)	Lou Gehrig	40.00	20.00	12.00
(3)	Carl Hubbell	15.00	7.50	4.50
(4)	Art Kores	10.00	5.00	3.00
(5)	Bill Leard	10.00	5.00	3.00
(6)	Babe Ruth	50.00	25.00	15.00
(7)	Dazzy Vance	10.00	5.00	3.00
(8)	Elmer Zacher	10.00	5.00	3.00

1931 Metropolitan Studio St. Louis Cardinals

Members of the St. Louis Cardinals are featured in this 30-card set. The cards were printed on heavy paper and feature sepia-toned photos. The player's name appears along the bottom white border below the photo. The cards measure 6-1/4" x 9-1/2" and are not numbered. Most cards feature the logo of Metropolitan Studio in a bottom corner, while others have "Sid Whiting St. Louis MO," and a few have no sponsor's credit.

		NM	EX	VG
	Complete Set (30):	1,800	810.00	450.00
	Common Player:	45.00	20.00	12.00
(1)	Earl "Sparky" Adams	45.00	20.00	12.00
(2)	Ray Blades	45.00	20.00	12.00
(3)	James Bottomley	95.00	45.00	25.00
(4)	Sam Breadon	45.00	20.00	12.00
(5)	James "Rip" Collins	45.00	20.00	12.00
(6)	Dizzy Dean	225.00	100.00	55.00
(7)	Paul Derringer	45.00	20.00	12.00
(8)	Jake Flowers	45.00	20.00	12.00
(9)	Frank Frisch	95.00	45.00	25.00
(10)	Charles Gelbert	45.00	20.00	12.00
(11)	Miguel Gonzales (Gonzalez)	80.00	35.00	20.00
(12)	Burleigh Grimes	95.00	45.00	25.00
(13)	Charles "Chick" Hafey	95.00	45.00	25.00
(14)	William Hallahan	45.00	20.00	12.00
(15)	Jesse Haines	95.00	45.00	25.00
(16)	Andrew High	45.00	20.00	12.00
(17)	Sylvester Johnson	45.00	20.00	12.00
(18)	Tony Kaufmann	45.00	20.00	12.00
(19)	James Lindsey	45.00	20.00	12.00
(20)	Gus Mancuso	45.00	20.00	12.00
(21)	John Leonard "Pepper" Martin	80.00	35.00	20.00
(22)	Ernest Orsatti	45.00	20.00	12.00
(23)	Charles Flint Rhem	45.00	20.00	12.00
(24)	Branch Rickey	125.00	55.00	35.00
(25)	Walter Roettger	45.00	20.00	12.00
(26)	Allyn Stout	45.00	20.00	12.00
(27)	"Gabby" Street	45.00	20.00	12.00
(28)	Clyde Wares	45.00	20.00	12.00
(29)	George Watkins	45.00	20.00	12.00
(30)	James Wilson	45.00	20.00	12.00

1979 Michigan Sports Collectors

Former Detroit Tigers, along with several baseball writers and announcers, including some who were appearing as auto-

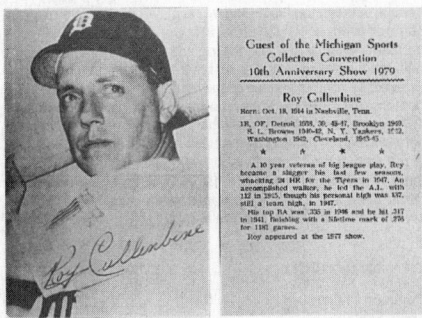

graph guests were featured in this collectors set issued in conjunction with the 1979 Troy, Mich. show. Cards are 3-1/2" x 5-1/16" black-and-white. Backs have personal data and a career summary of the pictured player, along with mention of the show. The unnumbered cards are checklisted here alphabetically.

		NM	EX	VG
Complete Set (20):		20.00	10.00	6.00
Common Player:		3.00	1.50	.90
(1)	Gates Brown	3.00	1.50	.90
(2)	Norm Cash	5.00	2.50	1.50
(3)	Al Cicotte	3.00	1.50	.90
(4)	Roy Cullenbine	3.00	1.50	.90
(5)	Gene Desautels	3.00	1.50	.90
(6)	Hoot Evers	3.00	1.50	.90
(7)	Joe Falls	3.00	1.50	.90
(8)	Joe Ginsberg	3.00	1.50	.90
(9)	Ernie Harwell	3.00	1.50	.90
(10)	Ray Herbert	3.00	1.50	.90
(11)	John Hiller	3.00	1.50	.90
(12)	Billy Hoeft	3.00	1.50	.90
(13)	Ralph Houk	4.00	2.00	1.25
(14)	Cliff Kachline	3.00	1.50	.90
(15)	George Kell	5.00	2.50	1.50
(16)	Ron LeFlore	4.00	2.00	1.25
(17)	Barney McCosky	3.00	1.50	.90
(18)	Jim Northrup	3.00	1.50	.90
(19)	Dick Radatz	3.00	1.50	.90
(20)	Tom Timmermann	3.00	1.50	.90

1940 Michigan Sportservice Detroit Tigers

Apparently a team issue sent to persons who wrote the team or players for photos, these blank-back cards measure 4-1/8" x 6-1/4" and are printed in black-and-white. A facsimile autograph is printed over the central portrait, which is surrounded by a border of baseballs. A few career notes are printed under the photo. At bottom-left is a union printing label. At bottom-right is printed, "Copyrighted 1939, Michigan Sportservice, Inc. Unauthorized Reproduction Prohibited." The unnumbered cards are checklisted here alphabetically.

		NM	EX	VG
Complete Set (21):		5,400	2,700	1,650
Common Player:		300.00	150.00	90.00
(1)	Earl Averill	300.00	150.00	90.00
(2)	Dick Bartell	350.00	175.00	105.00
(3)	Roy "Beau" Bell	300.00	150.00	90.00
(4)	Al Benton	300.00	150.00	90.00
(5)	Tommy Bridges	300.00	150.00	90.00
(6)	Frank Croucher	300.00	150.00	90.00
(7)	Pete Fox	300.00	150.00	90.00
(8)	Charlie Gehringer	400.00	200.00	120.00
(9)	Hank Greenberg	550.00	275.00	165.00
(10)	John Gorsica	300.00	150.00	90.00
(11)	Pinky Higgins	300.00	150.00	90.00
(12)	Fred Hutchinson	300.00	150.00	90.00
(13)	Ralph "Red" Kress	300.00	150.00	90.00
(14)	Barney McCosky	300.00	150.00	90.00
(15)	Archie R. McKain	300.00	150.00	90.00
(16)	Hal Newhouser	350.00	175.00	105.00
(17)	Louis "Buck" Newsom	300.00	150.00	90.00
(18)	Schoolboy Rowe	300.00	150.00	90.00
(19)	Birdie Tebbetts	300.00	150.00	90.00
(20)	Dizzy Trout	300.00	150.00	90.00
(21)	Rudy York	300.00	150.00	90.00

1975 Mid-Atlantic Sports Collectors Assn.

This "Baseball Royalty" collectors' set was issued in conjunction with the 1975 convention of the Mid-Atlantic Sports Collectors Association in Pikesville, Md. The blank-backed, 2-1/2" x 4-3/4" cards are printed in red and blue on white with player pho-

tos in blue. Each of the players in the set has a name or nickname pertaining to royalty. The unnumbered cards are checklisted here in alphabetical order.

		NM	EX	VG
Complete Set (8):		20.00	10.00	6.00
Common Player:		3.00	1.50	.90
(1)	Paul (Duke) Derringer	3.00	1.50	.90
(2)	Elroy (Baron of the Bullpen) Face	3.00	1.50	.90
(3)	Rogers (Rajah) Hornsby	5.00	2.50	1.50
(4)	(King) Carl Hubbell	4.00	2.00	1.25
(5)	Charley (King Kong) Keller	3.00	1.50	.90
(6)	Babe (Sultan of Swat) Ruth	10.00	5.00	3.00
(7)	(Prince) Hal Schumacher	3.00	1.50	.90
(8)	Edwin (Duke) Snider	7.50	3.75	2.25

1927 Middy Bread Browns/Cardinals Die-Cuts

St. Louis Cardinals and St. Louis Browns players comprise this set. Black-and-white, blank-backed and unnumbered, the cards are known only in die-cut form, and vary in size according to the player pose, with a typical card measuring 2-1/4" x 4" or so. The checklist, arranged here alphabetically, consists of 22 players from each team, but may be subject to future additions. Similar to the previous year's issue of Kut Outs Yankees and Giants die-cut cards, this issue features posed action photos with the backgrounds cut away and the player and team name printed at the bottom of the photo. Unlike the earlier New York issue, however, these cards carry an advertisement at bottom for Midday Bread, and were presumably issued in the St. Louis area, though the exact method of their distribution is unknown. Cards are blank-backed and unnumbered. As with all die-cut cards, various appendages and bat ends were easily torn off and cards with such defects suffer severe loss of value.

		NM	EX	VG
Complete Set (44):		13,500	6,750	4,250
Common Player:		300.00	150.00	60.00
St. Louis Browns				
(1)	Spencer Adams	450.00	180.00	90.00
(2)	Win Ballou	300.00	120.00	60.00
(3)	Walter Beck	300.00	120.00	60.00
(4)	Herschel Bennett	300.00	120.00	60.00
(5)	Stewart Bolen	300.00	120.00	60.00
(6)	Leo Dixon	300.00	120.00	60.00
(7)	Chester Falk	300.00	120.00	60.00
(8)	Milton Gaston	300.00	120.00	60.00
(9)	Walter Gerber	300.00	120.00	60.00
(10)	Sam Jones	300.00	120.00	60.00
(11)	Oscar Melillo	300.00	120.00	60.00
(12)	Bing Miller	300.00	120.00	60.00
(13)	Otis Miller	300.00	120.00	60.00
(14)	Billie Mullen	300.00	120.00	60.00
(15)	Ernie Nevers	600.00	240.00	120.00
(16)	Steve O'Neill	300.00	120.00	60.00
(17)	Harry Rice	300.00	120.00	60.00
(18)	George Sisler	500.00	200.00	100.00
(19)	Walter Stewart	300.00	120.00	60.00
(20)	Elam VanGilder	300.00	120.00	60.00
(21)	Ken Williams	300.00	120.00	60.00
(22)	Ernie Wingard	300.00	120.00	60.00
St. Louis Cardinals				
(1)	Grover Alexander	600.00	240.00	120.00
(2)	Herman Bell	300.00	120.00	60.00
(3)	Lester Bell	300.00	120.00	60.00
(4)	Ray Blades	300.00	120.00	60.00
(5)	Jim Bottomley	500.00	200.00	100.00
(6)	Danny Clark	300.00	120.00	60.00
(7)	Taylor Douthit	300.00	120.00	60.00
(8)	Frank Frisch	500.00	200.00	100.00
(9)	Chick Hafey	500.00	200.00	100.00
(10)	Jesse Haines	500.00	200.00	100.00
(11)	Vic Keen	300.00	120.00	60.00
(12)	Carlise Littlejohn	300.00	120.00	60.00
(13)	Bob McGraw	300.00	120.00	60.00
(14)	Bob O'Farrell	300.00	120.00	60.00
(15)	Art Reinhardt	300.00	120.00	60.00
(16)	Jimmy Ring	300.00	120.00	60.00
(17)	Walter Roettger	300.00	120.00	60.00
(18)	Robert Schang	300.00	120.00	60.00
(19)	Willie Sherdel	300.00	120.00	60.00
(20)	Billy Southworth	300.00	120.00	60.00
(21)	Tommy Thevenow	300.00	120.00	60.00
(22)	George Toporcer	300.00	120.00	60.00

1976 Midwest Sports Collectors Convention

 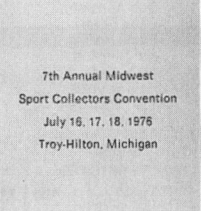

This collectors' issue was produced in conjunction with the 7th annual convention of the Midwest Sports Collectors in Troy, Mich. Former members of the Detroit Tigers, with an emphasis on the 1930s, are featured on the black-and-white, 2-3/8" x 2-7/8" cards. Players are depicted in portrait and action drawings, with personal data and career highlights added in either written or comic form. Backs advertise the show. The unnumbered cards are checklisted here in alphabetical order.

		NM	EX	VG
Complete Set (23):		15.00	7.50	4.50
Common Player:		3.00	1.50	.90
(1)	Eldon Auker	3.00	1.50	.90
(2)	Tommy Bridges	3.00	1.50	.90
(3)	Flea Clifton	3.00	1.50	.90
(4)	Mickey Cochrane	7.50	3.75	2.25
(5)	General Crowder	3.00	1.50	.90
(6)	Frank Doljack	3.00	1.50	.90
(7)	Carl Fischer	3.00	1.50	.90
(8)	Pete Fox	3.00	1.50	.90
(9)	Charlie Gehringer	6.00	3.00	1.75
(10)	Goose Goslin	4.50	2.25	1.25
(11)	Hank Greenberg	9.00	4.50	2.75
(12)	Luke Hamlin	3.00	1.50	.90
(13)	Ray Hayworth	3.00	1.50	.90
(14)	Chief Hogsett	3.00	1.50	.90
(15)	Firpo Marberry	3.00	1.50	.90
(16)	Marvin Owen	3.00	1.50	.90
(17)	Cy Perkins	3.00	1.50	.90
(18)	Bill Rogell	3.00	1.50	.90
(19)	Schoolboy Rowe	3.00	1.50	.90
(20)	Heinie Schuble	3.00	1.50	.90
(21)	Vic Sorrell	3.00	1.50	.90
(22)	Gee Walker	3.00	1.50	.90
(23)	Jo Jo White	3.00	1.50	.90

1980 Midwest Sports Collectors Convention

Reprints of a number of the player postcards of J.D. McCarthy were produced in conjunction with the 1980 Detroit show. The blank-backed, black-and-white postcards are 3-1/4" x 5-1/2" and all feature former Detroit Tigers. The unnumbered cards are checklisted here alphabetically.

	NM	EX	VG
Complete Set (11):	7.50	3.75	2.25
Common Player:	1.00	.50	.30
(1) Bob Anderson	1.00	.50	.30
(2) Babe Birrer	1.00	.50	.30
(3) Frank Bolling	1.00	.50	.30
(4) Jim Bunning	2.00	1.00	.60
(5) Al Cicotte	1.00	.50	.30
(6) Paul Foytack	1.00	.50	.30
(7) Joe Ginsberg	1.00	.50	.30
(8) Steve Gromek	1.00	.50	.30
(9) Art Houtteman	1.00	.50	.30
(10) Al Kaline	5.00	2.50	1.50
(11) Harvey Kuenn	2.00	1.00	.60

1971 Milk Duds

These cards were issued on the backs of five-cent packages of Milk Duds candy. Most collectors prefer complete boxes, rather than cut-out cards, which measure approximately 1-13/16" x 2-5/8" when trimmed tightly. Values quoted below are for complete boxes. Cut cards will bring 50-75 percent of the quoted values. The set includes 37 National League and 32 American League players. Card numbers appear on the box flap, with each number from 1 through 24 being shared by three different players. A suffix (a, b and c) has been added for the collector's convenience. Harmon Killebrew, Brooks Robinson and Pete Rose were double-printed.

	NM	EX	VG
Complete Set, Boxes:	1,750	900.00	550.00
Complete Set, Singles (72):	900.00	450.00	275.00
Common Player:	18.00	8.00	5.00
1a Frank Howard	20.00	10.00	6.00
1b Fritz Peterson	18.00	8.00	5.00
1c Pete Rose	100.00	50.00	30.00
2a Johnny Bench	25.00	12.00	8.00
2b Rico Carty	18.00	8.00	5.00
2c Pete Rose	100.00	50.00	30.00
3a Ken Holtzman	18.00	8.00	5.00
3b Willie Mays	100.00	50.00	30.00
3c Cesar Tovar	18.00	8.00	5.00
4a Willie Davis	18.00	8.00	5.00
4b Harmon Killebrew	25.00	12.00	8.00
4c Felix Millan	18.00	8.00	5.00
5a Billy Grabarkewitz	18.00	8.00	5.00
5b Andy Messersmith	18.00	8.00	5.00
5c Thurman Munson	80.00	40.00	25.00
6a Luis Aparicio	25.00	12.00	8.00
6b Lou Brock	20.00	10.00	6.00
6c Bill Melton	18.00	8.00	5.00
7a Ray Culp	18.00	8.00	5.00
7b Willie McCovey	35.00	18.00	10.00
7c Luke Walker	18.00	8.00	5.00
8a Roberto Clemente	200.00	100.00	60.00
8b Jim Merritt	18.00	8.00	5.00
8c Claud Osteen (Claude)	18.00	8.00	5.00
9a Stan Bahnsen	18.00	8.00	5.00
9b Sam McDowell	18.00	8.00	5.00
9c Billy Williams	25.00	15.00	8.00
10a Jim Hickman	18.00	8.00	5.00
10b Dave McNally	18.00	8.00	5.00
10c Tony Perez	35.00	20.00	12.00
11a Hank Aaron	70.00	35.00	20.00
11b Glen Beckert (Glenn)	18.00	8.00	5.00
11c Ray Fosse	18.00	8.00	5.00
12a Alex Johnson	18.00	8.00	5.00
12b Gaylord Perry	20.00	10.00	6.00
12c Wayne Simpson	18.00	8.00	5.00
13a Dave Johnson	18.00	8.00	5.00
13b George Scott	18.00	8.00	5.00
13c Tom Seaver	40.00	20.00	12.00
14a Bill Freehan	18.00	8.00	5.00
14b Bud Harrelson	18.00	8.00	5.00
14c Manny Sanguillen	18.00	8.00	5.00
15a Bob Gibson	25.00	12.00	8.00
15b Rusty Staub	20.00	10.00	6.00
15c Roy White	18.00	8.00	5.00
16a Jim Fregosi	18.00	8.00	5.00
16b Catfish Hunter	25.00	12.00	8.00
16c Mel Stottlemyer (Stottlemyre)	18.00	8.00	5.00
17a Tommy Harper	18.00	8.00	5.00
17b Frank Robinson	35.00	20.00	12.00
17c Reggie Smith	18.00	8.00	5.00
18a Orlando Cepeda	35.00	20.00	12.00
18b Rico Petrocelli	18.00	8.00	5.00
18c Brooks Robinson	35.00	20.00	12.00
19a Tony Oliva	20.00	10.00	6.00
19b Milt Pappas	18.00	8.00	5.00

19c Bobby Tolan	18.00	8.00	5.00
20a Ernie Banks	55.00	25.00	15.00
20b Don Kessinger	18.00	8.00	5.00
20c Joe Torre	20.00	10.00	6.00
21a Fergie Jenkins	25.00	12.00	8.00
21b Jim Palmer	25.00	12.00	8.00
21c Ron Santo	20.00	10.00	6.00
22a Randy Hundley	18.00	8.00	5.00
22b Dennis Menke (Denis)	18.00	8.00	5.00
22c Boog Powell	20.00	10.00	6.00
23a Dick Dietz	10.00	5.00	3.00
23b Tommy John	10.00	5.00	3.00
23c Brooks Robinson	20.00	10.00	6.00
24a Danny Cater	10.00	5.00	3.00
24b Harmon Killebrew	25.00	15.00	10.00
24c Jim Perry	20.00	10.00	6.00

1933 George C. Miller (R300)

George C. Miller & Co. of Boston, Mass., issued a 32-card set in one-cent packs of toffee in 1933. The set, which received limited distribution, consists of 16 National League and 16 American League players. The cards are color art reproductions of actual photographs and measure 2-3/8" x 2-7/8". Two distinct variations can be found for each card in the set. Type 1 cards have the names "Fox" and "Klien" misspelled on the back, while Type 2 cards have them correctly as "Foxx" and "Klein". Collectors were advised on the card backs to collect all 32 cards and return them for prizes. (Ivy Andrews' card was short-printed to avoid giving out too many prizes.) The cancelled cards were returned to the collector with the prize. Two forms of cancellation were used; one involved the complete trimming of the bottom one-quarter of the card, the other a diamond-shaped series of punch holes. Cancelled cards have a significantly decreased value.

	NM	EX	VG
Complete Set (32):	125,000	62,500	37,500
Common Player:	2,000	1,000	600.00
(1) Dale Alexander	2,000	1,000	600.00
(2) "Ivy" Paul Andrews	9,000	4,500	2,700
Cut-cancelled: 975.00			
Punch-cancelled: 2,400			
(3) Earl Averill	4,000	2,000	1,200
(4) Dick Bartell	2,000	1,000	600.00
(5) Walter Berger	2,000	1,000	600.00
(6) Jim Bottomley	4,000	2,000	1,200
(7) Joe Cronin	4,000	2,000	1,200
(8) Jerome "Dizzy" Dean	4,750	2,400	1,400
(9) William Dickey	4,000	2,000	1,200
(10) Jimmy Dykes	2,000	1,000	600.00
(11) Wesley Ferrell	2,000	1,000	600.00
(12) Jimmy Foxx	6,000	3,000	1,800
(13) Frank Frisch	4,000	2,000	1,200
(14) Charlie Gehringer	4,000	2,000	1,200
(15) Leon "Goose" Goslin	4,000	2,000	1,200
(16) Charlie Grimm	2,000	1,000	600.00
(17) Bob "Lefty" Grove	4,750	2,400	1,400
(18) Charles "Chick" Hafey	4,000	2,000	1,200
(19) Ray Hayworth	2,000	1,000	600.00
(20) Charles "Chuck" Klein	4,000	2,000	1,200
(21) Walter "Rabbit" Maranville	4,000	2,000	1,200
(22) Oscar Melillo	2,000	1,000	600.00
(23) Frank "Lefty" O'Doul	3,250	1,600	975.00
(24) Melvin Ott	5,000	2,500	1,500
(25) Carl Reynolds	2,000	1,000	600.00
(26) Charles Ruffing	4,000	2,000	1,200
(27) Al Simmons	4,000	2,000	1,200
(28) Joe Stripp	2,000	1,000	600.00
(29) Bill Terry	4,000	2,000	1,200
(30) Lloyd Waner	4,000	2,000	1,200
(31) Paul Waner	4,000	2,000	1,200
(32) Lonnie Warneke	2,000	1,000	600.00

1969 Milton Bradley

The first of three sets issued by Milton Bradley over a four-year period, these cards were part of a baseball board game. The unnumbered cards measure 2" x 3" and have a white bor-

der surrounding the black-and-white player photo. The player's name appears above the photo in upper case letters. There are no team designations and the photos are airbrushed to eliminate team logos. Backs display biographical data along the top followed by a list of various game situations used in playing the board game. The cards have square corners. The 1969 and 1972 game cards are virtually identical in format. They can be differentiated by looking on the back at any numeral "1" in a line of red type. If the "1" does not have a base, it is a 1969 card; if there is a base, the card is a 1972. Besides individual player cards, there was a non-photographic team cards for each of the contemporary 24 Major League teams.

	NM	EX	VG
Complete Boxed Set:	400.00	200.00	120.00
Complete Set (296):	150.00	75.00	45.00
Common Player:	.50	.25	.15
Team Card:	2.00	1.00	.60
(1) Hank Aaron	30.00	15.00	9.00
(2) Ted Abernathy	.50	.25	.15
(3) Jerry Adair	.50	.25	.15
(4) Tommy Agee	.50	.25	.15
(5) Bernie Allen	.50	.25	.15
(6) Hank Allen	.50	.25	.15
(7) Richie Allen	5.00	2.50	1.50
(8) Gene Alley	.50	.25	.15
(9) Bob Allison	.50	.25	.15
(10) Felipe Alou	1.00	.50	.30
(11) Jesus Alou	.50	.25	.15
(12) Matty Alou	.50	.25	.15
(13) Max Alvis	.50	.25	.15
(14) Mike Andrews	.50	.25	.15
(15) Luis Aparicio	10.00	5.00	3.00
(16) Jose Arcia	.50	.25	.15
(17) Bob Aspromonte	.50	.25	.15
(18) Joe Azcue	.50	.25	.15
(19) Ernie Banks	20.00	10.00	6.00
(20) Steve Barber	.50	.25	.15
(21) John Bateman	.50	.25	.15
(22) Glen Beckert (Glenn)	.50	.25	.15
(23) Gary Bell	.50	.25	.15
(24) John Bench	15.00	7.50	4.50
(25) Ken Berry	.50	.25	.15
(26) Frank Bertaina	.50	.25	.15
(27) Paul Blair	.50	.25	.15
(28) Wade Blasingame	.50	.25	.15
(29) Curt Blefary	.50	.25	.15
(30) John Boccabella	.50	.25	.15
(31) Bobby Lee Bonds	1.00	.50	.30
(32) Sam Bowens	.50	.25	.15
(33) Ken Boyer	1.00	.50	.30
(34) Charles Bradford	.50	.25	.15
(35) Darrell Brandon	.50	.25	.15
(36) Jim Brewer	.50	.25	.15
(37) John Briggs	.50	.25	.15
(38) Nelson Briles	.50	.25	.15
(39) Ed Brinkman	.50	.25	.15
(40) Lou Brock	10.00	5.00	3.00
(41) Gates Brown	.50	.25	.15
(42) Larry Brown	.50	.25	.15
(43) George Brunet	.50	.25	.15
(44) Jerry Buchek	.50	.25	.15
(45) Don Buford	.50	.25	.15
(46) Jim Bunning	7.50	3.75	2.25
(47) Johnny Callison	.50	.25	.15
(48) Campy Campaneris	.50	.25	.15
(49) Jose Cardenal	.50	.25	.15
(50) Leo Cardenas	.50	.25	.15
(51) Don Cardwell	.50	.25	.15
(52) Rod Carew	12.50	6.25	3.75
(53) Paul Casanova	.50	.25	.15
(54) Norm Cash	1.50	.70	.45
(55) Danny Cater	.50	.25	.15
(56) Orlando Cepeda	10.00	5.00	3.00
(57) Dean Chance	.50	.25	.15
(58) Ed Charles	.50	.25	.15
(59) Horace Clarke	.50	.25	.15
(60) Roberto Clemente	45.00	22.00	13.50
(61) Donn Clendenon	.50	.25	.15
(62) Ty Cline	.50	.25	.15
(63) Nate Colbert	.50	.25	.15
(64) Joe Coleman	.50	.25	.15
(65) Bob Cox	.50	.25	.15
(66) Mike Cuellar	.50	.25	.15
(67) Ray Culp	.50	.25	.15
(68) Clay Dalrymple	.50	.25	.15
(69) Vic Davalillo	.50	.25	.15
(70) Jim Davenport	.50	.25	.15
(71) Ron Davis	.50	.25	.15
(72) Tommy Davis	.50	.25	.15
(73) Willie Davis	.50	.25	.15
(74) Chuck Dobson	.50	.25	.15
(75) John Donaldson	.50	.25	.15
(76) Al Downing	.50	.25	.15
(77) Moe Drabowsky	.50	.25	.15
(78) Dick Ellsworth	.50	.25	.15
(79) Mike Epstein	.50	.25	.15
(80) Andy Etchebarren	.50	.25	.15
(81) Ron Fairly	.50	.25	.15
(82) Dick Farrell	.50	.25	.15
(83) Curt Flood	1.00	.50	.30
(84) Joe Foy	.50	.25	.15
(85) Tito Francona	.50	.25	.15
(86) Bill Freehan	.75	.40	.25
(87) Jim Fregosi	.50	.25	.15
(88) Woodie Fryman	.50	.25	.15
(89) Len Gabrielson	.50	.25	.15
(90) Cito Gaston	.50	.25	.15
(91) Jake Gibbs	.50	.25	.15
(92) Russ Gibson	.50	.25	.15
(93) Dave Giusti	.50	.25	.15
(94) Tony Gonzalez	.50	.25	.15
(95) Jim Gosger	.50	.25	.15
(96) Julio Gotay	.50	.25	.15
(97) Dick Green	.50	.25	.15
(98) Jerry Grote	.50	.25	.15

(99)	Jimmie Hall	.50	.25	.15
(100)	Tom Haller	.50	.25	.15
(101)	Steve Hamilton	.50	.25	.15
(102)	Ron Hansen	.50	.25	.15
(103)	Jim Hardin	.50	.25	.15
(104)	Tommy Harper	.50	.25	.15
(105)	Bud Harrelson	.50	.25	.15
(106)	Ken Harrelson	.50	.25	.15
(107)	Jim Hart	.50	.25	.15
(108)	Woodie Held	.50	.25	.15
(109)	Tommy Helms	.50	.25	.15
(110)	Elrod Hendricks	.50	.25	.15
(111)	Mike Hershberger	.50	.25	.15
(112)	Jack Hiatt	.50	.25	.15
(113)	Jim Hickman	.50	.25	.15
(114)	John Hiller	.50	.25	.15
(115)	Chuck Hinton	.50	.25	.15
(116)	Ken Holtzman	.50	.25	.15
(117)	Joel Horlen	.50	.25	.15
(118)	Tony Horton	.50	.25	.15
(119)	Willie Horton	.50	.25	.15
(120)	Frank Howard	1.00	.50	.30
(121)	Dick Howser	.50	.25	.15
(122)	Randy Hundley	.50	.25	.15
(123)	Ron Hunt	.50	.25	.15
(124)	Catfish Hunter	7.50	3.75	2.25
(125)	Al Jackson	.50	.25	.15
(126)	Larry Jackson	.50	.25	.15
(127)	Reggie Jackson	30.00	15.00	9.00
(128)	Sonny Jackson	.50	.25	.15
(129)	Pat Jarvis	.50	.25	.15
(130)	Julian Javier	.50	.25	.15
(131)	Ferguson Jenkins	7.50	3.75	2.25
(132)	Manny Jimenez	.50	.25	.15
(133)	Tommy John	1.00	.50	.30
(134)	Bob Johnson	.50	.25	.15
(135)	Dave Johnson	.50	.25	.15
(136)	Deron Johnson	.50	.25	.15
(137)	Lou Johnson	.50	.25	.15
(138)	Jay Johnstone	.50	.25	.15
(139)	Cleon Jones	.50	.25	.15
(140)	Dalton Jones	.50	.25	.15
(141)	Duane Josephson	.50	.25	.15
(142)	Jim Kaat	1.50	.70	.45
(143)	Al Kaline	15.00	7.50	4.50
(144)	Don Kessinger	.50	.25	.15
(145)	Harmon Killebrew	12.50	6.25	3.75
(146)	Harold King	.50	.25	.15
(147)	Ed Kirkpatrick	.50	.25	.15
(148)	Fred Klages	.50	.25	.15
(149)	Ron Kline	.50	.25	.15
(150)	Bobby Knoop	.50	.25	.15
(151)	Gary Kolb	.50	.25	.15
(152)	Andy Kosco	.50	.25	.15
(153)	Ed Kranepool	.50	.25	.15
(154)	Lew Krausse	.50	.25	.15
(155)	Harold Lanier	.50	.25	.15
(156)	Jim Lefebvre	.50	.25	.15
(157)	Denny Lemaster	.50	.25	.15
(158)	Dave Leonhard	.50	.25	.15
(159)	Don Lock	.50	.25	.15
(160)	Mickey Lolich	1.50	.70	.45
(161)	Jim Lonborg	.75	.40	.25
(162)	Mike Lum	.50	.25	.15
(163)	Al Lyle	.50	.25	.15
(164)	Jim Maloney	.50	.25	.15
(165)	Juan Marichal	8.00	4.00	2.50
(166)	J.C. Martin	.50	.25	.15
(167)	Marty Martinez	.50	.25	.15
(168)	Tom Matchick	.50	.25	.15
(169)	Ed Mathews	12.50	6.25	3.75
(170)	Dal Maxvill	.50	.25	.15
(171)	Jerry May	.50	.25	.15
(172)	Lee May	.50	.25	.15
(173)	Lee Maye	.50	.25	.15
(174)	Willie Mays	30.00	15.00	9.00
(175)	Bill Mazeroski	12.50	6.25	3.75
(176)	Richard McAuliffe	.50	.25	.15
(177)	Al McBean	.50	.25	.15
(178)	Tim McCarver	.75	.40	.25
(179)	Bill McCool	.50	.25	.15
(180)	Mike McCormick	.50	.25	.15
(181)	Willie McCovey	12.50	6.25	3.75
(182)	Tom McCraw	.50	.25	.15
(183)	Lindy McDaniel	.50	.25	.15
(184)	Sam McDowell	.75	.40	.25
(185)	Orlando McFarlane	.50	.25	.15
(186)	Jim McGlothlin	.50	.25	.15
(187)	Denny McLain	1.25	.60	.40
(188)	Ken McMullen	.50	.25	.15
(189)	Dave McNally	.50	.25	.15
(190)	Gerry McNertney	.50	.25	.15
(191)	Dennis Menke (Denis)	.50	.25	.15
(192)	Felix Millan	.50	.25	.15
(193)	Don Mincher	.50	.25	.15
(194)	Rick Monday	.50	.25	.15
(195)	Joe Morgan	10.00	5.00	3.00
(196)	Bubba Morton	.50	.25	.15
(197)	Manny Mota	.50	.25	.15
(198)	Jim Nash	.50	.25	.15
(199)	Dave Nelson	.50	.25	.15
(200)	Dick Nen	.50	.25	.15
(201)	Phil Niekro	7.50	3.75	2.25
(202)	Jim Northrup	.50	.25	.15
(203)	Richard Nye	.50	.25	.15
(204)	Johnny Odom	.50	.25	.15
(205)	Tony Oliva	1.00	.50	.30
(206)	Gene Oliver	.50	.25	.15
(207)	Phil Ortega	.50	.25	.15
(208)	Claude Osteen	.50	.25	.15
(209)	Ray Oyler	.50	.25	.15
(210)	Jose Pagan	.50	.25	.15
(211)	Jim Pagliaroni	.50	.25	.15
(212)	Milt Pappas	.50	.25	.15
(213)	Wes Parker	.50	.25	.15
(214)	Camilo Pascual	.50	.25	.15
(215)	Don Pavletich	.50	.25	.15
(216)	Joe Pepitone	.50	.25	.15

(217)	Tony Perez	10.00	5.00	3.00
(218)	Gaylord Perry	7.50	3.75	2.25
(219)	Jim Perry	.50	.25	.15
(220)	Gary Peters	.50	.25	.15
(221)	Rico Petrocelli	.50	.25	.15
(222)	Adolfo Phillips	.50	.25	.15
(223)	Tom Phoebus	.50	.25	.15
(224)	Vada Pinson	2.00	1.00	.60
(225)	Boog Powell	2.00	1.00	.60
(226)	Frank Quilici	.50	.25	.15
(227)	Doug Rader	.50	.25	.15
(228)	Rich Reese	.50	.25	.15
(229)	Phil Regan	.50	.25	.15
(230)	Rick Reichardt	.50	.25	.15
(231)	Rick Renick	.50	.25	.15
(232)	Roger Repoz	.50	.25	.15
(233)	Dave Ricketts	.50	.25	.15
(234)	Bill Robinson	.50	.25	.15
(235)	Brooks Robinson	15.00	7.50	4.50
(236)	Frank Robinson	15.00	7.50	4.50
(237)	Bob Rodgers	.50	.25	.15
(238)	Cookie Rojas	.50	.25	.15
(239)	Rich Rollins	.50	.25	.15
(240)	Phil Roof	.50	.25	.15
(241)	Pete Rose	30.00	15.00	9.00
(242)	John Roseboro	.50	.25	.15
(243)	Chico Ruiz	.50	.25	.15
(244)	Ray Sadecki	.50	.25	.15
(245)	Chico Salmon	.50	.25	.15
(246)	Jose Santiago	.50	.25	.15
(247)	Ron Santo	2.50	1.25	.70
(248)	Tom Satriano	.50	.25	.15
(249)	Paul Schaal	.50	.25	.15
(250)	Tom Seaver	15.00	7.50	4.50
(251)	Art Shamsky	.50	.25	.15
(252)	Mike Shannon	.50	.25	.15
(253)	Chris Short	.50	.25	.15
(254)	Dick Simpson	.50	.25	.15
(255)	Duke Sims	.50	.25	.15
(256)	Reggie Smith	.50	.25	.15
(257)	Willie Smith	.50	.25	.15
(258)	Russ Snyder	.50	.25	.15
(259)	Al Spangler	.50	.25	.15
(260)	Larry Stahl	.50	.25	.15
(261)	Lee Stange	.50	.25	.15
(262)	Fred Stanley	.50	.25	.15
(263)	Willie Stargell	10.00	5.00	3.00
(264)	Rusty Staub	1.00	.50	.30
(265)	Mel Stottlemyre	.50	.25	.15
(266)	Ed Stroud	.50	.25	.15
(267)	Don Sutton	7.50	3.75	2.25
(268)	Ron Swoboda	.50	.25	.15
(269)	Jose Tartabull	.50	.25	.15
(270)	Tony Taylor	.50	.25	.15
(271)	Luis Tiant	1.00	.50	.30
(272)	Bob Tillman	.50	.25	.15
(273)	Bobby Tolan	.50	.25	.15
(274)	Jeff Torborg	.50	.25	.15
(275)	Joe Torre	2.50	1.25	.70
(276)	Cesar Tovar	.50	.25	.15
(277)	Dick Tracewski	.50	.25	.15
(278)	Tom Tresh	.75	.40	.25
(279)	Ted Uhlaender	.50	.25	.15
(280)	Del Unser	.50	.25	.15
(281)	Hilario Valdespino	.50	.25	.15
(282)	Fred Valentine	.50	.25	.15
(283)	Bob Veale	.50	.25	.15
(284)	Zoilo Versalles	.50	.25	.15
(285)	Pete Ward	.50	.25	.15
(286)	Al Weis	.50	.25	.15
(287)	Don Wert	.50	.25	.15
(288)	Bill White	.50	.25	.15
(289)	Roy White	.50	.25	.15
(290)	Fred Whitfield	.50	.25	.15
(291)	Hoyt Wilhelm	7.50	3.75	2.25
(292)	Billy Williams	10.00	5.00	3.00
(293)	Maury Wills	.75	.40	.25
(294)	Earl Wilson	.50	.25	.15
(295)	Wilbur Wood	.50	.25	.15
(296)	Jerry Zimmerman	.50	.25	.15

1970 Milton Bradley

TONY TAYLOR

IF 12/19/35 5-9 TR BR

3	CATCHER
4	1ST BASEMAN
5	LEFT FIELDER
6	2ND BASEMAN
8	3RD BASEMAN
9	SHORTSTOP
10	CENTER FIELDER
11	RIGHT FIELDER
12	PITCHER

Except for the slightly larger (2-3/8" x 3-1/2") size, the format of the 1970 Milton Bradley set is similar to the 1969 Milton Bradley issue. Again designed for use with a baseball board game, the unnumbered black-and-white cards have rounded corners and wide white borders. The player's name appears in capital letters beneath the photo with his position, birthdate, height and batting and throwing preference on a line below. The back of the card shows the player's name along the top followed by a list of possible game situations used in playing the board game. There are no team designations on the cards and all team insignias have been airbrushed from the photos.

	NM	EX	VG
Complete Boxed Set:	175.00	85.00	45.00

Complete Card Set (28):	120.00	55.00	30.00
Common Player:	1.50	.70	.45
(1) Hank Aaron	15.00	7.50	4.50
(2) Ernie Banks	10.00	5.00	3.00
(3) Lou Brock	7.50	3.75	2.25
(4) Rod Carew	9.00	4.50	2.75
(5) Roberto Clemente	15.00	7.50	4.50
(6) Tommy Davis	1.50	.70	.45
(7) Bill Freehan	1.50	.70	.45
(8) Jim Fregosi	1.50	.70	.45
(9) Tom Haller	1.50	.70	.45
(10) Frank Howard	2.00	1.00	.60
(11) Reggie Jackson	10.00	5.00	3.00
(12) Harmon Killebrew	9.00	4.50	2.75
(13) Mickey S. Lolich	1.50	.70	.45
(14) Juan Marichal	6.00	3.00	1.75
(15) Willie Mays	15.00	7.50	4.50
(16) Willie McCovey	7.50	3.75	2.25
(17) Sam McDowell	1.50	.70	.45
(18) Dennis Menke (Denis)	1.50	.70	.45
(19) Don Mincher	1.50	.70	.45
(20) Phil Niekro	6.00	3.00	1.75
(21) Rico Petrocelli	1.50	.70	.45
(22) Boog Powell	2.00	1.00	.60
(23) Frank Robinson	9.00	4.50	2.75
(24) Pete Rose	15.00	7.50	4.50
(25) Ron Santo	3.00	1.50	.90
(26) Tom Seaver	9.00	4.50	2.75
(27) Mel Stottlemyre	1.50	.70	.45
(28) Tony Taylor	1.50	.70	.45

1972 Milton Bradley

ROBERTO CLEMENTE

ROBERTO CLEMENTE			
			OF
8/18/34	5-11		TR-BR
2	TRIPLE		
3	HOME RUN		
4	FOUL OUT		RH
5	SINGLE		RA2
6	FLY OUT		3BS
7	DOUBLE		RA3
8	GROUND OUT		RA1
9	GROUND OUT		RA1
10	FLY OUT		RH
11	SINGLE		RA2
12	SINGLE		RA2

The 1972 Milton Bradley set was again designed for use with a baseball table game. The 1972 cards are similar to the 1969 and 1970 issues. The unnumbered black-and-white cards measure 2" x 3" and display the player's name along the top of the card. Again, all team insignias have been eliminated by airbrushing, and there are no team designations indicated. Backs carry the player's name and personal data followed by a list of possible game situations used in playing the game. To differentiate a 1972 card from a 1969, look on back for a line of red type which contains the numeral "1." If the digit has a base, the card is a '72; if there is no base to the red "1", it is a 1969. Besides individual player cards, non-photographic team cards were issued for each of the contemporary 24 Major League teams.

	NM	EX	VG
Complete Boxed Set:	400.00	200.00	120.00
Complete Card Set (378):	350.00	175.00	110.00
Common Player:	.50	.25	.15
Team Card:	2.00	1.00	.60
(1) Hank Aaron	25.00	12.50	7.50
(2) Tommie Aaron	.50	.25	.15
(3) Ted Abernathy	.50	.25	.15
(4) Jerry Adair	.50	.25	.15
(5) Tommy Agee	.50	.25	.15
(6) Bernie Allen	.50	.25	.15
(7) Hank Allen	.50	.25	.15
(8) Richie Allen	1.50	.70	.45
(9) Gene Alley	.50	.25	.15
(10) Bob Allison	.50	.25	.15
(11) Sandy Alomar	.50	.25	.15
(12) Felipe Alou	.75	.40	.25
(13) Jesus Alou	.50	.25	.15
(14) Matty Alou	.50	.25	.15
(15) Max Alvis	.50	.25	.15
(16) Brant Alyea	.50	.25	.15
(17) Mike Andrews	.50	.25	.15
(18) Luis Aparicio	9.00	4.50	2.75
(19) Jose Arcia	.50	.25	.15
(20) Gerald Arrigo	.50	.25	.15
(21) Bob Aspromonte	.50	.25	.15
(22) Joe Azcue	.50	.25	.15
(23) Robert Bailey	.50	.25	.15
(24) Sal Bando	.50	.25	.15
(25) Ernie Banks	17.50	8.75	5.25
(26) Steve Barber	.50	.25	.15
(27) Robert Barton	.50	.25	.15
(28) John Bateman	.50	.25	.15
(29) Glen Beckert (Glenn)	.50	.25	.15
(30) John Bench	12.50	6.25	3.75
(31) Ken Berry	.50	.25	.15
(32) Frank Bertaina	.50	.25	.15
(33) Paul Blair	.50	.25	.15
(34) Stephen Blass	.50	.25	.15
(35) Curt Blefary	.50	.25	.15
(36) Bobby Bolin	.50	.25	.15
(37) Bobby Lee Bonds	1.00	.50	.30
(38) Donald Bosch	.50	.25	.15
(39) Richard Bosman	.50	.25	.15
(40) Dave Boswell	.50	.25	.15
(41) Kenneth Boswell	.50	.25	.15
(42) Cletis Boyer	.50	.25	.15
(43) Ken Boyer	1.25	.60	.40
(44) Charles Bradford	.50	.25	.15

(45)	Ronald Brand	.50	.25	.15
(46)	Ken Brett	.50	.25	.15
(47)	Jim Brewer	.50	.25	.15
(48)	John Briggs	.50	.25	.15
(49)	Nelson Briles	.50	.25	.15
(50)	Ed Brinkman	.50	.25	.15
(51)	James Britton	.50	.25	.15
(52)	Lou Brock	9.00	4.50	2.75
(53)	Gates Brown	.50	.25	.15
(54)	Larry Brown	.50	.25	.15
(55)	Ollie Brown	.50	.25	.15
(56)	George Brunet	.50	.25	.15
(57)	Don Buford	.50	.25	.15
(58)	Wallace Bunker	.50	.25	.15
(59)	Jim Bunning	6.00	3.00	1.75
(60)	William Butler	.50	.25	.15
(61)	Johnny Callison	.50	.25	.15
(62)	Campy Campaneris	.50	.25	.15
(63)	Jose Cardenal	.50	.25	.15
(64)	Leo Cardenas	.50	.25	.15
(65)	Don Cardwell	.50	.25	.15
(66)	Rod Carew	9.00	4.50	2.75
(67)	Cisco Carlos	.50	.25	.15
(68)	Steve Carlton	9.00	4.50	2.75
(69)	Clay Carroll	.50	.25	.15
(70)	Paul Casanova	.50	.25	.15
(71)	Norm Cash	1.50	.70	.45
(72)	Danny Cater	.50	.25	.15
(73)	Orlando Cepeda	9.00	4.50	2.75
(74)	Dean Chance	.50	.25	.15
(75)	Horace Clarke	.50	.25	.15
(76)	Roberto Clemente	30.00	15.00	9.00
(77)	Donn Clendenon	.50	.25	.15
(78)	Ty Cline	.50	.25	.15
(79)	Nate Colbert	.50	.25	.15
(80)	Joe Coleman	.50	.25	.15
(81)	William Conigliaro	.75	.40	.25
(82)	Casey Cox	.50	.25	.15
(83)	Mike Cuellar	.50	.25	.15
(84)	Ray Culp	.50	.25	.15
(85)	George Culver	.50	.25	.15
(86)	Vic Davalillo	.50	.25	.15
(87)	Jim Davenport	.50	.25	.15
(88)	Tommy Davis	.50	.25	.15
(89)	Willie Davis	.50	.25	.15
(90)	Larry Dierker	.50	.25	.15
(91)	Richard Dietz	.50	.25	.15
(92)	Chuck Dobson	.50	.25	.15
(93)	Pat Dobson	.50	.25	.15
(94)	John Donaldson	.50	.25	.15
(95)	Al Downing	.50	.25	.15
(96)	Moe Drabowsky	.50	.25	.15
(97)	John Edwards	.50	.25	.15
(98)	Thomas Egan	.50	.25	.15
(99)	Dick Ellsworth	.50	.25	.15
(100)	Mike Epstein	.50	.25	.15
(101)	Andy Etchebarren	.50	.25	.15
(102)	Ron Fairly	.50	.25	.15
(103)	Frank Fernandez	.50	.25	.15
(104)	Alfred Ferrara	.50	.25	.15
(105)	Michael Fiore	.50	.25	.15
(106)	Curt Flood	1.00	.50	.30
(107)	Vern Fuller	.50	.25	.15
(108)	Joe Foy	.50	.25	.15
(109)	Tito Francona	.50	.25	.15
(110)	Bill Freehan	.50	.25	.15
(111)	Jim Fregosi	.50	.25	.15
(112)	Woodie Fryman	.50	.25	.15
(113)	Len Gabrielson	.50	.25	.15
(114)	Philip Gagliano	.50	.25	.15
(115)	Cito Gaston	.50	.25	.15
(116)	Jake Gibbs	.50	.25	.15
(117)	Russ Gibson	.50	.25	.15
(118)	Dave Giusti	.50	.25	.15
(119)	Fred Gladding	.50	.25	.15
(120)	Tony Gonzalez	.50	.25	.15
(121)	Jim Gosger	.50	.25	.15
(122)	James Grant	.50	.25	.15
(123)	Thomas Griffin	.50	.25	.15
(124)	Dick Green	.50	.25	.15
(125)	Jerry Grote	.50	.25	.15
(126)	Tom Hall	.50	.25	.15
(127)	Tom Haller	.50	.25	.15
(128)	Steve Hamilton	.50	.25	.15
(129)	William Hands	.50	.25	.15
(130)	James Hannan	.50	.25	.15
(131)	Ron Hansen	.50	.25	.15
(132)	Jim Hardin	.50	.25	.15
(133)	Steve Hargan	.50	.25	.15
(134)	Tommy Harper	.50	.25	.15
(135)	Bud Harrelson	.50	.25	.15
(136)	Ken Harrelson	.50	.25	.15
(137)	Jim Hart	.50	.25	.15
(138)	Rich Hebner	.50	.25	.15
(139)	Michael Hedlund	.50	.25	.15
(140)	Tommy Helms	.50	.25	.15
(141)	Elrod Hendricks	.50	.25	.15
(142)	Ronald Herbel	.50	.25	.15
(143)	Jack Hernandez	.50	.25	.15
(144)	Mike Hershberger	.50	.25	.15
(145)	Jack Hiatt	.50	.25	.15
(146)	Jim Hickman	.50	.25	.15
(147)	Dennis Higgins	.50	.25	.15
(148)	John Hiller	.50	.25	.15
(149)	Chuck Hinton	.50	.25	.15
(150)	Larry Hisle	.50	.25	.15
(151)	Ken Holtzman	.50	.25	.15
(152)	Joel Horlen	.50	.25	.15
(153)	Tony Horton	.50	.25	.15
(154)	Willie Horton	.50	.25	.15
(155)	Frank Howard	.75	.40	.25
(156)	Robert Humphreys	.50	.25	.15
(157)	Randy Hundley	.50	.25	.15
(158)	Ron Hunt	.50	.25	.15
(159)	Catfish Hunter	6.00	3.00	1.75
(160)	Grant Jackson	.50	.25	.15
(161)	Reggie Jackson	15.00	7.50	4.50
(162)	Sonny Jackson	.50	.25	.15

(163)	Pat Jarvis	.50	.25	.15
(164)	Larry Jaster	.50	.25	.15
(165)	Julian Javier	.50	.25	.15
(166)	Ferguson Jenkins	6.00	3.00	1.75
(167)	Tommy John	1.00	.50	.30
(168)	Alexander Johnson	.50	.25	.15
(169)	Bob Johnson	.50	.25	.15
(170)	Dave Johnson	.50	.25	.15
(171)	Deron Johnson	.50	.25	.15
(172)	Jay Johnstone	.50	.25	.15
(173)	Cleon Jones	.50	.25	.15
(174)	Dalton Jones	.50	.25	.15
(175)	Mack Jones	.50	.25	.15
(176)	Richard Joseph	.50	.25	.15
(177)	Duane Josephson	.50	.25	.15
(178)	Jim Kaat	2.00	1.00	.60
(179)	Al Kaline	12.50	6.25	3.75
(180)	Richard Kelley	.50	.25	.15
(181)	Harold Kelly	.50	.25	.15
(182)	Gerald Kenney	.50	.25	.15
(183)	Don Kessinger	.50	.25	.15
(184)	Harmon Killebrew	9.00	4.50	2.75
(185)	Ed Kirkpatrick	.50	.25	.15
(186)	Bobby Knoop	.50	.25	.15
(187)	Calvin Koonce	.50	.25	.15
(188)	Jerry Koosman	.50	.25	.15
(189)	Andy Kosco	.50	.25	.15
(190)	Ed Kranepool	.50	.25	.15
(191)	Ted Kubiak	.50	.25	.15
(192)	Jose Laboy	.50	.25	.15
(193)	Joseph Lahoud	.50	.25	.15
(194)	William Landis	.50	.25	.15
(195)	Harold Lanier	.50	.25	.15
(196)	Fred Lasher	.50	.25	.15
(197)	John Lazar	.50	.25	.15
(198)	Jim Lefebvre	.50	.25	.15
(199)	Denny Lemaster	.50	.25	.15
(200)	Dave Leonhard	.50	.25	.15
(201)	Frank Linzy	.50	.25	.15
(202)	Mickey Lolich	.50	.25	.15
(203)	Jim Lonborg	.50	.25	.15
(204)	Mike Lum	.50	.25	.15
(205)	Al Lyle	.50	.25	.15
(206)	Jim Maloney	.50	.25	.15
(207)	Juan Marichal	7.50	3.75	2.25
(208)	David Marshall	.50	.25	.15
(209)	J.C. Martin	.50	.25	.15
(210)	Marty Martinez	.50	.25	.15
(211)	Tom Matchick	.50	.25	.15
(212)	Dal Maxvill	.50	.25	.15
(213)	Carlos May	.50	.25	.15
(214)	Jerry May	.50	.25	.15
(215)	Lee May	.50	.25	.15
(216)	Lee Maye	.50	.25	.15
(217)	Willie Mays	25.00	12.50	7.50
(218)	Bill Mazeroski	9.00	4.50	2.75
(219)	Richard McAuliffe	.50	.25	.15
(220)	Al McBean	.50	.25	.15
(221)	Tim McCarver	.75	.40	.25
(222)	Bill McCool	.50	.25	.15
(223)	Mike McCormick	.50	.25	.15
(224)	Willie McCovey	9.00	4.50	2.75
(225)	Tom McCraw	.50	.25	.15
(226)	Lindy McDaniel	.50	.25	.15
(227)	Sam McDowell	.50	.25	.15
(228)	Leon McFadden	.50	.25	.15
(229)	Daniel McGinn	.50	.25	.15
(230)	Jim McGlothlin	.50	.25	.15
(231)	Fred McGraw	.50	.25	.15
(232)	Denny McLain	.75	.40	.25
(233)	Ken McMullen	.50	.25	.15
(234)	Dave McNally	.50	.25	.15
(235)	Gerry McNertney	.50	.25	.15
(236)	William Melton	.50	.25	.15
(237)	Dennis Menke (Denis)	.50	.25	.15
(238)	John Messersmith	.50	.25	.15
(239)	Felix Millan	.50	.25	.15
(240)	Norman Miller	.50	.25	.15
(241)	Don Mincher	.50	.25	.15
(242)	Rick Monday	.50	.25	.15
(243)	Donald Money	.50	.25	.15
(244)	Barry Moore	.50	.25	.15
(245)	Bob Moose	.50	.25	.15
(246)	David Morehead	.50	.25	.15
(247)	Joe Morgan	9.00	4.50	2.75
(248)	Curt Motton	.50	.25	.15
(249)	Manny Mota	.50	.25	.15
(250)	Bob Murcer	.50	.25	.15
(251)	Thomas Murphy	.50	.25	.15
(252)	Ivan Murrell	.50	.25	.15
(253)	Jim Nash	.50	.25	.15
(254)	Joe Niekro	1.25	.60	.40
(255)	Phil Niekro	6.00	3.00	1.75
(256)	Gary Nolan	.50	.25	.15
(257)	Jim Northrup	.50	.25	.15
(258)	Richard Nye	.50	.25	.15
(259)	Johnny Odom	.50	.25	.15
(260)	John O'Donaghue	.50	.25	.15
(261)	Tony Oliva	1.00	.50	.30
(262)	Al Oliver	1.00	.50	.30
(263)	Robert Oliver	.50	.25	.15
(264)	Claude Osteen	.50	.25	.15
(265)	Ray Oyler	.50	.25	.15
(266)	Jose Pagan	.50	.25	.15
(267)	Jim Palmer	9.00	4.50	2.75
(268)	Milt Pappas	.50	.25	.15
(269)	Wes Parker	.50	.25	.15
(270)	Fred Patek	.50	.25	.15
(271)	Mike Paul	.50	.25	.15
(272)	Joe Pepitone	.50	.25	.15
(273)	Tony Perez	7.50	3.75	2.25
(274)	Gaylord Perry	6.00	3.00	1.75
(275)	Jim Perry	.50	.25	.15
(276)	Gary Peters	.50	.25	.15
(277)	Rico Petrocelli	.50	.25	.15
(278)	Tom Phoebus	.50	.25	.15
(279)	Lou Piniella	1.00	.50	.30
(280)	Vada Pinson	1.50	.70	.45

(281)	Boog Powell	1.50	.70	.45
(282)	Jim Price	.50	.25	.15
(283)	Frank Quilici	.50	.25	.15
(284)	Doug Rader	.50	.25	.15
(285)	Ron Reed	.50	.25	.15
(286)	Rich Reese	.50	.25	.15
(287)	Phil Regan	.50	.25	.15
(288)	Rick Reichardt	.50	.25	.15
(289)	Rick Renick	.50	.25	.15
(290)	Roger Repoz	.50	.25	.15
(291)	Mervin Rettenmund	.50	.25	.15
(292)	Dave Ricketts	.50	.25	.15
(293)	Juan Rios	.50	.25	.15
(294)	Bill Robinson	.50	.25	.15
(295)	Brooks Robinson	12.50	6.25	3.75
(296)	Frank Robinson	12.50	6.25	3.75
(297)	Aurelio Rodriguez	.50	.25	.15
(298)	Ellie Rodriguez	.50	.25	.15
(299)	Cookie Rojas	.50	.25	.15
(300)	Rich Rollins	.50	.25	.15
(301)	Vicente Romo	.50	.25	.15
(302)	Phil Roof	.50	.25	.15
(303)	Pete Rose	25.00	12.50	7.50
(304)	John Roseboro	.50	.25	.15
(305)	Chico Ruiz	.50	.25	.15
(306)	Mike Ryan	.50	.25	.15
(307)	Ray Sadecki	.50	.25	.15
(308)	Chico Salmon	.50	.25	.15
(309)	Manuel Sanguillen	.50	.25	.15
(310)	Ron Santo	3.00	1.50	.90
(311)	Tom Satriano	.50	.25	.15
(312)	Theodore Savage	.50	.25	.15
(313)	Paul Schaal	.50	.25	.15
(314)	Dick Schofield	.50	.25	.15
(315)	George Scott	.50	.25	.15
(316)	Tom Seaver	12.50	6.25	3.75
(317)	Art Shamsky	.50	.25	.15
(318)	Mike Shannon	.50	.25	.15
(319)	Chris Short	.50	.25	.15
(320)	Sonny Siebert	.50	.25	.15
(321)	Duke Sims	.50	.25	.15
(322)	William Singer	.50	.25	.15
(323)	Reggie Smith	.50	.25	.15
(324)	Willie Smith	.50	.25	.15
(325)	Russ Snyder	.50	.25	.15
(326)	Al Spangler	.50	.25	.15
(327)	James Spencer	.50	.25	.15
(328)	Ed Spiezio	.50	.25	.15
(329)	Larry Stahl	.50	.25	.15
(330)	Lee Stange	.50	.25	.15
(331)	Mickey Stanley	.50	.25	.15
(332)	Willie Stargell	9.00	4.50	2.75
(333)	Rusty Staub	2.00	1.00	.60
(334)	James Stewart	.50	.25	.15
(335)	George Stone	.50	.25	.15
(336)	William Stoneman	.50	.25	.15
(337)	Mel Stottlemyre	.50	.25	.15
(338)	Ed Stroud	.50	.25	.15
(339)	Ken Suarez	.50	.25	.15
(340)	Gary Sutherland	.50	.25	.15
(341)	Don Sutton	6.00	3.00	1.75
(342)	Ron Swoboda	.50	.25	.15
(343)	Fred Talbot	.50	.25	.15
(344)	Jose Tartabull	.50	.25	.15
(345)	Kenneth Tatum	.50	.25	.15
(346)	Tony Taylor	.50	.25	.15
(347)	Luis Tiant	.75	.40	.25
(348)	Bob Tillman	.50	.25	.15
(349)	Bobby Tolan	.50	.25	.15
(350)	Jeff Torborg	.50	.25	.15
(351)	Joe Torre	3.00	1.50	.90
(352)	Cesar Tovar	.50	.25	.15
(353)	Tom Tresh	.75	.40	.25
(354)	Ted Uhlaender	.50	.25	.15
(355)	Del Unser	.50	.25	.15
(356)	Bob Veale	.50	.25	.15
(357)	Zoilo Versalles	.50	.25	.15
(358)	Luke Walker	.50	.25	.15
(359)	Pete Ward	.50	.25	.15
(360)	Eddie Watt	.50	.25	.15
(361)	Ramon Webster	.50	.25	.15
(362)	Al Weis	.50	.25	.15
(363)	Don Wert	.50	.25	.15
(364)	Bill White	.50	.25	.15
(365)	Roy White	.50	.25	.15
(366)	Hoyt Wilhelm	6.00	3.00	1.75
(367)	Billy Williams	9.00	4.50	2.75
(368)	Walter Williams	.50	.25	.15
(369)	Maury Wills	.75	.40	.25
(370)	Don Wilson	.50	.25	.15
(371)	Earl Wilson	.50	.25	.15
(372)	Robert Wine	.50	.25	.15
(373)	Richard Wise	.50	.25	.15
(374)	Wilbur Wood	.50	.25	.15
(375)	William Woodward	.50	.25	.15
(376)	Clyde Wright	.50	.25	.15
(377)	James Wynn	.50	.25	.15
(378)	Jerry Zimmerman	.50	.25	.15

1957 Milwaukee Braves Picture Pack

HENRY AARON, Outfielder

Prior to the Jay Publishing Co. photo packs which dominated the market from 1958-62, the Braves issued this souvenir stand picture pack of 5" x 7" black-and-white, blank-back, player pictures. In the wide bottom border player names are printed in all-caps with the position indicated in upper- and lower-case letters. The unnumbered pictures are listed here in alphabetical order.

		NM	EX	VG
Complete Set (12):		100.00	50.00	30.00
Common Player:		7.50	3.75	2.25
(1)	Hank Aaron	30.00	15.00	9.00
(2)	Joe Adcock	7.50	3.75	2.25
(3)	Lew Burdette	7.50	3.75	2.25
(4)	Wes Covington	7.50	3.75	2.25
(5)	Del Crandall	7.50	3.75	2.25
(6)	Bob Hazle	7.50	3.75	2.25
(7)	Johnny Logan	7.50	3.75	2.25
(8)	Edwin Mathews	12.50	6.25	3.75
(9)	Don McMahon	7.50	3.75	2.25
(10)	Andy Pafko	7.50	3.75	2.25
(11)	Red Schoendienst	10.00	5.00	3.00
(12)	Warren Spahn	12.50	6.25	3.75

1965 Milwaukee Braves Picture Pack

HANK AARON, Braves

These 4-7/8" x 7-1/8" blank-back, black-and-white pictures were sold in groups of 12 in a white paper window envelope and possibly also as a complete set of 24. Besides the slight size difference, the team-issued pictures differ from the contemporary Jay Publishing pictures in that the city name is not included in the typography in the bottom border.

		NM	EX	VG
Complete Set (24):		75.00	37.50	22.50
Common Player:		3.00	1.50	.90
(1)	Hank Aaron	15.00	7.50	4.50
(2)	Sandy Alomar	3.00	1.50	.90
(3)	Felipe Alou	3.00	1.50	.90
(4)	Wade Blasingame	3.00	1.50	.90
(5)	Frank Bolling	3.00	1.50	.90
(6)	Bobby Bragan	3.00	1.50	.90
(7)	Rico Carty	3.00	1.50	.90
(8)	Ty Cline	3.00	1.50	.90
(9)	Tony Cloninger	3.00	1.50	.90
(10)	Mike de la Hoz	3.00	1.50	.90
(11)	Hank Fischer	3.00	1.50	.90
(12)	Mack Jones	3.00	1.50	.90
(13)	Gary Kolb	3.00	1.50	.90
(14)	Denny LeMaster	3.00	1.50	.90
(15)	Eddie Mathews	6.00	3.00	1.75
(16)	Lee Maye	3.00	1.50	.90
(17)	Denis Menke	3.00	1.50	.90
(18)	Billy O'Dell	3.00	1.50	.90
(19)	Gene Oliver	3.00	1.50	.90
(20)	Chi Chi Olivo	3.00	1.50	.90
(21)	Dan Osinki (Osinski)	3.00	1.50	.90
(22)	Bob Sadowski	3.00	1.50	.90
(23)	Bobby Tiefenauer	3.00	1.50	.90
(24)	Joe Torre	4.50	2.25	1.25

1980 Milwaukee Brewers/Pepsi Fan Club

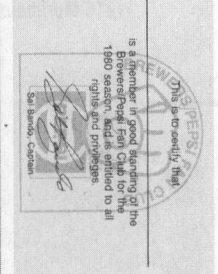

Star Milwaukee infielder Sal Bando is featured on this 2-1/2" x 3-1/2" membership card in a blue-bordered action pose. The back is printed in blue on white with both the team and soda logo.

	NM	EX	VG
Sal Bando	6.00	3.00	1.80

1912 Miner's Extra Series of Champions (T227)

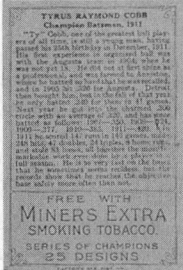

(See 1912 T227 Series of Champions for checklist, price guide.)

1977 Minneapolis Star Twins Scrapbook

Between July 4-August 12, the Star printed one player "Scrapbook" picture each day in the sports section. While sizes vary somewhat, most are about 4-3/16" x 10-3/16". Enclosed in a dotted-line border are a player portrait photo, facsimile autograph, position, uniform number, team logo, career highlights and full stats. Because they are printed on newsprint, the pictures are subject to rapid deterioration.

		NM	EX	VG
Complete Set (36):		100.00	50.00	30.00
Common Player:		4.00	2.00	1.25
7/4	Rod Carew	12.00	6.00	3.50
7/5	Geoff Zahn	4.00	2.00	1.25
7/6	Luis Gomez	4.00	2.00	1.25
7/7	Glenn Adams	4.00	2.00	1.25
7/8	Lyman Bostock	6.00	3.00	1.75
7/9	Bob Gorinski	4.00	2.00	1.25
7/11	Butch Wynegar	4.00	2.00	1.25
7/12	Rob Wilfong	4.00	2.00	1.25
7/13	Dave Goltz	4.00	2.00	1.25
7/14	Bill Butler	4.00	2.00	1.25
7/15	Bob Randall	4.00	2.00	1.25
7/16	Jeff Holly	4.00	2.00	1.25
7/18	Gene Mauch	4.00	2.00	1.25
7/19	Walt Terrell	4.00	2.00	1.25
7/20	Rich Chiles	4.00	2.00	1.25
7/21	Paul Thormodsgard	4.00	2.00	1.25
7/22	Dave Johnson	4.00	2.00	1.25
7/23	Mike Cubbage	4.00	2.00	1.25
7/25	Larry Hisle	4.00	2.00	1.25
7/26	Don McMahon	4.00	2.00	1.25
7/27	Glenn Borgmann	4.00	2.00	1.25
7/28	Craig Kusick	4.00	2.00	1.25
7/29	Ron Schueler	4.00	2.00	1.25
7/30	Karl Kuehl	4.00	2.00	1.25
8/1	Roy Smalley	4.00	2.00	1.25
8/2	Tony Oliva	7.50	3.75	2.25
8/3	Jerry Zimmerman	4.00	2.00	1.25
8/4	Dan Ford	4.00	2.00	1.25
8/5	Don Carrithers	4.00	2.00	1.25
8/6	Tom Johnson	4.00	2.00	1.25
8/8	Pete Redfern	4.00	2.00	1.25
8/9	Tom Burgmeier	4.00	2.00	1.25
8/10	Bud Bulling	4.00	2.00	1.25
8/11	Gary Serum	4.00	2.00	1.25
8/12	Calvin Griffith	4.00	2.00	1.25

1977-78 Minnesota Twins Team Issue

Produced by collector Barry Fritz, and sold by the team through its normal concession outlets, this set consists of two 25-card series. Cards 1-25 were issued in 1977; cards 26-50 in 1978. Measuring 2-5/8" x 3-3/4", card fronts feature quality color player poses with no other graphics. Backs are in black-and-white and have all player data, stats with the Twins and overall major league numbers, plus career highlights. Besides being sold as sets, the cards were also offered in uncut sheet form.

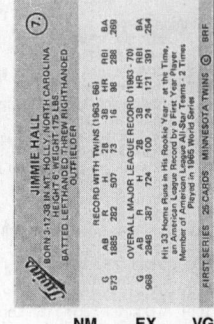

		NM	EX	VG
Complete Set (50):		35.00	17.50	10.00
Common Player:				
1	Bob Allison	1.00	.50	.30
2	Earl Battey	1.00	.50	.30
3	Dave Boswell	1.00	.50	.30
4	Dean Chance	1.25	.60	.40
5	Jim Grant	1.25	.60	.40
6	Calvin Griffith	1.25	.60	.40
7	Jimmie Hall	1.00	.50	.30
8	Harmon Killebrew	6.00	3.00	1.75
9	Jim Lemon	1.00	.50	.30
10	Billy Martin	3.00	1.50	.90
11	Gene Mauch	1.00	.50	.30
12	Sam Mele	1.00	.50	.30
13	Metropolitan Stadium	1.50	.70	.45
14	Don Mincher	1.00	.50	.30
15	Tony Oliva	3.00	1.50	.90
16	Camilo Pascual	1.25	.60	.40
17	Jim Perry	1.25	.60	.40
18	Frank Quilici	1.00	.50	.30
19	Rich Reese	1.00	.50	.30
20	Bill Rigney	1.00	.50	.30
21	Cesar Tovar	1.00	.50	.30
22	Zoilo Versalles	1.00	.50	.30
23	Al Worthington	1.00	.50	.30
24	Jerry Zimmerman	1.00	.50	.30
25	Checklist / Souvenir List	1.00	.50	.30
26	Bernie Allen	1.00	.50	.30
27	Leo Cardenas	1.00	.50	.30
28	Ray Corbin	1.00	.50	.30
29	Joe Decker	1.00	.50	.30
30	Johnny Goryl	1.00	.50	.30
31	Tom Hall	1.00	.50	.30
32	Bill Hands	1.00	.50	.30
33	Jim Holt	1.00	.50	.30
34	Randy Hundley	1.00	.50	.30
35	Jerry Kindall	1.00	.50	.30
36	Johnny Klippstein	1.00	.50	.30
37	Jack Kralick	1.00	.50	.30
38	Jim Merritt	1.00	.50	.30
39	Joe Nossek	1.00	.50	.30
40	Ron Perranoski	1.00	.50	.30
41	Bill Pleis	1.00	.50	.30
42	Rick Renick	1.00	.50	.30
43	Jim Roland	1.00	.50	.30
44	Lee Stange	1.00	.50	.30
45	Dick Stigman	1.00	.50	.30
46	Danny Thompson	1.00	.50	.30
47	Ted Uhlaender	1.00	.50	.30
48	Sandy Valdespino	1.00	.50	.30
49	Dick Woodson	1.00	.50	.30
50	Checklist #26-50	1.00	.50	.30

1911-16 Mino Cigarettes (T216)

Wagner, 2b. Pittsburgh Nat'l

The T216 baseball card set, issued by several brands of the Peoples Tobacco Co., is the last of the Louisiana cigarette sets and the most confusing. Apparently issued over a period of several years between 1911 and 1916, the set employs the same pictures as several contemporary caramel and bakery sets. Positive identification can be made by the back of the cards. The Peoples Tobacco cards carry advertising for one of three brands of cigarettes: Kotton, Mino or Virginia Extra. The Kotton brand is the most common, while the Virginia Extra and Mino backs command a premium. T216 cards are found in two types; one has a glossy front finish, while a second scarcer type is printed on a thin paper. The thin paper cards command an additional 15% premium. The cards represent players from the American, National and Federal Leagues. Cards measure a nominal 1-1/2" x 2-5/8", though reasonable allowance for variance must be made on consideration of cutting.

		NM	EX	VG
	Common Player:	1,920	870.00	480.00
(1)	Jack Barry/Btg	1,920	870.00	480.00
(2)	Jack Barry/Fldg	1,920	870.00	480.00
(3)	Harry Bemis	1,920	870.00	480.00
(4a)	Chief Bender (Philadelphia, striped cap.)	4,200	1,890	1,050
(4b)	Chief Bender (Baltimore, striped cap.)	4,200	1,890	1,050
(5a)	Chief Bender (Philadelphia, white cap.)	4,200	1,890	1,050
(5b)	Chief Bender (Baltimore, white cap.)	4,200	1,890	1,050
(6)	Bill Bergen	1,920	870.00	480.00
(7a)	Bob Bescher (Cincinnati)	1,920	870.00	480.00
(7b)	Bob Bescher (St. Louis)	1,920	870.00	480.00
(8)	Roger Bresnahan	4,200	1,890	1,050
(9)	Al Bridwell/Btg	1,920	870.00	480.00
(10a)	Al Bridwell/Sliding (New York)	1,920	870.00	480.00
(10b)	Al Bridwell/Sliding (St. Louis)	1,920	870.00	480.00
(11)	Donie Bush	1,920	870.00	480.00
(12)	Doc Casey	1,920	870.00	480.00
(13)	Frank Chance	4,200	1,890	1,050
(14a)	Hal Chase/Fldg (New York)	1,920	870.00	480.00
(14b)	Hal Chase/Fldg (Buffalo)	1,920	870.00	480.00
(15)	Hal Chase/Portrait	1,920	870.00	480.00
(16a)	Ty Cobb/Standing (Detroit Am.)	40,000	20,000	12,000
(16b)	Ty Cobb/Standing (Detroit Am.)	40,000	20,000	12,000
(17)	Ty Cobb/Btg (Detroit Am.)	40,000	20,000	12,000
(18a)	Eddie Collins (Phila. Am.)	4,200	1,890	1,050
(18b)	Eddie Collins (Phila. Amer.)	4,200	1,890	1,050
(19)	Eddie Collins (Chicago)	4,200	1,890	1,050
(20a)	Sam Crawford (Small print.)	4,200	1,890	1,050
(20b)	Sam Crawford (Large print.)	4,200	1,890	1,050
(21)	Harry Davis	1,920	870.00	480.00
(22)	Ray Demmitt	1,920	870.00	480.00
(23)	Art Devlin	1,920	870.00	480.00
(24a)	Wild Bill Donovan (Detroit)	1,920	870.00	480.00
(24b)	Wild Bill Donovan (New York)	1,920	870.00	480.00
(25a)	Red Dooin (Philadelphia)	1,920	870.00	480.00
(25b)	Red Dooin (Cincinnati)	1,920	870.00	480.00
(26a)	Mickey Doolan (Philadelphia)	1,920	870.00	480.00
(26b)	Mickey Doolan (Baltimore)	1,920	870.00	480.00
(27)	Patsy Dougherty	1,920	870.00	480.00
(28a)	Larry Doyle (N.Y. Nat'l,)(W/bat.)	1,920	870.00	480.00
(28b)	Larry Doyle (New York Nat'l)(W/bat.)	1,920	870.00	480.00
(29)	Larry Doyle/Throwing	1,920	870.00	480.00
(30)	Clyde Engle	1,920	870.00	480.00
(31a)	Johnny Evers (Chicago)	4,200	1,890	1,050
(31b)	Johnny Evers (Boston)	4,200	1,890	1,050
(32)	Art Fromme	1,920	870.00	480.00
(33a)	George Gibson (Pittsburg Nat'l., back view.)	1,920	870.00	480.00
(33b)	George Gibson (Pittsburg Nat'l., back view.)	1,920	870.00	480.00
(34a)	George Gibson (Pittsburg Nat'l., front view.)	1,920	870.00	480.00
(34b)	George Gibson (Pittsburg Nat'l., front view.)	1,920	870.00	480.00
(35a)	Topsy Hartsel (Phila. Am.)	1,920	870.00	480.00
(35b)	Topsy Hartsel (Phila. Amer.)	1,920	870.00	480.00
(36)	Roy Hartzell/Btg	1,920	870.00	480.00
(37)	Roy Hartzell/Catching	1,920	870.00	480.00
(38a)	Fred Jacklitsch (Philadelphia)	1,920	870.00	480.00
(38b)	Fred Jacklitsch (Baltimore)	1,920	870.00	480.00
(39a)	Hughie Jennings (Orange background.)	4,200	1,890	1,050
(39b)	Hughie Jennings (Red background.)	4,200	1,890	1,050
(40)	Red Kleinow	1,920	870.00	480.00
(41a)	Otto Knabe (Philadelphia)	1,920	870.00	480.00
(41b)	Otto Knabe (Baltimore)	1,920	870.00	480.00
(42)	Jack Knight	1,920	870.00	480.00
(43a)	Nap Lajoie/Fldg (Philadelphia)	4,800	2,160	1,200
(43b)	Nap Lajoie/Fldg (Cleveland)	4,800	2,160	1,200
(44)	Nap Lajoie/Portrait	4,800	2,160	1,200
(45a)	Hans Lobert (Cincinnati)	1,920	870.00	480.00
(45b)	Hans Lobert (New York)	1,920	870.00	480.00
(46)	Sherry Magee	1,920	870.00	480.00
(47)	Rube Marquard	4,200	1,890	1,050
(48a)	Christy Matthewson (Mathewson) (Large print.)	20,000	10,000	6,000
(48b)	Christy Matthewson (Mathewson) (Small print.)	20,000	10,000	6,000
(49a)	John McGraw (Large print.)	4,200	1,890	1,050
(49b)	John McGraw (Small print.)	4,200	1,890	1,050
(50)	Larry McLean	1,920	870.00	480.00
(51)	George McQuillan	1,920	870.00	480.00
(52)	Dots Miller/Btg	1,920	870.00	480.00
(53a)	Dots Miller/Fldg (Pittsburg)	1,920	870.00	480.00
(53b)	Dots Miller/Fldg (St. Louis)	1,920	870.00	480.00
(54a)	Danny Murphy (Philadelphia)	1,920	870.00	480.00
(54b)	Danny Murphy (Brooklyn)	1,920	870.00	480.00
(55)	Rebel Oakes	1,920	870.00	480.00
(56)	Bill O'Hara	1,920	870.00	480.00
(57)	Eddie Plank	5,400	2,430	1,350
(58a)	Germany Schaefer (Washington)	1,920	870.00	480.00
(58b)	Germany Schaefer (Newark)	1,920	870.00	480.00
(59)	Admiral Schlei	1,920	870.00	480.00
(60)	Boss Schmidt	1,920	870.00	480.00
(61)	Johnny Seigle	1,920	870.00	480.00
(62)	Dave Shean	1,920	870.00	480.00
(63)	Boss Smith (Schmidt)	1,920	870.00	480.00
(64)	Tris Speaker	7,800	3,510	1,950
(65)	Oscar Stanage	1,920	870.00	480.00
(66)	George Stovall	1,920	870.00	480.00
(67)	Jeff Sweeney	1,920	870.00	480.00

		NM	EX	VG
(68a)	Joe Tinker/Btg (Chicago Nat'l)	4,200	1,890	1,050
(68b)	Joe Tinker/Btg (Chicago Feds)	4,200	1,890	1,050
(69)	Joe Tinker/Portrait	4,200	1,890	1,050
(70a)	Honus Wagner/Btg (S.S.)	35,000	17,500	10,500
(70b)	Honus Wagner/Btg (2b.)	35,000	17,500	10,500
(71a)	Honus Wagner/Throwing (S.S.)	35,000	17,500	10,500
(71b)	Honus Wagner/Throwing (2b.)	35,000	17,500	10,500
(72)	Hooks Wiltse	1,920	870.00	480.00
(73)	Cy Young	15,000	6,750	3,750
(74a)	Heinie Zimmerman (2b.)	1,920	870.00	480.00
(74b)	Heinie Zimmerman (3b.)	1,920	870.00	480.00

1962 Molinari's Restaurant Frank Malzone

This black-and-white J.D. McCarthy postcard of the former Red Sox infielder was given to patrons of an Oneonta, N.Y., restaurant in which Malzone was a partner with his brother-in-law. The card measures 3-1/4" x 5-1/2" and has a facsimile autograph on front. A similar promotional postcard is listed under Ticoa Tires.

	NM	EX	VG
Frank Malzone	15.00	7.50	4.50

1911 Monarch Typewriter Philadelphia A's

 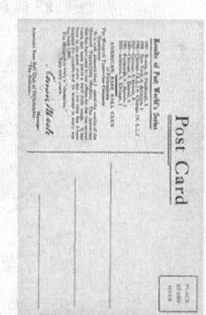

These black-and-white postcards (about 3-1/2" x 5") depict the World Champion 1910 Philadelphia A's. Fronts have posed player photos with a black pin stripe and white borders. The player's name and position are printed in the bottom border. "Compliments of THE MONARCH TYPEWRITER COMPANY" appears in the top border. Backs are rather standard postcard fare, but include data on the World Series between 1903-1910.

		NM	EX	VG
Complete Set (6):		14,000	7,000	4,200
Common Player:		2,000	1,000	600.00
(1)	John J. Barry	2,000	1,000	600.00
(2)	Chief Bender	2,750	1,400	850.00
(3)	Eddie Collins	2,750	1,400	850.00
(4)	Rube Oldring	2,000	1,000	600.00
(5)	Eddie Plank	2,750	1,400	850.00
(6)	Ira Thomas	2,000	1,000	600.00

1948 Montreal Royals Team-Issue Photos

It is unknown for what purpose these 5" x 7" blank-back black-and-white photos were produced for the 1948 Montreal Royals, champions of the International League that season. Without player identification or facsimile autographs, they likely weren't a concession stand souvenir picture pack, but may have been used for media and promotional purposes. It is unknown whether the checklist here is complete.

		NM	EX	VG
(1)	Jack Banta	20.00	12.00	6.00
(2)	Chuck Connors	50.00	30.00	15.00
(3)	Cliff Dapper	20.00	12.00	6.00
(4)	Al Gianfriddo	30.00	18.00	9.00
(5)	Oscar Grimes	20.00	12.00	6.00
(6)	Clay Hopper	20.00	12.00	6.00
(7)	Sam Jethroe	30.00	18.00	9.00
(8)	Clyde King	20.00	12.00	6.00
(9)	Frank Laga	20.00	12.00	6.00
(10)	Gene Mauch	30.00	18.00	9.00
(11)	Bobby Morgan	20.00	12.00	6.00
(12)	Don Newcombe	50.00	30.00	15.00
(13)	Bud Podbielan	20.00	12.00	6.00
(14)	Mike Sandlock	20.00	12.00	6.00
(15)	John Simmons	20.00	12.00	6.00
(16)	Duke Snider	100.00	60.00	30.00
(17)	Louis Welaj	20.00	12.00	6.00

1970 Montreal Expos Player Pins

Produced by "Best in Sports" for sale in the Montreal area for 35¢ apiece, these 1-3/4" diameter pinbacks feature action poses of the players set against a white background. The player's name at top is in black.

		NM	EX	VG
Complete Set (16):		350.00	175.00	100.00
Common Player:		25.00	12.50	7.50
(1)	John Bateman	25.00	12.50	7.50
(2)	Ron Brand	25.00	12.50	7.50
(3)	Ron Fairly	25.00	12.50	7.50
(4)	Mack Jones	25.00	12.50	7.50
(5)	Coco Laboy	25.00	12.50	7.50
(6)	Gene Mauch	25.00	12.50	7.50
(7)	Dan McGinn	25.00	12.50	7.50
(8)	Adolfo Phillips	25.00	12.50	7.50
(9)	Claude Raymond	25.00	12.50	7.50
(10)	Steve Renko	25.00	12.50	7.50
(11)	Marv Staehle	25.00	12.50	7.50
(12)	Rusty Staub	40.00	20.00	12.00
(13)	Bill Stoneman	25.00	12.50	7.50
(14)	Gary Sutherland	25.00	12.50	7.50
(15)	Bobby Wine	25.00	12.50	7.50
(16)	Expos team logo	10.00	5.00	3.00

1972-76 Montreal Expos Matchbook Covers

In 1972, 1973 and 1976, the Eddy Match Co., Montreal, issued series of seven matchbook covers featuring action photos. Fronts have a red, white and blue team logo on a white background. Backs have a bluetone action photo with the match-striking surface across the lower portion. The player in the photo is not identified on the matchbook. Inside of the 2-1/8" x 4-3/8" cover, printed in blue, is the team home schedule for that season. The unnumbered matchbook covers are checklisted here alphabetically by year. Values shown are for empty matchbooks; full matchbooks would be valued at 2-3X.

		NM	EX	VG
Complete Set (21):		40.00	20.00	12.00
Common Player:		4.00	2.00	1.25
1972				
(1)	Boots Day	4.00	2.00	1.25
(2)	Ron Fairly	4.00	2.00	1.25
(3)	Ron Hunt	4.00	2.00	1.25
(4)	Steve Renko	4.00	2.00	1.25
(5)	Rusty Staub	6.00	3.00	1.75
(6)	Bobby Wine	4.00	2.00	1.25
(7)	Hunt's 50th HBP (Scoreboard)	4.00	2.00	1.25
1973				
(1)	Tim Foli	4.00	2.00	1.25
(2)	Ron Hunt	4.00	2.00	1.25
(3)	Mike Jorgensen	4.00	2.00	1.25
(4)	Gene Mauch	4.00	2.00	1.25
(5)	Balor Moore	4.00	2.00	1.25
(6)	Ken Singleton	4.00	2.00	1.25
(7)	Bill Stoneman	4.00	2.00	1.25
1976				
(1)	Barry Foote	4.00	2.00	1.25
(2)	Mike Jorgensen	4.00	2.00	1.25
(3)	Pete Mackanin	4.00	2.00	1.25
(4)	Dale Murray	4.00	2.00	1.25
(5)	Larry Parrish	4.00	2.00	1.25
(6)	Steve Rogers	4.00	2.00	1.25
(7)	Dan Warthen	4.00	2.00	1.25

1916 Morehouse Baking Co.

BOYS and GIRLS

Here's your chance to get a complete set of 200 of the Best Ball Players in the Big Leagues. These photos will be wrapped in SUNLIGHT 10c BREAD When you get fifty, with no two alike, you may keep the photos but show them at our office and get a Dandy baseball bat, or a nice long jumprope FREE

MOREHOUSE BAKING CO.

OFFICE 7 MILL STREET LAWRENCE : MASS.

While this 200-card set is most often found with blank backs or with the advertising of "The Sporting News" on the back, a number of scarcer regional advertisers also can be found. This Massachusetts baker inserted the cards into bread loaves and offered a redemption program. Since cards are known that correspond to both versions of the parent M101 Blank Backs, it not known whether the bakery's version parallels M101-4 and M101-5 or is a hybrid of the two.

PREMIUM: 2-4X
(See 1916 M101-4 and M101-5 Blank Backs for checklist and price guide.)

1907 Morgan Stationery "Red Belt" Postcards

Only one player is individually identified in this series of postcards, though the identities of others have been discovered over the years. The 3-1/2" x 5-1/2" cards have colorized player and group photos on front with a title printed in white in the lower-left corner. Some photos were taken at the Reds ballpark, then known as the Palace of Fans. Cards include pictures of Reds and Pirates of the National League, and Toledo of the minors. Many of the players have bright red belts, thus the set's nickname. Postcard backs have a credit line: "The Morgan Stationery Co., Cincinnati, O., Publishers." The unnumbered cards are checklisted here alphabetically by title.

		NM	EX	VG
Complete Set (12):		3,250	1,625	950.00
Common Card:		275.00	135.00	80.00
(1)	After A High One	275.00	135.00	80.00
(2)	A Home Run	275.00	135.00	80.00
(3)	Hit & Run	275.00	135.00	80.00
(4)	In Consultation	275.00	135.00	80.00
(5)	It's All in the Game - "Noise"	275.00	135.00	80.00
(6)	Huggins Second Baseman Par Excellence (Miller Huggins) (Stadium background.)	325.00	160.00	95.00
(7)	Huggins Second Baseman Par Excellance (Miller Huggins) (Low buildings in background.)	325.00	160.00	95.00
(8)	Opening of the Season 1907	275.00	135.00	80.00
(9)	Out to the Long Green	275.00	135.00	80.00
(10)	Practise (Practice) Makes Perfect (Sam Leever)	275.00	135.00	80.00
(11)	Safe	275.00	135.00	80.00
(12)	Use Two If Necessary (Hans Lobert)	275.00	135.00	80.00

1959 Morrell Meats Dodgers

This set of Los Angeles Dodgers was the first issue of a three-year run for the Southern California meat company. The 12 cards in this 2-1/2" x 3-1/2" set are unnumbered and feature full-frame, unbordered color photos. Card backs feature a company ad and list only the player's name, birthdate and birthplace. Two errors exist in the set; the cards naming Clem Labine and Norm Larker show photos of Stan Williams and Joe Pignatano, respectively.

		NM	EX	VG
Complete Set (12):		3,500	1,750	1,000
Common Player:		100.00	50.00	30.00
(1)	Don Drysdale	200.00	100.00	60.00
(2)	Carl Furillo	150.00	75.00	45.00
(3)	Jim Gilliam	125.00	60.00	35.00
(4)	Gil Hodges	200.00	100.00	60.00
(5)	Sandy Koufax	2,000	1,000	600.00
(6)	Clem Labine (Photo actually Stan Williams.)	100.00	50.00	30.00

(7)	Norm Larker (Photo actually Joe Pignatano.)	100.00	50.00	30.00
(8)	Charlie Neal	100.00	50.00	30.00
(9)	Johnny Podres	125.00	60.00	35.00
(10)	John Roseboro	100.00	50.00	30.00
(11)	Duke Snider	200.00	100.00	60.00
(12)	Don Zimmer	125.00	60.00	35.00

1960 Morrell Meats Dodgers

This 12-card set is the same 2-1/2" x 3-1/2" size as the 1959 set, and again features unbordered color card fronts. Five of the players included are new to the Morrell's sets. Card backs in 1960 list player statistics and brief personal data on each player. Cards of Gil Hodges, Carl Furillo and Duke Snider are apparently scarcer than others in the set.

		NM	EX	VG
Complete Set (12):		2,200	1,100	650.00
Common Player:		80.00	40.00	24.00
(1)	Walt Alston	90.00	45.00	27.50
(2)	Roger Craig	80.00	40.00	24.00
(3)	Don Drysdale	120.00	60.00	35.00
(4)	Carl Furillo	225.00	110.00	65.00
(5)	Gil Hodges	400.00	200.00	120.00
(6)	Sandy Koufax	500.00	250.00	150.00
(7)	Wally Moon	80.00	40.00	24.00
(8)	Charlie Neal	80.00	40.00	24.00
(9)	Johnny Podres	80.00	40.00	24.00
(10)	John Roseboro	80.00	40.00	24.00
(11)	Larry Sherry	80.00	40.00	24.00
(12)	Duke Snider	450.00	225.00	135.00

1961 Morrell Meats Dodgers

The Morrell set shrunk to just six cards in 1961, with a format almost identical to the 1960 cards. Card fronts are again full-color, unbordered photos. Player statistics appear on the backs. The unnumbered cards measure a slightly smaller 2-1/4" x 3-1/4", and comparison of statistical information can also distinguish the cards from the 1960 version.

		NM	EX	VG
Complete Set (6):		900.00	450.00	275.00
Common Player:		90.00	45.00	27.50
(1)	Tommy Davis	90.00	45.00	27.50
(2)	Don Drysdale	120.00	60.00	36.00
(3)	Frank Howard	90.00	45.00	27.50
(4)	Sandy Koufax	450.00	225.00	135.00
(5)	Norm Larker	90.00	45.00	27.50
(6)	Maury Wills	90.00	45.00	27.00

1910 Morton's Buster Brown Bread Tigers Pins (PD2)

Dating of these two issues is arbitrary, since there is no indication on the pins of vintage. Both sets feature members of the Detroit Tigers, American League champions of 1907-09. The Buster Brown Bread pins measure 1-1/4" in diameter and have a small black-and-white player portrait photo surrounded by a yellow border. Artwork to the left depicts Buster

Brown with a tiger holding a blue banner with the Morton's name. The player photos carry no identification, which may make the checklist presented here somewhat tentative. Some collectors feel the pin identified as Jimmy Archer is actually Jim Delahanty."

		NM	EX	VG
Complete Set (15):		10,000	5,000	3,000
Common Player:		450.00	225.00	135.00
(1)	Jimmy Archer	450.00	225.00	135.00
(2)	Heinie Beckendorf	450.00	225.00	135.00
(3)	Donie Bush	450.00	225.00	135.00
(4)	Ty Cobb	4,000	2,000	1,200
(5)	Sam Crawford	750.00	375.00	225.00
(6)	Wild Bill Donovan	450.00	225.00	135.00
(7)	Hughie Jennings	750.00	375.00	225.00
(8)	Tom Jones	450.00	225.00	135.00
(9)	Red Killefer	450.00	225.00	135.00
(10)	George Moriarty	450.00	225.00	135.00
(11)	George Mullin	450.00	225.00	135.00
(12)	Claude Rossman	450.00	225.00	135.00
(13)	"Germany" Schaefer	450.00	225.00	135.00
(14)	Ed Summers	450.00	225.00	135.00
(15)	Ed Willett	450.00	225.00	135.00

1910 Morton's Pennant Winner Bread Tigers Pins

The American League champion Detroit Tigers (1907-1909) are featured on this set of pins advertising -- appropriately -- Pennant Winner Bread. The 1-1/4" pins have black-and-white player photos surrounded by a yellow border. A Detroit banner with tiger head superimposed is at bottom. The players are not identified anywhere on the pins, which may make this checklist somewhat arbitrary.

		NM	EX	VG
Complete Set (16):		12,000	6,000	3,500
Common Player:		500.00	250.00	150.00
(1)	Jimmy Archer	500.00	250.00	150.00
(2)	Heinie Beckendorf	500.00	250.00	150.00
(3)	Donie Bush	500.00	250.00	150.00
(4)	Ty Cobb	4,000	2,000	1,200
(5)	Sam Crawford	750.00	375.00	225.00
(6)	Wild Bill Donovan	500.00	250.00	150.00
(7)	Hughie Jennings	750.00	375.00	225.00
(8)	Davy Jones	500.00	250.00	150.00
(9)	Matty McIntyre	500.00	250.00	150.00
(10)	George Moriarty	500.00	250.00	150.00
(11)	George Mullin	500.00	250.00	150.00
(12)	Claude Rossman	500.00	250.00	150.00
(13)	Herman Schaeffer (Schaefer)	500.00	250.00	150.00
(14)	Charles Schmidt	500.00	250.00	150.00
(15)	Ed Summers	500.00	250.00	150.00
(16)	Ed Willett	500.00	250.00	150.00

1916 Mothers' Bread (D303)

Apparently issued in 1916 by the New Orleans branch of the General Baking Co., these unnumbered cards measure 1-1/2" x 2-3/4". The player pictures and format of the cards are identical to the 1915 American Caramel (E106) and 1914 General Baking Co. (D303) sets, but this issue carries an advertisement for Mothers' Bread on back. This version is much scarcer than the General Baking or American Caramel types. It is known that at least one player appears in this set who is not found in E106/D303 and many players are found with team, league and postion changes. The checklist here is incomplete and additions are welcome. Gaps have been left in the assigned numbering for future additions.

Common Player:	NM	EX	VG
(1)	Chief Bender (Brooklyn Nat'l.)	2,500 6,000	1,500 2,700	900.00 1,500
(2)	Bob Bescher (St. Louis Nat'l)	2,500	1,500	900.00
(3)	Rube Bressler (Phila. Am.)	2,500	1,500	900.00
(4)	Donie Bush (Detroit American)	2,500	1,500	900.00
(5)	Hal Chase/Portrait (Cincinnati Nat'l.)	3,900	1,750	950.00
(6)	Bill Donovan (N.Y. Amer.)	2,500	1,500	900.00
(7)	Larry Doyle (N.Y. Nat'l)	2,500	1,500	900.00
(8)	Happy Felsch (Chicago Am.) (Picture actually Ray Demmitt.)	7,500	3,375	1,875
(9)	George Gibson (Front view)	2,500	1,500	900.00
(11)	Roy Hartzell	2,500	1,500	900.00
(15)	Nap Lajoie (Phila. Americans)	6,000	2,700	1,500
(16)	Hans Lobert (New York Nat'l)	2,500	1,500	900.00
(17)	William Louden (Cincinnati Nat'l)(Picture is Otto Knabe.)	2,500	1,500	900.00
(20)	Rube Marquard (Brooklyn Nat'l)	6,000	2,700	1,500
(21)	Christy Matthewson (Mathewson)	15,000	8,000	5,000
(22)	Billy Meyer (Phila. Am.) (Picture is Fred Jacklitsch.)	2,500	1,500	900.00
(24)	Ray Morgan (Washington Am.) (Picture is Mike Doolan.)	2,500	1,500	900.00
(26)	Eddie Plank (St. Louis Am.)	12,000	6,000	3,500
(28)	Tris Speaker (Cleveland Am.)	8,000	4,000	2,000
(30)	Joe Tinker/Portrait (Mgr. Chicago Am.)	6,000	2,700	1,500
(33)	Honus Wagner/Btg	45,000	22,000	13,500
(35)	Buck Weaver/Btg (Picture is Joe Tinker.)	8,500	4,250	2,550

1920-21 Mother's Bread

Essentially a version of the W514 strip cards with an advertisement on the back, the Mother's Bread cards are much scarcer than the blank-backs with which they share a checklist. The cards are 1-1/2" x 2-1/2" with color drawings of the players on front, along with name, position, team, league and card number.

(See 1920-21 W514 for checklist.)
PREMIUM: 5-7X

1955 Motorola Bob Feller Premium Photo

Dating of this promotional photo is approximate, based on the uniform details. The 8" x 10" glossy black-and-white photo features a facsimile autograph. Feller is described on the picture as "CONSULTANT ON YOUTH ACTIVITIES" for Motorola, Inc. The picture is blank-backed and its method of distribution is unknown.

	NM	EX	VG
Bob Feller	60.00	30.00	18.00

1976 Motorola

This set of (mostly) Hall of Famers was issued in conjunction with the annual convention of Motorola electronics dealers. Cards were issued singly in a wax wrapper with a piece of bubblegum. Sepia player photos are featured in an oval at center. Player identification and a career highlight are in the white frame around the photo. A sales message appears in a white box at bottom. Overall borders are rust colored. Backs have information about various Motorola products.

	NM	EX	VG
Complete Set (11):	25.00	12.50	7.50
Common Player:	2.50	1.25	.70
1 Honus Wagner	4.00	2.00	1.25
2 Nap Lajoie	2.50	1.25	.70
3 Ty Cobb	7.50	3.75	2.25
4 William Wambsganss	2.50	1.25	.70
5 Three Finger Brown	2.50	1.25	.70
6 Ray Schalk	2.50	1.25	.70
7 Frank Frisch	2.50	1.25	.70
8 Pud Galvin	2.50	1.25	.70
9 Babe Ruth	15.00	7.50	4.50
10 Grover Cleveland Alexander	3.00	1.50	.90
11 Frank L. Chance	2.50	1.25	.70

1931-32 Movie Exhibits (W412-7)

A series of postcard-back Exhibits related to Western movies was listed in the American Card Catalog as W412-7. Because of the subjects depicted, the set can be dated to 1931-32. In the standard 3-3/8" x 5-3/8" format, each card is found in a number of different color tints on fronts. Among the subjects in the set is Jim Thorpe, who appeared in a number of Grade B Western movies in the early 1930s. The same pictures used on the Exhibit cards can be found on a set of smaller cards, in which format they are much scarcer.

	NM	EX	VG
Jim Thorpe	1,000	500.00	300.00

1943 M.P. & Co. (R302-1)

One of the few baseball card sets issued during World War II, this set of unnumbered cards, measuring approximately 2-5/8" x 2-1/4" was produced in two major types and at least five sub-types. The cards feature crude color drawings that have little resemblance to the player named. They were originally produced in strips and sold inexpensively in candy stores. The backs contain brief player write-ups. One major type has the player's full name, team and position on back. The second type has only the player's first and last name and position on back; no team. Variations in ink color and wording of the biographies on back are also seen. M.P. & Co. stands for Michael Pressner and Co., a New York City novelty and carnival supply firm.

		NM	EX	VG
Complete Set (24):		1,750	625.00	275.00
Common Player:		40.00	15.00	5.00
(1)	Ernie Bonham	40.00	15.00	5.00
(2)	Lou Boudreau	60.00	20.00	10.00
(3)	Dolph Camilli	40.00	15.00	5.00
(4)	Mort Cooper	40.00	15.00	5.00
(5)	Walker Cooper	40.00	15.00	5.00
(6)	Joe Cronin	60.00	20.00	10.00
(7)	Hank Danning	40.00	15.00	5.00
(8)	Bill Dickey	75.00	25.00	10.00
(9)	Joe DiMaggio	300.00	100.00	45.00
(10)	Bobby Feller	100.00	35.00	15.00
(11)	Jimmy Foxx	75.00	25.00	10.00
(12)	Hank Greenberg	100.00	35.00	15.00
(13)	Stan Hack	40.00	15.00	5.00
(14)	Tom Henrich	40.00	15.00	5.00
(15)	Carl Hubbell	60.00	20.00	10.00
(16)	Joe Medwick	60.00	20.00	10.00
(17)	John Mize	60.00	20.00	10.00
(18)	Lou Novikoff	40.00	15.00	5.00
(19)	Mel Ott	60.00	20.00	10.00
(20)	Pee Wee Reese	75.00	25.00	10.00
(21)	Pete Reiser	40.00	15.00	5.00
(22)	Charlie Ruffing	60.00	20.00	10.00
(23)	Johnny VanderMeer	40.00	15.00	5.00
(24)	Ted Williams	250.00	85.00	35.00

1949 M.P. & Co. (R302-2)

This set appears to be a re-issue of M.P. & Co.'s 1943 cards with several different players (although reusing the same pictures as the '43s). The cards, which measure about 2-11/16" x 2-1/4", feature crude drawings of generic baseball players which have little resemblance to the player named. Most backs include card

number and player information. The numbering sequence begins with card 100. Numbers 104, 118, and 120 are unknown, while three of the cards are unnumbered. The set is assigned the American Card Catalog number R302-2.

	NM	EX	VG
Complete Set (25):	1,750	575.00	275.00
Common Player:	45.00	16.00	7.00
100 Lou Boudreau	60.00	20.00	9.00
101 Ted Williams	250.00	85.00	35.00
102 Buddy Kerr	45.00	16.00	7.00
103 Bobby Feller	75.00	25.00	10.00
104 Unknown			
105 Joe DiMaggio	325.00	115.00	50.00
106 Pee Wee Reese	75.00	25.00	10.00
107 Ferris Fain	45.00	16.00	7.00
108 Andy Pafko	45.00	16.00	7.00
109 Del Ennis	45.00	16.00	7.00
110 Ralph Kiner	60.00	20.00	9.00
111 Nippy Jones	45.00	16.00	7.00
112 Del Rice	45.00	16.00	7.00
113 Hank Sauer	45.00	16.00	7.00
114 Gil Coan	45.00	16.00	7.00
115 Eddie Joost	45.00	16.00	7.00
116 Alvin Dark	45.00	16.00	7.00
117 Larry Berra	75.00	25.00	10.00
118 Unknown			
119 Bob Lemon	60.00	20.00	9.00
120 Unknown			
121 Johnny Pesky	45.00	16.00	7.00
122 Johnny Sain	45.00	16.00	7.00
123 Hoot Evers	45.00	16.00	7.00
124 Larry Doby	60.00	20.00	9.00
---- Jimmy Foxx	100.00	35.00	15.00
---- Tom Henrich	45.00	16.00	7.00
---- Al Kozar	45.00	16.00	7.00

1948-49 M.P. & Co. Photoprints

One of several 1930s-1940s kits for do-it-yourself production of photos, this issue was produced in New York City by the novelty firm M.P. & Co. A complete outfit consists of a film negative and a piece of light-sensitive paper for producing the photo. The negative and resulting print measure about 2" x 2-1/4". The issue includes 13 subjects, mostly non-sport, but includes Babe Ruth.

	NM	EX	VG
Babe Ruth (Negative)	300.00	150.00	90.00
Babe Ruth (Print)	75.00	37.50	22.00

1976 Mr. Softee Iron-Ons

Anecdotal evidence connects these iron-on transfers with the Mr. Softee dairy chain. About 4-1/2" x 6" inches, the color transfers have a player portrait on a baseball background, very similar in format to the 1978 Royal Crown Cola iron-ons. Like the RC pieces, the pictures have team logos removed from caps. The Mr. Softees include the team nickname beneath the player picture, along with a Players Association logo and an undated Quaker copyright line. The extent of the checklist is unknown.

		NM	EX	VG
Common Player:		4.00	2.00	1.25
(1)	George Brett	10.00	5.00	3.00
(2)	Jim Hunter	6.00	3.00	1.75
(3)	Randy Jones	4.00	2.00	1.25
(4)	Dave Kingman	5.00	2.50	1.50
(5)	Jerry Koosman	4.00	2.00	1.25
(6)	Fred Lynn	5.00	2.50	1.50
(7)	Joe Morgan	6.00	3.00	1.75
(8)	Thurman Munson	10.00	5.00	3.00
(9)	Amos Otis	4.00	2.00	1.25
(10)	Bill Russell	4.00	2.00	1.25
(11)	Nolan Ryan	12.00	6.00	3.60
(12)	Mike Schmidt	10.00	5.00	3.00
(13)	Tom Seaver	10.00	5.00	3.00

1977 Mrs. Carter's Bread Sports Illustrated Covers

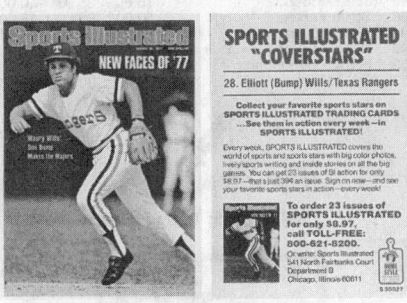

This two-sport set was issued by Mrs. Carter's Bread. Fronts of the 3-1/2" x 4-3/4" cards reproduce SI covers in full color, surrounded by a white border. Backs have a special offer for SI subscriptions, and are printed in black and blue on white. Despite the higher card numbers, it does not appear any more than five were ever issued.

	NM	EX	VG
Complete Set (5):	35.00	17.50	10.00
Common Card:	3.00	1.50	.90
(1) George Brett	25.00	12.50	7.50
(2) George Foster	4.00	2.00	1.25
(3) Bump Wills	4.00	2.00	1.25
(4) Oakland Wins a Big One (Football)	4.00	2.00	1.25
(5) Michigan is No. 1 (Football)	6.00	3.00	1.75

1921 Mrs. Sherlock's Bread Pins

The date of issue for these pins is uncertain. The 7/8" diameter pins feature black-and-white player photos with a red border. The player's last name and team are printed beneath the photo; above is "Mrs. Sherlock's Home Made Bread." The set is one of several sponsored by the Toledo bakery. The Babe Ruth pin was reproduced circa 1999 in 1-3/4" size; it has no collectible value.

	NM	EX	VG
Complete Set (10):	4,750	2,400	1,400
Common Player:	100.00	50.00	30.00
(1) Grover Alexander	350.00	175.00	100.00
(2) Ty Cobb	1,700	850.00	425.00
(3) Rogers Hornsby	375.00	185.00	110.00
(4) Walter Johnson	375.00	185.00	110.00
(5) Rabbit Maranville	300.00	150.00	90.00
(6) Pat Moran	100.00	50.00	30.00
(7) "Babe" Ruth	2,200	1,100	650.00
(8) George Sisler	300.00	150.00	90.00
(9) Tris Speaker	375.00	185.00	110.00
(10) Honus Wagner	700.00	350.00	210.00

1975-96 MSA

(See listings under Michael Schechter Associates.)

1916 M101-5 Blank Backs

JIM THORPE
R. F.—New York Giants
176

The Chicago printing and publishing firm of Felix Mendelsohn was the originator of this card set, which is often found bearing advertising on back of several businesses from around the country. Mendelsohn is not mentioned on the cards, which are blank-backed. Fronts of the 1-5/8" x 3" black-and-white cards have a player photo, name, position abbreviation, team and card number. The set was prepared in advance of the 1916 season and offered in ads in The Sporting News for $1, or a framed uncut sheet for $2.50. The blank-backs are the most common version of M101-5. There were at least two printings of the set, creating several variations to correct errors or replace players.

	NM	EX	VG
Complete Set (200):	13,000	65,000	40,000
Common Player:	90.00	45.00	30.00
1 Babe Adams	100.00	35.00	20.00
2 Sam Agnew	90.00	45.00	30.00
3 Eddie Ainsmith	90.00	45.00	30.00
4 Grover Alexander	550.00	275.00	165.00
5 Leon Ames	90.00	45.00	30.00
6 Jimmy Archer	90.00	45.00	30.00
7 Jimmy Austin	90.00	45.00	30.00
8 J. Franklin Baker	360.00	175.00	105.00
9 Dave Bancroft	360.00	175.00	105.00
10 Jack Barry	90.00	45.00	30.00
11 Zinn Beck	90.00	45.00	30.00
12a Beals Becker	275.00	135.00	80.00
12b Lute Boone	90.00	45.00	30.00
13 Joe Benz	90.00	45.00	30.00
14 Bob Bescher	90.00	45.00	30.00
15 Al Betzel	90.00	45.00	30.00
16 Roger Bresnahan	360.00	175.00	105.00
17 Eddie Burns	90.00	45.00	30.00
18 Geo. J. Burns	90.00	45.00	30.00
19 Joe Bush	90.00	45.00	30.00
20 Owen Bush	90.00	45.00	30.00
21 Art Butler	90.00	45.00	30.00
22 Bobbie Byrne	90.00	45.00	30.00
23a Forrest Cady	1,200	600.00	350.00
23b Forrest Cady (no number)	1,200	600.00	350.00
23c Mordecai Brown	1,100	550.00	325.00
24 Jimmy Callahan	90.00	45.00	30.00
25 Ray Caldwell	90.00	45.00	30.00
26 Max Carey	360.00	175.00	105.00
27 George Chalmers	90.00	45.00	30.00
28 Frank Chance	360.00	175.00	105.00
29 Ray Chapman	110.00	55.00	35.00
30 Larry Cheney	90.00	45.00	30.00
31 Eddie Cicotte	360.00	175.00	105.00
32 Tom Clarke	90.00	45.00	30.00
33 Eddie Collins	360.00	175.00	105.00
34 "Shauno" Collins	90.00	45.00	30.00
35 Charles Comisky (Comiskey)	360.00	175.00	105.00
36 Joe Connolly	90.00	45.00	30.00
37 Luther Cook	90.00	45.00	30.00
38 Jack Coombs	90.00	45.00	30.00
39 Dan Costello	90.00	45.00	30.00
40 Harry Coveleskie (Coveleski)	90.00	45.00	30.00
41 Gavvy Cravath	90.00	45.00	30.00
42 Sam Crawford	360.00	175.00	105.00
43 Jean Dale	90.00	45.00	30.00
44 Jake Daubert	90.00	45.00	30.00
45 Geo. A. Davis Jr.	90.00	45.00	30.00
46 Charles Deal	90.00	45.00	30.00
47 Al Demaree	90.00	45.00	30.00
48 William Doak	90.00	45.00	30.00
49 Bill Donovan	90.00	45.00	30.00
50 Charles Dooin	90.00	45.00	30.00
51 Mike Doolan	90.00	45.00	30.00
52 Larry Doyle	90.00	45.00	30.00
53 Jean Dubuc	90.00	45.00	30.00
54 Oscar Dugey	90.00	45.00	30.00
55 Johnny Evers	360.00	175.00	105.00
56 Urban Faber	360.00	175.00	105.00
57 "Hap" Felsch	2,000	415.00	250.00
58 Bill Fischer	90.00	45.00	30.00
59 Ray Fisher	90.00	45.00	30.00
60 Max Flack	90.00	45.00	30.00
61 Art Fletcher	90.00	45.00	30.00
62 Eddie Foster	90.00	45.00	30.00
63 Jacques Fournier	90.00	45.00	30.00
64 Del Gainer (Gainor)	90.00	45.00	30.00
65 Larry Gardner	90.00	45.00	30.00
66 Joe Gedeon	90.00	45.00	30.00
67 Gus Getz	90.00	45.00	30.00
68 Geo. Gibson	90.00	45.00	30.00
69 Wilbur Good	90.00	45.00	30.00
70 Hank Gowdy	90.00	45.00	30.00
71 John Graney	90.00	45.00	30.00
72 Tom Griffith	90.00	45.00	30.00
73 Heinie Groh	90.00	45.00	30.00
74 Earl Hamilton	90.00	45.00	30.00
75 Bob Harmon	90.00	45.00	30.00
76 Roy Hartzell	90.00	45.00	30.00
77 Claude Hendrix	90.00	45.00	30.00
78 Olaf Henriksen	90.00	45.00	30.00
79 John Henry	90.00	45.00	30.00
80 "Buck" Herzog	90.00	45.00	30.00
81 Hugh High	90.00	45.00	30.00
82 Dick Hoblitzell	90.00	45.00	30.00
83 Harry Hooper	360.00	175.00	105.00
84 Ivan Howard	90.00	45.00	30.00
85 Miller Huggins	360.00	175.00	105.00
86 Joe Jackson	15,000	4,950	2,970
87 William James	90.00	45.00	30.00
88 Harold Janvrin	90.00	45.00	30.00
89 Hugh Jennings	360.00	175.00	105.00
90 Walter Johnson	1,500	550.00	330.00
91 Fielder Jones	90.00	45.00	30.00
92 Bennie Kauff	90.00	45.00	30.00
93 Wm. Killefer Jr.	90.00	45.00	30.00
94 Ed. Konetchy	90.00	45.00	30.00
95 Napoleon Lajoie	360.00	175.00	105.00
96 Jack Lapp	90.00	45.00	30.00
97a John Lavan (Correct spelling)	90.00	45.00	30.00
97b John Lavin (Incorrect spelling)	90.00	45.00	30.00
98 Jimmy Lavender	90.00	45.00	30.00
99 "Nemo" Leibold	90.00	45.00	30.00
100 H.B. Leonard	90.00	45.00	30.00
101 Duffy Lewis	90.00	45.00	30.00
102 Hans Lobert	90.00	45.00	30.00
103 Tom Long	90.00	45.00	30.00
104 Fred Luderus	90.00	45.00	30.00
105 Connie Mack	360.00	175.00	105.00
106 Lee Magee	90.00	45.00	30.00
107 Al. Mamaux	90.00	45.00	30.00
108 Leslie Mann	90.00	45.00	30.00
109 "Rabbit" Maranville	360.00	175.00	105.00
110 Rube Marquard	360.00	175.00	105.00
111 Armando Marsans	100.00	50.00	30.00
112 J. Erskine Mayer	90.00	45.00	30.00
113 George McBride	90.00	45.00	30.00
114 John J. McGraw	360.00	175.00	105.00
115 Jack McInnis	90.00	45.00	30.00
116 Fred Merkle	90.00	45.00	30.00
117 Chief Meyers	90.00	45.00	30.00
118 Clyde Milan	90.00	45.00	30.00
119 Otto Miller	90.00	45.00	30.00
120 Willie Mitchel (Mitchell)	90.00	45.00	30.00
121 Fred Mollwitz	90.00	45.00	30.00
122 J. Herbert Moran	90.00	45.00	30.00
123 Pat Moran	90.00	45.00	30.00
124 Ray Morgan	90.00	45.00	30.00
125 Geo. Moriarty	90.00	45.00	30.00
126 Guy Morton	90.00	45.00	30.00
127 Ed. Murphy (Photo actually Danny Murphy.)	90.00	45.00	30.00
128 John Murray	90.00	45.00	30.00
129 "Hy" Myers	90.00	45.00	30.00
130 J.A. Niehoff	90.00	45.00	30.00
131 Leslie Nunamaker	90.00	45.00	30.00
132 Rube Oldring	90.00	45.00	30.00
133 Oliver O'Mara	90.00	45.00	30.00
134 Steve O'Neill	90.00	45.00	30.00
135 "Dode" Paskert	90.00	45.00	30.00
136 Roger Peckinpaugh (Photo actually Gavvy Cravath.)	90.00	45.00	30.00
137 E.J. Pfeffer (Photo actually Jeff Pfeffer.)	90.00	45.00	30.00
138 Geo. Pierce (Pearce)	90.00	45.00	30.00
139 Walter Pipp	90.00	45.00	30.00
140 Derril Pratt (Derrill)	90.00	45.00	30.00
141 Bill Rariden	90.00	45.00	30.00
142 Eppa Rixey	360.00	175.00	105.00
143 Davey Robertson	90.00	45.00	30.00
144 Wilbert Robinson	360.00	175.00	105.00
145 Bob Roth	90.00	45.00	30.00
146 Ed. Roush	360.00	175.00	105.00
147 Clarence Rowland	90.00	45.00	30.00
148 "Nap" Rucker	90.00	45.00	30.00
149 Dick Rudolph	90.00	45.00	30.00
150 Reb Russell	90.00	45.00	30.00
151 Babe Ruth	75,000	37,000	22,000
152 Vic Saier	90.00	45.00	30.00
153 "Slim" Sallee	90.00	45.00	30.00
154 "Germany" Schaefer	90.00	45.00	30.00
155 Ray Schalk	360.00	175.00	105.00
156 Walter Schang	90.00	45.00	30.00
157 Chas. Schmidt	90.00	45.00	30.00
158 Frank Schulte	90.00	45.00	30.00
159 Jim Scott	90.00	45.00	30.00
160 Everett Scott	90.00	45.00	30.00
161 Tom Seaton	90.00	45.00	30.00
162 Howard Shanks	90.00	45.00	30.00
163 Bob Shawkey (Photo actually Jack McInnis.)	90.00	45.00	30.00
164 Ernie Shore	90.00	45.00	30.00
165 Burt Shotton	90.00	45.00	30.00
166 George Sisler	360.00	175.00	105.00
167 J. Carlisle Smith	90.00	45.00	30.00
168 Fred Snodgrass	90.00	45.00	30.00
169 Geo. Stallings	90.00	45.00	30.00
170 Oscar Stanage (Photo actually Chas. Schmidt.)	90.00	45.00	30.00
171 Charles Stengel	1,200	600.00	350.00
172 Milton Stock	90.00	45.00	30.00
173 Amos Strunk (Photo actually Olaf Henriksen.)	90.00	45.00	30.00
174 Billy Sullivan	90.00	45.00	30.00
175 Chas. Tesreau	90.00	45.00	30.00
176 Jim Thorpe	22,500	11,250	6,750
177 Joe Tinker	360.00	175.00	105.00
178 Fred Toney	90.00	45.00	30.00
179 Terry Turner	90.00	45.00	30.00
180 Jim Vaughn	90.00	45.00	30.00
181 Bob Veach	90.00	45.00	30.00
182 James Viox	90.00	45.00	30.00
183 Oscar Vitt	90.00	45.00	30.00
184 Hans Wagner	3,000	660.00	395.00
185 Clarence Walker (Photo not Walker.)	90.00	45.00	30.00
186a Bobby Wallace	5,500	2,750	1,650
186b Zach Wheat	360.00	175.00	105.00
187 Ed. Walsh	360.00	175.00	105.00
188 Buck Weaver	2,000	360.00	215.00
189 Carl Weilman	90.00	45.00	30.00
190 Geo. Whitted	90.00	45.00	30.00
191 Fred Williams	90.00	45.00	30.00
192 Art Wilson	90.00	45.00	30.00
193 J. Owen Wilson	90.00	45.00	30.00
194 Ivy Wingo	90.00	45.00	30.00
195 "Mel" Wolfgang	90.00	45.00	30.00
196 Joe Wood	500.00	110.00	65.00
197 Steve Yerkes	90.00	45.00	30.00
198 Rollie Zeider	90.00	45.00	30.00
199 Heiny Zimmerman	90.00	45.00	30.00
200 Ed. Zwilling	90.00	45.00	30.00

1916 M101-4 Blank Backs

The "update" version of this set is nearly identical to the earlier cards. The 200 black-and-white cards once again are printed with player photo, name, position, team and card number on front and blank backs. This version appears to have been sold directly to consumers by the manufacturer, Felix Mendelsohn of Chicago. The same cards can be found with

JOE JACKSON
L. F.—Chicago White Sox
87

advertising on back from several businesses around the country. Most of the players included on the 1-5/8" x 3" cards also appear in the prior edition. Despite being labeled in the American Card Catalog as M101-4, this version was issued after the M101-5 version, with the first advertising appearing in August 1916. The complete set price does not include variations.

		NM	EX	VG
Complete Set (200):		100,000	50,000	30,000
Common Player:		60.00	30.00	18.00
1	Babe Adams	75.00	30.00	18.00
2	Sam Agnew	60.00	30.00	18.00
3	Eddie Ainsmith	60.00	30.00	18.00
4	Grover Alexander	375.00	185.00	110.00
5	Leon Ames	60.00	30.00	18.00
6	Jimmy Archer	60.00	30.00	18.00
7	Jimmy Austin	60.00	30.00	18.00
8	H.D. Baird	60.00	30.00	18.00
9	J. Franklin Baker	300.00	150.00	90.00
10	Dave Bancroft	300.00	150.00	90.00
11	Jack Barry	60.00	30.00	18.00
12	Zinn Beck	60.00	30.00	18.00
13	"Chief" Bender	300.00	150.00	90.00
14	Joe Benz	60.00	30.00	18.00
15	Bob Bescher	60.00	30.00	18.00
16	Al Betzel	60.00	30.00	18.00
17	Mordecai Brown	300.00	150.00	90.00
18	Eddie Burns	60.00	30.00	18.00
19	George Burns	60.00	30.00	18.00
20	Geo. J. Burns	60.00	30.00	18.00
21	Joe Bush	60.00	30.00	18.00
22	"Donie" Bush	60.00	30.00	18.00
23	Art Butler	60.00	30.00	18.00
24	Bobbie Byrne	60.00	30.00	18.00
25	Forrest Cady	60.00	30.00	18.00
26	Jimmy Callahan	60.00	30.00	18.00
27	Ray Caldwell	60.00	30.00	18.00
28	Max Carey	300.00	150.00	90.00
29	George Chalmers	60.00	30.00	18.00
30	Ray Chapman	90.00	45.00	25.00
31	Larry Cheney	60.00	30.00	18.00
32	Eddie Cicotte	300.00	150.00	90.00
33	Tom Clarke	60.00	30.00	18.00
34	Eddie Collins	300.00	150.00	90.00
35	"Shauno" Collins	60.00	30.00	18.00
36	Charles Comiskey	300.00	150.00	90.00
37	Joe Connolly	60.00	30.00	18.00
38	Ty Cobb	2,500	1,250	750.00
39	Harry Coveleskie (Coveleski)	60.00	30.00	18.00
40	Gavvy Cravath	60.00	30.00	18.00
41	Sam Crawford	300.00	150.00	90.00
42	Jean Dale	60.00	30.00	18.00
43	Jake Daubert	60.00	30.00	18.00
44	Charles Deal	60.00	30.00	18.00
45	Al Demaree	60.00	30.00	18.00
46	Josh Devore	60.00	30.00	18.00
47	William Doak	60.00	30.00	18.00
48	Bill Donovan	60.00	30.00	18.00
49	Charles Dooin	60.00	30.00	18.00
50	Mike Doolan	60.00	30.00	18.00
51	Larry Doyle	60.00	30.00	18.00
52	Jean Dubuc	60.00	30.00	18.00
53	Oscar Dugey	60.00	30.00	18.00
54	Johnny Evers	300.00	150.00	90.00
55	Urban Faber	300.00	150.00	90.00
56	"Hap" Felsch	2,000	375.00	225.00
57	Bill Fischer	60.00	30.00	18.00
58	Ray Fisher	60.00	30.00	18.00
59	Max Flack	60.00	30.00	18.00
60	Art Fletcher	60.00	30.00	18.00
61	Eddie Foster	60.00	30.00	18.00
62	Jacques Fournier	60.00	30.00	18.00
63	Del Gainer (Gainor)	60.00	30.00	18.00
64	"Chic" Gandil	500.00	250.00	150.00
65	Larry Gardner	60.00	30.00	18.00
66	Joe Gedeon	60.00	30.00	18.00
67	Gus Getz	60.00	30.00	18.00
68	Geo. Gibson	60.00	30.00	18.00
69	Wilbur Good	60.00	30.00	18.00
70	Hank Gowdy	60.00	30.00	18.00
71	John Graney	60.00	30.00	18.00
72	Clark Griffith	300.00	150.00	90.00
73	Tom Griffith	60.00	30.00	18.00
74	Heinie Groh	60.00	30.00	18.00
75	Earl Hamilton	60.00	30.00	18.00
76	Bob Harmon	60.00	30.00	18.00
77	Roy Hartzell	60.00	30.00	18.00
78	Claude Hendrix	60.00	30.00	18.00

79	Olaf Henriksen	60.00	30.00	18.00
80	John Henry	60.00	30.00	18.00
81	"Buck" Herzog	60.00	30.00	18.00
82	Hugh High	60.00	30.00	18.00
83	Dick Hoblitzell	60.00	30.00	18.00
84	Harry Hooper	300.00	150.00	90.00
85	Ivan Howard	60.00	30.00	18.00
86	Miller Huggins	300.00	150.00	90.00
87	Joe Jackson	10,000	5,000	3,000
88	William James	60.00	30.00	18.00
89	Harold Janvrin	60.00	30.00	18.00
90	Hugh Jennings	300.00	150.00	90.00
91	Walter Johnson	800.00	400.00	240.00
92	Fielder Jones	60.00	30.00	18.00
93	Joe Judge	60.00	30.00	18.00
94	Bennie Kauff	60.00	30.00	18.00
95	Wm. Killefer Jr.	60.00	30.00	18.00
96	Ed. Konetchy	60.00	30.00	18.00
97	Napoleon Lajoie	550.00	270.00	165.00
98	Jack Lapp	60.00	30.00	18.00
99	John Lavan	60.00	30.00	18.00
100	Jimmy Lavender	60.00	30.00	18.00
101	"Nemo" Leibold	60.00	30.00	18.00
102	H.B. Leonard	60.00	30.00	18.00
103	Duffy Lewis	60.00	30.00	18.00
104	Hans Lobert	60.00	30.00	18.00
105	Tom Long	60.00	30.00	18.00
106	Fred Luderus	60.00	30.00	18.00
107	Connie Mack	300.00	150.00	90.00
108	Lee Magee	60.00	30.00	18.00
109	Sherwood Magee	60.00	30.00	18.00
110	Al. Mamaux	60.00	30.00	18.00
111	Leslie Mann	60.00	30.00	18.00
112	"Rabbit" Maranville	300.00	150.00	90.00
113	Rube Marquard	300.00	150.00	90.00
114	J. Erskine Mayer	125.00	65.00	35.00
115	George McBride	60.00	30.00	18.00
116	John J. McGraw	300.00	150.00	90.00
117	Jack McInnis	60.00	30.00	18.00
118	Fred Merkle	60.00	30.00	18.00
119	Chief Meyers	60.00	30.00	18.00
120	Clyde Milan	60.00	30.00	18.00
121	John Miller	60.00	30.00	18.00
122	Otto Miller	60.00	30.00	18.00
123	Willie Mitchell	60.00	30.00	18.00
124	Fred Mollwitz	60.00	30.00	18.00
125	Pat Moran	60.00	30.00	18.00
126	Ray Morgan	60.00	30.00	18.00
127	Geo. Moriarty	60.00	30.00	18.00
128	Guy Morton	60.00	30.00	18.00
129	Mike Mowrey	60.00	30.00	18.00
130	Ed. Murphy	60.00	30.00	18.00
131	"Hy" Myers	60.00	30.00	18.00
132	J.A. Niehoff	60.00	30.00	18.00
133	Rube Oldring	60.00	30.00	18.00
134	Oliver O'Mara	60.00	30.00	18.00
135	Steve O'Neill	60.00	30.00	18.00
136	"Dode" Paskert	60.00	30.00	18.00
137	Roger Peckinpaugh	60.00	30.00	18.00
138	Walter Pipp	75.00	37.50	22.50
139	Derril Pratt (Derrill)	60.00	30.00	18.00
140	Pat Ragan	60.00	30.00	18.00
141	Bill Rariden	60.00	30.00	18.00
142	Eppa Rixey	300.00	150.00	90.00
143	Davey Robertson	60.00	30.00	18.00
144	Wilbert Robinson	300.00	150.00	90.00
145	Bob Roth	60.00	30.00	18.00
146	Ed. Roush	300.00	150.00	90.00
147	Clarence Rowland	60.00	30.00	18.00
148	"Nap" Rucker	60.00	30.00	18.00
149	Dick Rudolph	60.00	30.00	18.00
150	Reb Russell	60.00	30.00	18.00
151	Babe Ruth	75,000	37,000	22,000
152	Vic Saier	60.00	30.00	18.00
153	"Slim" Sallee	60.00	30.00	18.00
154	Ray Schalk	300.00	150.00	90.00
155	Walter Schang	60.00	30.00	18.00
156	Frank Schulte	60.00	30.00	18.00
157	Everett Scott	60.00	30.00	18.00
158	Jim Scott	60.00	30.00	18.00
159	Tom Seaton	60.00	30.00	18.00
160	Howard Shanks	60.00	30.00	18.00
161	Bob Shawkey	60.00	30.00	18.00
162	Ernie Shore	60.00	30.00	18.00
163	Burt Shotton	60.00	30.00	18.00
164	Geo. Sisler	300.00	150.00	90.00
165	J. Carlisle Smith	60.00	30.00	18.00
166	Fred Snodgrass	60.00	30.00	18.00
167	Geo. Stallings	60.00	30.00	18.00
168a	Oscar Stanage/Catching	60.00	30.00	24.00
168b	Oscar Stanage (Portrait to thighs.)	750.00	375.00	225.00
169	Charles Stengel	1,100	550.00	325.00
170	Milton Stock	60.00	30.00	18.00
171	Amos Strunk	60.00	30.00	18.00
172	Billy Sullivan	60.00	30.00	18.00
173	"Jeff" Tesreau	60.00	30.00	18.00
174	Joe Tinker	300.00	150.00	90.00
175	Fred Toney	60.00	30.00	18.00
176	Terry Turner	60.00	30.00	18.00
177	George Tyler	60.00	30.00	18.00
178	Jim Vaughn	60.00	30.00	18.00
179	Bob Veach	60.00	30.00	18.00
180	James Viox	60.00	30.00	18.00
181	Oscar Vitt	60.00	30.00	18.00
182	Hans Wagner	2,500	1,250	750.00
183	Clarence Walker	60.00	30.00	18.00
184	Ed. Walsh	300.00	150.00	90.00
185	W. Wambsganss (Photo actually Fritz Coumbe.)	60.00	30.00	18.00
186	Buck Weaver	600.00	300.00	180.00
187	Carl Weilman	60.00	30.00	18.00
188	Zach Wheat	300.00	150.00	90.00
189	Geo. Whitted	60.00	30.00	18.00
190	Fred Williams	60.00	30.00	18.00
191	Art Wilson	60.00	30.00	18.00
192	J. Owen Wilson	60.00	30.00	18.00
193	Ivy Wingo	60.00	30.00	18.00

194	"Mel" Wolfgang	60.00	30.00	18.00
195	Joe Wood	175.00	85.00	50.00
196	Steve Yerkes	60.00	30.00	18.00
197	"Pep" Young	60.00	30.00	18.00
198	Rollie Zeider	60.00	30.00	18.00
199	Heiny Zimmerman	60.00	30.00	18.00
200	Ed. Zwilling	60.00	30.00	18.00

N

1969 Nabisco Team Flakes

Frank Robinson—OF
Baltimore Orioles

This set of cards is seen in two different sizes: 1-15/16" x 3" and 1-3/4" x 2-15/16". This is explained by the varying widths of the card borders on the backs of Nabisco cereal packages. Cards are action color photos bordered in yellow. Twenty-four of the top players in the game are included in the set, which was issued in three series of eight cards each. No team insignias are visible on any of the cards. Packages described the cards as "Mini Posters."

		NM	EX	VG
Complete Set (24):		1,200	600.00	375.00
Common Player:		20.00	10.00	6.00
(1)	Hank Aaron	120.00	60.00	40.00
(2)	Richie Allen	35.00	20.00	12.00
(3)	Lou Brock	50.00	25.00	15.00
(4)	Paul Casanova	20.00	10.00	6.00
(5)	Roberto Clemente	250.00	125.00	75.00
(6)	Al Ferrara	20.00	10.00	6.00
(7)	Bill Freehan	20.00	10.00	6.00
(8)	Jim Fregosi	20.00	10.00	6.00
(9)	Bob Gibson	50.00	25.00	15.00
(10)	Tony Horton	20.00	10.00	6.00
(11)	Tommy John	20.00	10.00	6.00
(12)	Al Kaline	65.00	35.00	20.00
(13)	Jim Lonborg	20.00	10.00	6.00
(14)	Juan Marichal	50.00	25.00	15.00
(15)	Willie Mays	120.00	60.00	40.00
(16)	Rick Monday	20.00	10.00	6.00
(17)	Tony Oliva	20.00	10.00	6.00
(18)	Brooks Robinson	65.00	35.00	20.00
(19)	Frank Robinson	65.00	35.00	20.00
(20)	Pete Rose	90.00	45.00	25.00
(21)	Ron Santo	35.00	20.00	12.00
(22)	Tom Seaver	65.00	35.00	20.00
(23)	Rusty Staub	20.00	10.00	6.00
(24)	Mel Stottlemyre	20.00	10.00	6.00

1923-1924 Nacionales Cigarros

The baseball players in this mid-20s Cuban issue are part of a larger set which included boxers, actresses, actors, nudes, soccer players and others. The cards measure about 1-5/8" x 2-1/4" and have a distinctive wide black border on front. Backs identify the issue. An album was issued to house the set. The cards are printed on thin cardboard with a glossy finish.

		NM	EX	VG
Complete Baseball Set (40):		60,000	24,000	12,000
Common Player:		500.00	200.00	100.00
21	Rafael Almeida	1,500	600.00	300.00
22	Isidro Fabre	1,125	450.00	225.00
23	Eugenio Morin	500.00	200.00	100.00
24	Oscar Rodriguez	500.00	200.00	100.00

		NM	EX	VG
25	Joseito Rodriguez	500.00	200.00	100.00
26	Papo Gonzalez	500.00	200.00	100.00
27	Gutierrez	500.00	200.00	100.00
28	Valentin Dreke (Photo actually Lucas Boada.)	1,125	450.00	225.00
29	Jose Maria Fernandez	750.00	300.00	150.00
30	(Cheo) Ramos	500.00	200.00	100.00
31	Paito (Ramon Herrera)	500.00	200.00	100.00
32	Bernardo Baro	1,125	450.00	225.00
33	Manuel Cueto	750.00	300.00	150.00
34	(Oscar) Tuero	500.00	200.00	100.00
35	Kakin Gonzalez	500.00	200.00	100.00
36	Armando Marsans	1,500	600.00	300.00
37	Andy Cooper	9,000	3,600	1,800
38	Dolf Luque	2,500	1,000	500.00
39	Marcelino Guerra	500.00	200.00	100.00
40	Manzanillo (Tatic Campos)	500.00	200.00	100.00
41	Oscar Levis	750.00	300.00	150.00
42	Eufemio Abreu	500.00	200.00	100.00
43	Cristobal Torriente	12,000	4,800	2,400
44	Juanelo Mirabal	750.00	300.00	150.00
45	Merito Acosta	500.00	200.00	100.00
46	Jose Acostica (Acosta)	500.00	200.00	100.00
47	Rogelio Crespo	500.00	200.00	100.00
48	(Jacinto) Calvo	750.00	300.00	150.00
49	(Emilio) Palmero	750.00	300.00	150.00
50	Jose Mendez	9,000	3,600	1,800
51	Alejandro Oms	3,750	1,500	750.00
52	Pedro Dibut	750.00	300.00	150.00
53	Strike (Valentin "Sirique" Gonzalez)	500.00	200.00	100.00
54	Magrinat (Hector Magrinut)	500.00	200.00	100.00
55	Raphael Quintana	500.00	200.00	100.00
56	Bienvenido Jimenez	750.00	300.00	150.00
57	Bartolo Portuando (Portuondo)	1,500	600.00	300.00
58	(Pelayo) Chacon	1,500	600.00	300.00
59	Riant (Red Ryan)	1,500	600.00	300.00
60	Perico El Mano (Mascot)	500.00	200.00	100.00

1909 Nadja Caramels (E92)

 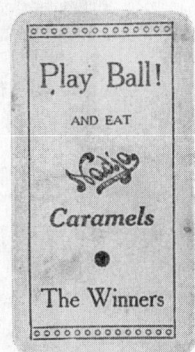

One of several 1909-10 issues produced for Nadja Caramels, this set can be distinguished by the players in the checklist (alphabetized here) and the type beneath the color player lithograph. In this set, the player's last name is in upper- and lower-case letters, and his position is given, along with the team. Backs of these 1-1/2" x 2-3/4" cards are identical to later Nadja issues, featuring an ad for the candy brand. Cataloged (along with the cards of Croft's Candy/Cocoa and Dockman Gum) as E92 in the "American Card Catalog," the Nadja set checklist differs from those issues in that it is larger and contains a group of St. Louis players not found in the other sets. Nadja was a brand name of the Blake-Wenneker Candy Co. of St. Louis.

		NM	EX	VG
Complete Set (62):		55,000	27,000	16,500
Common Player:		600.00	300.00	180.00
(1)	Bill Bailey	600.00	300.00	180.00
(2)	Jack Barry	600.00	300.00	180.00
(3)	Harry Bemis	600.00	300.00	180.00
(4)	Chief Bender (Striped cap.)	1,200	600.00	350.00
(5)	Chief Bender (White cap.)	1,200	600.00	350.00
(6)	Bill Bergen	600.00	300.00	180.00
(7)	Bob Bescher	600.00	300.00	180.00
(8)	Roger Bresnahan	1,200	600.00	350.00
(9)	Al Bridwell	600.00	300.00	180.00
(10)	Doc Casey	600.00	300.00	180.00
(11)	Frank Chance	1,200	600.00	350.00
(12)	Hal Chase	900.00	450.00	270.00
(13)	Ty Cobb	8,500	4,200	2,500
(14)	Eddie Collins	1,200	600.00	350.00
(15)	Sam Crawford	1,200	600.00	350.00
(16)	Harry Davis	600.00	300.00	180.00
(17)	Art Devlin	600.00	300.00	180.00
(18)	Bill Donovan	600.00	300.00	180.00
(19)	Red Dooin	600.00	300.00	180.00
(20)	Mickey Doolan	600.00	300.00	180.00
(21)	Patsy Dougherty	600.00	300.00	180.00
(22)	Larry Doyle/Throwing	600.00	300.00	180.00
(23)	Larry Doyle (With bat.)	600.00	300.00	180.00
(24)	Rube Ellis	600.00	300.00	180.00
(25)	Johnny Evers	1,200	600.00	350.00
(26)	George Gibson	600.00	300.00	180.00
(27)	Topsy Hartsel	600.00	300.00	180.00
(28)	Roy Hartzell/Btg	600.00	300.00	180.00
(29)	Roy Hartzell/Fldg	600.00	300.00	180.00
(30)	Harry Howell (Ready to pitch.)	600.00	300.00	180.00
(31)	Harry Howell (Follow-through.)	600.00	300.00	180.00
(32)	Fred Jacklitsch	600.00	300.00	180.00
(33)	Hugh Jennings	1,200	600.00	350.00
(34)	Red Kleinow	600.00	300.00	180.00

		NM	EX	VG
(35)	Otto Knabe	600.00	300.00	180.00
(36)	Jack Knight	600.00	300.00	180.00
(37)	Nap Lajoie	1,200	600.00	350.00
(38)	Hans Lobert	600.00	300.00	180.00
(39)	Sherry Magee	600.00	300.00	180.00
(40)	Christy Matthewson (Mathewson)	5,500	2,700	1,650
(41)	John McGraw	1,200	600.00	350.00
(42)	Larry McLean	600.00	300.00	180.00
(43)	Dots Miller (Batting)	600.00	300.00	180.00
(44)	Dots Miller (Fielding)	600.00	300.00	180.00
(45)	Danny Murphy	600.00	300.00	180.00
(46)	Rebel Oakes	600.00	300.00	180.00
(47)	Bill O'Hara	600.00	300.00	180.00
(48)	Eddie Phelps	600.00	300.00	180.00
(49)	Germany Schaefer	600.00	300.00	180.00
(50)	Admiral Schlei	600.00	300.00	180.00
(51)	Boss Schmidt	600.00	300.00	180.00
(52)	Johnny Seigle (Siegle)	600.00	300.00	180.00
(53)	Dave Shean	600.00	300.00	180.00
(54)	Boss Smith (Schmidt)	600.00	300.00	180.00
(55)	George Stone (Blue background.)	600.00	300.00	180.00
(56)	George Stone (Green background.)	600.00	300.00	180.00
(57)	Joe Tinker	1,200	600.00	350.00
(58)	Honus Wagner/Btg	7,000	3,500	2,100
(59)	Honus Wagner/Throwing	7,500	3,700	2,200
(60)	Bobby Wallace	1,200	600.00	350.00
(61)	Cy Young	3,000	1,500	900.00
(62)	Heinie Zimmerman	600.00	300.00	180.00

1910 Nadja Caramels Philadelphia Athletics (E104-1)

 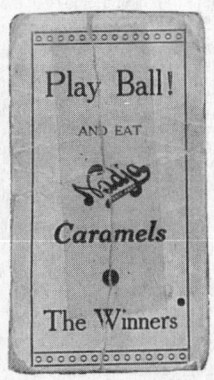

The 18 Philadelphia Athletics players in this set, can each be found in three different variations. Each of the approximately 1-1/2" x 2-3/4" cards can be found with a plain portrait lithograph on front, and either a blank back or a back containing a Nadja ad. Each player can also be found with a black overprint on front, comprised of a white elephant figure on the uniform and the notation "World's Champions 1910" above. The overprinted cards are known only with blank backs, and are somewhat scarcer than the plain cards of either type. Nadja-back cards should be valued about the same as the overprinted type.

		NM	EX	VG
Complete Set, No O/P, Blank Back (18):		36,000	18,000	10,000
Complete Set, With O/P or Ad Back:		45,000	22,500	13,500
Common Player:		1,800	900.00	550.00
(1a)	Home Run Baker	3,200	1,600	1,000
(1b)	Home Run Baker ("World's Champions")	6,500	3,250	2,000
(2a)	Jack Barry	1,800	900.00	550.00
(2b)	Jack Barry ("World's Champions")	6,500	3,250	2,000
(3a)	Chief Bender	3,200	1,600	1,000
(3b)	Chief Bender ("World's Champions")	6,500	3,250	2,000
(4a)	Eddie Collins	3,200	1,600	1,000
(4b)	Eddie Collins ("World's Champions")	6,500	3,250	2,000
(5a)	Harry Davis	1,800	900.00	550.00
(5b)	Harry Davis ("World's Champions")	6,500	3,250	2,000
(6a)	Jimmy Dygert (1910 above head)	1,800	900.00	550.00
(6b-1)	Jimmy Dygert ("World's Champions" 1910 above head)	6,500	3,250	2,000
(6b-2)	Jimmy Dygert (1910 at right)	6,500	3,250	2,000
(7a)	Topsy Hartsel	1,800	900.00	550.00
(7b)	Topsy Hartsel ("World's Champions")	6,500	3,250	2,000
(8a)	Harry Krause	1,800	900.00	550.00
(8b)	Harry Krause ("World's Champions")	6,500	3,250	2,000
(9a)	Jack Lapp	1,800	900.00	550.00
(9b)	Jack Lapp ("World's Champions")	6,500	3,250	2,000
(10a)	Paddy Livingstone (Livingston)	1,800	900.00	550.00
(10b)	Paddy Livingstone (Livingston) ("World's Champions")	6,500	3,250	2,000
(11a)	Bris Lord	1,800	900.00	550.00
(11b)	Bris Lord ("World's Champions")	6,500	3,250	2,000
(12a)	Connie Mack	10,000	5,000	3,000
(12b)	Connie Mack ("World's Champions")	22,000	11,000	7,000
(13a)	Cy Morgan	1,800	900.00	550.00
(13b)	Cy Morgan ("World's Champions")	6,500	3,250	2,000
(14a)	Danny Murphy	1,800	900.00	550.00
(14b)	Danny Murphy ("World's Champions")	6,500	3,250	2,000
(15a)	Rube Oldring	1,800	900.00	550.00
(15b)	Rube Oldring ("World's Champions")	6,500	3,250	2,000
(16a)	Eddie Plank	16,000	8,000	4,750
(16b)	Eddie Plank ("World's Champions")	27,500	13,500	8,250
(17a)	Amos Strunk	1,800	900.00	550.00
(17b)	Amos Strunk ("World's Champions")	6,500	3,250	2,000
(18a)	Ira Thomas	1,800	900.00	550.00
(18b-1)	Ira Thomas ("World's Champions") (1910 above head)	6,500	3,250	2,000
(18b-2)	Ira Thomas (1910 at right)	6,500	3,250	2,000

1910 Nadja Caramels Pittsburgh Pirates (E104-2)

Similar to the contemporary American Caramel issue, this set of 1-1/2" x 2-3/4" cards features portrait color lithographs of the 1909 World's Champion Pittsburgh (spelled "Pittsburg") Pirates. Each card was issued with both blank back and with a back bearing a Nadja ad. The Nadja-backed cards are scarcer but command little premium.

		NM	EX	VG
Complete Set (11):		30,000	15,000	9,000
Common Player:		1,325	665.00	400.00
Ad Back: 1.25X				
(1)	Babe Adams	1,325	665.00	400.00
(2)	Fred Clarke	3,000	1,500	900.00
(3)	George Gibson	1,325	665.00	400.00
(4)	Ham Hyatt	1,325	665.00	400.00
(5)	Tommy Leach	1,325	665.00	400.00
(6)	Sam Leever	1,325	665.00	400.00
(7)	Nick Maddox	1,325	665.00	400.00
(8)	Dots Miller	1,325	665.00	400.00
(9)	Deacon Phillippe	1,325	665.00	400.00
(10)	Honus Wagner	20,000	10,000	6,000
(11)	Owen Wilson	1,325	665.00	400.00

1910 Nadja Caramels (E104-3)

 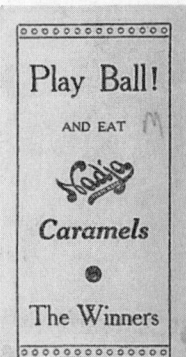

The cards in this issue can each be found with or without a Nadja ad on back; the latter being somewhat scarcer and carrying a premium over the values shown. These 1-1/2" x 2-3/4" cards can be distinguished from the 1909 issue by the line of type beneath the player portrait. On the 1910 cards, the player's last name is in all blue capital letters and there is no position designation given. This checklist is likely incomplete.

		NM	EX	VG
Common Player:		2,750	1,350	825.00
Ad Back: 1.25X				
(1)	Bill Abstein	2,750	1,350	825.00
(2)	Red Ames	2,750	1,350	825.00
(3)	Johnny Bates	2,750	1,350	825.00
(4)	Kitty Bransfield	2,750	1,350	825.00

(5)	Al Bridwell	2,750	1,350	825.00
(6)	Hal Chase	5,750	2,875	1,725
(7)	Doc Crandall	2,750	1,350	825.00
(8)	Sam Crawford	7,750	3,875	2,325
(9)	Jim Delehanty (Delahanty)	2,750	1,350	825.00
(10)	Art Devlin	2,750	1,350	825.00
(11)	Red Dooin	2,750	1,350	825.00
(12)	Mickey Doolan	2,750	1,350	825.00
(13)	Larry Doyle	2,750	1,350	825.00
(14)	Eddie Grant	2,750	1,350	825.00
(15)	Fred Jacklitsch	2,750	1,350	825.00
(16)	Hugh Jennings	7,750	3,875	2,325
(17)	Davy Jones	2,750	1,350	825.00
(18)	Tom Jones	2,750	1,350	825.00
(19)	Otto Knabe	2,750	1,350	825.00
(201)	Sherry Magee	2,750	1,350	825.00
(21)	John McGraw	7,750	3,875	2,325
(22)	Matty McIntyre	2,750	1,350	825.00
(23)	Earl Moore	2,750	1,350	825.00
(24)	Pat Moren (Moran)	2,750	1,350	825.00
(25)	George Moriarity	2,750	1,350	825.00
(26)	George Mullin	2,750	1,350	825.00
(27)	Red Murray	2,750	1,350	825.00
(28)	Simon Nicholls	2,750	1,350	825.00
(29)	Charley O'Leary	2,750	1,350	825.00
(30)	Admiral Schlei	2,750	1,350	825.00
(31)	Boss Schmidt	2,750	1,350	825.00
(32)	Cy Seymore (Seymour)	2,750	1,350	825.00
(33)	Tully Sparks	2,750	1,350	825.00
(34)	Ed Summers	2,750	1,350	825.00
(35)	Ed Willetts (Willett)	2,750	1,350	825.00
(36)	Vic Willis	7,750	3,875	2,325
(37)	Hooks Wiltse	2,750	1,350	825.00

1912 Napoleon Little Cigars

While this cigarette brand advertising on the backs of T207 cards is less commonly encountered than Recruit, collectors do not attach a commensurate premium to them, largely because each of the players can be found with more common back ads.

PREMIUM: 2X
(See T207 for checklist and base card values.)

1963 Nassau County Boy Scouts

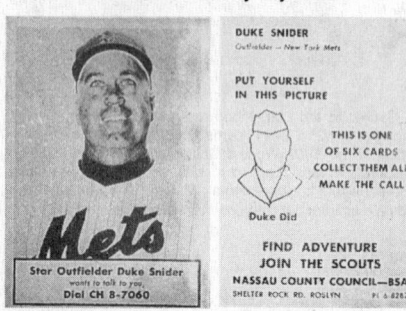

According to the text on the back, six cards were issued in this set. The other subjects are unknown, and may not feature any additional baseball players. The standard-size cards are printed in blue-and-white, both front and back, including a duo-tone photo of Snider in his only season with the Mets.

		NM	EX	VG
(1)	Duke Snider	150.00	75.00	45.00

1974 Nassau Tuberculosis and Respiratory Disease Assn.

The date attributed to these cards is arbitrary. The black-and-white 2-1/2" x 3-1/2" cards have a photo of the Yankees pitcher on front and a career summary on back, along with an anti-smoking message.

	NM	EX	VG
Whitey Ford	45.00	22.50	13.50
(Facing his right.)			
Whitey Ford (Follow-through.)	45.00	22.50	13.50

1921-23 National Caramel (E220)

Issued circa 1921 to 1923, this 120-card set is sometimes confused with contemporary American Caramel issues, but is easy to identify because of the words "Made only by National Caramel Company" on the back. With due consideration to normal cutting variances on cards of this era and type, E220s measure about 2" x 3-1/4" and feature black-and-white photos with the player's name, position and team at the bottom. In addition to the line indicating the manufacturer, the backs read

"This set consists of pictures of 120 of the leading Base Ball Stars of the American and National Leagues," There are 115 different players included in the set, with five players shown on two cards each. About half of the photos in the set are identical to those used in various American Caramel sets, leading to some confusion regarding the three sets.

		NM	EX	VG
Complete Set (120):		110,000	55,000	32,500
Common Player:		400.00	200.00	120.00
(1)	Charles "Babe" Adams	400.00	200.00	120.00
(2)	G.C. Alexander	1,600	800.00	475.00
(3)	James Austin	400.00	200.00	120.00
(4)	Jim Bagbyk (Bagby)	400.00	200.00	120.00
(5)	Franklin "Home Run" Baker	1,200	600.00	350.00
(6)	Dave Bancroft	1,200	600.00	350.00
(7)	Turner Barber	400.00	200.00	120.00
(8)	George Burns (Cincinnati)	400.00	200.00	120.00
(9)	George Burns (Cleveland)	400.00	200.00	120.00
(10)	Joe Bush	400.00	200.00	120.00
(11)	Leon Cadore	400.00	200.00	120.00
(12)	Max Carey	1,200	600.00	350.00
(13)	Ty Cobb	7,000	3,500	2,100
(14)	Eddie Collins	1,200	600.00	350.00
(15)	John Collins	400.00	200.00	120.00
(16)	Wilbur Cooper	400.00	200.00	120.00
(17)	S. Coveleskie (Coveleski)	1,200	600.00	350.00
(18)	Walton Cruise	400.00	200.00	120.00
(19)	Wm. Cunningham	400.00	200.00	120.00
(20)	George Cutshaw	400.00	200.00	120.00
(21)	Jake Daubert	400.00	200.00	120.00
(22)	Chas. A. Deal	400.00	200.00	120.00
(23)	Bill Doak	400.00	200.00	120.00
(24)	Joe Dugan	400.00	200.00	120.00
(25)	Jimmy Dykes/Btg	400.00	200.00	120.00
(26)	Jimmy Dykes/Fldg	400.00	200.00	120.00
(27)	"Red" Faber	1,200	600.00	350.00
(28)	"Chick" Fewster	400.00	200.00	120.00
(29)	Wilson Fewster	400.00	200.00	120.00
(30)	Ira Flagstead	400.00	200.00	120.00
(31)	Arthur Fletcher	400.00	200.00	120.00
(32)	Frank Frisch	1,200	600.00	350.00
(33)	Larry Gardner	400.00	200.00	120.00
(34)	Walter Gerber	400.00	200.00	120.00
(35)	Charles Glazner	400.00	200.00	120.00
(36)	Hank Gowdy	400.00	200.00	120.00
(37)	J.C. Graney (Should be J.G.)	400.00	200.00	120.00
(38)	Tommy Griffith	400.00	200.00	120.00
(39)	Charles Grimm	400.00	200.00	120.00
(40)	Heinie Groh	400.00	200.00	120.00
(41)	Byron Harris	400.00	200.00	120.00
(42)	Sam Harris (Bucky)	1,200	600.00	350.00
(43)	Harry Heilman (Heilmann)	1,200	600.00	350.00
(44)	Claude Hendrix	400.00	200.00	120.00
(45)	Walter Henline	400.00	200.00	120.00
(46)	Chas. Hollocher	400.00	200.00	120.00
(47)	Harry Hooper	1,200	600.00	350.00
(48)	Rogers Hornsby	1,600	800.00	475.00
(49)	Waite Hoyt	1,200	600.00	350.00
(50)	Wilbert Hubbell	400.00	200.00	120.00
(51)	Wm. Jacobson	400.00	200.00	120.00
(52)	Walter Johnson	3,400	1,700	1,000
(53)	Jimmy Johnston	400.00	200.00	120.00
(54)	Joe Judge	400.00	200.00	120.00
(55)	Geo. "Bingo" Kelly	1,200	600.00	350.00
(56)	Dick Kerr	400.00	200.00	120.00
(57)	Pete Kilduff/Bending	400.00	200.00	120.00
(58)	Pete Kilduff/Leaping	400.00	200.00	120.00
(59)	Larry Kopf	400.00	200.00	120.00
(60)	H.B. Leonard	400.00	200.00	120.00
(61)	Harry Liebold (Leibold)	400.00	200.00	120.00
(62)	Walter "Buster" Mails ("Duster")	400.00	200.00	120.00
(63)	Walter "Rabbit" Maranville	1,200	600.00	350.00
(64)	Carl Mays	400.00	200.00	120.00
(65)	Lee Meadows	400.00	200.00	120.00
(66)	Bob Meusel	400.00	200.00	120.00
(67)	Emil Meusel	400.00	200.00	120.00
(68)	J.C. Milan	400.00	200.00	120.00
(69)	Earl Neale	500.00	250.00	150.00
(70)	Robert Nehf (Arthur)	400.00	200.00	120.00
(71)	Bernie Neis	400.00	200.00	120.00
(72)	Joe Oeschger	400.00	200.00	120.00
(73)	Robert O'Farrell	400.00	200.00	120.00
(74)	Ivan Olson	400.00	200.00	120.00
(75)	Steve O'Neill	400.00	200.00	120.00
(76)	Geo. Paskert	400.00	200.00	120.00
(77)	Roger Peckinpaugh	400.00	200.00	120.00
(78)	Herb Pennock	1,200	600.00	350.00
(79)	Ralph "Cy" Perkins	400.00	200.00	120.00
(80)	Scott Perry (Photo actually Ed Rommel.)	400.00	200.00	120.00
(81)	Jeff Pfeffer	400.00	200.00	120.00
(82)	V.J. Picinich	400.00	200.00	120.00
(83)	Walter Pipp	460.00	230.00	140.00
(84)	Derrill Pratt	400.00	200.00	120.00
(85)	Goldie Rapp	400.00	200.00	120.00

(86)	Edgar Rice	1,200	600.00	350.00
(87)	Jimmy Ring	400.00	200.00	120.00
(88)	Eddie Rousch (Roush)	1,200	600.00	350.00
(89)	Babe Ruth	20,000	10,000	6,000
(90)	Raymond Schmandt	400.00	200.00	120.00
(91)	Everett Scott	400.00	200.00	120.00
(92)	Joe Sewell	1,200	600.00	350.00
(93)	Wally Shang (Schang)	400.00	200.00	120.00
(94)	Maurice Shannon	400.00	200.00	120.00
(95)	Bob Shawkey	400.00	200.00	120.00
(96)	Urban Shocker	400.00	200.00	120.00
(97)	George Sisler	1,200	600.00	350.00
(98)	Earl Smith	400.00	200.00	120.00
(99)	John Smith	400.00	200.00	120.00
(100)	Sherrod Smith	400.00	200.00	120.00
(101)	Frank Snyder/Crouching	400.00	200.00	120.00
(102)	Frank Snyder/Standing	400.00	200.00	120.00
(103)	Tris Speaker	1,600	800.00	475.00
(104)	Vernon Spencer	400.00	200.00	120.00
(105)	Chas. "Casey" Stengle (Stengel)	1,400	700.00	425.00
(106)	Milton Stock/Btg	400.00	200.00	120.00
(107)	Milton Stock/Fldg	400.00	200.00	120.00
(108)	James Vaughn	400.00	200.00	120.00
(109)	Robert Veach	400.00	200.00	120.00
(110)	Wm. Wambsgauss (Wambsganss)	400.00	200.00	120.00
(111)	Aaron Ward	400.00	200.00	120.00
(112)	Zach Wheat	1,200	600.00	350.00
(113)	George Whitted/Btg	400.00	200.00	120.00
(114)	George Whitted/Fldg	400.00	200.00	120.00
(115)	Fred C. Williams	400.00	200.00	120.00
(116)	Arthur Wilson	400.00	200.00	120.00
(117)	Ivy Wingo	400.00	200.00	120.00
(118)	Lawton Witt	400.00	200.00	120.00
(119)	"Pep" Young (Photo actually Ralph Young.)	400.00	200.00	120.00
(120)	Ross Young (Youngs)	1,200	600.00	350.00

1936 National Chicle "Fine Pens" (R313)

Issued in 1936 by the National Chicle Co., this set consists of 120 cards, measuring 3-1/4" x 5-3/8". The black-and-white cards are blank-backed and unnumbered. Although issued by National Chicle, the name of the company does not appear on the cards. The set includes individual player portraits with facsimilie autographs, multi-player cards and action photos. The cards, known in the hobby as "Fine Pen" because of the thin style of writing used for the facsimilie autographs, were originally available as an in-store premium.

		NM	EX	VG
Complete Set (120):		6,500	3,250	1,950
Common Player:		40.00	20.00	12.00
(1)	Melo Almada	45.00	22.50	13.50
(2)	Nick Altrock, Al Schacht	40.00	20.00	12.00
(3)	Paul Andrews	40.00	20.00	12.00
(4)	Elden Auker (Eldon)	40.00	20.00	12.00
(5)	Earl Averill	75.00	37.50	22.50
(6)	John Babich, James Bucher	40.00	20.00	12.00
(7)	Jim Becher (Bucher)	40.00	20.00	12.00
(8)	Moe Berg	350.00	175.00	105.00
(9)	Walter Berger	40.00	20.00	12.00
(10)	Charles Berry	40.00	20.00	12.00
(11)	Ralph Birkhofer (Birkofer)	40.00	20.00	12.00
(12)	Cy Blanton	40.00	20.00	12.00
(13)	O. Bluege	40.00	20.00	12.00
(14)	Cliff Bolton	40.00	20.00	12.00
(15)	Zeke Bonura	40.00	20.00	12.00
(16)	Stan Bordagaray, George Earnshaw	40.00	20.00	12.00
(17)	Jim Bottomley, Charley Gelbert	50.00	25.00	15.00
(18)	Thos. Bridges	40.00	20.00	12.00
(19)	Sam Byrd	40.00	20.00	12.00
(20)	Dolph Camilli	40.00	20.00	12.00
(21)	Dolph Camilli, Billy Jurges	40.00	20.00	12.00
(22)	Bruce Campbell	40.00	20.00	12.00
(23)	Walter "Kit" Carson	40.00	20.00	12.00
(24)	Ben Chapman	40.00	20.00	12.00
(25)	Harlond Clift, Luke Sewell	40.00	20.00	12.00
(26)	Mickey Cochrane, Jimmy Fox (Foxx), Al Simmons	90.00	45.00	27.50
(27)	"Rip" Collins	40.00	20.00	12.00
(28)	Joe Cronin	75.00	37.50	22.50
(29)	Frank Crossetti (Crosetti)	40.00	20.00	12.00
(30)	Frank Crosetti, Jimmy Dykes	40.00	20.00	12.00
(31)	Kiki Cuyler, Gabby Hartnett	85.00	40.00	25.00
(32)	Paul Derringer	40.00	20.00	12.00
(33)	Bill Dickey, Hank Greenberg	90.00	45.00	27.50
(34)	Bill Dietrich	40.00	20.00	12.00
(35)	Joe DiMaggio, Hank Erickson	750.00	375.00	225.00

		NM	EX	VG
(36)	Carl Doyle	40.00	20.00	12.00
(37)	Charles Dressen, Bill Myers	40.00	20.00	12.00
(38)	Jimmie Dykes	40.00	20.00	12.00
(39)	Rick Ferrell, Wess Ferrell (Wes)	75.00	37.50	22.50
(40)	Pete Fox	40.00	20.00	12.00
(41)	Frankie Frisch	75.00	37.50	22.50
(42)	Milton Galatzer	40.00	20.00	12.00
(43)	Chas. Gehringer	75.00	37.50	22.50
(44)	Charley Gelbert	40.00	20.00	12.00
(45)	Joe Glenn	40.00	20.00	12.00
(46)	Jose Gomez	40.00	20.00	12.00
(47)	Lefty Gomez, Red Ruffing	90.00	45.00	27.50
(48)	Vernon Gomez	75.00	37.50	22.50
(49)	Leon Goslin	75.00	37.50	22.50
(50)	Hank Gowdy	40.00	20.00	12.00
(51)	"Hank" Greenberg	90.00	45.00	27.50
(52)	"Lefty" Grove	90.00	45.00	27.50
(53)	Stan Hack	40.00	20.00	12.00
(54)	Odell Hale	40.00	20.00	12.00
(55)	Wild Bill Hallahan	40.00	20.00	12.00
(56)	Mel Harder	40.00	20.00	12.00
(57)	Stanley Bucky Harriss (Harris)	75.00	37.50	22.50
(58)	Gabby Hartnett, Rip Radcliff	75.00	37.50	22.50
(59)	Gabby Hartnett, L. Waner	45.00	22.50	13.50
(60)	Gabby Hartnett, Lon Warnecke (Warneke)	40.00	20.00	12.00
(61)	Buddy Hassett	40.00	20.00	12.00
(62)	Babe Herman	40.00	20.00	12.00
(63)	Frank Higgins	40.00	20.00	12.00
(64)	Oral C. Hildebrand	40.00	20.00	12.00
(65)	Myril Hoag	40.00	20.00	12.00
(66)	Rogers Hornsby	90.00	45.00	27.50
(67)	Waite Hoyt	75.00	37.50	22.50
(68)	Willis G. Hudlin	40.00	20.00	12.00
(69)	"Woody" Jensen	40.00	20.00	12.00
(70)	Woody Jenson (Jensen)	40.00	20.00	12.00
(71)	William Knickerbocker	40.00	20.00	12.00
(72)	Joseph Kuhel	40.00	20.00	12.00
(73)	Cookie Lavagetto	40.00	20.00	12.00
(74)	Thornton Lee	40.00	20.00	12.00
(75)	Ernie Lombardi	75.00	37.50	22.50
(76)	Red Lucas	40.00	20.00	12.00
(77)	Connie Mack, John McGraw	75.00	37.50	22.50
(78)	Pepper Martin	40.00	20.00	12.00
(79)	George McQuinn	40.00	20.00	12.00
(80)	George McQuinn, Lee Stine	40.00	20.00	12.00
(81)	Joe Medwick	75.00	37.50	22.50
(82)	Oscar Melillo	40.00	20.00	12.00
(83)	"Buddy" Meyer (Myer)	40.00	20.00	12.00
(84)	Randy Moore	40.00	20.00	12.00
(85)	T. Moore, Jimmie Wilson	40.00	20.00	12.00
(86)	Wallace Moses	40.00	20.00	12.00
(87)	V. Mungo	40.00	20.00	12.00
(88)	Lamar Newsom (Newsome)	40.00	20.00	12.00
(89)	Lewis "Buck" Newsom (Louis)	40.00	20.00	12.00
(90)	Steve O'Neill	40.00	20.00	12.00
(91)	Tommie Padden	40.00	20.00	12.00
(92)	E. Babe Philips (Phelps)	40.00	20.00	12.00
(93)	Bill Rogel (Rogell)	40.00	20.00	12.00
(94)	Lynn "Schoolboy" Rowe	40.00	20.00	12.00
(95)	Luke Sewell	40.00	20.00	12.00
(96)	Al Simmons	75.00	37.50	22.50
(97)	Casey Stengel	80.00	40.00	24.00
(98)	Bill Swift	40.00	20.00	12.00
(99)	Cecil Travis	40.00	20.00	12.00
(100)	"Pie" Traynor	75.00	37.50	22.50
(101)	William Urbansky (Urbanski)	40.00	20.00	12.00
(102)	Arky Vaughn (Vaughan)	75.00	37.50	22.50
(103)	Joe Vosmik	40.00	20.00	12.00
(104)	Honus Wagner	135.00	65.00	40.00
(105)	Rube Walberg	40.00	20.00	12.00
(106)	Bill Walker	40.00	20.00	12.00
(107)	Gerald Walker	40.00	20.00	12.00
(108)	L. Waner, P. Waner, Big Jim Weaver	75.00	37.50	22.50
(109)	George Washington	40.00	20.00	12.00
(110)	Bill Werber	40.00	20.00	12.00
(111)	Sam West	40.00	20.00	12.00
(112)	Pinkey Whitney	40.00	20.00	12.00
(113)	Vernon Wiltshere (Wilshere)	40.00	20.00	12.00
(114)	"Pep" Young	40.00	20.00	12.00
(115)	Chicago White Sox 1936	40.00	20.00	12.00
(116)	Fence Busters	40.00	20.00	12.00
(117)	Talking It Over (Leo Durocher)	40.00	20.00	12.00
(118)	There She Goes! Chicago City Series	40.00	20.00	12.00
(119)	Ump Says No - Cleveland vs. Detroit	40.00	20.00	12.00
(120)	World Series 1935 (Phil Cavarretta, Goose Goslin, Lon Warneke)	40.00	20.00	12.00

1936 National Chicle Rabbit Maranville 'How To'

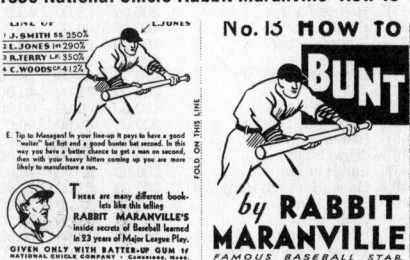

Issued by National Chicle in 1936, this 20-card set was a paper issue distributed with Batter-Up Gum. Unfolded, each paper measured 3-5/8" x 6". The numbered set featured a series of baseball tips from Rabbit Maranville and are illustrated with line drawings. American Card Catalog designation was R344.

		NM	EX	VG
Complete Set (20):		700.00	350.00	210.00
Common Card:		35.00	17.50	10.00
1	How to Pitch the Out Shoot	35.00	17.50	10.00
2	How to Throw the In Shoot	35.00	17.50	10.00
3	How to Pitch the Drop	35.00	17.50	10.00
4	How to Pitch the Floater	35.00	17.50	10.00
5	How to Run Bases	35.00	17.50	10.00
6	How to Slide	35.00	17.50	10.00
7	How to Catch Flies	35.00	17.50	10.00
8	How to Field Grounders	35.00	17.50	10.00
9	How to Tag A Man Out	35.00	17.50	10.00
10	How to Cover A Base	35.00	17.50	10.00
11	How to Bat	35.00	17.50	10.00
12	How to Steal Bases	35.00	17.50	10.00
13	How to Bunt	35.00	17.50	10.00
14	How to Coach Base Runner	35.00	17.50	18.00
15	How to Catch Behind the Bat	35.00	17.50	10.00
16	How to Throw to Bases	35.00	17.50	10.00
17	How to Signal	35.00	17.50	10.00
18	How to Umpire Balls and Strikes	35.00	17.50	10.00
19	How to Umpire Bases	35.00	17.50	10.00
20	How to Lay Out a Ball Field	35.00	17.50	10.00

1911 National Circulation System

Three cards of this type were discovered in the 1980s, each unique (only the Jimmy Archer card has been thus far publicly identified). It is believed they are salesman's sample produced to showcase the idea of handing out baseball cards with purchases at candy retailers. The hand-cut sample cards are approximately 1-7/8" x 3-3/8" in black-and-white. In the basic format that would become standard for candy cards later in the decade, fronts have a player photo with player name, position, date and team in three lines below. The back has printed, "A Picture with Every / 5 CENTS / In Trade at." Rubber-stamped in purple below is "Any Confectionary", presumably to give potential customers an idea where their specific business establishment's name and address could be printed. At the left end, also rubber-stamped, is "National Circulation System / DUBUQUE IOWA," probably the name of firm selling the concept. The only recent public sale of this type was a Jimmy Archer card in Good condition that brought $6,275 in a 2007 auction.

	NM	EX	VG
Jimmy Archer			

1898-99 National Copper Plate Co. Portraits

Besides supplying The Sporting News with the player portrait supplements issued during 1899-1900, this Grand Rapids, Mich., firm also sold nearly identical pieces in portfolios of 50 in a hard-cover, string-bound book. Approximately 10" x 13", the pictures feature the players at the turn of the century in formal portrait poses; some are in uniform, some in civilian clothes. The pictures are vignetted on a white background with the player's full name, team and year of issue printed at bottom. At lower-left on most, but not all, of the pictures is National Copper Plate's credit line. Backs have a player biographies in elaborate scrollwork frames.

		NM	EX	VG
Complete Set (50):		60,000	30,000	18,000
Common Player:		1,100	425.00	200.00
(1)	M.F. Amole (M.G. "Doc")	1,100	425.00	200.00
(2)	A.C. Anson	2,400	950.00	480.00
(3)	Robert Becker	1,100	425.00	200.00
(4)	Martin Bergen	1,100	425.00	200.00
(5)	James J. Collins	2,100	850.00	425.00
(6)	Joe Corbett	1,100	425.00	200.00
(7)	Louis Criger	1,100	425.00	200.00
(8)	Lave Cross	1,100	425.00	200.00
(9)	Montford Cross	1,100	425.00	200.00
(10)	Eugene DeMontreville	1,100	425.00	200.00
(11)	Charlie Dexter	1,100	425.00	200.00
(12)	P.J. Donovan	1,100	425.00	200.00
(13)	Thomas Dowd	1,100	425.00	200.00
(14)	John J. Doyle	1,100	425.00	200.00
(15)	Hugh Duffy	1,800	700.00	350.00
(16)	Frank Dwyer	1,100	425.00	200.00
(17)	Fred Ely ("Bones")	1,100	425.00	200.00
(18)	A.F. Esterquest	1,100	425.00	200.00
(19)	Wm. Ewing	1,800	700.00	350.00
(20)	Elmer Harrison Flick	1,800	700.00	350.00
(21)	Daniel Friend	1,100	425.00	200.00
(22)	Geo. F. Gilpatrick (Gillpatrick)	1,100	425.00	200.00
(23)	J.M. Goar	1,100	425.00	200.00
(24)	Mike Griffin	1,100	425.00	200.00
(25)	Clark C. Griffith	1,800	700.00	350.00
(26)	Wm. Hill	1,100	425.00	200.00
(27)	Wm. E. Hoy (Dummy)	2,100	850.00	400.00
(28)	James Hughes	1,100	425.00	200.00

		NM	EX	VG
(29)	William Joyce	1,100	425.00	200.00
(30)	William Keeler	1,800	700.00	350.00
(31)	Joseph J. Kelley	1,800	700.00	350.00
(32)	William Kennedy	1,100	425.00	200.00
(33)	William Lange	1,100	425.00	200.00
(34)	John J. McGraw	1,800	700.00	350.00
(35)	W.B. Mercer (George B. "Win")	1,100	425.00	200.00
(36)	Charles A. Nichols	2,100	850.00	400.00
(37)	Jerry Nops	1,100	425.00	200.00
(38)	John O'Connor	1,100	425.00	200.00
(39)	Richard Padden	1,100	425.00	200.00
(40)	Wilber Robinson (Wilbert)	1,800	700.00	350.00
(41)	William Shindle	1,000	425.00	200.00
(42)	Charles Stahl	1,000	425.00	200.00
(43)	E.P. Stein	1,100	425.00	200.00
(44)	S.L. Thompson	2,100	850.00	400.00
(45)	John Wagner	2,900	1,150	575.00
(46)	R.J. Wallace	1,800	700.00	350.00
(47)	Victor L. Willis	1,800	700.00	350.00
(48)	Parke Wilson	1,100	425.00	200.00
(49)	George Yeager	1,100	425.00	200.00
(50)	C.L. Zimmer	1,100	425.00	200.00

1913 National Game (WG5)

The patent date on the ornate red-and-white backs identify this as a 1913 issue. Fronts of the 2-1/2" x 3-1/2" cards have a black-and-white photo and a pair of baseball play scenarios used to play the card game. Corners are rounded. The set contains 43 identified player cards, a group of nine action photos in which the players are not identified and two header cards. The unnumbered cards are checklisted in alphabetical order. This set carries the ACC designation of WG5.

		NM	EX	VG
Complete Set (54):		6,000	3,000	1,800
Common Player:		55.00	30.00	20.00
Action Photo Card:		16.50	8.25	5.00
(1)	Grover Alexander	800.00	100.00	60.00
(2)	Frank Baker	150.00	50.00	30.00
(3)	Chief Bender	150.00	50.00	30.00
(4)	Bob Bescher	55.00	30.00	20.00
(5)	Joe Birmingham	55.00	30.00	20.00
(6)	Roger Bresnahan	150.00	50.00	30.00
(7)	Nixey Callahan	55.00	30.00	20.00
(8)	Frank Chance	150.00	50.00	30.00
(9)	Hal Chase	75.00	37.50	22.50
(10)	Fred Clarke	150.00	50.00	30.00
(11)	Ty Cobb	1,000	300.00	180.00
(12)	Sam Crawford	150.00	50.00	30.00
(13)	Bill Dahlen	55.00	30.00	20.00
(14)	Jake Daubert	55.00	30.00	20.00
(15)	Red Dooin	55.00	30.00	20.00
(16)	Johnny Evers	150.00	50.00	30.00
(17)	Vean Gregg	55.00	30.00	20.00
(18)	Clark Griffith	150.00	50.00	30.00
(19)	Dick Hoblitzel	55.00	30.00	20.00
(20)	Miller Huggins	150.00	50.00	30.00
(21)	Joe Jackson	3,500	800.00	480.00
(22)	Hughie Jennings	150.00	50.00	30.00
(23)	Walter Johnson	500.00	125.00	75.00
(24)	Ed Konetchy	55.00	30.00	20.00
(25)	Nap Lajoie	150.00	50.00	30.00
(26)	Connie Mack	150.00	50.00	30.00
(27)	Rube Marquard	150.00	50.00	30.00
(28)	Christy Mathewson	500.00	125.00	75.00
(29)	John McGraw	150.00	50.00	30.00
(30)	Larry McLean	55.00	30.00	20.00
(31)	Clyde Milan	55.00	30.00	20.00
(32)	Marty O'Toole	55.00	30.00	20.00
(33)	Nap Rucker	55.00	30.00	20.00
(34)	Tris Speaker	200.00	75.00	45.00
(35)	Jake Stahl	55.00	30.00	20.00
(36)	George Stallings	55.00	30.00	20.00
(37)	George Stovall	55.00	30.00	20.00
(38)	Bill Sweeney	55.00	30.00	20.00
(39)	Joe Tinker	150.00	50.00	30.00
(40)	Honus Wagner	1,000	200.00	120.00
(41)	Ed Walsh	150.00	50.00	30.00
(42)	Joe Wood	55.00	50.00	30.00
(43)	Cy Young	500.00	125.00	75.00
(---)	Rules Card	55.00	30.00	20.00
(---)	Score Card	55.00	30.00	20.00
(1A)	Batter swinging, looking forward	15.00	7.50	4.50
(2A)	Batter swinging, looking back	15.00	7.50	4.50
(3A)	Runner sliding, fielder at bag	15.00	7.50	4.50
(4A)	Runner sliding, umpire behind (Some collectors believe the player in the picture is Ty Cobb and are willing to pay a premium for this card.)	75.00	37.50	22.50
(5A)	Runner sliding, hugging base	15.00	7.50	4.50
(6A)	Sliding play at plate, umpire at left	15.00	7.50	4.50

(7A)	Sliding play at plate, umpire at right	15.00	7.50	4.50
(8A)	Play at plate, runner standing	15.00	7.50	4.50
(9A)	Runner looking backwards	15.00	7.50	4.50

1952 National Tea Labels

Another set of bread end-labels, this checklist now comprises 44 players, although there is speculation that others remain to be cataloged. The unnumbered labels measure approximately 2-3/4" x 2-11/16" and are sometimes referred to as "Red Borders" because of their wide, red margins. The player's name and team are printed alongside his photo, and the slogan "Eat More Bread for Health" also appears on some labels.

		NM	EX	VG
Complete Set (44):		10,000	5,000	3,000
Common Player:		200.00	100.00	60.00
(1)	Gene Bearden	200.00	100.00	60.00
(2)	Yogi Berra	450.00	225.00	135.00
(3)	Lou Brissie	200.00	100.00	60.00
(4)	Sam Chapman	200.00	100.00	60.00
(5)	Chuck Diering	200.00	100.00	60.00
(6)	Dom DiMaggio	250.00	125.00	75.00
(7)	Bruce Edwards	200.00	100.00	60.00
(8)	Del Ennis	200.00	100.00	60.00
(9)	Ferris Fain	200.00	100.00	60.00
(10)	Bob Feller	375.00	185.00	110.00
(11)	Howie Fox	200.00	100.00	60.00
(12)	Sid Gordon	200.00	100.00	60.00
(13)	John Groth	200.00	100.00	60.00
(14)	Granny Hamner	200.00	100.00	60.00
(15)	Jim Hegan	200.00	100.00	60.00
(16)	Sheldon Jones	200.00	100.00	60.00
(17)	Howie Judson	200.00	100.00	60.00
(18)	Sherman Lollar	200.00	100.00	60.00
(19)	Clarence Marshall	200.00	100.00	60.00
(20)	Don Mueller	200.00	100.00	60.00
(21)	Danny Murtaugh	200.00	100.00	60.00
(22)	Dave Philley	200.00	100.00	60.00
(23)	Jerry Priddy	200.00	100.00	60.00
(24)	Bill Rigney	200.00	100.00	60.00
(25)	Robin Roberts	350.00	175.00	100.00
(26)	Eddie Robinson	200.00	100.00	60.00
(27)	Preacher Roe	225.00	110.00	65.00
(28)	Stan Rojek	200.00	100.00	60.00
(29)	Al Rosen	225.00	110.00	65.00
(30)	Bob Rush	200.00	100.00	60.00
(31)	Hank Sauer	200.00	100.00	60.00
(32)	Johnny Schmitz	200.00	100.00	60.00
(33)	Enos Slaughter	350.00	175.00	100.00
(34)	Duke Snider	400.00	200.00	120.00
(35)	Warren Spahn	375.00	185.00	110.00
(36)	Gerry Staley	200.00	100.00	60.00
(37)	Virgil Stallcup	200.00	100.00	60.00
(38)	George Stirnweiss	200.00	100.00	60.00
(39)	Earl Torgeson	200.00	100.00	60.00
(40)	Dizzy Trout	200.00	100.00	60.00
(41)	Mickey Vernon	200.00	100.00	60.00
(42)	Wally Westlake	200.00	100.00	60.00
(43)	Johnny Wyrostek	200.00	100.00	60.00
(44)	Eddie Yost	200.00	100.00	60.00

1922 Neilson's Chocolate Type 1 (V61)

This set is closely related to the popular 1922 American Caramels (E120). The 120-card set was issued in Canada by Neilson's Chocolate Bars and carries the American Card Catalog designation V61. The front of the approximately 2" x 3-1/2" black-and-white cards has oval posed action photos with a dec-

orative border. In the bottom border is the player name, position and team. Backs contain an ad for Neilson's Chocolates. Two types of cards exist. Type 1 is printed on heavy paper (similar to E120), has a card number in the lower-left corner and features Old English typography of the sponsor's name on back. Type 2 is printed on cardboard, has no card numbers and has no Old English typography on back.

		NM	EX	VG
Complete Set (120):		27,500	11,000	5,500
Common Player:		115.00	45.00	22.50
1	George Burns	115.00	45.00	22.50
2	John Tobin	115.00	45.00	22.50
3	J.T. Zachary	115.00	45.00	22.50
4	"Bullet" Joe Bush	115.00	45.00	22.50
5	Lu Blue	115.00	45.00	22.50
6	Clarence (Tillie) Walker	115.00	45.00	22.50
7	Carl Mays	115.00	45.00	22.50
8	Leon Goslin	300.00	120.00	60.00
9	Ed Rommel	115.00	45.00	22.50
10	Charles Robertson	115.00	45.00	22.50
11	Ralph (Cy) Perkins	115.00	45.00	22.50
12	Joe Sewell	300.00	120.00	60.00
13	Harry Hooper	300.00	120.00	60.00
14	Urban (Red) Faber	300.00	120.00	60.00
15	Bib Falk (Bibb)	115.00	45.00	22.50
16	George Uhle	115.00	45.00	22.50
17	Emory Rigney	115.00	45.00	22.50
18	George Dauss	115.00	45.00	22.50
19	Herman Pillette	115.00	45.00	22.50
20	Wallie Schang	115.00	45.00	22.50
21	Lawrence Woodall	115.00	45.00	22.50
22	Steve O'Neill	115.00	45.00	22.50
23	Edmund (Bing) Miller	115.00	45.00	22.50
24	Sylvester Johnson	115.00	45.00	22.50
25	Henry Severeid	115.00	45.00	22.50
26	Dave Danforth	115.00	45.00	22.50
27	Harry Heilmann	300.00	120.00	60.00
28	Bert Cole	115.00	45.00	22.50
29	Eddie Collins	300.00	120.00	60.00
30	Ty Cobb	3,500	1,400	700.00
31	Bill Wambsganss	115.00	45.00	22.50
32	George Sisler	300.00	120.00	60.00
33	Bob Veach	115.00	45.00	22.50
34	Earl Sheely	115.00	45.00	22.50
35	T.P. (Pat) Collins	115.00	45.00	22.50
36	Frank (Dixie) Davis	115.00	45.00	22.50
37	Babe Ruth	7,500	3,700	2,200
38	Bryan Harris	115.00	45.00	22.50
39	Bob Shawkey	115.00	45.00	22.50
40	Urban Shocker	115.00	45.00	22.50
41	Martin McManus	115.00	45.00	22.50
42	Clark Pittenger	115.00	45.00	22.50
43	"Deacon" Sam Jones	115.00	45.00	22.50
44	Waite Hoyt	300.00	120.00	60.00
45	Johnny Mostil	115.00	45.00	22.50
46	Mike Menosky	115.00	45.00	22.50
47	Walter Johnson	600.00	240.00	120.00
48	Wallie Pipp (Wally)	115.00	45.00	22.50
49	Walter Gerber	115.00	45.00	22.50
50	Ed Gharrity	115.00	45.00	22.50
51	Frank Ellerbe	115.00	45.00	22.50
52	Kenneth Williams	115.00	45.00	22.50
53	Joe Hauser	175.00	70.00	35.00
54	Carson Bigbee	115.00	45.00	22.50
55	Emil (Irish) Meusel	115.00	45.00	22.50
56	Milton Stock	115.00	45.00	22.50
57	Wilbur Cooper	115.00	45.00	22.50
58	Tom Griffith	115.00	45.00	22.50
59	Walter (Butch) Henline	115.00	45.00	22.50
60	Gene (Bubbles) Hargrave	115.00	45.00	22.50
61	Russell Wrightstone	115.00	45.00	22.50
62	Frank Frisch	300.00	120.00	60.00
63	Frank Parkinson	115.00	45.00	22.50
64	Walter (Dutch) Reuther (Ruether)	115.00	45.00	22.50
65	Bill Doak	115.00	45.00	22.50
66	Marty Callaghan	115.00	45.00	22.50
67	Sammy Bohne	175.00	70.00	35.00
68	Earl Hamilton	115.00	45.00	22.50
69	Grover C. Alexander	325.00	130.00	65.00
70	George Burns	115.00	45.00	22.50
71	Max Carey	300.00	120.00	60.00
72	Adolfo Luque	145.00	58.00	29.00
73	Dave (Beauty) Bancroft	300.00	120.00	60.00
74	Vic Aldridge	115.00	45.00	22.50
75	Jack Smith	115.00	45.00	22.50
76	Bob O'Farrell	115.00	45.00	22.50
77	Pete Donohue	115.00	45.00	22.50
78	Ralph Pinelli	115.00	45.00	22.50
79	Eddie Roush	300.00	120.00	60.00
80	Norman Boeckel	115.00	45.00	22.50
81	Rogers Hornsby	400.00	160.00	80.00
82	George Toporcer	115.00	45.00	22.50
83	Ivy Wingo	115.00	45.00	22.50
84	Virgil Cheeves	115.00	45.00	22.50
85	Vern Clemons	115.00	45.00	22.50
86	Lawrence (Hack) Miller	115.00	45.00	22.50
87	Johnny Kelleher	115.00	45.00	22.50
88	Heinie Groh	115.00	45.00	22.50
89	Burleigh Grimes	300.00	120.00	60.00
90	"Rabbit" Maranville	300.00	120.00	60.00
91	Charles (Babe) Adams	115.00	45.00	22.50
92	Lee King	115.00	45.00	22.50
93	Art Nehf	115.00	45.00	22.50
94	Frank Snyder	115.00	45.00	22.50
95	Raymond Powell	115.00	45.00	22.50
96	Wilbur Hubbell	115.00	45.00	22.50
97	Leon Cadore	115.00	45.00	22.50
98	Joe Oeschger	115.00	45.00	22.50
99	Jake Daubert	115.00	45.00	22.50
100	Will Sherdel	115.00	45.00	22.50
101	Hank DeBerry	115.00	45.00	22.50
102	Johnny Lavan	115.00	45.00	22.50
103	Jesse Haines	300.00	120.00	60.00
104	Joe (Goldie) Rapp	115.00	45.00	22.50
105	Oscar Ray Grimes	115.00	45.00	22.50

106	Ross Young (Youngs)	300.00	120.00	60.00
107	Art Fletcher	115.00	45.00	22.50
108	Clyde Barnhart	115.00	45.00	22.50
109	Louis (Pat) Duncan	115.00	45.00	22.50
110	Charlie Hollocher	115.00	45.00	22.50
111	Horace Ford	115.00	45.00	22.50
112	Bill Cunningham	115.00	45.00	22.50
113	Walter Schmidt	115.00	45.00	22.50
114	Joe Schultz	115.00	45.00	22.50
115	John Morrison	115.00	45.00	22.50
116	Jimmy Caveney	115.00	45.00	22.50
117	Zach Wheat	300.00	120.00	60.00
118	Fred (Cy) Williams	115.00	45.00	22.50
119	George Kelly	300.00	120.00	60.00
120	Jimmy Ring	115.00	45.00	22.50

1922 Neilson's Chocolate Type 2 (V61)

This set is closely related to the popular 1922 American Caramels (E120). The 120-card set was issued in Canada by Neilson's Chocolate Bars and carries the American Card Catalog designation V61. The front of the approximately 2" x 3-1/2" black-and-white cards has oval posed action photos with a decorative border. In the bottom border is the player name, position and team. Backs contain and ad for Neilson's Chocolates. Two types of cards exist. Type 1 is printed on heavy paper (similar to E120), has a card number in the lower-left corner and features Old English typography of the sponsor's name on back. Type 2 is printed on cardboard, has no card numbers and has no Old English typography on back.

		NM	EX	VG
Complete Set (120):		42,500	17,000	8,500
Common Player:		200.00	85.00	40.00
(1)	Charles (Babe) Adams	200.00	85.00	40.00
(2)	Vic Aldridge	200.00	85.00	40.00
(3)	Grover C. Alexander	750.00	300.00	150.00
(4)	Dave (Beauty) Bancroft	450.00	180.00	90.00
(5)	Clyde Barnhart	200.00	85.00	40.00
(6)	Carson Bigbee	200.00	85.00	40.00
(7)	Lu Blue	200.00	85.00	40.00
(8)	Norman Boeckel	200.00	85.00	40.00
(9)	Sammy Bohne	250.00	100.00	50.00
(10)	George Burns (Boston)	200.00	85.00	40.00
(11)	George Burns (Cincinnati)	200.00	85.00	40.00
(12)	"'Bullet" Joe Bush	200.00	85.00	40.00
(13)	Leon Cadore	200.00	85.00	40.00
(14)	Marty Callaghan	200.00	85.00	40.00
(15)	Max Carey	450.00	180.00	90.00
(16)	Jimmy Caveney	200.00	85.00	40.00
(17)	Virgil Cheeves	200.00	85.00	40.00
(18)	Vern Clemons	200.00	85.00	40.00
(19)	Ty Cobb	5,500	2,200	1,100
(20)	Bert Cole	200.00	85.00	40.00
(21)	Eddie Collins	450.00	180.00	90.00
(22)	T.P. (Pat) Collins	200.00	85.00	40.00
(23)	Wilbur Cooper	200.00	85.00	40.00
(24)	Bill Cunningham	200.00	85.00	40.00
(25)	Dave Danforth	200.00	85.00	40.00
(26)	Jake Daubert	200.00	85.00	40.00
(27)	George Dauss	200.00	85.00	40.00
(28)	Frank (Dixie) Davis	200.00	85.00	40.00
(29)	Hank DeBerry	200.00	85.00	40.00
(30)	Bill Doak	200.00	85.00	40.00
(31)	Pete Donohue	200.00	85.00	40.00
(32)	Louis (Pat) Duncan	200.00	85.00	40.00
(33)	Frank Ellerbe	200.00	85.00	40.00
(34)	Urban (Red) Faber	450.00	180.00	90.00
(35)	Bib (Bibb) Falk	200.00	85.00	40.00
(36)	Art Fletcher	200.00	85.00	40.00
(37)	Horace Ford	200.00	85.00	40.00
(38)	Frank Frisch	450.00	180.00	90.00
(39)	Walter Gerber	200.00	85.00	40.00
(40)	Ed Gharrity	200.00	85.00	40.00
(41)	Leon Goslin	450.00	180.00	90.00
(42)	Tom Griffith	200.00	85.00	40.00
(43)	Burleigh Grimes	450.00	180.00	90.00
(44)	Oscar Ray Grimes	200.00	85.00	40.00
(45)	Heinie Groh	200.00	85.00	40.00
(46)	Jesse Haines	450.00	180.00	90.00
(47)	Earl Hamilton	200.00	85.00	40.00
(48)	Gene (Bubbles) Hargrave	200.00	85.00	40.00
(49)	Bryan Harris	200.00	85.00	40.00
(50)	Joe Hauser	350.00	140.00	70.00
(51)	Harry Heilmann	450.00	180.00	90.00
(52)	Walter (Butch) Henline	200.00	85.00	40.00
(53)	Charlie Hollocher	200.00	85.00	40.00
(54)	Harry Hooper	450.00	180.00	90.00
(55)	Rogers Hornsby	550.00	220.00	110.00
(56)	Waite Hoyt	450.00	180.00	90.00
(57)	Wilbert Hubbell	200.00	85.00	40.00
(58)	Sylvester Johnson	200.00	85.00	40.00
(59)	Walter Johnson	800.00	320.00	160.00
(60)	"Deacon" Sam Jones	200.00	85.00	40.00

(61)	Johnny Kelleher	200.00	85.00	40.00
(62)	George Kelly	450.00	180.00	90.00
(63)	Lee King	200.00	85.00	40.00
(64)	Johnny Lavan	200.00	85.00	40.00
(65)	Adolfo Luque	250.00	100.00	50.00
(66)	"Rabbit" Maranville	450.00	180.00	90.00
(67)	Carl Mays	200.00	85.00	40.00
(68)	Martin McManus	200.00	85.00	40.00
(69)	Mike Menosky	200.00	85.00	40.00
(70)	Emil (Irish) Meusel	200.00	85.00	40.00
(71)	Edmund (Bing) Miller	200.00	85.00	40.00
(72)	Lawrence (Hack) Miller	200.00	85.00	40.00
(73)	John Morrison	200.00	85.00	40.00
(74)	Johnny Mostil	200.00	85.00	40.00
(75)	Art Nehf	200.00	85.00	40.00
(76)	Joe Oeschger	200.00	85.00	40.00
(77)	Bob O'Farrell	200.00	85.00	40.00
(78)	Steve O'Neill	200.00	85.00	40.00
(79)	Frank Parkinson	200.00	85.00	40.00
(80)	Ralph (Cy) Perkins	200.00	85.00	40.00
(81)	Herman Pillette	200.00	85.00	40.00
(82)	Ralph Pinelli	200.00	85.00	40.00
(83)	Wallie (Wally) Pipp	200.00	85.00	40.00
(84)	Clark Pittinger	200.00	85.00	40.00
(85)	Raymond Powell	200.00	85.00	40.00
(86)	Joe (Goldie) Rapp	200.00	85.00	40.00
(87)	Walter (Dutch) Reuther	200.00	85.00	40.00
(88)	Emory Rigney	200.00	85.00	40.00
(89)	Jimmy Ring	200.00	85.00	40.00
(90)	Charles Robertson	200.00	85.00	40.00
(91)	Ed Rommel	200.00	85.00	40.00
(92)	Eddie Roush	450.00	180.00	90.00
(93)	Babe Ruth	10,000	5,000	3,000
(94)	Wallie (Wally) Schang	200.00	85.00	40.00
(95)	Walter Schmidt	200.00	85.00	40.00
(96)	Joe Schultz	200.00	85.00	40.00
(97)	Hank Severeid	200.00	85.00	40.00
(98)	Joe Sewell	450.00	180.00	90.00
(99)	Bob Shawkey	200.00	85.00	40.00
(100)	Earl Sheely	200.00	85.00	40.00
(101)	Will Sherdel	200.00	85.00	40.00
(102)	Urban Shocker	200.00	85.00	40.00
(103)	George Sisler	450.00	180.00	90.00
(104)	Jack Smith	200.00	85.00	40.00
(105)	Frank Snyder	200.00	85.00	40.00
(106)	Milton Stock	200.00	85.00	40.00
(107)	John Tobin	200.00	85.00	40.00
(108)	George Torporcer	200.00	85.00	40.00
(109)	George Uhle	200.00	85.00	40.00
(110)	Bob Veach	200.00	85.00	40.00
(111)	Clarence (Tillie) Walker	200.00	85.00	40.00
(112)	Bill Wambsganss	200.00	85.00	40.00
(113)	Zach Wheat	450.00	180.00	90.00
(114)	Fred (Cy) Williams	200.00	85.00	40.00
(115)	Kenneth Williams	200.00	85.00	40.00
(116)	Ivy Wingo	200.00	85.00	40.00
(117)	Lawrence Woodall	200.00	85.00	40.00
(118)	Russell Wrightstone	200.00	85.00	40.00
(119)	Ross Young (Youngs)	450.00	180.00	90.00
(120)	J.T. Zachary	200.00	85.00	40.00

1923 "Neilson's Chocolates"

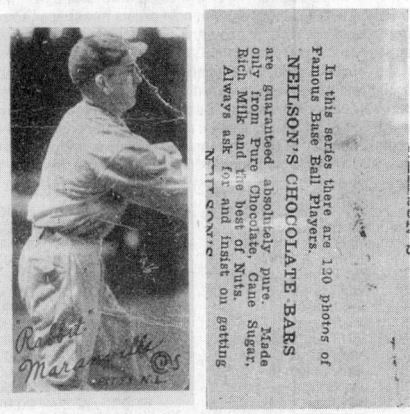

This issue, purporting to come from the Canadian candy maker which had produced a 1922 set, was first reported in 1996. The cards appear to be genuine W572 strip cards which have had a Neilson's ad overprinted on the back many years later in an apparent effort to defraud collectors. These altered W572s would have to be significantly downgraded to adjust for the defacing. It can be expected that any card that appears in W572 can be found with the Neilson's back, but the "discovery" contained only 47 different players.

(See W572 for checklist.)

1959 Neptune Sardines Jimmy Piersall

Like the earlier advertising postcards he did for various Cain's food products, this 3-1/2" x 5-1/2" black-and-white postcard carries the endorsement of the popular Indians outfielder for Neptune brand sardines. The front has a borderless photo of the player in a batting pose with a facsimile autograph at top. The back has standard postcard indicia along with the ad message and a product picture.

	NM	EX	VG
Jimmy Piersall	50.00	25.00	15.00

1976-81 New England Sports Collectors

From the period 1976-81, the New England Sports Collectors club issued a series of postcard-size (3-1/2" x 5-1/4")

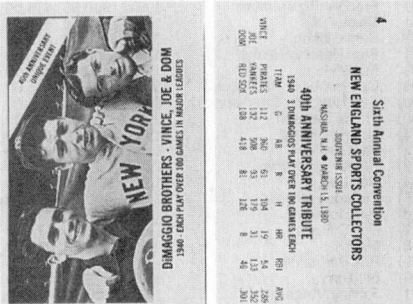

black-and-white card promoting their annual shows in Nashua, N.H. No card was issued in 1978.

		NM	EX	VG
Complete Set (5):		30.00	15.00	9.00
Common Player:		6.00	3.00	1.75
1	Joe DiMaggio (1976)	8.00	4.00	2.50
2	Jackie Robinson (1977)	6.00	3.00	1.75
3	Ted Williams (1979)	7.00	3.50	2.00
4	Vince DiMaggio, Joe DiMaggio, Dom DiMaggio (1980)	6.00	3.00	1.75
5	Mickey Mantle (1981)	9.00	4.50	2.75

1895 Newsboy Cabinets (N566)

Issued in the 1890s by the National Tobacco Works, this massive cabinet card set was distributed as a premium with the Newsboy tobacco brand. Although the set contained over 500 popular actresses, athletes, politicians and other celebrities of the day, only about a dozen cards of baseball players have been found. The cards measure 4-1/4" x 6-1/2" and feature sepia-toned photographs mounted on a backing that usually has "Newsboy New York" printed at bottom. Each portrait photograph is numbered and a few of the photos are round. The ballplayers in the set are mostly members of the 1894 New York Giants with a couple of Brooklyn players. There are two known poses of John Ward. Cards have been seen with advertising on the back for Keystone cigars and Red Indian tobacco, and on front for "Baum & Bernstein, Clothiers."

		NM	EX	VG
Common Player:		8,250	4,125	2,475
174	W.H. Murphy	8,250	4,125	2,475
175	Amos Rusie	25,000	12,500	7,500
176	Michael Tiernan	8,250	4,125	2,475
177	E.D. Burke	8,250	4,125	2,475
178	J.J. Doyle	8,250	4,125	2,475
179	W.B. Fuller	8,250	4,125	2,475
180	George Van Haltren	8,250	4,125	2,475
181	Dave Foutz	8,250	4,125	2,475
182	Jouett Meekin	8,250	4,125	2,475
183	Michael Griffin	8,250	4,125	2,475
201	W.H. (Dad) Clark (Clarke)	8,250	4,125	2,475
202	Parke Wilson	8,250	4,125	2,475
586	John Ward (Arms folded.)	40,000	20,000	12,000
587	John Ward (Bat at side.)	13,500	6,750	4,050

1886 New York Baseball Club (H812)

This rare 19th Century baseball issue can be classified under the general category of "trade" cards, a popular advertising vehicle of the period. The cards measure 3" x 4-3/4" and feature blue line-drawing portraits of members of the "New York Base Ball Club," which is printed along the top. As was common with this type of trade card, the bottom was left blank to accomodate various messages. The known examples of this set carry ads for local tobacco merchants and other businesses. The portraits are all based on the photographs used in the 1886 Old Judge set. The cards, which have been assigned an ACC designation of H812, are printed on thin paper rather than cardboard.

		NM	EX	VG
Complete Set (8):		84,000	37,200	20,400
Common Player:		7,200	3,200	1,450
(1)	T. Dealsey	7,200	3,200	1,450
(2)	M. Dorgan	7,200	3,200	1,450
(3)	T. Esterbrook	7,200	3,200	1,450
(4)	W. Ewing	16,200	8,100	4,800
(5)	J. Gerhardt	7,200	3,200	1,450
(6)	J. O'Rourke	16,200	8,100	4,800
(7)	D. Richardson	7,200	3,200	1,450
(8)	M. Welch	16,200	8,100	4,800

1969 N.Y. Boy Scouts

Cards featuring N.Y. Mets and Yankees players were used as a recruitment incentive in 1969. Cards are 2-1/2" x 3-1/2" and printed in black-and-white on thin cardboard. It is unknown, but likely, that players other than those checklisted here were also issued.

		NM	EX	VG
Common Player:		175.00	85.00	50.00
(1)	Tommy Agee	175.00	85.00	50.00
(2)	Bud Harrelson	175.00	85.00	50.00
(3)	Cleon Jones	175.00	85.00	50.00
(4)	Bobby Murcer	260.00	130.00	75.00
(5)	Joe Pepitone	260.00	130.00	75.00
(6)	Art Shamsky	175.00	85.00	50.00
(7)	Tom Seaver	700.00	350.00	210.00
(8)	Mel Stottlemyre	260.00	130.00	75.00
(9)	Ron Swoboda	175.00	85.00	50.00

1879-80 N.Y. Clipper Woodcuts

The N.Y. Clipper was a weekly newspaper devoted to theater and sports (primarily baseball) coverage in New York City between 1853-1923. Like many contemporary papers, the Clipper featured woodcut engravings in its pages in a time before photographic reproduction of pictures was feasible. Between April 1879, and November 1880, the paper printed a series of baseball player portraits. The early pieces were titled "The Clipper Prize Winners." and numbered. All of the woodcuts are about 4-1/2" x 5-3/4" in size featuring portraits within ornate frames with identification and biographical details below. Collectors prefer the woodcuts to be neatly trimmed from the newspaper page, with the biography at bottom intact. Because of the rarity of surviving examples, catalog values are undetermined. Many of these early stars of the game appear on no other contempary cards or memorabilia issues.

1879

1	M.C. Dorgan (4/12)
2	H.F. McCormick (4/19)
3	Stephen A. Libby (4/26)
4	Roscoe C. Barnes (5/3)
5	David W. Force (5/10)
6	Herman Doescher (Dosher) (5/17)
7a	Joseph Hornung (5/24)
7b	William H. McGunnigle (5/31)
9	Harding Richardson (6/7)
(10)	James L. White (7/14)
(11)	Levi S. Meyerle (6/21)
(12)	Joe Start (6/28)
(13)	T.H. Mumam (Murnane) (7/5)
(14)	Thomas York (7/12)
(15)	Fred Dunlap (7/19)
(16)	A.J. Leonard (7/26)
(17)	J. Lee Richmond (8/2)
(18)	Charles N. Snyder (8/9)
(19)	John Cassidy (8/16)
(20)	Charles Fulmer (8/23)
(21)	Thomas Poorman (8/30)
(22)	John Ward (9/6)
(23)	Larry Corcoran (9/13)
(24)	Douglas Allison (9/20)
(25)	John J. Farrow (9/27)
(26)	E.N. Williamson (10/4)
(27)	George Wright (10/11)
(28)	John J. Burdock (10/18)
(29)	James O'Rourke (10/25)
(30)	Philip Baker (11/1)

(31) Samuel W. Trott (11/8)
(32) John Lynch (11/15)
(33) A.G. Spalding (11/22)
(34) John C. Chapman (11/29)
(35) Paul A. Hines (12/6)
(36) Frank C. Bancroft (12/13)
(37) John T. O'Conner (12/20)
(38) Andrew J. Piercy (12/27)
1880
(39) Harold M. McClure (1/3)
(40) J.H. Gifford (1/24)
(41) Sam Wright (5/15)
(42) T.J. Keefe (5/22)
(43) M.J. Kelly (5/29)
(44) John Troy (6/5)
(45) Joe Quest (6/12)
(46) Alonzo Knight (6/19)
(47) Charles E. Mason (6/26)
(48) F.E. Goldsmith (7/3)
(49) R.E. McKelvy (7/10)
(50) Wm. McLean (Umpire)(7/17)
(51) C.A. McVey (7/24)
(52) John Manning (7/31)
(53) Harry D. Stovey (8/7)
(54) George A. Wood (8/14)
(55) Robert T. Mathews (8/21)
(56) D. Brouthers (8/28)
(57) C.M. Smith (9/4)
(58) James L. Clinton (9/11)
(59) A.J. Bushong (9/18)
(60) William J. Sweeney (9/25)
(61) Roger Connor (10/2)
(62) William Hawes (10/9)
(63) Frank S. Flint (10/16)
(64) William L. Haug (10/23)
(65) M. Welch (10/30)
(66) Aaron B. Clapp (11/6)
(67) John J. Smith (11/13)
(68) George Creamer (11/20)

1905 N.Y. Giants Scorecard Postcard

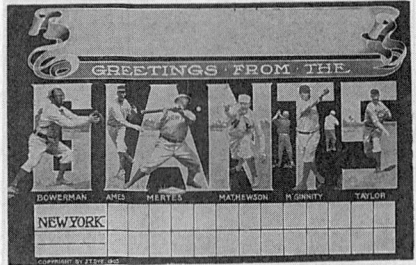

Two versions, black-and-white and color, of this standard size (about 5-1/2" x 3-1/2") postcard were apparently available for several years as it is copyrighted 1905 but postally used examples from years later are often seen. The card has a black background with large cut-out letters "GIANTS" at center featuring action poses of six players. A grid at bottom allows by-inning scores of a game to be posted before mailing. The undivided back has an embellished double-ruled stamp box and a large ornate "Post Card" at top-center.

	NM	EX	VG
Black-and-White:	300.00	150.00	90.00
Color:	400.00	200.00	125.00

Frank Bowerman, Red Ames, Sam Mertes, Christy Mathewson, Iron Man McGinnity, Luther Taylor

1932 N.Y. Giants Schedule Postcards

 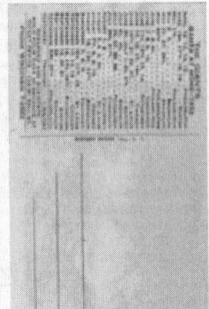

These postcard-size (3-1/2" x 5-1/2") black-and-white cards have an action pose on front with the player's identification and previous season's stats. At bottom is information about ladies' days, directions to the Polo Grounds and an offer to receive a free picture of a favorite player. The divided back has the team's 1932 schedule at left and space for addressing at right. There is also a credit line to Minden Press. The Carl Hubbell card is far more common than all others and can be found on either a thick or thin card stock that is unlike the stock on which the other players are found.

	NM	EX	VG
Complete Set (22):	35,000	17,500	10,500
Common Player:	1,600	800.00	475.00
(1) Ethan Allen	1,600	800.00	475.00
(2) Herman Bell	1,600	800.00	475.00
(3) Hugh Critz	1,600	800.00	475.00
(4) Freddie Fitzsimmons	1,600	800.00	475.00
(5) Chick Fullis	1,600	800.00	475.00
(6) Sam Gibson	1,600	800.00	475.00
(7) Fran Healey (Healy)	1,600	800.00	475.00
(8) Frank Hogan	1,600	800.00	475.00
(9a) Carl Hubbell (Thin stock.)	250.00	125.00	75.00
(9b) Carl Hubbell (Thick stock.)	3,000	1,500	900.00
(10) Travis Jackson	2,400	1,200	725.00
(11) Len Koenecke	1,600	800.00	475.00
(12) Sam Leslie	1,600	800.00	475.00
(13) Freddy Lindstrom	2,400	1,200	725.00
(14) Dolf Luque	1,600	800.00	475.00
(15) Clarence Mitchell	1,600	800.00	475.00
(16) Jim Mooney	1,600	800.00	475.00
(17) Bob O'Farrell	1,600	800.00	475.00
(18) Mel Ott	3,250	1,600	975.00
(19) Roy Parmelee	1,600	800.00	475.00
(20) Bill Terry	2,400	1,200	725.00
(21) Johnny Vergez	1,600	800.00	475.00
(22) Bill Walker	1,600	800.00	475.00

1948 N.Y. Giants Photo Pack

This set of player photos was sold at Polo Grounds souvenir stands. Pictures have player portraits in a 6-1/2" x 9" format. The black-and-white photos are blank-backed and have facsimile autographs printed near the bottom on front. A white border surrounds the front. The unnumbered photos are checklisted here in alphabetical order. It is possible the specific lineup of the packs changed over the course of the season to reflect roster moves.

	NM	EX	VG
Complete Set (27):	200.00	100.00	60.00
Common Player:	5.00	2.50	1.50
(1) Jack Conway	5.00	2.50	1.50
(2) Walker Cooper	5.00	2.50	1.50
(3) Leo Durocher	9.00	4.50	2.75
(4) Sid Gordon	7.50	3.75	2.25
(5) Andy Hansen	5.00	2.50	1.50
(6) Clint Hartung	5.00	2.50	1.50
(7) Larry Jansen	5.00	2.50	1.50
(8) Sheldon Jones	5.00	2.50	1.50
(9) Monte Kennedy	5.00	2.50	1.50
(10) Buddy Kerr	5.00	2.50	1.50
(11) Dave Koslo	5.00	2.50	1.50
(12) Thornton Lee	5.00	2.50	1.50
(13) Mickey Livingston	5.00	2.50	1.50
(14) Whitey Lockman	5.00	2.50	1.50
(15) Jack Lohrke	5.00	2.50	1.50
(16) Willard Marshall	5.00	2.50	1.50
(17) Johnnie McCarthy	5.00	2.50	1.50
(18) Earl McGowan	7.50	3.75	2.25
(19) Johnny Mize	12.50	6.25	3.75
(20) Bobo Newsom	5.00	2.50	1.50
(21) Mel Ott	25.00	12.50	7.50
(22) Ray Poat	5.00	2.50	1.50
(23) Bobby Rhawn	5.00	2.50	1.50
(24) Bill Rigney	5.00	2.50	1.50
(25) Bobby Thomson	10.00	5.00	3.00
(26) Ken Trinkle	5.00	2.50	1.50
(27) Wesley N. Westrum	5.00	2.50	1.50

1949 N.Y. Giants Photo Pack

This set of player photos was sold at Polo Grounds souvenir stands. Pictures have player portraits in a 6-1/2" x 9" format. The black-and-white photos are blank-backed and have facsimile autographs printed near the bottom on front. A white border surrounds the front. The unnumbered photos are checklisted here in alphabetical order.

	NM	EX	VG
Complete Set (25):	200.00	100.00	60.00
Common Player:	5.00	2.50	1.50
(1) Hank Behrman	5.00	2.50	1.50
(2) Walker Cooper	5.00	2.50	1.50
(3) Leo Durocher	9.00	4.50	2.75
(4) Fred Fitzsimmons	5.00	2.50	1.50
(5) Frank Frisch	12.50	6.25	3.75
(6) Augie Galan	5.00	2.50	1.50
(7) Sid Gordon	7.50	3.75	2.25
(8) Bert Haas	5.00	2.50	1.50
(9) Andy Hansen	5.00	2.50	1.50
(10) Clint Hartung	5.00	2.50	1.50
(11) Bob Hofman	5.00	2.50	1.50
(12) Larry Jansen	5.00	2.50	1.50
(13) Sheldon Jones	5.00	2.50	1.50
(14) Monte Kennedy	5.00	2.50	1.50
(15) Buddy Kerr	5.00	2.50	1.50
(16) Dave Koslo	5.00	2.50	1.50
(17) Mickey Livingston	5.00	2.50	1.50
(18) Whitey Lockman	5.00	2.50	1.50
(19) Willard Marshall	5.00	2.50	1.50
(20) Johnny Mize	12.50	6.25	3.75
(21) Don Mueller	5.00	2.50	1.50
(22) Ray Poat	5.00	2.50	1.50
(23) Bobby Rhawn	5.00	2.50	1.50
(24) Bill Rigney	5.00	2.50	1.50
(25) Bobby Thomson	10.00	5.00	3.00

1954 N.Y. Journal-American

Issued during the Golden Age of baseball in New York City, this 59-card set features only players from the Giants, Yankees and Dodgers. The 2" x 4" cards were issued at newsstands with the purchase of the now-extinct newspaper. Card fronts have promotional copy and a contest serial number in addition to the player's name. Cards are printed in black-and-white on colored stock and unnumbered. Backs feature team schedules. It has been theorized that a 60th card should exist, probably a Brooklyn Dodger. Each card can be found with the word "OFFERS" printed in either red or black, depending on the contest number at bottom. Numbers beginning with "0" have the word in black. Numbers 100000-150000 have the word in red or black, and numbers over 150000 have the word in red.

	NM	EX	VG
Complete Set (59):	4,750	2,400	1,400
Common Player:	40.00	20.00	12.00
(1) Johnny Antonelli	40.00	20.00	12.00
(2) Hank Bauer	45.00	22.50	13.50
(3) Yogi Berra	125.00	65.00	35.00
(4) Joe Black	65.00	32.50	20.00
(5) Harry Byrd	40.00	20.00	12.00
(6) Roy Campanella	200.00	100.00	60.00
(7) Andy Carey	40.00	20.00	12.00
(8) Jerry Coleman	40.00	20.00	12.00
(9) Joe Collins	40.00	20.00	12.00
(10) Billy Cox	65.00	32.50	20.00
(11) Al Dark	40.00	20.00	12.00
(12) Carl Erskine	65.00	32.50	20.00
(13) Whitey Ford	125.00	65.00	35.00
(14) Carl Furillo	90.00	45.00	27.50
(15) Junior Gilliam	90.00	45.00	27.50
(16) Ruben Gomez	40.00	20.00	12.00
(17) Marv Grissom	40.00	20.00	12.00
(18) Jim Hearn	40.00	20.00	12.00
(19) Gil Hodges	125.00	65.00	35.00
(20) Bobby Hofman	40.00	20.00	12.00
(21) Jim Hughes	65.00	32.50	20.00
(22) Monte Irvin	90.00	45.00	27.50
(23) Larry Jansen	40.00	20.00	12.00
(24) Ray Katt	40.00	20.00	12.00
(25) Steve Kraly	40.00	20.00	12.00
(26) Bob Kuzava	40.00	20.00	12.00
(27) Clem Labine	65.00	32.50	20.00
(28) Frank Leja	40.00	20.00	12.00
(29) Don Liddle	40.00	20.00	12.00
(30) Whitey Lockman	40.00	20.00	12.00
(31) Billy Loes	65.00	32.50	20.00
(32) Eddie Lopat	40.00	20.00	12.00
(33) Sal Maglie	40.00	20.00	12.00
(34) Mickey Mantle	800.00	400.00	240.00
(35) Willie Mays	375.00	185.00	110.00
(36) Gil McDougald	45.00	22.50	13.50
(37) Russ Meyer	65.00	32.50	20.00
(38) Bill Miller	40.00	20.00	12.00
(39) Tom Morgan	40.00	20.00	12.00
(40) Don Mueller	40.00	20.00	12.00

(41)	Don Newcombe	75.00	37.50	22.50
(42)	Irv Noren	40.00	20.00	12.00
(43)	Erv Palica	65.00	32.50	20.00
(44)	Pee Wee Reese	130.00	65.00	40.00
(45)	Allie Reynolds	40.00	20.00	12.00
(46)	Dusty Rhodes	40.00	20.00	12.00
(47)	Phil Rizzuto	125.00	65.00	35.00
(48)	Ed Robinson	40.00	20.00	12.00
(49)	Jackie Robinson	250.00	125.00	75.00
(50)	Preacher Roe	65.00	32.50	20.00
(51)	George Shuba	65.00	32.50	20.00
(52)	Duke Snider	200.00	100.00	60.00
(53)	Hank Thompson	40.00	20.00	12.00
(54)	Wes Westrum	40.00	20.00	12.00
(55)	Hoyt Wilhelm	90.00	45.00	27.00
(56)	Davey Williams	40.00	20.00	12.00
(57)	Dick Williams	65.00	32.50	20.00
(58)	Gene Woodling	45.00	22.50	13.50
(59)	Al Worthington	40.00	20.00	12.00

1969 N.Y. News Mets Portfolio of Stars

To commemorate the N.Y. Mets miracle season of 1969, one of the city's daily newspapers, The News, issued a portfolio of player portraits done by editorial cartoonist Bruce Stark. The 9" x 12" pencil drawings are printed on heavy textured paper and were sold as a set in a folder labeled, "The 1969 Mets / A Portfolio of Stars." The black-and-white drawings are on a white background. A facsimile player autograph is printed at lower-left. At lower-right is the signature of the artist, Stark, along with the paper's logo and a union label. The blank-backed, unnumbered pieces are checklisted here alphabetically.

		NM	EX	VG
	Complete Set (20):	225.00	110.00	70.00
	Common Player:	7.50	3.75	2.25
(1)	Tommie Agee	7.50	3.75	2.25
(2)	Ken Boswell	7.50	3.75	2.25
(3)	Don Cardwell	7.50	3.75	2.25
(4)	Donn Clendenon	10.00	5.00	3.00
(5)	Wayne Garrett	7.50	3.75	2.25
(6)	Gary Gentry	7.50	3.75	2.25
(7)	Jerry Grote	7.50	3.75	2.25
(8)	Bud Harrelson	10.00	5.00	3.00
(9)	Gil Hodges	20.00	10.00	6.00
(10)	Cleon Jones	7.50	3.75	2.25
(11)	Jerry Koosman	7.50	3.75	2.25
(12)	Ed Kranepool	7.50	3.75	2.25
(13)	Jim McAndrew	7.50	3.75	2.25
(14)	Tug McGraw	10.00	5.00	3.00
(15)	Nolan Ryan	150.00	75.00	45.00
(16)	Tom Seaver	40.00	20.00	12.00
(17)	Art Shamsky	7.50	3.75	2.25
(18)	Ron Swoboda	7.50	3.75	2.25
(19)	Ron Taylor	7.50	3.75	2.25
(20)	Al Weis	7.50	3.75	2.25

1973 N.Y. News Mets/Yankees Caricatures

Between June 17 and August 26, the Sunday color comics section of the N.Y. News carried a centerspread picturing one Mets and one Yankees player as caricatured by artist Bruce Stark. Each player picture is printed on newsprint in approximately 10-1/2" x 14-1/2", the pictures have a page of comics or other matter on their backs. Values shown are for single pages. Intact pairs or complete comics section would command a premium.

		NM	EX	VG
	Complete Set (22):	200.00	100.00	60.00
	Common Player:	6.00	3.00	1.75
	METS			

		NM	EX	VG
(1)	Yogi Berra (6/17)	17.50	8.75	5.25
(2)	Tom Seaver (6/24)	15.00	7.50	4.50
(3)	John Milner (7/1)	6.00	3.00	1.75
(4)	Felix Millan (7/8)	6.00	3.00	1.75
(5)	Bud Harrelson (7/15)	6.00	3.00	1.75
(6)	Jim Fregosi (7/22)	6.00	3.00	1.75
(7)	Jerry Grote (7/29)	6.00	3.00	1.75
(8)	Cleon Jones (8/5)	6.00	3.00	1.75
(9)	Willie Mays (8/12)	25.00	12.50	7.50
(10)	Rusty Staub (8/19)	9.00	4.50	2.75
(11)	Tug McGraw (8/26)	7.50	3.75	2.25
	YANKEES			
(12)	Ralph Houk (6/17)	7.50	3.75	2.25
(13)	Mel Stottlemyre (6/24)	7.50	3.75	2.25
(14)	Ron Blomberg (7/1)	6.00	3.00	1.75
(15)	Horace Clarke (7/8)	6.00	3.00	1.75
(16)	Gene Michael (7/15)	6.00	3.00	1.75
(17)	Graig Nettles (7/22)	7.50	3.75	2.25
(18)	Thurman Munson (7/29)	15.00	7.50	4.50
(19)	Roy White (8/5)	9.00	4.50	2.75
(20)	Bobby Murcer (8/12)	9.00	4.50	2.75
(21)	Matty Alou (8/19)	6.00	3.00	1.75
(22)	Sparky Lyle (8/26)	9.00	4.50	2.75

1916 N.Y. World Leaders in Baseball

This set of large-format (about 9" x 4") sepia-tone cards was issued to demonstrate the dominance of the World in New York City's newspaper wars. Each card has a portrait photo of a New York player. Most of the card is devoted to stats to boost the paper's claim as the "Pennant Winner in Advertising and Circulation." A note at left identifies the series as "'Leaders in Baseball' Series II." It is not known whether this checklist is complete.

		NM	EX	VG
	Common Player:	600.00	300.00	180.00
(1)	Home Run Baker	750.00	375.00	225.00
(2)	Jake Daubert	600.00	300.00	180.00
(3)	Buck Herzog	600.00	300.00	180.00
(4)	Dave Robertson	600.00	300.00	180.00

1944 N.Y. Yankees Stamps

One of the few paper collectibles issued during World War II, this set includes several players who do not appear on any other contemporary baseball card issue. The 1-3/4" x 2-3/8" stamps were issued on a single sheet with an album marking the Yankees 1943 World Series win. Stamps are in full color with the player's name in white on a red strip at bottom. The unnumbered stamps are checklisted here alphabetically. An album, about 6-1/2" x 3-1/2", was issued to display the stamps.

		NM	EX	VG
	Complete Set (30):	100.00	50.00	30.00
	Common Player:	12.00	6.00	3.50
	Uncut Sheet:	145.00	75.00	45.00
	Album:	40.00	20.00	12.00
(1)	Ernie Bonham	12.00	6.00	3.50
(2)	Hank Borowy	12.00	6.00	3.50
(3)	Marvin Breuer	12.00	6.00	3.50
(4)	Tommy Byrne	12.00	6.00	3.50
(5)	Spud Chandler	15.00	7.50	4.50
(6)	Earl Combs (Earle)	25.00	12.50	7.50
(7)	Frank Crosetti	20.00	10.00	6.00
(8)	Bill Dickey	35.00	17.50	10.50
(9)	Atley Donald	12.00	6.00	3.50
(10)	Nick Etten	12.00	6.00	3.50
(11)	Art Fletcher	12.00	6.00	3.50
(12)	Joe Gordon	25.00	12.50	7.50
(13)	Oscar Grimes	12.00	6.00	3.50
(14)	Rollie Hemsley	12.00	6.00	3.50
(15)	Bill Johnson	12.00	6.00	3.50
(16)	Charlie Keller	15.00	7.50	4.50
(17)	John Lindell	15.00	7.50	4.50
(18)	Joe McCarthy	25.00	12.50	7.50
(19)	Bud Metheny	12.00	6.00	3.50
(20)	Johnny Murphy	12.00	6.00	3.50
(21)	Pat O'Daugherty	12.00	6.00	3.50
(22)	Marius Russo	12.00	6.00	3.50
(23)	John Schulte	12.00	6.00	3.50
(24)	Ken Sears	12.00	6.00	3.50
(25)	Tuck Stainback	12.00	6.00	3.50
(26)	George Stirnweiss	12.00	6.00	3.50
(27)	Jim Turner	12.00	6.00	3.50
(28)	Roy Weatherly	12.00	6.00	3.50
(29)	Charley Wensloff	12.00	6.00	3.50
(30)	Bill Zuber	12.00	6.00	3.50

1947-50 N.Y. Yankees Picture Pack

These team-issued sets offered fans at the souvenir stand more than two dozen pictures of the players and staff. The 6-1/2" x 9" pictures are in black-and-white with a white border and a facsimile autograph. Backs are blank. Players repeated over the years were represented by the same picture. The unnumbered pictures are listed in alphabetical order by year of issue.

		NM	EX	VG
	Common Player:	4.00	2.00	1.25
	Complete 1947 Set (25):	100.00	50.00	30.00
(1)	Yogi Berra	20.00	10.00	6.00
(2)	Bill Bevens	4.00	2.00	1.25
(3)	Bobby Brown	4.00	2.00	1.25
(4)	Spud Chandler	4.00	2.00	1.25
(5)	Frank Colman	4.00	2.00	1.25
(6)	John Corriden	4.00	2.00	1.25
(7)	Frank Crosetti	5.00	2.50	1.50
(8)	Joe DiMaggio	40.00	20.00	12.00
(9)	Chuck Dressen	4.00	2.00	1.25
(10)	Randy Gumpert	4.00	2.00	1.25
(11)	Bucky Harris	5.00	2.50	1.50
(12)	Tommy Henrich	4.00	2.00	1.25
(13)	Ralph Houk	5.00	2.50	1.50
(14)	Don Johnson	4.00	2.00	1.25
(15)	Bill Johnson	4.00	2.00	1.25
(16)	Charlie Keller	5.00	2.50	1.50
(17)	John Lindell	4.00	2.00	1.25
(18)	George McQuinn	4.00	2.00	1.25
(19)	Joe Page	4.00	2.00	1.25
(20)	Allie Reynolds	5.00	2.50	1.50
(21)	Phil Rizzuto	12.50	6.25	3.75
(22)	Aaron Robinson	4.00	2.00	1.25
(23)	Frank Shea	4.00	2.00	1.25
(24)	Ken Silvestri	4.00	2.00	1.25
(25)	George Stirnweiss	4.00	2.00	1.25
	Complete 1948 Set (26):	100.00	50.00	30.00
(1)	Yogi Berra	20.00	10.00	6.00
(2)	Bobby Brown	4.00	2.00	1.25
(3)	Red Corriden	4.00	2.00	1.25
(4)	Frank Crosetti	5.00	2.50	1.50
(5)	Joe DiMaggio	40.00	20.00	12.00
(6)	Chuck Dressen	4.00	2.00	1.25
(7)	Karl Drews	4.00	2.00	1.25
(8)	Red Embree	4.00	2.00	1.25
(9)	Randy Gumpert	4.00	2.00	1.25
(10)	Bucky Harris	5.00	2.50	1.50
(11)	Tommy Henrich	4.00	2.00	1.25
(12)	Frank Hiller	4.00	2.00	1.25
(13)	Bill Johnson	4.00	2.00	1.25
(14)	Charlie Keller	5.00	2.50	1.50
(15)	John Lindell	4.00	2.00	1.25
(16)	Eddie Lopat	5.00	2.50	1.50
(17)	Cliff Mapes	4.00	2.00	1.25
(18)	George McQuinn	4.00	2.00	1.25
(19)	Gus Niarhos	4.00	2.00	1.25
(20)	George McQuinn	4.00	2.00	1.25
(21)	Joe Page	4.00	2.00	1.25
(22)	Vic Raschi	5.00	2.50	1.50
(23)	Allie Reynolds	5.00	2.50	1.50
(24)	Phil Rizzuto	12.50	6.25	3.75
(25)	Frank Shea	4.00	2.00	1.25
(26)	Snuffy Stirnweiss	4.00	2.00	1.25
	Complete 1949 Set (25):	100.00	50.00	30.00
(1)	Mel Allen	8.00	4.00	2.50
(2)	Larry Berra	20.00	10.00	6.00
(3)	Bobby Brown	4.00	2.00	1.25
(4)	Tommy Byrne	4.00	2.00	1.25
(5)	Jerry Coleman	4.00	2.00	1.25
(6)	Frank Crosetti	5.00	2.50	1.50
(7)	Bill Dickey	10.00	5.00	3.00
(8)	Joe DiMaggio	40.00	20.00	12.00
(9)	Tommy Henrich	4.00	2.00	1.25
(10)	Bill Johnson	4.00	2.00	1.25
(11)	Charlie Keller	5.00	2.50	1.50
(12)	John Lindell	4.00	2.00	1.25
(13)	Ed Lopat	5.00	2.50	1.50
(14)	Gus Niarhos	4.00	2.00	1.25
(15)	Joe Page	4.00	2.00	1.25
(16)	Bob Porterfield	4.00	2.00	1.25
(17)	Vic Raschi	5.00	2.50	1.50
(18)	Allie Reynolds	5.00	2.50	1.50
(19)	Phil Rizzuto	12.50	6.25	3.75
(20)	Fred Sanford	4.00	2.00	1.25
(21)	Frank Shea	4.00	2.00	1.25
(22)	Casey Stengel	15.00	7.50	4.50
(23)	George Stirnweiss	4.00	2.00	1.25
(24)	Jim Turner	4.00	2.00	1.25
(25)	Gene Woodling	5.00	2.50	1.50
	Complete 1950 Set (25):	100.00	50.00	30.00
(1)	Mel Allen	8.00	4.00	2.50
(2)	Hank Bauer	5.00	2.50	1.50
(3)	Larry Berra	20.00	10.00	6.00

		NM	EX	VG
(4)	Bobby Brown	4.00	2.00	1.25
(5)	Tommy Byrne	4.00	2.00	1.25
(6)	Jerry Coleman	4.00	2.00	1.25
(7)	Frank Crosetti	5.00	2.50	1.50
(8)	Bill Dickey	10.00	5.00	3.00
(9)	Joe DiMaggio	40.00	20.00	12.00
(10)	Tommy Henrich	4.00	2.00	1.25
(11)	Jack Jensen	7.50	3.75	2.25
(12)	Bill Johnson	4.00	2.00	1.25
(13)	Ed Lopat	5.00	2.50	1.50
(14)	Cliff Mapes	4.00	2.00	1.25
(15)	Joe Page	4.00	2.00	1.25
(16)	Bob Porterfield	4.00	2.00	1.25
(17)	Vic Raschi	5.00	2.50	1.50
(18)	Allie Reynolds	5.00	2.50	1.50
(19)	Phil Rizzuto	12.50	6.25	3.75
(20)	Fred Sanford	4.00	2.00	1.25
(21)	Charlie Silvera	5.00	2.50	1.50
(22)	Casey Stengel	15.00	7.50	4.50
(23)	George Stirnweiss	4.00	2.00	1.25
(24)	Jim Turner	4.00	2.00	1.25
(25)	Gene Woodling	5.00	2.50	1.50

1955-1957 N.Y. Yankees Picture Pack

The checklist for this set of 5" x 7" black-and-white, blank-back pictures does not allow pinpointing its year of issue more closely. Similar in format to the later Jay Publishing photo packs, this issue differs in that only the team name (in upper- and lower-case letters), and not the city, is presented along with the player name (all-caps) in the identification line in the bottom border. The set was sold for 25 cents in a manila envelope. The unnumbered pictures are listed here alphabetically.

		NM	EX	VG
Complete Set (12):		75.00	37.50	22.50
Common Player:		4.00	2.00	1.25
(1)	Hank Bauer	5.00	2.50	1.50
(2)	Yogi Berra	7.50	3.75	2.25
(3)	Tommy Byrne	4.00	2.00	1.25
(4)	Andy Carey	4.00	2.00	1.25
(5)	Joe Collins	4.00	2.00	1.25
(6)	Whitey Ford	7.50	3.75	2.25
(7)	Elston Howard	5.00	2.50	1.50
(8)	Mickey Mantle	35.00	17.50	10.00
(9)	Billy Martin	5.00	2.50	1.50
(10)	Gil McDougald	4.00	2.00	1.25
(11)	Casey Stengel	7.50	3.75	2.25
(12)	Bob Turley	4.00	2.00	1.25

1956 N.Y. Yankees "Action Pictures"

This set of 8" x 10" black-and-white pictures was sold for 75 cents in a paper envelope marked "12 ACTION / PICTURES." The white-bordered pictures have facsimile autographs or printed names on front and are blank-backed.

		NM	EX	VG
Complete Set (12):		125.00	65.00	49.00
Common Player:		6.00	3.00	1.75
(1)	Hank Bauer	7.50	3.75	2.25
(2)	Yogi Berra	15.00	7.50	4.50
(3)	Andy Carey	6.00	3.00	1.75
(4)	Joe Collins	6.00	3.00	1.75
(5)	Whitey Ford	15.00	7.50	4.50
(6)	Elston Howard	9.00	4.50	2.75
(7)	Mickey Mantle	75.00	37.00	22.00
(8)	Billy Martin	9.00	4.50	2.75
(9)	Gil McDougald	7.50	3.75	2.25
(10)	Phil Rizzuto	15.00	7.50	4.50
(11)	Bill Skowron	9.00	4.50	2.75
(12)	Bob Turley	7.50	3.75	2.25

1956 N.Y. Yankees Picture Pack

This set was issued, probably for sale at Yankee Stadium souvenir stands, in 1956, though some of the photos date as far back as 1951, and a few appear to have been taken during the

---

1955 World Series at Ebbets Field. Printed in black-and-white on semi-gloss paper, the pictures measure about 6" x 8-7/8". There is a 1/4" white border around the photo and a white strip at the bottom of each photo with the player's name. Backs are blank. The pictures are checklisted here in alphabetical order, but the list may not be complete. Some of the photos are familiar from their use on baseball cards, including the 1951 Bowman Mantle.

		NM	EX	VG
Complete Set (22):		275.00	135.00	80.00
Common Player:		8.00	4.00	2.50
(1)	Hank Bauer	10.00	5.00	3.00
(2)	Larry "Yogi" Berra	20.00	10.00	6.00
(3)	Tommy Byrne	8.00	4.00	2.50
(4)	Andy Carey	8.00	4.00	2.50
(5)	Bob Cerv	8.00	4.00	2.50
(6)	Gerry Coleman	8.00	4.00	2.50
(7)	Joe Collins	8.00	4.00	2.50
(8)	Ed "Whitey" Ford	20.00	10.00	6.00
(9)	Bob Grim	8.00	4.00	2.50
(10)	Elston Howard	10.00	5.00	3.00
(11)	Johnny Kucks	8.00	4.00	2.50
(12)	Don Larsen	12.50	6.25	3.75
(13)	Jerry Lumpe	8.00	4.00	2.50
(14)	Mickey Mantle	130.00	65.00	39.00
(15)	Billy Martin	15.00	7.50	4.50
(16)	Mickey McDermott	8.00	4.00	2.50
(17)	Gil McDougald	10.00	5.00	3.00
(18)	Tom Morgan	8.00	4.00	2.50
(19)	Irv Noren	8.00	4.00	2.50
(20)	Charlie Silvera	8.00	4.00	2.50
(21)	Bill Skowron	10.00	5.00	3.00
(22)	Bob Turley	10.00	5.00	3.00

1957 N.Y. Yankees Picture Pack

Nominally 8" x 10", the actual size on these blank-back, black-and-white pictures varies from about 7-1/2" to 8" wide by 9-7/8" x 10-1/8" tall. The player poses are surrounded with a white border. The player name is printed within the picture. Some of the photos used considerably pre-date the period of issue.

		NM	EX	VG
Complete Set (12):		125.00	65.00	40.00
Common Player:		10.00	5.00	3.00
(1)	Hank Bauer	12.50	6.25	3.75
(2)	Larry Berra	20.00	10.00	6.00
(3)	Andy Carey	10.00	5.00	3.00
(4)	Whitey Ford	20.00	10.00	6.00
(5)	Elston Howard	12.50	6.25	3.75
(6)	Tony Kubek	15.00	7.50	4.50
(7)	Don Larsen	12.50	6.25	3.75
(8)	Mickey Mantle	60.00	30.00	18.00
(9)	Gil McDougald	12.50	6.25	3.75
(10)	Bill Skowron	12.50	6.25	3.75
(11)	Bob Turley	12.50	6.25	3.75
(12)	Frank Crosetti, Bill Dickey, Casey Stengel, Jim Turner	10.00	5.00	3.00

1960 N.Y. Yankees "Action Pictures"

This set of 8" x 10" black-and-white pictures was sold for 75 cents in a paper envelope marked "12 ACTION / PICTURES." The white bordered pictures have facsimile autographs or printed names on front and are blank-backed.

		NM	EX	VG
Complete Set (12):		200.00	100.00	60.00
Common Player:		10.00	5.00	3.00
(1)	Larry Berra	20.00	10.00	6.00
(2)	Art Ditmar	10.00	5.00	3.00
(3)	Whitey Ford	20.00	10.00	6.00
(4)	Elston Howard	12.50	6.25	3.75
(5)	Tony Kubek	15.00	7.50	4.50
(6)	Hector Lopez	10.00	5.00	3.00
(7)	Mickey Mantle	60.00	30.00	18.00
(8)	Roger Maris	35.00	17.50	10.50
(9)	Bobby Richardson	12.50	6.25	3.75
(10)	Bill Skowron	12.50	6.25	3.75
(11)	Casey Stengel	15.00	7.50	4.50
(12)	Bob Turley	12.50	6.25	3.75

1970 N.Y. Yankees Clinic Schedule Postcards

This series of postcards was issued in conjunction with a series of baseball clinics which the Yankees put on for youngsters prior to selected home games. Fronts of the 3-1/2 x 5-1/2" glossy color cards have player portraits with a facsimile autograph in a white panel at bottom. Backs have player identification and career highlights, a schedule of the clinic days and credit line for Howard Photo Service. White and Murcer cards are scarce because of rainouts on their scheduled clinic appearance days. Cards are checklisted here in alphabetical order.

		NM	EX	VG
Complete Set (13):		130.00	65.00	40.00
Common Player:		3.00	1.50	.90
(1)	Stan Bahnsen	3.00	1.50	.90
(2)	Curt Blefary	3.00	1.50	.90
(3)	Danny Cater	3.00	1.50	.90
(4)	Horace Clarke	3.00	1.50	.90
(5)	Joe DiMaggio, Mickey Mantle	25.00	12.50	7.50
(6)	John Ellis	3.00	1.50	.90
(7)	Jerry Kenney	3.00	1.50	.90
(8)	Gene Michael	3.00	1.50	.90
(9)	Thurman Munson	30.00	15.00	9.00
(10)	Bobby Murcer	15.00	7.50	4.50
(11)	Fritz Peterson	3.00	1.50	.90
(12)	Mel Stottlemyre	4.50	2.25	1.25
(13)	Roy White	35.00	17.50	10.50

1971 N.Y. Yankees Clinic Schedule Postcards

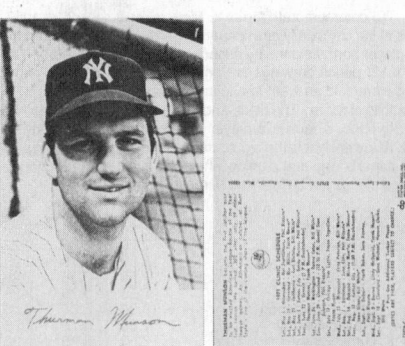

These postcards were issued in conjunction with a series of baseball clinics which the Yankees put on for youngsters prior to selected home games. Fronts of the 3-1/2" x 5-1/2" glossy color cards have player portraits with a facsimile autograph in a white panel at bottom. Backs are printed in blue, have player identification and career highlights and a schedule of the clinic days. Cards are checklisted here in alphabetical order.

		NM	EX	VG
Complete Set (16):		90.00	45.00	27.00
Common Player:		3.00	1.50	.90
(1)	Felipe Alou, Jim Lyttle	3.00	1.50	.90
(2)	Stan Bahnsen	3.00	1.50	.90
(3)	Frank Baker, Jerry Kenney	3.00	1.50	.90
(4)	Curt Blefary	3.00	1.50	.90
(5)	Danny Cater	3.00	1.50	.90
(6)	Horace Clarke, Gene Michael	3.00	1.50	.90
(7)	John Ellis	3.00	1.50	.90
(8)	Jake Gibbs	3.00	1.50	.90
(9)	Ralph Houk	3.00	1.50	.90
(10)	Mickey Mantle	30.00	15.00	9.00
(11)	Lindy McDaniel	3.00	1.50	.90
(12)	Thurman Munson	15.00	7.50	4.50
(13)	Bobby Murcer	4.50	2.25	1.25
(14)	Fritz Peterson	3.00	1.50	.90
(15)	Mel Stottlemyre	3.00	1.50	.90
(16)	Roy White	3.00	1.50	.90

1972 N.Y. Yankees Schedule Cards

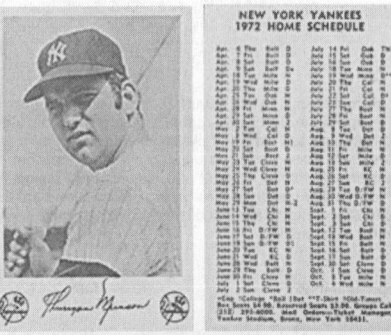

The origins and distribution of these cards is unclear. They may have been a collector issue. The 2-1/4" x 3-1/2" cards are printed in blue and sepia. Fronts have player photos with a facsimile autograph in the white border at bottom, between a pair of team insignia. Backs have the team schedule. The unnumbered cards are listed here alphabetically.

		NM	EX	VG
Complete Set (8):		350.00	175.00	100.00
Common Player:		30.00	15.00	9.00
(1)	Felipe Alou	35.00	17.50	10.50
(2)	Ron Blomberg	30.00	15.00	9.00
(3)	Thurman Munson	225.00	110.00	67.00
(4)	Bobby Murcer	35.00	17.50	10.50
(5)	Mel Stottlemyre	30.00	15.00	9.00
(6)	Ron Swoboda	30.00	15.00	9.00
(7)	Roy White	35.00	17.50	10.50
(8)	Frank Messer, Phil Rizzuto, Bill White/Announcers	30.00	15.00	9.00

1909 Niagara Baking Co.

Dooin, c. Phila. Nat.

THIS CARD IS ONE OF A SET OF 50 Base Ball Players

PROMINENT MEMBERS OF NATIONAL AND AMERICAN LEAGUES,

One of these pictures given with Tip-Top, Family, Butternut or Boomdeal Breads. NIAGARA BAKING CO., Lockport, N.Y.

This is a version of the set known as E101 "Set of 50" which has been rubber-stamped on back with an advertisement for Niagara Baking Co., of Lockport, N.Y. It is unclear whether all 50 cards in E101 can be found with the overprint. Because of the ease with which this regional variation could be faked, collectors must exercise extreme caution. Collectors can expect to pay a considerable premium over E101 prices for this version, especially for common players.

Values Undetermined
(See 1909 E101 for checklist.)

1953 Northland Bread Labels

BREAD for ENERGY

GUS BELL Cincinnati Red Legs

This bread end-label set consists of 32 players - two from each major league team. The unnumbered black and white labels measure approximately 2-11/16" square and include the slogan "Bread for Energy" along the top. An album to house the labels was also part of the promotion. All labels were also issued with "Top Taste" at top in place of the Bread for Energy slogan.

		NM	EX	VG
Complete Set (32):		16,500	8,250	4,950
Common Player:		400.00	200.00	120.00
(1)	Cal Abrams	400.00	200.00	120.00
(2)	Richie Ashburn	800.00	400.00	240.00
(3)	Gus Bell	400.00	200.00	120.00
(4)	Jim Busby	400.00	200.00	120.00
(5)	Clint Courtney	400.00	200.00	120.00
(6)	Billy Cox	400.00	200.00	120.00
(7)	Jim Dyck	400.00	200.00	120.00
(8)	Nellie Fox	800.00	400.00	240.00
(9)	Sid Gordon	400.00	200.00	120.00
(10)	Warren Hacker	400.00	200.00	120.00
(11)	Jim Hearn	400.00	200.00	120.00
(12)	Fred Hutchinson	400.00	200.00	120.00
(13)	Monte Irvin	800.00	400.00	240.00
(14)	Jackie Jensen	450.00	225.00	135.00
(15)	Ted Kluszewski	700.00	350.00	210.00
(16)	Bob Lemon	800.00	400.00	240.00
(17)	Maury McDermott	400.00	200.00	120.00
(18)	Minny Minoso	700.00	350.00	210.00
(19)	Johnny Mize	800.00	400.00	240.00
(20)	Mel Parnell	400.00	200.00	120.00
(21)	Howie Pollet	400.00	200.00	120.00
(22)	Jerry Priddy	400.00	200.00	120.00
(23)	Allie Reynolds	400.00	200.00	120.00
(24)	Preacher Roe	500.00	250.00	150.00
(25)	Al Rosen	500.00	250.00	150.00
(26)	Connie Ryan	400.00	200.00	120.00
(27)	Hank Sauer	400.00	200.00	120.00
(28)	Red Schoendienst	800.00	400.00	240.00
(29)	Bobby Shantz	400.00	200.00	120.00
(30)	Enos Slaughter	800.00	400.00	240.00
(31)	Warren Spahn	800.00	400.00	240.00
(32)	Gus Zernial	400.00	200.00	120.00

1978 North Shore Dodge Cecil Cooper

Cecil Cooper
Infielder — No. 15

Cecil Cooper
BORN: Dec. 20, 1949 | WEIGHT: 190
BATS & THROWS: Left | HEIGHT: 6' 2"
NICKNAME: Coop or CC

Traded to Brewers on December 6, 1976 for George Scott and Bernie Carbo ... hit .300 with 20 homers and 78 RBI and topped the Brewers in seven categories in 1977 ... 4 for 4 performance on the final day of '77 gave him a club record on 193 hits in a season ... earned the first Harvey Kuehn Batting Award from the local Milwaukee baseball scribes ... also named American League Player of the Week the final week of the season ... first Brewer .300 hitter since 1973.

North Shore Dodge
14th at Silver Spring   228-9300

As part of his work as promotional spokesman for a local auto dealership, popular Brewers first baseman Cecil Cooper appears on a one-card set which was given to fans and collectors during public appearances. The card is printed in black-and-white in standard 2-1/2" x 3-1/2" size and is often found with a genuine autograph on the front.

	NM	EX	VG
Cecil Cooper	6.00	3.00	1.75
Cecil Cooper/Auto.	15.00	7.50	4.50

1980 Nostalgic Enterprises 1903 N.Y. Highlanders

JESSE NILES TANNEHILL
B: JULY 14,1874   D: SEPT. 22,1956
B/B   T:L   H:5'8"   W:150 lbs
Pitcher

JESSE TANNEHILL
Pitcher

New York City's first team in the American League, the 1903 Highlanders, are featured in this collectors' issue. Fronts of the 2-1/2" x 3-1/2" cards have black-and-white portrait photos with ornate graphics, highlighted in yellow, and a white border. Backs have season and lifetime stats, player data and an extensive career summary. The unnumbered cards are checklisted here in alphabetical order. Sets originally sold for about $2.50.

		NM	EX	VG
Complete Set (17):		15.00	7.50	4.50
Common Player:		2.00	1.00	.60
(1)	Monte Beville	2.50	1.25	.70
(2)	Jack Chesbro	2.00	1.00	.60
(3)	Wid Conroy	2.00	1.00	.60
(4)	Lefty Davis	2.00	1.00	.60
(5)	Jim Deering	2.50	1.25	.70
(6)	Kid Elberfeld	2.00	1.00	.60
(7)	Dave Fultz	2.00	1.00	.60
(8)	John Ganzel	2.00	1.00	.60
(9)	Clark Griffith	2.00	1.00	.60
(10)	Harry Howell	2.00	1.00	.60
(11)	Willie Keeler	2.00	1.00	.60
(12)	Herm McFarland	2.00	1.00	.60
(13)	Jack O'Connor	2.00	1.00	.60
(14)	Jesse Tannehill	2.00	1.00	.60
(15)	Jimmy Williams	2.00	1.00	.60
(16)	Jack Zalusky	2.50	1.25	.70
(17)	Header Card/Checklist	2.00	1.00	.60

1907-09 Novelty Cutlery Postcards (PC805)

WALTER JOHNSTON

An ornately bordered black-and-white or sepia portrait or action pose of the day's great players identifies these postcards from a Canton, Ohio, knife company. Cards measure the standard 3-1/2" x 5-1/2" size with postcard indicia on the back. The sponsor is identified in a tiny line of type beneath the lower-right corner of the player photo.

		NM	EX	VG
Complete Set (26):		120,000	60,000	35,000
Common Player:		2,800	1,400	840.00
(1)	Roger Bresnahan	3,600	1,800	1,080
(2)	Al Bridwell	2,800	1,400	840.00
(3)	Three Finger Brown	3,600	1,800	1,080
(4)	Frank Chance	3,600	1,800	1,080
(5)	Hal Chase	3,200	1,600	960.00
(6)	Ty Cobb	18,000	9,000	5,500
(7)	Eddie Collins	3,600	1,800	1,080
(8)	Sam Crawford	3,600	1,800	1,080
(9)	Art Devlin	2,800	1,400	840.00
(10)	Red Dooin	2,800	1,400	840.00
(11)	Elmer Flick	3,600	1,800	1,080
(12)	Sam Frock	2,800	1,400	840.00
(13)	George Gibson	2,800	1,400	840.00
(14)	Solly Hofman	2,800	1,400	840.00
(15)	Walter Johnston (Johnson)	6,000	3,000	1,800
(16)	Nap Lajoie	3,600	1,800	1,080
(17)	Bris Lord	2,800	1,400	840.00
(18)	Christy Mathewson	6,000	3,000	1,800
(19)	Orval Overall	2,800	1,400	840.00
(20)	Eddie Plank	3,600	1,800	1,080
(21)	Tris Speaker	5,000	2,500	1,500
(22)	Charley Street	2,800	1,400	840.00
(23)	Honus Wagner	12,000	6,000	3,500
(24)	Ed Walsh	3,600	1,800	1,080
(25)	Ty Cobb, Honus Wagner	13,000	6,500	3,900
(26)	Johnny Evers, Germany Schaefer	3,200	1,600	960.00

1960 Nu-Card Baseball Hi-Lites

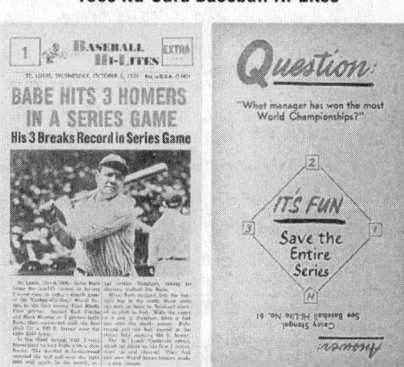

BASEBALL HI-LITES   EXTRA
BABE HITS 3 HOMERS IN A SERIES GAME
His 3 Breaks Record in Series Game

Question
"What manager has won the most World Championships?"

IT'S FUN
Save the Entire Series

These large, 3-1/4" x 5-3/8" cards are printed in a mock newspaper format, with a headline, picture and story describing one of baseball's greatest moments. Cards are printed in red-and-black on front, and green-and-black on back. Cards #1-18 that are printed only in black and are blank-backed are cataloged under 1960 CVC Baseball Hi-Lites." Each card is numbered in the upper-left corner. Backs offer a quiz question and answer.

		NM	EX	VG
Complete Set (72):		750.00	350.00	250.00
Common Player:		8.00	4.00	2.50
1	Babe Hits 3 Homers In A Series Game	60.00	30.00	20.00
2	Podres Pitching Wins Series	12.00	6.00	4.00
3	Bevans Pitches No Hitter, Almost	8.00	4.00	2.50
4	Box Score Devised By Reporter	8.00	4.00	2.50
5	VanderMeer Pitches 2 No Hitters	8.00	4.00	2.50
6	Indians Take Bums	8.00	4.00	2.50
7	DiMag Comes Thru	35.00	20.00	12.00
8	Mathewson Pitches 3 W.S. Shutouts	10.00	5.00	3.00
9	Haddix Pitches 12 Perfect Innings	8.00	4.00	2.50
10	Thomson's Homer Sinks Dodgers	12.00	6.00	4.00
11	Hubbell Strikes Out 5 A.L. Stars	8.00	4.00	2.50
12	Pickoff Ends Series (Marty Marion)	8.00	4.00	2.50
13	Cards Take Series From Yanks (Grover Cleveland Alexander)	8.00	4.00	2.50
14	Dizzy And Daffy Win Series	15.00	8.00	5.00
15	Owen Drops 3rd Strike	8.00	4.00	2.50
16	Ruth Calls His Shot	60.00	30.00	20.00
17	Merkle Pulls Boner	8.00	4.00	2.50
18	Larsen Hurls Perfect World Series Game	15.00	8.00	5.00
19	Bean Ball Ends Career of Mickey Cochrane	8.00	4.00	2.50
20	Banks Belts 47 Homers, Earns MVP Honors	8.00	4.00	2.50
21	Stan Musial Hits 5 Homers In 1 Day	18.00	9.00	5.00
22	Mickey Mantle Hits Longest Homer	80.00	40.00	25.00
23	Sievers Captures Home Run Title	8.00	4.00	2.50
24	Gehrig Consecutive Game Record Ends	35.00	20.00	12.00

		NM	EX	VG
25	Red Schoendienst Key Player In Victory	8.00	4.00	2.50
26	Midget Pinch-Hits For St. Louis Browns (Eddie Gaedel)	15.00	8.00	5.00
27	Willie Mays Makes Greatest Catch	35.00	20.00	12.00
28	Homer By Berra Puts Yanks In 1st Place	8.00	4.00	2.50
29	Campy National League's MVP	8.00	4.00	2.50
30	Bob Turley Hurls Yanks To Championship	8.00	4.00	2.50
31	Dodgers Take Series From Sox In Six	8.00	4.00	2.50
32	Furillo Hero As Dodgers Beat Chicago	8.00	4.00	2.50
33	Adcock Gets Four Homers And A Double	8.00	4.00	2.50
34	Dickey Chosen All Star Catcher	8.00	4.00	2.50
35	Burdette Beats Yanks In 3 Series Games	8.00	4.00	2.50
36	Umpires Clear White Sox Bench	8.00	4.00	2.50
37	Reese Honored As Greatest Dodger S.S.	10.00	5.00	3.00
38	Joe DiMaggio Hits In 56 Straight Games	40.00	20.00	12.00
39	Ted Williams Hits .406 For Season	35.00	20.00	12.00
40	Johnson Pitches 56 Scoreless Innings	8.00	4.00	2.50
41	Hodges Hits 4 Home Runs In Nite Game	8.00	4.00	2.50
42	Greenberg Returns To Tigers From Army	15.00	8.00	5.00
43	Ty Cobb Named Best Player Of All Time	20.00	10.00	6.00
44	Robin Roberts Wins 28 Games	8.00	4.00	2.50
45	Rizzuto's 2 Runs Save 1st Place	8.00	4.00	2.50
46	Tigers Beat Out Senators For Pennant (Hal Newhouser)	8.00	4.00	2.50
47	Babe Ruth Hits 60th Home Run	60.00	30.00	20.00
48	Cy Young Honored	8.00	4.00	2.50
49	Killebrew Starts Spring Training	8.00	4.00	2.50
50	Mantle Hits Longest Homer At Stadium	80.00	40.00	25.00
51	Braves Take Pennant (Hank Aaron)	8.00	4.00	2.50
52	Ted Williams Hero Of All Star Game	40.00	20.00	12.00
53	Robinson Saves Dodgers For Playoffs (Jackie Robinson)	18.00	9.00	5.00
54	Snodgrass Muffs A Fly Ball	8.00	4.00	2.50
55	Snider Belts 2 Homers	8.00	4.00	2.50
56	New York Giants Win 26 Straight Games (Christy Mathewson)	8.00	4.00	2.50
57	Ted Kluszewski Stars In 1st Game Win	8.00	4.00	2.50
58	Ott Walks 5 Times In A Single Game (Mel Ott)	8.00	4.00	2.50
59	Harvey Kuenn Takes Batting Title	8.00	4.00	2.50
60	Bob Feller Hurls 3rd No-Hitter Of Career	8.00	4.00	2.50
61	Yanks Champs Again! (Casey Stengel)	8.00	4.00	2.50
62	Aaron's Bat Beats Yankees In Series	15.00	8.00	5.00
63	Warren Spahn Beats Yanks in World Series	8.00	4.00	2.50
64	Ump's Wrong Call Helps Dodgers	8.00	4.00	2.50
65	Kaline Hits 3 Homers, 2 In Same Inning	8.00	4.00	2.50
66	Bob Allison Named A.L. Rookie of Year	8.00	4.00	2.50
67	McCovey Blasts Way Into Giant Lineup	8.00	4.00	2.50
68	Colavito Hits Four Homers In One Game	15.00	8.00	5.00
69	Erskine Sets Strike Out Record In W.S.	8.00	4.00	2.50
70	Sal Maglie Pitches No-Hit Game	8.00	4.00	2.50
71	Early Wynn Victory Crushes Yanks	8.00	4.00	2.50
72	Nellie Fox American League's M.V.P.	8.00	4.00	2.50

1961 Nu-Card Baseball Scoops

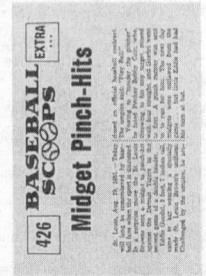

Very similar in style to their set of the year before, the Nu-Card Baseball Scoops were issued in a smaller 2-1/2" x 3-1/2"

size, but still featured the mock newspaper card front. This 80-card set is numbered from 401 to 480, with numbers shown on both the card front and back. These cards, which commemorate great moments in individual players' careers, included only the headline and black and white photo on the fronts, with the descriptive story on the card backs. Cards are again printed in red and black. It appears the set may have been counterfeited, though when is not known. These reprinted cards can be determined by examining the card photo for unusual blurring and fuzziness.

		NM	EX	VG
Complete Set (80):		550.00	275.00	165.00
Common Player:		4.00	2.00	1.25
Wax Pack (7):		100.00	.00	.00
401	Gentile Powers Birds Into 1st	10.00	6.00	3.00
402	Warren Spahn Hurls No-Hitter, Whiffs 15	7.00	3.50	2.00
403	Mazeroski's Homer Wins Series For Bucs	15.00	8.00	5.00
404	Willie Mays' 3 Triples Paces Giants	20.00	10.00	6.00
405	Woodie Held Slugs 2 Homers, 6 RBIs	4.00	2.00	1.25
406	Vern Law Winner Of Cy Young Award	4.00	2.00	1.25
407	Runnels Makes 9 Hits in Twin-Bill	4.00	2.00	1.25
408	Braves' Lew Burdette Wins No-Hitter	4.00	2.00	1.25
409	Dick Stuart Hits 3 Homers, Single	4.00	2.00	1.25
410	Don Cardwell Of Cubs Pitches No-Hit Game	4.00	2.00	1.25
411	Camilo Pascual Strikes Out 15 Bosox	4.00	2.00	1.25
412	Eddie Mathews Blasts 300th Big League HR	4.00	2.00	1.25
413	Groat, NL Bat King, Named Loop's MVP	4.00	2.00	1.25
414	AL Votes To Expand To 10 Teams (Gene Autry)	4.00	2.00	1.25
415	Bobby Richardson Sets Series Mark	4.00	2.00	1.25
416	Maris Nips Mantle For AL MVP Award	15.00	8.00	5.00
417	Merkle Pulls Boner	4.00	2.00	1.25
418	Larsen Hurls Perfect World Series Game	7.00	3.50	2.00
419	Bean Ball Ends Career Of Mickey Cochrane	4.00	2.00	1.25
420	Banks Belts 47 Homers, Earns MVP Award	10.00	5.00	3.00
421	Stan Musial Hits 5 Homers In 1 Day	12.00	6.00	4.00
422	Mickey Mantle Hits Longest Homer	50.00	25.00	15.00
423	Sievers Captures Home Run Title	4.00	2.00	1.25
424	Gehrig Consecutive Game Record Ends	20.00	10.00	6.00
425	Red Schoendienst Key Player In Victory	4.00	2.00	1.25
426	Midget Pinch-Hits For St. Louis Browns (Eddie Gaedel)	7.00	3.50	2.00
427	Willie Mays Makes Greatest Catch	30.00	15.00	9.00
428	Robinson Saves Dodgers For Playoffs	12.00	6.00	4.00
429	Campy Most Valuable Player	4.00	2.00	1.25
430	Turley Hurls Yanks To Championship	4.00	2.00	1.25
431	Dodgers Take Series From Sox In Six (Larry Sherry)	4.00	2.00	1.25
432	Furillo Hero In 3rd World Series Game	4.00	2.00	1.25
433	Adcock Gets Four Homers, Double	4.00	2.00	1.25
434	Dickey Chosen All Star Catcher	4.00	2.00	1.25
435	Burdette Beats Yanks In 3 Series Games	4.00	2.00	1.25
436	Umpires Clear White Sox Bench	4.00	2.00	1.25
437	Reese Honored As Greatest Dodgers S.S.	4.00	2.00	1.25
438	Joe DiMaggio Hits In 56 Straight Games	30.00	15.00	9.00
439	Ted Williams Hits .406 For Season	30.00	15.00	9.00
440	Johnson Pitches 56 Scoreless Innings	4.00	2.00	1.25
441	Hodges Hits 4 Home Runs In Nite Game	4.00	2.00	1.25
442	Greenberg Returns To Tigers From Army	4.00	2.00	1.25
443	Ty Cobb Named Best Player Of All Time	15.00	8.00	5.00
444	Robin Roberts Wins 28 Games	4.00	2.00	1.25
445	Rizzuto's 2 Runs Save 1st Place	4.00	2.00	1.25
446	Tigers Beat Out Senators For Pennant (Hal Newhouser)	4.00	2.00	1.25
447	Babe Ruth Hits 60th Home Run	30.00	15.00	9.00
448	Cy Young Honored	6.00	3.00	2.00
449	Killebrew Starts Spring Training	4.00	2.00	1.25
450	Mantle Hits Longest Homer At Stadium	50.00	25.00	15.00
451	Braves Take Pennant	4.00	2.00	1.25
452	Ted Williams Hero Of All Star Game	30.00	15.00	9.00
453	Homer By Berra Puts Yanks In 1st Place	6.00	3.00	2.00
454	Snodgrass Muffs A Fly Ball	4.00	2.00	1.25
455	Babe Hits 3 Homers In A Series Game	35.00	20.00	12.00
456	New York Wins 26 Straight Games	4.00	2.00	1.25
457	Ted Kluszewski Stars In 1st Series Win	4.00	2.00	1.25
458	Ott Walks 5 Times In A Single Game	4.00	2.00	1.25
459	Harvey Kuenn Takes Batting Title	4.00	2.00	1.25
460	Bob Feller Hurls 3rd No-Hitter Of Career	4.00	2.00	1.25
461	Yanks Champs Again! (Casey Stengel)	4.00	2.00	1.25
462	Aaron's Bat Beats Yankees In Series	15.00	8.00	5.00
463	Warren Spahn Beats Yanks In World Series	4.00	2.00	1.25
464	Ump's Wrong Call Helps Dodgers	4.00	2.00	1.25
465	Kaline Hits 3 Homers, 2 In Same Inning	4.00	2.00	1.25
466	Bob Allison Named A.L. Rookie Of Year	4.00	2.00	1.25
467	DiMag Comes Thru	30.00	15.00	9.00
468	Colavito Hits Four Homers In One Game	5.00	2.50	1.50
469	Erskine Sets Strike Out Record In W.S.	4.00	2.00	1.25
470	Sal Maglie Pitches No-Hit Game	4.00	2.00	1.25
471	Early Wynn Victory Crushes Yanks	4.00	2.00	1.25
472	Nellie Fox American League's MVP	4.00	2.00	1.25
473	Pickoff Ends Series (Marty Marion)	4.00	2.00	1.25
474	Podres Pitching Wins Series	4.00	2.00	1.25
475	Owen Drops 3rd Strike	4.00	2.00	1.25
476	Dizzy And Daffy Win Series	12.00	6.00	4.00
477	Mathewson Pitches 3 W.S. Shutouts	15.00	8.00	5.00
478	Haddix Pitches 12 Perfect Innings	4.00	2.00	1.25
479	Hubbell Strike Out 5 A.L. Stars	4.00	2.00	1.25
480	Homer Sinks Dodgers (Bobby Thomson)	8.00	4.00	2.50

1889 Number 7 Cigars (N526)

Three versions of this set picturing Boston Beaneaters (N.L.) players were issued in 1889. Number 7 and Diamond S brand cigars are the most commonly encountered advertising printed on the cards' backs. Cards with "C.S. White & Co." at top front are also known. The cards measure approximately 3-1/8" x 4-1/2" and feature black-and-white portrait drawings of the players with their name printed below in capital letters along with the team name. Backs carry ads for either Number 7 Cigars, a product of H.W.S. & Co. Howard W. Spurr & Co.), or Diamond S Cigars, advertised as the "Best 10 cent Cigar in America."

		NM	EX	VG
Complete Set (15):		40,000	20,000	12,000
Common Player:		2,200	1,100	650.00
(1)	C.W. Bennett	2,200	1,100	650.00
(2)	Dennis Brouthers	5,000	2,500	1,500
(3)	T.T. Brown	2,200	1,100	650.00
(4)	John G. Clarkson	5,000	2,500	1,500
(5)	C.W. Ganzel	2,200	1,100	650.00
(6)	James A. Hart	2,200	1,100	650.00
(7)	R.F. Johnston	2,200	1,100	650.00
(8)	M.J. Kelly	7,000	3,500	2,100
(9)	M.J. Madden	2,200	1,100	650.00
(10)	Wm. Nash	2,200	1,100	650.00
(11)	Jos. Quinn	2,200	1,100	650.00
(12)	Chas. Radbourn	5,000	2,500	1,500
(13)	J.B. Ray (Should be I.B.)	2,200	1,100	650.00
(14)	Hardie Richardson	2,200	1,100	650.00
(15)	Wm. Sowders	2,200	1,100	650.00

1949-1950 Num Num Cleveland Indians

The 6-1/2" x 9" photopack pictures sold at Municipal Stadium in 1949 did double duty when they were also used as a premium for Num Num snack foods. A rubber-stamped notice on the back of the black-and-white photos offered two pictures for 10 cents and a box top, while encouraging trading. The pictures generally feature posed action shots with a facsimile autograph and white border. Backs are blank except for the rubber stamping. The unnumbered cards are checklisted here alphabetically.

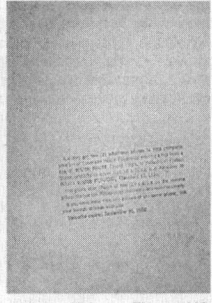

	NM	EX	VG
Complete Set (36):	1,850	925.00	550.00
Common Player:	35.00	17.50	10.00
(1) Bob Avila	35.00	17.50	10.00
(2) Gene Bearden	35.00	17.50	10.00
(3) Al Benton	35.00	17.50	10.00
(4) John Berardino	45.00	22.50	13.50
(5) Ray Boone	35.00	17.50	10.00
(6) Lou Boudreau	65.00	30.00	15.00
(7) Allie Clark	35.00	17.50	10.00
(8) Larry Doby	65.00	30.00	15.00
(9) Luke Easter	35.00	17.50	10.00
(10) Bob Feller	125.00	60.00	30.00
(11) Jess Flores	35.00	17.50	10.00
(12) Mike Garcia	35.00	17.50	10.00
(13) Joe Gordon	35.00	17.50	10.00
(14) Hank Greenberg	125.00	65.00	35.00
(15) Steve Gromek	35.00	17.50	10.00
(16) Jim Hegan	35.00	17.50	10.00
(17) Ken Keltner	35.00	17.50	10.00
(18) Bob Kennedy	35.00	17.50	10.00
(19) Bob Lemon	65.00	30.00	15.00
(20) Dale Mitchell	35.00	17.50	10.00
(21) Ray Murray	35.00	17.50	10.00
(22) Satchell Paige	200.00	90.00	50.00
(23) Frank Papish	35.00	17.50	10.00
(24) Hal Peck	35.00	17.50	10.00
(25) Chick Pieretti	35.00	17.50	10.00
(26) Al Rosen	45.00	22.50	13.50
(27) Dick Rozek (Glove out front.)	35.00	17.50	10.00
(28) Dick Rozek (Glove under leg.)	35.00	17.50	10.00
(29) Mike Tresh	35.00	17.50	10.00
(30) Thurman Tucker	35.00	17.50	10.00
(31) Bill Veeck	65.00	30.00	15.00
(32) Mickey Vernon	35.00	17.50	10.00
(33) Early Wynn	65.00	30.00	15.00
(34) Sam Zoldak	35.00	17.50	10.00
(35) Coaches (George Susce, Herold Ruel, Bill McKechnie, Steve O'Neill, Mel Harder)	35.00	17.50	10.00
(36) Municipal Stadium	35.00	17.50	10.00

1952 Num Num Cleveland Indians

Distributed with packages of Num Num potato chips, pretzels and other snack foods, this black-and-white set, like the 1950 issue, was also issued in a slightly different format directly by the team. The Num Num cards have a 1" tab at the bottom which could be redeemed, when a complete set was collected, for an autographed baseball. The team-issued version of the cards was printed without the tabs. Also like the 1950 Num Nums, Bob Kennedy's card is unaccountably scarce in the 1952 set. The 52 cards measure 3-1/2" x 5-1/2" including the tab, which has the card number on front, along with redemption details. Backs, also printed in black-and-white, repeat the card number in the upper-left corner. There is significant player biographical information and some 1951 season highlights. Cards with no tabs are worth about 1/3 less than the values quoted.

	NM	EX	VG
Complete Set, With Tabs (20):	8,100	4,000	2,500
Common Player, With Tab:	200.00	100.00	60.00
Complete Set, No Tabs (20):	4,600	2,300	1,400
Common Player, No Tab:	160.00	80.00	50.00
WITH TABS			
1 Lou Brissie	200.00	100.00	60.00
2 Jim Hegan	200.00	100.00	60.00
3 Birdie Tebbetts	200.00	100.00	60.00
4 Bob Lemon	420.00	220.00	125.00
5 Bob Feller	1,300	650.00	400.00
6 Early Wynn	420.00	220.00	125.00
7 Mike Garcia	200.00	100.00	60.00
8 Steve Gromek	200.00	100.00	60.00
9 Bob Chakales	200.00	100.00	60.00
10 Al Rosen	250.00	125.00	75.00

		NM	EX	VG
11	Dick Rozek	200.00	100.00	60.00
12	Luke Easter	250.00	125.00	75.00
13	Ray Boone	200.00	100.00	60.00
14	Bobby Avila	200.00	100.00	60.00
15	Dale Mitchell	200.00	100.00	60.00
16	Bob Kennedy/SP	2,250	1,100	700.00
17	Harry Simpson	200.00	100.00	60.00
18	Larry Doby	420.00	220.00	125.00
19	Sam Jones	200.00	100.00	60.00
20	Al Lopez	420.00	220.00	125.00
	NO TABS			
1	Lou Brissie	160.00	80.00	50.00
2	Jim Hegan	160.00	80.00	50.00
3	Birdie Tebbetts	160.00	80.00	50.00
4	Bob Lemon	280.00	140.00	85.00
5	Bob Feller	850.00	425.00	250.00
6	Early Wynn	280.00	140.00	85.00
7	Mike Garcia	160.00	80.00	50.00
8	Steve Gromek	160.00	80.00	50.00
9	Bob Chakales	160.00	80.00	50.00
10	Al Rosen	175.00	90.00	50.00
11	Dick Rozek	160.00	80.00	50.00
12	Luke Easter	175.00	90.00	50.00
13	Ray Boone	160.00	80.00	50.00
14	Bobby Avila	160.00	80.00	50.00
15	Dale Mitchell	160.00	80.00	50.00
16	Bob Kennedy/SP	1,750	875.00	550.00
17	Harry Simpson	160.00	80.00	50.00
18	Larry Doby	280.00	140.00	85.00
19	Sam Jones	160.00	80.00	50.00
20	Al Lopez	280.00	140.00	85.00

O

1937 O-Pee-Chee

Kind of a combination of 1934 Goudeys and 1934-36 Batter Ups, the '37 OPC "Baseball Stars" set features black-and-white action photos against a stylized ballpark. About halfway up the 2-5/8" x 2-15/16" cards, the background was die-cut to allow it to be folded back to create a stand-up card. Backs are printed in English and French. The 40 cards in "Series A" are all American Leaguers, leading to speculation that a Series B of National League players was to have been issued at a later date. The set carries the American Card Catalog designation of V300.

		NM	EX	VG
	Complete Set (40):	24,000	12,000	7,250
	Common Player:	450.00	225.00	135.00
101	John Lewis	450.00	225.00	135.00
102	"Jack" Hayes	450.00	225.00	135.00
103	Earl Averill	650.00	320.00	195.00
104	Harland Clift (Harland)	450.00	225.00	135.00
105	"Beau" Bell	450.00	225.00	135.00
106	Jimmy Foxx (Jimmie)	1,200	600.00	350.00
107	Hank Greenberg	1,325	660.00	400.00
108	George Selkirk	450.00	225.00	135.00
109	Wally Moses	450.00	225.00	135.00
110	"Gerry" Walker	450.00	225.00	135.00
111	"Goose" Goslin	650.00	320.00	195.00
112	Charlie Gehringer	425.00	210.00	125.00
113	Hal Trosky	450.00	225.00	135.00
114	"Buddy" Myer	450.00	225.00	135.00
115	Luke Appling	650.00	320.00	195.00
116	"Zeke" Bonura	425.00	210.00	125.00
117	Tony Lazzeri	450.00	225.00	135.00
118	Joe DiMaggio	7,500	3,700	2,200
119	Bill Dickey	600.00	300.00	180.00
120	Bob Feller	1,300	650.00	400.00
121	Harry Kelley	450.00	225.00	135.00
122	Johnny Allen	450.00	225.00	135.00
123	Bob Johnson	450.00	225.00	135.00
124	Joe Cronin	400.00	200.00	120.00
125	"Rip" Radcliff	450.00	225.00	135.00
126	Cecil Travis	450.00	225.00	135.00
127	Joe Kuhel	450.00	225.00	135.00
128	Odell Hale	450.00	225.00	135.00
129	Sam West	450.00	225.00	135.00
130	Ben Chapman	450.00	225.00	135.00
131	Monte Pearson	450.00	225.00	135.00
132	"Rick" Ferrell	650.00	320.00	195.00
133	Tommy Bridges	450.00	225.00	135.00
134	"Schoolboy" Rowe	450.00	225.00	135.00
135	Vernon Kennedy	450.00	225.00	135.00
136	"Red" Ruffing	650.00	320.00	195.00
137	"Lefty" Grove	500.00	250.00	150.00
138	Wes Farrell	450.00	225.00	135.00
139	"Buck" Newsom	450.00	225.00	135.00
140	Rogers Hornsby	750.00	375.00	225.00

1960 O-Pee-Chee Tattoos

Though much scarcer than the contemporary Topps version, this Canadian specialty bubblegum issue does not currently enjoy any price premium. The OPC type is identifiable by its imprint on the outside of the wrapper.

(See 1960 Topps Tattoos for description, checklist and price guide.)

1965 O-Pee-Chee

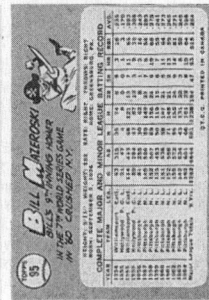

Identical in design to the 1965 Topps set, the Canadian-issued 1965 O-Pee-Chee set was printed on gray stock and consists of 283 cards, each measuring the standard 2-1/2" x 3-1/2". The words "Printed in Canada" appear along the bottom of the back of the cards. The checklist for '65 OPC parallels the first 283 cards in 1965 Topps.

	NM	EX	VG
Complete Set (283):	3,150	1,575	950.00
Common Player (1-196):	3.00	1.50	9.00
Common Player (197-283):	6.00	3.00	1.80
Stars: 2-3X Topps			

(See 1965 Topps #1-283 for checklist and star card values.)

1966 O-Pee-Chee

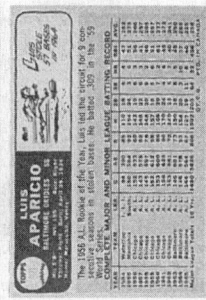

Utilizing the same design as the 1966 Topps set, the 1966 O-Pee-Chee set consists of 196 cards, measuring 2-1/2" x 3-1/2". The words "Ptd. in Canada" appear along the bottom on the back of the cards. The '66 OPC checklist parallels the first 196 cards in the Topps version.

	NM	EX	VG
Complete Set (196):	1,600	800.00	475.00
Common Player (1-196):	2.50	1.25	.75
Stars: 2-3X Topps			

(See 1966 Topps #1-196 for checklist and base star card values.)

1967 O-Pee-Chee

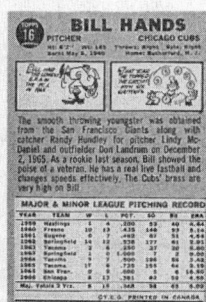

Cards in the 196-card Canadian set are nearly identical in design to the 1967 Topps set, except the words "Printed in Canada" are found on the back in the lower-right corner. Cards measure 2-1/2" x 3-1/2". The '67 OPC set parallels the first 196 cards on the Topps checklist, including "corrected" versions of the checklists and McCormick card.

	NM	EX	VG
Complete Set (196):	1,100	550.00	330.00
Common Player (1-109):	2.00	1.00	.60
Common Player (110-196):	2.50	1.25	.75
Stars: 2-3X Topps			

(See 1967 Topps #1-196 for checklist and base star card values.)

1968 O-Pee-Chee

The O-Pee-Chee set for 1968 again consists of 196 cards, in the standard 2-1/2" x 3-1/2". The design is identical to the 1968 Topps set, except the color of the backs is slightly different and the words "Prd. in Canada" appear in the lower-right corner of the back. The checklist parallels the first 196 cards in '68 Topps, though only the "b" versions of the checklists and name-color variations are found in OPC.

	NM	EX	VG
Complete Set (196):	3,000	1,500	900.00
Common Player:	2.00	1.00	.60
Stars: 2-3X Topps			

(See 1968 Topps #1-196 for checklist and base star card values.)

		NM	EX	VG
177	Mets Rookies (Jerry Koosman, Nolan Ryan)	1,600	800.00	475.00

1968 O-Pee-Chee Posters

The 5" x 7" "All Star Pin-ups" were inserts to 1968 OPC wax packs, but are virtually identical to the Topps version issued in 1967. The OPC posters have a small "Ptd. in Canada" line at bottom. They feature a full-color picture with the player's name, position and team in a circle in the lower-right corner on front. The numbered set consists of 32 players (generally big names). Because the large paper pin-ups had to be folded several times to fit into the wax packs, they are almost never found in technical Mint or NM condition.

		NM	EX	VG
Complete Set (32):		300.00	150.00	90.00
Common Player:		3.00	1.50	.90
1	Brooks Robinson	12.00	6.00	3.50
2	Bert Campaneris	3.00	1.50	.90
3	Carl Yastrzemski	12.00	6.00	3.50
4	Roberto Clemente	25.00	12.50	7.50
5	Cleon Jones	3.00	1.50	.90
6	Don Drysdale	12.00	6.00	3.50
7	Orlando Cepeda	9.00	4.50	2.75
8	Hank Aaron	25.00	12.50	7.50
9	Tommie Agee	6.00	3.00	1.75
10	Boog Powell	4.50	2.25	1.25
11	Mickey Mantle	40.00	20.00	12.00
12	Chico Cardenas	3.00	1.50	.90
13	John Callison	3.00	1.50	.90
14	Frank Howard	3.75	2.00	1.25
15	Willie Mays	25.00	12.50	7.50
16	Sam McDowell	4.50	2.25	1.25
17	Al Kaline	12.00	6.00	3.50
18	Juan Marichal	9.00	4.50	2.75
19	Denny McLain	4.50	2.25	1.25
20	Matty Alou	3.00	1.50	.90
21	Felipe Alou	4.50	2.25	1.25
22	Joe Pepitone	4.50	2.25	1.25
23	Leon Wagner	3.00	1.50	.90
24	Bobby Knoop	3.00	1.50	.90
25	Tony Oliva	4.50	2.25	1.25
26	Joe Torre	4.50	2.25	1.25
27	Ron Santo	6.00	3.00	1.75
28	Willie McCovey	12.00	6.00	3.50
29	Frank Robinson	12.00	6.00	3.50
30	Ron Hunt	3.00	1.50	.90
31	Harmon Killebrew	12.00	6.00	3.50
32	Joe Morgan	12.00	6.00	3.50

1969 O-Pee-Chee

O-Pee-Chee increased the number of cards in its 1969 set to 218, maintaining the standard 2-1/2" x 3-1/2" size. The card design is identical to the 1969 Topps set, except for the appearance of an OPC logo on back, a slightly different color on the back and the words "Ptd. in Canada," which appear along the bottom. The checklist for '69 OPC parallels the

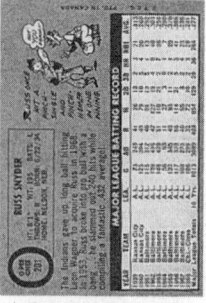

Topps version, but includes only the later-printed "b" versions of the variation cards. This was the first year for the N.L. expansion Montreal Expos, and the Canadian versions of their cards generally sell for a modest premium.

	NM	EX	VG
Complete Set (218):	775.00	375.00	225.00
Common Player:	2.50	1.25	.75
Stars: 1-2X Topps			
Expos: 1.5X Topps			

(See 1969 Topps #1-218 for checklist and base star card values.)

1969 O-Pee-Chee Deckle

Very similar in design to the Topps Deckle Edge set of the same year, the 1969 O-Pee-Chee set consists of 24 (rather than Topps' 33) unnumbered black-and-white cards. The Canadian version measures 2-1/8" x 3-1/8", slightly smaller than the Topps set, but features the same "deckle cut" borders. The OPC set is blank-backed and has the facsimile autographs in black ink, rather than blue.

		NM	EX	VG
Complete Set (24):		160.00	80.00	45.00
Common Player:		2.50	1.25	.75
(1)	Rich Allen	3.00	1.50	.90
(2)	Luis Aparicio	7.50	3.75	2.25
(3)	Rodney Carew	12.50	6.25	3.75
(4)	Roberto Clemente	30.00	15.00	9.00
(5)	Curt Flood	2.50	1.25	.75
(6)	Bill Freehan	2.50	1.25	.75
(7)	Robert Gibson	7.50	3.75	2.25
(8)	Ken Harrelson	2.50	1.25	.75
(9)	Tommy Helms	2.50	1.25	.75
(10)	Tom Haller	2.50	1.25	.75
(11)	Willie Horton	2.50	1.25	.70
(12)	Frank Howard	2.50	1.25	.75
(13)	Willie McCovey	10.00	5.00	3.00
(14)	Denny McLain	2.50	1.25	.75
(15)	Juan Marichal	7.50	3.75	2.25
(16)	Willie Mays	25.00	12.50	7.50
(17)	John "Boog" Powell	3.00	1.50	.90
(18)	Brooks Robinson	12.50	6.25	3.75
(19)	Ronald Santo	3.00	1.50	.90
(20)	Rusty Staub	3.00	1.50	.90
(21)	Mel Stottlemyre	2.50	1.25	.75
(22)	Luis Tiant	2.50	1.25	.75
(23)	Maurie Wills	2.50	1.25	.75
(24)	Carl Yastrzemski	12.50	6.25	3.75

1970 O-Pee-Chee

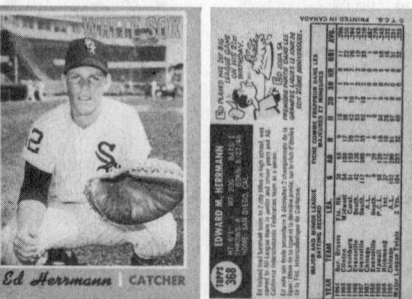

The 1970 O-Pee-Chee set, identical in design to the 1970 Topps set, expanded to 546 cards, measuring 2-1/2" x 3-1/2".

The Canadian-issued O-Pee-Chee set is easy to distinguish because the backs are printed in both French and English and include the words "Printed in Canada." The '70 OPC checklist parallels the Topps versions. Besides the star cards generally bringing a premium over the Topps version due to scarcity, collectors pay a modest premium for OPC cards of Expos players.

	NM	EX	VG
Complete Set (546):	1,750	875.00	525.00
Common Player (1-459):	1.50	.75	.45
Common Player (460-546):	2.50	1.25	.75
Stars: 1-2X Topps			
Expos: 1.5X Topps			

(See 1970 Topps #1-546 for checklist and base card values.)

1971 O-Pee-Chee

For 1971 O-Pee-Chee increased the number of cards in its set to 752, the same as the 1971 Topps set, which shares the same black-bordered design. The backs of the OPC are printed in yellow, rather than green, in a slightly different format and (except card numbers 524-752) are printed in both French and English. The words "Printed in Canada" appear on the back. Fourteen of the OPC cards have different photos from their corresponding Topps' cards or list the player with a different team. The '71 OPC checklist parallels the Topps version. Because of relative scarcity, superstars in the OPC set command a premium, as do cards of the "local" Expos players.

	NM	EX	VG
Complete Set (752):	3,000	1,500	900.00
Common Player (1-523):	2.75	1.50	.80
Common Player (524-643):	4.50	2.25	1.25
Common Player (644-752):	6.50	3.25	2.00
Stars: 1-2X Topps			
Expos: 1.5X Topps			

(See 1971 Topps for checklist and base card values.)

1972 O-Pee-Chee

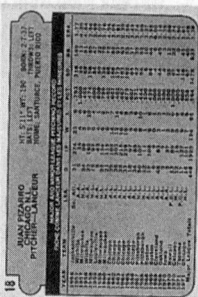

Identical in design to the Topps cards of the same year, the Canadian-issued 1972 O-Pee-Chee set numbers 525 cards, measuring 2-1/2" x 3-1/2". The backs state "Printed in Canada" and are identical in both French and English. The O-Pee-Chee card of Gil Hodges notes the Mets' manager's death. The '72 OPC set parallels the first 525 cards on the '72 Topps checklist, though without any of the scarcer "a" variations. Because of relative scarcity, superstars in the OPC brand bring a premium over Topps cards, while increased demand for Expos players causes their cards to bring a similar modest premium.

	NM	EX	VG
Complete Set (525):	875.00	425.00	250.00
Common Player (1-263):	.60	.30	.20
Common Player (264-394):	.90	.45	.25
Common Player (395-525):	1.00	.50	.30
Stars: 1-2X Topps			
Expos: 1.5X Topps			

(See 1972 Topps #1-525 for checklist and base card values.)

1973 O-Pee-Chee

The 1973 Canadian-issued O-Pee-Chee set numbers 660 cards and is identical in design and checklist (including only the later-printed "b" variations) to the 1973 Topps set. The backs of the OPC cards are written in both French and English and contain the line "Printed in Canada" along the bottom. The cards measure 2-1/2" x 3-1/2". Unlike the '73 Topps set, which was issued in series of increasing scarcity throughout the summer, the '73 OPC cards were issued in a single series, with cards #529-660 being somewhat short-printed. OPC star cards generally sell for more than the Topps version due to relative scarcity, while Expos players in OPC rate a similar premium due to increased "local" demand.

STEVE STONE
SAN FRANCISCO GIANTS   PITCHER

	NM	EX	VG
Complete Set (660):	500.00	250.00	150.00
Common Player (1-528):	.75	.35	.20
Common Player (529-660):	1.25	.60	.40
Stars/Expos: 1.5X Topps			
Wax Pack (10):	55.00		
Wax Box (36):	1,900		

(See 1973 Topps for checklist and base card values.)

1973 O-Pee-Chee Team Checklists

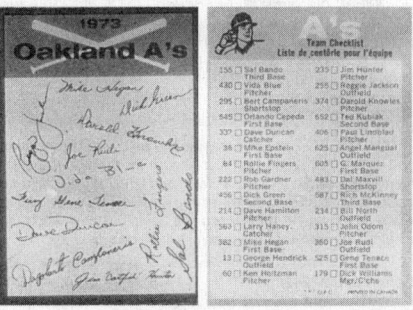

Similar to the 1973 Topps team checklist cards, this set was produced in Canada. The set consists of 24 unnumbered cards (2-1/2" x 3-1/2") with blue borders. The card fronts contain facsimile autographs of players from the same team. The backs contain team checklists of players found in the 1973 O-Pee-Chee regular issue set. The card backs contain the French translation for Team Checklist plus a copyright line "O.P.C. Printed in Canada."

		NM	EX	VG
Complete Set (24):		40.00	20.00	12.00
Common Card:		3.00	1.50	.90
(1)	Atlanta Braves	3.00	1.50	.90
(2)	Baltimore Orioles	3.00	1.50	.90
(3)	Boston Red Sox	3.00	1.50	.90
(4)	California Angels	3.00	1.50	.90
(5)	Chicago Cubs	3.00	1.50	.90
(6)	Chicago White Sox	3.00	1.50	.90
(7)	Cincinnati Reds	4.00	2.00	1.25
(8)	Cleveland Indians	3.00	1.50	.90
(9)	Detroit Tigers	4.00	2.00	1.25
(10)	Houston Astros	3.00	1.50	.90
(11)	Kansas City Royals	3.00	1.50	.90
(12)	Los Angeles Dodgers	3.00	1.50	.90
(13)	Milwaukee Brewers	3.00	1.50	.90
(14)	Minnesota Twins	3.00	1.50	.90
(15)	Montreal Expos	6.00	3.00	1.75
(16)	New York Mets	4.00	2.00	1.25
(17)	New York Yankees	3.00	1.50	.90
(18)	Oakland A's	4.50	2.25	1.25
(19)	Philadelphia Phillies	3.00	1.50	.90
(20)	Pittsburgh Pirates	3.00	1.50	.90
(21)	St. Louis Cardinals	3.00	1.50	.90
(22)	San Diego Padres	3.00	1.50	.90
(23)	San Francisco Giants	3.00	1.50	.90
(24)	Texas Rangers	3.00	1.50	.90

1974 O-Pee-Chee

SAN FRANCISCO   PITCHER
RON BRYANT   GIANTS

Again numbering 660 cards, the 1974 O-Pee-Chee set borrows its design and, except for 10 of the cards, shares its checklist with the Topps set of the same year. The cards measure the standard 2-1/2" x 3-1/2" and the backs are printed in both French and English and state "Printed in Canada." Because the OPC cards were printed later than Topps, there are no "Washington, Nat'l. League" variations in the Canadian set. Superstar cards and Expos players in OPC command a

modest premium over the Topps version due to relative scarcity and increased local demand, respectively. Those OPC cards which differ from Topps are listed below, with the Topps version of each card number shown parenthetically.

		NM	EX	VG
Complete Set (660):		950.00	475.00	275.00
Common Player:		.50	.25	.15
Stars/Expos: 1.5X Topps				
Wax Pack (8):		65.00	.00	.00
Wax Box (36):		2,150	.00	.00
3	Aaron Special 1958-1959 (Aaron Special 1958-1961)	7.00	3.50	2.00
4	Aaron Special 1960-1961 (Aaron Special 1962-1965)	7.00	3.50	2.00
5	Aaron Special 1962-1963 (Aaron Special 1966-1969)	7.00	3.50	2.00
6	Aaron Special 1964-1965 (Aaron Special 1970-1973)	7.00	3.50	2.00
7	Aaron Special 1966-1967 (Jim Hunter)	7.00	3.50	2.00
8	Aaron Special 1968-1969 (George Theodore)	7.00	3.50	2.00
9	Aaron Special 1970-1973 (Mickey Lolich)	7.00	3.50	2.00
99	George Theodore (Brewers Mgr./Coaches)	1.50	.70	.45
166	Mickey Lolich (Royals Mgr./Coaches)	2.00	1.00	.60
196	Jim Hunter (Jim Fregosi)	7.50	3.75	2.25

(See 1974 Topps for checklist and base card values.)

1974 O-Pee-Chee Team Checklists

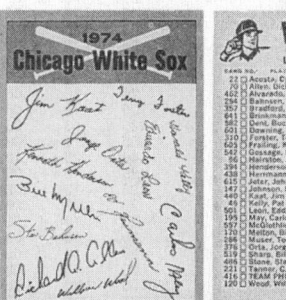

The 1974 O-Pee-Chee Team Checklists set is nearly identical to its Topps counterpart of the same year. Twenty-four unnumbered cards that measure 2-1/2" x 3-1/2" make up the set. The card fronts contain facsimile autographs while the backs carry a team checklist of players found in the regular issue O-Pee-Chee set of 1974. The cards have red borders and can be differentiated from the U.S. version by the "O.P.C. Printed in Canada" line on the back.

		NM	EX	VG
Complete Set (24):		25.00	12.50	7.50
Common Checklist:		1.50	.70	.40
(1)	Atlanta Braves	1.50	.70	.45
(2)	Baltimore Orioles	1.50	.70	.45
(3)	Boston Red Sox	1.50	.70	.45
(4)	California Angels	1.50	.70	.45
(5)	Chicago Cubs	1.50	.70	.45
(6)	Chicago White Sox	1.50	.70	.45
(7)	Cincinnati Reds	1.50	.70	.45
(8)	Cleveland Indians	1.50	.70	.45
(9)	Detroit Tigers	1.50	.70	.45
(10)	Houston Astros	1.50	.70	.45
(11)	Kansas City Royals	1.50	.70	.45
(12)	Los Angeles Dodgers	1.50	.70	.45
(13)	Milwaukee Brewers	1.50	.70	.45
(14)	Minnesota Twins	1.50	.70	.45
(15)	Montreal Expos	3.00	1.50	.90
(16)	New York Mets	1.50	.70	.45
(17)	New York Yankees	1.50	.70	.45
(18)	Oakland A's	1.50	.70	.45
(19)	Philadelphia Phillies	1.50	.70	.45
(20)	Pittsburgh Pirates	1.50	.70	.45
(21)	St. Louis Cardinals	1.50	.70	.45
(22)	San Diego Padres	1.50	.70	.45
(23)	San Francisco Giants	1.50	.70	.45
(24)	Texas Rangers	1.50	.70	.45

1975 O-Pee-Chee

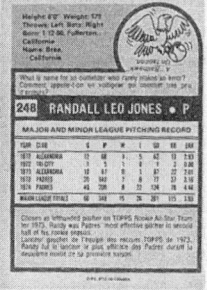

RANDALL LEO JONES • P
PADRES   RANDY JONES   Pitcher

The 1975 O-Pee-Chee set was again complete at 660 cards, each measuring 2-1/2" x 3-1/2", and using the same design as the 1975 Topps set. The backs of the O-Pee-Chee cards are written in both French and English and state that the

cards were printed in Canada. The checklist for OPC and Topps are identical in '75. Because they are relatively scarcer, OPC superstars sell for a premium over Topps. Expos players also enjoy a premium due to increased local demand.

	NM	EX	VG
Complete Set (660):	625.00	325.00	200.00
Common Player:	.45	.25	.15
Stars: 2X Topps			
Expos: 1.5X Topps			
Wax Pack (8):	30.00		
Wax Box (48):	1,200		

(See 1975 Topps for checklist and base card values.)

1976 O-Pee-Chee

TOM CARROLL   REDS   PITCHER

Identical in design to, and sharing a checklist with, the 1976 Topps set, the Canadian-issued 1976 O-Pee-Chees comprise 660 cards, each 2-1/2" x 3-1/2". The backs are printed in both French and English and state "Ptd. in Canada." Stars and Expos players enjoy a modest premium over the Topps versions due to relative scarcity and increased local demand, respectively.

	NM	EX	VG
Complete Set (660):	700.00	350.00	210.00
Common Player:	.20	.10	.05
Stars/Expos 2X Topps			
Wax Pack (8):	30.00		
Wax Box (48):	750.00		

(See 1976 Topps for checklist and base card values.)

1977 O-Pee-Chee

EXPOS   C-OF
GARY CARTER

The 1977 O-Pee-Chee set represents a change in philosophy for the Canadian company. The design of the set is still identical to the Topps set of the same year, but the number of cards was reduced to 264 with more emphasis on players from the two Canadian teams. The backs are printed in both French and English and state "O-Pee-Chee Printed in Canada." About 1/3 of the photos in the OPC set differ from the corresponding Topps cards either with entirely different photos, airbrushed uniform changes, the removal of All-Star and Rookie Team designations, or significant photo cropping variations. Cards measure the standard 2-1/2" x 3-1/2".

		NM	EX	VG
Complete Set (264):		125.00	65.00	40.00
Common Player:		.25	.13	.08
Wax Pack (8):		12.00		
Wax Box (48):		285.00		
1	Batting Leaders (George Brett, Bill Madlock)	4.00	2.00	1.25
2	Home Run Leaders (Graig Nettles, Mike Schmidt)	2.75	1.50	.80
3	Runs Batted In Leaders (George Foster, Lee May)	.25	.13	.08
4	Stolen Base Leaders (Dave Lopes, Bill North)	.25	.13	.08
5	Victory Leaders (Randy Jones, Jim Palmer)	1.00	.50	.30
6	Strikeout Leaders (Nolan Ryan, Tom Seaver)	12.50	6.25	3.75
7	Earned Run Avg. Leaders (John Denny, Mark Fidrych)	.25	.13	.08
8	Leading Firemen (Bill Campbell, Rawly Eastwick)	.25	.13	.08
9	Mike Jorgensen	.25	.13	.08
10	Jim Hunter	4.00	2.00	1.25
11	Ken Griffey	.25	.13	.08
12	Bill Campbell	.25	.13	.08
13	Otto Velez	.25	.13	.08
14	Milt May	.25	.13	.08
15	Dennis Eckersley	4.00	2.00	1.25
16	John Mayberry	.25	.13	.08
17	Larry Bowa	.25	.13	.08
18	Don Carrithers	.25	.13	.08

#	Player	NM	EX	VG
19	Ken Singleton	.25	.13	.08
20	Bill Stein	.25	.13	.08
21	Ken Brett	.25	.13	.08
22	Gary Woods	.25	.13	.08
23	Steve Swisher	.25	.13	.08
24	Don Sutton	4.00	2.00	1.25
25	Willie Stargell	4.00	2.00	1.25
26	Jerry Koosman	.25	.13	.08
27	Del Unser	.25	.13	.08
28	Bob Grich	.25	.13	.08
29	Jim Slaton	.25	.13	.08
30	Thurman Munson	4.00	2.00	1.25
31	Dan Driessen	.25	.13	.08
32	Tom Bruno (Not in Topps.)	.25	.13	.08
33	Larry Hisle	.25	.13	.08
34	Phil Garner	.25	.13	.08
35	Mike Hargrove	.25	.13	.08
36	Jackie Brown	.25	.13	.08
37	Carl Yastrzemski	7.50	3.75	2.25
38	Dave Roberts	.25	.13	.08
39	Ray Fosse	.25	.13	.08
40	Dave McKay	.25	.13	.08
41	Paul Splittorff	.25	.13	.08
42	Garry Maddox	.25	.13	.08
43	Phil Niekro	4.00	2.00	1.25
44	Roger Metzger	.25	.13	.08
45	Gary Carter	7.50	3.75	2.25
46	Jim Spencer	.25	.13	.08
47	Ross Grimsley	.25	.13	.08
48	Bob Bailor	.25	.13	.08
49	Chris Chambliss	.25	.13	.08
50	Will McEnaney	.25	.13	.08
51	Lou Brock	4.50	2.25	1.25
52	Rollie Fingers	4.00	2.00	1.25
53	Chris Speier	.25	.13	.08
54	Bombo Rivera	.25	.13	.08
55	Pete Broberg	.25	.13	.08
56	Bill Madlock	.25	.13	.08
57	Rick Rhoden	.25	.13	.08
58	Blue Jay Coaches (Don Leppert, Bob Miller, Jackie Moore, Harry Warner)	.50	.25	.15
59	John Candelaria	.25	.13	.08
60	Ed Kranepool	.25	.13	.08
61	Dave LaRoche	.25	.13	.08
62	Jim Rice	.75	.40	.25
63	Don Stanhouse	.25	.13	.08
64	Jason Thompson	.25	.13	.08
65	Nolan Ryan	25.00	12.50	7.50
66	Tom Poquette	.25	.13	.08
67	Leon Hooten	.25	.13	.08
68	Bob Boone	.25	.13	.08
69	Mickey Rivers	.25	.13	.08
70	Gary Nolan	.25	.13	.08
71	Sixto Lezcano	.25	.13	.08
72	Larry Parrish	.25	.13	.08
73	Dave Goltz	.25	.13	.08
74	Bert Campaneris	.25	.13	.08
75	Vida Blue	.25	.13	.08
76	Rick Cerone	.25	.13	.08
77	Ralph Garr	.25	.13	.08
78	Ken Forsch	.25	.13	.08
79	Willie Montanez	.25	.13	.08
80	Jim Palmer	4.50	2.25	1.25
81	Jerry White	.25	.13	.08
82	Gene Tenace	.25	.13	.08
83	Bobby Murcer	.25	.13	.08
84	Garry Templeton	.25	.13	.08
85	Bill Singer	.25	.13	.08
86	Buddy Bell	.25	.13	.08
87	Luis Tiant	.25	.13	.08
88	Rusty Staub	.25	.13	.08
89	Sparky Lyle	.25	.13	.08
90	Jose Morales	.25	.13	.08
91	Dennis Leonard	.25	.13	.08
92	Tommy Smith	.25	.13	.08
93	Steve Carlton	5.50	2.75	1.75
94	John Scott	.25	.13	.08
95	Bill Bonham	.25	.13	.08
96	Dave Lopes	.25	.13	.08
97	Jerry Reuss	.25	.13	.08
98	Dave Kingman	.35	.20	.11
99	Dan Warthen	.25	.13	.08
100	Johnny Bench	7.50	3.75	2.25
101	Bert Blyleven	.25	.13	.08
102	Cecil Cooper	.25	.13	.08
103	Mike Willis	.25	.13	.08
104	Dan Ford	.25	.13	.08
105	Frank Tanana	.25	.13	.08
106	Bill North	.25	.13	.08
107	Joe Ferguson	.25	.13	.08
108	Dick Williams	.25	.13	.08
109	John Denny	.25	.13	.08
110	Willie Randolph	.25	.13	.08
111	Reggie Cleveland	.25	.13	.08
112	Doug Howard	.25	.13	.08
113	Randy Jones	.25	.13	.08
114	Rico Carty	.25	.13	.08
115	Mark Fidrych	2.75	1.50	.80
116	Darrell Porter	.25	.13	.08
117	Wayne Garrett	.25	.13	.08
118	Greg Luzinski	.25	.13	.08
119	Jim Barr	.25	.13	.08
120	George Foster	.25	.13	.08
121	Phil Roof	.25	.13	.08
122	Bucky Dent	.25	.13	.08
123	Steve Braun	.25	.13	.08
124	Checklist 1-132	.40	.20	.12
125	Lee May	.25	.13	.08
126	Woodie Fryman	.25	.13	.08
127	Jose Cardenal	.25	.13	.08
128	Doug Rau	.25	.13	.08
129	Rennie Stennett	.25	.13	.08
130	Pete Vuckovich	.25	.13	.08
131	Cesar Cedeno	.25	.13	.08
132	Jon Matlack	.25	.13	.08
133	Don Baylor	.30	.15	.09
134	Darrel Chaney	.25	.13	.08
135	Tony Perez	4.00	2.00	1.25
136	Aurelio Rodriguez	.25	.13	.08
137	Carlton Fisk	4.00	2.00	1.25
138	Wayne Garland	.25	.13	.08
139	Dave Hilton	.25	.13	.08
140	Rawly Eastwick	.25	.13	.08
141	Amos Otis	.25	.13	.08
142	Tug McGraw	.25	.13	.08
143	Rod Carew	5.50	2.75	1.75
144	Mike Torrez	.25	.13	.08
145	Sal Bando	.25	.13	.08
146	Dock Ellis	.25	.13	.08
147	Jose Cruz	.25	.13	.08
148	Alan Ashby	.25	.13	.08
149	Gaylord Perry	4.00	2.00	1.25
150	Keith Hernandez	.25	.13	.08
151	Dave Pagan	.25	.13	.08
152	Richie Zisk	.25	.13	.08
153	Steve Rogers	.25	.13	.08
154	Mark Belanger	.25	.13	.08
155	Andy Messersmith	.25	.13	.08
156	Dave Winfield	6.00	3.00	1.75
157	Chuck Hartenstein	.25	.13	.08
158	Manny Trillo	.25	.13	.08
159	Steve Yeager	.25	.13	.08
160	Cesar Geronimo	.25	.13	.08
161	Jim Rooker	.25	.13	.08
162	Tim Foli	.25	.13	.08
163	Fred Lynn	.25	.13	.08
164	Ed Figueroa	.25	.13	.08
165	Johnny Grubb	.25	.13	.08
166	Pedro Garcia	.25	.13	.08
167	Ron LeFlore	.25	.13	.08
168	Rich Hebner	.25	.13	.08
169	Larry Herndon	.25	.13	.08
170	George Brett	15.00	7.50	4.50
171	Joe Kerrigan	.25	.13	.08
172	Bud Harrelson	.25	.13	.08
173	Bobby Bonds	.25	.13	.08
174	Bill Travers	.25	.13	.08
175	John Lowenstein	.25	.13	.08
176	Butch Wynegar	.25	.13	.08
177	Pete Falcone	.25	.13	.08
178	Claudell Washington	.25	.13	.08
179	Checklist 133-264	.40	.20	.12
180	Dave Cash	.25	.13	.08
181	Fred Norman	.25	.13	.08
182	Roy White	.25	.13	.08
183	Marty Perez	.25	.13	.08
184	Jesse Jefferson	.25	.13	.08
185	Jim Sundberg	.25	.13	.08
186	Dan Meyer	.25	.13	.08
187	Fergie Jenkins	6.00	3.00	1.75
188	Tom Veryzer	.25	.13	.08
189	Dennis Blair	.25	.13	.08
190	Rick Manning	.25	.13	.08
191	Doug Bird	.25	.13	.08
192	Al Bumbry	.25	.13	.08
193	Dave Roberts	.25	.13	.08
194	Larry Christenson	.25	.13	.08
195	Chet Lemon	.25	.13	.08
196	Ted Simmons	.25	.13	.08
197	Ray Burris	.25	.13	.08
198	Expos Coaches (Jim Brewer, Billy Gardner, Mickey Vernon, Ozzie Virgil)	.25	.13	.08
199	Ron Cey	.25	.13	.08
200	Reggie Jackson	12.50	6.25	3.75
201	Pat Zachry	.25	.13	.08
202	Doug Ault	.25	.13	.08
203	Al Oliver	.25	.13	.08
204	Robin Yount	5.50	2.75	1.75
205	Tom Seaver	7.50	3.75	2.25
206	Joe Rudi	.25	.13	.08
207	Barry Foote	.25	.13	.08
208	Toby Harrah	.25	.13	.08
209	Jeff Burroughs	.25	.13	.08
210	George Scott	.25	.13	.08
211	Jim Mason	.25	.13	.08
212	Vern Ruhle	.25	.13	.08
213	Fred Kendall	.25	.13	.08
214	Rick Reuschel	.25	.13	.08
215	Hal McRae	.25	.13	.08
216	Chip Lang	.25	.13	.08
217	Graig Nettles	.30	.15	.09
218	George Hendrick	.25	.13	.08
219	Glenn Abbott	.25	.13	.08
220	Joe Morgan	4.50	2.25	1.25
221	Sam Ewing	.25	.13	.08
222	George Medich	.25	.13	.08
223	Reggie Smith	.25	.13	.08
224	Dave Hamilton	.25	.13	.08
225	Pepe Frias	.25	.13	.08
226	Jay Johnstone	.25	.13	.08
227	J.R. Richard	.25	.13	.08
228	Doug DeCinces	.25	.13	.08
229	Dave Lemanczyk	.25	.13	.08
230	Rick Monday	.25	.13	.08
231	Manny Sanguillen	.25	.13	.08
232	John Montefusco	.25	.13	.08
233	Duane Kuiper	.25	.13	.08
234	Ellis Valentine	.25	.13	.08
235	Dick Tidrow	.25	.13	.08
236	Ben Oglivie	.25	.13	.08
237	Rick Burleson	.25	.13	.08
238	Roy Hartsfield	.25	.13	.08
239	Lyman Bostock	.25	.13	.08
240	Pete Rose	13.50	6.75	4.00
241	Mike Ivie	.25	.13	.08
242	Dave Parker	.35	.20	.11
243	Bill Greif	.25	.13	.08
244	Freddie Patek	.25	.13	.08
245	Mike Schmidt	15.00	7.50	4.50
246	Brian Downing	.25	.13	.08
247	Steve Hargan	.25	.13	.08
248	Dave Collins	.25	.13	.08
249	Felix Millan	.25	.13	.08
250	Don Gullett	.25	.13	.08
251	Jerry Royster	.25	.13	.08
252	Earl Williams	.25	.13	.08
253	Frank Duffy	.25	.13	.08
254	Tippy Martinez	.25	.13	.08
255	Steve Garvey	2.75	1.50	.80
256	Alvis Woods	.25	.13	.08
257	John Hiller	.25	.13	.08
258	Dave Concepcion	.25	.13	.08
259	Dwight Evans	.25	.13	.08
260	Pete MacKanin	.25	.13	.08
261	George Brett (Record Breaker)	5.00	2.50	1.50
262	Minnie Minoso (Record Breaker)	.25	.13	.08
263	Jose Morales (Record Breaker)	.25	.13	.08
264	Nolan Ryan (Record Breaker)	12.50	6.25	3.75

1978 O-Pee-Chee

The 1978 O-Pee-Chee set was further reduced to 242 cards and again had heavy representation from the two Canadian teams. The cards measure the standard 2-1/2" x 3-1/2" and the backs are printed in both French and English. The cards use the same design as the 1978 Topps set. Some of the cards contain an extra line on the front indicating a team change.

		NM	EX	VG
	Complete Set (242):	120.00	60.00	35.00
	Common Player:	.25	.13	.08
	Wax Pack (10):	8.00		
	Wax Box (36):	200.00		
1	Batting Leaders (Rod Carew, Dave Parker)	.75	.40	.25
2	Home Run Leaders (George Foster, Jim Rice)	.25	.13	.08
3	Runs Batted In Leaders (George Foster, Larry Hisle)	.25	.13	.08
4	Stolen Base Leaders (Freddie Patek, Frank Taveras)	.25	.13	.08
5	Victory Leaders (Steve Carlton, Dave Goltz, Dennis Leonard, Jim Palmer)	.45	.25	.14
6	Strikeout Leaders (Phil Niekro, Nolan Ryan)	1.50	.70	.45
7	Earned Run Avg. Ldrs. (John Candelaria, Frank Tanana)	.25	.13	.08
8	Leading Firemen (Bill Campbell, Rollie Fingers)	.45	.25	.14
9	Steve Rogers	.25	.13	.08
10	Graig Nettles	.25	.13	.08
11	Doug Capilla	.25	.13	.08
12	George Scott	.25	.13	.08
13	Gary Woods	.25	.13	.08
14	Tom Veryzer	.25	.13	.08
15	Wayne Garland	.25	.13	.08
16	Amos Otis	.25	.13	.08
17	Larry Christenson	.25	.13	.08
18	Dave Cash	.25	.13	.08
19	Jim Barr	.25	.13	.08
20	Ruppert Jones	.25	.13	.08
21	Eric Soderholm	.25	.13	.08
22	Jesse Jefferson	.25	.13	.08
23	Jerry Morales	.25	.13	.08
24	Doug Rau	.25	.13	.08
25	Rennie Stennett	.25	.13	.08
26	Lee Mazzilli	.25	.13	.08
27	Dick Williams	.25	.13	.08
28	Joe Rudi	.25	.13	.08
29	Robin Yount	2.00	1.00	.60
30	Don Gullett	.25	.13	.08
31	Roy Howell	.25	.13	.08
32	Cesar Geronimo	.25	.13	.08
33	Rick Langford	.25	.13	.08
34	Dan Ford	.25	.13	.08
35	Gene Tenace	.25	.13	.08
36	Santo Alcala	.25	.13	.08
37	Rick Burleson	.25	.13	.08
38	Dave Rozema	.25	.13	.08
39	Duane Kulper	.25	.13	.08
40	Ron Fairly	.25	.13	.08
41	Dennis Leonard	.25	.13	.08
42	Greg Luzinski	.25	.13	.08
43	Willie Montanez	.25	.13	.08
44	Enos Cabell	.25	.13	.08
45	Ellis Valentine	.25	.13	.08
46	Steve Stone	.25	.13	.08
47	Lee May	.25	.13	.08
48	Roy White	.25	.13	.08
49	Jerry Garvin	.25	.13	.08
50	Johnny Bench	2.00	1.00	.60
51	Garry Templeton	.25	.13	.08
52	Doyle Alexander	.25	.13	.08
53	Steve Henderson	.25	.13	.08
54	Stan Bahnsen	.25	.13	.08
55	Dan Meyer	.25	.13	.08
56	Rick Reuschel	.25	.13	.08

#	Player	NM	EX	VG
57	Reggie Smith	.25	.13	.08
58	Blue Jays Team	.50	.25	.15
59	John Montefusco	.25	.13	.08
60	Dave Parker	.25	.13	.08
61	Jim Bibby	.25	.13	.08
62	Fred Lynn	.25	.13	.08
63	Jose Morales	.25	.13	.08
64	Aurelio Rodriguez	.25	.13	.08
65	Frank Tanana	.25	.13	.08
66	Darrell Porter	.25	.13	.08
67	Otto Velez	.25	.13	.08
68	Larry Bowa	.25	.13	.08
69	Jim Hunter	1.50	.70	.45
70	George Foster	.25	.13	.08
71	Cecil Cooper	.25	.13	.08
72	Gary Alexander	.25	.13	.08
73	Paul Thormodsgard	.25	.13	.08
74	Toby Harrah	.25	.13	.08
75	Mitchell Page	.25	.13	.08
76	Alan Ashby	.25	.13	.08
77	Jorge Orta	.25	.13	.08
78	Dave Winfield	3.00	1.50	.90
79	Andy Messersmith	.25	.13	.08
80	Ken Singleton	.25	.13	.08
81	Will McEnaney	.25	.13	.08
82	Lou Piniella	.25	.13	.08
83	Bob Forsch	.25	.13	.08
84	Dan Driessen	.25	.13	.08
85	Dave Lemanczyk	.25	.13	.08
86	Paul Dade	.25	.13	.08
87	Bill Campbell	.25	.13	.08
88	Ron LeFlore	.25	.13	.08
89	Bill Madlock	.25	.13	.08
90	Tony Perez	.25	.13	.08
91	Freddie Patek	.25	.13	.08
92	Glenn Abbott	.25	.13	.08
93	Garry Maddox	.25	.13	.08
94	Steve Staggs	.25	.13	.08
95	Bobby Murcer	.25	.13	.08
96	Don Sutton	1.50	.70	.45
97	Al Oliver	.25	.13	.08
98	Jon Matlack	.25	.13	.08
99	Sam Mejias	.25	.13	.08
100	Pete Rose	6.00	3.00	1.75
101	Randy Jones	.25	.13	.08
102	Sixto Lezcano	.25	.13	.08
103	Jim Clancy	.25	.13	.08
104	Butch Wynegar	.25	.13	.08
105	Nolan Ryan	15.00	7.50	4.50
106	Wayne Gross	.25	.13	.08
107	Bob Watson	.25	.13	.08
108	Joe Kerrigan	.25	.13	.08
109	Keith Hernandez	.25	.13	.08
110	Reggie Jackson	5.00	2.50	1.50
111	Denny Doyle	.25	.13	.08
112	Sam Ewing	.25	.13	.08
113	Bert Blyleven	.25	.13	.08
114	Andre Thornton	.25	.13	.08
115	Milt May	.25	.13	.08
116	Jim Colborn	.25	.13	.08
117	Warren Cromartie	.25	.13	.08
118	Ted Sizemore	.25	.13	.08
119	Checklist 1-121	.35	.20	.11
120	Tom Seaver	2.50	1.25	.70
121	Luis Gomez	.25	.13	.08
122	Jim Spencer	.25	.13	.08
123	Leroy Stanton	.25	.13	.08
124	Luis Tiant	.25	.13	.08
125	Mark Belanger	.25	.13	.08
126	Jackie Brown	.25	.13	.08
127	Bill Buckner	.25	.13	.08
128	Bill Robinson	.25	.13	.08
129	Rick Cerone	.25	.13	.08
130	Ron Cey	.25	.13	.08
131	Jose Cruz	.25	.13	.08
132	Len Randle	.25	.13	.08
133	Bob Grich	.25	.13	.08
134	Jeff Burroughs	.25	.13	.08
135	Gary Carter	6.00	3.00	1.75
136	Milt Wilcox	.25	.13	.08
137	Carl Yastrzemski	2.50	1.25	.70
138	Dennis Eckersley	1.50	.70	.45
139	Tim Nordbrook	.25	.13	.08
140	Ken Griffey	.25	.13	.08
141	Bob Boone	.25	.13	.08
142	Dave Goltz	.25	.13	.08
143	Al Cowens	.25	.13	.08
144	Bill Atkinson	.25	.13	.08
145	Chris Chambliss	.25	.13	.08
146	Jim Slaton	.25	.13	.08
147	Bill Stein	.25	.13	.08
148	Bob Bailor	.25	.13	.08
149	J.R. Richard	.25	.13	.08
150	Ted Simmons	.25	.13	.08
151	Rick Manning	.25	.13	.08
152	Lerrin LaGrow	.25	.13	.08
153	Larry Parrish	.25	.13	.08
154	Eddie Murray	15.00	7.50	4.50
155	Phil Niekro	1.50	.70	.45
156	Bake McBride	.25	.13	.08
157	Pete Vuckovich	.25	.13	.08
158	Ivan DeJesus	.25	.13	.08
159	Rick Rhoden	.25	.13	.08
160	Joe Morgan	2.00	1.00	.60
161	Ed Ott	.25	.13	.08
162	Don Stanhouse	.25	.13	.08
163	Jim Rice	.50	.25	.15
164	Bucky Dent	.25	.13	.08
165	Jim Kern	.25	.13	.08
166	Doug Rader	.25	.13	.08
167	Steve Kemp	.25	.13	.08
168	John Mayberry	.25	.13	.08
169	Tim Foli	.25	.13	.08
170	Steve Carlton	2.00	1.00	.60
171	Pepe Frias	.25	.13	.08
172	Pat Zachry	.25	.13	.08
173	Don Baylor	.25	.13	.08
174	Sal Bando	.25	.13	.08

#	Player	NM	EX	VG
175	Alvis Woods	.25	.13	.08
176	Mike Hargrove	.25	.13	.08
177	Vida Blue	.25	.13	.08
178	George Hendrick	.25	.13	.08
179	Jim Palmer	2.00	1.00	.60
180	Andre Dawson	10.00	5.00	3.00
181	Paul Moskau	.25	.13	.08
182	Mickey Rivers	.25	.13	.08
183	Checklist 122-242	.35	.20	.11
184	Jerry Johnson	.25	.13	.08
185	Willie McCovey	2.00	1.00	.60
186	Enrique Romo	.25	.13	.08
187	Butch Hobson	.25	.13	.08
188	Rusty Staub	.45	.25	.14
189	Wayne Twitchell	.25	.13	.08
190	Steve Garvey	1.00	.50	.30
191	Rick Waits	.25	.13	.08
192	Doug DeCinces	.25	.13	.08
193	Tom Murphy	.25	.13	.08
194	Rich Hebner	.25	.13	.08
195	Ralph Garr	.25	.13	.08
196	Bruce Sutter	1.50	.70	.45
197	Tom Poquette	.25	.13	.08
198	Wayne Garrett	.25	.13	.08
199	Pedro Borbon	.25	.13	.08
200	Thurman Munson	2.00	1.00	.60
201	Rollie Fingers	1.50	.70	.45
202	Doug Ault	.25	.13	.08
203	Phil Garner	.25	.13	.08
204	Lou Brock	2.00	1.00	.60
205	Ed Kranepool	.25	.13	.08
206	Bobby Bonds	.25	.13	.08
207	Expos Team	.25	.13	.08
208	Bump Wills	.25	.13	.08
209	Gary Matthews	.25	.13	.08
210	Carlton Fisk	2.00	1.00	.60
211	Jeff Byrd	.25	.13	.08
212	Jason Thompson	.25	.13	.08
213	Larvell Blanks	.25	.13	.08
214	Sparky Lyle	.25	.13	.08
215	George Brett	6.00	3.00	1.75
216	Del Unser	.25	.13	.08
217	Manny Trillo	.25	.13	.08
218	Roy Hartsfield	.25	.13	.08
219	Carlos Lopez	.25	.13	.08
220	Dave Concepcion	.25	.13	.08
221	John Candelaria	.25	.13	.08
222	Dave Lopes	.25	.13	.08
223	Tim Blackwell	.25	.13	.08
224	Chet Lemon	.25	.13	.08
225	Mike Schmidt	6.00	3.00	1.75
226	Cesar Cedeno	.25	.13	.08
227	Mike Willis	.25	.13	.08
228	Willie Randolph	.25	.13	.08
229	Doug Bair	.25	.13	.08
230	Rod Carew	2.00	1.00	.60
231	Mike Flanagan	.25	.13	.08
232	Chris Speier	.25	.13	.08
233	Don Aase	.25	.13	.08
234	Buddy Bell	.25	.13	.08
235	Mark Fidrych	.30	.15	.09
236	Lou Brock (Record Breaker)	.75	.40	.25
237	Sparky Lyle (Record Breaker)	.25	.13	.08
238	Willie McCovey (Record Breaker)	.45	.25	.14
239	Brooks Robinson (Record Breaker)	.90	.45	.25
240	Pete Rose (Record Breaker)	2.00	1.00	.60
241	Nolan Ryan (Record Breaker)	10.00	5.00	3.00
242	Reggie Jackson (Record Breaker)	1.50	.70	.45

1979 O-Pee-Chee

The 1979 O-Pee-Chee cards are nearly identical in design to the Topps set of the same year, but display the O-Pee-Chee logo inside the baseball in the lower-left corner of the front. The number of cards in the set was increased to 374, each measuring 2-1/2" x 3-1/2".

	NM	EX	VG
Complete Set (374):	80.00	40.00	24.00
Common Player:	.25	.13	.08
Wax Pack (10):	10.00		
Wax Box (36):	175.00		

#	Player	NM	EX	VG
1	Lee May	.25	.13	.08
2	Dick Drago	.25	.13	.08
3	Paul Dade	.25	.13	.08
4	Ross Grimsley	.25	.13	.08
5	Joe Morgan	2.00	1.00	.60
6	Kevin Kobel	.25	.13	.08
7	Terry Forster	.25	.13	.08
8	Paul Molitor	12.00	6.00	3.50
9	Steve Carlton	2.00	1.00	.60
10	Dave Goltz	.25	.13	.08
11	Dave Winfield	3.00	1.50	.90
12	Dave Rozema	.25	.13	.08
13	Ed Figueroa	.25	.13	.08
14	Alan Ashby	.25	.13	.08

#	Player	NM	EX	VG
15	Dale Murphy	2.50	1.25	.70
16	Dennis Eckersley	1.50	.70	.45
17	Ron Blomberg	.25	.13	.08
18	Wayne Twitchell	.25	.13	.08
19	Al Hrabosky	.25	.13	.08
20	Fred Norman	.25	.13	.08
21	Steve Garvey	1.00	.50	.30
22	Willie Stargell	2.00	1.00	.60
23	John Hale	.25	.13	.08
24	Mickey Rivers	.25	.13	.08
25	Jack Brohamer	.25	.13	.08
26	Tom Underwood	.25	.13	.08
27	Mark Belanger	.25	.13	.08
28	Elliott Maddox	.25	.13	.08
29	John Candelaria	.25	.13	.08
30	Shane Rawley	.25	.13	.08
31	Steve Yeager	.25	.13	.08
32	Warren Cromartie	.25	.13	.08
33	Jason Thompson	.25	.13	.08
34	Roger Erickson	.25	.13	.08
35	Gary Matthews	.25	.13	.08
36	Pete Falcone	.25	.13	.08
37	Dick Tidrow	.25	.13	.08
38	Bob Boone	.25	.13	.08
39	Jim Bibby	.25	.13	.08
40	Len Barker	.25	.13	.08
41	Robin Yount	2.00	1.00	.60
42	Sam Mejias	.25	.13	.08
43	Ray Burris	.25	.13	.08
44	Tom Seaver	2.50	1.25	.70
45	Roy Howell	.25	.13	.08
46	Jim Todd	.25	.13	.08
47	Frank Duffy	.25	.13	.08
48	Joel Youngblood	.25	.13	.08
49	Vida Blue	.25	.13	.08
50	Cliff Johnson	.25	.13	.08
51	Nolan Ryan	15.00	7.50	4.50
52	Ozzie Smith	20.00	10.00	6.00
53	Jim Sundberg	.25	.13	.08
54	Mike Paxton	.25	.13	.08
55	Lou Whitaker	1.00	.50	.30
56	Dan Schatzeder	.25	.13	.08
57	Rick Burleson	.25	.13	.08
58	Doug Bair	.25	.13	.08
59	Ted Martinez	.25	.13	.08
60	Bob Watson	.25	.13	.08
61	Jim Clancy	.25	.13	.08
62	Rowland Office	.25	.13	.08
63	Bobby Murcer	.25	.13	.08
64	Don Gullett	.25	.13	.08
65	Tom Paciorek	.25	.13	.08
66	Rick Rhoden	.25	.13	.08
67	Duane Kuiper	.25	.13	.08
68	Bruce Boisclair	.25	.13	.08
69	Manny Sarmiento	.25	.13	.08
70	Wayne Cage	.25	.13	.08
71	John Hiller	.25	.13	.08
72	Rick Cerone	.25	.13	.08
73	Dwight Evans	.25	.13	.08
74	Buddy Solomon	.25	.13	.08
75	Roy White	.25	.13	.08
76	Mike Flanagan	.25	.13	.08
77	Tom Johnson	.25	.13	.08
78	Glenn Burke	.25	.13	.08
79	Frank Taveras	.25	.13	.08
80	Don Sutton	1.50	.70	.45
81	Leon Roberts	.25	.13	.08
82	George Hendrick	.25	.13	.08
83	Aurelio Rodriguez	.25	.13	.08
84	Ron Reed	.25	.13	.08
85	Alvis Woods	.25	.13	.08
86	Jim Beattie	.25	.13	.08
87	Larry Hisle	.25	.13	.08
88	Mike Garman	.25	.13	.08
89	Tim Johnson	.25	.13	.08
90	Paul Splittorff	.25	.13	.08
91	Darrel Chaney	.25	.13	.08
92	Mike Torrez	.25	.13	.08
93	Eric Soderholm	.25	.13	.08
94	Ron Cey	.25	.13	.08
95	Randy Jones	.25	.13	.08
96	Bill Madlock	.25	.13	.08
97	Steve Kemp	.25	.13	.08
98	Bob Apodaca	.25	.13	.08
99	Johnny Grubb	.25	.13	.08
100	Larry Milbourne	.25	.13	.08
101	Johnny Bench	2.00	1.00	.60
102	Dave Lemanczyk	.25	.13	.08
103	Reggie Cleveland	.25	.13	.08
104	Larry Bowa	.25	.13	.08
105	Denny Martinez	1.00	.50	.30
106	Bill Travers	.25	.13	.08
107	Willie McCovey	2.00	1.00	.60
108	Wilbur Wood	.25	.13	.08
109	Dennis Leonard	.25	.13	.08
110	Roy Smalley	.25	.13	.08
111	Cesar Geronimo	.25	.13	.08
112	Jesse Jefferson	.25	.13	.08
113	Dave Revering	.25	.13	.08
114	Rich Gossage	.30	.15	.09
115	Steve Stone	.25	.13	.08
116	Doug Flynn	.25	.13	.08
117	Bob Forsch	.25	.13	.08
118	Paul Mitchell	.25	.13	.08
119	Toby Harrah	.25	.13	.08
120	Steve Rogers	.25	.13	.08
121	Checklist 1-125	.25	.13	.08
122	Balor Moore	.25	.13	.08
123	Rick Reuschel	.25	.13	.08
124	Jeff Burroughs	.25	.13	.08
125	Willie Randolph	.25	.13	.08
126	Bob Stinson	.25	.13	.08
127	Rick Wise	.25	.13	.08
128	Luis Gomez	.25	.13	.08
129	Tommy John	.25	.13	.08
130	Richie Zisk	.25	.13	.08
131	Mario Guerrero	.25	.13	.08
132	Oscar Gamble	.25	.13	.08

#	Player	NM	EX	VG
133	Don Money	.25	.13	.08
134	Joe Rudi	.25	.13	.08
135	Woodie Fryman	.25	.13	.08
136	Butch Hobson	.25	.13	.08
137	Jim Colborn	.25	.13	.08
138	Tom Grieve	.25	.13	.08
139	Andy Messersmith	.25	.13	.08
140	Andre Thornton	.25	.13	.08
141	Kevin Kravec	.25	.13	.08
142	Bobby Bonds	.25	.13	.08
143	Jose Cruz	.25	.13	.08
144	Dave Lopes	.25	.13	.08
145	Jerry Garvin	.25	.13	.08
146	Pepe Frias	.25	.13	.08
147	Mitchell Page	.25	.13	.08
148	Ted Sizemore	.25	.13	.08
149	Rich Gale	.25	.13	.08
150	Steve Ontiveros	.25	.13	.08
151	Rod Carew	2.00	1.00	.60
152	Lary Sorensen	.25	.13	.08
153	Willie Montanez	.25	.13	.08
154	Floyd Bannister	.25	.13	.08
155	Bert Blyleven	.25	.13	.08
156	Ralph Garr	.25	.13	.08
157	Thurman Munson	1.00	.50	.30
158	Bob Robertson	.25	.13	.08
159	Jon Matlack	.25	.13	.08
160	Carl Yastrzemski	2.50	1.25	.70
161	Gaylord Perry	1.50	.70	.45
162	Mike Tyson	.25	.13	.08
163	Cecil Cooper	.25	.13	.08
164	Pedro Borbon	.25	.13	.08
165	Art Howe	.25	.13	.08
166	Joe Coleman	.25	.13	.08
167	George Brett	6.00	3.00	1.75
168	Gary Alexander	.25	.13	.08
169	Chet Lemon	.25	.13	.08
170	Craig Swan	.25	.13	.08
171	Chris Chambliss	.25	.13	.08
172	John Montague	.25	.13	.08
173	Ron Jackson	.25	.13	.08
174	Jim Palmer	2.00	1.00	.60
175	Willie Upshaw	.75	.40	.25
176	Tug McGraw	.25	.13	.08
177	Bill Buckner	.25	.13	.08
178	Doug Rau	.25	.13	.08
179	Andre Dawson	3.50	1.75	1.00
180	Jim Wright	.25	.13	.08
181	Garry Templeton	.25	.13	.08
182	Bill Bonham	.25	.13	.08
183	Lee Mazzilli	.25	.13	.08
184	Alan Trammell	2.00	1.00	.60
185	Amos Otis	.25	.13	.08
186	Tom Dixon	.25	.13	.08
187	Mike Cubbage	.25	.13	.08
188	Sparky Lyle	.25	.13	.08
189	Juan Bernhardt	.25	.13	.08
190	Bump Wills	.25	.13	.08
191	Dave Kingman	.25	.13	.08
192	Lamar Johnson	.25	.13	.08
193	Lance Rautzhan	.25	.13	.08
194	Ed Herrmann	.25	.13	.08
195	Bill Campbell	.25	.13	.08
196	Gorman Thomas	.25	.13	.08
197	Paul Moskau	.25	.13	.08
198	Dale Murray	.25	.13	.08
199	John Mayberry	.25	.13	.08
200	Phil Garner	.25	.13	.08
201	Dan Ford	.25	.13	.08
202	Gary Thomasson	.25	.13	.08
203	Rollie Fingers	1.50	.70	.45
204	Al Oliver	.25	.13	.08
205	Doug Ault	.25	.13	.08
206	Scott McGregor	.25	.13	.08
207	Dave Cash	.25	.13	.08
208	Bill Plummer	.25	.13	.08
209	Ivan DeJesus	.25	.13	.08
210	Jim Rice	.75	.40	.25
211	Ray Knight	.25	.13	.08
212	Paul Hartzell	.25	.13	.08
213	Tim Foli	.25	.13	.08
214	Butch Wynegar	.25	.13	.08
215	Darrell Evans	.25	.13	.08
216	Ken Griffey	.25	.13	.08
217	Doug DeCinces	.25	.13	.08
218	Ruppert Jones	.25	.13	.08
219	Bob Montgomery	.25	.13	.08
220	Rick Manning	.25	.13	.08
221	Chris Speier	.25	.13	.08
222	Bobby Valentine	.25	.13	.08
223	Dave Parker	.25	.13	.08
224	Larry Biittner	.25	.13	.08
225	Ken Clay	.25	.13	.08
226	Gene Tenace	.25	.13	.08
227	Frank White	.25	.13	.08
228	Rusty Staub	.35	.20	.11
229	Lee Lacy	.25	.13	.08
230	Doyle Alexander	.25	.13	.08
231	Bruce Bochte	.25	.13	.08
232	Steve Henderson	.25	.13	.08
233	Jim Lonborg	.25	.13	.08
234	Dave Concepcion	.25	.13	.08
235	Jerry Morales	.25	.13	.08
236	Len Randle	.25	.13	.08
237	Bill Lee	.25	.13	.08
238	Bruce Sutter	1.50	.70	.45
239	Jim Essian	.25	.13	.08
240	Graig Nettles	.25	.13	.08
241	Otto Velez	.25	.13	.08
242	Checklist 126-250	.25	.13	.08
243	Reggie Smith	.25	.13	.08
244	Stan Bahnsen	.25	.13	.08
245	Garry Maddox	.25	.13	.08
246	Joaquin Andujar	.25	.13	.08
247	Dan Driessen	.25	.13	.08
248	Bob Grich	.25	.13	.08
249	Fred Lynn	.25	.13	.08
250	Skip Lockwood	.25	.13	.08
251	Craig Reynolds	.25	.13	.08
252	Willie Horton	.25	.13	.08
253	Rick Waits	.25	.13	.08
254	Bucky Dent	.25	.13	.08
255	Bob Knepper	.25	.13	.08
256	Miguel Dilone	.25	.13	.08
257	Bob Owchinko	.25	.13	.08
258	Al Cowens	.25	.13	.08
259	Bob Bailor	.25	.13	.08
260	Larry Christenson	.25	.13	.08
261	Tony Perez	1.50	.70	.45
262	Blue Jays Team	.25	.13	.08
263	Glenn Abbott	.25	.13	.08
264	Ron Guidry	.50	.25	.15
265	Ed Kranepool	.25	.13	.08
266	Charlie Hough	.25	.13	.08
267	Ted Simmons	.25	.13	.08
268	Jack Clark	.25	.13	.08
269	Enos Cabell	.25	.13	.08
270	Gary Carter	6.00	3.00	1.75
271	Sam Ewing	.25	.13	.08
272	Tom Burgmeier	.25	.13	.08
273	Freddie Patek	.25	.13	.08
274	Frank Tanana	.25	.13	.08
275	Leroy Stanton	.25	.13	.08
276	Ken Forsch	.25	.13	.08
277	Ellis Valentine	.25	.13	.08
278	Greg Luzinski	.25	.13	.08
279	Rick Bosetti	.25	.13	.08
280	John Stearns	.25	.13	.08
281	Enrique Romo	.25	.13	.08
282	Bob Bailey	.25	.13	.08
283	Sal Bando	.25	.13	.08
284	Matt Keough	.25	.13	.08
285	Biff Pocoroba	.25	.13	.08
286	Mike Lum	.25	.13	.08
287	Jay Johnstone	.25	.13	.08
288	John Montefusco	.25	.13	.08
289	Ed Ott	.25	.13	.08
290	Dusty Baker	.25	.13	.08
291	Rico Carty	.25	.13	.08
292	Nino Espinosa	.25	.13	.08
293	Rich Hebner	.25	.13	.08
294	Cesar Cedeno	.25	.13	.08
295	Darrell Porter	.25	.13	.08
296	Rod Gilbreath	.25	.13	.08
297	Jim Kern	.25	.13	.08
298	Claudell Washington	.25	.13	.08
299	Luis Tiant	.25	.13	.08
300	Mike Parrott	.25	.13	.08
301	Pete Broberg	.25	.13	.08
302	Greg Gross	.25	.13	.08
303	Darold Knowles	.25	.13	.08
304	Paul Blair	.25	.13	.08
305	Julio Cruz	.25	.13	.08
306	Hal McRae	.25	.13	.08
307	Ken Reitz	.25	.13	.08
308	Tom Murphy	.25	.13	.08
309	Terry Whitfield	.25	.13	.08
310	J.R. Richard	.25	.13	.08
311	Mike Hargrove	.25	.13	.08
312	Rick Dempsey	.25	.13	.08
313	Phil Niekro	1.50	.70	.45
314	Bob Stanley	.25	.13	.08
315	Jim Spencer	.25	.13	.08
316	George Foster	.25	.13	.08
317	Dave LaRoche	.25	.13	.08
318	Rudy May	.25	.13	.08
319	Jeff Newman	.25	.13	.08
320	Rick Monday	.25	.13	.08
321	Omar Moreno	.25	.13	.08
322	Dave McKay	.25	.13	.08
323	Mike Schmidt	6.00	3.00	1.75
324	Ken Singleton	.25	.13	.08
325	Jerry Remy	.25	.13	.08
326	Bert Campaneris	.25	.13	.08
327	Pat Zachry	.25	.13	.08
328	Larry Herndon	.25	.13	.08
329	Mark Fidrych	.25	.13	.08
330	Del Unser	.25	.13	.08
331	Gene Garber	.25	.13	.08
332	Bake McBride	.25	.13	.08
333	Jorge Orta	.25	.13	.08
334	Don Kirkwood	.25	.13	.08
335	Don Baylor	.25	.13	.08
336	Bill Robinson	.25	.13	.08
337	Manny Trillo	.25	.13	.08
338	Eddie Murray	3.00	1.50	.90
339	Tom Hausman	.25	.13	.08
340	George Scott	.25	.13	.08
341	Rick Sweet	.25	.13	.08
342	Lou Piniella	.25	.13	.08
343	Pete Rose	15.00	7.50	4.50
344	Stan Papi	.25	.13	.08
345	Jerry Koosman	.25	.13	.08
346	Hosken Powell	.25	.13	.08
347	George Medich	.25	.13	.08
348	Ron LeFlore	.25	.13	.08
349	Expos Team	.75	.40	.25
350	Lou Brock	2.00	1.00	.60
351	Bill North	.25	.13	.08
352	Jim Hunter	1.50	.70	.45
353	Checklist 251-374	.25	.13	.08
354	Ed Halicki	.25	.13	.08
355	Tom Hutton	.25	.13	.08
356	Mike Caldwell	.25	.13	.08
357	Larry Parrish	.25	.13	.08
358	Geoff Zahn	.25	.13	.08
359	Derrel Thomas	.25	.13	.08
360	Carlton Fisk	2.00	1.00	.60
361	John Henry Johnson	.25	.13	.08
362	Dave Chalk	.25	.13	.08
363	Dan Meyer	.25	.13	.08
364	Sixto Lezcano	.25	.13	.08
365	Rennie Stennett	.25	.13	.08
366	Mike Willis	.25	.13	.08
367	Buddy Bell	.25	.13	.08
368	Mickey Stanley	.25	.13	.08
369	Dave Rader	.25	.13	.08
370	Burt Hooton	.25	.13	.08
371	Keith Hernandez	.25	.13	.08
372	Bill Stein	.25	.13	.08
373	Hal Dues	.25	.13	.08
374	Reggie Jackson	3.00	1.50	.90

1980 O-Pee-Chee

The 1980 Canadian-issued O-Pee-Chee set was again complete at 374 cards, which measure 2-1/2" x 3-1/2" and share the same design as the 1980 Topps set. The OPC cards are printed on a white stock, rather than the traditional gray stock used by Topps, and their backs are written in both French and English. Some of the cards include an extra line on the front indicating a new team designation.

	NM	EX	VG
Complete Set (374):	110.00	55.00	32.50
Common Player:	.15	.08	.05
Wax Pack (10):	10.00		
Wax Box (36):	290.00		

#	Player	NM	EX	VG
1	Craig Swan	.15	.08	.05
2	Denny Martinez	.15	.08	.05
3	Dave Cash	.15	.08	.05
4	Bruce Sutter	1.50	.70	.45
5	Ron Jackson	.15	.08	.05
6	Balor Moore	.15	.08	.05
7	Dan Ford	.15	.08	.05
8	Pat Putnam	.15	.08	.05
9	Derrel Thomas	.15	.08	.05
10	Jim Slaton	.15	.08	.05
11	Lee Mazzilli	.15	.08	.05
12	Del Unser	.15	.08	.05
13	Mark Wagner	.15	.08	.05
14	Vida Blue	.15	.08	.05
15	Jay Johnstone	.15	.08	.05
16	Julio Cruz	.15	.08	.05
17	Tony Scott	.15	.08	.05
18	Jeff Newman	.15	.08	.05
19	Luis Tiant	.15	.08	.05
20	Carlton Fisk	1.50	.70	.45
21	Dave Palmer	.15	.08	.05
22	Bombo Rivera	.15	.08	.05
23	Bill Fahey	.15	.08	.05
24	Frank White	.15	.08	.05
25	Rico Carty	.15	.08	.05
26	Bill Bonham	.15	.08	.05
27	Rick Miller	.15	.08	.05
28	J.R. Richard	.15	.08	.05
29	Joe Ferguson	.15	.08	.05
30	Bill Madlock	.15	.08	.05
31	Pete Vuckovich	.15	.08	.05
32	Doug Flynn	.15	.08	.05
33	Bucky Dent	.15	.08	.05
34	Mike Ivie	.15	.08	.05
35	Bob Stanley	.15	.08	.05
36	Al Bumbry	.15	.08	.05
37	Gary Carter	5.00	2.50	1.50
38	John Milner	.15	.08	.05
39	Sid Monge	.15	.08	.05
40	Bill Russell	.15	.08	.05
41	John Stearns	.15	.08	.05
42	Dave Stieb	1.25	.60	.40
43	Ruppert Jones	.15	.08	.05
44	Bob Owchinko	.15	.08	.05
45	Ron LeFlore	.15	.08	.05
46	Ted Sizemore	.15	.08	.05
47	Ted Simmons	.15	.08	.05
48	Pepe Frias	.15	.08	.05
49	Ken Landreaux	.15	.08	.05
50	Manny Trillo	.15	.08	.05
51	Rick Dempsey	.15	.08	.05
52	Cecil Cooper	.15	.08	.05
53	Bill Lee	.15	.08	.05
54	Victor Cruz	.15	.08	.05
55	Johnny Bench	1.50	.70	.45
56	Rich Dauer	.15	.08	.05
57	Frank Tanana	.15	.08	.05
58	Francisco Barrios	.15	.08	.05
59	Bob Horner	.30	.15	.09
60	Fred Lynn	.15	.08	.05
61	Bob Knepper	.15	.08	.05
62	Sparky Lyle	.15	.08	.05
63	Larry Cox	.15	.08	.05
64	Dock Ellis	.15	.08	.05
65	Phil Garner	.15	.08	.05
66	Greg Luzinski	.15	.08	.05
67	Checklist 1-125	.25	.13	.08
68	Dave Lemanczyk	.15	.08	.05
69	Tony Perez	1.50	.70	.45
70	Gary Thomasson	.15	.08	.05
71	Craig Reynolds	.15	.08	.05
72	Amos Otis	.15	.08	.05
73	Biff Pocoroba	.15	.08	.05
74	Matt Keough	.15	.08	.05
75	Bill Buckner	.15	.08	.05
76	John Castino	.15	.08	.05

#	Player			
77	Rich Gossage	.25	.13	.08
78	Gary Alexander	.15	.08	.05
79	Phil Huffman	.15	.08	.05
80	Bruce Bochte	.15	.08	.05
81	Darrell Evans	.15	.08	.05
82	Terry Puhl	.15	.08	.05
83	Jason Thompson	.15	.08	.05
84	Lary Sorenson	.15	.08	.05
85	Jerry Remy	.15	.08	.05
86	Tony Brizzolara	.15	.08	.05
87	Willie Wilson	.15	.08	.05
88	Eddie Murray	3.00	1.50	.90
89	Larry Christenson	.15	.08	.05
90	Bob Randall	.15	.08	.05
91	Greg Pryor	.15	.08	.05
92	Glenn Abbott	.15	.08	.05
93	Jack Clark	.15	.08	.05
94	Rick Waits	.15	.08	.05
95	Luis Gomez	.15	.08	.05
96	Burt Hooton	.15	.08	.05
97	John Henry Johnson	.15	.08	.05
98	Ray Knight	.15	.08	.05
99	Rick Reuschel	.15	.08	.05
100	Champ Summers	.15	.08	.05
101	Ron Davis	.15	.08	.05
102	Warren Cromartie	.15	.08	.05
103	Ken Reitz	.15	.08	.05
104	Hal McRae	.15	.08	.05
105	Alan Ashby	.15	.08	.05
106	Kevin Kobel	.15	.08	.05
107	Buddy Bell	.15	.08	.05
108	Dave Goltz	.15	.08	.05
109	John Montefusco	.15	.08	.05
110	Lance Parrish	.65	.35	.20
111	Mike LaCoss	.15	.08	.05
112	Jim Rice	.30	.15	.09
113	Steve Carlton	1.50	.70	.45
114	Sixto Lezcano	.15	.08	.05
115	Ed Halicki	.15	.08	.05
116	Jose Morales	.15	.08	.05
117	Dave Concepcion	.15	.08	.05
118	Joe Cannon	.15	.08	.05
119	Willie Montanez	.15	.08	.05
120	Lou Piniella	.15	.08	.05
121	Bill Stein	.15	.08	.05
122	Dave Winfield	3.00	1.50	.90
123	Alan Trammell	.30	.15	.09
124	Andre Dawson	4.00	2.00	1.25
125	Marc Hill	.15	.08	.05
126	Don Aase	.15	.08	.05
127	Dave Kingman	.15	.08	.05
128	Checklist 126-250	.25	.13	.08
129	Dennis Lamp	.15	.08	.05
130	Phil Niekro	1.00	.50	.30
131	Tim Foli	.15	.08	.05
132	Jim Clancy	.15	.08	.05
133	Bill Atkinson	.15	.08	.05
134	Paul Dade	.15	.08	.05
135	Dusty Baker	.15	.08	.05
136	Al Oliver	.15	.08	.05
137	Dave Chalk	.15	.08	.05
138	Bill Robinson	.15	.08	.05
139	Robin Yount	1.50	.70	.45
140	Dan Schatzeder	.15	.08	.05
141	Mike Schmidt	5.00	2.50	1.50
142	Ralph Garr	.15	.08	.05
143	Dale Murphy	1.00	.50	.30
144	Jerry Koosman	.15	.08	.05
145	Tom Veryzer	.15	.08	.05
146	Rick Bosetti	.15	.08	.05
147	Jim Spencer	.15	.08	.05
148	Gaylord Perry	1.00	.50	.30
149	Paul Blair	.15	.08	.05
150	Don Baylor	.15	.08	.05
151	Dave Rozema	.15	.08	.05
152	Steve Garvey	.50	.25	.15
153	Elias Sosa	.15	.08	.05
154	Larry Gura	.15	.08	.05
155	Tim Johnson	.15	.08	.05
156	Steve Henderson	.15	.08	.05
157	Ron Guidry	.20	.10	.06
158	Mike Edwards	.15	.08	.05
159	Butch Wynegar	.15	.08	.05
160	Randy Jones	.15	.08	.05
161	Denny Walling	.15	.08	.05
162	Mike Hargrove	.15	.08	.05
163	Dave Parker	.15	.08	.05
164	Roger Metzger	.15	.08	.05
165	Johnny Grubb	.15	.08	.05
166	Steve Kemp	.15	.08	.05
167	Bob Lacey	.15	.08	.05
168	Chris Speier	.15	.08	.05
169	Dennis Eckersley	1.00	.50	.30
170	Keith Hernandez	.15	.08	.05
171	Claudell Washington	.15	.08	.05
172	Tom Underwood	.15	.08	.05
173	Dan Driessen	.15	.08	.05
174	Al Cowens	.15	.08	.05
175	Rich Hebner	.15	.08	.05
176	Willie McCovey	1.50	.70	.45
177	Carney Lansford	.15	.08	.05
178	Ken Singleton	.15	.08	.05
179	Jim Essian	.15	.08	.05
180	Mike Vail	.15	.08	.05
181	Randy Lerch	.15	.08	.05
182	Larry Parrish	.15	.08	.05
183	Checklist 251-374	.25	.13	.08
184	George Hendrick	.15	.08	.05
185	Bob Davis	.15	.08	.05
186	Gary Matthews	.15	.08	.05
187	Lou Whitaker	.15	.08	.05
188	Darrell Porter	.15	.08	.05
189	Wayne Gross	.15	.08	.05
190	Bobby Murcer	.15	.08	.05
191	Willie Aikens	.15	.08	.05
192	Jim Kern	.15	.08	.05
193	Cesar Cedeno	.15	.08	.05
194	Joel Youngblood	.15	.08	.05
195	Ross Grimsley	.15	.08	.05
196	Jerry Mumphrey	.15	.08	.05
197	Kevin Bell	.15	.08	.05
198	Garry Maddox	.15	.08	.05
199	Dave Freisleben	.15	.08	.05
200	Ed Ott	.15	.08	.05
201	Enos Cabell	.15	.08	.05
202	Pete LaCock	.15	.08	.05
203	Fergie Jenkins	1.50	.70	.45
204	Milt Wilcox	.15	.08	.05
205	Ozzie Smith	5.00	2.50	1.50
206	Ellis Valentine	.15	.08	.05
207	Dan Meyer	.15	.08	.05
208	Barry Foote	.15	.08	.05
209	George Foster	.15	.08	.05
210	Dwight Evans	.15	.08	.05
211	Paul Molitor	5.00	2.50	1.50
212	Tony Solaita	.15	.08	.05
213	Bill North	.15	.08	.05
214	Paul Splittorff	.15	.08	.05
215	Bobby Bonds	.15	.08	.05
216	Butch Hobson	.15	.08	.05
217	Mark Belanger	.15	.08	.05
218	Grant Jackson	.15	.08	.05
219	Tom Hutton	.15	.08	.05
220	Pat Zachry	.15	.08	.05
221	Duane Kuiper	.15	.08	.05
222	Larry Hisle	.15	.08	.05
223	Mike Krukow	.15	.08	.05
224	Johnnie LeMaster	.15	.08	.05
225	Billy Almon	.15	.08	.05
226	Joe Niekro	.15	.08	.05
227	Dave Revering	.15	.08	.05
228	Don Sutton	1.00	.50	.30
229	John Hiller	.15	.08	.05
230	Alvis Woods	.15	.08	.05
231	Mark Fidrych	.15	.08	.05
232	Duffy Dyer	.15	.08	.05
233	Nino Espinosa	.15	.08	.05
234	Doug Bair	.15	.08	.05
235	George Brett	5.00	2.50	1.50
236	Mike Torrez	.15	.08	.05
237	Frank Taveras	.15	.08	.05
238	Bert Blyleven	.15	.08	.05
239	Willie Randolph	.15	.08	.05
240	Mike Sadek	.15	.08	.05
241	Jerry Royster	.15	.08	.05
242	John Denny	.15	.08	.05
243	Rick Monday	.15	.08	.05
244	Jesse Jefferson	.15	.08	.05
245	Aurelio Rodriguez	.15	.08	.05
246	Bob Boone	.15	.08	.05
247	Cesar Geronimo	.15	.08	.05
248	Bob Shirley	.15	.08	.05
249	Expos Team	.25	.13	.08
250	Bob Watson	.15	.08	.05
251	Mickey Rivers	.15	.08	.05
252	Mike Tyson	.15	.08	.05
253	Wayne Nordhagen	.15	.08	.05
254	Roy Howell	.15	.08	.05
255	Lee May	.15	.08	.05
256	Jerry Martin	.15	.08	.05
257	Bake McBride	.15	.08	.05
258	Silvio Martinez	.15	.08	.05
259	Jim Mason	.15	.08	.05
260	Tom Seaver	2.00	1.00	.60
261	Rick Wortham	.15	.08	.05
262	Mike Cubbage	.15	.08	.05
263	Gene Garber	.15	.08	.05
264	Bert Campaneris	.15	.08	.05
265	Tom Buskey	.15	.08	.05
266	Leon Roberts	.15	.08	.05
267	Ron Cey	.15	.08	.05
268	Steve Ontiveros	.15	.08	.05
269	Mike Caldwell	.15	.08	.05
270	Nelson Norman	.15	.08	.05
271	Steve Rogers	.15	.08	.05
272	Jim Morrison	.15	.08	.05
273	Clint Hurdle	.15	.08	.05
274	Dale Murray	.15	.08	.05
275	Jim Barr	.15	.08	.05
276	Jim Sundberg	.15	.08	.05
277	Willie Horton	.15	.08	.05
278	Andre Thornton	.15	.08	.05
279	Bob Forsch	.15	.08	.05
280	Joe Strain	.15	.08	.05
281	Rudy May	.15	.08	.05
282	Pete Rose	9.00	4.50	2.75
283	Jeff Burroughs	.15	.08	.05
284	Rick Langford	.15	.08	.05
285	Ken Griffey	.15	.08	.05
286	Bill Nahorodny	.15	.08	.05
287	Art Howe	.15	.08	.05
288	Ed Figueroa	.15	.08	.05
289	Joe Rudi	.15	.08	.05
290	Alfredo Griffin	.15	.08	.05
291	Dave Lopes	.15	.08	.05
292	Rick Manning	.15	.08	.05
293	Dennis Leonard	.15	.08	.05
294	Bud Harrelson	.15	.08	.05
295	Skip Lockwood	.15	.08	.05
296	Roy Smalley	.15	.08	.05
297	Kent Tekulve	.15	.08	.05
298	Scot Thompson	.15	.08	.05
299	Ken Kravec	.15	.08	.05
300	Blue Jays Team	.25	.13	.08
301	Scott Sanderson	.15	.08	.05
302	Charlie Moore	.15	.08	.05
303	Nolan Ryan	20.00	10.00	6.00
304	Bob Bailor	.15	.08	.05
305	Bob Stinson	.15	.08	.05
306	Al Hrabosky	.15	.08	.05
307	Mitchell Page	.15	.08	.05
308	Garry Templeton	.15	.08	.05
309	Chet Lemon	.15	.08	.05
310	Jim Palmer	1.50	.70	.45
311	Rick Cerone	.15	.08	.05
312	Jon Matlack	.15	.08	.05
313	Don Money	.15	.08	.05
314	Reggie Jackson	5.00	2.50	1.50
315	Brian Downing	.15	.08	.05
316	Woodie Fryman	.15	.08	.05
317	Alan Bannister	.15	.08	.05
318	Ron Reed	.15	.08	.05
319	Willie Stargell	1.50	.70	.45
320	Jerry Garvin	.15	.08	.05
321	Cliff Johnson	.15	.08	.05
322	Doug DeCinces	.15	.08	.05
323	Gene Richards	.15	.08	.05
324	Joaquin Andujar	.15	.08	.05
325	Richie Zisk	.15	.08	.05
326	Bob Grich	.15	.08	.05
327	Gorman Thomas	.15	.08	.05
328	Chris Chambliss	.15	.08	.05
329	Blue Jays Future Stars (Butch Edge, Pat Kelly, Ted Wilborn)	.25	.13	.08
330	Larry Bowa	.15	.08	.05
331	Barry Bonnell	.15	.08	.05
332	John Candelaria	.15	.08	.05
333	Toby Harrah	.15	.08	.05
334	Larry Biittner	.15	.08	.05
335	Mike Flanagan	.15	.08	.05
336	Ed Kranepool	.15	.08	.05
337	Ken Forsch	.15	.08	.05
338	John Mayberry	.15	.08	.05
339	Rick Burleson	.15	.08	.05
340	Milt May	.15	.08	.05
341	Roy White	.15	.08	.05
342	Joe Morgan	1.50	.70	.45
343	Rollie Fingers	1.00	.50	.30
344	Mario Mendoza	.15	.08	.05
345	Stan Bahnsen	.15	.08	.05
346	Tug McGraw	.15	.08	.05
347	Rusty Staub	.15	.08	.05
348	Tommy John	.15	.08	.05
349	Ivan DeJesus	.15	.08	.05
350	Reggie Smith	.15	.08	.05
351	Expos Future Stars (Tony Bernazard, Randy Miller, John Tamargo)	.40	.20	.12
352	Floyd Bannister	.15	.08	.05
353	Rod Carew	1.50	.70	.45
354	Otto Velez	.15	.08	.05
355	Gene Tenace	.15	.08	.05
356	Freddie Patek	.15	.08	.05
357	Elliott Maddox	.15	.08	.05
358	Pat Underwood	.15	.08	.05
359	Graig Nettles	.15	.08	.05
360	Rodney Scott	.15	.08	.05
361	Terry Whitfield	.15	.08	.05
362	Fred Norman	.15	.08	.05
363	Sal Bando	.15	.08	.05
364	Greg Gross	.15	.08	.05
365	Carl Yastrzemski	2.00	1.00	.60
366	Paul Hartzell	.15	.08	.05
367	Jose Cruz	.15	.08	.05
368	Shane Rawley	.15	.08	.05
369	Jerry White	.15	.08	.05
370	Rick Wise	.15	.08	.05
371	Steve Yeager	.15	.08	.05
372	Omar Moreno	.15	.08	.05
373	Bump Wills	.15	.08	.05
374	Craig Kusick	.15	.08	.05

1938 Oakland Oaks Stamps

The manner in which these stamps were issued is unknown, as if the extent of this probably incomplete checklist. The stamps measure 1-5/8" x 2-3/8" and are printed on semi-gloss stock in black-and-white, with the player name and position beneath a posed action photo. On back "PRODUXS-TAMP" / TRADE MARK is repeated in light blue. Gaps have been left in the checklist to accommodate future discoveries..

Common Player:		60.00	35.00	17.50
(1)	Joe Abreu	60.00	35.00	17.50
(5)	Bob Gibson	60.00	35.00	17.50
(7)	Bob Joyce	60.00	35.00	17.50
(9)	Hugh Luby	60.00	35.00	17.50
(12)	Bill Raimondi	60.00	35.00	17.50
(15)	Dutch Zwilling	60.00	35.00	17.50

1969 Oakland A's (Andersen)

5. Joe DiMaggio—coach

OAKLAND A's

Though they are sometimes identified as an issue of Jack in the Box restaurants, there is no identifier of that nature on these cards. In fact, they are a collectors' fantasy issue sold only within the hobby by Boston photographer Mike Andersen.

The blank-back black-and-white cards measure 2-1/8" x 3-5/8". Beneath the portrait photo on front is the player's name, position and uniform number. The team name is in gothic script at bottom. Cards are checklisted here by uniform number.

		NM	EX	VG
	Complete Set (21):	80.00	40.00	24.00
	Common Player:	2.50	1.25	.75
1	Dick Green	2.50	1.25	.75
2	Danny Cater	2.50	1.25	.75
3	Mike Hershberger	2.50	1.25	.75
4	Phil Roof	2.50	1.25	.75
5	Joe DiMaggio (Coach)	30.00	15.00	9.00
6	Sal Bando	2.50	1.25	.75
7	Rick Monday	2.50	1.25	.75
9a	Bert Campaneris	5.00	2.50	1.50
9b	Reggie Jackson	45.00	22.00	13.50
13	Blue Moon Odom	3.50	1.75	1.00
17	Jim Pagliaroni	2.50	1.25	.75
19	Bert Campaneris	2.50	1.25	.75
20	Lew Krausse	2.50	1.25	.75
24	Joe Nossek	2.50	1.25	.75
25	Paul Lindblad	2.50	1.25	.75
27	Catfish Hunter	7.50	3.75	2.25
29	Chuck Dobson	2.50	1.25	.75
30	Jim Nash	2.50	1.25	.75
31	Ramon Webster	2.50	1.25	.75
35	Tom Reynolds	2.50	1.25	.75
42	Hank Bauer	2.50	1.25	.70

1969 Oakland A's (Broder)

Reggie Jackson
OAKLAND A's

A second issue of black-and-white collector cards featuring the 1969 A's was produced by West Coast collector/dealer Ed Broder. In larger (2-3/4" x 4") format the Broder issue is considerably scarcer than that produced by Mike Andersen. Availability of the Broders was advertised at 100 sets. The blank-back Broder cards have the player name in the wide white border beneath the photo. At bottom the city name is in gothic script with the A's logo on a baseball flying out of a stadium. The unnumbered cards are checklisted here alphabetically.

		NM	EX	VG
	Complete Set (14):	65.00	32.50	20.00
	Common Player:	2.00	1.00	.60
(1)	Sal Bando	2.00	1.00	.60
(2)	Hank Bauer	2.00	1.00	.60
(3)	Bert Campaneris	3.00	1.50	.90
(4)	Dan Cater	2.00	1.00	.60
(5)	Joe DiMaggio	15.00	7.50	4.50
(6)	Chuck Dobson	2.00	1.00	.60
(7)	Dick Green	2.00	1.00	.60
(8)	Mike Hershberger	2.00	1.00	.60
(9)	Jim Hunter	8.00	4.00	2.50
(10)	Reggie Jackson	25.00	12.50	7.50
(11)	Bob Johnson	2.00	1.00	.60
(12)	Rick Monday	2.00	1.00	.60
(13)	Johnny Moon Odom	4.00	2.00	1.25
(14)	Phil Roof	2.00	1.00	.60

1970 Oakland A's (Andersen)

45 - ROBERTO RODRIQUEZ
Oakland A's

Boston baseball photographer Mike Andersen produced a second collectors' issue of Oakland A's cards in 1970. Nearly identical in format to his 1969 issue, the '70 team set measures 2-1/4" x 3-5/8" with black-and-white player poses at

center. Uniform number, name and team are in the bottom border. Backs are blank. Cards are checklisted here by uniform number.

		NM	EX	VG
	Complete Set (24):	30.00	15.00	9.00
	Common Player:	1.50	.75	.45
1	Dick Green	1.50	.75	.45
6	Sal Bando	1.50	.75	.45
8	Rick Monday	1.50	.75	.45
8	Felipe Alou	2.00	1.00	.60
9	Reggie Jackson	15.00	7.50	4.50
10	Dave Duncan	1.50	.75	.45
11	John McNamera (McNamara)	1.50	.75	.45
12	Larry Haney	1.50	.75	.45
13	Blue Moon Odom	2.00	1.00	.60
17	Roberto Pena	1.50	.75	.45
19	Bert Campaneris	2.00	1.00	.60
24	Diego Segui	1.50	.75	.45
25	Paul Lindblad	1.50	.75	.45
27	Catfish Hunter	4.00	2.00	1.25
28	Mudcat Grant	1.50	.75	.45
29	Chuck Dobson	1.50	.75	.45
30	Don Mincher	1.50	.75	.45
31	Jose Tartabull	1.50	.75	.45
33	Jim Roland	1.50	.75	.45
34	Rollie Fingers	4.00	2.00	1.25
36	Tito Francona	1.50	.75	.45
38	Al Downing	1.50	.75	.45
39	Frank Fernandez	1.50	.75	.45
45	Roberto Rodriguez	1.50	.75	.45

1968 Official Major League Players Baseball Marbles

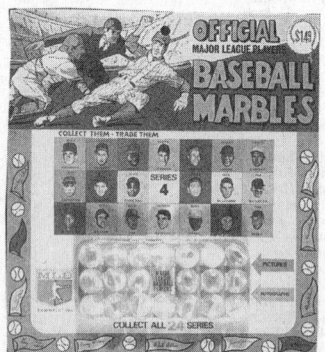

Produced by Creative Creations Inc., though not so identified on the marbles themselves, these approximately 3/4" hard plastic marbles have a player portrait photo (with cap logos removed) on one side and a facsimile autograph on the other, with "JAPAN" beneath. The marbles were issued in series of 20 on colorful cardboard packaging which pictures each player in the series. While the packaging says "Collect All 24 Series" only 120 marbles were actually issued. Suggested retail price at issue was $1.49 per series.

		NM	EX	VG
	Complete Set (115):	675.00	325.00	200.00
	Common Player:	4.00	2.00	1.25
(1)	Hank Aaron	40.00	20.00	12.00
(2)	Tommie Aaron	4.00	2.00	1.25
(3)	Tommy Agee	4.00	2.00	1.25
(4)	Richie Allen	7.00	3.50	2.00
(5)	Gene Alley	4.00	2.00	1.25
(6)	Bob Allison	4.00	2.00	1.25
(7)	Felipe Alou	5.00	2.50	1.50
(8)	Jesus Alou	4.00	2.00	1.25
(9)	Matty Alou	4.00	2.00	1.25
(10)	Max Alvis	4.00	2.00	1.25
(11)	Mike Andrews	4.00	2.00	1.25
(12)	Luis Aparicio	12.50	6.25	3.75
(13)	Bob Aspromonte	4.00	2.00	1.25
(14)	Stan Bahnsen	4.00	2.00	1.25
(15)	Bob Bailey	4.00	2.00	1.25
(16)	Ernie Banks	25.00	12.50	7.50
(17)	Glenn Beckert	4.00	2.00	1.25
(18)	Gary Bell	4.00	2.00	1.25
(19)	Johnny Bench	30.00	15.00	9.00
(20)	Ken Berry	4.00	2.00	1.25
(21)	Paul Blair	4.00	2.00	1.25
(22)	Bob Bolin	4.00	2.00	1.25
(23)	Dave Boswell	4.00	2.00	1.25
(24)	Nelson Briles	4.00	2.00	1.25
(25)	Lou Brock	12.50	6.25	3.75
(26)	Wally Bunker	4.00	2.00	1.25
(27)	Johnny Callison	4.00	2.00	1.25
(28)	Norm Cash	5.00	2.50	1.50
(29)	Orlando Cepeda	12.50	6.25	3.75
(30)	Dean Chance	4.00	2.00	1.25
(31)	Roberto Clemente	50.00	25.00	15.00
(32)	Donn Clendenon	4.00	2.00	1.25
(33)	Tony Cloninger	4.00	2.00	1.25
(34)	Tommy Davis	4.00	2.00	1.25
(35)	Al Downing	4.00	2.00	1.25
(36)	Curt Flood	4.00	2.00	1.25
(37)	Bill Freehan	4.00	2.00	1.25
(38)	Jim Fregosi	4.00	2.00	1.25
(39)	Bob Gibson	12.50	6.25	3.75
(40)	Jim "Mudcat" Grant	4.00	2.00	1.25
(41)	Jerry Grote	4.00	2.00	1.25
(42)	Jimmie Hall	4.00	2.00	1.25
(43)	Tom Haller	4.00	2.00	1.25
(44)	Ron Hansen	4.00	2.00	1.25
(45)	Steve Hargan	4.00	2.00	1.25

		NM	EX	VG
(46)	Ken Harrelson	4.00	2.00	1.25
(47)	Jim Hart	4.00	2.00	1.25
(48)	Jimmie Holt	4.00	2.00	1.25
(49)	Joe Horlen	4.00	2.00	1.25
(50)	Willie Horton	4.00	2.00	1.25
(51)	Frank Howard	5.00	2.50	1.50
(52)	Dick Hughes	4.00	2.00	1.25
(53)	Randy Hundley	4.00	2.00	1.25
(54)	Ron Hunt	4.00	2.00	1.25
(55)	Jim "Catfish" Hunter	12.50	6.25	3.75
(56)	Pat Jarvis	4.00	2.00	1.25
(57)	Julian Javier	4.00	2.00	1.25
(58)	Tommy John	6.00	3.00	1.75
(59)	Deron Johnson	4.00	2.00	1.25
(60)	Mack Jones	4.00	2.00	1.25
(61)	Jim Kaat	5.00	2.50	1.50
(62)	Al Kaline	20.00	10.00	6.00
(63)	Don Kessinger	4.00	2.00	1.25
(64)	Harmon Killebrew	20.00	10.00	6.00
(65)	Jerry Koosman	4.00	2.00	1.25
(66)	Jim Lefebvre	4.00	2.00	1.25
(67)	Mickey Lolich	4.00	2.00	1.25
(68)	Jim Lonborg	4.00	2.00	1.25
(69)	Juan Marichal	12.50	6.25	3.75
(70)	Roger Maris	30.00	15.00	9.00
(71)	Ed Mathews	20.00	10.00	6.00
(72)	Jerry May	4.00	2.00	1.25
(73)	Willie Mays	40.00	20.00	12.00
(74)	Dick McAuliffe	4.00	2.00	1.25
(75)	Tim McCarver	5.00	2.50	1.50
(76)	Willie McCovey	12.50	6.25	3.75
(77)	Sam McDowell	4.00	2.00	1.25
(78)	Denny McLain	5.00	2.50	1.50
(79)	Dave McNally	4.00	2.00	1.25
(80)	Denis Menke	4.00	2.00	1.25
(81)	Jim Merritt	4.00	2.00	1.25
(82)	Bob Miller	4.00	2.00	1.25
(83)	Rick Monday	4.00	2.00	1.25
(84)	Joe Morgan	12.50	6.25	3.75
(85)	Gary Nolan	4.00	2.00	1.25
(86)	Jim Northrup	4.00	2.00	1.25
(87)	Rich Nye	4.00	2.00	1.25
(88)	Tony Oliva	5.00	2.50	1.50
(89)	Milt Pappas	4.00	2.00	1.25
(90)	Camilo Pascual	4.00	2.00	1.25
(91)	Joe Pepitone	5.00	2.50	1.50
(92)	Tony Perez	12.50	6.25	3.75
(93)	Jim Perry	4.00	2.00	1.25
(94)	Gary Peters	4.00	2.00	1.25
(95)	Fritz Peterson	4.00	2.00	1.25
(96)	Rico Petrocelli	4.00	2.00	1.25
(97)	Vada Pinson	5.00	2.50	1.50
(98)	Boog Powell	5.00	2.50	1.50
(99)	Rick Reichardt	4.00	2.00	1.25
(100)	Brooks Robinson	15.00	7.50	4.50
(101)	Frank Robinson	15.00	7.50	4.50
(102)	Pete Rose	40.00	20.00	12.00
(103)	Chico Salmon	4.00	2.00	1.25
(104)	Ron Santo	5.00	2.50	1.50
(105)	George Scott	4.00	2.00	1.25
(106)	Tom Seaver	15.00	7.50	4.50
(107)	Dick Selma	4.00	2.00	1.25
(108)	Mike Shannon	4.00	2.00	1.25
(109)	Joe Sparma	4.00	2.00	1.25
(110)	Willie Stargell	12.50	6.25	3.75
(111)	Mel Stottlemyre	4.00	2.00	1.25
(113)	Luis Tiant	4.00	2.00	1.25
(114)	Cesar Tovar	4.00	2.00	1.25
(115)	Tom Tresh	4.50	2.25	1.25
(116)	Pete Ward	4.00	2.00	1.25
(117)	Billy Williams	12.50	6.25	3.75
(118)	Maury Wills	4.00	2.00	1.25
(119)	Earl Wilson	4.00	2.00	1.25
(120)	Dooley Womack	4.00	2.00	1.25

1974 Oh Henry! Henry Aaron Premium Photo

This 8" x 10" black-and-white photo was prepared as a premium for Oh Henry! candy. It features a full-length pose of Aaron and has a facsimile inscribed autographed on front.

	NM	EX	VG
Henry Aaron	20.00	10.00	6.00

1959 Oklahoma Today Major Leaguers

Contemporary and former ballplayers from the Sooner State were featured in this "card set" which was printed on the back cover of the Summer, 1959, issue of "Oklahoma Today" magazine. If cut from the cover, the cards measure about 1-11/16" x 2-3/4". Fronts have black-and-white photos on green, gold or aqua backgrounds. A white strip at bottom has the player name, position and number. Gray backs have the player name, position, team and league. The unnumbered cards are checklisted here in alphabetical order.

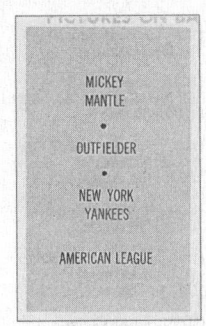

MICKEY MANTLE
•
OUTFIELDER
•
NEW YORK YANKEES
•
AMERICAN LEAGUE

	NM	EX	VG
Complete Magazine:	1,350	675.00	400.00
Complete Set, Singles (20):	1,350	675.00	400.00
Common Player:	45.00	22.50	13.50
(1) Jerry Adair	45.00	22.00	13.50
(2) Harry Brecheen	45.00	22.00	13.50
(3) Johnny Callison	45.00	22.00	13.50
(4) Alvin Dark	45.00	22.50	13.50
(5) "Dizzy" Dean	60.00	30.00	18.00
(6) Paul Dean	45.00	22.50	13.50
(7) Don Demeter	45.00	22.50	13.50
(8) Carl Hubbell	50.00	25.00	15.00
(9) Mickey Mantle	500.00	250.00	150.00
(10) "Pepper" Martin	45.00	22.00	13.50
(11) Lindy McDaniel	45.00	22.00	13.50
(12) Von McDaniel	45.00	22.50	13.50
(13) Cal McLish	45.00	22.00	13.50
(14) Dale Mitchel (Mitchell)	45.00	22.50	13.50
(15) Allie Reynolds	45.00	22.50	13.50
(16) Warren Spahn	45.00	22.00	13.50
(17) Tom Sturdivant	45.00	22.50	13.50
(18) Jerry Walker	45.00	22.50	13.50
(19) Lloyd Waner	45.00	22.00	13.50
(20) Paul Waner	45.00	22.00	13.50

1948 Old Gold Jackie Robinson

JACKIE ROBINSON, first baseman of the Brooklyn Dodgers, was born in Cairo, Georgia, 28 years ago. After his family moved to Pasadena, Calif., he entered the University of California, where he distinguished himself as a star athlete in baseball, football, basketball and track.

At 23, Jackie entered the Army, rising to second lieutenant. For 31 months he served overseas, and then joined the Kansas City Monarchs baseball team, but when he failed to conclusively that he attracted the attention of organized baseball. Impressed with his performance, Branch Rickey, president of the Brooklyn Dodgers, signed him for the Montreal Royals, a Dodger "farm."

So outstanding was Jackie's record with the Montreal Royals that President Rickey signed him to the Dodgers early in 1947. In that way, he became the first Negro to enter the big leagues. He is noted for his speed and batting skill.

A good-looking six-footer, Jackie weighs about 195, and is even-tempered and modest. Cliff comes to Jim in Los Angeles with his wife, a former trained nurse, and their young son, Jackie, Jr. His chief ambition is that success comes to pass as a tribute to the achievement and recognition of the Negro race.

These postcard-size (3-1/2" x 5-1/2") advertising pieces picture Jackie Robinson and a pack of Old Gold cigarettes on their black-and-white fronts, along with an endorsement from the player and his facsimile autograph. Each back has a different presentation of biography and career summary.

	NM	EX	VG
Jackie Robinson/Fldg	800.00	400.00	240.00
Jackie Robinson (In dugout.)	600.00	300.00	180.00

1886 Old Judge New York Giants (N167)

Produced in 1886, the rare N167 Old Judge tobacco cards were the first to be issued by New York's Goodwin & Co., the parent firm of Old Judge Cigarettes. The 1-1/2" x 2-1/2" sepia-toned cards were printed on thin paper and featured only members of the New York National League club. Twelve subjects are known to exist, six of whom are Hall of Famers. The front of each card lists the player's name, position and team and has the words "Old Judge" at the top. The backs contain another ad for the Old Judge brand and also include a line noting that the player poses were "copied from photo by J. Wood, 208 Bowery, N.Y."

	NM	EX	VG
Common Player:	50,000	25,000	15,000
(1) Roger Connor	112,500	56,250	33,750
(2) Larry Corcoran	50,000	25,000	15,000
(3) Mike Dorgan	50,000	25,000	15,000

(4) Dude Esterbrook	50,000	25,000	15,000
(5) Buck Ewing	120,000	60,000	30,000
(6) Joe Gerhardt	50,000	25,000	15,000
(7) Pete Gillespie	50,000	25,000	15,000
(8) Tim Keefe	112,500	56,250	33,750
(9) Orator Jim O'Rourke	112,500	56,250	33,750
(10) Danny Richardson	50,000	25,000	15,000
(11) John Ward	112,500	56,250	33,750
(12) Mickey Welsh (Welch)	112,500	56,250	33,750

1887-1890 Old Judge (N172)

This is one of the most fascinating of all card sets, being not only one of the first, but also the largest ever. The number of cards issued may never be finally determined. These cards were issued by the Goodwin & Co. tobacco firm in their Old Judge and, to a lesser extent, Gypsy Queen cigarettes. Players from more than 40 major and minor league teams are pictured on the nominally 1-7/16" x 2-1/2" cards (actual size varies), with some 500 different players known to exist. Up to 20 different pose, team and caption variations exist for some players. Cards were issued both with and without dates, numbered and unnumbered, and with both script and machine-printed identification. Known variations number over 3,500. The cards themselves are black-and-white (many now toned sepia or even pink) photographs pasted onto thick cardboard. They are blank-backed. Values shown here are for the most common examples of a specific player's cards, unless otherwise indicated. Demand for various photo, team, league, etc., variations can significantly affect value and, because of the relatively "thin" nature of the market for Old Judge cards, is subject to rapid fluctuations as collectors enter and leave the arena. These listings are presented alphabetically. Few Old Judge cards were issued with the player's first name, or even initial. Where verifiable, the first names have been added to these listings in the form most often encountered at the time of issue. Misspellings were common among the issue. Cases in which all of a player's cards were incorrectly spelled are listed by the misspelling, with the correct spelling in parentheses following. In cases where the name was sometimes spelled correctly, and sometimes not, the incorrect spellings are provided thus: "(Also: ...)". For each player, the number of different photo/team combinations known is indicated. Minor changes in the player identification caption, such as addition of an initial, presence or absence of period or comma, abbreviation of position, or spelling of team name, are not included in the number of cards listed. Team designations for each player are listed, where known. Pose/designation variations which have historically attracted increased collector interest are specified. These include such subsets as the Brown's Champions and Mets "spotted tie" portrait cards of 1887, the Player's League designations of 1890 and some other popularly collected subsets, such as the dual-player cards. Cards which depict and name both players are listed here under each player's name and are numbered with a "DP" prefix. League designations found in the listings include: AA - American Association; NL - National League; PL - Player's League; WA - Western Association. Gaps have been left in the assigned numbering to accommodate future additions.

	NM	EX	VG
Common Card:	800.00	350.00	200.00
(1) Gus Albert (Alberts) 7			
1 (a) (Cleveland)	800.00	350.00	200.00
1 (b) (Milwaukee)	800.00	350.00	200.00
(2) Charles Alcott 6			
2 (a) (Mansfield)	1,500	300.00	175.00
2 (b) (St. Louis Whites WA)	975.00	425.00	250.00
(3) Daniel Alexander 4			
3 (a) (Des Moines)	950.00	470.00	280.00
(4) Bob Allen 7			
4 (a) (Philadelphia NL)	800.00	350.00	200.00
4 (a) (Pittsburgh)	800.00	350.00	200.00
(5) Myron Allen 6			
5 (a) (Kansas City)	1,650	825.00	495.00

(6) Billy Alvord 3			
6 (a) (Des Moines)	800.00	350.00	200.00
6 (b) (Toledo)	975.00	425.00	250.00
(7) Varney Anderson 3			
7 (a) (St. Paul)	11,500	300.00	175.00
(8) Ed Andrews 6			
8 (a) (Philadelphia NL)	800.00	350.00	200.00
DP 1 (Being tagged by Buster Hoover.)	1,000	500.00	300.00
(9) Wally Andrews 3			
9 (a) (Omaha)	850.00	375.00	200.00
(10) Bill Annis 4			
10 (a) (Omaha)	900.00	400.00	230.00
10 (b) (Worcester)	800.00	350.00	200.00
(11) Cap Anson See Hall of Fame Section Following			
(12) Joe Ardner 4			
12 (a) (Kansas City)	800.00	350.00	200.00
12 (b) (St. Joseph)	1,150	500.00	275.00
(13) Tug Arundel 5			
13 (a) (Indianapolis)	800.00	350.00	200.00
(14) Jersey Bakley (Bakely) 5			
14 (a) (Cleveland)	850.00	375.00	200.00
(15) Kid Baldwin 5			
15 (a) (Cincinnati)	800.00	350.00	200.00
(16) Lady Baldwin 4			
16 (a) (Detroit)	2,200	975.00	550.00
(17) Mark Baldwin 10			
17 (a) (Chicago NL)	850.00	375.00	200.00
17 (b) (Chicago NL)(Portrait)	2,500	1,250	750.00
17 (c) (Chicago PL)	2,250	1,000	750.00
17 (d) (Columbus)	800.00	350.00	200.00
(18) Jim Banning 5			
18 (a) (Washington)	800.00	350.00	200.00
(19) Sam Barkley 8			
19 (a) (Kansas City)	975.00	425.00	250.00
19 (b) (Pittsburg)	920.00	400.00	230.00
DP 6 (Watching Jocko Fields field.)	1,250	575.00	300.00
DP 7 (Tagged by Jocko Fields.)	1,250	575.00	300.00
(20) John Barnes (Also: Barns) 2			
20 (a) (St. Paul)	1,400	600.00	350.00
(21) Billy Barnie 1			
21 (a) (Baltimore)	2,700	1,350	810.00
21 (a)	920.00	400.00	250.00
(22) Charley Bassett 3			
22 (a) (Indianapolis)	800.00	350.00	200.00
22 (b) (New York NL)	800.00	350.00	200.00
(23) Charlie Bastian 6			
23 (a) (Chicago NL)	800.00	350.00	200.00
23 (b) (Chicago PL)	2,700	1,200	600.00
23 (c) (Philadelphia NL)	600.00	275.00	150.00
DP 2 (Being tagged by Pop Schriver.)	1,150	500.00	275.00
(24) Ed Beatin (Also: Beattin) 3			
24 (a) (Cleveland)	800.00	350.00	200.00
(25) Jake Beckley See Hall of Fame Section Following			
(26) Stephen Behel 1			
26 (a) (New York AA "dotted tie")	16,000	8,000	4,750
(27) Charlie Bennett 1			
27 (a) (Boston NL)	800.00	350.00	200.00
(28) Lou Bierbauer (Also: Bierbaur) 5			
28 (a) (Philadelphia AA)	1,250	625.00	375.00
DP 3 (Tagging Bob Gamble.)	1,800	900.00	550.00
(29) Bill Bishop 4			
29 (a) (Pittsburgh)	800.00	350.00	200.00
29 (b) (Syracuse)	800.00	350.00	200.00
(30) Bill Blair 5			
30 (a) (Hamilton)	1,025	500.00	400.00
30 (b) (Philadelphia AA)	800.00	350.00	200.00
(31) Ned Bligh 6			
31 (a) (Columbus)	800.00	350.00	200.00
(32) Walter Bogart 5			
32 (a) (Indianapolis)	800.00	350.00	200.00
(33) Boyce 4			
33 (a) (Washington) (Never played for Wash.)	950.00	470.00	280.00
(34) Boyd 2			
34 (a) (Chicago Maroons WA)	2,000	900.00	500.00
(35) Henry Boyle 6			
35 (a) (Indianapolis)	800.00	350.00	200.00
35 (b) (New York NL) (Never played for N.Y.)	800.00	350.00	200.00
(36) Jack Boyle 6			
36 (a) (Chicago PL)	6,000	2,700	1,500
36 (b) (St. Louis AA)	875.00	350.00	200.00
(37) George Bradley 5			

37 (a)	(Sioux City)	800.00	350.00	200.00
(38)	**Nick Bradley 4**			
38 (a)	(Kansas City)	800.00	350.00	200.00
38 (b)	(Worcester)	800.00	350.00	200.00
(39)	**Steve Brady 1**			
39 (a)	(New York AA "dotted tie")	3,375	1,525	850.00
(40)	**E.L. Breckenridge 1**			
40 (a)	(Sacramento)			
	(Value Undetermined)			
	Willie Breslin - See Mascot			
(41)	**Timothy Brosnan**			
	(Also: Brosman) 8			
41 (a)	(Minneapolis)	800.00	350.00	200.00
41 (b)	(Sioux City)	800.00	350.00	200.00
(42)	**Cal Broughton 5**			
42 (a)	(St. Paul)	800.00	350.00	200.00
(43)	**Dan Brouthers**			
	See Hall of Fame Section Following			
(44)	**Tom Brown 7**			
44 (a)	(Boston NL)	800.00	350.00	200.00
44 (b)	(Boston PL)	2,700	1,200	700.00
44 (c)	(Pittsburgh)	600.00	275.00	150.00
(45)	**Willard (California) Brown 6**			
45 1	(New York NL)	800.00	350.00	200.00
45 1	(New York PL)	2,250	1,000	550.00
(46)	**Pete Browning 5**			
46 (a)	(Louisville)	7,000	3,500	2,100
(47)	**Charlie Brynan (Also: Bryn) 6**			
47 (a)	(Chicago NL)	800.00	350.00	200.00
47 (b)	(Des Moines)	800.00	350.00	200.00
(48)	**Al Buckenberger 2**			
48 (a)	(Columbus)	3,000	1,500	900.00
(49)	**Dick Buckley 7**			
49 (a)	(Indianapolis)	800.00	350.00	200.00
49 (b)	(New York NL)	800.00	350.00	200.00
(50)	**Charlie Buffinton**			
	(Also: Buffington) 4			
50 (a)	(Philadelphia NL)	800.00	350.00	200.00
50 (b)	(Philadelphia PL)	2,700	1,200	600.00
(51)	**Ernie Burch 8**			
51 (a)	(Brooklyn)	2,300	1,025	575.00
51 (b)	(St. Louis Whites WA)	800.00	350.00	200.00
(52)	**Bill Burdick 4**			
52 (a)	(Indianapolis)	800.00	350.00	200.00
52 (b)	(Omaha)	850.00	375.00	200.00
(53)	**Jack Burdock 5**			
53 (a)	(Boston NL)	2,000	1,000	600.00
(54)	**Bob Burks (Burk) 3**			
54 (a)	(Sioux City)	950.00	470.00	280.00
(55)	**Watch Burnham 1**			
55 (a)	(Indianapolis)	800.00	400.00	300.00
(56)	**Jim Burns 8**			
56 (a)	(Kansas City)	950.00	470.0 0	.280.00
56 (b)	(Omaha)	800.00	350.00	200.00
(58)	**Oyster Burns 5**			
58 (a)	(Baltimore)	800.00	350.00	200.00
58 (b)	(Brooklyn)	850.00	375.00	200.00
DP 22	(Being tagged by Sam Trott.)	1,150	500.00	275.00
(59)	**Tom Burns (Also: "E. Burns") 4**			
59 (a)	(Chicago NL)	800.00	350.00	200.00
(60)	**Doc Bushong 6**			
60 (a)	(Brooklyn)	850.00	375.00	200.00
60 2	(St. Louis AA "Brown's Champions")	1,000	450.00	300.00
(61)	**John (Patsy) Cahill 2**			
61 (a)	(Indianapolis)	800.00	350.00	200.00
(62)	**Count Campau 7**			
62 (a)	(Detroit)	800.00	350.00	200.00
62 (b)	(Kansas City)	800.00	350.00	200.00
(63)	**Jimmy Canavan 3**			
63 (a)	(Omaha)	800.00	350.00	200.00
(64)	**Bart Cantz (Also: McCantz) 5**			
64 (a)	(Baltimore)	800.00	350.00	200.00
64 (b)	(St. Louis Whites WA)	800.00	350.00	200.00
(65)	**Jack Carney 5**			
65 (a)	(Washington)	800.00	350.00	200.00
(66)	**Hick Carpenter 5**			
66 (a)	(Cincinnati)	800.00	350.00	200.00
66 (b)	(Tagging player.)	1,150	575.00	345.00
(67)	**Cliff Carroll 2**			
67 (a)	(Washington)	800.00	350.00	200.00
(68)	**Fred Carroll 3**			
68 (a)	(Pittsburgh)	800.00	350.00	200.00
(69)	**Scrappy Carroll 8**			
69 (a)	(Chicago NL)	800.00	350.00	200.00
69 (b)	(St. Paul)	800.00	350.00	200.00
(70)	**Ed Cartwright 5**			

70 (a)	(Kansas City)	800.00	350.00	200.00
70 (b)	(St. Joseph)	800.00	350.00	200.00
(71)	**Bob Caruthers 7**			
71 (a)	(Brooklyn)	800.00	400.00	240.00
71 (b)	(St. Louis AA "Brown's Champions")	1,875	850.00	450.00
(72)	**Dan Casey 3**			
72 (a)	(Philadelphia NL)	950.00	475.00	285.00
(73)	**Elton Chamberlain 6**			
73 (a)	(St. Louis)	800.00	350.00	200.00
(74)	**Cupid Childs 5**			
74 (a)	(Philadelphia NL)	1,150	500.00	275.00
74 (b)	(Syracuse)	950.00	475.00	285.00
	Chreve - See Shreve			
(75)	**Bob Clark 6**			
75 (a)	(Brooklyn)	800.00	350.00	200.00
DP 4	(Tagging Mickey Hughes.)	2,300	1,025	575.00
(76)	**Spider Clark 4**			
76 (a)	(Washington)	1,100	550.00	325.00
(77)	**Dad Clarke (Also: Clark) 11**			
77 (a)	(Chicago NL)	800.00	350.00	200.00
77 (b)	(Omaha)	850.00	375.00	200.00
(78)	**John Clarkson**			
	See Hall of Fame Section Following			
(79)	**Jack Clements 3**			
79 (a)	(Philadelphia NL)	1,400	700.00	425.00
(80)	**Elmer Cleveland 6**			
80 (a)	(New York NL)	800.00	350.00	200.00
(81)	**Monk Cline 5**			
81 (a)	(Sioux City)	800.00	350.00	200.00
(82)	**Mike Cody 4**			
82 (a)	(Des Moines)	950.00	470.00	280.00
(83)	**John Coleman 5**			
83 (a)	(Pittsburgh)	800.00	350.00	200.00
(84)	**Bill Collins 13**			
84 (a)	(Lowell)	800.00	350.00	200.00
84 (b)	(Newark)	950.00	470.00	280.00
84 (c)	(New York) (Never played for N.Y.)	900.00	400.00	230.00
(85)	**Hub Collins 6**			
85 (a)	(Brooklyn)	800.00	350.00	200.00
85 (b)	(Louisville)	975.00	425.00	250.00
(86)	**Charlie Comiskey**			
	(Also: Commiskey)			
86 (a)	See Hall of Fame Section Following			
(87)	**Pete Connell 2**			
87 (a)	(Des Moines, 3B, dark uniform.)	800.00	350.00	200.00
87 (b)	(Des Moines, 1B, light uniform. Photo actually P.J. O'Connell.)	800.00	350.00	200.00
(88)	**Roger Connor (Also: Conner)**			
	See Hall of Fame Section Following			
(89)	**Dick Conway 6**			
89 (a)	(Boston NL)	1,025	450.00	250.00
89 (b)	(Worcester)	800.00	350.00	200.00
(90)	**Jim Conway 5**			
90 (a)	(Kansas City)	800.00	350.00	200.00
(91)	**Pete Conway 10**			
91 (a)	(Detroit)	800.00	350.00	200.00
91 (b)	(Pittsburgh)	800.00	350.00	200.00
91 (c)	(Indianapolis)	800.00	350.00	200.00
(92)	**Paul Cook 4**			
92 (a)	(Louisville)	800.00	350.00	200.00
(93)	**Jimmy Cooney 5**			
93 (a)	(Chicago NL)	800.00	350.00	200.00
93 (b)	(Omaha)	850.00	375.00	200.00
(94)	**Larry Corcoran 4**			
94 (a)	(Indianapolis)	850.00	375.00	200.00
94 (b)	(London)	850.00	375.00	200.00
(95)	**Pop Corkhill 7**			
95 (a)	(Brooklyn)	800.00	350.00	200.00
95 (b)	(Cincinnati)	800.00	350.00	200.00
(96)	**Cannonball Crane 7**			
96 (a)	(New York NL)	800.00	350.00	200.00
96 (b)	(New York PL)	2,700	1,200	600.00
(97)	**Sam Crane 3**			
97 (a)	(Washington)	800.00	350.00	200.00
(98)	**Jack Crogan (Croghan) 5**			
98 (a)	(Chicago Maroons WA)	2,000	900.00	500.00
(99)	**John Crooks 7**			
99 (a)	(Omaha)	850.00	375.00	200.00
99 (b)	(St. Louis Whites WA)	800.00	350.00	200.00
(100)	**Lave Cross 6**			
100 (a)	(Louisville)	800.00	350.00	200.00
100 (b)	(Philadelphia AA)	950.00	470.00	280.00
100 (c)	(Philadelphia PL)	2,700	1,200	600.00

(101)	**William Crossley 5**			
101 (a)	(Milwaukee)	750.00	325.00	200.00
(102)	**Joe Crotty 5**			
102 (a)	(New York AA "dotted tie")	2,800	1,250	700.00
102 (b)	(Sioux City)	1,400	700.000	425.00
(103)	**Billy Crowell 9**			
103 (a)	(Cleveland)	800.00	350.00	200.00
103 (b)	(St. Joseph)	800.00	350.00	200.00
(104)	**Jim Cudworth 4**			
104 (a)	(Worcester)	800.00	350.00	200.00
(105)	**Bert Cunningham 6**			
105 (a)	(Baltimore)	850.00	375.00	200.00
105 (b)	(Philadelphia PL)	2,700	1,200	600.00
(106)	**Tacks Curtis 5**			
106 (a)	(St. Joseph)	950.00	470.00	280.00
(107)	**Ed Cushman 3**			
107 (a)	(New York AA "dotted tie")	2,800	1,250	600.00
107 (b)	(New York AA)	2,300	300.00	175.00
107 (c)	(Toledo)	4,250	2,100	1,250
(108)	**Tony Cusick 2**			
108 (a)	(Milwaukee)	5,750	300.00	175.00
(109)	**Edward Dailey (Also: Daley) 7**			
109 (a)	(Columbus)	800.00	350.00	200.00
109 (b)	(Philadelphia NL)	800.00	350.00	200.00
109 (c)	(Washington)	800.00	350.00	200.00
(110)	**Vincent Dailey 1**			
110 (a)	(Oakland)(SGC-graded Poor auctioned for $101,100 12/05.)			
(111)	**Bill Daley 2**			
111 (a)	(Boston NL)	800.00	400.00	240.00
111 (b)	(Boston PL)	2,400	1,100	600.00
(112)	**Con Daley (Daily) 9**			
112 (a)	(Boston NL)	800.00	350.00	200.00
112 (b)	(No name, team, etc.)	2,600	1,150	650.00
112 (c)	(Indianapolis)	800.00	350.00	200.00
(113)	**Abner Dalrymple 7**			
113 (a)	(Denver)	1,050	475.00	250.00
113 (b)	(Pittsburgh)	800.00	350.00	200.00
113 (c)	(Pittsburgh) ("Dolrynicle")	3,500	1,750	1,050
(114)	**Sun Daly 5**			
114 (a)	(Minneapolis)	900.00	400.00	225.00
(115)	**Tom Daly 7**			
115 (a)	(Chicago NL)	800.00	350.00	200.00
115 (b)	(Chicago NL)(Portrait)	1,200	600.00	350.00
115 (c)	(Cleveland) (Never played with Cleveland.)	800.00	350.00	200.00
(116)	**Law Daniels 5**			
116 (a)	(Kansas City)	800.00	350.00	200.00
(117)	**Dell Darling 6**			
117 (a)	(Chicago NL)	1,400	700.00	425.00
117 (b)	(Portrait)	2,000	1,000	600.00
117 (c)	(Chicago PL)	2,700	1,200	600.00
(118)	**William Darnbrough 2**			
118 (a)	(Denver)	850.00	375.00	200.00
(119)	**D.J. Davin 2**			
119 (a)	(Milwaukee)	5,750	300.00	175.00
(120)	**Jumbo Davis 5**			
120 (a)	(Kansas City)	800.00	350.00	200.00
(121)	**Pat Dealey (Also: Dealy) 6**			
121 (a)	(Washington)	800.00	400.00	240.00
(122)	**Tom Deasley 20**			
122 (a)	(New York NL)	800.00	350.00	200.00
122 (b)	(Washington)	800.00	350.00	200.00
(123)	**Harry Decker 5**			
123 (a)	(Philadelphia NL)	800.00	400.00	240.00
(124)	**Ed Delahanty**			
	See Hall of Fame Section Following			
(125)	**Jerry Denny 4**			
125 (a)	(Indianapolis)	800.00	350.00	200.00
125 (b)	(New York NL)	800.00	350.00	200.00
(126)	**Jim Devlin (Also: Delvin) 5**			
126 (a)	(St. Louis AA)	800.00	350.00	200.00
(127)	**Tom Dolan 5**			
127 (a)	(Denver)	800.00	350.00	200.00
127 (b)	(St. Louis AA)	800.00	350.00	200.00
(128)	**Jack Donahue 1**			
128 (a)	(San Francisco) (SGC-certified Poor, $52,240, 12/04 auction.)			
(129)	**Jim Donahue**			
	(Also: Donohue) 7			
129 (a)	(New York AA "dotted tie")	3,375	1,525	850.00
129 (b)	(Kansas City)	800.00	350.00	200.00
(130)	**Jim Donnelly 3**			
130 (a)	(Washington)	850.00	375.00	200.00
(131)	**Charlie Dooley 1**			

131 (a) (Oakland)(SGC-certified
Poor, $52,240, 12/04 auction.)

(132) John Doran 2
132 (a) (Omaha)   4,500   2,200   1,350

(133) Mike Dorgan 17
133 (a) (New York NL)   800.00   350.00   200.00
(Sliding)   1,100   500.00   250.00

(134) Con Doyle 1
134 (a) (San Francisco)
(Value Undetermined)

(135) Charlie Duffe (Duffee) 5
135 (a) (St. Louis AA)   1,150   575.00   345.00

(136) Hugh Duffy
See Hall of Fame Section Following

(137) Dan Dugdale 7
137 (a) (Chicago Maroons WA)   1,025   450.00   250.00
137 (b) (Minneapolis)   800.00   400.00   240.00

(138) Martin Duke 5
138 (a) (Minneapolis)   800.00   350.00   200.00

(139) Fred Dunlap 9
139 (b) (Pittsburgh)   825.00   375.00   200.00

(140) J.E. Dunn 5
140 (a) (Chicago Maroons WA)   2,300   1,100   600.00

(141) Jesse Duryea 4
141 (a) (Cincinnati)   800.00   350.00   200.00
141 (b) (St. Paul)   800.00   350.00   200.00

(142) Frank Dwyer 5
142 (a) (Chicago NL)   800.00   350.00   200.00
142 (b) (Chicago Maroons WA)   2,300   1,100   600.00

(143) Billy Earle (Also: Earl) 4
143 (a) (Cincinnati)   800.00   350.00   200.00
143 (b) (St. Paul)   800.00   350.00   200.00

(144) Hi Ebright 2
144 (a) (Washington)   800.00   350.00   200.00

(145) Red Ehret 4
145 (a) (Louisville)   800.00   350.00   200.00

Eidner - See Weidner

(146) R. Emmerke 5
146 (a) (Des Moines)   800.00   350.00   200.00

(147) Dude Esterbrook 11
147 (a) (Indianapolis)   800.00   350.00   200.00
147 (b) (Louisville)   800.00   350.00   200.00
147 (c) (New York AA)   1,300   575.00   325.00
147 (d) (New York NL)   800.00   350.00   200.00

(148) Henry Esterday (Easterday) 6
148 (a) (Columbus)   1,400   700.00   425.00
148 (b) (Kansas City)   1,150   575.00   345.00

(149) Buck Ewing
See Hall of Fame Section Following

(150) John Ewing 4
150 (a) (Louisville)   800.00   350.00   200.00

(151) Jay Faatz 3
151 (a) (Cleveland)   800.00   350.00   200.00

(152) Bill Fagan 5
152 (a) (Denver)   950.00   470.00   280.00
152 (b) (Kansas City)   950.00   470.00   280.00

(153) Bill Farmer 7
153 (a) (Pittsburgh)   800.00   350.00   200.00
153 (b) (St. Paul)   850.00   375.00   200.00

(154) Sid Farrar
(Also: Farrer, Faraer) 8
154 (a) (Philadelphia NL)   800.00   350.00   200.00
154 (b) (Philadelphia PL)   2,700   1,200   600.00

(155) Duke Farrell (Also: Farrel) 5
155 (a) (Chicago NL)   900.00   450.00   270.00
155 (b) (Chicago PL)   2,700   1,200   600.00

(156) Jack Farrell 12
156 (a) (Baltimore)   800.00   350.00   200.00
156 (b) (Washington)   800.00   350.00   200.00
156 (c) (Washington)   875.00   400.00   230.00
(Tagging Paul Hines.)

(157) Frank Fennelly 5
157 (a) (Cincinnati)   800.00   350.00   200.00
157 (b) (Philadelphia AA)   800.00   350.00   200.00

(158) Charlie Ferguson 4
158 (a) (Philadelphia NL)   950.00   470.00   280.00

(159) Alex Ferson 5
159 (a) (Washington)   850.00   375.00   200.00

(160) Wallace Fessenden 4
160 1 (Umpire)   1,850   825.00   450.00

(161) Jocko Fields (Also: Field) 6
161 (a) (Pittsburgh)   800.00   350.00   200.00
DP 6 (Fielding, Sam Barkley   1,250   575.00   300.00
looking on.)
DP 7 (Tagging Sam Barkley.)   1,250   575.00   300.00

(162) Fischer 3

(162) (a) (Chicago Maroons WA)   25,875   11,500   6,475

(163) Thomas Flanigan
(Flanagan) 4
163 (a) (Cleveland)   950.00   470.00   280.00
(Never played for Cleveland.)
163 (b) (Sioux City)   800.00   350.00   200.00

(164) Silver Flint 5
164 (a) (Chicago NL)   950.00   470.00   280.00
164 (b) (Chicago NL) (Portrait, street   1,500   750.00   450.00
clothes)

(165) Thomas Flood 5
165 (a) (St. Joseph)   800.00   350.00   200.00

(166) Jocko Flynn 2
166 (a) (Omaha)(Two known.)   11,500

(167) Jim Fogarty (Also: Fogerty) 5
167 (a) (Philadelphia NL)   800.00   350.00   200.00

(168) Frank Foreman 6
168 (a) (Baltimore)   800.00   350.00   200.00
168 (b) (Cincinnati)   1,250   575.00   300.00

(169) Tom Forster
(Also: "F.W. Foster") 3
169 (a) (Hartford)   800.00   350.00   200.00
169 (b) (Milwaukee, squatting.)   850.00   375.00   200.00
169 (c) (New York AA "dotted tie")   3,375   1,525   850.00
169 (d) Tom Forester   800.00   400.00   240.00
(Milwaukee, standing.)

(170) Elmer Foster 7
170 (a) (New York AA "dotted tie")   6,200   2,750   1,550
170 (b) (New York NL)   800.00   350.00   200.00
170 (c) (Minneapolis)   800.00   350.00   200.00

(171) Dave Foutz 5
171 (a) (Brooklyn)   800.00   400.00   240.00
171 (b) (St. Louis AA "Brown's   1,700   750.00   400.00
Champions")

(172) Julie Freeman 5
172 (a) (Milwaukee)   850.00   375.00   200.00

(173) Will Fry 4
173 (a) (St. Joseph)   850.00   375.00   250.00

(174) Frank Fudger 1
174 (a) (Oakland)
(Value Undetermined)

(175) Shorty Fuller 5
175 (a) (St. Louis AA)   850.00   375.00   200.00

(176) William Fuller 5
176 (a) (Milwaukee)   800.00   400.00   240.00

(177) Chris Fulmer (Also: Fullmer) 6
177 (a) (Baltimore)   800.00   350.00   200.00
DP 8 (Tagging Tom Tucker.)   3,000   1,500   900.00

(178) John Gaffney 1
178 (a) (Washington)   875.00   400.00   225.00
DP 21 (Behind George Shoch.)   1,150   500.00   300.00

(179) Pud Galvin
See Hall of Fame Section Following

(180) Bob Gamble 3
180 (a) (Philadelphia AA)   800.00   350.00   200.00
DP 3 (Being tagged by Lou   1,800   900.00   550.00
Bierbaur.) (Bierbauer)

(181) Charlie Ganzel
(Also: Gauzel) 5
181 (a) (Boston)   800.00   350.00   200.00
181 (b) (Detroit)   800.00   350.00   200.00

(182) Gid Gardner 5
182 (a) (Philadelphia NL)   800.00   350.00   200.00
182 (b) (Washington)   1,025   450.00   250.00
DP 9 (Tagging Miah Murray.)   2,875   1,300   700.00

(183) Hank Gastreich (Gastright) 5
183 (a) (Columbus)   800.00   350.00   200.00

(184) Emil Geiss 6
184 (a) (Chicago NL)   800.00   350.00   200.00
184 (b) (Chicago NFL) (Portrait)   1,200   600.00   350.00

(185) Frank Genins (Also: Genius) 5
185 (a) (Sioux City)   800.00   400.00   240.00

(186) Bill George 5
186 (a) (New York NL)   800.00   350.00   200.00

(187) Joe Gerhardt 4
187 (a) (Jersey City)   800.00   325.00   200.00
187 (b) (New York NL)   1,400   625.00   350.00

(188) Charlie Getzein (Getzien) 6
188 (a) (Detroit)   800.00   350.00   200.00
188 (b) (Indianapolis)   800.00   350.00   200.00

(189) Whitey Gibson 1
189 (a) (Philadelphia AA, two known.) 11,500   3,800

(190) Bob Gilks 6
190 (a) (Cleveland)   800.00   350.00   200.00

(191) Pete Gillespie 5
191 (a) (New York NL)   850.00   375.00   200.00

(192) Barney Gilligan 3
192 (a) (Detroit)   800.00   350.00   200.00

192 (b) (Washington)   800.00   400.00   240.00

(193) Frank Gilmore 5
193 (a) (Washington)   1,025   450.00   250.00

(194) Jack Glasscock (Also:
Glassock, Glass, Cock) 5
194 (a) (Indianapolis)   800.00   400.00   240.00
194 (b) (New York NL)   800.00   350.00   200.00

(195) Bill Gleason 5
195 (a) (Louisville)   800.00   350.00   200.00
195 (b) (Philadelphia AA)   800.00   350.00   200.00
195 (c) (St. Louis AA "Brown's   2,200   1,000   550.00
Champions")
DP 23 (W/ Curt Welch.)   2,300   1,100   600.00

(196) Kid Gleason 5
196 (a) (Philadelphia NL)   800.00   350.00   200.00

(197) Ed Glenn 5
197 (a) (Sioux City)   850.00   375.00   200.00

(198) Mike Goodfellow 9
198 (a) (Cleveland)   950.00   470.00   280.00
198 (b) (Detroit)   900.00   450.00   270.00

(199) George Gore 10
199 (a) (New York NL)   1,025   450.00   250.00
199 (b) (New York PL)   2,700   1,200   600.00

(200) Frank Graves 6
200 (a) (Minneapolis)   800.00   350.00   200.00

(201) Bill Greenwood 8
201 (a) (Baltimore)   1,250   575.00   300.00
201 (b) (Columbus)   800.00   350.00   200.00

(202) Ed Greer 3
202 (a) (Brooklyn)   850.00   375.00   200.00
DP 10 (Catching, Hardie   1,150   500.00   300.00
Henderson batting.)

(203) Mike Griffin 6
203 (a) (Baltimore)   1,150   500.00   300.00
203 (b) (Philadelphia PL)   2,700   1,200   600.00

(204) Clark Griffith
See Hall of Fame Section Following

(205) Henry Gruber 4
205 (a) (Cleveland)   800.00   350.00   200.00

(206) Ad Gumbert 5
206 (a) (Chicago NL)   800.00   350.00   200.00
206 (b) (Boston PL)   2,700   1,200   600.00

(207) Tom Gunning 4
207 (a) (Philadelphia AA)   800.00   350.00   200.00
207 (b) (Philadelphia NL)   800.00   350.00   200.00

(208) Joe Gunson 4
208 (a) (Kansas City)   800.00   400.00   240.00

(209) George Haddock 5
209 (a) (Washington)   800.00   350.00   200.00

(210) Frank Hafner 5
210 (a) (Kansas City)   800.00   400.00   240.00

(211) Willie Hahn (Mascot) 5
211 (a) (Chicago NL)   850.00   375.00   200.00
DP 24 (W/ Ned Williamson.)   4,000   1,800   1,000

Halliday - See Holliday

(212) Bill Hallman 6
212 (a) (Philadelphia NL)   850.00   375.00   200.00
212 (b) (Philadelphia PL)   2,700   1,200   600.00

(213) Billy Hamilton
See Hall of Fame Section Following

(214) Frank Hankinson 1
214 (a) (New York AA "dotted tie")   27,000   12,150   6,750

(215) Ned Hanlon 6
See Hall of Fame Section Following

Hannon - See Shannon

(216) Bill Hanrahan 9
216 (a) (Chicago Maroons WA)   1,025   450.00   250.00
216 (b) (Minneapolis)   800.00   350.00   200.00

(217) Al Hapeman 1
217 (a) (Sacramento)
(Value Undetermined)

(218) John Harkins
(Also: Harkens) 9
218 (a) (Baltimore)   800.00   350.00   200.00
218 (b) (Brooklyn)   800.00   350.00   200.00

(219) Bill Hart 5
219 (a) (Cincinnati)   800.00   350.00   200.00
(Never played for Cincinnati.)
219 (b) (Des Moines)   850.00   375.00   200.00

(220) Bill Hasamdear
(Hassamaer) 3
220 (a) (Kansas City)   800.00   350.00   200.00

(221) Gil Hatfield 5
221 (a) (New York NL)   800.00   350.00   200.00
221 (b) (New York PL)   2,700   1,200   600.00

(222) Bill Hawes (Also Howes) 5

222 (a) (Minneapolis)	800.00	350.00	200.00
222 (b) (St. Paul)	875.00	400.00	225.00

(223) John J. "Egyptian" Healey (Healy) 5

223 (a) (Indianapolis)	800.00	400.00	240.00
223 (b) (Washington)	950.00	470.00	280.00
223 (c) (Washington, portrait, w/ moustache, no cap, possibly unique.)	34,500	15,525	8,625

(224) John C. "Jack" Healy (Also: Healey) 8

224 (a) (Denver)	1,050	475.00	275.00
224 (b) (Omaha)	850.00	375.00	200.00

(225) Guy Hecker 5

225 (a) (Louisville)	2,200	975.00	550.00

(226) Tony Hellman 5

226 (a) (Sioux City)	1,000	500.00	300.00

(227) Hardie Henderson 13

227 (a) (Brooklyn)	800.00	350.00	200.00
227 (b) (Pittsburgh)	800.00	350.00	200.00
DP 10 (Batting, Ed Greer catching.)	1,150	500.00	300.00
DP 11 (Tagging Jimmy Peoples.)	1,600	725.00	400.00

(228) Moxie Hengle 10

228 (a) (Chicago Maroons WA)	950.00	470.00	280.00
228 (b) (Minneapolis)	950.00	470.00	280.00

(229) John Henry 5

229 (a) (Philadelphia) (Never actually played for Philadelphia.)	800.00	350.00	200.00

(230) Ed Herr 7

230 (a) (Milwaukee)	950.00	470.00	280.00
230 (b) (St. Louis Whites WA)	1,300	650.00	400.00

(231) Hunkey Hines 4

231 (a) (St. Louis Whites WA)	1,400	600.00	350.00

(232) Paul Hines 7

232 (a) (Indianapolis)	950.00	470.00	280.00
232 (b) (Washington)	1,500	750.00	450.00

(233) Frank Hoffman 4

233 (a) (Denver)	975.00	425.00	250.00

(234) Eddie Hogan 5

234 (a) (Cleveland)	800.00	400.00	240.00

(235) Bill Holbert 10

235 (a) (Brooklyn)	1,025	450.00	250.00
235 (b) (Jersey City)	1,025	450.00	250.00
235 (c) (New York AA "dotted tie")	10,700	4,800	2,650
235 (d) (New York AA)	2,250	1,125	675.00

(236) Bug Holliday (Also: Halliday) 7

236 (a) (Cincinnati)	800.00	350.00	200.00
236 (b) (Des Moines)	800.00	350.00	200.00

(238) Buster Hoover 3

238 (a) (Philadelphia)	800.00	350.00	200.00
238 (b) (Toronto) (Never played for Phila. in N172 era.)	800.00	400.00	240.00
DP 1 (Hoover tagging Ed Andrews.)	1,000	500.00	300.00

(239) Charlie Hoover 7

239 (a) (Chicago) (Never played for Chicago.)	800.00	350.00	200.00
239 (b) (Kansas City)	800.00	350.00	200.00

(240) Jack Horner (Also: Hodner) 6

240 (a) (Milwaukee)	800.00	350.00	200.00
240 (b) (New Haven)	800.00	350.00	200.00
240 (c) (Photo actually E.H. Warner.)	800.00	350.00	200.00
DP 5 (W/ Ed Warner.)	1,150	500.00	300.00

(241) Joe Hornung (Also: Horning) 6

241 (a) (Baltimore)	800.00	350.00	200.00
241 (b) (Boston)	1,000	500.00	300.00
241 (c) (New York NL)	800.00	350.00	200.00

(242) Pete Hotaling (Also: Hotoling) 4

242 (a) (Cleveland)	800.00	350.00	200.00

Howes - See Hawes

(243) Dummy Hoy 5

243 (a) (Washington)	8,625	3,900	2,150

(244) Nat Hudson 6

244 (a) (St. Louis AA "Brown's Champions")	2,250	1,125	675.00
244 (b) (St. Louis AA)	1,100	550.00	325.00

(245) Mickey Hughes 7

245 (a) (Brooklyn)	800.00	350.00	200.00
DP 4 (Being tagged by Bob Clark.)	2,300	1,100	600.00

(246) Al Hungler 4

246 (a) (Sioux City)	800.00	350.00	200.00

(247) Bill Hutchinson 4

247 (a) (Chicago NL)	1,400	600.00	350.00

(248) Arthur Irwin 13

248 (a) (Boston PL)	1,200	550.00	300.00
248 (b) (Philadelphia NL)	875.00	400.00	225.00
(Portrait, cap off.)	2,300	1,100	600.00
248 (c) (Washington)	800.00	350.00	200.00

(249) John Irwin 5

249 (a) (Washington)	800.00	350.00	200.00

249 (b) (Wilkes-Barre)	875.00	400.00	225.00

(250) A.C. Jantzen 5

250 (a) (Minneapolis)	1,350	675.00	405.00

(251) Frederick Jevne 5

251 (a) (Minneapolis)	900.00	450.00	270.00

(252) Spud Johnson 6

252 (a) (Columbus)	800.00	350.00	200.00
252 (b) (Kansas City)	950.00	470.00	280.00

(253) Dick Johnston 7

253 (a) (Boston NL)	1,300	650.00	400.00
253 (b) (Boston PL)	2,700	1,200	600.00

(254) W.T. Jordan 5

254 (a) (Minneapolis)	950.00	470.00	280.00

(255) Heinie Kappell (Kappel) 8

255 (a) (Cincinnati)	800.00	350.00	200.00
255 (b) (Columbus)	800.00	350.00	200.00

(256) Tim (Also: Jim) Keefe, (Also: Keef, Keefep) See Hall of Fame Section Following

(257) George Keefe 5

257 (a) (Washington)	800.00	350.00	200.00

(258) Jim Keenan 5

258 (a) (Cincinnati)	800.00	350.00	200.00

(259) Charlie Kelly 5

259 (a) (Philadelphia AA)	1,850	825.00	450.00

(260) Honest John Kelly 4

260 (a) (Louisville)	800.00	350.00	200.00
260 (b) (Umpire WA)	1,800	800.00	450.00
DP 14 (W/ Jim Powell.)	1,150	500.00	275.00

(261) King Kelly See Hall of Fame Section Following

(262) Rudy Kemmler (Also: Kemler) 2

262 (a) (St. Louis AA "Brown's Champions")	1,425	650.00	350.00
262 (b) (St. Paul)	800.00	350.00	200.00

(263) Ted Kennedy 9

263 (a) (Des Moines)	850.00	375.00	200.00
263 (b) (Omaha)	1,150	500.00	275.00

(264) J.J. Kenyon 7

264 (a) (Des Moines)	800.00	350.00	200.00
264 (b) (St. Louis Whites WA)	900.00	450.00	250.00

(265) John Kerins 6

265 (a) (Louisville)	850.00	375.00	200.00

(266) Matt Kilroy 7

266 (a) (Baltimore)	1,400	600.00	350.00
266 (b) (Boston PL)	2,700	1,200	600.00

(267) Silver King 3

267 (a) (Chicago PL)	2,700	1,200	600.00
267 (b) (St. Louis AA)	800.00	350.00	200.00

(268) Gus Kloff (Klopf) 7

268 (a) (Minneapolis)	800.00	350.00	200.00
268 (b) (St. Joseph)	800.00	350.00	200.00
DP 15 (W/ Bill Krieg.)	1,150	500.00	275.00

(269) Billy Klusman 7

269 (a) (Denver)	1,100	500.00	250.00
269 (b) (Milwaukee)	800.00	350.00	200.00

(270) Phil Knell 5

270 (a) (St. Joseph)	950.00	475.00	250.00

(271) Ed Knouff 5

271 (a) (St. Louis AA)	800.00	350.00	200.00

(272) Charles Kremmeyer (Krehmeyer) 1

272 (a) (Sacramento)(SGC-certified Fair, $50,233 12/04 auction.)			

(273) Bill Krieg (Also: Kreig) 14

273 (a) (Minneapolis)	800.00	400.00	220.00
273 (b) (St. Joseph)	800.00	400.00	220.00
273 (c) (Washington)	800.00	350.00	200.00
DP 15 (W/ Gus Kloff.) (Klopf)	1,150	500.00	300.00

(274) Gus Krock 5

274 (a) (Chicago NL)	800.00	350.00	200.00

(275) Willie Kuehne (Also: Kuchne) 5

275 (a) (Pittsburgh)	800.00	350.00	200.00

(276) Fred Lange 5

276 (a) (Chicago Maroons WA)	2,100	900.00	500.00

(277) Henry Larkin 4

277 (a) (Philadelphia AA)	800.00	350.00	200.00

(278) Arlie Latham 7

278 (a) (St. Louis AA "Brown's Champions")	2,800	1,400	850.00
278 (b) (St. Louis AA)	800.00	350.00	200.00
278 (c) (Chicago PL)	2,700	1,200	600.00

(279) Chuck Lauer 4

279 (a) (Pittsburgh)	800.00	350.00	200.00

(280) John Leighton 5

280 (a) (Omaha)	850.00	375.00	200.00

(281) Levy 1

281 (a) (San Francisco) (Value Undetermined)			

(282) Tom Loftus 2

282 (a) (Cleveland)	800.00	350.00	200.00
282 (b) (St. Louis Whites WA)	1,200.	600.00	375.00

(283) Danny Long 1

283 (a) (Oakland) (Value Undetermined)			

(284) Herman Long 7

284 (a) (Chicago Maroons WA)	3,100	1,400	775.00
284 (b) (Kansas City)	900.00	400.00	250.00

(285) Tom Lovett 6

285 (a) (Brooklyn)	900.00	400.00	250.00
285 (b) (Omaha)	850.00	375.00	200.00

(286) Bobby Lowe 6

286 (a) (Milwaukee)	1,300	650.00	400.00
DP 18 (About to be tagged by Pat Pettee.)	1,400	600.00	350.00

(287) Jack Lynch 5

287 (a) (New York AA "dotted tie")	3,375	1,500	850.00
287 (b) (New York AA)	800.00	350.00	200.00

(288) Denny Lyons 4

288 (a) (Philadelphia AA)	800.00	350.00	200.00

(289) Harry Lyons 6

289 (a) (St. Louis AA)	800.00	350.00	200.00
289 (b) (Jersey City)	800.00	350.00	200.00

(290) Connie Mack 3 See Hall of Fame Section Following

(291) Reddy Mack 6

291 (a) (Baltimore)	800.00	350.00	200.00
291 (b) (Louisville)	2,100	1,100	650.00

(292) Jimmy Macullar 7

292 (a) (Des Moines)	1,400	600.00	350.00
292 (b) (Milwaukee)	800.00	350.00	200.00

(293) Kid Madden 9

293 (a) (Boston NL)	800.00	350.00	200.00
293 (b) (Boston NL)(Portrait)	2,875	1,300	700.00
293 (c) (Boston PL)	2,700	1,200	600.00

(294) Danny Mahoney 1

294 (a) (St. Joseph)	2,525	1,125	600.00

(295) Willard Maines (Mains) 5

295 (a) (St. Paul)	800.00	350.00	200.00

(296) Fred Mann 5

296 (a) (Hartford)	800.00	350.00	200.00
296 (b) (St. Louis AA) (Never played for St. Louis.)	1,350	675.00	400.00

(297) Jimmy Manning 6

297 (a) (Kansas City)	850.00	375.00	200.00

(298) Lefty Marr 7

298 (a) (Cincinnati)	800.00	350.00	200.00
298 (b) (Columbus)	900.00	450.00	275.00

(299) Mascot (Willie Breslin) 1

299 (a) New York NL (Caption reads "New York Mascot.")	1,850	1,000	600.00

(300) Leech Maskrey 5

300 (a) (Des Moines)	800.00	350.00	200.00
300 (b) (Milwaukee)	800.00	350.00	200.00
300 (c) (Photo actually Jimmy Macullar.)	800.00	350.00	200.00

Massitt - See Messitt

(301) Bobby Mathews 3

301 (a) (Philadelphia AA)	900.00	400.00	250.00

(302) Mike Mattimore (Also: Mattemore) 19

302 (a) (New York NL)	800.00	350.00	200.00
302 (b) (Philadelphia AA)	800.00	350.00	250.00

(303) Al Maul 7

303 (a) (Pittsburgh)	800.00	350.00	200.00

(304) Al Mays 5

304 (a) (New York AA "dotted tie")	4,250	2,150	1,275
304 (b) (Columbus)	800.00	350.00	200.00

(305) Jimmy McAleer 4

305 (a) (Cleveland)	800.00	350.00	200.00

(306) John McCarthy (McCarty) 3

306 (a) (Kansas City)	900.00	400.00	250.00

(307) Tommy McCarthy See Hall of Fame Section Following

(308) Jim McCauley 3

308 (a) (Chicago Maroons WA)	2,100	900.00	500.00

(309) Bill McClellan (Also: McClennan) 3

309 (a) (Brooklyn)	800.00	350.00	200.00
309 (b) (Denver)	1,400	600.00	350.00

(310) Jim McCormack 4

310 (a) (St. Louis Whites WA)	800.00	350.00	200.00

(311) Jim McCormick 10
311 (a) (Chicago) — 2,000 1,000 600.00
311 (b) (Portrait) — 7,500 3,750 2,250
311 (c) (Pittsburgh) — 850.00 375.00 200.00

(312) McCreachery 1
312 (a) (Indianapolis)
(Value Undetermined)
(Nobody named McCreachery ever managed Indianapolis. Photo actually Deacon White.)

(313) Tom McCullum (McCallum) 4
313 (a) (Minneapolis) — 800.00 350.00 200.00

(314) Jim McDonald 1
314 (a) (Oakland)
(Value Undetermined)

(315) Chippy McGarr 5
315 (a) (Kansas City) — 800.00 350.00 200.00
315 (b) (St. Louis AA) — 800.00 350.00 200.00
315 (c) (St. Louis AA, batting, umpire behind.) — 875.00 400.00 225.00

(316) Jack McGeachy 4
316 (a) (Indianapolis) — 850.00 375.00 200.00

(317) John McGlone 7
317 (a) (Cleveland) — 800.00 350.00 200.00
317 (b) (Detroit) — 800.00 350.00 200.00

(318) Deacon McGuire 5
318 (a) (Philadelphia NL) — 800.00 400.00 250.00
318 (b) (Toronto) — 900.00 450.00 300.00

(319) Bill McGunnigle 1
319 (a) (Brooklyn) — 1,800 775.00 425.00

(320) Ed McKean 5
320 (a) (Cleveland) — 800.00 350.00 200.00

(321) Alex McKinnon 4
321 (a) (Pittsburgh) — 800.00 350.00 200.00

(322) Tom McLaughlin 1
322 (a) (New York AA "dotted tie") — 7,875 3,550 1,975

(323) Bid McPhee
See Hall of Fame Section Following

(324) Jack McQuaid 1
324 (a) (Umpire) — 2,300 1,025 575.00

(325) James McQuaid 3
325 (a) (Denver) — 1,800 775.00 425.00

(326) Jim McTamany
(Also: McTammany) 6
326 (a) (Brooklyn) — 1,800 775.00 425.00
326 (b) (Columbus) — 1,800 775.00 425.00
326 (c) (Kansas City) — 1,800 775.00 425.00

(327) George McVey 9
327 (a) (Denver) — 800.00 350.00 200.00
327 (b) (Milwaukee) — 800.00 350.00 200.00
327 (c) (St. Joseph) — 750.00 325.00 200.00

(328) Pete Meegan 1
328 (a) (San Francisco)
(Value Undetermined)

(329) John Messitt
(Also: Massitt, Wassitt) 3
329 (a) (Omaha) — 1,325 600.00 325.00

Micholson - See Nicholson

(330) Doggie Miller 5
330 (a) (Pittsburgh) — 800.00 350.00 200.00

(331) Joe Miller 4
331 (a) (Minneapolis) — 800.00 350.00 200.00
331 (b) (Omaha) — 850.00 425.00 250.00

(332) Jocko Milligan 6
332 (a) (Philadelphia PL) — 2,700 1,200 600.00
332 (b) (St. Louis AA) — 800.00 350.00 200.00

(333) E.L. Mills 5
333 (a) (Milwaukee) — 800.00 350.00 200.00

(334) Daniel Minnehan (Minahan) 4
334 (a) (Minneapolis) — 800.00 350.00 200.00

(335) Sam Moffet 3
335 (a) (Indianapolis) — 800.00 350.00 200.00

(336) John Morrill (Also: Morrell) 4
336 (a) (Boston NL) — 1,250 550.00 300.00
336 (b) (Boston NL)(Portrait) — 2,100 900.00 500.00
336 (c) (Washington) — 2,100 1,050. 650.00

(337) Ed Morris 6
337 (a) (Pittsburgh) — 800.00 350.00 200.00

(338) Tony Mullane 7
338 (a) (Cincinnati) — 1,250 625.00 400.00

(339) Joe Mulvey 4
339 (a) (Philadelphia NL) — 800.00 350.00 200.00
339 (b) (Philadelphia PL) — 2,700 1,200 600.00

(340) Pat Murphy 3
340 (a) (New York NL) — 800.00 350.00 200.00

(341) P.L. Murphy 5
341 (a) (St. Paul) — 1,200. 600.00 400.00

(342) Miah Murray 5
342 (a) (Washington) — 800.00 350.00 200.00
DP 9 (Being tagged by Gid Gardner.) — 2,875 1,300 700.00

(343) Jim Mutrie 3
343 (a) (New York NL) — 2,400 1,200 750.00

(344) Al Myers 6
344 (a) (Philadelphia NL) — 800.00 350.00 200.00
344 (b) (Washington) — 800.00 400.00 250.00

(345) George Myers 3
345 (a) (Indianapolis) — 800.00 350.00 200.00

(346) Tom Nagle 6
346 (a) (Chicago NL) — 800.00 350.00 200.00
346 (b) (Omaha) — 850.00 425.00 275.00

(347) Billy Nash 7
347 (a) (Boston NL) — 1,375 700.00 425.00
347 (b) (Tagging (unnamed) Old Hoss Radbourn.) — 2,000 1,000 600.00
347 (c) (Boston PL) — 2,700 1,200 600.00

(348) Jack Nelson 1
348 (a) (New York AA "dotted tie") — 7,875 3,550 1,975

(349) Kid Nichols
SEE HALL OF FAME SECTION FOLLOWING

(350) Samuel Nichols (Nichol) 4
350 (a) (Pittsburgh) — 800.00 350.00 200.00

(351) J.W. Nicholson 6
351 (a) (Chicago Maroons WA) — 4,000 2,000 1,200

(352) Parson Nicholson (Also: Micholson) 7
352 (a) (Cleveland) — 800.00 350.00 200.00
(Never played for Cleveland.)
352 (b) (St. Louis Whites WA) — 800.00 350.00 200.00

(353) Hugh Nicol (Also: Nicoll) 8
353 (a) (St. Louis AA "Brown's Champions") — 1,600 800.00 480.00
353 (b) (Cincinnati) — 825.00 375.00 200.00
DP 16 (Side by side w/ John Reilly.) — 2,300 1,025 575.00
DP 17 (Facing John Reilly.) — 2,525 1,125 625.00

(354) Frederick Nyce 4
354 (a) (Burlington) — 800.00 350.00 200.00
354 (b) (St. Louis Whites WA) — 800.00 350.00 200.00

(355) Doc Oberlander 8
355 (a) (Cleveland) — 800.00 350.00 200.00
355 (b) (Syracuse) — 800.00 350.00 200.00

(356) Billy O'Brien 5
356 (a) (Washington) — 900.00 400.00 250.00

(357) Darby O'Brien 5
357 (a) ("Brooklyns" or "Bk'ns") — 800.00 350.00 200.00

(358) Jack O'Brien 8
358 (a) (Baltimore) — 800.00 350.00 200.00
358 (b) ("Brooklyn") — 800.00 350.00 200.00
358 (c) ("Mini" photo.) — 5,750 2,600 1,425

(359) John O'Brien 4
359 (a) (Cleveland) — 900.00 400.00 250.00

(360) P.J. O'Connell 5
360 (a) (Des Moines) — 800.00 400.00 250.00
360 (b) (Omaha) — 800.00 350.00 200.00

(361) Jack O'Connor 8
361 (a) (Cincinnati) — 800.00 350.00 200.00
361 (b) (Columbus) — 800.00 350.00 200.00

(362) Hank O'Day 3
362 (a) (Washington) — 1,250 625.00 375.00

(363) Harry O'Day 1
363 (a) (Sacramento)(VALUE UNDETERMINED)

(364) Norris O'Neill 1
364 (a) (Oakland)(VALUE UNDETERMINED)

(365) Tip O'Neill (Also: O'Neil) 11
365 (a) (Chicago PL) — 2,500 1,100 625.00
365 (b) (St. Louis AA "Brown's Champions") — 1,875 850.00 475.00
365 (c) (St. Louis AA) — 800.00 350.00 200.00
365 (d) (Photo actually Bill White.) — 975.00 425.00 250.00
(W/moustasche, stooping to field grounder.)

(366) Orator Jim O'Rourke
SEE HALL OF FAME SECTION FOLLOWING

(367) Tom O'Rourke (Also: Rourke) 8
367 (a) (Boston NL) — 850.00 375.00 200.00
367 (b) (Jersey City) — 800.00 350.00 200.00

(368) Dave Orr 10
368 (a) (Brooklyn) — 900.00 400.00 250.00
368 (b) (Columbus) — 3,500 1,750 1,050
368 (c) (New York AA "dotted tie") — 15,750 7,100 3,925
368 (d) (New York AA) — 800.00 350.00 200.00

(369) Charlie Parsons 4
369 (a) (Minneapolis) — 800.00 350.00 200.00

(370) Owen Patton 8
370 (a) (Des Moines) — 1,000 500.00 300.00
370 (b) (Minneapolis) — 850.00 375.00 200.00

(371) Jimmy Peeples (Peoples) 4
371 (a) (Brooklyn) — 800.00 350.00 200.00
371 (b) (Columbus) — 800.00 350.00 200.00
DP 11 (Being tagged by Hardie Henderson.) — 1,600 725.00 400.00

(372) Hip Perrier 1
372 (a) (San Francisco)(VALUE UNDETERMINED)

(373) Pat Pettee 4
373 (a) (London) — 3,000 1,500 600.00
373 (b) (Milwaukee) — 800.00 350.00 200.00
DP 18 (About to tag Bobby Lowe.) — 1,400 600.00 350.00

(374) Fred Pfeffer 5
374 (a) (Chicago NL) — 1,300 650.00 400.00

(375) Dick Phelan 5
375 (a) (Des Moines) — 800.00 350.00 200.00

(376) Bill Phillips 7
376 (a) (Brooklyn, large photo.) — 1,400 600.00 350.00
376 (b) (Brooklyn, mini photo.) — 5,175 2,325 1,300
376 (c) (Kansas City) — 800.00 350.00 200.00

(377) John Pickett 12
377 (a) (Kansas City) — 800.00 350.00 200.00
377 (b) (Philadelphia PL) — 900.00 400.00 225.00
377 (c) (St. Paul) — 800.00 350.00 200.00

(378) George Pinkney (Pinckney) 5
378 (a) (Brooklyn) — 800.00 350.00 200.00

(379) Tom Poorman (Also: Poor Man, Porrman) 7
379 (a) (Milwaukee) — 800.00 350.00 200.00
379 (b) (Philadelphia AA) — 800.00 350.00 200.00

(380) Henry Porter 7
380 (a) (Brooklyn) — 1,100 550.00 350.00
380 (b) (Kansas City) — 1,125 500.00 275.00

(381) Jim Powell 5
381 (a) (Sioux City) — 900.00 400.00 250.00
DP 14 (w/ Honest John Kelly.) — 1,600 725.00 400.00

(382) Thomas Powers (Power) 1
382 (a) (San Francisco)(VALUE UNDETERMINED)

(383) Blondie Purcell 7
383 (b) (Baltimore) — 800.00 350.00 200.00
383 (b) (Philadelphia AA) — 800.00 350.00 200.00

(384) Tom Quinn 5
384 (a) (Baltimore) — 950.00 475.00 300.00

(385) Joe Quinn 3
385 (a) (Boston NL) — 1,400 600.00 350.00
385 (b) (Des Moines) — 800.00 350.00 200.00

(386) Old Hoss Radbourn
SEE HALL OF FAME SECTION FOLLOWING

(387) Paul Radford 8
387 (a) (Brooklyn) — 800.00 350.00 200.00
387 (b) (Cleveland) — 800.00 350.00 200.00

(388) Tom Ramsey 3
388 (a) (Louisville) — 1,050 450.00 300.00

(389) Rehse 5
389 (a) (Minneapolis) — 800.00 350.00 200.00

(390) Charlie Reilly (Also: Riley) 4
390 (a) (St. Paul) — 800.00 350.00 200.00

(391) Long John Reilly 3
391 (a) (Cincinnati) — 1,050 450.00 250.00
DP 16 (Side by side w/ Hugh Nicol.) — 2,300 1,125 575.00
DP 17 (Facing Hugh Nicol.) — 2,600 1,150 625.00

(392) Charlie Reynolds 4
392 (a) (Kansas City) — 800.00 350.00 200.00

(393) Danny Richardson (Also: Richards) 5
393 (a) (New York NL) — 800.00 350.00 200.00
393 (b) (New York PL) — 2,700 1,200 600.00
DP 12 (Being tagged by Tim Keefe) — 2,600 1,150 625.00
DP 13 (Sliding, Tim Keefe fielding ball.) — 4,250 2,150 1,300

(394) Hardy Richardson 5
394 (a) (Boston NL) — 800.00 350.00 200.00
394 (b) (Detroit) — 800.00 350.00 200.00

(395) Charlie Ripslager (Reipschlager) 1
395 (a) (New York AA "dotted tie") — 9,000 4,050 2,250

(396) John Roach 6
396 (a) (New York NL) — 800.00 400.00 250.00

(397) M.C. Robinson 6
397 (a) (Minneapolis) — 800.00 350.00 200.00

(398) Wilbert Robinson

SEE HALL OF FAME
SECTION FOLLOWING

(399)   Yank Robinson 6
399 (a) (St. Louis AA "Brown's
        Champions")   1,500   675.00   375.00
399 (b) (St. Louis AA)   800.00 350.00 200.00

(400)   George Rooks 6
400 (a) (Chicago Maroons WA)   1,050   450.00   250.00
400 (b) (Detroit)   800.00 350.00 200.00
        (Never played for Detroit.)

(401)   Chief Roseman 1
401 (a) (New York AA "dotted tie") 7,850 3,525 1,950

        Rourke - See Tom O'Rourke

(402)   Dave Rowe 8
402 (a) (Denver)   1,600   725.00   400.00
402 (b) (Kansas City, portrait.) 6,325 2,850   1,600
402 (c) (Kansas City)   1,050   450.00   250.00

(403)   Jack Rowe 3
403 (a) (Detroit)   875.00 400.00 225.00

(404)   Amos Rusie (Also: Russie)
        SEE HALL OF FAME
        SECTION FOLLOWING

(405)   Jimmy Ryan 8
405 (a) (Chicago NL)   1,000   500.00   300.00
405 (b) (Chicago PL)   2,700   1,200   600.00
405 (c) (Philadelphia)(Never player 800.00 350.00 200.00
        for Phila.)

(406)   Harry Sage 6
406 (a) (Des Moines)   800.00 350.00 200.00
406 (b) (Toledo)   1,750   800.00   425.00
DP 19 (W/ Bill Van Dyke.) (Des 1,150 500.00   300.00
        Moines)
DP 20 (W/ Bill Van Dyke.) (Toledo) 1,150 500.00 300.00

(407)   Ben Sanders 5
407 (a) (Philadelphia NL)   800.00 350.00 200.00
407 (b) (Philadelphia PL)   2,700   1,200   600.00

(408)   Frank Scheibeck 4
408 (a) (Detroit)   850.00 375.00 200.00

(409)   Al Schellhase 5
409 (a) (St. Joseph)   900.00 400.00 250.00

(410)   Bill Schenkel (Also:
        Schenkle) 4
410 (a) (Milwaukee)   800.00 350.00 200.00

(411)   L. Schildknecht 4
411 (a) (Des Moines)   800.00 350.00 200.00
411 (b) (Milwaukee)   800.00 350.00 200.00

(412)   Gus Schmelz 2
412 (a) (Cincinnati)   1,800   775.00   425.00

        Schoch - See Shoch

(413)   Jumbo Schoeneck 8
413 (a) (Chicago Maroons WA)   1,300   650.00   400.00
413 (b) (Indianapolis)   800.00 350.00 200.00

(414)   Pop Schriver 5
414 (a) (Philadelphia NL)   800.00 350.00 200.00
DP 2   (Tagging Charlie Bastian.) 1,150 500.00 300.00

        Schwartwood - See
        Swartwood

(415)   Emmett Seery 4
415 (a) (Indianapolis)   800.00 350.00 200.00

(416)   Billy Serad 5
416 (a) (Cincinnati)   800.00 350.00 200.00
416 (b) (Toronto)   850.00 375.00 200.00

(417)   Ed Seward 3
417 (a) (Philadelphia AA)   1,600   800.00   450.00

(418)   Orator Shafer (Shaffer) 4
418 (a) (Des Moines)   800.00 350.00 200.00

(419)   Taylor Shafer (Shaffer) 3
419 (a) (St. Louis Whites WA)   800.00 350.00 200.00
419 (b) (St. Paul)   800.00 350.00 200.00

(420)   Daniel Shannon (Also:
        Hannon) 6
420 (a) (Louisville)   800.00 350.00 200.00
420 (b) (Omaha)   800.00 350.00 200.00
420 (c) (Philadelphia PL)   2,700   1,200   600.00

(421)   Bill Sharsig 1
421 (a) (Philadelphia AA)   800.00 350.00 200.00

(422)   John Shaw 5
422 (a) (Minneapolis)   800.00 350.00 200.00

(423)   Samuel Shaw 4
423 (a) (Baltimore)   1,050   450.00   250.00
423 (b) (Newark)   1,150   500.00   300.00

(424)   Bill Shindle (Also: Shindel) 7
424 (a) (Baltimore)   850.00 375.00 200.00
424 (b) (Philadelphia PL)   3,300   1,500   825.00
        ("PL" not on card.)

(425)   George Shoch
        (Also: Schoch) 4
425 (a) (Washington)   800.00 350.00 200.00

DP 21 (Batting, John Gaffney   1,150   500.00   300.00
        behind.)

(426)   Otto Shomberg
        (Schomberg) 3
426 (a) (Indianapolis)   800.00 350.00 200.00

(427)   Lev Shreve 7
427 (a) (Indianapolis)   800.00 350.00 200.00

(428)   Ed Silch 8
428 (a) (Brooklyn)   800.00 350.00 200.00
428 (b) (Denver)   900.00 450.00 250.00

(429)   Mike Slattery 6
429 (a) (New York NL)   1,100   550.00   350.00
429 (b) (New York PL)   2,700   1,200   600.00

(430)   Elmer Smith 5
430 (a) (Cincinnati)   800.00 350.00 200.00

(431)   Fred Smith 5
431 (a) (Des Moines)   800.00 350.00 200.00

(432)   Germany (Geo.) Smith 5
432 (a) (Brooklyn)   800.00 350.00 200.00

(433)   Nick Smith 5
433 (a) (St. Joseph)   900.00 450.00 300.00

(434)   Phenomenal Smith 10
434 (a) (Baltimore)   900.00 450.00 300.00
434 (b) (Baltimore, portrait.) 9,775 4,400   2,450
        (No team designation.)
434 (c) (Philadelphia AA)   1,750   875.00   550.00

(435)   Pop Smith 5
435 (a) (Boston NL)   775.00 350.00 200.00
435 (b) (Pittsburgh)   1,100   550.00   350.00

(436)   Skyrocket (Sam) Smith 4
436 (a) (Louisville)   800.00 350.00 200.00

(437)   Pete Somers 5
437 (a) (St. Louis AA)   800.00 350.00 200.00
        (Never played for St. Louis.)

(438)   Joe Sommer (Also:
        Sommers) 5
438 (a) (Baltimore)   1,050   450.00   250.00

(439)   Pete Sommers 7
439 (a) (Chicago NL)   800.00 350.00 200.00
439 (b) (New York NL)   800.00 350.00 200.00

(440)   Bill Sowders 7
440 (a) (Boston NL)   800.00 350.00 200.00

(441)   John Sowders 4
441 (a) (Kansas City)   850.00 425.00 275.00
441 (b) (St. Paul)   800.00 350.00 200.00

(442)   Charlie Sprague 9
442 (a) (Chicago NL)   850.00 425.00 250.00
442 (b) (Chicago Maroons WA)   1,050   450.00   250.00
442 (c) (Cleveland)   800.00 400.00 250.00

(443)   Ed Sproat 5
443 (a) (St. Louis Whites WA)   975.00 425.00 250.00

(444)   Harry Staley (Also: Stoley) 7
444 (a) (Pittsburgh)   800.00 350.00 200.00
444 (b) (St. Louis Whites WA)   900.00 450.00 300.00

(445)   Dan Stearns (Also: Tearns) 4
445 (a) (Des Moines)   800.00 350.00 200.00
445 (b) (Kansas City)   1,000   500.00   300.00

(446)   Bill Stemmeyer
        (Also: Stemmyer) 6
446 (a) (Boston NL)   800.00 350.00 200.00
446 (b) (Cleveland)   1,050   450.00   250.00

(447)   B.F. Stephens 3
447 (a) (Milwaukee)   800.00 350.00 200.00

(448)   John Sterling 4
448 (a) (Minneapolis)   800.00 350.00 200.00

(449)   Len Stockwell 1
449 (a) (San Francisco)
        (Value Undetermined)

        Stoley - See Staley

(450)   Harry Stovey 9
450 (a) (Boston PL)   2,700   1,200   600.00
450 (b) (Philadelphia AA)   1,600   725.00   400.00

(451)   Scott Stratton 5
451 (a) (Louisville)   800.00 350.00 200.00

(452)   Joe Strauss (Also: Straus) 8
452 (a) (Milwaukee)   800.00 350.00 200.00
452 (b) (Omaha)   1,600   800.00   500.00

(453)   Cub Stricker 3
453 (a) (Cleveland)   800.00 350.00 200.00

(454)   Marty Sullivan 7
454 (a) (Chicago NL)   800.00 350.00 200.00
454 (b) (Indianapolis)   800.00 350.00 200.00

(455)   Mike Sullivan 3
455 (a) (Philadelphia AA)   800.00 350.00 200.00

(457)   Billy Sunday 10
457 (a) (Chicago NL)   2,350   1,200   725.00

(457) (b) (Pittsburgh)   1,800   775.00   425.00

(458)   Sy Sutcliffe 5
458 (a) (Cleveland)   900.00 400.00 250.00

(459)   Ezra Sutton 8
459 (a) (Boston NL)   800.00 350.00 200.00
459 (b) (Milwaukee)   850.00 425.00 275.00

(460)   Ed Swartwood
        (Also: Schwartwood) 7
460 (a) (Brooklyn)   800.00 350.00 200.00
460 (b) (Des Moines)   800.00 350.00 200.00
460 (c) (Hamilton)   950.00 475.00 325.00

(461)   Park Swartzel 6
461 (a) (Kansas City)   800.00 350.00 200.00

(462)   Pete Sweeney
        (Also: Sweeny) 5
462 (a) (Washington)   1,050   450.00   250.00

(463)   Louis Sylvester 1
463 (a) (Sacramento)
        (Value Undetermined)

(464)   Pop Tate 6
464 (a) (Baltimore)   800.00 350.00 200.00
464 (b) (Boston NL)   800.00 350.00 200.00

(465)   Patsy (Oliver) Tebeau 8
465 (a) (Chicago NL)   800.00 350.00 200.00
465 (b) (Cleveland)   950.00 475.00 325.00

        Tearns - See Stearns

(466)   John Tener 5
466 (a) (Chicago NL)   1,425   650.00   350.00

(467)   Adonis Terry 5
467 (a) (Brooklyn)   900.00 450.00 300.00

(468)   Sam Thompson
        See Hall of Fame Section Following

(469)   Mike Tiernan 6
469 (a) (New York NL)   800.00 350.00 200.00

(470)   Cannonball Titcomb 5
470 (a) (New York NL)   800.00 350.00 200.00

(471)   Phil Tomney 4
471 (a) (Louisville)   800.00 350.00 200.00

(472)   Steve Toole 7
472 (a) (Brooklyn)   850.00 375.00 225.00
472 (b) (Kansas City)   800.00 350.00 200.00
472 (c) (Rochester)   900.00 450.00 300.00

(473)   George Townsend 3
473 (a) (Philadelphia AA)   800.00 350.00 200.00

(474)   Bill Traffley 4
474 (a) (Des Moines)   800.00 350.00 200.00

(475)   George Treadway
        (Also: Tredway) 6
475 (a) (Denver)   1,000   500.00   300.00
475 (b) (St. Paul)   850.00 450.00 275.00

(476)   Sam Trott 10
476 (a) (Baltimore)   800.00 350.00 200.00
476 (b) (Newark)   800.00 350.00 200.00
DP 22 (Tagging Oyster Burns.) 1,150   500.00   300.00

(477)   Tommy Tucker 5
477 (a) (Baltimore)   1,400   600.00   350.00
DP 8   (Being tagged by Chris 3,000   1,500   1,000
        Fulmer.)

(478)   A.M. Tuckerman 5
478 (a) (St. Paul)   800.00 350.00 200.00

(479)   George Turner 5
479 (a) (Minneapolis)   800.00 350.00 200.00

(480)   Larry Twitchell 6
480 (a) (Cleveland)   800.00 350.00 200.00
480 (b) (Detroit)   800.00 350.00 200.00

(481)   Jim Tyng 4
481 (a) (Philadelphia NL)   800.00 350.00 200.00

(482)   Bill Van Dyke 3
482 (a) (Des Moines)   800.00 350.00 200.00
482 (b) (Toledo)   800.00 350.00 200.00
DP 19 (W/ Harry Sage.)   1,150   500.00   300.00
        (Des Moines)
DP 20 (W/ Harry Sage.) (Toledo) 1,150 500.00 300.00

(483)   George Van Haltren 4
483 (a) (Chicago NL)   1,725   875.00   525.00

(484)   Farmer Vaughn 7
484 (a) (Louisville)   800.00 350.00 200.00
484 (b) (New York PL)   2,700   1,200   600.00

(485)   Peek-A-Boo Veach 4
485 (a) (Sacramento)
        (Value Undetermined)
485 (b) (St. Paul)   800.00 350.00 200.00

(486)   Leon Viau 5
486 (a) (Cincinnati)   800.00 400.00 275.00

(487)   Bill Vinton 4
487 (a) (Minneapolis)   800.00 350.00 200.00

		NM	EX	VG
(488)	Joe Visner 5			
488 (a)	(Brooklyn)	800.00	350.00	200.00
(489)	Chris Von Der Ahe 1			
489 (a)	St. Louis AA "Brown's Champions")	5,500	2,750	1,650
(490)	Reddy Walsh 5			
490 (a)	(Omaha)	850.00	375.00	225.00
(491)	John Ward 5			
	See Hall of Fame Section Following			
(492)	Ed Warner 2			
492 (a)	(Milwaukee)	800.00	350.00	200.00
DP 5	(W/ Jack Horner.)	1,150	500.00	300.00
	Wassitt - See Messitt			
(493)	Bill Watkins 2			
493 (a)	(Detroit)	800.00	350.00	200.00
493 (b)	(Kansas City)	900.00	400.00	250.00
(494)	Farmer Weaver 4			
494 (a)	(Louisville)	1,800	900.00	450.00
(495)	Charlie Weber 5			
495 (a)	(Sioux City)	900.00	400.00	250.00
(496)	Stump Weidman (Wiedman) 4			
496 (a)	(Detroit)	800.00	350.00	200.00
(497)	Wild Bill Weidner (Widner) 5			
497 (a)	(Columbus)	900.00	400.00	250.00
(498)	Curt Welch (Also: Welsh) 7			
498 (a)	(St. Louis AA "Brown's Champions")	1,875	850.00	475.00
498 (b)	(Philadelphia AA)	800.00	350.00	200.00
DP 23	(W/ Bill Gleason.)	2,300	1,050	575.00
(499)	Mickey Welch (Also: Welsh)			
	See Hall of Fame Section Following			
(500)	Jake Wells 2			
500 (a)	(Kansas City)	1,325	600.00	325.00
(501)	Frank Wells 1			
501 (a)	(Milwaukee)	850.00	375.00	225.00
(502)	Joe Werrick 5			
502 (a)	(Louisville)	800.00	350.00	200.00
502 (b)	(St. Paul)	975.00	450.00	250.00
(503)	Buck West 5			
503 (a)	(Minneapolis)	850.00	375.00	225.00
(504)	Gus Weyhing 3			
504 (a)	(Philadelphia AA)	800.00	350.00	200.00
(505)	John Weyhing 4			
505 (a)	(Columbus)	800.00	350.00	200.00
505 (b)	(Philadelphia AA) (Never played for Phila.)	1,100	500.00	300.00
(506)	Bobby Wheelock 9			
506 (a)	(Boston NL)	800.00	350.00	200.00
506 (b)	(Detroit) (Never played for Detroit.)	800.00	350.00	200.00
506 (c)	(Photo actually Con Daily.)	800.00	350.00	200.00
(508)	Pat Whitaker (Also: Whitacre) 7			
508 (a)	(Baltimore)	800.00	350.00	200.00
508 (b)	(Philadelphia AA) (Never played for Philadelphia.)	800.00	350.00	200.00
(509)	Bill White 5			
509 (a)	(Louisville)	800.00	350.00	200.00
(510)	Deacon White 10			
510 (a)	(Detroit)	1,550	700.00	375.00
510 (b)	(Pittsburgh)	800.00	350.00	200.00
(511)	Art Whitney 7			
511 (a)	(New York NL)	800.00	350.00	200.00
511 (b)	(New York PL)	2,700	1,200	600.00
511 (c)	(Pittsburgh)	800.00	350.00	200.00
511 (d)	(W/dog.)	4,800	2,150	1,200
(512)	G. Whitney 5			
512 (a)	(St. Joseph)	850.00	375.00	225.00
(513)	Jim Whitney 4			
513 (a)	(Indianapolis)	800.00	350.00	200.00
513 (b)	(Washington)	950.00	475.00	300.00
	E. Williams, W. Williams - See Ned Williamson			
(514)	Jimmy Williams 2			
514 (a)	(Cleveland)	1,050	450.00	250.00
(515)	Ned Williamson 8			
515 (a)	(Chicago NL)	1,250	625.00	400.00
515 (c)	(in dress clothes)	5,175	2,325	1,300
515 (c)	(Chicago PL)	3,000	1,350	750.00
DP 24	(W/ Willie Hahn. (Mascot)	4,000	1,800	1,200
(516)	Tit Willis 5			
516 (a)	(Omaha)	800.00	350.00	200.00
(517)	Walt Wilmot 8			
517 (a)	(Chicago NL)	800.00	350.00	200.00
517 (b)	(Washington)	800.00	400.00	250.00

		NM	EX	VG
(518)	George Winkleman (Winkelman) 4			
518 (a)	(Hartford)	2,500	400.00	225.00
518 (b)	(Minneapolis)	2,500	400.00	225.00
(519)	Sam Wise 5			
519 (a)	(Boston NL)	2,000	1,000	600.00
519 (b)	(Washington)	800.00	350.00	200.00
(520)	Chicken Wolf 5			
520 (a)	(Louisville)	750.00	325.00	200.00
(521)	George Wood 5 (L.F.)			
521 (a)	(Philadelphia NL)	800.00	350.00	200.00
521 (b)	(Philadelphia PL)	2,700	1,200	600.00
(522)	Pete Wood 5 (P)			
522 (a)	(Philadelphia NL)	875.00	400.00	225.00
(523)	Harry Wright 5			
	See Hall of Fame Section Following			
(524)	Chief Zimmer 4			
524 (a)	(Cleveland)	800.00	400.00	225.00
(525)	Frank Zinn 3			
525 (a)	(Philadelphia AA)	800.00	350.00	200.00

1887-1890 Old Judge Hall of Famers Pose Variations

Because of the popularity of collecting Old Judge cards of Hall of Famers, and the sometimes widely varying market values of different poses for those players, this appendix lists each known pose and/or caption variation. These listings disregard the presence, absence or placement of Old Judge advertising within the photo area. Caption variations consider only those machine-printed captions outside of the photo area.

		NM	EX	VG
(11)	Cap Anson			
11 (a)	Street Clothes			
	(A.C. ANSON, Chicago's.)	11,000	5,500	3,300
	(Chicago's.)	10,200	4,600	2,550
	(ANSON, CAPT., Chicagos (N L)	15,000	6,750	3,750
11 (b)	In Uniform			
	(Chicago N L)	250,000	75,000	40,000
(25)	Jake Beckley			
25 (a)	Pittsburgh			
	(Batting, "O" just visible on jersey, Pittsburghs.)	5,400	2,430	1,350
	(Batting, "O" just visible on jersey, Pittsburgs.)	5,400	2,425	1,350
	(Fielding, ball knee-high, "BECKLEY, 1st B., Pittsburgs.")	5,400	2,430	1,350
	(Fielding, hands neck-high, Pittsburgh.)	5,400	2,430	1,350
	(Fielding, hands neck-high, "J. BECKLEY, 1st B., Pittsburghs.")	7,800	3,500	1,950
	(Fielding, hands neck-high, Pittsburgs.)	5,400	2,430	1,350
25 (b)	St. Louis Whites			
	(Batting, "O" just visible on jersey.)	7,800	3,500	1,950
	(Batting, "TLO" visible on jersey.)	7,800	3,500	1,950
	(Fielding, ball knee-high, "J. BECKLEY, 1st B., St. Louis Whites.")	10,200	4,600	2,550
	(Fielding, hands neck-high, "J. BECKLEY.")	6,000	2,700	1,500
(43)	Dan Brouthers			
43 (a)	Boston, N.L.			
	(Bat at ready, looking to right, "1st B., Bostons.")	3,600	1,620	900.00
	(Fielding, Brouthers on front, Bostons.)	3,120	1,400	780.00
43 (b)	Boston, P.L.			
	(Pose unrecorded.)	7,200	3,240	1,800
43 (c)	Detroit			
	(Bat at ready, looking down at ball.)	4,800	2,160	1,200
	(Bat at ready, looking to right, "1st B., Detroits.")	4,500	2,000	1,125

		NM	EX	VG
	(Fielding, "BROUTHERS, 1st B. Detroits.")	5,100	2,280	1,260
	(Fielding, "D. BROUTHERS.")	4,800	2,160	1,200
(78)	John Clarkson			
78 (a)	Boston			
	(Batting, Bostons.)	2,280	1,025	570.00
	(Right arm forward, left hand on thigh, Boston.)	2,280	1,025	570.00
	(Right arm forward, left hand on thigh, "P., Bostons.")	2,280	1,025	570.00
	(Right arm back, left hand clear of thigh, "P., Bostons.")	3,300	1,470	825.00
	(Right hand hip-high, Bostons.)	1,620	725.00	400.00
78 (b)	Chicago			
	(Ball in hands at chest, "P. Chicago.")	3,000	1,350	750.00
	(Batting, "P. Chicago.")	3,600	1,620	900.00
	(Fielding, hands head-high, "P. Chicago.")	3,600	1,620	900.00
	(Right arm forward, left hand on thigh, "P. Chicago.")	4,080	1,830	1,020
	(Right arm back, left hand clear of thigh, "P. Chicago.")	3,000	1,350	750.00
	(Right arm back, left hand on thigh, "P. Chicago.")	3,000	1,350	750.00
	(Right hand hip-high, "P. Chicago.")	3,000	1,350	750.00
(86)	Charlie Comiskey			
86 (a)	St. Louis Browns ("Brown's Champions")	9,500	4,750	2,850
86 (b)	St. Louis Browns (Arms folded.)	.00	.00	.00
	(Arms folded.)	5,100	2,300	1,275
	(Batting, "COMISKEY, Capt. St. Louis Browns.")	8,000	4,000	2,400
	(Fielding, hands head-high, "CHAS. COMISKEY, 1st B., Capt. St. Louis Browns.")	5,100	2,280	1,260
	(Fielding, hands shoulder-high, "COMISKEY, Capt. St. Louis.")	5,100	2,280	1,260
	(Fielding, hands shoulder-high, "C. COMMISKEY, 1st B., St. L. B's.")	4,800	2,160	1,200
	(Sliding, "CHAS. COMISKEY, 1st B., Capt. St. Louis Brown.")	4,800	2,160	1,200
	(Sliding, "COMISKEY, Capt., St. Louis.")	4,800	2,160	1,200
86 (c)	Chicago, P.L. (Arms folded, "COMMISKEY, 1st B., Chicagos.")	24,000	10,800	6,000
(88)	Roger Connor			
88 (a)	New York, N.L.			
	(Batter's box on floor, script name.)	6,900	3,100	1,700
	(Bat on shoulder, name in script.)	6,900	3,100	1,700
	(Bat on shoulder, N Y's.)	5,100	2,400	1,200
	(Fielding, "B. CONNOR," New Yorks.)	5,100	2,400	1,200
	(Fielding, hands at waist, "CONNER, 1st B., New Yorks.")	5,100	2,400	1,200
	(Hands on knees, name in script.)	6,900	3,100	1,700
	(Hands on knees, New York.)	4,800	2,160	1,200
	(Hands on knees, New Yorks.)	4,800	2,160	1,200
	(Hands on knees, N Y's.)	4,800	2,160	1,200
(124)	Ed Delahanty			
124 (a)	Philadelphia			
	(Bat on right shoulder, "2d B., Phila.")	14,000	10,000	6,000
	(Bat on right shoulder, "2d B., Phila's")	14,000	10,000	6,000
	(Bat nearly horizontal, "2d B., Phila.")	14,000	10,000	6,000
	(Fielding grounder, Phila.)	13,000	9,000	4,800
	(Fielding, hands at waist, "2d B., Phila.")	12,000	7,600	4,200
	(Fielding, hands at waist, Phila's.)	13,000	7,600	4,200
	(Throwing, "2d B., Phila.")	15,000	10,500	5,900
	(Throwing, Phila's.)	15,000	10,500	5,900
(136)	Hugh Duffy			
136 (a)	Chicago, N.L.			
	(Batting, S.S. Chicago.)	4,500	2,250	1,350
	(Batting, "H. DUFFY, S.S., Chicagos.")	4,500	2,250	1,350
	(Batting, "DUFFY, S.S., Chicago's.")	4,500	2,250	1,350
	(Fielding grounder, "H. DUFFY, S.S., Chicago.")	4,500	2,250	1,350
	(Fielding grounder, Chicagos.)	4,500	2,250	1,350
	(Fielding, hands chin-high, right heel behind left leg, Chicago.)	4,500	2,250	1,350
	(Fielding, hands chin-high, right heel behind left leg, Chicagos.)	4,500	2,250	1,350
	(Fielding, hands chin-high, right heel behind left leg, Chicago's.)	4,500	2,250	1,350
	(Fielding, hands neck-high, feet apart, Chicago.)	4,500	2,250	1,350
	(Throwing, right hand head-high, Chicago.)	4,500	2,250	1,350
	(Throwing, right hand head-high, Chicago's.)	4,500	2,250	1,350
136 (b)	Chicago, P.L. (Pose unrecorded.) (Value Undetermined)			

(149) Buck Ewing
149 (a)New York, N.L.

(Bat at 45 degrees, New Yorks.)	3,600	1,800	1,100
(Bat at 45 degrees, N Y's.)	3,600	1,800	1,100
(Bat in hand at side, New Yorks.)	3,600	1,800	1,100
(Bat nearly horizontal, Capt. New Yorks.)	3,600	1,800	1,100
(Bat nearly horizontal, Captain, New Yorks.)	3,600	1,800	1,100
(Fielding grounder, "BUCK EWING, Capt., New Yorks.")	3,600	1,800	1,100
(Fielding grounder, "EWING, C., New Yorks.")	3,600	1,800	1,100
(Fielding, hands head-high, New Yorks.)	3,600	1,800	1,100
(Fielding, hands head-high, N Y's.)	3,600	1,800	1,100
(Hands on knees, C. New Yorks.)	3,600	1,800	900.00
(Hands on knees, Captain, New Yorks.)	3,600	1,800	900.00
(Hands on knees, Capt. N Y's.)	3,600	1,800	900.00
(Running to left, C., New Yorks.)	3,600	1,620	900.00
(Running to left, Captain, New Yorks.)	3,600	1,620	900.00
(Sliding, C., New York.)	3,600	1,620	900.00
(Sliding, C., New Yorks.)	3,600	1,620	900.00
(Sliding, Capt., New Y's.)	3,600	1,620	900.00
(Throwing, right arm forward, C., New Yorks.)	4,200	1,900	1,050
(Throwing, right arm forward, Captain, New Yorks.)	4,200	1,900	1,050
(Throwing, right hand waist-high at side, "EWING, Captain, New Yorks.")	4,800	2,160	1,200

149 (b)New York, P.L.

(Hands on knees, C. New York.(PL)	7,800	3,500	1,950

149 (c)With mascot Willie Breslin.

("EWING & MASCOT, New Yorks")	.00	.00	.00
	7,500	3,750	2,250
(N. Y's)	7,500	3,750	2,250

149 (c)"EWING, MASCOT New York P L" (A Fair-Good example sold at auction 5/05 for $7,475.)

(179) Pud Galvin
179 (a)Pittsburg

(Arms at sides, P. Pittsburg.)	5,400	2,430	1,350
(Arms at sides, P. Pittsburgs.)	5,400	2,430	1,350
(Arms at sides, P. Pittsburgh.)	5,400	2,430	1,350
(Arms at sides, Pitcher.)	5,400	2,430	1,350
(Ball in hands above waist, P.)	4,500	2,000	1,125
(Ball in hands above waist, Pitcher.)	4,500	2,000	1,125
(Bat at ready, P.)	5,000	2,500	1,500
(Bat at ready, Pitcher.)	5,000	2,500	1,500
(Bat in hand at side, "GALVIN, P. Pittsburg.")	11,000	5,500	3,300
(Bat in hand at side, "GALVIN, Pitcher Pittsburg.")	9,000	4,500	2,800
(Bat in hand at side "GALVIN, P., Pittsburgs.")	9,000	4,500	2,800
(Bat in hand at side, "J. GALVIN, P., Pittsburghs.")	9,000	4,500	2,800
(Bat in hand at side, "JIM GALVIN.")	9,000	4,500	2,800

(204) Clark Griffith
204 (a)Milwaukee

(Ball in hands at chest.)	5,500	2,750	1,650
(Batting, looking at ball.)	5,500	2,750	1,650
(Batting, looking at camera, Milwaukee.)	5,500	2,750	1,650
(Batting, looking at camera, Milwaukees.)	6,000	3,000	1,800
(Pitching, hands at neck, Milwaukees.)	5,500	2,750	1,650
(Pitching, right hand head-high, Milwaukees.)	5,500	2,750	1,650

(213) Billy Hamilton
213 (a)Kansas City

(Batting, looking at camera, Kansas Citys.)	4,500	2,250	1,350
(Batting, looking up at ball, "L.F. KANSAS CITYS.")	4,500	2,250	1,350
(Batting, looking up at ball, K.C.s.)	4,500	2,250	1,350
(Fielding grounder.)	4,500	2,250	1,350
(Fielding, hands above waist, "L.F. Kansas Citys.")	4,500	2,250	1,350
(Fielding, hands neck-high, "L.F. Kansas Citys.")	4,500	2,250	1,350

213 (b)Philadelphia, N.L.

(Fielding, hands above waist, Philadelphia N.L.)	3,250	1,650	975.00
(Fielding, hands neck-high, Philadelphia N.L.)	3,250	1,650	975.00

(215) Ned Hanlon
215 (a)Boston
(Never played for Boston.)

(Bat in hand at sides, Bostons.)	3,600	1,620	900.00

215 (b)Detroit

(Bat in hand at side, C.F. Detroits.)	3,600	1,620	900.00
(Batting, Detroits.)	3,600	1,620	900.00
(Fielding, Detroits.)	3,600	1,620	900.00

215 (c)Pittsburgh

	.00	.00	.00
(Batting, Pittsburgs.)	3,900	1,620	975.00
(Fielding, C.F., Pittsburghs.)	3,900	1,620	975.00

(256) Tim Keefe
256 (a)New York, N.L.

(Ball in hands, front view, "KEEFE, P., New Yorks.")	3,360	1,500	840.00
(Ball in hands, front view, TIM KEEFE, P. N.Y's.")	3,360	1,500	840.00
(Ball in hands, side view, "JIM KEEFE," New Yorks.)	3,360	1,500	840.00
(Ball in hands, side view "TIM KEEFE," New Yorks.)	3,360	1,500	840.00
(Ball in hands, side view, "TIM KEEFE, P. N.Y's.")	3,360	1,500	840.00
(Bat nearly horizontal, "KEEFE, P., New Yorks.")	3,360	1,500	840.00
(Bat nearly horizontal, "TIM KEEF," New Yorks.)	3,360	1,500	840.00
(Bat nearly horizontal, "TIM KEEFE," New Yorks.")	3,360	1,500	840.00
(Bat nearly horizontal, "TIM KEEFE," N. Y's.)	3,360	1,500	840.00
(Bat nearly vertical, "TIM KEEFE, P. New Yorks.")	3,500	1,750	1,000
(Bat nearly vertical, "TIM...)	3,500	1,750	1,000
(Pitching, right hand at back, "JIM KEEFE," New Yorks.)	3,600	1,620	900.00
(Pitching, right hand at back, "TIM KEEF," New Yorks.)	3,600	1,620	900.00
(Pitching, right hand at back, "TIM KEEFE," New Yorks.)	3,600	1,620	900.00
(Pitching, right hand at back, "TIM KEEFE," N. Y's.)	3,600	1,620	900.00
(Pitching, right hand head-high, "KEEFE P., New Yorks.")	3,600	1,620	900.00
(Pitching, right hand head-high, "TIM KEEFE, P. N. Y's.")	3,600	1,620	900.00
(Pitching, right hand waist-high, "KEEFE, P., New Yorks.")	2,880	1,300	720.00
(Pitching, right hand waist-high, "TIM KEEFE, P. N.Y's.")	2,880	1,300	720.00

256 (b)New York, P.L.
(Pose unrecorded.) (VALUE UNDETERMINED)

DP 12 Tagging Danny Richardson.

("KEEFE, P., New Yorks")	2,700	1,225	675.00
("Keefe & Richardson")	2,700	1,200	675.00
("Keefe and Richardson Stealing 2d, N.Y's")	2,700	1,200	675.00

DP 13 Fielding Ball, Danny Richardson Sliding.

("Keefe and Richardson Stealing 2d, N.Y's")	4,250	2,100	1,300

(261) King Kelly
261 (a)Chicago

(Bat at 45 degrees, left-handed, "$10,000 KELLY" Chicago on jersey.)	8,750	4,400	2,600
(Portrait, bare head, "$10,000 KELLY," Chicago on jersey.)	9,300	3,970	2,300
(Portrait in cap, "$10,000 KELLY," Chicago on jersey.)	7,800	3,500	1,950

261 (b)Boston, N.L.

(Bat at 45 degrees, "$10,000 KELLY.")	9,000	4,500	2,700
(Bat at 45 degrees, no position, Boston.)	6,000	2,700	1,500
(Bat at 45 degrees, "Kelly, C., Boston.")	4,800	2,160	1,200
(Bat at 45 degrees, "Kelly, C., Bostons.")	4,800	2,160	1,200
(Bat horizontal, "$10,000 KELLY.")	7,250	3,600	2,200
(Bat in left hand at side, "$10,000 KELLY.")	6,000	2,700	1,500
(Bat on right shoulder, "$10,000 KELLY.")	7,200	3,240	1,800
(Fielding, hands chest-high, "$10,000 KELLY.")	6,000	2,700	1,500
(Fielding, hands head-high, "$10,000 KELLY.")	6,000	2,700	1,500
(Portrait, bare head, "$10,000 KELLY," Boston on jersey.)	11,400	5,130	2,850

261 (c)Boston, P.L.
(Bat at 45 degrees, no position, Boston. (PL) (Value Undetermined)

(290) Connie Mack
290 (a)Washington

(Batting, C.)	10,800	4,860	2,700
(Batting, Catcher.)	10,800	4,860	2,700
(Stooping, hands on knees, C. Washington.)	10,800	4,860	2,700
(Stooping, hands on knees, Catcher.)	10,800	4,860	2,700
(Throwing, C.)	10,800	4,860	2,700
(Throwing, Catcher, "C. MACK.")	10,800	4,860	2,700
(Throwing, Catcher, "MACK.")	10,800	4,860	2,700

(307) Tommy McCarthy
307 (a)Philadelphia, N.L.

(Batting, indoor background, "2d B. Phila.")	4,200	1,900	1,050
(Batting, indoor background, "McCARTHY, Second Base, Philadelphia.")	4,200	1,900	1,050
(Fielding, hands chest-high, "McCARTHY, 2d B. Phila.")	5,400	2,430	1,350
(Fielding, hands chest-high, Philadelphia.)	5,400	2,430	1,350
(Sliding, indoor background, 2d B. Phila.)	4,800	2,160	1,200
(Sliding, Philadelphia.)	4,800	2,160	1,200
(Tagging player, Phila.)	4,200	1,900	1,050
(Tagging player, Philadelphia.)	4,200	1,900	1,050
(Throwing, 2d B. Phila.)	4,200	1,900	1,050
(Throwing, Philadelphia.)	4,200	1,900	1,050

307 (b)St. Louis Browns

	.00	.00	.00
(Batting, indoor background, St. Louis Browns.)	4,250	2,100	1,300
(Batting, outdoor background, St. Louis.)	4,250	2,100	1,300
(Batting, outdoor background, St. Louis Browns.)	4,250	2,100	1,300
(Fielding, hands chest-high, 2d B. St. Louis.)	4,250	2,100	1,300
(Fielding, hands chest-high, C.F.)	4,250	2,100	1,300
(Fielding, hands head-high, "TOMMY CARTHY," St. Louis Brown.)	4,250	2,100	1,300
(Fielding, hands head-high, "TOMMY McCARTHY," St. Louis Brown.)	4,250	2,100	1,300
(Fielding, hands head-high, "cCARTHY, C. F. St. Louis Brown.")	4,250	2,100	1,300
(Fielding, hands head-high, "TOMMY McCARTHY" St. Louis Browns.)	4,250	2,100	1,300
(Fielding, hands head-high, "T. McCARTHY, C.F., St. Louis Browns.)	4,250	2,100	1,300
(Sliding, indoor background, "McCARTHY, 2d B. St. Louis.")	4,250	2,100	1,300
(Sliding, indoor background, C.F., St. Louis.)	4,250	2,100	1,300
(Sliding, outdoor background, St. Louis.)	4,250	2,100	1,300
(Sliding, outdoor background, C.F. St. Louis Browns.)	4,250	2,100	1,300
(Tagging player, 2d B.)	4,250	2,100	1,300
(Tagging player, C.F.)	4,250	2,100	1,300
(Throwing, "T. McCARTHY," St. Louis.)	4,500	2,250	1,350
(Throwing, "T. McCARTHY," St. Louis Browns.)	4,500	2,250	1,350
(Throwing, "McCARTHY," St. Louis Browns.)	4,500	2,250	1,350
(Throwing, "McCARTHY, C.F., St. Louis.")	4,500	2,250	1,350

(323) Bid McPhee
323 (a)Cincinnati

(Batting, looking at ball, "McPHEE.")	18,500	9,300	5,550
(Batting, looking at ball, "JOHN McPHEE.")	18,500	9,300	5,550
(Batting, looking at camera, Cincinnati.)	18,500	9,300	5,550
(Batting, looking at camera, Cincinnati. (NL)	18,500	9,300	5,550
(Batting, looking at camera, Cincinnatti.)	18,500	9,300	5,550
(Fielding, hands ankle-high, "McPHEE, 2d B., Cincinnat.")	18,500	9,300	5,550
(Fielding, hands ankle-high, "JOHN McPHEE, 2d B., Cincinnatis.")	18,500	9,300	5,550
(Fielding, hands head-high, "McPHEE, 2d B., Cincinnati.")	18,500	9,300	5,550
(Fielding, hands head-high, "JOHN McPHEE, 2d B. Cincinnatti.")	18,500	9,300	5,550
(Fielding, hands head-high, "McPHEE, 2d B., Cincinnatis.")	18,500	9,300	5,550
(Fielding, hands head-high, Cincinnatti.)	18,500	9,300	5,550
(Throwing, Cincinnati.)	18,500	9,300	5,550
(Throwing, Cincinnatti.)	18,500	9,300	5,550

(349) Kid Nichols
349 (a)Omaha

(Batting, looking at ball, Omaha.)	9,000	4,050	2,250
(Batting, looking at camera, Omaha.)	9,000	4,050	2,250
(Batting, looking at camera, "NICHOLS, P., Omahas.")	9,000	4,050	2,250
(Pitching, hands at chest, Omaha.)	9,000	4,050	2,250
(Pitching, right hand behind back, Omaha.)	9,600	4,320	2,400
(Pitching, right hand behind back, "NICHOLS, P., Omahas.)	9,600	4,320	2,400
(Pitching, right hand forward, P., Omaha.)	9,600	4,320	2,400
(Pitching, right hand forward, P., Omahas.)	9,600	4,320	2,400

(366) Orator Jim O'Rourke
366 (a)New York, N.L.

(Bat in hand at side, C., New Yorks.)	6,000	2,700	1,500
(Bat in hand at side, 3d B., New Yorks.)	6,000	2,700	1,500
(Bat in hand at side, 3d B. N.Y's.)	6,000	2,700	1,500
(Bat in hand at side, 3d B., N. Y's.)	6,000	2,700	1,500
(Batting, 3d B., New Yorks.)	6,000	2,700	1,500
(Batting, 3d B., N. Y's.)	6,000	2,700	1,500
(Fielding, "JIM O'ROURKE, 3d B. N. Y's.")	4,200	1,900	1,050
(Throwing, 3d B., N. Y's.)	4,800	2,160	1,200

(386) Old Hoss Radbourn

386 (a)Boston, N.L.

(Bat on shoulder, P., Boston.)	3,900	1,740	975.00
(Bat on shoulder, P., Bostons.)	3,900	1,750	975.00
(Bat on shoulder, Pitcher, Boston.)	3,900	1,740	975.00
(Bat on shoulder, Pitcher, Bostons.)	3,900	1,740	975.00
(Hands at waist, no space visible between hands and belt, P.)	3,600	1,620	900.00
(Hands at waist, no space visible between hands and belt, Pitcher.)	3,600	1,620	900.00
(Hands at waist, white uniform visible between hands and belt, P.)	4,800	2,160	1,200
(Hands at waist, white uniform visible between hands and belt, Pitcher.)	4,800	2,160	1,200
(Hands on hips, P.)	10,800	4,860	2,700
(Hands on hips, Pitcher.)	10,800	4,860	2,700
(Portrait, P., Boston.)	9,600	4,320	2,400
(Portrait, Pitcher, Boston.)	9,900	4,440	2,430
(Tagging Billy Nash, P., Boston.)	5,400	2,430	1,350
(Tagging Billy Nash, Pitcher.)	5,400	2,430	1,350

386 (b)Boston, P.L.

(Hands on hips, Pitcher, Boston.(PL) (VALUE UNDETERMINED)			

(398) Wilbert Robinson
398 (a)Philadelphia Athletics

(Batting)	4,800	2,150	1,200
(Fielding, hands above head, C. Athletics.)	4,800	2,160	1,200
(Fielding, hands above head, C., Athletics.)	4,800	2,160	1,200
(Fielding, hands neck-high, C. Athletics.)	4,800	2,160	1,200
(Fielding, hands thigh-high.)	4,800	2,160	1,200
(Throwing)	4,800	2,160	1,200

(404) Amos Rusie
404 (a)Indianapolis

(Batting, P., Indianapolis.)	4,200	1,900	1,050
(Pitching, hands at neck.)	4,200	1,900	1,050
(Pitching, right hand forward chin-high.)	4,200	1,900	1,050
(Pitching, right hand head-high to side, "RUSIE, P., Indianapolis.")	7,000	3,500	2,100
(Pitching, right hand head-high to side, "RUSSIE.")	7,000	3,500	2,100
(Ball in right hand, thigh-high "P., Indianapolis.")	9,000	4,500	2,700

404 (b)New York, N.L.

(Pitching, hands at neck, New Yorks.(NL)	.00	.00	.00
(Pitching, right hand forward chin-high, New Yorks.(NL)	24,000	10,800	6,000

(468) Sam Thompson
468 (a)Detroit

(Arms folded, R.F. Detroits.)	3,900	2,000	1,200
(Bat at 45 degrees, Detroits.)	5,000	2,500	1,500
(Bat in hand at side, Detroits.)	4,200	1,900	1,050
(Batting, ball above head, Detroits.)	3,000	1,350	750.00
(Batting, ball chest-high, R.F. Detroits.)	3,000	1,350	750.00

468 (b)Philadelphia, N.L.

(Arms folded, Phil'a.(NL)	.00	.00	.00
	3,000	1,500	900.00
(Bat in hand at side, Philadelphia.)	3,000	1,500	900.00
(Bat in hand at side, R.F., Philadelphias.)	3,000	1,500	900.00
(Bat in hand at side, Phila's.)	3,000	1,500	900.00

(491) John Ward
491 (a)New York, N.L.

(Batting, New Yorks.)	2,880	1,300	720.00
(Batting, "Capt. JOHN WARD, S.S. N Y's.")	2,880	1,300	720.00
(Cap in hand at side, "Capt. JOHN WARD.")	4,200	1,900	1,050
(Cap in hand at side, "J. WARD, S.S., New Yorks.")	4,200	1,900	1,050
(Cap in hand at side, "JOHN WARD.")	4,200	1,900	1,050
(Hands behind back, New Yorks.)	3,000	1,350	750.00
(Hands behind back, "Capt. JOHN WARD, S.S. N. Y's.")	3,000	1,350	750.00
(Hands on hips, "J.M. WARD, S.S. New Yorks.")	4,500	2,000	1,125
(Hands on hips, "Capt. JOHN WARD, S.S. N. Y's.")	6,600	2,970	1,650
(Portrait, "Capt. JOHN WARD.")	5,400	2,430	1,350
(Portrait, "J. WARD, S.S., New Yorks.")	5,400	2,430	1,350
(Portrait, "J.M. WARD, S.S., New Yorks.")	5,400	2,430	1,350
(Sliding, left hand raised, "Capt. JOHN WARD, S.S. N Y's.")	2,640	1,190	660.00
(Sliding, left hand raised, "J.M. WARD, S.S., New Yorks.")	2,640	1,190	660.00
(Sliding, left hand raised, "WARD.")	2,640	1,190	660.00
(Sliding, right hand raised, New Yorks.)	3,000	1,350	750.00
(Sliding, right hand raised, "Capt. JOHN WARD, S.S. N Y's.")	3,000	1,350	750.00

(Throwing, left profile, New Yorks.)	4,200	1,900	1,050
(Throwing, left profile, "Capt. JOHN WARD, S.S. N. Y's.")	4,200	1,900	1,050
(Throwing, right profile, "Capt. JOHN WARD, S.S. N. Y's.")	4,200	1,900	1,050
(Throwing, right profile, "JOHN WARD.")	4,200	1,900	1,050

(499) Mickey Welch
499 (a)New York, N.L.

(Ball in hands above waist, "SMILING MICKEY.")	6,000	3,000	1,800
(Ball in hands above waist, "WELSH.")	6,000	3,000	1,800
(Right arm extended forward, "SMILING MICKEY.")	6,000	3,000	1,800
(Right hand at right thigh, "WELCH," New Yorks.)	6,000	3,000	1,800
(Right hand at right thigh, "WELCH," New Yorks.(NL)	6,000	3,000	1,800
(Right hand at right thigh, "WELSH," New Yorks.)	6,000	3,000	1,800
(Right hand head-high, "WELCH," New York.)	6,000	3,000	1,800
(Right hand head-high, "WELCH," N.Y's.)	6,000	3,000	1,800
(Right hand head-high, "WELCH," New York.)	6,000	3,000	1,800

(523) Harry Wright
523 (a)Philadelphia, N.L.

(Portrait, looking to his right, beard clear of right side of collar, "HARRY WRIGHT, Man'g. Philas.")	18,000	8,100	4,500
(Portrait, looking to his right, beard just over right side of collar, "Mgr., Phila. N L.")	18,000	8,100	4,500
(Portrait, looking to his right, beard just over right side of collar, "Man'g. Phila.")	18,000	8,100	4,500
(Portrait, looking to his right, beard just over right side of collar, "Mgr. Phila's.")	18,000	8,100	4,500
(Portrait, looking to his left, "Man'g. Phila.")	18,000	8,100	4,500
(Portrait, looking to his left, "Man'g. Philas.")	18,000	8,100	4,500
(Portrait, looking to his left, Phila. (NL))	19,200	8,640	4,800
(Portrait, looking to his left, "Mgr. Phila's.")	18,000	8,100	5,400

1888-1889 Old Judge Cabinets (N173)

OLD JUDGE CIGARETTES

These cabinet cards were issued by Goodwin & Co. in 1888-89 as a premium available by exchanging coupons found in Old Judge or Dogs Head brand cigarettes. The cabinet cards consist of approximately 3-3/4" x 5-3/4" photographs affixed to a cardboard backing that measures approximately 4-1/4" x 6-1/2". The mounting is usually pale yellow with gold-leaf trimmings, but backings have also been found in red, blue or black. An ad for Old Judge Cigarettes appears along the bottom of the cabinet. Cabinets obtained by exchanging coupons from Dogs Head cigarettes include an ad for both Old Judge and Dogs Head, and are scarcer. According to an advertising sheet, cabinets were available of "every prominent player in the National League, Western League and American Association." There will continue to be additions to this checklist. This list includes all confirmed photo and team variations; minor differences in spelling of team name, position abbreviations or punctuation are not recorded, except in the case of Hall of Famers. Several Old Judge cabinets are not known to exist in the standard N172 format.

	NM	EX	VG
Common Player:	2,200	1,300	975.00
Black or Colored Mount: 3-5X			
Unlisted Dogs Head: 2-3X			

(4) Bob Allen

4 (a)	Pittsburgh, hands clasped at waist	2,200	1,300	975.00
4 (b)	Pittsburgh, batting, Dogs Head	4,500	2,250	1,350

(7) Varney Anderson

7 (a)	pitching, right hand head-high	2,200	1,300	975.00

(8) Ed Andrews

8 (a)	Philadelphia, both hands shoulder-high	2,200	1,300	975.00

8 (b)	Philadelphia, one hand above head	2,200	1,300	975.00
DP 1	being tagged by Buster Hoover	3,750	2,250	1,625

(9) Wally Andrews

9 (a)	Omaha, hands shoulder-high	2,200	1,300	975.00

(11) Cap Anson

11 (a)	portrait	20,250	12,150	8,700
11 (b)	portrait, Dogs Head	45,000	27,000	18,750

(15) Kid Baldwin

15 (a)	ball in hands, head-high	2,200	1,300	975.00

(16) Lady Baldwin

16 (a)	Detroit, pitching, left hand head-high	2,200	1,300	975.00

(17) Mark Baldwin

17 (a)	Chicago, batting, heels together	2,750	1,400	975.00
17 (b)	Chicago, pitching, right hand above head	2,750	1,400	975.00
17 (c)	Chicago, pitching, right hand waist-high	2,750	1,400	975.00

(20) John Barnes

20 (a)	portrait	5,500	2,250	1,650
		5,500	2,250	1,650

(21) Billy Barnie

21 (a)	portrait	3,000	1,800	1,300

(22) Charley Bassett

22 (a)	Indianapolis, bat at ready	2,200	1,300	975.00

(23) Charlie Bastian

23 (a)	Chicago, bat over shoulder	2,200	1,300	975.00
23 (b)	Chicago, fielding, hands chest-high	2,200	1,300	975.00
23 (c)	Philadelphia, stooping to field low ball	2,200	1,300	975.00
DP 2	Philadelphia, tagging Pop Schriver	3,750	2,250	1,625

(24) Ed Beatin

24 (a)	pitching, right arm forward	2,200	1,300	975.00
		2,200	1,300	975.00

(27) Charlie Bennett

27 (a)	batting	2,200	1,300	975.00
27 (b)	batting, Dogs Head	5,250	3,150	2,250

(28) Lou Bierbauer

28 (a)	fielding grounder	2,200	1,300	975.00
28 (b)	fielding, hands chest-high	3,375	2,000	1,450
28 (c)	throwing	3,750	2,250	1,650

(31) Ned Bligh

31 (a)	fielding, hands head-high	2,200	1,300	975.00
		2,200	1,300	975.00

(32) Bogart

32 (a)	fielding, hands chest-high	2,200	1,300	975.00

(35) Henry Boyle

35 (a)	Indianapolis, pitch., right arm extended	2,200	1,300	975.00

(36) Jack Boyle

36 (a)	St. Louis, bat at side	2,200	1,300	975.00
36 (b)	St. Louis, bat at ready	2,200	1,300	975.00
36 (c)	St. Louis, catching, hands knee-high	2,200	1,300	975.00

(37) George Bradley

37 (a)	Sioux City, fielding, looking up at ball	2,200	1,300	975.00

(43) Dan Brouthers

43 (a)	Boston, batting	5,625	3,375	2,400
43 (b)	Boston, batting, Dogs Head	9,750	5,850	4,200
43 (c)	Boston, fielding, hands at waist	6,750	3,400	2,400
43 (d)	Boston, throwing, horizontal format	6,000	3,600	2,600
	Detroit, batting	5,625	3,375	2,400

(44) Tom Brown

44 (a)	Boston, bat at ready	2,200	1,300	975.00
44 (b)	Boston, bat at side	2,200	1,300	975.00
44 (c)	Boston, bat at side Dogs Head	4,500	2,300	1,350
44 (d)	Boston, fielding	2,200	1,300	975.00

(45) Willard (California) Brown

45 (a)	New York, bat at side	2,200	1,300	975.00
45 (b)	New York, throwing, mask in left hand	2,200	1,300	975.00

(46) Pete Browning

46 (a)	batting, feet together	5,625	3,375	2,400

(47) Charlie Brynan

47 (a)	Chicago, pitching, right arm neck-high	2,200	1,300	975.00
47 (b)	Des Moines, pitching, right arm forward	2,200	1,300	975.00

(48) Al Buckenberger

48 (a)	portrait, looking right	2,200	1,300	975.00

(49) Dick Buckley

49 (a)	Indianapolis, fielding, hands chest-high	2,200	1,300	975.00

(50) Charlie Buffinton

50 (a)	fielding, hands chest-high	2,200	1,300	975.00
50 (b)	pitch., right hand above head, Dogs Head	9,000	5,400	3,850

(52) Jack Burdock

52 (a)	fielding grounder	2,200	1,300	975.00

(56) Jim Burns

56 (a)	Kansas City, fielding grounder	2,200	1,300	975.00

(58) Oyster Burns

58 (a)	Brooklyn, bat at ready vertically	2,200	1,300	975.00
58 (b)	Brooklyn, throwing, right hand head-high	2,200	1,300	975.00

(59) Tom Burns

59 (a)	Chicago, bat at side	2,200	1,300	975.00
59 (b)	Chicago, bat at ready	2,200	1,300	975.00
59 (b)	Chicago, fielding	2,200	1,300	975.00
59 (c)	Chicago, tagging player	2,850	1,725	1,225

(60) Doc Bushong

60 (a)	stooping, hands waist-high	2,200	1,300	975.00
60 (b)	throwing	3,750	2,250	1,625

(63) Jimmy Canavan

63 (a)	batting	2,200	1,300	975.00

(66) Hick Carpenter

66 (a)	batting	2,200	1,300	975.00

(68) Fred Carroll

68 (a)	Pittsburgh, throwing	2,200	1,300	975.00

(69) Scrappy Carroll

69 (a)	St. Paul, fielding, hands chest-high	3,375	2,000	1,450

(70) Ed Cartwright

70 (a)	St. Joseph, throwing	2,200	1,300	975.00

(71) Bob Caruthers

71 (a)	batting, feet apart	2,200	1,300	975.00
71 (b)	holding ball in left hand, neck-high	7,125	4,275	3,000

(72) Daniel Casey

72 (a)	pitching, left hand shoulder-high	2,200	1,300	975.00

(73) Elton Chamberlain

73 (a)	batting, looking at camera	2,200	1,300	975.00
73 (b)	pitching, hands chest-high	2,200	1,300	975.00
73 (c)	pitching, right hand head-high	2,200	1,300	975.00

(74) Cupid Childs

74 (a)	fielding	2,200	1,300	975.00

(75) Bob Clark

75 (a)	Brookyln, fielding, hands shoulder-high	2,200	1,300	975.00
75 (b)	Brooklyn, throwing	2,200	1,300	975.00
DP 4	Brooklyn, tagging Mickey Hughes	6,750	4,050	2,875
DP 4	Brooklyn, tagging M. Hughes, Dogs Head	8,250	4,950	3,550
	Clark, Chicago - See Dad Clarke	2,200	1,300	975.00

(76) Spider Clark

76 (a)	Washington, pose unrecorded	2,200	1,300	975.00

(77) Dad Clark (Clarke)

77 (a)	Chicago, right arm extended forward	2,200	1,300	975.00
77 (b)	Omaha, batting	2,200	1,300	975.00

(78) John Clarkson

78 (a)	Boston, batting	5,250	3,150	2,250
78 (b)	Boston, right arm forward, left on thigh	7,125	4,275	3,075
78 (c)	Boston, pitching, right arm back	5,250	3,150	2,250
78 (d)	Boston, pitching, arm back, Dogs Head	10,500	6,300	4,500

(79) Jack Clements

79 (a)	batting	2,200	1,300	975.00
79 (b)	fielding	3,225	1,950	1,375
79 (c)	hands on knees	2,200	1,300	975.00

(80) Elmer Cleveland

80 (a)	pose unrecorded	2,200	1,300	975.00

(81) Monk Cline

81 (a)	bat nearly vertical	2,200	1,300	975.00

(83) John Coleman

83 (a)	ball in hands at waist	2,200	1,300	975.00
83 (b)	bat in hands below waist	2,200	1,300	975.00

(85) Hub Collins

85 (a)	Brooklyn, batting	2,200	1,300	975.00
85 (b)	Brooklyn, fielding, hands chest-high	2,200	1,300	975.00

(86) Charlie Comiskey

86 (a)	arms folded	7,500	4,500	3,225
86 (b)	fielding, hands neck-high, ball visible	7,500	4,500	3,225
86 (c)	fielding, hands shoulder-high, no ball	11,250	6,750	4,825
86 (d)	sliding	14,250	8,550	6,100

(88) Roger Connor

88 (a)	batting, home plate, batter's boxes on floor	11,250	6,750	4,825
88 (b)	batting, outdoors scene on backdrop	9,750	6,000	4,200
88 (c)	fielding, hands at waist	7,500	4,500	3,225
88 (d)	hands on knees	7,500	4,500	3,225

(89) Dick Conway

90 (a)	Boston, bat in hand at side	4,500	2,700	1,950

(90) Jim Conway

90 (a)	Kansas City, pitching, left ear visible	3,600	1,800	1,100
90 (b)	K.C., pitching, left ear not visible	3,600	1,800	1,100

(91) Pete Conway

91 (a)	Detroit, pitching, right hand extended	2,200	1,300	975.00
91 (b)	Detroit, pitching, hands at chest	2,200	1,300	975.00

(92) Paul Cook

92 (a)	fielding in mask	2,200	1,300	975.00
92 (b)	tagging baserunner	2,200	1,300	975.00

(93) Jimmy Cooney

93 (a)	batting, Omaha, Dogs Head	5,250	3,150	2,250

(95) Pop Corkhill

95 (a)	Brooklyn, batting	2,200	1,300	975.00
95 (b)	Brooklyn, fielding, hands neck-high	2,200	1,300	975.00

(96) Cannonball Crane

96 (a)	New York, pitching, right hand head-high	2,200	1,300	975.00

(99) John Crooks

99 (a)	Omaha, pose unrecorded	2,200	1,300	975.00

(100) Lave Cross

100 (a)	Louisville, hands on thighs	2,200	1,300	975.00
100 (b)	Athletics, right arm head high	2,200	1,300	975.00

(105) Bert Cunningham

105 (a)	both arms waist level	2,200	1,300	975.00

(109) Edward Dailey

109 (a)	Columbus, pitching, right hand head-high	2,200	1,300	975.00
109 (b)	Washington, pitch., right hand head-high	2,200	1,300	975.00

(111) Bill Daley

111 (a)	Boston, pitching, hands above waist	2,200	1,300	975.00

(112) Con Daley (Daily)

112 (a)	Indianapolis, right hand on hip	2,200	1,300	975.00

(113) Abner Dalrymple

113 (a)	Pittsburgh, hands on hips, feet apart	2,200	1,300	975.00

(114) Sun Daly

114 (a)	Minneapolis, fielding, hands chest-high	2,200	1,300	975.00

(115) Tom Daly

115 (a)	Chicago, fielding, hands chest-high	3,000	1,500	1,000
115 (b)	Chicago, hands on knees	3,000	1,500	1,000
115 (c)	Washington, fielding, hands chest-high	3,000	1,500	1,000

(117) Dell Darling

117 (a)	fielding, hands waist-high	2,200	1,300	975.00
117 (b)	standing, arms crossed	2,200	1,300	975.00

(118) William Darnbrough

118 (a)	pitching	2,200	1,300	975.00

(123) Harry Decker

123 (a)	bat nearly horizontal	2,200	1,300	975.00

(124) Ed Delehanty

124 (a)	bat by shoulder	31,250	5,400	3,875
124 (b)	bat horizontal	9,000	5,400	3,875
124 (c)	fielding	22,500	13,500	9,675

(125) Jerry Denny

125 (a)	Indianapolis, batting	2,200	1,300	975.00
125 (b)	Indianapolis, fielding	2,200	1,300	975.00

(126) Jim Devlin

126 (a)	pitching, left hand shoulder-high	2,200	1,300	975.00
126 (b)	sliding	2,200	1,300	975.00

(130) Jim Donnelly

130 (a)	batting	2,200	1,300	975.00

132 John Doran

132 (a)	fielding	24,000	12,000	7,200

(133) Mike Dorgan

133 (a)	sliding, horizontal format	3,375	2,000	1,450

(135) Charlie Duffe (Duffee)

135 (a)	batting	2,200	1,300	975.00
135 (b)	fielding, bending to left	2,200	1,300	975.00
135 (c)	fielding grounder	2,200	1,300	975.00
135 (d)	fielding, standing upright	2,200	1,300	975.00

(136) Hugh Duffy

136 (a)	batting	4,875	2,925	2,100
136 (b)	fielding, hands chin-high	4,875	2,925	2,100
136 (c)	fielding grounder	6,000	3,600	2,600

(138) Martin Duke

138 (a)	ball in hands, chest-high	3,750	2,250	1,625

(139) Fred Dunlap

139 (a)	arms at side	2,200	1,300	975.00
139 (b)	holding ball aloft	2,200	1,300	975.00
139 (c)	holding ball aloft, Dogs Head	4,500	2,700	1,950
139 (d)	sliding, right arm up	4,000	2,000	1,200

(141) Jesse Duryea

141 (a)	batting	2,200	1,300	975.00

(142) Frank Dwyer

142 (a)	bat at side	3,750	2,250	1,625
142 (b)	bat in air	2,200	1,300	975.00
142 (c)	fielding	2,200	1,300	975.00

(143) Billy Earle

143 (a)	Cincinnati, fielding, hands over head	2,200	1,300	975.00

(145) Red Ehret

145 (a)	batting	2,200	1,300	975.00

(147) Dude Esterbrook

147 (a)	Indianapolis, fielding grounder	2,200	1,300	975.00
147 (b)	Indianapolis, fielding, hands chest-high	2,200	1,300	975.00
147 (c)	Louisville, fielding, hands chest high	2,200	1,300	975.00

(149) Buck Ewing

149 (a)	New York, bat at side	6,000	3,600	2,600
149 (b)	New York, bat in air	6,000	3,600	2,600
149 (c)	New York, fielding, hands head-high	6,000	3,600	2,600
149 (d)	New York, hands on knees	6,000	3,600	2,600
149 (e)	New York, throwing, right arm extended forward	9,000	5,400	3,875
149 (f)	New York, with mascot Willie Breslin	17,500	9,500	5,500
149 (g)	New York, w/ mascot, Dogs Head	26,250	15,750	11,275

(150) John Ewing

150 (a)	Louisville, bat almost vertical	2,200	1,300	975.00

(151) Jay Faatz

151 (a)	throwing	2,200	1,300	975.00
151 (b)	batting	2,200	1,300	975.00

(152) Bill Farmer

152 (a)	Pittsburgh, hands on knees	2,200	1,300	975.00

(154) Sid Farrar

154 (a)	fielding grounder	2,200	1,300	975.00
154 (b)	fielding, hands head-high	2,200	1,300	975.00

(155) Duke Farrell

155 (a)	Chicago, fielding grounder	3,000	1,500	975.00
155 (b)	Chicago, hands on knees	3,000	1,500	975.00

(157) Frank Fennelly

157 (a)	Cincinnati, fielding grounder	2,200	1,300	975.00

(158) Charlie Ferguson

158 (a)	pitching, hands at chest	2,200	1,300	975.00

(159) Alex Ferson

159 (a)	pitching, hands neck-high, looking front	2,200	1,300	975.00

(161) Jocko Fields

161 (a)	hands on thighs	2,200	1,300	975.00

(164) Silver Flint

164 (a)	batting	2,200	1,300	975.00
164 (b)	catching, with mask, hands waist-high	3,000	1,800	1,300

(167) Jim Fogarty

167 (a)	batting	2,200	1,300	975.00
167 (b)	fielding, hands neck-high	2,200	1,300	975.00
167 (c)	running to left	2,200	1,300	975.00
167 (d)	sliding	2,200	1,300	975.00

(168) Frank Foreman

168 (a)	Baltimore, ball in hands by right thigh	3,375	2,000	1,450

(170) Elmer Foster

170 (a)	Minneapolis, batting	2,200	1,300	975.00
170 (b)	New York, fielding	2,200	1,300	975.00

(171) Dave Foutz

171 (a)	bat at 45 degrees	2,200	1,300	975.00
171 (b)	throwing	2,200	1,300	975.00

(175) Shorty Fuller

175 (a)	bat on shoulder	2,200	1,300	975.00
175 (b)	fielding	2,200	1,300	975.00
175 (c)	hands on knees	2,200	1,300	975.00
175 (d)	swinging bat	2,200	1,300	975.00

(177) Chris Fulmer

DP 8	tagging Tom Tucker, Dogs Head	6,750	4,050	2,875

(179) Pud Galvin

179 (a)	batting	5,625	3,375	2,400

(181) Charlie Ganzel

181 (a)	Boston, batting	2,200	1,300	975.00
181 (b)	Boston, fielding, hands shoulder-high	3,750	2,250	1,625
181 (c)	Boston, fielding, hands thigh-high	2,200	1,300	975.00

(182) Gid Gardner

182 (a)	Philadelphia, fielding low ball	2,200	1,300	975.00

(183) Hank Gastreich
183 (a) pitching, left hand by thigh — 2,200 1,300 975.00

(185) Frank Genins
185 (a) batting, looking at ball — 2,200 1,300 975.00
185 (b) batting, looking at camera — 2,200 1,300 975.00

(186) Bill George
186 (a) bat at side — 2,200 1,300 975.00

(188) Charlie Getzein (Getzien)
188 (a) pitching, hands above waist — 2,200 1,300 975.00

(190) Bobby Gilks
190 (a) batting — 2,200 1,300 975.00

(192) Barney Gilligan
192 (a) Washington, fielding — 2,200 1,300 975.00

(193) Frank Gilmore
193 (a) pitching, hands neck-high — 2,200 1,300 975.00

(194) Jack Glasscock
194 (a) Indianapolis, bat at side, Dogs Head — 5,250 3,150 2,250
194 (b) Indianapolis, hands on knees
194 (c) Indianapolis, throwing — 2,200 1,300 975.00

(195) Bill Gleason
195 (a) Louisville, batting — 2,200 1,300 975.00
195 (b) Louisville, stooping, hands clasped — 2,200 1,300 975.00
DP 23 with Curt Welch — 3,375 2,025 1,450

(196) Kid Gleason
196 (a) Philadelphia, fielding grounder — 3,375 2,025 1,450
196 (b) Philadelphia, ball in hands at chin — 3,375 2,025 1,450

(197) Ed Glenn
197 (a) fielding, hands neck-high — 2,200 1,300 975.00

(199) George Gore
199 (a) bat nearly horizontal — 2,200 1,300 975.00
199 (b) bat at ready over left shoulder — 2,200 1,300 975.00
199 (c) fielding grounder — 2,200 1,300 975.00

(205) Henry Gruber
205 (a) pitching, right hand chin-high — 2,200 1,300 975.00

(206) Ad Gumbert
206 (a) pitching, right hand eye-high — 3,150 1,875 1,350
206 (b) pitching, right hand waist-high — 2,200 1,300 975.00

(207) Tom Gunning
207 (a) bending forward, hands by right knee — 2,200 1,300 975.00

(208) Joe Gunson
208 (a) wearing jacket — 2,200 1,300 975.00

(212) Bill Hallman
212 (a) leaning left to catch ball chest-high — 2,200 1,300 975.00

(213) Billy Hamilton
213 (a) Kansas City, batting: looking at camera — 9,000 5,400 3,875
213 (b) Kansas City, fielding, hands neck-high — 9,000 5,400 3,875
213 (c) Kansas City, fielding grounder — 9,000 5,400 3,875

(215) Ned Hanlon
215 (a) Detroit, batting — 4,500 2,700 1,950
215 (b) Pittsburgh, fielding — 4,875 2,925 2,100

(216) Bill Hanrahan
216 (a) bat at side — 2,200 1,300 975.00

(221) Gil Hatfield
221 (a) bat at waist — 2,200 1,300 975.00
221 (b) bat over shoulder — 2,200 1,300 975.00
221 (c) fielding, hands chest-high — 2,200 1,300 975.00

(223) Egyptian Healey (Healy)
223 (a) Indianapolis, pitching, hands at chest — 2,200 1,300 975.00

(227) Hardie Henderson
227 (a) Brooklyn, outdoors, throwing, right hand head-high — 3,000 1,800 1,300

(228) Moxie Hengle
228 (a) Minneapolis, hands on knees — 2,200 1,300 975.00

(229) John Henry
229 (a) throwing, right hand neck-high — 2,200 1,300 975.00

(231) Hunkey Hines
231 (a) St. Louis Whites, fielding — 2,200 1,300 975.00

(232) Paul Hines
232 (a) Washington, arms at side — 2,200 1,300 975.00

(233) Frank Hoffman
233 (a) pitching, right hand head-high — 2,200 1,300 975.00

(235) Bill Holbert
235 (a) throwing — 2,200 1,300 975.00

(236) Bug Holliday
236 (a) Cincinnati, arms at side — 2,200 1,300 975.00
236 (b) Cincinnati, ball in hands at shoulder — 2,200 1,300 975.00

(238) Buster Hoover
238 (a) Philadelphia, fielding, hands head-high — 2,200 1,300 975.00
DP 1 being tagged by Ed Andrews — 3,750 2,250 1,625

(239) Charlie Hoover
239 (a) Chicago, fielding grounder (Never played for Chicago) — 2,200 1,300 975.00
239 (b) Kansas City, pose unrecorded — 2,200 1,300 975.00

(241) Joe Hornung
241 (a) Boston, batting — 2,200 1,300 975.00

(243) Dummy Hoy
243 (a) fielding grounder — 6,750 4,050 2,875

(244) Nat Hudson
244 (a) ball in hands waist-high — 2,200 1,300 975.00
244 (b) pitching, right hand head-high — 2,200 1,300 975.00
244 (c) pitching, right hand waist-high — 2,200 1,300 975.00

(245) Mickey Hughes
245 (a) holding ball at chest — 2,200 1,300 975.00
245 (b) holding ball at side — 2,200 1,300 975.00
245 (c) right hand extended — 2,200 1,300 975.00
DP 4 being tagged by Bob Clark — 5,625 3,375 2,400

(247) Bill Hutchinson
247 (a) ball in hand, right heel hidden — 2,200 1,300 975.00
247 (b) ball in hand, right heel visible — 2,200 1,300 975.00
247 (c) batting — 2,200 1,300 975.00

(248) Arthur Irwin
248 (a) Philadelphia, fielding, hands chest-high — 2,200 1,300 975.00
248 (b) Phila., throwing, right hand head-high — 2,200 1,300 975.00

(249) John Irwin
249 (a) Washington, hands on knees — 2,200 1,300 975.00
249 (b) Washington, throwing — 2,200 1,300 975.00

(250) A.C. Jantzen
250 (a) batting, looking at camera — 2,200 1,300 975.00

(252) Spud Johnson
252 (a) Columbus, pose unrecorded — 2,200 1,300 975.00

(253) Dick Johnston
253 (a) batting, looking at ball — 2,200 1,300 975.00
253 (b) batting, looking at camera — 2,200 1,300 975.00
253 (c) hands on hips — 2,200 1,300 975.00
253 (d) throwing right hand head high — 2,200 1,300 975.00

(256) Tim Keefe
256 (a) bat nearly horizontal, Old Judge — 4,500 2,700 1,950
256 (b) bat nearly horizontal, Dogs Head — 18,750 11,250 8,100
256 (c) ball in hands at chest — 3,750 2,250 1,625
256 (d) pitching, right hand head-high — 4,500 2,700 1,950
256 (e) pitching, right hand waist-high — 4,500 2,700 1,950

(259) Charlie Kelly
259 (a) Philadelphia, fielding, hands head-high — 2,200 1,300 975.00

(261) King Kelly
261 (a) "Kelly, Boston.", bat at 45-degree angle — 15,000 7,500 4,500
261 (b) "Kelly, Boston.", bat at 45-degree angle, Dogs Head — 17,500 8,750 5,300
261 (c) "Mike Kelly, C, Bostons", bat at 45-degree angle — 9,000 5,400 3,875
261 (d) "Kelly, Capt.", bat at 45-degree angle — 9,000 5,400 3,875

(262) Rudy Kemmler
262 (a) fielding, hands chest-high — 2,200 1,300 975.00

(263) Ted Kennedy
263 (a) Omaha, pose unrecorded — 2,200 1,300 975.00

(264) J.J. Kenyon
264 (a) Des Moines, right hand in glove, head-high — 2,200 1,300 975.00

(265) John Kerins
265 (a) hands on thighs — 2,200 1,300 975.00

(266) Matt Kilroy
266 (a) pitching, hands waist-high to left — 2,200 1,300 975.00

(267) Silver King
267 (a) St. Louis, pitching, hands chest-high — 2,200 1,300 975.00
267 (b) St. Louis, pitching, hands chin-high — 2,200 1,300 975.00

(269) Billy Klusman
269 (a) fielding grounder — 2,200 1,300 975.00

(274) Gus Krock
274 (a) ball in hands above waist — 2,650 1,400 975.00
274 (b) batting — 2,650 1,400 975.00
274 (c) pitching, right hand chin-high — 2,650 1,400 975.00

(275) Willie Kuehne
275 (a) fielding grounder — 2,200 1,300 975.00

(277) Henry Larkin
277 (a) fielding, hands thigh-high — 2,200 1,300 975.00
277 (b) right hand shoulder-high — 2,200 1,300 975.00

(278) Arlie Latham
278 (a) batting — 2,200 1,300 975.00
278 (b) throwing — 3,950 2,000 1,250

(279) Chuck Lauer
279 (a) fielding, hands chest-high — 2,200 1,300 975.00

(280) John Leighton
280 (a) batting — 2,200 1,300 975.00
280 (b) fielding — 2,200 1,300 975.00

(284) Herman Long
284 (a) Kansas City, bat at side — 2,200 1,300 975.00
284 (b) Kansas City, fielding, hands chest-high — 2,200 1,300 975.00

(285) Tom Lovett
285 (a) Brooklyn, bat on shoulder — 2,200 1,300 975.00
285 (b) Brooklyn, pitching, hands over head — 2,200 1,300 975.00
285 (c) Brooklyn, right hand extended — 2,200 1,300 975.00

(288) Denny Lyons
288 (a) Philadelphia AA, bat at ready — 2,200 1,300 975.00
288 (b) Phila. AA, fielding, left hand over head — 2,200 1,300 975.00

(289) Harry Lyons
289 (a) St. Louis, at first base — 2,200 1,300 975.00

(290) Connie Mack
290 (a) Washington, batting — 31,250 11,250 8,100
290 (b) Washington, squatting, hands on knees — 31,250 13,500 9,675

(292) Jimmy Macullar
292 (a) Des Moines, fielding, hands head-high — 2,200 1,300 975.00

(293) Kid Madden
293 (a) ball in hand over head — 2,200 1,300 975.00
293 (b) ball in hands, neck-high — 2,200 1,300 975.00
293 (c) ball in left hand, eye-high — 2,200 1,300 975.00

(297) Jimmy Manning
297 (a) bat at side — 2,200 1,300 975.00
297 (b) fielding grounder — 2,200 1,300 975.00

(298) Lefty Marr
298 (a) Columbus, left hand neck-high — 2,200 1,300 975.00

(299) Mascot (Willie Breslin)
299 (a) New York — 3,500 1,750 1,050

(300) Leech Maskrey
300 (a) Des Moines, ball in hands chin-high — 2,200 1,300 975.00

(302) Mike Mattimore
302 (a) Phila. AA, sliding, left hand raised — 2,200 1,300 975.00

(303) Al Maul
303 (a) pitching, hands at chest — 2,200 1,300 975.00

(304) Al Mays
304 (a) pitching, hands chest-high — 2,200 1,300 975.00

(305) Jimmy McAleer
305 (a) batting, looking at ball — 2,200 1,300 975.00

(307) Tommy McCarthy
307 (a) St. Louis, batting, indoors — 5,250 3,150 2,250
307 (b) St. Louis, right hand head-high, indoors — 5,250 3,150 2,250
307 (c) tagging player — 6,900 4,125 2,950

(318) Deacon McGuire
318 (a) Phila., fielding, hands shoulder-high — 2,200 1,300 975.00

(319) Bill McGunnigle
319 (a) looking to right — 2,200 1,300 975.00

(320) Ed McKean
320 (a) batting, looking at camera — 2,200 1,300 975.00
320 (b) fielding, hands over head — 2,200 1,300 975.00

(325) James McQuaid
325 (a) fielding, hands near chin — 2,200 1,300 975.00

(330) Doggie Miller
330 (a) Pittsburgh, ball in hands, Dogs Head — 8,250 4,950 3,550
330 (b) Pittsburgh, bat at side — 2,200 1,300 975.00
330 (c) fielding, hands chest-high — 2,200 1,300 975.00

(331) Joe Miller
331 (a) Minneapolis, bat at side — 2,200 1,300 975.00
331 (b) Minneapolis, fielding — 2,200 1,300 975.00

(332) Jocko Milligan
332 (a) bat at side — 2,200 1,300 975.00
332 (b) bat in air — 2,200 1,300 975.00
332 (c) fielding — 2,200 1,300 975.00
332 (d) throwing — 2,200 1,300 975.00

(334) Daniel Minnehan (Minahan)
334 (a) batting, looking at camera — 2,200 1,300 975.00

(335) Sam Moffet
335 (a) pose unrecorded — 2,200 1,300 975.00

(336) John Morrill
336 (a) Boston, batting — 2,200 1,300 975.00

(338) Tony Mullane
338 (a) ball in hands above waist — 4,125 2,475 1,750

(339) Joe Mulvey
339 (a) batting — 2,200 1,300 975.00
339 (b) fielding — 2,200 1,300 975.00

Card	Description			
(340) Pat Murphy				
340 (a)	New York, fielding, hands chin-high	3,000	1,500	1,000
(341) P.L. Murphy				
341 (a)	St. Paul, batting	3,000	1,800	1,300
(342) Miah Murray				
342 (a)	on knee, hands at shoulder	2,200	1,300	975.00
(343) Jim Mutrie				
343 (a)	seated	2,200	1,300	975.00
343 (b)	standing	2,200	1,300	975.00
(344) Al Myers				
344 (a)	Wash., right hand at side, left at back	2,200	1,300	975.00
(345) George Myers				
345 (a)	Indianpolis, batting	2,200	1,300	975.00
(346) Tom Nagle				
346 (a)	Omaha, batting	2,200	1,300	975.00
346 (b)	fielding, Dogs Head	9,000	5,400	3,875
(347) Billy Nash				
347 (a)	hands atop vertical bat	2,200	1,300	975.00
347 (b)	hands atop vertical, Dogs Head	7,500	3,750	2,250
347 (c)	hands on knees	3,375	2,025	1,450
347 (d)	throwing	2,200	1,300	975.00
(349) Kid Nichols				
349 (a)	Omaha, batting, looking at ball	6,375	3,825	2,750
349 (b)	Omaha, pitching, right hand forward	6,375	3,825	2,750
(353) Hugh Nicol				
DP 16	side by side with Reilly, "Long & Short"	3,375	2,025	1,450
(357) Darby O'Brien				
357 (a)	Brooklyn, batting, looking at camera	2,200	1,300	975.00
(359) John O'Brien				
359 (a)	Cleveland, batting	2,200	1,300	975.00
359 (b)	Cleveland, pose unrecorded, Dogs Head	7,125	4,275	3,075
(361) Jack O'Connor				
361 (a)	Columbus, throwing	2,200	1,300	975.00
(362) Hank O'Day				
362 (a)	ball in right hand, head-high	2,200	1,300	975.00
(365) Tip O'Neill				
365 (a)	bat held horizontally	3,250	1,650	1,000
365 (b)	bat over shoulder	3,250	1,650	1,000
365 (c)	batting, facing camera	6,000	3,000	1,800
365 (d)	fielding grounder	3,250	1,650	1,000
365 (e)	throwing	6,000	3,000	1,800
(366) Orator Jim O'Rourke				
366 (a)	New York, bat in hand at side	6,000	3,600	2,600
366 (b)	New York, batting	7,125	4,275	3,075
366 (c)	New York, throwing, hand head-high	5,250	3,150	2,250
(367) Tom O'Rourke				
367 (a)	Boston, fielding, hands thigh-high	3,375	2,025	1,450
(368) Dave Orr				
368 (a)	Columbus, bat at ready, nearly vertical	2,200	1,300	975.00
(370) Owen Patton				
370 (a)	Des Moines, bat at head	2,200	1,300	975.00
(374) Fred Pfeffer				
374 (a)	batting, looking at ball	2,200	1,300	975.00
374 (b)	tagging player	2,850	1,725	1,225
374 (c)	throwing, right-hand neck-high	2,200	1,300	975.00
(375) Dick Phelan				
375 (a)	batting, looking at ball	2,200	1,300	975.00
(377) Jack Pickett				
377 (a)	St. Paul, bat over shoulder	2,200	1,300	975.00
377 (b)	St. Paul, fielding grounder	2,200	1,300	975.00
377 (c)	St. Paul, throwing, right hand head-high	2,200	1,300	975.00
(378) George Pinkney (Pinckny)				
378 (a)	bat in air, nearly vertical	2,200	1,300	975.00
378 (b)	bat over shoulder	2,200	1,300	975.00
378 (c)	fielding	5,250	2,650	1,600
DP 25	(w/ Steve Toole)	6,750	4,050	2,875
(381) Jim Powell				
381 (a)	batting, looking at camera	2,200	1,300	975.00
(383) Blondie Purcell				
383 (a)	throwing	2,200	1,300	975.00
(385) Joe Quinn				
385 (a)	ball in hands by chin	2,200	1,300	975.00
385 (b)	ready to run	2,200	1,300	975.00
385 (c)	ready to run, Dogs Head	4,500	2,250	1,400
(386) Old Hoss Radbourn				
386 (a)	hands at waist, Dogs Head	9,750	5,850	4,200
386 (b)	hands on hips, bat on left	4,500	2,700	1,950
386 (c)	tagging player	5,250	3,150	2,250
(388) Tom Ramsey				
388 (a)	bat at ready, nearly vertical	2,200	1,300	975.00
388 (b)	bat over right shoulder, Dogs Head	6,000	3,600	2,600
(390) Charlie Reilly				
390 (a)	St. Paul, throwing	2,200	1,300	975.00
(391) Long John Reilly				
391 (a)	Cincinnati, fielding	2,200	1,300	975.00
DP 16	side by side w/Nicol, "Long & Short"	3,375	2,025	1,450
(393) Danny Richardson				
393 (a)	New York, moving left, arms at side	2,200	1,300	975.00
393 (b)	New York, throwing	2,200	1,300	975.00
(394) Hardy Richardson				
394 (a)	Boston, bat over shoulder	2,200	1,300	975.00
394 (b)	Detroit, bat over shoulder	2,200	1,300	975.00
394 (c)	Boston, fielding, hands head-high	2,200	1,300	975.00
(398) Wilbert Robinson				
398 (a)	Philadelphia AA, batting	5,625	3,375	2,475
398 (b)	Phila. AA, catching, hands neck-high	5,625	3,375	2,475
398 (c)	Philadelphia AA, throwing	5,625	3,375	2,475
(399) Yank Robinson				
399 (a)	St. Louis, batting	3,150	1,875	1,350
399 (b)	St. Louis, fielding grounder	3,150	1,875	1,350
399 (c)	St. Louis, hands at chest	3,150	1,875	1,350
(402) Dave Rowe				
402 (a)	Kansas City, fielding, Dogs Head	5,250	3,150	2,250
(403) Jack Rowe				
403 (a)	Detroit, batting, looking at camera	2,200	1,300	975.00
403 (b)	Detroit, bat on shoulder, looking at ball	2,200	1,300	975.00
(404) Amos Rusie				
404 (a)	Indianapolis, ball in right hand, thigh-high	11,250	6,750	4,875
(405) Jimmy Ryan				
405 (a)	bat at side	4,250	2,150	1,400
405 (b)	batting	4,250	2,150	1,400
405 (c)	stooping for knee-high catch	4,250	2,150	1,400
405 (d)	throwing, left hand head-high	4,250	2,150	1,400
(407) Ben Sanders				
407 (a)	batting	2,200	1,300	975.00
407 (b)	fielding	2,200	1,300	975.00
407 (c)	right hand head-high	2,200	1,300	975.00
(408) Frank Scheibeck				
408 (a)	fielding, hand over head	2,200	1,300	975.00
(412) Gus Schmelz				
412 (a)	portrait	2,200	1,300	975.00
(413) Jumbo Schoeneck				
413 (a)	fielding, hands chin-high	2,200	1,300	975.00
(414) Pop Schriver				
414 (a)	fielding, hands ankle-high	2,200	1,300	975.00
414 (b)	hands cupped chest-high	1,750	1,050	750.00
DP 2	being tagged by Charlie Bastian	3,750	2,250	1,750
(415) Emmett Seery				
415 (a)	arms folded	2,200	1,300	975.00
(417) Ed Seward				
417 (a)	ball in hands neck-high	2,200	1,300	975.00
(420) Daniel Shannon				
420 (a)	Louisville, leaning to tag player	2,200	1,300	975.00
(421) Bill Sharsig				
421 (a)	full length in bowler hat	2,200	1,300	975.00
(425) George Shoch				
425 (a)	fielding grounder	2,200	1,300	975.00
(426) Otto Shomberg (Schomberg)				
426 (a)	fielding, hands head-high	2,200	1,300	975.00
(427) Lev Shreve				
427 (a)	right hand eye-high, looking at camera	2,200	1,300	975.00
(429) Mike Slattery				
429 (a)	fielding, hands chest-high	2,200	1,300	975.00
(430) Elmer Smith				
(431) Germany Smith				
431 (a)	Cincinnati, pitching, left hand head-high, looking at camera	2,200	1,300	975.00
431 (a)	Brooklyn, batting, looking at ball	2,200	1,300	975.00
431 (b)	Brooklyn, hands on knees	2,200	1,300	975.00
431 (c)	Brooklyn, right hand head-high	2,200	1,300	975.00
(435) Pop Smith				
435 (a)	Boston, batting	2,200	1,300	975.00
435 (b)	Pittsburgh, batting	2,200	1,300	975.00
435 (c)	hands on knees	2,200	1,300	975.00
(439) Pete Sommers				
439 (a)	portrait	3,375	2,025	1,450
(440) Bill Sowders				
440 (a)	Boston, pitching, hands at throat	2,200	1,300	975.00
440 (b)	Boston, pitching, right hand cap-high, left hand waist-high	3,000	1,800	1,300
(442) Charlie Sprague				
442 (a)	Chicago, left hand at back head-high	2,200	1,300	975.00
442 (b)	Cleveland, left hand at back head-high	2,200	1,300	975.00
(444) Harry Staley				
444 (a)	pitching, right hand chest-high	2,200	1,300	975.00
(445) Dan Stearns				
445 (a)	Kansas City, fielding, hands neck-high	3,750	2,250	1,750
(450) Harry Stovey				
450 (a)	bat at ready by head	3,375	2,025	1,450
450 (b)	fielding, hands chest-high, Dogs Head	18,000	10,800	7,725
450 (c)	hands on knees	2,200	1,300	975.00
(451) Scott Stratton				
451 (a)	batting	2,200	1,300	975.00
(452) Joe Straus (Strauss)				
452 (a)	Milwaukee, kneeling, looking to right	2,200	1,300	975.00
452 (b)	Omaha, batting	3,500	1,750	1,100
452 (c)	Omaha, throwing	3,000	1,500	1,000
(453) Cub Stricker				
453 (a)	fielding, hands over head	2,200	1,300	975.00
(454) Marty Sullivan				
454 (a)	Chicago, batting, looking at ball	2,200	1,300	975.00
454 (b)	Indianapolis, hands chest-high	2,200	1,300	975.00
(457) Billy Sunday				
457 (a)	Pittsburgh, bat at side	5,250	3,150	2,250
457 (b)	Pittsburgh, batting	7,500	4,500	3,225
457 (c)	Pittsburgh, fielding, hands thigh-high	5,250	3,150	2,250
(459) Ezra Sutton				
459 (a)	batting, looking down at ball	2,200	1,300	975.00
459 (b)	fielding, hands shoulder-high	2,200	1,300	975.00
(461) Park Swartzel				
461 (a)	arms at side	2,200	1,300	975.00
(464) Pop Tate				
464 (a)	Boston, batting	2,200	1,300	975.00
(465) Patsy Tebeau				
465 (a)	Chicago, fielding grounder	3,000	1,500	1,000
(466) John Tener				
466 (a)	ball in right hand chin-high	3,750	2,250	1,750
466 (b)	batting	3,750	2,250	1,750
(467) Adonis Terry				
467 (a)	arms extended horizontally	2,200	1,300	975.00
467 (b)	bat on shoulder	2,200	1,300	975.00
(468) Sam Thompson				
468 (a)	Detroit, bat ready at 45 degree angle	9,750	5,850	4,200
468 (b)	Philadelphia, batting, ball above head	9,750	5,850	4,200
(469) Mike Tiernan				
469 (a)	batting	2,200	1,300	975.00
469 (b)	sliding	3,375	2,025	1,450
469 (c)	throwing, left hand chin-high	2,200	1,300	975.00
(470) Cannonball Titcomb				
470 (a)	pitching, hands chin-high	2,200	1,300	975.00
(471) Phil Tomney				
471 (a)	fielding, hands over head	2,200	1,300	975.00
(472) Steve Toole				
DP 25	(w/ George Pinkney (Pinckney))	6,750	4,050	2,875
(473) George Townsend				
473 (a)	bat at ready by head	2,200	1,300	975.00
473 (b)	fielding. hands chest-high	2,200	1,300	975.00
(474) Bill Traffley				
474 (a)	hands on thighs	2,200	1,300	975.00
(477) Tommy Tucker				
477 (a)	ball in hands at chest	2,200	1,300	975.00
DP 8	being tagged by Chris Fulmer	6,750	4,050	2,875
(479) George Turner				
479 (a)	fielding, hands head-high	2,200	1,300	975.00
(480) Larry Twitchell				
480 (a)	Cleveland, pitching, hands at chest	2,200	1,300	975.00
480 (b)	Detroit, pitching, hands at chest	2,200	1,300	975.00
(481) Jim Tyng				
481 (a)	pitching	2,200	1,300	975.00
(483) George Van Haltren				
483 (a)	batting	5,250	2,700	1,950
483 (b)	ball in hands at waist	5,250	2,700	1,950
482 (c)	right hand at thigh	5,250	2,700	1,950
(484) Farmer Vaughn				

484 (a)	bat at ready, looking at camera	2,200	1,300	975.00
486	Leon Viau			
486 (a)	right hand cap-high	2,200	1,300	975.00
(488)	Joe Visner			
488 (a)	arms at side	2,200	1,300	975.00
488 (b)	batting	2,200	1,300	975.00
488 (c)	throwing	2,200	1,300	975.00
(490)	Reddy Walsh			
490 (a)	batting	2,200	1,300	975.00
(491)	John Ward			
491 (a)	hands behind back	6,000	3,600	2,600
491 (b)	hands on hips	10,500	6,300	4,500
491 (c)	portrait in dress clothes) (Value Undetermine)	2,200	1,300	975.00
491 (d)	sliding, left arm in air	6,000	3,600	2,600
491 (e)	throwing, right profile	6,000	3,600	2,600
491 (f)	cap in right hand at side	6,000	3,600	2,600
491 (g)	cap in right hand at side, Dogs Head	9,000	5,400	3,875
(493)	Bill Watkins			
493 (a)	Detroit, portrait	2,200	1,300	975.00
493 (b)	Kansas City, portrait	2,200	1,300	975.00
(494)	Farmer Weaver			
494 (a)	fielding, left hand over head	2,200	1,300	975.00
(496)	Stump Weidman (Wiedman)			
496 (a)	New York, batting	2,200	1,300	975.00
(497)	Wild Bill Weidner (Widner)			
497 (a)	batting	2,200	1,300	975.00
(498)	Curt Welch			
498 (a)	Philadelphia AA, fielding grounder	2,200	1,300	975.00
DP 23	with Will Gleason	3,375	2,025	1,450
(499)	Mickey Welch			
499 (a)	N.Y., pitching, right arm extended forward, name incorrect (Welsh)	4,500	2,700	1,950
499 (b)	N.Y., pitching, right arm extended forward, name correct	4,500	2,700	1,950
499 (c)	N.Y., pitching, right arm behind head, Dogs Head	22,500	13,500	9,675
(504)	A.C. (Gus) Weyhing			
504 (a)	right hand cap-high	2,200	1,300	975.00
504 (b)	Philadelphia AA, right hand chest-high	2,200	1,300	975.00
(505)	John Weyhing			
505 (a)	Philadelphia AA, left hand chest-high (Never played for Philadelphia)	2,200	1,300	975.00
(510)	Deacon White			
510 (a)	Detroit, hands above head	2,200	1,300	975.00
510 (b)	looking down at ball	2,200	1,300	975.00
(511)	Art Whitney			
511 (a)	New York, with dog	18,750	11,250	8,100
511 (b)	New York, fielding, hands thigh-high	2,200	1,300	975.00
511 (c)	Pittsburgh, fielding, hands thigh-high	2,200	1,300	975.00
(512)	G. Whitney			
512 (a)	St. Joseph, batting, looking at ball	2,200	1,300	975.00
(513)	Jim Whitney			
513 (a)	Wash., pitching, right hand waist-high	2,200	1,300	975.00
(515)	Ned Williamson			
515 (a)	arms folded	3,000	1,500	1,000
515 (b)	batting, looking at ball	3,000	1,500	1,000
515 (c)	fielding	3,000	1,500	1,000
515 (d)	throwing	3,000	1,500	1,000
(516)	Tit Willis			
516 (a)	pitching, arms head-high	2,200	1,300	975.00
(517)	Walt Wilmot			
517 (a)	Washington, fielding, hands at chest	2,200	1,300	975.00
(519)	Sam Wise			
519 (a)	Boston, bat at side	2,200	1,300	975.00
519 (b)	Boston, hands on knees	3,000	1,800	1,300
(520)	Chicken Wolf			
520 (a)	bat at ready, team name visible on shirt	2,200	1,300	975.00
(521)	George Wood (L.F.)			
521 (a)	both hands neck-high	2,200	1,300	975.00
521 (b)	right hand head-high	2,200	1,300	975.00
(522)	Pete Wood (P.)			
522 (a)	bat on shoulder	2,200	1,300	975.00
(523)	Harry Wright			
523 (a)	portrait, looking to his left	30,000	18,000	13,000
(524)	Chief Zimmer			
524 (a)	fielding, hands at chest	2,200	1,300	975.00
524 (b)	throwing	2,200	1,300	975.00

1965 Old London Coins

These 1-1/2" diameter metal coins were included in Old London snack food packages. The 40 coins in this set feature two players from each of the major leagues' 20 teams, except St. Louis (3) and the New York Mets (1). Coin fronts have color photos and player names, while the silver-colored backs give a brief biography. An Old London logo is also displayed on each coin back. Space Magic Ltd. produced the coins. This is the same company which produced similar sets for Topps in 1964 and 1971.

		NM	EX	VG
Complete Set (40):		475.00	240.00	140.00
Common Player:		3.00	1.50	.90
Unopened Set:		1,800	900.00	525.00
Unopened Coin: 3-4X				
(1)	Henry Aaron	35.00	17.50	10.50
(2)	Richie Allen	7.50	3.75	2.25
(3)	Bob Allison	3.00	1.50	.90
(4)	Ernie Banks	25.00	12.50	7.50
(5)	Ken Boyer	4.50	2.25	1.25
(6)	Jim Bunning	15.00	7.50	4.50
(7)	Orlando Cepeda	12.50	6.25	3.75
(8)	Dean Chance	3.00	1.50	.90
(9)	Rocky Colavito	10.00	5.00	3.00
(10)	Vic Davalillo	3.00	1.50	.90
(11)	Tommy Davis	3.00	1.50	.90
(12)	Ron Fairly	3.00	1.50	.90
(13)	Dick Farrell	3.00	1.50	.90
(14)	Jim Fregosi	3.00	1.50	.90
(15)	Bob Friend	3.00	1.50	.90
(16)	Dick Groat	3.00	1.50	.90
(17)	Ron Hunt	3.00	1.50	.90
(18)	Chuck Hinton	3.00	1.50	.90
(19)	Ken Johnson	3.00	1.50	.90
(20)	Al Kaline	20.00	10.00	6.00
(21)	Harmon Killebrew	20.00	10.00	6.00
(22)	Don Lock	3.00	1.50	.90
(23)	Mickey Mantle	100.00	50.00	30.00
(24)	Roger Maris	30.00	15.00	9.00
(25)	Willie Mays	35.00	17.50	10.50
(26)	Bill Mazeroski	12.50	6.25	3.75
(27)	Gary Peters	3.00	1.50	.90
(28)	Vada Pinson	3.50	1.75	1.00
(29)	Boog Powell	4.50	2.25	1.25
(30)	Dick Radatz	3.00	1.50	.90
(31)	Brooks Robinson	20.00	10.00	6.00
(32)	Frank Robinson	20.00	10.00	6.00
(33)	Tracy Stallard	3.00	1.50	.90
(34)	Joe Torre	7.50	3.75	2.25
(35)	Leon Wagner	3.00	1.50	.90
(36)	Pete Ward	3.00	1.50	.90
(37)	Dave Wickersham	3.00	1.50	.90
(38)	Billy Williams	15.00	7.50	4.50
(39)	John Wyatt	3.00	1.50	.90
(40)	Carl Yastrzemski	25.00	12.50	7.50

1909-11 Old Mill Cigarettes

T206 cards bearing the Old Mill advertising are, with a major exception, among the most common of the set's back variations. Two styles of Old Mill T206 backs are found. One, which appears on cards of major league players and minor leaguers other than those from the Southern leagues, mentions a "BASE BALL / SUBJECTS / LARGE ASSORTMENT." The other specifies the four Southern leagues from which the players depicted originate. In recent years advanced T206 specialists have become aware of a brown-ink version of the Southern leagues back, much rarer than the black-ink version usually found on both types of Old Mill backs. All of the confirmed brown-ink cards appear to have been hand-cut from a sheet, leading to speculation as to whether they represent an actual issued variation or were salvaged from a scrapped printing. Some brown-ink Southern League cards are found with a red overprint on back, "Facotry 649 - District 1 - State N.Y." Cards showing a similar overprint in black have been fraudulently

altered. Contemporary with the T206 issues, Old Mill also produced a lengthy series of red-bordered minor league player cards in 1910. Those are listed in the minor league section of this book.

PREMIUMS
Common: 1.25X
Stars/So. Leagues: 1X
Red overprint: 20X
Brown-ink So. Leagues: 10X
   (See S74, T3, T206.)

1910 Old Put Cigar

This is a version of the anonymous E98 "Set of 30" on which an advertisement for "OLD PUT / 5 ct. CIGAR" has been rubber-stamped in purple. Cards can be found with either red or blue backgrounds on front. Because of the ease with which these could be faked, collectors must exercise extreme caution.

		NM	EX	VG
Common Player:		3,750	1,875	1,125
(1)	Christy Matthewson (Mathewson)	13,500	6,500	4,000
(2)	John McGraw	6,000	3,000	1,800
(3)	Johnny Kling	3,750	1,875	1,025
(4)	Frank Chance	6,000	3,000	1,800
(5)	Hans Wagner	16,500	8,250	5,000
(6)	Fred Clarke	3,750	1,875	1,025
(7)	Roger Bresnahan	3,750	1,875	1,025
(8)	Hal Chase	6,000	3,000	1,800
(9)	Russ Ford	3,750	1,875	1,025
(10)	"Ty" Cobb	20,000	10,000	6,000
(11)	Hughey Jennings	3,750	1,875	1,025
(12)	Chief Bender	6,000	3,000	1,800
(13)	Ed Walsh	3,750	1,875	1,025
(14)	Cy Young	12,000	6,000	3,600
(15)	Al Bridwell	3,750	1,875	1,025
(16)	Miner Brown	3,750	1,875	1,025
(17)	George Mullin	3,750	1,875	1,025
(18)	Chief Meyers	3,750	1,875	1,025
(19)	Hippo Vaughn	3,750	1,875	1,025
(20)	Red Dooin	3,750	1,875	1,025
(21)	Fred Tenny (Tenney)	3,750	1,875	1,025
(22)	Larry McLean	3,750	1,875	1,025
(23)	Nap Lajoie	6,000	3,000	1,800
(24)	Joe Tinker	6,000	3,000	1,800
(25)	Johnny Evers	6,000	3,000	1,800
(26)	Harry Davis	3,750	1,875	1,025
(27)	Eddie Collins	6,000	3,000	1,800
(28)	Bill Dahlen	3,750	1,875	1,025
(29)	Connie Mack	6,000	3,000	1,800
(30)	Jack Coombs	3,750	1,875	1,025

1951 Olmes Studio Postcards

This line of Philadelphia player postcards (all but one from the A's) was produced by a local photographer, probably for player use in satisfying fans' autograph requests. The 3-1/2" x 5-1/2" cards have a glossy black-and-white player photo on front. Backs have only standard postcard indicia and the Olmes credit line. Other players may remain to be checklisted. The unnumbered cards are listed here alphabetically.

		NM	EX	VG
Common Player:		75.00	37.50	22.50
(1)	Sam Chapman	75.00	37.50	22.50
(2)	Ferris Fain (Ready to hit, on grass.)	100.00	50.00	30.00
(3)	Ferris Fain/Btg (Choking up.)	100.00	50.00	30.00

(4)	Ferris Fain/Btg (Follow-through.)	100.00	50.00	30.00
(5)	Ferris Fain/Kneeling	100.00	50.00	30.00
(6)	Dick Fowler	75.00	37.50	22.50
(7)	Bob Hooper	75.00	37.50	22.50
(8)	Skeeter Kell	75.00	37.00	22.50
(9)	Paul Lehner	75.00	37.50	22.50
(10)	Lou Limmer	75.00	37.50	22.50
(11)	Barney McCosky	75.00	37.50	22.50
(12)	Robin Roberts	275.00	135.00	80.00
(13)	Carl Scheib	75.00	37.50	22.50
(14)	Bobby Shantz	75.00	37.50	22.50
(15)	Joe Tipton	75.00	37.50	22.50
(16)	Gus Zernial/Btg	100.00	50.00	30.00
(17)	Gus Zernial/Kneeling	100.00	50.00	30.00

1979 Open Pantry/Lake to Lake MACC

 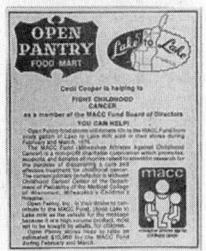

To benefit Milwaukee Athletes Against Childhood Cancer the Open Pantry convenience stores in Wisconsin teamed with Lake to Lake Dairy to produce this card set. Red, white and black fronts of the 5" x 6" cards have a player photo, fac-simile autograph and team logo. Backs are printed in red with a message from the player about the MACC fund. Besides members of the Milwaukee Brewers listed here, the set fea-tures Green Bay Packers and Milwaukee Bucks players. The unnumbered cards are checklisted here alphabetically.

		NM	EX	VG
Complete Set (12):		10.00	5.00	3.00
Common (Baseball) Player:		2.00	1.00	.60
(1)	Jerry Augustine	3.00	1.50	.90
(2)	Sal Bando	3.00	1.50	.90
(3)	Cecil Cooper	4.00	2.00	1.25
(4)	Larry Hisle	3.00	1.50	.90
(5)	Lary Sorensen	3.00	1.50	.90

1910 "Orange Borders"

Known in the hobby as "Orange Borders," these 1-1/2" x 2-7/16" cards were issued in 1910 and were printed on candy boxes that displayed the words "American Sports and Candy and Jewelry." The end flaps indicate the producers as the "Geo. Davis Co., Inc." and the "P.R. Warren Co., Warrenville Lowell, Mass." According to the box, the complete set includes "144 leading ballplayers," but to date just over two dozen dif-ferent subjects are known. When found today, these black and white photos, in reality, were part of the candy box. One of the team cards was found on each box, with a player card on the other side. Similar in format to the "Baseball Bats" cards, Orange Borders have player names which are hand-lettered, rather than type-set. Gaps have been left in the assigned numbering to acco-modate future additions to the checklist.

		NM	EX	VG
Common Player:		725.00	375.00	220.00
(1)	Jack Barry	725.00	375.00	220.00
(2)	Bill Bergen	725.00	375.00	220.00
(3)	Bill Bradley	725.00	375.00	220.00
(4)	Bill Carrigan	725.00	375.00	220.00
(5)	Hal Chase	900.00	450.00	240.00
(6)	Fred Clark (Clarke)	1,100	575.00	300.00
(7)	Ty Cobb	9,000	4,500	2,400
(8)	Sam Crawford	900.00	450.00	240.00
(9)	Lou Criger	725.00	375.00	220.00
(10)	Harry Davis	725.00	375.00	220.00
(11)	Art Devlin	725.00	375.00	220.00
(12)	Mickey Doolan	725.00	375.00	220.00
(13)	Larry Doyle	725.00	375.00	220.00
(14)	George Gibson	725.00	375.00	220.00
(15)	Addie Joss	1,200	600.00	300.00
(16)	Nap Lajoie	1,100	575.00	300.00
(17)	Frank LaPorte	725.00	375.00	220.00

(18)	Harry Lord	725.00	375.00	220.00
(19)	Christy Mathewson	4,100	2,100	1,250
(20)	Amby McConnell	725.00	375.00	220.00
(21)	John McGraw	1,100	575.00	300.00
(22)	Dots Miller	725.00	375.00	220.00
(23)	George Mullin	725.00	375.00	220.00
(24)	Larry Niles	725.00	375.00	220.00
(25)	Eddie Plank	1,110	575.00	300.00
(26)	Tris Speaker	1,300	675.00	350.00
(27)	Jake Stahl	725.00	375.00	220.00
(28)	Harry Steinfeldt	725.00	375.00	220.00
(29)	Honus Wagner/Btg	6,750	3,400	2,000
(30)	Honus Wagner/Portrait	6,750	3,400	2,000
(31)	Jack Warhop	725.00	375.00	220.00
(32)	American League Champions, 1909 (Detroit)	1,800	900.00	550.00
(33)	National League Champions, 1909 (Pittsburgh)	1,800	900.00	550.00

1976 Orbaker's Discs

One of several regional sponsors of player disc sets in 1976 was the Orbaker's restaurant chain. The discs are 3-3/8" diameter with a black-and-white player portrait photo in the center of the baseball design. A line of red stars is above, while the left and right panels feature one of several bright col-ors. Produced by Michael Schecter Associates under license from the Major League Baseball Players Association, the player photos have had uniform and cap logos removed. Backs are printed in red and purple. The unnumbered check-list here is presented in alphabetical order.

		NM	EX	VG
Complete Set (70):		50.00	25.00	15.00
Common Player:		1.00	.50	.30
(1)	Henry Aaron	20.00	10.00	6.00
(2)	Johnny Bench	6.00	3.00	1.75
(3)	Vida Blue	1.00	.50	.30
(4)	Larry Bowa	1.00	.50	.30
(5)	Lou Brock	4.00	2.00	1.25
(6)	Jeff Burroughs	1.00	.50	.30
(7)	John Candelaria	1.00	.50	.30
(8)	Jose Cardenal	1.00	.50	.30
(9)	Rod Carew	4.00	2.00	1.25
(10)	Steve Carlton	4.00	2.00	1.25
(11)	Dave Cash	1.00	.50	.30
(12)	Cesar Cedeno	1.00	.50	.30
(13)	Ron Cey	1.00	.50	.30
(14)	Carlton Fisk	4.00	2.00	1.25
(15)	Tito Fuentes	1.00	.50	.30
(16)	Steve Garvey	2.00	1.00	.60
(17)	Ken Griffey	1.00	.50	.30
(18)	Don Gullett	1.00	.50	.30
(19)	Willie Horton	1.00	.50	.30
(20)	Al Hrabosky	1.00	.50	.30
(21)	Catfish Hunter	3.00	1.50	.90
(22)	Reggie Jackson (A's)	12.00	6.00	3.50
(23)	Randy Jones	1.00	.50	.30
(24)	Jim Kaat	1.00	.50	.30
(25)	Don Kessinger	1.00	.50	.30
(26)	Dave Kingman	1.00	.50	.30
(27)	Jerry Koosman	1.00	.50	.30
(28)	Mickey Lolich	1.00	.50	.30
(29)	Greg Luzinski	1.00	.50	.30
(30)	Fred Lynn	1.00	.50	.30
(31)	Bill Madlock	1.00	.50	.30
(32)	Carlos May	1.00	.50	.30
(33)	John Mayberry	1.00	.50	.30
(34)	Bake McBride	1.00	.50	.30
(35)	Doc Medich	1.00	.50	.30
(36)	Andy Messersmith	1.00	.50	.30
(37)	Rick Monday	1.00	.50	.30
(38)	John Montefusco	1.00	.50	.30
(39)	Jerry Morales	1.00	.50	.30
(40)	Joe Morgan	4.00	2.00	1.25
(41)	Thurman Munson	3.00	1.50	.90
(42)	Bobby Murcer	1.00	.50	.30
(43)	Al Oliver	1.00	.50	.30
(44)	Jim Palmer	4.00	2.00	1.25
(45)	Dave Parker	1.00	.50	.30
(46)	Tony Perez	3.00	1.50	.90
(47)	Jerry Reuss	1.00	.50	.30
(48)	Brooks Robinson	6.00	3.00	1.75
(49)	Frank Robinson	6.00	3.00	1.75
(50)	Steve Rogers	1.00	.50	.30
(51)	Pete Rose	17.50	8.75	5.25
(52)	Nolan Ryan	25.00	12.50	7.50
(53)	Manny Sanguillen	1.00	.50	.30
(54)	Mike Schmidt	15.00	7.50	4.50
(55)	Tom Seaver	6.00	3.00	1.75
(56)	Ted Simmons	1.00	.50	.30
(57)	Reggie Smith	1.00	.50	.30
(58)	Willie Stargell	4.00	2.00	1.25
(59)	Rusty Staub	1.50	.70	.45
(60)	Rennie Stennett	1.00	.50	.30
(61)	Don Sutton	3.00	1.50	.90
(62)	Andy Thornton	1.00	.50	.30
(63)	Luis Tiant	1.00	.50	.30
(64)	Joe Torre	1.00	.50	.30
(65)	Mike Tyson	1.00	.50	.30
(66)	Bob Watson	1.00	.50	.30
(67)	Wilbur Wood	1.00	.50	.30

(68)	Jimmy Wynn	1.00	.50	.30
(69)	Carl Yastrzemski	6.00	3.00	1.75
(70)	Richie Zisk	1.00	.50	.30

1932 Orbit Gum Pins - Numbered (PR2)

Issued circa 1932, this skip-numbered set of small (13/16" diameter) pins was produced by Orbit Gum and carries the Amerian Card Catalog designation of PR2. A color player litho-graph is set against a green background with the player's name and team printed on a strip of yellow below. The pin number is at the very bottom; pins after #40 are skip-numbered.

		NM	EX	VG
Complete Set (53):		2,500	1,250	750.00
Common Player:		30.00	15.00	9.00
1	Ivy Andrews	30.00	15.00	9.00
2	Carl Reynolds	30.00	15.00	9.00
3	Riggs Stephenson	30.00	15.00	9.00
4	Lon Warneke	30.00	15.00	9.00
5	Frank Grube	30.00	15.00	9.00
6	"Kiki" Cuyler	60.00	30.00	18.00
7	Marty McManus	30.00	15.00	9.00
8	Lefty Clark	30.00	15.00	9.00
9	George Blaeholder	30.00	15.00	9.00
10	Willie Kamm	30.00	15.00	9.00
11	Jimmy Dykes	30.00	15.00	9.00
12	Earl Averill	60.00	30.00	18.00
13	Pat Malone	30.00	15.00	9.00
14	Dizzy Dean	200.00	100.00	60.00
15	Dick Bartell	30.00	15.00	9.00
16	Guy Bush	30.00	15.00	9.00
17	Bud Tinning	30.00	15.00	9.00
18	Jimmy Foxx	150.00	75.00	45.00
19	Mule Haas	30.00	15.00	9.00
20	Lew Fonseca	30.00	15.00	9.00
21	Pepper Martin	40.00	20.00	12.00
22	Phil Collins	30.00	15.00	9.00
23	Bill Cissell	30.00	15.00	9.00
24	Bump Hadley	30.00	15.00	9.00
25	Smead Jolley	30.00	15.00	9.00
26	Burleigh Grimes	60.00	30.00	18.00
27	Dale Alexander	30.00	15.00	9.00
28	Mickey Cochrane	60.00	30.00	18.00
29	Mel Harder	30.00	15.00	9.00
30	Mark Koenig	30.00	15.00	9.00
31a	Lefty O'Doul (Dodgers)	50.00	25.00	15.00
31b	Lefty O'Doul (Giants)	90.00	45.00	27.00
32a	Woody English (With bat.)	30.00	15.00	9.00
32b	Woody English (Without bat.)	80.00	40.00	24.00
33a	Billy Jurges (With bat.)	30.00	15.00	9.00
33b	Billy Jurges (Without bat.)	80.00	40.00	24.00
34	Bruce Campbell	30.00	15.00	9.00
35	Joe Vosmik	30.00	15.00	9.00
36	Dick Porter	30.00	15.00	9.00
37	Charlie Grimm	30.00	15.00	9.00
38	George Earnshaw	30.00	15.00	9.00
39	Al Simmons	60.00	30.00	18.00
40	Red Lucas	30.00	15.00	9.00
51	Wally Berger	30.00	15.00	9.00
55	Jim Levey	30.00	15.00	9.00
58	Ernie Lombardi	60.00	30.00	18.00
64	Jack Burns	30.00	15.00	9.00
67	Billy Herman	60.00	30.00	18.00
72	Bill Hallahan	30.00	15.00	9.00
92	Don Brennan	30.00	15.00	9.00
96	Sam Byrd	30.00	15.00	9.00
99	Ben Chapman	30.00	15.00	9.00
103	John Allen	30.00	15.00	9.00
107	Tony Lazzeri	60.00	30.00	18.00
111	Earl Combs (Earle)	60.00	30.00	18.00
116	Joe Sewell	60.00	30.00	18.00
120	Vernon Gomez	60.00	30.00	18.00

1932 Orbit Gum Pins - Unnumbered (PR3)

This set, issued by Orbit Gum circa 1932, has the Ameri-can Card Catalog designation PR3. The pins are identical to the PR2 set, except they are unnumbered.

	NM	EX	VG
Complete Set (60):	3,750	1,850	1,100
Common Player:	60.00	30.00	9.00

(1)	Dale Alexander	60.00	30.00	18.00
(2)	Ivy Andrews	60.00	30.00	18.00
(3)	Earl Averill	100.00	50.00	30.00
(4)	Dick Bartell	60.00	30.00	18.00
(5)	Wally Berger	60.00	30.00	18.00
(6)	George Blaeholder	60.00	30.00	18.00
(7)	Jack Burns	60.00	30.00	18.00
(8)	Guy Bush	60.00	30.00	18.00
(9)	Bruce Campbell	60.00	30.00	18.00
(10)	Bill Cissell	60.00	30.00	18.00
(11)	Lefty Clark	60.00	30.00	18.00
(12)	Mickey Cochrane	100.00	50.00	30.00
(13)	Phil Collins	60.00	30.00	18.00
(14)	"Kiki" Cuyler	100.00	50.00	30.00
(15)	Dizzy Dean	175.00	87.00	52.00
(16)	Jimmy Dykes	60.00	30.00	18.00
(17)	George Earnshaw	60.00	30.00	18.00
(18)	Woody English	60.00	30.00	18.00
(19)	Lew Fonseca	60.00	30.00	18.00
(20)	Jimmy (Jimmie) Foxx	175.00	87.00	52.00
(21)	Burleigh Grimes	100.00	50.00	30.00
(22)	Charlie Grimm	60.00	30.00	18.00
(23)	Lefty Grove	100.00	50.00	30.00
(24)	Frank Grube	60.00	30.00	18.00
(25)	Mule Haas	60.00	30.00	18.00
(26)	Bump Hadley	60.00	30.00	18.00
(27)	Chick Hafey	100.00	50.00	30.00
(28)	Jesse Haines	100.00	50.00	30.00
(29)	Bill Hallahan	60.00	30.00	18.00
(30)	Mel Harder	60.00	30.00	18.00
(31)	Gabby Hartnett	100.00	50.00	30.00
(32)	Babe Herman	65.00	32.00	19.50
(33)	Billy Herman	100.00	50.00	30.00
(34)	Rogers Hornsby	135.00	67.00	40.00
(35)	Roy Johnson	60.00	30.00	18.00
(36)	Smead Jolley	60.00	30.00	18.00
(37)	Billy Jurges	60.00	30.00	18.00
(38)	Willie Kamm	60.00	30.00	18.00
(39)	Mark Koenig	60.00	30.00	18.00
(40)	Jim Levey	60.00	30.00	18.00
(41)	Ernie Lombardi	100.00	50.00	30.00
(42)	Red Lucas	60.00	30.00	18.00
(43)	Ted Lyons	100.00	50.00	30.00
(44)	Connie Mack	100.00	50.00	30.00
(45)	Pat Malone	60.00	30.00	18.00
(46)	Pepper Martin	75.00	37.00	22.00
(47)	Marty McManus	60.00	30.00	18.00
(48)	Lefty O'Doul	80.00	40.00	24.00
(49)	Dick Porter	60.00	30.00	18.00
(50)	Carl Reynolds	60.00	30.00	18.00
(51)	Charlie Root	60.00	30.00	18.00
(52)	Bob Seeds	60.00	30.00	18.00
(53)	Al Simmons	100.00	50.00	30.00
(54)	Riggs Stephenson	60.00	30.00	18.00
(55)	Bud Tinning	60.00	30.00	18.00
(56)	Joe Vosmik	60.00	30.00	18.00
(57)	Rube Walberg	60.00	30.00	18.00
(58)	Paul Waner	100.00	50.00	30.00
(59)	Lon Warneke	60.00	30.00	18.00
(60)	Pinky Whitney	60.00	30.00	18.00

1937-39 Orcajo Cincinnati Reds Postcards (PC786)

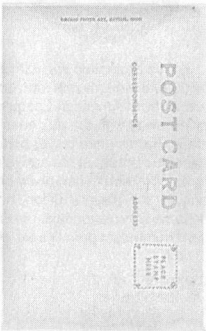

Orcajo, a Dayton, Ohio, photo firm, issued a series of Reds player postcards (plus, inexplicably, Joe DiMaggio) from 1937-39. Besides those found with just the issuer's imprint on the back, some or all of the players' cards can be found with the advertising on front of the Val Decker Packing Co., a meat dealer, Metropolitan Clothing Co., and an inset photo of WHIO radio announcer Si Burick (the latter are the 1937 cards and have no Orcajo imprint on back, utilizing different photos than the 1938-39 cards). The 3-1/2" x 5-1/2" cards have glossy black-and-white player poses on front with the player's name overprinted. Backs have standard postcard indicia. A number of spelling errors and several variations exist. The unnumbered cards are checklisted here alphabetically; those with ads for the meat company, men's store or radio station are appropriately noted.

		NM	EX	VG
Complete Set (37):		3,775	1,700	945.00
Common Player:		100.00	45.00	25.00
(1)	Wally Berger	100.00	45.00	25.00
(2)	Bongiovanni (First name Nino.)	100.00	45.00	25.00
(3)	Frenchy Bordagaray	100.00	45.00	25.00
(4)	Joe Cascarella, Gene Schott (Val Decker only.)	100.00	45.00	25.00
(5)	Allan Cooke (Allen) (Val Decker only.)	100.00	45.00	25.00
(6)	Harry Craft (Also Val Decker.)	100.00	45.00	25.00
(7)	Kiki Cuyler (WHIO only.)	160.00	72.00	40.00

(8)	Ray Davis	100.00	45.00	25.00
(9)	Virgil Davis (Val Decker only.)	100.00	45.00	25.00
(10)	Paul Derringer (Also Val Decker.)	100.00	45.00	25.00
(11)	Joe DiMaggio	825.00	370.00	205.00
(12a)	Linus Frey (Also Val Decker.) (No right foot, large caption.)	100.00	45.00	25.00
(12b)	Linus Frey (Also Val Decker.) (Right foot shows, small caption.)	100.00	45.00	25.00
(13)	Lee Gamble	100.00	45.00	25.00
(14)	Ivan Goodman (Ival) (Also Val Decker.)	100.00	45.00	25.00
(15)	Hank Gowdy	100.00	45.00	25.00
(16)	Lee Grissom	100.00	45.00	25.00
(17a)	Willard Hershberger (Hershberger, name in white.) (Also Val Decker.)	100.00	45.00	25.00
(17b)	Willard Hershberger (Name in black.)	100.00	45.00	25.00
(18a)	Al Hollingsworth	100.00	45.00	25.00
(18b)	Al Hollingsworth (WHIO)	100.00	45.00	25.00
(18c)	Al Hollingsworth (Val Decker)	100.00	45.00	25.00
(19)	Hank Johnson	100.00	45.00	25.00
(20)	Edwin Joost	100.00	45.00	25.00
(21a)	Ernie Lombardi (Plain letters.) (Also Val Decker, Metro.)	160.00	72.00	40.00
(21b)	Ernie Lombardi (Fancy letters.) (Also Val Decker, Metro.)	160.00	72.00	40.00
(22)	Frank McCormick (Also Val Decker, Metro.)	100.00	45.00	25.00
(23)	Bill McKecknie (McKechnie)	145.00	65.00	36.00
(24)	Billy Meyers (Myers) (Also Val Decker.)	100.00	45.00	25.00
(25a)	Whitey Moore (Photo actually Bucky Walters.)			
(25b)	Whitey Moore (Correct photo.)	100.00	45.00	25.00
(26)	Lew Riggs	100.00	45.00	25.00
(27)	Edd Roush (Val Decker only.)	145.00	65.00	36.00
(28a)	Leo Scarsella (Les)	160.00	72.00	40.00
(28b)	Les Scarsella (WHIO)	100.00	45.00	25.00
(29)	Gene Schott (WHIO)	100.00	45.00	25.00
(30)	Milburn Shoffner	100.00	45.00	25.00
(31)	Junior Thompson	100.00	45.00	25.00
(32a)	Johnny VanderMeer/Throwing (Also Metro, Val Decker.)	175.00	79.00	44.00
(32b)	Johnny VanderMeer (Fielding)(Also Metro.)	175.00	79.00	44.00
(33)	Bucky Walters	100.00	45.00	25.00
(34)	Bill Werber	100.00	45.00	25.00
(35)	Dick West	100.00	45.00	25.00
(36)	Jimmie Wilson	100.00	45.00	25.00
(37)	Cincinnati Reds composite team card.	100.00	45.00	25.00

1933 Oriental Theatre

To advertise its movie schedule for the week of June 17-23, as well as a Father's Day prize drawing, the Oriental Theatre (location unknown, possibly Dorchester, Mass., or Chicago) printed its message on the back of a 1929 Kashin Publications (R316) card or cards. The extent to which this overprinting was undertaken is unknown.

	NM	EX	VG
Ed "Bing" Miller	125.00	62.50	37.50

1912 A.F. Orr Louis Sockalexis Photocard

This 3-1/2" x 5-1/2" sepia photocard carries the copyright of A.F. Orr of Old Town, Maine, hometown of the original Cleveland Indian. At the time of the card's issue, the fallen diamond star was operating a ferry and probably commissioned this image for sale to tourists.

	NM	EX	VG
Louis Sockalexis	2,000	1,000	600.00

1963 Otto Milk

The attributed issue date of this commemorative milk carton is approximate. A 4" x 8" panel on the front of the milk carton has a picture and history of Honus Wagner printed in red and blue. Wagner is the only ballplayer in the milk carton series honoring Western Pennsylvania celebrities.

		NM	EX	VG
(1)	Honus Wagner (Complete carton.)	250.00	125.00	75.00
(1)	Honus Wagner (Cut panel.)	60.00	30.00	18.00

1938 Our National Game Pins

This unnumbered 30-pin set issued circa 1938 carries the American Card Catalog designation of PM8. The pins, which measure 7/8" in diameter, have a bendable "tab" rather than a pin back. The player photo is printed in blue-and-white. The player's name and team are printed at bottom. The pins were originally sold on a square of cardboard decorated with stars and stripes and imprinted "OUR NATIONAL GAME" above the pin, and "A BASEBALL HERO" below. A large number of the pins, complete with their cardboard backing, were found in a hoard in Oklahoma in the early 1990s.

		NM	EX	VG
Complete Set (30):		1,200	600.00	350.00
Common Player:		20.00	10.00	6.00
(1)	Wally Berger	20.00	10.00	6.00
(2)	Lou Chiozza	20.00	10.00	6.00
(3)	Joe Cronin	40.00	20.00	12.00
(4)	Frank Crosetti	25.00	12.50	7.50
(5)	Jerome (Dizzy) Dean	75.00	37.00	22.00
(6)	Frank DeMaree (Demaree)	20.00	10.00	6.00
(7)	Joe DiMaggio	100.00	50.00	30.00
(8)	Bob Feller	65.00	32.00	19.50
(9)	Jimmy Foxx (Jimmie)	75.00	37.00	22.00
(10)	Lou Gehrig	100.00	50.00	30.00
(11)	Charles Gehringer	50.00	25.00	15.00
(12)	Lefty Gomez	40.00	20.00	12.00
(13)	Hank Greenberg	65.00	32.00	19.50
(14)	Irving (Bump) Hadley	20.00	10.00	6.00
(15)	Leo Hartnett	40.00	20.00	12.00
(16)	Carl Hubbell	50.00	25.00	15.00
(17)	John (Buddy) Lewis	20.00	10.00	6.00
(18)	Gus Mancuso	20.00	10.00	6.00
(19)	Joe McCarthy	40.00	20.00	12.00
(20)	Joe Medwick	40.00	20.00	12.00
(21)	Joe Moore	20.00	10.00	6.00
(22)	Mel Ott	50.00	25.00	15.00
(23)	Jake Powell	20.00	10.00	6.00
(24)	Jimmy Ripple	20.00	10.00	6.00
(25)	Red Ruffing	40.00	20.00	12.00
(26)	Hal Schumacher	20.00	10.00	6.00
(27)	George Selkirk	20.00	10.00	6.00
(28)	"Al" Simmons	40.00	20.00	12.00
(29)	Bill Terry	40.00	20.00	12.00
(30)	Harold Trosky	20.00	10.00	6.00

1936 Overland Candy Co. (R301)

Used as wrappers for a piece of penny candy, these 5" x 5-1/4" waxed papers are usually found with resultant folds and creases, though unfolded examples are known. Printed in dark blue, the top of the wrapper features a line drawing portrait of the player, his formal name and nickname, team, position and career summary. The unnumbered wrappers are checklisted here alphabetically.

	NM	EX	VG
Complete Set (60):	45,000	20,000	9,000
Common Player:	650.00	300.00	130.00
(1) Melo (Mel) Almada	650.00	300.00	130.00
(2) Lucius B. (Luke) Appling	900.00	400.00	180.00
(3) Howard Earl Averill	900.00	400.00	180.00
(4) Walter Antone (Wally) Berger	650.00	300.00	130.00
(5) Henry John (Zeke) Bonura	650.00	300.00	130.00
(6) Dolph Camilli	650.00	300.00	130.00
(7) Philip Joseph (Phil) Cavarretta	650.00	300.00	130.00
(8) William Ben (Chappy) Chapman	650.00	300.00	130.00
(9) Harland Clift (First name Harlond.)	650.00	300.00	130.00
(10a) John Walter (Johnny) Cooney (Bees)	650.00	300.00	130.00
(10b) John Walter (Johnny) Cooney (Dodgers)	650.00	300.00	130.00
(11) Harry Danning	650.00	300.00	130.00
(12) William N. (Bill) Dickey (Middle initial is N.)	950.00	425.00	190.00
(13a) William J. (Bill) Dietrich (Athletics)	650.00	300.00	130.00
(13b) William J. (Bill) Dietrich (White Sox)	650.00	300.00	130.00
(14) Joseph (Deadpan Joe) DiMaggio	3,000	1,350	600.00
(15) Wesley Cheek Ferrell	650.00	300.00	130.00
(16) James Emory (Jimmie) Foxx	1,200	540.00	240.00
(17) Henry Louis (Lou) Gehrig	3,150	1,425	630.00
(18) Charles Leonard (Charley) Gehringer	900.00	400.00	180.00
(19) Jose Luis (Chile) Gomez	650.00	300.00	130.00
(20) Vernon (Lefty) Gomez	900.00	400.00	180.00
(21) Joe Gordon	650.00	300.00	130.00
(22) Henry (Hank) Greenberg	1,200	540.00	240.00
(23) Robert Moses (Lefty) Grove	950.00	425.00	190.00
(24) George W. (Mule) Haas	650.00	300.00	130.00
(25) Ralston Burdett (Rollie) Hemsley	650.00	300.00	130.00
(26) Michael Francis (Pinky) Higgins (Middle name Franklin.)	650.00	300.00	130.00
(27) Oral Clyde (Hildy) Hildebrand	650.00	300.00	130.00
(28) Robert Lee (Cherokee) Johnson	650.00	300.00	130.00
(29) Baxter Byerly (Buck) Jordan	650.00	300.00	130.00
(30) Ken Keltner	650.00	300.00	130.00
(31) Fabian Kowalik	650.00	300.00	130.00
(32) Harry A. Lavagetto	650.00	300.00	130.00
(33) Anthony Michael (Poosh 'em Up) Lazzeri	900.00	400.00	180.00
(34) Samuel A. Leslie	650.00	300.00	130.00
(35) Dan (Slug) Lithwhiler (Last name Litwhiler.)	650.00	300.00	130.00
(36) Theodore A. (Ted) Lyons	900.00	400.00	180.00
(37) George McQuinn	650.00	300.00	130.00
(38) John Robert (Skippy) Mize	900.00	400.00	180.00
(39) Terry Moore	650.00	300.00	130.00
(40) Charles Solomon (Buddy) Myer	650.00	300.00	130.00
(41) Louis Norman (Buck) Newsom	650.00	300.00	130.00
(42) Bill Nicholson	650.00	300.00	130.00
(43) Raymond Pepper	650.00	300.00	130.00
(44) Frank A. (Pity) Pytlak	650.00	300.00	130.00
(45) Raymond Allen (Rip) Radcliff	650.00	300.00	130.00
(46) Peter (Pete) Reiser (Correct name Harold Patrick.)	650.00	300.00	130.00
(47) Carl Nettles (Sheeps) Reynolds	650.00	300.00	130.00
(48) Robert Abial (Red) Rolfe	650.00	300.00	130.00
(49) Lynwood Thomas (Schoolboy) Rowe	650.00	300.00	130.00
(50) Aloysius Harry (Al) Simmons	900.00	400.00	180.00
(51) Cecil Howard Travis (Middle name is Howell.)	650.00	300.00	130.00
(52) Harold Arthus (Hal) Trosky	650.00	300.00	130.00
(53) Joseph Franklin (Joe) Vosmik	650.00	300.00	130.00
(54) Harold Burton (Rabbit) Warstler	650.00	300.00	130.00
(55) William M. (Bill) Werber	650.00	300.00	130.00
(56) Max West	650.00	300.00	130.00
(57) Samuel F. (Sam) West	650.00	300.00	130.00
(58) Whitlow (Whit) Wyatt	650.00	300.00	130.00

1921 Oxford Confectionery (E253)

Issued in 1921 by Oxford Confectionery of Oxford, Pa., this 20-card set was printed on thin paper and distributed with caramels. Each card measures 1-5/8" x 2-3/4" and features a black-and-white player photo with the player's name and team printed in a white band along the bottom. The back carries a checklist of the players in the set, 14 of whom are now in the Hall of Fame. The set is designated as E253 in the ACC.

	NM	EX	VG
Complete Set (20):	35,000	15,750	7,000
Common Player:	1,000	450.00	200.00
(1) Grover Alexander	1,800	810.00	360.00
(2) Dave Bancroft	1,200	540.00	240.00
(3) Max Carey	1,200	540.00	240.00
(4) Ty Cobb	6,000	2,700	1,200
(5) Eddie Collins	1,200	540.00	240.00
(6) Frankie Frisch	1,200	540.00	240.00
(7) Burleigh Grimes	1,200	540.00	240.00
(8) "Bill" Holke (Walter)	1,000	450.00	200.00
(9) Rogers Hornsby	1,800	810.00	360.00
(10) Walter Johnson	3,000	1,350	600.00
(11) Lee Meadows	1,000	450.00	200.00
(12) Cy Perkins	1,000	450.00	200.00
(13) Derrill Pratt	1,000	450.00	200.00
(14) Ed Rousch (Roush)	1,200	540.00	240.00
(15) "Babe" Ruth	12,000	5,400	2,400
(16) Ray Schalk	1,200	540.00	240.00
(17) George Sisler	1,200	540.00	240.00
(18) Tris Speaker	1,800	810.00	360.00
(19) Cy Williams	1,000	450.00	200.00
(20) Whitey Witt	1,000	450.00	200.00

P

1958 Packard-Bell

Issued by the "world's largest seller of TVs, radios and hi-fis," this set was distributed in California and features members of the newly arrived Los Angeles Dodgers and San Francisco Giants. The 3-1/2" x 5-1/2" black-and-white cards are unnumbered, checklisted here alphabetically.

	NM	EX	VG
Complete Set (7):	1,500	750.00	450.00
Common Player:	100.00	50.00	30.00
(1) Walter Alston	125.00	65.00	35.00
(2) John A. Antonelli	100.00	50.00	30.00
(3) Jim Gilliam	125.00	65.00	35.00
(4) Gil Hodges	200.00	100.00	60.00
(5) Willie Mays	800.00	400.00	240.00
(6) Bill Rigney	100.00	50.00	30.00
(7) Hank Sauer	100.00	50.00	30.00

1949 Page's Pittsburgh Milk Co.

These cards are identical in format to the issue long known as 1947 Bond Bread cards. Printed by Chicago playing card manufacturer Arrco, the cards are the same size as contemporary playing cards, 2-1/4" x 3-3/8" with rounded corners. The backs carry a printed (purple and black ink have been seen) advertisement in four lines, "Page's / Pittsburgh Milk Co. / The Sweetest Milk / Ever Sold." An offer card, which specified a Sept. 1, 1949 closing date, details a promotion by which a complete set of 48 cards - carrying the Page Milk stamp - could be redeemed for a "Roadmaster Luxury Liner" bicycle with a retail value of $69.95. It should be assumed that to avoid giving away too many bicycles, at least one of the cards was distributed in very limited quantities, though the rarity of any surviving examples of this issue makes determination of which card was short-printed impossible. The unnumbered cards are checklisted here alphabetically.

	NM	EX	VG
Common Player:	250.00	150.00	75.00
(1) Rex Barney	250.00	150.00	75.00

	NM	EX	VG
(2) Yogi Berra			
(3) Ewell Blackwell	250.00	150.00	75.00
(4) Lou Boudreau	275.00	165.00	85.00
(5) Ralph Branca	250.00	150.00	75.00
(6) Harry Brecheen	250.00	150.00	75.00
(7) Dom DiMaggio	275.00	165.00	85.00
(8) Joe DiMaggio	550.00	350.00	175.00
(9) Bobbie Doerr (Bobby)	275.00	165.00	85.00
(10) Bruce Edwards	250.00	150.00	75.00
(11) Bob Elliott	250.00	150.00	75.00
(12) Del Ennis	250.00	150.00	75.00
(13) Bob Feller	300.00	180.00	90.00
(14) Carl Furillo	250.00	150.00	75.00
(15) Cid Gordon (Sid)	250.00	150.00	75.00
(16) Joe Gordon	275.00	165.00	85.00
(17) Joe Hatten	250.00	150.00	75.00
(18) Gil Hodges	275.00	165.00	85.00
(19) Tommy Holmes	250.00	150.00	75.00
(20) Larry Janson (Jansen)	250.00	150.00	75.00
(21) Sheldon Jones	250.00	150.00	75.00
(22) Edwin Joost	250.00	150.00	75.00
(23) Charlie Keller	250.00	150.00	75.00
(24) Ken Keltner	250.00	150.00	75.00
(25) Buddy Kerr	250.00	150.00	75.00
(26) Ralph Kiner	275.00	165.00	85.00
(27) John Lindell	250.00	150.00	75.00
(28) Whitey Lockman	250.00	150.00	75.00
(29) Willard Marshall	250.00	150.00	75.00
(30) Johnny Mize	275.00	165.00	85.00
(31) Stan Musial	400.00	250.00	125.00
(32) Andy Pafko	250.00	150.00	75.00
(33) Johnny Pesky	250.00	150.00	75.00
(34) Pee Wee Reese	350.00	225.00	125.00
(35) Phil Rizzuto	350.00	225.00	125.00
(36) Aaron Robinson	250.00	150.00	75.00
(37) Jackie Robinson	500.00	300.00	150.00
(38) John Sain	250.00	150.00	75.00
(39) Enos Slaughter	275.00	165.00	85.00
(40) Vern Stephens	250.00	150.00	75.00
(41) George Tebbetts	250.00	150.00	75.00
(42) Bob Thomson	250.00	150.00	75.00
(43) Johnny Vandermeer (VanderMeer)	250.00	150.00	75.00
(44) Ted Williams	500.00	300.00	150.00
BOXERS			
(45) Primo Carnera	200.00	125.00	60.00
(46) Marcel Cerdan	200.00	125.00	60.00
(47) Jake LaMotta	250.00	150.00	75.00
(48) Joe Louis	400.00	250.00	125.00

1978 Papa Gino's Discs

 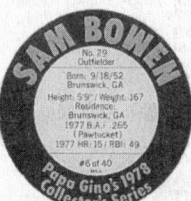

This promotion was largely confined to the Boston area, as 25 of the 40 players represented are Red Sox, the other 15 are all from American League teams. The 3-3/8" discs were given away with the purchase of soft drinks at the restaurant chain. Fronts have player portraits at center with name in the dark blue border at top and team below. Photos have the uniform logos airbrushed away because the discs were licensed only by the players' union, not MLB. Backs retain the color scheme with player data, previous season's stats, uniform and card numbers, sponsor's ad, etc.

	NM	EX	VG
Complete Set (40):	20.00	10.00	6.00
Common Player:	2.00	1.00	.60
1 Allen Ripley	2.00	1.00	.60
2 Jerry Remy	2.00	1.00	.60
3 Jack Brohamer	2.00	1.00	.60
4 Butch Hobson	2.00	1.00	.60
5 Dennis Eckersley	3.50	1.75	1.00
6 Sam Bowen	2.00	1.00	.60
7 Rick Burleson	2.00	1.00	.60
8 Carl Yastrzemski	5.00	2.50	1.50
9 Bill Lee	2.00	1.00	.60
10 Bob Montgomery	2.00	1.00	.60
11 Dick Drago	2.00	1.00	.60
12 Bob Stanley	2.00	1.00	.60
13 Fred Kendall	2.00	1.00	.60
14 Jim Rice	3.00	1.50	.90
15 George Scott	2.00	1.00	.60
16 Tom Burgmeier	2.00	1.00	.60
17 Frank Duffy	2.00	1.00	.60
18 Jim Wright	2.00	1.00	.60
19 Fred Lynn	2.00	1.00	.60
20 Bob Bailey	2.00	1.00	.60
21 Mike Torrez	2.00	1.00	.60
22 Bill Campbell	2.00	1.00	.60
23 Luis Tiant	2.00	1.00	.60
24 Dwight Evans	2.00	1.00	.60
25 Carlton Fisk	4.00	2.00	1.25
26 Reggie Jackson	5.00	2.50	1.50
27 Thurman Munson	3.50	1.75	1.00
28 Ron Guidry	2.00	1.00	.60
29 Bruce Bochte	2.00	1.00	.60
30 Richie Zisk	2.00	1.00	.60
31 Jim Palmer	4.00	2.00	1.25
32 Mark Fidrych	2.50	1.25	.70
33 Frank Tanana	2.00	1.00	.60
34 Buddy Bell	2.00	1.00	.60

		NM	EX	VG
35	Rod Carew	4.00	2.00	1.25
36	George Brett	7.50	3.75	2.25
37	Ralph Garr	2.00	1.00	.60
38	Larry Hisle	2.00	1.00	.60
39	Mitchell Page	2.00	1.00	.60
40	John Mayberry	2.00	1.00	.60

1974 Bob Parker 2nd Best

Star players who came in second, often to lesser-known players, in various statistical categories between 1899-1955 are featured in this collectors issue from Bob Parker. The blank-backed, black-and-white cards measure an unusual 3" x 8" and feature the story of the 1-2 finish in cartoon form. The unnumbered cards are listed here in chronological order.

		NM	EX	VG
	Complete Set (25):	55.00	25.00	15.00
	Common Player:	3.00	1.50	.90
(1)	Jesse Burkett, Ed Delahanty (1899)	3.00	1.50	.90
(2)	Hans Wagner, Cy Seymour (1905)	4.00	2.00	1.25
(3)	Gavvy Cravath, Jake Daubert (1913)	3.00	1.50	.90
(4)	Joe Jackson, Ty Cobb (1913)	10.00	5.00	3.00
(5)	Eddie Collins, Ty Cobb (1914)	4.00	2.00	1.25
(6)	Babe Ruth, Heinie Manush (1926)	7.50	3.75	2.25
(7)	Chick Hafey, Jim Bottomley, Hack Wilson (1928)	3.00	1.50	.90
(8)	Paul Waner, Rogers Hornsby (1928)	3.00	1.50	.90
(9)	Babe Herman, Lefty O'Doul (1929)	3.00	1.50	.90
(10)	Al Simmons, Lew Fonseca (1929)	3.00	1.50	.90
(11)	Lou Gehrig, Babe Ruth (1930)	10.00	5.00	3.00
(12)	Babe Herman, Bill Terry (1930)	3.00	1.50	.90
(13)	Chuck Klein, Hack Wilson (1930)	3.00	1.50	.90
(14)	Jim Bottomley, Bill Terry, Chick Hafey (1931)	3.00	1.50	.90
(15)	Jimmy (Jimmie) Foxx, Dale Alexander (1932)	3.00	1.50	.90
(16)	Spud Davis, Chuck Klein (1933)	3.00	1.50	.90
(17)	Heinie Manush, Jimmy Foxx (1933)	3.00	1.50	.90
(18)	Mel Ott, Wally Berger (1935)	3.00	1.50	.90
(19)	Joe Vosmik, Buddy Myer (1935)	3.00	1.50	.90
(20)	Blimp Phelps, Paul Waner (1936)	3.00	1.50	.90
(21)	Bobby Doerr, Lou Boudreau (1944)	3.00	1.50	.90
(22)	Stan Musial, Dixie Walker (1944)	4.00	2.00	1.25
(23)	George Kell, Billy Goodman (1950)	3.00	1.50	.90
(24)	Al Rosen, Mickey Vernon (1953)	3.00	1.50	.90
(25)	Vic Power, Al Kaline (1955)	3.00	1.50	.90

1976 Bob Parker More Baseball Cartoons

This collectors' issue showcased the pen and ink artwork of Ohio cartoonist Bob Parker on cards featuring current and former ballplayers from the great to the obscure. Cards are in 3-1/2" x 5" format with black-and-white fronts and blank backs.

		NM	EX	VG
	Complete Set (24):	65.00	32.50	20.00
	Common Card:	3.00	1.50	.90
1	Hank Aaron, Babe Ruth (All-Time HR Specialists)	7.50	3.75	2.25
2	Ernie Banks	4.00	2.00	1.25
3	Rod Carew	3.00	1.50	.90
4	Joe DiMaggio	15.00	7.50	4.50
5	Doug Flynn	3.00	1.50	.90
6	Mike Garcia	3.00	1.50	.90
7	Steve Garvey, Greg Luzinski (All-Stars)	3.00	1.50	.90
8	Lou Gehrig	15.00	7.50	4.50
9	Chuck Klein, Hack Wilson (Hall of Famers?)	3.00	1.50	.90
10	Don Larsen	3.00	1.50	.90
11	Fred Lynn	3.00	1.50	.90
12	Roy Majtyka	3.00	1.50	.90
13	Pepper Martin	3.00	1.50	.90
14	Christy Mathewson	5.00	2.50	1.50
15	Cal McVey	3.00	1.50	.90
16	Tony Perez	3.00	1.50	.90
17	Lou Gehrig, Babe Ruth (Great Moments)	15.00	7.50	4.50
18	Everett Scott	3.00	1.50	.90
19	Bobby Thomson	3.00	1.50	.90
20	Ted Williams (1939)	7.50	3.75	2.25
21	Ted Williams (Great Moments)	7.50	3.75	2.25
22	Bill Madlock	3.00	1.50	.90
23	Henry Chadwick, Buck Ewing, Albert Spalding, Honus Wagner (Hall of Famers)	3.00	1.50	.90
---	Checklist	3.00	1.50	.90

1977 Bob Parker Cincinnati Reds

In the late 1970s, Ohio cartoonist Bob Parker drew a series of Reds feature cartoons for the weekly "Reds Alert." Later, he assembled two groups of those cartoons into collectors' issue card sets. The cards are black-and-white with blank backs. Fronts have portraits and/or action main drawings, usually with some cartoon figures included to draw attention to the player's career highlights. Size is 3-1/2" x 5". The unnumbered series is listed in alphabetical order.

		NM	EX	VG
	Complete Set (48):	110.00	55.00	32.50
	Common Player:	3.00	1.50	.90
	UNNUMBERED SERIES (24):	55.00	25.00	15.00
(1)	Sparky Anderson	4.00	2.00	1.25
(2)	Wally Berger	3.00	1.50	.90
(3)	Pedro Borbon	3.00	1.50	.90
(4)	Rube Bressler	3.00	1.50	.90
(5)	Gordy Coleman	3.00	1.50	.90
(6)	Dave Concepcion	3.00	1.50	.90
(7)	Harry Craft	3.00	1.50	.90
(8)	Hugh Critz	3.00	1.50	.90
(9)	Dan Driessen	3.00	1.50	.90
(10)	Pat Duncan	3.00	1.50	.90
(11)	Lonnie Frey	3.00	1.50	.90
(12)	Ival Goodman	3.00	1.50	.90
(13)	Heinie Groh	3.00	1.50	.90
(14)	Noodles Hahn	3.00	1.50	.90
(15)	Mike Lum	3.00	1.50	.90
(16)	Bill McKechnie	3.00	1.50	.90
(17)	Pat Moran	3.00	1.50	.90
(18)	Billy Myers	3.00	1.50	.90
(19)	Gary Nolan	3.00	1.50	.90
(20)	Fred Norman	3.00	1.50	.90
(21)	Jim O'Toole	3.00	1.50	.90
(22)	Vada Pinson	4.00	2.00	1.25
(23)	Bucky Walters	3.00	1.50	.90
(24)	Checklist	3.00	1.50	.90
	NUMBERED SERIES (24):	60.00	30.00	18.00
1	Ted Kluszewski	6.00	3.00	1.75
2	Johnny Bench	10.00	5.00	3.00
3	Jim Maloney	3.00	1.50	.90
4	Bubbles Hargrave	3.00	1.50	.90
5	Don Gullett	3.00	1.50	.90
6	Joe Nuxhall	4.00	2.00	1.25
7	Edd Roush	3.00	1.50	.90
8	Wally Post	3.00	1.50	.90
9	George Wright	3.00	1.50	.90
10	George Foster	3.00	1.50	.90
11	Pete Rose	15.00	7.50	4.50
12	Red Lucas	3.00	1.50	.90
13	Joe Morgan	4.00	2.00	1.25
14	Eppa Rixey	3.00	1.50	.90
15	Bill Werber	3.00	1.50	.90
16	Frank Robinson	6.00	3.00	1.75
17	Dolf Luque	4.00	2.00	1.25
18	Paul Derringer	3.00	1.50	.90
19	Frank McCormick	3.00	1.50	.90
20	Ken Griffey	3.00	1.50	.90
21	Jack Billingham	3.00	1.50	.90
22	Larry Kopf	3.00	1.50	.90
23	Ernie Lombardi	3.00	1.50	.90
24	Johnny Vander Meer	3.00	1.50	.90

1977-81 Bob Parker Hall of Fame

This is one of many collectors issues produced in the mid to late 1970s by midwestern sports artist Bob Parker. The 3-3/8" x 5-1/2" cards are printed in sepia on tan cardboard; they are blank-backed. Fronts have a portrait drawing of the player, with career highlights in cartoon form. Three series were issued: #1-54 in 1977; #55-77 in 1980 and #78-100 in 1981. A header card was issued with each series.

		NM	EX	VG
	Complete Set (103):	125.00	65.00	35.00
	Common Player:	3.00	1.50	.90
	First Series Set (55):	50.00	25.00	15.00
---	First Series Header	1.00	.50	.30
1	Grover Alexander	3.00	1.50	.90
2	Cap Anson	3.00	1.50	.90
3	Luke Appling	3.00	1.50	.90
4	Ernie Banks	4.00	2.00	1.25
5	Chief Bender	3.00	1.50	.90
6	Jim Bottomley	3.00	1.50	.90
7	Dan Brouthers	3.00	1.50	.90
8	Morgan Bulkeley	3.00	1.50	.90
9	Roy Campanella	7.50	3.75	2.25
10	Alexander Cartwright	3.00	1.50	.90
11	Henry Chadwick	3.00	1.50	.90
12	John Clarkson	3.00	1.50	.90
13	Ty Cobb	10.00	5.00	3.00
14	Eddie Collins	3.00	1.50	.90
16	Charles Comiskey	3.00	1.50	.90
17	Sam Crawford	3.00	1.50	.90
18	Dizzy Dean	4.00	2.00	1.25
19	Joe DiMaggio	16.00	8.00	4.75
20	Buck Ewing	3.00	1.50	.90
21	Bob Feller	4.00	2.00	1.25
22	Lou Gehrig	16.00	8.00	4.75
23	Goose Goslin	3.00	1.50	.90
24	Burleigh Grimes	3.00	1.50	.90
25	Chick Hafey	3.00	1.50	.90
26	Rogers Hornsby	3.00	1.50	.90
27	Carl Hubbell	3.00	1.50	.90
28	Miller Huggins	3.00	1.50	.90
29	Tim Keefe	3.00	1.50	.90
30	Mike Kelly	3.00	1.50	.90
31	Nap Lajoie	3.00	1.50	.90
32	Freddie Lindstrom	3.00	1.50	.90
33	Connie Mack	3.00	1.50	.90
34	Mickey Mantle	25.00	12.50	7.50
35	Heinie Manush	3.00	1.50	.90
36	Joe McGinnity	3.00	1.50	.90
37	John McGraw	3.00	1.50	.90
38	Ed Plank	3.00	1.50	.90
39	Eppa Rixey	3.00	1.50	.90
40	Jackie Robinson	12.00	6.00	3.50
41	Edd Roush	3.00	1.50	.90
42	Babe Ruth	20.00	10.00	6.00
43	Al Simmons	3.00	1.50	.90
44	Al Spalding	3.00	1.50	.90
45	Tris Speaker	3.00	1.50	.90
46	Casey Stengel	3.00	1.50	.90
47	Bill Terry	3.00	1.50	.90
48	Rube Waddell	3.00	1.50	.90
49	Honus Wagner	5.00	2.50	1.50
50	Paul Waner	3.00	1.50	.90
51	John Montgomery Ward	3.00	1.50	.90
52	Ted Williams	10.00	5.00	3.00
53	George Wright	3.00	1.50	.90
54	Harry Wright	3.00	1.50	.90
	Second Series Set (24):	40.00	20.00	12.00
---	Second Series Header	1.00	.50	.30
55	Mordecai Brown	3.00	1.50	.90
56	Frank Chance	3.00	1.50	.90
57	Candy Cummings	3.00	1.50	.90
58	Frank Frisch	3.00	1.50	.90
59	Gabby Hartnett	3.00	1.50	.90
60	Billy Herman	3.00	1.50	.90
61	Waite Hoyt	3.00	1.50	.90
62	Walter Johnson	5.00	2.50	1.50
63	Kenesaw Landis	3.00	1.50	.90
64	Rube Marquard	3.00	1.50	.90
65	Christy Mathewson	6.00	3.00	1.75
66	Eddie Mathews	3.00	1.50	.90
67	Willie Mays	10.00	5.00	3.00
68	Bill McKechnie	3.00	1.50	.90
69	Stan Musial	7.50	3.75	2.25
70	Mel Ott	3.00	1.50	.90
71	Satchel Paige	7.50	3.75	2.25
72	Robin Roberts	3.00	1.50	.90

73	George Sisler	3.00	1.50	.90
74	Warren Spahn	3.00	1.50	.90
75	Joe Tinker	3.00	1.50	.90
76	Dazzy Vance	3.00	1.50	.90
77	Cy Young	6.00	3.00	1.75
	Third Series Set (24):	40.00	20.00	12.00
---	Third Series Header	1.00	.50	.30
78	Home Run Baker	3.00	1.50	.90
79	Yogi Berra	4.00	2.00	1.25
80	Max Carey	3.00	1.50	.90
81	Roberto Clemente	16.00	8.00	4.75
82	Mickey Cochrane	3.00	1.50	.90
83	Roger Connor	3.00	1.50	.90
84	Joe Cronin	3.00	1.50	.90
85	Kiki Cuyler	3.00	1.50	.90
86	Johnny Evers	3.00	1.50	.90
87	Jimmie Foxx	3.00	1.50	.90
88	Charlie Gehringer	3.00	1.50	.90
89	Lefty Gomez	3.00	1.50	.90
90	Jesse Haines	3.00	1.50	.90
91	Will Harridge	3.00	1.50	.90
92	Monte Irvin	3.00	1.50	.90
93	Addie Joss	3.00	1.50	.90
94	Al Kaline	3.00	1.50	.90
95	Sandy Koufax	10.00	5.00	3.00
96	Rabbit Maranville	3.00	1.50	.90
97	Jim O'Rourke	3.00	1.50	.90
98	Wilbert Robinson	3.00	1.50	.90
99	Pie Traynor	3.00	1.50	.90
100	Zack Wheat	3.00	1.50	.90

1968-70 Partridge Meats Reds

These cards were produced in conjunction with Reds' autograph appearances at Kroger food stores in the Cincinnati area. Players' service with the Reds indicates this set was issued over a period of several years. Similar cards are known for other Cincinnati pro sports teams. The 1968 cards measure 4" x 5" and feature a black-and-white player photo set against a borderless white background. The player's name and team and the word "Likes" are printed in black, the ad for the issuing meat company at bottom is printed in red. Cards have a blank back. The 1969-70 cards are in the same format but in 3-3/4" x 5-1/2" format. The unnumbered cards are checklisted here in alphabetical order.

		NM	EX	VG
	Complete Set (11):	1,000	500.00	300.00
	Common Player:	40.00	20.00	12.00
(1)	Ted Abernathy	80.00	40.00	25.00
(2)	John Bench	100.00	50.00	30.00
(3)	Jimmy Bragan	40.00	20.00	12.00
(4)	Dave Bristol	80.00	40.00	25.00
(5)	Tommy Helms	80.00	40.00	25.00
(6)	Gary Nolan	40.00	20.00	12.00
(7)	Milt Pappas	80.00	40.00	25.00
(8)	Don Pavletich	80.00	40.00	25.00
(9)	Mel Queen	80.00	40.00	25.00
(10)	Pete Rose	300.00	150.00	90.00
(11)	Jim Stewart	80.00	40.00	25.00

1972 Partridge Meats Reds

Similar in format to the meat company's 1968-70 issue, these later cards are in a slightly different size - 3-3/4" x 5-1/2". The ad on the '72 cards reads "Photo courtesy of Partridge Meats."

		NM	EX	VG
	Complete Set (7):	225.00	110.00	65.00
	Common Player:	30.00	15.00	9.00
(1)	Don Gullett	30.00	15.00	9.00
(2)	Lee May	30.00	15.00	9.00
(3)	Denis Menke	30.00	15.00	9.00
(4)	Jim Merritt	30.00	15.00	9.00
(5)	Gary Nolan	30.00	15.00	9.00
(6)	Tony Perez	60.00	30.00	18.00
(7)	Bob Tolan	30.00	15.00	9.00

1913 Pastime Novelty Christy Mathewson

This postcard features a photo taken Oct. 6, 1913, the day of Matty's victory over Eddie Plank, the only game the Giants won in losing the 1913 World Series to the Philadelphia A's. The black-and-white card is in standard postcard size of about 3-1/2" x 5-1/2", with typical postcard markings on back. It does not appear to be part of a series.

	NM	EX	VG
Christy Mathewson	1,500	900.00	450.00

1922 Wm. Paterson

Believed to have been a Canadian candy premium, this 50-card set of 2" x 3-1/4" cards features portrait or posed action photos with wide white borders. Beneath the photo is a card number, player name, team, and in two lines, "Wm. Paterson, Limited / Brantford, Canada." Backs are blank. Two distinct types are seen, black-and-white and sepia, though the reason for the variations is unknown.

		NM	EX	VG
	Complete Set (50):	120,000	50,000	25,000
	Common Player:	950.00	400.00	200.00
1	Eddie Roush	2,000	800.00	400.00
2	Rube Marquard	2,000	800.00	400.00
3	Del Gainor	950.00	400.00	200.00
4	George Sisler	2,000	800.00	400.00
5	Joe Bush	950.00	400.00	200.00
6	Joe Oeschger	950.00	400.00	200.00
7	Willie Kamm	950.00	400.00	200.00
8	John Watson	950.00	400.00	200.00
9	Dolf Luque	1,100	450.00	225.00
10	Miller Huggins	2,000	800.00	400.00
11	Wally Schang	950.00	400.00	200.00
12	Bob Shawkey	950.00	400.00	200.00
13	Tris Speaker	3,500	1,400	700.00
14	Hugh McQuillan	950.00	400.00	200.00
15	"Long George" Kelly	2,000	800.00	400.00
16	Ray Schalk	2,000	800.00	400.00
17	Sam Jones	950.00	400.00	200.00
18	Grover Alexander	3,500	1,400	700.00
19	Bob Meusel	950.00	400.00	200.00
20	"Irish" Emil Meusel	950.00	400.00	200.00
21	Rogers Hornsby	3,500	1,400	700.00
22	Harry Heilmann	2,000	800.00	400.00
23	Heinie Groh	950.00	400.00	200.00
24	Frank Frisch	2,000	800.00	400.00
25	Babe Ruth	30,000	12,000	6,000
26	Jack Bentley	950.00	400.00	200.00
27	Everett Scott	950.00	400.00	200.00
28	Max Carey	2,000	800.00	400.00
29	Chick Fewster	950.00	400.00	200.00
30	Cy Williams	950.00	400.00	200.00
31	Burleigh Grimes	2,000	800.00	400.00
32	Waite Hoyt	2,000	800.00	400.00
33	Frank Snyder	950.00	400.00	200.00
34	Clyde Milan	950.00	400.00	200.00
35	Eddie Collins	2,000	800.00	400.00
36	Travis Jackson	2,000	800.00	400.00
37	Ken Williams	2,000	800.00	400.00
38	Dave Bancroft	2,000	800.00	400.00
39	Mike McNally	950.00	400.00	200.00
40	John McGraw	2,000	800.00	400.00
41	Art Nehf	950.00	400.00	200.00
42	"Rabbit" Maranville	2,000	800.00	400.00
43	Charlie Grimm	950.00	400.00	200.00
44	Joe Judge	950.00	400.00	200.00
45	Wally Pipp	950.00	400.00	200.00
46	Ty Cobb	20,000	8,000	4,000
47	Walter Johnson	6,000	2,500	1,200
48	Jake Daubert	950.00	400.00	200.00
49	Zack Wheat	2,000	800.00	400.00
50	Herb Pennock	2,000	800.00	400.00

1921 Pathe Freres Phonograph Co.

One of the rarest early-1920s Babe Ruth items is this premium photo issued by Pathe Freres Phonograph Co. of Brooklyn. Ruth is pictured bare-headed in a pinstriped uniform on the front of this approximately 7" x 9-1/4" card, printed in green and gray tones with a white border. A photo credit to White Studios of New York is given on the front and there is a facsimile autograph at bottom front. The black-and-white back has a listing of Ruth's 1920 homers in a box at left, and a Pathe ad at bottom-right.

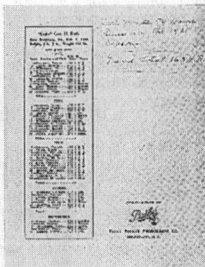

	NM	EX	VG
Babe Ruth	3,500	1,750	1,050

1910 PC796 Sepia Postcards

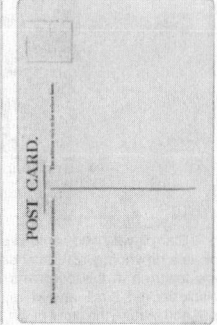

The manufacturer of these sepia-toned 3-1/2" x 5-1/2" postcards is unknown, but most of the photos utilized are familiar from other card issues of the era. Fronts have the player name at bottom in fancy capital letters. Backs have a standard divided postcard indicia. The set was given the PC796 designation in the "American Card Catalog." The unnumbered cards are checklisted here alphabetically.

		NM	EX	VG
	Complete Set (25):	68,000	27,000	14,500
	Common Player:	900.00	360.00	180.00
(1)	Roger Bresnahan	1,800	720.00	360.00
(2)	Al Bridwell	900.00	360.00	180.00
(3)	Mordecai Brown	1,800	720.00	360.00
(4)	Frank Chance	1,800	720.00	360.00
(5)	Hal Chase	1,350	550.00	270.00
(6)	Ty Cobb	12,750	5,100	2,500
(7)	Ty Cobb, Hanus Wagner	11,250	4,500	2,250
(8)	Eddie Collins	1,800	720.00	360.00
(9)	Sam Crawford	1,800	720.00	360.00
(10)	Art Devlin	900.00	360.00	180.00
(11)	Red Dooin	900.00	360.00	180.00
(12)	Johnny Evers, Germany Schaefer	1,200	480.00	240.00
(13)	Sam Frock	900.00	360.00	180.00
(14)	George Gibson	900.00	360.00	180.00
(15)	Artie Hoffman (Hofman)	900.00	360.00	180.00
(16)	Walter Johnson	3,600	1,500	720.00
(17)	Nap Lajoie	1,800	720.00	360.00
(18)	Harry Lord	900.00	360.00	180.00
(19)	Christy Mathewson	6,000	2,400	1,200
(20)	Orval Overall	900.00	360.00	180.00
(21)	Eddie Plank	1,800	720.00	360.00
(22)	Tris Speaker	2,250	1,000	450.00
(23)	Gabby Street	900.00	360.00	180.00
(24)	Honus Wagner	9,000	3,600	1,800
(25)	Ed Walsh	1,800	720.00	360.00

1869 Peck & Snyder Cincinnati Red Stockings - Small

Many consider this to be the first true baseball card in that it was produced in large quantities (relative to the cabinets and carte de visites of the era) and offered to firms wishing to place their advertising on the back. The 3-15/16" x 2-3/8" card features a sepia team photo on front of baseball's first real professional team, including Hall of Famers George and Harry

Wright. The Peck & Snyder ad back is the most commonly found, but others are known, including a back which lists only the team's line-up.

	NM	EX	VG
Cincinnati Red Stocking Team		30,000	18,000

1869 Peck & Snyder Cincinnati Red Stockings - Large

Many consider this to be the first true baseball card in that it was produced in large quantities (relative to the cabinets and carte de visites of the era) and offered to firms wishing to place their advertising on the back. The 4-3/16" x 3-5/16" card features a sepia team photo on front of baseball's first real professional team, including Hall of Famers George and Harry Wright. On this larger format, the players are identified on front with the team name in ornate black or red (slightly scarcer) type at bottom. Backs have been seen with ads for New York "Sportsman's "Emporium" along with a caricature of a bearded ballplayer, and for "The New York City Base Ball & Skate Emporium," with a large illsutration of an ice skate.

	NM	EX	VG
Cincinnati Red Stocking Team		45,000	27,500

1870 Peck & Snyder Chicago White Stockings

Using popular baseball teams of the day as an advertising medium, this apporoximately 4" x 2-3/4" black-and-white card pictures and identifies on front the 1870 Chicago White Stockings of pre-National Association days. On back is an ad for Peck & Snyder of New York City.

	NM	EX	VG
Chicago White Stockings		35,000	21,000

1870 Peck & Snyder New York Mutuals

Using popular baseball teams of the day as an advertising medium, this apporoximately 4" x 2-3/4" black-and-white card pictures and identifies on front the 1870 New York Mutuals of pre-National Association days. On back is a cartoon ad for Peck & Snyder of New York City.

	NM	EX	VG
New York Mutuals		35,000	21,000
James Creighton			

1870 Peck & Snyder Philadelphia Athletics

A composite photo of the players in street clothes is featured on this promotional card for the New York City sporting goods dealer whose advertising appears on back.

Philadelphia Athletics (Sold for $2,780 in 10/01 auction in Poor condition.)

1920 Peggy Popcorn

Whether the rarity of this Canadian card issue is attributablwe to limited original distribution or to the issuer's ground-breaking use of the cards in a prize redemption program is unknown. Currently only six of the what the card back advertised as a set of 20 cards are checklisted, with only a single example known of each player. The cards are printed in black-and-white on thin cream-colored cardboard stock in a size of approximately 2-1/4" x 3-1/4", though the size of the known cards varies somewhat, as do the particulars of the front design, which generally features a player picture with a graphic embellishment. Only the player name appears on the front. Backs provide details of the promotion which offered baseball equipment or other prizes for the redemption of a set. A card number appears on back. The cards were issued by The Peggy Popcorn and Food Products, Ltd., Winnipeg, Manitoba, though the manner of their distribution is unrecorded. The only example known to have been publicly sold since the cards' discovery in May, 2008, was an SGC-certified Joe Dugan in VG condition that brought $2,644 in a 2000 auction.

		NM	EX	VG
VALUES UNDETERMINED				
(1)	Joe Dugan			
(2)	Harry Heilmann			
(3)	Chick Gandil			
(5)	Kid Gleason			
(7)	Babe Ruth			
(16)	Dazzy Vance			

1963 Pepsi-Cola Colt .45's

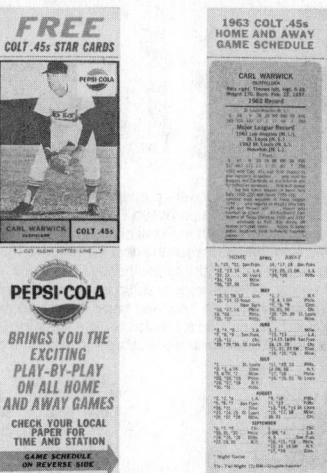

This issue was distributed regionally in Texas in bottled six-packs of Pepsi. The cards were issued on 2-3/8" x 9-1/8" panels. A 2-3/8" x 3-3/4" card was printed on each panel, which also included promos for Pepsi and the Colt .45's, as well as a team schedule. Card fronts are black-and-white posed action photos with blue and red trim. Backs offer player statistics and career highlights. The John Bateman card was apparently never distributed publicly and is among the rarest baseball cards of the 1960s. The unnumbered cards are checklisted here alphabetically. Values shown are for complete panels with top and bottom tabs; those without are valued about 25 percent.

		NM	EX	VG
Common Player:		10.00	5.00	3.00
(1)	Bob Aspromonte	10.00	5.00	3.00
(2)	John Bateman/SP value undetermined			
(3)	Bob Bruce	10.00	5.00	3.00
(4)	Jim Campbell	10.00	5.00	3.00
(5)	Dick Farrell	10.00	5.00	3.00
(6)	Ernie Fazio	10.00	5.00	3.00
(7)	Carroll Hardy	10.00	5.00	3.00
(8)	J.C. Hartman	10.00	5.00	3.00
(9)	Ken Johnson	10.00	5.00	3.00
(10)	Bob Lillis/SP	1,200	600.00	375.00
(11)	Don McMahon	10.00	5.00	3.00

		NM	EX	VG
(12)	Pete Runnels	10.00	5.00	3.00
(13)	Al Spangler	10.00	5.00	3.00
(14)	Rusty Staub	35.00	17.50	10.00
(15)	Johnny Temple	10.00	5.00	3.00
(16)	Carl Warwick/SP	1,000	500.00	300.00

1977 Pepsi-Cola Baseball Stars

An Ohio regional promotion (the checklist is extra heavy with Indians and Reds players), large numbers of these cards found their way into hobby dealers' hands. Designed to be inserted into cartons of soda, the cards have a 3-3/8" diameter central disc attached with perforations to a baseball glove design. A tab beneath the glove contains the checklist (the card discs themselves are unnumbered) and a coupon on back for ordering a player t-shirt, the offer for which is made on the back of the player disc. The Players Association logo appears on front, but the producer, Mike Schechter Associates, did not seek licensing by Major League Baseball, with the result that uniform logos have been removed from the black-and-white player photos. Prices shown are for complete glove/disc/tab cards. Values for unattached player discs would be no more than one-half of those shown. The discs of Reggie Jackson and Mike Schmidt can be found with either orange, green, purple, light blue or sky blue side panels; the other player discs are known in only one color each.

		NM	EX	VG
Complete Set (72):		35.00	17.50	10.00
W/Color Variations (80):		75.00	37.50	22.50
Common Player:		1.00	.50	.30
1	Robin Yount	4.00	2.00	1.25
2	Rod Carew	4.00	2.00	1.25
3	Butch Wynegar	1.00	.50	.30
4	Manny Sanguillen	1.00	.50	.30
5	Mike Hargrove	1.00	.50	.30
6	Larvel (Larvell) Blanks	1.00	.50	.30
7	Jim Kern	1.00	.50	.30
8	Pat Dobson	1.00	.50	.30
9	Rico Carty	1.00	.50	.30
10	John Grubb	1.00	.50	.30
11	Buddy Bell	1.00	.50	.30
12	Rick Manning	1.00	.50	.30
13	Dennis Eckersley	4.00	2.00	1.25
14	Wayne Garland	1.00	.50	.30
15	Dave LaRoche	1.00	.50	.30
16	Rick Waits	1.00	.50	.30
17	Ray Fosse	1.00	.50	.30
18	Frank Duffy	1.00	.50	.30
19	Duane Kuiper	1.00	.50	.30
20	Jim Palmer	4.00	2.00	1.25
21	Fred Lynn	1.00	.50	.30
22	Carlton Fisk	4.00	2.00	1.25
23	Carl Yastrzemski	6.00	3.00	1.75
24	Nolan Ryan	17.50	8.75	5.25
25	Bobby Grich	1.00	.50	.30
26	Ralph Garr	1.00	.50	.30
27	Richie Zisk	1.00	.50	.30
28	Ron LeFlore	1.00	.50	.30
29	Rusty Staub	1.00	.50	.30
30	Mark Fidrych	1.50	.70	.45
31	Willie Horton	1.00	.50	.30
32	George Brett	10.00	5.00	3.00
33	Amos Otis	1.00	.50	.30
34a	Reggie Jackson (Green)	7.50	3.75	2.25
34b	Reggie Jackson (Light blue.)	7.50	3.75	2.25
34c	Reggie Jackson (Orange)	7.50	3.75	2.25
34d	Reggie Jackson (Purple)	7.50	3.75	2.25
34e	Reggie Jackson (Sky blue.)	7.50	3.75	2.25
35	Don Gullett	1.00	.50	.30
36	Thurman Munson	3.00	1.50	.90
37	Al Hrabosky	1.00	.50	.30
38	Mike Tyson	1.00	.50	.30
39	Gene Tenace	1.00	.50	.30
40	George Hendrick	1.00	.50	.30
41	Chris Speier	1.00	.50	.30
42	John Montefusco	1.00	.50	.30
43	Pete Rose	10.00	5.00	3.00
44	Johnny Bench	5.00	2.50	1.50
45	Dan Driessen	1.00	.50	.30
46	Joe Morgan	4.00	2.00	1.25
47	Dave Concepcion	1.00	.50	.30
48	George Foster	1.00	.50	.30
49	Cesar Geronimo	1.00	.50	.30
50	Ken Griffey	1.00	.50	.30
51	Gary Nolan	1.00	.50	.30
52	Santo Alcala	1.00	.50	.30
53	Jack Billingham	1.00	.50	.30
54	Pedro Borbon	1.00	.50	.30
55	Rawly Eastwick	1.00	.50	.30

		NM	EX	VG
56	Fred Norman	1.00	.50	.30
57	Pat Zachary (Zachry)	1.00	.50	.30
58	Jeff Burroughs	1.00	.50	.30
59	Manny Trillo	1.00	.50	.30
60	Bob Watson	1.00	.50	.30
61	Steve Garvey	1.50	.70	.45
62	Don Sutton	4.00	2.00	1.25
63	John Candelaria	1.00	.50	.30
64	Willie Stargell	4.00	2.00	1.25
65	Jerry Reuss	1.00	.50	.30
66	Dave Cash	1.00	.50	.30
67	Tom Seaver	5.00	2.50	1.50
68	Jon Matlock	1.00	.50	.30
69	Dave Kingman	1.00	.50	.30
70a	Mike Schmidt (Green)	7.50	3.75	2.25
70b	Mike Schmidt (Light blue.)	7.50	3.75	2.25
70c	Mike Schmidt (Orange)	7.50	3.75	2.25
70d	Mike Schmidt (Purple)	7.50	3.75	2.25
70e	Mike Schmidt (Sky blue.)	7.50	3.75	2.25
71	Jay Johnstone	1.00	.50	.30
72	Greg Luzinski	1.00	.50	.30

1977 Pepsi-Cola Cincinnati Reds Playing Cards

Similar to a multi-sport series produced by Cubic Corp. (see also), these playing cards sets feature on back the pencil drawings of Al Landsman. Each boxed deck featured one Reds star player within a red border. Also on each card back are a facsimile autograph and Pepsi logo. Cards are standard bridge size (2-1/4" x 3-1/2") with rounded corners. Decks were available by sending in 250 16-oz. Pepsi cap liners or a combination of cash and cap liners.

		NM	EX	VG
(1)	Johnny Bench (Boxed deck.)	35.00	17.50	10.00
(1)	Johnny Bench (Single card.)	1.50	.70	.45
(2)	Joe Morgan (Boxed deck.)	20.00	10.00	6.00
(2)	Joe Morgan (Single card.)	1.00	.50	.30
(3)	Pete Rose (Boxed deck.)	55.00	27.50	16.50
(3)	Pete Rose (Single card.)	4.00	2.00	1.25

1978 Pepsi-Cola Superstars

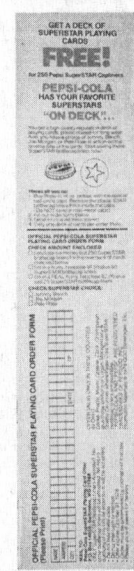

In its second year of producing carton-stuffer baseball cards, Cincinnati area Pepsi bottlers issued a 40-card set featuring 25 Reds players and 15 other major league stars. The entire carton insert measures 2-1/8" x 9-1/2". Besides the baseball card at top, there is a checklist and mail-in offer for playing cards featuring Johnny Bench, Joe Morgan and Pete Rose. The card element at the top measures 2-1/8" x 2-1/2". A player portrait, with uniform logos airbrushed off, is featured in black-and-white in a white star on a red background. The Major League Baseball Players Association logo appears in dark blue in the upper-left. Printed in black below are the player's name, team, position, birthdate and place and a few 1977 stats. In

back, printed in red, white and blue, is part of the offer for the playing cards. Large quantities of this set found their way into hobby hands and they remain common today.

		NM	EX	VG
Complete Set (40):		30.00	15.00	9.00
Common Player:		.75	.35	.20
(1)	Sparky Anderson	2.00	1.00	.60
(2)	Rick Auerbach	.75	.35	.20
(3)	Doug Bair	.75	.35	.20
(4)	Buddy Bell	.75	.35	.20
(5)	Johnny Bench	4.00	2.00	1.25
(6)	Bill Bonham	.75	.35	.20
(7)	Pedro Borbon	.75	.35	.20
(8)	Larry Bowa	.75	.35	.20
(9)	George Brett	7.50	3.75	2.25
(10)	Jeff Burroughs	.75	.35	.20
(11)	Rod Carew	3.00	1.50	.90
(12)	Dave Collins	.75	.35	.20
(13)	Dave Concepcion	.75	.35	.20
(14)	Dan Driessen	.75	.35	.20
(15)	George Foster	.75	.35	.20
(16)	Steve Garvey	1.50	.70	.45
(17)	Cesar Geronimo	.75	.35	.20
(18)	Ken Griffey	.75	.35	.20
(19)	Ken Henderson	.75	.35	.20
(20)	Tom Hume	.75	.35	.20
(21)	Reggie Jackson	7.50	3.75	2.25
(22)	Junior Kennedy	.75	.35	.20
(23)	Dave Kingman	.75	.40	.25
(24)	Ray Knight	.75	.35	.20
(25)	Jerry Koosman	.75	.35	.20
(26)	Mike Lum	.75	.35	.20
(27)	Bill Madlock	.75	.35	.20
(28)	Joe Morgan	3.00	1.50	.90
(29)	Paul Moskau	.75	.35	.20
(30)	Fred Norman	.75	.35	.20
(31)	Jim Palmer	3.00	1.50	.90
(32)	Pete Rose	10.00	5.00	3.00
(33)	Nolan Ryan	12.50	6.25	3.75
(34)	Manny Sarmiento	.75	.35	.20
(35)	Tom Seaver	4.00	2.00	1.25
(36)	Ted Simmons	.75	.35	.20
(37)	Dave Tomlin	.75	.35	.20
(38)	Don Werner	.75	.35	.20
(39)	Carl Yastrzemski	4.00	2.00	1.25
(40)	Richie Zisk	.75	.35	.20

1980 Pepsi-Cola All-Stars Prototypes

These prototype cards were prepared by Topps and Mike Schechter Associates for a proposed Pepsi promotion. Three sets of the cards were given to Pepsi officials for consideration but only two were returned when the deal fell through. The third sheet was cut up and sold into the hobby. The Pepsi cards share the format of Topps' regular 1980 issue, although Pepsi logos have been added on front and back, name and banner colors changed on front and a position circle added. In 2005, a number of the individual cards were offered on eBay by Topps.

		NM	EX	VG
Common Player:		250.00	125.00	75.00
1	Rod Carew	1,000	500.00	300.00
2	Paul Molitor	1,000	500.00	300.00
3	George Brett	1,500	750.00	450.00
4	Robin Yount	1,000	500.00	300.00
5	Reggie Jackson	1,500	750.00	450.00
6	Fred Lynn	250.00	125.00	75.00
7	Ken Landreaux	250.00	125.00	75.00
8	Jim Sundberg	250.00	125.00	75.00
9	Ron Guidry (One known, other two cut from sheets and destroyed; negatives reversed.)	1,450	725.00	435.00
10	Jim Palmer	1,000	500.00	300.00
11	Goose Gossage	250.00	125.00	75.00
12	Keith Hernandez	250.00	125.00	75.00
13	Dave Lopes	250.00	125.00	75.00
14	Mike Schmidt	1,500	750.00	450.00
15	Garry Templeton	250.00	125.00	75.00
16	Dave Parker	250.00	125.00	75.00
17	George Foster	250.00	125.00	75.00
18	Dave Winfield	1,000	500.00	300.00
19	Ted Simmons	250.00	125.00	75.00
20	Steve Carlton	1,000	500.00	300.00
21	J.R. Richard	400.00	200.00	120.00
22	Bruce Sutter	1,000	500.00	300.00

1966 Gaylord Perry Insurance

The attributed date is arbitrary, near the middle of his stay with the S.F. Giants in whose uniform he is pictured on this approximately 3-1/2" x 5-1/2", blank-backed, black-and-white "business" card for his insurance agency.

	NM	EX	VG
Gaylord Perry	40.00	20.00	12.00

1971 Pete Rose & Johnny Bench Lincoln-Mercury Postcards

This series of promotional postcards was issued in 1970-71 in conjunction with a Dayton, Ohio, Lincoln-Mercury auto dealership owned by Reds teammates Rose and Bench. Fronts of the 5-1/2" x 3-1/2" postcards feature color photos of new cars. Black-and-white backs have portraits of the players, a description of the auto, the address of the dealership and a credit line for the postcard's printer. Besides those listed here, other auto fronts may exist.

		NM	EX	VG
Common Card:		50.00	25.00	15.00
(1)	Johnny Bench, Pete Rose (1971 Lincoln Continental Sedan)	50.00	25.00	15.00
(2)	Johnny Bench, Pete Rose (1971 Mercury Cougar Convertible)	50.00	25.00	15.00
(3)	Johnny Bench, Pete Rose (1971 Mercury Montego)	50.00	25.00	15.00
(4)	Johnny Bench, Peter Rose (1971 Mercury Monterrey)	50.00	25.00	15.00

1972 Pete Rose & Johnny Bench Lincoln-Mercury Postcards

This series of promotional postcards was issued in 1971-72 in conjunction with a Dayton, Ohio, Lincoln-Mercury auto dealership owned by Reds teammates Rose and Bench. Fronts of the 5-1/2" x 3-1/2" postcards feature color photos of new cars. Black, white and backs have portraits of the players, a description of the auto, the address of the dealership and a credit line for the postcard's printer. Besides those listed here, other auto fronts may exist.

		NM	EX	VG
(1)	Pete Rose, Johnny Bench (1972 Mercury Marquis Brougham Colony Park Station Wagon)	50.00	25.00	15.00

1961 Peters Meats Twins

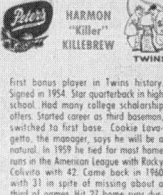

THE TWINS PLAYERS PICTURES CAN ALSO BE FOUND ON THE BACKS OF ALL Peter's PORKETTE PACKAGES #18 (COLLECT ALL 26)

HARMON "Killer" KILLEBREW — TWINS

First bonus player in Twins history. Signed in 1954. Star quarterback in high school. Had many college scholarship offers. Started career as third baseman, switched to first base. Cookie Lavagetto, the manager, says he will be a natural. In 1959 he tied for most home runs in the American League with Rocky Colivito with 42. Came back in 1960 with 31 in spite of missing about a third of games. Hit 27 home runs during last half of season. Bats and throws right handed.

Age 25 — Height 6' — Weight 185

This set, featuring the first-year 1961 Minnesota Twins, is in a large, 4-5/8" x 3-1/2", format. Cards are on thick cardboard and heavily waxed, as they were used as partial packaging for the company's meat products. Card fronts feature full-color photos, team and Peters logos, and biographical information. The cards are blank-backed. Prices shown are for cards with the surrounding packaging panel. Cut cards are worth about 50-75 percent of the prices shown.

	NM	EX	VG
Complete Set, Panels (26):	1,600	800.00	475.00
Complete Set, Cards (26):	1,500	750.00	450.00
Common Player, Panel:	80.00	40.00	24.00
Common Player, Card:	50.00	25.00	15.00
1 Zoilo Versalles	160.00	80.00	48.00
2 Eddie Lopat	80.00	40.00	24.00
3 Pedro Ramos	160.00	80.00	48.00
4 Charles "Chuck" Stobbs	80.00	40.00	24.00
5 Don Mincher	80.00	40.00	24.00
6 Jack Kralick	80.00	40.00	24.00
7 Jim Kaat	125.00	65.00	35.00
8 Hal Naragon	80.00	40.00	24.00
9 Don Lee	80.00	40.00	24.00
10 Harry "Cookie" Lavagetto	80.00	40.00	24.00
11 Tom "Pete" Whisenant	80.00	40.00	24.00
12 Elmer Valo	80.00	40.00	24.00
13 Ray Moore	80.00	40.00	24.00
14 Billy Gardner	80.00	40.00	24.00
15 Lenny Green	80.00	40.00	24.00
16 Sam Mele	80.00	40.00	24.00
17 Jim Lemon	80.00	40.00	24.00
18 Harmon "Killer" Killebrew	400.00	200.00	120.00
19 Paul Giel	80.00	40.00	24.00
20 Reno Bertoia	80.00	40.00	24.00
21 Clyde McCullough	80.00	40.00	24.00
22 Earl Battey	80.00	40.00	24.00
23 Camilo Pascual	160.00	80.00	48.00
24 Dan Dobbek	80.00	40.00	24.00
25 Joe "Valvy" Valdivielso	80.00	40.00	24.00
26 Billy Consolo	80.00	40.00	24.00

1938-53 Philadelphia A's Team-Issue Photos

For a decade and a half the Philadelphia A's issued souvenir sets of black-and-white player photos. All are in a 7" x 10" format but the size of picture, the use of posed action and portrait photos and the type style of the name printed in the bottom border differ among the years. In many cases, pictures were re-issued year after year making it impossible 50 years later to reconstruct the composition of any particular year's issue. The unnumbered pictures are checklisted here alphabetically. Multiple player listings are the result of known pose variations. Gaps have been left in the assigned numbering for future additions.

	NM	EX	VG
Common Player:	12.00	6.00	3.50
(1) Joe Astroth	12.00	6.00	3.50
(2) Loren Babe	12.00	6.00	3.50
(3) Johnny Babich	12.00	6.00	3.50
(4) Bill Beckman	12.00	6.00	3.50
(5) Joe Berry	12.00	6.00	3.50
(6) Herman Besse	12.00	6.00	3.50
(7) Hal Bevan	12.00	6.00	3.50
(8) Henry Biasatti	12.00	6.00	3.50
(9) Don Black	12.00	6.00	3.50

(10) Lena Blackburne	12.00	6.00	3.50
(11) Buddy Blair	12.00	6.00	3.50
(12) Don Bollweg	12.00	6.00	3.50
(13) Al Brancato	12.00	6.00	3.50
(14) Lou Brissie	12.00	6.00	3.50
(15) Earle Brucker	12.00	6.00	3.50
(16) Earle Brucker	12.00	6.00	3.50
(17) Earle Brucker	12.00	6.00	3.50
(18) William Burgo	15.00	7.50	4.50
(19) Joe Burns	12.00	6.00	3.50
(20) Ed Burtschy	12.00	6.00	3.50
(21) Edgar Busch	12.00	6.00	3.50
(22) Harry Byrd	12.00	6.00	3.50
(23) Fred Caligiuri	18.00	9.00	5.50
(24) George Caster	12.00	6.00	3.50
(25) Jim Castiglia	12.00	6.00	3.50
(27) Sam Chapman	12.00	6.00	3.50
(28) Sam Chapman	12.00	6.00	3.50
(29) Sam Chapman	12.00	6.00	3.50
(30) Russ Christopher	12.00	6.00	3.50
(31) Joe Coleman	12.00	6.00	3.50
(32) Eddie Collins Jr.	15.00	7.50	4.50
(33) Lawrence Davis	12.00	6.00	3.50
(34) Tom Davis	12.00	6.00	3.50
(35) Chubby Dean	12.00	6.00	3.50
(36) Joe DeMaestri	12.00	6.00	3.50
(37) Russ Derry	12.00	6.00	3.50
(38) Gene Desautels	12.00	6.00	3.50
(39) Art Ditmar	12.00	6.00	3.50
(40) Jimmy Dykes	12.00	6.00	3.50
(41) Bob Estalella	12.00	6.00	3.50
(42) Nick Etten	12.00	6.00	3.50
(43) Ferris Fain	18.00	9.00	5.50
(44) Tom Ferrick	12.00	6.00	3.50
(45) Jim Finigan	12.00	6.00	3.50
(46) Lewis Flick	12.00	6.00	3.50
(47) Jesse Flores	12.00	6.00	3.50
(48) Richard Fowler	12.00	6.00	3.50
(49) Nelson Fox	30.00	15.00	9.00
(51) Marion Fricano	12.00	6.00	3.50
(52) Joe Gantenbein	12.00	6.00	3.50
(53) Ford Garrison	12.00	6.00	3.50
(54) Mike Guerra	12.00	6.00	3.50
(55) Irv Hadley	12.00	6.00	3.50
(56) Irv Hall	12.00	6.00	3.50
(57) Luke Hamlin	12.00	6.00	3.50
(58) Gene Handley	12.00	6.00	3.50
(59) Bob Harris	12.00	6.00	3.50
(60) Charlie Harris	12.00	6.00	3.50
(61) Luman C. Harris (Full-length.)	12.00	6.00	3.50
(62) Luman Harris	12.00	6.00	3.50
(63) Frank Hayes	12.00	6.00	3.50
(64) Bob Johnson	15.00	7.50	4.50
(65) Bob Johnson	15.00	7.50	4.50
(66) Eddie Joost	12.00	6.00	3.50
(67) David Keefe	12.00	6.00	3.50
(68) George Kell	20.00	10.00	6.00
(69) Everett Kell	15.00	7.50	4.50
(70) Alex Kellner	12.00	6.00	3.50
(71) Alex Kellner	12.00	6.00	3.50
(72) Lou Klein	12.00	6.00	3.50
(73) Bill Knickerbocker	12.00	6.00	3.50
(74) Jack Knott	12.00	6.00	3.50
(75) Mike Kreevich	12.00	6.00	3.50
(76) John Kucab	12.00	6.00	3.50
(77) Paul Lehner	12.00	6.00	3.50
(78) Bill Lillard	12.00	6.00	3.50
(79) Lou Limmer	12.00	6.00	3.50
(80) Lou Limmer	12.00	6.00	3.50
(81) Dario Lodigiani	12.00	6.00	3.50
(82) Connie Mack	20.00	10.00	6.00
(83) Connie Mack	20.00	10.00	6.00
(84) Connie Mack	20.00	10.00	6.00
(85) Connie Mack	20.00	10.00	6.00
(86) Earle Mack	15.00	7.50	4.50
(87) Earle Mack	15.00	7.50	4.50
(88) Felix Mackiewicz	12.00	6.00	3.50
(89) Hank Majeski	12.00	6.00	3.50
(90) Hank Majeski	12.00	6.00	3.50
(91) Phil Marchildon	12.00	6.00	3.50
(92) Phil Marchildon	12.00	6.00	3.50
(93) Phil Marchildon	12.00	6.00	3.50
(94) Morris Martin	12.00	6.00	3.50
(95) Barney McCosky	12.00	6.00	3.50
(96) Bennie McCoy	12.00	6.00	3.50
(97) Les McCrabb	12.00	6.00	3.50
(98) Bill McGhee	18.00	9.00	5.50
(99) George McQuinn	12.00	6.00	3.50
(101) Charlie Metro	12.00	6.00	3.50
(102) Cass Michaels	12.00	6.00	3.50
(103) Dee Miles	12.00	6.00	3.50
(104) Wally Moses	12.00	6.00	3.50
(105) Wally Moses	12.00	6.00	3.50
(106) Ray Murray	12.00	6.00	3.50
(107) Bill Nagel	12.00	6.00	3.50
(108) Bobo Newsom	12.00	6.00	3.50
(109) Skeeter Newsome	12.00	6.00	3.50
(110) Hal Peck	12.00	6.00	3.50
(111) Dave Philley	12.00	6.00	3.50
(112) Cotton Pippen	12.00	6.00	3.50
(113) Arnie Portocarrero	12.00	6.00	3.50
(114) Nelson Potter	12.00	6.00	3.50
(115) Vic Power	15.00	7.50	4.50
(116) Jim Pruett	12.00	6.00	3.50
(117) Bill Renna	12.00	6.00	3.50
(118) Al Robertson	12.00	6.00	3.50
(119) Ed Robinson	12.00	6.00	3.50
(120) Buddy Rosar	12.00	6.00	3.50
(121) Buddy Rosar	12.00	6.00	3.50
(122) Al Rubeling	12.00	6.00	3.50
(123) Joseph Rullo	18.00	9.00	5.50
(124) Carl Scheib	12.00	6.00	3.50
(125) Bill Shantz	15.00	7.50	4.50
(126) Bob Shantz	18.00	9.00	5.50
(127) Newman Shirley	12.00	6.00	3.50
(128) Dick Siebert (Thigh-to-cap.)	12.00	6.00	3.50
(129) Dick Siebert	12.00	6.00	3.50
(130) Al Simmons	25.00	12.50	7.50

(131) Al Simmons	25.00	12.50	7.50
(132) Tuck Stainback	12.00	6.00	3.50
(133) Pete Suder (Waist-to-cap.)	12.00	6.00	3.50
(134) Pete Suder	12.00	6.00	3.50
(135) Bob Swift	12.00	6.00	3.50
(136) Keith Thomas	12.00	6.00	3.50
(137) Eric Tipton	12.00	6.00	3.50
(138) Bob Trice	12.00	6.00	3.50
(139) Elmer Valo (Portrait to waist.)	12.00	6.00	3.50
(140) Elmer Valo	12.00	6.00	3.50
(141) Ozzie Van Brabant	18.00	9.00	5.50
(142) Porter Vaughan	12.00	6.00	3.50
(143) Harold Wagner	12.00	6.00	3.50
(144) Harold Wagner	12.00	6.00	3.50
(145) Jack Wallaesa	12.00	6.00	3.50
(146) Johnny Welaj	12.00	6.00	3.50
(147) Elwood Wheaton	15.00	7.50	4.50
(148) Don White	12.00	6.00	3.50
(149) Jo Jo White	12.00	6.00	3.50
(151) Roger Wolff	12.00	6.00	3.50
(152) Tom Wright	12.00	6.00	3.50
(153) Gus Zernial	17.50	8.75	5.25
(154) 1938 A's Team	30.00	15.00	9.00
(155) 1939 A's Team	30.00	15.00	9.00
(156) 1940 A's Team	30.00	15.00	9.00
(157) 1941 A's Team	30.00	15.00	9.00
(158) 1942 A's Team	30.00	15.00	9.00
(159) 1943 A's Team	30.00	15.00	9.00
(160) 1944 A's Team	30.00	15.00	9.00
(161) 1945 A's Team	30.00	15.00	9.00
(162) 1946 A's Team	24.00	12.00	7.25
(163) 1948 A's Team	24.00	12.00	7.25
(164) 1949 A's Team	24.00	12.00	7.25
(165) Shibe Park	30.00	15.00	9.00

1941 Philadelphia Phillies Photo Pack

This set features 26 player photos in black-and-white with facsimile autographs on a 6" x 8-1/2" format. They appear to have been issued as a concession stand souvenir item. Backs are blanks. The unnumbered cards are checklisted here in alphabetical order..

	NM	EX	VG
Complete Set (26):	200.00	100.00	60.00
Common Player:	8.00	4.00	2.50
(1) Morrie Arnovich	8.00	4.00	2.50
(2) Bill Atwood	8.00	4.00	2.50
(3) Walter Beck	8.00	4.00	2.50
(4) Stan Benjamin	8.00	4.00	2.50
(5) Bob Bragan	8.00	4.00	2.50
(6) Roy Bruner	8.00	4.00	2.50
(7) Kirby Higbe	8.00	4.00	2.50
(8) Frank Hoerst	8.00	4.00	2.50
(9) Si Johnson	8.00	4.00	2.50
(10) Syl Johnson	8.00	4.00	2.50
(11) Chuck Klein	30.00	15.00	9.00
(12) Ed Levy	8.00	4.00	2.50
(13) Dan Litwhiler	8.00	4.00	2.50
(14) Hans Iobert	8.00	4.00	2.50
(15) Hershel Martin	8.00	4.00	2.50
(16) Joe Marty	8.00	4.00	2.50
(17) Merrill May	8.00	4.00	2.50
(18) Walt Millies	8.00	4.00	2.50
(19) Hugh Mulcahy	8.00	4.00	2.50
(20) Ike Pearson	8.00	4.00	2.50
(21) Doc Prothro	8.00	4.00	2.50
(22) George Scharein	8.00	4.00	2.50
(23) Clyde Smoll	8.00	4.00	2.50
(24) Gus Suhr	8.00	4.00	2.50
(25) Ben Warren	8.00	4.00	2.50
(26) Del Young	8.00	4.00	2.50

1954 Philadelphia A's Stickers

JOE ASTROTH

The issuer of this novelty set and the exact scope of its checklist are currently unknown. The pieces are printed in black-and-white on 4-1/2" x 6-1/2" to 8-1/4" (depending on pose) gummed-back paper. Instructions on front say, "(Moisten back. Paste on Cardboard and cut out.)" Only the player name is printed beneath the photo.

	NM	EX	VG
Common Player:	25.00	12.50	7.50
(1) Joe Astroth	25.00	12.50	7.50
(2) Don Bollweg	25.00	12.50	7.50
(3) Bob Cain	25.00	12.50	7.50
(4) Joe DeMaestri	25.00	12.50	7.50
(5) Marion Fricano	25.00	12.50	7.50

(6)	Forrest Jacobs	25.00	12.50	7.50
(7)	Eddie Joost	25.00	12.50	7.50
(8)	Alex Kellner	25.00	12.50	7.50
(9)	Morrie Martin	25.00	12.50	7.50
(10)	Ed McGhee	25.00	12.50	7.50
(11)	Arnold Portocarrero	25.00	12.50	7.50
(12)	Vic Power	35.00	17.50	10.50
(13)	Bill Renna	25.00	12.50	7.50
(14)	Jim Robertson	25.00	12.50	7.50
(15)	Bob Shantz	35.00	17.50	10.50
(16)	Pete Suder	25.00	12.50	7.50
(17)	Bob Trice	25.00	12.50	7.50
(18)	Elmer Valo	25.00	12.50	7.50
(19)	Leroy Wheat	25.00	12.50	7.50
(20)	Gus zernial	35.00	18.00	10.00

1952 Philadelphia A's/Phillies Player Pins

Only players on the Philadelphia A's and Phillies are found in this series of player pinbacks. The 1-3/4" diameter celluloid pins have black-and-white player portraits on front. The player name is printed in block letters across his shoulders, while the team name is printed in script across the chest. It is possible other player pins may exist. The unnumbered pieces are checklisted here in alphabetical order.

		NM	EX	VG
Common Player:		150.00	75.00	45.00
	Philadelphia Athletics			
(1)	Ferris Fain	200.00	100.00	60.00
(2)	Bobby Shantz	200.00	100.00	60.00
(3)	Gus Zernial	200.00	100.00	60.00
	Philadelphia Phillies			
(1)	Richie Ashburn	300.00	150.00	90.00
(2)	Del Ennis	150.00	75.00	45.00
(3)	Granny Hamner	150.00	75.00	45.00
(4)	Willie Jones	150.00	75.00	45.00
(5)	Jim Konstanty	150.00	75.00	45.00
(6)	Robin Roberts	300.00	150.00	90.00
(7)	Andy Seminick	150.00	75.00	45.00
(8)	Curt Simmons	150.00	75.00	45.00
(9)	Eddie Waitkus	150.00	75.00	45.00

1948 Philadelphia Bulletin Stand-Ups

These player pictures were printed in the "Fun Book" color section of the Sunday paper. The full-body pose cutouts carry facsimile autographs and were printed four per week on a page of about 9-1/2" x 14". While the individual pictures vary is size according to the pose, most are about 3" to 4" x 6-1/2" to 7". The player pictures are in black-and-white with a blue background and red base. They were intended to be cut out around the heavy black line, pasted to cardboard and folded at their base to create a stand-up figure. Values shown here are for well trimmed pieces without evidence of mounting. Complete pages carry a premium somewhat greater than the sum of the players present.

		NM	EX	VG
Common Player:		15.00	7.50	4.50
	PHILADELPHIA A's			
	June 13	75.00	37.00	22.00
(1)	Ferris Fain	15.00	7.50	4.50
(2)	Eddie Joost	15.00	7.50	4.50
(3)	Hank Majeski	15.00	7.50	4.50

(4)	Pete Suder	15.00	7.50	4.50
	June 20	75.00	37.00	22.00
(5)	Sam Chapman	15.00	7.50	4.50
(6)	Barney McCosky	15.00	7.50	4.50
(7)	Buddy Rosar	15.00	7.50	4.50
(8)	Elmer Valo	15.00	7.50	4.50
	June 27	75.00	37.00	22.00
(9)	Mike Guerra	15.00	7.50	4.50
(10)	Dick Fowler	15.00	7.50	4.50
(11)	Phil Marchildon	15.00	7.50	4.50
(12)	Carl Sheib	15.00	7.50	4.50
	July 4	75.00	37.00	22.00
(13)	Joe Coleman	15.00	7.50	4.50
(14)	Bob Savage	15.00	7.50	4.50
(15)	Don White	15.00	7.50	4.50
(16)	Rudy York	15.00	7.50	4.50
	July 11	75.00	37.00	22.00
(17)	Herman Franks	15.00	7.50	4.50
(18)	Charlie Harris	15.00	7.50	4.50
(19)	Bill McCahan	15.00	7.50	4.50
(20)	Skeeter Webb	15.00	7.50	4.50
	July 18	75.00	37.00	22.00
(21)	Lou Brissie	15.00	7.50	4.50
(22)	Ray Coleman	15.00	7.50	4.50
(23)	Billy DeMars	15.00	7.50	4.50
(24)	Skeeter Webb	15.00	7.50	4.50
	(Photo no Webb.)			
	PHILADELPHIA PHILLIES			
	July 25	90.00	45.00	27.00
(1)	Don Padgett	15.00	7.50	4.50
(2)	Schoolboy Rowe	15.00	7.50	4.50
(3)	Andy Seminick	15.00	7.50	4.50
(4)	Curt Simmons	20.00	10.00	6.00
	August 1	225.00	110.00	67.00
(5)	Richie Ashburn	150.00	75.00	45.00
(6)	Johnny Blatnik	15.00	7.50	4.50
(7)	Del Ennis	20.00	10.00	6.00
(8)	Harry Walker	15.00	7.50	4.50
	August 8	75.00	37.00	22.00
(9)	Bert Haas	15.00	7.50	4.50
(10)	Granny Hamner	15.00	7.50	4.50
(11)	Eddie Miller	15.00	7.50	4.50
(12)	Dick Sisler	15.00	7.50	4.50
	August 15	200.00	100.00	60.00
(13)	Ralph Caballero	15.00	7.50	4.50
(14)	Ed Heusser	15.00	7.50	4.50
(15)	Robin Roberts	125.00	62.00	37.00
(16)	Emil Verban	15.00	7.50	4.50
	August 22	75.00	37.00	22.00
(17)	Blix Donnelly	15.00	7.50	4.50
(18)	Walt Dubiel	15.00	7.50	4.50
(19)	Ken Heintzelman	15.00	7.50	4.50
(20)	Dutch Leonard	15.00	7.50	4.50
	August 29	75.00	37.00	22.00
(21)	Charlie Bicknell	15.00	7.50	4.50
(22)	Al Lakeman	15.00	7.50	4.50
(23)	Sam Nahem	15.00	7.50	4.50
(24)	Carvel "Bama" Rowell	15.00	7.50	4.50

1949 Philadelphia Bulletin A's/Phillies

Each Sunday between May 22 and July 24, 1949, the "Fun Book" rotogravure section of the Bulletin included a page of (usually) six baseball "cards" of the hometeam A's and Phillies which could be cut out and pasted to cardboard. The left side (front) of each card has a sepia portrait of the player, while a colored box at right (back) has biographical and career information. Uncut and unfolded, each card measures about 4-1/2" x 3-5/8". If cut out and pasted onto cardboard, the created cards would measure about 2-1/4" x 3-5/8". Complete pages measure about 9-1/2" x 13-3/8". Values shown are for single "cards" which have been cut off the page, but not pasted onto a backing.

		NM	EX	VG
Complete Set (60):		1,600	800.00	480.00
Common Player:		25.00	12.50	7.50
	MAY 22			
(1)	Richie Ashburn	265.00	130.00	79.00
(2)	Granny Hamner	25.00	12.50	7.50
(3)	Eddie Joost	25.00	12.50	7.50
(4)	Bill Nicholson	25.00	12.50	7.50
(5)	Buddy Rosar	25.00	12.50	7.50
(6)	Pete Suder	25.00	12.50	7.50
	MAY 29			
(7)	Hank Borowy	25.00	12.50	7.50
(8)	Del Ennis	35.00	17.50	10.50
(9)	Ferris Fain	35.00	17.50	10.50
(10)	Phil Marchildon	25.00	12.50	7.50
(11)	Wally Moses	25.00	12.50	7.50
(12)	Eddie Waitkus	25.00	12.50	7.50
	JUNE 5			
(13)	Dick Fowler	25.00	12.50	7.50

(14)	Willie Jones	25.00	12.50	7.50
(15)	Stan Lopata	25.00	12.50	7.50
(16)	Hank Majeski	25.00	12.50	7.50
(17)	Schoolboy Rowe	25.00	12.50	7.50
(18)	Elmer Valo	25.00	12.50	7.50
	JUNE 12			
(19)	Joe Coleman	25.00	12.50	7.50
(20)	Charley Harris	25.00	12.50	7.50
(21)	Russ Meyer	25.00	12.50	7.50
(22)	Eddie Miller	25.00	12.50	7.50
(23)	Robin Roberts	265.00	130.00	79.00
(24)	Taft Wright	25.00	12.50	7.50
	JUNE 19			
(25)	Lou Brissie	25.00	12.50	7.50
(26)	Ralph Caballero	25.00	12.50	7.50
(27)	Sam Chapman	25.00	12.50	7.50
(28)	Fermin (Mike) Guerra	25.00	12.50	7.50
(29)	Jim Konstanty	35.00	17.50	10.50
(30)	Curt Simmons	35.00	17.50	10.50
	JUNE 26			
(31)	Charles Bicknell	25.00	12.50	7.50
(32)	Ken Heintzelman	25.00	12.50	7.50
(33)	Alex Kellner	25.00	12.50	7.50
(34)	Barney McCosky	25.00	12.50	7.50
(35)	Bobby Shantz	35.00	17.50	10.50
(36)	Ken Trinkle	25.00	12.50	7.50
	JULY 3			
(37)	Blix Donnelly	25.00	12.50	7.50
(38)	Bill McCahan	25.00	12.50	7.50
(39)	Carl Scheib	25.00	12.50	7.50
(40)	Andy Seminick	25.00	12.50	7.50
(41)	Dick Sisler	25.00	12.50	7.50
(42)	Don White	25.00	12.50	7.50
	JULY 10			
(43)	Joe Astroth	25.00	12.50	7.50
(44)	Henry Biasetti	25.00	12.50	7.50
(45)	Buddy Blattner	25.00	12.50	7.50
(46)	Thomas O. Davis	25.00	12.50	7.50
(47)	Stan Hollmig	25.00	12.50	7.50
(48)	Jackie Mayo	25.00	12.50	7.50
	JULY 17			
(49)	Benny Bengough	25.00	12.50	7.50
(50)	Earle Brucker	25.00	12.50	7.50
(51)	Dusty Cooke	25.00	12.50	7.50
(52)	Jimmy Dykes	25.00	12.50	7.50
(53)	Cy Perkins	25.00	12.50	7.50
(54)	Al Simmons	40.00	20.00	12.00
	JULY 24			
(55)	Nellie Fox	265.00	130.00	79.00
(56)	Connie Mack	200.00	100.00	60.00
(57)	Earle Mack	25.00	12.50	7.50
(58)	Eddie Sawyer	25.00	12.50	7.50
(59)	Ken Silvestri	25.00	12.50	7.50
(60)	Phillies/ A's Pennants	25.00	12.50	7.50

1950 Philadelphia Bulletin Pin-Ups

This series of 8" x 10" black-and-white portraits of Phillies players, coaches, and manager was produced in two versions. A (mostly) numbered newsprint version was issued one per day in the paper, between September 13-30. A premium version, printed on heavy paper with a semi-gloss finish and blank back, was made available to fans for a nickel at the newspaper's office or a dime by mail. Each of the pictures is a cap-less portrait with facsimile autograph on front. A number of players in the premium version were not issued in the newsprint style.

		NM	EX	VG
Complete Set (26):		900.00	450.00	275.00
Common Player:		40.00	20.00	12.00
(1)	Rich Ashburn	75.00	37.00	22.00
(2)	Jimmy Bloodworth	40.00	20.00	12.00
(3)	Ralph Caballero	40.00	20.00	12.00
(4)	Milo Candini	40.00	20.00	12.00
(5)	Emory Church	40.00	20.00	12.00
(6)	Sylvester (Blix) Donnelly	40.00	20.00	12.00
(7)	Del Ennis	50.00	25.00	15.00
(8)	Mike Goliat	40.00	20.00	12.00
(9)	Gran Hamner	40.00	20.00	12.00
(10)	Ken Heintzelman	40.00	20.00	12.00
(11)	Stan Hollmig	40.00	20.00	12.00
(12)	Ken Johnson	40.00	20.00	12.00
(13)	Willie Jones	40.00	20.00	12.00
(14)	Jim Konstanty	40.00	20.00	12.00
(15)	Stan Lopata	40.00	20.00	12.00
(16)	Russ Meyer	40.00	20.00	12.00
(17)	Bob Miller	40.00	20.00	12.00
(18)	Bill Nicholson	40.00	20.00	12.00
(19)	Robin Roberts	65.00	32.00	19.50
(20)	Eddie Sawyer	40.00	20.00	12.00
(21)	Andy Seminick	40.00	20.00	12.00
(22)	Ken Silvestri	40.00	20.00	12.00
(23)	Curtis T. Simmons	50.00	25.00	15.00
(24)	Dick Sisler	40.00	20.00	12.00
(25)	Eddie Waitkus	40.00	20.00	12.00
(26)	Dick Whitman	40.00	20.00	12.00

1964 Philadelphia Bulletin Phillies Album (Paper)

This series of newspaper features was the basis for the more often-encountered mail-in premiums. About 5-1/2" x 9", these pieces are printed in black-and-white in the sports section of the daily paper. The artwork is by staff artist Jim Porter. While the newspaper pieces are numbered, they are checklisted here in alphabetical order due to uncertainty about the original issue sequence.

		NM	EX	VG
Complete Set (27):		400.00	200.00	120.00
Common Player:		15.00	7.50	4.50
(1)	Richie Allen	40.00	20.00	12.00
(2)	Ruben Amaro	15.00	7.50	4.50
(3)	Jack Baldschun	15.00	7.50	4.50
(4)	Dennis Bennett	15.00	7.50	4.50
(5)	John Boozer	15.00	7.50	4.50
(6)	Johnny Briggs	15.00	7.50	4.50
(7)	Jim Bunning	50.00	25.00	15.00
(8)	Johnny Callison	15.00	7.50	4.50
(9)	Danny Cater	15.00	7.50	4.50
(10)	Wes Covington	15.00	7.50	4.50
(11)	Ray Culp	15.00	7.50	4.50
(12)	Clay Dalrymple	15.00	7.50	4.50
(13)	Tony Gonzalez	15.00	7.50	4.50
(14)	John Herrnstein	15.00	7.50	4.50
(15)	Alex Johnson	15.00	7.50	4.50
(16)	Art Mahaffey	15.00	7.50	4.50
(17)	Gene Mauch	15.00	7.50	4.50
(18)	Vic Power	15.00	7.50	4.50
(19)	Ed Roebuck	15.00	7.50	4.50
(20)	Cookie Rojas	15.00	7.50	4.50
(21)	Bobby Shantz	15.00	7.50	4.50
(22)	Chris Short	15.00	7.50	4.50
(23)	Tony Taylor	15.00	7.50	4.50
(24)	Frank Thomas	15.00	7.50	4.50
(25)	Gus Triandos	15.00	7.50	4.50
(26)	Bobby Wine	15.00	7.50	4.50
(27)	Rick Wise	15.00	7.50	4.50

1964 Philadelphia Bulletin Phillies Album

Color artwork by Jim Ponter is featured in this series of newspaper inserts. Portrait and action figures are combined on a blank-backed 8" x 10" format, along with a facsimile autograph. The unnumbered pictures are checklisted here alphabetically, two varieties of Jim Bunning's picture have been reported.

		NM	EX	VG
Complete Set (28):		550.00	275.00	175.00
Common Player:		20.00	10.00	6.00
(1)	Richie Allen	60.00	30.00	18.00
(2)	Ruben Amaro	20.00	10.00	6.00
(3)	Jack Baldschun	20.00	10.00	6.00
(4)	Dennis Bennett	20.00	10.00	6.00
(5)	John Boozer	20.00	10.00	6.00
(6)	Johnny Briggs	20.00	10.00	6.00
(7)	Jim Bunning/Pitching	75.00	37.00	22.00
(8)	Jim Bunning/Portrait	60.00	30.00	18.00
(9)	Johnny Callison	20.00	10.00	6.00
(10)	Danny Cater	20.00	10.00	6.00
(11)	Wes Covington	20.00	10.00	6.00
(12)	Ray Culp	20.00	10.00	6.00
(13)	Clay Dalrymple	20.00	10.00	6.00
(14)	Tony Gonzalez	20.00	10.00	6.00
(15)	John Herrnstein	20.00	10.00	6.00
(16)	Alex Johnson	20.00	10.00	6.00
(17)	Art Mahaffey	20.00	10.00	6.00
(18)	Gene Mauch	20.00	10.00	6.00
(19)	Vic Power	20.00	10.00	6.00
(20)	Ed Roebuck	20.00	10.00	6.00
(21)	Cookie Rojas	20.00	10.00	6.00
(22)	Bobby Shantz	20.00	10.00	6.00
(23)	Chris Short	20.00	10.00	6.00
(24)	Tony Taylor	20.00	10.00	6.00
(25)	Frank Thomas	20.00	10.00	6.00
(26)	Gus Triandos	20.00	10.00	6.00
(27)	Bobby Wine	20.00	10.00	6.00
(28)	Rick Wise	20.00	10.00	6.00

1909 Philadelphia Caramel (E95)

Similar in style to several other early candy and caramel cards, the set designated as E95 by the American Card Catalog is a 25-card issue produced by the Philadelphia Caramel Co., Camden, N.J., in 1909. The cards measure approximately 1-1/2" x 2-5/8" and contain a full-color player drawing. The back, which differentiates the set from other similar issues, checklists the 25 players in black ink and displays the Philadelphia Caramel Co. name at the bottom. Blank-back cards printed on thinner stock exist; these are not proofs, but were cut off a "Base Ball Series" notebook cover, they are valued about 25-50 percent of a corresponding regular-issue card.

		NM	EX	VG
Complete Set (25):		50,000	20,000	10,000
Common Player:		850.00	350.00	125.00
1	Honus Wagner	10,000	5,000	3,000
2	Nick Maddox	850.00	350.00	125.00
3	Fred Merkle	850.00	350.00	125.00
4	Cy Morgan	850.00	350.00	125.00
5	Chief Bender	2,000	1,000	600.00
6	Harry Krause	850.00	350.00	125.00
7	Art Devlin	850.00	350.00	125.00
8	Matty McIntyre	850.00	350.00	125.00
9	Ty Cobb	12,000	6,000	3,500
10	Ed Willetts (Willett)	850.00	350.00	125.00
11	Sam Crawford	2,000	1,000	600.00
12	Christy Matthewson (Mathewson)	9,500	4,750	2,500
13	Hooks Wiltse	850.00	350.00	125.00
14	Larry Doyle	850.00	350.00	125.00
15	Tommy Leach	850.00	350.00	125.00
16	Harry Lord	850.00	350.00	125.00
17	Ed Cicotte	2,730	780.00	350.00
18	Bill Carrigan	850.00	350.00	125.00
19	Vic Willis	2,000	1,000	600.00
20	Johnny Evers	2,000	1,000	600.00
21	Frank Chance	2,000	1,000	600.00
22	Solly Hoffman (Hofman)	850.00	350.00	125.00
23	Eddie Plank	4,500	2,250	1,350
24	Eddie Collins	2,000	1,000	600.00
25	Ed Reulbach	850.00	350.00	125.00

1910 Philadelphia Caramel (E96)

This set of 30 subjects, known by the ACC designation E96, was issued in 1910 by the Philadelphia Caramel Co. The approximately 1-1/2" x 2-5/8" size and front design remained the same, but the two issues can be identified by the backs. The backs of E96 cards are printed in red and carry a checklist of 30 players. There is also a line at the bottom advising "Previous series 25, making total issue 55 cards." Just below that appears "Philadelphia Caramel Co./Camden, N.J." Blank-back cards printed on thinner stock are not proofs, but rather were cut off a "Base Ball Series" notebook cover. They are valued about 25-50 percent of a corresponding regular-issue card.

	NM	EX	VG
Complete Set (30):	38,500	15,500	9,500

		NM	EX	VG
Common Player:		2,000	1,000	600.00
1	Harry Davis	2,000	1,000	600.00
2	Connie Mack	3,000	1,500	900.00
3	Ira Thomas	2,000	1,000	600.00
4	Home Run Baker	3,000	1,500	900.00
5	Red Dooin	2,000	1,000	600.00
6	George McQuillan	2,000	1,000	600.00
7	Ed Konetchy	2,000	1,000	600.00
8	Ed Karger	2,000	1,000	600.00
9	Mike Mowrey	2,000	1,000	600.00
10	Red Murray	2,000	1,000	600.00
11	Nap Lajoie	3,250	1,600	925.00
12	Claude Rossman	2,000	1,000	600.00
13	Nap Rucker	2,000	1,000	600.00
14	Hugh Jennings	3,000	1,500	900.00
15	Wild Bill Donovan	2,000	1,000	600.00
16	Jim Delahanty	2,000	1,000	600.00
17	George Mullin	2,000	1,000	600.00
18	Frank Arrelanes (Arellanes)	2,000	1,000	600.00
19	Tubby Spencer	2,000	1,000	600.00
20	Johnny Kling	2,000	1,000	600.00
21	Jack Pfister (Pfiester)	2,000	1,000	600.00
22	Mordecai Brown	3,000	1,500	900.00
23	Joe Tinker	3,000	1,500	900.00
24	Fred Clark (Clarke)	3,000	1,500	900.00
25	George Gibson	2,000	1,000	600.00
26	Babe Adams	2,000	1,000	600.00
27	Red Ames	2,000	1,000	600.00
28	Rube Marquard	3,000	1,500	900.00
29	Buck Herzog	2,000	1,000	600.00
30	Chief Myers (Meyers)	2,000	1,000	600.00

1913 Philadelphia Caramel Proofs

The attribution of these cards to Philadelphia Caramel is speculative, since no advertising is found on their blank backs. The three known pieces, however, have pictures and color identical to the players' cards in the 1910 E96 Philadelphia Caramel issue. These proofs differ only in the team designations. Nominally 1-1/2" x 2-5/8", the known examples were hand-cut from a sheet and are, at present, each unique. The Kling card was offered at auction in 2003 without meeting a $500 reserve.

Frank Chance (New York, A.L.)
Harry Davis (Cleveland)
Johnny Kling (Boston, A.L.)

1913 Philadelphia Evening Telegraph Postcards

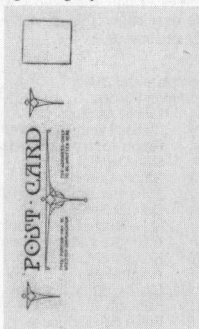

The attributed date of issue is speculative, about midway through Phillies manager Red Dooin's tenure. Issued by one of the city's daily newspapers, these 3-1/2" x 5-1/2" black-and-white postcards picture the managers of the Phils and A's in large portrait photos. The postcard-style back has ornate typography and embellishments.

		NM	EX	VG
Complete Set (2):		1,100	550.00	325.00
Common Card:		500.00	250.00	150.00
(1)	Charles Dooin	500.00	250.00	150.00
(2)	Connie Mack	650.00	325.00	200.00

1913 Philadelphia Evening Times Supplements

The checklist comprised almost entirely of Connie Mack's A's and John McGraw's Giants suggests this series of newspaper supplements was issued around World Series time. The blank-backed, sepia-toned pictures have posed action photos, are printed on light cardboard stock and measure about 7-1/2" x 9-1/2". This checklist may be incomplete.

		NM	EX	VG
Common Player:		200.00	100.00	60.00
(1)	Home Run Baker	400.00	200.00	120.00
(2)	Jack Barry	200.00	100.00	60.00
(3)	Chief Bender	400.00	200.00	120.00
(4)	George Burns	200.00	100.00	60.00
(5)	Ty Cobb	1,200	600.00	360.00
(6)	Eddie Collins	400.00	200.00	120.00
(7)	Al Demaree	200.00	100.00	60.00
(8)	Larry Doyle	200.00	100.00	60.00
(9)	Walter Johnson	800.00	400.00	240.00
(10)	Rube Marquard	400.00	200.00	120.00
(11)	Christy Mathewson	800.00	400.00	240.00
(12)	Stuffy McInnis	200.00	100.00	60.00
(13)	Chief Meyers	200.00	100.00	60.00
(14)	Rube Oldring	200.00	100.00	60.00
(15)	Eddie Plank	400.00	200.00	120.00
(16)	Jeff Tesreau	200.00	100.00	60.00

1950 Philadelphia Inquirer Fightin' Phillies

As the Whiz Kids battled to a National League pennant the "Philadelphia Inquirer" instituted a set of cut-out baseball cards in the Sunday rotogravure editions during September. The 4-7/8" x 6-7/8" cards have colored portrait photos surrounded with a white border. A facsimile autograph is printed across the chest. In the bottom border are the player's formal name, position, career summary and the line, "Inquirer Fightin' Phillies Album." Backs have whatever articles or ads were on the next page. The unnumbered cards are printed here in alphabetical order.

		NM	EX	VG
Complete Set (24):		350.00	175.00	105.00
Common Player:		15.00	7.50	4.50
(1)	Richie Ashburn	35.00	17.50	10.50
(2)	James Henry Bloodworth	15.00	7.50	4.50
(3)	Ralph Joseph Caballero	15.00	7.50	4.50
(4)	Milo Candini	15.00	7.50	4.50
(5)	Emory Church	15.00	7.50	4.50
(6)	Sylvester Urban Donnelly	15.00	7.50	4.50
(7)	Delmer Ennis	15.00	7.50	4.50
(8)	Mike Mitchel Goliat (Mitchell)	15.00	7.50	4.50
(9)	Granville Wilbur Hamner	15.00	7.50	4.50
(10)	Kenneth Alphonse Heintzelman	15.00	7.50	4.50
(11)	Stanley Ernst Hollmig	15.00	7.50	4.50
(12)	Kenneth W. Johnson	15.00	7.50	4.50
(13)	Willie Edward Jones	15.00	7.50	4.50
(14)	Stanley Edward Lopata	15.00	7.50	4.50
(15)	Russell Charles Meyer	15.00	7.50	4.50
(16)	Robert Miller	15.00	7.50	4.50
(17)	William Beck Nicholson	15.00	7.50	4.50
(18)	Robin Evan Roberts	35.00	17.50	10.50
(19)	Andrew Wasal Seminick	15.00	7.50	4.50
(20)	Kenneth Joseph Silvestri	15.00	7.50	4.50
(21)	Curtis Thomas Simmons	15.00	7.50	4.50
(22)	Richard Alan Sisler	15.00	7.50	4.50
(23)	Edward Stephen Waitkus	15.00	7.50	4.50
(24)	Dick Whitman	15.00	7.50	4.50

1954 Philadelphia Inquirer Album of Baseball Stars

A series of four baseball players from each of Philadelphia's teams appeared on a pair of pages in the Colorama color rotogravure section of the Sunday. Philadelphia Inquirer. Each picture is about 6-3/4" x 9-3/4" and was separated from

the other three on its "ALBUM OF SPORTS" page by a black dotted line, indicative of an intention for them to be cut out and saved. Under the portrait is a brief career summary. Backs have other newspaper content as printed each Sunday.

		NM	EX	VG
Complete Set (8):		75.00	37.50	22.50
Common Player:		8.00	4.00	2.50
JULY 25				
(1)	Richie Ashburn	25.00	12.50	7.50
(2)	Jim Finigan	8.00	4.00	2.50
(3)	Gran Hamner	8.00	4.00	2.50
(4)	Bill Shantz	8.00	4.00	2.50
SEPT. 12				
(1)	Smoky Burgess	10.00	5.00	3.00
(2)	Arnold Portocarrero	8.00	4.00	2.50
(3)	Robin Roberts	16.00	8.00	4.75
(4)	Curt Simmons	10.00	5.00	3.00

1940 Philadelphia Phillies Photo Pack

This set of 25 photos show players in poses on the field with the Quaker figure and "PHILADELPHIA NATIONAL LEAGUE BASE BALL CLUB" around it in a circular logo in the upper right hand corner. Size is 6" x 8-1/2".

		NM	EX	VG
Complete Set (25):		150.00	75.00	30.00
Common Player:		7.50	3.75	2.25
(1)	Morrie Arnovich	7.50	3.75	2.25
(2)	Bill Atwood	7.50	3.75	2.25
(3)	Walter Beck	7.50	3.75	2.25
(4)	Stan Benjamin	7.50	3.75	2.25
(5)	Bob Bragan	7.50	3.75	2.25
(6)	Roy Bruner	7.50	3.75	2.25
(7)	Kirby Higbie	7.50	3.75	2.25
(8)	Si Johnson	7.50	3.75	2.25
(9)	Syl Johnson	7.50	3.75	2.25
(10)	Chuck Klein	7.50	3.75	2.25
(11)	Ed Levy	7.50	3.75	2.25
(12)	Dan Litwhiler	7.50	3.75	2.25
(13)	Hans Lobert	7.50	3.75	2.25
(14)	Herschel Martin	7.50	3.75	2.25
(15)	Joe Marty	7.50	3.75	2.25
(16)	Maerrill May	7.50	3.75	2.25
(17)	Walk Millies	7.50	3.75	2.25
(18)	Hugh Mulcahy	7.50	3.75	2.25
(19)	Ike Pearson	7.50	3.75	2.25
(20)	Doc Prothro	7.50	3.75	2.25
(21)	George Scharen	7.50	3.75	2.25
(22)	Clyde Smoll	7.50	3.75	2.25
(23)	Gus Suhr	7.50	3.75	2.25
(24)	Ben Warren	7.50	3.75	2.25
(25)	Del Young	7.50	3.75	2.25

1943 Philadelphia Phillies Photo Pack

Like many teams in that era, the Phillies issued souvenir photo packs for sale at the stadium and by mail-order. This team issue is in a 6" x 8-1/2", blank-back, black-and-white format. The player picture is bordered in white with the player name in all-caps in the bottom border. From the large number of players known, it is evident that the composition of the photo packs was changed from time to time as the team roster changed. It is possible this checklist is not complete. The unnumbered pictures have been listed here alphabetically.

		NM	EX	VG
Complete Set (40):		300.00	150.00	90.00
Common Player:		8.00	4.00	2.50
(1)	Buster Adams	8.00	4.00	2.50
(2)	Walter Beck	8.00	4.00	2.50
(3)	Stan Benjamin	8.00	4.00	2.50
(4)	Cy Blanton	8.00	4.00	2.50
(5)	Bobby Bragan	8.00	4.00	2.50

		NM	EX	VG
(6)	Charlie Brewster	8.00	4.00	2.50
(7)	Paul Busby	8.00	4.00	2.50
(8)	Ben Culp	8.00	4.00	2.50
(9)	Babe Dahlgren	8.00	4.00	2.50
(10)	Lloyd Dietz	8.00	4.00	2.50
(11)	Nick Etten	8.00	4.00	2.50
(12)	George Eyrich	8.00	4.00	2.50
(13)	Charlie Fuchs	8.00	4.00	2.50
(14)	Al Glossop	8.00	4.00	2.50
(15)	Al Gerheauser	8.00	4.00	2.50
(16)	"Bucky" Harris	12.00	6.00	3.50
(17)	Frank Hoerst	8.00	4.00	2.50
(18)	Si Johnson	8.00	4.00	2.50
(19)	Chuck Klein	15.00	7.50	4.50
(20)	Ernie Koy	8.00	4.00	2.50
(21)	Tex Kraus	8.00	4.00	2.50
(22)	Danny Litwhiler	8.00	4.00	2.50
(23)	Mickey Livingston	8.00	4.00	2.50
(24)	Hans Lobert	8.00	4.00	2.50
(25)	Henry Marnie	8.00	4.00	2.50
(26)	Merrill May	8.00	4.00	2.50
(27)	Rube Melton	8.00	4.00	2.50
(28)	Danny Murtaugh	10.00	5.00	3.00
(29)	Sam Nahem	8.00	4.00	2.50
(30)	Earl Naylor	8.00	4.00	2.50
(31)	Ron Northey	8.00	4.00	2.50
(32)	Tommy Padden	8.00	4.00	2.50
(33)	Ike Pearson	8.00	4.00	2.50
(34)	Johnny Podgajny	8.00	4.00	2.50
(35)	Schoolboy Rowe	10.00	5.00	3.00
(36)	Glen Stewart	8.00	4.00	2.50
(37)	Coaker Triplett	8.00	4.00	2.50
(38)	Lloyd Waner	15.00	7.50	4.50
(39)	Ben Warren	8.00	4.00	2.50
(40)	Jimmy Wasdell	8.00	4.00	2.50

1958 Philadelphia Phillies Picture Pack

This set of 5" x 7" blank-backed, black-and-white player pictures was most likely issued in 1958, though it is also possible the set was issued in 1957 (or both). This team-issue set differs from the contemporary Jay Publishing picture packs in that it does not have the city name in the identication line, only the player name in all-caps and "Phillies." The unnumbered pictures are listed here alphabetically.

		NM	EX	VG
Complete Set (12):		75.00	40.00	22.50
Common Player:		7.50	3.75	2.25
(1)	Harry Anderson	7.50	3.75	2.25
(2)	Richie Ashburn	15.00	7.50	4.50
(3)	Bob Bowman	7.50	3.75	2.25
(4)	Turk Farrell	7.50	3.75	2.25
(5)	Chico Fernandez	7.50	3.75	2.25
(6)	Granny Hamner	7.50	3.75	2.25
(7)	Stan Lopata	7.50	3.75	2.25
(8)	Rip Repulski	7.50	3.75	2.25
(9)	Robin Roberts	15.00	7.50	4.50
(10)	Jack Sanford	7.50	3.75	2.25
(11)	Curt Simmons	7.50	3.75	2.25
(12)	Mayo Smith	7.50	3.75	2.25

1958-60 Philadelphia Phillies Team Issue

Thus far 22 different cards have been discovered in this format; it is likely the checklist here is not yet complete. Like many teams, the Phillies issued these cards to players and staff to honor fan requests for photos and autographs. The cards are 3-1/4" x 5-1/2" and have black-and-white portrait photos with white borders. Backs are blank. The unnumbered cards are listed here alphabetically.

		NM	EX	VG
Common Player:		6.00	3.00	1.75
(1)	Harry Anderson	6.00	3.00	1.75
(2)	Richie Ashburn	12.00	6.00	3.50
(3)	Ed Bouchee	6.00	3.00	1.75
(4)	Smoky Burgess	7.50	3.75	2.25
(5)	Johnny Callison	8.00	4.00	2.50
(6)	Jim Coker	6.00	3.00	1.75
(7)	Clay Dalrymple	6.00	3.00	1.75
(8)	Del Ennis	7.50	3.75	2.25
(9)	Tony Gonzalez	6.00	3.00	1.75
(10)	Granny Hamner	6.00	3.00	1.75
(11)	Willie Jones	6.00	3.00	1.75
(12)	Stan Lopata	6.00	3.00	1.75
(13)	Art Mahaffey	6.00	3.00	1.75
(14)	Gene Mauch	6.00	3.00	1.75
(15)	Bob Morgan	6.00	3.00	1.75
(16)	Wally Post	6.00	3.00	1.75
(17)	Robin Roberts	12.00	6.00	3.50
(18)	Eddie Sawyer	6.00	3.00	1.75
(19)	Andy Seminick	6.00	3.00	1.50
(20)	Ray Semproch	6.00	3.00	1.75
(21)	Chris Short	6.00	3.00	1.75
(22)	Curt Simmons	8.00	4.00	2.50
(23)	Earl Torgeson	6.00	3.00	1.75

1964 Philadelphia Phillies Player Pins

Only four players are checklisted in this series, but it is expected more will be added in the future. These pinbacks are 2-3/16" in diameter and have black-and-white player portraits on front, on a white background. The player's name is printed at bottom in block letters.

		NM	EX	VG
Common Player:		45.00	22.50	13.50
(1)	Dick Allen	90.00	45.00	27.50
(2)	Jim Bunning	90.00	45.00	27.50
(3)	Chris Short	45.00	22.50	13.50
(4)	Roy Sievers	45.00	22.50	13.50

1965 Go! Phillies Go! Pins

These large (3-1/2" diameter) pinback buttons feature a dozen members of the '65 Phils. Player portraits are on a white background and have had the cap and pinstripes colored in red. At top, the title is printed in red and blue. The facsimile autograph at bottom is printed in blue.

		NM	EX	VG
Complete Set (12):		750.00	375.00	225.00
Common Player:		50.00	25.00	15.00
(1)	Rich Allen	100.00	50.00	30.00
(2)	Ruben Amaro	50.00	25.00	15.00
(3)	Bo Belinsky	65.00	32.50	20.00
(4)	Jim Bunning	100.00	50.00	30.00
(5)	Johnny Callison	65.00	32.50	20.00
(6)	Wes Covington	50.00	25.00	15.00
(7)	Ray Culp	50.00	25.00	15.00
(8)	Cookie Rojas	50.00	25.00	15.00
(9)	Chris Short	50.00	25.00	15.00
(10)	Dick Stuart	50.00	25.00	15.00
(11)	Tony Taylor	50.00	25.00	15.00
(12)	Bobby Wine	50.00	25.00	15.00

1965 Philadelphia Phillies Tiles

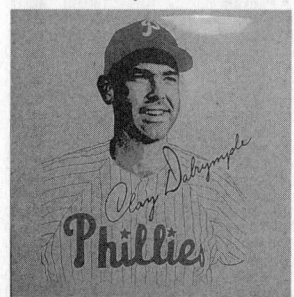

These decorative heavy ceramic tiles feature color portraits and facsimile autographs on a white background. In 6" x 6" format the tiles were made in England, but decorated in the U.S. They appear to have been originally issued with cork backing and some have been seen with a hangar attached on back.

		NM	EX	VG
Complete Set (12):		600.00	300.00	180.00
Common Player:		40.00	20.00	12.00
(1)	Richie Allen	100.00	50.00	30.00
(2)	Bo Belinsky	60.00	30.00	18.00
(3)	Jim Bunning	125.00	65.00	35.00
(4)	Johnny Callison	60.00	30.00	18.00
(5)	Wes Covington	40.00	20.00	12.00
(6)	Clay Dalrymple	40.00	20.00	12.00
(7)	Gene Mauch	40.00	20.00	12.00
(8)	Cookie Rojas	40.00	20.00	12.00
(9)	Tony Taylor	40.00	20.00	12.00
(10)	Chris Short	40.00	20.00	12.00
(11)	Dick Stuart	40.00	20.00	12.00
(12)	Bobby Wine	40.00	20.00	12.00

1967 Philadelphia Phillies Safe Driving

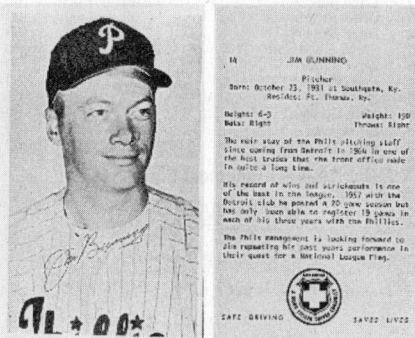

The honor of producing the only safety set of the 1960s goes to the Phillies for this traffic safety set. Measuring 2-3/4" x 4-1/2", the cards have a black-and-white front featuring the standard publicity photo of the player, with a facsimile autograph superimposed. Backs are printed in blue and include a few career and biographical details, along with the player's uniform number, by which the set is checklisted here. At bottom is a circle and shield design with the safety message.

		NM	EX	VG
Complete Set (13):		95.00	47.00	28.00
Common Player:		8.00	4.00	2.50
4	Gene Mauch	8.00	4.00	2.50
6	Johnny Callison	10.00	5.00	3.00
10	Bill White	10.00	5.00	3.00
11	Clay Dalrymple	8.00	4.00	2.50
12	Johnny Briggs	8.00	4.00	2.50
14	Jim Bunning	20.00	10.00	6.00
15	Dick Allen	18.00	9.00	5.50
16	Cookie Rojas	8.00	4.00	2.50
24	Dick Groat	10.00	5.00	3.00
25	Tony Gonzalez	8.00	4.00	2.50
37	Dick Ellsworth	8.00	4.00	2.50
41	Chris Short	8.00	4.00	2.50
46	Larry Jackson	8.00	4.00	2.50

1964 Philadelphia Phillies Picture Pack

This souvenir set of Phillies pictures features black-and-white portrait photos in a white border on a 4-1/4" x 7" format. The player's name and team are printed in the top border. The unnumbered pictures are checklisted here in alphabetical order.

		NM	EX	VG
Complete Set (12):		60.00	30.00	18.00
Common Player:		5.00	2.50	1.50
(1)	Richie Allen	7.50	3.75	2.25
(2)	John Callison	6.00	3.00	1.80
(3)	Woody Fryman	5.00	2.50	1.50
(4)	Larry Hisle	5.00	2.50	1.50
(5)	Deron Johnson	5.00	2.50	1.50
(6)	Don Money	5.00	2.50	1.50
(7)	Cookie Rojas	5.00	2.50	1.50
(8)	Mike Ryan	5.00	2.50	1.50
(9)	Chris Short	5.00	2.50	1.50
(10)	Bob Skinner	5.00	2.50	1.50
(11)	Tony Taylor	5.00	2.50	1.50
(12)	Rick Wise	5.00	2.50	1.50

1975 Philadelphia Phillies Photocards

JOE HOERNER

These 3-1/4" x 5-1/2" blank-back, black-and-white cards feature player portrait photos with only the player name in the white border at bottom. Fronts have a semi-gloss finish. It is likely the checklist, presented here alphabetically, is incomplete.

		NM	EX	VG
Common Player:		3.00	1.50	.90
(1)	Tom Hilgendorf	3.00	1.50	.90
(2)	Terry Harmon	3.00	1.50	.90
(3)	Joe Hoerner	3.00	1.50	.90
(4)	Tommy Hutton	3.00	1.50	.90
(5)	Jim Lonborg	4.00	2.00	1.25
(6)	John Oates	3.00	1.50	.90

1961 Phillies Cigar Mickey Mantle

This 6-1/2" x 9" blank-back color photo card of Mickey Mantle was part of a redemption program for Phillies cigars. For $3.39 and 20 cigar bands, a person could receive a Mickey Mantle model baseball glove and this "autographed" (facsimile) photo.

	NM	EX	VG
Mickey Mantle	225.00	110.00	65.00

1912 Photo Art Shop Boston Red Sox

Two postcards are currently known to have been produced, according to the legend on the back, by The Photo Art Shop of Swampscott, Mass. The standard-size (about 3-1/2" x 5-1/2") cards are printed in black-and-white. A vertically formatted card shows opposing World Series aces Joe Wood and Walter Johnson. A horizontal team-photo card has each player's last name printed over his picture and describes the team as "Champions of the American League". The Red Sox went on to defeat the Giants in the World Series.

	NM	EX	VG
Joe Wood, Walter Johnson	1,800	900.00	540.00
1912 Boston Red Sox	900.00	450.00	275.00

1964 Photo Linen Emblems

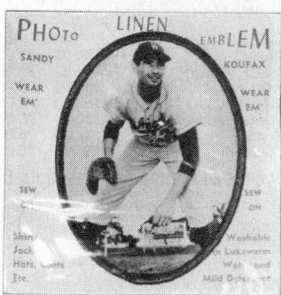

The attributed date of issue is only approximate. About 3-1/2" x 4-1/2", these sew-on patches feature black-and-white photos with an embroidered red border. The patches were sold in a cellowrapped package. The checklist presented here in alphabetical order is not complete.

		NM	EX	VG
Complete Set (10):		625.00	300.00	180.00
Common Player:		30.00	15.00	9.00
(1)	Yogi Berra	50.00	25.00	15.00
(2)	Clete Boyer	30.00	15.00	9.00
(3)	Elston Howard	30.00	15.00	9.00
(4)	Sandy Koufax	175.00	87.00	52.00
(5)	Tony Kubek	30.00	15.00	9.00
(6)	Mickey Mantle	250.00	125.00	75.00
(7)	Roger Maris	90.00	45.00	27.00
(8)	Joe Pepitone	30.00	15.00	9.00
(9)	Bobby Richardson	30.00	15.00	9.00
(10)	Tom Tresh	30.00	15.00	9.00

1972 Photo Sports Co. L.A. Dodgers

This is the first known issue of a sports novelty marketed by Photo Sports Co., Los Angeles. The company is best known to collectors for its 1974 McDonald's promotional "Foto Balls" with player discs. The Dodgers set is similar in concept with a hinged plastic baseball which opens to reveal player discs. A "keyhole" punched at the bottom of the discs keeps them in place within the ball. The Dodgers never rolled out the project and surviving sets are extremely rare. Discs are 2-5/8" diameter with borderless color photos on front. Backs have player stats and the team logo. The unnumbered discs are checklisted here in alphabetical order.

		NM	EX	VG
Complete Set (Ball and Discs):		300.00	150.00	90.00
Common Player:		16.00	8.00	4.75
(1)	Red Adams	16.00	8.00	4.75
(2)	Walt Alston	35.00	17.50	10.50
(3)	Willie Crawford	16.00	8.00	4.75
(4)	Willie Davis	24.00	12.00	7.25
(5)	Al Downing	16.00	8.00	4.75
(6)	Jim Gilliam	24.00	12.00	7.25
(7)	Bill Grabarkewitz	16.00	8.00	4.75
(8)	Jim Lefebvre	16.00	8.00	4.75
(9)	Pete Mikkelsen	16.00	8.00	4.75
(10)	Manny Mota	18.00	9.00	5.50
(11)	Claude Osteen	16.00	8.00	4.75
(12)	Wes Parker	16.00	8.00	4.75
(13)	Duke Sims	16.00	8.00	4.75
(14)	Bill Singer	16.00	8.00	4.75
(15)	Bill Sudakis	16.00	8.00	4.75
(16)	Don Sutton	30.00	15.00	9.00
(17)	Bob Valentine	18.00	9.00	5.50
(18)	Maury Wills	22.00	11.00	6.50

1953 Pictsweet Milwaukee Braves

This black-and-white mini-poster (8-1/2" x 11-1/4") depicts a player holding a package of frozen vegetables. They were probably intended for grocery store window or aisle display. Backs are blank. It's unknown how many players are in the set. See also, Top Taste Bread.

		NM	EX	VG
Common Player:		150.00	75.00	45.00
(1)	"Bullet Bill" Bruton	150.00	75.00	45.00
(2)	Walker Cooper	150.00	75.00	45.00
(3)	Sid Gordon	150.00	75.00	45.00
(4)	Charlie Grimm	150.00	75.00	45.00
(5)	Sibby Sisti	150.00	75.00	45.00
(6)	Max Surkont	150.00	75.00	45.00

1970 Pictures of Champions Baltimore Orioles

Issued in 1970 in the Baltimore area, this 16-card set pictures members of the Baltimore Orioles. The 2-1/8" x 2-3/4" cards feature black and white player photos on orange card stock. The method of distribution is unknown.

		NM	EX	VG
Complete Set (16):		80.00	40.00	25.00
Common Player:		2.00	1.00	.60
4	Earl Weaver	7.50	3.75	2.25
5	Brooks Robinson	25.00	12.50	7.50
7	Mark Belanger	2.00	1.00	.60
8	Andy Etchebarren	2.00	1.00	.60
9	Don Buford	2.00	1.00	.60
10	Ellie Hendricks	2.00	1.00	.60
12	Dave May	2.00	1.00	.60
15	Dave Johnson	2.00	1.00	.60
16	Dave McNally	2.00	1.00	.60
20	Frank Robinson	20.00	10.00	6.00
22	Jim Palmer	20.00	10.00	6.00
24	Pete Richert	2.00	1.00	.60
29	Dick Hall	2.00	1.00	.60
35	Mike Cuellar	2.00	1.00	.60
39	Eddie Watt	2.00	1.00	.60
40	Dave Leonhard	2.00	1.00	.60

1909-11 Piedmont Cigarettes

In both T205 and T206, Piedmont is the brand found most often on the cards' backs. In T205, Piedmonts backs are printed in blue with either Factory 25 and 42 designation, the latter of which is much scarcer but commands little premium, more due to collector indifference than relative scarcity. In T206, the familiar blue Piedmont logo is found in all three series. In the "150 Subjects" and "350 Subjects" series, only Factory 25 (Va.) is seen. In the "350-460 Subjects" series, both Factory 25 and Factory 42 (N.C.) are seen. The latter is much scarcer and commands a premium over the more common Factory 25 version.

FACTORY 42 OVERPRINTS PREMIUM:
Common Players: 5-7X
Hall of Famers: 2X
(See T205, T206)

1914 Piedmont Art Stamps (T330-2)

This series of "Piedmont Art Stamps" looks like a fragile version of the more popular T205 Gold Border tobacco cards of 1911, employing the same basic design on front. The Piedmont stamps measure 1-1/2" x 2-5/8". Though the backs advertise "100 designs," more than 110 different players are known. And, because some of the players are pictured in two separate poses, there are actually 118 different stamps known, with new discoveries still being made. All but three of the subjects in the Piedmont set were taken from the T205 set; the exceptions being Joe Wood, Walt Blair and Bill Killifer. Because of their fragile composition, and since they are stamps that were frequently stuck to album pages, examples of Piedmont Art Stamps in Near Mint or better condition are very scarce. The back of the stamps offered a "handsome" album in exchange for 25 Piedmont coupons. The set has an American Card Catalog designation of T330-2. Gaps have been left in the assigned numbering to accommodate future additions.

		NM	EX	VG
Common Player:		150.00	60.00	30.00
(1)	Leon K. Ames	150.00	60.00	30.00
(2)	Jimmy Archer	150.00	60.00	30.00
(3)	Jimmy Austin	150.00	60.00	30.00
(4)	Home Run Baker	450.00	180.00	90.00
(5)	Cy Barger (Full "B" on cap.)	150.00	60.00	30.00
(6)	Cy Barger (Partial "B" on cap.)	150.00	60.00	30.00
(7)	Jack Barry	150.00	60.00	30.00
(8)	Johnny Bates	150.00	60.00	30.00
(9)	Fred Beck	150.00	60.00	30.00
(10)	Beals Becker	150.00	60.00	30.00
(11)	Chief Bender	450.00	180.00	90.00
(12)	Bob Bescher	150.00	60.00	30.00
(13)	Joe Birmingham	150.00	60.00	30.00
(14)	Walt Blair	150.00	60.00	30.00
(15)	Roger Bresnahan	450.00	180.00	90.00
(16)	Al Bridwell	150.00	60.00	30.00
(17)	Mordecai Brown	450.00	180.00	90.00
(18)	Bobby Byrne	150.00	60.00	30.00
(19)	Howie Camnitz	150.00	60.00	30.00
(20)	Bill Carrigan	150.00	60.00	30.00
(21)	Frank Chance	450.00	180.00	90.00
(22)	Hal Chase ("Chase" on front.)	250.00	100.00	50.00
(23)	Hal Chase ("Hal Chase" on front.)	300.00	120.00	60.00
(24)	Ed Cicotte	375.00	150.00	75.00
(25)	Fred Clarke	450.00	180.00	90.00
(26)	Ty Cobb	5,500	2,200	1,100
(27)	Eddie Collins (Mouth closed.)	450.00	180.00	90.00
(28)	Eddie Collins (Mouth open.)	450.00	180.00	90.00
(29)	Otis "Doc" Crandall	150.00	60.00	30.00
(30)	Bill Dahlen	150.00	60.00	30.00
(31)	Jake Daubert	150.00	60.00	30.00
(32)	Jim Delahanty	150.00	60.00	30.00
(33)	Josh Devore	150.00	60.00	30.00
(34)	Red Dooin	150.00	60.00	30.00
(35)	Mickey Doolan	150.00	60.00	30.00
(36)	Tom Downey	150.00	60.00	30.00
(37)	Larry Doyle	150.00	60.00	30.00
(38)	Dick Egan	150.00	60.00	30.00
(39)	Kid Elberfield (Elberfeld)	150.00	60.00	30.00
(40)	Clyde Engle	150.00	60.00	30.00
(41)	Louis Evans	150.00	60.00	30.00
(42)	Johnny Evers	450.00	180.00	90.00
(43)	Ray Fisher	150.00	60.00	30.00
(44)	Art Fletcher	150.00	60.00	30.00
(45)	Russ Ford (Dark cap.)	150.00	60.00	30.00
(46)	Russ Ford (White cap.)	150.00	60.00	30.00
(47)	Art Fromme	150.00	60.00	30.00
(48)	George Gibson	150.00	60.00	30.00
(49)	William Goode (Wilbur Good)	150.00	60.00	30.00
(51)	Eddie Grant	225.00	90.00	45.00
(52)	Clark Griffith	450.00	180.00	90.00
(53)	Bob Groom	150.00	60.00	30.00
(54)	Bob Harmon	150.00	60.00	30.00
(55)	Arnold Hauser	150.00	60.00	30.00
(56)	Buck Herzog	150.00	60.00	30.00
(57)	Dick Hoblitzell	150.00	60.00	30.00
(58)	Miller Huggins	450.00	180.00	90.00
(59)	John Hummel	150.00	60.00	30.00
(60)	Hughie Jennings	450.00	180.00	90.00
(61)	Walter Johnson	750.00	300.00	150.00
(62)	Davy Jones	150.00	60.00	30.00
(63)	Bill Killifer (Killefer)	150.00	60.00	30.00
(64)	Jack Knight	150.00	60.00	30.00
(65)	Ed Konetchy	150.00	60.00	30.00
(66)	Frank LaPorte	150.00	60.00	30.00
(67)	Thomas Leach	150.00	60.00	30.00
(68)	Edgar Lennox	150.00	60.00	30.00
(69)	Hans Lobert	150.00	60.00	30.00
(70)	Harry Lord	150.00	60.00	30.00
(71)	Sherry Magee	150.00	60.00	30.00
(72)	Rube Marquard	450.00	180.00	90.00
(73)	Christy Mathewson	1,250	500.00	250.00
(74)	George McBride	150.00	60.00	30.00
(76)	J.J. McGraw	450.00	180.00	90.00
(77)	Larry McLean	150.00	60.00	30.00
(78)	Fred Merkle	150.00	60.00	30.00
(79)	Chief Meyers	150.00	60.00	30.00
(80)	Clyde Milan	150.00	60.00	30.00
(81)	Dots Miller	150.00	60.00	30.00
(82)	Mike Mitchell	150.00	60.00	30.00
(83)	Pat Moran	150.00	60.00	30.00
(84)	George Moriarity (Moriarty)	150.00	60.00	30.00
(85)	George Mullin	150.00	60.00	30.00
(86)	Danny Murphy	150.00	60.00	30.00
(87)	Jack "Red" Murray	150.00	60.00	30.00
(88)	Tom Needham	150.00	60.00	30.00
(89)	Rebel Oakes	150.00	60.00	30.00
(90)	Rube Oldring	150.00	60.00	30.00
(91)	Fred Parent	325.00	160.00	100.00
(92)	Dode Paskert	150.00	60.00	30.00
(93)	Jack Quinn	150.00	60.00	30.00
(94)	Ed Reulbach	150.00	60.00	30.00
(95)	Lewis Ritchie	150.00	60.00	30.00
(96)	Jack Rowan	150.00	60.00	30.00
(97)	Nap Rucker	150.00	60.00	30.00
(98)	Germany Schaefer	150.00	60.00	30.00
(99)	Wildfire Schulte	150.00	60.00	30.00
(101)	Jim Scott	150.00	60.00	30.00
(102)	Fred Snodgrass	150.00	60.00	30.00
(103)	Tris Speaker	600.00	240.00	120.00
(104)	Oscar Stamage (Stanage)	150.00	60.00	30.00
(105)	George Stovall	150.00	60.00	30.00
(106)	George Suggs	150.00	60.00	30.00
(107)	Jeff Sweeney	150.00	60.00	30.00
(108)	Ira Thomas	150.00	60.00	30.00
(109)	Joe Tinker	450.00	180.00	90.00
(110)	Terry Turner	150.00	60.00	30.00
(111)	Hippo Vaughn	150.00	60.00	30.00
(112)	Heinie Wagner	150.00	60.00	30.00
(113)	Bobby Wallace (No cap.)	450.00	180.00	90.00
(114)	Bobby Wallace (With cap.)	450.00	180.00	90.00
(115)	Ed Walsh	450.00	180.00	90.00
(116)	Zach Wheat	450.00	180.00	90.00
(117)	Irwin "Kaiser" Wilhelm	150.00	60.00	30.00
(118)	Ed Willett	150.00	60.00	30.00
(119)	Owen Wilson	150.00	60.00	30.00
(120)	Hooks Wiltse	150.00	60.00	30.00
(121)	Joe Wood	150.00	60.00	30.00

1939 Piel's Beer Coasters

New York Giants manager Bill Terry was the only baseball player among a trio of local celebrities endoring the beer brand in this series of approximately 4" diameter bar coasters. The printing is in black-and-red.

This set can be considerd a British version of the T215 Red Cross Type 1 set. Distributed by Pirate brand cigarettes of Bristol and London, England, the fronts of the cards are identical to the Red Cross cards, but the green backs carry advertising for Pirate Cigarettes. It is believed that the Pirate cards were printed for distribution to U.S. servicemen in the South Seas. There is reason to believe the "standard" tobacco card length of 2-5/8" (width 1-7/16") may not be universally applicable to the Pirate cards, possibly because of packaging considerations.

1910 Pittsburgh Gazette Times Honus Wagner Postcard

Describing him as "The Worlds' Greatest Base Ball Player," the local newspaper published this black-and-white standard size, typically marked, photographic postcard picturing the Flying Dutchman and landmarks from his Carnegie, Pa., hometown.

	NM	EX	VG
Honus Wagner	750.00	375.00	225.00

1904 Pittsburg Leader Honus Wagner Schedule

This 3-3/4" x 1-3/4" celluloid pocket schedule for the 1904 Pirates features on its front a black-and-white photographic portrait of the "KING OF BALL PLAYERS," Honus Wagner. Much of the remainder of the front and back printing is in regal purple typography.

	NM	EX	VG
Honus Wagner	4,000	2,000	1,200

1908 Pittsburgh Pirates Vignette Postcards

It has been reliably reported that 15 postcards and an album were produced for this souvenir issue sold at Pittsburgh's Exhibition Field. Only Pirates are pictured in this series of black-and-white standard-format postcards published locally by J.B. Coyle. Cards have an irregularly shaped posed photo of the player at center with his last name (or nickname), position and "PGH-08" crudely printed in white. Divided postcard backs have a stamp box and publisher's credit line. The incomplete checklist presented here is alphabetically arranged. Later editions of the American Card Catalog listed this set as PC800.

	Common Player:	NM	EX	VG
(1)	Abby (Ed Abbaticchio)	250.00	125.00	75.00
(2)	Howie Camnitz	250.00	125.00	75.00
(3)	Fred Clarke	350.00	175.00	105.00
(4)	George Gibson	250.00	125.00	75.00
(5)	Tommy Leach	250.00	125.00	75.00
(6)	Dan Moeller	250.00	125.00	75.00
(10)	Allen Storke	250.00	125.00	75.00
(14)	Honus Wagner	3,000	1,500	1,000
(15)	Owen Wilson	250.00	125.00	75.00

	NM	EX	VG
Bill Terry	30.00	15.00	9.00

1913-1915 Pinkerton Score/Photo/Post Cards

The picture portions of the T5 Pinkerton cabinets have also been seen in other formats, in printed rather than photographic presentation. The most desirable of these have backs printed for use as baseball scorecards. These measure a nominal 3-1/2" x 5-1/2", give or take 1/4". They are believed to have been printed some years after the cabinet cards. It is unknown to what extent the checklist of T5 can be found in this format. Postcard-style backs have also been seen for some Pinkerton pictures, as well as blank-backed versions; they are considerably discounted from the scorecard type. Confirmed examples are listed here.

	Common Player:	NM	EX	VG
	SCORECARD BACKS	300.00	150.00	90.00
153	Hughie Jennings	7,500	3,750	2,250
159	Ty Cobb	5,000	2,500	1,500
203	King Cole	500.00	250.00	150.00
205	Heinie Zimmerman	500.00	250.00	150.00
206	Wildfire Schulte	500.00	250.00	150.00
208	Joe Tinker	1,000	500.00	300.00
251	Christy Mathewson	3,000	1,500	1,000
252	Fred Merkle	500.00	250.00	75.00
260	Larry Doyle	500.00	250.00	75.00
303	Red Dooin	500.00	250.00	75.00
420	R.C. Hoblitzell	500.00	250.00	75.00
424	Mike Mitchell	500.00	250.00	75.00
505	Connie Mack	1,000	500.00	300.00
511	Eddie Collins	1,000	500.00	300.00
512	Frank Baker	1,000	500.00	300.00
872	Hans Wagner	5,500	2,750	1,650
	POSTCARD OR BLANK BACKS			
159	Ty Cobb	4,500	2,250	1,350
203	King Cole	300.00	150.00	90.00
206	Frank Schulte	300.00	150.00	90.00
208	Joe Tinker	500.00	250.00	150.00
251	Christy Mathewson	1,800	900.00	550.00
260	Larry Doyle	300.00	150.00	90.00
264	Chief Myers (Meyers)	300.00	150.00	90.00
419	Clark Griffith	500.00	250.00	150.00
424	Mike Mitchell	300.00	150.00	90.00
501	Chas. Bender	500.00	250.00	150.00
511	Eddie Collins	500.00	250.00	150.00
512	Frank Baker	500.00	250.00	150.00
627	Napoleon Lajoie	500.00	250.00	150.00
855	Fred Clarke	500.00	250.00	150.00
865	Babe Adams	300.00	150.00	90.00
872	Hans Wagner	3,250	1,600	1,000

1912 Pirate Cigarettes (T215)

		NM	EX	VG
	Common Player:	11,000	5,500	3,300
(1)	Red Ames	11,000	5,500	3,300
(2)	Home Run Baker	16,000	8,000	4,800
(3)	Neal Ball	11,000	5,500	3,300
(4)	Chief Bender	16,000	8,000	4,800
(5)	Al Bridwell	11,000	5,500	3,300
(6)	Bobby Byrne (St. Louis)	11,000	5,500	3,300
(7)	Mordecai Brown (Chicago on shirt.)	16,000	8,000	4,800
(8)	Howie Camnitz	11,000	5,500	3,300
(9)	Frank Chance	9,800	4,900	2,950
(10)	Hal Chase	14,500	7,250	4,350
(11)	Eddie Collins	16,000	8,000	4,800
(12)	Doc Crandall	11,000	5,500	3,300
(13)	Sam Crawford	16,000	8,000	4,800
(14)	Birdie Cree	11,000	5,500	3,300
(15)	Harry Davis	11,000	5,500	3,300
(16)	Josh Devore	11,000	5,500	3,300
(17)	Mike Donlin	11,000	5,500	3,300
(18)	Mickey Doolan/Btg	11,000	5,500	3,300
(19)	Mickey Doolan/Fldg	11,000	5,500	3,300
(20)	Patsy Dougherty	11,000	5,500	3,300
(21)	Larry Doyle/Btg	11,000	5,500	3,300
(22)	Larry Doyle/Portrait	11,000	5,500	3,300
(23)	Jean Dubuc	11,000	5,500	3,300
(24)	Kid Elberfeld	11,000	5,500	3,300
(25)	Steve Evans	11,000	5,500	3,300
(26)	Johnny Evers	16,000	8,000	4,800
(27)	Russ Ford	11,000	5,500	3,300
(28)	Art Fromme	11,000	5,500	3,300
(29)	Clark Griffith	16,000	8,000	4,800
(30)	Bob Groom	11,000	5,500	3,300
(31)	Topsy Hartsel	11,000	5,500	3,300
(32)	Buck Herzog	11,000	5,500	3,300
(33)	Dick Hoblitzell	11,000	5,500	3,300
(34)	Solly Hofman	11,000	5,500	3,300
(35)	Del Howard	11,000	5,500	3,300
(36)	Miller Huggins (Hands at mouth.)	16,000	8,000	4,800
(37)	Miller Huggins/Portrait	16,000	8,000	4,800
(38)	John Hummel	11,000	5,500	3,300
(39)	Hughie Jennings (Both hands showing.)	16,000	8,000	4,800
(40)	Hughie Jennings (One hand showing.)	16,000	8,000	4,800
(41)	Walter Johnson	35,000	17,500	10,500
(42)	Joe Kelley	16,000	8,000	4,800
(43)	Ed Konetchy	11,000	5,500	3,300
(44)	Harry Krause	11,000	5,500	3,300
(45)	Nap Lajoie	16,000	8,000	4,800
(46)	Joe Lake	11,000	5,500	3,300
(47)	Lefty Leifield	11,000	5,500	3,300
(48)	Harry Lord	11,000	5,500	3,300
(49)	Sherry Magee	11,000	5,500	3,300
(50)	Rube Marquard/Pitching	16,000	8,000	4,800
(51)	Rube Marquard/Portrait	16,000	8,000	4,800
(52)	Christy Mathewson (Black cap.)	20,000	10,000	5,000
(53)	Joe McGinnity	16,000	8,000	4,800
(54)	John McGraw (Glove at side.)	16,000	8,000	4,800
(55)	John McGraw/Portrait	16,000	8,000	4,800
(56)	Harry McIntyre (Chicago)	11,000	5,500	3,300
(57)	Harry McIntyre (Brooklyn & Chicago)	11,000	5,500	3,300
(58)	Matty McIntyre (Detroit)	11,000	5,500	3,300
(59)	Larry McLean	11,000	5,500	3,300
(60)	Fred Merkle	11,000	5,500	3,300
(61)	Chief Meyers	11,000	5,500	3,300
(62)	Mike Mitchell	11,000	5,500	3,300
(63)	Dots Miller	11,000	5,500	3,300
(64)	Mike Mowrey	11,000	5,500	3,300
(65)	George Mullin	11,000	5,500	3,300
(66)	Danny Murphy	11,000	5,500	3,300
(67)	Red Murray	11,000	5,500	3,300
(68)	Rebel Oakes	11,000	5,500	3,300
(69)	Rube Oldring	11,000	5,500	3,300
(70)	Charley O'Leary	11,000	5,500	3,300
(71)	Dode Paskert	11,000	5,500	3,300
(72)	Barney Pelty	11,000	5,500	3,300
(73)	Billy Purtell	11,000	5,500	3,300
(74)	Jack Quinn	11,000	5,500	3,300
(75)	Ed Reulbach	11,000	5,500	3,300
(76)	Nap Rucker	11,000	5,500	3,300
(77)	Germany Schaefer	11,000	5,500	3,300
(78)	Wildfire Schulte	11,000	5,500	3,300
(79)	Jimmy Sheckard	11,000	5,500	3,300
(80)	Frank Smith	11,000	5,500	3,300
(81)	Tris Speaker	18,000	9,000	5,400
(82)	Jake Stahl	11,000	5,500	3,300
(83)	Harry Steinfeldt	11,000	5,500	3,300
(84)	Gabby Street	11,000	5,500	3,300
(85)	Ed Summers	11,000	5,500	3,300
(86)	Jeff Sweeney	11,000	5,500	3,300
(87)	Lee Tannehill	11,000	5,500	3,300
(88)	Ira Thomas	11,000	5,500	3,300
(89)	Joe Tinker	16,000	8,000	4,800
(90)	Heinie Wagner	11,000	5,500	3,300
(91)	Jack Warhop	11,000	5,500	3,300
(92)	Zack Wheat	16,000	8,000	4,800
(93)	Ed Willetts (Willett)	11,000	5,500	3,300
(94)	Owen Wilson	11,000	5,500	3,300
(95)	Hooks Wiltse/Pitching	11,000	5,500	3,300
(96)	Hooks Wiltse/Portrait	11,000	5,500	3,300

1909 Pittsburgh Pirates Extension Postcard

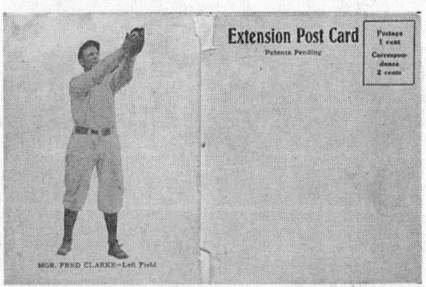

One of many novelty souvenirs commemorating the Bucs' World Championship season of 1909 was this uniquely formatted postcard. Picturing manager Fred Clarke on front, the 3-1/4" x 5-1/2" postcard opens up accordian fashion to a length of 14", revealing small action photos of 17 players each on a white background and identified by last name and position. The card was produced by W.M. Dick Co., Pittsburgh.

	NM	EX	VG
1909 Pittsburgh Pirates	3,000	1,500	900.00

1950-60s Pittsburgh Pirates Postcards

 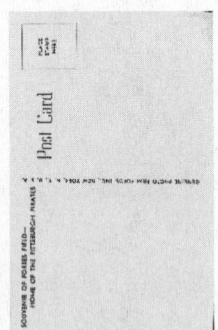

This listing encompasses the issues of several different postcard publishers who supplied black-and-white cards to the players for use in answering fan mail. Several different types of card stock are found, both matte and glossy. Some cards have postcard markings on back, others do not, especially those picturing players in the 1960s style sleeveless style uniforms. Because it is likely other players and poses will be reported, a description of each pose is included.

		NM	EX	VG
Common Player:		15.00	7.50	4.50
(1)	Gair Allie (Ready to hit.)	15.00	7.50	4.50
(2)	Toby Atwell (Squatting w/glove.)	15.00	7.50	4.50
(3)	Tony Bartirome (Stretching at 1B.)	15.00	7.50	4.50
(4)	Carlos Bernier/Btg	15.00	7.50	4.50
(5)	Ron Blackburn/Pitching (Left leg up.)	15.00	7.50	4.50
(6)	Ron Brand (Kneeling w/glove.)	15.00	7.50	4.50
(7)	Jim Bunning/Pitching (To letters.)	25.00	12.50	7.50
(8)	Don (Swede) Carlson/Pitching (By wall.)	15.00	7.50	4.50
(9)	Pete Castiglione (Ready to hit.)	15.00	7.50	4.50
(10)	Pete Castiglione (Kneeling w/bat.)	15.00	7.50	4.50
(12)	Cliff Chambers/Pitching (Leg up.)	15.00	7.50	4.50
(13)	Bob Chesnes (Follow-through.)	15.00	7.50	4.50
(14)	Roberto Clemente (Kneeling w/bat.)	125.00	65.00	35.00
(15)	Dick Cole/Fldg	15.00	7.50	4.50
(16)	Dale Coogan (Ready to hit.)	15.00	7.50	4.50
(18)	Bobby Del Greco (Batting follow-through.)	15.00	7.50	4.50
(20)	Elroy Face (Follow-through, cloth cap, sleeves.)	17.50	8.75	5.25
(21)	Elroy Face (Follow-through, cloth cap, no sleeves.)	17.50	8.75	5.25
(22)	Elroy Face (Follow-through, helmet, sleeves.)	17.50	8.75	5.25
(23)	Elroy Face (Follow-through, helmet, no sleeves.)	17.50	8.75	5.25
(24)	Hank Foiles/Squatting	15.00	7.50	4.50
(25)	Gene Freese (Ready to hit.)	15.00	7.50	4.50
(26)	Bob Friend (Follow-through.)	15.00	7.50	4.50
(27)	Bob Friend/Pitching (Leg up.)	15.00	7.50	4.50
(28)	Bob Friend (Standing in dugout.)	15.00	7.50	4.50
(29)	Dick Groat (Ready to hit.)	17.50	8.75	5.25
(30)	Fred Haney (Arms folded.)	15.00	7.50	4.50
(31)	John Hetki (Follow-through.)	15.00	7.50	4.50
(32)	Johnny Hopp (Stretching at 1B.)	15.00	7.50	4.50
(34)	Ralph Kiner/Btg (Two decks.)	25.00	12.50	7.50
(35)	Nellie King (Follow-through.)	15.00	7.50	4.50
(36)	Ron Kline (Follow-through.)	15.00	7.50	4.50
(37)	Ron Kline/Pitching (Leg up.)	15.00	7.50	4.50

		NM	EX	VG
(38)	Ted Kluszewski (Kneeling with bat.)	20.00	10.00	6.00
(39)	Ted Kluszewski (Pose to chest.)	20.00	10.00	6.00
(41)	Nick Koback/Kneeling	15.00	7.50	4.50
(42)	Clem Koshorek/Fldg	15.00	7.50	4.50
(43)	Danny Kravitz (Ready to hit.)	15.00	7.50	4.50
(44)	Vern Law (Follow-through, bleachers.)	17.50	8.75	5.25
(45)	Vern Law (Follow-through, trees.)	17.50	8.75	5.25
(46)	Vern Law (Follow-through, right foot cut off.)	17.50	8.75	5.25
(47)	Vern Law/Kneeling	17.50	8.75	5.25
(48)	Vern Law/Pitching (Leg up.)	17.50	8.75	5.25
(49)	Lenny Levy/Catching	15.00	7.50	4.50
(50)	Lenny Levy (Standing in dugout.)	15.00	7.50	4.50
(51)	Dale Long/Btg	15.00	7.50	4.50
(52)	Dale Long (Kneeling w/bat.)	15.00	7.50	4.50
(53)	Jerry Lynch/Btg (Sleeves.)	15.00	7.50	4.50
(54)	Jerry Lynch/Btg (No sleeves.)	15.00	7.50	4.50
(55)	Bill MacDonald/Pitching (Leg up.)	15.00	7.50	4.50
(56)	Bill Mazeroski/Fldg (Ball in glove, horizontal.)	25.00	12.50	7.50
(57)	Bill Mazeroski/Fldg (Ball in hand.)	25.00	12.50	7.50
(58)	Danny Murtaugh/Fldg	15.00	7.50	4.50
(59)	Danny Murtaugh/Portrait (Helmet)	15.00	7.50	4.50
(60)	George "Red" Munger/Pitching	15.00	7.50	4.50
(61)	Johnny O'Brien/Jumping	15.00	7.50	4.50
(63)	Danny O'Connell/Btg	15.00	7.50	4.50
(64)	Bob Oldis (Portrait to belt.)	15.00	7.50	4.50
(65)	Laurin Pepper (Follow-through.)	15.00	7.50	4.50
(66)	Pete Peterson/Catching	15.00	7.50	4.50
(68)	Buddy Pritchard/Btg	15.00	7.50	4.50
(69)	Bob Purkey (Follow-through.)	15.00	7.50	4.50
(70)	Bob Purkey/Portrait	15.00	7.50	4.50
(71)	Mel Quee/Pitching (Leg up.)	15.00	7.50	4.50
(72)	Curt Raydon (Follow-through, horizontal.)	15.00	7.50	4.50
(74)	Dino Restelli/Btg	15.00	7.50	4.50
(75)	Stan Rojek/Btg	15.00	7.50	4.50
(76)	Stan Rojek (Standing in dugout.)	15.00	7.50	4.50
(78)	Tom Saffell/Btg	15.00	7.50	4.50
(80)	Don Schwall/Pitching (No cap.)	15.00	7.50	4.50
(81)	Bob Skinner/Btg	15.00	7.50	4.50
(82)	Bob Smith (Follow-through.)	15.00	7.50	4.50
(83)	Paul Smith/Btg	15.00	7.50	4.50
(84)	Art Swanson (Hands on hips.)	15.00	7.50	4.50
(86)	Frank Thomas/Btg (Cap)	17.50	8.75	5.25
(87)	Frank Thomas/Btg (Helmet)	17.50	8.75	5.25
(90)	Bill Virdon/Btg (Matte)	17.50	8.75	5.25
(91)	Bill Virdon/Btg (Glossy)	17.50	8.75	5.25
(92)	Bill Virdon/Kneeling	17.50	8.75	5.25
(93)	Harry Walker/Portrait	15.00	7.50	4.50
(94)	Lee Walls/Btg (Glove in pocket.)	15.00	7.50	4.50
(95)	Lee Walls/Btg (Trees)	15.00	7.50	4.50
(96)	Jim Walsh (Follow-through, horizontal.)	15.00	7.50	4.50
(97)	Preston Ward/Btg (#44 in background.)	15.00	7.50	4.50
(98)	Preston Ward/Btg (No #44.)	15.00	7.50	4.50
(99)	Fred Waters/Pitching (Leg up.)	15.00	7.50	4.50
(100)	Bill Werle/Pitching	15.00	7.50	4.50

1950 Pittsburgh Pirates Photo Pack

The player photos in this picture pack that was sold at Forbes Field measure 6-1/2" x 9" and are printed in black-and-white on heavy, blank-backed paper. A facsimile "autograph" is printed on front of each picture, though all were written in the same hand. Several of the photos from this set were the basis for the color paintings found on 1951 Bowman cards. The unnumbered pictures are checklisted here alphabetically.

		NM	EX	VG
Complete Set (26):		250.00	125.00	75.00
Common Player:		12.00	6.00	3.50
(1)	Ted Beard	12.00	6.00	3.50
(2)	Gus Bell	20.00	10.00	6.00
(3)	Pete Castiglione	12.00	6.00	3.50
(4)	Cliff Chambers	12.00	6.00	3.50
(5)	Dale Coogan	12.00	6.00	3.50
(6)	Murry Dickson	12.00	6.00	3.50
(7)	Bob Dillinger	12.00	6.00	3.50

		NM	EX	VG
(8)	Froilan Fernandez	12.00	6.00	3.50
(9)	Johnny Hopp	12.00	6.00	3.50
(10)	Ralph Kiner	30.00	15.00	9.00
(11)	Vernon Law	20.00	10.00	6.00
(12)	Vic Lombardi	12.00	6.00	3.50
(13)	Bill MacDonald	12.00	6.00	3.50
(14)	Clyde McCullough	12.00	6.00	3.50
(15)	Bill Meyer	12.00	6.00	3.50
(16)	Ray Mueller	12.00	6.00	3.50
(17)	Danny Murtaugh	12.00	6.00	3.50
(18)	Jack Phillips	12.00	6.00	3.50
(19)	Mel Queen	12.00	6.00	3.50
(20)	Stan Rojek	12.00	6.00	3.50
(21)	Henry Schenz	12.00	6.00	3.50
(22)	George Strickland	12.00	6.00	3.50
(23)	Earl Turner	12.00	6.00	3.50
(24)	Jim Walsh	12.00	6.00	3.50
(25)	Bill Werle	12.00	6.00	3.50
(26)	Wally Westlake	12.00	6.00	3.50

1967 Pittsburgh Pirates Autograph Cards

A souvenir stand item introduced by the Pirates in 1967 was a series of color player cards bearing facsimile autographs. The 3-1/4" x 4-1/4" cards identify the player with a line of type beneath the photo giving name, position and uniform number. Backs are blank. The cards are checklisted here in alphabetical order.

		NM	EX	VG
Complete Set (24):		200.00	100.00	60.00
Common Player:		8.00	4.00	2.50
	SERIES A	.00	.00	.00
(1)	Gene Alley	8.00	4.00	2.50
(2)	Steve Blass	8.00	4.00	2.50
(3)	Roberto Clemente	70.00	35.00	20.00
(4)	Donn Clendenon	10.00	5.00	3.00
(5)	Roy Face	10.00	5.00	3.00
(6)	Jesse Gonder	8.00	4.00	2.50
(7)	Jerry May	8.00	4.00	2.50
(8)	Manny Mota	10.00	5.00	3.00
(9)	Jose Pagan	8.00	4.00	2.50
(10)	Dennis Ribant	8.00	4.00	2.50
(11)	Tommie Sisk	8.00	4.00	2.50
(12)	Bob Veale	8.00	4.00	2.50
	SERIES B	.00	.00	.00
(13)	Matty Alou	8.00	4.00	2.50
(14)	Woody Fryman	8.00	4.00	2.50
(15)	Vernon Law	10.00	5.00	3.00
(16)	Bill Mazeroski	35.00	18.00	12.00
(17)	Al McBean	8.00	4.00	2.50
(18)	Pete Mikkelsen	8.00	4.00	2.50
(19)	Jim Pagliaroni	8.00	4.00	2.50
(20)	Juan Pizarro	8.00	4.00	2.50
(21)	Andy Rodgers	8.00	4.00	2.50
(22)	Willie Stargell	35.00	18.00	12.00
(23)	Harry Walker	8.00	4.00	2.50
(24)	Maury Wills	14.00	7.00	4.00

1968 Pittsburgh Pirates Autograph Cards

These team-issued autograph cards were sold in packages at Forbes Field. The 3-1/4" x 4-1/4" cards feature a color player photo and facsimile autograph. They are blank-backed. Cards were issued in Series A and Series B, with header cards in each series providing a checklist. Cards are listed by series according to the uniform number found on the card.

		NM	EX	VG
Complete Set (26):		90.00	45.00	28.00
Common Player:		4.00	2.00	1.25
	SERIES A			
7	Larry Shepard	4.00	2.00	1.25
11	Jose Pagan	4.00	2.00	1.25
12	Jerry May	4.00	2.00	1.25

14	Jim Bunning	15.00	8.00	4.50
15	Manny Mota	4.00	2.00	1.25
17	Donn Clendenon	6.00	3.00	2.00
21	Roberto Clemente	30.00	15.00	10.00
22	Gene Alley	4.00	2.00	1.25
25	Tommie Sisk	4.00	2.00	1.25
26	Roy Face	4.00	2.00	1.25
28	Steve Blass	4.00	2.00	1.25
39	Bob Veale	4.00	2.00	1.25
--	Checklist Card, Series A	4.00	2.00	1.25
SERIES B				
8	Willie Stargell	16.00	8.00	4.50
9	Bill Mazeroski	18.00	9.00	5.00
10	Gary Kolb	4.00	2.00	1.25
18	Matty Alou	5.00	2.50	1.50
27	Ronnie Kline	4.00	2.00	1.25
29	Juan Pizzaro	4.00	2.00	1.25
30	Maury Wills	8.00	4.00	2.50
34	Al McBean	4.00	2.00	1.25
35	Manny Sanguillen	4.00	2.00	1.25
38	Bob Moose	4.00	2.00	1.25
40	Dave Wickersham	4.00	2.00	1.25
--	Jim Shellenback	4.00	2.00	1.25
--	Checklist Card, Series B	4.00	2.00	1.25

1969 Pittsburgh Pirates Autograph Cards

Sold in Series A with a blue header card/checklist and Series B with a pink header card/checklist, these team-issue autograph cards were available at Forbes Field. Identical in format to the previous year's issue, the 3-1/4" x 4-1/4" cards are blank-backed and feature a color player photo on front with a facsimile autograph in the wide white bottom border. Cards are checklisted here by series and uniform number (found on card fronts) within series.

		NM	EX	VG
Complete Set:		100.00	50.00	30.00
Common Player:		4.00	2.00	1.25
Series A				
2	Fred Patek	4.00	2.00	1.25
4	Larry Shepard	4.00	2.00	1.25
8	Willie Stargell	12.00	6.00	3.50
9	Bill Mazeroski	18.00	9.00	6.00
10	Gary Kolb	4.00	2.00	1.25
23	Luke Walker	4.00	2.00	1.25
28	Steve Blass	4.00	2.00	.1.25
29	Al Oliver	8.00	4.00	2.50
35	Manny Sanguillen	5.00	2.50	1.50
38	Bob Moose	4.00	2.00	1.25
39	Bob Veale	4.00	2.00	1.25
42	Chuck Hartenstein	4.00	2.00	1.25
Series B				
7	Bill Virdon	5.00	2.50	1.50
11	Jose Pagan	4.00	2.00	1.25
12	Jerry May	4.00	2.00	1.25
14	Jim Bunning	15.00	7.50	5.00
18	Matty Alou	5.00	2.50	1.50
20	Richie Hebner	6.00	3.00	2.00
21	Roberto Clemente	30.00	15.00	9.00
22	Gene Alley	4.00	2.00	1.25
32	Vernon Law	5.00	2.50	1.50
36	Carl Taylor	4.00	2.00	1.25
40	Dock Ellis	5.00	2.50	1.50
43	Bruce Dal Canton	4.00	2.00	1.25

1970 Pittsburgh Pirates (Andersen)

Boston baseball photographer Mike Andersen is believed to have produced this collectors' issue of Pirates cards. Nearly identical in format to his 1969-70 Oakland A's issues, the '70 Pirates measures 2-1/4" x 3-5/8" with black-and-white player poses at center. Player identification and 1969 stats are in the bottom border. Backs are blank. Cards are checklisted here alphabetically.

		NM	EX	VG
Complete Set (12):		40.00	20.00	12.00
Common Player:		2.00	1.00	.60
(1)	Gene Alley	2.00	1.00	.60
(2)	Dave Cash	2.00	1.00	.60
(3)	Dock Ellis	2.00	1.00	.60
(4)	Dave Giusti	2.00	1.00	.60
(5)	Jerry May	2.00	1.00	.60
(6)	Bill Mazeroski	12.00	6.00	3.50
(7)	Al Oliver	4.00	2.00	1.25
(8)	Jose Pagan	2.00	1.00	.60
(9)	Fred Patek	2.00	1.00	.60
(10)	Bob Robertson	2.00	1.00	.60
(11)	Manny Sanguillen	2.00	1.00	.60
(12)	Willie Stargell	12.00	6.00	3.50

1970 Pittsburgh Pirates Autograph Cards

Retaining the 3-1/4" x 4-1/4" format from previous years, these team-issued autograph cards can be distinguished from the 1968-69 issues by the Three Rivers Stadium photo back-

ground on each card. The Pirates moved from Forbes Field in June, 1970. The set is checklisted here by uniform number without regard to Series A and B.

		NM	EX	VG
Complete Set (25):		180.00	90.00	55.00
Common Player:		6.00	3.00	2.00
2	Fred Patek	6.00	3.00	2.00
5	Dave Ricketts	6.00	3.00	2.00
8	Willie Stargell	25.00	12.50	8.00
9	Bill Mazeroski	25.00	12.50	8.00
10	Richie Hebner	6.00	3.00	2.00
11	Jose Pagan	6.00	3.00	2.00
12	Jerry May	6.00	3.00	2.00
16	Al Oliver	10.00	5.00	3.00
17	Dock Ellis	6.00	3.00	2.00
18	Matty Alou	6.00	3.00	2.00
19	Joe Gibbon	6.00	3.00	2.00
21	Roberto Clemente	50.00	25.00	15.00
22	Gene Alley	6.00	3.00	2.00
22	Orlando Pena	6.00	3.00	2.00
23	Luke Walker	6.00	3.00	2.00
25	John Jeter	6.00	3.00	2.00
25	Bob Robertson	6.00	3.00	2.00
30	Dave Cash	6.00	3.00	2.00
31	Dave Giusti	6.00	3.00	2.00
35	Manny Sanguillen	6.00	3.00	2.00
36	Dick Calpaert (Colpaert)	6.00	3.00	2.00
38	Bob Moose	6.00	3.00	2.00
39	Bob Veale	6.00	3.00	2.00
40	Danny Murtaugh	6.00	3.00	2.00
50	Jim Nelson	6.00	3.00	2.00

1971 Pittsburgh Pirates Autograph Cards

The '71 team-issued Pirates autograph cards are distinguished by the appearance of mustard-yellow caps on the players' portraits. Otherwise the blank-back 3-1/4" x 4-1/2" photocards are identical in format to those of earlier seasons. Players are checklisted here alphabetically within series.

		NM	EX	VG
Complete Set (20):		90.00	45.00	28.00
Common Player:		4.00	2.00	1.25
Series A				
(1)	Gene Alley	4.00	2.00	1.25
(2)	Nelson Briles	4.00	2.00	1.25
(3)	Dave Cash	4.00	2.00	1.25
(4)	Dock Ellis	4.00	2.00	1.25
(5)	Mudcat Grant	5.00	2.50	1.50
(6)	Bill Mazeroski	18.00	9.00	5.50
(7)	Jim Nelson	4.00	2.00	1.25
(8)	Al Oliver	8.00	4.00	2.50
(9)	Manny Sanguillen	5.00	2.50	1.50
(10)	Luke Walker	4.00	2.00	1.25
Series B				
(11)	Steve Blass	4.00	2.00	1.25
(12)	Bob Clemente	30.00	15.00	10.00
(13)	Dave Giusti	4.00	2.00	1.25
(14)	Richie Hebner	5.00	2.50	1.50
(15)	Bob Johnson	4.00	2.00	1.25
(16)	Bob Moose	4.00	2.00	1.25
(17)	Jose Pagan	4.00	2.00	1.25
(18)	Bob Robertson	4.00	2.00	1.25
(19)	Willie Stargell	16.00	8.00	5.00
(20)	Bob Veale	4.00	2.00	1.25

1973 Pittsburgh Post-Gazette Pirates

This set of Pirates pictures was printed on newspaper stock one per day in the sports section of the daily paper. The black-bordered black-and-white photos are 5-1/4" x 9-1/4". At top is "'73 Pirate Album" and a short career summary. At bottom are 1972 and career stats. The first six pictures are unnumbered, the others are numbered alphabetically.

	NM	EX	VG
Complete Set (25):	125.00	60.00	35.00
Common Player:	6.00	3.00	1.75

		NM	EX	VG
	Gene Alley	6.00	3.00	1.75
	Steve Blass	6.00	3.00	1.75
	Nellie Briles	6.00	3.00	1.75
	Dave Cash	6.00	3.00	1.75
	Roberto Clemente	40.00	20.00	12.00
	Gene Clines	6.00	3.00	1.75
6	Vic Davalillo	6.00	3.00	1.75
7	Dock Ellis	6.00	3.00	1.75
8	Dave Giusti	6.00	3.00	1.75
9	Richie Hebner	6.00	3.00	1.75
10	Jackie Hernandez	6.00	3.00	1.75
11	Ramon Hernandez	6.00	3.00	1.75
12	Bob Johnson	6.00	3.00	1.75
13	Bruce Kison	6.00	3.00	1.75
14	Milt May	6.00	3.00	1.75
15	Bob Miller	6.00	3.00	1.75
16	Bob Moose	6.00	3.00	1.75
17	Al Oliver	7.50	3.75	2.25
18	Bob Robertson	6.00	3.00	1.75
19	Charlie Sands	6.00	3.00	1.75
20	Manny Sanguillen	6.00	3.00	1.75
21	Willie Stargell	12.00	6.00	3.50
22	Rennie Stennett	6.00	3.00	1.75
23	Luke Walker	6.00	3.00	1.75
24	Bill Virdon	7.50	3.75	2.25

1972 Pittsburgh Press "Buc-A-Day" Pirates

Through the month of March 1972, the daily Pittsburgh Press carried a "Buc-A-Day" feature highlighting members of the team. The feature was intended to be cut out of the paper and saved. Individual pieces measure 3-3/8" wide and vary in length from 9-1/4" to 11-1/16" depending on the length of the biographical information provided. Each player is pictured in a black-and-white photo in street clothes. Some are pictured with golf clubs, fishing poles, with their children, etc. Because of the nature of their distribution and their fragile nature, complete sets are very scarce.

		NM	EX	VG
Complete Set (25):		100.00	50.00	30.00
Common Player:		2.50	1.25	.70
1	Willie Stargell	7.50	3.75	2.25
2	Steve Blass	2.50	1.25	.70
3	Al Oliver	3.00	1.50	.90
4	Bob Moose	2.50	1.25	.70
5	Dave Cash	2.50	1.25	.70
6	Bill Mazeroski	7.50	3.75	2.25
7	Bob Johnson	2.50	1.25	.70
8	Nellie Briles	2.50	1.25	.70
9	Manny Sanguillen	3.00	1.50	.90
10	Vic Davalillo	2.50	1.25	.70
11	Dave Giusti	2.50	1.25	.70
12	Luke Walker	2.50	1.25	.70
13	Gene Clines	2.50	1.25	.70
14	Milt May	2.50	1.25	.70
15	Bob Robertson	2.50	1.25	.70
16	Roberto Clemente	15.00	7.50	4.50
17	Gene Alley	2.50	1.25	.70
18	Bruce Kison	2.50	1.25	.70
19	Jose Pagan	2.50	1.25	.70
20	Dock Ellis	2.50	1.25	.70
21	Richie Hebner	2.50	1.25	.70
22	Bob Miller	2.50	1.25	.70
23	Jackie Hernandez	2.50	1.25	.70
24	Rennie Stennett	2.50	1.25	.70
25	Bob Veale	2.50	1.25	.70

1948 Pittsburgh Provision & Packing Co.

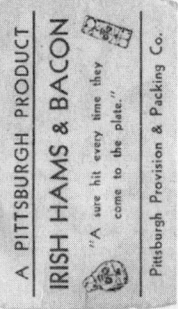

The attributed date is totally arbitrary, based on the photo shown. Also unknown are the scope of the issue and its manner of distribution. Hobby history would suggest the card was created to promote Wagner's ties to the meat company as a spokesman, or perhaps the card was created for Wagner to distribute at appearances on behalf of the packing company. The dark green-printed card measures about 4" x 2-1/2" and is printed on rather thin cardboard. It is not known whether similar cards exist for other players.

	NM	EX	VG
Honus Wagner	400.00	200.00	120.00

1936 Pittsburgh Sun-Telegraph Sport Stamps

Similar to several contemporary issues, the Sport Stamps were printed in a single edition of the daily newspaper. Thirteen players were printed for each of the 16 Major League teams. About 2" x 3", depending on the length of the biography and how well they were cut off the paper, they are printed in black-and-white. A tightly cropped player portrait is centered on a 1-3/4" x 2-1/4" stamp design with the paper's name above and the player's name, position and team below. This checklist is incomplete.

		NM	EX	VG
Complete Set:				
Common Player:		12.00	6.00	3.50
(1)	Ralph Birkofer	12.00	6.00	3.50
(2)	Cy Blanton	12.00	6.00	3.50
(3)	Bill Brubaker	12.00	6.00	3.50
(4)	Guy Bush	12.00	6.00	3.50
(5)	Ty Cobb	25.00	12.50	7.50
(6)	Jerome "Dizzy" Dean	25.00	12.50	7.50
(7)	Joe DiMaggio	75.00	37.00	22.00
(8)	Hank Greenberg	25.00	12.50	7.50
(9)	Waite Hoyt	20.00	10.00	6.00
(10)	Carl Hubbell	20.00	10.00	6.00
(11)	Woody Jensen	12.00	6.00	3.50
(12)	Red Lucas	12.00	6.00	3.50
(13)	Joe Medwick	20.00	10.00	6.00
(13)	Tommy Padden	12.00	6.00	3.50
(14)	Casey Stengel	20.00	10.00	6.00
(15)	Clarence Strass	12.00	6.00	3.50
(16)	Gus Suhr	12.00	6.00	3.50
(17)	Bill Swift	12.00	6.00	3.50
(18)	John Tising	12.00	6.00	3.50
(19)	Al Todd	12.00	6.00	3.50
(20)	Pie Traynor	20.00	10.00	6.00
(21)	Honus Wagner	25.00	12.50	7.50
(22)	Lloyd Waner	20.00	10.00	6.00
(23)	Paul Waner	20.00	10.00	6.00
(24)	Jim Weaver	12.00	6.00	3.50
(25)	Floyd Young	12.00	6.00	3.50

1954 Plankinton Milwaukee Braves Playing Tips

This set of "How to Play Better Baseball" poster booklets was apparently distributed in packages of hot dogs on a regional basis. Folded, the booklet measures 2-7/8" x 4-3/8" and has a black-and-white player portrait photo with a red background. When opened, the booklet forms an 11" x 17" poster offering big league tips from Braves players. The tips are well illustrated with many photos. There is a booklet for each position as well as one for right- and left-handed pitchers, a coach and even a team trainer.

	NM	EX	VG
Complete Set (12):	800.00	400.00	240.00
Common Player:	75.00	37.50	22.50
1 Joe Adcock	90.00	45.00	27.50
2 Danny O'Connell	75.00	37.50	22.50
3 Eddie Mathews	150.00	75.00	45.00
4 Johnny Logan	75.00	37.50	22.50
5 Bobby Thomson	90.00	45.00	27.50
6 Bill Bruton	75.00	37.50	22.50
7 Andy Pafko	75.00	37.50	22.50
8 Del Crandall	75.00	37.50	22.50
9 Warren Spahn	150.00	75.00	45.00
10 Gene Conley	75.00	37.50	22.50
11 Charlie Grimm	75.00	37.50	22.50
12 Joe Taylor	75.00	37.50	22.50

1939 Play Ball Samples

Each of the first 115 cards in the 1939 Play Ball set can be found with red overprinting on the back indicating sample card status. The overprint reads: FREE / SAMPLE CARD / GET YOUR PICTURES OF / LEADING BASEBALL PLAYERS. / THREE PICTURE CARDS PACKED / IN EACH PACKAGE OF / "PLAY BALL AMERICA" / BUBBLE GUM. / AT YOUR CANDY STORE / 1c." Collectors will pay a small premium for a type card of a common player. Sample cards of most star players sell for about double the price of the regular-issue cards, while DiMaggio and Williams samples sell for about the same price as their regular-issue cards.

		NM	EX	VG
Common Player:		35.00	17.50	10.00
26	Joe DiMaggio	1,300	650.00	390.00
92	Ted Williams	2,550	1,275	775.00

1939 Play Ball (R334)

With the issue of this card set by Gum Inc., a new era of baseball cards was born. Although the cards are black-and-white, the photos on front are of better quality than previously seen, and the 2-1/2" x 3-1/8" size was larger than virtually all of the tobacco and caramel cards of the early 20th Century. Card backs feature full player names, "Joseph Paul DiMaggio" instead of "Joe DiMaggio" and extensive biographies. Players are listed here by their most commonly used name. There are 161 cards in the set; card #126 was never issued. The complete set price does not include all back variations found in the low-numbered series. Many of the cards between #2-115 (indicated with an asterisk) can be found with the player name either in all capital letters, or in both upper- and lower-case letters. Minor differences in typography, along with variations in details of the biographical data, or within the wording of the career summary may be found on those cards that exist in two versions. No premium currently attaches to either version, though the cards with name in upper- and lower-case are somewhat scarcer.

		NM	EX	VG
Complete Set (161):		10,000	4,750	2,750
Common Player (1-115):		25.00	12.50	7.50
Common Player (116-162):		55.00	27.50	16.50
1	Jake Powell	135.00	15.00	7.50
2	Lee Grissom	25.00	12.50	7.50
3	Red Ruffing (*)	100.00	50.00	30.00
4	Eldon Auker (*)	25.00	12.50	7.50
5	Luke Sewell (*)	25.00	12.50	7.50
6	Leo Durocher (*)	100.00	50.00	30.00
7	Bobby Doerr (*)	100.00	50.00	30.00
8	Cotton Pippen	25.00	12.50	7.50
9	Jim Tobin (*)	25.00	12.50	7.50
10	Jimmie DeShong	25.00	12.50	7.50
11	Johnny Rizzo	25.00	12.50	7.50
12	Hersh Martin	25.00	12.50	7.50
13	Luke Hamlin (*)	25.00	12.50	7.50
14	Jim Tabor (*)	25.00	12.50	7.50
15	Paul Derringer (*)	25.00	12.50	7.50
16	Johnny Peacock	25.00	12.50	7.50
17	Emerson Dickman	25.00	12.50	7.50
18	Harry Danning (*)	25.00	12.50	7.50

19	Paul Dean	50.00	25.00	15.00
20	Joe Heving	25.00	12.50	7.50
21	Dutch Leonard (*)	25.00	12.50	7.50
22	Bucky Walters (*)	25.00	12.50	7.50
23	Burgess Whitehead	25.00	12.50	7.50
24	Dick Coffman (*)	25.00	12.50	7.50
25	George Selkirk (*)	25.00	12.50	7.50
26	Joe DiMaggio (*)	1,400	575.00	300.00
27	Fritz Ostermueller (*)	25.00	12.50	7.50
28	Syl Johnson	25.00	12.50	7.50
29	Jack Wilson (*)	25.00	12.50	7.50
30	Bill Dickey (*)	175.00	85.00	55.00
31	Sammy West (*)	25.00	12.50	7.50
32	Bob Seeds	25.00	12.50	7.50
33	Del Young	25.00	12.50	7.50
34	Frank Demaree (*)	25.00	12.50	7.50
35	Bill Jurges (*)	25.00	12.50	7.50
36	Frank McCormick (*)	25.00	12.50	7.50
37	Spud Davis	25.00	12.50	7.50
38	Billy Myers (*)	25.00	12.50	7.50
39	Rick Ferrell (*)	100.00	50.00	30.00
40	Jim Bagby Jr.	25.00	12.50	7.50
41	Lon Warneke (*)	25.00	12.50	7.50
42	Arndt Jorgens	25.00	12.50	7.50
43	Mel Almada	35.00	17.50	10.00
44	Don Heffner	25.00	12.50	7.50
45	Pinky May (*)	25.00	12.50	7.50
46	Morrie Arnovich (*)	40.00	20.00	12.00
47	Buddy Lewis (*)	25.00	12.50	7.50
48	Lefty Gomez (*)	100.00	50.00	30.00
49	Eddie Miller	25.00	12.50	7.50
50	Charlie Gehringer (*)	110.00	55.00	35.00
51	Mel Ott (*)	135.00	65.00	40.00
52	Tommy Henrich (*)	60.00	30.00	18.00
53	Carl Hubbell (*)	125.00	65.00	35.00
54	Harry Gumbert (*)	25.00	12.50	7.50
55	Arky Vaughan (*)	100.00	50.00	30.00
56	Hank Greenberg (*)	250.00	125.00	75.00
57	Buddy Hassett (*)	25.00	12.50	7.50
58	Lou Chiozza	25.00	12.50	7.50
59	Ken Chase	25.00	12.50	7.50
60	Schoolboy Rowe (*)	25.00	12.50	7.50
61	Tony Cuccinello (*)	25.00	12.50	7.50
62	Tom Carey	25.00	12.50	7.50
63	Heinie Mueller	25.00	12.50	7.50
64	Wally Moses (*)	25.00	12.50	7.50
65	Harry Craft (*)	25.00	12.50	7.50
66	Jimmy Ripple	25.00	12.50	7.50
67	Eddie Joost	25.00	12.50	7.50
68	Fred Sington	25.00	12.50	7.50
69	Elbie Fletcher	25.00	12.50	7.50
70	Fred Frankhouse	25.00	12.50	7.50
71	Monte Pearson (*)	25.00	12.50	7.50
72	Debs Garms (*)	25.00	12.50	7.50
73	Hal Schumacher (*)	25.00	12.50	7.50
74	Cookie Lavagetto (*)	25.00	12.50	7.50
75	Frenchy Bordagaray (*)	25.00	12.50	7.50
76	Goody Rosen	40.00	20.00	12.00
77	Lew Riggs	25.00	12.50	7.50
78	Moose Solters (*)	25.00	12.50	7.50
79	Joe Moore (*)	25.00	12.50	7.50
80	Pete Fox (*)	25.00	12.50	7.50
81	Babe Dahlgren (*)	25.00	12.50	7.50
82	Chuck Klein (*)	100.00	50.00	30.00
83	Gus Suhr (*)	25.00	12.50	7.50
84	Skeeter Newsome	25.00	12.50	7.50
85	Johnny Cooney	25.00	12.50	7.50
86	Dolph Camilli (*)	25.00	12.50	7.50
87	Milt Shoffner	25.00	12.50	7.50
88	Charlie Keller	35.00	17.50	10.00
89	Lloyd Waner (*)	100.00	50.00	30.00
90	Bob Klinger (*)	25.00	12.50	7.50
91	Jack Knott (*)	25.00	12.50	7.50
92	Ted Williams (*)	2,550	1,275	800.00
93	Charley Gelbert	25.00	12.50	7.50
94	Heinie Manush (*)	100.00	50.00	30.00
95	Whit Wyatt (*)	25.00	12.50	7.50
96	Babe Phelps (*)	25.00	12.50	7.50
97	Bob Johnson (*)	25.00	12.50	7.50
98	Pinky Whitney	25.00	12.50	7.50
99	Wally Berger (*)	25.00	12.50	7.50
100	Buddy Myer (*)	25.00	12.50	7.50
101	Doc Cramer (*)	25.00	12.50	7.50
102	Pep Young (*)	25.00	12.50	7.50
103	Moe Berg	140.00	75.00	45.00
104	Tommy Bridges (*)	25.00	12.50	7.50
105	Eric McNair (*)	25.00	12.50	7.50
106	Dolly Stark	50.00	25.00	15.00
107	Joe Vosmik	25.00	12.50	7.50
108	Frankie Hayes (*)	25.00	12.50	7.50
109	Myril Hoag (*)	25.00	12.50	7.50
110	Freddie Fitzsimmons (*)	25.00	12.50	7.50
111	Van Lingle Mungo (*)	35.00	17.50	10.00
112	Paul Waner (*)	100.00	50.00	30.00
113	Al Schacht	50.00	25.00	15.00
114	Cecil Travis (*)	25.00	12.50	7.50
115	Red Kress (*)	25.00	12.50	7.50
116	Gene Desautels	55.00	27.50	16.50
117	Wayne Ambler	55.00	27.50	16.50
118	Lynn Nelson	55.00	27.50	16.50
119	Will Hershberger	55.00	27.50	16.50
120	Rabbit Warstler	55.00	27.50	16.50
121	Bill Posedel	55.00	27.50	16.50
122	George McQuinn	55.00	27.50	16.50
123	Peaches Davis	55.00	27.50	16.50
124	Jumbo Brown	55.00	27.50	16.50
125	Cliff Melton	55.00	27.50	16.50
126	Not Issued			
127	Gil Brack	55.00	27.50	16.50
128	Joe Bowman	55.00	27.50	16.50
129	Bill Swift	55.00	27.50	16.50
130	Bill Brubaker	55.00	27.50	16.50
131	Mort Cooper	55.00	27.50	16.50
132	Jimmy Brown	55.00	27.50	16.50
133	Lynn Myers	55.00	27.50	16.50
134	Tot Pressnell	55.00	27.50	16.50
135	Mickey Owen	55.00	27.50	16.50
136	Roy Bell	55.00	27.50	16.50

		NM	EX	VG
137	Pete Appleton	55.00	27.50	16.50
138	George Case	55.00	27.50	16.50
139	Vito Tamulis	55.00	27.50	16.50
140	Ray Hayworth	55.00	27.50	16.50
141	Pete Coscarart	55.00	27.50	16.50
142	Ira Hutchinson	55.00	27.50	16.50
143	Earl Averill	225.00	110.00	65.00
144	Zeke Bonura	55.00	27.50	16.50
145	Hugh Mulcahy	55.00	27.50	16.50
146	Tom Sunkel	55.00	27.50	16.50
147	George Coffman	55.00	27.50	16.50
148	Bill Trotter	55.00	27.50	16.50
149	Max West	55.00	27.50	16.50
150	Jim Walkup	55.00	27.50	16.50
151	Hugh Casey	55.00	27.50	16.50
152	Roy Weatherly	55.00	27.50	16.50
153	Dizzy Trout	55.00	27.50	16.50
154	Johnny Hudson	55.00	27.50	16.50
155	Jimmy Outlaw	55.00	27.50	16.50
156	Ray Berres	55.00	27.50	16.50
157	Don Padgett	55.00	27.50	16.50
158	Bud Thomas	55.00	27.50	16.50
159	Red Evans	55.00	27.50	16.50
160	Gene Moore Jr.	55.00	27.50	16.50
161	Lonny Frey	60.00	27.50	17.50
162	Whitey Moore	200.00	30.00	17.50

1940 Play Ball (R335)

Following the success of its initial effort in 1939, Gum Inc. issued a bigger and better set in 1940. The 240 black-and-white cards are once again in 2-1/2" x 3-1/8" size, but the front photos are enclosed by a frame with the player's name. Backs again offer extensive biographies and are dated. A number of former stars were issued along with contemporary players, and many Hall of Famers are included. The final 60 cards of the set are more difficult to obtain.

		NM	EX	VG
	Complete Set (240):	22,500	11,000	6,500
	Common Player (1-180):	35.00	17.50	10.00
	Common Player (181-240):	60.00	30.00	18.00
1	Joe DiMaggio	5,350	2,675	1,600
2	"Art" Jorgens	35.00	17.50	10.00
3	"Babe" Dahlgren	35.00	17.50	10.00
4	"Tommy" Henrich	60.00	30.00	18.00
5	"Monte" Pearson	35.00	17.50	10.00
6	"Lefty" Gomez	130.00	65.00	40.00
7	"Bill" Dickey	160.00	80.00	45.00
8	"Twinkletoes" Selkirk	35.00	17.50	10.00
9	"Charley" Keller	35.00	17.50	10.00
10	"Red" Ruffing	130.00	65.00	40.00
11	"Jake" Powell	35.00	17.50	10.00
12	"Johnny" Schulte	35.00	17.50	10.00
13	"Jack" Knott	35.00	17.50	10.00
14	"Rabbit" McNair	35.00	17.50	10.00
15	George Case	35.00	17.50	10.00
16	Cecil Travis	35.00	17.50	10.00
17	"Buddy" Myer	35.00	17.50	10.00
18	"Charley" Gelbert	35.00	17.50	10.00
19	Ken Chase	35.00	17.50	10.00
20	"Buddy" Lewis	35.00	17.50	10.00
21	"Rick" Ferrell	130.00	65.00	40.00
22	"Sammy" West	35.00	17.50	10.00
23	"Dutch" Leonard	35.00	17.50	10.00
24	Frank "Blimp" Hayes	35.00	17.50	10.00
25	"Cherokee" Bob Johnson	35.00	17.50	10.00
26	"Wally" Moses	35.00	17.50	10.00
27	"Ted" Williams	1,950	550.00	280.00
28	"Gene" Desautels	35.00	17.50	10.00
29	"Doc" Cramer	35.00	17.50	10.00
30	"Moe" Berg	160.00	80.00	45.00
31	Jack Wilson	35.00	17.50	10.00
32	"Jim" Bagby	35.00	17.50	10.00
33	"Fritz" Ostermueller	35.00	17.50	10.00
34	John Peacock	35.00	17.50	10.00
35	"Joe" Heving	35.00	17.50	10.00
36	"Jim" Tabor	35.00	17.50	10.00
37	Emerson Dickman	35.00	17.50	10.00
38	"Bobby" Doerr	130.00	65.00	40.00
39	"Tom" Carey	35.00	17.50	10.00
40	"Hank" Greenberg	450.00	225.00	135.00
41	"Charley" Gehringer	180.00	90.00	55.00
42	"Bud" Thomas	35.00	17.50	10.00
43	Pete Fox	35.00	17.50	10.00
44	"Dizzy" Trout	35.00	17.50	10.00
45	"Red" Kress	35.00	17.50	10.00
46	Earl Averill	130.00	65.00	40.00
47	"Old Os" Vitt	35.00	17.50	10.00
48	"Luke" Sewell	35.00	17.50	10.00
49	"Stormy Weather" Weatherly	35.00	17.50	10.00
50	"Hal" Trosky	35.00	17.50	10.00
51	"Don" Heffner	35.00	17.50	10.00
52	Myril Hoag	35.00	17.50	10.00
53	"Mac" McQuinn	35.00	17.50	10.00
54	"Bill" Trotter	35.00	17.50	10.00
55	"Slick" Coffman	35.00	17.50	10.00
56	"Eddie" Miller	35.00	17.50	10.00
57	Max West	35.00	17.50	10.00
58	"Bill" Posedel	35.00	17.50	10.00
59	"Rabbit" Warstler	35.00	17.50	10.00
60	John Cooney	35.00	17.50	10.00
61	"Tony" Cuccinello	35.00	17.50	10.00
62	"Buddy" Hassett	35.00	17.50	10.00
63	"Pete" Cascarart (Coscarart)	35.00	17.50	10.00
64	"Van" Mungo	40.00	20.00	12.00
65	"Fitz" Fitzsimmons	35.00	17.50	10.00
66	"Babe" Phelps	35.00	17.50	10.00
67	"Whit" Wyatt	35.00	17.50	10.00
68	"Dolph" Camilli	35.00	17.50	10.00
69	"Cookie" Lavagetto	35.00	17.50	10.00
70	"Hot Potato" Hamlin	35.00	17.50	10.00
71	Mel Almada	40.00	20.00	12.00
72	"Chuck" Dressen	35.00	17.50	10.00
73	"Bucky" Walters	35.00	17.50	10.00
74	"Duke" Derringer	35.00	17.50	10.00
75	"Buck" McCormick	35.00	17.50	10.00
76	"Lonny" Frey	35.00	17.50	10.00
77	"Bill" Hershberger	60.00	30.00	18.00
78	"Lew" Riggs	35.00	17.50	10.00
79	"Wildfire" Craft	35.00	17.50	10.00
80	"Bill" Myers	35.00	17.50	10.00
81	"Wally" Berger	35.00	17.50	10.00
82	"Hank" Gowdy	35.00	17.50	10.00
83	"Clif" Melton (Cliff)	35.00	17.50	10.00
84	"Jo-Jo" Moore	35.00	17.50	10.00
85	"Hal" Schumacher	35.00	17.50	10.00
86	Harry Gumbert	35.00	17.50	10.00
87	Carl Hubbell	160.00	80.00	45.00
88	"Mel" Ott	225.00	110.00	65.00
89	"Bill" Jurges	35.00	17.50	10.00
90	Frank Demaree	35.00	17.50	10.00
91	Bob "Suitcase" Seeds	35.00	17.50	10.00
92	"Whitey" Whitehead	35.00	17.50	10.00
93	Harry "The Horse" Danning	35.00	17.50	10.00
94	"Gus" Suhr	35.00	17.50	10.00
95	"Mul" Mulcahy	35.00	17.50	10.00
96	"Heinie" Mueller	35.00	17.50	10.00
97	"Morry" Arnovich	35.00	17.50	10.00
98	"Pinky" May	35.00	17.50	10.00
99	"Syl" Johnson	35.00	17.50	10.00
100	"Hersh" Martin	35.00	17.50	10.00
101	"Del" Young	35.00	17.50	10.00
102	"Chuck" Klein	130.00	65.00	40.00
103	"Elbie" Fletcher	35.00	17.50	10.00
104	"Big Poison" Waner	130.00	65.00	40.00
105	"Little Poison" Waner	130.00	65.00	40.00
106	"Pep" Young	35.00	17.50	10.00
107	"Arky" Vaughan	130.00	65.00	40.00
108	"Johnny" Rizzo	35.00	17.50	10.00
109	Don Padgett	35.00	17.50	10.00
110	"Tom" Sunkel	35.00	17.50	10.00
111	"Mickey" Owen	35.00	17.50	10.00
112	"Jimmy" Brown	35.00	17.50	10.00
113	"Mort" Cooper	35.00	17.50	10.00
114	"Lon" Warneke	35.00	17.50	10.00
115	"Mike" Gonzales (Gonzalez)	40.00	20.00	12.00
116	"Al" Schacht	60.00	30.00	18.00
117	"Dolly" Stark	75.00	37.50	22.50
118	"Schoolboy" Hoyt	130.00	65.00	40.00
119	"Ol Pete" Alexander	130.00	65.00	40.00
120	Walter "Big Train" Johnson	275.00	135.00	80.00
121	Atley Donald	35.00	17.50	10.00
122	"Sandy" Sundra	35.00	17.50	10.00
123	"Hildy" Hildebrand	35.00	17.50	10.00
124	"Colonel" Combs	120.00	60.00	35.00
125	"Art" Fletcher	35.00	17.50	10.00
126	"Jake" Solters	35.00	17.50	10.00
127	"Muddy" Ruel	35.00	17.50	10.00
128	"Pete" Appleton	35.00	17.50	10.00
129	"Bucky" Harris	120.00	60.00	35.00
130	"Deerfoot" Milan	35.00	17.50	10.00
131	"Zeke" Bonura	35.00	17.50	10.00
132	Connie Mack	120.00	60.00	35.00
133	"Jimmie" Foxx	300.00	150.00	90.00
134	"Joe" Cronin	130.00	65.00	40.00
135	"Line Drive" Nelson	35.00	17.50	10.00
136	"Cotton" Pippen	35.00	17.50	10.00
137	"Bing" Miller	35.00	17.50	10.00
138	"Beau" Bell	35.00	17.50	10.00
139	Elden Auker (Eldon)	35.00	17.50	10.00
140	"Dick" Coffman	35.00	17.50	10.00
141	"Casey" Stengel	175.00	85.00	50.00
142	"Highpockets" Kelly	120.00	60.00	35.00
143	"Gene" Moore	35.00	17.50	10.00
144	"Joe" Vosmik	35.00	17.50	10.00
145	"Vito" Tamulis	35.00	17.50	10.00
146	"Tot" Pressnell	35.00	17.50	10.00
147	"Johnny" Hudson	35.00	17.50	10.00
148	"Hugh" Casey	35.00	17.50	10.00
149	"Pinky" Shoffner	35.00	17.50	10.00
150	"Whitey" Moore	35.00	17.50	10.00
151	Edwin Joost	35.00	17.50	10.00
152	Jimmy Wilson	35.00	17.50	10.00
153	"Bill" McKechnie	120.00	60.00	35.00
154	"Jumbo" Brown	35.00	17.50	10.00
155	"Ray" Hayworth	35.00	17.50	10.00
156	"Daffy" Dean	65.00	32.50	20.00
157	"Lou" Chiozza	35.00	17.50	10.00
158	"Stonewall" Jackson	120.00	60.00	35.00
159	"Pancho" Snyder	35.00	17.50	10.00
160	"Hans" Lobert	35.00	17.50	10.00
161	"Debs" Garms	35.00	17.50	10.00
162	Joe Bowman	35.00	17.50	10.00
163	"Spud" Davis	35.00	17.50	10.00
164	"Ray" Berres	35.00	17.50	10.00
165	"Bob" Klinger	35.00	17.50	10.00
166	"Bill" Brubaker	35.00	17.50	10.00
167	"Frankie" Frisch	130.00	65.00	40.00
168	"Honus" Wagner	300.00	150.00	90.00
169	"Gabby" Street	35.00	17.50	10.00
170	"Tris" Speaker	135.00	70.00	40.00
171	Harry Heilmann	120.00	60.00	35.00
172	"Chief" Bender	120.00	60.00	35.00
173	"Larry" Lajoie	120.00	60.00	35.00
174	"Johnny" Evers	120.00	60.00	35.00
175	"Christy" Mathewson	250.00	125.00	75.00
176	"Heinie" Manush	130.00	65.00	40.00
177	Frank "Homerun" Baker	120.00	60.00	35.00
178	Max Carey	120.00	60.00	35.00
179	George Sisler	120.00	60.00	35.00
180	"Mickey" Cochrane	175.00	90.00	50.00
181	"Spud" Chandler	60.00	30.00	18.00
182	"Knick" Knickerbocker	60.00	30.00	18.00
183	Marvin Breuer	60.00	30.00	18.00
184	"Mule" Haas	60.00	30.00	18.00
185	"Joe" Kuhel	60.00	30.00	18.00
186	Taft Wright	60.00	30.00	18.00
187	"Jimmy" Dykes	60.00	30.00	18.00
188	"Joe" Krakauskas	60.00	30.00	18.00
189	"Jim" Bloodworth	60.00	30.00	18.00
190	"Charley" Berry	60.00	30.00	18.00
191	John Babich	60.00	30.00	18.00
192	"Dick" Siebert	60.00	30.00	18.00
193	"Chubby" Dean	60.00	30.00	18.00
194	Sam Chapman	60.00	30.00	18.00
195	"Dee" Miles	60.00	30.00	18.00
196	"Nonny" Nonnenkamp	60.00	30.00	18.00
197	"Lou" Finney	60.00	30.00	18.00
198	"Denny" Galehouse	60.00	30.00	18.00
199	"Pinky" Higgins	60.00	30.00	18.00
200	"Soupy" Campbell	60.00	30.00	18.00
201	Barney McCosky	60.00	30.00	18.00
202	Al Milnar	60.00	30.00	18.00
203	"Bad News" Hale	60.00	30.00	18.00
204	Harry Eisenstat	75.00	37.50	22.50
205	"Rollie" Hemsley	60.00	30.00	18.00
206	"Chet" Laabs	60.00	30.00	18.00
207	"Gus" Mancuso	60.00	30.00	18.00
208	Lee Gamble	60.00	30.00	18.00
209	"Hy" Vandenberg	60.00	30.00	18.00
210	"Bill" Lohrman	60.00	30.00	18.00
211	"Pop" Joiner	60.00	30.00	18.00
212	"Babe" Young	60.00	30.00	18.00
213	John Rucker	60.00	30.00	18.00
214	"Ken" O'Dea	60.00	30.00	18.00
215	"Johnnie" McCarthy	60.00	30.00	18.00
216	"Joe" Marty	60.00	30.00	18.00
217	Walter Beck	60.00	30.00	18.00
218	"Wally" Millies	60.00	30.00	18.00
219	Russ Bauers	60.00	30.00	18.00
220	Mace Brown	60.00	30.00	18.00
221	Lee Handley	60.00	30.00	18.00
222	"Max" Butcher	60.00	30.00	18.00
223	Hugh "Ee-Yah" Jennings	140.00	70.00	40.00
224	"Pie" Traynor	140.00	70.00	40.00
225	"Shoeless Joe" Jackson	2,900	1,250	700.00
226	Harry Hooper	140.00	70.00	40.00
227	"Pop" Haines	140.00	70.00	40.00
228	"Charley" Grimm	60.00	30.00	18.00
229	"Buck" Herzog	60.00	30.00	18.00
230	"Red" Faber	140.00	70.00	40.00
231	"Dolf" Luque	75.00	37.50	22.50
232	"Goose" Goslin	140.00	70.00	40.00
233	"Moose" Earnshaw	60.00	30.00	18.00
234	Frank "Husk" Chance	140.00	70.00	40.00
235	John J. McGraw	140.00	70.00	40.00
236	"Sunny Jim" Bottomley	140.00	70.00	40.00
237	"Wee Willie" Keeler	140.00	70.00	40.00
238	"Poosh 'Em Up Tony" Lazzeri	175.00	85.00	50.00
239	George Uhle	60.00	30.00	18.00
240	"Bill" Atwood	120.00	40.00	20.00

1940 Play Ball Colorized Proofs

Probably created as part of the process which resulted in the introduction of color cards in 1941, these 1940 Play Balls have very muted color tones. It is unknown how many other players' cards from 1940 PB were created or survive in this form. The Mungo and Dean cards, authenticated and graded Excellent by SGC, sold in a 12/04 auction for $2,221.

Common player:		1,000	500.00	300.00
64	"Van" Mungo			
66	"Babe" Phelps			
76	"Lonny" Frey			
86	Harry Gumbert			
90	Frank Demaree			
92	"Whitey" Whitehead			
141	"Casey" Stengel			
150	"Whitey" Moore			
156	"Daffy" Dean			

1941 Play Ball (R336)

While the backs are quite similar to the black-and-white cards Gum Inc. issued in 1940, the card fronts in the 1941 set are printed in color. Many of the card photos, however, are just colorized versions of the player's 1940 card. The cards are still in the 2-1/2" x 3-1/8" size, but only 72 cards are included in the set. Card numbers 49-72 are rarer than the lower-numbered cards. The cards were printed in sheets of 12, and can still be found that way. Cards #1-48 can be found with or without the 1941 copyright date at lower-left; cards 49-72 are not found with the 1941 date. Some believe this indicates that a revised (no copyright) version of the low numbers and all of the high numbers were issued in 1942.

		NM	EX	VG
Complete Set (72):		15,000	7,500	4,500
Common Player (1-48):		75.00	37.50	22.50
Common Player (49-72):		100.00	50.00	30.00
1	"Eddie" Miller	340.00	60.00	25.00
2	Max West	110.00	37.50	22.50
3	"Bucky" Walters	75.00	37.50	22.50
4	"Duke" Derringer	75.00	37.50	22.50
5	"Buck" McCormick	75.00	37.50	22.50
6	Carl Hubbell	300.00	150.00	90.00
7	"The Horse" Danning	75.00	37.50	22.50
8	"Mel" Ott	340.00	170.00	100.00
9	"Pinky" May	75.00	37.50	22.50
10	"Arky" Vaughan	190.00	95.00	55.00
11	Debs Garms	75.00	37.50	22.50
12	"Jimmy" Brown	75.00	37.50	22.50
13	"Jimmie" Foxx	500.00	250.00	150.00
14	"Ted" Williams	1,500	750.00	450.00
15	"Joe" Cronin	190.00	95.00	55.00
16	"Hal" Trosky	75.00	37.50	22.50
17	"Stormy" Weatherly	75.00	37.50	22.50
18	"Hank" Greenberg	500.00	250.00	150.00
19	"Charley" Gehringer	275.00	140.00	85.00
20	"Red" Ruffing	190.00	95.00	55.00
21	"Charlie" Keller	150.00	75.00	45.00
22	"Indian Bob" Johnson	75.00	37.50	22.50
23	"Mac" McQuinn	75.00	37.50	22.50
24	"Dutch" Leonard	75.00	37.50	22.50
25	"Gene" Moore	75.00	37.50	22.50
26	Harry "Gunboat" Gumbert	75.00	37.50	22.50
27	"Babe" Young	75.00	37.50	22.50
28	"Joe" Marty	75.00	37.50	22.50
29	Jack Wilson	75.00	37.50	22.50
30	"Lou" Finney	75.00	37.50	22.50
31	"Joe" Kuhel	75.00	37.50	22.50
32	Taft Wright	75.00	37.50	22.50
33	"Happy" Milnar	75.00	37.50	22.50
34	"Rollie" Hemsley	75.00	37.50	22.50
35	"Pinky" Higgins	75.00	37.50	22.50
36	Barney McCosky	75.00	37.50	22.50
37	"Soupy" Campbell	75.00	37.50	22.50
38	Atley Donald	75.00	37.50	22.50
39	"Tommy" Henrich	150.00	75.00	45.00
40	"Johnny" Babich	75.00	37.50	22.50
41	Frank "Blimp" Hayes	75.00	37.50	22.50
42	"Wally" Moses	75.00	37.50	22.50
43	Albert "Bronk" Brancato	75.00	37.50	22.50
44	Sam Chapman	75.00	37.50	22.50
45	Elden Auker (Eldon)	75.00	37.50	22.50
46	"Sid" Hudson	75.00	37.50	22.50
47	"Buddy" Lewis	75.00	37.50	22.50
48	Cecil Travis	75.00	37.50	22.50
49	"Babe" Dahlgren	100.00	50.00	30.00
50	"Johnny" Cooney	100.00	50.00	30.00
51	"Dolph" Camilli	100.00	50.00	30.00
52	Kirby Higbe	100.00	50.00	30.00
53	Luke "Hot Potato" Hamlin	100.00	50.00	30.00
54	"Pee Wee" Reese	600.00	300.00	180.00
55	"Whit" Wyatt	100.00	50.00	30.00
56	"Vandy" Vander Meer	100.00	50.00	30.00
57	"Moe" Arnovich	125.00	65.00	35.00
58	"Frank" Demaree	100.00	50.00	30.00
59	"Bill" Jurges	100.00	50.00	30.00
60	"Chuck" Klein	300.00	150.00	90.00
61	"Vince" DiMaggio	300.00	150.00	90.00
62	"Elbie" Fletcher	100.00	50.00	30.00
63	"Dom" DiMaggio	400.00	200.00	120.00
64	"Bobby" Doerr	300.00	150.00	90.00
65	"Tommy" Bridges	100.00	50.00	30.00
66	Harland Clift (Harland)	100.00	50.00	30.00
67	"Walt" Judnich	100.00	50.00	30.00
68	"Jack" Knott	100.00	50.00	30.00
69	George Case	100.00	50.00	30.00
70	"Bill" Dickey	350.00	175.00	100.00
71	"Joe" DiMaggio	3,000	1,300	700.00
72	"Lefty" Gomez	425.00	180.00	60.00

1941 Play Ball Paper Version

As cardboard became a critical commodity during the months prior to the United States' entry into WWII, Play Ball experimented by issuing a version of the first 24 cards in the 1941 set on paper sheets of 12, comprising the color-printed layer of the regular cards and the backs. These paper versions, understandably, did not stand up to handling as well as the cardboard cards and survivors are much scarcer today.

		NM	EX	VG
Complete Set (24):		10,000	5,000	3,000
Common Player:		160.00	55.00	30.00
Complete Sheet 1-12:		3,000	700.00	325.00
Complete Sheet 13-24:		7,000	3,500	2,100
1	Eddie Miller	160.00	55.00	30.00
2	Max West	160.00	55.00	30.00
3	Bucky Walters	160.00	55.00	30.00
4	"Duke" Derringer	160.00	55.00	30.00
5	"Buck" McCormick	160.00	55.00	30.00
6	Carl Hubbell	600.00	210.00	120.00
7	"The Horse" Danning	160.00	55.00	30.00
8	Mel Ott	650.00	225.00	130.00
9	"Pinky" May	160.00	55.00	30.00
10	"Arky" Vaughan	400.00	140.00	80.00
11	Debs Garms	160.00	55.00	30.00
12	"Jimmy" Brown	160.00	55.00	30.00
13	Jimmie Foxx	1,100	385.00	220.00
14	Ted Williams	3,200	1,125	640.00
15	Joe Cronin	400.00	140.00	80.00
16	Hal Trosky	160.00	55.00	30.00
17	Roy Weatherly	160.00	55.00	30.00
18	Hank Greenberg	1,100	385.00	220.00
19	Charley Gehringer	600.00	210.00	120.00
20	"Red" Ruffing	400.00	140.00	80.00
21	Charlie Keller	180.00	65.00	35.00
22	Bob Johnson	160.00	55.00	30.00
23	"Mac" McQuinn	160.00	55.00	30.00
24	Dutch Leonard	160.00	55.00	30.00

1976 Playboy Press Who Was Harry Steinfeldt?

(Babe Ruth)

What left-handed Hall of Famer had the most victories by the time he turned 23?

ARE YOU READY FOR THIS ONE? WHO WAS HARRY STEINFELDT & OTHER BASEBALL TRIVIA

A Playboy Press paperback - Available at your bookstore

This 12-card set was issued in 1976 by Playboy Press to promote author Bert Randolph Sugar's book "Who Was Harry Steinfeldt? & Other Baseball Trivia Questions." (Steinfeldt was the third baseman in the Cubs' famous infield that featured Hall of Famers Tinker, Evers and Chance). The black and white cards measure the standard 2-1/2" x 3-1/2" with a player photo on the front and a trivia question and ad for the book on the back.

		NM	EX	VG
Complete Set (12):		150.00	75.00	45.00
Common Player:		9.00	4.50	2.75
(1)	Frankie Baumholtz	9.00	4.50	2.75
(2)	Jim Bouton	12.00	6.00	3.50
(3)	Tony Conigliaro	9.00	4.50	2.75
(4)	Don Drysdale	17.50	8.75	5.25
(5)	Hank Greenberg	15.00	7.50	4.50
(6)	Walter Johnson	25.00	12.50	7.50
(7)	Billy Loes	9.00	4.50	2.75
(8)	Johnny Mize	15.00	7.50	4.50
(9)	Frank "Lefty" O'Doul	12.00	6.00	3.50
(10)	Babe Ruth	50.00	25.00	15.00
(11)	Johnny Sain	12.00	6.00	3.50
(12)	Jim Thorpe	40.00	20.00	12.00

1947 Pleetwood Slacks Jackie Robinson

JACKIE ROBINSON, famous Brooklyn Dodger Baseball Star, says: "Make mine PLEETWOOD - the Biggest Hit in Smart SLACKS!"

The date of issue cited is conjectural. This card, about 5" x 8", depicts Jackie Robinson in a coat and tie in a black-and-white photo on front, along with a facsimile autograph. In a strip at bottom is his name and an endorsement for "Pleetwood Slacks." The back is blank. The card was probably used as an autograph vehicle for personal appearances by Robinson at clothing stores.

	NM	EX	VG
Jackie Robinson	600.00	300.00	180.00

1910-12 Plow Boy Tobacco

EXTRA VALUE COUPONS
PLOW BOY TOBACCO
FOR
SMOKE OR CHEW
SAVE THE PIPE COUPONS

Plowboy Tobacco, a product of the Spaulding & Merrick Co., issued a set of cabinet-size cards in the Chicago area featuring members of the Cubs and White Sox. From the checklist, it appears the bulk of the set was originally issued in 1910 with a few additional cards appearing over the next several years. Measuring approximately 5-3/4" x 8", the Plow Boys feature sepia-toned player photos in poses not found on other tobacco issues. The player's name appears in the lower-left corner, while the team name appears in the lower-right. Two different backs are known. One consists of a simple advertisement for Plow Boy Tobacco, while a second, more difficult, variety includes a list of premiums available in exchange for coupons. The set is among the rarest of all 20th Century tobacco issues.

		NM	EX	VG
Common Player:		3,650	1,450	725.00
Premium Back: 1.5X				
(1)	Jimmy Archer	3,650	1,450	725.00
(2)	Ginger Beaumont	3,650	1,450	725.00
(3)	Lena Blackburne	3,650	1,450	725.00
(4)	Bruno Block	3,650	1,450	725.00
(5)	Ping Bodie	3,650	1,450	725.00
(6)	Mordecai Brown	5,500	2,200	1,100
(7)	Al Carson	3,650	1,450	725.00
(8)	Frank Chance	5,500	2,200	1,100
(9)	Ed Cicotte	5,250	2,100	1,050
(10)	King Cole	3,650	1,450	725.00
(11)	Shano Collins	3,650	1,450	725.00
(12)	George Davis	5,500	2,200	1,100
(13)	Patsy Dougherty	3,650	1,450	725.00
(14)	Johnny Evers	5,500	2,200	1,100
(15)	Chick Gandel (Gandil)	5,250	2,100	1,050
(16)	Ed Hahn	3,650	1,450	725.00
(17)	Solly Hoffman (Hofman)	3,650	1,450	725.00
(18)	Del Howard	3,650	1,450	725.00
(19)	Bill Jones	3,650	1,450	725.00
(20)	Johnny Kling	3,650	1,450	725.00
(21)	Rube Kroh	3,650	1,450	725.00
(22)	Frank Lange	3,650	1,450	725.00
(23)	Fred Luderus	3,650	1,450	725.00
(24)	Harry McIntyre (McIntire)	3,650	1,450	725.00
(25)	Ward Miller	3,650	1,450	725.00
(26)	Charlie Mullen	3,650	1,450	725.00
(27)	Tom Needham	3,650	1,450	725.00
(28)	Fred Olmstead	3,650	1,450	725.00
(29)	Orval Overall	3,650	1,450	725.00
(30)	Fred Parent	3,650	1,450	725.00
(31)	Fred Payne	3,650	1,450	725.00
(32)	Francis "Big Jeff" Pfeffer	3,650	1,450	725.00
(33)	Jake Pfeister	3,650	1,450	725.00
(34)	Billy Purtell	3,650	1,450	725.00
(35)	Ed Reulbach	3,650	1,450	725.00
(36)	Lew Richie	3,650	1,450	725.00
(37)	Jimmy Scheckard (Sheckard)	3,650	1,450	725.00
(38)	Wildfire Schulte	3,650	1,450	725.00
(39a)	Jim Scot (Name incorrect.)	3,650	1,450	725.00
(39b)	Jim Scott (Name correct.)	3,650	1,450	725.00
(40)	Frank Smith	3,650	1,450	725.00
(41)	Harry Steinfeldt	3,650	1,450	725.00
(42)	Billy Sullivan	3,650	1,450	725.00
(43)	Lee Tannehill	3,650	1,450	725.00
(44)	Joe Tinker	5,500	2,200	1,100
(45)	Ed Walsh	5,500	2,200	1,100
(46)	Doc White	3,650	1,450	725.00
(47)	Irv Young	3,650	1,450	725.00
(48)	Rollie Zeider	3,650	1,450	725.00
(49)	Heinie Zimmerman	3,650	1,450	725.00

1912 Plow's Candy (E300)

PLOW'S CANDY COLLECTION

DELEHANTY
DETROIT AMERICANS

An extremely rare candy issue, cards in this 1912 set measure 3" x 4" and feature sepia-toned photos surrounded by a wide border. The player's name and team appear in the border below the photo, while the words "Plow's Candy Collection" appear at the top. The backs are blank. Not even known to exist until the late 1960s, this set has been assigned the designation of E300 and additions to the checklist continue to appear every few years.

		NM	EX	VG
Common Player:		3,000	1,500	900.00
(1)	Babe Adams	3,000	1,500	900.00
(2)	Home Run Baker	4,800	2,400	1,440
(3)	Cy Barger	3,000	1,500	900.00
(4)	Jack Barry	3,000	1,150	900.00
(5)	Johnny Bates	3,000	1,500	900.00
(7)	Joe Benz	3,000	1,150	900.00
(8)	Bill Berger (Bergen)	3,000	1,500	900.00
(9)	Roger Bresnahan	4,800	2,400	1,440
(10)	Mordecai Brown	4,800	2,400	1,440
(11)	Donie Bush	3,000	1,500	900.00
(12)	Bobby Byrne	3,000	1,500	900.00
(13)	Nixey Callahan	3,000	1,500	900.00
(14)	Hal Chase	4,500	2,250	1,350
(15)	Fred Clarke	4,800	2,400	1,440
(16)	Ty Cobb	40,000	16,500	9,900
(17)	King Cole	3,000	1,500	900.00
(18)	Eddie Collins	4,800	2,400	1,440
(19)	Jack Coombs	3,000	1,500	900.00
(20)	Bill Dahlen	3,000	1,500	900.00
(21)	Bert Daniels	3,000	1,500	900.00
(22)	Harry Davis	3,000	1,500	900.00
(23)	Jim Delehanty	3,000	1,500	900.00
(24)	Josh Devore	3,000	1,500	900.00
(25)	Wild Bill Donovan	3,000	1,500	900.00
(26)	Red Dooin	3,000	1,500	900.00
(27)	Larry Doyle	3,000	1,500	900.00
(28)	Johnny Evers	4,800	2,400	1,440
(29)	Russ Ford	3,000	1,500	900.00
(30)	Del Gainor	3,000	1,500	900.00
(31)	Vean Gregg	3,000	1,500	900.00
(32)	Bob Harmon	3,000	1,500	900.00
(33)	Arnold Hauser	3,000	1,500	900.00
(34)	Dick Hoblitzelle (Hoblitzell)	3,000	1,500	900.00
(35)	Solly Hofman	3,000	1,500	900.00
(36)	Miller Huggins	4,800	2,400	1,440
(37)	John Hummel	3,000	1,500	900.00
(38)	Walter Johnson	7,200	3,600	2,160
(39)	Johnny Kling	3,000	1,500	900.00
(41)	Nap Lajoie	5,400	2,700	1,620
(42)	Jack Lapp	3,000	1,500	900.00
(43)	Fred Luderus	3,000	1,500	900.00
(44)	Sherry Magee	3,000	1,500	900.00
(45)	Rube Marquard	4,800	2,400	1,440
(46)	Christy Mathewson	25,000	4,500	2,700
(47)	Stuffy McInnes (McInnis)	3,000	1,500	900.00
(48)	Larry McLean	3,000	1,500	900.00
(49)	Fred Merkle	3,000	1,500	900.00
(50)	Cy Morgan	3,000	1,500	900.00
(51)	George Moriarty	3,000	1,500	900.00
(52)	Mike Mowrey	3,000	1,500	900.00
(53)	Chief Myers (Meyers)	3,000	1,500	900.00
(54)	Rube Oldring	3,000	1,500	900.00
(55)	Marty O'Toole	3,000	1,500	900.00
(56)	Eddie Plank	5,400	2,700	1,620
(57)	Nap Rucker	3,000	1,500	900.00
(58)	Slim Sallee	3,000	1,500	900.00
(59)	Boss Schmidt	3,000	1,500	900.00
(60)	Jimmy Sheckard	3,000	1,500	900.00
(61)	Tris Speaker	5,400	2,700	1,620
(62)	Billy Sullivan	3,000	1,500	900.00
(63)	Ira Thomas	3,000	1,500	900.00
(64)	Joe Tinker	4,800	2,400	1,440
(65)	John Titus	3,000	1,500	900.00
(66)	Hippo Vaughan (Vaughn)	3,000	1,500	900.00
(67)	Honus Wagner	50,000	15,000	9,000
(68)	Ed Walsh	4,800	2,400	1,440
(69)	Bob Williams	3,000	1,500	900.00

1915 PM1 Ornate-Frame Pins

Little is known about these tiny (approximately 1-1/16" x 1") pins, such as who issued them, when and how they were distributed and how many are in the set. The pins feature a sepia-tone player photo surrounded by an ornate gilded metal frame. The player's name is usually printed in a black strip at the bottom of the photo. The pins were originally sold for 19 cents. Gaps have been left in the assigned numbering for future additions to the checklist.

		NM	EX	VG
Common Pin:		600.00	300.00	170.00
(1a)	Jimmy Archer	600.00	300.00	170.00
(1b)	Jimmy Archer (No name.)	775.00	380.00	235.00
(2)	Frank Baker	1,500	750.00	500.00
(3)	Jack Barry	600.00	300.00	170.00
(4a)	Chief Bender (No name.)	1,500	750.00	500.00

(4b)	Chief Bender (With name.)	1,500	750.00	500.00
(5)	Frank Chance	1,500	750.00	500.00
(6)	Ty Cobb	7,400	3,700	2,220
(7)	Jake Daubert	600.00	300.00	170.00
(8)	Al Demaree	600.00	300.00	170.00
(9a)	Johnny Evers (Name only.)	1,500	750.00	500.00
(9b)	Johnny Evers (Name and city.)	1,500	750.00	500.00
(10)	Rube Foster	600.00	300.00	170.00
(11)	Dick Hoblitzell	600.00	300.00	170.00
(12)	Walter Johnson	2,700	1,350	800.00
(13)	Benny Kauff	600.00	300.00	170.00
(14)	Johnny Kling (No name.)	600.00	300.00	170.00
(15)	Ed Konetchy	600.00	300.00	170.00
(16)	Nap Lajoie	1,500	750.00	500.00
(17)	Sherry Magee	600.00	300.00	170.00
(18)	Rube Marquard	1,500	750.00	500.00
(19)	Christy Mathewson	3,400	1,700	1,000
(21)	John McGraw	1,500	750.00	500.00
(22)	Ed Reulbach	600.00	300.00	170.00
(23)	Eppa Rixey	1,500	750.00	500.00
(24)	Babe Ruth	19,500	10,000	5,850
(25)	Tris Speaker/Btg (Facing forward.)	1,500	750.00	500.00
(26)	Tris Speaker/Btg (Side view.)	1,500	750.00	500.00
(27)	Jeff Tesreau	600.00	300.00	170.00
(28)	Joe Tinker	1,500	750.00	500.00
(29)	Honus Wagner	3,600	1,800	1,075

1928 PM6 Baseball Player Pins

The method of distribution for these small (3/8" diameter) pin-backs is unknown, but it has been reported they were given away in cereal boxes. The black-and-white photographic pins have the player name in a black arc at bottom. The extent of the checklist is unknown.

		NM	EX	VG
Common Player:		375.00	185.00	110.00
(1)	Grover Alexander	450.00	225.00	135.00
(2)	Ty Cobb	900.00	450.00	275.00
(3)	Bucky Harris	350.00	175.00	100.00
(4)	Rogers Hornsby	550.00	275.00	165.00
(5)	Walter Johnson	600.00	300.00	180.00
(6)	Babe Ruth	1,200	600.00	360.00
(7)	Geo. Sisler	350.00	175.00	100.00
(8)	Tris Speaker	450.00	225.00	135.00

1940 PM10 Baseball Player Pins

This was the first of two issues that share a nearly identical format. The 1-3/4" celluloid pin-back buttons feature a black-and-white player photo surrounded by a white border. The player's name is in black capital letters at bottom, and his team nickname in the same type size and style at top. These pins were originally sold at ballparks and other souvenir outlets. The checklist, arranged here in alphabetical order, is not complete.

		NM	EX	VG
Common Player:		30.00	15.00	9.00
	Dick Bartell	30.00	15.00	9.00
	Dolph Camilli	30.00	15.00	9.00
	Bill Dickey	50.00	25.00	15.00
	Joe DiMaggio	275.00	135.00	85.00
	Lou Gehrig	700.00	350.00	210.00
	Lou Gehrig (Black border, "NEVER FORGOTTEN" at top.)	650.00	325.00	195.00
	Lefty Gomez	50.00	25.00	15.00
	Carl Hubbell	100.00	50.00	30.00
	Cliff Melton	30.00	15.00	9.00
	Pete Reiser	30.00	15.00	9.00
	Dixie Walker	30.00	15.00	9.00
	Whitlow Wyatt	30.00	15.00	9.00

1951 PM10 Baseball Player Pins

This was the second of two issues that share a nearly identical format. The 1-3/4" celluloid pin-back buttons feature a black-and-white player photo surrounded by a white border. The player's name is in black capital letters at bottom, and full team name in the same type size and style at top. These pins were originally sold at ballparks and other souvenir outlets. The checklist, arranged here in alphabetical order, is likely not complete. Note that the woeful Pittsburgh Pirates represent more than half the known players in this issue.

	NM	EX	VG
Common Player:	50.00	25.00	15.00
Luke Easter	75.00	37.50	22.50
Ned Garver	50.00	25.00	15.00
Monte Irvin	100.00	50.00	30.00
Ralph Kiner	100.00	50.00	30.00
Bob Lemon	100.00	50.00	30.00
Willie Mays	175.00	87.00	52.00
Clyde McCullouhg (McCullough)	50.00	25.00	15.00
Billy Meyer	50.00	25.00	15.00
Danny Murtaugh	50.00	25.00	15.00
Don Newcombe	50.00	25.00	15.00
Saul Rogovin	50.00	25.00	15.00
Stan Rojek	50.00	25.00	15.00
Hank Thompson	50.00	25.00	15.00
Bill Werle	50.00	25.00	15.00

1950s-60s PM10 Baseball Player Pins - Name at Bottom

Issued over a period of years in a variety of styles, these celluloid pinback buttons have in common their approximately 1-3/4" diameter and the appearance of the player name at bottom. Black-and-white player portrait photos are found on a variety of backgrounds. In this checklist, the color of the background is listed, where known, immediately after the team name (where known). Other distinguishing characteristics may also be noted. The pins were usually originally sold with a red, white and blue swallow-tailed silk pennant attached and a brass chain with a baseball, bat or glove charms, or similar plastic toys. Values shown are for pins alone. The checklist here is incomplete.

	NM	EX	VG
Common Player:	20.00	10.00	6.00
Hank Aaron (Blue, script name, team above.)	100.00	50.00	30.00
Sandy Amoros (Brooklyn, blue.)	60.00	30.00	18.00
Harry Anderson (Phillies, photo.)	125.00	65.00	35.00
John Antonelli (NY cap, "floating head.")	20.00	10.00	6.00
John Antonelli (SF cap, ring around photo.)	20.00	10.00	6.00
Luis Aparicio (White Sox, white.)	75.00	37.00	22.00
Ernest Banks (Cubs, white, no cap logo.)	475.00	235.00	140.00
Bo Belinsky (Phillies, white.)	40.00	20.00	12.00
Gus Bell (White)	20.00	10.00	6.00
Gus Bell ("CINCINNATI REDLEGS" beneath name.)	100.00	50.00	30.00
Larry Berra (White)	90.00	45.00	27.00
Larry Berra (Blue)	100.00	50.00	30.00
Yogi Berra	80.00	40.00	24.00

Joe Black (Brooklyn, photo.)	40.00	20.00	12.00
Joe Black (Brooklyn, white, facing front.)	40.00	20.00	12.00
Joe Black (Brooklyn, white, facing his left.)	25.00	12.50	7.50
Don Bollweg (A's, photo.)	20.00	10.00	6.00
Lou Boudreau (Photo, script name.)	60.00	30.00	18.00
Lou Boudreau (Red Sox, white.)	50.00	25.00	15.00
Jackie Brandt (Orioles, photo.)	40.00	20.00	12.00
Eddie Bressoud	20.00	10.00	6.00
Bill Bruton (Braves, white.)	100.00	50.00	30.00
Jim Bunning (Phillies.)	40.00	20.00	12.00
Roy Campanella (Brooklyn, blue.)	90.00	45.00	27.50
Roy Campanella (Brooklyn, yellow.)	80.00	40.00	24.00
Roy Campanella (Brooklyn, white, cap backwards.)	75.00	37.50	22.50
Roy Campanella (Brooklyn, white, name across photo.)	60.00	30.00	18.00
Roy Campanella (Brooklyn, white, name under photo.)	60.00	30.00	18.00
Roy Campanella (Brooklyn, white, name in strip.)	100.00	50.00	30.00
Roy Campanella (Brooklyn, white circle border, team at top.)	250.00	125.00	75.00
Chico Carrasquel (Name in script, team at top.)	50.00	25.00	15.00
Phil Cavarretta (Cubs, script name, stars above.)	150.00	75.00	45.00
Orlando Cepeda (Gray)	30.00	15.00	9.00
Orlando Cepeda (S.F., name in strip, photo.)	30.00	15.00	9.00
Gerry Coleman (Dark)	40.00	20.00	12.00
Gerry Coleman (Light)	40.00	20.00	12.00
Tony Conigliaro (Red Sox, gray.)	40.00	20.00	12.00
Morton Cooper (Cardinals, white/black background.)	40.00	20.00	12.00
Billy Cox (Brooklyn, white, neck-to-cap.)	95.00	47.50	28.00
Billy Cox (Brooklyn, white, chest-to-cap.)	60.00	30.00	18.00
Alvin Dark (NY cap, "floating head.")	20.00	10.00	6.00
Jerome (Dizzy) Dean (Black)	90.00	45.00	27.50
Dom DiMaggio (White)	40.00	20.00	12.00
Dom DiMaggio (Dark)	40.00	20.00	12.00
Joe DiMaggio (Black)	475.00	235.00	140.00
Joe DiMaggio (Dark blue, name beyond shoulders.)	250.00	125.00	75.00
Joe DiMaggio (Light blue, name within shoulders.)	150.00	75.00	45.00
Joe DiMaggio (Light blue, name "ear to ear" - modern fantasy, no collectible value.)			
Joe DiMaggio (Green border.)	325.00	160.00	100.00
Joe DiMaggio (White, name in strip.)	200.00	100.00	60.00
Joe DiMaggio (White, name not in strip.)	215.00	100.00	65.00
Joe DiMaggio (Yellow, "YANKEES" under name.)	350.00	175.00	100.00
Larry Doby (Dark)	60.00	30.00	18.00
Larry Doby (Indians, white.)	90.00	45.00	27.50
Carl Erskine (Brooklyn, white.)	75.00	37.50	22.50
Bob Feller (Indians, white.)	80.00	40.00	24.00
Bob Feller (Brown, name in script.)	325.00	160.00	100.00
Whitey Ford (White.)	80.00	40.00	24.00
Whitey Ford (White, name in strip, 3-1/2".)	200.00	100.00	60.00
Nelson Fox (White Sox, fox figures at top.)	350.00	175.00	100.00
Carl Furillo (Brooklyn, blue.)	75.00	37.50	22.50
Carl Furillo (Brooklyn, gray.)	65.00	32.50	20.00
Carl Furillo (Brooklyn, photo, dark sleeves.)	100.00	50.00	30.00
Carl Furillo (Brooklyn, photo, no sleeves.)	115.00	60.00	35.00
Ned Garver (Browns, white, belly-to-cap.)	30.00	15.00	9.00
Ned Garver (Browns, white, chest-to-cap.)	30.00	15.00	9.00
Junior Gilliam (Brooklyn, white.)	100.00	50.00	30.00
Junior Gilliam (Brooklyn, photo.)	100.00	50.00	30.00
Ruben Gomez (SF cap, ring around photo.)	30.00	15.00	9.00
Billy Goodman (White)	100.00	50.00	30.00
Ron Hansen (Orioles, photo.)	40.00	20.00	12.00
Gabby Hartnett (Cubs, black.)	40.00	20.00	12.00
Mike Hegan (Indians, white border, script name.)	450.00	225.00	135.00
Tom Henrich (Gray)	40.00	20.00	12.00
Mike Higgins (Red Sox, dark.)	45.00	22.50	13.50
Gil Hodges (Brooklyn, blue.)	100.00	50.00	30.00
Gil Hodges (Brooklyn, red/orange.)	50.00	25.00	15.00
Gil Hodges (Brooklyn, photo.)	40.00	20.00	12.00
Gil Hodges (Brooklyn, white, name across photo.)	60.00	30.00	18.00
Gil Hodges (Brooklyn, white, name in strip.)	200.00	100.00	60.00
Gil Hodges (Brooklyn, white, name under photo.)	40.00	20.00	12.00
Gil Hodges (Mets, 3-1/2", name in strip.)	150.00	75.00	45.00
Roger Hornsby (Rogers) (Browns, white circle border.)	150.00	75.00	45.00
Monte Irvin (Giants, dark.)	80.00	40.00	24.00
Ransom Jackson (Cubs, stars above.)	150.00	75.00	45.00
Forrest "Spook" Jacobs (Gray)	20.00	10.00	6.00

Forrest "Spook" Jacobs (A's, photo.)	20.00	10.00	6.00
Jackie Jensen (Dark)	50.00	25.00	15.00
Jackie Jensen (White)	50.00	25.00	15.00
Ed Joost (A's, photo.)	20.00	10.00	6.00
Harmon Killebrew ("W" on cap, photo.)	375.00	185.00	110.00
Harmon Killebrew (Twins, name in black script	250.00	125.00	75.00
Ralph Kiner (Color, facsimile autograph.)	40.00	20.00	12.00
Ralph Kiner (Cubs, hearts above.)	600.00	300.00	180.00
Ted Kluszewski (Dark, name overprinted horizontally.)	200.00	100.00	60.00
Ted Kluszewski (Reds, white, name in strip.)	40.00	20.00	12.00
Ed Kranepool (White)	50.00	25.00	15.00
Big Bill Lee (Cubs, black/gray.)	20.00	10.00	6.00
Bob Lemon (Light)	40.00	20.00	12.00
Whitey Lockman (NY cap, gray.)	25.00	12.50	7.50
Peanuts Lowrey (Cardinals, white.)	25.00	12.50	7.50
Sal Maglie (Brooklyn, photo.)	50.00	25.00	15.00
Frank Malzone	40.00	20.00	12.00
Mickey Mantle (White, batting to waist, name from elbow to armpit.)	275.00	135.00	80.00
Mickey Mantle (White, batting to waist, name from wrist to shoulder.)	300.00	150.00	90.00
Mickey Mantle (Blue, batting, left hand not visible, 1-3/4".)	350.00	175.00	100.00
Mickey Mantle (Baseball background, name in strip.)	200.00	100.00	60.00
Mickey Mantle (Blue, name in strip.) (Modern replicas are commonly encountered .)	250.00	125.00	75.00
Mickey Mantle (Blue, name in strip, looking over left shoulder, 3-1/2".)	150.00	75.00	45.00
Mickey Mantle (Yellow, name in strip, looking over left shoulder, 3-1/2".)	300.00	150.00	90.00
Mickey Mantle (White, portrait.)	300.00	150.00	90.00
Mickey Mantle (Blue, portrait, 3-1/2".)	1,750	875.00	525.00
Juan Marichal (SF cap, uncentered black border.)	60.00	30.00	18.00
Marty Marion (Browns, white circle border.)	300.00	150.00	90.00
Roger Maris (Blue, bat behind head, name in white strip, 3-1/2".)	100.00	50.00	30.00
Roger Maris (White, looking over shoulder, no cap insignia.)	125.00	60.00	35.00
Roger Maris (Orange, bat behind head, 3-1/2".)	100.00	50.00	30.00
Roger Maris (Yellow, bat behind head, 1-3/4".)	75.00	37.50	22.50
Roger Maris (Yellow, blue or purple, bat behind head, 2-1/4" - modern replica, no collectible value.)			
Roger Maris (Yellow, bat behind head, 3-1/2".)	100.00	50.00	30.00
Willie Mays (S.F. Giants, gray.)	325.00	160.00	97.00
Willie Mays (Photo, N.Y. cap.)	300.00	150.00	90.00
Willie Mays (Photo, grass background, S.F. cap.)	300.00	150.00	90.00
Willie Mays (Photo, stadium background, S.F. cap.)	300.00	150.00	90.00
Willie Mays (White, N.Y. cap.)	230.00	115.00	70.00
Willie Mays (White, S.F. cap.)	150.00	75.00	45.00
Willie McCovey (Pats on shoulder, no cap logo.)	200.00	100.00	60.00
Willie McCovey (SF cap, name in ear-to-ear white stripe.)	40.00	20.00	12.00
Gil McDougald (Yankees, gray.)	45.00	22.50	13.50
"Vinegar Bend" Mizell (Cardinals, white.)	30.00	15.00	9.00
Bill Monbouquette	40.00	20.00	12.00
Don Mueller (White, "floating head.")	40.00	20.00	12.00
Bobby Murcer (White)	30.00	15.00	9.00
Stan MUSIAL (Cardinals, white, MUSIAL at bottom, "STAN" THE MAN at top.)	125.00	65.00	40.00
Stan Musial (Cardinals, white, piping shows.)	100.00	50.00	30.00
Stan Musial (Cardinals, white, no piping.)	100.00	50.00	30.00
Stan Musial (White, team name above photo, facsimile autograph.) (Modern replica exists in 2-3/16" size; no collectible value.)	100.00	50.00	30.00
Stan Musial (Yellow)	125.00	65.00	35.00
Don Newcombe (Brooklyn, blue.)	450.00	225.00	135.00
Don Newcombe (Brooklyn, white, name in strip.)	30.00	15.00	9.00
Don Newcombe (Brooklyn, white, name under photo.)	30.00	20.00	12.00
Don Newcombe (Brooklyn, white circle border, team at top.)	60.00	30.00	18.00
Don Newcombe (Yellow)	50.00	25.00	15.00
Dan O'Connell (SF cap, ring around photo.)	40.00	20.00	12.00
Andy Pafko (Brooklyn, black.)	30.00	15.00	9.00
Joe Page (White)	50.00	25.00	15.00

Leroy (Satchel) Paige (White)	175.00	85.00	50.00
Mel Parnell (Red Sox, white.)	45.00	22.50	13.50
Joe Pepitone (White)	30.00	15.00	9.00
Johnny Pesky (Red Sox, white.)	100.00	50.00	30.00
Billy Pierce (Name in serif type.)	40.00	20.00	12.00
Jimmy Piersall (Light)	50.00	25.00	15.00
Johnny Podres (Brooklyn, white.)	45.00	22.00	13.50
Wally Post ("CINCINNATI REDLEGS" beneath name.)	50.00	25.00	15.00
Vic Power (A's, photo.)	25.00	12.50	7.50
Bob Purkey (Reds, white background)	200.00	100.00	60.00
Dick Radatz (Red Sox, gray.)	30.00	15.00	9.00
Vic Raschi (Yankees, white.)	60.00	30.00	18.00
PeeWee Reese (Brooklyn, gray, name in strip.)	200.00	100.00	60.00
"Pee Wee" Reese (Brooklyn, gray, name across photo.)	60.00	30.00	18.00
"Pee Wee" Reese (Brooklyn, white, large photo.)	125.00	65.00	35.00
"Pee Wee" Reese (Brooklyn, white, small photo.)	100.00	50.00	30.00
"Pee Wee" Reese (Brooklyn, photo, name in strip.)	60.00	30.00	18.00
Bill Rigney (NY cap, dark background.)	20.00	10.00	6.00
Phil Rizzuto (White)	80.00	40.00	24.00
Robin Roberts (Phillies, photo.)	50.00	25.00	15.00
Frank Robinson ("Cincinnati Redlegs" at bottom.)	250.00	125.00	75.00
Jackie Robinson (Brooklyn, blue.)	300.00	150.00	90.00
Jackie Robinson (Brooklyn, yellow.)	190.00	95.00	55.00
Jackie Robinson (Brooklyn, white, chest-to-cap.)	200.00	100.00	60.00
Jackie Robinson (Brooklyn, white, neck-to-cap.)	250.00	125.00	75.00
Jackie Robinson (Brooklyn, white, name across bottom, facing his left.)	200.00	100.00	60.00
Jackie Robinson (Brooklyn, gray, name across photo, facing his left.)	200.00	100.00	60.00
Jackie Robinson (Brooklyn, white, name in strip, cap logo not visible.)	600.00	300.00	180.00
Jackie Robinson (Brooklyn, photo.)	275.00	135.00	80.00
Preacher Roe (Brooklyn, wind-up pose.)	90.00	45.00	27.50
Al Rosen (Light background.)	40.00	20.00	12.00
Charles Herbert Ruffing (Yankees, gray.)	40.00	20.00	12.00
Pete Runnels	40.00	20.00	12.00
Ron Santo (Cubs, white.)	40.00	20.00	12.00
Hank Sauer (Cubs, script name, stars above.)	150.00	75.00	45.00
Chuck Schilling	40.00	20.00	12.00
George Scott (White, "floating head.")	20.00	10.00	6.00
Bobby Shantz (A's, white.)	30.00	15.00	9.00
Frank Shea (Yankees, gray.)	50.00	25.00	15.00
Harry Simpson (Indians, white, team name at top, script name at bottom.)	650.00	325.00	195.00
Enos Slaughter (Cardinals, white.)	50.00	25.00	15.00
Enos Slaughter (Cardinals, black.)	50.00	25.00	15.00
Roy Smalley (Cubs, script name, stars above.)	150.00	75.00	45.00
Duke Snider (Brooklyn, white.)	80.00	40.00	24.00
Duke Snider (Brooklyn, blue.)	65.00	35.00	20.00
Duke Snider (Brooklyn, blue, 3-1/2".)	200.00	100.00	60.00
Duke Snider (Brooklyn, gray.)	75.00	37.50	22.50
Duke Snider (Brooklyn, photo.)	150.00	75.00	45.00
Gerald Staley (Cardinals, white.)	20.00	10.00	6.00
Bobby Thomson (NY cap, white, uniform shows.)	40.00	20.00	12.00
Bobby Thomson (NY cap, white, "floating head.")	30.00	15.00	9.00
Gus Triandos (Orioles, photo.)	40.00	20.00	12.00
Robt. Lee Trice (A's, photo.)	25.00	12.50	7.50
Sam White (Red Sox, white.)	30.00	15.00	9.00
James Hoyt Wilhelm (Orioles)	200.00	100.00	60.00
Ted Williams (Name beneath bust, white.)	200.00	100.00	60.00
Ted Williams (Name in strip, black.)	450.00	225.00	135.00
Ted Williams (Name in strip, white.)	400.00	200.00	120.00
Ted Williams (Name in strip, photo, belt-up.)	90.00	45.00	27.50
Ted Williams (Belt-up photo, name in strip at top, team in script at bottom) 1-1/4"	50.00	25.00	15.00
Ted Williams (Belt-up photo, name in strip at top, team in strip at bottom) 1-3/4"	100.00	50.00	30.00
Ted Williams (Name in strip, photo, close-up.)	100.00	50.00	30.00
Carl Yastrzemski	100.00	50.00	30.00

1950s-60s PM10 Baseball Player Pins - Name at Top

This series of baseball player pins is similar to contemporary issues in its 1-3/4" (unless otherwise noted) black-and-white celluloid format, but differs in that the player name appears at top. Players known in the series indicate the buttons were issued over a period of several years, probably for sale in stadium concession stands and other souvenir outlets. The alphabetical checklist here is not complete.

Common Player:	NM	EX	VG
Felipe Alou (Script name.)	60.00	30.00	18.00
Luis Arroyo	40.00	20.00	12.00
Hank Bauer	20.00	10.00	6.00
Yogi Berra	60.00	30.00	18.00
Johnny Blanchard	135.00	67.00	40.00
Cletis Boyer	60.00	30.00	18.00
Roy Campanella (2-1/4")	75.00	37.00	22.00
Andy Carey	450.00	225.00	135.00
(2", Yankees, white)	125.00	65.00	37.50
Joe Collins	60.00	30.00	18.00
Del Crandall (2-1/8")	40.00	20.00	12.00
Whitey Ford (2")	150.00	75.00	45.00
Whitey Ford (3-1/2" diameter)	400.00	200.00	120.00
Carl Furillo	75.00	37.00	22.00
(2", Brooklyn, white)			
Junior Gilliam	75.00	37.00	22.00
Ruben Gomez	40.00	20.00	12.00
Ken Harrelson	50.00	25.00	15.00
(Red Sox, white.)			
Don Hoak (Brooklyn, white.)	60.00	30.00	18.00
Elston Howard	75.00	37.00	22.00
Jackie Jensen	75.00	37.00	22.00
(Red Sox, white.)			
Clem Labine (Brooklyn, white.)	60.00	30.00	18.00
Billy Loes (2", Brooklyn, white)	130.00	65.00	40.00
Ed Lopat	60.00	30.00	18.00
Hector Lopez	40.00	20.00	12.00
Frank Malzone	50.00	25.00	15.00
(Red Sox, white.)			
Mickey Mantle (1-5/8")	500.00	250.00	150.00
Mickey Mantle (2-1/4"")	300.00	150.00	90.00
Roger Maris (2", yellow)	150.00	75.00	45.00
Roger Maris (2-1/4", white)	3.00	1.00	1.00
Billy Martin	75.00	37.00	22.00
Willie Mays (2-1/4", white)	450.00	225.00	135.00
Gil McDougald	100.00	50.00	30.00
(2", Yankees, white)			
Bill Monbouquette	50.00	25.00	15.00
(Red Sox, white.)			
Walt Moryn	250.00	125.00	75.00
(1-1/2", Brooklyn, white)			
Don Newcombe	125.00	62.00	37.00
(2", Brooklyn, white.)			
Irv Noren	60.00	30.00	18.00
Johnny Podres	60.00	30.00	18.00
(2", Brooklyn, white)			
Allie Reynolds	60.00	30.00	18.00
Jackie Robinson	1,600	800.00	475.00
(2-1/16", Brooklyn, white)			
Preacher Roe	60.00	30.00	18.00
(Brooklyn, white.)			
Pete Runnels	50.00	25.00	15.00
(Red Sox, white.)			
Chuck Schilling	50.00	25.00	15.00
(Red Sox, white.)			
Bill Skowron	60.00	30.00	18.00
Enos Slaughter	60.00	30.00	18.00
Duke Snider	135.00	67.00	40.00
(2-1/4", Brooklyn, white)			
Warren Spahn	120.00	60.00	36.00
Don Thompson	200.00	100.00	60.00
(2", Brooklyn, white)			
Bob Turley	60.00	30.00	18.00
Ted Williams	80.00	40.00	25.00
(1-3/4", name in strip at top, team in strip at bottom)			
Ted Williams	550.00	275.00	165.00
(2-1/4", name at top)			
Gene Woodling	60.00	30.00	18.00
Carl Yastrzemski	200.00	100.00	60.00
Don Zimmer (Brooklyn, white.)	75.00	37.50	22.50

1956 PM15 Yellow Basepath Pins

These pins were issued circa 1956; the sponsor of this 32-pin set is not indicated. The set, which has been assigned the American Card Catalog designation PM15, is commonly called "Yellow Basepaths" because of the design of the pin,

which features a black-and-white player photo set inside a green infield with yellow basepaths. The unnumbered pins measure 7/8" in diameter.

		NM	EX	VG
Complete Set (32):		4,500	2,250	1,350
Common Player:		85.00	40.00	25.00
(1)	Hank Aaron	400.00	200.00	120.00
(2)	Joe Adcock	85.00	40.00	25.00
(3)	Luis Aparicio	140.00	70.00	40.00
(4)	Richie Ashburn	150.00	75.00	45.00
(5)	Gene Baker	85.00	40.00	25.00
(6)	Ernie Banks	225.00	110.00	65.00
(7)	Yogi Berra	245.00	120.00	75.00
(8)	Bill Bruton	85.00	40.00	25.00
(9)	Larry Doby	140.00	70.00	40.00
(10)	Bob Friend	85.00	40.00	25.00
(11)	Nellie Fox	140.00	70.00	40.00
(12)	Ted Greengrass (Jim)	85.00	40.00	25.00
(13)	Steve Gromek	85.00	40.00	25.00
(14)	Johnny Groth	85.00	40.00	25.00
(15)	Gil Hodges	200.00	100.00	60.00
(16)	Al Kaline	150.00	75.00	45.00
(17)	Ted Kluzewski (Kluszewski)	140.00	70.00	40.00
(18)	Johnny Logan	85.00	40.00	25.00
(19)	Dale Long	85.00	40.00	25.00
(20)	Mickey Mantle	600.00	300.00	180.00
(21)	Ed Matthews (Mathews)	150.00	75.00	45.00
(22)	Minnie Minoso	100.00	50.00	30.00
(23)	Stan Musial	350.00	175.00	100.00
(24)	Don Newcombe	140.00	70.00	40.00
(25)	Bob Porterfield	85.00	40.00	25.00
(26)	Pee Wee Reese	200.00	100.00	60.00
(27)	Robin Roberts	140.00	70.00	40.00
(28)	Red Schoendienst	140.00	70.00	40.00
(29)	Duke Snider	225.00	110.00	65.00
(30)	Vern Stephens	85.00	40.00	25.00
(31)	Gene Woodling	100.00	50.00	30.00
(32)	Gus Zernial	85.00	40.00	25.00

1973 Pogue's Postcards

This 3-1/2" x 5-1/2" semi-glossy, blank-back photocard was issued by Pogue's department store in Cincinnati, presumably in conjunction with a player autograph appearance. Whether there were other players issued in unknown. The card is virtually identical to the team-issued photocard of 1973, with the exception of the red store logo at bottom.

		NM	EX	VG
(1)	Joe Morgan	40.00	20.00	12.00

1909-11 Polar Bear Tobacco

The most distinctive advertising-back found on 1909-11 T206 is that of Polar Bear with its dark blue background and white topography. A more conventional style of ad was used on 1911 T205 cards, also printed in blue. Because the cards were packaged loose among the tobacco leaves in Polar Bear pouches, stains on surviving cards are frequently seen. Polar Bear is among the most common brands found in both series.

PREMIUMS:
T205: 1X
T206: 1-1.5X
(See T205, T206 for checklists and card values.)

1889 Police Gazette Cabinets

Issued in the late 1880s through early 1890s as a premium by Police Gazette, a popular newspaper of the day, these cabinet cards are very rare. The 4-1/4" x 6-1/2" cards consist of sepia-toned photographs mounted on cardboard of various colors. Only about two dozen players are currently known. Some photographs correspond to those used in the S.F. Hess card series and many players are depicted in suit and tie, rather than baseball uniform. Each card displays the name of the player beneath his portrait, along with the signature of "Richard K. Fox" and a line identifying him as "Editor and Proprietor / Police Gazette / Franklin Square, New York."

	NM	EX	VG
Common Player:	8,800	4,400	2,650
Hick Carpenter	8,800	4,400	2,650
Fred Carroll	8,800	4,400	2,650
Bob Clark	8,800	4,400	2,650
John Coleman	8,800	4,400	2,650
Roger Conner (Connor)	11,000	5,500	3,500
Pete Conway	8,800	4,400	2,650
John Corkhill	8,800	4,400	2,650
Jerry Denny	8,800	4,400	2,650
Jas. A. Donohue (Donahue)	8,800	4,400	2,650
Buck Ewing	11,000	5,500	3,500
Bob Ferguson	8,800	4,400	2,650
Jocko Fields	8,800	4,400	2,650
Elmer Foster	8,800	4,400	2,650
Charlie Getzein (Getzien)	8,800	4,400	2,650
Pebbly Jack Glasscock	8,800	4,400	2,650
Bill Gleason	8,800	4,400	2,650
George Gore	8,800	4,400	2,650
Tim Keefe	11,000	5,500	3,500
Gus Krock	8,800	4,400	2,650
A.J. Maul	8,800	4,400	2,650
Ed Morris	8,800	4,400	2,650
Tip O'Neil (O'Neill)	8,800	4,400	2,650
N. (Fred) Pfeffer	8,800	4,400	2,650
Danny Richardson	8,800	4,400	2,650
A.B. Sanders	8,800	4,400	2,650
Charley (Pop) Smith	8,800	4,400	2,650
Elmer Smith	8,800	4,400	2,650
Harry Staley	8,800	4,400	2,650
William Swett (San Francisco)	11,000	5,500	3,500
George Tebeau	8,800	4,400	2,650
John Tener	9,900	5,000	3,000
Billy Terry (Adonis)	8,800	4,400	2,650
Sam Thompson	11,000	5,500	3,500
Curt Welch	8,800	4,400	2,650
Mickey Welsh	11,000	5,500	3,500
Wheeler C. Wikoff (Wykoff)	8,800	4,400	2,650
(Pres. American Association)			

1895 Police Gazette Supplement

Captains of the Twelve Clubs in the National League.

The 12 captains of the National League's teams, collectively termed "Our Baseball Heroes," are pictured in sepia lithographic portraits surrounding a colorful baseball action scene on this supplement issued with the June 1 edition of the men's newspaper. Overall the supplement measures about 21-1/2" x 15-1/2" and is the most impressive of the baseball items issued by the paper prior to the turn of the 20th Century.

	NM	EX	VG
Supplement:	15,000	7,000	4,000
Cap Anson			
Jack Boyle			
Ed Cartwright			
George Davis			
Buck Ewing			
Jack Glasscock			
Mike Griffin			
Connie Mack			
Doggie Miller			
Billy Nash			
Patsy Tebeau			
Wilbert Robinson			

1901-1917 Police Gazette Supplements

Each issue of the weekly men's magazine included a large-format (about 11-1/4" x 16-1/4") blank-backed, black-and-white supplement. In keeping with the publication's editorial focus at the time, the pictures featured baseball players, boxers, other atheletes, actresses and female models. The photos appear in a frame design and measure about 8-1/2" x 12-1/2". The supplements are designated as such by a line of type at top or bottom that names the publication, issue number and issue date. The subject is identified in capital letters beneath the photo and there are a few lines of information at bottom. The magazine sometimes printed the same pictures in nearly identical format within its regular pages. These can be differentiated from the supplements in that they are on pink paper, have advertising or other editorial material on back and are not marked as supplements. Such pages do not enjoy the same popularity and value as the supplements. In this possibly incomplete checklist, the card number shown is the issue number in which the supplement was inserted. The player name or title may not always exactly correspond to that printed on the piece. Because of their large size, the supplements are often found trimmed to remove evidence of corner creases and edge damage. This checklist includes only the baseball subjects.

		NM	EX	VG
Common Player:		100.00	50.00	30.00
1901				
	George Davis (Issue date unknown.)	200.00	100.00	60.00
1251	Christy Mathewson	2,000	1,000	600.00
1903				
1351	Roy Thomas	100.00	50.00	30.00
1353	Red Dooin	100.00	50.00	30.00
1357	Tommy Leach	100.00	50.00	30.00
1359	John McGraw	200.00	100.00	60.00
1361	Cy Seymour	100.00	50.00	30.00
1363	Joe McGinnity	200.00	100.00	60.00
1365	Jack Cronin	100.00	50.00	30.00
1904				
1400	Dan McGann	100.00	50.00	30.00
1403	Red Ames	100.00	50.00	30.00
1407	Jack Warner	100.00	50.00	30.00
1411	Frank Bowerman	100.00	50.00	30.00
1413	Roger Bresnahan	200.00	100.00	60.00
1905				
1450	Joe McGinnity	200.00	100.00	60.00
1451	Napoleon Lajoie	250.00	125.00	75.00
1452	Hans Wagner	1,250	625.00	375.00
1453	Malachi Kittredge	100.00	50.00	30.00
1457	Jack Chesbro	200.00	100.00	60.00
1459	Roger Bresnahan	200.00	100.00	60.00
1461	1905 Pittsburg Team	900.00	450.00	275.00
1463	Willie Keeler	200.00	100.00	60.00
1465	Sam Mertes	100.00	50.00	30.00
1466	Dave Fultz	100.00	50.00	30.00
1467	Carlisle University Team	150.00	75.00	45.00
1468	Bill Hogg	100.00	50.00	30.00
1906				
1502	Aleck Smith	100.00	50.00	30.00
1504	Jack Kleinow	100.00	50.00	30.00
1505	Rube Waddell	200.00	100.00	60.00
1507	Clark Griffith	200.00	100.00	60.00
1510	Nap Shea	100.00	50.00	30.00
1516	Jimmy Casey	100.00	50.00	30.00
1518	Hal Chase	200.00	100.00	60.00
1907				
1548	Harry Davis	100.00	50.00	30.00
1549	Mike Powers	100.00	50.00	30.00
1551	Willie Keeler, Jack Kleinow	150.00	75.00	45.00
1554	Eddie Plank	250.00	125.00	75.00
1557	George Moriarty	100.00	50.00	30.00
1559	Bill Dahlen	100.00	50.00	30.00
1562	Cecil Ferguson	100.00	50.00	30.00
1564	Sammy Strang	100.00	50.00	30.00
1567	Hal Chase, Charlie Armbruster	150.00	75.00	45.00
1571	Mordecai Brown	200.00	100.00	60.00
1572	Danny Hoffman	100.00	50.00	30.00
1908				
1607	Harry Bay	100.00	50.00	30.00
1613	Harry Lunn	100.00	50.00	30.00
1615	Charley Hemphill	100.00	50.00	30.00
1909				
1655	Buck Herzog	100.00	50.00	30.00
1657	Al Bridwell	100.00	50.00	30.00
1660	Hans Lobert	100.00	50.00	30.00
1663	Bugs Raymond	100.00	50.00	30.00
1664	Harry Coveleski	100.00	50.00	30.00
1665	Chief Meyers	100.00	50.00	30.00
1667	Orval Overall	100.00	50.00	30.00
1673	Al Burch	100.00	50.00	30.00
1674	Mike Donlin	100.00	50.00	30.00
1676	Del Howard	100.00	50.00	30.00
1678	Dick Morris (Amateur)	100.00	50.00	30.00
1910				
1716	Jack Warhop	100.00	50.00	30.00
1717	George Mullen (Mullin)	100.00	50.00	30.00
1720	Russ Ford	100.00	50.00	30.00
1721	Owen Bush	100.00	50.00	30.00
1722	Sherry Magee	100.00	50.00	30.00
1724	Jack Dalton	100.00	50.00	30.00
1726	Bert Daniels	100.00	50.00	30.00
1727	Birdie Cree	100.00	50.00	30.00
1729	Josh Devore	100.00	50.00	30.00

		NM	EX	VG
1730	Louis Drucke	100.00	50.00	30.00
1911				
1771	Christy Mathewson	750.00	375.00	225.00
1779	Arthur Wilson	100.00	50.00	30.00
1782	Hans Wagner, Roger Bresnahan	750.00	375.00	225.00
1791	Home Run Baker	200.00	100.00	60.00
1912				
1812	Zach Wheat	200.00	100.00	60.00
1814	Rube Marquard	200.00	100.00	60.00
1821	Tex Erwin	100.00	50.00	30.00
1823	Heinie Zimmerman	100.00	50.00	30.00
1825	Jake Stahl	100.00	50.00	30.00
1913				
1856	Frank Chance	200.00	100.00	60.00
1861	Joe Wood	125.00	62.50	37.50
1867	Jim Thorpe	3,000	1,500	900.00
1872	Jake Daubert	100.00	50.00	30.00
1877	Nap Rucker	100.00	50.00	30.00
1883	Joe Jackson	2,000	1,000	600.00
1888	Walter Johnson	750.00	375.00	225.00
1914				
1920	Ty Cobb	1,500	750.00	450.00
1926	Sam Crawford	200.00	100.00	60.00
1932	Dave Robertson	100.00	50.00	30.00
1938	Fritz Maisel	100.00	50.00	30.00
1942	Boston N.L. Team	200.00	100.00	60.00
1943	Philadelphia A.L. Team	200.00	100.00	60.00
1915				
1961	Ray Caldwell	100.00	50.00	30.00
1966	Rabbit Maranville	200.00	100.00	60.00
1970	Sherry Magee	100.00	50.00	30.00
1975	Hans Lobert	100.00	50.00	30.00
1982	Eddie Collins	200.00	100.00	60.00
1985	Dick Hoblitzell	100.00	50.00	30.00
1989	Grover Alexander	500.00	250.00	150.00
1916				
2011	Larry Doyle	100.00	50.00	30.00
2018	Fred Luderus	100.00	50.00	30.00
2020	Jimmy Archer	100.00	50.00	30.00
2023	Dick Rudolph	100.00	50.00	30.00
2026	Benny Kauff	100.00	50.00	30.00
2029	Sam Crawford	200.00	100.00	60.00
2035	Nick Cullop	100.00	50.00	30.00
2040	Clarence Mitchell	100.00	50.00	30.00
2042	George Sisler	200.00	100.00	60.00
2046	Pol Perritt	100.00	50.00	30.00
1917				
2064	Ping Bodie	100.00	50.00	30.00
2070	Benny Kauff	100.00	50.00	30.00
2074	Hans Lobert	100.00	50.00	30.00
2078	Harry Coveleskie (Coveleski)	100.00	50.00	30.00
2081	Jack Coombs	100.00	50.00	30.00

1887 Polka Dot Nine Trade Cards

This series of late 1880s (the specific attributed date is speculative) trade cards is related to the "Polka Dot Nine" cabinet cards that were a coupon-redemption premium for Allen & Ginter's Virginia Bright Cigarettes (see related listing). This version uses the same posed sepia-toned action photos of women in baseball uniforms with a polka-dot neckerchief. These trade cards are in a size of about 2-1/4" x 3-3/8". Examples have been seen with advertising on their backs for a men's clothing store in Binghamton, N.Y., and for Residio Cigars. The number of poses issued is unknown, but presumably numbers at least nine.

	NM	EX	VG
Common Card:	600.00	300.00	180.00

1914 Polo Grounds Game (WG4)

Called the "Polo Grounds Game" for the green-and-white photo of that stadium on each card's back, this set was officially issued as "All Star Card Base Ball" by The Card Baseball Co. of Norfolk, Va. Fronts of the round-cornered 2-1/2" x 3-1/2" cards have a black-and-white player photo and a baseball play scenario that is used to play the game. The set as issued includes 30 different players cards and 24 duplicate cards on which different game plays are displayed. The unnumbered cards are checklisted here alphabetically.

		NM	EX	VG
Complete Boxed Set (54):		6,650	3,325	2,000
Complete Set (30):		3,000	1,500	900.00
Common Player:		40.00	20.00	12.00
(1)	Jimmy Archer	40.00	20.00	12.00
(2)	Frank Baker	125.00	50.00	30.00
(3)	Frank Chance	125.00	50.00	30.00

		NM	EX	VG
(4)	Larry Cheney	40.00	20.00	12.00
(5)	Ty Cobb	1,000	275.00	165.00
(6)	Eddie Collins	100.00	50.00	30.00
(7)	Larry Doyle	40.00	20.00	12.00
(8)	Art Fletcher	40.00	20.00	12.00
(9)	Claude Hendrix	40.00	20.00	12.00
(10)	Joe Jackson	1,500	385.00	230.00
(11)	Hughie Jennings	125.00	50.00	30.00
(12)	Nap Lajoie	125.00	50.00	30.00
(13)	Jimmy Lavender	40.00	20.00	12.00
(14)	Fritz Maisel	40.00	20.00	12.00
(15)	Rabbit Maranville	125.00	50.00	30.00
(16)	Rube Marquard	125.00	50.00	30.00
(17)	Matty (Christy Mathewson)	500.00	100.00	60.00
(18)	John McGraw	125.00	50.00	30.00
(19)	Stuffy McInnis	40.00	20.00	12.00
(20)	Chief Meyers	40.00	20.00	12.00
(21)	Red Murray	40.00	20.00	12.00
(22)	Ed Plank	150.00	50.00	30.00
(23)	Nap Rucker	40.00	20.00	12.00
(24)	Reb Russell	40.00	20.00	12.00
(25)	Wildfire Schulte	40.00	20.00	12.00
(26)	Jim Scott	40.00	20.00	12.00
(27)	Tris Speaker	175.00	62.00	37.00
(28)	Honus Wagner	875.00	450.00	275.00
(29)	Ed Walsh	125.00	50.00	30.00
(30)	Joe Wood	100.00	30.00	18.00

1952 Ponca City Dodgers Team Issue

This set from the Globe Printing Co. line-up of minor league issues presents the 1952 Ponca City (Okla.) Dodgers, the Class D farm club of the Brooklyn Dodgers in the Kansas-Oklahoma-Missouri League's final season. The blank-backed, black-and-white cards are printed on thin cardboard and measure about 2-1/4" x 3-3/8". All but one of the known cards has one of seven local sponsor's names in the identical box on front. This checklist is likely incomplete. The set probably having been comprised of about 18 cards when issued.

		NM	EX	VG
Common Player:		75.00	40.00	25.00
(1)	Boyd Bartley	75.00	40.00	25.00
(2)	Tony DeVelis	75.00	40.00	25.00
(3)	Clyde Girrens	75.00	40.00	25.00
(4)	Russ Greenbush	75.00	40.00	25.00
(5)	Al Jarvis	75.00	40.00	25.00
(6)	Morris Mack	75.00	40.00	25.00
(7)	Mike Ryan	75.00	40.00	25.00
(8)	Don Stuart	75.00	40.00	25.00
(9)	Duke Stewart	75.00	40.00	25.00

1952 Ponca Dodgers/K-O-M Managers Team Issues

This set from the Globe Printing Co. line-up of minor league issues was issued by the Ponca City (Okla.) Dodgers, the Class D farm club of the Brooklyn Dodgers in the Kansas-Oklahoma-Missouri League's final season. It is unusual in that, besides Ponca City players and manager Boyd Bartley, the set included some (perhaps all) of the other K-O-M League managers. The blank-backed, black-and-white cards are printed on thin cardboard and measure about 2-1/4" x 3-3/8". Each of the known PC players has one of seven local sponsor's names in the identification box on front. This checklist may be incomplete.

		NM	EX	VG
(1)	Boyd Bartley (Ponca City mgr.)	75.00	40.00	25.00
(2)	Fred "Rip" Collins (Independence Browns mgr.)	75.00	40.00	25.00
(3)	Tony DeVelis	75.00	40.00	25.00
(4)	Clyde Girrens	75.00	40.00	25.00
(5)	Russ Greenbush	75.00	40.00	25.00
(6)	Al Jarvis	75.00	40.00	25.00
(7)	Morris Mack	75.00	40.00	25.00
(8)	Hershel Martin (Bartlesville-Pittsburg Pirates mgr.)	75.00	40.00	25.00
(9)	Al Reitz (Blackwell Broncos mgr.)	75.00	40.00	25.00
(10)	Mike Ryan	75.00	40.00	25.00
(11)	Don Stewart	75.00	40.00	25.00
(12)	Duke Stuart	75.00	40.00	25.00

1915 Postaco Stamps

A small find of these early stamps in complete sheets of 12 in the mid-1990s made the issue collectible, rather than impossibly rare. Individual stamps are 1-3/4" x 2-1/8" and feature black-and-white player portraits set against a bright background of either yellow or red-orange. The player name, position (in most cases), team and league are designated at the bottom of the picture. In the black frame between the picture and the perforated white border is a copyright symbol and "Postaco." Backs are, of course, blank. Stamps are checklisted here in alphabetical order within color group.

	NM	EX	VG
Complete Set, Sheets (3):	3,000	1,500	900.00
Complete Set, Singles (36):	2,500	1,250	750.00
Common Player:	30.00	15.00	9.00

Red-Orange Background

		NM	EX	VG
(1)	Home Run Baker	100.00	50.00	30.00
(2)	Chief Bender	100.00	50.00	30.00
(3)	George Burns	40.00	20.00	12.00
(4)	John Evers	100.00	50.00	30.00
(5)	Max Flack	40.00	20.00	12.00
(6)	Hank Gawdy (Gowdy)	40.00	20.00	12.00
(7)	Claude Ray Hendrix	40.00	20.00	12.00
(8)	Walter Johnson	200.00	100.00	60.00
(9)	Nap Lajoie	100.00	50.00	30.00
(10)	Hans Lobert	40.00	20.00	12.00
(11)	Sherwood Magee	40.00	20.00	12.00
(12)	Rabbit Maranville	100.00	50.00	30.00
(13)	Christy Mathewson	250.00	125.00	75.00
(14)	George McBride	40.00	20.00	12.00
(15)	John McGraw	100.00	50.00	30.00
(16)	Fred Merkle	40.00	20.00	12.00
(17)	Jack Miller	40.00	20.00	12.00
(18)	Emiliano Palmero	40.00	20.00	12.00
(19)	Pol Perritt	40.00	20.00	12.00
(20)	Derrill Pratt	40.00	20.00	12.00
(21)	Richard Rudolph	40.00	20.00	12.00
(22)	Butch Schmidt	40.00	20.00	12.00
(23)	Joe Tinker	100.00	50.00	30.00
(24)	Honus Wagner	300.00	150.00	90.00

Yellow Background

		NM	EX	VG
(25)	G.C. Alexander	100.00	50.00	30.00
(26)	J.P. Archer	30.00	15.00	9.00
(27)	Ty Cobb	300.00	150.00	90.00
(28)	Eugene Cocreham	30.00	15.00	9.00
(29)	E.S. Cottrell	30.00	15.00	9.00
(30)	Josh Devore	30.00	15.00	9.00
(31)	A. Hartzell (Roy)	30.00	15.00	9.00
(32)	Wm. H. James (middle initial actually L)	30.00	15.00	9.00
(33)	Connie Mack	75.00	37.50	22.50
(34)	M. McHale	30.00	15.00	9.00
(35)	Geo. T. Stallings	30.00	15.00	9.00
(36)	Ed. Sweeney	30.00	15.00	9.00

1930 Post Cereal Famous North Americans

CHRISTY MATHEWSON (1880-1925)—Greatest of all baseball pitchers.

The year of issue is unconfirmed. Mathewson is the only baseball player from a group of cereal-box cards printed in panels of four and featuring presidents, generals, Indian chiefs, explorers, etc. The front is printed in red and blue, the back is blank. The card measures about 2-5/8" x 3-1/2".

	NM	EX	VG
Christy Mathewson	600.00	300.00	180.00

1960 Post Cereal

These cards were issued on the backs of Grape Nuts Flakes cereal and measure an oversized 7" x 8-3/4". The nine cards in the set include five baseball players two football (Frank Gifford and John Unitas) and two basketball players (Bob Cousy and Bob Pettit). The full-color photos are bordered by a wood frame design. The cards covered the entire back of the cereal box and are blank backed. Card fronts include the player's name, team and a facsimile autograph. A panel on the side of the box has biographical information.

		NM	EX	VG
Common Player:		400.00	200.00	120.00
(1)	Don Drysdale	400.00	200.00	120.00
(2)	Al Kaline	400.00	200.00	120.00
(3)	Harmon Killebrew	400.00	200.00	120.00
(4)	Ed Mathews	400.00	200.00	120.00
(5)	Mickey Mantle	2,500	1,250	750.00

1961 Post Cereal

Two hundred different players are included in this set, but with variations the number of different cards exceeds 350. Cards were issued singly and in various panel configurations on the backs of cereal boxes, as well as on thinner stock in 10-card team sheets available from Post via a mail-in offer.

BASEBALL STAR CARD No. 73

Chuck Estrada

BALTIMORE ORIOLES—PITCHER

Ht.—6'; Wt.—185; Bats—Right; Throws—Right
Born—Feb. 15, 1938; Home—San Margarita, Calif.

Following a brief minor career (1959), Chuck lost no time in exhibiting his blazing fast ball, slider and sharp curve to his teammates. His fast ball accounted for 178 strike outs in 183 innings of Coast League play and was a big factor in bringing him to the Orioles. Selected for 1960 All Star Game.

MAJOR LEAGUE PITCHING RECORD

	Games	IP	Won	Lost	Pct	Hits	Runs	ER	SO	Walks	ERA
1960	36	209	18	11	.621	162	87	83	142	101	3.57
LIFE	36	209	18	11	.621	162	87	83	142	101	3.57

Because of placement on less popular sizes and brands of cereal, or because they were issued only on box backs or company sheets, some cards were issued in significantly smaller quantities, making their prices much higher than other comparable players in the set. Well-cut individual cards measure about 3-1/2" x 2-1/2". All cards are numbered in the upper-right corner. Card fronts have full-color portait photos of the player, along with biographical information and 1960 and career statistics. Backs are blank. The complete set price includes only the most common variation of each player.

		NM	EX	VG
Complete Set (200):		2,000	1,000	600.00
Common Player:		4.00	2.00	1.25
1a	Yogi Berra (Box)	40.00	16.00	10.00
1b	Yogi Berra (Company)	25.00	10.00	6.00
2a	Elston Howard (Box)	7.50	3.00	2.00
2b	Elston Howard (Company)	7.50	3.00	2.00
3a	Bill Skowron (Box)	7.50	3.00	2.00
3b	Bill Skowron (Company)	7.50	3.00	2.00
4a	Mickey Mantle (Box)	160.00	65.00	40.00
4b	Mickey Mantle (Company)	110.00	45.00	25.00
5	Bob Turley (Company)	40.00	16.00	10.00
6a	Whitey Ford (Box)	20.00	8.00	5.00
6b	Whitey Ford (Company)	12.50	5.00	3.00
7a	Roger Maris (Box)	35.00	15.00	9.00
7b	Roger Maris (Company)	35.00	15.00	9.00
8a	Bobby Richardson (Box)	15.00	6.00	4.00
8b	Bobby Richardson (Company)	10.00	4.00	2.50
9a	Tony Kubek (Box)	25.00	10.00	6.25
9b	Tony Kubek (Company)	35.00	15.00	9.00
10	Gil McDougald (Box)	60.00	25.00	15.00
11	Cletis Boyer (Box)	6.00	2.50	1.50
12a	Hector Lopez (Box)	12.50	5.00	3.00
12b	Hector Lopez (Company)	7.50	3.00	2.00
13	Bob Cerv (Box)	4.00	1.50	1.00
14	Ryne Duren (Box)	4.00	1.50	1.00
15	Bobby Shantz (Box)	4.00	1.50	1.00
16	Art Ditmar (Box)	4.00	1.50	1.00
17	Jim Coates (Box)	4.00	1.50	1.00
18	John Blanchard (Box)	4.00	1.50	1.00
19a	Luis Aparicio (Box)	7.50	3.00	2.00
19b	Luis Aparicio (Company)	15.00	6.00	4.00
20a	Nelson Fox (Box)	22.50	9.00	5.75
20b	Nelson Fox (Company)	20.00	8.00	5.00
21a	Bill Pierce (Box)	20.00	8.00	5.00
21b	Bill Pierce (Company)	9.00	3.50	2.25
22a	Early Wynn (Box)	17.50	7.00	4.50
22b	Early Wynn (Company)	25.00	10.00	6.25
23	Bob Shaw (Box)	125.00	50.00	30.00
24a	Al Smith (Box)	20.00	8.00	5.00
24b	Al Smith (Company)	17.50	7.00	4.50
25a	Minnie Minoso (Box)	15.00	6.00	4.00
25b	Minnie Minoso (Company)	10.00	4.00	2.50
26a	Roy Sievers (Box)	4.00	1.50	1.00
26b	Roy Sievers (Company)	7.50	3.00	2.00
27a	Jim Landis (Box)	15.00	6.00	3.75
27b	Jim Landis (Company)	7.50	3.00	2.00
28a	Sherman Lollar (Box)	4.00	1.50	1.00
28b	Sherman Lollar (Company)	7.50	3.00	2.00
29	Gerry Staley (Box)	4.00	1.50	1.00
30a	Gene Freese (Box, White Sox.)	4.00	1.50	1.00
30b	Gene Freese (Company, Reds.)	9.00	3.50	2.25
31	Ted Kluszewski (Box)	15.00	6.00	4.00
32	Turk Lown (Box)	4.00	1.50	1.00
33a	Jim Rivera (Box)	4.00	1.50	1.00
33b	Jim Rivera (Company)	7.50	3.00	2.00
34	Frank Baumann (Box)	4.00	1.50	1.00
35a	Al Kaline (Box)	25.00	10.00	6.25
35b	Al Kaline (Company)	30.00	12.00	7.50
36a	Rocky Colavito (Box)	30.00	12.00	7.50
36b	Rocky Colavito (Company)	22.50	9.00	5.75
37a	Charley Maxwell (Box)	20.00	8.00	5.00
37b	Charley Maxwell (Company)	15.00	6.00	3.75
38a	Frank Lary (Box)	4.00	1.50	1.00
38b	Frank Lary (Company)	9.00	3.50	2.00
39a	Jim Bunning (Box)	20.00	8.00	5.00
39b	Jim Bunning (Company)	15.00	6.00	4.00
40a	Norm Cash (Box)	4.00	1.50	1.00
40b	Norm Cash (Company)	12.50	5.00	3.00
41a	Frank Bolling (Box, Tigers.)	15.00	6.00	3.75
41b	Frank Bolling (Company, Braves.)	9.00	3.50	2.00
42a	Don Mossi (Box)	10.00	4.00	2.50
42b	Don Mossi (Company)	9.00	3.50	2.00
43a	Lou Berberet (Box)	10.00	4.00	2.50
43b	Lou Berberet (Company)	9.00	3.50	2.00
44	Dave Sisler (Box)	4.00	1.50	1.00
45	Ed Yost (Box)	4.00	1.50	1.00
46	Pete Burnside (Box)	4.00	1.50	1.00
47a	Pete Runnels (Box)	20.00	8.00	5.00
47b	Pete Runnels (Company)	17.50	7.00	4.50
48a	Frank Malzone (Box)	12.50	5.00	3.00
48b	Frank Malzone (Company)	7.50	3.00	2.00

		NM	EX	VG
49a	Vic Wertz (Box)	15.00	6.00	3.75
49b	Vic Wertz (Company)	20.00	8.00	5.00
50a	Tom Brewer (Box)	4.00	1.50	1.00
50b	Tom Brewer (Company)	7.50	3.00	2.00
51a	Willie Tasby (Box, no sold line.)	7.50	3.00	2.00
51b	Willie Tasby (Company, sold line.)	15.00	6.00	4.00
52a	Russ Nixon (Box)	4.00	1.50	1.00
52b	Russ Nixon (Company)	7.50	3.00	2.00
53a	Don Buddin (Box)	4.00	1.50	1.00
53b	Don Buddin (Company)	7.50	3.00	2.00
54a	Bill Monbouquette (Box)	4.00	1.50	1.00
54b	Bill Monbouquette (Company)	7.50	3.00	2.00
55a	Frank Sullivan (Box, Red Sox.)	4.00	1.50	1.00
55b	Frank Sullivan (Company, Phillies.)	25.00	10.00	6.25
56a	Haywood Sullivan (Box)	4.00	1.50	1.00
56b	Haywood Sullivan (Company)	7.50	3.00	2.00
57a	Harvey Kuenn (Box, Indians.)	25.00	10.00	6.25
57b	Harvey Kuenn (Company, Giants.)	9.00	3.50	2.00
58a	Gary Bell (Box)	7.50	3.00	2.00
58b	Gary Bell (Company)	7.50	3.00	2.00
59a	Jim Perry (Box)	4.00	1.50	1.00
59b	Jim Perry (Company)	7.50	3.00	2.00
60a	Jim Grant (Box)	4.00	1.50	1.00
60b	Jim Grant (Company)	20.00	8.00	5.00
61a	Johnny Temple (Box)	4.00	1.50	1.00
61b	Johnny Temple (Company)	7.50	3.00	2.00
62a	Paul Foytack (Box)	4.00	1.50	1.00
62b	Paul Foytack (Company)	7.50	3.00	2.00
63a	Vic Power (Box)	15.00	6.00	3.75
63b	Vic Power (Company)	7.50	3.00	2.00
64a	Tito Francona (Box)	4.00	1.50	1.00
64b	Tito Francona (Company)	7.50	3.00	2.00
65a	Ken Aspromonte (Box, no sold line.)	9.00	3.50	2.00
65b	Ken Aspromonte (Company, sold line.)	9.00	3.50	2.00
66	Bob Wilson (Box)	4.00	1.50	1.00
67a	John Romano (Box)	4.00	1.50	1.00
67b	John Romano (Company)	7.50	3.00	2.00
68a	Jim Gentile (Box)	4.00	1.50	1.00
68b	Jim Gentile (Company)	9.00	3.50	2.00
69a	Gus Triandos (Box)	4.00	1.50	1.00
69b	Gus Triandos (Company)	9.00	3.50	2.00
70	Gene Woodling (Box)	30.00	12.00	7.50
71a	Milt Pappas (Box)	4.00	1.50	1.00
71b	Milt Pappas (Company)	17.50	7.00	4.50
72a	Ron Hansen (Box)	4.00	1.50	1.00
72b	Ron Hansen (Company)	9.00	3.50	2.00
73	Chuck Estrada (Company)	110.00	45.00	27.50
74a	Steve Barber (Box)	12.00	4.75	3.00
74b	Steve Barber (Company)	9.00	3.50	2.00
75a	Brooks Robinson (Box)	35.00	15.00	9.00
75b	Brooks Robinson (Company)	35.00	15.00	9.00
76a	Jackie Brandt (Box)	4.00	1.50	1.00
76b	Jackie Brandt (Company)	9.00	3.50	2.00
77a	Marv Breeding (Box)	4.00	1.50	1.00
77b	Marv Breedding (Company)	9.00	3.50	2.00
78	Hal Brown (Box)	4.00	1.50	1.00
79	Billy Klaus (Box)	4.00	1.50	1.00
80a	Hoyt Wilhelm (Box)	7.50	3.00	2.00
80b	Hoyt Wilhelm (Company)	12.50	5.00	3.00
81a	Jerry Lumpe (Box)	9.00	3.50	2.00
81b	Jerry Lumpe (Company)	7.50	3.00	2.00
82a	Norm Siebern (Box)	4.00	1.50	1.00
82b	Norm Siebern (Company)	7.50	3.00	2.00
83a	Bud Daley (Box)	15.00	6.00	4.00
83b	Bud Daley (Company)	25.00	10.00	6.25
84a	Bill Tuttle (Box)	4.00	1.50	1.00
84b	Bill Tuttle (Company)	7.50	3.00	2.00
85a	Marv Throneberry (Box)	4.00	1.50	1.00
85b	Marv Throneberry (Company)	7.50	3.00	2.00
86a	Dick Williams (Box)	15.00	6.00	3.75
86b	Dick Williams (Company)	7.50	3.00	2.00
87a	Ray Herbert (Box)	4.00	1.50	1.00
87b	Ray Herbert (Company)	7.50	3.00	2.00
88a	Whitey Herzog (Box)	7.00	3.50	2.00
88b	Whitey Herzog (Company)	12.50	6.25	3.75
89a	Ken Hamlin (Box, no sold line.)	4.00	1.50	1.00
89b	Ken Hamlin (Company, sold line.)	9.00	3.50	2.00
90a	Hank Bauer (Box)	15.00	6.00	3.75
90b	Hank Bauer (Company)	9.00	3.50	2.00
91a	Bob Allison (Box, Minneapolis.)	9.00	3.50	2.00
91b	Bob Allison (Company, Minnesota.)	20.00	8.00	5.00
92a	Harmon Killebrew (Box, Minneapolis.)	50.00	20.00	12.50
92b	Harmon Killebrew (Company, Minnesota.)	60.00	24.00	15.00
93a	Jim Lemon (Box, Minneapolis.)	65.00	25.00	15.00
93b	Jim Lemon (Company, Minnesota.)	30.00	12.00	7.50
94	Chuck Stobbs (Company)	150.00	60.00	35.00
95a	Reno Bertoia (Box, Minneapolis.)	4.00	1.50	1.00
95b	Reno Bertoia (Company, Minnesota.)	20.00	8.00	5.00
96a	Billy Gardner (Box, Minneapolis.)	4.00	1.50	1.00
96b	Billy Gardner (Company, Minnesota.)	20.00	8.00	5.00
97a	Earl Battey (Box, Minneapolis.)	6.00	2.50	1.50
97b	Earl Battey (Company, Minnesota.)	20.00	8.00	5.00
98a	Pedro Ramos (Box, Minneapolis.)	4.00	1.50	1.00
98b	Pedro Ramos (Company, Minnesota.)	20.00	8.00	5.00

		NM	EX	VG
99a	Camilio Pascual (Camilo) (Box, Minneapolis.)	4.00	1.50	1.00
99b	Camilio Pascual (Camilo) (Company, Minnesota.)	20.00	8.00	5.00
100a	Billy Consolo (Box, Minneapolis.)	4.00	1.50	1.00
100b	Billy Consolo (Company, Minnesota.)	22.50	9.00	5.75
101a	Warren Spahn (Box)	35.00	14.00	9.00
101b	Warren Spahn (Company)	25.00	10.00	6.00
102a	Lew Burdette (Box)	4.00	1.50	1.00
102b	Lew Burdette (Company)	7.50	3.00	2.00
103a	Bob Buhl (Box)	4.00	1.50	1.00
103b	Bob Buhl (Company)	12.50	5.00	3.25
104a	Joe Adcock (Box)	12.50	5.00	3.25
104b	Joe Adcock (Company)	7.50	3.00	2.00
105a	John Logan (Box)	6.00	2.50	1.50
105b	John Logan (Company)	15.00	6.00	4.00
106	Ed Mathews (Company)	40.00	16.00	10.00
107a	Hank Aaron (Box)	30.00	12.00	7.50
107b	Hank Aaron (Company)	30.00	12.00	7.50
108a	Wes Covington (Box)	4.00	1.50	1.00
108b	Wes Covington (Company)	7.50	3.00	2.00
109a	Bill Bruton (Box, Braves.)	25.00	10.00	6.25
109b	Bill Bruton (Company, Tigers.)	12.50	5.00	3.00
110a	Del Crandall (Box)	6.00	2.50	1.50
110b	Del Crandall (Company)	7.50	3.00	2.00
111	Red Schoendienst (Box)	12.50	5.00	3.00
112	Juan Pizarro (Box)	4.00	1.50	1.00
113	Chuck Cottier (Box)	15.00	6.00	4.00
114	Al Spangler (Cox)	4.00	1.50	1.00
115a	Dick Farrell (Box)	25.00	10.00	6.25
115b	Dick Farrell (Company)	7.50	3.00	2.00
116a	Jim Owens (Box)	15.00	6.00	3.75
116b	Jim Owens (Company)	7.50	3.00	2.00
117a	Robin Roberts (Box)	12.50	5.00	3.00
117b	Robin Roberts (Company)	12.50	5.00	3.00
118a	Tony Taylor (Box)	4.00	1.50	1.00
118b	Tony Taylor (Company)	7.50	3.00	2.00
119a	Lee Walls (Box)	4.00	1.50	1.00
119b	Lee Walls (Company)	7.50	3.00	2.00
120a	Tony Curry (Box)	4.00	1.50	1.00
120b	Tony Curry (Company)	7.50	3.00	2.00
121a	Pancho Herrera (Box)	4.00	1.50	1.00
121b	Pancho Herrera (Company)	7.50	3.00	2.00
122a	Ken Walters (Box)	4.00	1.50	1.00
122b	Ken Walters (Company)	7.50	3.00	2.00
123a	John Callison (Box)	4.00	1.50	1.00
123b	John Callison (Company)	7.50	3.00	2.00
124a	Gene Conley (Box, Phillies.)	4.00	1.50	1.00
124b	Gene Conley (Company, Red Sox.)	20.00	8.00	5.00
125a	Bob Friend (Box)	5.00	2.00	1.25
125b	Bob Friend (Company)	7.50	3.00	2.00
126a	Vernon Law (Box)	5.00	2.00	1.25
126b	Vernon Law (Company)	7.50	3.00	2.00
127a	Dick Stuart (Box)	4.00	1.50	1.00
127b	Dick Stuart (Company)	7.50	3.00	2.00
128a	Bill Mazeroski (Box)	20.00	8.00	5.00
128b	Bill Mazeroski (Company)	12.50	5.00	3.00
129a	Dick Groat (Box)	4.00	1.50	1.00
129b	Dick Groat (Company)	10.00	4.00	2.50
130a	Don Hoak (Box)	4.00	1.50	1.00
130b	Don Hoak (Company)	7.50	3.00	2.00
131a	Bob Skinner (Box)	4.00	1.50	1.00
131b	Bob Skinner (Company)	7.50	3.00	2.00
132a	Bob Clemente (Box)	50.00	20.00	12.50
132b	Bob Clemente (Company)	70.00	28.00	17.50
133	Roy Face (Box)	15.00	6.00	4.00
134	Harvey Haddix (Box)	10.00	4.00	2.50
135	Bill Virdon (Box)	40.00	16.00	10.00
136a	Gino Cimoli (Box)	4.00	1.50	1.00
136b	Gino Cimoli (Company)	7.50	3.00	2.00
137	Rocky Nelson (Box)	6.00	2.50	1.50
138a	Smoky Burgess (Box)	4.00	1.50	1.00
138b	Smoky Burgess (Company)	7.50	3.00	2.00
139	Hal Smith (Box)	6.00	2.50	1.50
140	Wilmer Mizell (Box)	12.50	4.75	3.00
141a	Mike McCormick (Box)	4.00	1.50	1.00
141b	Mike McCormick (Company)	7.50	3.00	2.00
142a	John Antonelli (Box, Giants.)	4.00	1.50	1.00
142b	John Antonelli (Company, Indians.)	9.00	3.50	2.00
143a	Sam Jones (Box)	5.00	2.00	1.25
143b	Sam Jones (Company)	7.50	3.00	2.00
144a	Orlando Cepeda (Box)	22.50	9.00	5.75
144b	Orlando Cepeda (Company)	12.50	5.00	3.00
145a	Willie Mays (Box)	55.00	22.50	13.50
145b	Willie Mays (Company)	45.00	18.00	10.00
146a	Willie Kirkland (Box, Giants.)	60.00	24.00	15.00
146b	Willie Kirkland (Company, Indians.)	25.00	10.00	6.25
147a	Willie McCovey (Box)	20.00	8.00	5.00
147b	Willie McCovey (Company)	25.00	10.00	6.00
148a	Don Blasingame (Box)	4.00	1.50	1.00
148b	Don Blasingame (Company)	7.50	3.00	2.00
149a	Jim Davenport (Box)	4.00	1.50	1.00
149b	Jim Davenport (Company)	7.50	3.00	2.00
150a	Hobie Landrith (Box)	4.00	1.50	1.00
150b	Hobie Landrith (Company)	7.50	3.00	2.00
151	Bob Schmidt (Box)	9.00	3.50	2.00
152a	Ed Bressoud (Box)	4.00	1.50	1.00
152b	Ed Bressoud (Company)	7.50	3.00	2.00
153a	Andre Rodgers (Box, no traded line.)	9.00	3.50	2.00
153b	Andre Rodgers (Box, traded line.)	4.00	1.50	1.00
154	Jack Sanford (Box)	20.00	8.00	5.00
155	Billy O'Dell (Box)	4.00	1.50	1.00
156a	Norm Larker (Box)	7.50	3.00	2.00
156b	Norm Larker (Company)	7.50	3.00	2.00
157a	Charlie Neal (Box)	4.00	1.50	1.00
157b	Charlie Neal (Company)	7.50	3.00	2.00
158a	Jim Gilliam (Box)	7.50	3.00	2.00
158b	Jim Gilliam (Company)	7.50	3.00	2.00
159a	Wally Moon (Box)	20.00	8.00	5.00
159b	Wally Moon (Company)	12.00	4.75	3.00
160a	Don Drysdale (Box)	20.00	8.00	5.00

		NM	EX	VG
160b	Don Drysdale (Company)	20.00	8.00	5.00
161a	Larry Sherry (Box)	4.00	1.50	1.00
161b	Larry Sherry (Company)	7.50	3.00	2.00
162	Stan Williams (Box)	7.50	3.00	2.00
163	Mel Roach (Box)	55.00	22.50	13.50
164a	Maury Wills (Box)	20.00	8.00	5.00
164b	Maury Wills (Company)	35.00	14.00	9.00
165	Tom Davis (Box)	4.00	1.50	1.00
166a	John Roseboro (Box)	4.00	1.50	1.00
166b	John Roseboro (Company)	7.50	3.00	2.00
167a	Duke Snider (Box)	15.00	6.00	3.75
167b	Duke Snider (Company)	20.00	8.00	5.00
168a	Gil Hodges (Box)	7.50	3.00	2.00
168b	Gil Hodges (Company)	12.50	5.00	3.00
169	John Podres (Box)	4.00	1.50	1.00
170	Ed Roebuck (Box)	4.00	1.50	1.00
171a	Ken Boyer (Box)	15.00	6.00	3.75
171b	Ken Boyer (Company)	7.50	3.00	2.00
172a	Joe Cunningham (Box)	12.50	5.00	3.00
172b	Joe Cunningham (Company)	9.00	3.50	2.00
173a	Daryl Spencer (Box)	4.00	1.50	1.00
173b	Daryl Spencer (Company)	7.50	3.00	2.00
174a	Larry Jackson (Box)	12.50	5.00	3.00
174b	Larry Jackson (Company)	7.50	3.00	2.00
175a	Lindy McDaniel (Box)	7.50	3.00	2.00
175b	Lindy McDaniel (Company)	7.50	3.00	2.00
176a	Bill White (Box)	4.00	1.50	1.00
176b	Bill White (Company)	7.50	3.00	2.00
177a	Alex Grammas (Box)	20.00	8.00	5.00
177b	Alex Grammas (Company)	7.50	3.00	2.00
178a	Curt Flood (Box)	4.00	1.50	1.00
178b	Curt Flood (Company)	12.50	5.00	3.00
179a	Ernie Broglio (Box)	4.00	1.50	1.00
179b	Ernie Broglio (Company)	8.00	3.25	2.00
180a	Hal Smith (Box)	8.00	3.25	2.00
180b	Hal Smith (Company)	12.50	5.00	3.00
181a	Vada Pinson (Box)	20.00	8.00	5.00
181b	Vada Pinson (Company)	7.50	3.00	2.00
182a	Frank Robinson (Box)	30.00	12.00	7.50
182b	Frank Robinson (Company)	35.00	15.00	9.00
183	Roy McMillan (Box)	100.00	40.00	25.00
184a	Bob Purkey (Box)	4.00	1.50	1.00
184b	Bob Purkey (Company)	7.50	3.00	2.00
185a	Ed Kasko (Box)	7.50	3.00	2.00
185b	Ed Kasko (Company)	7.50	3.00	2.00
186a	Gus Bell (Box)	4.00	1.50	1.00
186b	Gus Bell (Company)	7.50	3.00	2.00
187a	Jerry Lynch (Box)	4.00	1.50	1.00
187b	Jerry Lynch (Company)	7.50	3.00	2.00
188a	Ed Bailey (Box)	4.00	1.50	1.00
188b	Ed Bailey (Company)	7.50	3.00	2.00
189a	Jim O'Toole (Box)	4.00	1.50	1.00
189b	Jim O'Toole (Company)	7.50	3.00	2.00
190a	Billy Martin (Box, no sold line.)	6.00	2.50	1.50
190b	Billy Martin (Company, sold line.)	12.50	5.00	3.00
191a	Ernie Banks (Box)	35.00	15.00	9.00
191b	Ernie Banks (Company)	20.00	8.00	5.00
192a	Richie Ashburn (Box)	12.50	5.00	3.00
192b	Richie Ashburn (Company)	22.50	9.00	5.75
193a	Frank Thomas (Box)	100.00	40.00	25.00
193b	Frank Thomas (Company)	40.00	16.00	10.00
194a	Don Cardwell (Box)	6.00	2.50	1.50
194b	Don Cardwell (Company)	7.50	3.00	2.00
195a	George Altman (Box)	15.00	6.00	3.75
195b	George Altman (Company)	7.50	3.00	2.00
196a	Ron Santo (Box)	6.00	2.50	1.50
196b	Ron Santo (Company)	30.00	12.00	7.50
197a	Glen Hobbie (Box)	4.00	1.50	1.00
197b	Glen Hobbie (Company)	7.50	3.00	2.00
198a	Sam Taylor (Box)	4.00	1.50	1.00
198b	Sam Taylor (Company)	7.50	3.00	2.00
199a	Jerry Kindall (Box)	8.00	3.25	2.00
199b	Jerry Kindall (Company)	7.50	3.00	2.00
200a	Don Elston (Box)	12.00	4.75	3.00
200b	Don Elston (Company)	7.50	3.00	2.00

1961 Post Cereal Company Sheets

Via a mail-in offer, sheets of 10 cards from each team could be ordered from the cereal company. Known to collectors as "company" cards, the sheets were issued in a perforated format on cardboard that is somewhat thinner than box-back cards. Sheet cards have perforations on one, two, or three sides, depending on their original placement on the sheet. Because of player movements between the time the box-back cards and sheet cards were printed, some cards are only found on the mail-in sheets, while others could not be obtained via the mail-in offer, and some are shown on the sheets of the "wrong" team.

		NM	EX	VG
	Complete Set (16):	5,250	2,625	1,575
	Common Team:	300.00	150.00	90.00
(1)	Baltimore Orioles	300.00	150.00	90.00
(2)	Boston Red Sox	300.00	150.00	90.00
(3)	Chicago Cubs	300.00	150.00	90.00
(4)	Chicago White Sox	300.00	150.00	90.00
(5)	Cincinnati Reds	300.00	150.00	90.00
(6)	Cleveland Indians	300.00	150.00	90.00
(7)	Detroit Tigers	300.00	150.00	90.00
(8)	Kansas City Athletics	300.00	150.00	90.00
(9)	Los Angeles Dodgers	375.00	185.00	110.00
(10)	Milwaukee Braves	375.00	185.00	110.00
(11)	Minnesota Twins	475.00	235.00	140.00
(12)	New York Yankees	600.00	300.00	180.00
(13)	Philadelphia Phillies	300.00	150.00	90.00
(14)	Pittsburgh Pirates	375.00	185.00	110.00
(15)	San Francisco Giants	375.00	185.00	110.00
(16)	St. Louis Cardinals	300.00	150.00	90.00

1961 Post Cereal Display Pinwheel

Designed for use in grocery stores to promote sales of Post cereal with baseball cards on the back, this display features double-sided, oversize (about 8-1/2" x 6") examples of

nine of the cards arranged in a circle. At center was a cardboard cutout of a youngster and accommodation for an electric motor.

	NM	EX	VG
Complete Display:	6,500	3,750	2,000

Ken Boyer, Lew Burdette, Roy Face, Whitey Ford, Nellie Fox, Jim Gentile, Jim Lemon, Willie Mays, Pete Runnels

1962 Post Cereal

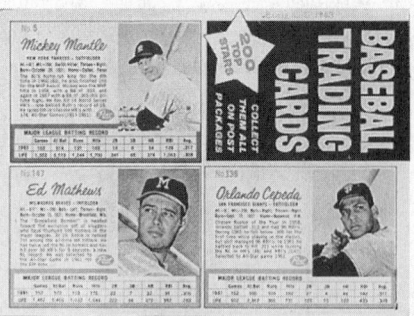

Like the 1961 Post set, there are 200 players pictured in this set of 3-1/2" x 2-1/2" cards. Differences include a Post logo on the card fronts and the player's name in script lettering. Cards are again blank backed and were issued in panels of five to seven cards on cereal boxes. American League players are numbered 1-100 and National League players 101-200. With variations there are 210 cards known. Some of the '62 cards, usually those printed on the backs of less popular brands or sizes, were issued in smaller quantities and sell for more than players of star caliber. The cards of Mickey Mantle and Roger Maris were reproduced in a special two-card panel for a Life magazine insert. The card stock for this insert is slightly thinner, with white margins. The 1962 Post Canadian and Jell-O sets have virtually the same checklist as this set. The complete set price does not include the scarcer variations. The #5 Mickey Mantle card has been extensively counterfeited in recent years by pasting a reproduction of the Life magazine promo card (no lines in the stats area) to a piece of blank cardboard. All genuine cereal-box Mantle cards have a grid of lines in the stats area.

		NM	EX	VG
	Complete Set (200):	1,000	500.00	250.00
	Common Player:	4.00	1.50	1.00
	April 13 Life magazine w/ad panel:	100.00	50.00	25.00
1	Bill Skowron	10.00	4.00	2.50
2	Bobby Richardson	12.50	5.00	3.00
3	Cletis Boyer	7.50	3.00	2.00
4	Tony Kubek	9.00	3.50	2.00
5a	Mickey Mantle (From box, no printing on back.)	70.00	35.00	17.50
5b	Mickey Mantle (From ad, printing on back.)	50.00	25.00	12.50
6a	Roger Maris (From box, no printing on back.)	35.00	14.00	9.00
6b	Roger Maris (From ad, printing on back.)	30.00	12.00	7.50
7	Yogi Berra	27.50	11.00	7.00
8	Elston Howard	20.00	8.00	5.00
9	Whitey Ford	22.50	9.00	6.00
10	Ralph Terry	10.00	4.00	2.50
11	John Blanchard	4.00	1.50	1.00
12	Luis Arroyo	20.00	8.00	5.00
13	Bill Stafford	4.00	1.50	1.00
14a	Norm Cash (Throws: Right)	30.00	12.00	7.50
14b	Norm Cash (Throws: Left)	10.00	4.00	2.50
15	Jake Wood	7.50	3.00	2.00
16	Steve Boros	10.00	4.00	2.50
17	Chico Fernandez	4.00	1.50	1.00
18	Bill Bruton	4.00	1.50	1.00
19	Rocky Colavito	16.00	6.50	4.00
20	Al Kaline	20.00	8.00	5.00
21	Dick Brown	4.00	1.50	1.00
22	Frank Lary	4.00	1.50	1.00
23	Don Mossi	4.00	1.50	1.00
24	Phil Regan	4.00	1.50	1.00
25	Charley Maxwell	7.50	3.00	2.00
26	Jim Bunning	30.00	12.00	7.50

		NM	EX	VG
27a	Jim Gentile (Home: Baltimore)	4.00	1.50	1.00
27b	Jim Gentile (Home: San Lorenzo)	6.00	2.50	1.50
28	Marv Breeding	4.00	1.50	1.00
29	Brooks Robinson	17.50	7.00	4.50
30	Ron Hansen	4.00	1.50	1.00
31	Jackie Brandt	4.00	1.50	1.00
32	Dick Williams	4.00	1.50	1.00
33	Gus Triandos	4.00	1.50	1.00
34	Milt Pappas	7.50	3.00	2.00
35	Hoyt Wilhelm	15.00	6.00	3.50
36	Chuck Estrada	12.50	5.00	3.00
37	Vic Power	4.00	1.50	1.00
38	Johnny Temple	4.00	1.50	1.00
39	Bubba Phillips	4.00	1.50	1.00
40	Tito Francona	9.00	3.50	2.00
41	Willie Kirkland	4.00	1.50	1.00
42	John Romano	4.00	1.50	1.00
43	Jim Perry	4.00	1.50	1.00
44	Woodie Held	4.00	1.50	1.00
45	Chuck Essegian	4.00	1.50	1.00
46	Roy Sievers	4.00	1.50	1.00
47	Nellie Fox	7.50	3.00	2.00
48	Al Smith	4.00	1.50	1.00
49	Luis Aparicio	12.50	5.00	3.25
50	Jim Landis	7.50	3.00	2.00
51	Minnie Minoso	10.00	4.00	2.50
52	Andy Carey	7.50	3.00	2.00
53	Sherman Lollar	4.00	1.50	1.00
54	Bill Pierce	7.50	3.00	2.00
55	Early Wynn	50.00	20.00	12.50
56	Chuck Schilling	7.50	3.00	2.00
57	Pete Runnels	15.00	6.00	3.75
58	Frank Malzone	4.00	1.50	1.00
59	Don Buddin	4.00	1.50	1.00
60	Gary Geiger	25.00	10.00	6.25
61	Carl Yastrzemski	40.00	20.00	10.00
62	Jackie Jensen	7.50	3.00	2.00
63	Jim Pagliaroni	4.00	1.50	1.00
64	Don Schwall	4.00	1.50	1.00
65	Dale Long	4.00	1.50	1.00
66	Chuck Cottier	4.00	1.50	1.00
67	Billy Klaus	9.00	3.50	2.00
68	Coot Veal	9.00	3.50	2.00
69	Marty Keough	60.00	30.00	15.00
70	Willie Tasby	9.00	3.50	2.00
71	Gene Woodling	4.00	1.50	1.00
72	Gene Green	4.00	1.50	1.00
73	Dick Donovan	4.00	1.50	1.00
74	Steve Bilko	4.00	1.50	1.00
75	Rocky Bridges	4.00	1.50	1.00
76	Eddie Yost	4.00	1.50	1.00
77	Leon Wagner	4.00	1.50	1.00
78	Albie Pearson	7.50	3.00	2.00
79	Ken Hunt	4.00	1.50	1.00
80	Earl Averill	4.00	1.50	1.00
81	Ryne Duren	4.00	1.50	1.00
82	Ted Kluszewski	6.00	2.50	1.50
83	Bob Allison	90.00	35.00	20.00
84	Billy Martin	9.00	3.50	2.00
85	Harmon Killebrew	40.00	16.00	10.00
86	Zoilo Versalles	20.00	8.00	5.00
87	Lenny Green	10.00	4.00	2.50
88	Bill Tuttle	4.00	1.50	1.00
89	Jim Lemon	4.00	1.50	1.00
90	Earl Battey	4.00	1.50	1.00
91	Camilo Pascual	4.00	1.50	1.00
92	Norm Siebern	55.00	27.50	13.75
93	Jerry Lumpe	4.00	1.50	1.00
94	Dick Howser	4.00	1.50	1.00
95a	Gene Stephens (Born: Jan. 5)	4.00	1.50	1.00
95b	Gene Stephens (Born: Jan. 20)	20.00	8.00	5.00
96	Leo Posada	4.00	1.50	1.00
97	Joe Pignatano	7.50	3.00	2.00
98	Jim Archer	4.00	1.50	1.00
99	Haywood Sullivan	4.00	1.50	1.00
100	Art Ditmar	6.00	2.50	1.50
101	Gil Hodges	50.00	25.00	12.50
102	Charlie Neal	4.00	1.50	1.00
103	Daryl Spencer	25.00	10.00	6.00
104	Maury Wills	4.00	1.50	1.00
105	Tommy Davis	4.00	1.50	1.00
106	Willie Davis	4.00	1.50	1.00
107	John Roseboro	7.50	3.00	2.00
108	John Podres	4.00	1.50	1.00
109a	Sandy Koufax (Blue lines around stats.)	2,250	1,125	700.00
109b	Sandy Koufax (Red lines around stats.)	30.00	15.00	7.50
110	Don Drysdale	20.00	8.00	5.00
111	Larry Sherry	4.00	1.50	1.00
112	Jim Gilliam	7.50	3.00	2.00
113	Norm Larker	65.00	32.50	16.25
114	Duke Snider	20.00	8.00	5.00
115	Stan Williams	4.00	1.50	1.00
116	Gordy Coleman	55.00	27.50	13.75
117	Don Blasingame	12.50	5.00	3.00
118	Gene Freese	4.00	1.50	1.00
119	Ed Kasko	4.00	1.50	1.00
120	Gus Bell	4.00	1.50	1.00
121	Vada Pinson	7.50	3.00	2.00
122	Frank Robinson	50.00	20.00	12.50
123	Bob Purkey	4.00	1.50	1.00
124a	Joey Jay (Blue lines around stats.)	300.00	150.00	90.00
124b	Joey Jay (Red lines around stats.)	6.00	2.50	1.50
125	Jim Brosnan	45.00	22.50	11.25
126	Jim O'Toole	4.00	1.50	1.00
127	Jerry Lynch	55.00	27.50	13.75
128	Wally Post	4.00	1.50	1.00
129	Ken Hunt	4.00	1.50	1.00
130	Jerry Zimmerman	4.00	1.50	1.00
131	Willie McCovey	55.00	27.50	13.75
132	Jose Pagan	4.00	1.50	1.00
133	Felipe Alou	4.00	1.50	1.00
134	Jim Davenport	4.00	1.50	1.00
135	Harvey Kuenn	4.00	1.50	1.00
136	Orlando Cepeda	15.00	6.00	3.75
137	Ed Bailey	4.00	1.50	1.00
138	Sam Jones	4.00	1.50	1.00
139	Mike McCormick	4.00	1.50	1.00
140	Juan Marichal	55.00	27.50	13.75
141	Jack Sanford	4.00	1.50	1.00
142	Willie Mays	35.00	17.50	8.75
143	Stu Miller (Photo actually Chuck Hiller.)	5.00	2.00	1.25
144	Joe Amalfitano	35.00	14.00	9.00
145a	Joe Adock (Name incorrect.)	65.00	32.50	16.25
145b	Joe Adcock (Name correct.)	4.00	1.50	1.00
146	Frank Bolling	4.00	1.50	1.00
147	Ed Mathews	17.50	7.00	4.50
148	Roy McMillan	4.00	1.50	1.00
149	Hank Aaron	40.00	20.00	10.00
150	Gino Cimoli	4.00	1.50	1.00
151	Frank Thomas	4.00	1.50	1.00
152	Joe Torre	25.00	10.00	6.25
153	Lou Burdette	4.00	1.50	1.00
154	Bob Buhl	10.00	4.00	2.50
155	Carlton Willey	20.00	8.00	5.00
156	Lee Maye	20.00	8.00	5.00
157	Al Spangler	7.50	3.00	2.00
158	Bill White	30.00	15.00	7.50
159	Ken Boyer	6.00	2.50	1.50
160	Joe Cunningham	4.00	1.50	1.00
161	Carl Warwick	4.00	1.50	1.00
162	Carl Sawatski	4.00	1.50	1.00
163	Lindy McDaniel	4.00	1.50	1.00
164	Ernie Broglio	4.00	1.50	1.00
165	Larry Jackson	4.00	1.50	1.00
166	Curt Flood	4.00	1.50	1.00
167	Curt Simmons	4.00	1.50	1.00
168	Alex Grammas	4.00	1.50	1.00
169	Dick Stuart	10.00	4.00	2.50
170	Bill Mazeroski	20.00	8.00	5.00
171	Don Hoak	20.00	8.00	5.00
172	Dick Groat	4.00	1.50	1.00
173a	Roberto Clemente (Blue lines around stats.)	1,500	750.00	450.00
173b	Roberto Clemente (Red lines around stats.)	30.00	15.00	7.50
174	Bob Skinner	4.00	1.50	1.00
175	Bill Virdon	4.00	1.50	1.00
176	Smoky Burgess	9.00	3.50	2.25
177	Elroy Face	4.00	1.50	1.00
178	Bob Friend	4.00	1.50	1.00
179	Vernon Law	4.00	1.50	1.00
180	Harvey Haddix	4.00	1.50	1.00
181	Hal Smith	7.50	3.00	2.00
182	Ed Bouchee	4.00	1.50	1.00
183	Don Zimmer	4.00	1.50	1.00
184	Ron Santo	7.50	3.00	2.00
185	Andre Rodgers	4.00	1.50	1.00
186	Richie Ashburn	12.50	5.00	3.00
187a	George Altman (Last line is "...1955.")	6.00	2.50	1.50
187b	George Altman (Last line is "...1955.")	7.50	3.00	2.00
188	Ernie Banks	17.50	7.00	4.50
189	Sam Taylor	25.00	10.00	6.25
190	Don Elston	7.50	3.00	2.00
191	Jerry Kindall	4.00	1.50	1.00
192	Pancho Herrera	4.00	1.50	1.00
193	Tony Taylor	4.00	1.50	1.00
194	Ruben Amaro	9.00	3.50	2.00
195	Don Demeter	4.00	1.50	1.00
196	Bobby Gene Smith	4.00	1.50	1.00
197	Clay Dalrymple	4.00	1.50	1.00
198	Robin Roberts	10.00	4.00	2.50
199	Art Mahaffey	4.00	1.50	1.00
200	John Buzhardt	4.00	1.50	1.00

1962 Post Cereal - Canadian

This Post set is scarce due to the much more limited distribution in Canada. Most cards were printed on the back of the cereal boxes and contain a full-color player photo with biography and statistics given in both French and English. Card backs are blank. Cards measure 3-1/2" x 2-1/2". This 200-card set is very similar to the Post Cereal cards printed in the United States. The Post logo appears at the upper-left corner in the Canadian issue. Several cards are scarce because of limited distribution and there are two Whitey Ford cards, the corrected version being the most scarce. The complete set price does not include the scarcer variations. Certain cereal brands had the cards packaged inside the box on perforated panels, and will be found with perforated edges on one side or other.

		NM	EX	VG
	Complete Set (200):	5,000	2,005	1,250
	Common Player:	8.00	3.25	2.00
1	Bill Skowron	35.00	14.00	9.00
2	Bobby Richardson	12.00	4.75	3.00
3	Cletis Boyer	10.00	4.00	2.50
4	Tony Kubek	12.00	4.75	3.00
5a	Mickey Mantle (Stats list 153 hits.)	215.00	85.00	55.00
5b	Mickey Mantle (163 hits; first line of bio ends: "4th time in")	120.00	50.00	30.00
5c	Mickey Mantle (163 hits; first line of bio ends: "4th time")	125.00	50.00	30.00
6a	Roger Maris (First line of French bio has large "P" in "Pour les circuits.")	65.00	25.00	15.00
6b	Roger Maris (French text reads, "Residence." Small "p" in "pour.")	55.00	22.50	13.50
6c	Roger Maris (French text reads, "a," not "Residence." Small "p" in "pour.")	55.00	22.50	13.50
7	Yogi Berra	40.00	16.00	10.00
8	Elston Howard	12.00	4.75	3.00
9a	Whitey Ford (Dodgers)	55.00	22.50	13.50
9b	Whitey Ford (Yankees)	80.00	32.00	20.00
10	Ralph Terry	95.00	38.00	24.00
11	John Blanchard	8.00	3.25	2.00
12	Luis Arroyo	8.00	3.25	2.00
13	Bill Stafford	8.00	3.25	2.00
14	Norm Cash	10.00	4.00	2.50
15	Jake Wood	8.00	3.25	2.00
16	Steve Boros	8.00	3.25	2.00
17	Chico Fernandez	8.00	3.25	2.00
18	Bill Bruton	8.00	3.25	2.00
19a	Rocky Colavito (Script name large.)	17.50	7.00	4.50
19b	Rocky Colavito (Script name small.)	17.50	7.00	4.50
20	Al Kaline	85.00	35.00	20.00
21	Dick Brown	12.00	4.75	3.00
22a	Frank Lary ("Residence-Northport, Alabama.")	17.50	7.00	4.50
22b	Frank Lary ("a Northport, Alabama.")	65.00	25.00	15.00
23	Don Mossi	8.00	3.25	2.00
24	Phil Regan	8.00	3.25	2.00
25	Charley Maxwell	8.00	3.25	2.00
26	Jim Bunning	25.00	10.00	6.25
27a	Jim Gentile (French bio begins "Le 8 mai, Jim ...")	13.50	5.50	3.50
27b	Jim Gentile (Begins, "Le 8 mai 1961, Jim ...")	13.50	5.50	3.50
28	Marv Breeding	17.50	7.00	4.50
29	Brooks Robinson	50.00	20.00	12.50
30	Ron Hansen	8.00	3.25	2.00
31	Jackie Brandt	8.00	3.25	2.00
32	Dick Williams	55.00	22.50	13.50
33	Gus Triandos	10.00	4.00	2.50
34	Milt Pappas	10.00	4.00	2.50
35	Hoyt Wilhelm	95.00	38.00	24.00
36	Chuck Estrada	8.00	3.25	2.00
37	Vic Power	8.00	3.25	2.00
38	Johnny Temple	8.00	3.25	2.00
39	Bubba Phillips	55.00	22.50	13.50
40	Tito Francona	55.00	22.50	13.50
41	Willie Kirkland	13.50	5.50	3.50
42	John Romano	13.50	5.50	3.50
43	Jim Perry	10.00	4.00	2.50
44	Woodie Held	8.00	3.25	2.00
45	Chuck Essegian	8.00	3.25	2.00
46	Roy Sievers	40.00	16.00	10.00
47	Nellie Fox	25.00	10.00	6.25
48	Al Smith	8.00	3.25	2.00
49	Luis Aparicio	100.00	40.00	25.00
50	Jim Landis	13.50	5.50	3.50
51	Minnie Minoso	55.00	22.50	13.50
52	Andy Carey	12.00	4.75	3.00
53	Sherman Lollar	8.00	3.25	2.00
54	Bill Pierce	10.00	4.00	2.50
55	Early Wynn	30.00	12.00	7.50
56	Chuck Schilling	10.00	4.00	2.50
57	Pete Runnels	10.00	4.00	2.50
58	Frank Malzone	8.00	3.25	2.00
59	Don Buddin	12.00	4.75	3.00
60	Gary Geiger	8.00	3.25	2.00
61	Carl Yastrzemski	60.00	25.00	15.00
62	Jackie Jensen	40.00	16.00	10.00
63	Jim Pagliaroni	8.00	3.25	2.00
64	Don Schwall	25.00	10.00	6.25
65	Dale Long	20.00	8.00	5.00
66	Chuck Cottier	8.00	3.25	2.00
67	Billy Klaus	8.00	3.25	2.00
68	Coot Veal	8.00	3.25	2.00
69	Marty Keough	8.00	3.25	2.00
70	Willie Tasby	125.00	50.00	30.00
71	Gene Woodling (Photo reversed.)	10.00	4.00	2.50
72	Gene Green	12.00	4.75	3.00
73	Dick Donovan	8.00	3.25	2.00
74	Steve Bilko	13.50	5.50	3.50
75	Rocky Bridges	12.00	4.75	3.00
76	Eddie Yost	8.00	3.25	2.00
77	Leon Wagner	65.00	25.00	15.00
78	Albie Pearson	13.50	5.50	3.50
79	Ken Hunt	8.00	3.25	2.00
80	Earl Averill	8.00	3.25	2.00
81	Ryne Duren	10.00	4.00	2.50
82	Ted Kluszewski	30.00	12.00	7.50
83	Bob Allison	13.50	5.50	3.50
84	Billy Martin	17.50	7.00	4.50
85	Harmon Killebrew	125.00	50.00	30.00
86	Zoilo Versalles	8.00	3.25	2.00
87	Lenny Green	95.00	38.00	24.00
88	Bill Tuttle	8.00	3.25	2.00
89	Jim Lemon	8.00	3.25	2.00
90	Earl Battey	13.50	5.50	3.50
91	Camilo Pascual	10.00	4.00	2.50
92	Norm Siebern	8.00	3.25	2.00
93	Jerry Lumpe	8.00	3.25	2.00
94	Dick Howser	80.00	32.00	20.00
95	Gene Stephens	8.00	3.25	2.00
96	Leo Posada	8.00	3.25	2.00

97	Joe Pignatano	8.00	3.25	2.00
98	Jim Archer	8.00	3.25	2.00
99	Haywood Sullivan	125.00	50.00	30.00
100	Art Ditmar	25.00	10.00	6.25
101	Gil Hodges	35.00	15.00	9.00
102	Charlie Neal	8.00	3.25	2.00
103	Daryl Spencer	8.00	3.25	2.00
104	Maury Wills	17.50	7.00	4.50
105	Tommy Davis	55.00	22.50	13.50
106	Willie Davis	12.00	4.75	3.00
107	John Rosboro (Roseboro)	10.00	4.00	2.50
108	John Podres	10.00	4.00	2.50
109	Sandy Koufax	80.00	32.00	20.00
110	Don Drysdale	35.00	15.00	9.00
111	Larry Sherry	55.00	22.50	13.50
112	Jim Gilliam	55.00	22.50	13.50
113	Norm Larker	8.00	3.25	2.00
114	Duke Snider	30.00	12.00	7.50
115	Stan Williams	13.50	5.50	3.50
116	Gordy Coleman	8.00	3.25	2.00
117	Don Blasingame	160.00	65.00	40.00
118	Gene Freese	40.00	16.00	10.00
119	Ed Kasko	13.50	5.50	3.50
120	Gus Bell	8.00	3.25	2.00
121	Vada Pinson	10.00	4.00	2.50
122	Frank Robinson	50.00	20.00	12.50
123	Bob Purkey	55.00	22.50	13.50
124	Joey Jay	8.00	3.25	2.00
125	Jim Brosnan	17.50	7.00	4.50
126	Jim O'Toole	8.00	3.25	2.00
127	Jerry Lynch	15.00	6.00	3.75
128	Wally Post	135.00	55.00	35.00
129	Ken Hunt	8.00	3.25	2.00
130	Jerry Zimmerman	8.00	3.25	2.00
131	Willie McCovey	40.00	16.00	10.00
132	Jose Pagan	12.00	4.75	3.00
133	Felipe Alou	10.00	4.00	2.50
134	Jim Davenport	8.00	3.25	2.00
135	Harvey Kuenn	10.00	4.00	2.50
136	Orlando Cepeda	25.00	10.00	6.25
137	Ed Bailey	75.00	30.00	18.50
138	Sam Jones	55.00	22.50	13.50
139	Mike McCormick	8.00	3.25	2.00
140	Juan Marichal	35.00	15.00	9.00
141	Jack Sanford	8.00	3.25	2.00
142a	Willie Mays (Big head.)	80.00	32.00	20.00
142b	Willie Mays (Small head.)	60.00	24.00	15.00
143	Stu Miller	8.00	3.25	2.00
144	Joe Amalfitano	100.00	40.00	25.00
145	Joe Adcock	13.50	5.50	3.50
146	Frank Bolling	13.50	5.50	3.50
147	Ed Mathews	30.00	12.00	7.50
148	Roy McMillan	24.00	9.50	6.00
149a	Hank Aaron (Script name large.)	80.00	32.00	20.00
149b	Hank Aaron (Script name small.)	60.00	24.00	15.00
150	Gino Cimoli	8.00	3.25	2.00
151	Frank Thomas	8.00	3.25	2.00
152	Joe Torre	25.00	10.00	6.25
153	Lou Burdette	25.00	10.00	6.25
154	Bob Buhl	10.00	4.00	2.50
155	Carlton Willey	12.00	4.75	3.00
156	Lee Maye	8.00	3.25	2.00
157	Al Spangler	8.00	3.25	2.00
158	Bill White	10.00	4.00	2.50
159	Ken Boyer	40.00	16.00	10.00
160	Joe Cunningham	8.00	3.25	2.00
161	Carl Warwick	55.00	22.50	13.50
162	Carl Sawatski	8.00	3.25	2.00
163	Lindy McDaniel	8.00	3.25	2.00
164	Ernie Broglio	8.00	3.25	2.00
165	Larry Jackson	8.00	3.25	2.00
166	Curt Flood	25.00	10.00	6.25
167	Curt Simmons	17.50	7.00	4.50
168	Alex Grammas	8.00	3.25	2.00
169	Dick Stuart	25.00	10.00	6.25
170	Bill Mazeroski	40.00	16.00	10.00
171	Don Hoak	8.00	3.25	2.00
172	Dick Groat	17.50	7.00	4.50
173	Roberto Clemente	100.00	40.00	25.00
174	Bob Skinner	8.00	3.25	2.00
175	Bill Virdon	10.00	4.00	2.50
176	Smoky Burgess	40.00	16.00	10.00
177	Elroy Face	17.50	7.00	4.50
178	Bob Friend	10.00	4.00	2.50
179	Vernon Law	10.00	4.00	2.50
180	Harvey Haddix	10.00	4.00	2.50
181	Hal Smith	85.00	35.00	20.00
182	Ed Bouchee	100.00	40.00	25.00
183	Don Zimmer	10.00	4.00	2.50
184	Ron Santo	13.50	5.50	3.50
185	Andre Rogers (Rodgers)	8.00	3.25	2.00
186	Richie Ashburn	30.00	12.00	7.50
187	George Altman	8.00	3.25	2.00
188	Ernie Banks	40.00	16.00	10.00
189	Sam Taylor	30.00	12.00	7.50
190	Don Elston	8.00	3.25	2.00
191	Jerry Kindall	8.00	3.25	2.00
192	Pancho Herrera	8.00	3.25	2.00
193	Tony Taylor	8.00	3.25	2.00
194	Ruben Amaro	8.00	3.25	2.00
195	Don Demeter	55.00	22.50	13.50
196	Bobby Gene Smith	8.00	3.25	2.00
197	Clay Dalrymple	8.00	3.25	2.00
198	Robin Roberts	45.00	18.00	11.00
199	Art Mahaffey	8.00	3.25	2.00
200	John Buzhardt	10.00	4.00	2.50

1963 Post Cereal

Another 200-player, 3-1/2" x 2-1/2" set that, with variations, totals more than 205 cards. Numerous color variations also exist due to the different cereal boxes on which the cards were printed. More than any of the other 1960s Post baseball issues, the set is rife with short-prints and other scarcities which make it more difficult to complete than earlier years'

sets. The 1963 Post cards are almost identical to the '63 Jell-O set, which is a slight 1/4" narrower. Cards are blank-backed, with a color player photo, biographies and statistics on the numbered card fronts. No Post logo appears on the '63 cards. The complete set price does not include the scarcer variations. An album to hold the cards was given away at grocery stores in a display featuring Mickey Mantle.

		NM	EX	VG
Complete Set (200):		3,300	1,650	825.00
Common Player:		5.00	2.00	1.25
1	Vic Power	6.00	2.50	1.50
2	Bernie Allen	6.00	2.50	1.50
3	Zoilo Versalles	7.50	3.00	2.00
4	Rich Rollins	5.00	2.00	1.25
5	Harmon Killebrew	25.00	10.00	6.00
6	Lenny Green	30.00	15.00	7.50
7	Bob Allison	9.00	3.50	2.00
8	Earl Battey	12.50	5.00	3.00
9	Camilo Pascual	15.00	6.00	3.50
10a	Jim Kaat (Light pole in background.)	15.00	6.00	3.50
10b	Jim Kaat (No light pole.)	10.00	4.00	2.50
11	Jack Kralick	7.50	3.00	2.00
12	Bill Skowron	15.00	6.00	3.50
13	Bobby Richardson	15.00	6.00	3.50
14	Cletis Boyer	6.00	2.50	1.50
15	Mickey Mantle	300.00	120.00	75.00
16	Roger Maris	115.00	45.00	30.00
17	Yogi Berra	30.00	12.00	7.50
18	Elston Howard	13.50	5.50	3.50
19	Whitey Ford	15.00	6.00	3.50
20	Ralph Terry	6.00	2.50	1.50
21	John Blanchard	10.00	4.00	2.50
22	Bill Stafford	5.00	2.00	1.25
23	Tom Tresh	9.00	3.50	2.00
24	Steve Bilko	15.00	6.00	3.50
25	Bill Moran	5.00	2.00	1.25
26a	Joe Koppe (1962 Avg. is .277)	17.50	7.00	4.50
26b	Joe Koppe (1962 Avg. is .227)	45.00	22.50	11.25
27	Felix Torres	7.50	3.00	2.00
28a	Leon Wagner (Lifetime Avg. is .278.)	15.00	6.00	3.50
28b	Leon Wagner (Lifetime Avg. is .272.)	25.00	10.00	6.00
29	Albie Pearson	5.00	2.00	1.25
30	Lee Thomas (Photo actually George Thomas.)	90.00	45.00	30.00
31	Bob Rodgers	5.00	2.00	1.25
32	Dean Chance	5.00	2.00	1.25
33	Ken McBride	7.50	3.00	2.00
34	George Thomas (Photo actually Lee Thomas.)	9.00	3.50	2.00
35	Joe Cunningham	5.00	2.00	1.25
36a	Nelson Fox (No bat showing.)	30.00	12.00	7.50
36b	Nelson Fox (Part of bat showing.)	25.00	10.00	6.00
37	Luis Aparicio	15.00	6.00	3.75
38	Al Smith	40.00	20.00	10.00
39	Floyd Robinson	175.00	90.00	50.00
40	Jim Landis	5.00	2.00	1.25
41	Charlie Maxwell	5.00	2.00	1.25
42	Sherman Lollar	5.00	2.00	1.25
43	Early Wynn	9.00	3.50	2.00
44	Juan Pizarro	5.00	2.00	1.25
45	Ray Herbert	5.00	2.00	1.25
46	Norm Cash	25.00	10.00	6.25
47	Steve Boros	5.00	2.00	1.25
48	Dick McAuliffe	35.00	15.00	9.00
49	Bill Bruton	12.50	5.00	3.00
50	Rocky Colavito	25.00	10.00	6.25
51	Al Kaline	25.00	10.00	6.25
52	Dick Brown	5.00	2.00	1.25
53	Jim Bunning	95.00	42.50	21.25
54	Hank Aguirre	5.00	2.00	1.25
55	Frank Lary	5.00	2.00	1.25
56	Don Mossi	7.50	3.00	2.00
57	Jim Gentile	9.00	3.50	2.00
58	Jackie Brandt	7.50	3.00	2.00
59	Brooks Robinson	25.00	10.00	6.00
60	Ron Hansen	5.00	2.00	1.25
61	Jerry Adair	275.00	140.00	85.00
62	John (Boog) Powell	15.00	6.00	3.75
63	Russ Snyder	5.00	2.00	1.25
64	Steve Barber	7.50	3.00	2.00

65	Milt Pappas	5.00	2.00	1.25
66	Robin Roberts	10.00	4.00	2.50
67	Tito Francona	5.00	2.00	1.25
68	Jerry Kindall	12.50	5.00	3.00
69	Woodie Held	5.00	2.00	1.25
70	Bubba Phillips	25.00	10.00	6.00
71	Chuck Essegian	5.00	2.00	1.25
72	Willie Kirkland	5.00	2.00	1.25
73	Al Luplow	5.00	2.00	1.25
74	Ty Cline	5.00	2.00	1.25
75	Dick Donovan	5.00	2.00	1.25
76	John Romano	5.00	2.00	1.25
77	Pete Runnels	6.00	2.50	1.50
78	Ed Bressoud	5.00	2.00	1.25
79	Frank Malzone	10.00	4.00	2.50
80	Carl Yastrzemski	325.00	160.00	90.00
81	Gary Geiger	5.00	2.00	1.25
82	Lou Clinton	5.00	2.00	1.25
83	Earl Wilson	7.50	3.00	2.00
84	Bill Monbouquette	5.00	2.00	1.25
85	Norm Siebern	5.00	2.00	1.25
86	Jerry Lumpe	75.00	37.50	18.75
87	Manny Jimenez	75.00	37.50	18.75
88	Gino Cimoli	9.00	3.50	2.00
89	Ed Charles	5.00	2.00	1.25
90	Ed Rakow	5.00	2.00	1.25
91	Bob Del Greco	5.00	2.00	1.25
92	Haywood Sullivan	5.00	2.00	1.25
93	Chuck Hinton	5.00	2.00	1.25
94	Ken Retzer	12.50	5.00	3.00
95	Harry Bright	5.00	2.00	1.25
96	Bob Johnson	7.50	3.00	2.00
97	Dave Stenhouse	20.00	8.00	5.00
98	Chuck Cottier	25.00	10.00	6.25
99	Tom Cheney	7.50	3.00	2.00
100	Claude Osteen	35.00	15.00	9.00
101	Orlando Cepeda	7.50	3.00	2.00
102	Charley Hiller	7.50	3.00	2.00
103	Jose Pagan	5.00	2.00	1.25
104	Jim Davenport	5.00	2.00	1.25
105	Harvey Kuenn	15.00	6.00	3.50
106	Willie Mays	35.00	17.50	8.75
107	Felipe Alou	7.50	3.00	2.00
108	Tom Haller	75.00	37.50	18.75
109	Juan Marichal	10.00	4.00	2.50
110	Jack Sanford	5.00	2.00	1.25
111	Bill O'Dell	5.00	2.00	1.25
112	Willie McCovey	12.50	5.00	3.00
113	Lee Walls	10.00	4.00	2.50
114	Jim Gilliam	15.00	6.00	3.50
115	Maury Wills	17.50	7.00	4.50
116	Ron Fairly	5.00	2.00	1.25
117	Tommy Davis	5.00	2.00	1.25
118	Duke Snider	25.00	10.00	6.25
119	Willie Davis	150.00	75.00	40.00
120	John Roseboro	5.00	2.00	1.25
121	Sandy Koufax	35.00	17.50	8.75
122	Stan Williams	9.00	3.50	2.00
123	Don Drysdale	20.00	8.00	5.00
124a	Daryl Spencer (No arm showing.)	7.50	3.00	2.00
124b	Daryl Spencer (Part of arm showing.)	15.00	6.00	3.50
125	Gordy Coleman	7.50	3.00	2.00
126	Don Blasingame	5.00	2.00	1.25
127	Leo Cardenas	5.00	2.00	1.25
128	Eddie Kasko	150.00	75.00	37.50
129	Jerry Lynch	35.00	15.00	9.75
130	Vada Pinson	15.00	6.00	3.50
131a	Frank Robinson (No stripes on cap.)	30.00	12.00	7.50
131b	Frank Robinson (Stripes on cap.)	115.00	60.00	35.00
132	John Edwards	15.00	6.00	3.50
133	Joey Jay	5.00	2.00	1.25
134	Bob Purkey	5.00	2.00	1.25
135	Marty Keough	15.00	6.00	3.50
136	Jim O'Toole	5.00	2.00	1.25
137	Dick Stuart	7.50	3.00	2.00
138	Bill Mazeroski	12.50	5.00	3.00
139	Dick Groat	6.00	2.50	1.50
140	Don Hoak	25.00	10.00	6.00
141	Bob Skinner	25.00	10.00	6.25
142	Bill Virdon	5.00	2.00	1.25
143	Roberto Clemente	125.00	65.00	40.00
144	Smoky Burgess	15.00	6.00	3.50
145	Bob Friend	5.00	2.00	1.25
146	Al McBean	5.00	2.00	1.25
147	El Roy Face (Elroy)	20.00	8.00	5.00
148	Joe Adcock	13.50	5.50	3.50
149	Frank Bolling	5.00	2.00	1.25
150	Roy McMillan	7.50	3.00	2.00
151	Eddie Mathews	22.50	9.00	5.75
152	Hank Aaron	65.00	35.00	20.00
153	Del Crandall	25.00	10.00	6.25
154a	Bob Shaw (Third sentence has "In 1959" twice.)	10.00	4.00	2.50
154b	Bob Shaw (Third sentence has "In 1959" once.)	9.00	3.50	2.00
155	Lew Burdette	20.00	8.00	5.00
156	Joe Torre	7.50	3.00	2.00
157	Tony Cloninger	5.00	2.00	1.25
158a	Bill White (Ht. 6')	6.00	2.50	1.50
158b	Bill White (Ht. 6'0")	6.00	2.50	1.50
159	Julian Javier	5.00	2.00	1.25
160	Ken Boyer	7.50	3.00	2.00
161	Julio Gotay	5.00	2.00	1.25
162	Curt Flood	85.00	42.50	21.25
163	Charlie James	9.00	3.50	2.00
164	Gene Oliver	5.00	2.00	1.25
165	Ernie Broglio	15.00	6.00	3.50
166	Bob Gibson	45.00	18.00	11.00
167a	Lindy McDaniel (Asterisk before trade line.)	10.00	4.00	2.50
167b	Lindy McDaniel (No asterisk before trade line.)	12.50	5.00	3.25
168	Ray Washburn	5.00	2.00	1.25
169	Ernie Banks	17.50	7.00	4.50

		NM	EX	VG
170	Ron Santo	25.00	10.00	6.25
171	George Altman	7.50	3.00	2.00
172	Billy Williams	235.00	120.00	70.00
173	Andre Rodgers	10.00	4.00	2.50
174	Ken Hubbs	25.00	10.00	6.00
175	Don Landrum	5.00	2.00	1.25
176	Dick Bertell	20.00	8.00	5.00
177	Roy Sievers	7.50	3.00	2.00
178	Tony Taylor	12.50	5.00	3.50
179	John Callison	5.00	2.00	1.25
180	Don Demeter	5.00	2.00	1.25
181	Tony Gonzalez	25.00	10.00	6.25
182	Wes Covington	35.00	15.00	9.00
183	Art Mahaffey	5.00	2.00	1.25
184	Clay Dalrymple	7.50	3.00	2.00
185	Al Spangler	6.00	2.50	1.50
186	Roman Mejias	7.50	3.00	2.00
187	Bob Aspromonte	350.00	175.00	87.50
188	Norm Larker	25.00	10.00	6.00
189	Johnny Temple	7.50	3.00	2.00
190	Carl Warwick	15.00	6.00	3.50
191	Bob Lillis	9.00	3.50	2.00
192	Dick Farrell	5.00	2.00	1.25
193	Gil Hodges	15.00	6.00	3.50
194	Marv Throneberry	7.50	3.00	2.00
195	Charlie Neal	30.00	12.00	7.50
196	Frank Thomas	175.00	87.50	43.75
197	Richie Ashburn	35.00	15.00	9.00
198	Felix Mantilla	10.00	4.00	2.50
199	Rod Kanehl	45.00	22.50	11.25
200	Roger Craig	10.00	4.00	2.50

1963 Post/Jell-O Album

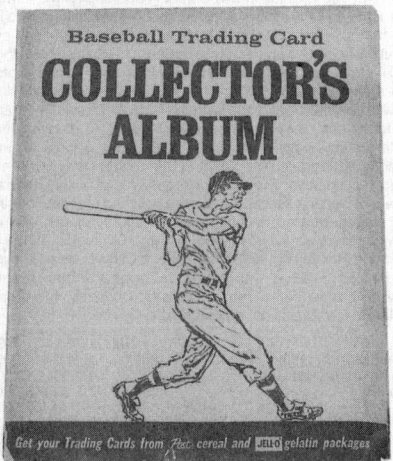

The baseball history and other printed matter in this back are reprinted from the Seattle Post-Intelligencer newspaper. The 2-3/8" x 5" cards are printed in black-and-white on semi-gloss cardboard. Fronts feature a pencil caricature of the player and include major and

The baseball history and other printed matter in this 26-page 8-1/2" x 11" album seems to point to 1963 as the issue date, though 1962 would not be impossible. Each major league team has a page on which the box-back cards from Post cereals and Jell-O could be pasted. The front cover is printed in red-and-white while the interior pages are in black-and-white.

	NM	EX	VG
Post/Jell-O Album	90.00	45.00	25.00

1978 Post Cereal Steve Garvey Baseball Tips

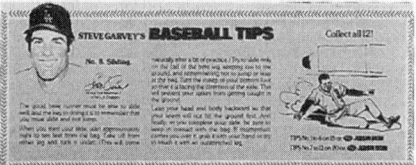

These 7-1/8" x 2-5/8" cut-out panels bordered in red "baseball" stitching were printed on the backs of 15-oz. (#1-6) and 20-oz. (#7-12) packages of Post Raisin Brand cereal. The panels have a green background with black-and-white artwork of a generic player illustrating the tip and a color portrait of Garvey.

		NM	EX	VG
	Complete Set (12):	30.00	15.00	9.00
	Common Panel:	3.00	1.50	.90
1	The Batting Stance	3.00	1.50	.90
2	Bunting	3.00	1.50	.90
3	Rounding First Base	3.00	1.50	.90
4	The Grip in Throwing	3.00	1.50	.90
5	Fielding a Pop-Up	3.00	1.50	.90
6	Proper Fielding Stances	3.00	1.50	.90
7	On-Deck Observation	3.00	1.50	.90
8	Sliding	3.00	1.50	.90
9	Hitting to the Opposite Field	3.00	1.50	.90
10	Throwing From the Outfield	3.00	1.50	.90
11	Mental Preparation for Each Play	3.00	1.50	.90
12	Total Conditioning	3.00	1.50	.90

1978 Post-Intelligencer 1969 Pilot Profiles

This series of cards of the one-year American League team states on its back they are reprinted from the Seattle Post-Intelligencer newspaper. The 2-3/8" x 5" cards are printed in black-and-white on semi-gloss cardboard. Fronts feature a pencil caricature of the player and include major and

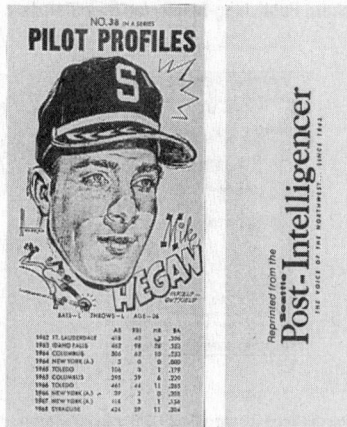

minor league stats. A card number is at top. Backs have the newspaper's ad. The cards were a collectors' issue produced by long-time minor league card maker Frank Caruso, with the paper's permission. The cartoons originally ran in a 3" x 6-3/8" format within the pages of the newspaper and are themselves highly collectible, with values about 2X-3X those of the reprints listed here. Reprint sets were originally sold for $6.

		NM	EX	VG
	Complete Set (39):	100.00	50.00	30.00
	Common Player:	4.00	3.00	1.50
1	Don Mincher	4.00	3.00	1.50
2	Tommy Harper	5.00	2.50	1.50
3	Ray Oyler	4.00	3.00	1.50
4	Jerry McNertney	4.00	3.00	1.50
5	Not Issued	4.00	3.00	1.50
6	Tommy Davis	5.00	2.50	1.50
7	Gary Bell	4.00	3.00	1.50
8	Chico Salmon	4.00	3.00	1.50
9	Jack Aker	4.00	3.00	1.50
10	Rich Rollins	4.00	3.00	1.50
11	Diego Segui	4.00	3.00	1.50
12	Steve Barber	5.00	2.50	1.50
13	Wayne Comer	4.00	3.00	1.50
14	John Kennedy	4.00	3.00	1.50
15	Buzz Stephen	4.00	3.00	1.50
16	Jim Gosger	4.00	3.00	1.50
17	Mike Ferraro	4.00	3.00	1.50
18	Marty Pattin	4.00	3.00	1.50
19	Gerry Schoen	4.00	3.00	1.50
20	Steve Hovely	4.00	3.00	1.50
21	Frank Crosetti	5.00	2.50	1.50
22	Charles Bates	4.00	3.00	1.50
23	Jose Vidal	4.00	3.00	1.50
24	Bob Richmond	4.00	3.00	1.50
25	Lou Piniella	6.00	3.00	1.75
26	John Miklos	4.00	3.00	1.50
27	John Morris	4.00	3.00	1.50
28	Larry Haney	4.00	3.00	1.50
29	Mike Marshall	5.00	2.50	1.50
30	Marv Staehle	4.00	3.00	1.50
31	Gus Gil	4.00	3.00	1.50
32	Sal Maglie	5.00	2.50	1.50
33	Ron Plaza	4.00	3.00	1.50
34	Ed O'Brien	4.00	3.00	1.50
35	Jim Bouton	6.00	3.00	1.75
36	Bill Stafford	4.00	3.00	1.50
37	Darrell Brandon	4.00	3.00	1.50
38	Mike Hegan	4.00	3.00	1.50
39	Dick Baney	4.00	3.00	1.50

1910 Doc Powers Day Postcard

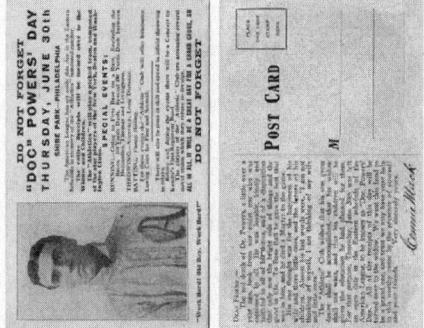

To announce to fans the forthcoming "'Doc' Powers' Day" benefit game, the Philadelphia A's produced this standard-sized (about 5-1/2" x 3-1/2") black-and-white postcard. Front has a photo of the late A's catcher and information about the special events to be held June 30. On back is a message over the facsimile autograph of Connie Mack asking fans to remember the widow and children of their fallen star.

	NM	EX	VG
Doc Powers	750.00	375.00	225.00

1975 Praeger Publishers Ty Cobb

This set was produced by Washington state collector Stephen Mitchell in conjunction with Praeger Publishers of

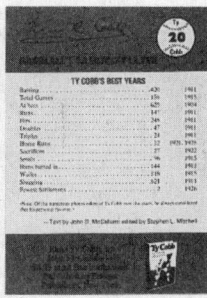

New York to promote the book "Ty Cobb" by John McCallum. Slightly larger than the current 2-1/2" x 3-1/2" standard, the cards featured black-and-white photos on front surrounded by a woodgrain-effect frame and with a plaque at bottom bearing the card title. Backs have an excerpt from the book, an ad for the book and a facsimile autograph. Cards are numbered in a baseball at upper-right. Sets originally sold for $3.25.

		NM	EX	VG
	Complete Set (20):	25.00	12.50	7.50
	Common Card:	2.00	1.00	.60
1	Ty Breaks In	3.00	1.50	.90
2	Four Inches of the Plate	2.00	1.00	.60
3	Slashing into Third	2.00	1.00	.60
4	Inking Another Contract	2.00	1.00	.60
5	Captain Tyrus R. Cobb	2.00	1.00	.60
6	Ty with "The Big Train" (With Walter Johnson.)	4.00	2.00	1.25
7	The End of an Era (With Babe Ruth.)	6.00	3.00	1.75
8	All-Time Centerfielder	2.00	1.00	.60
9	Ty Could "Walk 'em down"	2.00	1.00	.60
10	Menacing Batsman	2.00	1.00	.60
11	With Brother Paul	2.00	1.00	.60
12	Thomas Edison, Cobb Fan	3.00	1.50	.90
13	Ty Tangles with Muggsy McGraw	2.50	1.25	.70
14	Author McCallum with Cy Young	2.00	1.00	.60
15	Speaker - DiMaggio - Cobb	5.00	2.50	1.50
16	Ted Gets a Lesson (With Ted Williams.)	5.00	2.50	1.50
17	Five for Five!	2.00	1.00	.60
18	"I have but one regret ..."	2.00	1.00	.60
19	Excellence: The Cobb Standard	2.00	1.00	.60
20	His Favorite Photo	3.00	1.50	.90

1954 Preferred Products Milwaukee Braves

Sold as a 12-piece set in an envelope marked "Braves Team Autographed Portraits," this portfolio was one of several issued in the team's early years in Milwaukee. The artwork is apparently by Scott Douglas, whose copyright appears on the outer envelope. The same pictures can be found on Preferred Product felt patches and t-shirts. These 8" x 10" portraits are printed in sepia on cream-colored heavy textured paper and feature facsimile autographs. Backs are blank. The unnumbered portraits are checklisted here alphabetically.

		NM	EX	VG
	Complete Set (12):	300.00	150.00	90.00
	Common Player:	25.00	12.50	7.50
(1)	Joe Adcock	25.00	12.50	7.50
(2)	Bill Bruton	25.00	12.50	7.50
(3)	Bob Buhl	25.00	12.50	7.50
(4)	Lew Burdette	25.00	12.50	7.50
(5)	Del Crandall	25.00	12.50	7.50
(6)	Johnny Logan	25.00	12.50	7.50
(7)	Ed Mathews	40.00	20.00	12.00
(8)	Danny O'Connell	25.00	12.50	7.50
(9)	Andy Pafko	25.00	12.50	7.50
(10)	Jim Pendleton	25.00	12.50	7.50
(11)	Warren Spahn	40.00	20.00	12.00
(12)	Bob Thomson	25.00	12.50	7.50

1954 Preferred Products Milwaukee Braves Patches

While they are not so identified, the use of the same portraits and facsimile autographs found on the company's player pictures pinpoint this as a Preferred Products issue, as does a paper tag enclosed in the cellophane wrapper in which the patch was sold. The patches are of heavy felt, with blue or sepia pictures and red "stitching" on the baseball background. At 4-7/8" in diameter, they were intended to be sewn to jackets, etc. While only a handful of players have been confirmed to date, it is possible, even likely, that all 12 of the players from the picture set were also issued in this format.

		NM	EX	VG
Common Player:		175.00	85.00	50.00
(1)	Joe Adcock	175.00	85.00	50.00
(2)	Bill Bruton	175.00	85.00	50.00
(3)	Bob Buhl	175.00	90.00	50.00
(4)	Lew Burdette	175.00	85.00	50.00
(5)	Del Crandall	175.00	85.00	50.00
(6)	Johnny Logan	175.00	85.00	50.00
(7)	Eddie Mathews	225.00	110.00	70.00
(8)	Danny O'Connell	175.00	85.00	50.00
(9)	Andy Pafko	175.00	85.00	50.00
(11)	Warren Spahn	225.00	110.00	70.00

1957-60 Preferred Products Milwaukee Braves

CARL SAWATSKI

Similar in format to the company's 1954 issue, these 8" x 10" portraits are printed in sepia on cream-colored heavy textured paper with player names printed beneath. Backs are blank. The unnumbered portraits are checklisted here alphabetically, but the list may not be complete.

		NM	EX	VG
Common Player:		25.00	12.50	7.50
(1)	Hank Aaron	100.00	50.00	30.00
(2)	Joe Adcock	25.00	12.50	7.50
(3)	Bill Bruton	25.00	12.50	7.50
(4)	Bob Buhl			
(5)	Lew Burdette	25.00	12.50	7.50
(6)	Wes Covington	25.00	12.50	7.50
(7)	Johnny Logan	25.00	12.50	7.50
(8)	Andy Pafko			
(9)	Carl Sawatski	25.00	12.50	7.50
(10)	Red Schoendienst	35.00	17.50	10.50
(11)	Warren Spahn			
(12)	Frank Torre	25.00	12.50	7.50

1950 Prest-O-lite

The attributed date of issue is approximate for this multi-sport promotional postcard issue. Besides the two baseball players, football stars Doak Walker and Leon Hart also exist. The black-and-white, approximately 3-1/2" x 5-1/2" cards on front have a borderless action pose with a salutation and facsimile autograph. The postcard-style divided back has a pre-printed message over the player's facsimile autograph, asking the recipient to view ads for the battery manufacturer in various magazines.

	NM	EX	VG
Tommy Henrich	200.00	100.00	60.00
Ted Williams	400.00	200.00	120.00

1914 Pritchard Publishing Giants/Yankees Stamps

These colorful large-format (about 1-7/8" x 2-5/8") stamps are copyrighted 1914 by Pritchard Publishing Co., New York. All players are N.Y. Giants or Yankees. A similar issue of Yale baseball players is listed in the minor league section. The unnumbered stamps are listed alphabetically by team.

		NM	EX	VG
Common Player:		200.00	100.00	60.00
N.Y. GIANTS				
(1)	Bob Bescher	200.00	100.00	60.00
(2)	George Burns	200.00	100.00	60.00
(3)	Josh Devore	200.00	100.00	60.00
(4)	Larry Doyle	200.00	100.00	60.00
(5)	Art Fletcher	200.00	100.00	60.00
(6)	Christy Mathewson	900.00	450.00	270.00
(7)	Fred Merkle	200.00	100.00	60.00
(8)	Chief Meyers	200.00	100.00	60.00
(9)	Red Murray	200.00	100.00	60.00
(10)	Fred Snodgrass	200.00	100.00	60.00
N.Y. YANKEES				
(1)	Ray Caldwell	200.00	100.00	60.00
(2)	Les Channell	200.00	100.00	60.00
(3)	Roy Hartzell	200.00	100.00	60.00
(4)	Bill Holden	200.00	100.00	60.00
(5)	Fritz Maisel	200.00	100.00	60.00
(6)	Roger Peckinpaugh	200.00	100.00	60.00
(7)	Jeff Sweeney	200.00	100.00	60.00
(8)	Jimmy Walsh	200.00	100.00	60.00
(9)	Harry Williams	200.00	100.00	60.00

1956 Prize Frankies Cleveland Indians

Though the back of the cards says 24 Indians' cards were issued, only one player has ever been seen - and precious few of him. The 2-1/4" x 3-3/8" cards have a black-and-white photo on front with the player's name and number in black in the white border at bottom. Backs have an Indian logo and instructions to redeem complete sets of the cards for a pair of box seats. It is unlikely this alone accounts for the scarcity of the cards. More likely this card was made as a prototype for a promotion that never materialized.

 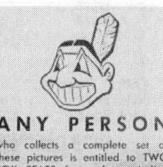

VIC WERTZ - 10

		NM	EX	VG
10	Vic Wertz	600.00	300.00	180.00

1924 Proctor's Theatre Babe Ruth

COMPLIMENTS OF
Mr. F. F. Proctor
TO
BABE RUTH'S
MANY MT. VERNON
FRIENDS

APPEARING AT
PROCTOR'S
MOUNT VERNON
Nov. 3rd-4th-5th

This 1-5/8" x 2-7/8" black-and-white card was issued to promote a vaudeville appearance by Babe Ruth in upstate New York during November 1924. The front has a photo with a facsimile autograph inscribed, "To My Mount Vernon Admirers." Back has details of his appearance.

	NM	EX	VG
Babe Ruth	16,000	8,000	4,800

1946-47 Propagandas Montiel Los Reyes del Deporte

The 180 athletes in this issue of "Sporting Kings" cards are featured in a couple of different styles. Most cards from #1-101 have only the athlete's photo on front, surrounded by a yellow or orange border. Most cards #100-180 also have the card number and player ID on front, with a chest-to-cap photo set a colored frame. All are roughly 2-1/8" x 3-1/8". Backs have biographical data, the issuer's name and, sometimes, an ad for a Cuban novelty store or radio program. Most examples in the hobby today were once pasted in the colorful album accompanying the issue and it is rare to find cards in better than VG condition. The set opens with a run of boxers, then a group of Cuban baseball stars of the past and present, former big league greats and contemporary major leaguers, plus a few wrestlers. Cards #100-180 (except 101) feature players from the Florida International League, a Class B circuit within Organized Baseball with teams in Havana, Miami, Miami Beach, Lakeland and Tampa included. Curiously, the West Palm Beach team is not represented.

		NM	EX	VG
Complete Set (180):		20,000	8,800	4,000
Common Baseball Player:		45.00	20.00	9.00
Album:		300.00	135.00	60.00
1	John L. Sullivan (Boxer)	135.00	60.00	27.50
2	James J. Corbett (Boxer)	85.00	37.50	17.50
3	Bob Fitzsimmons (Boxer)	70.00	30.00	15.00
4	James J. Jeffries (Boxer)	85.00	37.50	17.50
5	Tommy Burns (Boxer)	70.00	30.00	15.00
6	Jack Johnson (Boxer)	90.00	40.00	18.00
7	Jess Willard (Boxer)	75.00	35.00	15.00
8	Jack Dempsey (Boxer)	135.00	60.00	27.50
9	Gene Tunney (Boxer)	75.00	35.00	15.00
10	Max Schmeling (Boxer)	75.00	35.00	15.00
11	Jack Sharkey (Boxer)	70.00	30.00	15.00
12	Primo Carnera (Boxer)	70.00	30.00	15.00
13	Max Baer (Boxer)	70.00	30.00	15.00
14	James J. Braddock (Boxer)	70.00	30.00	15.00
15	Joe Louis (Boxer)	135.00	60.00	27.50
16	Georges Carpentier (Boxer)	70.00	30.00	15.00
17	Tommy Loughran (Boxer)	70.00	30.00	15.00
18	Tony Zale (Boxer)	70.00	30.00	15.00
19	Johnny Dundee (Boxer)	55.00	25.00	10.00
20	Billy Conn (Boxer)	70.00	30.00	15.00
21	Holman Williams (Boxer)	55.00	25.00	10.00
22	Kid Tuncro (Tunero) (Boxer)	55.00	25.00	10.00
23	Lazaro Salazar	300.00	135.00	60.00
24	Napoleon Reyes	120.00	55.00	25.00
25	Roberto Estalella	110.00	50.00	22.50
26	Juan Oliva (Boxer)	55.00	25.00	10.00
27	Gilberto Torres	75.00	35.00	15.00
28	Heberto Blanco	75.00	35.00	15.00
29	Adolfo Luque	375.00	175.00	75.00
30	Luis Galvani (Boxer)	55.00	25.00	10.00
31	Miguel Angel Gonzalez	195.00	90.00	40.00
32	Chuck Klein	110.00	50.00	22.50
33	Joe Legon (Boxer)	55.00	25.00	10.00
34	Carlos Blanco	75.00	35.00	15.00
35	Santos Amaro	225.00	100.00	45.00
36	Kid Chocolate (Boxer)	85.00	37.50	17.50
37	Henry Armstrong (Boxer)	55.00	25.00	10.00
38	Silvio Garcia	300.00	135.00	60.00
39	Martin Dihigo	3,750	1,800	1,150
40	Fermin Guerra	120.00	55.00	25.00
41	Babe Ruth	1,250	560.00	250.00
42	Ty Cobb	1,000	500.00	300.00
43	Alejandro Crespo	75.00	35.00	15.00
44	Ted Williams	2,000	1,000	600.00
45	Jose Maria Fernandez	85.00	37.50	17.50
46	Dom DiMaggio	110.00	50.00	22.50
47	Julio Rojo	75.00	35.00	15.00
48	Armando Marsans	110.00	50.00	22.50
49	Dick Sisler	75.00	35.00	15.00
50	Antonio Rodriguez	75.00	35.00	15.00
51	Joscito Rodriguez	75.00	35.00	15.00
52	Antonio Ordenana	80.00	35.00	15.00
53	Armandito Pi (Boxer)	55.00	25.00	10.00
54	Paul Derringer	75.00	35.00	15.00
55	Bob Feller	185.00	85.00	37.50
56a	Bill Dickey (Photo is Gabby Hartnett.) (Light cap.)	150.00	65.00	30.00
56b	Bill Dickey (Corrected photo.) (Dark cap.)	225.00	100.00	45.00

57	Lou Gehrig	750.00	335.00	150.00
58	Joe DiMaggio	2,250	1,125	675.00
59	Hank Greenberg	165.00	75.00	35.00
60	Red Ruffing	110.00	50.00	22.50
61	Tex Hughson	75.00	35.00	15.00
62	Bucky Walters	75.00	35.00	15.00
63	Stanley Hack	75.00	35.00	15.00
64	Stanley Musial	1,900	1,000	550.00
65	Melvin Ott	135.00	60.00	27.50
66	Dutch Leonard	75.00	35.00	15.00
67	Frank Overmire	75.00	35.00	15.00
68	Mort Cooper	75.00	35.00	15.00
69	Edward Miller	75.00	35.00	15.00
70	Jimmie Foxx	165.00	75.00	35.00
71	Joseph Cronin	110.00	50.00	22.50
72	James Vernon	75.00	35.00	15.00
73	Carl Hubbell	165.00	75.00	35.00
74	Andrew Pafko	75.00	35.00	15.00
75	David Ferris	75.00	35.00	15.00
76	John Mize	110.00	50.00	22.50
77	Spud Chandler	75.00	35.00	15.00
78	Joseph Medwick	110.00	50.00	22.50
79	Christy Mathewson	450.00	200.00	90.00
80	Nelson Potter	75.00	35.00	15.00
81	James Tabor	75.00	35.00	15.00
82	Martin Marion	75.00	35.00	15.00
83	Rip Sewell	75.00	35.00	15.00
84	Philip Cavaretta (Cavarretta)	75.00	35.00	15.00
85	Al Lopez	110.00	50.00	22.50
86	Rudy York	75.00	35.00	15.00
87	Walter Masterson	75.00	35.00	15.00
88	Roger Wolff	75.00	35.00	15.00
89	Jacob Early	75.00	35.00	15.00
90	Oswald Bluege	75.00	35.00	15.00
91	Zoco Godoy (Wrestler)	45.00	20.00	9.00
92	John Kelly Lewis	75.00	35.00	15.00
93	Well Stewart (Wrestler)	45.00	20.00	9.00
94	Bruce Campbell	75.00	35.00	15.00
95	Sherrod Robertson	75.00	35.00	15.00
96	Rose Evans (Wrestler)	45.00	20.00	9.00
97	Maurice "El Angel" Tillet (Wrestler)	45.00	20.00	9.00
98	Nicholas Altrock	75.00	35.00	15.00
99	Helen Willis (Tennis)	70.00	30.00	15.00
100	Borrest Smith	45.00	20.00	9.00
101	Merito Acosta	80.00	35.00	15.00
102	Oscar Rodriguez	45.00	20.00	9.00
103	Octavio Rubert	45.00	20.00	9.00
104	Antonio Lorenzo	45.00	20.00	9.00
105	Agustin del Toro	45.00	20.00	9.00
106	Hector Arago	45.00	20.00	9.00
107	Agustin de la Ville	45.00	20.00	9.00
108	Valeriano (Lilo) Fano	45.00	20.00	9.00
109	Orlando Moreno	45.00	20.00	9.00
110	"Bicho" Dunabeitia	45.00	20.00	9.00
111	Rafael Rivas	45.00	20.00	9.00
112	Jose Traspuestro	45.00	20.00	9.00
113	Mario Diaz	45.00	20.00	9.00
114	Armando Valdes	45.00	20.00	9.00
115	Alberto Matos	45.00	20.00	9.00
116	Humberto Baez	45.00	20.00	9.00
117	Orlando (Tango) Suarez	45.00	20.00	9.00
118	Manuel (Chino) Hidalgo	45.00	20.00	9.00
119	Fernando Rodriguez	45.00	20.00	9.00
120	Jose Cendan	45.00	20.00	9.00
121	Francisco Gallardo	45.00	20.00	9.00
122	Orlando Mejido	45.00	20.00	9.00
123	Julio (Jiqui) Moreno	45.00	20.00	9.00
124	Efrain Vinajcras	45.00	20.00	9.00
125	Luis Suarez	45.00	20.00	9.00
126	Oscar del Calvo	45.00	20.00	9.00
127	Julio Gomez	45.00	20.00	9.00
128	Ernesto Morillas	45.00	20.00	9.00
129	Leonardo Goicochea	45.00	20.00	9.00
130	Max Rosenfeld	300.00	135.00	60.00
131	Oscar Garmendia	45.00	20.00	9.00
132	Fernando Solis	45.00	20.00	9.00
133	Oliverio Ortiz	55.00	25.00	10.00
134	Osmaro Blanco	45.00	20.00	9.00
135	Oral Ratliff	45.00	20.00	9.00
136	Deo Grose	45.00	20.00	9.00
137	Homer Daugherty	45.00	20.00	9.00
138	Frank Matthews	45.00	20.00	9.00
139	Roger LaFrance	45.00	20.00	9.00
140	Harold Cowan	45.00	20.00	9.00
141	Harold Henton	45.00	20.00	9.00
142	Banks McDowell	45.00	20.00	9.00
143	Harold Graham	45.00	20.00	9.00
144	Jack Sweeting	45.00	20.00	9.00
145	Bill Wixted	45.00	20.00	9.00
146	Larry Graham	45.00	20.00	9.00
147	Ralph Brown	45.00	20.00	9.00
148	Felipe Jimenez	45.00	20.00	9.00
149	John Ippolito	45.00	20.00	9.00
150	Joe Benito	45.00	20.00	9.00
151	Bernardo Fernandez	45.00	20.00	9.00
152	Buckey Winkler	45.00	20.00	9.00
153	Carl Armstrong	45.00	20.00	9.00
154	Jack Bearden	45.00	20.00	9.00
155	George Bucci	45.00	20.00	9.00
156	John Pere (Pare)	45.00	20.00	9.00
157	Mickey O'Brien	45.00	20.00	9.00
158	Lamar Murphy	45.00	20.00	9.00
159	Devon Chaptman (Choptman)	45.00	20.00	9.00
160	Hal Johnson	45.00	20.00	9.00
161	"Bitsy" Mott	45.00	20.00	9.00
162	Charles Cuellar	45.00	20.00	9.00
163	Chester Covington	45.00	20.00	9.00
164	Howard Ermisch	45.00	20.00	9.00
165	Bill Lewis	45.00	20.00	9.00
166	Roy Knepper	45.00	20.00	9.00
167	Bull Enos	45.00	20.00	9.00
168	Joe Wilder	45.00	20.00	9.00
169	Jake Baker	45.00	20.00	9.00
170	Joe Bodner	45.00	20.00	9.00
171	Jackie Myer	45.00	20.00	9.00
172	Mel Fisher	45.00	20.00	9.00
173	Larry Baldwin	45.00	20.00	9.00

174	Richard Farkas	45.00	20.00	9.00
175	Alston McGahgin	45.00	20.00	9.00
176	Ray Weiss	45.00	20.00	9.00
177	Paul Waner	400.00	180.00	80.00
178	Frank Miller	45.00	20.00	9.00
179	John Sabatie	45.00	20.00	9.00
180	John Maire	45.00	20.00	9.00

1966 Pro's Pizza Chicago Cubs

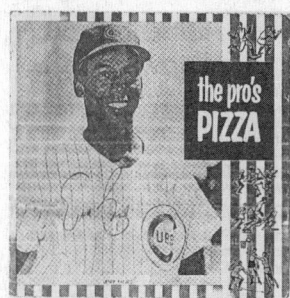

These black-and-white player cards were printed on boxes in which individual-serving pizzas were sold, reportedly only at Wrigley Field. The panel measures 6" x 6" and has a black-and-white player photo at left, with his name in a white strip at bottom. At right are drawn sports action scenes and toward the top is a black box with "the pro's PIZZA" in white. The backs are blank. The unnumbered pieces are listed here alphabetically. The example pictured was autographed by the player, no facsimile signature was printed originally.

		NM	EX	VG
Complete Set (16):		3,250	1,600	975.00
Common Player:		160.00	80.00	50.00
(1)	Ted Abernathy	160.00	80.00	50.00
(2)	Joe Amalfitano	160.00	80.00	50.00
(3)	George Altman	160.00	80.00	50.00
(4)	Ernie Banks	650.00	325.00	200.00
(5)	Ernie Broglio	160.00	80.00	50.00
(6)	Billy Connors	160.00	80.00	50.00
(7)	Dick Ellsworth	160.00	80.00	50.00
(8)	Bill Faul	160.00	80.00	50.00
(9)	Bill Hoeft	160.00	80.00	50.00
(10)	Ken Holtzman	160.00	80.00	50.00
(11)	Randy Hundley	160.00	80.00	50.00
(12)	Ferguson Jenkins	325.00	160.00	100.00
(13)	Chris Krug	160.00	80.00	50.00
(14)	Ron Santo	245.00	120.00	75.00
(15)	Carl Warwick	160.00	80.00	50.00
(16)	Billy Williams	400.00	200.00	120.00

1967 Pro's Pizza - B & W

For a second year, Chicago players - Cubs and White Sox - were featured on boxes of individual-serving pizza reportedly sold only at the ballparks. The panel on which the player photos (black-and-white) are printed measures 4-3/4" x 5-3/4" and is similar in design to the 1966 issue, except there is a vertical perforation allowing most of the player photo to be torn away in a 3-1/16" x 5-3/4" size. Cards are unnumbered and listed here alphabetically. Values are for unseparated panels. Those separated at the perforation line are worth 60-75%.

		NM	EX	VG
Complete Set (10):		1,500	750.00	450.00
Common Player:		125.00	65.00	35.00
(1)	Ernie Banks	325.00	160.00	100.00
(2)	Glenn Beckert	125.00	65.00	35.00
(3)	Byron Browne	125.00	65.00	35.00
(4)	Don Buford	125.00	65.00	35.00
(5)	Joel Horlen	125.00	65.00	35.00
(6)	Randy Hundley	125.00	65.00	35.00
(7)	Don Kessinger	125.00	65.00	35.00
(8)	Gary Peters	125.00	65.00	35.00
(9)	Ron Santo	175.00	85.00	50.00
(10)	Billy Williams	200.00	100.00	60.00

1967 Pro's Pizza - Color

Only Chicago Cubs are included in this set of cards printed on the top of individual serving pizza boxes, reportedly sold only at Wrigley Field. The color player poses are printed in a 4-3/4" diameter circle on top of the box, with the player's name in a white panel at bottom. The player's name was also printed in large black letters on one side of the box. Values shown here for the unnumbered cards are for the complete box top. A similar issue of Chicago Bears players was also produced.

		NM	EX	VG
Complete Set (12):		5,000	2,500	1,500
Common Player:		400.00	200.00	120.00
(1)	Joe Amalfitano	400.00	200.00	120.00
(2)	Ernie Banks	1,100	550.00	330.00
(3)	Glenn Beckert	400.00	200.00	120.00
(4)	John Boccabella	400.00	200.00	120.00
(5)	Bill Hands	400.00	200.00	120.00
(6)	Ken Holtzman	400.00	200.00	120.00
(7)	Randy Hundley	400.00	200.00	120.00
(8)	Ferguson Jenkins	675.00	335.00	200.00
(9)	Don Kessinger	400.00	200.00	120.00
(10)	Adolfo Phillips	400.00	200.00	120.00
(11)	Ron Santo	600.00	300.00	180.00
(12)	Billy Williams	850.00	425.00	255.00

1972 Pro Star Promotions

This set of postcard-sized (3-1/2" x 5-1/2") color photo-cards features players from 14 major league teams, with a heavy emphasis on Montreal Expos. Uniforms in the photos have had team logos removed. Cards have a facsimile autograph on front. In the white border at bottom is the player name, league, copyright notice and "Printed in Canada." The unnumbered cards are checklisted here in alphabetical order.

		NM	EX	VG
Complete Set (40):		275.00	135.00	85.00
Common Player:		3.00	1.50	.90
(1)	Hank Aaron	17.50	8.75	5.25
(2)	Bob Bailey	3.00	1.50	.90
(3)	Johnny Bench	12.50	6.25	3.75
(4)	Vida Blue	3.00	1.50	.90
(5)	John Boccabella	3.00	1.50	.90
(6)	Roberto Clemente	20.00	10.00	6.00
(7)	Boots Day	3.00	1.50	.90
(8)	Jim Fairey	3.00	1.50	.90
(9)	Tim Foli	3.00	1.50	.90
(10)	Ron Hunt	3.00	1.50	.90
(11)	Catfish Hunter	7.50	3.75	2.25
(12)	Reggie Jackson	15.00	7.50	4.50
(13)	Fergy Jenkins	10.00	5.00	3.00
(14)	Mike Jorgensen	3.00	1.50	.90
(15)	Al Kaline	12.50	6.25	3.75
(16)	Harmon Killebrew	12.50	6.25	3.75
(17)	Mickey Lolich	3.00	1.50	.90
(18)	Juan Marichal	7.50	3.75	2.25
(19)	Willie Mays	17.50	8.75	5.25
(20)	Willie McCovey	10.00	5.00	3.00
(21)	Ernie McAnally	3.00	1.50	.90
(22)	Dave McNally	3.00	1.50	.90
(23)	Bill Melton	3.00	1.50	.90
(24)	Carl Morton	3.00	1.50	.90
(25)	Bobby Murcer	3.00	1.50	.90
(26)	Fritz Peterson	3.00	1.50	.90
(27)	Boog Powell	6.00	3.00	1.75
(28)	Steve Renko	3.00	1.50	.90
(29)	Merv Rettenmund	3.00	1.50	.90
(30)	Brooks Robinson	12.50	6.25	3.75
(31)	Frank Robinson	12.50	6.25	3.75
(32)	Pete Rose	17.50	8.75	5.25
(33)	Tom Seaver	12.50	6.25	3.75
(34)	Ken Singleton	3.00	1.50	.90
(35)	Willie Stargell	10.00	5.00	3.00
(36)	Bill Stoneman	3.00	1.50	.90
(37)	Joe Torre	6.00	3.00	1.75
(38)	Checklist - American League	1.50	.70	.45
(39)	Checklist - National League	1.50	.70	.45
(40)	Checklist - Montreal Expos	1.50	.70	.45

1971 Pro Stars Publications Montreal Expos

Posed action photos of the Expos are featured on this postcard-size (3-1/2" x 5-1/2") issue. The color photos are surrounded by a white border and have a facsimile autograph.

Printed in the bottom border is, "Copyright Pro Stars Publications 1971 Printed in Canada." Backs are blank. The unnumbered cards are checklisted here in alphabetical order.

		NM	EX	VG
	Complete Set (28):	175.00	85.00	50.00
	Common Player:	6.00	3.00	1.80
(1)	Bob Bailey	6.00	3.00	1.80
(2)	John Bateman	6.00	3.00	1.80
(3)	John Boccabella	6.00	3.00	1.80
(4)	Ron Brand	6.00	3.00	1.80
(5)	Boots Day	6.00	3.00	1.80
(6)	Jim Fairey	6.00	3.00	1.80
(7)	Ron Fairly	7.50	3.75	2.25
(8)	Jim Gosger	6.00	3.00	1.80
(9)	Don Hahn	6.00	3.00	1.80
(10)	Ron Hunt	6.00	3.00	1.80
(11)	Mack Jones	6.00	3.00	1.80
(12)	Coco Laboy	6.00	3.00	1.80
(13)	Mike Marshall	7.50	3.75	2.25
(14)	Clyde Mashore	6.00	3.00	1.80
(15)	Gene Mauch	7.50	3.75	2.25
(16)	Dan McGinn	6.00	3.00	1.80
(17)	Carl Morton	6.00	3.00	1.80
(18)	John O'Donoghue	6.00	3.00	1.80
(19)	Adolfo Phillips	6.00	3.00	1.80
(20)	Claude Raymond	6.00	3.00	1.80
(21)	Howie Reed	6.00	3.00	1.80
(22)	Steve Renko	6.00	3.00	1.80
(23)	Rusty Staub	10.00	5.00	3.00
(24)	Bill Stoneman	6.00	3.00	1.80
(25)	John Strohmayer	6.00	3.00	1.80
(26)	Gary Sutherland	6.00	3.00	1.80
(27)	Mike Wegener	6.00	3.00	1.80
(28)	Bobby Wine	6.00	3.00	1.80

1950s Publix Markets

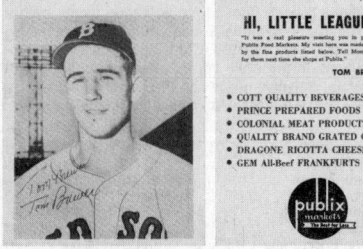

"HI, LITTLE LEAGUERS"

"It was a real pleasure meeting you in person at Publix Food Markets. My visit here was made possible by the fine products listed below. Tell Mom to look for them next time she shops at Publix."

TOM BREWER

• COTT QUALITY BEVERAGES
• PRINCE PREPARED FOODS
• COLONIAL MEAT PRODUCTS
• QUALITY BRAND GRATED CHEESE
• DRAGONE RICOTTA CHEESE
• GEM All-Beef FRANKFURTS

publix markets

It is not known whether this is a one-card set or whether similar cards exist for other players. Without information on other subjects it is impossible to date the issue more precisely. The black-and-white card is printed on thin, semi-gloss cardboard in 4" x 4-3/4" format. The front has a facsimile autograph. The back has a message to Little Leaguers from the Red Sox pitcher and a list of sponsors, along with the Publix logo.

	NM	EX	VG
Tom Brewer	150.00	75.00	45.00

1972 Puerto Rican League Stickers

BASEBALL
DE PUERTO RICO

64

MIKE SCHMIDT

Jardinero corto y tercera base. Tira y batea a la derecha. Bateó para .267 con 9 cuadrangulares y 24 carreras empujadas en la pasada temporada. Pertenece a los Phillies de Philadelphia.

Ediciones EYA   Printed in Spain

Often mistakenly called "minor league" cards, this issue consists of 231 ungummed stickers pertinent to the Puerto Rican winter baseball league. A colorful album was available in which to paste the stickers, though obviously stickers that have evidence of glue or torn paper have little collector value. Besides individual player photos, there are stickers of "old-timers" and groups of stickers which make up composite photos

of all-star teams and of the island's god of baseball, Roberto Clemente. Team emblem stickers are also included. Many big league stars who were either beginning or ending their pro careers can be found in the set, including some current and future Hall of Famers. Stickers have color photos on the front, with backs printed in Spanish. They measure 2-1/4" x 3".

		NM	EX	VG
	Complete Set (231):	1,000	500.00	300.00
	Complete Set in Album:	1,200	600.00	350.00
	Common Player:	5.00	2.50	1.50
	Album:	200.00	100.00	60.00
	Unopened Pack:	50.00		
1	Santurce All-Star Team Composite Photo	10.00	5.00	3.00
2	Santurce All-Star Team Composite Photo	10.00	5.00	3.00
3	Santurce All-Star Team Composite Photo	10.00	5.00	3.00
4	Santurce All-Star Team Composite Photo	10.00	5.00	3.00
5	Santurce All-Star Team Composite Photo	10.00	5.00	3.00
6	Santurce All-Star Team Composite Photo	10.00	5.00	3.00
7	Santurce All-Star Team Composite Photo	10.00	5.00	3.00
8	Santurce All-Star Team Composite Photo	10.00	5.00	3.00
9	Santurce All-Star Team Composite Photo	10.00	5.00	3.00
10	Ponce All-Star Team Composite Photo	10.00	5.00	3.00
11	Ponce All-Star Team Composite Photo	10.00	5.00	3.00
12	Ponce All-Star Team Composite Photo	10.00	5.00	3.00
13	Ponce All-Star Team Composite Photo	10.00	5.00	3.00
14	Ponce All-Star Team Composite Photo	10.00	5.00	3.00
15	Ponce All-Star Team Composite Photo	10.00	5.00	3.00
16	Ponce All-Star Team Composite Photo	10.00	5.00	3.00
17	Ponce All-Star Team Composite Photo	10.00	5.00	3.00
18	Ponce All-Star Team Composite Photo	10.00	5.00	3.00
19	Arecibo Team Emblem	5.00	2.50	1.50
20	Caguas-Guayana Team Emblem	5.00	2.50	1.50
21	Mayaguez Team Emblem	5.00	2.50	1.50
22	Ponce Team Emblem	5.00	2.50	1.50
23	San Juan Team Emblem	5.00	2.50	1.50
24	Santurce Team Emblem	5.00	2.50	1.50
25	Steve Boros	5.00	2.50	1.50
26	Luis Isaac	5.00	2.50	1.50
27	Emmanuel Toledo	5.00	2.50	1.50
28	Gregorio Perez	5.00	2.50	1.50
29	Rosario Llanos	5.00	2.50	1.50
30	Jose Geigel	5.00	2.50	1.50
31	Eduardo Figueroa	5.00	2.50	1.50
32	Julian Muniz	5.00	2.50	1.50
33	Fernando Gonzalez	5.00	2.50	1.50
34	Bennie Ayala	5.00	2.50	1.50
35	Miguel Villaran	5.00	2.50	1.50
36	Efrain Vazquez	5.00	2.50	1.50
37	Ramon Ariles	5.00	2.50	1.50
38	Angel Alcaraz	5.00	2.50	1.50
39	Henry Cruz	5.00	2.50	1.50
40	Jose Silva	5.00	2.50	1.50
41	Jose Alcaide	5.00	2.50	1.50
42	Pepe Mangual	5.00	2.50	1.50
43	Mike Jackson	5.00	2.50	1.50
44	Lynn McGlothen	5.00	2.50	1.50
45	Frank Ortenzio	5.00	2.50	1.50
46	Norm Angelini	5.00	2.50	1.50
47	Richard Coggins	5.00	2.50	1.50
48	Lance Clemons	5.00	2.50	1.50
49	Mike Kelleher	5.00	2.50	1.50
50	Ken Wright	5.00	2.50	1.50
51	Buck Martinez	5.00	2.50	1.50
52	Billy De Mars	5.00	2.50	1.50
53	Elwood Huyke	5.00	2.50	1.50
54	Pedro Garcia	5.00	2.50	1.50
55	Bob Boone	15.00	7.50	4.50
56	Jose Laboy	5.00	2.50	1.50
57	Eduardo Rodriguez	5.00	2.50	1.50
58	Jesus Hernaiz	5.00	2.50	1.50
59	Joaquin Quintana	5.00	2.50	1.50
60	Domingo Figueroa	5.00	2.50	1.50
61	Juan Lopez	5.00	2.50	1.50
62	Luis Alvarado	5.00	2.50	1.50
63	Otoniel Velez	5.00	2.50	1.50
64	Mike Schmidt	400.00	200.00	120.00
65	Felix Millan	5.00	2.50	1.50
66	Guillermo Montanez	5.00	2.50	1.50
67	Ivan de Jesus	7.50	3.75	2.25
68	Sixto Lezcano	5.00	2.50	1.50
69	Jerry Morales	5.00	2.50	1.50
70	Bombo Rivera	5.00	2.50	1.50
71	Mike Ondina	5.00	2.50	1.50
72	Grant Jackson	5.00	2.50	1.50
73	Roger Freed	5.00	2.50	1.50
74	Steve Rogers	5.00	2.50	1.50
75	Mac Scarce	5.00	2.50	1.50
76	Mike Jorgensen	5.00	2.50	1.50
77	Jerry Crider	5.00	2.50	1.50
78	Fred Beene	5.00	2.50	1.50
79	Carl Ermer	5.00	2.50	1.50
80	Luis Marquez	5.00	2.50	1.50
81	Hector Valle	5.00	2.50	1.50
82	Ramon Vega	5.00	2.50	1.50
83	Cirito Cruz	5.00	2.50	1.50
84	Fernando Vega	5.00	2.50	1.50
85	Porfiro Sanchez	5.00	2.50	1.50
86	Jose Sevillano	5.00	2.50	1.50
87	Felix Roque	5.00	2.50	1.50
88	Enrique Rivera	5.00	2.50	1.50
89	Wildredo Rios	5.00	2.50	1.50
90	Javier Andino	5.00	2.50	1.50
91	Milton Ramirez	5.00	2.50	1.50
92	Max Oliveras	5.00	2.50	1.50
93	Jose Calero	5.00	2.50	1.50
94	Esteban Vazquez	5.00	2.50	1.50
95	Hector Cruz	5.00	2.50	1.50
96	Felix Arce	5.00	2.50	1.50
97	Gilberto Rivera	5.00	2.50	1.50
98	Rafael Rodriguez	5.00	2.50	1.50
99	Julio Gonzalez	5.00	2.50	1.50
100	Rosendo Cedeno	5.00	2.50	1.50
101	Pedro Cintron	5.00	2.50	1.50
102	Osvaldo Ortiz	5.00	2.50	1.50
103	Frank Verdi	5.00	2.50	1.50
104	Carlos Santiago	5.00	2.50	1.50
105	Ramon Conde	5.00	2.50	1.50
106	Pat Corrales	5.00	2.50	1.50
107	Jose Morales	5.00	2.50	1.50
108	Jack Whillock	5.00	2.50	1.50
109	Raul Mercado	5.00	2.50	1.50
110	Bonifacio Aponte	5.00	2.50	1.50
111	Angel Alicea	5.00	2.50	1.50
112	Santos Alomar	10.00	5.00	3.00
113	Francisco Libran	5.00	2.50	1.50
114	Edwin Pacheco	5.00	2.50	1.50
115	Luis Gonzalez	5.00	2.50	1.50
116	Juan Rios	5.00	2.50	1.50
117	Jorge Roque	5.00	2.50	1.50
118	Carlos Velez	5.00	2.50	1.50
119	David Gonzalez	5.00	2.50	1.50
120	Jose Cruz	7.50	3.75	2.25
121	Luis Melendez	5.00	2.50	1.50
122	Jose Ortiz	5.00	2.50	1.50
123	David Rosello	5.00	2.50	1.50
124	Juan Veintidos	5.00	2.50	1.50
125	Arnaldo Nazario	5.00	2.50	1.50
126	Dave Lemonds	5.00	2.50	1.50
127	Jim Magnuson	5.00	2.50	1.50
128	Tom Kelley	7.50	3.75	2.25
129	Chris Zachary	5.00	2.50	1.50
130	Hal Breeden	5.00	2.50	1.50
131	Jackie Hernandez	5.00	2.50	1.50
132	Rick Gossage	30.00	15.00	9.00
133	Frank Luchessi	5.00	2.50	1.50
134	Nino Escalera	5.00	2.50	1.50
135	Julio Navarro	5.00	2.50	1.50
136	Manny Sanguillen	15.00	7.50	4.50
137	Bob Johnson	5.00	2.50	1.50
138	Chuck Coggins	5.00	2.50	1.50
139	Orlando Gomez	5.00	2.50	1.50
140	William Melendez	5.00	2.50	1.50
141	Jose Del Moral	5.00	2.50	1.50
142	Jacinto Camacho	5.00	2.50	1.50
143	Emiliano Rivera	5.00	2.50	1.50
144	Luis Peraza	5.00	2.50	1.50
145	Carlos Velazquez	5.00	2.50	1.50
146	Luis Raul Garcia	5.00	2.50	1.50
147	Eliseo Rodriguez	5.00	2.50	1.50
148	Santiago Rosario	5.00	2.50	1.50
149	Ruben Castillo	5.00	2.50	1.50
150	Sergio Ferrer	5.00	2.50	1.50
151	Jose Pagan	5.00	2.50	1.50
152	Raul Colon	5.00	2.50	1.50
153	Robert Rauch	5.00	2.50	1.50
154	Luis Rosado	5.00	2.50	1.50
155	Francisco Lopez	5.00	2.50	1.50
156	Richard Zisk	5.00	2.50	1.50
157	Orlando Alvarez	5.00	2.50	1.50
158	Jaime Rosario	5.00	2.50	1.50
159	Rosendo Torres	5.00	2.50	1.50
160	Jim McKee	5.00	2.50	1.50
161	Mike Nagy	5.00	2.50	1.50
162	Brent Strom	5.00	2.50	1.50
163	Tom Walker	5.00	2.50	1.50
164	Angel Davila	5.00	2.50	1.50
165	Jose Cruz	5.00	2.50	1.50
166	Frank Robinson	25.00	12.50	7.50
167	German Rivera	5.00	2.50	1.50
168	Reinaldo Oliver	5.00	2.50	1.50
169	Geraldo Rodriguez	5.00	2.50	1.50
170	Elrod Hendricks	5.00	2.50	1.50
171	Gilberto Flores	5.00	2.50	1.50
172	Ruben Gomez	5.00	2.50	1.50
173	Juan Pizarro	5.00	2.50	1.50
174	William De Jesus	5.00	2.50	1.50
175	Rogelio Morel	5.00	2.50	1.50
176	Victor Agosto	5.00	2.50	1.50
177	Esteban Texidor	5.00	2.50	1.50
178	Ramon Hernandez	5.00	2.50	1.50
179	Gilberto Rondon Olivo	5.00	2.50	1.50
180	Juan Beniquez	5.00	2.50	1.50
181	Arturo Miranda	5.00	2.50	1.50
182	Manuel Ruiz	5.00	2.50	1.50
183	Julio Gotay	5.00	2.50	1.50
184	Arsenio Rodriguez	5.00	2.50	1.50
185	Luis Delgado	5.00	2.50	1.50
186	Jorge Rivera	5.00	2.50	1.50
187	Willie Crawford	5.00	2.50	1.50
188	Angel Mangual	5.00	2.50	1.50
189	Mike Strahler	5.00	2.50	1.50
190	Doyle Alexander	5.00	2.50	1.50
191	Bob Reynolds	5.00	2.50	1.50
192	Ron Cey	7.50	3.75	2.25
193	Jerr Da Vanon	5.00	2.50	1.50
194	Don Baylor	12.50	6.25	3.75
195	Tony Perez	25.00	12.50	7.50
196	Lloyd Allen	5.00	2.50	1.50
197	Orlando Cepeda	20.00	10.00	6.00
198	Roberto Clemente Composite Photo	15.00	7.50	4.50
199	Roberto Clemente Composite Photo	15.00	7.50	4.50
200	Roberto Clemente Composite Photo	15.00	7.50	4.50

		NM	EX	VG
201	Roberto Clemente Composite Photo	15.00	7.50	4.50
202	Roberto Clemente Composite Photo	15.00	7.50	4.50
203	Roberto Clemente Composite Photo	15.00	7.50	4.50
204	Roberto Clemente Composite Photo	15.00	7.50	4.50
205	Roberto Clemente Composite Photo	15.00	7.50	4.50
206	Roberto Clemente Composite Photo	15.00	7.50	4.50
207	Jaime Almendro	5.00	2.50	1.50
208	Jose R. Santiago	5.00	2.50	1.50
209	Luis Cabrera	5.00	2.50	1.50
210	Jorge Tirado	5.00	2.50	1.50
211	Radames Lopez	5.00	2.50	1.50
212	Juan Vargas	5.00	2.50	1.50
213	Francisco Coimbre	5.00	2.50	1.50
214	Freddie Thon	5.00	2.50	1.50
215	Manuel Alvarez	5.00	2.50	1.50
216	Luis Olmo	5.00	2.50	1.50
217	Jose Santiago	7.50	3.75	2.25
218	Hiram Bithorn	12.50	6.25	3.75
219	Willard Brown	30.00	15.00	9.00
220	Robert Thurman	10.00	5.00	3.00
221	Buster Clarkson	7.50	3.75	2.25
222	Satchel Paige	40.00	20.00	12.00
223	Raymond Brown	30.00	15.00	9.00
224	Alonso Perry	7.50	3.75	2.25
225	Quincy Trouppe	12.50	6.25	3.75
226	Santiago Muratti	5.00	2.50	1.50
227	Johnny Davis	5.00	2.50	1.50
228	Lino Suarez	5.00	2.50	1.50
229	Demetrio Pesante	5.00	2.50	1.50
230	Luis Arroyo	5.00	2.50	1.50
231	Jose Garcia	5.00	2.50	1.50

1905 Harry Pulliam Cigar Label

The attributed dated is speculative. Pulliam was the first president of the modern National League. These colorful gold-leaf highlighted lithographed cigar box labels measure 4-1/4" square with clipped corners. Since all examples seen appear to be unused it is believed that the cigar brand never materialized, possibly having been aborted when Pulliam commited suicide in 1909.

	NM	EX	VG
Harry Pulliam	100.00	50.00	30.00

1910 Punch Cigars

By virtue of its age, scarcity and checklist, this is among the most popular of the Cuban card sets. Issued contemporary with a visit by the Detroit Tigers and Philadelphia A's for an exhibition series in Cuba, these cards feature an approximately 1-1/4" x 1-7/8" black-and-white portrait photo attached to a decorative cardboard backing of about 1-3/4" x 2-1/4". Known cards include a dozen each of the Major League teams and, it is speculated, an equal number from Cuba's professional Almendares and Havana clubs; though the complete checklist remains unknown. The scarcity of surviving specimens may be traced to the copy on the original cardboard backing that offers an album for anybody turning in a complete set. Only a tiny percentage of Punch cards are known with their cardboard backing attached. Because most cards seen to date have been in wretched condition, no values are quoted above VG condition. Cards with backing should command a 3X premium.

	NM	EX	VG
Common Cuban Player:			750.00
Common Major Leaguer:			1,125
ALMENDARES			
(1) Armando Cabanas			1,125
(2) Alfredo Cabrera			750.00
(3) Gervasio Gonzalez			1,500
(4) Eleadoro Hidalgo			1,500
(5) Armando Marzans (Marsans)			2,250
(6) Jose Mendez			30,000
(7) Evaristo Pia/Trainer			750.00
(8) Carlos Roggers (Royer)			1,125
(9) Rogelio Valdes			750.00
(10) Juan Viola			1,125
			500.00
HAVANA			
(1) P. (Pete) Hill			5,250
(2) Carlos Moran			2,250
(3) Agustin Molina			4,500
(4) Luis Padron			2,250
(5) Agustin Parpetti			1,500
			500.00
DETROIT TIGERS			
(1) Joe Casey			1,125
(2) Ty Cobb			11,250
(3) Sam Crawford			5,250
(4) Tom Jones			1,125
(5) Matty McIntyre			1,125
(6) George Moriarty			1,125
(7) George Mullin			1,125
(8) Charley O'Leary			1,125
(9) Germany Schaefer			1,125
(10) Oscar Stanage			1,125
(11) Ed Summers			1,125
(12) Ed Willetts (Willett)			1,125
			500.00
PHILADELPHIA A'S			
(1) Jack Barry			1,125
(2) Chief Bender			5,250
(3) Jack Coombs			1,125
(4) Harry Davis			1,125
(5) Claude Derrick			1,125
(6) Topsy Hartsel			1,125
(7) Jack Lapp			1,125
(8) Bris Lord			1,125
(9) Stuffy McInnis			1,125
(10) Danny Murphy			1,125
(11) Eddie Plank			6,000
(12) Ira Thomas			1,125
			500.00

1966 Pure Oil Atlanta Braves

 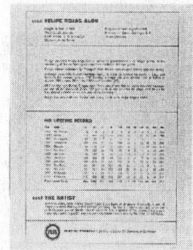

In their first year in Atlanta a set of Braves premium pictures done by noted portrait artist Nicholas Volpe was sponsored by Pure Oil. The 8-1/2" x 11" pictures were given away with gas purchases. Fronts featured a large pastel portrait and smaller full-figure action picture of the player set against a black background. A facsimile player autograph was pencilled at the bottom, along with the artist's signature. The player's name was printed in black in the white bottom border. Backs are printed in black-and-white and include biographical and career notes, full major and minor league stats, a short biography of the artist and the sponsoring company's logo. The unnumbered cards are checklisted here alphabetically.

	NM	EX	VG
Complete Set (12):	75.00	37.50	22.00
Common Player:	5.00	2.50	1.50
(1) Hank Aaron	25.00	12.50	7.50
(2) Felipe Alou	6.00	3.00	1.75
(3) Frank Bolling	5.00	2.50	1.50
(4) Bobby Bragan	5.00	2.50	1.50
(5) Rico Carty	5.00	2.50	1.50
(6) Tony Cloninger	5.00	2.50	1.50
(7) Mack Jones	5.00	2.50	1.50
(8) Denny LeMaster	5.00	2.50	1.50
(9) Eddie Mathews	15.00	7.50	4.50
(10) Denis Menke	5.00	2.50	1.50
(11) Lee Thomas	5.00	2.50	1.50
(12) Joe Torre	7.50	3.75	2.25

1933 PX3 Double Header Coins

Issued by Gum Inc. circa 1933, this unnumbered set consists of 43 metal discs approximately 1-1/4" in diameter. The front lists the player's name and team beneath his picture. The numbers "1" or "2" also appear inside a small circle at the bottom of the disc, and the wrapper advised collectors to "put 1 and 2 together and make a double header." Some players are found in more than one color. The set is designated as PX3 in the American Card Catalog.

	NM	EX	VG
Complete Set (43):	1,750	875.00	525.00
Common Player:	40.00	20.00	12.00
(1) Sparky Adams	40.00	20.00	12.00
(2) Dale Alexander	40.00	20.00	12.00
(3) Earl Averill	75.00	37.00	22.00
(4) Dick Bartell	40.00	20.00	12.00
(5) Walter Berger	40.00	20.00	12.00
(6) Jim Bottomley	75.00	37.00	22.00
(7) Lefty Brandt	40.00	20.00	12.00
(8) Owen Carroll	40.00	20.00	12.00
(9) Lefty Clark	40.00	20.00	12.00
(10) Mickey Cochrane	75.00	37.00	22.00
(11) Joe Cronin	75.00	37.00	22.00
(12) Jimmy Dykes	40.00	20.00	12.00
(13) George Earnshaw	40.00	20.00	12.00
(14) Wes Ferrell	40.00	20.00	12.00
(15) Neal Finn	40.00	20.00	12.00
(16) Lew Fonseca	40.00	20.00	12.00
(17) Jimmy Foxx	100.00	50.00	30.00
(18) Frankie Frisch	75.00	37.00	22.00
(19) Chick Fullis	40.00	20.00	12.00
(20) Charley Gehringer	75.00	37.00	22.00
(21) Goose Goslin	75.00	37.00	22.00
(22) Johnny Hodapp	40.00	20.00	12.00
(23) Frank Hogan	40.00	20.00	12.00
(24) Si Johnson	40.00	20.00	12.00
(25) Joe Judge	40.00	20.00	12.00
(26) Chuck Klein	75.00	37.00	22.00
(27) Al Lopez	75.00	37.00	22.00
(28) Ray Lucas	40.00	20.00	12.00
(29) Red Lucas	40.00	20.00	12.00
(30) Ted Lyons	75.00	37.00	22.00
(31) Firpo Marberry	40.00	20.00	12.00
(32) Oscar Melillo	40.00	20.00	12.00
(33) Lefty O'Doul	50.00	25.00	15.00
(34) George Pipgras	40.00	20.00	12.00
(35) Flint Rhem	40.00	20.00	12.00
(36) Sam Rice	75.00	37.00	22.00
(37) Muddy Ruel	40.00	20.00	12.00
(38) Harry Seibold	40.00	20.00	12.00
(39) Al Simmons	75.00	37.00	22.00
(40) Joe Vosmik	40.00	20.00	12.00
(41) Gerald Walker	40.00	20.00	12.00
(42) Pinky Whitney	40.00	20.00	12.00
(43) Hack Wilson	75.00	37.00	22.00

Q

1934 Quaker Oats Babe Ruth Premium Photo (8x10)

Members of the cereal company's Babe Ruth Baseball Club could obtain this souvenir photo among many other promotional items endorsed by the slugger. This 8" x 10" black-and-white photo has a facsimile autograph and is inscribed, "To My Pal." Advertising for Quaker Oats appears in the white border at bottom.

	NM	EX	VG
Babe Ruth	600.00	350.00	150.00

1954 Quaker Sports Oddities

Available both as cereal-box premiums and a mail-away set, this issue of horizontal-format 3-1/2" x 2-1/2", round-corner cards depicts "Odd but True" moments in sports. Fronts of the multi-sports set feature portrait and action color art. Backs describe the sports oddity.

	NM	EX	VG
Complete Set (27):	200.00	100.00	60.00
Common Card:	3.00	1.50	.90
1 Johnny Miller (Football)	4.00	2.00	1.25
2 Fred Snite Jr. (Golf)	3.00	1.50	.90

		NM	EX	VG
3	George Quam (Handball)	3.00	1.50	.90
4	John B. Maypole (Speed boating.)	3.00	1.50	.90
5	Harold (Bunny) Leavitt (Basketball)	5.00	2.50	1.50
6	Wake Forest College (Football)	5.00	2.50	1.50
7	Amos Alonzo Stagg (Football)	20.00	10.00	6.00
8	Catherine Fellmuth (Bowling)	3.00	1.50	.90
9	Bill Wilson (Golf)	3.00	1.50	.90
10	Chicago Blackhawks (Hockey)	20.00	10.00	6.00
11	Betty Robinson (Track)	3.00	1.50	.90
12	Dartmouth College/ University of Utah (Basketball)	5.00	2.50	1.50
13	Ab Jenkins (Auto racing.)	3.00	1.50	.90
14	Capt. Eddie Rickenbacker (Auto racing.)	5.00	2.50	1.50
15	Jackie LaVine (Swimming)	3.00	1.50	.90
16	Jack Riley (Wrestling)	3.00	1.50	.90
17	Carl Stockton (Biking)	3.00	1.50	.90
18	Jimmy Smilgoff (Baseball)	3.00	1.50	.90
19	George Halas (Football)	20.00	10.00	6.00
20	Joyce Rosenbom (Basketball)	5.00	2.50	1.50
21	Squatters Rights (Baseball)	3.00	1.50	.90
22	Richard Dwyer (Skating)	3.00	1.50	.90
23	Harlem Globetrotters (Basketball)	25.00	12.50	7.50
24	Everett Dean (Basketball)	3.00	1.50	.90
25	Texas U./Northwestern U. (Football)	5.00	2.50	1.50
26	Bronko Nagurski (Football)	25.00	12.50	7.50
27	Yankee Stadium (Baseball)	20.00	10.00	6.00

R

1909 Ramly Cigarettes (T204)

While issued with both Ramly and T.T.T. brand Turkish tobacco cigarettes, the cards in this set take their name from the more common of the two brands. By whatever name, the set is one of the more interesting and attractive of the early 20th Century. The 2" x 2-1/2" cards carry black-and-white photographic portraits with impressive gold embossed frames and borders on the front. Toward the bottom appears the player's last name, position, team and league. The backs carry only the most basic information on the cigarette company. The complete set price does not include the scarce variations of some players' cards on which the photos are square and surrounded by a heavy gold frame with white borders.

		NM	EX	VG
Complete Set (121):		125,000	50,000	25,000
Common Player:		1,750	875.00	525.00
T.T.T.: 4-5X				
(1)	Whitey Alperman	1,750	875.00	525.00
(2a)	John Anderson (Photo inside oval frame.)	1,750	875.00	525.00
(2b)	John Anderson (Photo inside square frame.)	22,500	9,000	4,500
(3)	Jimmy Archer	1,750	875.00	525.00
(4)	Frank Arrelanes (Arellanes)	1,750	875.00	525.00
(5)	Jim Ball	1,750	875.00	525.00
(6)	Neal Ball	1,750	875.00	525.00
(7a)	Frank C. Bancroft (Photo inside oval frame.)	1,750	875.00	525.00
(7b)	Frank C. Bancroft (Photo inside square frame.)	30,000	12,000	6,000
(8)	Johnny Bates	1,750	875.00	525.00
(9)	Fred Beebe	1,750	875.00	525.00
(10)	George Bell	1,750	875.00	525.00
(11)	Chief Bender	5,500	2,700	1,650
(12)	Walter Blair	1,750	875.00	525.00
(13)	Cliff Blankenship	1,750	875.00	525.00
(14)	Frank Bowerman	1,750	875.00	525.00
(15a)	Wm. Bransfield (Photo inside oval frame.)	1,750	875.00	525.00
(15b)	Wm. Bransfield (Photo inside square frame.)	22,500	9,000	4,500
(16)	Roger Bresnahan	5,500	2,700	1,650
(17)	Al Bridwell	1,750	875.00	525.00
(18)	Mordecai Brown	5,500	2,700	1,650
(19)	Fred Burchell	1,750	875.00	525.00
(20a)	Jesse C. Burkett (Photo inside oval frame.)	15,625	6,250	3,125
(20b)	Jesse C. Burkett (Photo inside square frame.)	22,500	9,000	4,500
(21)	Bobby Byrnes (Byrne)	1,750	875.00	525.00
(22)	Bill Carrigan	1,750	875.00	525.00
(23)	Frank Chance	5,500	2,700	1,650
(24)	Charlie Chech	1,750	875.00	525.00
(25)	Ed Cicolte (Cicotte)	3,000	1,200	600.00

		NM	EX	VG
(26)	Otis Clymer	1,750	875.00	525.00
(27)	Andy Coakley	1,750	875.00	525.00
(28)	Jimmy Collins	5,500	2,700	1,650
(29)	Ed. Collins	5,500	2,700	1,650
(30)	Wid Conroy	1,750	875.00	525.00
(31)	Jack Coombs	1,750	875.00	525.00
(32)	Doc Crandall	1,750	875.00	525.00
(33)	Lou Criger	1,750	875.00	525.00
(34)	Harry Davis	1,750	875.00	525.00
(35)	Art Devlin	1,750	875.00	525.00
(36a)	Wm. H. Dineen (Dinneen) (Photo inside oval frame.)	1,750	875.00	525.00
(36b)	Wm. H. Dineen (Dinneen) (Photo inside square frame.)	22,500	9,000	4,500
(37)	Pat Donahue	1,750	875.00	525.00
(38)	Mike Donlin	1,750	875.00	525.00
(39)	Wild Bill Donovan	1,750	875.00	525.00
(40)	Gus Dorner	1,750	875.00	525.00
(41)	Joe Dunn	1,750	875.00	525.00
(42)	Kid Elberfield (Elberfeld)	1,750	875.00	525.00
(43)	Johnny Evers	5,500	2,700	1,650
(44)	Bob Ewing	1,750	875.00	525.00
(45)	Cecil Ferguson	1,750	875.00	525.00
(46)	Hobe Ferris	1,750	875.00	525.00
(47)	Jerry Freeman	1,750	875.00	525.00
(48)	Art Fromme	1,750	875.00	525.00
(49)	Bob Ganley	1,750	875.00	525.00
(50)	Doc Gessler	1,750	875.00	525.00
(51)	Peaches Graham	1,750	875.00	525.00
(52)	Clark Griffith	5,500	2,700	1,650
(53)	Roy Hartzell	1,750	875.00	525.00
(54)	Charlie Hemphill	1,750	875.00	525.00
(55)	Dick Hoblitzel (Hoblitzell)	1,750	875.00	525.00
(56a)	Geo. Howard (Photo inside oval frame.)	1,750	875.00	525.00
(56b)	Geo. Howard (Photo inside square frame.)	22,500	9,000	4,500
(57)	Harry Howell	1,750	875.00	525.00
(58)	Miller Huggins	5,500	2,700	1,650
(59)	John Hummell (Hummel)	1,750	875.00	525.00
(60)	Walter Johnson	40,000	20,000	12,000
(61)	Thos. Jones	1,750	875.00	525.00
(62)	Mike Kahoe	1,750	875.00	525.00
(63)	Ed Kargar	1,750	875.00	525.00
(64)	Wee Willie Keeler	5,500	2,700	1,650
(65)	Red Kleinon (Kleinow)	1,750	875.00	525.00
(66)	Jack Knight	1,750	875.00	525.00
(67)	Ed Konetchey	1,750	875.00	525.00
(68)	Vive Lindaman	1,750	875.00	525.00
(69)	Hans Loebert (Lobert)	1,750	875.00	525.00
(70)	Harry Lord	1,750	875.00	525.00
(71)	Harry Lumley	1,750	875.00	525.00
(72)	Johnny Lush	1,750	875.00	525.00
(73)	Rube Manning	1,750	875.00	525.00
(74)	Jimmy McAleer	1,750	875.00	525.00
(75)	Amby McConnell	1,750	875.00	525.00
(76)	Moose McCormick	1,750	875.00	525.00
(77)	Harry McIntyre	1,750	875.00	525.00
(78)	Larry McLean	1,750	875.00	525.00
(79)	Fred Merkle	1,750	875.00	525.00
(80)	Clyde Milan	1,750	875.00	525.00
(81)	Mike Mitchell	1,750	875.00	525.00
(82a)	Pat Moran (Photo inside oval frame.)	1,750	875.00	525.00
(82b)	Pat Moran (Photo inside square frame.)	22,500	9,000	4,500
(83)	Cy Morgan	1,750	875.00	525.00
(84)	Tim Murname (Murnane)	1,750	875.00	525.00
(85)	Danny Murphy	1,750	875.00	525.00
(86)	Red Murray	1,750	875.00	525.00
(87)	Doc Newton	1,750	875.00	525.00
(88)	Simon Nichols (Nicholls)	1,750	875.00	525.00
(89)	Harry Niles	1,750	875.00	525.00
(90)	Bill O'Hare (O'Hara)	1,750	875.00	525.00
(91)	Charley O'Leary	1,750	875.00	525.00
(92)	Dode Paskert	1,750	875.00	525.00
(93)	Barney Pelty	1,750	875.00	525.00
(94)	Jake Pfeister	1,750	875.00	525.00
(95)	Ed Plank	17,250	8,625	5,175
(96)	Jack Powell	1,750	875.00	525.00
(97)	Bugs Raymond	1,750	875.00	525.00
(98)	Tom Reilly	1,750	875.00	525.00
(99)	Claude Ritchey	1,750	875.00	525.00
(100)	Nap Rucker	1,750	875.00	525.00
(101)	Ed Ruelbach (Reulbach)	1,750	875.00	525.00
(102)	Slim Sallee	1,750	875.00	525.00
(103)	Germany Schaefer	1,750	875.00	525.00
(104)	Jimmy Schekard (Sheckard)	1,750	875.00	525.00
(105)	Admiral Schlei	1,750	875.00	525.00
(106)	Wildfire Schulte	1,750	875.00	525.00
(107)	Jimmy Sebring	1,750	875.00	525.00
(108)	Bill Shipke	1,750	875.00	525.00
(109)	Charlie Smith	1,750	875.00	525.00
(110)	Tubby Spencer	1,750	875.00	525.00
(111)	Jake Stahl	1,750	875.00	525.00
(112)	Jim Stephens	1,750	875.00	525.00
(113)	Harry Stienfeldt (Steinfeldt)	1,750	875.00	525.00
(114)	Gabby Street	1,750	875.00	525.00
(115)	Bill Sweeney	1,750	875.00	525.00
(116)	Fred Tenney	1,750	875.00	525.00
(117)	Ira Thomas	1,750	875.00	525.00
(118)	Joe Tinker	5,500	2,700	1,650
(119)	Bob Unglane (Unglaub)	1,750	875.00	525.00
(120)	Heinie Wagner	1,750	875.00	525.00
(121)	Bobby Wallace	5,500	2,700	1,650

1910 Ramly Team Composite Premiums

At least two versions of coupons found in boxes of Ramly (and possibly T.T.T.) cigarettes offered a large-format (about 23" x 18-1/2") black-and-white photogravure premium featuring a composite of player portraits for five, or six, popular teams of the era. Players are identified in the bottom border, which also has a credit line for the tobacco company. To date, only the 1909 pennant winners' premiums have been confirmed as surviving.

(1)	Boston Red Sox (Unconfirmed)	.00	.00	.00
(2)	Boston Rustlers	.00	.00	.00
(3)	Detroit Tigers	.00	.00	.00
(4)	New York Giants (Unconfirmed)	.00	.00	.00
(5)	Philadelphia A's (unconfirmed)	.00	.00	.00
(6)	Pittsburgh Pirates (5/04 auction, trimmed, $3,163)	.00	.00	.00

1881 Randall Studio Cabinets

What the players of the 1881 Boston Beaneaters were doing posing in their Sunday best suits at the Detroit studio of Randall the photographer is open to speculation, as is the question of whether other teams' players were also photographed there. These cabinets are about 4-1/4" x 6-1/2" and blank-backed. On most of them the player name and city and in small type on the portrait.

		NM	EX	VG
Common Player:		2,000	1,000	600.00
(1)	Tommy Bond	2,000	1,000	600.00
(2)	Tom Deasley	2,000	1,000	600.00
(3)	John Morrill	2,000	1,000	600.00
(4)	John Richmond	2,000	1,000	600.00
(5)	Ezra Sutton	2,000	1,000	600.00
(6)	Jim Whitney	2,000	1,000	600.00
(7)	Harry Wright	8,000	4,000	2,500

1950s-70s Rawlings Advisory Staff Photos

Advisory staff photos were a promtional item which debuted in the early 1950s, flourished in the Sixties and died in the early 1970s. Generally 8" x 10" (sometimes a little larger), these black-and-white (a few later were color) glossy photos picture players who had contracted with a major baseball equipment company to endorse and use their product. Usually the product - most often a glove - was prominently displayed in the photo. The pictures were often displayed in the windows of sporting goods stores or the walls of sports departments and were sometimes made available to customers. Because the companies tended to stick with players over the years, some photos were reissued, sometimes with and sometimes without a change of team, pose or style. All advisory staff photos of the era are checklisted here in alphabetical order. A pose description is given for each known picture. The photos are checklisted here in alphabetical order. It is unlikely this list is complete. In general, Rawlings advisory staff photos feature a white box within the photo which contains the glove-company logo and a facsimile autograph of the player. Gaps have been left in the checklist numbering to accommodate possible additions.

		NM	EX	VG
Common Player:		25.00	12.50	7.50
(1)	Joe Adcock/Kneeling (Braves)	35.00	17.50	10.50
(2)	Joe Adcock (Braves, locker room.)	25.00	12.50	7.50
(3)	Joe Adcock (Braves, upper body.)	25.00	12.50	7.50
(4)	Hank Aguirre (Tigers, glove on knee.)	25.00	12.50	7.50
(5)	Bobby Avila (Indians, upper body.)	25.00	12.50	7.50
(6)	Bob Bailey/Kneeling (Pirates)	25.00	12.50	7.50
(7)	Ed Bailey (Reds, gearing up in dugout.)	25.00	12.50	7.50
(8)	Ed Bailey (Giants, catching crouch.)	25.00	12.50	7.50

		NM	EX	VG
(9)	Earl Battey (Twins, catching crouch.)	25.00	12.50	7.50
(10)	Earl Battey (Twins, kneeling w/bat.)	25.00	12.50	7.50
(11)	Johnny Bench (Crouching, no catcher's gear.)	45.00	22.00	13.50
(12)	Dick Bertell (Cubs, catching crouch.)	25.00	12.50	7.50
(13)	John Blanchard (Yankees, catching crouch.)	25.00	12.50	7.50
(14)	John Blanchard (Yankees, dugout step.)	25.00	12.50	7.50
(15)	"Clete" Boyer/Fldg (Yankees)	25.00	12.50	7.50
(16)	Ken Boyer (Cardinals, in front of locker.)	25.00	12.50	7.50
(17)	Ken Boyer/Kneeling (Cardinals, b/w)	25.00	12.50	7.50
(18)	Ken Boyer (Mets, b/w, full-length.)	25.00	12.50	7.50
(19)	Ken Boyer (Mets, color, leaning on bat.)	25.00	12.50	7.50
(20)	Ken Boyer (White Sox, upper body.)	30.00	15.00	9.00
(21)	Lew Burdette (Braves, beginning wind-up.)	25.00	12.50	7.50
(22)	Lew Burdette (Braves, upper body w/ball.)	35.00	17.50	10.50
(23)	Bob Cerv (A's, at bat rack.)	25.00	12.50	7.50
(24)	Gordon Coleman (Reds, kneeling w/bat.)	25.00	12.50	7.50
(25)	Tony Conigliaro (Red Sox, glove at chest.)	45.00	22.00	13.50
(26)	Wes Covington (Braves, upper body.)	25.00	12.50	7.50
(27)	Joe Cunningham (White Sox, glove at knee.)	25.00	12.50	7.50
(28)	Joe Cunningham (Cardinals, chest-up.)	25.00	12.50	7.50
(29)	Tommy Davis (Dodgers, dugout step.)	25.00	12.50	7.50
(30)	Don Demeter (Dodgers, upper body.)	25.00	12.50	7.50
(31)	Don Demeter (Phillies, hands on knees.)	25.00	12.50	7.50
(32)	Dick Dietz (Giants, catching pose.)	25.00	12.50	7.50
(33)	Tito Francona (Indians, sitting w/glove.)	25.00	12.50	7.50
(34)	Steve Garvey (Dodgers, horizontal, pose and action.)	25.00	12.50	7.50
(35)	Mudcat Grant (Indians, horizontal, upper body.)	25.00	12.50	7.50
(36)	Dick Groat (Pirates, b/w, full-length.)	25.00	12.50	7.50
(37)	Dick Groat (Pirates, b/w, upper body.)	25.00	12.50	7.50
(38)	Dick Groat (Cardinals, b/w, kneeling w/bat.)	25.00	12.50	7.50
(39)	Dick Groat/Kneeling (Cardinals, b/w)	25.00	12.50	7.50
(40)	Harvey Haddix/Kneeling (Pirates)	25.00	12.50	7.50
(41)	Harvey Haddix (Pirates, locker room.)	25.00	12.50	7.50
(42)	Ken Holtzman (Cubs, hands on knees.)	25.00	12.50	7.50
(43)	Ken Holtzman (A's, horizontal, two poses.)	25.00	12.50	7.50
(44)	Elston Howard (Yankees, catching crouch.)	30.00	15.00	9.00
(45)	Al Hrabosky (Cardinals, upper body.)	25.00	12.50	7.50
(46)	Larry Jackson/Kneeling (Cubs)	25.00	12.50	7.50
(47)	Larry Jackson/Fldg (Cardinals)	25.00	12.50	7.50
(48)	Larry Jackson (Cardinals, full-length on mound.)	25.00	12.00	7.50
(49)	Reggie Jackson (A's, full-length.)	40.00	20.00	12.00
(50)	Joey Jay (Reds, dugout step, glove on rail.)	25.00	12.50	7.50
(51)	Fergie Jenkins (Cubs, hands on knees.)	25.00	12.50	7.50
(52)	Ed Kranepool/Btg (Mets, color.)	25.00	12.50	7.50
(53)	Tony Kubek/Fldg (Full-length)	25.00	12.50	7.50
(54)	Tony Kubek/Kneeling (No bat.)	25.00	12.50	7.50
(55)	Tony Kubek (Kneeling w/bat.)	25.00	12.50	7.50
(56)	Tony Kubek (Horizontal, upper body.)	25.00	12.50	7.50
(57)	Vern Law (Locker room.)	25.00	12.50	7.50
(58)	Jim Lefebvre (Dodgers, kneeling, bat on shoulder.)	25.00	12.50	7.50
(59)	Sherman Lollar (White Sox, throwing from crouch.)	25.00	12.50	7.50
(60)	Art Mahaffey (Phillies, upper body.)	25.00	12.50	7.50
(61)	Mickey Mantle (Upper body, road uniform.)	150.00	75.00	45.00
(62)	Mickey Mantle (Leaning, hands on knees.)	100.00	50.00	30.00
(63)	Mickey Mantle (Seated w/bat, glove on knee.)	130.00	65.00	40.00
(64)	Mickey Mantle/Kneeling	150.00	75.00	45.00
(65)	Mickey Mantle (Seated at locker, pointing to glove.)	150.00	75.00	45.00
(66)	Eddie Mathews (Braves, full-length.)	45.00	22.00	13.50
(67)	Eddie Mathews (Braves, sepia, upper body.)	45.00	22.00	13.50
(68)	Eddie Mathews (Braves, upper body, glove in front.)	45.00	22.00	13.50
(69)	Eddie Mathews (Braves, upper body, looking at glove.)	45.00	22.00	13.50
(70)	Dal Maxvill (Cardinals, bat on shoulder.)	25.00	12.50	7.50
(71)	Dal Maxvill/Fldg (Cardinals)	25.00	12.50	7.50
(72)	Charlie Maxwell (Tigers, horizontal, upper body.)	25.00	12.50	7.50
(73)	Tim McCarver (Cardinals, catching crouch.)	25.00	12.50	7.50
(74)	Lindy McDaniel (Cardinals, b/w, on dugout steps.)	25.00	12.50	7.50
(75)	Dave McNally (Orioles, upper body.)	25.00	12.50	7.50
(76)	Wilmer Mizell (Cardinals, upper body.)	25.00	12.50	7.50
(77)	Wally Moon/Kneeling (Dodgers)	25.00	12.50	7.50
(78)	Wally Moon/Standing (Dodgers)	25.00	12.50	7.50
(79)	Stan Musial (Upper body.)	50.00	25.00	15.00
(80)	Stan Musial/Btg (Horizontal)	50.00	25.00	15.00
(81)	Stan Musial (Full-length holding glove and bat.)	50.00	25.00	15.00
(82)	Stan Musial (Kneeling on bat.)	50.00	25.00	15.00
(83)	Stan Musial (Kneeling on bat, glove on ground.)	50.00	25.00	15.00
(84)	Stan Musial (Kneeling, glove in front, Busch Stadium.)	50.00	25.00	15.00
(85)	Stan Musial (Full-length, hands on knees.)	80.00	40.00	24.00
(86)	Stan Musial (Socks to cap, white background, in proposed '56 road uniform.)	125.00	62.00	37.00
(87)	Charlie Neal/Kneeling (Dodgers)	25.00	12.50	7.50
(88)	Charlie Neal (Dodgers, looking into glove.)	25.00	12.50	7.50
(89)	Rocky Nelson/Kneeling (Pirates)	25.00	12.50	7.50
(90)	Rocky Nelson/Fldg (Pirates)	25.00	12.50	7.50
(91)	Amos Otis (Royals, upper body.)	25.00	12.50	7.50
(92)	Jim Perry/Pitching (Indians, pitching.	25.00	12.50	7.50
(93)	Boog Powell (Orioles, full-length.)	25.00	12.50	7.50
(94)	Rick Reichardt (Angels, full-length.)	25.00	12.50	7.50
(95)	Brooks Robinson (Dugout step.)	45.00	22.00	13.50
(96)	Brooks Robinson/Throwing	45.00	22.00	13.50
(97)	Brooks Robinson (Standing w/glove.)	45.00	22.00	13.50
(98)	Brooks Robinson (Tying shoe.)	45.00	22.00	13.50
(99)	John Romano (Indians, adjusting shinguard.)	25.00	12.50	7.50
(101)	Manny Sanguillen (Pirates, catching crouch.)	25.00	12.50	7.50
(102)	Chuck Schilling (Full-length.)	25.00	12.50	7.50
(103)	Herb Score (Indians, pitching.)	25.00	12.50	7.50
(104)	Norm Siebern (A's, vest.)	25.00	12.50	7.50
(105)	Norm Siebern (A's, jersey.)	25.00	12.50	7.50
(106)	Roy Sievers (Senators, full-length.)	25.00	12.50	7.50
(107)	Roy Sievers (White Sox, drinking fountain.)	25.00	12.50	7.50
(108)	Roy Sievers/Kneeling (Phillies)	25.00	12.50	7.50
(109)	Bob Skinner (Pirates, upper body.)	25.00	12.50	7.50
(110)	Duke Snider (Brooklyn Dodgers, full-length.)	45.00	22.00	13.50
(111)	Duke Snider (L.A. Dodgers, upper body.)	45.00	22.00	13.50
(112)	Warren Spahn (Braves, b/w, wind-up.)	45.00	22.00	13.50
(114)	Willie Stargell (Upper body.)	35.00	17.50	10.50
(115)	Willie Stargell (Full-length.)	35.00	17.50	10.50
(116)	Tom Tresh/Fldg (Yankees)	25.00	12.50	7.50
(117)	Tom Tresh (Yankees, full-length.)	25.00	12.50	7.50
(119)	Bob Turley (Yankees, upper body.)	25.00	12.50	7.50
(120)	Bob Turley (At water fountain.)	25.00	12.50	7.50
(121)	Bill White (Cardinals, glove over rail.)	25.00	12.50	7.50
(122)	Bill White (Phillies, b/w, full-length.)	25.00	12.50	7.50
(123)	Bill White (Phillies, color, full-length.)	25.00	12.50	7.50
(124)	Billy Williams (Cubs, full-length.)	35.00	17.50	10.50
(126)	Steve Yeager (Dodgers, upper body.)	25.00	12.50	7.50

1952 Rawlings Stan Musial Premium Photo

In this black-and-white, blank-backed premium photo, Musial is shown in a batting stance superimposed over a game-action photo at Sportsman's Park. A white facsimile autograph is at lower-right. The wide bottom border of the 5" x 7" picture has the Rawlings logoscript and address.

	NM	EX	VG
Stan Musial	40.00	20.00	12.00

1954 Rawlings Stan Musial

The date of issue is speculation although the picture is certainly from 1955 or earlier. This 5-1/2" x 7-1/2" colorized photo is actually part of a cardboard Rawlings glove box. The panel at lower-right of the card identifies it as "A GENUINE RAWLINGS FACSIMILE AUTOGRAPH PICTURE." Back is blank.

	NM	EX	VG
Stan Musial	300.00	150.00	90.00

1955 Rawlings Stan Musial

Though missing from Topps and Bowman card sets from 1954-57, Cardinals superstar Stan Musial wasn't entirely unavailable on baseball cards. About 1955 he appeared on a series of six cards found on boxes of Rawlings baseball gloves carrying Musial's endorsement. The cards feature black-and-white photos of Musial set against a blue background. Because the cards were part of a display box, they are blank-backed. Depending on the position on the box, the cards measure approximately 2" x 3" (#1A and 2A) or 2-1/2" x 3-3/4" (#1-4). Cards are numbered in a yellow star at upper left.

		NM	EX	VG
Complete Set (6):		2,500	1,250	750.00
Complete Box:		3,000	1,500	900.00
Common Card:		450.00	225.00	125.00
1	Stan Musial/Portrait	450.00	225.00	125.00
1A	Stan Musial (Portrait with bat.)	450.00	225.00	125.00
2	Stan Musial/Kneeling	450.00	225.00	125.00
2A	Stan Musial/Portrait	450.00	225.00	125.00
3	Stan Musial /Swinging (Horizontal)	450.00	225.00	125.00
4	Stan Musial (Batting pose.)	450.00	225.00	125.00

1963 Rawlings Stan Musial Premium

This premium was available by mail and commemorates the career of long-time Rawlings spokesman Stan Musial upon his retirement. The package contains an approximately 9" x 10" color portrait photo of Musial with a facsimile autograph, a sheet illustrated with four portraits of Musial during his career and listing his many records, and a note from the company indicating future availability of Musial gloves.

	NM	EX	VG
Complete Package:			
Stan Musial	60.00	30.00	18.00

1964 Rawlings Glove Box

Measuring about 2-3/8" x 4" when properly cut off the glove boxes on which they were printed, these full-color cards show stars of the day posing with their Rawlings glove prominently displayed. The blank-backed unnumbered cards are checklisted here alphabetically. The quality of cutting should be considered in grading these cards. In actuality, the cards were not meant to be cut from the boxes, but rather to show which premium photo was packed inside the glove box. Two cards of each player appear on the box.

		NM	EX	VG
Complete Set (8):		450.00	225.00	135.00
Common Player:		25.00	12.50	7.50
Complete Box:		750.00	375.00	225.00
(1)	Ken Boyer	35.00	17.50	10.50
(2)	Tommy Davis	25.00	12.50	7.50
(3)	Dick Groat	25.00	12.50	7.50
(4)	Mickey Mantle	200.00	100.00	60.00
(5)	Brooks Robinson	60.00	30.00	18.00
(6)	Warren Spahn	50.00	25.00	15.00
(7)	Tom Tresh	25.00	12.50	7.50
(8)	Billy Williams	45.00	22.00	13.50

1964-66 Rawlings Premium Photos

One premium photo was inserted into each baseball glove box sold by Rawlings beginning in 1964 and continuing at least into 1966, when some changes in players and pictures were added. The 8" x 9-1/2" full-color photos were advertised on the outside of the boxes in miniature form. Each of the photos pictures a player posed with his Rawlings leather prominently displayed. A black facsimile autograph is printed on the front.

		NM	EX	VG
Complete Set (12):		600.00	300.00	180.00
Common Player:		20.00	10.00	6.00
(1a)	Ken Boyer (Cardinals, 1964.)	25.00	12.50	7.50
(1b)	Ken Boyer (Mets, 1966.)	25.00	12.50	7.50
(2)	Tommy Davis	20.00	10.00	6.00
(3)	Dick Groat	20.00	10.00	6.00
(4a)	Mickey Mantle (No undershirt, 1964.)	150.00	75.00	45.00
(4b)	Mickey Mantle (Black undershirt, 1966.)	150.00	75.00	45.00
(5a)	Brooks Robinson (Full-bird cap, 1964.)	70.00	35.00	21.00
(5b)	Brooks Robinson (Bird's-head cap, 1966.)	85.00	42.00	25.00
(6)	Warren Spahn	75.00	37.00	22.00
(7)	Tom Tresh	20.00	10.00	6.00
(8)	Bill White (1966)	20.00	10.00	6.00
(9)	Billy Williams	50.00	25.00	15.00

1965 Rawlings MVP Premiums

The American and National League MVPs are featured in this pair of 8-1/8" x 10-1/4" premium pictures sponsored by the sporting goods manufacturer. The manner of their distribution is unknown. Printed on thin card stock, the premiums feature the artwork of Amadee Wohlschlaeger.

		NM	EX	VG
Complete Set (2):		125.00	65.00	40.00
(1)	Ken Boyer	65.00	35.00	20.00
(2)	Brooks Robinson	75.00	40.00	25.00

1969 Rawlings

How these cards were distributed is not certain today, nor is the extent of the series known. The approximately 3" x 5" black-and-white cards feature a portrait photo on front, with a wide white border at bottom that holds a facsimile autograph. The back has complete major and minor league stats, career highlights and a Rawlings ad.

	NM	EX	VG
Reggie Jackson	900.00	450.00	275.00
Mickey Mantle	2,500	1,250	750.00

1930 Ray-O-Print Photo Kits

This was one of several contemporary kits for do-it-yourself production of photo prints. The outfits were produced by M.P. & Co., of New York. The novelty kit consists of a 4-1/8" x 2-1/2" kraft paper envelope with production instructions printed on the outside and the name of the subject rubber-stamped on one end. Inside was a film negative, a piece of light-sensitive photo paper (each 1-7/8" x 2-15/16") and a tin stand for exposing and displaying the photo. Values shown are for complete kits. Individual components would be pro-rated, with the negative being the most valuable of the pieces. Anyone with a negative could make unlimited prints today, and even make them look old; collectors should use caution in purchasing prints alone.

		NM	EX	VG
Complete Set (8):		1,000	500.00	300.00
Common Kit:		125.00	67.00	38.00
Card: 20 Percent		.00	.00	.00
(1)	Lou Gehrig	250.00	125.00	75.00
(2)	Babe Ruth	400.00	200.00	120.00
(3)	Jack Dempsey (Boxer)	100.00	50.00	30.00
(4)	Herbert Hoover (President)	75.00	37.00	22.00
(5)	"Lindy" (Charles Lindbergh) (Aviator)	150.00	75.00	45.00
(6)	Mary Pickford (Actress)	50.00	25.00	15.00
(7)	Will Rogers (Humorist)	50.00	25.00	15.00
(8)	We (Charles Lindbergh) (W/ plane, Spirit of St. Louis.)	150.00	75.00	45.00

1899 Henry Reccius Cigars Honus Wagner

The date of this card's issue is probable, though it could have been issued anytime between 1897-99 during Wagner's stay in Louisville. The 3-3/8" x 4-11/16" card is printed in black-on-orange with an oval photograph of Wagner at center. Advertising for the company that marketed cigars under his name is around the border. The back has a lengthy pro-trade union poem. Only one example of the card is known. It was graded by PSA sometime after 1998 and given a Poor-Fair designation. The card was auctioned in November, 2001, for $21,850, and again in April, 2006, for $52,040.

Honus Wagner

1912 Recruit Little Cigars

This is the most common of the back advertisements found in T207. Factory 606 (Maryland) backs are much scarcer than those with Factory 240 (Pennsylvania), but currently carry little premium on that basis. Back printing is usually found in black, but several examples have been authenticated with brown ink printing on back. Their value is undetermined.

(See 1912 T207.)

1976 Red Barn Discs

The scarcest among the several regional sponsors of player disc sets issued in 1976 are those of the Red Barn family restaurant chain in Southeastern Wisconsin. The discs are 3-3/8" diameter with a black-and-white player portrait photo in the center of the baseball design. A line of red stars is above, while the left and right panels feature one of several bright colors. Produced by Michael Schecter Associates under license from the Major League Baseball Players Association, the player photos have had uniform and cap logos removed. Backs are printed in red and purple. The unnumbered checklist here is presented in alphabetical order.

		NM	EX	VG
Complete Set (70):		500.00	250.00	150.00
Common Player:		8.00	4.00	2.50
(1)	Henry Aaron	65.00	32.00	19.50
(2)	Johnny Bench	25.00	12.50	7.50
(3)	Vida Blue	8.00	4.00	2.50
(4)	Larry Bowa	8.00	4.00	2.50
(5)	Lou Brock	20.00	10.00	6.00
(6)	Jeff Burroughs	8.00	4.00	2.50
(7)	John Candelaria	8.00	4.00	2.50
(8)	Jose Cardenal	8.00	4.00	2.50
(9)	Rod Carew	20.00	10.00	6.00
(10)	Steve Carlton	25.00	12.50	7.50
(11)	Dave Cash	8.00	4.00	2.50
(12)	Cesar Cedeno	8.00	4.00	2.50
(13)	Ron Cey	8.00	4.00	2.50
(14)	Carlton Fisk	20.00	10.00	6.00
(15)	Tito Fuentes	8.00	4.00	2.50
(16)	Steve Garvey	12.00	6.00	3.50
(17)	Ken Griffey	8.00	4.00	2.50
(18)	Don Gullett	8.00	4.00	2.50
(19)	Willie Horton	8.00	4.00	2.50
(20)	Al Hrabosky	8.00	4.00	2.50
(21)	Catfish Hunter	20.00	10.00	6.00
(22)	Reggie Jackson	40.00	20.00	12.00
(23)	Randy Jones	8.00	4.00	2.50
(24)	Jim Kaat	8.00	4.00	2.50
(25)	Don Kessinger	8.00	4.00	2.50
(26)	Dave Kingman	8.00	4.00	2.50
(27)	Jerry Koosman	8.00	4.00	2.50
(28)	Mickey Lolich	8.00	4.00	2.50
(29)	Greg Luzinski	8.00	4.00	2.50
(30)	Fred Lynn	10.00	5.00	3.00
(31)	Bill Madlock	8.00	4.00	2.50
(32)	Carlos May	8.00	4.00	2.50
(33)	John Mayberry	8.00	4.00	2.50
(34)	Bake McBride	8.00	4.00	2.50
(35)	Doc Medich	8.00	4.00	2.50
(36)	Andy Messersmith	8.00	4.00	2.50
(37)	Rick Monday	8.00	4.00	2.50
(38)	John Montefusco	8.00	4.00	2.50
(39)	Jerry Morales	8.00	4.00	2.50
(40)	Joe Morgan	20.00	10.00	6.00
(41)	Thurman Munson	15.00	7.50	4.50
(42)	Bobby Murcer	8.00	4.00	2.50
(43)	Al Oliver	8.00	4.00	2.50
(44)	Jim Palmer	20.00	10.00	6.00
(45)	Dave Parker	8.00	4.00	2.50
(46)	Tony Perez	20.00	10.00	6.00
(47)	Jerry Reuss	8.00	4.00	2.50
(48)	Brooks Robinson	25.00	12.50	7.50
(49)	Frank Robinson	25.00	12.50	7.50

(50)	Steve Rogers	8.00	4.00	2.50
(51)	Pete Rose	65.00	32.00	19.50
(52)	Nolan Ryan	100.00	50.00	30.00
(53)	Manny Sanguillen	8.00	4.00	2.50
(54)	Mike Schmidt	45.00	22.00	13.50
(55)	Tom Seaver	25.00	12.50	7.50
(56)	Ted Simmons	8.00	4.00	2.50
(57)	Reggie Smith	8.00	4.00	2.50
(58)	Willie Stargell	20.00	10.00	6.00
(59)	Rusty Staub	12.00	6.00	3.50
(60)	Rennie Stennett	8.00	4.00	2.50
(61)	Don Sutton	20.00	10.00	6.00
(62)	Andy Thornton	8.00	4.00	2.50
(63)	Luis Tiant	8.00	4.00	2.50
(64)	Joe Torre	12.00	6.00	3.50
(65)	Mike Tyson	8.00	4.00	2.50
(66)	Bob Watson	8.00	4.00	2.50
(67)	Wilbur Wood	8.00	4.00	2.50
(68)	Jimmy Wynn	8.00	4.00	2.50
(69)	Carl Yastrzemski	25.00	12.50	7.50
(70)	Richie Zisk	8.00	4.00	2.50

1912 Red Cross Tobacco (T207)

Russell Blackburne

Russell Blackburn, the $10,000 White Sox beauty, who faded early through illness, was lifted by the White Sox from Providence in 1910, when Comiskey paid a young fortune for his services. In 1910 Blackburn played brilliantly, but unsteadily, and early in 1911 was forced to quit the game on account of an operation for a floating cartilage. He was over-anxious to make good and this cut in upon his worth. He was out practically all of 1911, so no record is shown, as he failed to take part in a big league contest. In 1912 he was turned back to the Eastern League for further seasoning.

SMOKE CHEW
RED CROSS
TOBACCO

Among the rarest back variations known in the tobacco card series is the Red Cross back on T207. Only a handful of examples have ever been seen. Determination of values is an inexact science.

	NM	EX	VG
(See T207 for checklist. A Fair-condition "common" was bid to $3,500 in a 12/00 auction but was not sold.)			
Russell Blackburne (4/02 auction G-VG)			
George Weaver		10,187	
(9/02 auction - Fair)			

1910-12 Red Cross Tobacco Type 1 (T215)

The T215 set issued by Red Cross Tobacco is another of the Louisiana regional sets closely related to the T206 "White Border" tobacco cards. Very similar to the T213 Coupon cards, the Red Cross Tobacco cards are found in two distinct types, both featuring color player lithographs and measuring approximately 1-1/2" x 2-5/8", the standard tobacco card size. Type 1 Red Cross cards, issued from 1910 to 1912, have brown captions; while Type 2 cards, most of which appear to be from 1912-13, have blue printing. The backs of both types are identical, displaying the Red Cross name and emblem, which can be used to positively identify the set and differentiate it from the other Louisiana sets of the same period. Several variations have been found, most of them involving caption changes. Gaps have been left in the assigned numbering to accommodate future additions to these checklists.

		NM	EX	VG
Common Player:		825.00	330.00	165.00
(1)	Red Ames	825.00	330.00	165.00
(2)	Home Run Baker	2,500	1,000	500.00
(3)	Neal Ball	825.00	330.00	165.00
(4)	Chief Bender (No trees in background.)	3,000	1,500	900.00
(5)	Chief Bender (Trees in background.)	3,000	1,500	900.00
(6)	Al Bridwell	825.00	330.00	165.00
(7)	Bobby Byrne	825.00	330.00	165.00
(8)	Howie Camnitz	825.00	330.00	165.00
(9)	Frank Chance	3,000	1,500	900.00
(10)	Hal Chase (Holding trophy)	3,500	1,750	1,050
(11)	Ty Cobb	12,500	6,250	3,750
(12)	Eddie Collins	3,000	1,500	900.00
(13)	Wid Conroy	825.00	330.00	165.00
(14)	Doc Crandall	825.00	330.00	165.00
(15)	Sam Crawford	3,000	1,500	900.00
(16)	Birdie Cree	825.00	330.00	165.00
(17)	Harry Davis	825.00	330.00	165.00
(18)	Josh Devore	825.00	330.00	165.00
(19)	Mike Donlin	825.00	330.00	165.00
(20)	Mickey Doolan	825.00	330.00	165.00
(21)	Patsy Dougherty	825.00	330.00	165.00
(22)	Larry Doyle/Btg	825.00	330.00	165.00
(23)	Larry Doyle/Portrait	825.00	330.00	165.00
(24)	Kid Elberfeld	825.00	330.00	165.00
(25)	Russ Ford	825.00	330.00	165.00
(26)	Art Fromme	825.00	330.00	165.00
(27)	Clark Griffith	3,000	1,500	900.00
(28)	Topsy Hartsel	825.00	330.00	165.00
(29)	Dick Hoblitzell	825.00	330.00	165.00
(30)	Solly Hofman	825.00	330.00	165.00

(31)	Del Howard	825.00	330.00	165.00
(32)	Miller Huggins (Hands at mouth.)	3,000	1,500	900.00
(33)	Miller Huggins/Portrait	3,000	1,500	900.00
(34)	John Hummel	825.00	330.00	165.00
(35)	Hughie Jennings (Both hands showing.)	3,000	1,500	900.00
(36)	Hughie Jennings (One hand showing.)	3,000	1,500	900.00
(37)	Walter Johnson	4,500	2,200	1,350
(38)	Ed Konetchy	825.00	330.00	165.00
(39)	Harry Krause	825.00	330.00	165.00
(41)	Nap Lajoie	3,000	1,500	900.00
(42)	Joe Lake	825.00	330.00	165.00
(43)	Arlie Latham	825.00	330.00	165.00
(44)	Tommy Leach	825.00	330.00	165.00
(45)	Lefty Leifield	825.00	330.00	165.00
(46)	Harry Lord	825.00	330.00	165.00
(47)	Sherry Magee	825.00	330.00	165.00
(48)	Rube Marquard/Pitching	3,000	1,500	900.00
(49)	Rube Marquard/Portrait	3,000	1,500	900.00
(51)	Christy Mathewson (Dark cap.)	7,500	3,700	2,200
(52)	Christy Mathewson (White cap.)	7,500	3,700	2,200
(53)	Joe McGinnity	3,000	1,500	900.00
(54)	John McGraw (Glove at hip.)	3,000	1,500	900.00
(55)	John McGraw/Portrait	3,000	1,500	900.00
(56)	Harry McIntyre	825.00	330.00	165.00
(57)	Fred Merkle	825.00	330.00	165.00
(58)	Chief Meyers	825.00	330.00	165.00
(59)	Dots Miller	825.00	330.00	165.00
(61)	Mike Mowrey	825.00	330.00	165.00
(62)	Danny Murphy	825.00	330.00	165.00
(63)	Red Murray	825.00	330.00	165.00
(64)	Rebel Oakes	825.00	330.00	165.00
(65)	Charley O'Leary	825.00	330.00	165.00
(66)	Dode Paskert	825.00	330.00	165.00
(67)	Barney Pelty	825.00	330.00	165.00
(68)	Jack Quinn	825.00	330.00	165.00
(69)	Ed Reulbach	825.00	330.00	165.00
(71)	Nap Rucker	825.00	330.00	165.00
(72)	Germany Schaefer	825.00	330.00	165.00
(73)	Wildfire Schulte	825.00	330.00	165.00
(74)	Jimmy Sheckard	825.00	330.00	165.00
(75)	Frank Smith	825.00	330.00	165.00
(76)	Frank Smither (Smith)	825.00	330.00	165.00
(77)	Tris Speaker	3,500	1,750	1,050
(78)	Jake Stahl	825.00	330.00	165.00
(79)	Harry Steinfeldt	825.00	330.00	165.00
(81)	Gabby Street/Catching	825.00	330.00	165.00
(82)	Gabby Street/Portrait	825.00	330.00	165.00
(83)	Jeff Sweeney	825.00	330.00	165.00
(84)	Lee Tannehill	825.00	330.00	165.00
(85)	Joe Tinker (Bat off shoulder.)	3,000	1,500	900.00
(86)	Joe Tinker (Bat on shoulder.)	3,000	1,500	900.00
(87)	Heinie Wagner	825.00	330.00	165.00
(88)	Jack Warhop	825.00	330.00	165.00
(89)	Zach Wheat	3,000	1,500	900.00
(91)	Doc White	825.00	330.00	165.00
(92)	Ed Willetts (Willett)	825.00	330.00	165.00
(93)	Owen Wilson	825.00	330.00	165.00
(94)	Hooks Wiltse/Pitching	825.00	330.00	165.00
(95)	Hooks Wiltse/Portrait	825.00	330.00	165.00
(96)	Cy Young	8,500	4,200	2,500

1912-13 Red Cross Tobacco Type 2 (T215)

		NM	EX	VG
Common Player:		1,250	500.00	250.00
(1)	Red Ames	1,250	500.00	250.00
(2)	Neal Ball	1,250	500.00	250.00
(3)	Home Run Baker	3,600	1,450	725.00
(4)	Chief Bender (No trees in background.)	3,600	1,450	725.00
(5)	Chief Bender (Trees in background.)	3,600	1,450	725.00
(6)	Roger Bresnahan	3,600	1,450	725.00
(7)	Al Bridwell	1,250	500.00	250.00
(8)	Mordecai Brown	3,600	1,450	725.00
(9)	Bobby Byrne	1,250	500.00	250.00
(10)	Howie Camnitz	1,250	500.00	250.00
(11)	Frank Chance	3,600	1,450	725.00
(12)	Hal Chase	2,250	900.00	450.00
(13)	Ty Cobb	14,000	7,000	3,000
(14)	Eddie Collins	3,600	1,450	725.00
(15)	Doc Crandall	1,250	500.00	250.00
(16)	Sam Crawford	3,600	1,450	725.00
(17)	Birdie Cree	1,250	500.00	250.00
(18)	Harry Davis	1,250	500.00	250.00
(19)	Josh Devore	1,250	500.00	250.00
(21)	Mike Donlin	1,250	500.00	250.00
(22)	Mickey Doolan/Btg	1,250	500.00	250.00
(23)	Mickey Doolan/Fldg	1,250	500.00	250.00
(24)	Patsy Dougherty	1,250	500.00	250.00

(25)	Larry Doyle/Btg	1,250	500.00	250.00
(26)	Larry Doyle/Portrait	1,250	500.00	250.00
(27)	Jean Dubuc	1,250	500.00	250.00
(28)	Kid Elberfeld	1,250	500.00	250.00
(29)	Johnny Evers	3,600	1,450	725.00
(30)	Russ Ford	1,250	500.00	250.00
(31)	Art Fromme	1,250	500.00	250.00
(32)	Clark Griffith	3,600	1,450	725.00
(33)	Bob Groom	1,250	500.00	250.00
(34)	Topsy Hartsel	1,250	500.00	250.00
(35)	Buck Herzog	1,250	500.00	250.00
(36)	Dick Hoblitzell	1,250	500.00	250.00
(37)	Solly Hofman	1,250	500.00	250.00
(38)	Miller Huggins (Hands at mouth.)	3,600	1,450	725.00
(39)	Miller Huggins/Portrait	3,600	1,450	725.00
(41)	John Hummel	1,250	500.00	250.00
(42)	Hughie Jennings	3,600	1,450	725.00
(43)	Walter Johnson	4,700	1,900	950.00
(44)	Joe Kelley	3,600	1,450	725.00
(45)	Ed Konetchy	1,250	500.00	250.00
(46)	Harry Krause	1,250	500.00	250.00
(47)	Nap Lajoie	3,600	1,450	725.00
(48)	Joe Lake	1,250	500.00	250.00
(49)	Tommy Leach	1,250	500.00	250.00
(50)	Lefty Leifield	1,250	500.00	250.00
(51)	Harry Lord	1,250	500.00	250.00
(52)	Sherry Magee	1,250	500.00	250.00
(53)	Rube Marquard/Pitching	3,600	1,450	725.00
(54)	Rube Marquard/Portrait	3,600	1,450	725.00
(55)	Christy Mathewson	5,200	2,100	1,100
(56)	John McGraw (Glove at side.)	3,600	1,450	725.00
(57)	John McGraw/Portrait	3,600	1,450	725.00
(58)	Harry McIntire	1,250	500.00	250.00
(59)	Larry McLean	1,250	500.00	250.00
(61)	Fred Merkle	1,250	500.00	250.00
(62)	Dots Miller	1,250	500.00	250.00
(63)	Mike Mitchell	1,250	500.00	250.00
(64)	Mike Mowrey	1,250	500.00	250.00
(65)	George Mullin	1,250	500.00	250.00
(66)	Danny Murphy	1,250	500.00	250.00
(67)	Red Murray	1,250	500.00	250.00
(68)	Rebel Oakes	1,250	500.00	250.00
(69)	Rube Oldring	1,250	500.00	250.00
(70)	Charley O'Leary	1,250	500.00	250.00
(71)	Dode Paskert	1,250	500.00	250.00
(72)	Barney Pelty	1,250	500.00	250.00
(73)	Billy Purtell	1,250	500.00	250.00
(74)	Ed Reulbach	1,250	500.00	250.00
(75)	Nap Rucker	1,250	500.00	250.00
(76)	Germany Schaefer (Chicago)	1,250	500.00	250.00
(77)	Germany Schaefer (Washington)	1,250	500.00	250.00
(78)	Wildfire Schulte	1,250	500.00	250.00
(79)	Frank Smith	1,250	500.00	250.00
(80)	Frank Smither (Smith)	1,250	500.00	250.00
(82)	Tris Speaker	3,600	1,450	725.00
(83)	Jake Stahl	1,250	500.00	250.00
(84)	Harry Steinfeldt	1,250	500.00	250.00
(85)	Ed Summers	1,250	500.00	250.00
(86)	Jeff Sweeney	1,250	500.00	250.00
(87)	Ira Thomas	1,250	500.00	250.00
(88)	Joe Tinker (Bat off shoulder.)	3,600	1,450	725.00
(89)	Joe Tinker (Bat on shoulder.)	3,600	1,450	725.00
(90)	Heinie Wagner	1,250	500.00	250.00
(91)	Jack Warhop	1,250	500.00	250.00
(92)	Doc White	1,250	500.00	250.00
(93)	Hooks Wiltse/Pitching	1,250	500.00	250.00
(94)	Hooks Wiltse/Portrait	1,250	500.00	250.00

1954 Red Heart Dog Food

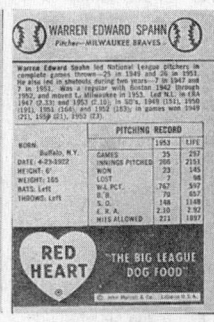

WARREN EDWARD SPAHN
Pitcher - MILWAUKEE BRAVES

WARREN SPAHN
MILWAUKEE BRAVES

RED HEART — "THE BIG LEAGUE DOG FOOD"

This set of 33 cards was issued in three color-coded series by the Red Heart Dog Food Co. Card fronts feature hand-colored photos on either a green, or red background. The 11 red-background cards are scarcer than the 11-card blue or green series. Backs of the 2-5/8" x 3-3/4" cards contain biographical and statistical information along with a Red Heart ad. Each 11-card series was available via a mail-in offer. As late as the early 1970s, the company was still sending cards to collectors who requested them.

		NM	EX	VG
Complete Set (33):		3,300	1,650	990.00
Common Player:		45.00	25.00	15.00
(1)	Richie Ashburn	150.00	60.00	30.00
(2)	Frankie Baumholtz	60.00	25.00	12.00
(3)	Gus Bell	45.00	25.00	15.00
(4)	Billy Cox	60.00	25.00	12.00
(5)	Alvin Dark	45.00	25.00	15.00
(6)	Carl Erskine	125.00	50.00	30.00
(7)	Ferris Fain	60.00	25.00	15.00
(8)	Dee Fondy	45.00	25.00	15.00
(9)	Nelson Fox	125.00	60.00	35.00
(10)	Jim Gilliam	75.00	30.00	15.00
(11)	Jim Hegan	60.00	25.00	12.00
(12)	George Kell	125.00	65.00	30.00

(13)	Ted Kluszewski	100.00	50.00	30.00
(14)	Ralph Kiner	90.00	45.00	25.00
(15)	Harvey Kuenn	45.00	25.00	15.00
(16)	Bob Lemon	80.00	35.00	20.00
(17)	Sherman Lollar	45.00	25.00	15.00
(18)	Mickey Mantle	625.00	310.00	190.00
(19)	Billy Martin	100.00	50.00	30.00
(20)	Gil McDougald	80.00	40.00	20.00
(21)	Roy McMillan	45.00	25.00	15.00
(22)	Minnie Minoso	75.00	30.00	15.00
(23)	Stan Musial	425.00	210.00	125.00
(24)	Billy Pierce	60.00	25.00	12.00
(25)	Al Rosen	65.00	30.00	15.00
(26)	Hank Sauer	45.00	25.00	15.00
(27)	Red Schoendienst	115.00	50.00	25.00
(28)	Enos Slaughter	100.00	50.00	30.00
(29)	Duke Snider	300.00	150.00	75.00
(30)	Warren Spahn	100.00	50.00	30.00
(31)	Sammy White	45.00	25.00	15.00
(32)	Eddie Yost	45.00	25.00	15.00
(33)	Gus Zernial	45.00	25.00	15.00

1952 Red Man Tobacco

This was the first national set of tobacco cards produced since the golden days of tobacco sets in the early part of the century. There are 52 cards in the set, with 25 top players and one manager from each league. Player selection was made by editor J.G. Taylor Spink of The Sporting News. Cards measure 3-1/2" x 4", including a 1/2" tab at the bottom of each card. These tabs were redeemable for a free baseball cap from Red Man. Cards are harder to find with tabs intact, and thus more valuable in that form. Values quoted here are for cards with tabs. Cards with the tabs removed would be valued about 25-35 percent of the quoted figures. Card fronts are full color paintings of each player with biographical information inset in the portrait area. Card backs contain company advertising. Cards are numbered and dated only on the tabs. The 1952 Red Man cards can be found with either of two expiration dates on back, March 31 or June 1, 1953; neither commands a premium.

	NM	EX	VG
Complete Set, W/Tab (52):	10,000	4,000	2,000
Common Player, W/Tab:	100.00	40.00	20.00
Complete Set, No Tab (52):	2,250	550.00	275.00
Common Player, No Tab:	20.00	8.00	4.00
WITH TAB			
1A Casey Stengel	250.00	100.00	50.00
1N Leo Durocher	200.00	80.00	40.00
2A Roberto Avila	100.00	40.00	20.00
2N Richie Ashburn	240.00	95.00	45.00
3A Larry "Yogi" Berra	375.00	150.00	75.00
3N Ewell Blackwell	120.00	45.00	25.00
4A Gil Coan	100.00	40.00	20.00
4N Cliff Chambers	100.00	40.00	20.00
5A Dom DiMaggio	140.00	55.00	27.50
5N Murry Dickson	100.00	40.00	20.00
6A Larry Doby	215.00	85.00	45.00
6N Sid Gordon	100.00	40.00	20.00
7A Ferris Fain	100.00	40.00	20.00
7N Granny Hamner	100.00	40.00	20.00
8A Bob Feller	325.00	130.00	65.00
8N Jim Hearn	100.00	40.00	20.00
9A Nelson Fox	215.00	85.00	45.00
9N Monte Irvin	215.00	85.00	45.00
10A Johnny Groth	100.00	40.00	20.00
10N Larry Jansen	100.00	40.00	20.00
11A Jim Hegan	100.00	40.00	20.00
11N Willie Jones	100.00	40.00	20.00
12A Eddie Joost	100.00	40.00	20.00
12N Ralph Kiner	215.00	85.00	45.00
13A George Kell	215.00	85.00	45.00
13N Whitey Lockman	100.00	40.00	20.00
14A Gil McDougald	100.00	40.00	20.00
14N Sal Maglie	100.00	40.00	20.00
15A Orestes Minoso	100.00	40.00	20.00
15N Willie Mays	600.00	240.00	120.00
16A Bill Pierce	100.00	40.00	20.00
16N Stan Musial	575.00	230.00	115.00
17A Bob Porterfield	100.00	40.00	20.00
17N Pee Wee Reese	340.00	135.00	65.00
18A Eddie Robinson	100.00	40.00	20.00
18N Robin Roberts	215.00	85.00	45.00
19A Saul Rogovin	100.00	40.00	20.00
19N Al Schoendienst	215.00	85.00	45.00
20A Bobby Shantz	100.00	40.00	20.00
20N Enos Slaughter	215.00	85.00	45.00
21A Vern Stephens	100.00	40.00	20.00
21N Duke Snider	275.00	110.00	55.00
22A Vic Wertz	100.00	40.00	20.00
22N Warren Spahn	215.00	85.00	45.00
23A Ted Williams	1,800	725.00	360.00
23N Eddie Stanky	100.00	40.00	20.00
24A Early Wynn	215.00	85.00	45.00
24N Bobby Thomson	100.00	40.00	20.00
25A Eddie Yost	100.00	40.00	20.00
25N Earl Torgeson	100.00	40.00	20.00
26A Gus Zernial	100.00	40.00	20.00
26N Wes Westrum	100.00	40.00	20.00

NO TAB			
1A Casey Stengel	45.00	18.00	9.00
1N Leo Durocher	35.00	14.00	7.00
2A Roberto Avila	20.00	8.00	4.00
2N Richie Ashburn	55.00	22.00	11.00
3A Larry "Yogi" Berra	85.00	35.00	17.50
3N Ewell Blackwell	25.00	10.00	5.00
4A Gil Coan	20.00	8.00	4.00
4N Cliff Chambers	20.00	8.00	4.00
5A Dom DiMaggio	30.00	12.00	6.00
5N Murry Dickson	20.00	8.00	4.00
6A Larry Doby	45.00	18.00	9.00
6N Sid Gordon	20.00	8.00	4.00
7A Ferris Fain	20.00	8.00	4.00
7N Granny Hamner	20.00	8.00	4.00
8A Bob Feller	80.00	32.00	16.00
8N Jim Hearn	20.00	8.00	4.00
9A Nelson Fox	50.00	20.00	10.00
9N Monte Irvin	45.00	18.00	9.00
10A Johnny Groth	20.00	8.00	4.00
10N Larry Jansen	20.00	8.00	4.00
11A Jim Hegan	20.00	8.00	4.00
11N Willie Jones	20.00	8.00	4.00
12A Eddie Joost	20.00	8.00	4.00
12N Ralph Kiner	45.00	18.00	9.00
13A George Kell	45.00	18.00	9.00
13N Whitey Lockman	20.00	8.00	4.00
14A Gil McDougald	25.00	10.00	5.00
14N Sal Maglie	20.00	8.00	4.00
15A Orestes Minoso	30.00	12.00	6.00
15N Willie Mays	200.00	80.00	40.00
16A Bill Pierce	20.00	8.00	4.00
16N Stan Musial	175.00	70.00	35.00
17A Bob Porterfield	20.00	8.00	4.00
17N Pee Wee Reese	70.00	28.00	14.00
18A Eddie Robinson	20.00	8.00	4.00
18N Robin Roberts	45.00	18.00	9.00
19A Saul Rogovin	20.00	8.00	4.00
19N Al Schoendienst	45.00	18.00	9.00
20A Bobby Shantz	20.00	8.00	4.00
20N Enos Slaughter	45.00	18.00	9.00
21A Vern Stephens	20.00	8.00	4.00
21N Duke Snider	85.00	35.00	17.50
22A Vic Wertz	20.00	8.00	4.00
22N Warren Spahn	45.00	18.00	9.00
23A Ted Williams	375.00	150.00	75.00
23N Eddie Stanky	20.00	8.00	4.00
24A Early Wynn	45.00	18.00	9.00
24N Bobby Thomson	20.00	8.00	4.00
25A Eddie Yost	20.00	8.00	4.00
25N Earl Torgeson	20.00	8.00	4.00
26A Gus Zernial	20.00	8.00	4.00
26N Wes Westrum	20.00	8.00	4.00

1953 Red Man Tobacco

This was the chewing tobacco company's second annual set of 3-1/2" x 4" cards, including the tabs at the bottom of the cards. Formats for front and back are similar to the '52 edition. The 1953 Red Man cards, however, include card numbers within the player biographical section, and the card backs are headlined "New for '53." Once again, cards with intact tabs (which were redeemable for a free cap) are more valuable. Prices below are for cards with tabs. Cards with tabs removed are worth about 25-35 percent of the stated values. Each league is represented by 25 players and a manager on the full-color cards, a total of 52. Values quoted here are for cards with tabs. Cards with the tabs removed would be valued about 35-40 percent of the quoted figures. The 1953 Red Man cards can be found with either of two expiration dates on back, March 31 or May 31, 1954; neither commands a premium.

	NM	EX	VG
Complete Set, W/Tab (52):	5,500	2,200	1,100
Common Player:	60.00	24.00	12.00
Complete Set, No Tab (52):	1,400	550.00	275.00
Common Player, No Tab:	12.50	5.00	2.50
WITH TAB			
1A Casey Stengel	150.00	60.00	30.00
1N Charlie Dressen	75.00	30.00	15.00
2A Hank Bauer	75.00	30.00	15.00
2N Bobby Adams	60.00	24.00	12.00
3A Larry "Yogi" Berra	300.00	120.00	60.00
3N Richie Ashburn	125.00	50.00	25.00
4A Walt Dropo	60.00	24.00	12.00
4N Joe Black	100.00	40.00	20.00
5A Nelson Fox	125.00	50.00	25.00
5N Roy Campanella	300.00	120.00	60.00
6A Jackie Jensen	75.00	30.00	15.00
6N Ted Kluszewski	95.00	40.00	20.00
7A Eddie Joost	60.00	24.00	12.00
7N Whitey Lockman	60.00	24.00	12.00
8A George Kell	125.00	50.00	25.00
8N Sal Maglie	60.00	24.00	12.00
9A Dale Mitchell	60.00	24.00	12.00
9N Andy Pafko	60.00	24.00	12.00
10A Phil Rizzuto	225.00	90.00	45.00
10N Pee Wee Reese	250.00	100.00	50.00
11A Eddie Robinson	60.00	24.00	12.00
11N Robin Roberts	125.00	50.00	25.00
12A Gene Woodling	70.00	28.00	14.00
12N Red Schoendienst	125.00	50.00	25.00
13A Gus Zernial	60.00	24.00	12.00
13N Enos Slaughter	125.00	50.00	25.00
14A Early Wynn	125.00	50.00	25.00
14N Edwin "Duke" Snider	300.00	120.00	60.00
15A Joe Dobson	60.00	24.00	12.00
15N Ralph Kiner	125.00	50.00	25.00
16A Billy Pierce	60.00	24.00	12.00
16N Hank Sauer	60.00	24.00	12.00
17A Bob Lemon	125.00	50.00	25.00
17N Del Ennis	60.00	24.00	12.00
18A Johnny Mize	145.00	60.00	30.00
18N Granny Hamner	60.00	24.00	12.00
19A Bob Porterfield	60.00	24.00	12.00
19N Warren Spahn	145.00	60.00	30.00
20A Bobby Shantz	60.00	24.00	12.00
20N Wes Westrum	60.00	24.00	12.00
21A "Mickey" Vernon	60.00	24.00	12.00
21N Hoyt Wilhelm	125.00	50.00	25.00
22A Dom DiMaggio	75.00	30.00	15.00
22N Murry Dickson	60.00	24.00	12.00
23A Gil McDougald	70.00	28.00	14.00
23N Warren Hacker	60.00	24.00	12.00
24A Al Rosen	70.00	28.00	14.00
24N Gerry Staley	60.00	24.00	12.00
25A Mel Parnell	60.00	24.00	12.00
25N Bobby Thomson	60.00	24.00	12.00
26A Roberto Avila	60.00	24.00	12.00
26N Stan Musial	700.00	280.00	140.00

NO TAB			
1A Casey Stengel	35.00	14.00	7.00
1N Charlie Dressen	17.50	7.00	3.50
2A Hank Bauer	17.50	7.00	3.50
2N Bobby Adams	12.50	5.00	2.50
3A Larry "Yogi" Berra	65.00	26.00	13.00
3N Richie Ashburn	40.00	16.00	8.00
4A Walt Dropo	12.50	5.00	2.50
4N Joe Black	20.00	8.00	4.00
5A Nelson Fox	40.00	16.00	8.00
5N Roy Campanella	65.00	26.00	13.00
6A Jackie Jensen	20.00	8.00	4.00
6N Ted Kluszewski	25.00	10.00	5.00
7A Eddie Joost	12.50	5.00	2.50
7N Whitey Lockman	12.50	5.00	2.50
8A George Kell	40.00	16.00	8.00
8N Sal Maglie	15.00	6.00	3.00
9A Dale Mitchell	12.50	5.00	2.50
9N Andy Pafko	12.50	5.00	2.50
10A Phil Rizzuto	50.00	20.00	10.00
10N Pee Wee Reese	60.00	24.00	12.00
11A Eddie Robinson	12.50	5.00	2.50
11N Robin Roberts	40.00	16.00	8.00
12A Gene Woodling	15.00	6.00	3.00
12N Red Schoendienst	40.00	16.00	8.00
13A Gus Zernial	12.50	5.00	2.50
13N Enos Slaughter	40.00	16.00	8.00
14A Early Wynn	40.00	16.00	8.00
14N Edwin "Duke" Snider	75.00	30.00	15.00
15A Joe Dobson	12.50	5.00	2.50
15N Ralph Kiner	40.00	16.00	8.00
16A Billy Pierce	15.00	6.00	3.00
16N Hank Sauer	12.50	5.00	2.50
17A Bob Lemon	40.00	16.00	8.00
17N Del Ennis	12.50	5.00	2.50
18A Johnny Mize	40.00	16.00	8.00
18N Granny Hamner	12.50	5.00	2.50
19A Bob Porterfield	12.50	5.00	2.50
19N Warren Spahn	45.00	18.00	9.00
20A Bobby Shantz	12.50	5.00	2.50
20N Wes Westrum	12.50	5.00	2.50
21A "Mickey" Vernon	12.50	5.00	2.50
21N Hoyt Wilhelm	35.00	14.00	7.00
22A Dom DiMaggio	25.00	10.00	5.00
22N Murry Dickson	12.50	5.00	2.50
23A Gil McDougald	15.00	6.00	3.00
23N Warren Hacker	12.50	5.00	2.50
24A Al Rosen	17.50	7.00	3.50
24N Gerry Staley	12.50	5.00	2.50
25A Mel Parnell	12.50	5.00	2.50
25N Bobby Thomson	12.50	5.00	2.50
26A Roberto Avila	12.50	5.00	2.50
26N Stan Musial	125.00	50.00	25.00

1954 Red Man Tobacco

In 1954, the Red Man set eliminated managers from the set, and issued only 25 player cards for each league. There are, however, four variations which bring the total set size to 54 full-color cards. Two cards exist for Gus Bell and Enos Slaughter, while American Leaguers George Kell, Sam Mele and Dave Philley are each shown with two different teams. Complete set prices quoted below do not include the scarcer of the variation pairs. Cards measure 3-1/2" x 4" with tabs intact. Cards without tabs are worth about 25-35 percent of the values quoted below. Formats for the cards remain virtually unchanged, with card numbers included within the player information boxes as well as on the tabs. Cards can be found with either of two expiration dates on back, March 31 or May 31, 1955; neither commands a premium.

		NM	EX	VG
	Complete Set, W/Tab (50):	4,000	1,600	800.00
	Common Player, W/Tab:	45.00	18.00	9.00
	Complete Set, No Tab (50):	1,400	550.00	275.00
	Common Player, No Tab:	15.00	6.00	3.00
	WITH TAB			
1A	Bobby Avila	45.00	18.00	9.00
1N	Richie Ashburn	90.00	36.00	18.00
2A	Jim Busby	45.00	18.00	9.00
2N	Billy Cox	55.00	22.00	11.00
3A	Nelson Fox	90.00	36.00	18.00
3N	Del Crandall	45.00	18.00	9.00
4Aa	George Kell (Boston)	125.00	50.00	25.00
4Ab	George Kell (Chicago)	180.00	70.00	35.00
4N	Carl Erskine	60.00	24.00	12.00
5A	Sherman Lollar	45.00	18.00	9.00
5N	Monte Irvin	90.00	36.00	18.00
6Aa	Sam Mele (Baltimore)	90.00	36.00	18.00
6Ab	Sam Mele (Chicago)	110.00	44.00	22.00
6N	Ted Kluszewski	100.00	40.00	20.00
7A	Orestes Minoso	65.00	26.00	13.00
7N	Don Mueller	45.00	18.00	9.00
8A	Mel Parnell	45.00	18.00	9.00
8N	Andy Pafko	45.00	18.00	9.00
9Aa	Dave Philley (Cleveland)	75.00	30.00	15.00
9Ab	Dave Philley (Philadelphia)	145.00	60.00	30.00
9N	Del Rice	45.00	18.00	9.00
10A	Billy Pierce	45.00	18.00	9.00
10N	Al Schoendienst	90.00	36.00	18.00
11A	Jim Piersall	60.00	24.00	12.00
11N	Warren Spahn	100.00	40.00	20.00
12A	Al Rosen	50.00	20.00	10.00
12N	Curt Simmons	45.00	18.00	9.00
13A	"Mickey" Vernon	45.00	18.00	9.00
13N	Roy Campanella	215.00	85.00	45.00
14A	Sammy White	45.00	18.00	9.00
14N	Jim Gilliam	60.00	24.00	12.00
15A	Gene Woodling	60.00	24.00	12.00
15N	"Pee Wee" Reese	160.00	64.00	32.00
16A	Ed "Whitey" Ford	140.00	56.00	28.00
16N	Edwin "Duke" Snider	215.00	85.00	45.00
17A	Phil Rizzuto	140.00	56.00	28.00
17N	Rip Repulski	45.00	18.00	9.00
18A	Bob Porterfield	45.00	18.00	9.00
18N	Robin Roberts	90.00	36.00	18.00
19A	Al "Chico" Carrasquel	45.00	18.00	9.00
19Na	Enos Slaughter	215.00	85.00	45.00
19Nb	Gus Bell	190.00	75.00	35.00
20A	Larry "Yogi" Berra	200.00	80.00	40.00
20N	Johnny Logan	45.00	18.00	9.00
21A	Bob Lemon	90.00	36.00	18.00
21N	Johnny Antonelli	45.00	18.00	9.00
22A	Ferris Fain	45.00	18.00	9.00
22N	Gil Hodges	90.00	36.00	18.00
23A	Hank Bauer	50.00	20.00	10.00
23N	Eddie Mathews	100.00	40.00	20.00
24A	Jim Delsing	45.00	18.00	9.00
24N	Lew Burdette	45.00	18.00	9.00
25A	Gil McDougald	55.00	22.00	11.00
25N	Willie Mays	425.00	170.00	85.00
	NO TAB			
1A	Bobby Avila	15.00	6.00	3.00
1N	Richie Ashburn	35.00	14.00	7.00
2A	Jim Busby	15.00	6.00	3.00
2N	Billy Cox	20.00	8.00	4.00
3A	Nelson Fox	35.00	14.00	7.00
3N	Del Crandall	15.00	6.00	3.00
4Aa	George Kell (Boston)	50.00	20.00	10.00
4Ab	George Kell (Chicago)	65.00	26.00	13.00
4N	Carl Erskine	22.50	9.00	4.50
5A	Sherman Lollar	15.00	6.00	3.00
5N	Monte Irvin	35.00	14.00	7.00
6Aa	Sam Mele (Baltimore)	30.00	12.00	6.00
6Ab	Sam Mele (Chicago)	55.00	22.00	11.00
6N	Ted Kluszewski	30.00	12.00	6.00
7A	Orestes Minoso	25.00	10.00	5.00
7N	Don Mueller	15.00	6.00	3.00
8A	Mel Parnell	15.00	6.00	3.00
8N	Andy Pafko	15.00	6.00	3.00
9Aa	Dave Philley (Cleveland)	30.00	12.00	6.00
9Ab	Dave Philley (Philadelphia)	65.00	26.00	13.00
9N	Del Rice	15.00	6.00	3.00
10A	Billy Pierce	15.00	6.00	3.00
10N	Al Schoendienst	35.00	14.00	7.00
11A	Jim Piersall	20.00	8.00	4.00
11N	Warren Spahn	35.00	14.00	7.00
12A	Al Rosen	20.00	8.00	4.00
12N	Curt Simmons	15.00	6.00	3.00
13A	"Mickey" Vernon	15.00	6.00	3.00
13N	Roy Campanella	65.00	26.00	13.00
14A	Sammy White	15.00	6.00	3.00
14N	Jim Gilliam	22.50	9.00	4.50
15A	Gene Woodling	22.50	9.00	4.50
15N	"Pee Wee" Reese	55.00	22.00	11.00
16A	Ed "Whitey" Ford	45.00	18.00	9.00
16N	Edwin "Duke" Snider	65.00	26.00	13.00
17A	Phil Rizzuto	50.00	20.00	10.00
17N	Rip Repulski	15.00	6.00	3.00
18A	Bob Porterfield	15.00	6.00	3.00
18N	Robin Roberts	35.00	14.00	7.00
19A	Al "Chico" Carrasquel	20.00	8.00	4.00
19Na	Enos Slaughter	70.00	28.00	14.00
19Nb	Gus Bell	70.00	28.00	14.00
20A	Larry "Yogi" Berra	65.00	26.00	13.00
20N	Johnny Logan	15.00	6.00	3.00
21A	Bob Lemon	35.00	14.00	7.00
21N	Johnny Antonelli	15.00	6.00	3.00
22A	Ferris Fain	15.00	6.00	3.00
22N	Gil Hodges	35.00	14.00	7.00
23A	Hank Bauer	20.00	8.00	4.00
23N	Eddie Mathews	35.00	14.00	7.00
24A	Jim Delsing	15.00	6.00	3.00
24N	Lew Burdette	15.00	6.00	3.00
25A	Gil McDougald	20.00	8.00	4.00
25N	Willie Mays	130.00	55.00	25.00

1955 Red Man Tobacco

These 50 cards are quite similar to the 1954 edition, with card fronts virtually unchanged except for the data in the biographical box on the color picture area. This set of the 3-1/2" x 4" cards includes 25 players from each league, with no known variations. As with all Red Man sets, those cards complete with the redeemable tabs are more valuable. Values quoted below are for cards with tabs. Cards with the tabs removed are worth about 25-35 percent of those figures. Each card can be found with two different expiration dates on back, April 15 or June 15, 1956; neither version commands a premium.

		NM	EX	VG
	Complete Set, W/Tab (50):	3,750	1,500	750.00
	Common Player, W/Tab:	60.00	24.00	12.00
	Complete Set, No Tab (50):	900.00	360.00	180.00
	Common Player, No Tab:	10.00	4.00	2.00
	WITH TAB			
1A	Ray Boone	60.00	24.00	12.00
1N	Richie Ashburn	95.00	38.00	19.00
2A	Jim Busby	60.00	24.00	12.00
2N	Del Crandall	60.00	24.00	12.00
3A	Ed "Whitey" Ford	125.00	50.00	25.00
3N	Gil Hodges	90.00	36.00	18.00
4A	Nelson Fox	90.00	36.00	18.00
4N	Brooks Lawrence	60.00	24.00	12.00
5A	Bob Grim	60.00	24.00	12.00
5N	Johnny Logan	60.00	24.00	12.00
6A	Jack Harshman	60.00	24.00	12.00
6N	Sal Maglie	60.00	24.00	12.00
7A	Jim Hegan	60.00	24.00	12.00
7N	Willie Mays	250.00	100.00	50.00
8A	Bob Lemon	90.00	36.00	18.00
8N	Don Mueller	60.00	24.00	12.00
9A	Irv Noren	60.00	24.00	12.00
9N	Bill Sarni	60.00	24.00	12.00
10A	Bob Porterfield	60.00	24.00	12.00
10N	Warren Spahn	90.00	36.00	18.00
11A	Al Rosen	75.00	30.00	15.00
11N	Henry Thompson	60.00	24.00	12.00
12A	"Mickey" Vernon	60.00	24.00	12.00
12N	Hoyt Wilhelm	90.00	36.00	18.00
13A	Vic Wertz	60.00	24.00	12.00
13N	Johnny Antonelli	60.00	24.00	12.00
14A	Early Wynn	90.00	36.00	18.00
14N	Carl Erskine	75.00	30.00	15.00
15A	Bobby Avila	60.00	24.00	12.00
15N	Granny Hamner	60.00	24.00	12.00
16A	Larry "Yogi" Berra	165.00	65.00	35.00
16N	Ted Kluszewski	75.00	30.00	15.00
17A	Joe Coleman	60.00	24.00	12.00
17N	Pee Wee Reese	125.00	50.00	25.00
18A	Larry Doby	90.00	36.00	18.00
18N	Al Schoendienst	90.00	36.00	18.00
19A	Jackie Jensen	65.00	26.00	13.00
19N	Duke Snider	165.00	65.00	35.00
20A	Pete Runnels	60.00	24.00	12.00
20N	Frank Thomas	60.00	24.00	12.00
21A	Jim Piersall	60.00	24.00	12.00
21N	Ray Jablonski	60.00	24.00	12.00
22A	Hank Bauer	65.00	26.00	13.00
22N	James "Dusty" Rhodes	60.00	24.00	12.00
23A	"Chico" Carrasquel	60.00	24.00	12.00
23N	Gus Bell	60.00	24.00	12.00
24A	Orestes Minoso	75.00	30.00	15.00
24N	Curt Simmons	60.00	24.00	12.00
25A	Sandy Consuegra	60.00	24.00	12.00
25N	Marvin Grissom	60.00	24.00	12.00
	NO TAB			
1A	Ray Boone	10.00	4.00	2.00
1N	Richie Ashburn	30.00	12.00	6.00
2A	Jim Busby	10.00	4.00	2.00
2N	Del Crandall	10.00	4.00	2.00
3A	Ed "Whitey" Ford	35.00	14.00	7.00
3N	Gil Hodges	30.00	12.00	6.00
4A	Nelson Fox	30.00	12.00	6.00
4N	Brooks Lawrence	10.00	4.00	2.00
5A	Bob Grim	10.00	4.00	2.00
5N	Johnny Logan	10.00	4.00	2.00
6A	Jack Harshman	10.00	4.00	2.00
6N	Sal Maglie	10.00	4.00	2.00
7A	Jim Hegan	10.00	4.00	2.00
7N	Willie Mays	100.00	40.00	20.00
8A	Bob Lemon	30.00	12.00	6.00
8N	Don Mueller	10.00	4.00	2.00
9A	Irv Noren	10.00	4.00	2.00
9N	Bill Sarni	10.00	4.00	2.00
10A	Bob Porterfield	10.00	4.00	2.00
10N	Warren Spahn	30.00	12.00	6.00
11A	Al Rosen	13.50	5.50	2.75
11N	Henry Thompson	10.00	4.00	2.00
12A	"Mickey" Vernon	10.00	4.00	2.00
12N	Hoyt Wilhelm	30.00	12.00	6.00
13A	Vic Wertz	10.00	4.00	2.00
13N	Johnny Antonelli	10.00	4.00	2.00
14A	Early Wynn	30.00	12.00	6.00
14N	Carl Erskine	15.00	6.00	3.00
15A	Bobby Avila	10.00	4.00	2.00

		NM	EX	VG
15N	Granny Hamner	10.00	4.00	2.00
16A	Larry "Yogi" Berra	50.00	20.00	10.00
16N	Ted Kluszewski	20.00	8.00	4.00
17A	Joe Coleman	10.00	4.00	2.00
17N	Pee Wee Reese	50.00	20.00	10.00
18A	Larry Doby	30.00	12.00	6.00
18N	Al Schoendienst	30.00	12.00	6.00
19A	Jackie Jensen	13.50	5.50	2.75
19N	Duke Snider	55.00	22.00	11.00
20A	Pete Runnels	10.00	4.00	2.00
20N	Frank Thomas	10.00	4.00	2.00
21A	Jim Piersall	13.50	5.50	2.75
21N	Ray Jablonski	10.00	4.00	2.00
22A	Hank Bauer	13.50	5.50	2.75
22N	James "Dusty" Rhodes	10.00	4.00	2.00
23A	"Chico" Carrasquel	10.00	4.00	2.00
23N	Gus Bell	10.00	4.00	2.00
24A	Orestes Minoso	15.00	6.00	3.00
24N	Curt Simmons	10.00	4.00	2.00
25A	Sandy Consuegra	10.00	4.00	2.00
25N	Marvin Grissom	10.00	4.00	2.00

1952-1954 Red Man Posters

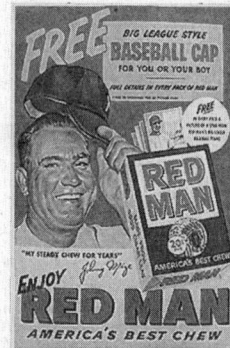

These colorful lithographed paper posters, 11" x 15-1/2", were intended as point-of-purchase displays to encourage sales of the chewing tobacco and offer a baseball cap in exchange for the tabs found on the bottom of each card. The posters were reproduced in 11" x 16" format on cardboard in the 1980s.

		NM	EX	VG
1952	Ralph Kiner (11" x 15")	200.00	100.00	60.00
1953	Enos Slaughter (11" x 15")	300.00	150.00	90.00
1954	Johnny Mize (12" x 15-1/2")	325.00	160.00	95.00

"1952-54" Red Man Posters

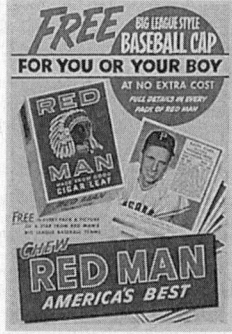

Some 30 years after the original 11" x 15-1/2" paper posters were used to advertise Red Man chewing tobacco and the baseball cards and caps available as premiums, three of the pieces were reproduced. Posters which are printed on cardboard and in a 11" x 16" size are modern reproductions with only decorative, rather than collectible, value.

NO COLLECTOR VALUE
1952 Ralph Kiner
1953 Enos Slaughter
1954 Johnny Mize

1976 Redpath Sugar Expos

Among the more unusual baseball collectibles of the late 1970s are the Montreal Expos sugar packs produced by Redpath Sugar for distribution in Quebec. About 1-1/2" x 2-3/4" in size, the sugar packs feature color portraits of the players on front, along with bi-lingual personal information and a uniform number. Backs have a color team logo and career highlights. Uncut sheets or the packaging are known which indicate several players were double- or triple-printed. The checklist here is arranged by uniform number.

		NM	EX	VG
Complete Set (36):		75.00	37.00	22.00
Common Player:		2.00	1.00	.60
1	Osvaldo Jose Virgil	2.00	1.00	.60
5	Peter Mackanin, Jr.	2.00	1.00	.60
6	Karl Otto Kuehl	2.00	1.00	.60
8	Gary Edmund Carter	15.00	7.50	4.50
9	Barry Clifton Foote	2.00	1.00	.60
11	Jose Manuel Mangual	2.00	1.00	.60
14	Lawrence Eugene Doby	6.00	3.00	1.75
15	Larry Alton Parrish	2.00	1.00	.60
16	Michael Jorgensen	2.00	1.00	.60
17	Andre Thornton	4.00	2.00	1.25
18	Joseph Thomas Kerrigan	2.00	1.00	.60
19	Timothy John Foli (DP)	2.00	1.00	.60
20	James Lawrence Lyttle, Jr.	2.00	1.00	.60
21	Frederick John Scherman, Jr.	2.00	1.00	.60
22	Ellis Clarence Valentine	2.00	1.00	.60
26	Donald Joseph Stanhouse	2.00	1.00	.60
27	Dale Albert Murray	2.00	1.00	.60
31	Clayton Laws Kirby, Jr.	2.00	1.00	.60
33	Robert David Lang	2.00	1.00	.60
34	Jose Manuel Morales	2.00	1.00	.60
35	Woodrow Thompson Fryman	3.00	1.50	.90
36	Steven John Dunning	2.00	1.00	.60
37	Jerome Cardell White	2.00	1.00	.60
38	Jesus Maria Frias (Andujar)	2.00	1.00	.60
39	Daniel Dean Warthen	2.00	1.00	.60
40	Donald George Carrithers (3P)	2.00	1.00	.60
41	Ronald Jacques Piche	2.00	1.00	.60
43	James Edward Dwyer	2.00	1.00	.60
44	Jesus Rivera (Torres), Jr.	2.00	1.00	.60
45	Stephen Douglas Rogers (DP)	2.00	1.00	.60
46	Marion Danne Adair	2.00	1.00	.60
47	Wayne Allen Granger	2.00	1.00	.60
48	Lawrence Donald Bearnarth	2.00	1.00	.60
---	Roland Wayne Garrett	2.00	1.00	.60
---	Charles Gilbert Taylor	2.00	1.00	.60
---	Delbert Bernard Unser	2.00	1.00	.60

1977 Redpath Sugar Expos

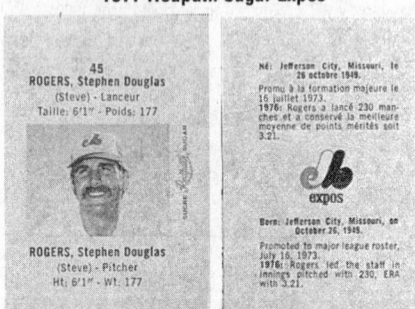

One of the more obscure regional Canadian issues, this 30-player set features members of the Expos and was printed on sugar packets distributed in the Montreal area in 1977. The front of the packet features a color photo of the player with his name, uniform number, position, height and weight listed in both English and French. A line identifying Redpath Sugar appears alongside the photo. The backs display the Expos logo and brief player highlights (again printed in both French and English). The set has been seen in uncut sheets, revealing that the packets of Steve Rogers and David Cash, Jr. were double printed.

		NM	EX	VG
Complete Set (30):		75.00	37.00	22.00
Common Player:		1.50	.70	.45
1	Osvaldo Jose Virgil	1.50	.70	.45
3	James Thomas Brewer	1.50	.70	.45
3	James Barton Vernon	1.50	.70	.45
4	Chris Edward Speier	1.50	.70	.45
5	Peter Mackanin Jr.	1.50	.70	.45
8	William Frederick Gardner	1.50	.70	.45
8	Gary Edmund Carter	15.00	7.50	4.50
9	Barry Clifton Foote	1.50	.70	.45
10	Andre Dawson	6.00	3.00	1.75
11	Ronald Wayne Garrett	1.50	.70	.45
14	Samuel Elias Mejias	1.50	.70	.45
15	Larry Alton Parrish	2.00	1.00	.60
16	Michael Jorgensen	1.50	.70	.45
17	Ellis Clarence Valentine	1.50	.70	.45
18	Joseph Thomas Kerrigan	1.50	.70	.45
20	William Henry McEnaney	1.50	.70	.45
23	Richard Hirshfield Williams	2.00	1.00	.60
24	Atanasio Rigal Perez	3.00	1.50	.90
25	Delbert Bernard Unser	1.50	.70	.45
26	Donald Joseph Stanhouse	1.50	.70	.45
30	David Cash, Jr.	1.50	.70	.45
31	Jackie Gene Brown	1.50	.70	.45
34	Jose Manual Morales	1.50	.70	.45
35	Gerald Ellis Hannahs	1.50	.70	.45
38	Jesus Maria Frias (Andujar)	1.50	.70	.45
39	Daniel Dean Warthen	1.50	.70	.45
42	William Cecil Glenn Atkinson	1.50	.70	.45
45	Stephen Douglas Rogers	2.25	1.25	.70
48	Jeffrey Michael Terpko	1.50	.70	.45
49	Warren Livingston Cromartie	1.50	.70	.45

1886 Red Stocking Cigars

This set of Boston Red Stockings schedule cards was issued in 1886, and the three known cards measure 6-1/2" x 3-3/4". The cards were printed in black and red. One side carries the 1886 Boston schedule, while the other side features a full-length player drawing. Both sides include advertising for "Red Stocking" cigars. Only three different players are known.

		NM	EX	VG
Complete Set (3):		55,000	27,500	16,500
Common Player:		45,000	16,000	10,000
(1)	C.G. Buffington	45,000	16,000	10,000
(2)	Capt. John F. Morrill	45,000	16,000	10,000
(3)	Charles Radbourn	100,000	10,000	5,000

1972 Regent Glove Hang Tag

This 2-1/4" x 3" card was distributed as an attachment to baseball gloves sold at retail outlets. A hole punched at top allowed the card to be strung to the glove. Front has a blue background and black-and-white portrait photo of 1971 MVP Vida Blue. His facsimile autograph is on back.

	NM	EX	VG
Vida Blue	15.00	7.50	4.50

1964-68 Requena N.Y. Yankees Postcards

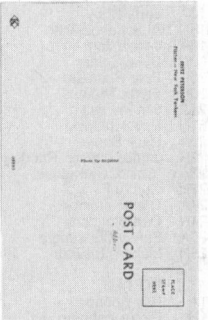

Over a period of several years in the 1960s a series of Yankee color player postcards was issued with the identifier "Photo by Requena." Similar in format, the 3-1/2" x 5-1/2" cards have borderless color photos on front. Except for facsimile autographs on some players' cards, there are no other front graphics. Backs are printed in dark green with player ID at upper-left, a "K"-within-diamond Kodachrome logo at bottom-left, a card number centered at bottom, the Requena line vertically at center and standard postcard markings at right.

		NM	EX	VG
Complete Set (17):		300.00	150.00	90.00
Common Player:		15.00	7.50	4.50
66443	Phil Linz	15.00	7.50	4.50
66880	Clete Boyer	15.00	7.50	4.50
66881	Jim Bouton	20.00	10.00	6.00
66882	Tom Tresh	20.00	10.00	6.00
66883	Joe Pepitone	20.00	10.00	6.00
66884	Tony Kubek	20.00	10.00	6.00
66885	Elston Howard	20.00	10.00	6.00
66886	Ralph Terry	15.00	7.50	4.50
66887	Bill Stafford	15.00	7.50	4.50
66888	Whitey Ford	30.00	15.00	9.00
66889	Bob Richardson	20.00	10.00	6.00
69891	Yogi Berra (Signature at top.)	30.00	15.00	9.00
69891	Yogi Berra (Signature at bottom.)	30.00	15.00	9.00
74284	John Blanchard	15.00	7.50	4.50
78909	Pedro Ramos	15.00	7.50	4.50
78910	Mel Stottlemyre	15.00	7.50	4.50
98553	Fritz Peterson	15.00	7.50	4.50
101461	Steve Barber	15.00	7.50	4.50

1964-66 Requena N.Y. Yankees 8x10s

Many of the same Yankees players and poses which appear in the standard (3-1/2" x 5-1/2") Requena postcard series can also be found, along with additional subjects, in an 8" x 10" blank-back format. The large format cards are listed here in alphabetical order.

		NM	EX	VG
Complete Set (21):		300.00	150.00	90.00
Common Player:		9.00	4.50	2.75
(1)	Yogi Berra	20.00	10.00	6.00
(2)	John Blanchard	9.00	4.50	2.75
(3)	Jim Bouton	12.50	6.25	3.75
(4)	Clete Boyer	9.00	4.50	2.75
(5)	Al Downing	9.00	4.50	2.75
(6)	Whitey Ford	20.00	10.00	6.00
(7)	Ralph Houk	9.00	4.50	2.75
(8)	Elston Howard	12.50	6.25	3.75
(9)	Tony Kubek	12.50	6.25	3.75
(10)	Phil Linz	9.00	4.50	2.75
(11)	Mickey Mantle	35.00	17.50	10.00
(12)	Mickey Mantle, Roger Maris	30.00	15.00	9.00
(13a)	Roger Maris (Facsimile autograph.)	25.00	12.50	7.50
(13b)	Roger Maris (No facsimile autograph.)	25.00	12.50	7.50
(14)	Joe Pepitone	12.50	6.25	3.75
(15)	Pedro Ramos	9.00	4.50	2.75
(16)	Bobby Richardson	12.50	6.25	3.75
(17)	Bill Stafford	9.00	4.50	2.75
(18)	Mel Stottlemyre	9.00	4.50	2.75
(19)	Ralph Terry	9.00	4.50	2.75
(20)	Tom Tresh	12.50	6.25	3.75

1953 R.G. Dun Cigars Milwaukee Braves

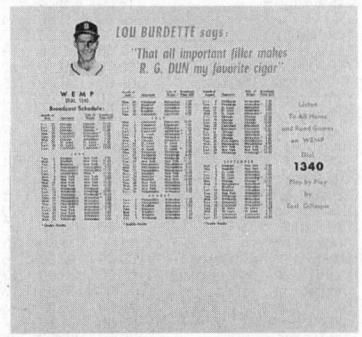

This series of counter cards was issued by a cigar company and features the radio schedule for the 1953 Braves. The cards are printed in red and black on cream cardboard and measure 10" x 9-1/2". They are unnumbered and blank-backed. The cards have vertical slits from bottom to about 1/3 the height of the cards, probably so they could be inserted into some type of counter display for Dun cigars. It's unknown how many players were represented in the series.

		NM	EX	VG
Common Player:		35.00	17.50	10.00
(1)	Lew Burdette	35.00	17.50	10.00
(2)	Jim Wilson	35.00	17.50	10.00

1933 Rialto Theater

The usually blank backs of 1929 Kashin Publications (R316) cards were used by the Rialto Theater (location unknown) as a coupon for a bring-a-friend movie matinee promotion. The number at the bottom of the 3-1/2" x 4-1/2" black-and-white card was probably used for prize drawings at the matinee. The extent to which the Kashin checklist was used in this fashion is unknown.

	NM	EX	VG
Common Player:	125.00	62.50	37.50
Stars:2X			

1935 Rice-Stix (UM7)

This two-card set was distributed in packages of shirts from a St. Louis firm. Measuring about 2-1/4" x 3", the cards feature color painting of the pitchers on front, along with a fac-simile autograph and photo credits. Backs have a short career summary and an ad for the issuer.

		NM	EX	VG
Complete Set (2):		3,250	1,600	975.00
(1)	Dizzy Dean	2,500	1,250	750.00
(2)	Paul Dean	950.00	470.00	280.00

1927 Rinkeydink Stamps

These 1-1/4" x 1-1/2" pieces are not actually stamps, but rather are printed on newsprint with unrelated matter on back. The printing is in red, green and black and each stamp has a "denomination" of 2 in a baseball design at top. The "stamps" were featured in the heading of the "Winnie Winkle" comic strip in the Sunday funnies section of newspapers.

		NM	EX	VG
Complete Set (10):		450.00	225.00	135.00
Common Player:		30.00	15.00	9.00
(1)	Grover C. Alexander	40.00	20.00	12.00
(2)	Ty Cobb	75.00	37.50	22.00
(3)	Eddie Collins	30.00	15.00	9.00
(4)	Bucky Harris	30.00	15.00	9.00
(5)	Rogers Hornsby	40.00	20.00	12.00
(6)	Walter Johnson	50.00	25.00	15.00
(7)	George Kelly	30.00	15.00	9.00
(8)	Herb Pennock	30.00	15.00	9.00
(9)	Babe Ruth	100.00	50.00	30.00
(10)	Tris Speaker	40.00	20.00	12.00

1933 Rittenhouse Candy (E285)

Designed to resemble a set of playing cards, this set, issued circa 1933 by the Rittenhouse Candy Company of Phil-adelphia, carries the ACC designation E285 and is generally considered to be the last of the E-card issues. Each card mea-sures 1-7/16" x 2-1/4" and features a small player photo in the center of the playing card design. Cards are known printed in red, orange, blue and green. The backs of the cards usually consist of just one single letter and were part of a promotion in which collectors were instructed to find enough different let-ters to spell "Rittenhouse Candy Co." Other backs explaining the contest and the prizes available were also issued, as were backs with numbers. Because it was designed as a deck of playing cards, the set is complete at 52 cards, featuring 46 dif-ferent players (six are pictured on two cards each).

		NM	EX	VG
Complete Set (52):		16,000	8,000	4,800
Common Player:		175.00	90.00	55.00
(1)	Dick Bartell	175.00	90.00	55.00
(2)	Walter Berger	175.00	90.00	55.00
(3)	Max Bishop	175.00	90.00	55.00
(4)	James Bottomley	350.00	175.00	100.00
(5)	Fred Brickell	175.00	90.00	55.00
(6)	Sugar Cain	175.00	90.00	55.00
(7)	Ed. Cihocki	175.00	90.00	55.00
(8)	Phil Collins	175.00	90.00	55.00

(9)	Roger Cramer	175.00	90.00	55.00
(10)	Hughie Critz	175.00	90.00	55.00
(11)	Joe Cronin	350.00	175.00	100.00
(12)	Hazen (Kiki) Cuyler	350.00	175.00	100.00
(13)	Geo. Davis	175.00	90.00	55.00
(14)	Spud Davis	175.00	90.00	55.00
(15)	Jimmy Dykes	175.00	90.00	55.00
(16)	George Earnshaw	175.00	90.00	55.00
(17)	Jumbo Elliot	175.00	90.00	55.00
(18)	Lou Finney	175.00	90.00	55.00
(19)	Jimmy Foxx	500.00	250.00	150.00
(20)	Frankie Frisch (3 of Spades)	350.00	175.00	100.00
(21)	Frankie Frisch (7 of Spades)	350.00	175.00	100.00
(22)	Robert (Lefty) Grove	360.00	180.00	110.00
(23)	Mule Haas	175.00	90.00	55.00
(24)	Chick Hafey	350.00	175.00	100.00
(25)	Chas. Leo Hartnett	350.00	175.00	100.00
(26)	Babe Herman	185.00	90.00	55.00
(27)	Wm. Herman	350.00	175.00	100.00
(28)	Kid Higgins	175.00	90.00	55.00
(29)	Rogers Hornsby	425.00	200.00	125.00
(30)	Don Hurst (Jack of Diamonds)	175.00	90.00	55.00
(31)	Don Hurst (6 of Spades)	175.00	90.00	55.00
(32)	Chuck Klein	350.00	175.00	100.00
(33)	Leroy Mahaffey	175.00	90.00	55.00
(34)	Gus Mancuso	175.00	90.00	55.00
(35)	Rabbit McNair	175.00	90.00	55.00
(36)	Bing Miller	175.00	90.00	55.00
(37)	Frank (Lefty) O'Doul	185.00	90.00	55.00
(38)	Mel Ott	350.00	175.00	100.00
(39)	Babe Ruth (Ace of Spades)	1,750	875.00	525.00
(40)	Babe Ruth (King of Clubs)	1,750	875.00	525.00
(41)	Al Simmons	350.00	175.00	100.00
(42)	Bill Terry	350.00	175.00	100.00
(43)	Pie Traynor	350.00	175.00	100.00
(44)	Rube Wallberg (Walberg)	175.00	90.00	55.00
(45)	Lloyd Waner	350.00	175.00	100.00
(46)	Paul Waner	350.00	175.00	100.00
(47)	Lloyd Warner (Waner)	350.00	175.00	100.00
(48)	Paul Warner (Waner)	350.00	175.00	100.00
(49)	Pinkey Whitney	175.00	90.00	55.00
(50)	Dib Williams	175.00	90.00	55.00
(51)	Hack Wilson (9 of Spades)	350.00	175.00	100.00
(52)	Hack Wilson (9 of Clubs)	350.00	175.00	100.00

1948 R.K.O. Theaters Babe Ruth Premium

 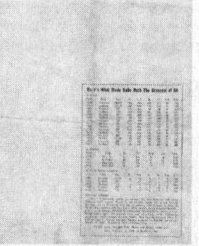

The attributed date is speculative, based on the similarity of the back copy to the 1948 American Association Babe Ruth memorial card. Apparently issued as a premium at moviehouses, this 8" x 9-1/2" picture is printed on thin cardboard. On front is a sepia action photo of Ruth in the 1932 World Series. In the bot-tom border is the R.K.O. attribution. Back has biographical details, career highlights and complete major league stats.

	NM	EX	VG
Babe Ruth	800.00	400.00	240.00

1949-1951 Roadmaster Photos

Black-and-white glossy photos of at least two major league stars were available as a premium from Roadmaster bicycles. Contemporary ads said that for a dime, an 8" x 10" photo could be obtained. The photos show the uniformed players seated on Roadmaster bikes inside a ballpark. There is a facsimile autograph on each. Backs may be found either blank, or with advertising from the sponsor. It's possible other player photos may yet be seen.

		NM	EX	VG
(1)	Bob Feller ("C" on jersey)	300.00	150.00	90.00
(2)	Bob Feller ("Indians" on jersey)	300.00	150.00	90.00
(3)	Pee Wee Reese	400.00	200.00	120.00

1920-21 H.A. Robinson Peanut Co.

This Lynchburg, Va., regional issue is a parallel to the 120-card strip card set known as W514, though it is not known whether all or only some of the W514 cards can be found with peanut company's advertising printed on the backs. The cards were originally issued in strips of 10, cut horizontally from larger sheets. Well-cut cards should measure about 1-3/8" x 2-1/2".

The back printing on each card indicates the cards were distrib-uted in five-cent bags of Our Hero and Robinson Cruso brand peanuts. See W514 for checklist and base price information.

	NM	EX	VG
Common Player:	600.00	250.00	125.00
Stars: 4-6X corresponding W514			

1947 Jackie Robinson Pins

In his historic debut season with the Brooklyn Dodgers, a number of celluloid pinback buttons featuring Jackie Robinson were issued. Ranging in size from about 1-1/4" to 1-3/4", the pins usually feature a black-and-white portrait photo at center and were originally sold with a silk pennant and plastic or pot-metal baseball charms attached.

		NM	EX	VG
(1)	Brooklyn 1947 Dodgers Congratulations "Jackie" (1-1/4" white background)	600.00	300.00	180.00
(2)	HI TEAMMATES (1-3/8", batting, blue background)	250.00	125.00	75.00
(3)	I'M FOR JACKIE (Blue type on white ball, no photo.)	200.00	100.00	60.00
(4)	I'm Rooting for Jackie Robinson (1-3/4", red border)	275.00	135.00	80.00
(5)	I'm Rooting for Jackie Robinson (1-1/4", white background)	350.00	175.00	100.00
(6)	I'm Rooting for Jackie Robinson (1-3/4", gray background)	300.00	150.00	90.00
(7)	JACKIE ROBINSON / DODGERS (1-3/4", b/w photo batting in pinstripes and plain cap)	400.00	200.00	125.00
(8)	JACKIE ROBINSON / DODGERS (1-1/4", white background)	200.00	100.00	60.00
(9)	Jackie Robinson Outstanding Rookie (3-3/8" white border)	200.00	100.00	60.00
(10)	19 Rookie of the Year 47 (1-3/4" red border)(Modern reproductions exist.)	325.00	160.00	100.00

1950s Jackie Robinson WNBC Photocard

This black-and-white 5-3/4" x 7-1/2" photocard pictures Robinson in his post-playing days career as a broadcaster for the NBC radio network's flagship station in New York.

	NM	EX	VG
Jackie Robinson	35.00	17.50	10.50

1911 Rochester Baking Philadelphia A's (D359)

The 1911 Rochester Baking set, an 18-card Philadelphia Athletics set, is among the scarcest of early 20th Century bakery issues. The set commemorates the Athletics' 1910 Championship season, and, except for pitcher Jack Coombs, the checklist includes nearly all key members of the club, including manager Connie Mack. The cards are the standard size for the era, 1-1/2" x 2-5/8". The front of each card features a player portrait set against a colored background. The player's name and the word "Athletics" appear at the bottom, while "World's Champions 1910" is printed along the top. The backs of the cards advertise the set as the "Athletics Series." Collectors should be aware that the same checklist was used for a similar Athletics set issued by Williams Baking and Cullivan's Fireside tobacco (T208), and also that blank-backed versions are also known to exist, but these are classified as E104 cards in the American Card Catalog.

		NM	EX	VG
Complete Set (18):		70,000	35,000	21,000
Common Player:		2,000	1,000	600.00
(1)	Home Run Baker	7,000	3,500	1,750
(2)	Jack Barry	2,000	1,000	600.00
(3)	Chief Bender	7,000	3,500	1,750
(4)	Eddie Collins	7,000	3,500	1,750
(5)	Harry Davis	2,000	1,000	600.00
(6)	Jimmy Dygert	2,000	1,000	600.00
(7)	Topsy Hartsel	2,000	1,000	600.00
(8)	Harry Krause	2,000	1,000	600.00
(9)	Jack Lapp	2,000	1,000	600.00
(10)	Paddy Livingston	2,000	1,000	600.00
(11)	Bris Lord	2,000	1,000	600.00
(12)	Connie Mack	14,000	7,900	4,575
(13)	Cy Morgan	2,000	1,000	600.00
(14)	Danny Murphy	2,000	1,000	600.00
(15)	Rube Oldring	2,000	1,000	600.00
(16)	Eddie Plank	14,000	7,900	4,575
(17)	Amos Strunk	2,000	1,000	600.00
(18)	Ira Thomas	2,000	1,000	600.00

1955 Rodeo Meats Athletics

This set of 2-1/2" x 3-1/2" color cards was issued by a local meat company to commemorate the first year of the Athletics in Kansas City. There are 38 different players included in the set, with nine players known to appppear in two different variations for a total of 47 cards in the set. Most variations are in background colors, although Bobby Shantz is also listed incorrectly as "Schantz" on one variation. The cards are unnumbered, with the Rodeo logo and player name on the fronts, and an ad for a scrapbook album listed on the backs.

		NM	EX	VG
Complete Set (47):		12,500	6,250	3,750
Common Player:		225.00	110.00	45.00
Album:		550.00	275.00	125.00
(1)	Joe Astroth	225.00	110.00	45.00
(2)	Harold Bevan	275.00	135.00	55.00
(3)	Charles Bishop	275.00	135.00	55.00
(4)	Don Bollweg	275.00	135.00	55.00
(5)	Lou Boudreau	600.00	300.00	120.00
(6)	Cloyd Boyer (Blue background.)	275.00	135.00	55.00
(7)	Cloyd Boyer (Pink background.)	225.00	110.00	45.00
(8)	Ed Burtschy	275.00	135.00	55.00
(9)	Art Ceccarelli	225.00	110.00	45.00
(10)	Joe DeMaestri (Pea green background.)	275.00	135.00	55.00
(11)	Joe DeMaestri (Light green background.)	225.00	110.00	45.00
(12)	Art Ditmar	225.00	110.00	45.00
(13)	John Dixon	275.00	135.00	55.00
(14)	Jim Finigan	225.00	110.00	45.00
(15)	Marion Fricano	275.00	135.00	55.00
(16)	Tom Gorman	275.00	135.00	55.00
(17)	John Gray	225.00	110.00	45.00
(18)	Ray Herbert	225.00	110.00	45.00
(19)	Forest "Spook" Jacobs (Forrest)	275.00	135.00	55.00
(20)	Alex Kellner	275.00	135.00	55.00
(21)	Harry Kraft (Craft)	225.00	110.00	45.00
(22)	Jack Littrell	225.00	110.00	45.00
(23)	Hector Lopez	275.00	135.00	55.00
(24)	Oscar Melillo	225.00	110.00	45.00
(25)	Arnold Portocarrero (Purple background.)	275.00	135.00	55.00
(26)	Arnold Portocarrero (Gray background.)	225.00	110.00	45.00
(27)	Vic Power (Pink background.)	275.00	135.00	55.00
(28)	Vic Power (Yellow background.)	250.00	125.00	50.00
(29)	Vic Raschi	275.00	135.00	55.00
(30)	Bill Renna (Dark pink background.)	275.00	135.00	55.00
(31)	Bill Renna (Light pink background.)	225.00	110.00	45.00
(32)	Al Robertson	275.00	135.00	55.00

(33)	Johnny Sain	275.00	135.00	55.00
(34a)	Bobby Schantz (Incorrect spelling.)	900.00	450.00	180.00
(34b)	Bobby Shantz (Correct spelling.)	300.00	150.00	60.00
(35)	Wilmer Shantz (Orange background.)	275.00	135.00	55.00
(36)	Wilmer Shantz (Purple background.)	225.00	110.00	45.00
(37)	Harry Simpson	225.00	110.00	45.00
(38)	Enos Slaughter	650.00	325.00	130.00
(39)	Lou Sleater	225.00	110.00	45.00
(40)	George Susce	225.00	110.00	45.00
(41)	Bob Trice	275.00	135.00	55.00
(42)	Elmer Valo (Yellow background.)	275.00	135.00	55.00
(43)	Elmer Valo (Green background.)	225.00	110.00	45.00
(44)	Bill Wilson (Yellow background.)	275.00	135.00	55.00
(45)	Bill Wilson (Purple background.)	225.00	110.00	45.00
(46)	Gus Zernial	250.00	125.00	50.00

1956 Rodeo Meats Athletics

Gus' Zernial

Hey Kids...

Rodeo Meats issued another Kansas City Athletics set in 1956, but this one was a much smaller 13-card set. The 2-1/2" x 3-1/2" cards are again unnumbered, with the player name and Rodeo logo on the fronts. Card backs feature some of the same graphics and copy as the 1955 cards, but the album offer is omitted. The full-color cards were only available in packages of Rodeo hot dogs.

		NM	EX	VG
Complete Set (12):		2,750	1,100	550.00
Common Player:		200.00	80.00	40.00
(1)	Joe Astroth	200.00	80.00	40.00
(2)	Lou Boudreau	350.00	140.00	70.00
(3)	Joe DeMaestri	200.00	80.00	40.00
(4)	Art Ditmar	200.00	80.00	40.00
(5)	Jim Finigan	200.00	80.00	40.00
(6)	Hector Lopez	200.00	80.00	40.00
(7)	Vic Power	200.00	80.00	40.00
(8)	Bobby Shantz	225.00	90.00	45.00
(9)	Harry Simpson	200.00	80.00	40.00
(10)	Enos Slaughter	475.00	190.00	95.00
(11)	Elmer Valo	200.00	80.00	40.00
(12)	Gus Zernial	200.00	80.00	40.00

1976 Rodeo Meats Athletics Commemorative

Bobby Shantz

This collectors' issue essentially reprints many of the 1955-56 Rodeo Meats cards in a 2-1/2" x 3-1/2" black-and-white format. Fronts have player photos, the Rodeo logo and the player name in the white border at bottom. Backs, instead of the original Rodeo ads, have player identification, biographical information and career summary, along with a reprint notice.

		NM	EX	VG
Complete Set (30):		20.00	10.00	6.00
Common Player:		2.00	1.00	.60
1	Header Card	.50	.25	.15
2	Checklist Card	.50	.25	.15
3	Joe Astroth	2.00	1.00	.60
4	Lou Boudreau	3.00	1.50	.90
5	Cloyd Boyer	2.00	1.00	.60
6	Art Ceccarelli	2.00	1.00	.60
7	Harry Craft	2.00	1.00	.60
8	Joe DeMaestri	2.00	1.00	.60
9	Art Ditmar	2.00	1.00	.60
10	Jim Finigan	2.00	1.00	.60
11	Ray Herbert	2.00	1.00	.60
12	Tom Gorman	2.00	1.00	.60
13	Alex Kellner	2.00	1.00	.60
14	Jack Littrell	2.00	1.00	.60
15	Hector Lopez	2.00	1.00	.60
16	Oscar Melillo	2.00	1.00	.60
17	Arnie Portocarrero	2.00	1.00	.60
18	Vic Power	2.50	1.25	.70
19	Vic Raschi	2.50	1.25	.70
20	Bill Renna	2.00	1.00	.60
21	Johnny Sain	2.50	1.25	.70
22	Bobby Shantz	2.50	1.25	.70
23	Wilmer Shantz	2.00	1.00	.60
24	Harry Simpson	2.50	1.25	.70
25	Enos Slaughter	4.00	2.00	1.25
26	Lou Sleator	2.00	1.00	.60
27	George Susce	2.00	1.00	.60
28	Elmer Valo	2.00	1.00	.60
29	Bill Wilson	2.00	1.00	.60
30	Gus Zernial	2.50	1.25	.70

1930s Rogers Peet Sport Album

18.— Herb Pennock

This is one of the scarcest multi-sport issues of the 1930s. It was the promotion of a New York-Boston chain of stores (boys' clothing?) in the form of a frequent customer program. Boys visiting the store with a parent could receive a set of four cards to be placed in a 14-page 4-1/2" x 7-1/4" album. Individual cards are about 1-7/8" x 2-1/2" and feature black-and-white photos with a white border. The athlete's name and card number are printed in the bottom border. Numbers correspond to spaces in the album. Only the "Baseball Stars" from the issue are checklisted here. Others include hockey, football, track, swimming, golf, tennis, aviation, etc.

		NM	EX	VG
Complete Set (44):		7,500	3,750	2,250
Complete Set in Album:		5,000	2,500	1,500
Common Sticker:		30.00	15.00	9.00
Album:		500.00	250.00	150.00
5	Dazzy Vance	225.00	110.00	65.00
13	Walter Johnson	650.00	325.00	195.00
16	Rogers Hornsby	450.00	225.00	135.00
18	Herb Pennock	225.00	110.00	65.00
28	Lou Gehrig	1,600	800.00	480.00
34	Ty Cobb	800.00	400.00	240.00
38	Tris Speaker	450.00	225.00	135.00
48	Babe Ruth	1,750	875.00	525.00

1960s Rogers Printing Co. Postcards

 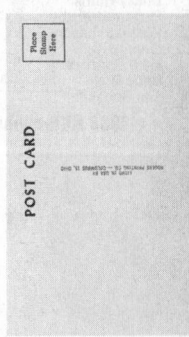

The extent to which this Columbus, Ohio, firm may have provided baseball players with postcards to answer fan mail requests is unknown. At present, only a single card is known, that of Bob Wills, who played his entire major league career (1957-63) with the Cubs. The card is printed in black-and-white on glossy stock in a 3-1/2" x 5-1/2" format. A facsimile autograph message is printed on front. Postcard-style backs have the imprint of the printer.

		NM	EX	VG
Bob Will		3.00	1.50	.90

1970 Rold Gold Pretzels

BABE RUTH

The 1970 Rold Gold Pretzels set of 15 cards honors the "Greatest Players Ever" in the first 100 years of baseball as chosen by the Baseball Writers of America. The cards, which measure 2-1/4" x 3-1/2" in size, feature a simulated 3-D effect. The set was re-released in 1972 by Kellogg's in packages of Danish-Go-Rounds. Rold Gold cards can be differentiated from the Kellogg's cards of 1972 by the 1970 copyright date found on the card reverse.

		NM	EX	VG
	Complete Set (15):	50.00	25.00	15.00
	Common Player:	2.00	1.00	.60
1	Walter Johnson	6.00	3.00	1.75
2	Rogers Hornsby	3.00	1.50	.90
3	John McGraw	2.00	1.00	.60
4	Mickey Cochrane	2.00	1.00	.60
5	George Sisler	2.00	1.00	.60
6	Babe Ruth ("Greatest Ever")	15.00	7.50	4.50
7	Robert "Lefty" Grove	2.00	1.00	.60
8	Harold "Pie" Traynor	2.00	1.00	.60
9	Honus Wagner	7.50	3.75	2.25
10	Eddie Collins	2.00	1.00	.60
11	Tris Speaker	3.00	1.50	.90
12	Cy Young	5.00	2.50	1.50
13	Lou Gehrig	10.00	5.00	3.00
14	Babe Ruth ("Greatest Right Fielder")	15.00	7.50	4.50
15	Ty Cobb	9.00	4.50	2.75

1908-1909 Rose Company Postcards

 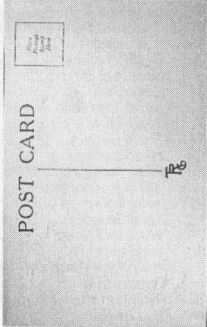

Among the most ornate and attractive baseball cards of the pre-1910 period is the set of postcards produced by The Rose Co., between 1908-09. The 3-1/2" x 5-1/2" cards feature a black-and-white player portrait photo at center, surrounded by an embossed round gold frame. The player's surname and (usually) team are in a white panel under the photo. The background of the card's front is in green and includes crossed bats and a baseball, a diamond diagram and pictures of a fielder and batter. The postcard-format back is printed in black-and-white with a TRC logo at bottom-center. The unnumbered postcards are checklisted here alphabetically; including 11 minor league players from Scranton in the New York State League. It is possible future discoveries will be added to this checklist; gaps have been left in the numbering to accommodate them.

		NM	EX	VG
	Common Player:	2,400	1,000	500.00
(1)	Ed Abbaticchio	2,400	1,000	500.00
(2)	Bill Abstein	2,400	1,000	500.00
(3)	Whitey Alperman	2,400	1,000	500.00
(4)	Nick Altrock	2,400	1,000	500.00
(5)	John Anderson	2,400	1,000	500.00
(6)	Shad Barry	2,400	1,000	500.00
(7)	Ginger Beaumont	2,400	1,000	500.00
(8)	Heinie Beckendorf	2,400	1,000	500.00
(9)	Fred Beebe	2,400	1,000	500.00
(10)	Harry Bemis	2,400	1,000	500.00
(11)	Chief Bender	6,000	3,400	1,750
(12)	Bills	2,400	1,000	500.00
(13)	Joe Birmingham	2,400	1,000	500.00
(14)	Frank Bowerman	2,400	1,000	500.00
(15)	Bill Bradley	2,400	1,000	500.00
(16)	Kitty Bransfield	2,400	1,000	500.00
(17)	Roger Bresnahan	6,000	3,400	1,750
(18)	Al Bridwell	2,400	1,000	500.00
(19)	Buster Brown (Philadelphia) (Photo actually Mordecai Brown.)	2,400	1,000	500.00
(20)	Samuel Brown (Boston)	2,400	1,000	500.00
(21)	Mordecai Brown (Chicago)	6,000	3,400	1,750
(22)	Bobby Byrne	2,400	1,000	500.00
(23)	Howie Camnitz	2,400	1,000	500.00
(24)	Billy Campbell	2,400	1,000	500.00
(25)	Frank Chance	6,000	3,400	1,750
(26)	Hal Chase	2,400	1,000	500.00
(27)	Charlie Chech	2,400	1,000	500.00
(28)	Jack Chesbro	6,000	3,400	1,750
(29)	Fred Clarke (Pittsburgh)	6,000	3,400	1,750
(30)	Nig Clarke (Cleveland)	2,400	1,000	500.00
(31)	Otis Clymer	2,400	1,000	500.00
(32)				
(33a)	Andy Coakley (Cincinnati)	2,400	1,000	500.00
(33b)	Andy Coakley (No team name.)	2,400	1,000	500.00
(34)	Ty Cobb	24,000	13,600	7,000
(35)	Jimmy Collins	6,000	3,400	1,750
(36)	Wid Conroy	2,400	1,000	500.00
(37)	Jack Coombs	2,400	1,000	500.00
(38)	Frank Corridon	2,400	1,000	500.00
(39)	Bill Coughlin	2,400	1,000	500.00
(40)	Sam Crawford	6,000	3,400	1,750
(41a)	Lou Criger (Boston)	2,400	1,000	500.00
(41b)	Lou Criger (No team.)	2,400	1,000	500.00

		NM	EX	VG
(42)	Bill Dahlen	2,400	1,000	500.00
(43)	Harry Davis	2,400	1,000	500.00
(44)	Joe Delahanty (St. Louis)	2,400	1,000	500.00
(45)	Frank Delehanty (Delahanty) (Washington; team actually N.Y., A.L.)	2,400	1,000	500.00
(46)	Art Devlin	2,400	1,000	500.00
(47)	Mike Donlin	2,400	1,000	500.00
(48)	Jiggs Donohue (Donahue)	2,400	1,000	500.00
(49)	Wild Bill Donovan	2,400	1,000	500.00
(51)	Red Dooin	2,400	1,000	500.00
(52)	Mickey Doolan	2,400	1,000	500.00
(53)	Larry Doyle	2,400	1,000	500.00
(54)	Jimmy Dygert	2,400	1,000	500.00
(55)	Kid Elberfeld	2,400	1,000	500.00
(56)	Eley	2,400	1,000	500.00
(57)	Johnny Evers	6,000	3,400	1,750
(58)	Bob Ewing	2,400	1,000	500.00
(59)	George Ferguson	2,400	1,000	500.00
(60)	Hobe Ferris	2,400	1,000	500.00
(61)	Jerry Freeman	2,400	1,000	500.00
(62)	Bob Ganley	2,400	1,000	500.00
(63)	John Ganzel	2,400	1,000	500.00
(64)	Doc Gessler	2,400	1,000	500.00
(65)	George Gibson	2,400	1,000	500.00
(66)	Billy Gilbert	2,400	1,000	500.00
(67)	Fred Glade	2,400	1,000	500.00
(68)	Ralph Glaze	2,400	1,000	500.00
(69)	Graham	2,400	1,000	500.00
(70)	Eddie Grant	2,400	1,000	500.00
(71)	Groh	2,400	1,000	500.00
(72)	Charley Hale (Hall)	2,400	1,000	500.00
(73)	Halligan	2,400	1,000	500.00
(74)	Topsy Hartsel	2,400	1,000	500.00
(75)	Charlie Hemphill	2,400	1,000	500.00
(76)	Bill Hinchman	2,400	1,000	500.00
(77)	Art Hoelskoetter	2,400	1,000	500.00
(78)	Danny Hoffman	2,400	1,000	500.00
(79)	Solly Hofmann	2,400	1,000	500.00
(80)	Houser	2,400	1,000	500.00
(81)	Harry Howell	2,400	1,000	500.00
(82)	Miller Huggins	6,000	3,400	1,750
(83)	Rudy Hulswitt	2,400	1,000	500.00
(84)	John Hummel	2,400	1,000	500.00
(85a)	Frank Isbel (Isbell)(Chicago)	2,400	1,000	500.00
(85b)	Frank Isbel (Isbell) (No team.)	2,400	1,000	500.00
(86)	Walter Johnson	12,000	6,800	3,500
(87)	Fielder Jones (Chicago)	2,400	1,000	500.00
(88)	Tom Jones (St. Louis)	2,400	1,000	500.00
(89)	Tim Jordan	2,400	1,000	500.00
(90)	Addie Joss	12,000	6,800	3,500
(91)	Johnny Kane	2,400	1,000	500.00
(92)	Ed Karger	2,400	1,000	500.00
(93)	Wee Willie Keeler	6,000	3,400	1,750
(94)	Kellogg	2,400	1,000	500.00
(95)	Ed Killian	2,400	1,000	500.00
(96)	Malachi Kittredge (Kittridge)	2,400	1,000	500.00
(97)	Red Kleinow	2,400	1,000	500.00
(98)	Johnny Kling	2,400	1,000	500.00
(99)	Otto Knabe	2,400	1,000	500.00
(100)	John Knight	2,400	1,000	500.00
(102)	Ed Konetchy	2,400	1,000	500.00
(103)	Nap Lajoie	12,000	6,800	3,500
(104)	Frank LaPorte	2,400	1,000	500.00
(105)	Tommy Leach	2,400	1,000	500.00
(106)	Glenn Leibhardt (Liebhardt)	2,400	1,000	500.00
(107)	Phil Lewis	2,400	1,000	500.00
(108)	Vive Lindamann (Lindaman)	2,400	1,000	500.00
(109)	Hans Lobert	2,400	1,000	500.00
(110)	Harry Lord	2,400	1,000	500.00
(111)	Harry Lumley	2,400	1,000	500.00
(112)	Johnny Lush	2,400	1,000	500.00
(113)	Nick Maddox	2,400	1,000	500.00
(114)	Sherry Magee	2,400	1,000	500.00
(115)	Billy Maloney	2,400	1,000	500.00
(116)	Christy Mathewson	12,000	6,800	3,500
(117)	George McBride	2,400	1,000	500.00
(118)	Joe McGinnity	6,000	3,400	1,750
(119)	Stoney McGlynn	2,400	1,000	500.00
(120)	Harry McIntyre (McIntire)(Brooklyn)	2,400	1,000	500.00
(121)	Matty McIntyre (Detroit)	2,400	1,000	500.00
(122)	Larry McLean	2,400	1,000	500.00
(123)	George McQuillen (McQuillan)	2,400	1,000	500.00
(124)	Clyde Milan	2,400	1,000	500.00
(126)	Mike Mitchell	2,400	1,000	500.00
(127)	Moran	2,400	1,000	500.00
(128)	Mike Mowrey	2,400	1,000	500.00
(129)	George Mullin	2,400	1,000	500.00
(130)	Danny Murphy	2,400	1,000	500.00
(131)	J.J. Murray	2,400	1,000	500.00
(132)	Doc Newton	2,400	1,000	500.00
(133)	Simon Nicholls	2,400	1,000	500.00
(134)	Harry Niles	2,400	1,000	500.00
(135)	Rebel Oakes	2,400	1,000	500.00
(136)	Rube Oldring	2,400	1,000	500.00
(137)	Charley O'Leary	2,400	1,000	500.00
(138)	Patsy O'Rourke	2,400	1,000	800.00
(139)	Al Orth	2,400	1,000	800.00
(140)	Fred Osborne (Osborn)	2,400	1,000	500.00
(141)	Orval Overall	2,400	1,000	500.00
(142)	Freddy Parent	2,400	1,000	500.00
(143)	George Paskert	2,400	1,000	500.00
(144)	Case Patten	2,400	1,000	500.00
(145)	Jeff Pfeffer	2,400	1,000	500.00
(146)	Deacon Phillippi (Phillippe)	2,400	1,000	500.00
(147)	Eddie Plank	12,000	6,800	3,500
(148)	Jack Powell	2,400	1,000	500.00
(149)	Tex Pruiett	2,400	1,000	500.00
(150)	Ed Reulbach	2,400	1,000	500.00
(151)	Bob Rhoades (Rhoads)	2,400	1,000	500.00
(152)	Claude Ritchey	2,400	1,000	500.00
(153)	Claude Rossman	2,400	1,000	500.00
(154)	Nap Rucker	2,400	1,000	500.00
(155)	Germany Schaefer	2,400	1,000	500.00
(156)	George Schlei	2,400	1,000	500.00
(157)	Boss Schmidt	2,400	1,000	500.00

		NM	EX	VG
(158)	Ossie Schreck	2,400	1,000	500.00
(159)	Wildfire Schulte	2,400	1,000	500.00
(160)	Schultz	2,400	1,000	500.00
(161)	Socks Seybold	2,400	1,000	500.00
(162)	Cy Seymour	2,400	1,000	500.00
(163)	Spike Shannon	2,400	1,000	500.00
(164)	Jimmy Sheckard	2,400	1,000	500.00
(165)	Tommy Sheehan	2,400	1,000	500.00
(166)	Bill Shipke	2,400	1,000	500.00
(167)	Jimmy Slagle	2,400	1,000	500.00
(168)	Charlie Smith (Chicago)	2,400	1,000	500.00
(169)	Frank Smith (Washington)	2,400	1,000	500.00
(170)	Bob Spade	2,400	1,000	500.00
(171)	Tully Sparks	2,400	1,000	500.00
(172)	Tris Speaker	6,000	3,400	1,750
(173)	Tubby Spencer	2,400	1,000	500.00
(174)	Jake Stahl	2,400	1,000	500.00
(176)	Steele	2,400	1,000	500.00
(177)	Harry Steinfeldt	2,400	1,000	500.00
(178)	George Stone	2,400	1,000	500.00
(179)	George Stovall	2,400	1,000	500.00
(180)	Billy Sullivan	2,400	1,000	500.00
(181)	Ed Summers	2,400	1,000	500.00
(182)	Bill Sweeney	2,400	1,000	500.00
(183)	Lee Tannehill	2,400	1,000	500.00
(184)	Dummy Taylor	2,400	1,000	500.00
(185)	Fred Tenney	2,400	1,000	500.00
(186)	Ira Thomas (No team.)	2,400	1,000	500.00
(187)	Roy Thomas (Pittsburg)	2,400	1,000	500.00
(188)	Jack Thoney	2,400	1,000	500.00
(189)	Joe Tinker	6,000	3,400	1,750
(190)	John Titus	2,400	1,000	500.00
(191)	Terry Turner	2,400	1,000	500.00
(192)	Bob Unglaub	2,400	1,000	500.00
(193)	Rube Waddell	6,000	3,400	1,750
(194)	Heinie Wagner (Boston)	2,400	1,000	500.00
(195)	Honus Wagner (Pittsburg)	24,000	13,600	7,000
(196)	Ed Walsh	6,000	3,400	1,750
(197)	Jack Warner	2,400	1,000	500.00
(198a)	Jake Weimer (Cincinnati)	2,400	1,000	500.00
(198b)	Jake Weimer (No team.)	2,400	1,000	500.00
(199)	Doc White	2,400	1,000	500.00
(201)	Jimmy Williams	2,400	1,000	500.00
(202)	Chief Wilson	2,400	1,000	500.00
(203)	Hooks Wiltse	2,400	1,000	500.00
(204)	George Winter	2,400	1,000	500.00
(205)	Cy Young (Boston)	12,000	6,800	3,500
(206)	Harley Young (Pittsburg)	2,400	1,000	500.00

1905 Rotograph Postcards

Only New York players have been seen on this series of 3-1/4" x 5-3/8" black-and-white or blue-and-white duotone postcards. Cards have player portrait photos with a white strip at bottom identifying the player; a "Rotograph / Series" notation is at left. Backs have typical postcard markings. This checklist may not be complete. The set was listed in the American Card Catalog under the number PC782.

		NM	EX	VG
	Common Player:	1,200	600.00	360.00
(1)	Geo. Brown (Browne)	1,200	600.00	360.00
(2)	J.D. Chesbro	1,500	750.00	450.00
(3)	Wm. F. Dahlen	1,200	600.00	360.00
(4)	Clark Griffill (Griffith)	2,000	1,000	600.00
(5)	Joseph McGinnity	1,500	750.00	450.00
(6)	John McGraw	2,250	1,125	675.00
(7)	A. Puttmann	1,200	600.00	360.00
(8)	Luther Taylor	1,900	950.00	600.00

1977 Jim Rowe 4-on-1 Exhibits

This collectors' edition set harkens back to the four-player cards issued in the 1930s by Exhibit Supply Co. The 1977 version is printed in black on yellow in a 3-1/4" x 5-1/2" format. Backs are blank. Each of the four player photos on front is identified by name. The cards are checklisted here in order of team name.

		NM	EX	VG
Complete Set (16):		90.00	45.00	27.00
Common Card:		5.00	2.50	1.50
(1)	Boston Braves (Al Lopez, Rabbit Maranville, Warren Spahn, Casey Stengel)	5.00	2.50	1.50
(2)	Boston Red Sox (Joe Cronin, Herb Pennock, Babe Ruth, Ted Williams)	15.00	7.50	4.50
(3)	Brooklyn Dodgers (Max Carey, Burleigh Grimes, Joe Medwick, Dazzy Vance)	5.00	2.50	1.50
(4)	Chicago Cubs (Kiki Cuyler, Gabby Hartnett, Billy Herman, Freddy Lindstrom)	5.00	2.50	1.50
(5)	Chicago White Sox (Luke Appling, Red Faber, Ted Lyons, Red Ruffing)	5.00	2.50	1.50
(6)	Cincinnati Reds (Chick Hafey, George Kelly, Bill McKechnie, Edd Roush)	5.00	2.50	1.50
(7)	Cleveland Indians (Earl Averill, Lou Boudreau, Bob Feller, Bob Lemon)	5.00	2.50	1.50
(8)	Detroit Tigers (Ty Cobb, Charlie Gehringer, Goose Goslin, Hank Greenberg)	11.00	5.50	3.25
(9)	New York Giants (Dave Bancroft, Carl Hubbell, Mel Ott, Bill Terry)	5.00	2.50	1.50
(10)	New York Yankees (Bill Dickey, Joe DiMaggio, Lou Gehrig, Lefty Gomez)	12.00	6.00	3.50
(11)	Philadelphia Athletics (Mickey Cochrane, Eddie Collins, Lefty Grove, Al Simmons)	5.00	2.50	1.50
(12)	Philadelphia Phillies (Grover Alexander, Jimmie Foxx, Eppa Rixey, Robin Roberts)	5.00	2.50	1.50
(13)	Pittsburgh Pirates (Pie Traynor, Honus Wagner, Lloyd Waner, Paul Waner)	6.00	3.00	1.75
(14)	St. Louis Browns (Jim Bottomley, Earle Combs, Rogers Hornsby, George Sisler)	5.00	2.50	1.50
(15)	St. Louis Cardinals (Dizzy Dean, Frankie Frisch, Jesse Haines, Stan Musial)	5.00	2.50	1.50
(16)	Washington Senators (Bucky Harris, Walter Johnson, Heinie Manush, Sam Rice)	6.00	3.00	1.75

1977 Jim Rowe 1929 Cubs Postcards

Originally retailed for $3 per set, these collector-issue postcards feature on front borderless black-and-white photos in 3-1/2" x 5-7/16" format. Backs are standard Kodak postcard style, with no mention of the issuer. The player name is usually found penned at top.

		NM	EX	VG
Complete Set (13):		30.00	20.00	12.00
Common Player:		3.00	1.50	.90
(1)	Guy Bush	3.00	1.50	.90
(2)	Kiki Cuyler	3.00	1.50	.90
(3)	Woody English	3.00	1.50	.90
(4)	Charlie Grimm	3.00	1.50	.90
(5)	Gabby Hartnett	3.00	1.50	.90
(6)	Rogers Hornsby	3.00	1.50	.90
(7)	Pat Malone	3.00	1.50	.90
(8)	Norman McMillan	3.00	1.50	.90
(9)	Charlie Root	3.00	1.50	.90
(10)	Riggs Stephenson	3.00	1.50	.90
(11)	Zach Taylor	3.00	1.50	.90
(12)	Hack Wilson	3.00	1.50	.90
(13)	Team photo	3.00	1.50	.90

1977 Jim Rowe 1956 Braves Postcards

Originally retailed for $4 per set, these collector-issue postcards feature on front borderless black-and-white photos in 3-1/2" x 5-7/16" format. Backs are standard Kodak postcard style, with no mention of the issuer. The player name is usually found penned at top.

	NM	EX	VG
Complete Set (16):	35.00	17.50	10.50

		NM	EX	VG
Common Player:		3.00	1.50	.90
(1)	Hank Aaron	4.00	2.00	1.25
(2)	Joe Adcock	3.00	1.50	.90
(3)	Bill Bruton	3.00	1.50	.90
(4)	Bob Buhl	3.00	1.50	.90
(5)	Lew Burdette	3.00	1.50	.90
(6)	Gene Conley	3.00	1.50	.90
(7)	Del Crandall	3.00	1.50	.90
(8)	Charlie Grimm	3.00	1.50	.90
(9)	Fred Haney	3.00	1.50	.90
(10)	Joey Jay	3.00	1.50	.90
(11)	Johnny Logan	3.00	1.50	.90
(12)	Chet Nichols	3.00	1.50	.90
(13)	Danny O'Connell	3.00	1.50	.90
(14)	Andy Pafko	3.00	1.50	.90
(15)	Warren Spahn	3.00	1.50	.90
(16)	Bobby Thomson	3.00	1.50	.90

1951 Royal Desserts Advertising Cards

The "10/51" printed on the backs of these sample cards appears to place their issue within the three-year (1950-52) span in which box-back cards of baseball players and movie stars were issued on Royal dessert products. The back message encourages collecting of a complete set. The sample cards are about 3-3/8" x 2-7/8", printed in black and red on white. Fronts of the known sample cards appear identical to the original 1950 issued versions. Whether any players other than the two listed here were issued in sample versions is unknown..

		NM	EX	VG
2	"Pee Wee" Reese	1,500	750.00	450.00
3	George Kell	1,000	500.00	300.00

1978 Royal Crown Cola Iron-Ons

These iron-on color transfers were available in team strips of five players for 50 cents and six bottle cap liners. Because they were licensed only by the Players' Association, and not MLB, the approximately 4-1/4" x 6-1/4" transfers do not show team logos or nicknames.

		NM	EX	VG
Complete Set (130):		750.00	375.00	225.00
Common Player:		6.00	3.00	1.75
	Atlanta Strip	25.00	12.50	7.50
(1)	Jeff Burroughs	6.00	3.00	1.75
(2)	Gary Matthews	6.00	3.00	1.75
(3)	Phil Niekro	7.50	3.75	2.25
(4)	Biff Pocoroba	6.00	3.00	1.75
(5)	Dick Ruthven	6.00	3.00	1.75
	Baltimore Strip	50.00	25.00	15.00
(6)	Al Bumbry	6.00	3.00	1.75
(7)	Lee May	6.00	3.00	1.75
(8)	Eddie Murray	30.00	15.00	9.00
(9)	Jim Palmer	15.00	7.50	4.50
(10)	Ken Singleton	6.00	3.00	1.75
	Boston Strip	40.00	20.00	12.00
(11)	Bill Campbell	6.00	3.00	1.75
(12)	Fred Lynn	6.00	3.00	1.75
(13)	Jim Rice	7.50	3.75	2.25
(14)	George Scott	6.00	3.00	1.75
(15)	Carl Yastrzemski	25.00	12.50	7.50
	California Strip	75.00	37.50	22.50
(16)	Dave Chalk	6.00	3.00	1.75
(17)	Bobby Grich	6.00	3.00	1.75
(18)	Joe Rudi	6.00	3.00	1.75
(19)	Nolan Ryan	60.00	30.00	18.00
(20)	Frank Tanana	6.00	3.00	1.75
	Chicago (Cubs) Strip	30.00	15.00	9.00
(21)	Bill Buckner	6.00	3.00	1.75
(22)	Dave Kingman	6.00	3.00	1.75
(23)	Steve Ontiveros	6.00	3.00	1.75
(24)	Bruce Sutter	7.50	3.75	2.25
(25)	Manny Trillo	6.00	3.00	1.75
	Chicago (White Sox) Strip	25.00	12.50	7.50
(26)	Ron Blomberg	6.00	3.00	1.75
(27)	Bobby Bonds	6.00	3.00	1.75
(28)	Ralph Garr	6.00	3.00	1.75
(29)	Jorge Orta	6.00	3.00	1.75
(30)	Eric Soderholm	6.00	3.00	1.75
	Cincinnati Strip			
(31)	Johnny Bench	15.00	7.50	4.50
(32)	Unknown	.00	.00	.00
(33)	Joe Morgan	15.00	7.50	4.50
(34)	Unknown			
(35)	Pete Rose	40.00	20.00	12.00
	Cleveland Strip	25.00	12.50	7.50
(36)	Buddy Bell	6.00	3.00	1.75
(37)	Wayne Garland	6.00	3.00	1.75
(38)	Johnny Grubb	6.00	3.00	1.75
(39)	Rick Manning	6.00	3.00	1.75
(40)	Andre Thornton	6.00	3.00	1.75

		NM	EX	VG
	Detroit Strip	25.00	12.50	7.50
(41)	Mark Fidrych	6.00	3.00	1.75
(42)	John Hiller	6.00	3.00	1.75
(43)	Ron LeFlore	6.00	3.00	1.75
(44)	Milt May	6.00	3.00	1.75
(45)	Jason Thompson	6.00	3.00	1.75
	Houston Strip	25.00	12.50	7.50
(46)	Enos Cabell	6.00	3.00	1.75
(47)	Cesar Cedeno	6.00	3.00	1.75
(48)	Joe Ferguson	6.00	3.00	1.75
(49)	J.R. Richard	6.00	3.00	1.75
(50)	Bobby Watson	6.00	3.00	1.75
	Kansas City Strip	45.00	22.50	13.50
(51)	George Brett	30.00	15.00	9.00
(52)	Al Cowens	6.00	3.00	1.75
(53)	Hal McRae	6.00	3.00	1.75
(54)	Amos Otis	6.00	3.00	1.75
(55)	Fred Patek	6.00	3.00	1.75
	Los Angeles Strip	30.00	15.00	9.00
(56)	Ron Cey	6.00	3.00	1.75
(57)	Steve Garvey	7.50	3.75	2.25
(58)	Tommy John	6.00	3.00	1.75
(59)	Bill Russell	6.00	3.00	1.75
(60)	Don Sutton	7.50	3.75	2.25
	Milwaukee Strip	30.00	15.00	9.00
(61)	Sal Bando	6.00	3.00	1.75
(62)	Ray Fosse	6.00	3.00	1.75
(63)	Larry Hisle	6.00	3.00	1.75
(64)	Sixto Lezcano	6.00	3.00	1.75
(65)	Robin Yount	15.00	7.50	4.50
	Minnesota Strip	30.00	15.00	9.00
(66)	Rod Carew	15.00	7.50	4.50
(67)	Dan Ford	6.00	3.00	1.75
(68)	Dave Goltz	6.00	3.00	1.75
(69)	Roy Smalley	6.00	3.00	1.75
(70)	Butch Wynegar	6.00	3.00	1.75
	Montreal Strip	30.00	15.00	9.00
(71)	Dave Cash	6.00	3.00	1.75
(72)	Andre Dawson	7.50	3.75	2.25
(73)	Tony Perez	7.50	3.75	2.25
(74)	Steve Rogers	6.00	3.00	1.75
(75)	Ellis Valentine	6.00	3.00	1.75
	New York (Mets) Strip	25.00	12.50	7.50
(76)	Steve Henderson	6.00	3.00	1.75
(77)	Jerry Koosman	6.00	3.00	1.75
(78)	Elliott Maddox	6.00	3.00	1.75
(79)	Willie Montanez	6.00	3.00	1.75
(80)	Lenny Randle	6.00	3.00	1.75
	New York (Yankees) Strip	30.00	15.00	9.00
(81)	Sparky Lyle	6.00	3.00	1.75
(82)	Thurman Munson	7.50	3.75	2.25
(83)	Lou Piniella	6.00	3.00	1.75
(84)	Willie Randolph	6.00	3.00	1.75
(85)	Mickey Rivers	6.00	3.00	1.75
	Oakland Strip	25.00	12.50	7.50
(86)	Wayne Gross	6.00	3.00	1.75
(87)	Rick Langford	6.00	3.00	1.75
(88)	Bill North	6.00	3.00	1.75
(89)	Mitchell Page	6.00	3.00	1.75
(90)	Gary Thomasson	6.00	3.00	1.75
	Philadelphia Strip	60.00	30.00	18.00
(91)	Larry Bowa	6.00	3.00	1.75
(92)	Steve Carlton	15.00	7.50	4.50
(93)	Greg Luzinski	6.00	3.00	1.75
(94)	Garry Maddox	6.00	3.00	1.75
(95)	Mike Schmidt	35.00	17.50	10.50
	Pittsburgh Strip	30.00	15.00	9.00
(96)	John Candelaria	6.00	3.00	1.75
(97)	Dave Parker	6.00	3.00	1.75
(98)	Bill Robinson	6.00	3.00	1.75
(99)	Willie Stargell	15.00	7.50	4.50
(100)	Rennie Stennett	6.00	3.00	1.75
	San Diego Strip	35.00	17.50	10.00
(101)	Rollie Fingers	7.50	3.75	2.25
(102)	Oscar Gamble	6.00	3.00	1.75
(103)	Randy Jones	6.00	3.00	1.75
(104)	Gene Tenace	6.00	3.00	1.75
(105)	Dave Winfield	15.00	7.50	4.50
	San Francisco Strip	30.00	15.00	9.00
(106)	Vida Blue	6.00	3.00	1.75
(107)	Gary Lavelle	6.00	3.00	1.75
(108)	Bill Madlock	6.00	3.00	1.75
(109)	Willie McCovey	15.00	7.50	4.50
(110)	John Montefusco	6.00	3.00	1.75
	Seattle Strip	25.00	12.50	7.50
(111)	Bruce Bochte	6.00	3.00	1.75
(112)	Ruppert Jones	6.00	3.00	1.75
(113)	Dan Meyer	6.00	3.00	1.75
(114)	Lee Stanton	6.00	3.00	1.75
(115)	Bill Stein	6.00	3.00	1.75
	St. Louis Strip	30.00	15.00	9.00
(116)	Lou Brock	15.00	7.50	4.50
(117)	Bob Forsch	6.00	3.00	1.75
(118)	Ken Reitz	6.00	3.00	1.75
(119)	Ted Simmons	6.00	3.00	1.75
(120)	Garry Templeton	6.00	3.00	1.75
	Texas Strip	25.00	12.50	7.50
(121)	Mike Hargrove	6.00	3.00	1.75
(122)	Toby Harrah	6.00	3.00	1.75
(123)	Jon Matlack	6.00	3.00	1.75
(124)	Jim Sundberg	6.00	3.00	1.75
(125)	Richie Zisk	6.00	3.00	1.75
	Toronto Strip	25.00	12.50	7.50
(126)	Doug Ault	6.00	3.00	1.75
(127)	Bob Bailor	6.00	3.00	1.75
(128)	Jerry Garvin	6.00	3.00	1.75
(129)	Roy Howell	6.00	3.00	1.75
(130)	Al Woods	6.00	3.00	1.75

1950-52 Royal Desserts

This set was issued one per box on the backs of various Royal Dessert products over a period of three years. The basic set contains 24 players, however a number of variations create the much higher total for the set. In 1950, Royal issued cards with two different tints - black and white with red, or blue and white with red. Over the next two years, various sen-

ROYAL STARS OF BASEBALL No. 21

VIRGIL TRUCKS

Detroit Tigers' great master of the speedball, Virgil is known around the American League as "Fire" Trucks.

Born in Birmingham, Ala., April 26, 1919, the 198 lb., 5' 11" pitcher has been a Tiger since 1941, except for a hitch in military service.

Trucks' string of 19 wins in 1949 was his top big league mark to date. He was also official winner of the All Star game that year.

Send for a Plastic Album to Hold Your Royal Stars Collection!

Eight clear envelopes, bound with colorful cover; displays 16 photographs. Mail 15¢ and 3 Royal Desserts package fronts to Royal, Box 89, New York 46, N. Y.

...ences of the cards' biographies were updated; up to three ...imes in some cases. Some players from the set left the ...majors after 1950 and others were apparently never updated, ...but the 23 biography updates that do exist, added to the orig-...nal 24 cards issued in 1950, give the set a total of 47 cards. ...he 2-5/8" x 3-1/4" cards are blank-backed with personal and ...laying biographies alongside the card front photos. Some ...sample cards can be found with advertising for the desserts ...on back; they are valued at about double regular card prices. ...A comb-bound album with seven pages to hold 14 cards was ...also issued in a 3-1/4" x 3-3/8" format with "Royal Stars" and ...a crown logo printed in red on white.

		NM	EX	VG
Common Player:		125.00	55.00	25.00
Album:		200.00	90.00	40.00
1a	Stan Musial (2nd paragraph begins "Musial's 207...")	525.00	235.00	100.00
1b	Stan Musial (2nd paragraph begins "Musial batted...")	525.00	235.00	100.00
2a	Pee Wee Reese (2nd paragraph begins "Pee Wee's...)	330.00	150.00	65.00
2b	Pee Wee Reese (2nd paragraph begins "Captain...")	330.00	150.00	65.00
2c	Pee Wee Reese (Ad card.)	330.00	150.00	65.00
3a	George Kell (2nd paragraph ends "...in 1945, '46.")	200.00	90.00	40.00
3b	George Kell (2nd paragraph ends "...two base hits, 56.")	200.00	90.00	40.00
3c	George Kell (Ad card.)	200.00	90.00	40.00
4a	Dom DiMaggio (2nd paragraph ends "...during 1947.")	165.00	75.00	35.00
4b	Dom DiMaggio (2nd paragraph ends "...with 11.")	165.00	75.00	35.00
5a	Warren Spahn (2nd paragraph ends "...shutouts 7.")	265.00	120.00	55.00
5b	Warren Spahn (2nd paragraph ends "...with 191.")	265.00	120.00	55.00
6a	Andy Pafko (2nd paragraph ends "...7 games.")	125.00	56.00	25.00
6b	Andy Pafko (2nd paragraph ends "...National League.")	125.00	55.00	25.00
6c	Andy Pafko (2nd paragraph ends "...weighs 190.")	125.00	55.00	25.00
7a	Andy Seminick (2nd paragraph ends "...as outfield.")	125.00	55.00	25.00
7b	Andy Seminick (2nd paragraph ends "...since 1916.")	125.00	55.00	25.00
7c	Andy Seminick (2nd paragraph ends "...in the outfield.")	125.00	55.00	25.00
7d	Andy Seminick (2nd paragraph ends "...right handed.")	125.00	55.00	25.00
8a	Lou Brissie (2nd paragraph ends "...when pitching.")	125.00	55.00	25.00
8b	Lou Brissie (2nd paragraph ends "...weighs 215.")	125.00	55.00	25.00
9a	Ewell Blackwell (2nd paragraph begins "Despite recent illness...")	145.00	65.00	30.00
9b	Ewell Blackwell (2nd paragraph begins "Blackwell's...")	145.00	65.00	30.00
10a	Bobby Thomson (2nd paragraph begins "In 1949...")	165.00	75.00	35.00
10b	Bobby Thomson (2nd paragraph begins "Thomson is...")	165.00	75.00	35.00
11a	Phil Rizzuto (2nd paragraph ends "...one 1942 game.")	330.00	150.00	65.00
11b	Phil Rizzuto (2nd paragraph ends "...Most Valuable Player.")	330.00	150.00	65.00
12	Tommy Henrich	155.00	70.00	30.00
13	Joe Gordon	200.00	100.00	60.00
14a	Ray Scarborough (Senators)	125.00	55.00	25.00
14b	Ray Scarborough (White Sox, 2nd paragraph ends "...military service.")	125.00	55.00	25.00
14c	Ray Scarborough (White Sox, 2nd paragraph ends "...the season.")	125.00	55.00	25.00
14d	Ray Scarborough (Red Sox)	125.00	55.00	25.00
15a	Stan Rojek (Pirates)	125.00	55.00	25.00
15b	Stan Rojek (Browns)	125.00	55.00	25.00
16	Luke Appling	180.00	80.00	35.00
17	Willard Marshall	125.00	55.00	25.00
18	Alvin Dark	125.00	55.00	25.00

		NM	EX	VG
19a	Dick Sisler (2nd paragraph ends "...service record.")	125.00	55.00	25.00
19b	Dick Sisler (2nd paragraph ends "...National League flag.")	125.00	55.00	25.00
19c	Dick Sisler (2nd paragraph ends "...Nov. 2, 1920.")	125.00	55.00	25.00
19d	Dick Sisler (2nd paragraph ends "...from '46 to '48.")	125.00	55.00	25.00
20a	Johnny Ostrowski (White Sox)	125.00	55.00	25.00
20b	Johnny Ostrowski (Senators)	125.00	55.00	25.00
21a	Virgil Trucks (2nd paragraph ends "...in military service.")	125.00	55.00	25.00
21b	Virgil Trucks (2nd paragraph ends "...that year.")	125.00	55.00	25.00
21c	Virgil Trucks (2nd paragraph ends "...for military service.")	125.00	55.00	25.00
22	Eddie Robinson	125.00	55.00	25.00
23	Nanny Fernandez	125.00	55.00	25.00
24	Ferris Fain	125.00	55.00	25.00

1952 Royal Desserts

This set, issued as a premium by Royal Desserts in 1952, consists of 16 unnumbered black and white cards, each measuring 5" x 7". The cards include the inscription "To A Royal Fan" along with the player's facsimile autograph. Backs are blank.

		NM	EX	VG
Complete Set (16):		1,400	625.00	275.00
Common Player:		55.00	25.00	10.00
(1)	Ewell Blackwell	55.00	25.00	10.00
(2)	Leland V. Brissie Jr.	55.00	25.00	10.00
(3)	Alvin Dark	55.00	25.00	10.00
(4)	Dom DiMaggio	100.00	45.00	20.00
(5)	Ferris Fain	55.00	25.00	10.00
(6)	George Kell	100.00	45.00	20.00
(7)	Stan Musial	280.00	125.00	55.00
(8)	Andy Pafko	55.00	25.00	10.00
(9)	Pee Wee Reese	175.00	80.00	35.00
(10)	Phil Rizzuto	160.00	70.00	30.00
(11)	Eddie Robinson	55.00	25.00	10.00
(12)	Ray Scarborough	55.00	25.00	10.00
(13)	Andy Seminick	55.00	25.00	10.00
(14)	Dick Sisler	55.00	25.00	10.00
(15)	Warren Spahn	140.00	65.00	25.00
(16)	Bobby Thomson	80.00	35.00	15.00

1920 Babe Ruth "Headin' Home"

This was one of several series of promotional cards issued to advertise the Bambino's starring role in the 1920 silent film, "Headin' Home." The black-and-white cards measure about 1-1/2" x 2-7/16". They feature borderless photos with the three-line caption: BABE RUTH / IN / "HEADIN' HOME." The cards are frequently found miscut with a portion of another card showing at one or more of the edges. Backs may be blank or carry the advertising of a local theater.

		NM	EX	VG
Complete Set (6):		16,000	8,000	4,750
Common Card:		3,000	1,500	900.00
(1)	Babe Ruth (Bat at shoulder, crotch-to-cap.)	3,000	1,500	900.00
(2)	Babe Ruth (Bat extended to his right.)	3,000	1,500	900.00
(3)	Babe Ruth (Bat on shoulder, full-length.)	3,000	1,500	900.00
(4)	Babe Ruth (Follow-through, bat head-high.)	3,000	1,500	900.00
(5)	Babe Ruth (Follow-through, bat below waist.)	3,000	1,500	900.00
(6)	Babe Ruth (Horizontal card, holding bat.)	3,000	1,500	900.00

1920 Babe Ruth "Headin' Home" Theater Cards

To promote the showing of "Headin' Home," a silent movie starring Babe Ruth, theaters had these cards printed up with details of show dates. Fronts of the 1-3/4" x 3-1/4" cards have a sepia photo of Ruth swinging the bat. On back is an advertisement from a local theater. This is one of the first cards ever to picture Ruth as a N.Y. Yankee.

	NM	EX	VG
Babe Ruth (Both hands on bat.)	2,750	1,375	825.00
Babe Ruth (One hand on bat.)	2,750	1,375	825.00

1920 Babe Ruth "Headin' Home" (Tex Rickard)

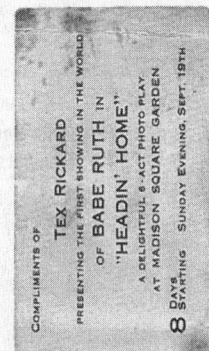

Taking advantage of the Babe's enormous popularity in the pinstripes of his new team, he was given a starring role in a 1920 silent movie titled "Headin Home." To promote the flick, a small set of cards was issued. The 1-7/8" x 3-1/4" black-and-white cards have posed photos of Ruth on front. Dropped out in white in the lower portion of the photo is his name and movie title. Backs have an ad for the movie (some cards are known with blank backs, as well). Tex Rickard was the Ebbets Field announcer for the Brooklyn Dodgers for over 30 years.

		NM	EX	VG
Common Card:		5,000	2,500	1,500
(1)	Babe Ruth (Bat on shoulder, crotch to cap.)	5,000	2,500	1,500
(2)	Babe Ruth (Bat on shoulder, full-length.)	5,000	2,500	1,500
(3)	Babe Ruth (Batting follow-through.)	5,000	2,500	1,500

1920s Babe Ruth Postcard

There is no indication of publisher or specific date of issue on this standard-size, typically marked black-and-white photo postcard which pictures the Babe in street clothes informally posed with a cane chair. The number "210" near the bottom of the photo indicates it was part of a series. The horizontal divided back has typical postcard markings.

		NM	EX	VG
210	Babe Ruth	750.00	375.00	225.00

1920s Babe Ruth Underwear Premium Photo

While the product itself and the boxes and display pieces are collectibles in their own right, among the scarcest pieces associated with the Babe Ruth brand underwear is this approximately 8" x 10" premium photo which was apparently only included in some forms of packaging. The blank-back photo shows a buff Babe in the product and has a facsimile autograph on his right bicep.

	NM	EX	VG
Babe Ruth	500.00	250.00	150.00

1927 "Babe Comes Home" Strip Cards (R94)

This strip card set of unknown scope (at least 75 known) was cataloged as "Movie Stars and Scenes (R94)" in the American Card Catalog. At least two of the cards depict Babe Ruth as "Babe Dugan" in scenes from his silent film. Cards are nominally about 2-7/8" x 2-5/16" and can be found printed in black-and-white or as red, blue or green duotones. The name of the movie is printed in white at bottom. Backs and blank.

	NM	EX	VG
Babe Ruth (In suit w/police.)	1,350	675.00	400.00
Babe Ruth (In uniform, locker room.)	1,350	675.00	400.00

1928 Babe Ruth Home Run Candy Club Membership Card

In conjunction with his candy bar, Ruth created the "Babe Ruth Home Run Candy Club," and issued this membership card. Front has a black-and-white portrait photo. Back of the 2-3/4" x 4" card has 10 rules of sportsmanship for members. The card folds open to reveal a membership certificate with a facsimile autograph.

	NM	EX	VG
Babe Ruth	2,500	1,250	750.00

1928 George Ruth Candy Co.

This circa 1928 issue features sepia-toned photos of Babe Ruth. According to the back of the cards, it was issued by the Geo. H. Ruth Candy Co. Cards measure 1-7/8" x 4" and picture Ruth during a 1924 promotional West Coast tour and in scenes from the movie "Babe Comes Home." The cards are numbered and include photo captions at the bottom. The backs of most cards contain an offer to exchange the six cards for an autographed baseball, which may explain their scarcity today. Cards have been seen with the address to mail for

exchange as Cleveland and as San Francisco. Cards can also be found with blank backs. This issue was deceptively counterfeited in the early 21st Century.

		NM	EX	VG
Complete Set (6):		7,000	3,150	1,400
Common Card:		1,250	650.00	300.00
Wrapper:		3,500	2,000	1,250
1	"Babe" Ruth ("King of them all...")	1,250	650.00	300.00
2	"Babe" Ruth ("Knocked out 60 Home Runs...")	1,250	650.00	300.00
3	"Babe" Ruth ("The only player...")	1,250	650.00	300.00
4	"Babe" Ruth ("The Popular Bambino...")	1,250	650.00	300.00
5	"Babe" Ruth ("A favorite with the Kiddies...")	1,250	650.00	300.00
6	"Babe" Ruth ("The King of Swat...")	1,250	650.00	300.00

1948 Babe Ruth Memorial Pin

Likely issued following Ruth's death in 1948, this 1-3/4" celluloid pinback has a black-and-white photo of Ruth swinging a bat on a black background with his name in capital letters in a white arc below.

	NM	EX	VG
Babe Ruth	300.00	150.00	90.00

1936 R311 Glossy Finish

The cards in this 28-card set, which was available as a premium in 1936, measure 6" x 8" and were printed on a glossy cardboard. The photos are either black and white or sepia-toned and include a facsimile autograph. The unnumbered set includes individual players and team photos. The Boston Red Sox team card can be found in two varieties; one shows the sky above the building on the card's right side, while the other does not. Some of the cards are scarcer than others in the set and command a premium. Babe Ruth is featured on the Boston Braves team card.

		NM	EX	VG
Complete Set (27):		3,750	1,850	1,100
Common Player:		60.00	30.00	18.00
(1)	Earl Averill	100.00	50.00	30.00
(2)	James L. "Jim" Bottomley	100.00	50.00	30.00
(3)	Gordon S. "Mickey" Cochrane	100.00	50.00	30.00
(4)	Joe Cronin	100.00	50.00	30.00
(5)	Jerome "Dizzy" Dean	150.00	75.00	45.00
(6)	Jimmy Dykes	60.00	30.00	18.00
(7)	Jimmy Foxx	125.00	65.00	35.00
(8)	Frankie Frisch	100.00	50.00	30.00
(9)	Henry "Hank" Greenberg	120.00	60.00	35.00
(10)	Mel Harder/SP	120.00	60.00	35.00
(11)	Pepper Martin/SP	225.00	110.00	65.00
(12)	Lynwood "Schoolboy" Rowe/SP	120.00	60.00	35.00
(13)	William "Bill" Terry	100.00	50.00	30.00
(14)	Harold "Pie" Traynor	100.00	50.00	30.00
(15)	Amer. League All-Stars - 1935	275.00	135.00	80.00
(16)	American League Pennant Winners - 1934 (Detroit Tigers)	125.00	65.00	35.00
(17)	Boston Braves - 1935	300.00	150.00	90.00
(18a)	Boston Red Sox (Sky visible above building at right.)	100.00	50.00	30.00
(18b)	Boston Red Sox (No sky visible.)	180.00	90.00	55.00
(19)	Brooklyn Dodgers - 1935/SP	225.00	110.00	65.00
(20)	Chicago White Sox - 1935	100.00	50.00	30.00

		NM	EX	VG
(21)	Columbus Red Birds (1934 Pennant Winners of American Association)/SP	150.00	75.00	45.00
(22)	National League All-Stars - 1935	180.00	90.00	55.00
(23)	National League Champions - 1935 (Chicago Cubs)	100.00	50.00	30.00
(24)	New York Yankees - 1935	180.00	90.00	55.00
(25)	Pittsburgh Pirates - 1935/SP	200.00	100.00	60.00
(26)	St. Louis Browns - 1935	100.00	50.00	30.00
(27)	The World Champions, 1934 (St. Louis Cardinals)	100.00	50.00	30.00

1936 R311 Leather Finish

This set of 15 unnumbered cards, issued as a premium in 1936, is distinctive because of its uneven, leather-like surface. The cards measure 6" x 8" and display a facsimile autograph on the black and white photo surrounded by a plain border. The cards are unnumbered and include individual player photos, multi-player photos and team photos of the 1935 pennant winners.

		NM	EX	VG
Complete Set (15):		2,750	1,325	825.00
Common Player:		90.00	45.00	25.00
(1)	Frank Crosetti, Joe DiMaggio, Tony Lazzeri	825.00	410.00	245.00
(2)	Paul Derringer	90.00	45.00	25.00
(3)	Wes Ferrell	90.00	45.00	25.00
(4)	Jimmy (Jimmie) Foxx	180.00	90.00	55.00
(5)	Charlie Gehringer	165.00	80.00	50.00
(6)	Mel Harder	90.00	45.00	25.00
(7)	Gabby Hartnett	165.00	80.00	50.00
(8)	Rogers Hornsby	190.00	95.00	55.00
(9)	Connie Mack	165.00	80.00	50.00
(10)	Van Mungo	90.00	45.00	25.00
(11)	Steve O'Neill	90.00	45.00	25.00
(12)	Charles Ruffing	165.00	80.00	50.00
(13)	Arky Vaughan, Honus Wagner	245.00	120.00	75.00
(14)	American League Pennant Winners - 1935 (Detroit Tigers)	165.00	80.00	50.00
(15)	National League Pennant Winners - 1935 (Chicago Cubs)	165.00	80.00	50.00

1936 R312

The 50 cards in this set of 4" x 5-3/8" point-of-purchase premiums are black-and-white photos that have been tinted in soft pastel colors. The set includes 25 individual player portraits, 14 multi-player cards and 11 action photos. Six of the action photos include facsimile autographs, while the other five have printed legends. The Allen card is scarcer than the others in the set.

		NM	EX	VG
Complete Set (50):		8,500	4,250	2,500
Common Player:		90.00	35.00	20.00
(1)	John Thomas Allen	90.00	35.00	20.00
(2)	Nick Altrock, Al Schacht	140.00	55.00	35.00
(3)	Ollie Bejma, Rolly Hemsley	90.00	35.00	20.00
(4)	Les Bell, Zeke Bonura	90.00	35.00	20.00
(5)	Cy Blanton	90.00	35.00	20.00
(6)	Cliff Bolton, Earl Whitehill	90.00	35.00	20.00
(7)	Frenchy Bordagaray, George Earnshaw	90.00	35.00	20.00
(8)	Mace Brown	90.00	35.00	20.00
(9)	Dolph Camilli	90.00	35.00	20.00
(10)	Phil Cavaretta (Cavarretta), Frank Demaree, Augie Galan, Stan Hack, Gabby Hartnett, Billy Herman, Billy Jurges, Chuck Klein, Fred Lindstrom	185.00	75.00	45.00
(11)	Phil Cavaretta (Cavarretta), Stan Hack, Billy Herman, Billy Jurges	185.00	75.00	45.00
(12)	Gordon Cochrane	185.00	75.00	45.00

		NM	EX	VG
(13)	Jim Collins, Stan Hack	90.00	35.00	20.00
(14)	Rip Collins	90.00	35.00	20.00
(15)	Joe Cronin, Buckey Harris (Bucky)	125.00	50.00	30.00
(16)	Alvin Crowder	90.00	35.00	20.00
(17)	Kiki Cuyler	185.00	75.00	45.00
(18)	Kiki Cuyler, Tris Speaker, Danny Taylor	225.00	90.00	55.00
(19)	"Bill" Dickey	185.00	75.00	45.00
(20)	Joe DiMagio (DiMaggio)	2,200	850.00	550.00
(21)	"Chas." Dressen	90.00	35.00	20.00
(22)	Rick Ferrell, Russ Van Atta	125.00	50.00	30.00
(23)	Pete Fox, Goose Goslin, "Jo Jo" White	165.00	65.00	40.00
(24)	Jimmey Foxx, Luke Sewell	215.00	85.00	55.00
(25)	Benny Frey	90.00	35.00	20.00
(26)	Augie Galan, "Pie" Traynor	165.00	65.00	40.00
(27)	Lefty Gomez, Myril Hoag	165.00	65.00	40.00
(28)	"Hank" Greenberg	185.00	75.00	45.00
(29)	Lefty Grove, Connie Mack	250.00	100.00	65.00
(30)	Muel Haas (Mule), Mike Kreevich, Dixie Walker	90.00	35.00	20.00
(31)	Mel Harder	90.00	35.00	20.00
(32)	Gabby Hartnett (Mickey Cochrane, Frank Demaree, Ernie Quigley (ump) in photo)	165.00	65.00	40.00
(33)	Gabby Hartnett, Lonnie Warnecke (Warneke)	135.00	55.00	35.00
(34)	Roger Hornsby (Rogers)	250.00	100.00	65.00
(35)	Rogers Hornsby, Allen Sothoren (Sothoron)	185.00	75.00	45.00
(36)	Ernie Lombardi	185.00	75.00	45.00
(37)	Al Lopez	185.00	75.00	45.00
(38)	Pepper Martin	110.00	45.00	25.00
(39)	"Johnny" Mize	185.00	75.00	45.00
(40)	Van L. Mungo	100.00	40.00	25.00
(41)	Bud Parmelee	90.00	35.00	20.00
(42)	Schoolboy Rowe	90.00	35.00	20.00
(43)	Chas. Ruffing	185.00	75.00	45.00
(44)	Eugene Schott	90.00	35.00	20.00
(45)	Casey Stengel	185.00	75.00	45.00
(46)	Bill Sullivan	90.00	35.00	20.00
(47)	Bill Swift	90.00	35.00	20.00
(48)	Floyd Vaughan, Hans Wagner	225.00	90.00	55.00
(49)	L. Waner, P. Waner, Big Jim Weaver	215.00	85.00	55.00
(50)	Ralph Winegarner	90.00	35.00	20.00

1936 R313

(See 1936 National Chicle "Fine Pens.)

1936 R314

(See 1936 Goudey "Wide Pen" Premiums.)

1929-1930 R315

Bob Shawkey "Yankees" — Andrew Reese "Giants"

Apparently issued over a period of at least two years, based on observed player/team combinations, the 58 cards in this set can be found in either black-and-white or yellow-and-black. The unnumbered, blank-backed cards measure a nominal 3-1/4" x 5-1/4" though original cutting variances abound. The cards feature either portraits or posed action photos. The set includes several different types of cards, depending on the caption. Cards can be found with the player's name and team inside a white box in a lower corner; other cards add the position and team in small type in the bottom border; a third type has the player's name in hand lettering near the bottom; and the final type includes the position and team printed in small type along the bottom border.

		NM	EX	VG
	Complete Set (46):	6,000	2,400	1,200
	Common Player:	45.00	20.00	10.00
1)	Earl Averill	90.00	35.00	25.00
2)	"Benny" Bengough	45.00	20.00	10.00
3)	Laurence Benton (Lawrence)	45.00	20.00	10.00
4)	"Max" Bishop	45.00	20.00	10.00
5)	"Sunny Jim" Bottomley	90.00	35.00	20.00
6)	Bill Cissell	45.00	20.00	10.00
7)	Bud Clancey (Clancy)	45.00	20.00	10.00
8)	"Freddy" Fitzsimmons	45.00	20.00	10.00
9)	"Jimmy" Foxx	260.00	100.00	65.00
10)	"Johnny" Fredericks (Frederick)	45.00	20.00	10.00
11)	Frank Frisch	110.00	45.00	25.00
12)	"Lou" Gehrig	3,000	1,500	900.00
13)	"Goose" Goslin	90.00	35.00	20.00
14)	Burleigh Grimes	90.00	35.00	20.00
15)	"Lefty" Grove	110.00	45.00	25.00
16)	"Mule" Haas	45.00	20.00	10.00
17)	Harvey Hendricks (Hendrick)	45.00	20.00	10.00
18)	"Babe" Herman	60.00	25.00	15.00
19)	"Roger" Hornsby (Rogers)	135.00	55.00	35.00

(20)	Karl Hubbell (Carl)	90.00	35.00	20.00
(21)	"Stonewall" Jackson	90.00	35.00	20.00
(22)	Smead Jolley	45.00	20.00	10.00
(23)	"Chuck" Klein	90.00	35.00	20.00
(24)	Mark Koenig	45.00	20.00	10.00
(25)	"Tony" Lazerri (Lazzeri)	90.00	35.00	20.00
(26)	Fred Leach	45.00	20.00	10.00
(27)	"Freddy" Lindstrom	90.00	35.00	20.00
(28)	Fred Marberry	45.00	20.00	10.00
(29)	"Bing" Miller	45.00	20.00	10.00
(30)	"Bob" O'Farrell	45.00	20.00	10.00
(31)	Frank O'Doul	75.00	30.00	18.50
(32)	"Herbie" Pennock	90.00	35.00	20.00
(33)	George Pipgras	45.00	20.00	10.00
(34)	Andrew Reese	45.00	20.00	10.00
(35)	Carl Reynolds	45.00	20.00	10.00
(36)	"Babe" Ruth	3,200	1,600	960.00
(37)	"Bob" Shawkey	45.00	20.00	10.00
(38)	Art Shires	45.00	20.00	10.00
(39)	"Al" Simmons	90.00	35.00	20.00
(40)	"Riggs" Stephenson	45.00	20.00	10.00
(41)	"Bill" Terry	90.00	35.00	20.00
(42)	"Pie" Traynor	90.00	35.00	20.00
(43)	"Dazzy" Vance	90.00	35.00	20.00
(44)	Paul Waner	90.00	35.00	20.00
(45)	Hack Wilson	90.00	35.00	20.00
(46)	"Tom" Zachary	45.00	20.00	10.00

1929 R316

(See Kashin Publications.)

1929 R316 5x7 Photos

There is nothing concrete to connect this set of player photos with the Kashin Publications card set which carried the R316 designation in the American Card Catalog except that these 4-7/8" x 6-3/4" heavy-paper pictures use the same photos and graphics as the smaller cards. It is thought that the photos are the work of Charles M. Conlon and that the 5x7s may have some connection to the Spalding sporting goods company for whom he worked. Pictures feature white borders and facsimile autographs on front, along with the player's city and league on two lines of type at bottom. While the photos are all the same as seen on R316, the city/league designation on some of the photos is sometimes in black instead of white as on the card, or vice versa. Because almost every card from R316 is known in the 5x7 series, it is reasonable to expect that pictures of Frank Hogan and Jimmy Welsh may also exist. A number of players in the 5x7 set do not appear in the Kashin Publications set, and are noted here with an asterisk.

		NM	EX	VG
	Complete Set (111):	7,000	3,500	2,100
	Common Player:	50.00	25.00	15.00
(1)	Dale Alexander	50.00	25.00	15.00
(2)	Ethan N. Allen	50.00	25.00	15.00
(3)	Ray Benge (*)	50.00	25.00	15.00
(4)	Larry Benton	50.00	25.00	15.00
(5)	Moe Berg	65.00	32.50	20.00
(6)	Max Bishop	50.00	25.00	15.00
(7)	Del Bissonette	50.00	25.00	15.00
(8)	Lucerne A. Blue	50.00	25.00	15.00
(9)	James Bottomley	75.00	37.50	22.50
(10)	Raymond B. Bressler (*)	50.00	25.00	15.00
(11)	Fred Brickell (*)	50.00	25.00	15.00
(12)	Guy T. Bush	50.00	25.00	15.00
(13)	Harold G. Carlson	50.00	25.00	15.00
(14)	Owen Carroll	50.00	25.00	15.00
(15)	Chalmers W. Cissell (Chalmer)	50.00	25.00	15.00
(16)	Mickey Cochrane (*)	85.00	45.00	25.00
(17)	Earl (Earle) Combs	75.00	37.50	22.50
(18)	Hugh M. Critz	50.00	25.00	15.00
(19)	H.J. DeBerry	50.00	25.00	15.00
(20)	Pete Donohue	50.00	25.00	15.00
(21)	Taylor Douthit	50.00	25.00	15.00
(22)	Chas. W. Dressen	50.00	25.00	15.00
(23)	Clise Dudley (*)	50.00	25.00	15.00
(24)	Jimmy Dykes	50.00	25.00	15.00
(25)	Howard Ehmke	50.00	25.00	15.00
(26)	Elwood English	50.00	25.00	15.00
(27)	Urban Faber	75.00	37.50	22.50
(28)	Fred Fitzsimmons	50.00	25.00	15.00
(29)	Lewis A. Fonseca	50.00	25.00	15.00
(30)	Horace H. Ford	50.00	25.00	15.00
(31)	Jimmy Foxx	85.00	45.00	25.00
(32)	Frank Frisch	75.00	37.50	22.50
(33)	Lou Gehrig	335.00	165.00	100.00
(34)	Charles Gehringer	75.00	37.50	22.50
(35)	Walter Gilbert (*)	50.00	25.00	15.00
(36)	Leon Goslin	75.00	37.50	22.50
(37)	George Grantham	50.00	25.00	15.00
(38)	Burleigh Grimes	75.00	37.50	22.50

(39)	Robert Grove	85.00	45.00	25.00
(40)	Bump Hadley	50.00	25.00	15.00
(41)	Charlie Hafey	75.00	37.50	22.50
(42)	Jesse J. Haines	75.00	37.50	22.50
(43)	Harvey Hendrick	50.00	25.00	15.00
(44)	Floyd C. Herman	50.00	25.00	15.00
(45)	Andy High	50.00	25.00	15.00
(46)	Urban J. Hodapp	50.00	25.00	15.00
(47)	Frank Hogan			
(48)	Rogers Hornsby	90.00	45.00	25.00
(49)	Waite Hoyt	75.00	37.50	22.50
(50)	Willis Hudlin	50.00	25.00	15.00
(51)	Frank O. Hurst	50.00	25.00	15.00
(52)	Charlie Jamieson	50.00	25.00	15.00
(53)	Roy C. Johnson	50.00	25.00	15.00
(54)	Percy Jones	50.00	25.00	15.00
(55)	Sam Jones	50.00	25.00	15.00
(56)	Joseph Judge	50.00	25.00	15.00
(57)	Willie Kamm	50.00	25.00	15.00
(58)	Charles Klein	75.00	37.50	22.50
(59)	Mark Koenig	50.00	25.00	15.00
(60)	Ralph Kress	50.00	25.00	15.00
(61)	Fred M. Leach	50.00	25.00	15.00
(62)	Carl Lind (*)	50.00	25.00	15.00
(63)	Fred Lindstrom	75.00	37.50	22.50
(64)	Ad Liska	50.00	25.00	15.00
(65)	Fred Lucas (Red)	50.00	25.00	15.00
(66)	Fred Maguire	50.00	25.00	15.00
(67)	Perce L. Malone	50.00	25.00	15.00
(68)	Harry Manush (Henry)	75.00	37.50	22.50
(69)	Walter Maranville	75.00	37.50	22.50
(70)	Earl McNeely (*)	50.00	25.00	15.00
(71)	Douglas McWeeney (McWeeny)	50.00	25.00	15.00
(72)	Oscar Melillo	50.00	25.00	15.00
(73)	Alex Metzler (*)	50.00	25.00	15.00
(74)	Ed "Bing" Miller	50.00	25.00	15.00
(75)	Clarence Mitchell (*)	50.00	25.00	15.00
(76)	Ed Morgan (*)	50.00	25.00	15.00
(77)	Chas. S. Myer (*)	50.00	25.00	15.00
(78)	Frank O'Doul	65.00	32.50	20.00
(79)	Melvin Ott	85.00	45.00	25.00
(80)	Herbert Pennock	75.00	37.50	22.50
(81)	William W. Regan	50.00	25.00	15.00
(82)	Harry F. Rice	50.00	25.00	15.00
(83)	Sam Rice	75.00	37.50	22.50
(84)	Lance Richbourgh (Richbourg)	50.00	25.00	15.00
(85)	Eddie Rommel	50.00	25.00	15.00
(86)	Chas. H. Root	50.00	25.00	15.00
(87)	Ed Roush	75.00	37.50	22.50
(88)	Harold Ruel (Herold)	50.00	25.00	15.00
(89)	Charles Ruffing	75.00	37.50	22.50
(90)	Jack Russell	50.00	25.00	15.00
(91)	Babe Ruth	425.00	210.00	125.00
(92)	Fred Schulte	50.00	25.00	15.00
(93)	Harry Seibold	50.00	25.00	15.00
(94)	Joe Sewell	75.00	37.50	22.50
(95)	Luke Sewell	50.00	25.00	15.00
(96)	Art Shires	50.00	25.00	15.00
(97)	Al Simmons	75.00	37.50	22.50
(98)	Bob Smith	50.00	25.00	15.00
(99)	Riggs Stephenson	50.00	25.00	15.00
(100)	Wm. H. Terry	75.00	37.50	22.50
(101)	Alphonse Thomas	50.00	25.00	15.00
(102)	Lafayette F. Thompson	50.00	25.00	15.00
(103)	Phil Todt	50.00	25.00	15.00
(104)	Harold J. Traynor	75.00	37.50	22.50
(105)	Dazzy Vance	75.00	37.50	22.50
(106)	Lloyd Waner	75.00	37.50	22.50
(107)	Paul Waner	75.00	37.50	22.50
(108)	Jimmy Welsh (Existence unconfirmed.)			
(109)	Earl Whitehill	50.00	25.00	15.00
(110)	A.C. Whitney	50.00	25.00	15.00
(111)	Claude Willoughby	50.00	25.00	15.00
(112)	Hack Wilson	75.00	37.50	22.50
(113)	Tom Zachary	50.00	25.00	15.00

1933 R337

(See 1933 Eclipse Import.)

1948 R346 Blue Tint

JACKIE ROBINSON BROOKLYN 36

Issued circa 1948-49, the cards in this set derive their name from the distinctive blue coloring used to tint the black-and-white photos. The cards have blank backs and measure 2" x 2-5/8". The set has a high percentage of New York players and was originally issued in strips of six or eight cards each and therefore would have been more appropriately cataloged as a "W" strip card set. The set includes several variations of team designations. It appears that all cards #25-48, along with possibly some of the team variations can also be found in black-and-white, rather than blue printing. The complete set price does not include the variations. Proof cards have been found with printing on the back indicating they were photographed by Al Weinstein of Brooklyn.

	NM	EX	VG
Complete Set (48):	1,300	650.00	375.00
Common Player:	15.00	7.50	4.50
Black-and-White: 1.5-3X			
1 Bill Johnson	15.00	7.50	4.50
2a Leo Durocher (Brooklyn)	30.00	15.00	9.00
2b Leo Durocher (New York)	30.00	15.00	9.00
3 Marty Marion	20.00	10.00	6.00
4 Ewell Blackwell	15.00	7.50	4.50
5 John Lindell	15.00	7.50	4.50
6 Larry Jansen	15.00	7.50	4.50
7 Ralph Kiner	30.00	15.00	9.00
8 Chuck Dressen	15.00	7.50	4.50
9 Bobby Brown	15.00	7.50	4.50
10 Luke Appling	30.00	15.00	9.00
11 Bill Nicholson	15.00	7.50	4.50
12 Phil Masi	15.00	7.50	4.50
13 Frank Shea	15.00	7.50	4.50
14 Bob Dillinger	15.00	7.50	4.50
15 Pete Suder	15.00	7.50	4.50
16 Joe DiMaggio	385.00	195.00	115.00
17 John Corriden	15.00	7.50	4.50
18a Mel Ott (New York)	40.00	20.00	12.00
18b Mel Ott (No team.)	40.00	20.00	12.00
19 Warren Rosar	15.00	7.50	4.50
20 Warren Spahn	35.00	17.50	10.00
21 Allie Reynolds	20.00	10.00	6.00
22 Lou Boudreau	30.00	15.00	9.00
23 Harry Majeski (Hank)(Photo actually Randy Gumpert.)	15.00	7.50	4.50
24 Frank Crosetti	15.00	7.50	4.50
25 Gus Niarhos	15.00	7.50	4.50
26 Bruce Edwards	15.00	7.50	4.50
27 Rudy York	15.00	7.50	4.50
28 Don Black	15.00	7.50	4.50
29 Lou Gehrig	225.00	110.00	65.00
30 Johnny Mize	30.00	15.00	9.00
31 Ed Stanky	15.00	7.50	4.50
32 Vic Raschi	20.00	10.00	6.00
33 Cliff Mapes	15.00	7.50	4.50
34 Enos Slaughter	30.00	15.00	9.00
35 Hank Greenberg	35.00	17.50	10.00
36 Jackie Robinson	225.00	110.00	65.00
37 Frank Hiller	15.00	7.50	4.50
38 Bob Elliot (Elliott)	15.00	7.50	4.50
39 Harry Walker	15.00	7.50	4.50
40 Ed Lopat	15.00	7.50	4.50
41 Bobby Thomson	20.00	10.00	6.00
42 Tommy Henrich	20.00	10.00	6.00
43 Bobby Feller	35.00	17.50	10.00
44 Ted Williams	125.00	62.50	37.50
45 Dixie Walker	15.00	7.50	4.50
46 Johnnie Vander Meer	20.00	10.00	6.00
47 Clint Hartung	15.00	7.50	4.50
(48) Charlie Keller	20.00	10.00	6.00

1950 R423

102. AL SIMMONS
Ball

These tiny (5/8" x 7/8") cards are numbered roughly in alphabetical order from 1 through 120. They were issued in 13-card perforated strips from vending machines. The black-and-white cards are printed on thin stock and include the player's name beneath his photo. The backs - most commonly printed in orange, but sometimes purple or green - display a rough drawing of a baseball infield with tiny figures at the various positions. It appears the cards were intended to be used to play a game of baseball. Many of the cards were printed on more than one strip, creating varying levels of scarcity not necessarily reflected in pricing.

	NM	EX	VG
Complete Set (119):	850.00	425.00	250.00
Common Player:	6.00	3.00	1.75
1 Richie Ashburn	12.50	6.25	3.75
2 Grover Alexander	10.00	5.00	3.00
3 Frank Baumholtz	6.00	3.00	1.75
4 Ralph Branca	6.00	3.00	1.75
5 Yogi Berra	15.00	7.50	4.50
6 Ewell Blackwell	7.50	3.75	2.25
7 Lou Boudreau	7.50	3.75	2.25
8 Harry Brecheen	6.00	3.00	1.75
9 Chico Carrasquel	6.00	3.00	1.75
10 Jerry Coleman	6.00	3.00	1.75
11 Walker Cooper	6.00	3.00	1.75
12 Roy Campanella	17.50	8.75	5.25
13 Phil Cavaretta (Cavarretta)	6.00	3.00	1.75
14a Ty Cobb (W/ facsimile autograph.)	30.00	15.00	9.00
14b Ty Cobb (No facsimile autograph.)	40.00	20.00	12.00
15 Mickey Cochrane	7.50	3.75	2.25
16 Ed Collins	7.50	3.75	2.25
17 Frank Crosetti	7.50	3.75	2.25
18 Larry Doby	7.50	3.75	2.25
19 Walter Dropo	6.00	3.00	1.75
20 Alvin Dark	6.00	3.00	1.75
21 Dizzy Dean	17.50	8.75	5.25
22 Bill Dickey	15.00	7.50	4.50

	NM	EX	VG
23 Murray Dickson (Murry)	6.00	3.00	1.75
24 Dom DiMaggio	7.50	3.75	2.25
25 Joe DiMaggio	50.00	25.00	15.00
26 Leo Durocher	7.50	3.75	2.25
27 Luke Easter	6.00	3.00	1.75
28 Bob Elliott	6.00	3.00	1.75
29 Del Ennis	6.00	3.00	1.75
30 Ferris Fain	6.00	3.00	1.75
31 Bob Feller	15.00	7.50	4.50
32 Frank Frisch	7.50	3.75	2.25
33 Billy Goodman	6.00	3.00	1.75
34 Lefty Gomez	7.50	3.75	2.25
35 Lou Gehrig	40.00	20.00	12.00
36 Joe Gordon	6.00	3.00	1.75
37 Sid Gordon	6.00	3.00	1.75
38 Hank Greenberg	15.00	7.50	4.50
39 Lefty Grove	10.00	5.00	3.00
40 Art Houtteman	6.00	3.00	1.75
41 Sid Hudson	6.00	3.00	1.75
42 Ken Heintzelman	6.00	3.00	1.75
43 Gene Hermanski	6.00	3.00	1.75
44 Jim Hearn	6.00	3.00	1.75
45 Gil Hodges	12.50	6.25	3.75
46 Harry Heilman (Heilmann)	7.50	3.75	2.25
47 Tommy Henrich	7.50	3.75	2.25
48 Roger Hornsby (Rogers)	10.00	5.00	3.00
49 Carl Hubbell	10.00	5.00	3.00
50 Edwin Joost	6.00	3.00	1.75
51 John Jorgensen	6.00	3.00	1.75
52 Larry Jansen	6.00	3.00	1.75
53 Nippy Jones	6.00	3.00	1.75
54 Walter Johnson	12.50	6.25	3.75
55 Ellis Kinder	6.00	3.00	1.75
56 Jim Konstanty	6.00	3.00	1.75
57 George Kell	7.50	3.75	2.25
58 Ralph Kiner	7.50	3.75	2.25
59 Bob Lemon	7.50	3.75	2.25
60 Whitey Lockman	6.00	3.00	1.75
61 Ed Lopat	7.50	3.75	2.25
62 Tony Lazzeri	7.50	3.75	2.25
63 Cass Michaels	6.00	3.00	1.75
64 Cliff Mapes	6.00	3.00	1.75
65 Willard Marshall	6.00	3.00	1.75
66 Clyde McCullough	6.00	3.00	1.75
67 Connie Mack	7.50	3.75	2.25
68 Christy Mathewson	17.50	8.75	5.25
69 Joe Medwick	7.50	3.75	2.25
70 Johnny Mize	7.50	3.75	2.25
71 Terry Moore	6.00	3.00	1.75
72 Stan Musial	20.00	10.00	6.00
73 Hal Newhouser	7.50	3.75	2.25
74 Don Newcombe	7.50	3.75	2.25
75 Lefty O'Doul	7.50	3.75	2.25
76 Mel Ott	10.00	5.00	3.00
77 Mel Parnell	6.00	3.00	1.75
78 Johnny Pesky	6.00	3.00	1.75
79 Gerald Priddy	6.00	3.00	1.75
80 Dave Philley	6.00	3.00	1.75
81 Bob Porterfield	6.00	3.00	1.75
82 Andy Pafko	6.00	3.00	1.75
83 Howie Pollet	6.00	3.00	1.75
84 Herb Pennock	7.50	3.75	2.25
85 Al Rosen	7.50	3.75	2.25
86 Pee Wee Reese	15.00	7.50	4.50
87 Del Rice	6.00	3.00	1.75
88 Vic Raschi	7.50	3.75	2.25
89 Allie Reynolds	7.50	3.75	2.25
90 Phil Rizzuto	15.00	7.50	4.50
91 Jackie Robinson	35.00	17.50	10.50
92 Babe Ruth	40.00	20.00	12.00
93 Casey Stengel	15.00	7.50	4.50
94 Vern Stephens	6.00	3.00	1.75
95 Duke Snider	15.00	7.50	4.50
96 Enos Slaughter	7.50	3.75	2.25
97 Al Schoendienst	7.50	3.75	2.25
98 Gerald Staley	6.00	3.00	1.75
99 Clyde Shoun	6.00	3.00	1.75
100 Unknown	.00	.00	.00
101 Hank Sauer	6.00	3.00	1.75
102 Al Simmons	7.50	3.75	2.25
103 George Sisler	7.50	3.75	2.25
104 Tris Speaker	12.50	6.25	3.75
105 Ed Stanky	6.00	3.00	1.75
106 Virgil Trucks	6.00	3.00	1.75
107 Henry Thompson	6.00	3.00	1.75
108 Bobby Thomson	7.50	3.75	2.25
109 Dazzy Vance	7.50	3.75	2.25
110 Lloyd Waner	7.50	3.75	2.25
111 Paul Waner	7.50	3.75	2.25
112 Gene Woodling	7.50	3.75	2.25
113 Ted Williams	35.00	17.50	10.50
114 Vic Wertz	6.00	3.00	1.75
115 Wes Westrom (Westrum)	6.00	3.00	1.75
116 Johnny Wyrostek	6.00	3.00	1.75
117 Eddie Yost	6.00	3.00	1.75
118 Allen Zarilla	6.00	3.00	1.75
119 Gus Zernial	6.00	3.00	1.75
120 Sam Zoldack (Zoldak)	6.00	3.00	1.75

S

1936 S and S Game

Small black-and-white player photos are featured on the fronts of this 52-card game set. Measuring about 2-1/4" x 3-1/2", with rounded corners, the cards feature plain green or cream-colored backs. Besides the player photo on front, there are a few biographical details and stats, and a pair of game scenarios. The cards are unnumbered and are checklisted here alphabetically. The complete game included a special scoreboard, at least two "directions" cards and a contest card.

PIE TRAYNOR
Pittsburgh N. L.   Infielder
Bats R. H.   Hgt. 6.00½
Throws R. H.   Wgt. 175

	NM	EX	VG
Complete Set (52):	750.00	370.00	220.00
Complete Boxed Set:	1,325	665.00	400.00
Common Player:	12.50	6.25	3.75
(1) Luke Appling	30.00	15.00	9.00
(2) Earl Averill	30.00	15.00	9.00
(3) Zeke Bonura	12.50	6.25	3.75
(4) Dolph Camilli	12.50	6.25	3.75
(5) Ben Cantwell	12.50	6.25	3.75
(6) Phil Cavaretta (Cavarretta)	12.50	6.25	3.75
(7) Rip Collins	12.50	6.25	3.75
(8) Joe Cronin	30.00	15.00	9.00
(9) Frank Crosetti	20.00	10.00	6.00
(10) Kiki Cuyler	30.00	15.00	9.00
(11) Virgil Davis	12.50	6.25	3.75
(12) Frank Demaree	12.50	6.25	3.75
(13) Paul Derringer	12.50	6.25	3.75
(14) Bill Dickey	50.00	25.00	15.00
(15) Woody English	12.50	6.25	3.75
(16) Fred Fitzsimmons	12.50	6.25	3.75
(17) Richard Ferrell	30.00	15.00	9.00
(18) Pete Fox	12.50	6.25	3.75
(19) Jimmy (Jimmie) Foxx	60.00	30.00	18.00
(20) Larry French	12.50	6.25	3.75
(21) Frank Frisch	30.00	15.00	9.00
(22) August Galan	12.50	6.25	3.75
(23) Chas. Gehringer	30.00	15.00	9.00
(24) John Gill	12.50	6.25	3.75
(25) Charles Grimm	12.50	6.25	3.75
(26) Mule Haas	12.50	6.25	3.75
(27) Stanley Hack	12.50	6.25	3.75
(28) Bill Hallahan	12.50	6.25	3.75
(29) Melvin Harder	12.50	6.25	3.75
(30) Gabby Hartnett	30.00	15.00	9.00
(31) Ray Hayworth	12.50	6.25	3.75
(32) Ralston Hemsley	12.50	6.25	3.75
(33) Bill Herman	30.00	15.00	9.00
(34) Frank Higgins	12.50	6.25	3.75
(35) Carl Hubbell	40.00	20.00	12.00
(36) Bill Jurges	12.50	6.25	3.75
(37) Vernon Kennedy	12.50	6.25	3.75
(38) Chuck Klein	30.00	15.00	9.00
(39) Mike Kreevich	12.50	6.25	3.75
(40) Bill Lee	12.50	6.25	3.75
(41) Jos. Medwick	30.00	15.00	9.00
(42) Van Mungo	12.50	6.25	3.75
(43) James O'Dea	12.50	6.25	3.75
(44) Mel Ott	50.00	25.00	15.00
(45) Rip Radcliff	12.50	6.25	3.75
(46) Pie Traynor	30.00	15.00	9.00
(47) Arky Vaughan (Vaughn)	30.00	15.00	9.00
(48) Joe Vosmik	12.50	6.25	3.75
(49) Lloyd Waner	30.00	15.00	9.00
(50) Paul Waner	30.00	15.00	9.00
(51) Lon Warneke	12.50	6.25	3.75
(52) Floyd Young	12.50	6.25	3.75

1948-50 Safe-T-Card

 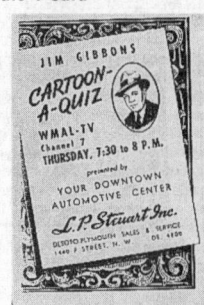

The earliest known safety issue is this series sponsored by a children's television show which was in turn sponsored by a Washington, D.C. auto dealer. Player selection and team indications on the cards point to a three-year (1948-50) range of issue dates for the cards. Minor differences in typography and information printed on the front probably differentiate the years of issue. All cards are about 2-1/2" x 3-1/2" with rounded corners. Fronts feature rather crude black-and-white drawings of the players with a facsimile autograph superimposed. A safety message is at top and, on most cards, the player's position and team are printed at bottom. Backs are printed in one of several colors and have a picture of the TV host and an ad for the program and its sponsors. The set is checklisted here alphabetically, though it's possible other cards may be added in the future. Only the baseball players from the set are listed here. Cards featuring football, basketball and other sports figures were also produced, along with cards for team executives, sports reporters and broadcasters.

	NM	EX	VG
Complete (Baseball) Set (21):	2,925	1,450	875.00
Common Player:	125.00	65.00	35.00
(1) Ossie Bluege	125.00	65.00	35.00
(2) Gil Coan	125.00	65.00	35.00
(3) Sam Dente	125.00	65.00	35.00
(4) Jake Early	125.00	65.00	35.00
(5) Al Evans	125.00	65.00	35.00
(6) Calvin Griffith	250.00	125.00	75.00
(7) Clark Griffith	150.00	75.00	45.00
(8) Bucky Harris	150.00	75.00	45.00
(9) Sid Hudson	125.00	65.00	35.00
(10) Joe Kuhel	125.00	65.00	35.00
(11) Bob Lemon	150.00	75.00	45.00
(12) Bill McGowan	400.00	200.00	120.00
(13) George McQuinn	125.00	65.00	35.00
(14) Don Newcombe	250.00	125.00	75.00
(15) Joe Ostrowski	125.00	65.00	35.00
(16) Sam Rice	150.00	75.00	45.00
(17) Bert Shepard	150.00	75.00	45.00
(18) Ray Scarborough	125.00	65.00	35.00
(19) Mickey Vernon	125.00	65.00	35.00
(20) Early Wynn	150.00	75.00	45.00
(21) Eddie Yost	125.00	65.00	35.00

1976 Safelon Discs

One of several regional sponsors of player disc sets in 1976, Safelon, of New York, advertised its "Super Star Lunch Bags" in red and purple on the backs of its discs. The discs are 3-3/8" diameter with a black-and-white player portrait photo in the center of the baseball design. A line of red stars is above, while the left and right panels feature one of several bright colors. Produced by Michael Schechter Associates under license from the Major League Baseball Players Association, the player photos have had uniform and cap logos removed. The unnumbered checklist here is presented in alphabetical order.

	NM	EX	VG
Complete Set (70):	100.00	50.00	30.00
Common Player:	3.00	1.50	.90
(1) Henry Aaron	20.00	10.00	6.00
(2) Johnny Bench	8.00	4.00	2.50
(3) Vida Blue	3.00	1.50	.90
(4) Larry Bowa	3.00	1.50	.90
(5) Lou Brock	6.00	3.00	1.75
(6) Jeff Burroughs	3.00	1.50	.90
(7) John Candelaria	3.00	1.50	.90
(8) Jose Cardenal	3.00	1.50	.90
(9) Rod Carew	6.00	3.00	1.75
(10) Steve Carlton	6.00	3.00	1.75
(11) Dave Cash	3.00	1.50	.90
(12) Cesar Cedeno	3.00	1.50	.90
(13) Ron Cey	3.00	1.50	.90
(14) Carlton Fisk	6.00	3.00	1.75
(15) Tito Fuentes	3.00	1.50	.90
(16) Steve Garvey	4.00	2.00	1.25
(17) Ken Griffey	3.00	1.50	.90
(18) Don Gullett	3.00	1.50	.90
(19) Willie Horton	3.00	1.50	.90
(20) Al Hrabosky	3.00	1.50	.90
(21) Catfish Hunter	6.00	3.00	1.75
(22) Reggie Jackson (A's)	12.00	6.00	3.50
(23) Randy Jones	3.00	1.50	.90
(24) Jim Kaat	3.00	1.50	.90
(25) Don Kessinger	3.00	1.50	.90
(26) Dave Kingman	3.00	1.50	.90
(27) Jerry Koosman	3.00	1.50	.90
(28) Mickey Lolich	3.00	1.50	.90
(29) Greg Luzinski	3.00	1.50	.90
(30) Fred Lynn	3.00	1.50	.90
(31) Bill Madlock	3.00	1.50	.90
(32) Carlos May (White Sox)	3.00	1.50	.90
(33) John Mayberry	3.00	1.50	.90
(34) Bake McBride	3.00	1.50	.90
(35) Doc Medich	3.00	1.50	.90
(36) Andy Messersmith	3.00	1.50	.90
(37) Rick Monday	3.00	1.50	.90
(38) John Montefusco	3.00	1.50	.90
(39) Jerry Morales	3.00	1.50	.90
(40) Joe Morgan	6.00	3.00	1.75
(41) Thurman Munson	5.00	2.50	1.50
(42) Bobby Murcer	3.00	1.50	.90
(43) Al Oliver	3.00	1.50	.90
(44) Jim Palmer	6.00	3.00	1.75
(45) Dave Parker	3.00	1.50	.90
(46) Tony Perez	6.00	3.00	1.75
(47) Jerry Reuss	3.00	1.50	.90
(48) Brooks Robinson	9.00	4.50	2.75
(49) Frank Robinson	9.00	4.50	2.75
(50) Steve Rogers	3.00	1.50	.90
(51) Pete Rose	15.00	7.50	4.50
(52) Nolan Ryan	40.00	20.00	12.00
(53) Manny Sanguillen	3.00	1.50	.90
(54) Mike Schmidt	12.00	6.00	3.50
(55) Tom Seaver	9.00	4.50	2.75
(56) Ted Simmons	3.00	1.50	.90
(57) Reggie Smith	3.00	1.50	.90
(58) Willie Stargell	6.00	3.00	1.75
(59) Rusty Staub	3.00	1.50	.90
(60) Rennie Stennett	3.00	1.50	.90
(61) Don Sutton	6.00	3.00	1.75

	NM	EX	VG
(62) Andy Thornton (Cubs)	3.00	1.50	.90
(63) Luis Tiant	3.00	1.50	.90
(64) Joe Torre	3.00	1.50	.90
(65) Mike Tyson	3.00	1.50	.90
(66) Bob Watson	3.00	1.50	.90
(67) Wilbur Wood	3.00	1.50	.90
(68) Jimmy Wynn	3.00	1.50	.90
(69) Carl Yastrzemski	9.00	4.50	2.75
(70) Richie Zisk	3.00	1.50	.90

1977 Saga Discs

Virtually identical in format to the several locally sponsored disc sets of the previous year, these 3-3/8" diameter player discs were given away with the purchase of school lunches in the Philadelphia area. They are the scarcest of the 1977 disc sets. Discs once again feature black-and-white player portrait photos in the center of a baseball design. The left and right panels are in one of several bright colors. Licensed by the Players Association through Mike Schechter Associates, the player photos carry no uniform logos. Backs are printed in orange with background art of a sunrise over the mountains. The unnumbered discs are checklisted here alphabetically.

	NM	EX	VG
Complete Set (70):	850.00	425.00	250.00
Common Player:	12.50	6.25	3.75
(1) Sal Bando	12.50	6.25	3.75
(2) Buddy Bell	12.50	6.25	3.75
(3) Johnny Bench	40.00	20.00	12.00
(4) Larry Bowa	12.50	6.25	3.75
(5) Steve Braun	12.50	6.25	3.75
(6) George Brett	125.00	62.00	37.00
(7) Lou Brock	35.00	17.50	10.50
(8) Jeff Burroughs	12.50	6.25	3.75
(9) Bert Campaneris	12.50	6.25	3.75
(10) John Candelaria	12.50	6.25	3.75
(11) Jose Cardenal	12.50	6.25	3.75
(12) Rod Carew	35.00	17.50	10.50
(13) Steve Carlton	35.00	17.50	10.50
(14) Dave Cash	12.50	6.25	3.75
(15) Cesar Cedeno	12.50	6.25	3.75
(16) Ron Cey	12.50	6.25	3.75
(17) Dave Concepcion	12.50	6.25	3.75
(18) Dennis Eckersley	35.00	17.50	10.50
(19) Mark Fidrych	17.50	8.75	5.25
(20) Rollie Fingers	35.00	17.50	10.50
(21) Carlton Fisk	35.00	17.50	10.50
(22) George Foster	12.50	6.25	3.75
(23) Wayne Garland	12.50	6.25	3.75
(24) Ralph Garr	12.50	6.25	3.75
(25) Steve Garvey	25.00	12.50	7.50
(26) Cesar Geronimo	12.50	6.25	3.75
(27) Bobby Grich	12.50	6.25	3.75
(28) Ken Griffey Sr.	12.50	6.25	3.75
(29) Don Gullett	12.50	6.25	3.75
(30) Mike Hargrove	12.50	6.25	3.75
(31) Al Hrabosky	12.50	6.25	3.75
(32) Jim Hunter	35.00	17.50	10.50
(33) Reggie Jackson	50.00	25.00	15.00
(34) Randy Jones	12.50	6.25	3.75
(35) Dave Kingman	15.00	7.50	4.50
(36) Jerry Koosman	12.50	6.25	3.75
(37) Dave LaRoche	12.50	6.25	3.75
(38) Greg Luzinski	12.50	6.25	3.75
(39) Fred Lynn	12.50	6.25	3.75
(40) Bill Madlock	12.50	6.25	3.75
(41) Rick Manning	12.50	6.25	3.75
(42) Jon Matlock	12.50	6.25	3.75
(43) John Mayberry	12.50	6.25	3.75
(44) Hal McRae	12.50	6.25	3.75
(45) Andy Messersmith	12.50	6.25	3.75
(46) Rick Monday	12.50	6.25	3.75
(47) John Montefusco	12.50	6.25	3.75
(48) Joe Morgan	35.00	17.50	10.50
(49) Thurman Munson	30.00	15.00	9.00
(50) Bobby Murcer	12.50	6.25	3.75
(51) Bill North	12.50	6.25	3.75
(52) Jim Palmer	35.00	17.50	10.50
(53) Tony Perez	35.00	17.50	10.50
(54) Jerry Reuss	12.50	6.25	3.75
(55) Brooks Robinson	40.00	20.00	12.00
(56) Pete Rose	110.00	55.00	33.00
(57) Joe Rudi	12.50	6.25	3.75
(58) Nolan Ryan	135.00	67.00	40.00
(59) Manny Sanguillen	12.50	6.25	3.75
(60) Mike Schmidt	75.00	37.00	22.00
(61) Tom Seaver	40.00	20.00	12.00
(62) Bill Singer	12.50	6.25	3.75
(63) Willie Stargell	35.00	17.50	10.50
(64) Rusty Staub	15.00	7.50	4.50
(65) Luis Tiant	12.50	6.25	3.75
(66) Bob Watson	12.50	6.25	3.75
(67) Butch Wynegar	12.50	6.25	3.75
(68) Carl Yastrzemski	40.00	20.00	12.00
(69) Robin Yount	35.00	17.50	10.50
(70) Richie Zisk	12.50	6.25	3.75

1978 Saga Discs

One player from each major league team was selected for inclusion in this disc set distributed by Saga, a provider of school lunches; discs were given one per lunch purchase at

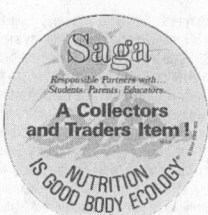

selected schools. The 3-3/8" diameter discs have a sepia-toned player portrait photo at center within a white diamond and surrounded by a brightly colored border with four colored stars at top. Licensed by the Players Association through Michael Schechter Associates, the photos have had uniform logos removed. Backs are nearly identical to the previous year, but printed in red. The unnumbered Saga discs are checklisted here according to the numbers found on the Big T/Tastee Freeze versions.

	NM	EX	VG
Complete Set (26):	130.00	65.00	40.00
Common Player:	6.00	3.00	1.75
(1) Buddy Bell	6.00	3.00	1.75
(2) Jim Palmer	12.50	6.25	3.75
(3) Steve Garvey	7.50	3.75	2.25
(4) Jeff Burroughs	6.00	3.00	1.75
(5) Greg Luzinski	6.00	3.00	1.75
(6) Lou Brock	12.50	6.25	3.75
(7) Thurman Munson	10.00	5.00	3.00
(8) Rod Carew	12.50	6.25	3.75
(9) George Brett	50.00	25.00	15.00
(10) Tom Seaver	15.00	7.50	4.50
(11) Willie Stargell	12.50	6.25	3.75
(12) Jerry Koosman	6.00	3.00	1.75
(13) Bill North	6.00	3.00	1.75
(14) Richie Zisk	6.00	3.00	1.75
(15) Bill Madlock	6.00	3.00	1.75
(16) Carl Yastrzemski	15.00	7.50	4.50
(17) Dave Cash	6.00	3.00	1.75
(18) Bob Watson	6.00	3.00	1.75
(19) Dave Kingman	6.50	3.25	2.00
(20) Gene Tenance (Tenace)	6.00	3.00	1.75
(21) Ralph Garr	6.00	3.00	1.75
(22) Mark Fidrych	6.50	3.25	2.00
(23) Frank Tanana	6.00	3.00	1.75
(24) Larry Hisle	6.00	3.00	1.75
(25) Bruce Bochte	6.00	3.00	1.75
(26) Bob Bailor	6.00	3.00	1.75

1962 John Sain Spinner Promotional Postcard

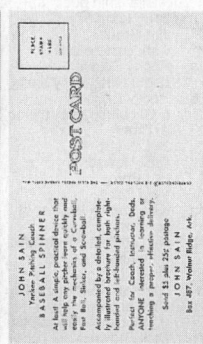

The attributed date of issue is approximate. This 3-7/16" x 5-7/16" color postcard was issued to promote the John Sain Spinner, a device to teach pitching mechanics. The front pictures the Yankees pitching coach in four views demonstrating the device, which is itself pictured at top. Black-and-white back is in traditional postcard divided-back format with information on the spinner and ordering information.

	NM	EX	VG
John Sain	15.00	7.50	4.50

1962 Salada-Junket Coins

These 1-3/8" diameter plastic coins were issued in packages of Salada Tea and Junket Pudding mix. There are 221 different players available, with variations bringing the total of different coins to 265. Each coin has a paper color photo inserted in the front which contains the player's name and position plus the coin number. The plastic rims come in six different colors, coded by team. Production began with 180 coins, but the addition of the New York Mets and Houston Colt .45's to the National League allowed the company to expand the set's size. Twenty expansion players were added along with 21 other players. Several players' coins were dropped after the initial 180 run, causing some scarcities. Embossed green plastic shields into which 10 coins could be placed were available via a mail-in offer. About 9" x 10-1/2", the shields have a banner near the top with the team name. Many of the players in the 180 series can be found with variations in the placement of the front typography relative to the colored portrait. Though these variations seem to affect a tiny percentage of some players' 180 coins, they are in most cases too difficult to distinguish except by direct comparison between specimens and are of interest only to the most dedicated Salada collectors.

		NM	EX	VG
	Complete Set, no variations (221):	3,000	1,500	900.00
	Complete Set, w/ variations (266):	6,500	3,250	2,000
	Complete Boxed Presentation Set (180):	1,900	950.00	575.00
	Complete Boxed Presentation Set (200):	2,600	1,300	800.00
	Uncut Sheet (180):	1,800	900.00	550.00
	Common Player (1-180):	4.00	2.00	1.25
	Common Player (181-221):	10.00	5.00	3.00
	Team Shield (Empty):	60.00	30.00	18.00
1	Jim Gentile	5.00	2.50	1.50
2	Bill Pierce	65.00	32.50	20.00
3a	Chico Fernandez (Light blue jersey piping.)	4.00	2.00	1.25
3b	Chico Fernandez (Dark blue jersey piping.)	12.00	6.00	3.50
4	Tom Brewer	15.00	7.50	4.50
5	Woody Held	4.00	2.00	1.25
6	Ray Herbert	22.50	11.00	7.00
7a	Ken Aspromonte (Angels)	10.00	5.00	3.00
7b	Ken Aspromonte (Indians)	10.00	5.00	3.00
8	Whitey Ford	20.00	10.00	6.00
9	Jim Lemon	4.00	2.00	1.25
10	Billy Klaus	4.00	2.00	1.25
11	Steve Barber	27.50	13.50	8.25
12	Nellie Fox	17.50	8.75	5.25
13	Jim Bunning	15.00	7.50	4.50
14	Frank Malzone	5.00	2.50	1.50
15	Tito Francona	4.00	2.00	1.25
16	Bobby Del Greco	4.00	2.00	1.25
17a	Steve Bilko (Red shirt buttons.)	9.00	4.50	2.75
17b	Steve Bilko (White shirt buttons.)	9.00	4.50	2.75
18	Tony Kubek	35.00	17.50	10.00
19	Earl Battey	4.00	2.00	1.25
20	Chuck Cottier	4.00	2.00	1.25
21	Willie Tasby	4.00	2.00	1.25
22	Bob Allison	6.00	3.00	1.75
23	Roger Maris	25.00	12.50	7.50
24a	Earl Averill (Red shirt buttons.)	9.00	4.50	2.75
24b	Earl Averill (White shirt buttons.)	5.00	2.50	1.50
25	Jerry Lumpe	4.00	2.00	1.25
26	Jim Grant	17.50	8.75	5.25
27	Carl Yastrzemski	30.00	15.00	9.00
28a	Rocky Colavito (Light blue jersey piping.)	20.00	10.00	6.00
28b	Rocky Colavito (Dark blue jersey piping.)	12.50	6.25	3.75
29	Al Smith	4.00	2.00	1.25
30	Jim Busby	30.00	15.00	9.00
31	Dick Howser	4.00	2.00	1.25
32	Jim Perry	4.00	2.00	1.25
33	Yogi Berra	25.00	12.50	7.50
34a	Ken Hamlin (Red shirt buttons.)	7.00	3.50	2.00
34b	Ken Hamlin (White shirt buttons.)	4.00	2.00	1.25
35	Dale Long	4.00	2.00	1.25
36	Harmon Killebrew	20.00	10.00	6.00
37a	Dick Brown (Light blue jersey piping.)	12.00	6.00	3.50
37b	Dick Brown (Dark blue jersey piping.)	4.00	2.00	1.25
38	Gary Geiger	4.00	2.00	1.25
39a	Minnie Minoso (White Sox)	20.00	10.00	6.00
39b	Minnie Minoso (Cardinals)	9.00	4.50	2.75
40	Brooks Robinson	20.00	10.00	6.00
41	Mickey Mantle	70.00	35.00	20.00
42	Bennie Daniels	4.00	2.00	1.25
43	Billy Martin	12.00	6.00	3.50
44	Vic Power	5.00	2.50	1.50
45	Joe Pignatano	4.00	2.00	1.25
46a	Ryne Duren (Red shirt buttons.)	9.00	4.50	2.75
46b	Ryne Duren (White shirt buttons.)	8.00	4.00	2.50
47a	Pete Runnels (2B)	12.00	6.00	3.50
47b	Pete Runnels (1B)	7.50	3.75	2.25
48a	Dick Williams (Name on right.)	1,800	900.00	550.00
48b	Dick Williams (Name on left.)	4.00	2.00	1.25
49	Jim Landis	4.00	2.00	1.25
50	Steve Boros	4.00	2.00	1.25
51a	Zoilo Versalles (Red shirt buttons.)	7.00	3.50	2.00
51b	Zoilo Versalles (White shirt buttons.)	7.00	3.50	2.00
52a	Johnny Temple (Indians)	12.50	6.25	3.75
52b	Johnny Temple (Orioles)	2,125	1,060	640.00
53a	Jackie Brandt (Oriole)	15.00	7.50	4.50
53b	Jackie Brandt (Orioles)	1,600	800.00	475.00
54	Joe McClain	4.00	2.00	1.25
55	Sherman Lollar	5.00	2.50	1.50
56	Gene Stephens	4.00	2.00	1.25
57a	Leon Wagner (Red shirt buttons.)	7.00	3.50	2.00
57b	Leon Wagner (White shirt buttons.)	5.00	2.50	1.50
58	Frank Lary	6.00	3.00	1.75
59	Bill Skowron	10.00	5.00	3.00
60	Vic Wertz	20.00	10.00	6.00
61	Willie Kirkland	4.00	2.00	1.25
62	Leo Posada	4.00	2.00	1.25
63a	Albie Pearson (Red shirt buttons.)	9.00	4.50	2.75
63b	Albie Pearson (White shirt buttons.)	8.00	4.00	2.50
64	Bobby Richardson	15.00	7.50	4.50
65a	Marv Breeding (SS)	9.00	4.50	2.75
65b	Marv Breeding (2B)	12.00	6.00	3.50
66	Roy Sievers	70.00	35.00	20.00
67	Al Kaline	25.00	12.50	7.50
68a	Don Buddin (Red Sox)	15.00	7.50	4.50
68b	Don Buddin (Colts)	5.00	2.50	1.50
69a	Lenny Green (Red shirt buttons.)	8.00	4.00	2.50
69b	Lenny Green (White shirt buttons.)	6.00	3.00	1.75
70	Gene Green	40.00	20.00	12.00
71	Luis Aparicio	12.00	6.00	3.50
72	Norm Cash	16.00	8.00	4.75
73	Jackie Jensen	20.00	10.00	6.00
74	Bubba Phillips	6.00	3.00	1.75
75	Jim Archer	4.00	2.00	1.25
76a	Ken Hunt (Red shirt buttons.)	9.00	4.50	2.75
76b	Ken Hunt (White shirt buttons.)	4.00	2.00	1.25
77	Ralph Terry	4.00	2.00	1.25
78	Camilo Pascual	4.00	2.00	1.25
79	Marty Keough	27.50	13.50	8.25
80	Cletis Boyer	10.00	5.00	3.00
81	Jim Pagliaroni	4.00	2.00	1.25
82a	Gene Leek (Red shirt buttons.)	9.00	4.50	2.75
82b	Gene Leek (White shirt buttons.)	4.00	2.00	1.25
83	Jake Wood	5.00	2.50	1.50
84	Coot Veal	25.00	12.50	7.50
85	Norm Siebern	5.00	2.50	1.50
86a	Andy Carey (White Sox)	25.00	12.50	7.50
86b	Andy Carey (Phillies)	9.00	4.50	2.75
87a	Bill Tuttle (Red shirt buttons.)	9.00	4.50	2.75
87b	Bill Tuttle (White shirt buttons.)	25.00	12.50	7.50
88a	Jimmy Piersall (Indians)	20.00	10.00	6.00
88b	Jimmy Piersall (Senators)	20.00	10.00	6.00
89	Ron Hansen	25.00	12.50	7.50
90a	Chuck Stobbs (Red shirt buttons.)	8.00	4.00	2.50
90b	Chuck Stobbs (White shirt buttons.)	4.00	2.00	1.25
91a	Ken McBride (Red shirt buttons.)	9.00	4.50	2.75
91b	Ken McBride (White shirt buttons.)	7.50	3.75	2.25
92	Bill Bruton	4.00	2.00	1.25
93	Gus Triandos	4.00	2.00	1.25
94	John Romano	4.00	2.00	1.25
95	Elston Howard	10.00	5.00	3.00
96	Gene Woodling	6.00	3.00	1.75
97a	Early Wynn (Pitching pose.)	45.00	22.00	13.50
97b	Early Wynn (Portrait)	15.00	7.50	4.50
98	Milt Pappas	4.00	2.00	1.25
99	Bill Monbouquette	4.00	2.00	1.25
100	Wayne Causey	4.00	2.00	1.25
101	Don Elston	4.00	2.00	1.25
102a	Charlie Neal (Dodgers)	12.00	6.00	3.50
102b	Charlie Neal (Mets)	4.00	2.00	1.25
103	Don Blasingame	4.00	2.00	1.25
104	Frank Thomas	30.00	15.00	9.00
105	Wes Covington	4.00	2.00	1.25
106	Chuck Hiller	5.00	2.50	1.50
107	Don Hoak	4.00	2.00	1.25
108a	Bob Lillis (Cardinals)	27.50	13.50	8.25
108b	Bob Lillis (Colts)	4.00	2.00	1.25
109	Sandy Koufax	30.00	15.00	9.00
110	Gordy Coleman	4.00	2.00	1.25
111	Ed Matthews (Mathews)	20.00	10.00	6.00
112	Art Mahaffey	4.00	2.00	1.25
113a	Ed Bailey (Partial left shoulder; "C" level w/ear.)	1,750	875.00	525.00
113b	Ed Bailey (Full left shoulder; second button red.)	10.00	5.00	3.00
113c	Ed Bailey (Full left shoulder; second button white.)	4.00	2.00	1.25
114	Smoky Burgess	7.00	3.50	2.00
115	Bill White	6.00	3.00	1.75
116	Ed Bouchee	25.00	12.50	7.50
117	Bob Buhl	8.00	4.00	2.50
118	Vada Pinson	4.00	2.00	1.25
119	Carl Sawatski	4.00	2.00	1.25
120	Dick Stuart	6.00	3.00	1.75
121	Harvey Kuenn	40.00	20.00	12.00
122	Pancho Herrera	4.00	2.00	1.25
123a	Don Zimmer (Cubs)	12.50	6.25	3.75
123b	Don Zimmer (Mets)	5.00	2.50	1.50
124	Wally Moon	6.00	3.00	1.75
125	Joe Adcock	9.00	4.50	2.75
126	Joey Jay	4.00	2.00	1.25
127a	Maury Wills (Blue "3" on shirt.)	10.00	5.00	3.00
127b	Maury Wills (Red "3" on shirt.)	10.00	5.00	3.00
128	George Altman	4.00	2.00	1.25
129a	John Buzhardt (Phillies)	30.00	15.00	9.00
129b	John Buzhardt (White Sox)	10.00	5.00	3.00
130	Felipe Alou	4.00	2.00	1.25
131	Bill Mazeroski	15.00	7.50	4.50
132	Ernie Broglio	4.00	2.00	1.25
133	John Roseboro	4.00	2.00	1.25
134	Mike McCormick	4.00	2.00	1.25
135a	Chuck Smith (Phillies)	15.00	7.50	4.50
135b	Chuck Smith (White Sox)	10.00	5.00	3.00
136	Ron Santo	12.00	6.00	3.50
137	Gene Freese	4.00	2.00	1.25
138	Dick Groat	5.00	2.50	1.50
139	Curt Flood	4.00	2.00	1.25
140	Frank Bolling	4.00	2.00	1.25
141	Clay Dalrymple	4.00	2.00	1.25
142	Willie McCovey	16.00	8.00	4.75
143	Bob Skinner	4.00	2.00	1.25
144	Lindy McDaniel	4.00	2.00	1.25
145	Glen Hobbie	4.00	2.00	1.25
146a	Gil Hodges (Dodgers)	30.00	15.00	9.00
146b	Gil Hodges (Mets)	22.50	11.00	6.75
147	Eddie Kasko	4.00	2.00	1.25
148	Gino Cimoli	25.00	12.50	7.50
149	Willie Mays	30.00	15.00	9.00
150	Roberto Clemente	55.00	27.50	16.50
151	Red Schoendienst	15.00	7.50	4.50
152	Joe Torre	5.00	2.50	1.50
153	Bob Purkey	4.00	2.00	1.25
154a	Tommy Davis (3B)	7.50	3.75	2.25
154b	Tommy Davis (OF)	12.00	6.00	3.50
155a	Andre Rogers (Incorrect spelling, 1B.)	7.50	3.75	2.25
155b	Andre Rodgers (Correct spelling, SS.)	12.00	6.00	3.50
156	Tony Taylor	4.00	2.00	1.25
157	Bob Friend	4.00	2.00	1.25
158a	Gus Bell (Redlegs)	20.00	10.00	6.00
158b	Gus Bell (Mets)	4.00	2.00	1.25
159	Roy McMillan	4.00	2.00	1.25
160	Carl Warwick	4.00	2.00	1.25
161	Willie Davis	4.00	2.00	1.25
162	Sam Jones	60.00	30.00	18.00
163	Ruben Amaro	6.00	3.00	1.75
164	Sam Taylor	4.00	2.00	1.25
165	Frank Robinson	15.00	7.50	4.50
166	Lou Burdette	5.00	2.50	1.50
167	Ken Boyer	13.50	6.75	4.00
168	Bill Virdon	4.00	2.00	1.25
169	Jim Davenport	4.00	2.00	1.25
170	Don Demeter	4.00	2.00	1.25
171	Richie Ashburn	40.00	20.00	12.00
172	John Podres	8.00	4.00	2.50
173a	Joe Cunningham (Cardinals)	30.00	15.00	9.00
173b	Joe Cunningham (White Sox)	12.50	6.25	3.75
174	ElRoy Face	5.00	2.50	1.50
175	Orlando Cepeda	12.00	6.00	3.50
176a	Bobby Gene Smith (Phillies)	15.00	7.50	4.50
176b	Bobby Gene Smith (Mets)	6.00	3.00	1.75
177a	Ernie Banks (OF)	25.00	12.50	7.50
177b	Ernie Banks (SS)	20.00	10.00	6.00
178a	Daryl Spencer (3B)	20.00	10.00	6.00
178b	Daryl Spencer (1B)	12.00	6.00	3.50
179	Bob Schmidt	25.00	12.50	7.50
180	Hank Aaron	35.00	17.50	10.50
181	Hobie Landrith	10.00	5.00	3.00
182a	Ed Broussard (Bressoud)	425.00	210.00	125.00
182b	Ed Bressoud	25.00	12.50	7.50
183	Felix Mantilla	10.00	5.00	3.00
184	Dick Farrell	10.00	5.00	3.00
185	Bob Miller	10.00	5.00	3.00
186	Don Taussig	15.00	7.50	4.50
187	Pumpsie Green	10.00	5.00	3.00
188	Bobby Shantz	10.00	5.00	3.00
189	Roger Craig	10.00	5.00	3.00
190	Hal Smith	10.00	5.00	3.00
191	John Edwards	10.00	5.00	3.00
192	John DeMerit	10.00	5.00	3.00
193	Joe Amalfitano	10.00	5.00	3.00
194	Norm Larker	10.00	5.00	3.00
195	Al Heist	10.00	5.00	3.00
196	Al Spangler	10.00	5.00	3.00
197	Alex Grammas	10.00	5.00	3.00
198	Gerry Lynch	10.00	5.00	3.00
199	Jim McKnight	15.00	7.50	4.50
200	Jose Pagen (Pagan)	10.00	5.00	3.00
201	Junior Gilliam	20.00	10.00	6.00
202	Art Ditmar	10.00	5.00	3.00
203	Pete Daley	10.00	5.00	3.00
204	Johnny Callison	20.00	10.00	6.00
205	Stu Miller	10.00	5.00	3.00
206	Russ Snyder	10.00	5.00	3.00
207	Billy Williams	25.00	12.50	7.50
208	Walter Bond	10.00	5.00	3.00
209	Joe Koppe	10.00	5.00	3.00
210	Don Schwall	16.00	8.00	4.75
211	Billy Gardner	15.00	7.50	4.50
212	Chuck Estrada	10.00	5.00	3.00
213	Gary Bell	15.00	7.50	4.50
214	Floyd Robinson	10.00	5.00	3.00
215	Duke Snider	25.00	12.50	7.50
216	Lee Maye	10.00	5.00	3.00
217	Howie Bedell	10.00	5.00	3.00
218	Bob Will	10.00	5.00	3.00
219	Dallas Green	15.00	7.50	4.50
220	Carroll Hardy	15.00	7.50	4.50
221	Danny O'Connell	10.00	5.00	3.00

1962 Salada-Junket Coins - Clip Back

A very rare version of the Salada Tea/Junket Dessert plastic coins exists in a clip-back format. An extruded tab at back center would allow the coin to be slid onto a cap bill or shirt flap as a decoration. With the exception of Averill (Angels), all clip-back Saladas confirmed thus far depict Boston Red Sox players. It has been reported that the clip-back coins were created for use in Opening Day stadium promotions by the Red Sox, Yankees and Mets.

		NM	EX	VG
	Common Player:	450.00	225.00	135.00
14	Frank Malzone	450.00	225.00	135.00
24	Earl Averill	450.00	225.00	135.00
27	Carl Yastrzemski	600.00	300.00	180.00
38	Gary Geiger	450.00	225.00	135.00
47	Pete Runnels	450.00	225.00	135.00

		NM	EX	VG
73	Jackie Jensen	450.00	225.00	135.00
81	Jim Pagliaroni	450.00	225.00	135.00
99	Bill Monbouquette	450.00	225.00	135.00
182	Ed Broussard (Bressoud)	450.00	225.00	135.00
187	Pumpsie Green	450.00	225.00	135.00
210	Don Schwall	450.00	225.00	135.00
220	Carroll Hardy	450.00	225.00	135.00

1963 Salada-Junket Coins

A much smaller set of baseball coins was issued by Salada/Junket in 1963. The 63 coins issued were called "All-Star Baseball Coins" and included most of the top players of the day. Unlike 1962, the coins were made of metal and measured a slightly larger 1-1/2" diameter. American League players have blue rims on their coins, while National Leaguers are rimmed in red. Coin fronts contain no printing on the full-color player photos, while backs list coin number, player name, team and position, along with brief statistics and the sponsors' logos.

		NM	EX	VG
	Complete Set (63):	1,000	500.00	300.00
	Common Player:	9.00	4.50	3.00
1	Don Drysdale	20.00	10.00	6.00
2	Dick Farrell	9.00	4.50	3.00
3	Bob Gibson	20.00	10.00	6.00
4	Sandy Koufax	55.00	30.00	15.00
5a	Juan Marichal (No buttons.)	20.00	10.00	6.00
5b	Juan Marichal (Jersey buttons.)	15.00	8.00	5.00
6	Bob Purkey	9.00	4.50	3.00
7	Bob Shaw	9.00	4.50	3.00
8	Warren Spahn	20.00	10.00	6.00
9	Johnny Podres	12.00	6.00	4.00
10	Art Mahaffey	9.00	4.50	3.00
11	Del Crandall	9.00	4.50	3.00
12	John Roseboro	9.00	4.50	3.00
13	Orlando Cepeda	15.00	8.00	5.00
14	Bill Mazeroski	15.00	8.00	5.00
15	Ken Boyer	12.00	6.00	4.00
16	Dick Groat	9.00	4.50	3.00
17	Ernie Banks	25.00	12.00	8.00
18	Frank Bolling	9.00	4.50	3.00
19	Jim Davenport	9.00	4.50	3.00
20	Maury Wills	12.00	6.00	4.00
21	Tommy Davis	9.00	4.50	3.00
22	Willie Mays	55.00	30.00	15.00
23	Roberto Clemente	70.00	35.00	20.00
24	Henry Aaron	45.00	25.00	15.00
25	Felipe Alou	12.00	6.00	4.00
26	Johnny Callison	9.00	4.50	3.00
27	Richie Ashburn	20.00	10.00	6.00
28	Eddie Mathews	20.00	10.00	6.00
29	Frank Robinson	15.00	8.00	5.00
30	Billy Williams	15.00	8.00	5.00
31	George Altman	9.00	4.50	3.00
32	Hank Aguirre	9.00	4.50	3.00
33	Jim Bunning	15.00	8.00	5.00
34	Dick Donovan	9.00	4.50	3.00
35	Bill Monbouquette	9.00	4.50	3.00
36	Camilo Pascual	9.00	4.50	3.00
37	David Stenhouse	9.00	4.50	3.00
38	Ralph Terry	9.00	4.50	3.00
39	Hoyt Wilhelm	15.00	8.00	5.00
40	Jim Kaat	12.00	6.00	4.00
41	Ken McBride	9.00	4.50	3.00
42	Ray Herbert	9.00	4.50	3.00
43	Milt Pappas	9.00	4.50	3.00
44	Earl Battey	9.00	4.50	3.00
45	Elston Howard	12.00	6.00	4.00
46	John Romano	9.00	4.50	3.00
47	Jim Gentile	9.00	4.50	3.00
48	Billy Moran	9.00	4.50	3.00
49	Rich Rollins	9.00	4.50	3.00
50	Luis Aparicio	15.00	8.00	5.00
51	Norm Siebern	9.00	4.50	3.00
52	Bobby Richardson	12.00	6.00	4.00
53	Brooks Robinson	25.00	12.00	8.00
54	Tom Tresh	12.00	6.00	4.00
55	Leon Wagner	9.00	4.50	3.00
56	Mickey Mantle	125.00	65.00	40.00
57	Roger Maris	35.00	18.00	10.00
58	Rocky Colavito	30.00	15.00	9.00
59	Lee Thomas	9.00	4.50	3.00
60	Jim Landis	9.00	4.50	3.00
61	Pete Runnels	9.00	4.50	3.00
62	Yogi Berra	35.00	18.00	6.75
63	Al Kaline	15.00	7.50	4.50

1961 Sam's Family Restaurants Roger Maris

This postcard was issued to commemorate the presentation of Roger Maris' historic 61st home run ball back to the slugger. Pictured with Maris on this color 3-1/2" x 5-1/2" postcard is Sam Gordon, owner of a chain of family restaurants in northern California. Gordon purchased the ball from the fan who caught it, Sal Durante, and flew Durante and his wife, and Maris to Sacramento where he paid $5,000 for the ball and presented it to Maris, who later donated it to the Hall of Fame. On front is a borderless color photo of the presentation. Back has the historical details and the traditional postcard indicia.

		NM	EX	VG
61	Roger Maris, Sam Gordon	50.00	25.00	15.00

1886 W.H. Sanders New York Baseball Club (H812)

This rare 19th Century baseball issue can be classified under the general category of "trade" cards, a popular advertising vehicle of the period. The cards measure 3" x 4-3/4" and feature blue line-drawing portraits of members of the "New York Base Ball Club," which is printed along the top. As was common with this type of trade card, the bottom was left blank to accomodate various messages. The known examples of this set carry ads for local tobacco merchants and other businesses. The portraits are all based on the photographs used in the 1886 Old Judge set. The cards, which have been assigned an ACC designation of H812, are printed on thin paper rather than cardboard.

(See 1889 New York Baseball Club for checklist and values.)

1969 San Diego Padres Premium Pictures

Unlike most of the contemporary large-format (8-1/2" x 11") premium pictures, this issue carries no advertising and appears to have been a team-issue in the Padres inaugural year. Fronts feature large portraits and smaller action pictures of the player against a dark background with a facsimile autograph at the bottom and the player's name printed in the white bottom border. The signature of the artist appears in the lower-left corner. The artwork was done by Nicholas Volpe, who produced many similar items for teams in all sports in the '60s, '70s and '80s. Backs have a large team logo at center and a sketch of the artist at bottom. There is evidence to suggest that the picture of Cito Gaston is scarcer than the other seven.

		NM	EX	VG
	Complete Set (8):	60.00	30.00	18.00
	Common Player:	7.50	3.75	2.25
(1)	Ollie Brown	7.50	3.75	2.25
(2)	Tommy Dean	7.50	3.75	2.25
(3)	Al Ferrara	7.50	3.75	2.25
(4)	Clarence Gaston	10.00	5.00	3.00
(5)	Preston Gomez	7.50	3.75	2.25
(6)	Johnny Podres	9.00	4.50	2.75
(7)	Al Santorini	7.50	3.75	2.25
(8)	Ed Spiezio	7.50	3.75	2.25

1977 San Diego Padres Schedule Cards

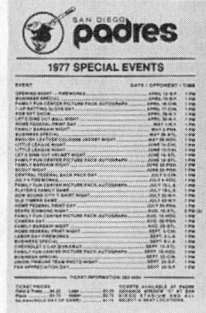

Members of the 1977 San Diego Padres, players and management, are featured in this set. The 2-1/4" x 3-3/8" cards are printed in brown on thin white stock. Fronts have a player photo with a pinstripe around and the team and player name at bottom. Backs have the team logo at top, a list of promotional dates in the center and ticket information at bottom. While some card backs state "One in a Series of 40 Player Photos," more than 80 variations are known, including some poses with blank backs. The unnumbered cards are checklisted here in alphabetical order, within three types differentiated by back printing.

		NM	EX	VG
	Complete Set (89):	60.00	30.00	18.00
	Common Player:	1.00	.50	.30
Type 1 - "Series of 40"				
(1)	Bill Almon	1.00	.50	.30
(2)	Joe Amalfitano	1.00	.50	.30
(3)	Buzzy Bavasi (General Manager)	1.00	.50	.30
(4)	Vic Bernal	1.00	.50	.30
(5)	Mike Champion	1.00	.50	.30
(6)	Billy Champion, Bill Almon	1.00	.50	.30
(7)	Roger Craig	1.00	.50	.30
(8)	John D'Acquisto	1.00	.50	.30
(9)	Bob Davis	1.00	.50	.30
(10)	Rollie Fingers	3.00	1.50	.90
(11)	Dave Freisleben	1.00	.50	.30
(12)	Tom Griffin	1.00	.50	.30
(13)	George Hendrick	1.00	.50	.30
(14)	Enzo Hernandez	1.00	.50	.30
(15)	Mike Ivie	1.00	.50	.30
(16)	Randy Jones (Follow-through.)	1.00	.50	.30
(17)	Randy Jones (Cy Young Award)	1.00	.50	.30
(18)	John McNamara	1.00	.50	.30
(19)	Luis Melendez	1.00	.50	.30
(20)	Butch Metzger	1.00	.50	.30
(21)	Bob Owchinko	1.00	.50	.30
(22)	Doug Rader	1.00	.50	.30
(23)	Merv Rettenmund	1.00	.50	.30
(24)	Gene Richards	1.00	.50	.30
(25)	Dave Roberts	1.00	.50	.30
(26)	Rick Sawyer	1.00	.50	.30
(27)	Bob Shirley	1.00	.50	.30
(28)	Bob Skinner	1.00	.50	.30
(29)	Dan Spillner	1.00	.50	.30
(30)	Brent Strom	1.00	.50	.30
(31)	Gary Sutherland	1.00	.50	.30
(32)	Gene Tenace	1.00	.50	.30
(33)	Dave Tomlin	1.00	.50	.30
(34)	Jerry Turner	1.00	.50	.30
(35)	Bobby Valentine	1.00	.50	.30
(36)	Dan Wehrmeister	1.00	.50	.30
(37)	Whitey Wietelmann	1.00	.50	.30
(38)	Don Williams	1.00	.50	.30
(39)	Dave Winfield (One bat.)	10.00	5.00	3.00
(40)	Dave Winfield (Two bats.)	5.00	2.50	1.50
Type 2 - No "Series of 40"				
(1)	Bill Almon	1.00	.50	.30
(2)	Matty Alou	1.00	.50	.30
(3)	Steve Arlin (Glove to chest.)	1.00	.50	.30
(4)	Steve Arlin (Follow-through.)	1.00	.50	.30
(5)	Bob Barton	1.00	.50	.30
(6)	Glenn Beckert	1.50	.75	.45
(7)	Ollie Brown	1.00	.50	.30
(8)	Dave Campbell (Bat on shoulder.)	1.00	.50	.30
(9)	Dave Campbell/Kneeling	1.00	.50	.30
(10)	Enzo Hernandez, Nate Colbert	1.00	.50	.30
(11)	Nate Colbert	1.00	.50	.30
(12)	Colbert and Friend (With child.)	1.00	.50	.30
(13)	Jerry Coleman/Announcer	1.00	.50	.30
(14)	Willie Davis	1.00	.50	.30
(15)	Jim Eakle ("TUBA MAN")	1.00	.50	.30
(16)	Rollie Fingers	3.00	1.50	.90
(17)	Cito Gaston (Bare hands.)	1.00	.50	.30
(18)	Cito Gaston (Batting gloves.)	1.00	.50	.30
(19)	Johnny Grubb	1.00	.50	.30
(20)	George Hendrick	1.00	.50	.30
(21)	Mike Ivie	1.00	.50	.30
(22)	Fred Kendall/Btg	1.00	.50	.30
(23)	Fred Kendall (Holding ball.)	1.00	.50	.30
(24)	Clay Kirby (Follow-through.)	1.00	.50	.30
(25)	Clay Kirby (Glove to chest.)	1.00	.50	.30
(26)	Dave Marshall	1.00	.50	.30
(27)	Willie McCovey (Moustache)	5.00	2.50	1.50
(28)	John McNamara	1.00	.50	.30
(29)	Bob Miller	1.00	.50	.30
(30)	Fred Norman (Arms above head.)	1.00	.50	.30

		NM	EX	VG
(31)	Fred Norman/Kneeling	1.00	.50	.30
(32)	Gene Richards	1.00	.50	.30
(33)	Ballard Smith (General Manager)	1.00	.50	.30
(34)	Ed Spiezio	1.00	.50	.30
(35)	Derrell (Darrel) Thomas (Glasses)	1.00	.50	.30
(36)	Derrel Thomas (No glasses.)	1.00	.50	.30
(37)	Bobby Tolan (Batting)	1.00	.50	.30
(38)	Bobby Tolan (Kneeling)	1.00	.50	.30
(39)	Jerry Turner	1.00	.50	.30
(40)	Dave Winfield	5.00	2.50	1.50

Type 3 - Blank back

(1)	Nate Colbert	1.00	.50	.30
(2)	Dave Freisleben	1.00	.50	.30
(3)	Mike Ivie	1.00	.50	.30
(4)	Randy Jones and Bowie Kuhn	1.00	.50	.30
(5)	Mike Kilkenny	1.00	.50	.30
(6)	Ray Kroc/Owner	1.00	.50	.30
(7)	Willie McCovey	5.00	2.50	1.50
(8)	John McNamara (Facing his right.)	1.00	.50	.30
(9)	Dave Winfield	7.50	3.75	2.25

1932 Sanella Margarine

One of several "foreign" Babe Ruth cards issued during his prime was included in a 112-card set produced as premiums for Sanella margarine in Germany. Ruth is the only major league ballplayer in the issue. Cards are in full color, measuring 2-3/4" x 4-1/8". Backs of the unnumbered cards are printed in German. Three types of backs can be found on the Ruth card. Type 1 has the Sanella name nearly centered. The Type 2 back has the brand name printed closer to the bottom of the card, with only four lines of type under it. Type 3 is a variation of Type 2 on which the appropriate page number (83) of the accompanying album is mentioned on the line immediately above "Handbuch des Sports" near the top. Type 1 cards also mention the page number; current hobby data suggests that no Sanellas with centered logos do not mention the page. One card was given with the purchase of each 1/2 pound of margarine and the album could be ordered by mail. See also Astra Margarine.

		NM	EX	VG
Type 1	Babe Ruth (Centered w/83)	200.00	100.00	60.00
Type 2	Babe Ruth (At bottom.)	140.00	70.00	42.00
Type 3	Babe Ruth (At bottom w/83.)	200.00	100.00	60.00

1958 San Francisco Call-Bulletin Giants

These unnumbered cards, picturing members of the San Francisco Giants, were inserted in copies of the San Francisco Call-Bulletin newspaper as part of a promotional contest. The 25 cards in the set measure 2" x 4" and were printed on orange paper. The top of the card contains a black and white player photo, while the bottom contains a perforated stub with a serial number used to win prizes. (Cards without the stub intact are approximately 50 percent of the prices listed.) The contest name, "Giant Payoff," appears prominently on both sides of the stub. The back of the card contains a 1958 Giants schedule.

		NM	EX	VG
Complete Set (25):		1,800	900.00	550.00
Common Player:		25.00	12.50	7.50
(1)	Johnny Antonelli	25.00	12.50	7.50
(2)	Curt Barclay	25.00	12.50	7.50

		NM	EX	VG
(3)	Tom Bowers/SP	400.00	200.00	120.00
(4)	Ed Bressoud/SP	150.00	75.00	45.00
(5)	Orlando Cepeda	250.00	125.00	75.00
(6)	Ray Crone	25.00	12.50	7.50
(7)	Jim Davenport	25.00	12.50	7.50
(8)	Paul Giel	25.00	12.50	7.50
(9)	Ruben Gomez	25.00	12.50	7.50
(10)	Marv Grissom	25.00	12.50	7.50
(11)	Ray Jablonski/SP	150.00	75.00	45.00
(12)	Willie Kirkland/SP	150.00	75.00	45.00
(13)	Whitey Lockman	25.00	12.50	7.50
(14)	Willie Mays	250.00	125.00	75.00
(15)	Mike McCormick	25.00	12.50	7.50
(16)	Stu Miller	25.00	12.50	7.50
(17)	Ramon Monzant	25.00	12.50	7.50
(18)	Danny O'Connell	25.00	12.50	7.50
(19)	Bill Rigney	25.00	12.50	7.50
(20)	Hank Sauer	25.00	12.50	7.50
(21)	Bob Schmidt	25.00	12.50	7.50
(22)	Daryl Spencer	25.00	12.50	7.50
(23)	Valmy Thomas	25.00	12.50	7.50
(24)	Bobby Thomson	45.00	22.50	13.50
(25)	Allan Worthington	25.00	12.50	7.50

1971-1982 San Francisco Giants Autograph Cards

RANDY MOFFITT

Chris Arnold — Infielder

Giants autograph card courtesy of Redwood City Tribune

For more than 10 years the Giants issued a number of different types of cards bearing facsimile autographs that the players could use to respond to fan mail. The cards vary in size from 3" x 5" to 3" x 6" and have a black-and-white photo (usually a portrait). The cards are black-backed. Besides the cards with pre-printed autographs, a number of special cards in similar format were issued without facsimile signature. The listings are presented here in two major styles, those with player name in all-capital letters and those with names in upper and lower case.

		NM	EX	VG
Common Player:		6.00	3.00	1.75

NAME IN ALL-CAPITAL LETTERS
TYPE 1 - Name only, letters 1/8" wide.

(1)	Doyle Alexander	6.00	3.00	1.75
(2)	Gary Alexander	6.00	3.00	1.75
(3)	Joe Altobelli	6.00	3.00	1.75
(4)	Rob Andrews/Portrait	6.00	3.00	1.75
(5)	Rob Andrews/Fldg	6.00	3.00	1.75
(6)	Jim Barr/Pitching	6.00	3.00	1.75
(7)	Dave Bergman	6.00	3.00	1.75
(8)	Vida Blue/Portrait	8.00	4.00	2.50
(9)	Vida Blue/Pitching	8.00	4.00	2.50
(10)	Bill Bordley	6.00	3.00	1.75
(11)	Fred Breining	6.00	3.00	1.75
(12)	Dave Bristol	6.00	3.00	1.75
(13)	Enos Cabell	6.00	3.00	1.75
(14)	Jack Clark (Ready to bat.)	8.00	4.00	2.50
(15)	Jack Clark (Swinging bat.)	8.00	4.00	2.50
(16)	Terry Cornutt	6.00	3.00	1.75
(17)	Heity Cruz	6.00	3.00	1.75
(18)	John Curtis	6.00	3.00	1.75
(19)	Jim Dwyer	6.00	3.00	1.75
(20)	Randy Elliott	6.00	3.00	1.75
(21)	Darrell Evans/Portrait	8.00	4.00	2.50
(22)	Darrell Evans/Btg	8.00	4.00	2.50
(23)	Tim Foli/Fldg	6.00	3.00	1.75
(24)	Tom Griffin	6.00	3.00	1.75
(25)	Ed Halicki/Portrait	6.00	3.00	1.75
(26)	Ed Halicki/Pitching	6.00	3.00	1.75
(27)	Vic Harris	6.00	3.00	1.75
(28)	Dave Heaverlo/Action	6.00	3.00	1.75
(29)	Tom Heintzelman	6.00	3.00	1.75
(30)	Larry Herndon	6.00	3.00	1.75
(31)	Marc Hill	6.00	3.00	1.75
(32)	Al Holland	6.00	3.00	1.75
(33)	Mike Ivie (Looks to side.)	6.00	3.00	1.75
(34)	Mike Ivie (Looks to front.)	6.00	3.00	1.75
(35)	Skip James	6.00	3.00	1.75
(36)	Bob Knepper	6.00	3.00	1.75
(37)	Gary Lavelle/Portrait	6.00	3.00	1.75
(38)	Gary Lavelle/Pitching	6.00	3.00	1.75
(39)	Johnnie Lemaster/Fldg	6.00	3.00	1.75
(40)	Dennis Littlejohn	6.00	3.00	1.75
(41)	Bill Madlock (Picture reversed.)	8.00	4.00	2.50
(42)	Bill Madlock (Corrected)	8.00	4.00	2.50
(43)	Jerry Martin	6.00	3.00	1.75
(44)	Milt May	6.00	3.00	1.75
(45)	Willie McCovey/Portrait	15.00	7.50	4.50
(46)	Willie McCovey/Btg	15.00	7.50	4.50
(47)	Lynn McGlothen/Pitching	6.00	3.00	1.75

(48)	Roger Metzger	6.00	3.00	1.75
(49)	Greg Minton	6.00	3.00	1.75
(50)	Randy Moffitt/Portrait	6.00	3.00	1.75
(51)	Randy Moffitt/Pitching	6.00	3.00	1.75
(52)	John Montefusco (To neck.)	6.00	3.00	1.75
(53)	John Montefusco (To letters.)	6.00	3.00	1.75
(54)	Joe Morgan	15.00	7.50	4.50
(55)	Rich Murray	6.00	3.00	1.75
(56)	Phil Nastu	6.00	3.00	1.75
(57)	Bill North	6.00	3.00	1.75
(58)	Joe Pettini	6.00	3.00	1.75
(59)	Allen Ripley	6.00	3.00	1.75
(60)	Dave Roberts	6.00	3.00	1.75
(61)	Frank Robinson	20.00	10.00	6.00
(62)	Mike Sadek (To neck.)	6.00	3.00	1.75
(63)	Mike Sadek (To letters.)	6.00	3.00	1.75
(64)	Billy Smith	6.00	3.00	1.75
(65)	Rennie Stennett	6.00	3.00	1.75
(66)	Joe Strain	6.00	3.00	1.75
(67)	John Tamargo	6.00	3.00	1.75
(68)	Derrel Thomas/Throwing	6.00	3.00	1.75
(69)	Gary Thomasson	6.00	3.00	1.75
(70)	Max Venable	6.00	3.00	1.75
(71)	Terry Whitfield	6.00	3.00	1.75
(72)	Ed Whitson	6.00	3.00	1.75
(73)	Charlie Williams	6.00	3.00	1.75
(74)	Jim Wohlford	6.00	3.00	1.75

TYPE 2 - Name only, letters 1/16" wide.

(1)	Jim Barr (Mouth closed.)	6.00	3.00	1.75
(2)	Jim Barr (Mouth open, fence.)	6.00	3.00	1.75
(3)	Jim Barr (Mouth open, no fence.)	6.00	3.00	1.75
(4)	Bobby Bonds	9.00	4.50	2.75
(5)	Tom Bradley	6.00	3.00	1.75
(6)	Ron Bryant	6.00	3.00	1.75
(7)	Don Carrithers (To neck.)	6.00	3.00	1.75
(8)	Don Carrithers (To letters.)	6.00	3.00	1.75
(9)	Pete Falcone	6.00	3.00	1.75
(10)	Charlie Fox	6.00	3.00	1.75
(11)	Tito Fuentes (To neck.)	6.00	3.00	1.75
(12)	Tito Fuentes (To letters.)	6.00	3.00	1.75
(13)	Alan Gallagher	6.00	3.00	1.75
(14)	Russ Gibson	6.00	3.00	1.75
(15)	Ed Goodson	6.00	3.00	1.75
(16)	Ed Halicki/Pitching	6.00	3.00	1.75
(17)	Marc Hill	6.00	3.00	1.75
(18)	Jim Howarth	6.00	3.00	1.75
(19)	Jerry Johnson	6.00	3.00	1.75
(20)	Von Joshua	6.00	3.00	1.75
(21)	Gary Lavelle/Pitching	6.00	3.00	1.75
(22)	Garry Maddox	6.00	3.00	1.75
(23)	Juan Marichal	15.00	7.50	4.50
(24)	Gary Matthews	8.00	4.00	2.50
(25)	Randy Moffitt	6.00	3.00	1.75
(26)	Willie McCovey	15.00	7.50	4.50
(27)	Willie Montanez	6.00	3.00	1.75
(28)	John Montefusco/Pitching	6.00	3.00	1.75
(29)	Bobby Murcer/Btg	8.00	4.00	2.50
(30)	Dave Rader	6.00	3.00	1.75
(31)	Ken Reitz/Btg	6.00	3.00	1.75
(32)	Bill Rigney	6.00	3.00	1.75
(33)	Mike Sadek	6.00	3.00	1.75
(34)	Elias Sosa	6.00	3.00	1.75
(35)	Chris Speier (To neck.)	6.00	3.00	1.75
(36)	Chris Speier (To shoulders.)	6.00	3.00	1.75
(37)	Steve Stone	8.00	4.00	2.50
(38)	Derrel Thomas	6.00	3.00	1.75
(39)	Gary Thomasson	6.00	3.00	1.75
(40)	Jim Willoughby	6.00	3.00	1.75

TYPE 3 - 25th Anniversary Logo

(1)	Jim Barr	6.00	3.00	1.75
(2)	Bob Brenly	6.00	3.00	1.75
(3)	Don Buford (1-1/2" autograph)	6.00	3.00	1.75
(4)	Don Buford (2-1/2" autograph)	6.00	3.00	1.75
(5)	Jim Davenport	6.00	3.00	1.75
(6)	Chili Davis	8.00	4.00	2.50
(7)	Alan Fowlkes	6.00	3.00	1.75
(8)	Rich Gale	6.00	3.00	1.75
(9)	Atlee Hammaker	6.00	3.00	1.75
(10)	Al Holland	6.00	3.00	1.75
(11)	Duane Kuiper	6.00	3.00	1.75
(12)	Bill Laskey	6.00	3.00	1.75
(13)	Jim Lefebvre	6.00	3.00	1.75
(14)	Johnnie Lemaster	6.00	3.00	1.75
(15)	Jeff Leonard (Chain in background.)	8.00	4.00	2.50
(16)	Jeff Leonard (No chain.)	8.00	4.00	2.50
(17)	Renie Martin	6.00	3.00	1.75
(18)	Willie McCovey	15.00	7.50	4.50
(19)	Don McMahon (2-3/8" autograph)	6.00	3.00	1.75
(20)	Don McMahon (2-5/8" autograph)	6.00	3.00	1.75
(21)	Greg Minton	6.00	3.00	1.75
(22)	Joe Morgan	15.00	7.50	4.50
(23)	Tom O'Malley	6.00	3.00	1.75
(24)	Frank Robinson	20.00	10.00	6.00
(25)	Mike Sadek	6.00	3.00	1.75
(26)	Reggie Smith	6.00	3.00	1.75
(27)	Guy Sularz	6.00	3.00	1.75
(28)	Champ Summers	6.00	3.00	1.75
(29)	John Van Ornum (2" autograph)	6.00	3.00	1.75
(30)	John Van Ornum (2-1/4" autograph)	6.00	3.00	1.75
(31)	Jim Wohlford	6.00	3.00	1.75

TYPE 4 - Position after name, no autograph

(1)	Chris Speier	6.00	3.00	1.75

TYPE 5 - Courtesy Chevrolet, no autograph

(1)	Bobby Bonds	9.00	4.50	2.75
(2)	Dick Dietz	6.00	3.00	1.75
(3)	Tito Fuentes	6.00	3.00	1.75
(4)	Ken Henderson	6.00	3.00	1.75

	TYPE 6 - West Valley Bicycles, no autograph			
(1)	Alan Gallagher	6.00	3.00	1.75
	TYPE 7 - Best Chevrolet, no autograph			
(1)	Tito Fuentes	6.00	3.00	1.75
(2)	Chris Speier	6.00	3.00	1.75
	TYPE 8 - Redwood City Tribune, no autograph			
(1)	Jim Barr	6.00	3.00	1.75
	NAME IN UPPER- AND LOWER CASE LETTERS			
	TYPE A - Name only			
(1)	John D'Acquisto	6.00	3.00	1.75
(2)	Mike Caldwell	6.00	3.00	1.75
(3)	Ed Goodson	6.00	3.00	1.75
(4)	Dave Kingman	8.00	4.00	2.50
(5)	Steve Ontiveros	6.00	3.00	1.75
(6)	Mike Phillips	6.00	3.00	1.75
(7)	"Wes" Westrum	6.00	3.00	1.75
(8)	Charlie Williams	6.00	3.00	1.75
	TYPE B - Team after name, no autograph			
(1)	Rich Robertson	6.00	3.00	1.75
	TYPE C - Courtesy Chevrolet, no autograph			
(1)	Rich Robertson	6.00	3.00	1.75
	TYPE D - Position after name			
(1)	Garry Maddox	6.00	3.00	1.75
	TYPE E - Redwood City Tribune, no logo, no autograph			
(1)	Chris Arnold	6.00	3.00	1.75
(2)	Jim Barr	6.00	3.00	1.75
(3)	Jim Howarth	6.00	3.00	1.75
(4)	Garry Maddox	6.00	3.00	1.75
(5)	Dave Rader	6.00	3.00	1.75
(6)	Chris Speier	6.00	3.00	1.75
	TYPE F - Redwood City Tribune, with newspaper logo, no autograph			
(1)	Chris Arnold	6.00	3.00	1.75
(2)	Jim Barr	6.00	3.00	1.75
(3)	Ed Goodson	6.00	3.00	1.75
	TYPE G - Name only, old Giants logo	.00	.00	.00
(1)	Dave Kingman	8.00	4.00	2.50
(2)	Juan Marichal	15.00	7.50	4.50

1977 San Francisco Giants Team Issue

These 3-1/2" x 5" blank-back cards feature black-and-white player photos surrounded by an orange frame with black borders. The manager, coaches and instructors are featured along with players in the issue. The unnumbered cards are checklisted here in alphabetical order.

		NM	EX	VG
	Complete Set (25):	15.00	7.50	4.50
	Common Player:	1.50	.75	.45
(1)	Joe Altobelli	1.50	.75	.45
(2)	Jim Barr	1.50	.75	.45
(3)	Jack Clark	2.50	1.25	.70
(4)	Terry Cornutt	1.50	.75	.45
(5)	Rob Dressler	1.50	.75	.45
(6)	Darrell Evans	2.50	1.25	.70
(7)	Frank Funk	1.50	.75	.45
(8)	Ed Halicki	1.50	.75	.45
(9)	Tom Haller	1.50	.75	.45
(10)	Marc Hill	1.50	.75	.45
(11)	Skip James	1.50	.75	.45
(12)	Bob Knepper	1.50	.75	.45
(13)	Gary Lavelle	1.50	.75	.45
(14)	Bill Madlock	1.75	.90	.50
(15)	Willie McCovey	6.00	3.00	1.75
(16)	Randy Moffitt	1.50	.75	.45
(17)	John Montefusco	1.50	.75	.45
(18)	Marty Perez	1.50	.75	.45
(19)	Frank Riccelli	1.50	.75	.45
(20)	Mike Sadek	1.50	.75	.45
(21)	Hank Sauer	1.50	.75	.45
(22)	Chris Speier	1.50	.75	.45
(23)	Gary Thomasson	1.50	.75	.45
(24)	Tommy Toms	1.50	.75	.45
(25)	Bobby Winkles	1.50	.75	.45

1979 San Francisco Giants Police

Each of the full-color cards measures 2-5/8" x 4-1/8" and is numbered by player uniform number. The set includes players and coaches. The player's name, position and facsimile autograph are on front, along with the Giants logo. Backs have a "Tip from the Giants" and sponsor logos for the Giants and radio station KNBR, all printed in orange and black. Half of the

set was distributed as a ballpark promotion, while the other cards were available from police agencies in several San Francisco Bay area counties.

		NM	EX	VG
	Complete Set (29):	10.00	5.00	3.00
	Common Player:	.50	.25	.15
1	Dave Bristol	.50	.25	.15
2	Marc Hill	.50	.25	.15
3	Mike Sadek	.50	.25	.15
5	Tom Haller	.50	.25	.15
6	Joe Altobelli	.50	.25	.15
8	Larry Shepard	.50	.25	.15
9	Heity Cruz	.50	.25	.15
10	Johnnie LeMaster	.50	.25	.15
12	Jim Davenport	.50	.25	.15
14	Vida Blue	.75	.40	.25
15	Mike Ivie	.50	.25	.15
16	Roger Metzger	.50	.25	.15
17	Randy Moffitt	.50	.25	.15
18	Bill Madlock	.60	.30	.20
21	Rob Andrews	.50	.25	.15
22	Jack Clark	.75	.40	.25
25	Dave Roberts	.50	.25	.15
26	John Montefusco	.50	.25	.15
28	Ed Halicki	.50	.25	.15
30	John Tamargo	.50	.25	.15
31	Larry Herndon	.50	.25	.15
36	Bill North	.50	.25	.15
39	Bob Knepper	.50	.25	.15
40	John Curtis	.50	.25	.15
41	Darrell Evans	.75	.40	.25
43	Tom Griffin	.50	.25	.15
44	Willie McCovey	5.00	2.50	1.50
46	Gary Lavelle	.50	.25	.15
49	Max Venable	.50	.25	.15

1980 San Francisco Giants Police

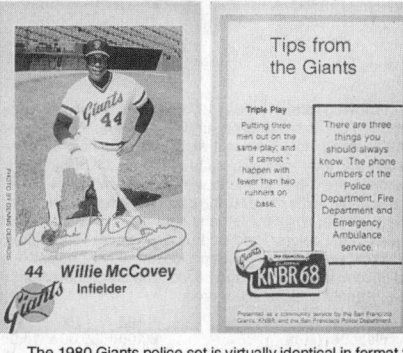

The 1980 Giants police set is virtually identical in format to its 1979 forerunner, with radio station KNBR and the San Francisco Police Department once again co-sponsors. The 2-5/8" x 4-1/8" cards feature full-color photos and facsimile autographs. Backs are in the team's orange and black colors. The set includes players and coaches, with each card numbered by uniform number. As in 1979, half of the cards were distributed as a stadium promotion, with the remainder available only from police officers.

		NM	EX	VG
	Complete Set (31):	9.00	4.50	2.75
	Common Player:	.50	.25	.15
1	Dave Bristol	.50	.25	.15
2	Marc Hill	.50	.25	.15
3	Mike Sadek	.50	.25	.15
4	Jim Lefebvre	.50	.25	.15
6	Rennie Stennett	.50	.25	.15
7	Milt May	.50	.25	.15
8	Vern Benson	.50	.25	.15
9	Jim Wohlford	.50	.25	.15
10	Johnnie LeMaster	.50	.25	.15
12	Jim Davenport	.50	.25	.15
14	Vida Blue	.75	.40	.25
15	Mike Ivie	.50	.25	.15
16	Roger Metzger	.50	.25	.15
17	Randy Moffitt	.50	.25	.15
19	Al Holland	.50	.25	.15
20	Joe Strain	.50	.25	.15
22	Jack Clark	.75	.40	.25
26	John Montefusco	.50	.25	.15
28	Ed Halicki	.50	.25	.15
31	Larry Herndon	.50	.25	.15
32	Ed Whitson	.50	.25	.15
36	Bill North	.50	.25	.15

38	Greg Minton	.50	.25	.15
39	Bob Knepper	.50	.25	.15
41	Darrell Evans	.60	.30	.20
42	John Van Ornum	.50	.25	.15
43	Tom Griffin	.50	.25	.15
44	Willie McCovey	4.00	2.00	1.25
45	Terry Whitfield	.50	.25	.15
46	Gary Lavelle	.50	.25	.15
47	Don McMahon	.50	.25	.15

1940s Sarra Trade Cards

While the cards are undated, one of the uniforms shown places its issue between 1940-1950. These ad cards are about 3-1/2" x 5-3/8" and printed in sepia on thick cream-colored paper stock. The backs picture examples of the company's personal care products, including cologne, available in sizes up to one quart!

	NM	EX	VG
Ralph Kiner	250.00	125.00	75.00
Stan Musial	350.00	175.00	100.00
Babe Ruth	550.00	275.00	165.00

1938 Sawyer Biscuit Cubs/White Sox

In the late 1930s, a local baker ran a promotion by which fans could redeem a coupon found in its product along with a dime for a matted black-and-white portrait photo of a favorite Chicago ballplayer. The photo was delivered in a thick textured maroon frame about 4-3/4" x 5-3/4" in size that had a punch-out stand on back. The Sawyer company name is not found on the actual photo, but is seen on the envelope and cover letter which are sometimes found with the pictures. It is unknown whether the list presented here is complete.

		NM	EX	VG
	Common Player:	600.00	300.00	180.00
	CHICAGO CUBS			
(1)	Jim Asbell	600.00	300.00	180.00
(2)	Clay Bryant	600.00	300.00	180.00
(3)	Tex Carleton	600.00	300.00	180.00
(4)	Phil Cavarretta	600.00	300.00	180.00
(5)	Rip Collins	600.00	300.00	180.00
(6)	Jerome "Dizzy" Dean	1,200	600.00	360.00
(7)	Frank Demaree	600.00	300.00	180.00
(8)	Al Epperly	600.00	300.00	180.00
(9)	Larry French	600.00	300.00	180.00
(10)	Augie Galan	600.00	300.00	180.00
(11)	Bob Garbark	600.00	300.00	180.00
(12)	Charlie Grimm	600.00	300.00	180.00
(13)	Stan Hack	650.00	325.00	195.00
(14)	Gabby Hartnett	750.00	375.00	225.00
(15)	Billy Herman	750.00	375.00	225.00
(16)	Bill Jurges	600.00	300.00	180.00
(17)	Tony Lazzeri	750.00	375.00	225.00
(18)	Bill Lee	600.00	300.00	180.00
(19)	Bob Logan	600.00	300.00	180.00
(20)	Joe Marty	600.00	300.00	180.00
(21)	Ken O'Dea	600.00	300.00	180.00
(22)	Carl Reynolds	600.00	300.00	180.00
(23)	Charlie Root	600.00	300.00	180.00
(24)	Jack Russell	600.00	300.00	180.00
	CHICAGO WHITE SOX			
(1)	Luke Appling	750.00	375.00	225.00
(2)	Boze Berger	600.00	300.00	180.00
(3)	Clint Brown	600.00	300.00	180.00
(4)	Frog Dietrich	600.00	300.00	180.00
(5)	Jimmie Dykes	600.00	300.00	180.00
(6)	Frank Gabler	600.00	300.00	180.00
(7)	Jackie Hayes	600.00	300.00	180.00
(8)	Jack Knott	600.00	300.00	180.00
(9)	Mike Kreevich	600.00	300.00	180.00
(10)	Joe Kuhel	600.00	300.00	180.00
(11)	Thornton Lee	600.00	300.00	180.00

		NM	EX	VG
(12)	Ted Lyons	750.00	375.00	225.00
(13)	Marv Owen	600.00	300.00	180.00
(14)	Tony Rensa	600.00	300.00	180.00
(15)	Dunc Rigney	600.00	300.00	180.00
(16)	Larry Rosenthal	600.00	300.00	180.00
(17)	Norm Schlueter	600.00	300.00	180.00
(18)	Luke Sewell	600.00	300.00	180.00
(19)	Henk Steinbacher	600.00	300.00	180.00
(20)	Monty Stratton	625.00	310.00	185.00
(21)	Gee Gee Walker	600.00	300.00	180.00
(22)	Porkshops Whitehead	600.00	300.00	180.00

BROADCASTER

	Bob Elson	600.00	300.00	180.00

1921-22 Schapira Bros. Big Show Candy

The players known, with the teams on which they are pictured, can pinpoint the issue date no closer than 1921-22. Nominally about 1-3/4" or 1-7/8" x 2-3/8" (size varies because the cards were printed without borders in sheet form, and are often found crudely cut), the cards were one of several types of insert cards and toys found in boxes of Schapira's "Big Show" candy. The cards have black-and-white borderless photos on which the player name is (usually) printed diagonally in script at lower right. Most cards have an Underwood & Underwood credit line on front, as well. Backs are blank. The unnumbered cards are listed here alphabetically, though the checklist may not be complete. Most cards are found with a horizontal crease at center, possibly to get them into the tight-fitting candy box.

		NM	EX	VG
	Common Player:	300.00	150.00	90.00
(1)	George J. Burns	300.00	150.00	90.00
(2)	Ty Cobb	2,700	1,350	800.00
(3)	Stan Coveleski	375.00	190.00	120.00
(4)	(Jake) Daubert	300.00	150.00	90.00
(5)	Joe Dugan	300.00	150.00	90.00
(6)	Jimmy Dykes	300.00	150.00	90.00
(7)	Walter Holke	300.00	150.00	90.00
(8)	Walter Johnson	900.00	450.00	270.00
(9)	Joe Judge	300.00	150.00	90.00
(10)	Geo. Kelly	575.00	275.00	175.00
(11)	Dick Kerr	300.00	150.00	90.00
(12)	Rabbit Maranville	375.00	190.00	120.00
(13)	(Bob) Meusel	300.00	150.00	90.00
(14)	Hy Meyers (Myers)	300.00	150.00	90.00
(15)	O'Neil (Mickey?)	300.00	150.00	90.00
(16)	Roger Peckinpaugh	300.00	150.00	90.00
(17)	Edd Rousch (Roush)	375.00	190.00	120.00
(18)	Ray Schalk	300.00	150.00	90.00
(19)	Everett Scott	300.00	150.00	90.00
(20)	Aaron Ward	300.00	150.00	90.00

1921 Schapira Bros. Candy Babe Ruth

The date assigned to this rare candy issue is a best guess based on the uniform in which the Babe is shown on the various cards. The blank-back cards measure between 1-5/8" and 1-3/4" in width, and are 2-1/2" tall. Printed in red, white and blue the cards were printed on a candy box and come in two types. Apparently each box contained a portrait card of Ruth which offered "a base ball autographed by Babe Ruth" for 250 of the pictures, plus one of five action photos. The portrait card would thus be much more common than any particular action pose, unless great numbers of them were redeemed. The cards illustrated here are not front and back, but show a typical action card and the portrait card. The unnumbered cards are checklisted here in alphabetical order based on the card's caption.

	NM	EX	VG
Complete Set (6):	11,00	5,500	3,300

		NM	EX	VG
(1)	Cleared the Bags (Babe Ruth)	2,000	1,000	600.00
(2)	Home Run (Babe Ruth)	2,000	1,000	600.00
(3)	Over the Fence (Babe Ruth)	2,000	1,000	600.00
(4)	They Passed Him (Babe Ruth)	2,000	1,000	600.00
(5)	Waiting for a High One (Babe Ruth)	2,000	1,000	600.00
(6a)	Babe Ruth/Portrait (Arrows point to top of ball.)	1,400	700.00	425.00
(6b)	Babe Ruth (No arrows.)	1,400	700.00	425.00

1975 Michael Schechter Associates Test Discs

Prior to rolling out its 70-disc set in 1976, Michael Schecter Associates issued this sample set of discs the previous year. Slightly larger, at 3-9/16" diameter, than the '76 issues, the '75 sample discs share a similar format. Fronts have a black-and-white player photo from which uniform logo details have been removed due to lack of licensing by Major League Baseball. Backs are blank. The Seaver and Bench discs are considerably scarcer than the other four players in the set.

		NM	EX	VG
	Complete Set (6):	175.00	90.00	55.00
	Common Player:	6.00	3.00	1.75
(1)	Hank Aaron	15.00	7.50	4.50
(2)	Johnny Bench	60.00	30.00	18.00
(3)	Catfish Hunter	6.00	3.00	1.75
(4)	Fred Lynn	6.00	3.00	1.75
(5)	Pete Rose	10.00	5.00	3.00
(6)	Tom Seaver	100.00	50.00	30.00

1976 Michael Schechter Associates Discs

Following its test issue of 1975, Michael Schechter Associates ran out its baseball player disc issues on a large scale in 1976. While most were sold with specific sponsor advertising on back, they were also made available with blank backs. The discs are 3-3/8" diameter with a black-and-white player portrait photo in the center of the baseball design. A line of red stars is above, while the left and right panels feature one of several bright colors. Produced by MSA under license from the Major League Players Association, the player photos have had uniform and cap logos removed. The unnumbered discs are presented in alphabetical order.

		NM	EX	VG
	Complete Set (70):	60.00	30.00	18.00
	Common Player:	.50	.25	.15
(1)	Henry Aaron	12.50	6.25	3.75
(2)	Johnny Bench	6.00	3.00	1.75
(3)	Vida Blue	.50	.25	.15
(4)	Larry Bowa	.50	.25	.15
(5)	Lou Brock	4.50	2.25	1.25
(6)	Jeff Burroughs	.50	.25	.15
(7)	John Candelaria	.50	.25	.15
(8)	Jose Cardenal	.50	.25	.15
(9)	Rod Carew	6.00	3.00	1.75
(10)	Steve Carlton	4.50	2.25	1.25
(11)	Dave Cash	.50	.25	.15
(12)	Cesar Cedeno	.50	.25	.15
(13)	Ron Cey	.50	.25	.15
(14)	Carlton Fisk	4.50	2.25	1.25
(15)	Tito Fuentes	.50	.25	.15
(16)	Steve Garvey	3.00	1.50	.90
(17)	Ken Griffey	.50	.25	.15
(18)	Don Gullett	.50	.25	.15
(19)	Willie Horton	.50	.25	.15
(20)	Al Hrabosky	.50	.25	.15
(21)	Catfish Hunter	4.50	2.25	1.25
(22)	Reggie Jackson (A's)	9.00	4.50	2.75
(23)	Randy Jones	.50	.25	.15
(24)	Jim Kaat	.50	.25	.15
(25)	Don Kessinger	.50	.25	.15
(26)	Dave Kingman	.50	.25	.15
(27)	Jerry Koosman	.50	.25	.15
(28)	Mickey Lolich	.60	.30	.20
(29)	Greg Luzinski	.50	.25	.15
(30)	Fred Lynn	.50	.25	.15
(31)	Bill Madlock	.50	.25	.15
(32)	Carlos May (White Sox)	.50	.25	.15
(33)	John Mayberry	.50	.25	.15
(34)	Bake McBride	.50	.25	.15
(35)	Doc Medich	.50	.25	.15
(36)	Andy Messersmith	.50	.25	.15
(37)	Rick Monday	.50	.25	.15
(38)	John Montefusco	.50	.25	.15
(39)	Jerry Morales	.50	.25	.15
(40)	Joe Morgan	4.50	2.25	1.25
(41)	Thurman Munson	4.50	2.25	1.25
(42)	Bobby Murcer	.50	.25	.15
(43)	Al Oliver	.50	.25	.15
(44)	Jim Palmer	4.50	2.25	1.25
(45)	Dave Parker	.50	.25	.15
(46)	Tony Perez	4.50	2.25	1.25
(47)	Jerry Reuss	.50	.25	.15
(48)	Brooks Robinson	6.00	3.00	1.75
(49)	Frank Robinson	6.00	3.00	1.75
(50)	Steve Rogers	.50	.25	.15
(51)	Pete Rose	10.00	5.00	3.00
(52)	Nolan Ryan	15.00	7.50	4.50
(53)	Manny Sanguillen	.50	.25	.15
(54)	Mike Schmidt	10.00	5.00	3.00
(55)	Tom Seaver	6.00	3.00	1.75
(56)	Ted Simmons	.50	.25	.15
(57)	Reggie Smith	.50	.25	.15
(58)	Willie Stargell	4.50	2.25	1.25
(59)	Rusty Staub	.75	.40	.25
(60)	Rennie Stennett	.50	.25	.15
(61)	Don Sutton	4.50	2.25	1.25
(62)	Andy Thornton	.50	.25	.15
(63)	Luis Tiant	.50	.25	.15
(64)	Joe Torre	.50	.25	.15
(65)	Mike Tyson	.50	.25	.15
(66)	Bob Watson	.50	.25	.15
(67)	Wilbur Wood	.50	.25	.15
(68)	Jimmy Wynn	.50	.25	.15
(69)	Carl Yastrzemski	6.00	3.00	1.75
(70)	Richie Zisk	.50	.25	.15

1977 Michael Schechter Associates Cup Lids

One of MSA's early baseball novelty issues was a set of drink-cup lids. The 3-1/2" diameter pieces are made of pressed and waxed cardboard. They are 3/16" thick and have a 3/8" die-cut hole for inserting a straw. Design is similar to other MSA issues of the era, with a black-and-white player portrait photo at center of a simulated baseball design. Personal data is printed in colored panels at left and right, and there is a row of colored stars above the photo. Player caps do not show team insignia because the issue was licensed only by the players' union, and not the owners. The unnumbered lids are checklisted here in alphabetical order.

		NM	EX	VG
	Complete Set (49):	700.00	350.00	225.00
	Common Player:	10.00	5.00	3.00
(1)	Sal Bando	10.00	5.00	3.00
(2)	Johnny Bench	30.00	15.00	9.00
(3)	Larry Bowa	10.00	5.00	3.00
(4)	Steve Braun	10.00	5.00	3.00
(5)	George Brett	100.00	50.00	30.00
(6)	Lou Brock	30.00	15.00	9.00
(7)	Bert Campaneris	10.00	5.00	3.00
(8)	Bill Campbell	10.00	5.00	3.00
(9)	Jose Cardenal	10.00	5.00	3.00
(10)	Rod Carew	30.00	15.00	9.00
(11)	Dave Cash	10.00	5.00	3.00
(12)	Cesar Cedeno	10.00	5.00	3.00
(13)	Chris Chambliss	10.00	5.00	3.00
(14)	Dave Concepcion	10.00	5.00	3.00
(15)	Mark Fidrych	10.00	5.00	3.00
(16)	Rollie Fingers	20.00	10.00	6.00
(17)	George Foster	10.00	5.00	3.00
(18)	Wayne Garland	10.00	5.00	3.00
(19)	Steve Garvey	20.00	10.00	6.00
(20)	Cesar Geronimo	10.00	5.00	3.00
(21)	Bobby Grich	10.00	5.00	3.00
(22)	Don Gullett	10.00	5.00	3.00
(23)	Mike Hargrove	10.00	5.00	3.00
(24)	Catfish Hunter	20.00	10.00	6.00
(25)	Randy Jones	10.00	5.00	3.00
(26)	Dave Kingman	15.00	7.50	4.50
(27)	Dave LaRoche	10.00	5.00	3.00
(28)	Greg Luzinski	10.00	5.00	3.00
(29)	Fred Lynn	10.00	5.00	3.00
(30)	Jon Matlack	10.00	5.00	3.00
(31)	Bake McBride	10.00	5.00	3.00
(32)	Joe Morgan	25.00	12.50	7.50
(33)	Phil Niekro	20.00	10.00	6.00
(34)	Jim Palmer	25.00	12.50	7.50
(35)	Dave Parker	10.00	5.00	3.00
(36)	Fred Patek	10.00	5.00	3.00
(37)	Mickey Rivers	10.00	5.00	3.00
(38)	Brooks Robinson	30.00	15.00	9.00
(39)	Pete Rose	75.00	37.00	22.00
(40)	Nolan Ryan	100.00	50.00	30.00
(41)	Tom Seaver (1976)	60.00	30.00	18.00
(42)	Mike Schmidt	50.00	25.00	15.00
(43)	Bill Singer	10.00	5.00	3.00

		NM	EX	VG
(44)	Chris Speier	10.00	5.00	3.00
(45)	Willie Stargell	25.00	12.50	7.50
(46)	Luis Tiant	12.50	6.25	3.75
(47)	Butch Wynegar	10.00	5.00	3.00
(48)	Robin Yount	20.00	10.00	6.00
(49)	Richie Zisk	10.00	5.00	3.00

1977 Mike Schechter Associates Customized Sports Discs

Virtually identical in format to the several locally sponsored disc sets of the previous year, these 3-3/8" diameter player discs once again feature black-and-white player portrait photos in the center of a baseball design. The left and right panels are in one of several bright colors. Licensed by the Players' Association, the photos carry no uniform logos. Backs of the discs are printed in dark blue and carry an ad from MSA for "Customized Sports Discs" and novelties for which Schechter held the licenses. The unnumbered discs are checklisted here alphabetically.

		NM	EX	VG
Complete Set (70):		350.00	175.00	100.00
Common Player:		3.00	1.50	.90
(1)	Sal Bando	3.00	1.50	.90
(2)	Buddy Bell	3.00	1.50	.90
(3)	Johnny Bench	20.00	10.00	6.00
(4)	Larry Bowa	3.00	1.50	.90
(5)	Steve Braun	3.00	1.50	.90
(6)	George Brett	125.00	62.00	37.00
(7)	Lou Brock	15.00	7.50	4.50
(8)	Jeff Burroughs	3.00	1.50	.90
(9)	Bert Campaneris	3.00	1.50	.90
(10)	John Candelaria	3.00	1.50	.90
(11)	Jose Cardenal	3.00	1.50	.90
(12)	Rod Carew	20.00	10.00	6.00
(13)	Steve Carlton	20.00	10.00	6.00
(14)	Dave Cash	3.00	1.50	.90
(15)	Cesar Cedeno	3.00	1.50	.90
(16)	Ron Cey	3.00	1.50	.90
(17)	Dave Concepcion	3.00	1.50	.90
(18)	Dennis Eckersley	15.00	7.50	4.50
(19)	Mark Fidrych	6.00	3.00	1.75
(20)	Rollie Fingers	15.00	7.50	4.50
(21)	Carlton Fisk	15.00	7.50	4.50
(22)	George Foster	3.00	1.50	.90
(23)	Wayne Garland	3.00	1.50	.90
(24)	Ralph Garr	3.00	1.50	.90
(25)	Steve Garvey	12.50	6.25	3.75
(26)	Cesar Geronimo	3.00	1.50	.90
(27)	Bobby Grich	3.00	1.50	.90
(28)	Ken Griffey Sr.	3.00	1.50	.90
(29)	Don Gullett	3.00	1.50	.90
(30)	Mike Hargrove	3.00	1.50	.90
(31)	Al Hrabosky	3.00	1.50	.90
(32)	Jim Hunter	15.00	7.50	4.50
(33)	Reggie Jackson	30.00	15.00	9.00
(34)	Randy Jones	3.00	1.50	.90
(35)	Dave Kingman	5.00	2.50	1.50
(36)	Jerry Koosman	3.00	1.50	.90
(37)	Dave LaRoche	3.00	1.50	.90
(38)	Greg Luzinski	3.00	1.50	.90
(39)	Fred Lynn	3.00	1.50	.90
(40)	Bill Madlock	3.00	1.50	.90
(41)	Rick Manning	3.00	1.50	.90
(42)	Jon Matlock	3.00	1.50	.90
(43)	John Mayberry	3.00	1.50	.90
(44)	Hal McRae	3.00	1.50	.90
(45)	Andy Messersmith	3.00	1.50	.90
(46)	Rick Monday	3.00	1.50	.90
(47)	John Montefusco	3.00	1.50	.90
(48)	Joe Morgan	15.00	7.50	4.50
(49)	Thurman Munson	12.50	6.25	3.75
(50)	Bobby Murcer	3.00	1.50	.90
(51)	Bill North	3.00	1.50	.90
(52)	Jim Palmer	15.00	7.50	4.50
(53)	Tony Perez	15.00	7.50	4.50
(54)	Jerry Reuss	3.00	1.50	.90
(55)	Brooks Robinson	20.00	10.00	6.00
(56)	Pete Rose	75.00	37.00	22.00
(57)	Joe Rudi	3.00	1.50	.90
(58)	Nolan Ryan	125.00	62.00	37.00
(59)	Manny Sanguillen	3.00	1.50	.90
(60)	Mike Schmidt	100.00	50.00	30.00
(61)	Tom Seaver	20.00	10.00	6.00
(62)	Bill Singer	3.00	1.50	.90
(63)	Willie Stargell	15.00	7.50	4.50
(64)	Rusty Staub	5.00	2.50	1.50
(65)	Luis Tiant	3.00	1.50	.90
(66)	Bob Watson	3.00	1.50	.90
(67)	Butch Wynegar	3.00	1.50	.90
(68)	Carl Yastrzemski	20.00	10.00	6.00
(69)	Robin Yount	15.00	7.50	4.50
(70)	Richie Zisk	3.00	1.50	.90

1915 Schmelzer's Sporting Goods Pins

The date of issue attributed is speculative, based on the limited checklist currently available. These pin-back celluloid buttons measure about 1-1/4" in diameter. A color lithographed figure of a generic ballplayer shares the front with a smaller inset black-and-white photo of an actual player and a

fancy script position designation. The player's last name appears at the bottom of the photo. Issuer identification is on back. It is presumed at least one pinback was issued for each of the nine positions.

		NM	EX	VG
Common Player:		3,000	1,500	900.00
RF	"Ty" Cobb	26,250	13,125	7,500
3B	Charlie Deal	3,000	1,500	900.00
C	Hank Gowdy	3,000	1,500	900.00
LF	Hoffman	3,000	1,500	900.00
CF	Joe Jackson	12,000	6,000	3,600
P	Christy Mathewson	6,750	3,375	2,025
SS	Rabbit Maranville	3,000	1,500	900.00
1B	Butch Schmidt	3,000	1,500	900.00

1921 C. Shulz Baseball Card Game

While this catalog generally does not attempt to list game cards which do not depict actual ballplayers, this set is considered exceptional due to its format similarity to the popularly collected 1922 American Caramel issue known as E120. Backs of the game cards are printed in blue on white and reproduce the border design of the National League cards of E120. The unnamed photo of Heinie Groh on back is identical to that to E120, except uniform lettering has been airbrushed away on the game card. Backs are printed in red with a ballgame situation. The credit line on back reads, "Instructions Copyrighted 1921 by C. Shulz." The game cards measure about 2-1/2" x 3-1/2".

	NM	EX	VG
Common Card:	35.00	17.50	10.00

1949 Schumacher Service Station

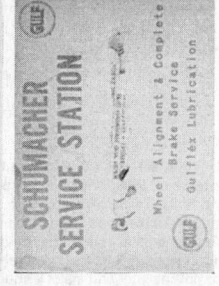

GEORGE (RED) MUNGER CARDINALS

Because some of these cards have been found with the advertising of Schumacher Service Station (location unknown) printed in red on the back, the issue is so designated for cataloging purposes. Given that the (living) players from this set were with their respective teams in 1949-1950, the issue date could be either year. Measuring 2-5/8" x 3-9/16", the cards are black-and-white on the front. It is unknown whether other players were issued in this series.

		NM	EX	VG
Complete Set (9):		2,200	1,100	650.00
Common Player:		200.00	100.00	60.00
(1)	Joe Garagiola	250.00	125.00	75.00
(2)	Marty Marion	225.00	110.00	65.00
(3)	Les Moss	200.00	100.00	60.00
(4)	George (Red) Munger	200.00	100.00	60.00
(5)	Don Newcomb (Newcombe)	250.00	125.00	75.00
(6)	Howard Pollet	200.00	100.00	60.00
(7)	George Herman (Babe) Ruth	600.00	300.00	180.00
(8)	Red Schoendienst	250.00	125.00	75.00
(9)	Vernon Stephens	200.00	100.00	60.00

1935 Schutter-Johnson (R332)

This 50-card set was issued by the Schutter-Johnson Candy Corp. of Chicago and Brooklyn circa 1930 and features drawings of major league players offering baseball playing tips. The cards measure 2-1/4" x 2-7/8". The drawings on the front are set against a red background while the backs are titled "Major League Secrets" and give the player's advice on some aspect of the game. The Scutter-Johnson name appears at the bottom.

		NM	EX	VG
Complete Set (50):		17,500	7,000	3,500
Common Player:		200.00	100.00	50.00
1	Al Simmons	350.00	140.00	70.00
2	Lloyd Waner	275.00	110.00	55.00
3	Kiki Cuyler	275.00	110.00	55.00
4	Frank Frisch	275.00	110.00	55.00
5	Chick Hafey	275.00	110.00	55.00
6	Bill Klem/Umpire	450.00	180.00	90.00
7	Rogers Hornsby	300.00	120.00	60.00
8	Carl Mays	200.00	100.00	50.00
9	Chas. Wrigley/Umpire	275.00	110.00	55.00
10	Christy Mathewson	900.00	360.00	180.00
11	Bill Dickey	275.00	110.00	55.00
12	Walter Berger	200.00	100.00	50.00
13	George Earnshaw	200.00	100.00	50.00
14	Hack Wilson	275.00	110.00	55.00
15	Charley Grimm	200.00	100.00	50.00
16	Lloyd Waner, Paul Waner	275.00	110.00	55.00
17	Chuck Klein	275.00	110.00	55.00
18	Woody English	200.00	100.00	50.00
19	Grover Alexander	350.00	175.00	105.00
20	Lou Gehrig	3,000	1,500	900.00
21	Wes Ferrell	200.00	100.00	50.00
22	Carl Hubbell	300.00	120.00	60.00
23	Pie Traynor	275.00	110.00	55.00
24	Gus Mancuso	200.00	100.00	50.00
25	Ben Cantwell	200.00	100.00	50.00
26	Babe Ruth	4,750	2,400	1,400
27	"Goose" Goslin	275.00	110.00	55.00
28	Earle Combs	275.00	110.00	55.00
29	"Kiki" Cuyler	275.00	110.00	55.00
30	Jimmy Wilson	200.00	100.00	50.00
31	Dizzy Dean	450.00	180.00	90.00
32	Mickey Cochrane	275.00	110.00	55.00
33	Ted Lyons	275.00	110.00	55.00
34	Si Johnson	200.00	100.00	50.00
35	Dizzy Dean	475.00	240.00	140.00
36	Pepper Martin	225.00	90.00	45.00
37	Joe Cronin	275.00	110.00	55.00
38	Gabby Hartnett	275.00	110.00	55.00
39	Oscar Melillo	200.00	100.00	50.00
40	Ben Chapman	200.00	100.00	50.00
41	John McGraw	275.00	110.00	55.00
42	Babe Ruth	2,350	940.00	470.00
43	"Red" Lucas	200.00	100.00	50.00
44	Charley Root	200.00	100.00	50.00
45	Dazzy Vance	275.00	110.00	55.00
46	Hugh Critz	200.00	100.00	50.00
47	"Firpo" Marberry	200.00	100.00	50.00
48	Grover Alexander	300.00	120.00	60.00
49	Lefty Grove	325.00	130.00	65.00
50	Heinie Meine	200.00	100.00	50.00

1888 "Scrapps Tobacco" Die-Cuts

The origin of these die-cut, embossed player busts is not known, but they were apparently part of a book of "punch-outs" issued in the late 1880s. When out of their original album, they apparently resembled scraps of paper, presumably leading to their unusual name. An earlier theory that they were issued by "Scrapps Tobacco" has since been disocunted after research indicated there never was such a company. The die-cuts include 18 different players - nine members of the American Association St. Louis Browns and nine from the National League Detroit Wolverines. Although they vary slightly in size, the player busts are generally about 2" wide and 3" high. The drawings for the St. Louis player busts were taken from the Old Judge "Brown's Champions" set. The player's name appears along the bottom.

		NM	EX	VG
Complete Set (18):		35,000	14,000	7,000
Common Player:		1,800	725.00	360.00
(1)	C.W. Bennett	1,800	725.00	360.00
(2)	D. Brouthers	2,400	960.00	480.00
(3)	A.J. Bushong	1,800	725.00	360.00
(4)	Robert L. Caruthers	1,800	725.00	360.00
(5)	Charles Comiskey	2,400	960.00	480.00
(6)	F. Dunlap	1,800	725.00	360.00
(7)	David L. Foutz	1,800	725.00	360.00
(8)	C.H. Getzen (Getzien)	1,800	725.00	360.00

		NM	EX	VG
(9)	Wm. Gleason	1,800	725.00	360.00
(10)	E. Hanlon	2,400	960.00	500.00
(11)	Walter A. Latham	1,800	725.00	360.00
(12)	James O'Neill	1,800	725.00	360.00
(13)	H. Richardson	1,800	725.00	360.00
(14)	Wm. Robinson	2,400	960.00	480.00
(15)	J.C. Rowe	1,800	725.00	360.00
(16)	S. Thompson	2,400	960.00	480.00
(17)	Curtis Welch	1,800	725.00	360.00
(18)	J.L. White	1,800	725.00	360.00

1949 Sealtest Phillies Stickers

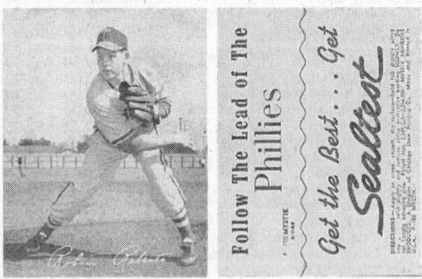

This regional Phillies set was issued in the Philadelphia area in 1949 by Sealtest Dairy. It consisted of 12 large (3-1/2" by 4-1/4") sticker cards with peel-off backs. The front of the unnumbered cards featured an action photo with facsimile autograph, while the back has an advertisement for Sealtest products. The same format, photos and checklist were also used for the Lummis Peanut Butter card set issued in Philadelphia the same year.

		NM	EX	VG
Complete Set (12):		4,000	2,000	1,200
Common Player:		250.00	125.00	75.00
(1)	Rich Ashburn	950.00	470.00	280.00
(2)	Hank Borowy	250.00	125.00	75.00
(3)	Del Ennis	350.00	175.00	105.00
(4)	Granny Hamner	250.00	125.00	75.00
(5)	Puddinhead Jones	250.00	125.00	75.00
(6)	Russ Meyer	250.00	125.00	75.00
(7)	Bill Nicholson	250.00	125.00	75.00
(8)	Robin Roberts	950.00	470.00	280.00
(9)	"Schoolboy" Rowe	250.00	125.00	75.00
(10)	Andy Seminick	250.00	125.00	75.00
(11)	Curt Simmons	300.00	150.00	90.00
(12)	Eddie Waitkus	250.00	125.00	75.00

1946 Sears St. Louis Browns/Cardinals Postcards

One of the more popular issues of the immediate post-war period are the black-and-white postcards of St. Louis Browns and Cardinals players issued by Sears in East St. Louis. The 3-1/2" x 5-3/8" postcards have posed player portraits on front with the player's name and Sears "Compliments of" line in the white border beneath. Backs are stamped "POST CARD / ACTUAL PHOTOGRAPH." The cards were reported to have been issued in groups of five on a bi-weekly basis, sold both at the Sears store and through the mail. The unnumbered cards are checklisted here alphabetically within team.

		NM	EX	VG
Complete Set (69):		16,000	8,000	4,750
Common Player:		200.00	100.00	60.00
	St. Louis Browns Set (33):	6,000	3,000	1,800
(1)	John Berardino	400.00	200.00	120.00
(2)	Frank Biscan	200.00	100.00	60.00
(3)	Mark Christman	200.00	100.00	60.00
(4)	Babe Dahlgren	200.00	100.00	60.00
(5)	Bob Dillinger	200.00	100.00	60.00
(6)	Stanley Ferens	200.00	100.00	60.00
(7)	Denny Galehouse	200.00	100.00	60.00
(8)	Joe Grace	200.00	100.00	60.00
(9)	Jeff Heath	200.00	100.00	60.00
(10)	Henry Helf	200.00	100.00	60.00
(11)	Fred Hoffman	200.00	100.00	60.00
(12)	Walt Judnich	200.00	100.00	60.00
(13)	Ellis Kinder	200.00	100.00	60.00
(14)	Jack Kramer	200.00	100.00	60.00
(15)	Chet Laabs	200.00	100.00	60.00
(16)	Al LaMacchia	250.00	125.00	75.00
(17)	John Lucadello	200.00	100.00	60.00
(18)	Frank Mancuso	200.00	100.00	60.00
(19)	Glenn McQuillen	200.00	100.00	60.00
(20)	John Miller	200.00	100.00	60.00
(21)	Al Milnar	300.00	150.00	90.00
(22)	Bob Muncrief	200.00	100.00	60.00
(23)	Nelson Potter	200.00	100.00	60.00

		NM	EX	VG
(24)	Ken Sears	200.00	100.00	60.00
(25)	Len Schulte	200.00	100.00	60.00
(26)	Luke Sewell	200.00	100.00	60.00
(27)	Joe Schultz	200.00	100.00	60.00
(28)	Tex Shirley	200.00	100.00	60.00
(29)	Vern Stephens	200.00	100.00	60.00
(30)	Chuck Stevens	200.00	100.00	60.00
(31)	Zack Taylor	200.00	100.00	60.00
(32)	Al Zarilla	200.00	100.00	60.00
(33)	Sam Zoldak	200.00	100.00	60.00
	St. Louis Cardinals Set (36):	10,000	5,000	3,000
(1)	Buster Adams	200.00	100.00	60.00
(2)	Red Barrett	200.00	100.00	60.00
(3)	Johnny Beazley	200.00	100.00	60.00
(4)	Al Brazle	200.00	100.00	60.00
(5)	Harry Brecheen	200.00	100.00	60.00
(6)	Ken Burkhart	200.00	100.00	60.00
(7)	Joffre Cross	200.00	100.00	60.00
(8)	Murray Dickson	200.00	100.00	60.00
(9)	George Dockins	200.00	100.00	60.00
(10)	Blix Donnelly	300.00	150.00	90.00
(11)	Erv Dusak	200.00	100.00	60.00
(12)	Eddie Dyer	200.00	100.00	60.00
(13)	Bill Endicott	200.00	100.00	60.00
(14)	Joe Garagiola	800.00	400.00	240.00
(15)	Mike Gonzales (Gonzalez)	250.00	125.00	75.00
(16)	Lou Klein	200.00	100.00	60.00
(17)	Clyde Kluttz	200.00	100.00	60.00
(18)	Howard Krist	200.00	100.00	60.00
(19)	George Kurowski	200.00	100.00	60.00
(20)	Danny Litwhiler	200.00	100.00	60.00
(21)	Marty Marion	300.00	150.00	90.00
(22)	Fred Martin	200.00	100.00	60.00
(23)	Terry Moore	250.00	125.00	75.00
(24)	Stan Musial	2,000	1,000	600.00
(25)	Ken O'Dea	200.00	100.00	60.00
(26)	Howard Pollet	200.00	100.00	60.00
(27)	Del Rice	200.00	100.00	60.00
(28)	Red Schoendienst	600.00	300.00	180.00
(29)	Walt Sessi	200.00	100.00	60.00
(30)	Dick Sisler	200.00	100.00	60.00
(31)	Enos Slaughter	600.00	300.00	180.00
(32)	Max Surkont	200.00	100.00	60.00
(33)	Harry Walker	200.00	100.00	60.00
(34)	Buzzy Wares	200.00	100.00	60.00
(35)	Ernie White	200.00	100.00	60.00
(36)	Ted Wilks	200.00	100.00	60.00

1969 Seattle Pilots Premium Pictures

This set of 8-1/2" x 11" premium pictures is based on the artwork of John Wheeldon, who did contemporary issues for the Mets, Twins and Red Sox, as well. The pastels feature large portraits and smaller action pictures with a large facsimile autograph at bottom. Backs are in black-and-white and feature biographical data, comprehensive career summary and complete minor and major league stats. There is a self-portrait and biographical sketch of the artist on back, as well. The premiums were given away at selected Pilots home games during their lone season in Seattle. They were later sold for 25 cents each in the concession stand. The unnumbered pictures are checklisted here in alphabetical order.

		NM	EX	VG
Complete Set (8):		75.00	37.00	22.00
Common Player:		8.00	4.00	2.50
(1)	Wayne Comer	8.00	4.00	2.50
(2)	Tommy Harper	10.00	5.00	3.00
(3)	Mike Hegan	8.00	4.00	2.50
(4)	Jerry McNertney	8.00	4.00	2.50
(5)	Don Mincher	8.00	4.00	2.50
(6)	Ray Oyler	8.00	4.00	2.50
(7)	Marty Pattin	8.00	4.00	2.50
(8)	Diego Segui	8.00	4.00	2.50

1963 Mickey Sego S.F. Giants

These self-framing pictures feature the artwork of Mickey Sego, but the method of their distribution is unknown. Measuring 7" x 8-1/2", the pieces have a dark frame around a large black-and-white portrait and smaller cartoon drawing of the player. There are also a few words about the player's career. A simulated plaque at the bottom of the frame bears a facsimile autograph. Each picture has a hole at top for hanging.

		NM	EX	VG
Common Player:		15.00	7.50	4.50
(1)	Chuck Hiller	15.00	7.50	4.50
(2)	Harvey Kuenn	20.00	10.00	6.00
(3)	Willie Mays	85.00	42.00	25.00
(4)	Billy Pierce	17.50	8.75	5.25

1914 Lawrence Semon Postcards

RICHARD (RUBE) W. MARQUARD

Seven players are currently known in this series, but it's possible others remain to be reported. The approximately 3-1/2" x 5-1/2" postcards feature on their fronts either portrait or action drawings of star players by Lawrence Semon. A few biographical and career details are printed at bottom, which have allowed the assignment of 1914 as the year of issue. Backs are standard postcard style. The unnumbered cards are checklisted here alphabetically.

		NM	EX	VG
Common Player:		500.00	250.00	150.00
(1)	George Burns	500.00	250.00	150.00
(2)	Frank Chance	1,000	500.00	300.00
(3)	Ty Cobb	9,500	4,700	2,800
(4)	Walter Johnson	4,500	2,250	1,350
(5)	Cornelius McGillicuddy (Connie Mack)	800.00	400.00	240.00
(6)	Richard (Rube) Marquard	800.00	400.00	240.00
(7)	John J. McGraw	800.00	400.00	240.00

1946-1947 Sensacion Premiums

Two types of baseball premium pictures were issued by the magazine "Sensacion" during the winter league season of 1946-47. One series of 27 features Cuban stars (some of whom played in the Major Leagues), while a series of 11 Major League stars was also issued. Printed in color on newspaper stock, the pictures measure about 7-3/4" x 11". Fronts have large portraits or posed action photos with the player name in a fancy bottom border. Backs have lengthy career summaries and full stats, along with a small ad. The premiums were issued in magazines as well as in a complete album of each type. They are numbered according to the apparent order of their appearance.

		NM	EX	VG
Complete Set, Cubans (27):		1,500	750.00	450.00
Complete Set, Major Leaguers (11):		600.00	300.00	175.00
Common Cuban Player:		30.00	15.00	9.00
Common Major Leaguer:		45.00	22.50	13.50
	Estrellas del Base Ball Cubano			
(1)	Napoleon Reyes	45.00	22.50	13.50
(2)	Fermin Guerra	30.00	15.00	9.00
(3)	Gilberto Torres	30.00	15.00	9.00
(4)	Martin Dihigo	750.00	375.00	225.00
(5)	Lazaro Salazar	100.00	50.00	30.00
(6)	Silvio Garcia	100.00	50.00	30.00
(7)	Pollo Rodriguez	30.00	15.00	9.00
(8)	Herberto Blanco	30.00	15.00	9.00
(9)	Andres Fleitas	30.00	15.00	9.00
(10)	Jorge J. Torres	30.00	15.00	9.00

		NM	EX	VG
(11)	Salvador Hernandez	30.00	15.00	9.00
(12)	Agapito Mayor	30.00	15.00	9.00
(13)	Tomas de la Cruz	30.00	15.00	9.00
(14)	Gilberto Valdivia	30.00	15.00	9.00
(15)	Julio Moreno	30.00	15.00	9.00
(16)	Regino Otero	30.00	15.00	9.00
(17)	Claro Duany	50.00	25.00	15.00
(18)	Pedro Jimenez	30.00	15.00	9.00
(19)	Tony Castanos	30.00	15.00	9.00
(20)	Alberto Hernandez	30.00	15.00	9.00
(21)	Hector Rodriguez	40.00	20.00	12.00
(22)	Carlos Blanco	30.00	15.00	9.00
(23)	Roberto Ortiz	50.00	25.00	15.00
(24)	Rene Monteagudo	30.00	15.00	9.00
(25)	Pedro Pages	30.00	15.00	9.00
(26)	Conrado Marrero	40.00	20.00	12.00
(27)	Chino Hidalgo	30.00	15.00	9.00

Estrellas de las Grandes Ligas

		NM	EX	VG
(1)	Stan Musial	150.00	75.00	45.00
(2)	Jim (Mickey) Vernon	50.00	25.00	15.00
(3)	Dave Ferris	45.00	22.50	13.50
(4)	Johnny Pesky	45.00	22.50	13.50
(5)	Howie Pollett	45.00	22.50	13.50
(6)	Ted Williams	200.00	100.00	60.00
(7)	Johnny Hopp	45.00	22.50	13.50
(8)	Dom DiMaggio	75.00	37.00	22.00
(9)	Tex Hughson	45.00	22.50	13.50
(10)	Johnny Beazley	45.00	22.00	13.50
(11)	Tommy Holmes	45.00	22.50	13.50

1977 Sertoma Stars

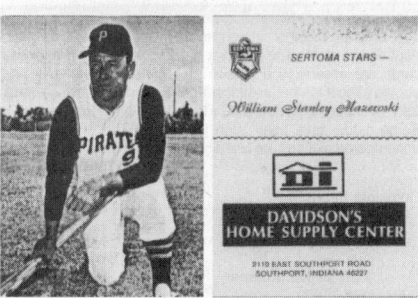

This collectors' issue was produced by an Indianapolis service club. The 3" x 4" cards are printed in black on a textured yellow stock. Fronts have borderless player poses, many of which were lifted from earlier-issued cards. Backs have the Sertoma logo, set name and player name at top. Beneath a squiggly line is a business-card size ad for different members of the organization.

		NM	EX	VG
	Complete Set (24):	45.00	22.50	13.50
	Common Player:	2.00	1.00	.60
(1)	Hank Aaron	10.00	5.00	3.00
(2)	Bob Allison	2.00	.75	.60
(3)	Clete Boyer	2.00	.75	.60
(4)	Don Buford	2.00	.75	.60
(5)	Rod Carew	3.00	1.50	.90
(6)	Rico Carty	2.00	.75	.60
(7)	Roberto Clemente	15.00	7.50	4.50
(8)	Jim Ray Hart	2.00	.75	.60
(9)	Dave Johnson	2.00	.75	.60
(10)	Harmon Killebrew	3.00	1.50	.90
(11)	Mickey Mantle	20.00	10.00	6.00
(12)	Juan Marichal	3.00	1.50	.90
(13)	Bill Mazeroski	3.00	1.50	.90
(14)	Joe Morgan	3.00	1.50	.90
(15)	Phil Niekro	2.50	1.25	.70
(16)	Tony Oliva	2.00	1.00	.60
(17)	Gaylord Perry	2.50	1.25	.70
(18)	Boog Powell	2.00	1.00	.60
(19)	Brooks Robinson	3.50	1.75	1.00
(20)	Frank Robinson	3.50	1.75	1.00
(21)	John Roseboro	2.00	.75	.60
(22)	Rusty Staub	2.00	.75	.60
(23)	Joe Torre	2.00	1.00	.60
(24)	Jim Wynn	2.00	.75	.60

1977 Sertoma Stars - Puzzle Backs

This collectors set was issued in conjunction with the Indianapolis Sports Collectors Convention in 1977. The set was sold for $3 with proceeds benefiting the local Sertoma (Service to Mankind) Club's charity works. Cards measure 2-3/4" x 4-1/8". A 2-1/2" black circle at center contains a black-and-white

player photo. The background on front is yellow, with red and black printing. Backs are borderless and form an old Pittsburgh Pirates team photo puzzle. Sets were originally sold for $3.50.

		NM	EX	VG
	Complete Set (25):	75.00	37.50	22.50
	Common Player:	2.00	1.00	.60
(1)	Bernie Allen	2.00	1.00	.60
(2)	Home Run Baker	2.00	1.00	.60
(3)	Ted Beard	2.00	1.00	.60
(4)	Don Buford	2.00	1.00	.60
(5)	Eddie Cicotte	4.00	2.00	1.25
(6)	Roberto Clemente	20.00	10.00	6.00
(7)	Dom Dallessandro	2.00	1.00	.60
(8)	Carl Erskine	2.00	1.00	.60
(9)	Nellie Fox	6.00	3.00	1.75
(10)	Lou Gehrig	20.00	10.00	6.00
(11)	Joe Jackson	20.00	10.00	6.00
(12)	Len Johnston	2.00	1.00	.60
(13)	Benny Kauff	2.00	1.00	.60
(14)	Dick Kenworthy	2.00	1.00	.60
(15)	Harmon Killebrew	6.00	3.00	1.75
(16)	"Lefty Bob" Logan	2.00	1.00	.60
(17)	Willie Mays	15.00	7.50	4.50
(18)	Satchel Paige	9.00	4.50	2.75
(19)	Edd Roush	2.00	1.00	.60
(20)	Chico Ruiz	2.00	1.00	.60
(21)	Babe Ruth	20.00	10.00	6.00
(22)	Herb Score	2.00	1.00	.60
(23)	George Sisler	2.00	1.00	.60
(24)	Buck Weaver	5.00	2.50	1.50
(25)	Early Wynn	2.00	1.00	.60

1961 7-11

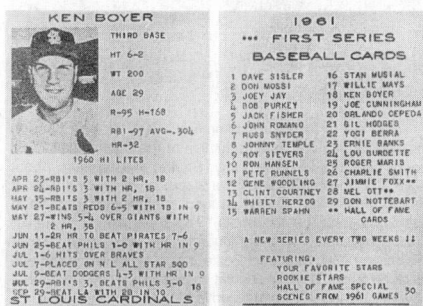

The first of 7-11's baseball card issues was a crude attempt which was abruptly halted. The checklist for the 30-card set indicated that it was the first of planned series to be issued two weeks apart. No follow-up to the first series was ever distributed. The 2-7/16" x 3-3/8" cards are printed on pink cardboard stock, with blank backs. Small black-and-white player portraits appear in the upper-left, with the player name at top, team name at bottom and card number in the lower-right corner. There are a few biographical bits and stats to the right of the photo, and several lines of 1960 season highlights below. The cards were sold seven for a nickel in vending machines.

		NM	EX	VG
	Complete Set (30):	2,400	1,200	725.00
	Common Player:	50.00	25.00	15.00
1	Dave Sisler	50.00	25.00	15.00
2	Don Mossi	50.00	25.00	15.00
3	Joey Jay	50.00	25.00	15.00
4	Bob Purkey	50.00	25.00	15.00
5	Jack Fisher	50.00	25.00	15.00
6	John Romano	50.00	25.00	15.00
7	Russ Snyder	50.00	25.00	15.00
8	Johnny Temple	50.00	25.00	15.00
9	Roy Sievers	50.00	25.00	15.00
10	Ron Hansen	50.00	25.00	15.00
11	Pete Runnels	50.00	25.00	15.00
12	Gene Woodling	50.00	25.00	15.00
13	Clint Courtney	50.00	25.00	15.00
14	Whitey Herzog	50.00	25.00	15.00
15	Warren Spahn	120.00	60.00	35.00
16	Stan Musial	250.00	125.00	75.00
17	Willie Mays	400.00	200.00	120.00
18	Ken Boyer	60.00	30.00	18.00
19	Joe Cunningham	50.00	25.00	15.00
20	Orlando Cepeda	90.00	45.00	27.00
21	Gil Hodges	125.00	65.00	35.00
22	Yogi Berra	150.00	75.00	45.00
23	Ernie Banks	200.00	100.00	60.00
24	Lou Burdette	50.00	25.00	15.00
25	Roger Maris	250.00	125.00	75.00
26	Charlie Smith	50.00	25.00	15.00
27	Jimmie Foxx	50.00	25.00	15.00
28	Mel Ott	50.00	25.00	15.00
29	Don Nottebart	50.00	25.00	15.00
----	Checklist	50.00	25.00	15.00

1975 Shakey's Pizza West Coast Greats

This collectors' issue was sponsored by Seattle area Shakey's Pizza restaurants in conjunction with the 1975 convention of the Washington State Sports Collectors Assn. Two thousand sets were produced featuring players who were born and/or played on the West Coast. The first 1,000 attendees at the convention were given a free sample of card #1, DiMaggio. Cards are 2-3/4" x about 3-5/8". Fronts have a black-and-white photo at center with black and red graphics. A large Shakey's logo is at lower-left. The card number, player name, position and connection to the West Coast are printed at lower-right. Backs are in red and white with the pizza chain's logo and a list of four Seattle-area locations.

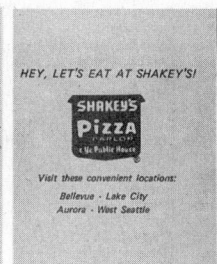

		NM	EX	VG
	Complete Set (18):	30.00	15.00	9.00
	Common Player:	4.00	2.00	1.25
1	Joe DiMaggio	15.00	7.50	4.50
2	Paul Waner	4.00	2.00	1.25
3	Lefty Gomez	4.00	2.00	1.25
4	Earl Averill	4.00	2.00	1.25
5	Ernie Lombardi	4.00	2.00	1.25
6	Joe Cronin	4.00	2.00	1.25
7	George Burns	4.00	2.00	1.25
8	Casey Stengel	5.00	2.50	1.50
9	Wahoo Sam Crawford	4.00	2.00	1.25
10	Ted Williams	12.50	6.25	3.75
11	Fred Hutchinson	4.00	2.00	1.25
12	Duke Snider	7.50	3.75	2.25
13	Hal Chase	4.00	2.00	1.25
14	Bobby Doerr	4.00	2.00	1.25
15	Arky Vaughan	4.00	2.00	1.25
16	Tony Lazzeri	4.00	2.00	1.25
17	Lefty O'Doul	4.00	2.00	1.25
18	Stan Hack	4.00	2.00	1.25

1976 Shakey's Pizza Hall of Fame

Between 1975-77 the Washington State Sports Collectors Assn. worked with the Shakey's pizza chain in the Seattle area to produce and distribute several sets of "old timers" cards. Generally one card from the set was given away to hobbyists attending the club's annual convention, with other cards available at the pizza places. Complete sets were also widely sold within the hobby. Interpretation of whether these are "legitimate" cards or a collector issue is up to each collector. The 1976 cards were issued in four series: Hall of Fame, Greatest Players, Immortals and All-Time Greats. The format was identical, with the (approximately) 2-1/2" x 3-1/2" cards featuring black-and-white player photos on front, surrounded by a red frame and bright blue border. Backs are in red, black and white with large Shakey ads at top and bottom. Also on back are player biographies and career stats. The cards were issued in order of the players' induction into the Hall of Fame. All four series are skip-numbered. Cards of Sam Thompson and Robin Roberts were re-issued in Series 2 to correct errors.

		NM	EX	VG
	Complete Set (160):	100.00	50.00	30.00
	Complete Set, no coupons (158):	75.00	37.50	22.00
	Common Player:	2.00	1.00	.60
	Series 1 - Baseball's Hall of Fame	35.00	17.50	10.50
A	Earl Averill	4.00	2.00	1.25
	($1 off pizza coupon on back; card show giveaway)			
1	Ty Cobb	7.50	3.75	2.25
3	Walter Johnson	3.00	1.50	.90
12	Connie Mack	2.00	1.00	.60
18	Lou Gehrig	9.00	4.50	2.75
20	George Sisler	2.00	1.00	.60
21	Cap Anson	2.00	1.00	.60
36	Mike "King" Kelly	2.00	1.00	.60
41	Jack Chesbro	2.00	1.00	.60
50	Mickey Cochrane	2.00	1.00	.60
52	Lefty Grove	2.00	1.00	.60
54	Herb Pennock	2.00	1.00	.60
55	Pie Traynor	2.00	1.00	.60
56	Charlie Gehringer	2.00	1.00	.60
57	Three-Finger Brown	2.00	1.00	.60
58	Kid Nichols	2.00	1.00	.60
59	Jimmie Foxx	2.00	1.00	.60
64	Al Simmons	2.00	1.00	.60
72	Rabbit Maranville	2.00	1.00	.60
73	Bill Terry	2.00	1.00	.60
80	Joe Cronin	2.00	1.00	.60
83	Joe McCarthy	2.00	1.00	.60
86	Bill Hamilton	2.00	1.00	.60
89	Jackie Robinson	7.50	3.75	2.25
89	Bill McKechnie	2.00	1.00	.60
93	Sam Rice	2.00	1.00	.60
95	Luke Appling	2.00	1.00	.60
103	Ted Williams	7.50	3.75	2.25

		NM	EX	VG
104	Casey Stengel	2.00	1.00	.60
107	Lloyd Waner	2.00	1.00	.60
108	Joe Medwick	2.00	1.00	.60
115	Lou Boudreau	2.00	1.00	.60
122	Harry Hooper	2.00	1.00	.60
127	Yogi Berra	3.00	1.50	.90
129	Lefty Gomez	2.00	1.00	.60
131	Sandy Koufax	7.50	3.75	2.25
143	Jocko Conlan	2.00	1.00	.60
144	Whitey Ford	2.00	1.00	.60
146	Sam Thompson	2.00	1.00	.60
147	Earl Averill	2.00	1.00	.60
149	Billy Herman	2.00	1.00	.60
154	Cal Hubbard	2.00	1.00	.60
156	Fred Lindstrom	2.00	1.00	.60
157	Robin Roberts	2.00	1.00	.60
	Series 2 - Baseball's Greatest Players	35.00	17.50	10.50
A	Earl Averill (Card show giveaway, coupon on back.)	2.00	1.00	.60
4	Christy Mathewson	3.00	1.50	.90
6	Nap Lajoie	2.00	1.00	.60
7	Tris Speaker	2.00	1.00	.60
9	Morgan Bulkeley	2.00	1.00	.60
10	Ban Johnson	2.00	1.00	.60
11	John McGraw	2.00	1.00	.60
14	Grover Alexander	2.00	1.00	.60
17	Eddie Collins	2.00	1.00	.60
19	Willie Keeler	2.00	1.00	.60
22	Charles Comiskey	2.00	1.00	.60
24	Buck Ewing	2.00	1.00	.60
31	Fred Clarke	2.00	1.00	.60
32	Jimmy Collins	2.00	1.00	.60
34	Hugh Duffy	2.00	1.00	.60
35	Hugh Jennings	2.00	1.00	.60
38	Wilbert Robinson	2.00	1.00	.60
40	Frank Chance	2.00	1.00	.60
42	John Evers	2.00	1.00	.60
43	Clark Griffith	2.00	1.00	.60
47	Joe Tinker	2.00	1.00	.60
51	Frank Frisch	2.00	1.00	.60
53	Carl Hubbell	2.00	1.00	.60
65	Ed Barrow	2.00	1.00	.60
66	Chief Bender	2.00	1.00	.60
67	Tommy Connolly	2.00	1.00	.60
74	Joe DiMaggio	12.50	6.25	3.75
75	Gabby Hartnett	2.00	1.00	.60
78	Home Run Baker	2.00	1.00	.60
81	Hank Greenberg	3.00	1.50	.90
87	Bob Feller	2.00	1.00	.60
90	Edd Roush	2.00	1.00	.60
109	Kiki Cuyler	2.00	1.00	.60
111	Roy Campanella	4.00	2.00	1.25
113	Stan Coveleski	2.00	1.00	.60
116	Earle Combs	2.00	1.00	.60
120	Jake Beckley	2.00	1.00	.60
125	Satchel Paige	4.00	2.00	1.25
128	Josh Gibson	3.00	1.50	.90
135	Roberto Clemente	10.00	5.00	3.00
141	Cool Papa Bell	2.00	1.00	.60
142	Jim Bottomley	2.00	1.00	.60
146	Sam Thompson	2.00	1.00	.60
150	Judy Johnson	2.00	1.00	.60
152	Oscar Charleston	2.00	1.00	.60
158	Robin Roberts	2.00	1.00	.60
	Series 3 - Baseball's Immortals	25.00	12.50	7.50
5	Honus Wagner	3.50	1.75	1.00
13	George Wright	2.00	1.00	.60
15	Alexander Cartwright	2.00	1.00	.60
16	Henry Chadwick	2.00	1.00	.60
23	Candy Cummings	2.00	1.00	.60
25	Old Hoss Radbourne	2.00	1.00	.60
26	Al Spalding	2.00	1.00	.60
28	Judge Landis	2.00	1.00	.60
29	Roger Bresnahan	2.00	1.00	.60
30	Dan Brouthers	2.00	1.00	.60
33	Ed Delahanty	2.00	1.00	.60
37	Jim O'Rourke	2.00	1.00	.60
39	Jesse Burkett	2.00	1.00	.60
44	Tommy McCarthy	2.00	1.00	.60
45	Joe McGinnity	2.00	1.00	.60
46	Eddie Plank	2.00	1.00	.60
49	Ed Walsh	2.00	1.00	.60
61	Harry Heilmann	2.00	1.00	.60
68	Bill Klem	2.00	1.00	.60
70	Harry Wright	2.00	1.00	.60
85	Max Carey	2.00	1.00	.60
91	John Clarkson	2.00	1.00	.60
92	Elmer Flick	2.00	1.00	.60
96	Red Faber	2.00	1.00	.60
97	Burleigh Grimes	2.00	1.00	.60
98	Miller Huggins	2.00	1.00	.60
99	Tim Keefe	2.00	1.00	.60
101	Monte Ward	2.00	1.00	.60
102	Pud Galvin	2.00	1.00	.60
110	Goose Goslin	2.00	1.00	.60
114	Waite Hoyt	2.00	1.00	.60
117	Ford Frick	2.00	1.00	.60
118	Jesse Haines	2.00	1.00	.60
126	George Weiss	2.00	1.00	.60
130	William Harridge	2.00	1.00	.60
132	Buck Leonard	2.00	1.00	.60
133	Early Wynn	2.00	1.00	.60
136	Billy Evans	2.00	1.00	.60
137	Monte Irvin	2.00	1.00	.60
138	George Kelly	2.00	1.00	.60
140	Mickey Welch	2.00	1.00	.60
148	Bucky Harris	2.00	1.00	.60
151	Ralph Kiner	2.00	1.00	.60
153	Roger Connor	2.00	1.00	.60
	Series 4 - Ball's All-Time Greats	20.00	10.00	6.00
2	Babe Ruth	12.50	6.25	3.75
8	Cy Young	2.50	1.25	.70
27	Rogers Hornsby	2.00	1.00	.60
48	Rube Waddell	2.00	1.00	.60
62	Paul Waner	2.00	1.00	.60

		NM	EX	VG
63	Dizzy Dean	2.50	1.25	.70
69	Bobby Wallace	2.00	1.00	.60
71	Bill Dickey	2.00	1.00	.60
77	Dazzy Vance	2.00	1.00	.60
79	Ray Schalk	2.00	1.00	.60
82	Sam Crawford	2.00	1.00	.60
84	Zack Wheat	2.00	1.00	.60
94	Eppa Rixey	2.00	1.00	.60
100	Heinie Manush	2.00	1.00	.60
105	Red Ruffing	2.00	1.00	.60
106	Branch Rickey	2.00	1.00	.60
112	Stan Musial	5.00	2.50	1.50
119	Dave Bancroft	2.00	1.00	.60
121	Chick Hafey	2.00	1.00	.60
123	Joe Kelley	2.00	1.00	.60
124	Rube Marquard	2.00	1.00	.60
134	Ross Youngs	2.00	1.00	.60
139	Warren Spahn	2.00	1.00	.60
145	Mickey Mantle	16.00	8.00	4.75
155	Bob Lemon	2.00	1.00	.60

1977 Shakey's All-Time Superstars

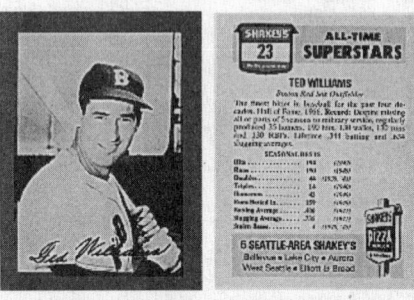

This set of baseball's all-time greatest (at least through the 1950s) was the final production of the Washington State Sports Collectors Assn. and local Shakey's restaurants. About 2-3/8" x 3", the cards feature black-and-white player photos at center with a red border around. A facsimile autograph appears in blue on the photo. Backs are similar to earlier Shakey's issues, with large logos for the pizza chain, player information and "Seasonal Bests" stats, all printed in red and black on white. Several special cards were produced for distribution at the 1977 annual convention and other venues.

		NM	EX	VG
	Complete Set (28):	35.00	17.50	10.00
	Complete Set (25):	25.00	12.50	7.50
	Common Player:	2.00	1.00	.60
	Welcome to WSSCA Show Card (Collectibles collage.)	3.00	1.50	.90
A	Earl Averill	3.00	1.50	.90
B	John Mize ($1 coupon on back)	3.00	1.50	.90
C	Robert Lee Johnson	3.00	1.50	.90
1	Connie Mack	2.00	1.00	.60
2	John J. McGraw	2.00	1.00	.60
3	Denton T. (Cy) Young	4.00	2.00	1.25
4	Walter Johnson	4.00	2.00	1.25
5	G.C. Alexander	2.00	1.00	.60
6	Christy Mathewson	4.00	2.00	1.25
7	Lefty Grove	2.00	1.00	.60
8	Mickey Cochrane	2.00	1.00	.60
9	Bill Dickey	2.00	1.00	.60
10	Lou Gehrig	7.50	3.75	2.25
11	George Sisler	2.00	1.00	.60
12	Cap Anson	2.00	1.00	.60
13	Jimmie Foxx	2.00	1.00	.60
14	Rogers Hornsby	2.00	1.00	.60
15	Nap Lajoie	2.00	1.00	.60
16	Eddie Collins	2.00	1.00	.60
17	Pie Traynor	2.00	1.00	.60
18	Honus Wagner	4.00	2.00	1.25
19	Ty Cobb	7.50	3.75	2.25
20	Babe Ruth	10.00	5.00	3.00
21	Joe Jackson	10.00	5.00	3.00
22	Tris Speaker	2.00	1.00	.60
23	Ted Williams	6.00	3.00	1.75
24	Joe DiMaggio	7.50	3.75	2.25
25	Stan Musial	5.00	2.50	1.50
---	WSSCA Club Information Card	4.00	2.00	1.25

1952 Shelby Bicycles

The year of issue stated is conjectural, based on the familiar picture of Berra used for this promotional photo. The photo shows Yogi kneeling in full catcher's gear, except mask, ready to throw the ball; it is seen on his '50 Bowman card, among others. The blank-back, black-and-white photos are 5" x 7" with a white border all around. Scripted at bottom is, "Ride Shelby / The Winner's Bike / Sincerely / Yogi Berra."

	NM	EX	VG
Yogi Berra	150.00	75.00	45.00

1958-1959 Shillito's Boys' Shop Cincinnati Reds

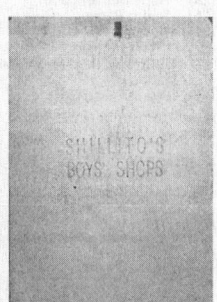

This rare regional set was issued by a Cincinnati-area chain department store. The 2-1/2" x 3-1/2" black-and-white glossy cards are essentially a version of contemporary team-issued photos except for the presence (usually) on the otherwise blank back of a purple "SHILLITO'S / BOYS' SHOPS" rubber-stamp. Some cards have been seen wuthout the ad on back. The unnumbered pictures are listed here in alphabetical order.

		NM	EX	VG
	Complete Set (23):	3,500	1,750	1,050
	Common Player:	200.00	100.00	60.00
(1)	Tom Acker	200.00	100.00	60.00
(2)	Ed Bailey	200.00	100.00	60.00
(3)	Gus Bell	200.00	100.00	60.00
(4)	John "Dutch" Dotterer	200.00	100.00	60.00
(5)	Walt Dropo	200.00	100.00	60.00
(6)	Del Ennis	200.00	100.00	60.00
(7)	Jay Hook	200.00	100.00	60.00
(8)	Hal Jeffcoat	200.00	100.00	60.00
(9)	Eddie Kasko	200.00	100.00	60.00
(10)	Brooks Lawrence	200.00	100.00	60.00
(11)	Jerry Lynch	200.00	100.00	60.00
(12)	Roy McMillan	200.00	100.00	60.00
(13)	Eddie Miksis	200.00	100.00	60.00
(14)	Don Newcombe	230.00	115.00	69.00
(15)	Joe Nuxhall	250.00	125.00	75.00
(16)	Jim O'Toole	200.00	100.00	60.00
(17)	Vada Pinson	250.00	125.00	75.00
(18)	Bob Purkey	200.00	100.00	60.00
(19)	Frank Robinson	500.00	250.00	150.00
(20)	Frank Thomas	200.00	100.00	60.00
(21)	Johnny Temple	200.00	100.00	60.00
(22)	Bob Thurman	200.00	100.00	60.00
(23)	Pete Whisenant	200.00	100.00	60.00

1975 Shillito's Pete Rose

Probably issued in conjunction with an autograph-signing appearance at the Cincinnati department store, this glossy black-and-white, blank-back photo measures 5-1/2" x 8". The autograph on the example shown is genuine, the photo does not have a facsimile signature.

	NM	EX	VG
Pete Rose	150.00	75.00	45.00

1976 Shillito's Kahn's Reds Clubhouse

Though the format for each photo differs, this series of Reds player photos was issued under the sponsorship of the Shillito's department store and Kahn's meats. In about 5" x 7-3/16" format, the blank-back photos are black-and-white with at least one (Bench) having red highlights. The pictures were given out at player autograph appearances at various Shillito's locations between June 21 and August 18. Youngsters enrolled in the club received a membership card, probably entitling them to an autograph at each event.

		NM	EX	VG
(1)	Johnny Bench (Kenwood Plaza)	100.00	50.00	30.00
(2)	Dave Concepcion (No sponsor)	30.00	15.00	9.00
(3)	Doug Flynn (Kahn's - WLW Radio)	12.00	6.00	3.50
(4)	George Foster (Three sponsors listed.)	25.00	12.50	7.50
(5)	Pete Rose (Shillito's)	100.00	50.00	30.00
---	Membership Card	10.00	5.00	3.00

1962 Shirriff Coins

This is a Canadian version of the better-known Salada-Junket plastic player coins issued in the U.S. Backs specify an issue of 200; 21 of the players from the Salada set were not issued by Shirriff. Because the Canadian coins were produced after the U.S. version they are not found with all the variations known in Salada, nor the differing levels of scarcity. Shirriff coins were packed in bags of potato chips, with each coin sealed in a clear cellophane wrapper. Although the Canadian coins are much scarcer than the U.S., significantly less demand keeps prices lower, as well.

		NM	EX	VG
	Complete Set (200):	1,600	800.00	525.00
	Common Player:	6.00	3.00	1.75
1	Jim Gentile	7.00	3.50	2.00
2	Not Issued (Bill Pierce)			
3	Chico Fernandez (Light blue piping.)	6.00	3.00	1.75
4	Not Issued (Tom Brewer)			
5	Woody Held	6.00	3.00	1.75
6	Not Issued (Ray Herbert)	.00	.00	.00
7	Ken Aspromonte (Indians)	6.00	3.00	1.75
8	Whitey Ford	40.00	20.00	12.00
9	Jim Lemon	6.00	3.00	1.75
10	Billy Klaus	6.00	3.00	1.75
11	Not Issued (Steve Barber)			
12	Nellie Fox	25.00	12.50	7.50
13	Jim Bunning	25.00	12.50	7.50
14	Frank Malzone	6.00	3.00	1.75
15	Tito Francona	6.00	3.00	1.75
16	Bobby Del Greco	6.00	3.00	1.75
17	Steve Bilko	6.00	3.00	1.75
18	Not Issued (Tony Kubek)			
19	Earl Battey	6.00	3.00	1.75
20	Chuck Cottier	6.00	3.00	1.75
21	Willie Tasby	6.00	3.00	1.75
22	Bob Allison	7.00	3.50	2.00
23	Roger Maris	40.00	20.00	12.00
24	Earl Averill	6.00	3.00	1.75
25	Jerry Lumpe	6.00	3.00	1.75
26	Not Issued (Jim Grant)			
27	Carl Yastrzemski	50.00	25.00	15.00
28	Rocky Colavito (Blue piping.)	20.00	10.00	6.00
29	Al Smith	6.00	3.00	1.75
30	Not Issued (Jim Busby)			
31	Dick Howser	6.00	3.00	1.75
32	Jim Perry	6.00	3.00	1.75
33	Yogi Berra	50.00	25.00	15.00
34	Ken Hamlin	6.00	3.00	1.75
35	Dale Long	6.00	3.00	1.75
36	Harmon Killebrew	35.00	17.50	10.50
37	Dick Brown	6.00	3.00	1.75
38	Gary Geiger	6.00	3.00	1.75
39	Minnie Minoso (Cardinals)	9.00	4.50	2.75
40	Brooks Robinson	35.00	17.50	10.50
41	Mickey Mantle	180.00	90.00	54.00
42	Bennie Daniels	6.00	3.00	1.75
43	Billy Martin	15.00	7.50	4.50
44	Vic Power	7.00	3.50	2.00
45	Joe Pignatano	6.00	3.00	1.75
46	Ryne Duren	7.00	3.50	2.00
47	Pete Runnels (1B)	6.00	3.00	1.75
48	Dick Williams	6.00	3.00	1.75
49	Jim Landis	6.00	3.00	1.75
50	Steve Boros	6.00	3.00	1.75
51	Zoilo Versalles	7.00	3.50	2.00
52	Johnny Temple (Orioles)	6.00	3.00	1.75
53	Jackie Brandt	6.00	3.00	1.75
54	Joe McClain	6.00	3.00	1.75

55	Sherman Lollar	6.00	3.00	1.75
56	Gene Stephens	6.00	3.00	1.75
57	Leon Wagner	6.00	3.00	1.75
58	Frank Lary	6.00	3.00	1.75
59	Bill Skowron	12.00	6.00	3.50
60	Not Issued (Vic Wertz)			
61	Willie Kirkland	6.00	3.00	1.75
62	Leo Posada	6.00	3.00	1.75
63	Albie Pearson	7.00	3.50	2.00
64	Bobby Richardson	15.00	7.50	4.50
65	Marv Breeding (SS)	6.00	3.00	1.75
66	Not Issued (Roy Sievers)			
67	Al Kaline	35.00	17.50	10.50
68	Don Buddin (Colts)	6.00	3.00	1.75
69	Lenny Green (White top button.)	6.00	3.00	1.75
70	Not Issued (Gene Green)			
71	Luis Aparicio	25.00	12.50	7.50
72	Norm Cash	12.00	6.00	3.50
73	Not Issued (Jackie Jensen)			
74	Bubba Phillips	6.00	3.00	1.75
75	Jim Archer	6.00	3.00	1.75
76	Ken Hunt	6.00	3.00	1.75
77	Ralph Terry	6.00	3.00	1.75
78	Camilo Pascual	6.00	3.00	1.75
79	Not Issued (Marty Keough)			
80	Cletis Boyer	9.00	4.50	2.75
81	Jim Pagliaroni	6.00	3.00	1.75
82	Gene Leek	6.00	3.00	1.75
83	Jake Wood	6.00	3.00	1.75
84	Not Issued (Coot Veal)			
85	Norm Siebern	6.00	3.00	1.75
86	Andy Carey (Phillies)	6.00	3.00	1.75
87	Bill Tuttle (White top button.)	6.00	3.00	1.75
88	Jimmy Piersall	6.00	3.00	1.75
89	Not Issued (Ron Hansen)			
90	Chuck Stobbs	6.00	3.00	1.75
91	Ken McBride	6.00	3.00	1.75
92	Bill Bruton	6.00	3.00	1.75
93	Gus Triandos	6.00	3.00	1.75
94	John Romano	6.00	3.00	1.75
95	Elston Howard	12.00	6.00	3.50
96	Gene Woodling	6.00	3.00	1.75
97	Early Wynn (Portrait)	20.00	10.00	6.00
98	Milt Pappas	6.00	3.00	1.75
99	Bill Monbouquette	6.00	3.00	1.75
100	Wayne Causey	6.00	3.00	1.75
101	Don Elston	6.00	3.00	1.75
102	Charlie Neal	6.00	3.00	1.75
103	Don Blasingame	6.00	3.00	1.75
104	Not Issued (Frank Thomas)			
105	Wes Covington	6.00	3.00	1.75
106	Chuck Hiller	6.00	3.00	1.75
107	Don Hoak	6.00	3.00	1.75
108	Bob Lillis (Colts)	6.00	3.00	1.75
109	Sandy Koufax	65.00	32.00	19.50
110	Gordy Coleman	6.00	3.00	1.75
111	Ed Matthews (Mathews)	30.00	15.00	9.00
112	Art Mahaffey	6.00	3.00	1.75
113	Ed Bailey (Name above ear.)	6.00	3.00	1.75
114	Smoky Burgess	7.00	3.50	2.00
115	Bill White	7.00	3.50	2.00
116	Not Issued (Ed Bouchee)			
117	Bob Buhl	6.00	3.00	1.75
118	Vada Pinson	7.00	3.50	2.00
119	Carl Sawatski	6.00	3.00	1.75
120	Dick Stuart	7.00	3.50	2.00
121	Not Issued (Harvey Kuenn)			
122	Pancho Herrera	6.00	3.00	1.75
123	Don Zimmer	7.00	3.50	2.00
124	Wally Moon	7.00	3.50	2.00
125	Joe Adcock	7.00	3.50	2.00
126	Joey Jay	6.00	3.00	1.75
127	Maury Wills (Red 3 on uniform.)	12.00	6.00	3.50
128	George Altman	6.00	3.00	1.75
129	John Buzhardt	6.00	3.00	1.75
130	Felipe Alou	7.00	3.50	2.00
131	Bill Mazeroski	25.00	12.50	7.50
132	Ernie Broglio	6.00	3.00	1.75
133	John Roseboro	7.00	3.50	2.00
134	Mike McCormick	6.00	3.00	1.75
135	Chuck Smith (White Sox)	6.00	3.00	1.75
136	Ron Santo	12.00	6.00	3.50
137	Gene Freese	6.00	3.00	1.75
138	Dick Groat	7.00	3.50	2.00
139	Curt Flood	7.00	3.50	2.00
140	Frank Bolling	6.00	3.00	1.75
141	Clay Dalrymple	6.00	3.00	1.75
142	Willie McCovey	30.00	15.00	9.00
143	Bob Skinner	6.00	3.00	1.75
144	Lindy McDaniel	6.00	3.00	1.75
145	Glen Hobbie	6.00	3.00	1.75
146	Gil Hodges	20.00	10.00	6.00
147	Eddie Kasko	6.00	3.00	1.75
148	Not Issued (Gino Cimoli)			
149	Willie Mays	75.00	37.00	22.00
150	Roberto Clemente	90.00	45.00	27.00
151	Red Schoendienst	25.00	12.50	7.50
152	Joe Torre	9.00	4.50	2.75
153	Bob Purkey	6.00	3.00	1.75
154	Tommy Davis (3B)	7.50	3.75	2.25
155	Andre Rogers (Rodgers)	6.00	3.00	1.75
156	Tony Taylor	6.00	3.00	1.75
157	Bob Friend	6.00	3.00	1.75
158	Gus Bell	6.00	3.00	1.75
159	Roy McMillan	6.00	3.00	1.75
160	Carl Warwick	6.00	3.00	1.75
161	Willie Davis	6.00	3.00	1.75
162	Not Issued (Sam Jones)			
163	Ruben Amaro	6.00	3.00	1.75
164	Sam Taylor	6.00	3.00	1.75
165	Frank Robinson	35.00	17.50	10.50
166	Lou Burdette	6.00	3.00	1.75
167	Ken Boyer	10.00	5.00	3.00
168	Bill Virdon	6.00	3.00	1.75
169	Jim Davenport	6.00	3.00	1.75
170	Don Demeter	6.00	3.00	1.75

171	Not Issued (Richie Ashburn)			
172	John Podres	7.50	3.75	2.25
173	Joe Cunningham (White Sox)	6.00	3.00	1.75
174	ElRoy Face	6.00	3.00	1.75
175	Orlando Cepeda	25.00	12.50	7.50
176	Bobby Gene Smith	6.00	3.00	1.75
177	Ernie Banks (SS)	50.00	25.00	15.00
178	Daryl Spencer (1B)	6.00	3.00	1.75
179	Not Issued (Bob Schmidt)			
180	Hank Aaron	75.00	37.00	22.00
181	Hobie Landrith	6.00	3.00	1.75
182	Ed Bressoud	6.00	3.00	1.75
183	Felix Mantilla	6.00	3.00	1.75
184	Dick Farrell	6.00	3.00	1.75
185	Bob Miller	6.00	3.00	1.75
186	Don Taussig	6.00	3.00	1.75
187	Pumpsie Green	6.00	3.00	1.75
188	Bobby Shantz	7.50	3.75	2.25
189	Roger Craig	6.00	3.00	1.75
190	Hal Smith	6.00	3.00	1.75
191	John Edwards	6.00	3.00	1.75
192	John DeMerit	6.00	3.00	1.75
193	Joe Amalfitano	6.00	3.00	1.75
194	Norm Larker	6.00	3.00	1.75
195	Al Heist	6.00	3.00	1.75
196	Al Spangler	6.00	3.00	1.75
197	Alex Grammas	6.00	3.00	1.75
198	Gerry Lynch	6.00	3.00	1.75
199	Jim McKnight	6.00	3.00	1.75
200	Jose Pagen (Pagan)	6.00	3.00	1.75
201	Junior Gilliam	7.50	3.75	2.25
202	Art Ditmar	6.00	3.00	1.75
203	Pete Daley	6.00	3.00	1.75
204	Johnny Callison	6.00	3.00	1.75
205	Stu Miller	6.00	3.00	1.75
206	Russ Snyder	6.00	3.00	1.75
207	Billy Williams	25.00	12.50	7.50
208	Walter Bond	6.00	3.00	1.75
209	Joe Koppe	6.00	3.00	1.75
210	Don Schwall	6.00	3.00	1.75
211	Billy Gardner	6.00	3.00	1.75
212	Chuck Estrada	6.00	3.00	1.75
213	Gary Bell	6.00	3.00	1.75
214	Floyd Robinson	6.00	3.00	1.75
215	Duke Snider	35.00	17.50	10.50
216	Lee Maye	6.00	3.00	1.75
217	Howie Bedell	6.00	3.00	1.75
218	Bob Will	6.00	3.00	1.75
219	Dallas Green	7.50	3.75	2.25
220	Carroll Hardy	6.00	3.00	1.75
221	Danny O'Connell	6.00	3.00	1.75

1929 Shonen Club Babe Ruth Postcard

This card, which the Japanese inscription describes as picturing Babe Ruth hitting his first home run of 1926, was part of a multi-sport premium issue by the Japanese magazine Shonen Kubulu ("Youth Club"). The front has a colorized black-and-white photo, with blue inscriptions at right. Back is in blue with standard international postcard indicia.

	NM	EX	VG
Babe Ruth	500.00	250.00	150.00

1949 Sealtest Phillies Stickers

This regional Phillies set was issued in the Philadelphia area in 1949 by Sealtest Dairy. It consisted of 12 large (3-1/2" by 4-1/4") sticker cards with peel-off backs. The front of the unnumbered cards featured an action photo with facsimilie autograph, while the back has an advertisement for Sealtest products. The same format, photos and checklist were also used for the Lummis Peanut Butter card set issued in Philadelphia the same year.

	NM	EX	VG
Complete Set (12):	4,000	2,000	1,200

Common Player:		350.00	175.00	105.00
(1)	Rich Ashburn	950.00	470.00	280.00
(2)	Hank Borowy	250.00	125.00	75.00
(3)	Del Ennis	350.00	175.00	105.00
(4)	Granny Hamner	250.00	125.00	75.00
(5)	Puddinhead Jones	250.00	125.00	75.00
(6)	Russ Meyer	250.00	125.00	75.00
(7)	Bill Nicholson	250.00	125.00	75.00
(8)	Robin Roberts	950.00	470.00	280.00
(9)	"Schoolboy" Rowe	250.00	125.00	75.00
(10)	Andy Seminick	250.00	125.00	75.00
(11)	Curt Simmons	300.00	150.00	90.00
(12)	Eddie Waitkus	250.00	125.00	75.00

1921 Shotwell

It is not known to what extent this issue actually parallels the 1921 American Caramel Co. Series of 80 (E121), with which it shares a format. The cards are printed in black-and-white, approximately 2" x 3-1/4". Since only two cards with this back advertising are known, each currently unique, it is possible they were part of a prototype printing intended to sell the concept of baseball card inserts to Shotwell Mfg. Co., a Chicago-based confectionery company that competed with Cracker Jack. Cards are listed here in conformity with the numbering assigned to 1921 American Caramel Series of 80.

		NM	EX	VG
Common Player:		2,000	1,000	600.00
(48)	Wm. C. Jacobson	2,000	1,000	600.00
(86a)	Babe Ruth (PSA-graded Fair, auctioned for $6,143 in 8/09)			

1889 G. Waldon Smith Boston Beaneaters Cabinets

Boston photographer G. Waldon Smith immortalized the players of the 1889 Nation League club ("Beaneaters") in this series of 4-1/4" x 6-1/2" cabinet cards. Each sepia toned photo is a capless, chest-up portrait. The studio's name and location are printed in red in the bottom border. The players are not identified on the cards, though most examples have the name added by hand on either front or back. The cards from the 1889 N.L. series can be distinguished from the studio's 1890 issue of Players League subjects by the plain typography used for the studio address in the lower-right; the 1890 cards have a more ornate presentation of that information. It is not known if the checklist here is complete; gaps have been left in the assigned numbering for possible future additions.

		NM	EX	VG
Common Player:		4,000	2,000	1,200
(1)	Charlie Bennett	4,000	2,000	1,200
(2)	Tom Brown	4,000	2,000	1,200
(3)	John Clarkson	7,500	3,750	2,250
(5)	Harry Ganzel	4,000	2,000	1,200
(7)	Kid Madden	4,000	2,000	1,200
(8)	Billy Nash	4,000	2,000	1,200
(10)	Charley Radbourn	7,500	3,750	2,250
(11)	Pop Smith	4,000	2,000	1,200
(13)	The Boston Base Ball Club (Team photo, 21" x 18".)	15,000	7,500	4,500

1890 G. Waldon Smith Boston Players League Cabinets

Boston photographer G. Waldon Smith immortalized the players of the 1890 Players League Boston Red Stockings and Brooklyn Wonders in this series of 4-1/4" x 6-1/2" cabinet cards. Each sepia toned photo is a (usually) capless and mustachioed chest-up portrait. The studio's name and location are printed in the bottom border. The players are not identified on the cards, though most examples have the name added by hand on either front or back. The cards from the 1890 P.L. series can be distinguished from the studio's 1889 issue of Boston National League subjects by the ornate typography used for the studio address in the lower-right; the 1889 cards have a more austere presentation of that information. It is not known if the checklist here is complete; gaps have been left in the assigned numbering for possible future additions.

		NM	EX	VG
Common Player:		4,500	2,250	1,350
BOSTON RED STOCKINGS				
(2)	Tom Brown	4,500	2,250	1,350
(3)	Dan Brouthers	7,500	3,750	2,250
(5)	Bill Dailey	4,500	2,250	1,350
(7)	Ad Gumbert	4,500	2,250	1,350

(8)	Arthur Irwin	4,500	2,250	1,350
(9)	Dick Johnston	4,500	2,250	1,350
(11)	John Morrill	4,500	2,250	1,350
(12)	Morgan Murphy	4,500	2,250	1,350
(13)	Billy Nash	4,500	2,250	1,350
(15)	Joe Quinn	4,500	2,250	1,350
(16)	Irv Ray	4,500	2,250	1,350
(17)	Hardy Richardson	4,500	2,250	1,350
(19)	Harry Stovey	4,500	2,250	1,350
(20)	Boston Base Ball Club / Players League (Team photo, 22" x 18")	20,000	10,000	6,000
BROOKLYN WONDERS				
(2)	Ben Conry	4,500	2,250	1,350
(3)	Paul Cook	4,500	2,250	1,350
(4)	Con Dailey	4,500	2,250	1,350
(6)	Jackie Hayes	4,500	2,250	1,350
(7)	Bill Joyce	4,500	2,250	1,350
(8)	Tom Kinslow	4,500	2,250	1,350
(10)	Con Murphy	4,500	2,250	1,350
(11)	Dave Orr	4,500	2,250	1,350
(13)	Emmett Seery	4,500	2,250	1,350
(15)	George Van Haltren	4,500	2,250	1,350
(16)	Gus Weyhing	4,500	2,250	1,350

1904 G. Waldon Smith Cabinets

Following a move down Tremont St. to No. 164A, this Boston photographer was still producing baseball player cabinet photos. Like his earlier photos, the circa 1904 pieces have black-and-white photographs mounted on stiff 4-1/4" x 6-1/2" cardboard backings. The only currently known picture in this series is a full-length portrait of Kip Selbach. Others almost certainly exist.

	NM	EX	VG
Kip Selbach	2,500	1,250	750.00

1909 W.W. Smith Postcards

THE MIGHTY HONUS

Only two subjects are known in this series of postcards issued contemporary with the 1909 World Series between the Tigers and Pirates, though it is possible a card of Ty Cobb might have also been issued. The 3-1/2" x 5-1/2" black-and-white cards have pencil portraits by W.W. Smith. Backs have standard postcard markings.

		NM	EX	VG
Complete Set (2):		2,000	1,000	600.00
(1)	The Mighty Honus (Honus Wagner)	1,500	750.00	450.00
(2)	Two of a Kind (Ty Cobb, Honus Wagner)	6,000	3,000	1,800

1957 Sohio Gas Indians/Reds

In 1957 Sohio (Standard Oil of Ohio) gas stations in Ohio issued sets of Cleveland Indians and Cincinnati Reds photocards and team albums. The blank-backed cards are 5" x 7" and printed in black-and-white with one perforated edge. The cards have a facsimile autograph as the only identification. The unnumbered cards are checklisted here alphabetically within team.

		NM	EX	VG
Complete Set (36):		650.00	325.00	195.00
Common Player:		10.00	5.00	3.00
CLEVELAND INDIANS				
	Complete Set (18):	300.00	150.00	90.00
(1)	Bob Avila	10.00	5.00	3.00
(2)	Jim Busby	10.00	5.00	3.00
(3)	Chico Carrasquel	10.00	5.00	3.00

(4)	Rocky Colavito	75.00	37.00	22.00
(5)	Mike Garcia	10.00	5.00	3.00
(6)	Jim Hegan	10.00	5.00	3.00
(7)	Bob Lemon	20.00	10.00	6.00
(8)	Roger Maris	150.00	75.00	45.00
(9)	Don Mossi	10.00	5.00	3.00
(10)	Ray Narleski	10.00	5.00	3.00
(11)	Russ Nixon	10.00	5.00	3.00
(12)	Herb Score	15.00	7.50	4.50
(13)	Al Smith	10.00	5.00	3.00
(14)	George Strickland	10.00	5.00	3.00
(15)	Bob Usher	10.00	5.00	3.00
(16)	Vic Wertz	10.00	5.00	3.00
(17)	Gene Woodling	10.00	5.00	3.00
(18)	Early Wynn	20.00	10.00	6.00
----	Cleveland Indians Album	60.00	30.00	18.00
CINCINNATI REDS				
	Complete Set (18):	325.00	160.00	97.00
(1)	Ed Bailey	10.00	5.00	3.00
(2)	Gus Bell	10.00	5.00	3.00
(3)	Rocky Bridges	10.00	5.00	3.00
(4)	Smoky Burgess	10.00	5.00	3.00
(5)	Hersh Freeman	10.00	5.00	3.00
(6)	Alex Grammas	10.00	5.00	3.00
(7)	Don Gross	10.00	5.00	3.00
(8)	Warren Hacker	10.00	5.00	3.00
(9)	Don Hoak	10.00	5.00	3.00
(10)	Hal Jeffcoat	10.00	5.00	3.00
(11)	Johnny Klippstein	10.00	5.00	3.00
(12)	Ted Kluszewski	60.00	30.00	18.00
(13)	Brooks Lawrence	10.00	5.00	3.00
(14)	Roy McMillan	10.00	5.00	3.00
(15)	Joe Nuxhall	12.50	6.25	3.75
(16)	Wally Post	10.00	5.00	3.00
(17)	Frank Robinson	150.00	75.00	45.00
(18)	Johnny Temple	10.00	5.00	3.00
----	Cincinnati Redlegs Album	60.00	30.00	18.00

1969 Solon Kansas City Royals

LOU PINIELLA
Outfielder

This collectors' issue is believed to have originated with Illinois hobbyist Bob Solon. The black-and-white, blank-back cards feature members of the expansion Royals. The border beneath the posed photos features a team logo and player identification at bottom. Cards measure 2-1/8" x 3-5/8". The checklist here is arranged alphabetically, as the cards are unnumbered.

		NM	EX	VG
Complete Set (15):		16.00	8.00	4.75
Common Player:		2.00	1.00	.60
(1)	Jerry Adair	2.00	1.00	.60
(2)	Wally Bunker	2.00	1.00	.60
(3)	Moe Drabowsky	3.00	1.50	.90
(4)	Dick Drago	2.00	1.00	.60
(5)	Joe Foy	2.00	1.00	.60
(6)	Joe Gordon	2.00	1.00	.60
(7)	Chuck Harrison	2.00	1.00	.60
(8)	Mike Hedlund	2.00	1.00	.60
(9)	Jack Hernandez	2.00	1.00	.60
(10)	Pat Kelly	2.00	1.00	.60
(11)	Roger Nelson	2.00	1.00	.60
(12)	Bob Oliver	2.00	1.00	.60
(13)	Lou Piniella	6.00	3.00	1.75
(14)	Ellie Rodriguez	2.00	1.00	.60
(15)	Dave Wickersham	2.00	1.00	.60

1905 Souvenir Post Card Shop of Cleveland

CLEVELAND

CHARLES C. CARR.

SOUVENIR POST CARD SHOP OF CLEVELAND

POST CARD

Formal portraits of the 1905 Cleveland Naps are featured in this set of black-and-white postcards. The 3-1/4" x 5-1/2" cards have a wide white border at bottom which carries the legend, "SOUVENIR POST CARD SHOP OF CLEVELAND." The player name is in white at the bottom of the photo. Backs have postage rate information and a notice, "NOTHING BUT ADDRESS ON THIS SIDE."

		NM	EX	VG
Complete Set (19):		16,500	8,250	5,000
Common Player:		950.00	475.00	285.00
(1)	Harry Bay	950.00	475.00	285.00
(2)	Harry Bemis	950.00	475.00	285.00
(3)	Bill Bernhard	950.00	475.00	285.00
(4)	Bill Bradley	950.00	475.00	285.00
(5)	Fred Buelow	950.00	475.00	285.00
(6)	Charles C. Carr	950.00	475.00	285.00
(7)	Frank Donahue	950.00	475.00	285.00
(8)	Elmer Flick	1,425	710.00	425.00
(9)	Otto Hess	950.00	475.00	285.00
(10)	Jay Jackson	950.00	475.00	285.00
(11)	Addie Joss	2,750	1,375	825.00
(12)	Nick Kahl	950.00	475.00	285.00
(13)	Napoleon Lajoie	2,000	1,000	600.00
(14)	Earl Moore	950.00	475.00	285.00
(15)	Robert Rhoads	950.00	475.00	285.00
(16)	George Stovall	950.00	475.00	285.00
(17)	Terry Turner	950.00	475.00	285.00
(18)	Ernest Vinson	950.00	475.00	285.00
(19)	Team Portraits Composite	1,500	750.00	450.00

1909-11 Sovereign Cigarettes

Premiums shown are for common-player cards. Hall of Famers or other high-demand cards generally realize little or no premium with Sovereign back. On T205s, the backs are printed in green.

PREMIUMS
T205: 1.25X
T206 150 Subjects: 1X
T206 350 Subjects: 1.5X
T206 460 Subjects: 1.5X
(See T205, T206 for checklists and base card values.)

1949 Spalding Joe DiMaggio Glove Premium Photos

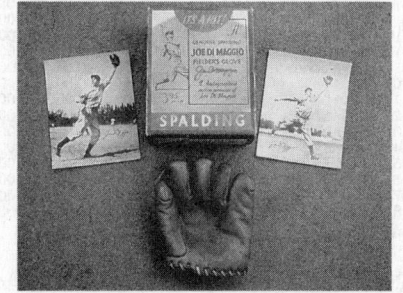

The attributed date is only approximate. Lucky youngsters who received a Spalding Joe DiMaggio fielder's glove also got a pair of 8" x 10" black-and-white posed action photos of the Yankee Clipper. Each blank-back, borderless photo has a facsimile autograph.

		NM	EX	VG
(1)	Joe DiMaggio (No ball in photo.)	125.00	65.00	40.00
(2)	Joe DiMaggio (Ball in photo.)	125.00	65.00	40.00

1950s-70s Spalding Advisory Staff Photos

Advisory staff photos were a promtional item which debuted in the early 1950s, flourished in the 1960s and died in the early 1970s. Generally 8" x 10" (sometimes a little larger), these black-and-white (a few later were color) glossy photos picture players who had contracted with a major baseball equipment company to endorse and use their product. Usually the product - most often a glove - was prominently displayed in the photo. The pictures were often displayed in the windows of sporting goods stores or the walls of sports departments and were sometimes made available to customers. Because the companies tended to stick with players over the years, some photos were reissued, sometimes with and sometimes without a change of team, pose or typography. Spalding staff photos of the era are checklisted here in alphabetical order. Team designation and pose description is given for each known picture. The photos are checklisted here in alphabetical order. It is unlikely this list is complete. Several arrangements of typography in the bottom border are seen for Spalding advisory staff pictures.

		NM	EX	VG
Common Player:		12.00	6.00	3.50
(1)	Richie Allen (Phillies, batting helmet.)	20.00	10.00	6.00
(2)	Gene Alley (Pirates, upper body.)	12.00	6.00	3.50
(3)	Mike Andrews (Red Sox, upper body.)	12.00	6.00	3.50
(4)	Bob Aspromonte (Dodgers, upper body.)	12.00	6.00	3.50
(5)	Sal Bando (A's, upper body.)	12.00	6.00	3.50
(7)	Steve Barber (Orioles, chest-to-cap.)	12.00	6.00	3.50
(8)	John Bateman (Colt .45s, upper body.)	12.00	6.00	3.50
(9)	Yogi Berra (Yankees, batting.)	30.00	15.00	9.00
(10)	Yogi Berra (Mets, upper body.)	30.00	15.00	9.00
(11)	Don Bessent (Brooklyn, follow-through.)	20.00	10.00	6.00
(12a)	Frank Bolling/Fldg (Tigers)	15.00	7.50	4.50
(12b)	Frank Bolling (Braves, chest up.)	15.00	7.50	4.50
(13)	Jim Bouton (Yankees, upper body.)	15.00	7.50	4.50
(14)	Jim Bunning (Phillies, upper body.)	20.00	10.00	6.00
(16)	John Callison (Phillies, batson shoulder.)	12.00	6.00	3.50
(17)	Rocky Colavito/Btg (Tigers)	25.00	12.50	7.50
(18)	Roger Craig (Brooklyn, follow-through.)	15.00	7.50	4.50
(19)	Clay Dalrymple (Phillies, upper body.)	12.00	6.00	3.50
(20)	Alvin Dark (Cardinals, batting follow-through.)	20.00	10.00	6.00
(21)	Don Drysdale (Dodgers, pitching follow-through.)	25.00	12.50	7.50
(22)	Sam Esposito (White Sox, hands on knees.)	12.00	6.00	3.50
(23)	Ron Fairly (Dodgers, upper body.)	12.00	6.00	3.50
(24)	Dick Farrell (Phillies, follow-through.)	25.00	12.50	7.50
(25)	Whitey Ford (Yankees, hands over head.) (Picture frame.)	30.00	15.00	9.00
(26)	Jim Fregosi (L.A. Angels, upper body.)	15.00	7.50	4.50
(27)	Jim Fregosi (California Angels, upper body, looking front.)	15.00	7.50	4.50
(28)	Jim Fregosi (California Angels, upper body, looking right.)	15.00	7.50	4.50
(29)	Jim Fregosi (Angels, green borders, b/w portrait.)	15.00	7.50	4.50
(30)	Bob Gibson (Color, stretch position.)	25.00	12.50	7.50
(33)	Tom Haller (Giants, catching crouch.)	12.00	6.00	3.50
(34)	Richie Hebner (Pirates, full-length.)	12.00	6.00	3.50
(35)	Mike Hegan (Brewers, upper body.)	12.00	6.00	3.50
(36)	Jim Hickman (Mets, upper body.)	12.00	6.00	3.50
(37)	Ken Hunt (Reds, follow-through.)	20.00	10.00	6.00
(38)	Jerry Koosman (Mets, ready to pitch.)	15.00	7.50	4.50
(39)	Jerry Koosman (Mets, upper body.)	15.00	7.50	4.50
(40)	Don Larsen (Yankees, follow-through.)	25.00	12.50	7.50
(41)	Charlie Lau (Braves, upper body.)	15.00	7.50	4.50
(42)	Mickey Lolich (Tigers, upper body, ready to pitch.)	15.00	7.50	4.50
(43)	Jerry Lumpe (Tigers, belt-up.)	12.00	6.00	3.50
(45)	Roger Maris/Btg (Yankees)	30.00	15.00	9.00
(46)	Roger Maris (Yankees, full-length.)	30.00	15.00	9.00
(47)	Roger Maris (Cardinals, "picture-frame," b/w photo.)	30.00	15.00	9.00
(49)	Dick McAuliffe/Portrait (Tigers)	12.00	6.00	3.50
(50)	Bill Monbouquette (Red Sox, wind-up.)	12.00	6.00	3.50
(51)	Bobby Murcer (Yankees, upper body.)	12.00	6.00	3.50
(53)	Jim Northrup/Btg (Tigers)	12.00	6.00	3.50
(56)	Jim Pagliaroni/Btg (Pirates)	12.00	6.00	3.50
(58)	Jim Palmer (Upper body.)	25.00	12.50	7.50
(60)	Joe Pepitone/Btg (Yankees)	15.00	7.50	4.50

		NM	EX	VG
(61)	Gary Peters (White Sox, green borders, b/w portrait.)	12.00	6.00	3.50
(62)	Rico Petrocelli (Red Sox, upper body.)	12.00	6.00	3.50
(64)	Joe Pignatano (A's, hands on hips.)	12.00	6.00	3.50
(66)	Bob Rodgers/Portrait (Angels)	12.00	6.00	3.50
(67)	Rich Rollins (Twins, arms crossed.)	12.00	6.00	3.50
(69)	Nolan Ryan/Pitching (Angels, color.)	75.00	37.00	22.00
(72)	Tom Seaver (Mets, waist-to-cap.)	30.00	15.00	9.00
(73)	Tom Seaver/Pitching (Mets, color.)	30.00	15.00	9.00
(75)	Mel Stottlemyre (Yankees, rust borders, b/w pitching pose .)	12.00	6.00	3.50
(76)	Dick Stuart/Btg (Pirates)	15.00	7.50	4.50
(78)	Joe Torre (Braves, upper body.)	15.00	7.50	4.50
(79)	Joe Torre (Cardinals, red borders, b/w portrait.)	15.00	7.50	4.50
(85)	Pete Ward/Portrait (White Sox)	12.00	6.00	3.50
(86)	Fred Whitfield/Portrait (Indians)	12.00	6.00	3.50
(87)	Carlton Willey (Braves, full-length.)			
(88)	Maury Wills (Dodgers, chest-to-cap.)	15.00	7.50	4.50
(89)	Maury Wills (No team, full-length batting.)	12.00	6.00	3.50
(90)	Carl Yastrzemski (Kneeling w/ bats.)	30.00	15.00	9.00
(91)	Carl Yastrzemski (Picture-frame border, b/w portrait.)	30.00	15.00	9.00

1969 Spare-Time Products Minnesota Twins Discs

The intended use and manner of distribution of these 8" uniface color discs is unknown. The hard composition discs have a baseball design on which is centered a player portrait. A facsimile autograph is at bottom and there is a hole at top for hanging. Copyright information appears at lower-right.

		NM	EX	VG
Complete Set (8):		400.00	200.00	125.00
Common Player:		30.00	15.00	9.00
(1)	Dave Boswell	30.00	22.00	9.00
(2)	Leo Cardenas	30.00	15.00	9.00
(3)	Dean Chance	30.00	15.00	9.00
(4)	Jim Kaat	45.00	22.00	13.50
(5)	Tony Oliva/SP	150.00	75.00	45.00
(6)	Ron Perranoski	30.00	22.00	9.00
(7)	Jim Perry	30.00	15.00	9.00
(8)	John Roseboro	30.00	15.00	9.00

1948 Speedway 79 Tiger of the Week Photos

This set of blank-back, black-and-white 8" x 10" photos was issued by one of the Tigers radio sponsors. One photo, bearing a facsimile autograph on front, was given away each week to honor the outstanding Tigers performer. The photos have no markings identifying the issuer and they are unnumbered. They are checklisted here alphabetically.

		NM	EX	VG
Complete Set (14):		350.00	175.00	100.00
Common Player:		30.00	15.00	9.00
(1)	Neil Berry	30.00	15.00	9.00
(2)	"Hoot" Evers	30.00	15.00	9.00
(3)	Ted Gray	30.00	15.00	9.00
(4)	Art Houtteman	30.00	15.00	9.00
(5)	Fred Hutchinson	30.00	15.00	9.00
(6)	George Kell	50.00	25.00	15.00
(7)	Eddie Lake	30.00	15.00	9.00
(8)	Johnny Lipon	30.00	15.00	9.00
(9)	Hal Newhouser	50.00	25.00	15.00

		NM	EX	VG
(10)	Dizzy Trout	30.00	15.00	9.00
(11)	Virgil Trucks	30.00	15.00	9.00
(12)	George Vico	30.00	15.00	9.00
(13)	Dick Wakefield	30.00	15.00	9.00
(14)	Bill Wertz	30.00	15.00	9.00

1936 Spencer Shoes Jimmie Foxx Premium Photo

The attributed date is speculative, based on the uniform in which the player is pictured on this 7" x 9", blank-back, black-and-white premium photo. The picture has a facsimile autograph at left. At bottom-right in script is, "Courtesy of Spencer Shoes."

	NM	EX	VG
Jimmie Foxx	350.00	175.00	105.00

1953-55 Spic and Span Braves

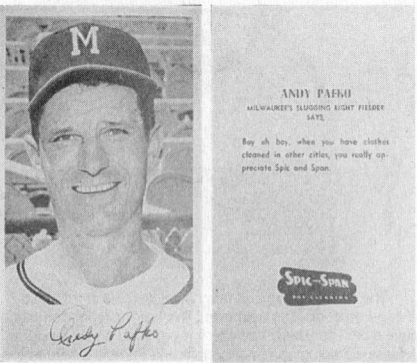

The first of several regional issues from a Milwaukee dry cleaner, the 1953-55 Spic and Span Braves set consists of black-and-white cards, 3-1/4" x 5-1/2". The fronts of the card have a facsimile autograph beneath the player photo. Cards are found with blank backs or with a Spic and Span advertising message on the back. Blank-backed cards are believed to have been issued by Wisco gas stations.

		NM	EX	VG
Complete Set (29):		1,800	900.00	540.00
Common Player:		50.00	25.00	15.00
(1)	Hank Aaron	600.00	300.00	180.00
(2)	Joe Adcock	50.00	25.00	15.00
(3)	John Antonelli	50.00	25.00	15.00
(4)	Vern Bickford	50.00	25.00	15.00
(5)	Bill Bruton	50.00	25.00	15.00
(6)	Bob Buhl	50.00	25.00	15.00
(7)	Lew Burdette	50.00	25.00	15.00
(8)	Dick Cole	50.00	25.00	15.00
(9)	Walker Cooper	50.00	25.00	15.00
(10)	Del Crandall	50.00	25.00	15.00
(11)	George Crowe	50.00	25.00	15.00
(12)	Jack Dittmer	50.00	25.00	15.00
(13)	Sid Gordon	50.00	25.00	15.00
(14)	Ernie Johnson	50.00	25.00	15.00
(15)	Dave Jolly	50.00	25.00	15.00
(16)	Don Liddle	50.00	25.00	15.00
(17)	John Logan	50.00	25.00	15.00
(18)	Ed Mathews	200.00	100.00	60.00
(19)	Chet Nichols	50.00	25.00	15.00
(20)	Dan O'Connell	50.00	25.00	15.00
(21)	Andy Pafko	50.00	25.00	15.00
(22)	Jim Pendleton	50.00	25.00	15.00
(23)	Ebba St. Claire	50.00	25.00	15.00
(24)	Warren Spahn	200.00	100.00	60.00
(25)	Max Surkont	50.00	25.00	15.00
(26)	Bob Thomson	75.00	37.50	22.00
(27)	Bob Thorpe	50.00	25.00	15.00
(28)	Roberto Vargas	50.00	25.00	15.00
(29)	Jim Wilson	50.00	25.00	15.00

1953-57 Spic and Span Braves 7x10 Photos

This regional set was issued by Spic and Span Dry Cleaners of Milwaukee over a four-year period and consists of large (7" x 10") photos of Braves players. Of all the various Spic and Span sets, this one seems to be the easiest to find. The fronts feature a player photo with a facsimile autograph below. The Spic and Span logo also appears on the fronts, while the backs are blank. A header card picturing Milwaukee County Stadium also exists.

		NM	EX	VG
Complete Set (14):		335.00	165.00	100.00
Common Player:		25.00	12.50	7.50
(1)	Joe Adcock	25.00	12.50	7.50
(2)	William H. Bruton	25.00	12.50	7.50
(3)	Robert Buhl	25.00	12.50	7.50
(4)	Lou Burdette	25.00	12.50	7.50
(5)	Del Crandall	25.00	12.50	7.50
(6)	Jack Dittmer	25.00	12.50	7.50
(7)	Johnny Logan	25.00	12.50	7.50
(8)	Edwin L. Mathews, Jr.	75.00	37.50	22.00
(9)	Chet Nichols	25.00	12.50	7.50
(10)	Danny O'Connell	25.00	12.50	7.50
(11)	Andy Pafko	25.00	12.50	7.50
(12)	Warren E. Spahn	75.00	37.50	22.00
(13)	Bob Thomson	35.00	17.50	10.00
(14)	Milwaukee County Stadium	35.00	17.50	10.00

1954 Spic and Span Braves

Player selection points to 1954 as the date of this issue, making it contemporary with several other card sets produced by the chain of Wisconsin dry cleaners. These cards are printed in blue on 5-1/2" x 8-1/2" yellow cardstock. Fronts have player portraits by an artist signed as "Warmuth," facsimile autographs, a promotional quote from the player and the sponsor's logo. Backs are blank. It is not known whether the set is complete at 13.

		NM	EX	VG
Complete Set (13):		1,200	600.00	350.00
Common Player:		75.00	37.50	22.50
(1)	Joe Adcock	90.00	45.00	27.50
(2)	William H. Bruton	75.00	37.50	22.50
(3)	Robert Buhl	75.00	37.50	22.50
(4)	Lou Burdette	75.00	37.50	22.50
(5)	Del Crandall	75.00	37.50	22.50
(6)	Jack Dittmer	75.00	37.50	22.50
(7)	Johnny Logan	75.00	37.50	22.50
(8)	Edwin L. Mathews Jr.	225.00	110.00	70.00
(9)	Chet Nichols	75.00	37.50	22.50
(10)	Danny O'Connell	75.00	37.50	22.50
(11)	Andy Pafko	75.00	37.50	22.50
(12)	Warren E. Spahn	225.00	110.00	70.00
(13)	Bob Thomson	90.00	45.00	27.50

1954-56 Spic and Span Braves

Issued during the three-year period from 1954-1956, this Spic and Span set consists of 18 postcard-size (4" x 6") cards. The front of the cards include a facsimile autograph printed in white and the Spic and Span logo.

		NM	EX	VG
Complete Set (18):		1,350	675.00	400.00
Common Player:		35.00	17.50	10.00
(1)	Hank Aaron	400.00	200.00	120.00
(2)	Joe Adcock	35.00	17.50	10.00
(3)	William H. Bruton	35.00	17.50	10.00
(4)	Robert Buhl	35.00	17.50	10.00
(5)	Lou Burdette	35.00	17.50	10.00
(6)	Gene Conley	35.00	17.50	10.00
(7)	Del Crandall	35.00	17.50	10.00
(8)	Ray Crone	35.00	17.50	10.00
(9)	Jack Dittmer	35.00	17.50	10.00
(10)	Ernie Johnson	35.00	17.50	10.00
(11)	Dave Jolly	35.00	17.50	10.00
(12)	Johnny Logan	35.00	17.50	10.00
(13)	Edwin L. Mathews, Jr.	225.00	110.00	70.00
(14)	Chet Nichols	35.00	17.50	10.00
(15)	Danny O'Connell	35.00	17.50	10.00
(16)	Andy Pafko	35.00	17.50	10.00
(17)	Warren E. Spahn	220.00	110.00	70.00
(18)	Bob Thomson	60.00	30.00	18.00

1955 Spic and Span Braves Die-Cuts

This 17-card, die-cut set is the rarest of all the Spic and Span issues. The stand-ups, which measure approximately 7-1/2" x 7", picture the players in action poses and were designed to be punched out, allowing them to stand up. Most cards were used in this fashion, making better-condition cards very rare today. The front of the card includes a facsimile autograph and the Spic and Span logo.

		NM	EX	VG
Complete Set (18):		4,400	2,200	1,250
Common Player:		175.00	90.00	55.00
(1)	Hank Aaron	900.00	450.00	275.00
(2)	Joe Adcock	175.00	90.00	55.00
(3)	Bill Bruton	175.00	90.00	55.00
(4)	Bob Buhl	175.00	90.00	55.00
(5)	Lew Burdette	175.00	90.00	55.00
(6)	Gene Conley	175.00	90.00	55.00
(7)	Del Crandall	175.00	90.00	55.00
(8)	Jack Dittmer	175.00	90.00	55.00
(9)	Ernie Johnson	175.00	90.00	55.00
(10)	Dave Jolly	175.00	90.00	55.00
(11)	John Logan	175.00	90.00	55.00
(12)	Ed Mathews	450.00	225.00	135.00
(13)	Chet Nichols	175.00	90.00	55.00
(14)	Dan O'Connell	175.00	90.00	55.00
(15)	Andy Pafko	175.00	90.00	55.00
(16)	Warren Spahn	450.00	225.00	135.00
(17)	Bob Thomson	225.00	110.00	65.00
(18)	Jim Wilson	175.00	90.00	55.00

1957 Spic and Span Braves

This 20-card set was issued in 1957, the year the Braves were World Champions and is a highly desirable set. The cards measure 4" x 5" and have a wide white border surrounding the player photo. A blue Spic and Span logo appears in the lower-right corner and the card includes a salutation and facsimile autograph, also in blue.

		NM	EX	VG
Complete Set (20):		1,250	625.00	375.00
Common Player:		25.00	12.50	7.50
(1)	Hank Aaron	400.00	200.00	120.00
(2)	Joe Adcock	25.00	12.50	7.50

		NM	EX	VG
(3)	Bill Bruton	25.00	12.50	7.50
(4)	Bob Buhl	25.00	12.50	7.50
(5)	Lew Burdette	25.00	12.50	7.50
(6)	Gene Conley	25.00	12.50	7.50
(7)	Wes Covington/SP	50.00	25.00	15.00
(8)	Del Crandall	25.00	12.50	7.50
(9)	Ray Crone	25.00	12.50	7.50
(10)	Fred Haney	25.00	12.50	7.50
(11)	Ernie Johnson	25.00	12.50	7.50
(12)	John Logan	25.00	12.50	7.50
(13)	Felix Mantilla/SP	50.00	25.00	15.00
(14)	Ed Mathews	85.00	45.00	25.00
(15)	Dan O'Connell	25.00	12.50	7.50
(16)	Andy Pafko	25.00	12.50	7.50
(17)	Red Schoendienst/SP	110.00	55.00	35.00
(18)	Warren Spahn	85.00	45.00	25.00
(19)	Bob Thomson	45.00	22.50	13.50
(20)	Bob Trowbridge/SP	50.00	25.00	15.00

1960 Spic and Span Braves

PHOTOGRAPHED AND AUTOGRAPHED EXCLUSIVELY FOR SPIC AND SPAN

Spic and Span's final Milwaukee Braves issue consists of 26 cards, each measuring 2-3/4" x 3-1/8". The fronts contain a white-bordered photo with no printing, while the backs include a facsimile autograph and the words "Photographed and Autographed Exclusively for Spic and Span." The 1960 set includes the only known variation in the Spic and Span sets; a "flopped" negative error showing catcher Del Crandall batting left-handed was later corrected.

		NM	EX	VG
Complete Set (26):		1,650	825.00	500.00
Common Player:		35.00	17.50	10.00
(1)	Hank Aaron	650.00	325.00	200.00
(2)	Joe Adcock	35.00	17.50	10.00
(3)	Bill Bruton	35.00	17.50	10.00
(4)	Bob Buhl	35.00	17.50	10.00
(5)	Lew Burdette	35.00	17.50	10.00
(6)	Chuck Cottier	35.00	17.50	10.00
(7a)	Del Crandall (Photo reversed.)	60.00	30.00	18.00
(7b)	Del Crandall (Correct photo.)	35.00	17.50	10.00
(8)	Chuck Dressen	35.00	17.50	10.00
(9)	Joey Jay	35.00	17.50	10.00
(10)	John Logan	35.00	17.50	10.00
(11)	Felix Mantilla	35.00	17.50	10.00
(12)	Ed Mathews	125.00	65.00	35.00
(13)	Lee Maye	35.00	17.50	10.00
(14)	Don McMahon	35.00	17.50	10.00
(15)	George Myatt	35.00	17.50	10.00
(16)	Andy Pafko	35.00	17.50	10.00
(17)	Juan Pizarro	35.00	17.50	10.00
(18)	Mel Roach	35.00	17.50	10.00
(19)	Bob Rush	35.00	17.50	10.00
(20)	Bob Scheffing	35.00	17.50	10.00
(21)	Red Schoendienst	90.00	45.00	27.50
(22)	Warren Spahn	125.00	65.00	35.00
(23)	Al Spangler	35.00	17.50	10.00
(24)	Frank Torre	35.00	17.50	10.00
(25)	Carl Willey	35.00	17.50	10.00
(26)	Whit Wyatt	35.00	17.50	10.00

1960s Spokane Indians Team Issue

The year of issue, its manner of distribution and the extent of this set of team-issued player pictures are unknown. Only a single example of the approximately 5" x 7" black-and-white, blank-back player pictures has thus far been cataloged. The known example pictures John Werhas in the uniform of the L.A. Dodgers, the parent club of the Pacific Coast League Spokane Indians in the early 1960s. Since Werhas played with Spokane each season between 1962-66, a more specific date of issue cannot be determined.

	NM	EX	VG
Common Player:	40.00	20.00	12.00
John Werhas	40.00	20.00	12.00

1964-67 Sport Hobbyist Famous Card Series

These very early collectors issues were produced over a period of several years in the mid-1960s during Frank Nagy's ownership of the "Sport Hobbyist" magazine. The 2-1/4" x 3-3/4" black-and-white cards picture on their fronts reproductions of rare and famous baseball cards from Nagy's unequaled collection, including eight of the very rare Tarzan Bread issue of the mid-1930s which few collectors even today have seen. Backs have identification of the pictured card, utilizing the then-standard "American Card Catalog" set designations.

		NM	EX	VG
Complete Set (30):		90.00	45.00	27.50
Common Player:		5.00	2.50	1.50
1	T206 Honus Wagner	12.50	6.25	3.75
2	T212 Henley	5.00	2.50	1.50
3	C46 Simmons	5.00	2.50	1.50
4	M116 Christy Mathewson	5.00	2.50	1.50
5	M101-5 Jack Barry	5.00	2.50	1.50
6	T204 Mordecai Brown	5.00	2.50	1.50
7	D322 Tip Top Bread Webb	5.00	2.50	1.50
8	S74 Lou Criger	5.00	2.50	1.50
9	R333 DeLong Kiki Cuyler	5.00	2.50	1.50
10	R319 Nap Lajoie	7.50	3.75	2.25
11	T205 John McGraw	5.00	2.50	1.50
12	E107 Addie Joss	5.00	2.50	1.50
13	W502 George Sisler	5.00	2.50	1.50
14	Allen & Ginter N29 Buck Ewing	5.00	2.50	1.50
15	E90 Chief Bender	5.00	2.50	1.50
16	E104 George Mullin	5.00	2.50	1.50
17	E95 Fred Merkle	5.00	2.50	1.50
18	E121 Walter Schang	5.00	2.50	1.50
19	Allen & Ginter N28 Tim Keefe	5.00	2.50	1.50
20	E120 Harold (Muddy) Ruel	5.00	2.50	1.50
21	D382 Irving (Jack) Burns	5.00	2.50	1.50
22	D382 George Connally	5.00	2.50	1.50
23	D382 Myril Hoag	5.00	2.50	1.50
24	D382 Willie Kamm	5.00	2.50	1.50
25	D382 Dutch Leonard	5.00	2.50	1.50
26	D382 Clyde Manion	5.00	2.50	1.50
27	D382 Johnny Vergez	5.00	2.50	1.50
28	D382 Tom Zachary	5.00	2.50	1.50
29	E145 Ty Cobb	7.50	3.75	2.25
30	Playing Card, Richardson	5.00	2.50	1.50

1971 Sport Hobbyist Famous Card Series

A new series of collector cards, designed as the first-ever attempt to reproduce the T206 tobacco set, was begun under the hobby paper's new ownership but quickly abandoned. The 2" x 3" cards have a black-and-white picture of a card at center, surrounded by a red frame (except Bescher, which has a black frame). Backs identify the card and include a card number.

		NM	EX	VG
Complete Set (21):		90.00	45.00	27.50
Common Card:		5.00	2.50	1.50
31	T206 Abbaticchio	5.00	2.50	1.50
32	T206 Barbeau	5.00	2.50	1.50
33	T206 Burch	5.00	2.50	1.50
34	T206 M. Brown	5.00	2.50	1.50
35	T206 Chase	5.00	2.50	1.50
36	T206 Ball	5.00	2.50	1.50
37	T206 Abstein	5.00	2.50	1.50
38	T206 Bowerman	5.00	2.50	1.50
39	T206 Chase	5.00	2.50	1.50
40	T206 Criss	5.00	2.50	1.50
41	T206 Beck	5.00	2.50	1.50
42	T206 Bresnahan	5.00	2.50	1.50
43	T206 Bradley	5.00	2.50	1.50
44	T206 Berger	5.00	2.50	1.50
45	T206 Bransfield	5.00	2.50	1.50
46	T206 Bescher	5.00	2.50	1.50
47	T206 Bell	5.00	2.50	1.50
48	T206 Bergen	5.00	2.50	1.50
49	T206 Bender	5.00	2.50	1.50
50	T206 Bush	5.00	2.50	1.50
51	T206 Chesbro	5.00	2.50	1.50

1975 Sport Hobbyist

This was one of several series of collectors issues produced in the 1960s and 1970s by the Sport Hobbyist, one of the card hobby's earliest periodicals. This series features the past greats of the game in postcard size (3-1/2" x 5-1/2"). Cards are found either blank-backed or with an ad over various new-card products. Fronts of cards numbered through 115 have watercolor portraits in an oval frame. A box below offers a career summary. Higher number cards feature photos and/or artwork, sometimes with a caption, and sometimes with no identification. Cards are numbered with an SH prefix. Each series of 18 were originally sold for $1.50.

JOE DIMAGGIO

Joe DiMaggio hit safely in 56 consecutive games for a major league record. Was MVP in 1939-41 and 47. Batted over 300 11 times in 13 seasons, seven times consecutively. Elected to Hall of Fame in 1955.

		NM	EX	VG
Complete Set (48):		150.00	75.00	45.00
Common Player:		5.00	2.50	1.50
98	Lou Gehrig	15.00	7.50	4.50
99	Ty Cobb	12.50	6.25	3.75
100	Joe DiMaggio	15.00	7.50	4.50
101	Mel Ott	5.00	2.50	1.50
102	Carl Hubbell	5.00	2.50	1.50
103	Babe Ruth	20.00	10.00	6.00
104	Rogers Hornsby	7.50	3.75	2.25
105	Tris Speaker	7.50	3.75	2.25
106	Hank Greenberg	7.50	3.75	2.25
107	Jimmy (Jimmie) Foxx	7.50	3.75	2.25
108	Ted Williams	15.00	7.50	4.50
109	Mickey Cochrane	5.00	2.50	1.50
110	Bob Feller	7.50	3.75	2.25
111	Cy Young	9.00	4.50	2.75
112	George Sissler (Sisler)	5.00	2.50	1.50
113	Honus Wagner	9.00	4.50	2.75
114	Lefty Grove	5.00	2.50	1.50
115	Dizzy Dean	7.50	3.75	2.25
116	Babe Ruth (Farewell address.)	9.00	4.50	2.75
117	Jackie Robinson	7.50	3.75	2.25
118	Mike Kelly (Woodcut)	5.00	2.50	1.50
119	Honus Wagner (Portrait and action.)	5.00	2.50	1.50
120	Babe Ruth (W/mascot Ray Kelly.)	9.00	4.50	2.75
121	Babe Ruth (Photos/artwork.)	5.00	2.50	1.50
122	John M. Ward (Newsboy cabinet.)	5.00	2.50	1.50
123	Babe Ruth (Photos/artwork.)	5.00	2.50	1.50
124	Babe Ruth (Artwork)	5.00	2.50	1.50
125	Hall of Fame Dedication, 1939	5.00	2.50	1.50
126	Babe Ruth (At microphone.)	5.00	2.50	1.50
127	Babe Ruth, Jacob Ruppert	7.50	3.75	2.25
128	Stan Musial	7.50	3.75	2.25
129	Babe Ruth (W/others.)	5.00	2.50	1.50
130	George Kell	5.00	2.50	1.50
131	Luke Appling	5.00	2.50	1.50
132	Cecil Travis	5.00	2.50	1.50
133	Larry "Yogi" Berra	7.50	3.75	2.25
134	Harry Heilman (Heilmann)	5.00	2.50	1.50
135	Johnny Mize	5.00	2.50	1.50
136	Christy Mathewson	7.50	3.75	2.25
137	Ralph Kiner	5.00	2.50	1.50
138	Bill Dickey	5.00	2.50	1.50
139	Hank Sauer	5.00	2.50	1.50
140	Hank Greenberg	7.50	3.75	2.25
141	Charlie Gehringer	5.00	2.50	1.50
142	Walter Evers	5.00	2.50	1.50
143	John Pepper Martin	5.00	2.50	1.50
144	Vern Stephens	5.00	2.50	1.50
145	Bobbie (Bobby) Doerr	5.00	2.50	1.50

1975 Sport Hobbyist Team Composites

This was one of several series of collectors issues produced in the 1960s and 1970s by the Sport Hobbyist, one of the card hobby's earliest periodicals. This series features black-and-white postcard size (about 3-1/2" x 5-1/4") reproductions of team composite photos from the 1931 Spalding Guide. Cards are blank-backed. Most of the cards are numbered, with an SH prefix, though some are not.

		NM	EX	VG
Common Card:		6.00	3.00	1.80
70	Chicago Cubs	6.00	3.00	1.80
71	Philadelphia Athletics	6.00	3.00	1.80
72	N.Y. Giants	6.00	3.00	1.80

73				
74	Pittsburgh Pirates	6.00	3.00	1.80
75	Chicago Cubs	6.00	3.00	1.80
76				
77	Boston Braves	6.00	3.00	1.80
78	Cincinnati Reds	6.00	3.00	1.80
79	Brooklyn Dodgers	6.00	3.00	1.80
80				
81	Philadelphia A's	6.00	3.00	1.80
82	Cleveland Indians	6.00	3.00	1.80
83	Detroit Tigers	6.00	3.00	1.80
84	Chicago White Sox	6.00	3.00	1.80
85	Chicago White Sox	6.00	3.00	1.80
86	Boston Red Sox	6.00	3.00	1.80
87	Boston Red Sox	6.00	3.00	1.80
88	N.Y. Yankees	10.00	5.00	3.00
89	Cleveland Indians	6.00	3.00	1.80
90	St. Louis Browns	6.00	3.00	1.80
91	Washington Senators	6.00	3.00	1.80
92	Boston Braves	6.00	3.00	1.80
93	St. Louis Browns	6.00	3.00	1.80
94	Washington Senators	6.00	3.00	1.80
95	Philadelphia Phillies	6.00	3.00	1.80
96	Cincinnati Reds	6.00	3.00	1.80
97	Philadelphia Phillies	6.00	3.00	1.80
	UNNUMBERED			
---	Brooklyn Dodgers	6.00	3.00	1.80
---	Detroit Tigers	6.00	3.00	1.80
---	N.Y. Yankees	10.00	5.00	3.00
---	Pittsburgh Pirates	6.00	3.00	1.80

1888-1889 Sporting Extra World Tour Imperial Cabinets

These large-format (about 9-3/4" x 6-1/2") imperial cabinet cards were issued in conjunction with "Spalding's World Base Ball Tour" of 1888-1889, though their method of distribution is unknown. The cards feature team portraits on a heavy cardboard, gilt-edge mount. At top is the name of the sponsoring cigarette brand, at bottom is the team name, printed in red. Backs are blank. Each of the cards that appeared in a 12/05 auction is believed unique.

(1)   THE ALL AMERICA B.B. TOURISTS
(2)   THE CHICAGO B.B. TOURISTS
      Pair sold in 12/05 auction for $27,709.

1902-11 Sporting Life Cabinets (W600)

From 1902 through 1911, Sporting Life, a weekly newspaper published in Philadelphia, produced and sold a lengthy run of 5" x 7-1/2" "Cabinet Phototypes of Well-known Baseball Players." They were collectively given the catalog number of W600 in "The American Card Catalog." Because many players were issued with different team designations as they moved about over the years, and because there are new discoveries from this issue being made even today, it is likely this checklist will remain in flux for some time to come. For that reason, gaps in the assigned card numbers in this checklist have been left to accommodate additions. Several different styles and colors of mattes were used over the years, with many players issued in more than one of them. Many of the earliest cabinets picture the players in suit-and-tie, while later issues show them in uniform. Where verified, cabinets showing players in street clothes are noted. The black-and-white player portraits are mounted on heavy cardboard mattes. The player's name, position, team and league are printed beneath the photo. Backs are blank. Each cabinet was issued in a transparent envelope. They were originally given away for three two-cents stamps and a coupon found in the paper; later they were offered for sale for 10 cents apiece; 12 for a dollar. The checklist here is presented in alphabetical order. Most of the names are presented as they appeared in contemporary ads from the newspaper; rife with misspellings and misidentifications, and may or may not represent the actual spelling shown on the cards. The year shown in parentheses indicates the first year the player was issued with that team. Because these cards were sold individually upon fan request, this is an issue in which the superstars of the day are more common than the benchwarmers. It is also likely that some of the cards on this list were never issued or do not survive.

		NM	EX	VG
	Common Player:	2,400	1,200	720.00
(1)	Edward Abbatichio (Abbaticchio) (Boston NL, 1903.)	3,600	1,800	1,100
(2)	Edward Abbatichio (Pittsburg, 1907.)	2,400	1,200	720.00
(3)	William Abstein (St. Louis AL, 1910.)	2,400	1,200	720.00
(4)	Charles B. Adams (Pittsburg, 1909.)	2,400	1,200	720.00
(5)	C.A. Alperman (Brooklyn, 1906.)	2,400	1,200	720.00
(6)	David Altizer (Washington, 1907.)	2,400	1,200	720.00
(7)	Nick Altrock (Chicago AL, 1903.)	4,300	2,150	1,300
(8)	Leon Ames (New York, NL, 1904.)	2,400	1,200	720.00
(9)	John Anderson (St. Louis AL, 1902, street.)	3,600	1,800	1,100
(10)	John Anderson (New York AL, 1904.)	2,400	1,200	720.00
(11)	John Anderson (Washington, 1905.)	2,400	1,200	720.00
(12)	Frank Arelanes (Arellanes) (Boston AL, 1910.)	2,400	1,200	720.00
(13)	Charles Armbruster (Boston AL, 1906.)	2,400	1,200	720.00
(14)	William R. Armour (Detroit, 1906.)	2,400	1,200	720.00
(15)	Harry Arndt (St. Louis NL, 1906.)	2,400	1,200	720.00
(16)	Harry J. Aubrey (Boston NL, 1903.)	3,600	1,800	1,100
(17)	James Austin (New York AL, 1910.)	2,400	1,200	720.00
(18)	Charles Babb (New York NL, 1903.)	3,600	1,800	1,100
(19)	Charles Babb (Brooklyn, 1904.)	2,400	1,200	720.00
(20)	William Bailey (St. Louis AL, 1910.)	2,400	1,200	720.00
(21)	Frank Baker (Philadelphia AL, 1910.)	6,500	3,250	1,950
(22)	J. Barbeau (Cleveland, 1906.)	2,400	1,200	720.00
(23)	G.O. Barclay (Boston NL, 1904.)	2,400	1,200	720.00
(24)	Edward Barger (First name Eros.) (Brooklyn, 1910.)	2,400	1,200	720.00
(25)	James Barrett (Detroit, 1902, street.)	3,600	1,800	1,100
(26)	James Barrett (Boston AL, 1906.)	2,400	1,200	720.00
(27)	John C. Barry (Philadelphia NL, 1902.)	3,600	1,800	1,100
(28)	John C. Barry (Chicago NL, 1904.)	2,400	1,200	720.00
(29)	John C. Barry (Cincinnati, 1905.)	2,400	1,200	720.00
(30)	John C. Barry (St. Louis NL, 1906.)	2,400	1,200	720.00
(31)	John J. Barry (Philadelphia AL, 1910.)	2,400	1,200	720.00
(32)	Harry L. Barton (Philadelphia AL, 1905.)	2,400	1,200	720.00
(33)	Henry Batch (Brooklyn, 1906.)	2,400	1,200	720.00
(34)	Joseph Bates (Johnny) (Boston NL, 1907.)	2,400	1,200	720.00
(35)	Harry Bay (Cleveland, 1903.)	3,600	1,800	1,100
(36)	Clarence H. Beaumont (Pittsburg, 1902, street.)	3,600	1,800	1,100
(37)	Clarence H. Beaumont (Pittsburg, 1902, uniform.)	3,600	1,800	1,100
(38)	Clarence H. Beaumont (Boston NL, 1907.)	2,400	1,200	720.00
(39)	Fred Beck (Boston NL, 1910.)	2,400	1,200	720.00
(40)	Harry Beckendorf (Detroit, 1910.)	2,400	1,200	720.00
(41)	Jacob Beckley (Cincinnati, 1902.)	7,900	4,000	2,375
(42)	Jacob Beckley (St. Louis NL, 1904.)	6,500	3,250	1,950
(43)	Fred L. Beebe (St. Louis NL, 1906.)	2,400	1,200	720.00
(44)	George C. Bell (Brooklyn, 1910.)	2,400	1,200	720.00
(45)	Harry Bemis (Cleveland, 1903.)	3,600	1,800	1,100
(46)	Charles Bender (Philadelphia AL, 1903, street.)	7,900	4,000	2,375
(47)	Charles Bender (Philadelphia AL, 1903, uniform.)	7,900	4,000	2,375
(48)	Justin J. Bennett (St. Louis AL, 1907.)	2,400	1,200	720.00
(49)	William Bergen (Brooklyn, 1904.)	2,400	1,200	720.00
(50)	Charles Berger (Cleveland, 1907.)	2,400	1,200	720.00
(51)	William Bernhardt (Bernhard) (Cleveland, 1902, street.)	3,000	1,500	900.00
(52)	Robert Bescher (Cincinnati, 1910.)	2,400	1,200	720.00
(53)	Walter Beville (Henry "Monte")(New York, AL 1903.)	3,600	1,800	1,100
(54)	Walter Beville (Henry "Monte") (Detroit, 1904.)	2,400	1,200	720.00
(55)	Russell Blackburne (Chicago AL, 1910.)	2,400	1,200	720.00
(56)	Elmer Bliss (St. Louis NL, 1910.)	2,400	1,200	720.00
(57)	Frank Bowerman (New York NL, 1903.)	3,600	1,800	1,100
(58)	Frank (William J.) Bradley (Cleveland, 1903.)	3,600	1,800	1,100
(59)	William J. Bradley (Cleveland, 1903.)	3,600	1,800	1,100
(60)	David L. Brain (St. Louis NL, 1903.)	3,600	1,800	1,100
(61)	David L. Brain (Pittsburg, 1905.)	2,400	1,200	720.00
(62)	David L. Brain (Boston NL, 1906.)	2,400	1,200	720.00
(63)	William Bransfield (Pittsburg, 1902, street.)	3,600	1,800	1,100
(64)	William Bransfield (Pittsburg, 1902, uniform.)	3,600	1,800	1,100
(65)	William Bransfield (Philadelphia NL, 1905.)	2,400	1,200	720.00
(66)	Roger Bresnahan (New York NL, 1903.)	7,900	4,000	2,375
(67)	Roger Bresnahan (St. Louis NL, 1909.)	6,750	3,375	2,025
(68)	Albert Bridwell (Boston NL, 1906.)	2,400	1,200	720.00
(69)	Herbert Briggs (Chicago NL, 1905.)	2,400	1,200	720.00
(70)	Herbert Briggs (Brooklyn, 1906.)	2,400	1,200	720.00
(71)	Charles E. Brown (St. Louis NL, 1906.)	2,400	1,200	720.00
(72)	Charles E. Brown (Philadelphia NL, 1907.)	2,400	1,200	720.00
(73)	Mordecai Brown (Chicago NL, 1904.)	6,500	3,250	1,950
(74)	Samuel Brown (Boston NL, 1907.)	2,400	1,200	720.00
(75)	George Browne (New York NL, 1903.)	3,600	1,800	1,100
(76)	Fred Buelow (Detroit, 1903.)	3,600	1,800	1,100
(77)	Fred Buelow (Cleveland, 1904.)	2,400	1,200	720.00
(78)	James T. Burke (St. Louis NL, 1903.)	3,600	1,800	1,100
(79)	James T. Burke (Philadelphia NL, 1906.)	2,400	1,200	720.00
(80)	Jesse Burkett (St. Louis AL, 1903.)	53,500	26,750	16,050
(81)	Jesse Burkett (Boston AL, 1905.)	6,500	3,250	1,950
(82)	James J. Callahan (Chicago AL, 1903.)	3,000	1,500	900.00
(83)	Howard Camnitz (Pittsburg, 1910.)	2,400	1,200	720.00
(84)	Wirt V. Cannell (Virgin Wirt) (Boston NL, 1903.)	3,600	1,800	1,100
(85)	Joseph Cantillion (Washington, 1907.)	2,400	1,200	720.00
(86)	George Carey (Washington, 1903.)	3,600	1,800	1,100
(87)	P.J. Carney (Boston NL, 1903.)	3,600	1,800	1,100
(88)	Charles C. Carr (Cleveland, 1904.)	2,400	1,200	720.00
(89)	Charles C. Carr (Cincinnati, 1906.)	2,400	1,200	720.00
(90)	William Carrigan (Boston AL, 1910.)	2,400	1,200	720.00
(91)	James P. Casey (Chicago NL, 1902, street.)	3,600	1,800	1,100
(92)	James P. Casey (Brooklyn, 1906.)	2,400	1,200	720.00
(93)	Joseph Cassidy (Washington, 1904.)	2,400	1,200	720.00
(94)	Luis Castro (Philadelphia AL, 1902, street.)	2,400	1,200	720.00
(95)	Frank Chance (Chicago NL, 1902, street.)	7,900	4,000	2,375
(96)	Frank Chance (Chicago NL, 1902, uniform.)	7,900	4,000	2,375
(97)	Harold Chase (New York AL, 1906.)	5,000	2,600	1,400
(98)	John Chesbro (Pittsburg, 1902, street.)	6,750	3,375	2,025
(99)	John Chesbro (New York AL, 1903, uniform.)	7,900	4,000	2,375
(100)	Edw. V. Cicotte (Boston AL, 1910.)	6,500	3,250	1,950
(101)	William Clark (Clarke) (Washington, 1903.)	3,600	1,800	1,100
(102)	William Clark (Clarke) (New York NL, 1905.)	2,400	1,200	720.00
(103)	Fred Clarke (Pittsburg, 1902, street.)	7,900	4,000	2,375
(104)	Fred Clarke (Pittsburg, 1902, uniform.)	7,900	4,000	2,375
(104)	Justin J. Clarke (Cleveland, 1906.)	2,400	1,200	720.00
(105)	Thomas Clarke (Cincinnati, 1910.)	2,400	1,200	720.00
(106)	Walter Clarkson (New York AL, 1906.)	2,400	1,200	720.00
(107)	Walter Clarkson (Cleveland, 1907.)	2,400	1,200	720.00
(108)	Otis Clymer (Pittsburg, 1905.)	2,400	1,200	720.00
(109)	Otis Clymer (Washington, 1907.)	2,400	1,200	720.00
(110)	Andrew Coakley (Philadelphia AL, 1905.)	2,400	1,200	720.00
(111)	Andrew Coakley (Cincinnati, 1907.)	2,400	1,200	720.00
(112)	Tyrus R. Cobb (Detroit, 1907.)	21,600	10,800	6,500
(115)	Edward Collins (Philadelphia AL, 1907.)	6,500	3,250	1,950
(116)	James Collins (Boston AL, 1902, uniform.)	6,250	3,125	1,875
(117)	W.M. Congalton (Cleveland, 1906.)	2,400	1,200	720.00
(118)	W.A. Congalton (Boston AL, 1907.)	2,400	1,200	720.00
(119)	William Conroy (New York AL, 1903.)	3,600	1,800	1,100
(120)	Richard Cooley (Boston NL, 1902, street.)	3,600	1,800	1,100
(121)	Richard Cooley (Detroit, 1905.)	2,400	1,200	720.00
(122)	John W. Coombs (Philadelphia AL, 1910.)	2,400	1,200	720.00
(123)	T.W. Corcoran (Cincinnati, 1904.)	2,400	1,200	720.00
(124)	T.W. Corcoran (New York NL, 1907.)	2,400	1,200	720.00
(125)	Frank J. Corridon (Philadelphia NL, 1907.)	2,400	1,200	720.00
(126)	William Coughlin (Washington, 1903.)	3,000	1,500	900.00

No.	Name			
(127)	William Coughlin (Detroit, 1904.)	2,400	1,200	720.00
(128)	Ernest Courtney (Philadelphia NL, 1905.)	2,400	1,200	720.00
(129)	Otis Crandall (New York NL, 1910.)	2,400	1,200	720.00
(130)	Samuel Crawford (Cincinnati, 1902, street.)	7,900	4,000	2,375
(131)	Samuel Crawford (Detroit, 1903.)	7,900	4,000	2,375
(132)	Burde Cree (Birdie) (New York AL, 1911.)	2,400	1,200	720.00
(134)	Louis Criger (Boston AL, 1903.)	3,600	1,800	1,100
(135)	Dode Criss (St. Louis AL, 1910.)	2,400	1,200	720.00
(136)	John Cronin (New York NL, 1903.)	3,600	1,800	1,100
(137)	John Cronin (Brooklyn, 1904.)	2,400	1,200	720.00
(138)	Lafayette Cross (Philadelphia AL, 1902, street.)	3,600	1,800	1,100
(139)	Lafayette Cross (Washington, 1906.)	2,400	1,200	720.00
(140)	Monte Cross (Philadelphia AL, 1902.)	3,600	1,800	1,100
(142)	Clarence Currie (St. Louis NL, 1903.)	3,600	1,800	1,100
(143)	Clarence Currie (Chicago NL, 1903.)	3,600	1,800	1,100
(145)	William Dahlen (Brooklyn, 1902, street.)	4,300	2,150	1,300
(146)	William Dahlen (New York NL, 1904.)	2,400	1,200	720.00
(147)	Thomas Daly (Chicago AL, 1903, street.)	3,600	1,800	1,100
(148)	Thomas Daly (Cincinnati, 1903.)	3,600	1,800	1,100
(148)	George Davis (Chicago AL, 1902.)	7,900	4,000	2,375
(150)	Harry Davis (Philadelphia AL, 1902, street.)	3,600	1,800	1,100
(152)	Edward J. Delahanty (Washington, 1902, street.)	19,400	9,700	5,825
(153)	James Delahanty (Boston NL, 1904.)	2,400	1,200	720.00
(154)	James Delahanty (Cincinnati, 1906.)	2,400	1,200	720.00
(155)	James Delahanty (St. Louis AL, 1907.)	2,400	1,200	720.00
(156)	James Delahanty (Washington, 1907.)	2,400	1,200	720.00
(158)	Arthur Devlin (New York NL, 1905.)	2,400	1,200	720.00
(159)	Joshua Devore (New York NL, 1911.)	2,400	1,200	720.00
(160)	Charles Dexter (Boston NL, 1903.)	3,600	1,800	1,100
(161)	Frank Dillon (Brooklyn, 1903.)	3,600	1,800	1,100
(162)	William Dinneen (Boston AL, 1903.)	3,000	1,500	900.00
(163)	William Dineen (St. Louis AL, 1907.)	2,400	1,200	720.00
(164)	John Dobbs (Brooklyn, 1903.)	3,600	1,800	1,100
(164)	Edward Doheny (Pittsburg, 1903.)	3,600	1,800	1,100
(165)	Harry Dolan (Patrick Henry "Cozy")(Cincinnati, 1904.)	2,400	1,200	720.00
(166)	Harry Dolan (Patrick Henry "Cozy")(Boston NL, 1905.)	2,400	1,200	720.00
(167)	Frank Donahue (St. Louis AL, 1903.)	3,600	1,800	1,100
(168)	Frank Donahue (Cleveland, 1903.)	3,600	1,800	1,100
(169)	Frank Donahue (Detroit, 1906.)	2,400	1,200	720.00
(170)	J. "Jiggs" Donahue (Chicago AL, 1903.)	3,600	1,800	1,100
(171)	Michael Donlin (Cincinnati, 1902, street.)	3,600	1,800	1,100
(172)	Michael Donlin (New York NL, 1904.)	2,400	1,200	720.00
(173)	P.J. (Patrick) Donovan (St. Louis NL, 1902, street.)	3,600	1,800	1,100
(174)	Patrick J. Donovan (Washington, 1904.)	2,400	1,200	720.00
(175)	Patrick J. Donovan (Brooklyn, 1906, street.)	2,400	1,200	720.00
(176)	William Donovan (Detroit, 1903.)	3,000	1,500	900.00
(177)	Charles Dooin (Philadelphia NL, 1903.)	3,600	1,800	1,100
(178)	Michael Doolin (Doolan) (Philadelphia NL, 1906.)	2,400	1,200	720.00
(180)	Thomas Doran (Boston AL, 1904.)	2,400	1,200	720.00
(181)	Thomas Doran (Detroit, 1905.)	2,400	1,200	720.00
(182)	August Dorner (Boston NL, 1907.)	2,400	1,200	720.00
(183)	Patrick Dougherty (Boston AL, 1903.)	3,600	1,800	1,100
(184)	Patrick Dougherty (New York AL, 1904.)	2,400	1,200	720.00
(185)	Patrick Dougherty (Chicago AL, 1906.)	2,400	1,200	720.00
(186)	William Douglas (Douglass) (Philadelphia NL, 1902.)	3,600	1,800	1,100
(187)	Thomas Downey (Cincinnati, 1910.)	2,400	1,200	720.00
(188)	J.W. Downs (Detroit, 1907.)	2,400	1,200	720.00
(189)	Joe Doyle (New York AL, 1907.)	2,400	1,200	720.00
(190)	John Doyle (Brooklyn, 1903.)	3,600	1,800	1,100
(191)	John Doyle (Philadelphia NL, 1904.)	2,400	1,200	720.00
(192)	Larry J. Doyle (New York NL, 1908.)	2,400	1,200	720.00
(194)	Louis Drill (Washington, 1903.)	3,600	1,800	1,100
(195)	Louis Drill (Detroit, 1904.)	2,400	1,200	720.00
(196)	Hugh Duffy (Philadelphia NL, 1905.)	6,500	3,250	1,950
(197)	William Duggleby (Philadelphia NL, 1903.)	3,600	1,800	1,100
(198)	William Duggleby (Pittsburg, 1907.)	2,400	1,200	720.00
(199)	August Dundon (Chicago AL, 1904.)	2,400	1,200	720.00
(200)	Edward Dunkle (Washington, 1903.)	3,600	1,800	1,100
(201)	James Dunleavy (John) (St. Louis NL, 1904.)	2,400	1,200	720.00
(202)	John Dunn (New York NL, 1903.)	3,600	1,800	1,100
(203)	James H. Dygert (Philadelphia AL, 1905.)	3,600	1,800	1,100
(204)	Malcolm Eason (Brooklyn, 1906.)	2,400	1,200	720.00
(205)	Harry Eells (Cleveland, 1906.)	2,400	1,200	720.00
(206)	Richard J. Egan (Cincinnati, 1910.)	2,400	1,200	720.00
(207)	Norman Elberfeld (Detroit, 1903.)	3,600	1,800	1,100
(208)	Norman Elberfeld (New York AL, 1903.)	3,600	1,800	1,100
(209)	Claude Elliott (New York NL, 1904.)	2,400	1,200	720.00
(210)	George W. Ellis (St. Louis NL, 1910.)	2,400	1,200	720.00
(212)	John Eubank (Detroit, 1906.)	2,400	1,200	720.00
(213)	John Evers (Chicago NL, 1903.)	7,900	4,000	2,375
(214)	Robert Ewing (George L.) (Cincinnati, 1904.)	2,400	1,200	720.00
(216)	Fred Falkenberg (Washington, 1906.)	2,400	1,200	720.00
(217)	Charles Farrell (Brooklyn, 1902, street.)	3,600	1,800	1,100
(218)	Charles Farrell (Boston AL, 1903.)	3,600	1,800	1,100
(219)	John S. Farrell (St. Louis NL, 1903.)	3,600	1,800	1,100
(220)	Cecil Ferguson (George) (New York NL, 1906.)	2,400	1,200	720.00
(221)	Hobe Ferris (Boston AL, 1903.)	3,600	1,800	1,100
(222)	Thomas S. Fisher (Middle initial C.)(Boston NL, 1904.)	2,400	1,200	720.00
(223)	Patrick Flaherty (Chicago AL, 1903.)	3,600	1,800	1,100
(224)	Patrick Flaherty (Pittsburg, 1904.)	2,400	1,200	720.00
(225)	Patrick Flaherty (Boston NL, 1907.)	2,400	1,200	720.00
(226)	Elmer Flick (Cleveland, 1903.)	5,750	2,875	1,725
(227)	John Flynn (Pittsburg, 1910.)	2,400	1,200	720.00
(229)	William Foxen (Chicago NL, 1910.)	2,400	1,200	720.00
(231)	Charles Fraser (Philadelphia NL, 1903, street.)	3,600	1,800	1,100
(232)	Charles Fraser (Boston NL, 1905.)	2,400	1,200	720.00
(233)	Charles Fraser (Chicago NL, 1907.)	2,400	1,200	720.00
(234)	John ("Buck") Freeman (Boston AL, 1902.)	4,300	2,150	1,300
(235)	William Friel (St. Louis AL, 1903.)	3,600	1,800	1,100
(236)	Arthur Fromme (Cincinnati, 1910.)	2,400	1,200	720.00
(237)	David L. Fultz (Philadelphia AL, 1902, street.)	3,600	1,800	1,100
(238)	David L. Fultz (New York AL, 1903.)	3,600	1,800	1,100
(240)	Robert S. Ganley (Pittsburg, 1906.)	2,400	1,200	720.00
(241)	Robert S. Ganley (Washington, 1907.)	2,400	1,200	720.00
(242)	John Ganzell (Ganzel) (New York AL, 1903.)	3,600	1,800	1,100
(243)	John Ganzel (Ganzel) (Cincinnati, 1907.)	2,400	1,200	720.00
(244)	Virgil Garvin (Brooklyn, 1903.)	3,600	1,800	1,100
(245)	Harry L. Gaspar (Cincinnati, 1910.)	2,400	1,200	720.00
(246)	Philip Geier (Boston NL, 1904.)	2,400	1,200	720.00
(247)	Harry Gessler (Brooklyn, 1903.)	3,600	1,800	1,100
(248)	Harry Gessler (Chicago NL, 1906.)	2,400	1,200	720.00
(250)	George Gibson (Pittsburg, 1905.)	2,400	1,200	720.00
(251)	Norwood Gibson (Boston AL, 1903.)	3,600	1,800	1,100
(252)	William Gilbert (New York NL, 1903.)	3,600	1,800	1,100
(253)	Frederick Glade (St. Louis AL, 1904.)	2,400	1,200	720.00
(254)	Harry Gleason (Boston AL, 1903.)	3,600	1,800	1,100
(255)	Harry Gleason (St. Louis AL, 1904.)	2,400	1,200	720.00
(256)	William Gleason (Philadelphia NL, 1903.)	3,600	1,800	1,100
(258)	William Gochnauer (John Gochnaur) (Cleveland, 1903.)	3,600	1,800	1,100
(259)	Michael Grady (St. Louis NL, 1904.)	2,400	1,200	720.00
(260)	Edward L. Grant (Philadelphia NL, 1910.)	3,450	1,725	1,050
(262)	Daniel Green (Chicago AL, 1903.)	3,600	1,800	1,100
(263)	E.W. Greminger (Boston NL, 1903.)	3,600	1,800	1,100
(264)	E.W. Greminger (Detroit, 1904.)	2,400	1,200	720.00
(265)	Clarke Griffith (Clark) (Chicago AL, 1902.)	7,900	4,000	2,375
(266)	Clarke Griffith (Clark) (New York AL, 1903.)	7,900	4,000	2,375
(267)	Myron Grimshaw (Boston AL, 1906.)	2,400	1,200	720.00
(269)	James Hackett (St. Louis NL, 1903.)	3,600	1,800	1,100
(270)	Edgar Hahn (Chicago AL, 1906.)	2,400	1,200	720.00
(271)	Frank Hahn (Cincinnati, 1902, street.)	2,400	1,200	720.00
(272)	Frank Hahn (New York AL, 1905.)	2,400	1,200	720.00
(273)	Charles Hall (Cincinnati, 1907.)	2,400	1,200	720.00
(274)	William H. Hallman (Philadelphia NL, 1903.)	3,600	1,800	1,100
(275)	William H. Hallman (Pittsburg, 1906.)	2,400	1,200	720.00
(276)	Edward Hanlon (Brooklyn, 1905, street.)	6,500	3,250	1,950
(277)	Edward Hanlon (Cincinnati, 1906.)	6,500	3,250	1,950
(278)	Richard Harley (Chicago NL, 1903.)	3,600	1,800	1,100
(279)	Robert Harmon (St. Louis NL, 1910.)	2,400	1,200	720.00
(280)	Charles Harper (Cincinnati, 1903.)	3,600	1,800	1,100
(281)	Charles Harper (Chicago NL, 1906.)	2,400	1,200	720.00
(282)	Joseph Harris (Boston AL, 1906.)	2,400	1,200	720.00
(283)	Harry Hart (Chicago AL, 1906.)	2,400	1,200	720.00
(284)	Frederick L. Hartzell (Hartsel) (Philadelphia AL, 1902.)	3,600	1,800	1,100
(285)	Roy A. Hartzell (St. Louis AL, 1906.)	2,400	1,200	720.00
(287)	J.E. Heidrick (St. Louis AL, 1903.)	3,600	1,800	1,100
(288)	Charles Hemphill (St. Louis AL, 1903.)	3,600	1,800	1,100
(289)	Weldon Henley (Philadelphia AL, 1903, street.)	3,600	1,800	1,100
(290)	Otto Hess (Cleveland, 1904.)	2,400	1,200	720.00
(291)	Edward Heydon (Mike)(Washington, 1906.)	2,400	1,200	720.00
(292)	Charles Hickman (Cleveland, 1903.)	3,600	1,800	1,100
(293)	Charles Hickman (Detroit, 1904.)	2,400	1,200	720.00
(294)	Charles Hickman (Washington, 1905.)	2,400	1,200	720.00
(295)	Charles Hickman (Chicago AL, 1907.)	2,400	1,200	720.00
(296)	Hunter Hill (St. Louis AL, 1903.)	3,600	1,800	1,100
(297)	Hunter Hill (Washington, 1904.)	2,400	1,200	720.00
(298)	Homer Hillebrand (Pittsburg, 1905.)	2,400	1,200	720.00
(299)	Harry Hinchman (Cleveland, 1907.)	2,400	1,200	720.00
(300)	William Hinchman (Cleveland, 1907.)	2,400	1,200	720.00
(303)	R. C. Hoblitzel (Cincinnati, 1910.)	2,400	1,200	720.00
(304)	Daniel Hoffman (Philadelphia AL, 1903.)	3,600	1,800	1,100
(305)	Daniel Hoffman (New York AL, 1906.)	2,400	1,200	720.00
(306)	Arthur Hofman (Chicago NL, 1906.)	2,400	1,200	720.00
(307)	William Hogg (New York AL, 1906.)	2,400	1,200	720.00
(308)	A. Holesketter (St. Louis NL, 1907.)	2,400	1,200	720.00
(309)	William Holmes (James Wm. "Ducky") (Chicago AL, 1903.)	3,600	1,800	1,100
(310)	George Howard (Pittsburg, 1905.)	2,400	1,200	720.00
(311)	George Howard (Boston NL, 1906.)	2,400	1,200	720.00
(312)	Harry Howell (Baltimore, 1902, street.)	3,600	1,800	1,100
(313)	Harry Howell (New York AL, 1903, street.)	3,600	1,800	1,100
(314)	Harry Howell (St. Louis AL, 1904.)	2,400	1,200	720.00
(315)	Miller Huggins (Cincinnati, 1906.)	6,500	3,250	1,950
(316)	James Hughes (Brooklyn, 1902, street.)	3,600	1,800	1,100
(317)	Thomas Hughes (Boston AL, 1902.)	3,600	1,800	1,100
(318)	Thomas Hughes (New York AL, 1904.)	2,400	1,200	720.00
(319)	Thomas Hughes (Washington, 1904.)	2,400	1,200	720.00
(320)	John Hulseman (Frank Huelsman) (Washington, 1904.)	2,400	1,200	720.00
(321)	Rudolph Hulswitt (Philadelphia NL, 1903.)	3,600	1,800	1,100
(322)	John Hummell (Hummel)(Brooklyn, 1906.)	2,400	1,200	720.00
(323)	Berthold J. Husting (Philadelphia AL, 1902, street.)	3,600	1,800	1,100
(324)	Hamilton Hyatt (Pittsburg, 1909.)	2,400	1,200	720.00
(325)	Frank Isbell (Chicago AL, 1903.)	3,600	1,800	1,100

No.	Name			
(326)	Fred Jacklitsch (Brooklyn, 1903, street.)	3,600	1,800	1,100
(327)	Fred Jacklitsch (Philadelphia NL, 1907.)	2,400	1,200	720.00
(328)	James Jackson (Cleveland, 1906.)	2,400	1,200	720.00
(329)	Harry Jacobson (Albert "Beany") (Washington, 1904.)	2,400	1,200	720.00
(330)	Harry Jacobson (Albert "Beany") (St. Louis AL, 1906.)	2,400	1,200	720.00
(331)	Harry Jacobson (Albert "Beany")(Boston AL, 1907.)	2,400	1,200	720.00
(333)	Hugh Jennings (Philadelphia NL, 1902.)	7,900	4,000	2,375
(334)	Hugh Jennings (Detroit, 1907.)	6,500	3,250	1,950
(335)	Charles Jones (Washington, 1905.)	2,400	1,200	720.00
(336)	David Jones (Chicago NL, 1904.)	2,400	1,200	720.00
(337)	David Jones (Detroit, 1906.)	2,400	1,200	720.00
(338)	Fielder Jones (Chicago AL, 1902.)	3,600	1,800	1,100
(339)	Oscar Jones (Brooklyn, 1903.)	3,600	1,800	1,100
(340)	Thomas Jones (St. Louis AL, 1904.)	2,400	1,200	720.00
(341)	Otto Jordan ("Dutch") (Brooklyn, 1903.)	3,600	1,800	1,100
(342)	Otto Jordan ("Dutch") (Cleveland, 1905.)	2,400	1,200	720.00
(343)	Tim Jordan (Brooklyn, 1906.)	2,400	1,200	720.00
(344)	Adrian Joss (Cleveland, 1903.)	8,600	4,300	2,600
(345)	Michael Kahoe (St. Louis AL, 1903.)	3,600	1,800	1,100
(346)	Michael Kahoe (Philadelphia NL, 1905.)	2,400	1,200	720.00
(347)	Michael Kahoe (Chicago NL, 1907.)	2,400	1,200	720.00
(348)	Michael Kahoe (Washington, 1907.)	2,400	1,200	720.00
(349)	Edward Karger (Edwin) (Boston AL, 1910.)	2,400	1,200	720.00
(350)	Robert Keefe (New York AL, 1906.)	2,400	1,200	720.00
(351)	William Keeler (Brooklyn, 1902, street.)	7,900	4,000	2,375
(352)	William Keeler (New York, AL 1903, street.)	8,350	4,175	2,500
(353)	William Keister (Philadelphia NL, 1903.)	3,600	1,800	1,100
(355)	Joseph J. Kelley (Cincinnati, 1902, street.)	11,000	5,500	3,250
(356)	William Kennedy (Pittsburg, 1903, street.)	3,600	1,800	1,100
(357)	Edward Killian (Detroit, 1904.)	2,400	1,200	720.00
(358)	James Kissinger (Chas. "Rube" Kisinger) (Detroit, 1903.)	3,600	1,800	1,100
(359)	Frank Kitson (Brooklyn, 1902, street.)	3,600	1,800	1,100
(360)	Frank Kitson (Detroit, 1903.)	3,600	1,800	1,100
(361)	Frank Kitson (Washington, 1906.)	2,400	1,200	720.00
(362)	Frank Kitson (New York AL, 1907.)	2,400	1,200	720.00
(363)	Malachi Kittridge (Washington, 1903.)	3,600	1,800	1,100
(365)	John Kleinow (New York AL, 1905, street.)	2,400	1,200	720.00
(366)	John Kleinow (New York AL, 1905, uniform.)	2,400	1,200	720.00
(367)	John Kling (Chicago NL, 1903.)	3,600	1,800	1,100
(368)	F. Otto Knabe (Philadelphia NL, 1910.)	2,400	1,200	720.00
(369)	John Knight (Philadelphia AL, 1905.)	2,400	1,200	720.00
(370)	John Knight (Boston AL, 1907.)	2,400	1,200	720.00
(371)	Bernard Koehler (St. Louis AL, 1906.)	2,400	1,200	720.00
(372)	Edward Konetchy (St. Louis NL, 1907.)	2,400	1,200	720.00
(373)	Harry Krause (Philadelphia AL, 1910.)	2,400	1,200	720.00
(374)	Otto Krueger (Pittsburg, 1903.)	3,600	1,800	1,100
(375)	Otto Krueger (Philadelphia NL, 1905.)	2,400	1,200	720.00
(376)	George LaChance (Boston AL, 1903.)	3,600	1,800	1,100
(377)	Napoleon Lajoie (Cleveland, 1902, street.)	7,900	4,000	2,375
(378)	Napoleon Lajoie (Cleveland, 1902, uniform.)	9,500	4,700	2,800
(379)	Joseph Lake (St. Louis AL, 1910.)	2,400	1,200	720.00
(380)	Frank Laporte (LaPorte) (New York AL, 1906.)	2,400	1,200	720.00
(381)	Louis Laroy (LeRoy)	2,400	1,200	720.00
(382)	William Lauder (New York NL, 1903.)	3,600	1,800	1,100
(383)	Thomas Leach (Pittsburg, 1902.)	3,600	1,800	1,100
(384)	Wyatt Lee (Washington, 1903.)	3,600	1,800	1,100
(385)	Wyatt Lee (Pittsburg, 1904.)	2,400	1,200	720.00
(386)	Samuel Leever (Pittsburg, 1902, street.)	3,600	1,800	1,100
(387)	Samuel Leever (Pittsburg, 1902, uniform.)	2,400	1,200	720.00
(388)	Philip Lewis (Brooklyn, 1908.)	2,400	1,200	720.00
(389)	Vive A. Lindaman (Boston NL, 1906.)	2,400	1,200	720.00
(390)	Paddy Livingstone (Livingston) (Philadelphia AL, 1910.)	2,400	1,200	720.00
(391)	John Lobert (Cincinnati, 1907.)	2,400	1,200	720.00
(392)	Herman Long (Boston NL, 1902.)	3,600	1,800	1,100
(393)	Herman Long (Detroit, 1903.)	3,600	1,800	1,100
(394)	Herman Long (New York AL, 1903.)	3,600	1,800	1,100
(395)	Briscoe Lord (Philadelphia AL, 1905.)	2,400	1,200	720.00
(396)	Harry D. Lord (Chicago AL, 1910.)	2,400	1,200	720.00
(397)	Robert H. Lowe (Detroit, 1907.)	2,400	1,200	720.00
(398)	Harry Lumley (Brooklyn, 1904.)	2,400	1,200	720.00
(399)	Carl Lundgren (Chicago NL, 1903.)	3,600	1,800	1,100
(400)	John Lush	2,400	1,200	720.00
(401)	William L. Lush (Detroit, 1903.)	3,600	1,800	1,100
(402)	William L. Lush (Cleveland, 1904.)	2,400	1,200	720.00
(403)	Michael M. Lynch (Pittsburg, 1906.)	2,400	1,200	720.00
(404)	Michael M. Lynch (New York NL, 1907.)	2,400	1,200	720.00
(405)	Connie Mack (Philadelphia AL, 1902, street.)	7,900	4,000	2,375
(406)	Nick Maddox (Pittsburg, 1909.)	2,400	1,200	720.00
(407)	Sherwood Magee (Philadelphia NL, 1905.)	2,400	1,200	720.00
(408)	George H. Magoon (Chicago AL, 1903.)	3,600	1,800	1,100
(409)	John Malarkey (Boston NL, 1903.)	3,600	1,800	1,100
(410)	William Maloney (Chicago NL, 1905.)	2,400	1,200	720.00
(411)	William Maloney (Brooklyn, 1906.)	2,400	1,200	720.00
(412)	William R. Marshall (New York NL, 1905.)	2,400	1,200	720.00
(413)	William R. Marshall (St. Louis NL, 1906.)	2,400	1,200	720.00
(414)	William R. Marshall (Brooklyn, 1909.)	2,400	1,200	720.00
(415)	Christopher Matthewson (Mathewson) (New York NL, 1902, street.)	21,600	10,800	6,500
(416a)	Christopher Matthewson (Mathewson) (New York NL, 1902, uniform.)	19,400	9,700	5,825
(416b)	Christopher Mathewson (New York, NL, uniform, corrected.)	17,280	8,600	5,200
(417)	James A. McAleer (St. Louis AL, 1906.)	2,400	1,200	720.00
(418)	Louis McAllister (Lewis) (Detroit, 1903.)	3,600	1,800	1,100
(419)	John McCarthy (Cleveland, 1903.)	3,600	1,800	1,100
(420)	John McCarthy (Chicago NL, 1903.)	3,600	1,800	1,100
(421)	John McCarthy (Brooklyn, 1906.)	2,400	1,200	720.00
(422)	John J. McCloskey (St. Louis NL, 1906.)	2,400	1,200	720.00
(423)	Ambrose McConnell (Boston AL, 1910.)	2,400	1,200	720.00
(424)	George W. McQuillan (Philadelphia NL, 1907.)	2,400	1,200	720.00
(425)	Barry McCormick (St. Louis NL, 1903.)	3,600	1,800	1,100
(426)	Barry McCormick (Washington, 1903.)	3,600	1,800	1,100
(427)	Michael McCormick (Brooklyn, 1904.)	2,400	1,200	720.00
(428)	Charles McFarland (St. Louis NL, 1903.)	3,600	1,800	1,100
(429)	Charles McFarland (Pittsburg, 1906.)	2,400	1,200	720.00
(430)	Edward McFarland (Chicago AL, 1902, street.)	3,600	1,800	1,100
(431)	Herm McFarland (Hermas) (New York AL, 1903.)	3,600	1,800	1,100
(432)	John McFetridge (Philadelphia NL, 1903.)	3,600	1,800	1,100
(433)	Dan McGann (New York NL, 1903.)	3,600	1,800	1,100
(434)	Joseph McGinnity (New York NL, 1902, street.)	7,900	4,000	2,375
(435)	Joseph McGinnity (New York NL, 1902, uniform.)	7,900	4,000	2,375
(436)	John J. McGraw (Infielder, New York NL, 1902, street.)	7,900	4,000	2,375
(437)	John J. McGraw (Manager, New York NL, 1902, street.)	9,500	4,700	2,800
(438)	James McGuire (Detroit, 1903.)	2,400	1,200	720.00
(439)	James McGuire (New York AL, 1904.)	2,400	1,200	720.00
(440)	James McGuire (Boston AL, 1907.)	2,400	1,200	720.00
(441)	Harry McIntyre (McIntire) (Brooklyn, 1905.)	2,400	1,200	720.00
(442)	Matty McIntyre (Detroit, 1904, street.)	2,400	1,200	720.00
(443)	John B. McLean (Cincinnati, 1910.)	2,400	1,200	720.00
(444)	John Menefee (Chicago NL, 1903.)	3,600	1,800	1,100
(445)	Fred Merkle (New York NL, 1908.)	2,400	1,200	720.00
(446)	Samuel Mertes (New York NL, 1903.)	3,600	1,800	1,100
(447)	Samuel Mertes (St. Louis NL, 1906.)	2,400	1,200	720.00
(448)	Samuel Mertes (Boston NL, 1907.)	2,400	1,200	720.00
(451)	Clyde Milan (Washington, 1910.)	2,400	1,200	720.00
(452)	John B. Miller (Pittsburg, 1909.)	2,400	1,200	720.00
(453)	Roscoe Miller (Photo actually George Mullin) (New York NL, 1903.)	3,600	1,800	1,100
(454)	Roscoe Miller (Pittsburg, 1903.)	3,600	1,800	1,100
(455)	William Milligan (New York NL, 1904.)	2,400	1,200	720.00
(456)	Frederick Mitchell (Philadelphia NL, 1903, street.)	3,600	1,800	1,100
(457)	Frederick Mitchell (Brooklyn, 1904.)	2,400	1,200	720.00
(458)	M.F. Mitchell (Cincinnati, 1910.)	2,400	1,200	720.00
(461)	Earl Moore (Cleveland, 1903.)	3,600	1,800	1,100
(462)	Earl Moore (New York AL, 1907.)	2,400	1,200	720.00
(463)	Charles P. Moran (Middle initial V.) (Washington, 1904.)	2,400	1,200	720.00
(464)	Charles P. Moran (Middle initial V.) (St. Louis AL, 1904.)	2,400	1,200	720.00
(465)	Patrick J. Moran (Boston NL, 1902, street.)	3,600	1,800	1,100
(466)	Patrick J. Moran (Chicago NL, 1906.)	2,400	1,200	720.00
(467)	Lewis Moren (Philadelphia NL, 1910.)	2,400	1,200	720.00
(468)	Harry R. Morgan (Philadelphia AL, 1910.)	2,400	1,200	720.00
(469)	Eugene Moriarty (George) (New York AL, 1906.)	2,400	1,200	720.00
(470)	John Morrissey (Cincinnati, 1903.)	3,600	1,800	1,100
(471)	Michael Mowery (Cincinnati, 1907.)	2,400	1,200	720.00
(472)	George Mullin (Detroit, 1903.)	3,600	1,800	1,100
(473)	Daniel Murphy (Philadelphia AL, 1902, street.)	3,600	1,800	1,100
(474)	John J. Murray (St. Louis NL, 1907.)	2,400	1,200	720.00
(475)	William Murray (Boston NL, 1907.)	2,400	1,200	720.00
(477)	Joseph Nealon (Jim) (Pittsburg, 1906.)	2,400	1,200	720.00
(478)	Daniel Needham (Thomas) (Boston NL, 1904.)	2,400	1,200	720.00
(479)	Eustace J. Newton (New York AL, 1906.)	2,400	1,200	720.00
(481)	Simon Nicholls (Philadelphia AL, 1907.)	2,400	1,200	720.00
(482)	Harry Niles (St. Louis AL, 1906.)	2,400	1,200	720.00
(483)	George Nill (Washington, 1906.)	2,400	1,200	720.00
(484)	George Nill (Cleveland, 1907.)	2,400	1,200	720.00
(485)	Pete Noonan (St. Louis AL, 1906.)	2,400	1,200	720.00
(486)	John O'Brien (Boston AL, 1903.)	3,600	1,800	1,100
(487)	Peter O'Brien (St. Louis AL, 1906.)	2,400	1,200	720.00
(488)	Peter O'Brien (Cleveland, 1907.)	2,400	1,200	720.00
(489)	Peter O'Brien (Washington, 1907.)	2,400	1,200	720.00
(490)	John O'Connor (Pittsburg, 1902.)	3,600	1,800	1,100
(491)	John O'Connor (New York AL, 1903.)	3,600	1,800	1,100
(492)	John O'Connor (St. Louis AL, 1904.)	2,400	1,200	720.00
(493)	Reuben Oldring (Philadelphia AL, 1906.)	2,400	1,200	720.00
(494)	Charles O'Leary (Detroit, 1904.)	2,400	1,200	720.00
(495)	John J. O'Neil (O'Neill) (St. Louis NL, 1903.)	3,000	1,500	900.00
(496)	John J. O'Neil (O'Neill) (Chicago NL, 1904.)	2,400	1,200	720.00
(497)	John O'Neil (O'Neill) (Boston NL, 1906.)	2,400	1,200	720.00
(498)	Michael J. O'Neil (O'Neill) (St. Louis NL, 1903.)	3,600	1,800	1,100
(499)	Michael J. O'Neil (O'Neill)(Brooklyn, 1906.)	2,400	1,200	720.00
(500)	Albert Orth (Washington, 1903.)	3,000	1,500	900.00
(501)	Albert Orth (New York AL, 1904.)	2,400	1,200	720.00
(502)	Orville Overall (Orval) (Chicago NL, 1906.)	2,400	1,200	720.00
(503)	Frank Owen (Chicago AL, 1903.)	3,600	1,800	1,100
(504)	Richard Padden (St. Louis AL, 1903.)	3,600	1,800	1,100
(505)	Frederick Parent (Boston AL, 1902.)	3,600	1,800	1,100
(506)	Frederick Parent (Chicago AL, 1908.)	2,400	1,200	720.00
(508)	George Paskert (Cincinnati, 1910.)	2,400	1,200	720.00
(509)	James Pastorious (Brooklyn, 1906.)	2,400	1,200	720.00
(510)	Case Patten (Washington, 1903.)	3,600	1,800	1,100
(511)	Roy Patterson (Chicago AL, 1903.)	3,600	1,800	1,100
(512)	Frederick Payne (Detroit, 1906.)	2,400	1,200	720.00
(513)	Henry Peitz (Cincinnati, 1904.)	2,400	1,200	720.00
(514)	Henry Peitz (Pittsburg, 1905.)	2,400	1,200	720.00
(515)	Barney Pelty (St. Louis AL, 1904.)	2,400	1,200	720.00

No.	Name (team, year)			
(516)	Frank Pfeiffer ("Big Jeff" Pfeffer)(Chicago NL, 1905.)	2,400	1,200	720.00
(517)	Frank Pfeiffer ("Big Jeff" Pfeffer)(Boston NL, 1906.)	2,400	1,200	720.00
(518)	John Pfiester (Chicago NL, 1907.)	2,400	1,200	720.00
(519)	Edward Phelps (Pittsburg, 1903.)	3,000	1,500	900.00
(520)	Edward Phelps (Cincinnati, 1905.)	2,400	1,200	720.00
(521)	Charles Phillippe (Pittsburg, 1903.)	3,600	1,800	1,100
(522)	William Phillips (Cincinnati, 1902, street.)	3,600	1,800	1,100
(523)	Wiley Piatt (Boston NL, 1903.)	3,600	1,800	1,100
(524)	Oliver Pickering (Philadelphia AL, 1903.)	3,600	1,800	1,100
(525)	Oliver Pickering (St. Louis AL, 1906.)	2,400	1,200	720.00
(526)	Charles Pittinger (Boston NL, 1903.)	3,600	1,800	1,100
(527)	Charles Pittinger (Philadelphia NL, 1905.)	2,400	1,200	720.00
(528)	Edward S. Plank (Philadelphia AL, 1902 street.)	12,250	6,125	3,675
(529)	Edward S. Plank (Philadelphia AL, 1902, uniform.)	12,250	6,125	3,675
(530)	Edward Poole (Cincinnati, 1903.)	3,600	1,800	1,100
(531)	Edward Poole (Brooklyn, 1904.)	2,400	1,200	720.00
(532)	John Powell (St. Louis AL, 1903.)	3,600	1,800	1,100
(533)	John Powell (New York AL, 1904.)	2,400	1,200	720.00
(534)	Maurice R. Powers (Michael) (Philadelphia AL, 1902, street.)	3,600	1,800	1,100
(535)	William Purtell (Boston AL, 1910.)	2,400	1,200	720.00
(536)	Ambrose Puttmann (New York AL, 1905.)	2,400	1,200	720.00
(539)	Thomas Raub (Chicago NL, 1903.)	3,600	1,800	1,100
(540)	Frederick Raymer (Boston NL, 1904.)	2,400	1,200	720.00
(541)	William Reidy (Brooklyn, 1903.)	3,600	1,800	1,100
(542)	Ed Reulbach (Chicago NL, 1907.)	2,400	1,200	720.00
(543)	R.B. Rhoades (Rhoads) (Cleveland, 1903.)	3,600	1,800	1,100
(544)	Lewis Richie (Chicago NL, 1910.)	2,400	1,200	720.00
(545)	Branch Rickey (New York AL, 1907.)	6,500	3,250	1,950
(546)	Claude Ritchey (Pittsburg, 1902, street.)	3,600	1,800	1,100
(547)	Claude Ritchey (Boston NL, 1907.)	2,400	1,200	720.00
(548)	Louis Ritter (Lewis) (Brooklyn, 1903.)	3,600	1,800	1,100
(549)	Clyde Robinson (Detroit, 1904.)	2,400	1,200	720.00
(550)	George Rohe (Chicago AL, 1906.)	2,400	1,200	720.00
(553)	Claude Rossman (Cleveland, 1906.)	2,400	1,200	720.00
(554)	Claude Rossman (Detroit, 1907.)	2,400	1,200	720.00
(555)	Frank Roth (Philadelphia NL, 1903.)	3,600	1,800	1,100
(556)	Frank Roth (St. Louis AL, 1905.)	2,400	1,200	720.00
(557)	Frank Roth (Chicago AL, 1906.)	2,400	1,200	720.00
(558)	John A. Rowan (Cincinnati, 1910.)	2,400	1,200	720.00
(559)	James Ryan (Washington, 1902, street.)	3,600	1,800	1,100
(562)	Harry Sallee (St. Louis NL, 1910.)	2,400	1,200	720.00
(563)	Herman Schaefer (Detroit, 1907.)	2,400	1,200	720.00
(564)	George Schlei (Cincinnati, 1906.)	2,400	1,200	720.00
(565)	Charles Schmidt (Detroit, 1906.)	2,400	1,200	720.00
(566)	Harry S. Schmidt (Henry M.) (Brooklyn, 1903.)	3,600	1,800	1,100
(567)	Osee F. Schreckengost (Ossee) (Philadelphia AL, 1902, street.)	3,600	1,800	1,100
(568)	Osee F. Schreckengost (Ossee) (Philadelphia AL, 1902, uniform.)	3,600	1,800	1,100
(569)	Frank Schulte (Chicago NL, 1905.)	2,400	1,200	720.00
(570)	Al Schweitzer (St. Louis AL, 1910.)	2,400	1,200	720.00
(571)	James Sebring (Pittsburg, 1903.)	3,600	1,800	1,100
(572)	James Sebring (Cincinnati, 1904.)	2,400	1,200	720.00
(573)	James Sebring (Chicago NL, 1905.)	2,400	1,200	720.00
(575)	Albert Selbach (Washington, 1903.)	3,600	1,800	1,100
(576)	Albert Selbach (Boston AL, 1904.)	2,400	1,200	720.00
(577)	Ralph O. "Socks" Seybold (Philadelphia AL, 1902, street.)	3,600	1,800	1,100
(578)	J. Bentley Seymour (Cincinnati, 1903.)	3,600	1,800	1,100
(579)	J. Bentley Seymour (New York NL, 1906.)	2,400	1,200	720.00
(580)	Arthur Shafer (New York NL, 1910.)	2,400	1,200	720.00
(581)	W.P. Shannon (St. Louis NL, 1904.)	2,400	1,200	720.00
(582)	W.P. Shannon (New York NL, 1906.)	2,400	1,200	720.00
(583)	Daniel Shay (St. Louis NL, 1904.)	2,400	1,200	720.00
(586)	David Shean (Boston NL, 1910.)	2,400	1,200	720.00
(587)	James Sheckard (Brooklyn, 1902, street.)	3,600	1,800	1,100
(588)	James Sheckard (Chicago NL, 1906.)	2,400	1,200	720.00
(589)	Edward Siever (Detroit, 1903.)	3,600	1,800	1,100
(590)	Edward Siever (St. Louis AL, 1903.)	3,600	1,800	1,100
(591)	James Slagle (Chicago NL, 1903.)	3,600	1,800	1,100
(592)	John Slattery (Chicago AL, 1903.)	3,600	1,800	1,100
(593)	Alexander Smith ("Broadway Aleck")(Boston AL, 1903.)	3,600	1,800	1,100
(594)	Alexander Smith ("Broadway Aleck")(Chicago NL, 1904.)	2,400	1,200	720.00
(595)	Alexander Smith ("Broadway Aleck") (New York NL, 1906.)	2,400	1,200	720.00
(596)	Charles Smith (Boston AL, 1910.)	2,400	1,200	720.00
(597)	Edward Smith (St. Louis AL, 1906.)	2,400	1,200	720.00
(598)	Frank Smith (Chicago AL, 1904.)	2,400	1,200	720.00
(599)	Harry Smith (Pittsburg, 1902, street.)	3,600	1,800	1,100
(600)	Heinie Smith (Detroit, 1903, street.)	3,600	1,800	1,100
(602)	Homer Smoot (St. Louis NL, 1903.)	3,600	1,800	1,100
(603)	Homer Smoot (Cincinnati, 1906.)	2,400	1,200	720.00
(604)	Frank Sparks (T. Frank "Tully") (Philadelphia, NL, 1903 .)	3,600	1,800	1,100
(605)	Charles ("Chic") Stahl (Boston AL, 1902.)	4,000	1,950	1,200
(606)	Jacob G. Stahl (Washington, 1904.)	2,400	1,200	720.00
(607)	Jacob G. Stahl (Washington)	2,400	1,200	720.00
(609)	J.B. Stanley (Boston NL, 1903.)	3,600	1,800	1,100
(610)	J.B. Stanley (Washington, 1905.)	2,400	1,200	720.00
(611)	Harry Steinfeldt (Cincinnati, 1902, street.)	3,600	1,800	1,100
(612)	Harry Steinfeldt (Chicago NL, 1905.)	2,400	1,200	720.00
(615)	James Stephens (St. Louis AL, 1910.)	2,400	1,200	720.00
(616)	George Stone (St. Louis AL, 1905.)	2,400	1,200	720.00
(617)	George Stovall (Cleveland, 1904.)	2,400	1,200	720.00
(618)	Jesse Stovall (Detroit, 1904.)	2,400	1,200	720.00
(619)	Samuel Strang (Brooklyn, 1903.)	3,600	1,800	1,100
(620)	Samuel Strang (New York NL, 1905.)	2,400	1,200	720.00
(621)	Elmer Stricklett (Brooklyn, 1906.)	2,400	1,200	720.00
(622)	Willie Sudhoff (St. Louis AL, 1903.)	3,600	1,800	1,100
(623)	Willie Sudhoff (Washington, 1906.)	2,400	1,200	720.00
(624)	Joseph Sugden (St. Louis AL, 1903.)	3,600	1,800	1,100
(625)	George Suggs (Cincinnati, 1910.)	2,400	1,200	720.00
(628)	William D. Sullivan (Middle initial J.)(Chicago AL, 1902.)	3,600	1,800	1,100
(629)	Edgar Summers (Detroit, 1909.)	2,400	1,200	720.00
(630)	William J. Sweeney (Boston NL, 1910.)	2,400	1,200	720.00
(632)	Jesse Tannehill (New York AL, 1903.)	3,600	1,800	1,100
(633)	Jesse Tannehill (Boston AL, 1904.)	2,400	1,200	720.00
(634)	Lee Tannehill (Chicago AL, 1903.)	3,600	1,800	1,100
(636)	John Taylor (Chicago NL, 1902.)	3,600	1,800	1,100
(637)	John Taylor (St. Louis NL, 1904.)	2,400	1,200	720.00
(638)	Luther H. Taylor (New York NL, 1903.)	7,900	4,000	2,375
(639)	Fred Tenney (Boston NL, 1903.)	3,600	1,800	1,100
(640)	Ira Thomas (New York AL, 1906.)	2,400	1,200	720.00
(641)	Roy Thomas (Philadelphia NL, 1903.)	3,600	1,800	1,100
(642)	John Thoney (Cleveland, 1903.)	3,600	1,800	1,100
(643)	John Thoney (Washington, 1904.)	2,400	1,200	720.00
(644)	John Thoney (New York AL, 1904.)	2,400	1,200	720.00
(645)	Joseph B. Tinker (Chicago NL, 1903.)	6,600	3,300	1,980
(646)	John Townsend (Washington, 1903.)	3,600	1,800	1,100
(647)	John Townsend (Cleveland, 1906.)	2,400	1,200	720.00
(648)	Terrence Turner (Cleveland, 1904.)	2,400	1,200	720.00
(650)	Robert Unglaub (Boston AL, 1905.)	2,400	1,200	720.00
(652)	George Van Haltren (New York NL, 1902, street.)	3,250	1,625	975.00
(653)	George Van Haltren (New York NL, 1902, uniform.)	3,250	1,625	975.00
(654)	Fred Veil (Pittsburg, 1903.)	3,600	1,800	1,100
(655)	Ernest Vinson (Cleveland, 1905.)	2,400	1,200	720.00
(656)	Ernest Vinson (Chicago AL, 1905.)	2,400	1,200	720.00
(660)	George Edward "Rube" Waddell (Philadelphia AL, 1902, street.)	7,900	4,000	2,375
(661)	George Edward Waddell (St. Louis AL, 1908.)	6,500	3,250	1,950
(663)	Charles Wagner (Boston AL, 1910.)	2,400	1,200	720.00
(664)	John ("Hans") Wagner (Pittsburg, 1902, street.)	19,400	9,700	5,825
(665)	John ("Hans") Wagner (Pittsburg, 1905, uniform.)	22,500	11,250	6,750
(666)	Robert Wallace (St. Louis AL, 1902.)	7,900	4,000	2,375
(668)	Edward A. Walsh (Chicago AL, 1904.)	6,500	3,250	1,950
(670)	John Warner (New York NL, 1903.)	3,600	1,800	1,100
(671)	John Warner (St. Louis NL, 1905.)	2,400	1,200	720.00
(672)	John Warner (Detroit, 1905.)	2,400	1,200	720.00
(673)	John Warner (Washington, 1906.)	2,400	1,200	720.00
(674)	Arthur Weaver (Pittsburg, 1903.)	3,600	1,800	1,100
(675)	Arthur Weaver (St. Louis AL, 1905.)	2,400	1,200	720.00
(676)	Jacob Weimer (Chicago NL, 1903.)	3,600	1,800	1,100
(677)	Jacob Weimer (Cincinnati, 1906.)	2,400	1,200	720.00
(678)	G. Harry White (G. Harris "Doc") (Chicago AL, 1903.)	3,600	1,800	1,100
(679)	Robert Wicker (Chicago NL, 1903.)	3,600	1,800	1,100
(680)	Robert Wicker (Cincinnati, 1906.)	2,400	1,200	720.00
(681)	Fredrick Wilhelm (Irvin "Kaiser") (Pittsburg, 1903.)	3,600	1,800	1,100
(682)	Fredrick Wilhelm (Irvin "Kaiser")(Boston NL, 1904.)	2,400	1,200	720.00
(683)	Edgar Willett (Detroit, 1907.)	2,400	1,200	720.00
(684)	James Williams (Baltimore, 1902, street.)	3,600	1,800	1,100
(685)	James Williams (New York AL, 1903, street.)	3,600	1,800	1,100
(686)	James Williams (New York AL, 1903, uniform.)	3,600	1,800	1,100
(687)	Otto G. Williams (Chicago NL, 1904.)	2,400	1,200	720.00
(688)	Otto G. Williams (Philadelphia AL, 1905.)	2,400	1,200	720.00
(689)	Otto G. Williams (Washington, 1906.)	2,400	1,200	720.00
(692)	Victor J. Willis (Boston NL, 1903.)	7,900	4,000	2,375
(693)	Victor J. Willis (Pittsburg, 1906.)	6,500	2,350	1,950
(694)	Howard P. Wilson (Philadelphia AL, 1902, street.)	3,600	1,800	1,100
(695)	Howard P. Wilson (Washington, 1903.)	3,600	1,800	1,100
(696)	Howard P. Wilson (Cleveland, 1906.)	2,400	1,200	720.00
(698)	J. Owen Wilson (Pittsburg, 1910.)	2,400	1,200	720.00
(699)	George Wiltse (New York NL, 1904.)	2,400	1,200	720.00
(700)	Louis Wiltse (Lewis) (Baltimore, 1902.)	3,600	1,800	1,100
(701)	Louis Wiltse (Lewis) (New York AL, 1903.)	3,600	1,800	1,100
(702)	George Winters (Winter) (Boston AL, 1902, street.)	3,000	1,500	900.00
(705)	William Wolfe (Wilbert) (Washington, 1904.)	2,400	1,200	720.00
(706)	Harry Wolverton (Philadelphia NL, 1902, street.)	3,600	1,800	1,100
(707)	Harry Wolverton (Boston NL, 1905.)	2,400	1,200	720.00
(708)	Robert Wood (Detroit, 1904.)	2,400	1,200	720.00
(710)	Eugene Wright (Clarence Eugene)(Cleveland, 1903.)	3,600	1,800	1,100
(711)	Eugene Wright (Clarence Eugene) (St. Louis AL, 1903.)	3,600	1,800	1,100
(712)	Joseph Yeager (Detroit, 1902, street.)	3,600	1,800	1,100
(713)	Joseph Yeager (New York AL, 1905.)	2,400	1,200	720.00
(714)	Joseph Yeager (St. Louis AL, 1907.)	2,400	1,200	720.00
(715)	Denton ("Cy") Young (Boston AL, 1903.)	22,250	11,125	6,675
(716)	Irving Young (Boston NL, 1905.)	2,400	1,200	720.00
(717)	David Zearfoss (St. Louis NL, 1904.)	2,400	1,200	720.00
(718)	Charles Zimmer (Pittsburg, 1902.)	3,600	1,800	1,100
(719)	Charles Zimmer (Philadelphia NL, 1903.)	3,600	1,800	1,100
(720)	H. Zimmerman (Chicago NL, 1910.)	2,400	1,200	720.00

TRAP SHOOTERS

No.	Name			
(T1)	Neas Apgar	950.00	500.00	300.00
(T2)	Chas. W. Budd	950.00	500.00	300.00
(T3)	W.R. Crosby	950.00	500.00	300.00
(T4)	J.A.R. Elliott	950.00	500.00	300.00
(T5)	J.S. Fanning	950.00	500.00	300.00
(T6)	Fred Gilbert	950.00	500.00	300.00
(T7)	Rolla O. Heikes	950.00	500.00	300.00

(T8)	H.C. Hirschy	950.00	500.00	300.00
(T9)	Tom A. Marshall	950.00	500.00	300.00
(T10)	Harvey McMurchy	950.00	500.00	300.00
(T11)	Ralph Trimble	950.00	500.00	300.00

1902 Sporting Life Team Composites (W601)

Printed on heavy 13" x 14" paper and featuring a composite of player photos arranged around that of the manager and a notice of league championship status, these prints were offered to readers of the weekly sports paper for six cents in postage stamps or 50 cents per dozen. The art was often found on the covers of "Sporting Life." While the prints were issued in 1902, they specify the teams as champions "for 1903." The Buck Weaver shown on the Butte composite is not the future Black Sox shortstop.

		NM	EX	VG
Complete Set:		4,500	2,200	1,350
Common Team:		300.00	150.00	90.00
(1)	Philadelphia, American League	500.00	250.00	150.00
(2)	Pittsburg, National League	500.00	250.00	150.00
(3)	Albany, New York State League	300.00	150.00	90.00
(4)	Butte, Pacific Northwest League	400.00	200.00	120.00
(5)	Indianapolis, American Association	400.00	200.00	120.00
(6)	Kansas City, Western League	400.00	200.00	120.00
(7)	Manchester, New England League	300.00	150.00	90.00
(8)	Nashville, Southern League	350.00	175.00	105.00
(9)	New Haven, Connecticut League	300.00	150.00	90.00
(10)	Rockford, Illinois-Indiana-Iowa League	300.00	150.00	90.00
(11)	Toronto, Eastern League	400.00	200.00	120.00

1903 Sporting Life Team Composites (W601)

Portraits of the individual players, usually identified by name and position, surround the manager's portrait in this series of team composites sold by Sporting Life newspaper. The 1903 series is the first in which all major league team composites were available. The 13" x 14" pictures are printed on heavy enamel paper and were sold for six cents in postage stamps, 50 cents per dozen. In some years bound portfolio complete sets were also offered, as were some of the more popular minor league teams. Notations of league and World Championships were incorporated into the design where appropriate. While issued in 1903, the pictures of league championship teams carry the notation "For 1904."

		NM	EX	VG
Complete Set (25):		5,550	2,700	1,650
Common (Major League) Team:		400.00	200.00	120.00
(1)	Boston, National League	400.00	200.00	120.00
(2)	Brooklyn, National League	400.00	200.00	120.00
(3)	Chicago, National League	600.00	300.00	180.00
(4)	Cincinnati, National League	400.00	200.00	120.00
(5)	New York, National League	500.00	250.00	150.00
(6)	Philadelphia, National League	400.00	200.00	120.00
(7)	Pittsburgh, National League	500.00	250.00	150.00
(8)	St. Louis, National League	400.00	200.00	120.00
(9)	Boston, American League	450.00	225.00	135.00
(10)	Chicago, American League	400.00	200.00	120.00
(11)	Cleveland, American League	400.00	200.00	120.00
(12)	Detroit, American League	400.00	200.00	120.00
(13)	New York, American League	450.00	225.00	135.00
(14)	Philadelphia, American League	450.00	225.00	135.00
(15)	St. Louis, American League	400.00	200.00	120.00
(16)	Washington, American League	400.00	200.00	120.00
(17)	Ft. Wayne, Central League	250.00	125.00	75.00
(18)	Holyoke, Connecticut League	250.00	125.00	75.00
(19)	Jersey City, Eastern League	300.00	150.00	90.00
(20)	Los Angeles, Pacific Coast League	300.00	150.00	90.00
(21)	Lowell, New England League	250.00	125.00	75.00
(22)	Memphis, Southern League	250.00	125.00	75.00
(23)	Schenectady, New York State League	250.00	125.00	75.00
(24)	Sedalia, Missouri Valley League	250.00	125.00	75.00
(25)	St. Paul, American Association	300.00	150.00	90.00

1904 Sporting Life Team Composites (W601)

Portraits of the individual players, usually identified by name and position, surround the manager's portrait in this series of team composites sold by Sporting Life newspaper. The 13" x 14" pictures are printed on heavy enamel paper and were sold for a dime apiece postpaid. In some years bound portfolio complete sets were also offered, as were some of the more popular minor league teams. Notations of league and World Championships were incorporated into the design where appropriate.

		NM	EX	VG
Complete Set (24):		5,550	2,700	1,650
Common (Major League) Team:		400.00	200.00	120.00
(1)	Boston, National League	400.00	200.00	120.00
(2)	Brooklyn, National League	400.00	200.00	120.00
(3)	Chicago, National League	600.00	300.00	180.00
(4)	Cincinnati, National League	400.00	200.00	120.00
(5)	New York, National League	500.00	250.00	150.00
(6)	Philadelphia, National League	400.00	200.00	120.00
(7)	Pittsburgh, National League	550.00	275.00	165.00
(8)	St. Louis, National League	400.00	200.00	120.00
(9)	Boston, American League	450.00	225.00	135.00
(10)	Chicago, American League	400.00	200.00	120.00
(11)	Cleveland, American League	400.00	200.00	120.00
(12)	Detroit, American League	400.00	200.00	120.00
(13)	New York, American League	450.00	225.00	135.00
(14)	Philadelphia, American League	450.00	225.00	135.00
(15)	St. Louis, American League	400.00	200.00	120.00
(16)	Washington, American League	400.00	200.00	120.00
(17)	Buffalo, Eastern League	300.00	150.00	90.00
(18)	Ft. Wayne, Central League	200.00	100.00	60.00
(19)	Haverhill, New England League	200.00	100.00	60.00
(20)	Macon, South Atlantic League	200.00	100.00	60.00
(21)	Memphis, Southern League	200.00	100.00	60.00
(22)	Springfield, Indiana-Illinois-Iowa League	200.00	100.00	60.00
(23)	St. Paul, American Association	250.00	125.00	75.00
(24)	Syracuse, New York League (1903 Indiana-Illinois-Iowa League Champs)	200.00	100.00	60.00

1905 Sporting Life Team Composites (W601)

Portraits of the individual players, usually identified by name and position, surround the manager's portrait in this series of team composites sold by Sporting Life newspaper. The 13" x 14" pictures are printed on heavy enamel paper and were sold for a dime apiece postpaid. In some years bound portfolio complete sets were also offered, as were some of the more popular minor league teams. Notations of league and World Championships were incorporated into the design where appropriate.

		NM	EX	VG
Complete Set (23):		5,500	2,700	1,650
Common (Major League) Team:		400.00	200.00	120.00
(1)	Boston, National League	400.00	200.00	120.00
(2)	Brooklyn, National League	400.00	200.00	120.00
(3)	Chicago, National League	600.00	300.00	180.00
(4)	Cincinnati, National League	400.00	200.00	120.00
(5)	New York, National League	450.00	225.00	135.00
(6)	Philadelphia, National League	400.00	200.00	120.00
(7)	Pittsburgh, National League	750.00	375.00	225.00
(8)	St. Louis, National League	400.00	200.00	120.00
(9)	Boston, American League	400.00	200.00	120.00
(10)	Chicago, American League	400.00	200.00	120.00
(11)	Cleveland, American League	400.00	200.00	120.00
(12)	Detroit, American League	400.00	200.00	120.00
(13)	New York, American League	600.00	300.00	180.00
(14)	Philadelphia, American League	600.00	300.00	180.00
(15)	St. Louis, American League	400.00	200.00	120.00

(16)	Washington, American League	400.00	200.00	120.00
(17)	A., J. & G., New York League	200.00	100.00	60.00
(18)	Columbus, American Association	250.00	125.00	75.00
(19)	Concord, New England League	200.00	100.00	60.00
(20)	Des Moines, Western League	200.00	100.00	60.00
(21)	Macon, South Atlantic League	200.00	100.00	60.00
(22)	New Orleans, Southern League	250.00	125.00	75.00
(23)	Providence, Eastern League	250.00	125.00	75.00

1906-07 Sporting Life Team Composite Postcards

A miniature version of the Sporting Life's team composite lithographs was utilized to create a postcard set. In 3-5/8" x 5-7/16" format, the postcards have a composite of player portraits surrounding that of the manager, with a wide white right margin. Backs have standard postcard indicia. Some cards have been found with backs containing an ad offering either league's set for 10 cents in stamps.

		NM	EX	VG
Complete Set (16):		13,500	6,750	4,150
Common Team:		675.00	335.00	200.00
(1)	Boston, National League	675.00	335.00	200.00
(2)	Brooklyn, National League	900.00	450.00	270.00
(3)	Chicago, National League	900.00	450.00	270.00
(4)	Cincinnati, National League	850.00	425.00	255.00
(5)	New York, National League	850.00	425.00	255.00
(6)	Philadelphia, National League	675.00	335.00	200.00
(7)	Pittsburg, National League	1,000	500.00	300.00
(8)	St. Louis, National League	675.00	335.00	200.00
(9)	Boston, American League	700.00	350.00	210.00
(10)	Chicago, American League	750.00	375.00	225.00
(11)	Cleveland, American League	1,100	550.00	330.00
(12)	Detroit, American League	1,200	600.00	360.00
(13)	New York, American League	1,100	550.00	330.00
(14)	Philadelphia, American League	900.00	450.00	270.00
(15)	St. Louis, American League	900.00	450.00	270.00
(16)	Washington, American League	800.00	400.00	240.00

1906 Sporting Life Team Composites (W601)

Originally sold as a string-bound "Premier Art Portfolio" containing 24 major and minor league team composite pictures, single pieces from this premium issue are not uncommonly found as they were later offered individually for 10 cents apiece. The individual pieces measure 13" x 14" and are printed in black-and-white on heavy enameled paper. Individual player pictures are arranged around a baseball containing the manager's picture. Each player is identified beneath his photo by name and position. By 1906 the year printed on the pictures corresponds to the year of issue.

	NM	EX	VG
Complete Set (24):	12,000	6,000	3,500
Common Major League Team:	550.00	275.00	165.00
Common Minor League Team:	300.00	150.00	90.00
(1) Boston, National League	750.00	375.00	225.00
(2) Brooklyn, National League	550.00	275.00	165.00
(3) Chicago, National League	800.00	400.00	240.00
(4) Cincinnati, National League	550.00	275.00	165.00
(5) New York, National League	650.00	325.00	195.00
(6) Philadelphia, National League	675.00	335.00	200.00
(7) Pittsburg, National League	650.00	325.00	195.00
(8) St. Louis, National League	550.00	275.00	165.00
(9) Boston, American League	800.00	400.00	240.00
(10) Chicago, American League	650.00	325.00	195.00
(11) Cleveland, American League	1,200	600.00	360.00
(12) Detroit, American League	1,200	600.00	360.00
(13) New York, American League	800.00	400.00	240.00
(14) Philadelphia, American League	800.00	400.00	240.00
(15) St. Louis, American League	550.00	275.00	165.00
(16) Washington, American League	550.00	275.00	165.00
(17) National League president, managers	600.00	300.00	180.00
(18) American League president, managers	600.00	300.00	180.00
(19) Birmingham, Southern League	300.00	150.00	90.00
(20) Buffalo, Eastern League	300.00	150.00	90.00
(21) Columbus, American Assoc.	300.00	150.00	90.00
(22) Grand Rapids, Central League	300.00	150.00	90.00
(23) Norwich, Connecticut League	300.00	150.00	90.00
(24) Scranton, New York League	300.00	150.00	90.00

1907 Sporting Life Team Composites (W601)

Portraits of the individual players, usually identified by name and position, surround the manager's portrait in this series of team composites sold by Sporting Life newspaper. The 13" x 14" pictures are printed on heavy enamel paper and were sold for a dime apiece postpaid. In some years bound portfolio complete sets were also offered, as were some of the more popular minor league teams. Notations of league and World Championships were incorporated into the design where appropriate.

	NM	EX	VG
Complete Set (23):	5,500	2,700	1,600
Common (Major League) Team:	400.00	200.00	120.00
(1) Boston, National League	400.00	200.00	120.00
(2) Brooklyn, National League	400.00	200.00	120.00
(3) Chicago, National League	500.00	250.00	150.00
(4) Cincinnati, National League	400.00	200.00	120.00
(5) New York, National League	500.00	250.00	150.00
(6) Philadelphia, National League	400.00	200.00	120.00
(7) Pittsburgh, National League	450.00	225.00	135.00
(8) St. Louis, National League	400.00	200.00	120.00
(9) Boston, American League	400.00	200.00	120.00
(10) Chicago, American League	400.00	200.00	120.00
(11) Cleveland, American League	400.00	200.00	120.00
(12) Detroit, American League	600.00	300.00	180.00
(13) New York, American League	450.00	225.00	135.00
(14) Philadelphia, American League	400.00	200.00	120.00
(15) St. Louis, American League	400.00	200.00	120.00
(16) Washington, American League	500.00	250.00	150.00
(17) Toronto, Eastern League	300.00	150.00	90.00
(18) Columbus, American Assoc.	300.00	150.00	90.00
(19) Williamsport, Tri-State League	200.00	100.00	60.00
(20) Albany, New York League	200.00	100.00	60.00
(21) Atlanta, Southern League	200.00	100.00	60.00
(22) Holyoke, Connecticut League	200.00	100.00	60.00
(23) Norfolk, Virginia League	200.00	100.00	60.00

1908 Sporting Life Team Composites (W601)

Portraits of the individual players, usually identified by name and position, surround the manager's portrait in this series of team composites sold by Sporting Life newspaper. The 13" x 14" pictures are printed on heavy enamel paper and were sold for a dime apiece postpaid. In some years bound portfolio complete sets were also offered, as were some of the more popular minor league teams. Notations of league and World Championships were incorporated into the design where appropriate.

	NM	EX	VG
Complete Set (16):	4,500	2,250	1,350
Common Team:	400.00	200.00	120.00
(1) Boston, National League	400.00	200.00	120.00
(2) Brooklyn, National League	400.00	200.00	120.00
(3) Chicago, National League	500.00	250.00	150.00
(4) Cincinnati, National League	400.00	200.00	120.00
(5) New York, National League	425.00	210.00	125.00
(6) Philadelphia, National League	400.00	200.00	120.00
(7) Pittsburgh, National League	450.00	225.00	135.00

(8) St. Louis, National League	400.00	200.00	120.00
(9) Boston, American League	400.00	200.00	120.00
(10) Chicago, American League	400.00	200.00	120.00
(11) Cleveland, American League	400.00	200.00	120.00
(12) Detroit, American League	600.00	300.00	180.00
(13) New York, American League	450.00	225.00	135.00
(14) Philadelphia, American League	400.00	200.00	120.00
(15) St. Louis, American League	400.00	200.00	120.00
(16) Washington, American League	450.00	225.00	135.00

1909 Sporting Life Team Composites (W601)

Portraits of the individual players, usually identified by name and position, surround the manager's portrait in this series of team composites sold by Sporting Life newspaper. The 13" x 14" pictures are printed on heavy enamel paper and were sold for a dime apiece postpaid. In some years bound portfolio complete sets were also offered, as were some of the more popular minor league teams. Notations of league and World Championships were incorporated into the design where appropriate.

	NM	EX	VG
Complete Set (16):	6,500	3,250	1,850
Common Team:	600.00	300.00	180.00
(1) Boston, National League	600.00	300.00	180.00
(2) Brooklyn, National League	600.00	300.00	180.00
(3) Chicago, National League	750.00	375.00	225.00
(4) Cincinnati, National League	600.00	300.00	180.00
(5) New York, National League	675.00	335.00	200.00
(6) Philadelphia, National League	600.00	300.00	180.00
(7) Pittsburgh, National League	1,125	560.00	335.00
(8) St. Louis, National League	1,000	500.00	300.00
(9) Boston, American League	600.00	300.00	180.00
(10) Chicago, American League	600.00	300.00	180.00
(11) Cleveland, American League	600.00	300.00	180.00
(12) Detroit, American League	900.00	450.00	270.00
(13) New York, American League	675.00	335.00	200.00
(14) Philadelphia, American League	600.00	300.00	180.00
(15) St. Louis, American League	600.00	300.00	180.00
(16) Washington, American League	675.00	335.00	200.00

1910 Sporting Life Team Composites (W601)

After several years of issuing composite team photos for all major league teams (and some minor league teams), Sporting Life in 1910 began issuing them only for the league and World's Champions. Like the others, they are 13" x 14", printed on heavy enamel paper with individual player portrait photos surrounding the manager at center.

	NM	EX	VG
Complete Set (2):	1,200	600.00	350.00
Common Team:	300.00	150.00	90.00
(1) Chicago Cubs (N.L. Champs)	450.00	225.00	135.00
(2) Philadelphia Athletics (World's Champions)	750.00	375.00	225.00

1910-11 Sporting Life (M116)

This set of nominally 1-1/2" x 2-5/8" (individual card sizes vary even moreso than typically found on early 20th Century cards, notably with the "high numbers" often found somewhat larger) cards was offered to subscribers to "Sporting Life," a major competitor of "The Sporting News" in the early part of the century. The cards were issued in 24 series of 12 cards each, sold by mail for four cents per series. Card fronts feature color-tinted black-and-white portrait photos with the name and team printed below. Backs have various ads for the weekly paper. The last three 24-card series are scarcer than the earlier cards. These 72 cards have "Over 300 subjects" printed on back. Val-

 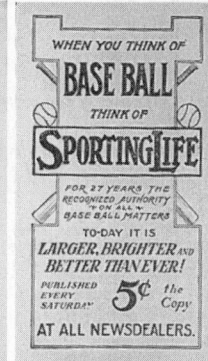

Hans Wagner, Pitts. Nationals

ues in this checklist are adjusted according to that scarcity. The scarce blue-background cards appear to have been a second printing of the first two 12-card series which no doubt sold out quickly in the original pastel-background version due to the popularity of the players included. The 12 players in the Third Series can be found in an original printing with the ad on back printed in black, and a later version with a blue back. Each of the Third Series cards also exhibits on front subtle differences in the size and coloring of the player portrait. The complete set price does not include variations. Early series cards with over 300 subjects back should have 30% premium.

	NM	EX	VG
Common Player:	360.00	180.00	110.00
(1) Ed Abbaticchio	360.00	180.00	110.00
(2a) Babe Adams (Black back.)	360.00	180.00	110.00
(2b) Babe Adams (Blue back.)	520.00	260.00	155.00
(3) Red Ames	1,000	500.00	300.00
(4) Jimmy Archer	1,000	500.00	300.00
(5) Frank Arrelanes (Arellanes)	360.00	180.00	110.00
(6) Tommy Atkins	1,000	500.00	300.00
(7) Jimmy Austin	1,000	500.00	300.00
(8) Les Bachman (Backman)	360.00	180.00	110.00
(9) Bill Bailey	360.00	180.00	110.00
(10a) Home Run Baker (Black back.)	1,600	800.00	480.00
(10b) Home Run Baker (Blue back.)	2,400	1,200	720.00
(11) Cy Barger	360.00	180.00	110.00
(12) Jack Barry	360.00	180.00	110.00
(13a) Johnny Bates (Philadelphia)	360.00	180.00	110.00
(13b) Johnny Bates (Cincinnati) (A G-VG example sold at auction 4/06 for $22,987.)			
(14) Ginger Beaumont	360.00	180.00	110.00
(15) Fred Beck	360.00	180.00	110.00
(16) Heinie Beckendorf	360.00	180.00	110.00
(17) Fred Beebe	360.00	180.00	110.00
(18) George Bell	360.00	180.00	110.00
(19) Harry Bemis	360.00	180.00	110.00
(20a) Chief Bender (Blue background.)	2,400	1,200	720.00
(20b) Chief Bender (Pastel background.)	1,600	800.00	480.00
(21) Bill Bergen	360.00	180.00	110.00
(22) Heinie Berger	360.00	180.00	110.00
(23) Bob Bescher	360.00	180.00	110.00
(24) Joe Birmingham	360.00	180.00	110.00
(25) Lena Blackburn (Blackburne)	360.00	180.00	110.00
(26) John Bliss	1,000	500.00	300.00
(27) Bruno Block	1,000	500.00	300.00
(28) Bill Bradley	360.00	180.00	110.00
(29) Kitty Bransfield	360.00	180.00	110.00
(30a) Roger Bresnahan (Blue)	2,400	1,200	720.00
(30b) Roger Bresnahan (Pastel)	1,600	800.00	480.00
(31) Al Bridwell	360.00	180.00	110.00
(32) Buster Brown (Boston)	360.00	180.00	110.00
(33a) Mordecai Brown (Blue; Chicago.)	2,400	1,200	720.00
(33b) Mordecai Brown (Pastel, Chicago.)	1,600	800.00	480.00
(34) Al Burch	360.00	180.00	110.00
(35) Donie Bush	360.00	180.00	110.00
(36) Bobby Byrne	360.00	180.00	110.00
(37) Howie Camnitz	360.00	180.00	110.00
(38) Vin Campbell	1,000	500.00	300.00
(39) Bill Carrigan	360.00	180.00	110.00
(40a) Frank Chance (Blue)	2,400	1,200	720.00
(40b) Frank Chance (Pastel)	1,600	800.00	480.00
(41) Chappy Charles	360.00	180.00	110.00
(42a) Hal Chase (Blue)	1,600	800.00	480.00
(42b) Hal Chase (Pastel)	1,100	550.00	330.00
(43) Ed Cicotte	1,800	900.00	540.00
(44a) Fred Clarke (Pittsburgh, black back.)	1,600	800.00	480.00
(44b) Fred Clarke (Pittsburgh, blue back.)	2,400	1,200	720.00
(45) Nig Clarke (Cleveland)	360.00	180.00	110.00
(46) Tommy Clarke (Cincinnati)	1,000	500.00	300.00
(47a) Ty Cobb (Blue)	6,000	3,000	1,800
(47b) Ty Cobb (Pastel)	18,000	9,000	5,400
(48a) Eddie Collins (Blue)	2,400	1,200	720.00
(48b) Eddie Collins (Pastel)	1,600	800.00	480.00
(49) Ray Collins	1,000	500.00	300.00
(50) Wid Conroy	360.00	180.00	110.00
(51) Jack Coombs	360.00	180.00	110.00
(52) Frank Corridon	360.00	180.00	110.00
(53) Harry Coveleskie (Coveleski)	2,000	1,000	600.00
(54) Doc Crandall	360.00	180.00	110.00
(55a) Sam Crawford (Blue)	2,400	1,200	720.00
(55b) Sam Crawford (Pastel)	1,600	800.00	480.00
(56) Birdie Cree	360.00	180.00	110.00
(57) Lou Criger	360.00	180.00	110.00

(58)	Dode Criss	1,000	500.00	300.00
(59)	Cliff Curtis	1,000	500.00	300.00
(60)	Bill Dahlen	360.00	180.00	110.00
(62)	Bill Davidson	1,000	500.00	300.00
(62a)	Harry Davis (Blue)	1,000	500.00	300.00
(62b)	Harry Davis (Pastel)	360.00	180.00	110.00
(63)	Jim Delehanty (Delahanty)	360.00	180.00	110.00
(64)	Ray Demmitt	1,000	500.00	300.00
(65)	Rube Dessau	1,000	500.00	300.00
(66a)	Art Devlin (Black back.)	360.00	180.00	110.00
(66b)	Art Devlin (Blue back.)	520.00	260.00	155.00
(67)	Josh Devore	1,000	500.00	300.00
(68)	Pat Donahue	360.00	180.00	110.00
(69)	Patsy Donovan	1,000	500.00	300.00
(70a)	Wild Bill Donovan (Blue)	1,000	500.00	300.00
(70b)	Wild Bill Donovan (Pastel)	360.00	180.00	110.00
(71a)	Red Dooin (Blue)	1,000	500.00	300.00
(71b)	Red Dooin (Pastel)	360.00	180.00	110.00
(72)	Mickey Doolan	360.00	180.00	110.00
(73)	Patsy Dougherty	360.00	180.00	110.00
(74)	Tom Downey	360.00	180.00	110.00
(75)	Jim Doyle	360.00	180.00	110.00
(76a)	Larry Doyle (Blue)	1,000	500.00	300.00
(76b)	Larry Doyle (Pastel)	360.00	180.00	110.00
(77)	Hugh Duffy	1,600	800.00	480.00
(78)	Jimmy Dygert	360.00	180.00	110.00
(79)	Dick Eagan (Egan)	360.00	180.00	110.00
(80)	Kid Elberfeld	360.00	180.00	110.00
(81)	Rube Ellis	360.00	180.00	110.00
(82)	Clyde Engle	360.00	180.00	110.00
(83)	Tex Erwin	1,000	500.00	300.00
(84)	Steve Evans	1,000	500.00	300.00
(85a)	Johnny Evers (Black back.)	1,600	800.00	480.00
(85b)	Johnny Evers (Blue back.)	2,400	1,200	720.00
(86)	Bob Ewing	360.00	180.00	110.00
(87)	Cy Falkenberg	360.00	180.00	110.00
(88)	George Ferguson	360.00	180.00	110.00
(89)	Art Fletcher	1,000	500.00	300.00
(90)	Elmer Flick	1,600	800.00	480.00
(91)	John Flynn	1,000	500.00	300.00
(92)	Russ Ford	1,000	500.00	300.00
(93)	Eddie Foster	1,000	500.00	300.00
(94)	Bill Foxen	360.00	180.00	110.00
(95)	John Frill	1,000	500.00	300.00
(96)	Sam Frock	1,000	500.00	300.00
(97)	Art Fromme	360.00	180.00	110.00
(98)	Earl Gardner (New York)	1,000	500.00	300.00
(99)	Larry Gardner (Boston)	1,000	500.00	300.00
(100)	Harry Gaspar	1,000	500.00	300.00
(101)	Doc Gessler	360.00	180.00	110.00
(102a)	George Gibson (Blue)	1,000	500.00	300.00
(102b)	George Gibson (Pastel)	360.00	180.00	110.00
(103)	Bill Graham (St. Louis)	360.00	180.00	110.00
(104)	Peaches Graham (Boston)	360.00	180.00	110.00
(105)	Eddie Grant	360.00	180.00	110.00
(106)	Clark Griffith	1,600	800.00	480.00
(107)	Ed Hahn	360.00	180.00	110.00
(108)	Charley Hall	360.00	180.00	110.00
(109)	Bob Harmon	1,000	500.00	300.00
(110)	Topsy Hartsel	360.00	180.00	110.00
(111)	Roy Hartzell	360.00	180.00	110.00
(112)	Heinie Heitmuller	360.00	180.00	110.00
(113)	Buck Herzog	360.00	180.00	110.00
(114)	Dick Hoblitzel (Hoblitzell)	360.00	180.00	110.00
(115)	Danny Hoffman	360.00	180.00	110.00
(116)	Solly Hofman	360.00	180.00	110.00
(117)	Harry Hooper	1,600	800.00	480.00
(118)	Harry Howell	360.00	180.00	110.00
(119)	Miller Huggins	1,600	800.00	480.00
(120)	Long Tom Hughes	1,000	500.00	300.00
(121)	Rudy Hulswitt	360.00	180.00	110.00
(122)	John Hummel	360.00	180.00	110.00
(123)	George Hunter	360.00	180.00	110.00
(124)	Ham Hyatt	360.00	180.00	110.00
(125)	Fred Jacklitsch	360.00	180.00	110.00
(126a)	Hughie Jennings (Blue)	2,400	1,200	720.00
(126b)	Hughie Jennings (Pastel)	1,600	800.00	480.00
(127)	Walter Johnson	7,000	3,500	2,100
(128a)	Davy Jones (Blue)	1,000	500.00	300.00
(128b)	Davy Jones (Pastel)	360.00	180.00	110.00
(129)	Tom Jones	360.00	180.00	110.00
(130a)	Tim Jordan (Blue)	1,000	500.00	300.00
(130b)	Tim Jordan (Pastel)	360.00	180.00	110.00
(131)	Addie Joss	1,800	900.00	540.00
(132)	Johnny Kane	360.00	180.00	110.00
(133)	Ed Karger	360.00	180.00	110.00
(134)	Red Killifer (Killefer)	1,000	500.00	300.00
(135)	Johnny Kling	360.00	180.00	110.00
(136)	Otto Knabe	360.00	180.00	110.00
(137)	John Knight	1,000	500.00	300.00
(138)	Ed Konetchy	360.00	180.00	110.00
(139)	Harry Krause	360.00	180.00	110.00
(140)	Rube Kroh	360.00	180.00	110.00
(141)	Art Krueger	1,600	800.00	480.00
(142a)	Nap Lajoie (Blue)	2,400	1,200	720.00
(142b)	Nap Lajoie (Pastel)	1,600	800.00	480.00
(143)	Fred Lake (Boston)	360.00	180.00	110.00
(144)	Joe Lake (St. Louis)	1,000	500.00	300.00
(145)	Frank LaPorte	360.00	180.00	110.00
(146)	Jack Lapp	1,000	500.00	300.00
(147)	Chick Lathers	1,000	500.00	300.00
(148a)	Tommy Leach (Blue)	1,000	500.00	300.00
(148b)	Tommy Leach (Pastel)	360.00	180.00	110.00
(149)	Sam Leever	360.00	180.00	110.00
(150)	Lefty Leifeld	360.00	180.00	110.00
(151)	Ed Lennox	360.00	180.00	110.00
(152)	Fred Linke (Link)	1,000	500.00	300.00
(153)	Paddy Livingstone (Livingston)	360.00	180.00	110.00
(154)	Hans Lobert	360.00	180.00	110.00
(155)	Bris Lord	1,000	500.00	300.00
(156a)	Harry Lord (Blue)	1,000	500.00	300.00
(156b)	Harry Lord (Pastel)	360.00	180.00	110.00
(157)	Johnny Lush	360.00	180.00	110.00
(158)	Connie Mack	1,600	800.00	480.00
(159)	Tom Madden	1,000	500.00	300.00
(160)	Nick Maddox	360.00	180.00	110.00
(161)	Sherry Magee	360.00	180.00	110.00
(162a)	Christy Mathewson (Blue)	10,000	5,000	3,000

(162b)	Christy Mathewson (Pastel)	5,400	2,700	1,625
(163)	Al Mattern	360.00	180.00	110.00
(164)	Jimmy McAleer	360.00	180.00	110.00
(165)	George McBride	1,000	500.00	300.00
(166a)	Amby McConnell (Boston)	360.00	180.00	110.00
(166b)	Amby McConnell (Chicago)	10,000	5,000	3,000
(167)	Pryor McElveen	360.00	180.00	110.00
(168)	John McGraw	1,600	800.00	480.00
(169)	Deacon McGuire	360.00	180.00	110.00
(170)	Stuffy McInnes (McInnis)	1,000	500.00	300.00
(171)	Harry McIntire (McIntyre)	360.00	180.00	110.00
(172)	Matty McIntyre	360.00	180.00	110.00
(173)	Larry McLean	360.00	180.00	110.00
(174)	Tommy McMillan	360.00	180.00	110.00
(175a)	George McQuillan (Blue, Philadelphia.)	1,000	500.00	300.00
(175b)	George McQuillan (Pastel, Philadelphia.)	360.00	180.00	110.00
(175c)	George McQuillan (Cincinnati)	5,000	2,500	1,500
(176)	Paul Meloan	1,000	500.00	300.00
(177)	Fred Merkle	360.00	180.00	110.00
(178)	Clyde Milan	360.00	180.00	110.00
(179)	Dots Miller (Pittsburgh)	360.00	180.00	110.00
(180)	Warren Miller (Washington)	1,000	500.00	300.00
(181)	Fred Mitchell	1,000	500.00	300.00
(182)	Mike Mitchell	360.00	180.00	110.00
(183)	Earl Moore	360.00	180.00	110.00
(184)	Pat Moran	360.00	180.00	110.00
(185a)	Lew Moren (Black back.)	520.00	260.00	155.00
(185b)	Lew Moren (Blue back.)	360.00	180.00	110.00
(186)	Cy Morgan	360.00	180.00	110.00
(187)	George Moriarty	360.00	180.00	110.00
(188)	Mike Mowery (Mowrey)	1,000	500.00	300.00
(189a)	George Mullin (Black back.)	360.00	180.00	110.00
(189b)	George Mullin (Blue back.)	520.00	260.00	155.00
(190)	Danny Murphy	360.00	180.00	110.00
(191)	Red Murray	360.00	180.00	110.00
(192)	Chief Myers (Meyers)	1,000	500.00	300.00
(193)	Tom Needham	360.00	180.00	110.00
(194)	Harry Niles	360.00	180.00	110.00
(195)	Rebel Oakes	1,000	500.00	300.00
(196)	Jack O'Connor	360.00	180.00	110.00
(197)	Paddy O'Connor	360.00	180.00	110.00
(198)	Bill O'Hara	1,000	500.00	300.00
(199)	Rube Oldring	360.00	180.00	110.00
(200)	Charley O'Leary	360.00	180.00	110.00
(201)	Orval Overall	360.00	180.00	110.00
(202)	Freddy Parent	360.00	180.00	110.00
(203)	Dode Paskert	1,000	500.00	300.00
(204)	Fred Payne	1,000	500.00	300.00
(205)	Barney Pelty	360.00	180.00	110.00
(206)	Hub Pernoll	1,000	500.00	300.00
(207)	George Perring	1,000	500.00	300.00
(208)	Big Jeff Pfeffer	1,000	500.00	300.00
(209)	Jack Pfiester	360.00	180.00	110.00
(210)	Art Phelan	1,000	500.00	300.00
(211)	Ed Phelps	360.00	180.00	110.00
(212)	Deacon Phillippe	360.00	180.00	110.00
(213)	Eddie Plank	4,800	2,400	1,450
(214)	Jack Powell	360.00	180.00	110.00
(215)	Billy Purtell	360.00	180.00	110.00
(216)	Farmer Ray	1,000	500.00	300.00
(217)	Bugs Raymond	360.00	180.00	110.00
(218)	Doc Reisling	360.00	180.00	110.00
(219)	Ed Reulbach	360.00	180.00	110.00
(220)	Lew Richie	360.00	180.00	110.00
(221)	Jack Rowan	360.00	180.00	110.00
(222a)	Nap Rucker (Black back.)	360.00	180.00	110.00
(222b)	Nap Rucker (Blue back.)	520.00	260.00	155.00
(223)	Slim Sallee	360.00	180.00	110.00
(224)	Doc Scanlon	360.00	180.00	110.00
(225)	Germany Schaefer	360.00	180.00	110.00
(226)	Lou Schettler	1,000	500.00	300.00
(227)	Admiral Schlei	360.00	180.00	110.00
(228)	Boss Schmidt	360.00	180.00	110.00
(229)	Wildfire Schulte	360.00	180.00	110.00
(230)	Al Schweitzer	360.00	180.00	110.00
(231)	Jim Scott	1,000	500.00	300.00
(232a)	Cy Seymour (N.Y.)	360.00	180.00	110.00
(232b)	Cy Seymour (Baltimore) (Two known; 4/04 auction $18,000+ Fair-Good.)			
(233)	Tillie Shafer	360.00	180.00	110.00
(234)	Bud Sharpe	1,000	500.00	300.00
(235)	Dave Shean	1,000	500.00	300.00
(236)	Jimmy Sheckard	360.00	180.00	110.00
(237)	Mike Simon	1,000	500.00	300.00
(238)	Charlie Smith (Boston)	1,000	500.00	300.00
(239)	Frank Smith (Chicago)	360.00	180.00	110.00
(240)	Harry Smith (Boston)	360.00	180.00	110.00
(241)	Fred Snodgrass	360.00	180.00	110.00
(242)	Bob Spade	360.00	180.00	110.00
(243)	Tully Sparks	360.00	180.00	110.00
(244)	Tris Speaker	3,000	1,500	900.00
(245)	Jake Stahl	360.00	180.00	110.00
(246)	George Stallings	360.00	180.00	110.00
(247)	Oscar Stanage	360.00	180.00	110.00
(248)	Harry Steinfeldt	360.00	180.00	110.00
(249)	Jim Stephens	360.00	180.00	110.00
(250)	George Stone	360.00	180.00	110.00
(251)	George Stovall	360.00	180.00	110.00
(252)	Gabby Street	360.00	180.00	110.00
(253)	Sailor Stroud	1,000	500.00	300.00
(254)	Amos Strunk	1,000	500.00	300.00
(255)	George Suggs	360.00	180.00	110.00
(256)	Billy Sullivan	360.00	180.00	110.00
(257a)	Ed Summers (Black back.)	360.00	180.00	110.00
(257b)	Ed Summers (Blue back.)	520.00	260.00	155.00
(258)	Bill Sweeney (Boston)	360.00	180.00	110.00
(259)	Jeff Sweeney (New York)	1,000	500.00	300.00
(260)	Lee Tannehill	360.00	180.00	110.00
(261a)	Fred Tenney (Blue)	1,000	500.00	300.00
(261b)	Fred Tenney (Pastel)	360.00	180.00	110.00
(262a)	Ira Thomas (Blue)	1,000	500.00	300.00
(262b)	Ira Thomas (Pastel)	360.00	180.00	110.00
(263)	Jack Thoney	360.00	180.00	110.00
(264a)	Joe Tinker (Black back.)	1,600	800.00	480.00

(264b)	Joe Tinker (Blue back.)	2,400	1,200	720.00
(265)	John Titus	1,000	500.00	300.00
(266)	Terry Turner	360.00	180.00	110.00
(267)	Bob Unglaub	360.00	180.00	110.00
(268a)	Rube Waddell (Black back.)	1,600	800.00	480.00
(268b)	Rube Waddell (Blue back.)	2,400	1,200	720.00
(269a)	Hans Wagner (Pittsburgh, blue.)	9,000	5,500	3,000
(269b)	Hans Wagner (Pittsburgh, pastel.)	7,000	3,500	2,000
(270)	Heinie Wagner (Boston)	360.00	180.00	110.00
(271)	Bobby Wallace	1,600	800.00	480.00
(272)	Ed Walsh (Chicago)	1,600	800.00	480.00
(273a)	Jimmy Walsh (Gray background, Philadelphia.)	1,400	700.00	420.00
(273b)	Jimmy Walsh (White background, Philadelphia.)	1,400	700.00	420.00
(274)	Doc White	360.00	180.00	110.00
(275)	Kaiser Wilhelm	360.00	180.00	110.00
(276)	Ed Willett	360.00	180.00	110.00
(277)	Vic Willis	1,600	800.00	480.00
(278)	Art Wilson (New York)	1,000	500.00	300.00
(279)	Owen Wilson (Pittsburgh)	360.00	180.00	110.00
(280)	Hooks Wiltse	360.00	180.00	110.00
(281)	Harry Wolter	360.00	180.00	110.00
(282)	Smokey Joe Wood	2,700	1,350	810.00
(283)	Ralph Works	360.00	180.00	110.00
(284a)	Cy Young (Black back.)	3,600	1,800	1,100
(284b)	Cy Young (Blue back.)	4,800	2,400	1,500
(285)	Irv Young	360.00	180.00	110.00
(286)	Heinie Zimmerman	1,000	500.00	300.00
(287)	Dutch Zwilling	360.00	180.00	110.00

1911 Sporting Life Cabinets (M110)

This set of 5-5/8" x 7-1/2" premium photos is similar to, but much scarcer than, the contemporary T3 Turkey Red cabinets. Like those, the Sporting Life cabinets feature a pastel player picture surrounded by a gray frame with a "gold" nameplate at bottom. Backs have advertising for the weekly sports paper printed in blue.

		NM	EX	VG
Complete Set (6):		150,000	75,000	45,000
Common Player:		18,000	9,000	5,500
(1)	Frank Chance	20,000	10,000	6,000
(2)	Hal Chase	18,000	9,000	5,500
(3)	Ty Cobb	40,000	20,000	12,000
(4)	Napoleon Lajoie	22,500	11,250	6,750
(5)	Christy Mathewson	27,500	13,500	8,250
(6)	Honus Wagner	35,000	17,500	8,750

1911 Sporting Life Team Composites (W601)

After several years of issuing composite team photos for all major league teams (and some minor league teams), Sporting Life in 1910 began issuing them only for the league and World's Champions. Like the others, they are 13" x 14", printed on heavy enamel paper with individual player portrait photos surrounding the manager at center.

		NM	EX	VG
Complete Set (2):		1,200	600.00	350.00
Common Team:		300.00	150.00	90.00
(1)	New York Giants (N.L. Champs)	600.00	300.00	180.00
(2)	Philadelphia Athletics (World's Champions)	750.00	375.00	225.00

1899-1900 Sporting News Supplements (M101-1)

For much of 1899 and 1900, the weekly issues of The Sporting News included a baseball player portrait supplement. About 8-3/4" x 11", the pictures offered vignetted photos of the era's stars on a glossy paper stock. Virtually all pictures were formal head-and-shoulders portraits; some in uniform, some in civilian clothes. A handful of players are depicted in full-length poses. The pictures were produced for the sports paper by National Copper Plate Co., (which issued its own set of prints listed elsewhere in this catalog). The TSN supplements have a logotype above the photo and the date in which it was included in the paper. Full player name and team/year are printed at bottom. Backs have a small box offering career information. Besides offering the pictures with weekly issues, portfolios of 50 could be had by starting or renewing a subscription for $2 a year.

	NM	EX	VG
Complete Set (62):	90,000	36,000	18,000
Common Player:	1,125	450.00	225.00
1899			
(1) William Lange (Apr. 22)	1,125	450.00	225.00
(2) Hugh Duffy (Apr. 29)	1,875	750.00	375.00
(3) Charles A. Nichols (May 6)	1,875	750.00	375.00
(4) Martin Bergen (May 13)	1,125	450.00	225.00
(5) Michael Griffin (May 20)	1,125	450.00	225.00
(6) Wilbert Robinson (May 27)	1,875	750.00	375.00
(7) Clark C. Griffith (June 3)	1,875	750.00	375.00
(8) John J. Doyle (June 10)	1,125	450.00	225.00
(9) R.J. Wallace (June 17)	1,875	750.00	375.00
(10) John O'Connor (June 24)	1,125	450.00	225.00
(11) Louis Criger (July 1)	1,125	450.00	225.00
(12) Jerry H. Nops (July 8)	1,125	450.00	225.00
(13) William Kennedy (July 15)	1,125	450.00	225.00
(14) P.J. Donovan (July 22)	1,125	450.00	225.00
(15) William H. Keeler (July 29)	1,875	750.00	375.00
(16) John J. McGraw (Aug. 5)	1,875	750.00	375.00
(17) James Hughes (Aug. 12)	1,125	450.00	225.00
(18) John Wagner (Aug. 19)	11,250	4,500	2,250
(19) Victor G. Willis (Aug. 26)	1,875	750.00	375.00
(20) James J. Collins (Sept. 2)	1,875	750.00	375.00
(21) Eugene DeMontreville (Sept. 9)	1,125	450.00	225.00
(22) Joseph J. Kelley (Sept. 16)	1,875	750.00	375.00
(23) Frank L. Donahue (Francis R. "Red")(Sept. 23)	1,125	450.00	225.00
(24) Edward J. Delehanty (Delahanty)(Sept. 30)	1,125	450.00	225.00
(25) Fred C. Clark (Clarke)(Oct. 7)	1,875	750.00	375.00
(26) Napoleon Lajoie (Oct. 14)	1,875	750.00	375.00
(27) Edward Hanlon (Oct. 21)	1,875	750.00	375.00
(28) Charles Stahl (Oct. 28)	1,125	450.00	225.00
(29) Lave N. Cross (Nov. 4)	1,125	450.00	225.00
(30) Elmer H. Flick (Nov. 11)	1,875	750.00	375.00
(31) Frank LeRoy Chance (Nov. 18)	1,875	750.00	375.00
(32) George S. Davis (Nov. 25)	1,875	750.00	375.00
(33) Hugh J. Jennings (Dec. 2)	1,875	750.00	375.00
(34) Denton T. Young (Dec. 9)	3,750	1,500	750.00
1900			
(35) George E. Waddell (Apr. 14)	1,875	750.00	375.00
(36) John Dunn (Apr. 21)	1,125	450.00	225.00
(37) Clarence Beaumont (Apr. 28)	1,125	450.00	225.00
(38) James T. McGuire (May 5)	1,125	450.00	225.00
(39) William H. Dineen (May 12)	1,125	450.00	225.00
(40) James T. Williams (May 19)	1,125	450.00	225.00
(41) Thomas W. Corcoran (May 26)	1,125	450.00	225.00
(42) John Freeman (June 2)	1,125	450.00	225.00
(43) Henry Peitz (June 9)	1,125	450.00	225.00
(44) Charles Phillippe (June 16)	1,125	450.00	225.00
(45) Frank Hahn (June 23)	1,125	450.00	225.00
(46) J. Emmet Heidrick (June 30)	1,125	450.00	225.00
(47) Joseph McGinnity (July 7)	1,875	750.00	375.00
(48) John D. Chesbro (July 14)	1,875	750.00	375.00
(49) William R. Hamilton (July 21)	1,875	750.00	375.00
(50) Samuel Leever (July 28)	1,125	450.00	225.00
(51) Mike Donlin (Aug. 4)	1,125	450.00	225.00
(52) William F. Dahlen (Aug. 11)	1,125	450.00	225.00
(53) Frederick Tenney (Aug. 18)	1,125	450.00	225.00
(54) Edward P. Scott (Aug. 25)	1,125	450.00	225.00
(55) Edward M. Lewis (Sept. 1)	1,125	450.00	225.00
(56) Theodore Breitenstein (Sept. 8)	1,125	450.00	225.00
(57) Herman C. Long (Sept. 15)	1,125	450.00	225.00
(58) Jesse Tannehill (Sept. 22)	1,125	450.00	225.00
(59) Burt E. Jones (Sept. 29)	1,125	450.00	225.00
(60) J. Callahan (Nixey)(Oct. 6)	1,125	450.00	225.00
(61) Claude Ritchey (Oct. 13)	1,125	450.00	225.00
(62) Roy Thomas (Oct. 20)	1,125	450.00	225.00

1909-1913 Sporting News Supplements (M101-2)

Among the finest large-format baseball collectibles published in the early part of the 20th Century was the 100-piece series of sepia-toned supplements issued by The Sporting News. Initially issued in a size of about 7-1/2" x 10", by late 1909 the size evolved to about 8-1/2" x 10" with the team photos issued in a 16" x 10" format. The series was begun with the insertion of a supplement in the July 22, 1909, issue of TSN. One supplement was issued with each week's paper through April 7, 1910. There were several gaps over the course of the next several years, until the final piece was issued with the TSN dated Dec. 11, 1913. Most of the supplements feature full-length poses of the players. Each is labeled "Supplement

to The Sporting News" with the issue date at top. At bottom is a box with the player's name and team. Backs are usually blank, but some supplements are found with colored advertising on back for various other collectibles from the newspaper. The TSN supplements were printed on heavy paper and are usually found with corner creases or other signs of wear.

	NM	EX	VG
Complete Set (100):	25,000	12,500	7,500
Common Player:	80.00	40.00	25.00
Ad backs: 3X			
1909			
(1) Roger Bresnahan (7/22)	600.00	300.00	180.00
(2) Denton Young, Louis Criger (7/29)	450.00	225.00	135.00
(3) Christopher Mathewson (8/5)	1,000	500.00	300.00
(4) Tyrus R. Cobb (8/12)	1,200	600.00	360.00
(5) Napoleon Lajoie (8/19)	550.00	275.00	165.00
(6) Sherwood N. Magee (8/26)	80.00	40.00	25.00
(7) Frank L. Chance (9/2)	500.00	250.00	150.00
(8) Edward Walsh (9/9)	500.00	250.00	150.00
(9) Nap Rucker (9/16)	80.00	40.00	25.00
(10) Honus Wagner (9/23)	1,000	500.00	300.00
(11) Hugh Jennings (9/30)	550.00	275.00	165.00
(12) Fred C. Clarke (10/7)	550.00	275.00	165.00
(13) Byron Bancroft Johnson (10/14)	550.00	275.00	165.00
(14) Charles A. Comiskey (10/21)	550.00	275.00	165.00
(15) Edward Collins (10/28)	550.00	275.00	165.00
(16) James A. McAleer (11/4)	160.00	80.00	50.00
(17) Pittsburgh Team (11/11)	350.00	175.00	100.00
(18) Detroit Team (11/18)	350.00	175.00	100.00
(19) George Bell (11/25)	160.00	80.00	50.00
(20) Tris Speaker (12/2)	650.00	325.00	195.00
(21) Mordecai Brown (12/9)	550.00	275.00	165.00
(22) Hal Chase (12/16)	550.00	275.00	165.00
(23) Thomas W. Leach (12/23)	160.00	80.00	50.00
(24) Owen Bush (12/30)	160.00	80.00	50.00
1910			
(25) John J. Evers (1/6)	400.00	200.00	120.00
(26) Harry Krause (1/13)	80.00	40.00	25.00
(27) Chas. B. Adams (1/20)	80.00	40.00	25.00
(28) Addie Joss (1/27)	400.00	200.00	120.00
(29) Orval Overall (2/3)	80.00	40.00	25.00
(30) Samuel E. Crawford (2/10)	400.00	200.00	120.00
(31) Fred Merkle (2/17)	90.00	45.00	25.00
(32) George Mullin (2/24)	80.00	40.00	25.00
(33) Edward Konetchy (3/3)	80.00	40.00	25.00
(34) George Gibson, Arthur Raymond (3/10)	80.00	40.00	25.00
(35) Ty Cobb, Hans Wagner (3/17)	2,000	1,000	600.00
(36) Connie Mack (3/24)	400.00	200.00	120.00
(37) Wm. Evans, "Silk" O'Loughlin, William Klem, Wm. Johnston (3/31)	550.00	275.00	165.00
(38) Edward Plank (4/7)	325.00	160.00	95.00
(39) Walter Johnson, Charles E. Street (9/1)	500.00	250.00	150.00
(40) John C. Kling (9/8)	80.00	40.00	25.00
(41) Frank Baker (9/15)	400.00	200.00	120.00
(42) Charles S. Dooin (9/22)	80.00	40.00	25.00
(43) Wm. F. Carrigan (9/29)	80.00	40.00	25.00
(44) John B. McLean (10/6)	80.00	40.00	25.00
(45) John W. Coombs (10/13)	80.00	40.00	25.00
(46) Jos. B. Tinker (10/20)	350.00	175.00	100.00
(47) John I. Taylor (10/27)	80.00	40.00	25.00
(48) Russell Ford (11/3)	80.00	40.00	25.00
(49) Leonard L. Cole (11/10)	80.00	40.00	25.00
(50) Harry Lord (11/17)	80.00	40.00	25.00
(51) Philadelphia-A Team (11/24)	130.00	65.00	40.00
(52) Chicago-N Team (12/1)	130.00	65.00	40.00
(53) Charles A. Bender (12/8)	400.00	200.00	120.00
(54) Arthur Hofman (12/15)	80.00	40.00	25.00
(55) Bobby Wallace (12/21)	325.00	160.00	95.00
(56) Jno. J. McGraw (12/28)	325.00	160.00	95.00
1911			
(57) Harry L. Davis (1/5)	80.00	40.00	25.00
(58) James P. Archer (1/12)	80.00	40.00	25.00
(59) Ira Thomas (1/19)	80.00	40.00	25.00
(60) Robert Byrnes (1/26)	80.00	40.00	25.00
(61) Clyde Milan (2/2)	80.00	40.00	25.00
(62) John T. Meyer (2/9)(Meyers)	80.00	40.00	25.00
(63) Robert Bescher (2/16)	80.00	40.00	25.00
(64) John J. Barry (2/23)	80.00	40.00	25.00
(65) Frank Schulte (3/2)	80.00	40.00	25.00
(66) C. Harris White (3/9)	80.00	40.00	25.00
(67) Lawrence Doyle (3/16)	80.00	40.00	25.00
(68) Joe Jackson (3/23)	2,500	1,250	750.00
(69) Martin O'Toole, William Kelly (10/26)	80.00	40.00	25.00
(70) Vean Gregg (11/2)	80.00	40.00	25.00
(71) Richard W. Marquard (11/9)	325.00	160.00	95.00
(72) John E. McInnis (11/16)	80.00	40.00	25.00
(73) Grover C. Alexander (11/23)	350.00	175.00	100.00
(74) Del Gainor (11/30)	80.00	40.00	25.00
(75) Fred Snodgrass (12/7)	80.00	40.00	25.00
(76) James J. Callahan (12/14)	80.00	40.00	25.00
(77) Robert Harmon (12/21)	80.00	40.00	25.00
(78) George Stovall (12/28)	80.00	40.00	25.00
1912			
(79) Zack D. Wheat (1/4)	325.00	160.00	95.00
(80) Frank "Ping" Bodie (1/11)	80.00	40.00	25.00
(81) Boston-A Team (10/10)	130.00	65.00	40.00
(82) New York-N Team (10/17)	130.00	65.00	40.00
(83) Jake Stahl (10/24)	80.00	40.00	25.00
(84) Joe Wood (10/31)	275.00	135.00	80.00
(85) Charles Wagner (11/7)	80.00	40.00	25.00
(86) Lew Ritchie (11/14)	80.00	40.00	25.00
(87) Clark Griffith (11/21)	325.00	160.00	95.00
(88) Arnold Hauser (11/28)	80.00	40.00	25.00
(89) Charles Herzog (12/5)	80.00	40.00	25.00
(90) James Lavender (12/12)	80.00	40.00	25.00
(91) Jeff Tesreau (12/19)	80.00	40.00	25.00
(92) August Herrmann (12/26)	110.00	55.00	30.00
1913			
(93) Jake Daubert (10/23)	80.00	40.00	25.00
(94) Heinie Zimmerman (10/30)	80.00	40.00	25.00
(95) Ray Schalk (11/6)	325.00	160.00	95.00
(96) Hans Lobert (11/13)	80.00	40.00	25.00
(97) Albert W. Demaree (11/20)	80.00	40.00	25.00
(98) Arthur Fletcher (11/27)	80.00	40.00	25.00
(99) Charles A. Somers (12/4)	80.00	40.00	25.00
(100) Joe Birmingham (12/11)	80.00	40.00	25.00

1913 Sporting News Postcards (M101-3)

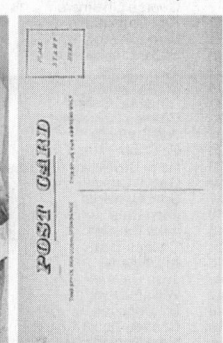

This six-card set was issued as a premium by the weekly sports newspaper. The 3-1/2" x 5-1/2" cards have borderless front photos printed in duotone color. Along with the player and team names at bottom is a "Published by The Sporting News" tag line. Postcard-format backs are in black-and-white. The unnumbered cards are checklisted here alphabetically.

	NM	EX	VG
Complete Set (6):	8,500	4,250	2,500
Common Player:	550.00	270.00	165.00
(1) Roger Bresnahan	900.00	450.00	270.00
(2) Ty Cobb	4,000	2,000	1,200
(3) Eddie Collins	900.00	450.00	270.00
(4) Vean Gregg	550.00	270.00	165.00
(5) Walter Johnson, Gabby Street	1,500	750.00	450.00
(6) Rube Marquard	900.00	450.00	270.00

1916 The Sporting News (M101-5)

(Though listed in catalogs for more than 25 years, it is now believed M101-5 cards with Sporting News backs do not exist.)

1916 The Sporting News (M101-4)

The "update" version of the promotional premium issued by The Sporting News is nearly identical to the earlier cards. The 200 black-and-white cards once again are printed with player photo, name, position, team and card number on front and advertising on the backs. The set checklist and, generally, values are the same for sets issued by several other businesses around the country. Most of the players included on the 1-5/8" x 3" cards also appear in the prior edition. Despite being labeled in the American Card Catalog as M101-4, this version was issued after the M101-5 version, with the first advertising appearing in August 1916. Cards could be ordered in series of 20 for a dime, or the complete set was free with a $2 subscription. The complete set price does not include variations.

	NM	EX	VG
Complete Set (200):	65,000	32,000	19,500
Common Player:	95.00	50.00	30.00
1 Babe Adams	110.00	50.00	30.00

#	Player			
2	Sam Agnew	95.00	50.00	30.00
3	Eddie Ainsmith	95.00	50.00	30.00
4	Grover Alexander	600.00	300.00	180.00
5	Leon Ames	95.00	50.00	30.00
6	Jimmy Archer	95.00	50.00	30.00
7	Jimmy Austin	95.00	50.00	30.00
8	H.D. Baird	95.00	50.00	30.00
9	J. Franklin Baker	390.00	190.00	115.00
10	Dave Bancroft	390.00	190.00	115.00
11	Jack Barry	95.00	50.00	30.00
12	Zinn Beck	95.00	50.00	30.00
13	"Chief" Bender	390.00	190.00	115.00
14	Joe Benz	95.00	50.00	30.00
15	Bob Bescher	95.00	50.00	30.00
16	Al Betzel	95.00	50.00	30.00
17	Mordecai Brown	390.00	190.00	115.00
18	Eddie Burns	95.00	50.00	30.00
19	George Burns	95.00	50.00	30.00
20	Geo. J. Burns	95.00	50.00	30.00
21	Joe Bush	95.00	50.00	30.00
22	"Donie" Bush	95.00	50.00	30.00
23	Art Butler	95.00	50.00	30.00
24	Bobbie Byrne	95.00	50.00	30.00
25	Forrest Cady	95.00	50.00	30.00
26	Jimmy Callahan	95.00	50.00	30.00
27	Ray Caldwell	95.00	50.00	30.00
28	Max Carey	390.00	190.00	115.00
29	George Chalmers	95.00	50.00	30.00
30	Ray Chapman	95.00	50.00	30.00
31	Larry Cheney	95.00	50.00	30.00
32	Eddie Cicotte	390.00	190.00	115.00
33	Tom Clarke	95.00	50.00	30.00
34	Eddie Collins	390.00	190.00	155.00
35	"Shauno" Collins	95.00	50.00	30.00
36	Charles Comiskey	390.00	190.00	115.00
37	Joe Connolly	95.00	50.00	30.00
38	Ty Cobb	5,500	2,700	1,650
39	Harry Coveleskie (Coveleski)	95.00	50.00	30.00
40	Gavvy Cravath	95.00	50.00	30.00
41	Sam Crawford	390.00	190.00	115.00
42	Jean Dale	95.00	50.00	30.00
43	Jake Daubert	95.00	50.00	30.00
44	Charles Deal	95.00	50.00	30.00
45	Al Demaree	95.00	50.00	30.00
46	Josh Devore	95.00	50.00	30.00
47	William Doak	95.00	50.00	30.00
48	Bill Donovan	95.00	50.00	30.00
49	Charles Dooin	95.00	50.00	30.00
50	Mike Doolan	95.00	50.00	30.00
51	Larry Doyle	95.00	50.00	30.00
52	Jean Dubuc	95.00	50.00	30.00
53	Oscar Dugey	95.00	50.00	30.00
54	Johnny Evers	390.00	190.00	115.00
55	Urban Faber	390.00	190.00	115.00
56	"Hap" Felsch	1,000	285.00	170.00
57	Bill Fischer	95.00	50.00	30.00
58	Ray Fisher	95.00	50.00	30.00
59	Max Flack	95.00	50.00	30.00
60	Art Fletcher	95.00	50.00	30.00
61	Eddie Foster	95.00	50.00	30.00
62	Jacques Fournier	95.00	50.00	30.00
63	Del Gainer (Gainor)	95.00	50.00	30.00
64	"Chic" Gandil	1,000	190.00	115.00
65	Larry Gardner	95.00	50.00	30.00
66	Joe Gedeon	95.00	50.00	30.00
67	Gus Getz	95.00	50.00	30.00
68	Geo. Gibson	95.00	50.00	30.00
69	Wilbur Good	95.00	50.00	30.00
70	Hank Gowdy	95.00	50.00	30.00
71	John Graney	95.00	50.00	30.00
72	Clark Griffith	390.00	190.00	115.00
73	Tom Griffith	95.00	50.00	30.00
74	Heinie Groh	95.00	50.00	30.00
75	Earl Hamilton	95.00	50.00	30.00
76	Bob Harmon	95.00	50.00	30.00
77	Roy Hartzell	95.00	50.00	30.00
78	Claude Hendrix	95.00	50.00	30.00
79	Olaf Henriksen	95.00	50.00	30.00
80	John Henry	95.00	50.00	30.00
81	"Buck" Herzog	95.00	50.00	30.00
82	Hugh High	95.00	50.00	30.00
83	Dick Hoblitzell	95.00	50.00	30.00
84	Harry Hooper	390.00	190.00	115.00
85	Ivan Howard	95.00	50.00	30.00
86	Miller Huggins	390.00	190.00	115.00
87	Joe Jackson	37,500	18,500	11,000
88	William James	95.00	50.00	30.00
89	Harold Janvrin	95.00	50.00	30.00
90	Hugh Jennings	390.00	190.00	115.00
91	Walter Johnson	1,140	570.00	345.00
92	Fielder Jones	95.00	50.00	30.00
93	Joe Judge	95.00	50.00	30.00
94	Bennie Kauff	95.00	50.00	30.00
95	Wm. Killefer Jr.	95.00	50.00	30.00
96	Ed. Konetchy	95.00	50.00	30.00
97	Napoleon Lajoie	390.00	190.00	115.00
98	Jack Lapp	95.00	50.00	30.00
99	John Lavan	95.00	50.00	30.00
100	Jimmy Lavender	95.00	50.00	30.00
101	"Nemo" Leibold	95.00	50.00	30.00
102	H.B. Leonard	95.00	50.00	30.00
103	Duffy Lewis	95.00	50.00	30.00
104	Hans Lobert	95.00	50.00	30.00
105	Tom Long	95.00	50.00	30.00
106	Fred Luderus	95.00	50.00	30.00
107	Connie Mack	390.00	190.00	115.00
108	Lee Magee	95.00	50.00	30.00
109	Sherwood Magee	95.00	50.00	30.00
110	Al. Mamaux	95.00	50.00	30.00
111	Leslie Mann	95.00	50.00	30.00
112	"Rabbit" Maranville	390.00	190.00	115.00
113	Rube Marquard	390.00	190.00	115.00
114	J. Erskine Mayer	150.00	80.00	45.00
115	George McBride	95.00	50.00	30.00
116	John J. McGraw	390.00	190.00	115.00
117	Jack McInnis	95.00	50.00	30.00
118	Fred Merkle	95.00	50.00	30.00
119	Chief Meyers	95.00	50.00	30.00

#	Player			
120	Clyde Milan	95.00	50.00	30.00
121	John Miller	95.00	50.00	30.00
122	Otto Miller	95.00	50.00	30.00
123	Willie Mitchell	95.00	50.00	30.00
124	Fred Mollwitz	95.00	50.00	30.00
125	Pat Moran	95.00	50.00	30.00
126	Ray Morgan	95.00	50.00	30.00
127	Geo. Moriarty	95.00	50.00	30.00
128	Guy Morton	95.00	50.00	30.00
129	Mike Mowrey	95.00	50.00	30.00
130	Ed. Murphy	95.00	50.00	30.00
131	"Hy" Myers	95.00	50.00	30.00
132	J.A. Niehoff	95.00	50.00	30.00
133	Rube Oldring	95.00	50.00	30.00
134	Oliver O'Mara	95.00	50.00	30.00
135	Steve O'Neill	95.00	50.00	30.00
136	"Dode" Paskert	95.00	50.00	30.00
137	Roger Peckinpaugh	95.00	50.00	30.00
138	Walter Pipp	95.00	50.00	30.00
139	Derril Pratt (Derrill)	95.00	50.00	30.00
140	Pat Ragan	95.00	50.00	30.00
141	Bill Rariden	95.00	50.00	30.00
142	Eppa Rixey	390.00	190.00	115.00
143	Davey Robertson	95.00	50.00	30.00
144	Wilbert Robinson	390.00	190.00	115.00
145	Bob Roth	95.00	50.00	30.00
146	Ed. Roush	390.00	190.00	115.00
147	Clarence Rowland	95.00	50.00	30.00
148	"Nap" Rucker	95.00	50.00	30.00
149	Dick Rudolph	95.00	50.00	30.00
150	Reb Russell	95.00	50.00	30.00
151	Babe Ruth	30,000	15,000	9,000
152	Vic Saier	95.00	50.00	30.00
153	"Slim" Sallee	95.00	50.00	30.00
154	Ray Schalk	390.00	190.00	115.00
155	Walter Schang	95.00	50.00	30.00
156	Frank Schulte	95.00	50.00	30.00
157	Everett Scott	95.00	50.00	30.00
158	Jim Scott	95.00	50.00	30.00
159	Tom Seaton	95.00	50.00	30.00
160	Howard Shanks	95.00	50.00	30.00
161	Bob Shawkey	95.00	50.00	30.00
162	Ernie Shore	95.00	50.00	30.00
163	Burt Shotton	95.00	50.00	30.00
164	Geo. Sisler	390.00	190.00	115.00
165	J. Carlisle Smith	95.00	50.00	30.00
166	Fred Snodgrass	95.00	50.00	30.00
167	Geo. Stallings	95.00	50.00	30.00
168a	Oscar Stanage/Catching	95.00	50.00	30.00
168b	Oscar Stanage (Portrait to thighs.)	900.00	450.00	270.00
169	Charles Stengel	390.00	190.00	115.00
170	Milton Stock	95.00	50.00	30.00
171	Amos Strunk	95.00	50.00	30.00
172	Billy Sullivan	95.00	50.00	30.00
173	"Jeff" Tesreau	95.00	50.00	30.00
174	Joe Tinker	390.00	190.00	115.00
175	Fred Toney	95.00	50.00	30.00
176	Terry Turner	95.00	50.00	30.00
177	George Tyler	95.00	50.00	30.00
178	Jim Vaughn	95.00	50.00	30.00
179	Bob Veach	95.00	50.00	30.00
180	James Viox	95.00	50.00	30.00
181	Oscar Vitt	95.00	50.00	30.00
182	Hans Wagner	2,500	660.00	395.00
183	Clarence Walker	95.00	50.00	30.00
184	Ed. Walsh	390.00	190.00	115.00
185	W. Wambsganss (Photo actually Fritz Coumbe.)	95.00	50.00	30.00
186	Buck Weaver	1,000	285.00	170.00
187	Carl Weilman	95.00	50.00	30.00
188	Zach Wheat	390.00	190.00	115.00
189	Geo. Whitted	95.00	50.00	30.00
190	Fred Williams	95.00	50.00	30.00
191	Art Wilson	95.00	50.00	30.00
192	J. Owen Wilson	95.00	50.00	30.00
193	Ivy Wingo	95.00	50.00	30.00
194	"Mel" Wolfgang	95.00	50.00	30.00
195	Joe Wood	500.00	120.00	75.00
196	Steve Yerkes	95.00	50.00	30.00
197	"Pep" Young	95.00	50.00	30.00
198	Rollie Zeider	95.00	50.00	30.00
199	Heiny Zimmerman	95.00	50.00	30.00
200	Ed. Zwilling	95.00	50.00	30.00

1919 Sporting News (M101-6)

(The issue listed in previous editions as 1919 Sporting News Supplements (M101-6) is now listed as 1917-1920 Felix Mendelsohn.)

1926 Sporting News Supplements (M101-7)

This set of 11 player photos was issued as a post-World Series weekly supplement by The Sporting News in 1926. Sepia-toned portrait or posed photos are featured on the 7" x 10" supplements. The player's name and team are printed at the bottom, while a line indentifying The Sporting News and the date appear in the upper left corner. The unnumbered set includes a half-dozen Hall of Famers. Large-format (10" x 14-1/4") team photos of the 1926 Yankees (October 28) and Cardinals were also issued in the weeks preceding the start of issue for the weekly player supplements.

	NM	EX	VG
Complete Set (13):	2,000	800.00	400.00
Common Player:	40.00	16.00	8.00
(1) Hazen "Kiki" Cuyler	100.00	40.00	20.00
(2) Rogers Hornsby	125.00	50.00	25.00
(3) Tony Lazzeri	100.00	40.00	20.00
(4) Harry E. Manush (Henry)	100.00	40.00	20.00
(5) John Mostil	40.00	16.00	8.00
(6) Harry Rice	40.00	16.00	8.00
(7) George Herman "Babe" Ruth	1,200	480.00	240.00
(8) Al Simmons	100.00	40.00	20.00
(9) Harold "Pie" Traynor	100.00	40.00	20.00
(10) George Uhle	40.00	16.00	8.00
(11) Glenn Wright	40.00	16.00	8.00
(12) 1926 Cardinals Team Photo	100.00	40.00	20.00
(13) 1926 Yankees Team Photo	200.00	80.00	40.00

1927-1928 Sporting News Ad-Back Supplements (M101-7)

 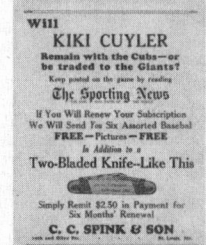

Evidently faced with a surplus of player supplements from its 1926 issue, The Sporting News recycled at least some of them in subsequent years as subscription sales advertising. Fronts of the supplements differ in that the sports paper's logo and the original issue date from 1926 have been removed from the upper-left border. Instead of blank backs, however, the re-issues have color (blue or red seen to date) advertising on back. Respond-by dates in 1927 have been seen rubber-stamped on the back of some pieces, while that of Kiki Cuyler mentions his team as being the Cubs, who he joined in 1928.

	NM	EX	VG
Kiki Cuyler	300.00	125.00	65.00
Babe Ruth	1,500	600.00	300.00

1932 Sporting News Supplements (M101-8)

 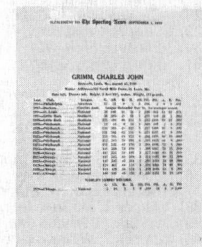

This issue of player-picture supplements from TSN is unusual not only in its brevity - only four were issued - but also in that the pictures have printed matter on back, consisting of player personal data and complete major/minor league stats. Only the Grimm piece has an issue date: Sept. 1, 1932. The pictures are on thin card stock in an 8-1/4" x 10-1/2" format. Fronts have a black-and-white photo with the player named in the wide bottom border.

	NM	EX	VG
Complete Set (4):	2,000	1,000	600.00
Common Player:	250.00	125.00	75.00
(1) Jerome H. (Dizzy) Dean	900.00	450.00	270.00
(2) Vernon Gomez	600.00	300.00	180.00
(3) Charles John Grimm	250.00	125.00	75.00
(4) Lonnie Warneke	250.00	125.00	75.00

1939 Sporting News Supplements (M101-9)

These dated supplements feature a trio of team photos and two star players as individuals. The team pictures are about 15" x 10-1/2" and comprise double-page spreads; the single players are 7-1/2" x 10".

		NM	EX	VG
Complete Set (5):		800.00	400.00	240.00
Common:		150.00	75.00	45.00
(1)	Joseph DiMaggio (Oct. 26)	200.00	100.00	60.00
(2)	Robert Feller (Nov. 9)	150.00	75.00	45.00
(3)	Cincinnati Reds Team (Nov. 2)	150.00	75.00	45.00
(4)	N.Y. Yankees Team (Oct. 19)	200.00	100.00	60.00
(5)	St. Louis Cardinals Team (Nov. 16)	150.00	75.00	45.00

1888 Sporting Times (M117)

Examples of these cards, issued in 1888 and 1889 by the Sporting Times weekly newspaper, are very rare. The complete set price includes all variations. The cabinet-size cards (7-1/4" x 4-1/2") feature line drawings of players in action poses on soft cardboard stock. The cards came in a variety of pastel colors surrounded by a 1/4" white border. The player's last name is printed on each drawing, as are the words "Courtesy Sporting Times New York." A pair of crossed bats and a baseball appear along the bottom of the card. Twenty-seven different players are known to exist. The drawing of Cap Anson is the same one used in the N28 Allen & Ginter series, and some of the other drawings are based on photos used in the popular Old Judge series.

		NM	EX	VG
Common Player:		15,000	10,000	6,000
(1)	Cap Anson	35,000	17,500	10,000
(2)	Jersey Bakely	15,000	10,000	6,000
(3)	Dan Brouthers	25,000	12,500	7,500
(4)	Doc Bushong	15,000	10,000	6,000
(5)	Jack Clements	15,000	10,000	6,000
(6)	Charlie Comiskey	25,000	12,500	7,500
(7)	Jerry Denny	15,000	10,000	6,000
(8)	Buck Ewing	25,000	12,500	7,500
(9)	Dude Esterbrook	15,000	10,000	6,000
(10)	Jay Faatz	15,000	10,000	6,000
(11)	Pud Galvin	25,000	12,500	7,500
(12)	Jack Glasscock	15,000	10,000	6,000
(13)	Tim Keefe	25,000	12,500	7,500
(14)	King Kelly	30,000	15,000	9,000
(15)	Matt Kilroy	15,000	10,000	6,000
(16)	Arlie Latham	15,000	10,000	6,000
(17)	Doggie Miller	15,000	10,000	6,000
(18)	Hank O'Day	15,000	10,000	6,000
(19)	Fred Pfeffer	15,000	10,000	6,000
(20)	Henry Porter	15,000	10,000	6,000
(21)	Toad Ramsey	15,000	10,000	6,000
(22)	Long John Reilly	15,000	10,000	6,000
(23)	Mike Smith	15,000	10,000	6,000
(24)	Harry Stovey	15,000	10,000	6,000
(25)	Sam Thompson	25,000	12,500	7,500
(26)	John Ward	25,000	12,500	7,500
(27)	Mickey Welch	25,000	12,500	7,500

1933 Sport Kings (R338)

This 48-card set features athletes at the top of several sports such as boxing, football, skiing, dogsled racing, and swimming, as well as three hall-of-fame baseball players. the cards measure 2-3/8" x 2-7/8" and feature waist-up portrait artwork.

	NM	EX	VG
Complete Set (48):	30,000	15,000	9,000
Common Player (1-24):	200.00	100.00	60.00
Common Player (25-48):	250.00	125.00	75.00
1 Ty Cobb	4,250	2,100	1,250

		NM	EX	VG
2	Babe Ruth	8,750	4,375	2,625
3	Nat Holman	900.00	450.00	270.00
4	Harold "Red" Grange	1,000	500.00	300.00
5	Ed Wachter	900.00	450.00	270.00
6	Jim Thorpe	1,500	750.00	450.00
7	Bobby Walthour, Jr.	200.00	100.00	60.00
8	Walter Hagen	800.00	400.00	240.00
9	Ed Blood	200.00	100.00	60.00
10	Anton Lekang	200.00	100.00	60.00
11	Charles Jewtraw	200.00	100.00	60.00
12	Bobby McLean	200.00	100.00	60.00
13	LaVerne Fatour	200.00	100.00	60.00
14	Jim Londos	200.00	100.00	60.00
15	Reggie McNamara	200.00	100.00	60.00
16	William Tilden	200.00	100.00	60.00
17	Jack Dempsey	500.00	250.00	150.00
18	Gene Tunney	400.00	200.00	120.00
19	Eddie Shore	600.00	300.00	180.00
20	Duke Kahanamoku	600.00	300.00	180.00
21	Johnny Weissmuller	500.00	250.00	150.00
22	Gene Sarazen	500.00	250.00	150.00
23	Vincent Richards	200.00	100.00	60.00
24	Howie Morenz	600.00	300.00	180.00
25	Ralph Snoddy	250.00	125.00	75.00
26	James R. Wedell	250.00	125.00	75.00
27	Roscoe Turner	250.00	125.00	75.00
28	Jimmy Doolittle	250.00	125.00	75.00
29	Ace Bailey	600.000	300.00	180.00
30	Ching Johnson	600.00	300.00	180.00
31	Bobby Walthour, Jr.	250.00	125.00	75.00
32	Joe Lopchick	900.00	450.00	270.00
33	Eddie Burke	900.00	450.00	270.00
34	Irving Jaffee	250.00	125.00	75.00
35	Knute Rockne	1,000	500.00	300.00
36	Willie Hoppe	250.00	125.00	75.00
37	Helene Madison	250.00	125.00	75.00
38	Bobby Jones	2,600	1,300	780.00
39	Jack Westrope	250.00	125.00	75.00
40	Don George	250.00	125.00	75.00
41	Jim Browning	250.00	125.00	75.00
42	Carl Hubbell	500.00	250.00	150.00
43	Primo Carnera	250.00	125.00	75.00
44	Max Baer	250.00	125.00	75.00
45	Babe Didrickson	1,100	550.00	325.00
46	Ellsworth Vines	250.00	125.00	75.00
47	J. Hubert Stevens	250.00	125.00	75.00
48	Leonhard Seppala	250.00	125.00	75.00

1947 Sport Magazine Premium

This 8-1/2" x 11", blank-back, paper-stock picture appears to have been a premium issued in conjunction with Sport magazine's premiere issue in March 1947, perhaps as a send-away offer. The picture has a black-and-white portrait photo on a bright orange background, surrounded with a white border. In the lower-left corner is "March '47." "15 Sport" appears at lower-right.

		NM	EX	VG
15	Joe DiMaggio	35.00	17.50	10.50

1953 Sport Magazine All-Star Portfolio

This set of 5-3/8" x 7" glossy color pictures was used by Sport Magazine as a subscription premium. Featuring the outstanding photography of Ozzie Sweet, all but the Bob Mathias pictures are portraits, surrounded with a white border and the player name at bottom. Backs are blank. The heavy cardboard mailing envelope contains short athlete biographies.

		NM	EX	VG
Complete Set (10):		350.00	175.00	100.00
Common Player:		30.00	15.00	9.00
(1)	Joe Black	40.00	20.00	12.00
(2)	Robert Cousy (Basketball)	30.00	15.00	9.00

		NM	EX	VG
(3)	Elroy Hirsch (Football)	30.00	15.00	9.00
(4)	Rocky Marciano (Boxing)	45.00	25.00	15.00
(5)	Robert Bruce Mathias (Track and field.)	30.00	15.00	9.00
(6)	Stanley Frank Musial	70.00	35.00	20.00
(7)	John Olszewski (Football)	30.00	15.00	9.00
(8)	Allie Pierce Reynolds	30.00	15.00	9.00
(9)	Robin Evan Roberts	45.00	25.00	15.00
(10)	Robert Clayton Shantz	30.00	15.00	9.00

1964 Sports Heroes Stickers

These red, white and blue 2-3/4" diameter were issued circa 1964 by Hunter Publishing Co., Winston-Salem, N.C. Besides their suitability to be used as wall, notebook, locker, etc., decorations, there were cardboard display pages issued on which the stickers could be placed. Currently only four teams are known to be represented, with the likelihood that four players were issued for each team. The teams represented in the issue are: Cardinals, Tigers, Pirates and Yankees. Gaps have been left in the assigned numbering to accommodate future additions to the checklist.

		NM	EX	VG
Common Player:		75.00	40.00	25.00
(1)	Ernie Broglio	75.00	40.00	25.00
(2)	Roberto Clemente	400.00	200.00	125.00
(3)	Donn Clendenon	100.00	50.00	30.00
(4)	Don Demeter	75.00	40.00	25.00
(6)	Curt Flood	100.00	50.00	30.00
(7)	Bill Freehan	100.00	50.00	30.00
(8)	Bob Friend	75.00	40.00	25.00
(10)	Elston Howard	100.00	50.00	30.00
(11)	Al Kaline	200.00	100.00	60.00
(13)	Mickey Mantle	600.00	300.00	180.00
(14)	Roger Maris	200.00	100.00	60.00
(15)	Bill Mazeroski	150.00	75.00	45.00
(16)	Tom Tresh	100.00	50.00	30.00

1968-69 Sports Cards for Collectors

These Myron Aronstein-drawn 3-1/2" x 4-1/4" postcards feature 78 pre-1950 players. Cards 1-36 feature blank backs, and 37-78 have brief biographical and statistical data. The last four are checklists.

		NM	EX	VG
Complete Set (82):		100.00	50.00	30.00
Common Player:		2.00	1.00	.60
1	Babe Ruth	15.00	7.50	5.00
2	Rube Marquard	2.00	1.00	.60
3	Zack Wheat	2.00	1.00	.60
4	John Clarkson	2.00	1.00	.60
5	Honus Wagner	2.00	1.00	.60
6	Johnny Evers	2.00	1.00	.60
7	Bill Dickey	2.00	1.00	.60
8	Elmer Smith	2.00	1.00	.60
9	Ty Cobb	10.00	5.00	3.00
10	Jack Chesbro	2.00	1.00	.60
11	George Gibson	2.00	1.00	.60
12	Bullet Joe Bush	2.00	1.00	.60
13	George Mullin	2.00	1.00	.60
14	Buddy Meyer	2.00	1.00	.60
15	Jimmy Collins	2.00	1.00	.60
16	Bill Wambsganss	2.00	1.00	.60
17	Jack Barry	2.00	1.00	.60
18	Dickie Kerr	2.00	1.00	.60
19	Connie Mack	2.00	1.00	.60
20	Rabbit Maranville	2.00	1.00	.60
21	Roger Peckinpaugh	2.00	1.00	.60
22	Mickey Cochrane	2.00	1.00	.60
23	George Kelly	2.00	1.00	.60
24	Frank "Home Rune" Baker	2.00	1.00	.60
25	Wally Schang	2.00	1.00	.60
26	Eddie Plank	2.00	1.00	.60
27	Bill Donovan	2.00	1.00	.60
28	Red Faber	2.00	1.00	.60
29	Hack Wilson	2.00	1.00	.60
30	Mordecai "3 Finger" Brown	2.00	1.00	.60
31	Fred Merkle	2.00	1.00	.60
32	Heinie Groh	2.00	1.00	.60
33	Stuffy McInnis	2.00	1.00	.60
34	Hal Chase	2.00	1.00	.60
35	Judge Kenesaw Mountain Landis	2.00	1.00	.60
36	Chief Bender	2.00	1.00	.60
37	Fred Snodgrass	2.00	1.00	.60
38	Tony Lazzeri	2.00	1.00	.60
39	John McGraw	2.00	1.00	.60
40	Mel Ott	10.00	5.00	3.00
41	Grover Alexander	2.00	1.00	.60
42	Rube Waddell	2.00	1.00	.60
43	Wilbert Robinson	2.00	1.00	.60
44	Cap Anson	2.00	1.00	.60
45	Eddie Cicotte	2.00	1.00	.60
46	Hank Gowdy	2.00	1.00	.60
47	Frankie Frisch	2.00	1.00	.60
48	Charles Comiskey	2.00	1.00	.60
49	Clyde Milan	2.00	1.00	.60
50	Jimmy Wilson	2.00	1.00	.60
51	Christy Mathewson	10.00	5.00	3.00
52	Tim Keefe	2.00	1.00	.60
53	Abner Doubleday	2.00	1.00	.60
54	Ed Walsh	2.00	1.00	.60
55	Jim Thorpe	10.00	5.00	3.00
56	Roger Bresnahan	2.00	1.00	.60
57	Frank Chance	2.00	1.00	.60
58	Heinie Manush	2.00	1.00	.60
59	Max Carey	2.00	1.00	.60
60	Joe Tinker	2.00	1.00	.60
61	Benny Kauff	2.00	1.00	.60
62	Fred Clarke	2.00	1.00	.60
63	Smokey Joe Wood	2.00	1.00	.60
64	George Burns	2.00	1.00	.60
65	Walter Johnson	10.00	5.00	3.00
66	Ferdie Schupp	2.00	1.00	.60

		NM	EX	VG
67	Jimmy McAleer	2.00	1.00	.60
68	Larry Gardner	2.00	1.00	.60
69	Buck Ewing	2.00	1.00	.60
70	George Sisler	2.00	1.00	.60
71	Charley Robertson	2.00	1.00	.60
72	Bill Dineen	2.00	1.00	.60
73	Kid Gleason	2.00	1.00	.60
74	Jim Bottomley	2.00	1.00	.60
75	Sam Crawford	2.00	1.00	.60
76	Kid Nichols	2.00	1.00	.60
77	Dick Rudolph	2.00	1.00	.60
78	Bill Klem	2.00	1.00	.60
79	Checklist			
80	Checklist			
81	Checklist			
82	Checklist			

1970 Sports Cards for Collectors Old Timer Postcards

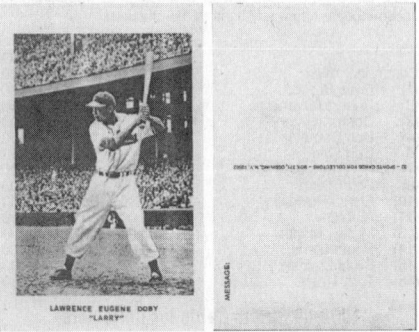

LAWRENCE EUGENE DOBY "LARRY"

The date of issue given here is approximate. This collectors issue "Old Timer Postcard Series" features black-and-white photos bordered in white in a 3-1/2" x 5-1/2" format. Player identification in the bottom border usually offers his complete name on one line and his nickname below. Backs are divided by a card number and the name and address of the issuer. At left is a space for "MESSAGE:."

		NM	EX	VG
Complete Set (32):		75.00	37.50	22.00
Common Player:		4.00	2.00	1.25
1	Babe Ruth, Lou Gehrig	12.00	6.00	3.50
2	Larry Doby	6.00	3.00	1.75
3	Mike Garcia	4.00	2.00	1.25
4	Bob Feller	10.00	5.00	3.00
5	Early Wynn	4.00	2.00	1.25
6	Burleigh Grimes	4.00	2.00	1.25
7	Rabbit Maranville	4.00	2.00	1.25
8	Babe Ruth	15.00	7.50	4.50
9	Lou Gehrig	12.00	6.00	3.50
10	Joe DiMaggio	12.00	6.00	3.50
11	Ty Cobb	10.00	5.00	3.00
12	Lou Boudreau	4.00	2.00	1.25
13	Jimmie Foxx	4.00	2.00	1.25
14	Casey Stengel	6.00	3.00	1.75
15	Kenesaw M. Landis	4.00	2.00	1.25
16	Max Carey	4.00	2.00	1.25
17	Wilbert Robinson	4.00	2.00	1.25
18	Paul Richards	4.00	2.00	1.25
19	Zack Wheat	4.00	2.00	1.25
20	Rube Marquard	4.00	2.00	1.25
21	Dave Bancroft	4.00	2.00	1.25
22	Bobby Thomson	4.00	2.00	1.25
23	Mel Ott	4.00	2.00	1.25
24	Bobo Newsom	4.00	2.00	1.25
25	Johnny Mize	4.00	2.00	1.25
26	Walker Cooper	4.00	2.00	1.25
27	Fred "Dixie" Walker	4.00	2.00	1.25
28	Augie Galan	4.00	2.00	1.25
29	"Snuffy" Sturnweiss (Stirnweiss)	4.00	2.00	1.25
30	Floyd Caves "Babe" Herman	4.00	2.00	1.25
31	Babe Ruth	15.00	7.50	4.50
32	Babe Ruth	15.00	7.50	4.50

1970 Sports Cards for Collectors Sports Stuff

This set includes 10 Myron Aronsten-drawn 3-1/2" x 4-1/4" postcards depicting pre-1920 baseball luminaries, trivia, and legends.

		NM	EX	VG
Complete Set (10):		20.00	10.00	6.00
Common Player:		2.00	1.00	.60
1	Manager Trivia	2.00	1.00	.60
2	1914 Miracle Braves	2.00	1.00	.60
3	1919 Black Sox	2.00	1.00	.60
4	Eddie Plank, Fred Clarke, Roger Bresnahan, Babe Ruth	5.00	2.50	1.50
5	Bobby Lowe	2.00	1.00	.60
6	$100,000 Athletics Infield	2.00	1.00	.60
7	Joe Bush, Eddie Plank, Chief Bender	2.00	1.00	.60
8	Joe Tinker, Johnny Evers, Frank Chance	2.00	1.00	.60
9	Wilbert Robinson, John McGraw, Roger Peckinpaugh	2.00	1.00	.60
10	Ty Cobb	5.00	2.50	1.50

1977-79 Sportscaster

This massive set of full-color cards includes players from dozens of different sports - some of them very obscure - among more than 2,000 different subjects, making it one of the biggest sets of trading cards ever issued. Available by mail subscription from 1977 through 1979, the Sportscaster cards are large, measuring 4-3/4" x 6-1/4". Subscribers were mailed one series of 24 cards for $1.89 plus postage every month or so. The set has an international flavor to it, including such sports as rugby, soccer, lawn bowling, fencing, karate, bicycling, curling, skiing, bullfighting, auto racing, mountain climbing, hang gliding, yachting, sailing, badminton, bobsledding, etc. Each card has a series of icons in the upper-right corner to assist collectors in the various methods of sorting. Most popular among American collectors are the baseball, football and basketball stars in the set, which includes the 140 baseball subjects listed here. The checklist includes many Hall of Famers. Backs contain detailed write-ups of the player featured. Because the set was issued in series, and many collectors dropped out of the program before the end, cards in the higher series are especially scarce. This accounts for prices on some of the superstar cards, issued in early series, being lower than for some of the lesser-known players. The cards of Aaron and Bench are quite common because they were mailed to large numbers of persons as samples to introduce the program. The cards were also sold in several European countries and can be found with backs printed in French, Swedish and other languages.

		NM	EX	VG
Complete (Baseball) Set (140):		350.00	175.00	100.00
Common Player:		1.00	.50	.30
(1)	Henry Aaron	4.00	2.00	1.25
(2)	Danny Ainge	30.00	15.00	9.00
(3)	Emmett Ashford/Umpire	2.50	1.25	.70
(4)	Ernie Banks	2.75	1.50	.80
(5)	Johnny Bench	7.50	3.75	2.25
(6)	Vida Blue	1.75	.90	.50
(7)	Bert Blyleven	1.25	.60	.40
(8)	Bobby Bonds	3.25	1.75	1.00
(9)	Lyman Bostock	1.25	.60	.40
(10)	George Brett	5.00	2.50	1.50
(11)	Lou Brock	3.25	1.75	1.00
(12)	Jeff Burroughs	1.25	.60	.40
(13)	Roy Campanella	8.00	4.00	2.50
(14)	John Candelaria	1.25	.60	.40
(15)	Rod Carew	3.25	1.75	1.00
(16)	Steve Carlton	4.00	2.00	1.25
(17)	Ron Cey	1.00	.50	.30
(18)	Roberto Clemente	10.00	5.00	3.00
(19)	Steve Dembowski	2.25	1.25	.70
(20)	Joe DiMaggio	5.00	2.50	1.50
(21)	Dennis Eckersley	4.00	2.00	1.25
(22)	Mark Fidrych	1.75	.90	.50
(23)	Carlton Fisk	6.00	3.00	1.75
(24)	Mike Flanagan	3.00	1.50	.90
(25)	Steve Garvey	5.00	2.50	1.50
(26)	Ron Guidry	3.00	1.50	.90
(27)	Gil Hodges	4.00	2.00	1.25
(28)	Catfish Hunter	4.00	2.00	1.25
(29)	Tommy John	1.25	.60	.40
(30)	Randy Jones	1.00	.50	.30
(31)	Dave Kingman	1.75	.90	.50
(32)	Sandy Koufax	6.00	3.00	1.75
(33)	Tommy Lasorda	6.50	3.25	2.00
(34)	Ron LeFlore	1.25	.60	.40
(35)	Greg Luzinski	1.00	.50	.30
(36)	Billy Martin	3.25	1.75	1.00
(37)	Willie Mays	4.00	2.00	1.25
(38)	Lee Mazzilli	5.00	2.50	1.50
(39)	Willie McCovey	3.75	2.00	1.25
(40)	Joe Morgan	2.75	1.50	.80
(41)	Thurman Munson	4.00	2.00	1.25
(42)	Stan Musial	5.00	2.50	1.50
(43)	Phil Niekro	4.00	2.00	1.25
(44)	Jim Palmer	3.00	1.50	.90
(45)	Dave Parker	1.75	.90	.50
(46)	Freddie Patek	1.25	.60	.40
(47)	Gaylord Perry	2.25	1.25	.70
(48)	Jim Piersall	2.75	1.50	.80
(49)	Vada Pinson	1.25	.60	.40
(50)	Rick Reuschel	1.25	.60	.40
(51)	Jim Rice	6.00	3.00	1.75
(52)	J.R. Richard	2.25	1.25	.70
(53)	Brooks Robinson	3.75	2.00	1.25
(54)	Frank Robinson	5.00	2.50	1.50
(55)	Jackie Robinson	5.00	2.50	1.50
(56)	Pete Rose	6.00	3.00	1.75
(57)	Joe Rudi	1.00	.50	.30
(58)	Babe Ruth	6.00	3.00	1.75
(59)	Nolan Ryan	7.00	3.50	2.00
(60)	Tom Seaver	3.75	2.00	1.25
(61)	Warren Spahn	3.75	2.00	1.25
(62)	Monty Stratton	2.25	1.25	.70
(63)	Craig Swan	1.75	.90	.50
(64)	Frank Tanana	1.00	.50	.30
(65)	Ron Taylor	2.25	1.25	.70
(66)	Garry Templeton	1.00	.50	.30
(67)	Gene Tenace	1.00	.50	.30
(68)	Bobby Thomson	1.75	.90	.50
(69)	Andre Thornton	1.25	.60	.40
(70)	Johnny VanderMeer	1.75	.90	.50
(71)	Ted Williams	7.00	3.50	2.00
(72)	Maury Wills	1.00	.50	.30
(73)	Hack Wilson	3.25	1.75	1.00
(74)	Dave Winfield/Htg	8.00	4.00	2.50
(75)	Dave Winfield/Portrait	4.00	2.00	1.25
(76)	Cy Young	2.75	1.50	.80
(77)	The 1927 Yankees	2.75	1.50	.80
(78)	1969 Mets	6.50	3.25	2.00
(79)	All-Star Game (Steve Garvey, Joe Morgan)	2.75	1.50	.80
(80)	Amateur Draft (Rick Monday)	1.25	.60	.40
(81)	At-A-Glance Reference (Tom Seaver)	5.00	2.50	1.50
(82)	Babe Ruth Baseball (Ed Figueroa)	6.50	3.25	2.00
(83)	Baltimore Memorial Stadium	3.00	1.50	.90
(84)	Boston's Fenway Park	5.00	2.50	1.50
(85)	Brother vs. Brother (Joe Niekro)	2.75	1.50	.80
(86)	Busch Memorial Stadium	2.50	1.25	.70
(87)	Candlestick Park	2.00	1.00	.60
(88)	Cape Cod League (Jim Beattie)	3.00	1.50	1.75
(89)	A Century and a Half of Baseball (Johnny Bench)	1.75	.90	.50
(90)	Cy Young Award (Tom Seaver)	2.75	1.50	.80
(91)	The Dean Brothers (Dizzy Dean, Paul Dean)	5.00	2.50	1.50
(92)	Designated Hitter (Rusty Staub)	2.25	1.25	.70
(93)	Dodger Stadium	2.75	1.50	.80
(94)	Perfect Game (Don Larsen)	3.25	1.75	1.00
(95)	The Double Steal (Davey Lopes)	5.00	2.50	1.50
(96)	Fenway Park	4.00	2.00	1.25
(97)	The Firemen (Goose Gossage)	4.00	2.00	1.25
(98)	Forever Blowing Bubbles (Davey Lopes)	2.00	1.00	.60
(99)	The Forsch Brothers (Bob Forsch, Ken Forsch)	5.00	2.50	1.50
(100)	Four Home Runs In A Game (Mike Schmidt)	6.50	3.25	2.00
(101)	400-Homer Club (Duke Snider)	5.00	2.50	1.50
(102)	Great Moments (Bob Gibson)	3.25	1.75	1.00
(103)	Great Moments (Ferguson Jenkins)	2.25	1.25	.70
(104)	Great Moments (Mickey Lolich)	1.75	.90	.50
(105)	Great Moments (Carl Yastrzemski)	3.25	1.75	1.00
(106)	Hidden Ball Trick (Carl Yastrzemski)	2.75	1.50	.80
(107)	Hit And Run (George Foster)	1.25	.60	.40
(108)	Hitting The Cutoff Man	1.00	.50	.30
(109)	Hitting Pitchers (Don Drysdale)	3.25	1.75	1.00
(110)	Infield Fly Rule (Bobby Grich)	1.25	.60	.40
(111)	Instruction (Rod Carew)	2.75	1.50	.80
(112)	Interference (Johnny Bench)	2.75	1.50	.80
(113)	Iron Mike (Pitching Machine)	2.75	1.50	.80
(114)	Keeping Score	1.75	.90	.50
(115)	Like Father, Like Son (Roy Smalley)	3.75	2.00	1.25
(116)	Lingo I (Gary Carter)	1.75	.90	.50
(117)	Lingo II (Earl Weaver)	2.75	1.50	.80
(118)	Little Leagues To Big Leagues (Hector Torres)	1.75	.90	.50
(119)	Maris and Mantle (Mickey Mantle, Roger Maris)	4.00	2.00	1.25
(120)	Measurements (Memorial Stadium)	1.00	.50	.30
(121)	The Money Game (Dennis Eckersley)	6.00	3.00	1.75
(122)	NCAA Tournament (Aggies-Longhorns)	1.75	.90	.50
(123)	The Oakland A's, 1971-75	3.00	1.50	.90
(124)	The Perfect Game (Sandy Koufax)	3.50	1.75	1.00
(125)	Pickoff (Luis Tiant)	1.25	.60	.40
(126)	The Presidential Ball (William Howard Taft)	1.75	.90	.50
(127)	Relief Pitching (Mike Marshall)	1.25	.60	.40
(128)	The Rules (Hank Aaron)	2.75	1.50	.80
(129)	Rundown (Mets vs. Astros)	1.75	.90	.50
(130)	7th Game of the World Series (Bert Campaneris)	2.25	1.25	.70
(131)	Shea Stadium	2.50	1.25	.70
(132)	The 3000 Hit Club (Roberto Clemente)	8.00	4.00	2.50
(133)	Training Camps (Orioles)	2.75	1.50	.80
(134)	Triple Crown (Carl Yastrzemski)	16.00	8.00	4.75
(135)	Triple Play (Rick Burleson)	2.75	1.50	.80
(136)	Triple Play (Bill Wambsganss)	1.75	.90	.50
(137)	Umpires Strike	1.75	.90	.50
(138)	Veterans Stadium	2.50	1.25	.70
(139)	Wrigley Marathon (Mike Schmidt)	8.00	4.00	2.50
(140)	Yankee Stadium	1.00	.50	.30
Beyond Sports (Baseball) Set: (6):		.00	.00	.00
(1)	Clemente Award (Andre Thornton)	5.00	2.50	1.50
(2)	Clowns (Al Schact, Nick Altrock)	4.00	2.00	1.25
(3)	Fellowship of Christian Athletes (Don Kessinger)	4.00	2.00	1.25

		NM	EX	VG
(4)	High School Record Book (David Clyde)	2.50	1.25	.70
(5)	Hutchinson Award (Al Kaline)	40.00	20.00	12.00
(6)	Walkie-Talkie (Yogi Berra)	5.00	2.50	1.50

1977 Sports Challenge Records

Taped highlights and an interview with the player are featured on this series of 33-1/3 RPM records. The 6" diameter records have a centerhole to be punched out to play the record. Fronts have a stylized picture of the player, his name and a title. Backs describe the highlight and give other career details.

		NM	EX	VG
	Complete Set (12):	250.00	125.00	75.00
	Common Player:	20.00	10.00	6.00
(1)	Henry Aaron (Hits 715th Homer)	45.00	22.50	13.50
(2)	Johnny Bench (Beats Pirates in '72 Playoff)	30.00	15.00	9.00
(3)	Jerry Koosman, Don Clendenon (1969 Miracle Mets)	20.00	10.00	6.00
(4)	Don Larsen ('56 World Series Perfect Game)	20.00	10.00	6.00
(5)	Fred Lynn (Has Incredible Day in Detroit)	20.00	10.00	6.00
(6)	Willie Mays (Hits 1st Met Homer)	35.00	17.50	10.50
(7)	Bill Mazeroski (Wins 1960 World Series)	25.00	12.50	7.50
(8)	Frank Robinson (Homers 1st Time as Indian)	20.00	10.00	6.00
(9)	Nolan Ryan (4th No Hitter)	45.00	22.50	13.50
(10)	Tom Seaver (Cubs Ruin Perfect Game)	25.00	12.50	7.50
(11)	Bobby Thomson (Shot Heard 'Round the World)	20.00	10.00	6.00
(12)	Ted Williams (Last Time at Bat in Boston)	35.00	17.50	10.50

1926 Sports Co. of America Champions

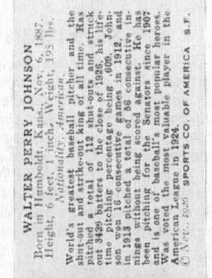

Little was known of these small (1-1/2" x 2-1/4") black-and-white cards until an original store display was discovered in the late 1980s. Carrying a copyright date of November 1926, from Sports Co. of America, a San Francisco publishing firm, these cards were produced for A. G. Spalding & Bros., the sporting goods firm. Each card was issued in a wax paper baggie with a like-sized red, white and blue "Sport-Scrip" which was serial numbered for use in a candy prize drawing at the store or could be redeemed for 10 cents on Spalding equipment. The cards themselves feature ornately framed photos at center, with "CHAMPIONS" in a cartouche at top and the player's name and sport in a second ornate frame at bottom. Most backs have biographical data and career notes, but some are seen with advertising offering an album for the pieces. Nearly 50 baseball players are known from a list of over 175 male and female athletes from sports as diverse as fishing, chess and balloon racing. The unnumbered baseball players from the set are checklisted here in alphabetical order.

		NM	EX	VG
	Common Baseball Player:	45.00	20.00	10.00
	Ad Back: 2X			
(1)	"Babe" Adams	45.00	20.00	10.00
(2)	Grover Alexander	275.00	110.00	55.00
(3)	Nick Altrock	45.00	20.00	10.00
(4)	Dave Bancroft	220.00	90.00	45.00
(5)	Jesse Barnes	45.00	20.00	10.00
(6)	Oswald Bluege	45.00	20.00	10.00
(7)	Jim Bottomley	220.00	90.00	45.00
(8)	Max Carey	220.00	90.00	45.00
(9)	Ty Cobb (Possibly Unique)			
(10)	Mickey Cochrane	220.00	90.00	45.00
(11)	Eddie Collins	220.00	90.00	45.00
(12)	Stan Coveleskie (Coveleski)	220.00	90.00	45.00
(13)	Kiki Cuyler	220.00	90.00	45.00
(14)	Hank DeBerry	45.00	20.00	10.00
(15)	Jack Fournier	45.00	20.00	10.00
(16)	Goose Goslin	220.00	90.00	45.00
(17)	Charlie Grimm	45.00	20.00	10.00
(18)	Bucky Harris	220.00	90.00	45.00
(19)	Gabby Hartnett	220.00	90.00	45.00
(20)	Fred Hofmann	45.00	20.00	10.00
(21)	Rogers Hornsby	275.00	110.00	55.00
(22)	Waite Hoyt	220.00	90.00	45.00
(23)	Walter Johnson	715.00	290.00	145.00
(24)	Joe Judge	45.00	20.00	10.00
(25)	Willie Kamm	45.00	20.00	10.00
(26)	Tony Lazzeri	220.00	90.00	45.00
(27)	Rabbit Maranville	220.00	90.00	45.00
(28)	Fred Marberry	45.00	20.00	10.00
(29)	Rube Marquard	220.00	90.00	45.00
(30)	"Stuffy" McInnis	45.00	20.00	10.00
(31)	"Babe" Pinelli	45.00	20.00	10.00
(32)	Wally Pipp	45.00	20.00	10.00
(33)	Sam Rice	220.00	90.00	45.00
(34)	Emory Rigney	45.00	20.00	10.00
(35)	Dutch Ruether	45.00	20.00	10.00
(36a)	Babe Ruth (1926 Copyright)	1,850	925.00	555.00
(36b)	Babe Ruth (1927 Copyright)	7,500	3,750	2,200
(37)	Ray Schalk	220.00	90.00	45.00
(38)	Joey Sewell	220.00	90.00	45.00
(39)	Urban Shocker	45.00	20.00	10.00
(40)	Al Simmons	220.00	90.00	45.00
(41)	George Sisler	220.00	90.00	45.00
(42)	Tris Speaker	275.00	110.00	55.00
(43)	Pie Traynor	220.00	90.00	45.00
(44)	George Uhle	45.00	20.00	10.00
(45)	Paul Waner	220.00	90.00	45.00
(46)	Aaron L. Ward	45.00	20.00	10.00
(47)	Ken Williams	45.00	20.00	10.00
(48)	Glenn Wright	45.00	20.00	10.00
(49)	Emil Yde	45.00	20.00	10.00

1946-49 Sports Exchange All-Star Picture File

Jesse Peter "Honus" Wagner
Facts and Figures

Produced and sold (originally at 50 cents per series) by "The Trading Post," one of the first card collectors' publications, over a period which spanned several years in the late 1940s, this 113-card set was issued in 12 series. Most of the series were nine cards each, printed in black-and-white, unnumbered and blank-backed in a 7" x 10" format. The first 27 cards carry no series designation but were advertised as Series 1A and 1B and Series 2. Series 3 features 11 cards and is printed in sepia tones rather than black-and-white. The fourth series is also unmarked. The final two series consist of 12 cards each, printed two per sheet in smaller format. The photos are labeled as originating with the International News Service. Most of the same players and photos appearing in this set are also found in the Sports Exchange Baseball Miniatures set. Because this was one of the first baseball card sets issued after World War II, it contains cards of several players not found in other issues. The set carries a W603 designation in the "American Card Catalog." Cards are listed alphabetically within series in the checklist which follows.

		NM	EX	VG
	Complete Set (113):	2,750	1,350	825.00
	Common Card:	15.00	7.50	4.50
SERIES 1A				
(1)	Phil Cavaretta	15.00	7.50	4.50
(2)	Walker Cooper	15.00	7.50	4.50
(3)	Dave Ferriss	15.00	7.50	4.50
(4)	Les Fleming	15.00	7.50	4.50
(5)	Whitey Kurowski	15.00	7.50	4.50
(6)	Marty Marion	20.00	10.00	6.00
(7)	Rip Sewell	15.00	7.50	4.50
(8)	Eddie Stanky	20.00	10.00	6.00
(9)	Dixie Walker	15.00	7.50	4.50
SERIES 1B				
(10)	Bill Dickey	40.00	20.00	12.00
(11)	Bobby Doerr	30.00	15.00	9.00
(12)	Bob Feller	40.00	20.00	12.00
(13)	Hank Greenberg	75.00	37.00	22.00
(14)	George McQuinn	15.00	7.50	4.50
(15)	Ray Mueller	15.00	7.50	4.50
(16)	Hal Newhouser	30.00	15.00	9.00
(17)	Dick Wakefield	15.00	7.50	4.50
(18)	Ted Williams	150.00	75.00	45.00
SERIES 2				
(19)	Al Benton	15.00	7.50	4.50
(20)	Lou Boudreau	30.00	15.00	9.00
(21)	Spud Chandler	15.00	7.50	4.50
(22)	Jeff Heath	15.00	7.50	4.50
(23)	Kirby Higbe	15.00	7.50	4.50
(24)	Tex Hughson	15.00	7.50	4.50
(25)	Stan Musial	175.00	90.00	55.00
(26)	Howie Pollet	15.00	7.50	4.50
(27)	Enos Slaughter	40.00	20.00	12.00
SERIES 3				
(28)	Harry Brecheen	15.00	7.50	4.50
(29)	Dom DiMaggio	30.00	15.00	9.00
(30)	Del Ennis	15.00	7.50	4.50
(31)	Al Evans	15.00	7.50	4.50
(32)	Johnny Lindell	15.00	7.50	4.50
(33)	Johnny Mize	35.00	17.50	10.50
(34)	Johnny Pesky	15.00	7.50	4.50
(35)	Pete Reiser	15.00	7.50	4.50
(36a)	Aaron Robinson/Throwing	15.00	7.50	4.50
(36b)	Aaron Robinson/Fldg	15.00	7.50	4.50
(37)	1946 Boston Red Sox Team	30.00	15.00	9.00
(38)	1946 St. Louis Cardinals Team	30.00	15.00	9.00
SERIES 4				
(39)	Jimmie Foxx	45.00	22.00	13.50
(40)	Frank Frisch	30.00	15.00	9.00
(41)	Lou Gehrig	150.00	75.00	45.00
(42)	Lefty Grove	35.00	17.50	10.50
(43)	Bill Hallahan	15.00	7.50	4.50
(44)	Rogers "Rajah" Hornsby	45.00	22.00	13.50
(45)	Carl Hubbell	30.00	15.00	9.00
(46)	Babe Ruth	250.00	125.00	75.00
(47)	Hack Wilson	30.00	15.00	9.00
SERIES 5				
(48)	Eddie Dyer	15.00	7.50	4.50
(49)	Charlie Grimm	15.00	7.50	4.50
(50)	Billy Herman	30.00	15.00	9.00
(51)	Ted Lyons	30.00	15.00	9.00
(52)	Lefty O'Doul	25.00	12.50	7.50
(53)	Steve O'Neill	15.00	7.50	4.50
(54)	Herb Pennock	30.00	15.00	9.00
(55)	Luke Sewell	15.00	7.50	4.50
(56)	Billy Southworth	15.00	7.50	4.50
SERIES 6				
(57)	Ewell Blackwell	25.00	12.50	7.50
(58)	Jimmy Outlaw	15.00	7.50	4.50
(59)	Andy Pafko	15.00	7.50	4.50
(60)	Pee Wee Reese	75.00	37.00	22.00
(61)	Phil Rizzuto	60.00	30.00	18.00
(62)	Buddy Rosar	15.00	7.50	4.50
(63)	Johnny Sain	25.00	12.50	7.50
(64)	Dizzy Trout	15.00	7.50	4.50
(65)	Harry Walker	15.00	7.50	4.50
SERIES 7				
(66)	Floyd Bevens	15.00	7.50	4.50
(67)	Hugh Casey	15.00	7.50	4.50
(68)	Sam Chapman	15.00	7.50	4.50
(69)	Joe DiMaggio	150.00	75.00	45.00
(70)	Tommy Henrich	25.00	12.50	7.50
(71)	Ralph Kiner	30.00	15.00	9.00
(72)	Cookie Lavagetto	15.00	7.50	4.50
(73)	Vic Lombardi	15.00	7.50	4.50
(74)	Cecil Travis	15.00	7.50	4.50
SERIES 8				
(75)	Nick Altrock	20.00	10.00	6.00
(76)	Mark Christman	15.00	7.50	4.50
(77)	Earle Combs	30.00	15.00	9.00
(78)	Travis Jackson	30.00	15.00	9.00
(79)	Bob Muncrief	15.00	7.50	4.50
(80)	Earl Neale	25.00	12.50	7.50
(81)	Joe Page	15.00	7.50	4.50
(82)	Honus Wagner	75.00	37.00	22.00
(83)	Mickey Witek	15.00	7.50	4.50
SERIES 9				
(84)	George Case	15.00	7.50	4.50
(85)	Jake Early	15.00	7.50	4.50
(86)	Carl Furillo	30.00	15.00	9.00
(87)	Augie Galan	15.00	7.50	4.50
(88)	Bert Haas	15.00	7.50	4.50
(89)	Johnny Hopp	15.00	7.50	4.50
(90)	Ray Lamanno	15.00	7.50	4.50
(91)	Buddy Lewis	15.00	7.50	4.50
(92)	Warren Spahn	40.00	20.00	12.00
SERIES 10				
(93)	Lu Blue	15.00	7.50	4.50
q94)	Bruce Edwards	15.00	7.50	4.50
(95)	Elbie Fletcher	15.00	7.50	4.50
(96)	Joe Gordon	15.00	7.50	4.50
(97)	Tommy Holmes	15.00	7.50	4.50
(98)	Billy Johnson	15.00	7.50	4.50
(99)	Phil Masi	15.00	7.50	4.50
(100)	Red Munger	15.00	7.50	4.50
(101)	Vern Stephens	15.00	7.50	4.50
SERIES 11				
(102)	Ralph Branca, Ken Keltner	20.00	10.00	6.00
(103)	Mickey Cochrane, Bob Dillinger	40.00	20.00	12.00
(104)	Dizzy Dean, Eddie Joost	80.00	40.00	24.00
(105)	Joe Jackson, Wally Westlake	400.00	200.00	120.00
(106)	Larry Jansen, Yogi Berra	80.00	40.00	24.00
(107)	Peanuts Lowrey, Heinie Manush	40.00	20.00	12.00
SERIES 12				
(108)	Gene Bearden, Dale Mitchell	45.00	22.00	13.50
(109)	Steve Gromek, Earl Torgeson	45.00	22.00	13.50
(110)	Jim Hegan, Mickey Vernon	45.00	22.00	13.50
(111)	Bob Lemon, Red Rolfe	100.00	50.00	30.00
(112)	Billy Meyer, Ben Chapman	45.00	22.00	13.50
(113)	Sibbi Sisti, Zach Taylor	45.00	22.00	13.50

1947 Sports Exchange Baseball Miniatures

Heinie Manush

Produced and sold (originally at $1 per series) by one of the hobby's first periodicals, "The Trading Post," this 108-card set was released in three series, designated by red, green and gold borders. The blank-back, unnumbered cards are printed in black-and-white and were sold in sheets of six. When cut from the sheets, individual cards in the red- and green-bordered series measure 2-1/2" x 3", while the gold-bordered cards measure 2-1/2" x 3-1/8". The set is checklisted here alphabetically within series. The set carries an American Card Catalog designation of W602.

		NM	EX	VG
	Complete Set (108):	4,750	2,400	1,400
	Common Player:	15.00	7.50	4.50

GREEN BORDER SERIES

		NM	EX	VG
(1)	Nick Altrock	20.00	10.00	6.00
(2)	Floyd Bevens	15.00	7.50	4.50
(3)	Ewell Blackwell	20.00	10.00	6.00
(4)	Lou Boudreau	35.00	17.50	10.50
(5)	Harry Brecheen	15.00	7.50	4.50
(6)	Hugh Casey	15.00	7.50	4.50
(7)	Phil Cavaretta	15.00	7.50	4.50
(8)	Sam Chapman	15.00	7.50	4.50
(9)	Mark Christman	15.00	7.50	4.50
(10)	Bill Dickey	40.00	20.00	12.00
(11)	Dom DiMaggio	25.00	12.50	7.50
(12)	Joe DiMaggio	400.00	200.00	120.00
(13)	Eddie Dyer	15.00	7.50	4.50
(14)	Frank Frisch	40.00	20.00	12.00
(15)	Lou Gehrig	275.00	135.00	82.00
(16)	Charlie Grimm	15.00	7.50	4.50
(17)	Lefty Grove	40.00	20.00	12.00
(18)	Tommy Henrich	20.00	10.00	6.00
(19)	Ralph Kiner	35.00	17.50	10.50
(20)	Cookie Lavagetto	15.00	7.50	4.50
(21)	Vic Lombardi	15.00	7.50	4.50
(22)	Ted Lyons	35.00	17.50	10.50
(23)	Bob Muncrief	15.00	7.50	4.50
(24)	Stan Musial	160.00	80.00	48.00
(25)	Steve O'Neill	15.00	7.50	4.50
(26)	Jimmy Outlaw	15.00	7.50	4.50
(27)	Joe Page	15.00	7.50	4.50
(28)	Pee Wee Reese	65.00	32.00	19.50
(29)	Phil Rizzuto	65.00	32.00	19.50
(30)	Buddy Rosar	15.00	7.50	4.50
(31)	Johnny Sain	20.00	10.00	6.00
(32)	Billy Southworth	15.00	7.50	4.50
(33)	Cecil Travis	15.00	7.50	4.50
(34)	Honus Wagner	90.00	45.00	27.00
(35)	Harry Walker	15.00	7.50	4.50
(36)	Mickey Witek	15.00	7.50	4.50

RED BORDER SERIES

		NM	EX	VG
(37)	Yogi Berra	80.00	40.00	24.00
(38)	Lu Blue	15.00	7.50	4.50
(39)	Ben Chapman	15.00	7.50	4.50
(40)	Mickey Cochrane	35.00	17.50	10.50
(41)	Earle Combs	35.00	17.50	10.50
(42)	Dizzy Dean	95.00	47.00	28.00
(43)	Bob Dillinger	15.00	7.50	4.50
(44)	Bobby Doerr	35.00	17.50	10.50
(45)	Al Evans	15.00	7.50	4.50
(46)	Jimmy (Jimmie) Foxx	50.00	25.00	15.00
(47)	Joe Gordon	15.00	7.50	4.50
(48)	Bill Hallahan	15.00	7.50	4.50
(49)	Tommy Holmes	15.00	7.50	4.50
(50)	Rogers Hornsby	50.00	25.00	15.00
(51)	Carl Hubbell	45.00	22.00	13.50
(52)	Travis Jackson	35.00	17.50	10.50
(53)	Bill Johnson	15.00	7.50	4.50
(54)	Ken Keltner	15.00	7.50	4.50
(55)	Whitey Kurowski	15.00	7.50	4.50
(56)	Ray Lamanno	15.00	7.50	4.50
(57)	Johnny Lindell	15.00	7.50	4.50
(58)	Peanuts Lowrey	15.00	7.50	4.50
(59)	Phil Masi	15.00	7.50	4.50
(60)	Earl Neale	20.00	10.00	6.00
(61)	Hal Newhouser	35.00	17.50	10.50
(62)	Lefty O'Doul	25.00	12.50	7.50
(63)	Herb Pennock	35.00	17.50	10.50
(64)	Red Rolfe	35.00	17.50	10.50
(65)	Babe Ruth	450.00	225.00	135.00
(66)	Luke Sewell	15.00	7.50	4.50
(67)	Rip Sewell	15.00	7.50	4.50
(68)	Warren Spahn	60.00	30.00	18.00
(69)	Vern Stephens	15.00	7.50	4.50
(70)	Dizzy Trout	15.00	7.50	4.50
(71)	Wally Westlake	15.00	7.50	4.50
(72)	Hack Wilson	50.00	25.00	15.00

GOLD BORDER SERIES

		NM	EX	VG
(73)	Al Benton	30.00	15.00	9.00
(74)	Ralph Branca	25.00	12.50	7.50
(75)	George Case	30.00	15.00	9.00
(76)	Spud Chandler	30.00	15.00	9.00
(77)	Jake Early	30.00	15.00	9.00
(78)	Bruce Edwards	30.00	15.00	9.00
(79)	Del Ennis	30.00	15.00	9.00
(80)	Bob Feller	80.00	40.00	24.00
(81)	Dave Ferriss	30.00	15.00	9.00
(82)	Les Fleming	30.00	15.00	9.00
(83)	Carl Furillo	150.00	75.00	45.00
(84)	Augie Galan	30.00	15.00	9.00
(85)	Hank Greenberg	100.00	50.00	30.00
(86)	Bert Haas	30.00	15.00	9.00
(87)	Jeff Heath	30.00	15.00	9.00
(88)	Billy Herman	60.00	30.00	18.00
(89)	Kirby Higbe	30.00	15.00	9.00
(90)	Tex Hughson	30.00	15.00	9.00
(91)	Johnny Hopp	30.00	15.00	9.00
(92)	Joe Jackson	650.00	325.00	195.00
(93)	Larry Jansen	30.00	15.00	9.00
(94)	Eddie Joost	30.00	15.00	9.00
(95)	Buddy Lewis	30.00	15.00	9.00
(96)	Heinie Manush	60.00	30.00	18.00
(97)	Marty Marion	30.00	15.00	9.00
(98)	George McQuinn	30.00	15.00	9.00
(99)	Johnny Mize	60.00	30.00	18.00
(100)	Red Munger	30.00	15.00	9.00
(101)	Andy Pafko	30.00	15.00	9.00
(102)	Johnny Pesky	30.00	15.00	9.00
(103)	Howie Pollet	30.00	15.00	9.00
(104)	Pete Reiser	30.00	15.00	9.00
(105)	Aaron Robinson	30.00	15.00	9.00
(106)	Enos Slaughter	60.00	30.00	18.00
(107)	Dixie Walker	30.00	15.00	9.00
(108)	Ted Williams (Photo actually Bobby Doerr.)	200.00	100.00	60.00

1963 Sports "Hall of Fame" Busts

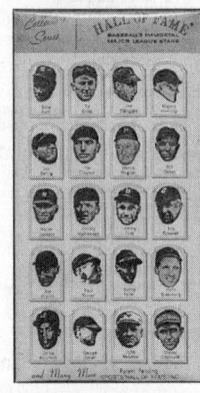

Licensed by the National Baseball Hall of Fame, this set of 20 plastic player busts was produced by Sports "Hall of Fame," Inc., of New York. Each six-inch statue has a white player figure atop a wood-look pedestal with a plaque providing career details. The busts were sold in a red, white and gold display box with photos of the players on the back. Though the box back promised "Many More," only the 20 players pictured were ever issued. Retail price at issue was $1-1.25. The first 12 busts are more common than the final eight, with Foxx and Greenberg especially scarce. Values quoted are for busts alone, add $25 for accompanying box and $50 or more for unopened box with cellophane.

		NM	EX	VG
	Complete Set (20):	3,000	1,500	900.00
	Common Player:	75.00	35.00	20.00
(1)	Babe Ruth	110.00	55.00	30.00
(2)	Ty Cobb	90.00	45.00	25.00
(3)	Joe DiMaggio	110.00	55.00	30.00
(4)	Rogers Hornsby	80.00	40.00	24.00
(5)	Lou Gehrig	100.00	50.00	30.00
(6)	Pie Traynor	75.00	35.00	20.00
(7)	Honus Wagner	150.00	75.00	45.00
(8)	Bill Dickey	110.00	55.00	30.00
(9)	Walter Johnson	135.00	65.00	40.00
(10)	Christy Mathewson	110.00	55.00	30.00
(11)	Jimmie Foxx	335.00	165.00	100.00
(12)	Tris Speaker	75.00	35.00	20.00
(13)	Joe Cronin	180.00	90.00	50.00
(14)	Paul Waner	165.00	80.00	45.00
(15)	Bobby Feller	225.00	110.00	65.00
(16)	Hank Greenberg	350.00	175.00	105.00
(17)	Jackie Robinson	260.00	130.00	75.00
(18)	George Sisler	225.00	110.00	65.00
(19)	John McGraw	225.00	110.00	65.00
(20)	Mickey Cochrane	250.00	125.00	75.00

1954 Sports Illustrated Topps Foldouts

To illustrate a feature about baseball card collecting in its very first issue, Sports Illustrated included a three-page foldout featuring 27 contemporary Topps cards. Printed on glossy paper stock in full color, the paper cards are exact front and back reproductions of the real thing. The foldout panel is found in the Aug. 16, 1954, issue of SI which features on its cover a photo of Eddie Mathews at bat during a night game. The magazine's second issue also contains a 27-card foldout of New York Yankees. The insert reproduces all of Topps' 1954 Yankees cards in full color, and supplements them with black-and-white "cards" in the general style of '54 Topps for those Yankees who appeared only on Bowman cards or on no cards in 1954. The August 23 issue of SI features a stand of golf clubs on its cover. Survivng examples of SI issue #2 are actually scarcer than the debut issue. Singles of the paper cards are rarely encountered. In 2001, SI reprinted 50,000 copies of issue #1 as a subscription premium. These copies are unmarked as reprints and difficult to distinguish from the originals. Many surviving original copies have a mail-in subscription offer card which the reprint does not.

		NM	EX	VG
	Aug. 16, 1954 Issue (Original)	175.00	87.5	52.50
	Aug. 16, 1954 Issue (2001 Reprint)	30.00	15.00	9.00
1	Ted Williams			
2	Gus Zernial			
4	Hank Sauer			
6	Pete Runnels			
7	Ted Kluszewski			
9	Harvey Haddix			
10	Jackie Robinson			
15	Al Rosen			
24	Granny Hamner			
25	Harvey Kuenn			
26	Ray Jablonski			
27	Ferris Fain			
29	Jim Hegan			
30	Ed Mathews			
32	Duke Snider			
34	Jim Rivera			
40	Mel Parnell			
45	Richie Ashburn			
70	Larry Doby			
77	Ray Boone			
85	Bob Turley			
90	Willie Mays			
100	Bob Keegan			
102	Gil Hodges			
119	Johnny Antonelli			
137	Wally Moon			
235	Vern Law			
	Aug. 23, 1954 Issue	225.00	110.00	65.00
5	Ed Lopat			
17	Phil Rizzuto			
37	Whitey Ford			
50	Yogi Berra			
56	Willie Miranda			
62	Eddie Robinson			
83	Joe Collins			
96	Charlie Silvera			
101	Gene Woodling			
105	Andy Carey			
130	Hank Bauer			
175	Frank Leja			
205	Johnny Sain			
230	Bob Kuzava			
239	Bill Skowron			
	Harry Byrd			
	Bob Cerv			
	Jerry Coleman			
	Tom Gorman			
	Bob Grim			
	Mickey Mantle			
	Jim McDonald			
	Gil McDougald			
	Tom Morgan			
	Irv Noren			
	Allie Reynolds			
	Enos Slaughter			

1955 Sports Illustrated Topps Foldouts

SI kicked off the 1955 baseball season by including a page of 1955 Topps card reproductions in its April 11 and April 18 issues. Unlike the tri-fold panels of 1954, the 1955 issues contain only eight reproductions per magazine. Printed in full size in full color on glossy magazine paper, the pages are exact front and back replicas of regular-issue 1955 Topps cards. The April 11 issue features on its cover Willie Mays, Leo Durocher and Lorraine Day (Mrs. D.); the April 18 issue has Al Rosen at bat. Surviving examples of these 1955 SI issues are scarce and the paper cards are seldom seen as singles.

		NM	EX	VG
	April 11, 1955 Issue	200.00	100.00	60.00
1	Dusty Rhodes			
26	Dick Groat			
28	Ernie Banks			
31	Warren Spahn			
56	Ray Jablonski			
67	Wally Moon			
79	Danny Schell			
90	Karl Spooner			
	April 18, 1955 Issue	60.00	30.00	18.00
8	Hal Smith			
10	Bob Keegan			
11	Ferris Fain			
16	Roy Sievers			
38	Bob Turley			
70	Al Rosen			
77	Arnie Portocarrero			
106	Frank Sullivan			

1968-70 Sports Illustrated Posters

Between 1968-70, Sports Illustrated issued a series of baseball player posters. The 2' x 3' blank-back posters have borderless color action or posed photos. In an upper corner are the player identification, copyright, poster number, etc., in small type. Values for the posters issued in 1969 and 1970 are higher than those produced in 1968. Current market values reflect the fact that many superstars' posters were sold in larger quantities than those of journeymen players and survive in greater numbers. The posters are listed here alphabetically within year of issue. Original selling price of the posters was $1.50 each, plus postage.

	NM	EX	VG
Complete Set (86):	2,500	1,250	750.00
Common Player:	10.00	5.00	3.00
1968			
(1) Hank Aaron	45.00	22.50	13.50
(2) Rich Allen	30.00	15.00	9.00
(3) Gene Alley	15.00	7.50	4.50
(4) Felipe Alou	15.00	7.50	4.50
(5) Max Alvis	10.00	5.00	3.00
(6) Bob Aspromonte	10.00	5.00	3.00
(7) Ernie Banks (Photo actually Billy Williams.)	35.00	17.50	10.50
(8) Clete Boyer	12.50	6.25	3.75
(9) Lou Brock	15.00	7.50	4.50
(10) John Callison	15.00	7.50	4.50
(11) Campy Campaneris	12.50	6.25	3.75
(12) Leo Cardenas	12.50	6.25	3.75
(13) Paul Casanova	17.50	8.75	5.25
(14) Orlando Cepeda	17.50	8.75	5.25
(15) Roberto Clemente	185.00	95.00	55.00
(16) Tony Conigliaro	20.00	10.00	6.00
(17) Willie Davis	15.00	7.50	4.50
(18) Don Drysdale	17.50	8.75	5.25
(19) Al Ferrara	12.50	6.25	3.75
(20) Curt Flood	15.00	7.50	4.50
(21) Bill Freehan	30.00	15.00	9.00
(22) Jim Fregosi	10.00	5.00	3.00
(23) Bob Gibson	15.00	7.50	4.50
(24) Bud Harrelson (Photo actually Ken Harrelson.)	20.00	10.00	6.00
(25) Joe Horlen	10.00	5.00	3.00
(26) Tony Horton	15.00	7.50	4.50
(27) Tommy John	12.50	6.25	3.75
(28) Al Kaline	40.00	20.00	12.00
(29) Harmon Killebrew	17.50	8.75	5.25
(30) Jim Lonborg	17.50	8.75	5.25
(31) Jim Maloney	12.50	6.25	3.75
(32) Mickey Mantle	185.00	92.00	55.00
(33) Juan Marichal	17.50	8.75	5.25
(34) Willie Mays	110.00	55.00	35.00
(35) Bill Mazeroski	25.00	12.50	7.50
(36) Tim McCarver	17.50	8.75	5.25
(37) Mike McCormick	15.00	7.50	4.50
(38) Willie McCovey	45.00	22.50	13.50
(39a) Don Mincher (Angels)	15.00	7.50	4.50
(39b) Don Mincher (Pilots)	20.00	10.00	6.00
(40) Rick Monday	12.50	6.25	3.75
(41) Tony Oliva	15.00	7.50	4.50
(42) Rick Reichardt	10.00	5.00	3.00
(43) Brooks Robinson	175.00	90.00	50.00
(44) Frank Robinson	75.00	37.50	22.00
(45) Pete Rose	100.00	50.00	30.00
(46) Ron Santo	17.50	8.75	5.25
(47) Tom Seaver	130.00	65.00	39.00
(48) Chris Short	15.00	7.50	4.50
(49) Reggie Smith	12.50	6.25	3.75
(50) Rusty Staub	17.50	8.75	5.25
(51) Mel Stottlemyre	20.00	10.00	6.00
(52) Ron Swoboda	25.00	12.50	7.50
(53) Cesar Tovar	15.00	7.50	4.50
(54) Earl Wilson	17.50	8.75	5.25
(55) Jim Wynn	10.00	5.00	3.00
(56) Carl Yastrzemski	25.00	12.50	7.50
1969			
(1) Tommie Agee	17.50	8.75	5.25
(2) Mike Andrews	12.50	6.25	3.75
(3) Ernie Banks/Btg	15.00	7.50	4.50
(4a) Gary Bell (Indians)	20.00	10.00	6.00
(4b) Gary Bell (Pilots)	20.00	10.00	6.00
(5a) Tommy Davis (White Sox)	17.50	8.75	5.25
(5b) Tommy Davis (Pilots)	20.00	10.00	6.00
(6) Frank Howard	20.00	10.00	6.00
(7) Reggie Jackson	95.00	47.00	28.00
(8) Fergie Jenkins	45.00	22.00	13.50
(9) Let's Go Mets (Tommie Agee, Jerry Grote, Cleon Jones, Jerry Koosman, Ed Kranepool, Tom Seaver, Ron Swoboda)	20.00	10.00	6.00
(10) Denny McLain	15.00	7.50	4.50
(11) Bobby Murcer	45.00	22.00	13.50
(12) John Odom	17.50	8.75	5.25
(13) Rico Petrocelli	17.50	8.75	5.25
(14) Boog Powell	20.00	10.00	6.00
(15) Roy White	25.00	12.50	7.50
1970			
(1) Glenn Beckert	17.50	8.75	5.25
(2) Bobby Bonds	20.00	10.00	6.00
(3) Rod Carew	17.50	8.75	5.25
(4) Mike Cuellar	17.50	8.75	5.25
(5) Mike Epstein	15.00	7.50	4.50
(6) Ken Holtzman	15.00	7.50	4.50
(7) Cleon Jones	15.00	7.50	4.50
(8) Mickey Lolich	15.00	7.50	4.50
(9) Sam McDowell	20.00	10.00	6.00
(10) Phil Niekro	35.00	17.50	10.50
(11) Wes Parker	17.50	8.75	5.25
(12) Tony Perez	25.00	12.50	7.50
(13) Bill Singer	10.00	5.00	3.00
(14) Walt Williams	10.00	5.00	3.00

1968 Sports Memorabilia All Time Baseball Team

This is one of the earliest collectors' issue baseball card sets created for distribution solely within the hobby. The 2-1/2" x 3-1/2" cards feature the artwork of Art Oulette done in sepia

tones on a white background and surrounded by a yellow border. Backs have career information, copyright and player identification. Issue price was $2.50.

	NM	EX	VG
Complete Set (15):	35.00	17.50	10.00
Common Player:	2.00	1.00	.60
1 Checklist	.50	.25	.15
2 "Connie" Mack	2.00	1.00	.60
3 Walter Johnson	4.00	2.00	1.25
4 Warren Spahn	2.00	1.00	.60
5 Christy Mathewson	4.00	2.00	1.25
6 Lefty Grove	2.00	1.00	.60
7 Mickey Cochrane	2.00	1.00	.60
8 Bill Dickey	2.00	1.00	.60
9 "Tris" Speaker	2.50	1.25	.75
10 "Ty" Cobb	6.00	3.00	2.00
11 "Babe" Ruth	10.00	5.00	3.00
12 "Lou" Gehrig	7.50	3.75	2.25
13 Rogers Hornsby	2.50	1.25	.75
14 "Honus" Wagner	5.00	2.50	1.50
15 "Pie" Traynor	2.00	1.00	.60

1960 Sports Novelties Inc. Genuine Baseball Photos

(See 1960 Leaf for checklist and price guide.)

1960s Sports Pix Premiums

These black-and-white blank-back pictures were distributed as a premium for Sports Pix magazine in the early 1960s. Two sizes are known: A smaller (about 8" x 10") style was issued in the early 1960s, while a larger (about 8-1/2" x 10-1/2") format was produced after 1963. Both styles have the photo bordered in white, with the player name centered at bottom. In the bottom-right corner is a three-line credit to the magazine and its Washington, D.C. address. Gaps have been left in the assigned numbering to accommodate future additions.

	NM	EX	VG
Common Player:	10.00	5.00	3.00
(1) Ty Cobb (Large)	7.50	3.75	2.25
(2) Mickey Cochrane (Large)	3.00	1.50	.90
(3) Rocky Colavito (Large)	5.00	2.50	1.50
(4) Joe Cronin (Large)	3.00	1.50	.90
(5) Bill Dickey (Large)	3.00	2.00	1.00
(6) Joe DiMaggio (Large, glossy, w/caption)	7.50	3.75	2.25
(7) Bob Feller (Large)	3.00	2.00	1.00
(8) Lou Gehrig (Large)	7.50	3.75	2.25
(9) Charlie Gehringer (Large)	3.00	2.00	1.00
(11) "Lefty" Grove (Large)	.00	2.00	1.00
(12) Rogers Hornsby (Large)	3.00	2.00	1.00
(13) Walter Johnson (Large)	5.00	2.50	1.50
(14) Sandy Koufax (Small)	5.00	2.50	1.50
(15) Sandy Koufax (Large)	5.00	2.50	1.50

	NM	EX	VG
(16) Mickey Mantle (Large)	15.00	7.50	4.50
(17) Mickey Mantle (Small)	15.00	7.50	4.50
(18) Roger Maris (Large)	4.50	2.25	1.25
(19) Willie Mays (Large)	7.50	3.75	2.25
(20) Willie Mays (Small)	7.50	3.75	2.25
(21) John McGraw (Large)	3.00	2.00	1.00
(22) Stan Musial (Large)	5.00	2.50	1.50
(24) Babe Ruth (Large)	7.50	3.75	2.25
(25) George Sisler (Large)	3.00	2.00	1.00
(26) Warren Spahn (Large)	3.00	2.00	1.00
(27) "Casey" Stengel (Large)	3.00	2.00	1.00
(28) "Pie" Traynor (Large)	3.00	2.00	1.00
(30) "Honus" Wagner (Large)	4.50	2.25	1.25
(32) Ted Williams (Large)	7.50	3.75	2.25

1979 Sports Reading Series

This set of large-format (about 8-1/2" x 14") was designed to encourage youthful readers. The black-and-white cards have one or more photos and lengthy text describing the player and/or action depicted.

	NM	EX	VG
Complete Set (50):	250.00	125.00	75.00
Common Player:	5.00	2.50	1.50
1 Carlos May	5.00	2.50	1.50
2 Babe Ruth	10.00	5.00	3.00
3 Eddie Gaedel	6.00	3.00	1.75
4 Cesar Gutierrez	5.00	2.50	1.50
5 Ted Williams	7.50	3.75	2.25
6 Pete Gray	6.00	3.00	1.75
7 Hank Aaron	7.50	3.75	2.25
8 Lou Brock	5.00	2.50	1.50
9 Virgil Trucks	5.00	2.50	1.50
10 Cesar Tovar	5.00	2.50	1.50
11 Wrigley Field	5.00	2.50	1.50
12 Ron Guidry	5.00	2.50	1.50
13 Bill Davis	5.00	2.50	1.50
14 Jimmy Piersall	5.00	2.50	1.50
15 Eddie Gaedel	6.00	3.00	1.75
16 Reggie Jackson	7.50	3.75	2.25
17 Mark Fidrych	5.00	2.50	1.50
18 Sandy Koufax	7.50	3.75	2.25
19 Dale Long	5.00	2.50	1.50
20 Herb Score	5.00	2.50	1.50
21 Dizzy Dean, Daffy Dean	5.00	2.50	1.50
22 Stan Musial	7.50	3.75	2.25
23 1903 N.Y. Giants	5.00	2.50	1.50
24 Pete Rose	7.50	3.75	2.25
25 Cy Young	5.00	2.50	1.50
26 Ferguson Jenkins	5.00	2.50	1.50
27 Minnie Minoso	5.00	2.50	1.50
28 Mort Cooper, Walker Cooper	5.00	2.50	1.50
29 Jim Thorpe	7.50	3.75	2.25
30 Lefty Grove	5.00	2.50	1.50
31 Roberto Clemente	9.00	4.50	2.75
32 Pres. Coolidge Throws Out First Ball	5.00	2.50	1.50
33 Lou Gehrig	7.50	3.75	2.25
34 Nolan Ryan	10.00	5.00	3.00
35 1969 N.Y. Mets	5.00	2.50	1.50
36 Yankee Stadium	5.00	2.50	1.50
37 Jackie Robinson	7.50	3.75	2.25
38 Carl Hubbell	5.00	2.50	1.50
39 Willie Mays	7.50	3.75	2.25
40 Mike Schmidt	6.00	3.00	1.75
41 Harvey Haddix	5.00	2.50	1.50
42 Pete Reiser	5.00	2.50	1.50
43 Gary Cooper (Pride of the Yankees)	5.00	2.50	1.50
44 Jackie Robinson	7.50	3.75	2.25
45 Walter Johnson	5.00	2.50	1.50
46 Hall of Fame	5.00	2.50	1.50
47 Jose Morales	5.00	2.50	1.50
48 Rod Carew	5.00	2.50	1.50
49 Lou Boudreau	5.00	2.50	1.50
50 Hank Greenberg	5.00	2.50	1.50

1950 Sport Stars Luckee Key Charms

This series of 1-3/8" square, diamond-format aluminum tags depicts on front an action picture of a player along with his facsimile autograph. A good luck and sportsmanship message appears on back. The charms are holed at the top to accomodate a beaded chain. While the charms themselves are not so marked, they were produced by Ralpat Co., of Cleveland, and sold on an approximately 3" x 5" cardboard backing card which has a line-art portrait of the player, his name, "Sport Stars" and "Luckee Key Charm." Values shown are for complete card/charm combinations. The metal charms themselves would be valued at about 35-50 percent.

1976
BASEBALL CARDS
Complete Set of 630 Cards
$12.99 + $1.00 Postage

You get the complete set of 630 cards in full color. In depth biography and uniform number on the back of every card.

NOT AVAILABLE IN STORES

All the players on your favorite team - $1.00 + 50¢ postage.

SPORTS STARS PUBLISHING CO.
P. O. BOX #132 DEPT JG
Valley Cottage, N. Y. 10989

	NM	EX	VG
Complete Set (5):	150.00	75.00	45.00
Common Player:	15.00	7.50	4.50
(1) Ewell Blackwell	15.00	7.50	4.50
(2) Bob Feller	30.00	15.00	9.00
(3) Ralph Kiner	20.00	10.00	6.00
(4) Hal Newhouser	17.50	8.75	5.25
(5) Ted Williams	100.00	50.00	30.00

1976 Sportstix

These peel-off player stickers were sold in five-piece plastic packs, with specific contents noted on the header. Stickers are found in three formats: 3-1/2" square, 3-1/2" square with clipped corners and 3" diameter round. The set includes 10 numbered current players and three retired baseball superstars identified as A, B and D. Stickers have full-color player pictures on front with no border. The player's name and sticker number are printed in black. Backs are blank. Besides the baseball players, there were stickers for football and basketball players, in a total issue of 30.

	NM	EX	VG
Complete Baseball Set (13):	40.00	20.00	12.00
Common Player:	1.00	.50	.30
A Willie Mays	10.00	5.00	3.00
C Roberto Clemente	12.50	6.25	3.75
D Mickey Mantle	15.00	7.50	4.50
1 Dave Kingman	1.00	.50	.30
2 Steve Busby	1.00	.50	.30
3 Bill Madlock	1.00	.50	.30
4 Jeff Burroughs	1.00	.50	.30
5 Ted Simmons	1.00	.50	.30
6 Randy Jones	1.00	.50	.30
7 Buddy Bell	1.00	.50	.30
8 Dave Cash	1.00	.50	.30
9 Jerry Grote	1.00	.50	.30
10 Davey Lopes	1.00	.50	.30

1975 SSPC Promo Cards

The six players in this sample set can each be found with three different backs. Some backs are similar to the cards issued in 1976, with player data and career summary. Some cards will have an ad message on back offering the complete 1976 SSPC set and team sets. Still others have blank backs. All cards are in 2-1/2" x 3-1/2" format with color photos on front surrounded by a white border and no extraneous graphics. Blank-back versions are worth 2-4X the values quoted here.

	NM	EX	VG
Complete Set (6):	15.00	7.50	4.50
Common Player:	1.50	.75	.45
(1) Hank Aaron	4.00	2.00	1.25
(2) Catfish Hunter	2.00	1.00	.60
(3) Dave Kingman	1.50	.75	.45
(4) Mickey Mantle	7.50	3.75	2.25
(5) Willie Mays	4.00	2.00	1.25
(6) Tom Seaver	3.00	1.50	.90

1975 SSPC Sample Cards

The Winter 1975 issue of "Collector's Quarterly" magazine (an advertising vehicle for Mike Aronstein, SSPC's principal) contained a two-page cardboard insert previewing the 1976 SSPC set. The cards could be cut apart into singles and represented something of a traded set, as each player or manager changed teams between the end of the 1975 season and the start of 1976. The cards have the players pictured on front in their old uniforms, with their new teams identified on back. Backs of the 2-1/2" x 3-1/2" cards are printed in red and black with a player biography and uniform number. "SAMPLE CARD 1975" is printed around the uniform number. A card number is in the lower-left corner, with 1975 copyright at bottom-right.

NEW YORK METS
41

GEORGE THOMAS SEAVER
Pitcher
6'1", 195 lbs. Bo. 11/17/44   Mets
BR-TR
His early '75 form indicated he has returned to this level that won him 2 Cy Young Awards and three times sees him 20 or more games. Moved into Mets' starting rotation after only one pro season, and has since compiled a 2.47 mark and a remarkable lifetime ERA of 2.47. Stamped in 11-11 with a 3.20 ERA last year, thanks to a hip injury, but still managed to strike out 201 men to become the first N.L. pitcher to K 200 or more 7 straight years.
© SSPC 1977

	NM	EX	VG
Complete Set, Uncut Sheet:	25.00	12.50	7.50
Complete Set, Singles (18):	20.00	10.00	6.00
Common Card:	1.50	.75	.45
1 Harry Parker	1.50	.75	.45
2 Jim Bibby	1.50	.75	.45
3 Mike Wallace	1.50	.75	.45
4 Tony Muser	1.50	.75	.45
5 Yogi Berra	7.50	3.75	2.25
6 Preston Gomez	1.50	.75	.45
7 Jack McKeon	1.50	.75	.45
8 Sam McDowell	1.50	.70	.45
9 Gaylord Perry	4.00	2.00	1.25
10 Fred Stanley	1.50	.75	.45
11 Willie Davis	1.50	.70	.45
12 Don Hopkins	1.50	.75	.45
13 Whitey Herzog	1.50	.70	.45
14 Ray Sadecki	1.50	.75	.45
15 Stan Bahnsen	1.50	.75	.45
16 Bob Oliver	1.50	.75	.45
17 Denny Doyle	1.50	.75	.45
18 Deron Johnson	1.50	.70	.45

1975 SSPC

KANSAS CITY ROYALS
5   Third Baseman
6', 190 lbs.
Bn. 5/15/53
BL-TR
GEORGE HOWARD BRETT
They stopped thinking of George as "Ken Brett's brother" in '75. He finished 6th in the A.L. with a .308 average, led the majors with 13 triples, and hit 35 doubles and 11 homers while knocking in 89 runs, and stealing 13 bases as well! Signed by the Royals in 1971, he advanced quickly, joining the Royals late in 1973 and taking over as the club's third baseman at age 21! He hit .282 as a rookie, foreshadowing his '75 success. A smooth fielder, he has experience at short, second and in the outfield. Has a .291 mark, 58 doubles, 18 triples, 13 homers, and 136 RBI.
CARD # 167   ★ SSPC 1975

This set, produced by the Sport Star Publishing Company in 1975 as a collectors' issue (though not actually issued until 1976), was withdrawn from the market because of legal entanglements. Because SSPC agreed never to reprint the issue, some collectors feel it has an air of legitimacy. The complete set contains 630 full-color cards, each 2-1/2" x 3-1/2" in size. The cards look similar to 1953 Bowmans, with only the player picture (no identification) on the fronts. Card backs are in a vertical format, with personal stats, brief biographies, uniform and card numbers printed in a variety of colors. Sets originally sold for $9.99.

	NM	EX	VG
Complete Set (630):	60.00	30.00	18.00
Common Player:	.10	.05	.03
1 Lee William (Buzz) Capra	.10	.05	.03
2 Thomas Ross House	.10	.05	.03
3 Maximino Leon	.10	.05	.03
4 Carl Wendle Morton	.10	.05	.03
5 Philip Henry Niekro	1.50	.70	.45
6 Michael Wayne Thompson	.10	.05	.03
7 Elias Sosa (Martinez)	.10	.05	.03
8 Larvell Blanks	.10	.05	.03
9 Darrell Wayne Evans	.10	.05	.03
10 Rodney Joe Gilbreath	.10	.05	.03
11 Michael Ken-Wai Lum	.10	.05	.03
12 Craig George Robinson	.10	.05	.03
13 Earl Craig Williams, Jr.	.10	.05	.03
14 Victor Crosby Correll	.10	.05	.03
15 Biff Pocoroba	.10	.05	.03
16 Johnny B. (Dusty) Baker, Jr.	.35	.20	.11
17 Ralph Allen Garr	.10	.05	.03
18 Clarence Edward (Cito) Gaston	.10	.05	.03
19 David LaFrance May	.10	.05	.03
20 Rowland Johnnie Office	.10	.05	.03
21 Robert Brooks Beall	.10	.05	.03
22 George Lee (Sparky) Anderson	1.00	.50	.30
23 John Eugene Billingham	.10	.05	.03
24 Pedro Rodriguez Borbon	.10	.05	.03
25 Clay Palmer Carroll	.10	.05	.03
26 Patrick Leonard Darcy	.10	.05	.03
27 Donald Edward Gullett	.10	.05	.03
28 Clayton Laws Kirby	.10	.05	.03
29 Gary Lynn Nolan	.10	.05	.03
30 Fredie Hubert Norman	.10	.05	.03
31 Johnny Lee Bench	2.50	1.25	.70
32 William Francis Plummer	.10	.05	.03
33 Darrel Lee Chaney	.10	.05	.03
34 David Ismael Concepcion	.10	.05	.03
35 Terrence Michael Crowley	.10	.05	.03

		NM	EX	VG
36	Daniel Driessen	.10	.05	.03
37	Robert Douglas Flynn, Jr.	.10	.05	.03
38	Joe Leonard Morgan	2.00	1.00	.60
39	Atanasio Rigal (Tony) Perez	1.50	.70	.45
40	George Kenneth (Ken) Griffey	.35	.20	.11
41	Peter Edward Rose	5.00	2.50	1.50
42	Edison Rosanda Armbrister	.10	.05	.03
43	John Christopher Vukovich	.10	.05	.03
44	George Arthur Foster	.10	.05	.03
45	Cesar Francisco Geronimo	.10	.05	.03
46	Mervin Weldon Rettenmund	.10	.05	.03
47	James Frederick Crawford	.10	.05	.03
48	Kenneth Roth Forsch	.10	.05	.03
49	Douglas James Konieczny	.10	.05	.03
50	Joseph Franklin Niekro	.10	.05	.03
51	Clifford Johnson	.10	.05	.03
52	Alfred Henry (Skip) Jutze	.10	.05	.03
53	Milton Scott May	.10	.05	.03
54	Robert Patrick Andrews	.10	.05	.03
55	Kenneth George Boswell	.10	.05	.03
56	Tommy Vann Helms	.10	.05	.03
57	Roger Henry Metzger	.10	.05	.03
58	Lawrence William Milbourne	.10	.05	.03
59	Douglas Lee Rader	.10	.05	.03
60	Robert Jose Watson	.10	.05	.03
61	Enos Milton Cabell, Jr.	.10	.05	.03
62	Jose Delan Cruz	.10	.05	.03
63	Cesar Cedeno	.10	.05	.03
64	Gregory Eugene Gross	.10	.05	.03
65	Wilbur Leon Howard	.10	.05	.03
66	Alphonso Erwin Downing	.10	.05	.03
67	Burt Carlton Hooton	.10	.05	.03
68	Charles Oliver Hough	.10	.05	.03
69	Thomas Edward John	.25	.13	.08
70	John Alexander Messersmith	.10	.05	.03
71	Douglas James Rau	.10	.05	.03
72	Richard Alan Rhoden	.10	.05	.03
73	Donald Howard Sutton	1.50	.70	.45
74	Frederick Steven Auerbach	.10	.05	.03
75	Ronald Charles Cey	.10	.05	.03
76	Ivan De Jesus	.10	.05	.03
77	Steven Patrick Garvey	1.00	.50	.30
78	Leonadus Lacy	.10	.05	.03
79	David Earl Lopes	.10	.05	.03
80	Kenneth Lee McMullen	.10	.05	.03
81	Joseph Vance Ferguson	.10	.05	.03
82	Paul Ray Powell	.10	.05	.03
83	Stephen Wayne Yeager	.10	.05	.03
84	Willie Murphy Crawford	.10	.05	.03
85	Henry Cruz	.10	.05	.03
86	Charles Fuqua Manuel	.10	.05	.03
87	Manuel Mota	.10	.05	.03
88	Thomas Marian Paciorek	.10	.05	.03
89	James Sherman Wynn	.10	.05	.03
90	Walter Emmons Alston	1.00	.50	.30
91	William Joseph Buckner	.10	.05	.03
92	James Leland Barr	.10	.05	.03
93	Ralph Michael (Mike) Caldwell	.10	.05	.03
94	John Francis D'Acquisto	.10	.05	.03
95	David Wallace Heaverlo	.10	.05	.03
96	Gary Robert Lavelle	.10	.05	.03
97	John Joseph Montefusco, Jr.	.10	.05	.03
98	Charles Prosek Williams	.10	.05	.03
99	Christopher Paul Arnold	.10	.05	.03
100	Mark Kevin Hill (Marc)	.10	.05	.03
101	David Martin Rader	.10	.05	.03
102	Charles Bruce Miller	.10	.05	.03
103	Guillermo Naranjo (Willie) Montanez	.10	.05	.03
104	Steven Robert Ontiveros	.10	.05	.03
105	Chris Edward Speier	.10	.05	.03
106	Derrel Osbon Thomas	.10	.05	.03
107	Gary Leah Thomasson	.10	.05	.03
108	Glenn Charles Adams	.10	.05	.03
109	Von Everett Joshua	.10	.05	.03
110	Gary Nathaniel Matthews	.10	.05	.03
111	Bobby Ray Murcer	.10	.05	.03
112	Horace Arthur Speed III	.10	.05	.03
113	Wesley Noreen Westrum	.10	.05	.03
114	Richard Nevin Folkers	.10	.05	.03
115	Alan Benton Foster	.10	.05	.03
116	David James Freisleben	.10	.05	.03
117	Daniel Vincent Frisella	.10	.05	.03
118	Randall Leo Jones	.10	.05	.03
119	Daniel Ray Spillner	.10	.05	.03
120	Howard Lawrence (Larry) Hardy	.10	.05	.03
121	Cecil Randolph (Randy) Hundley	.10	.05	.03
122	Fred Lyn Kendall	.10	.05	.03
123	John Francis McNamara	.10	.05	.03
124	Rigoberto (Tito) Fuentes	.10	.05	.03
125	Enzo Octavio Hernandez	.10	.05	.03
126	Stephen Michael Huntz	.10	.05	.03
127	Michael Wilson Ivie	.10	.05	.03
128	Hector Epitacio Torres	.10	.05	.03
129	Theodore Rodger Kubiak	.10	.05	.03
130	John Maywood Grubb, Jr.	.10	.05	.03
131	John Henry Scott	.10	.05	.03
132	Robert Tolan	.10	.05	.03
133	David Mark Winfield	2.50	1.25	.70
134	William Joseph Gogolewski	.10	.05	.03
135	Danny L. Osborn	.10	.05	.03
136	James Lee Kaat	.25	.13	.08
137	Claude Wilson Osteen	.10	.05	.03
138	Cecil Lee Upshaw, Jr.	.10	.05	.03
139	Wilbur Forrester Wood, Jr.	.10	.05	.03
140	Lloyd Cecil Allen	.10	.05	.03
141	Brian Jay Downing	.10	.05	.03
142	James Sarkis Essian, Jr.	.10	.05	.03
143	Russell Earl (Bucky) Dent	.50	.25	.15
144	Jorge Orta	.10	.05	.03
145	Lee Edward Richard	.10	.05	.03
146	William Allen Stein	.10	.05	.03
147	Kenneth Joseph Henderson	.10	.05	.03
148	Carlos May	.10	.05	.03
149	Nyls Wallace Rex Nyman	.10	.05	.03
150	Robert Pasquali Coluccio, Jr.	.10	.05	.03

#	Name			
151	Charles William Tanner, Jr.	.10	.05	.03
152	Harold Patrick (Pat) Kelly	.10	.05	.03
153	Jerry Wayne Hairston Sr.	.10	.05	.03
154	Richard Fred (Pete) Varney, Jr.	.10	.05	.03
155	William Edwin Melton	.10	.05	.03
156	Richard Michael Gossage	.50	.25	.15
157	Terry Jay Forster	.10	.05	.03
158	Richard Alan Hinton	.10	.05	.03
159	Nelson Kelley Briles	.10	.05	.03
160	Alan James Fitzmorris	.10	.05	.03
161	Stephen Bernard Mingori	.10	.05	.03
162	Martin William Pattin	.10	.05	.03
163	Paul William Splittorff, Jr.	.10	.05	.03
164	Dennis Patrick Leonard	.10	.05	.03
165	John Albert (Buck) Martinez	.10	.05	.03
166	Gorrell Robert (Bob) Stinson III	.10	.05	.03
167	George Howard Brett	7.50	3.75	2.25
168	Harmon Clayton Killebrew, Jr.	2.50	1.25	.70
169	John Claiborn Mayberry	.10	.05	.03
170	Freddie Joe Patek	.10	.05	.03
171	Octavio (Cookie) Rojas	.10	.05	.03
172	Rodney Darrell Scott	.10	.05	.03
173	Tolia (Tony) Solaita	.10	.05	.03
174	Frank White, Jr.	.10	.05	.03
175	Alfred Edward Cowens, Jr.	.10	.05	.03
176	Harold Abraham McRae	.10	.05	.03
177	Amos Joseph Otis	.10	.05	.03
178	Vada Edward Pinson, Jr.	.50	.25	.15
179	James Eugene Wohlford	.10	.05	.03
180	James Douglas Bird	.10	.05	.03
181	Mark Alan Littell	.10	.05	.03
182	Robert McClure	.10	.05	.03
183	Steven Lee Busby	.10	.05	.03
184	Francis Xavier Healy	.10	.05	.03
185	Dorrel Norman Elvert (Whitey) Herzog	.10	.05	.03
186	Andrew Earl Hassler	.10	.05	.03
187	Lynn Nolan Ryan, Jr.	7.50	3.75	2.25
188	William Robert Singer	.10	.05	.03
189	Frank Daryl Tanana	.10	.05	.03
190	Eduardo Figueroa	.10	.05	.03
191	David S. Collins	.10	.05	.03
192	Richard Hirshfeld Williams	.10	.05	.03
193	Eliseo Rodriguez	.10	.05	.03
194	David Lee Chalk	.10	.05	.03
195	Winston Enriquillo Llenas	.10	.05	.03
196	Rudolph Bart Meoli	.10	.05	.03
197	Orlando Ramirez	.10	.05	.03
198	Gerald Peter Remy	.10	.05	.03
199	Billy Edward Smith	.10	.05	.03
200	Bruce Anton Bochte	.10	.05	.03
201	Joseph Michael Lahoud, Jr.	.10	.05	.03
202	Morris Nettles, Jr.	.10	.05	.03
203	John Milton (Mickey) Rivers	.10	.05	.03
204	Leroy Bobby Stanton	.10	.05	.03
205	Victor Albury	.10	.05	.03
206	Thomas Henry Burgmeier	.10	.05	.03
207	William Franklin Butler	.10	.05	.03
208	William Richard Campbell	.10	.05	.03
209	Alton Ray Corbin	.10	.05	.03
210	George Henry (Joe) Decker, Jr.	.10	.05	.03
211	James Michael Hughes	.10	.05	.03
212	Edward Norman Bane (Photo actually Mike Pazik.)	.10	.05	.03
213	Glenn Dennis Borgmann	.10	.05	.03
214	Rodney Cline Carew	2.50	1.25	.70
215	Stephen Robert Brye	.10	.05	.03
216	Darnell Glenn (Dan) Ford	.10	.05	.03
217	Antonio Oliva	.35	.20	.11
218	David Allan Goltz	.10	.05	.03
219	Rikalbert Blyleven	.25	.13	.08
220	Larry Eugene Hisle	.10	.05	.03
221	Stephen Russell Braun, III	.10	.05	.03
222	Jerry Wayne Terrell	.10	.05	.03
223	Eric Thane Soderholm	.10	.05	.03
224	Philip Anthony Roof	.10	.05	.03
225	Danny Leon Thompson	.10	.05	.03
226	James William Colborn	.10	.05	.03
227	Thomas Andrew Murphy	.10	.05	.03
228	Eduardo Rodriguez	.10	.05	.03
229	James Michael Slaton	.10	.05	.03
230	Edward Nelson Sprague	.10	.05	.03
231	Charles William Moore, Jr.	.10	.05	.03
232	Darrell Ray Porter	.10	.05	.03
233	Kurt Anthony Bevacqua	.10	.05	.03
234	Pedro Garcia	.10	.05	.03
235	James Michael (Mike) Hegan	.10	.05	.03
236	Donald Wayne Money	.10	.05	.03
237	George C. Scott, Jr.	.10	.05	.03
238	Robin R. Yount	5.00	2.50	1.50
239	Henry Louis Aaron	5.00	2.50	1.50
240	Robert Walker Ellis	.10	.05	.03
241	Sixto Lezcano	.10	.05	.03
242	Robert Vance Mitchell	.10	.05	.03
243	James Gorman Thomas, III	.10	.05	.03
244	William Edward Travers	.10	.05	.03
245	Peter Sven Broberg	.10	.05	.03
246	William Howard Sharp	.10	.05	.03
247	Arthur Bobby Lee Darwin (Photo actually Larry Anderson.)	.10	.05	.03
248	Rick Gerald Austin (Photo actually Larry Anderson.)	.10	.05	.03
249	Lawrence Dennis Anderson (Photo actually Rick Austin.)	.10	.05	.03
250	Thomas Antony Bianco	.10	.05	.03
251	DeLancy LaFayette Currence	.10	.05	.03
252	Steven Raymond Foucault	.10	.05	.03
253	William Alfred Hands, Jr.	.10	.05	.03
254	Steven Lowell Hargan	.10	.05	.03
255	Ferguson Arthur Jenkins	1.50	.70	.45
256	Bob Mitchell Sheldon	.10	.05	.03
257	James Umbarger	.10	.05	.03
258	Clyde Wright	.10	.05	.03
259	William Roger Fahey	.10	.05	.03
260	James Howard Sundberg	.10	.05	.03
261	Leonardo Alfonso Cardenas	.10	.05	.03
262	James Louis Fregosi	.10	.05	.03
263	Dudley Michael (Mike) Hargrove	.10	.05	.03
264	Colbert Dale (Toby) Harrah	.10	.05	.03
265	Roy Lee Howell	.10	.05	.03
266	Leonard Shenoff Randle	.10	.05	.03
267	Roy Frederick Smalley III	.10	.05	.03
268	James Lloyd Spencer	.10	.05	.03
269	Jeffrey Alan Burroughs	.10	.05	.03
270	Thomas Alan Grieve	.10	.05	.03
271	Joseph Lovitto, Jr.	.10	.05	.03
272	Frank Joseph Lucchesi	.10	.05	.03
273	David Earl Nelson	.10	.05	.03
274	Ted Lyle Simmons	.10	.05	.03
275	Louis Clark Brock	2.00	1.00	.60
276	Ronald Ray Fairly	.10	.05	.03
277	Arnold Ray (Bake) McBride	.10	.05	.03
278	Carl Reginald (Reggie) Smith	.10	.05	.03
279	William Henry Davis	.10	.05	.03
280	Kenneth John Reitz	.10	.05	.03
281	Charles William (Buddy) Bradford	.10	.05	.03
282	Luis Antonio Melendez	.10	.05	.03
283	Michael Ray Tyson	.10	.05	.03
284	Ted Crawford Sizemore	.10	.05	.03
285	Mario Miguel Guerrero	.10	.05	.03
286	Larry Lintz	.10	.05	.03
287	Kenneth Victor Rudolph	.10	.05	.03
288	Richard Arlin Billings	.10	.05	.03
289	Jerry Wayne Mumphrey	.10	.05	.03
290	Michael Sherman Wallace	.10	.05	.03
291	Alan Thomas Hrabosky	.10	.05	.03
292	Kenneth Lee Reynolds	.10	.05	.03
293	Michael Douglas Garman	.10	.05	.03
294	Robert Herbert Forsch	.10	.05	.03
295	John Allen Denny	.10	.05	.03
296	Harold R. Rasmussen	.10	.05	.03
297	Lynn Everratt McGlothen (Everett)	.10	.05	.03
298	Michael Roswell Barlow	.10	.05	.03
299	Gregory John Terlecky	.10	.05	.03
300	Albert Fred (Red) Schoendienst	1.00	.50	.30
301	Ricky Eugene Reuschel	.10	.05	.03
302	Steven Michael Stone	.10	.05	.03
303	William Gordon Bonham	.10	.05	.03
304	Oscar Joseph Zamora	.10	.05	.03
305	Kenneth Douglas Frailing	.10	.05	.03
306	Milton Edward Wilcox	.10	.05	.03
307	Darold Duane Knowles	.10	.05	.03
308	Rufus James (Jim) Marshall	.10	.05	.03
309	Bill Madlock, Jr.	.10	.05	.03
310	Jose Domec Cardenal	.10	.05	.03
311	Robert James (Rick) Monday, Jr.	.10	.05	.03
312	Julio Ruben (Jerry) Morales	.10	.05	.03
313	Timothy Kenneth Hosley	.10	.05	.03
314	Gene Taylor Hiser	.10	.05	.03
315	Donald Eulon Kessinger	.10	.05	.03
316	Jesus Manuel (Manny) Trillo	.10	.05	.03
317	Ralph Pierre (Pete) LaCock, Jr.	.10	.05	.03
318	George Eugene Mitterwald	.10	.05	.03
319	Steven Eugene Swisher	.10	.05	.03
320	Robert Walter Sperring	.10	.05	.03
321	Victor Lanier Harris	.10	.05	.03
322	Ronald Ray Dunn	.10	.05	.03
323	Jose Manuel Morales	.10	.05	.03
324	Peter MacKanin, Jr.	.10	.05	.03
325	James Charles Cox	.10	.05	.03
326	Larry Alton Parrish	.10	.05	.03
327	Michael Jorgensen	.10	.05	.03
328	Timothy John Foli	.10	.05	.03
329	Harold Noel Breeden	.10	.05	.03
330	Nathan Colbert, Jr.	.10	.05	.03
331	Jesus Maria (Pepe) Frias	.10	.05	.03
332	James Patrick (Pat) Scanlon	.10	.05	.03
333	Robert Sherwood Bailey	.10	.05	.03
334	Gary Edmund Carter	2.00	1.00	.60
335	Jose Mauel (Pepe) Mangual	.10	.05	.03
336	Lawrence David Biittner	.10	.05	.03
337	James Lawrence Lyttle, Jr.	.10	.05	.03
338	Gary Roenicke	.10	.05	.03
339	Anthony Scott	.10	.05	.03
340	Jerome Cardell White	.10	.05	.03
341	James Edward Dwyer	.10	.05	.03
342	Ellis Clarence Valentine	.10	.05	.03
343	Frederick John Scherman, Jr.	.10	.05	.03
344	Dennis Herman Blair	.10	.05	.03
345	Woodrow Thompson Fryman	.10	.05	.03
346	Charles Gilbert Taylor	.10	.05	.03
347	Daniel Dean Warthen	.10	.05	.03
348	Donald George Carrithers	.10	.05	.03
349	Stephen Douglas Rogers	.10	.05	.03
350	Dale Albert Murray	.10	.05	.03
351	Edwin Donald (Duke) Snider	3.00	1.50	.90
352	Ralph George Houk	.10	.05	.03
353	John Frederick Hiller	.10	.05	.03
354	Michael Stephen Lolich	.10	.05	.03
355	David Lawrence Lemancyzk	.10	.05	.03
356	Lerrin Harris LaGrow	.10	.05	.03
357	Fred Arroyo	.10	.05	.03
358	Joseph Howard Coleman	.10	.05	.03
359	Benjamin A. Oglivie	.10	.05	.03
360	Willie Wattison Horton	.10	.05	.03
361	John Clinton Knox	.10	.05	.03
362	Leon Kauffman Roberts	.10	.05	.03
363	Ronald LeFlore	.10	.05	.03
364	Gary Lynn Sutherland	.10	.05	.03
365	Daniel Thomas Meyer	.10	.05	.03
366	Aurelio Rodriguez	.10	.05	.03
367	Thomas Martin Veryzer	.10	.05	.03
368	Lavern Jack Pierce	.10	.05	.03
369	Eugene Richard Michael	.10	.05	.03
370	Robert (Billy) Baldwin	.10	.05	.03
371	William James Gates Brown	.10	.05	.03
372	Mitchell Jack (Mickey) Stanley	.10	.05	.03
373	Terryal Gene Humphrey	.10	.05	.03
374	Doyle Lafayette Alexander	.10	.05	.03
375	Miguel Angel (Mike) Cuellar	.10	.05	.03
376	Marcus Wayne Garland	.10	.05	.03
377	Ross Albert Grimsley III	.10	.05	.03
378	Grant Dwight Jackson	.10	.05	.03
379	Dyar K. Miller	.10	.05	.03
380	James Alvin Palmer	2.00	1.00	.60
381	Michael Augustine Torrez	.10	.05	.03
382	Michael Henry Willis	.10	.05	.03
383	David Edwin Duncan	.10	.05	.03
384	Elrod Jerome Hendricks	.10	.05	.03
385	James Neamon Hutto Jr.	.10	.05	.03
386	Robert Michael Bailor	.10	.05	.03
387	Douglas Vernon DeCinces	.10	.05	.03
388	Robert Anthony Grich	.10	.05	.03
389	Lee Andrew May	.10	.05	.03
390	Anthony Joseph Muser	.10	.05	.03
391	Timothy C. Nordbrook	.10	.05	.03
392	Brooks Calbert Robinson, Jr.	2.50	1.25	.70
393	Royle Stillman	.10	.05	.03
394	Don Edward Baylor	.10	.05	.03
395	Paul L.D. Blair	.10	.05	.03
396	Alonza Benjamin Bumbry	.10	.05	.03
397	Larry Duane Harlow	.10	.05	.03
398	Herman Thomas (Tommy) Davis, Jr.	.10	.05	.03
399	James Thomas Northrup	.10	.05	.03
400	Kenneth Wayne Singleton	.10	.05	.03
401	Thomas Michael Shopay	.10	.05	.03
402	Fredrick Michael Lynn	.75	.40	.25
403	Carlton Ernest Fisk	2.00	1.00	.60
404	Cecil Celester Cooper	.10	.05	.03
405	James Edward Rice	1.00	.50	.30
406	Juan Jose Beniquez	.10	.05	.03
407	Robert Dennis Doyle	.10	.05	.03
408	Dwight Michael Evans	.10	.05	.03
409	Carl Michael Yastrzemski	3.00	1.50	.90
410	Richard Paul Burleson	.10	.05	.03
411	Bernardo Carbo	.10	.05	.03
412	Douglas Lee Griffin, Jr.	.10	.05	.03
413	Americo P. Petrocelli	.10	.05	.03
414	Robert Edward Montgomery	.10	.05	.03
415	Timothy P. Blackwell	.10	.05	.03
416	Richard Alan Miller	.10	.05	.03
417	Darrell Dean Johnson	.10	.05	.03
418	Jim Scott Burton	.10	.05	.03
419	James Arthur Willoughby	.10	.05	.03
420	Rogelio (Roger) Moret	.10	.05	.03
421	William Francis Lee, III	.10	.05	.03
422	Richard Anthony Drago	.10	.05	.03
423	Diego Pablo Segui	.10	.05	.03
424	Luis Clemente Tiant	.10	.05	.03
425	James Augustus (Catfish) Hunter	1.50	.70	.45
426	Richard Clyde Sawyer	.10	.05	.03
427	Rudolph May Jr.	.10	.05	.03
428	Richard William Tidrow	.10	.05	.03
429	Albert Walter (Sparky) Lyle	.10	.05	.03
430	George Francis (Doc) Medich	.10	.05	.03
431	Patrick Edward Dobson, Jr.	.10	.05	.03
432	David Percy Pagan	.10	.05	.03
433	Thurman Lee Munson	2.00	1.00	.60
434	Carroll Christopher Chambliss	.10	.05	.03
435	Roy Hilton White	.10	.05	.03
436	Walter Allen Williams	.10	.05	.03
437	Graig Nettles	.10	.05	.03
438	John Rikard (Rick) Dempsey	.10	.05	.03
439	Bobby Lee Bonds	.25	.13	.08
440	Edward Martin Hermann (Herrmann)	.10	.05	.03
441	Santos Alomar	.10	.05	.03
442	Frederick Blair Stanley	.10	.05	.03
443	Terry Bertland Whitfield	.10	.05	.03
444	Richard Alan Bladt	.10	.05	.03
445	Louis Victor Piniella	.50	.25	.15
446	Richard Allen Coggins	.10	.05	.03
447	Edwin Albert Brinkman	.10	.05	.03
448	James Percy Mason	.10	.05	.03
449	Larry Murray	.10	.05	.03
450	Ronald Mark Blomberg	.10	.05	.03
451	Elliott Maddox	.10	.05	.03
452	Kerry Dineen	.10	.05	.03
453	Alfred Manuel (Billy) Martin	.50	.25	.15
454	Dave Bergman	.10	.05	.03
455	Otoniel Velez	.10	.05	.03
456	Joseph Walter Hoerner	.10	.05	.03
457	Frank Edwin (Tug) McGraw, Jr.	.10	.05	.03
458	Henry Eugene (Gene) Garber	.10	.05	.03
459	Steven Norman Carlton	2.00	1.00	.60
460	Larry Richard Christenson	.10	.05	.03
461	Thomas Gerald Underwood	.10	.05	.03
462	James Reynold Lonborg	.10	.05	.03
463	John William (Jay) Johnstone, Jr.	.10	.05	.03
464	Lawrence Robert Bowa	.10	.05	.03
465	David Cash, Jr.	.10	.05	.03
466	Ollie Lee Brown	.10	.05	.03
467	Gregory Michael Luzinski	.10	.05	.03
468	Johnny Lane Oates	.10	.05	.03
469	Michael Allen Anderson	.10	.05	.03
470	Michael Jack Schmidt	4.00	2.00	1.25
471	Robert Raymond Boone	.10	.05	.03
472	Thomas George Hutton	.10	.05	.03
473	Richard Anthony Allen	.50	.25	.15
474	Antonio Taylor	.10	.05	.03
475	Jerry Lindsey Martin	.10	.05	.03
476	Daniel Leonard Ozark	.10	.05	.03
477	Richard David Ruthven	.10	.05	.03
478	James Richard Todd, Jr.	.10	.05	.03
479	Paul Aaron Lindblad	.10	.05	.03
480	Roland Glen Fingers	1.50	.70	.45
481	Vida Blue, Jr.	.10	.05	.03
482	Kenneth Dale Holtzman	.10	.05	.03
483	Richard Allen Bosman	.10	.05	.03
484	Wilfred Charles (Sonny) Siebert	.10	.05	.03
485	William Glenn Abbott	.10	.05	.03
486	Stanley Raymond Bahnsen	.10	.05	.03

		NM	EX	VG
487	Michael Norris	.10	.05	.03
488	Alvin Ralph Dark	.10	.05	.03
489	Claudell Washington	.10	.05	.03
490	Joseph Oden Rudi	.10	.05	.03
491	William Alex North	.10	.05	.03
492	Dagoberto Blanco (Bert) Campaneris	.10	.05	.03
493	Fury Gene Tenace	.10	.05	.03
494	Reginald Martinez Jackson	4.00	2.00	1.25
495	Philip Mason Garner	.10	.05	.03
496	Billy Leo Williams	2.00	1.00	.60
497	Salvatore Leonard Bando	.10	.05	.03
498	James William Holt	.10	.05	.03
499	Teodoro Noel Martinez	.10	.05	.03
500	Raymond Earl Fosse	.10	.05	.03
501	Matthew Alexander	.10	.05	.03
502	Wallace Larry Haney	.10	.05	.03
503	Angel Luis Mangual	.10	.05	.03
504	Fred Ray Beene	.10	.05	.03
505	Thomas William Buskey	.10	.05	.03
506	Dennis Lee Eckersley	2.00	1.00	.60
507	Roric Edward Harrison	.10	.05	.03
508	Donald Harris Hood	.10	.05	.03
509	James Lester Kern	.10	.05	.03
510	David Eugene LaRoche	.10	.05	.03
511	Fred Ingels (Fritz) Peterson	.10	.05	.03
512	James Michael Strickland	.10	.05	.03
513	Michael Richard (Rick) Waits	.10	.05	.03
514	Alan Dean Ashby	.10	.05	.03
515	John Charles Ellis	.10	.05	.03
516	Rick Cerone	.10	.05	.03
517	David Gus (Buddy) Bell	.10	.05	.03
518	John Anthony Brohamer, Jr.	.10	.05	.03
519	Ricardo Adolfo Jacobo Carty	.10	.05	.03
520	Edward Carlton Crosby	.10	.05	.03
521	Frank Thomas Duffy	.10	.05	.03
522	Duane Eugene Kuiper (Photo actually Rick Manning.)	.10	.05	.03
523	Joseph Anthony Lis	.10	.05	.03
524	John Wesley (Boog) Powell	.50	.25	.15
525	Frank Robinson	2.50	1.25	.70
526	Oscar Charles Gamble	.10	.05	.03
527	George Andrew Hendrick	.10	.05	.03
528	John Lee Lowenstein	.10	.05	.03
529	Richard Eugene Manning (photo actually Duane Kuiper)	.10	.05	.03
530	Tommy Alexander Smith	.10	.05	.03
531	Leslie Charles (Charlie) Spikes	.10	.05	.03
532	Steve Jack Kline	.10	.05	.03
533	Edward Emil Kranepool	.10	.05	.03
534	Michael Vail	.10	.05	.03
535	Delbert Bernard Unser	.10	.05	.03
536	Felix Bernardo Martinez Millan	.10	.05	.03
537	Daniel Joseph (Rusty) Staub	.25	.13	.08
538	Jesus Maria Rojas Alou	.10	.05	.03
539	Ronald Wayne Garrett	.10	.05	.03
540	Michael Dwaine Phillips	.10	.05	.03
541	Joseph Paul Torre	.10	.05	.03
542	David Arthur Kingman	.10	.05	.03
543	Eugene Anthony Clines	.10	.05	.03
544	Jack Seale Heidemann	.10	.05	.03
545	Derrel McKinley (Bud) Harrelson	.10	.05	.03
546	John Hardin Stearns	.10	.05	.03
547	John David Milner	.10	.05	.03
548	Robert John Apodaca	.10	.05	.03
549	Claude Edward (Skip) Lockwood Jr.	.10	.05	.03
550	Kenneth George Sanders	.10	.05	.03
551	George Thomas (Tom) Seaver	3.00	1.50	.90
552	Ricky Alan Baldwin	.10	.05	.03
553	Jonathan Trumpbour Matlack	.10	.05	.03
554	Henry Gaylon Webb	.10	.05	.03
555	Randall Lee Tate	.10	.05	.03
556	Tom Edward Hall	.10	.05	.03
557	George Heard Stone Jr.	.10	.05	.03
558	Craig Steven Swan	.10	.05	.03
559	Gerald Allen Cram	.10	.05	.03
560	Roy J. Staiger	.10	.05	.03
561	Kenton C. Tekulve	.10	.05	.03
562	Jerry Reuss	.10	.05	.03
563	John R. Candelaria	.10	.05	.03
564	Lawrence C. Demery	.10	.05	.03
565	David John Giusti Jr.	.10	.05	.03
566	James Phillip Rooker	.10	.05	.03
567	Ramon Gonzalez Hernandez	.10	.05	.03
568	Bruce Eugene Kison	.10	.05	.03
569	Kenneth Alven Brett (Alvin)	.10	.05	.03
570	Robert Ralph Moose Jr.	.10	.05	.03
571	Manuel Jesus Sanguillen	.10	.05	.03
572	David Gene Parker	.10	.05	.03
573	Wilver Dornel Stargell	2.00	1.00	.60
574	Richard Walter Zisk	.10	.05	.03
575	Renaldo Antonio Stennett	.10	.05	.03
576	Albert Oliver Jr.	.25	.13	.08
577	William Henry Robinson Jr.	.10	.05	.03
578	Robert Eugene Robertson	.10	.05	.03
579	Richard Joseph Hebner	.10	.05	.03
580	Edgar Leon Kirkpatrick	.10	.05	.03
581	Don Robert (Duffy) Dyer	.10	.05	.03
582	Craig Reynolds	.10	.05	.03
583	Franklin Fabian Taveras	.10	.05	.03
584	William Larry Randolph	.10	.05	.03
585	Arthur H. Howe	.10	.05	.03
586	Daniel Edward Murtaugh	.10	.05	.03
587	Charles Richard (Rich) McKinney	.10	.05	.03
588	James Edward Goodson	.10	.05	.03
589	George Brett, Al Cowans/ Checklist	1.50	.70	.45
590	Keith Hernandez, Lou Brock/ Checklist	.15	.08	.05
591	Jerry Koosman, Duke Snider/ Checklist	.25	.13	.08
592	John Knox, Maury Wills/ Checklist	.10	.05	.03
593a	Catfish Hunter, Noland Ryan/ Checklist	4.00	2.00	1.25
593b	Catfish Hunter, Nolan Ryan/ Checklist	3.00	1.50	.90
594	Pee Wee Reese, Ralph Branca, Carl Erskine	1.00	.50	.30
595	Willie Mays, Herb Score/ Checklist	1.00	.50	.30
596	Larry Eugene Cox	.10	.05	.03
597	Eugene William Mauch	.10	.05	.03
598	William Frederick (Whitey) Wietelmann	.10	.05	.03
599	Wayne Kirby Simpson	.10	.05	.03
600	Melvin Erskine Thomason	.10	.05	.03
601	Issac Bernard (Ike) Hampton	.10	.05	.03
602	Kenneth S. Crosby	.10	.05	.03
603	Ralph Emanuel Rowe	.10	.05	.03
604	James Vernon Tyrone	.10	.05	.03
605	Michael Dennis Kelleher	.10	.05	.03
606	Mario Mendoza	.10	.05	.03
607	Michael George Rogodzinski	.10	.05	.03
608	Robert Collins Gallagher	.10	.05	.03
609	Jerry Martin Koosman	.10	.05	.03
610	Joseph Filmore Frazier	.10	.05	.03
611	Karl Kuehl	.10	.05	.03
612	Frank J. LaCorte	.10	.05	.03
613	Raymond Douglas Bare	.10	.05	.03
614	Billy Arnold Muffett	.10	.05	.03
615	William Harry Laxton	.10	.05	.03
616	Willie Howard Mays	5.00	2.50	1.50
617	Philip Joseph Cavaretta (Cavarretta)	.10	.05	.03
618	Theodore Bernard Kluszewski	.50	.25	.15
619	Elston Gene Howard	.10	.05	.03
620	Alexander Peter Grammas	.10	.05	.03
621	James Barton (Mickey) Vernon	.10	.05	.03
622	Richard Allan Sisler	.10	.05	.03
623	Harvey Haddix, Jr.	.10	.05	.03
624	Bobby Brooks Winkles	.10	.05	.03
625	John Michael Pesky	.10	.05	.03
626	James Houston Davenport	.10	.05	.03
627	David Allen Tomlin	.10	.05	.03
628	Roger Lee Craig	.10	.05	.03
629	John Joseph Amalfitano	.10	.05	.03
630	James Harrison Reese	.25	.13	.08

1975 SSPC Mets/Yankees

Team sets of the New York clubs were issued by SSPC bearing a 1975 copyright date and in the same "pure card" format as most of the company's other issues. The 2-1/2" x 3-1/2" cards have a posed color photo on front with a thin white border and no extraneous graphics - not even the player's name. Backs are printed in red and blue with personal data and a career summary, along with the player's full formal name. The checklist lists the player as he is best known. Issue price was $1.25 per team set.

		NM	EX	VG
	Complete Set (45):	15.00	7.50	4.50
	Common Player:	.25	.13	.08
	New York Mets Team Set:	9.00	4.50	2.75
1	John Milner	.25	.13	.08
2	Henry Webb	.25	.13	.08
3	Tom Hall	.25	.13	.08
4	Del Unser	.25	.13	.08
5	Wayne Garrett	.25	.13	.08
6	Jesus Alou	.25	.13	.08
7	Rusty Staub	.40	.20	.12
8	John Stearns	.25	.13	.08
9	Dave Kingman	.75	.40	.25
10	Ed Kranepool	.35	.20	.11
11	Cleon Jones	.40	.20	.12
12	Tom Seaver	4.00	2.00	1.25
13	George Stone	.25	.13	.08
14	Jerry Koosman	.35	.20	.11
15	Bob Apodaca	.25	.13	.08
16	Felix Millan	.25	.13	.08
17	Gene Clines	.25	.13	.08
18	Mike Phillips	.25	.13	.08
19	Yogi Berra	3.00	1.50	.90
20	Joe Torre	1.50	.70	.45
21	Jon Matlack	.25	.13	.08
22	Ricky Baldwin	.25	.13	.08
	New York Yankees Team Set:	9.00	4.50	2.75
1	Catfish Hunter	1.00	.50	.30
2	Bobby Bonds	.35	.20	.11
3	Ed Brinkman	.25	.13	.08
4	Ron Blomberg	.25	.13	.08
5	Thurman Munson	3.50	1.75	1.00
6	Roy White	.35	.20	.11
7	Larry Gura	.25	.13	.08
8	Ed Hermann	.25	.13	.08
9	Bill Virdon	.25	.13	.08
10	Elliott Maddox	.25	.13	.08
11	Lou Piniella	.50	.25	.15
12	Rick Dempsey	.25	.13	.08
13	Fred Stanley	.25	.13	.08
14	Chris Chambliss	.25	.13	.08
15	Doc Medich	.25	.13	.08
16	Pat Dobson	.25	.13	.08
17	Alex Johnson	.25	.13	.08
18	Jim Mason	.25	.13	.08
19	Sandy Alomar	.25	.13	.08
20	Graig Nettles	.50	.25	.15
21	Walt Williams	.25	.13	.08
22	Sparky Lyle	.35	.20	.11
23	Dick Tidrow	.25	.13	.08

1975 SSPC Puzzle Backs

A large black-and-white puzzle picture of Nolan Ryan and Catfish Hunter can be assembled with the backs of these cards. Fronts of the 3-9/16" x 4-1/4" cards have a color player pose with a white border. The player's name, position and team are printed at bottom. Fronts have a glossy surface. The SSPC identification only appears around the border of the puzzle. The unnumbered cards are checklisted here alphabetically. Issue price was $2.

		NM	EX	VG
	Complete Set, Uncut Sheet:	40.00	20.00	12.00
	Complete Set (24):	20.00	10.00	6.00
	Common Player:	.30	.15	.09
(1)	Hank Aaron	4.00	2.00	1.25
(2)	Johnny Bench	1.75	.90	.50
(3)	Bobby Bonds	.35	.20	.11
(4)	Jeff Burroughs	.30	.15	.09
(5)	Rod Carew	1.75	.90	.50
(6)	Dave Cash	.30	.15	.09
(7)	Cesar Cedeno	.30	.15	.09
(8)	Bucky Dent	.30	.15	.09
(9)	Rollie Fingers	1.25	.60	.40
(10)	Steve Garvey	1.00	.50	.30
(11)	John Grubb	.30	.15	.09
(12)	Reggie Jackson	2.00	1.00	.60
(13)	Jim Kaat	.30	.15	.09
(14)	Greg Luzinski	.30	.15	.09
(15)	Fred Lynn	.50	.25	.15
(16)	Bill Madlock	.30	.15	.09
(17)	Andy Messersmith	.30	.15	.09
(18)	Thurman Munson	1.50	.70	.45
(19)	Jim Palmer	1.25	.60	.40
(20)	Dave Parker	.30	.15	.09
(21)	Jim Rice	.50	.25	.15
(22)	Pete Rose	4.00	2.00	1.25
(23)	Tom Seaver	1.75	.90	.50
(24)	Chris Speier	.30	.15	.09

1975 SSPC Superstars

 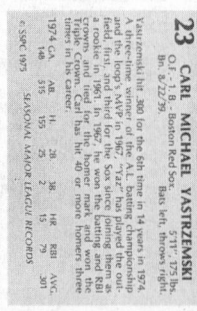

Nearly four dozen of the game's contemporary and former stars are featured in this set. Like other SSPC issues of 1975, fronts of the 2-1/2" x 3-1/2" cards have posed color photos with a white border. There are no other graphics, not even the player's name. The horizontal backs feature the player's full formal name (checklist here uses popular name) along with personal data, career summary and stats. Issue price was $4.

		NM	EX	VG
	Complete Set (42):	25.00	12.50	7.50
	Common Player:	.25	.13	.08
1	Wilbur Wood	.25	.13	.08
2	Johnny Sain	.25	.13	.08
3	Bill Melton	.25	.13	.08
4	Dick Allen	.50	.25	.15
5	Jim Palmer	1.00	.50	.30
6	Brooks Robinson	1.50	.70	.45
7	Tommy Davis	.25	.13	.08
8	Frank Robinson	1.50	.70	.45

9	Vada Pinson (Nolan Ryan in background of photo.)	1.00	.50	.30
10	Nolan Ryan	4.00	2.00	1.25
11	Reggie Jackson	3.00	1.50	.90
12	Vida Blue	.25	.13	.08
13	Sal Bando	.25	.13	.08
14	Bert Campaneris	.25	.13	.08
15	Tom Seaver	2.00	1.00	.60
16	Bud Harrelson	.25	.13	.08
17	Jerry Koosman	.25	.13	.08
18	Dave Nelson	.25	.13	.08
19	Ted Williams	3.50	1.75	1.00
20	Tony Oliva	.35	.20	.11
21	Mickey Lolich	.25	.13	.08
22	Amos Otis	.25	.13	.08
23	Carl Yastrzemski	2.00	1.00	.60
24	Mike Cuellar	.25	.13	.08
25	Doc Medich	.25	.13	.08
26	Cesar Cedeno	.25	.13	.08
27	Jeff Burroughs	.25	.13	.08
28	Ted Williams, Sparky Lyle	.75	.40	.25
29	Johnny Bench	2.00	1.00	.60
30	Gaylord Perry	1.00	.50	.30
31	John Mayberry	.25	.13	.08
32	Rod Carew	1.00	.50	.30
33	Whitey Ford	2.00	1.00	.60
34	Al Kaline	2.00	1.00	.60
35	Willie Mays	3.50	1.75	1.00
36	Warren Spahn	1.00	.50	.30
37	Mickey Mantle	5.00	2.50	1.50
38	Norm Cash	.35	.20	.11
39	Steve Busby	.25	.13	.08
40	Yogi Berra	2.00	1.00	.60
41	Harvey Kuenn	.25	.13	.08
42	Felipe Alou, Jesus Alou, Matty Alou	.60	.30	.20

1976 SSPC Yankees Old Timers Day

JOE DiMAGGIO

The Spring 1976 edition of "Collectors Quarterly" magazine contained a nine-card sheet of players who had appeared at an old timers' games in Yankees Stadium. The sheet could be cut into individual 2-1/2" x 3-1/2" cards with a color player photo and name on front. Backs form a black-and-white puzzle picture of Joe DiMaggio, Mickey Mantle, Whitey Ford, and Billy Martin. Cards are checklisted here alphabetically.

		NM	EX	VG
	Complete Magazine:	25.00	12.50	7.50
	Complete Set, Singles:	15.00	7.50	4.50
	Common Player:	.35	.20	.11
(1)	Earl Averill	.35	.20	.11
(2)	Joe DiMaggio	6.00	3.00	1.75
(3)	Tommy Henrich	.35	.20	.11
(4)	Billy Herman	.35	.20	.11
(5)	Monte Irvin	.35	.20	.11
(6)	Jim Konstanty	.35	.20	.11
(7)	Mickey Mantle	7.50	3.75	2.25
(8)	Pee Wee Reese	3.00	1.50	.90
(9)	Bobby Thompson (Thomson)	.50	.25	.15

1976 SSPC 1887 World Series

WORLD'S SERIES 1887
DETROIT vs. ST. LOUIS

BUSHONG, the veteran backstop, was given the task of educating young Boyle in the tricks of their trade, and did not see much action for St. Louis on the '87 nine. His infrequent performances were, however, typical of his considerable excellence.

ALBERT JOHN BUSHONG has a degree in dentistry, hence his nickname "Doc". He first made the big time in 1875, joining the old Brooklyn Atlantics. He has since caught for Philadelphia, Worcester, Cleveland, and the Browns, doing that club in '85, '87 saw him bat .280 in 53 contest, while swiping 14 bags. Bushong has gone to Brooklyn for 1888, where he will likely split the backstopping with the incumbent, Boyle. Never a strong hitter, he has made himself very valuable with his accurate pitch calling and agile fielding in back of the bat, and his willingness to have a go at other positions.

A.J. Bushong   C
NO. 13 of 18   * SSPC 1976

The history of the 1887 "World Series" between the Detroit Wolverines of the National League and the St. Louis Browns of the American Association is told on the backs of this collector's issue. The 2-1/2" x 3-1/2" cards were printed on a pair of uncut sheets inserted in the Fall 1976 issue of "Collectors Quarterly" magazine. Fronts of the cards reproduce in full color the Scrapps tobacco die-cut cards originally issued in 1888. Backs recount the individual players' performances in the series as well as giving a career summary; they are printed in red and black. Detroit won the Series, a best-of-15 contest.

	NM	EX	VG
Complete Magazine:	15.00	7.50	4.50

	Complete Set, Singles:	12.00	6.00	3.50
	Common Player:	.75	.40	.25
1	Bob Caruthers	.75	.40	.25
2	David Foutz	.75	.40	.25
3	W.A. Latham	.75	.40	.25
4	Charles H. Getzin (Getzien)	.75	.40	.25
5	J.C. Rowe	.75	.40	.25
6	Fred Dunlap	.75	.40	.25
7	James O'Neill	.75	.40	.25
8	Curtis Welch	.75	.40	.25
9	William Gleason	.75	.40	.25
10	Sam Thompson	.75	.40	.25
11	Ned Hanlon	.75	.40	.25
12	Dan Brothers (Brouthers)	.75	.40	.25
13	Albert Bushong	.75	.40	.25
14	Charles Comiskey	.75	.40	.25
15	Wm. Robinson	.75	.40	.25
16	Charles Bennett	.75	.40	.25
17	Hardy Richardson	.75	.40	.25
18	Deacon White	.75	.40	.25

1976 SSPC 1963 New York Mets

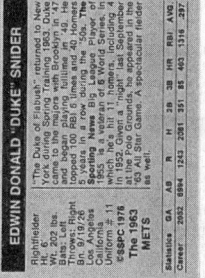

Issued in the Summer 1976 issue of "Collectors Quarterly" magazine as a two-page uncut sheet, this 18-card issue features the 1963 Mets. Like contemporary collectors' issues from SSPC, the cards feature white-bordered color photos on front with no other graphics or player identification. Backs are printed in black-and-white, contain player biographical data, a career summary and uniform number, by which the checklist is arranged. Size is standard 2-1/2" x 3-1/2".

		NM	EX	VG
	Complete Magazine:	25.00	12.50	7.50
	Complete Set, Singles (18):	15.00	7.50	4.50
	Common Player:	1.00	.50	.30
1	Duke Carmel	1.00	.50	.30
5	Norman Burt Sherry	1.00	.50	.30
7	Casey Stengel	5.00	2.50	1.50
9	Jim Hickman	1.00	.50	.30
10	Rod Kanehl	1.00	.50	.30
11	Duke Snider	7.50	3.75	2.25
12	Jesse Gonder	1.00	.50	.30
16	Dick Smith	1.00	.50	.30
17	Clarence Coleman	1.00	.50	.30
18	Pumpsie Green	1.00	.50	.30
23	Joe Christopher	1.00	.50	.30
36	Tracy Stallard	1.00	.50	.30
39	Steve Dillon	1.00	.50	.30
40	Rich Moran	1.00	.50	.30
41	Grover Powell	1.00	.50	.30
43	Ted Schreiber	1.00	.50	.30
53	Ernest White	1.00	.50	.30
56	Ed Bauta	1.00	.50	.30

1978 SSPC All Star Gallery

A series of team "Photo Fact Cards" was produced by Sports Stars Publishing Co., for insertion into its 48-page "All Star Gallery" magazine, sold for $2. Fully licensed by MLB and the Players Union, the 27 cards in each team set are printed on a triple-fold 24" x 10-7/8" cardboard sheet stapled into the center of the magazine. Cards are not perforated, though the back of each nine-card panel has dotted lines to guide the cutting of 2-1/2" x 3-1/2" single cards from the sheet. Fronts are full-color poses with no extraneous graphics. Backs are in black-and-white with a few vital data, a career summary, uniform number and a card number from within the overall issue of 270. Only eight teams are represented in the All Star Gallery magazine series. The Yankees (#001-027) and Phillies cards (#028-054) issued with other magazines that year may be considered part of the All-Star Gallery issue.

	NM	EX	VG
Complete Set, Magazines (8):	135.00	65.00	40.00
Complete Set, Singles (216):	125.00	60.00	35.00

	Common Player:	.50	.25	.15
	Los Angeles Dodgers Magazine:	15.00	7.50	4.50
0055	Burt Hooton	.50	.25	.15
0056	Bill Russell	.50	.25	.15
0057	Dusty Baker	.60	.30	.20
0058	Reggie Smith	.50	.25	.15
0059	Dick Rhoden	.50	.25	.15
0060	Jerry Grote	.50	.25	.15
0061	Bill Butler	.50	.25	.15
0062	Ron Cey	.50	.25	.15
0063	Ron Cey	.50	.25	.15
0064	Ted Martinez	.50	.25	.15
0065	Ed Goodson	.50	.25	.15
0066	Vic Davalillo	.50	.25	.15
0067	Davey Lopes	.50	.25	.15
0068	Terry Forster	.50	.25	.15
0069	Lee Lacy	.50	.25	.15
0070	Mike Garman	.50	.25	.15
0071	Steve Garvey	1.50	.70	.45
0072	Johnny Oates	.50	.25	.15
0073	Steve Yeager	.50	.25	.15
0074	Rafael Landestoy	.50	.25	.15
0075	Tommy John	.60	.30	.20
0076	Glenn Burke	.50	.25	.15
0077	Rick Monday	.50	.25	.15
0078	Doug Rau	.50	.25	.15
0079	Manny Mota	.50	.25	.15
0080	Don Sutton	2.00	1.00	.60
0081	Charlie Hough	.50	.25	.15
	Texas Rangers Magazine:	12.50	6.25	3.75
0082	Mike Hargrove	.50	.25	.15
0083	Jim Sundberg	.50	.25	.15
0084	Fergie Jenkins	2.00	1.00	.60
0085	Paul Lindblad	.50	.25	.15
0086	Sandy Alomar	.50	.25	.15
0087	John Lowenstein	.50	.25	.15
0088	Claudell Washington	.50	.25	.15
0089	Toby Harrah	.50	.25	.15
0090	Jim Umbarger	.50	.25	.15
0091	Len Barker	.50	.25	.15
0092	Dave May	.50	.25	.15
0093	Kurt Bevacqua	.50	.25	.15
0094	Jim Mason	.50	.25	.15
0095	Bump Wills	.50	.25	.15
0096	Dock Ellis	.50	.25	.15
0097	Bill Fahey	.50	.25	.15
0098	Richie Zisk	.50	.25	.15
0099	Jon Matlack	.50	.25	.15
0100	John Ellis	.50	.25	.15
0101	Bert Campaneris	.50	.25	.15
0102	Doc Medich	.50	.25	.15
0103	Juan Beniquez	.50	.25	.15
0104	Bill Hunter	.50	.25	.15
0105	Doyle Alexander	.50	.25	.15
0106	Roger Moret	.50	.25	.15
0107	Mike Jorgensen	.50	.25	.15
0108	Al Oliver	.60	.30	.20
	Cincinnati Reds Magazine:	15.00	7.50	4.50
0109	Fred Norman	.50	.25	.15
0110	Ray Knight	.50	.25	.15
0111	Pedro Borbon	.50	.25	.15
0112	Bill Bonham	.50	.25	.15
0113	George Foster	.60	.30	.20
0114	Doug Bair	.50	.25	.15
0115	Cesar Geronimo	.50	.25	.15
0116	Tom Seaver	3.50	1.75	1.00
0117	Mario Soto	.50	.25	.15
0118	Ken Griffey	.50	.25	.15
0119	Mike Lum	.50	.25	.15
0120	Tom Hume	.50	.25	.15
0121	Joe Morgan	2.50	1.25	.70
0122	Manny Sarmiento	.50	.25	.15
0123	Dan Driessen	.50	.25	.15
0124	Ed Armbrister	.50	.25	.15
0125	John Summers	.50	.25	.15
0126	Fred Auerbach	.50	.25	.15
0127	Doug Capilla	.50	.25	.15
0128	Johnny Bench	3.50	1.75	1.00
0129	Sparky Anderson	1.50	.70	.45
0130	Raul Ferreyra	.50	.25	.15
0131	Dale Murray	.50	.25	.15
0132	Pete Rose	7.50	3.75	2.25
0133	Dave Concepcion	.50	.25	.15
0134	Junior Kennedy	.50	.25	.15
0135	Dave Collins	.50	.25	.15
	Chicago White Sox Magazine:	12.50	6.25	3.75
0136	Mike Eden	.50	.25	.15
0137	Lamar Johnson	.50	.25	.15
0138	Ron Schueler	.50	.25	.15
0139	Bob Lemon	.75	.40	.25
0140	Thad Bosley	.50	.25	.15
0141	Bobby Bonds	.60	.30	.20
0142	Wilbur Wood	.50	.25	.15
0143	Jorge Orta	.50	.25	.15
0144	Francisco Barrios	.50	.25	.15
0145	Greg Pryor	.50	.25	.15
0146	Chet Lemon	.50	.25	.15
0147	Mike Squires	.50	.25	.15
0148	Eric Soderholm	.50	.25	.15
0149	Reggie Sanders	.50	.25	.15
0150	Kevin Bell	.50	.25	.15
0151	Alan Bannister	.50	.25	.15
0152	Henry Cruz	.50	.25	.15
0153	Larry Doby	2.00	1.00	.60
0154	Don Kessinger	.50	.25	.15
0155	Ralph Garr	.50	.25	.15
0156	Bill Nahorodny	.50	.25	.15
0157	Ron Blomberg	.50	.25	.15
0158	Bob Molinaro	.50	.25	.15
0159	Junior Moore	.50	.25	.15
0160	Minnie Minoso	1.50	.70	.45
0161	Lerrin LaGrow	.50	.25	.15
0162	Wayne Nordhagen	.50	.25	.15
	Boston Red Sox Magazine:	20.00	10.00	6.00
0163	Ramon Aviles	.50	.25	.15
0164	Bob Stanley	.50	.25	.15

0165	Reggie Cleveland	.50	.25	.15
0166	John Brohamer	.50	.25	.15
0167	Bill Lee	.50	.25	.15
0168	Jim Burton	.50	.25	.15
0169	Bill Campbell	.50	.25	.15
0170	Mike Torrez	.50	.25	.15
0171	Dick Drago	.50	.25	.15
0172	Butch Hobson	.50	.25	.15
0173	Bob Bailey	.50	.25	.15
0174	Fred Lynn	.50	.25	.15
0175	Rick Burleson	.50	.25	.15
0176	Luis Tiant	.50	.25	.15
0177	Ted Williams	6.00	3.00	1.75
0178	Dennis Eckersley	2.00	1.00	.60
0179	Don Zimmer	.50	.25	.15
0180	Carlton Fisk	2.50	1.25	.70
0181	Dwight Evans	.50	.25	.15
0182	Fred Kendall	.50	.25	.15
0183	George Scott	.50	.25	.15
0184	Frank Duffy	.50	.25	.15
0185	Bernie Carbo	.50	.25	.15
0186	Jerry Remy	.50	.25	.15
0187	Carl Yastrzemski	4.00	2.00	1.25
0188	Allen Ripley	.50	.25	.15
0189	Jim Rice	.90	.45	.25
California Angels Magazine:		20.00	10.00	6.00
0190	Ken Landreaux	.50	.25	.15
0191	Paul Hartzell	.50	.25	.15
0192	Ken Brett	.50	.25	.15
0193	Dave Garcia	.50	.25	.15
0194	Bobby Grich	.50	.25	.15
0195	Lyman Bostock	.50	.25	.15
0196	Isaac Hampton	.50	.25	.15
0197	Dave LaRoche	.50	.25	.15
0198	Dave Chalk	.50	.25	.15
0199	Rick Miller	.50	.25	.15
0200	Floyd Rayford	.50	.25	.15
0201	Willie Aikens	.50	.25	.15
0202	Balor Moore	.50	.25	.15
0203	Nolan Ryan	10.00	5.00	3.00
0204	Dan Goodwin	.50	.25	.15
0205	Ron Fairly	.50	.25	.15
0206	Dyar Miller	.50	.25	.15
0207	Carney Lansford	.50	.25	.15
0208	Don Baylor	.60	.30	.20
0209	Gil Flores	.50	.25	.15
0210	Terry Humphrey	.50	.25	.15
0211	Frank Tanana	.50	.25	.15
0212	Chris Knapp	.50	.25	.15
0213	Ron Jackson	.50	.25	.15
0214	Joe Rudi	.50	.25	.15
0215	Tony Solaita	.50	.25	.15
0216	Steve Mulliniks	.50	.25	.15
Kansas City Royals Magazine:		20.00	10.00	6.00
0217	George Brett	6.00	3.00	1.75
0218	Doug Bird	.50	.25	.15
0219	Hal McRae	.50	.25	.15
0220	Dennis Leonard	.50	.25	.15
0221	Darrell Porter	.50	.25	.15
0222	Randy McGilberry	.50	.25	.15
0223	Pete LaCock	.50	.25	.15
0224	Whitey Herzog	.50	.25	.15
0225	Andy Hassler	.50	.25	.15
0226	Joe Lahoud	.50	.25	.15
0227	Amos Otis	.50	.25	.15
0228	Al Hrabosky	.50	.25	.15
0229	Clint Hurdle	.50	.25	.15
0230	Paul Splittorff	.50	.25	.15
0231	Marty Pattin	.50	.25	.15
0232	Frank White	.50	.25	.15
0233	John Wathan	.50	.25	.15
0234	Freddie Patek	.50	.25	.15
0235	Rich Gale	.50	.25	.15
0236	U.L. Washington	.50	.25	.15
0237	Larry Gura	.50	.25	.15
0238	Jim Colburn	.50	.25	.15
0239	Tom Poquette	.50	.25	.15
0240	Al Cowens	.50	.25	.15
0241	Willie Wilson	.50	.25	.15
0242	Steve Mingori	.50	.25	.15
0243	Jerry Terrell	.50	.25	.15
Chicago Cubs Magazine:		12.50	6.25	3.75
0244	Larry Biitner	.50	.25	.15
0245	Rick Reuschel	.50	.25	.15
0246	Dave Rader	.50	.25	.15
0247	Paul Reuschel	.50	.25	.15
0248	Hector Cruz	.50	.25	.15
0249	Woody Fryman	.50	.25	.15
0250	Steve Ontiveros	.50	.25	.15
0251	Mike Gordon	.50	.25	.15
0252	Dave Kingman	.50	.25	.15
0253	Gene Clines	.50	.25	.15
0254	Bruce Sutter	2.00	1.00	.60
0255	Guillermo Hernandez	.50	.25	.15
0256	Ivan DeJesus	.50	.25	.15
0257	Greg Gross	.50	.25	.15
0258	Larry Cox	.50	.25	.15
0259	Joe Wallis	.50	.25	.15
0260	Dennis Lamp	.50	.25	.15
0261	Ray Burris	.50	.25	.15
0262	Bill Caudill	.50	.25	.15
0263	Donnie Moore	.50	.25	.15
0264	Bill Buckner	.60	.30	.20
0265	Bobby Murcer	.60	.30	.20
0266	Dave Roberts	.50	.25	.15
0267	Mike Krukow	.50	.25	.15
0268	Herman Franks	.50	.25	.15
0269	Mike Kelleher	.50	.25	.15
0270	Rudy Meoli	.50	.25	.15

1978 SSPC Baseball the Phillies Way

This team set was produced on a tri-fold insert in an SSPC magazine titled, "Baseball the Phillies Way." The magazine offered playing tips. Cards are in the contemporary SSPC format of a posed front photo with a white border and

no other graphics. Backs are printed in red, white and black with player ID, career data and card numbers between 0028-0054, continuing the sequence begun with the Yankees yearbook team set which continues with the All-Star Gallery set. Cards could be cut from the sheets into 2-1/2" x 3-1/2" singles.

		NM	EX	VG
Complete Magazine:		15.00	7.50	4.50
Complete Set, Singles (27):		12.00	6.00	3.50
Common Player:		.50	.25	.15
0028	Garry Maddox	.50	.25	.15
0029	Steve Carlton	2.50	1.25	.70
0030	Ron Reed	.50	.25	.15
0031	Greg Luzinski	.50	.25	.15
0032	Bobby Wine	.50	.25	.15
0033	Bob Boone	1.50	.70	.45
0034	Carroll Beringer	.50	.25	.15
0035	Dick Hebner	.50	.25	.15
0036	Ray Rippelmeyer	.50	.25	.15
0037	Terry Harmon	.50	.25	.15
0038	Gene Garber	.50	.25	.15
0039	Ted Sizemore	.50	.25	.15
0040	Barry Foote	.50	.25	.15
0041	Tony Taylor	.50	.25	.15
0042	Tug McGraw	.75	.40	.25
0043	Jay Johnstone	.65	.35	.20
0044	Randy Lerch	.50	.25	.15
0045	Billy DeMars	.50	.25	.15
0046	Mike Schmidt	5.00	2.50	1.50
0047	Larry Christenson	.50	.25	.15
0048	Tim McCarver	1.00	.50	.30
0049	Larry Bowa	.65	.35	.20
0050	Danny Ozark	.50	.25	.15
0051	Jerry Martin	.50	.25	.15
0052	Jim Lonborg	.50	.25	.15
0053	Bake McBride	.50	.25	.15
0054	Warren Brusstar	.50	.25	.15

1978 SSPC Yankees Yearbook

This team set was printed on a tri-fold insert found both in the 1978 Yankees yearbook and a magazine titled "Diary of a Champion Yankee," produced by SSPC. The nine cards on each sheet could be cut apart into 2-1/2" x 3-1/2" singles. Cards follow the basic SSPC format of a posed color photo on front with a white border and no graphic elements. Backs have player identification, career summary and "CHAMPIONSHIP SEASON" highlights, printed in black and blue on white. Cards are numbered from 0001-0027, and may be considered part of the larger All-Star Gallery issue.

		NM	EX	VG
Complete Magazine:		12.50	6.25	3.75
Complete Set, Singles (27):		10.00	5.00	3.00
Common Player:		.50	.25	.15
0001	Thurman Munson	3.00	1.50	.90
0002	Cliff Johnson	.50	.25	.15
0003	Lou Piniella	.75	.40	.25
0004	Dell Alston	.50	.25	.15
0005	Yankee Stadium	1.00	.50	.30
0006	Ken Holtzman	.50	.25	.15
0007	Chris Chambliss	.60	.30	.20
0008	Roy White	.60	.30	.20
0009	Ed Figueroa	.50	.25	.15
0010	Dick Tidrow	.50	.25	.15
0011	Sparky Lyle	.60	.30	.20
0012	Fred Stanley	.50	.25	.15
0013	Mickey Rivers	.50	.25	.15
0014	Billy Martin	.75	.40	.25
0015	George Zeber	.50	.25	.15
0016	Ken Clay	.50	.25	.15
0017	Ron Guidry	.75	.40	.25
0018	Don Gullett	.50	.25	.15
0019	Fran Healy	.50	.25	.15
0020	Paul Blair	.50	.25	.15
0021	Mickey Klutts	.50	.25	.15
0022	Yankee team	.50	.25	.15
0023	Catfish Hunter	1.50	.70	.45

0024	Bucky Dent	.75	.40	.25
0025	Graig Nettles	.75	.40	.25
0026	Reggie Jackson	3.00	1.50	.90
0027	Willie Randolph	.60	.30	.20

1889 "The Stage" Stars of the Diamond

Titled "Stars of the Diamond" and issued weekly between May 25-Aug. 31, 1889, these numbered supplements are printed in "The Stage" newspaper, a Philadelphia-based publication. Two types of supplements are found, those picturing New York players in uniforms (from Joseph Hall photos), and those picturing members of the Philadelphia National League and American Association teams in street clothes. The black-and-white portraits are printed in a 9" x 12" format on newsprint, making surviving examples very rare today.

		NM	EX	VG
Common Player:		250.00	125.00	75.00
1	Charles Buffington	250.00	125.00	75.00
2	John Clements	250.00	125.00	75.00
3	Harry D. Stovey	250.00	125.00	75.00
4	"Gus" Weyhing	250.00	125.00	75.00
5	L.M. Cross	250.00	125.00	75.00
6	Edward Seward	250.00	125.00	75.00
7	Wm. Robinson (Wilbert)	375.00	185.00	110.00
8	Denny Lyons	250.00	125.00	75.00
9	A.B. Sanders	250.00	125.00	75.00
10	William Schriver	250.00	125.00	75.00
11	Daniel M. Casey	250.00	125.00	75.00
12	"Tim" Keefe	375.00	185.00	110.00
13	"Buck" Ewing	375.00	185.00	110.00
14	John Ward	375.00	185.00	110.00

1953 Stahl-Meyer Franks

These nine cards, issued in packages of hot dogs by a New York area meat company, feature three players from each of the New York teams of the day - Dodgers Giants and Yankees. Cards in the set measure 3-1/4" x 4-1/2". The card fronts in this unnumbered set feature color photos with player name and facsimile autograph. The backs list both biographical and statistical information on half the card and a ticket offer promotion on the other half. The card corners are cut diagonally, although some cards (apparantly cut from sheets) with square corners have been seen. Cards are white-bordered.

		NM	EX	VG
Complete Set (9):		20,000	9,000	4,000
Common Player:		500.00	225.00	100.00
(1)	Hank Bauer	550.00	245.00	110.00
(2)	Roy Campanella	2,000	900.00	400.00
(3)	Gil Hodges	1,250	560.00	250.00
(4)	Monte Irvin	750.00	335.00	150.00
(5)	Whitey Lockman	500.00	225.00	100.00
(6)	Mickey Mantle	13,500	6,100	2,750
(7)	Phil Rizzuto	1,250	560.00	250.00
(8)	Duke Snider	2,000	900.00	400.00
(9)	Bobby Thomson	650.00	290.00	130.00

1954 Stahl-Meyer Franks

 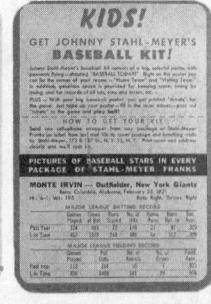

The 1954 set of Stahl-Meyer Franks was increased to 12 cards which retained the 3-1/4" x 4-1/2" size. The most prominent addition to the '54 set was New York Giants slugger Willie Mays. The card fronts are identical in format to the previous year's set. However, the backs are different as they are designed on a vertical format. The backs also contain an advertisement for a "Johnny Stahl-Meyer Baseball Kit." The cards in the set are unnumbered.

		NM	EX	VG
Complete Set (12):		30,000	13,500	6,000
Common Player:		650.00	290.00	130.00
(1)	Hank Bauer	750.00	335.00	150.00
(2)	Carl Erskine	750.00	335.00	150.00
(3)	Gil Hodges	2,000	900.00	400.00
(4)	Monte Irvin	1,000	450.00	200.00

		NM	EX	VG
(5)	Whitey Lockman	650.00	290.00	130.00
(6)	Gil McDougald	750.00	335.00	150.00
(7)	Mickey Mantle	12,000	5,400	2,400
(8)	Willie Mays	8,500	3,825	1,700
(9)	Don Mueller	650.00	290.00	130.00
(10)	Don Newcombe	750.00	335.00	150.00
(11)	Phil Rizzuto	2,000	900.00	400.00
(12)	Duke Snider	2,000	900.00	400.00

1955 Stahl-Meyer Franks

Eleven of the 12 players in the 1955 set are the same as those featured in 1954. The exception is the New York Giants' Dusty Rhodes, who replaced Willie Mays on the 3-1/4" x 4-1/2" cards. The card fronts are again full-color photos bordered in yellow with diagonal corners, and four players from each of the three New York teams are featured. The backs offer a new promotion, with a drawing of Mickey Mantle and advertisements selling pennants and caps. Player statistics are still included on the vertical card backs. The cards in the set are unnumbered.

		NM	EX	VG
Complete Set (12):		40,000	20,000	12,000
Common Player:		1,000	500.00	300.00
1)	Hank Bauer	1,200	600.00	350.00
2)	Carl Erskine	1,200	600.00	350.00
3)	Gil Hodges	3,000	1,500	900.00
4)	Monte Irvin	1,600	800.00	480.00
5)	Whitey Lockman	1,000	500.00	300.00
6)	Mickey Mantle	24,000	12,000	7,250
7)	Gil McDougald	1,200	600.00	350.00
8)	Don Mueller	1,000	500.00	300.00
9)	Don Newcombe	1,200	600.00	350.00
10)	Jim Rhodes	1,000	500.00	300.00
11)	Phil Rizzuto	3,000	1,500	900.00
12)	Duke Snider	3,000	1,500	900.00

1916 Standard Biscuit (D350-1)

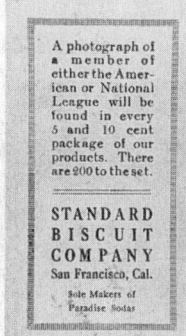

The range of cards in this issue is uncertain as examples can be found corresponding to the checklists of both of the 1916 sets known as M101-5 and M101-4 Blank Backs. Standard Biscuit cards in this format are also known that correspond to neither M101-5 nor M101-4. The approximately 1-5/8" x 3" black-and-white cards usually command a modest premium from collectors seeking to enhance a type collection or superstar collection. A trial checklist is begun herewith. Since D350-1 can be found corresponding to both M101-4 and M101-5, they have two different numerical checklists and should be split into D350-1a & D350-1b.

		NM	EX	VG
Common Player:		90.00	45.00	30.00
1	Babe Adams	90.00	45.00	30.00
3	Ed Ainsmith	90.00	45.00	30.00
6	Jimmy Archer	90.00	45.00	30.00
12	Beals Becker	90.00	45.00	30.00
12a	Beals Becker			
12b	Zinn Beck (May be unique) (Value undetermined)			
13	Joe Benz	90.00	45.00	30.00
14	Bob Bescher	90.00	45.00	30.00
15	Al Betzel	90.00	45.00	30.00
18	Eddie Burns	90.00	45.00	30.00
25	Forest Cady	90.00	45.00	30.00
27	George Chalmers	90.00	45.00	30.00
37	Joe Connolly	90.00	45.00	30.00
39	Harry Coveleskie (Coveleski)	90.00	45.00	30.00
	Sam Crawford	400.00	200.00	130.00
48	William Doak	90.00	45.00	30.00
50	Charles Dooin	90.00	45.00	30.00

		NM	EX	VG
54	Johnny Evers	500.00	250.00	150.00
57	Urban Faber	400.00	200.00	130.00
60	Max Flack	90.00	45.00	30.00
61	Art Fletcher	90.00	45.00	30.00
63	Jacques Fournier	90.00	45.00	30.00
64	"Chic" Gandil	900.00	450.00	300.00
66	Joe Gedeon	90.00	45.00	30.00
68	George Gibson	90.00	45.00	30.00
69	Wilbur Good	90.00	45.00	30.00
71	John Graney	90.00	45.00	30.00
72	Tom Griffith	90.00	45.00	30.00
73	Heinie Groh	90.00	45.00	30.00
75	Bob Harmon	90.00	45.00	30.00
77	Claude Hendrix	90.00	45.00	30.00
79	John Henry	90.00	45.00	30.00
80	Buck Herzog	90.00	45.00	30.00
82	Dick Hoblitzell	90.00	45.00	30.00
84	Ivan Howard	90.00	45.00	30.00
86	Joe Jackson	15,000	7,500	4,500
87	Joe Jackson	15,000	7,500	4,500
89	Hugh Jennings	400.00	200.00	130.00
131	Les Nunamaker	90.00	45.00	30.00
137	E.J. Pfeffer	90.00	45.00	30.00
151	Babe Ruth	30,000	15,000	9,000
164	Ernie Shore	90.00	45.00	30.00
172a	Milton Stock	90.00	45.00	30.00
172b	Billy Sullivan	90.00	45.00	30.00
176	Jim Thorpe	26,250	13,125	7,875
184	Honus Wagner	2,700	1,350	510.00
186	Bobby Wallace	600.00	300.00	200.00
191	Fred Williams	90.00	45.00	30.00
195	Joe Wood	600.00	300.00	180.00
196	Joe Wood	600.00	300.00	180.00
199	Heiny Zimmerman	90.00	45.00	30.00

1917 Standard Biscuit (D350-2)

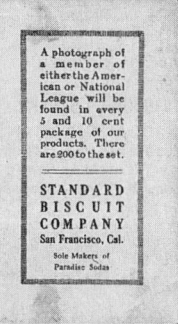

BOBBIE BYRNE 3rd B.—Philadelphia Nationals 23

The 200 cards in this set are more commonly found with the advertising of Collins-McCarthy Candy Co. on the back. The cards measure about 2" x 3-1/4" and are printed in black-and-white. Though the Standard Biscuit cards are scarcer than the Collins-McCarthy version, collectors do not attach much premium to them.

		NM	EX	VG
Complete Set (200):		70,000	35,000	21,000
Common Player:		150.00	75.00	45.00
1	Sam Agnew	150.00	75.00	45.00
2	Grover Alexander	1,000	700.00	300.00
3	W.S. Alexander (W.E.)	150.00	75.00	45.00
4	Leon Ames	150.00	75.00	45.00
5	Fred Anderson	150.00	75.00	45.00
6	Ed Appleton	150.00	75.00	45.00
7	Jimmy Archer	150.00	75.00	45.00
8	Jimmy Austin	150.00	75.00	45.00
9	Jim Bagby	150.00	75.00	45.00
10	H.D. Baird	150.00	75.00	45.00
11	J. Franklin Baker	1,000	700.00	300.00
12	Dave Bancroft	1,000	700.00	300.00
13	Jack Barry	150.00	75.00	45.00
14	Joe Benz	150.00	75.00	45.00
15	Al Betzel	150.00	75.00	45.00
16	Ping Bodie	150.00	75.00	45.00
17	Joe Boehling	150.00	75.00	45.00
18	Eddie Burns	150.00	75.00	45.00
19	George Burns	150.00	75.00	45.00
20	Geo. J. Burns	150.00	75.00	45.00
21	Joe Bush	150.00	75.00	45.00
22	Owen Bush	150.00	75.00	45.00
23	Bobby Byrne	150.00	75.00	45.00
24	Forrest Cady	150.00	75.00	45.00
25	Max Carey	1,000	700.00	300.00
26	Ray Chapman	200.00	100.00	60.00
27	Larry Cheney	150.00	75.00	45.00
28	Eddie Cicotte	1,000	700.00	300.00
29	Tom Clarke	150.00	75.00	45.00
30	Ty Cobb	5,000	3,000	2,000
31	Eddie Collins	1,000	700.00	300.00
32	"Shauno" Collins (Shano)	150.00	75.00	45.00
33	Fred Coumbe	150.00	75.00	45.00
34	Harry Coveleskie (Coveleski)	150.00	75.00	45.00
35	Gavvy Cravath	150.00	75.00	45.00
36	Sam Crawford	1,000	700.00	300.00
37	Geo. Cutshaw	150.00	75.00	45.00
38	Jake Daubert	150.00	75.00	45.00
39	Geo. Dauss	150.00	75.00	45.00
40	Charles Deal	150.00	75.00	45.00
41	"Wheezer" Dell	150.00	75.00	45.00
42	William Doak	150.00	75.00	45.00
43	Bill Donovan	150.00	75.00	45.00
44	Larry Doyle	150.00	75.00	45.00
45	Johnny Evers	1,000	700.00	300.00
46	Urban Faber	1,000	700.00	300.00
47	"Hap" Felsch	1,000	700.00	300.00
48	Bill Fischer	150.00	75.00	45.00
49	Ray Fisher	150.00	75.00	45.00
50	Art Fletcher	150.00	75.00	45.00
51	Eddie Foster	150.00	75.00	45.00
52	Jacques Fournier	150.00	75.00	45.00
53	Del Gainer (Gainor)	150.00	75.00	45.00
54	Bert Gallia	150.00	75.00	45.00
55	"Chic" Gandil (Chick)	1,000	700.00	300.00
56	Larry Gardner	150.00	75.00	45.00
57	Joe Gedeon	150.00	75.00	45.00
58	Gus Getz	150.00	75.00	45.00
59	Frank Gilhooley	150.00	75.00	45.00
60	Wm. Gleason	150.00	75.00	45.00
61	M.A. Gonzales (Gonzalez)	165.00	80.00	50.00
62	Hank Gowdy	150.00	75.00	45.00
63	John Graney	150.00	75.00	45.00
64	Tom Griffith	150.00	75.00	45.00
65	Heinie Groh	150.00	75.00	45.00
66	Bob Groom	150.00	75.00	45.00
67	Louis Guisto	150.00	75.00	45.00
68	Earl Hamilton	150.00	75.00	45.00
69	Harry Harper	150.00	75.00	45.00
70	Grover Hartley	150.00	75.00	45.00
71	Harry Heilmann	5,000	4,000	2,000
72	Claude Hendrix	150.00	75.00	45.00
73	Olaf Henriksen	150.00	75.00	45.00
74	John Henry	150.00	75.00	45.00
75	"Buck" Herzog	150.00	75.00	45.00
76	Hugh High	150.00	75.00	45.00
77	Dick Hoblitzell	150.00	75.00	45.00
78	Walter Holke	150.00	75.00	45.00
79	Harry Hooper	1,000	700.00	300.00
80	Rogers Hornsby	20,000	12,500	7,000
81	Ivan Howard	150.00	75.00	45.00
82	Joe Jackson	16,500	8,500	5,000
83	Harold Janvrin	150.00	75.00	45.00
84	William James	150.00	75.00	45.00
85	C. Jamieson	150.00	75.00	45.00
86	Hugh Jennings	1,000	700.00	300.00
87	Walter Johnson	3,000	2,000	1,000
88	James Johnston	150.00	75.00	45.00
89	Fielder Jones	150.00	75.00	45.00
90	Joe Judge	150.00	75.00	45.00
91	Hans Lobert	150.00	75.00	45.00
92	Benny Kauff	150.00	75.00	45.00
93	Wm. Killefer Jr.	150.00	75.00	45.00
94	Ed. Konetchy	150.00	75.00	45.00
95	John Lavan	150.00	75.00	45.00
96	Jimmy Lavender	150.00	75.00	45.00
97	"Nemo" Leibold	150.00	75.00	45.00
98	H.B. Leonard	150.00	75.00	45.00
99	Duffy Lewis	150.00	75.00	45.00
100	Tom Long	150.00	75.00	45.00
101	Wm. Louden	150.00	75.00	45.00
102	Fred Luderus	150.00	75.00	45.00
103	Lee Magee	150.00	75.00	45.00
104	Sherwood Magee	150.00	75.00	45.00
105	Al Mamaux	150.00	75.00	45.00
106	Leslie Mann	150.00	75.00	45.00
107	"Rabbit" Maranville	1,000	700.00	300.00
108	Rube Marquard	1,000	700.00	300.00
109	Armando Marsans	165.00	85.00	50.00
110	J. Erskine Mayer	175.00	85.00	50.00
111	George McBride	150.00	75.00	45.00
112	Lew McCarty	150.00	75.00	45.00
113	John J. McGraw	1,000	700.00	300.00
114	Jack McInnis	150.00	75.00	45.00
115	Lee Meadows	150.00	75.00	45.00
116	Fred Merkle	150.00	75.00	45.00
117	"Chief" Meyers	150.00	75.00	45.00
118	Clyde Milan	150.00	75.00	45.00
119	Otto Miller	150.00	75.00	45.00
120	Clarence Mitchell	150.00	75.00	45.00
121	Ray Morgan	150.00	75.00	45.00
122	Guy Morton	150.00	75.00	45.00
123	"Mike" Mowrey	150.00	75.00	45.00
124	Elmer Myers	150.00	75.00	45.00
125	"Hy" Myers	150.00	75.00	45.00
126	A.E. Neale	175.00	85.00	50.00
127	Arthur Nehf	150.00	75.00	45.00
128	J.A. Niehoff	150.00	75.00	45.00
129	Steve O'Neill	150.00	75.00	45.00
130	"Dode" Paskert	150.00	75.00	45.00
131	Roger Peckinpaugh	150.00	75.00	45.00
132	"Pol" Perritt	150.00	75.00	45.00
133	"Jeff" Pfeffer	150.00	75.00	45.00
134	Walter Pipp	150.00	75.00	45.00
135	Derril Pratt (Derrill)	150.00	75.00	45.00
136	Bill Rariden	150.00	75.00	45.00
137	E.C. Rice	350.00	175.00	100.00
138	Wm. A. Ritter (Wm. H.)	150.00	75.00	45.00
139	Eppa Rixey	1,000	700.00	300.00
140	Davey Robertson	150.00	75.00	45.00
141	"Bob" Roth	150.00	75.00	45.00
142	Ed. Roush	1,000	700.00	300.00
143	Clarence Rowland	150.00	75.00	45.00
144	Dick Rudolph	150.00	75.00	45.00
145	William Rumler	150.00	75.00	45.00
146	Reb Russell	150.00	75.00	45.00
147	"Babe" Ruth	12,500	6,250	3,750
148	Vic Saier	150.00	75.00	45.00
149	"Slim" Sallee	150.00	75.00	45.00
150	Ray Schalk	1,000	700.00	300.00
151	Walter Schang	150.00	75.00	45.00
152	Frank Schulte	150.00	75.00	45.00
153	Ferd Schupp	150.00	75.00	45.00
154	Everett Scott	150.00	75.00	45.00
155	Hank Severeid	150.00	75.00	45.00
156	Howard Shanks	150.00	75.00	45.00
157	Bob Shawkey	150.00	75.00	45.00
158	Jas. Sheckard	150.00	75.00	45.00
159	Ernie Shore	150.00	75.00	45.00
160	C.H. Shorten	150.00	75.00	45.00
161	Burt Shotton	150.00	75.00	45.00
162	Geo. Sisler	1,000	700.00	300.00
163	Elmer Smith	150.00	75.00	45.00
164	J. Carlisle Smith	150.00	75.00	45.00
165	Fred Snodgrass	150.00	75.00	45.00
166	Tris Speaker	2,000	1,500	1,000
167	Oscar Stanage	150.00	75.00	45.00

168	Charles Stengel	1,000	700.00	500.00
169	Milton Stock	150.00	75.00	45.00
170	Amos Strunk	150.00	75.00	45.00
171	"Zeb" Terry	150.00	75.00	45.00
172	"Jeff" Tesreau	150.00	75.00	45.00
173	Chester Thomas	150.00	75.00	45.00
174	Fred Toney	150.00	75.00	45.00
175	Terry Turner	150.00	75.00	45.00
176	George Tyler	150.00	75.00	45.00
177	Jim Vaughn	150.00	75.00	45.00
178	Bob Veach	150.00	75.00	45.00
179	Oscar Vitt	150.00	75.00	45.00
180	Hans Wagner	3,500	1,750	1,050
181	Clarence Walker	150.00	75.00	45.00
182	Jim Walsh	150.00	75.00	45.00
183	Al Walters	150.00	75.00	45.00
184	W. Wambsganss	150.00	75.00	45.00
185	Buck Weaver	1,000	500.00	300.00
186	Carl Weilman	150.00	75.00	45.00
187	Zack Wheat	1,000	700.00	300.00
188	Geo. Whitted	150.00	75.00	45.00
189	Joe Wilhoit	150.00	75.00	45.00
190	Claude Williams	750.00	375.00	225.00
191	Fred Williams	150.00	75.00	45.00
192	Art Wilson	150.00	75.00	45.00
193	Lawton Witt	150.00	75.00	45.00
194	Joe Wood	150.00	75.00	45.00
195	William Wortman	150.00	75.00	45.00
196	Steve Yerkes	150.00	75.00	45.00
197	Earl Yingling	150.00	75.00	45.00
198	"Pep" (Ralph) Young	150.00	75.00	45.00
199	Rollie Zeider	150.00	75.00	45.00
200	Henry Zimmerman	150.00	75.00	45.00

1921 Standard Biscuit (D350-3)

CHESTER THOMAS

A photograph of a member of either the American or National League will be found in every 5 and 10 cent package of our products. There are 80 to the set.

STANDARD BISCUIT COMPANY
San Francisco, Cal.
Sole Makers of Paradise Sodas

It is unknown to what extent this scarcest of the three Standard Biscuit advertising issues actually parallels the E121 Series of 80, on which American Caramel Co. backs are more commonly found. This uncertainty contributes to the relatively low premium value (about 2X) attached to the Standard Biscuit versions. Backs have been seen in two styles; one mentions "80 to the set," the other mentions "contains 80 photographs." Cards are printed in black-and-white in a size of about 2" x 3-1/4". A checklist has been started here in an effort to better understand the issue.

PREMIUM: 2-4X
(3) Jim Bagby
(4a) J. Franklin Baker
(12) Max Carey (Hands at hips.)
(14) Ty Cobb/Throwing (Looking front.)
(15b) Ty Cobb/Throwing (Looking right, manager on front.)
(16) Eddie Collins
(19) Dave Davenport
(37) Tom Griffith
(40) John Henry
(41) Clarence Hodge
(45) Rogers Hornsby
(52) James Johnston
(61) Al Mamaux
(62) "Rabbit" Maranville
(83) Eppa Rixey, Jr.
(86) Babe Ruth
(90) Ray Schalk
(103) Chester Thomas
(109) Jim Vaughn (Dark cap.)
(113) Oscar Vitt
(116) Zach Wheat
(120) Joe Wood

1910 Standard Caramel Co. (E93)

WILTSE, N. Y. Nat'l.

BASE BALL STARS
This card issued a series of stars from original photographs.
1. AMES, New York National
2. BENDER, Phila. American
3. BROWN, Chicago National
4. COLLINS, Phila. American
5. CHANCE, Chicago National
6. COVELESKIE, Cincinnati Nat'l
7. CHASE, Detroit American
8. COBB, Detroit American
9. CLARKE, Pittsburg National
10. DELEHANTY, Detroit American
11. DONOVAN, Detroit American
12. DOOIN, Philadelphia National
13. EVERS, Chicago National
14. GIBSON, Pittsburg National
15. GRIFFITH, Cincinnati National
16. JENNINGS, Detroit American
17. JONES, Detroit American
18. JOSS, Cleveland American
19. LAJOIE, Cleveland American
20. LEACH, Pittsburg National
21. MATHEWSON, N. Y. National
22. McGRAW, New York National
23. PHILLIPPI, Pittsburg American
24. PLANK, Philadelphia American
25. PASTORIOUS, Brooklyn Nat'l
26. TINKER, Chicago National
27. WADDELL, St. Louis American
28. WAGNER, Pittsburg National
29. WILTSE, New York National
30. CY. YOUNG, Cleveland Amer.
Manufactured only by
Standard Caramel Co., Lancaster, Pa.

This 30-card set issued in 1910 by Standard Caramel Co. of Lancaster, Pa., is closely related to several other candy sets from this period which share the same format and, in many cases, the same player poses. The cards measure 1-1/2" x 2-3/4" and utilize tinted black-and-white player photos. The back of each card contains an alphabetical checklist of the set plus a line indicating it was manufactured by Standard Caramel Co., Lancaster, Pa. The set carries the ACC designation of E93.

		NM	EX	VG
	Complete Set (30):	80,000	32,000	16,000
	Common Player:	1,200	480.00	240.00
(1)	Red Ames	1,200	480.00	240.00
(2)	Chief Bender	2,400	1,200	600.00
(3)	Mordecai Brown	2,400	1,200	600.00
(4)	Frank Chance	2,400	1,200	600.00
(5)	Hal Chase	1,800	880.00	440.00
(6)	Fred Clarke	2,400	1,200	600.00
(7)	Ty Cobb	12,000	6,000	3,000
(8)	Eddie Collins	2,400	1,200	600.00
(9)	Harry Coveleskie (Coveleski)	1,200	480.00	240.00
(10)	Jim Delehanty	1,600	800.00	450.00
(11)	Wild Bill Donovan	1,200	480.00	240.00
(12)	Red Dooin	1,200	480.00	240.00
(13)	Johnny Evers	2,400	1,200	600.00
(14)	George Gibson	1,200	480.00	240.00
(15)	Clark Griffith	2,400	1,200	600.00
(16)	Hugh Jennings	2,400	1,200	600.00
(17)	Davy Jones	1,200	480.00	240.00
(18)	Addie Joss	2,700	1,350	660.00
(19)	Nap Lajoie	2,400	120.00	600.00
(20)	Tommy Leach	1,200	480.00	240.00
(21)	Christy Mathewson	6,400	3,200	1,600
(22)	John McGraw	2,400	1,200	600.00
(23)	Jim Pastorious	1,200	480.00	240.00
(24)	Deacon Phillippi (Phillippe)	1,200	480.00	240.00
(25)	Eddie Plank	4,000	2,000	1,000
(26)	Joe Tinker	2,400	1,200	600.00
(27)	Rube Waddell	2,400	1,200	600.00
(28)	Honus Wagner	9,600	4,800	2,400
(29)	Hooks Wiltse	1,200	480.00	240.00
(30)	Cy Young	6,400	3,200	1,950

1960-70s Stan Musial & Biggie's Restaurant

These black-and-white photocards were prepared for Musial's use while glad-handing patrons at his St. Louis eatery. The pictures have a facsimile autograph. A "Compliments of . . ." message is printed in the bottom border. Backs are blank.

Compliments of
STAN MUSIAL & BIGGIE'S RESTAURANT
5130 Oakland Ave., St. Louis, Mo. 63110

COMPLIMENTS OF STAN MUSIAL & BIGGIE'S RESTAURANT

		NM	EX	VG
(1)	Stan Musial (Batting pose, 5" x 7".)	10.00	5.00	3.00
(2)	Stan Musial (Batting pose, 3-1/2" x 5-1/2".)	10.00	5.00	3.00
(3)	Stan Musial (Standing w/glove, 5" x 7".)	10.00	5.00	3.00

1952 Star-Cal Decals Type 1

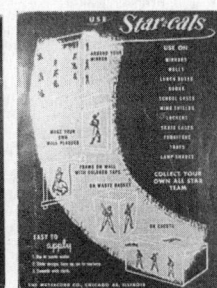

Mickey Mantle
Easy to apply with water

The Meyercord Co., of Chicago issued two sets of baseball player decals in 1952. The Type I Star-Cal Decal set consists of 68 players, each pictured on a large (4-1/8" x 6-1/8") decal. The player's name and facsimile autograph appear on the decal, along with the decal number listed on the checklist here. Values shown are for decals complete with outer directions envelope.

		NM	EX	VG
	Complete Set (68):	7,500	3,750	2,250
	Common Player:	45.00	22.50	13.50
70A	Allie Reynolds	50.00	25.00	15.00
70B	Ed Lopat	50.00	25.00	15.00
70C	Yogi Berra	200.00	100.00	60.00
70D	Vic Raschi	50.00	25.00	15.00
70E	Jerry Coleman	45.00	22.50	13.50
70F	Phil Rizzuto	110.00	55.00	35.00
70G	Mickey Mantle	1,750	875.00	525.00
71A	Mel Parnell	45.00	22.50	13.50

71B	Ted Williams	400.00	200.00	120.00
71C	Ted Williams	400.00	200.00	120.00
71D	Vern Stephens	45.00	22.50	13.50
71E	Billy Goodman	45.00	22.50	13.50
71F	Dom DiMaggio	50.00	25.00	15.00
71G	Dick Gernert	45.00	22.50	13.50
71H	Hoot Evers	45.00	22.50	13.50
72A	George Kell	50.00	25.00	15.00
72B	Hal Newhouser	50.00	25.00	15.00
72C	Hoot Evers	45.00	22.50	13.50
72D	Vic Wertz	45.00	22.50	13.50
72E	Fred Hutchinson	45.00	22.50	13.50
72F	Johnny Groth	45.00	22.50	13.50
73A	Al Zarilla	45.00	22.50	13.50
73B	Billy Pierce	45.00	22.50	13.50
73C	Eddie Robinson	45.00	22.50	13.50
73D	Chico Carrasquel	50.00	25.00	15.00
73E	Minnie Minoso	50.00	25.00	15.00
73F	Jim Busby	45.00	22.50	13.50
73G	Nellie Fox	55.00	27.50	16.50
73H	Sam Mele	45.00	22.50	13.50
74A	Larry Doby	55.00	27.50	16.50
74B	Al Rosen	50.00	25.00	15.00
74C	Bob Lemon	55.00	27.00	16.50
74D	Jim Hegan	45.00	22.50	13.50
74E	Bob Feller	90.00	45.00	27.00
74F	Dale Mitchell	45.00	22.50	13.50
75A	Ned Garver	45.00	22.50	13.50
76A	Gus Zernial	45.00	22.50	13.50
76B	Ferris Fain	45.00	22.50	13.50
76C	Bobby Shantz	45.00	22.50	13.50
77A	Richie Ashburn	60.00	30.00	18.00
77B	Ralph Kiner	55.00	27.50	16.50
77C	Curt Simmons	45.00	22.50	13.50
78A	Bobby Thomson	55.00	27.50	16.50
78B	Alvin Dark	45.00	22.50	13.50
78C	Sal Maglie	45.00	22.50	13.50
78D	Larry Jansen	45.00	22.50	13.50
78E	Willie Mays	425.00	210.00	125.00
78F	Monte Irvin	55.00	27.50	16.50
78G	Whitey Lockman	45.00	22.50	13.50
79A	Gil Hodges	90.00	45.00	27.00
79B	Pee Wee Reese	110.00	55.00	35.00
79C	Roy Campanella	110.00	55.00	35.00
79D	Don Newcombe	55.00	27.50	16.50
79E	Duke Snider	110.00	55.00	35.00
79F	Preacher Roe	50.00	25.00	15.00
79G	Jackie Robinson	350.00	175.00	105.00
80A	Eddie Miksis	45.00	22.50	13.50
80B	Dutch Leonard	45.00	22.50	13.50
80C	Randy Jackson	45.00	22.50	13.50
80D	Bob Rush	45.00	22.50	13.50
80E	Hank Sauer	45.00	22.50	13.50
80F	Phil Cavarretta	45.00	22.50	13.50
80G	Warren Hacker	45.00	22.50	13.50
81A	Red Schoendienst	55.00	27.50	16.50
81B	Wally Westlake	45.00	22.50	13.50
81C	Cliff Chambers	45.00	22.50	13.50
81D	Enos Slaughter	55.00	27.50	16.50
81E	Stan Musial	275.00	135.00	85.00
81F	Stan Musial	275.00	135.00	85.00
81G	Jerry Staley	45.00	22.50	13.50

1952 Star-Cal Decals Type 2

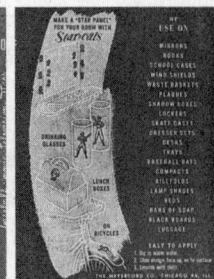

Also produced by Chicago's Meyercord Co. in 1952, these Star-Cal Decals are similar to the Type I variety, except the decal sheets are smaller, measuring 4-1/8" x 3-1/16", and each sheet features two players instead of one.

		NM	EX	VG
	Complete Set (32):	3,000	1,500	900.00
	Common Player:	45.00	22.50	13.50
84A	Vic Raschi, Allie Reynolds	80.00	40.00	25.00
84B	Yogi Berra, Ed Lopat	165.00	80.00	50.00
84C	Jerry Coleman, Phil Rizzuto	135.00	65.00	40.00
85A	Ted Williams, Ted Williams	450.00	225.00	135.00
85B	Dom DiMaggio, Mel Parnell	60.00	30.00	18.00
85C	Billy Goodman, Vern Stephens	45.00	22.50	13.50
86A	George Kell, Hal Newhouser	80.00	40.00	25.00
86B	Hoot Evers, Vic Wertz	45.00	22.50	13.50
86C	Johnny Groth, Fred Hutchinson	45.00	22.50	13.50
87A	Eddie Robinson, Eddie Robinson	45.00	22.50	13.50
87B	Chico Carrasquel, Minnie Minoso	60.00	30.00	18.00
87C	Nellie Fox, Billy Pierce	65.00	32.50	20.00
87D	Jim Busby, Al Zarilla	45.00	22.50	13.50
88A	Jim Hegan, Bob Lemon	65.00	32.50	20.00
88B	Larry Doby, Bob Feller	165.00	80.00	50.00
88C	Dale Mitchell, Al Rosen	45.00	22.50	13.50
89A	Ned Garver, Ned Garver	45.00	22.50	13.50
89B	Ferris Fain, Gus Zernial	45.00	22.50	13.50
89C	Richie Ashburn, Richie Ashburn	75.00	37.50	22.00
89D	Ralph Kiner, Ralph Kiner	75.00	37.50	22.00

		NM	EX	VG
90A	Monty Irvin, Willie Mays (Monte)	300.00	150.00	90.00
90B	Larry Jansen, Sal Maglie	45.00	22.50	13.50
90C	Al Dark, Bobby Thomson	55.00	27.50	16.50
91A	Gil Hodges, Pee Wee Reese	225.00	110.00	65.00
91B	Roy Campanella, Jackie Robinson	300.00	150.00	90.00
91C	Preacher Roe, Duke Snider	200.00	100.00	60.00
92A	Phil Cavarretta, Dutch Leonard	45.00	22.50	13.50
92B	Randy Jackson, Eddie Miksis	45.00	22.50	13.50
92C	Bob Rush, Hank Sauer	45.00	22.50	13.50
93A	Stan Musial, Stan Musial	350.00	175.00	105.00
93B	Red Schoendienst, Enos Slaughter	90.00	45.00	27.00
93C	Cliff Chambers, Wally Westlake	45.00	22.50	13.50

1976 Star Market Red Sox

Only Red Sox are featured in this set issued by the Star Market chain in the Boston area. Players are photographed hatless in jerseys which feature the Massachusetts Bicentennial logo. Pictures measure 5-7/8" x 9" and have a 3/16" white border all around. A facsimile autograph is printed on the front in black. Backs are blank. The unnumbered pictures are checklisted here alphabetically.

		NM	EX	VG
	Complete Set (16):	35.00	17.50	10.00
	Common Player:	1.50	.75	.45
(1)	Rick Burleson	1.50	.75	.45
(2)	Reggie Cleveland	1.50	.75	.45
(3)	Cecil Cooper	2.50	1.25	.70
(4)	Denny Doyle	1.50	.75	.45
(5)	Dwight Evans	2.50	1.25	.70
(6)	Carlton Fisk	5.00	2.50	1.50
(7)	Tom House	1.50	.75	.45
(8)	Fergie Jenkins	4.00	2.00	1.25
(9)	Bill Lee	1.50	.75	.45
(10)	Fred Lynn	2.50	1.25	.70
(11)	Rick Miller	1.50	.75	.45
(12)	Rico Petrocelli	2.50	1.25	.70
(13)	Jim Rice	3.50	1.75	1.00
(14)	Luis Tiant	2.50	1.25	.70
(15)	Rick Wise	1.50	.75	.45
(16)	Carl Yastrzemski	10.00	5.00	3.00

1928 Star Player Candy

WALLY SCHANG

Little is known about the origin of this set. The producer is not identified, but experienced collectors generally refer to it as the Star Player Candy set, possibly because it was distributed with a product of that name. The cards measure 1-7/8" x 2-7/8", are sepia-toned, blank-backed and printed on thin paper. The player's name (but no team designation) appears in the border below the photo in brown capital letters. To date the checklist of baseball players numbers 73, but more may exist, and cards of football players have also been found.

		NM	EX	VG
	Common Player:	1,800	900.00	550.00
(1)	Dave Bancroft	4,000	4,000	2,400
(2)	Emile Barnes	1,800	900.00	550.00
(3)	L.A. Blue	1,800	900.00	550.00
(4)	Garland Buckeye	1,800	900.00	550.00
(5)	George Burns	1,800	900.00	550.00
(6)	Guy T. Bush	1,800	900.00	550.00
(7)	Owen T. Carroll	1,800	900.00	550.00

		NM	EX	VG
(8)	Chalmer Cissell	1,800	900.00	550.00
(9)	Ty Cobb	20,000	8,000	4,000
(10)	Gordon Cochrane	4,000	2,000	1,200
(11)	Richard Coffman	1,800	900.00	550.00
(12)	Eddie Collins	4,000	2,000	1,200
(13)	Stanley Coveleskie (Coveleski)	4,000	2,000	1,200
(14)	Hugh Critz	1,800	900.00	550.00
(15)	Hazen Cuyler	2,000	800.00	400.00
(16)	Charles Dressen	1,800	900.00	550.00
(17)	Joe Dugan	1,800	900.00	550.00
(18)	Elwood English	1,800	900.00	550.00
(19)	Bib Falk (Bibb)	1,800	900.00	550.00
(20)	Ira Flagstead	1,800	900.00	550.00
(21)	Bob Fothergill	1,800	900.00	550.00
(22)	Frank T. Frisch	4,000	2,000	1,200
(23)	Foster Ganzel	1,800	900.00	550.00
(24)	Lou Gehrig	45,000	22,500	13,500
(25)	Chas. Gihringer (Gehringer)	4,000	2,000	1,200
(26)	George Gerken	1,800	900.00	550.00
(27)	Grant Gillis	1,800	900.00	550.00
(28)	Miguel Gonzales (Gonzalez)	1,800	900.00	550.00
(29)	Sam Gray	1,800	900.00	550.00
(30)	Chas. J. Grimm	1,800	900.00	550.00
(31)	Robert M. Grove	4,500	2,250	1,350
(32)	Chas. J. Hafey	4,000	2,000	1,200
(33)	Jesse Haines	4,000	2,000	1,200
(34)	Chas. L. Hartnett	4,000	2,000	1,200
(35)	Clifton Heathcote	1,800	900.00	550.00
(36)	Harry Heilmann	4,000	2,000	1,200
(37)	John Heving	1,800	900.00	550.00
(38)	Waite Hoyt	4,000	2,000	1,200
(39)	Chas. Jamieson	1,800	900.00	550.00
(40)	Joe Judge	1,800	900.00	550.00
(41)	Willie Kamm	1,800	900.00	550.00
(42)	George Kelly	4,000	2,000	1,200
(43)	Tony Lazzeri	4,000	2,000	1,200
(44)	Adolfo Luque	1,800	900.00	550.00
(45)	Ted Lyons	4,000	2,000	1,200
(46)	Hugh McMullen	1,800	900.00	550.00
(47)	Bob Meusel	1,800	900.00	550.00
(48)	Wilcey Moore (Wilcy)	1,800	900.00	550.00
(49)	Ed C. Morgan	1,800	900.00	550.00
(50)	Buddy Myer	1,800	900.00	550.00
(51)	Herb Pennock	4,000	2,000	1,200
(52)	Everett Purdy	1,800	900.00	550.00
(53)	William Regan	1,800	900.00	550.00
(54)	Eppa Rixey	4,000	2,000	1,200
(55)	Charles Root	1,800	900.00	550.00
(56)	Jack Rothrock	1,800	900.00	550.00
(57)	Harold Ruel (Herold)	1,800	900.00	550.00
(58)	Babe Ruth	32,500	13,000	6,500
(59)	Wally Schang	1,800	900.00	550.00
(60)	Joe Sewell	4,000	2,000	1,200
(61)	Luke Sewell	1,800	900.00	550.00
(62)	Joe Shaute	1,800	900.00	550.00
(63)	George Sisler	4,000	2,000	1,200
(64)	Tris Speaker	5,000	2,500	1,500
(65)	Riggs Stephenson	1,800	900.00	550.00
(66)	Jack Tavener	1,800	900.00	550.00
(67)	Al Thomas	1,800	900.00	550.00
(68)	Harold J. Traynor	4,000	2,000	1,200
(69)	George Uhle	1,800	900.00	550.00
(70)	Dazzy Vance	4,000	2,000	1,200
(71)	Cy Williams	1,800	900.00	550.00
(72)	Ken Williams	1,800	900.00	550.00
(73)	Lewis R. Wilson	4,000	2,000	1,200

1929 Star Player Candy

21

BABE RUTH, "Sultan of Swat," has reigned supreme as home run king for eight consecutive years. His record of 60 home runs in one season will probably remain unbroken for some years to come.

BABE RUTH

Three baseball players are included in this multi-subject set of cards that were sold in one-cent glassine envelopes with several dozen tiny pellets of bubblegum under the title "Dockman's 'Headliners & Gum'". Cards are about 1-7/8" x 2-7/8", printed in sepia on thin cardboard. Backs have a few words about the subject pictured on front and a card number.

		NM	EX	VG
21	Babe Ruth	12,000	6,000	3,500
32	Lou Gehrig	7,000	3,500	2,100
(# Unkn.)	Walter Johnson	6,000	3,000	1,800

1892 J.U. Stead Studio Cabinets

Only members of the N.Y. Giants are thus far known in this series of cabinet cards from New York City photographer J.U. Stead. About standard cabinet size (4-1/2" x 6-1/2") the cards have black-and-white portraits. On the thick cardboard mount's bottom border is the name and address of the studio. Backs repeat that information and have three lines of type at bottom extolling "Instantaneous Photographs." Unless the player name was penciled on the card by a previous owner, the players are not otherwise identified. Fortunately, the plethora of contemporary issues from other sources makes matching names and photos fairly easy. The issue date attributed is speculative.

J. U. STEAD.   383 6th Ave., N.Y.

	NM	EX	VG
Common Player:	3,000	1,500	900.00
Roger Connor	6,000	2,000	1,200
Willie Keeler	10,000	3,750	2,250
Mike Tiernan	3,000	1,500	900.00

1909-16 Max Stein Postcards (PC758)

Issued over a period of several years these sepia-toned photo postcards depict most of the stars of the day. In standard 3-1/2" x 5-1/2" format they have typical postcard indicia on the back. Some cards have been seen with a "United States Pub." legend on the back. Most of the subjects played in Stein's Chicago location. Besides the baseball players listed here, the series also included "Statesmen, etc.," Aeroplanes and Flyers, Fighters, etc.," and, "Dancing Girls," according to advertising found on the back of some cards. Wholesale prices when issued were 35 cents per hundred, $2.75 per thousand.

		NM	EX	VG
	Common Player:	400.00	200.00	120.00
	Advertising Back: 1.5X			
(1)	Ping Bodie	400.00	200.00	120.00
(2)	Frank Chance	800.00	400.00	240.00
(3)	Ty Cobb	4,500	2,250	1,350
(4)	Johnny Evers	800.00	400.00	240.00
(5)	Rube Marquard	800.00	400.00	240.00
(6)	Christy Mathewson	2,400	1,200	725.00
(7)	John McGraw	800.00	400.00	240.00
(8)	Chief Meyers	400.00	200.00	120.00
(9)	Marty O'Toole	400.00	200.00	120.00
(10)	Wildfire Schulte	400.00	200.00	120.00
(11)	Tris Speaker	900.00	450.00	270.00
(12)	Jake Stahl	400.00	200.00	120.00
(13)	Jim Thorpe	5,000	2,500	1,500
(14)	Joe Tinker	800.00	400.00	240.00
(15)	Honus Wagner	3,000	1,500	900.00
(16)	Ed Walsh	800.00	400.00	240.00
(17)	Buck Weaver	3,500	1,750	1,050
(18)	Joe Wood	400.00	200.00	120.00
(19)	Heinie Zimmerman	400.00	200.00	120.00
(20)	Chicago Cubs (Jimmy Archer, Roger Bresnahan, Johnny Evers, Mike Hechinger, Tom Needham)	400.00	200.00	120.00
(21)	Chicago Cubs (Bill Clymer, Wilbur Good, Ward Miller, Mike Mitchell, Wildfire Schulte)	400.00	200.00	120.00
(22)	Boston Americans Team Photo	400.00	200.00	120.00
(23)	1916 Chicago Cubs Team Photo	600.00	300.00	180.00
(24)	1916 Cincinnati Reds Team Photo	400.00	200.00	120.00
(25)	New York Nationals Team Photo	400.00	200.00	120.00
(26)	Johnny Coulon, Jess Willard (Boxers)	400.00	200.00	120.00

1904 Stenzel's Rooter Buttons

The extent of the checklist for this rare Cincinnati 1-1/4" pinback celluloid button issue is unknown. According to a paper label found in the back of well-preserved examples, the buttons are the issue of "Jake Stenzel B.B. Exchange located opposite Ball Park." Fronts have "STENZEL'S ROOTER BUTTON" at top and a player portrait photo at center with last name and position below.

		NM	EX	VG
(1)	Mike Donlin	750.00	375.00	225.00
(2)	Bob Ewing	600.00	300.00	180.00
(3)	Jack Harper	600.00	300.00	180.00
(4)	Joe Kelley	1,750	875.00	525.00
(5)	Win Kellum	600.00	300.00	180.00
(6)	Peaches O'Neil (O'Neill)	900.00	450.00	275.00
(7)	Heinie Pietz (Peitz)	600.00	300.00	180.00
(8)	Admiral Schlei	600.00	300.00	180.00
(9)	Cy Seymour	600.00	300.00	180.00
(10)	Jack Sutthoff	600.00	300.00	180.00
(11)	Sam Woodruff	600.00	300.00	180.00

1911 Stevens Firearms Philadelphia Athletics

Riding on the coattails of the A's American League pennant (and eventual World Series) win, Stevens Firearms created this set of cards to promote its rifles and shotguns. About 6-3/16" x 3-7/16", the blank-back, medium-weight cards have a black-and-white posed action photo at left with the player identified by name, position and team. At top right is advertising, at bottom-right is a box where local retailers' addresses could be stamped or printed. Cards have been seen printed on several different colors of stock. In actuality, these are really ink blotters from the old fountain pen days as opposed to "cards." Other players are likely to have been issued.

		NM	EX	VG
Common Player:		1,000	500.00	300.00
(1)	Frank Baker	3,000	1,500	900.00
(2)	Chief Bender	3,000	1,500	900.00
(3)	Bris Lord	1,000	500.00	300.00
(4)	Connie Mack	3,000	1,500	900.00
(5)	Danny Murphy	1,000	500.00	300.00
(6)	Rube Oldring	1,000	500.00	300.00
(7)	Harry Davis	1,000	500.00	300.00
(8)	Ira Thomas	1,000	500.00	300.00

1888-1889 Stevens Studio Australian Tour Cabinets

After the 1888 season, Albert Spalding toured to Australia with a group of major league players to increase interest in baseball Down Under (as well as to increase demand for the baseball equipment his firm sold). Prior to departure, many of the players gathered at Stevens Studio in Chicago for portrait photos to be made into cabinet cards, presumably for sale as souvenirs on the junket. Vignetted portraits present the players in their Sunday best. Below a decorative dividing line is "Spalding's Australian Base Ball Tour / Stevens 1888-89 Chicago." Back has a large ornate ad for the photographer. The full extent of the checklist is unknown.

	NM	EX	VG
Common Player:	3,500	1,750	1,000
Cap Anson	15,000	7,500	4,500

		NM	EX	VG
	Jim Donnelly	3,500	1,750	1,000
	Jim Fogarty	3,500	1,750	1,000
	Egyptian Healey	3,500	1,750	1,000
	Ned Williamson	3,500	1,750	1,000

1890 Stevens Studio Chicago Pirates Cabinets

The single-season players' revolution that spawned the Players League is marked with this issue of cabinet cards from the Stevens studio of Chicago. Only members of the Chicago Pirates P.L. team have been seen in this issue, all in street clothes and identified by a name penned on the front. A composite-photo card is also known, providing reasonable expectations that more individual player cabinets will be discovered. The studio advertising on back is ornately printed in maroon.

		NM	EX	VG
Common Player:		2,400	1,200	720.00
(1)	Mark Baldwin	2,400	1,200	720.00
(2)	Jack Boyle	2,400	1,200	720.00
(3)	Charles Comiskey	7,500	3,750	2,250
(4)	Del Darling	2,400	1,200	720.00
(5)	Hugh Duffy	7,500	3,750	2,250
(6)	Frank Dwyer	2,400	1,200	720.00
(7)	Silver Flint	2,400	1,200	720.00
(8)	Arlie Latham	2,400	1,200	720.00
(9)	Pat Luby	2,400	1,200	720.00
(10)	Jimmy Ryan	2,400	1,200	720.00
(11)	Team Composite	10,000	5,000	3,000

1890 Stevens Studio Chicago White Stockings Cabinets

Cabinet cards in the standard 4-1/4" x 6-1/2" format of at least three of the 1890 Chicago National Leaguers, as well as a team composite picture are known to have been produced by the Stevens Art Studio. Fronts have vignetted portraits of the players in dress clothes. Backs have an ornate ad for the photographer, which includes the note, "DUPLICATES OF THIS PICTURE CAN BE HAD AT ANY TIME, AT REDUCED RATES." Player names are often found penned on the cards, as the photos are otherwise unidentified. At least two styles of cardboard mounts are seen with the White Stockings cabinets. The extent of the checklist is also unknown.

		NM	EX	VG
Common Player:		1,800	900.00	550.00
(1)	Cap Anson	8,250	4,125	2,475
(2)	Mike Sullivan	1,800	900.00	550.00
(3)	Pat Wright	1,800	900.00	550.00
(4)	1890 Chicago White Stockings	4,400	2,200	1,325

1941 St. Louis Browns Team Issue (W753)

Measuring 2-1/8" x 2-5/8", this unnumbered boxed set of cards features the St. Louis Browns in black-and-white portrait photos on front. Backs have player name, position and personal and statistical information. There are also cards for coaches and one of the the club's two managers that season (Luke Sewell). As the Browns weren't much of a team in 1941 (or in most seasons for that matter) there are no major stars in the set. The issue was cataloged as W753 in the ACC.

		NM	EX	VG
Complete Set (30):		850.00	425.00	250.00
Common Player:		35.00	17.50	10.00
Box:		75.00	35.00	25.00
(1)	Johnny Allen	35.00	17.50	10.00
(2)	Elden Auker (Eldon)	35.00	17.50	10.00
(3)	Donald L Barnes	35.00	17.50	10.00
(4)	Johnny Berardino	50.00	25.00	15.00
(5)	George Caster	35.00	17.50	10.00
(6)	Harlond Benton (Darky) Clift	35.00	17.50	10.00
(7)	Roy J. Cullenbine	35.00	17.50	10.00
(8)	William O. DeWitt (Vice-President)	35.00	17.50	10.00

---

(9)	Roberto Estalella	35.00	17.50	10.00
(10)	Richard Benjamin (Rick) Ferrell	60.00	30.00	18.00
(11)	Dennis W. Galehouse	35.00	17.50	10.00
(12)	Joseph L. Grace	35.00	17.50	10.00
(13)	Frank Grube	35.00	17.50	10.00
(14)	Robert A. Harris	35.00	17.50	10.00
(15)	Donald Henry Heffner	35.00	17.50	10.00
(16)	Fred Hofmann	35.00	17.50	10.00
(17)	Walter Franklin Judnich	35.00	17.50	10.00
(18)	John Henry (Jack) Kramer	35.00	17.50	10.00
(19)	Chester (Chet) Laabs	35.00	17.50	10.00
(20)	John Lucadello	35.00	17.50	10.00
(21)	George Hartley McQuinn	35.00	17.50	10.00
(22)	Robert Cleveland Muncrief, Jr.	35.00	17.50	10.00
(23)	John Niggeling	35.00	17.50	10.00
(24)	Fred Raymond (Fritz) Ostermueller	35.00	17.50	10.00
(25)	James Luther (Luke) Sewell	35.00	17.50	10.00
(26)	Alan Cochran Strange (Cochrane)	35.00	17.50	10.00
(27)	Robert Virgil (Bob) Swift	35.00	17.50	10.00
(28)	James W. (Zack) Taylor	35.00	17.50	10.00
(29)	William Felix (Bill) Trotter	35.00	17.50	10.00
(30)	Presentation Card/Order Form	10.00	5.00	3.00

1952 St. Louis Browns Postcards

This series of player postcards features black-and-white glossy photos on front with a white border. The cards bear no player identification and were evidently intended for use in honoring fan requests for autographs. The 1952 issue can be differentiated from that of 1953 by the absence of a stamp box on back. The unnumbered cards are checklisted here alphabetically, though the list may be incomplete. Multiple player names indicate known different poses.

		NM	EX	VG
Common Player:		50.00	25.00	15.00
(1)	Tommy Byrne	50.00	25.00	15.00
(2)	Bob Cain	50.00	25.00	15.00
(3)	Bob Cain	50.00	25.00	15.00
(4)	Clint Courtney	50.00	25.00	15.00
(5)	Jim Delsing	50.00	25.00	15.00
(6)	Jim Dyck	50.00	25.00	15.00
(7)	Jim Dyck	50.00	25.00	15.00
(8)	Ned Garver	50.00	25.00	15.00
(9)	Marty Marion	60.00	30.00	18.00
(10)	Cass Michaels	50.00	25.00	15.00
(11)	Bob Nieman	50.00	25.00	15.00
(12)	Satchel Paige	200.00	100.00	60.00
(13)	Duane Pillette	50.00	25.00	15.00
(14)	Jim Rivera	50.00	25.00	15.00
(15)	Bill Veeck	75.00	37.00	22.00
(16)	Bobby Young	50.00	25.00	15.00

1953 St. Louis Browns Postcards

This series of player postcards from the team's final year in St. Louis features black-and-white glossy photos on front with a white border. The cards bear no player identification and were evidently intended for use in honoring fan requests for autographs. The 1953 issue can be differentiated from that of 1952 by the presence of a stamp box on back identifying the issuer as Deorite Peerless. The unnumbered cards are checklisted here alphabetically though the list is likely incomplete.

		NM	EX	VG
Common Player:		50.00	25.00	15.00
(1)	Connie Berry	50.00	25.00	15.00
(2)	Mike Blyzka	50.00	25.00	15.00
(3)	Harry Brecheen	50.00	25.00	15.00

		NM	EX	VG
(4)	Bob Cain	50.00	25.00	15.00
(5)	Clint Courtney	50.00	25.00	15.00
(6)	Jim Dyck	50.00	25.00	15.00
(7)	Hank Edwards	50.00	25.00	15.00
(8)	Ned Garver	50.00	25.00	15.00
(9)	Johnny Groth	50.00	25.00	15.00
(11)	Bobo Holloman	50.00	25.00	15.00
(12)	Billy Hunter	50.00	25.00	15.00
(13)	Dick Kokos	50.00	25.00	15.00
(14)	Dick Kryhoski	50.00	25.00	15.00
(15)	Max Lanier	50.00	25.00	15.00
(16)	Don Larsen	75.00	37.50	22.00
(17)	Don Lenhardt	50.00	25.00	15.00
(18)	Dick Littlefield	50.00	25.00	15.00
(19)	Marty Marion	60.00	30.00	18.00
(21)	Babe Martin	50.00	25.00	15.00
(22)	Willy Miranda	50.00	25.00	15.00
(23)	Les Moss	50.00	25.00	15.00
(24)	Bill Norman	50.00	25.00	15.00
(25)	Satchel Paige/Kneeling	200.00	100.00	60.00
(26)	Satchel Paige/Pitching	200.00	100.00	60.00
(27)	Duane Pillette	50.00	25.00	15.00
(28)	Bob Scheffing	50.00	25.00	15.00
(29)	Roy Sievers	60.00	30.00	18.00
(31)	Marlin Stuart	50.00	25.00	15.00
(32)	Virgil Trucks	65.00	32.00	19.50
(33)	Bill Veeck	75.00	37.00	22.00
(34)	Vic Wertz	50.00	25.00	15.00
(35)	Bobby Young	50.00	25.00	12.00

1941 St. Louis Cardinals Team Issue (W754)

 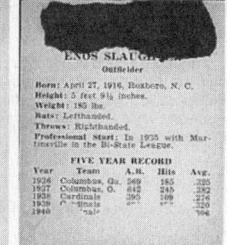

A companion set to W753, this time featuring the National League team in St. Louis. Cards measure 2-1/8" x 2-5/8" and are unnumbered. Like the Browns set, this issue features black-and-white portrait photos on front and the individual's name, position and personal and statistical information on back. One interesting addition to the set is a card of Branch Rickey which, coupled with cards of Enos Slaughter and Johnny Mize, gives the set a bit more appeal than the Browns set. ACC designation is W754.

		NM	EX	VG
Complete Set (30):		1,000	500.00	300.00
Common Player:		35.00	17.50	10.00
Box:		75.00	35.00	25.00
1)	Sam Breadon	35.00	17.50	10.00
2)	James Brown	35.00	17.50	10.00
3)	Morton Cooper	35.00	17.50	10.00
4)	William Walker Cooper	35.00	17.50	10.00
5)	Estel Crabtree	35.00	17.50	10.00
6)	Frank Crespi	35.00	17.50	10.00
7)	William Crouch	35.00	17.50	10.00
8)	Miguel Mike Gonzalez	50.00	25.00	15.00
9)	Harry Gumbert	35.00	17.50	10.00
10)	John Hopp	35.00	17.50	10.00
11)	Ira Hutchinson	35.00	17.50	10.00
12)	Howard Krist	35.00	17.50	10.00
13)	Edward E. Lake	35.00	17.50	10.00
14)	Hubert Max Lanier	35.00	17.50	10.00
15)	Gus Mancuso	35.00	17.50	10.00
16)	Martin Marion	55.00	27.50	16.50
17)	Steve Mesner	35.00	17.50	10.00
18)	John Mize	100.00	50.00	30.00
19)	Capt. Terry Moore	50.00	25.00	15.00
20)	Sam Nahem	35.00	17.50	10.00
21)	Don Padgett	35.00	17.50	10.00
22)	Branch Rickey (Vice-President)	60.00	30.00	18.00
23)	Clyde Shoun	35.00	17.50	10.00
24)	Enos Slaughter	100.00	50.00	30.00
25)	William H. (Billy) Southworth	35.00	17.50	10.00
26)	Herman Coaker Triplett	35.00	17.50	10.00
27)	Clyde Buzzy Wares	35.00	17.50	10.00
28)	Lon Warneke	35.00	17.50	10.00
29)	Ernest White	35.00	17.50	10.00
30)	Presentation Card/Order Form	10.00	5.00	3.00

1966 St. Louis Cardinals Busch Stadium Immortals Coins

A dozen all-time great Cardinals are included in this set of commemorative medallions. Each 1-1/2" bright bronze "coin" has a portrait and career summary. The coins were issued in a 9" x 10-1/2" cardinal-red cardboard holder with gold logo and graphics.

		NM	EX	VG
Complete Board/Coin Set:		75.00	37.50	22.50
Common Player:		7.50	3.75	2.25
(1)	Dizzy Dean	10.00	5.00	3.00
(2)	Frank Frisch	7.50	3.75	2.25
(3)	Chick Hafey	7.50	3.75	2.25
(4)	Jesse Haines	7.50	3.75	2.25
(5)	Marty Marion	7.50	3.75	2.25
(6)	Joe Medwick	7.50	3.75	2.25
(7)	Johnny Mize	7.50	3.75	2.25
(8)	Terry Moore	7.50	3.75	2.25
(9)	Stan Musial	15.00	7.50	4.50
(10)	Red Schoendienst	7.50	3.75	2.25
(11)	George Sisler	7.50	3.75	2.25
(12)	Enos Slaughter	7.50	3.75	2.25

1953 Stop & Shop Boston Red Sox

 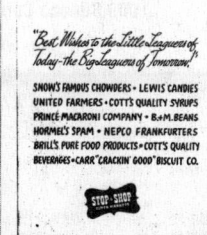

Four of the early 1950s Red Sox appear in this series issued by a Boston grocery chain. The cards may have been distributed in conjunction with players' in-store appearances. The cards measure 3-3/4" x 5" and are printed in black-and-white. A facsimile autograph appears on the front. Backs have the sponsor's advertising. The unnumbered cards are check-listed here alphabetically. See also 1953 First National Super Market Boston Red Sox.

		NM	EX	VG
Complete Set (4):		3,000	1,500	900.00
Common Player:		750.00	375.00	225.00
(1)	Billy Goodman	750.00	375.00	225.00
(2)	Ellis Kinder	750.00	375.00	225.00
(3)	Mel Parnell	750.00	375.00	225.00
(4)	Sammy White	750.00	375.00	225.00

1888 Sub Rosa Cigarettes Girl Baseball Players (N508)

(See 1888 Allen & Ginter Girl Baseball Players.)

1916 Successful Farming

Best known for its use as a promotional medium for The Sporting News (M101-5), this 200-card set can be found with ads on the back for several local and regional businesses. Among them is Successful Farming magazine of Des Moines, Iowa. Some collectors believe that cards with the magazine's advertising on back were promotional cards, and that the cards actually delivered with the subscription offer were blank-back M101-5s. This would account for the scarcity of the ad-back. Type card collectors and superstar collectors can expect to pay a modest premium for individual cards with the magazine's advertising. Cards measure about 1-5/8" x 3" and are printed in black-and-white.

PREMIUM: 6-8X
(See 1916 M101-5 Blank Backs for checklist and base card values.)

1976 Sugar Daddy Sports World

Two baseball related cards were issued as part of this multi-sport candy insert set. Each card is titled "BASEBALL" and they detail the 1974 and 1975 World Series and depict a player - though not naming him - in action. The cards are 1" x 2-3/4" and have a white-bordered color photo on front. Backs include various advertising details.

		NM	EX	VG
Complete Set (25):		60.00	30.00	18.00
12	Pete Rose (Series 1, 1974 World Series)	25.00	12.50	7.50
25	Bobby Murcer (Series 2, 1975 World Series)	17.50	9.00	5.00

1962 Sugardale Weiners

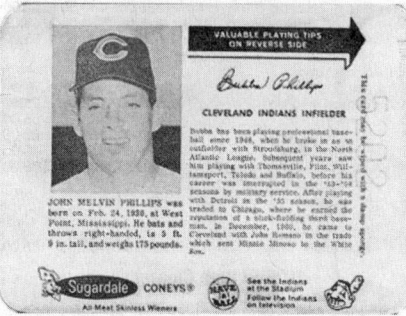

The Sugardale Meats set of black and white cards measure 5-1/8" x 3-3/4". The 22-card set includes 18 Cleveland Indians and four Pittsburgh Pirates players. The Indians cards are numbered from 1-19 with card number 6 not issued. The Pirates cards are lettered from A to D. The card fronts contain a relatively small player photo, with biographical information and Sugardale logo. The backs are printed in red and offer playing tips and another company logo. Card number 10 (Bob Nieman) is considerably more scarce than other cards in the set.

		NM	EX	VG
Complete Set (22):		10,000	4,000	2,000
Common Player:		325.00	130.00	65.00
A	Dick Groat	325.00	130.00	65.00
B	Roberto Clemente	3,250	1,300	650.00
C	Don Hoak	325.00	130.00	65.00
D	Dick Stuart	325.00	130.00	65.00
1	Barry Latman	325.00	130.00	65.00
2	Gary Bell	325.00	130.00	65.00
3	Dick Donovan	325.00	130.00	65.00
4	Frank Funk	325.00	130.00	65.00
5	Jim Perry	325.00	130.00	65.00
6	Not Issued			
7	Johnny Romano	325.00	130.00	65.00
8	Ty Cline	325.00	130.00	65.00
9	Tito Francona	325.00	130.00	65.00
10	Bob Nieman/SP	1,200	480.00	240.00
11	Willie Kirkland	325.00	130.00	65.00
12	Woodie Held	325.00	130.00	65.00
13	Jerry Kindall	325.00	130.00	65.00
14	Bubba Phillips	325.00	130.00	65.00
15	Mel Harder	325.00	130.00	65.00
16	Salty Parker	325.00	130.00	65.00
17	Ray Katt	325.00	130.00	65.00
18	Mel McGaha	325.00	130.00	65.00
19	Pedro Ramos	325.00	130.00	65.00

1963 Sugardale Weiners

Sugardale Meats again featured Cleveland and Pittsburgh players in its 1963 set, which grew to 31 cards. The black and white cards again measure 5-1/8" x 3-3/4", and consist of 28 Indians and five Pirates players. Card formats are virtually identical to the 1962 cards, with the only real difference being the information included in the player biographies. The cards are numbered 1-38, with numbers 6, 21, 22 and 29-32 not issued. Cards for Bob Skinner (#35) and Jim Perry (#5) are scarce as these two players were traded during the season and their cards withdrawn from distribution. The red card backs again offer playing tips.

		NM	EX	VG
Complete Set (31):		10,000	4,000	2,000
Common Player:		325.00	130.00	65.00
A	Don Cardwell	325.00	130.00	65.00
B	Robert R. Skinner/SP	600.00	240.00	120.00
C	Donald B. Schwall	325.00	130.00	65.00
D	Jim Pagliaroni	325.00	130.00	65.00
E	Dick Schofield	325.00	130.00	65.00
1	Barry Latman	325.00	130.00	65.00
2	Gary Bell	325.00	130.00	65.00
3	Dick Donovan	325.00	130.00	65.00
4	Joe Adcock	400.00	160.00	80.00
5	Jim Perry/SP	600.00	240.00	120.00
6	Not Issued			
7	Johnny Romano	325.00	130.00	65.00
8	Mike de la Hoz	325.00	130.00	65.00
9	Tito Francona	325.00	130.00	65.00
10	Gene Green	325.00	130.00	65.00
11	Willie Kirkland	325.00	130.00	65.00
12	Woodie Held	325.00	130.00	65.00
13	Jerry Kindall	325.00	130.00	65.00
14	Max Alvis	325.00	130.00	65.00
15	Mel Harder	325.00	130.00	65.00
16	George Strickland	325.00	130.00	65.00
17	Elmer Valo	325.00	130.00	65.00
18	Birdie Tebbetts	325.00	130.00	65.00
19	Pedro Ramos	325.00	130.00	65.00
20	Al Luplow	325.00	130.00	65.00
21	Not Issued			
22	Not Issued			
23	Jim Grant	325.00	130.00	65.00
24	Victor Davalillo	325.00	130.00	65.00
25	Jerry Walker	325.00	130.00	65.00
26	Sam McDowell	400.00	160.00	80.00
27	Fred Whitfield	325.00	130.00	65.00
28	Jack Kralick	325.00	130.00	65.00
29	Not Issued			
30	Not Issued			
31	Not Issued			
32	Not Issued			
33	Bob Allen	325.00	130.00	65.00

1933 Sulima Cigarettes

This is one of several early 1930s German cigarette cards to picture Babe Ruth. In this case he is pictured on the 1-5/8" x 2-3/8" black-and-white card with American comedic actor Harold Lloyd. The card is part of a numbered set of 272 movie star cards. Backs are printed in German. The card is identical in format to the Josetti cigarette cards.

		NM	EX	VG
151	Babe Ruth, Harold Lloyd	1,100	550.00	330.00

1936 Sunday Advertiser Sport Stamps

(See 1936 Boston American Sport Stamps.)

1974 Sun-Glo Pop Al Kaline

This 2-1/4" x 4-1/2" card was issued as an attachment to bottles of soda pop. The blank-back card features a modishly dressed portrait of the former Tigers great and his endorsement for the soda. Cards are printed in black on various brightly colored backgrounds.

	NM	EX	VG
Al Kaline	6.00	3.00	1.75

1969 Sunoco Cubs/Brewers Pins

Fans in Southern Wisconsin and Northern Illinois could acquire 1-1/8" lithographed steel baseball player pins of the Cubs and Brewers at participating Sunoco gas stations. The blue-and-white (Cubs) or red-and-white (Brewers) pins have black-and-white player portrait photos at center on which cap logos have been removed. The Brewers pins are somewhat scarcer than those of the Cubs.

		NM	EX	VG
Complete Set (18):		100.00	50.00	30.00
Common Player:		4.00	2.00	1.25
Chicago Cubs Team Set:		65.00	32.50	20.00
(1)	Ernie Banks	25.00	12.50	7.50
(2)	Glenn Beckert	4.00	2.00	1.25
(3)	Jim Hickman	4.00	2.00	1.25
(4)	Randy Hundley	4.00	2.00	1.25
(5)	Ferguson Jenkins	7.50	3.75	2.25
(6)	Don Kessinger	6.00	3.00	1.75
(7)	Joe Pepitone	6.00	3.00	1.75
(8)	Ron Santo	10.00	5.00	3.00
(9)	Billy Williams	12.50	6.25	3.75
Milwaukee Brewers Team Set:		50.00	25.00	15.00
(1)	Tommy Harper	6.00	3.00	1.75
(2)	Mike Hegan	6.00	3.00	1.75
(3)	Lew Krausse	6.00	3.00	1.75
(4)	Ted Kubiak	6.00	3.00	1.75
(5)	Marty Pattin	6.00	3.00	1.75
(6)	Phil Roof	6.00	3.00	1.75
(7)	Ken Sanders	6.00	3.00	1.75
(8)	Ted Savage	6.00	3.00	1.75
(9)	Danny Walton	6.00	3.00	1.75

1931 Sun Pictures Photo Kits

 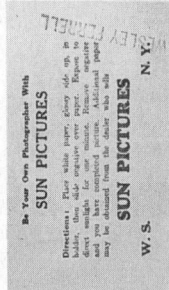

One of several contemporary kits for do-it-yourself production of photos, this issue was produced in New York City by a firm identified only as "W.S." A complete outfit consists of a 4-1/4" x 2-1/2" pink or kraft paper envelope with the name of the subject inside rubber-stamped on one end, a film negative, a piece of photo paper and a stand for producing/displaying the photo. The negative and resulting print measure 2-5/16" x 3-1/4". The set is listed in the American Card Catalog as W626. Prices shown are for complete kits; individual pieces would be pro-rated, with the negative the most valuable component. Because individual prints can be easily made even today, they have little collectible value. Only the baseball players are listed here.

	NM	EX	VG
Common Player Kit:	100.00	50.00	30.00

		NM	EX	VG
(1)	George Earnshaw	100.00	50.00	30.00
(2)	Wesley Ferrell	100.00	50.00	30.00
(3)	Lefty Grove	225.00	110.00	65.00
(4)	Leo Hartnett	200.00	100.00	60.00
(5)	Tony Lazzeri	225.00	110.00	65.00
(6)	Herb Pennock	200.00	100.00	60.00
(7)	Babe Ruth	2,000	1,000	600.00
(8)	Al Simmons	200.00	100.00	60.00
(9)	Dazzy Vance	200.00	100.00	60.00
(10)	Hack Wilson	225.00	110.00	65.00

1960s Sunny Ayr Farms Johnny Callison

 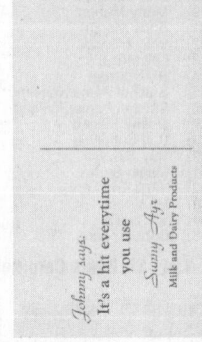

In the absence of other player cardsm, it is impossible to date this issue any more precisely than Callison's tenure with the Phillies which encompassed the 1960s. The 3-1/2" x 5-1/2" black-and-white card had a facsimile autograph on front. The divided back is printed in red.

	NM	EX	VG
Johnny Callison	100.00	50.00	30.00

1970 Superballs

Manufactured by Chemtoy (though not credited on the balls), these high-bouncing hard rubber balls are composed of see-through material in which is imbedded a disc with a baseball player's portrait and identification. About 1-1/8" in diameter, the balls identify the player by name, team and position and include a four-digit number. In this checklist, the balls are listed alphabetically for lack of access to a complete list of the actual numbers. It is also possible the checklist is incomplete.

		NM	EX	VG
Complete Set (286):		1,650	825.00	500.00
Common Player:		5.00	2.50	1.50
(1)	Hank Aaron	40.00	20.00	12.00
(2)	Jerry Adair	5.00	2.50	1.50
(3)	Tommie Agee	5.00	2.50	1.50
(4)	Bernie Allen	5.00	2.50	1.50
(5)	Lloyd Allen	5.00	2.50	1.50
(6)	Gene Alley	5.00	2.50	1.50
(7)	Bob Allison	5.00	2.50	1.50
(8)	Sandy Alomar	5.00	2.50	1.50
(9)	Jesus Alou	5.00	2.50	1.50
(10)	Matty Alou	5.00	2.50	1.50
(11)	Max Alvis	5.00	2.50	1.50
(12)	Mike Andrews	5.00	2.50	1.50
(13)	Luis Aparicio	17.50	8.75	5.25
(14)	Jose Arcia	5.00	2.50	1.50
(15)	Bob Aspromonte	5.00	2.50	1.50
(16)	Jose Azcue	5.00	2.50	1.50
(17)	Bob Bailey	5.00	2.50	1.50
(18)	Jack Baldschun	5.00	2.50	1.50
(19)	Sal Bando	5.00	2.50	1.50
(20)	Ernie Banks	25.00	12.50	7.50
(21)	John Bateman	5.00	2.50	1.50
(22)	Glenn Beckert	5.00	2.50	1.50
(23)	Mark Belanger	5.00	2.50	1.50
(24)	Ken Berry	5.00	2.50	1.50
(25)	Paul Blair	5.00	2.50	1.50
(26)	Curt Blefary	5.00	2.50	1.50
(27)	John Boccabella	5.00	2.50	1.50
(28)	Bobby Bonds	5.00	2.50	1.50
(29)	John Boozer	5.00	2.50	1.50
(30)	Ken Boswell	5.00	2.50	1.50
(31)	Clete Boyer	5.00	2.50	1.50
(32)	Gene Brabender	5.00	2.50	1.50
(33)	Ron Brand	5.00	2.50	1.50
(34)	Jim Brewer	5.00	2.50	1.50
(35)	Johnny Briggs	5.00	2.50	1.50
(36)	Nelson Briles	5.00	2.50	1.50
(37)	Ed Brinkman	5.00	2.50	1.50
(38)	Lou Brock	17.50	8.75	5.25
(39)	Don Buford	5.00	2.50	1.50
(40)	Tom Burgmeier	5.00	2.50	1.50
(41)	Bill Butler	5.00	2.50	1.50
(42)	Johnny Callison	5.00	2.50	1.50
(43)	Bert Campaneris	5.00	2.50	1.50
(44)	Jim Campanis	5.00	2.50	1.50

		NM	EX	VG
(45)	Chris Cannizzaro	5.00	2.50	1.50
(46)	Jose Cardenal	5.00	2.50	1.50
(47)	Leo Cardenas	5.00	2.50	1.50
(48)	Rod Carew	20.00	10.00	6.00
(49)	Clay Carroll	5.00	2.50	1.50
(50)	Rico Carty	5.00	2.50	1.50
(51)	Paul Casanova	5.00	2.50	1.50
(52)	Norm Cash	10.00	5.00	3.00
(53)	Orlando Cepeda	17.50	8.75	5.25
(54)	Billy Champion	5.00	2.50	1.50
(55)	Dean Chance	5.00	2.50	1.50
(56a)	Roberto Clemente (Red insert.)	60.00	30.00	18.00
(56b)	Roberto Clemente (Blue insert.)	50.00	25.00	15.00
(57)	Tony Cloninger	5.00	2.50	1.50
(58)	Nate Colbert	5.00	2.50	1.50
(59)	Joe Coleman	5.00	2.50	1.50
(60)	Kevin Collins	5.00	2.50	1.50
(61)	Wayne Comer	5.00	2.50	1.50
(62)	Tony Conigliaro	10.00	5.00	3.00
(63)	Billy Cowan	5.00	2.50	1.50
(64)	Casey Cox	5.00	2.50	1.50
(65)	Willie Crawford	5.00	2.50	1.50
(66)	Mike Cuellar	5.00	2.50	1.50
(67)	Al Dark	5.00	2.50	1.50
(68)	Vic Davalillo	5.00	2.50	1.50
(69)	Jim Davenport	5.00	2.50	1.50
(70)	Willie Davis	5.00	2.50	1.50
(71)	Tommy Dean	5.00	2.50	1.50
(72)	Larry Dierker	5.00	2.50	1.50
(73)	Dick Dietz	5.00	2.50	1.50
(74)	Moe Drabowsky	5.00	2.50	1.50
(75)	Leo Durocher	13.50	6.75	4.00
(76)	Johnny Edwards	5.00	2.50	1.50
(77)	Dock Ellis	5.00	2.50	1.50
(78)	Dick Ellsworth	5.00	2.50	1.50
(79)	Mike Epstein	5.00	2.50	1.50
(80)	Andy Etchebarren	5.00	2.50	1.50
(81)	Ron Fairly	5.00	2.50	1.50
(82)	Al Ferrara	5.00	2.50	1.50
(83)	Rollie Fingers	13.50	6.75	4.00
(84)	Mike Fiore	5.00	2.50	1.50
(85)	Eddie Fisher	5.00	2.50	1.50
(86)	Jack Fisher	5.00	2.50	1.50
(87)	Ray Fosse	5.00	2.50	1.50
(88)	Bill Freehan	5.00	2.50	1.50
(89)	Jim Fregosi	5.00	2.50	1.50
(90)	Tito Fuentes	5.00	2.50	1.50
(91)	Vern Fuller	5.00	2.50	1.50
(92)	Woody Fryman	5.00	2.50	1.50
(93)	Len Gabrielson	5.00	2.50	1.50
(94)	Gary Gentry	5.00	2.50	1.50
(95)	Jake Gibbs	5.00	2.50	1.50
(96)	Russ Gibson	5.00	2.50	1.50
(97)	Billy Grabarkewitz	5.00	2.50	1.50
(98)	Dick Green	5.00	2.50	1.50
(99)	Tom Griffin	5.00	2.50	1.50
(100)	Jerry Grote	5.00	2.50	1.50
(101)	Tom Haller	5.00	2.50	1.50
(102)	Steve Hamilton	5.00	2.50	1.50
(103)	Ron Hansen	5.00	2.50	1.50
(104)	Tommy Harmon	5.00	2.50	1.50
(105)	Tommy Harper	5.00	2.50	1.50
(106)	Bud Harrelson	5.00	2.50	1.50
(107)	Jim Ray Hart	5.00	2.50	1.50
(108)	Richie Hebner	5.00	2.50	1.50
(109)	Mike Hedlund	5.00	2.50	1.50
(110)	Mike Hegan	5.00	2.50	1.50
(111)	Tommy Helms	5.00	2.50	1.50
(112)	Angel Hermoso	5.00	2.50	1.50
(113)	Ed Herrmann	5.00	2.50	1.50
(114)	Mike Hershberger	5.00	2.50	1.50
(115)	Jim Hickman	5.00	2.50	1.50
(116)	Jim Hicks	5.00	2.50	1.50
(117)	Chuck Hinton	5.00	2.50	1.50
(118)	Larry Hisle	5.00	2.50	1.50
(119)	Gil Hodges	13.50	6.75	4.00
(120)	Ken Holtzman	5.00	2.50	1.50
(121)	Joel Horlen	5.00	2.50	1.50
(122)	Willie Horton	5.00	2.50	1.50
(123)	Ralph Houk	5.00	2.50	1.50
(124)	Frank Howard	7.50	3.75	2.25
(125)	Randy Hundley	5.00	2.50	1.50
(126)	Ron Hunt	5.00	2.50	1.50
(127)	Jim Hunter	13.50	6.75	4.00
(128)	Steve Huntz	5.00	2.50	1.50
(129)	Al Jackson	5.00	2.50	1.50
(130)	Reggie Jackson	35.00	17.50	10.50
(131)	Pat Jarvis	5.00	2.50	1.50
(132)	Julian Javier	5.00	2.50	1.50
(133)	Tommy John	10.00	5.00	3.00
(134)	Dave Johnson	5.00	2.50	1.50
(135)	Jerry Johnson	5.00	2.50	1.50
(136)	Jay Johnstone	5.00	2.50	1.50
(137)	Cleon Jones	5.00	2.50	1.50
(138)	Dalton Jones	5.00	2.50	1.50
(139)	Jim Kaat	7.50	3.75	2.25
(140)	Al Kaline	20.00	10.00	6.00
(141)	Dick Kelley	5.00	2.50	1.50
(142)	Pat Kelly	5.00	2.50	1.50
(143)	John Kennedy	5.00	2.50	1.50
(144)	Joe Keough	5.00	2.50	1.50
(145)	Don Kessinger	5.00	2.50	1.50
(146)	Harmon Killebrew	20.00	10.00	6.00
(147)	Clay Kirby	5.00	2.50	1.50
(148)	Darold Knowles	5.00	2.50	1.50
(149)	Jerry Koosman	5.00	2.50	1.50
(150)	Andy Kosco	5.00	2.50	1.50
(151)	Ed Kranepool	5.00	2.50	1.50
(152)	Lew Krausse	5.00	2.50	1.50
(153)	Coco Laboy	5.00	2.50	1.50
(154)	Hal Lanier	5.00	2.50	1.50
(155)	George Lauzerique	5.00	2.50	1.50
(156)	Denny Lemaster	5.00	2.50	1.50
(157)	Bob Locker	5.00	2.50	1.50
(158)	Mickey Lolich	5.00	2.50	1.50
(159)	Jim Lonborg	5.00	2.50	1.50
(160)	Mike Lum	5.00	2.50	1.50
(161)	Jim Maloney	5.00	2.50	1.50
(162)	Juan Marichal	13.50	6.75	4.00
(163)	Dal Maxvill	5.00	2.50	1.50
(164)	Carlos May	5.00	2.50	1.50
(165)	Lee May	5.00	2.50	1.50
(166)	Willie Mays	40.00	20.00	12.00
(167)	Bill Mazeroski	17.50	8.75	5.25
(168)	Dick McAuliffe	5.00	2.50	1.50
(169)	Mike McCormick	5.00	2.50	1.50
(170)	Willie McCovey	20.00	10.00	6.00
(171)	Denny McLain	5.00	2.50	1.50
(172)	Jerry McNertney	5.00	2.50	1.50
(173)	Bill Melton	5.00	2.50	1.50
(174)	Denis Menke	5.00	2.50	1.50
(175)	Jim Merritt	5.00	2.50	1.50
(176)	Gene Michael	5.00	2.50	1.50
(177)	Pete Mikkelsen	5.00	2.50	1.50
(178)	Felix Millan	5.00	2.50	1.50
(179)	Norm Miller	5.00	2.50	1.50
(180)	Don Mincher	5.00	2.50	1.50
(181)	George Mitterwald	5.00	2.50	1.50
(182)	Rick Monday	5.00	2.50	1.50
(183)	Don Money	5.00	2.50	1.50
(184)	Bob Moose	5.00	2.50	1.50
(185)	Dave Morehead	5.00	2.50	1.50
(186)	Joe Morgan	20.00	10.00	6.00
(187)	Bobby Mercer (Murcer)	7.50	3.75	2.25
(188)	Ivan Murrell	5.00	2.50	1.50
(189)	Phil Niekro	13.50	6.75	4.00
(190)	Jim Northrup	5.00	2.50	1.50
(191)	Tony Oliva	10.00	5.00	3.00
(192)	Al Oliver	5.00	2.50	1.50
(193)	Claude Osteen	5.00	2.50	1.50
(194)	Jose Pagan	5.00	2.50	1.50
(195)	Jim Pagliaroni	5.00	2.50	1.50
(196)	Jim Palmer	20.00	10.00	6.00
(197)	Lowell Palmer	5.00	2.50	1.50
(198)	Milt Pappas	5.00	2.50	1.50
(199)	Marty Pattin	5.00	2.50	1.50
(200)	Roberto Pena	5.00	2.50	1.50
(201)	Joe Pepitone	7.50	3.75	2.25
(202)	Tony Perez	17.50	8.75	5.25
(203)	Gaylord Perry	13.50	6.75	4.00
(204)	Jim Perry	5.00	2.50	1.50
(205)	Fritz Peterson	5.00	2.50	1.50
(206)	Rico Petrocelli (Petrocelli)	5.00	2.50	1.50
(207)	Lefty Phillips	5.00	2.50	1.50
(208)	Tom Phoebus	5.00	2.50	1.50
(209)	Lou Piniella	7.50	3.75	2.25
(210)	Vada Pinson	7.50	3.75	2.25
(211)	Boog Powell	10.00	5.00	3.00
(212)	Frank Quilici	5.00	2.50	1.50
(213)	Doug Rader	5.00	2.50	1.50
(214)	Ron Reed	5.00	2.50	1.50
(215)	Rich Reese	5.00	2.50	1.50
(216)	Rick Reichardt	5.00	2.50	1.50
(217)	Phil Regan	5.00	2.50	1.50
(218)	Roger Repoz	5.00	2.50	1.50
(219)	Juan Rios	5.00	2.50	1.50
(220)	Brooks Robinson	20.00	10.00	6.00
(221)	Frank Robinson	20.00	10.00	6.00
(222)	Cookie Rojas	5.00	2.50	1.50
(223)	Rich Rollins	5.00	2.50	1.50
(224)	Pete Rose	40.00	20.00	12.00
(225)	Gary Ross	5.00	2.50	1.50
(226)	Joe Rudi	5.00	2.50	1.50
(227)	Manny Sanguillen	5.00	2.50	1.50
(228)	Jose Santiago	5.00	2.50	1.50
(229)	Ron Santo	10.00	5.00	3.00
(230)	Tom Satriano	5.00	2.50	1.50
(231)	Richie Scheinblum	5.00	2.50	1.50
(232)	Red Schoendienst	13.50	6.75	4.00
(233)	George Scott	5.00	2.50	1.50
(234)	Tom Seaver	20.00	10.00	6.00
(235)	Norm Siebern	5.00	2.50	1.50
(236)	Sonny Siebert	5.00	2.50	1.50
(237)	Duke Sims	5.00	2.50	1.50
(238)	Tommie Sisk	5.00	2.50	1.50
(239)	Ted Sizemore	5.00	2.50	1.50
(240)	Mayo Smith	5.00	2.50	1.50
(241)	Reggie Smith	5.00	2.50	1.50
(242)	Willie Smith	5.00	2.50	1.50
(243)	Russ Snyder	5.00	2.50	1.50
(244)	Joe Sparma	5.00	2.50	1.50
(245)	Lee Stange	5.00	2.50	1.50
(246)	Mickey Stanley	5.00	2.50	1.50
(247)	Willie Stargell	17.50	8.75	5.25
(248)	Rusty Staub	7.50	3.75	2.25
(249)	Ron Stone	5.00	2.50	1.50
(250)	Bill Stoneman	5.00	2.50	1.50
(251)	Mel Stottlemyre	5.00	2.50	1.50
(252)	Ed Stroud	5.00	2.50	1.50
(253)	Bill Sudakis	5.00	2.50	1.50
(254)	Gary Sutherland	5.00	2.50	1.50
(255)	Ron Swoboda	5.00	2.50	1.50
(256)	Carl Taylor	5.00	2.50	1.50
(257)	Tony Taylor	5.00	2.50	1.50
(258)	Bob Tillman	5.00	2.50	1.50
(259)	Bobby Tolan	5.00	2.50	1.50
(260)	Cesar Tovar	5.00	2.50	1.50
(261)	Jeff Torborg	5.00	2.50	1.50
(262)	Joe Torre	10.00	5.00	3.00
(263)	Hector Torres	5.00	2.50	1.50
(264)	Tom Tresh	7.50	3.75	2.25
(265)	Ted Uhlaender	5.00	2.50	1.50
(266)	Del Unser	5.00	2.50	1.50
(267)	Bob Veale	5.00	2.50	1.50
(268)	Zoilo Versalles	5.00	2.50	1.50
(269)	Bill Voss	5.00	2.50	1.50
(270)	Pete Ward	5.00	2.50	1.50
(271)	Greg Washburn	5.00	2.50	1.50
(272)	Eddie Watt	5.00	2.50	1.50
(273)	Ramon Webster	5.00	2.50	1.50
(274)	Al Weis	5.00	2.50	1.50
(275)	Roy White	5.00	2.50	1.50
(276)	Billy Williams	17.50	8.75	5.25
(277)	Ted Williams	30.00	15.00	9.00
(278)	Walt Williams	5.00	2.50	1.50
(279)	Billy Wilson	5.00	2.50	1.50
(280)	Don Wilson	5.00	2.50	1.50
(281)	Earl Wilson	5.00	2.50	1.50
(282)	Rick Wise	5.00	2.50	1.50
(283)	Bobby Wine	5.00	2.50	1.50
(284)	Wilbur Wood	5.00	2.50	1.50
(285)	Woody Woodward	5.00	2.50	1.50
(286)	Billy Wynne	5.00	2.50	1.50

1980 Superstar

SUPERSTAR
18

SUPERSTAR

WILLIE HOWARD MAYS
Centerfielder, New York and
San Francisco Giants

In 1951 Willie Mays was the National League Rookie-of-the-Year and played in the World Series for the New York Giants. After several brilliant years with the Giants, in both New York and San Francisco, Willie was traded to the New York Mets in 1972. The following year, Willie ended his memorable career, by again appearing in the fall classic.

Willie lead the New York Giants to a stunning World Series Championship over the heavily favored Cleveland Indians in 1954. Ironically, although he had 660 lifetime homers to place him third on the all-time list he never homered in the World Series.

WILLIE MAYS

This collectors' issue, probably produced by Card Collectors Closet in Springfield, Mass., included up to five cards each of the most famous former players. The 2-1/2" x 3-1/2" cards have black-and-white photos on front, with yellow, white and blue graphics. Backs are in black-and-white with career narrative. The set sold originally for $3.50.

		NM	EX	VG
Complete Set (45):		20.00	10.00	6.00
Common Player:		.75	.35	.20
1	Babe Ruth	1.25	.60	.40
2	Roberto Clemente	1.00	.50	.30
3	Roberto Clemente	1.00	.50	.30
4	Roberto Clemente	1.00	.50	.30
5	Lou Gehrig, Joe DiMaggio	.75	.35	.20
6	Mickey Mantle, Roger Maris	1.75	.90	.50
7	Roger Maris, Yogi Berra, Mickey Mantle	1.25	.60	.40
8	Whitey Ford, Sandy Koufax	.75	.35	.20
9	Babe Ruth	1.25	.60	.40
10	Roger Maris, Mickey Mantle	1.75	.90	.50
11	Ted Williams, Stan Musial, Willie Mays	.75	.35	.20
12	Mickey Mantle, Hank Aaron	1.25	.60	.40
13	Sandy Koufax	.75	.35	.20
14	Sandy Koufax	.75	.35	.20
15	Thurman Munson	.75	.35	.20
16	Sandy Koufax	.75	.35	.20
17	Sandy Koufax	.75	.35	.20
18	Willie Mays	.75	.35	.20
19	Willie Mays	.75	.35	.20
20	Willie Mays	.75	.35	.20
21	Willie Mays	.75	.35	.20
22	Ted Williams	.75	.35	.20
23	Ted Williams	.75	.35	.20
24	Ted Williams	.75	.35	.20
25	Ted Williams	.75	.35	.20
26	Lou Gehrig	.75	.35	.20
27	Lou Gehrig	.75	.35	.20
28	Lou Gehrig	.75	.35	.20
29	Lou Gehrig	.75	.35	.20
30	Mickey Mantle	2.00	1.00	.60
31	Mickey Mantle	2.00	1.00	.60
32	Mickey Mantle	2.00	1.00	.60
33	Mickey Mantle	2.00	1.00	.60
34	Hank Aaron	.75	.35	.20
35	Joe DiMaggio	.75	.35	.20
36	Joe DiMaggio	.75	.35	.20
37	Joe DiMaggio	.75	.35	.20
38	Joe DiMaggio	.75	.35	.20
39	Roberto Clemente	1.00	.50	.30
40	Babe Ruth	1.25	.60	.40
41	Babe Ruth	1.25	.60	.40
42	Babe Ruth	1.25	.60	.40
43	Hank Aaron	.75	.35	.20
44	Hank Aaron	.75	.35	.20
45	Hank Aaron	.75	.35	.20

1970 Super Valu Minnesota Twins

One of many Minnesota Twins regional issues from the team's first decade, this set of player portraits was painted by noted celebrity artist John Wheeldon. Individual player pictures were given away at Super Valu grocery stores. The premiums feature large portraits and smaller action pictures, painted in pastels, against a pastel background. A facsimile autograph is printed below the pictures and the player's name is printed in the bottom border. At 7-3/4" x 9-3/8", the Twins portraits are somewhat smaller than similar contemporary issues. Backs are printed in black-and-white and include a self-portrait and biography of the artist. Player information includes biographical bits, a lengthy career summary and complete major and minor league stats. Team and sponsor logo are also included on the unnumbered card backs. The set is checklisted here alphabetically.

		NM	EX	VG
Complete Set (12):		90.00	45.00	27.50
Common Player:		6.00	3.00	1.75
(1)	Brant Alyea	6.00	3.00	1.75
(2)	Leo Cardenas	6.00	3.00	1.75
(3)	Rod Carew	20.00	10.00	6.00
(4)	Jim Kaat	9.00	4.50	2.75
(5)	Harmon Killebrew	20.00	10.00	6.00
(6)	George Mitterwald	6.00	3.00	1.75
(7)	Tony Oliva	9.00	4.50	2.75
(8)	Ron Perranoski	6.00	3.00	1.75
(9)	Jim Perry	6.00	3.00	1.75
(10)	Rich Reese	6.00	3.00	1.75
(11)	Luis Tiant	7.50	3.75	2.25
(12)	Cesar Tovar	6.00	3.00	1.75

1874 Suppards & Fennemore Cabinets

Only members of the hometown 1874 Athletics (National Association) have been reported in this issue of cabinet cards from the Philadelphia studio. The 4-1/4" x 6-1/2" cards have full-length poses on front. Backs carry an ornate ad for the photographer. The players are not identified on the cards, unless an earlier owner has written the name. Thus far the team's most famous player, Cap Anson, has not been reported.

		NM	EX	VG
Common Player:		3,750	1,875	1,125
(1)	Joe Battin (Bat on shoulder.)	3,750	1,875	1,125
(2)	John Clapp (Cap on floor to his right.)	3,750	1,875	1,125
(3)	Wes Fisler (Bat at right side, no cap on floor.)	3,750	1,875	1,125
(4)	Dick McBride (Ball in hands at waist.)	3,750	1,875	1,125
(5)	Mike McGeary (Bat in crook of arm.)	3,750	1,875	1,125
(6)	John McMullin (Bat at his left, cap on floor at left.)	3,750	1,875	1,125
(7)	Tim Murnane (Bat at his right, cap on floor at left.)	4,050	2,025	1,200

1966 Swap-N-Save Album

While this 4" x 9" album pictures 1965 and 1966 Topps cards in full color on front and back, it is not connected with Topps. The album's interior pages feature die-cuts which allow the central panel to be removed so both front and back of each card can be viewed. Informational pages include team rosters.

	NM	EX	VG
Album:	80.00	40.00	20.00

1909-11 Sweet Caporal

Among the most common of the American Tobacco Co. brands advertising on the backs of 1909-11 T206 and 1911 T205 is Sweet Caporal. T206s can be found with factory designations of No. 25, No. 30, No. 42 (overprinted), No. 649 and

No. 649 (overprinted). In T205, Sweet Cap backs can be found printed in red (no factory number, or No. 42) or black, No. 25, No. 42.

(See T205, T206.)

1909-12 Sweet Caporal Domino Discs (PX7)

Domino Discs, distributed by Sweet Caporal Cigarettes from 1909 to 1912, are among the more obscure 20th Century tobacco issues. Although the disc set contains many of the same players - some even pictured in the same poses - as the later Sweet Caporal pin set, the discs have always lagged behind the pins in collector appeal. The Domino Discs, so called because each disc has a large, white domino printed on the back, measure approximately 1-1/8" in diameter and are made of thin cardboard surrounded by a metal rim. The fronts of the discs contain a player portrait set against a background of either red, green or blue. The words "Sweet Caporal Cigarettes" appear on the front along with the player's last name and team. There are 129 different major leaguers featured in the set. Each player can be found with two picture variations involving uniform or cap details, or just the size of the portrait. Also known to exist as part of the set is a disc which pictures a generic player and contains the words "Home Team" against a red background on one side and "Visiting Team" with a green background on the reverse. Because each of the players can theoretically be found in two pictures, with three different background colors and with varying numbers of dots on the dominoes, there is almost an impossible number of variations available. Collectors, however, generally collect the discs without regard to background color or domino arrangement. The Domino Disc set was assigned the designation PX7 in the American Card Catalog.

		NM	EX	VG
Complete Set (129):		13,500	6,750	4,100
Common Player:		80.00	40.00	25.00
(1)	Red Ames	80.00	40.00	25.00
(2)	Jimmy Archer	80.00	40.00	25.00
(3)	Jimmy Austin	80.00	40.00	25.00
(4)	Home Run Baker	175.00	85.00	60.00
(5)	Neal Ball	80.00	40.00	25.00
(6)	Cy Barger	80.00	40.00	25.00
(7)	Jack Barry	80.00	40.00	25.00
(8)	Johnny Bates	80.00	40.00	25.00
(9)	Beals Becker	80.00	40.00	25.00
(10)	George Bell	80.00	40.00	25.00
(11)	Chief Bender	175.00	85.00	60.00
(12)	Bill Bergen	80.00	40.00	25.00
(13)	Bob Bescher	80.00	40.00	25.00
(14)	Joe Birmingham	80.00	40.00	25.00
(15)	Roger Bresnahan	175.00	85.00	60.00
(16)	Al Bridwell	80.00	40.00	25.00
(17)	Mordecai Brown	175.00	85.00	60.00
(18)	Bobby Byrne	80.00	40.00	25.00
(19)	Nixey Callahan	80.00	40.00	25.00
(20)	Howie Camnitz	80.00	40.00	25.00
(21)	Bill Carrigan	80.00	40.00	25.00
(22)	Frank Chance	175.00	85.00	60.00
(23)	Hal Chase	80.00	40.00	25.00
(24)	Ed Cicotte	80.00	40.00	25.00
(25)	Fred Clarke	175.00	85.00	60.00
(26a)	Ty Cobb ("D" on cap.)	800.00	400.00	250.00
(26b)	Ty Cobb (No "D" on cap.)	800.00	400.00	250.00
(27)	Eddie Collins	175.00	85.00	60.00
(28)	Doc Crandall	80.00	40.00	25.00
(29)	Birdie Cree	80.00	40.00	25.00
(30)	Bill Dahlen	80.00	40.00	25.00
(31)	Jim Delahanty	80.00	40.00	25.00
(32)	Art Devlin	80.00	40.00	25.00
(33)	Josh Devore	80.00	40.00	25.00
(34)	Red Dooin	80.00	40.00	25.00
(35)	Mickey Doolan	80.00	40.00	25.00
(36)	Patsy Dougherty	80.00	40.00	25.00
(37)	Tom Downey	80.00	40.00	25.00
(38)	Larry Doyle	80.00	40.00	25.00
(39)	Louis Drucke	80.00	40.00	25.00
(40)	Clyde Engle	80.00	40.00	25.00
(41)	Tex Erwin	80.00	40.00	25.00
(42)	Steve Evans	80.00	40.00	25.00
(43)	Johnny Evers	175.00	85.00	60.00
(44)	Cecil Ferguson	80.00	40.00	25.00
(45)	Russ Ford	80.00	40.00	25.00
(46)	Art Fromme	80.00	40.00	25.00
(47)	Harry Gaspar	80.00	40.00	25.00
(48)	George Gibson	80.00	40.00	25.00
(49)	Eddie Grant	90.00	45.00	25.00
(50)	Clark Griffith	175.00	85.00	60.00
(51)	Bob Groom	80.00	40.00	25.00
(52)	Bob Harmon	80.00	40.00	25.00
(53)	Topsy Hartsel	80.00	40.00	25.00
(54)	Arnold Hauser	80.00	40.00	25.00
(55)	Dick Hoblitzell	80.00	40.00	25.00
(56)	Danny Hoffman	80.00	40.00	25.00
(57)	Miller Huggins	175.00	85.00	60.00
(58)	John Hummel	80.00	40.00	25.00
(59)	Hugh Jennings	175.00	85.00	60.00
(60)	Walter Johnson	475.00	240.00	160.00
(61)	Ed Karger	80.00	40.00	25.00

		NM	EX	VG
(62a)	Jack Knight (Yankees)	80.00	40.00	25.00
(62b)	Jack Knight (Senators)	80.00	40.00	25.00
(63)	Ed Konetchy	80.00	40.00	25.00
(64)	Harry Krause	80.00	40.00	25.00
(65)	Frank LaPorte	80.00	40.00	25.00
(66)	Nap Lajoie	175.00	85.00	60.00
(67)	Tommy Leach	80.00	40.00	25.00
(68)	Sam Leever	80.00	40.00	25.00
(69)	Lefty Leifield	80.00	40.00	25.00
(70)	Paddy Livingston	80.00	40.00	25.00
(71)	Hans Lobert	80.00	40.00	25.00
(72)	Harry Lord	80.00	40.00	25.00
(73)	Nick Maddox	80.00	40.00	25.00
(74)	Sherry Magee	80.00	40.00	25.00
(75)	Rube Marquard	175.00	85.00	60.00
(76)	Christy Mathewson	550.00	275.00	185.00
(77)	Al Mattern	80.00	40.00	25.00
(78)	George McBride	80.00	40.00	25.00
(79)	John McGraw	175.00	85.00	60.00
(80)	Harry McIntire	80.00	40.00	25.00
(81)	Matty McIntyre	80.00	40.00	25.00
(82)	Larry McLean	80.00	40.00	25.00
(83)	Fred Merkle	80.00	40.00	25.00
(84)	Chief Meyers	80.00	40.00	25.00
(85)	Clyde Milan	80.00	40.00	25.00
(86)	Dots Miller	80.00	40.00	25.00
(87)	Mike Mitchell	80.00	40.00	25.00
(88a)	Pat Moran (Cubs)	80.00	40.00	25.00
(88b)	Pat Moran (Phillies)	80.00	40.00	25.00
(89)	George Mullen (Mullin)	80.00	40.00	25.00
(90)	Danny Murphy	80.00	40.00	25.00
(91)	Red Murray	80.00	40.00	25.00
(92)	Tom Needham	80.00	40.00	25.00
(93)	Rebel Oakes	80.00	40.00	25.00
(94)	Rube Oldring	80.00	40.00	25.00
(95)	Fred Parent	80.00	40.00	25.00
(96)	Dode Paskert	80.00	40.00	25.00
(97)	Barney Pelty	80.00	40.00	25.00
(98)	Eddie Phelps	80.00	40.00	25.00
(99)	Deacon Phillippe	80.00	40.00	25.00
(100)	Jack Quinn	80.00	40.00	25.00
(101)	Ed Reulbach	80.00	40.00	25.00
(102)	Lew Richie	80.00	40.00	25.00
(103)	Jack Rowan	80.00	40.00	25.00
(104)	Nap Rucker	80.00	40.00	25.00
(105a)	Doc Scanlon (Scanlan) (Superbas)	80.00	40.00	25.00
(105b)	Doc Scanlon (Scanlan) (Phillies)	80.00	40.00	25.00
(106)	Germany Schaefer	80.00	40.00	25.00
(107)	Boss Schmidt	80.00	40.00	25.00
(108)	Wildfire Schulte	80.00	40.00	25.00
(109)	Jimmy Sheckard	80.00	40.00	25.00
(110)	Hap Smith	80.00	40.00	25.00
(111)	Tris Speaker	200.00	100.00	60.00
(112)	Harry Stovall	80.00	40.00	25.00
(113a)	Gabby Street (Senators)	80.00	40.00	25.00
(113b)	Gabby Street (Yankees)	80.00	40.00	25.00
(114)	George Suggs	80.00	40.00	25.00
(115)	Ira Thomas	80.00	40.00	25.00
(116)	Joe Tinker	175.00	85.00	60.00
(117)	John Titus	80.00	40.00	25.00
(118)	Terry Turner	80.00	40.00	25.00
(119)	Heinie Wagner	80.00	40.00	25.00
(120)	Bobby Wallace	175.00	85.00	60.00
(121)	Ed Walsh	175.00	85.00	60.00
(122)	Jack Warhop	80.00	40.00	25.00
(123)	Zach Wheat	175.00	85.00	60.00
(124)	Doc White	80.00	40.00	25.00
(125a)	Art Wilson (Dark cap, Pirates.)	80.00	40.00	25.00
(125b)	Art Wilson (Dark cap, Giants.)	80.00	40.00	25.00
(126a)	Owen Wilson (White cap, Giants.)	80.00	40.00	25.00
(126b)	Owen Wilson (White cap, Pirates.)	80.00	40.00	25.00
(127)	Hooks Wiltse	80.00	40.00	25.00
(128)	Harry Wolter	80.00	40.00	25.00
(129)	Cy Young	550.00	275.00	165.00

1910-12 Sweet Caporal Pins (P2)

Expanding its premiums to include more than just trading cards, the American Tobacco Co. issued a series of baseball pins circa 1910-12. The sepia-colored pins measure 7/8" in diameter. The set includes 152 different players, but because of numerous "large letter" and "small letter" variations, collectors generally consider the set complete at 205 different pins. Fifty of the players are pictured on a second pin that usually displays the same photo but has the player's name and team designation printed in larger letters. Three players (Bresnahan, Mullin and Wallace) have three pins each. It is now generally accepted that there are 153 pins with "small letters" and another 52 "large letter" variations in a complete set. Research among advanced collectors has shown that 19 of the pins, including six of the "large letter" variations, are considered more difficult to find. The back of each pin has a variously colored paper insert advertising Sweet Caporal Cigarettes. The red backings are generally less common. The Sweet Caporal pins are closely related to the popular T20[ ]

Gold Border tobacco cards, also issued by the American Tobacco Co. about the same time. All but nine of the players featured in the pin set were also pictured on T205 cards, and in nearly all cases the photos are identical. The Sweet Caporal pins are designated as P2 in the American Card Catalog. The complete set price includes all variations.

	NM	EX	VG
Complete Set (204):	10,000	5,000	3,000
Common Player:	30.00	15.00	9.00
(1) Ed Abbaticchio	30.00	15.00	9.00
(2) Red Ames	30.00	15.00	9.00
(3a) Jimmy Archer (Small letters.)	30.00	15.00	9.00
(3b) Jimmy Archer (Large letters.)	35.00	17.50	10.00
(4a) Jimmy Austin (Small letters.)	30.00	15.00	9.00
(4b) Jimmy Austin (Large letters.)	35.00	17.50	10.00
(5) Home Run Baker	90.00	45.00	27.00
(6) Neal Ball	30.00	15.00	9.00
(7) Cy Barger	30.00	15.00	9.00
(8) Jack Barry	30.00	15.00	9.00
(9) Johnny Bates	30.00	15.00	9.00
(10) Beals Becker	30.00	15.00	9.00
(11) Fred Beebe	30.00	15.00	9.00
(12a) George Bell (Small letters.)	30.00	15.00	9.00
(12b) George Bell (Large letters.)	35.00	17.50	10.00
(13a) "Chief" Bender (Small letters.)	90.00	45.00	27.00
(13b) "Chief" Bender (Large letters.)	100.00	50.00	30.00
(14) Bill Bergen	30.00	15.00	9.00
(15) Bob Bescher	30.00	15.00	9.00
(16) Joe Birmingham	30.00	15.00	9.00
(17) Kitty Bransfield	65.00	32.50	20.00
(18a) Roger Bresnahan (Mouth closed, small letters.)	90.00	45.00	27.00
(18b) Roger Bresnahan (Mouth closed, large letters.)	100.00	50.00	30.00
(19) Roger Bresnahan (Mouth open.)	90.00	45.00	27.00
(20) Al Bridwell	30.00	15.00	9.00
(21a) Mordecai Brown (Small letters.)	90.00	45.00	27.00
(21b) Mordecai Brown (Large letters.)	100.00	50.00	30.00
(22) Bobby Byrne	30.00	15.00	9.00
(23) Nixey Callahan	30.00	15.00	9.00
(24a) Howie Camnitz (Small letters.)	30.00	15.00	9.00
(24b) Howie Camnitz (Large letters.)	35.00	17.50	10.00
(25a) Bill Carrigan (Small letters.)	30.00	15.00	9.00
(25b) Bill Carrigan (Large letters.)	35.00	17.50	10.00
(26a) Frank Chance (Small letters.)	90.00	45.00	27.00
(26b) Frank Chance (Large letters.)	100.00	50.00	30.00
(27) Hal Chase (Small letters.)	50.00	25.00	15.00
(28) Hal Chase (Large letters.)	90.00	45.00	27.00
(29) Ed Cicotte	90.00	45.00	27.00
(30a) Fred Clarke (Small letters.)	90.00	45.00	27.00
(30b) Fred Clarke (Large letters.)	100.00	50.00	30.00
(31a) Ty Cobb (Small letters, "D" on cap.)	600.00	300.00	180.00
(31b) Ty Cobb (Large letters, no "D" on cap.)	675.00	335.00	200.00
(32a) Eddie Collins (Small letters.)	90.00	45.00	27.00
(32b) Eddie Collins (Large letters.)	100.00	50.00	30.00
(33) Doc Crandall	30.00	15.00	9.00
(34) Birdie Cree	65.00	32.50	20.00
(35) Bill Dahlen	30.00	15.00	9.00
(36) Jim Delahanty	30.00	15.00	9.00
(37) Art Devlin	30.00	15.00	9.00
(38) Josh Devore	30.00	15.00	9.00
(39) Wild Bill Donovan	65.00	32.50	20.00
(40a) Red Dooin (Small letters.)	30.00	15.00	9.00
(40b) Red Dooin (Large letters.)	35.00	17.50	10.00
(41a) Mickey Doolan (Small letters.)	30.00	15.00	9.00
(41b) Mickey Doolan (Large letters.)	35.00	17.50	10.00
(42) Patsy Dougherty	30.00	15.00	9.00
(43a) Tom Downey (Small letters.)	30.00	15.00	9.00
(43b) Tom Downey (Large letters.)	35.00	17.50	10.00
(44a) Larry Doyle (Small letters.)	30.00	15.00	9.00
(44b) Larry Doyle (Large letters.)	35.00	17.50	10.00
(45) Louis Drucke	30.00	15.00	9.00
(46a) Hugh Duffy (Small letters.)	90.00	45.00	27.00
(46b) Hugh Duffy (Large letters.)	100.00	50.00	30.00
(47) Jimmy Dygert	30.00	15.00	9.00
(48a) Kid Elberfeld (Small letters.)	30.00	15.00	9.00
(48b) Kid Elberfeld (Large letters.)	35.00	17.50	10.00
(49a) Clyde Engle (Small letters.)	30.00	15.00	9.00
(49b) Clyde Engle (Large letters.)	35.00	17.50	10.00
(50) Tex Erwin	30.00	15.00	9.00
(51) Steve Evans	30.00	15.00	9.00
(52) Johnny Evers	90.00	45.00	27.00
(53) Cecil Ferguson	30.00	15.00	9.00
(54) John Flynn	30.00	15.00	9.00
(55a) Russ Ford (Small letters.)	30.00	15.00	9.00
(55b) Russ Ford (Large letters.)	35.00	17.50	10.00
(56) Art Fromme	30.00	15.00	9.00
(57) Harry Gaspar	30.00	15.00	9.00
(58a) George Gibson (Small letters.)	30.00	15.00	9.00
(58b) George Gibson (Large letters.)	35.00	17.50	10.00
(59) Eddie Grant	65.00	32.50	20.00
(60) Dolly Gray	30.00	15.00	9.00
(61a) Clark Griffith (Small letters.)	90.00	45.00	27.00
(61b) Clark Griffith (Large letters.)	100.00	50.00	30.00
(62) Bob Groom	30.00	15.00	9.00
(63) Bob Harmon	30.00	15.00	9.00
(64) Topsy Hartsel	30.00	15.00	9.00
(65) Arnold Hauser	65.00	32.50	20.00
(66) Ira Hemphill	30.00	15.00	9.00
(67a) Buck Herzog (Small letters.)	30.00	15.00	9.00
(67b) Buck Herzog (Large letters.)	35.00	17.50	10.00
(68) Dick Hoblitzell	30.00	15.00	9.00
(69) Danny Hoffman	30.00	15.00	9.00
(70) Harry Hooper	90.00	45.00	27.00
(71a) Miller Huggins (Small letters.)	90.00	45.00	27.00
(71b) Miller Huggins (Large letters.)	100.00	50.00	30.00
(72) John Hummel	30.00	15.00	9.00
(73) Hugh Jennings (Small letters.)	90.00	45.00	27.00
(74) Hugh Jennings (Large letters.)	100.00	50.00	30.00
(75a) Walter Johnson (Small letters.)	225.00	110.00	65.00
(75b) Walter Johnson (Large letters.)	275.00	135.00	85.00
(76) Tom Jones	65.00	32.50	20.00
(77) Ed Karger	30.00	15.00	9.00
(78) Ed Killian	65.00	32.50	20.00
(79a) Jack Knight (Small letters.)	30.00	15.00	9.00
(79b) Jack Knight (Large letters.)	35.00	17.50	10.00
(80) Ed Konetchy	30.00	15.00	9.00
(81) Harry Krause	30.00	15.00	9.00
(82) Rube Kroh	30.00	15.00	9.00
(83) Nap Lajoie	90.00	45.00	27.00
(84a) Frank LaPorte (Small letters.)	30.00	15.00	9.00
(84b) Frank LaPorte (Large letters.)	35.00	17.50	10.00
(85) Arlie Latham	30.00	15.00	9.00
(86a) Tommy Leach (Small letters.)	30.00	15.00	9.00
(86b) Tommy Leach (Large letters.)	35.00	17.50	10.00
(87) Sam Leever	30.00	15.00	9.00
(88) Lefty Leifield	30.00	15.00	9.00
(89) Hans Lobert	30.00	15.00	9.00
(90a) Harry Lord (Small letters.)	30.00	15.00	9.00
(90b) Harry Lord (Large letters.)	35.00	17.50	10.00
(91) Paddy Livingston	30.00	15.00	9.00
(92) Nick Maddox	30.00	15.00	9.00
(93) Sherry Magee	30.00	15.00	9.00
(94) Rube Marquard	90.00	45.00	27.00
(95a) Christy Mathewson (Small letters.)	225.00	110.00	65.00
(95b) Christy Mathewson (Large letters.)	275.00	135.00	80.00
(96a) Al Mattern (Small letters.)	30.00	15.00	9.00
(96b) Al Mattern (Large letters.)	35.00	17.50	10.00
(97) George McBride	30.00	15.00	9.00
(98a) John McGraw (Small letters.)	90.00	45.00	27.00
(98b) John McGraw (Large letters.)	100.00	50.00	30.00
(99) Harry McIntire (Cubs)	30.00	15.00	9.00
(100a) Matty McIntyre (White Sox, small letters.)	30.00	15.00	9.00
(100b) Matty McIntyre (White Sox, large letters.)	35.00	17.50	10.00
(101a) John McLean (Small letters.)	30.00	15.00	9.00
(101b) John McLean (Large letters.)	35.00	17.50	10.00
(102) Fred Merkle	30.00	15.00	9.00
(103) Chief Meyers	30.00	15.00	9.00
(104) Clyde Milan	30.00	15.00	9.00
(105) Dots Miller	30.00	15.00	9.00
(106) Mike Mitchell	30.00	15.00	9.00
(107) Pat Moran	30.00	15.00	9.00
(108a) George Mullen (Mullin) (Small letters.)	30.00	15.00	9.00
(108b) George Mullin (Large letters, white cap.)	90.00	45.00	27.00
(109) Danny Murphy	30.00	15.00	9.00
(110a) Red Murray (Small letters.)	35.00	17.50	10.00
(110b) Red Murray (Large letters.)	30.00	15.00	9.00
(111) Tom Needham	65.00	32.50	20.00
(112a) Rebel Oakes (Small letters.)	30.00	15.00	9.00
(112b) Rebel Oakes (Large letters.)	35.00	17.50	10.00
(113) Rube Oldring	30.00	15.00	9.00
(114) Charley O'Leary	30.00	15.00	9.00
(115) Orval Overall	65.00	32.50	20.00
(116) Fred Parent	30.00	15.00	9.00
(117a) Dode Paskert (Small letters.)	30.00	15.00	9.00
(117b) Dode Paskert (Large letters.)	35.00	17.50	10.00
(118) Barney Pelty	30.00	15.00	9.00
(119) Jake Pfeister	30.00	15.00	9.00
(120) Eddie Phelps	30.00	15.00	9.00
(121) Deacon Phillippe	30.00	15.00	9.00
(122) Jack Quinn	30.00	15.00	9.00
(123) Ed Reulbach	30.00	15.00	9.00
(124) Lew Richie	30.00	15.00	9.00
(125) Jack Rowan	30.00	15.00	9.00
(126a) Nap Rucker (Small letters.)	30.00	15.00	9.00
(126b) Nap Rucker (Large letters.)	35.00	17.50	10.00
(127) Doc Scanlon (Scanlan)	65.00	32.50	20.00
(128) Germany Schaefer	30.00	15.00	9.00
(129) Jimmy Scheckard (Sheckard)	30.00	15.00	9.00
(130a) Boss Schmidt (Small letters.)	30.00	15.00	9.00
(130b) Boss Schmidt (Large letters.)	35.00	17.50	10.00
(131) Wildfire Schulte	30.00	15.00	9.00
(132) Hap Smith	30.00	15.00	9.00
(133a) Tris Speaker (Small letters.)	150.00	75.00	45.00
(133b) Tris Speaker (Large letters.)	175.00	85.00	50.00
(134) Oscar Stanage	30.00	15.00	9.00
(135) Harry Steinfeldt	30.00	15.00	9.00
(136) George Stone	30.00	15.00	9.00
(137a) George Stoval (Stovall) (Small letters.)	30.00	15.00	9.00
(137b) George Stoval (Stovall) (Large letters.)	35.00	17.50	10.00
(138a) Gabby Street (Small letters.)	30.00	15.00	9.00
(138b) Gabby Street (Large letters.)	35.00	17.50	10.00
(139) George Suggs	30.00	15.00	9.00
(140a) Ira Thomas (Small letters.)	30.00	15.00	9.00
(140b) Ira Thomas (Large letters.)	35.00	17.50	10.00
(141a) Joe Tinker (Small letters.)	90.00	45.00	27.00
(141b) Joe Tinker (Large letters.)	100.00	50.00	30.00
(142a) John Titus (Small letters.)	30.00	15.00	9.00
(142b) John Titus (Large letters.)	35.00	17.50	10.00
(143) Terry Turner	30.00	15.00	9.00
(144) Heinie Wagner	30.00	15.00	9.00
(145a) Bobby Wallace (With cap, small letters.)	90.00	45.00	27.00
(145b) Bobby Wallace (With cap, large letters.)	100.00	50.00	30.00
(146) Bobby Wallace (Without cap.)	90.00	45.00	27.00
(147) Ed Walsh	90.00	45.00	27.00
(148) Jack Warhop	30.00	15.00	9.00
(149a) Zach Wheat (Small letters.)	90.00	45.00	27.00
(149b) Zach Wheat (Large letters.)	100.00	50.00	30.00
(150) Doc White	30.00	15.00	9.00
(151) Art Wilson (Giants)	30.00	15.00	9.00
(152) Owen Wilson (Pirates)	30.00	15.00	9.00
(153) Hooks Wiltse	30.00	15.00	9.00
(154) Harry Wolter	30.00	15.00	9.00
(155a) "Cy" Young ("C" on cap.)	200.00	100.00	60.00
(155b) Old Cy Young (Plain cap.)	225.00	110.00	65.00

1928 Sweetman

The cards of this St. Louis firm share the format - about 1-3/8" x 2-1/2", black-and-white with card number in parentheses to the left of player name on front - and checklist with the 1928 York Caramels Type 2 issue, but are less frequently encountered. Backs of the Sweetman cards offer an album for 15 cents in stamps. The type of business is which Sweetman Co., Inc., was engaged is unknown.

		NM	EX	VG
Complete Set (60):		25,000	12,500	7,500
Common Player:		250.00	125.00	75.00
1	Burleigh Grimes	400.00	200.00	120.00
2	Walter Reuther (Ruether)	250.00	125.00	75.00
3	Joe Dugan	250.00	125.00	75.00
4	Red Faber	400.00	200.00	120.00
5	Gabby Hartnett	400.00	200.00	120.00
6	Babe Ruth	6,000	3,000	1,800
7	Bob Meusel	250.00	125.00	75.00
8	Herb Pennock	400.00	200.00	120.00
9	George Burns	250.00	125.00	75.00
10	Joe Sewell	400.00	200.00	120.00
11	George Uhle	250.00	125.00	75.00
12	Bob O'Farrell	250.00	125.00	75.00
13	Rogers Hornsby	500.00	250.00	150.00
14	"Pie" Traynor	400.00	200.00	120.00
15	Clarence Mitchell	250.00	125.00	75.00
16	Eppa Jepha Rixey	400.00	200.00	120.00
17	Carl Mays	300.00	150.00	90.00
18	Adolfo Luque	250.00	125.00	75.00
19	Dave Bancroft	400.00	200.00	120.00
20	George Kelly	400.00	200.00	120.00
21	Earl (Earle) Combs	400.00	200.00	120.00
22	Harry Heilmann	400.00	200.00	120.00
23	Ray W. Schalk	400.00	200.00	120.00
24	Johnny Mostil	250.00	125.00	75.00
25	Hack Wilson	400.00	200.00	120.00
26	Lou Gehrig	4,000	2,000	1,200
27	Ty Cobb	4,000	2,000	1,200
28	Tris Speaker	500.00	250.00	150.00
29	Tony Lazzeri	400.00	200.00	120.00
30	Waite Hoyt	400.00	200.00	120.00
31	Sherwood Smith	250.00	125.00	75.00
32	Max Carey	400.00	200.00	120.00
33	Eugene Hargrave	250.00	125.00	75.00
34	Miguel L. Gonzales (Miguel A. Gonzalez)	250.00	125.00	75.00
35	Joe Judge	250.00	125.00	75.00
36	E.C. (Sam) Rice	400.00	200.00	120.00
37	Earl Sheely	250.00	125.00	75.00
38	Sam Jones	250.00	125.00	75.00
39	Bib (Bibb) A. Falk	250.00	125.00	75.00
40	Willie Kamm	250.00	125.00	75.00
41	Stanley Harris	400.00	200.00	120.00
42	John J. McGraw	400.00	200.00	120.00
43	Artie Nehf	250.00	125.00	75.00
44	Grover Alexander	500.00	250.00	150.00
45	Paul Waner	400.00	200.00	120.00
46	William H. Terry	400.00	200.00	120.00
47	Glenn Wright	250.00	125.00	75.00
48	Earl Smith	250.00	125.00	75.00
49	Leon (Goose) Goslin	400.00	200.00	120.00
50	Frank Frisch	400.00	200.00	120.00
51	Joe Harris	250.00	125.00	75.00
52	Fred (Cy) Williams	250.00	125.00	75.00
53	Eddie Roush	400.00	200.00	120.00
54	George Sisler	400.00	200.00	120.00
55	Ed. Rommel	250.00	125.00	75.00
56	Rogers Peckinpaugh (Roger)	250.00	125.00	75.00
57	Stanley Coveleskie (Coveleski)	400.00	200.00	120.00
58	Lester Bell	250.00	125.00	75.00
59	Clyde Barnhart	250.00	125.00	75.00
60	John P. McInnis	250.00	125.00	75.00

1948 Swell Babe Ruth Story

The Philadelphia Gum Co., in 1948, created a card set about the movie "The Babe Ruth Story," which starred William Bendix and Claire Trevor. The set, whose American Card Catalog designation is R421, contains 28 black and white, numbered cards which measure 2" x 2-1/2". The Babe Ruth Story set was originally intended to consist of sixteen cards. Twelve additional cards (#'s 17-28) were added when Ruth died before the release of the film. The card backs include an offer for an autographed photo of William Bendix, starring as the Babe, for five Swell Bubble Gum wrappers and five cents.

1948 Swell Babe Ruth Story

		NM	EX	VG
Complete Set (28):		2,750	1,100	550.00
Common Card (1-16):		45.00	20.00	10.00
Common Card (17-28):		125.00	55.00	30.00
1	"The Babe Ruth Story" in the Making	150.00	65.00	35.00
2	Batboy Becomes the Babe (William Bendix)	45.00	20.00	10.00
3	Claire Hodgson (Claire Trevor)	45.00	20.00	10.00
4	Babe Ruth and Claire Hodgson	45.00	20.00	10.00
5	Brother Mathias (Charles Bickford)	45.00	20.00	10.00
6	Phil Conrad (Sam Levene)	45.00	20.00	10.00
7	Nightclub Singer (Gertrude Niesen)	45.00	20.00	10.00
8	Baseball's Famous Deal, Jack Dunn (William Frawley)	45.00	20.00	10.00
9	Mr. and Mrs. Babe Ruth	45.00	20.00	10.00
10	Babe Ruth, Claire Ruth and Brother Mathias	45.00	20.00	10.00
11	Babe Ruth and Miller Huggins (Fred Lightner)	45.00	20.00	10.00
12	Babe at Bed of Ill Boy Johnny Sylvester (Gregory Marshall)	45.00	20.00	10.00
13	Sylvester Family Listening to Game	45.00	20.00	10.00
14	"When a Feller Needs a Friend" (With dog at police station)	45.00	20.00	10.00
15	Dramatic Home Run	45.00	20.00	10.00
16	The Homer That Set the Record - #60 (#60)	75.00	34.00	18.50
17	"The Slap That Started Baseball's Famous Career"	125.00	55.00	30.00
18	The Babe Plays Santa Claus	125.00	55.00	30.00
19	Meeting of Owner and Manager	125.00	55.00	30.00
20	"Broken Window Paid Off"	125.00	55.00	30.00
21	Babe in a Crowd of Autograph Collectors	200.00	90.00	50.00
22	Charley Grimm, William Bendix	125.00	55.00	30.00
23	Ted Lyons, William Bendix	125.00	55.00	30.00
24	Lefty Gomez, William Bendix, Bucky Harris	150.00	65.00	35.00
25	Babe Ruth, William Bendix	400.00	180.00	100.00
26	Babe Ruth, William Bendix	400.00	180.00	100.00
27	Babe Ruth, Claire Trevor	400.00	180.00	100.00
28	William Bendix, Babe Ruth, Claire Trevor	400.00	180.00	100.00

1948 Swell Sport Thrills

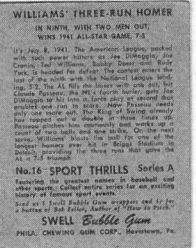

This is a set of black-and-white cards which depicts memorable events in baseball history. The cards measure 2-1/2" x 3" and have a picture frame border and event title on the card fronts. The card backs describe the event in detail. Twenty cards were produced in this set by the Swell Gum Co. of Philadelphia. Each card is numbered, and card numbers 9, 11, 16 and 20 are considered more difficult to obtain.

		NM	EX	VG
Complete Set (20):		2,400	1,200	720.00
Common Player:		50.00	25.00	15.00
1	Greatest Single Inning (Mickey Cochrane, Jimmy (Jimmie) Foxx, George Haas, Bing Miller, Al Simmons)	140.00	70.00	45.00
2	Amazing Record (Pete Reiser)	50.00	25.00	15.00
3	Dramatic Debut (Jackie Robinson)	280.00	140.00	85.00
4	Greatest Pitcher (Walter Johnson)	120.00	60.00	35.00
5	Three Strikes Not Out! (Tommy Henrich, Mickey Owen)	50.00	25.00	15.00
6	Home Run Wins Series (Bill Dickey)	55.00	25.00	15.00
7	Never Say Die Pitcher (Hal Schumacher)	50.00	25.00	15.00
8	Five Strikeouts! (Carl Hubbell)	65.00	35.00	20.00
9	Greatest Catch! (Al Gionfriddo)	90.00	45.00	30.00

10	No Hits! No Runs! (Johnny VanderMeer)	50.00	25.00	15.00
11	Bases Loaded! (Tony Lazzeri, Bob O'Farrell)	60.00	25.00	15.00
12	Most Dramatic Home Run (Lou Gehrig, Babe Ruth)	320.00	160.00	100.00
13	Winning Run (Tommy Bridges, Mickey Cochrane, Goose Goslin)	50.00	25.00	15.00
14	Great Slugging (Lou Gehrig)	360.00	180.00	110.00
15	Four Men to Stop Him! (Jim Bagby, Al Smith)	80.00	40.00	25.00
16	Three Run Homer in Ninth! (Joe DiMaggio, Joe Gordon, Ted Williams)	360.00	180.00	110.00
17	Football Block! (Whitey Kurowski, Johnny Lindell)	50.00	25.00	15.00
18	Home Run to Fame (Pee Wee Reese)	140.00	70.00	45.00
19	Strikout Record! (Bob Feller)	80.00	40.00	25.00
20	Rifle Arm! (Carl Furillo)	80.00	40.00	25.00

1957 Swift Meats

One of the really different baseball card issues of the 50s was the set of 18 3-D baseball player figures which could be punched out and assembled from cards included in packages of hot dogs. The unpunched cards measure approximately 3-1/2" x 4". Prices below are for unpunched cards. Values for assembled figures are problematical.

		NM	EX	VG
Complete Set, Singles (18):		1,500	750.00	450.00
Complete Set w/ Mailer, Playing Board:		3,000	1,500	1,000
Common Player:		60.00	30.00	18.00
1	John Podres	75.00	37.50	22.50
2	Gus Triandos	60.00	30.00	18.00
3	Dale Long	60.00	30.00	18.00
4	Billy Pierce	60.00	30.00	18.00
5	Ed Bailey	60.00	30.00	18.00
6	Vic Wertz	60.00	30.00	18.00
7	Nelson Fox	130.00	65.00	40.00
8	Ken Boyer	75.00	37.50	22.50
9	Gil McDougald	75.00	37.50	22.50
10	Junior Gilliam	75.00	37.50	22.50
11	Eddie Yost	60.00	30.00	18.00
12	Johnny Logan	60.00	30.00	18.00
13	Hank Aaron	200.00	100.00	60.00
14	Bill Tuttle	60.00	30.00	18.00
15	Jackie Jensen	60.00	30.00	18.00
16	Frank Robinson	200.00	100.00	60.00
17	Richie Ashburn	130.00	65.00	40.00
18	Rocky Colavito	200.00	100.00	60.00

1951 Sylvania Leo Durocher Postcard

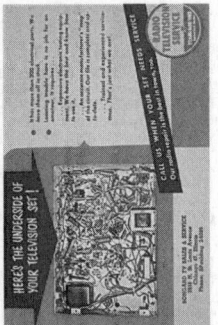

The N.Y. Giants manager endorses Sylvania radio/television service on this large-format (8-1/2" x 5-1/2") postcard. Color artwork features Durocher with a quotation endorsing Sylvania parts and service.

	NM	EX	VG
Leo Durocher	50.00	25.00	15.00

1910-11 S74 Silks - White

Designated as S74 in the "American Card Catalog," these delicate fabric collectibles are popular with advanced collectors. The silks were issued as premiums with several different brands of cigarettes: Turkey Red (with or without border around type), Old Mill, Red Sun, and, rarely, Helmar. The satin-like collectibles can be found in two different styles, either "white" or "colored." The white silks measure 1-7/8" x 3" and were originally issued with a brown paper backing that carried an advertisement for one of the cigarette brands. The backing also advised that the silks were "useful in making pillow covers and other fancy articles for home decoration." Many undoubt-

edly were used for such purposes, making silks with the paper backing still intact more difficult to find. White silks must have the backing intact to command top values shown here. Ninety-two subjects are known in the "white" silks. The silks feature the player pictures found in the popular T205 Gold Border tobacco card set.

		NM	EX	VG
Complete Set (87):		16,000	6,400	4,150
Common Player:		200.00	100.00	60.00
No Paper Backing: 50 Percent				
(1)	Home Run Baker	450.00	225.00	140.00
(2)	Cy Barger	200.00	100.00	60.00
(3)	Jack Barry	200.00	100.00	60.00
(4)	Johnny Bates	200.00	100.00	60.00
(5)	Fred Beck	200.00	100.00	60.00
(6)	Beals Becker	200.00	100.00	60.00
(7)	George Bell	200.00	100.00	60.00
(8)	Chief Bender	450.00	225.00	140.00
(9)	Roger Bresnahan	450.00	225.00	140.00
(10)	Al Bridwell	200.00	100.00	60.00
(11)	Mordecai Brown	450.00	225.00	140.00
(12)	Bobby Byrne	200.00	100.00	60.00
(13)	Howie Camnitz	200.00	100.00	60.00
(14)	Bill Carrigan	200.00	100.00	60.00
(15)	Frank Chance	450.00	225.00	140.00
(16)	Hal Chase	400.00	200.00	120.00
(17)	Fred Clarke	450.00	225.00	140.00
(18)	Ty Cobb	4,500	2,250	1,350
(19)	Eddie Collins	450.00	225.00	140.00
(20)	Doc Crandall	200.00	100.00	60.00
(21)	Lou Criger	200.00	100.00	60.00
(22)	Jim Delahanty	200.00	100.00	60.00
(23)	Art Devlin	200.00	100.00	60.00
(24)	Red Dooin	200.00	100.00	60.00
(25)	Mickey Doolan	200.00	100.00	60.00
(26)	Larry Doyle	200.00	100.00	60.00
(27)	Jimmy Dygert	200.00	100.00	60.00
(28)	Kid Elberfield (Elberfeld)	200.00	100.00	60.00
(29)	Steve Evans	200.00	100.00	60.00
(30)	Johnny Evers	450.00	225.00	140.00
(31)	Bob Ewing	200.00	100.00	60.00
(32)	Art Fletcher	200.00	100.00	60.00
(33)	John Flynn	200.00	100.00	60.00
(34)	Bill Foxen	200.00	100.00	60.00
(35)	George Gibson	200.00	100.00	60.00
(36)	Peaches Graham (Cubs) Existence now questioned			
(37)	Peaches Graham (Rustlers)	200.00	100.00	60.00
(38)	Clark Griffith	450.00	225.00	140.00
(39)	Topsy Hartsel	200.00	100.00	60.00
(40)	Arnold Hauser	200.00	100.00	60.00
(41)	Charlie Hemphill	200.00	100.00	60.00
(42)	Davy Jones	200.00	100.00	60.00
(43)	Jack Knight	200.00	100.00	60.00
(44)	Ed Konetchy	200.00	100.00	60.00
(45)	Harry Krause	200.00	100.00	60.00
(46)	Tommy Leach Existence now questioned			
(47)	Rube Marquard	450.00	225.00	140.00
(48)	Christy Mathewson	1,000	500.00	300.00
(49)	Al Mattern	200.00	100.00	60.00
(50)	Amby McConnell	200.00	100.00	60.00
(51)	John McGraw	450.00	225.00	140.00
(52)	Harry McIntire (McIntyre)	200.00	100.00	60.00
(53)	Fred Merkle	200.00	100.00	60.00
(54)	Chief Meyers	200.00	100.00	60.00
(55)	Dots Miller	200.00	100.00	60.00
(56)	Danny Murphy	200.00	100.00	60.00
(57)	Red Murray	200.00	100.00	60.00
(58)	Tom Needham	200.00	100.00	60.00
(59)	Rebel Oakes	200.00	100.00	60.00
(60)	Rube Oldring	200.00	100.00	60.00
(61)	Orval Overall	200.00	100.00	60.00
(62)	Fred Parent	200.00	100.00	60.00
(63)	Fred Payne	200.00	100.00	60.00
(64)	Barney Pelty	200.00	100.00	60.00
(65)	Deacon Phillippe	200.00	100.00	60.00
(66)	Jack Quinn	200.00	100.00	60.00
(67)	Bugs Raymond Existence now questioned			
(68)	Ed Reulbach	200.00	100.00	60.00
(69)	Doc Scanlon (Scanlan) Existence now questioned			
(70)	Germany Schaefer	200.00	100.00	60.00
(71)	Geo. Schlei	200.00	100.00	60.00
(72)	Wildfire Schulte	200.00	100.00	60.00
(73)	Dave Shean	200.00	100.00	60.00
(74)	Jimmy Sheckard	200.00	100.00	60.00
(75)	Tony Smith (Superbas)	200.00	100.00	60.00
(76)	Harry Smith (Rustlers)	500.00	200.00	125.00
(77)	Fred Snodgrass	200.00	100.00	60.00
(78)	Tris Speaker	525.00	265.00	160.00
(79)	Harry Steinfeldt (Cubs)	200.00	100.00	60.00
(80)	Harry Steinfeldt (Rustlers) Existence now questioned			
(81)	George Stone	200.00	100.00	60.00
(82)	Gabby Street	200.00	100.00	60.00
(83)	Ed Summers	200.00	100.00	60.00
(84)	Lee Tannehill	200.00	100.00	60.00
(85)	Joe Tinker	450.00	225.00	140.00

		NM	EX	VG
(86)	John Titus	200.00	100.00	60.00
(87)	Terry Turner	200.00	100.00	60.00
(88)	Bobby Wallace	450.00	225.00	140.00
(89)	Doc White	200.00	100.00	60.00
(90)	Ed Willett	200.00	100.00	60.00
(91)	Art Wilson	200.00	100.00	60.00
(92)	Harry Wolter	200.00	100.00	60.00

1911 S74 Silks - Colored

Designated as S74 in the "American Card Catalog," these delicate fabric collectibles are popular with advanced collectors. The silks were issued as premiums with several different brands of cigarettes: Turkey Red, Old Mill, Helmar, and, rarely, Red Sun. The satin-like silks can be found in two different styles, either "white" or "colored." The S74 "colored" silks, as their name indicates, were issued in a variety of colors. They are slightly larger than the white version, measuring 1-7/8" x 3-1/2", and were issued without a paper backing, carrying the cigarette brand name on the lower front of the fabric. (No color silks advertising the Helmar brand are known to exist.) In the colored silks, 120 subjects are known. The silks feature the same player pictures found in the popular T205 Gold Border tobacco card set.

		NM	EX	VG
Complete Set (120):		20,000	8,000	5,000
Common Player:		150.00	60.00	35.00
1)	Red Ames	150.00	60.00	35.00
2)	Jimmy Archer	150.00	60.00	35.00
3)	Home Run Baker	300.00	120.00	70.00
4)	Cy Barger	150.00	60.00	35.00
5)	Jack Barry	150.00	60.00	35.00
6)	Johnny Bates	150.00	60.00	35.00
7)	Beals Becker	150.00	60.00	35.00
8)	George Bell	150.00	60.00	35.00
9)	Chief Bender	300.00	120.00	70.00
10)	Bill Bergen	150.00	60.00	35.00
11)	Bob Bescher	150.00	60.00	35.00
12)	Roger Bresnahan (Mouth closed.)	300.00	120.00	70.00
13)	Roger Bresnahan (Mouth open.)	300.00	120.00	70.00
14)	Al Bridwell	150.00	60.00	35.00
15)	Mordecai Brown	300.00	120.00	70.00
16)	Bobby Byrne	150.00	60.00	35.00
17)	Howie Camnitz	150.00	60.00	35.00
18)	Bill Carrigan	150.00	60.00	35.00
19)	Frank Chance	300.00	120.00	70.00
20)	Hal Chase	225.00	90.00	55.00
21)	Ed Cicotte	300.00	120.00	70.00
22)	Fred Clarke	300.00	120.00	70.00
23)	Ty Cobb	1,200	480.00	290.00
24)	Eddie Collins	300.00	120.00	70.00
25)	Doc Crandall	150.00	60.00	35.00
26)	Bill Dahlen	150.00	60.00	35.00
27)	Jake Daubert	150.00	60.00	35.00
28)	Jim Delahanty	150.00	60.00	35.00
29)	Art Devlin	150.00	60.00	35.00
30)	Josh Devore	150.00	60.00	35.00
31)	Red Dooin	150.00	60.00	35.00
32)	Mickey Doolan	150.00	60.00	35.00
33)	Tom Downey	150.00	60.00	35.00
34)	Larry Doyle	150.00	60.00	35.00
35)	Hugh Duffy	300.00	120.00	70.00
36)	Jimmy Dygert	150.00	60.00	35.00
37)	Kid Elberfield (Elberfeld)	150.00	60.00	35.00
38)	Steve Evans	150.00	60.00	35.00
39)	Johnny Evers	300.00	120.00	70.00
40)	Bob Ewing	150.00	60.00	35.00
41)	Art Fletcher	150.00	60.00	35.00
42)	John Flynn	150.00	60.00	35.00
43)	Russ Ford	150.00	60.00	35.00
44)	Bill Foxen	150.00	60.00	35.00
45)	Art Fromme	150.00	60.00	35.00
46)	George Gibson	150.00	60.00	35.00
47)	Peaches Graham	150.00	60.00	35.00
48)	Eddie Grant	150.00	60.00	35.00
49)	Clark Griffith	300.00	120.00	70.00
50)	Topsy Hartsel	150.00	60.00	35.00
51)	Arnold Hauser	150.00	60.00	35.00
52)	Charlie Hemphill	150.00	60.00	35.00
53)	Dick Hoblitzell	150.00	60.00	35.00
54)	Miller Huggins	300.00	120.00	70.00
55)	John Hummel	150.00	60.00	35.00
56)	Walter Johnson	600.00	240.00	145.00
57)	Davy Jones	150.00	60.00	35.00
58)	Johnny Kling	150.00	60.00	35.00
59)	Jack Knight	150.00	60.00	35.00

		NM	EX	VG
(60)	Ed Konetchy	150.00	60.00	35.00
(61)	Harry Krause	150.00	60.00	35.00
(62)	Tommy Leach	150.00	60.00	35.00
(63)	Lefty Leifield	150.00	60.00	35.00
(64)	Hans Lobert	150.00	60.00	35.00
(65)	Rube Marquard	300.00	120.00	70.00
(66)	Christy Mathewson	750.00	300.00	180.00
(67)	Al Mattern	150.00	60.00	35.00
(68)	Amby McConnell	150.00	60.00	35.00
(69)	John McGraw	300.00	120.00	70.00
(70)	Harry McIntire (McIntyre)	150.00	60.00	35.00
(71)	Fred Merkle	150.00	60.00	35.00
(72)	Chief Meyers	150.00	60.00	35.00
(73)	Dots Miller	150.00	60.00	35.00
(74)	Mike Mitchell	150.00	60.00	35.00
(75)	Pat Moran	150.00	60.00	35.00
(76)	George Moriarty	150.00	60.00	35.00
(77)	George Mullin	150.00	60.00	35.00
(78)	Danny Murphy	150.00	60.00	35.00
(79)	Red Murray	150.00	60.00	35.00
(80)	Tom Needham	150.00	60.00	35.00
(81)	Rebel Oakes	150.00	60.00	35.00
(82)	Rube Oldring	150.00	60.00	35.00
(83)	Orval Overall	150.00	60.00	35.00
(84)	Fred Parent	150.00	60.00	35.00
(85)	Dode Paskert	150.00	60.00	35.00
(86)	Fred Payne	150.00	60.00	35.00
(87)	Barney Pelty	150.00	60.00	35.00
(88)	Deacon Phillippe	150.00	60.00	35.00
(89)	Jack Quinn	150.00	60.00	35.00
(90)	Bugs Raymond	150.00	60.00	35.00
(91)	Ed Reulbach	150.00	60.00	35.00
(92)	Jack Rowan	150.00	60.00	35.00
(93)	Nap Rucker	150.00	60.00	35.00
(94)	Doc Scanlon (Scanlan)	150.00	60.00	35.00
(95)	Germany Schaefer	150.00	60.00	35.00
(96)	Geo. Schlei	150.00	60.00	35.00
(97)	Wildfire Schulte	150.00	60.00	35.00
(98)	Dave Shean	150.00	60.00	35.00
(99)	Jimmy Sheckard	150.00	60.00	35.00
(100)	Happy Smith	150.00	60.00	35.00
(101)	Fred Snodgrass	150.00	60.00	35.00
(102)	Tris Speaker	400.00	160.00	95.00
(103)	Jake Stahl	150.00	60.00	35.00
(104)	Harry Steinfeldt	150.00	60.00	35.00
(105)	George Stone	150.00	60.00	35.00
(106)	Gabby Street	150.00	60.00	35.00
(107)	Ed Summers	150.00	60.00	35.00
(108)	Lee Tannehill	150.00	60.00	35.00
(109)	Joe Tinker	300.00	120.00	70.00
(110)	John Titus	150.00	60.00	35.00
(111)	Terry Turner	150.00	60.00	35.00
(112)	Bobby Wallace	300.00	120.00	70.00
(113)	Zack Wheat	300.00	120.00	70.00
(114)	Doc White (White Sox)	150.00	60.00	35.00
(115)	Kirby White (Pirates)	150.00	60.00	35.00
(116)	Ed Willett	150.00	60.00	35.00
(117)	Owen Wilson	150.00	60.00	35.00
(118)	Hooks Wiltse	150.00	60.00	35.00
(119)	Harry Wolter	150.00	60.00	35.00
(120)	Cy Young	750.00	300.00	180.00

1912 S81 Silks

The 1912 S81 "Silks," so-called because they featured pictures of baseball players on a satin-like fabric rather than paper or cardboard, are closely related to the better-known T3 Turkey Red cabinet cards of the same era. The silks, which featured 25 of the day's top baseball players among its other various subjects, were available as a premium with Helmar "Turkish Trophies" cigarettes. According to an advertising sheet, one silk could be obtained for 25 Helmar coupons. The silks measure about 6-3/4" x 8-3/4" and, with a few exceptions, used the same pictures featured on the popular Turkey Red cards. Five players (Rube Marquard, Rube Benton, Marty O'Toole, Grover Alexander and Russ Ford) appear in the "Silks" set that were not included in the T3 set. In addition, an error involving the Frank Baker card was corrected for the "Silks" set. (In the T3 set, Baker's card actually pictured Jack Barry.) Several years ago a pair of New England collectors found a small stack of Christy Mathewson "Silks," making his, by far, the most common. Otherwise, the "Silks" are generally so rare that it is difficult to determine the relative scarcity of the others. Baseball enthusiasts are usually only attracted to the 25 baseball players in the "Silks" premium set, but it is interesting to note that the promotion also offered dozens of other subjects, including "beautiful women in bathing and athletic costumes, charming dancers in gorgeous attire, natiional flags and generals on horseback."

		NM	EX	VG
Complete Set (25):		145,000	50,000	27,500
Common Player:		3,000	1,000	575.00
86	Rube Marquard	6,500	2,275	1,225

		NM	EX	VG
87	Marty O'Toole	3,000	1,000	575.00
88	Rube Benton	3,000	1,000	575.00
89	Grover Alexander	9,000	3,150	1,700
90	Russ Ford	3,000	1,000	575.00
91	John McGraw	6,500	2,275	1,225
92	Nap Rucker	3,000	1,000	575.00
93	Mike Mitchell	3,000	1,000	575.00
94	Chief Bender	6,500	2,275	1,225
95	Home Run Baker	6,500	2,275	1,225
96	Nap Lajoie	9,000	4,500	3,000
97	Joe Tinker	6,500	2,275	1,225
98	Sherry Magee	3,000	1,000	575.00
99	Howie Camnitz	3,000	1,000	575.00
100	Eddie Collins	6,500	2,275	1,225
101	Red Dooin	3,000	1,000	575.00
102	Ty Cobb	15,000	5,250	2,850
103	Hugh Jennings	6,500	2,275	1,225
104	Roger Bresnahan	6,500	2,275	1,225
105	Jake Stahl	3,000	1,000	575.00
106	Tris Speaker	10,000	5,000	3,000
107	Ed Walsh	6,500	2,275	1,225
108	Christy Mathewson	6,000	2,100	1,150
109	Johnny Evers	6,500	2,275	1,225
110	Walter Johnson	12,000	4,200	2,275

1912 S110 Baseball Player Silks Pillow Case

Closely related to the S81 silks, and issued as a premuim for 100 coupons, this approximately 23" x 23" pillow case shares the same designs as the individual silks of the players thereon. Cross-stich borders for the player images on the cloth pillow case would indicate the silks were meant to be sewn on as they were acquired. Besides the baseball players pillow cases, similar premiums are known for the other Turkey Red/Helmar silks — Indians, generals, etc.

		NM	EX	VG
(1)	Home Run Baker, Ty Cobb, Walter Johnson, Christy Mathewson, Tris Speaker	8,500	4,250	2,550
(2)	Home Run Baker, Ty Cobb, Christy Mathewson, Marty O'Toole, Tris Speaker	8,000	4,000	2,400

T

1928 Tabacalera la Morena

Believed to have been issued in El Salvador in the late 1920s, the extent of this card issue is not yet known. It is possible other American baseball players are included in the issue. Approximately 1-7/8" x 2-5/8", the cards are printed in black-and-white with some color tints added. The borderless front that includes the card number at bottom. Backs are printed in Spanish and repeat the card number along with player identification and a few words about the pictured players. An ad at bottom attributes the card (roughly): "Courtesy of Rich Brown Tobacco, the Champion among Consumers."

		NM	EX	VG
96	St. Louis Cardinals Team	100.00	50.00	30.00
97	Everett Scott	50.00	25.00	15.00
98	Babe Ruth	900.00	450.00	270.00
100	Lou Gehrig, Babe Ruth	500.00	250.00	150.00
101	George Kelly	100.00	50.00	30.00
103	Earl Webb	50.00	25.00	15.00

		NM	EX	VG
105	Ty Cobb, Babe Ruth	300.00	150.00	90.00
106	Jim Bottomley	100.00	50.00	30.00
107	Christy Mathewson, John McGraw	150.00	75.00	45.00
109	John J. Mc. Graw	100.00	50.00	30.00
110	Ullmann	50.00	25.00	15.00
111	Lee Todd, P Todd	50.00	25.00	15.00
114	St. Louis Cardinals/Brooklyn Robins	50.00	25.00	15.00
120	St. Louis Cardinals/Brooklyn Robins	50.00	25.00	15.00

1916 Tango Eggs

Ask your grocer for
"TANGO BRAND EGGS"
Every one guaranteed
to be of
"FINEST QUALITY"
Packed only by
L. FRANK & COMPANY
NEW ORLEANS, LA.

Chase, 1b. Cincinnati Nat'l.

Unknown until the discovery of a hoard of "fewer than 500" cards in 1991, this 18-card set was produced for L. Frank & Co. of New Orleans to be distributed in an as-yet unknown manner in connection with its Tango brand eggs. Similar in size (1-7/16" x 2-3/4") and format to contemporary caramel cards, the Tango set features familiar player pictures from those issues. In fact, several of the Tango cards have player designations which differ from the same pictures used in the E106 American Caramel issue of 1915. The Tango cards feature a glossy front surface, and are brightly colored. The hoard varied greatly in the number of each player's card. Some were found in quantities as low as one, while some were represented by more than 50 specimens. Because several of the cards exist in only a single specimen, no price for a complete set is quoted.

		NM	EX	VG
	Common Player:	240.00	95.00	50.00
(1)	Bob Bescher	240.00	95.00	50.00
(2)	Roger Bresnahan (Four known.)	2,400	960.00	480.00
(3)	Al Bridwell (Fewer than 10 known.)	870.00	350.00	175.00
(4)	Hal Chase	1,080	430.00	215.00
(5)	Ty Cobb (One known, VG, value undetermined.)			
(6)	Eddie Collins	2,250	1,125	750.00
(7)	Sam Crawford (Fewer than five known.)	2,400	960.00	480.00
(8)	Red Dooin	850.00	425.00	285.00
(9)	Johnny Evers (One known, G/VG, value undetermined.)			
(10)	Happy Felsch (Picture actually Ray Demmitt.) (2-3 known)	2,880	1,150	575.00
(11)	Hughie Jennings (20 known)	660.00	265.00	135.00
(12)	George McQuillen	775.00	400.00	260.00
(13)	Billy Meyer (Picture actually Fred Jacklitsch.)	775.00	400.00	260.00
(14)	Ray Morgan (Picture actually Mike Doolan.) (2-3 known)	1,920	770.00	385.00
(15)	Danny Murphy	485.00	245.00	160.00
(16)	Germany Schaefer (1-2 known)	2,400	960.00	480.00
(17)	Buck Weaver (Picture actually Joe Tinker.)	1,500	600.00	300.00
(28)	Heinie Zimmerman (Fewer than 10 known.)	870.00	350.00	175.00

1934 Tarzan Bread (D382)

TARZAN
thoro BREAD
BUILDS CHAMPIONS

CLYDE J. MANION
CINCINNATI REDS

A catcher obtained by the Cincinnati team from Milwaukee in 1932 by draft.

He is 37 years old, weighs 175 pounds, and is 5 feet, 11 inches in height. He makes his home at Detroit, Michigan.

He bats and throws right-handed. Last season he batted .167 for 56 games and had a fielding average of .981.

Among the rarest issues of the 1930s is this set sponsored by an unusually named brand of bread from a bakery whose location is unknown. The cards are printed in black-and-white in 2-1/4" x 3-1/4" format. Borderless front photos have the player name in capital letters. Backs have the sponsor's name and a short career summary. Some cards have a red "TROPHY" sticker at top on back, covering the "TARZAN". The checklist here, almost certainly incomplete, is arranged alphabetically; the cards are unnumbered.

		NM	EX	VG
	Common Player:	3,250	1,600	975.00
(1)	Sparky Adams	3,250	1,600	975.00
(2)	Walter Betts	3,250	1,600	975.00
(3)	George Blaeholder	3,250	1,600	975.00
(4)	Ed Brandt	3,250	1,600	975.00
(5)	Tommy Bridges	3,250	1,600	975.00
(6)	Irving "Jack" Burns	3,250	1,600	975.00
(7)	Bruce Campbell	3,250	1,600	975.00
(8)	Tex Carleton	3,250	1,600	975.00
(9)	Dick Coffman	3,250	1,600	975.00
(10)	George Connally	3,250	1,600	975.00
(11)	Tony Cuccinello	3,250	1,600	975.00
(12)	Debs Garms	3,250	1,600	975.00
(13)	Milt Gaston	3,250	1,600	975.00
(14)	Bill Hallahan	3,250	1,600	975.00
(15)	Myril Hoag	3,250	1,600	975.00
(16)	Chief Hogsett	3,250	1,600	975.00
(17)	Arndt Jorgens	3,250	1,600	975.00
(18)	Willie Kamm	3,250	1,600	975.00
(19)	Dutch Leonard	3,250	1,600	975.00
(20)	Clyde Manion	3,250	1,600	975.00
(21)	Eric McNair	3,250	1,600	975.00
(22)	Oscar Melillo	3,250	1,600	975.00
(23)	Randy Moore	3,250	1,600	975.00
(24)	Bob O'Farrell	3,250	1,600	975.00
(25)	Gus Suhr	3,250	1,600	975.00
(26)	Evar Swanson	3,250	1,600	975.00
(27)	Billy Urbanski	3,250	1,600	975.00
(28)	Johnny Vergez	3,250	1,600	975.00
(29)	Robert Worthington	3,250	1,600	975.00
(30)	Tom Zachary	3,250	1,600	975.00

1969 Tasco All-Star Collection Caricatures

This set of large - 11-1/2" x 16" - player posters features colorful caricatures with an emphasis on Tigers players, befitting the Detroit address of the publisher. Licensed by MLBPA, the pictures are listed here alphabetically. They were originally sold for less than $1 apiece.

		NM	EX	VG
	Complete Set (46):	450.00	225.00	135.00
	Common Player:	7.50	3.75	2.25
(1)	Hank Aaron	35.00	17.50	10.50
(2)	Richie Allen	12.50	6.25	3.75
(3)	Luis Aparicio	17.50	8.75	5.25
(4)	Ernie Banks	25.00	12.50	7.50
(5)	Glenn Beckert	7.50	3.75	2.25
(6)	Johnny Bench	20.00	10.00	6.00
(7)	Norm Cash	10.00	5.00	3.00
(8)	Danny Cater	7.50	3.75	2.25
(9)	Pat Dobson	7.50	3.75	2.25
(10)	Don Drysdale	17.50	8.75	5.25
(11)	Bill Freehan	7.50	3.75	2.25
(12)	Jim Fregosi	7.50	3.75	2.25
(13)	Bob Gibson	17.50	8.75	5.25
(14)	Bill Hands	7.50	3.75	2.25
(15)	Ken Holtzman	7.50	3.75	2.25
(16)	Willie Horton	7.50	3.75	2.25
(17)	Frank Howard	9.00	4.50	2.75
(18)	Randy Hundley	7.50	3.75	2.25
(19)	Ferguson Jenkins	17.50	8.75	5.25
(20)	Al Kaline	25.00	12.50	7.50
(21)	Don Kessinger	7.50	3.75	2.25
(22)	Jerry Koosman	7.50	3.75	2.25
(23)	Mickey Lolich	7.50	3.75	2.25
(24)	Juan Marichal	17.50	8.75	5.25
(25)	Willie Mays	35.00	17.50	10.50
(26)	Bill Mazeroski	17.50	8.75	5.25
(27)	Dick McAuliffe	7.50	3.75	2.25
(28)	Denny McLain	7.50	3.75	2.25
(29)	Dave McNally	7.50	3.75	2.25
(30)	Jim Northrup	7.50	3.75	2.25
(31)	Tony Oliva	9.00	4.50	2.75
(32)	Adolfo Phillips	7.50	3.75	2.25
(33)	Jim Price	7.50	3.75	2.25
(34)	Brooks Robinson	20.00	10.00	6.00
(35)	Pete Rose	35.00	17.50	10.50
(36)	Ron Santo	15.00	7.50	4.50
(37)	Joe Sparma	7.50	3.75	2.25
(38)	Mickey Stanley	7.50	3.75	2.25
(39)	Mel Stottlemyre	7.50	3.75	2.25
(40)	Luis Tiant	7.50	3.75	2.25
(41)	Joe Torre	9.00	4.50	2.75
(42)	Dick Tracewski	7.50	3.75	2.25
(43)	Don Wert	7.50	3.75	2.25
(44)	Billy Williams	17.50	8.75	5.25
(45)	Earl Wilson	7.50	3.75	2.25
(46)	Carl Yastrzemski	25.00	12.50	7.50

1970 Tasco Caricatures

JIM "CATFISH" HUNTER

This group of colorful player caricatures was sold in a four-pack featuring two each baseball and football players. The 8-1/2" x 10-7/8" blank-back pictures have central images surrounded by colorful borders.

		NM	EX	VG
	Complete Set (4):	150.00	75.00	45.00
	Common Player:	40.00	20.00	12.00
(1)	Jim "Catfish" Hunter	40.00	20.00	12.00
(2)	Al Kaline	50.00	25.00	15.00
(3)	Joe Namath	75.00	37.00	22.00
(4)	O.J. Simpson	50.00	25.00	15.00

1933 Tattoo Orbit (R305)

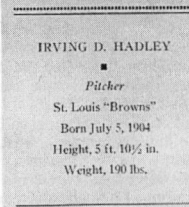

IRVING D. HADLEY
Pitcher
St. Louis "Browns"
Born July 5, 1904
Height, 5 ft. 10½ in.
Weight, 190 lbs.

Found in 1¢ packages of Tattoo gum, these 2" x 2-1/4" cards were produced by the Orbit Gum Co., of Chicago, a subsidiary of Wrigley's. Fronts feature a black-and-white photo which is tinted to give the skin some color. Stylized ballpark backgrounds are separated from the photograph by a black line. The rest of the background is printed in vivid red, yellow and green. Backs have player identification and vitals. Cards of Bump Hadley and George Blaeholder are the most elusive, followed by those of Ivy Andrews and Rogers Hornsby.

		NM	EX	VG
	Complete Set (60):	24,000	12,000	7,200
	Common Player:	300.00	150.00	100.00
(1)	Dale Alexander	300.00	150.00	100.00
(2)	Ivy Paul Andrews	1,100	550.00	330.00
(3)	Earl Averill	480.00	240.00	150.00
(4)	Richard Bartell	300.00	150.00	100.00
(5)	Walter Berger	300.00	150.00	100.00
(6)	George F. Blaeholder	1,200	600.00	360.00
(7)	Irving J. Burns	300.00	150.00	100.00
(8)	Guy T. Bush	300.00	150.00	100.00
(9)	Bruce D. Campbell	300.00	150.00	100.00
(10)	William Cissell	300.00	150.00	100.00
(11)	Lefty Clark	300.00	150.00	100.00
(12)	Mickey Cochrane	480.00	240.00	150.00
(13)	Phil Collins	300.00	150.00	100.00
(14)	Hazen Kiki Cuyler	480.00	240.00	150.00
(15)	Dizzy Dean	700.00	350.00	225.00
(16)	Jimmy Dykes	300.00	150.00	100.00
(17)	George L. Earnshaw	300.00	150.00	100.00
(18)	Woody English	300.00	150.00	100.00
(19)	Lewis A. Fonseca	300.00	150.00	100.00
(20)	Jimmy Foxx	900.00	450.00	270.00
(21)	Burleigh A. Grimes	480.00	240.00	150.00
(22)	Charles John Grimm	300.00	150.00	100.00
(23)	Robert M. Grove	600.00	300.00	180.00
(24)	Frank Grube	300.00	150.00	100.00
(25)	George W. Haas	300.00	150.00	100.00
(26)	Irving D. Hadley	1,200	600.00	360.00
(27)	Chick Hafey	480.00	240.00	150.00
(28)	Jesse Joseph Haines	480.00	240.00	150.00
(29)	William Hallahan	300.00	150.00	100.00
(30)	Melvin Harder	300.00	150.00	100.00
(31)	Gabby Hartnett	480.00	240.00	150.00
(32)	Babe Herman	300.00	150.00	100.00
(33)	William Herman	480.00	240.00	150.00
(34)	Rogers Hornsby	1,450	720.00	450.00
(35)	Roy C. Johnson	300.00	150.00	100.00
(36)	J. Smead Jolley	300.00	150.00	100.00
(37)	William Jurges	300.00	150.00	100.00
(38)	William Kamm	300.00	150.00	100.00
(39)	Mark A. Koenig	300.00	150.00	100.00
(40)	James J. Levey	550.00	275.00	200.00
(41)	Ernie Lombardi	480.00	240.00	150.00
(42)	Red Lucas	300.00	150.00	100.00
(43)	Ted Lyons	480.00	240.00	150.00
(44)	Connie Mack	480.00	240.00	150.00
(45)	Pat Malone	300.00	150.00	100.00
(46)	Pepper Martin	400.00	200.00	120.00
(47)	Marty McManus	300.00	150.00	100.00
(48)	Frank J. O'Doul	420.00	210.00	140.00
(49)	Richard Porter	300.00	150.00	100.00
(50)	Carl N. Reynolds	300.00	150.00	100.00
(51)	Charles Henry Root	300.00	150.00	100.00

		NM	EX	VG
(52)	Robert Seeds	300.00	150.00	100.00
(53)	Al H. Simmons	480.00	240.00	150.00
(54)	Jackson Riggs Stephenson	300.00	150.00	100.00
(55)	Bud Tinning	300.00	150.00	100.00
(56)	Joe Vosmik	300.00	150.00	100.00
(57)	Rube Walberg	300.00	150.00	100.00
(58)	Paul Waner	480.00	240.00	150.00
(59)	Lonnie Warneke	300.00	150.00	100.00
(60)	Arthur C. Whitney	300.00	150.00	100.00

1933 Tattoo Orbit (R308)

This obscure set of cards, issued with Tattoo Orbit gum, is numbered from 151 through 207, with a few of the numbers still unknown. Most surviving examples measure 1-7/8" x 1-1/4," but larger pieces (2-1/2" x 3-7/8") are also known with the same players and numbers. The player pictures on the cards "developed" when moistened and rubbed with a piece of blotting paper. Besides the baseball players, there were also pictures of movie stars and other celebrities.

		NM	EX	VG
Common Player:		200.00	90.00	50.00
Large-Format: 4X				
151	Vernon Gomez	500.00	225.00	125.00
152	Kiki Cuyler	500.00	225.00	125.00
153	Jimmy Foxx	850.00	380.00	210.00
154	Al Simmons	500.00	225.00	125.00
155	Chas. J. Grimm	200.00	90.00	50.00
156	William Jurges	200.00	90.00	50.00
157	Chuck Klein	500.00	225.00	125.00
158	Richard Bartell	200.00	90.00	50.00
159	Pepper Martin	275.00	125.00	69.00
160	Earl Averill	500.00	225.00	125.00
161	William Dickey	500.00	225.00	125.00
162	Wesley Ferrell	200.00	90.00	50.00
163	Oral Hildebrand	200.00	90.00	50.00
164	Wm. Kamm	200.00	90.00	50.00
165	Earl Whitehill	200.00	90.00	50.00
166	Charles Fullis	200.00	90.00	50.00
167	Jimmy Dykes	200.00	90.00	50.00
168	Ben Cantwell	200.00	90.00	50.00
169	George Earnshaw	200.00	90.00	50.00
170	Jackson Stephenson	200.00	90.00	50.00
171	Randolph Moore	200.00	90.00	50.00
172	Ted Lyons	500.00	225.00	125.00
173	Goose Goslin	500.00	225.00	125.00
174	E. Swanson	200.00	90.00	50.00
175	Lee Roy Mahaffey	200.00	90.00	50.00
176	Joe Cronin	500.00	225.00	125.00
177	Tom Bridges	200.00	90.00	50.00
178	Henry Manush	500.00	225.00	125.00
179	Walter Stewart	200.00	90.00	50.00
180	Frank Pytlak	200.00	90.00	50.00
181	Dale Alexander	200.00	90.00	50.00
182	Robert Grove	600.00	270.00	150.00
183	Charles Gehringer	500.00	225.00	125.00
184	Lewis Fonseca	200.00	90.00	50.00
185	Alvin Crowder	200.00	90.00	50.00
186	Mickey Cochrane	500.00	225.00	125.00
187	Max Bishop	200.00	90.00	50.00
188	Connie Mack	500.00	225.00	125.00
189	Guy Bush	200.00	90.00	50.00
190	Charlie Root	200.00	90.00	50.00
191a	Burleigh Grimes	500.00	225.00	125.00
191b	Gabby Hartnett	500.00	225.00	125.00
192	Pat Malone	200.00	90.00	50.00
193	Woody English	200.00	90.00	50.00
194	Lonnie Warneke	200.00	90.00	50.00
195	Babe Herman	275.00	125.00	69.00
196	Unknown			
197	Unknown			
198	Unknown			
199	Unknown			
200	Gabby Hartnett	500.00	225.00	125.00
201	Paul Waner	500.00	225.00	125.00
202	Dizzy Dean	750.00	335.00	185.00
203	Unknown			
204	Unknown			
205	Jim Bottomley	500.00	225.00	125.00
206	Unknown			
207	Charles Hafey	500.00	225.00	125.00
208	Unknown			
209	Unknown			
210	Unknown			

1907-09 H.M. Taylor Detroit Tigers Postcards

Various players and groups of players are featured in this issue of hometown heroes from H. M. Taylor in Detroit. The 5-1/2" 3-1/2" black-and-white cards have white borders on front. Undided backs have a gothic "Post Card" at top, a one-cent stamp box and, at bottom-left, "Rights reserved by H. M. Taylor, Detroit."

		NM	EX	VG
Complete Set (7):		5,000	2,500	1,500
Common Card:		525.00	260.00	150.00
(1)	Tyrus Cobb (At bat.)	1,800	900.00	550.00
(2)	Bill Coughlin/Btg	525.00	260.00	150.00
(3)	Sam Crawford (Ready for the Ball.)	750.00	375.00	225.00
(4)	Detroit Club (Team photo.)	850.00	425.00	250.00
(5)	Wild Bill Donovan (Floral horseshoe presented at Philadelphia.)	525.00	260.00	150.00
(6)	Hughie Jennings ("WEE'AH")	525.00	260.00	150.00
(7)	Hughie Jennings, Wild Bill Donovan, Frank Chance (In dugout.)	525.00	260.00	150.00

1972 TCMA The 1930's

Extending to over 500 cards, this was one of TCMA's first ventures into the business of creating collectors' edition card sets of former players. Over the length of the series there were a number of style differences. The set was issued in 21 series of 24 cards each. All cards were printed in black-and-white (except for Series 18-19 printed in blue) and feature player photos on usually borderless fronts. Dimensions were about 2" x 2-3/4" for most series, with Series 15-16 in a 2-1/2" x 3-1/2" format. Except for a TCMA copyright line on some of the earlier cards, there is no other printing on front. Backs have player identification, team affiliations, TCMA copyright and, after #72, a card number. Production is reported as 1,000 sets. Blank-bank versions and uncut panels of 12 exist.

		NM	EX	VG
Complete Set (504):		400.00	200.00	120.00
Common Player:		3.00	1.50	.90
(1)	Roy Bell	3.00	1.50	.90
(2)	Max Bishop	3.00	1.50	.90
(3)	Bob Boken	3.00	1.50	.90
(4)	Cliff Bolton	3.00	1.50	.90
(5)	John Broaca	3.00	1.50	.90
(6)	Bill Brubaker	3.00	1.50	.90
(7)	Slick Castleman	3.00	1.50	.90
(8)	Dick Coffman	3.00	1.50	.90
(9)	Phil Collins	3.00	1.50	.90
(10)	Earle Combs	3.00	1.50	.90
(11)	Doc Cramer	3.00	1.50	.90
(12)	Joe Cronin	3.00	1.50	.90
(13)	Jack Crouch	3.00	1.50	.90
(14)	Tony Cuccinello	3.00	1.50	.90
(15)	Babe Dahlgren	3.00	1.50	.90
(16)	Spud Davis	3.00	1.50	.90
(17)	Dizzy Dean	6.00	3.00	1.75
(18)	Paul Dean	3.00	1.50	.90
(19)	Bill Dickey	3.00	1.50	.90
(20)	Joe DiMaggio	10.00	5.00	3.00
(21)	George Earnshaw	3.00	1.50	.90
(22)	Woody English	3.00	1.50	.90
(23)	Woody English	3.00	1.50	.90
(24)	Hal Finney	3.00	1.50	.90
(25)	Freddie Fitzsimmons, Bump Hadley	3.00	1.50	.90
(26)	Tony Freitas	3.00	1.50	.90
(27)	Frank Frisch	3.00	1.50	.90
(28)	Milt Gaston	3.00	1.50	.90
(29)	Sid Gautreaux	3.00	1.50	.90
(30)	Charlie Gehringer	3.00	1.50	.90
(31)	Charley Gelbert	3.00	1.50	.90
(32)	Lefty Gomez	3.00	1.50	.90
(33)	Lefty Grove	5.00	2.50	1.50
(34)	Chick Hafey	3.00	1.50	.90
(35)	Jesse Haines	3.00	1.50	.90
(36)	Bill Hallahan	3.00	1.50	.90
(37)	Bucky Harris	3.00	1.50	.90
(38)	Ed Heusser	3.00	1.50	.90
(39)	Carl Hubbell	3.00	1.50	.90
(40)	Carl Hubbell	3.00	1.50	.90

		NM	EX	VG
(41)	Jimmy Jordan	3.00	1.50	.90
(42)	Joe Judge	3.00	1.50	.90
(43)	Len Koenecke	3.00	1.50	.90
(44)	Mark Koenig	3.00	1.50	.90
(45)	Cookie Lavagetto	3.00	1.50	.90
(46)	Roxie Lawson	3.00	1.50	.90
(47)	Tony Lazzeri	3.00	1.50	.90
(48)	Gus Mancuso	3.00	1.50	.90
(49)	John McCarthy	3.00	1.50	.90
(50)	Joe Medwick	3.00	1.50	.90
(51)	Cliff Melton	3.00	1.50	.90
(52)	Terry Moore	3.00	1.50	.90
(53)	John Murphy	3.00	1.50	.90
(54)	Ken O'Dea	3.00	1.50	.90
(55)	Bob O'Farrell	3.00	1.50	.90
(56)	Manuel Onis	3.00	1.50	.90
(57)	Monte Pearson	3.00	1.50	.90
(58)	Paul Richards	3.00	1.50	.90
(59)	Max Rosenfeld	6.00	3.00	1.75
(60)	Red Ruffing	3.00	1.50	.90
(61)	Red Ruffing	3.00	1.50	.90
(62)	Hal Schumacher	3.00	1.50	.90
(63)	George Selkirk	3.00	1.50	.90
(64)	Joe Shaute	3.00	1.50	.90
(65)	Gordon Slade	3.00	1.50	.90
(66)	Lindo Storti	3.00	1.50	.90
(67)	Smokey Sundra	3.00	1.50	.90
(68)	Bill Terry	3.00	1.50	.90
(69)	Jack Tising	3.00	1.50	.90
(70)	Sandy Vance	3.00	1.50	.90
(71)	Rube Walberg	3.00	1.50	.90
(72)	Sammy West	3.00	1.50	.90
73	Vito Tamulis	3.00	1.50	.90
74	Kemp Wicker	3.00	1.50	.90
75	Bob Seeds	3.00	1.50	.90
76	Jack Saltzgaver	3.00	1.50	.90
77	Walter Brown	3.00	1.50	.90
78	Spud Chandler	3.00	1.50	.90
79	Myril Hoag	3.00	1.50	.90
80	Joe Glenn	3.00	1.50	.90
81	Lefty Gomez	3.00	1.50	.90
82	Arndt Jorgens	3.00	1.50	.90
83	Jesse Hill	3.00	1.50	.90
84	Red Rolfe	3.00	1.50	.90
85	Wes Ferrell	3.00	1.50	.90
86	Joe Morrissey	3.00	1.50	.90
87	Tony Piet	3.00	1.50	.90
88	Fred Walker	3.00	1.50	.90
89	Bill Dietrich	3.00	1.50	.90
90	Lyn Lary	3.00	1.50	.90
91	Lyn Lary	3.00	1.50	.90
92	Lyn Lary	3.00	1.50	.90
93	Lyn Lary	3.00	1.50	.90
94	Buzz Boyle	3.00	1.50	.90
95	Tony Malinosky	3.00	1.50	.90
96	Al Lopez	3.00	1.50	.90
97	Linus Frey	3.00	1.50	.90
98	Tony Malinosky	3.00	1.50	.90
99	Owen Carroll	3.00	1.50	.90
100	Buddy Hassett	3.00	1.50	.90
101	Gib Brack	3.00	1.50	.90
102	Sam Leslie	3.00	1.50	.90
103	Fred Heimach	3.00	1.50	.90
104	Burleigh Grimes	3.00	1.50	.90
105	Ray Benge	3.00	1.50	.90
106	Joe Stripp	3.00	1.50	.90
107	Joe Becker	3.00	1.50	.90
108	Oscar Melillo	3.00	1.50	.90
109	Charley O'Leary, Rogers Hornsby	3.00	1.50	.90
110	Luke Appling	3.00	1.50	.90
111	Stan Hack	3.00	1.50	.90
112	Ray Hayworth	3.00	1.50	.90
113	Charles Wilson	3.00	1.50	.90
114	Hal Trosky	3.00	1.50	.90
115	Wes Ferrell	3.00	1.50	.90
116	Lyn Lary	3.00	1.50	.90
117	Milt Gaston	3.00	1.50	.90
118	Eldon Auker	3.00	1.50	.90
119	Heinie Manush	3.00	1.50	.90
120	Jimmie Foxx	6.00	3.00	1.75
121	Don Heffner	3.00	1.50	.90
122	George Pipgras	3.00	1.50	.90
123	Bump Hadley	3.00	1.50	.90
124	Tommy Henrich	3.00	1.50	.90
125	Joe McCarthy	3.00	1.50	.90
126	Joe Sewell	3.00	1.50	.90
127	Frank Crosetti	3.00	1.50	.90
128	Fred Walker	3.00	1.50	.90
129	Ted Kleinhans	3.00	1.50	.90
130	Jake Powell	3.00	1.50	.90
131	Ben Chapman	3.00	1.50	.90
132	John Murphy	3.00	1.50	.90
133	Lon Warneke	3.00	1.50	.90
134	Augie Galan	3.00	1.50	.90
135	Gene Lillard	3.00	1.50	.90
136	Stan Hack	3.00	1.50	.90
137	Frank Demaree	3.00	1.50	.90
138	Tony Piet	3.00	1.50	.90
139	Tony Piet	3.00	1.50	.90
140	Don Brennan	3.00	1.50	.90
141	Hal Schumacher, Lefty Gomez	3.00	1.50	.90
142	Bump Hadley	3.00	1.50	.90
143	Ollie Bejma	3.00	1.50	.90
144	Jim Bottomley	3.00	1.50	.90
145	Clay Bryant	3.00	1.50	.90
146	Charlie Grimm	3.00	1.50	.90
147	Flea Clifton	3.00	1.50	.90
148	Rollie Stiles	3.00	1.50	.90
149	Al Simmons	3.00	1.50	.90
150	Al Simmons	3.00	1.50	.90
151	Lyn Lary	3.00	1.50	.90
152	Roy Weatherly	3.00	1.50	.90
153	Whit Wyatt	3.00	1.50	.90
154	Oscar Vitt	3.00	1.50	.90
155	Jack Kroner	3.00	1.50	.90
156	Ted Lyons	3.00	1.50	.90
157	Joe Malay	3.00	1.50	.90

#	Name			
158	John McCarthy	3.00	1.50	.90
159	Hy Vandenberg	3.00	1.50	.90
160	Hank Leiber	3.00	1.50	.90
161	Joe Moore	3.00	1.50	.90
162	Cliff Melton	3.00	1.50	.90
163	Harry Danning	3.00	1.50	.90
164	Ray Harrell	3.00	1.50	.90
165	Bruce Ogrodowski	3.00	1.50	.90
166	Leo Durocher	3.00	1.50	.90
167	Leo Durocher	3.00	1.50	.90
168	William Walker	3.00	1.50	.90
169	Alvin Crowder	3.00	1.50	.90
170	Gus Suhr	3.00	1.50	.90
171	Monty Stratton	4.50	2.25	1.25
172	Boze Berger	3.00	1.50	.90
173	John Whitehead	3.00	1.50	.90
174	Joe Heving	3.00	1.50	.90
175	Merv Shea	3.00	1.50	.90
176	Ed Durham	3.00	1.50	.90
177	Buddy Myer	3.00	1.50	.90
178	Earl Whitehill	3.00	1.50	.90
179	Joe Cronin	3.00	1.50	.90
180	Zeke Bonura	3.00	1.50	.90
181	John Knott	3.00	1.50	.90
182	John Allen	3.00	1.50	.90
183	William Knickerbocker	3.00	1.50	.90
184	Earl Averill	3.00	1.50	.90
185	Bob Feller	4.50	2.25	1.25
186	Steve O'Neill	3.00	1.50	.90
187	Bruce Campbell	3.00	1.50	.90
188	Ivy Andrews	3.00	1.50	.90
189	Ivy Andrews	3.00	1.50	.90
190	Muddy Ruel	3.00	1.50	.90
191	Art Scharein	3.00	1.50	.90
192	Merv Shea	3.00	1.50	.90
193	George Myatt	3.00	1.50	.90
194	Bill Werber	3.00	1.50	.90
195	Red Lucas	3.00	1.50	.90
196	Hugh Luby	3.00	1.50	.90
197	Vic Sorrell	3.00	1.50	.90
198	Mickey Cochrane	3.00	1.50	.90
199	Rudy York	3.00	1.50	.90
200	Ray Mack	3.00	1.50	.90
201	Vince DiMaggio	4.50	2.25	1.25
202	Mel Ott	4.50	2.25	1.25
203	John Lucadello	3.00	1.50	.90
204	Debs Garms	3.00	1.50	.90
205	John Murphy, Pat Malone, Bump Hadley, Kemp Wicker, John Broaca	3.00	1.50	.90
206	Stan Sperry	3.00	1.50	.90
207	Hal Schumacher	3.00	1.50	.90
208	Blondy Ryan	3.00	1.50	.90
209	Bob Seeds	3.00	1.50	.90
210	Danny MacFayden	3.00	1.50	.90
211	Fran Healy	3.00	1.50	.90
212	Al Spohrer	3.00	1.50	.90
213	Ed Linke	3.00	1.50	.90
214	Joe Schultz	3.00	1.50	.90
215	Casey Stengel	3.00	1.50	.90
216	Casey Stengel	3.00	1.50	.90
217	Phil Hensick	3.00	1.50	.90
218	Rollie Hemsley	3.00	1.50	.90
219	Ace Parker	4.50	2.25	1.25
220	Henry Helf	3.00	1.50	.90
221	Bill Schuster	3.00	1.50	.90
222	Heinie Schuble	3.00	1.50	.90
223	John Salveson	3.00	1.50	.90
224	Robert Grace	3.00	1.50	.90
225	Sig Gryska	3.00	1.50	.90
226	Mickey Haslin	3.00	1.50	.90
227	Randy Gumpert	3.00	1.50	.90
228	Frank Gustine	3.00	1.50	.90
229	Marv Gudat	3.00	1.50	.90
230	Bob Logan	3.00	1.50	.90
231	Marvin Owen	3.00	1.50	.90
232	Bucky Walters	3.00	1.50	.90
233	Marty Hopkins	3.00	1.50	.90
234	Jimmy Dykes	3.00	1.50	.90
235	Lefty O'Doul	3.00	1.50	.90
236	Larry Rosenthal	3.00	1.50	.90
237	Mickey Haslin	3.00	1.50	.90
238	Eugene Schott	3.00	1.50	.90
239	Sad Sam Jones	3.00	1.50	.90
240	Edwin Rommel	3.00	1.50	.90
241	Rip Collins	3.00	1.50	.90
242	Rosy Ryan	3.00	1.50	.90
243	James Bucher	3.00	1.50	.90
244	Ethan Allen	3.00	1.50	.90
245	Dick Bartell	3.00	1.50	.90
246	Henry Leiber	3.00	1.50	.90
247	Lou Chiozza	3.00	1.50	.90
248	Babe Herman	3.00	1.50	.90
249	Tommy Henrich	3.00	1.50	.90
250	Thornton Lee	3.00	1.50	.90
251	Joe Kuhel	3.00	1.50	.90
252	George Pipgras	3.00	1.50	.90
253	Luke Sewell	3.00	1.50	.90
254	Tony Lazzeri	3.00	1.50	.90
255	Ival Goodman	3.00	1.50	.90
256	George Rensa	3.00	1.50	.90
257	Hal Newhouser	3.00	1.50	.90
258	Rogers Hornsby	5.00	2.50	1.50
259	Tuck Stainback	3.00	1.50	.90
260	Vance Page	3.00	1.50	.90
261	Art Scharein	3.00	1.50	.90
262	Mike Ryba	3.00	1.50	.90
263	James Lindsey	3.00	1.50	.90
264	Ed Parsons	3.00	1.50	.90
265	Elon Hogsett	3.00	1.50	.90
266	Bud Hafey	3.00	1.50	.90
267	John Gill	3.00	1.50	.90
268	Owen Bush	3.00	1.50	.90
269	Ethan Allen	3.00	1.50	.90
270	Jim Bagby	3.00	1.50	.90
271	Bill Atwood	3.00	1.50	.90
272	Phil Cavarretta	3.00	1.50	.90
273	Travis Jackson	3.00	1.50	.90
274	Ted Olson	3.00	1.50	.90
275	Boze Berger	3.00	1.50	.90
276	Norb Kleinke	3.00	1.50	.90
277	Rip Radcliff	3.00	1.50	.90
278	Mule Haas	3.00	1.50	.90
279	Julius Solters	3.00	1.50	.90
280	Ivey Shiver	3.00	1.50	.90
281	Wes Schulmerich	3.00	1.50	.90
282	Ray Kolp	3.00	1.50	.90
283	Si Johnson	3.00	1.50	.90
284	Al Hollingsworth	3.00	1.50	.90
285	D'Arcy Flowers	3.00	1.50	.90
286	Adam Comorosky	3.00	1.50	.90
287	Allen Cooke	3.00	1.50	.90
288	Clyde Kimsey	3.00	1.50	.90
289	Fred Ostermueller	3.00	1.50	.90
290	Angelo Giuliani	3.00	1.50	.90
291	John Wilson	3.00	1.50	.90
292	George Dickman	3.00	1.50	.90
293	Jim DeShong	3.00	1.50	.90
294	Red Evans	3.00	1.50	.90
295	Curtis Davis	3.00	1.50	.90
296	Charlie Berry	3.00	1.50	.90
297	George Gibson	3.00	1.50	.90
298	Fern Bell	3.00	1.50	.90
299	Irv Bartling	3.00	1.50	.90
300	Babe Barna	3.00	1.50	.90
301	Henry Johnson	3.00	1.50	.90
302	Harlond Clift	3.00	1.50	.90
303	Lu Blue	3.00	1.50	.90
304	George Hockette	3.00	1.50	.90
305	Walt Bashore	3.00	1.50	.90
306	Walter Beck	3.00	1.50	.90
307	Jewel Ens	3.00	1.50	.90
308	Doc Prothro	3.00	1.50	.90
309	Morrie Arnovich	3.00	1.50	.90
310	Bill Killefer	3.00	1.50	.90
311	Pete Appleton	3.00	1.50	.90
312	Fred Archer	3.00	1.50	.90
313	Bill Lohrman	3.00	1.50	.90
314	Fred Haney	3.00	1.50	.90
315	Jimmy Ripple	3.00	1.50	.90
316	Johnny Kerr	3.00	1.50	.90
317	Harry Gumbert	3.00	1.50	.90
318	Samuel Derringer	3.00	1.50	.90
319	Firpo Marberry	3.00	1.50	.90
320	Waite Hoyt	3.00	1.50	.90
321	Rick Ferrell	3.00	1.50	.90
322	Hank Greenberg	6.00	3.00	1.75
323	Carl Reynolds	3.00	1.50	.90
324	Roy Johnson	3.00	1.50	.90
325	Gil English	3.00	1.50	.90
326	Al Smith	3.00	1.50	.90
327	Dolph Camilli	3.00	1.50	.90
328	Oscar Grimes	3.00	1.50	.90
329	Ray Berres	3.00	1.50	.90
330	Norm Schlueter	3.00	1.50	.90
331	Joe Vosmik	3.00	1.50	.90
332	Jimmy Dykes	3.00	1.50	.90
333	Vern Washington	3.00	1.50	.90
334	"Bad News" Hale	3.00	1.50	.90
335	Lew Fonseca	3.00	1.50	.90
336	Mike Kreevich	3.00	1.50	.90
337	Bob Johnson	3.00	1.50	.90
338	"Jeep" Handley	3.00	1.50	.90
339	Gabby Hartnett	3.00	1.50	.90
340	Freddie Lindstrom	3.00	1.50	.90
341	Bert Haas	3.00	1.50	.90
342	Elbie Fletcher	3.00	1.50	.90
343	Tom Hafey	3.00	1.50	.90
344	Rip Collins	3.00	1.50	.90
345	John Babich	3.00	1.50	.90
346	Joe Beggs	3.00	1.50	.90
347	Bobo Newsom	3.00	1.50	.90
348	Wally Berger	3.00	1.50	.90
349	Bud Thomas	3.00	1.50	.90
350	Tom Heath	3.00	1.50	.90
351	Cecil Travis	3.00	1.50	.90
352	Jack Redmond	3.00	1.50	.90
353	Fred Schulte	3.00	1.50	.90
354	Pat Malone	3.00	1.50	.90
355	Hugh Critz	3.00	1.50	.90
356	Frank Pytlak	3.00	1.50	.90
357	Glenn Liebhardt	3.00	1.50	.90
358	Al Milnar	3.00	1.50	.90
359	Al Benton	3.00	1.50	.90
360	Moe Berg	6.00	3.00	1.75
361	Al Brancato	3.00	1.50	.90
362	Mark Christman	3.00	1.50	.90
363	Fabian Gaffke	3.00	1.50	.90
364	George Gill	3.00	1.50	.90
365	Oral Hildebrand	3.00	1.50	.90
366	Lou Fette	3.00	1.50	.90
367	Tex Carleton	3.00	1.50	.90
368	Don Gutteridge	3.00	1.50	.90
369	Pete Fox	3.00	1.50	.90
370	George Blaeholder	3.00	1.50	.90
371	George Caster	3.00	1.50	.90
372	Joe Cascarella	3.00	1.50	.90
373	Jimmy Hitchcock	3.00	1.50	.90
374	Frank Croucher	3.00	1.50	.90
375	LeRoy Parmelee	3.00	1.50	.90
376	Joe Mulligan	3.00	1.50	.90
377	John Welch	3.00	1.50	.90
378	Donald McNair	3.00	1.50	.90
379	Frenchy Bordagaray	3.00	1.50	.90
380	Denny Galehouse	3.00	1.50	.90
381	Robert Harris	3.00	1.50	.90
382	Max Butcher	3.00	1.50	.90
383	Sam Byrd	3.00	1.50	.90
384	Pete Coscarart	3.00	1.50	.90
385	George Case	3.00	1.50	.90
386	John Hudson	3.00	1.50	.90
387	Frank Crespi	3.00	1.50	.90
388	Gene Desautels	3.00	1.50	.90
389	Bill Cissell	3.00	1.50	.90
390	John Burns	3.00	1.50	.90
391	Larry Benton	3.00	1.50	.90
392	James Holbrook	3.00	1.50	.90
393	Ernie Koy	3.00	1.50	.90
394	Bobby Doerr	3.00	1.50	.90
395	Harry Boyles	3.00	1.50	.90
396	Pinky Higgins	3.00	1.50	.90
397	Mel Almada	3.00	1.50	.90
398	Carl Fischer	3.00	1.50	.90
399	Rabbit Maranville, Johnny Evers, Hank Gowdy	3.00	1.50	.90
400	Lou Gehrig	10.00	5.00	3.00
401	Lincoln Blakely	3.00	1.50	.90
402	James Henry	3.00	1.50	.90
403	Ed Holley	3.00	1.50	.90
404	Elmer Hodgin	3.00	1.50	.90
405	Bob Garbark	3.00	1.50	.90
406	John Burnett	3.00	1.50	.90
407	David Harris	3.00	1.50	.90
408	Johnny Dickshot	3.00	1.50	.90
409	Ray Mueller	3.00	1.50	.90
410	John Welaj	3.00	1.50	.90
411	Les McCrabb	3.00	1.50	.90
412	George Uhle	3.00	1.50	.90
413	Leo Mangum	3.00	1.50	.90
414	Howard Maple	3.00	1.50	.90
415	Syl Johnson	3.00	1.50	.90
416	Hershel Martin	3.00	1.50	.90
417	Joe Martin	3.00	1.50	.90
418	Phil Masi	3.00	1.50	.90
419	Bobby Mattick	3.00	1.50	.90
420	Marshall Mauldin	3.00	1.50	.90
421	Frank May	3.00	1.50	.90
422	Merrill May	3.00	1.50	.90
423	Bill McAfee	3.00	1.50	.90
424	Benny McCoy	3.00	1.50	.90
425	Charlie George	3.00	1.50	.90
426	Roy Hughes	3.00	1.50	.90
427	Bill Kerksieck	3.00	1.50	.90
428	Wes Kingdon	3.00	1.50	.90
429	Lynn King	3.00	1.50	.90
430	Harry Kinzy	3.00	1.50	.90
431	Harry Kimberlin	3.00	1.50	.90
432	Bob Klinger	3.00	1.50	.90
433	Wilfred Knothe	3.00	1.50	.90
434	Lou Finney	3.00	1.50	.90
435	Roy Johnson	3.00	1.50	.90
436	Woody Jensen	3.00	1.50	.90
437	George Jeffcoat	3.00	1.50	.90
438	Roy Joiner	3.00	1.50	.90
439	Baxter Jordan	3.00	1.50	.90
440	Edwin Joost	3.00	1.50	.90
441	Bubber Jonnard	3.00	1.50	.90
442	Bucky Jacobs	3.00	1.50	.90
443	Art Jacobs	3.00	1.50	.90
444	Orville Jorgens	3.00	1.50	.90
445	Hal Kelleher	3.00	1.50	.90
446	Harry Kelley	3.00	1.50	.90
447	Ken Keltner	3.00	1.50	.90
448	Paul Kardon	3.00	1.50	.90
449	Alex Kampouris	3.00	1.50	.90
450	Willie Kamm	3.00	1.50	.90
451	Bob Kahle	3.00	1.50	.90
452	Billy Jurges	3.00	1.50	.90
453	Ken Jungles	3.00	1.50	.90
454	John Juelich	3.00	1.50	.90
455	John Marcum	3.00	1.50	.90
456	Walt Masterson	3.00	1.50	.90
457	Clint Brown	3.00	1.50	.90
458	Buddy Lewis	3.00	1.50	.90
459	Watty Clark	3.00	1.50	.90
460	Johnny Cooney	3.00	1.50	.90
461	Mel Harder	3.00	1.50	.90
462	Justin McLaughlin	3.00	1.50	.90
463	Frank Grube	3.00	1.50	.90
464	Jeff Heath	3.00	1.50	.90
465	Cliff Heathcote	3.00	1.50	.90
466	Harvey Hendrick	3.00	1.50	.90
467	Johnny Hodapp	3.00	1.50	.90
468	Bob Holland	3.00	1.50	.90
469	Otto Huber	3.00	1.50	.90
470	Rudy Hulswitt	3.00	1.50	.90
471	Roy Johnson	3.00	1.50	.90
472	Smead Jolley	3.00	1.50	.90
473	Rollie Hemsley, Bob Smith, John Moore	3.00	1.50	.90
474	John Jones	3.00	1.50	.90
475	Harry Kelley	3.00	1.50	.90
476	George Kelly	3.00	1.50	.90
477	Chuck Klein	3.00	1.50	.90
478	Joe Krakauskas	3.00	1.50	.90
479	Mike Kreevich	3.00	1.50	.90
480	Dick Lanahan	3.00	1.50	.90
481	Emil "Dutch" Leonard	3.00	1.50	.90
482	Harl Maggert	3.00	1.50	.90
483	Cyrus Malis	3.00	1.50	.90
484	Dario Lodigiani	3.00	1.50	.90
485	Walt Masterson	3.00	1.50	.90
486	Rabbit Maranville	3.00	1.50	.90
487	Ed Marshall	3.00	1.50	.90
488	Tim McKeithan	3.00	1.50	.90
489	Patrick McLaughlin	3.00	1.50	.90
490	Bob McNamara	3.00	1.50	.90
491	Steve Mesner	3.00	1.50	.90
492	Clarence Mitchell	3.00	1.50	.90
493	Mal Moss	3.00	1.50	.90
494	Joe Murray	3.00	1.50	.90
495	Pete Naktenis	3.00	1.50	.90
496	Bill Nicholson	3.00	1.50	.90
497	John Rigney	3.00	1.50	.90
498	Clyde Sukeforth	3.00	1.50	.90
499	Evar Swanson	3.00	1.50	.90
500	Dan Taylor	3.00	1.50	.90
501	Sloppy Thurston	3.00	1.50	.90
502	Forrest Wright	3.00	1.50	.90
503	Ray Lucas	3.00	1.50	.90
504	Nig Lipscomb	3.00	1.50	.90

1973-80 TCMA All-Time Greats Postcards

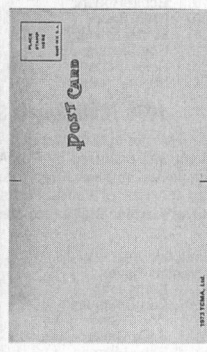

One of the longest collectors' series issued by TCMA in the 1970s was this set of player postcards. Measuring 3-1/2" x 5-1/2" the black-and-white cards have large photos on front, bordered in black and highlighted with banners and baseball equipment. Backs have postcard markings. Six series of cards were issued between 1973-80 and the unnumbered cards are checklisted here in alphabetical order within series.

		NM	EX	VG
Complete Set (156):		150.00	75.00	45.00
Common Player:		3.00	1.50	.90
SERIES 1				
(1)	Luke Appling	3.00	1.50	.90
(2)	Mickey Cochrane	3.00	1.50	.90
(3)	Eddie Collins	3.00	1.50	.90
(4)	Kiki Cuyler	3.00	1.50	.90
(5)	Bill Dickey	3.00	1.50	.90
(6)	Joe DiMaggio	7.50	3.75	2.25
(7)	Bob Feller	3.00	1.50	.90
(8)	Frank Frisch	3.00	1.50	.90
(9)	Lou Gehrig	7.50	3.75	2.25
(10)	Goose Goslin	3.00	1.50	.90
(11)	Chick Hafey	3.00	1.50	.90
(12)	Gabby Hartnett	3.00	1.50	.90
(13)	Rogers Hornsby	4.00	2.00	1.25
(14)	Ted Lyons	3.00	1.50	.90
(15)	Connie Mack	3.00	1.50	.90
(16)	Heinie Manush	3.00	1.50	.90
(17)	Rabbit Maranville	3.00	1.50	.90
(18)	Ducky Medwick	3.00	1.50	.90
(19)	Al Simmons	3.00	1.50	.90
(20)	Bill Terry	3.00	1.50	.90
(21)	Pie Traynor	3.00	1.50	.90
(22)	Dazzy Vance	3.00	1.50	.90
(23)	Cy Young	5.00	2.50	1.50
(24)	Gabby Hartnett, Babe Ruth	6.00	3.00	1.75
SERIES 2				
(1)	Roger Bresnahan	3.00	1.50	.90
(2)	Dizzy Dean	4.00	2.00	1.25
(3)	Buck Ewing & mascot	3.00	1.50	.90
(4)	Jimmie Foxx	4.50	2.25	1.25
(5)	Hank Greenberg	4.50	2.25	1.25
(6)	Burleigh Grimes	3.00	1.50	.90
(7)	Harry Heilmann	3.00	1.50	.90
(8)	Waite Hoyt	3.00	1.50	.90
(9)	Walter Johnson	5.00	2.50	1.50
(10)	George Kelly	3.00	1.50	.90
(11)	Christy Mathewson	5.00	2.50	1.50
(12)	John McGraw	3.00	1.50	.90
(13)	Stan Musial	4.00	2.00	1.25
(14)	Mel Ott	3.00	1.50	.90
(15)	Satchel Paige	6.00	3.00	1.75
(16)	Sam Rice	3.00	1.50	.90
(17)	Edd Roush	3.00	1.50	.90
(18)	Red Ruffing	3.00	1.50	.90
(19)	Casey Stengel	3.00	1.50	.90
(20)	Honus Wagner	6.00	3.00	1.75
(21)	Lloyd Waner	3.00	1.50	.90
(22)	Paul Waner	3.00	1.50	.90
(23)	Harry Wright	3.00	1.50	.90
(24)	Ross Youngs	3.00	1.50	.90
SERIES 3				
(1)	Home Run Baker	3.00	1.50	.90
(2)	Chief Bender	3.00	1.50	.90
(3)	Jim Bottomley	3.00	1.50	.90
(4)	Lou Boudreau	3.00	1.50	.90
(5)	Mordecai Brown	3.00	1.50	.90
(6)	Roy Campanella	3.50	1.75	1.00
(7)	Max Carey	3.00	1.50	.90
(8)	Ty Cobb	7.50	3.75	2.25
(9)	Earle Combs	3.00	1.50	.90
(10)	Jocko Conlan	3.00	1.50	.90
(11)	Hugh Duffy	3.00	1.50	.90
(12)	Red Faber	3.00	1.50	.90
(13)	Lefty Grove	3.00	1.50	.90
(14)	Judge K.M. Landis	3.00	1.50	.90
(15)	Eddie Plank	3.00	1.50	.90
(16)	Hoss Radbourne	3.00	1.50	.90
(17)	Eppa Rixey	3.00	1.50	.90
(18)	Jackie Robinson	6.00	3.00	1.75
(19)	Babe Ruth	7.50	3.75	2.25
(20)	George Sisler	3.00	1.50	.90
(21)	Zack Wheat	3.00	1.50	.90
(22)	Ted Williams	6.00	3.00	1.75
(23)	Mel Ott, Babe Ruth	6.00	3.00	1.75
(24)	Tris Speaker, Wilbert Robinson	3.00	1.50	.90
SERIES 4				
(1)	Grover C. Alexander	3.50	1.75	1.00
(2)	Cap Anson	3.00	1.50	.90
(3)	Earl Averill	3.00	1.50	.90
(4)	Ed Barrow	3.00	1.50	.90
(5)	Yogi Berra	3.50	1.75	1.00

(6)	Roberto Clemente	6.00	3.00	1.75
(7)	Jimmy Collins	3.00	1.50	.90
(8)	Whitey Ford	3.50	1.75	1.00
(9)	Ford Frick	3.00	1.50	.90
(10)	Vernon Gomez	3.00	1.50	.90
(11)	Bucky Harris	3.00	1.50	.90
(12)	Billy Herman	3.00	1.50	.90
(13)	Carl Hubbell	3.00	1.50	.90
(14)	Miller Huggins	3.00	1.50	.90
(15)	Monte Irvin	3.00	1.50	.90
(16)	Ralph Kiner	3.00	1.50	.90
(17)	Bill Klem	3.00	1.50	.90
(18)	Sandy Koufax	6.00	3.00	1.75
(19)	Napoleon Lajoie	3.00	1.50	.90
(20)	Bob Lemon	3.00	1.50	.90
(21)	Mickey Mantle	7.50	3.75	2.25
(22)	Rube Marquard	3.00	1.50	.90
(23)	Joe McCarthy	3.00	1.50	.90
(24)	Bill McKechnie	3.00	1.50	.90
(25)	Herb Pennock	3.00	1.50	.90
(26)	Warren Spahn	3.00	1.50	.90
(27)	Joe Tinker	3.00	1.50	.90
(28)	Early Wynn	3.00	1.50	.90
(29)	Joe Cronin, Honus Wagner, Bill Terry	3.00	1.50	.90
(30)	Jimmie Foxx, Lou Gehrig	6.00	3.00	1.75
(31)	Hank Greenberg, Ralph Kiner	3.00	1.50	.90
(32)	Walter Johnson, Connie Mack	3.00	1.50	.90
(33)	Connie Mack, Bob Feller	3.00	1.50	.90
(34)	Mel Ott, Lou Gehrig	6.00	3.00	1.75
(35)	Al Simmons, Tris Speaker, Ty Cobb	3.00	1.50	.90
(36)	Ted Williams, Lou Boudreau	3.00	1.50	.90
SERIES 5				
(1)	Dave Bancroft	3.00	1.50	.90
(2)	Ernie Banks	3.50	1.75	1.00
(3)	Frank Chance	3.00	1.50	.90
(4)	Stan Coveleski	3.00	1.50	.90
(5)	Billy Evans	3.00	1.50	.90
(6)	Clark Griffith	3.00	1.50	.90
(7)	Jesse Haines	3.00	1.50	.90
(8)	Will Harridge	3.00	1.50	.90
(9)	Harry Hooper	3.00	1.50	.90
(10)	Cal Hubbard	3.00	1.50	.90
(11)	Hugh Jennings	3.00	1.50	.90
(12)	Wee Willie Keeler	3.00	1.50	.90
(13)	Fred Lindstrom	3.00	1.50	.90
(14)	Pop Lloyd	3.00	1.50	.90
(15)	Al Lopez	3.00	1.50	.90
(16)	Robin Roberts	3.00	1.50	.90
(17)	Amos Rusie	3.00	1.50	.90
(18)	Ray Schalk	3.00	1.50	.90
(19)	Joe Sewell	3.00	1.50	.90
(20)	Rube Waddell	3.00	1.50	.90
(21)	George Weiss	3.00	1.50	.90
(22)	Dizzy Dean, Gabby Hartnett	3.00	1.50	.90
(23)	Joe DiMaggio, Mickey Mantle	7.50	3.75	2.25
(24)	Ted Williams, Joe DiMaggio	6.00	3.00	1.75
SERIES 6				
(1)	Jack Chesbro	3.00	1.50	.90
(2)	Tom Connolly	3.00	1.50	.90
(3)	Sam Crawford	3.00	1.50	.90
(4)	Elmer Flick	3.00	1.50	.90
(5)	Charlie Gehringer	3.00	1.50	.90
(6)	Warren Giles	3.00	1.50	.90
(7)	Ban Johnson	3.00	1.50	.90
(8)	Addie Joss	3.00	1.50	.90
(9)	Al Kaline	3.00	1.50	.90
(10)	Willie Mays	6.00	3.00	1.75
(11)	Joe McGinnity	3.00	1.50	.90
(12)	Larry McPhail (MacPhail)	3.00	1.50	.90
(13)	Branch Rickey	3.00	1.50	.90
(14)	Wilbert Robinson	3.00	1.50	.90
(15)	Duke Snider	3.00	1.50	.90
(16)	Tris Speaker	4.00	2.00	1.25
(17)	Bobby Wallace	3.00	1.50	.90
(18)	Hack Wilson	.45	.25	.14
(19)	Yogi Berra, Casey Stengel	4.00	2.00	1.25
(20)	Warren Giles, Roberto Clemente	4.50	2.25	1.25
(21)	Mickey Mantle, Willie Mays	6.00	3.00	1.75
(22)	John McGraw, Babe Ruth	6.00	3.00	1.75
(23)	Satchel Paige, Bob Feller	5.00	2.50	1.50
(24)	Paul Waner, Lloyd Waner	4.00	2.00	1.25

1973 TCMA All Time New York Yankees Team

Outfield-Mickey Mantle

Printed in black-and-white in 3-1/2" x 5-1/2" format, these cards have borderless photos on front with a white strip at bottom in which the player's position and name appear. Backs list the all-time roster but are not numbered or dated. Production was 1,000 sets.

		NM	EX	VG
Complete Set (12):		25.00	12.50	7.50
Common Player:		3.50	1.75	1.00
(1)	Bill Dickey	3.50	1.75	1.00

(2)	Joe DiMaggio	10.00	5.00	3.00
(3)	Whitey Ford	5.00	2.50	1.50
(4)	Lou Gehrig	10.00	5.00	3.00
(5)	Tony Lazzeri	3.50	1.75	1.00
(6)	Mickey Mantle	15.00	7.50	4.50
(7)	Johnny Murphy	3.50	1.75	1.00
(8)	Phil Rizzuto	5.00	2.50	1.50
(9)	Red Rolfe	3.50	1.75	1.00
(10)	Red Ruffing	3.50	1.75	1.00
(11)	Babe Ruth	10.00	5.00	3.00
(12)	Casey Stengel	3.50	1.75	1.00

1973 TCMA Autographs & Drawings Postcards

These black-and-white postcards feature drawings of the players, along with facsimile autographs.

		NM	EX	VG
Complete Set (12):		50.00	25.00	15.00
Common Player:		5.00	2.50	1.50
1	Mickey Cockran (Cochrane)	5.00	2.50	1.50
2	Christy Mathewson	5.00	2.50	1.50
3	Roberto Clemente	10.00	5.00	3.00
4	Rogers Hornsby	5.00	2.50	1.50
5	Pie Traynor	5.00	2.50	1.50
6	Frankie Frisch	5.00	2.50	1.50
7	Ty Cobb	7.50	3.75	2.25
8	Connie Mack	5.00	2.50	1.50
9	Babe Ruth	10.00	5.00	3.00
10	Lou Gehrig	8.00	4.00	2.50
11	Gil Hodges	5.00	2.50	1.50
12	Jackie Robinson	8.00	4.00	2.50

1973-1974 TCMA Autograph Series

These postcard-size black-and-white cards have borderless front photos with a wide white strip at bottom to accomodate an autograph. They are blank-backed.

		NM	EX	VG
Complete Set (36):		125.00	65.00	35.00
Common Player:		4.00	2.00	1.20
1	Satchel Paige	7.50	3.75	2.25
2	Phil Rizzuto	6.00	3.00	1.75
3	Sid Gordon	4.00	2.00	1.20
4	Ernie Lombardi	4.00	2.00	1.20
5	Jesse Haines	4.00	2.00	1.20
6	Joe Gordon	4.00	2.00	1.20
7	Bill Terry	4.00	2.00	1.20
8	Bill Dickey	6.00	3.00	1.75
9	Joe DiMaggio	12.00	6.00	3.50
10	Carl Hubbell	5.00	2.50	1.50
11	Fred Lindstrom	4.00	2.00	1.20
12	Ted Lyons	4.00	2.00	1.20
13	Red Ruffing	4.00	2.00	1.20
14	Joe Gordon	4.00	2.00	1.20
15	Bob Feller	6.00	3.00	1.75
16	Yogi Berra	7.50	3.75	2.25
17	Ford Frick, Whitey Ford	5.00	2.50	1.50
18	Sandy Koufax	12.00	6.00	3.50
19	Ted Williams	10.00	5.00	3.00
20	Warren Spahn	5.00	2.50	1.50
21	Al Rosen	4.00	2.00	1.20
22	Luke Appling	4.00	2.00	1.20
23	Joe Bush	4.00	2.00	1.20
24	Joe Medwick	4.00	2.00	1.20
25	Lou Boudreau	4.00	2.00	1.20
26	Ralph Kiner	4.00	2.00	1.20
27	Lloyd Waner	4.00	2.00	1.20
28	Pee Wee Reese	7.50	3.75	2.25
29	Duke Snider	7.50	3.75	2.25
30	Sal Maglie	4.00	2.00	1.20
31	Monte Irvin	4.00	2.00	1.20
32	Lefty Gomez	4.00	2.00	1.20
33	George Kelly	4.00	2.00	1.20
34	Joe Adcock	4.00	2.00	1.20
35	Max Carey	4.00	2.00	1.20
36	Rube Marquard	4.00	2.00	1.20

1973 TCMA "Bobo"

The major league travels of Bobo Newsom are chronicled in this set of 3-1/2" x 5-1/2" black-and-white cards depicting the pitcher in the uniforms of the nine teams for whom he played between 1929-53.

		NM	EX	VG
Complete Set (10):		25.00	12.50	7.50
Common Card:		4.00	2.00	1.25
(1)	Bobo Newsom (A's)	4.00	2.00	1.25
(2)	Bobo Newsom (A's, with Bobby Shantz.)	4.00	2.00	1.25
(3)	Bobo Newsom (Browns)	4.00	2.00	1.25
(4)	Bobo Newsom (Cubs)	4.00	2.00	1.25
(5)	Bobo Newsom (Dodgers, with Leo Durocher.)	4.00	2.00	1.25
(6)	Bobo Newsom (Giants)	4.00	2.00	1.25
(7)	Bobo Newsom (Red Sox)	4.00	2.00	1.25
(8)	Bobo Newsom (Senators, with Ossie Bluege.)	4.00	2.00	1.25
(9)	Bobo Newsom (Tigers, with Paul Derringer.)	4.00	2.00	1.25
(10)	Bobo Newsom (Yankees, with Vic Rashi, Bucky Harris.)	4.00	2.00	1.25

1973 TCMA Giants 1886

		NM	EX	VG
Complete Set (15):		40.00	20.00	12.00
Common Player:		2.00	1.00	.60
1	Roger Connor	2.00	1.00	.60
2	Larry Corcoran	2.00	1.00	.60
3	Tom Deasley	2.00	1.00	.60
4	Mike Dorgan	2.00	1.00	.60
5	Dude Esterbrook	2.00	1.00	.60
6	Buck Ewing	2.00	1.00	.60
7	Joe Gerhardt	2.00	1.00	.60
8	Pete Gillespie	2.00	1.00	.60
9	Tim Keefe	2.00	1.00	.60
10	Jim Mutrie	2.00	1.00	.60
11	Jim O'Rourke	2.00	1.00	.60
12	Daniel Richardson	2.00	1.00	.60
13	John M. Ward	2.00	1.00	.60
14	Mickey Welch	2.00	1.00	.60
15	Bat Boy	2.00	1.00	.60

1973 TCMA Pudge Gautreaux

This custom-published postcard of the Brooklyn Dodgers catcher (1936-37) was printed in black-and-white in a 3-1/2" x 6" format. The issue date is approximate.

	NM	EX	VG
Sid "Pudge" Gautreaux	4.00	2.00	1.25

1973-78 TCMA League Leaders

One of TCMA's earliest major series of collectors cards was this run of postcard-size (3-1/2" x 5-1/2") black-and-whites honoring various statistical leaders in each league from the 1920s through the 1950s. Backs have a list of the leaders by year within decade, with one of them pictured on the front. The unnumbered cards are checklisted here in alphabetical order within decade, as they were issued.

		NM	EX	VG
Complete Set (96):		190.00	95.00	55.00
Common Player:		5.00	2.50	1.50
	Complete Set, The 1920s	50.00	25.00	15.00
(1)	Grover C. Alexander	5.00	2.50	1.50
(2)	Jim Bagby, Sr.	5.00	2.50	1.50
(3)	Jim Bottomley	5.00	2.50	1.50
(4)	Eddie Collins	5.00	2.50	1.50
(5)	Earle Combs	5.00	2.50	1.50
(6)	Kiki Cuyler	5.00	2.50	1.50
(7)	Urban "Red" Faber	5.00	2.50	1.50
(8)	Johnny Frederick	5.00	2.50	1.50
(9)	Charlie Gehringer	5.00	2.50	1.50
(10)	Goose Goslin	5.00	2.50	1.50
(11)	Rogers Hornsby	5.00	2.50	1.50
(12)	Walter Johnson	6.00	3.00	1.75
(13)	Freddie Lindstrom	5.00	2.50	1.50
(14)	Bob Meusel	5.00	2.50	1.50
(15)	Charlie Root	5.00	2.50	1.50
(16)	Babe Ruth, Rogers Hornsby	7.50	3.75	2.25
(17)	Al Simmons, Babe Ruth	7.50	3.75	2.25
(18)	Tris Speaker	5.00	2.50	1.50
(19)	Dazzy Vance	5.00	2.50	1.50
(20)	Lloyd Waner	5.00	2.50	1.50
(21)	Cy Williams	5.00	2.50	1.50
(22)	Ken Williams	5.00	2.50	1.50
(23)	Hack Wilson	5.00	2.50	1.50
(24)	Ross Youngs	5.00	2.50	1.50
	Complete Set, The 1930s	50.00	25.00	15.00
(1)	Johnny Allen	5.00	2.50	1.50
(2)	Beau Bell	5.00	2.50	1.50
(3)	Cy Blanton	5.00	2.50	1.50
(4)	Ben Chapman	5.00	2.50	1.50
(5)	Joe Cronin	5.00	2.50	1.50
(6)	Dizzy Dean	6.50	3.25	2.00
(7)	Joe DiMaggio	20.00	10.00	6.00
(8)	Jimmie Foxx	5.00	2.50	1.50
(9)	Lou Gehrig	15.00	7.50	4.50
(10)	Charlie Gehringer	5.00	2.50	1.50
(11)	Lefty Gomez	5.00	2.50	1.50
(12)	Ival Goodman	5.00	2.50	1.50
(13)	Lefty Grove	5.00	2.50	1.50
(14)	Billy Herman	5.00	2.50	1.50
(15)	Ernie Lombardi	5.00	2.50	1.50
(16)	Chuck Klein	5.00	2.50	1.50
(17)	Heinie Manush	5.00	2.50	1.50
(18)	Pepper Martin	5.00	2.50	1.50
(19)	Joe Medwick	5.00	2.50	1.50
(20)	Van Mungo	5.00	2.50	1.50
(21)	Mel Ott	5.00	2.50	1.50
(22)	Bill Terry	5.00	2.50	1.50
(23)	Hal Trosky	5.00	2.50	1.50
(24)	Arky Vaughan	5.00	2.50	1.50
	Complete Set, The 1940s	50.00	25.00	15.00
(1)	Gene Bearden	5.00	2.50	1.50
(2)	Lou Boudreau	5.00	2.50	1.50
(3)	George Case	5.00	2.50	1.50
(4)	Phil Cavarretta	5.00	2.50	1.50
(5)	Bob Feller	6.00	3.00	1.75
(6)	Boo Ferriss	5.00	2.50	1.50
(7)	Hank Greenberg	9.00	4.50	2.75
(8)	Jeff Heath	5.00	2.50	1.50
(9)	Tommy Holmes	5.00	2.50	1.50
(10)	Larry Jansen	5.00	2.50	1.50
(11)	George Kell	5.00	2.50	1.50
(12)	Ralph Kiner	5.00	2.50	1.50
(13)	Marty Marion	5.00	2.50	1.50
(14)	Johnny Mize	5.00	2.50	1.50
(15)	Stan Musial	10.00	5.00	3.00
(16)	Bill Nicholson	5.00	2.50	1.50
(17)	Johnny Pesky	5.00	2.50	1.50
(18)	Jackie Robinson	10.00	5.00	3.00
(19)	Enos Slaughter	5.00	2.50	1.50
(20)	Snuffy Stirnweiss	5.00	2.50	1.50
(21)	Bill Voiselle	5.00	2.50	1.50
(22)	Bucky Walters	5.00	2.50	1.50
(23)	Ted Williams	10.00	5.00	3.00
(24)	Ted Williams, Joe DiMaggio	10.00	5.00	3.00
	Complete Set, The 1950s	50.00	25.00	15.00
(1)	Luis Aparicio	5.00	2.50	1.50
(2)	Ernie Banks	5.00	2.50	1.50
(3)	Bill Bruton	5.00	2.50	1.50
(4)	Lew Burdette	5.00	2.50	1.50
(5)	Rocky Colavito	5.00	2.50	1.50
(6)	Dom DiMaggio	5.00	2.50	1.50
(7)	Ferris Fain	5.00	2.50	1.50
(8)	Whitey Ford	5.00	2.50	1.50
(9)	Don Hoak	5.00	2.50	1.50
(10)	Sam Jethroe	5.00	2.50	1.50
(11)	Ted Kluszewski	5.00	2.50	1.50
(12)	Harvey Kuenn	5.00	2.50	1.50
(13)	Bob Lemon	5.00	2.50	1.50
(14)	Mickey Mantle	30.00	15.00	9.00
(15)	Willie Mays	15.00	7.50	4.50
(16)	Willie Mays, Bobby Avila	5.00	2.50	1.50
(17)	Minnie Minoso	5.00	2.50	1.50
(18)	Don Newcombe	5.00	2.50	1.50
(19)	Robin Roberts	5.00	2.50	1.50
(20)	Hank Sauer	5.00	2.50	1.50
(21)	Bobby Shantz	5.00	2.50	1.50
(22)	Roy Sievers	5.00	2.50	1.50
(23)	Duke Snider	6.00	3.00	1.75
(24)	Mickey Vernon	5.00	2.50	1.50

1973 TCMA Sports Scoop Hall of Fame

This set of large-format (3-1/2" x 5-1/2") black-and-white cards was produced by TCMA for the collectors' magazine Sports Scoop, which was promoting the players to be inducted into the Hall of Fame. Backs have information about the player's career and HoF credentials.

		NM	EX	VG
Complete Set (12):		20.00	10.00	6.00
Common Player:		2.00	1.00	.60
(1)	Earl Averill	2.50	1.25	.70
(2)	Ben Chapman	2.00	1.00	.60
(3)	Doc Cramer	2.00	1.00	.60
(4)	Spud Davis	2.00	1.00	.60
(5)	Babe Herman	2.00	1.00	.60
(6)	Billy Herman	2.50	1.25	.70
(7)	Chuck Klein	2.50	1.25	.70
(8)	Bob Meusel	2.00	1.00	.60
(9)	Johnny Mize	3.00	1.50	.90
(10)	Joe Sewell	2.50	1.25	.70
(11)	Enos Slaughter	3.00	1.50	.90
(12)	Hal Trosky	2.00	1.00	.60

1973 TCMA 1874 Philadelphia Athletics

This early collectors' issue reproduces woodcuts of the A's as they appeared in the July 25, 1874, edition of Harper's Weekly. The 3-1/16" x 4-1/2" cards are printed in black-and-white with the player name and position in the white border at bottom. Identical backs credit the pictures' original source and state "TCMA Reprint 1973." The unnumbered cards are checklisted here alphabetically.

		NM	EX	VG
Complete Set (9):		25.00	12.50	7.50
Common Player:		3.00	1.50	.90
(1)	Cap Anson	10.00	5.00	3.00
(2)	Joseph Battin	3.00	1.50	.90
(3)	John Clapp	3.00	1.50	.90
(4)	Wes Fisler	3.00	1.50	.90
(5)	Count Gedney	3.00	1.50	.90
(6)	Dick McBride	3.00	1.50	.90
(7)	Mike McGeary	3.00	1.50	.90
(8)	J.F. McMullen	3.00	1.50	.90
(9)	Ezra Sutton	3.00	1.50	.90

1973 TCMA 1890 Base-ball Season

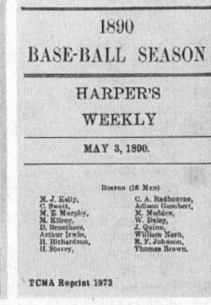

This set commemorates the baseball "war" of 1890 when many National League players - stars and journeymen alike - defected to a new player-owned league called, appropriately enough, the Players League. Fronts of these 3-1/8" x 4-1/2" black-and-white cards feature reproductions of woodcuts originally printed in Harper's Weekly. Backs have information about the teams in each league. The unnumbered cards are checklisted here in alphabetical order. Original issue price of the set was $3.

		NM	EX	VG
Complete Set (30):		48.00	24.00	14.50
Common Player:		2.00	1.00	.60
(1)	Cap Anson	2.00	1.00	.60
(2)	Dan Brouthers	2.00	1.00	.60
(3)	Thomas E. Burns	2.00	1.00	.60
(4)	John Clarkson	2.00	1.00	.60
(5)	C.A. Comiskey	2.00	1.00	.60
(6)	Roger Connor	2.00	1.00	.60
(7)	E.N. Crane	2.00	1.00	.60

		NM	EX	VG
(8)	Jeremiah Denny	2.00	1.00	.60
(9)	William B. Ewing	2.00	1.00	.60
(10)	D.L. Foutz	2.00	1.00	.60
(11)	John W. Glasscock	2.00	1.00	.60
(12)	W. Hallman	2.00	1.00	.60
(13)	Edward Hanlon	2.00	1.00	.60
(14)	Timothy J. Keefe	2.00	1.00	.60
(15)	M.J. Kelly	2.00	1.00	.60
(16)	M. Kilroy	2.00	1.00	.60
(17)	W.A. Latham	2.00	1.00	.60
(18)	J.A. McPhee	2.00	1.00	.60
(19)	Joseph Mulvey	2.00	1.00	.60
(20)	W.D. O'Brien	2.00	1.00	.60
(21)	David Orr	2.00	1.00	.60
(22)	John G. Reilly	2.00	1.00	.60
(23)	S.L. Thompson	2.00	1.00	.60
(24)	M. Tiernan	2.00	1.00	.60
(25)	John M. Ward	2.00	1.00	.60
(26)	M. Welsh (Welch)	2.00	1.00	.60
(27)	A. Weyhing	2.00	1.00	.60
(28)	Charles Zimmer	2.00	1.00	.60
(29)	A dive for second base	1.00	.50	.30
(30)	Brotherhood Players Header Card	1.00	.50	.30

1973 TCMA 1930's No Hit Pitchers and 6 for 6 Hitters

These large-format (3-1/2" x 5-1/2") cards feature the no-hit pitchers and 6-for-6 hitters of the 1930s. Borderless front photos are in black-and-white. On back of the pitchers' cards is a list of the decade's no-hitters, the date, score and opposing team. A similar list of the 6-for-6 hitters is on the back of their cards. The cards are unnumbered.

		NM	EX	VG
Complete Set (12):		40.00	20.00	12.00
Common Player:		4.00	2.00	1.25
	PITCHERS			
(1)	Paul Dean	6.00	3.00	1.75
(2)	Bill Dietrich	4.00	2.00	1.25
(3)	Vern Kennedy	4.00	2.00	1.25
(4)	Monte Pearson	4.00	2.00	1.25
(5)	Johnny Vander Meer	5.00	2.50	1.50
	HITTERS			
(6)	Jim Bottomley	6.00	3.00	1.75
(7)	Bruce Campbell	4.00	2.00	1.25
(8)	Doc Cramer	4.00	2.00	1.25
(9)	Myril Hoag	4.00	2.00	1.25
(10)	Cookie Lavagetto	4.00	2.00	1.25
(11)	Terry Moore	5.00	2.50	1.50
(12)	Henry Steinbacher	4.00	2.00	1.25

1973 TCMA 1941 Brooklyn Dodgers

These 3-3/8" x 2-1/2" cards are printed in blue-and-white. The unnumbered cards do not have player names on front.

		NM	EX	VG
Complete Set (32):		50.00	25.00	15.00
Common Player		2.00	1.00	.60
(1)	Title Card	1.00	.50	.30
(2)	John Allen	2.00	1.00	.60
(3)	Mace Brown	2.00	1.00	.60
(4)	Dolph Camilli	2.00	1.00	.60
(5)	Hugh Casey	2.00	1.00	.60
(6)	Curt Davis	2.00	1.00	.60
(7)	Tom Drake	2.00	1.00	.60
(8)	Leo Durocher	4.00	2.00	1.25
(9)	Fred Fitzsimmons	2.00	1.00	.60
(10)	Herman Franks	2.00	1.00	.60
(11)	Augie Galan	2.00	1.00	.60
(12)	Tony Giuliani	2.00	1.00	.60
(13)	Luke Hamlin	2.00	1.00	.60
(14)	Billy Herman	4.00	2.00	1.25
(15)	Kirby Higbe	2.00	1.00	.60
(16)	Alex Kampouris	2.00	1.00	.60
(17)	Newt Kimball	2.00	1.00	.60
(18)	Cookie Lavagetto	2.00	1.00	.60
(19)	Ducky Medwick	4.00	2.00	1.25
(20)	Van Mungo	2.00	1.00	.60
(21)	Mickey Owen	2.00	1.00	.60
(22)	Babe Phelps	2.00	1.00	.60
(23)	Pee Wee Reese	8.00	4.00	2.50
(24)	Pete Reiser	2.00	1.00	.60
(25)	Lew Riggs	2.00	1.00	.60
(26)	Bill Swift	2.00	1.00	.60
(27)	Vito Tamulis	2.00	1.00	.60
(28)	Joe Vosmik	2.00	1.00	.60
(29)	Dixie Walker	2.00	1.00	.60
(30)	Paul Waner	4.00	2.00	1.25
(31)	Jimmy Wasdell	2.00	1.00	.60
(32)	Whit Wyatt	2.00	1.00	.60

1973 TCMA Stan Martucci Postcards

This set of postcards was custom-produced by TCMA for card dealer Stan Martucci who apparently used them as "ride alongs" when filling orders. Approximately 3-1/2" x 5-1/2", the fronts have borderless, unidentified black-and-white photos of popular former stars. The back is in standard postcard format and had the player identified at top-left and a note from Martucci in the message area.

		NM	EX	VG
Complete Set (16):		15.00	7.50	4.50
Common Player:		1.00	.50	.30
(1)	Joe Cronin	1.00	.50	.30
(2)	Dizzy Dean	2.00	1.00	.60
(3)	Joe DiMaggio	5.00	2.50	1.50
(4)	Jimmie Foxx	2.00	1.00	.60
(5)	Lou Gehrig	5.00	2.50	1.50
(6)	Charlie Gehringer	1.00	.50	.30
(7)	Lefty Gomez	1.00	.50	.30
(8)	Lefty Grove	1.00	.50	.30
(9)	Carl Hubbell	1.00	.50	.30
(10)	Ted Lyons	1.00	.50	.30
(11)	Heinie Manush	1.00	.50	.30

		NM	EX	VG
(12)	Joe Medwick	1.00	.50	.30
(13)	Mel Ott	1.00	.50	.30
(14)	Red Ruffing	1.00	.50	.30
(15)	Bill Terry	1.00	.50	.30
(16)	Paul Waner	1.00	.50	.30

1974 TCMA Nicknames

"Nicknames"

WILD BILL

Nicknames of notable ballplayers of the 1930s-40s are featured in this early collectors' set. Fronts of the 2-5/16" x 3-1/2" cards have a black-and-white photo with the player's nickname in the bottom border and "Nicknames" in the top border, both printed in red. Backs have a card number, the player's full name, position and the teams and years he played in the major leagues. The set originally sold for $3.

		NM	EX	VG
Complete Set (28):		40.00	20.00	12.00
Common Player:		3.00	1.50	.90
1	Rapid Robert Feller	4.50	2.25	1.25
2	Babe Dahlgren	3.00	1.50	.90
3	Spud Chandler	3.00	1.50	.90
4	Ducky Medwick	3.00	1.50	.90
5	Silent Cal Benge	3.00	1.50	.90
6	Goose Goslin	3.00	1.50	.90
7	Mule Haas	3.00	1.50	.90
8	Dizzy Dean	6.00	3.00	1.75
9	Cowboy Harrell	3.00	1.50	.90
10	Buzz Boyle	3.00	1.50	.90
11	Coonskin Davis	3.00	1.50	.90
12	Moose Solters	3.00	1.50	.90
13	Sad Sam Jones	3.00	1.50	.90
14	Bad News Hale	3.00	1.50	.90
15	Bucky Harris	3.00	1.50	.90
16	Lord Jim Jordan	3.00	1.50	.90
17	Zeke Bonura	3.00	1.50	.90
18	Heave-o Hafey	3.00	1.50	.90
19	Spud Davis	3.00	1.50	.90
20	Bing Miller	3.00	1.50	.90
21	Preacher Roe	3.00	1.50	.90
22	Wild Bill Hallahan	3.00	1.50	.90
23	Indian Bob Johnson	3.00	1.50	.90
24	Flash Gordon	3.00	1.50	.90
25	Tot Pressnell	3.00	1.50	.90
26	Hot Potato Hamlin	3.00	1.50	.90
27	Old Reliable Henrich	3.00	1.50	.90
28	Tom Hafey	3.00	1.50	.90

1974 TCMA Sports Nostalgia Store Postcards

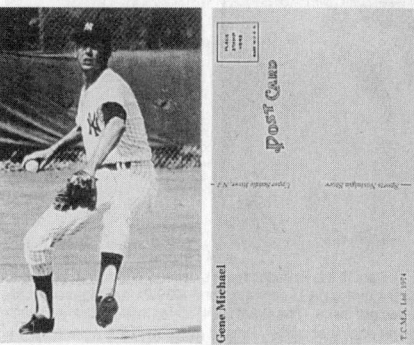

Gene Michael

To celebrate the opening of one of the first, if not the first, sports collectors' retail stores, TCMA issued a set of four 3-1/2" x 5-1/2" black-and-white postcards. The set includes one current N.Y. Yankees player and three former boxers. The set was issued in an edition of 1,000.

		NM	EX	VG
Complete Set (4):		20.00	10.00	6.00
Common Card:		5.00	2.50	1.50
(1)	Gene Michael	7.50	3.75	2.25
(2)	Emile Griffith	5.00	2.50	1.50
(3)	Floyd Patterson	5.00	2.50	1.50
(4)	Willie Pep	5.00	2.50	1.50

1974 TCMA Stadium Postcards

These 5" x 3-1/2" black-and-white postcards are not numbered and are listed here alphabetically.

		NM	EX	VG
Complete Set (12):		35.00	17.50	10.50
Common Card:		4.00	2.00	1.20
(1)	Baltimore Stadium	4.00	2.00	1.20

		NM	EX	VG
(2)	Boston Braves Field	4.00	2.00	1.20
(3)	Crosley Field	4.00	2.00	1.20
(4)	Ebbet's (Ebbets) Field	6.00	3.00	1.75
(5)	Forbes Field	4.00	2.00	1.20
(6)	Griffith Field	4.00	2.00	1.20
(7)	Milwaukee County Stadium	4.00	2.00	1.20
(8)	Narvin (Navin) Field	4.00	2.00	1.20
(9)	Polo Grounds	4.00	2.00	1.20
(10)	Shea Stadium	4.00	2.00	1.20
(11)	Wrigley Field	5.00	2.50	1.50
(12)	Yankee Stadium	7.50	3.75	2.25

1974-75 TCMA St. Louis Browns

St.Louis Browns 1902 - 1953

OSTERMUELLER, Frederick Raymond "Fritz"

	G.	W-L
1941	16	0-3
1942	10	3-1
1943	11	0-2

FRITZ OSTER MUELLER

THE BROWNS
2nd Series

1974 TCMA, Ltd.

Some of baseball's most loveable losers from about the 1930s through the team's flight to Baltimore in 1953 are presented in this multi-series collectors' issue. Cards are printed in a 2-1/4" x 3-7/8" format, with brown ink used on front and on back of Series 1 and 2; Series 3 cards have black ink on back. Some cards have player identification on front, some only on back. All cards have a TCMA copyright date line and a few player stats for his years with the Brownies. The unnumbered cards are checklisted here alphabetically by series.

		NM	EX	VG
Complete Set (108):		80.00	40.00	20.00
Common Player:		1.50	.75	.45
	Series 1 - 1974	25.00	12.50	7.50
(1)	Ethan Allen	1.50	.75	.45
(2)	Mel Almada	2.00	1.00	.60
(3)	Ed Baecht	1.50	.75	.45
(4)	John Berardino	4.00	2.00	1.25
(5)	Emil Bildilli	1.50	.75	.45
(6)	John Blake	1.50	.75	.45
(7)	Julio Bonetti	1.50	.75	.45
(8)	Earl Caldwell	1.50	.75	.45
(9)	Scoops Carey	1.50	.75	.45
(10)	Stinky Davis	1.50	.75	.45
(11)	Fred Haney	1.50	.75	.45
(12)	Jeff Heath	1.50	.75	.45
(13)	Don Heffner	1.50	.75	.45
(14)	Rollie Hemsley	1.50	.75	.45
(15)	Oral Hildebrand	1.50	.75	.45
(16)	Elon Hogsett	1.50	.75	.45
(17)	Ben Huffman	1.50	.75	.45
(18)	Sig Jakucki	1.50	.75	.45
(19)	Billy Knickerbocker	1.50	.75	.45
(20)	John Knott	1.50	.75	.45
(21)	Jack Kramer	1.50	.75	.45
(22)	Red Kress	1.50	.75	.45
(23)	Chet Laabs	1.50	.75	.45
(24)	Gerard "Nig" Lipscomb	1.50	.75	.45
(25)	John Lucadello	1.50	.75	.45
(26)	Mel Mazzera	1.50	.75	.45
(27)	Red McQuillen	1.50	.75	.45
(28)	George McQuinn	1.50	.75	.45
(29)	Oscar Melillo	1.50	.75	.45
(30)	Howard Mills	1.50	.75	.45
(31)	Bob Muncrief	1.50	.75	.45
(32)	Hank Thompson	1.50	.75	.45
(33)	Russell "Sheriff" Van Atta	1.50	.75	.45
(34)	Joe Vosmik	1.50	.75	.45
(35)	Jim Walkup	1.50	.75	.45
(36)	Sam West	1.50	.75	.45
	Series 2 - 1974	30.00	15.00	9.00
(37)	Floyd Baker	1.50	.75	.45
(38)	John Bassler	1.50	.75	.45
(39)	Ollie Bejma	1.50	.75	.45
(40)	Jim Bottomley	2.00	1.00	.60
(41)	Willard Brown	4.50	2.25	1.25
(42)	Bob Dillinger	1.50	.75	.45
(43)	Owen "Red" Friend	1.50	.75	.45
(44)	Eddie Gaedel	5.00	2.50	1.50
(45)	Dennis Galehouse	1.50	.75	.45
(46)	Joseph Gallagher	1.50	.75	.45
(47)	Ned Garver	1.50	.75	.45
(48)	Robert Harris	1.50	.75	.45
(49)	Al Hollingsworth	1.50	.75	.45
(50)	Walter Judnich	1.50	.75	.45
(51)	William "Lefty" Kennedy	1.50	.75	.45
(52)	Lou Kretlow	1.50	.75	.45
(53)	Martin Marion	1.50	.70	.45
(54)	Les Moss	1.50	.75	.45
(55)	Louis "Bobo" Newsom	1.50	.75	.45
(56)	Fritz Ostermueller	1.50	.75	.45
(57)	Joe Ostrowski	1.50	.75	.45
(58)	Edward Pellagrini	1.50	.75	.45
(59)	Duane Pillette	1.50	.75	.45
(60)	Nelson Potter	1.50	.75	.45
(61)	Raymond "Rip" Radcliff	1.50	.75	.45
(62)	Harry Rice	1.50	.75	.45
(63)	Jim Rivera	1.50	.75	.45
(64)	John "Fred" Sanford	1.50	.75	.45

(65)	Luke Sewell	1.50	.75	.45
(66)	Al Shirley	1.50	.75	.45
(67)	Junior Stephens	1.50	.75	.45
(68)	Thomas Turner	1.50	.75	.45
(69)	Ken Wood	1.50	.75	.45
(70)	Allen "Zeke" Zarilla	1.50	.75	.45
(71)	Samuel "Sad Sam" Zoldak	1.50	.75	.45
(72)	1944 Infield	1.50	.75	.45
	Series 3 - 1975	30.00	15.00	9.00
(73)	Bow-Wow Arft	1.50	.75	.45
(74)	Matthew Batts	1.50	.75	.45
(75)	Tommy Byrne	1.50	.75	.45
(76)	Skippy Byrnes	1.50	.75	.45
(77)	Raymond Coleman	1.50	.75	.45
(78)	Scrap Iron Courtney	1.50	.75	.45
(79)	James Delsing	1.50	.75	.45
(80)	William "Kid" DeMars	1.50	.75	.45
(81)	Clifford "Mule" Fannin	1.50	.75	.45
(82)	Tom Fine	1.50	.75	.45
(83)	Pete Gray	5.00	2.50	1.50
(84)	Red Hayworth	1.50	.70	.45
(85)	Procopio Herrera	1.50	.75	.45
(86)	Fred Hoffman	1.50	.75	.45
(87)	Walter "Union Man" Holke	1.50	.75	.45
(88)	Hal Hudson	1.50	.70	.45
(89)	Richard Kokos	1.50	.75	.45
(90)	Michael Kreevich	1.50	.75	.45
(91)	Richard Kryhoski	1.50	.75	.45
(92)	Paul "Peanuts" Lehner	1.50	.75	.45
(93)	Footsie Lenhardt	1.50	.75	.45
(94)	Joe Lutz	1.50	.75	.45
(95)	Robert Mahoney	1.50	.75	.45
(96)	Frank Mancuso	1.50	.75	.45
(97)	Clifford Mapes	1.50	.75	.45
(98)	Cass Michaels	1.50	.75	.45
(99)	Frank "Stubby" Overmire	1.50	.75	.45
(100)	Satchel Paige	5.00	2.50	1.50
(101)	Roy Sievers	1.50	.75	.45
(102)	Louis Sleator	1.50	.75	.45
(103)	Richard Starr	1.50	.75	.45
(104)	Thomas "Muscles" Upton	1.50	.75	.45
(105)	Jerome Witte	1.50	.75	.45
(106)	Robert Young	1.50	.75	.45
(107)	1951 Browns	1.50	.75	.45
(108)	1952 Browns	1.50	.75	.45

1974 TCMA The Babe Postcards

This set of black-and-white postcards features photos of Ruth with contemporary players and managers. Cards measure 5-1/2" x 3-1/2" and have standard postcard indicia on the backs.

		NM	EX	VG
Complete Set (6):		20.00	10.00	6.00
Common Card:		5.00	2.50	1.50
1	Babe Ruth, Bill Terry	5.00	2.50	1.50
2	Babe Ruth, Walter Johnson	5.00	2.50	1.50
3	Babe Ruth, Lou Gehrig, Joe McCarthy	5.00	2.50	1.50
4	Babe Ruth, Miller Huggins	5.00	2.50	1.50
5	Babe Ruth, Tony Lazzeri	5.00	2.50	1.50
6	Babe Ruth and 1934 All-Stars	5.00	2.50	1.50

1974 TCMA 1890 Brooklyn Club

The National League champion Brooklyn Bridegrooms are featured in this collectors issue. Fronts of the 3-1/2" x 3-3/4" black-and-white cards picture the players in dress suits with ornate designs around the border. The design was copied from an 1890 Brooklyn scorecard/yearbook. Backs have biographical information and career highlights, also copied from the earlier publication. The back also includes a 1974 TCMA reprint notice. The unnumbered cards are checklisted here in alphabetical order.

		NM	EX	VG
Complete Set (16):		30.00	15.00	9.00
Common Player:		3.00	1.50	.90
(1)	Thomas P. Burns	3.00	1.50	.90
(2)	Albert J. Bushong	3.00	1.50	.90
(3)	Robert Lee Caruthers	3.00	1.50	.90
(4)	Robert H. Clark	3.00	1.50	.90
(5)	Hubbert Collins	3.00	1.50	.90
(6)	John S. Corkhill	3.00	1.50	.90
(7)	Thomas P. Daly	3.00	1.50	.90
(8)	D.L. Foutz	3.00	1.50	.90
(9)	Michael F. Hughes	3.00	1.50	.90
(10)	Thomas J. Lovett	3.00	1.50	.90
(11)	W.H. McGunnigle	3.00	1.50	.90
(12)	Wm. D. O'Brien	3.00	1.50	.90
(13)	George Burton Pinkney	3.00	1.50	.90
(14)	George J. Smith	3.00	1.50	.90
(15)	George T. Stallings	3.00	1.50	.90
(16)	Wm. H. Terry	3.00	1.50	.90

1974 TCMA 1910-14 Philadelphia Athletics Postcards

This series of collectors' issue postcards (about 3-1/2" x 5-3/4") was issued in two forms; printed front and back in black-and-white or in blue-and-white. While numbered between 501 and 518, only 12 cards were issued. The cards are reproductions of the images from the 1911 Pinkerton cabinets (T5). The postcard-format backs have a "1974 TCMA Reprint" notice along with the list of the dynasty's league and world championships.

		NM	EX	VG
Complete Set (12):		10.00	5.00	3.00
Common Player:		1.00	.50	.30
501	Chas. Bender	1.50	.70	.45
502	John Coombs	1.00	.50	.30
503	Eddie Plank	1.50	.70	.45
504	Amos Strunk	1.00	.50	.30
506	Ira Thomas	1.00	.50	.30
508	Stuffy McInnis	1.00	.50	.30
510	Rube Oldring	1.00	.50	.30
511	Eddie Collins	1.50	.70	.45
512	Frank Baker	1.50	.70	.45
515	Jack Barry	1.00	.50	.30
516	Jack Lapp	1.00	.50	.30
518	Danny Murphy	1.00	.50	.30

1974 TCMA 1929-31 Athletics

Stars of the Philadelphia A's dynasty which won two World Series and an A.L. pennant from 1929-31 are featured in this collectors issue. The 2-5/8" x 4" cards have black-and-white player photos at center. Printed in green in the white border at top is "1929-31 Athletics." At bottom, printed in black, is the player's name and position. Backs are in black-and-white with stats for 1929, 1930 and 1931, as appropriate. The unnumbered cards are checklisted here in alphabetical order.

		NM	EX	VG
Complete Set (29):		30.00	15.00	9.00
Common Player:		2.00	1.00	.60
(1)	Max Bishop	2.00	1.00	.60
(2)	Joe Boley	2.00	1.00	.60
(3)	George Burns	2.00	1.00	.60
(4)	Mickey Cochrane	3.00	1.50	.90
(5)	Eddie Collins, Lew Krausse	2.00	1.00	.60
(6)	"Doc" Cramer	2.00	1.00	.60
(7)	Jimmy Dykes	2.00	1.00	.60
(8)	George Earnshaw	2.00	1.00	.60
(9)	Howard Ehmke	2.00	1.00	.60
(10)	Lou Finney, John Heving	2.00	1.00	.60
(11)	Jimmie Foxx	4.00	2.00	1.25
(12)	Walt French, Waite Hoyt	2.00	1.00	.60
(13)	"Lefty" Grove	3.00	1.50	.90
(14)	"Mule" Haas	2.00	1.00	.60
(15)	Sammy Hale	2.00	1.00	.60
(16)	"Pinky" Higgins, Phil Todt	2.00	1.00	.60
(17)	Earle Mack, Connie Mack	2.00	1.00	.60
(18)	Roy Mahaffey	2.00	1.00	.60
(19)	Eric McNair	2.00	1.00	.60
(20)	Bing Miller	2.00	1.00	.60
(21)	Jim Moore, Jim Peterson	2.00	1.00	.60
(22)	Jack Quinn	2.00	1.00	.60
(23)	Eddie Rommel	2.00	1.00	.60
(24)	Wally Schang	2.50	1.25	.70
(25)	Al Simmons	2.50	1.25	.70
(26)	Homer Summa	2.00	1.00	.60
(27)	Rube Walberg	2.00	1.00	.60
(28)	"Dib" Williams	2.00	1.00	.60
(29)	Team Photo Card (10" x 5")	10.00	5.00	3.00

1974 TCMA 1934 St. Louis Cardinals

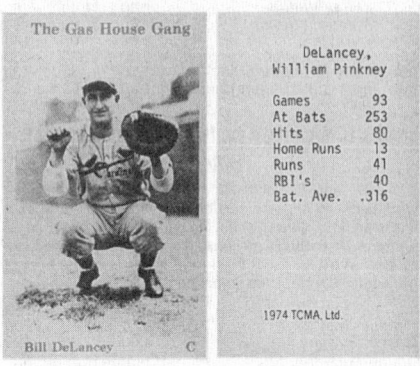

The "Gas House Gang" (as some of these cards are designated) is featured in this collectors' issue. Cards are 2-1/4" x 3-5/8" (#27-31 are 4-1/2" x 3-3/4") and feature black-and-white photos on front with red typography. Backs have a few stats in black-and-white. Some cards have a title at top front reading "1934 Cardinals." The unnumbered cards are checklisted here in alphabetical order.

		NM	EX	VG
Complete Set (31):		50.00	25.00	15.00
Common Player:		2.00	1.00	.60
(1)	"Tex" Carleton	2.00	1.00	.60
(2)	"Ripper" Collins	2.00	1.00	.60
(3)	"Pat" Crawford	2.00	1.00	.60
(4)	"Spud" Davis	2.00	1.00	.60
(5)	"Daffy" Dean	2.50	1.25	.70
(6)	"Dizzy" Dean	4.00	2.00	1.25
(7)	Bill DeLancey	2.00	1.00	.60
(8)	Leo Durocher	2.50	1.25	.70
(9)	Frank Frisch	2.50	1.25	.70
(10)	"Chick" Fullis	2.00	1.00	.60
(11)	"Mike" Gonzalez	2.50	1.25	.70
(12)	"Pop" Haines	2.50	1.25	.70
(13)	Bill Hallahan	2.00	1.00	.60
(14)	Francis Healey (Healy)	2.00	1.00	.60
(15)	Jim Lindsey	2.00	1.00	.60
(16)	"Pepper" Martin	2.50	1.25	.70
(17)	"Ducky" Medwick	2.50	1.25	.70
(18)	Jim Mooney	2.00	1.00	.60
(19)	Ernie Orsatti	2.00	1.00	.60
(20)	Flint Rhem	2.00	1.00	.60
(21)	John Rothrock	2.00	1.00	.60
(22)	"Dazzy" Vance	2.50	1.25	.70
(23)	Bill Walker	2.00	1.00	.60
(24)	"Buzzy" Wares	2.00	1.00	.60
(25)	"Whitey" Whitehead	2.00	1.00	.60
(26)	Jim Winford	2.00	1.00	.60
(27)	"Daffy" & "Dizzy" (Daffy Dean, Dizzy Dean)	6.00	3.00	1.75
(28)	Dizzy & Leo Celebrate (Dizzy Dean, Leo Durocher)	4.00	2.00	1.25
(29)	Durocher Scores (Leo Durocher) (1934 World Series)	4.00	2.00	1.25
(30)	Medwick Out Cochrane Catcher (Mickey Cochrane, Ducky Medwick) (1934 World Series)	4.00	2.00	1.25
(31)	1934 St. Louis Cardinals World Champions	4.00	2.00	1.25

1974 TCMA 1934-5 Detroit Tigers

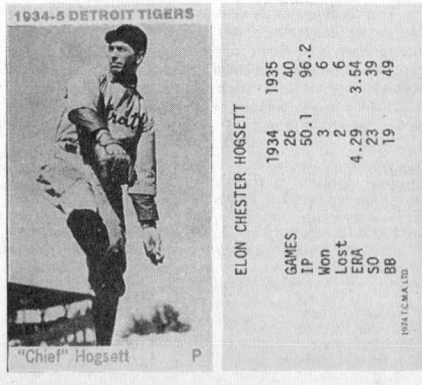

Members of the 1934 A.L. Champion and 1935 World's Champion teams are featured in this collectors issue team set. Except for a pair of large-format (4-1/4" x 3-3/4") cards, the cards measure about 2-1/8" x 3-5/8". Fronts have black-and-white photos. Above and below the photo are white stripes with the set title, player name and position. Backs are in black-and-white with 1934 and/or 1935 stats. The unnumbered cards are checklisted here alphabetically.

	NM	EX	VG
Complete Set (36):	35.00	17.50	10.00
Common Player:	2.00	1.00	.60
(1) Eldon Auker	2.00	1.00	.60
(2) Del Baker	2.00	1.00	.60
(3) Tommy Bridges	2.00	1.00	.60
(4) "Flea" Clifton	2.00	1.00	.60
(5) Mickey Cochrane	4.00	2.00	1.25
(6) "General" Crowder	2.00	1.00	.60
(7) Frank Doljack	2.00	1.00	.60
(8) Carl Fischer	2.00	1.00	.60
(9) Pete Fox	2.00	1.00	.60
(10) Vic Frasier	2.00	1.00	.60
(11) Charlie Gehringer	4.00	2.00	1.25
(12) Goose Goslin	2.00	1.00	.60
(13) Hank Greenberg	5.00	2.50	1.50
(14) Luke Hamlin	2.00	1.00	.60
(15) Clyde Hatter	2.00	1.00	.60
(16) Ray Hayworth	2.00	1.00	.60
(17) "Chief" Hogsett	2.00	1.00	.60
(18) Roxie Lawson	2.00	1.00	.60
(19) "Firpo" Marberry	2.00	1.00	.60
(20) Chet Morgan	2.00	1.00	.60
(21) Marv Owen	2.00	1.00	.60
(22) "Cy" Perkins	2.00	1.00	.60
(23) "Red" Phillips	2.00	1.00	.60
(24) Frank Reiber	2.00	1.00	.60
(25) Billy Rogell	2.00	1.00	.60
(26) "Schoolboy" Rowe	2.00	1.00	.60
(27) "Heinie" Schuble	2.00	1.00	.60
(28) Hugh Shelley	2.00	1.00	.60
(29) Vic Sorrell	2.00	1.00	.60
(30) Joe Sullivan	2.00	1.00	.60
(31) "Gee" Walker	2.00	1.00	.60
(32) "Hub" Walker	2.00	1.00	.60
(33) "Jo-Jo" White	2.00	1.00	.60
(34) Rudy York	2.00	1.00	.60
(35) 1934 Pitchers (Eldon Auker, Firpo Marberry, Tommy Bridges, Schoolboy Rowe) (4-1/4" x 3-3/4")	5.00	2.50	1.50
(36) 1935 Outfield (Goose Goslin, Jo-Jo White, Pete Fox) (4-1/4" x 3-3/4")	5.00	2.50	1.50

1974 TCMA 1936-37 New York Giants

This is the rarest of the TCMA Great Teams sets. Fewer than half of the 1,000 sets got into the hands of customers before legal action by Dick Bartell forced the company to halt sales and destroy more than 500 sets. The 2-5/8" x 3-3/8" cards are printed in black-and-orange. They are unnumbered and checklisted here in alphabetical order.

	NM	EX	VG
Complete Set (36):	90.00	45.00	27.50
Common Player:	2.50	1.25	.75
(1) Title card	1.00	.50	.30
(2) Tom Baker	2.50	1.25	.75
(3) Dick Bartell	2.50	1.25	.75
(4) Wally Berger	2.50	1.25	.75
(5) Don Brennan	2.50	1.25	.75
(6) Walter Brown	2.50	1.25	.75
(7) Clyde Castleman	2.50	1.25	.75
(8) Lou Chiozza	2.50	1.25	.70
(9) Dick Coffman	2.50	1.25	.75
(10) Harry Danning	2.50	1.25	.75
(11) George Davis	2.50	1.25	.75
(12) Charlie English	2.50	1.25	.75
(13) Freddie Fitzsimmons	2.50	1.25	.75
(14) Frank Gabler	2.50	1.25	.75
(15) Harry Gumbert	2.50	1.25	.75
(16) Mickey Haslin	2.50	1.25	.75
(17) Carl Hubbell	6.00	3.00	1.75
(18) Travis Jackson	4.00	2.00	1.25
(19) Mark Koenig	2.50	1.25	.75
(20) Hank Leiber	2.50	1.25	.75
(21) Sam Leslie	2.50	1.25	.75
(22) Bill Lohrman	2.50	1.25	.75
(23) Eddie Mayo	2.50	1.25	.75
(24) John McCarthy	2.50	1.25	.75
(25) Cliff Melton	2.50	1.25	.75
(26) Jo Jo Moore	2.50	1.25	.75
(27) Mel Ott	6.00	3.00	1.75
(28) Jimmy Ripple	2.50	1.25	.75
(29) Hal Schumacher	2.50	1.25	.75
(30) Al Smith	2.50	1.25	.75
(31) Roy Spencer	2.50	1.25	.75
(32) Bill Terry	5.00	2.50	1.50
(33) Hy Vandenberg	2.50	1.25	.75
(34) Phil Weintraub	2.50	1.25	.75
(35) Burgess Whitehead	2.50	1.25	.75
(36) Babe Young	2.50	1.25	.75

1974 TCMA 1936-1939 Yankee Dynasty

Many of the players who participated in one or more of the Yankees' four consecutive World Champion seasons in the late 1930s are included in this collectors' edition. Cards are 2-3/4" x 4" and feature black-and-white photos on front. In the white borders at top and bottom, the set name and player identification are printed in blue. Backs have stats for each season and are printed in black-and-white on a white background. A virtual reprint of this set was made circa 1983 with two player cards added and a brown background on back. The unnumbered cards are checklisted here alphabetically.

1936 - 1939 Yankee Dynasty

JOHN JOSEPH MURPHY

	1936	1937	1938	1939
Games	27	39	32	38
Won	3	13	8	3
Lost	3	4	2	6
Pct.	.750	.765	.800	.333
BB	36	50	41	30
SO	34	46	43	28
ERA	3.38	4.17	4.24	4.40

Johnny Murphy P

T.C.M.A. Ltd.

	NM	EX	VG
Complete Set (56):	75.00	37.50	22.50
Complete Set (51):	45.00	22.50	13.50
Common Player:	2.00	1.00	.60
(1) "Poison Ivy" Andrews	2.00	1.00	.60
(2) Joe Beggs	2.00	1.00	.60
(3) Marv Breuer	2.00	1.00	.60
(4) Johnny Broaca	2.00	1.00	.60
(5) "Jumbo" Brown	2.00	1.00	.60
(6) "Spud" Chandler	2.00	1.00	.60
(7) Ben Chapman	2.00	1.00	.60
(8) Earle Combs	2.00	1.00	.60
(9) Frankie Crosetti	2.00	1.00	.60
(10) "Babe" Dahlgren	2.00	1.00	.60
(11) Bill Dickey	2.50	1.25	.70
(12) Joe DiMaggio	10.00	5.00	3.00
(13) Atley Donald	2.00	1.00	.60
(14) Wes Ferrell	2.00	1.00	.60
(15) Artie Fletcher	2.00	1.00	.60
(16) Joe Gallagher	2.00	1.00	.60
(17) Lou Gehrig	10.00	5.00	3.00
(18) Joe Glenn	2.00	1.00	.60
(19) "Lefty" Gomez	2.00	1.00	.60
(20) Joe Gordon	2.00	1.00	.60
(21) "Bump" Hadley	2.00	1.00	.60
(22) Don Heffner	2.00	1.00	.60
(23) Tommy Henrich	2.00	1.00	.60
(24) Oral Hildebrand	2.00	1.00	.60
(25) Myril Hoag	2.00	1.00	.60
(26) Roy Johnson	2.00	1.00	.60
(27) Arndt Jorgens	2.00	1.00	.60
(28) Charlie Keller	2.00	1.00	.60
(29) Ted Kleinhans	2.00	1.00	.60
(30) Billy Knickerbocker	2.00	1.00	.60
(31) Tony Lazzeri	2.50	1.25	.70
(32) Frank Makosky	2.00	1.00	.60
(33) "Pat" Malone	2.00	1.00	.60
(34) Johnny Murphy	2.00	1.00	.60
(35) "Monty" Pearson	2.00	1.00	.60
(36) "Jake" Powell	2.00	1.00	.60
(37) "Red" Rolfe	2.00	1.00	.60
(38) "Buddy" Rosar	2.00	1.00	.60
(39) "Red" Ruffing	2.50	1.25	.70
(40) Marius Russo	2.00	1.00	.60
(41) "Jack" Saltzgaver	2.00	1.00	.60
(42) Paul Schreiber	2.00	1.00	.60
(43) Johnny Schulte	2.00	1.00	.60
(44) Bob Seeds	2.00	1.00	.60
(45) "Twinkletoes" Selkirk	2.00	1.00	.60
(46) Lee Stine	2.00	1.00	.60
(47) Steve Sundra	2.00	1.00	.60
(48) "Sandy" Vance	2.00	1.00	.60
(49) Dixie Walker	2.00	1.00	.60
(50) Kemp Wicker	2.00	1.00	.60
(51) Joe McCarthy, Jacob Ruppert	2.00	1.00	.60
5-1/2" x 4" FEATURE CARDS			
(52) Joe DiMaggio, Frank Crosetti, Tony Lazzeri, Bill Dickey, Lou Gehrig, Jake Powell, George Selkirk	5.00	2.50	1.50
(53) Lou Gehrig, Joe DiMaggio	7.50	3.75	2.25
(54) Gehrig Hits Another	6.00	3.00	1.75
(55) Red Rolfe, Tony Lazzeri, Lou Gehrig, Frank Crosetti	5.00	2.50	1.50
(56) World Champions - 1936	6.00	3.00	1.75

1974 TCMA 1952 Brooklyn Dodgers

1952 BROOKLYN DODGERS

ALBERT BLUFORD WALKER

Catcher #10

Games	46
AB	139
Hits	36
Runs	9
HR	0
RBI	19
BA	.259

Rube

T.C.M.A. 1974

The National League champion '52 Dodgers are featured in this collectors issue. Nominally 2-3/4" x 3-3/8", the cards are often found with minor variations in size. Fronts are printed in red and blue with a white border. The only identification on front is the player's first name or nickname. Backs are in black-and-white with the player's full name, position, uniform number, 1952 stats and TCMA copyright. Cards are checklisted here in alphabetical order.

	NM	EX	VG
Complete Set (40):	25.00	15.00	7.50

	NM	EX	VG
Common Player:	2.00	1.00	.60
(1) Header/Team History Card (Jackie Robinson, Gil Hodges, Roy Campanella, Billy Cox, Pee Wee Reese)	2.00	1.00	.60
(2) Cal Abrams	2.00	1.00	.60
(3) Sandy Amoros	2.00	1.00	.60
(4) Joe Black	2.00	1.00	.60
(5) Ralph Branca	2.00	1.00	.60
(6) Rocky Bridges	2.00	1.00	.60
(7) Roy Campanella	4.00	2.00	1.25
(8) Billy Cox	2.00	1.00	.60
(9) Chuck Dressen	2.00	1.00	.60
(10) Carl Erskine	2.00	1.00	.60
(11) Carl Furillo	3.00	1.50	.90
(12) Billy Herman	2.00	1.00	.60
(13) Gil Hodges	4.00	2.00	1.25
(14) Tommy Holmes	2.00	1.00	.60
(15) Jim Hughes	2.00	1.00	.60
(16) Clyde King	2.00	1.00	.60
(17) Clem Labine	2.00	1.00	.60
(18) Joe Landrum	2.00	1.00	.60
(19) Cookie Lavagetto	2.00	1.00	.60
(20) Ken Lehman	2.00	1.00	.60
(21) Steve Lembo	2.00	1.00	.60
(22) Billy Loes	2.00	1.00	.60
(23) Ray Moore	2.00	1.00	.60
(24) Bobby Morgan	2.00	1.00	.60
(25) Ron Negray	2.00	1.00	.60
(26) Rocky Nelson	2.00	1.00	.60
(27) Andy Pafko	2.00	1.00	.60
(28) Jake Pitler	2.00	1.00	.60
(29) Bud Podbielan	2.00	1.00	.60
(30) Pee Wee Reese	4.00	2.00	1.25
(31) Jackie Robinson	7.50	3.75	2.25
(32) Preacher Roe	2.00	1.00	.60
(33) Johnny Rutherford	2.00	1.00	.60
(34) Johnny Schmitz	2.00	1.00	.60
(35) George Shuba	2.00	1.00	.60
(36) Duke Snider	4.00	2.00	1.25
(37) Chris Van Cuyk	2.00	1.00	.60
(38) Ben Wade	2.00	1.00	.60
(39) Rube Walker	2.00	1.00	.60
(40) Dick Williams	2.00	1.00	.60

1975 TCMA All Time Brooklyn/Los Angeles Dodgers

LHP Sandy Koufax

ALL TIME BROOKLYN/LOS ANGELES DODGERS

1b	Gil Hodges
2b	Jackie Robinson
ss	Pee Wee Reese
3b	Junior Gilliam
OF	Duke Snider
OF	Dixie Walker
OF	Zack Wheat
C	Roy Campanella
RHP	Don Drysdale
LHP	Sandy Koufax
RP	Hugh Casey
Mgr	Walter Alston

T.C.M.A. Ltd. 1975

A picked team of former Dodgers stars is featured in this collectors issue team set. Cards are in black-and-white in the standard 2-1/2" x 3-1/2" format. Fronts have player identification in the border beneath the photo. Backs have a checklist by position and a TCMA copyright line. The unnumbered cards are checklisted here in the order presented on back.

	NM	EX	VG
Complete Set (12):	25.00	12.50	7.50
Common Player:	2.25	1.25	.70
(1) Gil Hodges	3.00	1.50	.90
(2) Jackie Robinson	10.00	5.00	3.00
(3) Pee Wee Reese	3.00	1.50	.90
(4) Junior Gilliam	2.25	1.25	.70
(5) Duke Snider	3.00	1.50	.90
(6) Dixie Walker	2.25	1.25	.70
(7) Zack Wheat	2.25	1.25	.70
(8) Roy Campanella	4.00	2.00	1.25
(9) Don Drysdale	3.00	1.50	.90
(10) Sandy Koufax	8.00	4.00	2.50
(11) Hugh Casey	2.25	1.25	.70
(12) Walter Alston	2.25	1.25	.70

1975 TCMA All-Time Greats

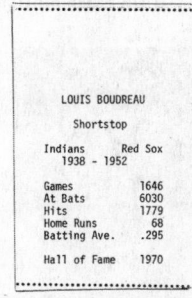

LOUIS BOUDREAU

Shortstop

Indians   Red Sox
1938 - 1952

Games	1646
At Bats	6030
Hits	1779
Home Runs	68
Batting Ave.	.295
Hall of Fame	1970

LOU BOUDREAU

This is a smaller - both in size and number - version of TCMA's Hall of Famer postcard set issued between 1973-80. These collectors' edition cards measure 2-3/8" x 3-3/4" and were issued in strips of six. Two printings were done, the first with blue-and-white fronts and red backs, the second in black-and-white, blank-backed. Surrounding the photo on front is a blue or black border with baseball equipment ornamentation. The unnumbered cards are checklisted here in alphabetical order.

		NM	EX	VG
Complete Set (39):		40.00	20.00	12.00
Common Player:		2.00	1.00	.60
(1)	"Luke" Appling	2.00	1.00	.60
(2)	Roger Bresnahan	2.00	1.00	.60
(3)	Ty Cobb	8.00	4.00	2.50
(4)	Mickey Cochrane	2.00	1.00	.60
(5)	Eddie Collins	2.00	1.00	.60
(6)	Kiki Cuyler	2.00	1.00	.60
(7)	Dizzy Dean	4.00	2.00	1.25
(8)	Bill Dickey	2.00	1.00	.60
(9)	Joe DiMaggio	8.00	4.00	2.50
(10)	Bob Feller	2.00	1.00	.60
(11)	Elmer Flick	2.00	1.00	.60
(12)	Frank Frisch	2.00	1.00	.60
(13)	Lou Gehrig	8.00	4.00	2.50
(14)	Hank Greenberg	4.00	2.00	1.25
(15)	Goose Goslin	2.00	1.00	.60
(16)	Chick Hafey	2.00	1.00	.60
(17)	Gabby Hartnett	2.00	1.00	.60
(18)	Harry Heilmann	2.00	1.00	.60
(19)	Rogers Hornsby	2.00	1.00	.60
(20)	Waite Hoyt	2.00	1.00	.60
(21)	Walter Johnson	4.00	2.00	1.25
(22)	George Kelly	2.00	1.00	.60
(23)	Ted Lyons	2.00	1.00	.60
(24)	Connie Mack	2.00	1.00	.60
(25)	Mickey Mantle	10.00	5.00	3.00
(26)	Rabbit Maranville	2.00	1.00	.60
(27)	Mel Ott	2.00	1.00	.60
(28)	Edd Roush	2.00	1.00	.60
(29)	Red Ruffing	2.00	1.00	.60
(30)	Babe Ruth	10.00	5.00	3.00
(31)	Al Simmons	2.00	1.00	.60
(32)	Casey Stengel	2.00	1.00	.60
(33)	Pie Traynor	2.00	1.00	.60
(34)	Dazzy Vance	2.00	1.00	.60
(35)	Honus Wagner	4.00	2.00	1.25
(36)	Lloyd Waner	2.00	1.00	.60
(37)	Paul Waner	2.00	1.00	.60
(38)	Ted Williams	6.00	3.00	1.75
(39)	Harry Wright	2.00	1.00	.60

1975 TCMA All Time New York Giants

ss Alvin Dark

ALL TIME NEW YORK GIANTS	
1b	Bill Terry
2b	Frankie Frisch
ss	Alvin Dark
3b	Fred Lindstrom
LF	Bobby Thomson
CF	Willie Mays
RF	Mel Ott
C	Wes Westrum
LHP	Carl Hubbell
RHP	Christy Mathewson
RP	Hoyt Wilhelm
Mgr	John McGraw

TCMA Ltd. 1975

An all-time line-up of Giants is presented in this collector issue. Fronts of the 2-1/2" x 3-1/2" cards have black-and-white player photos with the player's name and position printed in red in the white bottom border. Backs are in black-and-white and present the all-time roster. The unnumbered cards are checklisted here alphabetically.

		NM	EX	VG
Complete Set (12):		30.00	15.00	9.00
Common Player:		2.00	1.00	.60
(1)	Alvin Dark	2.00	1.00	.60
(2)	Frankie Frisch	2.00	1.00	.60
(3)	Carl Hubbell	2.00	1.00	.60
(4)	Freddie Lindstrom	2.00	1.00	.60
(5)	Christy Mathewson	4.00	2.00	1.25
(6)	Willie Mays	15.00	7.50	4.50
(7)	John McGraw	2.00	1.00	.60
(8)	Mel Ott	2.00	1.00	.60
(9)	Bill Terry	2.00	1.00	.60
(10)	Bobby Thomson	2.00	1.00	.60
(11)	Wes Westrum	2.00	1.00	.60
(12)	Hoyt Wilhelm	2.00	1.00	.60

1975 TCMA All Time New York Yankees

SS Phil Rizzuto

ALL TIME NEW YORK YANKEE TEAM	
1B	Lou Gehrig
2B	Tony Lazzeri
3B	Red Rolfe
SS	Phil Rizzuto
OF	Babe Ruth
OF	Mickey Mantle
OF	Joe DiMaggio
C	Bill Dickey
P	Red Ruffing
P	Whitey Ford
RP	Johnny Murphy
Mgr	Casey Stengel

T.C.M.A. LTD 1975

The best players on the best team in baseball history are featured in this collectors' edition. Cards measure 2-1/2" x 3-3/4" and feature black-and-white photos on front, with white borders.

Player name and position are printed in a white strip toward the bottom of the picture. Backs have a list of the all-time team. The unnumbered cards are listed here in that order.

		NM	EX	VG
Complete Set (12):		15.00	7.50	4.50
Common Player:		2.00	1.00	.60
(1)	Lou Gehrig	4.00	2.00	1.25
(2)	Tony Lazzeri	2.00	1.00	.60
(3)	Red Rolfe	2.00	1.00	.60
(4)	Phil Rizzuto	2.50	1.25	.70
(5)	Babe Ruth	5.00	2.50	1.50
(6)	Mickey Mantle	6.00	3.00	1.75
(7)	Joe DiMaggio	4.00	2.00	1.25
(8)	Bill Dickey	2.00	1.00	.60
(9)	Red Ruffing	2.00	1.00	.60
(10)	Whitey Ford	2.50	1.25	.70
(11)	Johnny Murphy	2.00	1.00	.60
(12)	Casey Stengel	2.00	1.00	.60

1975 TCMA Larry French Postcards

The career of National League pitcher Larry French is recounted in this set of 3-1/2" x 5-1/2" postcard-size cards. Fronts have photos of him with the Pirates, Cubs and Dodgers. Backs have a continuing biography.

		NM	EX	VG
Complete Set (6):		15.00	7.50	4.50
Common Card:		3.00	1.50	.90
1	Larry French (Pittsburgh Pirates)	3.00	1.50	.90
2	Larry French (Chicago Cubs)	3.00	1.50	.90
3	Larry French (W/Bill Lee, Charlie Root, Tuck Stainback .)	3.00	1.50	.90
4	Larry French (W/Charlie Grimm, Fred Lindstrom.)	3.00	1.50	.90
5	Larry French (Brooklyn Dodgers)	3.00	1.50	.90
6	Larry French (W/Mickey Owen.)	3.00	1.50	.90

1975 TCMA Guam WW2

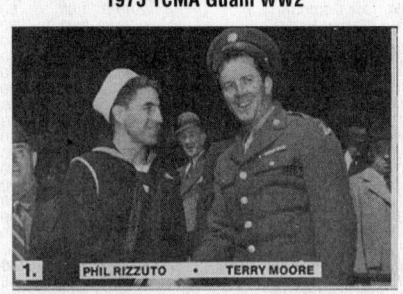

1. PHIL RIZZUTO • TERRY MOORE

This set of 3-1/2" x 5-1/2" black-and-white cards details the connection between Major League Baseball and the Pacific island of Guam during WWII. Some cards picture players in the their military uniforms, others shown them in baseball uniforms. Backs contain a narrative of the series.

		NM	EX	VG
Complete Set (18):		25.00	12.50	7.50
Common Card:		1.00	.50	.30
1	Phil Rizzuto, Terry Moore	5.00	2.50	1.50
2	Gab Gab Guam 1945	1.00	.50	.30
3	Team Photo	1.00	.50	.30
4	Merrill May, Pee Wee Reese, Johnny Vander Meer	2.50	1.25	.70
5	Team Photo	1.00	.50	.30
6	Team Photo	1.00	.50	.30
7	Del Ennis	2.00	1.00	.60
8	Mace Brown	2.00	1.00	.60
9	Pee Wee Reese, Joe Gordon, Bill Dickey	3.50	1.75	1.00
10	Glenn McQuillen	2.00	1.00	.60
11	Mike Budnick	2.00	1.00	.60
12	Team Photo	1.00	.50	.30
13	"Skeets" Dickey	2.00	1.00	.60
14	Connie Ryan	2.00	1.00	.60
15	Hal White	2.00	1.00	.60
16	Mickey Cochrane	7.50	3.75	2.25
17	Barney McCosky	2.00	1.00	.60
18	Ben Huffman	2.00	1.00	.60

1975 TCMA 1913 Philadelphia Athletics

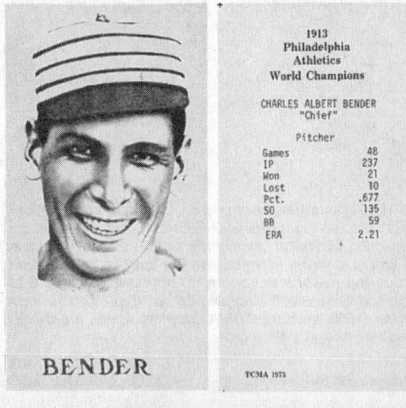

BENDER

1913 Philadelphia Athletics World Champions

CHARLES ALBERT BENDER "Chief"

Pitcher

Games	48
IP	237
Won	21
Lost	10
Pct.	.677
SO	135
BB	59
ERA	2.21

TCMA 1975

Members of the World Champion A's of 1913 are featured in this collectors' edition card set. In an unusual 3-1/8" x 5-11/16" format, the cards have black-and-white photos on front, with white borders and player identification at bottom. Backs feature season statistics. The unnumbered cards are checklisted here alphabetically.

		NM	EX	VG
Complete Set (16):		20.00	10.00	6.00
Common Player:		3.00	1.50	.90
(1)	Home Run Baker	3.00	1.50	.90
(2)	Jack Barry	3.00	1.50	.90
(3)	Chief Bender	3.00	1.50	.90
(4)	Joe Bush	3.00	1.50	.90
(5)	Eddie Collins	3.00	1.50	.90
(6)	Jack Coombs	3.00	1.50	.90
(7)	Jack Lapp	3.00	1.50	.90
(8)	Connie Mack	3.00	1.50	.90
(9)	Stuffy McInnis	3.00	1.50	.90
(10)	Dan Murphy	3.00	1.50	.90
(11)	Eddie Murphy	3.00	1.50	.90
(12)	Rube Oldring	3.00	1.50	.90
(13)	William Orr	3.00	1.50	.90
(14)	Ed Plank	3.00	1.50	.90
(15)	Walter Schang	3.00	1.50	.90
(16)	Amos Strunk	3.00	1.50	.90

1975 TCMA 1919 Chicago White Sox

Joe Jackson OF
1919 CHICAGO WHITE SOX

JOSEPH JEFFERSON JACKSON

Games	139
At Bats	516
Hits	181
Runs	79
Home Runs	7
RBI's	96
Bat. Ave.	.351

T.C.M.A. 1975

The infamous Black Sox who threw the 1919 World Series, and their teammates, are featured in this collectors' edition. The 2-1/2" x 3-1/2" cards are printed in black-and-white. Fronts have player photos with identification in the white border at bottom. Backs have 1919 season stats. The unnumbered cards are checklisted here alphabetically.

		NM	EX	VG
Complete Set (28):		35.00	17.50	10.00
Common Player:		1.00	.50	.30
(1)	Joe Benz	1.00	.50	.30
(2)	Eddie Cicotte	3.50	1.75	1.00
(3)	Eddie Collins	2.50	1.25	.70
(4)	Shano Collins	1.00	.50	.30
(5)	Dave Danforth	1.00	.50	.30
(6)	Red Faber	1.00	.40	.25
(7)	Happy Felsch	3.50	1.75	1.00
(8)	Chick Gandil	5.00	2.50	1.50
(9)	Kid Gleason	1.00	.50	.30
(10)	Joe Jackson	10.00	5.00	3.00
(11)	Bill James	1.00	.50	.30
(12)	Dickie Kerr	1.00	.50	.30
(13)	Nemo Leibold	1.00	.50	.30
(14)	Byrd Lynn	1.00	.50	.30
(15)	Erskine Mayer	2.00	1.00	.60
(16)	Harvey McClellan	1.00	.50	.30
(17)	Fred McMullin	4.00	2.00	1.25
(18)	Eddie Murphy	1.00	.50	.30
(19)	Pat Ragan	1.00	.50	.30
(20)	Swede Risberg	4.00	2.00	1.25
(21)	Charlie Robertson	1.00	.50	.30
(22)	Reb Russell	1.00	.50	.30
(23)	Ray Schalk	1.00	.40	.25
(24)	Buck Weaver	6.00	3.00	1.75
(25)	Roy Wilkinson	1.00	.50	.30
(26)	Lefty Williams	4.00	2.00	1.25
(27)	Frank Shellenback, Grover Lowdermilk, Joe Jenkins, Dickie Kerr, Ray Schalk	1.00	.50	.30
(28)	Team Photo (4-3/4" x 3-1/2")	7.50	3.75	2.25

1975 TCMA 1924-1925 Washington Senators

1924 - 1925 Washington Senators

Bennie Tate C

HENRY BENNETT TATE

	1924	1925
Games	21	16
At Bats	43	27
Hits	13	13
Runs	2	0
HR	0	0
RBI's	7	7
AVE.	.302	.481

T.C.M.A. Ltd. 1975

The back-to-back American League champion Senators of 1924-25 are featured in this collectors' edition card set. Cards measure 2-3/8" x 3-7/16". Fronts have black-and-white photos with blue captions and white borders. Backs have player stats for the two seasons. The unnumbered cards are checklisted here in alphabetical order.

		NM	EX	VG
Complete Set (42):		30.00	15.00	9.00
Common Player:		1.50	.75	.45
(1)	Spencer Adams	1.50	.75	.45
(2)	Nick Altrock	1.50	.75	.45
(3)	Ossie Bluege	1.50	.75	.45
(4)	Stan Coveleski	1.50	.75	.45
(5)	Alex Ferguson	1.50	.75	.45
(6)	Showboat Fisher	1.50	.75	.45
(7)	Goose Goslin	1.50	.75	.45
(8)	Bart Griffith	1.50	.75	.45
(9)	Pinky Hargrave	1.50	.75	.45
(10)	Bucky Harris	1.50	.75	.45
(11)	Joe Harris	1.50	.75	.45
(12)	Tex Jeanes	1.50	.75	.45
(13)	Walter Johnson	4.00	2.00	1.25
(14)	Joe Judge	1.50	.75	.45
(15)	Wade Lefler	1.50	.75	.45
(16)	Nemo Leibold	1.50	.75	.45
(17)	Firpo Marberry	1.50	.75	.45
(18)	Joe Martina	1.50	.75	.45
(19)	Wid Matthews	1.50	.75	.45
(20)	Mike McNally	1.50	.75	.45
(21)	Earl McNeely	1.50	.75	.45
(22)	Ralph Miller	1.50	.75	.45
(23)	George Mogridge	1.50	.75	.45
(24)	Buddy Myer	1.50	.75	.45
(25)	Curly Ogden	1.50	.75	.45
(26)	Roger Peckinpaugh	1.50	.75	.45
(27)	Spencer Pumpelly	1.50	.75	.45
(28)	Sam Rice	1.50	.75	.45
(29)	Muddy Ruel	1.50	.75	.45
(30)	Dutch Ruether	1.50	.75	.45
(31)	Allen Russell	1.50	.75	.45
(32)	Everett Scott	1.50	.75	.45
(33)	Hank Severeid	1.50	.75	.45
(34)	Mule Shirley	1.50	.75	.45
(35)	Byron Speece	1.50	.75	.45
(36)	Benny Tate	1.50	.75	.45
(37)	Bobby Veach	1.50	.75	.45
(38)	Tom Zachary	1.50	.75	.45
(39)	Paul Zahniser	1.50	.75	.45
	5" x 3-1/2" FEATURE CARDS	1.50	.75	.45
(40)	Bucky Harris, Bill McKechnie	2.00	1.00	.60
(41)	Ossie Bluege, Roger Peckinpaugh, Bucky Harris, Joe Judge	2.00	1.00	.60
(42)	Tom Zachary, Firpo Marberry, Alex Ferguson, Walter Johnson	2.50	1.25	.70

1975 TCMA 1927 New York Yankees

One of the greatest teams in baseball history is featured in this set of collectors' cards. The 2-1/2" x 3-1/2" cards have black-and-white photos with a white border. At top is the team identification, at bottom is player name and position. The back has the player's 1927 season stats. The unnumbered cards are checklisted here alphabetically.

		NM	EX	VG
Complete Set (30):		40.00	20.00	12.00
Common Player:		2.00	1.00	.60
(1)	Walter Beall	2.00	1.00	.60
(2)	Benny Bengough	2.00	1.00	.60
(3)	Pat Collins	2.00	1.00	.60
(4)	Earle Combs	2.00	1.00	.60
(5)	Joe Dugan	2.00	1.00	.60
(6)	Cedric Durst	2.00	1.00	.60
(7)	Mike Gazella	2.00	1.00	.60
(8)	Lou Gehrig	7.50	3.75	2.25
(9)	Joe Giard	2.00	1.00	.60
(10)	Johnny Grabowski	2.00	1.00	.60
(11)	Waite Hoyt	2.00	1.00	.60
(12)	Miller Huggins	2.00	1.00	.60
(13)	Mark Koenig	2.00	1.00	.60
(14)	Tony Lazzeri	2.00	1.00	.60
(15)	Bob Meusel	2.00	1.00	.60
(16)	Wilcy Moore	2.00	1.00	.60
(17)	Ray Morehart	2.00	1.00	.60
(18)	Ben Paschal	2.00	1.00	.60
(19)	Herb Pennock	2.00	1.00	.60
(20)	George Pipgras	2.00	1.00	.60
(21)	Dutch Ruether	2.00	1.00	.60
(22)	Jacob Ruppert	2.00	1.00	.60
(23)	Babe Ruth	12.00	6.00	3.50
(24)	Bob Shawkey	2.00	1.00	.60
(25)	Urban Shocker	2.00	1.00	.60
(26)	Myles Thomas	2.00	1.00	.60
(27)	Julie Wera	2.00	1.00	.60
(28)	Yankee Coaches and Manager (Charlie O'Leary, Miller Huggins, Artie Fletcher)			

(29)	Yankee Stadium	3.00	1.50	.90
(30)	Yankees infield (Lou Gehrig, Tony Lazzeri, Mark Koenig, Joe Dugan) (5" x 3-5/8")	9.00	4.50	2.75

1975 TCMA 1942-46 St. Louis Cardinals

1942 St. Louis Cardinals

This collectors' issue set features players and staff from the Cards' war-years dynasty. In 2-1/2" x 3-5/8" format, the cards have black-and-white photos with red printing on front. The unnumbered cards have statistics on back.

		NM	EX	VG
Complete Set (66):		40.00	20.00	12.00
Common Player:		1.00	.50	.30
(1)	Buster Adams	1.00	.50	.30
(2)	Red Barrett	1.00	.50	.30
(3)	John Beazley	1.00	.50	.30
(4)	Al Brazle	1.00	.50	.30
(5)	Harry Brecheen	1.00	.50	.30
(6)	Jimmy Brown	1.00	.50	.30
(7)	Ken Burkhart	1.00	.50	.30
(8)	Bud Byerly	1.00	.50	.30
(9)	Mort Cooper	1.00	.50	.30
(10)	Walker Cooper	1.00	.50	.30
(11)	Estel Crabtree	1.00	.50	.30
(12)	Creepy Crespi	1.00	.50	.30
(13)	Jeff Cross	1.00	.50	.30
(14)	Frank Demaree	1.00	.50	.30
(15)	Murrey Dickson (Murry)	1.00	.50	.30
(16)	Blix Donnelly	1.00	.50	.30
(17)	Erv Dusak	1.00	.50	.30
(18)	Eddie Dyer	1.00	.50	.30
(19)	Bill Endicott	1.00	.50	.30
(20)	George Fallon	1.00	.50	.30
(21)	Joe Garagiola	3.00	1.50	.90
(22)	Debs Garms	1.00	.50	.30
(23)	Mike Gonzalez	1.25	.60	.40
(24)	Johnny Grodzicki	1.00	.50	.30
(25)	Harry Gumbert	1.00	.50	.30
(26)	Johnny Hopp	1.00	.50	.30
(27)	Nippy Jones	1.00	.50	.30
(28)	Lou Klein	1.00	.50	.30
(29)	Clyde Kluttz	1.00	.50	.30
(30)	Howie Krist	1.00	.50	.30
(31)	Whitey Kurowski	1.00	.50	.30
(32)	Max Lanier	1.00	.50	.30
(33)	Danny Litwhiler	1.00	.50	.30
(34)	Bill Lohrman	1.00	.50	.30
(35)	Marty Marion	1.50	.70	.45
(36)	Freddie Martin	1.00	.50	.30
(37)	Pepper Martin	2.00	1.00	.60
(38)	Terry Moore	1.00	.50	.30
(39)	Red Munger	1.00	.50	.30
(40)	Stan Musial	5.00	2.50	1.50
(41)	Sam Narron	1.00	.50	.30
(42)	Ken O'Dea	1.00	.50	.30
(43)	Howie Pollet	1.00	.50	.30
(44)	Del Rice	1.00	.50	.30
(45)	Ray Sanders	1.00	.50	.30
(46)	Fred Schmidt	1.00	.50	.30
(47)	Red Schoendienst	3.00	1.50	.90
(48)	Walt Sessi	1.00	.50	.30
(49)	Clyde Shoun	1.00	.50	.30
(50)	Dick Sisler	1.00	.50	.30
(51)	Enos Slaughter	3.00	1.50	.90
(52)	Billy Southworth	1.00	.50	.30
(53)	Coaker Triplett	1.00	.50	.30
(54)	Emil Verban	1.00	.50	.30
(55)	Harry Walker	1.00	.50	.30
(56)	Buzzy Wares	1.00	.50	.30
(57)	Lon Warneke	1.00	.50	.30
(58)	Ernie White	1.00	.50	.30
(59)	Del Wilber	1.00	.50	.30
(60)	Ted Wilks	1.00	.50	.30
(61)	Leo Durocher, Eddie Dyer	1.00	.50	.30
(62)	Stan Musial, Billy Southworth, Johnny Hopp	1.00	.50	.30
(63)	Stan Musial, Billy Southworth, Ray Sanders	1.00	.50	.30
(64)	Red Ruffing, Johnny Beazley	1.00	.50	.30
(65)	1942 St. Louis Cardinals (5" x 3-1/2")	3.00	1.50	.90
(66)	Sportsman's Park (5" x 3-1/2")	2.50	1.25	.70

The Red Sox American League champions of 1946 are featured in this collectors' issue. Blue-and-white player photos appear on front, with the player's name and position in black below. At bottom-front is the team name in red. Backs of the 2-1/2" x 3-1/2" cards have the player's 1946 stats. The unnumbered cards are checklisted here in alphabetical order.

Ben Steiner 3b
1946 BOSTON RED SOX

BENJAMIN SAUNDERS STEINER

Games 3
At Bats 4
Hits 1
Runs 1
Home Runs 0
Runs Batted In 0
Batting Average .250

TCMA, Ltd. 1975

		NM	EX	VG
Complete Set (43):		45.00	22.50	13.50
Common Player:		1.50	.75	.45
(1)	Jim Bagby	1.50	.75	.45
(2)	Del Baker	1.50	.75	.45
(3)	Mace Brown	1.50	.75	.45
(4)	Bill Butland	1.50	.75	.45
(5)	Paul Campbell	1.50	.75	.45
(6)	Tom Carey	1.50	.75	.45
(7)	Joe Cronin	2.00	1.00	.60
(8)	Leon Culberson	1.50	.75	.45
(9)	Tom Daly	1.50	.75	.45
(10)	Dom DiMaggio	2.50	1.25	.70
(11)	Joe Dobson	1.50	.75	.45
(12)	Bobby Doerr	1.50	.75	.45
(13)	Clem Dreisewerd	1.50	.75	.45
(14)	"Boo" Ferriss	1.50	.75	.45
(15)	Andy Gilbert	1.50	.75	.45
(16)	Don Gutteridge	1.50	.75	.45
(17)	Mickey Harris	1.50	.75	.45
(18)	Randy Heflin	1.50	.75	.45
(19)	"Pinky" Higgins	1.50	.75	.45
(20)	"Tex" Hughson	1.50	.75	.45
(21)	Earl Johnson	1.50	.75	.45
(22)	Bob Klinger	1.50	.75	.45
(23)	Johnny Lazor	1.50	.75	.45
(24)	Tom McBride	1.50	.75	.45
(25)	Ed McGah	1.50	.75	.45
(26)	"Catfish" Metkovich	1.50	.75	.45
(27)	Wally Moses	1.50	.75	.45
(28)	Roy Partee	1.50	.75	.45
(29)	Eddie Pellagrini	1.50	.75	.45
(30)	Johnny Pesky	1.50	.75	.45
(31)	Frank Pytlak	1.50	.75	.45
(32)	"Rip" Russell	1.50	.75	.45
(33)	Mike Ryba	1.50	.75	.45
(34)	Ben Steiner	1.50	.70	.45
(35)	Charlie Wagner	1.50	.75	.45
(36)	Hal Wagner	1.50	.75	.45
(37)	Ted Williams	7.50	3.75	2.25
(38)	Larry Woodall	1.50	.75	.45
(39)	Rudy York	1.50	.75	.45
(40)	Bill Zuber	1.50	.75	.45
(41)	Team Photo	2.00	1.00	.60
(42)	Larry Woodall, Hal Wagner, Del Baker	1.50	.75	.45
(43)	Rudy York, Wally Moses, Dom DiMaggio, Bobby Doerr, Charlie Wagner (5" x 3-1/2")	4.00	2.00	1.25

1975 TCMA 1950 Philadelphia Phillies/Whiz Kids

Whiz Kids

Eddie Waitkus 1b

EDWARD STEPHEN WAITKUS

Games 154
At Bats 641
Hits 182
Runs 102
HR 2
RBI 44
Bat. Ave. .284

T.C.M.A Ltd. 1975

The National League Champion "Whiz Kids" are featured in this collectors' issue. The 2-1/2" x 3-1/2" cards have black-and-white photos on front with the player's name and position in red at bottom and either "Whiz Kids" or "1950 Philadelphia Phillies" in red at top. Black-and-white backs have 1950 season stats. The unnumbered cards are checklisted here alphabetically. The large-format multiple-player card was issued coincidentally with the set.

		NM	EX	VG
Complete Set (32):		45.00	22.50	13.50
Common Player:		2.00	1.00	.60
(1)	Richie Ashburn	11.00	5.50	3.25
(2)	Benny Bengough	2.00	1.00	.60
(3)	Jimmy Bloodworth	2.00	1.00	.60
(4)	Hank Borowy	2.00	1.00	.60
(5)	"Putsy" Caballero	2.00	1.00	.60
(6)	"Bubba" Church	2.00	1.00	.60
(7)	Dusty Cooke	2.00	1.00	.60
(8)	Blix Donnelly	2.00	1.00	.60
(9)	Del Ennis	2.00	1.00	.60
(10)	Mike Goliat	2.00	1.00	.60
(11)	Granny Hamner	2.00	1.00	.60
(12)	Ken Heintzelman	2.00	1.00	.60
(13)	Stan Hollmig	2.00	1.00	.60

(14)	Ken Johnson	2.00	1.00	.60
(15)	"Puddin'-Head" Jones	2.00	1.00	.60
(16)	Jim Konstanty	2.00	1.00	.60
(17)	Stan Lopata	2.00	1.00	.60
(18)	Jackie Mayo	2.00	1.00	.60
(19)	Russ Meyer	2.00	1.00	.60
(20)	Bob Miller	2.00	1.00	.60
(21)	Bill Nicholson	2.00	1.00	.60
(22)	Cy Perkins	2.00	1.00	.60
(23)	Robin Roberts	11.00	5.50	3.25
(24)	Eddie Sawyer	2.00	1.00	.60
(25)	Andy Seminick	2.00	1.00	.60
(26)	Ken Silvestri	2.00	1.00	.60
(27)	Curt Simmons	2.00	1.00	.60
(28)	Dick Sisler	2.00	1.00	.60
(29)	"Jocko" Thompson	2.00	1.00	.60
(30)	Eddie Waitkus	2.00	1.00	.60
(31)	Dick Whitman	2.00	1.00	.60
(32)	Russ Meyer, Hank Borowy, Bill Nicholson, Willie Jones (4-7/8" x 3-1/2")	15.00	7.50	4.50

1975 TCMA 1951 New York Giants

Artie Wilson   OF
1951 NEW YORK GIANTS

ARTHUR LEE WILSON
Infielder
Games   19
At Bats   44
Hits   4
Runs   2
HR   0
RBI   1
Bat.Ave.   .182

TCMA, Ltd. 1975

The National League Champion Giants of 1951 are honored in this collectors' issue card set. The 2-1/2" x 3-1/2" cards have black-and-white photos on front, with player name, team and position in the bottom border in red-orange ink. Backs are black-and-white with 1951 stats. The unnumbered cards are listed here in alphabetical order.

		NM	EX	VG
Complete Set (34):		35.00	17.50	10.00
Common Player:		1.50	.75	.45
(1)	George Bamberger	1.50	.75	.45
(2)	Roger Bowman	1.50	.75	.45
(3)	Al Corwin	1.50	.75	.45
(4)	Alvin Dark	2.00	1.00	.60
(5)	Allen Gettel	1.50	.75	.45
(6)	Clint Hartung	1.50	.75	.45
(7)	Jim Hearn	1.50	.75	.45
(8)	Monte Irvin	2.00	1.00	.60
(9)	Larry Jansen	1.50	.75	.45
(10)	Sheldon Jones	1.50	.75	.45
(11)	"Spider" Jorgensen	1.50	.75	.45
(12)	Monte Kennedy	1.50	.75	.45
(13)	Alex Konikowski	1.50	.70	.45
(14)	Dave Koslo	1.50	.75	.45
(15)	Jack Kramer	1.50	.75	.45
(16)	Whitey Lockman	1.50	.75	.45
(17)	"Lucky" Lohrke	1.50	.75	.45
(18)	Sal Maglie	1.50	.70	.45
(19)	Jack Maguire	1.50	.70	.45
(20)	Willie Mays	10.00	5.00	3.00
(21)	Don Mueller	1.50	.75	.45
(22)	Ray Noble	1.50	.75	.45
(23)	Earl Rapp	1.50	.75	.45
(24)	Bill Rigney	1.50	.75	.45
(25)	George Spencer	1.50	.75	.45
(26)	Eddie Stanky	1.50	.70	.45
(27)	Hank Thompson	1.50	.75	.45
(28)	Bobby Thomson	2.50	1.20	.70
(29)	Wes Westrum	1.50	.75	.45
(30)	Davey Williams	1.50	.75	.45
(31)	Artie Wilson	1.50	.75	.45
(32)	Sal Yvars	1.50	.75	.45
(33)	Leo Durocher, Willie Mays (3-5/8" x 5")	7.00	3.50	2.00
(34)	Durocher and coaches (3-5/8" x 5")	3.00	1.50	.90

1975 TCMA 1954 Cleveland Indians

Art Houtteman   P

1954 CLEVELAND INDIANS

ARTHUR JOSEPH HOUTTEMAN
Games   32
IP   188
Won   15
Lost   7
Pct.   6.82
BB   59
SO   68
ERA   3.35

T.C.M.A. 1975

The American League Champions of 1954 are featured in this collectors issue. Individual player cards are 2-1/2" x 3-1/2" printed in black-and-white. Backs have 1954 season stats.

Three large-format (3-3/4" x 5-1/8") multi-player cards were issued with the complete set. The unnumbered cards are checklisted here alphabetically.

		NM	EX	VG
Complete Set (39):		35.00	17.50	10.00
Common Player:		1.50	.75	.45
(1)	Bobby Avila	2.00	1.00	.60
(2)	Bob Chakales	1.50	.75	.45
(3)	Tony Cuccinello	1.50	.75	.45
(4)	Sam Dente	1.50	.75	.45
(5)	Larry Doby	3.50	1.75	1.00
(6)	Luke Easter	2.00	1.00	.60
(7)	Bob Feller	5.00	2.50	1.50
(8)	Mike Garcia	2.00	1.00	.60
(9)	Joe Ginsberg	1.50	.75	.45
(10)	Bill Glynn	1.50	.75	.45
(11)	Mickey Grasso	1.50	.75	.45
(12)	Mel Harder	1.50	.75	.45
(13)	Jim Hegan	1.50	.75	.45
(14)	Bob Hooper	1.50	.75	.45
(15)	Dave Hoskins	1.50	.75	.45
(16)	Art Houtteman	1.50	.75	.45
(17)	Bob Kennedy	1.50	.75	.45
(18)	Bob Lemon	2.50	1.25	.70
(19)	Al Lopez	2.50	1.25	.70
(20)	Hank Majeski	1.50	.75	.45
(21)	Dale Mitchell	1.50	.75	.45
(22)	Don Mossi	1.50	.75	.45
(23)	Hal Naragon	1.50	.75	.45
(24)	Ray Narleski	1.50	.75	.45
(25)	Rocky Nelson	1.50	.75	.45
(26)	Hal Newhouser	2.50	1.25	.70
(27)	Dave Philley	1.50	.75	.45
(28)	Dave Pope	1.50	.75	.45
(29)	Rudy Regaldo	1.50	.75	.45
(30)	Al Rosen	2.00	1.00	.60
(31)	Jose Santiago	1.50	.75	.45
(32)	Al Smith	1.50	.75	.45
(33)	George Strickland	1.50	.75	.45
(34)	Vic Wertz	1.50	.75	.45
(35)	Wally Westlake	1.50	.75	.45
(36)	Early Wynn	2.50	1.25	.70
	Large Format Cards	1.50	.75	.45
(37)	Al Lopez and Coaches	5.00	2.50	1.50
(38)	Al Lopez and Pitchers	5.00	2.50	1.50
(39)	Indians Outfielders	5.00	2.50	1.50

1975 TCMA/ASCCA Ad Card

To promote the American Sports Card Collectors Association Show in New York City, this 3-1/2" x 5-1/2" black-and-white card done in the format of the All-Time Greats postcards was issued. The front pictures two of the game's greatest pitchers and offers a discount on show admission. The back provides a detailed description of the show.

	NM	EX	VG
Dizzy Dean, Lefty Grove	6.00	3.00	1.80

1976 TCMA DiMaggio Brothers Postcard

This black-and-white postcard was issued singly circa the mid-1970s. It measures approximately 3-1/2" x 5-1/2".

	NM	EX	VG
Dom DiMaggio, Joe DiMaggio, Vince DiMaggio	12.00	6.00	3.50

1976 TCMA Larry Rosenthal

This custom-published card of the long-time American League outfielder (1936-1945) was printed in red, black and white in a 2-5/8" x 4-5/8" format. The issue date is approximate.

	NM	EX	VG
Larry Rosenthal	6.00	3.00	2.00

1976 TCMA Umpires

American League

Don Denkinger   Umpire

Eight of the better-known umpires of the era apparently commissioned TCMA to produce cards for them. The cards are black-and-white in the standard 2-1/2" x 3-1/2" format.

		NM	EX	VG
Complete Set (8):		25.00	12.50	7.50
Common Card:		4.00	2.00	1.25
(1)	Larry Barnett	4.00	2.00	1.25
(2)	Al Clark	4.00	2.00	1.25
(3)	Nick Colosi	4.00	2.00	1.25
(4)	Don Denkinger	4.00	2.00	1.25
(5)	Art Frantz	4.00	2.00	1.25
(6)	Marty Springstead	4.00	2.00	1.25
(7)	Ed Sudol	4.00	2.00	1.25
(8)	Bill Williams	4.00	2.00	1.25

1976 TCMA 1911 N.Y. Highlanders Postcard

This black-and-white postcard was issued singly circa the mid-1970s. It measures approximately 6" x 3-1/2".

	NM	EX	VG
1911 N.Y. Highlanders Team Photo	12.00	6.00	3.50

1976 TCMA 1938 Chicago Cubs

Augie Galan   OF

AUGUST JOHN GALAN
Games   110
At Bats   395
Hits   113
Runs   52
Home Runs   6
RBI   69
Bat.Ave.   .286

1938 CHICAGO CUBS
NATIONAL LEAGUE CHAMPIONS
1976 TCMA LTD.

The National League Champion Chicago Cubs of 1938 are featured in this collectors issue. The 2-1/2" x 3-1/2" cards have black-and-white player photos on front with the player's name and position in blue at bottom. Backs are in black-and-white with season stats. The unnumbered cards are checklisted here alphabetically.

		NM	EX	VG
Complete Set (33):		40.00	20.00	12.00
Common Player:		2.00	1.00	.60
(1)	Jim Asbell	2.00	1.00	.60
(2)	Clay Bryant	2.00	1.00	.60
(3)	Tex Carleton	2.00	1.00	.60
(4)	Phil Cavarretta	2.00	1.00	.60
(5)	Ripper Collins	2.00	1.00	.60
(6)	"Red" Corriden	2.00	1.00	.60
(7)	Dizzy Dean	7.50	3.75	2.25
(8)	Frank Demaree	2.00	1.00	.60
(9)	Al Epperly	2.00	1.00	.60
(10)	Larry French	2.00	1.00	.60
(11)	Augie Galan	2.00	1.00	.60
(12)	Bob Garbark	2.00	1.00	.60
(13)	Charlie Grimm	2.00	1.00	.60
(14)	Stan Hack	2.00	1.00	.60
(15)	Gabby Hartnett	3.00	1.50	.90
(16)	Billy Herman	3.00	1.50	.90
(17)	Kirby Higbe	2.00	1.00	.60
(18)	Hardrock Johnson	2.00	1.00	.60
(19)	Billy Jurges	2.00	1.00	.60
(20)	Newt Kimball	2.00	1.00	.60
(21)	Tony Lazzeri	3.00	1.50	.90
(22)	Bill Lee	2.00	1.00	.60
(23)	Bob Logan	2.00	1.00	.60
(24)	Joe Marty	2.00	1.00	.60
(25)	Bobby Mattick	2.00	1.00	.60
(26)	Steve Mesner	2.00	1.00	.60
(27)	Ken O'Dea	2.00	1.00	.60
(28)	Vance Page	2.00	1.00	.60
(29)	Carl Reynolds	2.00	1.00	.60
(30)	Charlie Root	2.00	1.00	.60
(31)	Jack Russell	2.00	1.00	.60
(32)	Coaker Triplett	2.00	1.00	.60
(33)	Team History Card	.70	.35	.20

1977 TCMA All-Time White Sox

Ray Schalk   C

All-Time
Chicago White Sox
Eddie Robinson   1B
Eddie Collins   2B
Willie Kamm   3B
Luke Appling   SS
Ray Schalk   C
Al Simmons   LF
Johnny Mostil   CF
Harry Hooper   RF
Ted Lyons   RHP
Billy Pierce   LHP
Gerry Staley   RP
Al Lopez   Mgr

Because this is one of the few early TCMA issues not to have a date printed on the back, the quoted year of issue is approximate. Fronts of the 2-1/2" x 3-1/2" cards have black-and-white player photos with name and position printed in red in the bottom border. Black-and-white backs have an all-time team roster of position players, pitchers and manager. The unnumbered cards are checklisted here in alphabetical order.

		NM	EX	VG
Complete Set (12):		24.00	12.00	7.25
Common Player:		2.00	1.00	.60
(1)	Luke Appling	2.50	1.25	.70
(2)	Eddie Collins	2.50	1.25	.70
(3)	Harry Hooper	2.00	1.00	.60
(4)	Willie Kamm	2.00	1.00	.60
(5)	Al Lopez	2.00	1.00	.60
(6)	Ted Lyons	2.00	1.00	.60
(7)	Johnny Mostil	2.00	1.00	.60
(8)	Billy Pierce	2.00	1.00	.60
(9)	Eddie Robinson	2.00	1.00	.60
(10)	Ray Schalk	2.00	1.00	.60
(11)	Al Simmons	2.00	1.00	.60
(12)	Gerry Staley	2.00	1.00	.60

1977 TCMA Chicago Cubs All Time Team

Chicago Cubs	
All Time Team	
1B - Charlie Grimm	
2B - Rogers Hornsby	
SS - Ernie Banks	
3B - Ron Santo	
C - Gabby Hartnett	
LF - Billy Williams	
RF - Kiki Cuyler	
CF - Hack Wilson	
RHP - Charlie Root	
LHR - Larry French	
RP - Emil Kush	
MGR - Charlie Grimm	
INF - Billy Herman	

The best of the Cubs are presented in this collectors issue. An all-time great at each position is featured on the 2-1/2" x 3-1/2" card. Fronts have black-and-white photos with orange graphics. Backs are in black-and-white and list the team by position. The unnumbered cards are checklisted here in that order.

		NM	EX	VG
Complete Set (12):		30.00	15.00	9.00
Common Player:		3.00	1.50	.90
(1)	Charlie Grimm	3.00	1.50	.90
(2)	Rogers Hornsby	4.00	2.00	1.25
(3)	Ernie Banks	4.00	2.00	1.25
(4)	Ron Santo	3.00	1.50	.90
(5)	Gabby Hartnett	3.00	1.50	.90
(6)	Billy Williams	3.00	1.50	.90
(7)	Kiki Cuyler	3.00	1.50	.90
(8)	Hack Wilson	4.00	2.00	1.25
(9)	Charlie Root	3.00	1.50	.90
(10)	Larry French	3.00	1.50	.90
(11)	Emil Kush	3.00	1.50	.90
(12)	Billy Herman	3.00	1.50	.90

1977 TCMA Stars of the Twenties

Six players are featured on this 22" x 11" triple-folder which was glued into issues of the Summer, 1977, "Baseball Quarterly" magazine from TCMA. The pictures feature artwork by John Anderson in sepia tones on heavy cream-colored textured paper stock. The pictures are back-to-back in pairs as listed here, with individual pictures varying in width from 7-1/4" to 7-1/2".

		NM	EX	VG
Complete Foldout:		10.00	5.00	3.00
Common Pair:		3.00	1.50	.90
(1/2)	Joe Bush, Gabby Hartnett	3.00	1.50	.90
(3/4)	Jim Bottomley, "Mule" Haas	3.00	1.50	.90
(5/6)	Sam Rice, Buddy Myer	3.00	1.50	.90

1977-80 TCMA The War Years

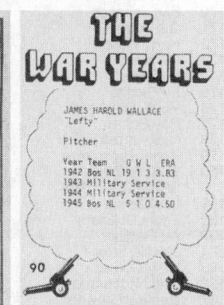

The decimated major league rosters circa 1942-46 are reflected in this collectors' card set. The 2-1/2" x 3-1/2" cards have black-and-white player photos on front, with a white border around. There is no typography on front. Backs have player identification, stats and the set title. Series 1, cards #1-45 was issued in 1977 and is much scarcer than Series 2, #46-90, which was issued in 1980.

		NM	EX	VG
Complete Set (90):		140.00	70.00	42.50
Common Player:		2.00	1.00	.60
1	Samuel Narron	3.00	1.50	.90
2	Raymond Mack	3.00	1.50	.90

3	Arnold (Mickey) Owen	3.00	1.50	.90
4	John Peacock	3.00	1.50	.90
5	Paul (Dizzy) Trout	3.00	1.50	.90
6	George (Birdie) Tebbetts	3.00	1.50	.90
7	Alfred Todd	3.00	1.50	.90
8	Harland Clift	3.00	1.50	.90
9	Don G.N. (Gil) Torres	3.00	1.50	.90
10	Alfonso Lopez	4.00	2.00	1.25
11	Ulysses (Tony) Lupien	3.00	1.50	.90
12	Lucius Appling	4.00	2.00	1.25
13	James (Pat) Seery	3.00	1.50	.90
14	Phil Masi	3.00	1.50	.90
15	Thomas Turner	3.00	1.50	.90
16	Nicholas Piccuito	3.00	1.50	.90
17	Mel Ott	7.50	3.75	2.25
18	Thadford Treadway	3.00	1.50	.90
19	Sam Naham (Neham)	3.00	1.50	.90
20	Truett (Rip) Sewell	3.00	1.50	.90
21	Roy Partee	3.00	1.50	.90
22	Richard Siebert	3.00	1.50	.90
23	Francis (Red) Barrett	3.00	1.50	.90
24	Paul O'Dea	3.00	1.50	.90
25	Lou Parisse	3.00	1.50	.90
26	Martin Marion	4.00	2.00	1.25
27	Eugene Moore	3.00	1.50	.90
28	Walter Beck	3.00	1.50	.90
29	Donald Manno	3.00	1.50	.90
30	Harold Newhouser	4.00	2.00	1.25
31	August Mancuso	3.00	1.50	.90
32	Merrill May	3.00	1.50	.90
33	Gerald Priddy	3.00	1.50	.90
34	Herman Besse	3.00	1.50	.90
35	Luis Olmo	3.00	1.50	.90
36	Robert O'Neill	3.00	1.50	.90
37	John Barrett	3.00	1.50	.90
38	Gordon Maltzberger	3.00	1.50	.90
39	William Nicholson	3.00	1.50	.90
40	Ron Northey	3.00	1.50	.90
41	Howard Pollet	3.00	1.50	.90
42	Aloysius Piechota	3.00	1.50	.90
43	Albert Shepard	7.50	3.75	2.25
44	Alfred Anderson	3.00	1.50	.90
45	Damon Phillips	3.00	1.50	.90
46	Herman Franks	2.00	1.00	.60
47	Aldon Wilke	2.00	1.00	.60
48	Max Macon	2.00	1.00	.60
49	Lester Webber	2.00	1.00	.60
50	Robert Swift	2.00	1.00	.60
51	Philip Weintraub	2.00	1.00	.60
52	Nicholas Strincevich	2.00	1.00	.60
53	Michael Tresh	2.00	1.00	.60
54	William Trotter	2.00	1.00	.60
55	1943 Yankees (Spud Chandler, Frank Crosetti, Bill Dickey, Nick Etten, Joe Gordon, Billy Johnson, Charlie Keller, John Lindell, Bud Metheny)	4.00	2.00	1.25
56	John Sturm	2.00	1.00	.60
57	Silas Johnson	2.00	1.00	.60
58	Donald Kolloway	2.00	1.00	.60
59	Cecil Vaughn (Vaughan)	2.00	1.00	.60
60	St. Louis Browns Bombers (Harlond Clift, Walt Judnich, Chet Laabs)	3.00	1.50	.90
61	Harold Wagner	2.00	1.00	.60
62	Alva Javery	2.00	1.00	.60
63	1941 Boston Bees Pitchers (George Barnicle, Ed Carnett, Art Johnson, Frank LaManna, Casey Stengel, Bob Williams)	3.00	1.50	.90
64	Adolph Camilli	2.00	1.00	.60
65	Myron McCormick	2.00	1.00	.60
66	Richard Wakefield	2.00	1.00	.60
67	James (Mickey) Vernon	3.00	1.50	.90
68	John Vander Meer	3.00	1.50	.90
69	James McDonnell	4.00	2.00	1.25
70	Thomas Jordan	2.00	1.00	.60
71	Maurice Van Robays	2.00	1.00	.60
72	Charles Stanceau	2.00	1.00	.60
73	Samuel Zoldak	2.00	1.00	.60
74	Raymond Starr	2.00	1.00	.60
75	Roger Wolff	2.00	1.00	.60
76	Cecil Travis	2.00	1.00	.60
77	Arthur Johnson	2.00	1.00	.60
78	Louis (Lewis) Riggs	2.00	1.00	.60
79	Peter Suder	2.00	1.00	.60
80	Thomas Warren	2.00	1.00	.60
81	John Welaj	2.00	1.00	.60
82	Gerald Walker	2.00	1.00	.60
83	Dewey Williams	2.00	1.00	.60
84	Leonard Merullo	2.00	1.00	.60
85	John Johnson	2.00	1.00	.60
86	Eugene Thompson	2.00	1.00	.60
87	William Zuber	2.00	1.00	.60
88	Earl Johnson	2.00	1.00	.60
89	Norman Young	2.00	1.00	.60
90	James Wallace	2.00	1.00	.60

1977 TCMA 1920 Cleveland Indians

The World Champion Indians are pictured on this collectors' issue team set. In standard 2-1/2" x 3-1/2" size with black-and-white photos, the cards are unnumbered. Some of the players are pictured in their 1921 uniforms with the "World Champions" lettering.

		NM	EX	VG
Complete Set (22):		25.00	12.50	7.50
Common Player:		2.00	1.00	.60
(1)	Jim Bagby	2.00	1.00	.60
(2)	George Burns	2.00	1.00	.60
(3)	Ray Caldwell	2.00	1.00	.60
(4)	Ray Chapman	3.00	1.50	.90
(5)	Stan Coveleski	2.50	1.25	.70
(6)	Joe Evans	2.00	1.00	.60
(7)	Larry Gardner	2.00	1.00	.60

(8)	Jack Graney	2.00	1.00	.60
(9)	Charlie Jamieson	2.00	1.00	.60
(10)	Doc Johnston	2.00	1.00	.60
(11)	Harry Lunte	2.00	1.00	.60
(12)	Duster Mails	2.00	1.00	.60
(13)	Guy Morton	2.00	1.00	.60
(14)	Les Nunamaker	2.00	1.00	.60
(15)	Steve O'Neill	2.00	1.00	.60
(16)	Joe Sewell	2.50	1.25	.70
(17)	Elmer Smith	2.00	1.00	.60
(18)	Tris Speaker	4.00	2.00	1.25
(19)	George Uhle	2.00	1.00	.60
(20)	Bill Wambsganss	2.50	1.25	.70
(21)	Joe Wood	2.50	1.25	.70
(22)	World Series Foes (Wilbert Robinson, Tris Speaker) (5-1/2" x 3")	4.00	2.00	1.25

1977 TCMA 1927 Yankees 50th Anniversary

As an insert in its inaugural issue of "Baseball Quarterly" magazine dated Winter, 1977, TCMA included a 16-3/4" x 11" cardboard panel with 18 black-and-white cards featuring members of the 1927 N.Y. Yankees. Measuring about 2-1/2" x 3-3/8" if cut apart, the individual cards have unadorned photos on front framed in black with a white border. Backs have player identification, a 50th anniversary logo, career summary and 1927 and career stats. The unnumbered cards are listed here in alphabetical order.

		NM	EX	VG
Complete Panel:		35.00	17.50	10.50
Complete Set (18):		25.00	12.50	7.50
Common Player:		2.00	1.00	.60
(1)	Bernard Oliver Bengough	2.00	1.00	.60
(2)	Tharon Patrick Collins	2.00	1.00	.60
(3)	Earle Bryan Combs	2.00	1.00	.60
(4)	Joseph Anthony Dugan	2.00	1.00	.60
(5)	Henry Louis Gehrig	6.00	3.00	1.75
(6)	John Patrick Grabowski	2.00	1.00	.60
(7)	Waite Charles Hoyt	2.00	1.00	.60
(8)	Miller James Huggins	2.00	1.00	.60
(9)	Mark Anthony Koenig	2.00	1.00	.60
(10)	Anthony Michael Lazzeri	2.00	1.00	.60
(11)	Robert Williams Meusel	2.00	1.00	.60
(12)	William Wiley Moore	2.00	1.00	.60
(13)	Herbert Jeffries Pennock	2.00	1.00	.60
(14)	George William Pipgras	2.00	1.00	.60
(15)	Walter Henry Ruether	2.00	1.00	.60
(16)	George Herman Ruth	8.00	4.00	2.50
(17)	James Robert Shawkey	2.00	1.00	.60
(18)	Urban James Shocker	2.00	1.00	.60

1977 TCMA 1939-40 Cincinnati Reds

The National League Champion Reds of 1939 and the World's Champion team of 1940 are featured in this collectors' issue. The 2-1/2" x 3-1/2" cards have black-and-white photos on front surrounded by red borders. Backs, also in black-and-white, have 1939 and/or 1940 season stats.

		NM	EX	VG
Complete Set (45):		35.00	17.50	10.00
Common Player:		1.50	.75	.45
1	Vince DiMaggio	2.50	1.25	.70
2	Wally Berger	1.50	.75	.45
3	Nolan Richardson (Nolen)	1.50	.75	.45
4	Ernie Lombardi	2.50	1.25	.70
5	Ival Goodman	1.50	.75	.45
6	Jim Turner	1.50	.75	.45
7	Bucky Walters	1.50	.75	.45
8	Jimmy Ripple	1.50	.75	.45
9	Hank Johnson	1.50	.75	.45
10	Bill Baker	1.50	.75	.45
11	Al Simmons	2.00	1.00	.60
12	Johnny Hutchings	1.50	.75	.45
13	Peaches Davis	1.50	.75	.45
14	Willard Hershberger	2.50	1.25	.70
15	Bill Werber	1.50	.75	.45

16	Harry Craft	1.50	.75	.45
17	Milt Galatzer	1.50	.75	.45
18	Dick West	1.50	.75	.45
19	Art Jacobs	1.50	.75	.45
20	Joe Beggs	1.50	.75	.45
21	Frenchy Bordagaray	1.50	.75	.45
22	Lee Gamble	1.50	.75	.45
23	Lee Grissom	1.50	.75	.45
24	Eddie Joost	1.50	.75	.45
25	Milt Shofner	1.50	.75	.45
26	Morrie Arnovich	1.50	.75	.45
27	Pete Naktenis	1.50	.75	.45
28	Jim Weaver	1.50	.75	.45
29	Mike McCormick	1.50	.75	.45
30	John Niggeling	1.50	.75	.45
31	Les Scarsella	1.50	.75	.45
32	Lonny Frey	1.50	.75	.45
33	Bill Myers	1.50	.75	.45
34	Frank McCormick	1.50	.75	.45
35	Lew Riggs	1.50	.75	.45
36	Nino Bongiovanni	1.50	.75	.45
37	Johnny Rizzo	1.50	.75	.45
38	Wes Livengood	1.50	.75	.45
39	Junior Thompson	1.50	.75	.45
40	Mike Dejan	1.50	.75	.45
41	Jimmy Wilson	1.50	.75	.45
42	Paul Derringer	1.50	.75	.45
43	Johnny Vander Meer	2.00	1.00	.60
44	Whitey Moore	1.50	.75	.45
45	Bill McKechnie	2.00	1.00	.60

1977 TCMA 1960 Pittsburgh Pirates

The World's Champions Pirates are featured on this collector issue. The 2-1/2" x 3-1/2" cards have black-and-white photos on front surrounded by orange borders. Backs, also in black-and-white, have a card number, player name and position at top and season stats.

		NM	EX	VG
	Complete Set (42):	100.00	50.00	30.00
	Common Player:	3.00	1.50	.90
1	Danny Murtaugh	3.00	1.50	.90
2	Dick Stuart	4.00	2.00	1.25
3	Bill Mazeroski	10.00	5.00	3.00
4	Dick Groat	4.00	2.00	1.25
5	Don Hoak	3.00	1.50	.90
6	Roberto Clemente	20.00	10.00	6.00
7	Bill Virdon	3.00	1.50	.90
8	Bob Skinner	3.00	1.50	.90
9	Smoky Burgess	3.00	1.50	.90
10	Gino Cimoli	3.00	1.50	.90
11	Rocky Nelson	3.00	1.50	.90
12	Hal Smith	3.00	1.50	.90
13	Dick Schofield	3.00	1.50	.90
14	Joe Christopher	3.00	1.50	.90
15	Gene Baker	3.00	1.50	.90
16	Bob Oldis	3.00	1.50	.90
17	Vern Law	3.00	1.50	.90
18	Bob Friend	3.00	1.50	.90
19	Wilmer Mizell	3.00	1.50	.90
20	Harvey Haddix	3.00	1.50	.90
21	Roy Face	3.00	1.50	.90
22	Fred Green	3.00	1.50	.90
23	Joe Gibbon	3.00	1.50	.90
24	Clem Labine	3.00	1.50	.90
25	Paul Giel	3.00	1.50	.90
26	Tom Cheney	3.00	1.50	.90
27	Earl Francis	3.00	1.50	.90
28	Jim Umbricht	3.00	1.50	.90
29	George Witt	3.00	1.50	.90
30	Bennie Daniels	3.00	1.50	.90
31	Don Gross	3.00	1.50	.90
32	Diomedes Olivo	4.00	2.00	1.25
33	Roman Mejias	3.00	1.50	.90
34	R.C. Stevens	3.00	1.50	.90
35	Mickey Vernon	3.00	1.50	.90
36	Danny Kravitz	3.00	1.50	.90
37	Harry Bright	3.00	1.50	.90
38	Dick Barone	3.00	1.50	.90
39	Bill Burwell	3.00	1.50	.90
40	Lenny Levy	4.00	2.00	1.25
41	Sam Narron	3.00	1.50	.90
42	Team Card (Bob Friend)	3.00	1.50	.90

1977 TCMA/ASCCA Ad Card

To promote the American Sports Card Collectors Association Show in New York City, this 2-1/2" x 3-1/2" black-and-white, gold highlighted card was issued. The front pictures Babe Ruth and offers a 25-cent discount on show admission. The back provides a detailed description of the show.

	NM	EX	VG
Babe Ruth	6.00	3.00	1.80

1977-84 TCMA/Renata Galasso

This issue of six 45-card series is in similar format but with different players, checklists and copyright dates pro-

MICKEY MANTLE
CENTER FIELDER—NEW YORK YANKEES

duced by TCMA and marketed by Renata Galasso. In 2-1/2" x 3-1/2" format the cards have black-and-white photos on front. Backs are printed in red and blue and include a career summary, large Galasso ad and TCMA dateline.

		NM	EX	VG
	Complete Set (270):	45.00	22.00	13.50
	Common Player:	.25	.13	.08
	SERIES 1 - 1977	12.50	6.25	3.75
1	Joe DiMaggio	4.00	2.00	1.25
2	Ralph Kiner	.25	.13	.08
3	Don Larsen	.25	.13	.08
4	Robin Roberts	.25	.13	.08
5	Roy Campanella	.50	.25	.15
6	Smoky Burgess	.25	.13	.08
7	Mickey Mantle	6.00	3.00	1.75
8	Willie Mays	3.00	1.50	.90
9	George Kell	.25	.13	.08
10	Ted Williams	3.00	1.50	.90
11	Carl Furillo	.25	.13	.08
12	Bob Feller	.25	.13	.08
13	Casey Stengel	.25	.13	.08
14	Richie Ashburn	.25	.13	.08
15	Gil Hodges	.25	.13	.08
16	Stan Musial	.75	.40	.25
17	Don Newcombe	.25	.13	.08
18	Jackie Jensen	.25	.13	.08
19	Lou Boudreau	.25	.13	.08
20	Jackie Robinson	2.00	1.00	.60
21	Billy Goodman	.25	.13	.08
22	Satchel Paige	1.00	.50	.30
23	Hoyt Wilhelm	.25	.13	.08
24	Duke Snider	.25	.13	.08
25	Whitey Ford	.25	.13	.08
26	Monte Irvin	.25	.13	.08
27	Hank Sauer	.25	.13	.08
28	Sal Maglie	.25	.13	.08
29	Ernie Banks	.25	.13	.08
30	Billy Pierce	.25	.13	.08
31	Pee Wee Reese	.25	.13	.08
32	Al Lopez	.25	.13	.08
33	Allie Reynolds	.25	.13	.08
34	Eddie Mathews	.25	.13	.08
35	Al Rosen	.25	.13	.08
36	Early Wynn	.25	.13	.08
37	Phil Rizzuto	.25	.13	.08
38	Warren Spahn	.25	.13	.08
39	Bobby Thomson	.25	.13	.08
40	Enos Slaughter	.25	.13	.08
41	Roberto Clemente	4.00	2.00	1.25
42	Luis Aparicio	.25	.13	.08
43	Roy Sievers	.25	.13	.08
44	Hank Aaron	4.00	2.00	1.25
45	Mickey Vernon	.25	.13	.08
	SERIES 2 - 1979	10.00	5.00	3.00
46	Lou Gehrig	3.00	1.50	.90
47	Lefty O'Doul	.25	.13	.08
48	Chuck Klein	.25	.13	.08
49	Paul Waner	.25	.13	.08
50	Mel Ott	.25	.13	.08
51	Riggs Stephenson	.25	.13	.08
52	Dizzy Dean	.50	.25	.15
53	Frankie Frisch	.25	.13	.08
54	Red Ruffing	.25	.13	.08
55	Lefty Grove	.25	.13	.08
56	Heinie Manush	.25	.13	.08
57	Jimmie Foxx	.25	.13	.08
58	Al Simmons	.25	.13	.08
59	Charlie Root	.25	.13	.08
60	Goose Goslin	.25	.13	.08
61	Mickey Cochrane	.25	.13	.08
62	Gabby Hartnett	.25	.13	.08
63	Ducky Medwick	.25	.13	.08
64	Ernie Lombardi	.25	.13	.08
65	Joe Cronin	.25	.13	.08
66	Pepper Martin	.25	.13	.08
67	Jim Bottomley	.25	.13	.08
68	Bill Dickey	.25	.13	.08
69	Babe Ruth	5.00	2.50	1.50
70	Joe McCarthy	.25	.13	.08
71	Doc Cramer	.25	.13	.08
72	Kiki Cuyler	.25	.13	.08
73	Johnny Vander Meer	.25	.13	.08
74	Paul Derringer	.25	.13	.08
75	Freddie Fitzsimmons	.25	.13	.08
76	Lefty Gomez	.25	.13	.08
77	Arky Vaughan	.25	.13	.08
78	Stan Hack	.25	.13	.08
79	Earl Averill	.25	.13	.08
80	Luke Appling	.25	.13	.08
81	Mel Harder	.25	.13	.08
82	Hank Greenberg	.25	.13	.08
83	Schoolboy Rowe	.25	.13	.08
84	Billy Herman	.25	.13	.08
85	Gabby Street	.25	.13	.08
86	Lloyd Waner	.25	.13	.08
87	Jocko Conlan	.25	.13	.08
88	Carl Hubbell	.25	.13	.08

89	Series 1 checklist	.25	.13	.08
90	Series 2 checklist	.25	.13	.08
	SERIES 3 - 1980	7.50	3.75	2.25
91	Babe Ruth	3.00	1.50	.90
92	Rogers Hornsby	.25	.13	.08
93	Edd Roush	.25	.13	.08
94	George Sisler	.25	.13	.08
95	Harry Heilmann	.25	.13	.08
96	Tris Speaker	.25	.13	.08
97	Burleigh Grimes	.25	.13	.08
98	John McGraw	.25	.13	.08
99	Eppa Rixey	.25	.13	.08
100	Ty Cobb	1.00	.50	.30
101	Zack Wheat	.25	.13	.08
102	Pie Traynor	.25	.13	.08
103	Max Carey	.25	.13	.08
104	Dazzy Vance	.25	.13	.08
105	Walter Johnson	.50	.25	.15
106	Herb Pennock	.25	.13	.08
107	Joe Sewell	.25	.13	.08
108	Sam Rice	.25	.13	.08
109	Earle Combs	.25	.13	.08
110	Ted Lyons	.25	.13	.08
111	Eddie Collins	.25	.13	.08
112	Bill Terry	.25	.13	.08
113	Hack Wilson	.25	.13	.08
114	Rabbit Maranville	.25	.13	.08
115	Charlie Grimm	.25	.13	.08
116	Tony Lazzeri	.25	.13	.08
117	Waite Hoyt	.25	.13	.08
118	Stan Coveleski	.25	.13	.08
119	George Kelly	.25	.13	.08
120	Jimmy Dykes	.25	.13	.08
121	Red Faber	.25	.13	.08
122	Dave Bancroft	.25	.13	.08
123	Judge Landis	.25	.13	.08
124	Branch Rickey	.25	.13	.08
125	Jesse Haines	.25	.13	.08
126	Carl Mays	.25	.13	.08
127	Fred Lindstrom	.25	.13	.08
128	Miller Huggins	.25	.13	.08
129	Sad Sam Jones	.25	.13	.08
130	Joe Judge	.25	.13	.08
131	Ross Young (Youngs)	.25	.13	.08
132	Bucky Harris	.25	.13	.08
133	Bob Meusel	.25	.13	.08
134	Billy Evans	.25	.13	.08
135	1927 N.Y. Yankees Team Photo/Checklist	.50	.25	.15
	SERIES 4 - 1981	7.50	3.75	2.25
136	Ty Cobb	1.00	.50	.30
137	Nap Lajoie	.25	.13	.08
138	Tris Speaker	.25	.13	.08
139	Heinie Groh	.25	.13	.08
140	Sam Crawford	.25	.13	.08
141	Clyde Milan	.25	.13	.08
142	Chief Bender	.25	.13	.08
143	Big Ed Walsh	.25	.13	.08
144	Walter Johnson	.50	.25	.15
145	Connie Mack	.25	.13	.08
146	Hal Chase	.25	.13	.08
147	Hugh Duffy	.25	.13	.08
148	Honus Wagner	.50	.25	.15
149	Tom Connolly	.25	.13	.08
150	Clark Griffith	.25	.13	.08
151	Zack Wheat	.25	.13	.08
152	Christy Mathewson	.50	.25	.15
153	Grover C. Alexander	.25	.13	.08
154	Joe Jackson	3.00	1.50	.90
155	Home Run Baker	.25	.13	.08
156	Ed Plank	.25	.13	.08
157	Larry Doyle	.25	.13	.08
158	Rube Marquard	.25	.13	.08
159	Johnny Evers	.25	.13	.08
160	Joe Tinker	.25	.13	.08
161	Frank Chance	.25	.13	.08
162	Wilbert Robinson	.25	.13	.08
163	Roger Peckinpaugh	.25	.13	.08
164	Fred Clarke	.25	.13	.08
165	Babe Ruth	3.00	1.50	.90
166	Wilbur Cooper	.25	.13	.08
167	Germany Schaefer	.25	.13	.08
168	Addie Joss	.25	.13	.08
169	Cy Young	.50	.25	.15
170	Ban Johnson	.25	.13	.08
171	Joe Judge	.25	.13	.08
172	Harry Hooper	.25	.13	.08
173	Bill Klem	.25	.13	.08
174	Ed Barrow	.25	.13	.08
175	Ed Cicotte	.25	.13	.08
176	Hughie Jennings	.25	.13	.08
177	Ray Schalk	.25	.13	.08
178	Nick Altrock	.25	.13	.08
179	Roger Bresnahan	.25	.13	.08
180	$100,000 Infield	.25	.13	.08
	SERIES 5 - 1983	7.50	3.75	2.25
181	Lou Gehrig	3.00	1.50	.90
182	Eddie Collins	.25	.13	.08
183	Art Fletcher	.25	.13	.08
184	Jimmie Foxx	.25	.13	.08
185	Lefty Gomez	.25	.13	.08
186	Oral Hildebrand	.25	.13	.08
187	General Crowder	.25	.13	.08
188	Bill Dickey	.25	.13	.08
189	Wes Ferrell	.25	.13	.08
190	Al Simmons	.25	.13	.08
191	Tony Lazzeri	.25	.13	.08
192	Sam West	.25	.13	.08
193	Babe Ruth	3.00	1.50	.90
194	Connie Mack	.25	.13	.08
195	Lefty Grove	.25	.13	.08
196	Eddie Rommel	.25	.13	.08
197	Ben Chapman	.25	.13	.08
198	Joe Cronin	.25	.13	.08
199	Rich Ferrell (Rick)	.25	.13	.08
200	Charlie Gehringer	.25	.13	.08
201	Jimmy Dykes	.25	.13	.08
202	Earl Averill	.25	.13	.08

		NM	EX	VG
203	Pepper Martin	.25	.13	.08
204	Bill Terry	.25	.13	.08
205	Pie Traynor	.25	.13	.08
206	Gabby Hartnett	.25	.13	.08
207	Frank Frisch	.25	.13	.08
208	Carl Hubbell	.25	.13	.08
209	Paul Waner	.25	.13	.08
210	Woody English	.25	.13	.08
211	Bill Hallahan	.25	.13	.08
212	Dick Bartell	.25	.13	.08
213	Bill McKechnie	.25	.13	.08
214	Max Carey	.25	.13	.08
215	John McGraw	.25	.13	.08
216	Jimmie Wilson	.25	.13	.08
217	Chick Hafey	.25	.13	.08
218	Chuck Klein	.25	.13	.08
219	Lefty O'Doul	.25	.13	.08
220	Wally Berger	.25	.13	.08
221	Hal Schumacher	.25	.13	.08
222	Lon Warneke	.25	.13	.08
223	Tony Cuccinello	.25	.13	.08
(224)	1933 A.L. All-Stars	.50	.25	.15
(225)	1933 N.L. All-Stars	.50	.25	.15
	SERIES 6 - 1984	15.00	7.50	4.50
226	Roger Maris	.75	.40	.25
227	Babe Ruth	3.00	1.50	.90
228	Jackie Robinson	2.00	1.00	.60
229	Pete Gray	.75	.40	.25
230	Ted Williams	3.00	1.50	.90
231	Hank Aaron	3.00	1.50	.90
232	Mickey Mantle	5.00	2.50	1.50
233	Gil Hodges	.25	.13	.08
234	Walter Johnson	.50	.25	.15
235	Joe DiMaggio	3.00	1.50	.90
236	Lou Gehrig	3.00	1.50	.90
237	Stan Musial	.75	.40	.25
238	Mickey Cochrane	.25	.13	.08
239	Denny McLain	.25	.13	.08
240	Carl Hubbell	.25	.13	.08
241	Harvey Haddix	.25	.13	.08
242	Christy Mathewson	.50	.25	.15
243	Johnny VanderMeer	.25	.13	.08
244	Sandy Koufax	3.00	1.50	.90
245	Willie Mays	3.00	1.50	.90
246	Don Drysdale	.25	.13	.08
247	Bobby Richardson	.25	.13	.08
248	Hoyt Wilhelm	.25	.13	.08
249	Yankee Stadium	.25	.13	.08
250	Bill Terry	.25	.13	.08
251	Roy Campanella	.50	.25	.15
252	Roberto Clemente	3.00	1.50	.90
253	Casey Stengel	.25	.13	.08
254	Ernie Banks	.50	.25	.15
255	Bobby Thomson	.25	.13	.08
256	Mel Ott	.25	.13	.08
257	Tony Oliva	.25	.13	.08
258	Satchel Paige	1.00	.50	.30
259	Joe Jackson	3.00	1.50	.90
260	Larry Lajoie	.25	.13	.08
261	Bill Mazeroski	.25	.13	.08
262	Bill Wambsganss	.25	.13	.08
263	Willie McCovey	.25	.13	.08
264	Warren Spahn	.25	.13	.08
265	Lefty Gomez	.25	.13	.08
266	Dazzy Vance	.25	.13	.08
267	Sam Crawford	.25	.13	.08
268	Tris Speaker	.25	.13	.08
269	Lou Brock	.25	.13	.08
270	Cy Young	.25	.13	.08

1978 TCMA Baseball Nostalgia Postcard

 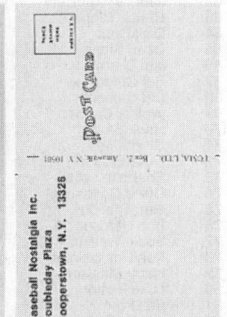

Vernon "Whitey" Wilshere

TCMA produced this card for Baseball Nostalgia, Inc., a Cooperstown, N.Y., hobby shop, in an edition of 500. The card pictures a Cooperstown resident who taught at the local high school following a short (1934-36) major league pitching career. The 3-1/2" x 5-1/2" black-and-white card has standard postcard markings on back.

	NM	EX	VG
Vernon "Whitey" Wilshere	6.00	3.00	1.80

1978 TCMA The 1960's

Nearly 300 players of the 1960s are featured in this collectors issue. Fronts of the 2-1/2" x 3-1/2" cards have a color photo with a black frameline and white border. There are no other graphics. Backs are printed in green and include a lengthy career summary. On some cards the set's title, "The 1960's" is printed at top. Several mistakes in card numbering are noted in the accompanying checklist.

MICKEY CHARLES (MICKEY MANTLE)
New York Yankees
Outfielder
Bats-B Throws-R
Ht 5-11½ Wt 195 Bn 10-20-31

		NM	EX	VG
	Complete Set (293):	32.50	16.00	9.75
	Common Player:	.25	.13	.08
1	Smoky Burgess	.25	.13	.08
2	Juan Marichal	1.00	.50	.30
3	Don Drysdale	1.00	.50	.30
4	Jim Gentile	.25	.13	.08
5	Roy Face	.25	.13	.08
6	Joe Pepitone	.25	.13	.08
7	Joe Christopher	.25	.13	.08
8	Wayne Causey	.25	.13	.08
9	Frank Bolling	.25	.13	.08
10	Jim Maloney	.25	.13	.08
11	Roger Maris	2.50	1.25	.70
12	Bill White	.25	.13	.08
13	Roberto Clemente	7.50	3.75	2.25
14	Bob Saverine	.25	.13	.08
15	Barney Schultz	.25	.13	.08
16	Albie Pearson	.25	.13	.08
17	Denny Lemaster	.25	.13	.08
18	Ernie Broglio	.25	.13	.08
19	Bobby Klaus	.25	.13	.08
20	Tony Cloninger	.25	.13	.08
21	Whitey Ford	1.50	.70	.45
22	Ron Santo	.60	.30	.20
23	Jim Duckworth	.25	.13	.08
24	Willie Davis	.25	.13	.08
25	Ed Charles	.25	.13	.08
26	Bob Allison	.25	.13	.08
27	Fritz Ackley	.25	.13	.08
28	Ruben Amaro	.25	.13	.08
29	Johnny Callison	.25	.13	.08
30	Greg Bollo	.25	.13	.08
31	Felix Millan	.25	.13	.08
32	Camilo Pascual	.25	.13	.08
33	Jackie Brandt	.25	.13	.08
34	Don Lock	.25	.13	.08
35	Chico Ruiz	.25	.13	.08
36	Joe Azcue	.25	.13	.08
37	Ed Bailey	.25	.13	.08
38	Pete Ramos	.25	.13	.08
39	Eddie Bressoud	.25	.13	.08
40	Al Kaline	1.50	.70	.45
41	Ron Brand	.25	.13	.08
42	Bob Lillis	.25	.13	.08
43	Not Issued (See #125.)	.25	.13	.08
44	Buster Narum	.25	.13	.08
45	Jim Gilliam	.25	.13	.08
46	Claude Raymond	.25	.13	.08
47	Billy Bryan	.25	.13	.08
48	Marshall Bridges	.25	.13	.08
49	Norm Cash	.45	.25	.14
50	Orlando Cepeda	1.00	.50	.30
51	Lee Maye	.25	.13	.08
52	Andre Rodgers	.25	.13	.08
53	Ken Berry	.25	.13	.08
54	Don Mincher	.25	.13	.08
55	Jerry Lumpe	.25	.13	.08
56	Milt Pappas	.25	.13	.08
57	Steve Barber	.25	.13	.08
58	Denis Menke	.25	.13	.08
59	Larry Maxie	.25	.13	.08
60	Bob Gibson	1.00	.50	.30
61	Larry Bearnarth	.25	.13	.08
62	Bill Mazeroski	1.00	.50	.30
63	Bob Rodgers	.25	.13	.08
64	Jerry Arrigo	.25	.13	.08
65	Joe Nuxhall	.25	.13	.08
66	Dean Chance	.25	.13	.08
67	Ken Boyer	.60	.30	.20
68	John Odom	.25	.13	.08
69	Chico Cardenas	.25	.13	.08
70	Maury Wills	.35	.20	.11
71	Tony Oliva	.45	.25	.14
72	Don Nottebart	.25	.13	.08
73	Joe Adcock	.25	.13	.08
74	Felipe Alou	.25	.13	.08
75	Matty Alou	.25	.13	.08
76	Dick Radatz	.25	.13	.08
77	Jim Bouton	.25	.13	.08
78	John Blanchard	.25	.13	.08
79	Juan Pizarro	.25	.13	.08
80	Boog Powell	.45	.25	.14
81	Earl Robinson	.25	.13	.08
82	Bob Chance	.25	.13	.08
83	Max Alvis	.25	.13	.08
84	Don Blasingame	.25	.13	.08
85	Tom Cheney	.25	.13	.08
86	Jerry Arrigo	.25	.13	.08
87	Tommy Davis	.25	.13	.08
88	Steve Boros	.25	.13	.08
89	Don Cardwell	.25	.13	.08
90	Harmon Killebrew	1.50	.70	.45
91	Jim Pagliaroni	.25	.13	.08
92	Jim O'Toole	.25	.13	.08
93	Dennis Bennett	.25	.13	.08
94	Dick McAuliffe	.25	.13	.08
95	Dick Brown	.25	.13	.08
96	Joe Amalfitano	.25	.13	.08
97	Phil Linz	.25	.13	.08
98	Not Issued (See #165.)	.25	.13	.08
99	Dave Nicholson	.25	.13	.08
100	Hoyt Wilhelm	1.00	.50	.30
101	Don Leppert	.25	.13	.08
102	Jose Pagan	.25	.13	.08
103	Sam McDowell	.25	.13	.08
104	Jack Baldschun	.25	.13	.08
105	Jim Perry	.25	.13	.08
106	Hal Reniff	.25	.13	.08
107	Lee Maye	.25	.13	.08
108	Joe Adcock	.25	.13	.08
109	Bob Bolin	.25	.13	.08
110	Don Leppert	.25	.13	.08
111	Bill Monbouquette	.25	.13	.08
112	Bobby Richardson	.45	.25	.14
113	Earl Battey	.25	.13	.08
114	Bob Veale	.25	.13	.08
115	Lou Jackson	.25	.13	.08
116	Frank Kreutzer	.25	.13	.08
117	Jerry Zimmerman	.25	.13	.08
118	Don Schwall	.25	.13	.08
119	Rich Rollins	.25	.13	.08
120	Pete Ward	.25	.13	.08
121	Moe Drabowsky	.25	.13	.08
122	Jesse Gonder	.25	.13	.08
123	Hal Woodeshick	.25	.13	.08
124	John Herrnstein	.25	.13	.08
125a	Gary Peters (Should be #43.)	.25	.13	.08
125b	Leon Wagner	.25	.13	.08
126	Dwight Siebler	.25	.13	.08
027	Gary Kroll	.25	.13	.08
128	Tony Horton	.25	.13	.08
129	John DeMerit	.25	.13	.08
130	Sandy Koufax	6.00	3.00	1.75
131	Jim Davenport	.25	.13	.08
132	Wes Covington	.25	.13	.08
133	Tony Taylor	.25	.13	.08
134	Jack Kralick	.25	.13	.08
135	Bill Pleis	.25	.13	.08
136	Russ Snyder	.25	.13	.08
137	Joe Torre	.75	.40	.25
138	Ted Wills	.25	.13	.08
139	Wes Stock	.25	.13	.08
140	Frank Robinson	1.50	.70	.45
141	Dave Stenhouse	.25	.13	.08
142	Ron Hansen	.25	.13	.08
143	Don Elston	.25	.13	.08
144	Del Crandall	.25	.13	.08
145	Bennie Daniels	.25	.13	.08
146	Vada Pinson	.45	.25	.14
147	Bill Spanswick	.25	.13	.08
148	Earl Wilson	.25	.13	.08
149	Ty Cline	.25	.13	.08
150	Dick Groat	.25	.13	.08
151	Jim Duckworth	.25	.13	.08
152	Jimmie Schaffer	.25	.13	.08
153	George Thomas	.25	.13	.08
154	Wes Stock	.25	.13	.08
155	Mike White	.25	.13	.08
156	John Podres	.25	.13	.08
157	Willie Crawford	.25	.13	.08
158	Fred Gladding	.25	.13	.08
159	John Wyatt	.25	.13	.08
160	Bob Friend	.25	.13	.08
161	Ted Uhlaender	.25	.13	.08
162	Dick Stigman	.25	.13	.08
163	Don Wert	.25	.13	.08
164	Eddie Bressoud	.25	.13	.08
165a	Ed Roebuck (Should be #98.)	.25	.13	.08
165b	Leon Wagner	.25	.13	.08
166	Al Spangler	.25	.13	.08
167	Bob Sadowski	.25	.13	.08
168	Ralph Terry	.25	.13	.08
169	Jimmie Schaffer	.25	.13	.08
170a	Jim Fregosi (Should be #180.)	.25	.13	.08
170b	Dick Hall	.25	.13	.08
171	Al Spangler	.25	.13	.08
172	Bob Tillman	.25	.13	.08
173	Ed Bailey	.25	.13	.08
174	Cesar Tovar	.25	.13	.08
175	Morrie Stevens	.25	.13	.08
176	Floyd Weaver	.25	.13	.08
177	Frank Malzone	.25	.13	.08
178	Norm Siebern	.25	.13	.08
179	Dick Phillips	.25	.13	.08
180	Not Issued (See #170.)	.25	.13	.08
181	Bobby Wine	.25	.13	.08
182	Masanori Murakami	.75	.40	.25
183	Chuck Schilling	.25	.13	.08
184	Jimmie Schaffer	.25	.13	.08
185	John Roseboro	.25	.13	.08
186	Jake Wood	.25	.13	.08
187	Dallas Green	.25	.13	.08
188	Tom Haller	.25	.13	.08
189	Chuck Cottier	.25	.13	.08
190	Brooks Robinson	1.50	.70	.45
191	Ty Cline	.25	.13	.08
192	Bubba Phillips	.25	.13	.08
193	Al Jackson	.25	.13	.08
194	Herm Starrette	.25	.13	.08
195	Dave Wickersham	.25	.13	.08
196	Vic Power	.25	.13	.08
197	Ray Culp	.25	.13	.08
198	Don Demeter	.25	.13	.08
199	Dick Schofield	.25	.13	.08
200	Stephen Grant	.25	.13	.08
201	Roger Craig	.25	.13	.08
202	Dick Farrell	.25	.13	.08
203	Clay Dalrymple	.25	.13	.08
204	Jim Duffalo	.25	.13	.08
205	Tito Francona	.25	.13	.08
206	Tony Conigliaro	.45	.25	.14
207	Jim King	.25	.13	.08
208	Joe Gibbon	.25	.13	.08
209	Arnold Earley	.25	.13	.08
210	Denny McLain	.25	.13	.08

		NM	EX	VG
211	Don Larsen	.25	.13	.08
212	Ron Hunt	.25	.13	.08
213	Deron Johnson	.25	.13	.08
214	Harry Bright	.25	.13	.08
215	Ernie Fazio	.25	.13	.08
216	Joey Jay	.25	.13	.08
217	Jim Coates	.25	.13	.08
218	Jerry Kindall	.25	.13	.08
219	Joe Gibbon	.25	.13	.08
220	Frank Howard	.35	.20	.11
221	Howie Koplitz	.25	.13	.08
222	Larry Jackson	.25	.13	.08
223	Dale Long	.25	.13	.08
224	Jimmy Dykes	.25	.13	.08
225	Hank Aguirre	.25	.13	.08
226	Earl Francis	.25	.13	.08
227	Vic Wertz	.25	.13	.08
228	Larry Haney	.25	.13	.08
229	Tony LaRussa	.45	.25	.14
230	Moose Skowron	.35	.20	.11
231a	Tito Francona (Should be #235.)	.25	.13	.08
231b	Lee Thomas	.25	.13	.08
232	Ken Johnson	.25	.13	.08
233	Dick Howser	.25	.13	.08
234	Bobby Knoop	.25	.13	.08
235	Not Issued (See #231.)	.25	.13	.08
236	Elston Howard	.35	.20	.11
237	Donn Clendenon	.25	.13	.08
238	Jesse Gonder	.25	.13	.08
239	Vern Law	.25	.13	.08
240	Curt Flood	.25	.13	.08
241	Dal Maxvill	.25	.13	.08
242	Roy Sievers	.25	.13	.08
243	Jim Brewer	.25	.13	.08
244	Harry Craft	.25	.13	.08
245	Dave Eilers	.25	.13	.08
246	Dave DeBusschere	.25	.13	.08
247	Ken Harrelson	.25	.13	.08
248	Not Issued (See #249.)	.25	.13	.08
249a	Jim Duffalo	.25	.13	.08
249b	Eddie Kasko (Should be #248.)	.25	.13	.08
250	Luis Aparicio	1.00	.50	.30
251	Ron Kline	.25	.13	.08
252	Chuck Hinton	.25	.13	.08
253	Frank Lary	.25	.13	.08
254	Stu Miller	.25	.13	.08
255	Ernie Banks	2.00	1.00	.60
256	Dick Farrell	.25	.13	.08
257	Bud Daley	.25	.13	.08
258	Luis Arroyo	.25	.13	.08
259	Bob Del Greco	.25	.13	.08
260	Ted Williams	6.00	3.00	1.75
261	Mike Epstein	.25	.13	.08
262	Mickey Mantle	10.00	5.00	3.00
263	Jim LeFebvre	.25	.13	.08
264	Pat Jarvis	.25	.13	.08
265	Chuck Hinton	.25	.13	.08
266	Don Larsen	.25	.13	.08
267	Jim Coates	.25	.13	.08
268	Gary Kolb	.25	.13	.08
269	Jim Ray Hart	.25	.13	.08
270	Dave McNally	.25	.13	.08
271	Jerry Kindall	.25	.13	.08
272	Hector Lopez	.25	.13	.08
273	Claude Osteen	.25	.13	.08
274	Jack Aker	.25	.13	.08
275	Mike Shannon	.25	.13	.08
276	Lew Burdette	.25	.13	.08
277	Mack Jones	.25	.13	.08
278	Art Shamsky	.25	.13	.08
279	Bob Johnson	.25	.13	.08
280	Willie Mays	6.00	3.00	1.75
281	Rich Nye	.25	.13	.08
282	Bill Cowan	.25	.13	.08
283	Gary Kolb	.25	.13	.08
284	Woody Held	.25	.13	.08
285	Bill Freehan	.25	.13	.08
286	Larry Jackson	.25	.13	.08
287	Mike Hershberger	.25	.13	.08
288	Julian Javier	.25	.13	.08
289	Charley Smith	.25	.13	.08
290	Hank Aaron	6.00	3.00	1.75
291	John Boccabella	.25	.13	.08
292	Charley James	.25	.13	.08
293	Sammy Ellis	.25	.13	.08

1978 TCMA 1941 Brooklyn Dodgers

The National League Champion Brooklyn Dodgers are featured in the collectors' edition card set. Measuring 2-1/2" x 3-1/2", the cards have blue duotone player photos on front with the name and position overprinted in black at bottom. A white border surrounds the photo. Backs are in black-and-white with a large championship logo and a few stats from the 1941 season.

	NM	EX	VG
Complete Set (43):	25.00	12.50	7.50

Common Player:		1.50	.75	.45
1	Mickey Owen	2.50	1.25	.70
2	Pee Wee Reese	7.50	3.75	2.25
3	Hugh Casey	1.50	.75	.45
4	Larry French	1.50	.75	.45
5	Tom Drake	1.50	.75	.45
6	Ed Albosta	1.50	.75	.45
7	Tommy Tatum	1.50	.75	.45
8	Paul Waner	3.50	1.75	1.00
9	Van Lingle Mungo	2.50	1.25	.70
10	Bill Swift	1.50	.75	.45
11	Dolph Camilli	2.50	1.25	.70
12	Pete Coscarart	1.50	.75	.45
13	Vito Tamulis	1.50	.75	.45
14	John Allen	1.50	.75	.45
15	Lee Grissom	1.50	.75	.45
16	Billy Herman	2.50	1.25	.70
17	Joe Vosmik	1.50	.75	.45
18	Babe Phelps	1.50	.75	.45
19	Mace Brown	1.50	.75	.45
20	Freddie Fitzsimmons	1.50	.75	.45
21	Angelo Guiliani	1.50	.75	.45
22	Lewis Riggs	1.50	.75	.45
23	Jimmy Wasdell	1.50	.75	.45
24	Herman Franks	1.50	.75	.45
25	Alex Kampouris	1.50	.75	.45
26	Kirby Higbe	1.50	.75	.45
27	Joe Medwick	2.50	1.25	.70
28	Newt Kimball	1.50	.75	.45
29	Curt Davis	1.50	.75	.45
30	Augie Galan	1.50	.75	.45
31	Luke Hamlin	1.50	.75	.45
32	Cookie Lavagetto	1.50	.75	.45
33	Joe Gallagher	1.50	.75	.45
34	Whitlow Wyatt	1.50	.75	.45
35	Dixie Walker	1.50	.75	.45
36	Pete Reiser	1.50	.75	.45
37	Leo Durocher	2.50	1.25	.70
38	Pee Wee Reese, Joe Medwick (3" x 5")	4.50	2.25	1.25
39	Dixie Walker, Joe Medwick, Dolph Camilli, Pete Reiser (3" x 5")	4.50	2.25	1.25
40	Team photo	3.00	1.50	.90
41	Kemp Wicker	1.50	.75	.45
42	George Pfister	2.00	1.00	.60
43	Chuck Dressen	1.50	.75	.45

1979 TCMA All Time Tigers

Utilizing a format similar to its several minor league team sets of the same year, this collectors' issue from TCMA features an "All Time" Tigers team selection of position players, pitchers and manager. The 2-1/2" x 3-1/2" cards have black-and-white photos on front with the player's name and position in an orange "wave" at bottom; the whole is surrounded by a white border. Backs are in black-and-white and detail the all-time line-up. The unnumbered cards are checklisted here alphabetically.

		NM	EX	VG
Complete Set (12):		20.00	10.00	6.00
Common Player:		1.50	.70	.45
(1)	Ty Cobb	6.00	3.00	1.75
(2)	Mickey Cochrane	1.50	.70	.45
(3)	Terry Fox	1.50	.70	.45
(4)	Charlie Gehringer	2.50	1.25	.70
(5)	Hank Greenberg	5.00	2.50	1.50
(6)	Harry Heilmann	1.50	.70	.45
(7)	Al Kaline	5.00	2.50	1.50
(8)	George Kell	1.50	.70	.45
(9)	Denny McLain	1.50	.70	.45
(10)	Hal Newhouser	1.50	.70	.45
(11)	Steve O'Neil (O'Neill)	1.50	.70	.45
(12)	Billy Rogell	1.50	.70	.45

1979 TCMA Baseball History Series: The Fifties

 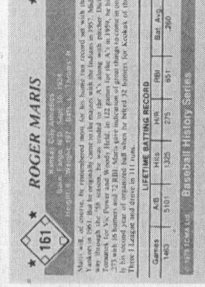

The "pure" format of the 1953 Bowman set was borrowed in this collectors' issue featuring the stars and journeymen of baseball in the 1950s. The 2-1/2" x 3-1/2" cards have color photos on front with white borders. Backs are in red and black with personal data and career summary and stats. Each set originally sold by TCMA came with two large-format (5" x 3-1/2") team-photo cards.

		NM	EX	VG
Complete Set (291):		27.50	13.50	8.25
Common Player:		.25	.13	.08
1	Joe DiMaggio	7.50	3.75	2.25
2	Yogi Berra	1.50	.70	.45
3	Warren Spahn	.75	.40	.25
4	Robin Roberts	.60	.30	.20
5	Ernie Banks	1.50	.70	.45
6	Willie Mays	5.00	2.50	1.50
7	Mickey Mantle	10.00	5.00	3.00
8	Roy Campanella	1.50	.70	.45
9	Stan Musial	4.00	2.00	1.25
10	Ted Williams	5.00	2.50	1.50
11	Ed Bailey	.25	.13	.08
12	Ted Kluszewski	.60	.30	.20
13	Ralph Kiner	.60	.30	.20
14	Dick Littlefield	.25	.13	.08
15	Nellie Fox	.60	.30	.20
16	Billy Pierce	.25	.13	.08
17	Richie Ashburn	.60	.30	.20
18	Del Ennis	.25	.13	.08
19	Bob Lemon	.50	.25	.15
20	Early Wynn	.50	.25	.15
21	Joe Collins	.25	.13	.08
22	Hank Bauer	.25	.13	.08
23	Roberto Clemente	6.00	3.00	1.75
24	Frank Thomas	.25	.13	.08
25	Alvin Dark	.25	.13	.08
26	Whitey Lockman	.25	.13	.08
27	Larry Doby	.60	.30	.20
28	Bob Feller	.75	.40	.25
29	Willie Jones	.25	.13	.08
30	Granny Hamner	.25	.13	.08
31	Clem Labine	.25	.13	.08
32	Ralph Branca	.25	.13	.08
33	Jack Harshman	.25	.13	.08
34	Dick Donovan	.25	.13	.08
35	Tommy Henrich	.25	.13	.08
36	Jerry Coleman	.25	.13	.08
37	Billy Hoeft	.25	.13	.08
38	Johnny Groth	.25	.13	.08
39	Harvey Haddix	.25	.13	.08
40	Gerry Staley	.25	.13	.08
41	Dale Long	.25	.13	.08
42	Vern Law	.25	.13	.08
43	Dodger Power	1.50	.70	.45
44	Sam Jethroe	.25	.13	.08
45	Vic Wertz	.25	.13	.08
46	Wes Westrum	.25	.13	.08
47	Dee Fondy	.25	.13	.08
48	Gene Baker	.25	.13	.08
49	Sandy Koufax	5.00	2.50	1.50
50	Billy Loes	.25	.13	.08
51	Chuck Diering	.25	.13	.08
52	Joe Ginsberg	.25	.13	.08
53	Jim Konstanty	.25	.13	.08
54	Curt Simmons	.25	.13	.08
55	Alex Kellner	.25	.13	.08
56	Charlie Dressen	.25	.13	.08
57	Frank Sullivan	.25	.13	.08
58	Mel Parnell	.25	.13	.08
59	Bobby Hofman	.25	.13	.08
60	Bill Connelly	.25	.13	.08
61	Corky Valentine	.25	.13	.08
62	Johnny Klippstein	.25	.13	.08
63	Chuck Tanner	.25	.13	.08
64	Dick Drott	.25	.13	.08
65	Dean Stone	.25	.13	.08
66	Jim Busby	.25	.13	.08
67	Sid Gordon	.25	.13	.08
68	Del Crandall	.25	.13	.08
69	Walker Cooper	.25	.13	.08
70	Hank Sauer	.25	.13	.08
71	Gil Hodges	.75	.40	.25
72	Duke Snider	1.00	.50	.30
73	Sherman Lollar	.25	.13	.08
74	Chico Carrasquel	.25	.13	.08
75	Gus Triandos	.25	.13	.08
76	Bob Harrison	.25	.13	.08
77	Eddie Waitkus	.25	.13	.08
78	Ken Heintzelman	.25	.13	.08
79	Harry Simpson	.25	.13	.08
80	Luke Easter	.25	.13	.08
81	Ed Dick	.25	.13	.08
82	Jim DePaola	.25	.13	.08
83	Billy Cox	.25	.13	.08
84	Pee Wee Reese	1.00	.50	.30
85	Virgil Trucks	.25	.13	.08
86	George Kell	.50	.25	.15
87	Mickey Vernon	.25	.13	.08
88	Eddie Yost	.25	.13	.08
89	Gus Bell	.25	.13	.08
90	Wally Post	.25	.13	.08
91	Ed Lopat	.25	.13	.08
92	Dick Wakefield	.25	.13	.08
93	Solly Hemus	.25	.13	.08
94	Al "Red" Schoendienst	.60	.30	.20
95	Sammy White	.25	.13	.08
96	Billy Goodman	.25	.13	.08
97	Jim Hearn	.25	.13	.08
98	Ruben Gomez	.25	.13	.08
99	Marty Marion	.25	.13	.08
100	Bill Virdon	.25	.13	.08
101	Chuck Stobbs	.25	.13	.08
102	Ron Samford	.25	.13	.08
103	Bill Tuttle	.25	.13	.08
104	Harvey Kuenn	.25	.13	.08
105	Joe Cunningham	.25	.13	.08
106	Bill Sarni	.25	.13	.08

#	Player			
107	Jack Kramer	.25	.13	.08
108	Eddie Stanky	.25	.13	.08
109	Carmen Mauro	.25	.13	.08
110	Wayne Belardi	.25	.13	.08
111	Preston Ward	.25	.13	.08
112	Jack Shepard	.25	.13	.08
113	Buddy Kerr	.25	.13	.08
114	Vern Bickford	.25	.13	.08
115	Ellis Kinder	.25	.13	.08
116	Walt Dropo	.25	.13	.08
117	Duke Maas	.25	.13	.08
118	Billy Hunter	.25	.13	.08
119	Ewell Blackwell	.25	.13	.08
120	Hershell Freeman	.25	.13	.08
121	Freddie Martin	.25	.13	.08
122	Erv Dusak	.25	.13	.08
123	Roy Hartsfield	.25	.13	.08
124	Willard Marshall	.25	.13	.08
125	Jack Sanford	.25	.13	.08
126	Herm Wehmeier	.25	.13	.08
127	Hal Smith	.25	.13	.08
128	Jim Finigan	.25	.13	.08
129	Bob Hale	.25	.13	.08
130	Jim Wilson	.25	.13	.08
131	Bill Wight	.25	.13	.08
132	Mike Fornieles	.25	.13	.08
133	Steve Gromek	.25	.13	.08
134	Herb Score	.35	.20	.11
135	Ryne Duren	.25	.13	.08
136	Bob Turley	.25	.13	.08
137	Wally Moon	.25	.13	.08
138	Fred Hutchinson	.25	.13	.08
139	Jim Hegan	.25	.13	.08
140	Dale Mitchell	.25	.13	.08
141	Walt Moryn	.25	.13	.08
142	Cal Neeman	.25	.13	.08
143	Billy Martin	.50	.25	.15
144	Phil Rizzuto	1.00	.50	.30
145	Preacher Roe	.25	.13	.08
146	Carl Erskine	.25	.13	.08
147	Vic Power	.25	.13	.08
148	Elmer Valo	.25	.13	.08
149	Don Mueller	.25	.13	.08
150	Hank Thompson	.25	.13	.08
151	Stan Lopata	.25	.13	.08
152	Dick Sisler	.25	.13	.08
153	Willard Schmidt	.25	.13	.08
154	Roy McMillan	.25	.13	.08
155	Gil McDougald	.25	.13	.08
156	Gene Woodling	.25	.13	.08
157	Eddie Mathews	.75	.40	.25
158	Johnny Logan	.25	.13	.08
159	Dan Bankhead	.25	.13	.08
160	Joe Black	.25	.13	.08
161	Roger Maris	1.50	.70	.45
162	Bob Cerv	.25	.13	.08
163	Paul Minner	.25	.13	.08
164	Bob Rush	.25	.13	.08
165	Gene Hermanski	.25	.13	.08
166	Harry Brecheen	.25	.13	.08
167	Davey Williams	.25	.13	.08
168	Monte Irvin	.60	.30	.20
169	Clint Courtney	.25	.13	.08
170	Sandy Consuegra	.25	.13	.08
171	Bobby Shantz	.25	.13	.08
172	Harry Byrd	.25	.13	.08
173	Marv Throneberry	.25	.13	.08
174	Woody Held	.25	.13	.08
175	Al Rosen	.25	.13	.08
176	Rance Pless	.25	.13	.08
177	Steve Bilko	.25	.13	.08
178	Joe Presko	.25	.13	.08
179	Ray Boone	.25	.13	.08
180	Jim Lemon	.25	.13	.08
181	Andy Pafko	.25	.13	.08
182	Don Newcombe	.35	.20	.11
183	Frank Lary	.25	.13	.08
184	Al Kaline	.75	.40	.25
185	Allie Reynolds	.25	.13	.08
186	Vic Raschi	.25	.13	.08
187	Dodger Braintrust	.50	.25	.15
188	Jim Piersall	.25	.13	.08
189	George Wilson	.25	.13	.08
190	Jim "Dusty" Rhodes	.25	.13	.08
191	Duane Pillette	.25	.13	.08
192	Dave Philley	.25	.13	.08
193	Bobby Morgan	.25	.13	.08
194	Russ Meyer	.25	.13	.08
195	Hector Lopez	.25	.13	.08
196	Arnie Portocarrero	.25	.13	.08
197	Joe Page	.25	.13	.08
198	Tommy Byrne	.25	.13	.08
199	Ray Monzant	.25	.13	.08
200	John "Windy" McCall	.25	.13	.08
201	Leo Durocher	.50	.25	.15
202	Bobby Thomson	.35	.20	.11
203	Jack Banta	.25	.13	.08
204	Joe Pignatano	.25	.13	.08
205	Carlos Paula	.25	.13	.08
206	Roy Sievers	.25	.13	.08
207	Mickey McDermott	.25	.13	.08
208	Ray Scarborough	.25	.13	.08
209	Bill Miller	.25	.13	.08
210	Bill Skowron	.25	.13	.08
211	Bob Nieman	.25	.13	.08
212	Al Pilarcik	.25	.13	.08
213	Jerry Priddy	.25	.13	.08
214	Frank House	.25	.13	.08
215	Don Mossi	.25	.13	.08
216	Rocky Colavito	.60	.30	.20
217	Brooks Lawrence	.25	.13	.08
218	Ted Wilks	.25	.13	.08
219	Zack Monroe	.25	.13	.08
220	Art Ditmar	.25	.13	.08
221	Cal McLish	.25	.13	.08
222	Gene Bearden	.25	.13	.08
223	Norm Siebern	.25	.13	.08
224	Bob Wiesler	.25	.13	.08

#	Player			
225	Foster Castleman	.25	.13	.08
226	Daryl Spencer	.25	.13	.08
227	Dick Williams	.25	.13	.08
228	Don Zimmer	.25	.13	.08
229	Jackie Jensen	.25	.13	.08
230	Billy Johnson	.25	.13	.08
231	Dave Koslo	.25	.13	.08
232	Al Corwin	.25	.13	.08
233	Erv Palica	.25	.13	.08
234	Bob Milliken	.25	.13	.08
235	Ray Katt	.25	.13	.08
236	Sammy Calderone	.25	.13	.08
237	Don Demeter	.25	.13	.08
238	Karl Olson	.25	.13	.08
239	The Veteran and The Rookie	.50	.25	.15
240	Enos Slaughter	.50	.25	.15
241	Dick Kryhoski	.25	.13	.08
242	Art Houtteman	.25	.13	.08
243	Andy Carey	.25	.13	.08
244	Tony Kubek	.35	.20	.11
245	Mike McCormick	.25	.13	.08
246	Bob Schmidt	.25	.13	.08
247	Nelson King	.25	.13	.08
248	Bob Skinner	.25	.13	.08
249	Dick Bokelmann	.25	.13	.08
250	Eddie Kazak	.25	.13	.08
251	Billy Klaus	.25	.13	.08
252	Norm Zauchin	.25	.13	.08
253	Art Schult	.25	.13	.08
254	Bob Martyn	.25	.13	.08
255	Larry Jansen	.25	.13	.08
256	Sal Maglie	.25	.13	.08
257	Bob Darnell	.25	.13	.08
258	Ken Lehman	.25	.13	.08
259	Jim Blackburn	.25	.13	.08
260	Bob Purkey	.25	.13	.08
261	Harry Walker	.25	.13	.08
262	Joe Garagiola	.35	.20	.11
263	Gus Zernial	.25	.13	.08
264	Walter "Hoot" Evers	.25	.13	.08
265	Mark Freeman	.25	.13	.08
266	Charlie Silvera	.25	.13	.08
267	Johnny Podres	.25	.13	.08
268	Jim Hughes	.25	.13	.08
269	Al Worthington	.25	.13	.08
270	Hoyt Wilhelm	.50	.25	.15
271	Elston Howard	.25	.13	.08
272	Don Larsen	.40	.20	.12
273	Don Hoak	.25	.13	.08
274	Chico Fernandez	.25	.13	.08
275	Gail Harris	.25	.13	.08
276	Valmy Thomas	.25	.13	.08
277	George Shuba	.25	.13	.08
278	Al "Rube" Walker	.25	.13	.08
279	Willard Ramsdell	.25	.13	.08
280	Lindy McDaniel	.25	.13	.08
281	Bob Wilson	.25	.13	.08
282	Chuck Templeton	.25	.13	.08
283	Eddie Robinson	.25	.13	.08
284	Bob Porterfield	.25	.13	.08
285	Larry Miggins	.25	.13	.08
286	Minnie Minoso	.25	.13	.08
287	Lou Boudreau	.50	.25	.15
288	Jim Davenport	.25	.13	.08
289	Bob Miller	.25	.13	.08
290	Jim Gilliam	.25	.13	.08
291	Jackie Robinson	4.00	2.00	1.25
Bonus 1	1955 Brooklyn Dodgers Team Card	10.00	5.00	3.00
Bonus 2	1957 Milwaukee Braves Team	10.00	5.00	3.00

1979 TCMA Japan Pro Baseball

Stars of Japan's Pacific and Central "major" leagues are featured in this collectors' issue. More than a dozen Americans playing or managing in Japan at the time are included in the set, as well as several Japanese Hall of Famers including home-run king Sadaharu Oh. Cards feature a color posed portrait with a light blue semi-circle at bottom containing the team and player name in royal blue. Backs are printed in red and black on white and have a few personal data, 1978 and career stats, plus league and team logos and TCMA copyright. Cards are nominally standard 2-1/2" x 3-1/2" in size, but actual size varies a bit due to cutting discrepancies.

	NM	EX	VG
Complete Set (90):	40.00	20.00	12.00
Common Player:	.50	.25	.15
1 Sadaharu Oh	15.00	7.50	4.50
2 Jinten Haku	.50	.25	.15
3 Toshizo Sakamoto	.50	.25	.15
4 Tony Muser	1.00	.50	.30
5 Makoto Matsubara	.50	.25	.15
6 Masayuki Nakaysuka	.50	.25	.15
7 Daisuke Yamashita	.50	.25	.15

#	Player	NM	EX	VG
8	Koji Yamamoto	.50	.25	.15
9	Sachio Kinugasa	4.00	2.00	1.25
10	Bernie Williams	.60	.30	.20
11	Bobby Marcano	.60	.30	.20
12	Koichi Tabuchi	.50	.25	.15
13	Katsuya Nomura	3.00	1.50	.90
14	Jack Maloof	.60	.30	.20
15	Masahiro Doi	.50	.25	.15
16	Hiroyuki Yamazaki	.50	.25	.15
17	Vernon Law	2.00	1.00	.60
18	Dave Hilton	.60	.30	.20
19	Katsuo Osugi	.50	.25	.15
20	Tsutomu Wakamatsu	.50	.25	.15
21	John Scott	.60	.30	.20
22	Toru Sugiura	.50	.25	.15
23	Akihiko Kondo	.50	.25	.15
24	Shintaro Mizutani	.50	.25	.15
25	Tatsuro Hirooka	.50	.25	.15
26	Kojiro Ikegaya	.50	.25	.15
27	Yutaka Enatsu	1.50	.70	.45
28	Tomehiro Kaneda	.50	.25	.15
29	Yoshihiko Takahashi	.50	.25	.15
30	Jitsuo Mizutani	.50	.25	.15
31	Adrian Garrett	.60	.30	.20
32	Jim Lyttle	.60	.30	.20
33	Takeshi Koba	.50	.25	.15
34	Sam Ewing	.60	.30	.20
35	Kazumi Takahashi	.50	.25	.15
36	Kazushi Saeki	.50	.25	.15
37	Masanori Murakami	7.50	3.75	2.25
38	Toshiro Kato	.50	.25	.15
39	Junichi Kashiwabara	.50	.25	.15
40	Masaru Tomita	.50	.25	.15
41	Bobby Mitchell	.60	.30	.20
42	Mikio Sendoh	.50	.25	.15
43	Chris Arnold	.60	.30	.20
44	Charlie Manuel	.60	.30	.20
45	Keiji Suzuki	.50	.25	.15
46	Toru Ogawa	.50	.25	.15
47	Shigeru Ishiwata	.50	.25	.15
48	Kyosuke Sasaki	.50	.25	.15
49	Iwao Ikebe	.50	.25	.15
50	Kaoru Betto	.50	.25	.15
51	Gene Martin	.60	.30	.20
52	Felix Millan	1.00	.50	.30
53	Mitsuo Motoi	.50	.25	.15
54	Tomio Tashiro	.50	.25	.15
55	Shigeo Nagashima	7.50	3.75	2.25
56	Yoshikazu Takagi	.50	.25	.15
57	Keiichi Nagasaki	.50	.25	.15
58	Rick Krueger	.60	.30	.20
59	John Sipin	.60	.30	.20
60	Osao Shibata	.50	.25	.15
61	Isao Harimoto	.50	.25	.15
62	Shigeru Takada	.50	.25	.15
63	Michiyo Arito	.50	.25	.15
64	Hisao Niura	.50	.25	.15
65	Teruhide Sakurai	.50	.25	.15
66	Yoshito Oda	.50	.25	.15
67	Leron Lee	.60	.30	.20
68	Carlos May	.60	.30	.20
69	Frank Ortenzio	.60	.30	.20
70	Leon Lee	.60	.30	.20
71	Mitsuru Fujiwara	.50	.25	.15
72	Senichi Hoshino	.50	.25	.15
73	Tatsuhiko Kimata	.50	.25	.15
74	Morimichi Takagi	.50	.25	.15
75	Yasunori Oshima	.50	.25	.15
76	Yasushi Tao	.50	.25	.15
77	Wayne Garrett	.60	.30	.20
78	Bob Jones	.60	.30	.20
79	Toshiro Naka	.50	.25	.15
80	Don Blasingame	3.00	1.50	.90
81	Mike Reinbach	.60	.30	.20
82	Masashi Takenouchi	.50	.25	.15
83	Masayuki Kakefu	.50	.25	.15
84	Katsuhiro Nakamura	.50	.25	.15
85	Shigeru Kobayashi	.50	.25	.15
86	Lee Stanton	.60	.30	.20
87	Takenori Emoto	.50	.25	.15
88	Sohachi Aniya	.50	.25	.15
89	Wally Yonamine	4.00	2.00	1.25
90	Kazuhiro Yamauchi	.50	.25	.15

1979 TCMA 1927 New York Yankees

Perhaps the finest baseball team of all time is featured in this collectors' set. The sepia oval photos at center are surrounded by black-and-white graphics of baseball equipment and other ornamentation. Player name and position are in a strip beneath the photo. Backs have personal data and a career summary. The cards are in standard 2-1/2" x 3-1/2".

	NM	EX	VG
Complete Set (32):	20.00	10.00	6.00
Common Player:	1.00	.50	.30
1 Babe Ruth	6.00	3.00	1.75
2 Lou Gehrig	4.00	2.00	1.25

3	Tony Lazzeri	1.00	.50	.30
4	Mark Koenig	1.00	.50	.30
5	Julie Wera	1.00	.50	.30
6	Ray Morehart	1.00	.50	.30
7	Art Fletcher	1.00	.50	.30
8	Joe Dugan	1.00	.50	.30
9	Charley O'Leary	1.00	.50	.30
10	Bob Meusel	1.00	.50	.30
11	Earle Combs	1.00	.50	.30
12	Cedric Durst	1.00	.50	.30
13	Johnny Grabowski	1.00	.50	.30
14	Mike Gazella	1.00	.50	.30
15	Pat Collins	1.00	.50	.30
16	Waite Hoyt	1.00	.50	.30
17	Myles Thomas	1.00	.50	.30
18	Benny Bengough	1.00	.50	.30
19	Herb Pennock	1.00	.50	.30
20	Wilcy Moore	1.00	.50	.30
21	Urban Shocker	1.00	.50	.30
22	Dutch Ruether	1.00	.50	.30
23	George Pipgras	1.00	.50	.30
24	Jacob Ruppert	1.00	.50	.30
25	Eddie Bennett	1.00	.50	.30
26	Ed Barrow	1.00	.50	.30
27	Ben Paschal	1.00	.50	.30
28	Miller Huggins	1.00	.50	.30
29	Joe Giard	1.00	.50	.30
30	Bob Shawkey	1.00	.50	.30
31	Walter Beall	1.00	.50	.30
32	Don Miller	1.00	.50	.30

1980 TCMA All-Time Teams

ERNIE BANKS

In 1980, TCMA began a new series of sets featuring 11 all-time great players and a manager from several of the 26 teams. In standard 2-1/2" x 3-1/2" format, most of the cards utilize black-and-white player photos, though some more recent stars are pictured in color. Several decorative borders, varying by team, surround the front photos. On most team sets there is an "All Time" designation at top, with the player name and (usually) position at bottom. Backs are fairly uniform, printed in blue or black, and offering a few biographical details and career highlights or a checklist. Besides hobby sales, these old-timers' sets were also sold in several major retail chains.

(Team sets listed individually.)

1980 TCMA All Time Brooklyn Dodgers

ZACH WHEAT

		NM	EX	VG
Complete Set (12):		6.00	3.00	1.80
Common Player:		.50	.25	.15
1	Gil Hodges	1.00	.50	.30
2	Jim Gilliam	.50	.25	.15
3	Pee Wee Reese	1.00	.50	.30
4	Jackie Robinson	3.00	1.50	.90
5	Sandy Koufax	3.00	1.50	.90
6	Zach Wheat	.50	.25	.15
7	Dixie Walker	.50	.25	.15
8	Hugh Casey	.50	.25	.15
9	Dazzy Vance	.50	.25	.15
10	Duke Snider	1.00	.50	.30
11	Roy Campanella	1.50	.70	.45
12	Walter Alston	.50	.25	.15

1980 TCMA All Time Cubs

		NM	EX	VG
Complete Set (12):		6.00	3.00	1.80
Common Player:		.50	.25	.15
1	Billy Williams	1.50	.70	.45
2	Charlie Root	.50	.25	.15
3	Ron Santo	1.50	.70	.45
4	Larry French	.50	.25	.15
5	Gabby Hartnett	.50	.25	.15
6	Emil Kush	.50	.25	.15
7	Charlie Grimm	.50	.25	.15
8	Kiki Cuyler	.50	.25	.15

9	Billy Herman	.50	.25	.15
10	Hack Wilson	1.00	.50	.30
11	Rogers Hornsby	1.00	.50	.30
12	Ernie Banks	4.00	2.00	1.25

1980 TCMA All Time N.Y. Giants

BILL TERRY

ALL TIME N.Y. GIANTS
BILL TERRY

Bill Terry, nicknamed "Memphis Bill" was one of the greatest hitters in baseball history. Over his fourteen year career he maintained a .341 batting average. Although he was not known as a slugger, he knocked home one hundred or more runs in six consecutive years. Terry is best remembered as the last .400 hitter in the National League, as he batted .401 in 1930. Terry, a Hall of Fame selection in 1954, also succeeded John McGraw as the Giant's manager. He led them to three pennants over a ten year period.

© TCMA Ltd 1980-0007

		NM	EX	VG
Complete Set (12):		6.00	3.00	1.80
Common Player:		.50	.25	.15
1	Willie Mays	4.00	2.00	1.25
2	Wes Westrum	.50	.25	.15
3	Carl Hubbell	.50	.25	.15
4	Hoyt Wilhelm	.50	.25	.15
5	Bobby Thomson	1.00	.50	.30
6	Frankie Frisch	.50	.25	.15
7	Bill Terry	.50	.25	.15
8	Alvin Dark	.50	.25	.15
9	Mel Ott	1.00	.50	.30
10	Christy Mathewson	2.50	1.25	.70
11	Freddie Lindstrom	.50	.25	.15
12	John McGraw	.50	.25	.15

1980 TCMA All Time Tigers

JOHN HILLER

ALL TIME TIGERS
JOHN HILLER

Sets printed with blue or red borders.

		NM	EX	VG
Complete Set (12):		6.00	3.00	1.80
Common Player:		.50	.25	.15
1	George Kell	.50	.25	.15
2	Billy Rogell	.50	.25	.15
3	Ty Cobb	4.00	2.00	1.25
4	Hank Greenberg	2.50	1.25	.70
5	Al Kaline	1.50	.70	.45
6	Charlie Gehringer	.75	.40	.25
7	Harry Heilmann	.50	.25	.15
8	Hal Newhouser	.50	.25	.15
9	Steve O'Neill	.50	.25	.15
10	Denny McLain	.50	.25	.15
11	Mickey Cochrane	.50	.25	.15
12	John Hiller	.50	.25	.15

1980 TCMA All Time White Sox

LUKE APPLING

ALL TIME WHITE SOX
LUKE APPLING

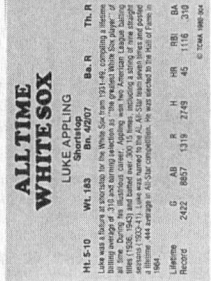

		NM	EX	VG
Complete Set (12):		6.00	3.00	1.80
Common Player:		.50	.25	.15
1	Ted Lyons	.50	.25	.15
2	Eddie Collins	2.00	1.00	.60
3	Al Lopez	.75	.40	.25
4	Luke Appling	2.00	1.00	.60
5	Billy Pierce	.75	.40	.25
6	Willie Kamm	.50	.25	.15
7	Johnny Mostil	.50	.25	.15
8	Al Simmons	.75	.40	.25
9	Ray Schalk	.50	.25	.15
10	Gerry Staley	.50	.25	.15
11	Harry Hooper	.50	.25	.15
12	Eddie Robinson	.50	.25	.15

1980 TCMA All Time Yankees

ALL TIME N.Y. YANKEES

1B	Lou Gehrig
2B	Tony Lazzeri
3B	Red Rolfe
SS	Phil Rizzuto
OF	Babe Ruth
OF	Mickey Mantle
OF	Joe DiMaggio
C	Bill Dickey
P	Red Ruffing
P	Whitey Ford
RP	Johnny Murphy
Mgr	Casey Stengel

Casey Stengel

TCMA 1980-010

		NM	EX	VG
Complete Set (12):		16.00	8.00	4.75
Common Player:		.50	.25	.15
1	Lou Gehrig	4.00	2.00	1.25
2	Tony Lazzeri	.50	.25	.15
3	Red Rolfe	.50	.25	.15
4	Phil Rizzuto	1.00	.50	.30
5	Babe Ruth	4.00	2.00	1.25
6	Mickey Mantle	5.00	2.50	1.50
7	Joe DiMaggio	4.00	2.00	1.25
8	Bill Dickey	.75	.40	.25
9	Red Ruffing	.50	.25	.15
10	Whitey Ford	1.00	.50	.30
11	Johnny Murphy	.50	.25	.15
12	Casey Stengel	.75	.40	.25

1980 TCMA 1914 Miracle (Boston) Braves

The 1914 Boston Braves team which went from dead last in the National League in mid-July to winning the pennant by 10-1/2 games and sweeping the Philadelphia A's in the World Series is featured on this collectors' issue. In standard 2-1/2" x 3-1/2" format, the cards feature sepia photos in fancy borders. Backs have details of the person's contribution to the "Miracle," along with stats and biographical data.

		NM	EX	VG
Complete Set (32):		30.00	15.00	9.00
Common Player:		1.00	.50	.30
1	Joe Connolly	1.00	.50	.30
2	Lefty Tyler	1.00	.50	.30
3	Tom Hughes	1.00	.50	.30
4	Hank Gowdy	1.00	.50	.30
5	Gene Cochreham (Cocreham)	1.25	.60	.40
6	Larry Gilbert	1.00	.50	.30
7	George Davis	1.00	.50	.30
8	Hub Perdue	1.00	.50	.30
9	Otto Hess	1.00	.50	.30
10	Clarence Kraft	1.25	.60	.40
11	Tommy Griffith	1.00	.50	.30
12	1914 World Series	1.00	.50	.30
13	Oscar Dugey	1.00	.50	.30
14	Josh Devore	1.00	.50	.30
15	George Stallings	1.00	.50	.30
16	Rabbit Maranville	1.50	.70	.45
17	Paul Strand	1.00	.50	.30
18	Charlie Deal	1.00	.50	.30
19	Dick Rudolph	1.00	.50	.30
20	Butch Schmidt	1.00	.50	.30
21	Johnny Evers	2.00	1.00	.60
22	Dick Crutcher	1.25	.60	.40
23	Possum Whitted	1.00	.50	.30
24	Fred Mitchell	1.00	.50	.30
25	Herbie Moran	1.00	.50	.30
26	Bill James	1.00	.50	.30
27	Ted Cather	1.00	.50	.30
28	Red Smith	1.00	.50	.30
29	Les Mann	1.00	.50	.30
30	Herbie Moran, Wally Schrang (Schang)	1.00	.50	.30
31	Not Issued			
32	Johnny Evers (1914 MVP)	1.00	.50	.30
33	Jim Gaffney	1.25	.60	.40

1980 TCMA 1950 Philadelphia Phillies/Whiz Kids

WHIZ KIDS

JACKIE MAYO

1950 PHILADELPHIA PHILLIES
JOHN LEWIS MAYO

The National League Champions of 1950 are featured in this collectors' issue team-set. The 2-1/2" x 3-1/2" cards have black-and-white player photo surrounded by red borders. Backs are in black-and-white with player personal data, career summary and 1950 and lifetime stats.

		NM	EX	VG
Complete Set (31):		20.00	10.00	6.00
Common Player:		.60	.30	.20
1	Ken Silvestri	.50	.25	.15
2	Hank Borowy	.50	.25	.15

#	Player	NM	EX	VG
3	Bob Miller	.50	.25	.15
4	Jocko Thompson	.50	.25	.15
5	Curt Simmons	.50	.25	.15
6	Dick Sisler	.50	.25	.15
7	Eddie Waitkus	.50	.25	.15
8	Dick Whitman	.50	.25	.15
9	Andy Seminick	.50	.25	.15
10	Richie Ashburn	5.00	2.50	1.50
11	Bubba Church	.50	.25	.15
12	Jackie Mayo	.50	.25	.15
13	Eddie Sawyer	.50	.25	.15
14	Benny Bengough	.50	.25	.15
15	Jim Konstanty	.50	.25	.15
16	Robin Roberts	5.00	2.50	1.50
17	Del Ennis	.50	.25	.15
18	Dusty Cooke	.50	.25	.15
19	Mike Goliat	.50	.25	.15
20	Russ Meyer	.50	.25	.15
21	Granny Hamner	.50	.25	.15
22	Stan Lopata	.50	.25	.15
23	Willie Jones	.50	.25	.15
24	Stan Hollmig	.50	.25	.15
25	Jimmy Bloodworth	.50	.25	.15
26	Ken Johnson	.50	.25	.15
27	Bill Nicholson	.50	.25	.15
28	Ken Heintzelman	.50	.25	.15
29	Blix Donnelly	.50	.25	.15
30	Putsy Caballero	.50	.25	.15
31	Cy Perkins	.50	.25	.15

1980 TCMA 1957 Milwaukee Braves

The World Champion Milwaukee Braves are featured in this collectors' issue. The 2-1/2" x 3-1/2" cards have blue-and-white player photos with white borders, blue typography and red graphics. Backs are in blue-and-white with a few bits of player data, career information and stats, along with a TCMA copyright line.

#	Player	NM	EX	VG
	Complete Set (42):	30.00	15.00	9.00
	Common Player:	.50	.25	.15
1	Don McMahon	.50	.25	.15
2	Joey Jay	.75	.40	.25
3	Phil Paine	.50	.25	.15
4	Bob Trowbridge	.50	.25	.15
5	Bob Buhl	.50	.25	.15
6	Lew Burdette	.75	.40	.25
7	Ernie Johnson	.50	.25	.15
8	Ray Crone	.50	.25	.15
9	Taylor Phillips	.50	.25	.15
10	Johnny Logan	.50	.25	.15
11	Frank Torre	.50	.25	.15
12	John DeMerit	.50	.25	.15
13	Red Murff	.50	.25	.15
14	Nippy Jones	.50	.25	.15
15	Bobby Thomson	.75	.40	.25
16	Chuck Tanner	.50	.25	.15
17	Charlie Root	.50	.25	.15
18	Juan Pizarro	.50	.25	.15
19	Hawk Taylor	.50	.25	.15
20	Mel Roach	.50	.25	.15
21	Bob Hazle	.75	.40	.25
22	Del Rice	.50	.25	.15
23	Felix Mantilla	.50	.25	.15
24	Andy Pafko	.50	.25	.15
25	Del Crandall	.75	.40	.25
26	Wes Covington	.50	.25	.15
27	Eddie Mathews	5.00	2.50	1.50
28	Joe Adcock	.75	.40	.25
29	Dick Cole	.50	.25	.15
30	Carl Sawatski	.50	.25	.15
31	Warren Spahn	5.00	2.50	1.50
32	Hank Aaron	10.00	5.00	3.00
33	Bob Keely	.50	.25	.15
34	Johnny Riddle	.50	.25	.15
35	Connie Ryan	.50	.25	.15
36	Harry Hanebrink	.50	.25	.15
37	Danny O'Connell	.50	.25	.15
38	Fred Haney	.50	.25	.15
39	Dave Jolly	.50	.25	.15
40	Red Schoendienst	3.50	1.75	1.00
41	Gene Conley	.50	.25	.15
42	Bill Bruton	.50	.25	.15

1980 TCMA 1959 L.A. Dodgers

This collectors' issue features the members of the 1959 World Champion L.A. Dodgers. The 2-1/2" x 3-1/2" cards can be found printed in either black-and-white or blue-and-white on front and back. Backs have personal data, 1959 and career stats and a few sentences about the player's performance in the championship season.

#	Player	NM	EX	VG
	Complete Set (40):	40.00	20.00	12.00
	Common Player:	1.00	.50	.30
1	Joe Pignatano	1.00	.50	.30
2	Carl Furillo	1.50	.70	.45
3	Bob Lillis	1.00	.50	.30
4	Chuck Essegian	1.00	.50	.30
5	Dick Gray	1.00	.50	.30
6	Rip Repulski	1.00	.50	.30
7	Jim Baxes	1.00	.50	.30
8	Frank Howard	2.50	1.25	.70
9	Solly Drake	1.00	.50	.30
10	Sandy Amoros	1.50	.70	.45
11	Norm Sherry	1.50	.70	.45
12	Tommy Davis	1.50	.70	.45
13	Jim Gilliam	1.50	.70	.45
14	Duke Snider	5.00	2.50	1.50
15	Maury Wills	2.50	1.25	.70
16	Don Demeter	1.00	.50	.30
17	Wally Moon	1.50	.70	.45
18	John Roseboro	1.50	.70	.45
19	Ron Fairly	1.50	.70	.45
20	Norm Larker	1.50	.70	.45
21	Charlie Neal	1.50	.70	.45
22	Don Zimmer	1.50	.70	.45
23	Chuck Dressen	1.00	.50	.30
24	Gil Hodges	4.00	2.00	1.25
25	Joe Becker	1.00	.50	.30
26	Walter Alston	1.50	.70	.45
27	Greg Mulleavy	1.00	.50	.30
28	Don Drysdale	4.00	2.00	1.25
29	Johnny Podres	1.50	.70	.45
30	Sandy Koufax	7.50	3.75	2.25
31	Roger Craig	1.50	.70	.45
32	Danny McDevitt	1.00	.50	.30
33	Bill Harris	1.00	.50	.30
34	Larry Sherry	1.00	.50	.30
35	Stan Williams	1.50	.70	.45
36	Clem Labine	1.50	.70	.45
37	Chuck Churn	1.00	.50	.30
38	Johnny Klippstein	1.00	.50	.30
39	Carl Erskine	1.50	.70	.45
40	Fred Kipp	1.00	.50	.30

1980 TCMA 1960 Pittsburgh Pirates

The World Champion 1960 Pirates are featured in this collectors issue team-set. Black-and-white player photos are bordered in gold on the fronts of the 2-1/2" x 3-1/2" cards. Backs are in black-and-white with personal data, career summary and stats for the 1960 season and career. The Cimoli error card #39 was pulled from distribution and replaced with the unnumbered corrected version.

#	Player	NM	EX	VG
	Complete Set (41):	30.00	15.00	9.00
	(No #39 Cimoli error.)			
	Common Player:	.50	.25	.15
1	Clem Labine	.50	.25	.15
2	Bob Friend	.75	.40	.25
3	Roy Face	.75	.40	.25
4	Vern Law	.75	.40	.25
5	Harvey Haddix	.75	.40	.25
6	Vinegar Bend Mizell	.50	.25	.15
7	Bill Burwell	.50	.25	.15
8	Diomedes Olivo	.50	.25	.15
9	Don Gross	.50	.25	.15
10	Fred Green	.50	.25	.15
11	Jim Umbricht	.50	.25	.15
12	George Witt	.50	.25	.15
13	Tom Cheney	.50	.25	.15
14	Bennie Daniels	.50	.25	.15
15	Earl Francis	.50	.25	.15
16	Joe Gibbon	.50	.25	.15
17	Paul Giel	.50	.25	.15
18	Danny Kravitz	.50	.25	.15
19	R.C. Stevens	.50	.25	.15
20	Roman Mejias	.50	.25	.15
21	Dick Barone	.50	.25	.15
22	Sam Narron	.50	.25	.15
23	Harry Bright	.50	.25	.15
24	Mickey Vernon	.50	.25	.15
25	Bob Skinner	.60	.30	.20
26	Smoky Burgess	.60	.30	.20
27	Bill Virdon	.60	.30	.20
28	Not Issued			
29	Don Hoak	.60	.30	.20
30	Bill Mazeroski	6.00	3.00	1.75
31	Dick Stuart	1.50	.70	.45
32	Dick Groat	1.50	.70	.45
33	Bob Oldis	.50	.25	.15
34	Gene Baker	.50	.25	.15
35	Joe Christopher	.50	.25	.15
36	Dick Schofield	.60	.30	.20
37	Hal Smith	.50	.25	.15
38	Rocky Nelson	.50	.25	.15
39	Gino Cimoli (Photo actually Dick Schofield.)	6.00	3.00	1.75
40	Danny Murtaugh	.50	.25	.15
41	Lenny Levy	.50	.25	.15
---	Gino Cimoli			
---	Roberto Clemente	12.00	6.00	3.50

1980 TCMA 1961 Cincinnati Reds

Virtually every member of the World Champion Cincinnati Reds team of 1961 is included in this collectors issue. Fronts of the 2-1/2" x 3-1/2" cards feature black-and-white player poses with red graphics. Backs are in black-and-white with personal data, 1961 and career stats and a short career summary.

#	Player	NM	EX	VG
	Complete Set (41):	30.00	15.00	9.00
	Common Player:	1.00	.50	.30
1	Eddie Kasko	1.00	.50	.30
2	Wally Post	1.00	.50	.30
3	Vada Pinson	2.50	1.25	.70
4	Frank Robinson	7.50	3.75	2.25
5	Pete Whisenant	1.00	.50	.30
6	Reggie Otero	1.00	.50	.30
7	Dick Sisler	1.00	.50	.30
8	Jim Turner	1.00	.50	.30
9	Fred Hutchinson	1.00	.50	.30
10	Gene Freese	1.00	.50	.30
11	Gordy Coleman	1.00	.50	.30
12	Don Blasingame	1.00	.50	.30
13	Gus Bell	1.00	.50	.30
14	Leo Cardenas	1.00	.50	.30
15	Elio Chacon	1.00	.50	.30
16	Dick Gernert	1.00	.50	.30
17	Jim Baumer	1.00	.50	.30
18	Willie Jones	1.00	.50	.30
19	Joe Gaines	1.00	.50	.30
20	Cliff Cook	1.00	.50	.30
21	Harry Anderson	1.00	.50	.30
22	Jerry Zimmerman	1.00	.50	.30
23	Johnny Edwards	1.00	.50	.30
24	Bob Schmidt	1.00	.50	.30
25	Darrell Johnson	1.00	.50	.30
26	Ed Bailey	1.00	.50	.30
27	Joey Jay	1.00	.50	.30
28	Jim O'Toole	1.00	.50	.30
29	Bob Purkey	1.00	.50	.30
30	Jim Brosnan	1.00	.50	.30
31	Ken Hunt	1.00	.50	.30
32	Ken Johnson	1.00	.50	.30
33	Jim Mahoney	1.00	.50	.30
34	Bill Henry	1.00	.50	.30
35	Jerry Lynch	1.00	.50	.30
36	Hal Bevan	1.00	.50	.30
37	Howie Nunn	1.00	.50	.30
38	Sherman Jones	1.00	.50	.30
39	Jay Hook	1.00	.50	.30
40	Claude Osteen	1.00	.50	.30
41	Marshall Bridges	1.00	.50	.30

1980 TCMA/Sports Nostalgia Store Babe Ruth

The same photo on the Babe Ruth card which appeared in TCMA's 1927 N.Y. Yankees set from 1979 was utilized by Sports Nostalgia as an advertising medium. On the back of the ad card is store information and an offer to redeem the card there for a free picture of Ruth. Production was 500 cards.

	NM	EX	VG
Babe Ruth	7.50	3.75	2.25

1978 Allen P. Terach Immortals of Baseball

These souvenir cards were issued as the first of what was intended to be a series honoring baseball's greatest players. No succeeding issues were forthcoming. The images on the 9" x 6-1/2" blank-back cards are printed in black-and-white and sepia. Fine print at the bottom states the card is part of an edition of 3,500. Issue price was just under $5 apiece.

Immortals of Baseball

	NM	EX	VG
Souvenir Card:			
1 Babe Ruth, Joe DiMaggio	9.00	4.50	2.75
2 Ty Cobb, Stan Musial	6.00	3.00	1.75

1914 Texas Tommy Type 1 (E224)

"TEXAS TOMMY"

John J. McGraw, the peppery manager of the New York Giants, is known wherever the national game is played. He began his career when scarcely sixteen years old and has been in the limelight ever since. In a small town in New York State, he drifted from one minor league club to another, till finally he landed as one of the great Baltimore team, by many experts considered the greatest team ever put together. As third baseman of the famous Orioles, he had Hughie Jennings as his shortstop side partner and the friendship thus formed has continued ever since. McGraw left Baltimore to become manager of the Giants July 19, 1902, when the team had an average of .315. His influence was soon felt and next year the team finished second. In 1904 the Giants won their first pennant in 15 years and the following year won both the National and World's Champion ships. Three times in succession, in 1911, 1912 and 1913 the Giants have finished first in their league, but were beaten twice by Philadelphia and once by Boston in the World's Series. McGraw, however, is still hopeful.

Designated as E224 in the American Card Catalog these cards measure about 2-3/8" x 3-1/2". Fronts feature sepia-toned action photos with the player's name in capital letters and his team below in parenthesis. The back carries a lengthy player biography and most cards, although not all, include year-by-year statistics at the bottom. The words "Texas Tommy" appear at the top. Texas Tommy was a candy bar brand from the Cardinet Candy Co., Oakland, Calif. The candy bar took its name from a popular dance of the era. Most examples of this set have been found in northern California. There is also a second variety of the set, smaller in size (1-7/8" x 3"), which have borderless pictures and a glossy finish. Gaps have been left in the assigned numbers on this checklist to accomo-date future additions.

		NM	EX	VG
Common Player:		5,850	2,925	1,755
(1)	Jimmy Archer	5,850	2,925	1,755
(2)	Jimmy Austin	5,850	2,925	1,755
(3)	Home Run Baker	9,750	4,875	2,925
(4)	Chief Bender	5,850	2,925	1,755
(5)	Bob Bescher	5,850	2,925	1,755
(6)	Ping Bodie	5,850	2,925	1,755
(7)	Donie Bush	5,850	2,925	1,755
(8)	Bobby Byrne	5,850	2,925	1,755
(9)	Nixey Callanan (Callahan)	5,850	2,925	1,755
(10)	Howie Camnitz	5,850	2,925	1,755
(11)	Frank Chance	9,750	4,875	2,925
(12)	Hal Chase	8,450	4,225	2,535
(13)	Ty Cobb	45,500	22,750	13,000
(14)	Jack Coombs	5,850	2,925	1,755
(15)	Sam Crawford	9,750	4,875	2,925
(16)	Birdie Cree	5,850	2,925	1,755
(17)	Al Demaree	5,850	2,925	1,755
(18)	Red Dooin	5,850	2,925	1,755
(19)	Larry Doyle	5,850	2,925	1,755
(20)	Johnny Evers	9,750	4,875	2,925
(21)	Vean Gregg	5,850	2,925	1,755
(22)	Bob Harmon	5,850	2,925	1,755
(23)	Joe Jackson	58,500	29,250	17,550
(24)	Walter Johnson	19,500	9,750	5,850
(25)	Otto Knabe	5,850	2,925	1,755
(26)	Nap Lajoie	9,750	4,875	2,925
(27)	Harry Lord	5,850	2,925	1,755
(28)	Connie Mack	9,750	4,875	2,925
(29)	Armando Marsans	5,850	2,925	1,755
(30)	Christy Mathewson	9,750	4,875	2,925
(31)	George McBride	5,850	2,925	1,755
(32)	John McGraw	9,750	4,875	2,925
(33)	Stuffy McInnis	5,850	2,925	1,755
(34)	Chief Meyers	5,850	2,925	1,755
(35)	Earl Moore	5,850	2,925	1,755
(36)	Mike Mowrey	5,850	2,925	1,755
(37)	Rebel Oakes	5,850	2,925	1,755
(38)	Marty O'Toole	5,850	2,925	1,755
(39)	Eddie Plank	13,000	6,500	3,900
(41)	Bud Ryan	5,850	2,925	1,755
(42)	Tris Speaker	16,250	8,125	4,875
(43)	Jake Stahl	5,850	2,925	1,755
(44)	Oscar Strange (Stanage)	5,850	2,925	1,755
(45)	Bill Sweeney	5,850	2,925	1,755
(46)	Honus Wagner	42,500	21,000	12,500
(47)	Ed Walsh	9,750	4,875	2,925
(48)	Zach Wheat	9,750	4,875	2,925
(49)	Harry Wolter	5,850	2,925	1,755
(50)	Joe Wood	7,150	3,575	2,145
(51)	Steve Yerkes	5,850	2,925	1,755
(52)	Heinie Zimmerman	5,850	2,925	1,755

1914 Texas Tommy Type 2 (E224)

YERKES (RED SOX)

Type 2 Texas Tommy cards are smaller in size, at about 1-7/8" x 3" to 3-1/16", have a glossy front surface and are blank-backed. Their only real link to the Type 1 Texas Tommy cards is the shared front on those players who appear in both checklists.

		NM	EX	VG
Common Player:		6,000	3,000	1,800
(1)	Ping Bodie	6,000	3,000	1,800
(2)	Larry Doyle	6,000	3,000	1,800
(3)	Vean Gregg	6,000	3,000	1,800
(4)	Harry Hooper	7,800	3,900	2,340
(5)	Walter Johnson	12,000	6,000	3,600
(6)	Connie Mack	7,800	3,900	2,340
(7)	Rube Marquard	7,800	3,900	2,340
(8)	Christy Mathewson	14,400	7,200	4,320
(9)	John McGraw	7,800	3,900	2,340
(10)	Chief Meyers	6,000	3,000	1,800
(11)	Fred Snodgrass	6,000	3,000	1,800
(12)	Jake Stahl	6,000	3,000	1,800
(13)	Honus Wagner	16,200	8,100	4,860
(14)	Joe Wood	6,600	3,300	1,980
(15)	Steve Yerkes	6,000	3,000	1,800

1928 Tharp's Ice Cream

(6) BABE RUTH

SAVE THESE PICTURES

One ice cream bar will be given free for each picture of Babe Ruth.

ALSO

One gallon of Tharp's ice cream will be delivered free to the holder of a complete set of sixty different Baseball Stars, upon surrender of same to any Tharp dealer.

Sharing the same format and checklist with several other contemporary ice cream sets this 60-card set includes all of the top stars of the day. Cards are printed in black-and-white on a 1-3/8" x 2-1/2" format. There appears to have been two different types issued, but the extent of each version is unknown. The variations are found in the player's name and card number which can appear either in a strip within the frame of the photo, or printed in the border beneath the photo. Card backs have a redemption offer that includes an ice cream bar in exchange for a Babe Ruth card, or a gallon of ice cream for a complete set of 60. Tharp's was located in Shamokin, Pa.

		NM	EX	VG
Complete Set (60):		20,000	8,000	4,000
Common Player:		115.00	45.00	20.00
1	Burleigh Grimes	225.00	90.00	45.00
2	Walter Reuther (Ruether)	115.00	45.00	20.00
3	Joe Dugan	115.00	45.00	20.00
4	Red Faber	225.00	90.00	45.00
5	Gabby Hartnett	225.00	90.00	45.00
6a	Babe Ruth (Portrait)	7,500	3,000	1,500
6b	Babe Ruth (Throwing)	7,500	3,000	1,500
7	Bob Meusel	115.00	45.00	20.00
8	Herb Pennock	225.00	90.00	45.00
9	George Burns	115.00	45.00	20.00
10	Joe Sewell	225.00	90.00	45.00
11	George Uhle	115.00	45.00	20.00
12	Bob O'Farrell	115.00	45.00	20.00
13	Rogers Hornsby	350.00	140.00	70.00
14	"Pie" Traynor	225.00	90.00	45.00
15	Clarence Mitchell	115.00	45.00	20.00
16a	Eppa Jepha Rixey	225.00	90.00	45.00
16b	Eppa Rixey	225.00	90.00	45.00
17	Carl Mays	115.00	45.00	20.00
18	Adolfo Luque	125.00	50.00	25.00

19	Dave Bancroft	225.00	90.00	45.00
20	George Kelly	225.00	90.00	45.00
21	Earl (Earle) Combs	225.00	90.00	45.00
22	Harry Heilmann	225.00	90.00	45.00
23a	Ray W. Schalk	225.00	90.00	45.00
23b	Ray Schalk	225.00	90.00	45.00
24	Johnny Mostil	115.00	45.00	20.00
25	Hack Wilson	225.00	90.00	45.00
26	Lou Gehrig	2,500	1,000	500.00
27	Ty Cobb	1,500	600.00	300.00
28	Tris Speaker	350.00	140.00	70.00
29	Tony Lazzeri	225.00	90.00	45.00
30	Waite Hoyt	225.00	90.00	45.00
31	Sherwood Smith	115.00	45.00	20.00
32	Max Carey	225.00	90.00	45.00
33	Eugene Hargrave	115.00	45.00	20.00
34	Miguel L. Gonzalez (Middle initial A.)	125.00	50.00	25.00
35	Joe Judge	115.00	45.00	20.00
36	E.C. (Sam) Rice	225.00	90.00	45.00
37	Earl Sheely	115.00	45.00	20.00
38	Sam Jones	115.00	45.00	20.00
39	Bib (Bibb) A. Falk	115.00	45.00	20.00
40	Willie Kamm	115.00	45.00	20.00
41	Stanley Harris	225.00	.90.00	45.00
42	John J. McGraw	225.00	90.00	45.00
43	Artie Nehf	115.00	45.00	20.00
44	Grover Alexander	700.00	280.00	140.00
45	Paul Waner	225.00	90.00	45.00
46	William H. Terry (Photo actually Zeb Terry.)	225.00	90.00	45.00
47	Glenn Wright	115.00	45.00	20.00
48	Earl Smith	115.00	45.00	20.00
49	Leon (Goose) Goslin	225.00	90.00	45.00
50	Frank Frisch	225.00	90.00	45.00
51	Joe Harris	115.00	45.00	20.00
52	Fred (Cy) Williams	115.00	45.00	20.00
53	Eddie Roush	225.00	90.00	45.00
54	George Sisler	225.00	90.00	45.00
55	Ed. Rommel	115.00	45.00	20.00
56	Rogers Peckinpaugh (Roger)	115.00	45.00	20.00
57	Stanley Coveleskie (Coveleski)	225.00	90.00	45.00
58	Lester Bell	115.00	45.00	20.00
59	L. Waner	225.00	90.00	45.00
60	John P. McInnis	115.00	45.00	20.00

1978 The Card Coach Milwaukee Braves Greats

JOE ADCOCK

MILWAUKEE BRAVES GREATS

9 JOE ADCOCK FIRST BASEMAN

Throws: Right   Height: 6' 4"
Bats: Right   Weight: 210 lbs.
Born: October 30, 1927, Coushatta, La.

A favorite with the fans, Joe Adcock seldom was a disappointment at the plate. The big hit was his specialty - Joe could hit the ball harder than anyone in the League. Adcock's best year was 1954 when he batted .308. He swatted 38 round-trippers in 1956, his personal high.

MAJOR LEAGUE RECORD (1950-1966)

Games 1959   Doubles 295
At Bats 6606   Triples 35
Hits 1832   H.R. 336
Batting Ave. 277   RBI's 1122

Years as a Milwaukee Brave - 1953-1962

© 1978, T.C.C.

Stars of the Milwaukee Braves from the early 1950s through the early 1960s are featured in this collectors' issue. The 2-1/2" x 3-1/2" cards have black-and-white player photos on front with the player name in the white border at bottom. Backs are also in black-and-white with personal data, career summary and stats. Cards are numbered by uniform number.

		NM	EX	VG
Complete Set (15):		10.00	5.00	3.00
Common Player:		2.00	1.00	.60
1	Del Crandall	2.00	1.00	.60
4	Red Schoendienst	2.00	1.00	.60
8	Bob Uecker	2.50	1.25	.70
9	Joe Adcock	2.00	1.00	.60
10	Bob Buhl	2.00	1.00	.60
15	Joe Torre	2.50	1.25	.70
16	Carlton Willey	2.00	1.00	.60
21	Warren Spahn	3.00	1.50	.90
22	Johnny Logan	2.00	1.00	.60
33	Lew Burdette	2.00	1.00	.60
34	Billy Bruton	2.00	1.00	.60
41	Eddie Mathews	3.00	1.50	.90
43	Wes Covington	2.00	1.00	.60
44	Hank Aaron	7.50	3.75	2.25
48	Andy Pafko (Checklist)	2.00	1.00	.60

1971 Ticketron L.A. Dodgers/S.F. Giants

Essentially large team schedule cards with promotional dates noted and an ad for the ticket service, the Ticketron Dodgers/Giants cards of 1971 are similar in format. Each has a color photo on front with facsimile autograph. The Dodgers cards are 4" x 6" with no borders on fronts; the 3-3/4" x 5-3/4" Giants cards have a white border. Backs are white with red and blue printing. The unnumbered cards are checklisted here alphabetically within team.

	NM	EX	VG
Complete Dodgers Set (20):	75.00	37.00	22.00
Complete Giants Set (10):	150.00	75.00	45.00
Common Dodger Player:	3.00	1.50	.90
Common Giant Player:	6.00	3.00	1.75

LOS ANGELES DODGERS

		NM	EX	VG
(1)	Richie Allen	15.00	7.50	4.50
(2)	Walter Alston	6.00	3.00	1.75
(3)	Jim Brewer	3.00	1.50	.90
(4)	Willie Crawford	3.00	1.50	.90
(5)	Willie Davis	4.50	2.25	1.25
(6)	Steve Garvey	20.00	10.00	6.00
(7)	Bill Grabarkewitz	3.00	1.50	.90
(8)	Jim Lefebvre	3.00	1.50	.90
(9)	Pete Mikkelsen	3.00	1.50	.90
(10)	Joe Moeller	3.00	1.50	.90
(11)	Manny Mota	4.50	2.25	1.25
(12)	Claude Osteen	3.00	1.50	.90
(13)	Wes Parker	3.00	1.50	.90
(14)	Bill Russell	4.50	2.25	1.25
(15)	Duke Sims	3.00	1.50	.90
(16)	Bill Singer	3.00	1.50	.90
(17)	Bill Sudakis	3.00	1.50	.90
(18)	Don Sutton	20.00	10.00	6.00
(19)	Maury Wills	7.50	3.75	2.25
(20)	Jerry Doggett, Vin Scully	3.00	1.50	.90

SAN FRANSICO GIANTS

		NM	EX	VG
(1)	Bobby Bonds	9.00	4.50	2.75
(2)	Dick Dietz	6.00	3.00	1.75
(3)	Charles Fox	6.00	3.00	1.75
(4)	Tito Fuentes	6.00	3.00	1.75
(5)	Ken Henderson	6.00	3.00	1.75
(6)	Juan Marichal	20.00	10.00	6.00
(7)	Willie Mays	60.00	30.00	18.00
(8)	Willie McCovey	25.00	12.50	7.50
(9)	Don McMahon	3.00	1.50	.90
(10)	Gaylord Perry	15.00	7.50	4.50

1972 Ticketron Phillies

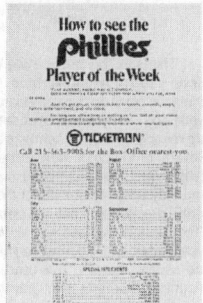

The Phillies' main off-site ticket outlet produced this set of schedule cards. Fronts are in horizontal 6" x 3-7/8" format with a color player photo at center. Backs are in black-and-white and include a Phillies home schedule and sponsor advertising. Because he was traded to the Expos in mid-season, the card of Tim McCarver is scarcer than the others.

		NM	EX	VG
Complete Set (10):		95.00	47.00	28.00
Common Player:		8.00	4.00	2.50
(1)	Mike Anderson	8.00	4.00	2.50
(2)	Larry Bowa	8.00	4.00	2.50
(3)	Steve Carlton	15.00	7.50	4.50
(4)	Deron Johnson	8.00	4.00	2.50
(5)	Frank Lucchesi	8.00	4.00	2.50
(6)	Greg Luzinski	10.00	5.00	3.00
(7)	Tim McCarver	35.00	17.50	10.50
(8)	Don Money	8.00	4.00	2.50
(9)	Willie Montanez	8.00	4.00	2.50
(10)	Dick Selma	8.00	4.00	2.50

1959 Ticoa Tires Frank Malzone

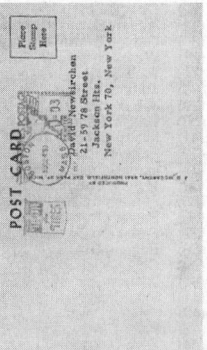

This black-and-white J.D. McCarthy postcard of the former Red Sox infielder was issued in conjunction with Malzone's endorsement of the Boston area tire store chain. The card measures 3-1/4" x 5-1/2" and has a blue facsimile autograph on front. A similar promotional postcard is listed under Molinari's Restaurant.

	NM	EX	VG
Frank Malzone	25.00	12.50	7.50

1910 Tip-Top Bread Pittsburgh Pirates (D322)

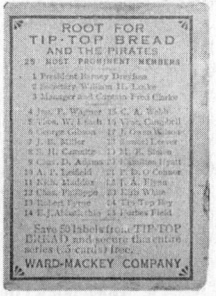

The previous season's World Champion Pittsburgh Pirates are featured in this issue. The cards have an unusual - for the era - nearly square (1-13/16" x 2-3/8") format. Fronts have pastel paintings of the subjects with identification in the white border below as "World's Champions." Backs have a checklist, ad for the bakery and offer to send the complete set of cards for 50 bread labels.

		NM	EX	VG
Complete Set (25):		120,000	60,000	36,000
Common Player:		1,400	700.00	425.00
1	Barney Dreyfuss (President)	15,000	7,500	4,500
2	William H. Locke (Secretary)	1,400	700.00	425.00
3	Fred Clarke	6,000	3,000	1,800
4	Honus Wagner	60,000	30,000	18,000
5	Tom Leach	1,400	700.00	425.00
6	George Gibson	1,400	700.00	425.00
7	Dots Miller	1,400	700.00	425.00
8	Howie Camnitz	1,400	700.00	425.00
9	Babe Adams	1,400	700.00	425.00
10	Lefty Leifield	1,400	700.00	425.00
11	Nick Maddox	1,400	700.00	425.00
12	Deacon Philippe	1,400	700.00	425.00
13	Bobby Byrne	1,400	700.00	425.00
14	Ed Abbaticchio	1,400	700.00	425.00
15	Lefty Webb	1,400	700.00	425.00
16	Vin Campbell	1,400	700.00	425.00
17	Owen Wilson	1,400	700.00	425.00
18	Sam Leever	1,400	700.00	425.00
19	Mike Simon	1,400	700.00	425.00
20	Ham Hyatt	1,400	700.00	425.00
21	Paddy O'Connor	1,400	700.00	425.00
22	John Flynn	1,400	700.00	425.00
23	Kirby White	1,400	700.00	425.00
24	Tip Top Boy Mascot	7,000	3,500	2,000
25	Forbes Field	4,000	2,000	1,250

1939 Tip-Top Bread Joe DiMaggio Pin

This 1-1/4" black-and-white photo portrait pin has a white background and printed endorsement for the Ward's brand. Similar pins were issued of boxer Billy Conn and hockey star Eddie Shore.

	NM	EX	VG
Joe DiMaggio	600.00	300.00	180.00

1947 Tip Top Bread

This 163-card set actually consists of a group of regional issues, some of which are scarcer than others. The 2-1/4" x 3" cards are borderless at top and sides, with a black-and-white player photo below which is a white strip containing the player identification. Backs carry an illustrated advertisement. The set is known for a quantity of obscure players, many of whom played during the talent-lean World War II seasons.

		NM	EX	VG
Complete Set (163):		16,000	6,400	3,200
Common Player:		60.00	25.00	12.50
(1)	Bill Ayers	60.00	25.00	12.50
(2)	Floyd Baker	100.00	40.00	20.00
(3)	Charles Barrett	100.00	40.00	20.00
(4)	Eddie Basinski	60.00	25.00	12.50
(5)	John Berardino	100.00	40.00	20.00
(6)	Larry Berra	500.00	200.00	100.00
(7)	Bill Bevens	100.00	40.00	20.00
(8)	Robert Blattner	60.00	25.00	12.50
(9)	Ernie Bonham	60.00	25.00	12.50
(10)	Bob Bragan	80.00	32.00	16.00
(11)	Ralph Branca	125.00	50.00	25.00
(12)	Alpha Brazle	60.00	25.00	12.50
(13)	Bobbie Brown (Bobby)	100.00	40.00	20.00
(14)	Mike Budnick	60.00	25.00	12.50
(15)	Ken Burkhart	60.00	25.00	12.50
(16)	Thomas Byrne	100.00	40.00	20.00
(17)	Earl Caldwell	100.00	40.00	20.00
(18)	"Hank" Camelli	100.00	40.00	20.00
(19)	Hugh Casey	80.00	32.00	16.00
(20)	Phil Cavarretta	100.00	40.00	20.00
(21)	Bob Chipman	100.00	40.00	20.00
(22)	Lloyd Christopher	100.00	40.00	20.00
(23)	Bill Cox	60.00	25.00	12.50
(24)	Bernard Creger	60.00	25.00	12.50
(25)	Frank Crosetti	100.00	40.00	20.00
(26)	Joffre Cross	60.00	25.00	12.50
(27)	Leon Culberson	100.00	40.00	20.00
(28)	Dick Culler	100.00	40.00	20.00
(29)	Dom DiMaggio	200.00	80.00	40.00
(30)	George Dickey	100.00	40.00	20.00
(31)	Chas. E. Diering	60.00	25.00	12.50
(32)	Joseph Dobson	100.00	40.00	20.00
(33)	Bob Doerr	260.00	105.00	52.00
(34)	Ervin Dusak	60.00	25.00	12.50
(35)	Bruce Edwards	60.00	24.00	12.00
(36)	Walter "Hoot" Evers	130.00	52.00	26.00
(37)	Clifford Fannin	60.00	25.00	12.50
(38)	"Nanny" Fernandez	100.00	40.00	20.00
(39)	Dave "Boo" Ferriss	100.00	40.00	20.00
(40)	Elbie Fletcher	60.00	25.00	12.50
(41)	Dennis Galehouse	60.00	25.00	12.50
(42)	Joe Garagiola	225.00	90.00	45.00
(43)	Sid Gordon	60.00	25.00	12.50
(44)	John Gorsica	100.00	40.00	20.00
(45)	Hal Gregg	60.00	24.00	12.00
(46)	Frank Gustine	60.00	25.00	12.50
(47)	Stanley Hack	100.00	40.00	20.00
(48)	Mickey Harris	100.00	40.00	20.00
(49)	Clinton Hartung	60.00	25.00	12.50
(50)	Joe Hatten	60.00	24.00	12.00
(51)	Frank Hayes	100.00	40.00	20.00
(52)	"Jeff" Heath	60.00	25.00	12.50
(53)	Tom Henrich	130.00	52.00	26.00
(54)	Gene Hermanski	60.00	24.00	12.00
(55)	Kirby Higbe	60.00	25.00	12.50
(56)	Ralph Hodgin	100.00	40.00	20.00
(57)	Tex Hughson	100.00	40.00	20.00
(58)	Fred Hutchinson	150.00	60.00	30.00
(59)	LeRoy Jarvis	60.00	25.00	12.50
(60)	"Si" Johnson	100.00	40.00	20.00
(61)	Don Johnson	100.00	40.00	20.00
(62)	Earl Johnson	80.00	32.00	16.00
(63)	John Jorgensen	60.00	24.00	12.00
(64)	Walter Judnick (Judnich)	60.00	25.00	12.50
(65)	Tony Kaufmann	60.00	25.00	12.50
(66)	George Kell	260.00	105.00	52.00
(67)	Charlie Keller	100.00	40.00	20.00
(68)	Bob Kennedy	100.00	40.00	20.00
(69)	Montia Kennedy	60.00	25.00	12.50
(70)	Ralph Kiner	140.00	56.00	28.00
(71)	Dave Koslo	60.00	25.00	12.50
(72)	Jack Kramer	60.00	25.00	12.50
(73)	Joe Kuhel	100.00	40.00	20.00
(74)	George Kurowski	60.00	25.00	12.50
(75)	Emil Kush	100.00	40.00	20.00
(76)	"Eddie" Lake	100.00	40.00	20.00
(77)	Harry Lavagetto	80.00	32.00	16.00
(78)	Bill Lee	100.00	40.00	20.00
(79)	Thornton Lee	100.00	40.00	20.00
(80)	Paul Lehner	60.00	25.00	12.50
(81)	John Lindell	100.00	40.00	20.00
(82)	Danny Litwhiler	100.00	40.00	20.00
(83)	"Mickey" Livingston	100.00	40.00	20.00
(84)	Carroll Lockman	60.00	25.00	12.50
(85)	Jack Lohrke	60.00	25.00	12.50
(86)	Ernie Lombardi	140.00	56.00	28.00
(87)	Vic Lombardi	60.00	24.00	12.00
(88)	Edmund Lopat	130.00	52.00	26.00
(89)	Harry Lowrey	100.00	40.00	20.00
(90)	Marty Marion	80.00	32.00	16.00
(91)	Willard Marshall	60.00	25.00	12.50
(92)	Phil Masi	100.00	40.00	20.00
(93)	Edward J. Mayo	100.00	40.00	20.00
(94)	Clyde McCullough	100.00	40.00	20.00
(95)	Frank Melton	100.00	40.00	20.00
(96)	Cass Michaels	100.00	40.00	20.00
(97)	Ed Miksis	100.00	40.00	20.00
(98)	Arthur Mills	100.00	40.00	20.00
(99)	Johnny Mize	140.00	56.00	28.00
(100)	Lester Moss	60.00	25.00	12.50
(101)	"Pat" Mullin	100.00	40.00	20.00
(102)	"Bob" Muncrief	60.00	25.00	12.50
(103)	George Munger	60.00	25.00	12.50
(104)	Fritz Ostermueller	60.00	25.00	12.50
(105)	James P. Outlaw	100.00	40.00	20.00
(106)	Frank "Stub" Overmire	100.00	40.00	20.00

		NM	EX	VG
(107)	Andy Pafko	100.00	40.00	20.00
(108)	Joe Page	100.00	40.00	20.00
(109)	Roy Partee	100.00	40.00	20.00
(110)	Johnny Pesky	100.00	40.00	20.00
(111)	Nelson Potter	60.00	25.00	12.50
(112)	Mel Queen	100.00	40.00	20.00
(113)	Marion Rackley	60.00	24.00	12.00
(114)	Al Reynolds	125.00	50.00	25.00
(115)	Del Rice	60.00	25.00	12.50
(116)	Marv Rickert	100.00	40.00	20.00
(117)	John Rigney	100.00	40.00	20.00
(118)	Phil Rizzuto	375.00	150.00	75.00
(119)	Aaron Robinson	100.00	40.00	20.00
(120)	"Preacher" Roe	80.00	32.00	16.00
(121)	Carvel Rowell	100.00	40.00	20.00
(122)	Jim Russell	60.00	25.00	12.50
(123)	Rip Russell	100.00	40.00	20.00
(124)	Connie Ryan	100.00	40.00	20.00
(125)	John Sain	100.00	40.00	20.00
(126)	Ray Sanders	100.00	40.00	20.00
(127)	Fred Sanford	60.00	25.00	12.50
(128)	Johnny Schmitz	100.00	40.00	20.00
(129)	Joe Schultz	60.00	25.00	12.50
(130)	"Rip" Sewell	60.00	25.00	12.50
(131)	Dick Sisler	60.00	25.00	12.50
(132)	"Sibby" Sisti	100.00	40.00	20.00
(133)	Enos Slaughter	130.00	52.00	26.00
(134)	"Billy" Southworth	100.00	40.00	20.00
(135)	Warren Spahn	475.00	190.00	95.00
(136)	Verne Stephens (Vern)	60.00	25.00	12.50
(137)	George Sternweiss (Stirnweiss)	100.00	40.00	20.00
(138)	Ed Stevens	60.00	24.00	12.00
(139)	Nick Strincevich	60.00	25.00	12.50
(140)	"Bobby" Sturgeon	100.00	40.00	20.00
(141)	Robt. "Bob" Swift	100.00	40.00	20.00
(142)	Geo. "Birdie" Tibbetts (Tebbetts)	100.00	40.00	20.00
(143)	"Mike" Tresh	100.00	40.00	20.00
(144)	Ken Trinkle	60.00	25.00	12.50
(145)	Paul "Diz" Trout	100.00	40.00	20.00
(146)	Virgil "Fire" Trucks	100.00	40.00	20.00
(147)	Thurman Tucker	100.00	40.00	20.00
(148)	Bill Voiselle	60.00	25.00	12.50
(149)	Hal Wagner	100.00	40.00	20.00
(150)	Honus Wagner	475.00	190.00	95.00
(151)	Eddy Waitkus	100.00	40.00	20.00
(152)	Richard "Dick" Wakefield	100.00	40.00	20.00
(153)	Jack Wallaesa	100.00	40.00	20.00
(154)	Charles Wensloff	100.00	40.00	20.00
(155)	Ted Wilks	60.00	25.00	12.50
(156)	Mickey Witek	60.00	25.00	12.50
(157)	"Jerry" Witte	60.00	25.00	12.50
(158)	Ed Wright	100.00	40.00	20.00
(159)	Taft Wright	100.00	40.00	20.00
(160)	Henry Wyse	100.00	40.00	20.00
(161)	"Rudy" York	100.00	40.00	20.00
(162)	Al Zarilla	60.00	25.00	12.50
(163)	Bill Zuber	125.00	50.00	25.00

1952 Tip Top Bread Labels

This unnumbered set of bread end-labels consists of 48 different labels, including two of Phil Rizzuto. The player's photo, name and team appear inside a star, with the words "Tip Top" printed above. The labels measure approximately 2-1/2" x 2-3/4". An advertising message appears in red on back. A large fold-out sheet to collect and display the labels was also issued. Each space is labeled with a player name and basic information, and is die-cut to allow the label to be slid in.

		NM	EX	VG
Complete Set (48):		27,500	13,750	9,200
Common Player:		550.00	275.00	185.00
Display Sheet:		350.00	175.00	120.00
(1)	Hank Bauer	625.00	300.00	200.00
(2)	Yogi Berra	975.00	500.00	300.00
(3)	Ralph Branca	625.00	300.00	200.00
(4)	Lou Brissie	550.00	275.00	185.00
(5)	Roy Campanella	975.00	500.00	300.00
(6)	Phil Cavarreta (Cavarretta)	550.00	275.00	185.00
(7)	Murray Dickson (Murry)	550.00	275.00	185.00
(8)	Ferris Fain	550.00	275.00	185.00
(9)	Carl Furillo	625.00	300.00	200.00
(10)	Ned Garver	550.00	275.00	185.00
(11)	Sid Gordon	550.00	275.00	185.00
(12)	John Groth	550.00	275.00	185.00
(13)	Gran Hamner	550.00	275.00	185.00
(14)	Jim Hearn	550.00	275.00	185.00
(15)	Gene Hermanski	550.00	275.00	185.00
(16)	Gil Hodges	775.00	400.00	240.00
(17)	Larry Jansen	550.00	275.00	185.00
(18)	Eddie Joost	550.00	275.00	185.00
(19)	George Kell	700.00	350.00	240.00
(20)	Dutch Leonard	550.00	275.00	185.00
(21)	Whitey Lockman	550.00	275.00	185.00

		NM	EX	VG
(22)	Ed Lopat	625.00	300.00	200.00
(23)	Sal Maglie	550.00	275.00	185.00
(24)	Mickey Mantle	6,200	3,100	2,100
(25)	Gil McDougald	625.00	300.00	200.00
(26)	Dale Mitchell	550.00	275.00	185.00
(27)	Don Mueller	550.00	275.00	185.00
(28)	Andy Pafko	550.00	275.00	185.00
(29)	Bob Porterfield	550.00	275.00	185.00
(30)	Ken Raffensberger	550.00	275.00	185.00
(31)	Allie Reynolds	625.00	300.00	200.00
(32a)	Phil Rizzuto (Rizzuto) ("NY" shows on shirt.)	825.00	425.00	275.00
(32b)	Phil Rizzuto (Rizzuto) (No "NY" visible on shirt.)	825.00	400.00	275.00
(33)	Robin Roberts	775.00	400.00	250.00
(34)	Saul Rogovin	550.00	275.00	185.00
(35)	Ray Scarborough	550.00	275.00	185.00
(36)	Red Schoendienst	700.00	350.00	225.00
(37)	Dick Sisler	550.00	275.00	185.00
(38)	Enos Slaughter	700.00	350.00	225.00
(39)	Duke Snider	825.00	400.00	225.00
(40)	Warren Spahn	825.00	400.00	225.00
(41)	Vern Stephens	550.00	275.00	185.00
(42)	Earl Torgeson	550.00	275.00	185.00
(43)	Mickey Vernon	550.00	275.00	185.00
(44)	Ed Waitkus	550.00	275.00	185.00
(45)	Wes Westrum	550.00	275.00	185.00
(46)	Eddie Yost	550.00	275.00	185.00
(47)	Al Zarilla	550.00	275.00	185.00

1887 Tobin Lithographs Color

The Tobin lithographs, measuring about 3" x 4-1/2", are typical of the "trade" cards that were popular advertising vehicles in the late 19th Century. Found in both black-and-white and color, the lithos include 10 cards depicting caricature action drawings of popular baseball players of the era. Each cartoon-like drawing is accompanied by a colorful caption along with the player's name in parenthesis below. The team affiliation is printed in the upper-left corner, while a large space in the upper-right corner was left blank to accomodate advertising messages. As a result, Tobin cards can be found with ads for various products and services or left blank. Similarly the backs of the cards are also found either blank or with advertising. The set takes its name from the manufacturer, whose name ("Tobin N.Y.") appears in the lower-right corner of each card.

		NM	EX	VG
Complete Set (10):		10,000	5,000	3,000
Common Player:		1,000	500	300.00
(1)	"Go It Old Boy" (Ed Andrews)	1,000	500	300.00
(2)	"Oh, Come Off!" (Cap Anson)	2,000	1,000	600.00
(3)	"Watch Me Soak it" (Dan Brouthers)	1,200	600.00	400.00
(4)	"Not Onto It" (Charlie Ferguson)	1,000	500	300.00
(5)	"Struck By A Cyclone" (Jack Glasscock)	1,000	500	300.00
(6)	"An Anxious Moment" (Paul Hines)	1,000	500	300.00
(7)	"Where'l You Have It?" (Tim Keefe)	1,200	600.00	400.00
(8)	"The Flower Of The Flock" (Our Own Kelly)	1,500	750.00	500.00
(9)	"A Slide For Home" (Jim M'Cormick) (McCormick)	1,000	500	300.00
(10)	"Ain't It A Daisy?" (Smiling Mickey Welch)	1,200	600.00	400.00

1887 Tobin Lithographs B/W

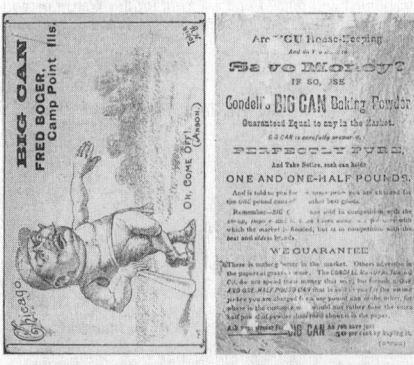

The black-and-white Tobin Lithographs were likely created to offer 19th Century advertisers a lower-cost venue than the lavishly colored version of the same cards. It appears,

however, that most advertisers opted for the color type and/or that the color cards were saved more often because the black-and-white cards are today many times scarcer than their color counterparts. Despite the disparity in rarity, the black-and-whites carry only a modest premium value over the color, again probably attributable to the grander overall appearance of the colored cards.

		NM	EX	VG
Complete Set (10):		19,000	9,500	6,350
Common Player:		1,900	950.00	650.00
(1)	"Go It Old Boy" (Ed Andrews)	1,900	950.00	650.00
(2)	"Oh, Come Off!" (Cap Anson)	3,750	1,875	1,250
(3)	"Watch Me Soak it" (Dan Brouthers)	2,250	1,150	750.00
(4)	"Not Onto It" (Charlie Ferguson)	1,900	950.00	650.00
(5)	"Struck By A Cyclone" (Jack Glasscock)	1,900	950.00	650.00
(6)	"An Anxious Moment" (Paul Hines)	1,900	950.00	650.00
(7)	"Where'l You Have It?" (Tim Keefe)	2,250	1,150	750.00
(8)	"The Flower Of The Flock" (Our Own Kelly)	2,850	1,425	950.00
(9)	"A Slide For Home" (Jim M'Cormick) (McCormick)	1,900	950.00	650.00
(10)	"Ain't It A Daisy?" (Smiling Mickey Welch)	2,250	1,150	750.00

1948-1949 Toleteros

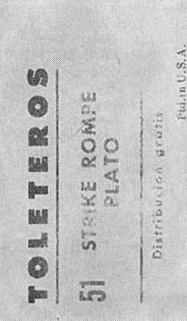

This was the first of three annual issues during the Puerto Rican League winter seasons. Cards are about 1-1/2" x 2-1/4", printed in sepia on thin cardboard. Backs are printed in black-and-white and have a "play" designation for use in a card game. They are numbered, but the numbers are not unique to specific players. Several of the cards were issued in photographic format, rather than printed. It is believed these are scarcer than the regular cards and may account for most of the seven cards which are not currently checklisted. They are designated here with a (P) notation. This checklist is presented alphabetically. An album was issued with the set, and like most contemporary Caribbean issues, cards are usually found in well-used condition with evidence of past mounting. Toleteros is roughly translated as "sluggers."

		NM	EX	VG
Complete Set (168):				
Value Undetermined				
Common Player:		150.00	75.00	45.00
Album:				
(1)	Yuyo Acosta	150.00	75.00	45.00
(2)	Hector Agosto	150.00	75.00	45.00
(3)	Alberto Alberdeston	150.00	75.00	45.00
(4)	Alberto Alicea	150.00	75.00	45.00
(5)	Jaime Almendro	150.00	75.00	45.00
(6)	Guinea Almaro	150.00	75.00	45.00
(7)	Pedro Alomar	150.00	75.00	45.00
(8)	Alfredo Alonso	150.00	75.00	45.00
(9)	Yiyo Alonso	150.00	75.00	45.00
(10)	Pablo Andino	150.00	75.00	45.00
(11)	Jueyito Andrade	150.00	75.00	45.00
(12)	Paday Anglero	150.00	75.00	45.00
(13)	Luis Arroyo	200.00	100.00	60.00
(14)	Pedro J. Arroyo	150.00	75.00	45.00
(15)	Joe Atkins (P)	300.00	150.00	90.00
(16)	Eugene Baker	300.00	150.00	90.00
(17)	Dan Bankhead	300.00	150.00	90.00
(18)	Bennett	150.00	75.00	45.00
(19)	Carlos Bernier	200.00	100.00	60.00
(20)	Hiram Bithorn	250.00	125.00	75.00
(21)	Efrain Blasini	150.00	75.00	45.00
(22)	Oswaldo Brau	150.00	75.00	45.00
(23)	Johnny Britton	150.00	75.00	45.00
(25)	George Brown	150.00	75.00	45.00
(26)	Willard Brown	4,500	2,250	1,350
(27)	Jose Burgos	150.00	75.00	45.00
(28)	Tommy Butts	1,200	600.00	360.00
(29)	Joe Buzas	150.00	75.00	45.00
(30)	Luis R. Cabrera	150.00	75.00	45.00
(31)	Marzo Cabrera	150.00	75.00	45.00
(32)	Eugenio Camara	150.00	75.00	45.00
(33)	Juan Carrero	150.00	75.00	45.00
(34)	Medina Chapman	150.00	75.00	45.00
(35)	Fernando Clara	150.00	75.00	45.00
(36)	Buster Clarkson (P)	800.00	400.00	240.00
(37)	Francisco Coimbre	1,000	500.00	300.00
(38)	Eugene Collins	400.00	200.00	120.00
(39)	Cefo Conde	150.00	75.00	45.00
(40)	Johnny Cox	150.00	75.00	45.00
(41)	Vitin Cruz	150.00	75.00	45.00
(42)	Johnny Davis	500.00	250.00	150.00
(43)	Piper Davis	500.00	250.00	150.00
(44)	Felle Delgado	150.00	75.00	45.00

		NM	EX	VG
(45)	Luke Easter	500.00	250.00	150.00
(46)	Howard Easterling	600.00	300.00	180.00
(47)	Saturnino Escalera	150.00	75.00	45.00
(49)	Teggy Espinosa	150.00	75.00	45.00
(50)	Coco Ferrer	150.00	75.00	45.00
(51)	Wilmer Fields	400.00	200.00	120.00
(52)	Tite Figueroa	150.00	75.00	45.00
(53)	Oscar Mir Flores	150.00	75.00	45.00
(54)	Jesus M. Freyre	150.00	75.00	45.00
(55)	Cinque Garcia	150.00	75.00	45.00
(56)	Alfonso Gerard	150.00	75.00	45.00
(57)	Jim Gilliam (P)	800.00	400.00	240.00
(58)	Charlie Glock	150.00	75.00	45.00
(59)	Ruben Gomez	250.00	125.00	75.00
(60)	David Gonzalez	150.00	75.00	45.00
(61)	Gely Goyco	150.00	75.00	45.00
(62)	Jack Graham	150.00	75.00	45.00
(63)	Roberto Griffith	600.00	300.00	180.00
(64)	Jesus Guilbe	150.00	75.00	45.00
(65)	Juan Guilbe	150.00	75.00	45.00
(66)	Hector Haddock	150.00	75.00	45.00
(67)	Sam Hairston	200.00	100.00	60.00
(68)	Van Harrington	150.00	75.00	45.00
(69)	Luman Harris	150.00	75.00	45.00
(70)	Manuel Hernandez	150.00	75.00	45.00
(71)	Efrain Hidalgo	150.00	75.00	45.00
(73)	Dixie Howell	150.00	75.00	45.00
(74)	Jim Lamarque (P)	800.00	400.00	240.00
(75)	Carlos Lanauze	150.00	75.00	45.00
(76)	Ramon Lasa	150.00	75.00	45.00
(77)	Lee Layton	150.00	75.00	45.00
(78)	Liebould	150.00	75.00	45.00
(79)	Royce Lint	150.00	75.00	45.00
(80)	Radames Lopez	150.00	75.00	45.00
(81)	Louis Louden	250.00	125.00	75.00
(82)	Robert Lynn	150.00	75.00	45.00
(83)	Caro Maldonado	150.00	75.00	45.00
(84)	Canena Marquez	500.00	250.00	150.00
(85)	Antonio Marrero	150.00	75.00	45.00
(86)	Gilberto Marrero	150.00	75.00	45.00
(87)	Humberto Marti	150.00	75.00	45.00
(88)	Millito Martinez	150.00	75.00	45.00
(89)	Jose E. Montalvo	150.00	75.00	45.00
(90)	Luis Morales	150.00	75.00	45.00
(91)	Willie Morales	150.00	75.00	45.00
(92)	Howard Moss	150.00	75.00	45.00
(93)	Chaguin Muratti	150.00	75.00	45.00
(94)	Domingo Navarro	150.00	75.00	45.00
(95)	Millito Navarro	200.00	100.00	60.00
(97)	Alfredo Olivencia	150.00	75.00	45.00
(98)	Guayubin Olivo	200.00	100.00	60.00
(99)	Noel Oquendo	150.00	75.00	45.00
(100)	Otoniel Ortiz	150.00	75.00	45.00
(101)	Rafaelito Ortiz	150.00	75.00	45.00
(102)	Alberto Padilla	150.00	75.00	45.00
(103)	Fernando Diaz Pedroso	200.00	100.00	60.00
(104)	Victor Pellot (Power)	250.00	125.00	75.00
(105)	Pedro Pena	150.00	75.00	45.00
(106)	Pepin Pereira	150.00	75.00	45.00
(107)	Ismael Perez	150.00	75.00	45.00
(108)	Juan Perez	150.00	75.00	45.00
(109)	Palomo Perez	150.00	75.00	45.00
(110)	Villodas Perez	150.00	75.00	45.00
(111)	Alonso Perry	500.00	250.00	150.00
(112)	Jose Polanco	150.00	75.00	45.00
(113)	Bill Powell	200.00	100.00	60.00
(114)	Tomas Quinones	200.00	100.00	60.00
(115)	R. Cuebas Quintana	150.00	75.00	45.00
(116)	Milton Ralat	150.00	75.00	45.00
(117)	Otto Ralat	150.00	75.00	45.00
(118)	Fernando Ramos	150.00	75.00	45.00
(119)	Xavier Rescigno	150.00	75.00	45.00
(121)	Miguel L. Rivera	150.00	75.00	45.00
(122)	Charlie Rivero	150.00	75.00	45.00
(123)	Bienvenido Rodriguez	150.00	75.00	45.00
(124)	Pedro Rodriguez	150.00	75.00	45.00
(125)	Anastasio Rosario	150.00	75.00	45.00
(126)	Jorge Rosas	150.00	75.00	45.00
(127)	Cafe Salaberrios	150.00	75.00	45.00
(128)	Wilfredo Salas	150.00	75.00	45.00
(129)	Juan Sanchez	150.00	75.00	45.00
(130)	Carlos M. Santiago	150.00	75.00	45.00
(131)	Jose G. Santiago (P)	400.00	200.00	120.00
(132)	Ed Sauer	150.00	75.00	45.00
(133)	George Scales	1,200	600.00	360.00
(134)	Kermit Schmidt	150.00	75.00	45.00
(135)	Ken Sears (P)	400.00	200.00	120.00
(136)	Herbert Sewell (Souell)	250.00	125.00	75.00
(137)	Dwain Sloat	150.00	75.00	45.00
(138)	Eugene Smith	200.00	100.00	60.00
(139)	Hilton Smith	20,000	10,000	6,000
(140)	John Ford Smith	400.00	200.00	120.00
(141)	Fernando Sola	150.00	75.00	45.00
(142)	Ismael Solla	150.00	75.00	45.00
(143)	Francisco Sostre	150.00	75.00	45.00
(144)	Earl Taborn	200.00	100.00	60.00
(145)	Freddie Thon	150.00	75.00	45.00
(146)	Bob Thurman	400.00	200.00	120.00
(147)	Griffin Tirado	150.00	75.00	45.00
(148)	Leon Tirado	150.00	75.00	45.00
(149)	Pedro J. Toro	150.00	75.00	45.00
(150)	Bin Torres	150.00	75.00	45.00
(151)	Carmelo Torres	150.00	75.00	45.00
(152)	Onofre Torres	150.00	75.00	45.00
(153)	Penpen Torres	150.00	75.00	45.00
(154)	Quincy Trouppe	1,000	500.00	300.00
(155)	Foca Valentin	150.00	75.00	45.00
(156)	Roberto Vargas	150.00	75.00	45.00
(157)	Tetelo Vargas	1,000	500.00	300.00
(158)	Rafael Vasquez	150.00	75.00	45.00
(159)	Guillermo Vega	150.00	75.00	45.00
(160)	Jose L. Velazquez	150.00	75.00	45.00
(161)	Laru Velazquez	150.00	75.00	45.00
(164)	Vicente Villafane	150.00	75.00	45.00
(165)	Luis Villodas	200.00	100.00	60.00
(166)	Jesse Williams	200.00	100.00	60.00
(167)	Artie Wilson	500.00	250.00	150.00
(168)	Rogelio Wiscovich	150.00	75.00	45.00

1949-1950 Toleteros

LEON DAY

The second of three annual issues during the Puerto Rican League winter seasons, these cards are similar in format to the previous year's set. Front photos are printed in black-and-white, and the backs are printed in red. Cards are about 1-1/2" x 2-1/4", printed on thin cardboard with a light gloss. Backs have a "play" designation for use in a card game and are numbered, though the numbers are not unique to specific players. This checklist is presented alphabetically. Some players can be found in two different poses. Where the variations are known, they are described parenthetically; where the poses are not known, an asterisk is shown. Players with a (P) designation were produced on photographic, rather than printed stock and are scarcer than the regular cards. An album was issued with the set, and like most contemporary Caribbean issues, cards are usually found in well-used condition with evidence of past mounting. Toleteros is roughly translated as "sluggers."

		NM	EX	VG
Complete Set (216):				
Value Undetermined				
Common Player:		100.00	50.00	30.00
Album:		600.00	300.00	180.00
(1)	Hector Agosto	100.00	50.00	30.00
(2)	Alberto Alberdeston	100.00	50.00	30.00
(3)	Alberto Alicea	100.00	50.00	30.00
(4)	Jaime Almendro (*)	100.00	50.00	30.00
(5)	Guinea Alomar	100.00	50.00	30.00
(6)	Pedro Alomar	100.00	50.00	30.00
(7)	Alfredo Alonso	100.00	50.00	30.00
(8)	Yiyo Alonso	100.00	50.00	30.00
(9)	Ismael Alvarado	100.00	50.00	30.00
(10)	Manuel Alvarez (*)	100.00	50.00	30.00
(11)	Pablo Andino	100.00	50.00	30.00
(12)	Jueyito Andrade	100.00	50.00	30.00
(13)	Paday Anglero	100.00	50.00	30.00
(14)	Luis Arroyo (*)	125.00	65.00	40.00
(15)	Pedro J. Arroyo	100.00	50.00	30.00
(16)	Eugene Baker	150.00	75.00	45.00
(17)	Dan Bankhead	150.00	75.00	45.00
(18)	Sammy Bankhead	475.00	240.00	140.00
(19)	Ramon Bayron	100.00	50.00	30.00
(20)	Carlos Bernier	160.00	80.00	47.50
(21)	Hiram Bithorn	275.00	135.00	82.50
(22)	Efrain Blasini	100.00	50.00	30.00
(23)	Anil Bonilla (*)	100.00	50.00	30.00
(24)	Stan Bread (Breard)	100.00	50.00	30.00
(25)	Chester Brewer	1,000	500.00	300.00
(26)	Johnny Britton	100.00	50.00	30.00
(27)	George Brown	100.00	50.00	30.00
(28)	Willard Brown (*)	3,750	1,850	1,100
(29)	J.A. Burgos (*)	100.00	50.00	30.00
(30)	Tommy Butts	225.00	110.00	70.00
(31)	Joe Buzas	100.00	50.00	30.00
(32)	Rafael Cabezudo	100.00	50.00	30.00
(33)	Luis R. Cabrera	100.00	50.00	30.00
(34)	Marzo Cabrera	100.00	50.00	30.00
(35)	Manolete Caceres (*)	100.00	50.00	30.00
(36)	Eugenio Camara	100.00	50.00	30.00
(37)	Maximo Casals	100.00	50.00	30.00
(38)	Rafael Casanovas	100.00	50.00	30.00
(39)	Nino Zurdo Castro	100.00	50.00	30.00
(40)	Perucho Cepeda (*)	500.00	250.00	150.00
(41)	Medina Chapman	100.00	50.00	30.00
(42)	T. Gomez Checo	100.00	50.00	30.00
(43)	Buster Clarkson	300.00	150.00	90.00
(44)	Francisco Coimbre	400.00	200.00	120.00
(45a)	Eugene Collins (Chest-up.)	200.00	100.00	60.00
(45b)	Eugene Collins (Waist-up.)	200.00	100.00	60.00
(46)	Luis Colmenero	100.00	50.00	30.00
(47)	Luis Colon	100.00	50.00	30.00
(48)	M. Concepcion (*)	125.00	65.00	40.00
(49)	Cefo Conde	100.00	50.00	30.00
(50)	Omar Cordero	100.00	50.00	30.00
(51)	Johnny Cox	100.00	50.00	30.00
(52)	Vitin Cruz	100.00	50.00	30.00
(53)	Johnny Davis	400.00	200.00	120.00
(54)	Lomax Davis	150.00	75.00	45.00
(55)	Piper Davis	200.00	100.00	60.00
(56)	Leon Day	12,000	6,000	3,600
(57)	Felle Delgado	100.00	50.00	30.00
(58)	Carmelo Delpin	100.00	50.00	30.00
(59)	Ruben Diaz	100.00	50.00	30.00
(60)	Lucius Easter	100.00	50.00	30.00
(61)	Howard Easterling	160.00	80.00	47.50
(62)	Saturnino Escalera	125.00	65.00	40.00
(63)	Teggy Espinosa	100.00	50.00	30.00
(64)	George Fallon	100.00	50.00	30.00
(65)	Coco Ferrer	100.00	50.00	30.00
(66)	Walter Fialla (Fiala)	100.00	50.00	30.00
(67)	Wilmer Fields (*)	300.00	150.00	90.00
(68)	Tite Figueroa	100.00	50.00	30.00
(69)	Oscar Mir Flores	100.00	50.00	30.00

		NM	EX	VG
(70)	Jesus M. Freyre	100.00	50.00	30.00
(71)	(Les) Fusselmann (Fusselman)	100.00	50.00	30.00
(72)	Cinque Garcia	100.00	50.00	30.00
(73)	Alfonso Gerard	100.00	50.00	30.00
(74)	Alban Glossopp (Glossop)	100.00	50.00	30.00
(75)	Ruben Gomez (*)	160.00	80.00	47.50
(76)	Faelo Gonzalez (P)	200.00	100.00	60.00
(77)	Rafael Gonzalez	100.00	50.00	30.00
(78)	Gely Goyco	100.00	50.00	30.00
(79)	Jack Graham	100.00	50.00	30.00
(80)	Bill Greason	125.00	65.00	40.00
(81)	Felo Guilbe	100.00	50.00	30.00
(82)	Jesus Guilbe	100.00	50.00	30.00
(83)	Juan Guilbe	100.00	50.00	30.00
(84)	Hector Haddock	100.00	50.00	30.00
(85)	Sam Hairston	150.00	75.00	45.00
(86)	Luman Harris	100.00	50.00	30.00
(87a)	Vic Harris (Black background.)	1,000	500.00	300.00
(87b)	Vic Harris (Outdoors background.)	1,000	500.00	300.00
(88)	Angel Hernaiz (P)	200.00	100.00	60.00
(89)	Manuel Hernandez	100.00	50.00	30.00
(90)	Efrain Hidalgo	100.00	50.00	30.00
(91)	Dixie Howell	100.00	50.00	30.00
(92)	Roy Hughes (*)	100.00	50.00	30.00
(93)	Natalio Irizarry	100.00	50.00	30.00
(94)	Walter James	100.00	50.00	30.00
(95)	Cecyl Kayser (P)	300.00	150.00	90.00
(96)	Jack Krauss	100.00	50.00	30.00
(97)	Jim Lamarque	160.00	80.00	47.50
(98)	Carlos Lanauze	100.00	50.00	30.00
(99)	Ramon Lasa	100.00	50.00	30.00
(100)	Rafael Lastra	100.00	50.00	30.00
(101)	Lee Layton	100.00	50.00	30.00
(102)	Lettish	100.00	50.00	30.00
(103)	Johnny Logan	100.00	50.00	30.00
(104)	Radames Lopez	100.00	50.00	30.00
(105)	Louis Louden	150.00	75.00	45.00
(106)	Robert Lynn	100.00	50.00	30.00
(107)	Al Lyons	100.00	50.00	30.00
(108)	Cirico Machuca	100.00	50.00	30.00
(109)	Caro Maldonado	100.00	50.00	30.00
(110)	Clifford Mapes	100.00	50.00	30.00
(111)	Jim Markland (P)	200.00	100.00	60.00
(112)	Canena Marquez	200.00	100.00	60.00
(113)	Leo Marquez	100.00	50.00	30.00
(114)	Antonio Marrero (*)	100.00	50.00	30.00
(115)	Gilberto Marrero	100.00	50.00	30.00
(116)	Humberto Marti	100.00	50.00	30.00
(117)	Achin Matos	100.00	50.00	30.00
(118)	Booker McDaniels	150.00	75.00	45.00
(119)	George McQuillen	100.00	50.00	30.00
(120)	Agustin Medina	100.00	50.00	30.00
(121)	John Medina	100.00	50.00	30.00
(122)	Vicente Medina	100.00	50.00	30.00
(123)	Henry Miller (P)	300.00	150.00	90.00
(124)	Jose E. Montalvo	100.00	50.00	30.00
(125a)	Luis A. Morales (*)	100.00	50.00	30.00
(125b)	Luis Morales	100.00	50.00	30.00
(126)	Pedroso Morales	100.00	50.00	30.00
(127)	Willie Morales	100.00	50.00	30.00
(128)	Howard Moss	100.00	50.00	30.00
(129)	Gallego Munoz	100.00	50.00	30.00
(130)	Digno Navarro	100.00	50.00	30.00
(131)	Domingo Navarro	100.00	50.00	30.00
(132)	Millito Navarro	160.00	80.00	47.50
(133)	Earl Naylor (P)	200.00	100.00	60.00
(134)	Alfredo Olivencia	100.00	50.00	30.00
(135)	Guayubin Olivo	125.00	65.00	40.00
(136)	Noel Oquendo	100.00	50.00	30.00
(137)	Otoniel Ortiz	100.00	50.00	30.00
(138)	Rafaelito Ortiz	100.00	50.00	30.00
(139)	Alberto Padilla	100.00	50.00	30.00
(140)	Miguel Payano (P)	200.00	100.00	60.00
(141)	Fernando Diaz Pedroso (*)	125.00	65.00	40.00
(142)	Victor Pellot (Power)	150.00	75.00	45.00
(143)	Pedro Pena	100.00	50.00	30.00
(144)	Pepin Pereira (*)	100.00	50.00	30.00
(145)	Ismael Perez	100.00	50.00	30.00
(146)	Juan Perez	100.00	50.00	30.00
(147)	Palomo Perez	100.00	50.00	30.00
(148)	Rogelio Perez	100.00	50.00	30.00
(149)	Villodas Perez	100.00	50.00	30.00
(150)	Alonso Perry	200.00	100.00	60.00
(151)	Russ Peters	100.00	50.00	30.00
(152)	Jose Polanco	100.00	50.00	30.00
(153)	(Bill) Powell	100.00	50.00	30.00
(154)	Thomas Quinones (*)	125.00	65.00	40.00
(155)	Milton Ralat	100.00	50.00	30.00
(156)	Otto Ralat	100.00	50.00	30.00
(157)	Fernando Ramos	100.00	50.00	30.00
(158)	Lionel Richards	100.00	50.00	30.00
(159)	Enrique Reinoso	100.00	50.00	30.00
(160)	Xavier Rescigno	100.00	50.00	30.00
(161)	Miguel A. Rivera	100.00	50.00	30.00
(162)	Bienvenido Rodriguez	100.00	50.00	30.00
(163)	Pedro Rodriguez	100.00	50.00	30.00
(164)	Jose M. Roque	100.00	50.00	30.00
(165)	Fachy Rosado	100.00	50.00	30.00
(166)	Jorge Rosas	100.00	50.00	30.00
(167)	Ramon Salgado (*)	100.00	50.00	30.00
(168)	Juan Sanchez	100.00	50.00	30.00
(169)	Carlos M. Santiago	100.00	50.00	30.00
(170)	Jose G. Santiago	100.00	50.00	30.00
(171)	Ed Sauer (*)	100.00	50.00	30.00
(172)	George Scales	800.00	400.00	240.00
(173)	Kermit Schmidt (*)	100.00	50.00	30.00
(174)	Ken Sears	100.00	50.00	30.00
(175)	Dick Seay	700.00	350.00	210.00
(176)	Jose Seda	100.00	50.00	30.00
(177)	Barney Serrell	200.00	100.00	60.00
(178)	McDuffie Sevilla (*)	100.00	50.00	30.00
(179)	Dwain Sloat	100.00	50.00	30.00
(180)	Eugene Smith	125.00	65.00	40.00
(181)	Hilton Smith	12,000	6,000	3,600
(182)	John F. Smith	150.00	75.00	45.00
(183)	Jerome Snider	100.00	50.00	30.00

(184)	Ismael Solla	100.00	50.00	30.00
(185)	Francisco Sostre	100.00	50.00	30.00
(186)	Herb Souell	100.00	50.00	30.00
(187)	Luis St. Clair	100.00	50.00	30.00
(188)	Tetelo Sterling	100.00	50.00	30.00
(189)	Lonnie Summers	125.00	65.00	40.00
(190)	Jim Tabor (*)	100.00	50.00	30.00
(191)	Earl Taborn	100.00	50.00	30.00
(192)	Israel Ten (*)	100.00	50.00	30.00
(193)	Leo Thomas	100.00	50.00	30.00
(194)	Freddie Thon	100.00	50.00	30.00
(195)	Bob Thurman (*)	200.00	100.00	60.00
(196)	Griffin Tirado (*)	100.00	50.00	30.00
(197)	Leon Tirado	100.00	50.00	30.00
(198)	Bin Torres	100.00	50.00	30.00
(199)	Carmelo Torres	100.00	50.00	30.00
(200)	Indian Torres	100.00	50.00	30.00
(201)	Quincy Trouppe	700.00	350.00	210.00
(202)	Hector Trussa	100.00	50.00	30.00
(203)	Foca Valentin	100.00	50.00	30.00
(204)	Roberto Vargas	100.00	50.00	30.00
(205)	Tetelo Vargas	300.00	150.00	90.00
(206)	Rafael Vazquez	100.00	50.00	30.00
(207)	Guillermo Vega	100.00	50.00	30.00
(208)	Jose L. Velazquez	100.00	50.00	30.00
(209)	Vicente Villafane (*)	100.00	50.00	30.00
(210)	Luis Villodas	100.00	50.00	30.00
(211)	Curley Williams (P)	300.00	150.00	90.00
(212)	Marvin Williams (P)	300.00	150.00	90.00
(213)	Artie Wilson	300.00	150.00	90.00
(214)	Robert Wilson (*)	100.00	50.00	30.00
(215)	Rogelio Wiscovich	100.00	50.00	30.00
(216)	Rafael Zavala	100.00	50.00	30.00

1950-1951 Toleteros

JOSHUA GIBSON

The last of three annual issues during the Puerto Rican League winter seasons, these cards are similar in format to the previous years' sets, with the principal difference being that the approximately 1-3/4" x 2-1/2" cards are printed in color rather than black-and-white. Most are printed on thin cardboard, but some are produced on photographic stock and believed to be scarcer than the others. Those are designated with a (P) in the checklist. Unlike the previous years' issues, backs are blank. This checklist is presented alphabetically. An album was issued with the set, and like most contemporary Caribbean issues, cards are usually found in well-used condition with evidence of past mounting. Toleteros is roughly translated as "sluggers."

		NM	EX	VG
Complete Set (192):		Value Undetermined		
Common Player:		60.00	30.00	18.00
Album:		300.00	150.00	90.00
(1)	Hector Agosto	60.00	30.00	18.00
(2)	Robert Alexander	60.00	30.00	18.00
(3)	Alberto Alicea	60.00	30.00	18.00
(4)	Jaime Almendro (Blue Senadores.)	75.00	37.00	22.00
(5)	Jaime Almendro (Red Senadores.)	60.00	30.00	18.00
(6)	Pedro Alomar	60.00	30.00	18.00
(7)	Ismael Alvarado (Ponce)	60.00	30.00	18.00
(8)	Ismael Alvarado (Aguadilla)	60.00	30.00	18.00
(9)	Jueyito Andrade	60.00	30.00	18.00
(10)	Nick Andromidas	60.00	30.00	18.00
(11)	Pacay Anglero	60.00	30.00	18.00
(12)	Luis (Tite) Arroyo	75.00	37.50	22.50
(13)	Pedro J. Arroyo	60.00	30.00	18.00
(14)	Dan Bankhead	100.00	50.00	30.00
(15)	Babe Barna	60.00	30.00	18.00
(16)	Carlos Bernier	75.00	37.50	22.50
(17)	John Bero	60.00	30.00	18.00
(18)	Wayne Blackburn	60.00	30.00	18.00
(19)	Efrain Blasini	60.00	30.00	18.00
(20)	Bill Boyd	75.00	37.50	22.50
(21)	Stan Breard	60.00	30.00	18.00
(22)	Willard Brown	4,000	2,000	1,200
(23)	Lou Burdette (P)	125.00	65.00	35.00
(24)	Jose A. Burgos	60.00	30.00	18.00
(25)	Rafael Cabezudo	60.00	30.00	18.00
(26)	Luis R. Cabrera	60.00	30.00	18.00
(27)	Marzo Cabrera	60.00	30.00	18.00
(28)	Manolete Caceres	60.00	30.00	18.00
(29)	Rafael Casanova	60.00	30.00	18.00
(30)	Medina Chapman	60.00	30.00	18.00
(31)	Al Cihosky (P)	125.00	65.00	35.00
(32)	Mike Clark	75.00	37.00	22.00
(33)	Buster Clarkson (Santurce)	250.00	125.00	75.00
(34)	Buster Clarkson (Ponce)	250.00	125.00	75.00
(35)	Francisco Coimbre	300.00	150.00	90.00
(36)	Rafael Colmenero	60.00	30.00	18.00
(37)	Luis Colon	60.00	30.00	18.00

(38)	Monchile Concepcion	75.00	37.50	22.50
(39)	Cefo Conde	60.00	30.00	18.00
(40)	Omar Cordero	60.00	30.00	18.00
(41)	William Costa	60.00	30.00	18.00
(42)	Clinton Courtney	75.00	37.50	22.50
(43)	George Crowe	75.00	37.50	22.50
(44)	Johnny Davis (Mayaguez)	150.00	75.00	45.00
(45)	Johnny Davis (San Juan)	150.00	75.00	45.00
(46)	Piper Davis	200.00	100.00	60.00
(47)	Ellis Deal	100.00	50.00	30.00
(48)	Felle Delgado	60.00	30.00	18.00
(49)	Luke Easter	175.00	85.00	50.00
(50)	Jaime A. Escalera	60.00	30.00	18.00
(51)	Saturnino Escalera	85.00	42.00	25.00
(52)	Luis Ferbe	60.00	30.00	18.00
(53)	L.E. Fernandez	60.00	30.00	18.00
(54)	Coco Ferrer	60.00	30.00	18.00
(55)	Walter Fialla (Fiala)	60.00	30.00	18.00
(56)	Wilmer Fields	150.00	75.00	45.00
(57)	Jose A. Figueroa	75.00	37.50	22.50
(58)	Oscar Mir Flores	60.00	30.00	18.00
(59)	Jesus M. Freyre	60.00	30.00	18.00
(60)	Dominic Galata	60.00	30.00	18.00
(61)	Felipe Garcia	60.00	30.00	18.00
(62)	Alfonso Gerard	60.00	30.00	18.00
(63)	Al Gerheauser (P)	225.00	110.00	70.00
(64)	Joshua Gibson	50,000	25,000	15,000
(65)	James Gilliam	325.00	160.00	97.50
(66)	Ruben Gomez	125.00	62.50	37.50
(67)	Rafael Gonzalez	60.00	30.00	18.00
(68)	Felo Guilbe (Ponce)	60.00	30.00	18.00
(69)	Felo Guilbe (San Juan)	60.00	30.00	18.00
(70)	Juan Guilbe	60.00	30.00	18.00
(71)	Hector Haddock	60.00	30.00	18.00
(72)	Red Hardy (P)	125.00	60.00	35.00
(73)	Van Harrington (P)	200.00	100.00	60.00
(74)	Ray Hathaway	60.00	30.00	18.00
(75)	Ralston Hemsley	75.00	37.50	22.50
(76)	Angel Hernaiz	60.00	30.00	18.00
(77)	Rudy Hernandez	125.00	60.00	35.00
(78)	Don Hoak	100.00	50.00	30.00
(79)	Rogers Hornsby	500.00	250.00	150.00
(80)	Dixie Howell	60.00	30.00	18.00
(81)	Natalio Irizarry (P)	125.00	60.00	35.00
(82)	Walter James	60.00	30.00	18.00
(83)	Stan Karpinsky (P)	125.00	60.00	35.00
(84)	Cecyl Kayser	100.00	50.00	30.00
(85)	Carlos Lanauze	60.00	30.00	18.00
(86)	Rafael Lastra	60.00	30.00	18.00
(87)	Quique Leon	60.00	30.00	18.00
(88)	George Lerchen (P)	125.00	60.00	35.00
(89)	Lou Limmer	150.00	75.00	45.00
(90)	Royce Lint	60.00	30.00	18.00
(91)	Al Lyons	60.00	30.00	18.00
(92)	Glenn MacQuillen	60.00	30.00	18.00
(93)	Jim Markland	60.00	30.00	18.00
(94)	Luis A. Marquez	225.00	110.00	65.00
(95)	Bob Marquis	60.00	30.00	18.00
(96)	Antonio Marrero	60.00	30.00	18.00
(97)	Humberto Marti	60.00	30.00	18.00
(98)	Vicente Medina	60.00	30.00	18.00
(99)	M. Monserrate Jr.	60.00	30.00	18.00
(100)	Jose E. Montalvo (Blue Senadores.)	60.00	30.00	18.00
(101)	Jose E. Montalvo (Red Senadores.)	90.00	45.00	27.00
(102)	Luis Morales	100.00	50.00	30.00
(103)	Pedroso Morales	60.00	30.00	18.00
(104)	Willie Morales	60.00	30.00	18.00
(105)	Luis M. Munoz (Blue Senadores.)	60.00	30.00	18.00
(106)	Luis M. Munoz (Red Senadores.)	60.00	30.00	18.00
(107)	Napier	75.00	37.50	22.50
(108)	Digno Navarro	60.00	30.00	18.00
(109)	Ernest Nevel	60.00	30.00	18.00
(110)	Alfredo Olivencia	60.00	30.00	18.00
(111)	L. Rodriguez Olmo	135.00	67.50	40.50
(112)	Noel Oquendo	60.00	30.00	18.00
(113)	Otoniel Ortiz	60.00	30.00	18.00
(114)	Rafaelito Ortiz	60.00	30.00	18.00
(115)	Roy Partlow	175.00	85.00	50.00
(116)	Miguel Payano (Red Senadores.)	60.00	30.00	18.00
(117)	Miguel Payano (Mayaguez)	60.00	30.00	18.00
(118)	Fernando Pedroso	75.00	37.50	22.50
(119)	Victor Pellot (Power)	100.00	50.00	30.00
(120)	Pedro Pena	60.00	30.00	18.00
(121)	Jose Pereira	60.00	30.00	18.00
(122)	Ismael Perez	60.00	30.00	18.00
(123)	Juan Perez	60.00	30.00	18.00
(124)	Villodas Perez	60.00	30.00	18.00
(125)	Alonso Perry	300.00	150.00	90.00
(126)	Alonso Perry	300.00	150.00	90.00
(127)	Jose D. Polanco	60.00	30.00	18.00
(128)	A. Portocarrero	125.00	62.50	37.50
(129)	Bill Powell	75.00	37.50	22.50
(130)	Tomas Quinones	75.00	37.50	22.50
(131)	Milton Ralat	60.00	30.00	18.00
(132)	Fernando Ramos	60.00	30.00	18.00
(133)	Henry Rementeria	60.00	30.00	18.00
(134)	Luis Renta	60.00	30.00	18.00
(135)	Herminio Reyes	60.00	30.00	18.00
(136)	Lionel Richards	60.00	30.00	18.00
(137)	Gene Richardson	75.00	37.50	22.50
(138)	Jim Rivera	125.00	62.50	37.50
(139)	Miguel A. Rivera	60.00	30.00	18.00
(140)	Roberto Rivera	60.00	30.00	18.00
(141)	Jack Robinson	60.00	30.00	18.00
(142)	Ministro Rodriguez	60.00	30.00	18.00
(143)	Pedro Rodriguez	60.00	30.00	18.00
(144)	Jorge Rosas	60.00	30.00	18.00
(145)	Miguel Ruiz	60.00	30.00	18.00
(146)	Ramon Salgado	60.00	30.00	18.00
(147)	Juan Sanchez	60.00	30.00	18.00
(148)	Carlos M. Santiago	60.00	30.00	18.00
(149)	Jose G. Santiago	150.00	75.00	45.00
(150)	George Scales	250.00	125.00	75.00

(151)	Scarpatte	60.00	30.00	18.00
(152)	Kermit Schmidt (Ponce)	60.00	30.00	18.00
(153)	Kermit Schmidt (Red Senadores.)	60.00	30.00	18.00
(154)	Ken Sears	60.00	30.00	18.00
(155)	Dick Seay	300.00	150.00	90.00
(156)	Pedro Seda	60.00	30.00	18.00
(157)	McDuffie Sevilla	60.00	30.00	18.00
(158)	Vincent Shuppe	60.00	30.00	18.00
(159)	William Skowron	150.00	75.00	45.00
(160)	Dwain Sloat	60.00	30.00	18.00
(161)	John Ford Smith	175.00	85.00	50.00
(162)	Francisco Sostre	60.00	30.00	18.00
(163)	Jose St. Clair (Looking forward.)	60.00	30.00	18.00
(164)	Jose St. Clair (Looking left.)	60.00	30.00	18.00
(165)	Luis St. Clair	60.00	30.00	18.00
(166)	Jimmy Starks	75.00	37.50	22.50
(167)	Israel Ten	60.00	30.00	18.00
(168)	Leo Thomas	60.00	30.00	18.00
(169)	Valmy Thomas (P)	375.00	185.00	110.00
(170)	Freddie Thon	60.00	30.00	18.00
(171)	Bob Thurman	200.00	100.00	60.00
(172)	Miguel A. Tineo	60.00	30.00	18.00
(173)	Griffin Tirado (Blue background.)	60.00	30.00	18.00
(174)	Griffin Tirado (Trees in background.)	160.00	80.00	47.50
(175)	Bin Torres	60.00	30.00	18.00
(176)	Clarkson Torres	60.00	30.00	18.00
(177)	Manuel Traboux	60.00	30.00	18.00
(178)	Gilberto Valentin	60.00	30.00	18.00
(179)	Roberto Vargas	60.00	30.00	18.00
(180)	Tetelo Vargas	425.00	210.00	125.00
(181)	Rafael Vazquez	60.00	30.00	18.00
(182)	Guillermo Vega	60.00	30.00	18.00
(183)	Jose L. Velazquez	60.00	30.00	18.00
(184)	Vicente Villafane	60.00	30.00	18.00
(185)	Luis Villodas	75.00	37.50	22.50
(186)	Curley Williams (P)	150.00	75.00	45.00
(187)	Artie Wilson	225.00	110.00	65.00
(188)	Robert Wilson (P)	150.00	75.00	45.00
(189)	Jerry Witte (P)	125.00	60.00	35.00
(190)	Pete Wojey	60.00	30.00	18.00
(191)	Andres Zabala	60.00	30.00	18.00
(192)	Rafael Zavala	60.00	30.00	18.00

1950-1951 Toleteros In Action

90. Piper intenta sacar a Tetelo- SAFE

		NM	EX	VG
Complete Set (178):		6,500	3,250	2,000
Common Card:		50.00	25.00	15.00
1	Pellot fildea con elegencia. (Victor Pellot (Power))	60.00	30.00	18.00
2	Burgos conecta hit de piernas. (Jose Burgos)	50.00	25.00	15.00
3	OUT por medio paso.	50.00	25.00	15.00
4	Te gusta el mamabo, Canena? (Canena Marquez)	65.00	32.50	20.00
5	OUT!!	50.00	25.00	15.00
6	Lanauze se eleva tras la bola. (Carlos Lanauze)	50.00	25.00	15.00
7	Simpson se escurre en tercera. . .	50.00	25.00	15.00
8	Si no se la cae la bola. . .	50.00	25.00	15.00
9	Escalera realiza brillante cogida. (Saturnino Escalera)	50.00	25.00	15.00
10	Lucha Grecoromana?	50.00	25.00	15.00
11	Gallego a punto deslizarse. . . (Gallego Munoz)	50.00	25.00	15.00
12	Parece. . .pero no lo empuja. . .	50.00	25.00	15.00
13	Ramos da out a Felo en primera. (Fernando Ramos)	50.00	25.00	15.00
14	El Chiquitin y El Magnifico.	50.00	25.00	15.00
15	Limmer llege de pie tras triple. (Lou Limmer)	50.00	25.00	15.00
16	Arroyo toca a Costa. . .OUT. (Luis Arroyo)	50.00	25.00	15.00
17	Thon a salvo en tercera. (Freddie Thon)	50.00	25.00	15.00
18	Thurman hacia home Scales lo felicita. (Bob Thurman, George Scales)	65.00	32.50	20.00
19	Not Issued			
20	Not Issued			
21	Coca trata de escurrirse - OUT. (Coco Ferrer)	50.00	25.00	15.00
22	Thurman out a manos de Lanauze (Bob Thurman, Carlos Lanauzue)	65.00	32.50	20.00
23	Santiago felicita a Atkins (Carlos M. Santiago, Joe Atkins)	50.00	25.00	15.00
24	Griffin captura a Miller en home. (Griffin Tirado, Henry Miller)	50.00	25.00	15.00

25	"Detente Villodas": Escalera. (Luis Villodas, Saturnino Escalera)	50.00	25.00	15.00
26	Felo se desliza. . .SAFE. (Felo Guilbe)	50.00	25.00	15.00
27	Gallego llega safe a Home. (Gallego Munoz)	50.00	25.00	15.00
28	Que pena! Se cayo la bola. . .	50.00	25.00	15.00
29	Easterling esperando la bola - OUT. (Howard Easterling)	80.00	40.00	24.00
30	Pitcher McDuffie anotando. (McDuffie Sevilla)	50.00	25.00	15.00
31	El raudo Roberto se desliza - SAFE. (Roberto Vargas)	50.00	25.00	15.00
32	Harris felicita Brown tras homerun (Willard Brown)	275.00	140.00	80.00
33	Burgos intenta sacar Easter - SAFE. (Jose Burgos, Luke Easter)	80.00	40.00	24.00
34	Los Leones felicitan a Clarkson. (Buster Clarkson)	65.00	32.50	20.00
35	Otoniel realiza dificil cogida. . . (Otoniel Ortiz)	65.00	32.50	20.00
36	Thurman safe en tercera. . . (Bob Thurman)	65.00	32.50	20.00
37	Bernier safe en home. (Carlos Bernier)	50.00	25.00	15.00
38	Chifflan Clark se va de homerun. (Chiflan Clark)	50.00	25.00	15.00
39	El gran Easter llega tras homerun. (Luke Easter)	65.00	32.50	20.00
40	Se cae bola a Fields; Graham safe. (Wilmer Fields, Jack Graham)	60.00	30.00	18.00
41	Otoniel trata sacar Taborn - SAFE. (Otoniel Ortiz, Earl Taborn)	50.00	25.00	15.00
42	McQuillen se desliza tercera - SAFE. (George McQuillen)	50.00	25.00	15.00
43	Uno, dos y tres. . .Y anota Coimbre (Francisco Coimbre)	90.00	45.00	27.50
44	Carlos Manuel llega trade. . .OUT. (Carlos M. Santiago)	50.00	25.00	15.00
45	Aprieta el paso, Griffin. . . (Griffin Tirado)	50.00	25.00	15.00
46	Pepe Lucas saca out a Resbaloso. (Pepe Lucas)	50.00	25.00	15.00
47	"No hay quien pase", dice Howell (Dixie Howell)	50.00	25.00	15.00
48	Y que dice el Umpiere?	50.00	25.00	15.00
49	Pedroso intenta robo home - OUT. (Fernando Pedroso)	50.00	25.00	15.00
50	Se formo el nudo. . .	50.00	25.00	15.00
51	Cogelo con calma, Leo. . . (Leo Thomas)	50.00	25.00	15.00
52	Tetelo galopando hacia primera. . . (Tetelo Vargas)	90.00	45.00	27.50
53	Haciendose burla?	50.00	25.00	15.00
54	Los tiburones felicitan. . .	50.00	25.00	15.00
55	La No. 29 de Bernier. (Carlos Bernier)	50.00	25.00	15.00
56	Jockey entra facilmente a primera.	50.00	25.00	15.00
57	Buzas felicita a Collins. (Joe Buzas, Eugene Collins)	50.00	25.00	15.00
58	Ya es tarde, Jose Enrique. . .	50.00	25.00	15.00
59	Lomax Davis entra tras homerun (Lomax Davis)	50.00	25.00	15.00
60	Haddock no puede sacar Villafane. (Hector Haddock)	50.00	25.00	15.00
61	Otoniel Ortiz se va de hom,erun. . . (Otoniel Ortiz)	50.00	25.00	15.00
62	Otra mas para Bernier (Carlos Bernier)	50.00	25.00	15.00
63	Montalvo se desliza en tercera (?) (Jose E. Montalvo)	50.00	25.00	15.00
64	Willie es todo ojos. . . (Willie Morales)	50.00	25.00	15.00
65	La Mucura esta llegando. . . (Johnny Davis)	60.00	30.00	18.00
66	Chapman da out espectacular. (Medina Chapman)	50.00	25.00	15.00
67	McQuilen pisa plato tras homerun (George McQuillen)	50.00	25.00	15.00
68	"Coimbre, Safe". . .dice el Umpire. (Francisco Coimbre)	90.00	45.00	27.50
69	Llega Perry despues de Homerun. . . (Alonso Perry)	65.00	32.50	20.00
70	Griffin, ya es tuyo. . . (Griffin Tirado)	50.00	25.00	15.00
71	Fields pisa plato tras Homerun. . . (Wilmer Fields)	50.00	25.00	15.00
72	EL HOMBRE ESE. . . (Willard Brown)	200.00	100.00	60.00
73	Jockey se desliza violentamente. . .	50.00	25.00	15.00
74	Montalvo esperando a Tite - OUT. (Jose E. Montalvo)	50.00	25.00	15.00
75	Perry anota transqueando. . . (Alonso Perry)	65.00	32.50	20.00
76	Fields pivotea para double-play. (Wilmer Fields)	60.00	30.00	18.00
77	Andando en la cuerda, Piper? (Piper Davis)	65.00	32.50	20.00
78	Montalvo en pie de combate. . . (Jose E. Montalvo)	50.00	25.00	15.00
79	EN GRAN EXPECTATIVA. . .	50.00	25.00	15.00
80	Indios reciben Gachito tras homer	50.00	25.00	15.00
81	Butts esquiva la bola - SAFE. (Pee Wee Butts)	50.00	25.00	15.00
82	Otro para el Gaucho Davis. . (Johnny Davis)	60.00	30.00	18.00
83	Los leones se alborotan. . . (Piper Davis)	60.00	30.00	18.00
84	Lanauze safe en home. (Carlos Lanauze)	50.00	25.00	15.00
85	Lanauze se alarga - OUT. (Carlos Lanauze)	50.00	25.00	15.00
86	Thurman llega tras homerun. (Bob Thurman)	65.00	32.50	20.00
87	Sauer roba home espectacularmente (Ed Sauer)	50.00	25.00	15.00
88	PERRY SE ESTIRA. . .OUT. (Alonso Perry)	65.00	32.50	20.00
89	Clarkson conecta otro homerun. (Buster Clarkson)	80.00	40.00	24.00
90	Piper intenta sacar a Tetelo - SAFE (Tetelo Vargas, Piper Davis)	90.00	45.00	27.50
91	QUE QUE USTED DICE. . .?	50.00	25.00	15.00
92	Bernier se roba el home. . . (Carlos Bernier)	50.00	25.00	15.00
93	UNA ESCENA DE RUTINA. . (Willard Brown)	400.00	200.00	120.00
94	Taborn trata de esquvarse - OUT. (Earl Taborn)	50.00	25.00	15.00
95	Pita Marti safe en tercera. (Humberto Marti)	50.00	25.00	15.00
96	PIE CONTRA PIE. . .(?)	50.00	25.00	15.00
97	NO QUIERE NI VERLO. . .	50.00	25.00	15.00
98	SUDOR Y ARENA. . .	50.00	25.00	15.00
99	Jueyito safe en primera. (Jueyito Andrade)	50.00	25.00	15.00
100	QUIEN LLEGO PRIMERO?	50.00	25.00	15.00
101	LLEGO TARDE EL TIRO..SAFE.	50.00	25.00	15.00
102	Escalera se estira. . .pero es SAFE. (Saturnino Escalera)	50.00	25.00	15.00
103	Howell aspera. . .Almendro observa. (Dixie Howell)	50.00	25.00	15.00
104	A todo vapor hacia tercera. . .	50.00	25.00	15.00
105	Buena cogida, pero es SAFE.	50.00	25.00	15.00
106	El arbitro dice. . .SAFE.	50.00	25.00	15.00
107	SAFE EN HOME.	50.00	25.00	15.00
108	Regreso a tiempo. . .SAFE.	50.00	25.00	15.00
109	Canena es felicitados tras Homer. (Canena Marquez)	65.00	32.50	20.00
110	"COC SAFE", canta el umpiere. (Coco Ferrer)	50.00	25.00	15.00
111	Taft Wright jonronen. . . (Taft Wright)	50.00	25.00	15.00
112	Esta solo. . .pero siempre gana.	50.00	25.00	15.00
113	????????, CANTE!	50.00	25.00	15.00
114	Casanovas quieto en tercera. . . (Rafael Casanovas)	50.00	25.00	15.00
115	Wilson espera pero no llega. . .SAFE. (Artie Wilson)	65.00	32.50	20.00
116	FELLE FELICITA MONTALVO (Felle Delgado, Jose E. Montalvo)	50.00	25.00	15.00
117	El tigre tambien se desliza. . .Safe.	50.00	25.00	15.00
118	Limmer se adelanta. . .Montalvo out. (Lou Limmer, Jose E. Montalvo)	50.00	25.00	15.00
119	TIRO MALO. . .BUTTS SAFE. (Pee Wee Butts)	50.00	25.00	15.00
120	SAFE EN TERCERA.	50.00	25.00	15.00
121	EL JIBARO CONECTA HIT. . .	50.00	25.00	15.00
122	Chapman no puede alcanzarla. . . (Medina Chapman)	50.00	25.00	15.00
123	Guinea Alomar da OUT en Home. (Guinea Alomar)	50.00	25.00	15.00
124	INDIO ANOTA EN SLIDE. . .	50.00	25.00	15.00
125	Miller saca a Serrel en primera. (Henry Miller, Barney Serrell)	50.00	25.00	15.00
126	El gran COIMBRE llega SAFE. (Francisco Coimbre)	90.00	45.00	27.50
127	El arbitro tome impulsa. . .OUT!	50.00	25.00	15.00
128	TROUPPE DA OUT EN HOME. (Quincy Trouppe)	90.00	45.00	27.50
129	BANKHEAD OUT EN PRIMERA. (Bankhead)	60.00	30.00	18.00
130	Tiene que pensarlo bien. . .	50.00	25.00	15.00
131	Escalera a salvo en tercera. . . (Saturnino Escalera)	50.00	25.00	15.00
132	DOS MANOS QUE BUSCAN. . .	50.00	25.00	15.00
133	FIGUEROA SE DESLIZA - SAFE (Tite Figueroa)	50.00	25.00	15.00
134	VIENE LA BOLA. . .OUT.	50.00	25.00	15.00
135	Esperando el tiro. . .OUT.	50.00	25.00	15.00
136	KAYSER SAFE EN PRIMERA. (Cecyl Kayser)	65.00	32.00	19.50
137	COCO FERRER DA OUT. (Coco Ferrer)	50.00	25.00	15.00
138	Lo atajaron a tiempo. . .OUT.	50.00	25.00	15.00
139	Limmer da su primer homer. (Lou Limmer)	50.00	25.00	15.00
140	Starks y Blasini alegan. . . (Jimmy Starks, Efrain Blasini)	50.00	25.00	15.00
141	BARNA SE VA DE HOMERUN. (Babe Barna)	65.00	32.00	19.50
142	"La antesala del gran choque. . . (George Scales)	60.00	30.00	18.00
143	"QUIETO". DICE EL UMPIER.	50.00	25.00	15.00
144	LO SACARON POR UN PELO. . .	50.00	25.00	15.00
145	Un recibimiento poco agradable.	50.00	25.00	15.00
146	Montalvo se desliza. . .OUT. (Jose E. Montalvo)	50.00	25.00	15.00
147	ALOMAR OUT EN HOME. . . (Alomar)	50.00	25.00	15.00
148	EASTER SAFE EN HOME. . (Luke Easter)	65.00	32.50	20.00
149	Grillo se anota hit de piernas. . .	50.00	25.00	15.00
150	BARNA SAFE EN TERCERA. (Babe Barna)	50.00	25.00	15.00
151	Esta en la base pero es OUT.	50.00	25.00	15.00
152	TYBOR DA OUT A TABORN. (Jim Tabor, Earl Taborn)	50.00	25.00	15.00
153	BUTTS OUT EN PRIMERA. (Pee Wee Butts)	50.00	25.00	15.00
154	Viene la bola. . .Hernaiz SAFE. (Angel Hernaiz)	50.00	25.00	15.00
155	VILLODAS LO ESPERA. . .OUT. (Luis Villodas)	50.00	25.00	15.00
156	TYBOR SACA A COCA FERRER. (Jim Tabor, Coco Ferrer)	50.00	25.00	15.00
157	LO FUSILAN EN TERCERA.	50.00	25.00	15.00
158	B L O Q U E A D O. . .	50.00	25.00	15.00
159	"Estoy firme en base", dice Coco. (Coco Ferrer)	50.00	25.00	15.00
160	Ruben Gomez se tira slide. . .SAFE. (Ruben Gomez)	50.00	25.00	15.00
161	HOWELL OUT EN PRIMERA. (Dixie Howell)	50.00	25.00	15.00
162	SAFE EN HOME.	50.00	25.00	15.00
163	PERRY ES ESCURRE. . .SAFE. (Alonso Perry)	65.00	32.50	20.00
164	PEDROSO SE LESIONA. (Fernando Pedroso)	50.00	25.00	15.00
165	LA APOTEOSIS DEL TRIUNFO.	50.00	25.00	15.00
166	Ruben jonroneo ganar su juego. (Ruben Gomez)	50.00	25.00	15.00
167	Primer homerun CANENA 1950-51 (Canena Marquez)	65.00	32.50	20.00
168	GOLPE DE IZQUIRDA? SAFE.	50.00	25.00	15.00
169	PELLOT OUT EN HOME. (Victor Pellot (Power))	65.00	32.50	20.00
170	Muchos ojos tras Scales y Mullens. (George Scales)	60.00	30.00	18.00
171	Nube de polvo en el Castillo. . .	50.00	25.00	15.00
172	Bero participa carnaval jonrones. (John Bero)	50.00	25.00	15.00
173	Lanauze completa out a Butts. (Carlos Lanauze, Pee Wee Butts)	50.00	25.00	15.00
174	SE LE ESCAPO LA PILDORA.	50.00	25.00	15.00
175	EL UMPIRE DECIDIRA. . .	50.00	25.00	15.00
176	Llego tarde el HOMBRE ESE. (Willard Brown)	200.00	100.00	60.00
177	THON SE DESLIZA. . .	50.00	25.00	15.00
178	AL REVES, PERO SAFE. . .SAFE. (Freddie Thon)	50.00	25.00	15.00
179	Hughes no puede sacar al corredor. (Roy Hughes)	50.00	25.00	15.00
180	"Chiflan Safe". . .dice el Umpiere. (Chiflan Clark)	50.00	25.00	15.00

1909-11 Tolstoi Cigarettes

PREMIUMS:
Commons: 1.5-2X
Hall of Famers: 1.5-2X
(See T206 for checklist and base values.)

1886 Tomlinson Studios Cabinets

The extent to which Detroit photographer Frank N. Tomlinson promulgated individual player cabinet cards of the 1886 Wolverines is unknown. However, since the known player portraits are the same as those found on a team-composite it is not unreasonable to expect that each of the 14 players on the team card may have been issued as individual portraits. In addition, posed action cabinets are currently known for 13 players. The cabinets are in typical 4-1/4" x 6-1/2" format, with the player's name and position appearing in script on the mount below the photo. Most are found with blank backs, though some cards have ornate advertising for the studio on back.

		NM	EX	VG
Common Player, Portrait		8,000	4,000	2,500
Common Player, Action		6,750	3,400	2,000
(1a)	C.B. Baldwin/Pitching	6,750	3,400	2,000
(2a)	C.W. Bennett/Btg	6,750	3,400	2,000
(2b)	C.W. Bennett/Portrait	8,000	4,000	2,500
(3a)	D. Brouthers/Btg	15,000	7,500	4,500
(3b)	D. Brouthers/Portrait	20,000	10,000	6,000
(4a)	S.N. Crane/Btg	6,750	3,400	2,000
(5a)	C.H. Getzein/Pitching	6,750	3,400	2,000
(5b)	C.H. Getzein/Portrait	8,000	4,000	2,500
(6a)	C.L. Hall/Btg	6,750	3,400	2,000
(7a)	E. Hanlon/Btg	15,000	7,500	4,500
(8a)	J.H. Manning/Btg	6,750	3,400	2,000
(8b)	J.H. Manning/Portrait	8,000	4,000	2,500
(9a)	H. Richardson/Btg	6,750	3,400	2,000
(10a)	J.C. Rowe/Btg	6,750	3,400	2,000
(11a)	S.L. Thompson/Btg	15,000	7,500	4,500
(12a)	L. Twitchell/Pitching	6,750	3,400	2,000
(13b)	W.H. Watkins/Portrait	10,000	5,000	3,000
(14a)	J.L. White/Btg	7,500	3,750	2,250
(14b)	J.L. White/Portrait	9,000	4,500	2,700

1953 Top Taste Bread Labels

(See 1953 Northland Bread Labels)

1909 Topping & Co. Detroit Tigers Postcards

This set of postcards features the members of the 1909 American League Champion Detroit Tigers. About 3-1/2" x 5-1/2" in size, vertically formatted fronts have black-and-white player portraits at center within a yellow six-pointed star. "Tiger Stars" appears in script in a yellow stripe at top, while the player name and position are in a similar strip at bottom. Black trim surrounds the design elements. Backs are black-and-white with standard postcard markings and a credit line for Topping and Publishers Co., Detroit. The unnumbered cards are listed here alphabetically.

		NM	EX	VG
Complete Set (21):		12,000	6,000	3,500
Common Player:		475.00	240.00	140.00
(1)	Henry Beckendorf	475.00	240.00	140.00
(2)	Donie Bush	475.00	240.00	140.00
(3)	Ty Cobb	4,000	2,000	1,200
(4)	Sam Crawford	1,000	500.00	300.00
(5)	Jim Delehanty	475.00	240.00	140.00
(6)	Bill Donovan	475.00	240.00	140.00
(7)	Hughie Jennings	1,000	500.00	300.00
(8)	Davy Jones	475.00	240.00	140.00
(9)	Tom Jones	475.00	240.00	140.00
(10)	Ed Killian	475.00	240.00	140.00
(11)	Matty McIntyre	475.00	240.00	140.00
(12)	George Moriarty	475.00	240.00	140.00
(13)	George Mullin	475.00	240.00	140.00
(14)	Charley O'Leary	475.00	240.00	140.00
(15)	Germany Schaefer	475.00	240.00	140.00
(16)	Charlie Schmidt	475.00	240.00	140.00
(17)	George Speer	475.00	240.00	140.00
(18)	Oscar Stanage	475.00	240.00	140.00
(19)	Eddie Summers	475.00	240.00	140.00
(20)	Ed Willett	475.00	240.00	140.00
(21)	Ralph Works	475.00	240.00	140.00

1948 Topps Magic Photos

The first Topps baseball cards appeared as a subset of 19 cards from an issue of 252 "Magic Photos." The set takes its name from the self-developing nature of the cards. The cards were blank on the front when first taken from the wrapper. By spitting on the wrapper and holding it to the card while exposing it to light the black-and-white photo appeared. Measuring 7/8" x 1-1/2", the cards are very similar to Topps 1955 and 1956 "Hocus Focus" issues.

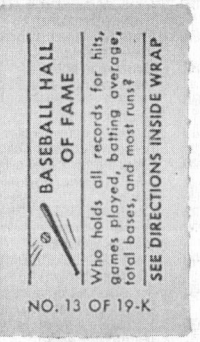

		NM	EX	VG
Complete Set (19):		2,400	1,200	725.00
Common Card:		60.00	30.00	18.00
1	Lou Boudreau	75.00	37.50	22.50
2	Cleveland Indians	60.00	30.00	18.00
3	Bob Eliott	75.00	37.50	22.50
4	Cleveland Indians 4-3	60.00	30.00	18.00
5	Cleveland Indians 4-1	60.00	30.00	18.00
6	Babe Ruth	450.00	225.00	135.00
7	Tris Speaker	90.00	45.00	27.50
8	Rogers Hornsby	90.00	45.00	27.50
9	Connie Mack	75.00	37.50	22.50
10	Christy Mathewson	150.00	75.00	45.00
11	Hans Wagner	100.00	50.00	30.00
12	Grover Alexander	90.00	45.00	27.50
13	Ty Cobb	275.00	135.00	80.00
14	Lou Gehrig	275.00	135.00	80.00
15	Walter Johnson	125.00	65.00	35.00
16	Cy Young	125.00	65.00	35.00
17	George Sisler	75.00	37.50	22.50
18	Tinker and Evers	125.00	65.00	35.00
19	Third Base Cleveland Indians	75.00	37.50	22.50

1951 Topps Red Backs

Like the Blue Backs, the Topps Red Backs which were sold at the same time came two to a package for 1¢. Their black-and-white photographs appear on a red, white, blue and yellow background. The back printing is red on white. Their 2" x 2-5/8" size is the same as Blue Backs. Also identical is the set size (52 cards) and the game situations to be found on the fronts of the cards, for use in playing a card game of baseball. Red Backs are more common than the Blue Backs by virtue of a 1980s discovery of a large hoard of unopened boxes. Red Backs are also known to have been sold in a plastic-bagged set along with a foldout paper game board for 29 cents.

		NM	EX	VG
Complete Set (52):		1,200	600.00	350.00
Common Player:		12.00	6.00	3.50
Wax Pack (2):		100.00		
1	Larry (Yogi) Berra	150.00	75.00	37.50
2	Sid Gordon	12.00	6.00	3.50
3	Ferris Fain	12.00	6.00	3.50
4	Verne Stephens	12.00	6.00	3.50
5	Phil Rizzuto	60.00	30.00	15.00
6	Allie Reynolds	30.00	15.00	7.50
7	Howie Pollet	12.00	6.00	3.50
8	Early Wynn	35.00	17.50	8.75
9	Roy Sievers	12.00	6.00	3.50
10	Mel Parnell	12.00	6.00	3.50
11	Gene Hermanski	12.00	6.00	3.50
12	Jim Hegan	12.00	6.00	3.50
13	Dale Mitchell	12.00	6.00	3.50
14	Wayne Terwilliger	12.00	6.00	3.50
15	Ralph Kiner	35.00	17.50	8.75
16	Preacher Roe	30.00	15.00	7.50
17	Dave Bell	12.00	6.00	3.50
18	Gerry Coleman	20.00	10.00	5.00
19	Dick Kokos	12.00	6.00	3.50
20	Dominick DiMaggio	30.00	15.00	7.50
21	Larry Jansen	12.00	6.00	3.50
22	Bob Feller	50.00	25.00	14.00
23	Ray Boone	12.00	6.00	3.50
24	Hank Bauer	20.00	10.00	5.00
25	Cliff Chambers	12.00	6.00	3.50
26	Luke Easter	20.00	10.00	5.00
27	Wally Westlake	12.00	6.00	3.50
28	Elmer Valo	12.00	6.00	3.50
29	Bob Kennedy	12.00	6.00	3.50
30	Warren Spahn	50.00	25.00	14.00
31	Gil Hodges	40.00	20.00	11.00
32	Henry Thompson	12.00	6.00	3.50
33	William Werle	12.00	6.00	3.50
34	Grady Hatton	12.00	6.00	3.50
35	Al Rosen	20.00	10.00	5.00
36a	Gus Zernial (Chicago in bio.)	50.00	25.00	15.00
36b	Gus Zernial (Philadelphia in bio.)	25.00	12.50	8.00
37	Wes Westrum	12.00	6.00	3.50
38	Ed (Duke) Snider	60.00	30.00	18.00
39	Ted Kluszewski	30.00	15.00	7.50
40	Mike Garcia	12.00	6.00	3.50
41	Whitey Lockman	12.00	6.00	3.50
42	Ray Scarborough	12.00	6.00	3.50
43	Maurice McDermott	12.00	6.00	3.50
44	Sid Hudson	12.00	6.00	3.50
45	Andy Seminick	12.00	6.00	3.50
46	Billy Goodman	12.00	6.00	3.50
47	Tommy Glaviano	12.00	6.00	3.50
48	Eddie Stanky	12.00	6.00	3.50
49	Al Zarilla	12.00	6.00	3.50
50	Monte Irvin	40.00	20.00	10.00
51	Eddie Robinson	12.00	6.00	3.50
52a	Tommy Holmes (Boston in bio.)	50.00	25.00	15.00
52b	Tommy Holmes (Hartford in bio.)	25.00	12.50	8.00

1951 Topps Blue Backs

Sold two cards in a package with a piece of candy for 1¢, the Topps Blue Backs are considerably scarcer than their Red Back counterparts. The 2" x 2-5/8" cards carry a black-and-white player photograph on a red, white, yellow and green background along with the player's name and other information including their 1950 record on the front. The back is printed in blue on a white background. The 52-card set has varied baseball situations on them, making the playing of a rather elementary game of baseball possible. Although scarce, Blue Backs were printed on thick cardboard and have survived quite well over the years. There are, however, few stars in the set.

		NM	EX	VG
Complete Set (52):		2,000	1,000	600.00
Common Player:		30.00	15.00	8.00
Wax Pack (2):		200.00		
1	Eddie Yost	40.00	20.00	10.00
2	Henry (Hank) Majeski	30.00	15.00	8.00
3	Richie Ashburn	200.00	100.00	50.00
4	Del Ennis	30.00	15.00	8.00
5	Johnny Pesky	30.00	15.00	8.00
6	Albert (Red) Schoendienst	100.00	50.00	25.00
7	Gerald Staley	30.00	15.00	8.00
8	Dick Sisler	30.00	15.00	8.00
9	Johnny Sain	40.00	20.00	10.00
10	Joe Page	30.00	15.00	8.00
11	Johnny Groth	30.00	15.00	8.00
12	Sam Jethroe	30.00	15.00	8.00
13	James (Mickey) Vernon	30.00	15.00	8.00
14	George Munger	30.00	15.00	8.00
15	Eddie Joost	30.00	15.00	8.00
16	Murry Dickson	30.00	15.00	8.00
17	Roy Smalley	30.00	15.00	8.00
18	Ned Garver	30.00	15.00	8.00
19	Phil Masi	30.00	15.00	8.00
20	Ralph Branca	40.00	20.00	10.00
21	Billy Johnson	30.00	15.00	8.00
22	Bob Kuzava	30.00	15.00	8.00
23	Paul (Dizzy) Trout	30.00	15.00	8.00
24	Sherman Lollar	30.00	15.00	8.00
25	Sam Mele	30.00	15.00	8.00
26	Chico Carrasquel	30.00	15.00	8.00
27	Andy Pafko	30.00	15.00	8.00
28	Harry (The Cat) Brecheen	30.00	15.00	8.00
29	Granville Hamner	30.00	15.00	8.00
30	Enos (Country) Slaughter	100.00	50.00	25.00
31	Lou Brissie	30.00	15.00	8.00
32	Bob Elliott	30.00	15.00	8.00
33	Don Lenhardt	30.00	15.00	8.00
34	Earl Torgeson	30.00	15.00	8.00
35	Tommy Byrne	30.00	15.00	8.00
36	Cliff Fannin	30.00	15.00	8.00
37	Bobby Doerr	100.00	50.00	25.00
38	Irv Noren	30.00	15.00	8.00
39	Ed Lopat	40.00	20.00	10.00
40	Vic Wertz	30.00	15.00	8.00
41	Johnny Schmitz	30.00	15.00	8.00
42	Bruce Edwards	30.00	15.00	8.00
43	Willie (Puddin' Head) Jones	30.00	15.00	8.00
44	Johnny Wyrostek	30.00	15.00	8.00
45	Bill Pierce	30.00	15.00	8.00
46	Gerry Priddy	30.00	15.00	8.00
47	Herman Wehmeier	30.00	15.00	8.00
48	Billy Cox	30.00	15.00	8.00
49	Henry (Hank) Sauer	30.00	15.00	8.00
50	Johnny Mize	100.00	50.00	25.00
51	Eddie Waitkus	30.00	15.00	8.00
52	Sam Chapman	30.00	15.00	8.00

1951 Topps Connie Mack's All-Stars

A set of die-cut, 2-1/16" x 5-1/4" cards, all 11 players are Hall of Famers. The cards feature a black-and-white action player photograph printed on a red background with a colored

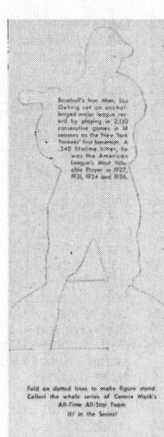

name plaque underneath. Like the "Current All-Stars," with which they were issued, the background could be folded, making it possible for the card to stand up. This practice, however, resulted in the card's mutilation and lowers its condition in the eyes of today's collectors. Connie Mack All-Stars are scarce today and, despite being relatively expensive, retain a certain popularity as one of Topps first issues.

		NM	EX	VG
Complete Set (11):		18,000	9,000	5,500
Common Player:		525.00	260.00	155.00
(1)	Grover Cleveland Alexander	900.00	450.00	275.00
(2)	Gordon Stanley Cochrane	600.00	300.00	180.00
(3)	Edward Trowbridge Collins	600.00	300.00	180.00
(4)	James J. Collins	600.00	300.00	180.00
(5)	Lou Gehrig	7,500	3,700	2,200
(6)	Walter Johnson	1,000	500.00	300.00
(7)	Connie Mack	600.00	300.00	180.00
(8)	Christopher Mathewson	1,125	560.00	335.00
(9)	George Herman Ruth	5,500	2,750	1,650
(10)	Tris Speaker	600.00	300.00	180.00
(11)	Honus Wagner	1,650	825.00	495.00

1951 Topps Major League All-Stars

The Topps Major League All-Stars are very similar to the Connie Mack All-Stars of the same year. The 2-1/16" x 5-1/4" cards have a black-and-white photograph on a red die-cut background. Most of the background could be folded over so that the card would stand up. A plaque at the base carries brief biographical information. The set was to contain 11 cards, but only eight were actually issued in gum packs. Those of Konstanty, Roberts and Stanky were not issued and are very rare, with only a handful of each known. A big problem with the set is that if the card was used as it was intended it was folded and, thus, damaged from a collector's viewpoint. That makes top quality examples of any players difficult to find and quite expensive.

		NM	EX	VG
Complete Set (11):		18,500	9,250	5,550
Common Player:		1,850	925.00	555.00
(1)	Yogi Berra	6,000	3,000	1,800
(2)	Larry Doby	4,000	2,000	1,200
(3)	Walt Dropo	900.00	450.00	270.00
(4)	"Hoot" Evers	900.00	450.00	270.00
(5)	George Clyde Kell	1,850	925.00	555.00
(6)	Ralph Kiner	1,850	925.00	555.00
(7)	Jim Konstanty	30,000	15,000	9,000
(8)	Bob Lemon	1,850	925.00	555.00
(9)	Phil Rizzuto	2,750	1,375	825.00
(10)	Robin Roberts	35,000	17,500	10,500
(11)	Ed Stanky	30,000	15,000	9,000

1951 Topps Teams

An innovative issue for 1951, the Topps team cards were a nine-card set, 5-1/4" x 2-1/16", which carry a black-and-white picture of a major league team surrounded by a yellow border on the front. The back identifies team members with red printing on white cardboard. There are two versions of each card, with and without the date "1950" in the banner that carries the team name. Undated versions are valued slightly

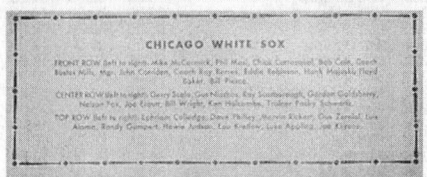

higher than the cards with dates. Strangely only nine teams were issued. Scarcity varies, with the Cardinals and Red Sox being the most difficult to obtain.

		NM	EX	VG
(1a)	Boston Red Sox (1950)	475.00	235.00	140.00
(1b)	Boston Red Sox (Undated)	500.00	250.00	150.00
(2a)	Brooklyn Dodgers (1950)	375.00	185.00	110.00
(2b)	Brooklyn Dodgers (Undated)	400.00	200.00	120.00
(3a)	Chicago White Sox (1950)	275.00	135.00	80.00
(3b)	Chicago White Sox (Undated)	250.00	125.00	75.00
(4a)	Cincinnati Reds (1950)	300.00	150.00	90.00
(4b)	Cincinnati Reds (Undated)	325.00	160.00	95.00
(5a)	New York Giants (1950)	300.00	150.00	90.00
(5b)	New York Giants (Undated)	325.00	160.00	95.00
(6a)	Philadelphia Athletics (1950)	225.00	110.00	65.00
(6b)	Philadelphia Athletics (Undated)	250.00	125.00	75.00
(7a)	Philadelphia Phillies (1950)	225.00	110.00	65.00
(7b)	Philadelphia Phillies (Undated)	400.00	200.00	120.00
(8a)	St. Louis Cardinals (1950)	400.00	200.00	120.00
(8b)	St. Louis Cardinals (Undated)	425.00	210.00	125.00
(9a)	Washington Senators (1950)	250.00	125.00	75.00
(9b)	Washington Senators (Undated)	300.00	150.00	90.00

1952 Topps

At 407 cards, the 1952 Topps set was the largest set of its day, both in number of cards and physical dimensions of the cards. Cards are 2-5/8" x 3-3/4" with a colorized black-and-white photograph on front. Major baseball card innovations presented in the set include the first-ever use of color team logos as part of the design, and the inclusion of stats for the previous season and career on the backs. The first 80 cards in the set can be found with backs printed entirely in black or black and red. While "Black Backs" used to command a significant premium over the "Red Back" version, that differential has diminished in recent years to the point of insignificance. Several cards in the #1-80 range can be found with noticeable color differences on front depending on whether they are Red Back or Black Back. Cards #311-407, known as the "high numbers," were distributed in limited areas and are extremely rare.

		NM	EX	VG
Complete Set (407):		120,000	55,000	30,000
Common Player (1-250):		45.00	22.50	13.50
Common Player (251-310):		60.00	30.00	18.00
Common Player (311-407):		400.00	200.00	120.00
1	Andy Pafko	7,500	625.00	225.00
2	James E. Runnels	2,700	140.00	25.00
3	Hank Thompson	200.00	30.00	15.00
4	Don Lenhardt	45.00	22.50	13.50
5	Larry Jansen	45.00	22.50	13.50
6	Grady Hatton	45.00	22.50	13.50
7	Wayne Terwilliger	55.00	27.50	16.50
8	Fred Marsh	45.00	22.50	13.50
9	Bobby Hogue	775.00	390.00	235.00
10	Al Rosen	80.00	40.00	20.00
11	Phil Rizzuto	600.00	300.00	180.00
12	Monty Basgall	45.00	22.50	13.50
13	Johnny Wyrostek	45.00	22.50	13.50
14	Bob Elliott	45.00	22.50	13.50
15	Johnny Pesky	45.00	22.50	13.50
16	Gene Hermanski	45.00	22.50	13.50
17	Jim Hegan	45.00	22.50	13.50
18	Merrill Combs	45.00	22.50	13.50
19	Johnny Bucha	45.00	22.50	13.50
20	Billy Loes	150.00	75.00	37.50
21	Ferris Fain	60.00	30.00	18.00
22	Dom DiMaggio	125.00	75.00	45.00
23	Billy Goodman	45.00	22.50	13.50
24	Luke Easter	60.00	30.00	18.00
25	Johnny Groth	45.00	22.50	13.50
26	Monty Irvin	230.00	115.00	70.00
27	Sam Jethroe	45.00	22.50	13.50
28	Jerry Priddy	45.00	22.50	13.50
29	Ted Kluszewski	150.00	75.00	37.50
30	Mel Parnell	45.00	22.50	13.50
31	Gus Zernial	100.00	50.00	25.00
32	Eddie Robinson	45.00	22.50	13.50
33	Warren Spahn	300.00	150.00	75.00
34	Elmer Valo	45.00	22.50	13.50
35	Hank Sauer	45.00	22.50	13.50
36	Gil Hodges	275.00	135.00	82.50
37	Duke Snider	450.00	220.00	135.00
38	Wally Westlake	45.00	22.50	13.50
39	"Dizzy" Trout	45.00	22.50	13.50
40	Irv Noren	45.00	22.50	13.50
41	Bob Wellman	45.00	22.50	13.50
42	Lou Kretlow	45.00	22.50	13.50
43	Ray Scarborough	45.00	22.50	13.50
44	Con Dempsey	45.00	22.50	13.50
45	Eddie Joost	45.00	22.50	13.50
46	Gordon Goldsberry	45.00	22.50	13.50
47	Willie Jones	45.00	22.50	13.50
48a	Joe Page (Wrong (Sain) back.)	1,200	600.00	350.00
48b	Joe Page (Correct back.)	350.00	175.00	105.00
49a	Johnny Sain (Wrong (Page) back.)	1,100	550.00	325.00
49b	Johnny Sain (Correct back.)	150.00	75.00	50.00
50	Marv Rickert	45.00	22.50	13.50
51	Jim Russell	55.00	27.50	16.50
52	Don Mueller	45.00	22.50	13.50
53	Chris Van Cuyk	55.00	27.50	16.50
54	Leo Kiely	45.00	22.50	13.50
55	Ray Boone	45.00	22.50	13.50
56	Tommy Glaviano	45.00	22.50	13.50
57	Ed Lopat	90.00	45.00	25.00
58	Bob Mahoney	45.00	22.50	13.50
59	Robin Roberts	200.00	100.00	60.00
60	Sid Hudson	45.00	22.50	13.50
61	"Tookie" Gilbert	45.00	22.50	13.50
62	Chuck Stobbs	45.00	22.50	13.50
63	Howie Pollet	45.00	22.50	13.50
64	Roy Sievers	45.00	22.50	13.50
65	Enos Slaughter	160.00	80.00	40.00
66	"Preacher" Roe	100.00	50.00	35.00
67	Allie Reynolds	120.00	60.00	35.00
68	Cliff Chambers	45.00	22.50	13.50
69	Virgil Stallcup	45.00	22.50	13.50
70	Al Zarilla	45.00	22.50	13.50
71	Tom Upton	45.00	22.50	13.50
72	Karl Olson	45.00	22.50	13.50
73	William Werle	45.00	22.50	13.50
74	Andy Hansen	45.00	22.50	13.50
75	Wes Westrum	45.00	22.50	13.50
76	Eddie Stanky	45.00	22.50	13.50
77	Bob Kennedy	45.00	22.50	13.50
78	Ellis Kinder	45.00	22.50	13.50
79	Gerald Staley	45.00	22.50	13.50
80	Herman Wehmeier	45.00	22.50	13.50
81	Vernon Law	45.00	22.50	13.50
82	Duane Pillette	45.00	22.50	13.50
83	Billy Johnson	45.00	22.50	13.50
84	Vern Stephens	45.00	22.50	13.50
85	Bob Kuzava	55.00	27.50	16.50
86	Ted Gray	45.00	22.50	13.50
87	Dale Coogan	45.00	22.50	13.50
88	Bob Feller	285.00	140.00	85.00
89	Johnny Lipon	45.00	22.50	13.50
90	Mickey Grasso	45.00	22.50	13.50
91	Al Schoendienst	140.00	70.00	40.00
92	Dale Mitchell	45.00	22.50	13.50
93	Al Sima	45.00	22.50	13.50
94	Sam Mele	45.00	22.50	13.50
95	Ken Holcombe	45.00	22.50	13.50
96	Willard Marshall	45.00	22.50	13.50
97	Earl Torgeson	45.00	22.50	13.50
98	Bill Pierce	55.00	27.50	16.50
99	Gene Woodling	80.00	40.00	24.00
100	Del Rice	45.00	22.50	13.50
101	Max Lanier	45.00	22.50	13.50
102	Bill Kennedy	45.00	22.50	13.50
103	Cliff Mapes	45.00	22.50	13.50
104	Don Kolloway	45.00	22.50	13.50
105	John Pramesa	45.00	22.50	13.50
106	Mickey Vernon	45.00	22.50	13.50
107	Connie Ryan	45.00	22.50	13.50
108	Jim Konstanty	45.00	22.50	13.50
109	Ted Wilks	45.00	22.50	13.50
110	Dutch Leonard	45.00	22.50	13.50
111	Harry Lowrey	45.00	22.50	13.50
112	Henry Majeski	45.00	22.50	13.50
113	Dick Sisler	45.00	22.50	13.50
114	Willard Ramsdell	45.00	22.50	13.50
115	George Munger	45.00	22.50	13.50
116	Carl Scheib	45.00	22.50	13.50
117	Sherman Lollar	45.00	22.50	13.50
118	Ken Raffensberger	45.00	22.50	13.50
119	Maurice McDermott	45.00	22.50	13.50
120	Bob Chakales	45.00	22.50	13.50
121	Gus Niarhos	45.00	22.50	13.50
122	Jack Jensen	100.00	50.00	30.00
123	Eddie Yost	45.00	22.50	13.50
124	Monte Kennedy	45.00	22.50	13.50
125	Bill Rigney	45.00	22.50	13.50
126	Fred Hutchinson	45.00	22.50	13.50
127	Paul Minner	45.00	22.50	13.50
128	Don Bollweg	55.00	27.50	16.50
129	Johnny Mize	140.00	70.00	35.00
130	Sheldon Jones	45.00	22.50	13.50
131	Morrie Martin	45.00	22.50	13.50
132	Clyde Kluttz	45.00	22.50	13.50
133	Al Widmar	45.00	22.50	13.50
134	Joe Tipton	45.00	22.50	13.50
135	Dixie Howell	45.00	22.50	13.50
136	Johnny Schmitz	45.00	22.50	13.50
137	Roy McMillan	50.00	25.00	15.00
138	Bill MacDonald	45.00	22.50	13.50
139	Ken Wood	45.00	22.50	13.50

#	Player	NM	EX	VG
140	John Antonelli	45.00	22.50	13.50
141	Clint Hartung	45.00	22.50	13.50
142	Harry Perkowski	45.00	22.50	13.50
143	Les Moss	45.00	22.50	13.50
144	Ed Blake	45.00	22.50	13.50
145	Joe Haynes	45.00	22.50	13.50
146	Frank House	45.00	22.50	13.50
147	Bob Young	45.00	22.50	13.50
148	Johnny Klippstein	45.00	22.50	13.50
149	Dick Kryhoski	45.00	22.50	13.50
150	Ted Beard	45.00	22.50	13.50
151	*Wally Post*	55.00	27.50	16.50
152	Al Evans	45.00	22.50	13.50
153	Bob Rush	45.00	22.50	13.50
154	Joe Muir	45.00	22.50	13.50
155	Frank Overmire	55.00	27.50	16.50
156	Frank Hiller	45.00	22.50	13.50
157	Bob Usher	45.00	22.50	13.50
158	Eddie Waitkus	45.00	22.50	13.50
159	Saul Rogovin	45.00	22.50	13.50
160	Owen Friend	45.00	22.50	13.50
161	Bud Byerly	45.00	22.50	13.50
162	Del Crandall	45.00	22.50	13.50
163	Stan Rojek	45.00	22.50	13.50
164	Walt Dubiel	45.00	22.50	13.50
165	Eddie Kazak	45.00	22.50	13.50
166	Paul LaPalme	45.00	22.50	13.50
167	Bill Howerton	45.00	22.50	13.50
168	*Charlie Silvera*	75.00	37.50	22.50
169	Howie Judson	45.00	22.50	13.50
170	Gus Bell	65.00	32.50	20.00
171	Ed Erautt	45.00	22.50	13.50
172	Eddie Miksis	45.00	22.50	13.50
173	Roy Smalley	45.00	22.50	13.50
174	Clarence Marshall	45.00	22.50	13.50
175	*Billy Martin*	675.00	340.00	200.00
176	Hank Edwards	45.00	22.50	13.50
177	Bill Wight	45.00	22.50	13.50
178	Cass Michaels	45.00	22.50	13.50
179	Frank Smith	45.00	22.50	13.50
180	*Charley Maxwell*	60.00	30.00	18.00
181	Bob Swift	45.00	22.50	13.50
182	Billy Hitchcock	45.00	22.50	13.50
183	Erv Dusak	45.00	22.50	13.50
184	Bob Ramazzotti	45.00	22.50	13.50
185	Bill Nicholson	45.00	22.50	13.50
186	Walt Masterson	45.00	22.50	13.50
187	Bob Miller	45.00	22.50	13.50
188	Clarence Podbielan	45.00	22.50	13.50
189	Pete Reiser	45.00	22.50	13.50
190	Don Johnson	45.00	22.50	13.50
191	Yogi Berra	900.00	450.00	270.00
192	Myron Ginsberg	45.00	22.50	13.50
193	Harry Simpson	45.00	22.50	13.50
194	Joe Hatten	45.00	22.50	13.50
195	*Orestes Minoso*	175.00	87.50	43.75
196	Solly Hemus	45.00	22.50	13.50
197	George Strickland	45.00	22.50	13.50
198	Phil Haugstad	50.00	25.00	15.00
199	George Zuverink	45.00	22.50	13.50
200	Ralph Houk	75.00	50.00	25.00
201	Alex Kellner	45.00	22.50	13.50
202	Joe Collins	60.00	30.00	18.00
203	Curt Simmons	45.00	22.50	13.50
204	Ron Northey	45.00	22.50	13.50
205	Clyde King	45.00	22.50	13.50
206	Joe Ostrowski	55.00	27.50	16.50
207	Mickey Harris	45.00	22.50	13.50
208	Marlin Stuart	45.00	22.50	13.50
209	Howie Fox	45.00	22.50	13.50
210	Dick Fowler	45.00	22.50	13.50
211	Ray Coleman	45.00	22.50	13.50
212	Ned Garver	45.00	22.50	13.50
213	Nippy Jones	45.00	22.50	13.50
214	Johnny Hopp	55.00	27.50	16.50
215	Hank Bauer	95.00	45.00	25.00
216	Richie Ashburn	225.00	112.50	56.25
217	George Stirnweiss	45.00	22.50	13.50
218	Clyde McCullough	45.00	22.50	13.50
219	Bobby Shantz	55.00	27.50	16.50
220	Joe Presko	45.00	22.50	13.50
221	Granny Hamner	45.00	22.50	13.50
222	"Hoot" Evers	45.00	22.50	13.50
223	Del Ennis	45.00	22.50	13.50
224	Bruce Edwards	45.00	22.50	13.50
225	Frank Baumholtz	45.00	22.50	13.50
226	Dave Philley	45.00	22.50	13.50
227	Joe Garagiola	100.00	50.00	25.00
228	Al Brazle	45.00	22.50	13.50
229	Gene Bearden	45.00	22.50	13.50
230	Matt Batts	45.00	22.50	13.50
231	Sam Zoldak	45.00	22.50	13.50
232	Billy Cox	90.00	45.00	25.00
233	*Bob Friend*	75.00	37.50	22.50
234	Steve Souchock	45.00	22.50	13.50
235	Walt Dropo	45.00	22.50	13.50
236	Ed Fitz Gerald	45.00	22.50	13.50
237	Jerry Coleman	60.00	30.00	18.00
238	Art Houtteman	45.00	22.50	13.50
239	*Rocky Bridges*	45.00	22.50	13.50
240	Jack Phillips	45.00	22.50	13.50
241	Tommy Byrne	45.00	22.50	13.50
242	Tom Poholsky	45.00	22.50	13.50
243	Larry Doby	100.00	50.00	25.00
244	Vic Wertz	45.00	22.50	13.50
245	Sherry Robertson	45.00	22.50	13.50
246	George Kell	100.00	50.00	25.00
247	Randy Gumpert	45.00	22.50	13.50
248	Frank Shea	45.00	22.50	13.50
249	Bobby Adams	45.00	22.50	13.50
250	Carl Erskine	100.00	50.00	25.00
251	Chico Carrasquel	95.00	47.50	27.50
252	Vern Bickford	60.00	30.00	18.00
253	Johnny Berardino	75.00	37.50	22.50
254	Joe Dobson	60.00	30.00	18.00
255	Clyde Vollmer	60.00	30.00	18.00
256	Pete Suder	60.00	30.00	18.00
257	Bobby Avila	60.00	30.00	18.00

#	Player	NM	EX	VG
258	Steve Gromek	60.00	30.00	18.00
259	Bob Addis	60.00	30.00	18.00
260	Pete Castiglione	60.00	30.00	18.00
261	Willie Mays	2,200	1,100	660.00
262	Virgil Trucks	60.00	30.00	18.00
263	Harry Brecheen	60.00	30.00	18.00
264	Roy Hartsfield	60.00	30.00	18.00
265	Chuck Diering	60.00	30.00	18.00
266	Murry Dickson	60.00	30.00	18.00
267	Sid Gordon	60.00	30.00	18.00
268	Bob Lemon	125.00	62.50	31.25
269	Willard Nixon	60.00	30.00	18.00
270	Lou Brissie	60.00	30.00	18.00
271	Jim Delsing	60.00	30.00	18.00
272	Mike Garcia	60.00	30.00	18.00
273	Erv Palica	70.00	35.00	20.00
274	Ralph Branca	125.00	62.50	31.25
275	Pat Mullin	60.00	30.00	18.00
276	Jim Wilson	60.00	30.00	18.00
277	Early Wynn	175.00	85.00	50.00
278	Al Clark	60.00	30.00	18.00
279	Ed Stewart	60.00	30.00	18.00
280	Cloyd Boyer	60.00	30.00	18.00
281	Tommy Brown	60.00	30.00	18.00
282	Birdie Tebbetts	60.00	30.00	18.00
283	Phil Masi	60.00	30.00	18.00
284	Hank Arft	60.00	30.00	18.00
285	Cliff Fannin	60.00	30.00	18.00
286	Joe De Maestri	60.00	30.00	18.00
287	Steve Bilko	60.00	30.00	18.00
288	Chet Nichols	60.00	30.00	18.00
289	Tommy Holmes	60.00	30.00	18.00
290	Joe Astroth	60.00	30.00	18.00
291	Gil Coan	60.00	30.00	18.00
292	Floyd Baker	60.00	30.00	18.00
293	Sibby Sisti	60.00	30.00	18.00
294	Walker Cooper	60.00	30.00	18.00
295	Phil Cavarretta	60.00	30.00	18.00
296	"Red" Rolfe	60.00	30.00	18.00
297	Andy Seminick	60.00	30.00	18.00
298	Bob Ross	60.00	30.00	18.00
299	Ray Murray	60.00	30.00	18.00
300	Barney McCosky	60.00	30.00	18.00
301	Bob Porterfield	60.00	30.00	18.00
302	Max Surkont	60.00	30.00	18.00
303	Harry Dorish	60.00	30.00	18.00
304	Sam Dente	60.00	30.00	18.00
305	Paul Richards	60.00	30.00	18.00
306	Lou Sleator	60.00	30.00	18.00
307a	Frank Campos (Black star on back to right of "TOPPS BASEBALL.")		8,000	3,200
307b	Frank Campos (Red star on back to right of "TOPPS BASEBALL.")	60.00	30.00	18.00
308	Luis Aloma	60.00	30.00	18.00
309	Jim Busby	60.00	30.00	18.00
310	George Metkovich	125.00	30.00	18.00
311	Mickey Mantle (DP)	29,500	17,000	8,000
312	Jackie Robinson (DP)	2,200	1,100	550.00
313	Bobby Thomson (DP)	340.00	170.00	85.00
314	Roy Campanella	2,500	1,250	625.00
315	Leo Durocher	600.00	300.00	150.00
316	Davey Williams	400.00	200.00	120.00
317	Connie Marrero	400.00	200.00	120.00
318	Hal Gregg	400.00	200.00	120.00
319	Al Walker	300.00	150.00	90.00
320	John Rutherford	300.00	150.00	90.00
321	*Joe Black*	400.00	200.00	100.00
322	Randy Jackson	400.00	200.00	120.00
323	Bubba Church	400.00	200.00	120.00
324	Warren Hacker	400.00	200.00	120.00
325	Bill Serena	400.00	200.00	120.00
326	George Shuba	400.00	200.00	100.00
327	Archie Wilson	400.00	200.00	120.00
328	Bob Borkowski	400.00	200.00	120.00
329	Ivan Delock	400.00	200.00	120.00
330	Turk Lown	400.00	200.00	120.00
331	Tom Morgan	400.00	200.00	120.00
332	Tony Bartirome	400.00	200.00	120.00
333	Pee Wee Reese	1,800	900.00	450.00
334	Wilmer Mizell	400.00	200.00	120.00
335	Ted Lepcio	400.00	200.00	120.00
336	Dave Koslo	400.00	200.00	120.00
337	Jim Hearn	400.00	200.00	120.00
338	Sal Yvars	400.00	200.00	120.00
339	Russ Meyer	400.00	200.00	120.00
340	Bob Hooper	400.00	200.00	120.00
341	Hal Jeffcoat	400.00	200.00	120.00
342	*Clem Labine*	500.00	250.00	125.00
343	Dick Gernert	400.00	200.00	120.00
344	Ewell Blackwell	400.00	200.00	120.00
345	Sam White	400.00	200.00	120.00
346	George Spencer	400.00	200.00	120.00
347	Joe Adcock	375.00	187.50	100.00
348	Bob Kelly	400.00	200.00	120.00
349	Bob Cain	400.00	200.00	120.00
350	Cal Abrams	400.00	200.00	120.00
351	Al Dark	300.00	150.00	90.00
352	Karl Drews	400.00	200.00	120.00
353	Bob Del Greco	400.00	200.00	120.00
354	Fred Hatfield	400.00	200.00	120.00
355	Bobby Morgan	300.00	150.00	90.00
356	Toby Atwell	400.00	200.00	120.00
357	Smoky Burgess	350.00	175.00	100.00
358	John Kucab	400.00	200.00	120.00
359	Dee Fondy	400.00	200.00	120.00
360	George Crowe	400.00	200.00	120.00
361	Bill Posedel	400.00	200.00	120.00
362	Ken Heintzelman	400.00	200.00	120.00
363	Dick Rozek	400.00	200.00	120.00
364	Clyde Sukeforth	400.00	200.00	120.00
365	"Cookie" Lavagetto	400.00	200.00	120.00
366	Dave Madison	400.00	200.00	120.00
367	Bob Thorpe	400.00	200.00	120.00
368	Ed Wright	400.00	200.00	120.00
369	*Dick Groat*	400.00	200.00	120.00
370	Billy Hoeft	400.00	200.00	120.00

#	Player	NM	EX	VG
371	Bob Hofman	400.00	200.00	120.00
372	*Gil McDougald*	500.00	250.00	150.00
373	Jim Turner	375.00	187.50	100.00
374	Al Benton	400.00	200.00	120.00
375	Jack Merson	400.00	200.00	120.00
376	Faye Throneberry	400.00	200.00	120.00
377	Chuck Dressen	400.00	200.00	120.00
378	Les Fusselman	400.00	200.00	120.00
379	Joe Rossi	400.00	200.00	120.00
380	Clem Koshorek	400.00	200.00	120.00
381	Milton Stock	400.00	200.00	120.00
382	Sam Jones	400.00	200.00	120.00
383	Del Wilber	400.00	200.00	120.00
384	Frank Crosetti	500.00	250.00	125.00
385	Herman Franks	400.00	200.00	120.00
386	Eddie Yuhas	400.00	200.00	120.00
387	Billy Meyer	400.00	200.00	120.00
388	Bob Chipman	400.00	200.00	120.00
389	Ben Wade	300.00	150.00	90.00
390	Glenn Nelson	300.00	150.00	90.00
391	Ben Chapman (Photo actually Sam Chapman.)	400.00	200.00	120.00
392	*Hoyt Wilhelm*	900.00	450.00	225.00
393	Ebba St. Claire	400.00	200.00	120.00
394	Billy Herman	450.00	225.00	120.00
395	Jake Pitler	300.00	150.00	90.00
396	*Dick Williams*	450.00	225.00	120.00
397	Forrest Main	400.00	200.00	120.00
398	Hal Rice	400.00	200.00	120.00
399	Jim Fridley	400.00	200.00	120.00
400	Bill Dickey	1,100	550.00	330.00
401	Bob Schultz	275.00	135.00	80.00
402	Earl Harrist	275.00	135.00	80.00
403	Bill Miller	300.00	150.00	90.00
404	Dick Brodowski	275.00	135.00	80.00
405	Eddie Pellagrini	275.00	135.00	80.00
406	*Joe Nuxhall*	450.00	225.00	120.00
407	*Eddie Mathews*	8,000	3,500	1,525

1952 Topps "Canadian"

Perhaps because the "gray back" 1954 Topps cards have long been known as the "Canadian" issue, there is growing hobby support for the belief that a similar abbreviated set was printed in Canada for distribution there. The cards differ from the regular 1952 Topps of the same numerical range in that they are printed on a gray-backed cardboard stock, distinctly different from the cream-colored stock found on most '52 Topps #131-190. Additionally, the fronts of most, but not all, of the "Canadian" cards have colors which are subjectively darker or more muted than the the "U.S.A." versions. The market is just beginning to differentiate values between the two types, though the gray-backs are considered scarcer.

#	Player	NM	EX	VG
Complete Set (60):		5,000	2,500	1,500
Common Player:		80.00	40.00	24.00
131	Morrie Martin	80.00	40.00	24.00
132	Clyde Kluttz	80.00	40.00	24.00
133	Al Widmar	80.00	40.00	24.00
134	Joe Tipton	80.00	40.00	24.00
135	Dixie Howell	80.00	40.00	24.00
136	Johnny Schmitz	85.00	42.50	25.00
137	Roy McMillan	80.00	40.00	24.00
138	Bill MacDonald	80.00	40.00	24.00
139	Ken Wood	80.00	40.00	24.00
140	John Antonelli	80.00	40.00	24.00
141	Clint Hartung	80.00	40.00	24.00
142	Harry Perkowski	80.00	40.00	24.00
143	Les Moss	80.00	40.00	24.00
144	Ed Blake	80.00	40.00	24.00
145	Joe Haynes	80.00	40.00	24.00
146	Frank House	80.00	40.00	24.00
147	Bob Young	80.00	40.00	24.00
148	Johnny Klippstein	80.00	40.00	24.00
149	Dick Kryhoski	80.00	40.00	24.00
150	Ted Beard	80.00	40.00	24.00
151	Wally Post	80.00	40.00	24.00
152	Al Evans	80.00	40.00	24.00
153	Bob Rush	80.00	40.00	24.00
154	Joe Muir	80.00	40.00	24.00
155	Frank Overmire	85.00	42.50	25.00
156	Frank Hiller	80.00	40.00	24.00
157	Bob Usher	80.00	40.00	24.00
158	Eddie Waitkus	80.00	40.00	24.00
159	Saul Rogovin	80.00	40.00	24.00
160	Owen Friend	80.00	40.00	24.00
161	Bud Byerly	80.00	40.00	24.00
162	Del Crandall	80.00	40.00	24.00
163	Stan Rojek	80.00	40.00	24.00
164	Walt Dubiel	80.00	40.00	24.00
165	Eddie Kazak	80.00	40.00	24.00
166	Paul LaPalme	80.00	40.00	24.00
167	Bill Howerton	80.00	40.00	24.00
168	Charlie Silvera	100.00	50.00	30.00
169	Howie Judson	80.00	40.00	24.00
170	Gus Bell	100.00	50.00	30.00
171	Ed Erautt	80.00	40.00	24.00
172	Eddie Miksis	80.00	40.00	24.00

		NM	EX	VG
173	Roy Smalley	80.00	40.00	24.00
174	Clarence Marshall	80.00	40.00	24.00
175	Billy Martin	500.00	250.00	150.00
176	Hank Edwards	80.00	40.00	24.00
177	Bill Wight	80.00	40.00	24.00
178	Cass Michaels	80.00	40.00	24.00
179	Frank Smith	80.00	40.00	24.00
180	Charley Maxwell	80.00	40.00	24.00
181	Bob Swift	80.00	40.00	24.00
182	Billy Hitchcock	80.00	40.00	24.00
183	Erv Dusak	80.00	40.00	24.00
184	Bob Ramazzotti	80.00	40.00	24.00
185	Bill Nicholson	80.00	40.00	24.00
186	Walt Masterson	80.00	40.00	24.00
187	Bob Miller	80.00	40.00	24.00
188	Clarence Podbielan	80.00	40.00	24.00
189	Pete Reiser	80.00	40.00	24.00
190	Don Johnson	80.00	40.00	24.00

1953 Topps

 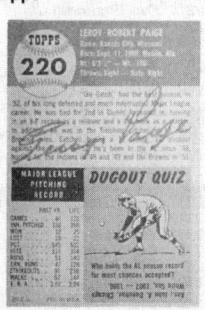

The 1953 Topps set reflects the company's continuing legal battles with Bowman. The set, originally intended to consist of 280 cards, is lacking six numbers (253, 261, 267, 268, 271 and 275) that represent players whose contracts were lost to the competition. The 2-5/8" x 3-3/4" cards feature painted player pictures. A color team logo appears at a bottom panel (red for American League and National). Card backs contain the first baseball-card trivia questions along with brief statistics and player biographies. In the red panel at the top, which lists the player's personal data, cards from the 2nd Series (#86-165 plus 10, 44, 61, 72 and 81) can be found with that data printed in either black or white, black being the marginally scarcer variety. Eighty-five cards between #1-165 were printed in noticeably larger quantities than the others, and are indicated in these listings with a double-print (DP) notation. Cards #221-280, the high numbers, were printed late in the season, in smaller quantities than the earlier series. Among the high numbers, even scarcer short-printed (SP) cards are interspersed in the series.

		NM	EX	VG
Complete Set (274):		30,000	15,000	9,000
Common Player (1-165):		30.00	15.00	9.00
Common Player (166-220):		35.00	17.50	10.00
Common Player (221-280):		60.00	30.00	18.00
Short-print Player (221-280):		90.00	45.00	27.50
1	Jackie Robinson (DP)	1,000	300.00	100.00
2	Luke Easter (DP)	40.00	20.00	12.00
3	George Crowe	40.00	20.00	12.00
4	Ben Wade	45.00	22.50	13.50
5	Joe Dobson	40.00	20.00	12.00
6	Sam Jones	40.00	20.00	12.00
7	Bob Borkowski (DP)	30.00	15.00	9.00
8	Clem Koshorek (DP)	30.00	15.00	9.00
9	Joe Collins	45.00	22.50	13.50
10	Smoky Burgess/SP	70.00	35.00	20.00
11	Sal Yvars	40.00	20.00	12.00
12	Howie Judson (DP)	30.00	15.00	9.00
13	Connie Marrero (DP)	30.00	15.00	9.00
14	Clem Labine (DP)	60.00	30.00	18.00
15	Bobo Newsom (DP)	30.00	15.00	9.00
16	Harry Lowrey (DP)	30.00	15.00	9.00
17	Billy Hitchcock	40.00	20.00	12.00
18	Ted Lepcio (DP)	30.00	15.00	9.00
19	Mel Parnell (DP)	30.00	15.00	9.00
20	Hank Thompson	40.00	20.00	12.00
21	Billy Johnson	40.00	20.00	12.00
22	Howie Fox	40.00	20.00	12.00
23	Toby Atwell (DP)	30.00	15.00	9.00
24	Ferris Fain	40.00	20.00	12.00
25	Ray Boone	40.00	20.00	12.00
26	Dale Mitchell (DP)	30.00	15.00	9.00
27	Roy Campanella (DP)	300.00	150.00	75.00
28	Eddie Pellagrini	40.00	20.00	12.00
29	Hal Jeffcoat	40.00	20.00	12.00
30	Willard Nixon	40.00	20.00	12.00
31	Ewell Blackwell	55.00	27.50	16.50
32	Clyde Vollmer	40.00	20.00	12.00
33	Bob Kennedy (DP)	30.00	15.00	9.00
34	George Shuba	60.00	30.00	18.00
35	Irv Noren (DP)	35.00	17.50	10.00
36	Jim Groth (DP)	30.00	15.00	9.00
37	Ed Mathews (DP)	275.00	187.50	100.00
38	Jim Hearn (DP)	30.00	15.00	9.00
39	Eddie Miksis	40.00	20.00	12.00
40	John Lipon	40.00	20.00	12.00
41	Enos Slaughter	80.00	40.00	24.00
42	Gus Zernial (DP)	30.00	15.00	9.00
43	Gil McDougald	75.00	37.50	22.50
44	Ellis Kinder (SP)	75.00	37.50	22.50
45	Grady Hatton (DP)	30.00	15.00	9.00
46	Johnny Klippstein (DP)	30.00	15.00	9.00
47	Bubba Church (DP)	30.00	15.00	9.00
48	Bob Del Greco (DP)	30.00	15.00	9.00
49	Faye Throneberry (DP)	30.00	15.00	9.00
50	Chuck Dressen (DP)	40.00	20.00	12.00
51	Frank Campos (DP)	30.00	15.00	9.00
52	Ted Gray (DP)	30.00	15.00	9.00
53	Sherman Lollar (DP)	30.00	15.00	9.00
54	Bob Feller (DP)	175.00	87.50	50.00
55	Maurice McDermott (DP)	30.00	15.00	9.00
56	Gerald Staley (DP)	30.00	15.00	9.00
57	Carl Scheib	40.00	20.00	12.00
58	George Metkovich	40.00	20.00	12.00
59	Karl Drews (DP)	30.00	15.00	9.00
60	Cloyd Boyer (DP)	30.00	15.00	9.00
61	Early Wynn (SP)	125.00	62.50	31.25
62	Monte Irvin (DP)	100.00	50.00	30.00
63	Gus Niarhos (DP)	30.00	15.00	9.00
64	Dave Philley	40.00	20.00	12.00
65	Earl Harrist	40.00	20.00	12.00
66	Orestes Minoso	70.00	35.00	20.00
67	Roy Sievers (DP)	30.00	15.00	9.00
68	Del Rice	40.00	20.00	12.00
69	Dick Brodowski	40.00	20.00	12.00
70	Ed Yuhas	40.00	20.00	12.00
71	Tony Bartirome	40.00	20.00	12.00
72	Fred Hutchinson (SP)	75.00	37.50	22.50
73	Eddie Robinson	40.00	20.00	12.00
74	Joe Rossi	40.00	20.00	12.00
75	Mike Garcia	40.00	20.00	12.00
76	Pee Wee Reese	200.00	100.00	60.00
77	Johnny Mize (DP)	75.00	37.50	22.50
78	Al Schoendienst	100.00	50.00	30.00
79	Johnny Wyrostek	40.00	20.00	12.00
80	Jim Hegan	40.00	20.00	12.00
81	Joe Black (SP)	80.00	40.00	20.00
82	Mickey Mantle	3,125	1,600	940.00
83	Howie Pollet	40.00	20.00	12.00
84	Bob Hooper (DP)	30.00	15.00	9.00
85	Bobby Morgan (DP)	35.00	17.50	10.00
86	Billy Martin	175.00	87.50	43.75
87	Ed Lopat	60.00	30.00	18.00
88	Willie Jones (DP)	30.00	15.00	9.00
89	Chuck Stobbs (DP)	30.00	15.00	9.00
90	Hank Edwards (DP)	30.00	15.00	9.00
91	Ebba St. Claire (DP)	30.00	15.00	9.00
92	Paul Minner (DP)	30.00	15.00	9.00
93	Hal Rice (DP)	30.00	15.00	9.00
94	William Kennedy (DP)	30.00	15.00	9.00
95	Willard Marshall (DP)	30.00	15.00	9.00
96	Virgil Trucks	40.00	20.00	12.00
97	Don Kolloway (DP)	30.00	15.00	9.00
98	Cal Abrams (DP)	30.00	15.00	9.00
99	Dave Madison	40.00	20.00	12.00
100	Bill Miller	40.00	20.00	12.00
101	Ted Wilks	40.00	20.00	12.00
102	Connie Ryan (DP)	30.00	15.00	9.00
103	Joe Astroth (DP)	30.00	15.00	9.00
104	Yogi Berra	400.00	200.00	100.00
105	Joe Nuxhall (DP)	35.00	17.50	10.00
106	John Antonelli	40.00	20.00	12.00
107	Danny O'Connell (DP)	30.00	15.00	9.00
108	Bob Porterfield (DP)	30.00	15.00	9.00
109	Alvin Dark	40.00	20.00	12.00
110	Herman Wehmeier (DP)	30.00	15.00	9.00
111	Hank Sauer (DP)	30.00	15.00	9.00
112	Ned Garver (DP)	30.00	15.00	9.00
113	Jerry Priddy	40.00	20.00	12.00
114	Phil Rizzuto	250.00	125.00	62.50
115	George Spencer	40.00	20.00	12.00
116	Frank Smith (DP)	30.00	15.00	9.00
117	Sid Gordon (DP)	30.00	15.00	9.00
118	Gus Bell (DP)	30.00	15.00	9.00
119	John Sain	75.00	37.50	22.50
120	Davey Williams	40.00	20.00	12.00
121	Walt Dropo	40.00	20.00	12.00
122	Elmer Valo	40.00	20.00	12.00
123	Tommy Byrne (DP)	30.00	15.00	9.00
124	Sibby Sisti (DP)	30.00	15.00	9.00
125	Dick Williams	35.00	17.50	10.00
126	Bill Connelly (DP)	30.00	15.00	9.00
127	Clint Courtney (DP)	30.00	15.00	9.00
128	Wilmer Mizell (DP)	30.00	15.00	9.00
129	Keith Thomas	40.00	20.00	12.00
130	Turk Lown (DP)	30.00	15.00	9.00
131	Harry Byrd (DP)	30.00	15.00	9.00
132	Tom Morgan	45.00	22.50	13.50
133	Gil Coan	40.00	20.00	12.00
134	Rube Walker	45.00	22.50	13.50
135	Al Rosen (DP)	45.00	22.50	13.50
136	Ken Heintzelman (DP)	30.00	15.00	9.00
137	John Rutherford (DP)	35.00	17.50	10.00
138	George Kell	55.00	27.50	16.50
139	Sammy White	40.00	20.00	12.00
140	Tommy Glaviano	40.00	20.00	12.00
141	Allie Reynolds (DP)	75.00	37.50	22.50
142	Vic Wertz	40.00	20.00	12.00
143	Billy Pierce	40.00	20.00	12.00
144	Bob Schultz (DP)	30.00	15.00	9.00
145	Harry Dorish (DP)	30.00	15.00	9.00
146	Granville Hamner	40.00	20.00	12.00
147	Warren Spahn	200.00	100.00	50.00
148	Mickey Grasso	40.00	20.00	12.00
149	Dom DiMaggio (DP)	65.00	32.50	20.00
150	Harry Simpson (DP)	30.00	15.00	9.00
151	Hoyt Wilhelm	100.00	50.00	25.00
152	Bob Adams (DP)	30.00	15.00	9.00
153	Andy Seminick (DP)	30.00	15.00	9.00
154	Dick Groat	40.00	20.00	12.00
155	Dutch Leonard	40.00	20.00	12.00
156	Jim Rivera (DP)	30.00	15.00	9.00
157	Bob Addis (DP)	30.00	15.00	9.00
158	John Logan	40.00	20.00	12.00
159	Wayne Terwilliger (DP)	30.00	15.00	9.00
160	Bob Young	40.00	20.00	12.00
161	Vern Bickford (DP)	30.00	15.00	9.00
162	Ted Kluszewski	80.00	40.00	24.00
163	Fred Hatfield (DP)	30.00	15.00	9.00
164	Frank Shea (DP)	30.00	15.00	9.00
165	Billy Hoeft	40.00	20.00	12.00
166	Bill Hunter	35.00	17.50	10.00
167	Art Schult	35.00	17.50	10.00
168	Willard Schmidt	35.00	17.50	10.00
169	Dizzy Trout	35.00	17.50	10.00
170	Bill Werle	35.00	17.50	10.00
171	Bill Glynn	35.00	17.50	10.00
172	Rip Repulski	35.00	17.50	10.00
173	Preston Ward	35.00	17.50	10.00
174	Billy Loes	45.00	22.50	13.50
175	Ron Kline	35.00	17.50	10.00
176	Don Hoak	40.00	20.00	12.00
177	Jim Dyck	35.00	17.50	10.00
178	Jim Waugh	35.00	17.50	10.00
179	Gene Hermanski	35.00	17.50	10.00
180	Virgil Stallcup	35.00	17.50	10.00
181	Al Zarilla	35.00	17.50	10.00
182	Bob Hofman	35.00	17.50	10.00
183	Stu Miller	35.00	17.50	10.00
184	Hal Brown	35.00	17.50	10.00
185	Jim Pendleton	35.00	17.50	10.00
186	Charlie Bishop	35.00	17.50	10.00
187	Jim Fridley	35.00	17.50	10.00
188	Andy Carey	60.00	30.00	18.00
189	Ray Jablonski	35.00	17.50	10.00
190	Dixie Walker	35.00	17.50	10.00
191	Ralph Kiner	75.00	37.50	18.75
192	Wally Westlake	35.00	17.50	10.00
193	Mike Clark	35.00	17.50	10.00
194	Eddie Kazak	35.00	17.50	10.00
195	Ed McGhee	35.00	17.50	10.00
196	Bob Keegan	35.00	17.50	10.00
197	Del Crandall	35.00	17.50	10.00
198	Forrest Main	35.00	17.50	10.00
199	Marion Fricano	35.00	17.50	10.00
200	Gordon Goldsberry	35.00	17.50	10.00
201	Paul La Palme	35.00	17.50	10.00
202	Carl Sawatski	35.00	17.50	10.00
203	Cliff Fannin	35.00	17.50	10.00
204	Dick Bokelman	35.00	17.50	10.00
205	Vern Benson	35.00	17.50	10.00
206	Ed Bailey	35.00	17.50	10.00
207	Whitey Ford	300.00	150.00	75.00
208	Jim Wilson	35.00	17.50	10.00
209	Jim Greengrass	35.00	17.50	10.00
210	Bob Cerv	45.00	22.20	13.50
211	J.W. Porter	35.00	17.50	10.00
212	Jack Dittmer	35.00	17.50	10.00
213	Ray Scarborough	35.00	17.50	10.00
214	Bill Bruton	35.00	17.50	10.00
215	Gene Conley	35.00	17.50	10.00
216	Jim Hughes	40.00	20.00	12.00
217	Murray Wall	35.00	17.50	10.00
218	Les Fusselman	35.00	17.50	10.00
219	Pete Runnels (Picture actually Don Johnson.)	35.00	17.50	10.00
220	Satchell Paige	950.00	470.00	280.00
221	Bob Milliken/SP	100.00	50.00	30.00
222	Vic Janowicz	100.00	50.00	30.00
223	Jim O'Brien	60.00	30.00	18.00
224	Lou Sleater	60.00	30.00	18.00
225	Bobby Shantz/SP	90.00	45.00	27.50
226	Ed Erautt/SP	90.00	45.00	27.50
227	Morris Martin/SP	90.00	45.00	27.50
228	Hal Newhouser/SP	150.00	75.00	37.50
229	Rocky Krsnich/SP	90.00	45.00	27.50
230	Johnny Lindell	60.00	30.00	18.00
231	Solly Hemus	60.00	30.00	18.00
232	Dick Kokos/SP	90.00	45.00	27.50
233	Al Aber/SP	90.00	45.00	27.50
234	Ray Murray	60.00	30.00	18.00
235	John Hetki	60.00	30.00	18.00
236	Harry Perkowski	60.00	30.00	18.00
237	Clarence Podbielan	60.00	30.00	18.00
238	Cal Hogue	60.00	30.00	18.00
239	Jim Delsing/SP	90.00	45.00	27.50
240	Freddie Marsh/SP	90.00	45.00	27.50
241	Al Sima	60.00	30.00	18.00
242	Charlie Silvera/SP	100.00	50.00	30.00
243	Carlos Bernier	60.00	30.00	18.00
244	Willie Mays/SP	2,500	1,000	400.00
245	Bill Norman	90.00	45.00	27.50
246	Roy Face	75.00	37.50	22.50
247	Mike Sandlock	60.00	30.00	18.00
248	Gene Stephens	60.00	30.00	18.00
249	Ed O'Brien/SP	90.00	45.00	27.50
250	Bob Wilson/SP	90.00	45.00	27.50
251	Sid Hudson/SP	90.00	45.00	27.50
252	Henry Foiles/SP	90.00	45.00	27.50
253	Not Issued			
254	Preacher Roe	100.00	50.00	25.00
255	Dixie Howell/SP	100.00	50.00	25.00
256	Les Peden/SP	90.00	45.00	27.50
257	Bob Boyd/SP	90.00	45.00	27.50
258	Jim Gilliam/SP	400.00	200.00	100.00
259	Roy McMillan	60.00	30.00	18.00
260	Sam Calderone/SP	90.00	45.00	27.50
261	Not Issued			
262	Bob Oldis/SP	90.00	45.00	27.50
263	Johnny Podres/SP	300.00	150.00	90.00
264	Gene Woodling	95.00	47.50	27.50
265	Jackie Jensen/SP	125.00	62.50	31.25
266	Bob Cain/SP	90.00	45.00	27.50
267	Not Issued			
268	Not Issued			
269	Duane Pillette/SP	90.00	45.00	27.50
270	Vern Stephens/SP	90.00	45.00	27.50
271	Not Issued			
272	Bill Antonello/SP	100.00	50.00	30.00
273	Harvey Haddix/SP	125.00	62.50	31.25
274	John Riddle/SP	90.00	45.00	27.50
275	Not Issued			
276	Ken Raffensberger/SP	90.00	45.00	27.50
277	Don Lund/SP	90.00	45.00	27.50
278	Willie Miranda/SP	90.00	45.00	27.50
279	Joe Coleman	60.00	30.00	18.00
280	Milt Bolling/SP	400.00		

1954 Topps

The first issue to use two player pictures on the front, the 1954 Topps set remains popular today. Solid color backgrounds frame both color portraits and black-and-white action pictures of the player. The player's name, position, team and team logo appear at the top. Backs include an "Inside Baseball" cartoon regarding the player as well as statistics and biography. The 250-card, 2-5/8" x 3-3/4", set includes manager and coaches cards. A gray-back version of cards #1-50 is known, distinguished by the use of dark gray cardboard on back. These are often attributed to Canadian issue and carry a modest premium.

		NM	EX	VG
Complete Set (250):		11,000	5,500	3,250
Common Player (1-50):		20.00	10.00	6.00
Common Player (51-75):		35.00	17.50	10.00
Common Player (76-250):		20.00	10.00	6.00
1	Ted Williams	900.00	250.00	90.00
2	Gus Zernial	35.00	10.00	6.00
3	Monte Irvin	60.00	30.00	18.00
4	Hank Sauer	20.00	10.00	6.00
5	Ed Lopat	25.00	12.50	7.50
6	Pete Runnels	20.00	10.00	6.00
7	Ted Kluszewski	35.00	17.50	10.00
8	Bobby Young	20.00	10.00	6.00
9	Harvey Haddix	20.00	10.00	6.00
10	Jackie Robinson	300.00	150.00	90.00
11	Paul Smith	20.00	10.00	6.00
12	Del Crandall	20.00	10.00	6.00
13	Billy Martin	100.00	50.00	25.00
14	Preacher Roe	35.00	17.50	10.00
15	Al Rosen	30.00	15.00	9.00
16	Vic Janowicz	25.00	12.50	7.50
17	Phil Rizzuto	125.00	62.50	31.25
18	Walt Dropo	20.00	10.00	6.00
19	Johnny Lipon	20.00	10.00	6.00
20	Warren Spahn	150.00	75.00	37.50
21	Bobby Shantz	20.00	10.00	6.00
22	Jim Greengrass	20.00	10.00	6.00
23	Luke Easter	25.00	12.50	7.50
24	Granny Hamner	20.00	10.00	6.00
25	Harvey Kuenn	35.00	17.50	10.00
26	Ray Jablonski	20.00	10.00	6.00
27	Ferris Fain	20.00	10.00	6.00
28	Paul Minner	20.00	10.00	6.00
29	Jim Hegan	20.00	10.00	6.00
30	Ed Mathews	100.00	50.00	25.00
31	Johnny Klippstein	20.00	10.00	6.00
32	Duke Snider	200.00	100.00	50.00
33	Johnny Schmitz	20.00	10.00	6.00
34	Jim Rivera	20.00	10.00	6.00
35	Junior Gilliam	35.00	17.50	10.00
36	Hoyt Wilhelm	40.00	20.00	12.00
37	Whitey Ford	200.00	100.00	50.00
38	Eddie Stanky	20.00	10.00	6.00
39	Sherm Lollar	20.00	10.00	6.00
40	Mel Parnell	20.00	10.00	6.00
41	Willie Jones	20.00	10.00	6.00
42	Don Mueller	20.00	10.00	6.00
43	Dick Groat	20.00	10.00	6.00
44	Ned Garver	20.00	10.00	6.00
45	Richie Ashburn	80.00	40.00	20.00
46	Ken Raffensberger	20.00	10.00	6.00
47	Ellis Kinder	20.00	10.00	6.00
48	Billy Hunter	20.00	10.00	6.00
49	Ray Murray	20.00	10.00	6.00
50	Yogi Berra	300.00	150.00	75.00
51	Johnny Lindell	35.00	17.50	10.00
52	Vic Power	40.00	20.00	12.00
53	Jack Dittmer	35.00	17.50	10.00
54	Vern Stephens	35.00	17.50	10.00
55	Phil Cavarretta	35.00	17.50	10.00
56	Willie Miranda	35.00	17.50	10.00
57	Luis Aloma	35.00	17.50	10.00
58	Bob Wilson	35.00	17.50	10.00
59	Gene Conley	35.00	17.50	10.00
60	Frank Baumholtz	35.00	17.50	10.00
61	Bob Cain	35.00	17.50	10.00
62	Eddie Robinson	40.00	20.00	12.00
63	Johnny Pesky	35.00	17.50	10.00
64	Hank Thompson	35.00	17.50	10.00
65	Bob Swift	35.00	17.50	10.00
66	Ted Lepcio	35.00	17.50	10.00
67	Jim Willis	35.00	17.50	10.00
68	Sammy Calderone	35.00	17.50	10.00
69	Bud Podbielan	35.00	17.50	10.00
70	Larry Doby	75.00	37.50	18.75
71	Frank Smith	35.00	17.50	10.00
72	Preston Ward	35.00	17.50	10.00
73	Wayne Terwilliger	35.00	17.50	10.00
74	Bill Taylor	35.00	17.50	10.00
75	Fred Haney	35.00	17.50	10.00
76	Bob Scheffing	20.00	10.00	6.00
77	Ray Boone	20.00	10.00	6.00
78	Ted Kazanski	20.00	10.00	6.00
79	Andy Pafko	20.00	10.00	6.00
80	Jackie Jensen	30.00	15.00	9.00
81	Dave Hoskins	20.00	10.00	6.00
82	Milt Bolling	20.00	10.00	6.00
83	Joe Collins	25.00	12.50	7.50
84	Dick Cole	20.00	10.00	6.00
85	Bob Turley	35.00	17.50	10.00
86	Billy Herman	45.00	22.50	13.50
87	Roy Face	20.00	10.00	6.00
88	Matt Batts	20.00	10.00	6.00
89	Howie Pollet	20.00	10.00	6.00
90	Willie Mays	500.00	250.00	150.00
91	Bob Oldis	20.00	10.00	6.00
92	Wally Westlake	20.00	10.00	6.00
93	Sid Hudson	20.00	10.00	6.00
94	Ernie Banks	1,150	575.00	345.00
95	Hal Rice	20.00	10.00	6.00
96	Charlie Silvera	25.00	12.50	7.50
97	Jerry Lane	20.00	10.00	6.00
98	Joe Black	60.00	30.00	20.00
99	Bob Hofman	20.00	10.00	6.00
100	Bob Keegan	20.00	10.00	6.00
101	Gene Woodling	50.00	25.00	15.00
102	Gil Hodges	90.00	45.00	22.50
103	Jim Lemon	25.00	12.50	7.50
104	Mike Sandlock	20.00	10.00	6.00
105	Andy Carey	25.00	12.50	7.50
106	Dick Kokos	20.00	10.00	6.00
107	Duane Pillette	20.00	10.00	6.00
108	Thornton Kipper	20.00	10.00	6.00
109	Bill Bruton	20.00	10.00	6.00
110	Harry Dorish	20.00	10.00	6.00
111	Jim Delsing	20.00	10.00	6.00
112	Bill Renna	20.00	10.00	6.00
113	Bob Boyd	20.00	10.00	6.00
114	Dean Stone	20.00	10.00	6.00
115	"Rip" Repulski	20.00	10.00	6.00
116	Steve Bilko	20.00	10.00	6.00
117	Solly Hemus	20.00	10.00	6.00
118	Carl Scheib	20.00	10.00	6.00
119	Johnny Antonelli	20.00	10.00	6.00
120	Roy McMillan	20.00	10.00	6.00
121	Clem Labine	45.00	22.50	13.50
122	Johnny Logan	20.00	10.00	6.00
123	Bobby Adams	20.00	10.00	6.00
124	Marion Fricano	20.00	10.00	6.00
125	Harry Perkowski	20.00	10.00	6.00
126	Ben Wade	25.00	12.50	7.50
127	Steve O'Neill	20.00	10.00	6.00
128	Hank Aaron	1,875	940.00	560.00
129	Forrest Jacobs	20.00	10.00	6.00
130	Hank Bauer	40.00	20.00	10.00
131	Reno Bertoia	20.00	10.00	6.00
132	Tom Lasorda	250.00	125.00	62.50
133	Del Baker	20.00	10.00	6.00
134	Cal Hogue	20.00	10.00	6.00
135	Joe Presko	20.00	10.00	6.00
136	Connie Ryan	20.00	10.00	6.00
137	Wally Moon	35.00	17.50	10.00
138	Bob Borkowski	20.00	10.00	6.00
139	Ed O'Brien, Johnny O'Brien	60.00	30.00	15.00
140	Tom Wright	20.00	10.00	6.00
141	Joe Jay	40.00	20.00	12.00
142	Tom Poholsky	20.00	10.00	6.00
143	Rollie Hemsley	20.00	10.00	6.00
144	Bill Werle	20.00	10.00	6.00
145	Elmer Valo	20.00	10.00	6.00
146	Don Johnson	20.00	10.00	6.00
147	John Riddle	20.00	10.00	6.00
148	Bob Trice	20.00	10.00	6.00
149	Jim Robertson	20.00	10.00	6.00
150	Dick Kryhoski	20.00	10.00	6.00
151	Alex Grammas	20.00	10.00	6.00
152	Mike Blyzka	20.00	10.00	6.00
153	Rube Walker	25.00	12.50	7.50
154	Mike Fornieles	20.00	10.00	6.00
155	Bob Kennedy	25.00	12.50	7.50
156	Joe Coleman	20.00	10.00	6.00
157	Don Lenhardt	20.00	10.00	6.00
158	"Peanuts" Lowrey	20.00	10.00	6.00
159	Dave Philley	20.00	10.00	6.00
160	"Red" Kress	20.00	10.00	6.00
161	John Hetki	20.00	10.00	6.00
162	Herman Wehmeier	20.00	10.00	6.00
163	Frank House	20.00	10.00	6.00
164	Stu Miller	20.00	10.00	6.00
165	Jim Pendleton	20.00	10.00	6.00
166	Johnny Podres	45.00	22.50	13.50
167	Don Lund	20.00	10.00	6.00
168	Morrie Martin	20.00	10.00	6.00
169	Jim Hughes	25.00	12.50	7.50
170	Jim Rhodes	40.00	20.00	12.00
171	Leo Kiely	20.00	10.00	6.00
172	Hal Brown	20.00	10.00	6.00
173	Jack Harshman	20.00	10.00	6.00
174	Tom Qualters	20.00	10.00	6.00
175	Frank Leja	25.00	12.50	7.50
176	Bob Keely	20.00	10.00	6.00
177	Bob Milliken	25.00	12.50	7.50
178	Bill Gynn (Glynn)	20.00	10.00	6.00
179	Gair Allie	20.00	10.00	6.00
180	Wes Westrum	20.00	10.00	6.00
181	Mel Roach	20.00	10.00	6.00
182	Chuck Harmon	20.00	10.00	6.00
183	Earle Combs	25.00	12.50	7.50
184	Ed Bailey	20.00	10.00	6.00
185	Chuck Stobbs	20.00	10.00	6.00
186	Karl Olson	20.00	10.00	6.00
187	"Heinie" Manush	25.00	12.50	7.50
188	Dave Jolly	20.00	10.00	6.00
189	Bob Ross	20.00	10.00	6.00
190	Ray Herbert	20.00	10.00	6.00
191	Dick Schofield	25.00	12.50	7.50
192	"Cot" Deal	20.00	10.00	6.00
193	Johnny Hopp	20.00	10.00	6.00
194	Bill Sarni	20.00	10.00	6.00
195	Bill Consolo	20.00	10.00	6.00
196	Stan Jok	20.00	10.00	6.00
197	"Schoolboy" Rowe	20.00	10.00	6.00
198	Carl Sawatski	20.00	10.00	6.00
199	"Rocky" Nelson	20.00	10.00	6.00
200	Larry Jansen	20.00	10.00	6.00
201	Al Kaline	700.00	350.00	175.00
202	Bob Purkey	20.00	10.00	6.00
203	Harry Brecheen	20.00	10.00	6.00
204	Angel Scull	20.00	10.00	6.00
205	Johnny Sain	30.00	15.00	9.00
206	Ray Crone	20.00	10.00	6.00
207	Tom Oliver	20.00	10.00	6.00
208	Grady Hatton	20.00	10.00	6.00
209	Charlie Thompson	25.00	12.50	7.50
210	Bob Buhl	25.00	12.50	7.50
211	Don Hoak	25.00	12.50	7.50
212	Mickey Micelotta	20.00	10.00	6.00
213	John Fitzpatrick	20.00	10.00	6.00
214	Arnold Portocarrero	20.00	10.00	6.00
215	Ed McGhee	20.00	10.00	6.00
216	Al Sima	20.00	10.00	6.00
217	Paul Schreiber	20.00	10.00	6.00
218	Fred Marsh	20.00	10.00	6.00
219	Charlie Kress	20.00	10.00	6.00
220	Ruben Gomez	20.00	10.00	6.00
221	Dick Brodowski	20.00	10.00	6.00
222	Bill Wilson	20.00	10.00	6.00
223	Joe Haynes	20.00	10.00	6.00
224	Dick Weik	20.00	10.00	6.00
225	Don Liddle	20.00	10.00	6.00
226	Jehosie Heard	20.00	10.00	6.00
227	Buster Mills	20.00	10.00	6.00
228	Gene Hermanski	20.00	10.00	6.00
229	Bob Talbot	20.00	10.00	6.00
230	Bob Kuzava	25.00	12.50	7.50
231	Roy Smalley	20.00	10.00	6.00
232	Lou Limmer	20.00	10.00	6.00
233	Augie Galan	20.00	10.00	6.00
234	Jerry Lynch	20.00	10.00	6.00
235	Vern Law	20.00	10.00	6.00
236	Paul Penson	20.00	10.00	6.00
237	Mike Ryba	20.00	10.00	6.00
238	Al Aber	20.00	10.00	6.00
239	Bill Skowron	90.00	45.00	22.50
240	Sam Mele	20.00	10.00	6.00
241	Bob Miller	20.00	10.00	6.00
242	Curt Roberts	20.00	10.00	6.00
243	Ray Blades	20.00	10.00	6.00
244	Leroy Wheat	20.00	10.00	6.00
245	Roy Sievers	20.00	10.00	6.00
246	Howie Fox	20.00	10.00	6.00
247	Eddie Mayo	20.00	10.00	6.00
248	Al Smith	20.00	10.00	6.00
249	Wilmer Mizell	20.00	10.00	6.00
250	Ted Williams	850.00	190.00	95.00

1954 Topps "Canadian"

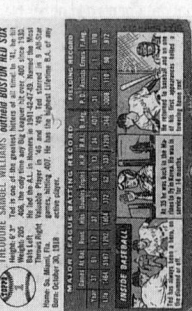

This version of the first 50 cards from 1954 Topps has long been known as the "Canadian" issue. It is widely believed that the abbreviated set was intended solely for Canadian distribution. The cards differ from the regular 1954 Topps in that they are printed on a gray-backed cardboard stock, distinctly different from the white stock found on most '54 Topps. Later series white-back Topps cards were sold in Canada in O-Pee-Chee marked wrappers at four for a nickel as opposed to six for five cents in the U.S.

		NM	EX	VG
Complete Set (50):		5,500	2,750	1,750
Common Player:		40.00	20.00	12.00
1	Ted Williams	1,500	700.00	450.00
2	Gus Zernial	60.00	20.00	12.00
3	Monte Irvin	115.00	55.00	35.00
4	Hank Sauer	40.00	20.00	12.00
5	Ed Lopat	50.00	25.00	15.00
6	Pete Runnels	40.00	20.00	12.00
7	Ted Kluszewski	75.00	35.00	22.50
8	Bobby Young	40.00	20.00	12.00
9	Harvey Haddix	40.00	20.00	12.00
10	Jackie Robinson	525.00	250.00	150.00
11	Paul Smith	40.00	20.00	12.00
12	Del Crandall	40.00	20.00	12.00
13	Billy Martin	225.00	100.00	65.00
14	Preacher Roe	75.00	35.00	22.50
15	Al Rosen	85.00	40.00	25.00
16	Vic Janowicz	45.00	22.00	13.50
17	Phil Rizzuto	225.00	110.00	65.00
18	Walt Dropo	40.00	20.00	12.00
19	Johnny Lipon	40.00	20.00	12.00
20	Warren Spahn	215.00	100.00	60.00
21	Bobby Shantz	45.00	22.50	13.50
22	Jim Greengrass	40.00	20.00	12.00
23	Luke Easter	40.00	20.00	12.00
24	Granny Hamner	40.00	20.00	12.00
25	Harvey Kuenn	75.00	35.00	22.50
26	Ray Jablonski	40.00	20.00	12.00
27	Ferris Fain	40.00	20.00	12.00
28	Paul Minner	40.00	20.00	12.00
29	Jim Hegan	40.00	20.00	12.00
30	Ed Mathews	165.00	80.00	47.50
31	Johnny Klippstein	40.00	20.00	12.00

		NM	EX	VG
32	Duke Snider	315.00	150.00	90.00
33	Johnny Schmitz	40.00	20.00	12.00
34	Jim Rivera	40.00	20.00	12.00
35	Junior Gilliam	85.00	40.00	25.00
36	Hoyt Wilhelm	115.00	55.00	32.50
37	Whitey Ford	215.00	100.00	60.00
38	Eddie Stanky	45.00	22.50	13.50
39	Sherm Lollar	40.00	20.00	12.00
40	Mel Parnell	40.00	20.00	12.00
41	Willie Jones	40.00	20.00	12.00
42	Don Mueller	40.00	20.00	12.00
43	Dick Groat	40.00	20.00	12.00
44	Ned Garver	40.00	20.00	12.00
45	Richie Ashburn	140.00	70.00	40.00
46	Ken Raffensberger	40.00	20.00	12.00
47	Ellis Kinder	40.00	20.00	12.00
48	Billy Hunter	40.00	20.00	12.00
49	Ray Murray	40.00	20.00	12.00
50	Yogi Berra	365.00	175.00	100.00

1954 Topps Look 'N See

Among the 135 historical figures in this set is only one baseball player - Babe Ruth. These 2-1/16" x 2-15/16" cards feature colorful portrait paintings on the front and biographies on the back. The answer to a trivia question on back can be discovered by laying a piece of red cellophane over the question box.

		NM	EX	VG
Complete Set (135):		3,000	1,500	900.00
Common Card:		4.00	2.00	1.25
15	Babe Ruth	150.00	75.00	45.00

1954 Topps Scoops

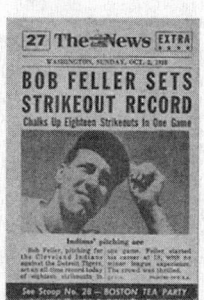

World - and sports - history from the mid-18th Century through October 1953, is chronicled in this 156-card set. Four baseball subjects are presented in the set. Cards are 2-1/16" x 2-15/16" and feature on the front a color painting with a dated caption box at bottom. Originally a black scratch-off ink covered the caption box (cards with the black ink removed can still be considered Mint as those with the ink currently command little premium value). Backs feature a simulated newspaper front page with banner headline and picture, along with a description of the event.

		NM	EX	VG
Complete Set (156):		3,500	1,750	1,050
Common Card:		6.00	3.00	1.75
27	Bob Feller Strikeout King, Oct. 2, 1938 (Bob Feller)	60.00	30.00	18.00
41	Babe Ruth Sets Record, Sept. 30, 1927 (Babe Ruth)	250.00	125.00	75.00
130	Braves Go to Milwaukee	40.00	20.00	12.00
154	26-Inning Tie Game May 1, 1920	60.00	30.00	18.00

1955 Topps

The 1955 Topps set is numerically the smallest of the regular annual issues. The 3-3/4" x 2-5/8" cards mark the first time that Topps used a horizontal format for the entire set. While that format was new, the design was not; they are very similar to the 1954 cards to the point many pictures appeared in both years. Although it was slated for a 210-card set, the 1955 Topps set turned out to be only 206 cards with numbers 175, 186, 203 and 209 never being released. The scarce high numbers in this set begin with #161.

		NM	EX	VG
Complete Set (206):		8,000	3,750	2,250
Common Player (1-150):		20.00	10.00	6.00
Common Player (151-160):		25.00	12.50	7.50
Common Player (161-210):		45.00	22.50	13.50
1	"Dusty" Rhodes	125.00	62.50	31.25
2	Ted Williams	500.00	250.00	150.00
3	Art Fowler	20.00	10.00	6.00
4	Al Kaline	150.00	75.00	45.00
5	Jim Gilliam	60.00	30.00	15.00
6	Stan Hack	25.00	12.50	7.50
7	Jim Hegan	20.00	10.00	6.00
8	Hal Smith	20.00	10.00	6.00
9	Bob Miller	20.00	10.00	6.00
10	Bob Keegan	20.00	10.00	6.00
11	Ferris Fain	20.00	10.00	6.00
12	"Jake" Thies	20.00	10.00	6.00
13	Fred Marsh	20.00	10.00	6.00
14	Jim Finigan	20.00	10.00	6.00
15	Jim Pendleton	20.00	10.00	6.00
16	Roy Sievers	20.00	10.00	6.00
17	Bobby Hofman	20.00	10.00	6.00
18	Russ Kemmerer	20.00	10.00	6.00
19	Billy Herman	40.00	20.00	10.00
20	Andy Carey	25.00	12.50	7.50
21	Alex Grammas	20.00	10.00	6.00
22	Bill Skowron	35.00	17.50	10.00
23	Jack Parks	20.00	10.00	6.00
24	Hal Newhouser	40.00	20.00	10.00
25	Johnny Podres	40.00	20.00	10.00
26	Dick Groat	20.00	10.00	6.00
27	Billy Gardner	20.00	10.00	6.00
28	Ernie Banks	250.00	125.00	62.50
29	Herman Wehmeier	20.00	10.00	6.00
30	Vic Power	20.00	10.00	6.00
31	Warren Spahn	150.00	75.00	37.50
32	Ed McGhee	20.00	10.00	6.00
33	Tom Qualters	20.00	10.00	6.00
34	Wayne Terwilliger	20.00	10.00	6.00
35	Dave Jolly	20.00	10.00	6.00
36	Leo Kiely	20.00	10.00	6.00
37	Joe Cunningham	20.00	10.00	6.00
38	Bob Turley	27.50	13.50	8.25
39	Bill Glynn	20.00	10.00	6.00
40	Don Hoak	25.00	12.50	7.50
41	Chuck Stobbs	20.00	10.00	6.00
42	"Windy" McCall	20.00	10.00	6.00
43	Harvey Haddix	20.00	10.00	6.00
44	"Corky" Valentine	20.00	10.00	6.00
45	Hank Sauer	20.00	10.00	6.00
46	Ted Kazanski	20.00	10.00	6.00
47	Hank Aaron	325.00	160.00	97.00
48	Bob Kennedy	20.00	10.00	6.00
49	J.W. Porter	20.00	10.00	6.00
50	Jackie Robinson	400.00	200.00	120.00
51	Jim Hughes	25.00	12.50	7.50
52	Bill Tremel	20.00	10.00	6.00
53	Bill Taylor	20.00	10.00	6.00
54	Lou Limmer	20.00	10.00	6.00
55	"Rip" Repulski	20.00	10.00	6.00
56	Ray Jablonski	20.00	10.00	6.00
57	Billy O'Dell	20.00	10.00	6.00
58	Jim Rivera	20.00	10.00	6.00
59	Gair Allie	20.00	10.00	6.00
60	Dean Stone	20.00	10.00	6.00
61	"Spook" Jacobs	20.00	10.00	6.00
62	Thornton Kipper	20.00	10.00	6.00
63	Joe Collins	25.00	12.50	7.50
64	Gus Triandos	25.00	12.50	7.50
65	Ray Boone	20.00	10.00	6.00
66	Ron Jackson	20.00	10.00	6.00
67	Wally Moon	20.00	10.00	6.00
68	Jim Davis	20.00	10.00	6.00
69	Ed Bailey	20.00	10.00	6.00
70	Al Rosen	40.00	20.00	12.00
71	Ruben Gomez	20.00	10.00	6.00
72	Karl Olson	20.00	10.00	6.00
73	Jack Shepard	20.00	10.00	6.00
74	Bob Borkowski	20.00	10.00	6.00
75	Sandy Amoros	50.00	25.00	12.50
76	Howie Pollet	20.00	10.00	6.00
77	Arnold Portocarrero	20.00	10.00	6.00
78	Gordon Jones	20.00	10.00	6.00
79	Danny Schell	20.00	10.00	6.00
80	Bob Grim	25.00	12.50	7.50
81	Gene Conley	20.00	10.00	6.00
82	Chuck Harmon	20.00	10.00	6.00
83	Tom Brewer	20.00	10.00	6.00
84	Camilo Pascual	35.00	17.50	10.00
85	Don Mossi	35.00	17.50	10.00
86	Bill Wilson	20.00	10.00	6.00
87	Frank House	20.00	10.00	6.00
88	Bob Skinner	20.00	10.00	6.00
89	Joe Frazier	20.00	10.00	6.00
90	Karl Spooner	25.00	12.50	7.50
91	Milt Bolling	20.00	10.00	6.00
92	Don Zimmer	50.00	25.00	12.50
93	Steve Bilko	20.00	10.00	6.00
94	Reno Bertoia	20.00	10.00	6.00
95	Preston Ward	20.00	10.00	6.00
96	Charlie Bishop	20.00	10.00	6.00
97	Carlos Paula	20.00	10.00	6.00
98	Johnny Riddle	20.00	10.00	6.00
99	Frank Leja	25.00	12.50	7.50
100	Monte Irvin	40.00	20.00	12.00
101	Johnny Gray	20.00	10.00	6.00
102	Wally Westlake	20.00	10.00	6.00
103	Charlie White	20.00	10.00	6.00
104	Jack Harshman	20.00	10.00	6.00
105	Chuck Diering	20.00	10.00	6.00
106	Frank Sullivan (Several variations exist in the size, shape and density of the dot over the "i" in the facsimile autograph.)	20.00	10.00	6.00
107	Curt Roberts	20.00	10.00	6.00
108	"Rube" Walker	25.00	12.50	7.50
109	Ed Lopat	30.00	15.00	9.00
110	Gus Zernial	20.00	10.00	6.00
111	Bob Milliken	25.00	12.50	7.50
112	Nelson King	20.00	10.00	6.00
113	Harry Brecheen	20.00	10.00	6.00
114	Lou Ortiz	20.00	10.00	6.00
115	Ellis Kinder	20.00	10.00	6.00
116	Tom Hurd	20.00	10.00	6.00
117	Mel Roach	20.00	10.00	6.00
118	Bob Purkey	20.00	10.00	6.00
119	Bob Lennon	20.00	10.00	6.00
120	Ted Kluszewski	45.00	22.50	13.50
121	Bill Renna	20.00	10.00	6.00
122	Carl Sawatski	20.00	10.00	6.00
123	"Sandy" Koufax	875.00	440.00	260.00
124	Harmon Killebrew	300.00	150.00	90.00
125	Ken Boyer	80.00	40.00	24.00
126	Dick Hall	20.00	10.00	6.00
127	Dale Long	20.00	10.00	6.00
128	Ted Lepcio	20.00	10.00	6.00
129	Elvin Tappe	20.00	10.00	6.00
130	Mayo Smith	20.00	10.00	6.00
131	Grady Hatton	20.00	10.00	6.00
132	Bob Trice	20.00	10.00	6.00
133	Dave Hoskins	20.00	10.00	6.00
134	Joe Jay	20.00	10.00	6.00
135	Johnny O'Brien	20.00	10.00	6.00
136	"Bunky" Stewart	20.00	10.00	6.00
137a	Harry Elliott (Last line in bio is, "the Cards in '53.")	20.00	10.00	6.00
137b	Harry Elliott (Last line in bio ends, "the Cards in (crescent mark).")	20.00	10.00	6.00
137c	Harry Elliott (Last line in bio ends, "the Cards in.")	20.00	10.00	6.00
138	Ray Herbert	20.00	10.00	6.00
139	Steve Kraly	25.00	12.50	7.50
140	Mel Parnell	20.00	10.00	6.00
141	Tom Wright	20.00	10.00	6.00
142	Jerry Lynch	20.00	10.00	6.00
143	Dick Schofield	20.00	10.00	6.00
144	Joe Amalfitano	20.00	10.00	6.00
145	Elmer Valo	20.00	10.00	6.00
146	Dick Donovan	20.00	10.00	6.00
147	Laurin Pepper	20.00	10.00	6.00
148	Hal Brown	20.00	10.00	6.00
149	Ray Crone	20.00	10.00	6.00
150	Mike Higgins	20.00	10.00	6.00
151	"Red" Kress	25.00	12.50	7.50
152	Harry Agganis	100.00	50.00	25.00
153	"Bud" Podbielan	25.00	12.50	7.50
154	Willie Miranda	25.00	12.50	7.50
155	Ed Mathews	200.00	100.00	50.00
156	Joe Black	60.00	30.00	18.00
157	Bob Miller	25.00	12.50	7.50
158	Tom Carroll	35.00	17.50	10.50
159	Johnny Schmitz	25.00	12.50	7.50
160	Ray Narleski	25.00	12.50	7.50
161	Chuck Tanner	50.00	25.00	15.00
162	Joe Coleman	45.00	22.50	13.50
163	Faye Throneberry	45.00	22.50	13.50
164	Roberto Clemente	2,250	1,125	675.00
165	Don Johnson	45.00	22.50	13.50
166	Hank Bauer	75.00	37.50	18.75
167	Tom Casagrande	45.00	22.50	13.50
168	Duane Pillette	45.00	22.50	13.50
169	Bob Oldis	45.00	22.50	13.50
170	Jim Pearce	45.00	22.50	13.50
171	Dick Brodowski	45.00	22.50	13.50
172	Frank Baumholtz	45.00	22.50	13.50
173	Bob Kline	45.00	22.50	13.50
174	Rudy Minarcin	45.00	22.50	13.50
175	Not Issued			
176	Norm Zauchin	45.00	22.50	13.50
177	Jim Robertson	45.00	22.50	13.50
178	Bobby Adams	45.00	22.50	13.50
179	Jim Bolger	45.00	22.50	13.50
180	Clem Labine	60.00	30.00	18.00
181	Roy McMillan	45.00	22.50	13.50
182	Humberto Robinson	45.00	22.50	13.50
183	Tony Jacobs	45.00	22.50	13.50
184	Harry Perkowski	45.00	22.50	13.50
185	Don Ferrarese	45.00	22.50	13.50
186	Not Issued			
187	Gil Hodges	175.00	87.50	43.75
188	Charlie Silvera	50.00	25.00	15.00
189	Phil Rizzuto	175.00	87.50	43.75
190	Gene Woodling	40.00	20.00	10.00
191	Ed Stanky	45.00	22.50	13.50
192	Jim Delsing	45.00	22.50	13.50
193	Johnny Sain	50.00	25.00	12.50
194	Willie Mays	600.00	300.00	150.00
195	Ed Roebuck	50.00	25.00	15.00
196	Gale Wade	45.00	22.50	13.50
197	Al Smith	45.00	22.50	13.50
198	Yogi Berra	300.00	150.00	75.00
199	Bert Hamric	50.00	25.00	15.00
200	Jack Jensen	60.00	30.00	18.00
201	Sherm Lollar	45.00	22.50	13.50
202	Jim Owens	45.00	22.50	13.50
203	Not Issued			
204	Frank Smith	45.00	22.50	13.50
205	Gene Freese	45.00	22.50	13.50
206	Pete Daley	45.00	22.50	13.50
207	Bill Consolo	45.00	22.50	13.50
208	Ray Moore	45.00	22.50	13.50
209	Not Issued			
210	Duke Snider	600.00	130.00	80.00

1955 Topps Doubleheaders

This set is a throwback to the 1911 T201 Mecca Double Folders. The cards are perforated through the middle, allowing them to be folded. Open, there is a color painting of a player set against a stadium background. When folded, a different player and stadium appears; both players share the same lower legs and feet. Backs have abbreviated career histories and stats. Placed side by side in reverse numerical order, the backgrounds form a continuous stadium scene. When open the cards measure 2-1/16" x 4-7/8". The 66 cards in the set mean 132 total players, all of whom also appeared in the lower numbers of the regular 1955 Topps set.

	NM	EX	VG
Complete Set (66):	4,000	2,000	1,200
Common Card:	45.00	22.50	13.50
Wax Pack:	240.00	.00	.00
1-2 Al Rosen, Chuck Diering	60.00	25.00	15.00
3-4 Monte Irvin, Russ Kemmerer	60.00	30.00	18.00
5-6 Ted Kazanski, Gordon Jones	45.00	22.50	13.50
7-8 Bill Taylor, Billy O'Dell	45.00	22.50	13.50
9-10 J.W. Porter, Thornton Kipper	45.00	22.50	13.50
11-12 Curt Roberts, Arnie Portocarrero	45.00	22.50	13.50
13-14 Wally Westlake, Frank House	45.00	22.50	13.50
15-16 Rube Walker, Lou Limmer	45.00	22.50	13.50
17-18 Dean Stone, Charlie White	45.00	22.50	13.50
19-20 Karl Spooner, Jim Hughes	50.00	25.00	15.00
21-22 Bill Skowron, Frank Sullivan	60.00	30.00	18.00
23-24 Jack Shepard, Stan Hack	45.00	22.50	13.50
25-26 Jackie Robinson, Don Hoak	325.00	160.00	100.00
27-28 Dusty Rhodes, Jim Davis	45.00	22.50	13.50
29-30 Vic Power, Ed Bailey	45.00	22.50	13.50
31-32 Howie Pollet, Ernie Banks	200.00	100.00	60.00
33-34 Jim Pendleton, Gene Conley	45.00	22.50	13.50
35-36 Karl Olson, Andy Carey	45.00	22.50	13.50
37-38 Wally Moon, Joe Cunningham	45.00	22.50	13.50
39-40 Fred Marsh, "Jake" Thies	45.00	22.50	13.50
41-42 Ed Lopat, Harvey Haddix	45.00	22.50	13.50
43-44 Leo Kiely, Chuck Stobbs	45.00	22.50	13.50
45-46 Al Kaline, "Corky" Valentine	225.00	110.00	65.00
47-48 "Spook" Jacobs, Johnny Gray	45.00	22.50	13.50
49-50 Ron Jackson, Jim Finigan	45.00	22.50	13.50
51-52 Ray Jablonski, Bob Keegan	45.00	22.50	13.50
53-54 Billy Herman, Sandy Amoros	60.00	30.00	18.00
55-56 Chuck Harmon, Bob Skinner	45.00	22.50	13.50
57-58 Dick Hall, Bob Grim	45.00	22.50	13.50
59-60 Bill Glynn, Bob Miller	45.00	22.50	13.50
61-62 Billy Gardner, John Hetki	45.00	22.50	13.50
63-64 Bob Borkowski, Bob Turley	45.00	22.50	13.50
65-66 Joe Collins, Jack Harshman	45.00	22.50	13.50
67-68 Jim Hegan, Jack Parks	45.00	22.50	13.50
69-70 Ted Williams, Hal Smith	425.00	210.00	125.00
71-72 Gair Allie, Grady Hatton	45.00	22.50	13.50
73-74 Jerry Lynch, Harry Brecheen	45.00	22.50	13.50
75-76 Tom Wright, "Bunky" Stewart	45.00	22.50	13.50
77-78 Dave Hoskins, Ed McGhee	45.00	22.50	13.50
79-80 Roy Sievers, Art Fowler	45.00	22.50	13.50
81-82 Danny Schell, Gus Triandos	45.00	22.50	13.50
83-84 Joe Frazier, Don Mossi	45.00	22.50	13.50
85-86 Elmer Valo, Hal Brown	45.00	22.50	13.50
87-88 Bob Kennedy, "Windy" McCall	45.00	22.50	13.50
89-90 Ruben Gomez, Jim Rivera	45.00	22.50	13.50
91-92 Lou Ortiz, Milt Bolling	45.00	22.50	13.50
93-94 Carl Sawatski, Elvin Tappe	45.00	22.50	13.50
95-96 Dave Jolly, Bobby Hofman	45.00	22.50	13.50
97-98 Preston Ward, Don Zimmer	45.00	22.50	13.50
99-100 Bill Renna, Dick Groat	45.00	22.50	13.50
101-102 Bill Wilson, Bill Tremel	45.00	22.50	13.50
103-104 Hank Sauer, Camilo Pascual	45.00	22.50	13.50
105-106 Hank Aaron, Ray Herbert	400.00	200.00	120.00
107-108 Alex Grammas, Tom Qualters	45.00	22.50	13.50
109-110 Hal Newhouser, Charlie Bishop	60.00	30.00	18.00
111-112 Harmon Killebrew, John Podres	225.00	110.00	65.00
113-114 Ray Boone, Bob Purkey	45.00	22.50	13.50
115-116 Dale Long, Ferris Fain	45.00	22.50	13.50
117-118 Steve Bilko, Bob Milliken	45.00	22.50	13.50
119-120 Mel Parnell, Tom Hurd	45.00	22.50	13.50
121-122 Ted Kluszewski, Jim Owens	60.00	30.00	18.00
123-124 Gus Zernial, Bob Trice	45.00	22.50	13.50
125-126 "Rip" Repulski, Ted Lepcio	45.00	22.50	13.50
127-128 Warren Spahn, Tom Brewer	150.00	75.00	45.00
129-130 Jim Gilliam, Ellis Kinder	60.00	30.00	18.00
131-132 Herm Wehmeier, Wayne Terwilliger	45.00	22.50	13.50

1955 Topps Hocus Focus

This set is a direct descendant of the 1948 "Topps Magic Photo" issue. Again, the baseball players were part of a larger overall series covering several topical areas. The cards, 7/8 x 1-3/8", state on the back that they are a series of 23, though only 14 are known. The photos on these cards were developed by wetting the card's surface and exposing to light. Prices below are for cards with well-developed pictures. Cards with poorly developed photos are worth significantly less.

	NM	EX	VG
Common Player:	250.00	125.00	75.00
1 Babe Ruth	3,500	1,750	1,000
2 Lou Gehrig	3,500	1,750	1,000
3 Dick Groat	275.00	135.00	80.00
4 Ed Lopat	400.00	200.00	120.00
5 Hank Sauer	250.00	125.00	75.00
6 "Dusty" Rhodes	250.00	125.00	75.00
7 Ted Williams	1,950	975.00	585.00
8 Harvey Haddix	250.00	125.00	75.00
9 Ray Boone	250.00	125.00	75.00
10 Al Rosen	450.00	225.00	135.00
11 Mayo Smith	250.00	125.00	75.00
12 Warren Spahn	600.00	300.00	180.00
13 Jim Rivera	250.00	125.00	75.00
14 Ted Kluszewski	600.00	300.00	180.00
15 Gus Zernial	250.00	125.00	75.00
16 Jackie Robinson	1,750	875.00	525.00
17 Unknown			
18 Johnny Schmitz	250.00	125.00	75.00
19 Wally Moon	250.00	125.00	75.00
20 Karl Spooner	275.00	135.00	80.00
21 Ed Mathews	600.00	300.00	180.00
22 "Spook" Jacobs	250.00	125.00	75.00
23 Unknown			

1955 Topps Stamps

An extremely rare and enigmatic test issue, these stamps are the same size as Topps' 1955 card issue and have a blank, gummed back. Most of the specimens currently known are imperforate along one of the sides. All of the known examples have counterparts in the regular set which range from card #6 through 108. The unnumbered stamps are checklisted here alphabetically, with gaps left in the numbering to accommodate future discoveries.

		NM	EX	VG
Common Player:		750.00	375.00	225.00
(1)	Ray Boone	750.00	375.00	225.00
(2)	Joe Cunningham	750.00	375.00	225.00
(3)	Jim Davis	750.00	375.00	225.00
(4)	Chuck Diering	750.00	375.00	225.00
(5)	Ruben Gomez	750.00	375.00	225.00
(6)	Alex Grammas	750.00	375.00	225.00
(7)	Stan Hack	750.00	375.00	225.00
(8)	Harvey Haddix	750.00	375.00	225.00
(9)	Bobby Hofman	750.00	375.00	225.00
(11)	Ray Jablonski	750.00	375.00	225.00
(12)	Dave Jolly	750.00	375.00	225.00
(13)	Ted Kazanski	750.00	375.00	225.00
(14)	Don Mossi	775.00	385.00	230.00
(15)	Jim Pendleton	750.00	375.00	225.00
(16)	Howie Pollet	750.00	375.00	225.00
(17)	Jack Shepard	750.00	375.00	225.00
(18)	Bob Skinner	750.00	375.00	225.00
(19)	Bill Skowron	975.00	485.00	290.00
(20)	Karl Spooner	775.00	385.00	230.00
(21)	Bill Tremel	750.00	375.00	225.00
(22)	Corky Valentine	750.00	375.00	225.00
(23)	Rube Walker	775.00	385.00	230.00
(24)	Charlie White	750.00	375.00	225.00

1956 Topps

This set is similar in format to the 1955 Topps set, again using both a portrait and an "action" picture. Some portraits are the same as those used in 1955 (and even 1954). Innovations found in the 1956 Topps set of 2-5/8" x 3-3/4" cards include team cards introduced as part of a regular set. Additionally, there are two unnumbered checklist cards (the complete set price quoted below does not include the checklist cards). Finally, there are cards of the two league presidents, William Harridge and Warren Giles. On the backs, a three-panel cartoon depicts big moments from the player's career while biographical information appears above the cartoon and the statistics below. Card backs for numbers 1-180 can be found with either white or gray cardboard. Some hobbyists feel a premium is warranted for gray backs between #1-100 and white backs from #101-180.

		NM	EX	VG
Complete Set (340):		9,000	4,250	2,550
Common Player (1-180):		15.00	7.50	4.50
Common Player (181-340):		20.00	10.00	6.00
1	William Harridge	125.00	25.00	15.00
2	Warren Giles	65.00	12.00	6.00
3	Elmer Valo	15.00	7.50	4.50
4	Carlos Paula	15.00	7.50	4.50
5	Ted Williams	450.00	220.00	135.00
6	Ray Boone	15.00	7.50	4.50
7	Ron Negray	15.00	7.50	4.50
8	Walter Alston	45.00	22.50	13.50
9	Ruben Gomez	15.00	7.50	4.50
10	Warren Spahn	125.00	62.50	31.25
11a	Chicago Cubs - 1955	80.00	40.00	20.00
11b	Chicago Cubs (No date, name centered.)	60.00	30.00	18.00
11c	Chicago Cubs (No date, name at left.)	70.00	35.00	20.00
12	Andy Carey	20.00	10.00	6.00
13	Roy Face	15.00	7.50	4.50
14	Ken Boyer	25.00	12.50	7.50
15	Ernie Banks	125.00	62.50	31.25
16	*Hector Lopez*	20.00	10.00	6.00
17	Gene Conley	15.00	7.50	4.50
18	Dick Donovan	15.00	7.50	4.50
19	Chuck Diering	15.00	7.50	4.50
20	Al Kaline	125.00	62.50	31.25
21	Joe Collins	20.00	10.00	6.00
22	Jim Finigan	15.00	7.50	4.50
23	Freddie Marsh	20.00	10.00	6.00
24	Dick Groat	20.00	10.00	6.00
25	Ted Kluszewski	35.00	17.50	10.00
26	Grady Hatton	15.00	7.50	4.50
27	Nelson Burbrink	15.00	7.50	4.50
28	Bobby Hofman	15.00	7.50	4.50
29	Jack Harshman	15.00	7.50	4.50
30	Jackie Robinson	300.00	150.00	90.00
31	Hank Aaron	300.00	150.00	90.00
32	Frank House	15.00	7.50	4.50
33	Roberto Clemente	400.00	200.00	120.00
34	Tom Brewer	15.00	7.50	4.50
35	Al Rosen	20.00	10.00	6.00
36	Rudy Minarcin	15.00	7.50	4.50
37	Alex Grammas	15.00	7.50	4.50
38	Bob Kennedy	15.00	7.50	4.50
39	Don Mossi	15.00	7.50	4.50
40	Bob Turley	25.00	12.50	7.50
41	Hank Sauer	15.00	7.50	4.50
42	Sandy Amoros	25.00	12.50	7.50
43	Ray Moore	15.00	7.50	4.50
44	"Windy" McCall	15.00	7.50	4.50
45	Gus Zernial	15.00	7.50	4.50
46	Gene Freese	15.00	7.50	4.50
47	Art Fowler	15.00	7.50	4.50
48	Jim Hegan	15.00	7.50	4.50
49	*Pedro Ramos*	20.00	10.00	6.00
50	"Dusty" Rhodes	15.00	7.50	4.50
51	Ernie Oravetz	15.00	7.50	4.50
52	Bob Grim	20.00	10.00	6.00
53	Arnold Portocarrero	15.00	7.50	4.50
54	Bob Keegan	15.00	7.50	4.50
55	Wally Moon	15.00	7.50	4.50
56	Dale Long	15.00	7.50	4.50
57	"Duke" Maas	15.00	7.50	4.50
58	Ed Roebuck	20.00	10.00	6.00
59	Jose Santiago	15.00	7.50	4.50
60	Mayo Smith	15.00	7.50	4.50
61	Bill Skowron	35.00	17.50	10.00
62	Hal Smith	15.00	7.50	4.50
63	*Roger Craig*	27.50	13.50	8.00
64	Luis Arroyo	15.00	7.50	4.50
65	Johnny O'Brien	15.00	7.50	4.50
66	Bob Speake	15.00	7.50	4.50
67	Vic Power	15.00	7.50	4.50
68	Chuck Stobbs	15.00	7.50	4.50
69	Chuck Tanner	15.00	7.50	4.50
70	Jim Rivera	15.00	7.50	4.50

71	Frank Sullivan	15.00	7.50	4.50
72a	Philadelphia Phillies - 1955	100.00	50.00	25.00
72b	Philadelphia Phillies (No date, name centered.)	40.00	20.00	12.00
72c	Philadelphia Phillies (No date, name at left.)	60.00	30.00	18.00
73	Wayne Terwilliger	15.00	7.50	4.50
74	Jim King	15.00	7.50	4.50
75	Roy Sievers	15.00	7.50	4.50
76	Ray Crone	15.00	7.50	4.50
77	Harvey Haddix	15.00	7.50	4.50
78	Herman Wehmeier	15.00	7.50	4.50
79	Sandy Koufax	350.00	175.00	87.50
80	Gus Triandos	15.00	7.50	4.50
81	Wally Westlake	15.00	7.50	4.50
82	Bill Renna	15.00	7.50	4.50
83	Karl Spooner	20.00	10.00	6.00
84	"Babe" Birrer	15.00	7.50	4.50
85a	Cleveland Indians - 1955	85.00	42.50	25.00
85b	Cleveland Indians (No date, name centered.)	50.00	25.00	15.00
85c	Cleveland Indians (No date, name at left.)	80.00	40.00	20.00
86	Ray Jablonski	15.00	7.50	4.50
87	Dean Stone	15.00	7.50	4.50
88	Johnny Kucks	20.00	10.00	6.00
89	Norm Zauchin	15.00	7.50	4.50
90a	Cincinnati Redlegs - 1955	100.00	50.00	30.00
90b	Cincinnati Redlegs (No date, name centered.)	45.00	22.50	13.50
90c	Cincinnati Redlegs (No date, name at left.)	90.00	45.00	27.50
91	Gail Harris	15.00	7.50	4.50
92	"Red" Wilson	15.00	7.50	4.50
93	George Susce, Jr.	15.00	7.50	4.50
94	Ronnie Kline	15.00	7.50	4.50
95a	Milwaukee Braves - 1955	100.00	50.00	25.00
95b	Milwaukee Braves (No date, name centered.)	60.00	30.00	18.00
95c	Milwaukee Braves (No date, name at left.)	55.00	27.50	16.50
96	Bill Tremel	15.00	7.50	4.50
97	Jerry Lynch	15.00	7.50	4.50
98	Camilo Pascual	15.00	7.50	4.50
99	Don Zimmer	30.00	15.00	9.00
100a	Baltimore Orioles - 1955	100.00	50.00	25.00
100b	Baltimore Orioles (No date, name centered.)	100.00	50.00	25.00
100c	Baltimore Orioles (No date, name at left.)	100.00	50.00	25.00
101	Roy Campanella	150.00	75.00	37.50
102	Jim Davis	15.00	7.50	4.50
103	Willie Miranda	15.00	7.50	4.50
104	Bob Lennon	15.00	7.50	4.50
105	Al Smith	15.00	7.50	4.50
106	Joe Astroth	15.00	7.50	4.50
107	Ed Mathews	100.00	50.00	25.00
108	Laurin Pepper	15.00	7.50	4.50
109	Enos Slaughter	32.50	16.00	10.00
110	Yogi Berra	180.00	90.00	45.00
111	Boston Red Sox	35.00	17.50	10.00
112	Dee Fondy	15.00	7.50	4.50
113	Phil Rizzuto	150.00	75.00	37.50
114	Jim Owens	15.00	7.50	4.50
115	Jackie Jensen	20.00	10.00	6.00
116	Eddie O'Brien	15.00	7.50	4.50
117	Virgil Trucks	15.00	7.50	4.50
118	"Nellie" Fox	50.00	25.00	15.00
119	*Larry Jackson*	15.00	7.50	4.50
120	Richie Ashburn	50.00	25.00	15.00
121	Pittsburgh Pirates	65.00	32.50	20.00
122	Willard Nixon	15.00	7.50	4.50
123	Roy McMillan	15.00	7.50	4.50
124	Don Kaiser	15.00	7.50	4.50
125	"Minnie" Minoso	30.00	15.00	9.00
126	Jim Brady	15.00	7.50	4.50
127	Willie Jones	15.00	7.50	4.50
128	Eddie Yost	15.00	7.50	4.50
129	"Jake" Martin	15.00	7.50	4.50
130	Willie Mays	300.00	150.00	90.00
131	Bob Roselli	15.00	7.50	4.50
132	Bobby Avila	15.00	7.50	4.50
133	Ray Narleski	15.00	7.50	4.50
134	St. Louis Cardinals	25.00	12.50	7.50
135	Mickey Mantle	1,150	575.00	345.00
136	Johnny Logan	15.00	7.50	4.50
137	Al Silvera	15.00	7.50	4.50
138	Johnny Antonelli	15.00	7.50	4.50
139	Tommy Carroll	20.00	10.00	6.00
140	*Herb Score*	35.00	17.50	10.00
141	Joe Frazier	15.00	7.50	4.50
142	Gene Baker	15.00	7.50	4.50
143	Jim Piersall	20.00	10.00	6.00
144	Leroy Powell	15.00	7.50	4.50
145	Gil Hodges	55.00	27.50	16.50
146	Washington Nationals	40.00	20.00	12.00
147	Earl Torgeson	15.00	7.50	4.50
148	Alvin Dark	15.00	7.50	4.50
149	"Dixie" Howell	15.00	7.50	4.50
150	"Duke" Snider	150.00	75.00	37.50
151	"Spook" Jacobs	15.00	7.50	4.50
152	Billy Hoeft	15.00	7.50	4.50
153	Frank Thomas	15.00	7.50	4.50
154	Dave Pope	15.00	7.50	4.50
155	Harvey Kuenn	15.00	7.50	4.50
156	Wes Westrum	15.00	7.50	4.50
157	Dick Brodowski	15.00	7.50	4.50
158	Wally Post	15.00	7.50	4.50
159	Clint Courtney	15.00	7.50	4.50
160	Billy Pierce	15.00	7.50	4.50
161	Joe De Maestri	15.00	7.50	4.50
162	"Gus" Bell	15.00	7.50	4.50
163	Gene Woodling	15.00	7.50	4.50
164	Harmon Killebrew	150.00	75.00	37.50
165	"Red" Schoendienst	35.00	17.50	10.00
166	Brooklyn Dodgers	200.00	100.00	50.00
167	Harry Dorish	15.00	7.50	4.50
68	Sammy White	15.00	7.50	4.50

169	Bob Nelson	15.00	7.50	4.50
170	Bill Virdon	15.00	7.50	4.50
171	Jim Wilson	15.00	7.50	4.50
172	*Frank Torre*	20.00	10.00	6.00
173	Johnny Podres	30.00	15.00	9.00
174	Glen Gorbous	15.00	7.50	4.50
175	Del Crandall	15.00	7.50	4.50
176	Alex Kellner	15.00	7.50	4.50
177	Hank Bauer	30.00	15.00	9.00
178	Joe Black	20.00	10.00	6.00
179	Harry Chiti	15.00	7.50	4.50
180	Robin Roberts	40.00	20.00	12.00
181	Billy Martin	100.00	50.00	25.00
182	Paul Minner	20.00	10.00	6.00
183	Stan Lopata	20.00	10.00	6.00
184	Don Bessent	25.00	12.50	7.50
185	Bill Bruton	20.00	10.00	6.00
186	Ron Jackson	20.00	10.00	6.00
187	Early Wynn	55.00	27.50	16.50
188	Chicago White Sox	60.00	30.00	15.00
189	Ned Garver	20.00	10.00	6.00
190	Carl Furillo	45.00	22.50	13.50
191	Frank Lary	20.00	10.00	6.00
192	"Smoky" Burgess	20.00	10.00	6.00
193	Wilmer Mizell	20.00	10.00	6.00
194	Monte Irvin	55.00	27.50	16.50
195	George Kell	45.00	22.50	13.50
196	Tom Poholsky	20.00	10.00	6.00
197	Granny Hamner	20.00	10.00	6.00
198	Ed Fitzgerald	20.00	10.00	6.00
199	Hank Thompson	20.00	10.00	6.00
200	Bob Feller	120.00	60.00	30.00
201	"Rip" Repulski	20.00	10.00	6.00
202	Jim Hearn	20.00	10.00	6.00
203	Bill Tuttle	20.00	10.00	6.00
204	Art Swanson	20.00	10.00	6.00
205	"Whitey" Lockman	20.00	10.00	6.00
206	Erv Palica	20.00	10.00	6.00
207	Jim Small	20.00	10.00	6.00
208	Elston Howard	45.00	22.50	13.50
209	Max Surkont	20.00	10.00	6.00
210	Mike Garcia	20.00	10.00	6.00
211	Murry Dickson	20.00	10.00	6.00
212	Johnny Temple	20.00	10.00	6.00
213	Detroit Tigers	60.00	30.00	18.00
214	Bob Rush	20.00	10.00	6.00
215	Tommy Byrne	25.00	12.50	7.50
216	Jerry Schoonmaker	20.00	10.00	6.00
217	Billy Klaus	20.00	10.00	6.00
218	Joe Nuxall (Nuxhall)	25.00	12.50	7.50
219	Lew Burdette	20.00	10.00	6.00
220	Del Ennis	20.00	10.00	6.00
221	Bob Friend	20.00	10.00	6.00
222	Dave Philley	20.00	10.00	6.00
223	Randy Jackson	25.00	12.50	7.50
224	"Bud" Podbielan	20.00	10.00	6.00
225	Gil McDougald	35.00	17.50	10.00
226	New York Giants	50.00	25.00	15.00
227	Russ Meyer	20.00	10.00	6.00
228	"Mickey" Vernon	20.00	10.00	6.00
229	Harry Brecheen	20.00	10.00	6.00
230	"Chico" Carrasquel	20.00	10.00	6.00
231	Bob Hale	20.00	10.00	6.00
232	"Toby" Atwell	20.00	10.00	6.00
233	Carl Erskine	30.00	15.00	9.00
234	"Pete" Runnels	20.00	10.00	6.00
235	Don Newcombe	55.00	27.50	16.50
236	Kansas City Athletics	35.00	17.50	10.00
237	Jose Valdivielso	20.00	10.00	6.00
238	Walt Dropo	20.00	10.00	6.00
239	Harry Simpson	20.00	10.00	6.00
240	"Whitey" Ford	125.00	62.50	31.25
241	Don Mueller	20.00	10.00	6.00
242	Hershell Freeman	20.00	10.00	6.00
243	Sherm Lollar	20.00	10.00	6.00
244	Bob Buhl	20.00	10.00	6.00
245	Billy Goodman	20.00	10.00	6.00
246	Tom Gorman	20.00	10.00	6.00
247	Bill Sarni	20.00	10.00	6.00
248	Bob Porterfield	20.00	10.00	6.00
249	Johnny Klippstein	20.00	10.00	6.00
250	Larry Doby	45.00	22.50	13.50
251	New York Yankees	250.00	125.00	75.00
252	Vernon Law	20.00	10.00	6.00
253	Irv Noren	25.00	12.50	7.50
254	George Crowe	20.00	10.00	6.00
255	Bob Lemon	35.00	17.50	10.00
256	Tom Hurd	20.00	10.00	6.00
257	Bobby Thomson	25.00	12.50	7.50
258	Art Ditmar	20.00	10.00	6.00
259	Sam Jones	20.00	10.00	6.00
260	"Pee Wee" Reese	150.00	75.00	37.50
261	Bobby Shantz	20.00	10.00	6.00
262	Howie Pollet	20.00	10.00	6.00
263	Bob Miller	20.00	10.00	6.00
264	Ray Monzant	20.00	10.00	6.00
265	Sandy Consuegra	20.00	10.00	6.00
266	Don Ferrarese	20.00	10.00	6.00
267	Bob Nieman	20.00	10.00	6.00
268	Dale Mitchell	20.00	10.00	6.00
269	Jack Meyer	20.00	10.00	6.00
270	Billy Loes	25.00	12.50	7.50
271	Foster Castleman	20.00	10.00	6.00
272	Danny O'Connell	20.00	10.00	6.00
273	Walker Cooper	20.00	10.00	6.00
274	Frank Baumholtz	20.00	10.00	6.00
275	Jim Greengrass	20.00	10.00	6.00
276	George Zuverink	20.00	10.00	6.00
277	Daryl Spencer	20.00	10.00	6.00
278	Chet Nichols	20.00	10.00	6.00
279	Johnny Groth	20.00	10.00	6.00
280	Jim Gilliam	45.00	22.50	13.50
281	Art Houtteman	20.00	10.00	6.00
282	Warren Hacker	20.00	10.00	6.00
283	Hal Smith	20.00	10.00	6.00
284	Ike Delock	20.00	10.00	6.00
285	Eddie Miksis	20.00	10.00	6.00
286	Bill Wight	20.00	10.00	6.00

287	Bobby Adams	20.00	10.00	6.00
288	Bob Cerv/SP	45.00	22.50	13.50
289	Hal Jeffcoat	20.00	10.00	6.00
290	Curt Simmons	20.00	10.00	6.00
291	Frank Kellert	20.00	10.00	6.00
292	*Luis Aparicio*	150.00	75.00	37.50
293	Stu Miller	20.00	10.00	6.00
294	Ernie Johnson	20.00	10.00	6.00
295	Clem Labine	30.00	15.00	9.00
296	Andy Seminick	20.00	10.00	6.00
297	Bob Skinner	20.00	10.00	6.00
298	Johnny Schmitz	20.00	10.00	6.00
299	Charley Neal/SP	35.00	17.50	10.00
300	Vic Wertz	20.00	10.00	6.00
301	Marv Grissom	20.00	10.00	6.00
302	Eddie Robinson	25.00	12.50	7.50
303	Jim Dyck	20.00	10.00	6.00
304	Frank Malzone	20.00	10.00	6.00
305	Brooks Lawrence	20.00	10.00	6.00
306	Curt Roberts	20.00	10.00	6.00
307	Hoyt Wilhelm	40.00	20.00	12.00
308	"Chuck" Harmon	20.00	10.00	6.00
309	*Don Blasingame*	25.00	12.50	7.50
310	Steve Gromek	20.00	10.00	6.00
311	Hal Naragon	20.00	10.00	6.00
312	Andy Pafko	20.00	10.00	6.00
313	Gene Stephens	20.00	10.00	6.00
314	Hobie Landrith	20.00	10.00	6.00
315	Milt Bolling	20.00	10.00	6.00
316	Jerry Coleman	25.00	12.50	7.50
317	Al Aber	20.00	10.00	6.00
318	Fred Hatfield	20.00	10.00	6.00
319	Jack Crimian	20.00	10.00	6.00
320	Joe Adcock	20.00	10.00	6.00
321	Jim Konstanty	25.00	12.50	7.50
322	Karl Olson	20.00	10.00	6.00
323	Willard Schmidt	20.00	10.00	6.00
324	"Rocky" Bridges	20.00	10.00	6.00
325	Don Liddle	20.00	10.00	6.00
326	Connie Johnson	20.00	10.00	6.00
327	Bob Wiesler	20.00	10.00	6.00
328	Preston Ward	20.00	10.00	6.00
329	Lou Berberet	20.00	10.00	6.00
330	Jim Busby	20.00	10.00	6.00
331	Dick Hall	20.00	10.00	6.00
332	Don Larsen	55.00	27.50	16.50
333	"Rube" Walker	25.00	12.50	7.50
334	Bob Miller	20.00	10.00	6.00
335	Don Hoak	20.00	10.00	6.00
336	Ellis Kinder	20.00	10.00	6.00
337	Bobby Morgan	20.00	10.00	6.00
338	Jim Delsing	20.00	10.00	6.00
339	Rance Pless	20.00	10.00	6.00
340	Mickey McDermott	85.00	15.00	8.00
----	Checklist 1/3	250.00	125.00	62.50
----	Checklist 2/4	250.00	125.00	62.50

1956 Topps Hocus Focus

Following its 1955 issue with a somewhat larger format (1" x 1-5/8") the following year, the baseball players in this set are part of a larger overall series covering several topical areas. Cards backs specify an issue of 18 baseball stars. The black-and-white photos on these cards were developed by wetting the card's surface and exposing to light. Prices below are for cards with well-developed pictures. Cards with poorly developed photos are worth significantly less.

		NM	EX	VG
Complete Set (18):		7,000	3,500	2,100
Common Player:		225.00	110.00	65.00
1	Dick Groat	225.00	110.00	65.00
2	Ed Lopat	425.00	210.00	125.00
3	Hank Sauer	225.00	110.00	65.00
4	"Dusty" Rhodes	225.00	110.00	65.00
5	Ted Williams	1,600	800.00	480.00
6	Harvey Haddix	225.00	110.00	65.00
7	Ray Boone	225.00	110.00	65.00
8	Al Rosen	250.00	125.00	75.00
9	Mayo Smith	225.00	110.00	65.00
10	Warren Spahn	550.00	275.00	165.00
11	Jim Rivera	225.00	110.00	65.00
12	Ted Kluszewski	450.00	225.00	135.00
13	Gus Zernial	225.00	110.00	65.00
14	Jackie Robinson	1,350	675.00	400.00
15	Hal Smith	225.00	110.00	65.00
16	Johnny Schmitz	225.00	110.00	65.00
17	"Spook" Jacobs	225.00	110.00	65.00
18	Mel Parnell	225.00	110.00	65.00

1956 Topps Pins

One of Topps first specialty issues, the 60-pin set of ball-players issued in 1956 contains a high percentage of big-name stars which, combined with the scarcity of the pins, makes collecting a complete set extremely challenging. Compounding the situation is the fact that some pins are seen far less often than others, though the reason is unknown. Chuck Stobbs, Hector Lopez and Chuck Diering are unaccountably scarce. Measuring 1-1/8" in diameter, the pins utilize the same portraits found on 1956 Topps baseball cards. The photos are set against a solid color background. The pins were sold in a box picturing the Ted Williams pin, with a piece of bubblegum for five cents.

		NM	EX	VG
Complete Set (60):		3,600	1,800	1,100
Common Player:		40.00	20.00	12.00
Box:		700.00	350.00	210.00
(1)	Hank Aaron	200.00	100.00	60.00
(2)	Sandy Amoros	50.00	25.00	15.00
(3)	Luis Arroyo	40.00	20.00	12.00
(4)	Ernie Banks	150.00	75.00	45.00
(5)	Yogi Berra	150.00	75.00	45.00
(6)	Joe Black	60.00	30.00	18.00
(7)	Ray Boone	40.00	20.00	12.00
(8)	Ken Boyer	45.00	22.50	13.50
(9)	Joe Collins	45.00	22.50	13.50
(10)	Gene Conley	40.00	20.00	12.00
(11)	Chuck Diering	275.00	135.00	85.00
(12)	Dick Donovan	40.00	20.00	12.00
(13)	Jim Finigan	40.00	20.00	12.00
(14)	Art Fowler	40.00	20.00	12.00
(15)	Ruben Gomez	40.00	20.00	12.00
(16)	Dick Groat	40.00	20.00	12.00
(17)	Harvey Haddix	40.00	20.00	12.00
(18)	Jack Harshman	40.00	20.00	12.00
(19)	Grady Hatton	40.00	20.00	12.00
(20)	Jim Hegan	40.00	20.00	12.00
(21)	Gil Hodges	100.00	50.00	30.00
(22)	Bobby Hofman	40.00	20.00	12.00
(23)	Frank House	40.00	20.00	12.00
(24)	Jackie Jensen	45.00	22.50	13.50
(25)	Al Kaline	100.00	50.00	30.00
(26)	Bob Kennedy	40.00	20.00	12.00
(27)	Ted Kluszewski	85.00	42.50	25.00
(28)	Dale Long	40.00	20.00	12.00
(29)	Hector Lopez	400.00	200.00	120.00
(30)	Ed Mathews	100.00	50.00	30.00
(31)	Willie Mays	200.00	100.00	60.00
(32)	Roy McMillan	40.00	20.00	12.00
(33)	Willie Miranda	40.00	20.00	12.00
(34)	Wally Moon	40.00	20.00	12.00
(35)	Don Mossi	40.00	20.00	12.00
(36)	Ron Negray	40.00	20.00	12.00
(37)	Johnny O'Brien	40.00	20.00	12.00
(38)	Carlos Paula	40.00	20.00	12.00
(39)	Vic Power	40.00	20.00	12.00
(40)	Jim Rivera	40.00	20.00	12.00
(41)	Phil Rizzuto	150.00	75.00	45.00
(42)	Jackie Robinson	180.00	90.00	55.00
(43)	Al Rosen	45.00	22.50	13.50
(44)	Hank Sauer	40.00	20.00	12.00
(45)	Roy Sievers	40.00	20.00	12.00
(46)	Bill Skowron	45.00	22.50	13.50
(47)	Al Smith	40.00	20.00	12.00
(48)	Hal Smith	40.00	20.00	12.00
(49)	Mayo Smith	40.00	20.00	12.00
(50)	Duke Snider	125.00	65.00	35.00
(51)	Warren Spahn	100.00	50.00	30.00
(52)	Karl Spooner	45.00	22.50	13.50
(53)	Chuck Stobbs	225.00	110.00	65.00
(54)	Frank Sullivan	40.00	20.00	12.00
(55)	Bill Tremel	40.00	20.00	12.00
(56)	Gus Triandos	40.00	20.00	12.00
(57)	Bob Turley	50.00	25.00	15.00
(58)	Herman Wehmeier	40.00	20.00	12.00
(59)	Ted Williams	225.00	110.00	65.00
(60)	Gus Zernial	40.00	20.00	12.00

1957 Topps

For 1957, Topps reduced the size of its cards to the now-standard 2-1/2" x 3-1/2". Set size was increased to 407 cards. Another change came in the form of the use of real color photographs as opposed to the hand-colored black and whites of previous years. For the first time since 1954, there were also cards with more than one player. The two, "Dodger Sluggers" and "Yankees' Power Hitters" began a trend toward the increased use of multiple-player cards. Another first-time innovation, found on the backs, is complete players statistics. The scarce cards in the set are not the highest numbers, but rather numbers 265-352. Four unnumbered checklist cards were issued along with the set. They are quite expensive and are not included in the complete set prices quoted below.

		NM	EX	VG
Complete Set (407):		13,500	6,750	4,050
Common Player (1-264):		12.00	6.00	3.50
Common Player (265-352):		25.00	12.50	7.50
Common Player (353-407):		12.00	6.00	3.50
1	Ted Williams	450.00	225.00	135.00
2	Yogi Berra	200.00	100.00	50.00
3	Dale Long	12.00	6.00	3.50
4	Johnny Logan	12.00	6.00	3.50
5	Sal Maglie	20.00	10.00	6.00
6	Hector Lopez	12.00	6.00	3.50
7	Luis Aparicio	40.00	20.00	12.00
8	Don Mossi	12.00	6.00	3.50
9	Johnny Temple	12.00	6.00	3.50
10	Willie Mays	300.00	150.00	90.00
11	George Zuverink	12.00	6.00	3.50
12	Dick Groat	12.00	6.00	3.50
13	Wally Burnette	12.00	6.00	3.50
14	Bob Nieman	12.00	6.00	3.50
15	Robin Roberts	50.00	25.00	15.00
16	Walt Moryn	12.00	6.00	3.50
17	Billy Gardner	12.00	6.00	3.50
18	*Don Drysdale*	250.00	125.00	62.50
19	Bob Wilson	12.00	6.00	3.50
20	Hank Aaron (Photo reversed.)	325.00	162.50	81.25
21	Frank Sullivan	12.00	6.00	3.50
22	Jerry Snyder (Photo actually Ed Fitz Gerald.)	12.00	6.00	3.50
23	Sherman Lollar	12.00	6.00	3.50
24	*Bill Mazeroski*	80.00	40.00	20.00
25	Whitey Ford	150.00	75.00	37.50
26	Bob Boyd	12.00	6.00	3.50
27	Ted Kazanski	12.00	6.00	3.50
28	Gene Conley	12.00	6.00	3.50
29	*Whitey Herzog*	30.00	15.00	9.00
30	Pee Wee Reese	75.00	37.50	22.50
31	Ron Northey	12.00	6.00	3.50
32	Hersh Freeman	12.00	6.00	3.50
33	Jim Small	12.00	6.00	3.50
34	Tom Sturdivant	15.00	7.50	4.50
35	*Frank Robinson*	300.00	150.00	75.00
36	Bob Grim	15.00	7.50	4.50
37	Frank Torre	12.00	6.00	3.50
38	Nellie Fox	40.00	20.00	12.00
39	Al Worthington	12.00	6.00	3.50
40	Early Wynn	30.00	15.00	9.00
41	Hal Smith	12.00	6.00	3.50
42	Dee Fondy	12.00	6.00	3.50
43	Connie Johnson	12.00	6.00	3.50
44	Joe DeMaestri	12.00	6.00	3.50
45	Carl Furillo	40.00	20.00	12.00
46	Bob Miller	12.00	6.00	3.50
47	Don Blasingame	12.00	6.00	3.50
48	Bill Bruton	12.00	6.00	3.50
49	Daryl Spencer	12.00	6.00	3.50
50	Herb Score	25.00	12.50	7.50
51	Clint Courtney	12.00	6.00	3.50
52	Lee Walls	12.00	6.00	3.50
53	Clem Labine	20.00	10.00	6.00
54	Elmer Valo	12.00	6.00	3.50
55	Ernie Banks	130.00	65.00	32.50
56	Dave Sisler	12.00	6.00	3.50
57	Jim Lemon	12.00	6.00	3.50
58	Ruben Gomez	12.00	6.00	3.50
59	Dick Williams	12.00	6.00	3.50
60	Billy Hoeft	12.00	6.00	3.50
61	Dusty Rhodes	12.00	6.00	3.50
62	Billy Martin	40.00	20.00	12.00
63	Ike Delock	12.00	6.00	3.50
64	Pete Runnels	12.00	6.00	3.50
65	Wally Moon	12.00	6.00	3.50
66	Brooks Lawrence	12.00	6.00	3.50
67	Chico Carrasquel	12.00	6.00	3.50
68	Ray Crone	12.00	6.00	3.50
69	Roy McMillan	12.00	6.00	3.50
70	Richie Ashburn	45.00	22.50	13.50
71	Murry Dickson	12.00	6.00	3.50
72	Bill Tuttle	12.00	6.00	3.50
73	George Crowe	12.00	6.00	3.50
74	Vito Valentinetti	12.00	6.00	3.50
75	Jim Piersall	15.00	7.50	4.50
76	Bob Clemente	250.00	125.00	75.00
77	Paul Foytack	12.00	6.00	3.50
78	Vic Wertz	12.00	6.00	3.50
79	*Lindy McDaniel*	15.00	7.50	4.50
80	Gil Hodges	45.00	22.50	13.50
81	Herm Wehmeier	12.00	6.00	3.50
82	Elston Howard	30.00	15.00	9.00
83	Lou Skizas	12.00	6.00	3.50
84	Moe Drabowsky	12.00	6.00	3.50
85	Larry Doby	40.00	20.00	12.00
86	Bill Sarni	12.00	6.00	3.50
87	Tom Gorman	12.00	6.00	3.50
88	Harvey Kuenn	15.00	7.50	4.50
89	Roy Sievers	12.00	6.00	3.50
90	Warren Spahn	100.00	50.00	25.00
91	Mack Burk	12.00	6.00	3.50
92	Mickey Vernon	12.00	6.00	3.50
93	Hal Jeffcoat	12.00	6.00	3.50
94	Bobby Del Greco	12.00	6.00	3.50
95	Mickey Mantle	775.00	390.00	235.00
96	*Hank Aguirre*	12.00	6.00	3.50
97	New York Yankees Team	100.00	50.00	25.00
98	Al Dark	12.00	6.00	3.50
99	Bob Keegan	12.00	6.00	3.50
100	League Presidents (Warren Giles, William Harridge)	60.00	30.00	18.00
101	Chuck Stobbs	12.00	6.00	3.50
102	Ray Boone	12.00	6.00	3.50
103	Joe Nuxhall	12.00	6.00	3.50
104	Hank Foiles	12.00	6.00	3.50
105	Johnny Antonelli	12.00	6.00	3.50
106	Ray Moore	12.00	6.00	3.50
107	Jim Rivera	12.00	6.00	3.50
108	Tommy Byrne	15.00	7.50	4.50
109	Hank Thompson	12.00	6.00	3.50
110	Bill Virdon	12.00	6.00	3.50
111	Hal Smith	12.00	6.00	3.50
112	Tom Brewer	12.00	6.00	3.50
113	Wilmer Mizell	12.00	6.00	3.50
114	Milwaukee Braves Team	30.00	15.00	9.00
115	Jim Gilliam	27.50	13.50	8.25
116	Mike Fornieles	12.00	6.00	3.50
117	Joe Adcock	12.00	6.00	3.50
118	Bob Porterfield	12.00	6.00	3.50
119	Stan Lopata	12.00	6.00	3.50
120	Bob Lemon	35.00	17.50	10.00
121	*Cletis Boyer*	30.00	15.00	9.00
122	Ken Boyer	20.00	10.00	6.00
123	Steve Ridzik	12.00	6.00	3.50
124	Dave Philley	12.00	6.00	3.50
125	Al Kaline	100.00	50.00	25.00
126	Bob Wiesler	12.00	6.00	3.50
127	Bob Buhl	12.00	6.00	3.50
128	Ed Bailey	12.00	6.00	3.50
129	Saul Rogovin	12.00	6.00	3.50
130	Don Newcombe	25.00	12.50	7.50
131	Milt Bolling	12.00	6.00	3.50
132	Art Ditmar	12.00	6.00	3.50
133	Del Crandall	12.00	6.00	3.50
134	Don Kaiser	12.00	6.00	3.50
135	Bill Skowron	30.00	15.00	9.00
136	Jim Hegan	12.00	6.00	3.50
137	Bob Rush	12.00	6.00	3.50
138	Minnie Minoso	25.00	12.50	7.50
139	Lou Kretlow	12.00	6.00	3.50
140	Frank Thomas	12.00	6.00	3.50
141	Al Aber	12.00	6.00	3.50
142	Charley Thompson	12.00	6.00	3.50
143	Andy Pafko	12.00	6.00	3.50
144	Ray Narleski	12.00	6.00	3.50
145	Al Smith	12.00	6.00	3.50
146	Don Ferrarese	12.00	6.00	3.50
147	Al Walker	15.00	7.50	4.50
148	Don Mueller	12.00	6.00	3.50
149	Bob Kennedy	12.00	6.00	3.50
150	Bob Friend	12.00	6.00	3.50
151	Willie Miranda	12.00	6.00	3.50
152	Jack Harshman	12.00	6.00	3.50
153	Karl Olson	12.00	6.00	3.50
154	Red Schoendienst	30.00	15.00	9.00
155	Jim Brosnan	12.00	6.00	3.50
156	Gus Triandos	12.00	6.00	3.50
157	Wally Post	12.00	6.00	3.50
158	Curt Simmons	12.00	6.00	3.50
159	Solly Drake	12.00	6.00	3.50
160	Billy Pierce	12.00	6.00	3.50
161	Pitsburgh Pirates Team	20.00	10.00	6.00
162	Jack Meyer	12.00	6.00	3.50
163	Sammy White	12.00	6.00	3.50
164	Tommy Carroll	15.00	7.50	4.50
165	Ted Kluszewski	80.00	40.00	20.00
166	Roy Face	12.00	6.00	3.50
167	Vic Power	12.00	6.00	3.50
168	Frank Lary	12.00	6.00	3.50
169	Herb Plews	12.00	6.00	3.50
170	Duke Snider	150.00	75.00	37.50
171	Boston Red Sox Team	32.50	16.00	10.00
172	Gene Woodling	12.00	6.00	3.50
173	Roger Craig	15.00	7.50	4.50
174	Willie Jones	12.00	6.00	3.50
175	Don Larsen	35.00	17.50	10.00
176a	Gene Baker	12.00	6.00	3.50
176b	Gene Baker (Error on back, "EUGENF W. BAKEP.")	850.00	420.00	250.00
177	Eddie Yost	12.00	6.00	3.50
178	Don Bessent	15.00	7.50	4.50
179	Ernie Oravetz	12.00	6.00	3.50
180	Gus Bell	12.00	6.00	3.50
181	Dick Donovan	12.00	6.00	3.50
182	Hobie Landrith	12.00	6.00	3.50
183	Chicago Cubs Team	25.00	12.50	7.50
184	*Tito Francona*	12.00	6.00	3.50
185	Johnny Kucks	15.00	7.50	4.50
186	Jim King	12.00	6.00	3.50
187	Virgil Trucks	12.00	6.00	3.50
188	Felix Mantilla	12.00	6.00	3.50
189	Willard Nixon	12.00	6.00	3.50
190	Randy Jackson	15.00	7.50	4.50
191	Joe Margoneri	12.00	6.00	3.50
192	Jerry Coleman	15.00	7.50	4.50
193	Del Rice	12.00	6.00	3.50
194	Hal Brown	12.00	6.00	3.50
195	Bobby Avila	12.00	6.00	3.50
196	Larry Jackson	12.00	6.00	3.50
197	Hank Sauer	12.00	6.00	3.50
198	Detroit Tigers Team	20.00	10.00	6.00
199	Vernon Law	12.00	6.00	3.50
200	Gil McDougald	25.00	12.50	7.50
201	Sandy Amoros	25.00	12.50	7.50
202	Dick Gernert	12.00	6.00	3.50
203	Hoyt Wilhelm	25.00	12.50	7.50
204	Kansas City A's Team	20.00	10.00	6.00
205	Charley Maxwell	12.00	6.00	3.50
206	Willard Schmidt	12.00	6.00	3.50
207	Billy Hunter	12.00	6.00	3.50
208	Lew Burdette	12.00	6.00	3.50
209	Bob Skinner	12.00	6.00	3.50
210	Roy Campanella	150.00	75.00	37.50
211	Camilo Pascual	12.00	6.00	3.50
212	*Rocky Colavito*	125.00	62.50	31.25
213	Les Moss	12.00	6.00	3.50
214	Philadelphia Phillies Team	25.00	12.50	7.50
215	Enos Slaughter	35.00	17.50	10.00
216	Marv Grissom	12.00	6.00	3.50

217	Gene Stephens	12.00	6.00	3.50
218	Ray Jablonski	12.00	6.00	3.50
219	Tom Acker	12.00	6.00	3.50
220	Jackie Jensen	17.50	8.75	5.25
221	Dixie Howell	12.00	6.00	3.50
222	Alex Grammas	12.00	6.00	3.50
223	Frank House	12.00	6.00	3.50
224	Marv Blaylock	12.00	6.00	3.50
225	Harry Simpson	12.00	6.00	3.50
226	Preston Ward	12.00	6.00	3.50
227	Jerry Staley	12.00	6.00	3.50
228	Smoky Burgess	12.00	6.00	3.50
229	George Susce	12.00	6.00	3.50
230	George Kell	25.00	12.50	7.50
231	Solly Hemus	12.00	6.00	3.50
232	Whitey Lockman	12.00	6.00	3.50
233	Art Fowler	12.00	6.00	3.50
234	Dick Cole	12.00	6.00	3.50
235	Tom Poholsky	12.00	6.00	3.50
236	Joe Ginsberg	12.00	6.00	3.50
237	Foster Castleman	12.00	6.00	3.50
238	Eddie Robinson	12.00	6.00	3.50
239	Tom Morgan	12.00	6.00	3.50
240	Hank Bauer	30.00	15.00	9.00
241	Joe Lonnett	12.00	6.00	3.50
242	Charley Neal	15.00	7.50	4.50
243	St. Louis Cardinals Team	20.00	10.00	6.00
244	Billy Loes	12.00	6.00	3.50
245	Rip Repulski	12.00	6.00	3.50
246	Jose Valdivielso	12.00	6.00	3.50
247	Turk Lown	12.00	6.00	3.50
248	Jim Finigan	12.00	6.00	3.50
249	Dave Pope	12.00	6.00	3.50
250	Ed Mathews	55.00	27.50	16.50
251	Baltimore Orioles Team	20.00	10.00	6.00
252	Carl Erskine	20.00	10.00	6.00
253	Gus Zernial	12.00	6.00	3.50
254	Ron Negray	12.00	6.00	3.50
255	Charlie Silvera	12.00	6.00	3.50
256	Ronnie Kline	12.00	6.00	3.50
257	Walt Dropo	12.00	6.00	3.50
258	Steve Gromek	12.00	6.00	3.50
259	Eddie O'Brien	12.00	6.00	3.50
260	Del Ennis	12.00	6.00	3.50
261	Bob Chakales	12.00	6.00	3.50
262	Bobby Thomson	15.00	7.50	4.50
263	George Strickland	12.00	6.00	3.50
264	Bob Turley	25.00	12.50	7.50
265	Harvey Haddix	25.00	12.50	7.50
266	Ken Kuhn	25.00	12.50	7.50
267	Danny Kravitz	25.00	12.50	7.50
268	Jackie Collum	25.00	12.50	7.50
269	Bob Cerv	25.00	12.50	7.50
270	Washington Senators Team	45.00	22.50	13.50
271	Danny O'Connell	25.00	12.50	7.50
272	Bobby Shantz	40.00	20.00	12.00
273	Jim Davis	25.00	12.50	7.50
274	Don Hoak	25.00	12.50	7.50
275	Cleveland Indians Team	40.00	20.00	12.00
276	Jim Pyburn	25.00	12.50	7.50
277	Johnny Podres	40.00	20.00	12.00
278	Fred Hatfield	25.00	12.50	7.50
279	Bob Thurman	25.00	12.50	7.50
280	Alex Kellner	25.00	12.50	7.50
281	Gail Harris	25.00	12.50	7.50
282	Jack Dittmer	25.00	12.50	7.50
283	*Wes Covington*	25.00	12.50	7.50
284	Don Zimmer	40.00	20.00	12.00
285	Ned Garver	25.00	12.50	7.50
286	*Bobby Richardson*	120.00	60.00	30.00
287	Sam Jones	25.00	12.50	7.50
288	Ted Lepcio	25.00	12.50	7.50
289	Jim Bolger	25.00	12.50	7.50
290	Andy Carey	35.00	17.50	10.00
291	Windy McCall	20.00	10.00	6.00
292	Billy Klaus	25.00	12.50	7.50
293	Ted Abernathy	25.00	12.50	7.50
294	Rocky Bridges	25.00	12.50	7.50
295	Joe Collins	35.00	17.50	10.50
296	Johnny Klippstein	25.00	12.50	7.50
297	Jack Crimian	25.00	12.50	7.50
298	Irv Noren	25.00	12.50	7.50
299	Chuck Harmon	25.00	12.50	7.50
300	Mike Garcia	25.00	12.50	7.50
301	Sam Esposito	25.00	12.50	7.50
302	Sandy Koufax	350.00	175.00	87.50
303	Billy Goodman	25.00	12.50	7.50
304	Joe Cunningham	25.00	12.50	7.50
305	Chico Fernandez	25.00	12.50	7.50
306	*Darrell Johnson*	35.00	17.50	10.00
307	Jack Phillips	25.00	12.50	7.50
308	Dick Hall	25.00	12.50	7.50
309	Jim Busby	25.00	12.50	7.50
310	Max Surkont	25.00	12.50	7.50
311	Al Pilarcik	25.00	12.50	7.50
312	*Tony Kubek*	90.00	45.00	22.50
313	Mel Parnell	25.00	12.50	7.50
314	Ed Bouchee	25.00	12.50	7.50
315	Lou Berberet	25.00	12.50	7.50
316	Billy O'Dell	25.00	12.50	7.50
317	New York Giants Team	60.00	30.00	15.00
318	Mickey McDermott	25.00	12.50	7.50
319	*Gino Cimoli*	30.00	15.00	9.00
320	Neil Chrisley	25.00	12.50	7.50
321	Red Murff	25.00	12.50	7.50
322	Cincinnati Redlegs Team	45.00	22.50	13.50
323	Wes Westrum	25.00	12.50	7.50
324	Brooklyn Dodgers Team	125.00	62.50	31.25
325	Frank Bolling	25.00	12.50	7.50
326	Pedro Ramos	25.00	12.50	7.50
327	Jim Pendleton	25.00	12.50	7.50
328	*Brooks Robinson*	400.00	200.00	100.00
329	Chicago White Sox Team	45.00	22.50	13.50
330	Jim Wilson	25.00	12.50	7.50
331	Ray Katt	25.00	12.50	7.50
332	Bob Bowman	25.00	12.50	7.50
333	Ernie Johnson	25.00	12.50	7.50
334	Jerry Schoonmaker	25.00	12.50	7.50

335	Granny Hamner	25.00	12.50	7.50
336	*Haywood Sullivan*	25.00	12.50	7.50
337	Rene Valdes (Valdez)	30.00	15.00	9.00
338	*Jim Bunning*	150.00	75.00	37.50
339	Bob Speake	25.00	12.50	7.50
340	Bill Wight	25.00	12.50	7.50
341	Don Gross	25.00	12.50	7.50
342	Gene Mauch	25.00	12.50	7.50
343	Taylor Phillips	25.00	12.50	7.50
344	Paul LaPalme	25.00	12.50	7.50
345	Paul Smith	25.00	12.50	7.50
346	Dick Littlefield	25.00	12.50	7.50
347	Hal Naragon	25.00	12.50	7.50
348	Jim Hearn	25.00	12.50	7.50
349	Nelson King	25.00	12.50	7.50
350	Eddie Miksis	25.00	12.50	7.50
351	Dave Hillman	25.00	12.50	7.50
352	Ellis Kinder	25.00	12.50	7.50
353	Cal Neeman	12.00	6.00	3.50
354	Rip Coleman	12.00	6.00	3.50
355	Frank Malzone	12.00	6.00	3.50
356	Faye Throneberry	12.00	6.00	3.50
357	Earl Torgeson	12.00	6.00	3.50
358	Jerry Lynch	12.00	6.00	3.50
359	Tom Cheney	12.00	6.00	3.50
360	Johnny Groth	12.00	6.00	3.50
361	Curt Barclay	12.00	6.00	3.50
362	Roman Mejias	12.00	6.00	3.50
363	Eddie Kasko	12.00	6.00	3.50
364	*Cal McLish*	12.00	6.00	3.50
365	Ossie Virgil	12.00	6.00	3.50
366	Ken Lehman	15.00	7.50	4.50
367	Ed FitzGerald	12.00	6.00	3.50
368	Bob Purkey	12.00	6.00	3.50
369	Milt Graff	12.00	6.00	3.50
370	Warren Hacker	12.00	6.00	3.50
371	Bob Lennon	12.00	6.00	3.50
372	Norm Zauchin	12.00	6.00	3.50
373	Pete Whisenant	12.00	6.00	3.50
374	Don Cardwell	12.00	6.00	3.50
375	*Jim Landis*	12.00	6.00	3.50
376	Don Elston	15.00	7.50	4.50
377	Andre Rodgers	12.00	6.00	3.50
378	Elmer Singleton	12.00	6.00	3.50
379	Don Lee	12.00	6.00	3.50
380	Walker Cooper	12.00	6.00	3.50
381	Dean Stone	12.00	6.00	3.50
382	Jim Brideweser	12.00	6.00	3.50
383	*Juan Pizarro*	12.00	6.00	3.50
384	Bobby Gene Smith	12.00	6.00	3.50
385	Art Houtteman	12.00	6.00	3.50
386	Lyle Luttrell	12.00	6.00	3.50
387	*Jack Sanford*	12.00	6.00	3.50
388	Pete Daley	12.00	6.00	3.50
389	Dave Jolly	12.00	6.00	3.50
390	Reno Bertoia	12.00	6.00	3.50
391	*Ralph Terry*	15.00	7.50	4.50
392	Chuck Tanner	12.00	6.00	3.50
393	Raul Sanchez	12.00	6.00	3.50
394	Luis Arroyo	12.00	6.00	3.50
395	Bubba Phillips	12.00	6.00	3.50
396	Casey Wise	12.00	6.00	3.50
397	Roy Smalley	12.00	6.00	3.50
398	Al Cicotte	15.00	7.50	4.50
399	Billy Consolo	12.00	6.00	3.50
400	Dodgers' Sluggers (Roy Campanella, Carl Furillo, Gil Hodges, Duke Snider)	200.00	100.00	60.00
401	*Earl Battey*	15.00	7.50	4.50
402	Jim Pisoni	12.00	6.00	3.50
403	Dick Hyde	12.00	6.00	3.50
404	Harry Anderson	12.00	6.00	3.50
405	Duke Maas	12.00	6.00	3.50
406	Bob Hale	12.00	6.00	3.50
407	Yankees' Power Hitters (Mickey Mantle, Yogi Berra)	500.00	250.00	125.00
----	Checklist Series 1-2 (Big Blony ad on back)	600.00	300.00	180.00
----	Checklist Series 1-2 (Bazooka ad on back)	600.00	300.00	180.00
----	Checklist Series 2-3 (Big Blony)	625.00	310.00	185.00
----	Checklist Series 2-3 (Bazooka)	625.00	310.00	185.00
----	Checklist Series 3-4 (Twin Blony)	1,300	650.00	390.00
----	Checklist Series 3-4 (Bazooka)	1,300	650.00	390.00
----	Checklist Series 4-5 (Twin Blony)	1,950	975.00	585.00
----	Checklist Series 4-5 (Bazooka)	1,950	975.00	585.00
----	Contest May 4	100.00	50.00	25.00
----	Contest May 25	135.00	65.00	40.00
----	Contest June 22	145.00	75.00	45.00
----	Contest July 19	200.00	100.00	60.00
----	Lucky Penny insert card	250.00	125.00	75.00

1958 Topps

Topps continued to expand its set size in 1958 with the release of a 494-card set. One card (#145) was not issued after Ed Bouchee was suspended from baseball. Cards retained the 2-1/2" x 3-1/2" size. There are a number of variations, including player or team names found in either yellow or white lettering on 33 cards between numbers 2-108 (higher priced yellow-letter variations checklisted below are not included in the complete set prices). The number of multiple-player cards was increased. A major innovation is the addition of 20 "All-Star" cards. For the first time, checklists were incorporated into the numbered series, on the backs of team cards.

		NM	EX	VG
	Complete Set (494):	8,500	4,250	2,500
	Common Player (1-495):	9.00	4.50	2.57
1	Ted Williams	600.00	175.00	80.00
2a	Bob Lemon (Yellow team.)	80.00	40.00	24.00
2b	Bob Lemon (White team.)	30.00	15.00	9.00
3	Alex Kellner	9.00	4.50	2.57
4	Hank Foiles	9.00	4.50	2.57
5	Willie Mays	325.00	162.50	81.25
6	George Zuverink	9.00	4.50	2.57
7	Dale Long	9.00	4.50	2.57
8a	Eddie Kasko (Yellow name.)	60.00	30.00	18.00
8b	Eddie Kasko (White name.)	9.00	4.50	2.57
9	Hank Bauer	20.00	10.00	6.00
10	Lou Burdette	9.00	4.50	2.57
11a	Jim Rivera (Yellow team.)	60.00	30.00	18.00
11b	Jim Rivera (White team.)	9.00	4.50	2.57
12	George Crowe	9.00	4.50	2.57
13a	Billy Hoeft (Yellow name.)	60.00	30.00	18.00
13b	Billy Hoeft (White name, orange triangle by foot.)	9.00	4.50	2.57
13c	Billy Hoeft (White name, red triangle by foot.)	9.00	4.50	2.57
14	Rip Repulski	9.00	4.50	2.57
15	Jim Lemon	9.00	4.50	2.57
16	Charley Neal	9.00	4.50	2.57
17	Felix Mantilla	9.00	4.50	2.57
18	Frank Sullivan	9.00	4.50	2.57
19	1957 Giants Team	40.00	20.00	12.00
20a	Gil McDougald (Yellow name.)	75.00	37.50	22.00
20b	Gil McDougald (White name.)	20.00	10.00	6.00
21	Curt Barclay	9.00	4.50	2.57
22	Hal Naragon	9.00	4.50	2.57
23a	Bill Tuttle (Yellow name.)	60.00	30.00	18.00
23b	Bill Tuttle (White name.)	9.00	4.50	2.57
24a	Hobie Landrith (Yellow name.)	60.00	30.00	18.00
24b	Hobie Landrith (White name.)	9.00	4.50	2.57
25	Don Drysdale	100.00	50.00	25.00
26	Ron Jackson	9.00	4.50	2.57
27	Bud Freeman	9.00	4.50	2.57
28	Jim Busby	9.00	4.50	2.57
29	Ted Lepcio	9.00	4.50	2.57
30a	Hank Aaron (Yellow name.)	460.00	230.00	140.00
30b	Hank Aaron (White name.)	225.00	112.50	56.25
31	Tex Clevenger	9.00	4.50	2.57
32a	J.W. Porter (Yellow name.)	60.00	30.00	18.00
32b	J.W. Porter (White name.)	9.00	4.50	2.57
33a	Cal Neeman (Yellow team.)	60.00	30.00	18.00
33b	Cal Neeman (White team.)	9.00	4.50	2.57
34	Bob Thurman	9.00	4.50	2.57
35a	Don Mossi (Yellow team.)	60.00	30.00	18.00
35b	Don Mossi (White team.)	9.00	4.50	2.57
36	Ted Kazanski	9.00	4.50	2.57
37	*Mike McCormick* (Photo actually Ray Monzant.)	9.00	4.50	2.57
38	Dick Gernert	9.00	4.50	2.57
39	Bob Martyn	9.00	4.50	2.57
40	George Kell	20.00	10.00	6.00
41	Dave Hillman	9.00	4.50	2.57
42	*John Roseboro*	25.00	12.50	7.50
43	Sal Maglie	12.50	6.25	3.75
44	Wash. Senators Team	20.00	10.00	6.00
45	Dick Groat	9.00	4.50	2.57
46a	Lou Sleater (Yellow name.)	60.00	30.00	18.00
46b	Lou Sleater (White name.)	9.00	4.50	2.57
47	*Roger Maris*	425.00	210.00	125.00
48	Chuck Harmon	9.00	4.50	2.57
49	Smoky Burgess	9.00	4.50	2.57
50a	Billy Pierce (Yellow team.)	60.00	30.00	18.00
50b	Billy Pierce (White team.)	9.00	4.50	2.57
51	Del Rice	9.00	4.50	2.57
52a	Bob Clemente (Yellow team.)	450.00	220.00	135.00
52b	Bob Clemente (White team.)	300.00	150.00	75.00
53a	Morrie Martin (Yellow name.)	60.00	30.00	18.00
53b	Morrie Martin (White name.)	9.00	4.50	2.57
54	*Norm Siebern*	12.50	6.25	3.75
55	Chico Carrasquel	9.00	4.50	2.57
56	Bill Fischer	9.00	4.50	2.57
57a	Tim Thompson (Yellow name.)	60.00	30.00	18.00
57b	Tim Thompson (White name.)	9.00	4.50	2.57
58a	Art Schult (Yellow team.)	60.00	30.00	18.00
58b	Art Schult (White team.)	9.00	4.50	2.57
59	Dave Sisler	9.00	4.50	2.57
60a	Del Ennis (Yellow name.)	60.00	30.00	18.00
60b	Del Ennis (White name.)	9.00	4.50	2.57
61a	Darrell Johnson (Yellow name.)	100.00	50.00	30.00
61b	Darrell Johnson (White name.)	15.00	7.50	4.50
62	Joe DeMaestri	9.00	4.50	2.57
63	Joe Nuxhall	9.00	4.50	2.57
64	Joe Lonnett	9.00	4.50	2.57
65a	Von McDaniel (Yellow name.)	60.00	30.00	18.00
65b	Von McDaniel (White name.)	9.00	4.50	2.57
66	Lee Walls	9.00	4.50	2.57
67	Joe Ginsberg	9.00	4.50	2.57
68	Daryl Spencer	9.00	4.50	2.57
69	Wally Burnette	9.00	4.50	2.57
70a	Al Kaline (Yellow name.)	300.00	150.00	90.00
70b	Al Kaline (White name.)	100.00	50.00	25.00
71	1957 Dodgers Team	80.00	40.00	20.00
72	Bud Byerly (Photo actually Hal Griggs.)	9.00	4.50	2.57
73	Pete Daley	9.00	4.50	2.57
74	Roy Face	9.00	4.50	2.57

#	Player			
75	Gus Bell	9.00	4.50	2.57
76a	Dick Farrell (Yellow team.)	60.00	30.00	18.00
76b	Dick Farrell (White team.)	9.00	4.50	2.57
77a	Don Zimmer (Yellow team.)	80.00	40.00	24.00
77b	Don Zimmer (White team.)	15.00	7.50	4.50
78a	Ernie Johnson (Yellow name.)	60.00	30.00	18.00
78b	Ernie Johnson (White name.)	9.00	4.50	2.57
79a	Dick Williams (Yellow team.)	60.00	30.00	18.00
79b	Dick Williams (White team.)	9.00	4.50	2.57
80	Dick Drott	9.00	4.50	2.57
81a	*Steve Boros* (Yellow team.)	60.00	30.00	18.00
81b	*Steve Boros* (White team.)	9.00	4.50	2.57
82	Ronnie Kline	9.00	4.50	2.57
83	*Bob Hazle*	9.00	4.50	2.57
84	Billy O'Dell	9.00	4.50	2.57
85a	Luis Aparicio (Yellow team.)	140.00	70.00	40.00
85b	Luis Aparicio (White team.)	30.00	15.00	9.00
86	Valmy Thomas	9.00	4.50	2.57
87	Johnny Kucks	10.00	5.00	3.00
88	Duke Snider	45.00	22.50	13.50
89	Billy Klaus	9.00	4.50	2.57
90	Robin Roberts	30.00	15.00	9.00
91	Chuck Tanner	9.00	4.50	2.57
92a	Clint Courtney (Yellow name.)	60.00	30.00	18.00
92b	Clint Courtney (White name.)	9.00	4.50	2.57
93	Sandy Amoros	12.00	6.00	3.50
94	Bob Skinner	9.00	4.50	2.57
95	Frank Bolling	9.00	4.50	2.57
96	Joe Durham	9.00	4.50	2.57
97a	Larry Jackson (Yellow name.)	60.00	30.00	18.00
97b	Larry Jackson (White name.)	9.00	4.50	2.57
98a	Billy Hunter (Yellow name.)	60.00	30.00	18.00
98b	Billy Hunter (White name.)	9.00	4.50	2.57
99	Bobby Adams	9.00	4.50	2.57
100a	Early Wynn (Yellow team.)	90.00	45.00	27.50
100b	Early Wynn (White team.)	20.00	10.00	6.00
101a	Bobby Richardson (Yellow name.)	100.00	50.00	30.00
101b	Bobby Richardson (White name.)	30.00	15.00	9.00
102	George Strickland	9.00	4.50	2.57
103	Jerry Lynch	9.00	4.50	2.57
104	Jim Pendleton	9.00	4.50	2.57
105	Billy Gardner	9.00	4.50	2.57
106	Dick Schofield	9.00	4.50	2.57
107	Ossie Virgil	9.00	4.50	2.57
108a	Jim Landis (Yellow team.)	60.00	30.00	18.00
108b	Jim Landis (White team.)	9.00	4.50	2.57
109	Herb Plews	9.00	4.50	2.57
110	Johnny Logan	9.00	4.50	2.57
111	Stu Miller	9.00	4.50	2.57
112	Gus Zernial	9.00	4.50	2.57
113	Jerry Walker	9.00	4.50	2.57
114	Irv Noren	9.00	4.50	2.57
115	Jim Bunning	20.00	10.00	6.00
116	Dave Philley	9.00	4.50	2.57
117	Frank Torre	9.00	4.50	2.57
118	Harvey Haddix	9.00	4.50	2.57
119	Harry Chiti	9.00	4.50	2.57
120	Johnny Podres	12.00	6.00	3.50
121	Eddie Miksis	9.00	4.50	2.57
122	Walt Moryn	9.00	4.50	2.57
123	Dick Tomanek	9.00	4.50	2.57
124	Bobby Usher	9.00	4.50	2.57
125	Al Dark	9.00	4.50	2.57
126	Stan Palys	9.00	4.50	2.57
127	Tom Sturdivant	10.00	5.00	3.00
128	*Willie Kirkland*	9.00	4.50	2.57
129	Jim Derrington	9.00	4.50	2.57
130	Jackie Jensen	10.00	5.00	3.00
131	Bob Henrich	9.00	4.50	2.57
132	Vernon Law	9.00	4.50	2.57
133	Russ Nixon	9.00	4.50	2.57
134	Phila. Phillies Team	16.00	8.00	4.75
135	Mike Drabowsky	9.00	4.50	2.57
136	Jim Finingan	9.00	4.50	2.57
137	Russ Kemmerer	9.00	4.50	2.57
138	Earl Torgeson	9.00	4.50	2.57
139	George Brunet	9.00	4.50	2.57
140	Wes Covington	9.00	4.50	2.57
141	Ken Lehman	9.00	4.50	2.57
142	Enos Slaughter	25.00	12.50	7.50
143	Billy Muffett	9.00	4.50	2.57
144	Bobby Morgan	9.00	4.50	2.57
145	Not Issued			
146	Dick Gray	9.00	4.50	2.57
147	*Don McMahon*	9.00	4.50	2.57
148	Billy Consolo	9.00	4.50	2.57
149	Tom Acker	9.00	4.50	2.57
150	Mickey Mantle	875.00	440.00	265.00
151	Buddy Pritchard	9.00	4.50	2.57
152	Johnny Antonelli	9.00	4.50	2.57
153	Les Moss	9.00	4.50	2.57
154	Harry Byrd	9.00	4.50	2.57
155	Hector Lopez	9.00	4.50	2.57
156	Dick Hyde	9.00	4.50	2.57
157	Dee Fondy	9.00	4.50	2.57
158	Cleve. Indians Team	25.00	12.50	7.50
159	Taylor Phillips	10.00	5.00	3.00
160	Don Hoak	9.00	4.50	2.57
161	Don Larsen	25.00	12.50	7.50
162	Gil Hodges	30.00	15.00	9.00
163	Jim Wilson	9.00	4.50	2.57
164	Bob Taylor	9.00	4.50	2.57
165	Bob Nieman	9.00	4.50	2.57
166	Danny O'Connell	9.00	4.50	2.57
167	Frank Baumann	9.00	4.50	2.57
168	Joe Cunningham	9.00	4.50	2.57
169	Ralph Terry	9.00	4.50	2.57
170	Vic Wertz	9.00	4.50	2.57
171	Harry Anderson	9.00	4.50	2.57
172	Don Gross	9.00	4.50	2.57
173	Eddie Yost	9.00	4.50	2.57
174	K.C. Athletics Team	20.00	10.00	6.00
175	*Marv Throneberry*	25.00	12.50	7.50
176	Bob Buhl	9.00	4.50	2.57
177	Al Smith	9.00	4.50	2.57
178	Ted Kluszewski	20.00	10.00	6.00
179	Willy Miranda	9.00	4.50	2.57
180	Lindy McDaniel	9.00	4.50	2.57
181	Willie Jones	9.00	4.50	2.57
182	Joe Caffie	9.00	4.50	2.57
183	Dave Jolly	9.00	4.50	2.57
184	Elvin Tappe	9.00	4.50	2.57
185	Ray Boone	9.00	4.50	2.57
186	Jack Meyer	9.00	4.50	2.57
187	Sandy Koufax	275.00	137.50	68.75
188	Milt Bolling (Photo actually Lou Berberet.)	9.00	4.50	2.57
189	George Susce	9.00	4.50	2.57
190	Red Schoendienst	20.00	10.00	6.00
191	Art Ceccarelli	9.00	4.50	2.57
192	Milt Graff	9.00	4.50	2.57
193	*Jerry Lumpe*	12.50	6.25	3.75
194	Roger Craig	9.00	4.50	2.57
195	Whitey Lockman	9.00	4.50	2.57
196	Mike Garcia	9.00	4.50	2.57
197	Haywood Sullivan	9.00	4.50	2.57
198	Bill Virdon	9.00	4.50	2.57
199	Don Blasingame	9.00	4.50	2.57
200	Bob Keegan	9.00	4.50	2.57
201	Jim Bolger	9.00	4.50	2.57
202	*Woody Held*	9.00	4.50	2.57
203	Al Walker	9.00	4.50	2.57
204	Leo Kiely	9.00	4.50	2.57
205	Johnny Temple	9.00	4.50	2.57
206	Bob Shaw	9.00	4.50	2.57
207	Solly Hemus	9.00	4.50	2.57
208	Cal McLish	9.00	4.50	2.57
209	Bob Anderson	9.00	4.50	2.57
210	Wally Moon	9.00	4.50	2.57
211	Pete Burnside	9.00	4.50	2.57
212	Bubba Phillips	9.00	4.50	2.57
213	Red Wilson	9.00	4.50	2.57
214	Willard Schmidt	9.00	4.50	2.57
215	Jim Gilliam	12.50	6.25	3.75
216	St. Louis Cards Team	25.00	12.50	7.50
217	Jack Harshman	9.00	4.50	2.57
218	Dick Rand	9.00	4.50	2.57
219	Camilo Pascual	9.00	4.50	2.57
220	Tom Brewer	9.00	4.50	2.57
221	Jerry Kindall	9.00	4.50	2.57
222	Bud Daley	9.00	4.50	2.57
223	Andy Pafko	9.00	4.50	2.57
224	Bob Grim	10.00	5.00	3.00
225	Billy Goodman	9.00	4.50	2.57
226	Bob Smith (Photo actually Bobby Gene Smith.)	9.00	4.50	2.57
227	Gene Stephens	9.00	4.50	2.57
228	Duke Maas	9.00	4.50	2.57
229	Frank Zupo	9.00	4.50	2.57
230	Richie Ashburn	30.00	15.00	9.00
231	Lloyd Merritt	9.00	4.50	2.57
232	Reno Bertoia	9.00	4.50	2.57
233	Mickey Vernon	9.00	4.50	2.57
234	Carl Sawatski	9.00	4.50	2.57
235	Tom Gorman	9.00	4.50	2.57
236	Ed FitzGerald	9.00	4.50	2.57
237	Bill Wight	9.00	4.50	2.57
238	Bill Mazeroski	30.00	15.00	9.00
239	Chuck Stobbs	9.00	4.50	2.57
240	Moose Skowron	20.00	10.00	6.00
241	Dick Littlefield	9.00	4.50	2.57
242	Johnny Klippstein	9.00	4.50	2.57
243	Larry Raines	9.00	4.50	2.57
244	*Don Demeter*	9.00	4.50	2.57
245	*Frank Lary*	9.00	4.50	2.57
246	New York Yankees Team	100.00	50.00	25.00
247	Casey Wise	9.00	4.50	2.57
248	Herm Wehmeier	9.00	4.50	2.57
249	Ray Moore	9.00	4.50	2.57
250	Roy Sievers	9.00	4.50	2.57
251	Warren Hacker	9.00	4.50	2.57
252	Bob Trowbridge	9.00	4.50	2.57
253	Don Mueller	9.00	4.50	2.57
254	Alex Grammas	9.00	4.50	2.57
255	Bob Turley	25.00	12.50	7.50
256	Chicago White Sox Team	20.00	10.00	6.00
257	Hal Smith	9.00	4.50	2.57
258	Carl Erskine	17.50	8.75	5.25
259	Al Pilarcik	9.00	4.50	2.57
260	Frank Malzone	9.00	4.50	2.57
261	Turk Lown	9.00	4.50	2.57
262	Johnny Groth	9.00	4.50	2.57
263	Eddie Bressoud	9.00	4.50	2.57
264	Jack Sanford	9.00	4.50	2.57
265	Pete Runnels	9.00	4.50	2.57
266	Connie Johnson	9.00	4.50	2.57
267	Sherm Lollar	9.00	4.50	2.57
268	Granny Hamner	9.00	4.50	2.57
269	Paul Smith	9.00	4.50	2.57
270	Warren Spahn	80.00	40.00	20.00
271	Billy Martin	20.00	10.00	6.00
272	Ray Crone	9.00	4.50	2.57
273	Hal Smith	9.00	4.50	2.57
274	Rocky Bridges	9.00	4.50	2.57
275	Elston Howard	20.00	10.00	6.00
276	Bobby Avila	9.00	4.50	2.57
277	Virgil Trucks	9.00	4.50	2.57
278	Mack Burk	9.00	4.50	2.57
279	Bob Boyd	9.00	4.50	2.57
280	Jim Piersall	9.00	4.50	2.57
281	Sam Taylor	9.00	4.50	2.57
282	Paul Foytack	9.00	4.50	2.57
283	Ray Shearer	9.00	4.50	2.57
284	Ray Katt	9.00	4.50	2.57
285	Frank Robinson	100.00	50.00	25.00
286	Gino Cimoli	9.00	4.50	2.57
287	Sam Jones	9.00	4.50	2.57
288	Harmon Killebrew	100.00	50.00	25.00
289	Series Hurling Rivals (Lou Burdette, Bobby Shantz)	25.00	12.50	7.50
290	Dick Donovan	9.00	4.50	2.57
291	Don Landrum	9.00	4.50	2.57
292	Ned Garver	9.00	4.50	2.57
293	Gene Freese	9.00	4.50	2.57
294	Hal Jeffcoat	9.00	4.50	2.57
295	Minnie Minoso	20.00	10.00	6.00
296	*Ryne Duren*	50.00	25.00	15.00
297	Don Buddin	9.00	4.50	2.57
298	Jim Hearn	9.00	4.50	2.57
299	Harry Simpson	9.00	4.50	2.57
300	League Presidents (Warren Giles, William Harridge)	35.00	17.50	10.00
301	Randy Jackson	9.00	4.50	2.57
302	Mike Baxes	9.00	4.50	2.57
303	Neil Chrisley	9.00	4.50	2.57
304	Tigers' Big Bats (Al Kaline, Harvey Kuenn)	35.00	17.50	10.00
305	Clem Labine	12.50	6.25	3.75
306	Whammy Douglas	9.00	4.50	2.57
307	Brooks Robinson	100.00	50.00	25.00
308	Paul Giel	9.00	4.50	2.57
309	Gail Harris	9.00	4.50	2.57
310	Ernie Banks	125.00	62.50	31.25
311	Bob Purkey	9.00	4.50	2.57
312	Boston Red Sox Team	25.00	12.50	7.50
313	Bob Rush	9.00	4.50	2.57
314	Dodgers' Boss & Power (Duke Snider, Walter Alston)	35.00	17.50	10.00
315	Bob Friend	9.00	4.50	2.57
316	Tito Francona	9.00	4.50	2.57
317	*Albie Pearson*	10.00	5.00	3.00
318	Frank House	9.00	4.50	2.57
319	Lou Skizas	9.00	4.50	2.57
320	Whitey Ford	80.00	40.00	20.00
321	Sluggers Supreme (Ted Kluszewski, Ted Williams)	100.00	50.00	25.00
322	Harding Peterson	9.00	4.50	2.57
323	Elmer Valo	9.00	4.50	2.57
324	Hoyt Wilhelm	20.00	10.00	6.00
325	Joe Adcock	9.00	4.50	2.57
326	Bob Miller	9.00	4.50	2.57
327	Chicago Cubs Team	20.00	10.00	6.00
328	Ike Delock	9.00	4.50	2.57
329	Bob Cerv	9.00	4.50	2.57
330	Ed Bailey	9.00	4.50	2.57
331	Pedro Ramos	9.00	4.50	2.57
332	Jim King	9.00	4.50	2.57
333	Andy Carey	10.00	5.00	3.00
334	Mound Aces (Bob Friend, Billy Pierce)	12.00	6.00	3.50
335	Ruben Gomez	9.00	4.50	2.57
336	Bert Hamric	9.00	4.50	2.57
337	Hank Aguirre	9.00	4.50	2.57
338	Walt Dropo	9.00	4.50	2.57
339	Fred Hatfield	9.00	4.50	2.57
340	Don Newcombe	25.00	12.50	7.50
341	Pittsburgh Pirates Team	30.00	15.00	9.00
342	Jim Brosnan	9.00	4.50	2.57
343	*Orlando Cepeda*	100.00	50.00	25.00
344	Bob Porterfield	9.00	4.50	2.57
345	Jim Hegan	9.00	4.50	2.57
346	Steve Bilko	9.00	4.50	2.57
347	Don Rudolph	9.00	4.50	2.57
348	Chico Fernandez	9.00	4.50	2.57
349	Murry Dickson	9.00	4.50	2.57
350	Ken Boyer	12.50	6.25	3.75
351	Braves' Fence Busters (Hank Aaron, Joe Adcock, Del Crandall, Eddie Mathews)	60.00	30.00	18.00
352	Herb Score	12.50	6.25	3.75
353	Stan Lopata	9.00	4.50	2.57
354	Art Ditmar	10.00	5.00	3.00
355	Bill Bruton	9.00	4.50	2.57
356	Bob Malkmus	9.00	4.50	2.57
357	Danny McDevitt	9.00	4.50	2.57
358	Gene Baker	9.00	4.50	2.57
359	Billy Loes	9.00	4.50	2.57
360	Roy McMillan	9.00	4.50	2.57
361	Mike Fornieles	9.00	4.50	2.57
362	Ray Jablonski	9.00	4.50	2.57
363	Don Elston	9.00	4.50	2.57
364	Earl Battey	9.00	4.50	2.57
365	Tom Morgan	9.00	4.50	2.57
366	Gene Green	9.00	4.50	2.57
367	Jack Urban	9.00	4.50	2.57
368	Rocky Colavito	50.00	25.00	15.00
369	Ralph Lumenti	9.00	4.50	2.57
370	Yogi Berra	120.00	60.00	30.00
371	Marty Keough	9.00	4.50	2.57
372	Don Cardwell	9.00	4.50	2.57
373	Joe Pignatano	9.00	4.50	2.57
374	Brooks Lawrence	9.00	4.50	2.57
375	Pee Wee Reese	45.00	22.50	13.50
376	Charley Rabe	9.00	4.50	2.57
377a	Milwaukee Braves Team (Alphabetical checklist.)	20.00	10.00	6.00
377b	Milwaukee Braves Team (Numerical checklist.)	140.00	70.00	40.00
378	Hank Sauer	9.00	4.50	2.57
379	Ray Herbert	9.00	4.50	2.57
380	Charley Maxwell	9.00	4.50	2.57
381	Hal Brown	9.00	4.50	2.57
382	Al Cicotte	10.00	5.00	3.00
383	Lou Berberet	9.00	4.50	2.57
384	John Goryl	9.00	4.50	2.57
385	Wilmer Mizell	9.00	4.50	2.57
386	Birdie's Young Sluggers (Ed Bailey, Frank Robinson, Birdie Tebbetts)	20.00	10.00	6.00
387	Wally Post	9.00	4.50	2.57
388	Billy Moran	9.00	4.50	2.57
389	Bill Taylor	9.00	4.50	2.57
390	Del Crandall	9.00	4.50	2.57
391	Dave Melton	9.00	4.50	2.57
392	Bennie Daniels	9.00	4.50	2.57
393	Tony Kubek	20.00	10.00	6.00
394	*Jim Grant*	10.00	5.00	3.00
395	Willard Nixon	9.00	4.50	2.57
396	Dutch Dotterer	9.00	4.50	2.57
397a	Detroit Tigers Team (Alphabetical checklist.)	15.00	7.50	4.50

		NM	EX	VG
397b	Detroit Tigers Team (Numerical checklist.)	125.00	65.00	35.00
398	Gene Woodling	9.00	4.50	2.57
399	Marv Grissom	9.00	4.50	2.57
400	Nellie Fox	25.00	12.50	7.50
401	Don Bessent	9.00	4.50	2.57
402	Bobby Gene Smith	9.00	4.50	2.57
403	Steve Korcheck	9.00	4.50	2.57
404	Curt Simmons	9.00	4.50	2.57
405	Ken Aspromonte	9.00	4.50	2.57
406	Vic Power	9.00	4.50	2.57
407	Carlton Willey	9.00	4.50	2.57
408a	Baltimore Orioles Team (Alphabetical checklist.)	15.00	7.50	4.50
408b	Baltimore Orioles Team (Numerical checklist.)	125.00	65.00	35.00
409	Frank Thomas	9.00	4.50	2.57
410	Murray Wall	9.00	4.50	2.57
411	*Tony Taylor*	9.00	4.50	2.57
412	Jerry Staley	9.00	4.50	2.57
413	*Jim Davenport*	9.00	4.50	2.57
414	Sammy White	9.00	4.50	2.57
415	Bob Bowman	9.00	4.50	2.57
416	Foster Castleman	9.00	4.50	2.57
417	Carl Furillo	15.00	7.50	4.50
418	World Series Foes (Hank Aaron, Mickey Mantle)	400.00	200.00	100.00
419	Bobby Shantz	15.00	7.50	4.50
420	*Vada Pinson*	20.00	10.00	6.00
421	Dixie Howell	9.00	4.50	2.57
422	Norm Zauchin	9.00	4.50	2.57
423	Phil Clark	9.00	4.50	2.57
424	Larry Doby	20.00	10.00	6.00
425	Sam Esposito	9.00	4.50	2.57
426	Johnny O'Brien	9.00	4.50	2.57
427	Al Worthington	9.00	4.50	2.57
428a	Cincinnati Redlegs Team (Alphabetical checklist.)	15.00	7.50	4.50
428b	Cincinnati Redlegs Team (Numerical checklist.)	125.00	65.00	35.00
429	Gus Triandos	9.00	4.50	2.57
430	Bobby Thomson	12.00	6.00	3.50
431	Gene Conley	9.00	4.50	2.57
432	John Powers	9.00	4.50	2.57
433	Pancho Herrera	9.00	4.50	2.57
433a	Pancho Herrera (Printing error, no "a" in Herrera.)	6,000	3,000	1,800
434	Harvey Kuenn	9.00	4.50	2.57
435	Ed Roebuck	9.00	4.50	2.57
436	Rival Fence Busters (Willie Mays, Duke Snider)	80.00	40.00	20.00
437	Bob Speake	9.00	4.50	2.57
438	Whitey Herzog	20.00	10.00	6.00
439	Ray Narleski	9.00	4.50	2.57
440	Ed Mathews	80.00	40.00	20.00
441	Jim Marshall	9.00	4.50	2.57
442	Phil Paine	9.00	4.50	2.57
443	Billy Harrell (SP)	15.00	7.50	4.50
444	Danny Kravitz	9.00	4.50	2.57
445	Bob Smith	9.00	4.50	2.57
446	Carroll Hardy (SP)	15.00	7.50	4.50
447	Ray Monzant	9.00	4.50	2.57
448	*Charlie Lau*	13.50	7.00	4.00
449	Gene Fodge	9.00	4.50	2.57
450	Preston Ward (SP)	15.00	7.50	4.50
451	Joe Taylor	9.00	4.50	2.57
452	Roman Mejias	9.00	4.50	2.57
453	Tom Qualters	9.00	4.50	2.57
454	Harry Hanebrink	9.00	4.50	2.57
455	Hal Griggs (Photo actually Bud Byerly.)	9.00	4.50	2.57
456	Dick Brown	9.00	4.50	2.57
457	*Milt Pappas*	10.00	5.00	3.00
458	Julio Becquer	9.00	4.50	2.57
459	Ron Blackburn	9.00	4.50	2.57
460	Chuck Essegian	9.00	4.50	2.57
461	Ed Mayer	9.00	4.50	2.57
462	Gary Geiger (SP)	15.00	7.50	4.50
463	Vito Valentinetti	9.00	4.50	2.57
464	*Curt Flood*	30.00	15.00	9.00
465	Arnie Portocarrero	9.00	4.50	2.57
466	Pete Whisenant	9.00	4.50	2.57
467	Glen Hobbie	9.00	4.50	2.57
468	Bob Schmidt	9.00	4.50	2.57
469	Don Ferrarese	9.00	4.50	2.57
470	R.C. Stevens	9.00	4.50	2.57
471	Lenny Green	9.00	4.50	2.57
472	Joe Jay	9.00	4.50	2.57
473	Bill Renna	9.00	4.50	2.57
474	Roman Semproch	9.00	4.50	2.57
475	All-Star Managers (Fred Haney, Casey Stengel)	30.00	15.00	9.00
476	Stan Musial (All-Star)	35.00	17.50	10.00
477	Bill Skowron (All-Star)	15.00	7.50	4.50
478	Johnny Temple (All-Star)	10.00	5.00	3.00
479	Nellie Fox (All-Star)	15.00	7.50	4.50
480	Eddie Mathews (All-Star)	25.00	12.50	7.50
481	Frank Malzone (All-Star)	10.00	5.00	3.00
482	Ernie Banks (All-Star)	30.00	15.00	9.00
483	Luis Aparicio (All-Star)	20.00	10.00	6.00
484	Frank Robinson (All-Star)	30.00	15.00	9.00
485	Ted Williams (All-Star)	150.00	75.00	37.50
486	Willie Mays (All-Star)	75.00	37.50	18.75
487	Mickey Mantle (All-Star)(Triple Print)	165.00	82.50	49.50
488	Hank Aaron (All-Star)	55.00	27.50	16.50
489	Jackie Jensen (All-Star)	12.00	6.00	3.50
490	Ed Bailey (All-Star)	10.00	5.00	3.00
491	Sherman Lollar (All-Star)	10.00	5.00	3.00
492	Bob Friend (All-Star)	10.00	5.00	3.00
493	Bob Turley (All-Star)	15.00	7.50	4.50
494	Warren Spahn (All-Star)	25.00	12.50	7.50
495	Herb Score (All-Star)	15.00	7.50	4.50
	Contest Card (All-Star Game, July 8)	70.00	35.00	20.00
	Felt Emblems Insert Card	45.00	22.50	13.50

1959 Topps

These 2-1/2" x 3-1/2" cards have a round photograph on front with a solid-color background above and below and a white border. A facsimile autograph is found across the photo. The 572-card set marks the largest set issued to that time. Card numbers below 507 have red and green printing on back with the card number in white in a green box. On high number cards beginning with #507, the printing is black and red and the card number is in a black box. Specialty cards include multiple-player cards, team cards with checklists on back, "All-Star" cards, "Baseball Thrills," and 31 "Rookie Stars." There is also a card of the commissioner, Ford Frick, and one of Roy Campanella in a wheelchair. A handful of cards can be found with and without lines added to the biographies on back indicating trades or demotions; those without the added lines are scarcer and more valuable and are not included in the complete set price. Card numbers 199-286 can be found with either white or gray backs, with the gray stock being the less common.

		NM	EX	VG
	Complete Set (572):	12,000	6,000	3,600
	Common Player (1-506):	7.00	3.50	2.00
	Common Player (507-572):	15.00	7.50	4.50
1	Ford Frick	80.00	40.00	20.00
2	Eddie Yost	12.00	3.50	2.00
3	Don McMahon	7.00	3.50	2.00
4	Albie Pearson	7.00	3.50	2.00
5	Dick Donovan	7.00	3.50	2.00
6	Alex Grammas	7.00	3.50	2.00
7	Al Pilarcik	7.00	3.50	2.00
8	Philadelphia Phillies Team (SP)	90.00	45.00	27.50
9	Paul Giel	7.00	3.50	2.00
10	Mickey Mantle	825.00	410.00	250.00
11	Billy Hunter	7.00	3.50	2.00
12	Vern Law	7.00	3.50	2.00
13	Dick Gernert	7.00	3.50	2.00
14	Pete Whisenant	7.00	3.50	2.00
15	Dick Drott	7.00	3.50	2.00
16	Joe Pignatano	7.00	3.50	2.00
17	Danny's All-Stars (Ted Kluszewski, Danny Murtaugh, Frank J. Thomas)	13.50	7.00	4.00
18	Jack Urban	7.00	3.50	2.00
19	Ed Bressoud	7.00	3.50	2.00
20	Duke Snider	40.00	20.00	12.00
21	Connie Johnson	7.00	3.50	2.00
22	Al Smith	7.00	3.50	2.00
23	Murry Dickson	7.00	3.50	2.00
24	Red Wilson	7.00	3.50	2.00
25	Don Hoak	7.00	3.50	2.00
26	Chuck Stobbs	7.00	3.50	2.00
27	Andy Pafko	7.00	3.50	2.00
28	Red Worthington	7.00	3.50	2.00
29	Jim Bolger	7.00	3.50	2.00
30	Nellie Fox	30.00	15.00	9.00
31	Ken Lehman	7.00	3.50	2.00
32	Don Buddin	7.00	3.50	2.00
33	Ed Fitz Gerald	7.00	3.50	2.00
34	Pitchers Beware (Al Kaline, Charlie Maxwell)	25.00	12.50	7.50
35	Ted Kluszewski	17.50	8.75	5.25
36	Hank Aguirre	7.00	3.50	2.00
37	Gene Green	7.00	3.50	2.00
38	Morrie Martin	7.00	3.50	2.00
39	Ed Bouchee	7.00	3.50	2.00
40a	Warren Spahn (Born 1931.)	100.00	50.00	25.00
40b	Warren Spahn (Born 1931, "3" partially obscured.)	100.00	50.00	25.00
40c	Warren Spahn (Born 1921.)	50.00	25.00	12.50
41	Bob Martyn	7.00	3.50	2.00
42	Murray Wall	7.00	3.50	2.00
43	Steve Bilko	7.00	3.50	2.00
44	Vito Valentinetti	7.00	3.50	2.00
45	Andy Carey	9.00	4.50	2.75
46	Bill Henry	7.00	3.50	2.00
47	Jim Finigan	7.00	3.50	2.00
48	Baltimore Orioles Team	17.50	8.75	5.25
49	Bill Hall	7.00	3.50	2.00
50	Willie Mays	150.00	75.00	45.00
51	Rip Coleman	7.00	3.50	2.00
52	Coot Veal	7.00	3.50	2.00
53	*Stan Williams*	20.00	10.00	6.00
54	Mel Roach	7.00	3.50	2.00
55	Tom Brewer	7.00	3.50	2.00
56	Carl Sawatski	7.00	3.50	2.00
57	Al Cicotte	7.00	3.50	2.00
58	Eddie Miksis	7.00	3.50	2.00
59	Irv Noren	7.00	3.50	2.00
60	Bob Turley	15.00	7.50	4.50
61	Dick Brown	7.00	3.50	2.00
62	Tony Taylor	7.00	3.50	2.00
63	Jim Hearn	7.00	3.50	2.00
64	Joe DeMaestri	7.00	3.50	2.00
65	Frank Torre	7.00	3.50	2.00

		NM	EX	VG
66	Joe Ginsberg	7.00	3.50	2.00
67	Brooks Lawrence	7.00	3.50	2.00
68	Dick Schofield	7.00	3.50	2.00
69	San Francisco Giants Team	17.50	8.75	5.25
70	Harvey Kuenn	7.00	3.50	2.00
71	Don Bessent	7.00	3.50	2.00
72	Bill Renna	7.00	3.50	2.00
73	Ron Jackson	7.00	3.50	2.00
74	Directing the Power (Cookie Lavagetto, Jim Lemon, Roy Sievers)	9.00	4.50	2.75
75	Sam Jones	7.00	3.50	2.00
76	Bobby Richardson	25.00	12.50	7.50
77	John Goryl	7.00	3.50	2.00
78	Pedro Ramos	7.00	3.50	2.00
79	Harry Chiti	7.00	3.50	2.00
80	Minnie Minoso	15.00	7.50	4.50
81	Hal Jeffcoat	7.00	3.50	2.00
82	Bob Boyd	7.00	3.50	2.00
83	Bob Smith	7.00	3.50	2.00
84	Reno Bertoia	7.00	3.50	2.00
85	Harry Anderson	7.00	3.50	2.00
86	Bob Keegan	7.00	3.50	2.00
87	Danny O'Connell	7.00	3.50	2.00
88	Herb Score	15.00	7.50	4.50
89	Billy Gardner	7.00	3.50	2.00
90	Bill Skowron (SP)	60.00	30.00	18.00
91	Herb Moford	7.00	3.50	2.00
92	Dave Philley	7.00	3.50	2.00
93	Julio Becquer	7.00	3.50	2.00
94	Chicago White Sox Team	17.50	8.75	5.25
95	Carl Willey	7.00	3.50	2.00
96	Lou Berberet	7.00	3.50	2.00
97	Jerry Lynch	7.00	3.50	2.00
98	Arnie Portocarrero	7.00	3.50	2.00
99	Ted Kazanski	7.00	3.50	2.00
100	Bob Cerv	7.00	3.50	2.00
101	Alex Kellner	7.00	3.50	2.00
102	*Felipe Alou*	25.00	12.50	7.50
103	Billy Goodman	7.00	3.50	2.00
104	Del Rice	7.00	3.50	2.00
105	Lee Walls	7.00	3.50	2.00
106	Hal Woodeshick	7.00	3.50	2.00
107	*Norm Larker*	10.00	5.00	3.00
108	Zack Monroe	9.00	4.50	2.75
109	Bob Schmidt	7.00	3.50	2.00
110	George Witt	7.00	3.50	2.00
111	Cincinnati Red Legs Team	16.00	8.00	4.75
112	Billy Consolo	7.00	3.50	2.00
113	Taylor Phillips	7.00	3.50	2.00
114	Earl Battey	7.00	3.50	2.00
115	Mickey Vernon	7.00	3.50	2.00
116	*Bob Allison*	13.50	7.00	4.00
117	*John Blanchard*	15.00	7.50	4.50
118	John Buzhardt	7.00	3.50	2.00
119	*John Callison*	12.50	6.25	3.75
120	Chuck Coles	7.00	3.50	2.00
121	Bob Conley	7.00	3.50	2.00
122	Bennie Daniels	7.00	3.50	2.00
123	Don Dillard	7.00	3.50	2.00
124	Dan Dobbek	7.00	3.50	2.00
125	*Ron Fairly*	13.50	6.75	4.00
126	Eddie Haas	7.00	3.50	2.00
127	Kent Hadley	7.00	3.50	2.00
128	Bob Hartman	7.00	3.50	2.00
129	Frank Herrera	7.00	3.50	2.00
130	Lou Jackson	7.00	3.50	2.00
131	*Deron Johnson*	10.00	5.00	3.00
132	Don Lee	7.00	3.50	2.00
133	*Bob Lillis*	7.00	3.50	2.00
134	Jim McDaniel	7.00	3.50	2.00
135	Gene Oliver	7.00	3.50	2.00
136	*Jim O'Toole*	7.50	3.75	2.25
137	Dick Ricketts	7.00	3.50	2.00
138	John Romano	7.00	3.50	2.00
139	Ed Sadowski	7.00	3.50	2.00
140	Charlie Secrest	7.00	3.50	2.00
141	Joe Shipley	7.00	3.50	2.00
142	Dick Stigman	7.00	3.50	2.00
143	Willie Tasby	7.00	3.50	2.00
144	Jerry Walker	7.00	3.50	2.00
145	Dom Zanni	7.00	3.50	2.00
146	Jerry Zimmerman	7.00	3.50	2.00
147	Cubs' Clubbers (Ernie Banks, Dale Long, Walt Moryn)	20.00	10.00	6.00
148	Mike McCormick	7.00	3.50	2.00
149	Jim Bunning	20.00	10.00	6.00
150	Stan Musial	150.00	75.00	37.50
151	Bob Malkmus	7.00	3.50	2.00
152	Johnny Klippstein	7.00	3.50	2.00
153	Jim Marshall	7.00	3.50	2.00
154	Ray Herbert	7.00	3.50	2.00
155	Enos Slaughter	20.00	10.00	6.00
156	Ace Hurlers (Billy Pierce, Robin Roberts)	12.50	6.25	3.75
157	Felix Mantilla	7.00	3.50	2.00
158	Walt Dropo	7.00	3.50	2.00
159	Bob Shaw	7.00	3.50	2.00
160	Dick Groat	7.00	3.50	2.00
161	Frank Baumann	7.00	3.50	2.00
162	Bobby G. Smith	7.00	3.50	2.00
163	Sandy Koufax	160.00	80.00	40.00
164	Johnny Groth	7.00	3.50	2.00
165	Bill Bruton	7.00	3.50	2.00
166	Destruction Crew (Rocky Colavito, Larry Doby, Minnie Minoso)	20.00	10.00	6.00
167	Duke Maas	7.00	3.50	2.00
168	Carroll Hardy	7.00	3.50	2.00
169	Ted Abernathy	7.00	3.50	2.00
170	Gene Woodling	7.00	3.50	2.00
171	Willard Schmidt	7.00	3.50	2.00
172	Kansas City Athletics Team	16.00	8.00	4.75
173	*Bill Monbouquette*	7.00	3.50	2.00
174	Jim Pendleton	7.00	3.50	2.00
175	Dick Farrell	7.00	3.50	2.00
176	Preston Ward	7.00	3.50	2.00

No.	Name			
177	Johnny Briggs	7.00	3.50	2.00
178	Ruben Amaro	7.00	3.50	2.00
179	Don Rudolph	7.00	3.50	2.00
180	Yogi Berra	100.00	50.00	25.00
181	Bob Porterfield	7.00	3.50	2.00
182	Milt Graff	7.00	3.50	2.00
183	Stu Miller	7.00	3.50	2.00
184	Harvey Haddix	7.00	3.50	2.00
185	Jim Busby	7.00	3.50	2.00
186	Mudcat Grant	7.00	3.50	2.00
187	Bubba Phillips	7.00	3.50	2.00
188	Juan Pizarro	7.00	3.50	2.00
189	Neil Chrisley	7.00	3.50	2.00
190	Bill Virdon	7.00	3.50	2.00
191	Russ Kemmerer	7.00	3.50	2.00
192	Charley Beamon	7.00	3.50	2.00
193	Sammy Taylor	7.00	3.50	2.00
194	Jim Brosnan	7.00	3.50	2.00
195	Rip Repulski	7.00	3.50	2.00
196	Billy Moran	7.00	3.50	2.00
197	Ray Semproch	7.00	3.50	2.00
198	Jim Davenport	7.00	3.50	2.00
199	Leo Kiely	7.00	3.50	2.00
200	Warren Giles	20.00	10.00	6.00
201	Tom Acker	7.00	3.50	2.00
202	Roger Maris	120.00	60.00	30.00
203	Ozzie Virgil	7.00	3.50	2.00
204	Casey Wise	7.00	3.50	2.00
205	Don Larsen	20.00	10.00	6.00
206	Carl Furillo	20.00	10.00	6.00
207	George Strickland	7.00	3.50	2.00
208	Willie Jones	7.00	3.50	2.00
209	Lenny Green	7.00	3.50	2.00
210	Ed Bailey	7.00	3.50	2.00
211	Bob Blaylock	7.00	3.50	2.00
212	Fence Busters (Hank Aaron, Eddie Mathews)	80.00	40.00	20.00
213	Jim Rivera	7.00	3.50	2.00
214	Marcelino Solis	7.00	3.50	2.00
215	Jim Lemon	7.00	3.50	2.00
216	Andre Rodgers	7.00	3.50	2.00
217	Carl Erskine	12.50	6.25	3.75
218	Roman Mejias	7.00	3.50	2.00
219	George Zuverink	7.00	3.50	2.00
220	Frank Malzone	7.00	3.50	2.00
221	Bob Bowman	7.00	3.50	2.00
222	Bobby Shantz	15.00	7.50	4.50
223	St. Louis Cardinals Team	20.00	10.00	6.00
224	*Claude Osteen*	7.50	3.75	2.25
225	Johnny Logan	7.00	3.50	2.00
226	Art Ceccarelli	7.00	3.50	2.00
227	Hal Smith	7.00	3.50	2.00
228	Don Gross	7.00	3.50	2.00
229	Vic Power	7.00	3.50	2.00
230	Bill Fischer	7.00	3.50	2.00
231	Ellis Burton	7.00	3.50	2.00
232	Eddie Kasko	7.00	3.50	2.00
233	Paul Foytack	7.00	3.50	2.00
234	Chuck Tanner	7.00	3.50	2.00
235	Valmy Thomas	7.00	3.50	2.00
236	Ted Bowsfield	7.00	3.50	2.00
237	Run Preventers (Gil McDougald, Bobby Richardson, Bob Turley)	20.00	10.00	6.00
238	Gene Baker	7.00	3.50	2.00
239	Bob Trowbridge	7.00	3.50	2.00
240	Hank Bauer	13.50	7.00	4.00
241	Billy Muffett	7.00	3.50	2.00
242	Ron Samford	7.00	3.50	2.00
243	Marv Grissom	7.00	3.50	2.00
244	Dick Gray	7.00	3.50	2.00
245	Ned Garver	7.00	3.50	2.00
246	J.W. Porter	7.00	3.50	2.00
247	Don Ferrarese	7.00	3.50	2.00
248	Boston Red Sox Team	16.00	8.00	4.75
249	Bobby Adams	7.00	3.50	2.00
250	Billy O'Dell	7.00	3.50	2.00
251	Cletis Boyer	15.00	7.50	4.50
252	Ray Boone	7.00	3.50	2.00
253	Seth Morehead	7.00	3.50	2.00
254	Zeke Bella	7.00	3.50	2.00
255	Del Ennis	7.00	3.50	2.00
256	Jerry Davie	7.00	3.50	2.00
257	*Leon Wagner*	9.00	4.50	2.75
258	Fred Kipp	7.00	3.50	2.00
259	Jim Pisoni	7.00	3.50	2.00
260	Early Wynn	20.00	10.00	6.00
261	Gene Stephens	7.00	3.50	2.00
262	Hitters' Foes (Don Drysdale, Clem Labine, Johnny Podres)	20.00	10.00	6.00
263	Buddy Daley	7.00	3.50	2.00
264	Chico Carrasquel	7.00	3.50	2.00
265	Ron Kline	7.00	3.50	2.00
266	Woody Held	7.00	3.50	2.00
267	John Romonosky	7.00	3.50	2.00
268	Tito Francona	7.00	3.50	2.00
269	Jack Meyer	7.00	3.50	2.00
270	Gil Hodges	20.00	10.00	6.00
271	*Orlando Pena*	7.00	3.50	2.00
272	Jerry Lumpe	9.00	4.50	2.75
273	Joe Jay	7.00	3.50	2.00
274	Jerry Kindall	7.00	3.50	2.00
275	Jack Sanford	7.00	3.50	2.00
276	Pete Daley	7.00	3.50	2.00
277	Turk Lown	7.00	3.50	2.00
278	Chuck Essegian	7.00	3.50	2.00
279	Ernie Johnson	7.00	3.50	2.00
280	Frank Bolling	7.00	3.50	2.00
281	Walt Craddock	7.00	3.50	2.00
282	R.C. Stevens	7.00	3.50	2.00
283	Russ Heman	7.00	3.50	2.00
284	Steve Korcheck	7.00	3.50	2.00
285	Joe Cunningham	7.00	3.50	2.00
286	Dean Stone	7.00	3.50	2.00
287	Don Zimmer	12.50	6.25	3.75
288	Dutch Dotterer	7.00	3.50	2.00
289	Johnny Kucks	9.00	4.50	2.75
290	Wes Covington	7.00	3.50	2.00
291	Pitching Partners (Camilo Pascual, Pedro Ramos)	9.00	4.50	2.75
292	Dick Williams	7.00	3.50	2.00
293	Ray Moore	7.00	3.50	2.00
294	Hank Foiles	7.00	3.50	2.00
295	Billy Martin	17.50	8.75	5.25
296	*Ernie Broglio*	7.00	3.50	2.00
297	*Jackie Brandt*	7.00	3.50	2.00
298	Tex Clevenger	7.00	3.50	2.00
299	Billy Klaus	7.00	3.50	2.00
300	Richie Ashburn	25.00	12.50	7.50
301	Earl Averill	7.00	3.50	2.00
302	Don Mossi	7.00	3.50	2.00
303	Marty Keough	7.00	3.50	2.00
304	Chicago Cubs Team	16.00	8.00	4.75
305	Curt Raydon	7.00	3.50	2.00
306	Jim Gilliam	12.00	6.00	3.50
307	Curt Barclay	7.00	3.50	2.00
308	Norm Siebern	9.00	4.50	2.75
309	Sal Maglie	7.00	3.50	2.00
310	Luis Aparicio	25.00	12.50	7.50
311	Norm Zauchin	7.00	3.50	2.00
312	Don Newcombe	9.00	4.50	2.75
313	Frank House	7.00	3.50	2.00
314	Don Cardwell	7.00	3.50	2.00
315	Joe Adcock	9.00	4.50	2.75
316a	Ralph Lumenti (No optioned statement.)	75.00	37.50	22.50
316b	Ralph Lumenti (Optioned statement.)	7.00	3.50	2.00
317	N.L. Hitting Kings (Richie Ashburn, Willie Mays)	45.00	22.50	13.50
318	Rocky Bridges	7.00	3.50	2.00
319	Dave Hillman	7.00	3.50	2.00
320	Bob Skinner	7.00	3.50	2.00
321a	Bob Giallombardo (No optioned statement.)	75.00	37.50	22.50
321b	Bob Giallombardo (Optioned statement.)	7.00	3.50	2.00
322a	Harry Hanebrink (No trade statement.)	90.00	45.00	27.50
322b	Harry Hanebrink (Trade statement.)	7.00	3.50	2.00
323	Frank Sullivan	7.00	3.50	2.00
324	Don Demeter	7.00	3.50	2.00
325	Ken Boyer	13.50	7.00	4.00
326	Marv Throneberry	10.00	5.00	3.00
327	*Gary Bell*	7.00	3.50	2.00
328	Lou Skizas	7.00	3.50	2.00
329	Detroit Tigers Team	17.50	8.75	5.25
330	Gus Triandos	7.00	3.50	2.00
331	Steve Boros	7.00	3.50	2.00
332	Ray Monzant	7.00	3.50	2.00
333	Harry Simpson	7.00	3.50	2.00
334	Glen Hobbie	7.00	3.50	2.00
335	Johnny Temple	7.00	3.50	2.00
336a	Billy Loes (No trade statement.)	75.00	37.50	22.50
336b	Billy Loes (Trade statement.)	7.00	3.50	2.00
337	George Crowe	7.00	3.50	2.00
338	*George Anderson* (Sparky)	30.00	15.00	9.00
339	Roy Face	7.00	3.50	2.00
340	Roy Sievers	7.00	3.50	2.00
341	Tom Qualters	7.00	3.50	2.00
342	Ray Jablonski	7.00	3.50	2.00
343	Billy Hoeft	7.00	3.50	2.00
344	Russ Nixon	7.00	3.50	2.00
345	Gil McDougald	12.50	6.25	3.75
346	Batter Bafflers (Tom Brewer, Dave Sisler)	9.00	4.50	2.75
347	Bob Buhl	7.00	3.50	2.00
348	Ted Lepcio	7.00	3.50	2.00
349	Hoyt Wilhelm	15.00	7.50	4.50
350	Ernie Banks	80.00	40.00	20.00
351	Earl Torgeson	7.00	3.50	2.00
352	Robin Roberts	20.00	10.00	6.00
353	Curt Flood	12.00	6.00	3.50
354	Pete Burnside	7.00	3.50	2.00
355	Jim Piersall	9.00	4.50	2.75
356	Bob Mabe	7.00	3.50	2.00
357	*Dick Stuart*	10.00	5.00	3.00
358	Ralph Terry	7.00	3.50	2.00
359	*Bill White*	12.50	6.25	3.75
360	Al Kaline	35.00	17.50	10.00
361	Willard Nixon	7.00	3.50	2.00
362a	Dolan Nichols (No optioned statement.)	80.00	40.00	24.00
362b	Dolan Nichols (Optioned statement.)	7.00	3.50	2.00
363	Bobby Avila	7.00	3.50	2.00
364	Danny McDevitt	7.00	3.50	2.00
365	Gus Bell	7.00	3.50	2.00
366	Humberto Robinson	7.00	3.50	2.00
367	Cal Neeman	7.00	3.50	2.00
368	Don Mueller	7.00	3.50	2.00
369	Dick Tomanek	7.00	3.50	2.00
370	Pete Runnels	7.00	3.50	2.00
371	Dick Brodowski	7.00	3.50	2.00
372	Jim Hegan	7.00	3.50	2.00
373	Herb Plews	7.00	3.50	2.00
374	Art Ditmar	9.00	4.50	2.75
375	Bob Nieman	7.00	3.50	2.00
376	Hal Naragon	7.00	3.50	2.00
377	Johnny Antonelli	7.00	3.50	2.00
378	Gail Harris	7.00	3.50	2.00
379	Bob Will	7.00	3.50	2.00
380	Hank Aaron	140.00	70.00	42.50
381	Mike Baxes	7.00	3.50	2.00
382	Curt Simmons	7.00	3.50	2.00
383	Words of Wisdom (Don Larsen, Casey Stengel)	16.00	8.00	4.75
384	Dave Sisler	7.00	3.50	2.00
385	Sherm Lollar	7.00	3.50	2.00
386	Jim Delsing	7.00	3.50	2.00
387	Don Drysdale	25.00	12.50	7.50
388	Bob Will	7.00	3.50	2.00
389	Joe Nuxhall	7.00	3.50	2.00
390	Orlando Cepeda	25.00	12.50	7.50
391	Milt Pappas	7.00	3.50	2.00
392	Whitey Herzog	20.00	10.00	6.00
393	Frank Lary	7.00	3.50	2.00
394	Randy Jackson	7.00	3.50	2.00
395	Elston Howard	15.00	7.50	4.50
396	Bob Rush	7.00	3.50	2.00
397	Washington Senators Team	16.00	8.00	4.75
398	Wally Post	7.00	3.50	2.00
399	Larry Jackson	7.00	3.50	2.00
400	Jackie Jensen	10.00	5.00	3.00
401	Ron Blackburn	7.00	3.50	2.00
402	Hector Lopez	7.00	3.50	2.00
403	Clem Labine	12.50	6.25	3.75
404	Hank Sauer	7.00	3.50	2.00
405	Roy McMillan	7.00	3.50	2.00
406	Solly Drake	7.00	3.50	2.00
407	Moe Drabowsky	7.00	3.50	2.00
408	Keystone Combo (Luis Aparicio, Nellie Fox)	20.00	10.00	6.00
409	Gus Zernial	7.00	3.50	2.00
410	Billy Pierce	7.00	3.50	2.00
411	Whitey Lockman	7.00	3.50	2.00
412	Stan Lopata	7.00	3.50	2.00
413	Camilo (Camilo) Pascual	7.00	3.50	2.00
414	Dale Long	7.00	3.50	2.00
415	Bill Mazeroski	20.00	10.00	6.00
416a	Haywood Sullivan (No circle around copyright symbol, no period after "A" in "U.S.A.")	15.00	7.50	4.50
416b	Haywood Sullivan (No circle around copyright symbol, period added after "A" in "U.S.A.")	7.00	3.50	2.00
416c	Haywood Sullivan (Circle around copyright symbol, period after "A" in "U.S.A.")	7.00	3.50	2.00
417	Virgil Trucks	7.00	3.50	2.00
418	Gino Cimoli	7.00	3.50	2.00
419	Milwaukee Braves Team	16.00	8.00	4.75
420	Rocky Colavito	20.00	10.00	6.00
421	Herm Wehmeier	7.00	3.50	2.00
422	Hobie Landrith	7.00	3.50	2.00
423	Bob Grim	7.00	3.50	2.00
424	Ken Aspromonte	7.00	3.50	2.00
425	Del Crandall	7.00	3.50	2.00
426	Jerry Staley	7.00	3.50	2.00
427	Charlie Neal	7.00	3.50	2.00
428	Buc Hill Aces (Roy Face, Bob Friend, Ron Kline, Vern Law)	9.00	4.50	2.75
429	Bobby Thomson	9.00	4.50	2.75
430	Whitey Ford	40.00	20.00	12.00
431	Whammy Douglas	7.00	3.50	2.00
432	Smoky Burgess	7.00	3.50	2.00
433	Billy Harrell	7.00	3.50	2.00
434	Hal Griggs	7.00	3.50	2.00
435	Frank Robinson	30.00	15.00	9.00
436	Granny Hamner	7.00	3.50	2.00
437	Ike Delock	7.00	3.50	2.00
438	Sam Esposito	7.00	3.50	2.00
439	Brooks Robinson	30.00	15.00	9.00
440	Lou Burdette	7.00	3.50	2.00
441	John Roseboro	7.00	3.50	2.00
442	Ray Narleski	7.00	3.50	2.00
443	Daryl Spencer	7.00	3.50	2.00
444	*Ronnie Hansen*	7.00	3.50	2.00
445	Cal McLish	7.00	3.50	2.00
446	Rocky Nelson	7.00	3.50	2.00
447	Bob Anderson	7.00	3.50	2.00
448	Vada Pinson	7.00	3.50	2.00
449	Tom Gorman	7.00	3.50	2.00
450	Ed Mathews	45.00	22.50	13.50
451	Jimmy Constable	7.00	3.50	2.00
452	Chico Fernandez	7.00	3.50	2.00
453	Les Moss	7.00	3.50	2.00
454	Phil Clark	7.00	3.50	2.00
455	Larry Doby	15.00	7.50	4.50
456	Jerry Casale	7.00	3.50	2.00
457	Los Angeles Dodgers Team	20.00	10.00	6.00
458	Gordon Jones	7.00	3.50	2.00
459	Bill Tuttle	7.00	3.50	2.00
460	Bob Friend	7.00	3.50	2.00
461	Mantle Hits 42nd Homer For Crown (Mickey Mantle)	115.00	57.50	34.50
462	Colavito's Great Catch Saves Game (Rocky Colavito)	12.50	6.25	3.75
463	Kaline Becomes Youngest Batting Champ (Al Kaline)	15.00	7.50	4.50
464	Mays' Catch Makes Series History (Willie Mays)	35.00	17.50	10.00
465	Sievers Sets Homer Mark (Roy Sievers)	7.00	3.50	2.00
466	Pierce All-Star Starter (Billy Pierce)	7.00	3.50	2.00
467	Aaron Clubs World Series Homer (Hank Aaron)	25.00	12.50	7.50
468	Snider's Play Brings L.A. Victory (Duke Snider)	15.00	7.50	4.50
469	Hustler Banks Wins M.V.P. Award (Ernie Banks)	16.00	8.00	5.00
470	Musial Raps Out 3,000th Hit (Stan Musial)	25.00	12.50	7.50
471	Tom Sturdivant	9.00	4.50	2.75
472	Gene Freese	7.00	3.50	2.00
473	Mike Fornieles	7.00	3.50	2.00
474	Moe Thacker	7.00	3.50	2.00
475	Jack Harshman	7.00	3.50	2.00
476	Cleveland Indians Team	16.00	8.00	4.75
477	Barry Latman	7.00	3.50	2.00
478	Bob Clemente	175.00	87.50	43.75
479	Lindy McDaniel	7.00	3.50	2.00
480	Red Schoendienst	20.00	10.00	6.00
481	Charley Maxwell	7.00	3.50	2.00
482	Russ Meyer	7.00	3.50	2.00
483	Clint Courtney	7.00	3.50	2.00
484	Willie Kirkland	7.00	3.50	2.00
485	Ryne Duren	10.00	5.00	3.00

		NM	EX	VG
486	Sammy White	7.00	3.50	2.00
487	Hal Brown	7.00	3.50	2.00
488	Walt Moryn	7.00	3.50	2.00
489	John C. Powers	7.00	3.50	2.00
490	Frank Thomas	7.00	3.50	2.00
491	Don Blasingame	7.00	3.50	2.00
492	Gene Conley	7.00	3.50	2.00
493	Jim Landis	7.00	3.50	2.00
494	Don Pavletich	7.00	3.50	2.00
495	Johnny Podres	11.00	5.50	3.25
496	Wayne Terwilliger	7.00	3.50	2.00
497	Hal R. Smith	7.00	3.50	2.00
498	Dick Hyde	7.00	3.50	2.00
499	Johnny O'Brien	7.00	3.50	2.00
500	Vic Wertz	7.00	3.50	2.00
501	Bobby Tiefenauer	7.00	3.50	2.00
502	Al Dark	7.00	3.50	2.00
503	Jim Owens	7.00	3.50	2.00
504	Ossie Alvarez	7.00	3.50	2.00
505	Tony Kubek	20.00	10.00	6.00
506	Bob Purkey	7.00	3.50	2.00
507	Bob Hale	15.00	7.50	4.50
508	Art Fowler	15.00	7.50	4.50
509	*Norm Cash*	80.00	40.00	20.00
510	New York Yankees Team	125.00	62.50	31.25
511	George Susce	15.00	7.50	4.50
512	George Altman	15.00	7.50	4.50
513	Tom Carroll	15.00	7.50	4.50
514	*Bob Gibson*	375.00	185.00	110.00
515	Harmon Killebrew	100.00	50.00	30.00
516	Mike Garcia	15.00	7.50	4.50
517	Joe Koppe	15.00	7.50	4.50
518	*Mike Cuellar*	20.00	10.00	6.00
519	Infield Power (Dick Gernert, Frank Malzone, Pete Runnels)	17.50	8.75	5.25
520	Don Elston	15.00	7.50	4.50
521	Gary Geiger	15.00	7.50	4.50
522	Gene Snyder	15.00	7.50	4.50
523	Harry Bright	15.00	7.50	4.50
524	Larry Osborne	15.00	7.50	4.50
525	Jim Coates	17.50	8.75	5.25
526	Bob Speake	15.00	7.50	4.50
527	Solly Hemus	15.00	7.50	4.50
528	Pittsburgh Pirates Team	40.00	20.00	12.00
529	*George Bamberger*	15.00	7.50	4.50
530	Wally Moon	15.00	7.50	4.50
531	Ray Webster	15.00	7.50	4.50
532	Mark Freeman	15.00	7.50	4.50
533	Darrell Johnson	17.50	8.75	5.25
534	Faye Throneberry	15.00	7.50	4.50
535	Ruben Gomez	15.00	7.50	4.50
536	Dan Kravitz	15.00	7.50	4.50
537	Rodolfo Arias	15.00	7.50	4.50
538	Chick King	15.00	7.50	4.50
539	Gary Blaylock	15.00	7.50	4.50
540	Willy Miranda	15.00	7.50	4.50
541	Bob Thurman	15.00	7.50	4.50
542	*Jim Perry*	30.00	15.00	9.00
543	Corsair Outfield Trio (Roberto Clemente, Bob Skinner, Bill Virdon)	100.00	50.00	25.00
544	Lee Tate	15.00	7.50	4.50
545	Tom Morgan	15.00	7.50	4.50
546	Al Schroll	15.00	7.50	4.50
547	Jim Baxes	15.00	7.50	4.50
548	Elmer Singleton	15.00	7.50	4.50
549	Howie Nunn	15.00	7.50	4.50
550	Roy Campanella (Symbol of Courage)	150.00	75.00	37.50
551	Fred Haney (All-Star)	15.00	7.50	4.50
552	Casey Stengel (All-Star)	25.00	12.50	7.50
553	Orlando Cepeda (All-Star)	25.00	12.50	7.50
554	Bill Skowron (All-Star)	22.50	11.00	6.75
555	Bill Mazeroski (All-Star)	25.00	12.50	7.50
556	Nellie Fox (All-Star)	27.50	13.50	8.25
557	Ken Boyer (All-Star)	20.00	10.00	6.00
558	Frank Malzone (All-Star)	15.00	7.50	4.50
559	Ernie Banks (All-Star)	45.00	22.50	13.50
560	Luis Aparicio (All-Star)	20.00	10.00	6.00
561	Hank Aaron (All-Star)	150.00	75.00	37.50
562	Al Kaline (All-Star)	30.00	15.00	9.00
563	Willie Mays (All-Star)	125.00	62.50	31.25
564	Mickey Mantle (All-Star)	250.00	125.00	75.00
565	Wes Covington (All-Star)	15.00	7.50	4.50
566	Roy Sievers (All-Star)	15.00	7.50	4.50
567	Del Crandall (All-Star)	15.00	7.50	4.50
568	Gus Triandos (All-Star)	15.00	7.50	4.50
569	Bob Friend (All-Star)	15.00	7.50	4.50
570	Bob Turley (All-Star)	17.50	8.75	5.25
571	Warren Spahn (All-Star)	27.50	13.50	8.25
572	Billy Pierce (All-Star)	150.00	10.00	6.00
--	Elect Your Favorite Rookie Insert (Paper stock, September 29 date on back.)	200.00	100.00	60.00
--	Felt Pennants Insert (paper stock)	30.00	15.00	9.00

1960 Topps

In 1960, Topps opted for a horizontal format in standard 3-1/2" x 2-1/2" size. Basic fronts have a large color portrait or pose at right and black-and-white action photograph at left. After a one-year hiatus, backs returned to the use of lifetime statistics along with a cartoon and short career summary or previous season highlights. Specialty cards in the 572-card set are multi-player cards, managers and coaches cards, and highlights of the 1959 World Series. Two groups of rookie cards are included. The first are numbers 117-148, which are the Sport Magazine rookies. The second group is called "Topps All-Star Rookies." Finally, there is a run of All-Star cards to close out the set in the scarcer high numbers. Cards #375-440 can be found with backs printed on either white or grey cardboard, with the white stock being the less common. Team cards have checklists on the back.

		NM	EX	VG
	Complete Set (572):	6,500	3,250	2,000
	Common Player (1-440):	6.00	3.00	1.75
	Common Player (441-506):	9.00	4.50	2.75
	Common Player (507-572):	15.00	7.50	4.50
1	Early Wynn	45.00	10.00	6.00
2	Roman Mejias	20.00	4.00	1.75
3	Joe Adcock	6.00	3.00	1.75
4	Bob Purkey	6.00	3.00	1.75
5	Wally Moon	6.00	3.00	1.75
6	Lou Berberet	6.00	3.00	1.75
7	Master and Mentor (Willie Mays, Bill Rigney)	20.00	10.00	6.00
8	Bud Daley	6.00	3.00	1.75
9	Faye Throneberry	6.00	3.00	1.75
10	Ernie Banks	70.00	35.00	17.50
11	Norm Siebern	6.00	3.00	1.75
12	Milt Pappas	6.00	3.00	1.75
13	Wally Post	6.00	3.00	1.75
14	Jim Grant	6.00	3.00	1.75
15	Pete Runnels	6.00	3.00	1.75
16	Ernie Broglio	6.00	3.00	1.75
17	Johnny Callison	6.00	3.00	1.75
18	Los Angeles Dodgers Team	35.00	17.50	10.00
19	Felix Mantilla	6.00	3.00	1.75
20	Roy Face	6.00	3.00	1.75
21	Dutch Dotterer	6.00	3.00	1.75
22	Rocky Bridges	6.00	3.00	1.75
23	Eddie Fisher	6.00	3.00	1.75
24	Dick Gray	6.00	3.00	1.75
25	Roy Sievers	6.00	3.00	1.75
26	Wayne Terwilliger	6.00	3.00	1.75
27	Dick Drott	6.00	3.00	1.75
28	Brooks Robinson	40.00	20.00	12.00
29	Clem Labine	8.00	4.00	2.50
30	Tito Francona	6.00	3.00	1.75
31	Sammy Esposito	6.00	3.00	1.75
32	Sophomore Stalwarts (Jim O'Toole, Vada Pinson)	9.00	4.50	2.75
33	Tom Morgan	6.00	3.00	1.75
34	George Anderson (Sparky)	20.00	10.00	6.00
35	Whitey Ford	35.00	17.50	10.00
36	Russ Nixon	6.00	3.00	1.75
37	Bill Bruton	6.00	3.00	1.75
38	Jerry Casale	6.00	3.00	1.75
39	Earl Averill	6.00	3.00	1.75
40	Joe Cunningham	6.00	3.00	1.75
41	Barry Latman	6.00	3.00	1.75
42	Hobie Landrith	6.00	3.00	1.75
43	Washington Senators Team	15.00	7.50	4.50
44	Bobby Locke	6.00	3.00	1.75
45	Roy McMillan	6.00	3.00	1.75
46	Jack Fisher	6.00	3.00	1.75
47	Don Zimmer	12.00	6.00	3.50
48	Hal Smith	6.00	3.00	1.75
49	Curt Raydon	6.00	3.00	1.75
50	Al Kaline	50.00	25.00	12.50
51	Jim Coates	6.00	3.00	1.75
52	Dave Philley	6.00	3.00	1.75
53	Jackie Brandt	6.00	3.00	1.75
54	Mike Fornieles	6.00	3.00	1.75
55	Bill Mazeroski	20.00	10.00	6.00
56	Steve Korcheck	6.00	3.00	1.75
57	Win-Savers (Turk Lown, Gerry Staley)	6.00	3.00	1.75
58	Gino Cimoli	6.00	3.00	1.75
59	Juan Pizarro	6.00	3.00	1.75
60	Gus Triandos	6.00	3.00	1.75
61	Eddie Kasko	6.00	3.00	1.75
62	Roger Craig	6.00	3.00	1.75
63	George Strickland	6.00	3.00	1.75
64	Jack Meyer	6.00	3.00	1.75
65	Elston Howard	15.00	7.50	4.50
66	Bob Trowbridge	6.00	3.00	1.75
67	*Jose Pagan*	6.00	3.00	1.75
68	Dave Hillman	6.00	3.00	1.75
69	Billy Goodman	6.00	3.00	1.75
70	Lou Burdette	6.00	3.00	1.75
71	Marty Keough	6.00	3.00	1.75
72	Detroit Tigers Team	15.00	7.50	4.50
73	Bob Gibson	50.00	25.00	15.00
74	Walt Moryn	6.00	3.00	1.75
75	Vic Power	6.00	3.00	1.75
76	Bill Fischer	6.00	3.00	1.75
77	Hank Foiles	6.00	3.00	1.75
78	Bob Grim	6.00	3.00	1.75
79	Walt Dropo	6.00	3.00	1.75
80	Johnny Antonelli	6.00	3.00	1.75
81	Russ Snyder	6.00	3.00	1.75
82	Ruben Gomez	6.00	3.00	1.75
83	Tony Kubek	25.00	12.50	7.50
84	Hal Smith	6.00	3.00	1.75
85	Frank Lary	6.00	3.00	1.75
86	Dick Gernert	6.00	3.00	1.75
87	John Romonosky	6.00	3.00	1.75
88	John Roseboro	6.00	3.00	1.75
89	Hal Brown	6.00	3.00	1.75
90	Bobby Avila	6.00	3.00	1.75
91	Bennie Daniels	6.00	3.00	1.75
92	Whitey Herzog	15.00	7.50	4.50

		NM	EX	VG
93	Art Schult	6.00	3.00	1.75
94	Leo Kiely	6.00	3.00	1.75
95	Frank Thomas	6.00	3.00	1.75
96	Ralph Terry	7.50	3.75	2.25
97	Ted Lepcio	6.00	3.00	1.75
98	Gordon Jones	6.00	3.00	1.75
99	Lenny Green	6.00	3.00	1.75
100	Nellie Fox	20.00	10.00	6.00
101	Bob Miller	6.00	3.00	1.75
102	Kent Hadley	6.00	3.00	1.75
103	Dick Farrell	6.00	3.00	1.75
104	Dick Schofield	6.00	3.00	1.75
105	*Larry Sherry*	12.00	6.00	3.50
106	Billy Gardner	6.00	3.00	1.75
107	Carl Willey	6.00	3.00	1.75
108	Pete Daley	6.00	3.00	1.75
109	Cletis Boyer	13.50	6.75	4.00
110	Cal McLish	6.00	3.00	1.75
111	Vic Wertz	6.00	3.00	1.75
112	Jack Harshman	6.00	3.00	1.75
113	Bob Skinner	6.00	3.00	1.75
114	Ken Aspromonte	6.00	3.00	1.75
115	Fork and Knuckler (Roy Face, Hoyt Wilhelm)	9.00	4.50	2.75
116	Jim Rivera	6.00	3.00	1.75
117	Tom Borland	6.00	3.00	1.75
118	Bob Bruce	6.00	3.00	1.75
119	*Chico Cardenas*	6.00	3.00	1.75
120	Duke Carmel	6.00	3.00	1.75
121	Camilo Carreon	6.00	3.00	1.75
122	Don Dillard	6.00	3.00	1.75
123	Dan Dobbek	6.00	3.00	1.75
124	Jim Donohue	6.00	3.00	1.75
125	*Dick Ellsworth*	6.00	3.00	1.75
126	*Chuck Estrada*	6.00	3.00	1.75
127	Ronnie Hansen	6.00	3.00	1.75
128	Bill Harris	6.00	3.00	1.75
129	Bob Hartman	6.00	3.00	1.75
130	Frank Herrera	6.00	3.00	1.75
131	Ed Hobaugh	6.00	3.00	1.75
132	*Frank Howard*	20.00	10.00	6.00
133	*Manuel Javier*	6.00	3.00	1.75
134	Deron Johnson	7.50	3.75	2.25
135	Ken Johnson	6.00	3.00	1.75
136	*Jim Kaat*	20.00	10.00	6.00
137	Lou Klimchock	6.00	3.00	1.75
138	*Art Mahaffey*	6.00	3.00	1.75
139	Carl Mathias	6.00	3.00	1.75
140	Julio Navarro	6.00	3.00	1.75
141	Jim Proctor	6.00	3.00	1.75
142	Bill Short	6.00	3.00	1.75
143	Al Spangler	6.00	3.00	1.75
144	Al Stieglitz	6.00	3.00	1.75
145	Jim Umbricht	6.00	3.00	1.75
146	Ted Wieand	6.00	3.00	1.75
147	Bob Will	6.00	3.00	1.75
148	*Carl Yastrzemski*	225.00	112.50	56.25
149	Bob Nieman	6.00	3.00	1.75
150	Billy Pierce	6.00	3.00	1.75
151	San Francisco Giants Team	15.00	7.50	4.50
152	Gail Harris	6.00	3.00	1.75
153	Bobby Thomson	7.50	3.75	2.25
154	Jim Davenport	6.00	3.00	1.75
155	Charlie Neal	6.00	3.00	1.75
156	Art Ceccarelli	6.00	3.00	1.75
157	Rocky Nelson	6.00	3.00	1.75
158	Wes Covington	6.00	3.00	1.75
159	Jim Piersall	8.00	4.00	2.50
160	Rival All-Stars (Ken Boyer, Mickey Mantle)	150.00	75.00	37.50
161	Ray Narleski	6.00	3.00	1.75
162	Sammy Taylor	6.00	3.00	1.75
163	Hector Lopez	6.00	3.00	1.75
164	Cincinnati Reds Team	15.00	7.50	4.50
165	Jack Sanford	6.00	3.00	1.75
166	Chuck Essegian	6.00	3.00	1.75
167	Valmy Thomas	6.00	3.00	1.75
168	Alex Grammas	6.00	3.00	1.75
169	Jake Striker	6.00	3.00	1.75
170	Del Crandall	6.00	3.00	1.75
171	Johnny Groth	6.00	3.00	1.75
172	Willie Kirkland	6.00	3.00	1.75
173	Billy Martin	10.00	5.00	3.00
174	Cleveland Indians Team	15.00	7.50	4.50
175	Pedro Ramos	6.00	3.00	1.75
176	Vada Pinson	10.00	5.00	3.00
177	Johnny Kucks	6.00	3.00	1.75
178	Woody Held	6.00	3.00	1.75
179	Rip Coleman	6.00	3.00	1.75
180	Harry Simpson	6.00	3.00	1.75
181	Billy Loes	6.00	3.00	1.75
182	Glen Hobbie	6.00	3.00	1.75
183	Eli Grba	6.00	3.00	1.75
184	Gary Geiger	6.00	3.00	1.75
185	Jim Owens	6.00	3.00	1.75
186	Dave Sisler	6.00	3.00	1.75
187	Jay Hook	6.00	3.00	1.75
188	Dick Williams	6.00	3.00	1.75
189	Don McMahon	6.00	3.00	1.75
190	Gene Woodling	6.00	3.00	1.75
191	Johnny Klippstein	6.00	3.00	1.75
192	Danny O'Connell	6.00	3.00	1.75
193	Dick Hyde	6.00	3.00	1.75
194	Bobby Gene Smith	6.00	3.00	1.75
195	Lindy McDaniel	6.00	3.00	1.75
196	Andy Carey	6.00	3.00	1.75
197	Ron Kline	6.00	3.00	1.75
198	Jerry Lynch	6.00	3.00	1.75
199	Dick Donovan	6.00	3.00	1.75
200	Willie Mays	125.00	62.50	31.25
201	Larry Osborne	6.00	3.00	1.75
202	Fred Kipp	6.00	3.00	1.75
203	Sammy White	6.00	3.00	1.75
204	Ryne Duren	7.50	3.75	2.25
205	Johnny Logan	6.00	3.00	1.75
206	Claude Osteen	6.00	3.00	1.75
207	Bob Boyd	6.00	3.00	1.75
208	Chicago White Sox Team	15.00	7.50	4.50

GIL HODGES — Los Angeles Dodgers—1B

#	Name			
209	Ron Blackburn	6.00	3.00	1.75
210	Harmon Killebrew	30.00	15.00	9.00
211	Taylor Phillips	6.00	3.00	1.75
212	Walt Alston	12.00	6.00	3.50
213	Chuck Dressen	6.00	3.00	1.75
214	Jimmie Dykes	6.00	3.00	1.75
215	Bob Elliott	6.00	3.00	1.75
216	Joe Gordon	6.00	3.00	1.75
217	Charley Grimm	6.00	3.00	1.75
218	Solly Hemus	6.00	3.00	1.75
219	Fred Hutchinson	6.00	3.00	1.75
220	Billy Jurges	6.00	3.00	1.75
221	Cookie Lavagetto	6.00	3.00	1.75
222	Al Lopez	10.00	5.00	3.00
223	Danny Murtaugh	6.00	3.00	1.75
224	Paul Richards	6.00	3.00	1.75
225	Bill Rigney	6.00	3.00	1.75
226	Eddie Sawyer	6.00	3.00	1.75
227	Casey Stengel	17.50	8.75	5.25
228	Ernie Johnson	6.00	3.00	1.75
229	Joe Morgan	6.00	3.00	1.75
230	Mound Magicians (Bob Buhl, Lou Burdette, Warren Spahn)	17.50	8.75	5.25
231	Hal Naragon	6.00	3.00	1.75
232	Jim Busby	6.00	3.00	1.75
233	Don Elston	6.00	3.00	1.75
234	Don Demeter	6.00	3.00	1.75
235	Gus Bell	6.00	3.00	1.75
236	Dick Ricketts	6.00	3.00	1.75
237	Elmer Valo	6.00	3.00	1.75
238	Danny Kravitz	6.00	3.00	1.75
239	Joe Shipley	6.00	3.00	1.75
240	Luis Aparicio	17.50	8.75	5.25
241	Albie Pearson	6.00	3.00	1.75
242	St. Louis Cardinals Team	15.00	7.50	4.50
243	Bubba Phillips	6.00	3.00	1.75
244	Hal Griggs	6.00	3.00	1.75
245	Eddie Yost	6.00	3.00	1.75
246	Lee Maye	6.00	3.00	1.75
247	Gil McDougald	12.00	6.00	3.50
248	Del Rice	6.00	3.00	1.75
249	*Earl Wilson*	6.00	3.00	1.75
250	Stan Musial	100.00	50.00	25.00
251	Bobby Malkmus	6.00	3.00	1.75
252	Ray Herbert	6.00	3.00	1.75
253	Eddie Bressoud	6.00	3.00	1.75
254	Arnie Portocarrero	6.00	3.00	1.75
255	Jim Gilliam	10.00	5.00	3.00
256	Dick Brown	6.00	3.00	1.75
257	Gordy Coleman	6.00	3.00	1.75
258	Dick Groat	6.00	3.00	1.75
259	George Altman	6.00	3.00	1.75
260	Power Plus (Rocky Colavito, Tito Francona)	11.00	5.50	3.25
261	Pete Burnside	6.00	3.00	1.75
262	Hank Bauer	7.50	3.75	2.25
263	Darrell Johnson	6.00	3.00	1.75
264	Robin Roberts	12.50	6.25	3.75
265	Rip Repulski	6.00	3.00	1.75
266	Joe Jay	6.00	3.00	1.75
267	Jim Marshall	6.00	3.00	1.75
268	Al Worthington	6.00	3.00	1.75
269	Gene Green	6.00	3.00	1.75
270	Bob Turley	10.00	5.00	3.00
271	Julio Becquer	6.00	3.00	1.75
272	Fred Green	6.00	3.00	1.75
273	Neil Chrisley	6.00	3.00	1.75
274	Tom Acker	6.00	3.00	1.75
275	Curt Flood	9.00	4.50	2.75
276	Ken McBride	6.00	3.00	1.75
277	Harry Bright	6.00	3.00	1.75
278	Stan Williams	6.00	3.00	1.75
279	Chuck Tanner	6.00	3.00	1.75
280	Frank Sullivan	6.00	3.00	1.75
281	Ray Boone	6.00	3.00	1.75
282	Joe Nuxhall	6.00	3.00	1.75
283	John Blanchard	7.50	3.75	2.25
284	Don Gross	6.00	3.00	1.75
285	Harry Anderson	6.00	3.00	1.75
286	Ray Semproch	6.00	3.00	1.75
287	Felipe Alou	7.50	3.75	2.25
288	Bob Mabe	6.00	3.00	1.75
289	Willie Jones	6.00	3.00	1.75
290	Jerry Lumpe	6.00	3.00	1.75
291	Bob Keegan	6.00	3.00	1.75
292	Dodger Backstops (Joe Pignatano, John Roseboro)	7.50	3.75	2.25
293	Gene Conley	6.00	3.00	1.75
294	Tony Taylor	6.00	3.00	1.75
295	Gil Hodges	15.00	7.50	4.50
296	Nelson Chittum	6.00	3.00	1.75
297	Reno Bertoia	6.00	3.00	1.75
298	George Witt	6.00	3.00	1.75
299	Earl Torgeson	6.00	3.00	1.75
300	Hank Aaron	140.00	70.00	35.00
301	Jerry Davie	6.00	3.00	1.75
302	Philadelphia Phillies Team	15.00	7.50	4.50
303	Billy O'Dell	6.00	3.00	1.75
304	Joe Ginsberg	6.00	3.00	1.75
305	Richie Ashburn	15.00	7.50	4.50
306	Frank Baumann	6.00	3.00	1.75
307	Gene Oliver	6.00	3.00	1.75
308	Dick Hall	6.00	3.00	1.75
309	Bob Hale	6.00	3.00	1.75
310	Frank Malzone	6.00	3.00	1.75
311	Raul Sanchez	6.00	3.00	1.75
312	Charlie Lau	6.00	3.00	1.75
313	Turk Lown	6.00	3.00	1.75
314	Chico Fernandez	6.00	3.00	1.75
315	Bobby Shantz	11.00	5.50	3.25
316	*Willie McCovey*	150.00	75.00	37.50
317	Pumpsie Green	7.50	3.75	2.25
318	Jim Baxes	6.00	3.00	1.75
319	Joe Koppe	6.00	3.00	1.75
320	Bob Allison	6.00	3.00	1.75
321	Ron Fairly	6.00	3.00	1.75
322	Willie Tasby	6.00	3.00	1.75
323	Johnny Romano	6.00	3.00	1.75
324	Jim Perry	7.50	3.75	2.25
325	Jim O'Toole	6.00	3.00	1.75
326	Bob Clemente	175.00	87.50	43.75
327	*Ray Sadecki*	6.00	3.00	1.75
328	Earl Battey	6.00	3.00	1.75
329	Zack Monroe	6.00	3.00	1.75
330	Harvey Kuenn	6.00	3.00	1.75
331	Henry Mason	6.00	3.00	1.75
332	New York Yankees Team	37.50	18.50	11.00
333	Danny McDevitt	6.00	3.00	1.75
334	Ted Abernathy	6.00	3.00	1.75
335	Red Schoendienst	12.50	6.25	3.75
336	Ike Delock	6.00	3.00	1.75
337	Cal Neeman	6.00	3.00	1.75
338	Ray Monzant	6.00	3.00	1.75
339	Harry Chiti	6.00	3.00	1.75
340	Harvey Haddix	6.00	3.00	1.75
341	Carroll Hardy	6.00	3.00	1.75
342	Casey Wise	6.00	3.00	1.75
343	Sandy Koufax	125.00	62.50	31.25
344	Clint Courtney	6.00	3.00	1.75
345	Don Newcombe	7.50	3.75	2.25
346	J.C. Martin (Photo actually Gary Peters.)	6.00	3.00	1.75
347	Ed Bouchee	6.00	3.00	1.75
348	Barry Shetrone	6.00	3.00	1.75
349	Moe Drabowsky	6.00	3.00	1.75
350	Mickey Mantle	425.00	210.00	125.00
351	Don Nottebart	6.00	3.00	1.75
352	Cincy Clouters (Gus Bell, Jerry Lynch, Frank Robinson)	12.00	6.00	3.50
353	Don Larsen	8.00	4.00	2.50
354	Bob Lillis	6.00	3.00	1.75
355	Bill White	6.00	3.00	1.75
356	Joe Amalfitano	6.00	3.00	1.75
357	Al Schroll	6.00	3.00	1.75
358	Joe De Maestri	6.00	3.00	1.75
359	Buddy Gilbert	6.00	3.00	1.75
360	Herb Score	7.50	3.75	2.25
361	Bob Oldis	6.00	3.00	1.75
362	Russ Kemmerer	6.00	3.00	1.75
363	Gene Stephens	6.00	3.00	1.75
364	Paul Foytack	6.00	3.00	1.75
365	Minnie Minoso	12.50	6.25	3.75
366	*Dallas Green*	9.00	4.50	2.75
367	Bill Tuttle	6.00	3.00	1.75
368	Daryl Spencer	6.00	3.00	1.75
369	Billy Hoeft	6.00	3.00	1.75
370	Bill Skowron	17.50	8.75	5.25
371	Bud Byerly	6.00	3.00	1.75
372	Frank House	6.00	3.00	1.75
373	Don Hoak	6.00	3.00	1.75
374	Bob Buhl	6.00	3.00	1.75
375	Dale Long	6.00	3.00	1.75
376	Johnny Briggs	6.00	3.00	1.75
377	Roger Maris	100.00	50.00	25.00
378	Stu Miller	6.00	3.00	1.75
379	Red Wilson	6.00	3.00	1.75
380	Bob Shaw	6.00	3.00	1.75
381	Milwaukee Braves Team	16.00	8.00	4.75
382	Ted Bowsfield	6.00	3.00	1.75
383	Leon Wagner	6.00	3.00	1.75
384	Don Cardwell	6.00	3.00	1.75
385	World Series Game 1 (Neal Steals Second)	10.00	5.00	3.00
386	World Series Game 2 (Neal Belts 2nd Homer)	10.00	5.00	3.00
387	World Series Game 3 (Furillo Breaks Up Game)	10.00	5.00	3.00
388	World Series Game 4 (Hodges' Winning Homer)	10.00	5.00	3.00
389	World Series Game 5 (Luis Swipes Base)	12.00	6.00	3.50
390	World Series Game 6 (Scrambling After Ball)	10.00	5.00	3.00
391	World Series Summary (The Champs Celebrate)	10.00	5.00	3.00
392	Tex Clevenger	6.00	3.00	1.75
393	Smoky Burgess	6.00	3.00	1.75
394	Norm Larker	6.00	3.00	1.75
395	Hoyt Wilhelm	13.50	6.75	4.00
396	Steve Bilko	6.00	3.00	1.75
397	Don Blasingame	6.00	3.00	1.75
398	Mike Cuellar	6.00	3.00	1.75
399	Young Hill Stars (Jack Fisher, Milt Pappas, Jerry Walker)	6.00	3.00	1.75
400	Rocky Colavito	20.00	10.00	6.00
401	Bob Duliba	6.00	3.00	1.75
402	Dick Stuart	6.00	3.00	1.75
403	Ed Sadowski	6.00	3.00	1.75
404	Bob Rush	6.00	3.00	1.75
405	Bobby Richardson	25.00	12.50	7.50
406	Billy Klaus	6.00	3.00	1.75
407	*Gary Peters* (Photo actually J.C. Martin.)	6.00	3.00	1.75
408	Carl Furillo	11.00	5.50	3.25
409	Ron Samford	6.00	3.00	1.75
410	Sam Jones	6.00	3.00	1.75
411	Ed Bailey	6.00	3.00	1.75
412	Bob Anderson	6.00	3.00	1.75
413	Kansas City Athletics Team	15.00	7.50	4.50
414	Don Williams	6.00	3.00	1.75
415	Bob Cerv	6.00	3.00	1.75
416	Humberto Robinson	6.00	3.00	1.75
417	Chuck Cottier	6.00	3.00	1.75
418	Don Mossi	6.00	3.00	1.75
419	George Crowe	6.00	3.00	1.75
420	Ed Mathews	25.00	12.50	7.50
421	Duke Maas	6.00	3.00	1.75
422	Johnny Powers	6.00	3.00	1.75
423	Ed Fitz Gerald	6.00	3.00	1.75
424	Pete Whisenant	6.00	3.00	1.75
425	Johnny Podres	10.00	5.00	3.00
426	Ron Jackson	6.00	3.00	1.75
427	Al Grunwald	6.00	3.00	1.75
428	Al Smith	6.00	3.00	1.75
429	American League Kings (Nellie Fox, Harvey Kuenn)	12.50	6.25	3.75
430	Art Ditmar	6.00	3.00	1.75
431	Andre Rodgers	6.00	3.00	1.75
432	Chuck Stobbs	6.00	3.00	1.75
433	Irv Noren	6.00	3.00	1.75
434	Brooks Lawrence	6.00	3.00	1.75
435	Gene Freese	6.00	3.00	1.75
436	Marv Throneberry	6.00	3.00	1.75
437	Bob Friend	6.00	3.00	1.75
438	Jim Coker	6.00	3.00	1.75
439	Tom Brewer	6.00	3.00	1.75
440	Jim Lemon	6.00	3.00	1.75
441	Gary Bell	9.00	4.50	2.75
442	Joe Pignatano	9.00	4.50	2.75
443	Charlie Maxwell	9.00	4.50	2.75
444	Jerry Kindall	9.00	4.50	2.75
445	Warren Spahn	35.00	17.50	10.00
446	Ellis Burton	9.00	4.50	2.75
447	Ray Moore	9.00	4.50	2.75
448	*Jim Gentile*	15.00	7.50	4.50
449	Jim Brosnan	9.00	4.50	2.75
450	Orlando Cepeda	30.00	15.00	9.00
451	Curt Simmons	9.00	4.50	2.75
452	Ray Webster	9.00	4.50	2.75
453	Vern Law	9.00	4.50	2.75
454	Hal Woodeshick	9.00	4.50	2.75
455	Baltimomre Orioles Coaches (Harry Brecheen, Lum Harris, Eddie Robinson)	9.00	4.50	2.75
456	Boston Red Sox Coaches (Del Baker, Billy Herman, Sal Maglie, Rudy York)	15.00	7.50	4.50
457	Chicago Cubs Coaches (Lou Klein, Charlie Root, Elvin Tappe)	9.00	4.50	2.75
458	Chicago White Sox Coaches (Ray Berres, Johnny Cooney, Tony Cuccinello, Don Gutteridge)	9.00	4.50	2.75
459	Cincinnati Reds Coaches (Cot Deal, Wally Moses, Reggie Otero)	9.00	4.50	2.75
460	Cleveland Indians Coaches (Mel Harder, Red Kress, Bob Lemon, Jo-Jo White)	10.00	5.00	3.00
461	Detroit Tigers Coaches (Luke Appling, Tom Ferrick, Billy Hitchcock)	10.00	5.00	3.00
462	Kansas City A's Coaches (Walker Cooper, Fred Fitzsimmons, Don Heffner)	9.00	4.50	2.75
463	L.A. Dodgers Coaches (Joe Becker, Bobby Bragan, Greg Mulleavy, Pete Reiser)	9.00	4.50	2.75
464	Milwaukee Braves Coaches (George Myatt, Andy Pafko, Bob Scheffing, Whitlow Wyatt)	9.00	4.50	2.75
465	N.Y. Yankees Coaches (Frank Crosetti, Bill Dickey, Ralph Houk, Ed Lopat)	20.00	10.00	6.00
466	Phila. Phillies Coaches (Dick Carter, Andy Cohen, Ken Silvestri)	9.00	4.50	2.75
467	Pitts. Pirates Coaches (Bill Burwell, Sam Narron, Frank Oceak, Mickey Vernon)	9.00	4.50	2.75
468	St. Louis Cards Coaches (Ray Katt, Johnny Keane, Howie Pollet, Harry Walker)	9.00	4.50	2.75
469	San Fran. Giants Coaches (Salty Parker, Bill Posedel, Wes Westrum)	9.00	4.50	2.75
470	Wash. Senators Coaches (Ellis Clary, Sam Mele, Bob Swift)	9.00	4.50	2.75
471	Ned Garver	9.00	4.50	2.75
472	Al Dark	9.00	4.50	2.75
473	Al Cicotte	9.00	4.50	2.75
474	Haywood Sullivan	9.00	4.50	2.75
475	Don Drysdale	35.00	17.50	10.00
476	Lou Johnson	9.00	4.50	2.75
477	Don Ferrarese	9.00	4.50	2.75
478	Frank Torre	9.00	4.50	2.75
479	Georges Maranda	9.00	4.50	2.75
480	Yogi Berra	90.00	45.00	22.50
481	Wes Stock	9.00	4.50	2.75
482	Frank Bolling	9.00	4.50	2.75
483	Camilo Pascual	9.00	4.50	2.75
484	Pittsburgh Pirates Team	25.00	12.50	7.50
485	Ken Boyer	15.00	7.50	4.50
486	Bobby Del Greco	9.00	4.50	2.75
487	Tom Sturdivant	9.00	4.50	2.75
488	Norm Cash	15.00	7.50	4.50
489	Steve Ridzik	9.00	4.50	2.75
490	Frank Robinson	40.00	20.00	12.00
491	Mel Roach	9.00	4.50	2.75
492	Larry Jackson	9.00	4.50	2.75
493	Duke Snider	50.00	25.00	12.50
494	Baltimore Orioles Team	20.00	10.00	6.00
495	Sherm Lollar	9.00	4.50	2.75
496	Bill Virdon	9.00	4.50	2.75
497	John Tsitouris	9.00	4.50	2.75
498	Al Pilarcik	9.00	4.50	2.75
499	Johnny James	9.00	4.50	2.75
500	Johnny Temple	9.00	4.50	2.75
501	Bob Schmidt	9.00	4.50	2.75
502	Jim Bunning	20.00	10.00	6.00
503	Don Lee	9.00	4.50	2.75
504	Seth Morehead	9.00	4.50	2.75
505	Ted Kluszewski	15.00	7.50	4.50
506	Lee Walls	9.00	4.50	2.75
507	Dick Stigman	15.00	7.50	4.50
508	Billy Consolo	15.00	7.50	4.50
509	*Tommy Davis*	20.00	10.00	6.00
510	Jerry Staley	15.00	7.50	4.50
511	Ken Walters	15.00	7.50	4.50
512	Joe Gibbon	15.00	7.50	4.50
513	Chicago Cubs Team	20.00	10.00	6.00
514	*Steve Barber*	17.50	8.75	5.25

		NM	EX	VG
515	Stan Lopata	15.00	7.50	4.50
516	Marty Kutyna	15.00	7.50	4.50
517	Charley James	15.00	7.50	4.50
518	*Tony Gonzalez*	15.00	7.50	4.50
519	Ed Roebuck	15.00	7.50	4.50
520	Don Buddin	15.00	7.50	4.50
521	Mike Lee	15.00	7.50	4.50
522	Ken Hunt	15.00	7.50	4.50
523	*Clay Dalrymple*	15.00	7.50	4.50
524	Bill Henry	15.00	7.50	4.50
525	Marv Breeding	15.00	7.50	4.50
526	Paul Giel	15.00	7.50	4.50
527	Jose Valdivielso	15.00	7.50	4.50
528	Ben Johnson	15.00	7.50	4.50
529	Norm Sherry	17.50	8.75	5.25
530	Mike McCormick	15.00	7.50	4.50
531	Sandy Amoros	15.00	7.50	4.50
532	Mike Garcia	15.00	7.50	4.50
533	Lu Clinton	15.00	7.50	4.50
534	Ken MacKenzie	15.00	7.50	4.50
535	Whitey Lockman	15.00	7.50	4.50
536	Wynn Hawkins	15.00	7.50	4.50
537	Boston Red Sox Team	25.00	12.50	7.50
538	Frank Barnes	15.00	7.50	4.50
539	Gene Baker	15.00	7.50	4.50
540	Jerry Walker	15.00	7.50	4.50
541	Tony Curry	15.00	7.50	4.50
542	Ken Hamlin	15.00	7.50	4.50
543	Elio Chacon	15.00	7.50	4.50
544	Bill Monbouquette	15.00	7.50	4.50
545	Carl Sawatski	15.00	7.50	4.50
546	Hank Aguirre	15.00	7.50	4.50
547	*Bob Aspromonte*	17.50	8.75	5.25
548	*Don Mincher*	15.00	7.50	4.50
549	John Buzhardt	15.00	7.50	4.50
550	Jim Landis	15.00	7.50	4.50
551	Ed Rakow	15.00	7.50	4.50
552	Walt Bond	15.00	7.50	4.50
553	Bill Skowron/AS	20.00	10.00	6.00
554	Willie McCovey/AS	35.00	17.50	10.00
555	Nellie Fox/AS	20.00	10.00	6.00
556	Charlie Neal/AS	17.50	8.75	5.25
557	Frank Malzone/AS	17.50	8.75	5.25
558	Eddie Mathews/AS	25.00	12.50	7.50
559	Luis Aparicio/AS	20.00	10.00	6.00
560	Ernie Banks/AS	35.00	17.50	10.00
561	Al Kaline/AS	30.00	15.00	9.00
562	Joe Cunningham/AS	17.50	8.75	5.25
563	Mickey Mantle/AS	275.00	137.50	68.75
564	Willie Mays/AS	100.00	50.00	25.00
565	Roger Maris/AS	100.00	50.00	25.00
566	Hank Aaron/AS	100.00	50.00	25.00
567	Sherm Lollar/AS	17.50	8.75	5.25
568	Del Crandall/AS	17.50	8.75	5.25
569	Camilo Pascual/AS	17.50	8.75	5.25
570	Don Drysdale/AS	25.00	12.50	7.50
571	Billy Pierce/AS	17.50	8.75	5.25
572	Johnny Antonelli/AS	25.00	9.00	5.25
----	Elect Your Favorite Rookie Insert (Paper stock, no date on back.)	30.00	15.00	9.00
----	Hot Iron Transfer Insert (Paper stock.)	30.00	15.00	9.00

1960 Topps Proofs

KENT HADLEY
NEW YORK YANKEES   FIRST BASE

Subsequent to a pair of December 1959 trades, the 1960 Topps cards of three players were significantly changed. Whether the change occurred prior to regular production printing and packaging or while the cards were still in the proofing stage is unknown. The changes affect the cards of Gino Cimoli, Kent Hadley and, reportedly, Marv Throneberry. In the very rare versions each player's card has at bottom left the logo of his team prior to the trade. The common regular-issue version has the new team logo. The front of Hadley's rare card names his team as the Yankees, while Cimoli's rare version says Cardinals.

		NM	EX	VG
58	Gino Cimoli (Cardinals logo.) (No recent sales.)			
102	Kent Hadley (A's logo.) (Nov., 1999 auction record.)	13,500	.00	.00
436	Marv Throneberry (Yankees logo.) (Existence not confirmed.)			

1960 Topps Tattoos

Probably the least popular of all Topps products among parents and teachers, the Tattoos were printed on the reverse of the wrappers of Topps "Tattoo Bubble Gum." The entire wrapper was 1-9/16" x 3-1/2". The owner moistened their skin and applied the back of the wrapper to the wet spot, producing a colorful "tattoo" (although often blurred by running colors). The set offered 96 tattoo possibilities of which 55 were play-

ers, 16 teams, 15 action pictures and 10 autographed balls. Because the packaged gum slides easily in and out of the "sealed" wrapper, allowing the tattoo to be easily seen, unopened packs command little premium.

		NM	EX	VG
	Complete Set (96):	2,750	1,350	825.00
	Common Player:	20.00	10.00	6.00
	Common Non-player:	12.00	6.00	3.50
(1)	Hank Aaron	150.00	75.00	45.00
(2)	Bob Allison	20.00	10.00	6.00
(3)	John Antonelli	20.00	10.00	6.00
(4)	Richie Ashburn	40.00	10.00	12.00
(5)	Ernie Banks	65.00	32.00	19.50
(6)	Yogi Berra	60.00	30.00	18.00
(7)	Lew Burdette	20.00	10.00	6.00
(8)	Orlando Cepeda	35.00	17.50	10.50
(9)	Rocky Colavito	35.00	17.50	10.50
(10)	Joe Cunningham	20.00	10.00	6.00
(11)	Buddy Daley	20.00	10.00	6.00
(12)	Don Drysdale	40.00	20.00	12.00
(13)	Ryne Duren	20.00	10.00	6.00
(14)	Roy Face	20.00	10.00	6.00
(15)	Whitey Ford	60.00	30.00	18.00
(16)	Nellie Fox	35.00	17.50	10.50
(17)	Tito Francona	20.00	10.00	6.00
(18)	Gene Freese	20.00	10.00	6.00
(19)	Jim Gilliam	20.00	10.00	6.00
(20)	Dick Groat	20.00	10.00	6.00
(21)	Ray Herbert	20.00	10.00	6.00
(22)	Glen Hobbie	20.00	10.00	6.00
(23)	Jackie Jensen	20.00	10.00	6.00
(24)	Sam Jones	20.00	10.00	6.00
(25)	Al Kaline	60.00	30.00	18.00
(26)	Harmon Killebrew	40.00	20.00	12.00
(27)	Harvey Kuenn	20.00	10.00	6.00
(28)	Frank Lary	20.00	10.00	6.00
(29)	Vernon Law	20.00	10.00	6.00
(30)	Frank Malzone	20.00	10.00	6.00
(31)	Mickey Mantle	300.00	150.00	90.00
(32)	Roger Maris	75.00	37.00	22.00
(33)	Ed Mathews	40.00	20.00	12.00
(34)	Willie Mays	150.00	75.00	45.00
(35)	Cal Mclish	20.00	10.00	6.00
(36)	Wally Moon	20.00	10.00	6.00
(37)	Walt Moryn	20.00	10.00	6.00
(38)	Don Mossi	20.00	10.00	6.00
(39)	Stan Musial	100.00	50.00	30.00
(40)	Charlie Neal	20.00	10.00	6.00
(41)	Don Newcombe	20.00	10.00	6.00
(42)	Milt Pappas	20.00	10.00	6.00
(43)	Camilo Pascual	20.00	10.00	6.00
(44)	Billie (Billy) Pierce	20.00	10.00	6.00
(45)	Robin Roberts	35.00	17.50	10.50
(46)	Frank Robinson	40.00	20.00	12.00
(47)	Pete Runnels	20.00	10.00	6.00
(48)	Herb Score	20.00	10.00	6.00
(49)	Warren Spahn	35.00	17.50	10.50
(50)	Johnny Temple	20.00	10.00	6.00
(51)	Gus Triandos	20.00	10.00	6.00
(52)	Jerry Walker	20.00	10.00	6.00
(53)	Bill White	20.00	10.00	6.00
(54)	Gene Woodling	20.00	10.00	6.00
(55)	Early Wynn	35.00	17.50	10.50
(56)	Chicago Cubs Logo	15.00	7.50	4.50
(57)	Cincinnati Reds Logo	15.00	7.50	4.50
(58)	Los Angeles Dodgers Logo	15.00	7.50	4.50
(59)	Milwaukee Braves Logo	15.00	7.50	4.50
(60)	Philadelphia Phillies Logo	15.00	7.50	4.50
(61)	Pittsburgh Pirates Logo	20.00	10.00	6.00
(62)	San Francisco Giants Logo	15.00	7.50	4.50
(63)	St. Louis Cardinals Logo	15.00	7.50	4.50
(64)	Baltimore Orioles Logo	15.00	7.50	4.50
(65)	Boston Red Sox Logo	15.00	7.50	4.50
(66)	Chicago White Sox Logo	15.00	7.50	4.50
(67)	Cleveland Indians Logo	15.00	7.50	4.50
(68)	Detroit Tigers Logo	15.00	7.50	4.50
(69)	Kansas City Athletics Logo	15.00	7.50	4.50
(70)	New York Yankees Logo	20.00	10.00	6.00
(71)	Washington Senators Logo	15.00	7.50	4.50
(72)	Autograph (Richie Ashburn)	20.00	10.00	6.00
(73)	Autograph (Rocky Colavito)	25.00	12.50	7.50
(74)	Autograph (Roy Face)	15.00	7.50	4.50
(75)	Autograph (Jackie Jensen)	15.00	7.50	4.50
(76)	Autograph (Harmon Killebrew)	25.00	12.50	7.50
(77)	Autograph (Mickey Mantle)	100.00	50.00	30.00
(78)	Autograph (Willie Mays)	50.00	25.00	15.00
(79)	Autograph (Stan Musial)	50.00	25.00	15.00
(80)	Autograph (Billy Pierce)	15.00	7.50	4.50
(81)	Autograph (Jerry Walker)	15.00	7.50	4.50
(82)	Run-Down	12.00	6.00	3.50
(83)	Out At First	12.00	6.00	3.50
(84)	The Final Word	12.00	6.00	3.50
(85)	Twisting Foul	12.00	6.00	3.50
(86)	Out At Home	12.00	6.00	3.50
(87)	Circus Catch	12.00	6.00	3.50
(88)	Great Catch	12.00	6.00	3.50
(89)	Stolen Base	12.00	6.00	3.50
(90)	Grand Slam Homer	12.00	6.00	3.50
(91)	Double Play	12.00	6.00	3.50
(92)	Left-Handed Follow Thru	12.00	6.00	3.50
(93)	Left-Handed High Leg Kick	12.00	6.00	3.50
(94)	Right-handed pitcher	12.00	6.00	3.50
(95)	Right-handed batter	12.00	6.00	3.50
(96)	Left-handed batter	12.00	6.00	3.50

1950s-60s Topps "PROMOTIONAL SAMPLES"

 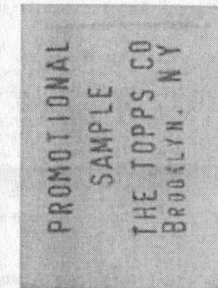

These mini sample cards are fantasy items created in the late 1990s to defraud collectors. Often sold grouped in an older frame or otherwise made to look old, they are pictures which have been cut out of the "Topps Baseball Cards" books or the team-issued Surf books which reproduced Topps cards in about 1-1/4" x 1-3/4" format. The color glossy pictures were then glued to a cardboard back which has been rubber-stamped "PROMOTIONAL / SAMPLE / THE TOPPS CO / BROOKLYN, N. Y." There were no legitimate miniature Topps promotional or sample cards produced.

(No Collectible Value.)

1961 Topps

Except for some of the specialty cards, Topps returned to a vertical format with their 1961 cards. The set is numbered through 589, however, only 587 cards were printed. No numbers 426, 587 and 588 were issued. Two cards numbered 463 exist (one a Braves team card and one a player card of Jack Fisher). Actually, the Braves team card is checklisted as #426. Designs for 1961 are basically large color portraits; the backs return to extensive statistics. A three-panel cartoon highlighting the player's career appears on the card backs. Innovations include numbered checklists, cards for statistical leaders, and 10 "Baseball Thrills" cards. The scarce high numbers are card numbers 523-589.

		NM	EX	VG
	Complete Set (587):	7,500	3,750	2,250
	Common Player (1-522):	6.00	3.00	1.75
	Common Player (523-589):	20.00	10.00	6.00
1	Dick Groat	25.00	6.00	2.00
2	Roger Maris	200.00	100.00	60.00
3	John Buzhardt	6.00	3.00	1.75
4	Lenny Green	6.00	3.00	1.75
5	Johnny Romano	6.00	3.00	1.75
6	Ed Roebuck	6.00	3.00	1.75
7	Chicago White Sox Team	10.00	5.00	3.00
8	Dick Williams	6.00	3.00	1.75
9	Bob Purkey	6.00	3.00	1.75
10	Brooks Robinson	50.00	25.00	12.50
11	Curt Simmons	6.00	3.00	1.75
12	Moe Thacker	6.00	3.00	1.75
13	Chuck Cottier	6.00	3.00	1.75
14	Don Mossi	6.00	3.00	1.75
15	Willie Kirkland	6.00	3.00	1.75
16	Billy Muffett	6.00	3.00	1.75
17	1st Series Checklist (1-88)	12.00	6.00	3.50
18	Jim Grant	6.00	3.00	1.75
19	Cletis Boyer	10.00	5.00	3.00
20	Robin Roberts	15.00	7.50	4.50
21	*Zoilo Versalles*	12.50	6.25	3.75
22	Clem Labine	6.00	3.00	1.75
23	Don Demeter	6.00	3.00	1.75
24	Ken Johnson	6.00	3.00	1.75

No.	Card			
25	Reds' Heavy Artillery (Gus Bell, Vada Pinson, Frank Robinson)	15.00	7.50	4.50
26	Wes Stock	6.00	3.00	1.75
27	Jerry Kindall	6.00	3.00	1.75
28	Hector Lopez	6.00	3.00	1.75
29	Don Nottebart	6.00	3.00	1.75
30	Nellie Fox	20.00	10.00	6.00
31	Bob Schmidt	6.00	3.00	1.75
32	Ray Sadecki	6.00	3.00	1.75
33	Gary Geiger	6.00	3.00	1.75
34	Wynn Hawkins	6.00	3.00	1.75
35	*Ron Santo*	50.00	25.00	12.50
36	Jack Kralick	6.00	3.00	1.75
37	Charlie Maxwell	6.00	3.00	1.75
38	Bob Lillis	6.00	3.00	1.75
39	Leo Posada	6.00	3.00	1.75
40	Bob Turley	10.00	5.00	3.00
41	N.L. Batting Leaders (Roberto Clemente, Dick Groat, Norm Larker, Willie Mays)	20.00	10.00	6.00
42	A.L. Batting Leaders (Minnie Minoso, Pete Runnels, Bill Skowron, Al Smith)	9.00	4.50	2.75
43	N.L. Home Run Leaders (Hank Aaron, Ernie Banks, Ken Boyer, Eddie Mathews)	17.50	8.75	5.25
44	A.L. Home Run Leaders (Rocky Colavito, Jim Lemon, Mickey Mantle, Roger Maris)	75.00	37.50	18.75
45	N.L. E.R.A. Leaders (Ernie Broglio, Don Drysdale, Bob Friend, Mike McCormick, Stan Williams)	7.00	3.50	2.00
46	A.L. E.R.A. Leaders (Frank Baumann, Hal Brown, Jim Bunning, Art Ditmar)	9.00	4.50	2.75
47a	N.L. Pitching Leaders (Ernie Broglio, Lou Burdette, Vern Law, Warren Spahn) (Vertical black bar in Burdette's box to right of 19.)	12.00	6.00	3.50
47b	N.L. Pitching Leaders (Ernie Broglio, Lew Burdette, Vern Law, Warren Spahn) (No black bar.)	12.00	6.00	3.50
48	A.L. Pitching Leaders (Bud Daley, Art Ditmar, Chuck Estrada, Frank Lary, Milt Pappas, Jim Perry)	7.00	3.50	2.00
49	N.L. Strikeout Leaders (Ernie Broglio, Don Drysdale, Sam Jones, Sandy Koufax)	16.00	8.00	4.75
50	A.L. Strikeout Leaders (Jim Bunning, Frank Lary, Pedro Ramos, Early Wynn)	12.00	6.00	3.50
51	Detroit Tigers Team	10.00	5.00	3.00
52	George Crowe	6.00	3.00	1.75
53	Russ Nixon	6.00	3.00	1.75
54	Earl Francis	6.00	3.00	1.75
55	Jim Davenport	6.00	3.00	1.75
56	Russ Kemmerer	6.00	3.00	1.75
57	Marv Throneberry	6.00	3.00	1.75
58	Joe Schaffernoth	6.00	3.00	1.75
59	Jim Woods	6.00	3.00	1.75
60	Woodie Held	6.00	3.00	1.75
61	Ron Piche	6.00	3.00	1.75
62	Al Pilarcik	6.00	3.00	1.75
63	Jim Kaat	9.00	4.50	2.75
64	Alex Grammas	6.00	3.00	1.75
65	Ted Kluszewski	10.00	5.00	3.00
66	Bill Henry	6.00	3.00	1.75
67	Ossie Virgil	6.00	3.00	1.75
68	Deron Johnson	6.00	3.00	1.75
69	Earl Wilson	6.00	3.00	1.75
70	Bill Virdon	6.00	3.00	1.75
71	Jerry Adair	6.00	3.00	1.75
72	Stu Miller	6.00	3.00	1.75
73	Al Spangler	6.00	3.00	1.75
74	Joe Pignatano	6.00	3.00	1.75
75	Lindy Shows Larry (Larry Jackson, Lindy McDaniel)	6.00	3.00	1.75
76	Harry Anderson	6.00	3.00	1.75
77	Dick Stigman	6.00	3.00	1.75
78	Lee Walls	6.00	3.00	1.75
79	Joe Ginsberg	6.00	3.00	1.75
80	Harmon Killebrew	25.00	12.50	7.50
81	Tracy Stallard	6.00	3.00	1.75
82	Joe Christopher	6.00	3.00	1.75
83	Bob Bruce	6.00	3.00	1.75
84	Lee Maye	6.00	3.00	1.75
85	Jerry Walker	6.00	3.00	1.75
86	Los Angeles Dodgers Team	11.00	5.50	3.25
87	Joe Amalfitano	6.00	3.00	1.75
88	Richie Ashburn	15.00	7.50	4.50
89	Billy Martin	9.00	4.50	2.75
90	Jerry Staley	6.00	3.00	1.75
91	Walt Moryn	6.00	3.00	1.75
92	Hal Naragon	6.00	3.00	1.75
93	Tony Gonzalez	6.00	3.00	1.75
94	Johnny Kucks	6.00	3.00	1.75
95	Norm Cash	12.50	6.25	3.75
96	Billy O'Dell	6.00	3.00	1.75
97	Jerry Lynch	6.00	3.00	1.75
98a	2nd Series Checklist (9-176) ("Checklist" in red on front.)	12.00	6.00	3.50
98b	2nd Series Checklist (89-176) ("Checklist" in yellow, 98 on back in black.)	12.00	6.00	3.50
98c	2nd Series Checklist (89-176) ("Checklist" in yellow, 98 on back in white.)	12.00	6.00	3.50
99	Don Buddin	6.00	3.00	1.75
100	Harvey Haddix	6.00	3.00	1.75
101	Bubba Phillips	6.00	3.00	1.75
102	Gene Stephens	6.00	3.00	1.75
103	Ruben Amaro	6.00	3.00	1.75
104	John Blanchard	7.50	3.75	2.25
105	Carl Willey	6.00	3.00	1.75
106	Whitey Herzog	12.50	6.25	3.75
107	Seth Morehead	6.00	3.00	1.75
108	Dan Dobbek	6.00	3.00	1.75
109	Johnny Podres	7.50	3.75	2.25
110	Vada Pinson	9.00	4.50	2.75
111	Jack Meyer	6.00	3.00	1.75
112	Chico Fernandez	6.00	3.00	1.75
113	Mike Fornieles	6.00	3.00	1.75
114	Hobie Landrith	6.00	3.00	1.75
115	Johnny Antonelli	6.00	3.00	1.75
116	Joe DeMaestri	6.00	3.00	1.75
117	Dale Long	6.00	3.00	1.75
118	Chris Cannizzaro	6.00	3.00	1.75
119	A's Big Armor (Hank Bauer, Jerry Lumpe, Norm Siebern)	9.00	4.50	2.75
120	Ed Mathews	20.00	10.00	6.00
121	Eli Grba	6.00	3.00	1.75
122	Chicago Cubs Team	10.00	5.00	3.00
123	Billy Gardner	6.00	3.00	1.75
124	J.C. Martin	6.00	3.00	1.75
125	Steve Barber	6.00	3.00	1.75
126	Dick Stuart	6.00	3.00	1.75
127	Ron Kline	6.00	3.00	1.75
128	Rip Repulski	6.00	3.00	1.75
129	Ed Hobaugh	6.00	3.00	1.75
130	Norm Larker	6.00	3.00	1.75
131	Paul Richards	6.00	3.00	1.75
132	Al Lopez	12.50	6.25	3.75
133	Ralph Houk	25.00	12.50	7.50
134	Mickey Vernon	6.00	3.00	1.75
135	Fred Hutchinson	6.00	3.00	1.75
136	Walt Alston	12.50	6.25	3.75
137	Chuck Dressen	6.00	3.00	1.75
138	Danny Murtaugh	6.00	3.00	1.75
139	Solly Hemus	6.00	3.00	1.75
140	Gus Triandos	6.00	3.00	1.75
141	*Billy Williams*	60.00	30.00	15.00
142	Luis Arroyo	6.00	3.00	1.75
143	Russ Snyder	6.00	3.00	1.75
144	Jim Coker	6.00	3.00	1.75
145	Bob Buhl	6.00	3.00	1.75
146	Marty Keough	6.00	3.00	1.75
147	Ed Rakow	6.00	3.00	1.75
148	Julian Javier	6.00	3.00	1.75
149	Bob Oldis	6.00	3.00	1.75
150	Willie Mays	120.00	60.00	30.00
151	Jim Donohue	6.00	3.00	1.75
152	Earl Torgeson	6.00	3.00	1.75
153	Don Lee	6.00	3.00	1.75
154	Bobby Del Greco	6.00	3.00	1.75
155	Johnny Temple	6.00	3.00	1.75
156	Ken Hunt	6.00	3.00	1.75
157	Cal McLish	6.00	3.00	1.75
158	Pete Daley	6.00	3.00	1.75
159	Baltimore Orioles Team	10.00	5.00	3.00
160	Whitey Ford	50.00	25.00	12.50
161	Sherman Jones	6.00	3.00	1.75
162	Jay Hook	6.00	3.00	1.75
163	Ed Sadowski	6.00	3.00	1.75
164	Felix Mantilla	6.00	3.00	1.75
165	Gino Cimoli	6.00	3.00	1.75
166	Danny Kravitz	6.00	3.00	1.75
167	San Francisco Giants Team	10.00	5.00	3.00
168	Tommy Davis	6.00	3.00	1.75
169	Don Elston	6.00	3.00	1.75
170	Al Smith	6.00	3.00	1.75
171	Paul Foytack	6.00	3.00	1.75
172	Don Dillard	6.00	3.00	1.75
173	Beantown Bombers (Jackie Jensen, Frank Malzone, Vic Wertz)	9.00	4.50	2.75
174	Ray Semproch	6.00	3.00	1.75
175	Gene Freese	6.00	3.00	1.75
176	Ken Aspromonte	6.00	3.00	1.75
177	Don Larsen	7.50	3.75	2.25
178	Bob Nieman	6.00	3.00	1.75
179	Joe Koppe	6.00	3.00	1.75
180	Bobby Richardson	15.00	7.50	4.50
181	Fred Green	6.00	3.00	1.75
182	*Dave Nicholson*	6.00	3.00	1.75
183	Andre Rodgers	6.00	3.00	1.75
184	Steve Bilko	6.00	3.00	1.75
185	Herb Score	6.00	3.00	1.75
186	Elmer Valo	6.00	3.00	1.75
187	Billy Klaus	6.00	3.00	1.75
188	Jim Marshall	6.00	3.00	1.75
189a	3rd Series Checklist (177-264) (No "4" on player at left.)	10.00	5.00	3.00
189b	3rd Series Checklist (177-264) ("4" shows on player on left)	10.00	5.00	3.00
190	Stan Williams	6.00	3.00	1.75
191	Mike de la Hoz	6.00	3.00	1.75
192	Dick Brown	6.00	3.00	1.75
193	Gene Conley	6.00	3.00	1.75
194	Gordy Coleman	6.00	3.00	1.75
195	Jerry Casale	6.00	3.00	1.75
196	Ed Bouchee	6.00	3.00	1.75
197	Dick Hall	6.00	3.00	1.75
198	Carl Sawatski	6.00	3.00	1.75
199	Bob Boyd	6.00	3.00	1.75
200	Warren Spahn	40.00	20.00	10.00
201	Pete Whisenant	6.00	3.00	1.75
202	Al Neiger	6.00	3.00	1.75
203	Eddie Bressoud	6.00	3.00	1.75
204	Bob Skinner	6.00	3.00	1.75
205	Bill Pierce	6.00	3.00	1.75
206	Gene Green	6.00	3.00	1.75
207	Dodger Southpaws (Sandy Koufax, Johnny Podres)	20.00	10.00	6.00
208	Larry Osborne	6.00	3.00	1.75
209	Ken McBride	6.00	3.00	1.75
210	Pete Runnels	6.00	3.00	1.75
211	Bob Gibson	25.00	12.50	7.50
212	Haywood Sullivan	6.00	3.00	1.75
213	*Bill Stafford*	6.00	3.00	1.75
214	Danny Murphy	6.00	3.00	1.75
215	Gus Bell	6.00	3.00	1.75
216	Ted Bowsfield	6.00	3.00	1.75
217	Mel Roach	6.00	3.00	1.75
218	Hal Brown	6.00	3.00	1.75
219	Gene Mauch	6.00	3.00	1.75
220	Al Dark	6.00	3.00	1.75
221	Mike Higgins	6.00	3.00	1.75
222	Jimmie Dykes	6.00	3.00	1.75
223	Bob Scheffing	6.00	3.00	1.75
224	Joe Gordon	6.00	3.00	1.75
225	Bill Rigney	6.00	3.00	1.75
226	Harry Lavagetto	6.00	3.00	1.75
227	Juan Pizarro	6.00	3.00	1.75
228	New York Yankees Team	60.00	30.00	15.00
229	Rudy Hernandez	6.00	3.00	1.75
230	Don Hoak	6.00	3.00	1.75
231	Dick Drott	6.00	3.00	1.75
232	Bill White	6.00	3.00	1.75
233	Joe Jay	6.00	3.00	1.75
234	Ted Lepcio	6.00	3.00	1.75
235	Camilo Pascual	6.00	3.00	1.75
236	Don Gile	6.00	3.00	1.75
237	Billy Loes	6.00	3.00	1.75
238	Jim Gilliam	7.50	3.75	2.25
239	Dave Sisler	6.00	3.00	1.75
240	Ron Hansen	6.00	3.00	1.75
241	Al Cicotte	6.00	3.00	1.75
242	Hal W. Smith	6.00	3.00	1.75
243	Frank Lary	6.00	3.00	1.75
244	Chico Cardenas	6.00	3.00	1.75
245	Joe Adcock	6.00	3.00	1.75
246	Bob Davis	6.00	3.00	1.75
247	Billy Goodman	6.00	3.00	1.75
248	Ed Keegan	6.00	3.00	1.75
249	Cincinnati Reds Team	10.00	5.00	3.00
250	Buc Hill Aces (Roy Face, Vern Law)	9.00	4.50	2.75
251	Bill Bruton	6.00	3.00	1.75
252	Bill Short	6.00	3.00	1.75
253	Sammy Taylor	6.00	3.00	1.75
254	Ted Sadowski	6.00	3.00	1.75
255	Vic Power	6.00	3.00	1.75
256	Billy Hoeft	6.00	3.00	1.75
257	Carroll Hardy	6.00	3.00	1.75
258	Jack Sanford	6.00	3.00	1.75
259	John Schaive	6.00	3.00	1.75
260	Don Drysdale	25.00	12.50	7.50
261	Charlie Lau	6.00	3.00	1.75
262	Tony Curry	6.00	3.00	1.75
263	Ken Hamlin	6.00	3.00	1.75
264	Glen Hobbie	6.00	3.00	1.75
265	Tony Kubek	15.00	7.50	4.50
266	Lindy McDaniel	6.00	3.00	1.75
267	Norm Siebern	6.00	3.00	1.75
268	Ike DeLock (Delock)	6.00	3.00	1.75
269	Harry Chiti	6.00	3.00	1.75
270	Bob Friend	6.00	3.00	1.75
271	Jim Landis	6.00	3.00	1.75
272	Tom Morgan	6.00	3.00	1.75
273a	4th Series Checklist (265-352) (Copyright ends opposite fifth name.)	12.00	6.00	3.50
273b	4th Series Checklist (265-352) (Copyright ends opposite top name.)	12.00	6.00	3.50
274	Gary Bell	6.00	3.00	1.75
275	Gene Woodling	6.00	3.00	1.75
276	Ray Rippelmeyer	6.00	3.00	1.75
277	Hank Foiles	6.00	3.00	1.75
278	Don McMahon	6.00	3.00	1.75
279	Jose Pagan	6.00	3.00	1.75
280	Frank Howard	9.00	4.50	2.75
281	Frank Sullivan	6.00	3.00	1.75
282	Faye Throneberry	6.00	3.00	1.75
283	Bob Anderson	6.00	3.00	1.75
284	Dick Gernert	6.00	3.00	1.75
285	Sherm Lollar	6.00	3.00	1.75
286	George Witt	6.00	3.00	1.75
287	Carl Yastrzemski	45.00	22.50	13.50
288	Albie Pearson	6.00	3.00	1.75
289	Ray Moore	6.00	3.00	1.75
290	Stan Musial	100.00	50.00	25.00
291	Tex Clevenger	6.00	3.00	1.75
292	Jim Baumer	6.00	3.00	1.75
293	Tom Sturdivant	6.00	3.00	1.75
294	Don Blasingame	6.00	3.00	1.75
295	Milt Pappas	6.00	3.00	1.75
296	Wes Covington	6.00	3.00	1.75
297	Kansas City Athletics Team	10.00	5.00	3.00
298	Jim Golden	6.00	3.00	1.75
299	Clay Dalrymple	6.00	3.00	1.75
300	Mickey Mantle	425.00	210.00	125.00
301	Chet Nichols	6.00	3.00	1.75
302	Al Heist	6.00	3.00	1.75
303	Gary Peters	6.00	3.00	1.75
304	Rocky Nelson	6.00	3.00	1.75
305	Mike McCormick	6.00	3.00	1.75
306	World Series Game 1 (Virdon Saves Game)	9.00	4.50	2.75
307	World Series Game 2 (Mantle Slams 2 Homers)	75.00	37.50	18.75
308	World Series Game 3 (Richardson Is Hero)	20.00	10.00	6.00
309	World Series Game 4 (Cimoli Safe In Crucial Play)	9.00	4.50	2.75
310	World Series Game 5 (Face Saves The Day)	10.00	5.00	3.00
311	World Series Game 6 (Ford Pitches Second Shutout)	15.00	7.50	4.50
312	World Series Game 7 (Mazeroski's Homer Wins It!)	25.00	12.50	7.50
313	World Series (The Winners Celebrate)	12.50	6.25	3.75
314	Bob Miller	6.00	3.00	1.75
315	Earl Battey	6.00	3.00	1.75
316	Bobby Gene Smith	6.00	3.00	1.75
317	*Jim Brewer*	6.00	3.00	1.75

318	Danny O'Connell	6.00	3.00	1.75
319	Valmy Thomas	6.00	3.00	1.75
320	Lou Burdette	6.00	3.00	1.75
321	Marv Breeding	6.00	3.00	1.75
322	Bill Kunkel	6.00	3.00	1.75
323	Sammy Esposito	6.00	3.00	1.75
324	Hank Aguirre	6.00	3.00	1.75
325	Wally Moon	6.00	3.00	1.75
326	Dave Hillman	6.00	3.00	1.75
327	*Matty Alou*	12.50	6.25	3.75
328	Jim O'Toole	6.00	3.00	1.75
329	Julio Becquer	6.00	3.00	1.75
330	Rocky Colavito	15.00	7.50	4.50
331	Ned Garver	6.00	3.00	1.75
332	Dutch Dotterer (Photo actually Tommy Dotterer.)	6.00	3.00	1.75
333	Fritz Brickell	6.00	3.00	1.75
334	Walt Bond	6.00	3.00	1.75
335	Frank Bolling	6.00	3.00	1.75
336	Don Mincher	6.00	3.00	1.75
337	Al's Aces (Al Lopez, Herb Score, Early Wynn)	9.00	4.50	2.75
338	Don Landrum	6.00	3.00	1.75
339	Gene Baker	6.00	3.00	1.75
340	Vic Wertz	6.00	3.00	1.75
341	Jim Owens	6.00	3.00	1.75
342	Clint Courtney	6.00	3.00	1.75
343	Earl Robinson	6.00	3.00	1.75
344	Sandy Koufax	100.00	50.00	25.00
345	Jim Piersall	7.50	3.75	2.25
346	Howie Nunn	6.00	3.00	1.75
347	St. Louis Cardinals Team	10.00	5.00	3.00
348	Steve Boros	6.00	3.00	1.75
349	Danny McDevitt	6.00	3.00	1.75
350	Ernie Banks	50.00	25.00	12.50
351	Jim King	6.00	3.00	1.75
352	Bob Shaw	6.00	3.00	1.75
353	Howie Bedell	6.00	3.00	1.75
354	Billy Harrell	6.00	3.00	1.75
355	Bob Allison	6.00	3.00	1.75
356	Ryne Duren	7.50	3.75	2.25
357	Daryl Spencer	6.00	3.00	1.75
358	Earl Averill	6.00	3.00	1.75
359	Dallas Green	7.50	3.75	2.25
360	Frank Robinson	25.00	12.50	7.50
361a	5th Series Checklist (353-429) ("Topps Baseball" in black on front.)	10.00	5.00	3.00
361b	5th Series Checklist (353-429) ("Topps Baseball" in yellow.)	12.00	6.00	3.50
362	Frank Funk	6.00	3.00	1.75
363	John Roseboro	6.00	3.00	1.75
364	Moe Drabowsky	6.00	3.00	1.75
365	Jerry Lumpe	6.00	3.00	1.75
366	Eddie Fisher	6.00	3.00	1.75
367	Jim Rivera	6.00	3.00	1.75
368	Bennie Daniels	6.00	3.00	1.75
369	Dave Philley	6.00	3.00	1.75
370	Roy Face	6.00	3.00	1.75
371	Bill Skowron (SP)	50.00	25.00	12.50
372	Bob Hendley	6.00	3.00	1.75
373	Boston Red Sox Team	10.00	5.00	3.00
374	Paul Giel	6.00	3.00	1.75
375	Ken Boyer	13.50	6.75	4.00
376	Mike Roarke	6.00	3.00	1.75
377	Ruben Gomez	6.00	3.00	1.75
378	Wally Post	6.00	3.00	1.75
379	Bobby Shantz	6.00	3.00	1.75
380	Minnie Minoso	9.00	4.50	2.75
381	Dave Wickersham	6.00	3.00	1.75
382	Frank Thomas	6.00	3.00	1.75
383	Frisco First Liners (Mike McCormick, Billy O'Dell, Jack Sanford)	7.50	3.75	2.25
384	Chuck Essegian	6.00	3.00	1.75
385	Jim Perry	6.00	3.00	1.75
386	Joe Hicks	6.00	3.00	1.75
387	Duke Maas	6.00	3.00	1.75
388	Bob Clemente	150.00	75.00	37.50
389	Ralph Terry	6.00	3.00	1.75
390	Del Crandall	6.00	3.00	1.75
391	Winston Brown	6.00	3.00	1.75
392	Reno Bertoia	6.00	3.00	1.75
393	Batter Bafflers (Don Cardwell, Glen Hobbie)	7.50	3.75	2.25
394	Ken Walters	6.00	3.00	1.75
395	Chuck Estrada	6.00	3.00	1.75
396	Bob Aspromonte	6.00	3.00	1.75
397	Hal Woodeshick	6.00	3.00	1.75
398	Hank Bauer	7.50	3.75	2.25
399	Cliff Cook	6.00	3.00	1.75
400	Vern Law	6.00	3.00	1.75
401	Babe Ruth Hits 60th Homer	50.00	25.00	15.00
402	Larsen Pitches Perfect Game (SP)	25.00	12.50	7.50
403	Brooklyn-Boston Play 26-Inning Tie	6.00	3.00	1.75
404	Hornsby Tops N.L. with .424 Average	9.00	4.50	2.75
405	Gehrig Benched After 2,130 Games	75.00	37.50	18.75
406	Mantle Blasts 565 ft. Home Run	100.00	50.00	25.00
407	Jack Chesbro Wins 41st Game	6.00	3.00	1.75
408	Mathewson Strikes Out 267 Batters (SP)	17.50	8.75	5.25
409	Johnson Hurls 3rd Shutout In 4 Days	9.00	4.50	2.75
410	Haddix Pitches 12 Perfect Innings	7.50	3.75	2.25
411	Tony Taylor	6.00	3.00	1.75
412	Larry Sherry	6.00	3.00	1.75
413	Eddie Yost	6.00	3.00	1.75
414	Dick Donovan	6.00	3.00	1.75
415	Hank Aaron	125.00	62.50	31.25
416	*Dick Howser* (SP)	12.50	6.25	3.75
417	*Juan Marichal*	100.00	50.00	25.00
418	Ed Bailey	6.00	3.00	1.75
419	Tom Borland	6.00	3.00	1.75
420	Ernie Broglio	6.00	3.00	1.75
421	Ty Cline (SP)	12.50	6.25	3.75
422	Bud Daley	6.00	3.00	1.75
423	Charlie Neal (SP)	12.50	6.25	3.75
424	Turk Lown	6.00	3.00	1.75
425	Yogi Berra	85.00	42.50	21.25
426	Not Issued (See #463.)			
427	Dick Ellsworth	6.00	3.00	1.75
428	Ray Barker (SP)	12.50	6.25	3.75
429	Al Kaline	50.00	25.00	12.50
430	Bill Mazeroski (SP)	50.00	25.00	12.50
431	Chuck Stobbs	6.00	3.00	1.75
432	Coot Veal	6.00	3.00	1.75
433	Art Mahaffey	6.00	3.00	1.75
434	Tom Brewer	6.00	3.00	1.75
435	Orlando Cepeda	15.00	7.50	4.50
436	*Jim Maloney* (SP)	20.00	10.00	6.00
437a	6th Series Checklist (430-506) (#440 is Louis Aparicio)	12.00	6.00	3.50
437b	6th Series Checklist (430-506) (#440 is Luis Aparicio)	10.00	5.00	3.00
438	Curt Flood	7.50	3.75	2.25
439	*Phil Regan*	6.00	3.00	1.75
440	Luis Aparicio	15.00	7.50	4.50
441	Dick Bertell	6.00	3.00	1.75
442	Gordon Jones	6.00	3.00	1.75
443	Duke Snider	30.00	15.00	9.00
444	Joe Nuxhall	6.00	3.00	1.75
445	Frank Malzone	6.00	3.00	1.75
446	Bob "Hawk" Taylor	6.00	3.00	1.75
447	Harry Bright	6.00	3.00	1.75
448	Del Rice	6.00	3.00	1.75
449	*Bobby Bolin*	6.00	3.00	1.75
450	Jim Lemon	6.00	3.00	1.75
451	Power For Ernie (Ernie Broglio, Daryl Spencer, Bill White)	7.50	3.75	2.25
452	Bob Allen	6.00	3.00	1.75
453	Dick Schofield	6.00	3.00	1.75
454	Pumpsie Green	6.00	3.00	1.75
455	Early Wynn	12.50	6.25	3.75
456	Hal Bevan	6.00	3.00	1.75
457	Johnny James	6.00	3.00	1.75
458	Willie Tasby	6.00	3.00	1.75
459	Terry Fox	6.00	3.00	1.75
460	Gil Hodges	12.50	6.25	3.75
461	Smoky Burgess	6.00	3.00	1.75
462	Lou Klimchock	6.00	3.00	1.75
463a	Milwaukee Braves Team (Should be card #426.)	10.00	5.00	3.00
463b	Jack Fisher	6.00	3.00	1.75
464	*Leroy Thomas*	6.00	3.00	1.75
465	Roy McMillan	6.00	3.00	1.75
466	Ron Moeller	6.00	3.00	1.75
467	Cleveland Indians Team	10.00	5.00	3.00
468	Johnny Callison	6.00	3.00	1.75
469	Ralph Lumenti	6.00	3.00	1.75
470	Roy Sievers	6.00	3.00	1.75
471	Phil Rizzuto (MVP)	30.00	15.00	7.50
472	Yogi Berra (MVP)	50.00	25.00	12.50
473	Bobby Shantz (MVP)	7.50	3.75	2.25
474	Al Rosen (MVP)	7.50	3.75	2.25
475	Mickey Mantle (MVP)	220.00	110.00	55.00
476	Jackie Jensen (MVP)	7.50	3.75	2.25
477	Nellie Fox (MVP)	17.50	8.75	5.25
478	Roger Maris (MVP)	60.00	30.00	15.00
479	Jim Konstanty (MVP)	6.00	3.00	1.75
480	Roy Campanella (MVP)	40.00	20.00	10.00
481	Hank Sauer (MVP)	6.00	3.00	1.75
482	Willie Mays (MVP)	50.00	25.00	12.50
483	Don Newcombe (MVP)	7.50	3.75	2.25
484	Hank Aaron (MVP)	50.00	25.00	12.50
485	Ernie Banks (MVP)	20.00	10.00	6.00
486	Dick Groat (MVP)	7.50	3.75	2.25
487	Gene Oliver	6.00	3.00	1.75
488	Joe McClain	6.00	3.00	1.75
489	Walt Dropo	6.00	3.00	1.75
490	Jim Bunning	12.50	6.25	3.75
491	Philadelphia Phillies Team	10.00	5.00	3.00
492	Ron Fairly	6.00	3.00	1.75
493	Don Zimmer	7.50	3.75	2.25
494	Tom Cheney	6.00	3.00	1.75
495	Elston Howard	15.00	7.50	4.50
496	Ken MacKenzie	6.00	3.00	1.75
497	Willie Jones	6.00	3.00	1.75
498	Ray Herbert	6.00	3.00	1.75
499	*Chuck Schilling*	6.00	3.00	1.75
500	Harvey Kuenn	6.00	3.00	1.75
501	John DeMerit	6.00	3.00	1.75
502	Clarence Coleman	6.00	3.00	1.75
503	Tito Francona	6.00	3.00	1.75
504	Billy Consolo	6.00	3.00	1.75
505	Red Schoendienst	12.50	6.25	3.75
506	*Willie Davis*	13.50	6.75	4.00
507	Pete Burnside	6.00	3.00	1.75
508	Rocky Bridges	6.00	3.00	1.75
509	Camilo Carreon	6.00	3.00	1.75
510	Art Ditmar	6.00	3.00	1.75
511	Joe Morgan	6.00	3.00	1.75
512	Bob Will	6.00	3.00	1.75
513	Jim Brosnan	6.00	3.00	1.75
514	Jake Wood	6.00	3.00	1.75
515	Jackie Brandt	6.00	3.00	1.75
516a	7th Series Checklist (507-587) (Second "C" of "CHECK" above #13's cap.)	12.00	6.00	3.50
516b	7th Series Checklist (506-587) (Second "C" of "CHECK" covers top of #13's cap.)	12.00	6.00	3.50
517	Willie McCovey	40.00	20.00	10.00
518	Andy Carey	6.00	3.00	1.75
519	Jim Pagliaroni	6.00	3.00	1.75
520	Joe Cunningham	6.00	3.00	1.75
521	Brother Battery (Larry Sherry, Norm Sherry)	10.00	5.00	3.00
522	Dick Farrell	6.00	3.00	1.75
523	Joe Gibbon	20.00	10.00	6.00
524	Johnny Logan	20.00	10.00	6.00
525	*Ron Perranoski*	60.00	30.00	15.00
526	R.C. Stevens	20.00	10.00	6.00
527	Gene Leek	20.00	10.00	6.00
528	Pedro Ramos	20.00	10.00	6.00
529	Bob Roselli	20.00	10.00	6.00
530	Bobby Malkmus	20.00	10.00	6.00
531	Jim Coates	20.00	10.00	6.00
532	Bob Hale	20.00	10.00	6.00
533	Jack Curtis	20.00	10.00	6.00
534	Eddie Kasko	20.00	10.00	6.00
535	Larry Jackson	20.00	10.00	6.00
536	Bill Tuttle	20.00	10.00	6.00
537	Bobby Locke	20.00	10.00	6.00
538	Chuck Hiller	20.00	10.00	6.00
539	Johnny Klippstein	20.00	10.00	6.00
540	Jackie Jensen	22.50	11.00	7.00
541	Roland Sheldon	20.00	10.00	6.00
542	Minnesota Twins Team	40.00	20.00	10.00
543	Roger Craig	20.00	10.00	6.00
544	George Thomas	20.00	10.00	6.00
545	Hoyt Wilhelm	60.00	30.00	15.00
546	Marty Kutyna	20.00	10.00	6.00
547	Leon Wagner	20.00	10.00	6.00
548	Ted Wills	20.00	10.00	6.00
549	Hal R. Smith	20.00	10.00	6.00
550	Frank Baumann	20.00	10.00	6.00
551	George Altman	20.00	10.00	6.00
552	Jim Archer	20.00	10.00	6.00
553	Bill Fischer	20.00	10.00	6.00
554	Pittsburgh Pirates Team	75.00	37.50	18.75
555	Sam Jones	20.00	10.00	6.00
556	Ken R. Hunt	20.00	10.00	6.00
557	Jose Valdivielso	20.00	10.00	6.00
558	Don Ferrarese	20.00	10.00	6.00
559	Jim Gentile	60.00	30.00	15.00
560	Barry Latman	20.00	10.00	6.00
561	Charley James	20.00	10.00	6.00
562	Bill Monbouquette	20.00	10.00	6.00
563	Bob Cerv	20.00	10.00	6.00
564	Don Cardwell	20.00	10.00	6.00
565	Felipe Alou	25.00	12.50	6.25
566	Paul Richards/AS	20.00	10.00	6.00
567	Danny Murtaugh/AS	20.00	10.00	6.00
568	Bill Skowron/AS	25.00	12.50	7.50
569	Frank Herrera/AS	20.00	10.00	6.00
570	Nellie Fox/AS	50.00	25.00	12.50
571	Bill Mazeroski/AS	50.00	25.00	12.50
572	Brooks Robinson/AS	60.00	30.00	15.00
573	Ken Boyer/AS	22.50	11.00	6.75
574	Luis Aparicio/AS	50.00	25.00	12.50
575	Ernie Banks/AS	100.00	50.00	25.00
576	Roger Maris/AS	150.00	75.00	37.50
577	Hank Aaron/AS	160.00	80.00	40.00
578	Mickey Mantle/AS	500.00	250.00	125.00
579	Willie Mays/AS	160.00	80.00	40.00
580	Al Kaline/AS	80.00	40.00	20.00
581	Frank Robinson/AS	90.00	45.00	22.50
582	Earl Battey/AS	20.00	10.00	6.00
583	Del Crandall/AS	20.00	10.00	6.00
584	Jim Perry/AS	20.00	10.00	6.00
585	Bob Friend/AS	20.00	10.00	6.00
586	Whitey Ford/AS	100.00	50.00	25.00
587	Not Issued			
588	Not Issued			
589	Warren Spahn/AS	100.00	50.00	25.00

1961 Topps Dice Game

One of the more obscure Topps test issues that may have never actually been issued is the 1961 Topps Dice Game. Eighteen black and white cards, each measuring 2-1/2" x 3-1/2" in size, comprise the set. Interestingly, there are no identifying marks, such as copyrights or trademarks, to indicate the set was produced by Topps. The card backs contain various baseball plays that occur when a certain pitch is called and a specific number of the dice is rolled.

		NM	EX	VG
	Common Player:	1,850	925.00	550.00
(1)	Earl Battey	1,850	925.00	550.00
(2)	Del Crandall	1,850	925.00	550.00
(3)	Jim Davenport	1,850	925.00	550.00
(4)	Don Drysdale	4,500	2,250	1,350
(5)	Dick Groat	1,850	925.00	550.00
(6)	Al Kaline	7,500	3,750	2,250
(7)	Tony Kubek	3,250	1,625	975.00
(8)	Mickey Mantle	45,000	22,500	13,500
(9)	Willie Mays	20,000	8,500	5,100
(10)	Bill Mazeroski	4,500	2,250	1,350
(11)	Stan Musial	20,000	10,000	6,000
(12)	Camilo Pascual	1,850	925.00	550.00
(13)	Bobby Richardson	3,500	1,750	1,050
(14)	Brooks Robinson	7,500	3,750	2,250

		NM	EX	VG
(15)	Frank Robinson	7,500	3,750	2,250
(16)	Norm Siebern	1,850	925.00	550.00
(17)	Leon Wagner	1,850	925.00	550.00
(18)	Bill White	1,850	925.00	550.00

1961 Topps Magic Rub-Offs

Not too different in concept from the tattoos of the previous year, the Topps Magic Rub-Off was designed to leave impressions of team themes or individual players when properly applied. Measuring 2-1/16" x 3-1/16", the Magic Rub-Off was not designed specifically for application to the owner's skin. The set features team themes that are a far cry from official logos, and the players (one per team) seem to have been included for their nicknames.

		NM	EX	VG
	Complete Set (36):	200.00	100.00	60.00
	Common Player:	6.00	3.00	1.75
(1)	Baltimore Orioles Pennant	6.00	3.00	1.75
(2)	Ernie "Bingo" Banks	15.00	7.50	4.50
(3)	Yogi Berra	15.00	7.50	4.50
(4)	Boston Red Sox Pennant	6.00	3.00	1.75
(5)	Jackie "Ozark" Brandt	6.00	3.00	1.75
(6)	Jim "Professor" Brosnan	6.00	3.00	1.75
(7)	Chicago Cubs Pennant	6.00	3.00	1.75
(8)	Chicago White Sox Pennant	6.00	3.00	1.75
(9)	Cincinnati Red Legs Pennant	6.00	3.00	1.75
(10)	Cleveland Indians Pennant	6.00	3.00	1.75
(11)	Detroit Tigers Pennant	6.00	3.00	1.75
(12)	Henry "Dutch" Dotterer	6.00	3.00	1.75
(13)	Joe "Flash" Gordon	6.00	3.00	1.75
(14)	Harvey "The Kitten" Haddix	6.00	3.00	1.75
(15)	Frank "Pancho" Hererra	6.00	3.00	1.75
(16)	Frank "Tower" Howard	7.50	3.75	2.25
(17)	"Sad" Sam Jones	6.00	3.00	1.75
(18)	Kansas City Athletics Pennant	6.00	3.00	1.75
(19)	Los Angeles Angels Pennant	7.50	3.75	2.25
(20)	Los Angeles Dodgers Pennant	7.50	3.75	2.25
(21)	Omar "Turk" Lown	6.00	3.00	1.75
(22)	Billy "The Kid" Martin	7.50	3.75	2.25
(23)	Duane "Duke" Mass (Maas)	6.00	3.00	1.75
(24)	Charlie "Paw Paw" Maxwell	6.00	3.00	1.75
(25)	Milwaukee Braves Pennant	6.00	3.00	1.75
(26)	Minnesota Twins Pennant	7.50	3.75	2.25
(27)	"Farmer" Ray Moore	6.00	3.00	1.75
(28)	Walt "Moose" Moryn	6.00	3.00	1.75
(29)	New York Yankees Pennant	9.00	4.50	2.75
(30)	Philadelphia Phillies Pennant	6.00	3.00	1.75
(31)	Pittsburgh Pirates Pennant	6.00	3.00	1.75
(32)	John "Honey" Romano	6.00	3.00	1.75
(33)	"Pistol Pete" Runnels	6.00	3.00	1.75
(34)	St. Louis Cardinals Pennant	6.00	3.00	1.75
(35)	San Francisco Giants Pennant	6.00	3.00	1.75
(36)	Washington Senators Pennant	9.00	4.50	2.75

1961 Topps Stamps

Issued as an added insert to 1961 Topps wax packs these 1-3/8" x 1-3/16" stamps were desigend to be collected and placed in an album which could be bought for an additional 10¢. Packs of cards contained two stamps. There are 208 stamps in a complete set which depict 207 different players (Al Kaline appears twice). There are 104 players on brown stamps and 104 on green. While there are many Hall of Famers on the stamps, prices remain low because there is relatively little interest in what is a non-card set.

	NM	EX	VG
Complete Set (208):	750.00	375.00	225.00
Common Player:	2.00	1.00	.60
Stamp Album (Green):	65.00	30.00	20.00

(1)	Hank Aaron	20.00	10.00	6.00
(2)	Joe Adcock	2.00	1.00	.60
(3)	Hank Aguirre	2.00	1.00	.60
(4)	Bob Allison	2.00	1.00	.60
(5)	George Altman	2.00	1.00	.60
(6)	Bob Anderson	2.00	1.00	.60
(7)	Johnny Antonelli	2.00	1.00	.60
(8)	Luis Aparicio	12.00	6.00	3.50
(9)	Luis Arroyo	2.00	1.00	.60
(10)	Richie Ashburn	13.50	6.75	4.00
(11)	Ken Aspromonte	2.00	1.00	.60
(12)	Ed Bailey	2.00	1.00	.60
(13)	Ernie Banks	13.50	6.75	4.00
(14)	Steve Barber	2.00	1.00	.60
(15)	Earl Battey	2.00	1.00	.60
(16)	Hank Bauer	2.00	1.00	.60
(17)	Gus Bell	2.00	1.00	.60
(18)	Yogi Berra	13.50	6.75	4.00
(19)	Reno Bertoia	2.00	1.00	.60
(20)	John Blanchard	2.00	1.00	.60
(21)	Don Blasingame	2.00	1.00	.60
(22)	Frank Bolling	2.00	1.00	.60
(23)	Steve Boros	2.00	1.00	.60
(24)	Ed Bouchee	2.00	1.00	.60
(25)	Bob Boyd	2.00	1.00	.60
(26)	Cletis Boyer	2.00	1.00	.60
(27)	Ken Boyer	3.00	1.50	.90
(28)	Jackie Brandt	2.00	1.00	.60
(29)	Marv Breeding	2.00	1.00	.60
(30)	Eddie Bressoud	2.00	1.00	.60
(31)	Jim Brewer	2.00	1.00	.60
(32)	Tom Brewer	2.00	1.00	.60
(33)	Jim Brosnan	2.00	1.00	.60
(34)	Bill Bruton	2.00	1.00	.60
(35)	Bob Buhl	2.00	1.00	.60
(36)	Jim Bunning	10.00	5.00	3.00
(37)	Smoky Burgess	2.00	1.00	.60
(38)	John Buzhardt	2.00	1.00	.60
(39)	Johnny Callison	2.00	1.00	.60
(40)	Chico Cardenas	2.00	1.00	.60
(41)	Andy Carey	2.00	1.00	.60
(42)	Jerry Casale	2.00	1.00	.60
(43)	Norm Cash	4.00	2.00	1.25
(44)	Orlando Cepeda	10.00	5.00	3.00
(45)	Bob Cerv	2.00	1.00	.60
(46)	Harry Chiti	2.00	1.00	.60
(47)	Gene Conley	2.00	1.00	.60
(48)	Wes Covington	2.00	1.00	.60
(49)	Del Crandall	2.00	1.00	.60
(50)	Tony Curry	2.00	1.00	.60
(51)	Bud Daley	2.00	1.00	.60
(52)	Pete Daley	2.00	1.00	.60
(53)	Clay Dalrymple	2.00	1.00	.60
(54)	Jim Davenport	2.00	1.00	.60
(55)	Tommy Davis	2.00	1.00	.60
(56)	Bobby Del Greco	2.00	1.00	.60
(57)	Ike Delock	2.00	1.00	.60
(58)	Art Ditmar	2.00	1.00	.60
(59)	Dick Donovan	2.00	1.00	.60
(60)	Don Drysdale	13.50	6.75	4.00
(61)	Dick Ellsworth	2.00	1.00	.60
(62)	Don Elston	2.00	1.00	.60
(63)	Chuck Estrada	2.00	1.00	.60
(64)	Roy Face	2.00	1.00	.60
(65)	Dick Farrell	2.00	1.00	.60
(66)	Chico Fernandez	2.00	1.00	.60
(67)	Curt Flood	2.00	1.00	.60
(68)	Whitey Ford	13.50	6.75	4.00
(69)	Tito Francona	2.00	1.00	.60
(70)	Gene Freese	2.00	1.00	.60
(71)	Bob Friend	2.00	1.00	.60
(72)	Billy Gardner	2.00	1.00	.60
(73)	Ned Garver	2.00	1.00	.60
(74)	Gary Geiger	2.00	1.00	.60
(75)	Jim Gentile	2.00	1.00	.60
(76)	Dick Gernert	2.00	1.00	.60
(77)	Tony Gonzalez	2.00	1.00	.60
(78)	Alex Grammas	2.00	1.00	.60
(79)	Jim Grant	2.00	1.00	.60
(80)	Dick Groat	2.00	1.00	.60
(81)	Dick Hall	2.00	1.00	.60
(82)	Ron Hansen	2.00	1.00	.60
(83)	Bob Hartman	2.00	1.00	.60
(84)	Woodie Held	2.00	1.00	.60
(85)	Ray Herbert	2.00	1.00	.60
(86)	Frank Herrera	2.00	1.00	.60
(87)	Whitey Herzog	2.00	1.00	.60
(88)	Don Hoak	2.00	1.00	.60
(89)	Elston Howard	5.00	2.50	1.50
(90)	Frank Howard	4.00	2.00	1.25
(91)	Ken Hunt	2.00	1.00	.60
(92)	Larry Jackson	2.00	1.00	.60
(93)	Julian Javier	2.00	1.00	.60
(94)	Joe Jay	2.00	1.00	.60
(95)	Jackie Jensen	2.00	1.00	.60
(96)	Jim Kaat	2.50	1.25	.70
(97a)	Al Kaline (Green)	25.00	12.50	7.50
(97b)	Al Kaline (Brown)	15.00	7.50	4.50
(98)	Eddie Kasko	2.00	1.00	.60
(99)	Russ Kemmerer	2.00	1.00	.60
(100)	Harmon Killebrew	13.50	6.75	4.00
(101)	Billy Klaus	2.00	1.00	.60
(102)	Ron Kline	2.00	1.00	.60
(103)	Johnny Klippstein	2.00	1.00	.60
(104)	Ted Kluszewski	10.00	5.00	3.00
(105)	Tony Kubek	5.00	2.50	1.50
(106)	Harvey Kuenn	2.00	1.00	.60
(107)	Jim Landis	2.00	1.00	.60
(108)	Hobie Landrith	2.00	1.00	.60
(109)	Norm Larker	2.00	1.00	.60
(110)	Frank Lary	2.00	1.00	.60
(111)	Barry Latman	2.00	1.00	.60
(112)	Vern Law	2.00	1.00	.60
(113)	Jim Lemon	2.00	1.00	.60
(114)	Sherman Lollar	2.00	1.00	.60
(115)	Dale Long	2.00	1.00	.60
(116)	Jerry Lumpe	2.00	1.00	.60
(117)	Jerry Lynch	2.00	1.00	.60

(118)	Art Mahaffey	2.00	1.00	.60
(119)	Frank Malzone	2.00	1.00	.60
(120)	Felix Mantilla	2.00	1.00	.60
(121)	Mickey Mantle	60.00	30.00	18.00
(122)	Juan Marichal	13.50	6.75	4.00
(123)	Roger Maris	25.00	12.50	7.50
(124)	Billy Martin	5.00	2.50	1.50
(125)	J.C. Martin	2.00	1.00	.60
(126)	Ed Mathews	13.50	6.75	4.00
(127)	Charlie Maxwell	2.00	1.00	.60
(128)	Willie Mays	20.00	10.00	6.00
(129)	Bill Mazeroski	12.00	6.00	3.50
(130)	Mike McCormick	2.00	1.00	.60
(131)	Willie McCovey	13.50	6.75	4.00
(132)	Lindy McDaniel	2.00	1.00	.60
(133)	Roy McMillan	2.00	1.00	.60
(134)	Minnie Minoso	3.00	1.50	.90
(135)	Bill Monbouquette	2.00	1.00	.60
(136)	Wally Moon	2.00	1.00	.60
(137)	Stan Musial	20.00	10.00	6.00
(138)	Charlie Neal	2.00	1.00	.60
(139)	Rocky Nelson	2.00	1.00	.60
(140)	Russ Nixon	2.00	1.00	.60
(141)	Billy O'Dell	2.00	1.00	.60
(142)	Jim O'Toole	2.00	1.00	.60
(143)	Milt Pappas	2.00	1.00	.60
(144)	Camilo Pascual	2.00	1.00	.60
(145)	Jim Perry	2.00	1.00	.60
(146)	Bubba Phillips	2.00	1.00	.60
(147)	Bill Pierce	2.00	1.00	.60
(148)	Jim Piersall	2.00	1.00	.60
(149)	Vada Pinson	3.00	1.50	.90
(150)	Johnny Podres	2.50	1.25	.70
(151)	Wally Post	2.00	1.00	.60
(152)	Vic Powers (Power)	2.00	1.00	.60
(153)	Pedro Ramos	2.00	1.00	.60
(154)	Robin Roberts	10.00	5.00	3.00
(155)	Brooks Robinson	13.50	6.75	4.00
(156)	Frank Robinson	13.50	6.75	4.00
(157)	Ed Roebuck	2.00	1.00	.60
(158)	John Romano	2.00	1.00	.60
(159)	John Roseboro	2.00	1.00	.60
(160)	Pete Runnels	2.00	1.00	.60
(161)	Ed Sadowski	2.00	1.00	.60
(162)	Jack Sanford	2.00	1.00	.60
(163)	Ron Santo	3.00	1.50	.90
(164)	Ray Semproch	2.00	1.00	.60
(165)	Bobby Shantz	2.00	1.00	.60
(166)	Bob Shaw	2.00	1.00	.60
(167)	Larry Sherry	2.00	1.00	.60
(168)	Norm Siebern	2.00	1.00	.60
(169)	Roy Sievers	2.00	1.00	.60
(170)	Curt Simmons	2.00	1.00	.60
(171)	Dave Sisler	2.00	1.00	.60
(172)	Bob Skinner	2.00	1.00	.60
(173)	Al Smith	2.00	1.00	.60
(174)	Hal Smith	2.00	1.00	.60
(175)	Hal Smith	2.00	1.00	.60
(176)	Duke Snider	13.50	6.75	4.00
(177)	Warren Spahn	13.50	6.75	4.00
(178)	Daryl Spencer	2.00	1.00	.60
(179)	Bill Stafford	2.00	1.00	.60
(180)	Jerry Staley	2.00	1.00	.60
(181)	Gene Stephens	2.00	1.00	.60
(182)	Chuck Stobbs	2.00	1.00	.60
(183)	Dick Stuart	2.00	1.00	.60
(184)	Willie Tasby	2.00	1.00	.60
(185)	Sammy Taylor	2.00	1.00	.60
(186)	Tony Taylor	2.00	1.00	.60
(187)	Johnny Temple	2.00	1.00	.60
(188)	Marv Throneberry	2.00	1.00	.60
(189)	Gus Triandos	2.00	1.00	.60
(190)	Bob Turley	2.00	1.00	.60
(191)	Bill Tuttle	2.00	1.00	.60
(192)	Zoilo Versalles	2.00	1.00	.60
(193)	Bill Virdon	2.00	1.00	.60
(194)	Lee Walls	2.00	1.00	.60
(195)	Vic Wertz	2.00	1.00	.60
(196)	Pete Whisenant	2.00	1.00	.60
(197)	Bill White	2.00	1.00	.60
(198)	Hoyt Wilhelm	10.00	5.00	3.00
(199)	Bob Will	2.00	1.00	.60
(200)	Carl Willey	2.00	1.00	.60
(201)	Billy Williams	12.00	6.00	3.50
(202)	Dick Williams	2.00	1.00	.60
(203)	Stan Williams	2.00	1.00	.60
(204)	Gene Woodling	2.00	1.00	.60
(205)	Early Wynn	10.00	5.00	3.00
(206)	Carl Yastrzemski	13.50	6.75	4.00
(207)	Eddie Yost	2.00	1.00	.60

1961 Topps Stamps Panels

Some advanced collectors pursue the 1961 Topps stamps in the form of the two-stamp panels in which they were issued. The 208 different stamps which make up the issue can be found on 182 different two-stamp panels. The unnumbered stamps are listed here alphabetically according to the name of the player which appears on the left end of the panel. Values shown are for complete panels of two players stamps plus the attached tab at left.

	NM	EX	VG
Complete Panel Set (182):	3,000	1,500	900.00
Common Panel:	9.00	4.50	2.75
(1) Hank Aguirre/Bob Boyd	9.00	4.50	2.75
(2) Bob Allison/Orlando Cepeda	20.00	10.00	6.00
(3) Bob Allison/Early Wynn	20.00	10.00	6.00
(4) George Altman/Andy Carey	9.00	4.50	2.75
(5) George Altman/ Lindy McDaniel	9.00	4.50	2.75
(6) Johnny Antonelli/Ken Hunt	9.00	4.50	2.75
(7) Richie Ashburn/Don Drysdale	30.00	15.00	9.00
(8) Richie Ashburn/Joe Jay	25.00	12.50	7.50
(9) Ken Aspromonte/ Chuck Estrada	9.00	4.50	2.75
(10) Ken Aspromonte/Jerry Lynch	9.00	4.50	2.75
(11) Ed Bailey/Marv Breeding	9.00	4.50	2.75
(12) Ed Bailey/Smoky Burgess	9.00	4.50	2.75
(13) Ernie Banks/Chico Fernandez	30.00	15.00	9.00
(14) Ernie Banks/Pedro Ramos	30.00	15.00	9.00
(15) Steve Barber/Eddie Kasko	9.00	4.50	2.75
(16) Steve Barber/Roy Sievers	9.00	4.50	2.75
(17) Earl Battey/Art Ditmar	9.00	4.50	2.75
(18) Earl Battey/Bill White	9.00	4.50	2.75
(19) Gus Bell/Gary Geiger	9.00	4.50	2.75
(20) Gus Bell/Early Wynn	20.00	10.00	6.00
(21) John Blanchard/Dick Donovan	9.00	4.50	2.75
(22) John Blanchard/ Ray Semproch	9.00	4.50	2.75
(23) Don Blasingame/ Elston Howard	12.00	6.00	3.50
(24) Don Blasingame/ Charlie Maxwell	9.00	4.50	2.75
(25) Frank Bolling/Luis Aparicio	20.00	10.00	6.00
(26) Frank Bolling/Whitey Herzog	9.00	4.50	2.75
(27) Steve Boros/Ike Delock	9.00	4.50	2.75
(28) Steve Boros/Russ Nixon	9.00	4.50	2.75
(29) Ed Bouchee/Larry Sherry	9.00	4.50	2.75
(30) Ed Bouchee/Willie Tasby	9.00	4.50	2.75
(31) Cletis Boyer/Johnny Klippstein	9.00	4.50	2.75
(32) Jim Brewer/Vern Law	9.00	4.50	2.75
(33) Jim Brewer/Camilo Pascual	9.00	4.50	2.75
(34) Tom Brewer/Tommy Davis	9.00	4.50	2.75
(35) Tom Brewer/Larry Sherry	9.00	4.50	2.75
(36) Jim Brosnan/Roy McMillan	9.00	4.50	2.75
(37) Jim Brosnan/Cair Willey	9.00	4.50	2.75
(38) Bill Bruton/Ken Boyer	12.00	6.00	3.50
(39) Bill Bruton/Mickey Mantle	200.00	100.00	60.00
(40) Bob Buhl/Willie Mays	60.00	30.00	18.00
(41) Bob Buhl/Roy Sievers	9.00	4.50	2.75
(42) Jim Bunning/Bob Boyd	20.00	10.00	6.00
(43) Jim Bunning/Ron Hansen	20.00	10.00	6.00
(44) John Buzhardt/ Brooks Robinson	30.00	15.00	9.00
(45) John Buzhardt/Dick Williams	9.00	4.50	2.75
(46) Johnny Callison/Jim Landis	9.00	4.50	2.75
(47) Johnny Callison/Ed Roebuck	9.00	4.50	2.75
(48) Harry Chiti/Jackie Brandt	9.00	4.50	2.75
(49) Harry Chiti/Gene Conley	9.00	4.50	2.75
(50) Del Crandall/Billy Gardner	9.00	4.50	2.75
(51) Bud Daley/Al Kaline	30.00	15.00	9.00
(52) Bud Daley/Dave Sisler	9.00	4.50	2.75
(53) Pete Daley/Dick Ellsworth	9.00	4.50	2.75
(54) Pete Daley/Hal (R.) Smith	9.00	4.50	2.75
(55) Clay Dalrymple/Norm Larker	9.00	4.50	2.75
(56) Clay Dalrymple/Stan Williams	9.00	4.50	2.75
(57) Jim Davenport/Reno Bertoia	9.00	4.50	2.75
(58) Jim Davenport/Jerry Lynch	9.00	4.50	2.75
(59) Bobby Del Greco/Roy Face	9.00	4.50	2.75
(60) Bobby Del Greco/ Frank Howard	12.00	6.00	3.50
(61) Gene Freese/Wes Covington	9.00	4.50	2.75
(62) Gene Freese/Vada Pinson	9.00	4.50	2.75
(63) Bob Friend/Hank Aaron	60.00	30.00	18.00
(64) Bob Friend/Lee Walls	9.00	4.50	2.75
(65) Jim Gentile/Chuck Estrada	9.00	4.50	2.75
(66) Jim Gentile/Billy O'Dell	9.00	4.50	2.75
(67) Dick Gernert/Russ Nixon	9.00	4.50	2.75
(68) Alex Grammas/ Eddie Bressoud	9.00	4.50	2.75
(69) Frank Herrera/Joe Jay	9.00	4.50	2.75
(70) Frank Herrera/Jim Landis	9.00	4.50	2.75
(71) Julian Javier/Eddie Kasko	9.00	4.50	2.75
(72) Jackie Jensen/Hank Bauer	15.00	7.50	4.50
(73) Jackie Jensen/Mickey Mantle	200.00	100.00	60.00
(74) Al Kaline/Dick Hall	30.00	15.00	9.00
(75) Al Kaline/Ray Herbert	30.00	15.00	9.00
(76) Russ Kemmerer/Ed Sadowski	9.00	4.50	2.75
(77) Harmon Killebrew/Bill Stafford	30.00	15.00	9.00
(78) Harmon Killebrew/Bill White	30.00	15.00	9.00
(79) Billy Klaus/Bob Anderson	9.00	4.50	2.75
(80) Ron Kline/Juan Marichal	20.00	10.00	6.00
(81) Ron Kline/Curt Simmons	9.00	4.50	2.75
(82) Tony Kubek/Reno Bertoia	12.00	6.00	3.50
(83) Frank Lary/Andy Carey	9.00	4.50	2.75
(84) Barry Latman/Hank Bauer	9.00	4.50	2.75
(85) Jim Lemon/Tony Curry	9.00	4.50	2.75
(86) Jim Lemon/Dick Williams	9.00	4.50	2.75
(87) Sherm Lollar/Willie Mays	60.00	30.00	18.00
(88) Sherm Lollar/Duke Snider	30.00	15.00	9.00
(89) Dale Long/Bob Anderson	9.00	4.50	2.75
(90) Dale Long/Don Elston	9.00	4.50	2.75
(91) Art Mahaffey/Vada Pinson	9.00	4.50	2.75
(92) Art Mahaffey/Robin Roberts	20.00	10.00	6.00
(93) Frank Malzone/Dick Hall	9.00	4.50	2.75
(94) Frank Malzone/Bob Hartman	9.00	4.50	2.75
(95) Felix Mantilla/Billy Gardner	9.00	4.50	2.75
(96) Felix Mantilla/Gary Geiger	9.00	4.50	2.75
(97) Roger Maris/Johnny Klippstein	45.00	22.00	13.50
(98) Roger Maris/Ray Semproch	45.00	22.00	13.50
(99) Billy Martin/Hank Aaron	60.00	30.00	18.00
(100) Billy Martin/Whitey Herzog	15.00	7.50	4.50
(101) J.C. Martin/Bob Cerv	9.00	4.50	2.75
(102) J.C. Martin/Eddie Yost	9.00	4.50	2.75
(103) Ed Mathews/Chico Cardenas	30.00	15.00	9.00
(104) Bill Mazeroski/Joe Adcock	20.00	10.00	6.00
(105) Bill Mazeroski/Elston Howard	20.00	10.00	6.00

	NM	EX	VG
(106) Mike McCormick/ Rocky Nelson	9.00	4.50	2.75
(107) Mike McCormick/ Curt Simmons	9.00	4.50	2.75
(108) Wille McCovey/ Smoky Burgess	30.00	15.00	9.00
(109) Minnie Minoso/ Ted Kluszewski	15.00	7.50	4.50
(110) Minnie Minoso/Eddie Yost	12.00	6.00	3.50
(111) Bikll Monbouquette/ Tony Curry	9.00	4.50	2.75
(112) Bill Monbouquette/ Sammy Taylor	9.00	4.50	2.75
(113) Wally Moon/Roy Face	9.00	4.50	2.75
(114) Stan Musial/Rocky Nelson	60.00	30.00	18.00
(115) Charlie Neal/Marv Breeding	9.00	4.50	2.75
(116) Charlie Neal/Jim Grant	9.00	4.50	2.75
(117) Jim O'Toole/Chico Cardenas	9.00	4.50	2.75
(118) Jim O'Toole/Roy McMillan	9.00	4.50	2.75
(119) Milt Pappas/Tito Francona	9.00	4.50	2.75
(120) Milt Pappas/Jim Piersall	9.00	4.50	2.75
(121) Jim Perry/Bob Cerv	9.00	4.50	2.75
(122) Jim Perry/Ken Hunt	9.00	4.50	2.75
(123) Bubba Phillips/Art Ditmar	9.00	4.50	2.75
(124) Bubba Phillips/Jim Kaat	15.00	7.50	4.50
(125) Johnny Podres/Dick Farrell	9.00	4.50	2.75
(126) Wally Post/Dick Farrell	9.00	4.50	2.75
(127) Wally Post/Robin Roberts	20.00	10.00	6.00
(128) Frank Robinson/Jim Grant	30.00	15.00	9.00
(129) Frank Robinson/Don Hoak	30.00	15.00	9.00
(130) John Romano/Al Kaline	30.00	15.00	9.00
(131) John Roseboro/Dick Groat	9.00	4.50	2.75
(132) Pete Runnels/Larry Jackson	9.00	4.50	2.75
(133) Jack Sanford/Whitey Ford	30.00	15.00	9.00
(134) Jack Sanford/Pedro Ramos	9.00	4.50	2.75
(135) Ron Santo/Harvey Kuenn	15.00	7.50	4.50
(136) Ron Santo/Vern Law	15.00	7.50	4.50
(137) Bobby Shantz/Joe Adcock	9.00	4.50	2.75
(138) Bobby Shantz/Dick Groat	9.00	4.50	2.75
(139) Bob Shaw/Jerry Casale	9.00	4.50	2.75
(140) Bob Shaw/Ned Garver	9.00	4.50	2.75
(141) Norm Siebem/Tony Gonzalez	9.00	4.50	2.75
(142) Norm Siebern/Woodie Held	9.00	4.50	2.75
(143) Bob Skinner/Hobie Landrith	9.00	4.50	2.75
(144) Bob Skinner/Juan Marichal	20.00	10.00	6.00
(145) Al Smith/Don Drysdale	25.00	12.50	7.50
(146) Hal (W.) Smith/ Eddie Bressoud	9.00	4.50	2.75
(147) Hal (W.) Smith/Harvey Kuenn	9.00	4.50	2.75
(148) Daryl Spencer/Norm Cash	9.00	4.50	2.75
(149) Daryl Spencer/ Vic Powers (Power)	9.00	4.50	2.75
(150) Jerry Staley/Ned Garver	9.00	4.50	2.75
(151) Jerry Staley/Ed Sadowski	9.00	4.50	2.75
(152) Gene Stephens/Gene Conley	9.00	4.50	2.75
(153) Gene Stephens/Ike Delock	9.00	4.50	2.75
(154) Chuck Stobbs/Ken Boyer	12.00	6.00	3.50
(155) Chuck Stobbs/Curt Flood	9.00	4.50	2.75
(156) Dick Stuart/Whitey Ford	30.00	15.00	9.00
(157) Dick Stuart/Larry Jackson	9.00	4.50	2.75
(158) Tony Taylor/Frank Howard	12.00	6.00	3.50
(159) Tony Taylor/Norm Larker	9.00	4.50	2.75
(160) Johnny Temple/Norm Cash	9.00	4.50	2.75
(161) Johnny Temple/Dave Sisler	9.00	4.50	2.75
(162) Marv Throneberry/Yogi Berra	45.00	22.00	13.50
(163) Marv Throneberry/ Tommy Davis	9.00	4.50	2.75
(164) Gus Triandos/Sammy Taylor	9.00	4.50	2.75
(165) Bob Turley/Luis Aparicio	20.00	10.00	6.00
(166) Bill Tuttle/Jerry Casale	9.00	4.50	2.75
(167) Bill Tuttle/Bill Pierce	9.00	4.50	2.75
(168) Zoilo Versalles/Bill Stafford	9.00	4.50	2.75
(169) Bill Virdon/Yogi Berra	30.00	15.00	9.00
(170) Vic Wertz/Bob Hartman	9.00	4.50	2.75
(171) Vic Wertz/Jerry Lumpe	9.00	4.50	2.75
(172) Pete Whisenant/Luis Arroyo	9.00	4.50	2.75
(173) Pete Whisenant/Dick Donovan	9.00	4.50	2.75
(174) Hoyt Wilhelm/Ron Hansen	20.00	10.00	6.00
(175) Hoyt Wilhelm/Jim Piersall	20.00	10.00	6.00
(176) Bob Will/Tony Gonzalez	9.00	4.50	2.75
(177) Bob Will/Lindy McDaniel	9.00	4.50	2.75
(178) Billy Williams/Warren Spahn	30.00	15.00	9.00
(179) Billy Williams/Carl Willey	25.00	12.50	7.50
(180) Gene Woodling/Don Elston	9.00	4.50	2.75
(181) Gene Woodling/Hal (R.) Smith	9.00	4.50	2.75
(182) Carl Yastrzemski/Jerry Lumpe	60.00	30.00	18.00

1962 Topps

The 1962 Topps set established another plateau for set size with 598 cards. The 2-1/2" x 3-1/2" cards feature a photograph set against a woodgrain background. The lower-right corner has been made to look like it is curling away. Many established specialty cards dot the set including statistical leaders, multi-player cards, team cards, checklists, World Series cards and All-Stars. Of note is that 1962 was the first year of the multi-player rookie card. There is a nine-card "In

Action" subset and a 10-card run of special Babe Ruth cards. Photo variations of several cards in the 2nd Series (#110-196) exist. All cards in the 2nd Series can be found with two distinct printing variations, an early printing with the cards containing a very noticeable greenish tint, having been corrected to clear photos in subsequent print runs. The complete set price in the checklist that follows does not include the higher-priced variations. Among the high numbers (#523-598) certain cards were "short-printed," produced in lesser quantities. These cards carry a higher value and are indicated in the checklist by the notation (SP) after the player name.

	NM	EX	VG
Complete Set (598):	7,000	3,500	2,100
Common Player (1-446):	4.00	2.00	1.25
Common Player (447-522):	7.00	3.50	2.00
Common Player (523-598):	10.00	5.00	3.00
1 Roger Maris	500.00	250.00	125.00
2 Jim Brosnan	4.00	2.00	1.25
3 Pete Runnels	4.00	2.00	1.25
4 John DeMerit	4.00	2.00	1.25
5 Sandy Koufax	150.00	75.00	37.50
6 Marv Breeding	4.00	2.00	1.25
7 Frank Thomas	4.00	2.00	1.25
8 Ray Herbert	4.00	2.00	1.25
9 Jim Davenport	4.00	2.00	1.25
10 Bob Clemente	200.00	100.00	50.00
11 Tom Morgan	4.00	2.00	1.25
12 Harry Craft	4.00	2.00	1.25
13 Dick Howser	4.00	2.00	1.25
14 Bill White	4.00	2.00	1.25
15 Dick Donovan	4.00	2.00	1.25
16 Darrell Johnson	4.00	2.00	1.25
17 Johnny Callison	4.00	2.00	1.25
18 Managers' Dream (Mickey Mantle, Willie Mays)	200.00	100.00	50.00
19 *Ray Washburn*	4.00	2.00	1.25
20 Rocky Colavito	15.00	7.50	4.50
21 Jim Kaat	6.00	3.00	1.75
22a 1st Series Checklist (1-88) (Numbers 121-176 on back.)	6.00	3.00	1.75
22b 1st Series Checklist (1-88) (Numbers 33-88 on back.)	9.00	4.50	2.75
23 Norm Larker	4.00	2.00	1.25
24 Detroit Tigers Team	7.00	3.50	2.00
25 Ernie Banks	65.00	32.50	16.25
26 Chris Cannizzaro	4.00	2.00	1.25
27 Chuck Cottier	4.00	2.00	1.25
28 Minnie Minoso	9.00	4.50	2.75
29 Casey Stengel	13.50	6.75	4.00
30 Ed Mathews	25.00	12.50	7.50
31 *Tom Tresh*	13.50	6.75	4.00
32 John Roseboro	4.00	2.00	1.25
33 Don Larsen	4.00	2.00	1.25
34 Johnny Temple	4.00	2.00	1.25
35 *Don Schwall*	4.00	2.00	1.25
36 Don Leppert	4.00	2.00	1.25
37 Tribe Hill Trio (Barry Latman, Jim Perry, Dick Stigman)	6.00	3.00	1.75
38 Gene Stephens	4.00	2.00	1.25
39 Joe Koppe	4.00	2.00	1.25
40 Orlando Cepeda	16.00	8.00	4.75
41 Cliff Cook	4.00	2.00	1.25
42 Jim King	4.00	2.00	1.25
43 Los Angeles Dodgers Team	10.00	5.00	3.00
44 Don Taussig	4.00	2.00	1.25
45 Brooks Robinson	25.00	12.50	7.50
46 *Jack Baldschun*	4.00	2.00	1.25
47 Bob Will	4.00	2.00	1.25
48 Ralph Terry	4.00	2.00	1.25
49 Hal Jones	4.00	2.00	1.25
50 Stan Musial	100.00	50.00	25.00
51 A.L. Batting Leaders (Norm Cash, Elston Howard, Al Kaline, Jim Piersall)	12.50	6.25	3.75
52 N.L. Batting Leaders (Ken Boyer, Roberto Clemente, Wally Moon, Vada Pinson)	15.00	7.50	4.50
53 A.L. Home Run Leaders (Jim Gentile, Harmon Killebrew, Mickey Mantle, Roger Maris)	100.00	50.00	25.00
54 N.L. Home Run Leaders (Orlando Cepeda, Willie Mays, Frank Robinson)	12.50	6.25	3.75
55 A.L. E.R.A. Leaders (Dick Donovan, Don Mossi, Milt Pappas, Bill Stafford)	6.00	3.00	1.75
56 N.L. E.R.A. Leaders (Mike McCormick, Jim O'Toole, Curt Simmons, Warren Spahn)	7.00	3.50	2.00
57 A.L. Win Leaders (Steve Barber, Jim Bunning, Whitey Ford, Frank Lary)	10.00	5.00	3.00
58 N.L. Win Leaders (Joe Jay, Jim O'Toole, Warren Spahn)	7.00	3.50	2.00
59 A.L. Strikeout Leaders (Jim Bunning, Whitey Ford, Camilo Pascual, Juan Pizzaro)	7.50	3.75	2.25
60 N.L. Strikeout Leaders (Don Drysdale, Sandy Koufax, Jim O'Toole, Stan Williams)	16.00	8.00	4.75
61 St. Louis Cardinals Team	7.00	3.50	2.00
62 Steve Boros	4.00	2.00	1.25
63 *Tony Cloninger*	7.00	3.50	2.00
64 Russ Snyder	4.00	2.00	1.25
65 Bobby Richardson	15.00	7.50	4.50
66 Cuno Barragon (Barragan)	4.00	2.00	1.25
67 Harvey Haddix	4.00	2.00	1.25
68 Ken L. Hunt	4.00	2.00	1.25
69 Phil Ortega	4.00	2.00	1.25
70 Harmon Killebrew	25.00	12.50	7.50
71 Dick LeMay	4.00	2.00	1.25
72 Bob's Pupils (Steve Boros, Bob Scheffing, Jake Wood)	4.50	2.25	1.25
73 Nellie Fox	16.00	8.00	4.75
74 Bob Lillis	4.00	2.00	1.25

No.	Player			
75	Milt Pappas	4.00	2.00	1.25
76	Howie Bedell	4.00	2.00	1.25
77	Tony Taylor	4.00	2.00	1.25
78	Gene Green	4.00	2.00	1.25
79	Ed Hobaugh	4.00	2.00	1.25
80	Vada Pinson	7.00	3.50	2.00
81	Jim Pagliaroni	4.00	2.00	1.25
82	Deron Johnson	4.00	2.00	1.25
83	Larry Jackson	4.00	2.00	1.25
84	Lenny Green	4.00	2.00	1.25
85	Gil Hodges	15.00	7.50	4.50
86	*Donn Clendenon*	6.00	3.00	1.75
87	Mike Roarke	4.00	2.00	1.25
88	Ralph Houk	10.00	5.00	3.00
89	Barney Schultz	4.00	2.00	1.25
90	Jim Piersall	6.00	3.00	1.75
91	J.C. Martin	4.00	2.00	1.25
92	Sam Jones	4.00	2.00	1.25
93	John Blanchard	5.00	2.50	1.50
94	Jay Hook	4.00	2.00	1.25
95	Don Hoak	4.00	2.00	1.25
96	Eli Grba	4.00	2.00	1.25
97	Tito Francona	4.00	2.00	1.25
98	2nd Series Checklist (89-176)	6.00	3.00	1.75
99	*John Powell* (Boog)	20.00	10.00	6.00
100	Warren Spahn	50.00	25.00	12.50
101	Carroll Hardy	4.00	2.00	1.25
102	Al Schroll	4.00	2.00	1.25
103	Don Blasingame	4.00	2.00	1.25
104	Ted Savage	4.00	2.00	1.25
105	Don Mossi	4.00	2.00	1.25
106	Carl Sawatski	4.00	2.00	1.25
107	Mike McCormick	4.00	2.00	1.25
108	Willie Davis	5.00	2.50	1.50
109	Bob Shaw	4.00	2.00	1.25
110	Bill Skowron	22.50	11.00	7.00
111	Dallas Green	4.00	2.00	1.25
112	Hank Foiles	4.00	2.00	1.25
113	Chicago White Sox Team	7.00	3.50	2.00
114	Howie Koplitz	4.00	2.00	1.25
115	Bob Skinner	4.00	2.00	1.25
116	Herb Score	4.00	2.00	1.25
117	Gary Geiger	4.00	2.00	1.25
118	Julian Javier	4.00	2.00	1.25
119	Danny Murphy	4.00	2.00	1.25
120	Bob Purkey	4.00	2.00	1.25
121	Billy Hitchcock	4.00	2.00	1.25
122	Norm Bass	4.00	2.00	1.25
123	Mike de la Hoz	4.00	2.00	1.25
124	Bill Pleis	4.00	2.00	1.25
125	Gene Woodling	4.00	2.00	1.25
126	Al Cicotte	4.00	2.00	1.25
127	Pride of the A's (Hank Bauer, Jerry Lumpe, Norm Siebern)	4.50	2.25	1.25
128	Art Fowler	4.00	2.00	1.25
129a	Lee Walls (Pinstriped jersey.)	20.00	10.00	6.00
129b	Lee Walls (Plain jersey.)	6.00	3.00	1.75
130	Frank Bolling	4.00	2.00	1.25
131	*Pete Richert*	4.00	2.00	1.25
132a	Los Angeles Angels Team (With inset photos.)	13.50	6.75	4.00
132b	Los Angeles Angels Team (No inset photos.)	7.00	3.50	2.00
133	Felipe Alou	9.00	4.50	2.75
134a	Billy Hoeft (Green sky.)	15.00	7.50	4.50
134b	Billy Hoeft (Blue sky.)	12.00	6.00	3.50
135	Babe as a Boy (Babe Ruth)	20.00	10.00	6.00
136	Babe Joins Yanks (Babe Ruth)	20.00	10.00	6.00
137	Babe and Mgr. Huggins (Babe Ruth)	20.00	10.00	6.00
138	The Famous Slugger (Babe Ruth)	20.00	10.00	6.00
139a	Hal Reniff (Pitching)	30.00	15.00	7.50
139b	Hal Reniff (Portrait)	15.00	7.50	4.50
139c	Babe Hits 60 (Babe Ruth) (Pole in background at left.)	50.00	25.00	12.50
139d	Babe Hits 60 (Babe Ruth) (No pole.)	35.00	17.50	10.00
140	Gehrig and Ruth (Babe Ruth)	35.00	17.50	10.00
141	Twilight Years (Babe Ruth)	20.00	10.00	6.00
142	Coaching for the Dodgers (Babe Ruth)	20.00	10.00	6.00
143	Greatest Sports Hero (Babe Ruth)	20.00	10.00	6.00
144	Farewell Speech (Babe Ruth)	20.00	10.00	6.00
145	Barry Latman	4.00	2.00	1.25
146	Don Demeter	4.00	2.00	1.25
147a	Bill Kunkel (Ball in hand.)	17.50	8.75	5.25
147b	Bill Kunkel (Portrait)	12.00	6.00	3.50
148	Wally Post	4.00	2.00	1.25
149	Bob Duliba	4.00	2.00	1.25
150	Al Kaline	50.00	25.00	12.50
151	Johnny Klippstein	4.00	2.00	1.25
152	Mickey Vernon	4.00	2.00	1.25
153	Pumpsie Green	4.00	2.00	1.25
154	Lee Thomas	4.00	2.00	1.25
155	Stu Miller	4.00	2.00	1.25
156	Merritt Ranew	4.00	2.00	1.25
157	Wes Covington	4.00	2.00	1.25
158	Milwaukee Braves Team	7.00	3.50	2.00
159	Hal Reniff	4.00	2.00	1.25
160	Dick Stuart	4.00	2.00	1.25
161	Frank Baumann	4.00	2.00	1.25
162	Sammy Drake	4.00	2.00	1.25
163	Hot Corner Guardians (Cletis Boyer, Billy Gardner)	10.00	5.00	3.00
164	Hal Naragon	4.00	2.00	1.25
165	Jackie Brandt	4.00	2.00	1.25
166	Don Lee	4.00	2.00	1.25
167	*Tim McCarver*	17.50	8.75	5.25
168	Leo Posada	4.00	2.00	1.25
169	Bob Cerv	4.00	2.00	1.25
170	Ron Santo	12.50	6.25	3.75
171	Dave Sisler	4.00	2.00	1.25
172	Fred Hutchinson	4.00	2.00	1.25
173	Chico Fernandez	4.00	2.00	1.25
174a	Carl Willey (With cap.)	15.00	7.50	4.50
174b	Carl Willey (No cap.)	8.00	4.00	2.50
175	Frank Howard	5.00	2.50	1.50
176a	Eddie Yost (Batting)	15.00	7.50	4.50
176b	Eddie Yost (Portrait)	4.00	2.00	1.25
177	Bobby Shantz	4.00	2.00	1.25
178	Camilo Carreon	4.00	2.00	1.25
179	Tom Sturdivant	4.00	2.00	1.25
180	Bob Allison	4.00	2.00	1.25
181	Paul Brown	4.00	2.00	1.25
182	Bob Nieman	4.00	2.00	1.25
183	Roger Craig	4.00	2.00	1.25
184	Haywood Sullivan	4.00	2.00	1.25
185	Roland Sheldon	4.00	2.00	1.25
186	*Mack Jones*	4.00	2.00	1.25
187	Gene Conley	4.00	2.00	1.25
188	Chuck Hiller	4.00	2.00	1.25
189	Dick Hall	4.00	2.00	1.25
190a	Wally Moon (With cap.)	20.00	10.00	6.00
190b	Wally Moon (No cap.)	6.00	3.00	1.75
191	Jim Brewer	4.00	2.00	1.25
192a	3rd Series Checklist (177-264) (192 is Check List, 3)	7.00	3.50	2.00
192b	3rd Series Checklist (177-264) (192 is Check List 3)	8.00	4.00	2.50
193	Eddie Kasko	4.00	2.00	1.25
194	*Dean Chance*	12.50	6.25	3.75
195	Joe Cunningham	4.00	2.00	1.25
196	Terry Fox	4.00	2.00	1.25
197	Daryl Spencer	4.00	2.00	1.25
198	Johnny Keane	4.00	2.00	1.25
199	*Gaylord Perry*	80.00	40.00	20.00
200	Mickey Mantle	525.00	260.00	160.00
201	Ike Delock	4.00	2.00	1.25
202	Carl Warwick	4.00	2.00	1.25
203	Jack Fisher	4.00	2.00	1.25
204	Johnny Weekly	4.00	2.00	1.25
205	Gene Freese	4.00	2.00	1.25
206	Washington Senators Team	7.00	3.50	2.00
207	Pete Burnside	4.00	2.00	1.25
208	Billy Martin	12.00	6.00	3.50
209	*Jim Fregosi*	15.00	7.50	4.50
210	Roy Face	4.00	2.00	1.25
211	Midway Masters (Frank Bolling, Roy McMillan)	4.50	2.25	1.25
212	Jim Owens	4.00	2.00	1.25
213	Richie Ashburn	20.00	10.00	6.00
214	Dom Zanni	4.00	2.00	1.25
215	Woody Held	4.00	2.00	1.25
216	Ron Kline	4.00	2.00	1.25
217	Walt Alston	10.00	5.00	3.00
218	*Joe Torre*	55.00	27.50	16.50
219	*Al Downing*	12.00	6.00	3.50
220	Roy Sievers	4.00	2.00	1.25
221	Bill Short	4.00	2.00	1.25
222	Jerry Zimmerman	4.00	2.00	1.25
223	Alex Grammas	4.00	2.00	1.25
224	Don Rudolph	4.00	2.00	1.25
225	Frank Malzone	4.00	2.00	1.25
226	San Francisco Giants Team	7.00	3.50	2.00
227	Bobby Tiefenauer	4.00	2.00	1.25
228	Dale Long	4.00	2.00	1.25
229	Jesus McFarlane	4.00	2.00	1.25
230	Camilo Pascual	4.00	2.00	1.25
231	Ernie Bowman	4.00	2.00	1.25
232	World Series Game 1 (Yanks Win Opener)	8.00	4.00	2.50
233	World Series Game 2 (Jay Ties It Up)	10.00	5.00	3.00
234	World Series Game 3 (Maris Wins It In the 9th)	22.50	11.00	7.00
235	World Series Game 4 (Ford Sets New Mark)	17.50	8.75	5.25
236	World Series Game 5 (Yanks Crush Reds in Finale)	7.00	3.50	2.00
237	World Series (The Winners Celebrate)	10.00	5.00	3.00
238	Norm Sherry	4.00	2.00	1.25
239	Cecil Butler	4.00	2.00	1.25
240	George Altman	4.00	2.00	1.25
241	Johnny Kucks	4.00	2.00	1.25
242	Mel McGaha	4.00	2.00	1.25
243	Robin Roberts	15.00	7.50	4.50
244	Don Gile	4.00	2.00	1.25
245	Ron Hansen	4.00	2.00	1.25
246	Art Ditmar	4.00	2.00	1.25
247	Joe Pignatano	4.00	2.00	1.25
248	Bob Aspromonte	4.00	2.00	1.25
249	Ed Keegan	4.00	2.00	1.25
250	Norm Cash	12.00	6.00	3.50
251	New York Yankees Team	50.00	25.00	12.50
252	Earl Francis	4.00	2.00	1.25
253	Harry Chiti	4.00	2.00	1.25
254	Gordon Windhorn	4.00	2.00	1.25
255	Juan Pizarro	4.00	2.00	1.25
256	Elio Chacon	4.00	2.00	1.25
257	Jack Spring	4.00	2.00	1.25
258	Marty Keough	4.00	2.00	1.25
259	Lou Klimchock	4.00	2.00	1.25
260	Bill Pierce	4.00	2.00	1.25
261	George Alusik	4.00	2.00	1.25
262	Bob Schmidt	4.00	2.00	1.25
263	The Right Pitch (Joe Jay, Bob Purkey, Jim Turner)	4.50	2.25	1.25
264	Dick Ellsworth	4.00	2.00	1.25
265	Joe Adcock	4.00	2.00	1.25
266	John Anderson	4.00	2.00	1.25
267	Dan Dobbek	4.00	2.00	1.25
268	Ken McBride	4.00	2.00	1.25
269	Bob Oldis	4.00	2.00	1.25
270	Dick Groat	4.00	2.00	1.25
271	Ray Rippelmeyer	4.00	2.00	1.25
272	Earl Robinson	4.00	2.00	1.25
273	Gary Bell	4.00	2.00	1.25
274	Sammy Taylor	4.00	2.00	1.25
275	Norm Siebern	4.00	2.00	1.25
276	Hal Kostad	4.00	2.00	1.25
277	4th Series Checklist (265-352)	7.00	3.50	2.00
278	Ken Johnson	4.00	2.00	1.25
279	Hobie Landrith	4.00	2.00	1.25
280	Johnny Podres	7.50	3.75	2.25
281	*Jake Gibbs*	7.50	3.75	2.25
282	Dave Hillman	4.00	2.00	1.25
283	Charlie Smith	4.00	2.00	1.25
284	Ruben Amaro	4.00	2.00	1.25
285	Curt Simmons	4.00	2.00	1.25
286	Al Lopez	9.00	4.50	2.75
287	George Witt	4.00	2.00	1.25
288	Billy Williams	35.00	17.50	8.75
289	Mike Krsnich	4.00	2.00	1.25
290	Jim Gentile	6.00	3.00	1.75
291	Hal Stowe	4.00	2.00	1.25
292	Jerry Kindall	4.00	2.00	1.25
293	Bob Miller	4.00	2.00	1.25
294	Philadelphia Phillies Team	7.50	3.75	2.25
295	Vern Law	4.00	2.00	1.25
296	Ken Hamlin	4.00	2.00	1.25
297	Ron Perranoski	4.00	2.00	1.25
298	Bill Tuttle	4.00	2.00	1.25
299	*Don Wert*	4.00	2.00	1.25
300	Willie Mays	250.00	125.00	62.50
301	Galen Cisco	4.00	2.00	1.25
302	*John Edwards*	4.00	2.00	1.25
303	Frank Torre	4.00	2.00	1.25
304	Dick Farrell	4.00	2.00	1.25
305	Jerry Lumpe	4.00	2.00	1.25
306	Redbird Rippers (Larry Jackson, Lindy McDaniel)	5.00	2.50	1.50
307	Jim Grant	4.00	2.00	1.25
308	Neil Chrisley	4.00	2.00	1.25
309	Moe Morhardt	4.00	2.00	1.25
310	Whitey Ford	50.00	25.00	12.50
311	Kubek Makes The Double Play (Tony Kubek)	12.00	6.00	3.50
312	Spahn Shows No-Hit Form (Warren Spahn)	15.00	7.50	4.50
313	Maris Blasts 61st (Roger Maris)	75.00	37.50	18.75
314	Colavito's Power (Rocky Colavito)	11.00	5.50	3.25
315	Ford Tosses a Curve (Whitey Ford)	20.00	10.00	6.00
316	Killebrew Sends One into Orbit (Harmon Killebrew)	20.00	10.00	6.00
317	Musial Plays 21st Season (Stan Musial)	17.50	8.75	5.25
318	The Switch Hitter Connects (Mickey Mantle)	150.00	75.00	37.50
319	McCormick Shows His Stuff (Mike McCormick)	6.00	3.00	1.75
320	Hank Aaron	175.00	87.50	43.75
321	Lee Stange	4.00	2.00	1.25
322	Al Dark	4.00	2.00	1.25
323	Don Landrum	4.00	2.00	1.25
324	Joe McClain	4.00	2.00	1.25
325	Luis Aparicio	15.00	7.50	4.50
326	Tom Parsons	4.00	2.00	1.25
327	Ozzie Virgil	4.00	2.00	1.25
328	Ken Walters	4.00	2.00	1.25
329	Bob Bolin	4.00	2.00	1.25
330	Johnny Romano	4.00	2.00	1.25
331	Moe Drabowsky	4.00	2.00	1.25
332	Don Buddin	4.00	2.00	1.25
333	Frank Cipriani	4.00	2.00	1.25
334	Boston Red Sox Team	9.00	4.50	2.75
335	Bill Bruton	4.00	2.00	1.25
336	Billy Muffett	4.00	2.00	1.25
337	Jim Marshall	4.00	2.00	1.25
338	Billy Gardner	4.00	2.00	1.25
339	Jose Valdivielso	4.00	2.00	1.25
340	Don Drysdale	50.00	25.00	12.50
341	Mike Hershberger	4.00	2.00	1.25
342	Ed Rakow	4.00	2.00	1.25
343	Albie Pearson	4.00	2.00	1.25
344	Ed Bauta	4.00	2.00	1.25
345	Chuck Schilling	4.00	2.00	1.25
346	Jack Kralick	4.00	2.00	1.25
347	Chuck Hinton	4.00	2.00	1.25
348	Larry Burright	4.00	2.00	1.25
349	Paul Foytack	4.00	2.00	1.25
350	Frank Robinson	50.00	25.00	12.50
351	Braves' Backstops (Del Crandall, Joe Torre)	12.00	6.00	3.50
352	Frank Sullivan	4.00	2.00	1.25
353	Bill Mazeroski	20.00	10.00	6.00
354	Roman Mejias	4.00	2.00	1.25
355	Steve Barber	4.00	2.00	1.25
356	Tom Haller	4.00	2.00	1.25
357	Jerry Walker	4.00	2.00	1.25
358	Tommy Davis	4.00	2.00	1.25
359	Bobby Locke	4.00	2.00	1.25
360	Yogi Berra	80.00	40.00	20.00
361	Bob Hendley	4.00	2.00	1.25
362	Ty Cline	4.00	2.00	1.25
363	Bob Roselli	4.00	2.00	1.25
364	Ken Hunt	4.00	2.00	1.25
365	Charley Neal	4.00	2.00	1.25
366	Phil Regan	4.00	2.00	1.25
367	5th Checklist (353-429)	8.00	4.00	2.50
368	Bob Tillman	4.00	2.00	1.25
369	Ted Bowsfield	4.00	2.00	1.25
370	Ken Boyer	7.50	3.75	2.25
371	Earl Battey	4.00	2.00	1.25
372	Jack Curtis	4.00	2.00	1.25
373	Al Heist	4.00	2.00	1.25
374	Gene Mauch	4.00	2.00	1.25
375	Ron Fairly	4.00	2.00	1.25
376	Bud Daley	4.00	2.00	1.25
377	Johnny Orsino	4.00	2.00	1.25
378	Bennie Daniels	4.00	2.00	1.25
379	Chuck Essegian	4.00	2.00	1.25
380	Lou Burdette	4.00	2.00	1.25
381	Chico Cardenas	4.00	2.00	1.25
382	Dick Williams	4.00	2.00	1.25
383	Ray Sadecki	4.00	2.00	1.25
384	Kansas City Athletics Team	8.00	4.00	2.50
385	Early Wynn	12.00	6.00	3.50
386	Don Mincher	4.00	2.00	1.25

		NM	EX	VG
387	*Lou Brock*	120.00	60.00	30.00
388	Ryne Duren	4.00	2.00	1.25
389	Smoky Burgess	4.00	2.00	1.25
390	Orlando Cepeda/AS	10.00	5.00	3.00
391	Bill Mazeroski/AS	12.00	6.00	3.50
392	Ken Boyer/AS	7.00	3.50	2.00
393	Roy McMillan/AS	4.00	2.00	1.25
394	Hank Aaron/AS	60.00	30.00	15.00
395	Willie Mays/AS	50.00	25.00	12.50
396	Frank Robinson/AS	13.50	6.75	4.00
397	John Roseboro/AS	4.00	2.00	1.25
398	Don Drysdale/AS	13.50	6.75	4.00
399	Warren Spahn/AS	13.50	6.75	4.00
400	Elston Howard	15.00	7.50	4.50
401	AL & NL Homer Kings (Roger Maris, Orlando Cepeda)	60.00	30.00	15.00
402	Gino Cimoli	4.00	2.00	1.25
403	Chet Nichols	4.00	2.00	1.25
404	Tim Harkness	4.00	2.00	1.25
405	Jim Perry	4.00	2.00	1.25
406	Bob Taylor	4.00	2.00	1.25
407	Hank Aguirre	4.00	2.00	1.25
408	Gus Bell	4.00	2.00	1.25
409	Pittsburgh Pirates Team	11.00	5.50	3.25
410	Al Smith	4.00	2.00	1.25
411	Danny O'Connell	4.00	2.00	1.25
412	Charlie James	4.00	2.00	1.25
413	Matty Alou	4.00	2.00	1.25
414	Joe Gaines	4.00	2.00	1.25
415	Bill Virdon	4.00	2.00	1.25
416	Bob Scheffing	4.00	2.00	1.25
417	Joe Azcue	4.00	2.00	1.25
418	Andy Carey	4.00	2.00	1.25
419	Bob Bruce	4.00	2.00	1.25
420	Gus Triandos	4.00	2.00	1.25
421	Ken MacKenzie	4.00	2.00	1.25
422	Steve Bilko	4.00	2.00	1.25
423	Rival League Relief Aces (Roy Face, Hoyt Wilhelm)	9.00	4.50	2.75
424	Al McBean	4.00	2.00	1.25
425	Carl Yastrzemski	125.00	62.50	31.25
426	Bob Farley	4.00	2.00	1.25
427	Jake Wood	4.00	2.00	1.25
428	Joe Hicks	4.00	2.00	1.25
429	Bill O'Dell	4.00	2.00	1.25
430	Tony Kubek	15.00	7.50	4.50
431	*Bob Rodgers*	4.00	2.00	1.25
432	Jim Pendleton	4.00	2.00	1.25
433	Jim Archer	4.00	2.00	1.25
434	Clay Dalrymple	4.00	2.00	1.25
435	Larry Sherry	4.00	2.00	1.25
436	Felix Mantilla	4.00	2.00	1.25
437	Ray Moore	4.00	2.00	1.25
438	Dick Brown	4.00	2.00	1.25
439	Jerry Buchek	4.00	2.00	1.25
440	Joe Jay	4.00	2.00	1.25
441a	6th Series Checklist (430-506) (Large "CHECKLIST.")	9.00	4.50	2.75
441b	6th Series Checklist (430-506) (Small "CHECKLIST.")	9.00	4.50	2.75
442	Wes Stock	4.00	2.00	1.25
443	Del Crandall	4.00	2.00	1.25
444	Ted Wills	4.00	2.00	1.25
445	Vic Power	4.00	2.00	1.25
446	Don Elston	4.00	2.00	1.25
447	Willie Kirkland	7.00	3.50	2.00
448	Joe Gibbon	7.00	3.50	2.00
449	Jerry Adair	7.00	3.50	2.00
450	Jim O'Toole	7.00	3.50	2.00
451	*Jose Tartabull*	7.00	3.50	2.00
452	Earl Averill	7.00	3.50	2.00
453	Cal McLish	7.00	3.50	2.00
454	Floyd Robinson	7.00	3.50	2.00
455	Luis Arroyo	7.00	3.50	2.00
456	Joe Amalfitano	7.00	3.50	2.00
457	Lou Clinton	7.00	3.50	2.00
458a	Bob Buhl ("M" on cap)	17.50	8.75	5.25
458b	Bob Buhl (Plain cap.)	15.00	7.50	4.50
459	Ed Bailey	7.00	3.50	2.00
460	Jim Bunning	20.00	10.00	6.00
461	*Ken Hubbs*	15.00	7.50	4.50
462a	Willie Tasby ("W" on cap)	17.50	8.75	5.25
462b	Willie Tasby (Plain cap.)	16.00	8.00	4.75
463	Hank Bauer	9.00	4.50	2.75
464	*Al Jackson*	7.00	3.50	2.00
465	Cincinnati Reds Team	11.00	5.50	3.25
466	Norm Cash/AS	13.50	6.75	4.00
467	Chuck Schilling/AS	7.00	3.50	2.00
468	Brooks Robinson/AS	15.00	7.50	4.50
469	Luis Aparicio/AS	11.00	5.50	3.25
470	Al Kaline/AS	20.00	10.00	6.00
471	Mickey Mantle/AS	225.00	112.50	56.25
472	Rocky Colavito/AS	12.00	6.00	3.50
473	Elston Howard/AS	10.00	5.00	3.00
474	Frank Lary/AS	7.00	3.50	2.00
475	Whitey Ford/AS	15.00	7.50	4.50
476	Baltimore Orioles Team	12.50	6.25	3.75
477	Andre Rodgers	7.00	3.50	2.00
478	Don Zimmer	12.50	6.25	3.75
479	*Joel Horlen*	7.00	3.50	2.00
480	Harvey Kuenn	7.00	3.50	2.00
481	Vic Wertz	7.00	3.50	2.00
482	Sam Mele	7.00	3.50	2.00
483	Don McMahon	7.00	3.50	2.00
484	Dick Schofield	7.00	3.50	2.00
485	Pedro Ramos	7.00	3.50	2.00
486	Jim Gilliam	12.00	6.00	3.50
487	Jerry Lynch	7.00	3.50	2.00
488	Hal Brown	7.00	3.50	2.00
489	Julio Gotay	7.00	3.50	2.00
490	Clete Boyer	13.50	6.75	4.00
491	Leon Wagner	7.00	3.50	2.00
492	Hal Smith	7.00	3.50	2.00
493	Danny McDevitt	7.00	3.50	2.00
494	Sammy White	7.00	3.50	2.00
495	Don Cardwell	7.00	3.50	2.00
496	Wayne Causey	7.00	3.50	2.00
497	Ed Bouchee	7.00	3.50	2.00
498	Jim Donohue	7.00	3.50	2.00
499	Zoilo Versalles	7.00	3.50	2.00
500	Duke Snider	60.00	30.00	15.00
501	Claude Osteen	7.00	3.50	2.00
502	Hector Lopez	7.00	3.50	2.00
503	Danny Murtaugh	7.00	3.50	2.00
504	Eddie Bressoud	7.00	3.50	2.00
505	Juan Marichal	40.00	20.00	10.00
506	Charley Maxwell	7.00	3.50	2.00
507	Ernie Broglio	7.00	3.50	2.00
508	Gordy Coleman	7.00	3.50	2.00
509	*Dave Giusti*	7.00	3.50	2.00
510	Jim Lemon	7.00	3.50	2.00
511	Bubba Phillips	7.00	3.50	2.00
512	Mike Fornieles	7.00	3.50	2.00
513	Whitey Herzog	12.50	6.25	3.75
514	Sherm Lollar	7.00	3.50	2.00
515	Stan Williams	7.00	3.50	2.00
516a	7th Series Checklist (507-598) (Boxes are yellow.)	9.00	4.50	2.75
516b	7th Series Checklist (507-598) (Boxes are white.)	9.00	4.50	2.75
517	Dave Wickersham	7.00	3.50	2.00
518	Lee Maye	7.00	3.50	2.00
519	Bob Johnson	7.00	3.50	2.00
520	Bob Friend	7.00	3.50	2.00
521	Jacke Davis	7.00	3.50	2.00
522	Lindy McDaniel	7.00	3.50	2.00
523	Russ Nixon/SP	15.00	7.50	4.50
524	Howie Nunn/SP	15.00	7.50	4.50
525	George Thomas	10.00	5.00	3.00
526	Hal Woodeshick/SP	15.00	7.50	4.50
527	*Dick McAuliffe*	10.00	5.00	3.00
528	Turk Lown	10.00	5.00	3.00
529	John Schaive/SP	15.00	7.50	4.50
530	Bob Gibson/SP	125.00	112.50	56.25
531	Bobby G. Smith	10.00	5.00	3.00
532	Dick Stigman	10.00	5.00	3.00
533	Charley Lau/SP	15.00	7.50	4.50
534	Tony Gonzalez/SP	15.00	7.50	4.50
535	Ed Roebuck	10.00	5.00	3.00
536	Dick Gernert	10.00	5.00	3.00
537	Cleveland Indians Team	20.00	10.00	6.00
538	Jack Sanford	10.00	5.00	3.00
539	Billy Moran	10.00	5.00	3.00
540	Jim Landis/SP	15.00	7.50	4.50
541	Don Nottebart/SP	15.00	7.50	4.50
542	Dave Philley	10.00	5.00	3.00
543	Bob Allen/SP	15.00	7.50	4.50
544	Willie McCovey/SP	120.00	60.00	30.00
545	Hoyt Wilhelm/SP	50.00	25.00	12.50
546	Moe Thacker/SP	15.00	7.50	4.50
547	Don Ferrarese	10.00	5.00	3.00
548	Bobby Del Greco	10.00	5.00	3.00
549	Bill Rigney/SP	15.00	7.50	4.50
550	Art Mahaffey/SP	15.00	7.50	4.50
551	Harry Bright	10.00	5.00	3.00
552	Chicago Cubs Team/SP	50.00	25.00	12.50
553	Jim Coates	10.00	5.00	3.00
554	Bubba Morton/SP	15.00	7.50	4.50
555	John Buzhardt/SP	15.00	7.50	4.50
556	Al Spangler	10.00	5.00	3.00
557	Bob Anderson/SP	15.00	7.50	4.50
558	John Goryl	10.00	5.00	3.00
559	Mike Higgins	10.00	5.00	3.00
560	Chuck Estrada/SP	15.00	7.50	4.50
561	Gene Oliver/SP	15.00	7.50	4.50
562	Bill Henry	10.00	5.00	3.00
563	Ken Aspromonte	10.00	5.00	3.00
564	Bob Grim	10.00	5.00	3.00
565	Jose Pagan	10.00	5.00	3.00
566	Marty Kutyna/SP	15.00	7.50	4.50
567	Tracy Stallard/SP	15.00	7.50	4.50
568	Jim Golden	10.00	5.00	3.00
569	Ed Sadowski/SP	15.00	7.50	4.50
570	Bill Stafford	10.00	5.00	3.00
571	Billy Klaus/SP	15.00	7.50	4.50
572	Bob Miller/SP	15.00	7.50	4.50
573	Johnny Logan	10.00	5.00	3.00
574	Dean Stone	10.00	5.00	3.00
575	Red Schoendienst	25.00	12.50	7.50
576	Russ Kemmerer/SP	15.00	7.50	4.50
577	Dave Nicholson/SP	15.00	7.50	4.50
578	Jim Duffalo	10.00	5.00	3.00
579	Jim Schaffer/SP	15.00	7.50	4.50
580	Bill Monbouquette	10.00	5.00	3.00
581	Mel Roach	10.00	5.00	3.00
582	Ron Piche	10.00	5.00	3.00
583	Larry Osborne	10.00	5.00	3.00
584	Minnesota Twins Team/SP	50.00	25.00	12.50
585	Glen Hobbie/SP	15.00	7.50	4.50
586	Sammy Esposito/SP	15.00	7.50	4.50
587	Frank Funk/SP	15.00	7.50	4.50
588	Birdie Tebbetts	10.00	5.00	3.00
589	Bob Turley	17.50	8.75	5.25
590	Curt Flood	17.50	8.75	5.25
591	Rookie Parade Pitchers (*Sam McDowell, Ron Nischwitz, Art Quirk, Dick Radatz, Ron Taylor*)	75.00	37.50	18.75
592	Rookie Parade Pitchers (Bo Belinsky, Joe Bonikowski, Jim Bouton, Dan Pfister, Dave Stenhouse)	75.00	37.50	18.75
593	Rookie Parade Pitchers (*Craig Anderson, Jack Hamilton, Jack Lamabe, Bob Moorhead, Bob Veale*)	40.00	20.00	12.00
594	Rookie Parade Catchers (*Doug Camilli, Doc Edwards, Don Pavletich, Ken Retzer, Bob Uecker*)	75.00	37.50	18.75
595	Rookie Parade Infielders (Ed Charles, Marlin Coughtry, Bob Sadowski, Felix Torres)	25.00	12.50	7.50
596	Rookie Parade Infielders (*Bernie Allen, Phil Linz, Joe Pepitone, Rich Rollins*)	80.00	40.00	20.00
597	Rookie Parade Infielders (Rod Kanehl, Jim McKnight, Denis Menke, Amado Samuel)	40.00	20.00	12.00
598	Rookie Parade Outfielders (*Howie Goss, Jim Hickman, Manny Jimenez, Al Luplow, Ed Olivares*)	80.00	40.00	20.00

1962 Topps Baseball Bucks

Issued in their own one-cent package, "Baseball Bucks" measure 4-1/8" x 1-3/4", were printed in black on green paper and designed to resemble dollar bills. The center player portrait has a banner underneath with the player's name. His home park is shown on the right and there is some biographical information at left. The back features a large denomination, with the player's league and team logo on either side. Poorly centered examples of this issue are the rule, rather than the exception. Sixty-two of the players appear on facsimile $1 notes. There are 24 $5 stars and 10 $10 superstars. Baseball Bucks are graded without regard to the vertical fold with which they were issued.

		NM	EX	VG
	Complete Set (96):	2,000	1,000	600.00
	Common Player:	7.50	3.75	2.25
	Wax Pack:	175.00		
(1)	Hank Aaron ($5)	50.00	25.00	15.00
(2)	Joe Adcock	7.50	3.75	2.25
(3)	George Altman	7.50	3.75	2.25
(4)	Jim Archer	7.50	3.75	2.25
(5)	Richie Ashburn ($5)	40.00	20.00	12.00
(6)	Ernie Banks ($10)	45.00	22.00	13.50
(7)	Earl Battey	7.50	3.75	2.25
(8)	Gus Bell	7.50	3.75	2.25
(9)	Yogi Berra ($5)	40.00	20.00	12.00
(10)	Ken Boyer ($10)	15.00	7.50	4.50
(11)	Jackie Brandt	7.50	3.75	2.25
(12)	Jim Bunning	15.00	7.50	4.50
(13)	Lou Burdette ($5)	7.50	3.75	2.25
(14)	Don Cardwell	7.50	3.75	2.25
(15)	Norm Cash ($5)	15.00	7.50	4.50
(16)	Orlando Cepeda ($5)	30.00	15.00	9.00
(17)	Roberto Clemente ($5)	200.00	100.00	60.00
(18)	Rocky Colavito ($5)	25.00	12.50	7.50
(19)	Chuck Cottier	7.50	3.75	2.25
(20)	Roger Craig	7.50	3.75	2.25
(21)	Bennie Daniels	7.50	3.75	2.25
(22)	Don Demeter	7.50	3.75	2.25
(23)	Don Drysdale	30.00	15.00	9.00
(24)	Chuck Estrada	7.50	3.75	2.25
(25)	Dick Farrell	7.50	3.75	2.25
(26)	Whitey Ford ($10)	40.00	20.00	12.00
(27)	Nellie Fox ($5)	30.00	15.00	9.00
(28)	Tito Francona	7.50	3.75	2.25
(29)	Bob Friend	7.50	3.75	2.25
(30)	Jim Gentile	7.50	3.75	2.25
(31)	Dick Gernert	7.50	3.75	2.25
(32)	Lenny Green	7.50	3.75	2.25
(33)	Dick Groat	7.50	3.75	2.25
(34)	Woody Held	7.50	3.75	2.25
(35)	Don Hoak	7.50	3.75	2.25
(36)	Gil Hodges ($5)	25.00	12.50	7.50
(37)	Frank Howard	10.00	5.00	3.00
(38)	Elston Howard	10.00	5.00	3.00
(39)	Dick Howser	7.50	3.75	2.25
(40)	Ken Hunt	7.50	3.75	2.25
(41)	Larry Jackson	7.50	3.75	2.25
(42)	Joe Jay	7.50	3.75	2.25
(43)	Al Kaline	30.00	15.00	9.00
(44)	Harmon Killebrew ($5)	40.00	20.00	12.00
(45)	Sandy Koufax ($5)	75.00	37.00	22.00
(46)	Harvey Kuenn	7.50	3.75	2.25
(47)	Jim Landis	7.50	3.75	2.25
(48)	Norm Larker	7.50	3.75	2.25
(49)	Frank Lary ($5)	7.50	3.75	2.25
(50)	Jerry Lumpe	7.50	3.75	2.25
(51)	Art Mahaffey	7.50	3.75	2.25
(52)	Frank Malzone	7.50	3.75	2.25
(53)	Felix Mantilla	7.50	3.75	2.25
(54)	Mickey Mantle ($10)	350.00	175.00	105.00
(55)	Roger Maris ($10)	45.00	22.00	13.50
(56)	Ed Mathews ($10)	35.00	17.50	10.50
(57)	Willie Mays ($10)	65.00	32.00	19.50
(58)	Ken McBride	7.50	3.75	2.25
(59)	Mike McCormick	7.50	3.75	2.25
(60)	Stu Miller	7.50	3.75	2.25
(61)	Minnie Minoso	10.00	5.00	3.00
(62)	Wally Moon ($5)	7.50	3.75	2.25
(63)	Stan Musial ($5)	60.00	30.00	18.00
(64)	Danny O'Connell	7.50	3.75	2.25
(65)	Jim O'Toole	7.50	3.75	2.25

		NM	EX	VG
(66)	Camilo Pascual ($5)	7.50	3.75	2.25
(67)	Jim Perry	7.50	3.75	2.25
(68)	Jimmy Piersall ($5)	12.00	6.00	3.50
(69)	Vada Pinson ($5)	12.00	6.00	3.50
(70)	Juan Pizarro	7.50	3.75	2.25
(71)	Johnny Podres	10.00	5.00	3.00
(72)	Vic Power ($5)	7.50	3.75	2.25
(73)	Bob Purkey	7.50	3.75	2.25
(74)	Pedro Ramos	7.50	3.75	2.25
(75)	Brooks Robinson ($5)	30.00	15.00	9.00
(76)	Floyd Robinson	7.50	3.75	2.25
(77)	Frank Robinson ($10)	35.00	17.50	10.50
(78)	Johnny Romano	7.50	3.75	2.25
(79)	Pete Runnels ($5)	7.50	3.75	2.25
(80)	Don Schwall	7.50	3.75	2.25
(81)	Bobby Shantz ($5)	7.50	3.75	2.25
(82)	Norm Siebern	7.50	3.75	2.25
(83)	Roy Sievers ($5)	7.50	3.75	2.25
(84)	Hal (W.) Smith	7.50	3.75	2.25
(85)	Warren Spahn ($10)	40.00	20.00	12.00
(86)	Dick Stuart	7.50	3.75	2.25
(87)	Tony Taylor	7.50	3.75	2.25
(88)	Lee Thomas	7.50	3.75	2.25
(89)	Gus Triandos	7.50	3.75	2.25
(90)	Leon Wagner	7.50	3.75	2.25
(91)	Jerry Walker	7.50	3.75	2.25
(92)	Bill White	7.50	3.75	2.25
(93)	Billy Williams	15.00	7.50	4.50
(94)	Gene Woodling	7.50	3.75	2.25
(95)	Early Wynn ($5)	15.00	7.50	4.50
(96)	Carl Yastrzemski	40.00	20.00	12.00

1962 Topps Stamps

CARL YASTRZEMSKI
BOST. RED SOX OUTFIELD

An artistic improvement over the somewhat drab Topps stamps of the previous year, the 1962 stamps, 1-3/8" x 1-7/8", had color player photographs set on red or yellow backgrounds. As in 1961, they were issued in two-stamp panels as insert with Topps baseball cards. A change from 1961 was the inclusion of team emblems in the set. A complete set consists of 201 stamps; Roy Sievers was originally portrayed on the wrong team - Athletics - and was later corrected to the Phillies.

		NM	EX	VG
Complete Set (200):		800.00	400.00	240.00
Common Player:		3.00	1.50	.90
Stamp Album (Red):		60.00	30.00	18.00
(1)	Hank Aaron	15.00	7.50	4.50
(2)	Jerry Adair	3.00	1.50	.90
(3)	Joe Adcock	3.00	1.50	.90
(4)	Bob Allison	3.00	1.50	.90
(5)	Felipe Alou	4.00	2.00	1.25
(6)	George Altman	3.00	1.50	.90
(7)	Joe Amalfitano	3.00	1.50	.90
(8)	Ruben Amaro	3.00	1.50	.90
(9)	Luis Aparicio	6.00	3.00	1.75
(10)	Jim Archer	3.00	1.50	.90
(11)	Bob Aspromonte	3.00	1.50	.90
(12)	Ed Bailey	3.00	1.50	.90
(13)	Jack Baldschun	3.00	1.50	.90
(14)	Ernie Banks	9.00	4.50	2.75
(15)	Earl Battey	3.00	1.50	.90
(16)	Gus Bell	3.00	1.50	.90
(17)	Yogi Berra	12.00	6.00	3.50
(18)	Dick Bertell	3.00	1.50	.90
(19)	Steve Bilko	3.00	1.50	.90
(20)	Frank Bolling	3.00	1.50	.90
(21)	Steve Boros	3.00	1.50	.90
(22)	Ted Bowsfield	3.00	1.50	.90
(23)	Clete Boyer	3.00	1.50	.90
(24)	Ken Boyer	4.00	2.00	1.25
(25)	Jackie Brandt	3.00	1.50	.90
(26)	Bill Bruton	3.00	1.50	.90
(27)	Jim Bunning	6.00	3.00	1.75
(28)	Lou Burdette	3.00	1.50	.90
(29)	Smoky Burgess	3.00	1.50	.90
(30)	Johnny Callizon (Callison)	3.00	1.50	.90
(31)	Don Cardwell	3.00	1.50	.90
(32)	Camilo Carreon	3.00	1.50	.90
(33)	Norm Cash	4.00	2.00	1.25
(34)	Orlando Cepeda	6.00	3.00	1.75
(35)	Roberto Clemente	20.00	10.00	6.00
(36)	Ty Cline	3.00	1.50	.90
(37)	Rocky Colavito	6.00	3.00	1.75
(38)	Gordon Coleman	3.00	1.50	.90
(39)	Chuck Cottier	3.00	1.50	.90
(40)	Roger Craig	3.00	1.50	.90
(41)	Del Crandall	3.00	1.50	.90
(42)	Pete Daley	3.00	1.50	.90
(43)	Clay Dalrymple	3.00	1.50	.90
(44)	Bennie Daniels	3.00	1.50	.90
(45)	Jim Davenport	3.00	1.50	.90
(46)	Don Demeter	3.00	1.50	.90
(47)	Dick Donovan	3.00	1.50	.90
(48)	Don Drysdale	10.00	5.00	3.00
(49)	John Edwards	3.00	1.50	.90
(50)	Dick Ellsworth	3.00	1.50	.90

		NM	EX	VG
(51)	Chuck Estrada	3.00	1.50	.90
(52)	Roy Face	3.00	1.50	.90
(53)	Ron Fairly	3.00	1.50	.90
(54)	Dick Farrell	3.00	1.50	.90
(55)	Whitey Ford	12.00	6.00	3.50
(56)	Mike Fornieles	3.00	1.50	.90
(57)	Nellie Fox	7.00	3.50	2.00
(58)	Tito Francona	3.00	1.50	.90
(59)	Gene Freese	3.00	1.50	.90
(60)	Bob Friend	3.00	1.50	.90
(61)	Gary Geiger	3.00	1.50	.90
(62)	Jim Gentile	3.00	1.50	.90
(63)	Tony Gonzalez	3.00	1.50	.90
(64)	Lenny Green	3.00	1.50	.90
(65)	Dick Groat	3.00	1.50	.90
(66)	Ron Hansen	3.00	1.50	.90
(67)	Al Heist	3.00	1.50	.90
(68)	Woody Held	3.00	1.50	.90
(69)	Ray Herbert	3.00	1.50	.90
(70)	Chuck Hinton	3.00	1.50	.90
(71)	Don Hoak	3.00	1.50	.90
(72)	Glen Hobbie	3.00	1.50	.90
(73)	Gil Hodges	6.00	3.00	1.75
(74)	Jay Hook	3.00	1.50	.90
(75)	Elston Howard	4.00	2.00	1.25
(76)	Frank Howard	3.00	1.50	.90
(77)	Dick Howser	3.00	1.50	.90
(78)	Ken Hunt	3.00	1.50	.90
(79)	Larry Jackson	3.00	1.50	.90
(80)	Julian Javier	3.00	1.50	.90
(81)	Joe Jay	3.00	1.50	.90
(82)	Bob Johnson	3.00	1.50	.90
(83)	Sam Jones	3.00	1.50	.90
(84)	Al Kaline	9.00	4.50	2.75
(85)	Eddie Kasko	3.00	1.50	.90
(86)	Harmon Killebrew	10.00	5.00	3.00
(87)	Sandy Koufax	15.00	7.50	4.50
(88)	Jack Kralick	3.00	1.50	.90
(89)	Tony Kubek	4.00	2.00	1.25
(90)	Harvey Kuenn	3.00	1.50	.90
(91)	Jim Landis	3.00	1.50	.90
(92)	Hobie Landrith	3.00	1.50	.90
(93)	Frank Lary	3.00	1.50	.90
(94)	Barry Latman	3.00	1.50	.90
(95)	Jerry Lumpe	3.00	1.50	.90
(96)	Art Mahaffey	3.00	1.50	.90
(97)	Frank Malzone	3.00	1.50	.90
(98)	Felix Mantilla	3.00	1.50	.90
(99)	Mickey Mantle	50.00	25.00	15.00
(100)	Juan Marichal	6.00	3.00	1.75
(101)	Roger Maris	13.50	6.75	4.00
(102)	J.C. Martin	3.00	1.50	.90
(103)	Ed Mathews	9.00	4.50	2.75
(104)	Willie Mays	15.00	7.50	4.50
(105)	Bill Mazeroski	6.00	3.00	1.75
(106)	Ken McBride	3.00	1.50	.90
(107)	Tim McCarver	3.00	1.50	.90
(108)	Joe McClain	3.00	1.50	.90
(109)	Mike McCormick	3.00	1.50	.90
(110)	Lindy McDaniel	3.00	1.50	.90
(111)	Roy McMillan	3.00	1.50	.90
(112)	Bob L. Miller	3.00	1.50	.90
(113)	Stu Miller	3.00	1.50	.90
(114)	Minnie Minoso	6.00	3.00	1.75
(115)	Bill Monbouquette	3.00	1.50	.90
(116)	Wally Moon	3.00	1.50	.90
(117)	Don Mossi	3.00	1.50	.90
(118)	Stan Musial	15.00	7.50	4.50
(119)	Russ Nixon	3.00	1.50	.90
(120)	Danny O'Connell	3.00	1.50	.90
(121)	Jim O'Toole	3.00	1.50	.90
(122)	Milt Pappas	3.00	1.50	.90
(123)	Camilo Pascual	3.00	1.50	.90
(124)	Albie Pearson	3.00	1.50	.90
(125)	Jim Perry	3.00	1.50	.90
(126)	Bubba Phillips	3.00	1.50	.90
(127)	Jimmy Piersall	3.00	1.50	.90
(128)	Vada Pinson	3.00	1.50	.90
(129)	Juan Pizarro	3.00	1.50	.90
(130)	Johnny Podres	3.00	1.50	.90
(131)	Leo Posada	3.00	1.50	.90
(132)	Vic Power	3.00	1.50	.90
(133)	Bob Purkey	3.00	1.50	.90
(134)	Pedro Ramos	3.00	1.50	.90
(135)	Bobby Richardson	3.00	1.50	.90
(136)	Brooks Robinson	10.00	5.00	3.00
(137)	Floyd Robinson	3.00	1.50	.90
(138)	Frank Robinson	10.00	5.00	3.00
(139)	Bob Rodgers	3.00	1.50	.90
(140)	Johnny Romano	3.00	1.50	.90
(141)	John Roseboro	3.00	1.50	.90
(142)	Pete Runnels	3.00	1.50	.90
(143)	Ray Sadecki	3.00	1.50	.90
(144)	Ron Santo	3.00	1.50	.90
(145)	Chuck Schilling	3.00	1.50	.90
(146)	Barney Schultz	3.00	1.50	.90
(147)	Don Schwall	3.00	1.50	.90
(148)	Bobby Shantz	3.00	1.50	.90
(149)	Bob Shaw	3.00	1.50	.90
(150)	Norm Siebern	3.00	1.50	.90
(151a)	Roy Sievers (Kansas City)	3.00	1.50	.90
(151b)	Roy Sievers (Philadelphia)	3.00	1.50	.90
(152)	Bill Skowron	4.00	2.00	1.25
(153)	Hal (W.) Smith	3.00	1.50	.90
(154)	Duke Snider	12.00	6.00	3.50
(155)	Warren Spahn	9.00	4.50	2.75
(156)	Al Spangler	3.00	1.50	.90
(157)	Daryl Spencer	3.00	1.50	.90
(158)	Gene Stephens	3.00	1.50	.90
(159)	Dick Stuart	3.00	1.50	.90
(160)	Haywood Sullivan	3.00	1.50	.90
(161)	Tony Taylor	3.00	1.50	.90
(162)	George Thomas	3.00	1.50	.90
(163)	Lee Thomas	3.00	1.50	.90
(164)	Bob Tiefenauer	3.00	1.50	.90
(165)	Joe Torre	6.00	3.00	1.75
(166)	Gus Triandos	3.00	1.50	.90
(167)	Bill Tuttle	3.00	1.50	.90

		NM	EX	VG
(168)	Zoilo Versalles	3.00	1.50	.90
(169)	Bill Virdon	3.00	1.50	.90
(170)	Leon Wagner	3.00	1.50	.90
(171)	Jerry Walker	3.00	1.50	.90
(172)	Lee Walls	3.00	1.50	.90
(173)	Bill White	3.00	1.50	.90
(174)	Hoyt Wilhelm	4.00	2.00	1.25
(175)	Billy Williams	6.00	3.00	1.75
(176)	Jake Wood	3.00	1.50	.90
(177)	Gene Woodling	3.00	1.50	.90
(178)	Early Wynn	4.00	2.00	1.25
(179)	Carl Yastrzemski	12.00	6.00	3.50
(180)	Don Zimmer	3.00	1.50	.90
(181)	Baltimore Orioles Logo	3.00	1.50	.90
(182)	Boston Red Sox Logo	3.00	1.50	.90
(183)	Chicago Cubs Logo	3.00	1.50	.90
(184)	Chicago White Sox Logo	3.00	1.50	.90
(185)	Cincinnati Reds Logo	3.00	1.50	.90
(186)	Cleveland Indians Logo	3.00	1.50	.90
(187)	Detroit Tigers Logo	3.00	1.50	.90
(188)	Houston Colts Logo	3.00	1.50	.90
(189)	Kansas City Athletics Logo	3.00	1.50	.90
(190)	Los Angeles Angels Logo	3.00	1.50	.90
(191)	Los Angeles Dodgers Logo	3.00	1.50	.90
(192)	Milwaukee Braves Logo	3.00	1.50	.90
(193)	Minnesota Twins Logo	3.00	1.50	.90
(194)	New York Mets Logo	3.00	1.50	.90
(195)	New York Yankees Logo	6.00	3.00	1.75
(196)	Philadelphia Phillies Logo	3.00	1.50	.90
(197)	Pittsburgh Pirates Logo	3.00	1.50	.90
(198)	St. Louis Cardinals Logo	3.00	1.50	.90
(199)	San Francisco Giants Logo	3.00	1.50	.90
(200)	Washington Senators Logo	3.00	1.50	.90

1962 Topps Stamps Panels

ELSTON HOWARD N.Y. YANKEES CATCHER **BOB CLEMENTE** PITT. PIRATES OUTFIELD

Some advanced collectors pursue the 1962 Topps stamps in the form of the two-stamp panels in which they were issued. The 200 different stamps which make up the issue can be found on 245 different two-stamp panels, flanked at left by a smaller tab advertising the accompanying album. The unnumbered stamps are listed here alphabetically according to the name of the player or team which apears on the left end of the panel. Values shown are for full three-piece panels.

		NM	EX	VG
Complete Panel Set (245):		2,750	1,375	825.00
Common Panel:		8.00	4.00	2.50
(1)	Hank Aaron/Ted Bowsfield	35.00	17.50	10.50
(2)	Jerry Adair/Tony Gonzalez	8.00	4.00	2.50
(3)	Joe Adcock/George Thomas	8.00	4.00	2.50
(4)	Bob Allison/Jim Davenport	8.00	4.00	2.50
(5)	Felipe Alou/Mickey Mantle	100.00	50.00	30.00
(6)	Felipe Alou/Chuck Schilling	9.00	4.50	2.50
(7)	George Altman/ Rocky Colavito	10.00	5.00	3.00
(8)	George Altman/Don Schwall	8.00	4.00	2.50
(9)	Joe Amalfitano/Jim Gentile	8.00	4.00	2.50
(10)	Joe Amalfitano/Vic Power	8.00	4.00	2.50
(11)	Ruben Amaro/ Carl Yastrzemski	30.00	15.00	9.00
(12)	Luis Aparicio/Dick Farrell	10.00	5.00	3.00
(13)	Luis Aparicio/Al Heist	10.00	5.00	3.00
(14)	Bob Aspromonte/Al Kaline	15.00	7.50	4.50
(15)	Ed Bailey/Jim Piersall	8.00	4.00	2.50
(16)	Ernie Banks/Milt Pappas	20.00	10.00	6.00
(17)	Earl Battey/Bob Clemente	35.00	17.50	10.50
(18)	Earl Battey/Ed Mathews	12.00	6.00	3.50
(19)	Gus Bell/Steve Boros	8.00	4.00	2.50
(20)	Gus Bell/Ty Cline	8.00	4.00	2.50
(21)	Yogi Berra/Roy Face	20.00	10.00	6.00
(22)	Yogi Berra/Jack Kralick	15.00	7.50	4.50
(23)	Dick Bertell/Hoyt Wilhelm	10.00	5.00	3.00
(24)	Dick Bertell/Don Zimmer	9.00	4.50	2.75
(25)	Steve Bilko/Ruben Amaro	8.00	4.00	2.50
(26)	Steve Bilko/Roy Sievers	8.00	4.00	2.50
(27)	Frank Bolling/Nellie Fox	10.00	5.00	3.00
(28)	Steve Boros/Art Mahaffey	8.00	4.00	2.50
(29)	Clete Boyer/Chuck Cottier	9.00	4.50	2.75
(30)	Ken Boyer/Bob Friend	9.00	4.50	2.75
(31)	Jackie Brandt/Frank Robinson	15.00	7.50	4.50
(32)	Bill Bruton/Ernie Banks	20.00	10.00	6.00
(33)	Bill Bruton/Jay Hook	8.00	4.00	2.50
(34)	Jim Bunning/Bob Miller	10.00	5.00	3.00
(35)	Jim Bunning/Jim O'Toole	10.00	5.00	3.00
(36)	Jim Bunning/Daryl Spencer	10.00	5.00	3.00
(37)	Lou Burdette/Ed Mathews	12.00	6.00	3.50
(38)	Lou Burdette/Willie Mays	35.00	17.50	10.50
(39)	Smoky Burgess/ Bobby Richardson	9.00	4.50	2.75
(40)	Johnny Callizon (Callison)/ Barry Latman	9.00	4.50	2.75
(41)	Johnny Callizon (Callison)/Frank Malzone	9.00	4.50	2.75
(42)	Johnny Callizon (Callison)/ Willie Mays	35.00	17.50	10.50
(43)	Don Cardwell/Hoyt Wilhelm	10.00	5.00	3.00
(44)	Norm Cash/Dick Bertell	9.00	4.50	2.75
(45)	Norm Cash/Don Cardwell	9.00	4.50	2.75
(46)	Norm Cash/Dick Howser	9.00	4.50	2.75
(47)	Ty Cline/Art Mahaffey	8.00	4.00	2.50
(48)	Rocky Colavito/Sam Jones	10.00	5.00	3.00

		NM	EX	VG
(49)	Gordon Coleman/Pete Daley	8.00	4.00	2.50
(50)	Gordon Coleman/Danny O'Connell	8.00	4.00	2.50
(51)	Roger Craig/Ted Bowsfield	8.00	4.00	2.50
(52)	Roger Craig/Minnie Minoso	9.00	4.50	2.75
(53)	Del Crandall/Clete Boyer	9.00	4.50	2.75
(54)	Del Crandall/Ray Sadecki	8.00	4.00	2.50
(55)	Pete Daley/Bob Friend	8.00	4.00	2.50
(56)	Pete Daley/Mike McCormick	8.00	4.00	2.50
(57)	Clay Dalrymple/Woody Held	8.00	4.00	2.50
(58)	Clay Dalrymple/Pedro Ramos	8.00	4.00	2.50
(59)	Bennie Daniels/Jerry Walker	8.00	4.00	2.50
(60)	Jim Davenport/Harmon Killebrew	15.00	7.50	4.50
(61)	Don Demeter/Haywood Sullivan	8.00	4.00	2.50
(62)	Don Demeter/Gus Triandos	8.00	4.00	2.50
(63)	Don Demeter/Lee Walls	8.00	4.00	2.50
(64)	Dick Donovan/Jerry Adair	8.00	4.00	2.50
(65)	Dick Donovan/Jim Perry	8.00	4.00	2.50
(66)	Dick Donovan/Vada Pinson	9.00	4.50	2.75
(67)	John Edwards/Jerry Walker	8.00	4.00	2.50
(68)	Dick Ellsworth/Glen Hobbie	8.00	4.00	2.50
(69)	Dick Ellsworth/Pete Runnels	8.00	4.00	2.50
(70)	Chuck Estrada/Don Drysdale	12.00	6.00	3.50
(71)	Chuck Estrada/Al Kaline	15.00	7.50	4.50
(72)	Roy Face/Minnie Minoso	9.00	4.50	2.75
(73)	Ron Fairly/Jim Landis	8.00	4.00	2.50
(74)	Dick Farrell/Frank Lary	8.00	4.00	2.50
(75)	Whitey Ford/Joe Torre	15.00	7.50	4.50
(76)	Nellie Fox/Willie Mays	35.00	17.50	10.50
(77)	Tito Francona/Ken Boyer	9.00	4.50	2.75
(78)	Tito Francona/Bob Johnson	8.00	4.00	2.50
(79)	Gene Freese/Bob Allison	8.00	4.00	2.50
(80)	Gene Freese/Ernie Banks	15.00	7.50	4.50
(81)	Gary Geiger/Bobby Richardson	9.00	4.50	2.75
(82)	Jim Gentile/Hal W. Smith	8.00	4.00	2.50
(83)	Dick Groat/Joe McClain	8.00	4.00	2.50
(84)	Al Heist/Frank Lary	8.00	4.00	2.50
(85)	Woody Held/Orlando Cepeda	10.00	5.00	3.00
(86)	Ray Herbert/Frank Bolling	8.00	4.00	2.50
(87)	Ray Herbert/Eddie Kasko	8.00	4.00	2.50
(88)	Chuck Hinton/Dick Groat	8.00	4.00	2.50
(89)	Chuck Hinton/Stu Miller	8.00	4.00	2.50
(90)	Don Hoak/Bob Allison	8.00	4.00	2.50
(91)	Gil Hodges/Bennie Daniels	10.00	5.00	3.00
(92)	Gil Hodges/John Edwards	10.00	5.00	3.00
(93)	Elston Howard/Bob Clemente	35.00	17.50	10.50
(94)	Dick Howser/Don Zimmer	9.00	4.50	2.75
(95)	Ken Hunt/Lenny Green	8.00	4.00	2.50
(96)	Larry Jackson/Smoky Burgess	8.00	4.00	2.50
(97)	Larry Jackson/Gary Geiger	8.00	4.00	2.50
(98)	Joe Jay/Johnny Romano	8.00	4.00	2.50
(99)	Bob Johnson/Bob Friend	8.00	4.00	2.50
(100)	Al Kaline/Don Hoak	15.00	7.50	4.50
(101)	Eddie Kasko/Nellie Fox	10.00	5.00	3.00
(102)	Sandy Koufax/Joe Adcock	30.00	15.00	9.00
(103)	Sandy Koufax/Hobie Landrith	30.00	15.00	9.00
(104)	Sandy Koufax/Bob Shaw	30.00	15.00	9.00
(105)	Jack Kralick/Minnie Minoso	9.00	4.50	2.75
(106)	Harvey Kuenn/Ken Hunt	8.00	4.00	2.50
(107)	Havey Kuenn/Gene Woodling	8.00	4.00	2.50
(108)	Hobie Landrith/Mike Fornieles	8.00	4.00	2.50
(109)	Barry Latman/Tony Kubek	9.00	4.50	2.75
(110)	Barry Latman/Johnny Podres	8.00	4.00	2.50
(111)	Frank Malzone/Johnny Podres	8.00	4.00	2.50
(112)	Frank Malzone/Duke Snider	15.00	7.50	4.50
(113)	Felix Mantilla/Camilo Carreon	8.00	4.00	2.50
(114)	Mickey Mantle/Hank Aaron	125.00	62.00	37.00
(115)	Mickey Mantle/Dick Stuart	110.00	55.00	33.00
(116)	Juan Marichal/Bill Bruton	12.00	6.00	3.50
(117)	Juan Marichal/Gene Freese	12.00	6.00	3.50
(118)	Juan Marichal/Don Hoak	12.00	6.00	3.50
(119)	Roger Maris/Lou Burdette	20.00	10.00	6.00
(120)	Roger Maris/Nellie Fox	20.00	10.00	6.00
(121)	Roger Maris/Lee Thomas	20.00	10.00	6.00
(122)	J.C. Martin/Felix Mantilla	8.00	4.00	2.50
(123)	J.C. Martin/Barney Schultz	8.00	4.00	2.50
(124)	Willie Mays/Tony Kubek	35.00	17.50	10.50
(125)	Bill Mazeroski/Earl Battey	10.00	5.00	3.00
(126)	Bill Mazeroski/Elston Howard	10.00	5.00	3.00
(127)	Bill Mazeroski/Early Wynn	12.00	6.00	3.50
(128)	Ken McBride/Joe Torre	9.00	4.50	2.75
(129)	Tim McCarver/Bill Tuttle	9.00	4.50	2.75
(130)	Lindy McDaniel/Jim Piersall	8.00	4.00	2.50
(131)	Roy McMillan/Bob Allison	8.00	4.00	2.50
(132)	Roy McMillan/Albie Pearson	8.00	4.00	2.50
(133)	Roy McMillan/Leon Wagner	8.00	4.00	2.50
(134)	Bob Miller/Ron Hansen	8.00	4.00	2.50
(135)	Stu Miller/Joe McCain	8.00	4.00	2.50
(136)	Bill Monbouquette/Don Hoak	8.00	4.00	2.50
(137)	Bill Monbouquette/Joe Torre	9.00	4.50	2.75
(138)	Wally Moon/Frank Malzone	8.00	4.00	2.50
(139)	Wally Moon/Juan Pizarro	8.00	4.00	2.50
(140)	Wally Moon/Brooks Robinson	20.00	10.00	6.00
(141)	Don Mossi/Bill Bruton	8.00	4.00	2.50
(142)	Don Mossi/Johnny Podres	8.00	4.00	2.50
(143)	Don Mossi/Al Spangler	8.00	4.00	2.50
(144)	Stan Musial/Whitey Ford	30.00	15.00	9.00
(145)	Stan Musial/Joe Torre	30.00	15.00	9.00
(146)	Russ Nixon/Ed Bailey	8.00	4.00	2.50
(147)	Russ Nixon/Lindy McDaniel	8.00	4.00	2.50
(148)	Danny O'Connell/Mike McCormick	8.00	4.00	2.50
(149)	Jim O'Toole/Ron Hansen	8.00	4.00	2.50
(150)	Jim O'Toole/Gene Stephens	8.00	4.00	2.50
(151)	Camilo Pascual/Pete Daley	8.00	4.00	2.50
(152)	Camilo Pascual/Tim McCarver	9.00	4.50	2.75
(153)	Camilo Pascual/Bill Virdon	8.00	4.00	2.50
(154)	Albie Pearson/Julian Javier	8.00	4.00	2.50
(155)	Jim Perry/Frank Howard	8.00	4.00	2.50
(156)	Bubba Phillips/Don Drysdale	12.00	6.00	3.50
(157)	Vada Pinson/Tony Gonzalez	9.00	4.50	2.75
(158)	Vada Pinson/Frank Howard	8.00	4.00	2.50
(159)	Juan Pizarro/Jack Baldschun	8.00	4.00	2.50
(160)	Johnny Podres/Jim Archer	8.00	4.00	2.50
(161)	Leo Posada/Milt Pappas	8.00	4.00	2.50
(162)	Leo Posada/Johnny Romano	8.00	4.00	2.50
(163)	Vic Power/Hal W. Smith	8.00	4.00	2.50
(164)	Bob Purkey/Harmon Killebrew	15.00	7.50	4.50
(165)	Pedro Ramos/Orlando Cepeda	10.00	5.00	3.00
(166)	Brooks Robinson/Jack Baldschun	15.00	7.50	4.50
(167)	Brooks Robinson/Duke Snider	20.00	10.00	6.00
(168)	Floyd Robinson/Ron Fairly	8.00	4.00	2.50
(169)	Floyd Robinson/Tony Taylor	8.00	4.00	2.50
(170)	Bob Rodgers/Hank Aaron	35.00	17.50	10.50
(171)	Bob Rodgers/Roger Craig	8.00	4.00	2.50
(172)	Bob Rodgers/Johnny Romano	8.00	4.00	2.50
(173)	Johnny Romano/Minnie Minoso	9.00	4.50	2.75
(174)	John Roseboro/Bob Aspromonte	8.00	4.00	2.50
(175)	John Roseboro/Chuck Estrada	8.00	4.00	2.50
(176)	John Roseboro/Bubba Phillips	8.00	4.00	2.50
(177)	Ray Sadecki/Chuck Cottier	8.00	4.00	2.50
(178)	Ron Santo/Ernie Banks	20.00	10.00	6.00
(179)	Ron Santo/Joe Jay	9.00	4.50	2.75
(180)	Ron Santo/Leo Posada	9.00	4.50	2.75
(181)	Chuck Schilling/Hank Aaron	35.00	17.50	10.50
(182)	Chuck Schilling/Dick Stuart	8.00	4.00	2.50
(183)	Barney Schultz/Camilo Carreon	8.00	4.00	2.50
(184)	Don Schwall/Sam Jones	8.00	4.00	2.50
(185)	Bobby Shantz/Pete Runnels	8.00	4.00	2.50
(186)	Bob Shaw/Mike Fornieles	8.00	4.00	2.50
(187)	Bob Shaw/George Thomas	8.00	4.00	2.50
(188)	Norm Siebern/Dick Ellsworth	8.00	4.00	2.50
(189)	Norm Siebern/Bobby Shantz	8.00	4.00	2.50
(190)	Norm Siebern/Early Wynn	10.00	5.00	3.00
(191)	Roy Sievers/Carl Yastrzemski	30.00	15.00	9.00
(192)	Bill Skowron/Jim Davenport	9.00	4.50	2.75
(193)	Bill Skowron/Bob Purkey	9.00	4.50	2.75
(194)	Warren Spahn/Whitey Ford	20.00	10.00	6.00
(195)	Al Spangler/Jim Archer	8.00	4.00	2.50
(196)	Al Spangler/Jay Hook	8.00	4.00	2.50
(197)	Daryl Spencer/Gene Stephens	8.00	4.00	2.50
(198)	Haywood Sullivan/Jerry Lumpe	8.00	4.00	2.50
(199)	Haywood Sullivan/Billy Williams	10.00	5.00	3.00
(200)	Tony Taylor/Jim Landis	8.00	4.00	2.50
(201)	Lee Thomas/Ed Mathews	12.00	6.00	3.50
(202)	Bob Tiefenauer/Jackie Brandt	8.00	4.00	2.50
(203)	Bob Tiefenauer/Jake Wood	8.00	4.00	2.50
(204)	Gus Triandos/Billy Williams	10.00	5.00	3.00
(205)	Zoilo Versalles/Whitey Ford	12.50	6.25	3.75
(206)	Zoilo Versalles/Stan Musial	30.00	15.00	9.00
(207)	Zoilo Verasalles/Warren Spahn	12.00	6.00	3.50
(208)	Bill Virdon/Bob Friend	8.00	4.00	2.50
(209)	Bill Virdon/Bill Tuttle	8.00	4.00	2.50
(210)	Leon Wagner/Jim Davenport	8.00	4.00	2.50
(211)	Leon Wagner/Julian Javier	8.00	4.00	2.50
(212)	Lee Walls/Jerry Lumpe	8.00	4.00	2.50
(213)	Bill White/Al Kaline	15.00	7.50	4.50
(214)	Bill White/Ken Mcbride	8.00	4.00	2.50
(215)	Bill White/Bill Monbouquette	8.00	4.00	2.50
(216)	Jake Wood/Frank Robinson	12.00	6.00	3.50
(217)	Gene Woodling/Lenny Green	8.00	4.00	2.50
(218)	Early Wynn/Glen Hobbie	10.00	5.00	3.00
(219)	Early Wynn/Ed Mathews	15.00	7.50	4.50
(220)	Angels/Athletics	8.00	4.00	2.50
(221)	Angels/Colts	9.00	4.50	2.75
(222)	Angels/Orioles	8.00	4.00	2.50
(223)	Athletics/Mets	10.00	5.00	3.00
(224)	Athletics/Pirates	9.00	4.50	2.75
(225)	Cardinals/Indians	9.00	4.50	2.75
(226)	Colts/Mets	12.00	6.00	3.50
(227)	Colts/Twins	9.00	4.50	2.75
(228)	Cubs/Senators	9.00	4.50	2.75
(229)	Giants/Red Sox	9.00	4.50	2.75
(230)	Giants/Tigers	9.00	4.50	2.75
(231)	Giants/White Sox	12.00	6.00	3.50
(232)	Indians/Reds	9.00	4.50	2.75
(233)	Mets/Dodgers	10.00	5.00	3.00
(234)	Orioles/Pirates	9.00	4.50	2.75
(235)	Phillies/Senators	9.00	4.50	2.75
(236)	Red Sox/Braves	9.00	4.50	2.75
(237)	Red Sox/Phillies	9.00	4.50	2.75
(238)	Reds/Indians	9.00	4.50	2.75
(239)	Reds/Yankees	12.50	6.25	3.75
(240)	Tigers/Braves	9.00	4.50	2.75
(241)	Twins/Dodgers	12.50	6.25	3.75
(242)	White Sox/Cubs	10.00	5.00	3.00
(243)	White Sox/Phillies	10.00	5.00	3.00
(244)	Yankees/Cardinals	12.50	6.25	3.75
(245)	Yankees/Reds	12.50	6.25	3.75

1963 Topps

Although the number of cards dropped to 576, the 1963 Topps set is among the most popular of the 1960s. A color photo dominates the 2-1/2" x 3-1/2" card, but a colored circle at the bottom carries a black and white portrait as well. A colored band gives the player's name, team and position. The backs again feature career statistics and a cartoon, career summary and brief biographical details. The set is somewhat unlike those immediately preceding it in that there are fewer specialty cards. The major groupings are statistical leaders, World Series highlights, and rookies. It is one rookie which makes the set special - Pete Rose. As one of most avidly sought cards in history and a high-numbered card at that, the Rose rookie card accounts for much of the value of a complete set.

		NM	EX	VG
	Complete Set (576):	5,500	2,750	1,375
	Common Player (1-446):	4.00	2.00	1.25
	Common Player (447-576):	12.50	6.25	3.25
1	N.L. Batting Leaders (Hank Aaron, Bill White, Frank Robinson, Tommy Davis, Stan Musial)	40.00	20.00	10.00
2	A.L. Batting Leaders (Chuck Hinton, Mickey Mantle, Floyd Robinson, Pete Runnels, Norm Siebern)	40.00	20.00	10.00
3	N.L. Home Run Leaders (Hank Aaron, Ernie Banks, Orlando Cepeda, Willie Mays, Frank Robinson)	40.00	20.00	12.00
4	A.L. Home Run Leaders (Norm Cash, Rocky Colavito, Jim Gentile, Harmon Killebrew, Roger Maris, Leon Wagner)	20.00	10.00	6.00
5	N.L. E.R.A. Leaders (Don Drysdale, Bob Gibson, Sandy Koufax, Bob Shaw, Bob Purkey)	17.50	8.75	5.25
6	A.L. E.R.A. Leaders (Hank Aguirre, Dean Chance, Eddie Fisher, Whitey Ford, Robin Roberts)	10.00	5.00	3.00
7	N.L. Pitching Leaders (Don Drysdale, Joe Jay, Art Mahaffey, Billy O'Dell, Bob Purkey, Jack Sanford)	12.00	6.00	3.50
8	A.L. Pitching Leaders (Jim Bunning, Dick Donovan, Ray Herbert, Camilo Pascual, Ralph Terry)	10.00	5.00	3.00
9	N.L. Strikeout Leaders (Don Drysdale, Dick Farrell, Bob Gibson, Sandy Koufax, Billy O'Dell)	20.00	10.00	6.00
10	A.L. Strikeout Leaders (Jim Bunning, Jim Kaat, Camilo Pascual, Juan Pizarro, Ralph Terry)	9.00	4.50	2.75
11	Lee Walls	4.00	2.00	1.25
12	Steve Barber	4.00	2.00	1.25
13	Philadelphia Phillies Team	7.00	3.50	2.00
14	Pedro Ramos	4.00	2.00	1.25
15	Ken Hubbs	10.00	5.00	3.00
16	Al Smith	4.00	2.00	1.25
17	Ryne Duren	4.00	2.00	1.25
18	Buc Blasters (Smoky Burgess, Roberto Clemente, Bob Skinner, Dick Stuart)	75.00	37.50	18.75
19	Pete Burnside	4.00	2.00	1.25
20	Tony Kubek	12.50	6.25	3.75
21	Marty Keough	4.00	2.00	1.25
22	Curt Simmons	4.00	2.00	1.25
23	Ed Lopat	4.00	2.00	1.25
24	Bob Bruce	4.00	2.00	1.25
25	Al Kaline	50.00	25.00	12.50
26	Ray Moore	4.00	2.00	1.25
27	Choo Choo Coleman	4.00	2.00	1.25
28	Mike Fornieles	4.00	2.00	1.25
29a	1962 Rookie Stars (**Sammy Ellis, Ray Culp, John Boozer, Jesse Gonder**)	6.00	3.00	1.75
29b	1963 Rookie Stars (**Sammy Ellis, Ray Culp, John Boozer, Jesse Gonder**)	4.00	2.00	1.25
30	Harvey Kuenn	4.00	2.00	1.25
31	Cal Koonce	4.00	2.00	1.25
32	Tony Gonzalez	4.00	2.00	1.25
33	Bo Belinsky	4.00	2.00	1.25
34	Dick Schofield	4.00	2.00	1.25
35	John Buzhardt	4.00	2.00	1.25
36	Jerry Kindall	4.00	2.00	1.25
37	Jerry Lynch	4.00	2.00	1.25
38	Bud Daley	4.00	2.00	1.25
39	Los Angeles Angels Team	7.00	3.50	2.00
40	Vic Power	4.00	2.00	1.25
41	Charlie Lau	4.00	2.00	1.25
42	Stan Williams	4.00	2.00	1.25
43	Veteran Masters (Casey Stengel, Gene Woodling)	7.50	3.75	2.25
44	Terry Fox	4.00	2.00	1.25
45	Bob Aspromonte	4.00	2.00	1.25
46	*Tommie Aaron*	5.00	2.50	1.50
47	Don Lock	4.00	2.00	1.25
48	Birdie Tebbetts	4.00	2.00	1.25
49	*Dal Maxvill*	4.00	2.00	1.25
50	Bill Pierce	4.00	2.00	1.25
51	George Alusik	4.00	2.00	1.25
52	Chuck Schilling	4.00	2.00	1.25
53	Joe Moeller	4.00	2.00	1.25
54a	1962 Rookie Stars (**Nelson Mathews, Harry Fanok, Jack Cullen, Dave DeBusschere**)	10.00	5.00	3.00
54b	1963 Rookie Stars (**Jack Cullen, Dave DeBusschere, Harry Fanok, Nelson Mathews**)	8.00	4.00	2.50

No.	Player			
55	Bill Virdon	4.00	2.00	1.25
56	Dennis Bennett	4.00	2.00	1.25
57	Billy Moran	4.00	2.00	1.25
58	Bob Will	4.00	2.00	1.25
59	Craig Anderson	4.00	2.00	1.25
60	Elston Howard	9.00	4.50	2.75
61	Ernie Bowman	4.00	2.00	1.25
62	Bob Hendley	4.00	2.00	1.25
63	Cincinnati Reds Team	7.00	3.50	2.00
64	Dick McAuliffe	4.00	2.00	1.25
65	Jackie Brandt	4.00	2.00	1.25
66	Mike Joyce	4.00	2.00	1.25
67	Ed Charles	4.00	2.00	1.25
68	Friendly Foes (Gil Hodges, Duke Snider)	15.00	7.50	4.50
69	Bud Zipfel	4.00	2.00	1.25
70	Jim O'Toole	4.00	2.00	1.25
71	Bobby Wine	4.00	2.00	1.25
72	Johnny Romano	4.00	2.00	1.25
73	Bobby Bragan	4.00	2.00	1.25
74	Denver Lemaster	4.00	2.00	1.25
75	Bob Allison	4.00	2.00	1.25
76	Earl Wilson	4.00	2.00	1.25
77	Al Spangler	4.00	2.00	1.25
78	Marv Throneberry	4.00	2.00	1.25
79	1st Series Checklist (1-88)	6.00	3.00	1.75
80	Jim Gilliam	6.00	3.00	1.75
81	Jimmie Schaffer	4.00	2.00	1.25
82	Ed Rakow	4.00	2.00	1.25
83	Charley James	4.00	2.00	1.25
84	Ron Kline	4.00	2.00	1.25
85	Tom Haller	4.00	2.00	1.25
86	Charley Maxwell	4.00	2.00	1.25
87	Bob Veale	4.00	2.00	1.25
88	Ron Hansen	4.00	2.00	1.25
89	Dick Stigman	4.00	2.00	1.25
90	Gordy Coleman	4.00	2.00	1.25
91	Dallas Green	4.00	2.00	1.25
92	Hector Lopez	4.00	2.00	1.25
93	Galen Cisco	4.00	2.00	1.25
94	Bob Schmidt	4.00	2.00	1.25
95	Larry Jackson	4.00	2.00	1.25
96	Lou Clinton	4.00	2.00	1.25
97	Bob Duliba	4.00	2.00	1.25
98	George Thomas	4.00	2.00	1.25
99	Jim Umbricht	4.00	2.00	1.25
100	Joe Cunningham	4.00	2.00	1.25
101	Joe Gibbon	4.00	2.00	1.25
102a	2nd Series Checklist (89-176) ("Checklist" in red on yellow.)	6.00	3.00	1.75
102b	2nd Series Checklist (89-176) ("Checklist" in white on red.)	10.00	5.00	3.00
103	Chuck Essegian	4.00	2.00	1.25
104	Lew Krausse	4.00	2.00	1.25
105	Ron Fairly	4.00	2.00	1.25
106	Bob Bolin	4.00	2.00	1.25
107	Jim Hickman	4.00	2.00	1.25
108	Hoyt Wilhelm	15.00	7.50	4.50
109	Lee Maye	4.00	2.00	1.25
110	Rich Rollins	4.00	2.00	1.25
111	Al Jackson	4.00	2.00	1.25
112	Dick Brown	4.00	2.00	1.25
113	Don Landrum (Photo actually Ron Santo.)	4.00	2.00	1.25
114	Dan Osinski	4.00	2.00	1.25
115	Carl Yastrzemski	40.00	20.00	12.00
116	Jim Brosnan	4.00	2.00	1.25
117	Jacke Davis	4.00	2.00	1.25
118	Sherm Lollar	4.00	2.00	1.25
119	Bob Lillis	4.00	2.00	1.25
120	Roger Maris	80.00	40.00	20.00
121	Jim Hannan	4.00	2.00	1.25
122	Julio Gotay	4.00	2.00	1.25
123	Frank Howard	4.00	2.00	1.25
124	Dick Howser	4.00	2.00	1.25
125	Robin Roberts	15.00	7.50	4.50
126	Bob Uecker	17.50	8.75	5.25
127	Bill Tuttle	4.00	2.00	1.25
128	Matty Alou	4.00	2.00	1.25
129	Gary Bell	4.00	2.00	1.25
130	Dick Groat	4.00	2.00	1.25
131	Washington Senators Team	7.00	3.50	2.00
132	Jack Hamilton	4.00	2.00	1.25
133	Gene Freese	4.00	2.00	1.25
134	Bob Scheffing	4.00	2.00	1.25
135	Richie Ashburn	15.00	7.50	4.50
136	Ike Delock	4.00	2.00	1.25
137	Mack Jones	4.00	2.00	1.25
138	Pride of N.L. (Willie Mays, Stan Musial)	80.00	40.00	20.00
139	Earl Averill	4.00	2.00	1.25
140	Frank Lary	4.00	2.00	1.25
141	Manny Mota	6.00	3.00	1.75
142	World Series Game 1 (Yanks' Ford Wins Series Opener)	11.00	5.50	3.25
143	World Series Game 2 (Sanford Flashes Shutout Magic)	5.00	2.50	1.50
144	World Series Game 3 (Maris Sparks Yankee Rally)	12.00	6.00	3.50
145	World Series Game 4 (Hiller Blasts Grand Slammer)	5.00	2.50	1.50
146	World Series Game 5 (Tresh's Homer Defeats Giants)	6.00	3.00	1.75
147	World Series Game 6 (Pierce Stars in 3-Hit Victory)	6.00	3.00	1.75
148	World Series Game 7 (Yanks Celebrate as Terry Wins)	7.00	3.50	2.00
149	Marv Breeding	4.00	2.00	1.25
150	Johnny Podres	6.00	3.00	1.75
151	Pittsburgh Pirates Team	10.00	5.00	3.00
152	Ron Nischwitz	4.00	2.00	1.25
153	Hal Smith	4.00	2.00	1.25
154	Walt Alston	7.50	3.75	2.25
155	Bill Stafford	4.00	2.00	1.25
156	Roy McMillan	4.00	2.00	1.25
157	Diego Segui	4.00	2.00	1.25
158	1963 Rookie Stars (Rogelio Alvarez, Tommy Harper, Dave Roberts, Bob Saverine)	6.00	3.00	1.75
159	Jim Pagliaroni	4.00	2.00	1.25
160	Juan Pizarro	4.00	2.00	1.25
161	Frank Torre	4.00	2.00	1.25
162	Minnesota Twins Team	7.00	3.50	2.00
163	Don Larsen	4.00	2.00	1.25
164	Bubba Morton	4.00	2.00	1.25
165	Jim Kaat	5.00	2.50	1.50
166	Johnny Keane	4.00	2.00	1.25
167	Jim Fregosi	4.00	2.00	1.25
168	Russ Nixon	4.00	2.00	1.25
169	1963 Rookie Stars (Dick Egan, Julio Navarro, Gaylord Perry, Tommie Sisk)	17.50	8.75	5.25
170	Joe Adcock	4.00	2.00	1.25
171	Steve Hamilton	4.00	2.00	1.25
172	Gene Oliver	4.00	2.00	1.25
173	Bombers' Best (Tom Tresh, Mickey Mantle, Bobby Richardson)	150.00	75.00	37.50
174	Larry Burright	4.00	2.00	1.25
175	Bob Buhl	4.00	2.00	1.25
176	Jim King	4.00	2.00	1.25
177	Bubba Phillips	4.00	2.00	1.25
178	Johnny Edwards	4.00	2.00	1.25
179	Ron Piche	4.00	2.00	1.25
180	Bill Skowron	10.00	5.00	3.00
181	Sammy Esposito	4.00	2.00	1.25
182	Albie Pearson	4.00	2.00	1.25
183	Joe Pepitone	10.00	5.00	3.00
184	Vern Law	4.00	2.00	1.25
185	Chuck Hiller	4.00	2.00	1.25
186	Jerry Zimmerman	4.00	2.00	1.25
187	Willie Kirkland	4.00	2.00	1.25
188	Eddie Bressoud	4.00	2.00	1.25
189	Dave Giusti	4.00	2.00	1.25
190	Minnie Minoso	6.00	3.00	1.75
191	3rd Series Checklist (177-264)	8.00	4.00	2.50
192	Clay Dalrymple	4.00	2.00	1.25
193	Andre Rodgers	4.00	2.00	1.25
194	Joe Nuxhall	4.00	2.00	1.25
195	Manny Jimenez	4.00	2.00	1.25
196	Doug Camilli	4.00	2.00	1.25
197	Roger Craig	4.00	2.00	1.25
198	Lenny Green	4.00	2.00	1.25
199	Joe Amalfitano	4.00	2.00	1.25
200	Mickey Mantle	525.00	260.00	160.00
201	Cecil Butler	4.00	2.00	1.25
202	Boston Red Sox Team	7.00	3.50	2.00
203	Chico Cardenas	4.00	2.00	1.25
204	Don Nottebart	4.00	2.00	1.25
205	Luis Aparicio	15.00	7.50	4.50
206	Ray Washburn	4.00	2.00	1.25
207	Ken Hunt	4.00	2.00	1.25
208	1963 Rookie Stars (Ron Herbel, John Miller, Ron Taylor, Wally Wolf)	4.00	2.00	1.25
209	Hobie Landrith	4.00	2.00	1.25
210	Sandy Koufax	150.00	75.00	37.50
211	Fred Whitfield	4.00	2.00	1.25
212	Glen Hobbie	4.00	2.00	1.25
213	Billy Hitchcock	4.00	2.00	1.25
214	Orlando Pena	4.00	2.00	1.25
215	Bob Skinner	4.00	2.00	1.25
216	Gene Conley	4.00	2.00	1.25
217	Joe Christopher	4.00	2.00	1.25
218	Tiger Twirlers (Jim Bunning, Frank Lary, Don Mossi)	7.50	3.75	2.25
219	Chuck Cottier	4.00	2.00	1.25
220	Camilo Pascual	4.00	2.00	1.25
221	Cookie Rojas	4.00	2.00	1.25
222	Chicago Cubs Team	7.00	3.50	2.00
223	Eddie Fisher	4.00	2.00	1.25
224	Mike Roarke	4.00	2.00	1.25
225	Joe Jay	4.00	2.00	1.25
226	Julian Javier	4.00	2.00	1.25
227	Jim Grant	4.00	2.00	1.25
228	1963 Rookie Stars (Max Alvis, Bob Bailey, Ed Kranepool, Tony Oliva)	50.00	25.00	12.50
229	Willie Davis	4.00	2.00	1.25
230	Pete Runnels	4.00	2.00	1.25
231	Eli Grba (Photo actually Ryne Duren.)	4.00	2.00	1.25
232	Frank Malzone	4.00	2.00	1.25
233	Casey Stengel	15.00	7.50	4.50
234	Dave Nicholson	4.00	2.00	1.25
235	Billy O'Dell	4.00	2.00	1.25
236	Bill Bryan	4.00	2.00	1.25
237	Jim Coates	4.00	2.00	1.25
238	Lou Johnson	4.00	2.00	1.25
239	Harvey Haddix	4.00	2.00	1.25
240	Rocky Colavito	17.50	8.75	5.25
241	Billy Smith	4.00	2.00	1.25
242	Power Plus (Hank Aaron, Ernie Banks)	60.00	30.00	15.00
243	Don Leppert	4.00	2.00	1.25
244	John Tsitouris	4.00	2.00	1.25
245	Gil Hodges	12.50	6.25	3.75
246	Lee Stange	4.00	2.00	1.25
247	New York Yankees Team	50.00	25.00	12.50
248	Tito Francona	4.00	2.00	1.25
249	Leo Burke	4.00	2.00	1.25
250	Stan Musial	100.00	50.00	25.00
251	Jack Lamabe	4.00	2.00	1.25
252	Ron Santo	13.50	6.75	4.00
253	1963 Rookie Stars (Len Gabrielson, Pete Jernigan, Deacon Jones, John Wojcik)	4.00	2.00	1.25
254	Mike Hershberger	4.00	2.00	1.25
255	Bob Shaw	4.00	2.00	1.25
256	Jerry Lumpe	4.00	2.00	1.25
257	Hank Aguirre	4.00	2.00	1.25
258	Alvin Dark	4.00	2.00	1.25
259	Johnny Logan	4.00	2.00	1.25
260	Jim Gentile	4.00	2.00	1.25
261	Bob Miller	4.00	2.00	1.25
262	Ellis Burton	4.00	2.00	1.25
263	Dave Stenhouse	4.00	2.00	1.25
264	Phil Linz	4.00	2.00	1.25
265	Vada Pinson	7.00	3.50	2.00
266	Bob Allen	4.00	2.00	1.25
267	Carl Sawatski	4.00	2.00	1.25
268	Don Demeter	4.00	2.00	1.25
269	Don Mincher	4.00	2.00	1.25
270	Felipe Alou	5.00	2.50	1.50
271	Dean Stone	4.00	2.00	1.25
272	Danny Murphy	4.00	2.00	1.25
273	Sammy Taylor	4.00	2.00	1.25
274	6th Series Checklist (265-352)	8.00	4.00	2.50
275	Ed Mathews	25.00	12.50	7.50
276	Barry Shetrone	4.00	2.00	1.25
277	Dick Farrell	4.00	2.00	1.25
278	Chico Fernandez	4.00	2.00	1.25
279	Wally Moon	4.00	2.00	1.25
280	Bob Rodgers	4.00	2.00	1.25
281	Tom Sturdivant	4.00	2.00	1.25
282	Bob Del Greco	4.00	2.00	1.25
283	Roy Sievers	4.00	2.00	1.25
284	Dave Sisler	4.00	2.00	1.25
285	Dick Stuart	4.00	2.00	1.25
286	Stu Miller	4.00	2.00	1.25
287	Dick Bertell	4.00	2.00	1.25
288	Chicago White Sox Team	8.00	4.00	2.50
289	Hal Brown	4.00	2.00	1.25
290	Bill White	4.00	2.00	1.25
291	Don Rudolph	4.00	2.00	1.25
292	Pumpsie Green	4.00	2.00	1.25
293	Bill Pleis	4.00	2.00	1.25
294	Bill Rigney	4.00	2.00	1.25
295	Ed Roebuck	4.00	2.00	1.25
296	Doc Edwards	4.00	2.00	1.25
297	Jim Golden	4.00	2.00	1.25
298	Don Dillard	4.00	2.00	1.25
299	1963 Rookie Stars (Tom Butters, Bob Dustal, Dave Morehead, Dan Schneider)	4.00	2.00	1.25
300	Willie Mays	160.00	80.00	40.00
301	Bill Fischer	4.00	2.00	1.25
302	Whitey Herzog	12.50	6.25	3.75
303	Earl Francis	4.00	2.00	1.25
304	Harry Bright	4.00	2.00	1.25
305	Don Hoak	4.00	2.00	1.25
306	Star Receivers (Earl Battey, Elston Howard)	5.00	2.50	1.50
307	Chet Nichols	4.00	2.00	1.25
308	Camilo Carreon	4.00	2.00	1.25
309	Jim Brewer	4.00	2.00	1.25
310	Tommy Davis	6.00	3.00	1.75
311	Joe McClain	4.00	2.00	1.25
312	Houston Colt .45s Team	13.50	6.75	4.00
313	Ernie Broglio	4.00	2.00	1.25
314	John Goryl	4.00	2.00	1.25
315	Ralph Terry	4.00	2.00	1.25
316	Norm Sherry	4.00	2.00	1.25
317	Sam McDowell	5.00	2.50	1.50
318	Gene Mauch	4.00	2.00	1.25
319	Joe Gaines	4.00	2.00	1.25
320	Warren Spahn	60.00	30.00	15.00
321	Gino Cimoli	4.00	2.00	1.25
322	Bob Turley	4.00	2.00	1.25
323	Bill Mazeroski	20.00	10.00	6.00
324	1963 Rookie Stars (Vic Davalillo, Phil Roof, Pete Ward, George Williams)	6.00	3.00	1.75
325	Jack Sanford	4.00	2.00	1.25
326	Hank Foiles	4.00	2.00	1.25
327	Paul Foytack	4.00	2.00	1.25
328	Dick Williams	4.00	2.00	1.25
329	Lindy McDaniel	4.00	2.00	1.25
330	Chuck Hinton	4.00	2.00	1.25
331	Series Foes (Bill Pierce, Bill Stafford)	7.00	3.50	2.00
332	Joel Horlen	4.00	2.00	1.25
333	Carl Warwick	4.00	2.00	1.25
334	Wynn Hawkins	4.00	2.00	1.25
335	Leon Wagner	4.00	2.00	1.25
336	Ed Bauta	4.00	2.00	1.25
337	Los Angeles Dodgers Team	15.00	7.50	4.50
338	Russ Kemmerer	4.00	2.00	1.25
339	Ted Bowsfield	4.00	2.00	1.25
340	Yogi Berra	100.00	50.00	25.00
341a	Jack Baldschun (White slash across body in inset photo.)	8.00	4.00	2.50
341b	Jack Baldschun (Slash repaired with red/mottling.)	4.00	2.00	1.25
342	Gene Woodling	4.00	2.00	1.25
343	Johnny Pesky	4.00	2.00	1.25
344	Don Schwall	4.00	2.00	1.25
345	Brooks Robinson	60.00	30.00	15.00
346	Billy Hoeft	4.00	2.00	1.25
347	Joe Torre	17.50	8.75	5.25
348	Vic Wertz	4.00	2.00	1.25
349	Zoilo Versalles	4.00	2.00	1.25
350	Bob Purkey	4.00	2.00	1.25
351	Al Luplow	4.00	2.00	1.25
352	Ken Johnson	4.00	2.00	1.25
353	Billy Williams	20.00	10.00	6.00
354	Dom Zanni	4.00	2.00	1.25
355	Dean Chance	4.00	2.00	1.25
356	John Schaive	4.00	2.00	1.25
357	George Altman	4.00	2.00	1.25
358	Milt Pappas	4.00	2.00	1.25
359	Haywood Sullivan	4.00	2.00	1.25
360	Don Drysdale	50.00	25.00	12.50
361	Clete Boyer	9.00	4.50	2.75
362	5th Series Checklist (353-429)	9.00	4.50	2.75
363	Dick Radatz	4.00	2.00	1.25
364	Howie Goss	4.00	2.00	1.25
365	Jim Bunning	13.50	6.75	4.00
366	Tony Taylor	4.00	2.00	1.25
367	Tony Cloninger	4.00	2.00	1.25
368	Ed Bailey	4.00	2.00	1.25

369	Jim Lemon	4.00	2.00	1.25
370	Dick Donovan	4.00	2.00	1.25
371	Rod Kanehl	4.00	2.00	1.25
372	Don Lee	4.00	2.00	1.25
373	Jim Campbell	4.00	2.00	1.25
374	Claude Osteen	4.00	2.00	1.25
375	Ken Boyer	10.00	5.00	3.00
376	Johnnie Wyatt	4.00	2.00	1.25
377	Baltimore Orioles Team	9.00	4.50	2.75
378	Bill Henry	4.00	2.00	1.25
379	Bob Anderson	4.00	2.00	1.25
380	Ernie Banks	100.00	50.00	25.00
381	Frank Baumann	4.00	2.00	1.25
382	Ralph Houk	6.00	3.00	1.75
383	Pete Richert	4.00	2.00	1.25
384	Bob Tillman	4.00	2.00	1.25
385	Art Mahaffey	4.00	2.00	1.25
386	1963 Rookie Stars (**John Bateman, Larry Bearnarth, Ed Kirkpatrick, Garry Roggenburk**)	5.00	2.50	1.50
387	Al McBean	4.00	2.00	1.25
388a	Jim Davenport (collar shadow above red box)	4.00	2.00	1.25
388b	Jim Davenport (collar shadow touches red box)	4.00	2.00	1.25
389	Frank Sullivan	4.00	2.00	1.25
390	Hank Aaron	185.00	92.50	46.25
391	Bill Dailey	4.00	2.00	1.25
392	Tribe Thumpers (Tito Francona, Johnny Romano)	4.50	2.25	1.25
393	Ken MacKenzie	4.00	2.00	1.25
394	Tim McCarver	9.00	4.50	2.75
395	Don McMahon	4.00	2.00	1.25
396	Joe Koppe	4.00	2.00	1.25
397	Kansas City Athletics Team	9.00	4.50	2.75
398	Boog Powell	12.50	6.25	3.75
399	Dick Ellsworth	4.00	2.00	1.25
400	Frank Robinson	60.00	30.00	15.00
401	Jim Bouton	12.00	6.00	3.50
402	Mickey Vernon	4.00	2.00	1.25
403	Ron Perranoski	4.00	2.00	1.25
404	Bob Oldis	4.00	2.00	1.25
405	Floyd Robinson	4.00	2.00	1.25
406	Howie Koplitz	4.00	2.00	1.25
407	1963 Rookie Stars (**Larry Elliot, Frank Kostro, Chico Ruiz, Dick Simpson**)	4.00	2.00	1.25
408	Billy Gardner	4.00	2.00	1.25
409	Roy Face	4.00	2.00	1.25
410	Earl Battey	4.00	2.00	1.25
411	Jim Constable	4.00	2.00	1.25
412	Dodgers' Big Three (Johnny Podres, Don Drysdale, Sandy Koufax)	50.00	25.00	12.50
413	Jerry Walker	4.00	2.00	1.25
414	Ty Cline	4.00	2.00	1.25
415	Bob Gibson	60.00	30.00	15.00
416	Alex Grammas	4.00	2.00	1.25
417	San Francisco Giants Team	9.00	4.50	2.75
418	Johnny Orsino	4.00	2.00	1.25
419	Tracy Stallard	4.00	2.00	1.25
420	Bobby Richardson	12.50	6.25	3.75
421	Tom Morgan	4.00	2.00	1.25
422	Fred Hutchinson	4.00	2.00	1.25
423	Ed Hobaugh	4.00	2.00	1.25
424	Charley Smith	4.00	2.00	1.25
425	Smoky Burgess	4.00	2.00	1.25
426	Barry Latman	4.00	2.00	1.25
427	Bernie Allen	4.00	2.00	1.25
428	Carl Boles	4.00	2.00	1.25
429	Lou Burdette	4.00	2.00	1.25
430	Norm Siebern	4.00	2.00	1.25
431a	6th Series Checklist (430-506) ("Checklist" in black on front.)	8.00	4.00	2.50
431b	6th Series Checklist (430-506) ("Checklist" in white.)	20.00	10.00	6.00
432	Roman Mejias	4.00	2.00	1.25
433	Denis Menke	4.00	2.00	1.25
434	Johnny Callison	4.00	2.00	1.25
435	Woody Held	4.00	2.00	1.25
436	Tim Harkness	4.00	2.00	1.25
437	Bill Bruton	4.00	2.00	1.25
438	Wes Stock	4.00	2.00	1.25
439	Don Zimmer	6.00	3.00	1.75
440	Juan Marichal	25.00	12.50	7.50
441	Lee Thomas	4.00	2.00	1.25
442	J.C. Hartman	4.00	2.00	1.25
443	Jim Piersall	7.00	3.50	2.00
444	Jim Maloney	4.00	2.00	1.25
445	Norm Cash	9.00	4.50	2.75
446	Whitey Ford	60.00	30.00	15.00
447	Felix Mantilla	12.50	6.25	3.25
448	Jack Kralick	12.50	6.25	3.25
449	Jose Tartabull	12.50	6.25	3.25
450	Bob Friend	12.50	6.25	3.25
451	Cleveland Indians Team	20.00	10.00	6.00
452	Barney Schultz	12.50	6.25	3.25
453	Jake Wood	12.50	6.25	3.25
454a	Art Fowler (Card # on orange background.)	12.50	6.25	3.25
454b	Art Fowler (Card # on white background.)	30.00	15.00	9.00
455	Ruben Amaro	12.50	6.25	3.25
456	Jim Coker	12.50	6.25	3.25
457	Tex Clevenger	12.50	6.25	3.25
458	Al Lopez	20.00	10.00	6.00
459	Dick LeMay	12.50	6.25	3.25
460	Del Crandall	12.50	6.25	3.25
461	Norm Bass	12.50	6.25	3.25
462	Wally Post	12.50	6.25	3.25
463	Joe Schaffernoth	12.50	6.25	3.25
464	Ken Aspromonte	12.50	6.25	3.25
465	Chuck Estrada	12.50	6.25	3.25
466	1963 Rookie Stars (**Bill Freehan, Tony Martinez, Nate Oliver, Jerry Robinson**)	60.00	30.00	15.00

467	Phil Ortega	12.50	6.25	3.25
468	Carroll Hardy	12.50	6.25	3.25
469	Jay Hook	12.50	6.25	3.25
470	Tom Tresh (SP)	40.00	20.00	10.00
471	Ken Retzer	12.50	6.25	3.25
472	Lou Brock	75.00	37.50	18.75
473	New York Mets Team	75.00	37.50	18.75
474	Jack Fisher	12.50	6.25	3.25
475	Gus Triandos	12.50	6.25	3.25
476	Frank Funk	12.50	6.25	3.25
477	Donn Clendenon	12.50	6.25	3.25
478	Paul Brown	12.50	6.25	3.25
479	*Ed Brinkman*	12.50	6.25	3.25
480	Bill Monbouquette	12.50	6.25	3.25
481	Bob Taylor	12.50	6.25	3.25
482	Felix Torres	12.50	6.25	3.25
483	Jim Owens	12.50	6.25	3.25
484	Dale Long (SP)	15.00	7.50	4.50
485	Jim Landis	12.50	6.25	3.25
486	Ray Sadecki	12.50	6.25	3.25
487	John Roseboro	12.50	6.25	3.25
488	Jerry Adair	12.50	6.25	3.25
489	Paul Toth	12.50	6.25	3.25
490	Willie McCovey	100.00	50.00	25.00
491	Harry Craft	12.50	6.25	3.25
492	Dave Wickersham	12.50	6.25	3.25
493	Walt Bond	12.50	6.25	3.25
494	Phil Regan	12.50	6.25	3.25
495	Frank Thomas (SP)	15.00	7.50	4.50
496	1963 Rookie Stars (**Carl Bouldin, Steve Dalkowski, Fred Newman, Jack Smith**)	20.00	10.00	6.00
497	Bennie Daniels	12.50	6.25	3.25
498	Eddie Kasko	12.50	6.25	3.25
499	J.C. Martin	12.50	6.25	3.25
500	Harmon Killebrew (SP)	150.00	75.00	37.50
501	Joe Azcue	12.50	6.25	3.25
502	Daryl Spencer	12.50	6.25	3.25
503	Milwaukee Braves Team	15.00	7.50	4.50
504	Bob Johnson	12.50	6.25	3.25
505	Curt Flood	15.00	7.50	4.50
506	Gene Green	12.50	6.25	3.25
507	Roland Sheldon	12.50	6.25	3.25
508	Ted Savage	12.50	6.25	3.25
509a	7th Series Checklist (507-576) (Copyright centered.)	17.50	8.75	5.25
509b	7th Series Checklist (509-576) (Copyright to right.)	17.50	8.75	5.25
510	Ken McBride	12.50	6.25	3.25
511	Charlie Neal	12.50	6.25	3.25
512	Cal McLish	12.50	6.25	3.25
513	Gary Geiger	12.50	6.25	3.25
514	Larry Osborne	12.50	6.25	3.25
515	Don Elston	12.50	6.25	3.25
516	Purnal Goldy	12.50	6.25	3.25
517	Hal Woodeshick	12.50	6.25	3.25
518	Don Blasingame	12.50	6.25	3.25
519	Claude Raymond	12.50	6.25	3.25
520	Orlando Cepeda	30.00	15.00	9.00
521	Dan Pfister	12.50	6.25	3.25
522	1963 Rookie Stars (**Mel Nelson, Gary Peters, Art Quirk, Jim Roland**)	12.50	6.25	3.25
523	Bill Kunkel	12.50	6.25	3.25
524	St. Louis Cardinals Team	20.00	10.00	6.00
525	Nellie Fox	50.00	25.00	12.50
526	Dick Hall	12.50	6.25	3.25
527	Ed Sadowski	12.50	6.25	3.25
528	Carl Willey	12.50	6.25	3.25
529	Wes Covington	12.50	6.25	3.25
530	Don Mossi	12.50	6.25	3.25
531	Sam Mele	12.50	6.25	3.25
532	Steve Boros	12.50	6.25	3.25
533	Bobby Shantz	12.50	6.25	3.25
534	Ken Walters	12.50	6.25	3.25
535	Jim Perry	12.50	6.25	3.25
536	Norm Larker	12.50	6.25	3.25
537	1963 Rookie Stars (*Pedro Gonzalez, Ken McMullen, Pete Rose, Al Weis*)	825.00	410.00	250.00
538	George Brunet	12.50	6.25	3.25
539	Wayne Causey	12.50	6.25	3.25
540	Bob Clemente	225.00	110.00	67.50
541	Ron Moeller	12.50	6.25	3.25
542	Lou Klimchock	12.50	6.25	3.25
543	Russ Snyder	12.50	6.25	3.25
544	1963 Rookie Stars (*Duke Carmel, Bill Haas, Dick Phillips, Rusty Staub*)	50.00	25.00	12.50
545	Jose Pagan	12.50	6.25	3.25
546	Hal Reniff	12.50	6.25	3.25
547	Gus Bell	12.50	6.25	3.25
548	Tom Satriano	12.50	6.25	3.25
549	1963 Rookie Stars (Marcelino Lopez, Pete Lovrich, Elmo Plaskett, Paul Ratliff)	13.00	6.50	3.25
550	Duke Snider	75.00	37.50	18.75
551	Billy Klaus	12.50	6.25	3.25
552	Detroit Tigers Team	50.00	25.00	12.50
553	1963 Rookie Stars (*Brock Davis, Jim Gosger, John Herrnstein, Willie Stargell*)	120.00	60.00	30.00
554	Hank Fischer	12.50	6.25	3.25
555	John Blanchard	15.00	7.50	3.75
556	Al Worthington	12.50	6.25	3.25
557	Cuno Barragan	12.50	6.25	3.25
558	1963 Rookie Stars (*Bill Faul, Ron Hunt, Bob Lipski, Al Moran*)	13.00	6.50	3.25
559	Danny Murtaugh	12.50	6.25	3.25
560	Ray Herbert	12.50	6.25	3.25
561	Mike de la Hoz	12.50	6.25	3.25
562	1963 Rookie Stars (*Randy Cardinal, Dave McNally, Don Rowe, Ken Rowe*)	25.00	12.50	7.50
563	Mike McCormick	12.50	6.25	3.25
564	George Banks	12.50	6.25	3.25
565	Larry Sherry	12.50	6.25	3.25

566	Cliff Cook	12.50	6.25	3.25
567	Jim Duffalo	12.50	6.25	3.25
568	Bob Sadowski	12.50	6.25	3.25
569	Luis Arroyo	12.50	6.25	3.25
570	Frank Bolling	12.50	6.25	3.25
571	Johnny Klippstein	12.50	6.25	3.25
572	Jack Spring	12.50	6.25	3.25
573	Coot Veal	12.50	6.25	3.25
574	Hal Kolstad	12.50	6.25	3.25
575	Don Cardwell	12.50	6.25	3.25
576	Johnny Temple	13.50	5.00	3.00

1963 Topps Famous Americans Stamps

Actually marketed as "Stamp Gum," this obscure test issue features 80 perforated stamps depicting great Americans from all walks of life, including two baseball players. The 2-9/16" x 1-3/8" stamps are printed in black, blue and yellow and combine a photographic portrait with a cartoon drawing. Centering is often a problem with these pieces. Only the baseball players are listed here.

		NM	EX	VG
50	Babe Ruth	300.00	150.00	90.00
60	Lou Gehrig	250.00	125.00	75.00

1963 Topps Mickey Mantle Plaque

Advertised as a "mask" on high-number 1963 Topps wax wrappers, this is actually a plastic plaque. About 6" x 8", the plaque features a color picture of Mantle in embossed plastic with a faux wood frame, also embossed plastic, around it. A holed tab at top allows hanging.

	NM	EX	VG
Mickey Mantle	3,500	1,750	1,050

1963 Topps Peel-Offs

JIM BUNNING
DET. TIGERS   PITCHER

Measuring 1-1/4" x 2-3/4", Topps Peel-Offs were an insert with 1963 Topps baseball cards. There are 46 players in the unnumbered set, each pictured in a color photo inside an oval with the player's name, team and position in a band below. The back of the Peel-Off is removable, with a sticky surface that made the Peel-Off a popular decorative item among youngsters of the day. Naturally, that makes them quite scarce today. The stickers can be found both blank-backed (much scarcer) and with instructions printed on the peel-off backing.

		NM	EX	VG
Complete Set (46):		525.00	275.00	160.00
Common Player:		4.00	2.00	1.25
(1)	Hank Aaron	35.00	17.50	10.00
(2)	Luis Aparicio	12.50	6.25	3.75
(3)	Richie Ashburn	17.50	8.75	5.25

(4)	Bob Aspromonte	4.00	2.00	1.25
(5)	Ernie Banks	22.50	11.00	6.75
(6)	Ken Boyer	7.50	3.75	2.25
(7)	Jim Bunning	10.00	5.00	3.00
(8)	Johnny Callison	4.00	2.00	1.25
(9)	Orlando Cepeda	10.00	5.00	3.00
(10)	Roberto Clemente	40.00	20.00	12.00
(11)	Rocky Colavito	9.00	4.50	2.75
(12)	Tommy Davis	4.00	2.00	1.25
(13)	Dick Donovan	4.00	2.00	1.25
(14)	Don Drysdale	15.00	7.50	4.50
(15)	Dick Farrell	4.00	2.00	1.25
(16)	Jim Gentile	4.00	2.00	1.25
(17)	Ray Herbert	4.00	2.00	1.25
(18)	Chuck Hinton	4.00	2.00	1.25
(19)	Ken Hubbs	7.50	3.75	2.25
(20)	Al Jackson	4.00	2.00	1.25
(21)	Al Kaline	17.50	8.75	5.25
(22)	Harmon Killebrew	17.50	8.75	5.25
(23)	Sandy Koufax	40.00	20.00	12.00
(24)	Jerry Lumpe	4.00	2.00	1.25
(25)	Art Mahaffey	4.00	2.00	1.25
(26)	Mickey Mantle	100.00	50.00	30.00
(27)	Willie Mays	35.00	17.50	10.00
(28)	Bill Mazeroski	12.50	6.25	3.75
(29)	Bill Monbouquette	4.00	2.00	1.25
(30)	Stan Musial	35.00	17.50	10.00
(31)	Camilo Pascual	4.00	2.00	1.25
(32)	Bob Purkey	4.00	2.00	1.25
(33)	Bobby Richardson	9.00	4.50	2.75
(34)	Brooks Robinson	17.50	8.75	5.25
(35)	Floyd Robinson	4.00	2.00	1.25
(36)	Frank Robinson	17.50	8.75	5.25
(37)	Bob Rodgers	4.00	2.00	1.25
(38)	Johnny Romano	4.00	2.00	1.25
(39)	Jack Sanford	4.00	2.00	1.25
(40)	Norm Siebern	4.00	2.00	1.25
(41)	Warren Spahn	17.50	8.75	5.25
(42)	Dave Stenhouse	4.00	2.00	1.25
(43)	Ralph Terry	4.00	2.00	1.25
(44)	Lee Thomas	4.00	2.00	1.25
(45)	Bill White	4.00	2.00	1.25
(46)	Carl Yastrzemski	20.00	10.00	6.00

1963 Topps Valentine Foldees

Featuring the artwork of 1960s cartoonist Jack Davis, this set of specialty cards had the left and right panels of the 4-1/2" x 2-3/8" pieces slit to allow either the top or the bottom half of the portrait to be folded over the central panel to create funny combinations. There were 55 cards in the series; Babe Ruth is the only baseball player included.

		NM	EX	VG
	Complete Set (55):	150.00	75.00	45.00
6	Babe Ruth	25.00	12.50	7.50

1964 Topps

The 1964 Topps set is a 587-card issue of 2-1/2" x 3-1/2" cards which is considered by many as being among the company's best efforts. Card fronts feature a large color photo which blends into a top panel which contains the team name, while a panel below the picture carries the player's name and position. An interesting innovation on the back is a baseball quiz question which required the rubbing of a white panel to

reveal the answer. As in 1963, specialty cards remained modest in number with a 12-card set of statistical leaders, a few multi-player cards, rookies and World Series highlights. An interesting card is an "In Memoriam" card for Ken Hubbs who was killed in an airplane crash.

		NM	EX	VG
	Complete Set (587):	4,250	2,125	1,250
	Common Player (1-370):	3.50	1.75	1.00
	Common Player (371-522):	6.00	3.00	1.75
	Common Player (523-587):	9.00	4.50	2.75
1	N.L. E.R.A. Leaders (Dick Ellsworth, Bob Friend, Sandy Koufax)	25.00	12.50	6.25
2	A.L. E.R.A. Leaders (Camilo Pascual, Gary Peters, Juan Pizarro)	12.00	3.00	2.00
3	N.L. Pitching Leaders (Sandy Koufax, Jim Maloney, Juan Marichal, Warren Spahn)	20.00	10.00	6.00
4a	A.L. Pitching Leaders (Jim Bouton, Whitey Ford, Camilo Pascual) (Apostrophe after "Pitching" on back.)	17.50	8.75	5.25
4b	A.L. Pitching Leaders (Jim Bouton, Whitey Ford, Camilo Pascual) (No apostrophe.)	17.50	8.75	5.25
5	N.L. Strikeout Leaders (Don Drysdale, Sandy Koufax, Jim Maloney)	20.00	10.00	6.00
6	A.L. Strikeout Leaders (Jim Bunning, Camilo Pascual, Dick Stigman)	12.50	6.25	3.75
7	N.L. Batting Leaders (Hank Aaron, Roberto Clemente, Tommy Davis, Dick Groat)	16.00	8.00	4.75
8	A.L. Batting Leaders (Al Kaline, Rich Rollins, Carl Yastrzemski)	12.50	6.25	3.75
9	N.L. Home Run Leaders (Hank Aaron, Orlando Cepeda, Willie Mays, Willie McCovey)	25.00	12.50	6.25
10	A.L. Home Run Leaders (Bob Allison, Harmon Killebrew, Dick Stuart)	12.00	6.00	3.50
11	N.L. R.B.I. Leaders (Hank Aaron, Ken Boyer, Bill White)	12.50	6.25	3.75
12	A.L. R.B.I. Leaders (Al Kaline, Harmon Killebrew, Dick Stuart)	13.50	6.75	4.00
13	Hoyt Wilhelm	15.00	7.50	4.50
14	Dodgers Rookies (Dick Nen, Nick Willhite)	3.50	1.75	1.00
15	Zoilo Versalles	3.50	1.75	1.00
16	John Boozer	3.50	1.75	1.00
17	Willie Kirkland	3.50	1.75	1.00
18	Billy O'Dell	3.50	1.75	1.00
19	Don Wart	3.50	1.75	1.00
20	Bob Friend	3.50	1.75	1.00
21	Yogi Berra	50.00	25.00	12.50
22	Jerry Adair	3.50	1.75	1.00
23	Chris Zachary	3.50	1.75	1.00
24	Carl Sawatski	3.50	1.75	1.00
25	Bill Monbouquette	3.50	1.75	1.00
26	Gino Cimoli	3.50	1.75	1.00
27	New York Mets Team	7.50	3.75	2.25
28	Claude Osteen	3.50	1.75	1.00
29	Lou Brock	40.00	20.00	10.00
30	Ron Perranoski	3.50	1.75	1.00
31	Dave Nicholson	3.50	1.75	1.00
32	Dean Chance	3.50	1.75	1.00
33	Reds Rookies (Sammy Ellis, Mel Queen)	3.50	1.75	1.00
34	Jim Perry	3.50	1.75	1.00
35	Ed Mathews	20.00	10.00	6.00
36	Hal Reniff	3.50	1.75	1.00
37	Smoky Burgess	3.50	1.75	1.00
38	Jim Wynn	5.00	2.50	1.50
39	Hank Aguirre	3.50	1.75	1.00
40	Dick Groat	3.50	1.75	1.00
41	Friendly Foes (Willie McCovey, Leon Wagner)	10.00	5.00	3.00
42	Moe Drabowsky	3.50	1.75	1.00
43	Roy Sievers	3.50	1.75	1.00
44	Duke Carmel	3.50	1.75	1.00
45	Milt Pappas	3.50	1.75	1.00
46	Ed Brinkman	3.50	1.75	1.00
47	Giants Rookies (Jesus Alou, Ron Herbel)	5.00	2.50	1.75
48	Bob Perry	3.50	1.75	1.00
49	Bill Henry	3.50	1.75	1.00
50	Mickey Mantle	375.00	185.00	110.00
51	Pete Richert	3.50	1.75	1.00
52	Chuck Hinton	3.50	1.75	1.00
53	Denis Menke	3.50	1.75	1.00
54	Sam Mele	3.50	1.75	1.00
55	Ernie Banks	45.00	22.50	11.25
56	Hal Brown	3.50	1.75	1.00
57	Tim Harkness	3.50	1.75	1.00
58	Don Demeter	3.50	1.75	1.00
59	Ernie Broglio	3.50	1.75	1.00
60	Frank Malzone	3.50	1.75	1.00
61	Angel Backstops (Bob Rodgers, Ed Sadowski)	3.50	1.75	1.00
62	Ted Savage	3.50	1.75	1.00
63	Johnny Orsino	3.50	1.75	1.00
64	Ted Abernathy	3.50	1.75	1.00
65	Felipe Alou	4.50	2.25	1.25
66	Eddie Fisher	3.50	1.75	1.00
67	Detroit Tigers Team	6.00	3.00	1.75
68	Willie Davis	3.50	1.75	1.00
69	Clete Boyer	10.00	5.00	3.00
70	Joe Torre	12.00	6.00	3.50
71	Jack Spring	3.50	1.75	1.00
72	Chico Cardenas	3.50	1.75	1.00

73	Jimmie Hall	3.50	1.75	1.00
74	Pirates Rookies (Tom Butters, Bob Priddy)	3.50	1.75	1.00
75	Wayne Causey	3.50	1.75	1.00
76	1st Series Checklist (1-88)	5.00	2.50	1.50
77	Jerry Walker	3.50	1.75	1.00
78	Merritt Ranew	3.50	1.75	1.00
79	Bob Heffner	3.50	1.75	1.00
80	Vada Pinson	9.00	4.50	2.75
81	All-Star Vets (Nellie Fox, Harmon Killebrew)	12.50	6.25	3.75
82	Jim Davenport	3.50	1.75	1.00
83	Gus Triandos	3.50	1.75	1.00
84	Carl Willey	3.50	1.75	1.00
85	Pete Ward	3.50	1.75	1.00
86	Al Downing	3.50	1.75	1.00
87	St. Louis Cardinals Team	6.00	3.00	1.75
88	John Roseboro	3.50	1.75	1.00
89	Boog Powell	7.50	3.75	2.25
90	Earl Battey	3.50	1.75	1.00
91	Bob Bailey	3.50	1.75	1.00
92	Steve Ridzik	3.50	1.75	1.00
93	Gary Geiger	3.50	1.75	1.00
94	Braves Rookies (Jim Britton, Larry Maxie)	3.50	1.75	1.00
95	George Altman	3.50	1.75	1.00
96	Bob Buhl	3.50	1.75	1.00
97	Jim Fregosi	3.50	1.75	1.00
98	Bill Bruton	3.50	1.75	1.00
99	Al Stanek	3.50	1.75	1.00
100	Elston Howard	12.50	6.25	3.75
101	Walt Alston	6.00	3.00	1.75
102	2nd Series Checklist (89-176)	6.00	3.00	1.75
103	Curt Flood	5.00	2.50	1.50
104	Art Mahaffey	3.50	1.75	1.00
105	Woody Held	3.50	1.75	1.00
106	Joe Nuxhall	3.50	1.75	1.00
107	White Sox Rookies (Bruce Howard, Frank Kreutzer)	3.50	1.75	1.00
108	John Wyatt	3.50	1.75	1.00
109	Rusty Staub	10.00	5.00	3.00
110	Albie Pearson	3.50	1.75	1.00
111	Don Elston	3.50	1.75	1.00
112	Bob Tillman	3.50	1.75	1.00
113	Grover Powell	3.50	1.75	1.00
114	Don Lock	3.50	1.75	1.00
115	Frank Bolling	3.50	1.75	1.00
116	Twins Rookies (Tony Oliva, Jay Ward)	9.00	4.50	2.75
117	Earl Francis	3.50	1.75	1.00
118	John Blanchard	5.00	2.50	1.50
119	Gary Kolb	3.50	1.75	1.00
120	Don Drysdale	17.50	8.75	5.25
121	Pete Runnels	3.50	1.75	1.00
122	Don McMahon	3.50	1.75	1.00
123	Jose Pagan	3.50	1.75	1.00
124	Orlando Pena	3.50	1.75	1.00
125	Pete Rose	250.00	125.00	62.50
126	Russ Snyder	3.50	1.75	1.00
127	Angels Rookies (Aubrey Gatewood, Dick Simpson)	3.50	1.75	1.00
128	Mickey Lolich	12.50	6.25	3.75
129	Amado Samuel	3.50	1.75	1.00
130	Gary Peters	3.50	1.75	1.00
131	Steve Boros	3.50	1.75	1.00
132	Milwaukee Braves Team	6.00	3.00	1.75
133	Jim Grant	3.50	1.75	1.00
134	Don Zimmer	5.00	2.50	1.50
135	Johnny Callison	3.50	1.75	1.00
136	World Series Game 1 (Koufax Strikes Out 15)	30.00	15.00	9.00
137	World Series Game 2 (Davis Sparks Rally)	9.00	4.50	2.75
138	World Series Game 3 (L.A. Takes 3rd Straight)	9.00	4.50	2.75
139	World Series Game 4 (Sealing Yanks' Doom)	7.00	3.50	2.00
140	World Series (The Dodgers Celebrate)	7.00	3.50	2.00
141	Danny Murtaugh	3.50	1.75	1.00
142	John Bateman	3.50	1.75	1.00
143	Bubba Phillips	3.50	1.75	1.00
144	Al Worthington	3.50	1.75	1.00
145	Norm Siebern	3.50	1.75	1.00
146	Indians Rookies (Bob Chance, Tommy John)	17.50	8.75	5.25
147	Ray Sadecki	3.50	1.75	1.00
148	J.C. Martin	3.50	1.75	1.00
149	Paul Foytack	3.50	1.75	1.00
150	Willie Mays	120.00	60.00	30.00
151	K.C. Athletics Team	6.00	3.00	1.75
152	Denver Lemaster	3.50	1.75	1.00
153	Dick Williams	3.50	1.75	1.00
154	Dick Tracewski	3.50	1.75	1.00
155	Duke Snider	15.00	7.50	4.50
156	Bill Dailey	3.50	1.75	1.00
157	Gene Mauch	3.50	1.75	1.00
158	Ken Johnson	3.50	1.75	1.00
159	Charlie Dees	3.50	1.75	1.00
160	Ken Boyer	8.00	4.00	2.50
161	Dave McNally	3.50	1.75	1.00
162	Hitting Area (Vada Pinson, Dick Sisler)	5.00	2.50	1.50
163	Donn Clendenon	3.50	1.75	1.00
164	Bud Daley	3.50	1.75	1.00
165	Jerry Lumpe	3.50	1.75	1.00
166	Marty Keough	3.50	1.75	1.00
167	Senators Rookies (Mike Brumley, Lou Piniella)	27.50	13.50	8.25
168	Al Weis	3.50	1.75	1.00
169	Del Crandall	3.50	1.75	1.00
170	Dick Radatz	3.50	1.75	1.00
171	Ty Cline	3.50	1.75	1.00
172	Cleveland Indians Team	6.00	3.00	1.75
173	Ryne Duren	3.50	1.75	1.00
174	Doc Edwards	3.50	1.75	1.00
175	Billy Williams	17.50	8.75	5.25
176	Tracy Stallard	3.50	1.75	1.00

#	Name			
177	Harmon Killebrew	25.00	12.50	6.25
178	Hank Bauer	4.50	2.25	1.25
179	Carl Warwick	3.50	1.75	1.00
180	Tommy Davis	3.50	1.75	1.00
181	Dave Wickersham	3.50	1.75	1.00
182	Sox Sockers (Chuck Schilling, Carl Yastrzemski)	17.50	8.75	5.25
183	Ron Taylor	3.50	1.75	1.00
184	Al Luplow	3.50	1.75	1.00
185	Jim O'Toole	3.50	1.75	1.00
186	Roman Mejias	3.50	1.75	1.00
187	Ed Roebuck	3.50	1.75	1.00
188	3rd Series Checklist (177-264)	5.00	2.50	1.50
189	Bob Hendley	3.50	1.75	1.00
190	Bobby Richardson	12.50	6.25	3.75
191	Clay Dalrymple	3.50	1.75	1.00
192	Cubs Rookies (**John Boccabella, Billy Cowan**)	3.50	1.75	1.00
193	Jerry Lynch	3.50	1.75	1.00
194	John Goryl	3.50	1.75	1.00
195	Floyd Robinson	3.50	1.75	1.00
196	Jim Gentile	3.50	1.75	1.00
197	Frank Lary	3.50	1.75	1.00
198	Len Gabrielson	3.50	1.75	1.00
199	Joe Azcue	3.50	1.75	1.00
200	Sandy Koufax	125.00	62.50	31.25
201	Orioles Rookies (**Sam Bowens, Wally Bunker**)	3.50	1.75	1.00
202	Galen Cisco	3.50	1.75	1.00
203	John Kennedy	3.50	1.75	1.00
204	Matty Alou	3.50	1.75	1.00
205	Nellie Fox	12.50	6.25	3.75
206	Steve Hamilton	3.50	1.75	1.00
207	Fred Hutchinson	3.50	1.75	1.00
208	Wes Covington	3.50	1.75	1.00
209	Bob Allen	3.50	1.75	1.00
210	Carl Yastrzemski	35.00	17.50	10.00
211	Jim Coker	3.50	1.75	1.00
212	Pete Lovrich	3.50	1.75	1.00
213	Los Angeles Angels Team	6.00	3.00	1.75
214	Ken McMullen	3.50	1.75	1.00
215	Ray Herbert	3.50	1.75	1.00
216	Mike de la Hoz	3.50	1.75	1.00
217	Jim King	3.50	1.75	1.00
218	Hank Fischer	3.50	1.75	1.00
219	Young Aces (Jim Bouton, Al Downing)	8.00	4.00	2.50
220	Dick Ellsworth	3.50	1.75	1.00
221	Bob Saverine	3.50	1.75	1.00
222	Bill Pierce	3.50	1.75	1.00
223	George Banks	3.50	1.75	1.00
224	Tommie Sisk	3.50	1.75	1.00
225	Roger Maris	60.00	30.00	15.00
226	Colts Rookies (**Gerald Grote, Larry Yellen**)	5.00	2.50	1.50
227	Barry Latman	3.50	1.75	1.00
228	Felix Mantilla	3.50	1.75	1.00
229	Charley Lau	3.50	1.75	1.00
230	Brooks Robinson	40.00	20.00	10.00
231	Dick Calmus	3.50	1.75	1.00
232	Al Lopez	6.00	3.00	1.75
233	Hal Smith	3.50	1.75	1.00
234	Gary Bell	3.50	1.75	1.00
235	Ron Hunt	3.50	1.75	1.00
236	Bill Faul	3.50	1.75	1.00
237	Chicago Cubs Team	6.50	3.25	2.00
238	Roy McMillan	3.50	1.75	1.00
239	Herm Starrette	3.50	1.75	1.00
240	Bill White	3.50	1.75	1.00
241	Jim Owens	3.50	1.75	1.00
242	Harvey Kuenn	3.50	1.75	1.00
243	Phillies Rookies (**Richie Allen, John Herrnstein**)	17.50	8.75	5.25
244	*Tony LaRussa*	17.50	8.75	5.25
245	Dick Stigman	3.50	1.75	1.00
246	Manny Mota	3.50	1.75	1.00
247	Dave DeBusschere	5.00	2.50	1.50
248	Johnny Pesky	3.50	1.75	1.00
249	Doug Camilli	3.50	1.75	1.00
250	Al Kaline	40.00	20.00	10.00
251	Choo Choo Coleman	3.50	1.75	1.00
252	Ken Aspromonte	3.50	1.75	1.00
253	Wally Post	3.50	1.75	1.00
254	Don Hoak	3.50	1.75	1.00
255	Lee Thomas	3.50	1.75	1.00
256	Johnny Weekly	3.50	1.75	1.00
257	San Francisco Giants Team	6.00	3.00	1.75
258	Garry Roggenburk	3.50	1.75	1.00
259	Harry Bright	3.50	1.75	1.00
260	Frank Robinson	40.00	20.00	10.00
261	Jim Hannan	3.50	1.75	1.00
262	Cardinals Rookies (*Harry Fanok, Mike Shannon*)	9.00	4.50	2.75
263	Chuck Estrada	3.50	1.75	1.00
264	Jim Landis	3.50	1.75	1.00
265	Jim Bunning	12.50	6.25	3.75
266	Gene Freese	3.50	1.75	1.00
267	*Wilbur Wood*	5.00	2.50	1.50
268	Bill's Got It (Danny Murtaugh, Bill Virdon)	3.50	1.75	1.00
269	Ellis Burton	3.50	1.75	1.00
270	Rich Rollins	3.50	1.75	1.00
271	Bob Sadowski	3.50	1.75	1.00
272	Jake Wood	3.50	1.75	1.00
273	Mel Nelson	3.50	1.75	1.00
274	4th Series Checklist (265-352)	6.00	3.00	1.75
275	John Tsitouris	3.50	1.75	1.00
276	Jose Tartabull	3.50	1.75	1.00
277	Ken Retzer	3.50	1.75	1.00
278	Bobby Shantz	3.50	1.75	1.00
279	Joe Koppe	3.50	1.75	1.00
280	Juan Marichal	12.50	6.25	3.75
281	Yankees Rookies (**Jake Gibbs, Tom Metcalf**)	5.00	2.50	1.50
282	Bob Bruce	3.50	1.75	1.00
283	*Tommy McCraw*	3.50	1.75	1.00
284	Dick Schofield	3.50	1.75	1.00
285	Robin Roberts	12.50	6.25	3.75
286	Don Landrum	3.50	1.75	1.00
287	Red Sox Rookies (**Tony Conigliaro, Bill Spanswick**)	50.00	25.00	12.50
288	Al Moran	3.50	1.75	1.00
289	Frank Funk	3.50	1.75	1.00
290	Bob Allison	3.50	1.75	1.00
291	Phil Ortega	3.50	1.75	1.00
292	Mike Roarke	3.50	1.75	1.00
293	Phillies Team	6.00	3.00	1.75
294	Ken Hunt	3.50	1.75	1.00
295	Roger Craig	3.50	1.75	1.00
296	Ed Kirkpatrick	3.50	1.75	1.00
297	Ken MacKenzie	3.50	1.75	1.00
298	Harry Craft	3.50	1.75	1.00
299	Bill Stafford	3.50	1.75	1.00
300	Hank Aaron	125.00	62.50	31.25
301	Larry Brown	3.50	1.75	1.00
302	Dan Pfister	3.50	1.75	1.00
303	Jim Campbell	3.50	1.75	1.00
304	Bob Johnson	3.50	1.75	1.00
305	Jack Lamabe	3.50	1.75	1.00
306	Giant Gunners (Orlando Cepeda, Willie Mays)	40.00	20.00	10.00
307	Joe Gibbon	3.50	1.75	1.00
308	Gene Stephens	3.50	1.75	1.00
309	Paul Toth	3.50	1.75	1.00
310	Jim Gilliam	5.00	2.50	1.50
311	Tom Brown	3.50	1.75	1.00
312	Tigers Rookies (**Fritz Fisher, Fred Gladding**)	3.50	1.75	1.00
313	Chuck Hiller	3.50	1.75	1.00
314	Jerry Buchek	3.50	1.75	1.00
315	Bo Belinsky	3.50	1.75	1.00
316	Gene Oliver	3.50	1.75	1.00
317	Al Smith	3.50	1.75	1.00
318	Twins Team	6.00	3.00	1.75
319	Paul Brown	3.50	1.75	1.00
320	Rocky Colavito	12.50	6.25	3.75
321	Bob Lillis	3.50	1.75	1.00
322	George Brunet	3.50	1.75	1.00
323	John Buzhardt	3.50	1.75	1.00
324	Casey Stengel	12.50	6.25	3.75
325	Hector Lopez	3.50	1.75	1.00
326	Ron Brand	3.50	1.75	1.00
327	Don Blasingame	3.50	1.75	1.00
328	Bob Shaw	3.50	1.75	1.00
329	Russ Nixon	3.50	1.75	1.00
330	Tommy Harper	3.50	1.75	1.00
331	A.L. Bombers (Norm Cash, Al Kaline, Mickey Mantle, Roger Maris)	150.00	75.00	37.50
332	Ray Washburn	3.50	1.75	1.00
333	Billy Moran	3.50	1.75	1.00
334	Lew Krausse	3.50	1.75	1.00
335	Don Mossi	3.50	1.75	1.00
336	Andre Rodgers	3.50	1.75	1.00
337	Dodgers Rookies (**Al Ferrara, Jeff Torborg**)	6.00	3.00	1.75
338	Jack Kralick	3.50	1.75	1.00
339	Walt Bond	3.50	1.75	1.00
340	Joe Cunningham	3.50	1.75	1.00
341	Jim Roland	3.50	1.75	1.00
342	Willie Stargell	30.00	15.00	7.50
343	Senators Team	6.00	3.00	1.75
344	Phil Linz	3.50	1.75	1.00
345	Frank Thomas	3.50	1.75	1.00
346	Joe Jay	3.50	1.75	1.00
347	Bobby Wine	3.50	1.75	1.00
348	Ed Lopat	3.50	1.75	1.00
349	Art Fowler	3.50	1.75	1.00
350	Willie McCovey	20.00	10.00	6.00
351	Dan Schneider	3.50	1.75	1.00
352	Eddie Bressoud	3.50	1.75	1.00
353	Wally Moon	3.50	1.75	1.00
354	Dave Giusti	3.50	1.75	1.00
355	Vic Power	3.50	1.75	1.00
356	Reds Rookies (**Bill McCool, Chico Ruiz**)	3.50	1.75	1.00
357	Charley James	3.50	1.75	1.00
358	Ron Kline	3.50	1.75	1.00
359	Jim Schaffer	3.50	1.75	1.00
360	Joe Pepitone	4.50	2.25	1.25
361	Jay Hook	3.50	1.75	1.00
362	5th Series Checklist (353-429)	6.00	3.00	1.75
363	Dick McAuliffe	3.50	1.75	1.00
364	Joe Gaines	3.50	1.75	1.00
365	Cal McLish	3.50	1.75	1.00
366	Nelson Mathews	3.50	1.75	1.00
367	Fred Whitfield	3.50	1.75	1.00
368	White Sox Rookies (**Fritz Ackley, Don Buford**)	5.50	2.75	1.75
369	Jerry Zimmerman	3.50	1.75	1.00
370	Hal Woodeshick	3.50	1.75	1.00
371	Frank Howard	7.50	3.75	2.25
372	Howie Koplitz	6.00	3.00	1.75
373	Pittsburgh Pirates Team	11.00	5.50	3.25
374	Bobby Bolin	6.00	3.00	1.75
375	Ron Santo	20.00	10.00	6.00
376	Dave Morehead	6.00	3.00	1.75
377	Bob Skinner	6.00	3.00	1.75
378	Braves Rookies (*Jack Smith, Woody Woodward*)	6.00	3.00	1.75
379	Tony Gonzalez	6.00	3.00	1.75
380	Whitey Ford	40.00	20.00	10.00
381	Bob Taylor	6.00	3.00	1.75
382	Wes Stock	6.00	3.00	1.75
383	Bill Rigney	6.00	3.00	1.75
384	Ron Hansen	6.00	3.00	1.75
385	Curt Simmons	6.00	3.00	1.75
386	Lenny Green	6.00	3.00	1.75
387	Terry Fox	6.00	3.00	1.75
388	Athletics Rookies (**John O'Donoghue, George Williams**)	6.00	3.00	1.75
389	Jim Umbricht	6.00	3.00	1.75
390	Orlando Cepeda	17.50	8.75	5.25
391	Sam McDowell	6.00	3.00	1.75
392	Jim Pagliaroni	6.00	3.00	1.75
393	Casey Teaches (Ed Kranepool, Casey Stengel)	12.50	6.25	3.75
394	Bob Miller	6.00	3.00	1.75
395	Tom Tresh	13.50	6.75	4.00
396	Dennis Bennett	6.00	3.00	1.75
397	Chuck Cottier	6.00	3.00	1.75
398	Mets Rookies (**Bill Haas, Dick Smith**)	6.00	3.00	1.75
399	Jackie Brandt	6.00	3.00	1.75
400	Warren Spahn	35.00	17.50	8.75
401	Charlie Maxwell	6.00	3.00	1.75
402	Tom Sturdivant	6.00	3.00	1.75
403	Cincinnati Reds Team	10.00	5.00	3.00
404	Tony Martinez	6.00	3.00	1.75
405	Ken McBride	6.00	3.00	1.75
406	Al Spangler	6.00	3.00	1.75
407	Bill Freehan	6.00	3.00	1.75
408	Cubs Rookies (**Fred Burdette, Jim Stewart**)	6.00	3.00	1.75
409	Bill Fischer	6.00	3.00	1.75
410	Dick Stuart	6.00	3.00	1.75
411	Lee Walls	6.00	3.00	1.75
412	Ray Culp	6.00	3.00	1.75
413	Johnny Keane	6.00	3.00	1.75
414	Jack Sanford	6.00	3.00	1.75
415	Tony Kubek	12.50	6.25	3.75
416	Lee Maye	6.00	3.00	1.75
417	Don Cardwell	6.00	3.00	1.75
418	Orioles Rookies (**Darold Knowles, Les Narum**)	6.00	3.00	1.75
419	*Ken Harrelson*	9.00	4.50	2.75
420	Jim Maloney	6.00	3.00	1.75
421	Camilo Carreon	6.00	3.00	1.75
422	Jack Fisher	6.00	3.00	1.75
423	Tops in N.L. (Hank Aaron, Willie Mays)	125.00	62.50	31.50
424	Dick Bertell	6.00	3.00	1.75
425	Norm Cash	12.00	6.00	3.50
426	Bob Rodgers	6.00	3.00	1.75
427	Don Rudolph	6.00	3.00	1.75
428	Red Sox Rookies (**Archie Skeen, Pete Smith**)	6.00	3.00	1.75
429	Tim McCarver	12.50	6.25	3.75
430	Juan Pizarro	6.00	3.00	1.75
431	George Alusik	6.00	3.00	1.75
432	Ruben Amaro	6.00	3.00	1.75
433	New York Yankees Team	40.00	20.00	10.00
434	Don Nottebart	6.00	3.00	1.75
435	Vic Davalillo	6.00	3.00	1.75
436	Charlie Neal	6.00	3.00	1.75
437	Ed Bailey	6.00	3.00	1.75
438	6th Series Checklist (430-506)	11.00	5.50	3.25
439	Harvey Haddix	6.00	3.00	1.75
440	Bob Clemente	200.00	100.00	50.00
441	Bob Duliba	6.00	3.00	1.75
442	Pumpsie Green	6.00	3.00	1.75
443	Chuck Dressen	6.00	3.00	1.75
444	Larry Jackson	6.00	3.00	1.75
445	Bill Skowron	9.00	4.50	2.75
446	Julian Javier	6.00	3.00	1.75
447	Ted Bowsfield	6.00	3.00	1.75
448	Cookie Rojas	6.00	3.00	1.75
449	Deron Johnson	6.00	3.00	1.75
450	Steve Barber	6.00	3.00	1.75
451	Joe Amalfitano	6.00	3.00	1.75
452	Giants Rookies (*Gil Garrido, Jim Hart*)	7.50	3.75	2.25
453	Frank Baumann	6.00	3.00	1.75
454	Tommie Aaron	6.00	3.00	1.75
455	Bernie Allen	6.00	3.00	1.75
456	Dodgers Rookies (**Wes Parker, John Werhas**)	6.00	3.00	1.75
457	Jesse Gonder	6.00	3.00	1.75
458	Ralph Terry	6.00	3.00	1.75
459	Red Sox Rookies (**Pete Charton, Dalton Jones**)	6.00	3.00	1.75
460	Bob Gibson	30.00	15.00	7.50
461	George Thomas	6.00	3.00	1.75
462	Birdie Tebbetts	6.00	3.00	1.75
463	Don Leppert	6.00	3.00	1.75
464	Dallas Green	6.00	3.00	1.75
465	Mike Hershberger	6.00	3.00	1.75
466	Athletics Rookies (**Dick Green, Aurelio Monteagudo**)	6.00	3.00	1.75
467	Bob Aspromonte	6.00	3.00	1.75
468	Gaylord Perry	40.00	20.00	10.00
469	Cubs Rookies (**Fred Norman, Sterling Slaughter**)	6.00	3.00	1.75
470	Jim Bouton	10.00	5.00	3.00
471	*Gates Brown*	6.50	3.25	2.00
472	Vern Law	6.00	3.00	1.75
473	Baltimore Orioles Team	9.00	4.50	3.75
474	Larry Sherry	6.00	3.00	1.75
475	Ed Charles	6.00	3.00	1.75
476	Braves Rookies (**Rico Carty, Dick Kelley**)	9.00	4.50	2.75
477	Mike Joyce	6.00	3.00	1.75
478	Dick Howser	6.00	3.00	1.75
479	Cardinals Rookies (**Dave Bakenhaster, Johnny Lewis**)	6.00	3.00	1.75
480	Bob Purkey	6.00	3.00	1.75
481	Chuck Schilling	6.00	3.00	1.75
482	Phillies Rookies (**John Briggs, Danny Cater**)	6.00	3.00	1.75
483	Fred Valentine	6.00	3.00	1.75
484	Bill Pleis	6.00	3.00	1.75
485	Tom Haller	6.00	3.00	1.75
486	Bob Kennedy	6.00	3.00	1.75
487	Mike McCormick	6.00	3.00	1.75
488	Yankees Rookies (**Bob Meyer, Pete Mikkelsen**)	6.00	3.00	1.75
489	Julio Navarro	6.00	3.00	1.75
490	Ron Fairly	6.00	3.00	1.75
491	Ed Rakow	6.00	3.00	1.75
492	Colts Rookies (**Jim Beauchamp, Mike White**)	6.00	3.00	1.75

#	Player	NM	EX	VG
493	Don Lee	6.00	3.00	1.75
494	Al Jackson	6.00	3.00	1.75
495	Bill Virdon	6.00	3.00	1.75
496	Chicago White Sox Team	9.00	4.50	2.75
497	Jeoff Long	6.00	3.00	1.75
498	Dave Stenhouse	6.00	3.00	1.75
499	Indians Rookies (Chico Salmon, Gordon Seyfried)	6.00	3.00	1.75
500	Camilo Pascual	6.00	3.00	1.75
501	Bob Veale	6.00	3.00	1.75
502	Angels Rookies (Bobby Knoop, Bob Lee)	6.00	3.00	1.75
503	Earl Wilson	6.00	3.00	1.75
504	Claude Raymond	6.00	3.00	1.75
505	Stan Williams	6.00	3.00	1.75
506	Bobby Bragan	6.00	3.00	1.75
507	John Edwards	6.00	3.00	1.75
508	Diego Segui	6.00	3.00	1.75
509	Pirates Rookies (Gene Alley, Orlando McFarlane)	6.00	3.00	1.75
510	Lindy McDaniel	6.00	3.00	1.75
511	Lou Jackson	6.00	3.00	1.75
512	Tigers Rookies (Willie Horton, Joe Sparma)	22.50	11.00	6.75
513	Don Larsen	6.00	3.00	1.75
514	Jim Hickman	6.00	3.00	1.75
515	Johnny Romano	6.00	3.00	1.75
516	Twins Rookies (Jerry Arrigo, Dwight Siebler)	6.00	3.00	1.75
517a	7th Series Checklist (507-587) (Wrong numbering on back.)	15.00	7.50	4.50
517b	7th Series Checklist (507-587) (Correct numbering on back.)	11.00	5.50	3.25
518	Carl Bouldin	6.00	3.00	1.75
519	Charlie Smith	6.00	3.00	1.75
520	Jack Baldschun	6.00	3.00	1.75
521	Tom Satriano	6.00	3.00	1.75
522	Bobby Tiefenauer	6.00	3.00	1.75
523	Lou Burdette	9.00	4.50	2.75
524	Reds Rookies (Jim Dickson, Bobby Klaus)	9.00	4.50	2.75
525	Al McBean	9.00	4.50	2.75
526	Lou Clinton	9.00	4.50	2.75
527	Larry Bearnarth	9.00	4.50	2.75
528	Athletics Rookies (Dave Duncan, Tom Reynolds)	9.00	4.50	2.75
529	Al Dark	9.00	4.50	2.75
530	Leon Wagner	9.00	4.50	2.75
531	L.A. Dodgers Team	17.50	8.75	5.25
532	Twins Rookies (Bud Bloomfield, Joe Nossek)	9.00	4.50	2.75
533	Johnny Klippstein	9.00	4.50	2.75
534	Gus Bell	9.00	4.50	2.75
535	Phil Regan	9.00	4.50	2.75
536	Mets Rookies (Larry Elliot, John Stephenson)	9.00	4.50	2.75
537	Dan Osinski	9.00	4.50	2.75
538	Minnie Minoso	13.50	6.75	4.00
539	Roy Face	9.00	4.50	2.75
540	Luis Aparicio	35.00	17.50	10.00
541	Braves Rookies (Phil Niekro, Phil Roof)	75.00	37.50	18.75
542	Don Mincher	9.00	4.50	2.75
543	Bob Uecker	40.00	20.00	10.00
544	Colts Rookies (Steve Hertz, Joe Hoerner)	9.00	4.50	2.75
545	Max Alvis	9.00	4.50	2.75
546	Joe Christopher	9.00	4.50	2.75
547	Gil Hodges	15.00	7.50	4.50
548	N.L. Rookies (Wayne Schurr, Paul Speckenbach)	9.00	4.50	2.75
549	Joe Moeller	9.00	4.50	2.75
550	Ken Hubbs - In Memoriam	30.00	15.00	7.50
551	Billy Hoeft	9.00	4.50	2.75
552	Indians Rookies (Tom Kelley, Sonny Siebert)	11.00	5.50	3.25
553	Jim Brewer	9.00	4.50	2.75
554	Hank Foiles	9.00	4.50	2.75
555	Lee Stange	9.00	4.50	2.75
556	Mets Rookies (Steve Dillon, Ron Locke)	9.00	4.50	2.75
557	Leo Burke	9.00	4.50	2.75
558	Don Schwall	9.00	4.50	2.75
559	Dick Phillips	9.00	4.50	2.75
560	Dick Farrell	9.00	4.50	2.75
561	Phillies Rookies (Dave Bennett, Rick Wise)	11.00	5.50	3.25
562	Pedro Ramos	9.00	4.50	2.75
563	Dal Maxvill	9.00	4.50	2.75
564	A.L. Rookies (Joe McCabe, Jerry McNertney)	9.00	4.50	2.75
565	Stu Miller	9.00	4.50	2.75
566	Ed Kranepool	9.00	4.50	2.75
567	Jim Kaat	12.50	6.25	3.75
568	N.L. Rookies (Phil Gagliano, Cap Peterson)	9.00	4.50	2.75
569	Fred Newman	9.00	4.50	2.75
570	Bill Mazeroski	40.00	20.00	10.00
571	Gene Conley	9.00	4.50	2.75
572	A.L. Rookies (Dick Egan, Dave Gray)	9.00	4.50	2.75
573	Jim Duffalo	9.00	4.50	2.75
574	Manny Jimenez	9.00	4.50	2.75
575	Tony Cloninger	9.00	4.50	2.75
576	Mets Rookies (Jerry Hinsley, Bill Wakefield)	9.00	4.50	2.75
577	Gordy Coleman	9.00	4.50	2.75
578	Glen Hobbie	9.00	4.50	2.75
579	Boston Red Sox Team	17.50	8.75	5.25
580	Johnny Podres	11.00	5.50	3.25
581	Yankees Rookies (Pedro Gonzalez, Archie Moore)	9.00	4.50	2.75
582	Rod Kanehl	9.00	4.50	2.75
583	Tito Francona	9.00	4.50	2.75
584	Joel Horlen	9.00	4.50	2.75
585	Tony Taylor	9.00	4.50	2.75
586	Jim Piersall	10.00	5.00	3.00
587	Bennie Daniels	12.00	6.00	3.50

1964 Topps Coins

The 164 metal coins in this set were issued by Topps as inserts in the company's baseball card wax packs. The series is divided into two principal types, 120 "regular" coins and 44 All-Star coins. The 1 1/2" diameter coins feature a full-color background for the player photos in the "regular" series, while the players in the All-Star series are featured against plain red or blue backgrounds. There are two variations each of the Mantle, Causey and Hinton coins among the All-Star subset.

		NM	EX	VG
Complete Set (164):		1,125	550.00	325.00
Common Player:		6.00	3.00	1.75
1	Don Zimmer	6.00	3.00	1.75
2	Jim Wynn	6.00	3.00	1.75
3	Johnny Orsino	6.00	3.00	1.75
4	Jim Bouton	7.50	3.75	2.25
5	Dick Groat	6.00	3.00	1.75
6	Leon Wagner	6.00	3.00	1.75
7	Frank Malzone	6.00	3.00	1.75
8	Steve Barber	6.00	3.00	1.75
9	Johnny Romano	6.00	3.00	1.75
10	Tom Tresh	7.50	3.75	2.25
11	Felipe Alou	6.00	3.00	1.75
12	Dick Stuart	6.00	3.00	1.75
13	Claude Osteen	6.00	3.00	1.75
14	Juan Pizarro	6.00	3.00	1.75
15	Donn Clendenon	6.00	3.00	1.75
16	Jimmie Hall	6.00	3.00	1.75
17	Larry Jackson	6.00	3.00	1.75
18	Brooks Robinson	15.00	7.50	4.50
19	Bob Allison	6.00	3.00	1.75
20	Ed Roebuck	6.00	3.00	1.75
21	Pete Ward	6.00	3.00	1.75
22	Willie McCovey	12.50	6.25	3.75
23	Elston Howard	7.00	3.50	2.00
24	Diego Segui	6.00	3.00	1.75
25	Ken Boyer	7.00	3.50	2.00
26	Carl Yastrzemski	20.00	10.00	6.00
27	Bill Mazeroski	12.50	6.25	3.75
28	Jerry Lumpe	6.00	3.00	1.75
29	Woody Held	6.00	3.00	1.75
30	Dick Radatz	6.00	3.00	1.75
31	Luis Aparicio	10.00	5.00	3.00
32	Dave Nicholson	6.00	3.00	1.75
33	Ed Mathews	15.00	7.50	4.50
34	Don Drysdale	15.00	7.50	4.50
35	Ray Culp	6.00	3.00	1.75
36	Juan Marichal	10.00	5.00	3.00
37	Frank Robinson	15.00	7.50	4.50
38	Chuck Hinton	6.00	3.00	1.75
39	Floyd Robinson	6.00	3.00	1.75
40	Tommy Harper	6.00	3.00	1.75
41	Ron Hansen	6.00	3.00	1.75
42	Ernie Banks	20.00	10.00	6.00
43	Jesse Gonder	6.00	3.00	1.75
44	Billy Williams	10.00	5.00	3.00
45	Vada Pinson	7.00	3.50	2.00
46	Rocky Colavito	9.00	4.50	2.75
47	Bill Monbouquette	6.00	3.00	1.75
48	Max Alvis	6.00	3.00	1.75
49	Norm Siebern	6.00	3.00	1.75
50	John Callison	6.00	3.00	1.75
51	Rich Rollins	6.00	3.00	1.75
52	Ken McBride	6.00	3.00	1.75
53	Don Lock	6.00	3.00	1.75
54	Ron Fairly	6.00	3.00	1.75
55	Roberto Clemente	30.00	15.00	9.00
56	Dick Ellsworth	6.00	3.00	1.75
57	Tommy Davis	6.00	3.00	1.75
58	Tony Gonzalez	6.00	3.00	1.75
59	Bob Gibson	15.00	7.50	4.50
60	Jim Maloney	6.00	3.00	1.75
61	Frank Howard	7.00	3.50	2.00
62	Jim Pagliaroni	6.00	3.00	1.75
63	Orlando Cepeda	10.00	5.00	3.00
64	Ron Perranoski	6.00	3.00	1.75
65	Curt Flood	6.00	3.00	1.75
66	Al McBean	6.00	3.00	1.75
67	Dean Chance	6.00	3.00	1.75
68	Ron Santo	7.50	3.75	2.25
69	Jack Baldschun	6.00	3.00	1.75
70	Milt Pappas	6.00	3.00	1.75
71	Gary Peters	6.00	3.00	1.75
72	Bobby Richardson	7.50	3.75	2.25
73	Lee Thomas	6.00	3.00	1.75
74	Hank Aguirre	6.00	3.00	1.75
75	Carl Willey	6.00	3.00	1.75
76	Camilo Pascual	6.00	3.00	1.75
77	Bob Friend	6.00	3.00	1.75
78	Bill White	6.00	3.00	1.75
79	Norm Cash	7.50	3.75	2.25
80	Willie Mays	30.00	15.00	9.00
81	Duke Carmel	6.00	3.00	1.75
82	Pete Rose	35.00	17.50	10.50
83	Hank Aaron	30.00	15.00	9.00
84	Bob Aspromonte	6.00	3.00	1.75
85	Jim O'Toole	6.00	3.00	1.75
86	Vic Davalillo	6.00	3.00	1.75
87	Bill Freehan	6.00	3.00	1.75
88	Warren Spahn	15.00	7.50	4.50

#	Player	NM	EX	VG
89	Ron Hunt	6.00	3.00	1.75
90	Denis Menke	6.00	3.00	1.75
91	Turk Farrell	6.00	3.00	1.75
92	Jim Hickman	6.00	3.00	1.75
93	Jim Bunning	9.00	4.50	2.75
94	Bob Hendley	6.00	3.00	1.75
95	Ernie Broglio	6.00	3.00	1.75
96	Rusty Staub	7.00	3.50	2.00
97	Lou Brock	10.00	5.00	3.00
98	Jim Fregosi	6.00	3.00	1.75
99	Jim Grant	6.00	3.00	1.75
100	Al Kaline	15.00	7.50	4.50
101	Earl Battey	6.00	3.00	1.75
102	Wayne Causey	6.00	3.00	1.75
103	Chuck Schilling	6.00	3.00	1.75
104	Boog Powell	7.50	3.75	2.25
105	Dave Wickersham	6.00	3.00	1.75
106	Sandy Koufax	30.00	15.00	9.00
107	John Bateman	6.00	3.00	1.75
108	Ed Brinkman	6.00	3.00	1.75
109	Al Downing	6.00	3.00	1.75
110	Joe Azcue	6.00	3.00	1.75
111	Albie Pearson	6.00	3.00	1.75
112	Harmon Killebrew	15.00	7.50	4.50
113	Tony Taylor	6.00	3.00	1.75
114	Alvin Jackson	6.00	3.00	1.75
115	Billy O'Dell	6.00	3.00	1.75
116	Don Demeter	6.00	3.00	1.75
117	Ed Charles	6.00	3.00	1.75
118	Joe Torre	7.50	3.75	2.25
119	Don Nottebart	6.00	3.00	1.75
120	Mickey Mantle	65.00	32.00	19.50
121	Joe Pepitone/AS	7.50	3.75	2.25
122	Dick Stuart/AS	6.00	3.00	1.75
123	Bobby Richardson/AS	7.50	3.75	2.25
124	Jerry Lumpe/AS	6.00	3.00	1.75
125	Brooks Robinson/AS	12.50	6.25	3.75
126	Frank Malzone/AS	6.00	3.00	1.75
127	Luis Aparicio/AS	9.00	4.50	2.75
128	Jim Fregosi/AS	6.00	3.00	1.75
129	Al Kaline/AS	12.50	6.25	3.75
130	Leon Wagner/AS	6.00	3.00	1.75
131a	Mickey Mantle/AS (Lefthanded)	45.00	22.00	13.50
131b	Mickey Mantle/AS (Righthanded)	50.00	25.00	15.00
132	Albie Pearson/AS	6.00	3.00	1.75
133	Harmon Killebrew/AS	12.50	6.25	3.75
134	Carl Yastrzemski/AS	17.50	8.75	5.25
135	Elston Howard/AS	7.00	3.50	2.00
136	Earl Battey/AS	6.00	3.00	1.75
137	Camilo Pascual/AS	6.00	3.00	1.75
138	Jim Bouton/AS	7.00	3.50	2.00
139	Whitey Ford/AS	15.00	7.50	4.50
140	Gary Peters/AS	6.00	3.00	1.75
141	Bill White/AS	6.00	3.00	1.75
142	Orlando Cepeda/AS	9.00	4.50	2.75
143	Bill Mazeroski/AS	10.00	5.00	3.00
144	Tony Taylor/AS	6.00	3.00	1.75
145	Ken Boyer/AS	7.00	3.50	2.00
146	Ron Santo/AS	7.50	3.75	2.25
147	Dick Groat/AS	6.00	3.00	1.75
148	Roy McMillan/AS	6.00	3.00	1.75
149	Hank Aaron/AS	27.50	13.50	8.25
150	Roberto Clemente/AS	27.50	13.50	8.25
151	Willie Mays/AS	27.50	13.50	8.25
152	Vada Pinson/AS	7.00	3.50	2.00
153	Tommy Davis/AS	6.00	3.00	1.75
154	Frank Robinson/AS	12.50	6.25	3.75
155	Joe Torre/AS	7.50	3.75	2.25
156	Tim McCarver/AS	6.00	3.00	1.75
157	Juan Marichal/AS	10.00	5.00	3.00
158	Jim Maloney/AS	6.00	3.00	1.75
159	Sandy Koufax/AS	27.50	13.50	8.25
160	Warren Spahn/AS	12.50	6.25	3.75
161a	Wayne Causey/AS (N.L. on back.)	20.00	10.00	6.00
161b	Wayne Causey/AS (A.L. on back.)	6.00	3.00	1.75
162a	Chuck Hinton/AS (N.L. on back.)	20.00	10.00	6.00
162b	Chuck Hinton/AS (A.L. on back.)	6.00	3.00	1.75
163	Bob Aspromonte/AS	6.00	3.00	1.75
164	Ron Hunt/AS	6.00	3.00	1.75

1964 Topps Giants

Measuring 3-1/8" x 5-1/4" the Topps Giants were the company's first postcard-size issue. The cards feature large color photographs surrounded by white borders with a white baseball containing the player's name, position and team. Card backs carry another photo of the player surrounded by a newspaper-style explanation of the depicted career highlight.

The 60-card set contains primarily stars which means it's an excellent place to find inexpensive cards of Hall of Famers. The '64 Giants were not printed in equal quantity and seven of the cards, including Sandy Koufax and Willie Mays, are significantly scarcer than the remainder of the set.

		NM	EX	VG
	Complete Set (60):	300.00	150.00	75.00
	Common Player:	3.00	1.50	.90
1	Gary Peters	3.00	1.50	.90
2	Ken Johnson	3.00	1.50	.90
3	Sandy Koufax/SP	40.00	20.00	10.00
4	Bob Bailey	3.00	1.50	.90
5	Milt Pappas	3.00	1.50	.90
6	Ron Hunt	3.00	1.50	.90
7	Whitey Ford	10.00	5.00	3.00
8	Roy McMillan	3.00	1.50	.90
9	Rocky Colavito	6.00	3.00	1.75
10	Jim Bunning	6.00	3.00	1.75
11	Roberto Clemente	30.00	15.00	7.50
12	Al Kaline	9.00	4.50	2.75
13	Nellie Fox	7.00	3.50	2.00
14	Tony Gonzalez	3.00	1.50	.90
15	Jim Gentile	3.00	1.50	.90
16	Dean Chance	3.00	1.50	.90
17	Dick Ellsworth	3.00	1.50	.90
18	Jim Fregosi	3.00	1.50	.90
19	Dick Groat	3.00	1.50	.90
20	Chuck Hinton	3.00	1.50	.90
21	Elston Howard	4.50	2.25	1.25
22	Dick Farrell	3.00	1.50	.90
23	Albie Pearson	3.00	1.50	.90
24	Frank Howard	4.00	2.00	1.25
25	Mickey Mantle	60.00	30.00	15.00
26	Joe Torre	5.00	2.50	1.50
27	Ed Brinkman	3.00	1.50	.90
28	Bob Friend/SP	12.50	6.25	3.75
29	Frank Robinson	8.00	4.00	2.50
30	Bill Freehan	3.00	1.50	.90
31	Warren Spahn	8.00	4.00	2.50
32	Camilo Pascual	3.00	1.50	.90
33	Pete Ward	3.00	1.50	.90
34	Jim Maloney	3.00	1.50	.90
35	Dave Wickersham	3.00	1.50	.90
36	Johnny Callison	3.00	1.50	.90
37	Juan Marichal	7.00	3.50	2.00
38	Harmon Killebrew	9.00	4.50	2.75
39	Luis Aparicio	7.00	3.50	2.00
40	Dick Radatz	3.00	1.50	.90
41	Bob Gibson	7.00	3.50	2.00
42	Dick Stuart/SP	15.00	7.50	4.50
43	Tommy Davis	3.00	1.50	.90
44	Tony Oliva	3.50	1.75	1.00
45	Wayne Causey/SP	15.00	7.50	4.50
46	Max Alvis	3.00	1.50	.90
47	Galen Cisco/SP	13.50	6.75	4.00
48	Carl Yastrzemski	9.00	4.50	2.75
49	Hank Aaron	35.00	17.50	8.75
50	Brooks Robinson	9.00	4.50	2.75
51	Willie Mays/SP	50.00	25.00	12.50
52	Billy Williams	8.00	4.00	2.50
53	Juan Pizarro	3.00	1.50	.90
54	Leon Wagner	3.00	1.50	.90
55	Orlando Cepeda	7.00	3.50	2.00
56	Vada Pinson	3.50	1.75	1.00
57	Ken Boyer	3.50	1.75	1.00
58	Ron Santo	5.00	2.50	1.50
59	John Romano	3.00	1.50	.90
60	Bill Skowron/SP	20.00	10.00	5.00

1964 Topps Photo Tatoos

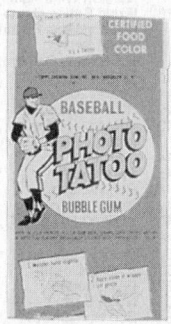

Apparently not content to leave the skin of American children without adornment, Topps jumped back into the tattoo field in 1964 with the release of a new series, measuring 1-9/16" x 3-1/2". The picture side for the 20 team tattoos gives the team logo and name.

		NM	EX	VG
	Complete Set (79):	3,000	1,500	900.00
	Common Player:	15.00	7.50	4.50
	Unopened Pack:	160.00		
(1)	Hank Aaron	135.00	65.00	40.00
(2)	Hank Aguirre	15.00	7.50	4.50
(3)	Max Alvis	15.00	7.50	4.50
(4)	Ernie Banks	80.00	40.00	24.00
(5)	Steve Barber	15.00	7.50	4.50
(6)	Ken Boyer	20.00	10.00	6.00
(7)	Johnny Callison	15.00	7.50	4.50
(8)	Norm Cash	20.00	10.00	6.00
(9)	Wayne Causey	15.00	7.50	4.50
(10)	Orlando Cepeda	50.00	25.00	15.00
(11)	Rocky Colavito	50.00	25.00	15.00
(12)	Ray Culp	15.00	7.50	4.50
(13)	Vic Davalillo	15.00	7.50	4.50

(14)	Moe Drabowsky	15.00	7.50	4.50
(15)	Dick Ellsworth	15.00	7.50	4.50
(16)	Curt Flood	15.00	7.50	4.50
(17)	Bill Freehan	15.00	7.50	4.50
(18)	Jim Fregosi	15.00	7.50	4.50
(19)	Bob Friend	15.00	7.50	4.50
(20)	Dick Groat	15.00	7.50	4.50
(21)	Woody Held	15.00	7.50	4.50
(22)	Frank Howard	20.00	10.00	6.00
(23)	Al Jackson	15.00	7.50	4.50
(24)	Larry Jackson	15.00	7.50	4.50
(25)	Ken Johnson	15.00	7.50	4.50
(26)	Al Kaline	60.00	30.00	18.00
(27)	Harmon Killebrew (Green background.)	60.00	30.00	18.00
(28)	Harmon Killebrew (Red background.)	60.00	30.00	18.00
(29)	Sandy Koufax (Horizontal band.)	135.00	65.00	40.00
(30)	Sandy Koufax (Diagonal band.)	145.00	75.00	45.00
(31)	Don Lock	15.00	7.50	4.50
(32)	Frank Malzone	15.00	7.50	4.50
(33)	Mickey Mantle (Diagonal yellow band.)	325.00	160.00	100.00
(34)	Mickey Mantle (Red triangle.)	325.00	160.00	100.00
(35)	Eddie Mathews	60.00	30.00	18.00
(36)	Willie Mays (Yellow background encompasses head.)	135.00	65.00	40.00
(37)	Willie Mays (Yellow background ears-to-chin.)	135.00	65.00	40.00
(38)	Bill Mazeroski	60.00	30.00	18.00
(39)	Ken McBride	15.00	7.50	4.50
(40)	Bill Monbouquette	15.00	7.50	4.50
(41)	Dave Nicholson	15.00	7.50	4.50
(42)	Claude Osteen	15.00	7.50	4.50
(43)	Milt Pappas	15.00	7.50	4.50
(44)	Camilio Pascual	15.00	7.50	4.50
(45)	Albie Pearson	15.00	7.50	4.50
(46)	Ron Perranoski	15.00	7.50	4.50
(47)	Gary Peters	15.00	7.50	4.50
(48)	Boog Powell	20.00	10.00	6.00
(49)	Frank Robinson	60.00	30.00	18.00
(50)	John Romano	15.00	7.50	4.50
(51)	Norm Siebern	15.00	7.50	4.50
(52)	Warren Spahn	60.00	30.00	18.00
(53)	Dick Stuart	15.00	7.50	4.50
(54)	Lee Thomas	15.00	7.50	4.50
(55)	Joe Torre	25.00	12.50	7.50
(56)	Pete Ward	15.00	7.50	4.50
(57)	Carlton Willey	15.00	7.50	4.50
(58)	Billy Williams	60.00	30.00	18.00
(59)	Carl Yastrzemski	75.00	37.50	22.50
(60)	Baltimore Orioles Logo	20.00	10.00	6.00
(61)	Boston Red Sox Logo	20.00	10.00	6.00
(62)	Chicago Cubs Logo	20.00	10.00	6.00
(63)	Chicago White Sox Logo	20.00	10.00	6.00
(64)	Cincinnati Reds Logo	20.00	10.00	6.00
(65)	Cleveland Indians Logo	20.00	10.00	6.00
(66)	Detroit Tigers Logo	20.00	10.00	6.00
(67)	Houston Colts Logo	25.00	12.50	7.50
(68)	Kansas City Athletics Logo	20.00	10.00	6.00
(69)	Los Angeles Angels Logo	20.00	10.00	6.00
(70)	Los Angeles Dodgers Logo	20.00	10.00	6.00
(71)	Milwaukee Braves Logo	20.00	10.00	6.00
(72)	Minnesota Twins Logo	20.00	10.00	6.00
(73)	New York Mets Logo	25.00	12.50	7.50
(74)	New York Yankees Logo	25.00	12.50	7.50
(75)	Philadelphia Phillies Logo	20.00	10.00	6.00
(76)	Pittsburgh Pirates Logo	20.00	10.00	6.00
(77)	St. Louis Cardinals Logo	20.00	10.00	6.00
(78)	San Francisco Giants Logo	20.00	10.00	6.00
(79)	Washington Senators Logo	20.00	10.00	6.00

1964 Topps Rookie All-Star Banquet

Since 1959, Topps has sponsored a formal post-season banquet to honor its annual Rookie All-Star team. In 1964, the gum company deviated from the tradition dinner program by issuing a 36-card boxed set. Each card is printed in black-and-white, with red or light blue graphic highlights. The first seven cards in the set feature Topps staff and baseball dignitaries involved in the selection of the rookie team. Cards #8-12 are composite photos of the 1959-63 Rookie All-Star team. Cards #13-34A showcase the '64 honorees. Each player's card is matched with a card from the team's public relations officer extolling the rookie's virtues. Each card in this unique dinner program measures 3" x 5-1/4" and is numbered as a "PAGE" in the lower-right corner.

	NM	EX	VG
Complete Boxed Set (36):	2,800	1,400	850.00

		NM	EX	VG
	Common Player:	17.50	8.75	5.25
1	"6th Annual Topps Rookie All-Star Team Awards" Header Card	17.50	8.75	5.25
2	The Baseball World Votes (Tommy Davis, Jeff Torborg, Ron Santo, Billy Williams)	17.50	8.75	5.25
3	The Baseball World Votes (Six more clubhouse scenes.)	17.50	8.75	5.25
4	Topps Rookie All-Star Team Honorary Election Committee (Photos of media and Hall of Famers Hank Greenberg and Fran Frisch.)	55.00	27.00	16.50
5	Topps Rookie All-Star Team Honorary Election Committee (Photos of five media, Topps' VP Joel Shorin and Jackie Robinson.)	120.00	60.00	35.00
6	Executive Director of the Committee and His Associates (Topps' Cy Berger, three others.)	17.50	8.75	5.25
7	Topps Salutes Joe Garagiola (Joe Garagiola)	95.00	45.00	25.00
8	The 1959 Topps Rookie All-Star Team (Willie McCovey, Pumpsie Green, Joe Koppe, Jim Baxes, Bobby Allison, Ron Fairly, Willie Tasby, John Romano, Jim Perry, Jim O'Toole)	225.00	110.00	65.00
9	The 1960 Topps Rookie All-Star Team (Jim Gentile, Julian Javier, Ron Hansen, Ron Santo, Tommy Davis, Frank Howard, Tony Curry, Jimmie Coker, Chuck Estrada, Dick Stigman)	225.00	110.00	65.00
10	The 1961 Topps Rookie All-Star Team (J.C. Martin, Jake Wood, Dick Howser, Charlie Smith, Billy Williams, Lee Thomas, Floyd Robinson, Joe Torre, Don Schwall, Jack Curtis)	185.00	90.00	55.00
11	The 1962 Topps Rookie All-Star Team (Fred Whitfield, Bernie Allen, Tom Tresh, Ed Charles, Manny Jiminez, Al Luplow, Boog Powell, Buck Rodgers, Dean Chance, Al Jackson)	185.00	90.00	55.00
12	The 1963 Topps Rookie All-Star Team (Pete Rose, Rusty Staub, Al Weis, Pete Ward, Jimmie Hall, Vic Davalillo, Tommy Harper, Jesse Gonder, Ray Culp, Gary Peters)	1,400	700.00	425.00
13	1964 Topps Rookie All-Star Team Header Card	17.50	8.75	5.25
14	Ed Uhas, Cleveland Indians PR	17.50	8.75	5.25
15	Bob Chance	135.00	65.00	40.00
16	Garry Schumacher, S.F. Giants PR	17.50	8.75	5.25
17	Hal Lanier	135.00	65.00	40.00
18	Larry Shenk, Phillies PR	17.50	8.75	5.25
19	Richie Allen	300.00	150.00	90.00
20	Jim Schaaf, Athletics PR	17.50	8.75	5.25
21	Bert Campaneris	160.00	80.00	45.00
22	Ernie Johnson, Braves PR	17.50	8.75	5.25
23	Rico Carty	160.00	80.00	45.00
24	Bill Crowley, Red Sox PR	17.50	8.75	5.25
25	Tony Conigliaro	345.00	175.00	100.00
26	Tom Mee, Twins PR	17.50	8.75	5.25
27	Tony Oliva	210.00	100.00	60.00
28	Burt Hawkins, Senators PR	17.50	8.75	5.25
29	Mike Brumley	135.00	65.00	40.00
30	Hank Zureick, Reds PR	17.50	8.75	5.25
31	Bill McCool	135.00	65.00	40.00
32	Rob Brown, Orioles PR	17.50	8.75	5.25
33	Wally Bunker	135.00	65.00	40.00
34	"5th Annual Topps Minor League Player of the Year" Header Card	17.50	8.75	5.25
34A	Luis Tiant (Minor League Player of the Year)	160.00	80.00	45.00
35	Rookie All-Star Trophy	17.50	8.75	5.25

1964 Topps Stand-Ups

These 2-1/2" x 3-1/2" cards were the first since the All-Star sets of 1951 to be die-cut. This made it possible for a folded card to stand on display. The 77-cards in the set feature color photographs of the player with yellow and green backgrounds. Directions for folding are on the yellow top background, and when folded only the green background remains. Of the 77 cards, 55 were double-printed while 22 were single-printed, making them twice as scarce.

	NM	EX	VG
Complete Set (77):	3,500	1,750	1,050
Common Player:	12.00	6.00	3.50
Wax Pack (1):	600.00		
(1) Hank Aaron	180.00	90.00	45.00
(2) Hank Aguirre	12.00	6.00	3.50
(3) George Altman	12.00	6.00	3.50
(4) Max Alvis	12.00	6.00	3.50
(5) Bob Aspromonte	12.00	6.00	3.50
(6) Jack Baldschun/SP	20.00	10.00	6.00
(7) Ernie Banks	100.00	50.00	25.00
(8) Steve Barber	12.00	6.00	3.50
(9) Earl Battey	12.00	6.00	3.50
(10) Ken Boyer	20.00	10.00	6.00
(11) Ernie Broglio	12.00	6.00	3.50
(12) Johnny Callison	12.00	6.00	3.50
(13) Norm Cash/SP	65.00	32.50	16.25
(14) Wayne Causey	12.00	6.00	3.50
(15) Orlando Cepeda	27.50	13.50	8.25
(16) Ed Charles	12.00	6.00	3.50
(17) Roberto Clemente	240.00	120.00	60.00
(18) Donn Clendenon/SP	20.00	10.00	6.00
(19) Rocky Colavito	25.00	12.50	7.50
(20) Ray Culp/SP	20.00	10.00	6.00
(21) Tommy Davis	12.00	6.00	3.50
(22) Don Drysdale/SP	140.00	70.00	35.00
(23) Dick Ellsworth	12.00	6.00	3.50
(24) Dick Farrell	12.00	6.00	3.50
(25) Jim Fregosi	12.00	6.00	3.50
(26) Bob Friend	12.00	6.00	3.50
(27) Jim Gentile	12.00	6.00	3.50
(28) Jesse Gonder/SP	20.00	10.00	6.00
(29) Tony Gonzalez/SP	20.00	10.00	6.00
(30) Dick Groat	12.50	6.25	3.75
(31) Woody Held	12.00	6.00	3.50
(32) Chuck Hinton	12.00	6.00	3.50
(33) Elston Howard	20.00	10.00	6.00
(34) Frank Howard/SP	27.50	13.50	8.25
(35) Ron Hunt	12.00	6.00	3.50
(36) Al Jackson	12.00	6.00	3.50
(37) Ken Johnson	12.00	6.00	3.50
(38) Al Kaline	100.00	50.00	25.00
(39) Harmon Killebrew	100.00	50.00	25.00
(40) Sandy Koufax	200.00	100.00	50.00
(41) Don Lock/SP	20.00	10.00	6.00
(42) Jerry Lumpe/SP	20.00	10.00	6.00
(43) Jim Maloney	12.00	6.00	3.50
(44) Frank Malzone	12.00	6.00	3.50
(45) Mickey Mantle	550.00	275.00	137.50
(46) Juan Marichal/SP	120.00	60.00	30.00
(47) Ed Mathews/SP	150.00	75.00	37.50
(48) Willie Mays	300.00	150.00	75.00
(49) Bill Mazeroski	22.50	11.00	7.00
(50) Ken McBride	12.00	6.00	3.50
(51) Willie McCovey/SP	120.00	60.00	30.00
(52) Claude Osteen	12.00	6.00	3.50
(53) Jim O'Toole	12.00	6.00	3.50
(54) Camilo Pascual	12.00	6.00	3.50
(55) Albie Pearson/SP	20.00	10.00	6.00
(56) Gary Peters	12.00	6.00	3.50
(57) Vada Pinson	15.00	7.50	4.50
(58) Juan Pizarro	12.00	6.00	3.50
(59) Boog Powell	20.00	10.00	6.00
(60) Bobby Richardson	20.00	10.00	6.00
(61) Brooks Robinson	100.00	50.00	25.00
(62) Floyd Robinson	12.00	6.00	3.50
(63) Frank Robinson	100.00	50.00	25.00
(64) Ed Roebuck/SP	20.00	10.00	6.00
(65) Rich Rollins	12.00	6.00	3.50
(66) Johnny Romano	12.00	6.00	3.50
(67) Ron Santo/SP	50.00	25.00	12.50
(68) Norm Siebern	12.00	6.00	3.50
(69) Warren Spahn/SP	150.00	75.00	37.50
(70) Dick Stuart/SP	20.00	10.00	6.00
(71) Lee Thomas	12.00	6.00	3.50
(72) Joe Torre	30.00	15.00	9.00
(73) Pete Ward	12.00	6.00	3.50
(74) Bill White/SP	25.00	12.50	7.50
(75) Billy Williams/SP	120.00	60.00	30.00
(76) Hal Woodeshick/SP	20.00	10.00	6.00
(77) Carl Yastrzemski/SP	500.00	250.00	125.00

1965 Topps

about the player. There are no multi-player cards in the 1965 set other than the usual team cards and World Series highlights. Rookie cards include team, as well as league groupings from two to four players per card. Also present in the 598-card set are statistical leaders. Certain cards in the high-number series (#523-598) were produced in lesser quantities than the rest of the series. Known as "short-prints," and valued somewhat higher than the other high numbers, they are indicated in the checklist by an (SP) after the player name.

		NM	EX	VG
Complete Set (598):		4,000	2,000	1,200
Common Player (1-370):		3.00	1.50	.90
Common Player (371-598):		6.00	3.00	1.75
1	A.L. Batting Leaders (Elston Howard, Tony Oliva, Brooks Robinson)	25.00	12.50	6.25
2	N.L. Batting Leaders (Hank Aaron, Rico Carty, Roberto Clemente)	20.00	10.00	5.00
3	A.L. Home Run Leaders (Harmon Killebrew, Mickey Mantle, Boog Powell)	40.00	20.00	10.00
4	N.L. Home Run Leaders (Johnny Callison, Orlando Cepeda, Jim Hart, Willie Mays, Billy Williams)	20.00	10.00	5.00
5	A.L. RBI Leaders (Harmon Killebrew, Mickey Mantle, Brooks Robinson, Dick Stuart)	35.00	17.50	10.00
6	N.L. RBI Leaders (Ken Boyer, Willie Mays, Ron Santo)	13.50	6.75	4.00
7	A.L. ERA Leaders (Dean Chance, Joel Horlen)	3.50	1.75	1.00
8	N.L. ERA Leaders (Don Drysdale, Sandy Koufax)	20.00	10.00	5.00
9	A.L. Pitching Leaders (Wally Bunker, Dean Chance, Gary Peters, Juan Pizarro, Dave Wickersham)	3.50	1.75	1.00
10	N.L. Pitching Leaders (Larry Jackson, Juan Marichal, Ray Sadecki)	4.50	2.25	1.25
11	A.L. Strikeout Leaders (Dean Chance, Al Downing, Camilo Pascual)	3.50	1.75	1.00
12	N.L. Strikeout Leaders (Don Drysdale, Bob Gibson, Bob Veale)	12.00	6.00	3.50
13	Pedro Ramos	3.00	1.50	.90
14	Len Gabrielson	3.00	1.50	.90
15	Robin Roberts	12.50	6.25	3.75
16	Astros Rookies (*Sonny Jackson, Joe Morgan*)	60.00	30.00	15.00
17	Johnny Romano	3.00	1.50	.90
18	Bill McCool	3.00	1.50	.90
19	Gates Brown	3.00	1.50	.90
20	Jim Bunning	10.00	5.00	3.00
21	Don Blasingame	3.00	1.50	.90
22	Charlie Smith	3.00	1.50	.90
23	Bob Tiefenauer	3.00	1.50	.90
24	Twins Team	7.50	3.75	2.25
25	Al McBean	3.00	1.50	.90
26	Bobby Knoop	3.00	1.50	.90
27	Dick Bertell	3.00	1.50	.90
28	Barney Schultz	3.00	1.50	.90
29	Felix Mantilla	3.00	1.50	.90
30	Jim Bouton	4.50	2.25	1.25
31	Mike White	3.00	1.50	.90
32	Herman Franks	3.00	1.50	.90
33	Jackie Brandt	3.00	1.50	.90
34	Cal Koonce	3.00	1.50	.90
35	Ed Charles	3.00	1.50	.90
36	Bobby Wine	3.00	1.50	.90
37	Fred Gladding	3.00	1.50	.90
38	Jim King	3.00	1.50	.90
39	Gerry Arrigo	3.00	1.50	.90
40	Frank Howard	4.50	2.25	1.25
41	White Sox Rookies (**Bruce Howard, Marv Staehle**)	3.00	1.50	.90
42	Earl Wilson	3.00	1.50	.90
43	Mike Shannon	3.00	1.50	.90
44	Wade Blasingame	3.00	1.50	.90
45	Roy McMillan	3.00	1.50	.90
46	Bob Lee	3.00	1.50	.90
47	Tommy Harper	3.00	1.50	.90
48	Claude Raymond	3.00	1.50	.90
49	Orioles Rookies (**Curt Blefary, John Miller**)	3.00	1.50	.90
50	Juan Marichal	13.50	6.75	4.00
51	Billy Bryan	3.00	1.50	.90
52	Ed Roebuck	3.00	1.50	.90
53	Dick McAuliffe	3.00	1.50	.90
54	Joe Gibbon	3.00	1.50	.90
55	Tony Conigliaro	12.00	6.00	3.50
56	Ron Kline	3.00	1.50	.90
57	Cards Team	7.50	3.75	2.25
58	Fred Talbot	3.00	1.50	.90
59	Nate Oliver	3.00	1.50	.90
60	Jim O'Toole	3.00	1.50	.90
61	Chris Cannizzaro	3.00	1.50	.90
62	Jim Katt (Kaat)	3.50	1.75	1.00
63	Ty Cline	3.00	1.50	.90
64	Lou Burdette	3.00	1.50	.90
65	Tony Kubek	11.00	5.50	3.25
66	Bill Rigney	3.00	1.50	.90
67	Harvey Haddix	3.00	1.50	.90
68	Del Crandall	3.00	1.50	.90
69	Bill Virdon	3.00	1.50	.90
70	Bill Skowron	3.50	1.75	1.00
71	John O'Donoghue	3.00	1.50	.90
72	Tony Gonzalez	3.00	1.50	.90
73	Dennis Ribant	3.00	1.50	.90
74	Red Sox Rookies (**Rico Petrocelli, Jerry Stephenson**)	13.50	6.75	4.00
75	Deron Johnson	3.00	1.50	.90
76	Sam McDowell	3.00	1.50	.90
77	Doug Camilli	3.00	1.50	.90
78	Dal Maxvill	3.00	1.50	.90
79a	1st Series Checklist (1-88) (61 is C. Cannizzaro)	3.50	1.75	1.00
79b	1st Series Checklist (1-88) (61 is Cannizzaro)	7.00	3.50	2.00
80	Turk Farrell	3.00	1.50	.90
81	Don Buford	3.00	1.50	.90
82	Braves Rookies (**Santos Alomar, John Braun**)	4.50	2.25	1.25
83	George Thomas	3.00	1.50	.90
84	Ron Herbel	3.00	1.50	.90
85	Willie Smith	3.00	1.50	.90
86	Les Narum	3.00	1.50	.90
87	Nelson Mathews	3.00	1.50	.90
88	Jack Lamabe	3.00	1.50	.90
89	Mike Hershberger	3.00	1.50	.90
90	Rich Rollins	3.00	1.50	.90
91	Cubs Team	7.50	3.75	2.25
92	Dick Howser	3.00	1.50	.90
93	Jack Fisher	3.00	1.50	.90
94	Charlie Lau	3.00	1.50	.90
95	Bill Mazeroski	12.50	6.25	3.75
96	Sonny Siebert	3.00	1.50	.90
97	Pedro Gonzalez	3.00	1.50	.90
98	Bob Miller	3.00	1.50	.90
99	Gil Hodges	9.00	4.50	2.75
100	Ken Boyer	4.50	2.25	1.25
101	Fred Newman	3.00	1.50	.90
102	Steve Boros	3.00	1.50	.90
103	Harvey Kuenn	3.00	1.50	.90
104	2nd Series Checklist (89-176)	4.00	2.00	1.25
105	Chico Salmon	3.00	1.50	.90
106	Gene Oliver	3.00	1.50	.90
107	Phillies Rookies (**Pat Corrales, Costen Shockley**)	4.00	2.00	1.25
108	Don Mincher	3.00	1.50	.90
109	Walt Bond	3.00	1.50	.90
110	Ron Santo	12.00	6.00	3.50
111	Lee Thomas	3.00	1.50	.90
112	Derrell Griffith	3.00	1.50	.90
113	Steve Barber	3.00	1.50	.90
114	Jim Hickman	3.00	1.50	.90
115	Bobby Richardson	20.00	10.00	5.00
116	Cardinals Rookies (*Dave Dowling, Bob Tolan*)	3.00	1.50	.90
117	Wes Stock	3.00	1.50	.90
118	*Hal Lanier*	3.00	1.50	.90
119	John Kennedy	3.00	1.50	.90
120	Frank Robinson	40.00	20.00	10.00
121	Gene Alley	3.00	1.50	.90
122	Bill Pleis	3.00	1.50	.90
123	Frank Thomas	3.00	1.50	.90
124	Tom Satriano	3.00	1.50	.90
125	Juan Pizarro	3.00	1.50	.90
126	Dodgers Team	7.50	3.75	2.25
127	Frank Lary	3.00	1.50	.90
128	Vic Davalillo	3.00	1.50	.90
129	Bennie Daniels	3.00	1.50	.90
130	Al Kaline	40.00	20.00	10.00
131	Johnny Keane	4.00	2.00	1.25
132	World Series Game 1 (Cards Take Opener)	10.00	5.00	3.00
133	World Series Game 2 (Stottlemyre Wins)	15.00	7.50	3.75
134	World Series Game 3 (Mantle's Clutch HR)	60.00	30.00	15.00
135	World Series Game 4 (Boyer's Grand-Slam)	10.00	5.00	3.00
136	World Series Game 5 (10th Inning Triumph)	7.00	3.50	2.00
137	World Series Game 6 (Bouton Wins Again)	10.00	5.00	3.00
138	World Series Game 7 (Gibson Wins Finale)	15.00	7.50	4.50
139	World Series (The Cards Celebrate)	9.00	4.50	2.75
140	Dean Chance	3.00	1.50	.90
141	Charlie James	3.00	1.50	.90
142	Bill Monbouquette	3.00	1.50	.90
143	Pirates Rookies (**John Gelnar, Jerry May**)	3.00	1.50	.90
144	Ed Kranepool	3.00	1.50	.90
145	*Luis Tiant*	20.00	10.00	5.00
146	Ron Hansen	3.00	1.50	.90
147	Dennis Bennett	3.00	1.50	.90
148	Willie Kirkland	3.00	1.50	.90
149	Wayne Schurr	3.00	1.50	.90
150	Brooks Robinson	40.00	20.00	10.00
151	Athletics Team	7.50	3.75	2.25
152	Phil Ortega	3.00	1.50	.90
153	Norm Cash	9.00	4.50	2.75
154	Bob Humphreys	3.00	1.50	.90
155	Roger Maris	50.00	25.00	15.00
156	Bob Sadowski	3.00	1.50	.90
157	Zoilo Versalles	3.00	1.50	.90
158	Dick Sisler	3.00	1.50	.90
159	Jim Duffalo	3.00	1.50	.90
160	Bob Clemente	200.00	100.00	50.00
161	Frank Baumann	3.00	1.50	.90
162	Russ Nixon	3.00	1.50	.90
163	John Briggs	3.00	1.50	.90
164	Al Spangler	3.00	1.50	.90
165	Dick Ellsworth	3.00	1.50	.90
166	Indians Rookies (**Tommie Agee, George Culver**)	9.00	4.50	2.75
167	Bill Wakefield	3.00	1.50	.90
168	Dick Green	3.00	1.50	.90
169	Dave Vineyard	3.00	1.50	.90
170	Hank Aaron	160.00	80.00	40.00
171	Jim Roland	3.00	1.50	.90
172	Jim Piersall	6.00	3.00	1.75
173	Tigers Team	8.00	4.00	2.50
174	Joe Jay	3.00	1.50	.90
175	Bob Aspromonte	3.00	1.50	.90
176	Willie McCovey	20.00	10.00	5.00
177	Pete Mikkelsen	3.00	1.50	.90
178	Dalton Jones	3.00	1.50	.90

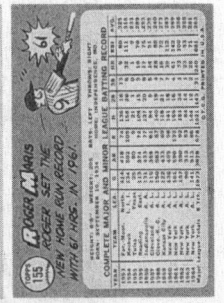

The 1965 Topps set features a large color photograph of the player surrounded by a colored, round-cornered frame and a white border. The bottom of the 2-1/2" x 3-1/2" cards includes a pennant with a color team logo and name over the left side of a rectangle which features the player's name and position. Backs feature statistics and, if space allowed, a cartoon and headline

#	Name			
179	Hal Woodeshick	3.00	1.50	.90
180	Bob Allison	3.00	1.50	.90
181	Senators Rookies (Don Loun, Joe McCabe)	3.00	1.50	.90
182	Mike de la Hoz	3.00	1.50	.90
183	Dave Nicholson	3.00	1.50	.90
184	John Boozer	3.00	1.50	.90
185	Max Alvis	3.00	1.50	.90
186	Billy Cowan	3.00	1.50	.90
187	Casey Stengel	12.50	6.25	3.75
188	Sam Bowens	3.00	1.50	.90
189	3rd Series Checklist (177-264)	6.50	3.25	2.00
190	Bill White	3.00	1.50	.90
191	Phil Regan	3.00	1.50	.90
192	Jim Coker	3.00	1.50	.90
193	Gaylord Perry	12.00	6.00	3.50
194	Angels Rookies (Bill Kelso, Rick Reichardt)	3.00	1.50	.90
195	Bob Veale	3.00	1.50	.90
196	Ron Fairly	3.00	1.50	.90
197	Diego Segui	3.00	1.50	.90
198	Smoky Burgess	3.00	1.50	.90
199	Bob Heffner	3.00	1.50	.90
200	Joe Torre	12.00	6.00	3.50
201	Twins Rookies (Cesar Tovar, Sandy Valdespino)	3.00	1.50	.90
202	Leo Burke	3.00	1.50	.90
203	Dallas Green	3.00	1.50	.90
204	Russ Snyder	3.00	1.50	.90
205	Warren Spahn	30.00	15.00	7.50
206	Willie Horton	3.00	1.50	.90
207	Pete Rose	160.00	80.00	40.00
208	Tommy John	6.00	3.00	1.75
209	Pirates Team	7.50	3.75	2.25
210	Jim Fregosi	3.00	1.50	.90
211	Steve Ridzik	3.00	1.50	.90
212	Ron Brand	3.00	1.50	.90
213	Jim Davenport	3.00	1.50	.90
214	Bob Purkey	3.00	1.50	.90
215	Pete Ward	3.00	1.50	.90
216	Al Worthington	3.00	1.50	.90
217	Walt Alston	9.00	4.50	2.75
218	Dick Schofield	3.00	1.50	.90
219	Bob Meyer	3.00	1.50	.90
220	Billy Williams	25.00	12.50	7.50
221	John Tsitouris	3.00	1.50	.90
222	Bob Tillman	3.00	1.50	.90
223	Dan Osinski	3.00	1.50	.90
224	Bob Chance	3.00	1.50	.90
225	Bo Belinsky	3.00	1.50	.90
226	Yankees Rookies (Jake Gibbs, Elvio Jimenez)	9.00	4.50	2.75
227	Bobby Klaus	3.00	1.50	.90
228	Jack Sanford	3.00	1.50	.90
229	Lou Clinton	3.00	1.50	.90
230	Ray Sadecki	3.00	1.50	.90
231	Jerry Adair	3.00	1.50	.90
232	Steve Blass	3.00	1.50	.90
233	Don Zimmer	6.00	3.00	1.75
234	White Sox Team	7.50	3.75	2.25
235	Chuck Hinton	3.00	1.50	.90
236	Dennis McLain	20.00	10.00	5.00
237	Bernie Allen	3.00	1.50	.90
238	Joe Moeller	3.00	1.50	.90
239	Doc Edwards	3.00	1.50	.90
240	Bob Bruce	3.00	1.50	.90
241	Mack Jones	3.00	1.50	.90
242	George Brunet	3.00	1.50	.90
243	Reds Rookies (Ted Davidson, Tommy Helms)	3.00	1.50	.90
244	Lindy McDaniel	3.00	1.50	.90
245	Joe Pepitone	10.00	5.00	3.00
246	Tom Butters	3.00	1.50	.90
247	Wally Moon	3.00	1.50	.90
248	Gus Triandos	3.00	1.50	.90
249	Dave McNally	3.00	1.50	.90
250	Willie Mays	150.00	75.00	37.50
251	Billy Herman	7.50	3.75	2.25
252	Pete Richert	3.00	1.50	.90
253	Danny Cater	3.00	1.50	.90
254	Roland Sheldon	3.00	1.50	.90
255	Camilo Pascual	3.00	1.50	.90
256	Tito Francona	3.00	1.50	.90
257	Jim Wynn	3.00	1.50	.90
258	Larry Bearnarth	3.00	1.50	.90
259	Tigers Rookies (Jim Northrup, Ray Oyler)	4.00	2.00	1.25
260	Don Drysdale	20.00	10.00	6.00
261	Duke Carmel	3.00	1.50	.90
262	Bud Daley	3.00	1.50	.90
263	Marty Keough	3.00	1.50	.90
264	Bob Buhl	3.00	1.50	.90
265	Jim Pagliaroni	3.00	1.50	.90
266	Bert Campaneris	15.00	7.50	4.50
267	Senators Team	7.50	3.75	2.25
268	Ken McBride	3.00	1.50	.90
269	Frank Bolling	3.00	1.50	.90
270	Milt Pappas	3.00	1.50	.90
271	Don Wert	3.00	1.50	.90
272	Chuck Schilling	3.00	1.50	.90
273	4th Series Checklist (265-352)	7.50	3.75	2.25
274	Lum Harris	3.00	1.50	.90
275	Dick Groat	3.00	1.50	.90
276	Hoyt Wilhelm	12.50	6.25	3.75
277	Johnny Lewis	3.00	1.50	.90
278	Ken Retzer	3.00	1.50	.90
279	Dick Tracewski	3.00	1.50	.90
280	Dick Stuart	3.00	1.50	.90
281	Bill Stafford	3.00	1.50	.90
282	Giants Rookies (Dick Estelle, Masanori Murakami)	20.00	10.00	6.00
283	Fred Whitfield	3.00	1.50	.90
284	Nick Willhite	3.00	1.50	.90
285	Ron Hunt	3.00	1.50	.90
286	Athletic Rookies (Jim Dickson, Aurelio Monteagudo)	3.00	1.50	.90
287	Gary Kolb	3.00	1.50	.90
288	Jack Hamilton	3.00	1.50	.90
289	Gordy Coleman	3.00	1.50	.90
290	Wally Bunker	3.00	1.50	.90
291	Jerry Lynch	3.00	1.50	.90
292	Larry Yellen	3.00	1.50	.90
293	Angels Team	7.50	3.75	2.25
294	Tim McCarver	8.00	4.00	2.50
295	Dick Radatz	3.00	1.50	.90
296	Tony Taylor	3.00	1.50	.90
297	Dave DeBusschere	4.00	2.00	1.25
298	Jim Stewart	3.00	1.50	.90
299	Jerry Zimmerman	3.00	1.50	.90
300	Sandy Koufax	100.00	50.00	25.00
301	Birdie Tebbetts	3.00	1.50	.90
302	Al Stanek	3.00	1.50	.90
303	Johnny Orsino	3.00	1.50	.90
304	Dave Stenhouse	3.00	1.50	.90
305	Rico Carty	3.00	1.50	.90
306	Bubba Phillips	3.00	1.50	.90
307	Barry Latman	3.00	1.50	.90
308	Mets Rookies (Cleon Jones, Tom Parsons)	8.00	4.00	2.50
309	Steve Hamilton	3.00	1.50	.90
310	Johnny Callison	3.00	1.50	.90
311	Orlando Pena	3.00	1.50	.90
312	Joe Nuxhall	3.00	1.50	.90
313	Jimmie Schaffer	3.00	1.50	.90
314	Sterling Slaughter	3.00	1.50	.90
315	Frank Malzone	3.00	1.50	.90
316	Reds Team	7.00	3.50	2.00
317	Don McMahon	3.00	1.50	.90
318	Matty Alou	3.00	1.50	.90
319	Ken McMullen	3.00	1.50	.90
320	Bob Gibson	30.00	15.00	7.50
321	Rusty Staub	7.50	3.75	2.25
322	Rick Wise	3.00	1.50	.90
323	Hank Bauer	3.00	1.50	.90
324	Bobby Locke	3.00	1.50	.90
325	Donn Clendenon	3.00	1.50	.90
326	Dwight Siebler	3.00	1.50	.90
327	Denis Menke	3.00	1.50	.90
328	Eddie Fisher	3.00	1.50	.90
329	Hawk Taylor	3.00	1.50	.90
330	Whitey Ford	50.00	25.00	12.50
331	Dodgers Rookies (Al Ferrara, John Purdin)	3.00	1.50	.90
332	Ted Abernathy	3.00	1.50	.90
333	Tommie Reynolds	3.00	1.50	.90
334	Vic Roznovsky	3.00	1.50	.90
335	Mickey Lolich	6.00	3.00	1.75
336	Woody Held	3.00	1.50	.90
337	Mike Cuellar	3.00	1.50	.90
338	Phillies Team	7.50	3.75	2.25
339	Ryne Duren	3.00	1.50	.90
340	Tony Oliva	15.00	7.50	4.50
341	Bobby Bolin	3.00	1.50	.90
342	Bob Rodgers	3.00	1.50	.90
343	Mike McCormick	3.00	1.50	.90
344	Wes Parker	3.00	1.50	.90
345	Floyd Robinson	3.00	1.50	.90
346	Bobby Bragan	3.00	1.50	.90
347	Roy Face	3.00	1.50	.90
348	George Banks	3.00	1.50	.90
349	Larry Miller	3.00	1.50	.90
350	Mickey Mantle	550.00	270.00	165.00
351	Jim Perry	3.00	1.50	.90
352	Alex Johnson	3.50	1.75	1.00
353	Jerry Lumpe	3.00	1.50	.90
354	Cubs Rookies (Billy Ott, Jack Warner)	3.00	1.50	.90
355	Vada Pinson	8.00	4.00	2.50
356	Bill Spanswick	3.00	1.50	.90
357	Carl Warwick	3.00	1.50	.90
358	Albie Pearson	3.00	1.50	.90
359	Ken Johnson	3.00	1.50	.90
360	Orlando Cepeda	20.00	10.00	6.00
361	5th Series Checklist (353-429)	9.00	4.50	2.75
362	Don Schwall	3.00	1.50	.90
363	Bob Johnson	3.00	1.50	.90
364	Galen Cisco	3.00	1.50	.90
365	Jim Gentile	3.00	1.50	.90
366	Dan Schneider	3.00	1.50	.90
367	Leon Wagner	3.00	1.50	.90
368	White Sox Rookies (Ken Berry, Joel Gibson)	3.00	1.50	.90
369	Phil Linz	3.00	1.50	.90
370	Tommy Davis	3.00	1.50	.90
371	Frank Kreutzer	7.50	3.75	2.25
372	Clay Dalrymple	7.50	3.75	2.25
373	Curt Simmons	7.50	3.75	2.25
374	Angels Rookies (Jose Cardenal, Dick Simpson)	9.00	4.50	2.75
375	Dave Wickersham	7.50	3.75	2.25
376	Jim Landis	7.50	3.75	2.25
377	Willie Stargell	20.00	10.00	6.00
378	Chuck Estrada	7.50	3.75	2.25
379	Giants Team	10.00	5.00	3.00
380	Rocky Colavito	12.00	6.00	3.50
381	Al Jackson	7.50	3.75	2.25
382	J.C. Martin	7.50	3.75	2.25
383	Felipe Alou	9.00	4.50	2.75
384	Johnny Klippstein	7.50	3.75	2.25
385	Carl Yastrzemski	40.00	20.00	10.00
386	Cubs Rookies (Paul Jaeckel, Fred Norman)	7.50	3.75	2.25
387	Johnny Podres	9.00	4.50	2.75
388	John Blanchard	7.50	3.75	2.25
389	Don Larsen	7.50	3.75	2.25
390	Bill Freehan	7.50	3.75	2.25
391	Mel McGaha	7.50	3.75	2.25
392	Bob Friend	7.50	3.75	2.25
393	Ed Kirkpatrick	7.50	3.75	2.25
394	Jim Hannan	7.50	3.75	2.25
395	Jim Hart	7.50	3.75	2.25
396	Frank Bertaina	7.50	3.75	2.25
397	Jerry Buchek	7.50	3.75	2.25
398	Reds Rookies (Dan Neville, Art Shamsky)	7.50	3.75	2.25
399	Ray Herbert	7.50	3.75	2.25
400	Harmon Killebrew	50.00	25.00	12.50
401	Carl Willey	7.50	3.75	2.25
402	Joe Amalfitano	7.50	3.75	2.25
403	Red Sox Team	10.00	5.00	3.00
404	Stan Williams	7.50	3.75	2.25
405	John Roseboro	7.50	3.75	2.25
406	Ralph Terry	7.50	3.75	2.25
407	Lee Maye	7.50	3.75	2.25
408	Larry Sherry	7.50	3.75	2.25
409	Astros Rookies (Jim Beauchamp, Larry Dierker)	9.00	4.50	2.75
410	Luis Aparicio	17.50	8.75	5.25
411	Roger Craig	7.50	3.75	2.25
412	Bob Bailey	7.50	3.75	2.25
413	Hal Reniff	7.50	3.75	2.25
414	Al Lopez	12.50	6.25	3.75
415	Curt Flood	12.50	6.25	3.75
416	Jim Brewer	7.50	3.75	2.25
417	Ed Brinkman	7.50	3.75	2.25
418	Johnny Edwards	7.50	3.75	2.25
419	Ruben Amaro	7.50	3.75	2.25
420	Larry Jackson	7.50	3.75	2.25
421	Twins Rookies (Gary Dotter, Jay Ward)	7.50	3.75	2.25
422	Aubrey Gatewood	7.50	3.75	2.25
423	Jesse Gonder	7.50	3.75	2.25
424	Gary Bell	7.50	3.75	2.25
425	Wayne Causey	7.50	3.75	2.25
426	Braves Team	10.00	5.00	3.00
427	Bob Saverine	7.50	3.75	2.25
428	Bob Shaw	7.50	3.75	2.25
429	Don Demeter	7.50	3.75	2.25
430	Gary Peters	7.50	3.75	2.25
431	Cardinals Rookies (Nelson Briles, Wayne Spiezio)	9.00	4.50	2.75
432	Jim Grant	7.50	3.75	2.25
433	John Bateman	7.50	3.75	2.25
434	Dave Morehead	7.50	3.75	2.25
435	Willie Davis	7.50	3.75	2.25
436	Don Elston	7.50	3.75	2.25
437	Chico Cardenas	7.50	3.75	2.25
438	Harry Walker	7.50	3.75	2.25
439	Moe Drabowsky	7.50	3.75	2.25
440	Tom Tresh	12.50	6.25	3.75
441	Denver Lemaster	7.50	3.75	2.25
442	Vic Power	7.50	3.75	2.25
443	6th Series Checklist (430-506)	9.00	4.50	2.75
444	Bob Hendley	7.50	3.75	2.25
445	Don Lock	7.50	3.75	2.25
446	Art Mahaffey	7.50	3.75	2.25
447	Julian Javier	7.50	3.75	2.25
448	Lee Stange	7.50	3.75	2.25
449	Mets Rookies (Jerry Hinsley, Gary Kroll)	7.50	3.75	2.25
450	Elston Howard	12.00	6.00	3.50
451	Jim Owens	7.50	3.75	2.25
452	Gary Geiger	7.50	3.75	2.25
453	Dodgers Rookies (Willie Crawford, John Werhas)	7.50	3.75	2.25
454	Ed Rakow	7.50	3.75	2.25
455	Norm Siebern	7.50	3.75	2.25
456	Bill Henry	7.50	3.75	2.25
457	Bob Kennedy	7.50	3.75	2.25
458	John Buzhardt	7.50	3.75	2.25
459	Frank Kostro	7.50	3.75	2.25
460	Richie Allen	25.00	12.50	6.25
461	Braves Rookies (Clay Carroll, Phil Niekro)	30.00	15.00	7.50
462	Lew Krausse (Photo actually Pete Lovrich.)	7.50	3.75	2.25
463	Manny Mota	7.50	3.75	2.25
464	Ron Piche	7.50	3.75	2.25
465	Tom Haller	7.50	3.75	2.25
466	Senators Rookies (Pete Craig, Dick Nen)	7.50	3.75	2.25
467	Ray Washburn	7.50	3.75	2.25
468	Larry Brown	7.50	3.75	2.25
469	Don Nottebart	7.50	3.75	2.25
470	Yogi Berra	60.00	30.00	15.00
471	Billy Hoeft	7.50	3.75	2.25
472	Don Pavletich	7.50	3.75	2.25
473	Orioles Rookies (Paul Blair, Dave Johnson)	12.50	6.25	3.75
474	Cookie Rojas	7.50	3.75	2.25
475	Clete Boyer	10.00	5.00	3.00
476	Billy O'Dell	7.50	3.75	2.25
477	Cardinals Rookies (Fritz Ackley, Steve Carlton)	175.00	87.50	43.75
478	Wilbur Wood	7.50	3.75	2.25
479	Ken Harrelson	7.50	3.75	2.25
480	Joel Horlen	7.50	3.75	2.25
481	Indians Team	10.00	5.00	3.00
482	Bob Priddy	7.50	3.75	2.25
483	George Smith	7.50	3.75	2.25
484	Ron Perranoski	7.50	3.75	2.25
485	Nellie Fox	15.00	7.50	4.50
486	Angels Rookies (Tom Egan, Pat Rogan)	7.50	3.75	2.25
487	Woody Woodward	7.50	3.75	2.25
488	Ted Wills	7.50	3.75	2.25
489	Gene Mauch	7.50	3.75	2.25
490	Earl Battey	7.50	3.75	2.25
491	Tracy Stallard	7.50	3.75	2.25
492	Gene Freese	7.50	3.75	2.25
493	Tigers Rookies (Bruce Brubaker, Bill Roman)	7.50	3.75	2.25
494	Jay Ritchie	7.50	3.75	2.25
495	Joe Christopher	7.50	3.75	2.25
496	Joe Cunningham	7.50	3.75	2.25
497	Giants Rookies (Ken Henderson, Jack Hiatt)	7.50	3.75	2.25
498	Gene Stephens	7.50	3.75	2.25
499	Stu Miller	7.50	3.75	2.25
500	Ed Mathews	30.00	15.00	7.50
501	Indians Rookies (Ralph Gagliano, Jim Rittwage)	7.50	3.75	2.25
502	Don Cardwell	7.50	3.75	2.25

		NM	EX	VG
503	Phil Gagliano	7.50	3.75	2.25
504	Jerry Grote	7.50	3.75	2.25
505	Ray Culp	7.50	3.75	2.25
506	Sam Mele	7.50	3.75	2.25
507	Sammy Ellis	7.50	3.75	2.25
508a	7th Series Checklist (507-598) (Large print on front.)	9.00	4.50	2.75
508b	7th Series Checklist (507-598) (Small print on front.)	9.00	4.50	2.75
509	Red Sox Rookies (Bob Guindon, Gerry Vezendy)	7.50	3.75	2.25
510	Ernie Banks	80.00	40.00	20.00
511	Ron Locke	7.50	3.75	2.25
512	Cap Peterson	7.50	3.75	2.25
513	Yankees Team	30.00	15.00	7.50
514	Joe Azcue	7.50	3.75	2.25
515	Vern Law	7.50	3.75	2.25
516	Al Weis	7.50	3.75	2.25
517	Angels Rookies (Paul Schaal, Jack Warner)	7.50	3.75	2.25
518	Ken Rowe	7.50	3.75	2.25
519	Bob Uecker	20.00	10.00	5.00
520	Tony Cloninger	7.50	3.75	2.25
521	Phillies Rookies (Dave Bennett, Morrie Stevens)	7.50	3.75	2.25
522	Hank Aguirre	7.50	3.75	2.25
523	Mike Brumley/SP	9.00	4.50	2.75
524	Dave Giusti/SP	9.00	4.50	2.75
525	Eddie Bressoud	7.50	3.75	2.25
526	Athletics Rookies (Catfish Hunter, Rene Lachemann, Skip Lockwood, Johnny Odom)/SP	80.00	40.00	20.00
527	Jeff Torborg/SP	9.00	4.50	2.75
528	George Altman	7.50	3.75	2.25
529	Jerry Fosnow/SP	9.00	4.50	2.75
530	Jim Maloney	7.50	3.75	2.25
531	Chuck Hiller	7.50	3.75	2.25
532	Hector Lopez	9.00	4.50	2.75
533	Mets Rookies(Jim Bethke, Tug McGraw, Dan Napolean, Ron Swoboda)/SP	25.00	12.50	6.25
534	John Herrnstein	7.50	3.75	2.25
535	Jack Kralick/SP	9.00	4.50	2.75
536	Andre Rodgers/SP	9.00	4.50	2.75
537	Angels Rookies (Marcelino Lopez, Rudy May, Phil Roof)	9.00	4.50	2.75
538	Chuck Dressen/SP	9.00	4.50	2.75
539	Herm Starrette	7.50	3.75	2.25
540	Lou Brock/SP	25.00	12.50	6.25
541	White Sox Rookies (Greg Bollo, Bob Locker)	7.50	3.75	2.25
542	Lou Klimchock	7.50	3.75	2.25
543	Ed Connolly/SP	9.00	4.50	2.75
544	Howie Reed	7.50	3.75	2.25
545	Jesus Alou/SP	9.00	4.50	2.75
546	Indians Rookies (Ray Barker, Bill Davis, Mike Hedlund, Floyd Weaver)	7.50	3.75	2.25
547	Jake Wood/SP	9.00	4.50	2.75
548	Dick Stigman	7.50	3.75	2.25
549	Cubs Rookies (Glenn Beckert, Roberto Pena)/SP	12.00	6.00	3.50
550	Mel Stottlemyre/SP	25.00	12.50	6.25
551	Mets Team/SP	16.00	8.00	4.75
552	Julio Gotay	7.50	3.75	2.25
553	Houston Rookies (Dan Coombs, Jack McClure, Gene Ratliff)	7.50	3.75	2.25
554	Chico Ruiz/SP	9.00	4.50	2.75
555	Jack Baldschun/SP	9.00	4.50	2.75
556	Red Schoendienst/SP	12.50	6.25	3.75
557	Jose Santiago	7.50	3.75	2.25
558	Tommie Sisk	7.50	3.75	2.25
559	Ed Bailey/SP	9.00	4.50	2.75
560	Boog Powell/SP	10.00	5.00	3.00
561	Dodgers Rookies (Dennis Daboll, Mike Kekich, Jim Lefebvre, Hector Valle)	12.00	6.00	3.50
562	Billy Moran	7.50	3.75	2.25
563	Julio Navarro	7.50	3.75	2.25
564	Mel Nelson	7.50	3.75	2.25
565	Ernie Broglio/SP	9.00	4.50	2.75
566	Yankees Rookies (Gil Blanco, Art Lopez, Ross Moschitto)/SP	10.00	5.00	3.00
567	Tommie Aaron	7.50	3.75	2.25
568	Ron Taylor/SP	9.00	4.50	2.75
569	Gino Cimoli/SP	9.00	4.50	2.75
570	Claude Osteen/SP	9.00	4.50	2.75
571	Ossie Virgil/SP	9.00	4.50	2.75
572	Orioles team/SP	15.00	7.50	4.50
573	Red Sox Rookies (Jim Lonborg, Gerry Moses, Mike Ryan, Bill Schlesinger)/SP	13.50	6.75	4.00
574	Roy Sievers	7.50	3.75	2.25
575	Jose Pagan	7.50	3.75	2.25
576	Terry Fox (SP)	9.00	4.50	2.75
577	A.L. Rookies (Jim Buschhorn, Darold Knowles, Richie Scheinblum)/SP	9.00	4.50	2.75
578	Camilo Carreon/SP	9.00	4.50	2.75
579	Dick Smith/SP	9.00	4.50	2.75
580	Jimmie Hall/SP	9.00	4.50	2.75
581	N.L. Rookies (Kevin Collins, Tony Perez, Dave Ricketts)/SP	80.00	40.00	20.00
582	Bob Schmidt/SP	9.00	4.50	2.75
583	Wes Covington/SP	9.00	4.50	2.75
584	Harry Bright	7.50	3.75	2.25
585	Hank Fischer	7.50	3.75	2.25
586	Tommy McCraw/SP	9.00	4.50	2.75
587	Joe Sparma	7.50	3.75	2.25
588	Lenny Green	7.50	3.75	2.25
589	Giants Rookies (Frank Linzy, Bob Schroder)/SP	9.00	4.50	2.75
590	Johnnie Wyatt	7.50	3.75	2.25

		NM	EX	VG
591	Bob Skinner/SP	9.00	4.50	2.75
592	Frank Bork/SP	9.00	4.50	2.75
593	Tigers Rookies (Jackie Moore, John Sullivan)/SP	9.00	4.50	2.75
594	Joe Gaines	7.50	3.75	2.25
595	Don Lee	7.50	3.75	2.25
596	Don Landrum/SP	9.00	4.50	2.75
597	Twins Rookies (Joe Nossek, Dick Reese, John Sevcik)	7.00	3.50	2.00
598	Al Downing/SP	25.00	6.00	3.00

1965 Topps Embossed

Inserted in regular packs, the 2-1/8" x 3-1/2" Topps Embossed cards feature a 3-D profile portrait on gold foil-like cardboard (some collectors report finding the cards with silver cardboard). The player's name, team and position are below the portrait - which is good, because most of the embossed portraits are otherwise unrecognizeable. There is a gold border with American League players framed in blue and National Leaguers in red.

		NM	EX	VG
	Complete Set (72):	400.00	140.00	60.00
	Common Player:	4.00	1.50	.60
1	Carl Yastrzemski	15.00	5.25	2.25
2	Ron Fairly	4.00	1.50	.60
3	Max Alvis	4.00	1.50	.60
4	Jim Ray Hart	4.00	1.50	.60
5	Bill Skowron	5.00	1.75	.70
6	Ed Kranepool	4.00	1.50	.60
7	Tim McCarver	5.00	1.75	.70
8	Sandy Koufax	25.00	9.00	4.00
9	Donn Clendenon	4.00	1.50	.60
10	John Romano	4.00	1.50	.60
11	Mickey Mantle	60.00	20.00	9.00
12	Joe Torre	6.00	2.00	.90
13	Al Kaline	15.00	5.25	2.25
14	Al McBean	4.00	1.50	.60
15	Don Drysdale	10.00	3.50	1.50
16	Brooks Robinson	12.50	4.50	2.00
17	Jim Bunning	9.00	3.25	1.25
18	Gary Peters	4.00	1.50	.60
19	Roberto Clemente	40.00	14.00	6.00
20	Milt Pappas	4.00	1.50	.60
21	Wayne Causey	4.00	1.50	.60
22	Frank Robinson	12.50	4.50	2.00
23	Bill Mazeroski	9.00	3.25	1.25
24	Diego Segui	4.00	1.50	.60
25	Jim Bouton	4.00	1.50	.60
26	Ed Mathews	10.00	3.50	1.50
27	Willie Mays	25.00	9.00	4.00
28	Ron Santo	6.00	2.00	.90
29	Boog Powell	6.00	2.00	.90
30	Ken McBride	4.00	1.50	.60
31	Leon Wagner	4.00	1.50	.60
32	John Callison	4.00	1.50	.60
33	Zoilo Versalles	4.00	1.50	.60
34	Jack Baldschun	4.00	1.50	.60
35	Ron Hunt	4.00	1.50	.60
36	Richie Allen	6.00	2.00	.90
37	Frank Malzone	4.00	1.50	.60
38	Bob Allison	4.00	1.50	.60
39	Jim Fregosi	4.00	1.50	.60
40	Billy Williams	9.00	3.25	1.25
41	Bill Freehan	4.00	1.50	.60
42	Vada Pinson	5.00	1.75	.70
43	Bill White	4.00	1.50	.60
44	Roy McMillan	4.00	1.50	.60
45	Orlando Cepeda	9.00	3.25	1.25
46	Rocky Colavito	7.50	2.75	1.25
47	Ken Boyer	5.00	1.75	.70
48	Dick Radatz	4.00	1.50	.60
49	Tommy Davis	4.00	1.50	.60
50	Walt Bond	4.00	1.50	.60
51	John Orsino	4.00	1.50	.60
52	Joe Christopher	4.00	1.50	.60
53	Al Spangler	4.00	1.50	.60
54	Jim King	4.00	1.50	.60
55	Mickey Lolich	4.00	1.50	.60
56	Harmon Killebrew	10.00	3.50	1.50
57	Bob Shaw	4.00	1.50	.60
58	Ernie Banks	15.00	5.25	2.25
59	Hank Aaron	25.00	9.00	4.00
60	Chuck Hinton	4.00	1.50	.60
61	Bob Aspromonte	4.00	1.50	.60
62	Lee Maye	4.00	1.50	.60
63	Joe Cunningham	4.00	1.50	.60
64	Pete Ward	4.00	1.50	.60
65	Bobby Richardson	6.00	2.00	.90
66	Dean Chance	4.00	1.50	.60
67	Dick Ellsworth	4.00	1.50	.60
68	Jim Maloney	4.00	1.50	.60
69	Bob Gibson	9.00	3.25	1.25
70	Earl Battey	4.00	1.50	.60

		NM	EX	VG
71	Tony Kubek	5.00	1.75	.70
72	Jack Kralick	4.00	1.50	.60

1965 Topps Push-Pull

Part of a 36-card set combining sports and non-sport subjects, the Push-Pull novelties have a louvered shutter attached to a tab at the bottom. When the tab is moved, from position to position, each of the underlying photos is revealed in turn. The cards measure 2-1/2" x 4-11/16". Backs are printed in black-and-white and contain biographical data. Three of the cards in the set feature baseball players.

		NM	EX	VG
	Complete Set (36):	3,650	1,800	1,050
(1)	Lou Gehrig, Babe Ruth	500.00	250.00	150.00
(2)	Casey Stengel Wins/Loses	75.00	37.00	22.00
(3)	Yogi Berra, Mickey Mantle	950.00	475.00	285.00

1965 Topps Transfers

Issued as strips of three players each as inserts in 1965, the Topps Transfers were 2" x 3" portraits of players. The transfers have blue or red bands at the top and bottom with the team name and position in the top band and the player's name in the bottom. As is so often the case, the superstars in the transfer set can be quite expensive, but like many of Topps non-card products, the common transfers are neither terribly expensive nor popular today.

		NM	EX	VG
	Complete Set (72):	750.00	375.00	225.00
	Common Player:	6.00	3.00	1.75
(1)	Hank Aaron	50.00	25.00	15.00
(2)	Richie Allen	12.00	6.00	3.50
(3)	Bob Allison	6.00	3.00	1.75
(4)	Max Alvis	6.00	3.00	1.75
(5)	Luis Aparicio	17.50	8.75	5.25
(6)	Bob Aspromonte	6.00	3.00	1.75
(7)	Walt Bond	6.00	3.00	1.75
(8)	Jim Bouton	9.00	4.50	2.75
(9)	Ken Boyer	10.00	5.00	3.00
(10)	Jim Bunning	17.50	8.75	5.25
(11)	John Callison	6.00	3.00	1.75
(12)	Rico Carty	6.00	3.00	1.75
(13)	Wayne Causey	6.00	3.00	1.75
(14)	Orlando Cepeda	17.50	8.75	5.25
(15)	Bob Chance	6.00	3.00	1.75
(16)	Dean Chance	6.00	3.00	1.75
(17)	Joe Christopher	6.00	3.00	1.75
(18)	Roberto Clemente	60.00	30.00	18.00
(19)	Rocky Colavito	15.00	7.50	4.50
(20)	Tony Conigliaro	10.00	5.00	3.00
(21)	Tommy Davis	6.00	3.00	1.75
(22)	Don Drysdale	17.50	8.75	5.25
(23)	Bill Freehan	6.00	3.00	1.75
(24)	Jim Fregosi	6.00	3.00	1.75
(25)	Bob Gibson	17.50	8.75	5.25
(26)	Dick Groat	6.00	3.00	1.75
(27)	Tom Haller	6.00	3.00	1.75
(28)	Chuck Hinton	6.00	3.00	1.75
(29)	Elston Howard	9.00	4.50	2.75
(30)	Ron Hunt	6.00	3.00	1.75
(31)	Al Jackson	6.00	3.00	1.75
(32)	Al Kaline	25.00	12.50	7.50
(33)	Harmon Killebrew	20.00	10.00	6.00
(34)	Jim King	6.00	3.00	1.75
(35)	Ron Kline	6.00	3.00	1.75

		NM	EX	VG
(36)	Bobby Knoop	6.00	3.00	1.75
(37)	Sandy Koufax	45.00	22.00	13.50
(38)	Ed Kranepool	6.00	3.00	1.75
(39)	Jim Maloney	6.00	3.00	1.75
(40)	Mickey Mantle	90.00	45.00	27.00
(41)	Juan Marichal	17.50	8.75	5.25
(42)	Lee Maye	6.00	3.00	1.75
(43)	Willie Mays	50.00	25.00	15.00
(44)	Bill Mazeroski	17.50	8.75	5.25
(45)	Tony Oliva	7.50	3.75	2.25
(46)	Jim O'Toole	6.00	3.00	1.75
(47)	Milt Pappas	6.00	3.00	1.75
(48)	Camilo Pascual	6.00	3.00	1.75
(49)	Gary Peters	6.00	3.00	1.75
(50)	Vada Pinson	6.00	3.00	1.75
(51)	Juan Pizarro	6.00	3.00	1.75
(52)	Boog Powell	10.00	5.00	3.00
(53)	Dick Radatz	6.00	3.00	1.75
(54)	Bobby Richardson	10.00	5.00	3.00
(55)	Brooks Robinson	20.00	10.00	6.00
(56)	Frank Robinson	20.00	10.00	6.00
(57)	Bob Rodgers	6.00	3.00	1.75
(58)	John Roseboro	6.00	3.00	1.75
(59)	Ron Santo	12.00	6.00	3.50
(60)	Diego Segui	6.00	3.00	1.75
(61)	Bill Skowron	9.00	4.50	2.75
(62)	Al Spangler	6.00	3.00	1.75
(63)	Dick Stuart	6.00	3.00	1.75
(64)	Luis Tiant	6.00	3.00	1.75
(65)	Joe Torre	12.00	6.00	3.50
(66)	Bob Veale	6.00	3.00	1.75
(67)	Leon Wagner	6.00	3.00	1.75
(68)	Pete Ward	6.00	3.00	1.75
(69)	Bill White	6.00	3.00	1.75
(70)	Dave Wickersham	6.00	3.00	1.75
(71)	Billy Williams	17.50	8.75	5.25
(72)	Carl Yastrzemski	25.00	12.50	7.50

1966 Topps

In 1966, Topps produced another 598-card set. The 2-1/2" x 3-1/2" cards feature the traditional color photograph with a diagonal strip in the upper left-hand corner carrying the team name. A band at the bottom carries the player's name and position. Multi-player cards returned in 1966 after a year's hiatus. The statistical leader cards feature the categorical leader and two runners-up. Most team managers have cards as well. The 1966 set features a handful of cards found with or without a notice of the player's sale or trade to another team. Cards without the notice bring higher prices and are not included in the complete set prices. Some cards in the high series (#523-598) were short-printed - produced in lesser quantities than the rest of the series. They are valued somewhat higher than the others and are indicated in the checklist by an (SP) notation following the player name.

	NM	EX	VG
Complete Set (598):	4,600	2,300	1,375
Common Player (1-370):	4.00	2.00	1.25
Common Player (371-446):	7.50	3.75	2.25
Common Player (447-522):	9.00	4.50	2.75
Common Player (523-598):	12.50	6.25	3.75

		NM	EX	VG
1	Willie Mays	250.00	125.00	62.50
2	Ted Abernathy	4.00	2.00	1.25
3	Sam Mele	4.00	2.00	1.25
4	Ray Culp	4.00	2.00	1.25
5	Jim Fregosi	4.00	2.00	1.25
6	Chuck Schilling	4.00	2.00	1.25
7	Tracy Stallard	4.00	2.00	1.25
8	Floyd Robinson	4.00	2.00	1.25
9	Clete Boyer	8.00	4.00	2.50
10	Tony Cloninger	4.00	2.00	1.25
11	Senators Rookies (Brant Alyea, Pete Craig)	4.00	2.00	1.25
12	John Tsitouris	4.00	2.00	1.25
13	Lou Johnson	4.00	2.00	1.25
14	Norm Siebern	4.00	2.00	1.25
15	Vern Law	4.00	2.00	1.25
16	Larry Brown	4.00	2.00	1.25
17	Johnny Stephenson	4.00	2.00	1.25
18	Roland Sheldon	4.00	2.00	1.25
19	Giants Team	7.50	3.75	2.25
20	Willie Horton	4.00	2.00	1.25
21	Don Nottebart	4.00	2.00	1.25
22	Joe Nossek	4.00	2.00	1.25
23	Jack Sanford	4.00	2.00	1.25
24	*Don Kessinger*	7.50	3.75	2.25
25	Pete Ward	4.00	2.00	1.25
26	Ray Sadecki	4.00	2.00	1.25
27	Orioles Rookies (Andy Etchebarren, Darold Knowles)	6.00	3.00	1.75
28	Phil Niekro	15.00	7.50	4.50
29	Mike Brumley	4.00	2.00	1.25
30	Pete Rose	80.00	40.00	20.00
31	Jack Cullen	4.00	2.00	1.25
32	Adolfo Phillips	4.00	2.00	1.25

		NM	EX	VG
33	Jim Pagliaroni	4.00	2.00	1.25
34	1st Series Checklist (1-88)	7.50	3.75	2.25
35	Ron Swoboda	4.00	2.00	1.25
36	Jim Hunter	15.00	7.50	4.50
37	Billy Herman	6.00	3.00	1.75
38	Ron Nischwitz	4.00	2.00	1.25
39	Ken Henderson	4.00	2.00	1.25
40	Jim Grant	4.00	2.00	1.25
41	Don LeJohn	4.00	2.00	1.25
42	Aubrey Gatewood	4.00	2.00	1.25
43a	Don Landrum (No button on pants.)	4.00	2.00	1.25
43b	Don Landrum (Partial button on pants.)	6.00	3.00	1.75
43c	Don Landrum (Full button on pants.)	6.00	3.00	1.75
44	Indians Rookies (Bill Davis, Tom Kelley)	4.00	2.00	1.25
45	Jim Gentile	4.00	2.00	1.25
46	Howie Koplitz	4.00	2.00	1.25
47	J.C. Martin	4.00	2.00	1.25
48	Paul Blair	4.00	2.00	1.25
49	Woody Woodward	4.00	2.00	1.25
50	Mickey Mantle	325.00	160.00	97.50
51	Gordon Richardson	4.00	2.00	1.25
52	Power Plus (Johnny Callison, Wes Covington)	4.00	2.00	1.25
53	Bob Duliba	4.00	2.00	1.25
54	Jose Pagan	4.00	2.00	1.25
55	Ken Harrelson	4.00	2.00	1.25
56	Sandy Valdespino	4.00	2.00	1.25
57	Jim Lefebvre	4.00	2.00	1.25
58	Dave Wickersham	4.00	2.00	1.25
59	Reds Team	7.00	3.50	2.00
60	Curt Flood	4.00	2.00	1.25
61	Bob Bolin	4.00	2.00	1.25
62a	Merritt Ranew (No sold statement.)	20.00	10.00	6.00
62b	Merritt Ranew (With sold statement.)	4.00	2.00	1.25
63	Jim Stewart	4.00	2.00	1.25
64	Bob Bruce	4.00	2.00	1.25
65	Leon Wagner	4.00	2.00	1.25
66	Al Weis	4.00	2.00	1.25
67	Mets Rookies (Cleon Jones, Dick Selma)	4.00	2.00	1.25
68	Hal Reniff	4.00	2.00	1.25
69	Ken Hamlin	4.00	2.00	1.25
70	Carl Yastrzemski	25.00	12.50	6.25
71	Frank Carpin	4.00	2.00	1.25
72	Tony Perez	25.00	12.50	6.25
73	Jerry Zimmerman	4.00	2.00	1.25
74	Don Mossi	4.00	2.00	1.25
75	Tommy Davis	4.00	2.00	1.25
76	Red Schoendienst	7.50	3.75	2.25
77	Johnny Orsino	4.00	2.00	1.25
78	Frank Linzy	4.00	2.00	1.25
79	Joe Pepitone	8.00	4.00	2.50
80	Richie Allen	6.00	3.00	1.75
81	Ray Oyler	4.00	2.00	1.25
82	Bob Hendley	4.00	2.00	1.25
83	Albie Pearson	4.00	2.00	1.25
84	Braves Rookies (Jim Beauchamp, Dick Kelley)	4.00	2.00	1.25
85	Eddie Fisher	4.00	2.00	1.25
86	John Bateman	4.00	2.00	1.25
87	Dan Napoleon	4.00	2.00	1.25
88	Fred Whitfield	4.00	2.00	1.25
89	Ted Davidson	4.00	2.00	1.25
90	Luis Aparicio	15.00	7.50	4.50
91a	Bob Uecker (No trade statement.)	60.00	30.00	18.00
91b	Bob Uecker (With trade statement.)	20.00	10.00	6.00
92	Yankees Team	15.00	7.50	4.50
93	Jim Lonborg	4.00	2.00	1.25
94	Matty Alou	4.00	2.00	1.25
95	Pete Richert	4.00	2.00	1.25
96	Felipe Alou	6.00	3.00	1.75
97	Jim Merritt	4.00	2.00	1.25
98	Don Demeter	4.00	2.00	1.25
99	Buc Belters (Donn Clendenon, Willie Stargell)	8.00	4.00	2.50
100	Sandy Koufax	100.00	50.00	25.00
101a	2nd Series Checklist (89-176) (115 is Spahn)	12.50	6.25	3.75
101b	2nd Series Checklist (89-176) (115 is Henry)	7.50	3.75	2.25
102	Ed Kirkpatrick	4.00	2.00	1.25
103a	Dick Groat (No trade statement.)	15.00	7.50	3.75
103b	Dick Groat (With trade statement.)	4.00	2.00	1.25
104a	Alex Johnson (No trade statement.)	20.00	10.00	6.00
104b	Alex Johnson (With trade statement.)	4.00	2.00	1.25
105	Milt Pappas	4.00	2.00	1.25
106	Rusty Staub	6.00	3.00	1.75
107	Athletics Rookies (Larry Stahl, Ron Tompkins)	4.00	2.00	1.25
108	Bobby Klaus	4.00	2.00	1.25
109	Ralph Terry	4.00	2.00	1.25
110	Ernie Banks	25.00	12.50	6.25
111	Gary Peters	4.00	2.00	1.25
112	Manny Mota	4.00	2.00	1.25
113	Hank Aguirre	4.00	2.00	1.25
114	Jim Gosger	4.00	2.00	1.25
115	Bill Henry	4.00	2.00	1.25
116	Walt Alston	6.00	3.00	1.75
117	Jake Gibbs	4.00	2.00	1.25
118	Mike McCormick	4.00	2.00	1.25
119	Art Shamsky	4.00	2.00	1.25
120	Harmon Killebrew	15.00	7.50	3.75
121	Ray Herbert	4.00	2.00	1.25
122	Joe Gaines	4.00	2.00	1.25
123	Pirates Rookies (Frank Bork, Jerry May)	4.00	2.00	1.25

		NM	EX	VG
124	Tug McGraw	4.00	2.00	1.25
125	Lou Brock	20.00	10.00	6.00
126	*Jim Palmer*	100.00	50.00	25.00
127	Ken Berry	4.00	2.00	1.25
128	Jim Landis	4.00	2.00	1.25
129	Jack Kralick	4.00	2.00	1.25
130	Joe Torre	6.00	3.00	1.75
131	Angels Team	7.50	3.75	2.25
132	Orlando Cepeda	15.00	7.50	4.50
133	Don McMahon	4.00	2.00	1.25
134	Wes Parker	4.00	2.00	1.25
135	Dave Morehead	4.00	2.00	1.25
136	Woody Held	4.00	2.00	1.25
137	Pat Corrales	4.00	2.00	1.25
138	Roger Repoz	4.00	2.00	1.25
139	Cubs Rookies (Byron Browne, Don Young)	4.00	2.00	1.25
140	Jim Maloney	4.00	2.00	1.25
141	Tom McCraw	4.00	2.00	1.25
142	Don Dennis	4.00	2.00	1.25
143	Jose Tartabull	4.00	2.00	1.25
144	Don Schwall	4.00	2.00	1.25
145	Bill Freehan	4.00	2.00	1.25
146	George Altman	4.00	2.00	1.25
147	Lum Harris	4.00	2.00	1.25
148	Bob Johnson	4.00	2.00	1.25
149	Dick Nen	4.00	2.00	1.25
150	Rocky Colavito	12.00	6.00	3.50
151	Gary Wagner	4.00	2.00	1.25
152	Frank Malzone	4.00	2.00	1.25
153	Rico Carty	4.00	2.00	1.25
154	Chuck Hiller	4.00	2.00	1.25
155	Marcelino Lopez	4.00	2.00	1.25
156	D P Combo (Hal Lanier, Dick Schofield)	4.00	2.00	1.25
157	Rene Lachemann	4.00	2.00	1.25
158	Jim Brewer	4.00	2.00	1.25
159	Chico Ruiz	4.00	2.00	1.25
160	Whitey Ford	35.00	17.50	8.75
161	Jerry Lumpe	4.00	2.00	1.25
162	Lee Maye	4.00	2.00	1.25
163	Tito Francona	4.00	2.00	1.25
164	White Sox Rookies (Tommie Agee, Marv Staehle)	4.00	2.00	1.25
165	Don Lock	4.00	2.00	1.25
166	Chris Krug	4.00	2.00	1.25
167	Boog Powell	6.00	3.00	1.75
168	Dan Osinski	4.00	2.00	1.25
169	Duke Sims	4.00	2.00	1.25
170	Cookie Rojas	4.00	2.00	1.25
171	Nick Willhite	4.00	2.00	1.25
172	Mets Team	6.00	3.00	1.75
173	Al Spangler	4.00	2.00	1.25
174	Ron Taylor	4.00	2.00	1.25
175	Bert Campaneris	4.00	2.00	1.25
176	Jim Davenport	4.00	2.00	1.25
177	Hector Lopez	4.00	2.00	1.25
178	Bob Tillman	4.00	2.00	1.25
179	Cardinals Rookies (Dennis Aust, Bob Tolan)	4.00	2.00	1.25
180	Vada Pinson	7.50	3.75	2.25
181	Al Worthington	4.00	2.00	1.25
182	Jerry Lynch	4.00	2.00	1.25
183a	3rd Series Checklist (177-264) (Large print on front.)	7.50	3.75	2.25
183b	3rd Series Checklist (177-264) (Small print on front.)	9.00	4.50	2.75
184	Denis Menke	4.00	2.00	1.25
185	Bob Buhl	4.00	2.00	1.25
186	Ruben Amaro	4.00	2.00	1.25
187	Chuck Dressen	4.00	2.00	1.25
188	Al Luplow	4.00	2.00	1.25
189	John Roseboro	4.00	2.00	1.25
190	Jimmie Hall	4.00	2.00	1.25
191	Darrell Sutherland	4.00	2.00	1.25
192	Vic Power	4.00	2.00	1.25
193	Dave McNally	4.00	2.00	1.25
194	Senators Team	6.00	3.00	1.75
195	Joe Morgan	25.00	12.50	7.50
196	Don Pavletich	4.00	2.00	1.25
197	Sonny Siebert	4.00	2.00	1.25
198	*Mickey Stanley*	6.00	3.00	1.75
199	Chisox Clubbers (Floyd Robinson, Johnny Romano, Bill Skowron)	6.00	3.00	1.75
200	Ed Mathews	20.00	10.00	6.00
201	Jim Dickson	4.00	2.00	1.25
202	Clay Dalrymple	4.00	2.00	1.25
203	Jose Santiago	4.00	2.00	1.25
204	Cubs Team	7.50	3.75	2.25
205	Tom Tresh	9.00	4.50	2.75
206	Alvin Jackson	4.00	2.00	1.25
207	Frank Quilici	4.00	2.00	1.25
208	Bob Miller	4.00	2.00	1.25
209	Tigers Rookies (Fritz Fisher, John Hiller)	4.00	2.00	1.25
210	Bill Mazeroski	17.50	8.75	5.25
211	Frank Kreutzer	4.00	2.00	1.25
212	Ed Kranepool	4.00	2.00	1.25
213	Fred Newman	4.00	2.00	1.25
214	Tommy Harper	4.00	2.00	1.25
215	N.L. Batting Leaders (Hank Aaron, Roberto Clemente, Willie Mays)	35.00	17.50	8.75
216	A.L. Batting Leaders (Vic Davalillo, Tony Oliva, Carl Yastrzemski)	16.00	8.00	4.75
217	N.L. Home Run Leaders (Willie Mays, Willie McCovey, Billy Williams)	15.00	7.50	3.75
218	A.L. Home Run Leaders (Norm Cash, Tony Conigliaro, Willie Horton)	12.50	6.25	3.75
219	N.L. RBI Leaders (Deron Johnson, Willie Mays, Frank Robinson)	15.00	7.50	3.75

No.	Player			
220	A.L. RBI Leaders (Rocky Colavito, Willie Horton, Tony Oliva)	12.00	6.00	3.50
221	N.L. ERA Leaders (Sandy Koufax, Vern Law, Juan Marichal)	15.00	7.50	4.50
222	A.L. ERA Leaders (Eddie Fisher, Sam McDowell, Sonny Siebert)	6.00	3.00	1.75
223	N.L. Pitching Leaders (Tony Cloninger, Don Drysdale, Sandy Koufax)	16.00	8.00	4.75
224	A.L. Pitching Leaders (Jim Grant, Jim Kaat, Mel Stottlemyre)	9.00	4.50	2.75
225	N.L. Strikeout Leaders (Bob Gibson, Sandy Koufax, Bob Veale)	15.00	7.50	4.50
226	A.L. Strikeout Leaders (Mickey Lolich, Sam McDowell, Denny McLain, Sonny Siebert)	10.00	5.00	3.00
227	Russ Nixon	4.00	2.00	1.25
228	Larry Dierker	4.00	2.00	1.25
229	Hank Bauer	4.50	2.25	1.25
230	Johnny Callison	4.00	2.00	1.25
231	Floyd Weaver	4.00	2.00	1.25
232	Glenn Beckert	4.00	2.00	1.25
233	Dom Zanni	4.00	2.00	1.25
234	Yankees Rookies (*Rich Beck, Roy White*)	15.00	7.50	4.50
235	Don Cardwell	4.00	2.00	1.25
236	Mike Hershberger	4.00	2.00	1.25
237	Billy O'Dell	4.00	2.00	1.25
238	Dodgers Team	9.00	4.50	2.75
239	Orlando Pena	4.00	2.00	1.25
240	Earl Battey	4.00	2.00	1.25
241	Dennis Ribant	4.00	2.00	1.25
242	Jesus Alou	4.00	2.00	1.25
243	Nelson Briles	4.00	2.00	1.25
244	Astros Rookies (Chuck Harrison, Sonny Jackson)	4.00	2.00	1.25
245	John Buzhardt	4.00	2.00	1.25
246	Ed Bailey	4.00	2.00	1.25
247	Carl Warwick	4.00	2.00	1.25
248	Pete Mikkelsen	4.00	2.00	1.25
249	Bill Rigney	4.00	2.00	1.25
250	Sam Ellis	4.00	2.00	1.25
251	Ed Brinkman	4.00	2.00	1.25
252	Denver Lemaster	4.00	2.00	1.25
253	Don Wert	4.00	2.00	1.25
254	Phillies Rookies (Fergie Jenkins, Bill Sorrell)	60.00	30.00	15.00
255	Willie Stargell	20.00	10.00	6.00
256	Lew Krausse	4.00	2.00	1.25
257	Jeff Torborg	4.00	2.00	1.25
258	Dave Giusti	4.00	2.00	1.25
259	Red Sox Team	7.50	3.75	2.25
260	Bob Shaw	4.00	2.00	1.25
261	Ron Hansen	4.00	2.00	1.25
262	Jack Hamilton	4.00	2.00	1.25
263	Tom Egan	4.00	2.00	1.25
264	Twins Rookies (Andy Kosco, Ted Uhlaender)	4.00	2.00	1.25
265	Stu Miller	4.00	2.00	1.25
266	Pedro Gonzalez	4.00	2.00	1.25
267	Joe Sparma	4.00	2.00	1.25
268	John Blanchard	4.00	2.00	1.25
269	Don Heffner	4.00	2.00	1.25
270	Claude Osteen	4.00	2.00	1.25
271	Hal Lanier	4.00	2.00	1.25
272	Jack Baldschun	4.00	2.00	1.25
273	Astro Aces (Bob Aspromonte, Rusty Staub)	6.00	3.00	1.75
274	Buster Narum	4.00	2.00	1.25
275	Tim McCarver	7.50	3.75	2.25
276	Jim Bouton	6.00	3.00	1.75
277	George Thomas	4.00	2.00	1.25
278	Calvin Koonce	4.00	2.00	1.25
279a	4th Series Checklist (265-352) (Player's cap black.)	7.00	3.50	2.00
279b	4th Series Checklist (265-352) (Player's cap red.)	7.50	3.75	2.25
280	Bobby Knoop	4.00	2.00	1.25
281	Bruce Howard	4.00	2.00	1.25
282	Johnny Lewis	4.00	2.00	1.25
283	Jim Perry	4.00	2.00	1.25
284	Bobby Wine	4.00	2.00	1.25
285	Luis Tiant	4.00	2.00	1.25
286	Gary Geiger	4.00	2.00	1.25
287	Jack Aker	4.00	2.00	1.25
288	Dodgers Rookies (*Bill Singer, Don Sutton*)	60.00	30.00	15.00
289	Larry Sherry	4.00	2.00	1.25
290	Ron Santo	12.50	6.25	3.75
291	Moe Drabowsky	4.00	2.00	1.25
292	Jim Coker	4.00	2.00	1.25
293	Mike Shannon	4.00	2.00	1.25
294	Steve Ridzik	4.00	2.00	1.25
295	Jim Hart	4.00	2.00	1.25
296	Johnny Keane	4.00	2.00	1.25
297	Jim Owens	4.00	2.00	1.25
298	Rico Petrocelli	6.00	3.00	1.75
299	Lou Burdette	4.00	2.00	1.25
300	Bob Clemente	150.00	75.00	37.50
301	Greg Bollo	4.00	2.00	1.25
302	Ernie Bowman	4.00	2.00	1.25
303a	Indians Team (Dot between "PLACE" and "AMERICAN.")	6.00	3.00	1.75
303b	Indians Team (No dot.)	6.00	3.00	1.75
304	John Herrnstein	4.00	2.00	1.25
305	Camilo Pascual	4.00	2.00	1.25
306	Ty Cline	4.00	2.00	1.25
307	Clay Carroll	4.00	2.00	1.25
308	Tom Haller	4.00	2.00	1.25
309	Diego Segui	4.00	2.00	1.25
310	Frank Robinson	30.00	15.00	7.50
311	Reds Rookies (Tommy Helms, Dick Simpson)	4.00	2.00	1.25
312	Bob Saverine	4.00	2.00	1.25
313	Chris Zachary	4.00	2.00	1.25
314	Hector Valle	4.00	2.00	1.25
315	Norm Cash	11.00	5.50	3.25
316	Jack Fisher	4.00	2.00	1.25
317	Dalton Jones	4.00	2.00	1.25
318	Harry Walker	4.00	2.00	1.25
319	Gene Freese	4.00	2.00	1.25
320	Bob Gibson	30.00	15.00	9.00
321	Rick Reichardt	4.00	2.00	1.25
322	Bill Faul	4.00	2.00	1.25
323	Ray Barker	4.00	2.00	1.25
324	John Boozer	4.00	2.00	1.25
325	Vic Davalillo	4.00	2.00	1.25
326a	Braves Team (Dot between "PLACE" and "NATIONAL.")	7.50	3.75	2.25
326b	Braves Team (No dot.)	7.50	3.75	2.25
327	Bernie Allen	4.00	2.00	1.25
328	Jerry Grote	4.00	2.00	1.25
329	Pete Charton	4.00	2.00	1.25
330	Ron Fairly	4.00	2.00	1.25
331	Ron Herbel	4.00	2.00	1.25
332	Billy Bryan	4.00	2.00	1.25
333	Senators Rookies (Joe Coleman, Jim French)	4.00	2.00	1.25
334	Marty Keough		4.00	2.00	1.25
335	Juan Pizarro		4.00	2.00	1.25
336	Gene Alley		4.00	2.00	1.25
337	Fred Gladding		4.00	2.00	1.25
338	Dal Maxvill		4.00	2.00	1.25
339	Del Crandall		4.00	2.00	1.25
340	Dean Chance	.	4.00	2.00	1.25
341	Wes Westrum		4.00	2.00	1.25
342	Bob Humphreys		4.00	2.00	1.25
343	Joe Christopher		4.00	2.00	1.25
344	Steve Blass		4.00	2.00	1.25
345	Bob Allison		4.00	2.00	1.25
346	Mike de la Hoz		4.00	2.00	1.25
347	Phil Regan		4.00	2.00	1.25
348	Orioles Team		8.00	4.00	2.50
349	Cap Peterson		4.00	2.00	1.25
350	Mel Stottlemyre		6.00	3.00	1.75
351	Fred Valentine		4.00	2.00	1.25
352	Bob Aspromonte		4.00	2.00	1.25
353	Al McBean		4.00	2.00	1.25
354	Smoky Burgess		4.00	2.00	1.25
355	Wade Blasingame		4.00	2.00	1.25
356	Red Sox Rookies (Owen Johnson, Ken Sanders)		4.00	2.00	1.25
357	Gerry Arrigo		4.00	2.00	1.25
358	Charlie Smith		4.00	2.00	1.25
359	Johnny Briggs		4.00	2.00	1.25
360	Ron Hunt		4.00	2.00	1.25
361	Tom Satriano		4.00	2.00	1.25
362	Gates Brown		4.00	2.00	1.25
363	5th Series Checklist (353-429)		9.00	4.50	2.75
364	Nate Oliver		4.00	2.00	1.25
365	Roger Maris		50.00	25.00	12.50
366	Wayne Causey		4.00	2.00	1.25
367	Mel Nelson		4.00	2.00	1.25
368	Charlie Lau		4.00	2.00	1.25
369	Jim King		4.00	2.00	1.25
370	Chico Cardenas		4.00	2.00	1.25
371	Lee Stange		7.50	3.75	2.25
372	Harvey Kuenn		7.50	3.75	2.25
373	Giants Rookies (Dick Estelle, Jack Hiatt)		7.50	3.75	2.25
374	Bob Locker		7.50	3.75	2.25
375	Donn Clendenon		7.50	3.75	2.25
376	Paul Schaal		7.50	3.75	2.25
377	Turk Farrell		7.50	3.75	2.25
378	Dick Tracewski		7.50	3.75	2.25
379	Cards Team		10.00	5.00	3.00
380	Tony Conigliaro		12.50	6.25	3.75
381	Hank Fischer		7.50	3.75	2.25
382	Phil Roof		7.50	3.75	2.25
383	Jackie Brandt		7.50	3.75	2.25
384	Al Downing		7.50	3.75	2.25
385	Ken Boyer		10.00	5.00	3.00
386	Gil Hodges		11.00	5.50	3.25
387	Howie Reed		7.50	3.75	2.25
388	Don Mincher		7.50	3.75	2.25
389	Jim O'Toole		7.50	3.75	2.25
390	Brooks Robinson		40.00	20.00	10.00
391	Chuck Hinton		7.50	3.75	2.25
392	Cubs Rookies (*Bill Hands, Randy Hundley*)		12.00	6.00	3.50
393	George Brunet		7.50	3.75	2.25
394	Ron Brand		7.50	3.75	2.25
395	Len Gabrielson		7.50	3.75	2.25
396	Jerry Stephenson		7.50	3.75	2.25
397	Bill White		7.50	3.75	2.25
398	Danny Cater		7.50	3.75	2.25
399	Ray Washburn		7.50	3.75	2.25
400	Zoilo Versalles		7.50	3.75	2.25
401	Ken McMullen		7.50	3.75	2.25
402	Jim Hickman		7.50	3.75	2.25
403	Fred Talbot		7.50	3.75	2.25
404a	Pirates Team (Dot between "PLACE" and "NATIONAL.")		12.50	6.25	3.75
404b	Pirates Team (No dot.)		12.50	6.25	3.75
405	Elston Howard		9.00	4.50	2.75
406	Joe Jay		7.50	3.75	2.25
407	John Kennedy		7.50	3.75	2.25
408	Lee Thomas		7.50	3.75	2.25
409	Billy Hoeft		7.50	3.75	2.25
410	Al Kaline		40.00	20.00	10.00
411	Gene Mauch		7.50	3.75	2.25
412	Sam Bowens		7.50	3.75	2.25
413	John Romano		7.50	3.75	2.25
414	Dan Coombs		7.50	3.75	2.25
415	Max Alvis		7.50	3.75	2.25
416	Phil Ortega		7.50	3.75	2.25
417	Angels Rookies (Jim McGlothlin, Ed Sukla)		7.50	3.75	2.25
418	Phil Gagliano		7.50	3.75	2.25
419	Mike Ryan	7.50	3.75	2.25
420	Juan Marichal	15.00	7.50	3.75
421	Roy McMillan	7.50	3.75	2.25
422	Ed Charles	7.50	3.75	2.25
423	Ernie Broglio	7.50	3.75	2.25
424	Reds Rookies (Lee May, Darrell Osteen)	10.00	5.00	3.00
425	Bob Veale	7.50	3.75	2.25
426	White Sox Team	10.00	5.00	3.00
427	John Miller	7.50	3.75	2.25
428	Sandy Alomar	7.50	3.75	2.25
429	Bill Monbouquette	7.50	3.75	2.25
430	Don Drysdale	20.00	10.00	6.00
431	Walt Bond	7.50	3.75	2.25
432	Bob Heffner	7.50	3.75	2.25
433	Alvin Dark	7.50	3.75	2.25
434	Willie Kirkland	7.50	3.75	2.25
435	Jim Bunning	15.00	7.50	4.50
436	Julian Javier	7.50	3.75	2.25
437	Al Stanek	7.50	3.75	2.25
438	Willie Smith	7.50	3.75	2.25
439	Pedro Ramos	7.50	3.75	2.25
440	Deron Johnson	7.50	3.75	2.25
441	Tommie Sisk	7.50	3.75	2.25
442	Orioles Rookies (Ed Barnowski, Eddie Watt)	7.50	3.75	2.25
443	Bill Wakefield	7.50	3.75	2.25
444a	6th Series Checklist (430-506) (456 is R. Sox Rookies)	7.50	3.75	2.25
444b	6th Series Checklist (430-506) (456 is Red Sox Rookies)	9.00	4.50	2.75
445	Jim Kaat	9.00	4.50	2.75
446	Mack Jones	7.50	3.75	2.25
447	Dick Ellsworth (Photo actually Ken Hubbs.)	12.50	6.25	3.75
448	Eddie Stanky	9.00	4.50	2.75
449	Joe Moeller	9.00	4.50	2.75
450	Tony Oliva	15.00	7.50	4.50
451	Barry Latman	9.00	4.50	2.75
452	Joe Azcue	9.00	4.50	2.75
453	Ron Kline	9.00	4.50	2.75
454	Jerry Buchek	9.00	4.50	2.75
455	Mickey Lolich	9.00	4.50	2.75
456	Red Sox Rookies (Darrell Brandon, Joe Foy)	9.00	4.50	2.75
457	Joe Gibbon	9.00	4.50	2.75
458	Manny Jiminez (Jimenez)	9.00	4.50	2.75
459	Bill McCool	9.00	4.50	2.75
460	Curt Blefary	9.00	4.50	2.75
461	Roy Face	9.00	4.50	2.75
462	Bob Rodgers	9.00	4.50	2.75
463	Phillies Team	12.00	6.00	3.50
464	Larry Bearnarth	9.00	4.50	2.75
465	Don Buford	9.00	4.50	2.75
466	Ken Johnson	9.00	4.50	2.75
467	Vic Roznovsky	9.00	4.50	2.75
468	Johnny Podres	9.00	4.50	2.75
469	Yankees Rookies (Bobby Murcer, Dooley Womack)	30.00	15.00	7.50
470	Sam McDowell	9.00	4.50	2.75
471	Bob Skinner	9.00	4.50	2.75
472	Terry Fox	9.00	4.50	2.75
473	Rich Rollins	9.00	4.50	2.75
474	Dick Schofield	9.00	4.50	2.75
475	Dick Radatz	9.00	4.50	2.75
476	Bobby Bragan	9.00	4.50	2.75
477	Steve Barber	9.00	4.50	2.75
478	Tony Gonzalez	9.00	4.50	2.75
479	Jim Hannan	9.00	4.50	2.75
480	Dick Stuart	9.00	4.50	2.75
481	Bob Lee	9.00	4.50	2.75
482	Cubs Rookies (John Boccabella, Dave Dowling)	9.00	4.50	2.75
483	Joe Nuxhall	9.00	4.50	2.75
484	Wes Covington	9.00	4.50	2.75
485	Bob Bailey	9.00	4.50	2.75
486	Tommy John	9.00	4.50	2.75
487	Al Ferrara	9.00	4.50	2.75
488	George Banks	9.00	4.50	2.75
489	Curt Simmons	9.00	4.50	2.75
490	Bobby Richardson	20.00	10.00	5.00
491	Dennis Bennett	9.00	4.50	2.75
492	Athletics Team	12.00	6.00	3.50
493	Johnny Klippstein	9.00	4.50	2.75
494	Gordon Coleman	9.00	4.50	2.75
495	Dick McAuliffe	9.00	4.50	2.75
496	Lindy McDaniel	9.00	4.50	2.75
497	Chris Cannizzaro	9.00	4.50	2.75
498	Pirates Rookies (Woody Fryman, Luke Walker)	9.00	4.50	2.75
499	Wally Bunker	9.00	4.50	2.75
500	Hank Aaron	125.00	62.50	31.25
501	John O'Donoghue	9.00	4.50	2.75
502	Lenny Green	9.00	4.50	2.75
503	Steve Hamilton	9.00	4.50	2.75
504	Grady Hatton	9.00	4.50	2.75
505	Jose Cardenal	9.00	4.50	2.75
506	Bo Belinsky	9.00	4.50	2.75
507	John Edwards	9.00	4.50	2.75
508	*Steve Hargan*	9.00	4.50	2.75
509	Jake Wood	9.00	4.50	2.75
510	Hoyt Wilhelm	16.00	8.00	4.75
511	Giants Rookies (*Bob Barton, Tito Fuentes*)	9.00	4.50	2.75
512	Dick Stigman	9.00	4.50	2.75
513	Camilo Carreon	9.00	4.50	2.75
514	Hal Woodeshick	9.00	4.50	2.75
515	Frank Howard	9.00	4.50	2.75
516	Eddie Bressoud	9.00	4.50	2.75
517a	7th Series Checklist (507-598) (529 is W. Sox Rookies)	11.00	5.50	3.25
517b	7th Series Checklist (507-598) (529 is White Sox Rookies)	13.50	6.75	4.00
518	Braves Rookies (Herb Hippauf, Arnie Umbach)	9.00	4.50	2.75
519	Bob Friend	9.00	4.50	2.75
520	Jim Wynn	9.00	4.50	2.75
521	John Wyatt	9.00	4.50	2.75

522	Phil Linz	9.00	4.50	2.75
523	Bob Sadowski	12.50	6.25	3.75
524	Giants Rookies	16.00	8.00	4.75
	(Ollie Brown, Don Mason)/SP			
525	Gary Bell/SP	16.00	8.00	4.75
526	Twins Team/SP	75.00	37.50	18.75
527	Julio Navarro	12.50	6.25	3.75
528	Jesse Gonder/SP	16.00	8.00	4.75
529	White Sox Rookies	12.50	6.25	3.75
	(Lee Elia, Dennis Higgins, Bill Voss)			
530	Robin Roberts	40.00	20.00	10.00
531	Joe Cunningham	12.50	6.25	3.75
532	Aurelio Monteagudo/SP	16.00	8.00	4.75
533	Jerry Adair/SP	16.00	8.00	4.75
534	Mets Rookies	12.50	6.25	3.75
	(Dave Eilers, Rob Gardner)			
535	Willie Davis/SP	16.00	8.00	4.75
536	Dick Egan	12.50	6.25	3.75
537	Herman Franks	12.50	6.25	3.75
538	Bob Allen/SP	16.00	8.00	4.75
539	Astros Rookies (Bill Heath, Carroll Sembera)	12.50	6.25	3.75
540	Denny McLain/SP	50.00	25.00	15.00
541	Gene Oliver/SP	16.00	8.00	4.75
542	George Smith	12.50	6.25	3.75
543	Roger Craig/SP	16.00	8.00	4.75
544	Cardinals Rookies	16.00	8.00	4.75
	(Joe Hoerner, George Kernek, Jimmy Williams)/SP			
545	Dick Green/SP	16.00	8.00	4.75
546	Dwight Siebler	12.50	6.25	3.75
547	*Horace Clarke*/SP	45.00	22.50	11.25
548	Gary Kroll/SP	16.00	8.00	4.75
549	Senators Rookies (Al Closter, Casey Cox)	12.50	6.25	3.75
550	Willie McCovey/SP	100.00	50.00	25.00
551	Bob Purkey/SP	16.00	8.00	4.75
552	Birdie Tebbetts/SP	16.00	8.00	4.75
553	Major League Rookies (Pat Garrett, Jackie Warner)	12.50	6.25	3.75
554	Jim Northrup/SP	16.00	8.00	4.75
555	Ron Perranoski/SP	16.00	8.00	4.75
556	Mel Queen/SP	16.00	8.00	4.75
557	Felix Mantilla/SP	16.00	8.00	4.75
558	Red Sox Rookies	20.00	10.00	6.00
	(*Guido Grilli, Pete Magrini, George Scott*)			
559	Roberto Pena/SP	16.00	8.00	4.75
560	Joel Horlen	12.50	6.25	3.75
561	Choo Choo Coleman/SP	25.00	12.50	6.25
562	Russ Snyder	12.50	6.25	3.75
563	Twins Rookies (Pete Cimino, Cesar Tovar)	12.50	6.25	3.75
564	Bob Chance/SP	16.00	8.00	4.75
565	Jimmy Piersall/SP	35.00	17.50	8.75
566	Mike Cuellar/SP	16.00	8.00	4.75
567	Dick Howser/SP	16.00	8.00	4.75
568	Athletics Rookies (Paul Lindblad, Ron Stone)	12.50	6.25	3.75
569	Orlando McFarlane/SP	16.00	8.00	4.75
570	Art Mahaffey/SP	16.00	8.00	4.75
571	Dave Roberts/SP	16.00	8.00	4.75
572	Bob Priddy	12.50	6.25	3.75
573	Derrell Griffith	12.50	6.25	3.75
574	Mets Rookies (Bill Hepler, Bill Murphy)	12.50	6.25	3.75
575	Earl Wilson	12.50	6.25	3.75
576	Dave Nicholson/SP	16.00	8.00	4.75
577	Jack Lamabe/SP	16.00	8.00	4.75
578	Chi Chi Olivo/SP	16.00	8.00	4.75
579	Orioles Rookies	20.00	10.00	5.00
	(Frank Bertaina, Gene Brabender, Dave Johnson)			
580	Billy Williams/SP	40.00	20.00	10.00
581	Tony Martinez	12.50	6.25	3.75
582	Garry Roggenburk	12.50	6.25	3.75
583	Tigers Team/SP	75.00	37.50	22.50
584	Yankees Rookies	15.00	7.50	4.50
	(*Frank Fernandez, Fritz Peterson*)			
585	Tony Taylor	12.50	6.25	3.75
586	Claude Raymond/SP	16.00	8.00	4.75
587	Dick Bertell	12.50	6.25	3.75
588	Athletics Rookies (Chuck Dobson, Ken Suarez)	12.50	6.25	3.75
589	Lou Klimchock/SP	16.00	8.00	4.75
590	Bill Skowron/SP	30.00	15.00	7.50
591	N.L. Rookies (Grant Jackson, Bart Shirley)/SP	16.00	8.00	4.75
592	Andre Rodgers	12.50	6.25	3.75
593	Doug Camilli/SP	16.00	8.00	4.75
594	Chico Salmon	12.50	6.25	3.75
595	Larry Jackson	12.50	6.25	3.75
596	Astros Rookies (Nate Colbert, Greg Sims)/SP	20.00	10.00	6.00
597	John Sullivan	12.50	6.25	3.75
598	Gaylord Perry/SP	170.00	85.00	42.50

1966 Topps Comic Book Foldees

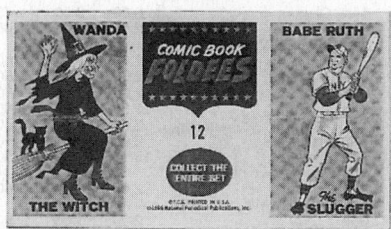

Comic book heroes and other fictional characters were the focus of this set of 44 "foldees." The pictures on the left and right ends of the 4-1/2" x 2-3/8" cards were cut through the middle to allow them to be folded over the central picture and each other to create funny combinations. Babe Ruth, in a rather generic drawing, is the only baseball player represented in the issue. A version of the set exists which carries a "T.G.C. PRINTED IN CANADA" copyright line; it is valued similarly.

		NM	EX	VG
Complete Set (44):		100.00	50.00	30.00
12	Babe Ruth	20.00	10.00	7.25

1966 Topps Punch-Outs

Only a handful of surviving examples of this issue are known. It is believed they represent a prototype for the 1967 Topps Punch-Outs which were themselves issued only on a test basis. The cards are blank-backed, measuring about 2-1/2" x 4-5/8" and perforated at center to allow the American League and National League to be separated for game play. A team captain is pictured in black-and-white on each half of the card. The A.L. side has a red background with 35 yellow baseballs to be punched out to determine game action. Background on the N.L. side is blue. Because of their rarity and lack of recent sales records, valuations for most pieces are not provided. This checklist is likely incomplete.

		NM	EX	VG
(1)	Ernie Banks, Mel Stottlemyre			
(2)	Johnny Callison, Jim Grant			
(3)	Donn Clendenon, Al Kaline			
(4)	Curt Flood, Bill Skowron			
(5)	Jim Ray Hart, Mickey Mantle			
(6)	Juan Marichal, Rich Rollins			
(7)	Sandy Koufax, Carl Yastrzemski (12/04 auction)	6,700		
(8)	Roy McMillan, Frank Robinson			
(9)	John Roseboro, Bobby Richardson			
(10)	Willie Stargell, Felix Mantilla			
(11)	Willie Mays, Tony Conigliaro			
(12)	Joe Torre, Harmon Killebrew			

1966 Topps Rub-Offs

Returning to a concept last tried in 1961, Topps tried an expanded version of Rub-Offs in 1966. Measuring 2-1/16" x 3", the Rub-Offs are in vertical format for the 100 players and

horizontal for the 20 team pennants. The player Rub-Offs feature a color photo. Cutting procedures left well-centered examples in the distinct minority.

		NM	EX	VG
Complete Set (120):		800.00	265.00	120.00
Common Player:		5.00	1.50	.75
(1)	Hank Aaron	30.00	11.00	5.00
(2)	Jerry Adair	5.00	1.50	.75
(3)	Richie Allen	6.00	2.00	.90
(4)	Jesus Alou	5.00	1.50	.75
(5)	Max Alvis	5.00	1.50	.75
(6)	Bob Aspromonte	5.00	1.50	.75
(7)	Ernie Banks	15.00	5.00	2.50
(8)	Earl Battey	5.00	1.50	.75
(9)	Curt Blefary	5.00	1.50	.75
(10)	Ken Boyer	6.00	2.00	.90
(11)	Bob Bruce	5.00	1.50	.75
(12)	Jim Bunning	10.00	3.50	1.50
(13)	Johnny Callison	5.00	1.50	.75
(14)	Bert Campaneris	5.00	1.50	.75
(15)	Jose Cardenal	5.00	1.50	.75
(16)	Dean Chance	5.00	1.50	.75
(17)	Ed Charles	5.00	1.50	.75
(18)	Bob Clemente	35.00	12.00	5.00
(19)	Tony Cloninger	5.00	1.50	.75
(20)	Rocky Colavito	6.00	2.00	.90
(21)	Tony Conigliaro	6.50	2.25	1.00
(22)	Vic Davillilo	5.00	1.50	.75
(23)	Willie Davis	5.00	1.50	.75
(24)	Don Drysdale	10.00	3.50	1.50
(25)	Sammy Ellis	5.00	1.50	.75
(26)	Dick Ellsworth	5.00	1.50	.75
(27)	Ron Fairly	5.00	1.50	.75
(28)	Dick Farrell	5.00	1.50	.75
(29)	Eddie Fisher	5.00	1.50	.75
(30)	Jack Fisher	5.00	1.50	.75
(31)	Curt Flood	5.00	1.50	.75
(32)	Whitey Ford	15.00	5.25	2.25
(33)	Bill Freehan	5.00	1.50	.75
(34)	Jim Fregosi	5.00	1.50	.75
(35)	Bob Gibson	10.00	3.50	1.50
(36)	Jim Grant	5.00	1.50	.75
(37)	Jimmie Hall	5.00	1.50	.75
(38)	Ken Harrelson	5.00	1.50	.75
(39)	Jim Hart	5.00	1.50	.75
(40)	Joel Horlen	5.00	1.50	.75
(41)	Willie Horton	5.00	1.50	.75
(42)	Frank Howard	6.00	2.00	.90
(43)	Deron Johnson	5.00	1.50	.75
(44)	Al Kaline	12.50	4.50	2.00
(45)	Harmon Killebrew	10.00	3.50	1.50
(46)	Bobby Knoop	5.00	1.50	.75
(47)	Sandy Koufax	30.00	10.00	5.00
(48)	Ed Kranepool	5.00	1.50	.75
(49)	Gary Kroll	5.00	1.50	.75
(50)	Don Landrum	5.00	1.50	.75
(51)	Vernon Law	5.00	1.50	.75
(52)	Johnny Lewis	5.00	1.50	.75
(53)	Don Lock	5.00	1.50	.75
(54)	Mickey Lolich	5.00	1.50	.75
(55)	Jim Maloney	5.00	1.50	.75
(56)	Felix Mantilla	5.00	1.50	.75
(57)	Mickey Mantle	55.00	20.00	8.00
(58)	Juan Marichal	10.00	3.50	1.50
(59)	Ed Mathews	10.00	3.50	1.50
(60)	Willie Mays	30.00	10.00	5.00
(61)	Bill Mazeroski	10.00	3.50	1.50
(62)	Dick McAuliffe	5.00	1.50	.75
(63)	Tim McCarver	6.00	2.00	.90
(64)	Willie McCovey	10.00	3.50	1.50
(65)	Sammy McDowell	5.00	1.50	.75
(66)	Ken McMullen	5.00	1.50	.75
(67)	Denis Menke	5.00	1.50	.75
(68)	Bill Monbouquette	5.00	1.50	.75
(69)	Joe Morgan	10.00	3.50	1.50
(70)	Fred Newman	5.00	1.50	.75
(71)	John O'Donoghue	5.00	1.50	.75
(72)	Tony Oliva	6.00	2.00	.90
(73)	Johnny Orsino	5.00	1.50	.75
(74)	Phil Ortega	5.00	1.50	.75
(75)	Milt Pappas	5.00	1.50	.75
(76)	Dick Radatz	5.00	1.50	.75
(77)	Bobby Richardson	6.50	2.25	1.00
(78)	Pete Richert	5.00	1.50	.75
(79)	Brooks Robinson	12.50	4.50	2.00
(80)	Floyd Robinson	5.00	1.50	.75
(81)	Frank Robinson	12.50	4.50	2.00
(82)	Cookie Rojas	5.00	1.50	.75
(83)	Pete Rose	25.00	9.00	4.00
(84)	John Roseboro	5.00	1.50	.75
(85)	Ron Santo	6.50	2.25	1.00
(86)	Bill Skowron	5.00	1.75	.70
(87)	Willie Stargell	10.00	3.50	1.50
(88)	Mel Stottlemyre	5.00	1.50	.75
(89)	Dick Stuart	5.00	1.50	.75
(90)	Ron Swoboda	5.00	1.50	.75
(91)	Fred Talbot	5.00	1.50	.75
(92)	Ralph Terry	5.00	1.50	.75
(93)	Joe Torre	6.50	2.25	1.00
(94)	Tom Tresh	5.00	1.50	.75
(95)	Bob Veale	5.00	1.50	.75
(96)	Pete Ward	5.00	1.50	.75
(97)	Bill White	5.00	1.50	.75
(98)	Billy Williams	10.00	3.50	1.50
(99)	Jim Wynn	5.00	1.50	.75
(100)	Carl Yastrzemski	15.00	5.25	2.25
(101)	Angels Pennant	7.00	2.50	1.00
(102)	Astros Pennant	7.00	2.50	1.00
(103)	Athletics Pennant	7.00	2.50	1.00
(104)	Braves Pennant	7.00	2.50	1.00
(105)	Cards Pennant	7.00	2.50	1.00
(106)	Cubs Pennant	7.00	2.50	1.00
(107)	Dodgers Pennant	7.00	2.50	1.00
(108)	Giants Pennant	7.00	2.50	1.00
(109)	Indians Pennant	7.00	2.50	1.00
(110)	Mets Pennant	7.00	2.50	1.00
(111)	Orioles Pennant	7.00	2.50	1.00

(112)	Phillies Pennant	7.00	2.50	1.00
(113)	Pirates Pennant	7.00	2.50	1.00
(114)	Red Sox Pennant	7.00	2.50	1.00
(115)	Reds Pennant	7.00	2.50	1.00
(116)	Senators Pennant	7.00	2.50	1.00
(117)	Tigers Pennant	7.00	2.50	1.00
(118)	Twins Pennant	7.00	2.50	1.00
(119)	White Sox Pennant	7.00	2.50	1.00
(120)	Yankees Pennant	9.00	3.25	1.25

1967 Topps

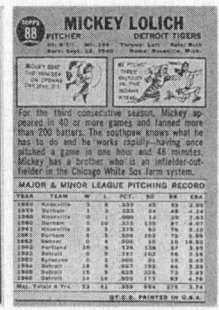

This 609-card set of 2-1/2" x 3-1/2" cards marked the largest set up to that time for Topps. Card fronts feature large color photographs bordered by white. The player's name and position are printed at the top with the team at the bottom. Across the front of the card with the exception of #254 (Milt Pappas) there is a facsimile autograph. The backs were the first to be done vertically, although they continued to carry familiar statistical and biographical information. The only subsets are statistical leaders and World Series highlights. Rookie cards are done by team or league with two players per card. The high numbers (#534-609) in '67 are quite scarce, and while it is known that some are even scarcer, by virtue of having been short-printed in relation to the rest of the series, there is no general agreement on which cards are involved. Cards in the high series which are generally believed to have been double-printed - and thus worth somewhat less than the other cards in the series - are indicated in the checklist by a (DP) notation following the player name.

		NM	EX	VG
	Complete Set (609):	4,500	2,250	1,350
	Common Player (1-370):	2.00	1.00	.60
	Common Player (371-457):	4.00	2.00	1.25
	Common Player (458-533):	7.00	3.50	2.00
	Common Player (534-609):	12.00	6.00	3.50
1	The Champs (Hank Bauer, Brooks Robinson, Frank Robinson)	20.00	9.00	5.00
2	Jack Hamilton	2.00	1.00	.60
3	Duke Sims	2.00	1.00	.60
4	Hal Lanier	2.00	1.00	.60
5	Whitey Ford	30.00	15.00	7.50
6	Dick Simpson	2.00	1.00	.60
7	Don McMahon	2.00	1.00	.60
8	Chuck Harrison	2.00	1.00	.60
9	Ron Hansen	2.00	1.00	.60
10	Matty Alou	2.00	1.00	.60
11	Barry Moore	2.00	1.00	.60
12	Dodgers Rookies (Jimmy Campanis, Bill Singer)	2.00	1.00	.60
13	Joe Sparma	2.00	1.00	.60
14	Phil Linz	2.00	1.00	.60
15	Earl Battey	2.00	1.00	.60
16	Bill Hands	2.00	1.00	.60
17	Jim Gosger	2.00	1.00	.60
18	Gene Oliver	2.00	1.00	.60
19	Jim McGlothlin	2.00	1.00	.60
20	Orlando Cepeda	10.00	5.00	2.50
21	Dave Bristol	2.00	1.00	.60
22	Gene Brabender	2.00	1.00	.60
23	Larry Elliot	2.00	1.00	.60
24	Bob Allen	2.00	1.00	.60
25	Elston Howard	7.00	3.50	2.00
26a	Bob Priddy (No trade statement.)	25.00	12.50	6.25
26b	Bob Priddy (With trade statement.)	2.00	1.00	.60
27	Bob Saverine	2.00	1.00	.60
28	Barry Latman	2.00	1.00	.60
29	Tommy McCraw	2.00	1.00	.60
30	Al Kaline	20.00	10.00	6.00
31	Jim Brewer	2.00	1.00	.60
32	Bob Bailey	2.00	1.00	.60
33	Athletics Rookies (Sal Bando, Randy Schwartz)	4.00	2.00	1.25
34	Pete Cimino	2.00	1.00	.60
35	Rico Carty	2.00	1.00	.60
36	Bob Tillman	2.00	1.00	.60
37	Rick Wise	2.00	1.00	.60
38	Bob Johnson	2.00	1.00	.60
39	Curt Simmons	2.00	1.00	.60
40	Rick Reichardt	2.00	1.00	.60
41	Joe Hoerner	2.00	1.00	.60
42	Mets Team	8.00	4.00	2.50
43	Chico Salmon	2.00	1.00	.60
44	Joe Nuxhall	2.00	1.00	.60
45a	Roger Maris (Cards on front.)	50.00	25.00	12.50
45b	Roger Maris (Yankees on front, blank-back proof.)	2,600	1,300	780.00
46	Lindy McDaniel	2.00	1.00	.60
47	Ken McMullen	2.00	1.00	.60
48	Bill Freehan	2.00	1.00	.60
49	Roy Face	2.00	1.00	.60

50	Tony Oliva	6.00	3.00	1.75
51	Astros Rookies (Dave Adlesh, Wes Bales)	2.00	1.00	.60
52	Dennis Higgins	2.00	1.00	.60
53	Clay Dalrymple	2.00	1.00	.60
54	Dick Green	2.00	1.00	.60
55	Don Drysdale	20.00	10.00	6.00
56	Jose Tartabull	2.00	1.00	.60
57	*Pat Jarvis*	2.00	1.00	.60
58a	Paul Schaal (Bat green above name.)	15.00	7.50	4.50
58b	Paul Schaal (Bat natural above name.)	2.00	1.00	.60
59	Ralph Terry	2.00	1.00	.60
60	Luis Aparicio	15.00	7.50	4.50
61	Gordy Coleman	2.00	1.00	.60
62a	1st Series Check List (1-109) (Frank Robinson) (Copyright symbol beneath T of Tribe.)	7.00	3.50	2.00
62b	1st Series Check List (1-109) (Frank Robinson) (Copyright symbol beneath r of Tribe.)	7.00	3.50	2.00
63	Cards Clubbers (Lou Brock, Curt Flood)	12.00	6.00	3.50
64	Fred Valentine	2.00	1.00	.60
65	Tom Haller	2.00	1.00	.60
66	Manny Mota	2.00	1.00	.60
67	Ken Berry	2.00	1.00	.60
68	Bob Buhl	2.00	1.00	.60
69	Vic Davalillo	2.00	1.00	.60
70	Ron Santo	6.00	3.00	1.75
71	Camilo Pascual	2.00	1.00	.60
72	Tigers Rookies (George Korince, John Matchick) (Korince photo actually James M. Brown.)	2.00	1.00	.60
73	Rusty Staub	3.00	1.50	.90
74	Wes Stock	2.00	1.00	.60
75	George Scott	2.00	1.00	.60
76	Jim Barbieri	2.00	1.00	.60
77	Dooley Womack	2.00	1.00	.60
78	Pat Corrales	2.00	1.00	.60
79	Bubba Morton	2.00	1.00	.60
80	Jim Maloney	2.00	1.00	.60
81	Eddie Stanky	2.00	1.00	.60
82	Steve Barber	2.00	1.00	.60
83	Ollie Brown	2.00	1.00	.60
84	Tommie Sisk	2.00	1.00	.60
85	Johnny Callison	2.00	1.00	.60
86a	Mike McCormick (No trade statement.)	30.00	15.00	9.00
86b	Mike McCormick (With trade statement.)	2.00	1.00	.60
87	George Altman	2.00	1.00	.60
88	Mickey Lolich	2.00	1.00	.60
89	*Felix Millan*	2.00	1.00	.60
90	Jim Nash	2.00	1.00	.60
91	Johnny Lewis	2.00	1.00	.60
92	Ray Washburn	2.00	1.00	.60
93	Yankees Rookies (*Stan Bahnsen, Bobby Murcer*)	12.00	6.00	3.50
94	Ron Fairly	2.00	1.00	.60
95	Sonny Siebert	2.00	1.00	.60
96	Art Shamsky	2.00	1.00	.60
97	Mike Cuellar	2.00	1.00	.60
98	Rich Rollins	2.00	1.00	.60
99	Lee Stange	2.00	1.00	.60
100	Frank Robinson	20.00	10.00	6.00
101	Ken Johnson	2.00	1.00	.60
102	Phillies Team	3.50	1.75	1.00
103a	2nd Series Check List (110-196) (Mickey Mantle) (170: Line after D)	25.00	12.50	7.50
103b	2nd Series Check List (110-196) (Mickey Mantle) (170: Period after D)	25.00	12.50	7.50
104	Minnie Rojas	2.00	1.00	.60
105	Ken Boyer	5.00	2.50	1.50
106	Randy Hundley	2.00	1.00	.60
107	Joel Horlen	2.00	1.00	.60
108	Alex Johnson	2.00	1.00	.60
109	Tribe Thumpers (Rocky Colavito, Leon Wagner)	9.00	4.50	2.75
110	Jack Aker	2.00	1.00	.60
111	John Kennedy	2.00	1.00	.60
112	Dave Wickersham	2.00	1.00	.60
113	Dave Nicholson	2.00	1.00	.60
114	Jack Baldschun	2.00	1.00	.60
115	Paul Casanova	2.00	1.00	.60
116	Herman Franks	2.00	1.00	.60
117	Darrell Brandon	2.00	1.00	.60
118	Bernie Allen	2.00	1.00	.60
119	Wade Blasingame	2.00	1.00	.60
120	Floyd Robinson	2.00	1.00	.60
121	Ed Bressoud	2.00	1.00	.60
122	George Brunet	2.00	1.00	.60
123	Pirates Rookies (Jim Price, Luke Walker)	2.00	1.00	.60
124	Jim Stewart	2.00	1.00	.60
125	Moe Drabowsky	2.00	1.00	.60
126	Tony Taylor	2.00	1.00	.60
127	John O'Donoghue	2.00	1.00	.60
128a	Ed Spiezio (Most of "SPIE" missing at top.)	75.00	37.50	22.50
128b	Ed Spiezio (Lettering all there.)	2.00	1.00	.60
129	Phil Roof	2.00	1.00	.60
130	Phil Regan	2.00	1.00	.60
131	Yankees Team	9.00	4.50	2.75
132	Ozzie Virgil	2.00	1.00	.60
133	Ron Kline	2.00	1.00	.60
134	Gates Brown	2.00	1.00	.60
135	Deron Johnson	2.00	1.00	.60
136	Carroll Sembera	2.00	1.00	.60
137	Twins Rookies (Ron Clark, Jim Ollom)	2.00	1.00	.60
138	Dick Kelley	2.00	1.00	.60
139	Dalton Jones	2.00	1.00	.60

140	Willie Stargell	20.00	10.00	6.00
141	John Miller	2.00	1.00	.60
142	Jackie Brandt	2.00	1.00	.60
143	Sox Sockers (Don Buford, Pete Ward)	2.00	1.00	.60
144	Bill Hepler	2.00	1.00	.60
145	Larry Brown	2.00	1.00	.60
146	Steve Carlton	40.00	20.00	10.00
147	Tom Egan	2.00	1.00	.60
148	Adolfo Phillips	2.00	1.00	.60
149a	Joe Moeller (White streak between "M" and cap.)	30.00	15.00	9.00
149b	Joe Moeller (No white streak.)	2.00	1.00	.60
150	Mickey Mantle	250.00	125.00	75.00
151	World Series Game 1 (Moe Mows Down 11)	6.00	3.00	1.75
152	World Series Game 2 (Palmer Blanks Dodgers)	11.00	5.50	3.25
153	World Series Game 3 (Blair's Homer Defeats L.A.)	6.00	3.00	1.75
154	World Series Game 4 (Orioles Win 4th Straight)	6.00	3.00	1.75
155	World Series (The Winners Celebrate)	7.50	3.75	2.25
156	Ron Herbel	2.00	1.00	.60
157	Danny Cater	2.00	1.00	.60
158	Jimmy Coker	2.00	1.00	.60
159	Bruce Howard	2.00	1.00	.60
160	Willie Davis	2.00	1.00	.60
161	Dick Williams	2.00	1.00	.60
162	Billy O'Dell	2.00	1.00	.60
163	Vic Roznovsky	2.00	1.00	.60
164	Dwight Siebler	2.00	1.00	.60
165	Cleon Jones	2.00	1.00	.60
166	Ed Mathews	20.00	10.00	6.00
167	Senators Rookies (Joe Coleman, Tim Cullen)	2.00	1.00	.60
168	Ray Culp	2.00	1.00	.60
169	Horace Clarke	2.00	1.00	.60
170	Dick McAuliffe	2.00	1.00	.60
171	Calvin Koonce	2.00	1.00	.60
172	Bill Heath	2.00	1.00	.60
173	Cards Team	5.00	2.50	1.50
174	Dick Radatz	2.00	1.00	.60
175	Bobby Knoop	2.00	1.00	.60
176	Sammy Ellis	2.00	1.00	.60
177	Tito Fuentes	2.00	1.00	.60
178	John Buzhardt	2.00	1.00	.60
179	Braves Rookies (Cecil Upshaw, Chas. Vaughan)	2.00	1.00	.60
180	Curt Blefary	2.00	1.00	.60
181	Terry Fox	2.00	1.00	.60
182	Ed Charles	2.00	1.00	.60
183	Jim Pagliaroni	2.00	1.00	.60
184	George Thomas	2.00	1.00	.60
185	*Ken Holtzman*	4.00	2.00	1.25
186	Mets Maulers (Ed Kranepool, Ron Swoboda)	3.50	1.75	1.00
187	Pedro Ramos	2.00	1.00	.60
188	Ken Harrelson	2.00	1.00	.60
189	Chuck Hinton	2.00	1.00	.60
190	Turk Farrell	2.00	1.00	.60
191a	3rd Series Check List (197-283) (Willie Mays) (214 is Dick Kelley)	9.00	4.50	2.75
191b	3rd Series Check List (197-283) (Willie Mays) (214 is Tom Kelley)	12.00	6.00	3.50
192	Fred Gladding	2.00	1.00	.60
193	Jose Cardenal	2.00	1.00	.60
194	Bob Allison	2.00	1.00	.60
195	Al Jackson	2.00	1.00	.60
196	Johnny Romano	2.00	1.00	.60
197	Ron Perranoski	2.00	1.00	.60
198	Chuck Hiller	2.00	1.00	.60
199	Billy Hitchcock	2.00	1.00	.60
200	Willie Mays	125.00	62.50	31.25
201	Hal Reniff	2.00	1.00	.60
202	Johnny Edwards	2.00	1.00	.60
203	Al McBean	2.00	1.00	.60
204	Orioles Rookies (Mike Epstein, Tom Phoebus)	2.00	1.00	.60
205	Dick Groat	2.00	1.00	.60
206	Dennis Bennett	2.00	1.00	.60
207	John Orsino	2.00	1.00	.60
208	Jack Lamabe	2.00	1.00	.60
209	Joe Nossek	2.00	1.00	.60
210	Bob Gibson	25.00	12.50	6.25
211	Twins Team	6.00	3.00	1.75
212	Chris Zachary	2.00	1.00	.60
213	*Jay Johnstone*	4.00	2.00	1.25
214	Tom Kelley	2.00	1.00	.60
215	Ernie Banks	25.00	12.50	7.50
216	Bengal Belters (Norm Cash, Al Kaline)	15.00	7.50	4.50
217	Rob Gardner	2.00	1.00	.60
218	Wes Parker	2.00	1.00	.60
219	Clay Carroll	2.00	1.00	.60
220	Jim Hart	2.00	1.00	.60
221	Woody Fryman	2.00	1.00	.60
222	Reds Rookies (Lee May, Darrell Osteen)	2.00	1.00	.60
223	Mike Ryan	2.00	1.00	.60
224	Walt Bond	2.00	1.00	.60
225	Mel Stottlemyre	4.00	2.00	1.25
226	Julian Javier	2.00	1.00	.60
227	Paul Lindblad	2.00	1.00	.60
228	Gil Hodges	9.00	4.50	2.75
229	Larry Jackson	2.00	1.00	.60
230	Boog Powell	6.00	3.00	1.75
231	John Bateman	2.00	1.00	.60
232	Don Buford	2.00	1.00	.60
233	A.L. ERA Leaders (Steve Hargan, Joel Horlen, Gary Peters)	3.00	1.50	.90
234	N.L. ERA Leaders (Mike Cuellar, Sandy Koufax, Juan Marichal)	12.00	6.00	3.50

#	Name			
235	A.L. Pitching Leaders (Jim Kaat, Denny McLain, Earl Wilson)	3.50	1.75	1.00
236	N.L. Pitching Leaders (Bob Gibson, Sandy Koufax, Juan Marichal, Gaylord Perry)	15.00	7.50	3.75
237	A.L. Strikeout Leaders (Jim Kaat, Sam McDowell, Earl Wilson)	3.50	1.75	1.00
238	N.L. Strikeout Leaders (Jim Bunning, Sandy Koufax, Bob Veale)	12.00	6.00	3.50
239	A.L. Batting Leaders (Al Kaline, Tony Oliva, Frank Robinson)	15.00	7.50	3.75
240	N.L. Batting Leaders (Felipe Alou, Matty Alou, Rico Carty)	11.00	5.50	3.25
241	A.L. RBI Leaders (Harmon Killebrew, Boog Powell, Frank Robinson)	11.00	5.50	3.25
242	N.L. RBI Leaders (Hank Aaron, Richie Allen, Bob Clemente)	15.00	7.50	3.75
243	A.L. Home Run Leaders (Harmon Killebrew, Boog Powell, Frank Robinson)	11.00	5.50	3.25
244	N.L. Home Run Leaders (Hank Aaron, Richie Allen, Willie Mays)	15.00	7.50	4.50
245	Curt Flood	5.00	2.50	1.50
246	Jim Perry	2.00	1.00	.60
247	Jerry Lumpe	2.00	1.00	.60
248	Gene Mauch	2.00	1.00	.60
249	Nick Willhite	2.00	1.00	.60
250	Hank Aaron	100.00	50.00	25.00
251	Woody Held	2.00	1.00	.60
252a	Bob Bolin (White streak between Bob and Bolin.)	60.00	30.00	18.00
252b	Bob Bolin (No white streak.)	2.00	1.00	.60
253	Indians Rookies (Bill Davis, Gus Gil)	2.00	1.00	.60
254	Milt Pappas	2.00	1.00	.60
255	Frank Howard	2.50	1.25	.70
256	Bob Hendley	2.00	1.00	.60
257	Charley Smith	2.00	1.00	.60
258	Lee Maye	2.00	1.00	.60
259	Don Dennis	2.00	1.00	.60
260	Jim Lefebvre	2.00	1.00	.60
261	John Wyatt	2.00	1.00	.60
262	Athletics Team	6.00	3.00	1.75
263	Hank Aguirre	2.00	1.00	.60
264	Ron Swoboda	2.00	1.00	.60
265	Lou Burdette	2.00	1.00	.60
266	Pitt Power (Donn Clendenon, Willie Stargell)	12.00	6.00	3.50
267	Don Schwall	2.00	1.00	.60
268	John Briggs	2.00	1.00	.60
269	Don Nottebart	2.00	1.00	.60
270	Zoilo Versalles	2.00	1.00	.60
271	Eddie Watt	2.00	1.00	.60
272	Cubs Rookies (Bill Connors, Dave Dowling)	2.00	1.00	.60
273	Dick Lines	2.00	1.00	.60
274	Bob Aspromonte	2.00	1.00	.60
275	Fred Whitfield	2.00	1.00	.60
276	Bruce Brubaker	2.00	1.00	.60
277	Steve Whitaker	2.00	1.00	.60
278	4th Series Check List (284-370) (Jim Kaat)	7.00	3.50	2.00
279	Frank Linzy	2.00	1.00	.60
280	Tony Conigliaro	9.00	4.50	2.75
281	Bob Rodgers	2.00	1.00	.60
282	Johnny Odom	2.00	1.00	.60
283	Gene Alley	2.00	1.00	.60
284	Johnny Podres	3.00	1.50	.90
285	Lou Brock	10.00	5.00	2.50
286	Wayne Causey	2.00	1.00	.60
287	Mets Rookies (Greg Goossen, Bart Shirley)	2.00	1.00	.60
288	Denver Lemaster	2.00	1.00	.60
289	Tom Tresh	6.00	3.00	1.75
290	Bill White	2.00	1.00	.60
291	Jim Hannan	2.00	1.00	.60
292	Don Pavletich	2.00	1.00	.60
293	Ed Kirkpatrick	2.00	1.00	.60
294	Walt Alston	7.00	3.50	2.00
295	Sam McDowell	2.00	.70	.60
296	Glenn Beckert	2.00	1.00	.60
297	Dave Morehead	2.00	1.00	.60
298	Ron Davis	2.00	1.00	.60
299	Norm Siebern	2.00	1.00	.60
300	Jim Kaat	4.00	2.00	1.25
301	Jesse Gonder	2.00	1.00	.60
302	Orioles Team	6.00	3.00	1.75
303	Gil Blanco	2.00	1.00	.60
304	Phil Gagliano	2.00	1.00	.60
305	Earl Wilson	2.00	1.00	.60
306	*Bud Harrelson*	7.00	3.50	2.00
307	Jim Beauchamp	2.00	1.00	.60
308	Al Downing	2.00	1.00	.60
309	Hurlers Beware (Richie Allen, Johnny Callison)	6.00	3.00	1.75
310	Gary Peters	2.00	1.00	.60
311	Ed Brinkman	2.00	1.00	.60
312	Don Mincher	2.00	1.00	.60
313	Bob Lee	2.00	1.00	.60
314	Red Sox Rookies (*Mike Andrews, Reggie Smith*)	12.00	6.00	3.50
315	Billy Williams	15.00	7.50	3.75
316	Jack Kralick	2.00	1.00	.60
317	Cesar Tovar	2.00	1.00	.60
318	Dave Giusti	2.00	1.00	.60
319	Paul Blair	2.00	1.00	.60
320	Gaylord Perry	15.00	7.50	4.50
321	Mayo Smith	2.00	1.00	.60
322	Jose Pagan	2.00	1.00	.60
323	Mike Hershberger	2.00	1.00	.60
324	Hal Woodeshick	2.00	1.00	.60
325	Chico Cardenas	2.00	1.00	.60
326	Bob Uecker	12.00	6.00	3.50
327	Angels Team	6.00	3.00	1.75
328	Clete Boyer	4.00	2.00	1.25
329	Charlie Lau	2.00	1.00	.60
330	Claude Osteen	2.00	1.00	.60
331	Joe Foy	2.00	1.00	.60
332	Jesus Alou	2.00	1.00	.60
333	Fergie Jenkins	10.00	5.00	2.50
334	Twin Terrors (Bob Allison, Harmon Killebrew)	15.00	7.50	4.50
335	Bob Veale	2.00	1.00	.60
336	Joe Azcue	2.00	1.00	.60
337	Joe Morgan	17.50	8.75	5.25
338	Bob Locker	2.00	1.00	.60
339	Chico Ruiz	2.00	1.00	.60
340	Joe Pepitone	4.00	2.00	1.25
341	Giants Rookies (Dick Dietz, Bill Sorrell)	2.00	1.00	.60
342	Hank Fischer	2.00	1.00	.60
343	Tom Satriano	2.00	1.00	.60
344	Ossie Chavarria	2.00	1.00	.60
345	Stu Miller	2.00	1.00	.60
346	Jim Hickman	2.00	1.00	.60
347	Grady Hatton	2.00	1.00	.60
348	Tug McGraw	3.00	1.50	.90
349	Bob Chance	2.00	1.00	.60
350	Joe Torre	7.00	3.50	2.00
351	Vern Law	2.00	1.00	.60
352	Ray Oyler	2.00	1.00	.60
353	Bill McCool	2.00	1.00	.60
354	Cubs Team	6.00	3.00	1.75
355	Carl Yastrzemski	60.00	30.00	15.00
356	Larry Jaster	2.00	1.00	.60
357	Bill Skowron	5.00	2.50	1.50
358	Ruben Amaro	2.00	1.00	.60
359	Dick Ellsworth	2.00	1.00	.60
360	Leon Wagner	2.00	1.00	.60
361	5th Series Check List (371-457) (Roberto Clemente)	9.00	4.50	2.75
362	Darold Knowles	2.00	1.00	.60
363	Dave Johnson	2.00	1.00	.60
364	Claude Raymond	2.00	1.00	.60
365	John Roseboro	2.00	1.00	.60
366	Andy Kosco	2.00	1.00	.60
367	Angels Rookies (Bill Kelso, Don Wallace)	2.00	1.00	.60
368	Jack Hiatt	2.00	1.00	.60
369	Jim Hunter	20.00	10.00	5.00
370	Tommy Davis	2.00	1.00	.60
371	Jim Lonborg	4.00	2.00	1.25
372	Mike de la Hoz	4.00	2.00	1.25
373	White Sox Rookies (Duane Josephson, Fred Klages)	4.00	2.00	1.25
374a	Mel Queen (Rule under stats totals nearly gone.)	4.00	2.00	1.25
374b	Mel Queen (Full rule.)	4.00	2.00	1.25
375	Jake Gibbs	4.00	2.00	1.25
376	Don Lock	4.00	2.00	1.25
377	Luis Tiant	4.00	2.00	1.25
378	Tigers Team	7.00	3.50	2.00
379	Jerry May	4.00	2.00	1.25
380	Dean Chance	4.00	2.00	1.25
381	Dick Schofield	4.00	2.00	1.25
382	Dave McNally	4.00	2.00	1.25
383	Ken Henderson	4.00	2.00	1.25
384	Cards Rookies (Jim Cosman, Dick Hughes)	4.00	2.00	1.25
385	Jim Fregosi	4.00	2.00	1.25
386	Dick Selma	4.00	2.00	1.25
387	Cap Peterson	4.00	2.00	1.25
388	Arnold Earley	4.00	2.00	1.25
389	Al Dark	4.00	2.00	1.25
390	Jim Wynn	4.00	2.00	1.25
391	Wilbur Wood	4.00	2.00	1.25
392	Tommy Harper	4.00	2.00	1.25
393	Jim Bouton	7.00	3.50	2.00
394	Jake Wood	4.00	2.00	1.25
395	Chris Short	4.00	2.00	1.25
396	Atlanta Aces (Tony Cloninger, Denis Menke)	7.00	3.50	2.00
397	Willie Smith	4.00	2.00	1.25
398	Jeff Torborg	4.00	2.00	1.25
399	Al Worthington	4.00	2.00	1.25
400	Roberto Clemente	125.00	62.50	31.25
401	Jim Coates	4.00	2.00	1.25
402a	Phillies Rookies (Grant Jackson, Billy Wilson) (Incomplete line under Wilson's stats.)	6.50	3.25	2.00
402b	Grant Jackson, Billy Wilson (Complete line.)	4.00	2.00	1.25
403	Dick Nen	4.00	2.00	1.25
404	Nelson Briles	4.00	2.00	1.25
405	Russ Snyder	4.00	2.00	1.25
406	Lee Elia	4.00	2.00	1.25
407	Reds Team	7.00	3.50	2.00
408	Jim Northrup	4.00	2.00	1.25
409	Ray Sadecki	4.00	2.00	1.25
410	Lou Johnson	4.00	2.00	1.25
411	Dick Howser	4.00	2.00	1.25
412	Astros Rookies (*Norm Miller, Doug Rader*)	5.00	2.50	1.50
413	Jerry Grote	4.00	2.00	1.25
414	Casey Cox	4.00	2.00	1.25
415	Sonny Jackson	4.00	2.00	1.25
416	Roger Repoz	4.00	2.00	1.25
417a	Bob Bruce (RBAVES on back.)	20.00	10.00	5.00
417b	Bob Bruce (Corrected)	4.00	2.00	1.25
418	Sam Mele	4.00	2.00	1.25
419	Don Kessinger	4.00	2.00	1.25
420	Denny McLain	7.00	3.50	2.00
421	Dal Maxvill	4.00	2.00	1.25
422	Hoyt Wilhelm	15.00	7.50	4.50
423	Fence Busters (Willie Mays, Willie McCovey)	25.00	12.50	7.50
424	Pedro Gonzalez	4.00	2.00	1.25
425	Pete Mikkelsen	4.00	2.00	1.25
426	Lou Clinton	4.00	2.00	1.25
427a	Ruben Gomez (Stats totals line nearly gone.)	12.00	6.00	3.50
427b	Ruben Gomez (Full stats totals line.)	4.00	2.00	1.25
428	Dodgers Rookies (*Tom Hutton, Gene Michael*)	6.00	3.00	1.75
429	Garry Roggenburk	4.00	2.00	1.25
430	Pete Rose	90.00	45.00	22.50
431	Ted Uhlaender	4.00	2.00	1.25
432	Jimmie Hall	4.00	2.00	1.25
433	Al Luplow	4.00	2.00	1.25
434	Eddie Fisher	4.00	2.00	1.25
435	Mack Jones	4.00	2.00	1.25
436	Pete Ward	4.00	2.00	1.25
437	Senators Team	7.00	3.50	2.00
438	Chuck Dobson	4.00	2.00	1.25
439	Byron Browne	4.00	2.00	1.25
440	Steve Hargan	4.00	2.00	1.25
441	Jim Davenport	4.00	2.00	1.25
442	Yankees Rookies (Bill Robinson, Joe Verbanic)	6.00	3.00	1.75
443	Tito Francona	4.00	2.00	1.25
444	George Smith	4.00	2.00	1.25
445	Don Sutton	15.00	7.50	4.50
446	Russ Nixon	4.00	2.00	1.25
447a	Bo Belinsky (1966 S.D. stats nearly gone.)	6.00	3.00	1.75
447b	Bo Belinsky (Full 1966 S.D. stats line.)	4.00	2.00	1.25
448	Harry Walker	4.00	2.00	1.25
449	Orlando Pena	4.00	2.00	1.25
450	Richie Allen	12.00	6.00	3.50
451	Fred Newman	4.00	2.00	1.25
452	Ed Kranepool	4.00	2.00	1.25
453	Aurelio Monteagudo	4.00	2.00	1.25
454a	6th Series Check List (458-533) (Juan Marichal) (Left ear shows.)	9.00	4.50	2.75
454b	6th Series Check List (458-533) (Juan Marichal) (No left ear.)	12.00	6.00	3.50
455	Tommie Agee	4.00	2.00	1.25
456	Phil Niekro	15.00	7.50	4.50
457	Andy Etchebarren	4.00	2.00	1.25
458	Lee Thomas	7.00	3.50	2.00
459	Senators Rookies (Dick Bosman, Pete Craig)	7.00	3.50	2.00
460	Harmon Killebrew	60.00	30.00	15.00
461	Bob Miller	7.00	3.50	2.00
462	Bob Barton	7.00	3.50	2.00
463	Hill Aces (Sam McDowell, Sonny Siebert)	11.00	5.50	3.25
464	Dan Coombs	7.00	3.50	2.00
465	Willie Horton	7.00	3.50	2.00
466	Bobby Wine	7.00	3.50	2.00
467	Jim O'Toole	7.00	3.50	2.00
468	Ralph Houk	7.00	3.50	2.00
469	Len Gabrielson	7.00	3.50	2.00
470	Bob Shaw	7.00	3.50	2.00
471	Rene Lachemann	7.00	3.50	2.00
472	Pirates Rookies (John Gelnar, George Spriggs)	7.00	3.50	2.00
473	Jose Santiago	7.00	3.50	2.00
474	Bob Tolan	7.00	3.50	2.00
475	Jim Palmer	75.00	37.50	18.75
476	Tony Perez/SP	40.00	20.00	12.00
477	Braves Team	11.00	5.50	3.25
478	Bob Humphreys	7.00	3.50	2.00
479	Gary Bell	7.00	3.50	2.00
480	Willie McCovey	30.00	15.00	7.50
481	Leo Durocher	12.00	6.00	3.50
482	Bill Monbouquette	7.00	3.50	2.00
483	Jim Landis	7.00	3.50	2.00
484	Jerry Adair	7.00	3.50	2.00
485	Tim McCarver	15.00	7.50	3.75
486	Twins Rookies (Rich Reese, Bill Whitby)	7.00	3.50	2.00
487	Tom Reynolds	7.00	3.50	2.00
488	Gerry Arrigo	7.00	3.50	2.00
489	Doug Clemens	7.00	3.50	2.00
490	Tony Cloninger	7.00	3.50	2.00
491	Sam Bowens	7.00	3.50	2.00
492	Pirates Team	15.00	7.50	3.75
493	Phil Ortega	7.00	3.50	2.00
494	Bill Rigney	7.00	3.50	2.00
495	Fritz Peterson	7.00	3.50	2.00
496	Orlando McFarlane	7.00	3.50	2.00
497	Ron Campbell	7.00	3.50	2.00
498	Larry Dierker	7.00	3.50	2.00
499	Indians Rookies (George Culver, Jose Vidal)	7.00	3.50	2.00
500	Juan Marichal	20.00	10.00	5.00
501	Jerry Zimmerman	7.00	3.50	2.00
502	Derrell Griffith	7.00	3.50	2.00
503	Dodgers Team	15.00	7.50	3.75
504	Orlando Martinez	7.00	3.50	2.00
505	Tommy Helms	7.00	3.50	2.00
506	Smoky Burgess	7.00	3.50	2.00
507	Orioles Rookies (Ed Barnowski, Larry Haney)	7.00	3.50	2.00
508	Dick Hall	7.00	3.50	2.00
509	Jim King	7.00	3.50	2.00
510	Bill Mazeroski	20.00	10.00	6.00
511	Don Wert	7.00	3.50	2.00
512	Red Schoendienst	15.00	7.50	4.50
513	Marcelino Lopez	7.00	3.50	2.00
514	John Werhas	7.00	3.50	2.00
515	Bert Campaneris	7.00	3.50	2.00
516	Giants Team	17.50	8.75	5.25
517	Fred Talbot	7.00	3.50	2.00
518	Denis Menke	7.00	3.50	2.00
519	Ted Davidson	7.00	3.50	2.00
520	Max Alvis	7.00	3.50	2.00
521	Bird Bombers (Curt Blefary, Boog Powell)	7.50	3.75	2.25
522	John Stephenson	7.00	3.50	2.00

523	Jim Merritt	7.00	3.50	2.00
524	Felix Mantilla	7.00	3.50	2.00
525	Ron Hunt	7.00	3.50	2.00
526	Tigers Rookies (Pat Dobson, George Korince)	11.00	5.50	3.25
527	Dennis Ribant	7.00	3.50	2.00
528	Rico Petrocelli	12.50	6.25	3.75
529	Gary Wagner	7.00	3.50	2.00
530	Felipe Alou	12.00	6.00	3.50
531	7th Series Check List (534-609) (Brooks Robinson)	12.00	6.00	3.50
532	Jim Hicks	7.00	3.50	2.00
533	Jack Fisher	7.00	3.50	2.00
534	Hank Bauer (DP)	8.00	4.00	2.50
535	Donn Clendenon	12.00	6.00	3.50
536	Cubs Rookies (Joe Niekro, Paul Popovich)	25.00	12.50	6.25
537	Chuck Estrada (DP)	8.00	4.00	2.50
538	J.C. Martin	12.00	6.00	3.50
539	Dick Egan (DP)	8.00	4.00	2.50
540	Norm Cash	50.00	25.00	12.50
541	Joe Gibbon	12.00	6.00	3.50
542	Athletics Rookies (Rick Monday, Tony Pierce) (DP)	12.50	6.25	3.75
543	Dan Schneider	12.00	6.00	3.50
544	Indians Team	20.00	10.00	5.00
545	Jim Grant	12.00	6.00	3.50
546	Woody Woodward	12.00	6.00	3.50
547	Red Sox Rookies (Russ Gibson, Bill Rohr) (DP)	8.00	4.00	2.50
548	Tony Gonzalez (DP)	8.00	4.00	2.50
549	Jack Sanford	12.00	6.00	3.50
550	Vada Pinson (DP)	12.00	6.00	3.50
551	Doug Camilli (DP)	8.00	4.00	2.50
552	Ted Savage	12.00	6.00	3.50
553	Yankees Rookies (Mike Hegan, Thad Tillotson)	30.00	15.00	7.50
554	Andre Rodgers (DP)	8.00	4.00	2.50
555	Don Cardwell	12.00	6.00	3.50
556	Al Weis (DP)	8.00	4.00	2.50
557	Al Ferrara	12.00	6.00	3.50
558	Orioles Rookies (Mark Belanger, Bill Dillman)	45.00	22.50	13.50
559	Dick Tracewski (DP)	8.00	4.00	2.50
560	Jim Bunning	45.00	22.50	11.25
561	Sandy Alomar	12.00	6.00	3.50
562	Steve Blass (DP)	8.00	4.00	2.50
563	Joe Adcock	15.00	7.50	4.50
564	Astros Rookies (Alonzo Harris, Aaron Pointer) (DP)	8.00	4.00	2.50
565	Lew Krausse	12.00	6.00	3.50
566	Gary Geiger (DP)	8.00	4.00	2.50
567	Steve Hamilton	12.00	6.00	3.50
568	John Sullivan	12.00	6.00	3.50
569	A.L. Rookies (**Hank Allen, Rod Carew**)	300.00	150.00	75.00
570	Maury Wills	50.00	25.00	12.50
571	Larry Sherry	12.00	6.00	3.50
572	Don Demeter	12.00	6.00	3.50
573	White Sox Team (Indians team stats on back)	20.00	10.00	5.00
574	Jerry Buchek	12.00	6.00	3.50
575	*Dave Boswell*	12.00	6.00	3.50
576	N.L. Rookies (Norm Gigon, Ramon Hernandez)	12.00	6.00	3.50
577	Bill Short	12.00	6.00	3.50
578	John Boccabella	12.00	6.00	3.50
579	Bill Henry	12.00	6.00	3.50
580	Rocky Colavito	150.00	75.00	37.50
581	Mets Rookies (**Bill Denehy, Tom Seaver**)	500.00	250.00	150.00
582	Jim Owens (DP)	8.00	4.00	2.50
583	Ray Barker	12.00	6.00	3.50
584	Jim Piersall	20.00	10.00	6.00
585	Wally Bunker	12.00	6.00	3.50
586	Manny Jimenez	12.00	6.00	3.50
587	N.L. Rookies (Don Shaw, Gary Sutherland)	12.00	6.00	3.50
588	Johnny Klippstein (DP)	8.00	4.00	2.50
589	Dave Ricketts (DP)	8.00	4.00	2.50
590	Pete Richert	12.00	6.00	3.50
591	Ty Cline	12.00	6.00	3.50
592	N.L. Rookies (Jim Shellenback, Ron Willis)	12.00	6.00	3.50
593	Wes Westrum	12.00	6.00	3.50
594	Dan Osinski	12.00	6.00	3.50
595	Cookie Rojas	12.00	6.00	3.50
596	Galen Cisco (DP)	8.00	4.00	2.50
597	Ted Abernathy	12.00	6.00	3.50
598	White Sox Rookies (Ed Stroud, Walt Williams)	12.00	6.00	3.50
599	Bob Duliba (DP)	8.00	4.00	2.50
600	Brooks Robinson/SP	250.00	125.00	62.50
601	Bill Bryan (DP)	8.00	4.00	2.50
602	Juan Pizarro	12.00	6.00	3.50
603	Athletics Rookies (Tim Talton, Ramon Webster)	12.00	6.00	3.50
604	Red Sox Team	100.00	50.00	25.00
605	Mike Shannon	50.00	25.00	12.50
606	Ron Taylor	12.00	6.00	3.50
607	Mickey Stanley	25.00	12.50	7.50
608	Cubs Rookies (Rich Nye, John Upham) (DP)	8.00	4.00	2.50
609	Tommy John	80.00	40.00	20.00

1967 Topps Discs

Similar to the more common 28-piece set of 1968, this set of all-stars is known only in proof form, evidently intended to be pressed onto a pin-back button issue which never materialized. Printed on blank-backed silver foil about 2-3/8" square, the pieces have a 2-1/4" diameter center with color player portrait with name and position printed in black across the chest. Some pieces have a name to the left and right of the player's picture. "JAPAN" is printed in tiny black letters at top-left, apparently intended to be folded under the rim of the button. The unnumbered discs are checklisted here alphabetically.

		NM	EX	VG
	Complete Set (24):	12,500	6,250	3,750
	Common Player:	185.00	90.00	55.00
(1)	Hank Aaron	1,400	700.00	420.00
(2)	Johnny Callison	185.00	90.00	55.00
(3)	Bert Campaneris	185.00	90.00	55.00
(4)	Leo Cardenas	185.00	90.00	55.00
(5)	Orlando Cepeda	600.00	300.00	180.00
(6)	Roberto Clemente	1,850	925.00	555.00
(7)	Frank Howard	210.00	105.00	63.00
(8)	Cleon Jones	185.00	90.00	55.00
(9)	Bobby Knoop	185.00	90.00	55.00
(10)	Sandy Koufax	1,150	575.00	345.00
(11)	Mickey Mantle	2,800	1,400	840.00
(12)	Juan Marichal	600.00	300.00	180.00
(13)	Willie Mays	1,400	700.00	420.00
(14)	Sam McDowell	185.00	90.00	55.00
(15)	Denny McLain	210.00	105.00	63.00
(16)	Joe Morgan	600.00	300.00	180.00
(17)	Tony Oliva	185.00	90.00	55.00
(18)	Boog Powell	225.00	110.00	67.00
(19)	Brooks Robinson	750.00	375.00	225.00
(20)	Frank Robinson	750.00	375.00	225.00
(21)	Johnny Romano	185.00	90.00	55.00
(22)	Ron Santo	210.00	105.00	63.00
(23)	Joe Torre	450.00	225.00	135.00
(24)	Carl Yastrzemski	750.00	375.00	225.00

1967 Topps S.F. Giants Discs

One of several prototypes for pinback button sets which were never issued. Generally found in the form of a silver-foil cardboard square, about 2-3/8" a side, the 2-1/4" round center features color player photos or team booster slogans. The player's name and position are printed across his chest, the team name at top. At top-left is a tiny black "JAPAN." The unnumbered discs are checklisted here alphabetically.

		NM	EX	VG
	Complete Set (24):	8,000	4,000	2,400
	Common Player:	185.00	92.00	55.00
(1)	Jesus Alou	185.00	92.00	55.00
(2)	Bob Bolin	185.00	92.00	55.00
(3)	Ollie Brown	185.00	92.00	55.00
(4)	Jim Davenport	185.00	92.00	55.00
(5)	Herman Franks	185.00	92.00	55.00
(6)	Len Gabrielson	185.00	92.00	55.00
(7)	Joe Gibbon	185.00	92.00	55.00
(8)	Tom Haller	185.00	92.00	55.00
(9)	Jim Ray Hart	185.00	92.00	55.00
(10)	Ron Herbel	185.00	92.00	55.00
(11)	Hal Lanier	185.00	92.00	55.00
(12)	Frank Linzy	185.00	92.00	55.00
(13)	Juan Marichal	925.00	460.00	275.00
(14)	Willie Mays	1,625	810.00	485.00
(15)	Willie McCovey	925.00	460.00	275.00
(16)	Lindy McDaniel	185.00	92.00	55.00
(17)	Gaylord Perry	825.00	410.00	245.00
(18)	Cap Peterson	185.00	92.00	55.00
(19)	Bob Priddy	185.00	92.00	55.00
(20)	Happiness is a Giant Win	115.00	57.00	34.00
(21)	I Love the Giants	115.00	57.00	34.00
(22)	Let's Go Giants	115.00	57.00	34.00
(23)	Willie Mays for Mayor (Willie Mays)	700.00	350.00	210.00
(24)	S.F. Giants Logo	115.00	57.00	34.00

1967 Topps Pin-Ups

The 5" x 7" "All Star Pin-ups" were wax pack inserts. They feature a full color picture with the player's name, position and team in a circle in one of the lower corners on the front. The numbered set consists of 32 players (generally big names). Because the large paper pin-ups had to be folded several times to fit into the wax packs, the factory-created folds are not considered when grading unless paper separations have developed along the seams. At least one of the pin-ups (Clemente) has been seen in an unnumbered version printed on better-quality sticker stock and not having fold lines.

		NM	EX	VG
	Complete Set (32):	150.00	65.00	35.00
	Common Player:	2.00	.70	.30
1	Boog Powell	2.50	.90	.40
2	Bert Campaneris	2.00	.70	.30
3	Brooks Robinson	9.00	3.25	1.25
4	Tommie Agee	2.00	.70	.30
5	Carl Yastrzemski	9.00	3.25	1.25
6	Mickey Mantle	40.00	14.00	6.00
7	Frank Howard	2.50	.90	.40
8	Sam McDowell	2.00	.70	.30
9	Orlando Cepeda	6.00	2.00	.90
10	Chico Cardenas	2.00	.70	.30
11	Roberto Clemente	20.00	7.00	3.00
12	Willie Mays	15.00	5.25	2.25
13	Cleon Jones	2.00	.70	.30
14	John Callison	2.00	.70	.30
15	Hank Aaron	15.00	5.25	2.25
16	Don Drysdale	7.50	2.75	1.25
17	Bobby Knoop	2.00	.70	.30
18	Tony Oliva	2.50	.90	.40
19	Frank Robinson	9.00	3.25	1.25
20	Denny McLain	2.50	.90	.40
21	Al Kaline	9.00	3.25	1.25
22	Joe Pepitone	3.00	1.00	.45
23	Harmon Killebrew	7.50	2.75	1.25
24	Leon Wagner	2.00	.70	.30
25	Joe Morgan	7.50	2.75	1.25
26	Ron Santo	3.00	1.00	.45
27	Joe Torre	4.50	1.50	.70
28	Juan Marichal	6.00	2.00	.90
29	Matty Alou	2.00	.70	.30
30	Felipe Alou	2.00	.70	.30
31	Ron Hunt	2.00	.70	.30
32	Willie McCovey	7.50	2.75	1.25

1967 Topps Punch-Outs

This test issue was reportedly released around Maryland in cello packs containing two perforated strips of three game cards each. Cards are printed in black, white and red and measure 2-1/2" x 4-2/3". Backs have instructions on how to play a baseball game by punching out the small squares. Only the "Team Captain" is pictured on the card; each captain can be found with at least two different line-ups on his team, creating a large number of collectible variations. Variations in some player photos have also been noted. The unnumbered issue is checklisted here in alphabetical order. Note, punch-outs of the following players are now believed not to exist: Campaneris, Gibson, Grote, McMillan, and Brooks Robinson.

		NM	EX	VG
	Complete Set (91):	19,000	9,500	5,750
	Common Player:	80.00	40.00	24.00
(1)	Hank Aaron	1,500	750.00	450.00
(2)	Richie Allen	150.00	75.00	45.00
(3)	Gene Alley	80.00	40.00	24.00
(4)	Felipe Alou	90.00	45.00	27.00
(5)	Matty Alou	80.00	40.00	24.00
(6)	Max Alvis	80.00	40.00	24.00
(7)	Luis Aparicio	200.00	100.00	60.00
(8)	Steve Barber	80.00	40.00	24.00
(9)	Earl Battey	80.00	40.00	24.00
(10)	Clete Boyer	100.00	50.00	30.00
(11)	Ken Boyer	100.00	50.00	30.00
(12)	Lou Brock	200.00	100.00	60.00
(13)	Jim Bunning	175.00	87.00	52.00
(14)	Johnny Callison	80.00	40.00	24.00

		NM	EX	VG
(15)	Bert Campaneris	80.00	40.00	24.00
	(Believed not to exist.)			
(16)	Leo Cardenas	80.00	40.00	24.00
(17)	Rico Carty	80.00	40.00	24.00
(18)	Norm Cash	90.00	45.00	27.00
(19)	Orlando Cepeda	175.00	87.00	52.00
(20)	Ed Charles	80.00	40.00	24.00
(21a)	Roberto Clemente	1,500	750.00	450.00
	(Plain background photo.)			
(21b)	Roberto Clemente (Stadium	2,000	1,000	600.00
	background photo.)			
(22)	Donn Clendenon	80.00	40.00	24.00
(23)	Rocky Colavito	150.00	75.00	45.00
(24)	Tony Conigliaro	90.00	45.00	27.00
(25)	Willie Davis	80.00	40.00	24.00
(26)	Johnny Edwards	80.00	40.00	24.00
(27)	Andy Etchebarren	80.00	40.00	24.00
(28)	Curt Flood	80.00	40.00	24.00
(29)	Bill Freehan	80.00	40.00	24.00
(30)	Jim Fregosi	80.00	40.00	24.00
(31)	Bob Gibson	300.00	150.00	90.00
	(Believed not to exist.)			
(32)	Dick Green	80.00	40.00	24.00
(33)	Dick Groat	80.00	40.00	24.00
(34)	Jerry Grote	80.00	40.00	24.00
	(Believed not to exist.)			
(35)	Tom Haller	80.00	40.00	24.00
(36)	Jim Ray Hart	80.00	40.00	24.00
(37)	Mike Hershberger	80.00	40.00	24.00
(38)	Elston Howard	100.00	50.00	30.00
(39)	Frank Howard	90.00	45.00	27.00
(40)	Ron Hunt	80.00	40.00	24.00
(41)	Sonny Jackson	80.00	40.00	24.00
(42)	Cleon Jones	80.00	40.00	24.00
(43)	Jim Kaat	100.00	50.00	30.00
(44)	Al Kaline	400.00	200.00	120.00
(45)	Harmon Killebrew	300.00	150.00	90.00
(46)	Bobby Knoop	80.00	40.00	24.00
(47)	Sandy Koufax	1,500	750.00	450.00
(48)	Ed Kranepool	80.00	40.00	24.00
(49)	Jim Lefebvre	80.00	40.00	24.00
(50)	Don Lock	80.00	40.00	24.00
(51)	Jerry Lumpe	80.00	40.00	24.00
(52)	Mickey Mantle	2,400	1,200	720.00
(53)	Juan Marichal	175.00	87.00	52.00
(54)	Willie Mays	1,500	750.00	450.00
(55)	Bill Mazeroski	175.00	87.00	52.00
(56)	Dick McAuliffe	80.00	40.00	24.00
(57)	Tim McCarver	90.00	45.00	27.00
(58)	Willie McCovey	200.00	100.00	60.00
(59)	Denny McLain	90.00	45.00	27.00
(60)	Roy McMillan	80.00	40.00	24.00
	(Believed not to exist.)			
(61)	Denis Menke	80.00	40.00	24.00
(62)	Joe Morgan	200.00	100.00	60.00
(63)	Tony Oliva	90.00	45.00	27.00
(64)	Joe Pepitone	100.00	50.00	30.00
(65)	Gaylord Perry	175.00	87.00	52.00
(66)	Vada Pinson	90.00	45.00	27.00
(67)	Boog Powell	100.00	50.00	30.00
(68)	Rick Reichardt	80.00	40.00	24.00
(69)	Brooks Robinson	400.00	200.00	120.00
	(Believed not to exist.)			
(70)	Floyd Robinson	80.00	40.00	24.00
(71)	Frank Robinson	400.00	200.00	120.00
(72)	Johnny Romano	80.00	40.00	24.00
(73)	Pete Rose	1,250	625.00	375.00
(74)	John Roseboro	80.00	40.00	24.00
(75)	Ron Santo	100.00	50.00	30.00
(76)	Chico Salmon	80.00	40.00	24.00
(77)	George Scott	80.00	40.00	24.00
(78)	Sonny Siebert	80.00	40.00	24.00
(79)	Russ Snyder	80.00	40.00	24.00
(80)	Willie Stargell	200.00	100.00	60.00
(81)	Mel Stottlemyre	80.00	40.00	24.00
(82)	Joe Torre	120.00	60.00	36.00
(83)	Cesar Tovar	80.00	40.00	24.00
(84)	Tom Tresh	90.00	45.00	27.00
(85)	Zoilo Versalles	80.00	40.00	24.00
(86)	Leon Wagner	80.00	40.00	24.00
(87)	Bill White	80.00	40.00	24.00
(88)	Fred Whitfield	80.00	40.00	24.00
(89)	Billy Williams	175.00	87.00	52.00
(90)	Jimmy Wynn	80.00	40.00	24.00
(91)	Carl Yastrzemski	450.00	225.00	135.00

1967 Topps Stand-Ups

Never actually issued, no more than a handful of each of these rare test issues have made their way into the hobby market. Designed so that the color photo of the player's head could be popped out of the black background and placed into a punch-out base to create a stand-up display, examples of these 3-1/8" x 5-1/4" cards can be found either on thick stock, die-cut around the portrait and with a die-cut stand, or as thin-stock proofs without the die-cutting. Blank-backed, there are 24 cards in the set, numbered on the front at bottom left.

		NM	EX	VG
Complete Set, Thick (24):		75,000	37,500	22,500
Complete Set, Thin (24):		60,000	30,000	18,000
Common Player, Thick:		1,250	625.00	375.00
Common Player, Thin:		1,000	500.00	300.00
THICK STOCK, DIE-CUT				
1	Pete Rose	4,750	2,375	1,425
2	Gary Peters	1,250	625.00	375.00
3	Frank Robinson	2,400	1,200	720.00
4	Jim Lonborg	1,250	625.00	375.00
5	Ron Swoboda	1,250	625.00	375.00
6	Harmon Killebrew	2,100	1,050	630.00
7	Roberto Clemente	8,500	4,250	2,550
8	Mickey Mantle	12,500	6,250	3,750
9	Jim Fregosi	1,250	625.00	375.00
10	Al Kaline	3,000	1,500	900.00
11	Don Drysdale	2,500	1,250	750.00
12	Dean Chance	1,250	625.00	375.00
13	Orlando Cepeda	1,750	875.00	525.00
14	Tim McCarver	1,400	700.00	420.00
15	Frank Howard	1,400	700.00	420.00
16	Max Alvis	1,250	625.00	375.00
17	Rusty Staub	1,400	700.00	420.00
18	Richie Allen	1,400	700.00	420.00
19	Willie Mays	8,500	4,250	2,550
20	Hank Aaron	8,500	4,250	2,550
21	Carl Yastrzemski	7,000	3,500	2,100
22	Ron Santo	1,400	700.00	420.00
23	Catfish Hunter	1,750	875.00	525.00
24	Jim Wynn	1,250	625.00	375.00
THIN STOCK, PROOFS				
1	Pete Rose	3,750	1,875	1,125
2	Gary Peters	1,000	500.00	300.00
3	Frank Robinson	1,900	950.00	570.00
4	Jim Lonborg	1,000	500.00	300.00
5	Ron Swoboda	1,000	500.00	300.00
6	Harmon Killebrew	1,650	825.00	495.00
7	Roberto Clemente	6,500	3,250	1,950
8	Mickey Mantle	10,000	5,000	3,000
9	Jim Fregosi	1,000	500.00	300.00
10	Al Kaline	2,500	1,250	750.00
11	Don Drysdale	2,000	1,000	600.00
12	Dean Chance	1,000	500.00	300.00
13	Orlando Cepeda	1,400	700.00	420.00
14	Tim McCarver	1,100	550.00	330.00
15	Frank Howard	1,100	550.00	330.00
16	Max Alvis	1,000	500.00	300.00
17	Rusty Staub	1,100	550.00	330.00
18	Richie Allen	1,100	550.00	330.00
19	Willie Mays	7,000	3,500	2,100
20	Hank Aaron	7,000	3,500	2,100
21	Carl Yastrzemski	5,500	2,750	1,650
22	Ron Santo	1,100	550.00	330.00
23	Catfish Hunter	1,400	700.00	420.00
24	Jim Wynn	1,000	500.00	300.00

1967 Topps Pirates Stickers

Considered a "test" issue, this 33-sticker set of 2-1/2" x 3-1/2" stickers is very similar to the Red Sox stickers which were produced the same year. Player stickers have a color picture (often just the player's head) and the player's name in large "comic book" letters. Besides the players, there are other topics such as "I Love the Pirates," "Bob Clemente for Mayor," and a number of similar sentiments. The stickers have blank backs and are rather scarce.

		NM	EX	VG
Complete Set (33):		750.00	375.00	225.00
Common Player:		15.00	7.50	4.50
1	Gene Alley	15.00	7.50	4.50
2	Matty Alou	15.00	7.50	4.50
3	Dennis Ribant	15.00	7.50	4.50
4	Steve Blass	15.00	7.50	4.50
5	Juan Pizarro	15.00	7.50	4.50
6	Bob Clemente	175.00	85.00	50.00
7	Donn Clendenon	15.00	7.50	4.50
8	Roy Face	15.00	7.50	4.50
9	Woody Fryman	15.00	7.50	4.50
10	Jesse Gonder	15.00	7.50	4.50
11	Vern Law	15.00	7.50	4.50
12	Al McBean	15.00	7.50	4.50
13	Jerry May	15.00	7.50	4.50
14	Bill Mazeroski	35.00	17.50	10.00
15	Pete Mikkelsen	15.00	7.50	4.50
16	Manny Mota	15.00	7.50	4.50
17	Billy O'Dell	15.00	7.50	4.50
18	Jose Pagan	15.00	7.50	4.50
19	Jim Pagliaroni	15.00	7.50	4.50
20	Johnny Pesky	15.00	7.50	4.50
21	Tommie Sisk	15.00	7.50	4.50
22	Willie Stargell	60.00	30.00	18.00
23	Bob Veale	15.00	7.50	4.50
24	Harry Walker	15.00	7.50	4.50
25	I Love The Pirates	20.00	10.00	6.00
26	Let's Go Pirates	20.00	10.00	6.00
27	Bob Clemente For Mayor	100.00	50.00	30.00
28	National League Batting Champion (Matty Alou)	15.00	7.50	4.50
29	Happiness Is A Pirate Win	20.00	10.00	6.00
30	Donn Clendenon Is My Hero	15.00	7.50	4.50
31	Pirates' Home Run Champion (Willie Stargell)	30.00	15.00	9.00
32	Pirates Logo	20.00	10.00	6.00
33	Pirates Pennant	25.00	12.50	7.50

1967 Topps Red Sox Stickers

Like the 1967 Pirates Stickers, the Red Sox Stickers were part of the same test procedure. The Red Sox Stickers have the same 2-1/2" x 3-1/2" dimensions, color picture and large player's name on the front. A set is complete at 33 stickers. The majority are players, but themes such as "Let's Go Red Sox" are also included.

		NM	EX	VG
Complete Set (33):		500.00	250.00	150.00
Common Player:		10.00	5.00	3.00
1	Dennis Bennett	10.00	5.00	3.00
2	Darrell Brandon	10.00	5.00	3.00
3	Tony Conigliaro	35.00	17.50	10.00
4	Don Demeter	10.00	5.00	3.00
5	Hank Fischer	10.00	5.00	3.00
6	Joe Foy	10.00	5.00	3.00
7	Mike Andrews	10.00	5.00	3.00
8	Dalton Jones	10.00	5.00	3.00
9	Jim Lonborg	10.00	5.00	3.00
10	Don McMahon	10.00	5.00	3.00
11	Dave Morehead	10.00	5.00	3.00
12	George Smith	10.00	5.00	3.00
13	Rico Petrocelli	15.00	7.50	4.50
14	Mike Ryan	10.00	5.00	3.00
15	Jose Santiago	10.00	5.00	3.00
16	George Scott	10.00	5.00	3.00
17	Sal Maglie	10.00	5.00	3.00
18	Reggie Smith	10.00	5.00	3.00
19	Lee Stange	10.00	5.00	3.00
20	Jerry Stephenson	10.00	5.00	3.00
21	Jose Tartabull	10.00	5.00	3.00
22	George Thomas	10.00	5.00	3.00
23	Bob Tillman	10.00	5.00	3.00
24	Johnnie Wyatt	10.00	5.00	3.00
25	Carl Yastrzemski	90.00	45.00	27.50
26	Dick Williams	10.00	5.00	3.00
27	I Love The Red Sox	12.50	6.25	3.75
28	Let's Go Red Sox	12.50	6.25	3.75
29	Carl Yastrzemski For Mayor	50.00	25.00	15.00
30	Tony Conigliaro Is My Hero	27.50	13.50	8.25
31	Happiness Is A Boston Win	12.50	6.25	3.75
32	Red Sox Logo	15.00	7.50	4.50
33	Red Sox Pennant	20.00	10.00	6.00

1967 Topps Who Am I?

A cartoon caption and goofy facial features were printed on the front of these 2-1/2" x 3-1/2" cards and were designed to be scratched off to reveal the portrait, name and claim to fame of the person beneath. This 44-card set includes all manner of U.S. and international historical figures, including four baseball players. Backs are printed in red and have a large question mark with several hints printed thereon. Unscratched cards are much rarer than scratched cards, though they carry only about a 50 percent premium.

	NM	EX	VG
Complete Set (44):	850.00	425.00	250.00
Wax Pack:	350.00		
12 Babe Ruth	100.00	50.00	30.00
22 Mickey Mantle	225.00	110.00	65.00
33 Willie Mays	100.00	50.00	30.00
41 Sandy Koufax	100.00	50.00	30.00

1968 Topps

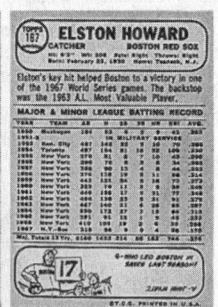

In 1968, Topps returned to a 598-card set of 2-1/2" x 3-1/2" cards. It is not, however, more of the same by way of appearance as the cards feature a color photograph on a background of what appears to be a burlap fabric. The player's name is below the photo but on the unusual background. A colored circle on the lower right carries the team and position. Backs were also changed, while retaining the vertical format introduced the previous year, with stats in the middle and cartoon at the bottom. The set features many of the old favorite subsets, including statistical leaders, World Series highlights, multi-player cards, checklists, rookie cards and the return of All-Star cards. Most checklist cards are double-printed, once in the series preceding the series it lists and once within the series it lists; subtle variations between the pairs are listed where known. It is now believed that the Yellow Team variations of cards #49 and 66 originated in the Milton Bradley Win-A-Card board game.

	NM	EX	VG
Complete Set (598):	3,000	1,500	900.00
Common Player (1-457):	2.00	1.00	.60
Common Player (458-598):	5.00	2.50	1.50
1 N.L. Batting Leaders (Matty Alou, Roberto Clemente, Tony Gonzalez)	15.00	7.50	3.75
2 A.L. Batting Leaders (Al Kaline, Frank Robinson, Carl Yastrzemski)	15.00	7.50	3.75
3 N.L. RBI Leaders (Hank Aaron, Orlando Cepeda, Roberto Clemente)	15.00	7.50	3.75
4 A.L. RBI Leaders (Harmon Killebrew, Frank Robinson, Carl Yastrzemski)	12.00	6.00	3.50
5 N.L. Home Run Leaders (Hank Aaron, Willie McCovey, Ron Santo, Jim Wynn)	20.00	10.00	6.00
6 A.L. Home Run Leaders (Frank Howard, Harmon Killebrew, Carl Yastrzemski)	12.00	6.00	3.50
7 N.L. ERA Leaders (Jim Bunning, Phil Niekro, Chris Short)	7.00	3.50	2.00
8 A.L. ERA Leaders (Joe Horlen, Gary Peters, Sonny Siebert)	2.00	1.00	.60
9 N.L. Pitching Leaders (Jim Bunning, Fergie Jenkins, Mike McCormick, Claude Osteen)	7.00	3.50	2.00
10a A.L. Pitching Leaders (Dean Chance, Jim Lonborg, Earl Wilson) ("Lonberg" on back.)	9.00	4.50	2.75
10b A.L. Pitching Leaders (Dean Chance, Jim Lonborg, Earl Wilson) ("Lonborg" on back.)	7.00	3.50	2.00
11 N.L. Strikeout Leaders (Jim Bunning, Fergie Jenkins, Gaylord Perry)	7.00	3.50	2.00
12 A.L. Strikeout Leaders (Dean Chance, Jim Lonborg, Sam McDowell)	7.00	3.50	2.00
13 Chuck Hartenstein	2.00	1.00	.60
14 Jerry McNertney	2.00	1.00	.60
15 Ron Hunt	2.00	1.00	.60
16 Indians Rookies (Lou Piniella, Richie Scheinblum)	5.00	2.50	1.50
17 Dick Hall	2.00	1.00	.60
18 Mike Hershberger	2.00	1.00	.60
19 Juan Pizarro	2.00	1.00	.60
20 Brooks Robinson	20.00	10.00	5.00
21 Ron Davis	2.00	1.00	.60
22 Pat Dobson	2.00	1.00	.60
23 Chico Cardenas	2.00	1.00	.60
24 Bobby Locke	2.00	1.00	.60
25 Julian Javier	2.00	1.00	.60
26 Darrell Brandon	2.00	1.00	.60
27 Gil Hodges	7.50	3.75	2.25
28 Ted Uhlaender	2.00	1.00	.60
29 Joe Verbanic	2.00	1.00	.60
30 Joe Torre	8.00	4.00	2.50
31 Ed Stroud	2.00	1.00	.60
32 Joe Gibbon	2.00	1.00	.60
33 Pete Ward	2.00	1.00	.60
34 Al Ferrara	2.00	1.00	.60
35 Steve Hargan	2.00	1.00	.60

36 Pirates Rookies (**Bob Moose, Bob Robertson**)	2.00	1.00	.60
37 Billy Williams	13.50	6.75	4.00
38 Tony Pierce	2.00	1.00	.60
39 Cookie Rojas	2.00	1.00	.60
40 Denny McLain	20.00	10.00	5.00
41 Julio Gotay	2.00	1.00	.60
42 Larry Haney	2.00	1.00	.60
43 Gary Bell	2.00	1.00	.60
44 Frank Kostro	2.00	1.00	.60
45 Tom Seaver	50.00	25.00	12.50
46 Dave Ricketts	2.00	1.00	.60
47 Ralph Houk	2.50	1.25	.70
48 Ted Davidson	2.00	1.00	.60
49a Ed Brinkman (Yellow team.)	50.00	25.00	12.50
49b Ed Brinkman (White team.)	2.00	1.00	.60
50 Willie Mays	60.00	30.00	15.00
51 Bob Locker	2.00	1.00	.60
52 Hawk Taylor	2.00	1.00	.60
53 Gene Alley	2.00	1.00	.60
54 Stan Williams	2.00	1.00	.60
55 Felipe Alou	5.00	2.50	1.50
56 Orioles Rookies (Dave Leonhard, Dave May)	2.00	1.00	.60
57 Dan Schneider	2.00	1.00	.60
58 Ed Mathews	15.00	7.50	3.75
59 Don Lock	2.00	1.00	.60
60 Ken Holtzman	2.00	1.00	.60
61 Reggie Smith	2.00	1.00	.60
62 Chuck Dobson	2.00	1.00	.60
63 Dick Kenworthy	2.00	1.00	.60
64 Jim Merritt	2.00	1.00	.60
65 John Roseboro	2.00	1.00	.60
66a Casey Cox (Yellow team.)	75.00	37.50	18.75
66b Casey Cox (White team.)	2.00	1.00	.60
67 1st Series Check List (1-109) (Jim Kaat)	5.00	2.50	1.50
68 Ron Willis	2.00	1.00	.60
69 Tom Tresh	6.00	3.00	1.75
70 Bob Veale	2.00	1.00	.60
71 Vern Fuller	2.00	1.00	.60
72 Tommy John	5.00	2.50	1.50
73 Jim Hart	2.00	1.00	.60
74 Milt Pappas	2.00	1.00	.60
75 Don Mincher	2.00	1.00	.60
76 Braves Rookies (**Jim Britton, Ron Reed**)	2.00	1.00	.60
77 **Don Wilson**	2.00	1.00	.60
78 Jim Northrup	2.00	1.00	.60
79 Ted Kubiak	2.00	1.00	.60
80 Rod Carew	50.00	25.00	12.50
81 Larry Jackson	2.00	1.00	.60
82 Sam Bowens	2.00	1.00	.60
83 John Stephenson	2.00	1.00	.60
84 Bob Tolan	2.00	1.00	.60
85 Gaylord Perry	9.00	4.50	2.75
86 Willie Stargell	12.00	6.00	3.50
87 Dick Williams	2.00	1.00	.60
88 Phil Regan	2.00	1.00	.60
89 Jake Gibbs	2.00	1.00	.60
90 Vada Pinson	5.00	2.50	1.50
91 Jim Ollom	2.00	1.00	.60
92 Ed Kranepool	2.00	1.00	.60
93 Tony Cloninger	2.00	1.00	.60
94 Lee Maye	2.00	1.00	.60
95 Bob Aspromonte	2.00	1.00	.60
96 Senators Rookies (Frank Coggins, Dick Nold)	2.00	1.00	.60
97 Tom Phoebus	2.00	1.00	.60
98 Gary Sutherland	2.00	1.00	.60
99 Rocky Colavito	7.00	3.50	2.00
100 Bob Gibson	20.00	10.00	5.00
101 Glenn Beckert	2.00	1.00	.60
102 Jose Cardenal	2.00	1.00	.60
103 Don Sutton	9.00	4.50	2.75
104 Dick Dietz	2.00	1.00	.60
105 Al Downing	2.00	1.00	.60
106 Dalton Jones	2.00	1.00	.60
107 2nd Series Check List (110-196) (Juan Marichal)	5.00	2.50	1.50
108 Don Pavletich	2.00	1.00	.60
109 Bert Campaneris	2.00	1.00	.60
110 Hank Aaron	80.00	40.00	20.00
111 Rich Reese	2.00	1.00	.60
112 Woody Fryman	2.00	1.00	.60
113 Tigers Rookies (Tom Matchick, Daryl Patterson)	2.00	1.00	.60
114 Ron Swoboda	2.00	1.00	.60
115 Sam McDowell	2.00	1.00	.60
116 Ken McMullen	2.00	1.00	.60
117 Larry Jaster	2.00	1.00	.60
118 Mark Belanger	2.00	1.00	.60
119 Ted Savage	2.00	1.00	.60
120 Mel Stottlemyre	5.00	2.50	1.50
121 Jimmie Hall	2.00	1.00	.60
122 Gene Mauch	2.00	1.00	.60
123 Jose Santiago	2.00	1.00	.60
124 Nate Oliver	2.00	1.00	.60
125 Joe Horlen	2.00	1.00	.60
126 Bobby Etheridge	2.00	1.00	.60
127 Paul Lindblad	2.00	1.00	.60
128 Astros Rookies (Tom Dukes, Alonzo Harris)	2.00	1.00	.60
129 Mickey Stanley	2.00	1.00	.60
130 Tony Perez	10.00	5.00	3.00
131 Frank Bertaina	2.00	1.00	.60
132 Bud Harrelson	2.00	1.00	.60
133 Fred Whitfield	2.00	1.00	.60
134 Pat Jarvis	2.00	1.00	.60
135 Paul Blair	2.00	1.00	.60
136 Randy Hundley	2.00	1.00	.60
137 Twins Team	5.00	2.50	1.50
138 Ruben Amaro	2.00	1.00	.60
139 Chris Short	2.00	1.00	.60
140 Tony Conigliaro	5.00	2.50	1.50
141 Dal Maxvill	2.00	1.00	.60
142 White Sox Rookies (Buddy Bradford, Bill Voss)	2.00	1.00	.60

143 Pete Cimino	2.00	1.00	.60
144 Joe Morgan	12.00	6.00	3.50
145 Don Drysdale	15.00	7.50	4.50
146 Sal Bando	2.00	1.00	.60
147 Frank Linzy	2.00	1.00	.60
148 Dave Bristol	2.00	1.00	.60
149 Bob Saverine	2.00	1.00	.60
150 Roberto Clemente	100.00	50.00	25.00
151 World Series Game 1 (Brock Socks 4 Hits in Opener)	6.00	3.00	1.75
152 World Series Game 2 (Yaz Smashes Two Homers)	12.00	6.00	3.00
153 World Series Game 3 (Briles Cools Off Boston)	3.00	1.50	.90
154 World Series Game 4 (Gibson Hurls Shutout)	9.00	4.50	2.75
155 World Series Game 5 (Lonborg Wins Again)	6.00	3.00	1.75
156 World Series Game 6 (Petrocelli Socks Two Homers)	6.00	3.00	1.75
157 World Series Game 7 (St. Louis Wins It)	6.00	3.00	1.75
158 1967 World Series (The Cardinals Celebrate)	5.00	2.50	1.50
159 Don Kessinger	2.00	1.00	.60
160 Earl Wilson	2.00	1.00	.60
161 Norm Miller	2.00	1.00	.60
162 Cards Rookies (**Hal Gilson, Mike Torrez**)	2.00	1.00	.60
163 Gene Brabender	2.00	1.00	.60
164 Ramon Webster	2.00	1.00	.60
165 Tony Oliva	5.00	2.50	1.50
166 Claude Raymond	2.00	1.00	.60
167 Elston Howard	5.00	2.50	1.50
168 Dodgers Team	5.00	2.50	1.50
169 Bob Bolin	2.00	1.00	.60
170 Jim Fregosi	2.00	1.00	.60
171 Don Nottebart	2.00	1.00	.60
172 Walt Williams	2.00	1.00	.60
173 John Boozer	2.00	1.00	.60
174 Bob Tillman	2.00	1.00	.60
175 Maury Wills	2.00	1.00	.60
176 Bob Allen	2.00	1.00	.60
177 Mets Rookies (**Jerry Koosman, Nolan Ryan**)	490.00	245.00	150.00
178 Don Wert	2.00	1.00	.60
179 Bill Stoneman	2.00	1.00	.60
180 Curt Flood	3.00	1.50	.90
181 Jerry Zimmerman	2.00	1.00	.60
182 Dave Giusti	2.00	1.00	.60
183 Bob Kennedy	2.00	1.00	.60
184 Lou Johnson	2.00	1.00	.60
185 Tom Haller	2.00	1.00	.60
186 Eddie Watt	2.00	1.00	.60
187 Sonny Jackson	2.00	1.00	.60
188 Cap Peterson	2.00	1.00	.60
189 Bill Landis	2.00	1.00	.60
190 Bill White	2.00	1.00	.60
191 Dan Frisella	2.00	1.00	.60
192a 3rd Series Check List (197-283) (Carl Yastrzemski) ("To increase the..." on back.)	6.00	3.00	1.75
192b 3rd Series Check List (197-283) (Carl Yastrzemski) ("To increase your..." on back.)	6.00	3.00	1.75
193 Jack Hamilton	2.00	1.00	.60
194 Don Buford	2.00	1.00	.60
195 Joe Pepitone	5.00	2.50	1.50
196 Gary Nolan	2.00	1.00	.60
197 Larry Brown	2.00	1.00	.60
198 Roy Face	2.00	1.00	.60
199 A's Rookies (Darrell Osteen, Roberto Rodriguez)	2.00	1.00	.60
200 Orlando Cepeda	11.00	5.50	3.25
201 **Mike Marshall**	3.00	1.50	.90
202 Adolfo Phillips	2.00	1.00	.60
203 Dick Kelley	2.00	1.00	.60
204 Andy Etchebarren	2.00	1.00	.60
205 Juan Marichal	9.00	4.50	2.75
206 Cal Ermer	2.00	1.00	.60
207 Carroll Sembera	2.00	1.00	.60
208 Willie Davis	2.00	1.00	.60
209 Tim Cullen	2.00	1.00	.60
210 Gary Peters	2.00	1.00	.60
211 J.C. Martin	2.00	1.00	.60
212 Dave Morehead	2.00	1.00	.60
213 Chico Ruiz	2.00	1.00	.60
214 Yankees Rookies (Stan Bahnsen, Frank Fernandez)	2.00	1.00	.60
215 Jim Bunning	9.00	4.50	2.75
216 Bubba Morton	2.00	1.00	.60
217 Turk Farrell	2.00	1.00	.60
218 Ken Suarez	2.00	1.00	.60
219 Rob Gardner	2.00	1.00	.60
220 Harmon Killebrew	15.00	7.50	3.75
221 Braves Team	5.00	2.50	1.50
222 Jim Hardin	2.00	1.00	.60
223 Ollie Brown	2.00	1.00	.60
224 Jack Aker	2.00	1.00	.60
225 Richie Allen	6.00	3.00	1.75
226 Jimmie Price	2.00	1.00	.60
227 Joe Hoerner	2.00	1.00	.60
228 Dodgers Rookies (**Jack Billingham**, Jim Fairey)	2.00	1.00	.60
229 Fred Klages	2.00	1.00	.60
230 Pete Rose	50.00	25.00	12.50
231 Dave Baldwin	2.00	1.00	.60
232 Denis Menke	2.00	1.00	.60
233 George Scott	2.00	1.00	.60
234 Bill Monbouquette	2.00	1.00	.60
235 Ron Santo	6.00	3.00	1.75
236 Tug McGraw	2.00	1.00	.60
237 Alvin Dark	2.00	1.00	.60
238 Tom Satriano	2.00	1.00	.60
239 Bill Henry	2.00	1.00	.60
240 Al Kaline	40.00	20.00	10.00
241 Felix Millan	2.00	1.00	.60

242	Moe Drabowsky	2.00	1.00	.60
243	Rich Rollins	2.00	1.00	.60
244	John Donaldson	2.00	1.00	.60
245	Tony Gonzalez	2.00	1.00	.60
246	Fritz Peterson	2.00	1.00	.60
247	Reds Rookies (**Johnny Bench**, Ron Tompkins)	125.00	62.50	31.25
248	Fred Valentine	2.00	1.00	.60
249	Bill Singer	2.00	1.00	.60
250	Carl Yastrzemski	20.00	10.00	6.00
251	*Manny Sanguillen*	4.50	2.25	1.25
252	Angels Team	5.00	2.50	1.50
253	Dick Hughes	2.00	1.00	.60
254	Cleon Jones	2.00	1.00	.60
255	Dean Chance	2.00	1.00	.60
256	Norm Cash	7.00	3.50	2.00
257	Phil Niekro	9.00	4.50	2.75
258	Cubs Rookies (Jose Arcia, Bill Schlesinger)	2.00	1.00	.60
259	Ken Boyer	5.00	2.50	1.50
260	Jim Wynn	2.00	1.00	.60
261	Dave Duncan	2.00	1.00	.60
262	Rick Wise	2.00	1.00	.60
263	Horace Clarke	2.00	1.00	.60
264	Ted Abernathy	2.00	1.00	.60
265	Tommy Davis	2.00	1.00	.60
266	Paul Popovich	2.00	1.00	.60
267	Herman Franks	2.00	1.00	.60
268	Bob Humphreys	2.00	1.00	.60
269	Bob Tiefenauer	2.00	1.00	.60
270	Matty Alou	2.00	1.00	.60
271	Bobby Knoop	2.00	1.00	.60
272	Ray Culp	2.00	1.00	.60
273	Dave Johnson	2.00	1.00	.60
274	Mike Cuellar	2.00	1.00	.60
275	Tim McCarver	5.00	2.50	1.50
276	Jim Roland	2.00	1.00	.60
277	Jerry Buchek	2.00	1.00	.60
278a	4th Series Check List (284-370) (Orlando Cepeda) (Copyright at right.)	5.00	2.50	1.50
278b	4th Series Check List (284-370) (Orlando Cepeda) (Copyright at left.)	5.50	2.75	1.75
279	Bill Hands	2.00	1.00	.60
280	Mickey Mantle	400.00	200.00	100.00
281	Jim Campanis	2.00	1.00	.60
282	Rick Monday	2.00	1.00	.60
283	Mel Queen	2.00	1.00	.60
284	John Briggs	2.00	1.00	.60
285	Dick McAuliffe	2.00	1.00	.60
286	Cecil Upshaw	2.00	1.00	.60
287	White Sox Rookies (Mickey Abarbanel, Cisco Carlos)	2.00	1.00	.60
288	Dave Wickersham	2.00	1.00	.60
289	Woody Held	2.00	1.00	.60
290	Willie McCovey	15.00	7.50	3.75
291	Dick Lines	2.00	1.00	.60
292	Art Shamsky	2.00	1.00	.60
293	Bruce Howard	2.00	1.00	.60
294	Red Schoendienst	7.00	3.50	2.00
295	Sonny Siebert	2.00	1.00	.60
296	Byron Browne	2.00	1.00	.60
297	Russ Gibson	2.00	1.00	.60
298	Jim Brewer	2.00	1.00	.60
299	Gene Michael	2.00	1.00	.60
300	Rusty Staub	2.50	1.25	.70
301	Twins Rookies (George Mitterwald, Rick Renick)	2.00	1.00	.60
302	Gerry Arrigo	2.00	1.00	.60
303	Dick Green	2.00	1.00	.60
304	Sandy Valdespino	2.00	1.00	.60
305	Minnie Rojas	2.00	1.00	.60
306	Mike Ryan	2.00	1.00	.60
307	John Hiller	2.00	1.00	.60
308	Pirates Team	6.00	3.00	1.75
309	Ken Henderson	2.00	1.00	.60
310	Luis Aparicio	11.00	5.50	3.25
311	Jack Lamabe	2.00	1.00	.60
312	Curt Blefary	2.00	1.00	.60
313	Al Weis	2.00	1.00	.60
314	Red Sox Rookies (Bill Rohr, George Spriggs)	2.00	1.00	.60
315	Zoilo Versalles	2.00	1.00	.60
316	Steve Barber	2.00	1.00	.60
317	Ron Brand	2.00	1.00	.60
318	Chico Salmon	2.00	1.00	.60
319	George Culver	2.00	1.00	.60
320	Frank Howard	2.50	1.25	.70
321	Leo Durocher	6.00	3.00	1.75
322	Dave Boswell	2.00	1.00	.60
323	Deron Johnson	2.00	1.00	.60
324	Jim Nash	2.00	1.00	.60
325	Manny Mota	2.00	1.00	.60
326	Dennis Ribant	2.00	1.00	.60
327	Tony Taylor	2.00	1.00	.60
328	Angels Rookies (Chuck Vinson, Jim Weaver)	2.00	1.00	.60
329	Duane Josephson	2.00	1.00	.60
330	Roger Maris	50.00	25.00	12.50
331	Dan Osinski	2.00	1.00	.60
332	Doug Rader	2.00	1.00	.60
333	Ron Herbel	2.00	1.00	.60
334	Orioles Team	5.00	2.50	1.50
335	Bob Allison	2.00	1.00	.60
336	John Purdin	2.00	1.00	.60
337	Bill Robinson	2.00	1.00	.60
338	Bob Johnson	2.00	1.00	.60
339	Rich Nye	2.00	1.00	.60
340	Max Alvis	2.00	1.00	.60
341	Jim Lemon	2.00	1.00	.60
342	Ken Johnson	2.00	1.00	.60
343	Jim Gosger	2.00	1.00	.60
344	Donn Clendenon	2.00	1.00	.60
345	Bob Hendley	2.00	1.00	.60
346	Jerry Adair	2.00	1.00	.60
347	George Brunet	2.00	1.00	.60
348	Phillies Rookies (Larry Colton, Dick Thoenen)	2.00	1.00	.60
349	Ed Spiezio	2.00	1.00	.60
350	Hoyt Wilhelm	9.00	4.50	2.75
351	Bob Barton	2.00	1.00	.60
352	Jackie Hernandez	2.00	1.00	.60
353	Mack Jones	2.00	1.00	.60
354	Pete Richert	2.00	1.00	.60
355	Ernie Banks	20.00	10.00	6.00
356a	5th Series Check List (371-457) (Ken Holtzman) (Top of cap away from black circle.)	5.00	2.50	1.50
356b	5th Series Check List (371-457) (Ken Holtzman) (Top of cap near black circle.)	5.00	2.50	1.50
357	Len Gabrielson	2.00	1.00	.60
358	Mike Epstein	2.00	1.00	.60
359	Joe Moeller	2.00	1.00	.60
360	Willie Horton	2.00	1.00	.60
361	Harmon Killebrew (All-Star)	7.50	3.75	2.25
362	Orlando Cepeda (All-Star)	5.00	2.50	1.50
363	Rod Carew (All-Star)	6.50	3.25	2.00
364	Joe Morgan (All-Star)	6.00	3.00	1.75
365	Brooks Robinson (All-Star)	7.50	3.75	2.25
366	Ron Santo (All-Star)	5.00	2.50	1.50
367	Jim Fregosi (All-Star)	2.00	1.00	.60
368	Gene Alley (All-Star)	2.00	1.00	.60
369	Carl Yastrzemski (All-Star)	7.50	3.75	2.25
370	Hank Aaron (All-Star)	25.00	12.50	6.25
371	Tony Oliva (All-Star)	2.50	1.25	.70
372	Lou Brock (All-Star)	6.00	3.00	1.75
373	Frank Robinson (All-Star)	7.50	3.75	2.25
374	Roberto Clemente (All-Star)	25.00	12.50	6.25
375	Bill Freehan (All-Star)	2.00	1.00	.60
376	Tim McCarver (All-Star)	3.00	1.50	.90
377	Joe Horlen (All-Star)	2.00	1.00	.60
378	Bob Gibson (All-Star)	7.00	3.50	2.00
379	Gary Peters (All-Star)	2.00	1.00	.60
380	Ken Holtzman (All-Star)	2.00	1.00	.60
381	Boog Powell	3.00	1.50	.90
382	Ramon Hernandez	2.00	1.00	.60
383	Steve Whitaker	2.00	1.00	.60
384	Red Rookies (*Bill Henry, Hal McRae*)	6.00	3.00	1.75
385	Jim Hunter	10.00	5.00	3.00
386	Greg Goossen	2.00	1.00	.60
387	Joe Foy	2.00	1.00	.60
388	Ray Washburn	2.00	1.00	.60
389	Jay Johnstone	2.00	1.00	.60
390	Bill Mazeroski	10.00	5.00	3.00
391	Bob Priddy	2.00	1.00	.60
392	Grady Hatton	2.00	1.00	.60
393	Jim Perry	2.00	1.00	.60
394	Tommie Aaron	2.00	1.00	.60
395	Camilo Pascual	2.00	1.00	.60
396	Bobby Wine	2.00	1.00	.60
397	Vic Davalillo	2.00	1.00	.60
398	Jim Grant	2.00	1.00	.60
399	Ray Oyler	2.00	1.00	.60
400a	Mike McCormick (White team.)	475.00	240.00	140.00
400b	Mike McCormick (Yellow team.)	2.00	1.00	.60
401	Mets Team	5.00	2.50	1.50
402	Mike Hegan	2.00	1.00	.60
403	John Buzhardt	2.00	1.00	.60
404	Floyd Robinson	2.00	1.00	.60
405	Tommy Helms	2.00	1.00	.60
406	Dick Ellsworth	2.00	1.00	.60
407	Gary Kolb	2.00	1.00	.60
408	Steve Carlton	20.00	10.00	5.00
409	Orioles Rookies (Frank Peters, Ron Stone)	2.00	1.00	.60
410	Fergie Jenkins	10.00	5.00	3.00
411	Ron Hansen	2.00	1.00	.60
412	Clay Carroll	2.00	1.00	.60
413	Tommy McCraw	2.00	1.00	.60
414	Mickey Lolich	2.00	1.00	.60
415	Johnny Callison	2.00	1.00	.60
416	Bill Rigney	2.00	1.00	.60
417	Willie Crawford	2.00	1.00	.60
418	Eddie Fisher	2.00	1.00	.60
419	Jack Hiatt	2.00	1.00	.60
420	Cesar Tovar	2.00	1.00	.60
421	Ron Taylor	2.00	1.00	.60
422	Rene Lachemann	2.00	1.00	.60
423	Fred Gladding	2.00	1.00	.60
424	White Sox Team	5.00	2.50	1.50
425	Jim Maloney	2.00	1.00	.60
426	Hank Allen	2.00	1.00	.60
427	Dick Calmus	2.00	1.00	.60
428	Vic Roznovsky	2.00	1.00	.60
429	Tommie Sisk	2.00	1.00	.60
430	Rico Petrocelli	2.00	1.00	.60
431	Dooley Womack	2.00	1.00	.60
432	Indians Rookies (Bill Davis, Jose Vidal)	2.00	1.00	.60
433	Bob Rodgers	2.00	1.00	.60
434	Ricardo Joseph	2.00	1.00	.60
435	Ron Perranoski	2.00	1.00	.60
436	Hal Lanier	2.00	1.00	.60
437	Don Cardwell	2.00	1.00	.60
438	Lee Thomas	2.00	1.00	.60
439	Luman Harris	2.00	1.00	.60
440	Claude Osteen	2.00	1.00	.60
441	Alex Johnson	2.00	1.00	.60
442	Dick Bosman	2.00	1.00	.60
443	Joe Azcue	2.00	1.00	.60
444	Jack Fisher	2.00	1.00	.60
445	Mike Shannon	2.00	1.00	.60
446	Ron Kline	2.00	1.00	.60
447	Tigers Rookies (George Korince, Fred Lasher)	2.00	1.00	.60
448	Gary Wagner	2.00	1.00	.60
449	Gene Oliver	2.00	1.00	.60
450	Jim Kaat	2.50	1.25	.70
451	Al Spangler	2.00	1.00	.60
452	Jesus Alou	2.00	1.00	.60
453	Sammy Ellis	2.00	1.00	.60
454a	6th Series Check List (458-533) (Frank Robinson) (Neck chain shows.)	6.00	3.00	1.75
454b	6th Series Check List (458-533) (Frank Robinson) (No neck chain.)	6.00	3.00	1.75
455	Rico Carty	2.00	1.00	.60
456	John O'Donoghue	2.00	1.00	.60
457	Jim Lefebvre	2.00	1.00	.60
458	Lew Krausse	5.00	2.50	1.50
459	Dick Simpson	5.00	2.50	1.50
460	Jim Lonborg	5.00	2.50	1.50
461	Chuck Hiller	5.00	2.50	1.50
462	Barry Moore	5.00	2.50	1.50
463	Jimmie Schaffer	5.00	2.50	1.50
464	Don McMahon	5.00	2.50	1.50
465	Tommie Agee	5.00	2.50	1.50
466	Bill Dillman	5.00	2.50	1.50
467	Dick Howser	5.00	2.50	1.50
468	Larry Sherry	5.00	2.50	1.50
469	Ty Cline	5.00	2.50	1.50
470	Bill Freehan	5.00	2.50	1.50
471	Orlando Pena	5.00	2.50	1.50
472	Walt Alston	8.00	4.00	2.50
473	Al Worthington	5.00	2.50	1.50
474	Paul Schaal	5.00	2.50	1.50
475	Joe Niekro	5.00	2.50	1.50
476	Woody Woodward	5.00	2.50	1.50
477	Phillies Team	6.00	3.00	1.75
478	Dave McNally	5.00	2.50	1.50
479	Phil Gagliano	5.00	2.50	1.50
480	Manager's Dream (Chico Cardenas, Roberto Clemente, Tony Oliva)	75.00	37.50	18.75
481	John Wyatt	5.00	2.50	1.50
482	Jose Pagan	5.00	2.50	1.50
483	Darold Knowles	5.00	2.50	1.50
484	Phil Roof	5.00	2.50	1.50
485	Ken Berry	5.00	2.50	1.50
486	Cal Koonce	5.00	2.50	1.50
487	Lee May	5.00	2.50	1.50
488	Dick Tracewski	5.00	2.50	1.50
489	Wally Bunker	5.00	2.50	1.50
490	Super Stars (Harmon Killebrew, Mickey Mantle, Willie Mays)	140.00	70.00	35.00
491	Denny Lemaster	5.00	2.50	1.50
492	Jeff Torborg	5.00	2.50	1.50
493	Jim McGlothlin	5.00	2.50	1.50
494	Ray Sadecki	5.00	2.50	1.50
495	Leon Wagner	5.00	2.50	1.50
496	Steve Hamilton	5.00	2.50	1.50
497	Cards Team	6.00	3.00	1.75
498	Bill Bryan	5.00	2.50	1.50
499	Steve Blass	5.00	2.50	1.50
500	Frank Robinson	25.00	12.50	7.50
501	John Odom	5.00	2.50	1.50
502	Mike Andrews	5.00	2.50	1.50
503	Al Jackson	5.00	2.50	1.50
504	Russ Snyder	5.00	2.50	1.50
505	Joe Sparma	5.00	2.50	1.50
506	Clarence Jones	5.00	2.50	1.50
507	Wade Blasingame	5.00	2.50	1.50
508	Duke Sims	5.00	2.50	1.50
509	Dennis Higgins	5.00	2.50	1.50
510	Ron Fairly	5.00	2.50	1.50
511	Bill Kelso	5.00	2.50	1.50
512	Grant Jackson	5.00	2.50	1.50
513	Hank Bauer	5.00	2.50	1.50
514	Al McBean	5.00	2.50	1.50
515	Russ Nixon	5.00	2.50	1.50
516	Pete Mikkelsen	5.00	2.50	1.50
517	Diego Segui	5.00	2.50	1.50
518a	7th Series Check List (534-598) (Clete Boyer) (539 is Maj. L. Rookies)	6.00	3.00	1.75
518b	7th Series Check List (534-598) (Clete Boyer) (539 is Amer. L. Rookies)	10.00	5.00	3.00
519	Jerry Stephenson	5.00	2.50	1.50
520	Lou Brock	15.00	7.50	3.75
521	Don Shaw	5.00	2.50	1.50
522	Wayne Causey	5.00	2.50	1.50
523	John Tsitouris	5.00	2.50	1.50
524	Andy Kosco	5.00	2.50	1.50
525	Jim Davenport	5.00	2.50	1.50
526	Bill Denehy	5.00	2.50	1.50
527	Tito Francona	5.00	2.50	1.50
528	Tigers Team	45.00	22.50	11.25
529	Bruce Von Hoff	5.00	2.50	1.50
530	Bird Belters (Brooks Robinson, Frank Robinson)	25.00	12.50	6.25
531	Chuck Hinton	5.00	2.50	1.50
532	Luis Tiant	5.00	2.50	1.50
533	Wes Parker	5.00	2.50	1.50
534	Bob Miller	5.00	2.50	1.50
535	Danny Cater	5.00	2.50	1.50
536	Bill Short	5.00	2.50	1.50
537	Norm Siebern	5.00	2.50	1.50
538	Manny Jimenez	5.00	2.50	1.50
539	Major League Rookies (Mike Ferraro, Jim Ray)	5.00	2.50	1.50
540	Nelson Briles	5.00	2.50	1.50
541	Sandy Alomar	5.00	2.50	1.50
542	John Boccabella	5.00	2.50	1.50
543	Bob Lee	5.00	2.50	1.50
544	Mayo Smith	5.00	2.50	1.50
545	Lindy McDaniel	5.00	2.50	1.50
546	Roy White	4.50	2.25	1.25
547	Dan Coombs	5.00	2.50	1.50
548	Bernie Allen	5.00	2.50	1.50
549	Orioles Rookies (Curt Motton, Roger Nelson)	5.00	2.50	1.50
550	Clete Boyer	5.00	2.50	1.50
551	Darrell Sutherland	5.00	2.50	1.50
552	Ed Kirkpatrick	5.00	2.50	1.50
553	Hank Aguirre	5.00	2.50	1.50

		NM	EX	VG
554	A's Team	6.00	3.00	1.75
555	Jose Tartabull	5.00	2.50	1.50
556	Dick Selma	5.00	2.50	1.50
557	Frank Quilici	5.00	2.50	1.50
558	John Edwards	5.00	2.50	1.50
559	Pirates Rookies	5.00	2.50	1.50
	(Carl Taylor, Luke Walker)			
560	Paul Casanova	5.00	2.50	1.50
561	Lee Elia	5.00	2.50	1.50
562	Jim Bouton	6.00	3.00	1.75
563	Ed Charles	5.00	2.50	1.50
564	Eddie Stanky	5.00	2.50	1.50
565	Larry Dierker	5.00	2.50	1.50
566	Ken Harrelson	5.00	2.50	1.50
567	Clay Dalrymple	5.00	2.50	1.50
568	Willie Smith	5.00	2.50	1.50
569	N.L. Rookies	5.00	2.50	1.50
	(Ivan Murrell, Les Rohr)			
570	Rick Reichardt	5.00	2.50	1.50
571	Tony LaRussa	6.00	3.00	1.75
572	Don Bosch	5.00	2.50	1.50
573	Joe Coleman	5.00	3.75	1.50
574	Reds Team	7.50	3.75	2.25
575	Jim Palmer	35.00	17.50	8.75
576	Dave Adlesh	5.00	2.50	1.50
577	Fred Talbot	5.00	2.50	1.50
578	Orlando Martinez	5.00	2.50	1.50
579	N.L. Rookies	5.00	2.50	1.50
	(*Larry Hisle, Mike Lum*)			
580	Bob Bailey	5.00	2.50	1.50
581	Garry Roggenburk	5.00	2.50	1.50
582	Jerry Grote	5.00	2.50	1.50
583	Gates Brown	6.00	3.00	1.75
584	Larry Shepard	5.00	2.50	1.50
585	Wilbur Wood	5.00	2.50	1.50
586	Jim Pagliaroni	5.00	2.50	1.50
587	Roger Repoz	5.00	2.50	1.50
588	Dick Schofield	5.00	2.50	1.50
589	Twins Rookies	5.00	2.50	1.50
	(Ron Clark, Moe Ogier)			
590	Tommy Harper	5.00	2.50	1.50
591	Dick Nen	5.00	2.50	1.50
592	John Bateman	5.00	2.50	1.50
593	Lee Stange	5.00	2.50	1.50
594	Phil Linz	5.00	2.50	1.50
595	Phil Ortega	5.00	2.50	1.50
596	Charlie Smith	5.00	2.50	1.50
597	Bill McCool	5.00	2.50	1.50
598	Jerry May	10.00	5.00	2.50

1968 Topps Action Stickers

Another of the many Topps test issues of the late 1960s, Action All-Star stickers were sold in a strip of three, with bubblegum, for 10 cents. The strip is comprised of three 3-1/4" x 5-1/4" panels, perforated at the joints for separation. The numbered central panel contains a large photo of a star player. While there are 16 numbered center panels, only 12 of them are different; panels 13-16 are double-prints. Similarly, the triple-player panels at top and bottom of stickers 13-16 repeat panels from #1-4. Prices below are for stickers which have all three panels still joined. Individual panels are priced signicantly lower.

		NM	EX	VG
Complete Set (16):		5,750	2,875	1,725
Common Panel:		130.00	65.00	45.00
1	Orlando Cepeda, Joe Horlen, Al Kaline, Bill Mazeroski, Claude Osteen, Mel Stottlemyre, Carl Yastrzemski	400.00	200.00	120.00
2	Don Drysdale, Harmon Killebrew, Mike McCormick, Tom Phoebus, George Scott, Ron Swoboda, Pete Ward	175.00	90.00	50.00

		NM	EX	VG
3	Hank Aaron, Paul Casanova, Jim Maloney, Joe Pepitone, Rick Reichardt, Frank Robinson, Tom Seaver	150.00	75.00	45.00
4	Bob Aspromonte, Johnny Callison, Dean Chance, Jim Lefebvre, Jim Lonborg, Frank Robinson, Ron Santo	200.00	100.00	60.00
5	Bert Campaneris, Al Downing, Willie Horton, Ed Kranepool, Willie Mays, Pete Rose, Ron Santo	500.00	250.00	150.00
6	Max Alvis, Ernie Banks, Al Kaline, Tim McCarver, Rusty Staub, Walt Williams, Carl Yastrzemski	400.00	200.00	120.00
7	Rod Carew, Tony Gonzalez, Steve Hargan, Mickey Mantle, Willie McCovey, Rick Monday, Billy Williams	1,750	875.00	525.00
8	Clete Boyer, Jim Bunning, Tony Conigliaro, Mike Cuellar, Joe Horlen, Ken McMullen, Don Mincher	130.00	65.00	45.00
9	Orlando Cepeda, Bob Clemente, Jim Fregosi, Harmon Killebrew, Willie Mays, Chris Short, Earl Wilson	400.00	200.00	120.00
10	Hank Aaron, Bob Gibson, Bud Harrelson, Jim Hunter, Mickey Mantle, Gary Peters, Vada Pinson	500.00	250.00	150.00
11	Don Drysdale, Bill Freehan, Frank Howard, Ferguson Jenkins, Tony Oliva, Bob Veale, Jim Wynn	300.00	150.00	90.00
12	Richie Allen, Bob Clemente, Sam McDowell, Jim McGlothlin, Tony Perez, Brooks Robinson, Joe Torre	900.00	450.00	275.00
13	Dean Chance, Don Drysdale, Jim Lefebvre, Tom Phoebus, Frank Robinson, George Scott, Carl Yastrzemski	400.00	200.00	120.00
14	Paul Casanova, Orlando Cepeda, Joe Horlen, Harmon Killebrew, Bill Mazeroski, Rick Reichardt, Tom Seaver	250.00	125.00	75.00
15	Bob Aspromonte, Johnny Callison, Jim Lonborg, Mike McCormick, Frank Robinson, Ron Swoboda, Pete Ward	175.00	90.00	50.00
16	Hank Aaron, Al Kaline, Jim Maloney, Claude Osteen, Joe Pepitone, Ron Santo, Mel Stottlemyre	300.00	150.00	90.00

1968 Topps "Batter Up" Game

The same cards which were issued as pack inserts in 1968 Topps were sold in a much scarcer boxed-set form. Packaged in a colorful cardboard box with game rules on back, the set is labeled "Batter Up" and can be found in versions with 10 or 15 original retail price.

	NM	EX	VG
Complete Boxed Set:	275.00	85.00	45.00
(See 1968 Topps Game for individual card checklist and values.)			

1968 Topps Deckle Edge Proofs

While most Topps proofs are so rare as to preclude their listing in this catalog, the 1968 Deckle Edge test set is an exception. Usually found in the form of a 7-3/4" x 11" uncut sheet of nine black-and-white cards, single cards are sometimes encountered. The blank-backed sheet and cards can be found with the players' facsimile autographs printed in red, black or blue. Unnumbered cards are checklisted here alphabetically.

		NM	EX	VG
Complete Set, Singles (9):		700.00	350.00	225.00
Uncut Sheet:		700.00	350.00	225.00
Common Player:		50.00	25.00	15.00
(1)	Dave Adlesh	50.00	25.00	15.00
(2)	Hank Aguirre	50.00	25.00	15.00
(3)	Sandy Alomar	50.00	25.00	15.00
(4)	Sonny Jackson	50.00	25.00	15.00
(5)	Bob Johnson	50.00	25.00	15.00
(6)	Claude Osteen	50.00	25.00	15.00
(7)	Juan Pizarro	50.00	25.00	15.00
(8)	Hal Woodeshick	50.00	25.00	15.00
(9)	Carl Yastrzemski	400.00	200.00	120.00

1968 Topps Discs

One of the scarcer Topps baseball collectibles, this set was apparently a never-completed test issue. These full-color, cardboard discs, which measure approximately 2-1/4" in diameter, were probably intended to be made into a pin set but production was never completed and no actual pins are known to exist. Uncut sheets of the player discs have been found. The discs include a player portrait photo with the name beneath and (usually) the city and team nickname along the sides.

		NM	EX	VG
Complete Set (28):		12,800	6,400	4,000
Common Player:		200.00	100.00	60.00
(1)	Hank Aaron	1,000	500.00	300.00
(2)	Richie Allen	225.00	110.00	65.00
(3)	Gene Alley	200.00	100.00	60.00
(4)	Rod Carew	560.00	280.00	175.00
(5)	Orlando Cepeda	480.00	240.00	150.00
(6)	Dean Chance	200.00	100.00	60.00
(7)	Roberto Clemente	1,400	700.00	400.00
(8)	Tommy Davis	200.00	100.00	60.00
(9)	Bill Freehan	200.00	100.00	60.00
(10)	Jim Fregosi	200.00	100.00	60.00
(11)	Steve Hargan	200.00	100.00	60.00
(12)	Frank Howard	200.00	100.00	60.00
(13)	Al Kaline	560.00	280.00	175.00
(14)	Harmon Killebrew	560.00	280.00	175.00
(15)	Mickey Mantle	6,000	3,000	1,800
(16)	Willie Mays	1,000	500.00	300.00
(17)	Mike McCormick	200.00	100.00	60.00
(18)	Rick Monday	200.00	100.00	60.00
(19)	Claude Osteen	200.00	100.00	60.00
(20)	Gary Peters	200.00	100.00	60.00
(21)	Brooks Robinson	560.00	280.00	175.00
(22)	Frank Robinson	560.00	280.00	175.00
(23)	Pete Rose	900.00	450.00	275.00
(24)	Ron Santo	250.00	125.00	75.00
(25)	Rusty Staub	220.00	110.00	70.00
(26)	Joe Torre	200.00	100.00	60.00
(27)	Bob Veale	200.00	100.00	60.00
(28)	Carl Yastrzemski	560.00	280.00	175.00

1968 Topps Game

A throwback to the Red and Blue Back sets of 1951, the 33-cards in the 1968 Topps Game set, inserted into packs of regular '68 Topps cards or purchases as a complete boxed set, enable the owner to play a game of baseball based on the game situations on each card. Also on the 2-1/4" x 3-1/4" cards were a color photograph of a player and his facsimile autograph. One redeeming social value of the set (assuming you're not mesmerized by the game) is that it affords an inexpensive way to get big-name cards as the set is loaded with stars, but not at all popular with collectors.

	NM	EX	VG
Complete Set (33):	115.00	55.00	35.00
Common Player:	2.00	1.00	.60
1 Mateo Alou	2.00	1.00	.60
2 Mickey Mantle	30.00	15.00	9.00
3 Carl Yastrzemski	10.00	5.00	3.00
4 Henry Aaron	12.00	6.00	3.50
5 Harmon Killebrew	9.00	4.50	2.75
6 Roberto Clemente	15.00	7.50	4.50
7 Frank Robinson	9.00	4.50	2.75
8 Willie Mays	12.00	6.00	3.50
9 Brooks Robinson	9.00	4.50	2.75
10 Tommy Davis	2.00	1.00	.60
11 Bill Freehan	2.00	1.00	.60
12 Claude Osteen	2.00	1.00	.60
13 Gary Peters	2.00	1.00	.60
14 Jim Lonborg	2.00	1.00	.60
15 Steve Hargan	2.00	1.00	.60
16 Dean Chance	2.00	1.00	.60
17 Mike McCormick	2.00	1.00	.60
18 Tim McCarver	3.00	1.50	.90
19 Ron Santo	6.00	3.00	1.75
20 Tony Gonzalez	2.00	1.00	.60
21 Frank Howard	3.00	1.50	.90
22 George Scott	2.00	1.00	.60
23 Rich Allen	6.00	3.00	1.75
24 Jim Wynn	2.00	1.00	.60
25 Gene Alley	2.00	1.00	.60
26 Rick Monday	2.00	1.00	.60
27 Al Kaline	9.00	4.50	2.75
28 Rusty Staub	3.00	1.50	.90
29 Rod Carew	9.00	4.50	2.75
30 Pete Rose	12.00	6.00	3.50
31 Joe Torre	6.00	3.00	1.75
32 Orlando Cepeda	6.00	3.00	1.75
33 Jim Fregosi	2.00	1.00	.60

1968 Topps Plaks

Among the scarcest Topps test issues of the late 1960s, the "All Star Baseball Plaks" were plastic busts of two dozen stars of the era which came packaged like model airplane parts. The busts had to be snapped off a sprue and could be inserted into a base which carried the player's name. Packed with the plastic plaks was one of two checklist cards which featured six color photos per side. The 2-1/8" x 4" checklist cards are popular with superstar collectors and are considerably easier to find today than the actual plaks. Wax packs of three plaks and two sticks of bubblegum were sold for a dime. "Despite their appearance on the checklist cards, it is now believed that no plaks were issued of Gary Peters, Frank Robinson, Hank Aaron, Don Drysdale or Willie Mays."

	NM	EX	VG
Complete Set (19):	15,000	7,500	4,500
Common Player:	250.00	125.00	75.00
(1) Max Alvis	250.00	125.00	75.00
(2) Dean Chance	250.00	125.00	75.00
(3) Jim Fregosi	250.00	125.00	75.00
(4) Frank Howard	350.00	175.00	105.00
(5) Jim Hunter	625.00	310.00	190.00
(6) Al Kaline	900.00	450.00	270.00
(7) Harmon Killebrew	900.00	450.00	270.00
(8) Jim Lonborg	250.00	125.00	75.00
(9a) Mickey Mantle (Big nose)	3,500	1,750	1,050
(9b) Mickey Mantle (Small nose)	3,500	1,750	1,050
(10) Carl Yastrzemski	900.00	450.00	270.00
(11) Richie Allen	350.00	175.00	105.00
(12) Orlando Cepeda	1,000	500.00	300.00
(13) Roberto Clemente	2,500	1,250	750.00
(14) Tommy Davis	350.00	175.00	105.00
(15) Tim McCarver	900.00	450.00	270.00
(16) Ron Santo	2,500	1,250	750.00
(17) Rusty Staub	350.00	175.00	105.00
(18) Pete Rose	2,200	1,100	650.00
(19) Jim Wynn	250.00	125.00	75.00
--- Checklist Card 1-12	1,375	687.50	412.50
--- Checklist Card 13-24	2,100	1,050	625.00

1968 Topps Posters

Yet another innovation from the creative minds at Topps appeared in 1968; a set of color player posters. Measuring 9-3/4" x 18-1/8", each poster was sold separately with its own piece of gum, rather than as an insert. The posters feature a large color photograph with a star at the bottom containing the player's name, position and team. There are 24 different posters which were folded numerous times to fit into the package they were sold in. Unless the paper has split at the folds, they are not considered in grading.

	NM	EX	VG
Complete Set (24):	650.00	325.00	200.00
Common Player:	15.00	7.50	4.50
Unopened Pack:	175.00	.00	.00
1 Dean Chance	15.00	7.50	4.50
2 Max Alvis	15.00	7.50	4.50
3 Frank Howard	17.50	8.75	5.25
4 Jim Fregosi	15.00	7.50	4.50
5 Catfish Hunter	20.00	10.00	6.00
6 Roberto Clemente	60.00	30.00	18.00
7 Don Drysdale	25.00	12.50	7.50
8 Jim Wynn	15.00	7.50	4.50
9 Al Kaline	25.00	12.50	7.50
10 Harmon Killebrew	25.00	12.50	7.50
11 Jim Lonborg	15.00	7.50	4.50
12 Orlando Cepeda	20.00	10.00	6.00
13 Gary Peters	15.00	7.50	4.50
14 Hank Aaron	50.00	25.00	15.00
15 Richie Allen	17.50	8.75	5.25
16 Carl Yastrzemski	30.00	15.00	9.00
17 Ron Swoboda	15.00	7.50	4.50
18 Mickey Mantle	80.00	40.00	24.00
19 Tim McCarver	15.00	7.50	4.50
20 Willie Mays	50.00	25.00	15.00
21 Ron Santo	17.50	8.75	5.25
22 Rusty Staub	17.50	8.75	5.25
23 Pete Rose	50.00	25.00	15.00
24 Frank Robinson	25.00	12.50	7.50

1968 Tipps From Topps Book

While the Bazooka brand is not referenced in this booklet, it presents the baseball playing tips that appeared on box backs of Bazooka gum. The player photo and cartoon tips are printed in blue in the interior pages of the 5-7/8" x 3" book. The front and back covers are black, white and green. The manner of distribution for this premium is not known.

	NM	EX	VG
Tipps From Topps Book	150.00	75.00	45.00

1968 Topps 3-D Prototype

Apparently produced as a prototype for the 3-D cards which Topps issued as a test in 1968, this prototype card is 2-1/4" x 3-1/4" with square corners. The team name is in red block letters at top. The back carries a rubber-stamped notice which identifies the card as a "Xograph 3-D" product from New York City.

	NM	EX	VG
Brooks Robinson	20,000	10,000	6,000

1968 Topps 3-D

These very rare test-issue cards measure 2-1/4" x 3-1/2" with rounded corners and blank backs. They simulate a three-dimensional effect with backgrounds purposely blurred, in front of which is a sharp color player photograph. The outer layer is a thin coating of ribbed plastic. The special process gives the picture the illusion of depth when the card is moved or tilted. As this was done two years before Kellogg's began its 3-D cards, this test issue really was breaking new ground. Production and distribution were limited, making the cards very tough to find. Some cards, said to have been the first produced, are stamped on back with a notice from Visual Panographics of New York. "This is an experimental XOGRAPH card produced as a limited edition. Not for public circulation or distribution. Not for resale. To be returned to:".

	NM	EX	VG
Common Player:	500.00	250.00	150.00
Wrapper:	900.00	450.00	275.00
(1) Bob Clemente	12,000	6,000	3,600
(2) Willie Davis	500.00	250.00	150.00
(3a) Ron Fairly (Dugout in background)	500.00	250.00	150.00
(3b) Ron Fairly (No dugout)	2,200	1,100	650.00
(4) Curt Flood	750.00	375.00	225.00
(5) Jim Lonborg	500.00	250.00	150.00
(6a) Jim Maloney (Dugout in background)	750.00	375.00	225.00
(6b) Jim Maloney (No dugout)	1,650	825.00	495.00
(7) John O'Donogue (No player or team designation)	5,000	2,500	1,500
(8) Tony Perez	1,200	600.00	360.00
(9) Boog Powell	750.00	375.00	225.00
(10) Bill Robinson	500.00	250.00	150.00
(11) Rusty Staub	1,200	600.00	360.00
(12) Mel Stottlemyre	1,200	600.00	360.00
(13) Ron Swoboda	500.00	250.00	150.00

1968 Topps/Milton Bradley

As part of a Win-A-Card trading card board game, Milton Bradley contracted with Topps to print 132 special versions of its 1968 baseball cards, 1967 football cards and hot rod cards. The baseball cards can be differentiated from regular-issue 1968 Topps in that the yellow ink on back is much lighter and brighter than the dark yellow/gold ink usually found on back. Also, some of the card fronts will show evidence of the white-bordered football and hot rod cards at one or more edges. Collectors currently will pay only a small premium for the MB version, but that gap is likely to widen in the future.

		NM	EX	VG
Complete (Baseball) Set (76):		600.00	300.00	180.00
Common Player:		2.00	1.00	.60
7	N.L. ERA Leaders (Jim Bunning, Phil Niekro, Chris Short)	7.00	3.50	2.00
8	A.L. ERA Leaders (Joe Horlen, Gary Peters, Sonny Siebert)	2.00	1.00	.60
10	A.L. Pitching Leaders (Dean Chance, Jim Lonborg, Earl Wilson)	9.00	4.50	2.75
13	Chuck Hartenstein	2.00	1.00	.60
16	Indians Rookies (Lou Piniella, Richie Scheinblum)	4.00	2.00	1.25
17	Dick Hall	2.00	1.00	.60
18	Mike Hershberger	2.00	1.00	.60
19	Juan Pizarro	2.00	1.00	.60
20	Brooks Robinson	15.00	7.50	4.50
24	Bobby Locke	2.00	1.00	.60
26	Darrell Brandon	2.00	1.00	.60
34	Al Ferrara	2.00	1.00	.60
36	Pirates Rookies (Bob Moose, Bob Robertson)	2.00	1.00	.60
38	Tony Pierce	2.00	1.00	.60
43	Gary Bell	2.00	1.00	.60
44	Frank Kostro	2.00	1.00	.60
45	Tom Seaver	30.00	15.00	9.00
48	Ted Davidson	2.00	1.00	.60
49	Ed Brinkman (Yellow team.)	50.00	25.00	15.00
53	Gene Alley	2.00	1.00	.60
57	Dan Schneider	2.00	1.00	.60

#	Player	NM	EX	VG
58	Ed Mathews	13.50	6.75	4.00
60	Ken Holtzman	2.00	1.00	.60
61	Reggie Smith	2.00	1.00	.60
62	Chuck Dobson	2.00	1.00	.60
64	Jim Merritt	2.00	1.00	.60
66	Casey Cox (Yellow team.)	50.00	25.00	15.00
68	Ron Willis	2.00	1.00	.60
72	Tommy John	4.00	2.00	1.25
74	Milt Pappas	2.00	1.00	.60
77	*Don Wilson*	2.00	1.00	.60
78	Jim Northrup	2.00	1.00	.60
80	Rod Carew	17.50	8.75	5.25
81	Larry Jackson	2.00	1.00	.60
85	Gaylord Perry	9.00	4.50	2.75
89	Jake Gibbs	2.00	1.00	.60
94	Lee Maye	2.00	1.00	.60
98	Gary Sutherland	2.00	1.00	.60
99	Rocky Colavito	7.00	3.50	2.00
100	Bob Gibson	17.50	8.75	5.25
105	Al Downing	2.00	1.00	.60
106	Dalton Jones	2.00	1.00	.60
107	2nd Series Check List (110-196) (Juan Marichal)	4.00	2.00	1.25
108	Don Pavletich	2.00	1.00	.60
110	Hank Aaron	40.00	20.00	12.00
112	Woody Fryman	2.00	1.00	.60
113	Tigers Rookies (Tom Matchick, Daryl Patterson)	2.00	1.00	.60
117	Larry Jaster	2.00	1.00	.60
118	Mark Belanger	2.00	1.00	.60
119	Ted Savage	2.00	1.00	.60
120	Mel Stottlemyre	4.00	2.00	1.25
121	Jimmie Hall	2.00	1.00	.60
124	Nate Oliver	2.00	1.00	.60
127	Paul Lindblad	2.00	1.00	.60
128	Astros Rookies (Tom Dukes, Alonzo Harris)	2.00	1.00	.60
129	Mickey Stanley	2.00	1.00	.60
136	Randy Hundley	2.00	1.00	.60
139	Chris Short	2.00	1.00	.60
143	Pete Cimino	2.00	1.00	.60
146	Sal Bando	2.00	1.00	.60
149	Bob Saverine	2.00	1.00	.60
155	World Series Game 5 (Lonborg Wins Again)	6.00	3.00	1.75
156	World Series Game 6 (Petrocelli Socks Two Homers)	6.00	3.00	1.75
165	Tony Oliva	4.00	2.00	1.25
168	Dodgers Team	5.00	2.50	1.50
172	Walt Williams	2.00	1.00	.60
175	Maury Wills	2.00	1.00	.60
176	Bob Allen	2.00	1.00	.60
177	Mets Rookies (*Jerry Koosman, Nolan Ryan*)	335.00	190.00	95.00
179	Bill Stoneman	2.00	1.00	.60
180	Curt Flood	3.00	1.50	.90
185	Tom Haller	2.00	1.00	.60
189	Bill Landis	2.00	1.00	.60
191	Dan Frisella	2.00	1.00	.60
193	Jack Hamilton	2.00	1.00	.60
195	Joe Pepitone	4.00	2.00	1.25

1969 Topps

The 1969 Topps set broke yet another record for quantity as the issue is officially a whopping 664 cards. With substantial numbers of variations, the number of possible cards runs closer to 700. The design of the 2-1/2" x 3-1/2" cards in the set feature a color photo with the team name printed in block letters underneath. A circle contains the player's name and position. Card backs returned to a horizontal format. Despite the size of the set, it contains no team cards. It does, however, have multi-player cards, All-Stars, statistical leaders, and World Series highlights. Most significant among the varieties are white and yellow letter cards from the run of #'s 440-511. The complete set prices below do not include the scarcer and more expensive "white letter" variations.

		NM	EX	VG
	Complete Set (664):	3,150	1,550	925.00
	Common Player (1-588):	2.00	1.00	.60
	Common Player (589-664):	3.00	1.50	.90
1	A.L. Batting Leaders (Danny Cater, Tony Oliva, Carl Yastrzemski)	15.00	7.50	4.50
2	N.L. Batting Leaders (Felipe Alou, Matty Alou, Pete Rose)	15.00	7.50	4.50
3	A.L. RBI Leaders (Ken Harrelson, Frank Howard, Jim Northrup)	2.50	1.25	.75
4	N.L. RBI Leaders (Willie McCovey, Ron Santo, Billy Williams)	10.00	5.00	2.50

#	Player	NM	EX	VG
5	A.L. Home Run Leaders (Ken Harrelson, Willie Horton, Frank Howard)	6.00	3.00	1.75
6	N.L. Home Run Leaders (Richie Allen, Ernie Banks, Willie McCovey)	8.00	4.00	2.50
7	A.L. ERA Leaders (Sam McDowell, Dave McNally, Luis Tiant)	3.00	1.50	.90
8	N.L. ERA Leaders (Bobby Bolin, Bob Gibson, Bob Veale)	4.00	2.00	1.25
9	A.L. Pitching Leaders (Denny McLain, Dave McNally, Mel Stottlemyre, Luis Tiant)	4.00	2.00	1.25
10	N.L. Pitching Leaders (Bob Gibson, Fergie Jenkins, Juan Marichal)	5.00	2.50	1.50
11	A.L. Strikeout Leaders (Sam McDowell, Denny McLain, Luis Tiant)	3.00	1.50	.90
12	N.L. Strikeout Leaders (Bob Gibson, Fergie Jenkins, Bill Singer)	5.00	2.50	1.50
13	Mickey Stanley	2.00	1.00	.60
14	Al McBean	2.00	1.00	.60
15	Boog Powell	3.00	1.50	.90
16	Giants Rookies (Cesar Gutierrez, Rich Robertson)	2.00	1.00	.60
17	Mike Marshall	2.00	1.00	.60
18	Dick Schofield	2.00	1.00	.60
19	Ken Suarez	2.00	1.00	.60
20	Ernie Banks	25.00	12.50	7.50
21	Jose Santiago	2.00	1.00	.60
22	Jesus Alou	2.00	1.00	.60
23	Lew Krausse	2.00	1.00	.60
24	Walt Alston	4.00	2.00	1.25
25	Roy White	2.00	1.00	.60
26	Clay Carroll	2.00	1.00	.60
27	Bernie Allen	2.00	1.00	.60
28	Mike Ryan	2.00	1.00	.60
29	Dave Morehead	2.00	1.00	.60
30	Bob Allison	2.00	1.00	.60
31	Mets Rookies (*Gary Gentry, Amos Otis*)	3.00	1.50	.90
32	Sammy Ellis	2.00	1.00	.60
33	Wayne Causey	2.00	1.00	.60
34	Gary Peters	2.00	1.00	.60
35	Joe Morgan	10.00	5.00	3.00
36	Luke Walker	2.00	1.00	.60
37	Curt Motton	2.00	1.00	.60
38	Zoilo Versalles	2.00	1.00	.60
39	Dick Hughes	2.00	1.00	.60
40	Mayo Smith	2.00	1.00	.60
41	Bob Barton	2.00	1.00	.60
42	Tommy Harper	2.00	1.00	.60
43	Joe Niekro	2.00	1.00	.60
44	Danny Cater	2.00	1.00	.60
45	Maury Wills	2.00	1.00	.60
46	Fritz Peterson	2.00	1.00	.60
47a	Paul Popovich (Emblem visible thru airbrush.)	15.00	7.50	4.50
47b	Paul Popovich (Helmet emblem completely airbrushed.)	2.00	1.00	.60
48	Brant Alyea	2.00	1.00	.60
49a	Royals Rookies (Steve Jones, Eliseo Rodriguez) (Rodriquez on front.)	15.00	7.50	4.50
49b	Royals Rookies (Steve Jones, Eliseo Rodriguez) (Rodriquez on front.)	2.00	1.00	.60
50	Roberto Clemente	60.00	30.00	15.00
51	Woody Fryman	2.00	1.00	.60
52	Mike Andrews	2.00	1.00	.60
53	Sonny Jackson	2.00	1.00	.60
54	Cisco Carlos	2.00	1.00	.60
55	Jerry Grote	2.00	1.00	.60
56	Rich Reese	2.00	1.00	.60
57	1st Series Check List (1-109) (Denny McLain)	4.00	2.00	1.25
58	Fred Gladding	2.00	1.00	.60
59	Jay Johnstone	2.00	1.00	.60
60	Nelson Briles	2.00	1.00	.60
61	Jimmie Hall	2.00	1.00	.60
62	Chico Salmon	2.00	1.00	.60
63	Jim Hickman	2.00	1.00	.60
64	Bill Monbouquette	2.00	1.00	.60
65	Willie Davis	2.00	1.00	.60
66	Orioles Rookies (*Mike Adamson, Merv Rettenmund*)	2.00	1.00	.60
67	Bill Stoneman	2.00	1.00	.60
68	Dave Duncan	2.00	1.00	.60
69	Steve Hamilton	2.00	1.00	.60
70	Tommy Helms	2.00	1.00	.60
71	Steve Whitaker	2.00	1.00	.60
72	Ron Taylor	2.00	1.00	.60
73	Johnny Briggs	2.00	1.00	.60
74	Preston Gomez	2.00	1.00	.60
75	Luis Aparicio	9.00	4.50	2.75
76	Norm Miller	2.00	1.00	.60
77a	Ron Perranoski (LA visible thru airbrush.)	10.00	5.00	2.50
77b	Ron Perranoski (Cap emblem completely airbrushed.)	2.00	1.00	.60
78	Tom Satriano	2.00	1.00	.60
79	Milt Pappas	2.00	1.00	.60
80	Norm Cash	6.00	3.00	1.75
81	Mel Queen	2.00	1.00	.60
82	Pirates Rookies (*Rich Hebner, Al Oliver*)	10.00	5.00	3.00
83	Mike Ferraro	2.00	1.00	.60
84	Bob Humphreys	2.00	1.00	.60
85	Lou Brock	20.00	10.00	6.00
86	Pete Richert	2.00	1.00	.60
87	Horace Clarke	2.00	1.00	.60
88	Rich Nye	2.00	1.00	.60
89	Russ Gibson	2.00	1.00	.60
90	Jerry Koosman	2.00	1.00	.60
91	Al Dark	2.00	1.00	.60
92	Jack Billingham	2.00	1.00	.60
93	Joe Foy	2.00	1.00	.60
94	Hank Aguirre	2.00	1.00	.60
95	Johnny Bench	60.00	30.00	15.00
96	Denver Lemaster	2.00	1.00	.60
97	Buddy Bradford	2.00	1.00	.60
98	Dave Giusti	2.00	1.00	.60
99a	Twins Rookies (*Danny Morris, Graig Nettles*) (Black loop above "Twins.")	13.50	6.75	4.00
99b	Twins Rookies (*Danny Morris, Graig Nettles*) (No black loop.)	10.00	5.00	2.50
100	Hank Aaron	60.00	30.00	15.00
101	Daryl Patterson	2.00	1.00	.60
102	Jim Davenport	2.00	1.00	.60
103	Roger Repoz	2.00	1.00	.60
104	Steve Blass	2.00	1.00	.60
105	Rick Monday	2.00	1.00	.60
106	Jim Hannan	2.00	1.00	.60
107a	2nd Series Check List (110-218) (Bob Gibson) (161 is Jim Purdin)	4.00	2.00	1.25
107b	2nd Series Check List (110-218) (Bob Gibson) (161 is John Purdin)	6.00	3.00	1.75
108	Tony Taylor	2.00	1.00	.60
109	Jim Lonborg	2.00	1.00	.60
110	Mike Shannon	2.00	1.00	.60
111	Johnny Morris	2.00	1.00	.60
112	J.C. Martin	2.00	1.00	.60
113	Dave May	2.00	1.00	.60
114	Yankees Rookies (Alan Closter, John Cumberland)	2.00	1.00	.60
115	Bill Hands	2.00	1.00	.60
116	Chuck Harrison	2.00	1.00	.60
117	Jim Fairey	2.00	1.00	.60
118	Stan Williams	2.00	1.00	.60
119	Doug Rader	2.00	1.00	.60
120	Pete Rose	40.00	20.00	10.00
121	Joe Grzenda	2.00	1.00	.60
122	Ron Fairly	2.00	1.00	.60
123	Wilbur Wood	2.00	1.00	.60
124	Hank Bauer	2.00	1.00	.60
125	Ray Sadecki	2.00	1.00	.60
126	Dick Tracewski	2.00	1.00	.60
127	Kevin Collins	2.00	1.00	.60
128	Tommie Aaron	2.00	1.00	.60
129	Bill McCool	2.00	1.00	.60
130	Carl Yastrzemski	32.50	16.00	9.75
131	Chris Cannizzaro	2.00	1.00	.60
132	Dave Baldwin	2.00	1.00	.60
133	Johnny Callison	2.00	1.00	.60
134	Jim Weaver	2.00	1.00	.60
135	Tommy Davis	2.00	1.00	.60
136	Cards Rookies (Steve Huntz, Mike Torrez)	2.00	1.00	.60
137	Wally Bunker	2.00	1.00	.60
138	John Bateman	2.00	1.00	.60
139	Andy Kosco	2.00	1.00	.60
140	Jim Lefebvre	2.00	1.00	.60
141	Bill Dillman	2.00	1.00	.60
142	Woody Woodward	2.00	1.00	.60
143	Joe Nossek	2.00	1.00	.60
144	Bob Hendley	2.00	1.00	.60
145	Max Alvis	2.00	1.00	.60
146	Jim Perry	2.00	1.00	.60
147	Leo Durocher	5.00	2.50	1.50
148	Lee Stange	2.00	1.00	.60
149	Ollie Brown	2.00	1.00	.60
150	Denny McLain	5.00	2.50	1.50
151a	Clay Dalrymple (Phillies)	15.00	7.50	3.75
151b	Clay Dalrymple (Orioles)	2.00	1.00	.60
152	Tommie Sisk	2.00	1.00	.60
153	Ed Brinkman	2.00	1.00	.60
154	Jim Britton	2.00	1.00	.60
155	Pete Ward	2.00	1.00	.60
156	Astros Rookies (Hal Gilson, Leon McFadden)	2.00	1.00	.60
157	Bob Rodgers	2.00	1.00	.60
158	Joe Gibbon	2.00	1.00	.60
159	Jerry Adair	2.00	1.00	.60
160	Vada Pinson	3.00	1.50	.90
161	John Purdin	2.00	1.00	.60
162	World Series Game 1 (Gibson Fans 17; Sets New Record)	15.00	7.50	4.50
163	World Series Game 2 (Tiger Homers Deck The Cards)	6.00	3.00	1.75
164	World Series Game 3 (McCarver's Homer Puts St. Louis Ahead)	7.00	3.50	2.00
165	World Series Game 4 (Brock's Lead-Off HR Starts Cards' Romp)	7.00	3.50	2.00
166	World Series Game 5 (Kaline's Key Hit Sparks Tiger Rally)	7.00	3.50	2.00
167	World Series Game 6 (Tiger 10-Run Inning Ties Mark)	6.00	3.00	1.75
168	World Series Game 7 (Lolich Series Hero Outduels Gibson)	9.00	4.50	2.75
169	World Series (Tigers Celebrate Their Victory)	12.00	6.00	3.50
170	Frank Howard	3.00	1.50	.90
171	Glenn Beckert	2.00	1.00	.60
172	Jerry Stephenson	2.00	1.00	.60
173	White Sox Rookies (Bob Christian, Gerry Nyman)	2.00	1.00	.60
174	Grant Jackson	2.00	1.00	.60
175	Jim Bunning	8.00	4.00	2.50
176	Joe Azcue	2.00	1.00	.60

#	Name			
177	Ron Reed	2.00	1.00	.60
178	Ray Oyler	2.00	1.00	.60
179	Don Pavletich	2.00	1.00	.60
180	Willie Horton	2.00	1.00	.60
181	Mel Nelson	2.00	1.00	.60
182	Bill Rigney	2.00	1.00	.60
183	Don Shaw	2.00	1.00	.60
184	Roberto Pena	2.00	1.00	.60
185	Tom Phoebus	2.00	1.00	.60
186	John Edwards	2.00	1.00	.60
187	Leon Wagner	2.00	1.00	.60
188	Rick Wise	2.00	1.00	.60
189	Red Sox Rookies (Joe Lahoud, John Thibdeau)	2.00	1.00	.60
190	Willie Mays	65.00	32.00	19.50
191	Lindy McDaniel	2.00	1.00	.60
192	Jose Pagan	2.00	1.00	.60
193	Don Cardwell	2.00	1.00	.60
194	Ted Uhlaender	2.00	1.00	.60
195	John Odom	2.00	1.00	.60
196	Lum Harris	2.00	1.00	.60
197	Dick Selma	2.00	1.00	.60
198	Willie Smith	2.00	1.00	.60
199	Jim French	2.00	1.00	.60
200	Bob Gibson	15.00	7.50	4.50
201	Russ Snyder	2.00	1.00	.60
202	Don Wilson	2.00	1.00	.60
203	Dave Johnson	2.00	1.00	.60
204	Jack Hiatt	2.00	1.00	.60
205	Rick Reichardt	2.00	1.00	.60
206	Phillies Rookies (Larry Hisle, Barry Lersch)	2.00	1.00	.60
207	Roy Face	2.00	1.00	.60
208a	Donn Clendenon (Expos)	20.00	10.00	5.00
208b	Donn Clendenon (Houston)	3.00	1.00	.60
209	Larry Haney (Photo reversed.)	2.00	1.00	.60
210	Felix Millan	2.00	1.00	.60
211	Galen Cisco	2.00	1.00	.60
212	Tom Tresh	6.00	3.00	1.75
213	Gerry Arrigo	2.00	1.00	.60
214	3rd Series Check List (219-327)	4.00	2.00	1.25
215	Rico Petrocelli	2.00	1.00	.60
216	Don Sutton	8.00	4.00	2.50
217	John Donaldson	2.00	1.00	.60
218	John Roseboro	2.00	1.00	.60
219	*Freddie Patek*	2.00	1.00	.60
220	Sam McDowell	2.00	1.00	.60
221	Art Shamsky	2.00	1.00	.60
222	Duane Josephson	2.00	1.00	.60
223	Tom Dukes	2.00	1.00	.60
224	Angels Rookies (Bill Harrelson, Steve Kealey)	2.00	1.00	.60
225	Don Kessinger	2.00	1.00	.60
226	Bruce Howard	2.00	1.00	.60
227	Frank Johnson	2.00	1.00	.60
228	Dave Leonhard	2.00	1.00	.60
229	Don Lock	2.00	1.00	.60
230	Rusty Staub	3.00	1.50	.90
231	Pat Dobson	2.00	1.00	.60
232	Dave Ricketts	2.00	1.00	.60
233	Steve Barber	2.00	1.00	.60
234	Dave Bristol	2.00	1.00	.60
235	Jim Hunter	15.00	7.50	3.75
236	Manny Mota	2.00	1.00	.60
237	*Bobby Cox*	17.50	8.75	5.25
238	Ken Johnson	2.00	1.00	.60
239	Bob Taylor	2.00	1.00	.60
240	Ken Harrelson	2.00	1.00	.60
241	Jim Brewer	2.00	1.00	.60
242	Frank Kostro	2.00	1.00	.60
243	Ron Kline	2.00	1.00	.60
244	Indians Rookies (**Ray Fosse**, George Woodson)	3.50	1.75	1.00
245	Ed Charles	2.00	1.00	.60
246	Joe Coleman	2.00	1.00	.60
247	Gene Oliver	2.00	1.00	.60
248	Bob Priddy	2.00	1.00	.60
249	Ed Spiezio	2.00	1.00	.60
250	Frank Robinson	25.00	12.50	7.50
251	Ron Herbel	2.00	1.00	.60
252	Chuck Cottier	2.00	1.00	.60
253	Jerry Johnson	2.00	1.00	.60
254	Joe Schultz	2.00	1.00	.60
255	Steve Carlton	20.00	10.00	5.00
256	Gates Brown	2.00	1.00	.60
257	Jim Ray	2.00	1.00	.60
258	Jackie Hernandez	2.00	1.00	.60
259	Bill Short	2.00	1.00	.60
260	*Reggie Jackson*	265.00	132.50	79.50
261	Bob Johnson	2.00	1.00	.60
262	Mike Kekich	2.00	1.00	.60
263	Jerry May	2.00	1.00	.60
264	Bill Landis	2.00	1.00	.60
265	Chico Cardenas	2.00	1.00	.60
266	Dodgers Rookies (Alan Foster, Tom Hutton)	2.00	1.00	.60
267	Vicente Romo	2.00	1.00	.60
268	Al Spangler	2.00	1.00	.60
269	Al Weis	2.00	1.00	.60
270	Mickey Lolich	2.00	1.00	.60
271	Larry Stahl	2.00	1.00	.60
272	Ed Stroud	2.00	1.00	.60
273	Ron Willis	2.00	1.00	.60
274	Clyde King	2.00	1.00	.60
275	Vic Davalillo	2.00	1.00	.60
276	Gary Wagner	2.00	1.00	.60
277	*Rod Hendricks*	2.00	1.00	.60
278	Gary Geiger	2.00	1.00	.60
279	Roger Nelson	2.00	1.00	.60
280	Alex Johnson	2.00	1.00	.60
281	Ted Kubiak	2.00	1.00	.60
282	Pat Jarvis	2.00	1.00	.60
283	Sandy Alomar	2.00	1.00	.60
284	Expos Rookies (Jerry Robertson, Mike Wegener)	2.00	1.00	.60
285	Don Mincher	2.00	1.00	.60
286	*Dock Ellis*	3.00	1.50	.90
287	Jose Tartabull	2.00	1.00	.60
288	Ken Holtzman	2.00	1.00	.60
289	Bart Shirley	2.00	1.00	.60
290	Jim Kaat	3.00	1.50	.90
291	Vern Fuller	2.00	1.00	.60
292	Al Downing	2.00	1.00	.60
293	Dick Dietz	2.00	1.00	.60
294	Jim Lemon	2.00	1.00	.60
295	Tony Perez	12.00	6.00	3.00
296	*Andy Messersmith*	3.00	1.50	.90
297	Deron Johnson	2.00	1.00	.60
298	Dave Nicholson	2.00	1.00	.60
299	Mark Belanger	2.00	1.00	.60
300	Felipe Alou	4.00	2.00	1.25
301	Darrell Brandon	2.00	1.00	.60
302	Jim Pagliaroni	2.00	1.00	.60
303	Cal Koonce	2.00	1.00	.60
304	Padres Rookies (*Bill Davis, Clarence Gaston*)	4.00	2.00	1.25
305	Dick McAuliffe	2.00	1.00	.60
306	Jim Grant	2.00	1.00	.60
307	Gary Kolb	2.00	1.00	.60
308	Wade Blasingame	2.00	1.00	.60
309	Walt Williams	2.00	1.00	.60
310	Tom Haller	2.00	1.00	.60
311	*Sparky Lyle*	6.00	3.00	1.75
312	Lee Elia	2.00	1.00	.60
313	Bill Robinson	2.00	1.00	.60
314	4th Series Check List (328-425) (Don Drysdale)	5.00	2.50	1.50
315	Eddie Fisher	2.00	1.00	.60
316	Hal Lanier	2.00	1.00	.60
317	Bruce Look	2.00	1.00	.60
318	Jack Fisher	2.00	1.00	.60
319	Ken McMullen	2.00	1.00	.60
320	Dal Maxvill	2.00	1.00	.60
321	Jim McAndrew	2.00	1.00	.60
322	Jose Vidal	2.00	1.00	.60
323	Larry Miller	2.00	1.00	.60
324	Tigers Rookies (Les Cain, Dave Campbell)	2.00	1.00	.60
325	Jose Cardenal	2.00	1.00	.60
326	Gary Sutherland	2.00	1.00	.60
327	Willie Crawford	2.00	1.00	.60
328	Joe Horlen	2.00	1.00	.60
329	Rick Joseph	2.00	1.00	.60
330	Tony Conigliaro	6.00	3.00	1.75
331	Braves Rookies (*Gil Garrido, Tom House*)	2.00	1.00	.60
332	Fred Talbot	2.00	1.00	.60
333	Ivan Murrell	2.00	1.00	.60
334	Phil Roof	2.00	1.00	.60
335	Bill Mazeroski	10.00	5.00	3.00
336	Jim Roland	2.00	1.00	.60
337	Marty Martinez	2.00	1.00	.60
338	*Del Unser*	2.00	1.00	.60
339	Reds Rookies (Steve Mingori, Jose Pena)	2.00	1.00	.60
340	Dave McNally	2.00	1.00	.60
341	Dave Adlesh	2.00	1.00	.60
342	Bubba Morton	2.00	1.00	.60
343	Dan Frisella	2.00	1.00	.60
344	Tom Matchick	2.00	1.00	.60
345	Frank Linzy	2.00	1.00	.60
346	Wayne Comer	2.00	1.00	.60
347	Randy Hundley	2.00	1.00	.60
348	Steve Hargan	2.00	1.00	.60
349	Dick Williams	2.00	1.00	.60
350	Richie Allen	4.00	2.00	1.25
351	Carroll Sembera	2.00	1.00	.60
352	Paul Schaal	2.00	1.00	.60
353	Jeff Torborg	2.00	1.00	.60
354	Nate Oliver	2.00	1.00	.60
355	Phil Niekro	8.00	4.00	2.50
356	Frank Quilici	2.00	1.00	.60
357	Carl Taylor	2.00	1.00	.60
358	Athletics Rookies (George Lauzerique, Roberto Rodriguez)	2.00	1.00	.60
359	Dick Kelley	2.00	1.00	.60
360	Jim Wynn	2.00	1.00	.60
361	Gary Holman	2.00	1.00	.60
362	Jim Maloney	2.00	1.00	.60
363	Russ Nixon	2.00	1.00	.60
364	Tommie Agee	2.00	1.00	.60
365	Jim Fregosi	2.00	1.00	.60
366	Bo Belinsky	2.00	1.00	.60
367	Lou Johnson	2.00	1.00	.60
368	Vic Roznovsky	2.00	1.00	.60
369	Bob Skinner	2.00	1.00	.60
370	Juan Marichal	8.00	4.00	2.50
371	Sal Bando	2.00	1.00	.60
372	Adolfo Phillips	2.00	1.00	.60
373	Fred Lasher	2.00	1.00	.60
374	Bob Tillman	2.00	1.00	.60
375	Harmon Killebrew	20.00	10.00	6.00
376	Royals Rookies (*Mike Fiore, Jim Rooker*)	2.00	1.00	.60
377	Gary Bell	2.00	1.00	.60
378	Jose Herrera	2.00	1.00	.60
379	Ken Boyer	2.00	1.00	.60
380	Stan Bahnsen	2.00	1.00	.60
381	Ed Kranepool	2.00	1.00	.60
382	Pat Corrales	2.00	1.00	.60
383	Casey Cox	2.00	1.00	.60
384	Larry Shepard	2.00	1.00	.60
385	Orlando Cepeda	10.00	5.00	3.00
386	Jim McGlothlin	2.00	1.00	.60
387	Bobby Klaus	2.00	1.00	.60
388	Tom McCraw	2.00	1.00	.60
389	Dan Coombs	2.00	1.00	.60
390	Bill Freehan	2.00	1.00	.60
391	Ray Culp	2.00	1.00	.60
392	Bob Burda	2.00	1.00	.60
393	Gene Brabender	2.00	1.00	.60
394	Pilots Rookies (Lou Piniella, Marv Staehle)	4.00	2.00	1.25
395	Chris Short	2.00	1.00	.60
396	Jim Campanis	2.00	1.00	.60
397	Chuck Dobson	2.00	1.00	.60
398	Tito Francona	2.00	1.00	.60
399	Bob Bailey	2.00	1.00	.60
400	Don Drysdale	15.00	7.50	4.50
401	Jake Gibbs	2.00	1.00	.60
402	Ken Boswell	2.00	1.00	.60
403	Bob Miller	2.00	1.00	.60
404	Cubs Rookies (Vic LaRose, Gary Ross)	2.00	1.00	.60
405	Lee May	2.00	1.00	.60
406	Phil Ortega	2.00	1.00	.60
407	Tom Egan	2.00	1.00	.60
408	Nate Colbert	2.00	1.00	.60
409	Bob Moose	2.00	1.00	.60
410	Al Kaline	15.00	7.50	3.75
411	Larry Dierker	2.00	1.00	.60
412	5th Series Check List (426-512) (Mickey Mantle)	20.00	10.00	5.00
413	Roland Sheldon	2.00	1.00	.60
414	Duke Sims	2.00	1.00	.60
415	Ray Washburn	2.00	1.00	.60
416	Willie McCovey (All-Star)	7.00	3.50	2.00
417	Ken Harrelson (All-Star)	2.00	1.00	.60
418	Tommy Helms (All-Star)	2.00	1.00	.60
419	Rod Carew (All-Star)	8.00	4.00	2.50
420	Ron Santo (All-Star)	4.00	2.00	1.25
421	Brooks Robinson (All-Star)	9.00	4.50	2.75
422	Don Kessinger (All-Star)	2.00	1.00	.60
423	Bert Campaneris (All-Star)	2.00	1.00	.60
424	Pete Rose (All-Star)	25.00	12.50	6.25
425	Carl Yastrzemski (All-Star)	15.00	7.50	3.75
426	Curt Flood (All-Star)	3.00	1.50	.90
427	Tony Oliva (All-Star)	3.00	1.50	.90
428	Lou Brock (All-Star)	7.00	3.50	2.00
429	Willie Horton (All-Star)	2.00	1.00	.60
430	Johnny Bench (All-Star)	17.50	8.75	5.25
431	Bill Freehan (All-Star)	2.00	1.00	.60
432	Bob Gibson (All-Star)	8.00	4.00	2.50
433	Denny McLain (All-Star)	3.00	1.50	.90
434	Jerry Koosman (All-Star)	2.00	1.00	.60
435	Sam McDowell (All-Star)	2.00	1.00	.60
436	Gene Alley	2.00	1.00	.60
437	Luis Alcaraz	2.00	1.00	.60
438	Gary Waslewski	2.00	1.00	.60
439	White Sox Rookies (Ed Herrmann, Dan Lazar)	2.00	1.00	.60
440a	Willie McCovey (Last name in white.)	150.00	75.00	45.00
440b	Willie McCovey (Last name in yellow.)	15.00	7.50	3.75
441a	Dennis Higgins (Last name in white.)	60.00	30.00	18.00
441b	Dennis Higgins (Last name in yellow.)	2.00	1.00	.60
442	Ty Cline	2.00	1.00	.60
443	Don Wert	2.00	1.00	.60
444a	Joe Moeller (Last name in white.)	60.00	30.00	18.00
444b	Joe Moeller (Last name in yellow.)	2.00	1.00	.60
445	Bobby Knoop	2.00	1.00	.60
446	Claude Raymond	2.00	1.00	.60
447a	Ralph Houk (Last name in white.)	80.00	40.00	24.00
447b	Ralph Houk (Last name in yellow.)	5.00	2.50	1.50
448	Bob Tolan	2.00	1.00	.60
449	Paul Lindblad	2.00	1.00	.60
450	Billy Williams	15.00	7.50	3.75
451a	Rich Rollins (First name in white.)	60.00	30.00	18.00
451b	Rich Rollins (First name in yellow.)	2.00	1.00	.60
452a	Al Ferrara (First name in white.)	60.00	30.00	18.00
452b	Al Ferrara (First name in yellow.)	2.00	1.00	.60
453	Mike Cuellar	2.00	1.00	.60
454a	Phillies Rookies (*Larry Colton, Don Money*) (Names in white.)	60.00	30.00	18.00
454b	Phillies Rookies (*Larry Colton, Don Money*) (Names in yellow.)	2.00	1.00	.60
455	Sonny Siebert	2.00	1.00	.60
456	Bud Harrelson	2.00	1.00	.60
457	Dalton Jones	2.00	1.00	.60
458	Curt Blefary	2.00	1.00	.60
459	Dave Boswell	2.00	1.00	.60
460	Joe Torre	5.00	2.50	1.50
461a	Mike Epstein (Last name in white.)	60.00	30.00	18.00
461b	Mike Epstein (Last name in yellow.)	2.00	1.00	.60
462	Red Schoendienst	7.00	3.50	2.00
463	Dennis Ribant	2.00	1.00	.60
464a	Dave Marshall	60.00	30.00	18.00
464b	Dave Marshall	2.00	1.00	.60
465	Tommy John	4.00	2.00	1.25
466	John Boccabella	2.00	1.00	.60
467	Tom Reynolds	2.00	1.00	.60
468a	Pirates Rookies (Bruce Dal Canton, Bob Robertson) (Names in white.)	60.00	30.00	18.00
468b	Pirates Rookies (Bruce Dal Canton, Bob Robertson) (Names in yellow.)			
469	Chico Ruiz	2.00	1.00	.60
470a	Mel Stottlemyre	60.00	30.00	18.00
470b	Mel Stottlemyre (Last name in yellow.)	3.00	1.50	.90
471a	Ted Savage (Last name in white.)	60.00	30.00	18.00

471b	Ted Savage (Last name in yellow.)	2.00	1.00	.60
472	Jim Price	2.00	1.00	.60
473a	Jose Arcia (First name in white.)	60.00	30.00	18.00
473b	Jose Arcia (First name in yellow.)	2.00	1.00	.60
474	Tom Murphy	2.00	1.00	.60
475	Tim McCarver	3.00	1.50	.90
476a	Red Sox Rookies (**Ken Brett**, Gerry Moses) (Names in white.)	60.00	30.00	18.00
476b	Red Sox Rookies (**Ken Brett**, Gerry Moses) (Names in yellow.)	3.00	1.50	.90
477	Jeff James	2.00	1.00	.60
478	Don Buford	2.00	1.00	.60
479	Richie Scheinblum	2.00	1.00	.60
480	Tom Seaver	60.00	30.00	18.00
481	*Bill Melton*	2.00	1.00	.60
482a	Jim Gosger (First name in white.)	60.00	30.00	18.00
482b	Jim Gosger (First name in yellow.)	2.00	1.00	.60
483	Ted Abernathy	2.00	1.00	.60
484	Joe Gordon	2.00	1.00	.60
485a	Gaylord Perry (Last name in white.)	90.00	45.00	27.50
485b	Gaylord Perry (Last name in yellow.)	8.00	4.00	2.50
486a	Paul Casanova (Last name in white.)	60.00	30.00	18.00
486b	Paul Casanova (Last name in yellow.)	2.00	1.00	.60
487	Denis Menke	2.00	1.00	.60
488	Joe Sparma	2.00	1.00	.60
489	Clete Boyer	3.00	1.50	.90
490	Matty Alou	2.00	1.00	.60
491a	Twins Rookies (Jerry Crider, George Mitterwald) (Names in white.)	60.00	30.00	18.00
491b	Twins Rookies (Jerry Crider, George Mitterwald) (Names in yellow.)	2.00	1.00	.60
492	Tony Cloninger	2.00	1.00	.60
493a	Wes Parker (Last name in white.)	60.00	30.00	18.00
493b	Wes Parker (Last name in yellow.)	2.00	1.00	.60
494	Ken Berry	2.00	1.00	.60
495	Bert Campaneris	2.00	1.00	.60
496	Larry Jaster	2.00	1.00	.60
497	Julian Javier	2.00	1.00	.60
498	Juan Pizarro	2.00	1.00	.60
499	Astros Rookies (Don Bryant, Steve Shea)	2.00	1.00	.60
500a	Mickey Mantle (Last name in white.)	1,750	875.00	525.00
500b	Mickey Mantle (Last name in yellow.)	250.00	125.00	75.00
501a	Tony Gonzalez (First name in white.)	60.00	30.00	18.00
501b	Tony Gonzalez (First name in yellow.)	2.00	1.00	.60
502	Minnie Rojas	2.00	1.00	.60
503	Larry Brown	2.00	1.00	.60
504	6th Series Check List (513-588) (Brooks Robinson)	7.00	3.50	2.00
505a	Bobby Bolin (Last name in white.)	60.00	30.00	18.00
505b	Bobby Bolin (Last name in yellow.)	2.00	1.00	.60
506	Paul Blair	2.00	1.00	.60
507	Cookie Rojas	2.00	1.00	.60
508	Moe Drabowsky	2.00	1.00	.60
509	Manny Sanguillen	2.00	1.00	.60
510	Rod Carew	30.00	15.00	7.50
511a	Diego Segui (First name in white.)	60.00	30.00	18.00
511b	Diego Segui (First name in yellow.)	2.00	1.00	.60
512	Cleon Jones	2.00	1.00	.60
513	Camilo Pascual	2.00	1.00	.60
514	Mike Lum	2.00	1.00	.60
515	Dick Green	2.00	1.00	.60
516	Earl Weaver	9.00	4.50	2.75
517	Mike McCormick	2.00	1.00	.60
518	Fred Whitfield	2.00	1.00	.60
519	Yankees Rookies (Len Boehmer, Gerry Kenney)	2.00	1.00	.60
520	Bob Veale	2.00	1.00	.60
521	George Thomas	2.00	1.00	.60
522	Joe Hoerner	2.00	1.00	.60
523	Bob Chance	2.00	1.00	.60
524	Expos Rookies (Jose Laboy, Floyd Wicker)	2.00	1.00	.60
525	Earl Wilson	2.00	1.00	.60
526	Hector Torres	2.00	1.00	.60
527	Al Lopez	6.00	3.00	1.75
528	Claude Osteen	2.00	1.00	.60
529	Ed Kirkpatrick	2.00	1.00	.60
530	Cesar Tovar	2.00	1.00	.60
531	Dick Farrell	2.00	1.00	.60
532	Bird Hill Aces (Mike Cuellar, Jim Hardin, Dave McNally, Tom Phoebus)	3.50	1.75	1.00
533	Nolan Ryan	200.00	100.00	60.00
534	Jerry McNertney	2.00	1.00	.60
535	Phil Regan	2.00	1.00	.60
536	Padres Rookies (*Danny Breeden, Dave Roberts*)	2.00	1.00	.60
537	Mike Paul	2.00	1.00	.60
538	Charlie Smith	2.00	1.00	.60
539	Ted Shows How (Mike Epstein, Ted Williams)	13.50	6.75	4.00
540	Curt Flood	3.00	1.50	.90
541	Joe Verbanic	2.00	1.00	.60
542	Bob Aspromonte	2.00	1.00	.60

543	Fred Newman	2.00	1.00	.60
544	Tigers Rookies (Mike Kilkenny, Ron Woods)	2.00	1.00	.60
545	Willie Stargell	12.00	6.00	3.00
546	Jim Nash	2.00	1.00	.60
547	Billy Martin	6.00	3.00	1.75
548	Bob Locker	2.00	1.00	.60
549	Ron Brand	2.00	1.00	.60
550	Brooks Robinson	25.00	12.50	7.50
551	Wayne Granger	2.00	1.00	.60
552	Dodgers Rookies (*Ted Sizemore, Bill Sudakis*)	3.00	1.50	.90
553	Ron Davis	2.00	1.00	.60
554	Frank Bertaina	2.00	1.00	.60
555	Jim Hart	2.00	1.00	.60
556	A's Stars (Sal Bando, Bert Campaneris, Danny Cater)	3.00	1.50	.90
557	Frank Fernandez	2.00	1.00	.60
558	*Tom Burgmeier*	2.00	1.00	.60
559	Cards Rookies (Joe Hague, Jim Hicks)	2.00	1.00	.60
560	Luis Tiant	2.00	1.00	.60
561	Ron Clark	2.00	1.00	.60
562	*Bob Watson*	4.00	2.00	1.25
563	Marty Pattin	2.00	1.00	.60
564	Gil Hodges	12.50	6.25	3.75
565	Hoyt Wilhelm	8.00	4.00	2.50
566	Ron Hansen	2.00	1.00	.60
567a	Pirates Rookies (Elvio Jimenez, Jim Shellenback) (No black outline around title letters.)	45.00	22.50	13.50
567b	Pirates Rookies (Elvio Jiminez, Jim Shellenback) (Title letters outlined in black.)	2.00	1.00	.60
568	Cecil Upshaw	2.00	1.00	.60
569	Billy Harris	2.00	1.00	.60
570	Ron Santo	15.00	7.50	3.75
571	Cap Peterson	2.00	1.00	.60
572	Giants Heroes (Juan Marichal, Willie McCovey)	9.00	4.50	2.75
573	Jim Palmer	15.00	7.50	4.50
574	George Scott	2.00	1.00	.60
575	Bill Singer	2.00	1.00	.60
576	Phillies Rookies (Ron Stone, Bill Wilson)	2.00	1.00	.60
577	Mike Hegan	2.00	1.00	.60
578	Don Bosch	2.00	1.00	.60
579	*Dave Nelson*	2.00	1.00	.60
580	Jim Northrup	2.00	1.00	.60
581	Gary Nolan	2.00	1.00	.60
582a	7th Series Check List (589-664) (Tony Oliva) (Red circle on back.)	4.50	2.25	1.25
582b	7th Series Check List (589-664) (Tony Oliva) (White circle on back.)	3.00	1.50	.90
583	*Clyde Wright*	2.00	1.00	.60
584	Don Mason	2.00	1.00	.60
585	Ron Swoboda	2.00	1.00	.60
586	Tim Cullen	2.00	1.00	.60
587	Joe Rudi	5.00	2.50	1.50
588	Bill White	3.00	1.50	.90
589	Joe Pepitone	6.00	3.00	1.75
590	Rico Carty	3.00	1.50	.90
591	Mike Hedlund	3.00	1.50	.90
592	Padres Rookies (Rafael Robles, Al Santorini)	3.00	1.50	.90
593	Don Nottebart	3.00	1.50	.90
594	Dooley Womack	3.00	1.50	.90
595	Lee Maye	3.00	1.50	.90
596	Chuck Hartenstein	3.00	1.50	.90
597	A.L. Rookies (Larry Burchart, **Rollie Fingers**, Bob Floyd)	35.00	17.50	8.75
598	Ruben Amaro	3.00	1.50	.90
599	John Boozer	3.00	1.50	.90
600	Tony Oliva	6.00	3.00	1.75
601	Tug McGraw	4.00	2.00	1.25
602	Cubs Rookies (Alec Distaso, Jim Qualls, Don Young)	3.00	1.50	.90
603	Joe Keough	3.00	1.50	.90
604	Bobby Etheridge	3.00	1.50	.90
605	Dick Ellsworth	3.00	1.50	.90
606	Gene Mauch	3.00	1.50	.90
607	Dick Bosman	3.00	1.50	.90
608	Dick Simpson	3.00	1.50	.90
609	Phil Gagliano	3.00	1.50	.90
610	Jim Hardin	3.00	1.50	.90
611	Braves Rookies (Bob Didier, Walt Hriniak, Gary Neibauer)	3.00	1.50	.90
612	Jack Aker	3.00	1.50	.90
613	Jim Beauchamp	3.00	1.50	.90
614	Astros Rookies (Tom Griffin, Skip Guinn)	3.00	1.50	.90
615	Len Gabrielson	3.00	1.50	.90
616	Don McMahon	3.00	1.50	.90
617	Jesse Gonder	3.00	1.50	.90
618	Ramon Webster	3.00	1.50	.90
619	Royals Rookies (Bill Butler, **Pat Kelly**, Juan Rios)	3.00	1.50	.90
620	Dean Chance	3.00	1.50	.90
621	Bill Voss	3.00	1.50	.90
622	Dan Osinski	3.00	1.50	.90
623	Hank Allen	3.00	1.50	.90
624	N.L. Rookies (Darrel Chaney, Duffy Dyer, Terry Harmon)	3.00	1.50	.90
625	Mack Jones	3.00	1.50	.90
626	Gene Michael	3.00	1.50	.90
627	George Stone	3.00	1.50	.90
628	Red Sox Rookies (**Bill Conigliaro**, Syd O'Brien, Fred Wenz)	4.00	2.00	1.25
629	Jack Hamilton	3.00	1.50	.90
630	*Bobby Bonds*	30.00	15.00	9.00
631	John Kennedy	3.00	1.50	.90

632	Jon Warden	3.00	1.50	.90
633	Harry Walker	3.00	1.50	.90
634	Andy Etchebarren	3.00	1.50	.90
635	George Culver	3.00	1.50	.90
636	Woodie Held	3.00	1.50	.90
637	Padres Rookies (Jerry DaVanon, Clay Kirby, Frank Reberger)	3.00	1.50	.90
638	Ed Sprague	3.00	1.50	.90
639	Barry Moore	3.00	1.50	.90
640	Fergie Jenkins	15.00	7.50	3.75
641	N.L. Rookies (Bobby Darwin, Tommy Dean, John Miller)	3.00	1.50	.90
642	John Hiller	3.00	1.50	.90
643	Billy Cowan	3.00	1.50	.90
644	Chuck Hinton	3.00	1.50	.90
645	George Brunet	3.00	1.50	.90
646	Expos Rookies (*Dan McGinn, Carl Morton*)	3.00	1.50	.90
647	Dave Wickersham	3.00	1.50	.90
648	Bobby Wine	3.00	1.50	.90
649	Al Jackson	3.00	1.50	.90
650	Ted Williams	25.00	12.50	6.25
651	Gus Gil	3.00	1.50	.90
652	Eddie Watt	3.00	1.50	.90
653	*Aurelio Rodriguez* (Photo actually batboy Leonard Garcia.)	6.00	3.00	1.75
654	White Sox Rookies (**Carlos May**, Rich Morales, Don Secrist)	3.50	1.75	1.00
655	Mike Hershberger	3.00	1.50	.90
656	Dan Schneider	3.00	1.50	.90
657	Bobby Murcer	6.00	3.00	1.75
658	A.L. Rookies (Bill Burbach, Tom Hall, Jim Miles)	3.00	1.50	.90
659	Johnny Podres	3.00	1.50	.90
660	Reggie Smith	3.00	1.50	.90
661	Jim Merritt	3.00	1.50	.90
662	Royals Rookies (Dick Drago, Bob Oliver, George Spriggs)	3.00	1.50	.90
663	Dick Radatz	4.50	2.25	1.25
664	Ron Hunt	13.50	3.00	1.00

1969 Topps Decals

Designed as an insert for 1969 regular issue card packs, these decals are virtually identical in format to the '69 cards. The 48 decals in the set measure 1" x 2-1/2", although they are mounted on white paper backing which measures 1-3/4" x 2-1/8". In March 2001, a hoard consisting of two original 10,000-piece rolls - 833 each of half the players in the set - was sold at auction. The players represented in that find are indicated in these listings with an asterisk.

		NM	EX	VG
Complete Set (48):		350.00	175.00	100.00
Common Player:		4.00	2.00	1.25
(1)	Hank Aaron	25.00	12.50	7.50
(2)	Richie Allen	7.00	3.50	2.00
(3)	Felipe Alou	5.00	2.50	1.50
(4)	Matty Alou	4.00	2.00	1.25
(5)	Luis Aparicio	9.00	4.50	2.75
(6)	Bob Clemente	30.00	15.00	9.00
(7)	Donn Clendenon	4.00	2.00	1.25
(8)	Tommy Davis (*)	4.00	2.00	1.25
(9)	Don Drysdale (*)	10.00	5.00	3.00
(10)	Joe Foy (*)	4.00	2.00	1.25
(11)	Jim Fregosi	4.00	2.00	1.25
(12)	Bob Gibson (*)	10.00	5.00	3.00
(13)	Tony Gonzalez	4.00	2.00	1.25
(14)	Tom Haller	4.00	2.00	1.25
(15)	Ken Harrelson	4.00	2.00	1.25
(16)	Tommy Helms	4.00	2.00	1.25
(17)	Willie Horton (*)	4.00	2.00	1.25
(18)	Frank Howard	4.50	2.25	1.25
(19)	Reggie Jackson (*)	20.00	10.00	6.00
(20)	Fergie Jenkins	9.00	4.50	2.75
(21)	Harmon Killebrew (*)	10.00	5.00	3.00
(22)	Jerry Koosman (*)	4.00	2.00	1.25
(23)	Mickey Mantle	40.00	20.00	12.00
(24)	Willie Mays (*)	20.00	10.00	6.00
(25)	Tim McCarver	4.50	2.25	1.25
(26)	Willie McCovey	10.00	5.00	3.00
(27)	Sam McDowell (*)	4.00	2.00	1.25
(28)	Denny McLain (*)	4.00	2.00	1.25
(29)	Dave McNally (*)	4.00	2.00	1.25
(30)	Don Mincher	4.00	2.00	1.25
(31)	Rick Monday	4.00	2.00	1.25
(32)	Tony Oliva (*)	4.50	2.25	1.25
(33)	Camilo Pascual	4.00	2.00	1.25
(34)	Rick Reichardt (*)	4.00	2.00	1.25
(35)	Frank Robinson (*)	10.00	5.00	3.00
(36)	Pete Rose (*)	20.00	10.00	6.00
(37)	Ron Santo (*)	5.00	2.50	1.50
(38)	Tom Seaver (*)	12.00	6.00	3.50
(39)	Dick Selma (*)	4.00	2.00	1.25
(40)	Chris Short (*)	4.00	2.00	1.25

		NM	EX	VG
(41)	Rusty Staub	4.00	2.00	1.25
(42)	Mel Stottlemyre	4.00	2.00	1.25
(43)	Luis Tiant (*)	4.00	2.00	1.25
(44)	Pete Ward	4.00	2.00	1.25
(45)	Hoyt Wilhelm (*)	7.50	3.75	2.25
(46)	Maury Wills (*)	4.00	2.00	1.25
(47)	Jim Wynn	4.00	2.00	1.25
(48)	Carl Yastrzemski (*)	12.00	6.00	3.50

1969 Topps Deckle Edge

 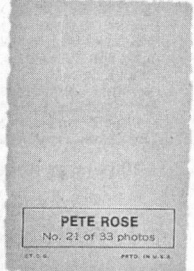

PETE ROSE
No. 21 of 33 photos

These 2-1/4" x 3-1/4" cards take their name from their borders which have a scalloped effect. Fronts have a black-and-white player photo along with a blue facsimile autograph. Backs have the player's name and the card number in light blue ink in a small box at the bottom of the card. While there are only 33 numbered cards, there are actually 35 possible players; both Jim Wynn and Hoyt Wilhelm cards are found as #11 while cards of Joe Foy and Rusty Staub as #22. Straight-edged proof cards are sometimes found but these were never formally issued; they carry a premium.

		NM	EX	VG
Complete Set (33):		80.00	40.00	25.00
Common Player:		1.00	.50	.30
Proofs: 6-8X				
1	Brooks Robinson	9.00	4.50	2.75
2	Boog Powell	1.50	.70	.45
3	Ken Harrelson	1.00	.50	.30
4	Carl Yastrzemski	9.00	4.50	2.75
5	Jim Fregosi	1.00	.50	.30
6	Luis Aparicio	7.50	3.75	2.25
7	Luis Tiant	1.00	.50	.30
8	Denny McLain	1.00	.50	.30
9	Willie Horton	1.00	.50	.30
10	Bill Freehan	1.00	.50	.30
11a	Hoyt Wilhelm	6.00	3.00	1.75
11b	Jim Wynn	12.00	6.00	3.50
12	Rod Carew	7.50	3.75	2.25
13	Mel Stottlemyre	1.00	.50	.30
14	Rick Monday	1.00	.50	.30
15	Tommy Davis	1.00	.50	.30
16	Frank Howard	1.50	.70	.45
17	Felipe Alou	1.00	.50	.30
18	Don Kessinger	1.00	.50	.30
19	Ron Santo	2.00	1.00	.60
20	Tommy Helms	1.00	.50	.30
21	Pete Rose	15.00	7.50	4.50
22a	Rusty Staub	2.00	1.00	.60
22b	Joe Foy	9.00	4.50	2.75
23	Tom Haller	1.00	.50	.30
24	Maury Wills	1.00	.50	.30
25	Jerry Koosman	1.00	.50	.30
26	Richie Allen	3.00	1.50	.90
27	Roberto Clemente	20.00	10.00	6.00
28	Curt Flood	1.00	.50	.30
29	Bob Gibson	7.50	3.75	2.25
30	Al Ferrara	1.00	.50	.30
31	Willie McCovey	7.50	3.75	2.25
32	Juan Marichal	6.00	3.00	1.75
33	Willie Mays	15.00	7.50	4.50

1969 Topps Stamps

Topps continued to refine its efforts at baseball stamps in 1969 with the release of 240 player stamps, each measuring 1" x 1-7/16". Each stamp has a color photo along with the player's name, position and team. Unlike prior stamp issues, the 1969 stamps have 24 separate albums (one per team). The stamps were issued in strips of 12, many players appearing on two different strips.

	NM	EX	VG
Complete Sheet Set (24):	200.00	100.00	60.00

		NM	EX	VG
Common Sheet:		5.00	2.50	1.50
Complete Stamp Album Set (24):		65.00	32.00	19.50
Single Stamp Album:		3.00	1.50	.90
Unopened Pack:		50.00	.00	.00
(1)	Tommie Agee, Sandy Alomar, Jose Cardenal, Dean Chance, Joe Foy, Jim Grant, Don Kessinger, Mickey Mantle, Jerry May, Bob Rodgers, Cookie Rojas, Gary Sutherland	55.00	27.50	16.50
(2)	Jesus Alou, Mike Andrews, Larry Brown, Moe Drabowsky, Alex Johnson, Lew Krausse, Jim Lefebvre, Dal Maxvill, John Odom, Claude Osteen, Rick Reichardt, Luis Tiant	5.00	2.50	1.50
(3)	Hank Aaron, Matty Alou, Max Alvis, Nelson Briles, Eddie Fisher, Bud Harrelson, Willie Horton, Randy Hundley, Larry Jaster, Jim Kaat, Gary Peters, Pete Ward	20.00	10.00	6.00
(4)	Don Buford, John Callison, Tommy Davis, Jackie Hernandez, Fergie Jenkins, Lee May, Denny McLain, Bob Oliver, Roberto Pena, Tony Perez, Joe Torre, Tom Tresh	7.50	3.75	2.25
(5)	Jim Bunning, Dean Chance, Joe Foy, Sonny Jackson, Don Kessinger, Rick Monday, Gaylord Perry, Roger Repoz, Cookie Rojas, Mel Stottlemyre, Leon Wagner, Jim Wynn	7.50	3.75	2.25
(6)	Felipe Alou, Gerry Arrigo, Bob Aspromonte, Gary Bell, Clay Dalrymple, Jim Fregosi, Tony Gonzalez, Duane Josephson, Dick McAuliffe, Tony Oliva, Brooks Robinson, Willie Stargell	20.00	10.00	6.00
(7)	Steve Barber, Donn Clendenon, Joe Coleman, Vic Davalillo, Russ Gibson, Jerry Grote, Tom Haller, Andy Kosco, Willie McCovey, Don Mincher, Joe Morgan, Don Wilson	7.50	3.75	2.25
(8)	George Brunet, Don Buford, John Callison, Danny Cater, Tommy Davis, Willie Davis, John Edwards, Jim Hart, Mickey Lolich, Willie Mays, Roberto Pena, Mickey Stanley	25.00	12.50	7.50
(9)	Ernie Banks, Glenn Beckert, Ken Berry, Horace Clarke, Roberto Clemente, Len Gabrielson, Jake Gibbs, Jerry Koosman, Sam McDowell, Tom Satriano, Bill Singer	25.00	12.50	7.50
(10)	Gene Alley, Lou Brock, Larry Brown, Moe Drabowsky, Frank Howard, Tommie John, Roger Nelson, Claude Osteen, Phil Regan, Rick Reichardt, Tony Taylor, Roy White	7.50	3.75	2.25
(11)	Bob Allison, John Bateman, Don Drysdale, Dave Johnson, Harmon Killebrew, Jim Maloney, Bill Mazeroski, Gerry McNertney, Ron Perranoski, Rico Petrocelli, Pete Rose, Billy Williams	35.00	17.50	10.50
(12)	Bernie Allen (Senators), Jose Arcia, Stan Bahnsen, Sal Bando, Jim Davenport, Tito Francona, Dick Green, Ron Hunt, Mack Jones, Vada Pinson, George Scott, Don Wert	5.00	2.50	1.50
(13)	Gerry Arrigo, Bob Aspromonte, Joe Azcue, Curt Blefary, Orlando Cepeda, Bill Freehan, Jim Fregosi, Dave Giusti, Duane Josephson, Tim McCarver, Jose Santiago, Bob Tolan	7.50	3.75	2.25
(14)	Jerry Adair, Johnny Bench, Clete Boyer, John Briggs, Bert Campaneris, Woody Fryman, Ron Kline, Bobby Knoop, Ken McMullen, Adolfo Phillips, John Roseboro, Tom Seaver	20.00	10.00	6.00
(15)	Norm Cash, Ron Fairly, Bob Gibson, Bill Hands, Cleon Jones, Al Kaline, Paul Schaal, Mike Shannon, Duke Sims, Reggie Smith, Steve Whitaker, Carl Yastrzemski	15.00	7.50	4.50
(16)	Steve Barber, Paul Casanova, Dick Dietz, Russ Gibson, Jerry Grote, Tom Haller, Ed Kranepool, Juan Marichal, Denis Menke, Jim Nash, Bill Robinson, Frank Robinson	7.50	3.75	2.25

		NM	EX	VG
(17)	Bobby Bolin, Ollie Brown, Rod Carew, Mike Epstein, Bud Harrelson, Larry Jaster, Dave McNally, Willie Norton, Milt Pappas, Gary Peters, Paul Popovich, Stan Williams	7.50	3.75	2.25
(18)	Ted Abernathy, Bob Allison, Ed Brinkman, Don Drysdale, Jim Hardin, Julian Javier, Hal Lanier, Jim McGlothlin, Ron Perranoski, Rich Rollins, Ron Santo, Billy Williams	15.00	7.50	4.50
(19)	Richie Allen, Luis Aparicio, Wally Bunker, Curt Flood, Ken Harrelson, Jim Hunter, Denver Lemaster, Felix Millan, Jim Northrop (Northrup), Art Shamsky, Larry Stahl, Ted Uhlaender	7.50	3.75	2.25
(20)	Bob Bailey, Johnny Bench, Woody Fryman, Jim Hannan, Ron Kline, Al McBean, Camilo Pascual, Joe Pepitone, Doug Rader, Ron Reed, John Roseboro, Sonny Siebert	7.50	3.75	2.25
(21)	Jack Aker, Tommy Harper, Tommy Helms, Dennis Higgins, Jim Hunter, Don Lock, Lee Maye, Felix Millan, Jim Northrop (Northrup), Larry Stahl, Don Sutton, Zoilo Versalles	7.50	3.75	2.25
(22)	Norm Cash, Ed Charles, Joe Horlen, Pat Jarvis, Jim Lonborg, Manny Mota, Boog Powell, Dick Selma, Mike Shannon, Duke Sims, Steve Whitaker, Hoyt Wilhelm	7.50	3.75	2.25
(23)	Bernie Allen (Senator), Ray Culp, Al Ferrara, Tito Francona, Dick Green, Ron Hunt, Ray Oyler, Tom Phoebus, Rusty Staub, Bob Veale, Maury Wills, Wilbur Wood	5.00	2.50	1.50
(24)	Ernie Banks, Mark Belanger, Steve Blass, Horace Clarke, Bob Clemente, Larry Dierker, Dave Duncan, Chico Salmon, Chris Short, Ron Swoboda, Cesar Tovar, Rick Wise	20.00	10.00	6.00

1969 Topps Super

 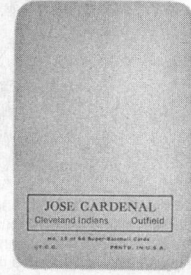

JOSE CARDENAL
Cleveland Indians   Outfield

These 2-1/4" x 3-1/4" cards are not the bigger "Super" cards which would be seen in following years. Rather, what enabled Topps to dub them "Super Baseball Cards" is their high-gloss finish which enhances the bright color photograph used on their fronts. The only other design element on the front is a facsimile autograph. The backs contain a box at the the bottom which carries the player's name, team, position, a copyright line and the card number. Another unusual feature is that the cards have rounded corners, although square-cornered proof cards are also known, completely printed on front and back.

		NM	EX	VG
Complete Set (66):		4,000	2,000	1,200
Common Player:		15.00	7.50	4.50
Proofs: 1.5-2X				
1	Dave McNally	15.00	7.50	4.50
2	Frank Robinson	125.00	62.50	37.50
3	Brooks Robinson	125.00	62.50	37.50
4	Ken Harrelson	15.00	7.50	4.50
5	Carl Yastrzemski	200.00	100.00	60.00
6	Ray Culp	15.00	7.50	4.50
7	James Fregosi	15.00	7.50	4.50
8	Rick Reichardt	15.00	7.50	4.50
9	Vic Davalillo	15.00	7.50	4.50
10	Luis Aparicio	75.00	37.00	22.00
11	Pete Ward	15.00	7.50	4.50
12	Joe Horlen	15.00	7.50	4.50
13	Luis Tiant	15.00	7.50	4.50
14	Sam McDowell	15.00	7.50	4.50
15	Jose Cardenal	15.00	7.50	4.50
16	Willie Horton	15.00	7.50	4.50
17	Denny McLain	15.00	7.50	4.50
18	Bill Freehan	15.00	7.50	4.50
19	Harmon Killebrew	125.00	62.50	37.50
20	Tony Oliva	15.00	7.50	4.50
21	Dean Chance	15.00	7.50	4.50
22	Joe Foy	15.00	7.50	4.50
23	Roger Nelson	15.00	7.50	4.50

		NM	EX	VG
24	Mickey Mantle	1,100	550.00	350.00
25	Mel Stottlemyre	15.00	7.50	4.50
26	Roy White	15.00	7.50	4.50
27	Rick Monday	15.00	7.50	4.50
28	Reggie Jackson	400.00	200.00	120.00
29	Bert Campaneris	15.00	7.50	4.50
30	Frank Howard	15.00	7.50	4.50
31	Camilo Pascual	15.00	7.50	4.50
32	Tommy Davis	15.00	7.50	4.50
33	Don Mincher	15.00	7.50	4.50
34	Henry Aaron	300.00	150.00	90.00
35	Felipe Alou	15.00	7.50	4.50
36	Joe Torre	20.00	10.00	6.00
37	Fergie Jenkins	75.00	37.00	22.00
38	Ronald Santo	20.00	10.00	6.00
39	Billy Williams	75.00	37.00	22.00
40	Tommy Helms	15.00	7.50	4.50
41	Pete Rose	300.00	150.00	90.00
42	Joe Morgan	75.00	37.00	22.00
43	Jim Wynn	15.00	7.50	4.50
44	Curt Blefary	15.00	7.50	4.50
45	Willie Davis	15.00	7.50	4.50
46	Don Drysdale	125.00	62.50	37.50
47	Tom Haller	15.00	7.50	4.50
48	Rusty Staub	20.00	10.00	6.00
49	Maurice Wills	15.00	7.50	4.50
50	Cleon Jones	15.00	7.50	4.50
51	Jerry Koosman	15.00	7.50	4.50
52	Tom Seaver	125.00	62.50	37.50
53	Rich Allen	20.00	10.00	6.00
54	Chris Short	15.00	7.50	4.50
55	Cookie Rojas	15.00	7.50	4.50
56	Mateo Alou	15.00	7.50	4.50
57	Steve Blass	15.00	7.50	4.50
58	Roberto Clemente	400.00	200.00	120.00
59	Curt Flood	15.00	7.50	4.50
60	Bob Gibson	100.00	50.00	30.00
61	Tim McCarver	20.00	10.00	6.00
62	Dick Selma	15.00	7.50	4.50
63	Ollie Brown	15.00	7.50	4.50
64	Juan Marichal	75.00	37.00	22.00
65	Willie Mays	300.00	150.00	90.00
66	Willie McCovey	100.00	50.00	30.00

1969 Topps Team Posters

Picking up where the 1968 posters left off, the 1969 poster is larger at about 12" x 20". The posters each have a team focus with a large pennant carrying the team name, along with nine or 10 photos of players. Each of the photos has a facsimile autograph. The size of posters meant they had to be folded to fit in their packages. These original folds are not considered when grading, unless the paper has split on those seams.

		NM	EX	VG
Complete Set (24):		2,250	1,125	675.00
Common Poster:		55.00	27.50	16.00
Unopened Pack:		190.00		
1	Detroit Tigers (Norm Cash, Bill Freehan, Willie Horton, Al Kaline, Mickey Lolich, Dick McAuliffe, Denny McLain, Jim Northrup, Mickey Stanley, Don Wert, Earl Wilson)	125.00	65.00	35.00
2	Atlanta Braves (Hank Aaron, Felipe Alou, Clete Boyer, Rico Carty, Tito Francona, Sonny Jackson, Pat Jarvis, Felix Millan, Phil Niekro, Milt Pappas, Joe Torre)	90.00	45.00	27.00
3	Boston Red Sox (Mike Andrews, Tony Conigliaro, Ray Culp, Russ Gibson, Ken Harrelson, Bill Hands, Rico Petrocelli, Jose Santiago, George Scott, Reggie Smith, Carl Yastrzemski)	100.00	50.00	30.00
4	Chicago Cubs (Ernie Banks, Glenn Beckert, Bill Hands, Jim Hickman, Ken Holtzman, Randy Hundley, Fergie Jenkins, Don Kessinger, Adolfo Phillips, Ron Santo, Billy Williams)	90.00	45.00	27.00

		NM	EX	VG
5	Baltimore Orioles (Mark Belanger, Paul Blair, Don Buford, Andy Etchebarren, Jim Hardin, Dave Johnson, Dave McNally, Tom Phoebus, Boog Powell, Brooks Robinson, Frank Robinson)	80.00	40.00	24.00
6	Houston Astros (Curt Blefary, Donn Clendenon, Larry Dierker, John Edwards, Denny Lemaster, Denis Menke, Norm Miller, Joe Morgan, Doug Rader, Don Wilson, Jim Wynn)	55.00	27.50	16.00
7	Kansas City Royals (Jerry Adair, Wally Bunker, Mike Fiore, Joe Foy, Jackie Hernandez, Pat Kelly, Dave Morehead, Roger Nelson, Dave Nicholson, Eliseo Rodriguez, Steve Whitaker)	55.00	27.50	16.00
8	Philadelphia Phillies (Richie Allen, Johnny Callison, Woody Fryman, Larry Hisle, Don Money, Cookie Rojas, Mike Ryan, Chris Short, Tony Taylor, Bill White, Rick Wise)	60.00	30.00	18.00
9	Seattle Pilots (Jack Aker, Steve Barber, Gary Bell, Tommy Davis, Jim Gosger, Tommy Harper, Gerry McNertney, Don Mincher, Ray Oyler, Rich Rollins, Chico Salmon)	150.00	75.00	45.00
10	Montreal Expos (Bob Bailey, John Bateman, Jack Billingham, Jim Grant, Larry Jaster, Mack Jones, Manny Mota, Rusty Staub, Gary Sutherland, Jim Williams, Maury Wills)	50.00	25.00	15.00
11	Chicago White Sox (Sandy Alomar, Luis Aparicio, Ken Berry, Buddy Bradford, Joe Horlen, Tommy John, Duane Josephson, Tom McCraw, Bill Melton, Pete Ward, Wilbur Wood)	55.00	27.50	16.00
12	San Diego Padres (Jose Arcia, Danny Breeden, Ollie Brown, Bill Davis, Ron Davis, Tony Gonzalez, Dick Kelley, Al McBean, Roberto Pena, Dick Selma, Ed Spiezio)	55.00	27.50	16.00
13	Cleveland Indians (Max Alvis, Joe Azcue, Jose Cardenal, Vern Fuller, Lou Johnson, Sam McDowell, Sonny Siebert, Duke Sims, Russ Snyder, Luis Tiant, Zoilo Versalles)	75.00	37.00	22.00
14	San Francisco Giants (Bobby Bolin, Jim Davenport, Dick Dietz, Jim Hart, Ron Hunt, Hal Lanier, Juan Marichal, Willie Mays, Willie McCovey, Gaylord Perry, Charlie Smith)	125.00	65.00	35.00
15	Minnesota Twins (Bob Allison, Chico Cardenas, Rod Carew, Dean Chance, Jim Kaat, Harmon Killebrew, Tony Oliva, Jim Perry, John Roseboro, Cesar Tovar, Ted Uhlaender)	100.00	50.00	30.00
16	Pittsburgh Pirates (Gene Alley, Matty Alou, Steve Blass, Jim Bunning, Bob Clemente, Rich Hebner, Jerry May, Bill Mazeroski, Bob Robertson, Willie Stargell, Bob Veale)	135.00	65.00	40.00
17	California Angels (Ruben Amaro, George Brunet, Bob Chance, Vic Davalillo, Jim Fregosi, Bobby Knoop, Jim McGlothlin, Rick Reichardt, Roger Repoz, Bob Rodgers, Hoyt Wilhelm)	60.00	30.00	18.00
18	St. Louis Cardinals (Nelson Briles, Lou Brock, Orlando Cepeda, Curt Flood, Bob Gibson, Julian Javier, Dal Maxvill, Tim McCarver, Vada Pinson, Mike Shannon, Ray Washburn)	75.00	37.50	22.00
19	New York Yankees (Stan Bahnsen, Horace Clarke, Bobby Cox, Jake Gibbs, Mickey Mantle, Joe Pepitone, Fritz Peterson, Bill Robinson, Mel Stottlemyre, Tom Tresh, Roy White)	165.00	82.00	49.00
20	Cincinnati Reds (Gerry Arrigo, Johnny Bench, Tommy Helms, Alex Johnson, Jim Maloney, Lee May, Gary Nolan, Tony Perez, Pete Rose, Bob Tolan, Woody Woodward)	110.00	55.00	33.00
21	Oakland Athletics (Sal Bando, Bert Campaneris, Danny Cater, Dick Green, Mike Hershberger, Jim Hunter, Reggie Jackson, Rick Monday, Jim Nash, John Odom, Jim Pagliaroni)	100.00	50.00	30.00

		NM	EX	VG
22	Los Angeles Dodgers (Willie Crawford, Willie Davis, Don Drysdale, Ron Fairly, Tom Haller, Andy Kosco, Jim Lefebvre, Claude Osteen, Paul Popovich, Bill Singer, Bill Sudakis)	80.00	40.00	24.00
23	Washington Senators (Bernie Allen, Brant Alyea, Ed Brinkman, Paul Casanova, Joe Coleman, Mike Epstein, Jim Hannan, Frank Howard, Ken McMullen, Camilo Pascual, Del Unser)	80.00	40.00	24.00
24	New York Mets (Tommie Agee, Ken Boswell, Ed Charles, Jerry Grote, Bud Harrelson, Cleon Jones, Jerry Koosman, Ed Kranepool, Jim McAndrew, Tom Seaver, Ron Swoboda)	150.00	75.00	45.00

1969 Topps (4-On-1) Mini Stickers

Another in the long line of Topps test issues, the 4-on-1s are 2-1/2" x 3-1/2" cards with blank backs featuring a quartet of miniature stickers in the design of the same cards from the 1969 Topps regular set. There are 25 different cards, for a total of 100 different stickers. As they are not common, Mint cards bring fairly strong prices on today's market. As the set was drawn from the 3rd Series of the regular cards, it includes some rookie stickers and World Series highlight stickers.

		NM	EX	VG
Complete Set (25):		2,250	1,125	675.00
Common 4-in-1:		50.00	25.00	15.00
Unopened Pack:		375.00		
(1)	Jerry Adair, Willie Mays, Johnny Morris, Don Wilson	400.00	200.00	120.00
(2)	Tommie Aaron, Jim Britton, Donn Clendenon, Woody Woodward	50.00	25.00	15.00
(3)	Tommy Davis, Don Pavletich, Vada Pinson, World Series Game 4 (Lou Brock)	75.00	37.50	22.00
(4)	Max Alvis, Glenn Beckett, Ron Fairly, Rick Wise	50.00	25.00	15.00
(5)	Johnny Callison, Jim French, Lum Harris, Dick Selma	50.00	25.00	15.00
(6)	Bob Gibson, Larry Haney, Rick Reichardt, World Series Game 3 (Tim McCarver)	125.00	65.00	35.00
(7)	Wally Bunker, Don Cardwell, Joe Gibbon, Astros Rookies (Gilsen, McFadden)	50.00	25.00	15.00
(8)	Ollie Brown, Jim Bunning, Andy Kosco, Ron Reed	50.00	25.00	15.00
(9)	Bill Dillman, Jim Lefebvre, John Purdin, John Roseboro	50.00	25.00	15.00
(10)	Bill Hands, Chuck Harrison, Lindy McDaniel, Felix Millan	50.00	25.00	15.00
(11)	Jack Hiatt, Dave Johnson, Mel Nelson, Tommie Sisk	50.00	25.00	15.00
(12)	Clay Dalrymple, Leo Durocher, John Odom, Wilbur Wood	50.00	25.00	15.00
(13)	Hank Bauer, Kevin Collins, Ray Oyler, Russ Snyder	50.00	25.00	15.00
(14)	Gerry Arrigo, Jim Perry, Red Sox Rookies (Lahoud, Thibdeau), World Series Game 7 (Mickey Lolich)	50.00	25.00	15.00
(15)	Bill McCool, Roberto Pena, Doug Rader, World Series Game 2 (Willie Horton)	75.00	37.50	22.00
(16)	Ed Brinkman, Roy Face, Willie Horton, Bob Rodgers	50.00	25.00	15.00
(17)	Dave Baldwin, J.C. Martin, Dave May, Ray Sadecki	50.00	25.00	15.00
(18)	Jose Pagan, Tom Phoebus, Mike Shannon, World Series Game 1 (Bob Gibson)	50.00	25.00	15.00
(19)	Pete Rose, Lee Stange, Don Sutton, Ted Uhlaender	500.00	250.00	150.00
(20)	Joe Grzenda, Frank Howard, Dick Tracewski, Jim Weaver	50.00	25.00	15.00
(21)	Joe Azcue, Grant Jackson, Denny McLain, White Sox Rookies (Christman, Nyman)	50.00	25.00	15.00
(22)	John Edwards, Jim Fairey, Phillies Rookies, Stan Williams	50.00	25.00	15.00
(23)	John Bateman, Willie Smith, Leon Wagner, World Series Summary	50.00	25.00	15.00

(24)	Chris Cannizzaro, Bob Hendley, World Series Game 5 (Al Kaline), Yankees Rookies (Closter, Cumberland)	50.00	25.00	15.00
(25)	Joe Nossek, Rico Petrocelli, Carl Yastrzemski, Cardinals Rookies (Huntz, Torrez)	350.00	175.00	105.00

1969 Topps Bowie Kuhn

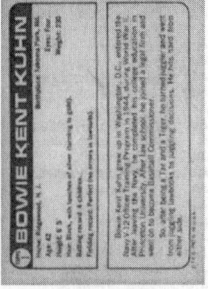

Following Kuhn's election as Commissioner in February 1969, Topps produced this special card, presumably for his personal use. In standard 2-1/2" x 3-1/2" format, but printed on thinner than usual card stock, the front has a photo of Kuhn's face composited with the drawing of a crowned baseball player sitting on top of the world. The horizontal back has a few personal data and a career summary.

		NM	EX	VG
1	Bowie Kuhn	90.00	45.00	27.50

1970 Topps

Topps established another set size record by coming out with 720 cards in 1970. The 2-1/2" x 3-1/2" cards have a color photo with a thin white frame. The photos have the player's team overprinted at the top, while the player's name in script and his position are at the bottom. A gray border surrounds the front. Card backs follow the normal design pattern, although they are more readable than some issues of the past. Team cards returned and were joined with many of the usual specialty cards. The World Series highlights were joined by cards with playoff highlights. Statistical leaders and All-Stars are also included in the set. High-numbered cards provide the most expensive cards in the set.

		NM	EX	VG
	Complete Set (720):	2,100	1,050	625.00
	Common Player (1-546):	1.50	.75	.45
	Common Player (547-633):	4.00	2.00	1.00
	Common Player (634-720):	8.00	4.00	2.25
1	World Champions (Mets Team)	25.00	12.50	7.50
2	Diego Segui	1.50	.75	.45
3	Darrel Chaney	1.50	.75	.45
4	Tom Egan	1.50	.75	.45
5	Wes Parker	1.50	.75	.45
6	Grant Jackson	1.50	.75	.45
7	Indians Rookies (Gary Boyd, Russ Nagelson)	1.50	.75	.45
8	Jose Martinez	1.50	.75	.45
9	1st Series Check List (1-132)	8.00	4.00	2.50
10	Carl Yastrzemski	20.00	10.00	5.00
11	Nate Colbert	1.50	.75	.45
12	John Hiller	1.50	.75	.45
13	Jack Hiatt	1.50	.75	.45
14	Hank Allen	1.50	.75	.45
15	Larry Dierker	1.50	.75	.45
16	Charlie Metro	1.50	.75	.45
17	Hoyt Wilhelm	6.00	3.00	1.75
18	Carlos May	1.50	.75	.45
19	John Boccabella	1.50	.75	.45
20	Dave McNally	1.50	.75	.45
21	Athletics Rookies (Vida Blue, Gene Tenace)	5.00	2.50	1.25
22	Ray Washburn	1.50	.75	.45
23	Bill Robinson	1.50	.75	.45
24	Dick Selma	1.50	.75	.45
25	Cesar Tovar	1.50	.75	.45
26	Tug McGraw	1.50	.75	.45
27	Chuck Hinton	1.50	.75	.45
28	Billy Wilson	1.50	.75	.45
29	Sandy Alomar	1.50	.75	.45
30	Matty Alou	1.50	.75	.45
31	Marty Pattin	1.50	.75	.45
32	Harry Walker	1.50	.75	.45

33	Don Wert	1.50	.75	.45
34	Willie Crawford	1.50	.75	.45
35	Joe Horlen	1.50	.75	.45
36	Reds Rookies (Danny Breeden, Bernie Carbo)	1.50	.75	.45
37	Dick Drago	1.50	.75	.45
38	Mack Jones	1.50	.75	.45
39	Mike Nagy	1.50	.75	.45
40	Rich Allen	3.00	1.50	.90
41	George Lauzerique	1.50	.75	.45
42	Tito Fuentes	1.50	.75	.45
43	Jack Aker	1.50	.75	.45
44	Roberto Pena	1.50	.75	.45
45	Dave Johnson	1.50	.75	.45
46	Ken Rudolph	1.50	.75	.45
47	Bob Miller	1.50	.75	.45
48	Gill Garrido (Gil)	1.50	.75	.45
49	Tim Cullen	1.50	.75	.45
50	Tommie Agee	1.50	.75	.45
51	Bob Christian	1.50	.75	.45
52	Bruce Dal Canton	1.50	.75	.45
53	John Kennedy	1.50	.75	.45
54	Jeff Torborg	1.50	.75	.45
55	John Odom	1.50	.75	.45
56	Phillies Rookies (Joe Lis, Scott Reid)	1.50	.75	.45
57	Pat Kelly	1.50	.75	.45
58	Dave Marshall	1.50	.75	.45
59	Dick Ellsworth	1.50	.75	.45
60	Jim Wynn	1.50	.75	.45
61	N.L. Batting Leaders (Roberto Clemente, Cleon Jones, Pete Rose)	15.00	7.50	3.75
62	A.L. Batting Leaders (Rod Carew, Tony Oliva, Reggie Smith)	6.00	3.00	1.75
63	N.L. RBI Leaders (Willie McCovey, Tony Perez, Ron Santo)	5.00	2.50	1.50
64	A.L. RBI Leaders (Reggie Jackson, Harmon Killebrew, Boog Powell)	10.00	5.00	3.00
65	N.L. Home Run Leaders (Hank Aaron, Lee May, Willie McCovey)	10.00	5.00	3.00
66	A.L. Home Run Leaders (Frank Howard, Reggie Jackson, Harmon Killebrew)	8.00	4.00	2.50
67	N.L. ERA Leaders (Steve Carlton, Bob Gibson, Juan Marichal)	8.00	4.00	2.50
68	A.L. ERA Leaders (Dick Bosman, Mike Cuellar, Jim Palmer)	4.00	2.00	1.25
69	N.L. Pitching Leaders (Fergie Jenkins, Juan Marichal, Phil Niekro, Tom Seaver)	10.00	5.00	3.00
70	A.L. Pitching Leaders (Dave Boswell, Mike Cuellar, Dennis McLain, Dave McNally, Jim Perry, Mel Stottlemyre)	4.00	2.00	1.25
71	N.L. Strikeout Leaders (Bob Gibson, Fergie Jenkins, Bill Singer)	6.00	3.00	1.75
72	A.L. Strikeout Leaders (Mickey Lolich, Sam McDowell, Andy Messersmith)	4.00	2.00	1.25
73	Wayne Granger	1.50	.75	.45
74	Angels Rookies (Greg Washburn, Wally Wolf)	1.50	.75	.45
75	Jim Kaat	1.50	.75	.45
76	Carl Taylor	1.50	.75	.45
77	Frank Linzy	1.50	.75	.45
78	Joe Lahoud	1.50	.75	.45
79	Clay Kirby	1.50	.75	.45
80	Don Kessinger	1.50	.75	.45
81	Dave May	1.50	.75	.45
82	Frank Fernandez	1.50	.75	.45
83	Don Cardwell	1.50	.75	.45
84	Paul Casanova	1.50	.75	.45
85	Max Alvis	1.50	.75	.45
86	Lum Harris	1.50	.75	.45
87	Steve Renko	1.50	.75	.45
88	Pilots Rookies (Dick Baney, Miguel Fuentes)	1.50	.75	.45
89	Juan Rios	1.50	.75	.45
90	Tim McCarver	3.00	1.50	.90
91	Rich Morales	1.50	.75	.45
92	George Culver	1.50	.75	.45
93	Rick Renick	1.50	.75	.45
94	Fred Patek	1.50	.75	.45
95	Earl Wilson	1.50	.75	.45
96	Cards Rookies (Leron Lee, Jerry Reuss)	3.00	1.50	.90
97	Joe Moeller	1.50	.75	.45
98	Gates Brown	1.50	.75	.45
99	Bobby Pfeil	1.50	.75	.45
100	Mel Stottlemyre	1.50	.75	.45
101	Bobby Floyd	1.50	.75	.45
102	Joe Rudi	1.50	.75	.45
103	Frank Reberger	1.50	.75	.45
104	Gerry Moses	1.50	.75	.45
105	Tony Gonzalez	1.50	.75	.45
106	Darold Knowles	1.50	.75	.45
107	Bobby Etheridge	1.50	.75	.45
108	Tom Burgmeier	1.50	.75	.45
109	Expos Rookies (Garry Jestadt, Carl Morton)	1.50	.75	.45
110	Bob Moose	1.50	.75	.45
111	Mike Hegan	1.50	.75	.45
112	Dave Nelson	1.50	.75	.45
113	Jim Ray	1.50	.75	.45
114	Gene Michael	1.50	.75	.45
115	Alex Johnson	1.50	.75	.45
116	Sparky Lyle	1.50	.75	.45
117	Don Young	1.50	.75	.45

118	George Mitterwald	1.50	.75	.45
119	Chuck Taylor	1.50	.75	.45
120	Sal Bando	1.50	.75	.45
121	Orioles Rookies (Fred Beene, Terry Crowley)	1.50	.75	.45
122	George Stone	1.50	.75	.45
123	Don Gutteridge	1.50	.75	.45
124	Larry Jaster	1.50	.75	.45
125	Deron Johnson	1.50	.75	.45
126	Marty Martinez	1.50	.75	.45
127	Joe Coleman	1.50	.75	.45
128a	2nd Series Check List (133-263) (226 is R Perranoski)	5.00	2.50	1.50
128b	2nd Series Check List (133-263) (226 is R. Perranoski)	5.00	2.50	1.50
129	Jimmie Price	1.50	.75	.45
130	Ollie Brown	1.50	.75	.45
131	Dodgers Rookies (Ray Lamb, Bob Stinson)	1.50	.75	.45
132	Jim McGlothlin	1.50	.75	.45
133	Clay Carroll	1.50	.75	.45
134	Danny Walton	1.50	.75	.45
135	Dick Dietz	1.50	.75	.45
136	Steve Hargan	1.50	.75	.45
137	Art Shamsky	1.50	.75	.45
138	Joe Foy	1.50	.75	.45
139	Rich Nye	1.50	.75	.45
140	Reggie Jackson	50.00	25.00	12.50
141	Pirates Rookies (Dave Cash, Johnny Jeter)	1.50	.75	.45
142	Fritz Peterson	1.50	.75	.45
143	Phil Gagliano	1.50	.75	.45
144	Ray Culp	1.50	.75	.45
145	Rico Carty	1.50	.75	.45
146	Danny Murphy	1.50	.75	.45
147	Angel Hermoso	1.50	.75	.45
148	Earl Weaver	4.00	2.00	1.25
149	Billy Champion	1.50	.75	.45
150	Harmon Killebrew	10.00	5.00	3.00
151	Dave Roberts	1.50	.75	.45
152	Ike Brown	1.50	.75	.45
153	Gary Gentry	1.50	.75	.45
154	Senators Rookies (Jan Dukes, Jim Miles)	1.50	.75	.45
155	Denis Menke	1.50	.75	.45
156	Eddie Fisher	1.50	.75	.45
157	Manny Mota	1.50	.75	.45
158	Jerry McNertney	1.50	.75	.45
159	Tommy Helms	1.50	.75	.45
160	Phil Niekro	6.00	3.00	1.75
161	Richie Scheinblum	1.50	.75	.45
162	Jerry Johnson	1.50	.75	.45
163	Syd O'Brien	1.50	.75	.45
164	Ty Cline	1.50	.75	.45
165	Ed Kirkpatrick	1.50	.75	.45
166	Al Oliver	2.00	1.00	.60
167	Bill Burbach	1.50	.75	.45
168	Dave Watkins	1.50	.75	.45
169	Tom Hall	1.50	.75	.45
170	Billy Williams	8.00	4.00	2.50
171	Jim Nash	1.50	.75	.45
172	Braves Rookies (Ralph Garr, Garry Hill)	2.00	1.00	.60
173	Jim Hicks	1.50	.75	.45
174	Ted Sizemore	1.50	.75	.45
175	Dick Bosman	1.50	.75	.45
176	Jim Hart	1.50	.75	.45
177	Jim Northrup	1.50	.75	.45
178	Denny Lemaster	1.50	.75	.45
179	Ivan Murrell	1.50	.75	.45
180	Tommy John	2.00	1.00	.60
181	Sparky Anderson	6.00	3.00	1.75
182	Dick Hall	1.50	.75	.45
183	Jerry Grote	1.50	.75	.45
184	Ray Fosse	1.50	.75	.45
185	Don Mincher	1.50	.75	.45
186	Rick Joseph	1.50	.75	.45
187	Mike Hedlund	1.50	.75	.45
188	Manny Sanguillen	1.50	.75	.45
189	Yankees Rookies (Dave McDonald, Thurman Munson)	85.00	42.00	25.00
190	Joe Torre	6.00	3.00	1.75
191	Vicente Romo	1.50	.75	.45
192	Jim Qualls	1.50	.75	.45
193	Mike Wegener	1.50	.75	.45
194	Chuck Manuel	1.50	.75	.45
195	N.L.C.S. Game 1 (Seaver Wins Opener!)	10.00	5.00	3.00
196	N.L.C.S. Game 2 (Mets Show Muscle!)	6.00	3.00	1.75
197	N.L.C.S. Game 3 (Ryan Saves the Day!)	25.00	12.50	6.25
198	Mets Celebrate (We're Number One!)(Nolan Ryan)	15.00	7.50	4.50
199	A.L.C.S. Game 1 (Orioles Win A Squeaker!)	4.00	2.00	1.25
200	A.L.C.S. Game 2 (Powell Scores Winning Run!)	4.00	2.00	1.25
201	A.L.C.S. Game 3 (Birds Wrap It Up!)	3.00	1.50	.90
202	Oriole Celebrate (Sweep Twins In Three!)	3.00	1.50	.90
203	Rudy May	1.50	.75	.45
204	Len Gabrielson	1.50	.75	.45
205	Bert Campaneris	1.50	.75	.45
206	Clete Boyer	1.50	.75	.45
207	Tigers Rookies (Norman McRae, Bob Reed)	1.50	.75	.45
208	Fred Gladding	1.50	.75	.45
209	Ken Suarez	1.50	.75	.45
210	Juan Marichal	6.00	3.00	1.75
211	Ted Williams	20.00	10.00	5.00
212	Al Santorini	1.50	.75	.45
213	Andy Etchebarren	1.50	.75	.45
214	Ken Boswell	1.50	.75	.45
215	Reggie Smith	1.50	.75	.45
216	Chuck Hartenstein	1.50	.75	.45

#	Name			
217	Ron Hansen	1.50	.75	.45
218	Ron Stone	1.50	.75	.45
219	Jerry Kenney	1.50	.75	.45
220	Steve Carlton	10.00	5.00	3.00
221	Ron Brand	1.50	.75	.45
222	Jim Rooker	1.50	.75	.45
223	Nate Oliver	1.50	.75	.45
224	Steve Barber	1.50	.75	.45
225	Lee May	1.50	.75	.45
226	Ron Perranoski	1.50	.75	.45
227	Astros Rookies (**John Mayberry**, Bob Watkins)	1.50	.75	.45
228	Aurelio Rodriguez	1.50	.75	.45
229	Rich Robertson	1.50	.75	.45
230	Brooks Robinson	15.00	7.50	3.75
231	Luis Tiant	1.50	.75	.45
232	Bob Didier	1.50	.75	.45
233	Lew Krausse	1.50	.75	.45
234	Tommy Dean	1.50	.75	.45
235	Mike Epstein	1.50	.75	.45
236	Bob Veale	1.50	.75	.45
237	Russ Gibson	1.50	.75	.45
238	Jose Laboy	1.50	.75	.45
239	Ken Berry	1.50	.75	.45
240	Fergie Jenkins	6.00	3.00	1.75
241	Royals Rookies (Al Fitzmorris, Scott Northey)	1.50	.75	.45
242	Walter Alston	4.00	2.00	1.25
243	Joe Sparma	1.50	.75	.45
244a	3rd Series Check List (264-372) (Red bat on front.)	6.00	3.00	1.75
244b	3rd Series Check List (264-372) (Brown bat on front.)	6.00	3.00	1.75
245	Leo Cardenas	1.50	.75	.45
246	Jim McAndrew	1.50	.75	.45
247	Lou Klimchock	1.50	.75	.45
248	Jesus Alou	1.50	.75	.45
249	Bob Locker	1.50	.75	.45
250	Willie McCovey	10.00	5.00	3.00
251	Dick Schofield	1.50	.75	.45
252	Lowell Palmer	1.50	.75	.45
253	Ron Woods	1.50	.75	.45
254	Camilo Pascual	1.50	.75	.45
255	*Jim Spencer*	1.50	.75	.45
256	Vic Davalillo	1.50	.75	.45
257	Dennis Higgins	1.50	.75	.45
258	Paul Popovich	1.50	.75	.45
259	Tommie Reynolds	1.50	.75	.45
260	Claude Osteen	1.50	.75	.45
261	Curt Motton	1.50	.75	.45
262	Padres Rookies (Jerry Morales, Jim Williams)	1.50	.75	.45
263	Duane Josephson	1.50	.75	.45
264	Rich Hebner	1.50	.75	.45
265	Randy Hundley	1.50	.75	.45
266	Wally Bunker	1.50	.75	.45
267	Twins Rookies (Herman Hill, Paul Ratliff)	1.50	.75	.45
268	Claude Raymond	1.50	.75	.45
269	Cesar Gutierrez	1.50	.75	.45
270	Chris Short	1.50	.75	.45
271	Greg Goossen	1.50	.75	.45
272	Hector Torres	1.50	.75	.45
273	Ralph Houk	4.00	2.00	1.25
274	Gerry Arrigo	1.50	.75	.45
275	Duke Sims	1.50	.75	.45
276	Ron Hunt	1.50	.75	.45
277	Paul Doyle	1.50	.75	.45
278	Tommie Aaron	1.50	.75	.45
279	*Bill Lee*	1.50	.75	.45
280	Donn Clendenon	1.50	.75	.45
281	Casey Cox	1.50	.75	.45
282	Steve Huntz	1.50	.75	.45
283	Angel Bravo	1.50	.75	.45
284	Jack Baldschun	1.50	.75	.45
285	Paul Blair	1.50	.75	.45
286	Dodgers Rookies (**Bill Buckner**, Jack Jenkins)	6.00	3.00	1.75
287	Fred Talbot	1.50	.75	.45
288	Larry Hisle	1.50	.75	.45
289	Gene Brabender	1.50	.75	.45
290	Rod Carew	10.00	5.00	3.00
291	Leo Durocher	4.00	2.00	1.25
292	Eddie Leon	1.50	.75	.45
293	Bob Bailey	1.50	.75	.45
294	Jose Azcue	1.50	.75	.45
295	Cecil Upshaw	1.50	.75	.45
296	Woody Woodward	1.50	.75	.45
297	Curt Blefary	1.50	.75	.45
298	Ken Henderson	1.50	.75	.45
299	Buddy Bradford	1.50	.75	.45
300	Tom Seaver	22.50	11.25	6.75
301	Chico Salmon	1.50	.75	.45
302	Jeff James	1.50	.75	.45
303	Brant Alyea	1.50	.75	.45
304	*Bill Russell*	4.00	2.00	1.25
305	World Series Game 1 (Buford Belts Leadoff Homer!)	4.00	2.00	1.25
306	World Series Game 2 (Clendenon's HR Breaks Ice!)	4.00	2.00	1.25
307	World Series Game 3 (Agee's Catch Saves The Day!)	4.00	2.00	1.25
308	World Series Game 4 (Martin's Bunt Ends Deadlock!)	4.00	2.00	1.25
309	World Series Game 5 (Koosman Shuts The Door!)	4.00	2.00	1.25
310	World Series Celebration (Mets Whoop It Up!)	8.00	4.00	2.50
311	Dick Green	1.50	.75	.45
312	Mike Torrez	1.50	.75	.45
313	Mayo Smith	1.50	.75	.45
314	Bill McCool	1.50	.75	.45
315	Luis Aparicio	8.00	4.00	2.50
316	Skip Guinn	1.50	.75	.45
317	Red Sox Rookies (Luis Alvarado, Billy Conigliaro)	1.50	.75	.45
318	Willie Smith	1.50	.75	.45
319	Clayton Dalrymple	1.50	.75	.45
320	Jim Maloney	1.50	.75	.45
321	Lou Piniella	3.00	1.50	.90
322	Luke Walker	1.50	.75	.45
323	Wayne Comer	1.50	.75	.45
324	Tony Taylor	1.50	.75	.45
325	Dave Boswell	1.50	.75	.45
326	Bill Voss	1.50	.75	.45
327	Hal King	1.50	.75	.45
328	George Brunet	1.50	.75	.45
329	Chris Cannizzaro	1.50	.75	.45
330	Lou Brock	10.00	5.00	3.00
331	Chuck Dobson	1.50	.75	.45
332	Bobby Wine	1.50	.75	.45
333	Bobby Murcer	3.00	1.50	.90
334	Phil Regan	1.50	.75	.45
335	Bill Freehan	1.50	.75	.45
336	Del Unser	1.50	.75	.45
337	Mike McCormick	1.50	.75	.45
338	Paul Schaal	1.50	.75	.45
339	Johnny Edwards	1.50	.75	.45
340	Tony Conigliaro	4.00	2.00	1.25
341	Bill Sudakis	1.50	.75	.45
342	Wilbur Wood	1.50	.75	.45
343a	4th Series Check List (373-459) (Red bat on front.)	5.00	2.50	1.50
343b	4th Series Check List (373-459) (Brown bat on front.)	5.00	2.50	1.50
344	Marcelino Lopez	1.50	.75	.45
345	Al Ferrara	1.50	.75	.45
346	Red Schoendienst	4.00	2.00	1.25
347	Russ Snyder	1.50	.75	.45
348	Mets Rookies (Jesse Hudson, Mike Jorgensen)	1.50	.75	.45
349	Steve Hamilton	1.50	.75	.45
350	Roberto Clemente	50.00	25.00	15.00
351	Tom Murphy	1.50	.75	.45
352	Bob Barton	1.50	.75	.45
353	Stan Williams	1.50	.75	.45
354	Amos Otis	1.50	.75	.45
355	Doug Rader	1.50	.75	.45
356	Fred Lasher	1.50	.75	.45
357	Bob Burda	1.50	.75	.45
358	*Pedro Borbon*	1.50	.75	.45
359	Phil Roof	1.50	.75	.45
360	Curt Flood	2.00	1.00	.60
361	Ray Jarvis	1.50	.75	.45
362	Joe Hague	1.50	.75	.45
363	Tom Shopay	1.50	.75	.45
364	Dan McGinn	1.50	.75	.45
365	Zoilo Versalles	1.50	.75	.45
366	Barry Moore	1.50	.75	.45
367	Mike Lum	1.50	.75	.45
368	Ed Herrmann	1.50	.75	.45
369	Alan Foster	1.50	.75	.45
370	Tommy Harper	1.50	.75	.45
371	Rod Gaspar	1.50	.75	.45
372	Dave Giusti	1.50	.75	.45
373	Roy White	2.50	1.25	.75
374	Tommie Sisk	1.50	.75	.45
375	Johnny Callison	1.50	.75	.45
376	Lefty Phillips	1.50	.75	.45
377	Bill Butler	1.50	.75	.45
378	Jim Davenport	1.50	.75	.45
379	Tom Tischinski	1.50	.75	.45
380	Tony Perez	8.00	4.00	2.50
381	Athletics Rookies (Bobby Brooks, Mike Olivo)	1.50	.75	.45
382	Jack DiLauro	1.50	.75	.45
383	Mickey Stanley	1.50	.75	.45
384	Gary Neibauer	1.50	.75	.45
385	George Scott	1.50	.75	.45
386	Bill Dillman	1.50	.75	.45
387	Baltimore Orioles Team	3.00	1.50	.90
388	Byron Browne	1.50	.75	.45
389	Jim Shellenback	1.50	.75	.45
390	Willie Davis	1.50	.75	.45
391	Larry Brown	1.50	.75	.45
392	Walt Hriniak	1.50	.75	.45
393	John Gelnar	1.50	.75	.45
394	Gil Hodges	6.00	3.00	1.75
395	Walt Williams	1.50	.75	.45
396	Steve Blass	1.50	.75	.45
397	Roger Repoz	1.50	.75	.45
398	Bill Stoneman	1.50	.75	.45
399	New York Yankees Team	8.00	4.00	2.50
400	Denny McLain	1.50	.70	.45
401	Giants Rookies (John Harrell, Bernie Williams)	1.50	.75	.45
402	Ellie Rodriguez	1.50	.75	.45
403	Jim Bunning	6.00	3.00	1.75
404	Rich Reese	1.50	.75	.45
405	Bill Hands	1.50	.75	.45
406	Mike Andrews	1.50	.75	.45
407	Bob Watson	1.50	.75	.45
408	Paul Lindblad	1.50	.75	.45
409	Bob Tolan	1.50	.75	.45
410	Boog Powell	5.00	2.50	1.50
411	Los Angeles Dodgers Team	6.00	3.00	1.75
412	Larry Burchart	1.50	.75	.45
413	Sonny Jackson	1.50	.75	.45
414	Paul Edmondson	1.50	.75	.45
415	Julian Javier	1.50	.75	.45
416	Joe Verbanic	1.50	.75	.45
417	John Bateman	1.50	.75	.45
418	John Donaldson	1.50	.75	.45
419	Ron Taylor	1.50	.75	.45
420	Ken McMullen	1.50	.75	.45
421	Pat Dobson	1.50	.75	.45
422	Kansas City Royals Team	3.00	1.50	.90
423	Jerry May	1.50	.75	.45
424	Mike Kilkenny	1.50	.75	.45
425	Bobby Bonds	3.00	1.50	.90
426	Bill Rigney	1.50	.75	.45
427	Fred Norman	1.50	.75	.45
428	Don Buford	1.50	.75	.45
429	Cubs Rookies (Randy Bobb, Jim Cosman)	1.50	.75	.45
430	A. Messersmith	1.50	.75	.45
431	Ron Swoboda	1.50	.75	.45
432a	5th Series Check List (460-546) ("Baseball" on front in yellow.)	4.00	2.00	1.25
432b	5th Series Check List (460-546) ("Baseball" on front in white.)	4.00	2.00	1.25
433	Ron Bryant	1.50	.75	.45
434	Felipe Alou	2.50	1.25	.75
435	Nelson Briles	1.50	.75	.45
436	Philadelphia Phillies Team	3.00	1.50	.90
437	Danny Cater	1.50	.75	.45
438	Pat Jarvis	1.50	.75	.45
439	Lee Maye	1.50	.75	.45
440	Bill Mazeroski	8.00	4.00	2.50
441	John O'Donoghue	1.50	.75	.45
442	Gene Mauch	1.50	.75	.45
443	Al Jackson	1.50	.75	.45
444	White Sox Rookies (Bill Farmer, John Matias)	1.50	.75	.45
445	Vada Pinson	2.00	1.00	.60
446	*Billy Grabarkewitz*	1.50	.75	.45
447	Lee Stange	1.50	.75	.45
448	Houston Astros Team	3.00	1.50	.90
449	Jim Palmer	8.00	4.00	2.50
450	Willie McCovey/AS	6.00	3.00	1.75
451	Boog Powell/AS	2.00	1.00	.60
452	Felix Millan/AS	1.50	.75	.45
453	Rod Carew/AS	6.00	3.00	1.75
454	Ron Santo/AS	3.00	1.50	.90
455	Brooks Robinson/AS	6.00	3.00	1.75
456	Don Kessinger/AS	1.50	.75	.45
457	Rico Petrocelli/AS	1.50	.75	.45
458	Pete Rose/AS	20.00	10.00	6.00
459	Reggie Jackson/AS	12.50	6.25	3.75
460	Matty Alou/AS	1.50	.75	.45
461	Carl Yastrzemski/AS	12.50	6.25	3.75
462	Hank Aaron/AS	27.50	13.50	8.25
463	Frank Robinson/AS	8.00	4.00	2.50
464	Johnny Bench/AS	22.50	11.25	6.75
465	Bill Freehan/AS	1.50	.75	.45
466	Juan Marichal/AS	6.00	3.00	1.75
467	Denny McLain/AS	1.50	.70	.45
468	Jerry Koosman/AS	1.50	.75	.45
469	Sam McDowell/AS	1.50	.75	.45
470	Willie Stargell	10.00	5.00	3.00
471	Chris Zachary	1.50	.75	.45
472	Atlanta Braves Team	3.00	1.50	.90
473	Don Bryant	1.50	.75	.45
474	Dick Kelley	1.50	.75	.45
475	Dick McAuliffe	1.50	.75	.45
476	Don Shaw	1.50	.75	.45
477	Orioles Rookies (Roger Freed, Al Severinsen)	1.50	.75	.45
478	Bob Heise	1.50	.75	.45
479	Dick Woodson	1.50	.75	.45
480	Glenn Beckert	1.50	.75	.45
481	Jose Tartabull	1.50	.75	.45
482	Tom Hilgendorf	1.50	.75	.45
483	Gail Hopkins	1.50	.75	.45
484	Gary Nolan	1.50	.75	.45
485	Jay Johnstone	1.50	.75	.45
486	Terry Harmon	1.50	.75	.45
487	Cisco Carlos	1.50	.75	.45
488	J.C. Martin	1.50	.75	.45
489	Eddie Kasko	1.50	.75	.45
490	Bill Singer	1.50	.75	.45
491	Graig Nettles	3.00	2.00	.90
492	Astros Rookies (Keith Lampard, Scipio Spinks)	1.50	.75	.45
493	Lindy McDaniel	1.50	.75	.45
494	Larry Stahl	1.50	.75	.45
495	Dave Morehead	1.50	.75	.45
496	Steve Whitaker	1.50	.75	.45
497	Eddie Watt	1.50	.75	.45
498	Al Weis	1.50	.75	.45
499	Skip Lockwood	1.50	.75	.45
500	Hank Aaron	50.00	25.00	12.50
501	Chicago White Sox Team	3.00	1.50	.90
502	Rollie Fingers	8.00	4.00	2.50
503	Dal Maxvill	1.50	.75	.45
504	Don Pavletich	1.50	.75	.45
505	Ken Holtzman	1.50	.75	.45
506	Ed Stroud	1.50	.75	.45
507	Pat Corrales	1.50	.75	.45
508	Joe Niekro	1.50	.75	.45
509	Montreal Expos Team	3.00	1.50	.90
510	Tony Oliva	3.50	1.75	1.00
511	Joe Hoerner	1.50	.75	.45
512	Billy Harris	1.50	.75	.45
513	Preston Gomez	1.50	.75	.45
514	Steve Hovley	1.50	.75	.45
515	Don Wilson	1.50	.75	.45
516	Yankees Rookies (John Ellis, Jim Lyttle)	1.50	.75	.45
517	Joe Gibbon	1.50	.75	.45
518	Bill Melton	1.50	.75	.45
519	Don McMahon	1.50	.75	.45
520	Willie Horton	1.50	.75	.45
521	Cal Koonce	1.50	.75	.45
522	California Angels Team	3.00	1.50	.90
523	Jose Pena	1.50	.75	.45
524	Alvin Dark	1.50	.75	.45
525	Jerry Adair	1.50	.75	.45
526	Ron Herbel	1.50	.75	.45
527	Don Bosch	1.50	.75	.45
528	Elrod Hendricks	1.50	.75	.45
529	Bob Aspromonte	1.50	.75	.45
530	Bob Gibson	15.00	7.50	3.75
531	Ron Clark	1.50	.75	.45
532	Danny Murtaugh	1.50	.75	.45
533	Buzz Stephen	1.50	.75	.45
534	Minnesota Twins Team	3.00	1.50	.90
535	Andy Kosco	1.50	.75	.45
536	Mike Kekich	1.50	.75	.45
537	Joe Morgan	10.00	5.00	3.00
538	Bob Humphreys	1.50	.75	.45

#	Player	NM	EX	VG
539	Phillies Rookies (Larry Bowa, Dennis Doyle)	6.00	3.00	1.75
540	Gary Peters	1.50	.75	.45
541	Bill Heath	1.50	.75	.45
542a	6th Series Check List (547-633) (Gray bat on front.)	5.00	2.50	1.50
542b	6th Series Check List (547-633) (Brown bat on front.)	5.00	2.50	1.50
543	Clyde Wright	1.50	.75	.45
544	Cincinnati Reds Team	5.00	2.50	1.50
545	Ken Harrelson	1.50	.75	.45
546	Ron Reed	1.50	.75	.45
547	Rick Monday	4.00	2.00	1.25
548	Howie Reed	3.00	1.50	.90
549	St. Louis Cardinals Team	6.00	3.00	1.75
550	Frank Howard	5.00	2.50	1.50
551	Dock Ellis	4.00	2.00	1.25
552	Royals Rookies (Don O'Riley, Dennis Paepke, Fred Rico)	4.00	2.00	1.25
553	Jim Lefebvre	4.00	2.00	1.25
554	Tom Timmermann	4.00	2.00	1.25
555	Orlando Cepeda	15.00	7.50	3.75
556	Dave Bristol	4.00	2.00	1.25
557	Ed Kranepool	4.00	2.00	1.25
558	Vern Fuller	4.00	2.00	1.25
559	Tommy Davis	4.00	2.00	1.25
560	Gaylord Perry	8.00	4.00	2.50
561	Tom McCraw	4.00	2.00	1.25
562	Ted Abernathy	4.00	2.00	1.25
563	Boston Red Sox Team	8.00	4.00	2.50
564	Johnny Briggs	4.00	2.00	1.25
565	Jim Hunter	8.00	4.00	2.50
566	Gene Alley	4.00	2.00	1.25
567	Bob Oliver	4.00	2.00	1.25
568	Stan Bahnsen	4.00	2.00	1.25
569	Cookie Rojas	4.00	2.00	1.25
570	Jim Fregosi	5.00	2.50	1.50
571	Jim Brewer	4.00	2.00	1.25
572	Frank Quilici	4.00	2.00	1.25
573	Padres Rookies (Mike Corkins, Rafael Robles, Ron Slocum)	4.00	2.00	1.25
574	Bobby Bolin	4.00	2.00	1.25
575	Cleon Jones	4.00	2.00	1.25
576	Milt Pappas	4.00	2.00	1.25
577	Bernie Allen	4.00	2.00	1.25
578	Tom Griffin	4.00	2.00	1.25
579	Detroit Tigers Team	8.00	4.00	2.50
580	Pete Rose	50.00	25.00	15.00
581	Tom Satriano	4.00	2.00	1.25
582	Mike Paul	4.00	2.00	1.25
583	Hal Lanier	4.00	2.00	1.25
584	Al Downing	5.00	2.50	1.50
585	Rusty Staub	6.00	3.00	1.75
586	Rickey Clark	4.00	2.00	1.25
587	Jose Arcia	4.00	2.00	1.25
588a	7th Series Check List (634-720) (666 is Adolpho Phillips)	6.00	3.00	1.75
588b	7th Series Check List (634-720) (666 is Adolfo Phillips)	6.00	3.00	1.75
589	Joe Keough	4.00	2.00	1.25
590	Mike Cuellar	4.00	2.00	1.25
591	Mike Ryan	4.00	2.00	1.25
592	Daryl Patterson	4.00	2.00	1.25
593	Chicago Cubs Team	8.00	4.00	2.50
594	Jake Gibbs	4.00	2.00	1.25
595	Maury Wills	6.00	3.00	1.75
596	Mike Hershberger	4.00	2.00	1.25
597	Sonny Siebert	4.00	2.00	1.25
598	Joe Pepitone	5.00	2.50	1.50
599	Senators Rookies (Gene Martin, Dick Stelmaszek, Dick Such)	4.00	2.00	1.25
600	Willie Mays	60.00	30.00	18.00
601	Pete Richert	4.00	2.00	1.25
602	Ted Savage	4.00	2.00	1.25
603	Ray Oyler	4.00	2.00	1.25
604	Clarence Gaston	6.00	3.00	1.75
605	Rick Wise	4.00	2.00	1.25
606	Chico Ruiz	4.00	2.00	1.25
607	Gary Waslewski	4.00	2.00	1.25
608	Pittsburgh Pirates Team	8.00	4.00	2.50
609	*Buck Martinez*	6.00	3.00	1.75
610	Jerry Koosman	6.00	3.00	1.75
611	Norm Cash	6.00	3.00	1.75
612	Jim Hickman	4.00	2.00	1.25
613	Dave Baldwin	4.00	2.00	1.25
614	Mike Shannon	4.00	2.00	1.25
615	Mark Belanger	4.00	2.00	1.25
616	Jim Merritt	4.00	2.00	1.25
617	Jim French	4.00	2.00	1.25
618	Billy Wynne	4.00	2.00	1.25
619	Norm Miller	4.00	2.00	1.25
620	Jim Perry	4.00	2.00	1.25
621	Braves Rookies (Darrell Evans, Rick Kester, Mike McQueen)	10.00	5.00	3.00
622	Don Sutton	8.00	4.00	2.50
623	Horace Clarke	4.00	2.00	1.25
624	Clyde King	4.00	2.00	1.25
625	Dean Chance	4.00	2.00	1.25
626	Dave Ricketts	4.00	2.00	1.25
627	Gary Wagner	4.00	2.00	1.25
628	Wayne Garrett	4.00	2.00	1.25
629	Merv Rettenmund	4.00	2.00	1.25
630	Ernie Banks	50.00	25.00	12.50
631	Oakland Athletics Team	8.00	4.00	2.50
632	Gary Sutherland	4.00	2.00	1.25
633	Roger Nelson	4.00	2.00	1.25
634	Bud Harrelson	8.00	4.00	2.50
635	Bob Allison	8.00	4.00	2.50
636	Jim Stewart	8.00	4.00	2.50
637	Cleveland Indians Team	12.00	6.00	3.50
638	Frank Bertaina	8.00	4.00	2.50
639	Dave Campbell	8.00	4.00	2.50
640	Al Kaline	50.00	25.00	12.50
641	Al McBean	8.00	4.00	2.50
642	Angels Rookies (Greg Garrett, Gordon Lund, Jarvis Tatum)	8.00	4.00	2.50
643	Jose Pagan	8.00	4.00	2.50
644	Gerry Nyman	8.00	4.00	2.50
645	Don Money	8.00	4.00	2.50
646	Jim Britton	8.00	4.00	2.50
647	Tom Matchick	8.00	4.00	2.50
648	Larry Haney	8.00	4.00	2.50
649	Jimmie Hall	8.00	4.00	2.50
650	Sam McDowell	10.00	5.00	3.00
651	Jim Gosger	8.00	4.00	2.50
652	Rich Rollins	10.00	5.00	3.00
653	Moe Drabowsky	8.00	4.00	2.50
654	N.L. Rookies (Boots Day, Oscar Gamble, Angel Mangual)	10.00	5.00	3.00
655	John Roseboro	8.00	4.00	2.50
656	Jim Hardin	8.00	4.00	2.50
657	San Diego Padres Team	15.00	7.50	4.50
658	Ken Tatum	8.00	4.00	2.50
659	Pete Ward	8.00	4.00	2.50
660	Johnny Bench	65.00	32.00	19.50
661	Jerry Robertson	8.00	4.00	2.50
662	Frank Lucchesi	8.00	4.00	2.50
663	Tito Francona	8.00	4.00	2.50
664	Bob Robertson	8.00	4.00	2.50
665	Jim Lonborg	8.00	4.00	2.50
666	Adolfo Phillips	8.00	4.00	2.50
667	Bob Meyer	8.00	4.00	2.50
668	Bob Tillman	8.00	4.00	2.50
669	White Sox Rookies (Bart Johnson, Dan Lazar, Mickey Scott)	8.00	4.00	2.50
670	Ron Santo	20.00	10.00	5.00
671	Jim Campanis	10.00	5.00	3.00
672	Leon McFadden	8.00	4.00	2.50
673	Ted Uhlaender	8.00	4.00	2.50
674	Dave Leonhard	8.00	4.00	2.50
675	Jose Cardenal	10.00	5.00	3.00
676	Washington Senators Team	15.00	7.50	4.50
677	Woodie Fryman	8.00	4.00	2.50
678	Dave Duncan	15.00	7.50	4.50
679	Ray Sadecki	8.00	4.00	2.50
680	Rico Petrocelli	10.00	5.00	3.00
681	Bob Garibaldi	8.00	4.00	2.50
682	Dalton Jones	8.00	4.00	2.50
683	Reds Rookies (Vern Geishert, Hal McRae, Wayne Simpson)	10.00	5.00	3.00
684	Jack Fisher	8.00	4.00	2.50
685	Tom Haller	8.00	4.00	2.50
686	Jackie Hernandez	8.00	4.00	2.50
687	Bob Priddy	8.00	4.00	2.50
688	Ted Kubiak	8.00	4.00	2.50
689	Frank Tepedino	8.00	4.00	2.50
690	Ron Fairly	8.00	4.00	2.50
691	Joe Grzenda	8.00	4.00	2.50
692	Duffy Dyer	8.00	4.00	2.50
693	Bob Johnson	8.00	4.00	2.50
694	Gary Ross	8.00	4.00	2.50
695	Bobby Knoop	8.00	4.00	2.50
696	San Francisco Giants Team	12.00	6.00	3.00
697	Jim Hannan	8.00	4.00	2.50
698	Tom Tresh	10.00	5.00	3.00
699	Hank Aguirre	8.00	4.00	2.50
700	Frank Robinson	50.00	25.00	12.50
701	Jack Billingham	8.00	4.00	2.50
702	A.L. Rookies (Bob Johnson, Ron Klimkowski, Bill Zepp)	8.00	4.00	2.50
703	Lou Marone	8.00	4.00	2.50
704	Frank Baker	8.00	4.00	2.50
705	Tony Cloninger	8.00	4.00	2.50
706	John McNamara	8.00	4.00	2.50
707	Kevin Collins	8.00	4.00	2.50
708	Jose Santiago	8.00	4.00	2.50
709	Mike Fiore	8.00	4.00	2.50
710	Felix Millan	8.00	4.00	2.50
711	Ed Brinkman	8.00	4.00	2.50
712	Nolan Ryan	200.00	100.00	60.00
713	Seattle Pilots Team	20.00	10.00	6.00
714	Al Spangler	8.00	4.00	2.50
715	Mickey Lolich	8.00	4.00	2.50
716	Cards Rookies (Sal Campisi, **Reggie Cleveland**, Santiago Guzman)	10.00	5.00	3.00
717	Tom Phoebus	8.00	4.00	2.50
718	Ed Spiezio	8.00	4.00	2.50
719	Jim Roland	8.00	4.00	2.50
720	Rick Reichardt	12.00	5.00	2.50

1970 Topps Candy Lids

The 1970 Topps Candy Lids are a test issue that was utilized again in 1973. The set is made up of 24 lids that measure 1-7/8" in diameter and were the tops of small 1.1 oz. tubs of "Baseball Stars Candy." Unlike the 1973 versions, the 1970 lids have no border surrounding the full-color photos. Frank Howard, Tom Seaver and Carl Yastrzemski photos are found on the top (outside) of the candy lid.

		NM	EX	VG
Complete Set (24):		3,200	1,600	900.00
Common Player:		45.00	25.00	15.00
(1)	Hank Aaron	400.00	200.00	125.00
(2)	Rich Allen	85.00	40.00	25.00
(3)	Luis Aparicio	160.00	80.00	50.00
(4)	Johnny Bench	260.00	130.00	75.00
(5)	Ollie Brown	45.00	25.00	15.00
(6)	Willie Davis	45.00	25.00	15.00
(7)	Jim Fregosi	45.00	25.00	15.00
(8)	Mike Hegan	45.00	25.00	15.00
(9)	Frank Howard	70.00	35.00	20.00
(10)	Reggie Jackson	320.00	160.00	100.00
(11)	Fergie Jenkins	150.00	75.00	45.00
(12)	Harmon Killebrew	200.00	100.00	60.00
(13)	Juan Marichal	160.00	80.00	50.00
(14)	Bill Mazeroski	160.00	80.00	50.00
(15)	Tim McCarver	70.00	35.00	20.00
(16)	Sam McDowell	45.00	25.00	15.00
(17)	Denny McLain	70.00	35.00	20.00
(18)	Lou Piniella	50.00	25.00	15.00
(19)	Frank Robinson	200.00	100.00	60.00
(20)	Tom Seaver	225.00	120.00	70.00
(21)	Rusty Staub	70.00	35.00	20.00
(22)	Mel Stottlemyre	45.00	25.00	15.00
(23)	Jim Wynn	45.00	25.00	15.00
(24)	Carl Yastrzemski	260.00	130.00	75.00

1970 Topps Cloth Stickers

The earliest and rarest of the Topps cloth sticker test issues, only 15 subjects are known, and a single specimen apiece is known for many of them. In the same 2-1/2" x 3-1/2" size, and with the same design as the 1970 Topps baseball cards, the stickers are blank-backed. The stickers of Denny Lemaster, Dennis Higgins and Rich Nye use photos that are different from their '70 Topps cards. It is quite likely that the checklist presented here is incomplete. The stickers are unnumbered and are checklisted alphabetically.

		NM	EX	VG
Common Player:		1,750	875.00	525.00
(1)	A.L. Playoff Game 2 (Boog Powell)	1,900	950.00	570.00
(2)	Bill Burbach	1,750	875.00	525.00
(3)	Gary Gentry	1,750	875.00	525.00
(4)	Tom Hall	1,750	875.00	525.00
(5)	Chuck Hartenstein	1,750	875.00	525.00
(6)	Dennis Higgins	1,750	875.00	525.00
(7)	Jose Laboy	1,750	875.00	525.00
(8)	Denny Lemaster	1,750	875.00	525.00
(9)	Juan Marichal	2,200	1,100	660.00
(10)	Willie McCovey	1,750	875.00	525.00
(11)	Jerry McNertney	1,750	875.00	525.00
(12)	Curt Motton	1,750	875.00	525.00
(13)	Ivan Murrell	1,750	875.00	525.00
(14)	N.L. Playoff Game 1 (Tom Seaver)	1,750	875.00	525.00
(15)	N.L. Playoff Game 3 (Nolan Ryan)	3,000	1,500	900.00
(16)	Phil Niekro	2,100	1,050	630.00
(17)	Jim Northrup	1,750	875.00	525.00
(18)	Rich Nye	1,750	875.00	525.00
(19)	Ron Perranoski	1,750	875.00	525.00
(20)	Al Santorini	1,750	875.00	525.00

1970 Topps Posters

Helping to ease a price increase, Topps included extremely fragile 8-11/16" x 9-5/8" posters in packs of regular cards. The posters feature color portraits and a smaller black and white "action" pose as well as the player's name, team and position at the top. Although there are Hall of Famers in the 24-poster set, all the top names are not represented. Folds from original packaging are not considered in grading unless they split the paper.

		NM	EX	VG
	Complete Set (24):	60.00	30.00	18.00
	Common Player:	3.00	1.50	.90
1	Joe Horlen	3.00	1.50	.90
2	Phil Niekro	6.00	3.00	1.75
3	Willie Davis	3.00	1.50	.90
4	Lou Brock	7.00	3.50	2.00
5	Ron Santo	4.00	2.00	1.25
6	Ken Harrelson	3.00	1.50	.90
7	Willie McCovey	7.00	3.50	2.00
8	Rick Wise	3.00	1.50	.90
9	Andy Messersmith	3.00	1.50	.90
10	Ron Fairly	3.00	1.50	.90
11	Johnny Bench	10.00	5.00	3.00
12	Frank Robinson	10.00	5.00	3.00
13	Tommie Agee	3.00	1.50	.90
14	Roy White	3.00	1.50	.90
15	Larry Dierker	3.00	1.50	.90
16	Rod Carew	9.00	4.50	2.75
17	Don Mincher	3.00	1.50	.90
18	Ollie Brown	3.00	1.50	.90
19	Ed Kirkpatrick	3.00	1.50	.90
20	Reggie Smith	3.00	1.50	.90
21	Roberto Clemente	25.00	12.50	7.50
22	Frank Howard	3.00	1.50	.90
23	Bert Campaneris	3.00	1.50	.90
24	Denny McLain	3.00	1.50	.90

1970 Topps Scratch-Offs

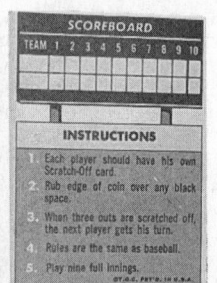

Not having given up on the idea of a game which could be played with baseball cards, Topps provided a new game - the baseball scratch-off - in 1970. Unfolded, cards measure 3-3/8" x 5", and reveal a baseball game played by rubbing the black ink off playing squares to determine the "action." Fronts have a player picture as "captain," while backs have instructions and a scoreboard. Inserts with white centers are from 1970 while those with red centers are from 1971.

		NM	EX	VG
	Complete Set (24):	60.00	30.00	18.00
	Common Player:	1.50	.75	.45
(1)	Hank Aaron	12.00	6.00	3.50
(2)	Rich Allen	2.50	1.25	.70
(3)	Luis Aparicio	3.50	1.75	1.00
(4)	Sal Bando	1.50	.75	.45
(5)	Glenn Beckert	1.50	.75	.45
(6)	Dick Bosman	1.50	.75	.45
(7)	Nate Colbert	1.50	.75	.45
(8)	Mike Hegan	1.50	.75	.45
(9)	Mack Jones	1.50	.75	.45
(10)	Al Kaline	4.50	2.25	1.25
(11)	Harmon Killebrew	4.50	2.25	1.25
(12)	Juan Marichal	3.50	1.75	1.00
(13)	Tim McCarver	2.50	1.25	.70
(14)	Sam McDowell	1.50	.75	.45
(15)	Claude Osteen	1.50	.75	.45
(16)	Tony Perez	3.50	1.75	1.00
(17)	Lou Piniella	1.50	.75	.45
(18)	Boog Powell	2.50	1.25	.70
(19)	Tom Seaver	4.50	2.25	1.25
(20)	Jim Spencer	1.50	.75	.45
(21)	Willie Stargell	3.50	1.75	1.00
(22)	Mel Stottlemyre	1.50	.75	.45
(23)	Jim Wynn	1.50	.75	.45
(24)	Carl Yastrzemski	6.00	3.00	1.75

1970 Topps Booklets

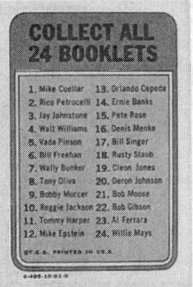

Measuring 2-1/2" x 3-7/16", the Topps Story Booklet was a 1970 regular pack insert. The booklet feature a photo, title and booklet number on the "cover." Inside are six pages of comic book story. The backs give a checklist of other available booklets. Not every star had a booklet as the set is only 24 in number.

		NM	EX	VG
	Complete Set (24):	65.00	32.50	20.00
	Common Player:	1.50	.75	.45
1	Mike Cuellar	1.50	.75	.45

2	Rico Petrocelli	1.50	.75	.45
3	Jay Johnstone	1.50	.75	.45
4	Walt Williams	1.50	.75	.45
5	Vada Pinson	2.25	1.25	.70
6	Bill Freehan	1.50	.75	.45
7	Wally Bunker	1.50	.75	.45
8	Tony Oliva	2.25	1.25	.70
9	Bobby Murcer	2.00	1.00	.60
10	Reggie Jackson	9.00	4.50	2.75
11	Tommy Harper	1.50	.75	.45
12	Mike Epstein	1.50	.75	.45
13	Orlando Cepeda	4.00	2.00	1.25
14	Ernie Banks	7.00	3.50	2.00
15	Pete Rose	10.00	5.00	3.00
16	Denis Menke	1.50	.75	.45
17	Bill Singer	1.50	.75	.45
18	Rusty Staub	2.00	1.00	.60
19	Cleon Jones	1.50	.75	.45
20	Deron Johnson	1.50	.75	.45
21	Bob Moose	1.50	.75	.45
22	Bob Gibson	5.00	2.50	1.50
23	Al Ferrara	1.50	.75	.45
24	Willie Mays	10.00	5.00	3.00

1970 Topps Super

Representing a refinement of the concept begun in 1969, the 1970 Topps Supers had a new 3-1/8" x 5-1/4" size. Printed on thick stock with rounded corners, card fronts feature a borderless color photograph and facsimile autograph. Backs are an enlarged version of the player's regular 1970 Topps card. Probably due to the press sheet configuration, eight of the 42 cards were short-printed. The most elusive is card #38 (Boog Powell). The set was more widely produced than was the case in 1969. Square-cornered proofs, either with blank or printed backs, are known, valued from 1X-2X the regular-card price.

		NM	EX	VG
	Complete Set (42):	250.00	125.00	75.00
	Common Player:	4.00	2.00	1.25
	Unopened Pack:	95.00	.00	.00
	Proofs: 1-2X			
1	Claude Osteen (SP)	10.00	5.00	3.00
2	Sal Bando (SP)	10.00	5.00	3.00
3	Luis Aparicio	9.00	4.50	2.75
4	Harmon Killebrew	15.00	7.50	4.50
5	Tom Seaver (SP)	25.00	12.50	7.50
6	Larry Dierker	4.00	2.00	1.25
7	Bill Freehan	4.00	2.00	1.25
8	Johnny Bench	20.00	10.00	6.00
9	Tommy Harper	4.00	2.00	1.25
10	Sam McDowell	4.00	2.00	1.25
11	Lou Brock	12.00	6.00	3.50
12	Roberto Clemente	40.00	20.00	12.00
13	Willie McCovey	12.00	6.00	3.50
14	Rico Petrocelli	4.00	2.00	1.25
15	Phil Niekro	9.00	4.50	2.75
16	Frank Howard	4.00	2.00	1.25
17	Denny McLain	4.00	2.00	1.25
18	Willie Mays	35.00	17.50	10.00
19	Willie Stargell	12.00	6.00	3.50
20	Joe Horlen	4.00	2.00	1.25
21	Ron Santo	6.00	3.00	1.75
22	Dick Bosman	4.00	2.00	1.25
23	Tim McCarver	5.00	2.50	1.50
24	Henry Aaron	35.00	17.50	10.00
25	Andy Messersmith	4.00	2.00	1.25
26	Tony Oliva	5.00	2.50	1.50
27	Mel Stottlemyre	4.00	2.00	1.25
28	Reggie Jackson	30.00	15.00	9.00
29	Carl Yastrzemski	20.00	10.00	6.00
30	James Fregosi	4.00	2.00	1.25
31	Vada Pinson	5.00	2.50	1.50
32	Lou Piniella	4.00	2.00	1.25
33	Robert Gibson	10.00	5.00	3.00
34	Pete Rose	35.00	17.50	10.00
35	Jim Wynn	4.00	2.00	1.25
36	Ollie Brown/SP	10.00	5.00	3.00
37	Frank Robinson/SP	35.00	17.50	10.00
38	Boog Powell/SP	60.00	30.00	18.00
39	Willie Davis/SP	10.00	5.00	3.00
40	Billy Williams/SP	20.00	10.00	6.00
41	Rusty Staub	5.00	2.50	1.50
42	Tommie Agee	4.00	2.00	1.25

1971 Topps

In 1971, Topps again increased the size of its set to 752 cards. These 2-1/2" x 3-1/2" cards feature a large color photo with a thin white frame. Above the picture, in the card's overall black border, is the player's name, team and position. A facsimile autograph completes the front. Backs feature a major change as a black-and-white "snapshot" of the player appears. Abbreviated statistics, a line giving the player's first

pro and major league games and a short biography complete the back. Specialty cards in this issue are limited. There are statistical leaders as well as World Series and playoff highlights. High-number cards #644-752 are scarce, with about half of the cards being short-printed.

		NM	EX	VG
	Complete Set (752):	3,000	1,500	900.00
	Common Player (1-523):	2.00	1.00	.60
	Common Player (524-643):	4.00	2.00	1.00
	Common Player (644-752):	6.00	3.00	1.75
1	World Champions (Orioles Team)	15.00	7.50	3.75
2	Dock Ellis	2.00	1.00	.60
3	Dick McAuliffe	2.00	1.00	.60
4	Vic Davalillo	2.00	1.00	.60
5	Thurman Munson	145.00	72.50	43.50
6	Ed Spiezio	2.00	1.00	.60
7	Jim Holt	2.00	1.00	.60
8	Mike McQueen	2.00	1.00	.60
9	George Scott	2.00	1.00	.60
10	Claude Osteen	2.00	1.00	.60
11	*Elliott Maddox*	2.00	1.00	.60
12	Johnny Callison	2.00	1.00	.60
13	White Sox Rookies (Charlie Brinkman, Dick Moloney)	2.00	1.00	.60
14	*Dave Concepcion*	15.00	7.50	4.50
15	Andy Messersmith	2.00	1.00	.60
16	*Ken Singleton*	4.00	2.00	1.25
17	Billy Sorrell	2.00	1.00	.60
18	Norm Miller	2.00	1.00	.60
19	Skip Pitlock	2.00	1.00	.60
20	Reggie Jackson	50.00	25.00	15.00
21	Dan McGinn	2.00	1.00	.60
22	Phil Roof	2.00	1.00	.60
23	Oscar Gamble	2.00	1.00	.60
24	Rich Hand	2.00	1.00	.60
25	Clarence Gaston	2.00	1.00	.60
26	*Bert Blyleven*	40.00	20.00	12.00
27	Pirates Rookies (Fred Cambria, Gene Clines)	2.00	1.00	.60
28	Ron Klimkowski	2.00	1.00	.60
29	Don Buford	2.00	1.00	.60
30	Phil Niekro	8.00	4.00	2.50
31	Eddie Kasko	2.00	1.00	.60
32	Jerry DaVanon	2.00	1.00	.60
33	Del Unser	2.00	1.00	.60
34	Sandy Vance	2.00	1.00	.60
35	Lou Piniella	4.00	2.00	1.25
36	Dean Chance	2.00	1.00	.60
37	Rich McKinney	2.00	1.00	.60
38	*Jim Colborn*	2.00	1.00	.60
39	Tigers Rookies (*Gene Lamont, Lerrin LaGrow*)	2.00	1.00	.60
40	Lee May	2.00	1.00	.60
41	Rick Austin	2.00	1.00	.60
42a	Boots Day (Stadium lights behind ear.)	8.00	4.00	2.50
42b	Boots Day (No stadium lights.)	8.00	4.00	2.50
43	Steve Kealey	2.00	1.00	.60
44	Johnny Edwards	2.00	1.00	.60
45	Jim Hunter	8.00	4.00	2.50
46	Dave Campbell	2.00	1.00	.60
47	Johnny Jeter	2.00	1.00	.60
48	Dave Baldwin	2.00	1.00	.60
49	Don Money	2.00	1.00	.60
50	Willie McCovey	10.00	5.00	3.00
51	Steve Kline	2.00	1.00	.60
52	Braves Rookies (*Oscar Brown, Earl Williams*)	2.00	1.00	.60
53	Paul Blair	2.00	1.00	.60
54	1st Series Checklist (1-132)	5.00	2.50	1.50
55	Steve Carlton	20.00	10.00	6.00
56	Duane Josephson	2.00	1.00	.60
57	Von Joshua	2.00	1.00	.60
58	Bill Lee	2.00	1.00	.60
59	Gene Mauch	2.00	1.00	.60
60	Dick Bosman	2.00	1.00	.60
61	A.L. Batting Leaders (Alex Johnson, Tony Oliva, Carl Yastrzemski)	8.00	4.00	2.50
62	N.L. Batting Leaders (Rico Carty, Manny Sanguillen, Joe Torre)	6.00	3.00	1.75
63	A.L. RBI Leaders (Tony Conigliaro, Frank Howard, Boog Powell)	6.00	3.00	1.75
64	N.L. RBI Leaders (Johnny Bench, Tony Perez, Billy Williams)	8.00	4.00	2.50
65	A.L. Home Run Leaders (Frank Howard, Harmon Killebrew, Carl Yastrzemski)	8.00	4.00	2.50
66	N.L. Home Run Leaders (Johnny Bench, Tony Perez, Billy Williams)	10.00	5.00	3.00

#	Player			
67	A.L. ERA Leaders (Jim Palmer, Diego Segui, Clyde Wright)	6.00	3.00	1.75
68	N.L. ERA Leaders (Tom Seaver, Wayne Simpson, Luke Walker)	6.00	3.00	1.75
69	A.L. Pitching Leaders (Mike Cuellar, Dave McNally, Jim Perry)	3.00	1.50	.90
70	N.L. Pitching Leaders (Bob Gibson, Fergie Jenkins, Gaylord Perry)	8.00	4.00	2.50
71	A.L. Strikeout Leaders (Bob Johnson, Mickey Lolich, Sam McDowell)	3.00	1.50	.90
72	N.L. Strikeout Leaders (Bob Gibson, Fergie Jenkins, Tom Seaver)	8.00	4.00	2.50
73	George Brunet	2.00	1.00	.60
74	Twins Rookies (Pete Hamm, Jim Nettles)	2.00	1.00	.60
75	Gary Nolan	2.00	1.00	.60
76	Ted Savage	2.00	1.00	.60
77	Mike Compton	2.00	1.00	.60
78	Jim Spencer	2.00	1.00	.60
79	Wade Blasingame	2.00	1.00	.60
80	Bill Melton	2.00	1.00	.60
81	Felix Millan	2.00	1.00	.60
82	Casey Cox	2.00	1.00	.60
83	Mets Rookies (Randy Bobb, Tim Foli)	2.00	1.00	.60
84	Marcel Lachemann	2.00	1.00	.60
85	Billy Grabarkewitz	2.00	1.00	.60
86	Mike Kilkenny	2.00	1.00	.60
87	Jack Heidemann	2.00	1.00	.60
88	Hal King	2.00	1.00	.60
89	Ken Brett	2.00	1.00	.60
90	Joe Pepitone	2.00	1.00	.60
91	Bob Lemon	4.00	2.00	1.25
92	Fred Wenz	2.00	1.00	.60
93	Senators Rookies (Norm McRae, Denny Riddleberger)	2.00	1.00	.60
94	Don Hahn	2.00	1.00	.60
95	Luis Tiant	2.00	1.00	.60
96	Joe Hague	2.00	1.00	.60
97	Floyd Wicker	2.00	1.00	.60
98	Joe Decker	2.00	1.00	.60
99	Mark Belanger	2.00	1.00	.60
100	Pete Rose	70.00	35.00	21.00
101	Les Cain	2.00	1.00	.60
102	Astros Rookies (Ken Forsch, Larry Howard)	2.00	1.00	.60
103	Rich Severson	2.00	1.00	.60
104	Dan Frisella	2.00	1.00	.60
105	Tony Conigliaro	6.00	3.00	1.75
106	Tom Dukes	2.00	1.00	.60
107	Roy Foster	2.00	1.00	.60
108	John Cumberland	2.00	1.00	.60
109	Steve Hovley	2.00	1.00	.60
110	Bill Mazeroski	10.00	5.00	3.00
111	Yankees Rookies (Loyd Colson, Bobby Mitchell)	2.00	1.00	.60
112	Manny Mota	2.00	1.00	.60
113	Jerry Crider	2.00	1.00	.60
114	Billy Conigliaro	2.00	1.00	.60
115	Donn Clendenon	2.00	1.00	.60
116	Ken Sanders	2.00	1.00	.60
117	Ted Simmons	8.00	4.00	2.50
118	Cookie Rojas	2.00	1.00	.60
119	Frank Lucchesi	2.00	1.00	.60
120	Willie Horton	2.00	1.00	.60
121	Cubs Rookies (Jim Dunegan, Roe Skidmore)	2.00	1.00	.60
122	Eddie Watt	2.00	1.00	.60
123a	2nd Series Checklist (133-263) (Card # on right, orange helmet.)	5.00	2.50	1.50
123b	2nd Series Checklist (133-263) (Card # on right, red helmet.)	5.00	2.50	1.50
123c	2nd Series Checklist (133-263) (Card # centered.)	5.00	2.50	1.50
124	Don Gullett	2.00	1.00	.60
125	Ray Fosse	2.00	1.00	.60
126	Danny Coombs	2.00	1.00	.60
127	Danny Thompson	2.00	1.00	.60
128	Frank Johnson	2.00	1.00	.60
129	Aurelio Monteagudo	2.00	1.00	.60
130	Denis Menke	2.00	1.00	.60
131	Curt Blefary	2.00	1.00	.60
132	Jose Laboy	2.00	1.00	.60
133	Mickey Lolich	2.00	1.00	.60
134	Jose Arcia	2.00	1.00	.60
135	Rick Monday	2.00	1.00	.60
136	Duffy Dyer	2.00	1.00	.60
137	Marcelino Lopez	2.00	1.00	.60
138	Phillies Rookies (Joe Lis, Willie Montanez)	2.00	1.00	.60
139	Paul Casanova	2.00	1.00	.60
140	Gaylord Perry	8.00	4.00	2.50
141	Frank Quilici	2.00	1.00	.60
142	Mack Jones	2.00	1.00	.60
143	Steve Blass	2.00	1.00	.60
144	Jackie Hernandez	2.00	1.00	.60
145	Bill Singer	2.00	1.00	.60
146	Ralph Houk	2.00	1.00	.60
147	Bob Priddy	2.00	1.00	.60
148	John Mayberry	2.00	1.00	.60
149	Mike Hershberger	2.00	1.00	.60
150	Sam McDowell	2.00	1.00	.60
151	Tommy Davis	2.00	1.00	.60
152	Angels Rookies (Lloyd Allen, Winston Llenas)	2.00	1.00	.60
153	Gary Ross	2.00	1.00	.60
154	Cesar Gutierrez	2.00	1.00	.60
155	Ken Henderson	2.00	1.00	.60
156	Bart Johnson	2.00	1.00	.60
157	Bob Bailey	2.00	1.00	.60
158	Jerry Reuss	2.00	1.00	.60
159	Jarvis Tatum	2.00	1.00	.60
160	Tom Seaver	25.00	12.50	7.50
161	Coins Checklist	4.00	2.00	1.25
162	Jack Billingham	2.00	1.00	.60
163	Buck Martinez	2.00	1.00	.60
164	Reds Rookies (Frank Duffy, Milt Wilcox)	2.00	1.00	.60
165	Cesar Tovar	2.00	1.00	.60
166	Joe Hoerner	2.00	1.00	.60
167	Tom Grieve	2.00	1.00	.60
168	Bruce Dal Canton	2.00	1.00	.60
169	Ed Herrmann	2.00	1.00	.60
170	Mike Cuellar	2.00	1.00	.60
171	Bobby Wine	2.00	1.00	.60
172	Duke Sims	2.00	1.00	.60
173	Gil Garrido	2.00	1.00	.60
174	Dave LaRoche	2.00	1.00	.60
175	Jim Hickman	2.00	1.00	.60
176	Red Sox Rookies (Doug Griffin, Bob Montgomery)	2.00	1.00	.60
177	Hal McRae	2.00	1.00	.60
178	Dave Duncan	2.00	1.00	.60
179	Mike Corkins	2.00	1.00	.60
180	Al Kaline	20.00	10.00	6.00
181	Hal Lanier	2.00	1.00	.60
182	Al Downing	2.00	1.00	.60
183	Gil Hodges	5.00	2.50	1.25
184	Stan Bahnsen	2.00	1.00	.60
185	Julian Javier	2.00	1.00	.60
186	Bob Spence	2.00	1.00	.60
187	Ted Abernathy	2.00	1.00	.60
188	Dodgers Rookies (Mike Strahler, Bob Valentine)	4.00	2.00	1.25
189	George Mitterwald	2.00	1.00	.60
190	Bob Tolan	2.00	1.00	.60
191	Mike Andrews	2.00	1.00	.60
192	Billy Wilson	2.00	1.00	.60
193	Bob Grich	5.00	2.50	1.50
194	Mike Lum	2.00	1.00	.60
195	A.L. Playoff Game 1 (Powell Muscles Twins!)	5.00	2.50	1.50
196	A.L. Playoff Game 2 (McNally Makes It Two Straight!)	3.00	1.50	.90
197	A.L. Playoff Game 3 (Palmer Mows 'Em Down!)	6.00	3.00	1.75
198	Orioles Celebrate! (A Team Effort!)	3.00	1.50	.90
199	N.L. Playoff Game 1 (Cline Pinch-Triple Decides It!)	3.00	1.50	.90
200	N.L. Playoff Game 2 (Tolan Scores For Third Time!)	3.00	1.50	.90
201	N.L. Playoff Game 3 (Cline Scores Winning Run!)	3.00	1.50	.90
202	Reds Celebrate! (World Series Bound!)	3.00	1.50	.90
203	Larry Gura	2.00	1.00	.60
204	Brewers Rookies (George Kopacz, Bernie Smith)	2.00	1.00	.60
205	Gerry Moses	2.00	1.00	.60
206a	3rd Series Checklist (264-393) (Orange helmet.)	6.00	3.00	1.75
206b	3rd Series Checklist (264-393) (Red helmet.)	6.00	3.00	1.75
207	Alan Foster	2.00	1.00	.60
208	Billy Martin	8.00	4.00	2.50
209	Steve Renko	2.00	1.00	.60
210	Rod Carew	15.00	7.50	4.50
211	Phil Hennigan	2.00	1.00	.60
212	Rich Hebner	2.00	1.00	.60
213	Frank Baker	2.00	1.00	.60
214	Al Ferrara	2.00	1.00	.60
215	Diego Segui	2.00	1.00	.60
216	Cards Rookies (Reggie Cleveland, Luis Melendez)	2.00	1.00	.60
217	Ed Stroud	2.00	1.00	.60
218	Tony Cloninger	2.00	1.00	.60
219	Elrod Hendricks	2.00	1.00	.60
220	Ron Santo	8.00	4.00	2.50
221	Dave Morehead	2.00	1.00	.60
222	Bob Watson	2.00	1.00	.60
223	Cecil Upshaw	2.00	1.00	.60
224	Alan Gallagher	2.00	1.00	.60
225	Gary Peters	2.00	1.00	.60
226	Bill Russell	2.00	1.00	.60
227	Floyd Weaver	2.00	1.00	.60
228	Wayne Garrett	2.00	1.00	.60
229	Jim Hannan	2.00	1.00	.60
230	Willie Stargell	15.00	7.50	4.50
231	Indians Rookies (Vince Colbert, John Lowenstein)	2.00	1.00	.60
232	John Strohmayer	2.00	1.00	.60
233	Larry Bowa	2.00	1.00	.60
234	Jim Lyttle	2.00	1.00	.60
235	Nate Colbert	2.00	1.00	.60
236	Bob Humphreys	2.00	1.00	.60
237	Cesar Cedeno	6.00	3.00	1.75
238	Chuck Dobson	2.00	1.00	.60
239	Red Schoendienst	6.00	3.00	1.75
240	Clyde Wright	2.00	1.00	.60
241	Dave Nelson	2.00	1.00	.60
242	Jim Ray	2.00	1.00	.60
243	Carlos May	2.00	1.00	.60
244	Bob Tillman	2.00	1.00	.60
245	Jim Kaat	3.00	1.50	.90
246	Tony Taylor	2.00	1.00	.60
247	Royals Rookies (Jerry Cram, Paul Splittorff)	2.00	1.00	.60
248	Hoyt Wilhelm	8.00	4.00	2.50
249	Chico Salmon	2.00	1.00	.60
250	Johnny Bench	50.00	25.00	12.50
251	Frank Reberger	2.00	1.00	.60
252	Eddie Leon	2.00	1.00	.60
253	Bill Sudakis	2.00	1.00	.60
254	Cal Koonce	2.00	1.00	.60
255	Bob Robertson	2.00	1.00	.60
256	Tony Gonzalez	2.00	1.00	.60
257	Nelson Briles	2.00	1.00	.60
258	Dick Green	2.00	1.00	.60
259	Dave Marshall	2.00	1.00	.60
260	Tommy Harper	2.00	1.00	.60
261	Darold Knowles	2.00	1.00	.60
262	Padres Rookies (Dave Robinson, Jim Williams)	2.00	1.00	.60
263	John Ellis	2.00	1.00	.60
264	Joe Morgan	10.00	5.00	2.50
265a	Jim Northrup (Black "dot" at right of photo.)	2.00	1.00	.60
265b	Jim Northrup (Black "blob" at right of photo.)	2.00	1.00	.60
266	Bill Stoneman	2.00	1.00	.60
267	Rich Morales	2.00	1.00	.60
268	Phillies Team	4.00	2.00	1.25
269	Gail Hopkins	2.00	1.00	.60
270	Rico Carty	2.00	1.00	.60
271	Bill Zepp	2.00	1.00	.60
272	Tommy Helms	2.00	1.00	.60
273	Pete Richert	2.00	1.00	.60
274	Ron Slocum	2.00	1.00	.60
275	Vada Pinson	5.00	2.50	1.50
276	Giants Rookies (Mike Davison, George Foster)	10.00	5.00	2.50
277	Gary Waslewski	2.00	1.00	.60
278	Jerry Grote	2.00	1.00	.60
279	Lefty Phillips	2.00	1.00	.60
280	Fergie Jenkins	10.00	5.00	3.00
281	Danny Walton	2.00	1.00	.60
282	Jose Pagan	2.00	1.00	.60
283	Dick Such	2.00	1.00	.60
284	Jim Gosger	2.00	1.00	.60
285	Sal Bando	2.00	1.00	.60
286	Jerry McNertney	2.00	1.00	.60
287	Mike Fiore	2.00	1.00	.60
288	Joe Moeller	2.00	1.00	.60
289	White Sox Team	4.00	2.00	1.25
290	Tony Oliva	10.00	5.00	2.50
291	George Culver	2.00	1.00	.60
292	Jay Johnstone	2.00	1.00	.60
293	Pat Corrales	2.00	1.00	.60
294	Steve Dunning	2.00	1.00	.60
295	Bobby Bonds	4.00	2.00	1.25
296	Tom Timmermann	2.00	1.00	.60
297	Johnny Briggs	2.00	1.00	.60
298	Jim Nelson	2.00	1.00	.60
299	Ed Kirkpatrick	2.00	1.00	.60
300	Brooks Robinson	20.00	10.00	6.00
301	Earl Wilson	2.00	1.00	.60
302	Phil Gagliano	2.00	1.00	.60
303	Lindy McDaniel	2.00	1.00	.60
304	Ron Brand	2.00	1.00	.60
305	Reggie Smith	2.00	1.00	.60
306a	Jim Nash (Black blob, left center.)	4.00	2.00	1.25
306b	Jim Nash (Blob airbrushed away.)	2.00	1.00	.60
307	Don Wert	2.00	1.00	.60
308	Cards Team	3.00	1.50	.90
309	Dick Ellsworth	2.00	1.00	.60
310	Tommie Agee	2.00	1.00	.60
311	Lee Stange	2.00	1.00	.60
312	Harry Walker	2.00	1.00	.60
313	Tom Hall	2.00	1.00	.60
314	Jeff Torborg	2.00	1.00	.60
315	Ron Fairly	2.00	1.00	.60
316	Fred Scherman	2.00	1.00	.60
317	Athletics Rookies (Jim Driscoll, Angel Mangual)	2.00	1.00	.60
318	Rudy May	2.00	1.00	.60
319	Ty Cline	2.00	1.00	.60
320	Dave McNally	2.00	1.00	.60
321	Tom Matchick	2.00	1.00	.60
322	Jim Beauchamp	2.00	1.00	.60
323	Billy Champion	2.00	1.00	.60
324	Graig Nettles	4.00	2.00	1.25
325	Juan Marichal	8.00	4.00	2.50
326	Richie Scheinblum	2.00	1.00	.60
327	World Series Game 1 (Powell Homers To Opposite Field!)	3.00	1.50	.90
328	World Series Game 2 (Buford Goes 2-For-4!)	2.00	1.00	.60
329	World Series Game 3 (F. Robinson Shows Muscle!)	6.00	3.00	1.75
330	World Series Game 4 (Reds Stay Alive!)	2.00	1.00	.60
331	World Series Game 5 (B. Robinson Commits Robbery!)	8.00	4.00	2.50
332	World Series Celebration! (Convincing Performance!)	5.00	2.50	1.50
333	Clay Kirby	2.00	1.00	.60
334	Roberto Pena	2.00	1.00	.60
335	Jerry Koosman	2.00	1.00	.60
336	Tigers Team	4.00	2.00	1.25
337	Jesus Alou	2.00	1.00	.60
338	Gene Tenace	2.00	1.00	.60
339	Wayne Simpson	2.00	1.00	.60
340	Rico Petrocelli	2.00	1.00	.60
341	Steve Garvey	35.00	17.50	8.75
342	Frank Tepedino	2.00	1.00	.60
343	Pirates Rookies (Ed Acosta, Milt May)	2.00	1.00	.60
344	Ellie Rodriguez	2.00	1.00	.60
345	Joe Horlen	2.00	1.00	.60
346	Lum Harris	2.00	1.00	.60
347	Ted Uhlaender	2.00	1.00	.60
348	Fred Norman	2.00	1.00	.60
349	Rich Reese	2.00	1.00	.60
350	Billy Williams	5.00	2.50	1.25
351	Jim Shellenback	2.00	1.00	.60
352	Denny Doyle	2.00	1.00	.60
353	Carl Taylor	2.00	1.00	.60
354	Don McMahon	2.00	1.00	.60
355	Bud Harrelson	2.00	1.00	.60

#	Name			
356	Bob Locker	2.00	1.00	.60
357	Reds Team	4.00	2.00	1.25
358	Danny Cater	2.00	1.00	.60
359	Ron Reed	2.00	1.00	.60
360	Jim Fregosi	2.00	1.00	.60
361	Don Sutton	8.00	4.00	2.50
362	Orioles Rookies (Mike Adamson, Roger Freed)	2.00	1.00	.60
363	Mike Nagy	2.00	1.00	.60
364	Tommy Dean	2.00	1.00	.60
365	Bob Johnson	2.00	1.00	.60
366	Ron Stone	2.00	1.00	.60
367	Dalton Jones	2.00	1.00	.60
368	Bob Veale	2.00	1.00	.60
369a	4th Series Checklist (394-523) (Orange helmet.)	5.00	2.50	1.50
369b	4th Series Checklist (394-523) (Red helmet, black line above ear.)	6.00	3.00	1.75
369c	4th Series Checklist (394-523) (Red helmet, no line.)	6.00	3.00	1.75
370	Joe Torre	6.00	3.00	1.75
371	Jack Hiatt	2.00	1.00	.60
372	Lew Krausse	2.00	1.00	.60
373	Tom McCraw	2.00	1.00	.60
374	Clete Boyer	2.00	1.00	.60
375	Steve Hargan	2.00	1.00	.60
376	Expos Rookies (Clyde Mashore, Ernie McAnally)	2.00	1.00	.60
377	Greg Garrett	2.00	1.00	.60
378	Tito Fuentes	2.00	1.00	.60
379	Wayne Granger	2.00	1.00	.60
380	Ted Williams	12.00	6.00	3.50
381	Fred Gladding	2.00	1.00	.60
382	Jake Gibbs	2.00	1.00	.60
383	Rod Gaspar	2.00	1.00	.60
384	Rollie Fingers	8.00	4.00	2.50
385	Maury Wills	4.00	2.00	1.25
386	Red Sox Team	4.00	2.00	1.25
387	Ron Herbel	2.00	1.00	.60
388	Al Oliver	2.00	1.00	.60
389	Ed Brinkman	2.00	1.00	.60
390	Glenn Beckert	2.00	1.00	.60
391	Twins Rookies (Steve Brye, Cotton Nash)	2.00	1.00	.60
392	Grant Jackson	2.00	1.00	.60
393	Merv Rettenmund	2.00	1.00	.60
394	Clay Carroll	2.00	1.00	.60
395	Roy White	2.00	1.00	.60
396	Dick Schofield	2.00	1.00	.60
397	Alvin Dark	2.00	1.00	.60
398	Howie Reed	2.00	1.00	.60
399	Jim French	2.00	1.00	.60
400	Hank Aaron	55.00	27.00	16.50
401	Tom Murphy	2.00	1.00	.60
402	Dodgers Team	4.00	2.00	1.25
403	Joe Coleman	2.00	1.00	.60
404	Astros Rookies (Buddy Harris, Roger Metzger)	2.00	1.00	.60
405	Leo Cardenas	2.00	1.00	.60
406	Ray Sadecki	2.00	1.00	.60
407	Joe Rudi	2.00	1.00	.60
408	Rafael Robles	2.00	1.00	.60
409	Don Pavletich	2.00	1.00	.60
410	Ken Holtzman	2.00	1.00	.60
411	George Spriggs	2.00	1.00	.60
412	Jerry Johnson	2.00	1.00	.60
413	Pat Kelly	2.00	1.00	.60
414	Woodie Fryman	2.00	1.00	.60
415	Mike Hegan	2.00	1.00	.60
416	Gene Alley	2.00	1.00	.60
417	Dick Hall	2.00	1.00	.60
418	Adolfo Phillips	2.00	1.00	.60
419	Ron Hansen	2.00	1.00	.60
420	Jim Merritt	2.00	1.00	.60
421	John Stephenson	2.00	1.00	.60
422	Frank Bertaina	2.00	1.00	.60
423	Tigers Rookies (Tim Marting, Dennis Saunders)	2.00	1.00	.60
424	Roberto Rodriquez (Rodriguez)	2.00	1.00	.60
425	Doug Rader	2.00	1.00	.60
426	Chris Cannizzaro	2.00	1.00	.60
427	Bernie Allen	2.00	1.00	.60
428	Jim McAndrew	2.00	1.00	.60
429	Chuck Hinton	2.00	1.00	.60
430	Wes Parker	2.00	1.00	.60
431	Tom Burgmeier	2.00	1.00	.60
432	Bob Didier	2.00	1.00	.60
433	Skip Lockwood	2.00	1.00	.60
434	Gary Sutherland	2.00	1.00	.60
435	Jose Cardenal	2.00	1.00	.60
436	Wilbur Wood	2.00	1.00	.60
437	Danny Murtaugh	2.00	1.00	.60
438	Mike McCormick	2.00	1.00	.60
439	Phillies Rookies (Greg Luzinski, Scott Reid)	5.00	2.50	1.50
440	Bert Campaneris	2.00	1.00	.60
441	Milt Pappas	2.00	1.00	.60
442	Angels Team	4.00	2.00	1.25
443	Rich Robertson	2.00	1.00	.60
444	Jimmie Price	2.00	1.00	.60
445	Art Shamsky	2.00	1.00	.60
446	Bobby Bolin	2.00	1.00	.60
447	Cesar Geronimo	3.00	1.50	.90
448	Dave Roberts	2.00	1.00	.60
449	Brant Alyea	2.00	1.00	.60
450	Bob Gibson	15.00	7.50	4.50
451	Joe Keough	2.00	1.00	.60
452	John Boccabella	2.00	1.00	.60
453	Terry Crowley	2.00	1.00	.60
454	Mike Paul	2.00	1.00	.60
455	Don Kessinger	2.00	1.00	.60
456	Bob Meyer	2.00	1.00	.60
457	Willie Smith	2.00	1.00	.60
458	White Sox Rookies (Dave Lemonds, Ron Lolich)	2.00	1.00	.60
459	Jim Lefebvre	2.00	1.00	.60
460	Fritz Peterson	2.00	1.00	.60
461	Jim Hart	2.00	1.00	.60
462	Senators Team	5.00	2.50	1.50
463	Tom Kelley	2.00	1.00	.60
464	Aurelio Rodriguez	2.00	1.00	.60
465	Tim McCarver	6.00	3.00	1.75
466	Ken Berry	2.00	1.00	.60
467	Al Santorini	2.00	1.00	.60
468	Frank Fernandez	2.00	1.00	.60
469	Bob Aspromonte	2.00	1.00	.60
470	Bob Oliver	2.00	1.00	.60
471	Tom Griffin	2.00	1.00	.60
472	Ken Rudolph	2.00	1.00	.60
473	Gary Wagner	2.00	1.00	.60
474	Jim Fairey	2.00	1.00	.60
475	Ron Perranoski	2.00	1.00	.60
476	Dal Maxvill	2.00	1.00	.60
477	Earl Weaver	5.00	2.50	1.50
478	Bernie Carbo	2.00	1.00	.60
479	Dennis Higgins	2.00	1.00	.60
480	Manny Sanguillen	2.00	1.00	.60
481	Daryl Patterson	2.00	1.00	.60
482	Padres Team	5.00	2.50	1.50
483	Gene Michael	2.00	1.00	.60
484	Don Wilson	2.00	1.00	.60
485	Ken McMullen	2.00	1.00	.60
486	Steve Huntz	2.00	1.00	.60
487	Paul Schaal	2.00	1.00	.60
488	Jerry Stephenson	2.00	1.00	.60
489	Luis Alvarado	2.00	1.00	.60
490	Deron Johnson	2.00	1.00	.60
491	Jim Hardin	2.00	1.00	.60
492	Ken Boswell	2.00	1.00	.60
493	Dave May	2.00	1.00	.60
494	Braves Rookies (Ralph Garr, Rick Kester)	2.00	1.00	.60
495	Felipe Alou	3.00	1.50	.90
496	Woody Woodward	2.00	1.00	.60
497	Horacio Pina	2.00	1.00	.60
498	John Kennedy	2.00	1.00	.60
499	5th Series Checklist (524-643)	6.00	3.00	1.75
500	Jim Perry	2.00	1.00	.60
501	Andy Etchebarren	2.00	1.00	.60
502	Cubs Team	5.00	2.50	1.50
503	Gates Brown	2.00	1.00	.60
504	Ken Wright	2.00	1.00	.60
505	Ollie Brown	2.00	1.00	.60
506	Bobby Knoop	2.00	1.00	.60
507	George Stone	2.00	1.00	.60
508	Roger Repoz	2.00	1.00	.60
509	Jim Grant	2.00	1.00	.60
510	Ken Harrelson	2.00	1.00	.60
511	Chris Short	2.00	1.00	.60
512	Red Sox Rookies (Mike Garman, Dick Mills)	2.00	1.00	.60
513	Nolan Ryan	120.00	60.00	35.00
514	Ron Woods	2.00	1.00	.60
515	Carl Morton	2.00	1.00	.60
516	Ted Kubiak	2.00	1.00	.60
517	Charlie Fox	2.00	1.00	.60
518	Joe Grzenda	2.00	1.00	.60
519	Willie Crawford	2.00	1.00	.60
520	Tommy John	5.00	2.50	1.50
521	Leron Lee	2.00	1.00	.60
522	Twins Team	4.00	2.00	1.25
523	John Odom	2.00	1.00	.60
524	Mickey Stanley	4.00	2.00	1.25
525	Ernie Banks	50.00	25.00	12.50
526	Ray Jarvis	4.00	2.00	1.25
527	Cleon Jones	4.00	2.00	1.25
528	Wally Bunker	4.00	2.00	1.25
529	N.L. Rookies (Bill Buckner, Enzo Hernandez, Marty Perez)	6.00	3.00	1.75
530	Carl Yastrzemski	25.00	12.50	7.50
531	Mike Torrez	4.00	2.00	1.25
532	Bill Rigney	4.00	2.00	1.25
533	Mike Ryan	4.00	2.00	1.25
534	Luke Walker	4.00	2.00	1.25
535	Curt Flood	5.00	2.50	1.50
536	Claude Raymond	4.00	2.00	1.25
537	Tom Egan	4.00	2.00	1.25
538	Angel Bravo	4.00	2.00	1.25
539	Larry Brown	4.00	2.00	1.25
540	Larry Dierker	4.00	2.00	1.25
541	Bob Burda	4.00	2.00	1.25
542	Bob Miller	4.00	2.00	1.25
543	Yankees Team	8.00	4.00	2.50
544	Vida Blue	5.00	2.50	1.50
545	Dick Dietz	4.00	2.00	1.25
546	John Matias	4.00	2.00	1.25
547	Pat Dobson	4.00	2.00	1.25
548	Don Mason	4.00	2.00	1.25
549	Jim Brewer	4.00	2.00	1.25
550	Harmon Killebrew	20.00	10.00	5.00
551	Frank Linzy	4.00	2.00	1.25
552	Buddy Bradford	4.00	2.00	1.25
553	Kevin Collins	4.00	2.00	1.25
554	Lowell Palmer	4.00	2.00	1.25
555	Walt Williams	4.00	2.00	1.25
556	Jim McGlothlin	4.00	2.00	1.25
557	Tom Satriano	4.00	2.00	1.25
558	Hector Torres	4.00	2.00	1.25
559	A.L. Rookies (Terry Cox, Bill Gogolewski, Gary Jones)	4.00	2.00	1.25
560	Rusty Staub	5.00	2.50	1.50
561	Syd O'Brien	4.00	2.00	1.25
562	Dave Giusti	4.00	2.00	1.25
563	Giants Team	10.00	5.00	3.00
564	Al Fitzmorris	4.00	2.00	1.25
565	Jim Wynn	4.00	2.00	1.25
566	Tim Cullen	4.00	2.00	1.25
567	Walt Alston	6.00	3.00	1.75
568	Sal Campisi	4.00	2.00	1.25
569	Ivan Murrell	4.00	2.00	1.25
570	Jim Palmer	25.00	12.50	7.50
571	Ted Sizemore	4.00	2.00	1.25
572	Jerry Kenney	4.00	2.00	1.25
573	Ed Kranepool	4.00	2.00	1.25
574	Jim Bunning	8.00	4.00	2.50
575	Bill Freehan	4.00	2.00	1.25
576	Cubs Rookies (Brock Davis, Adrian Garrett, Garry Jestadt)	4.00	2.00	1.25
577	Jim Lonborg	4.00	2.00	1.25
578	Ron Hunt	4.00	2.00	1.25
579	Marty Pattin	4.00	2.00	1.25
580	Tony Perez	15.00	7.50	3.75
581	Roger Nelson	4.00	2.00	1.25
582	Dave Cash	4.00	2.00	1.25
583	Ron Cook	4.00	2.00	1.25
584	Indians Team	10.00	5.00	3.00
585	Willie Davis	4.00	2.00	1.25
586	Dick Woodson	4.00	2.00	1.25
587	Sonny Jackson	4.00	2.00	1.25
588	Tom Bradley	4.00	2.00	1.25
589	Bob Barton	4.00	2.00	1.25
590	Alex Johnson	4.00	2.00	1.25
591	Jackie Brown	4.00	2.00	1.25
592	Randy Hundley	4.00	2.00	1.25
593	Jack Aker	4.00	2.00	1.25
594	Cards Rookies (Bob Chlupsa, Al Hrabosky, Bob Stinson)	6.00	3.00	1.75
595	Dave Johnson	4.00	2.00	1.25
596	Mike Jorgensen	4.00	2.00	1.25
597	Ken Suarez	4.00	2.00	1.25
598	Rick Wise	4.00	2.00	1.25
599	Norm Cash	6.00	3.00	1.75
600	Willie Mays	75.00	37.00	22.00
601	Ken Tatum	4.00	2.00	1.25
602	Marty Martinez	4.00	2.00	1.25
603	Pirates Team	8.00	4.00	2.50
604	John Gelnar	4.00	2.00	1.25
605	Orlando Cepeda	10.00	5.00	2.50
606	Chuck Taylor	4.00	2.00	1.25
607	Paul Ratliff	4.00	2.00	1.25
608	Mike Wegener	4.00	2.00	1.25
609	Leo Durocher	8.00	4.00	2.50
610	Amos Otis	4.00	2.00	1.25
611	Tom Phoebus	4.00	2.00	1.25
612	Indians Rookies (Lou Camilli, Ted Ford, Steve Mingori)	4.00	2.00	1.25
613	Pedro Borbon	4.00	2.00	1.25
614	Billy Cowan	4.00	2.00	1.25
615	Mel Stottlemyre	6.00	3.00	1.75
616	Larry Hisle	4.00	2.00	1.25
617	Clay Dalrymple	4.00	2.00	1.25
618	Tug McGraw	4.00	2.00	1.25
619a	6th Series Checklist (644-752) (No copyright on back.)	5.00	2.50	1.50
619b	6th Series Checklist (644-752) (With copyright, no wavy line on helmet brim.)	4.00	2.00	1.25
619c	6th Series Checklist (644-752) (With copyright, wavy line on helmet brim.)	4.00	2.00	1.25
620	Frank Howard	5.00	2.50	1.50
621	Ron Bryant	4.00	2.00	1.25
622	Joe Lahoud	4.00	2.00	1.25
623	Pat Jarvis	4.00	2.00	1.25
624	Athletics Team	10.00	5.00	3.00
625	Lou Brock	25.00	12.50	7.50
626	Freddie Patek	4.00	2.00	1.25
627	Steve Hamilton	4.00	2.00	1.25
628	John Bateman	4.00	2.00	1.25
629	John Hiller	4.00	2.00	1.25
630	Roberto Clemente	120.00	60.00	35.00
631	Eddie Fisher	4.00	2.00	1.25
632	Darrel Chaney	4.00	2.00	1.25
633	A.L. Rookies (Bobby Brooks, Pete Koegel, Scott Northey)	4.00	2.00	1.25
634	Phil Regan	4.00	2.00	1.25
635	Bobby Murcer	15.00	7.50	4.50
636	Denny Lemaster	4.00	2.00	1.25
637	Dave Bristol	4.00	2.00	1.25
638	Stan Williams	4.00	2.00	1.25
639	Tom Haller	4.00	2.00	1.25
640	Frank Robinson	40.00	20.00	12.00
641	Mets Team	10.00	5.00	3.00
642	Jim Roland	4.00	2.00	1.25
643	Rick Reichardt	4.00	2.00	1.25
644	Jim Stewart/SP	8.00	4.00	2.50
645	Jim Maloney/SP	8.00	4.00	2.50
646	Bobby Floyd/SP	8.00	4.00	2.50
647	Juan Pizarro	6.00	3.00	1.75
648	Mets Rookies (Rich Folkers, Ted Martinez, Jon Matlack)/SP	20.00	10.00	6.00
649	Sparky Lyle/SP	10.00	5.00	3.00
650	Rich Allen/SP	30.00	15.00	9.00
651	Jerry Robertson/SP	8.00	4.00	2.50
652	Braves Team	10.00	5.00	3.00
653	Russ Snyder/SP	8.00	4.00	2.50
654	Don Shaw/SP	8.00	4.00	2.50
655	Mike Epstein/SP	8.00	4.00	2.50
656	Gerry Nyman/SP	8.00	4.00	2.50
657	Jose Azcue	6.00	3.00	1.75
658	Paul Lindblad/SP	8.00	4.00	2.50
659	Byron Browne/SP	8.00	4.00	2.50
660	Ray Culp	6.00	3.00	1.75
661	Chuck Tanner/SP	8.00	4.00	2.50
662	Mike Hedlund/SP	8.00	4.00	2.50
663	Marv Staehle	6.00	3.00	1.75
664	Major League Rookies (Archie Reynolds, Bob Reynolds, Ken Reynolds)			
665	Ron Swoboda/SP	8.00	4.00	2.50
666	Gene Brabender/SP	8.00	4.00	2.50
667	Pete Ward	6.00	3.00	1.75
668	Gary Neibauer	6.00	3.00	1.75
669	Ike Brown/SP	8.00	4.00	2.50
670	Bill Hands	6.00	3.00	1.75
671	Bill Voss/SP	8.00	4.00	2.50
672	Ed Crosby/SP	8.00	4.00	2.50
673	Gerry Janeski/SP	8.00	4.00	2.50
674	Expos Team	10.00	5.00	2.50
675	Dave Boswell	6.00	3.00	1.75

676	Tommie Reynolds	6.00	3.00	1.75

		NM	EX	VG
676	Tommie Reynolds	6.00	3.00	1.75
677	Jack DiLauro/SP	8.00	4.00	2.50
678	George Thomas	6.00	3.00	1.75
679	Don O'Riley	6.00	3.00	1.75
680	Don Mincher/SP	8.00	4.00	2.50
681	Bill Butler	6.00	3.00	1.75
682	Terry Harmon	6.00	3.00	1.75
683	Bill Burbach/SP	8.00	4.00	2.50
684	Curt Motton	6.00	3.00	1.75
685	Moe Drabowsky	6.00	3.00	1.75
686	Chico Ruiz/SP	8.00	4.00	2.50
687	Ron Taylor/SP	8.00	4.00	2.50
688	Sparky Anderson/SP	25.00	12.50	7.50
689	Frank Baker	6.00	3.00	1.75
690	Bob Moose	6.00	3.00	1.75
691	Bob Heise	6.00	3.00	1.75
692	A.L. Rookies (Hal Haydel, Rogelio Moret, Wayne Twitchell)/SP	8.00	4.00	2.50
693	Jose Pena/SP	8.00	4.00	2.50
694	Rick Renick/SP	8.00	4.00	2.50
695	Joe Niekro	6.00	3.00	1.75
696	Jerry Morales	6.00	3.00	1.75
697	Rickey Clark/SP	8.00	4.00	2.50
698	Brewers Team/SP	15.00	7.50	3.75
699	Jim Britton	6.00	3.00	1.75
700	Boog Powell/SP	20.00	10.00	6.00
701	Bob Garibaldi	6.00	3.00	1.75
702	Milt Ramirez	6.00	3.00	1.75
703	Mike Kekich	6.00	3.00	1.75
704	J.C. Martin/SP	8.00	4.00	2.50
705	Dick Selma/SP	8.00	4.00	2.50
706	Joe Foy/SP	8.00	4.00	2.50
707	Fred Lasher	6.00	3.00	1.75
708	Russ Nagelson/SP	8.00	4.00	2.50
709	Major League Rookies (*Dusty Baker, Don Baylor, Tom Paciorek*)/SP	65.00	32.00	19.50
710	Sonny Siebert	6.00	3.00	1.75
711	Larry Stahl/SP	8.00	4.00	2.50
712	Jose Martinez	6.00	3.00	1.75
713	Mike Marshall/SP	8.00	4.00	2.50
714	Dick Williams/SP	8.00	4.00	2.50
715	Horace Clarke/SP	8.00	4.00	2.50
716	Dave Leonhard	6.00	3.00	1.75
717	Tommie Aaron/SP	8.00	4.00	2.50
718	Billy Wynne	6.00	3.00	1.75
719	Jerry May/SP	8.00	4.00	2.50
720	Matty Alou	6.00	3.00	1.75
721	John Morris	6.00	3.00	1.75
722	Astros Team/SP	15.00	7.50	4.50
723	Vicente Romo/SP	8.00	4.00	2.50
724	Tom Tischinski/SP	8.00	4.00	2.50
725	Gary Gentry/SP	8.00	4.00	2.50
726	Paul Popovich	6.00	3.00	1.75
727	Ray Lamb/SP	8.00	4.00	2.50
728	N.L. Rookies (Keith Lampard, Wayne Redmond, Bernie Williams)	6.00	3.00	1.75
729	Dick Billings	6.00	3.00	1.75
730	Jim Rooker	6.00	3.00	1.75
731	Jim Qualls/SP	8.00	4.00	2.50
732	Bob Reed	6.00	3.00	1.75
733	Lee Maye/SP	8.00	4.00	2.50
734	Rob Gardner/SP	8.00	4.00	2.50
735	Mike Shannon/SP	8.00	4.00	2.50
736	Mel Queen/SP	8.00	4.00	2.50
737	Preston Gomez/SP	8.00	4.00	2.50
738	Russ Gibson/SP	8.00	4.00	2.50
739	Barry Lersch/SP	8.00	4.00	2.50
740	Luis Aparicio/SP	25.00	12.50	7.50
741	Skip Guinn	6.00	3.00	1.75
742	Royals Team	10.00	5.00	3.00
743	John O'Donoghue/SP	8.00	4.00	2.50
744	Chuck Manuel/SP	8.00	4.00	2.50
745	Sandy Alomar/SP	8.00	4.00	2.50
746	Andy Kosco	6.00	3.00	1.75
747	N.L. Rookies (Balor Moore, Al Severinsen, Scipio Spinks)	6.00	3.00	1.75
748	John Purdin/SP	8.00	4.00	2.50
749	Ken Szotkiewicz	6.00	3.00	1.75
750	Denny McLain/SP	20.00	10.00	6.00
751	Al Weis/SP	6.00	3.00	1.75
752	Dick Drago	10.00	5.00	3.00

1971 Topps All-Star Rookies Artist's Proofs

There exists only one set of these artist's proofs for a proposed set of All-Star Rookie cards. The standard-size card fronts are pasted onto 9-1/2" x 6-1/2" cardboard backing. It may have been intended that these be issued in card form for Topps' annual banquet. There is a player for each position on the 1970 All-Rookie Team, plus right- and left-handed pitchers. Players are listed here in alphabetical order. Because each card is unique and there have been no reported sales in recent years, no current values can be assigned.

		NM	EX	VG
(1)	Larry Bowa			
(2)	Les Cain			
(3)	Bernie Carbo			
(4)	Dave Cash			
(5)	Billy Conigliaro			
(6)	John Ellis			
(7)	Roy Foster			
(8)	Alan Gallagher			
(9)	Carl Morton			
(10)	Thurman Munson			

1971 Topps Coins

Measuring 1-1/2" in diameter, the latest edition of the Topps coins was a 153-piece set. The coins feature a color photograph surrounded by a colored band on the front. The band carries the player's name, team, position and several stars. Backs have a short biography, the coin number and encouragement to collect the entire set. Back colors differ, with #s 1-51 having a brass back, #s 52-102 chrome backs, and the rest have blue backs. Most of the stars of the period are included in the set.

		NM	EX	VG
	Complete Set (153):	500.00	250.00	150.00
	Common Player:	2.00	1.00	.60
1	Cito Gaston	2.00	1.00	.60
2	Dave Johnson	2.00	1.00	.60
3	Jim Bunning	8.00	4.00	2.50
4	Jim Spencer	2.00	1.00	.60
5	Felix Millan	2.00	1.00	.60
6	Gerry Moses	2.00	1.00	.60
7	Fergie Jenkins	8.00	4.00	2.50
8	Felipe Alou	2.50	1.25	.70
9	Jim McGlothlin	2.00	1.00	.60
10	Dick McAuliffe	2.00	1.00	.60
11	Joe Torre	5.00	2.50	1.50
12	Jim Perry	2.00	1.00	.60
13	Bobby Bonds	2.00	1.00	.60
14	Danny Cater	2.00	1.00	.60
15	Bill Mazeroski	8.00	4.00	2.50
16	Luis Aparicio	8.00	4.00	2.50
17	Doug Rader	2.00	1.00	.60
18	Vada Pinson	3.00	1.50	.90
19	John Bateman	2.00	1.00	.60
20	Lew Krausse	2.00	1.00	.60
21	Billy Grabarkewitz	2.00	1.00	.60
22	Frank Howard	2.00	1.00	.60
23	Jerry Koosman	2.00	1.00	.60
24	Rod Carew	10.00	5.00	3.00
25	Al Ferrara	2.00	1.00	.60
26	Dave McNally	2.00	1.00	.60
27	Jim Hickman	2.00	1.00	.60
28	Sandy Alomar	2.00	1.00	.60
29	Lee May	2.00	1.00	.60
30	Rico Petrocelli	2.00	1.00	.60
31	Don Money	2.00	1.00	.60
32	Jim Rooker	2.00	1.00	.60
33	Dick Dietz	2.00	1.00	.60
34	Roy White	2.00	1.00	.60
35	Carl Morton	2.00	1.00	.60
36	Walt Williams	2.00	1.00	.60
37	Phil Niekro	8.00	4.00	2.50
38	Bill Freehan	2.00	1.00	.60
39	Julian Javier	2.00	1.00	.60
40	Rick Monday	2.00	1.00	.60
41	Don Wilson	2.00	1.00	.60
42	Ray Fosse	2.00	1.00	.60
43	Art Shamsky	2.00	1.00	.60
44	Ted Savage	2.00	1.00	.60
45	Claude Osteen	2.00	1.00	.60
46	Ed Brinkman	2.00	1.00	.60
47	Matty Alou	2.00	1.00	.60
48	Bob Oliver	2.00	1.00	.60
49	Danny Coombs	2.00	1.00	.60
50	Frank Robinson	10.00	5.00	3.00
51	Randy Hundley	2.00	1.00	.60
52	Cesar Tovar	2.00	1.00	.60
53	Wayne Simpson	2.00	1.00	.60
54	Bobby Murcer	2.00	1.00	.60
55	Tony Taylor	2.00	1.00	.60
56	Tommy John	3.00	1.50	.90
57	Willie McCovey	9.00	4.50	2.75
58	Carl Yastrzemski	13.50	6.75	4.00
59	Bob Bailey	2.00	1.00	.60
60	Clyde Wright	2.00	1.00	.60
61	Orlando Cepeda	8.00	4.00	2.50
62	Al Kaline	10.00	5.00	3.00
63	Bob Gibson	9.00	4.50	2.75
64	Bert Campaneris	2.00	1.00	.60
65	Ted Sizemore	2.00	1.00	.60
66	Duke Sims	2.00	1.00	.60
67	Bud Harrelson	2.00	1.00	.60
68	Jerry McNertney	2.00	1.00	.60
69	Jim Wynn	2.00	1.00	.60
70	Dick Bosman	2.00	1.00	.60
71	Roberto Clemente	30.00	15.00	9.00
72	Rich Reese	2.00	1.00	.60
73	Gaylord Perry	8.00	4.00	2.50
74	Boog Powell	3.00	1.50	.90
75	Billy Williams	9.00	4.50	2.75
76	Bill Melton	2.00	1.00	.60

77	Nate Colbert	2.00	1.00	.60
78	Reggie Smith	2.00	1.00	.60
79	Deron Johnson	2.00	1.00	.60
80	Catfish Hunter	8.00	4.00	2.50
81	Bob Tolan	2.00	1.00	.60
82	Jim Northrup	2.00	1.00	.60
83	Ron Fairly	2.00	1.00	.60
84	Alex Johnson	2.00	1.00	.60
85	Pat Jarvis	2.00	1.00	.60
86	Sam McDowell	2.00	1.00	.60
87	Lou Brock	9.00	4.50	2.75
88	Danny Walton	2.00	1.00	.60
89	Denis Menke	2.00	1.00	.60
90	Jim Palmer	9.00	4.50	2.75
91	Tommie Agee	2.00	1.00	.60
92	Duane Josephson	2.00	1.00	.60
93	Willie Davis	2.00	1.00	.60
94	Mel Stottlemyre	2.00	1.00	.60
95	Ron Santo	5.00	2.50	1.50
96	Amos Otis	2.00	1.00	.60
97	Ken Henderson	2.00	1.00	.60
98	George Scott	2.00	1.00	.60
99	Dock Ellis	2.00	1.00	.60
100	Harmon Killebrew	10.00	5.00	3.00
101	Pete Rose	20.00	10.00	6.00
102	Rick Reichardt	2.00	1.00	.60
103	Cleon Jones	2.00	1.00	.60
104	Ron Perranoski	2.00	1.00	.60
105	Tony Perez	9.00	4.50	2.75
106	Mickey Lolich	2.00	1.00	.60
107	Tim McCarver	3.00	1.50	.90
108	Reggie Jackson	15.00	7.50	4.50
109	Chris Cannizzaro	2.00	1.00	.60
110	Steve Hargan	2.00	1.00	.60
111	Rusty Staub	3.00	1.50	.90
112	Andy Messersmith	2.00	1.00	.60
113	Rico Carty	2.00	1.00	.60
114	Brooks Robinson	10.00	5.00	3.00
115	Steve Carlton	9.00	4.50	2.75
116	Mike Hegan	2.00	1.00	.60
117	Joe Morgan	9.00	4.50	2.75
118	Thurman Munson	8.00	4.00	2.50
119	Don Kessinger	2.00	1.00	.60
120	Joe Horlen	2.00	1.00	.60
121	Wes Parker	2.00	1.00	.60
122	Sonny Siebert	2.00	1.00	.60
123	Willie Stargell	9.00	4.50	2.75
124	Ellie Rodriguez	2.00	1.00	.60
125	Juan Marichal	8.00	4.00	2.50
126	Mike Epstein	2.00	1.00	.60
127	Tom Seaver	10.00	5.00	3.00
128	Tony Oliva	3.00	1.50	.90
129	Jim Merritt	2.00	1.00	.60
130	Willie Horton	2.00	1.00	.60
131	Rick Wise	2.00	1.00	.60
132	Sal Bando	2.00	1.00	.60
133	Ollie Brown	2.00	1.00	.60
134	Ken Harrelson	2.00	1.00	.60
135	Mack Jones	2.00	1.00	.60
136	Jim Fregosi	2.00	1.00	.60
137	Hank Aaron	25.00	12.50	7.50
138	Fritz Peterson	2.00	1.00	.60
139	Joe Hague	2.00	1.00	.60
140	Tommy Harper	2.00	1.00	.60
141	Larry Dierker	2.00	1.00	.60
142	Tony Conigliaro	4.00	2.00	1.25
143	Glenn Beckert	2.00	1.00	.60
144	Carlos May	2.00	1.00	.60
145	Don Sutton	8.00	4.00	2.50
146	Paul Casanova	2.00	1.00	.60
147	Bob Moose	2.00	1.00	.60
148	Leo Cardenas	2.00	1.00	.60
149	Johnny Bench	10.00	5.00	3.00
150	Mike Cuellar	2.00	1.00	.60
151	Donn Clendenon	2.00	1.00	.60
152	Lou Piniella	3.00	1.50	.90
153	Willie Mays	25.00	12.50	7.50

1971 Topps Greatest Moments

This 55-card set features highlights from the careers of top players of the day. The front of the 2-1/2" x 4-3/4" cards features a portrait photo of the player at left and deckle-edge action photo at right. There is a small headline on the white border of the action photo. The player's name and "One of Baseball's Greatest Moments" along with a black border complete the front. The back features a detail from the front photo and the story of the event. The newspaper style presentation includes the name of real newspapers. Relatively scarce, virtually every card in this set is a star or at least an above-average player. Because of their unusual size, 22 of the cards were double-printed, as indicated in the checklist here. Because of endemic centering problems there is a greater than usual value difference between NM and lower-grade cards.

		NM	EX	VG
	Complete Set (55):	6,750	3,850	2,000
	Common Player:	30.00	15.00	9.00
1	Thurman Munson (DP)	450.00	225.00	150.00
2	Hoyt Wilhelm	120.00	60.00	40.00
3	Rico Carty	100.00	50.00	30.00
4	Carl Morton (DP)	30.00	15.00	9.00
5	Sal Bando (DP)	30.00	15.00	9.00
6	Bert Campaneris (DP)	30.00	15.00	9.00
7	Jim Kaat	100.00	50.00	30.00
8	Harmon Killebrew	350.00	175.00	100.00
9	Brooks Robinson	375.00	190.00	120.00
10	Jim Perry	70.00	35.00	20.00
11	Tony Oliva	185.00	90.00	50.00
12	Vada Pinson	185.00	90.00	50.00
13	Johnny Bench	450.00	225.00	140.00
14	Tony Perez	150.00	75.00	40.00
15	Pete Rose (DP)	220.00	120.00	75.00
16	Jim Fregosi (DP)	30.00	15.00	9.00
17	Alex Johnson (DP)	30.00	15.00	9.00
18	Clyde Wright (DP)	30.00	15.00	9.00
19	Al Kaline (DP)	150.00	75.00	40.00
20	Denny McLain (DP)	75.00	40.00	25.00
21	Jim Northrup	70.00	35.00	20.00
22	Bill Freehan	75.00	40.00	25.00
23	Mickey Lolich	90.00	45.00	25.00
24	Bob Gibson (DP)	120.00	60.00	40.00
25	Tim McCarver (DP)	50.00	25.00	15.00
26	Orlando Cepeda (DP)	70.00	35.00	20.00
27	Lou Brock (DP)	90.00	45.00	25.00
28	Nate Colbert (DP)	30.00	15.00	9.00
29	Maury Wills	75.00	40.00	25.00
30	Wes Parker	100.00	50.00	30.00
31	Jim Wynn	80.00	40.00	25.00
32	Larry Dierker	90.00	45.00	25.00
33	Bill Melton	90.00	45.00	25.00
34	Joe Morgan	120.00	60.00	40.00
35	Rusty Staub	100.00	50.00	30.00
36	Ernie Banks (DP)	150.00	75.00	40.00
37	Billy Williams	120.00	60.00	40.00
38	Lou Piniella	120.00	60.00	40.00
39	Rico Petrocelli (DP)	50.00	25.00	15.00
40	Carl Yastrzemski (DP)	150.00	75.00	40.00
41	Willie Mays (DP)	260.00	130.00	75.00
42	Tommy Harper	65.00	35.00	20.00
43	Jim Bunning (DP)	35.00	18.00	10.00
44	Fritz Peterson	90.00	45.00	25.00
45	Roy White	120.00	60.00	40.00
46	Bobby Murcer	250.00	125.00	75.00
47	Reggie Jackson	900.00	450.00	300.00
48	Frank Howard	90.00	45.00	25.00
49	Dick Bosman	75.00	40.00	25.00
50	Sam McDowell (DP)	35.00	18.00	10.00
51	Luis Aparicio (DP)	70.00	35.00	20.00
52	Willie McCovey (DP)	100.00	50.00	30.00
53	Joe Pepitone	100.00	50.00	30.00
54	Jerry Grote	65.00	35.00	20.00
55	Bud Harrelson	140.00	70.00	40.00

1971 Topps Scratch-Offs

For a second year in 1971, Topps continued its scratch-off baseball card game with the same checklist of 24 players from the previous year. Unfolded, cards measure 3-3/8" x 5", and reveal a baseball game played by rubbing the black ink off squares to determine the "action." Fronts of the cards have a player picture as "captain," while backs have instructions and a scoreboard. Inserts with white centers are from 1970 while those with red centers are from 1971.

		NM	EX	VG
	Complete Set (24):	65.00	32.50	20.00
	Common Player:	1.50	.75	.45
(1)	Hank Aaron	7.50	3.75	2.25
(2)	Rich Allen	2.00	1.00	.60
(3)	Luis Aparicio	3.50	1.75	1.00
(4)	Sal Bando	1.50	.75	.45
(5)	Glenn Beckert	1.50	.75	.45
(6)	Dick Bosman	1.50	.75	.45
(7)	Nate Colbert	1.50	.75	.45
(8)	Mike Hegan	1.50	.75	.45
(9)	Mack Jones	1.50	.75	.45
(10)	Al Kaline	5.00	2.50	1.50
(11)	Harmon Killebrew	5.00	2.50	1.50
(12)	Juan Marichal	3.50	1.75	1.00
(13)	Tim McCarver	2.00	1.00	.60
(14)	Sam McDowell	1.50	.75	.45
(15)	Claude Osteen	1.50	.75	.45
(16)	Tony Perez	3.50	1.75	1.00
(17)	Lou Piniella	1.50	.75	.45

(18)	Boog Powell	2.00	1.00	.60
(19)	Tom Seaver	5.00	2.50	1.50
(20)	Jim Spencer	1.50	.75	.45
(21)	Willie Stargell	3.50	1.75	1.00
(22)	Mel Stottlemyre	1.50	.75	.45
(23)	Jim Wynn	1.50	.75	.45
(24)	Carl Yastrzemski	5.00	2.50	1.50

1971 Topps Super

Topps continued to produce its special oversized cards in 1971. Measuring 3-1/8" x 5-1/4" with rounded corners, they feature a borderless color photograph with a facsimile autograph on front. Backs are basically enlargements of the player's regular Topps card. The set size was enlarged to 63 cards in 1971, so there are no short-printed cards as in 1970. Proof cards with square corners and blank backs, measuring about 3-3/8" x 5-1/2", are known.

		NM	EX	VG
	Complete Set (63):	300.00	150.00	90.00
	Common Player:	3.00	1.50	.90
	Wax Pack (3):	50.00		
	Proofs: 1-2X			
1	Reggie Smith	3.00	1.50	.90
2	Gaylord Perry	7.50	3.75	2.25
3	Ted Savage	3.00	1.50	.90
4	Donn Clendenon	3.00	1.50	.90
5	Boog Powell	4.50	2.25	1.25
6	Tony Perez	7.50	3.75	2.25
7	Dick Bosman	3.00	1.50	.90
8	Alex Johnson	3.00	1.50	.90
9	Rusty Staub	3.50	1.75	1.00
10	Mel Stottlemyre	3.00	1.50	.90
11	Tony Oliva	4.00	2.00	1.25
12	Bill Freehan	3.00	1.50	.90
13	Fritz Peterson	3.00	1.50	.90
14	Wes Parker	3.00	1.50	.90
15	Cesar Cedeno	3.00	1.50	.90
16	Sam McDowell	3.00	1.50	.90
17	Frank Howard	3.00	1.50	.90
18	Dave McNally	3.00	1.50	.90
19	Rico Petrocelli	3.00	1.50	.90
20	Pete Rose	25.00	12.50	7.50
21	Luke Walker	3.00	1.50	.90
22	Nate Colbert	3.00	1.50	.90
23	Luis Aparicio	7.50	3.75	2.25
24	Jim Perry	3.00	1.50	.90
25	Louis Brock	9.00	4.50	2.75
26	Roy White	3.00	1.50	.90
27	Claude Osteen	3.00	1.50	.90
28	Carl W. Morton	3.00	1.50	.90
29	Rico Carty	3.00	1.50	.90
30	Larry Dierker	3.00	1.50	.90
31	Bert Campaneris	3.00	1.50	.90
32	Johnny Bench	10.00	5.00	3.00
33	Felix Millan	3.00	1.50	.90
34	Tim McCarver	3.50	1.75	1.00
35	Ronald Santo	6.00	3.00	1.75
36	Tommie Agee	3.00	1.50	.90
37	Roberto Clemente	40.00	20.00	12.00
38	Reggie Jackson	20.00	10.00	6.00
39	Clyde Wright	3.00	1.50	.90
40	Rich Allen	4.50	2.25	1.25
41	Curt Flood	3.50	1.75	1.00
42	Fergie Jenkins	7.50	3.75	2.25
43	Willie Stargell	9.00	4.50	2.75
44	Henry Aaron	25.00	12.50	7.50
45	Amos Otis	3.00	1.50	.90
46	Willie McCovey	9.00	4.50	2.75
47	William Melton	3.00	1.50	.90
48	Bob Gibson	9.00	4.50	2.75
49	Carl Yastrzemski	12.00	6.00	3.50
50	Glenn Beckert	3.00	1.50	.90
51	Ray Fosse	3.00	1.50	.90
52	Clarence Gaston	3.00	1.50	.90
53	Tom Seaver	10.00	5.00	3.00
54	Al Kaline	10.00	5.00	3.00
55	Jim Northrup	3.00	1.50	.90
56	Willie Mays	25.00	12.50	7.50
57	Sal Bando	3.00	1.50	.90
58	Deron Johnson	3.00	1.50	.90
59	Brooks Robinson	10.00	5.00	3.00
60	Harmon Killebrew	9.00	4.50	2.75
61	Joseph Torre	4.50	2.25	1.25
62	Lou Piniella	4.50	2.25	1.25
63	Tommy Harper	3.00	1.50	.90

1971 Topps Tattoos

Topps once again produced baseball tattoos in 1971. This time, the tattoos came in a variety of sizes, shapes and themes. The sheets of tattoos measure 3-1/2" x 14-1/4". Each sheet contains an assortment of tattoos in two sizes, 1-3/4" x 2-3/8", or 1-3/16" x 1-3/4". There are players, facsimile auto-

graphed baseballs, team pennants and assorted baseball cartoon figures carried on the 16 different sheets. Listings below are for complete sheets; with the exception of the biggest-name stars, individual tattoos have little or no collector value.

		NM	EX	VG
	Complete Sheet Set (16):	350.00	175.00	100.00
	Common Sheet:	10.00	5.00	3.00
	Unopened Pack:	25.00		
1	Brooks Robinson Autograph Montreal Expos Pennant San Francisco Giants Pennant (Sal Bando, Dick Bosman, Nate Colbert, Cleon Jones, Juan Marichal)	25.00	12.50	7.50
2	Red Sox Pennant Carl Yastrzemski Autograph New York Mets Pennant (Glenn Beckert, Tommy Harper, Ken Henderson, Fritz Peterson, Bob Robertson, Carl Yastrzemski)	35.00	17.50	10.00
3	Jim Fregosi Autograph New York Yankees Pennant Philadelphia Phillies Pennant (Orlando Cepeda, Jim Fregosi, Randy Hundley, Reggie Jackson, Jim Koosman, Jim Palmer)	35.00	17.50	10.00
4	Kansas City Royals Pennant Oakland Athletics Pennant Sam McDowell Autograph (Dick Dietz, Cito Gaston, Dave Johnson, Sam McDowell, Gary Nolan, Amos Otis)	10.00	5.00	3.00
5	Al Kaline Autograph Braves Pennant L.A. Dodgers Pennant (Bill Grabarkewitz, Al Kaline, Lee May, Tom Murphy, Vada Pinson, Manny Sanguillen)	20.00	10.00	6.00
6	Chicago Cubs Pennant Cincinnati Reds Pennant Harmon Kilebrew Autograph (Luis Aparicio, Paul Blair, Chris Cannizzaro, Donn Clendenon, Larry Dieker, Harmon Killebrew)	25.00	12.50	7.50
7	Boog Powell Autograph Cleveland Indians Pennant Milwaukee Brewers Pennant (Rich Allen, Bert Campaneris, Don Money, Boog Powell, Ted Savage, Rusty Staub)	15.00	7.50	4.50
8	Chicago White Sox Pennant Frank Howard Autograph San Diego Padres Pennant (Leo Cardenas, Bill Hands, Frank Howard, Wes Parker, Reggie Smith, Willie Stargell)	10.00	5.00	3.00
9	Detroit Tigers Pennant Henry Aaron Autograph (Hank Aaron, Tommy Agee, Jim Hunter, Dick McAuliffe, Tony Perez, Lou Piniella)	35.00	17.50	10.00
10	Baltimore Orioles Pennant Fergie Jenkins Autograph (Roberto Clemente, Tony Conigliaro, Fergie Jenkins, Thurman Munson, Gary Peters, Joe Torre)	50.00	25.00	15.00
11	Johnny Bench Autograph Washington Senators Pennant (Johnny Bench, Rico Carty, Bill Mazeroski, Bob Oliver, Rico Petrocelli, Frank Robinson)	35.00	17.50	10.00
12	Billy Williams Autograph Houston Astros Pennant (Bill Freehan, Dave McNally, Felix Millan, Mel Stottlemyre, Bob Tolan, Billy Williams)	15.00	7.50	4.50

#	Player	NM	EX	VG
13	Pittsburgh Pirates Pennant Willie McCovey Autograph (Ray Culp, Bud Harrelson, Mickey Lolich, Willie McCovey, Ron Santo, Roy White)	20.00	10.00	6.00
14	Minnesota Twins Pennant Tom Seaver Autograph (Bill Melton, Jim Perry, Pete Rose, Tom Seaver, Maury Wills, Clyde Wright)	45.00	22.00	13.50
15	Robert Gibson Autograph St. Louis Cardinals Pennant (Rod Carew, Bob Gibson, Alex Johnson, Don Kessinger, Jim Merritt, Rick Monday)	20.00	10.00	6.00
16	Angels Pennant Willie Mays Autograph (Larry Bowa, Mike Cuellar, Ray Fosse, Willie Mays, Carl Morton, Tony Oliva)	25.00	12.50	7.50

1972 Topps

The largest Topps issue of its time appeared in 1972, with the set size reaching the 787 mark. The 2-1/2" x 3-1/2" cards are something special as well. Their fronts have a color photo which is shaped into an arch and surrounded by two different color borders, all of which is inside the overall white border. The player's name is in a white panel below the picture while the team name is above the picture in what might best be described as "superhero" type in a variety of colors. No mention of the player's position appears on the front. Cards backs are tame by comparison, featuring statistics and a trivia question. The set features a record number of specialty cards including more than six dozen "In Action" (shown as "IA" in checklists below) cards featuring action shots of popular players. There are the usual statistical leaders, playoff and World Series highlights. Other innovations are 16 "Boyhood Photo" cards which depict scrapbook black and white photos of 1972's top players, and a group of cards depicting the trophies which comprise baseball's major awards. Finally, a group of seven "Traded" cards was included which feature a large "Traded" across the front of the card.

		NM	EX	VG
Complete Set (787):		1,800	900.00	500.00
Common Player (1-525):		1.50	.70	.45
Common Player (526-656):		4.00	2.00	1.00
Common Player (657-787):		12.00	6.00	3.00
1	Pirates Team (World Champions)	8.00	4.00	2.50
2	Ray Culp	1.50	.70	.45
3	Bob Tolan	1.50	.70	.45
4	1st Series Checklist (1-132)	4.00	2.00	1.25
5	John Bateman	1.50	.70	.45
6	Fred Scherman	1.50	.70	.45
7	Enzo Hernandez	1.50	.70	.45
8	Ron Swoboda	1.50	.70	.45
9	Stan Williams	1.50	.70	.45
10	Amos Otis	1.50	.70	.45
11	Bobby Valentine	1.50	.70	.45
12	Jose Cardenal	1.50	.70	.45
13	Joe Grzenda	1.50	.70	.45
14	Phillies Rookies (Mike Anderson, Pete Koegel, Wayne Twitchell)	1.50	.70	.45
15	Walt Williams	1.50	.70	.45
16	Mike Jorgensen	1.50	.70	.45
17	Dave Duncan	1.50	.70	.45
18a	Juan Pizarro (Green under "C" and "S.")	7.50	3.75	2.25
18b	Juan Pizarro (Yellow under "C" and "S.")	1.50	.70	.45
19	Billy Cowan	1.50	.70	.45
20	Don Wilson	1.50	.70	.45
21	Braves Team	3.00	1.50	.90
22	Rob Gardner	1.50	.70	.45
23	Ted Kubiak	1.50	.70	.45
24	Ted Ford	1.50	.70	.45
25	Bill Singer	1.50	.70	.45
26	Andy Etchebarren	1.50	.70	.45
27	Bob Johnson	1.50	.70	.45
28	Twins Rookies (Steve Brye, Bob Gebhard, Hal Haydel)	1.50	.70	.45
29a	Bill Bonham (Green under "C" and "S.")	7.50	3.75	2.25
29b	Bill Bonham (Yellow under "C" and "S.")	1.50	.70	.45
30	Rico Petrocelli	1.50	.70	.45
31	Cleon Jones	1.50	.70	.45
32	Cleon Jones (In Action)	1.50	.70	.45
33	Billy Martin	6.00	3.00	1.75
34	Billy Martin (In Action)	2.00	1.00	.60
35	Jerry Johnson	1.50	.70	.45
36	Jerry Johnson (In Action)	1.50	.70	.45

#	Player	NM	EX	VG
37	Carl Yastrzemski	10.00	5.00	2.50
38	Carl Yastrzemski (In Action)	5.00	2.50	1.50
39	Bob Barton	1.50	.70	.45
40	Bob Barton (In Action)	1.50	.70	.45
41	Tommy Davis	1.50	.70	.45
42	Tommy Davis (In Action)	1.50	.70	.45
43	Rick Wise	1.50	.70	.45
44	Rick Wise (In Action)	1.50	.70	.45
45a	Glenn Beckert (Green under "C" and "S.")	7.50	3.75	2.25
45b	Glenn Beckert (Yellow under "C" and "S.")	1.50	.70	.45
46	Glenn Beckert (In Action)	1.50	.70	.45
47	John Ellis	1.50	.70	.45
48	John Ellis (In Action)	1.50	.70	.45
49	Willie Mays	40.00	20.00	12.00
50	Willie Mays (In Action)	25.00	12.50	7.50
51	Harmon Killebrew	8.00	4.00	2.50
52	Harmon Killebrew (In Action)	5.00	2.50	1.50
53	Bud Harrelson	1.50	.70	.45
54	Bud Harrelson (In Action)	1.50	.70	.45
55	Clyde Wright	1.50	.70	.45
56	Rich Chiles	1.50	.70	.45
57	Bob Oliver	1.50	.70	.45
58	Ernie McAnally	1.50	.70	.45
59	*Fred Stanley*	1.50	.70	.45
60	Manny Sanguillen	1.50	.70	.45
61	Cubs Rookies (Gene Hiser, **Burt Hooton**, Earl Stephenson)	1.50	.70	.45
62	Angel Mangual	1.50	.70	.45
63	Duke Sims	1.50	.70	.45
64	Pete Broberg	1.50	.70	.45
65	Cesar Cedeno	1.50	.70	.45
66	Ray Corbin	1.50	.70	.45
67	Red Schoendienst	4.00	2.00	1.25
68	Jim York	1.50	.70	.45
69	Roger Freed	1.50	.70	.45
70	Mike Cuellar	1.50	.70	.45
71	Angels Team	3.00	1.50	.90
72	*Bruce Kison*	1.50	.70	.45
73	Steve Huntz	1.50	.70	.45
74	Cecil Upshaw	1.50	.70	.45
75	Bert Campaneris	1.50	.70	.45
76	Don Carrithers	1.50	.70	.45
77	Ron Theobald	1.50	.70	.45
78	Steve Arlin	1.50	.70	.45
79	Red Sox Rookies (**Cecil Cooper, Carlton Fisk**, Mike Garman)	40.00	20.00	12.00
80	Tony Perez	6.00	3.00	1.75
81	Mike Hedlund	1.50	.70	.45
82	Ron Woods	1.50	.70	.45
83	Dalton Jones	1.50	.70	.45
84	Vince Colbert	1.50	.70	.45
85	N.L. Batting Leaders (Glenn Beckert, Ralph Garr, Joe Torre)	4.00	2.00	1.25
86	A.L. Batting Leaders (Bobby Murcer, Tony Oliva, Merv Rettenmund)	3.00	1.50	.90
87	N.L. R.B.I. Leaders (Hank Aaron, Willie Stargell, Joe Torre)	6.00	3.00	1.75
88	A.L. R.B.I. Leaders (Harmon Killebrew, Frank Robinson, Reggie Smith)	3.00	1.50	.90
89	N.L. Home Run Leaders (Hank Aaron, Lee May, Willie Stargell)	6.00	3.00	1.75
90	A.L. Home Run Leaders (Norm Cash, Reggie Jackson, Bill Melton)	4.00	2.00	1.25
91	N.L. E.R.A. Leaders (Dave Roberts (picture is Denny Coombs), Tom Seaver, Don Wilson)	2.50	1.25	.70
92	A.L. E.R.A. Leaders (Vida Blue, Jim Palmer, Wilbur Wood)	2.00	1.00	.60
93	N.L. Pitching Leaders (Steve Carlton, Al Downing, Fergie Jenkins, Tom Seaver)	4.00	2.00	1.25
94	A.L. Pitching Leaders (Vida Blue, Mickey Lolich, Wilbur Wood)	1.50	.70	.45
95	N.L. Strikeout Leaders (Fergie Jenkins, Tom Seaver, Bill Stoneman)	4.00	2.00	1.25
96	A.L. Strikeout Leaders (Vida Blue, Joe Coleman, Mickey Lolich)	1.50	.70	.45
97	Tom Kelley	1.50	.70	.45
98	Chuck Tanner	1.50	.70	.45
99	*Ross Grimsley*	1.50	.70	.45
100	Frank Robinson	8.00	4.00	2.50
101	Astros Rookies (*Ray Busse, Bill Grief, J.R. Richard*)	4.00	2.00	1.25
102	Lloyd Allen	1.50	.70	.45
103	2nd Series Checklist (133-263)	2.00	1.00	.60
104	*Toby Harrah*	1.50	.70	.45
105	Gary Gentry	1.50	.70	.45
106	Brewers Team	3.00	1.50	.90
107	*Jose Cruz*	3.00	1.50	.90
108	Gary Waslewski	1.50	.70	.45
109	Jerry May	1.50	.70	.45
110	Ron Hunt	1.50	.70	.45
111	Jim Grant	1.50	.70	.45
112	Greg Luzinski	1.50	.70	.45
113	Rogelio Moret	1.50	.70	.45
114	Bill Buckner	1.50	.70	.45
115	Jim Fregosi	1.50	.70	.45
116	*Ed Farmer*	1.50	.70	.45
117a	Cleo James (Green under "C" and "S.")	7.50	3.75	2.25
117b	Cleo James (Yellow under "C" and "S.")	1.50	.70	.45

#	Player	NM	EX	VG
118	Skip Lockwood	1.50	.70	.45
119	Marty Perez	1.50	.70	.45
120	Bill Freehan	1.50	.70	.45
121	Ed Sprague	1.50	.70	.45
122	Larry Biittner	1.50	.70	.45
123	Ed Acosta	1.50	.70	.45
124	Yankees Rookies (Alan Closter, Roger Hambright, Rusty Torres)	1.50	.70	.45
125	Dave Cash	1.50	.70	.45
126	Bart Johnson	1.50	.70	.45
127	Duffy Dyer	1.50	.70	.45
128	Eddie Watt	1.50	.70	.45
129	Charlie Fox	1.50	.70	.45
130	Bob Gibson	8.00	4.00	2.50
131	Jim Nettles	1.50	.70	.45
132	Joe Morgan	8.00	4.00	2.50
133	Joe Keough	1.50	.70	.45
134	Carl Morton	1.50	.70	.45
135	Vada Pinson	2.50	1.25	.70
136	Darrel Chaney	1.50	.70	.45
137	Dick Williams	1.50	.70	.45
138	Mike Kekich	1.50	.70	.45
139	Tim McCarver	3.00	1.50	.90
140	Pat Dobson	1.50	.70	.45
141	Mets Rookies (Buzz Capra, Jon Matlack, Leroy Stanton)	1.50	.70	.45
142	*Chris Chambliss*	3.00	1.50	.90
143	Garry Jestadt	1.50	.70	.45
144	Marty Pattin	1.50	.70	.45
145	Don Kessinger	1.50	.70	.45
146	Steve Kealey	1.50	.70	.45
147	*Dave Kingman*	6.00	3.00	1.75
148	Dick Billings	1.50	.70	.45
149	Gary Neibauer	1.50	.70	.45
150	Norm Cash	2.50	1.25	.70
151	Jim Brewer	1.50	.70	.45
152	Gene Clines	1.50	.70	.45
153	Rick Auerbach	1.50	.70	.45
154	Ted Simmons	4.00	2.00	1.25
155	Larry Dierker	1.50	.70	.45
156	Twins Team	3.00	1.50	.90
157	Don Gullett	1.50	.70	.45
158	Jerry Kenney	1.50	.70	.45
159	John Boccabella	1.50	.70	.45
160	Andy Messersmith	1.50	.70	.45
161	Brock Davis	1.50	.70	.45
162	Brewers Rookies (Jerry Bell, Darrell Porter, Bob Reynolds) (Bell and Porter photos transposed)	1.50	.70	.45
163	Tug McGraw	1.50	.70	.45
164	Tug McGraw/IA	1.50	.70	.45
165	*Chris Speier*	1.50	.70	.45
166	Chris Speier/IA	1.50	.70	.45
167	Deron Johnson	1.50	.70	.45
168	Deron Johnson/IA	1.50	.70	.45
169	Vida Blue	4.00	2.00	1.25
170	Vida Blue/IA	2.00	1.00	.60
171	Darrell Evans	3.00	1.50	.90
172	Darrell Evans/IA	2.00	1.00	.60
173	Clay Kirby	1.50	.70	.45
174	Clay Kirby/IA	1.50	.70	.45
175	Tom Haller	1.50	.70	.45
176	Tom Haller/IA	1.50	.70	.45
177	Paul Schaal	1.50	.70	.45
178	Paul Schaal/IA	1.50	.70	.45
179	Dock Ellis	1.50	.70	.45
180	Dock Ellis/IA	1.50	.70	.45
181	Ed Kranepool	1.50	.70	.45
182	Ed Kranepool/IA	1.50	.70	.45
183	Bill Melton	1.50	.70	.45
184	Bill Melton/IA	1.50	.70	.45
185	Ron Bryant	1.50	.70	.45
186	Ron Bryant/IA	1.50	.70	.45
187	Gates Brown	1.50	.70	.45
188	Frank Lucchesi	1.50	.70	.45
189	Gene Tenace	1.50	.70	.45
190	Dave Giusti	1.50	.70	.45
191	*Jeff Burroughs*	3.00	1.50	.90
192	Cubs Team	4.00	2.00	1.25
193	*Kurt Bevacqua*	1.50	.70	.45
194	Fred Norman	1.50	.70	.45
195	Orlando Cepeda	6.00	3.00	1.75
196	Mel Queen	1.50	.70	.45
197	Johnny Briggs	1.50	.70	.45
198	Dodgers Rookies (**Charlie Hough**, Bob O'Brien, Mike Strahler)	5.00	2.50	1.50
199	Mike Fiore	1.50	.70	.45
200	Lou Brock	8.00	4.00	2.50
201	Phil Roof	1.50	.70	.45
202	Scipio Spinks	1.50	.70	.45
203	*Ron Blomberg*	2.50	1.25	.70
204	Tommy Helms	1.50	.70	.45
205	Dick Drago	1.50	.70	.45
206	Dal Maxvill	1.50	.70	.45
207	Tom Egan	1.50	.70	.45
208	Milt Pappas	1.50	.70	.45
209	Joe Rudi	1.50	.70	.45
210	Denny McLain	3.00	1.50	.90
211	Gary Sutherland	1.50	.70	.45
212	Grant Jackson	1.50	.70	.45
213	Angels Rookies (Art Kusnyer, Billy Parker, Tom Silverio)	1.50	.70	.45
214	Mike McQueen	1.50	.70	.45
215	Alex Johnson	1.50	.70	.45
216	Joe Niekro	1.50	.70	.45
217	Roger Metzger	1.50	.70	.45
218	Eddie Kasko	1.50	.70	.45
219	*Rennie Stennett*	1.50	.70	.45
220	Jim Perry	1.50	.70	.45
221	N.L. Playoffs (Bucs Champs)	4.00	2.00	1.25
222	A.L. Playoffs (Orioles Champs)	5.00	2.50	1.50
223	World Series Game 1	4.00	2.00	1.25
224	World Series Game 2	4.00	2.00	1.25
225	World Series Game 3	4.00	2.00	1.25

No.	Player			
226	World Series Game 4 (Roberto Clemente)	10.00	5.00	3.00
227	World Series Game 5	4.00	2.00	1.25
228	World Series Game 6	4.00	2.00	1.25
229	World Series Game 7	4.00	2.00	1.25
230	Series Celebration (On Top of the World)	4.00	2.00	1.25
231	Casey Cox	1.50	.70	.45
232	Giants Rookies (Chris Arnold, Jim Barr, Dave Rader)	1.50	.70	.45
233	Jay Johnstone	1.50	.70	.45
234	Ron Taylor	1.50	.70	.45
235	Merv Rettenmund	1.50	.70	.45
236	Jim McGlothlin	1.50	.70	.45
237	Yankees Team	4.00	2.00	1.25
238	Leron Lee	1.50	.70	.45
239	Tom Timmermann	1.50	.70	.45
240	Rich Allen	3.00	1.50	.90
241	Rollie Fingers	6.00	3.00	1.75
242	Don Mincher	1.50	.70	.45
243	Frank Linzy	1.50	.70	.45
244	Steve Braun	1.50	.70	.45
245	Tommie Agee	1.50	.70	.45
246	Tom Burgmeier	1.50	.70	.45
247	Milt May	1.50	.70	.45
248	Tom Bradley	1.50	.70	.45
249	Harry Walker	1.50	.70	.45
250	Boog Powell	2.00	1.00	.60
251a	3rd Series Checklist (264-394) (Small print on front.)	3.00	1.50	.90
251b	3rd Series Checklist (264-394) (Large print on front.)	3.00	1.50	.90
252	Ken Reynolds	1.50	.70	.45
253	Sandy Alomar	1.50	.70	.45
254	Boots Day	1.50	.70	.45
255	Jim Lonborg	1.50	.70	.45
256	George Foster	2.50	1.25	.70
257	Tigers Rookies (Jim Foor, Tim Hosley, Paul Jata)	1.50	.70	.45
258	Randy Hundley	1.50	.70	.45
259	Sparky Lyle	1.50	.70	.45
260	Ralph Garr	1.50	.70	.45
261	Steve Mingori	1.50	.70	.45
262	Padres Team	3.00	1.50	.90
263	Felipe Alou	2.00	1.00	.60
264	Tommy John	2.00	1.00	.60
265	Wes Parker	1.50	.70	.45
266	Bobby Bolin	1.50	.70	.45
267	Dave Concepcion	2.00	1.00	.60
268	A's Rookies (Dwain Anderson, Chris Floethe)	1.50	.70	.45
269	Don Hahn	1.50	.70	.45
270	Jim Palmer	8.00	4.00	2.50
271	Ken Rudolph	1.50	.70	.45
272	Mickey Rivers	2.00	1.00	.60
273	Bobby Floyd	1.50	.70	.45
274	Al Severinsen	1.50	.70	.45
275	Cesar Tovar	1.50	.70	.45
276	Gene Mauch	1.50	.70	.45
277	Elliott Maddox	1.50	.70	.45
278	Dennis Higgins	1.50	.70	.45
279	Larry Brown	1.50	.70	.45
280	Willie McCovey	8.00	4.00	2.50
281	Bill Parsons	1.50	.70	.45
282	Astros Team	4.00	2.00	1.25
283	Darrell Brandon	1.50	.70	.45
284	Ike Brown	1.50	.70	.45
285	Gaylord Perry	6.00	3.00	1.75
286	Gene Alley	1.50	.70	.45
287	Jim Hardin	1.50	.70	.45
288	Johnny Jeter	1.50	.70	.45
289	Syd O'Brien	1.50	.70	.45
290	Sonny Siebert	1.50	.70	.45
291	Hal McRae	2.50	1.25	.70
292	Hal McRae/IA	1.50	.70	.45
293	Danny Frisella	1.50	.70	.45
294	Danny Frisella/IA	1.50	.70	.45
295	Dick Dietz	1.50	.70	.45
296	Dick Dietz/IA	1.50	.70	.45
297	Claude Osteen	1.50	.70	.45
298	Claude Osteen/IA	1.50	.70	.45
299	Hank Aaron	50.00	25.00	12.50
300	Hank Aaron/IA	25.00	12.50	7.50
301	George Mitterwald	1.50	.70	.45
302	George Mitterwald/IA	1.50	.70	.45
303	Joe Pepitone	2.00	1.00	.60
304	Joe Pepitone/IA	1.50	.70	.45
305	Ken Boswell	1.50	.70	.45
306	Ken Boswell/IA	1.50	.70	.45
307	Steve Renko	1.50	.70	.45
308	Steve Renko/IA	1.50	.70	.45
309	Roberto Clemente	50.00	25.00	15.00
310	Roberto Clemente/IA	30.00	15.00	9.00
311	Clay Carroll	1.50	.70	.45
312	Clay Carroll/IA	1.50	.70	.45
313	Luis Aparicio	6.00	3.00	1.75
314	Luis Aparicio/IA	4.00	2.00	1.25
315	Paul Splittorff	1.50	.70	.45
316	Cardinals Rookies (Jim Bibby, Santiago Guzman, Jorge Roque)	1.50	.70	.45
317	Rich Hand	1.50	.70	.45
318	Sonny Jackson	1.50	.70	.45
319	Aurelio Rodriguez	1.50	.70	.45
320	Steve Blass	1.50	.70	.45
321	Joe Lahoud	1.50	.70	.45
322	Jose Pena	1.50	.70	.45
323	Earl Weaver	5.00	2.50	1.50
324	Mike Ryan	1.50	.70	.45
325	Mel Stottlemyre	1.50	.70	.45
326	Pat Kelly	1.50	.70	.45
327	Steve Stone	3.00	1.50	.90
328	Red Sox Team	5.00	2.50	1.50
329	Roy Foster	1.50	.70	.45
330	Jim Hunter	6.00	3.00	1.75
331	Stan Swanson	1.50	.70	.45
332	Buck Martinez	1.50	.70	.45
333	Steve Barber	1.50	.70	.45
334	Rangers Rookies (Bill Fahey, Jim Mason, Tom Ragland)	1.50	.70	.45
335	Bill Hands	1.50	.70	.45
336	Marty Martinez	1.50	.70	.45
337	Mike Kilkenny	1.50	.70	.45
338	Bob Grich	1.50	.70	.45
339	Ron Cook	1.50	.70	.45
340	Roy White	1.50	.70	.45
341	Joe Torre (Boyhood Photo)	2.50	1.25	.70
342	Wilbur Wood (Boyhood Photo)	1.50	.70	.45
343	Willie Stargell (Boyhood Photo)	2.00	1.00	.60
344	Dave McNally (Boyhood Photo)	1.50	.70	.45
345	Rick Wise (Boyhood Photo)	1.50	.70	.45
346	Jim Fregosi (Boyhood Photo)	1.50	.70	.45
347	Tom Seaver (Boyhood Photo)	3.00	1.50	.90
348	Sal Bando (Boyhood Photo)	1.50	.70	.45
349	Al Fitzmorris	1.50	.70	.45
350	Frank Howard	2.00	1.00	.60
351	Braves Rookies (Jimmy Britton, Tom House, Rick Kester)	1.50	.70	.45
352	Dave LaRoche	1.50	.70	.45
353	Art Shamsky	1.50	.70	.45
354	Tom Murphy	1.50	.70	.45
355	Bob Watson	1.50	.70	.45
356	Gerry Moses	1.50	.70	.45
357	Woodie Fryman	1.50	.70	.45
358	Sparky Anderson	4.00	2.00	1.25
359	Don Pavletich	1.50	.70	.45
360	Dave Roberts	1.50	.70	.45
361	Mike Andrews	1.50	.70	.45
362	Mets Team	4.00	2.00	1.25
363	Ron Klimkowski	1.50	.70	.45
364	Johnny Callison	1.50	.70	.45
365	Dick Bosman	1.50	.70	.45
366	Jimmy Rosario	1.50	.70	.45
367	Ron Perranoski	1.50	.70	.45
368	Danny Thompson	1.50	.70	.45
369	Jim Lefebvre	1.50	.70	.45
370	Don Buford	1.50	.70	.45
371	Denny Lemaster	1.50	.70	.45
372	Royals Rookies (Lance Clemons, Monty Montgomery)	1.50	.70	.45
373	John Mayberry	1.50	.70	.45
374	Jack Heidemann	1.50	.70	.45
375	Reggie Cleveland	1.50	.70	.45
376	Andy Kosco	1.50	.70	.45
377	Terry Harmon	1.50	.70	.45
378	4th Series Checklist (395-525)	3.00	1.50	.90
379	Ken Berry	1.50	.70	.45
380	Earl Williams	1.50	.70	.45
381	White Sox Team	3.00	1.50	.90
382	Joe Gibbon	1.50	.70	.45
383	Brant Alyea	1.50	.70	.45
384	Dave Campbell	1.50	.70	.45
385	Mickey Stanley	1.50	.70	.45
386	Jim Colborn	1.50	.70	.45
387	Horace Clarke	1.50	.70	.45
388	Charlie Williams	1.50	.70	.45
389	Bill Rigney	1.50	.70	.45
390	Willie Davis	1.50	.70	.45
391	Ken Sanders	1.50	.70	.45
392	Pirates Rookies (Fred Cambria, Richie Zisk)	2.00	1.00	.60
393	Curt Motton	1.50	.70	.45
394	Ken Forsch	1.50	.70	.45
395	Matty Alou	1.50	.70	.45
396	Paul Lindblad	1.50	.70	.45
397	Phillies Team	4.00	2.00	1.25
398	Larry Hisle	2.00	1.00	.60
399	Milt Wilcox	1.50	.70	.45
400	Tony Oliva	3.00	1.50	.90
401	Jim Nash	1.50	.70	.45
402	Bobby Heise	1.50	.70	.45
403	John Cumberland	1.50	.70	.45
404	Jeff Torborg	1.50	.70	.45
405	Ron Fairly	1.50	.70	.45
406	George Hendrick	2.00	1.00	.60
407	Chuck Taylor	1.50	.70	.45
408	Jim Northrup	1.50	.70	.45
409	Frank Baker	1.50	.70	.45
410	Fergie Jenkins	6.00	3.00	1.75
411	Bob Montgomery	1.50	.70	.45
412	Dick Kelley	1.50	.70	.45
413	White Sox Rookies (Don Eddy, Dave Lemonds)	1.50	.70	.45
414	Bob Miller	1.50	.70	.45
415	Cookie Rojas	1.50	.70	.45
416	Johnny Edwards	1.50	.70	.45
417	Tom Hall	1.50	.70	.45
418	Tom Shopay	1.50	.70	.45
419	Jim Spencer	1.50	.70	.45
420	Steve Carlton	15.00	7.50	4.50
421	Ellie Rodriguez	1.50	.70	.45
422	Ray Lamb	1.50	.70	.45
423	Oscar Gamble	1.50	.70	.45
424	Bill Gogolewski	1.50	.70	.45
425	Ken Singleton	1.50	.70	.45
426	Ken Singleton/IA	1.50	.70	.45
427	Tito Fuentes	1.50	.70	.45
428	Tito Fuentes/IA	1.50	.70	.45
429	Bob Robertson	1.50	.70	.45
430	Bob Robertson/IA	1.50	.70	.45
431	Clarence Gaston	1.50	.70	.45
432	Clarence Gaston/IA	1.50	.70	.45
433	Johnny Bench	25.00	12.50	6.25
434	Johnny Bench/IA	15.00	7.50	3.75
435	Reggie Jackson	25.00	12.50	7.50
436	Reggie Jackson/IA	10.00	5.00	2.50
437	Maury Wills	1.50	.70	.45
438	Maury Wills/IA	1.50	.70	.45
439	Billy Williams	8.00	4.00	2.50
440	Billy Williams/IA	5.00	2.50	1.50
441	Thurman Munson	25.00	12.50	6.25
442	Thurman Munson/IA	10.00	5.00	3.00
443	Ken Henderson	1.50	.70	.45
444	Ken Henderson/IA	1.50	.70	.45
445	Tom Seaver	25.00	12.50	7.50
446	Tom Seaver/IA	10.00	5.00	2.50
447	Willie Stargell	10.00	5.00	2.50
448	Willie Stargell/IA	5.00	2.50	1.50
449	Bob Lemon	4.00	2.00	1.25
450	Mickey Lolich	1.50	.70	.45
451	Tony LaRussa	2.50	1.25	.70
452	Ed Herrmann	1.50	.70	.45
453	Barry Lersch	1.50	.70	.45
454	A's Team	4.00	2.00	1.25
455	Tommy Harper	1.50	.70	.45
456	Mark Belanger	1.50	.70	.45
457	Padres Rookies (Darcy Fast, Mike Ivie, Derrel Thomas)	1.50	.70	.45
458	Aurelio Monteagudo	1.50	.70	.45
459	Rick Renick	1.50	.70	.45
460	Al Downing	1.50	.70	.45
461	Tim Cullen	1.50	.70	.45
462	Rickey Clark	1.50	.70	.45
463	Bernie Carbo	1.50	.70	.45
464	Jim Roland	1.50	.70	.45
465	Gil Hodges	4.00	2.00	1.25
466	Norm Miller	1.50	.70	.45
467	Steve Kline	1.50	.70	.45
468	Richie Scheinblum	1.50	.70	.45
469	Ron Herbel	1.50	.70	.45
470	Ray Fosse	1.50	.70	.45
471	Luke Walker	1.50	.70	.45
472	Phil Gagliano	1.50	.70	.45
473	Dan McGinn	1.50	.70	.45
474	Orioles Rookies (Don Baylor, Roric Harrison, Johnny Oates)	10.00	5.00	3.00
475	Gary Nolan	1.50	.70	.45
476	Lee Richard	1.50	.70	.45
477	Tom Phoebus	1.50	.70	.45
478a	5th Series Checklist (526-656) (Small print on front.)	2.50	1.25	.70
478b	5th Series Checklist (526-656) (Large printing on front.)	2.50	1.25	.70
479	Don Shaw	1.50	.70	.45
480	Lee May	1.50	.70	.45
481	Billy Conigliaro	1.50	.70	.45
482	Joe Hoerner	1.50	.70	.45
483	Ken Suarez	1.50	.70	.45
484	Lum Harris	1.50	.70	.45
485	Phil Regan	1.50	.70	.45
486	John Lowenstein	1.50	.70	.45
487	Tigers Team	5.00	2.50	1.50
488	Mike Nagy	1.50	.70	.45
489	Expos Rookies (Terry Humphrey, Keith Lampard)	1.50	.70	.45
490	Dave McNally	1.50	.70	.45
491	Lou Piniella (Boyhood Photo)	1.50	.70	.45
492	Mel Stottlemyre (Boyhood Photo)	1.50	.70	.45
493	Bob Bailey (Boyhood Photo)	1.50	.70	.45
494	Willie Horton (Boyhood Photo)	1.50	.70	.45
495	Bill Melton (Boyhood Photo)	1.50	.70	.45
496	Bud Harrelson (Boyhood Photo)	1.50	.70	.45
497	Jim Perry (Boyhood Photo)	1.50	.70	.45
498	Brooks Robinson (Boyhood Photo)	4.00	2.00	1.25
499	Vicente Romo	1.50	.70	.45
500	Joe Torre	5.00	2.50	1.50
501	Pete Hamm	1.50	.70	.45
502	Jackie Hernandez	1.50	.70	.45
503	Gary Peters	1.50	.70	.45
504	Ed Spiezio	1.50	.70	.45
505	Mike Marshall	1.50	.70	.45
506	Indians Rookies (Terry Ley, Jim Moyer, Dick Tidrow)	1.50	.70	.45
507	Fred Gladding	1.50	.70	.45
508	Ellie Hendricks	1.50	.70	.45
509	Don McMahon	1.50	.70	.45
510	Ted Williams	20.00	10.00	5.00
511	Tony Taylor	1.50	.70	.45
512	Paul Popovich	1.50	.70	.45
513	Lindy McDaniel	1.50	.70	.45
514	Ted Sizemore	1.50	.70	.45
515	Bert Blyleven	3.00	1.50	.90
516	Oscar Brown	1.50	.70	.45
517	Ken Brett	1.50	.70	.45
518	Wayne Garrett	1.50	.70	.45
519	Ted Abernathy	1.50	.70	.45
520	Larry Bowa	1.50	.70	.45
521	Alan Foster	1.50	.70	.45
522	Dodgers Team	4.00	2.00	1.25
523	Chuck Dobson	1.50	.70	.45
524	Reds Rookies (Ed Armbrister, Mel Behney)	1.50	.70	.45
525	Carlos May	1.50	.70	.45
526	Bob Bailey	4.00	2.00	1.00
527	Dave Leonhard	4.00	2.00	1.00
528	Ron Stone	4.00	2.00	1.00
529	Dave Nelson	4.00	2.00	1.00
530	Don Sutton	10.00	5.00	3.00
531	Freddie Patek	5.00	2.50	1.25
532	Fred Kendall	4.00	2.00	1.00
533	Ralph Houk	6.00	3.00	1.75
534	Jim Hickman	4.00	2.00	1.00
535	Ed Brinkman	4.00	2.00	1.00
536	Doug Rader	4.00	2.00	1.00
537	Bob Locker	4.00	2.00	1.00
538	Charlie Sands	4.00	2.00	1.00
539	Terry Forster	5.00	2.50	1.25
540	Felix Millan	4.00	2.00	1.00
541	Roger Repoz	4.00	2.00	1.00
542	Jack Billingham	4.00	2.00	1.00
543	Duane Josephson	4.00	2.00	1.00
544	Ted Martinez	4.00	2.00	1.00
545	Wayne Granger	4.00	2.00	1.00
546	Joe Hague	4.00	2.00	1.00

547	Indians Team	6.00	3.00	1.75
548	Frank Reberger	4.00	2.00	1.00
549	Dave May	4.00	2.00	1.00
550	Brooks Robinson	20.00	10.00	5.00
551	Ollie Brown	4.00	2.00	1.00
552	Ollie Brown/IA	4.00	2.00	1.00
553	Wilbur Wood	4.00	2.00	1.00
554	Wilbur Wood/IA	4.00	2.00	1.00
555	Ron Santo	8.00	4.00	2.50
556	Ron Santo/IA	5.00	2.50	1.25
557	John Odom	4.00	2.00	1.00
558	John Odom/IA	4.00	2.00	1.00
559	Pete Rose	32.50	16.00	9.75
560	Pete Rose/IA	17.50	8.75	5.25
561	Leo Cardenas	4.00	2.00	1.00
562	Leo Cardenas/IA	4.00	2.00	1.00
563	Ray Sadecki	4.00	2.00	1.00
564	Ray Sadecki/IA	4.00	2.00	1.00
565	Reggie Smith	4.00	2.00	1.00
566	Reggie Smith/IA	4.00	2.00	1.00
567	Juan Marichal	10.00	5.00	3.00
568	Juan Marichal/IA	5.00	2.50	1.50
569	Ed Kirkpatrick	4.00	2.00	1.00
570	Ed Kirkpatrick/IA	4.00	2.00	1.00
571	Nate Colbert	4.00	2.00	1.00
572	Nate Colbert/IA	4.00	2.00	1.00
573	Fritz Peterson	4.00	2.00	1.00
574	Fritz Peterson/IA	4.00	2.00	1.00
575	Al Oliver	5.00	2.50	1.25
576	Leo Durocher	5.00	2.50	1.50
577	Mike Paul	4.00	2.00	1.00
578	Billy Grabarkewitz	4.00	2.00	1.00
579	*Doyle Alexander*	5.00	2.50	1.25
580	Lou Piniella	5.00	2.50	1.50
581	Wade Blasingame	4.00	2.00	1.00
582	Expos Team	6.00	3.00	1.75
583	Darold Knowles	4.00	2.00	1.00
584	Jerry McNertney	4.00	2.00	1.00
585	George Scott	4.00	2.00	1.00
586	Denis Menke	4.00	2.00	1.00
587	Billy Wilson	4.00	2.00	1.00
588	Jim Holt	4.00	2.00	1.00
589	Hal Lanier	4.00	2.00	1.00
590	Graig Nettles	4.00	2.00	1.00
591	Paul Casanova	4.00	2.00	1.00
592	Lew Krausse	4.00	2.00	1.00
593	Rich Morales	4.00	2.00	1.00
594	Jim Beauchamp	4.00	2.00	1.00
595	Nolan Ryan	80.00	40.00	24.00
596	Manny Mota	4.00	2.00	1.00
597	Jim Magnuson	4.00	2.00	1.00
598	Hal King	4.00	2.00	1.00
599	Billy Champion	4.00	2.00	1.00
600	Al Kaline	20.00	10.00	5.00
601	George Stone	4.00	2.00	1.00
602	Dave Bristol	4.00	2.00	1.00
603	Jim Ray	4.00	2.00	1.00
604a	6th Series Checklist (657-787) (Copyright on right.)	6.00	3.00	1.75
604b	6th Series Checklist (657-787) (Copyright on left.)	6.00	3.00	1.75
605	Nelson Briles	4.00	2.00	1.00
606	Luis Melendez	4.00	2.00	1.00
607	Frank Duffy	4.00	2.00	1.00
608	Mike Corkins	4.00	2.00	1.00
609	Tom Grieve	4.00	2.00	1.00
610	Bill Stoneman	4.00	2.00	1.00
611	Rich Reese	4.00	2.00	1.00
612	Joe Decker	4.00	2.00	1.00
613	Mike Ferraro	4.00	2.00	1.00
614	Ted Uhlaender	4.00	2.00	1.00
615	Steve Hargan	4.00	2.00	1.00
616	*Joe Ferguson*	3.00	1.50	.90
617	Royals Team	6.00	3.00	1.75
618	Rich Robertson	4.00	2.00	1.00
619	Rich McKinney	4.00	2.00	1.00
620	Phil Niekro	10.00	5.00	3.00
621	Commissioners Award	4.00	2.00	1.00
622	Most Valuable Player Award	4.00	2.00	1.00
623	Cy Young Award	4.00	2.00	1.00
624	Minor League Player Of The Year Award	4.00	2.00	1.00
625	Rookie of the Year Award	4.00	2.00	1.00
626	Babe Ruth Award	4.00	2.00	1.00
627	Moe Drabowsky	4.00	2.00	1.00
628	Terry Crowley	4.00	2.00	1.00
629	Paul Doyle	4.00	2.00	1.00
630	Rich Hebner	4.00	2.00	1.00
631	John Strohmayer	4.00	2.00	1.00
632	Mike Hegan	4.00	2.00	1.00
633	Jack Hiatt	4.00	2.00	1.00
634	Dick Woodson	4.00	2.00	1.00
635	Don Money	4.00	2.00	1.00
636	Bill Lee	4.00	2.00	1.00
637	Preston Gomez	4.00	2.00	1.00
638	Ken Wright	4.00	2.00	1.00
639	J.C. Martin	4.00	2.00	1.00
640	Joe Coleman	4.00	2.00	1.00
641	Mike Lum	4.00	2.00	1.00
642	Denny Riddleberger	4.00	2.00	1.00
643	Russ Gibson	4.00	2.00	1.00
644	Bernie Allen	4.00	2.00	1.00
645	Jim Maloney	4.00	2.00	1.00
646	Chico Salmon	4.00	2.00	1.00
647	Bob Moose	4.00	2.00	1.00
648	Jim Lyttle	4.00	2.00	1.00
649	Pete Richert	4.00	2.00	1.00
650	Sal Bando	4.00	2.00	1.00
651	Reds Team	8.00	4.00	2.50
652	Marcelino Lopez	4.00	2.00	1.00
653	Jim Fairey	4.00	2.00	1.00
654	Horacio Pina	4.00	2.00	1.00
655	Jerry Grote	4.00	2.00	1.00
656	Rudy May	4.00	2.00	1.00
657	Bobby Wine	12.00	6.00	3.00
658	Steve Dunning	12.00	6.00	3.00
659	Bob Aspromonte	12.00	6.00	3.00
660	Paul Blair	12.00	6.00	3.00
661	Bill Virdon	12.00	6.00	3.00
662	Stan Bahnsen	12.00	6.00	3.00
663	Fran Healy	12.00	6.00	3.00
664	Bobby Knoop	12.00	6.00	3.00
665	Chris Short	12.00	6.00	3.00
666	Hector Torres	12.00	6.00	3.00
667	Ray Newman	12.00	6.00	3.00
668	Rangers Team	25.00	12.50	6.25
669	Willie Crawford	12.00	6.00	3.00
670	Ken Holtzman	12.00	6.00	3.00
671	Donn Clendenon	12.00	6.00	3.00
672	Archie Reynolds	12.00	6.00	3.00
673	Dave Marshall	12.00	6.00	3.00
674	John Kennedy	12.00	6.00	3.00
675	Pat Jarvis	12.00	6.00	3.00
676	Danny Cater	12.00	6.00	3.00
677	Ivan Murrell	12.00	6.00	3.00
678	Steve Luebber	12.00	6.00	3.00
679	Astros Rookies (Bob Fenwick, Bob Stinson)	12.00	6.00	3.00
680	Dave Johnson	12.00	6.00	3.00
681	Bobby Pfeil	12.00	6.00	3.00
682	Mike McCormick	12.00	6.00	3.00
683	Steve Hovley	12.00	6.00	3.00
684	Hal Breeden	12.00	6.00	3.00
685	Joe Horlen	12.00	6.00	3.00
686	Steve Garvey	25.00	12.50	7.50
687	Del Unser	12.00	6.00	3.00
688	Cardinals Team	15.00	7.50	3.75
689	Eddie Fisher	12.00	6.00	3.00
690	Willie Montanez	12.00	6.00	3.00
691	Curt Blefary	12.00	6.00	3.00
692	Curt Blefary/IA	12.00	6.00	3.00
693	Alan Gallagher	12.00	6.00	3.00
694	Alan Gallagher/IA	12.00	6.00	3.00
695	Rod Carew	50.00	25.00	15.00
696	Rod Carew/IA	25.00	12.50	7.50
697	Jerry Koosman	15.00	7.50	4.50
698	Jerry Koosman/IA	12.00	6.00	3.00
699	Bobby Murcer	13.00	6.50	3.75
700	Bobby Murcer/IA	12.00	6.00	3.00
701	Jose Pagan	12.00	6.00	3.00
702	Jose Pagan/IA	12.00	6.00	3.00
703	Doug Griffin	12.00	6.00	3.00
704	Doug Griffin/IA	12.00	6.00	3.00
705	Pat Corrales	12.00	6.00	3.00
706	Pat Corrales/IA	12.00	6.00	3.00
707	Tim Foli	12.00	6.00	3.00
708	Tim Foli/IA	12.00	6.00	3.00
709	Jim Kaat	15.00	7.50	4.50
710	Jim Kaat/IA	12.00	6.00	3.00
711	Bobby Bonds	12.00	6.00	3.00
712	Bobby Bonds/IA	12.00	6.00	3.00
713	Gene Michael	12.00	6.00	3.00
714	Gene Michael/IA	12.00	6.00	3.00
715	Mike Epstein	12.00	6.00	3.00
716	Jesus Alou	12.00	6.00	3.00
717	Bruce Dal Canton	12.00	6.00	3.00
718	Del Rice	12.00	6.00	3.00
719	Cesar Geronimo	12.00	6.00	3.00
720	Sam McDowell	12.00	6.00	3.00
721	Eddie Leon	12.00	6.00	3.00
722	Bill Sudakis	12.00	6.00	3.00
723	Al Santorini	12.00	6.00	3.00
724	A.L. Rookies (John Curtis, Rich Hinton, Mickey Scott)	12.00	6.00	3.00
725	Dick McAuliffe	12.00	6.00	3.00
726	Dick Selma	12.00	6.00	3.00
727	Jose Laboy	12.00	6.00	3.00
728	Gail Hopkins	12.00	6.00	3.00
729	Bob Veale	12.00	6.00	3.00
730	Rick Monday	12.00	6.00	3.00
731	Orioles Team	15.00	7.50	4.50
732	George Culver	12.00	6.00	3.00
733	Jim Hart	12.00	6.00	3.00
734	Bob Burda	12.00	6.00	3.00
735	Diego Segui	12.00	6.00	3.00
736	Bill Russell	12.00	6.00	3.00
737	*Lenny Randle*	12.00	6.00	3.00
738	Jim Merritt	12.00	6.00	3.00
739	Don Mason	12.00	6.00	3.00
740	Rico Carty	12.00	6.00	3.00
741	Major League Rookies (*Tom Hutton, Rick Miller, John Milner*)	12.00	6.00	3.00
742	Jim Rooker	12.00	6.00	3.00
743	Cesar Gutierrez	12.00	6.00	3.00
744	*Jim Slaton*	12.00	6.00	3.00
745	Julian Javier	12.00	6.00	3.00
746	Lowell Palmer	12.00	6.00	3.00
747	Jim Stewart	12.00	6.00	3.00
748	Phil Hennigan	12.00	6.00	3.00
749	Walter Alston	15.00	7.50	4.50
750	Willie Horton	12.00	6.00	3.00
751	Steve Carlton (Traded)	30.00	15.00	9.00
752	Joe Morgan (Traded)	30.00	15.00	9.00
753	Denny McLain (Traded)	15.00	7.50	4.50
754	Frank Robinson (Traded)	25.00	12.50	6.25
755	Jim Fregosi (Traded)	15.00	7.50	4.50
756	Rick Wise (Traded)	12.00	6.00	3.00
757	Jose Cardenal (Traded)	12.00	6.00	3.00
758	Gil Garrido	12.00	6.00	3.00
759	Chris Cannizzaro	12.00	6.00	3.00
760	Bill Mazeroski	20.00	10.00	6.00
761	A.L.-N.L. Rookies (**Ron Cey, Ben Oglivie,** Bernie Williams)	20.00	10.00	
762	Wayne Simpson	12.00	6.00	3.00
763	Ron Hansen	12.00	6.00	3.00
764	Dusty Baker	15.00	7.50	4.50
765	Ken McMullen	12.00	6.00	3.00
766	Steve Hamilton	12.00	6.00	3.00
767	Tom McCraw	12.00	6.00	3.00
768	Denny Doyle	12.00	6.00	3.00
769	Jack Aker	12.00	6.00	3.00
770	Jim Wynn	12.00	6.00	3.00
771	Giants Team	15.00	7.50	3.75
772	Ken Tatum	12.00	6.00	3.00
773	Ron Brand	12.00	6.00	3.00
774	Luis Alvarado	12.00	6.00	3.00
775	Jerry Reuss	12.00	6.00	3.00
776	Bill Voss	12.00	6.00	3.00
777	Hoyt Wilhelm	20.00	10.00	5.00
778	Twins Rookies (Vic Albury, **Rick Dempsey**, Jim Strickland)	15.00	7.50	3.75
779	Tony Cloninger	12.00	6.00	3.00
780	Dick Green	12.00	6.00	3.00
781	Jim McAndrew	12.00	6.00	3.00
782	Larry Stahl	12.00	6.00	3.00
783	Les Cain	12.00	6.00	3.00
784	Ken Aspromonte	12.00	6.00	3.00
785	Vic Davalillo	12.00	6.00	3.00
786	Chuck Brinkman	12.00	6.00	3.00
787	Ron Reed	12.00	6.00	3.00

1972 Topps Bubble Gum Lid Test Issue

Between the production of its regular-issue candy lid sets of 1970 and 1973, Topps was working on another issue that survives today in proof form, either as uncropped squares or cut to the 1-7/8" diameter tabbed lid form meant to cover a plastic bucket of bubblegum nuggets. The 1972 proofs are very close to the 1973 issue in format; the principal difference is the player portrait does not have a solid-color border as on the 1973s, and that the pictures of Seaver and Yaz on the front are set against green, rather than orange, stars.

		NM	EX	VG
Complete Set (55):		15,000	7,500	4,500
Common Player:		100.00	50.00	30.00
(1)	Hank Aaron	900.00	450.00	275.00
(2)	Dick Allen	150.00	75.00	45.00
(3)	Dusty Baker	100.00	50.00	35.00
(4)	Sal Bando	100.00	50.00	30.00
(5)	Johnny Bench	450.00	225.00	135.00
(6)	Bobby Bonds	100.00	50.00	30.00
(7)	Dick Bosman	100.00	50.00	30.00
(8)	Lou Brock	250.00	125.00	75.00
(9)	Rod Carew	300.00	150.00	90.00
(10)	Steve Carlton	300.00	150.00	90.00
(11)	Nate Colbert	100.00	50.00	30.00
(12)	Willie Davis	100.00	50.00	30.00
(13)	Larry Dierker	100.00	50.00	30.00
(14)	Mike Epstein	100.00	50.00	30.00
(15)	Carlton Fisk	300.00	150.00	90.00
(16)	Tim Foli	100.00	50.00	30.00
(17)	Ray Fosse	100.00	50.00	30.00
(18)	Bill Freehan	100.00	50.00	30.00
(19)	Bob Gibson	300.00	150.00	90.00
(20)	Bud Harrelson	100.00	50.00	30.00
(21)	Catfish Hunter	250.00	125.00	75.00
(22)	Reggie Jackson	650.00	325.00	195.00
(23)	Fergie Jenkins	250.00	125.00	75.00
(24)	Al Kaline	350.00	175.00	100.00
(25)	Harmon Killebrew	350.00	175.00	100.00
(26)	Clay Kirby	100.00	50.00	30.00
(27)	Mickey Lolich	100.00	50.00	30.00
(28)	Greg Luzinski	100.00	50.00	30.00
(29)	Mike Marshall	100.00	50.00	30.00
(30)	Lee May	100.00	50.00	30.00
(31)	John Mayberry	100.00	50.00	30.00
(32)	Willie Mays	900.00	450.00	275.00
(33)	Willie McCovey	250.00	125.00	75.00
(34)	Thurman Munson	300.00	150.00	90.00
(35)	Bobby Murcer	150.00	75.00	45.00
(36)	Gary Nolan	100.00	50.00	30.00
(37)	Amos Otis	100.00	50.00	30.00
(38)	Jim Palmer	250.00	125.00	75.00
(39)	Gaylord Perry	250.00	125.00	75.00
(40)	Lou Piniella	150.00	75.00	45.00
(41)	Brooks Robinson	350.00	175.00	100.00
(42)	Frank Robinson	350.00	175.00	100.00
(43)	Ellie Rodriguez	100.00	50.00	30.00
(44)	Pete Rose	900.00	450.00	275.00
(45)	Nolan Ryan	2,500	1,250	750.00
(46)	Manny Sanguillen	100.00	50.00	30.00
(47)	George Scott	100.00	50.00	30.00
(48)	Tom Seaver	350.00	175.00	100.00
(49)	Chris Speier	100.00	50.00	30.00
(50)	Willie Stargell	250.00	125.00	75.00
(51)	Don Sutton	250.00	125.00	75.00
(52)	Joe Torre	150.00	75.00	45.00
(53)	Billy Williams	250.00	125.00	75.00
(54)	Wilbur Wood	100.00	50.00	30.00
(55)	Carl Yastrzemski	450.00	225.00	135.00

1972 Topps Cloth Stickers

Despite the fact they were never actually issued, examples of this test issue can readily be found within the hobby. The set of 33 contains stickers with designs identical to cards found in three contiguous rows of a regular Topps card sheet that year; thus the inclusion of a meaningless checklist card. Sometimes found in complete 33-sticker strips, or 132-piece sheets, individual stickers nominally measure 2-1/2" x 3-1/2", though dimensions vary according to the care with which they were cut. Stickers are unnumbered and blank-backed; most are found without the original paper backing as the glue used did not hold up well over the years. Eleven of the stickers are prone to mis-cutting and are identified with an (SP) in the checklist.

	NM	EX	VG
Complete Set (33):	1,300	650.00	390.00
Common Player:	20.00	10.00	6.00
(1) Hank Aaron	200.00	100.00	60.00
(2) Luis Aparicio/IA/SP	60.00	30.00	18.00
(3) Ike Brown	20.00	10.00	6.00
(4) Johnny Callison	20.00	10.00	6.00
(5) Checklist 264-319	10.00	5.00	3.00
(6) Roberto Clemente/IA	300.00	150.00	90.00
(7) Dave Concepcion/SP	40.00	20.00	12.00
(8) Ron Cook	20.00	10.00	6.00
(9) Willie Davis	20.00	10.00	6.00
(10) Al Fitzmorris	20.00	10.00	6.00
(11) Bobby Floyd	20.00	10.00	6.00
(12) Roy Foster	20.00	10.00	6.00
(13) Jim Fregosi (Boyhood Photo)	20.00	10.00	6.00
(14) Danny Frisella/IA	20.00	10.00	6.00
(15) Woody Fryman/SP	25.00	12.50	7.50
(16) Terry Harmon	20.00	10.00	6.00
(17) Frank Howard/SP	40.00	20.00	12.00
(18) Ron Klimkowski	20.00	10.00	6.00
(19) Joe Lahoud	20.00	10.00	6.00
(20) Jim Lefebvre	20.00	10.00	6.00
(21) Elliott Maddox	20.00	10.00	6.00
(22) Marty Martinez	20.00	10.00	6.00
(23) Willie McCovey/SP	100.00	50.00	30.00
(24) Hal McRae/SP	30.00	15.00	9.00
(25) Syd O'Brien/SP	25.00	12.50	7.50
(26) Red Sox team	25.00	12.50	7.50
(27) Aurelio Rodriguez	20.00	10.00	6.00
(28) Al Severinsen	20.00	10.00	6.00
(29) Art Shamsky/SP	25.00	12.50	7.50
(30) Steve Stone/SP	30.00	15.00	9.00
(31) Stan Swanson/SP	25.00	12.50	7.50
(32) Bob Watson	20.00	10.00	6.00
(33) Roy White/SP	30.00	15.00	9.00

1972 Topps Posters

Issued as a separate set, rather than as a wax pack insert, these 9-7/16" x 18" posters feature a borderless full-color picture on the front with the player's name, team and position. Printed on very thin paper, the posters were folded for packaging, causing large creases that cannot be removed. Grading of these posters is done without regard to those packaging folds.

	NM	EX	VG
Complete Set (24):	700.00	350.00	200.00
Common Player:	12.00	6.00	3.50
Wax Pack:	50.00	.00	.00
1 Dave McNally	12.00	6.00	3.50
2 Carl Yastrzemski	45.00	22.50	13.50
3 Bill Melton	12.00	6.00	3.50
4 Ray Fosse	12.00	6.00	3.50
5 Mickey Lolich	12.00	6.00	3.50
6 Amos Otis	12.00	6.00	3.50
7 Tony Oliva	15.00	7.50	4.50
8 Vida Blue	12.00	6.00	3.50
9 Hank Aaron	75.00	37.50	22.00
10 Fergie Jenkins	30.00	15.00	9.00
11 Pete Rose	75.00	37.50	22.00
12 Willie Davis	12.00	6.00	3.50

13 Tom Seaver	40.00	20.00	12.00
14 Rick Wise	12.00	6.00	3.50
15 Willie Stargell	30.00	15.00	9.00
16 Joe Torre	17.50	8.75	5.25
17 Willie Mays	75.00	37.50	22.00
18 Andy Messersmith	12.00	6.00	3.50
19 Wilbur Wood	12.00	6.00	3.50
20 Harmon Killebrew	35.00	17.50	10.00
21 Billy Williams	30.00	15.00	9.00
22 Bud Harrelson	12.00	6.00	3.50
23 Roberto Clemente	125.00	65.00	35.00
24 Willie McCovey	30.00	15.00	9.00

1973 Topps

 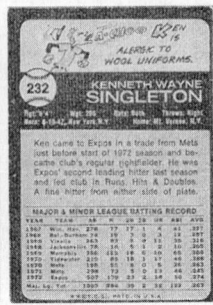

Topps cut back to 660 cards in 1973. The set is interesting for it marks the last time cards were issued by series, a procedure which had produced many a scarce high number card over the years. These 2-1/2" x 3-1/2" cards have a color photo, accented by a silhouette of a player on the front, indicative of his position. Card backs are vertical for the first time since 1968, with the usual statistical and biographical information. Specialty cards begin with card number 1, which depicted Ruth, Mays and Aaron as the all-time home run leaders. It was followed by statistical leaders, although there also were additional all-time leader cards. Also present are playoff and World Series highlights. From the age-and-youth department, the 1973 Topps set has coaches and managers as well as more "Boyhood Photos."

	NM	EX	VG
Complete Set (660):	825.00	420.00	250.00
Common Player (1-396):	.75	.40	.25
Common Player (397-528):	1.00	.50	.30
Common Player (529-660):	2.00	1.00	.60
Series 1/2/3 Wax Pack (10):	80.00		
Series 4 Wax Pack (10):	165.00		
Series 5 Wax Pack (10+1):	215.00		
1 All Time Home Run Leaders (Hank Aaron, Willie Mays, Babe Ruth)	35.00	17.50	8.75
2 Rich Hebner	.75	.40	.25
3 Jim Lonborg	.75	.40	.25
4 John Milner	.75	.40	.25
5 Ed Brinkman	.75	.40	.25
6 Mac Scarce	.75	.40	.25
7 Texas Rangers Team	1.00	.50	.30
8 Tom Hall	.75	.40	.25
9 Johnny Oates	.75	.40	.25
10 Don Sutton	3.00	1.50	.90
11 Chris Chambliss	.75	.40	.25
12a Padres Mgr./Coaches (Dave Garcia, Johnny Podres, Bob Skinner, Whitey Wietelmann, Don Zimmer) (Coaches background brown.)	1.00	.50	.30
12b Padres Mgr./Coaches (Dave Garcia, Johnny Podres, Bob Skinner, Whitey Wietelmann, Don Zimmer) (Coaches background orange.)	1.00	.50	.30
13 George Hendrick	.75	.40	.25
14 Sonny Siebert	.75	.40	.25
15 Ralph Garr	.75	.40	.25
16 Steve Braun	.75	.40	.25
17 Fred Gladding	.75	.40	.25
18 Leroy Stanton	.75	.40	.25
19 Tim Foli	.75	.40	.25
20 Stan Bahnsen	1.00	.50	.30
21 Randy Hundley	.75	.40	.25
22 Ted Abernathy	.75	.40	.25
23 Dave Kingman	1.00	.50	.30
24 Al Santorini	.75	.40	.25
25 Roy White	.75	.40	.25
26 Pittsburgh Pirates Team	2.00	1.00	.60
27 Bill Gogolewski	.75	.40	.25
28 Hal McRae	.75	.40	.25
29 Tony Taylor	.75	.40	.25
30 Tug McGraw	.75	.40	.25
31 *Buddy Bell*	6.00	3.00	1.75
32 Fred Norman	.75	.40	.25
33 Jim Breazeale	.75	.40	.25
34 Pat Dobson	.75	.40	.25
35 Willie Davis	.75	.40	.25
36 Steve Barber	.75	.40	.25
37 Bill Robinson	.75	.40	.25
38 Mike Epstein	.75	.40	.25
39 Dave Roberts	.75	.40	.25
40 Reggie Smith	.75	.40	.25
41 Tom Walker	.75	.40	.25
42 Mike Andrews	.75	.40	.25
43 *Randy Moffitt*	.75	.40	.25
44 Rick Monday	.75	.40	.25
45 Ellie Rodriguez (Photo actually Paul Ratliff.)	.75	.40	.25
46 Lindy McDaniel	.75	.40	.25

47 Luis Melendez	.75	.40	.25
48 Paul Splittorff	.75	.40	.25
49a Twins Mgr./Coaches (Vern Morgan, Frank Quilici, Bob Rodgers, Ralph Rowe, Al Worthington) (Coaches background brown.)	.75	.40	.25
49b Twins Mgr./Coaches (Vern Morgan, Frank Quilici, Bob Rodgers, Ralph Rowe, Al Worthington) (Coaches background orange.)	.75	.40	.25
50 Roberto Clemente	50.00	25.00	12.50
51 Chuck Seelbach	.75	.40	.25
52 Denis Menke	.75	.40	.25
53 Steve Dunning	.75	.40	.25
54 Checklist 1-132	1.00	.50	.30
55 Jon Matlack	.75	.40	.25
56 Merv Rettenmund	.75	.40	.25
57 Derrel Thomas	.75	.40	.25
58 Mike Paul	.75	.40	.25
59 *Steve Yeager*	.75	.40	.25
60 Ken Holtzman	.75	.40	.25
61 Batting Leaders (Rod Carew, Billy Williams)	1.00	.50	.30
62 Home Run Leaders (Dick Allen, Johnny Bench)	1.00	.50	.30
63 Runs Batted In Leaders (Dick Allen, Johnny Bench)	1.00	.50	.30
64 Stolen Base Leaders (Lou Brock, Bert Campaneris)	1.00	.50	.30
65 Earned Run Average Leaders (Steve Carlton, Luis Tiant)	1.00	.50	.30
66 Victory Leaders (Steve Carlton, Gaylord Perry, Wilbur Wood)	1.00	.50	.30
67 Strikeout Leaders (Steve Carlton, Nolan Ryan)	17.50	8.75	5.25
68 Leading Firemen (Clay Carroll, Sparky Lyle)	.75	.40	.25
69 Phil Gagliano	.75	.40	.25
70 Milt Pappas	.75	.40	.25
71 Johnny Briggs	.75	.40	.25
72 Ron Reed	.75	.40	.25
73 Ed Herrmann	.75	.40	.25
74 Billy Champion	.75	.40	.25
75 Vada Pinson	1.00	.50	.30
76 Doug Rader	.75	.40	.25
77 Mike Torrez	.75	.40	.25
78 Richie Scheinblum	.75	.40	.25
79 Jim Willoughby	.75	.40	.25
80 Tony Oliva ("MINNSEOTA" on front is uncorrected error.)	1.00	.50	.30
81a Cubs Mgr./Coaches (Hank Aguirre, Ernie Banks, Larry Jansen, Whitey Lockman, Pete Reiser) (Trees in coaches background.)	1.25	.60	.40
81b Cubs Mgr./Coaches (Hank Aguirre, Ernie Banks, Larry Jansen, Whitey Lockman, Pete Reiser) (Solid orange background.)	1.25	.60	.40
82 Fritz Peterson	.75	.40	.25
83 Leron Lee	.75	.40	.25
84 Rollie Fingers	3.00	1.50	.90
85 Ted Simmons	.75	.40	.25
86 Tom McCraw	.75	.40	.25
87 Ken Boswell	.75	.40	.25
88 Mickey Stanley	.75	.40	.25
89 Jack Billingham	.75	.40	.25
90 Brooks Robinson	10.00	5.00	2.50
91 Los Angeles Dodgers Team	2.00	1.00	.60
92 Jerry Bell	.75	.40	.25
93 Jesus Alou	.75	.40	.25
94 Dick Billings	.75	.40	.25
95 Steve Blass	.75	.40	.25
96 Doug Griffin	.75	.40	.25
97 Willie Montanez	.75	.40	.25
98 Dick Woodson	.75	.40	.25
99 Carl Taylor	.75	.40	.25
100 Hank Aaron	35.00	17.50	10.50
101 Ken Henderson	.75	.40	.25
102 Rudy May	.75	.40	.25
103 Celerino Sanchez	.75	.40	.25
104 Reggie Cleveland	.75	.40	.25
105 Carlos May	.75	.40	.25
106 Terry Humphrey	.75	.40	.25
107 Phil Hennigan	.75	.40	.25
108 Bill Russell	1.00	.50	.30
109 Doyle Alexander	.75	.40	.25
110 Bob Watson	.75	.40	.25
111 Dave Nelson	.75	.40	.25
112 Gary Ross	.75	.40	.25
113 Jerry Grote	.75	.40	.25
114 Lynn McGlothen	.75	.40	.25
115 Ron Santo	2.00	1.00	.60
116a Yankees Mgr./Coaches (Jim Hegan, Ralph Houk, Elston Howard, Dick Howser, Jim Turner) (Coaches background brown.)	2.00	1.00	.60
116b Yankees Mgr./Coaches (Jim Hegan, Ralph Houk, Elston Howard, Dick Howser, Jim Turner) (Coaches background orange.)	2.00	1.00	.60
117 Ramon Hernandez	.75	.40	.25
118 John Mayberry	.75	.40	.25
119 Larry Bowa	1.50	.70	.45
120 Joe Coleman	.75	.40	.25
121 Dave Rader	.75	.40	.25
122 Jim Strickland	.75	.40	.25
123 Sandy Alomar	.75	.40	.25
124 Jim Hardin	.75	.40	.25
125 Ron Fairly	.75	.40	.25

No.	Player			
126	Jim Brewer	.75	.40	.25
127	Milwaukee Brewers Team	2.00	1.00	.60
128	Ted Sizemore	.75	.40	.25
129	Terry Forster	.75	.40	.25
130	Pete Rose	20.00	10.00	6.00
131a	Red Sox Mgr./Coaches (Doug Camilli, Eddie Kasko, Don Lenhardt, Eddie Popowski, Lee Stange) (Coaches background brown.)	.75	.40	.25
131b	Red Sox Mgr./Coaches (Doug Camilli, Eddie Kasko, Don Lenhardt, Eddie Popowski, Lee Stange) (Coaches background orange.)	.75	.40	.25
132	Matty Alou	.75	.40	.25
133	Dave Roberts	.75	.40	.25
134	Milt Wilcox	.75	.40	.25
135	Lee May	.75	.40	.25
136a	Orioles Mgr./Coaches (George Bamberger, Jim Frey, Billy Hunter, George Staller, Earl Weaver) (Coaches background brown.)	2.00	1.00	.60
136b	Orioles Mgr./Coaches (George Bamberger, Jim Frey, Billy Hunter, George Staller, Earl Weaver) (Coaches background orange.)	2.00	1.00	.60
137	Jim Beauchamp	.75	.40	.25
138	Horacio Pina	.75	.40	.25
139	Carmen Fanzone	.75	.40	.25
140	Lou Piniella	2.00	1.00	.60
141	Bruce Kison	.75	.40	.25
142	Thurman Munson	20.00	10.00	5.00
143	John Curtis	.75	.40	.25
144	Marty Perez	.75	.40	.25
145	Bobby Bonds	2.00	1.00	.60
146	Woodie Fryman	.75	.40	.25
147	Mike Anderson	.75	.40	.25
148	Dave Goltz	.75	.40	.25
149	Ron Hunt	.75	.40	.25
150	Wilbur Wood	1.50	.70	.45
151	Wes Parker	.75	.40	.25
152	Dave May	.75	.40	.25
153	Al Hrabosky	1.50	.70	.45
154	Jeff Torborg	.75	.40	.25
155	Sal Bando	.75	.40	.25
156	Cesar Geronimo	.75	.40	.25
157	Denny Riddleberger	.75	.40	.25
158	Houston Astros Team	2.00	1.00	.60
159	Clarence Gaston	.75	.40	.25
160	Jim Palmer	8.00	4.00	2.00
161	Ted Martinez	.75	.40	.25
162	Pete Broberg	.75	.40	.25
163	Vic Davalillo	.75	.40	.25
164	Monty Montgomery	.75	.40	.25
165	Luis Aparicio	4.00	2.00	1.25
166	Terry Harmon	.75	.40	.25
167	Steve Stone	1.00	.50	.30
168	Jim Northrup	.75	.40	.25
169	Ron Schueler	.75	.40	.25
170	Harmon Killebrew	5.00	2.50	1.25
171	Bernie Carbo	.75	.40	.25
172	Steve Kline	.75	.40	.25
173	Hal Breeden	.75	.40	.25
174	Rich Gossage	15.00	7.50	4.50
175	Frank Robinson	8.00	4.00	2.50
176	Chuck Taylor	.75	.40	.25
177	Bill Plummer	.75	.40	.25
178	Don Rose	.75	.40	.25
179a	A's Mgr./Coaches (Jerry Adair, Vern Hoscheit, Irv Noren, Wes Stock, Dick Williams) (Coaches background brown.)	1.00	.50	.30
179b	A's Mgr./Coaches (Jerry Adair, Vern Hoscheit, Irv Noren, Wes Stock, Dick Williams) (Coaches background orange.)	1.00	.50	.30
180	Fergie Jenkins	5.00	2.50	1.25
181	Jack Brohamer	.75	.40	.25
182	Mike Caldwell	.75	.40	.25
183	Don Buford	.75	.40	.25
184	Jerry Koosman	1.00	.50	.30
185	Jim Wynn	.75	.40	.25
186	Bill Fahey	.75	.40	.25
187	Luke Walker	.75	.40	.25
188	Cookie Rojas	.75	.40	.25
189	Greg Luzinski	1.50	.70	.45
190	Bob Gibson	8.00	4.00	2.00
191	Detroit Tigers Team	2.00	1.00	.60
192	Pat Jarvis	.75	.40	.25
193	Carlton Fisk	10.00	5.00	2.50
194	Jorge Orta	.75	.40	.25
195	Clay Carroll	.75	.40	.25
196	Ken McMullen	.75	.40	.25
197	Ed Goodson	.75	.40	.25
198	Horace Clarke	.75	.40	.25
199	Bert Blyleven	1.50	.70	.45
200	Billy Williams	5.00	2.50	1.50
201	A.L. Playoffs (Hendrick Scores Winning Run.)	1.00	.50	.30
202	N.L. Playoffs (Foster's Run Decides It.)	1.00	.50	.30
203	World Series Game 1 (Tenace The Menace.)	1.00	.50	.30
204	World Series Game 2 (A's Make It Two Straight.)	1.00	.50	.30
205	World Series Game 3 (Reds Win Squeeker.)	1.00	.50	.30
206	World Series Game 4 (Tenace Singles In Ninth.)	1.00	.50	.30
207	World Series Game 5 (Odom Out At Plate.)	1.00	.50	.30
208	World Series Game 6 (Reds' Slugging Ties Series.)	4.00	2.00	1.25
209	World Series Game 7 (Campy Starts Winning Rally.)	1.00	.50	.30
210	A's Win! (World Champions.)	1.50	.70	.45
211	Balor Moore	.75	.40	.25
212	Joe Lahoud	.75	.40	.25
213	Steve Garvey	3.00	1.50	.90
214	Dave Hamilton	.75	.40	.25
215	Dusty Baker	1.00	.50	.30
216	Toby Harrah	.75	.40	.25
217	Don Wilson	.75	.40	.25
218	Aurelio Rodriguez	.75	.40	.25
219	St. Louis Cardinals Team	2.00	1.00	.60
220	Nolan Ryan	36.00	18.00	10.00
221	Fred Kendall	.75	.40	.25
222	Rob Gardner	.75	.40	.25
223	Bud Harrelson	.75	.40	.25
224	Bill Lee	.75	.40	.25
225	Al Oliver	1.00	.50	.30
226	Ray Fosse	.75	.40	.25
227	Wayne Twitchell	.75	.40	.25
228	Bobby Darwin	.75	.40	.25
229	Roric Harrison	.75	.40	.25
230	Joe Morgan	5.00	2.50	1.25
231	Bill Parsons	.75	.40	.25
232	Ken Singleton	.75	.40	.25
233	Ed Kirkpatrick	.75	.40	.25
234	Bill North	.75	.40	.25
235	Jim Hunter	3.00	1.50	.90
236	Tito Fuentes	.75	.40	.25
237a	Braves Mgr./Coaches (Lew Burdette, Jim Busby, Roy Hartsfield, Eddie Mathews, Ken Silvestri) (Coaches background brown.)	1.00	.50	.30
237b	Braves Mgr./Coaches (Lew Burdette, Jim Busby, Roy Hartsfield, Eddie Mathews, Ken Silvestri) (Coaches background orange.)	1.00	.50	.30
238	Tony Muser	.75	.40	.25
239	Pete Richert	.75	.40	.25
240	Bobby Murcer	1.00	.50	.30
241	Dwain Anderson	.75	.40	.25
242	George Culver	.75	.40	.25
243	California Angels Team	2.00	1.00	.60
244	Ed Acosta	.75	.40	.25
245	Carl Yastrzemski	15.00	7.50	4.50
246	Ken Sanders	.75	.40	.25
247	Del Unser	.75	.40	.25
248	Jerry Johnson	.75	.40	.25
249	Larry Biittner	.75	.40	.25
250	Manny Sanguillen	.75	.40	.25
251	Roger Nelson	.75	.40	.25
252a	Giants Mgr./Coaches (Joe Amalfitano, Charlie Fox, Andy Gilbert, Don McMahon, John McNamara) (Coaches background brown.)	.75	.40	.25
252b	Giants Mgr./Coaches (Joe Amalfitano, Charlie Fox, Andy Gilbert, Don McMahon, John McNamara) (Coaches background orange.)	.75	.40	.25
253	Mark Belanger	.75	.40	.25
254	Bill Stoneman	.75	.40	.25
255	Reggie Jackson	13.50	6.75	4.00
256	Chris Zachary	.75	.40	.25
257a	Mets Mgr./Coaches (Yogi Berra, Roy McMillan, Joe Pignatano, Rube Walker, Eddie Yost) (Coaches background brown.)	2.00	1.00	.60
257b	Mets Mgr./Coaches (Yogi Berra, Roy McMillan, Joe Pignatano, Rube Walker, Eddie Yost) (Coaches background orange.)	2.00	1.00	.60
258	Tommy John	1.00	.50	.30
259	Jim Holt	.75	.40	.25
260	Gary Nolan	.75	.40	.25
261	Pat Kelly	.75	.40	.25
262	Jack Aker	.75	.40	.25
263	George Scott	.75	.40	.25
264	Checklist 133-264	1.00	.50	.30
265	Gene Michael	.75	.40	.25
266	Mike Lum	.75	.40	.25
267	Lloyd Allen	.75	.40	.25
268	Jerry Morales	.75	.40	.25
269	Tim McCarver	1.50	.70	.45
270	Luis Tiant	.75	.40	.25
271	Tom Hutton	.75	.40	.25
272	Ed Farmer	.75	.40	.25
273	Chris Speier	.75	.40	.25
274	Darold Knowles	.75	.40	.25
275	Tony Perez	4.00	2.00	1.00
276	Joe Lovitto	.75	.40	.25
277	Bob Miller	.75	.40	.25
278	Baltimore Orioles Team	3.00	1.50	.90
279	Mike Strahler	.75	.40	.25
280	Al Kaline	8.00	4.00	2.50
281	Mike Jorgensen	.75	.40	.25
282	Steve Hovley	.75	.40	.25
283	Ray Sadecki	.75	.40	.25
284	Glenn Borgmann	.75	.40	.25
285	Don Kessinger	.75	.40	.25
286	Frank Linzy	.75	.40	.25
287	Eddie Leon	.75	.40	.25
288	Gary Gentry	.75	.40	.25
289	Bob Oliver	.75	.40	.25
290	Cesar Cedeno	.75	.40	.25
291	Rogelio Moret	.75	.40	.25
292	Jose Cruz	.75	.40	.25
293	Bernie Allen	.75	.40	.25
294	Steve Arlin	.75	.40	.25
295	Bert Campaneris	.75	.40	.25
296	Reds Mgr./Coaches (Sparky Anderson, Alex Grammas, Ted Kluszewski, George Scherger, Larry Shepard)	2.50	1.25	.70
297	Walt Williams	.75	.40	.25
298	Ron Bryant	.75	.40	.25
299	Ted Ford	.75	.40	.25
300	Steve Carlton	10.00	5.00	2.50
301	Billy Grabarkewitz	.75	.40	.25
302	Terry Crowley	.75	.40	.25
303	Nelson Briles	.75	.40	.25
304	Duke Sims	.75	.40	.25
305	Willie Mays	35.00	17.50	10.50
306	Tom Burgmeier	.75	.40	.25
307	Boots Day	.75	.40	.25
308	Skip Lockwood	.75	.40	.25
309	Paul Popovich	.75	.40	.25
310	Dick Allen	1.50	.70	.45
311	Joe Decker	.75	.40	.25
312	Oscar Brown	.75	.40	.25
313	Jim Ray	.75	.40	.25
314	Ron Swoboda	.75	.40	.25
315	John Odom	.75	.40	.25
316	San Diego Padres Team	2.00	1.00	.60
317	Danny Cater	.75	.40	.25
318	Jim McGlothlin	.75	.40	.25
319	Jim Spencer	.75	.40	.25
320	Lou Brock	8.00	4.00	2.00
321	Rich Hinton	.75	.40	.25
322	Garry Maddox	1.00	.50	.30
323	Tigers Mgr./Coaches (Art Fowler, Billy Martin, Joe Schultz, Charlie Silvera, Dick Tracewski)	1.00	.50	.30
324	Al Downing	.75	.40	.25
325	Boog Powell	1.00	.50	.30
326	Darrell Brandon	.75	.40	.25
327	John Lowenstein	.75	.40	.25
328	Bill Bonham	.75	.40	.25
329	Ed Kranepool	.75	.40	.25
330	Rod Carew	10.00	5.00	2.50
331	Carl Morton	.75	.40	.25
332	John Felske	.75	.40	.25
333	Gene Clines	.75	.40	.25
334	Freddie Patek	.75	.40	.25
335	Bob Tolan	.75	.40	.25
336	Tom Bradley	.75	.40	.25
337	Dave Duncan	1.00	.50	.30
338	Checklist 265-396	1.00	.50	.30
339	Dick Tidrow	.75	.40	.25
340	Nate Colbert	.75	.40	.25
341	Jim Palmer (Boyhood Photo)	1.50	.70	.45
342	Sam McDowell (Boyhood Photo)	.75	.40	.25
343	Bobby Murcer (Boyhood Photo)	.75	.40	.25
344	Jim Hunter (Boyhood Photo)	1.50	.70	.45
345	Chris Speier (Boyhood Photo)	.75	.40	.25
346	Gaylord Perry (Boyhood Photo)	1.50	.70	.45
347	Kansas City Royals Team	2.00	1.00	.60
348	Rennie Stennett	.75	.40	.25
349	Dick McAuliffe	.75	.40	.25
350	Tom Seaver	10.00	5.00	3.00
351	Jimmy Stewart	.75	.40	.25
352	Don Stanhouse	.75	.40	.25
353	Steve Brye	.75	.40	.25
354	Billy Parker	.75	.40	.25
355	Mike Marshall	.75	.40	.25
356	White Sox Mgr./Coaches (Joe Lonnett, Jim Mahoney, Al Monchak, Johnny Sain, Chuck Tanner)	.75	.40	.25
357	Ross Grimsley	.75	.40	.25
358	Jim Nettles	.75	.40	.25
359	Cecil Upshaw	.75	.40	.25
360	Joe Rudi (Photo actually Gene Tenace.)	.75	.40	.25
361	Fran Healy	.75	.40	.25
362	Eddie Watt	.75	.40	.25
363	Jackie Hernandez	.75	.40	.25
364	Rick Wise	.75	.40	.25
365	Rico Petrocelli	.75	.40	.25
366	Brock Davis	.75	.40	.25
367	Burt Hooton	.75	.40	.25
368	Bill Buckner	1.00	.50	.30
369	Lerrin LaGrow	.75	.40	.25
370	Willie Stargell	6.00	3.00	1.75
371	Mike Kekich	.75	.40	.25
372	Oscar Gamble	.75	.40	.25
373	Clyde Wright	.75	.40	.25
374	Darrell Evans	1.00	.50	.30
375	Larry Dierker	.75	.40	.25
376	Frank Duffy	.75	.40	.25
377	Expos Mgr./Coaches (Dave Bristol, Larry Doby, Gene Mauch, Cal McLish, Jerry Zimmerman)	1.00	.50	.30
378	Lenny Randle	.75	.40	.25
379	Cy Acosta	.75	.40	.25
380	Johnny Bench	15.00	7.50	3.75
381	Vicente Romo	.75	.40	.25
382	Mike Hegan	.75	.40	.25
383	Diego Segui	.75	.40	.25
384	Don Baylor	3.00	1.50	.90
385	Jim Perry	.75	.40	.25
386	Don Money	.75	.40	.25
387	Jim Barr	.75	.40	.25
388	Ben Oglivie	.75	.40	.25
389	New York Mets Team	4.00	2.00	1.25
390	Mickey Lolich	.75	.40	.25
391	Lee Lacy	.75	.40	.25
392	Dick Drago	.75	.40	.25
393	Jose Cardenal	.75	.40	.25
394	Sparky Lyle	.75	.40	.25
395	Roger Metzger	.75	.40	.25
396	Grant Jackson	.75	.40	.25
397	Dave Cash	1.00	.50	.30

#	Player			
398	Rich Hand	1.00	.50	.30
399	George Foster	1.00	.50	.30
400	Gaylord Perry	5.00	2.50	1.50
401	Clyde Mashore	1.00	.50	.30
402	Jack Hiatt	1.00	.50	.30
403	Sonny Jackson	1.00	.50	.30
404	Chuck Brinkman	1.00	.50	.30
405	Cesar Tovar	1.00	.50	.30
406	Paul Lindblad	1.00	.50	.30
407	Felix Millan	1.00	.50	.30
408	Jim Colborn	1.00	.50	.30
409	Ivan Murrell	1.00	.50	.30
410	Willie McCovey	5.00	2.50	1.25
411	Ray Corbin	1.00	.50	.30
412	Manny Mota	1.00	.50	.30
413	Tom Timmermann	1.00	.50	.30
414	Ken Rudolph	1.00	.50	.30
415	Marty Pattin	1.00	.50	.30
416	Paul Schaal	1.00	.50	.30
417	Scipio Spinks	1.00	.50	.30
418	Bobby Grich	1.00	.50	.30
419	Casey Cox	1.00	.50	.30
420	Tommie Agee	1.00	.50	.30
421	Angels Mgr./Coaches (Tom Morgan, Salty Parker, Jimmie Reese, John Roseboro, Bobby Winkles)	1.50	.70	.45
422	Bob Robertson	1.00	.50	.30
423	Johnny Jeter	1.00	.50	.30
424	Denny Doyle	1.00	.50	.30
425	Alex Johnson	1.00	.50	.30
426	Dave LaRoche	1.00	.50	.30
427	Rick Auerbach	1.00	.50	.30
428	Wayne Simpson	1.00	.50	.30
429	Jim Fairey	1.00	.50	.30
430	Vida Blue	1.50	.70	.45
431	Gerry Moses	1.00	.50	.30
432	Dan Frisella	1.00	.50	.30
433	Willie Horton	1.00	.50	.30
434	San Francisco Giants Team	3.00	1.50	.90
435	Rico Carty	1.00	.50	.30
436	Jim McAndrew	1.00	.50	.30
437	John Kennedy	1.00	.50	.30
438	Enzo Hernandez	1.00	.50	.30
439	Eddie Fisher	1.00	.50	.30
440	Glenn Beckert	1.00	.50	.30
441	Gail Hopkins	1.00	.50	.30
442	Dick Dietz	1.00	.50	.30
443	Danny Thompson	1.00	.50	.30
444	Ken Brett	1.00	.50	.30
445	Ken Berry	1.00	.50	.30
446	Jerry Reuss	1.00	.50	.30
447	Joe Hague	1.00	.50	.30
448	John Hiller	1.00	.50	.30
449a	Indians Mgr./Coaches (Ken Aspromonte, Rocky Colavito, Joe Lutz, Warren Spahn) (Spahn's ear pointed.)	1.50	.70	.45
449b	Indians Mgr./Coaches (Ken Aspromonte, Rocky Colavito, Joe Lutz, Warren Spahn) (Spahn's ear round.)	2.00	1.00	.60
450	Joe Torre	3.00	1.50	.90
451	John Vukovich	1.00	.50	.30
452	Paul Casanova	1.00	.50	.30
453	Checklist 397-528	1.25	.60	.40
454	Tom Haller	1.00	.50	.30
455	Bill Melton	1.00	.50	.30
456	Dick Green	1.00	.50	.30
457	John Strohmayer	1.00	.50	.30
458	Jim Mason	1.00	.50	.30
459	Jimmy Howarth	1.00	.50	.30
460	Bill Freehan	1.00	.50	.30
461	Mike Corkins	1.00	.50	.30
462	Ron Blomberg	1.00	.50	.30
463	Ken Tatum	1.00	.50	.30
464	Chicago Cubs Team	4.00	2.00	1.25
465	Dave Giusti	1.00	.50	.30
466	Jose Arcia	1.00	.50	.30
467	Mike Ryan	1.00	.50	.30
468	Tom Griffin	1.00	.50	.30
469	Dan Monzon	1.00	.50	.30
470	Mike Cuellar	1.00	.50	.30
471	All-Time Hit Leader (Ty Cobb)	8.00	4.00	2.00
472	All-Time Grand Slam Leader (Lou Gehrig)	12.00	6.00	3.50
473	All-Time Total Base Leader (Hank Aaron)	8.00	4.00	2.00
474	All-Time RBI Leader (Babe Ruth)	15.00	7.50	3.75
475	All-Time Batting Leader (Ty Cobb)	6.00	3.00	1.50
476	All-Time Shutout Leader (Walter Johnson)	3.00	1.50	.90
477	All-Time Victory Leader (Cy Young)	3.00	1.50	.90
478	All-Time Strikeout Leader (Walter Johnson)	3.00	1.50	.90
479	Hal Lanier	1.00	.50	.30
480	Juan Marichal	6.00	3.00	1.75
481	Chicago White Sox Team	3.00	1.50	.90
482	*Rick Reuschel*	2.00	1.00	.60
483	Dal Maxvill	1.00	.50	.30
484	Ernie McAnally	1.00	.50	.30
485	Norm Cash	1.50	.70	.45
486a	Phillies Mgr./Coaches (Carroll Berringer, Billy DeMars, Danny Ozark, Ray Rippelmeyer, Bobby Wine) (Coaches background brown-red.)	1.00	.50	.30
486b	Phillies Mgr./Coaches (Carroll Beringer, Billy DeMars, Danny Ozark, Ray Rippelmeyer, Bobby Wine) (Coaches background brown.)	1.00	.50	.30
487	Bruce Dal Canton	1.00	.50	.30
488	Dave Campbell	1.00	.50	.30
489	Jeff Burroughs	1.00	.50	.30
490	Claude Osteen	1.00	.50	.30
491	Bob Montgomery	1.00	.50	.30
492	Pedro Borbon	1.00	.50	.30
493	Duffy Dyer	1.00	.50	.30
494	Rich Morales	1.00	.50	.30
495	Tommy Helms	1.00	.50	.30
496	Ray Lamb	1.00	.50	.30
497	Cardinals Mgr./Coaches (Vern Benson, George Kissell, Red Schoendienst, Barney Schultz)	1.50	.70	.45
498	Graig Nettles	1.50	.70	.45
499	Bob Moose	1.00	.50	.30
500	Oakland A's Team	4.00	2.00	1.25
501	Larry Gura	1.00	.50	.30
502	Bobby Valentine	1.00	.50	.30
503	Phil Niekro	5.00	2.50	1.50
504	Earl Williams	1.25	.60	.40
505	Bob Bailey	1.00	.50	.30
506	Bart Johnson	1.00	.50	.30
507	Darrel Chaney	1.00	.50	.30
508	Gates Brown	1.00	.50	.30
509	Jim Nash	1.00	.50	.30
510	Amos Otis	1.00	.50	.30
511	Sam McDowell	1.00	.50	.30
512	Dalton Jones	1.00	.50	.30
513	Dave Marshall	1.00	.50	.30
514	Jerry Kenney	1.00	.50	.30
515	Andy Messersmith	1.00	.50	.30
516	Danny Walton	1.00	.50	.30
517a	Pirates Mgr./Coaches (Don Leppert, Bill Mazeroski, Dave Ricketts, Bill Virdon, Mel Wright) (Coaches background brown.)	1.50	.70	.45
517b	Pirates Mgr./Coaches (Don Leppert, Bill Mazeroski, Dave Ricketts, Bill Virdon, Mel Wright) (Coaches background orange.)	1.50	.70	.45
518	Bob Veale	1.00	.50	.30
519	John Edwards	1.00	.50	.30
520	Mel Stottlemyre	1.25	.60	.40
521	Atlanta Braves Team	4.00	2.00	1.25
522	Leo Cardenas	1.00	.50	.30
523	Wayne Granger	1.00	.50	.30
524	Gene Tenace	1.00	.50	.30
525	Jim Fregosi	1.00	.50	.30
526	Ollie Brown	1.00	.50	.30
527	Dan McGinn	1.00	.50	.30
528	Paul Blair	1.00	.50	.30
529	Milt May	2.00	1.00	.60
530	Jim Kaat	4.00	2.00	1.25
531	Ron Woods	2.00	1.00	.60
532	Steve Mingori	2.00	1.00	.60
533	Larry Stahl	2.00	1.00	.60
534	Dave Lemonds	2.00	1.00	.60
535	John Callison	2.00	1.00	.60
536	Philadelphia Phillies Team	6.00	3.00	1.75
537	Bill Slayback	2.00	1.00	.60
538	Jim Hart	2.00	1.00	.60
539	Tom Murphy	2.00	1.00	.60
540	Cleon Jones	2.00	1.00	.60
541	Bob Bolin	2.00	1.00	.60
542	Pat Corrales	2.00	1.00	.60
543	Alan Foster	2.00	1.00	.60
544	Von Joshua	2.00	1.00	.60
545	Orlando Cepeda	6.00	3.00	1.50
546	Jim York	2.00	1.00	.60
547	Bobby Heise	2.00	1.00	.60
548	Don Durham	2.00	1.00	.60
549	Rangers Mgr./Coaches (Chuck Estrada, Whitey Herzog, Chuck Hiller, Jackie Moore)	4.00	2.00	1.25
550	Dave Johnson	2.00	1.00	.60
551	Mike Kilkenny	2.00	1.00	.60
552	J.C. Martin	2.00	1.00	.60
553	Mickey Scott	2.00	1.00	.60
554	Dave Concepcion	2.00	1.00	.60
555	Bill Hands	2.00	1.00	.60
556	New York Yankees Team	8.00	4.00	2.00
557	Bernie Williams	2.00	1.00	.60
558	Jerry May	2.00	1.00	.60
559	Barry Lersch	2.00	1.00	.60
560	Frank Howard	3.00	1.50	.90
561	Jim Geddes	2.00	1.00	.60
562	Wayne Garrett	2.00	1.00	.60
563	Larry Haney	2.00	1.00	.60
564	Mike Thompson	2.00	1.00	.60
565	Jim Hickman	2.00	1.00	.60
566	Lew Krausse	2.00	1.00	.60
567	Bob Fenwick	2.00	1.00	.60
568	Ray Newman	2.00	1.00	.60
569	Dodgers Mgr./Coaches (Red Adams, Walt Alston, Monty Basgall, Jim Gilliam, Tom Lasorda)	5.00	2.50	1.50
570	Bill Singer	2.00	1.00	.60
571	Rusty Torres	2.00	1.00	.60
572	Gary Sutherland	2.00	1.00	.60
573	Fred Beene	2.00	1.00	.60
574	Bob Didier	2.00	1.00	.60
575	Dock Ellis	2.00	1.00	.60
576	Montreal Expos Team	5.00	2.50	1.50
577	*Eric Soderholm*	2.00	1.00	.60
578	Ken Wright	2.00	1.00	.60
579	Tom Grieve	2.00	1.00	.60
580	Joe Pepitone	2.00	1.00	.60
581	Steve Kealey	2.00	1.00	.60
582	Darrell Porter	2.00	1.00	.60
583	Bill Greif	2.00	1.00	.60
584	Chris Arnold	2.00	1.00	.60
585	Joe Niekro	2.00	1.00	.60
586	Bill Sudakis	2.00	1.00	.60
587	Rich McKinney	2.00	1.00	.60
588	Checklist 529-660	15.00	7.50	4.50
589	Ken Forsch	2.00	1.00	.60
590	Deron Johnson	2.00	1.00	.60
591	Mike Hedlund	2.00	1.00	.60
592	John Boccabella	2.00	1.00	.60
593	Royals Mgr./Coaches (Galen Cisco, Harry Dunlop, Charlie Lau, Jack McKeon)	2.00	1.00	.60
594	Vic Harris	2.00	1.00	.60
595	Don Gullett	2.00	1.00	.60
596	Boston Red Sox Team	5.00	2.50	1.50
597	Mickey Rivers	2.00	1.00	.60
598	Phil Roof	2.00	1.00	.60
599	Ed Crosby	2.00	1.00	.60
600	Dave McNally	2.00	1.00	.60
601	Rookie Catchers (George Pena, Sergio Robles, Rick Stelmaszek)	3.00	1.50	.90
602	Rookie Pitchers (*Mel Behney, Ralph Garcia, Doug Rau*)	3.00	1.50	.90
603	Rookie Third Basemen (*Terry Hughes, Bill McNulty, Ken Reitz*)	3.00	1.50	.90
604	Rookie Pitchers (Jesse Jefferson, Dennis O'Toole, Bob Strampe)	3.00	1.50	.90
605	Rookie First Basemen (Pat Bourque, **Enos Cabell**, Gonzalo Marquez)	3.00	1.50	.90
606	Rookie Outfielders (**Gary Matthews**, Tom Paciorek, Jorge Roque)	4.00	2.00	1.25
607	Rookie Shortstops (Ray Busse, Pepe Frias, Mario Guerrero)	3.00	1.50	.90
608	Rookie Pitchers (*Steve Busby, Dick Colpaert, George Medich*)	3.00	1.50	.90
609	Rookie Second Basemen (*Larvell Blanks, Pedro Garcia, Dave Lopes*)	5.00	2.50	1.50
610	Rookie Pitchers (Jimmy Freeman, Charlie Hough, Hank Webb)	4.00	2.00	1.25
611	Rookie Outfielders (Rich Coggins, Jim Wohlford, Richie Zisk)	3.00	1.50	.90
612	Rookie Pitchers (Steve Lawson, Bob Reynolds, Brent Strom)	3.00	1.50	.90
613	Rookie Catchers (**Bob Boone**, Mike Ivie, Skip Jutze)	12.00	6.00	3.00
614	Rookie Outfielders (**Al Bumbry, Dwight Evans**, Charlie Spikes)	20.00	10.00	6.00
615	Rookie Third Basemen (*Ron Cey, John Hilton, Mike Schmidt*)	130.00	65.00	40.00
616	Rookie Pitchers (Norm Angelini, Steve Blateric, Mike Garman)	3.00	1.50	.90
617	Rich Chiles	2.00	1.00	.60
618	Andy Etchebarren	2.00	1.00	.60
619	Billy Wilson	2.00	1.00	.60
620	Tommy Harper	2.00	1.00	.60
621	Joe Ferguson	2.00	1.00	.60
622	Larry Hisle	2.00	1.00	.60
623	Steve Renko	2.00	1.00	.60
624	Astros Mgr./Coaches (Leo Durocher, Preston Gomez, Grady Hatton, Hub Kittle, Jim Owens)	3.00	1.50	.90
625	Angel Mangual	2.00	1.00	.60
626	Bob Barton	2.00	1.00	.60
627	Luis Alvarado	2.00	1.00	.60
628	Jim Slaton	2.00	1.00	.60
629	Cleveland Indians Team	5.00	2.50	1.50
630	Denny McLain	6.00	3.00	1.75
631	Tom Matchick	2.00	1.00	.60
632	Dick Selma	2.00	1.00	.60
633	Ike Brown	2.00	1.00	.60
634	Alan Closter	2.00	1.00	.60
635	Gene Alley	2.00	1.00	.60
636	Rick Clark	2.00	1.00	.60
637	Norm Miller	2.00	1.00	.60
638	Ken Reynolds	2.00	1.00	.60
639	Willie Crawford	2.00	1.00	.60
640	Dick Bosman	2.00	1.00	.60
641	Cincinnati Reds Team	5.00	2.50	1.25
642	Jose Laboy	2.00	1.00	.60
643	Al Fitzmorris	2.00	1.00	.60
644	Jack Heidemann	2.00	1.00	.60
645	Bob Locker	2.00	1.00	.60
646	Brewers Mgr./Coaches (Del Crandall, Harvey Kuenn, Joe Nossek, Bob Shaw, Jim Walton)	2.00	1.00	.60
647	George Stone	2.00	1.00	.60
648	Tom Egan	2.00	1.00	.60
649	Rich Folkers	2.00	1.00	.60
650	Felipe Alou	4.00	2.00	1.25
651	Don Carrithers	2.00	1.00	.60
652	Ted Kubiak	2.00	1.00	.60
653	Joe Hoerner	2.00	1.00	.60
654	Minnesota Twins Team	4.00	2.00	1.25
655	Clay Kirby	2.00	1.00	.60
656	John Ellis	2.00	1.00	.60
657	Bob Johnson	2.00	1.00	.60
658	Elliott Maddox	2.00	1.00	.60
659	Jose Pagan	2.00	1.00	.60
660	Fred Scherman	2.00	1.00	.60

1973 Topps Bubble Gum Lids

A bit out of the ordinary, the Topps Candy Lids were the top of a product called "Baseball Stars Bubble Gum." The bo...

tom (inside) of the lids carry a color photo of a player with a ribbon containing the name, position and team. The lids are 1-7/8" in diameter. A total of 55 different lids were made, featuring most of the stars of the day.

		NM	EX	VG
Complete Set (55):		750.00	375.00	225.00
Common Player:		6.00	3.00	1.75
Unopened Tub:		135.00	.00	.00
(1)	Hank Aaron	60.00	30.00	18.00
(2)	Dick Allen	7.50	3.75	2.25
(3)	Dusty Baker	6.00	3.00	1.75
(4)	Sal Bando	6.00	3.00	1.75
(5)	Johnny Bench	30.00	15.00	9.00
(6)	Bobby Bonds	6.00	3.00	1.75
(7)	Dick Bosman	6.00	3.00	1.75
(8)	Lou Brock	15.00	7.50	4.50
(9)	Rod Carew	25.00	12.50	7.50
(10)	Steve Carlton	25.00	12.50	7.50
(11)	Nate Colbert	6.00	3.00	1.75
(12)	Willie Davis	6.00	3.00	1.75
(13)	Larry Dierker	6.00	3.00	1.75
(14)	Mike Epstein	6.00	3.00	1.75
(15)	Carlton Fisk	15.00	7.50	4.50
(16)	Tim Foli	6.00	3.00	1.75
(17)	Ray Fosse	6.00	3.00	1.75
(18)	Bill Freehan	6.00	3.00	1.75
(19)	Bob Gibson	25.00	12.50	7.50
(20)	Bud Harrelson	6.00	3.00	1.75
(21)	Catfish Hunter	15.00	7.50	4.50
(22)	Reggie Jackson	40.00	20.00	12.00
(23)	Fergie Jenkins	15.00	7.50	4.50
(24)	Al Kaline	30.00	15.00	9.00
(25)	Harmon Killebrew	30.00	15.00	9.00
(26)	Clay Kirby	6.00	3.00	1.75
(27)	Mickey Lolich	6.00	3.00	1.75
(28)	Greg Luzinski	6.00	3.00	1.75
(29)	Mike Marshall	6.00	3.00	1.75
(30)	Lee May	6.00	3.00	1.75
(31)	John Mayberry	6.00	3.00	1.75
(32)	Willie Mays	60.00	30.00	18.00
(33)	Willie McCovey	15.00	7.50	4.50
(34)	Thurman Munson	25.00	12.50	7.50
(35)	Bobby Murcer	12.50	6.25	3.75
(36)	Gary Nolan	6.00	3.00	1.75
(37)	Amos Otis	6.00	3.00	1.75
(38)	Jim Palmer	15.00	7.50	4.50
(39)	Gaylord Perry	15.00	7.50	4.50
(40)	Lou Piniella	7.50	3.75	2.25
(41)	Brooks Robinson	30.00	15.00	9.00
(42)	Frank Robinson	30.00	15.00	9.00
(43)	Ellie Rodriguez	6.00	3.00	1.75
(44)	Pete Rose	50.00	25.00	15.00
(45)	Nolan Ryan	200.00	100.00	60.00
(46)	Manny Sanguillen	6.00	3.00	1.75
(47)	George Scott	6.00	3.00	1.75
(48)	Tom Seaver	25.00	12.50	7.50
(49)	Chris Speier	6.00	3.00	1.75
(50)	Willie Stargell	15.00	7.50	4.50
(51)	Don Sutton	15.00	7.50	4.50
(52)	Joe Torre	7.50	3.75	2.25
(53)	Billy Williams	15.00	7.50	4.50
(54)	Wilbur Wood	6.00	3.00	1.75
(55)	Carl Yastrzemski	35.00	17.50	10.50

1973 Topps Comics

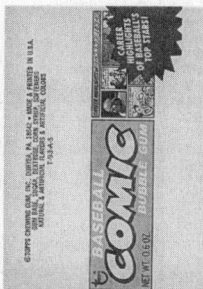

Strictly a test issue, if ever publicly distributed at all (most are found without any folding which would have occurred had they actually been used to wrap a piece of bubblegum), the 24 players in the 1973 Topps Comics issue appear on 4-5/8" x 3-7/16" waxed paper wrappers. The inside of the wrapper combines a color photo and facsimile autograph with a comic-style presentation of the player's career highlights. The Comics share a checklist with the 1973 Topps Pin-Ups, virtually all star players.

		NM	EX	VG
Complete Set (24):		15,000	7,500	4,500
Common Player:		200.00	100.00	60.00
1)	Hank Aaron	1,100	550.00	330.00
2)	Dick Allen	375.00	185.00	110.00
3)	Johnny Bench	675.00	335.00	200.00
4)	Steve Carlton	550.00	275.00	165.00

(5)	Nate Colbert	200.00	100.00	60.00
(6)	Willie Davis	200.00	100.00	60.00
(7)	Mike Epstein	200.00	100.00	60.00
(8)	Reggie Jackson	1,100	550.00	330.00
(9)	Harmon Killebrew	550.00	275.00	165.00
(10)	Mickey Lolich	200.00	100.00	60.00
(11)	Mike Marshall	200.00	100.00	60.00
(12)	Lee May	200.00	100.00	60.00
(13)	Willie McCovey	550.00	275.00	165.00
(14)	Bobby Murcer	300.00	150.00	90.00
(15)	Gaylord Perry	525.00	260.00	155.00
(16)	Lou Piniella	300.00	150.00	90.00
(17)	Brooks Robinson	900.00	450.00	270.00
(18)	Nolan Ryan	3,500	1,750	1,000
(19)	George Scott	200.00	100.00	60.00
(20)	Tom Seaver	750.00	375.00	225.00
(21)	Willie Stargell	550.00	275.00	165.00
(22)	Joe Torre	300.00	150.00	90.00
(23)	Billy Williams	525.00	260.00	155.00
(24)	Carl Yastrzemski	1,100	550.00	330.00

1973 Topps Pin-Ups

Another test issue of 1973, the 24 Topps Pin-Ups include the same basic format and the same checklist of star-caliber players as the Comics test issue of the same year. The 3-7/16" x 4-5/8" Pin-Ups are actually the inside of a wrapper for a piece of bubblegum. The color player photo features a decorative lozenge inserted at bottom with the player's name, team and position. There is also a facsimile autograph. Curiously, neither the Pin-Ups nor the Comics of 1973 bear team logos on the players' caps.

		NM	EX	VG
Complete Set (24):		12,000	6,000	4,000
Common Player:		350.00	175.00	100.00
(1)	Hank Aaron	1,100	550.00	320.00
(2)	Dick Allen	400.00	200.00	125.00
(3)	Johnny Bench	800.00	400.00	250.00
(4)	Steve Carlton	700.00	350.00	200.00
(5)	Nate Colbert	350.00	175.00	100.00
(6)	Willie Davis	350.00	175.00	100.00
(7)	Mike Epstein	350.00	175.00	100.00
(8)	Reggie Jackson	1,1000	550.00	320.00
(9)	Harmon Killebrew	750.00	375.00	225.00
(10)	Mickey Lolich	350.00	175.00	100.00
(11)	Mike Marshall	350.00	175.00	100.00
(12)	Lee May	350.00	175.00	100.00
(13)	Willie McCovey	750.00	375.00	225.00
(14)	Bobby Murcer	400.00	200.00	125.00
(15)	Gaylord Perry	700.00	350.00	200.00
(16)	Lou Piniella	400.00	200.00	125.00
(17)	Brooks Robinson	800.00	400.00	250.00
(18)	Nolan Ryan	1,200	600.00	400.00
(19)	George Scott	350.00	175.00	100.00
(20)	Tom Seaver	800.00	400.00	250.00
(21)	Willie Stargell	750.00	375.00	225.00
(22)	Joe Torre	375.00	185.00	120.00
(23)	Billy Williams	750.00	375.00	225.00
(24)	Carl Yastrzemski	875.00	440.00	275.00

1973 Topps Team Checklists

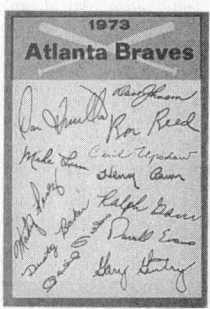

This is a 24-card unnumbered set of 2-1/2" x 3-1/2" cards that is generally believed to have been included with the high-numbered series in 1973, while also being made available in a mail-in offer. The front of the cards have the team name at the top and a white panel with various facsimile autographs takes up the rest of the space except for a blue border. Backs feature the team name and checklist. Relatively scarce, these somewhat mysterious cards are not included by many in their collections despite their obvious relationship to the regular set.

		NM	EX	VG
Complete Set (24):		200.00	100.00	60.00
Common Checklist:		7.00	3.50	2.00
(1)	Atlanta Braves	7.00	3.50	2.00
(2)	Baltimore Orioles	7.00	3.50	2.00
(3)	Boston Red Sox	10.00	5.00	3.00

(4)	California Angels	7.00	3.50	2.00
(5)	Chicago Cubs	7.00	3.50	2.00
(6)	Chicago White Sox	7.00	3.50	2.00
(7)	Cincinnati Reds	10.00	5.00	3.00
(8)	Cleveland Indians	7.00	3.50	2.00
(9)	Detroit Tigers	12.00	6.00	4.00
(10)	Houston Astros	7.00	3.50	2.00
(11)	Kansas City Royals	7.00	3.50	2.00
(12)	Los Angeles Dodgers	7.00	3.50	2.00
(13)	Milwaukee Brewers	7.00	3.50	2.00
(14)	Minnesota Twins	7.00	3.50	2.00
(15)	Montreal Expos	7.00	3.50	2.00
(16)	New York Mets	12.00	6.00	4.00
(17)	New York Yankees	1200	6.00	4.00
(18)	Oakland A's	12.00	6.00	4.00
(19)	Philadelphia Phillies	7.00	3.50	2.00
(20)	Pittsburgh Pirates	7.00	3.50	2.00
(21)	St. Louis Cardinals	7.00	3.50	2.00
(22)	San Diego Padres	7.00	3.50	2.00
(23)	San Francisco Giants	7.00	3.50	2.00
(24)	Texas Rangers	7.00	3.50	2.00

1973 Topps 1953 Reprints

Long before Topps reprinted virtually the entire 1953 set in its "Archives" program in 1991, selected cards from the '53 set had been reprinted in a rare eight-card issue. Some sources say the cards were produced as table favors at a Topps banquet, while at least one contemporary hobby periodical said they were sold on a test-issue basis in Brooklyn. It was said only 300 of the sets were made. Unlike the original cards in 2-5/8" x 3-3/4" format, the test issue cards are modern standard 2-1/2" x 3-1/2". Three of the players in the issue were misidentified. Card backs feature a career summary written as though in 1953; the backs are formatted differently than original 1953 Topps cards and are printed in black-and-white.

		NM	EX	VG
Complete Set (8):		750.00	375.00	225.00
Common Player:		35.00	17.50	10.00
1	Satchell Paige	225.00	110.00	65.00
2	Jackie Robinson	300.00	150.00	90.00
3	Carl Furillo (Picture actually Bill Antonello.)	50.00	25.00	15.00
4	Al Rosen (Picture actually Jim Fridley.)	35.00	17.50	10.00
5	Hal Newhouser	40.00	20.00	12.00
6	Clyde McCullough (Picture actually Vic Janowicz.)	35.00	17.50	10.00
7	"Peanuts" Lowrey	35.00	17.50	10.00
8	Johnny Mize	85.00	42.50	25.00

1974 Topps

Issued all at once at the beginning of the year, rather than by series throughout the baseball season as had been done since 1952, this 660-card '74 Topps set features a famous group of error cards. At the time the cards were printed, it was uncertain whether the San Diego Padres would move to Washington, D.C., and by the time a decision was made some Padres cards had appeared with a "Washington, Nat'l League" designation on the front. A total of 15 cards were affected, and those with the Washington designation bring prices well in excess of regular cards of the same players (the Washington variations are not included in the complete set prices quoted below). The 2-1/2" x 3-1/2" cards feature color photos (frequently game-action shots) along with the player's name, team and position. Specialty cards abound, starting with a Hank Aaron tribute and running through the usual managers, statistical leaders, playoff and World Series highlights, multi-player rookie cards and All-Stars.

	NM	EX	VG
Unopened Factory Set (704):	825.00	420.00	250.00
Complete Set (660):	275.00	135.00	82.50
Common Player:	.40	.20	.10

Wax Pack (2):	9.00		
Wax Pack (8+1 - B.T.C.):	50.00		
Wax Box (36):	2,000		
Wax Pack (12+1 - B.T.C.):	75.00		
Wax Box (24):	1,875		
Cello Pack (22):	115.00		
Rack Pack: (42):	250.00		
Vending Box (500):	925.00		

#	Player			
1	Hank Aaron (All-Time Home Run King)	50.00	25.00	15.00
2	Hank Aaron (Aaron Special 1954-57)	10.00	5.00	3.00
3	Hank Aaron (Aaron Special 1958-61)	10.00	5.00	3.00
4	Hank Aaron (Aaron Special 1962-65)	10.00	5.00	3.00
5	Hank Aaron (Aaron Special 1966-69)	10.00	5.00	3.00
6	Hank Aaron (Aaron Special 1970-73)	10.00	5.00	3.00
7	Jim Hunter	4.00	2.00	1.25
8	George Theodore	.40	.20	.10
9	Mickey Lolich	.40	.20	.09
10	Johnny Bench	20.00	10.00	6.00
11	Jim Bibby	.40	.20	.10
12	Dave May	.40	.20	.10
13	Tom Hilgendorf	.40	.20	.10
14	Paul Popovich	.40	.20	.10
15	Joe Torre	2.00	1.00	.60
16	Baltimore Orioles Team	2.00	1.00	.60
17	Doug Bird	.40	.20	.10
18	Gary Thomasson	.40	.20	.10
19	Gerry Moses	.40	.20	.10
20	Nolan Ryan	30.00	15.00	9.00
21	Bob Gallagher	.40	.20	.10
22	Cy Acosta	.40	.20	.10
23	Craig Robinson	.40	.20	.10
24	John Hiller	.40	.20	.10
25	Ken Singleton	.40	.20	.10
26	*Bill Campbell*	.40	.20	.10
27	George Scott	.40	.20	.10
28	Manny Sanguillen	.40	.20	.10
29	Phil Niekro	4.00	2.00	1.25
30	Bobby Bonds	.40	.20	.09
31	Astros Mgr./Coaches (Roger Craig, Preston Gomez, Grady Hatton, Hub Kittle, Bob Lillis)	.40	.20	.09
32a	John Grubb (Washington)	3.00	1.50	.90
32b	John Grubb (San Diego)	.40	.20	.10
33	Don Newhauser	.40	.20	.10
34	Andy Kosco	.40	.20	.10
35	Gaylord Perry	4.00	2.00	1.25
36	St. Louis Cardinals Team	2.00	1.00	.60
37	Dave Sells	.40	.20	.10
38	Don Kessinger	.40	.20	.10
39	Ken Suarez	.40	.20	.10
40	Jim Palmer	6.00	3.00	1.75
41	Bobby Floyd	.40	.20	.10
42	Claude Osteen	.40	.20	.10
43	Jim Wynn	.40	.20	.10
44	Mel Stottlemyre	.75	.40	.25
45	Dave Johnson	.40	.20	.10
46	Pat Kelly	.40	.20	.10
47	*Dick Ruthven*	.40	.20	.10
48	Dick Sharon	.40	.20	.10
49	Steve Renko	.40	.20	.10
50	Rod Carew	6.00	3.00	1.75
51	Bobby Heise	.40	.20	.10
52	Al Oliver	.50	.25	.15
53a	Fred Kendall (Washington)	3.00	1.50	.90
53b	Fred Kendall (San Diego)	.40	.20	.10
54	*Elias Sosa*	.40	.20	.10
55	Frank Robinson	8.00	4.00	2.50
56	New York Mets Team	1.50	.70	.45
57	Darold Knowles	.40	.20	.10
58	Charlie Spikes	.40	.20	.10
59	Ross Grimsley	.40	.20	.10
60	Lou Brock	8.00	4.00	2.50
61	Luis Aparicio	4.00	2.00	1.25
62	Bob Locker	.40	.20	.10
63	Bill Sudakis	.40	.20	.10
64	Doug Rau	.40	.20	.10
65	Amos Otis	.40	.20	.10
66	Sparky Lyle	.40	.20	.10
67	Tommy Helms	.40	.20	.10
68	Grant Jackson	.40	.20	.10
69	Del Unser	.40	.20	.10
70	Dick Allen	.75	.40	.25
71	Danny Frisella	.40	.20	.10
72	Aurelio Rodriguez	.40	.20	.10
73	Mike Marshall	.40	.20	.10
74	Minnesota Twins Team	1.00	.50	.30
75	Jim Colborn	.40	.20	.10
76	Mickey Rivers	.40	.20	.10
77a	Rich Troedson (Washington)	3.00	1.50	.90
77b	Rich Troedson (San Diego)	.40	.20	.10
78	Giants Mgr./Coaches (Joe Amalfitano, Charlie Fox, Andy Gilbert, Don McMahon, John McNamara)	.40	.20	.10
79	Gene Tenace	.40	.20	.10
80	Tom Seaver	10.00	5.00	3.00
81	Frank Duffy	.40	.20	.10
82	Dave Giusti	.40	.20	.10
83	Orlando Cepeda	4.00	2.00	1.25
84	Rick Wise	.40	.20	.10
85	Joe Morgan	6.00	3.00	1.75
86	Joe Ferguson	.40	.20	.10
87	Fergie Jenkins	4.00	2.00	1.25
88	Freddie Patek	.40	.20	.10
89	Jackie Brown	.40	.20	.10
90	Bobby Murcer	.50	.25	.15
91	Ken Forsch	.40	.20	.10
92	Paul Blair	.40	.20	.10
93	Rod Gilbreath	.40	.20	.10
94	Detroit Tigers Team	1.00	.50	.30
95	Steve Carlton	8.00	4.00	2.50

#	Player			
96	*Jerry Hairston Sr.*	.40	.20	.10
97	Bob Bailey	.40	.20	.10
98	Bert Blyleven	.75	.40	.25
99	Brewers Mgr./Coaches (Del Crandall, Harvey Kuenn, Joe Nossek, Jim Walton, Al Widmar)	.40	.20	.10
100	Willie Stargell	8.00	4.00	2.50
101	Bobby Valentine	.40	.20	.10
102a	Bill Greif (Washington)	3.00	1.50	.90
102b	Bill Greif (San Diego)	.40	.20	.10
103	Sal Bando	.40	.20	.10
104	Ron Bryant	.40	.20	.10
105	Carlton Fisk	10.00	5.00	3.00
106	Harry Parker	.40	.20	.10
107	Alex Johnson	.40	.20	.10
108	Al Hrabosky	.40	.20	.10
109	Bob Grich	.40	.20	.10
110	Billy Williams	5.00	2.50	1.50
111	Clay Carroll	.40	.20	.10
112	Dave Lopes	.40	.20	.10
113	Dick Drago	.40	.20	.10
114	California Angels Team	1.00	.50	.30
115	Willie Horton	.40	.20	.10
116	Jerry Reuss	.40	.20	.10
117	Ron Blomberg	.40	.20	.10
118	Bill Lee	.40	.20	.10
119	Phillies Mgr./Coaches (Carroll Beringer, Bill DeMars, Danny Ozark, Ray Ripplemeyer, Bobby Wine)	.40	.20	.10
120	Wilbur Wood	.40	.20	.10
121	Larry Lintz	.40	.20	.10
122	Jim Holt	.40	.20	.10
123	Nelson Briles	.40	.20	.10
124	Bob Coluccio	.40	.20	.10
125a	Nate Colbert (Washington)	3.00	1.50	.90
125b	Nate Colbert (San Diego)	.40	.20	.10
126	Checklist 1-132	.75	.40	.25
127	Tom Paciorek	.40	.20	.10
128	John Ellis	.40	.20	.10
129	Chris Speier	.40	.20	.10
130	Reggie Jackson	15.00	7.50	4.50
131	Bob Boone	1.50	.70	.45
132	Felix Millan	.40	.20	.10
133	*David Clyde*	.40	.20	.10
134	Denis Menke	.40	.20	.10
135	Roy White	.40	.20	.10
136	Rick Reuschel	.40	.20	.10
137	Al Bumbry	.40	.20	.10
138	Ed Brinkman	.40	.20	.10
139	Aurelio Monteagudo	.40	.20	.10
140	Darrell Evans	.75	.40	.25
141	Pat Bourque	.40	.20	.10
142	Pedro Garcia	.40	.20	.10
143	Dick Woodson	.40	.20	.10
144	Dodgers Mgr./Coaches (Red Adams, Walter Alston, Monty Basgall, Jim Gilliam, Tom Lasorda)	1.00	.50	.30
145	Dock Ellis	.40	.20	.10
146	Ron Fairly	.40	.20	.10
147	Bart Johnson	.40	.20	.10
148a	Dave Hilton (Washington)	3.00	1.50	.90
148b	Dave Hilton (San Diego)	.40	.20	.10
149	Mac Scarce	.40	.20	.10
150	John Mayberry	.40	.20	.10
151	Diego Segui	.40	.20	.10
152	Oscar Gamble	.40	.20	.10
153	Jon Matlack	.40	.20	.10
154	Houston Astros Team	1.50	.70	.45
155	Bert Campaneris	.40	.20	.10
156	Randy Moffitt	.40	.20	.10
157	Vic Harris	.40	.20	.10
158	Jack Billingham	.40	.20	.10
159	Jim Ray Hart	.40	.20	.10
160	Brooks Robinson	6.00	3.00	1.75
161	*Ray Burris*	.50	.20	.10
162	Bill Freehan	.40	.20	.10
163	Ken Berry	.40	.20	.10
164	Tom House	.40	.20	.10
165	Willie Davis	.40	.20	.10
166	Royals Mgr./Coaches (Galen Cisco, Harry Dunlop, Charlie Lau, Jack McKeon)	.40	.20	.10
167	Luis Tiant	1.00	.50	.30
168	Danny Thompson	.40	.20	.10
169	*Steve Rogers*	.40	.20	.10
170	Bill Melton	.40	.20	.10
171	Eduardo Rodriguez	.40	.20	.10
172	Gene Clines	.40	.20	.10
173a	*Randy Jones* (Washington)	3.00	1.50	.90
173b	*Randy Jones* (San Diego)	.40	.20	.10
174	Bill Robinson	.40	.20	.10
175	Reggie Cleveland	.40	.20	.10
176	John Lowenstein	.40	.20	.10
177	Dave Roberts	.40	.20	.10
178	Garry Maddox	.40	.20	.10
179	Mets Mgr./Coaches (Yogi Berra, Roy McMillan, Joe Pignatano, Rube Walker, Eddie Yost)	1.50	.70	.45
180	Ken Holtzman	.40	.20	.10
181	Cesar Geronimo	.40	.20	.10
182	Lindy McDaniel	.40	.20	.10
183	Johnny Oates	.40	.20	.10
184	Texas Rangers Team	1.00	.50	.30
185	Jose Cardenal	.40	.20	.10
186	Fred Scherman	.40	.20	.10
187	Don Baylor	1.00	.50	.30
188	Rudy Meoli	.40	.20	.10
189	Jim Brewer	.40	.20	.10
190	Tony Oliva	1.50	.70	.45
191	Al Fitzmorris	.40	.20	.10
192	Mario Guerrero	.40	.20	.10
193	Tom Walker	.40	.20	.10
194	Darrell Porter	.40	.20	.10
195	Carlos May	.40	.20	.10

#	Player			
196	Jim Fregosi	.75	.40	.25
197a	Vicente Romo (Washington)	3.00	1.50	.90
197b	Vicente Romo (San Diego)	.40	.20	.10
198	Dave Cash	.40	.20	.10
199	Mike Kekich	.40	.20	.10
200	Cesar Cedeno	.40	.20	.10
201	Batting Leaders (Rod Carew, Pete Rose)	6.00	3.00	1.75
202	Home Run Leaders (Reggie Jackson, Willie Stargell)	4.00	2.00	1.25
203	RBI Leaders (Reggie Jackson, Willie Stargell)	4.00	2.00	1.25
204	Stolen Base Leaders (Lou Brock, Tommy Harper)	1.50	.70	.45
205	Victory Leaders (Ron Bryant, Wilbur Wood)	1.00	.50	.30
206	Earned Run Average Leaders (Jim Palmer, Tom Seaver)	2.00	1.00	.60
207	Strikeout Leaders (Nolan Ryan, Tom Seaver)	10.00	5.00	3.00
208	Leading Firemen (John Hiller, Mike Marshall)	1.00	.50	.30
209	Ted Sizemore	.40	.20	.10
210	Bill Singer	.40	.20	.10
211	Chicago Cubs Team	1.00	.50	.30
212	Rollie Fingers	4.00	2.00	1.25
213	Dave Rader	.40	.20	.10
214	Billy Grabarkewitz	.40	.20	.10
215	Al Kaline	8.00	4.00	2.50
216	Ray Sadecki	.40	.20	.10
217	Tim Foli	.40	.20	.10
218	Johnny Briggs	.40	.20	.10
219	Doug Griffin	.40	.20	.10
220	Don Sutton	4.00	2.00	1.25
221	White Sox Mgr./Coaches (Joe Lonnett, Jim Mahoney, Alex Monchak, Johnny Sain, Chuck Tanner)	.40	.20	.10
222	Ramon Hernandez	.40	.20	.10
223	Jeff Burroughs	.40	.20	.10
224	Roger Metzger	.40	.20	.10
225	Paul Splittorff	.40	.20	.10
226a	Washington Nat'l. Team	12.00	6.00	3.50
226b	San Diego Padres Team	2.00	1.00	.60
227	Mike Lum	.40	.20	.10
228	Ted Kubiak	.40	.20	.10
229	Fritz Peterson	.40	.20	.10
230	Tony Perez	4.00	2.00	1.25
231	Dick Tidrow	.40	.20	.10
232	Steve Brye	.40	.20	.10
233	Jim Barr	.40	.20	.10
234	John Milner	.40	.20	.10
235	Dave McNally	.40	.20	.10
236	Cardinals Mgr./Coaches (Vern Benson, George Kissell, Johnny Lewis, Red Schoendienst, Barney Schultz)	.75	.40	.25
237	Ken Brett	.40	.20	.10
238	Fran Healy	.40	.20	.10
239	Bill Russell	.40	.20	.10
240	Joe Coleman	.40	.20	.10
241a	Glenn Beckert (Washington)	3.00	1.50	.90
241b	Glenn Beckert (San Diego)	.40	.20	.10
242	Bill Gogolewski	.40	.20	.10
243	Bob Oliver	.40	.20	.10
244	Carl Morton	.40	.20	.10
245	Cleon Jones	.40	.20	.10
246	Oakland A's Team	2.00	1.00	.60
247	Rick Miller	.40	.20	.10
248	Tom Hall	.40	.20	.10
249	George Mitterwald	.40	.20	.10
250a	Willie McCovey (Washington)	20.00	10.00	6.00
250b	Willie McCovey (San Diego)	15.00	7.50	4.50
251	Graig Nettles	1.50	.70	.45
252	*Dave Parker*	8.00	4.00	2.50
253	John Boccabella	.40	.20	.10
254	Stan Bahnsen	.40	.20	.10
255	Larry Bowa	1.00	.50	.30
256	Tom Griffin	.40	.20	.10
257	Buddy Bell	.40	.20	.10
258	Jerry Morales	.40	.20	.10
259	Bob Reynolds	.40	.20	.10
260	Ted Simmons	.75	.40	.25
261	Jerry Bell	.40	.20	.10
262	Ed Kirkpatrick	.40	.20	.10
263	Checklist 133-264	1.00	.50	.30
264	Joe Rudi	.40	.20	.10
265	Tug McGraw	.40	.20	.10
266	Jim Northrup	.40	.20	.10
267	Andy Messersmith	.40	.20	.10
268	Tom Grieve	.40	.20	.10
269	Bob Johnson	.40	.20	.10
270	Ron Santo	3.00	1.50	.90
271	Bill Hands	.40	.20	.10
272	Paul Casanova	.40	.20	.10
273	Checklist 265-396	.75	.40	.25
274	Fred Beene	.40	.20	.10
275	Ron Hunt	.40	.20	.10
276	Angels Mgr./Coaches (Tom Morgan, Salty Parker, Jimmie Reese, John Roseboro, Bobby Winkles)	.40	.20	.10
277	Gary Nolan	.40	.20	.10
278	Cookie Rojas	.40	.20	.10
279	Jim Crawford	.40	.20	.10
280	Carl Yastrzemski	10.00	5.00	3.00
281	San Francisco Giants Team	1.00	.50	.30
282	Doyle Alexander	.40	.20	.10
283	Mike Schmidt	15.00	7.50	4.50
284	Dave Duncan	.40	.20	.10
285	Reggie Smith	.40	.20	.10
286	Tony Muser	.40	.20	.10
287	Clay Kirby	.40	.20	.10
288	*Gorman Thomas*	2.00	1.00	.60
289	Rick Auerbach	.40	.20	.10
290	Vida Blue	1.00	.50	.30

#	Name			
291	Don Hahn	.40	.20	.10
292	Chuck Seelbach	.40	.20	.10
293	Milt May	.40	.20	.10
294	Steve Foucault	.40	.20	.10
295	Rick Monday	.40	.20	.10
296	Ray Corbin	.40	.20	.10
297	Hal Breeden	.40	.20	.10
298	Roric Harrison	.40	.20	.10
299	Gene Michael	.40	.20	.10
300	Pete Rose	15.00	7.50	4.50
301	Bob Montgomery	.40	.20	.10
302	Rudy May	.40	.20	.10
303	George Hendrick	.40	.20	.10
304	Don Wilson	.40	.20	.10
305	Tito Fuentes	.40	.20	.10
306	Orioles Mgr./Coaches (George Bamberger, Jim Frey, Billy Hunter, George Staller, Earl Weaver)	2.00	1.00	.60
307	Luis Melendez	.40	.20	.10
308	Bruce Dal Canton	.40	.20	.10
309a	Dave Roberts (Washington)	3.00	1.50	.90
309b	Dave Roberts (San Diego)	.40	.20	.10
310	Terry Forster	.40	.20	.10
311	Jerry Grote	.40	.20	.10
312	Deron Johnson	.40	.20	.10
313	Barry Lersch	.40	.20	.10
314	Milwaukee Brewers Team	1.00	.50	.30
315	Ron Cey	.50	.25	.15
316	Jim Perry	.40	.20	.10
317	Richie Zisk	.40	.20	.10
318	Jim Merritt	.40	.20	.10
319	Randy Hundley	.40	.20	.10
320	Dusty Baker	1.00	.50	.30
321	Steve Braun	.40	.20	.10
322	Ernie McAnally	.40	.20	.10
323	Richie Scheinblum	.40	.20	.10
324	Steve Kline	.40	.20	.10
325	Tommy Harper	.40	.20	.10
326	Reds Mgr./Coaches (Sparky Anderson, Alex Grammas, Ted Kluszewski, George Scherger, Larry Shepard)	2.00	1.00	.60
327	Tom Timmermann	.40	.20	.10
328	Skip Jutze	.40	.20	.10
329	Mark Belanger	.40	.20	.10
330	Juan Marichal	4.00	2.00	1.25
331	All-Star Catchers (Johnny Bench, Carlton Fisk)	4.00	2.00	1.25
332	All-Star First Basemen (Hank Aaron, Dick Allen)	6.00	3.00	1.75
333	All-Star Second Basemen (Rod Carew, Joe Morgan)	3.00	1.50	.90
334	All-Star Third Basemen (Brooks Robinson, Ron Santo)	2.00	1.00	.60
335	All-Star Shortstops (Bert Campaneris, Chris Speier)	1.00	.50	.30
336	All-Star Left Fielders (Bobby Murcer, Pete Rose)	5.00	2.50	1.50
337	All-Star Center Fielders (Cesar Cedeno, Amos Otis)	.75	.40	.25
338	All-Star Right Fielders (Reggie Jackson, Billy Williams)	4.00	2.00	1.25
339	All-Star Pitchers (Jim Hunter, Rick Wise)	2.00	1.00	.60
340	Thurman Munson	9.00	4.50	2.75
341	*Dan Driessen*	.40	.20	.10
342	Jim Lonborg	.40	.20	.10
343	Kansas City Royals Team	1.00	.50	.30
344	Mike Caldwell	.40	.20	.10
345	Bill North	.40	.20	.10
346	Ron Reed	.40	.20	.10
347	Sandy Alomar	.40	.20	.10
348	Pete Richert	.40	.20	.10
349	John Vukovich	.40	.20	.10
350	Bob Gibson	6.00	3.00	1.75
351	Dwight Evans	1.00	.50	.30
352	Bill Stoneman	.40	.20	.10
353	Rich Coggins	.40	.20	.10
354	Cubs Mgr./Coaches (Hank Aguirre, Whitey Lockman, Jim Marshall, J.C. Martin, Al Spangler)	.40	.20	.10
355	Dave Nelson	.40	.20	.10
356	Jerry Koosman	.40	.20	.10
357	Buddy Bradford	.40	.20	.10
358	Dal Maxvill	.40	.20	.10
359	Brent Strom	.40	.20	.10
360	Greg Luzinski	1.00	.50	.30
361	Don Carrithers	.40	.20	.10
362	Hal King	.40	.20	.10
363	New York Yankees Team	2.00	1.00	.60
364a	Clarence Gaston (Washington)	6.00	3.00	1.75
364b	Clarence Gaston (San Diego)	.40	.20	.10
365	Steve Busby	.40	.20	.10
366	Larry Hisle	.40	.20	.10
367	Norm Cash	1.00	.50	.30
368	Manny Mota	.40	.20	.10
369	Paul Lindblad	.40	.20	.10
370	Bob Watson	.40	.20	.10
371	Jim Slaton	.40	.20	.10
372	Ken Reitz	.40	.20	.10
373	John Curtis	.40	.20	.10
374	Marty Perez	.40	.20	.10
375	Earl Williams	.40	.20	.10
376	Jorge Orta	.40	.20	.10
377	Ron Woods	.40	.20	.10
378	Burt Hooton	.40	.20	.10
379	Rangers Mgr./Coaches (Art Fowler, Frank Lucchesi, Billy Martin, Jackie Moore, Charlie Silvera)	.45	.25	.15
380	Bud Harrelson	.40	.20	.10
381	Charlie Sands	.40	.20	.10
382	Bob Moose	.40	.20	.10
383	Philadelphia Phillies Team	1.00	.50	.30
384	Chris Chambliss	.75	.40	.25
385	Don Gullett	.40	.20	.10
386	Gary Matthews	.40	.20	.10
387a	Rich Morales (Washington)	3.00	1.50	.90
387b	Rich Morales (San Diego)	.40	.20	.10
388	Phil Roof	.40	.20	.10
389	Gates Brown	.40	.20	.10
390	Lou Piniella	2.00	1.00	.60
391	Billy Champion	.40	.20	.10
392	Dick Green	.40	.20	.10
393	Orlando Pena	.40	.20	.10
394	Ken Henderson	.40	.20	.10
395	Doug Rader	.40	.20	.10
396	Tommy Davis	.40	.20	.10
397	George Stone	.40	.20	.10
398	Duke Sims	.40	.20	.10
399	Mike Paul	.40	.20	.10
400	Harmon Killebrew	6.00	3.00	1.75
401	Elliott Maddox	.40	.20	.10
402	Jim Rooker	.40	.20	.10
403	Red Sox Mgr./Coaches (Don Bryant, Darrell Johnson, Eddie Popowski, Lee Stange, Don Zimmer)	.40	.20	.10
404	Jim Howarth	.40	.20	.10
405	Ellie Rodriguez	.40	.20	.10
406	Steve Arlin	.40	.20	.10
407	Jim Wohlford	.40	.20	.10
408	Charlie Hough	1.00	.50	.30
409	Ike Brown	.40	.20	.10
410	Pedro Borbon	.40	.20	.10
411	Frank Baker	.40	.20	.10
412	Chuck Taylor	.40	.20	.10
413	Don Money	.40	.20	.10
414	Checklist 397-528	2.00	1.00	.60
415	Gary Gentry	.40	.20	.10
416	Chicago White Sox Team	1.00	.50	.30
417	Rich Folkers	.40	.20	.10
418	Walt Williams	.40	.20	.10
419	Wayne Twitchell	.40	.20	.10
420	Ray Fosse	.40	.20	.10
421	Dan Fife	.40	.20	.10
422	Gonzalo Marquez	.40	.20	.10
423	Fred Stanley	.40	.20	.10
424	Jim Beauchamp	.40	.20	.10
425	Pete Broberg	.40	.20	.10
426	Rennie Stennett	.40	.20	.10
427	Bobby Bolin	.40	.20	.10
428	Gary Sutherland	.40	.20	.10
429	Dick Lange	.40	.20	.10
430	Matty Alou	.40	.20	.10
431	*Gene Garber*	.40	.20	.10
432	Chris Arnold	.40	.20	.10
433	Lerrin LaGrow	.40	.20	.10
434	Ken McMullen	.40	.20	.10
435	Dave Concepcion	1.00	.50	.30
436	Don Hood	.40	.20	.10
437	Jim Lyttle	.40	.20	.10
438	Ed Herrmann	.40	.20	.10
439	Norm Miller	.40	.20	.10
440	Jim Kaat	1.50	.70	.45
441	Tom Ragland	.40	.20	.10
442	Alan Foster	.40	.20	.10
443	Tom Hutton	.40	.20	.10
444	Vic Davalillo	.40	.20	.10
445	George Medich	.40	.20	.10
446	Len Randle	.40	.20	.10
447	Twins Mgr./Coaches (Vern Morgan, Frank Quilici, Bob Rodgers, Ralph Rowe)	.40	.20	.10
448	Ron Hodges	.40	.20	.10
449	Tom McCraw	.40	.20	.10
450	Rich Hebner	.40	.20	.10
451	Tommy John	1.00	.50	.30
452	Gene Hiser	.40	.20	.10
453	Balor Moore	.40	.20	.10
454	Kurt Bevacqua	.40	.20	.10
455	Tom Bradley	.40	.20	.10
456	*Dave Winfield*	36.00	18.00	10.00
457	Chuck Goggin	.40	.20	.10
458	Jim Ray	.40	.20	.10
459	Cincinnati Reds Team	1.50	.70	.45
460	Boog Powell	1.00	.50	.30
461	John Odom	.40	.20	.10
462	Luis Alvarado	.40	.20	.10
463	Pat Dobson	.40	.20	.10
464	Jose Cruz	.40	.20	.10
465	Dick Bosman	.40	.20	.10
466	Dick Billings	.40	.20	.10
467	Winston Llenas	.40	.20	.10
468	Pepe Frias	.40	.20	.10
469	Joe Decker	.40	.20	.10
470	A.L. Playoffs (Reggie Jackson)	4.00	2.00	1.25
471	N.L. Playoffs (Jon Matlack)	.50	.25	.15
472	World Series Game 1 (Darold Knowles)	.50	.25	.15
473	World Series Game 2 (Willie Mays)	6.00	3.00	1.75
474	World Series Game 3	1.00	.50	.30
475	World Series Game 4	1.00	.50	.30
476	World Series Game 5	1.00	.50	.30
477	World Series Game 6 (Reggie Jackson)	4.00	2.00	1.25
478	World Series Game 7	1.50	.75	.45
479	A's Celebrate (Win 2nd Consecutive Championship!)	1.00	.50	.30
480	Willie Crawford	.40	.20	.10
481	Jerry Terrell	.40	.20	.10
482	Bob Didier	.40	.20	.10
483	Atlanta Braves Team	1.00	.50	.30
484	Carmen Fanzone	.40	.20	.10
485	Felipe Alou	.50	.25	.15
486	Steve Stone	.40	.20	.10
487	Ted Martinez	.40	.20	.10
488	Andy Etchebarren	.40	.20	.10
489	Pirates Mgr./Coaches (Don Leppert, Bill Mazeroski, Danny Murtaugh, Don Osborn, Bob Skinner)	.75	.40	.25
490	Vada Pinson	1.00	.50	.30
491	Roger Nelson	.40	.20	.10
492	Mike Rogodzinski	.40	.20	.10
493	Joe Hoerner	.40	.20	.10
494	Ed Goodson	.40	.20	.10
495	Dick McAuliffe	.40	.20	.10
496	Tom Murphy	.40	.20	.10
497	Bobby Mitchell	.40	.20	.10
498	Pat Corrales	.40	.20	.10
499	Rusty Torres	.40	.20	.10
500	Lee May	.75	.40	.25
501	Eddie Leon	.40	.20	.10
502	Dave LaRoche	.40	.20	.10
503	Eric Soderholm	.40	.20	.10
504	Joe Niekro	.75	.40	.25
505	Bill Buckner	.75	.40	.25
506	Ed Farmer	.40	.20	.10
507	Larry Stahl	.40	.20	.10
508	Montreal Expos Team	1.00	.50	.30
509	Jesse Jefferson	.40	.20	.10
510	Wayne Garrett	.40	.20	.10
511	Toby Harrah	.40	.20	.10
512	Joe Lahoud	.40	.20	.10
513	Jim Campanis	.40	.20	.10
514	Paul Schaal	.40	.20	.10
515	Willie Montanez	.40	.20	.10
516	Horacio Pina	.40	.20	.10
517	Mike Hegan	.40	.20	.10
518	Derrel Thomas	.40	.20	.10
519	Bill Sharp	.40	.20	.10
520	Tim McCarver	1.50	.70	.45
521	Indians Mgr./Coaches (Ken Aspromonte, Clay Bryant, Tony Pacheco)	.40	.20	.10
522	J.R. Richard	1.00	.50	.30
523	Cecil Cooper	1.00	.50	.30
524	Bill Plummer	.40	.20	.10
525	Clyde Wright	.40	.20	.10
526	Frank Tepedino	.40	.20	.10
527	Bobby Darwin	.40	.20	.10
528	Bill Bonham	.40	.20	.10
529	Horace Clarke	.40	.20	.10
530	Mickey Stanley	.40	.20	.10
531	Expos Mgr./Coaches (Dave Bristol, Larry Doby, Gene Mauch, Cal McLish, Jerry Zimmerman)	.40	.20	.10
532	Skip Lockwood	.40	.20	.10
533	Mike Phillips	.40	.20	.10
534	Eddie Watt	.40	.20	.10
535	Bob Tolan	.40	.20	.10
536	Duffy Dyer	.40	.20	.10
537	Steve Mingori	.40	.20	.10
538	Cesar Tovar	.40	.20	.10
539	Lloyd Allen	.40	.20	.10
540	Bob Robertson	.40	.20	.10
541	Cleveland Indians Team	1.00	.50	.30
542	Rich Gossage	4.00	2.00	1.25
543	Danny Cater	.40	.20	.10
544	Ron Schueler	.40	.20	.10
545	Billy Conigliaro	.40	.20	.10
546	Mike Corkins	.40	.20	.10
547	Glenn Borgmann	.40	.20	.10
548	Sonny Siebert	.40	.20	.10
549	Mike Jorgensen	.40	.20	.10
550	Sam McDowell	.40	.20	.10
551	Von Joshua	.40	.20	.10
552	Denny Doyle	.40	.20	.10
553	Jim Willoughby	.40	.20	.10
554	Tim Johnson	.40	.20	.10
555	Woodie Fryman	.40	.20	.10
556	Dave Campbell	.40	.20	.10
557	Jim McGlothlin	.40	.20	.10
558	Bill Fahey	.40	.20	.10
559	Darrel Chaney	.40	.20	.10
560	Mike Cuellar	.40	.20	.10
561	Ed Kranepool	.40	.20	.10
562	Jack Aker	.40	.20	.10
563	Hal McRae	.75	.40	.25
564	Mike Ryan	.40	.20	.10
565	Milt Wilcox	.40	.20	.10
566	Jackie Hernandez	.40	.20	.10
567	Boston Red Sox Team	1.50	.75	.45
568	Mike Torrez	.40	.20	.10
569	Rick Dempsey	.40	.20	.10
570	Ralph Garr	.40	.20	.10
571	Rich Hand	.40	.20	.10
572	Enzo Hernandez	.40	.20	.10
573	Mike Adams	.40	.20	.10
574	Bill Parsons	.40	.20	.10
575	Steve Garvey	2.00	1.00	.60
576	Scipio Spinks	.40	.20	.10
577	Mike Sadek	.40	.20	.10
578	Ralph Houk	.75	.40	.25
579	Cecil Upshaw	.40	.20	.10
580	Jim Spencer	.40	.20	.10
581	Fred Norman	.40	.20	.10
582	*Bucky Dent*	2.00	1.00	.60
583	Marty Pattin	.40	.20	.10
584	Ken Rudolph	.40	.20	.10
585	Merv Rettenmund	.40	.20	.10
586	Jack Brohamer	.40	.20	.10
587	*Larry Christenson*	.40	.20	.10
588	Hal Lanier	.40	.20	.10
589	Boots Day	.40	.20	.10
590	Rogelio Moret	.40	.20	.10
591	Sonny Jackson	.40	.20	.10
592	Ed Bane	.40	.20	.10
593	Steve Yeager	.40	.20	.10
594	Leroy Stanton	.40	.20	.10
595	Steve Blass	.40	.20	.10
596	Rookie Pitchers (Wayne Garland, Fred Holdsworth, Mark Littell, Dick Pole)	.40	.20	.10
597	Rookie Shortstops (Dave Chalk, John Gamble, Pete Mackanin, Manny Trillo)	1.00	.50	.30

598	Rookie Outfielders (*Dave Augustine, Ken Griffey, Steve Ontiveros, Jim Tyrone*)	10.00	5.00	3.00
599a	Rookie Pitchers (Ron Diorio, Dave Freisleben, Frank Riccelli, Greg Shanahan) (Freisleben- Washington)	1.00	.50	.30
599b	Rookie Pitchers (Ron Diorio, Dave Freisleben, Frank Riccelli, Greg Shanahan) (Freisleben- San Diego large print.)	5.00	2.50	1.50
599c	Rookie Pitchers (Ron Diorio, Dave Freisleben, Frank Riccelli, Greg Shanahan) (Freisleben- San Diego small print.)	5.00	2.50	1.50
600	Rookie Infielders (*Ron Cash, Jim Cox, Bill Madlock, Reggie Sanders*)	5.00	2.50	1.50
601	Rookie Outfielders (*Ed Armbrister, Rich Bladt, Brian Downing, Bake McBride*)	2.00	1.00	.60
602	Rookie Pitchers (Glenn Abbott, Rick Henninger, Craig Swan, Dan Vossler)	.75	.40	.25
603	Rookie Catchers (Barry Foote, Tom Lundstedt, Charlie Moore, Sergio Robles)	.75	.40	.25
604	Rookie Infielders (*Terry Hughes, John Knox, Andy Thornton, Frank White*)	4.00	2.00	1.25
605	Rookie Pitchers (*Vic Albury, Ken Frailing, Kevin Kobel, Frank Tanana*)	3.00	1.50	.90
606	Rookie Outfielders (Jim Fuller, Wilbur Howard, Tommy Smith, Otto Velez)	.75	.40	.25
607	Rookie Shortstops (*Leo Foster, Tom Heintzelman, Dave Rosello, Frank Taveras*)	.75	.40	.25
608a	Rookie Pitchers (Bob Apodaco, Dick Baney, John D'Acquisto, Mike Wallace) (Apodaca incorrect)	1.50	.75	.45
608b	Rookie Pitchers (Bob Apodaca, Dick Baney, John D'Acquisto, Mike Wallace) (Corrected)	.75	.40	.25
609	Rico Petrocelli	1.00	.50	.30
610	Dave Kingman	.75	.40	.25
611	Rick Stelmaszek	.40	.20	.10
612	Luke Walker	.40	.20	.10
613	Dan Monzon	.40	.20	.10
614	Adrian Devine	.40	.20	.10
615	Johnny Jeter	.40	.20	.10
616	Larry Gura	.40	.20	.10
617	Ted Ford	.40	.20	.10
618	Jim Mason	.40	.20	.10
619	Mike Anderson	.40	.20	.10
620	Al Downing	.40	.20	.10
621	Bernie Carbo	.40	.20	.10
622	Phil Gagliano	.40	.20	.10
623	Celerino Sanchez	.40	.20	.10
624	Bob Miller	.40	.20	.10
625	Ollie Brown	.40	.20	.10
626	Pittsburgh Pirates Team	1.00	.50	.30
627	Carl Taylor	.40	.20	.10
628	Ivan Murrell	.40	.20	.10
629	Rusty Staub	.75	.40	.25
630	Tommie Agee	.40	.20	.10
631	Steve Barber	.40	.20	.10
632	George Culver	.40	.20	.10
633	Dave Hamilton	.40	.20	.10
634	Braves Mgr./Coaches (Jim Busby, Eddie Mathews, Connie Ryan, Ken Silvestri, Herm Starrette)	2.00	1.00	.60
635	John Edwards	.40	.20	.10
636	Dave Goltz	.40	.20	.10
637	Checklist 529-660	1.00	.50	.30
638	Ken Sanders	.40	.20	.10
639	Joe Lovitto	.40	.20	.10
640	Milt Pappas	.40	.20	.10
641	Chuck Brinkman	.40	.20	.10
642	Terry Harmon	.40	.20	.10
643	Los Angeles Dodgers Team	2.50	1.25	.75
644	Wayne Granger	.40	.20	.10
645	Ken Boswell	.40	.20	.10
646	George Foster	.75	.40	.25
647	*Juan Beniquez*	.40	.20	.10
648	Terry Crowley	.40	.20	.10
649	Fernando Gonzalez	.40	.20	.10
650	Mike Epstein	.40	.20	.10
651	Leron Lee	.40	.20	.10
652	Gail Hopkins	.40	.20	.10
653	Bob Stinson	.40	.20	.10
654a	Jesus Alou (No position.)	4.00	2.00	1.25
654b	Jesus Alou ("Outfield")	.40	.20	.10
655	Mike Tyson	.40	.20	.10
656	Adrian Garrett	.40	.20	.10
657	Jim Shellenback	.40	.20	.10
658	Lee Lacy	.40	.20	.10
659	Joe Lis	.40	.20	.10
660	Larry Dierker	1.50	.70	.45

1974 Topps Traded

Appearing late in the season, these 2-1/2" x 3-1/2" cards share the format of the regular-issue Topps cards. The major change is a large yellow panel with the word "Traded" in red, added below the player photo. Backs feature a "Baseball News" design that contains the details of the trade. Card numbers correspond to the player's regular card number in 1974

except that the suffix "T" is added. The set consists of 43 player cards and a checklist. In most cases, Topps did not obtain pictures of the players in their new uniforms. Instead, the Topps artists simply provided the needed changes to existing photos.

		NM	EX	VG
Complete Set (44):		15.00	7.50	4.50
Common Player:		.50	.25	.15
23T	Craig Robinson	.50	.25	.15
42T	Claude Osteen	.50	.25	.15
43T	Jim Wynn	.50	.25	.15
51T	Bobby Heise	.50	.25	.15
59T	Ross Grimsley	.50	.25	.15
62T	Bob Locker	.50	.25	.15
63T	Bill Sudakis	.50	.25	.15
73T	Mike Marshall	.50	.25	.15
123T	Nelson Briles	.50	.25	.15
139T	Aurelio Monteagudo	.50	.25	.15
151T	Diego Segui	.50	.25	.15
165T	Willie Davis	.50	.25	.15
175T	Reggie Cleveland	.50	.25	.15
182T	Lindy McDaniel	.50	.25	.15
186T	Fred Scherman	.50	.25	.15
249T	George Mitterwald	.50	.25	.15
262T	Ed Kirkpatrick	.50	.25	.15
269T	Bob Johnson	.50	.25	.15
270T	Ron Santo	3.00	1.50	.90
313T	Barry Lersch	.50	.25	.15
319T	Randy Hundley	.50	.25	.15
330T	Juan Marichal	4.00	2.00	1.25
348T	Pete Richert	.50	.25	.15
373T	John Curtis	.50	.25	.15
390T	Lou Piniella	2.00	1.00	.60
428T	Gary Sutherland	.50	.25	.15
454T	Kurt Bevacqua	.50	.25	.15
458T	Jim Ray	.50	.25	.15
485T	Felipe Alou	.75	.40	.25
486T	Steve Stone	.75	.40	.25
496T	Tom Murphy	.50	.25	.15
516T	Horacio Pina	.50	.25	.15
534T	Eddie Watt	.50	.25	.15
538T	Cesar Tovar	.50	.25	.15
544T	Ron Schueler	.50	.25	.15
579T	Cecil Upshaw	.50	.25	.15
585T	Merv Rettenmund	.50	.25	.15
612T	Luke Walker	.50	.25	.15
616T	Larry Gura	.50	.25	.15
618T	Jim Mason	.50	.25	.15
630T	Tommie Agee	.50	.25	.15
648T	Terry Crowley	.50	.25	.15
649T	Fernando Gonzalez	.50	.25	.15
----	Traded Checklist	.50	.25	.15

1974 Topps Action Emblem Cloth Stickers

This enigmatic Topps test issue has never found favor with collectors because no actual ballplayers are pictured. In fact, official team logos are not used either, negating the necessity of licensing from either Major League Baseball or the Players Association. The 2-1/2" x 3-1/2" cloth stickers were sold with a rub-off baseball game card in a Topps white test wrapper with a sticker describing them as "Topps Baseball Action Emblems Cloth Stickers." Each sticker features a generic ballplayer on front with a city (not team) name. At bottom is a pennant with another major league city named and a generic baseball symbol at its left. Backs are blank. This issue can be found in either a cloth sticker version or cardboard version. The cardboard pieces are worth about 4X the cloth type.

		NM	EX	VG
Complete Set (24):		900.00	450.00	275.00
Common Sticker:		40.00	20.00	12.00
Wax Pack:		75.00		
Cardboard: 4X				
(1)	Atlanta/Baltimore	40.00	20.00	12.00
(2)	Baltimore/Montreal	40.00	20.00	12.00
(3)	Boston/Oakland	40.00	20.00	12.00
(4)	California/St. Louis	40.00	20.00	12.00
(5)	Chicago/Houston	40.00	20.00	12.00
(6)	Chicago/Pittsburgh	40.00	20.00	12.00
(7)	Cincinnati/Minnesota	40.00	20.00	12.00
(8)	Cleveland/San Diego	40.00	20.00	12.00
(9)	Detroit/New York	40.00	20.00	12.00
(10)	Houston/Chicago	40.00	20.00	12.00
(11)	Kansas City/Philadelphia	40.00	20.00	12.00
(12)	Los Angeles/Milwaukee	40.00	20.00	12.00
(13)	Milwaukee/New York	40.00	20.00	12.00
(14)	Minnesota/California	40.00	20.00	12.00
(15)	Montreal/San Francisco	40.00	20.00	12.00
(16)	New York/Cincinnati	40.00	20.00	12.00
(17)	New York/Texas	40.00	20.00	12.00
(18)	Oakland/Boston	40.00	20.00	12.00
(19)	Philadelphia/Los Angeles	40.00	20.00	12.00
(20)	Pittsburgh/Cleveland	40.00	20.00	12.00
(21)	St. Louis/Kansas City	40.00	20.00	12.00
(22)	San Diego/Detroit	40.00	20.00	12.00
(23)	San Francisco/Chicago	40.00	20.00	12.00
(24)	Texas/Atlanta	40.00	20.00	12.00

1974 Topps (Deckle Edge) Photos

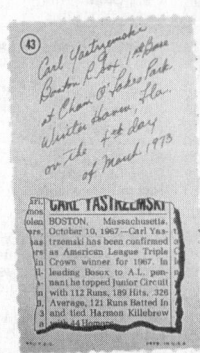

These borderless 2-7/8" x 5" cards feature a black-and-white photograph with a blue facsimile autograph on the front. The backs have in handwritten script the player's name, team, position and the date and location of the picture. Below is a mock newspaper clipping providing a detail from the player's career. Backs can be found in either gray or white (somewhat scarcer). The cards take their names from their specially cut edges which give them a scalloped appearance. The 72-card set was a test issue and received rather limited distribution around Massachusetts. The cards were sold three per pack for five cents with a piece of gum, or in two-card pack with no gum. Proof versions with straight edges and white or gray backs are known; they are slightly larger, at about 3-1/8" x 5-1/4".

		NM	EX	VG
Complete Set (72):		5,000	2,500	1,500
Common Player:		20.00	10.00	6.00
White Backs: 1.5X				
Proofs: .75-1X				
Wax Pack (5):		375.00		
1	Amos Otis	20.00	10.00	6.00
2	Darrell Evans	20.00	10.00	6.00
3	Bob Gibson	135.00	65.00	40.00
4	David Nelson	20.00	10.00	6.00
5	Steve Carlton	135.00	65.00	40.00
6	Catfish Hunter	90.00	45.00	27.50
7	Thurman Munson	175.00	87.50	52.50
8	Bob Grich	20.00	10.00	6.00
9	Tom Seaver	150.00	75.00	45.00
10	Ted Simmons	20.00	10.00	6.00
11	Bobby Valentine	20.00	10.00	6.00
12	Don Sutton	90.00	45.00	27.50
13	Wilbur Wood	20.00	10.00	6.00
14	Doug Rader	20.00	10.00	6.00
15	Chris Chambliss	20.00	10.00	6.00
16	Pete Rose	275.00	135.00	80.00
17	John Hiller	20.00	10.00	6.00
18	Burt Hooton	20.00	10.00	6.00
19	Tim Foli	20.00	10.00	6.00
20	Lou Brock	100.00	50.00	30.00
21	Ron Bryant	20.00	10.00	6.00
22	Manuel Sanguillen	20.00	10.00	6.00
23	Bobby Tolan	20.00	10.00	6.00
24	Greg Luzinski	20.00	10.00	6.00
25	Brooks Robinson	150.00	75.00	45.00
26	Felix Millan	20.00	10.00	6.00
27	Luis Tiant	20.00	10.00	6.00
28	Willie McCovey	100.00	50.00	30.00
29	Chris Speier	20.00	10.00	6.00
30	George Scott	20.00	10.00	6.00
31	Willie Stargell	100.00	50.00	30.00
32	Rod Carew	135.00	65.00	40.00
33	Charlie Spikes	20.00	10.00	6.00
34	Nate Colbert	20.00	10.00	6.00
35	Richie Hebner	20.00	10.00	6.00
36	Bobby Bonds	20.00	10.00	6.00
37	Buddy Bell	20.00	10.00	6.00
38	Claude Osteen	20.00	10.00	6.00
39	Rich Allen	55.00	27.50	16.50
40	Bill Russell	20.00	10.00	6.00
41	Nolan Ryan	900.00	450.00	275.00
42	Willie Davis	20.00	10.00	6.00
43	Carl Yastrzemski	160.00	80.00	45.00
44	Jon Matlack	20.00	10.00	6.00
45	Jim Palmer	135.00	65.00	40.00
46	Bert Campaneris	20.00	10.00	6.00
47	Bert Blyleven	20.00	10.00	6.00
48	Jeff Burroughs	20.00	10.00	6.00

49	Jim Colborn	20.00	10.00	6.00
50	Dave Johnson	20.00	10.00	6.00
51	John Mayberry	20.00	10.00	6.00
52	Don Kessinger	20.00	10.00	6.00
53	Joe Coleman	20.00	10.00	6.00
54	Tony Perez	90.00	45.00	27.50
55	Jose Cardenal	20.00	10.00	6.00
56	Paul Splittorff	20.00	10.00	6.00
57	Henry Aaron	275.00	135.00	80.00
58	David May	20.00	10.00	6.00
59	Fergie Jenkins	90.00	45.00	27.50
60	Ron Blomberg	20.00	10.00	6.00
61	Reggie Jackson	175.00	85.00	50.00
62	Tony Oliva	40.00	20.00	12.00
63	Bobby Murcer	45.00	22.50	13.50
64	Carlton Fisk	100.00	50.00	30.00
65	Steve Rogers	20.00	10.00	6.00
66	Frank Robinson	150.00	75.00	45.00
67	Joe Ferguson	20.00	10.00	6.00
68	Bill Melton	20.00	10.00	6.00
69	Bob Watson	20.00	10.00	6.00
70	Larry Bowa	20.00	10.00	6.00
71	Johnny Bench	150.00	75.00	45.00
72	Willie Horton	20.00	10.00	6.00

1974 Topps Puzzles

One of many test issues by Topps in the mid-1970s, the 2-player jigsaw puzzle set was an innovation which never caught on with collectors. The 40-piece puzzles (4-3/4" x 7-1/2") feature color photos with a decorative lozenge at bottom naming the player, team and position. The 25-cent or 29-cent puzzles came in individual wrappers picturing Tom Seaver. Centering, particularly of the Ryan puzzle, is a plague with the puzzles, accounting for the greater than usual spread betwern NM and lower- grade values.

		NM	EX	VG
Complete Set (12):		2,000	700.00	300.00
Common Player:		65.00	32.50	20.00
Wax Pack:		225.00		
Wrapper:		20.00		
(1)	Hank Aaron	250.00	90.00	35.00
(2)	Dick Allen	75.00	30.00	15.00
(3)	Johnny Bench	125.00	44.00	18.50
(4)	Bobby Bonds	65.00	25.00	10.00
(5)	Bob Gibson	125.00	44.00	18.50
(6)	Reggie Jackson	200.00	70.00	30.00
(7)	Bobby Murcer	65.00	25.00	10.00
(8)	Jim Palmer	100.00	35.00	15.00
(9)	Nolan Ryan	650.00	225.00	100.00
(10)	Tom Seaver	125.00	44.00	18.50
(11)	Willie Stargell	100.00	35.00	15.00
(12)	Carl Yastrzemski	250.00	87.00	37.00

1974 Topps Stamps

Topps continued to market baseball stamps in 1974 through the release of 240 unnumbered stamps featuring color player portraits. The player's name, team and position are found in an oval at the bottom of the 1" x 1-1/2" stamps. The stamps, sold separately rather than issued as an insert, came in panels of 12. Two dozen team albums designed to hold 10 stamps were also issued.

	NM	EX	VG
Complete Sheet Set (24):	90.00	45.00	25.00
Common Sheet:	2.00	1.00	.60
Complete Stamp Album Set (24):	300.00	150.00	90.00
Single Stamp Album:	5.00	2.50	1.50

(1)	Hank Aaron, Luis Aparicio, Bob Bailey, Johnny Bench, Ron Blomberg, Bob Boone, Lou Brock, Bud Harrelson, Randy Jones, Dave Rader, Nolan Ryan, Joe Torre	15.00	7.50	4.50
(2)	Buddy Bell, Steve Braun, Jerry Grote, Tommy Helms, Bill Lee, Mike Lum, Dave May, Brooks Robinson, Bill Russell, Del Unser, Wilbur Wood, Carl Yastrzemski	9.00	4.50	2.75
(3)	Jerry Bell, Jim Colborn, Toby Harrah, Ken Henderson, John Hiller, Randy Hundley, Don Kessinger, Jerry Koosman, Dave Lopes, Felix Millan, Thurman Munson, Ted Simmons	6.00	3.00	1.75
(4)	Jerry Bell, Bill Buckner, Jim Colborn, Ken Henderson, Don Kessinger, Felix Millan, George Mitterwald, Dave Roberts, Ted Simmons, Jim Slaton, Charlie Spikes, Paul Splittorff	2.00	1.00	.60
(5)	Glenn Beckert, Jim Bibby, Bill Buckner, Jim Lonborg, George Mitterwald, Dave Parker, Dave Roberts, Jim Slaton, Reggie Smith, Charlie Spikes, Paul Splittorff, Bob Watson	2.00	1.00	.60
(6)	Paul Blair, Bobby Bonds, Ed Brinkman, Norm Cash, Mike Epstein, Tommy Harper, Mike Marshall, Phil Niekro, Cookie Rojas, George Scott, Mel Stottlemyre, Jim Wynn	2.00	1.00	.60
(7)	Jack Billingham, Reggie Cleveland, Bobby Darwin, Dave Duncan, Tim Foli, Ed Goodson, Cleon Jones, Mickey Lolich, George Medich, John Milner, Rick Monday, Bobby Murcer	2.00	1.00	.60
(8)	Steve Carlton, Orlando Cepeda, Joe Decker, Reggie Jackson, Dave Johnson, John Mayberry, Bill Melton, Roger Metzger, Dave Nelson, Jerry Reuss, Jim Spencer, Bobby Valentine	10.00	5.00	3.00
(9)	Dan Driessen, Pedro Garcia, Grant Jackson, Al Kaline, Clay Kirby, Carlos May, Willie Montanez, Rogelio Moret, Jim Palmer, Doug Rader, J. R. Richard, Frank Robinson	7.50	3.75	2.25
(10)	Pedro Garcia, Ralph Garr, Wayne Garrett, Ron Hunt, Al Kaline, Fred Kendall, Carlos May, Jim Palmer, Doug Rader, Frank Robinson, Rick Wise, Richie Zisk	7.50	3.75	2.25
(11)	Dusty Baker, Larry Bowa, Steve Busby, Chris Chambliss, Dock Ellis, Cesar Geronimo, Fran Healy, Deron Johnson, Jorge Orta, Joe Rudi, Mickey Stanley, Rennie Stennett	2.00	1.00	.60
(12)	Bob Coluccio, Ray Corbin, John Ellis, Oscar Gamble, Dave Giusti, Bill Greif, Alex Johnson, Mike Jorgensen, Andy Messersmith, Bill Robinson, Elias Sosa, Willie Stargell	2.00	1.00	.60
(13)	Ron Bryant, Nate Colbert, Jose Cruz, Dan Driessen, Billy Grabarkewitz, Don Gullett, Willie Horton, Grant Jackson, Clay Kirby, Willie Montanez, Rogelio Moret, J. R. Richard	2.00	1.00	.60
(14)	Carlton Fisk, Bill Freehan, Bobby Grich, Vic Harris, George Hendrick, Ed Herrmann, Jim Holt, Ken Holtzman, Fergie Jenkins, Lou Piniella, Steve Rogers, Ken Singleton	5.00	2.50	1.50
(15)	Stan Bahnsen, Sal Bando, Mark Belanger, David Clyde, Willie Crawford, Burt Hooton, Jon Matlack, Tim McCarver, Joe Morgan, Gene Tenace, Dick Tidrow, Dave Winfield	7.50	3.75	2.25
(16)	Hank Aaron, Stan Bahnsen, Bob Bailey, Johnny Bench, Bob Boone, Jon Matlack, Tim McCarver, Joe Morgan, Dave Rader, Gene Tenace, Dick Tidrow, Joe Torre	10.00	5.00	3.00
(17)	John Boccabella, Frank Duffy, Darrell Evans, Sparky Lyle, Lee May, Don Money, Bill North, Ted Sizemore, Chris Speier, Wayne Twitchell, Billy Williams, Earl Williams	2.00	1.00	.60
(18)	John Boccabella, Bobby Darwin, Frank Duffy, Dave Duncan, Tim Foli, Cleon Jones, Mickey Lolich, Sparky Lyle, Lee May, Rick Monday, Bill North, Billy Williams	2.00	1.00	.60
(19)	Don Baylor, Vida Blue, Tom Bradley, Jose Cardenal, Ron Cey, Greg Luzinski, Johnny Oates, Tony Oliva, Al Oliver, Tony Perez, Darrell Porter, Roy White	3.00	1.50	.90
(20)	Pedro Borbon, Rod Carew, Roric Harrison, Jim Hunter, Ed Kirkpatrick, Garry Maddox, Gene Michael, Rick Miller, Claude Osteen, Amos Otis, Rich Reuschel, Mike Tyson	5.00	2.50	1.50
(21)	Sandy Alomar, Bert Campaneris, Dave Concepcion, Tommy Davis, Joe Ferguson, Tito Fuentes, Jerry Morales, Carl Morton, Gaylord Perry, Vada Pinson, Dave Roberts, Ellie Rodriguez	2.00	1.00	.60
(22)	Dick Allen, Jeff Burroughs, Joe Coleman, Terry Forster, Bob Gibson, Harmon Killebrew, Tug McGraw, Bob Oliver, Steve Renko, Pete Rose, Luis Tiant, Otto Velez	12.00	6.00	3.50
(23)	Johnny Briggs, Willie Davis, Jim Fregosi, Rich Hebner, Pat Kelly, Dave Kingman, Willie McCovey, Graig Nettles, Freddie Patek, Marty Pattin, Manny Sanguillen, Richie Scheinblum	5.00	2.50	1.50
(24)	Bert Blyleven, Nelson Briles, Cesar Cedeno, Ron Fairly, Johnny Grubb, Dave McNally, Aurelio Rodriguez, Ron Santo, Tom Seaver, Bill Singer, Bill Sudakis, Don Sutton	6.00	3.00	1.75

1974 Topps Team Checklists

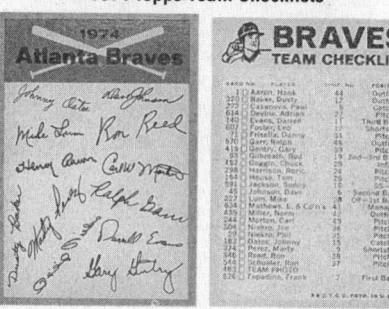

This set is a repeat of the 1973 set in the form of 24 unnumbered 2-1/2" x 3-1/2" checklist cards. Cards feature a team name on the front at the top with a white panel and a number of facsimile autographs below. Backs feature the team name and a checklist. The big difference between the 1973 and 1974 checklists is that the 1973s have busy borders while the 1974s have red borders. The 1974s were inserted into packages of the regular issue Topps cards and were also available in uncut sheet form as a wrapper redemption.

		NM	EX	VG
Complete Set (24):		40.00	20.00	12.00
Common Checklist:		2.50	1.25	.75
Uncut Sheet:		40.00	20.00	12.00
(1)	Atlanta Braves	2.50	1.25	.75
(2)	Baltimore Orioles	2.50	1.25	.75
(3)	Boston Red Sox	2.50	1.25	.75
(4)	California Angels	2.50	1.25	.75
(5)	Chicago Cubs	2.50	1.25	.75
(6)	Chicago White Sox	2.50	1.25	.75
(7)	Cincinnati Reds	2.50	1.25	.75
(8)	Cleveland Indians	2.50	1.25	.75
(9)	Detroit Tigers	2.50	1.25	.75
(10)	Houston Astros	2.50	1.25	.75
(11)	Kansas City Royals	2.50	1.25	.75
(12)	Los Angeles Dodgers	2.50	1.25	.75
(13)	Milwaukee Brewers	2.50	1.25	.75
(14)	Minnesota Twins	2.50	1.25	.75
(15)	Montreal Expos	2.50	1.25	.75
(16)	New York Mets	2.50	1.25	.75
(17)	New York Yankees	2.50	1.25	.75
(18)	Oakland A's	2.50	1.25	.75
(19)	Philadelphia Phillies	2.50	1.25	.75
(20)	Pittsburgh Pirates	2.50	1.25	.75
(21)	St. Louis Cardinals	2.50	1.25	.75
(22)	San Diego Padres	2.50	1.25	.75
(23)	San Francisco Giants	2.50	1.25	.75
(24)	Texas Rangers	2.50	1.25	.75

1975 Topps

What was once seen as the strongest rookie card crop of any modern card set made this a collector favorite from the out-set. Featuring the most colorful designs since 1972, cards feature large front photos with facsimile autographs. Red-and-green backs include a cartoon trivia fact and complete stats. A subset of 1951-74 MVP cards which reproduces or creates contemporary cards of past stars is one of several special features of the set, as are a group of four-on-one rookie cards. While the cards were all issued at one time, the first 132 cards have been discovered to have been printed in somewhat lesser quantities than the rest of the issue. This scarcity is not noted among the mini-version of the set which was produced as a test issue. Team/manager cards are sometimes found on thinner, white cardboard stock; these are a special version produced for a mail-in offer.

	NM	EX	VG
Complete Set (660):	650.00	325.00	162.50
Common Player:	.40	.20	.10
Mini Stars/Rookies: 1-1.5X			
Wax Pack (10):	40.00		
Wax Box (36):	2,400		
Cello Pack (18):	85.00		
Rack Pack (42):	190.00		
Vending Box (500):	.00		
1 Hank Aaron ('74 Highlights)	30.00	15.00	9.00
2 Lou Brock ('74 Highlights)	2.00	1.00	.60
3 Bob Gibson ('74 Highlights)	2.00	1.00	.60
4 Al Kaline ('74 Highlights)	4.00	2.00	1.25
5 Nolan Ryan ('74 Highlights)	12.00	6.00	3.50
6 Mike Marshall ('74 Highlights)	.40	.20	.10
7 Dick Bosman, Steve Busby, Nolan Ryan ('74 Highlights)	8.00	4.00	2.50
8 Rogelio Moret	.40	.20	.10
9 Frank Tepedino	.40	.20	.10
10 Willie Davis	.40	.20	.10
11 Bill Melton	.40	.20	.10
12 David Clyde	.40	.20	.10
13 Gene Locklear	.40	.20	.10
14 Milt Wilcox	.40	.20	.10
15 Jose Cardenal	.40	.20	.10
16 Frank Tanana	.40	.20	.10
17 Dave Concepcion	.40	.20	.10
18 Tigers team (Ralph Houk)	1.50	.70	.45
19 Jerry Koosman	.40	.20	.10
20 Thurman Munson	12.00	6.00	3.00
21 Rollie Fingers	3.00	1.50	.90
22 Dave Cash	.40	.20	.10
23 Bill Russell	.75	.40	.25
24 Al Fitzmorris	.40	.20	.10
25 Lee May	.75	.40	.25
26 Dave McNally	.40	.20	.10
27 Ken Reitz	.40	.20	.10
28 Tom Murphy	.40	.20	.10
29 Dave Parker	1.50	.70	.45
30 Bert Blyleven	1.50	.70	.45
31 Dave Rader	.40	.20	.10
32 Reggie Cleveland	.40	.20	.10
33 Dusty Baker	1.50	.70	.45
34 Steve Renko	.40	.20	.10
35 Ron Santo	2.00	1.00	.60
36 Joe Lovitto	.40	.20	.10
37 Dave Freisleben	.40	.20	.10
38 Buddy Bell	.75	.40	.25
39 Andy Thornton	.75	.40	.25
40 Bill Singer	.40	.20	.10
41 Cesar Geronimo	.40	.20	.10
42 Joe Coleman	.40	.20	.10
43 Cleon Jones	.40	.20	.10
44 Pat Dobson	.40	.20	.10
45 Joe Rudi	.40	.20	.10
46 Phillies Team (Danny Ozark)	1.50	.70	.45
47 Tommy John	1.50	.70	.45
48 Freddie Patek	.40	.20	.10
49 Larry Dierker	.75	.40	.25
50 Brooks Robinson	10.00	5.00	2.50
51 Bob Forsch	.75	.40	.25
52 Darrell Porter	.75	.40	.25
53 Dave Giusti	.40	.20	.10
54 Eric Soderholm	.40	.20	.10
55 Bobby Bonds	1.50	.70	.45
56 Rick Wise	.40	.20	.10
57 Dave Johnson	.75	.40	.25
58 Chuck Taylor	.40	.20	.10
59 Ken Henderson	.40	.20	.10
60 Fergie Jenkins	3.00	1.50	.90
61 Dave Winfield	12.00	6.00	3.50
62 Fritz Peterson	.40	.20	.10
63 Steve Swisher	.40	.20	.10
64 Dave Chalk	.40	.20	.10
65 Don Gullett	.40	.20	.10
66 Willie Horton	.40	.20	.10
67 Tug McGraw	.40	.20	.10
68 Ron Blomberg	.40	.20	.10
69 John Odom	.40	.20	.10
70 Mike Schmidt	20.00	10.00	6.00
71 Charlie Hough	.75	.40	.25
72 Royals Team (Jack McKeon)	1.00	.50	.30
73 J.R. Richard	.40	.20	.10
74 Mark Belanger	.40	.20	.10
75 Ted Simmons	1.00	.50	.30
76 Ed Sprague	.40	.20	.10
77 Richie Zisk	.40	.20	.10
78 Ray Corbin	.40	.20	.10
79 Gary Matthews	.40	.20	.10
80 Carlton Fisk	6.00	3.00	1.75
81 Ron Reed	.40	.20	.10
82 Pat Kelly	.40	.20	.10
83 Jim Merritt	.40	.20	.10
84 Enzo Hernandez	.40	.20	.10
85 Bill Bonham	.40	.20	.10
86 Joe Lis	.40	.20	.10
87 George Foster	1.00	.50	.30
88 Tom Egan	.40	.20	.10
89 Jim Ray	.40	.20	.10
90 Rusty Staub	1.00	.50	.30
91 Dick Green	.40	.20	.10
92 Cecil Upshaw	.40	.20	.10
93 Dave Lopes	1.00	.50	.30
94 Jim Lonborg	.75	.40	.25
95 John Mayberry	.75	.40	.25
96 Mike Cosgrove	.40	.20	.10
97 Earl Williams	.40	.20	.10
98 Rich Folkers	.40	.20	.10
99 Mike Hegan	.40	.20	.10
100 Willie Stargell	5.00	2.50	1.25
101 Expos Team (Gene Mauch)	1.00	.50	.30
102 Joe Decker	.40	.20	.10
103 Rick Miller	.40	.20	.10
104 Bill Madlock	.75	.40	.25
105 Buzz Capra	.40	.20	.10
106 *Mike Hargrove*	2.00	1.00	.60
107 Jim Barr	.40	.20	.10
108 Tom Hall	.40	.20	.10
109 George Hendrick	.40	.20	.10
110 Wilbur Wood	.40	.20	.10
111 Wayne Garrett	.40	.20	.10
112 Larry Hardy	.40	.20	.10
113 Elliott Maddox	.40	.20	.10
114 Dick Lange	.40	.20	.10
115 Joe Ferguson	.40	.20	.10
116 Lerrin LaGrow	.40	.20	.10
117 Orioles Team (Earl Weaver)	3.00	1.50	.90
118 Mike Anderson	.40	.20	.10
119 Tommy Helms	.40	.20	.10
120 Steve Busby (Photo actually Fran Healy.)	.40	.20	.10
121 Bill North	.40	.20	.10
122 Al Hrabosky	.75	.40	.25
123 Johnny Briggs	.40	.20	.10
124 Jerry Reuss	.75	.40	.25
125 Ken Singleton	.75	.40	.25
126 Checklist 1-132	2.00	1.00	.60
127 Glen Borgmann	.40	.20	.10
128 Bill Lee	.40	.20	.10
129 Rick Monday	.40	.20	.10
130 Phil Niekro	3.00	1.50	.90
131 Toby Harrah	.40	.20	.10
132 Randy Moffitt	.40	.20	.10
133 Dan Driessen	.40	.20	.10
134 Ron Hodges	.40	.20	.10
135 Charlie Spikes	.40	.20	.10
136 Jim Mason	.40	.20	.10
137 Terry Forster	.40	.20	.10
138 Del Unser	.40	.20	.10
139 Horacio Pina	.40	.20	.10
140 Steve Garvey	2.00	1.00	.60
141 Mickey Stanley	.40	.20	.10
142 Bob Reynolds	.40	.20	.10
143 *Cliff Johnson*	.40	.20	.10
144 Jim Wohlford	.40	.20	.10
145 Ken Holtzman	.40	.20	.10
146 Padres Team (John McNamara)	1.00	.50	.30
147 Pedro Garcia	.40	.20	.10
148 Jim Rooker	.40	.20	.10
149 Tim Foli	.40	.20	.10
150 Bob Gibson	5.00	2.50	1.50
151 Steve Brye	.40	.20	.10
152 Mario Guerrero	.40	.20	.10
153 Rick Reuschel	.40	.20	.10
154 Mike Lum	.40	.20	.10
155 Jim Bibby	.40	.20	.10
156 Dave Kingman	1.00	.50	.30
157 Pedro Borbon	.40	.20	.10
158 Jerry Grote	.40	.20	.10
159 Steve Arlin	.40	.20	.10
160 Graig Nettles	1.00	.50	.30
161 Stan Bahnsen	.40	.20	.10
162 Willie Montanez	.40	.20	.10
163 Jim Brewer	.40	.20	.10
164 Mickey Rivers	.40	.20	.10
165 Doug Rader	.40	.20	.10
166 Woodie Fryman	.40	.20	.10
167 Rich Coggins	.40	.20	.10
168 Bill Greif	.40	.20	.10
169 Cookie Rojas	.40	.20	.10
170 Bert Campaneris	.40	.20	.10
171 Ed Kirkpatrick	.40	.20	.10
172 Red Sox Team (Darrell Johnson)	1.50	.70	.45
173 Steve Rogers	.40	.20	.10
174 Bake McBride	.40	.20	.10
175 Don Money	.40	.20	.10
176 Burt Hooton	.40	.20	.10
177 Vic Correll	.40	.20	.10
178 Cesar Tovar	.40	.20	.10
179 Tom Bradley	.40	.20	.10
180 Joe Morgan	6.00	3.00	1.50
181 Fred Beene	.40	.20	.10
182 Don Hahn	.40	.20	.10
183 Mel Stottlemyre	.40	.20	.10
184 Jorge Orta	.40	.20	.10
185 Steve Carlton	6.00	3.00	1.50
186 Willie Crawford	.40	.20	.10
187 Denny Doyle	.40	.20	.10
188 Tom Griffin	.40	.20	.10
189 1951-MVPs (Yogi Berra, Roy Campanella)	3.00	1.50	.90
190 1952-MVPs (Hank Sauer, Bobby Shantz)	1.00	.50	.30
191 1953-MVPs (Roy Campanella, Al Rosen)	1.50	.70	.45
192 1954-MVPs (Yogi Berra, Willie Mays)	4.00	2.00	1.25
193 1955-MVPs (Yogi Berra, Roy Campanella)	3.00	1.50	.90
194 1956-MVPs (Mickey Mantle, Don Newcombe)	8.00	4.00	2.00
195 1957-MVPs (Hank Aaron, Mickey Mantle)	10.00	5.00	2.50
196 1958-MVPs (Ernie Banks, Jackie Jensen)	2.50	1.25	.70
197 1959-MVPs (Ernie Banks, Nellie Fox)	2.00	1.00	.60
198 1960-MVPs (Dick Groat, Roger Maris)	1.50	.70	.45
199 1961-MVPs (Roger Maris, Frank Robinson)	2.00	1.00	.60
200 1962-MVPs (Mickey Mantle, Maury Wills)	8.00	4.00	2.50
201 1963-MVPs (Elston Howard, Sandy Koufax)	2.50	1.25	.70
202 1964-MVPs (Ken Boyer, Brooks Robinson)	1.00	.50	.30
203 1965-MVPs (Willie Mays, Zoilo Versalles)	2.00	1.00	.60
204 1966-MVPs (Roberto Clemente, Frank Robinson)	5.00	2.50	1.50
205 1967-MVPs (Orlando Cepeda, Carl Yastrzemski)	1.50	.70	.45
206 1968-MVPs (Bob Gibson, Denny McLain)	1.50	.70	.45
207 1969-MVPs (Harmon Killebrew, Willie McCovey)	2.00	1.00	.60
208 1970-MVPs (Johnny Bench, Boog Powell)	2.00	1.00	.60
209 1971-MVPs (Vida Blue, Joe Torre)	1.00	.50	.30
210 1972-MVPs (Rich Allen, Johnny Bench)	2.00	1.00	.60
211 1973-MVPs (Reggie Jackson, Pete Rose)	4.00	2.00	1.25
212 1974-MVPs (Jeff Burroughs, Steve Garvey)	1.00	.50	.30
213 Oscar Gamble	.40	.20	.10
214 Harry Parker	.40	.20	.10
215 Bobby Valentine	.40	.20	.10
216 Giants Team (Wes Westrum)	1.00	.50	.30
217 Lou Piniella	1.50	.70	.45
218 Jerry Johnson	.40	.20	.10
219 Ed Herrmann	.40	.20	.10
220 Don Sutton	3.00	1.50	.90
221 Aurelio Rodriquez (Rodriguez)	.40	.20	.10
222 Dan Spillner	.40	.20	.10
223 *Robin Yount*	40.00	20.00	12.00
224 Ramon Hernandez	.40	.20	.10
225 Bob Grich	.75	.40	.25
226 Bill Campbell	.40	.20	.10
227 Bob Watson	.40	.20	.10
228 *George Brett*	65.00	32.00	19.50
229 Barry Foote	.40	.20	.10
230 Jim Hunter	5.00	2.50	1.25
231 Mike Tyson	.40	.20	.10
232 Diego Segui	.40	.20	.10
233 Billy Grabarkewitz	.40	.20	.10
234 Tom Grieve	.40	.20	.10
235 Jack Billingham	.40	.20	.10
236 Angels Team (Dick Williams)	1.00	.50	.30
237 Carl Morton	.40	.20	.10
238 Dave Duncan	.75	.40	.25
239 George Stone	.40	.20	.10
240 Garry Maddox	.40	.20	.10
241 Dick Tidrow	.40	.20	.10
242 Jay Johnstone	.40	.20	.10
243 Jim Kaat	1.50	.70	.45
244 Bill Buckner	.75	.40	.25
245 Mickey Lolich	1.00	.50	.30
246 Cardinals Team (Red Schoendienst)	1.00	.50	.30
247 Enos Cabell	.40	.20	.10
248 Randy Jones	.40	.20	.10
249 Danny Thompson	.40	.20	.10
250 Ken Brett	.40	.20	.10
251 Fran Healy	.40	.20	.10
252 Fred Scherman	.40	.20	.10
253 Jesus Alou	.40	.20	.10
254 Mike Torrez	.40	.20	.10
255 Dwight Evans	1.00	.50	.30
256 Billy Champion	.40	.20	.10
257 Checklist 133-264	2.00	1.00	.60
258 Dave LaRoche	.40	.20	.10
259 Len Randle	.40	.20	.10
260 Johnny Bench	12.00	6.00	3.00
261 Andy Hassler	.40	.20	.10
262 Rowland Office	.40	.20	.10
263 Jim Perry	.40	.20	.10
264 John Milner	.40	.20	.10
265 Ron Bryant	.40	.20	.10
266 Sandy Alomar	.40	.20	.10
267 Dick Ruthven	.40	.20	.10
268 Hal McRae	.75	.40	.25
269 Doug Rau	.40	.20	.10
270 Ron Fairly	.40	.20	.10
271 Jerry Moses	.40	.20	.10
272 Lynn McGlothen	.40	.20	.10
273 Steve Braun	.40	.20	.10
274 Vicente Romo	.40	.20	.10
275 Paul Blair	.40	.20	.10
276 White Sox Team (Chuck Tanner)	1.00	.50	.30
277 Frank Taveras	.40	.20	.10
278 Paul Lindblad	.40	.20	.10
279 Milt May	.40	.20	.10
280 Carl Yastrzemski	10.00	5.00	3.00
281 Jim Slaton	.40	.20	.10
282 Jerry Morales	.40	.20	.10
283 Steve Foucault	.40	.20	.10
284 Ken Griffey	2.00	1.00	.60
285 Ellie Rodriguez	.40	.20	.10
286 Mike Jorgensen	.40	.20	.10
287 Roric Harrison	.40	.20	.10
288 Bruce Ellingsen	.40	.20	.10
289 Ken Rudolph	.40	.20	.10
290 Jon Matlack	.40	.20	.10
291 Bill Sudakis	.40	.20	.10
292 Ron Schueler	.40	.20	.10
293 Dick Sharon	.40	.20	.10
294 *Geoff Zahn*	.40	.20	.10

#	Player			
295	Vada Pinson	1.50	.70	.45
296	Alan Foster	.40	.20	.10
297	Craig Kusick	.40	.20	.10
298	Johnny Grubb	.40	.20	.10
299	Bucky Dent	1.00	.50	.30
300	Reggie Jackson	12.00	6.00	3.50
301	Dave Roberts	.40	.20	.10
302	*Rick Burleson*	.75	.40	.25
303	Grant Jackson	.40	.20	.10
304	Pirates Teamz (Danny Murtaugh)	1.50	.70	.45
305	Jim Colborn	.40	.20	.10
306	Batting Leaders (Rod Carew, Ralph Garr)	1.50	.70	.45
307	Home Run Leaders (Dick Allen, Mike Schmidt)	3.00	1.50	.90
308	Runs Batted In Leaders (Johnny Bench, Jeff Burroughs)	1.50	.70	.45
309	Stolen Base Leaders (Lou Brock, Bill North)	1.50	.70	.45
310	Victory Leaders (Jim Hunter, Fergie Jenkins, Andy Messersmith, Phil Niekro)	1.50	.70	.45
311	Earned Run Average Leaders (Buzz Capra, Jim Hunter)	1.50	.70	.45
312	Strikeout Leaders (Steve Carlton, Nolan Ryan)	10.00	5.00	3.00
313	Leading Firemen (Terry Forster, Mike Marshall)	1.00	.50	.30
314	Buck Martinez	.40	.20	.10
315	Don Kessinger	.40	.20	.10
316	Jackie Brown	.40	.20	.10
317	Joe Lahoud	.40	.20	.10
318	Ernie McAnally	.40	.20	.10
319	Johnny Oates	.40	.20	.10
320	Pete Rose	25.00	12.50	7.50
321	Rudy May	.40	.20	.10
322	Ed Goodson	.40	.20	.10
323	Fred Holdsworth	.40	.20	.10
324	Ed Kranepool	.40	.20	.10
325	Tony Oliva	1.50	.70	.45
326	Wayne Twitchell	.40	.20	.10
327	Jerry Hairston Sr.	.40	.20	.10
328	Sonny Siebert	.40	.20	.10
329	Ted Kubiak	.40	.20	.10
330	Mike Marshall	.40	.20	.10
331	Indians Team (Frank Robinson)	1.50	.75	.45
332	Fred Kendall	.40	.20	.10
333	Dick Drago	.40	.20	.10
334	*Greg Gross*	.40	.20	.10
335	Jim Palmer	4.00	2.00	1.25
336	Rennie Stennett	.40	.20	.10
337	Kevin Kobel	.40	.20	.10
338	Rick Stelmaszek	.40	.20	.10
339	Jim Fregosi	1.00	.50	.30
340	Paul Splittorff	.40	.20	.10
341	Hal Breeden	.40	.20	.10
342	Leroy Stanton	.40	.20	.10
343	Danny Frisella	.40	.20	.10
344	Ben Oglivie	1.00	.50	.30
345	Clay Carroll	.40	.20	.10
346	Bobby Darwin	.40	.20	.10
347	Mike Caldwell	.40	.20	.10
348	Tony Muser	.40	.20	.10
349	Ray Sadecki	.40	.20	.10
350	Bobby Murcer	.75	.40	.25
351	Bob Boone	1.50	.70	.45
352	Darold Knowles	.40	.20	.10
353	Luis Melendez	.40	.20	.10
354	Dick Bosman	.40	.20	.10
355	Chris Cannizzaro	.40	.20	.10
356	Rico Petrocelli	.75	.40	.25
357	Ken Forsch	.40	.20	.10
358	Al Bumbry	.40	.20	.10
359	Paul Popovich	.40	.20	.10
360	George Scott	.40	.20	.10
361	Dodgers Team (Walter Alston)	1.50	.75	.45
362	Steve Hargan	.40	.20	.10
363	Carmen Fanzone	.40	.20	.10
364	Doug Bird	.40	.20	.10
365	Bob Bailey	.40	.20	.10
366	Ken Sanders	.40	.20	.10
367	Craig Robinson	.40	.20	.10
368	Vic Albury	.40	.20	.10
369	Merv Rettenmund	.40	.20	.10
370	Tom Seaver	10.00	5.00	3.00
371	Gates Brown	.40	.20	.10
372	John D'Acquisto	.40	.20	.10
373	Bill Sharp	.40	.20	.10
374	Eddie Watt	.40	.20	.10
375	Roy White	.45	.25	.15
376	Steve Yeager	.40	.20	.10
377	Tom Hilgendorf	.40	.20	.10
378	Derrel Thomas	.40	.20	.10
379	Bernie Carbo	.40	.20	.10
380	Sal Bando	.40	.20	.10
381	John Curtis	.40	.20	.10
382	Don Baylor	1.50	.70	.45
383	Jim York	.40	.20	.10
384	Brewers Team (Del Crandall)	1.50	.70	.45
385	Dock Ellis	.40	.20	.10
386	Checklist 265-396	2.00	1.00	.60
387	Jim Spencer	.40	.20	.10
388	Steve Stone	.75	.40	.25
389	Tony Solaita	.40	.20	.10
390	Ron Cey	1.00	.50	.30
391	Don DeMola	.40	.20	.10
392	Bruce Bochte	.40	.20	.10
393	Gary Gentry	.40	.20	.10
394	Larvell Blanks	.40	.20	.10
395	Bud Harrelson	.40	.20	.10
396	Fred Norman	.40	.20	.10
397	Bill Freehan	.75	.40	.25
398	Elias Sosa	.40	.20	.10
399	Terry Harmon	.40	.20	.10
400	Dick Allen	1.00	.50	.30
401	Mike Wallace	.40	.20	.10
402	Bob Tolan	.40	.20	.10
403	Tom Buskey	.40	.20	.10
404	Ted Sizemore	.40	.20	.10
405	John Montague	.40	.20	.10
406	Bob Gallagher	.40	.20	.10
407	*Herb Washington*	1.00	.50	.30
408	Clyde Wright	.40	.20	.10
409	Bob Robertson	.40	.20	.10
410	Mike Cueller (Cuellar)	.40	.20	.10
411	George Mitterwald	.40	.20	.10
412	Bill Hands	.40	.20	.10
413	Marty Pattin	.40	.20	.10
414	Manny Mota	.40	.20	.10
415	John Hiller	.40	.20	.10
416	Larry Lintz	.40	.20	.10
417	Skip Lockwood	.40	.20	.10
418	Leo Foster	.40	.20	.10
419	Dave Goltz	.40	.20	.10
420	Larry Bowa	1.50	.70	.45
421	Mets Team (Yogi Berra)	2.50	1.25	.70
422	Brian Downing	.40	.20	.10
423	Clay Kirby	.40	.20	.10
424	John Lowenstein	.40	.20	.10
425	Tito Fuentes	.40	.20	.10
426	George Medich	.40	.20	.10
427	Clarence Gaston	.40	.20	.10
428	Dave Hamilton	.40	.20	.10
429	*Jim Dwyer*	.40	.20	.10
430	Luis Tiant	1.00	.50	.30
431	Rod Gilbreath	.40	.20	.10
432	Ken Berry	.40	.20	.10
433	Larry Demery	.40	.20	.10
434	Bob Locker	.40	.20	.10
435	Dave Nelson	.40	.20	.10
436	Ken Frailing	.40	.20	.10
437	*Al Cowens*	.40	.20	.10
438	Don Carrithers	.40	.20	.10
439	Ed Brinkman	.40	.20	.10
440	Andy Messersmith	.40	.20	.10
441	Bobby Heise	.40	.20	.10
442	Maximino Leon	.40	.20	.10
443	Twins Team (Frank Quilici)	1.00	.50	.30
444	Gene Garber	.40	.20	.10
445	Felix Millan	.40	.20	.10
446	Bart Johnson	.40	.20	.10
447	Terry Crowley	.40	.20	.10
448	Frank Duffy	.40	.20	.10
449	Charlie Williams	.40	.20	.10
450	Willie McCovey	5.00	2.50	1.50
451	Rick Dempsey	.40	.20	.10
452	Angel Mangual	.40	.20	.10
453	Claude Osteen	.40	.20	.10
454	Doug Griffin	.40	.20	.10
455	Don Wilson	.40	.20	.10
456	Bob Coluccio	.40	.20	.10
457	Mario Mendoza	.40	.20	.10
458	Ross Grimsley	.40	.20	.10
459	A.L. Championships (Brooks Robinson)	1.00	.50	.30
460	N.L. Championships (Steve Garvey)	1.00	.50	.30
461	World Series Game 1 (Reggie Jackson)	2.00	1.00	.60
462	World Series Game 2 (Joe Ferguson)	.75	.40	.25
463	World Series Game 3 (Rollie Fingers)	1.50	.70	.45
464	World Series Game 4	.75	.40	.25
465	World Series Game 5	.75	.40	.25
466	A's Do It Again! (Win 3rd Straight World Series!)	1.50	.70	.45
467	Ed Halicki	.40	.20	.10
468	Bobby Mitchell	.40	.20	.10
469	Tom Dettore	.40	.20	.10
470	Jeff Burroughs	.40	.20	.10
471	Bob Stinson	.40	.20	.10
472	Bruce Dal Canton	.40	.20	.10
473	Ken McMullen	.40	.20	.10
474	Luke Walker	.40	.20	.10
475	Darrell Evans	1.00	.50	.30
476	*Ed Figueroa*	.40	.20	.10
477	Tom Hutton	.40	.20	.10
478	Tom Burgmeier	.40	.20	.10
479	Ken Boswell	.40	.20	.10
480	Carlos May	.40	.20	.10
481	*Will McEnaney*	.40	.20	.10
482	Tom McCraw	.40	.20	.10
483	Steve Ontiveros	.40	.20	.10
484	Glenn Beckert	.40	.20	.10
485	Sparky Lyle	.40	.20	.10
486	Ray Fosse	.40	.20	.10
487	Astros Team (Preston Gomez)	1.00	.50	.30
488	Bill Travers	.40	.20	.10
489	Cecil Cooper	1.00	.50	.30
490	Reggie Smith	.75	.40	.25
491	Doyle Alexander	.40	.20	.10
492	Rich Hebner	.40	.20	.10
493	Don Stanhouse	.40	.20	.10
494	*Pete LaCock*	.40	.20	.10
495	Nelson Briles	.40	.20	.10
496	Pepe Frias	.40	.20	.10
497	Jim Nettles	.40	.20	.10
498	Al Downing	.40	.20	.10
499	Marty Perez	.40	.20	.10
500	Nolan Ryan	40.00	20.00	12.00
501	Bill Robinson	.40	.20	.10
502	Pat Bourque	.40	.20	.10
503	Fred Stanley	.40	.20	.10
504	Buddy Bradford	.40	.20	.10
505	Chris Speier	.40	.20	.10
506	Leron Lee	.40	.20	.10
507	Tom Carroll	.40	.20	.10
508	Bob Hansen	.40	.20	.10
509	Dave Hilton	.40	.20	.10
510	Vida Blue	.75	.40	.25
511	Rangers Team (Billy Martin)	1.50	.75	.45
512	Larry Milbourne	.40	.20	.10
513	Dick Pole	.40	.20	.10
514	Jose Cruz	.40	.20	.10
515	Manny Sanguillen	.40	.20	.10
516	Don Hood	.40	.20	.10
517	Checklist 397-528	2.00	1.00	.60
518	Leo Cardenas	.40	.20	.10
519	Jim Todd	.40	.20	.10
520	Amos Otis	.40	.20	.10
521	Dennis Blair	.40	.20	.10
522	Gary Sutherland	.40	.20	.10
523	Tom Paciorek	.40	.20	.10
524	John Doherty	.40	.20	.10
525	Tom House	.40	.20	.10
526	Larry Hisle	.40	.20	.10
527	Mac Scarce	.40	.20	.10
528	Eddie Leon	.40	.20	.10
529	Gary Thomasson	.40	.20	.10
530	Gaylord Perry	3.00	1.50	.90
531	Reds Team (Sparky Anderson)	5.00	2.50	1.50
532	Gorman Thomas	.40	.20	.10
533	Rudy Meoli	.40	.20	.10
534	Alex Johnson	.40	.20	.10
535	Gene Tenace	.40	.20	.10
536	Bob Moose	.40	.20	.10
537	Tommy Harper	.40	.20	.10
538	Duffy Dyer	.40	.20	.10
539	Jesse Jefferson	.40	.20	.10
540	Lou Brock	5.00	2.50	1.50
541	Roger Metzger	.40	.20	.10
542	Pete Broberg	.40	.20	.10
543	Larry Biittner	.40	.20	.10
544	Steve Mingori	.40	.20	.10
545	Billy Williams	5.00	2.50	1.50
546	John Knox	.40	.20	.10
547	Von Joshua	.40	.20	.10
548	Charlie Sands	.40	.20	.10
549	Bill Butler	.40	.20	.10
550	Ralph Garr	.40	.20	.10
551	Larry Christenson	.40	.20	.10
552	Jack Brohamer	.40	.20	.10
553	John Boccabella	.40	.20	.10
554	Rich Gossage	1.50	.70	.45
555	Al Oliver	1.00	.50	.30
556	Tim Johnson	.40	.20	.10
557	Larry Gura	.40	.20	.10
558	Dave Roberts	.40	.20	.10
559	Bob Montgomery	.40	.20	.10
560	Tony Perez	5.00	2.50	1.25
561	A's Team (Alvin Dark)	1.00	.50	.30
562	Gary Nolan	.40	.20	.10
563	Wilbur Howard	.40	.20	.10
564	Tommy Davis	.40	.20	.10
565	Joe Torre	2.00	1.00	.60
566	Ray Burris	.40	.20	.10
567	*Jim Sundberg*	1.00	.50	.30
568	Dale Murray	.40	.20	.10
569	Frank White	.40	.20	.10
570	Jim Wynn	.40	.20	.10
571	Dave Lemanczyk	.40	.20	.10
572	Roger Nelson	.40	.20	.10
573	Orlando Pena	.40	.20	.10
574	Tony Taylor	.40	.20	.10
575	Gene Clines	.40	.20	.10
576	Phil Roof	.40	.20	.10
577	John Morris	.40	.20	.10
578	Dave Tomlin	.40	.20	.10
579	Skip Pitlock	.40	.20	.10
580	Frank Robinson	8.00	4.00	2.00
581	Darrel Chaney	.40	.20	.10
582	Eduardo Rodriguez	.40	.20	.10
583	Andy Etchebarren	.40	.20	.10
584	Mike Garman	.40	.20	.10
585	Chris Chambliss	.75	.40	.25
586	Tim McCarver	1.00	.50	.30
587	Chris Ward	.40	.20	.10
588	Rick Auerbach	.40	.20	.10
589	Braves Team (Clyde King)	1.00	.50	.30
590	Cesar Cedeno	.40	.20	.10
591	Glenn Abbott	.40	.20	.10
592	Balor Moore	.40	.20	.10
593	Gene Lamont	.40	.20	.10
594	Jim Fuller	.40	.20	.10
595	Joe Niekro	.40	.20	.10
596	Ollie Brown	.40	.20	.10
597	Winston Llenas	.40	.20	.10
598	Bruce Kison	.40	.20	.10
599	Nate Colbert	.40	.20	.10
600	Rod Carew	6.00	3.00	1.75
601	Juan Beniquez	.40	.20	.10
602	John Vukovich	.40	.20	.10
603	Lew Krausse	.40	.20	.10
604	Oscar Zamora	.40	.20	.10
605	John Ellis	.40	.20	.10
606	Bruce Miller	.40	.20	.10
607	Jim Holt	.40	.20	.10
608	Gene Michael	.40	.20	.10
609	Ellie Hendricks	.40	.20	.10
610	Ron Hunt	.40	.20	.10
611	Yankees Team (Bill Virdon)	2.00	1.00	.60
612	Terry Hughes	.40	.20	.10
613	Bill Parsons	.40	.20	.10
614	Rookie Pitchers (Jack Kucek, Dyar Miller, Vern Ruhle, Paul Siebert)	.40	.20	.10
615	Rookie Pitchers (*Pat Darcy, Dennis Leonard, Tom Underwood, Hank Webb*)	.40	.20	.10
616	Rookie Outfielders (*Dave Augustine, Pepe Mangual, Jim Rice, John Scott*)	20.00	10.00	6.00
617	Rookie Infielders (Mike Cubbage, Doug DeCinces, Reggie Sanders, Manny Trillo)	1.50	.70	.45

		NM	EX	VG
618	Rookie Pitchers (*Jamie Easterly, Tom Johnson, Scott McGregor, Rick Rhoden*)	2.00	1.00	.60
619	Rookie Outfielders (Benny Ayala, Nyls Nyman, Tommy Smith, Jerry Turner)	.40	.20	.10
620	Rookie Catchers-Outfielders (*Gary Carter, Marc Hill, Danny Meyer, Leon Roberts*)	20.00	10.00	5.00
621	Rookie Pitchers (**John Denny**, Rawly Eastwick, Jim Kern, Juan Veintidos)	.50	.25	.15
622	Rookie Outfielders (*Ed Armbrister, Fred Lynn, Tom Poquette, Terry Whitfield*)	8.00	4.00	2.50
623	Rookie Infielders (*Phil Garner, Keith Hernandez, Bob Sheldon, Tom Veryzer*)	10.00	5.00	2.50
624	Rookie Pitchers (Doug Konieczny, Gary Lavelle, Jim Otten, Eddie Solomon)	.40	.20	.10
625	Boog Powell	1.00	.50	.30
626	Larry Haney	.40	.20	.10
627	Tom Walker	.40	.20	.10
628	*Ron LeFlore*	.75	.40	.25
629	Joe Hoerner	.40	.20	.10
630	Greg Luzinski	1.00	.50	.30
631	Lee Lacy	.40	.20	.10
632	Morris Nettles	.40	.20	.10
633	Paul Casanova	.40	.20	.10
634	Cy Acosta	.40	.20	.10
635	Chuck Dobson	.40	.20	.10
636	Charlie Moore	.40	.20	.10
637	Ted Martinez	.40	.20	.10
638	Cubs Team (Jim Marshall)	1.50	.70	.45
639	Steve Kline	.40	.20	.10
640	Harmon Killebrew	6.00	3.00	1.75
641	Jim Northrup	.40	.20	.10
642	Mike Phillips	.40	.20	.10
643	Brent Strom	.40	.20	.10
644	Bill Fahey	.40	.20	.10
645	Danny Cater	.40	.20	.10
646	Checklist 529-660	1.00	.50	.30
647	*Claudell Washington*	.75	.40	.25
648	Dave Pagan	.40	.20	.10
649	Jack Heidemann	.40	.20	.10
650	Dave May	.40	.20	.10
651	John Morlan	.40	.20	.10
652	Lindy McDaniel	.40	.20	.10
653	Lee Richards	.40	.20	.10
654	Jerry Terrell	.40	.20	.10
655	Rico Carty	.40	.20	.10
656	Bill Plummer	.40	.20	.10
657	Bob Oliver	.40	.20	.10
658	Vic Harris	.40	.20	.10
659	Bob Apodaca	.40	.20	.10
660	Hank Aaron	30.00	15.00	9.00

1975 Topps Mini

RICK REUSCHEL

This popular set was actually a test issue to see how collectors would react to cards which were 20 percent smaller than the standard 2-1/2" x 3-1/2". Other than their 2-1/4" x 3-1/8" size, they are exactly the same front and back as the regular-issue '75 Topps. The experimental cards were sold in Michigan and on the West Coast, where they were quickly gobbled up by collectors, dealers and speculators. While the minis for many years enjoyed a 2X premium over regular 1975 Topps values, that differential has shrunk in recent years.

	NM	EX	VG
Complete Set (660):	425.00	210.00	125.00
Common Player:	.50	.25	.15
Wax Pack (10):	40.00		
Wax Box (36):	1,350		
Cello Pack (18):	100.00		
Rack Pack (42):	200.00		

(Stars and rookies valued 1X to 1.5X regular 1975 Topps.)

1975 Topps Team Checklist Sheet

Via a mail-in wrapper redemption, collectors could receive an uncut sheet of the 24 team photo/checklist cards from the 1975 Topps baseball set. Measuring about 10-1/2" x 20-1/8", the sheet could be cut into individual team cards of standard size. The sheet-cut cards differ from issued versions in that they have white backs and are printed on thinner stock than the pack-issued versions.

	NM	EX	VG
Complete Sheet:	50.00	25.00	15.00

1976 Topps

 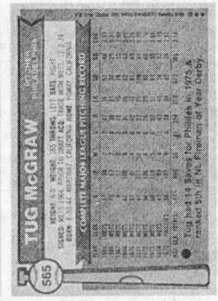

TUG McGRAW
PHILLIES

These 2-1/2" x 3-1/2" cards begin a design trend for Topps. The focus was more on the photo quality than in past years with a corresponding trend toward simplicity in the borders. The front of the cards has the player's name and team in two strips while his position is in the lower-left corner under a drawing of a player representing that position. The backs have a bat and ball with the card number on the left; statistics and personal information and career highlights on the right. The 660-card set features a number of specialty sets including record-setting performances, statistical leaders, playoff and World Series highlights, the Sporting News All-Time All-Stars and father and son combinations.

		NM	EX	VG
Complete Set (660):		250.00	125.00	75.00
Common Player:		.40	.20	.10
Wax Pack (6):		30.00		
Wax Box (36 six-card):		1,200		
Wax Pack (10):		50.00		
Wax Box (36 10-card):		2,000		
Cello Pack (18):		60.00		
Cello Box (24):		1,950		
Rack Pack (42):		105.00		
Vending Box (500):		510.00		
1	Hank Aaron (Record Breaker)	15.00	7.50	4.50
2	Bobby Bonds (Record Breaker)	1.50	.70	.45
3	Mickey Lolich (Rzecord Breaker)	.40	.20	.10
4	Dave Lopes (Record Breaker)	.40	.20	.10
5	Tom Seaver (Record Breaker)	3.00	1.50	.90
6	Rennie Stennett (Record Breaker)	.40	.20	.10
7	Jim Umbarger	.40	.20	.10
8	Tito Fuentes	.40	.20	.10
9	Paul Lindblad	.40	.20	.10
10	Lou Brock	5.00	2.50	1.50
11	Jim Hughes	.40	.20	.10
12	Richie Zisk	.40	.20	.10
13	Johnny Wockenfuss	.40	.20	.10
14	Gene Garber	.40	.20	.10
15	George Scott	.40	.20	.10
16	Bob Apodaca	.40	.20	.10
17	New York Yankees Team (Billy Martin)	1.50	.70	.45
18	Dale Murray	.40	.20	.10
19	George Brett	22.50	11.25	6.75
20	Bob Watson	.40	.20	.10
21	Dave LaRoche	.40	.20	.10
22	Bill Russell	1.00	.50	.30
23	Brian Downing	.40	.20	.10
24	Cesar Geronimo	.40	.20	.10
25	Mike Torrez	.40	.20	.10
26	Andy Thornton	.75	.40	.25
27	Ed Figueroa	.40	.20	.10
28	Dusty Baker	1.50	.70	.45
29	Rick Burleson	.40	.20	.10
30	*John Montefusco*	.40	.20	.10
31	Len Randle	.40	.20	.10
32	Danny Frisella	.40	.20	.10
33	Bill North	.40	.20	.10
34	Mike Garman	.40	.20	.10
35	Tony Oliva	1.00	.50	.30
36	Frank Taveras	.40	.20	.10
37	John Hiller	.40	.20	.10
38	Garry Maddox	.40	.20	.10
39	Pete Broberg	.40	.20	.10
40	Dave Kingman	.75	.40	.25
41	*Tippy Martinez*	.75	.40	.25
42	Barry Foote	.40	.20	.10
43	Paul Splittorff	.40	.20	.10
44	Doug Rader	.40	.20	.10
45	Boog Powell	.75	.40	.25
46	Los Angeles Dodgers Team (Walter Alston)	1.00	.50	.30
47	Jesse Jefferson	.40	.20	.10
48	Dave Concepcion	.40	.20	.10
49	Dave Duncan	.40	.20	.10
50	Fred Lynn	.75	.40	.25
51	Ray Burris	.40	.20	.10
52	Dave Chalk	.40	.20	.10
53	Mike Beard	.40	.20	.10
54	Dave Rader	.40	.20	.10
55	Gaylord Perry	3.00	1.50	.90
56	Bob Tolan	.40	.20	.10
57	Phil Garner	.40	.20	.10
58	Ron Reed	.40	.20	.10
59	Larry Hisle	.40	.20	.10
60	Jerry Reuss	.40	.20	.10
61	Ron LeFlore	.40	.20	.10
62	Johnny Oates	.40	.20	.10
63	Bobby Darwin	.40	.20	.10
64	Jerry Koosman	.40	.20	.10
65	Chris Chambliss	.40	.20	.10

		NM	EX	VG
66	Father & Son (Buddy Bell, Gus Bell)	.40	.20	.10
67	Father & Son (Bob Boone, Ray Boone)	.40	.20	.12
68	Father & Son (Joe Coleman, Joe Coleman, Jr.)	.40	.20	.10
69	Father & Son (Jim Hegan, Mike Hegan)	.40	.20	.10
70	Father & Son (Roy Smalley, III, Roy Smalley, Jr.)	.40	.20	.10
71	Steve Rogers	.40	.20	.10
72	Hal McRae	.40	.20	.10
73	Baltimore Orioles Team (Earl Weaver)	1.00	.50	.30
74	Oscar Gamble	.40	.20	.10
75	Larry Dierker	.40	.20	.10
76	Willie Crawford	.40	.20	.10
77	Pedro Borbon	.40	.20	.10
78	Cecil Cooper	.40	.20	.10
79	Jerry Morales	.40	.20	.10
80	Jim Kaat	.75	.40	.25
81	Darrell Evans	.75	.40	.25
82	Von Joshua	.40	.20	.10
83	Jim Spencer	.40	.20	.10
84	Brent Strom	.40	.20	.10
85	Mickey Rivers	.40	.20	.10
86	Mike Tyson	.40	.20	.10
87	Tom Burgmeier	.40	.20	.10
88	Duffy Dyer	.40	.20	.10
89	Vern Ruhle	.40	.20	.10
90	Sal Bando	.40	.20	.10
91	Tom Hutton	.40	.20	.10
92	Eduardo Rodriguez	.40	.20	.10
93	Mike Phillips	.40	.20	.10
94	Jim Dwyer	.40	.20	.10
95	Brooks Robinson	6.00	3.00	1.75
96	Doug Bird	.40	.20	.10
97	Wilbur Howard	.40	.20	.10
98	*Dennis Eckersley*	25.00	12.50	7.50
99	Lee Lacy	.40	.20	.10
100	Jim Hunter	4.00	2.00	1.00
101	Pete LaCock	.40	.20	.10
102	Jim Willoughby	.40	.20	.10
103	Biff Pocoroba	.40	.20	.10
104	Cincinnati Reds Team (Sparky Anderson)	1.00	.50	.30
105	Gary Lavelle	.40	.20	.10
106	Tom Grieve	.40	.20	.10
107	Dave Roberts	.40	.20	.10
108	Don Kirkwood	.40	.20	.10
109	Larry Lintz	.40	.20	.10
110	Carlos May	.40	.20	.10
111	Danny Thompson	.40	.20	.10
112	*Kent Tekulve*	.75	.40	.25
113	Gary Sutherland	.40	.20	.10
114	Jay Johnstone	.40	.20	.10
115	Ken Holtzman	.40	.20	.10
116	Charlie Moore	.40	.20	.10
117	Mike Jorgensen	.40	.20	.10
118	Boston Red Sox Team (Darrell Johnson)	1.00	.50	.30
119	Checklist 1-132	1.00	.50	.30
120	Rusty Staub	.75	.40	.25
121	Tony Solaita	.40	.20	.10
122	Mike Cosgrove	.40	.20	.10
123	Walt Williams	.40	.20	.10
124	Doug Rau	.40	.20	.10
125	Don Baylor	1.50	.70	.45
126	Tom Dettore	.40	.20	.10
127	Larvell Blanks	.40	.20	.10
128	Ken Griffey	1.00	.50	.30
129	Andy Etchebarren	.40	.20	.10
130	Luis Tiant	1.00	.50	.30
131	Bill Stein	.40	.20	.10
132	Don Hood	.40	.20	.10
133	Gary Matthews	.40	.20	.10
134	Mike Ivie	.40	.20	.10
135	Bake McBride	.40	.20	.10
136	Dave Goltz	.40	.20	.10
137	Bill Robinson	.40	.20	.10
138	Lerrin LaGrow	.40	.20	.10
139	Gorman Thomas	.75	.40	.25
140	Vida Blue	1.00	.50	.30
141	*Larry Parrish*	1.00	.50	.30
142	Dick Drago	.40	.20	.10
143	Jerry Grote	.40	.20	.10
144	Al Fitzmorris	.40	.20	.10
145	Larry Bowa	1.00	.50	.30
146	George Medich	.40	.20	.10
147	Houston Astros Team (Bill Virdon)	1.00	.50	.30
148	Stan Thomas	.40	.20	.10
149	Tommy Davis	.40	.20	.10
150	Steve Garvey	2.00	1.00	.60
151	Bill Bonham	.40	.20	.10
152	Leroy Stanton	.40	.20	.10
153	Buzz Capra	.40	.20	.10
154	Bucky Dent	.40	.20	.10
155	Jack Billingham	.40	.20	.10
156	Rico Carty	.40	.20	.10
157	Mike Caldwell	.40	.20	.10
158	Ken Reitz	.40	.20	.10
159	Jerry Terrell	.40	.20	.10
160	Dave Winfield	8.00	4.00	2.50
161	Bruce Kison	.40	.20	.10
162	Jack Pierce	.40	.20	.10
163	Jim Slaton	.40	.20	.10
164	Pepe Mangual	.40	.20	.10
165	Gene Tenace	.40	.20	.10
166	Skip Lockwood	.40	.20	.10
167	Freddie Patek	.40	.20	.10
168	Tom Hilgendorf	.40	.20	.10
169	Graig Nettles	.75	.40	.2
170	Rick Wise	.40	.20	.10
171	Greg Gross	.40	.20	.10
172	Texas Rangers Team (Frank Lucchesi)	1.00	.50	.30
173	Steve Swisher	.40	.20	.10

#	Player			
174	Charlie Hough	.75	.40	.25
175	Ken Singleton	.40	.20	.10
176	Dick Lange	.40	.20	.10
177	Marty Perez	.40	.20	.10
178	Tom Buskey	.40	.20	.10
179	George Foster	.75	.40	.25
180	Rich Gossage	1.00	.50	.30
181	Willie Montanez	.40	.20	.10
182	Harry Rasmussen	.40	.20	.10
183	Steve Braun	.40	.20	.10
184	Bill Greif	.40	.20	.10
185	Dave Parker	1.00	.50	.30
186	Tom Walker	.40	.20	.10
187	Pedro Garcia	.40	.20	.10
188	Fred Scherman	.40	.20	.10
189	Claudell Washington	.40	.20	.10
190	Jon Matlack	.40	.20	.10
191	N.L. Batting Leaders (Bill Madlock, Manny Sanguillen, Ted Simmons)	.75	.40	.25
192	A.L. Batting Leaders (Rod Carew, Fred Lynn, Thurman Munson)	1.00	.50	.30
193	N.L. Home Run Leaders (Dave Kingman, Greg Luzinski, Mike Schmidt)	2.00	1.00	.60
194	A.L. Home Run Leaders (Reggie Jackson, John Mayberry, George Scott)	2.00	1.00	.60
195	N.L. RBI Leaders (Johnny Bench, Greg Luzinski, Tony Perez)	1.00	.50	.30
196	A.L. RBI Leaders (Fred Lynn, John Mayberry, George Scott)	.40	.20	.10
197	N.L. Stolen Base Leaders (Lou Brock, Dave Lopes, Joe Morgan)	1.50	.70	.45
198	A.L. Stolen Base Leaders (Amos Otis, Mickey Rivers, Claudell Washington)	.40	.20	.10
199	N.L. Victory Leaders (Randy Jones, Andy Messersmith, Tom Seaver)	2.00	1.00	.60
200	A.L. Victory Leaders (Vida Blue, Jim Hunter, Jim Palmer)	1.00	.50	.30
201	N.L. ERA Leaders (Randy Jones, Andy Messersmith, Tom Seaver)	1.00	.50	.30
202	A.L. ERA Leaders (Dennis Eckersley, Jim Hunter, Jim Palmer)	2.00	1.00	.60
203	N.L. Strikeout Leaders (Andy Messersmith, John Montefusco, Tom Seaver)	1.50	.70	.45
204	A.L. Strikeout Leaders (Bert Blyleven, Gaylord Perry, Frank Tanana)	1.00	.50	.30
205	Major League Leading Firemen (Rich Gossage, Al Hrabosky)	.75	.40	.25
206	Manny Trillo	.40	.20	.10
207	Andy Hassler	.40	.20	.10
208	Mike Lum	.40	.20	.10
209	Alan Ashby	.40	.20	.10
210	Lee May	.40	.20	.10
211	Clay Carroll	.40	.20	.10
212	Pat Kelly	.40	.20	.10
213	Dave Heaverlo	.40	.20	.10
214	Eric Soderholm	.40	.20	.10
215	Reggie Smith	.40	.20	.10
216	Montreal Expos Team (Karl Kuehl)	1.00	.50	.30
217	Dave Freisleben	.40	.20	.10
218	John Knox	.40	.20	.10
219	Tom Murphy	.40	.20	.10
220	Manny Sanguillen	.40	.20	.10
221	Jim Todd	.40	.20	.10
222	Wayne Garrett	.40	.20	.10
223	Ollie Brown	.40	.20	.10
224	Jim York	.40	.20	.10
225	Roy White	.40	.20	.10
226	Jim Sundberg	.40	.20	.10
227	Oscar Zamora	.40	.20	.10
228	John Hale	.40	.20	.10
229	*Jerry Remy*			
230	Carl Yastrzemski	8.00	4.00	2.00
231	Tom House	.40	.20	.10
232	Frank Duffy	.40	.20	.10
233	Grant Jackson	.40	.20	.10
234	Mike Sadek	.40	.20	.10
235	Bert Blyleven	1.00	.50	.30
236	Kansas City Royals Team (Whitey Herzog)	1.00	.50	.30
237	Dave Hamilton	.40	.20	.10
238	Larry Biittner	.40	.20	.10
239	John Curtis	.40	.20	.10
240	Pete Rose	20.00	10.00	5.00
241	Hector Torres	.40	.20	.10
242	Dan Meyer	.40	.20	.10
243	Jim Rooker	.40	.20	.10
244	Bill Sharp	.40	.20	.10
245	Felix Millan	.40	.20	.10
246	Cesar Tovar	.40	.20	.10
247	Terry Harmon	.40	.20	.10
248	Dick Tidrow	.40	.20	.10
249	Cliff Johnson	.40	.20	.10
250	Fergie Jenkins	3.00	1.50	.90
251	Rick Monday	.40	.20	.10
252	Tim Nordbrook	.40	.20	.10
253	Bill Buckner	.75	.40	.25
254	Rudy Meoli	.40	.20	.10
255	Fritz Peterson	.40	.20	.10
256	Rowland Office	.40	.20	.10
257	Ross Grimsley	.40	.20	.10
258	Nyls Nyman	.40	.20	.10
259	Darrel Chaney	.40	.20	.10
260	Steve Busby	.40	.20	.10
261	Gary Thomasson	.40	.20	.10

#	Player			
262	Checklist 133-264	1.00	.50	.30
263	*Lyman Bostock*	.75	.40	.25
264	Steve Renko	.40	.20	.10
265	Willie Davis	.40	.20	.10
266	Alan Foster	.40	.20	.10
267	Aurelio Rodriguez	.40	.20	.10
268	Del Unser	.40	.20	.10
269	Rick Austin	.40	.20	.10
270	Willie Stargell	4.00	2.00	1.25
271	Jim Lonborg	.40	.20	.10
272	Rick Dempsey	.40	.20	.10
273	Joe Niekro	.40	.20	.10
274	Tommy Harper	.40	.20	.10
275	*Rick Manning*	.75	.40	.25
276	Mickey Scott	.40	.20	.10
277	Chicago Cubs Team (Jim Marshall)	1.00	.50	.30
278	Bernie Carbo	.40	.20	.10
279	Roy Howell	.40	.20	.10
280	Burt Hooton	.40	.20	.10
281	Dave May	.40	.20	.10
282	Dan Osborn	.40	.20	.10
283	Merv Rettenmund	.40	.20	.10
284	Steve Ontiveros	.40	.20	.10
285	Mike Cuellar	.40	.20	.10
286	Jim Wohlford	.40	.20	.10
287	Pete Mackanin	.40	.20	.10
288	Bill Campbell	.40	.20	.10
289	Enzo Hernandez	.40	.20	.10
290	Ted Simmons	.40	.20	.10
291	Ken Sanders	.40	.20	.10
292	Leon Roberts	.40	.20	.10
293	Bill Castro	.40	.20	.10
294	Ed Kirkpatrick	.40	.20	.10
295	Dave Cash	.40	.20	.10
296	Pat Dobson	.40	.20	.10
297	Roger Metzger	.40	.20	.10
298	Dick Bosman	.40	.20	.10
299	Champ Summers	.40	.20	.10
300	Johnny Bench	10.00	5.00	3.00
301	Jackie Brown	.40	.20	.10
302	Rick Miller	.40	.20	.10
303	Steve Foucault	.40	.20	.10
304	California Angels Team (Dick Williams)	1.00	.50	.30
305	Andy Messersmith	.40	.20	.10
306	Rod Gilbreath	.40	.20	.10
307	Al Bumbry	.40	.20	.10
308	Jim Barr	.40	.20	.10
309	Bill Melton	.40	.20	.10
310	Randy Jones	.40	.20	.10
311	Cookie Rojas	.40	.20	.10
312	Don Carrithers	.40	.20	.10
313	*Dan Ford*	.40	.20	.10
314	Ed Kranepool	.40	.20	.10
315	Al Hrabosky	.40	.20	.10
316	Robin Yount	10.00	5.00	2.50
317	*John Candelaria*	1.00	.50	.30
318	Bob Boone	.75	.40	.25
319	Larry Gura	.40	.20	.10
320	Willie Horton	.40	.20	.10
321	Jose Cruz	.75	.40	.25
322	Glenn Abbott	.40	.20	.10
323	Rob Sperring	.40	.20	.10
324	Jim Bibby	.40	.20	.10
325	Tony Perez	4.00	2.00	1.25
326	Dick Pole	.40	.20	.10
327	Dave Moates	.40	.20	.10
328	Carl Morton	.40	.20	.10
329	Joe Ferguson	.40	.20	.10
330	Nolan Ryan	15.00	7.50	4.50
331	San Diego Padres Team (John McNamara)	1.00	.50	.30
332	Charlie Williams	.40	.20	.10
333	Bob Coluccio	.40	.20	.10
334	Dennis Leonard	.40	.20	.10
335	Bob Grich	.75	.40	.25
336	Vic Albury	.40	.20	.10
337	Bud Harrelson	.40	.20	.10
338	Bob Bailey	.40	.20	.10
339	John Denny	.40	.20	.10
340	Jim Rice	3.00	1.50	.90
341	Lou Gehrig (All Time 1B)	10.00	5.00	3.00
342	Rogers Hornsby (All Time 2B)	2.50	1.25	.70
343	Pie Traynor (All Time 3B)	1.00	.50	.30
344	Honus Wagner (All Time SS)	5.00	2.50	1.50
345	Babe Ruth (All Time OF)	15.00	7.50	4.50
346	Ty Cobb (All Time OF)	10.00	5.00	3.00
347	Ted Williams (All Time OF)	10.00	5.00	3.00
348	Mickey Cochrane (All Time C)	1.00	.50	.30
349	Walter Johnson" (All Time RHP)	4.00	2.00	1.25
350	Lefty Grove (All Time LHP)	1.00	.50	.30
351	Randy Hundley	.40	.20	.10
352	Dave Giusti	.40	.20	.10
353	*Sixto Lezcano*	.75	.40	.25
354	Ron Blomberg	.40	.20	.10
355	Steve Carlton	4.00	2.00	1.25
356	Ted Martinez	.40	.20	.10
357	Ken Forsch	.40	.20	.10
358	Buddy Bell	.40	.20	.10
359	Rick Reuschel	.40	.20	.10
360	Jeff Burroughs	.40	.20	.10
361	Detroit Tigers Team (Ralph Houk)	1.00	.50	.30
362	Will McEnaney	.40	.20	.10
363	*Dave Collins*	.40	.20	.12
364	Elias Sosa	.40	.20	.10
365	Carlton Fisk	5.00	2.50	1.50
366	Bobby Valentine	.40	.20	.10
367	Bruce Miller	.40	.20	.10
368	Wilbur Wood	.40	.20	.10
369	Frank White	.75	.40	.25
370	Ron Cey	.75	.40	.25
371	Ellie Hendricks	.40	.20	.10
372	Rick Baldwin	.40	.20	.10
373	Johnny Briggs	.40	.20	.10
374	Dan Warthen	.40	.20	.10

#	Player			
375	Ron Fairly	.40	.20	.10
376	Rich Hebner	.40	.20	.10
377	Mike Hegan	.40	.20	.10
378	Steve Stone	.40	.20	.10
379	Ken Boswell	.40	.20	.10
380	Bobby Bonds	1.00	.50	.30
381	Denny Doyle	.40	.20	.10
382	Matt Alexander	.40	.20	.10
383	John Ellis	.40	.20	.10
384	Philadelphia Phillies Team (Danny Ozark)	1.00	.50	.30
385	Mickey Lolich	.75	.40	.25
386	Ed Goodson	.40	.20	.10
387	Mike Miley	.40	.20	.10
388	Stan Perzanowski	.40	.20	.10
389	Glenn Adams	.40	.20	.10
390	Don Gullett	.40	.20	.10
391	Jerry Hairston Sr.	.40	.20	.10
392	Checklist 265-396	1.00	.50	.30
393	Paul Mitchell	.40	.20	.10
394	Fran Healy	.40	.20	.10
395	Jim Wynn	.40	.20	.10
396	Bill Lee	.40	.20	.10
397	Tim Foli	.40	.20	.10
398	Dave Tomlin	.40	.20	.10
399	Luis Melendez	.40	.20	.10
400	Rod Carew	5.00	2.50	1.50
401	Ken Brett	.40	.20	.10
402	Don Money	.40	.20	.10
403	Geoff Zahn	.40	.20	.10
404	Enos Cabell	.40	.20	.10
405	Rollie Fingers	3.00	1.50	.90
406	Ed Herrmann	.40	.20	.10
407	Tom Underwood	.40	.20	.10
408	Charlie Spikes	.40	.20	.10
409	Dave Lemanczyk	.40	.20	.10
410	Ralph Garr	.40	.20	.10
411	Bill Singer	.40	.20	.10
412	Toby Harrah	.40	.20	.10
413	Pete Varney	.40	.20	.10
414	Wayne Garland	.40	.20	.10
415	Vada Pinson	1.00	.50	.30
416	Tommy John	1.00	.50	.30
417	Gene Clines	.40	.20	.10
418	Jose Morales	.40	.20	.10
419	Reggie Cleveland	.40	.20	.10
420	Joe Morgan	4.00	2.00	1.25
421	Oakland A's Team	1.00	.50	.30
422	Johnny Grubb	.40	.20	.10
423	Ed Halicki	.40	.20	.10
424	Phil Roof	.40	.20	.10
425	Rennie Stennett	.40	.20	.10
426	Bob Forsch	.40	.20	.10
427	Kurt Bevacqua	.40	.20	.10
428	Jim Crawford	.40	.20	.10
429	Fred Stanley	.40	.20	.10
430	Jose Cardenal	.40	.20	.10
431	Dick Ruthven	.40	.20	.10
432	Tom Veryzer	.40	.20	.10
433	Rick Waits	.40	.20	.10
434	Morris Nettles	.40	.20	.10
435	Phil Niekro	3.00	1.50	.90
436	Bill Fahey	.40	.20	.10
437	Terry Forster	.40	.20	.10
438	Doug DeCinces	.40	.20	.10
439	Rick Rhoden	.40	.20	.10
440	John Mayberry	.40	.20	.10
441	Gary Carter	6.00	3.00	1.75
442	Hank Webb	.40	.20	.10
443	San Francisco Giants Team	1.00	.50	.30
444	Gary Nolan	.40	.20	.10
445	Rico Petrocelli	.40	.20	.10
446	Larry Haney	.40	.20	.10
447	Gene Locklear	.40	.20	.10
448	Tom Johnson	.40	.20	.10
449	Bob Robertson	.40	.20	.10
450	Jim Palmer	4.00	2.00	1.25
451	Buddy Bradford	.40	.20	.10
452	Tom Hausman	.40	.20	.10
453	Lou Piniella	1.50	.70	.45
454	Tom Griffin	.40	.20	.10
455	Dick Allen	.75	.40	.25
456	Joe Coleman	.40	.20	.10
457	Ed Crosby	.40	.20	.10
458	Earl Williams	.40	.20	.10
459	Jim Brewer	.40	.20	.10
460	Cesar Cedeno	.40	.20	.10
461	NL & AL Championships	.75	.40	.25
462	1975 World Series	.75	.40	.25
463	Steve Hargan	.40	.20	.10
464	Ken Henderson	.40	.20	.10
465	Mike Marshall	.40	.20	.10
466	Bob Stinson	.40	.20	.10
467	Woodie Fryman	.40	.20	.10
468	Jesus Alou	.40	.20	.10
469	Rawly Eastwick	.40	.20	.10
470	Bobby Murcer	.75	.40	.25
471	Jim Burton	.40	.20	.10
472	Bob Davis	.40	.20	.10
473	Paul Blair	.40	.20	.10
474	Ray Corbin	.40	.20	.10
475	Joe Rudi	.40	.20	.10
476	Bob Moose	.40	.20	.10
477	Cleveland Indians Team (Frank Robinson)	1.50	.70	.45
478	Lynn McGlothen	.40	.20	.10
479	Bobby Mitchell	.40	.20	.10
480	Mike Schmidt	12.00	6.00	3.00
481	Rudy May	.40	.20	.10
482	Tim Hosley	.40	.20	.10
483	Mickey Stanley	.40	.20	.10
484	Eric Raich	.40	.20	.10
485	Mike Hargrove	.40	.20	.10
486	Bruce Dal Canton	.40	.20	.10
487	Leron Lee	.40	.20	.10
488	Claude Osteen	.40	.20	.10
489	Skip Jutze	.40	.20	.10
490	Frank Tanana	.40	.20	.10

491	Terry Crowley	.40	.20	.10
492	Marty Pattin	.40	.20	.10
493	Derrel Thomas	.40	.20	.10
494	Craig Swan	.40	.20	.10
495	Nate Colbert	.40	.20	.10
496	Juan Beniquez	.40	.20	.10
497	Joe McIntosh	.40	.20	.10
498	Glenn Borgmann	.40	.20	.10
499	Mario Guerrero	.40	.20	.10
500	Reggie Jackson	10.00	5.00	3.00
501	Billy Champion	.40	.20	.10
502	Tim McCarver	1.00	.50	.30
503	Elliott Maddox	.40	.20	.10
504	Pittsburgh Pirates Team (Danny Murtaugh)	1.00	.50	.30
505	Mark Belanger	.40	.20	.10
506	George Mitterwald	.40	.20	.10
507	Ray Bare	.40	.20	.10
508	*Duane Kuiper*	.40	.20	.10
509	Bill Hands	.40	.20	.10
510	Amos Otis	.40	.20	.10
511	Jamie Easterly	.40	.20	.10
512	Ellie Rodriguez	.40	.20	.10
513	Bart Johnson	.40	.20	.10
514	Dan Driessen	.40	.20	.10
515	Steve Yeager	.40	.20	.10
516	Wayne Granger	.40	.20	.10
517	John Milner	.40	.20	.10
518	*Doug Flynn*	.40	.20	.10
519	Steve Brye	.40	.20	.10
520	Willie McCovey	4.00	2.00	1.25
521	Jim Colborn	.40	.20	.10
522	Ted Sizemore	.40	.20	.10
523	Bob Montgomery	.40	.20	.10
524	Pete Falcone	.40	.20	.10
525	Billy Williams	3.00	1.50	.75
526	Checklist 397-528	1.00	.50	.30
527	Mike Anderson	.40	.20	.10
528	Dock Ellis	.40	.20	.10
529	Deron Johnson	.40	.20	.10
530	Don Sutton	3.00	1.50	.90
531	New York Mets Team (Joe Frazier)	1.00	.50	.30
532	Milt May	.40	.20	.10
533	Lee Richard	.40	.20	.10
534	Stan Bahnsen	.40	.20	.10
535	Dave Nelson	.40	.20	.10
536	Mike Thompson	.40	.20	.10
537	Tony Muser	.40	.20	.10
538	Pat Darcy	.40	.20	.10
539	John Balaz	.40	.20	.10
540	Bill Freehan	.40	.20	.10
541	Steve Mingori	.40	.20	.10
542	Keith Hernandez	1.00	.50	.30
543	Wayne Twitchell	.40	.20	.10
544	Pepe Frias	.40	.20	.10
545	Sparky Lyle	.40	.20	.10
546	Dave Rosello	.40	.20	.10
547	Roric Harrison	.40	.20	.10
548	Manny Mota	.40	.20	.10
549	Randy Tate	.40	.20	.10
550	Hank Aaron	25.00	12.50	7.50
551	Jerry DaVanon	.40	.20	.10
552	Terry Humphrey	.40	.20	.10
553	Randy Moffitt	.40	.20	.10
554	Ray Fosse	.40	.20	.10
555	Dyar Miller	.40	.20	.10
556	Minnesota Twins Team (Gene Mauch)	1.00	.50	.30
557	Dan Spillner	.40	.20	.10
558	Clarence Gaston	.40	.20	.10
559	Clyde Wright	.40	.20	.10
560	Jorge Orta	.40	.20	.10
561	Tom Carroll	.40	.20	.10
562	Adrian Garrett	.40	.20	.10
563	Larry Demery	.40	.20	.10
564	Kurt Bevacqua (Bubble Gum Blowing Champ)	.40	.20	.10
565	Tug McGraw	.75	.40	.25
566	Ken McMullen	.40	.20	.10
567	George Stone	.40	.20	.10
568	Rob Andrews	.40	.20	.10
569	Nelson Briles	.40	.20	.10
570	George Hendrick	.40	.20	.10
571	Don DeMola	.40	.20	.10
572	Rich Coggins	.40	.20	.10
573	Bill Travers	.40	.20	.10
574	Don Kessinger	.40	.20	.10
575	Dwight Evans	.75	.40	.25
576	Maximino Leon	.40	.20	.10
577	Marc Hill	.40	.20	.10
578	Ted Kubiak	.40	.20	.10
579	Clay Kirby	.40	.20	.10
580	Bert Campaneris	.40	.20	.10
581	St. Louis Cardinals Team (Red Schoendienst)	1.50	.70	.45
582	Mike Kekich	.40	.20	.10
583	Tommy Helms	.40	.20	.10
584	Stan Wall	.40	.20	.10
585	Joe Torre	1.50	.70	.45
586	Ron Schueler	.40	.20	.10
587	Leo Cardenas	.40	.20	.10
588	Kevin Kobel	.40	.20	.10
589	Rookie Pitchers (Santo Alcala, Mike Flanagan, Joe Pactwa, Pablo Torrealba)	1.00	.50	.30
590	Rookie Outfielders (**Henry Cruz, Chet Lemon, Ellis Valentine, Terry Whitfield**)	.75	.40	.25
591	Rookie Pitchers (Steve Grilli, Craig Mitchell, Jose Sosa, George Throop)	.40	.20	.10
592	Rookie Infielders (*Dave McKay, Willie Randolph, Jerry Royster, Roy Staiger*)	6.00	3.00	1.75

593	Rookie Pitchers (*Larry Anderson, Ken Crosby, Mark Littell, Butch Metzger*)	.40	.20	.10
594	Rookie Catchers & Outfielders (Andy Merchant, Ed Ott, Royle Stillman, Jerry White)	.40	.20	.10
595	Rookie Pitchers (Steve Barr, Art DeFilippis, Randy Lerch, Sid Monge)	.40	.20	.10
596	Rookie Infielders (*Lamar Johnson, Johnny LeMaster, Jerry Manuel, Craig Reynolds*)	.40	.20	.10
597	Rookie Pitchers (Don Aase, Jack Kucek, Frank LaCorte, Mike Pazik)	.40	.20	.10
598	Rookie Outfielders (Hector Cruz, *Jamie Quirk*, Jerry Turner, Joe Wallis)	.40	.20	.10
599	Rookie Pitchers (*Rob Dressler, Ron Guidry, Bob McClure, Pat Zachry*)	10.00	5.00	2.50
600	Tom Seaver	8.00	4.00	2.50
601	Ken Rudolph	.40	.20	.10
602	Doug Konieczny	.40	.20	.10
603	Jim Holt	.40	.20	.10
604	Joe Lovitto	.40	.20	.10
605	Al Downing	.40	.20	.10
606	Milwaukee Brewers Team (Alex Grammas)	1.00	.50	.30
607	Rich Hinton	.40	.20	.10
608	Vic Correll	.40	.20	.10
609	Fred Norman	.40	.20	.10
610	Greg Luzinski	.75	.40	.25
611	Rich Folkers	.40	.20	.10
612	Joe Lahoud	.40	.20	.10
613	Tim Johnson	.40	.20	.10
614	Fernando Arroyo	.40	.20	.10
615	Mike Cubbage	.40	.20	.10
616	Buck Martinez	.40	.20	.10
617	Darold Knowles	.40	.20	.10
618	Jack Brohamer	.40	.20	.10
619	Bill Butler	.40	.20	.10
620	Al Oliver	.75	.40	.25
621	Tom Hall	.40	.20	.10
622	Rick Auerbach	.40	.20	.10
623	Bob Allietta	.40	.20	.10
624	Tony Taylor	.40	.20	.10
625	J.R. Richard	.40	.20	.10
626	Bob Sheldon	.40	.20	.10
627	Bill Plummer	.40	.20	.10
628	John D'Acquisto	.40	.20	.10
629	Sandy Alomar	.40	.20	.10
630	Chris Speier	.40	.20	.10
631	Atlanta Braves Team (Dave Bristol)	1.00	.50	.30
632	Rogelio Moret	.40	.20	.10
633	*John Stearns*	.40	.20	.10
634	Larry Christenson	.40	.20	.10
635	Jim Fregosi	.40	.20	.10
636	Joe Decker	.40	.20	.10
637	Bruce Bochte	.40	.20	.10
638	Doyle Alexander	.40	.20	.10
639	Fred Kendall	.40	.20	.10
640	Bill Madlock	.75	.40	.25
641	Tom Paciorek	.40	.20	.10
642	Dennis Blair	.40	.20	.10
643	Checklist 529-660	1.00	.50	.30
644	Tom Bradley	.40	.20	.10
645	Darrell Porter	.40	.20	.10
646	John Lowenstein	.40	.20	.10
647	Ramon Hernandez	.40	.20	.10
648	Al Cowens	.40	.20	.10
649	Dave Roberts	.40	.20	.10
650	Thurman Munson	8.00	4.00	2.00
651	John Odom	.40	.20	.10
652	Ed Armbrister	.40	.20	.10
653	*Mike Norris*	.40	.20	.10
654	Doug Griffin	.40	.20	.10
655	Mike Vail	.40	.20	.10
656	Chicago White Sox Team (Chuck Tanner)	1.00	.50	.30
657	*Roy Smalley*	.40	.20	.10
658	Jerry Johnson	.40	.20	.10
659	Ben Oglivie	.40	.20	.10
660	Dave Lopes	1.00	.50	.30

1976 Topps Traded

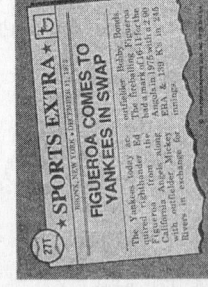

Similar to the Topps Traded set of 1974, the 2-1/2" x 3-1/2" cards feature photos of players traded after the printing dead-line. The style of the cards is essentially the same as the regular issue, but with a large "Sports Extra" headline announcing the trade and its date. The backs continue in newspaper style to detail the specifics of the trade. There are 43 player cards and one checklist in the set. Numbers remain the same as the player's regular card, with the addition of a "T" suffix.

		NM	EX	VG
Complete Set (44):		20.00	10.00	6.00
Common Player:		.75	.35	.20
27T	Ed Figueroa	.75	.35	.20
28T	Dusty Baker	1.25	.60	.40
44T	Doug Rader	.75	.35	.20
58T	Ron Reed	.75	.35	.20
74T	Oscar Gamble	.75	.35	.20
80T	Jim Kaat	.75	.35	.20
83T	Jim Spencer	.75	.35	.20
85T	Mickey Rivers	.75	.35	.20
99T	Lee Lacy	.75	.35	.20
120T	Rusty Staub	.75	.35	.20
127T	Larvell Blanks	.75	.35	.20
146T	George Medich	.75	.35	.20
158T	Ken Reitz	.75	.35	.20
208T	Mike Lum	.75	.35	.20
211T	Clay Carroll	.75	.35	.20
231T	Tom House	.75	.35	.20
250T	Fergie Jenkins	3.00	1.50	.90
259T	Darrel Chaney	.75	.35	.20
292T	Leon Roberts	.75	.35	.20
296T	Pat Dobson	.75	.35	.20
309T	Bill Melton	.75	.35	.20
338T	Bob Bailey	.75	.35	.20
380T	Bobby Bonds	.75	.35	.20
383T	John Ellis	.75	.35	.20
385T	Mickey Lolich	.75	.35	.20
401T	Ken Brett	.75	.35	.20
410T	Ralph Garr	.75	.35	.20
411T	Bill Singer	.75	.35	.20
428T	Jim Crawford	.75	.35	.20
434T	Morris Nettles	.75	.35	.20
464T	Ken Henderson	.75	.35	.20
497T	Joe McIntosh	.75	.35	.20
524T	Pete Falcone	.75	.35	.20
527T	Mike Anderson	.75	.35	.20
528T	Dock Ellis	.75	.35	.20
532T	Milt May	.75	.35	.20
554T	Ray Fosse	.75	.35	.20
579T	Clay Kirby	.75	.35	.20
583T	Tommy Helms	.75	.35	.20
592T	Willie Randolph	.75	.35	.20
618T	Jack Brohamer	.75	.35	.20
632T	Rogelio Moret	.75	.35	.20
649T	Dave Roberts	.75	.35	.20
----	Traded Checklist	.75	.35	.20

1976 Topps Cloth Sticker Prototypes

Apparently produced to test different materials for the cloth sticker set which would be issued the following year, these pro-totypes were never issued. Each of the players can be found on four different types of material. The blank-backed stickers feature the card fronts as they appeared in the regular 1976 issue. It is unknown whether other players were produced for the test.

		NM	EX	VG
Common Player:		30.00	15.00	9.00
(1a)	Bob Apodaca (Silk)	30.00	15.00	9.00
(1b)	Bob Apodaca (Thin felt.)	30.00	15.00	9.00
(1c)	Bob Apodaca (Textured felt.)	60.00	30.00	18.00
(1d)	Bob Apodaca (Thick felt.)	30.00	15.00	9.00
(2a)	Duffy Dyer (Silk)	30.00	15.00	9.00
(2b)	Duffy Dyer (Thin felt.)	30.00	15.00	9.00
(2c)	Duffy Dyer (Textured felt.)	60.00	30.00	18.00
(2d)	Duffy Dyer (Thick felt.)	30.00	15.00	9.00

1976 Topps Team Checklist Sheet

Via a mail-in redemption (50¢ and a wrapper), collectors could receive an uncut sheet of the 24 team photo/checklist cards from the 1976 Topps baseball set. Measuring about 10-1/2" x 20-1/8", the sheet could be cut into individual team cards of standard size, though printed on stock that is lighter than pack-issued versions.

	NM	EX	VG
Complete Sheet:	35.00	17.50	10.00

1976 Topps Joe Garagiola

Topps produced this personal business card for long-time NBC announcer and former major leaguer Joe Garagiola. The front is in the format of a 1973 Topps card and has a color portrait. The back resembles the 1976 Topps card, is in black-and-white and provides contact information.

	NM	EX	VG
Joe Garagiola	20.00	10.00	6.00

1976 Topps/Dynamite Magazine Panels

In at least one issue of its "Dynamite" kids' magazine, Scholastic Book Club teamed with Topps to insert a six-card panel of its 1976 baseball issue. Values shown are for just the uncut panel; complete magazines would bear a small premium.

	NM	EX	VG
Complete Panel:	20.00	10.00	6.00
469 Rawly Eastwick			
471 Jim Burton			
474 Ray Corbin			
481 Rudy May			
482 Tim Hosley			
22 Ted Sizemore			

1977 Topps

 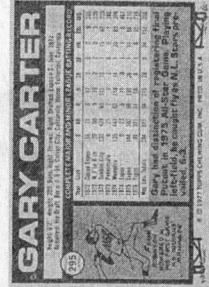

The 1977 Topps Set is a 660-card effort featuring front designs dominated by a color photograph on which there is a facsimile autograph. Above the picture are the player's name, team and position. The backs of the 2-1/2" x 3-1/2" cards include personal and career statistics along with newspaper-style highlights and a cartoon. Specialty cards include statistical leaders, record performances, a new "Turn Back The Clock" feature which highlighted great past moments and a "Big League Brothers" feature.

	NM	EX	VG
Complete Set (660):	200.00	95.00	55.00
Common Player:	.25	.10	.06
Wax Pack (10):	22.50		
Wax Box (36):	525.00		
Cello Pack (18):	40.00		
Cello Box (24):	1,200		
Rack Pack (39):	65.00		
Rack Box (24):	2,000		
Vending Box (500):	350.00		
1 Batting Leaders (George Brett, Bill Madlock)	6.00	3.00	1.75
2 Home Run Leaders (Graig Nettles, Mike Schmidt)	2.00	1.00	.60
3 RBI Leaders (George Foster, Lee May)	.75	.40	.25
4 Stolen Base Leaders (Dave Lopes, Bill North)	.50	.25	.15
5 Victory Leaders (Randy Jones, Jim Palmer)	1.00	.50	.30
6 Strikeout Leaders (Nolan Ryan, Tom Seaver)	10.00	5.00	3.00
7 ERA Leaders (John Denny, Mark Fidrych)	.50	.25	.15
8 Leading Firemen (Bill Campbell, Rawly Eastwick)	.25	.10	.06
9 Doug Rader	.25	.10	.06
10 Reggie Jackson	8.00	4.00	2.50
11 Rob Dressler	.25	.10	.06
12 Larry Haney	.25	.10	.06
13 Luis Gomez	.25	.10	.06
14 Tommy Smith	.25	.10	.06
15 Don Gullett	.25	.10	.06
16 Bob Jones	.25	.10	.06
17 Steve Stone	.25	.10	.06
18 Indians Team (Frank Robinson)	1.50	.70	.45
19 John D'Acquisto	.25	.10	.06
20 Graig Nettles	.75	.40	.25
21 Ken Forsch	.25	.10	.06
22 Bill Freehan	.25	.10	.06
23 Dan Driessen	.25	.10	.06
24 Carl Morton	.25	.10	.06
25 Dwight Evans	.75	.40	.25
26 Ray Sadecki	.25	.10	.06
27 Bill Buckner	.75	.40	.25
28 Woodie Fryman	.25	.10	.06
29 Bucky Dent	.50	.25	.15
30 Greg Luzinski	.50	.25	.15
31 Jim Todd	.25	.10	.06
32 Checklist 1-132	1.00	.50	.30
33 Wayne Garland	.25	.10	.06
34 Angels Team (Norm Sherry)	1.00	.50	.30
35 Rennie Stennett	.25	.10	.06
36 John Ellis	.25	.10	.06
37 Steve Hargan	.25	.10	.06
38 Craig Kusick	.25	.10	.06
39 Tom Griffin	.25	.10	.06
40 Bobby Murcer	.50	.25	.15
41 Jim Kern	.25	.10	.06
42 Jose Cruz	.25	.10	.06

		NM	EX	VG
43	Ray Bare	.25	.10	.06
44	Bud Harrelson	.25	.10	.06
45	Rawly Eastwick	.25	.10	.06
46	Buck Martinez	.25	.10	.06
47	Lynn McGlothen	.25	.10	.06
48	Tom Paciorek	.25	.10	.06
49	Grant Jackson	.25	.10	.06
50	Ron Cey	.50	.25	.15
51	Brewers Team (Alex Grammas)	1.00	.50	.30
52	Ellis Valentine	.25	.10	.06
53	Paul Mitchell	.25	.10	.06
54	Sandy Alomar	.25	.10	.06
55	Jeff Burroughs	.25	.10	.06
56	Rudy May	.25	.10	.06
57	Marc Hill	.25	.10	.06
58	Chet Lemon	.25	.10	.06
59	Larry Christenson	.25	.10	.06
60	Jim Rice	2.00	1.00	.60
61	Manny Sanguillen	.25	.10	.06
62	Eric Raich	.25	.10	.06
63	Tito Fuentes	.25	.10	.06
64	Larry Biittner	.25	.10	.06
65	Skip Lockwood	.25	.10	.06
66	Roy Smalley	.25	.10	.06
67	*Joaquin Andujar*	.50	.25	.15
68	Bruce Bochte	.25	.10	.06
69	Jim Crawford	.25	.10	.06
70	Johnny Bench	8.00	4.00	2.00
71	Dock Ellis	.25	.10	.06
72	Mike Anderson	.25	.10	.06
73	Charlie Williams	.25	.10	.06
74	A's Team (Jack McKeon)	1.00	.50	.30
75	Dennis Leonard	.25	.10	.06
76	Tim Foli	.25	.10	.06
77	Dyar Miller	.25	.10	.06
78	Bob Davis	.25	.10	.06
79	Don Money	.25	.10	.06
80	Andy Messersmith	.25	.10	.06
81	Juan Beniquez	.25	.10	.06
82	Jim Rooker	.25	.10	.06
83	Kevin Bell	.25	.10	.06
84	Ollie Brown	.25	.10	.06
85	Duane Kuiper	.25	.10	.06
86	Pat Zachry	.25	.10	.06
87	Glenn Borgmann	.25	.10	.06
88	Stan Wall	.25	.10	.06
89	*Butch Hobson*	.25	.10	.06
90	Cesar Cedeno	.25	.10	.06
91	John Verhoeven	.25	.10	.06
92	Dave Rosello	.25	.10	.06
93	Tom Poquette	.25	.10	.06
94	Craig Swan	.25	.10	.06
95	Keith Hernandez	.75	.40	.25
96	Lou Piniella	.75	.40	.25
97	Dave Heaverlo	.25	.10	.06
98	Milt May	.25	.10	.06
99	Tom Hausman	.25	.10	.06
100	Joe Morgan	3.00	1.50	.90
101	Dick Bosman	.25	.10	.06
102	Jose Morales	.25	.10	.06
103	Mike Bacsik	.25	.10	.06
104	*Omar Moreno*	.50	.25	.15
105	Steve Yeager	.50	.25	.15
106	Mike Flanagan	.50	.25	.15
107	Bill Melton	.25	.10	.06
108	Alan Foster	.25	.10	.06
109	Jorge Orta	.25	.10	.06
110	Steve Carlton	4.00	2.00	1.25
111	Rico Petrocelli	.50	.25	.15
112	Bill Greif	.25	.10	.06
113	Blue Jays Mgr./Coaches (Roy Hartsfield, Don Leppert, Bob Miller, Jackie Moore, Harry Warner)	.75	.40	.25
114	Bruce Dal Canton	.25	.10	.06
115	Rick Manning	.25	.10	.06
116	Joe Niekro	.25	.10	.06
117	Frank White	.25	.10	.06
118	Rick Jones	.25	.10	.06
119	John Stearns	.25	.10	.06
120	Rod Carew	4.00	2.00	1.00
121	Gary Nolan	.25	.10	.06
122	Ben Oglivie	.25	.10	.06
123	Fred Stanley	.25	.10	.06
124	George Mitterwald	.25	.10	.06
125	Bill Travers	.25	.10	.06
126	Rod Gilbreath	.25	.10	.06
127	Ron Fairly	.25	.10	.06
128	Tommy John	.50	.25	.15
129	Mike Sadek	.25	.10	.06
130	Al Oliver	.75	.40	.25
131	Orlando Ramirez	.25	.10	.06
132	Chip Lang	.25	.10	.06
133	Ralph Garr	.25	.10	.06
134	Padres Team (John McNamara)	.75	.40	.25
135	Mark Belanger	.25	.10	.06
136	*Jerry Mumphrey*	.25	.10	.06
137	Jeff Terpko	.25	.10	.06
138	Bob Stinson	.25	.10	.06
139	Fred Norman	.25	.10	.06
140	Mike Schmidt	10.00	5.00	3.00
141	Mark Littell	.25	.10	.06
142	Steve Dillard	.25	.10	.06
143	Ed Herrmann	.25	.10	.06
144	*Bruce Sutter*	15.00	7.50	4.50
145	Tom Veryzer	.25	.10	.06
146	Dusty Baker	1.00	.50	.30
147	Jackie Brown	.25	.10	.06
148	Fran Healy	.25	.10	.06
149	Mike Cubbage	.25	.10	.06
150	Tom Seaver	6.00	3.00	1.75
151	Johnnie LeMaster	.25	.10	.06
152	Gaylord Perry	2.50	1.25	.70
153	Ron Jackson	.25	.10	.06
154	Dave Giusti	.25	.10	.06
155	Joe Rudi	.25	.10	.06

		NM	EX	VG
156	Pete Mackanin	.25	.10	.06
157	Ken Brett	.25	.10	.06
158	Ted Kubiak	.25	.10	.06
159	Bernie Carbo	.25	.10	.06
160	Will McEnaney	.25	.10	.06
161	*Garry Templeton*	1.00	.50	.30
162	Mike Cuellar	.25	.10	.06
163	Dave Hilton	.25	.10	.06
164	Tug McGraw	.25	.10	.06
165	Jim Wynn	.25	.10	.06
166	Bill Campbell	.25	.10	.06
167	Rich Hebner	.25	.10	.06
168	Charlie Spikes	.25	.10	.06
169	Darold Knowles	.25	.10	.06
170	Thurman Munson	6.00	3.00	1.75
171	Ken Sanders	.25	.10	.06
172	John Milner	.25	.10	.06
173	Chuck Scrivener	.25	.10	.06
174	Nelson Briles	.25	.10	.06
175	*Butch Wynegar*	.25	.10	.06
176	Bob Robertson	.25	.10	.06
177	Bart Johnson	.25	.10	.06
178	Bombo Rivera	.25	.10	.06
179	Paul Hartzell	.25	.10	.06
180	Dave Lopes	.50	.25	.15
181	Ken McMullen	.25	.10	.06
182	Dan Spillner	.25	.10	.06
183	Cardinals Team (Vern Rapp)	1.00	.50	.30
184	Bo McLaughlin	.25	.10	.06
185	Sixto Lezcano	.25	.10	.06
186	Doug Flynn	.25	.10	.06
187	Dick Pole	.25	.10	.06
188	Bob Tolan	.25	.10	.06
189	Rick Dempsey	.25	.10	.06
190	Ray Burris	.25	.10	.06
191	Doug Griffin	.25	.10	.06
192	Clarence Gaston	.25	.10	.06
193	Larry Gura	.25	.10	.06
194	Gary Matthews	.25	.10	.06
195	Ed Figueroa	.25	.10	.06
196	Len Randle	.25	.10	.06
197	Ed Ott	.25	.10	.06
198	Wilbur Wood	.25	.10	.06
199	Pepe Frias	.25	.10	.06
200	Frank Tanana	.25	.10	.06
201	Ed Kranepool	.25	.10	.06
202	Tom Johnson	.25	.10	.06
203	Ed Armbrister	.25	.10	.06
204	Jeff Newman	.25	.10	.06
205	Pete Falcone	.25	.10	.06
206	Boog Powell	.75	.40	.25
207	Glenn Abbott	.25	.10	.06
208	Checklist 133-264	.75	.40	.25
209	Rob Andrews	.25	.10	.06
210	Fred Lynn	.50	.25	.15
211	Giants Team (Joe Altobelli)	.75	.40	.25
212	Jim Mason	.25	.10	.06
213	Maximino Leon	.25	.10	.06
214	Darrell Porter	.25	.10	.06
215	Butch Metzger	.25	.10	.06
216	Doug DeCinces	.25	.10	.06
217	Tom Underwood	.25	.10	.06
218	*John Wathan*	.25	.10	.06
219	Joe Coleman	.25	.10	.06
220	Chris Chambliss	.50	.25	.15
221	Bob Bailey	.25	.10	.06
222	Francisco Barrios	.25	.10	.06
223	Earl Williams	.25	.10	.06
224	Rusty Torres	.25	.10	.06
225	Bob Apodaca	.25	.10	.06
226	Leroy Stanton	.25	.10	.06
227	*Joe Sambito*	.25	.10	.06
228	Twins Team (Gene Mauch)	1.00	.50	.30
229	Don Kessinger	.25	.10	.06
230	Vida Blue	.25	.10	.06
231	George Brett (Record Breaker)	6.00	3.00	1.50
232	Minnie Minoso (Record Breaker)	.50	.25	.15
233	Jose Morales (Record Breaker)	.50	.25	.15
234	Nolan Ryan (Record Breaker)	12.00	6.00	3.00
235	Cecil Cooper	.25	.10	.06
236	Tom Buskey	.25	.10	.06
237	Gene Clines	.25	.10	.06
238	Tippy Martinez	.25	.10	.06
239	Bill Plummer	.25	.10	.06
240	Ron LeFlore	.25	.10	.06
241	Dave Tomlin	.25	.10	.06
242	Ken Henderson	.25	.10	.06
243	Ron Reed	.25	.10	.06
244	John Mayberry	.25	.10	.06
245	Rick Rhoden	.25	.10	.06
246	Mike Vail	.25	.10	.06
247	Chris Knapp	.25	.10	.06
248	Wilbur Howard	.25	.10	.06
249	Pete Redfern	.25	.10	.06
250	Bill Madlock	.50	.25	.15
251	Tony Muser	.25	.10	.06
252	Dale Murray	.25	.10	.06
253	John Hale	.25	.10	.06
254	Doyle Alexander	.25	.10	.06
255	George Scott	.25	.10	.06
256	Joe Hoerner	.25	.10	.06
257	Mike Miley	.25	.10	.06
258	Luis Tiant	.50	.25	.15
259	Mets Team (Joe Frazier)	1.00	.50	.30
260	J.R. Richard	.25	.10	.06
261	Phil Garner	.50	.25	.15
262	Al Cowens	.25	.10	.06
263	Mike Marshall	.25	.10	.06
264	Tom Hutton	.25	.10	.06
265	*Mark Fidrych*	5.00	2.50	1.50
266	Derrel Thomas	.25	.10	.06
267	Ray Fosse	.25	.10	.06
268	Rick Sawyer	.25	.10	.06
269	Joe Lis	.25	.10	.06
270	Dave Parker	.50	.25	.15
271	Terry Forster	.25	.10	.06

No.	Player			
272	Lee Lacy	.25	.10	.06
273	Eric Soderholm	.25	.10	.06
274	Don Stanhouse	.25	.10	.06
275	Mike Hargrove	.25	.10	.06
276	A.L. Championship (Chambliss' Dramatic Homer Decides It)	.25	.13	.08
277	N.L. Championship (Reds Sweep Phillies 3 In Row)	3.00	1.50	.90
278	Danny Frisella	.25	.10	.06
279	Joe Wallis	.25	.10	.06
280	Jim Hunter	2.50	1.25	.70
281	Roy Staiger	.25	.10	.06
282	Sid Monge	.25	.10	.06
283	Jerry DaVanon	.25	.10	.06
284	Mike Norris	.25	.10	.06
285	Brooks Robinson	4.00	2.00	1.25
286	Johnny Grubb	.25	.10	.06
287	Reds Team (Sparky Anderson)	1.00	.50	.30
288	Bob Montgomery	.25	.10	.06
289	Gene Garber	.25	.10	.06
290	Amos Otis	.25	.10	.06
291	Jason Thompson	.25	.10	.06
292	Rogelio Moret	.25	.10	.06
293	Jack Brohamer	.25	.10	.06
294	George Medich	.25	.10	.06
295	Gary Carter	3.00	1.50	.90
296	Don Hood	.25	.10	.06
297	Ken Reitz	.25	.10	.06
298	Charlie Hough	.25	.10	.06
299	Otto Velez	.25	.10	.06
300	Jerry Koosman	.25	.10	.06
301	Toby Harrah	.25	.10	.06
302	Mike Garman	.25	.10	.06
303	Gene Tenace	.25	.10	.06
304	Jim Hughes	.25	.10	.06
305	Mickey Rivers	.25	.10	.06
306	Rick Waits	.25	.10	.06
307	Gary Sutherland	.25	.10	.06
308	Gene Pentz	.25	.10	.06
309	Red Sox Team (Don Zimmer)	1.50	.70	.45
310	Larry Bowa	.50	.25	.15
311	Vern Ruhle	.25	.10	.06
312	Rob Belloir	.25	.10	.06
313	Paul Blair	.25	.10	.06
314	Steve Mingori	.25	.10	.06
315	Dave Chalk	.25	.10	.06
316	Steve Rogers	.25	.10	.06
317	Kurt Bevacqua	.25	.10	.06
318	Duffy Dyer	.25	.10	.06
319	Rich Gossage	.75	.40	.25
320	Ken Griffey	.75	.40	.25
321	Dave Goltz	.25	.10	.06
322	Bill Russell	.50	.25	.15
323	Larry Lintz	.25	.10	.06
324	John Curtis	.25	.10	.06
325	Mike Ivie	.25	.10	.06
326	Jesse Jefferson	.25	.10	.06
327	Astros Team (Bill Virdon)	.75	.40	.25
328	Tommy Boggs	.25	.10	.06
329	Ron Hodges	.25	.10	.06
330	George Hendrick	.25	.10	.06
331	Jim Colborn	.25	.10	.06
332	Elliott Maddox	.25	.10	.06
333	Paul Reuschel	.25	.10	.06
334	Bill Stein	.25	.10	.06
335	Bill Robinson	.25	.10	.06
336	Denny Doyle	.25	.10	.06
337	Ron Schueler	.25	.10	.06
338	Dave Duncan	.25	.10	.06
339	Adrian Devine	.25	.10	.06
340	Hal McRae	.50	.25	.15
341	Joe Kerrigan	.25	.10	.06
342	Jerry Remy	.25	.10	.06
343	Ed Halicki	.25	.10	.06
344	Brian Downing	.25	.10	.06
345	Reggie Smith	.25	.10	.06
346	Bill Singer	.25	.10	.06
347	George Foster	.25	.10	.06
348	Brent Strom	.25	.10	.06
349	Jim Holt	.25	.10	.06
350	Larry Dierker	.25	.10	.06
351	Jim Sundberg	.25	.10	.06
352	Mike Phillips	.25	.10	.06
353	Stan Thomas	.25	.10	.06
354	Pirates Team (Chuck Tanner)	.75	.40	.25
355	Lou Brock	3.00	1.50	.90
356	Checklist 265-396	.75	.40	.25
357	Tim McCarver	.75	.40	.25
358	Tom House	.25	.10	.06
359	Willie Randolph	.75	.40	.25
360	Rick Monday	.25	.10	.06
361	Eduardo Rodriguez	.25	.10	.06
362	Tommy Davis	.25	.10	.06
363	Dave Roberts	.25	.10	.06
364	Vic Correll	.25	.10	.06
365	Mike Torrez	.25	.10	.06
366	Ted Sizemore	.25	.10	.06
367	Dave Hamilton	.25	.10	.06
368	Mike Jorgensen	.25	.10	.06
369	Terry Humphrey	.25	.10	.06
370	John Montefusco	.25	.10	.06
371	Royals Team (Whitey Herzog)	1.00	.50	.30
372	Rich Folkers	.25	.10	.06
373	Bert Campaneris	.25	.10	.06
374	Kent Tekulve	.25	.10	.06
375	Larry Hisle	.25	.10	.06
376	Nino Espinosa	.25	.10	.06
377	Dave McKay	.25	.10	.06
378	Jim Umbarger	.25	.10	.06
379	Larry Cox	.25	.10	.06
380	Lee May	.25	.10	.06
381	Bob Forsch	.25	.10	.06
382	Charlie Moore	.25	.10	.06
383	Stan Bahnsen	.25	.10	.06
384	Darrel Chaney	.25	.10	.06
385	Dave LaRoche	.25	.10	.06
386	Manny Mota	.25	.10	.06
387	Yankees Team (Billy Martin)	2.00	1.00	.60
388	Terry Harmon	.25	.10	.06
389	Ken Kravec	.25	.10	.06
390	Dave Winfield	3.00	1.50	.90
391	Dan Warthen	.25	.10	.06
392	Phil Roof	.25	.10	.06
393	John Lowenstein	.25	.10	.06
394	Bill Laxton	.25	.10	.06
395	Manny Trillo	.25	.10	.06
396	Tom Murphy	.25	.10	.06
397	Larry Herndon	.25	.10	.06
398	Tom Burgmeier	.25	.10	.06
399	Bruce Boisclair	.25	.10	.06
400	Steve Garvey	2.00	1.00	.60
401	Mickey Scott	.25	.10	.06
402	Tommy Helms	.25	.10	.06
403	Tom Grieve	.25	.10	.06
404	Eric Rasmussen	.25	.10	.06
405	Claudell Washington	.25	.10	.06
406	Tim Johnson	.25	.10	.06
407	Dave Freisleben	.25	.10	.06
408	Cesar Tovar	.25	.10	.06
409	Pete Broberg	.25	.10	.06
410	Willie Montanez	.25	.10	.06
411	World Series Games 1 & 2 (Joe Morgan, Johnny Bench)	2.00	1.00	.60
412	World Series Games 3 & 4 (Johnny Bench)	2.00	1.00	.60
413	World Series Summary	.75	.40	.25
414	Tommy Harper	.25	.10	.06
415	Jay Johnstone	.25	.10	.06
416	Chuck Hartenstein	.25	.10	.06
417	Wayne Garrett	.25	.10	.06
418	White Sox Team (Bob Lemon)	1.00	.50	.30
419	Steve Swisher	.25	.10	.06
420	Rusty Staub	.50	.25	.15
421	Doug Rau	.25	.10	.06
422	Freddie Patek	.25	.10	.06
423	Gary Lavelle	.25	.10	.06
424	Steve Brye	.25	.10	.06
425	Joe Torre	1.00	.50	.30
426	Dick Drago	.25	.10	.06
427	Dave Rader	.25	.10	.06
428	Rangers Team (Frank Lucchesi)	.75	.40	.25
429	Ken Boswell	.25	.10	.06
430	Fergie Jenkins	2.50	1.25	.70
431	Dave Collins	.25	.10	.06
432	Buzz Capra	.25	.10	.06
433	Nate Colbert (Turn Back The Clock)	.25	.10	.06
434	Carl Yastrzemski (Turn Back The Clock)	1.50	.70	.45
435	Maury Wills (Turn Back The Clock)	.50	.25	.15
436	Bob Keegan (Turn Back The Clock)	.25	.10	.06
437	Ralph Kiner (Turn Back The Clock)	.75	.40	.25
438	Marty Perez	.25	.10	.06
439	Gorman Thomas	.25	.10	.06
440	Jon Matlack	.25	.10	.06
441	Larvell Blanks	.25	.10	.06
442	Braves Team (Dave Bristol)	1.00	.50	.30
443	Lamar Johnson	.25	.10	.06
444	Wayne Twitchell	.25	.10	.06
445	Ken Singleton	.25	.10	.06
446	Bill Bonham	.25	.10	.06
447	Jerry Turner	.25	.10	.06
448	Ellie Rodriguez	.25	.10	.06
449	Al Fitzmorris	.25	.10	.06
450	Pete Rose	15.00	7.50	4.50
451	Checklist 397-528	1.00	.50	.30
452	Mike Caldwell	.25	.10	.06
453	Pedro Garcia	.25	.10	.06
454	Andy Etchebarren	.25	.10	.06
455	Rick Wise	.25	.10	.06
456	Leon Roberts	.25	.10	.06
457	Steve Luebber	.25	.10	.06
458	Leo Foster	.25	.10	.06
459	Steve Foucault	.25	.10	.06
460	Willie Stargell	4.00	2.00	1.25
461	Dick Tidrow	.25	.10	.06
462	Don Baylor	.30	.15	.10
463	Jamie Quirk	.25	.10	.06
464	Randy Moffitt	.25	.10	.06
465	Rico Carty	.25	.10	.06
466	Fred Holdsworth	.25	.10	.06
467	Phillies Team (Danny Ozark)	.50	.25	.15
468	Ramon Hernandez	.25	.10	.06
469	Pat Kelly	.25	.10	.06
470	Ted Simmons	.50	.25	.15
471	Del Unser	.25	.10	.06
472	Rookie Pitchers (Don Aase, Bob McClure, Gil Patterson (Photo is Sheldon Gill.), Dave Wehrmeister)	.25	.10	.06
473	Rookie Outfielders (Andre Dawson, Gene Richards, John Scott, Denny Walling)	20.00	10.00	5.00
474	Rookie Shortstops (Bob Bailor, Kiko Garcia, Craig Reynolds, Alex Taveras)	.25	.10	.06
475	Rookie Pitchers (Chris Batton, Rick Camp, Scott McGregor, Manny Sarmiento)	.25	.10	.06
476	Rookie Catchers (Gary Alexander, Rick Cerone, Dale Murphy, Kevin Pasley)	15.00	7.50	3.75
477	Rookie Infielders (Doug Ault, Rich Dauer, Orlando Gonzalez, Phil Mankowski)	.25	.10	.06
478	Rookie Pitchers (Jim Gideon, Leon Hooten, Dave Johnson, Mark Lemongello)	.25	.10	.06
479	Rookie Outfielders (Brian Asselstine, Wayne Gross, Sam Mejias, Alvis Woods)	.25	.10	.06
480	Carl Yastrzemski	6.00	3.00	1.75
481	Roger Metzger	.25	.10	.06
482	Tony Solaita	.25	.10	.06
483	Richie Zisk	.25	.10	.06
484	Burt Hooton	.25	.10	.06
485	Roy White	.25	.10	.06
486	Ed Bane	.25	.10	.06
487	Rookie Pitchers (Larry Anderson, Ed Glynn, Joe Henderson, Greg Terlecky)	.25	.10	.06
488	Rookie Outfielders (Jack Clark, Ruppert Jones, Lee Mazzilli, Dan Thomas)	3.00	1.50	.90
489	Rookie Pitchers (Len Barker, Randy Lerch, Greg Minton, Mike Overy)	.75	.40	.25
490	Rookie Shortstops (Billy Almon, Mickey Klutts, Tommy McMillan, Mark Wagner)	.25	.10	.06
491	Rookie Pitchers (Mike Dupree, Dennis Martinez, Craig Mitchell, Bob Sykes)	3.00	1.50	.90
492	Rookie Outfielders (Tony Armas, Steve Kemp, Carlos Lopez, Gary Woods)	.75	.40	.25
493	Rookie Pitchers (Mike Krukow, Jim Otten, Gary Wheelock, Mike Willis)	.25	.10	.06
494	Rookie Infielders (Juan Bernhardt, Mike Champion, Jim Gantner, Bump Wills)	1.00	.50	.30
495	Al Hrabosky	.50	.25	.15
496	Gary Thomasson	.25	.10	.06
497	Clay Carroll	.25	.10	.06
498	Sal Bando	.25	.10	.06
499	Pablo Torrealba	.25	.10	.06
500	Dave Kingman	.75	.40	.25
501	Jim Bibby	.25	.10	.06
502	Randy Hundley	.25	.10	.06
503	Bill Lee	.25	.10	.06
504	Dodgers Team (Tom Lasorda)	1.50	.70	.45
505	Oscar Gamble	.50	.25	.15
506	Steve Grilli	.25	.10	.06
507	Mike Hegan	.25	.10	.06
508	Dave Pagan	.25	.10	.06
509	Cookie Rojas	.25	.10	.06
510	John Candelaria	.25	.10	.06
511	Bill Fahey	.25	.10	.06
512	Jack Billingham	.25	.10	.06
513	Jerry Terrell	.25	.10	.06
514	Cliff Johnson	.25	.10	.06
515	Chris Speier	.25	.10	.06
516	Bake McBride	.25	.10	.06
517	Pete Vuckovich	.50	.25	.15
518	Cubs Team (Herman Franks)	1.00	.50	.30
519	Don Kirkwood	.25	.10	.06
520	Garry Maddox	.50	.25	.15
521	Bob Grich	.25	.10	.06
522	Enzo Hernandez	.25	.10	.06
523	Rollie Fingers	2.50	1.25	.70
524	Rowland Office	.25	.10	.06
525	Dennis Eckersley	4.00	2.00	1.25
526	Larry Parrish	.25	.10	.06
527	Dan Meyer	.25	.10	.06
528	Bill Castro	.25	.10	.06
529	Jim Essian	.25	.10	.06
530	Rick Reuschel	.25	.10	.06
531	Lyman Bostock	.25	.10	.06
532	Jim Willoughby	.25	.10	.06
533	Mickey Stanley	.25	.10	.06
534	Paul Splittorff	.25	.10	.06
535	Cesar Geronimo	.25	.10	.06
536	Vic Albury	.25	.10	.06
537	Dave Roberts	.25	.10	.06
538	Frank Taveras	.25	.10	.06
539	Mike Wallace	.25	.10	.06
540	Bob Watson	.25	.10	.06
541	John Denny	.25	.10	.06
542	Frank Duffy	.25	.10	.06
543	Ron Blomberg	.25	.10	.06
544	Gary Ross	.25	.10	.06
545	Bob Boone	.25	.10	.06
546	Orioles Team (Earl Weaver)	1.50	.70	.45
547	Willie McCovey	3.00	1.50	.90
548	Joel Youngblood	.25	.10	.06
549	Jerry Royster	.25	.10	.06
550	Randy Jones	.25	.10	.06
551	Bill North	.25	.10	.06
552	Pepe Mangual	.25	.10	.06
553	Jack Heidemann	.25	.10	.06
554	Bruce Kimm	.25	.10	.06
555	Dan Ford	.25	.10	.06
556	Doug Bird	.25	.10	.06
557	Jerry White	.25	.10	.06
558	Elias Sosa	.25	.10	.06
559	Alan Bannister	.25	.10	.06
560	Dave Concepcion	.25	.10	.06
561	Pete LaCock	.25	.10	.06
562	Checklist 529-660	.75	.40	.25
563	Bruce Kison	.25	.10	.06
564	Alan Ashby	.25	.10	.06
565	Mickey Lolich	.50	.25	.15
566	Rick Miller	.25	.10	.06
567	Enos Cabell	.25	.10	.06
568	Carlos May	.25	.10	.06
569	Jim Lonborg	.25	.10	.06
570	Bobby Bonds	.75	.40	.25
571	Darrell Evans	.25	.10	.06
572	Ross Grimsley	.25	.10	.06
573	Joe Ferguson	.25	.10	.06
574	Aurelio Rodriguez	.25	.10	.06
575	Dick Ruthven	.25	.10	.06

576	Fred Kendall	.25	.10	.06
577	Jerry Augustine	.25	.10	.06
578	Bob Randall	.25	.10	.06
579	Don Carrithers	.25	.10	.06
580	George Brett	15.00	7.50	3.75
581	Pedro Borbon	.25	.10	.06
582	Ed Kirkpatrick	.25	.10	.06
583	Paul Lindblad	.25	.10	.06
584	Ed Goodson	.25	.10	.06
585	Rick Burleson	.25	.10	.06
586	Steve Renko	.25	.10	.06
587	Rick Baldwin	.25	.10	.06
588	Dave Moates	.25	.10	.06
589	Mike Cosgrove	.25	.10	.06
590	Buddy Bell	.25	.10	.06
591	Chris Arnold	.25	.10	.06
592	Dan Briggs	.25	.10	.06
593	Dennis Blair	.25	.10	.06
594	Biff Pocoroba	.25	.10	.06
595	John Hiller	.25	.10	.06
596	*Jerry Martin*	.25	.10	.06
597	Mariners Mgr./Coaches	1.00	.50	.30
	(Don Bryant, Jim Busby,			
	Darrell Johnson, Vada			
	Pinson, Wes Stock)			
598	Sparky Lyle	.25	.10	.06
599	Mike Tyson	.25	.10	.06
600	Jim Palmer	3.00	1.50	.90
601	Mike Lum	.25	.10	.06
602	Andy Hassler	.25	.10	.06
603	Willie Davis	.25	.10	.06
604	Jim Slaton	.25	.10	.06
605	Felix Millan	.25	.10	.06
606	Steve Braun	.25	.10	.06
607	Larry Demery	.25	.10	.06
608	Roy Howell	.25	.10	.06
609	Jim Barr	.25	.10	.06
610	Jose Cardenal	.25	.10	.06
611	Dave Lemanczyk	.25	.10	.06
612	Barry Foote	.25	.10	.06
613	Reggie Cleveland	.25	.10	.06
614	Greg Gross	.25	.10	.06
615	Phil Niekro	2.50	1.25	.70
616	Tommy Sandt	.25	.10	.06
617	Bobby Darwin	.25	.10	.06
618	Pat Dobson	.25	.10	.06
619	Johnny Oates	.25	.10	.06
620	Don Sutton	2.50	1.25	.70
621	Tigers Team (Ralph Houk)	1.00	.50	.30
622	Jim Wohlford	.25	.10	.06
623	Jack Kucek	.25	.10	.06
624	Hector Cruz	.25	.10	.06
625	Ken Holtzman	.25	.10	.06
626	Al Bumbry	.25	.10	.06
627	Bob Myrick	.25	.10	.06
628	Mario Guerrero	.25	.10	.06
629	Bobby Valentine	.25	.10	.06
630	Bert Blyleven	.75	.40	.25
631	Big League Brothers	5.00	2.50	1.50
	(George Brett, Ken Brett)			
632	Big League Brothers	.25	.10	.06
	(Bob Forsch, Ken Forsch)			
633	Big League Brothers	.25	.10	.06
	(Carlos May, Lee May)			
634	Big League Brothers (Paul	.25	.10	.06
	Reuschel, Rick Reuschel)			
	(Names switched.)			
635	Robin Yount	6.00	3.00	1.50
636	Santo Alcala	.25	.10	.06
637	Alex Johnson	.25	.10	.06
638	Jim Kaat	.50	.25	.15
639	Jerry Morales	.25	.10	.06
640	Carlton Fisk	4.00	2.00	1.25
641	Dan Larson	.25	.10	.06
642	Willie Crawford	.25	.10	.06
643	Mike Pazik	.25	.10	.06
644	Matt Alexander	.25	.10	.06
645	Jerry Reuss	.25	.10	.06
646	Andres Mora	.25	.10	.06
647	Expos Team (Dick Williams)	.75	.40	.25
648	Jim Spencer	.25	.10	.06
649	Dave Cash	.25	.10	.06
650	Nolan Ryan	20.00	10.00	6.00
651	Von Joshua	.25	.10	.06
652	Tom Walker	.25	.10	.06
653	Diego Segui	.25	.10	.06
654	Ron Pruitt	.25	.10	.06
655	Tony Perez	3.00	1.50	.90
656	Ron Guidry	1.00	.50	.30
657	Mick Kelleher	.25	.10	.06
658	Marty Pattin	.25	.10	.06
659	Merv Rettenmund	.25	.10	.06
660	Willie Horton	1.00	.50	.30

1977 Topps Proofs

Perhaps the most sought-after Topps proof card is the 1977 blank-back featuring Reggie Jackson in an Orioles uniform but designating his team as the Yankees, with whom he signed as a free agent prior to the 1977 season. Less well-known are a group of other players' cards that have uniform/team variations from the regularly issued versions. All of the handful of known examples were hand-cut from sheets. Backs are blank.

	NM	EX	VG
Don Baylor	350.00	175.00	100.00
Rollie Fingers	900.00	450.00	275.00
Al Fitzmorris	300.00	150.00	90.00
Wayne Garland	300.00	150.00	90.00
Bill Greif	200.00	100.00	60.00
Reggie Jackson (5/04 auction)	6,000		
Pat Kelly	300.00	150.00	90.00
Gary Matthews	450.00	225.00	135.00
Dan Meyer	300.00	150.00	90.00
Bill Singer	200.00	100.00	60.00
Steve Stone	350.00	175.00	100.00
Gene Tenace	425.00	210.00	125.00

1977 Topps Team Checklist Sheet

A redemption offer on packs of 1977 Topps cards offered an uncut sheet of the 26 team/checklist cards by mail. Besides the perforated team cards, the 10-1/2" x 22-1/2" sheet has a card offering collectors a card locker. The cards on the sheet are identical to the single team/checklist cards issued in packs, except they are printed on thinner card stock.

	NM	EX	VG
Uncut Sheet	35.00	17.50	10.50

1977 Topps/Dynamite Magazine Panels

In at least two issues of its "Dynamite" kids' magazine, Scholastic Book Club teamed with Topps to insert a six-card panel of its 1977 baseball issue. Values shown are for just the uncut panel; complete magazines would bear a small premium.

	NM	EX	VG
Complete Panel Set (2):	50.00	25.00	15.00
PANEL 1	25.00	12.50	7.50
215 Butch Metzger			
335 Bill Robinson			
599 Mike Tyson			
625 Ken Holtzman			
630 Bert Blyleven			
641 Dan Larson			
PANEL 2	30.00	15.00	9.00
242 Ken Henderson			
294 George Medich			
415 Jay Johnstone			
535 Cesar Geronimo			
580 George Brett			
626 Al Bumbry			

1977 Topps Cloth Stickers

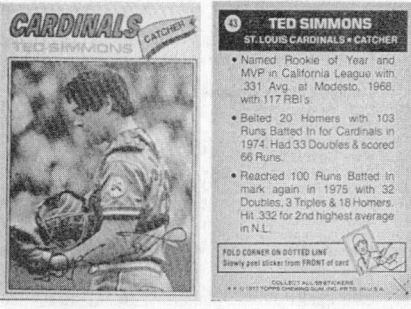

One of the few Topps specialty issues of the late 1970s, the 73-piece set of cloth stickers issued in 1977 includes 55 player stickers and 18 puzzle cards which could be joined to form a photo of the American League or National League All-Star teams. Issued as a separate issue, the 2-1/2" x 3-1/2" stickers have a paper backing which could be removed to allow the cloth to be adhered to a jacket, notebook, etc.

	NM	EX	VG
Complete Set (73):	75.00	37.70	22.50
Common Player:	1.00	.50	.30
Wax Pack:	12.50		
Wax Box (36):	325.00		
1 Alan Ashby	1.00	.50	.30
2 Buddy Bell	1.00	.50	.30

3	Johnny Bench	5.00	2.50	1.50
4	Vida Blue	1.00	.50	.30
5	Bert Blyleven	1.00	.50	.30
6	Steve Braun	1.00	.50	.30
7	George Brett	8.00	4.00	2.50
8	Lou Brock	4.00	2.00	1.25
9	Jose Cardenal	1.00	.50	.30
10	Rod Carew	5.00	2.50	1.50
11	Steve Carlton	4.00	2.00	1.25
12	Dave Cash	1.00	.50	.30
13	Cesar Cedeno	1.00	.50	.30
14	Ron Cey	1.00	.50	.30
15	Mark Fidrych	2.50	1.25	.70
16	Dan Ford	1.00	.50	.30
17	Wayne Garland	1.00	.50	.30
18	Ralph Garr	1.00	.50	.30
19	Steve Garvey	2.00	1.00	.60
20	Mike Hargrove	1.00	.50	.30
21	Catfish Hunter	3.00	1.50	.90
22	Reggie Jackson	8.00	4.00	2.50
23	Randy Jones	1.00	.50	.30
24	Dave Kingman	1.00	.50	.30
25	Bill Madlock	1.00	.50	.30
26	Lee May	1.00	.50	.30
27	John Mayberry	1.00	.50	.30
28	Andy Messersmith	1.00	.50	.30
29	Willie Montanez	1.00	.50	.30
30	John Montefusco	1.00	.50	.30
31	Joe Morgan	4.00	2.00	1.25
32	Thurman Munson	4.00	2.00	1.25
33	Bobby Murcer	1.00	.50	.30
34	Al Oliver	1.00	.50	.30
35	Dave Pagan	1.00	.50	.30
36	Jim Palmer	4.00	2.00	1.25
37	Tony Perez	3.00	1.50	.90
38	Pete Rose	10.00	5.00	3.00
39	Joe Rudi	1.00	.50	.30
40	Nolan Ryan	20.00	10.00	6.00
41	Mike Schmidt	8.00	4.00	2.50
42	Tom Seaver	5.00	2.50	1.50
43	Ted Simmons	1.00	.50	.30
44	Bill Singer	1.00	.50	.30
45	Willie Stargell	4.00	2.00	1.25
46	Rusty Staub	1.25	.60	.40
47	Don Sutton	3.00	1.50	.90
48	Luis Tiant	1.00	.50	.30
49	Bill Travers	1.00	.50	.30
50	Claudell Washington	1.00	.50	.30
51	Bob Watson	1.00	.50	.30
52	Dave Winfield	4.00	2.00	1.25
53	Carl Yastrzemski	7.00	3.50	2.00
54	Robin Yount	4.00	2.00	1.25
55	Richie Zisk	1.00	.50	.30
---	American League Nine-Piece Puzzle	6.00	3.00	1.75
---	National League Nine-Piece Puzzle	6.00	3.00	1.75

1978 Topps

JACK CLARK

At 726 cards, this was the largest issue from Topps since 1972. In design, the color player photo is slightly larger than usual, with the player's name and team at the bottom. In the upper right-hand corner of the 2-1/2" x 3-1/2" cards, there is a small white baseball with the player's position. Most of the starting All-Stars from the previous year had a red, white and blue shield instead of the baseball. Backs feature statistics and a baseball situation which made a card game of baseball possible. Specialty cards include baseball records, statistical leaders and the World Series and playoffs. As one row of cards per sheet had to be double-printed to accommodate the 726-card set size, some cards are more common, yet that seems to have no serious impact on their prices.

	NM	EX	VG
Complete Set (726):	200.00	100.00	45.00
Common Player:	.20	.10	.06
Wax Pack (14):	15.00		
Wax Box (36):	480.00		
Cello Pack (21):	25.00		
Cello Box (24):	475.00		
Rack Pack (39):	35.00		
Rack Box (24):	725.00		
Vending Box (500):	285.00		
1 Lou Brock (Record Breaker)	1.00	.50	.30
2 Sparky Lyle (Record Breaker)	.20	.10	.06
3 Willie McCovey (Record Breaker)	.50	.25	.15
4 Brooks Robinson (Record Breaker)	2.00	1.00	.60
5 Pete Rose (Record Breaker)	6.00	3.00	1.50
6 Nolan Ryan (Record Breaker)	15.00	7.50	3.75
7 Reggie Jackson (Record Breaker)	4.00	2.00	1.25
8 Mike Sadek	.20	.10	.06
9 Doug DeCinces	.20	.10	.06
10 Phil Niekro	3.00	1.50	.90

#	Name			
11	Rick Manning	.20	.10	.06
12	Don Aase	.20	.10	.06
13	Art Howe	.20	.10	.06
14	Lerrin LaGrow	.20	.10	.06
15	Tony Perez	4.00	2.00	1.25
16	Roy White	.20	.10	.06
17	Mike Krukow	.20	.10	.06
18	Bob Grich	.20	.10	.06
19	Darrell Porter	.20	.10	.06
20	Pete Rose	10.00	5.00	2.50
21	Steve Kemp	.20	.10	.06
22	Charlie Hough	.20	.10	.06
23	Bump Wills	.20	.10	.06
24	Don Money	.20	.10	.06
25	Jon Matlack	.20	.10	.06
26	Rich Hebner	.20	.10	.06
27	Geoff Zahn	.20	.10	.06
28	Ed Ott	.20	.10	.06
29	Bob Lacey	.20	.10	.06
30	George Hendrick	.20	.10	.06
31	Glenn Abbott	.20	.10	.06
32	Garry Templeton	.20	.10	.06
33	Dave Lemanczyk	.20	.10	.06
34	Willie McCovey	4.00	2.00	1.25
35	Sparky Lyle	.20	.10	.06
36	*Eddie Murray*	35.00	17.50	10.50
37	Rick Waits	.20	.10	.06
38	Willie Montanez	.20	.10	.06
39	*Floyd Bannister*	.45	.25	.14
40	Carl Yastrzemski	5.00	2.50	1.50
41	Burt Hooton	.20	.10	.06
42	Jorge Orta	.20	.10	.06
43	Bill Atkinson	.20	.10	.06
44	Toby Harrah	.20	.10	.06
45	Mark Fidrych	.30	.15	.09
46	Al Cowens	.20	.10	.06
47	Jack Billingham	.20	.10	.06
48	Don Baylor	.25	.13	.08
49	Ed Kranepool	.20	.10	.06
50	Rick Reuschel	.20	.10	.06
51	Charlie Moore	.20	.10	.06
52	Jim Lonborg	.20	.10	.06
53	Phil Garner	.20	.10	.06
54	Tom Johnson	.20	.10	.06
55	Mitchell Page	.20	.10	.06
56	Randy Jones	.20	.10	.06
57	Dan Meyer	.20	.10	.06
58	Bob Forsch	.20	.10	.06
59	Otto Velez	.20	.10	.06
60	Thurman Munson	5.00	2.50	1.25
61	Larvell Blanks	.20	.10	.06
62	Jim Barr	.20	.10	.06
63	Don Zimmer	.20	.10	.06
64	Gene Pentz	.20	.10	.06
65	Ken Singleton	.20	.10	.06
66	White Sox Team	.30	.15	.09
67	Claudell Washington	.20	.10	.06
68	Steve Foucault	.20	.10	.06
69	Mike Vail	.20	.10	.06
70	Rich Gossage	.20	.10	.06
71	Terry Humphrey	.20	.10	.06
72	Andre Dawson	3.00	1.50	.90
73	Andy Hassler	.20	.10	.06
74	Checklist 1-121	.20	.10	.06
75	Dick Ruthven	.20	.10	.06
76	Steve Ontiveros	.20	.10	.06
77	Ed Kirkpatrick	.20	.10	.06
78	Pablo Torrealba	.20	.10	.06
79	Darrell Johnson (DP)	.20	.10	.06
80	Ken Griffey	.20	.10	.06
81	Pete Redfern	.20	.10	.06
82	Giants Team	.30	.15	.09
83	Bob Montgomery	.20	.10	.06
84	Kent Tekulve	.20	.10	.06
85	Ron Fairly	.20	.10	.06
86	Dave Tomlin	.20	.10	.06
87	John Lowenstein	.20	.10	.06
88	Mike Phillips	.20	.10	.06
89	Ken Clay	.20	.10	.06
90	Larry Bowa	.20	.10	.06
91	Oscar Zamora	.20	.10	.06
92	Adrian Devine	.20	.10	.06
93	Bobby Cox	.40	.20	.12
94	Chuck Scrivener	.20	.10	.06
95	Jamie Quirk	.20	.10	.06
96	Orioles Team	.30	.15	.09
97	Stan Bahnsen	.20	.10	.06
98	Jim Essian	.20	.10	.06
99	*Willie Hernandez*	.30	.15	.09
100	George Brett	15.00	7.50	3.75
101	Sid Monge	.20	.10	.06
102	Matt Alexander	.20	.10	.06
103	Tom Murphy	.20	.10	.06
104	Lee Lacy	.20	.10	.06
105	Reggie Cleveland	.20	.10	.06
106	Bill Plummer	.20	.10	.06
107	Ed Halicki	.20	.10	.06
108	Von Joshua	.20	.10	.06
109	Joe Torre	.55	.30	.15
110	Richie Zisk	.20	.10	.06
111	Mike Tyson	.20	.10	.06
112	Astros Team	.30	.15	.09
113	Don Carrithers	.20	.10	.06
114	Paul Blair	.20	.10	.06
115	Gary Nolan	.20	.10	.06
116	Tucker Ashford	.20	.10	.06
117	John Montague	.20	.10	.06
118	Terry Harmon	.20	.10	.06
119	Denny Martinez	.20	.10	.06
120	Gary Carter	4.00	2.00	1.25
121	Alvis Woods	.20	.10	.06
122	Dennis Eckersley	4.00	2.00	1.25
123	Manny Trillo	.20	.10	.06
124	*Dave Rozema*	.20	.10	.06
125	George Scott	.20	.10	.06
126	Paul Moskau	.20	.10	.06
127	Chet Lemon	.20	.10	.06
128	Bill Russell	.20	.10	.06
129	Jim Colborn	.20	.10	.06
130	Jeff Burroughs	.20	.10	.06
131	Bert Blyleven	.20	.10	.06
132	Enos Cabell	.20	.10	.06
133	Jerry Augustine	.20	.10	.06
134	*Steve Henderson*	.20	.10	.06
135	Ron Guidry	.30	.15	.09
136	Ted Sizemore	.20	.10	.06
137	Craig Kusick	.20	.10	.06
138	Larry Demery	.20	.10	.06
139	Wayne Gross	.20	.10	.06
140	Rollie Fingers	3.00	1.50	.90
141	Ruppert Jones	.20	.10	.06
142	John Montefusco	.20	.10	.06
143	Keith Hernandez	.20	.10	.06
144	Jesse Jefferson	.20	.10	.06
145	Rick Monday	.20	.10	.06
146	Doyle Alexander	.20	.10	.06
147	Lee Mazzilli	.20	.10	.06
148	Andre Thornton	.20	.10	.06
149	Dale Murray	.20	.10	.06
150	Bobby Bonds	.20	.10	.06
151	Milt Wilcox	.20	.10	.06
152	*Ivan DeJesus*	.20	.10	.06
153	Steve Stone	.20	.10	.06
154	Cecil Cooper	.20	.10	.06
155	Butch Hobson	.20	.10	.06
156	Andy Messersmith	.20	.10	.06
157	Pete LaCock	.20	.10	.06
158	Joaquin Andujar	.20	.10	.06
159	Lou Piniella	.30	.15	.09
160	Jim Palmer	4.00	2.00	1.25
161	Bob Boone	.20	.10	.06
162	Paul Thormodsgard	.20	.10	.06
163	Bill North	.20	.10	.06
164	Bob Owchinko	.20	.10	.06
165	Rennie Stennett	.20	.10	.06
166	Carlos Lopez	.20	.10	.06
167	Tim Foli	.20	.10	.06
168	Reggie Smith	.20	.10	.06
169	Jerry Johnson	.20	.10	.06
170	Lou Brock	4.00	2.00	1.25
171	Pat Zachry	.20	.10	.06
172	Mike Hargrove	.20	.10	.06
173	Robin Yount	4.00	2.00	1.25
174	Wayne Garland	.20	.10	.06
175	Jerry Morales	.20	.10	.06
176	Milt May	.20	.10	.06
177	Gene Garber	.20	.10	.06
178	Dave Chalk	.20	.10	.06
179	Dick Tidrow	.20	.10	.06
180	Dave Concepcion	.20	.10	.06
181	Ken Forsch	.20	.10	.06
182	Jim Spencer	.20	.10	.06
183	Doug Bird	.20	.10	.06
184	Checklist 122-242	.20	.10	.06
185	Ellis Valentine	.20	.10	.06
186	*Bob Stanley*	.20	.10	.06
187	Jerry Royster	.20	.10	.06
188	Al Bumbry	.20	.10	.06
189	Tom Lasorda	.55	.30	.15
190	John Candelaria	.20	.10	.06
191	Rodney Scott	.20	.10	.06
192	Padres Team	.30	.15	.09
193	Rich Chiles	.20	.10	.06
194	Derrel Thomas	.20	.10	.06
195	Larry Dierker	.20	.10	.06
196	Bob Bailor	.20	.10	.06
197	Nino Espinosa	.20	.10	.06
198	Ron Pruitt	.20	.10	.06
199	Craig Reynolds	.20	.10	.06
200	Reggie Jackson	6.00	3.00	1.75
201	Batting Leaders (Rod Carew, Dave Parker)	.50	.25	.15
202	Home Run Leaders (George Foster, Jim Rice)	.25	.13	.08
203	RBI Leaders (George Foster, Larry Hisle)	.20	.10	.06
204	Stolen Base Leaders (Freddie Patek, Frank Taveras)	.20	.10	.06
205	Victory Leaders (Steve Carlton, Dave Goltz, Dennis Leonard, Jim Palmer)	.50	.25	.15
206	Strikeout Leaders (Phil Niekro, Nolan Ryan)	3.00	1.50	.90
207	ERA Leaders (John Candelaria, Frank Tanana)	.20	.10	.06
208	Leading Firemen (Bill Campbell, Rollie Fingers)	.25	.13	.08
209	Dock Ellis	.20	.10	.06
210	Jose Cardenal	.20	.10	.06
211	Earl Weaver (DP)	.50	.25	.15
212	Mike Caldwell	.20	.10	.06
213	Alan Bannister	.20	.10	.06
214	Angels Team	.30	.15	.09
215	Darrell Evans	.25	.13	.08
216	Mike Paxton	.20	.10	.06
217	Rod Gilbreath	.20	.10	.06
218	Marty Pattin	.20	.10	.06
219	Mike Cubbage	.20	.10	.06
220	Pedro Borbon	.20	.10	.06
221	Chris Speier	.20	.10	.06
222	Jerry Martin	.20	.10	.06
223	Bruce Kison	.20	.10	.06
224	Jerry Tabb	.20	.10	.06
225	Don Gullett	.20	.10	.06
226	Joe Ferguson	.20	.10	.06
227	Al Fitzmorris	.20	.10	.06
228	Manny Mota	.20	.10	.06
229	Leo Foster	.20	.10	.06
230	Al Hrabosky	.20	.10	.06
231	Wayne Nordhagen	.20	.10	.06
232	Mickey Stanley	.20	.10	.06
233	Dick Pole	.20	.10	.06
234	Herman Franks	.20	.10	.06
235	Tim McCarver	.30	.15	.09
236	Terry Whitfield	.20	.10	.06
237	Rich Dauer	.20	.10	.06
238	Juan Beniquez	.20	.10	.06
239	Dyar Miller	.20	.10	.06
240	Gene Tenace	.20	.10	.06
241	Pete Vuckovich	.20	.10	.06
242	Barry Bonnell	.20	.10	.06
243	Bob McClure	.20	.10	.06
244	Expos Team	.30	.15	.09
245	Rick Burleson	.20	.10	.06
246	Dan Driessen	.20	.10	.06
247	Larry Christenson	.20	.10	.06
248	Frank White	.20	.10	.06
249	Dave Goltz	.20	.10	.06
250	Graig Nettles	.25	.13	.08
251	Don Kirkwood	.20	.10	.06
252	Steve Swisher	.20	.10	.06
253	Jim Kern	.20	.10	.06
254	Dave Collins	.20	.10	.06
255	Jerry Reuss	.20	.10	.06
256	Joe Altobelli	.20	.10	.06
257	Hector Cruz	.20	.10	.06
258	John Hiller	.20	.10	.06
259	Dodgers Team	.50	.25	.15
260	Bert Campaneris	.20	.10	.06
261	Tim Hosley	.20	.10	.06
262	Rudy May	.20	.10	.06
263	Danny Walton	.20	.10	.06
264	Jamie Easterly	.20	.10	.06
265	Sal Bando	.20	.10	.06
266	*Bob Shirley*	.20	.10	.06
267	Doug Ault	.20	.10	.06
268	Gil Flores	.20	.10	.06
269	Wayne Twitchell	.20	.10	.06
270	Carlton Fisk	4.00	2.00	1.25
271	Randy Lerch	.20	.10	.06
272	Royle Stillman	.20	.10	.06
273	Fred Norman	.20	.10	.06
274	Freddie Patek	.20	.10	.06
275	Dan Ford	.20	.10	.06
276	Bill Bonham	.20	.10	.06
277	Bruce Boisclair	.20	.10	.06
278	Enrique Romo	.20	.10	.06
279	Bill Virdon	.20	.10	.06
280	Buddy Bell	.20	.10	.06
281	Eric Rasmussen	.20	.10	.06
282	Yankees Team	1.00	.50	.30
283	Omar Moreno	.20	.10	.06
284	Randy Moffitt	.20	.10	.06
285	Steve Yeager	.20	.10	.06
286	Ben Oglivie	.20	.10	.06
287	Kiko Garcia	.20	.10	.06
288	Dave Hamilton	.20	.10	.06
289	Checklist 243-363	.20	.10	.06
290	Willie Horton	.20	.10	.06
291	Gary Ross	.20	.10	.06
292	Gene Richard	.20	.10	.06
293	Mike Willis	.20	.10	.06
294	Larry Parrish	.20	.10	.06
295	Bill Lee	.20	.10	.06
296	Biff Pocoroba	.20	.10	.06
297	Warren Brusstar	.20	.10	.06
298	Tony Armas	.20	.10	.06
299	Whitey Herzog	.75	.40	.25
300	Joe Morgan	4.00	2.00	1.25
301	Buddy Schultz	.20	.10	.06
302	Cubs Team	.30	.15	.09
303	Sam Hinds	.20	.10	.06
304	John Milner	.20	.10	.06
305	Rico Carty	.20	.10	.06
306	Joe Niekro	.20	.10	.06
307	Glenn Borgmann	.20	.10	.06
308	Jim Rooker	.20	.10	.06
309	Cliff Johnson	.20	.10	.06
310	Don Sutton	3.00	1.50	.90
311	Jose Baez	.20	.10	.06
312	Greg Minton	.20	.10	.06
313	Andy Etchebarren	.20	.10	.06
314	Paul Lindblad	.20	.10	.06
315	Mark Belanger	.20	.10	.06
316	Henry Cruz	.20	.10	.06
317	Dave Johnson	.20	.10	.06
318	Tom Griffin	.20	.10	.06
319	Alan Ashby	.20	.10	.06
320	Fred Lynn	.20	.10	.06
321	Santo Alcala	.20	.10	.06
322	Tom Paciorek	.20	.10	.06
323	Jim Fregosi (DP)	.20	.10	.06
324	Vern Rapp	.20	.10	.06
325	Bruce Sutter	3.00	1.50	.90
326	Mike Lum	.20	.10	.06
327	Rick Langford	.20	.10	.06
328	Brewers Team	.30	.15	.09
329	John Verhoeven	.20	.10	.06
330	Bob Watson	.20	.10	.06
331	Mark Littell	.20	.10	.06
332	Duane Kuiper	.20	.10	.06
333	Jim Todd	.20	.10	.06
334	John Stearns	.20	.10	.06
335	Bucky Dent	.20	.10	.06
336	Steve Busby	.20	.10	.06
337	Tom Grieve	.20	.10	.06
338	Dave Heaverlo	.20	.10	.06
339	Mario Guerrero	.20	.10	.06
340	Bake McBride	.20	.10	.06
341	Mike Flanagan	.20	.10	.06
342	Aurelio Rodriguez	.20	.10	.06
343	John Wathan (DP)	.20	.10	.06
344	Sam Ewing	.20	.10	.06
345	Luis Tiant	.20	.10	.06
346	Larry Biittner	.20	.10	.06
347	Terry Forster	.20	.10	.06
348	Del Unser	.20	.10	.06
349	Rick Camp (DP)	.20	.10	.06
350	Steve Garvey	2.00	1.00	.60
351	Jeff Torborg	.20	.10	.06
352	Tony Scott	.20	.10	.06
353	Doug Bair	.20	.10	.06
354	Cesar Geronimo	.20	.10	.06
355	Bill Travers	.20	.10	.06

#	Name			
356	Mets Team	.60	.30	.20
357	Tom Poquette	.20	.10	.06
358	Mark Lemongello	.20	.10	.06
359	Marc Hill	.20	.10	.06
360	Mike Schmidt	8.00	4.00	2.00
361	Chris Knapp	.20	.10	.06
362	Dave May	.20	.10	.06
363	Bob Randall	.20	.10	.06
364	Jerry Turner	.20	.10	.06
365	Ed Figueroa	.20	.10	.06
366	Larry Milbourne (DP)	.20	.10	.06
367	Rick Dempsey	.20	.10	.06
368	Balor Moore	.20	.10	.06
369	Tim Nordbrook	.20	.10	.06
370	Rusty Staub	.25	.13	.08
371	Ray Burris	.20	.10	.06
372	Brian Asselstine	.20	.10	.06
373	Jim Willoughby	.20	.10	.06
374a	Jose Morales (Red stitching on position ball.)	.20	.10	.06
374b	Jose Morales (Black overprint on red stitching.)	.20	.10	.06
375	Tommy John	.30	.15	.09
376	Jim Wohlford	.20	.10	.06
377	Manny Sarmiento	.20	.10	.06
378	Bobby Winkles	.20	.10	.06
379	Skip Lockwood	.20	.10	.06
380	Ted Simmons	.20	.10	.06
381	Phillies Team	.35	.20	.11
382	Joe Lahoud	.20	.10	.06
383	Mario Mendoza	.20	.10	.06
384	Jack Clark	.30	.15	.09
385	Tito Fuentes	.20	.10	.06
386	Bob Gorinski	.20	.10	.06
387	Ken Holtzman	.20	.10	.06
388	Bill Fahey (DP)	.20	.10	.06
389	Julio Gonzalez	.20	.10	.06
390	Oscar Gamble	.20	.10	.06
391	Larry Haney	.20	.10	.06
392	Billy Almon	.20	.10	.06
393	Tippy Martinez	.20	.10	.06
394	Roy Howell	.20	.10	.06
395	Jim Hughes	.20	.10	.06
396	Bob Stinson	.20	.10	.06
397	Greg Gross	.20	.10	.06
398	Don Hood	.20	.10	.06
399	Pete Mackanin	.20	.10	.06
400	Nolan Ryan	20.00	10.00	6.00
401	Sparky Anderson	.55	.30	.15
402	Dave Campbell	.20	.10	.06
403	Bud Harrelson	.20	.10	.06
404	Tigers Team	.30	.15	.09
405	Rawly Eastwick	.20	.10	.06
406	Mike Jorgensen	.20	.10	.06
407	Odell Jones	.20	.10	.06
408	Joe Zdeb	.20	.10	.06
409	Ron Schueler	.20	.10	.06
410	Bill Madlock	.20	.10	.06
411	A.L. Championships (Yankees Rally To Defeat Royals)	.50	.25	.15
412	N.L. Championships (Dodgers Overpower Phillies In Four)	.50	.25	.15
413	World Series (Reggie & Yankees Reign Supreme)	2.00	1.00	.60
414	Darold Knowles (DP)	.20	.10	.06
415	Ray Fosse	.20	.10	.06
416	Jack Brohamer	.20	.10	.06
417	Mike Garman	.20	.10	.06
418	Tony Muser	.20	.10	.06
419	Jerry Garvin	.20	.10	.06
420	Greg Luzinski	.20	.10	.06
421	Junior Moore	.20	.10	.06
422	Steve Braun	.20	.10	.06
423	Dave Rosello	.20	.10	.06
424	Red Sox Team	.45	.25	.14
425	Steve Rogers	.20	.10	.06
426	Fred Kendall	.20	.10	.06
427	Mario Soto	.35	.20	.11
428	Joel Youngblood	.20	.10	.06
429	Mike Barlow	.20	.10	.06
430	Al Oliver	.30	.15	.09
431	Butch Metzger	.20	.10	.06
432	Terry Bulling	.20	.10	.06
433	Fernando Gonzalez	.20	.10	.06
434	Mike Norris	.20	.10	.06
435	Checklist 364-484	.20	.10	.06
436	Vic Harris (DP)	.20	.10	.06
437	Bo McLaughlin	.20	.10	.06
438	John Ellis	.20	.10	.06
439	Ken Kravec	.20	.10	.06
440	Dave Lopes	.20	.10	.06
441	Larry Gura	.20	.10	.06
442	Elliott Maddox	.20	.10	.06
443	Darrel Chaney	.20	.10	.06
444	Roy Hartsfield	.20	.10	.06
445	Mike Ivie	.20	.10	.06
446	Tug McGraw	.20	.10	.06
447	Leroy Stanton	.20	.10	.06
448	Bill Castro	.20	.10	.06
449	Tim Blackwell	.20	.10	.06
450	Tom Seaver	5.00	2.50	1.50
451	Twins Team	.30	.15	.09
452	Jerry Mumphrey	.20	.10	.06
453	Doug Flynn	.20	.10	.06
454	Dave LaRoche	.20	.10	.06
455	Bill Robinson	.20	.10	.06
456	Vern Ruhle	.20	.10	.06
457	Bob Bailey	.20	.10	.06
458	Jeff Newman	.20	.10	.06
459	Charlie Spikes	.20	.10	.06
460	Jim Hunter	3.00	1.50	.90
461	Rob Andrews	.20	.10	.06
462	Rogelio Moret	.20	.10	.06
463	Kevin Bell	.20	.10	.06
464	Jerry Grote	.20	.10	.06
465	Hal McRae	.20	.10	.06
466	Dennis Blair	.20	.10	.06
467	Alvin Dark	.20	.10	.06
468	Warren Cromartie	.20	.10	.06
469	Rick Cerone	.20	.10	.06
470	J.R. Richard	.20	.10	.06
471	Roy Smalley	.20	.10	.06
472	Ron Reed	.20	.10	.06
473	Bill Buckner	.20	.10	.06
474	Jim Slaton	.20	.10	.06
475	Gary Matthews	.20	.10	.06
476	Bill Stein	.20	.10	.06
477	Doug Capilla	.20	.10	.06
478	Jerry Remy	.20	.10	.06
479	Cardinals Team	.30	.15	.09
480	Ron LeFlore	.20	.10	.06
481	Jackson Todd	.20	.10	.06
482	Rick Miller	.20	.10	.06
483	Ken Macha	.20	.10	.06
484	Jim Norris	.20	.10	.06
485	Chris Chambliss	.20	.10	.06
486	John Curtis	.20	.10	.06
487	Jim Tyrone	.20	.10	.06
488	Dan Spillner	.20	.10	.06
489	Rudy Meoli	.20	.10	.06
490	Amos Otis	.20	.10	.06
491	Scott McGregor	.20	.10	.06
492	Jim Sundberg	.20	.10	.06
493	Steve Renko	.20	.10	.06
494	Chuck Tanner	.20	.10	.06
495	Dave Cash	.20	.10	.06
496	Jim Clancy	.20	.10	.06
497	Glenn Adams	.20	.10	.06
498	Joe Sambito	.20	.10	.06
499	Mariners Team	.30	.15	.09
500	George Foster	.20	.10	.06
501	Dave Roberts	.20	.10	.06
502	Pat Rockett	.20	.10	.06
503	Ike Hampton	.20	.10	.06
504	Roger Freed	.20	.10	.06
505	Felix Millan	.20	.10	.06
506	Ron Blomberg	.20	.10	.06
507	Willie Crawford	.20	.10	.06
508	Johnny Oates	.20	.10	.06
509	Brent Strom	.20	.10	.06
510	Willie Stargell	4.00	2.00	1.25
511	Frank Duffy	.20	.10	.06
512	Larry Herndon	.20	.10	.06
513	Barry Foote	.20	.10	.06
514	Rob Sperring	.20	.10	.06
515	Tim Corcoran	.20	.10	.06
516	Gary Beare	.20	.10	.06
517	Andres Mora	.20	.10	.06
518	Tommy Boggs (DP)	.20	.10	.06
519	Brian Downing	.20	.10	.06
520	Larry Hisle	.20	.10	.06
521	Steve Staggs	.20	.10	.06
522	Dick Williams	.20	.10	.06
523	Donnie Moore	.20	.10	.06
524	Bernie Carbo	.20	.10	.06
525	Jerry Terrell	.20	.10	.06
526	Reds Team	.45	.25	.14
527	Vic Correll	.20	.10	.06
528	Rob Picciolo	.20	.10	.06
529	Paul Hartzell	.20	.10	.06
530	Dave Winfield	4.00	2.00	1.25
531	Tom Underwood	.20	.10	.06
532	Skip Jutze	.20	.10	.06
533	Sandy Alomar	.20	.10	.06
534	Wilbur Howard	.20	.10	.06
535	Checklist 485-605	.20	.10	.06
536	Roric Harrison	.20	.10	.06
537	Bruce Bochte	.20	.10	.06
538	Johnnie LeMaster	.20	.10	.06
539	Vic Davalillo	.20	.10	.06
540	Steve Carlton	4.00	2.00	1.25
541	Larry Cox	.20	.10	.06
542	Tim Johnson	.20	.10	.06
543	Larry Harlow	.20	.10	.06
544	Len Randle	.20	.10	.06
545	Bill Campbell	.20	.10	.06
546	Ted Martinez	.20	.10	.06
547	John Scott	.20	.10	.06
548	Billy Hunter (DP)	.20	.10	.06
549	Joe Kerrigan	.20	.10	.06
550	John Mayberry	.20	.10	.06
551	Braves Team	.30	.15	.09
552	Francisco Barrios	.20	.10	.06
553	Terry Puhl	.25	.13	.08
554	Joe Coleman	.20	.10	.06
555	Butch Wynegar	.20	.10	.06
556	Ed Armbrister	.20	.10	.06
557	Tony Solaita	.20	.10	.06
558	Paul Mitchell	.20	.10	.06
559	Phil Mankowski	.20	.10	.06
560	Dave Parker	.20	.10	.06
561	Charlie Williams	.20	.10	.06
562	Glenn Burke	.20	.10	.06
563	Dave Rader	.20	.10	.06
564	Mick Kelleher	.20	.10	.06
565	Jerry Koosman	.20	.10	.06
566	Merv Rettenmund	.20	.10	.06
567	Dick Drago	.20	.10	.06
568	Tom Hutton	.20	.10	.06
569	Lary Sorensen	.20	.10	.06
570	Dave Kingman	.20	.10	.06
571	Buck Martinez	.20	.10	.06
572	Rick Wise	.20	.10	.06
573	Luis Gomez	.20	.10	.06
574	Bob Lemon	.50	.25	.15
575	Pat Dobson	.20	.10	.06
576	Sam Mejias	.20	.10	.06
577	A's Team	.30	.15	.09
578	Buzz Capra	.20	.10	.06
579	Rance Mulliniks	.25	.13	.08
580	Rod Carew	4.00	2.00	1.25
581	Lynn McGlothen	.20	.10	.06
582	Fran Healy	.20	.10	.06
583	George Medich	.20	.10	.06
584	John Hale	.20	.10	.06
585	Woodie Fryman	.20	.10	.06
586	Ed Goodson	.20	.10	.06
587	John Urrea	.20	.10	.06
588	Jim Mason	.20	.10	.06
589	Bob Knepper	.20	.10	.06
590	Bobby Murcer	.20	.10	.06
591	George Zeber	.20	.10	.06
592	Bob Apodaca	.20	.10	.06
593	Dave Skaggs	.20	.10	.06
594	Dave Freisleben	.20	.10	.06
595	Sixto Lezcano	.20	.10	.06
596	Gary Wheelock	.20	.10	.06
597	Steve Dillard	.20	.10	.06
598	Eddie Solomon	.20	.10	.06
599	Gary Woods	.20	.10	.06
600	Frank Tanana	.20	.10	.06
601	Gene Mauch	.20	.10	.06
602	Eric Soderholm	.20	.10	.06
603	Will McEnaney	.20	.10	.06
604	Earl Williams	.20	.10	.06
605	Rick Rhoden	.20	.10	.06
606	Pirates Team	.30	.15	.09
607	Fernando Arroyo	.20	.10	.06
608	Johnny Grubb	.20	.10	.06
609	John Denny	.20	.10	.06
610	Garry Maddox	.20	.10	.06
611	Pat Scanlon	.20	.10	.06
612	Ken Henderson	.20	.10	.06
613	Marty Perez	.20	.10	.06
614	Joe Wallis	.20	.10	.06
615	Clay Carroll	.20	.10	.06
616	Pat Kelly	.20	.10	.06
617	Joe Nolan	.20	.10	.06
618	Tommy Helms	.20	.10	.06
619	Thad Bosley	.20	.10	.06
620	Willie Randolph	.20	.10	.06
621	Craig Swan	.20	.10	.06
622	Champ Summers	.20	.10	.06
623	Eduardo Rodriguez	.20	.10	.06
624	Gary Alexander	.20	.10	.06
625	Jose Cruz	.20	.10	.06
626	Blue Jays Team	.30	.15	.09
627	Dave Johnson	.20	.10	.06
628	Ralph Garr	.20	.10	.06
629	Don Stanhouse	.20	.10	.06
630	Ron Cey	.20	.10	.06
631	Danny Ozark	.20	.10	.06
632	Rowland Office	.20	.10	.06
633	Tom Veryzer	.20	.10	.06
634	Len Barker	.20	.10	.06
635	Joe Rudi	.20	.10	.06
636	Jim Bibby	.20	.10	.06
637	Duffy Dyer	.20	.10	.06
638	Paul Splittorff	.20	.10	.06
639	Gene Clines	.20	.10	.06
640	Lee May	.20	.10	.06
641	Doug Rau	.20	.10	.06
642	Denny Doyle	.20	.10	.06
643	Tom House	.20	.10	.06
644	Jim Dwyer	.20	.10	.06
645	Mike Torrez	.20	.10	.06
646	Rick Auerbach	.20	.10	.06
647	Steve Dunning	.20	.10	.06
648	Gary Thomasson	.20	.10	.06
649	Moose Haas	.20	.10	.06
650	Cesar Cedeno	.20	.10	.06
651	Doug Rader	.20	.10	.06
652	Checklist 606-726	.20	.10	.06
653	Ron Hodges	.20	.10	.06
654	Pepe Frias	.20	.10	.06
655	Lyman Bostock	.20	.10	.06
656	Dave Garcia	.20	.10	.06
657	Bombo Rivera	.20	.10	.06
658	Manny Sanguillen	.20	.10	.06
659	Rangers Team	.30	.15	.09
660	Jason Thompson	.20	.10	.06
661	Grant Jackson	.20	.10	.06
662	Paul Dade	.20	.10	.06
663	Paul Reuschel	.20	.10	.06
664	Fred Stanley	.20	.10	.06
665	Dennis Leonard	.20	.10	.06
666	Billy Smith	.20	.10	.06
667	Jeff Byrd	.20	.10	.06
668	Dusty Baker	.35	.20	.11
669	Pete Falcone	.20	.10	.06
670	Jim Rice	.75	.40	.25
671	Gary Lavelle	.20	.10	.06
672	Don Kessinger	.20	.10	.06
673	Steve Brye	.20	.10	.06
674	Ray Knight	1.00	.50	.30
675	Jay Johnstone	.20	.10	.06
676	Bob Myrick	.20	.10	.06
677	Ed Herrmann	.20	.10	.06
678	Tom Burgmeier	.20	.10	.06
679	Wayne Garrett	.20	.10	.06
680	Vida Blue	.20	.10	.06
681	Rob Belloir	.20	.10	.06
682	Ken Brett	.20	.10	.06
683	Mike Champion	.20	.10	.06
684	Ralph Houk	.20	.10	.06
685	Frank Taveras	.20	.10	.06
686	Gaylord Perry	3.00	1.50	.90
687	Julio Cruz	.25	.13	.08
688	George Mitterwald	.20	.10	.06
689	Indians Team	.30	.15	.09
690	Mickey Rivers	.20	.10	.06
691	Ross Grimsley	.20	.10	.06
692	Ken Reitz	.20	.10	.06
693	Lamar Johnson	.20	.10	.06
694	Elias Sosa	.20	.10	.06
695	Dwight Evans	.20	.10	.06
696	Steve Mingori	.20	.10	.06
697	Roger Metzger	.20	.10	.06
698	Juan Bernhardt	.20	.10	.06
699	Jackie Brown	.20	.10	.06
700	Johnny Bench	6.00	3.00	1.50

701	Rookie Pitchers (**Tom Hume, Larry Landreth, Steve McCatty, Bruce Taylor**)	.20	.10	.06
702	Rookie Catchers (Bill Nahorodny, Kevin Pasley, Rick Sweet, Don Werner)	.20	.10	.06
703	Rookie Pitchers (*Larry Andersen, Tim Jones, Mickey Mahler, Jack Morris*)	4.00	2.00	1.00
704	Rookie 2nd Basemen (*Garth Iorg, Dave Oliver, Sam Perlozzo, Lou Whitaker*)	6.00	3.00	1.50
705	Rookie Outfielders (**Dave Bergman, Miguel Dilone, Clint Hurdle, Willie Norwood**)	.20	.10	.06
706	Rookie 1st Basemen (**Wayne Cage, Ted Cox, Pat Putnam, Dave Revering**)	.20	.10	.06
707	Rookie Shortstops (**Mickey Klutts, Paul Molitor, Alan Trammell, U.L. Washington**)	35.00	17.50	10.50
708	Rookie Catchers (**Bo Diaz, Dale Murphy, Lance Parrish, Ernie Whitt**)	4.00	2.00	1.00
709	Rookie Pitchers (**Steve Burke, Matt Keough, Lance Rautzhan, Dan Schatzeder**)	.20	.10	.06
710	Rookie Outfielders (Dell Alston, Rick Bosetti, Mike Easler, Keith Smith)	.20	.10	.06
711	Rookie Pitchers (Cardell Camper, Dennis Lamp, Craig Mitchell, Roy Thomas)	.20	.10	.06
712	Bobby Valentine	.20	.10	.06
713	Bob Davis	.20	.10	.06
714	Mike Anderson	.20	.10	.06
715	Jim Kaat	.20	.10	.06
716	Clarence Gaston	.20	.10	.06
717	Nelson Briles	.20	.10	.06
718	Ron Jackson	.20	.10	.06
719	Randy Elliott	.20	.10	.06
720	Fergie Jenkins	3.00	1.50	.90
721	Billy Martin	.50	.25	.15
722	Pete Broberg	.20	.10	.06
723	Johnny Wockenfuss	.20	.10	.06
724	Royals Team	.30	.15	.09
725	Kurt Bevacqua	.20	.10	.06
726	Wilbur Wood	.20	.10	.06

1978 Topps Team Checklist Sheet

A redemption offer on packs of 1978 Topps cards offered an uncut sheet of the 26 team/checklist cards by mail. Besides the team cards, the 10-1/2" x 22-1/2" sheet has a card offering collectors card boxes. The cards on the sheet are identical to the single team/checklist cards issued in packs.

	NM	EX	VG
Uncut Sheet	25.00	12.50	7.50

1978 Topps/Dynamite Magazine Panels

In issue No. 47 of its *Dynamite* kids' magazine, Scholastic Book Club teamed with Topps to insert a six-card panel of its 1978 baseball issue. Three such panels have been found thus far, one of which includes an Eddie Murray rookie card. Values shown are for just the uncut panel; complete magazines would bear a small premium.

		NM	EX	VG
Complete Panel Set (3):		60.00	30.00	18.00
PANEL 1		40.00	20.00	12.00
36	Eddie Murray			
125	George Scott			
141	Ruppert Jones			
150	Bobby Bonds			
490	Amos Otis			
550	John Mayberry			
	PANEL 2	10.00	5.00	3.00
21	Steve Kemp			

168	Reggie Smith			
200	Reggie Jackson			
245	Rick Burleson			
332	Duane Kuiper			
440	Davey Lopes			
	PANEL 3	15.00	7.50	4.50
44	Toby Harrah			
120	Gary Carter			
130	Jeff Burroughs			
320	Fred Lynn			
335	Bucky Dent			
670	Jim Rice			

1978 Topps/Zest Soap

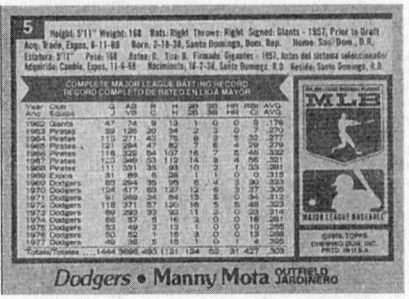

Produced by Topps for a Zest Soap promotion, the five cards in this set are almost identical to the regular issue, except the backs are printed in both Spanish and English, the game feature on back has been replaced by MLB and MLBPA logos and the card numbers are different. The cards measure 2-1/2" x 3-1/2". Because of the player selection and the bilingual backs, it seems obvious that this set was aimed at the Hispanic community. Cards were issued as complete sets in a cello package.

		NM	EX	VG
Complete Set (5):		9.00	4.50	2.75
Common Player:		1.50	.70	.45
1	Joaquin Andujar	2.00	1.00	.60
2	Bert Campaneris	4.50	2.25	1.25
3	Ed Figueroa	1.50	.70	.45
4	Willie Montanez	1.50	.70	.45
5	Manny Mota	4.50	2.25	1.25

1979 Topps

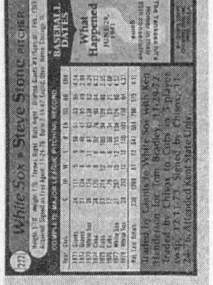

The size of this issue remained the same as in 1978 with 726 cards making their appearance. Actually, the 2-1/2" x 3-1/2" cards have a relatively minor design change from the previous year. The large color photo still dominates the front, with the player's name, team and position below it. The baseball with the player's position was moved to the lower left and the position replaced by a Topps logo. On the back, the printing color was changed and the game situation was replaced by a quiz called "Baseball Dates". Specialty cards include statistical leaders, major league records set during the season and eight cards devoted to career records. For the first time, rookies are arranged by teams under the heading of "Prospects." The key Ozzie Smith rookie card is usually seen with very poor centering.

		NM	EX	VG
Complete Set (726):		150.00	75.00	37.50
Common Player:		.15	.08	.05
Wax Pack (12):		10.00		
Wax Box (36):		300.00		
Cello Pack (18):		12.50		
Cello Box (24):		325.00		
Super Cello Pack (28):		.00		
Super Cello Box (24):		.00		
Rack Pack (39):		25.00		
Rack Box (24):		480.00		
Vending Box (500):		165.00		
1	Batting Leaders (Rod Carew, Dave Parker)	1.00	.50	.30
2	Home Run Leaders (George Foster, Jim Rice)	.15	.08	.05
3	RBI Leaders (George Foster, Jim Rice)	.15	.08	.05
4	Stolen Base Leaders (Ron LeFlore, Omar Moreno)	.15	.08	.05
5	Victory Leaders (Ron Guidry, Gaylord Perry)	.15	.08	.05
6	Strikeout Leaders (J.R. Richard, Nolan Ryan)	4.00	2.00	1.25
7	ERA Leaders (Ron Guidry, Craig Swan)	.15	.08	.05

8	Leading Firemen (Rollie Fingers, Rich Gossage)	.20	.10	.06
9	Dave Campbell	.15	.08	.05
10	Lee May	.15	.08	.05
11	Marc Hill	.15	.08	.05
12	Dick Drago	.15	.08	.05
13	Paul Dade	.15	.08	.05
14	Rafael Landestoy	.15	.08	.05
15	Ross Grimsley	.15	.08	.05
16	Fred Stanley	.15	.08	.05
17	Donnie Moore	.15	.08	.05
18	Tony Solaita	.15	.08	.05
19	Larry Gura	.15	.08	.05
20	Joe Morgan	3.00	1.50	.90
21	Kevin Kobel	.15	.08	.05
22	Mike Jorgensen	.15	.08	.05
23	Terry Forster	.15	.08	.05
24	Paul Molitor	8.00	4.00	2.00
25	Steve Carlton	3.00	1.50	.90
26	Jamie Quirk	.15	.08	.05
27	Dave Goltz	.15	.08	.05
28	Steve Brye	.15	.08	.05
29	Rick Langford	.15	.08	.05
30	Dave Winfield	3.00	1.50	.90
31	Tom House	.15	.08	.05
32	Jerry Mumphrey	.15	.08	.05
33	Dave Rozema	.15	.08	.05
34	Rob Andrews	.15	.08	.05
35	Ed Figueroa	.15	.08	.05
36	Alan Ashby	.15	.08	.05
37	Joe Kerrigan	.15	.08	.05
38	Bernie Carbo	.15	.08	.05
39	Dale Murphy	2.00	1.00	.60
40	Dennis Eckersley	2.50	1.25	.70
41	Twins Team (Gene Mauch)	.25	.13	.08
42	Ron Blomberg	.15	.08	.05
43	Wayne Twitchell	.15	.08	.05
44	Kurt Bevacqua	.15	.08	.05
45	Al Hrabosky	.15	.08	.05
46	Ron Hodges	.15	.08	.05
47	Fred Norman	.15	.08	.05
48	Merv Rettenmund	.15	.08	.05
49	Vern Ruhle	.15	.08	.05
50	Steve Garvey	1.50	.70	.45
51	Ray Fosse	.15	.08	.05
52	Randy Lerch	.15	.08	.05
53	Mick Kelleher	.15	.08	.05
54	Dell Alston	.15	.08	.05
55	Willie Stargell	3.00	1.50	.90
56	John Hale	.15	.08	.05
57	Eric Rasmussen	.15	.08	.05
58	Bob Randall	.15	.08	.05
59	John Denny	.15	.08	.05
60	Mickey Rivers	.15	.08	.05
61	Bo Diaz	.15	.08	.05
62	Randy Moffitt	.15	.08	.05
63	Jack Brohamer	.15	.08	.05
64	Tom Underwood	.15	.08	.05
65	Mark Belanger	.15	.08	.05
66	Tigers Team (Les Moss)	.25	.13	.08
67	Jim Mason	.15	.08	.05
68	Joe Niekro	.15	.08	.05
69	Elliott Maddox	.15	.08	.05
70	John Candelaria	.15	.08	.05
71	Brian Downing	.15	.08	.05
72	Steve Mingori	.15	.08	.05
73	Ken Henderson	.15	.08	.05
74	*Shane Rawley*	.15	.08	.05
75	Steve Yeager	.15	.08	.05
76	Warren Cromartie	.15	.08	.05
77	Dan Briggs	.15	.08	.05
78	Elias Sosa	.15	.08	.05
79	Ted Cox	.15	.08	.05
80	Jason Thompson	.15	.08	.05
81	Roger Erickson	.15	.08	.05
82	Mets Team (Joe Torre)	.75	.40	.25
83	Fred Kendall	.15	.08	.05
84	Greg Minton	.15	.08	.05
85	Gary Matthews	.15	.08	.05
86	Rodney Scott	.15	.08	.05
87	Pete Falcone	.15	.08	.05
88	Bob Molinaro	.15	.08	.05
89	Dick Tidrow	.15	.08	.05
90	Bob Boone	.15	.08	.05
91	Terry Crowley	.15	.08	.05
92	Jim Bibby	.15	.08	.05
93	Phil Mankowski	.15	.08	.05
94	Len Barker	.15	.08	.05
95	Robin Yount	4.00	2.00	1.00
96	Indians Team (Jeff Torborg)	.25	.13	.08
97	Sam Mejias	.15	.08	.05
98	Ray Burris	.15	.08	.05
99	John Wathan	.15	.08	.05
100	Tom Seaver	4.00	2.00	1.00
101	Roy Howell	.15	.08	.05
102	Mike Anderson	.15	.08	.05
103	Jim Todd	.15	.08	.05
104	Johnny Oates	.15	.08	.05
105	Rick Camp	.15	.08	.05
106	Frank Duffy	.15	.08	.05
107	Jesus Alou	.15	.08	.05
108	Eduardo Rodriguez	.15	.08	.05
109	Joel Youngblood	.15	.08	.05
110	Vida Blue	.15	.08	.05
111	Roger Freed	.15	.08	.05
112	Phillies Team (Danny Ozark)	.25	.13	.08
113	Pete Redfern	.15	.08	.05
114	Cliff Johnson	.15	.08	.05
115	Nolan Ryan	20.00	10.00	5.00
116	*Ozzie Smith*	40.00	20.00	12.00
117	Grant Jackson	.15	.08	.05
118	Bud Harrelson	.15	.08	.05
119	Don Stanhouse	.15	.08	.05
120	Jim Sundberg	.15	.08	.05
121	Checklist 1-121	.15	.08	.05
122	Mike Paxton	.15	.08	.05
123	Lou Whitaker	1.00	.50	.30
124	Dan Schatzeder	.15	.08	.05

No.	Name			
125	Rick Burleson	.15	.08	.05
126	Doug Bair	.15	.08	.05
127	Thad Bosley	.15	.08	.05
128	Ted Martinez	.15	.08	.05
129	Marty Pattin	.15	.08	.05
130	Bob Watson	.15	.08	.05
131	Jim Clancy	.15	.08	.05
132	Rowland Office	.15	.08	.05
133	Bill Castro	.15	.08	.05
134	Alan Bannister	.15	.08	.05
135	Bobby Murcer	.15	.08	.05
136	Jim Kaat	.15	.08	.05
137	Larry Wolfe	.15	.08	.05
138	Mark Lee	.15	.08	.05
139	Luis Pujols	.15	.08	.05
140	Don Gullett	.15	.08	.05
141	Tom Paciorek	.15	.08	.05
142	Charlie Williams	.15	.08	.05
143	Tony Scott	.15	.08	.05
144	Sandy Alomar	.15	.08	.05
145	Rick Rhoden	.15	.08	.05
146	Duane Kuiper	.15	.08	.05
147	Dave Hamilton	.15	.08	.05
148	Bruce Boisclair	.15	.08	.05
149	Manny Sarmiento	.15	.08	.05
150	Wayne Cage	.15	.08	.05
151	John Hiller	.15	.08	.05
152	Rick Cerone	.15	.08	.05
153	Dennis Lamp	.15	.08	.05
154	Jim Gantner	.15	.08	.05
155	Dwight Evans	.15	.08	.05
156	Buddy Solomon	.15	.08	.05
157	U.L. Washington	.15	.08	.05
158	Joe Sambito	.15	.08	.05
159	Roy White	.15	.08	.05
160	Mike Flanagan	.15	.08	.05
161	Barry Foote	.15	.08	.05
162	Tom Johnson	.15	.08	.05
163	Glenn Burke	.15	.08	.05
164	Mickey Lolich	.15	.08	.05
165	Frank Taveras	.15	.08	.05
166	Leon Roberts	.15	.08	.05
167a	Roger Metzger (Solid vertical black line between first and last names, through "A" of "GIANTS.")	.50	.25	.15
167b	Roger Metzger (Partial black line.)	.25	.13	.08
167c	Roger Metzger (No black line.)	.15	.08	.05
168	Dave Freisleben	.15	.08	.05
169	Bill Nahorodny	.15	.08	.05
170	Don Sutton	2.50	1.25	.70
171	Gene Clines	.15	.08	.05
172	Mike Bruhert	.15	.08	.05
173	John Lowenstein	.15	.08	.05
174	Rick Auerbach	.15	.08	.05
175	George Hendrick	.15	.08	.05
176	Aurelio Rodriguez	.15	.08	.05
177	Ron Reed	.15	.08	.05
178	Alvis Woods	.15	.08	.05
179	Jim Beattie	.15	.08	.05
180	Larry Hisle	.15	.08	.05
181	Mike Garman	.15	.08	.05
182	Tim Johnson	.15	.08	.05
183	Paul Splittorff	.15	.08	.05
184	Darrel Chaney	.15	.08	.05
185	Mike Torrez	.15	.08	.05
186	Eric Soderholm	.15	.08	.05
187	Mark Lemongello	.15	.08	.05
188	Pat Kelly	.15	.08	.05
189	Eddie Whitson	.25	.13	.08
190	Ron Cey	.15	.08	.05
191	Mike Norris	.15	.08	.05
192	Cardinals Team (Ken Boyer)	.25	.13	.08
193	Glenn Adams	.15	.08	.05
194	Randy Jones	.15	.08	.05
195	Bill Madlock	.15	.08	.05
196	Steve Kemp	.15	.08	.05
197	Bob Apodaca	.15	.08	.05
198	Johnny Grubb	.15	.08	.05
199	Larry Milbourne	.15	.08	.05
200	Johnny Bench	4.00	2.00	1.00
201	Mike Edwards (Record Breaker)	.15	.08	.05
202	Ron Guidry (Record Breaker)	.15	.08	.05
203	J.R. Richard (Record Breaker)	.15	.08	.05
204	Pete Rose (Record Breaker)	1.00	.50	.30
205	John Stearns (Record Breaker)	.15	.08	.05
206	Sammy Stewart (Record Breaker)	.15	.08	.05
207	Dave Lemanczyk	.15	.08	.05
208	Clarence Gaston	.15	.08	.05
209	Reggie Cleveland	.15	.08	.05
210	Larry Bowa	.15	.08	.05
211	Denny Martinez	.15	.08	.05
212	Carney Lansford	.60	.30	.20
213	Bill Travers	.15	.08	.05
214	Red Sox Team (Don Zimmer)	.25	.13	.08
215	Willie McCovey	3.00	1.50	.90
216	Wilbur Wood	.15	.08	.05
217	Steve Dillard	.15	.08	.05
218	Dennis Leonard	.15	.08	.05
219	Roy Smalley	.15	.08	.05
220	Cesar Geronimo	.15	.08	.05
221	Jesse Jefferson	.15	.08	.05
222	Bob Beall	.15	.08	.05
223	Kent Tekulve	.15	.08	.05
224	Dave Revering	.15	.08	.05
225	Rich Gossage	.25	.13	.08
226	Ron Pruitt	.15	.08	.05
227	Steve Stone	.15	.08	.05
228	Vic Davalillo	.15	.08	.05
229	Doug Flynn	.15	.08	.05
230	Bob Forsch	.15	.08	.05
231	Johnny Wockenfuss	.15	.08	.05
232	Jimmy Sexton	.15	.08	.05
233	Paul Mitchell	.15	.08	.05
234	Toby Harrah	.15	.08	.05
235	Steve Rogers	.15	.08	.05
236	Jim Dwyer	.15	.08	.05
237	Billy Smith	.15	.08	.05
238	Balor Moore	.15	.08	.05
239	Willie Horton	.15	.08	.05
240	Rick Reuschel	.15	.08	.05
241	Checklist 122-242	.15	.08	.05
242	Pablo Torrealba	.15	.08	.05
243	Buck Martinez	.15	.08	.05
244	Pirates Team (Chuck Tanner)	.25	.13	.08
245	Jeff Burroughs	.15	.08	.05
246	Darrell Jackson	.15	.08	.05
247	Tucker Ashford	.15	.08	.05
248	Pete LaCock	.15	.08	.05
249	Paul Thormodsgard	.15	.08	.05
250	Willie Randolph	.15	.08	.05
251	Jack Morris	.40	.20	.12
252	Bob Stinson	.15	.08	.05
253	Rick Wise	.15	.08	.05
254	Luis Gomez	.15	.08	.05
255	Tommy John	.30	.15	.09
256	Mike Sadek	.15	.08	.05
257	Adrian Devine	.15	.08	.05
258	Mike Phillips	.15	.08	.05
259	Reds Team (Sparky Anderson)	.75	.40	.25
260	Richie Zisk	.15	.08	.05
261	Mario Guerrero	.15	.08	.05
262	Nelson Briles	.15	.08	.05
263	Oscar Gamble	.15	.08	.05
264	*Don Robinson*	.15	.08	.05
265	Don Money	.15	.08	.05
266	Jim Willoughby	.15	.08	.05
267	Joe Rudi	.15	.08	.05
268	Julio Gonzalez	.15	.08	.05
269	Woodie Fryman	.15	.08	.05
270	Butch Hobson	.15	.08	.05
271	Rawly Eastwick	.15	.08	.05
272	Tim Corcoran	.15	.08	.05
273	Jerry Terrell	.15	.08	.05
274	Willie Norwood	.15	.08	.05
275	Junior Moore	.15	.08	.05
276	Jim Colborn	.15	.08	.05
277	Tom Grieve	.15	.08	.05
278	Andy Messersmith	.15	.08	.05
279	Jerry Grote	.15	.08	.05
280	Andre Thornton	.15	.08	.05
281	Vic Correll	.15	.08	.05
282	Blue Jays Team (Roy Hartsfield)	.25	.13	.08
283	Ken Kravec	.15	.08	.05
284	Johnnie LeMaster	.15	.08	.05
285	Bobby Bonds	.15	.08	.05
286	Duffy Dyer	.15	.08	.05
287	Andres Mora	.15	.08	.05
288	Milt Wilcox	.15	.08	.05
289	Jose Cruz	.15	.08	.05
290	Dave Lopes	.15	.08	.05
291	Tom Griffin	.15	.08	.05
292	Don Reynolds	.15	.08	.05
293	Jerry Garvin	.15	.08	.05
294	Pepe Frias	.15	.08	.05
295	Mitchell Page	.15	.08	.05
296	Preston Hanna	.15	.08	.05
297	Ted Sizemore	.15	.08	.05
298	Rich Gale	.15	.08	.05
299	Steve Ontiveros	.15	.08	.05
300	Rod Carew	3.00	1.50	.90
301	Tom Hume	.15	.08	.05
302	Braves Team (Bobby Cox)	.45	.25	.14
303	Lary Sorensen	.15	.08	.05
304	Steve Swisher	.15	.08	.05
305	Willie Montanez	.15	.08	.05
306	Floyd Bannister	.15	.08	.05
307	Larvell Blanks	.15	.08	.05
308	Bert Blyleven	.15	.08	.05
309	Ralph Garr	.15	.08	.05
310	Thurman Munson	5.00	2.50	1.50
311	Gary Lavelle	.15	.08	.05
312	Bob Robertson	.15	.08	.05
313	Dyar Miller	.15	.08	.05
314	Larry Harlow	.15	.08	.05
315	Jon Matlack	.15	.08	.05
316	Milt May	.15	.08	.05
317	*Jose Cardenal*	.15	.08	.05
318	*Bob Welch*	1.50	.70	.45
319	Wayne Garrett	.15	.08	.05
320	Carl Yastrzemski	4.00	2.00	1.00
321	Gaylord Perry	2.50	1.25	.70
322	Danny Goodwin	.15	.08	.05
323	Lynn McGlothen	.15	.08	.05
324	Mike Tyson	.15	.08	.05
325	Cecil Cooper	.15	.08	.05
326	Pedro Borbon	.15	.08	.05
327	Art Howe	.15	.08	.05
328	A's Team (Jack McKeon)	.25	.13	.08
329	Joe Coleman	.15	.08	.05
330	George Brett	8.00	4.00	2.00
331	Mickey Mahler	.15	.08	.05
332	Gary Alexander	.15	.08	.05
333	Chet Lemon	.15	.08	.05
334	Craig Swan	.15	.08	.05
335	Chris Chambliss	.15	.08	.05
336	Bobby Thompson	.15	.08	.05
337	John Montague	.15	.08	.05
338	Vic Harris	.15	.08	.05
339	Ron Jackson	.15	.08	.05
340	Jim Palmer	3.00	1.50	.90
341	*Willie Upshaw*	.20	.10	.06
342	Dave Roberts	.15	.08	.05
343	Ed Glynn	.15	.08	.05
344	Jerry Royster	.15	.08	.05
345	Tug McGraw	.15	.08	.05
346	Bill Buckner	.15	.08	.05
347	Doug Rau	.15	.08	.05
348	Andre Dawson	1.50	.70	.45
349	Jim Wright	.15	.08	.05
350	Garry Templeton	.15	.08	.05
351	Wayne Nordhagen	.15	.08	.05
352	Steve Renko	.15	.08	.05
353	Checklist 243-363	.15	.08	.05
354	Bill Bonham	.15	.08	.05
355	Lee Mazzilli	.15	.08	.05
356	Giants Team (Joe Altobelli)	.25	.13	.08
357	Jerry Augustine	.15	.08	.05
358	Alan Trammell	2.00	1.00	.60
359	Dan Spillner	.15	.08	.05
360	Amos Otis	.15	.08	.05
361	Tom Dixon	.15	.08	.05
362	Mike Cubbage	.15	.08	.05
363	Craig Skok	.15	.08	.05
364	Gene Richards	.15	.08	.05
365	Sparky Lyle	.15	.08	.05
366	Juan Bernhardt	.15	.08	.05
367	Dave Skaggs	.15	.08	.05
368	Don Aase	.15	.08	.05
369a	Bump Wills (Blue Jays)	2.00	1.00	.60
369b	Bump Wills (Rangers)	2.00	1.00	.60
370	Dave Kingman	.15	.08	.05
371	Jeff Holly	.15	.08	.05
372	Lamar Johnson	.15	.08	.05
373	Lance Rautzhan	.15	.08	.05
374	Ed Herrmann	.15	.08	.05
375	Bill Campbell	.15	.08	.05
376	Gorman Thomas	.15	.08	.05
377	Paul Moskau	.15	.08	.05
378	Rob Picciolo	.15	.08	.05
379	Dale Murray	.15	.08	.05
380	John Mayberry	.15	.08	.05
381	Astros Team (Bill Virdon)	.25	.13	.08
382	Jerry Martin	.15	.08	.05
383	Phil Garner	.15	.08	.05
384	Tommy Boggs	.15	.08	.05
385	Dan Ford	.15	.08	.05
386	Francisco Barrios	.15	.08	.05
387	Gary Thomasson	.15	.08	.05
388	Jack Billingham	.15	.08	.05
389	Joe Zdeb	.15	.08	.05
390	Rollie Fingers	2.50	1.25	.70
391	Al Oliver	.30	.15	.09
392	Doug Ault	.15	.08	.05
393	Scott McGregor	.15	.08	.05
394	Randy Stein	.15	.08	.05
395	Dave Cash	.15	.08	.05
396	Bill Plummer	.15	.08	.05
397	Sergio Ferrer	.15	.08	.05
398	Ivan DeJesus	.15	.08	.05
399	David Clyde	.15	.08	.05
400	Jim Rice	.50	.25	.15
401	Ray Knight	.15	.08	.05
402	Paul Hartzell	.15	.08	.05
403	Tim Foli	.15	.08	.05
404	White Sox Team (Don Kessinger)	.25	.13	.08
405	Butch Wynegar	.15	.08	.05
406	Joe Wallis	.15	.08	.05
407	Pete Vuckovich	.15	.08	.05
408	Charlie Moore	.15	.08	.05
409	*Willie Wilson*	2.00	1.00	.60
410	Darrell Evans	.15	.08	.05
411	All-Time Hits Leaders (Ty Cobb, George Sisler)	.50	.25	.15
412	All-Time RBI Leaders (Hank Aaron, Hack Wilson)	.50	.25	.15
413	All-Time Home Run Leaders (Hank Aaron, Roger Maris)	4.50	2.25	1.25
414	All-Time Batting Average Leaders (Ty Cobb, Roger Hornsby)	.50	.25	.15
415	All-Time Stolen Bases Leader (Lou Brock)	.30	.15	.09
416	All-Time Wins Leaders (Jack Chesbro, Cy Young)	.25	.13	.08
417	All-Time Strikeout Leaders (Walter Johnson, Nolan Ryan)	4.50	2.25	1.25
418	All-Time ERA Leaders (Walter Johnson, Dutch Leonard)	.20	.10	.06
419	Dick Ruthven	.15	.08	.05
420	Ken Griffey	.15	.08	.05
421	Doug DeCinces	.15	.08	.05
422	Ruppert Jones	.15	.08	.05
423	Bob Montgomery	.15	.08	.05
424	Angels Team (Jim Fregosi)	.25	.13	.08
425	Rick Manning	.15	.08	.05
426	Chris Speier	.15	.08	.05
427	Andy Replogle	.15	.08	.05
428	Bobby Valentine	.15	.08	.05
429	John Urrea	.15	.08	.05
430	Dave Parker	.15	.08	.05
431	Glenn Borgmann	.15	.08	.05
432	Dave Heaverlo	.15	.08	.05
433	Larry Biittner	.15	.08	.05
434	Ken Clay	.15	.08	.05
435	Gene Tenace	.15	.08	.05
436	Hector Cruz	.15	.08	.05
437	Rick Williams	.15	.08	.05
438	Horace Speed	.15	.08	.05
439	Frank White	.15	.08	.05
440	Rusty Staub	.15	.08	.05
441	Lee Lacy	.15	.08	.05
442	Doyle Alexander	.15	.08	.05
443	*Bruce Bochte*	.15	.08	.05
444	*Aurelio Lopez*	.15	.08	.05
445	Steve Henderson	.15	.08	.05
446	Jim Lonborg	.15	.08	.05
447	Manny Sanguillen	.15	.08	.05
448	Moose Haas	.15	.08	.05
449	Bombo Rivera	.15	.08	.05
450	Dave Concepcion	.15	.08	.05
451	Royals Team (Whitey Herzog)	.25	.13	.08
452	Jerry Morales	.15	.08	.05
453	Chris Knapp	.15	.08	.05
454	Len Randle	.15	.08	.05
455	Bill Lee	.15	.08	.05

#	Name	NM	EX	VG
456	Chuck Baker	.15	.08	.05
457	Bruce Sutter	2.50	1.25	.70
458	Jim Essian	.15	.08	.05
459	Sid Monge	.15	.08	.05
460	Graig Nettles	.15	.08	.05
461	Jim Barr	.15	.08	.05
462	Otto Velez	.15	.08	.05
463	Steve Comer	.15	.08	.05
464	Joe Nolan	.15	.08	.05
465	Reggie Smith	.15	.08	.05
466	Mark Littell	.15	.08	.05
467	Don Kessinger	.15	.08	.05
468	Stan Bahnsen	.15	.08	.05
469	Lance Parrish	.30	.15	.09
470	Garry Maddox	.15	.08	.05
471	Joaquin Andujar	.15	.08	.05
472	Craig Kusick	.15	.08	.05
473	Dave Roberts	.15	.08	.05
474	Dick Davis	.15	.08	.05
475	Dan Driessen	.15	.08	.05
476	Tom Poquette	.15	.08	.05
477	Bob Grich	.15	.08	.05
478	Juan Beniquez	.15	.08	.05
479	Padres Team (Roger Craig)	.25	.13	.08
480	Fred Lynn	.15	.08	.05
481	Skip Lockwood	.15	.08	.05
482	Craig Reynolds	.15	.08	.05
483	Checklist 364-484	.15	.08	.05
484	Rick Waits	.15	.08	.05
485	Bucky Dent	.15	.08	.05
486	Bob Knepper	.15	.08	.05
487	Miguel Dilone	.15	.08	.05
488	Bob Owchinko	.15	.08	.05
489	Larry Cox (Photo actually Dave Rader.)	.15	.08	.05
490	Al Cowens	.15	.08	.05
491	Tippy Martinez	.15	.08	.05
492	Bob Bailor	.15	.08	.05
493	Larry Christenson	.15	.08	.05
494	Jerry White	.15	.08	.05
495	Tony Perez	2.00	1.00	.60
496	Barry Bonnell	.15	.08	.05
497	Glenn Abbott	.15	.08	.05
498	Rich Chiles	.15	.08	.05
499	Rangers Team (Pat Corrales)	.25	.13	.08
500	Ron Guidry	.20	.10	.05
501	Junior Kennedy	.15	.08	.05
502	Steve Braun	.15	.08	.05
503	Terry Humphrey	.15	.08	.05
504	*Larry McWilliams*	.15	.08	.05
505	Ed Kranepool	.15	.08	.05
506	John D'Acquisto	.15	.08	.05
507	Tony Armas	.15	.08	.05
508	Charlie Hough	.15	.08	.05
509	Mario Mendoza	.15	.08	.05
510	Ted Simmons	.15	.08	.05
511	Paul Reuschel	.15	.08	.05
512	Jack Clark	.15	.08	.05
513	Dave Johnson	.15	.08	.05
514	Mike Proly	.15	.08	.05
515	Enos Cabell	.15	.08	.05
516	Champ Summers	.15	.08	.05
517	Al Bumbry	.15	.08	.05
518	Jim Umbarger	.15	.08	.05
519	Ben Oglivie	.15	.08	.05
520	Gary Carter	3.00	1.50	.90
521	Sam Ewing	.15	.08	.05
522	Ken Holtzman	.15	.08	.05
523	John Milner	.15	.08	.05
524	Tom Burgmeier	.15	.08	.05
525	Freddie Patek	.15	.08	.05
526	Dodgers Team (Tom Lasorda)	.60	.30	.20
527	Lerrin LaGrow	.15	.08	.05
528	Wayne Gross	.15	.08	.05
529	Brian Asselstine	.15	.08	.05
530	Frank Tanana	.15	.08	.05
531	Fernando Gonzalez	.15	.08	.05
532	Buddy Schultz	.15	.08	.05
533	Leroy Stanton	.15	.08	.05
534	Ken Forsch	.15	.08	.05
535	Ellis Valentine	.15	.08	.05
536	Jerry Reuss	.15	.08	.05
537	Tom Veryzer	.15	.08	.05
538	Mike Ivie	.15	.08	.05
539	John Ellis	.15	.08	.05
540	Greg Luzinski	.15	.08	.05
541	Jim Slaton	.15	.08	.05
542	Rick Bosetti	.15	.08	.05
543	Kiko Garcia	.15	.08	.05
544	Fergie Jenkins	2.00	1.00	.60
545	John Stearns	.15	.08	.05
546	Bill Russell	.15	.08	.05
547	Clint Hurdle	.15	.08	.05
548	Enrique Romo	.15	.08	.05
549	Bob Bailey	.15	.08	.05
550	Sal Bando	.15	.08	.05
551	Cubs Team (Herman Franks)	.25	.13	.08
552	Jose Morales	.15	.08	.05
553	Denny Walling	.15	.08	.05
554	Matt Keough	.15	.08	.05
555	Biff Pocoroba	.15	.08	.05
556	Mike Lum	.15	.08	.05
557	Ken Brett	.15	.08	.05
558	Jay Johnstone	.15	.08	.05
559	Greg Pryor	.15	.08	.05
560	John Montefusco	.15	.08	.05
561	Ed Ott	.15	.08	.05
562	Dusty Baker	.20	.10	.06
563	Roy Thomas	.15	.08	.05
564	Jerry Turner	.15	.08	.05
565	Rico Carty	.15	.08	.05
566	Nino Espinosa	.15	.08	.05
567	Rich Hebner	.15	.08	.05
568	Carlos Lopez	.15	.08	.05
569	Bob Sykes	.15	.08	.05
570	Cesar Cedeno	.15	.08	.05
571	Darrell Porter	.15	.08	.05
572	Rod Gilbreath	.15	.08	.05
573	Jim Kern	.15	.08	.05
574	Claudell Washington	.15	.08	.05
575	Luis Tiant	.15	.08	.05
576	Mike Parrott	.15	.08	.05
577	Brewers Team (George Bamberger)	.25	.13	.08
578	Pete Broberg	.15	.08	.05
579	Greg Gross	.15	.08	.05
580	Ron Fairly	.15	.08	.05
581	Darold Knowles	.15	.08	.05
582	Paul Blair	.15	.08	.05
583	Julio Cruz	.15	.08	.05
584	Jim Rooker	.15	.08	.05
585	Hal McRae	.15	.08	.05
586	*Bob Horner*	1.00	.50	.30
587	Ken Reitz	.15	.08	.05
588	Tom Murphy	.15	.08	.05
589	Terry Whitfield	.15	.08	.05
590	J.R. Richard	.15	.08	.05
591	Mike Hargrove	.15	.08	.05
592	Mike Krukow	.15	.08	.05
593	Rick Dempsey	.15	.08	.05
594	Bob Shirley	.15	.08	.05
595	Phil Niekro	2.00	1.00	.60
596	Jim Wohlford	.15	.08	.05
597	Bob Stanley	.15	.08	.05
598	Mark Wagner	.15	.08	.05
599	Jim Spencer	.15	.08	.05
600	George Foster	.15	.08	.05
601	Dave LaRoche	.15	.08	.05
602	Checklist 485-605	.15	.08	.05
603	Rudy May	.15	.08	.05
604	Jeff Newman	.15	.08	.05
605	Rick Monday	.15	.08	.05
606	Expos Team (Dick Williams)	.25	.13	.08
607	Omar Moreno	.15	.08	.05
608	Dave McKay	.15	.08	.05
609	Silvio Martinez	.15	.08	.05
610	Mike Schmidt	6.00	3.00	1.75
611	Jim Norris	.15	.08	.05
612	*Rick Honeycutt*	.25	.13	.08
613	Mike Edwards	.15	.08	.05
614	Willie Hernandez	.15	.08	.05
615	Ken Singleton	.15	.08	.05
616	Billy Almon	.15	.08	.05
617	Terry Puhl	.15	.08	.05
618	Jerry Remy	.15	.08	.05
619	*Ken Landreaux*	.15	.08	.05
620	Bert Campaneris	.15	.08	.05
621	Pat Zachry	.15	.08	.05
622	Dave Collins	.15	.08	.05
623	Bob McClure	.15	.08	.05
624	Larry Herndon	.15	.08	.05
625	Mark Fidrych	.20	.10	.06
626	Yankees Team (Bob Lemon)	.60	.30	.20
627	Gary Serum	.15	.08	.05
628	Del Unser	.15	.08	.05
629	Gene Garber	.15	.08	.05
630	Bake McBride	.15	.08	.05
631	Jorge Orta	.15	.08	.05
632	Don Kirkwood	.15	.08	.05
633	Rob Wilfong	.15	.08	.05
634	Paul Lindblad	.15	.08	.05
635	Don Baylor	.30	.15	.09
636	Wayne Garland	.15	.08	.05
637	Bill Robinson	.15	.08	.05
638	Al Fitzmorris	.15	.08	.05
639	Manny Trillo	.15	.08	.05
640	Eddie Murray	10.00	5.00	2.50
641	*Bobby Castillo*	.15	.08	.05
642	Wilbur Howard	.15	.08	.05
643	Tom Hausman	.15	.08	.05
644	Manny Mota	.15	.08	.05
645	George Scott	.15	.08	.05
646	Rick Sweet	.15	.08	.05
647	Bob Lacey	.15	.08	.05
648	Lou Piniella	.25	.13	.08
649	Jim Curtis	.15	.08	.05
650	Pete Rose	10.00	5.00	2.50
651	Mike Caldwell	.15	.08	.05
652	Stan Papi	.15	.08	.05
653	Warren Brusstar	.15	.08	.05
654	Rick Miller	.15	.08	.05
655	Jerry Koosman	.15	.08	.05
656	Hosken Powell	.15	.08	.05
657	George Medich	.15	.08	.05
658	Taylor Duncan	.15	.08	.05
659	Mariners Team (Darrell Johnson)	.25	.13	.08
660	Ron LeFlore	.15	.08	.05
661	Bruce Kison	.15	.08	.05
662	Kevin Bell	.15	.08	.05
663	Mike Vail	.15	.08	.05
664	Doug Bird	.15	.08	.05
665	Lou Brock	3.00	1.50	.90
666	Rich Dauer	.15	.08	.05
667	Don Hood	.15	.08	.05
668	Bill North	.15	.08	.05
669	Checklist 606-726	.15	.08	.05
670	Jim Hunter	3.00	1.50	.90
671	Joe Ferguson	.15	.08	.05
672	Ed Halicki	.15	.08	.05
673	Tom Hutton	.15	.08	.05
674	Dave Tomlin	.15	.08	.05
675	Tim McCarver	.25	.13	.08
676	Johnny Sutton	.15	.08	.05
677	Larry Parrish	.15	.08	.05
678	Geoff Zahn	.15	.08	.05
679	Derrel Thomas	.15	.08	.05
680	Carlton Fisk	3.00	1.50	.90
681	*John Henry Johnson*	.15	.08	.05
682	Dave Chalk	.15	.08	.05
683	Dan Meyer	.15	.08	.05
684	Jamie Easterly	.15	.08	.05
685	Sixto Lezcano	.15	.08	.05
686	Ron Schueler	.15	.08	.05
687	Rennie Stennett	.15	.08	.05
688	Mike Willis	.15	.08	.05
689	Orioles Team (Earl Weaver)	.60	.30	.20
690	Buddy Bell	.15	.08	.05
691	Dock Ellis	.15	.08	.05
692	Mickey Stanley	.15	.08	.05
693	Dave Rader	.15	.08	.05
694	Burt Hooton	.15	.08	.05
695	Keith Hernandez	.15	.08	.05
696	Andy Hassler	.15	.08	.05
697	Dave Bergman	.15	.08	.05
698	Bill Stein	.15	.08	.05
699	Hal Dues	.15	.08	.05
700	Reggie Jackson	5.00	2.50	1.25
701	Orioles Prospects (*Mark Corey, John Flinn, Sammy Stewart*)	.15	.08	.05
702	Red Sox Prospects (Joel Finch, Garry Hancock, Allen Ripley)	.15	.08	.05
703	Angels Prospects (Jim Anderson, Dave Frost, Bob Slater)	.15	.08	.05
704	White Sox Prospects (*Ross Baumgarten, Mike Colbern, Mike Squires*)	.15	.08	.05
705	Indians Prospects (*Alfredo Griffin*, Tim Norrid, Dave Oliver)	.25	.13	.08
706	Tigers Prospects (Dave Stegman, Dave Tobik, Kip Young)	.15	.08	.05
707	Royals Prospects (Randy Bass, Jim Gaudet, Randy McGilberry)	.15	.08	.05
708	Brewers Prospects (*Kevin Bass, Eddie Romero, Ned Yost*)	.25	.13	.08
709	Twins Prospects (Sam Perlozzo, Rick Sofield, Kevin Stanfield)	.15	.08	.05
710	Yankees Prospects (*Brian Doyle, Mike Heath, Dave Rajsich*)	.20	.10	.06
711	A's Prospects (*Dwayne Murphy, Bruce Robinson, Alan Wirth*)	.15	.08	.05
712	Mariners Prospects (Bud Anderson, Greg Biercevicz, Byron McLaughlin)	.15	.08	.05
713	Rangers Prospects (*Danny Darwin, Pat Putnam, Billy Sample*)	.25	.13	.08
714	Blue Jays Prospects (Victor Cruz, Pat Kelly, Ernie Whitt)	.15	.08	.05
715	Braves Prospects (*Bruce Benedict, Glenn Hubbard, Larry Whisenton*)	.25	.13	.08
716	Cubs Prospects (*Dave Geisel, Karl Pagel, Scot Thompson*)	.15	.08	.05
717	Reds Prospects (*Mike LaCoss, Ron Oester, Harry Spilman*)	.15	.08	.05
718	Astros Prospects (Bruce Bochy, Mike Fischlin, Don Pisker)	.15	.08	.05
719	Dodgers Prospects (*Pedro Guerrero, Rudy Law, Joe Simpson*)	1.50	.70	.45
720	Expos Prospects (*Jerry Fry, Jerry Pirtle, Scott Sanderson*)	.30	.15	.09
721	Mets Prospects (Juan Berenguer, Dwight Bernard, Dan Norman)	.15	.08	.05
722	Phillies Prospects (*Jim Morrison, Lonnie Smith, Jim Wright*)	.50	.25	.15
723	Pirates Prospects (Dale Berra, Eugenio Cotes, Ben Wiltbank)	.15	.08	.05
724	Cardinals Prospects (*Tom Bruno, George Frazier, Terry Kennedy*)	.20	.10	.06
725	Padres Prospects (Jim Beswick, Steve Mura, Broderick Perkins)	.15	.08	.05
726	Giants Prospects (Greg Johnston, Joe Strain, John Tamargo)	.15	.08	.05

1979 Topps Team Checklist Sheet

This uncut sheet of 26 team card/checklists was available via a mail-in offer. The sheet was mailed with two folds. The sheet cards are printed on lighter stock.

	NM	EX	VG
Uncut Sheet:	20.00	10.00	6.00

1979 Topps Comics

Issued as the 3" x 3-3/4" wax wrapper for a five-cent piece of bubblegum, this "test" issue was bought up in great quantities by speculators and remains rather common. It is also inexpensive, because the comic-style player representations were not popular with collectors. The set is complete at 33 pieces. Each wax box contains only 11 different players. Original packaging folds are not considered in grading.

		NM	EX	VG
	Complete Set (33):	15.00	7.50	4.50
	Common Player:	.25	.13	.08
	Wax Box (72):	55.00	.00	.00
1	Eddie Murray	1.50	.70	.45
2	Jim Rice	.60	.30	.20
3	Carl Yastrzemski	1.50	.70	.45
4	Nolan Ryan	5.00	2.50	1.50
5	Chet Lemon	.25	.13	.08
6	Andre Thornton	.25	.13	.08
7	Rusty Staub	.25	.13	.08
8	Ron LeFlore	.25	.13	.08
9	George Brett	3.00	1.50	.90
10	Larry Hisle	.25	.13	.08
11	Rod Carew	1.50	.70	.45
12	Reggie Jackson	2.50	1.25	.70
13	Ron Guidry	.25	.13	.08
14	Mitchell Page	.25	.13	.08
15	Leon Roberts	.25	.13	.08
16	Al Oliver	.25	.13	.08
17	John Mayberry	.25	.13	.08
18	Bob Horner	.25	.13	.08
19	Phil Niekro	1.00	.50	.30
20	Dave Kingman	.25	.13	.08
21	John Bench	1.50	.70	.45
22	Tom Seaver	1.50	.70	.45
23	J.R. Richard	.25	.13	.08
24	Steve Garvey	.60	.30	.20
25	Reggie Smith	.25	.13	.08
26	Ross Grimsley	.25	.13	.08
27	Craig Swan	.25	.13	.08
28	Pete Rose	3.50	1.75	1.00
29	Dave Parker	.25	.13	.08
30	Ted Simmons	.25	.13	.08
31	Dave Winfield	1.50	.70	.45
32	Jack Clark	.25	.13	.08
33	Vida Blue	.25	.13	.08

1979 Topps/Dynamite Magazine Panels

In at least two issue of its "Dynamite" kids' magazine, Scholastic Book Club teamed with Topps to insert a six-card panel of its 1979 baseball issue. Complete magazines would bear a small premium.

		NM	EX	VG
	Complete Panel:	20.00	10.00	6.00
2	Home Run Leaders			
	(Jim Rice, George Foster)			
5	Victory Leaders			
	(Ron Guidry, Gaylord Perry)			
6	Strikeout Leaders			
	(Nolan Ryan, J.R. Richard)			
201	Mike Edwards			
	(Record Breaker)			
202	Ron Guidry (Record Breaker)			
203	J.R. Richard (Record Breaker)			
	Complete Panel:	15.00	7.50	4.50
232	Jimmy Sexton			
292	Don Reynolds			
336	Bobby Thompson			
432	Dave Heaverlo			
532	Buddy Schultz			
539	John Ellis			

1980 Topps

Again numbering 726 cards measuring 2-1/2" x 3-1/2", Topps did make some design changes in 1980. Fronts have the usual color picture with a facsimile autograph. The player's name appears above the picture, while his position is on a pennant at the upper left and his team on another pennant in the lower right. Backs no longer feature games, returning instead to statistics, personal information, a few headlines and

a cartoon about the player. Specialty cards include statistical leaders, and previous season highlights. Many rookies again appear in team threesomes.

		NM	EX	VG
	Complete Set (726):	120.00	60.00	30.00
	Common Player:	.15	.08	.05
	Wax Pack (15):	10.00		
	Wax Box (36):	260.00		
	Cello Pack (25):	12.50		
	Cello Box (24):	275.00		
	Super Cello Pack (28):	14.00		
	Super Cello Box (24):	290.00		
	Rack Pack (42):	17.75		
	Rack Box (24):	360.00		
	Vending Box (500):	100.00		
1	Lou Brock, Carl Yastrzemski	1.00	.50	.30
	(Highlights)			
2	Willie McCovey (Highlights)	.30	.15	.09
3	Manny Mota (Highlights)	.15	.08	.05
4	Pete Rose (Highlights)	2.00	1.00	.60
5	Garry Templeton (Highlights)	.15	.08	.05
6	Del Unser (Highlights)	.15	.08	.05
7	Mike Lum	.15	.08	.05
8	Craig Swan	.15	.08	.05
9a	Steve Braun (Name in yellow.)	200.00	100.00	60.00
9b	Steve Braun (Name in red.)	.15	.08	.05
10	Denny Martinez	.15	.08	.05
11	Jimmy Sexton	.15	.08	.05
12	John Curtis	.15	.08	.05
13	Ron Pruitt	.15	.08	.05
14	Dave Cash	.15	.08	.05
15	Bill Campbell	.15	.08	.05
16	Jerry Narron	.15	.08	.05
17	Bruce Sutter	2.00	1.00	.60
18	Ron Jackson	.15	.08	.05
19	Balor Moore	.15	.08	.05
20	Dan Ford	.15	.08	.05
21	Manny Sarmiento	.15	.08	.05
22	Pat Putnam	.15	.08	.05
23	Derrel Thomas	.15	.08	.05
24	Jim Slaton	.15	.08	.05
25	Lee Mazzilli	.15	.08	.05
26	Marty Pattin	.15	.08	.05
27	Del Unser	.15	.08	.05
28	Bruce Kison	.15	.08	.05
29	Mark Wagner	.15	.08	.05
30	Vida Blue	.15	.08	.05
31	Jay Johnstone	.15	.08	.05
32	Julio Cruz	.15	.08	.05
33	Tony Scott	.15	.08	.05
34	Jeff Newman	.15	.08	.05
35	Luis Tiant	.15	.08	.05
36	Rusty Torres	.15	.08	.05
37	Kiko Garcia	.15	.08	.05
38	Dan Spillner	.15	.08	.05
39	Rowland Office	.15	.08	.05
40	Carlton Fisk	2.50	1.25	.70
41	Rangers Team (Pat Corrales)	.25	.13	.08
42	*Dave Palmer*	.15	.08	.05
43	Bombo Rivera	.15	.08	.05
44	Bill Fahey	.15	.08	.05
45	Frank White	.15	.08	.05
46	Rico Carty	.15	.08	.05
47	Bill Bonham	.15	.08	.05
48	Rick Miller	.15	.08	.05
49	Mario Guerrero	.15	.08	.05
50	J.R. Richard	.15	.08	.05
51	Joe Ferguson	.15	.08	.05
52	Warren Brusstar	.15	.08	.05
53	Ben Oglivie	.15	.08	.05
54	Dennis Lamp	.15	.08	.05
55	Bill Madlock	.15	.08	.05
56	Bobby Valentine	.15	.08	.05
57	Pete Vuckovich	.15	.08	.05
58	Doug Flynn	.15	.08	.05
59	Eddy Putman	.15	.08	.05
60	Bucky Dent	.20	.10	.06
61	Gary Serum	.15	.08	.05
62	Mike Ivie	.15	.08	.05
63	Bob Stanley	.15	.08	.05
64	Joe Nolan	.15	.08	.05
65	Al Bumbry	.15	.08	.05
66	Royals Team (Jim Frey)	.25	.13	.08
67	Doyle Alexander	.15	.08	.05
68	Larry Harlow	.15	.08	.05
69	Rick Williams	.15	.08	.05
70	Gary Carter	2.50	1.25	.70
71	John Milner	.15	.08	.05
72	Fred Howard	.15	.08	.05
73	Dave Collins	.15	.08	.05
74	Sid Monge	.15	.08	.05
75	Bill Russell	.15	.08	.05
76	John Stearns	.15	.08	.05
77	*Dave Stieb*	1.00	.50	.30
78	Ruppert Jones	.15	.08	.05
79	Bob Owchinko	.15	.08	.05
80	Ron LeFlore	.15	.08	.05

		NM	EX	VG
81	Ted Sizemore	.15	.08	.05
82	Astros Team (Bill Virdon)	.25	.13	.08
83	*Steve Trout*	.15	.08	.05
84	Gary Lavelle	.15	.08	.05
85	Ted Simmons	.15	.08	.05
86	Dave Hamilton	.15	.08	.05
87	Pepe Frias	.15	.08	.05
88	Ken Landreaux	.15	.08	.05
89	Don Hood	.15	.08	.05
90	Manny Trillo	.15	.08	.05
91	Rick Dempsey	.15	.08	.05
92	Rick Rhoden	.15	.08	.05
93	Dave Roberts	.15	.08	.05
94	*Neil Allen*	.15	.08	.05
95	Cecil Cooper	.15	.08	.05
96	A's Team (Jim Marshall)	.25	.13	.08
97	Bill Lee	.15	.08	.05
98	Jerry Terrell	.15	.08	.05
99	Victor Cruz	.15	.08	.05
100	Johnny Bench	3.00	1.50	.90
101	Aurelio Lopez	.15	.08	.05
102	Rich Dauer	.15	.08	.05
103	*Bill Caudill*	.15	.08	.05
104	Manny Mota	.15	.08	.05
105	Frank Tanana	.15	.08	.05
106	*Jeff Leonard*	.25	.13	.08
107	Francisco Barrios	.15	.08	.05
108	Bob Horner	.15	.08	.05
109	Bill Travers	.15	.08	.05
110	Fred Lynn	.15	.08	.05
111	Bob Knepper	.15	.08	.05
112	White Sox Team	.45	.25	.14
	(Tony LaRussa)			
113	Geoff Zahn	.15	.08	.05
114	Juan Beniquez	.15	.08	.05
115	Sparky Lyle	.15	.08	.05
116	Larry Cox	.15	.08	.05
117	Dock Ellis	.15	.08	.05
118	Phil Garner	.15	.08	.05
119	Sammy Stewart	.15	.08	.05
120	Greg Luzinski	.15	.08	.05
121	Checklist 1-121	.15	.08	.05
122	Dave Rosello	.15	.08	.05
123	Lynn Jones	.15	.08	.05
124	Dave Lemanczyk	.15	.08	.05
125	Tony Perez	2.00	1.00	.60
126	Dave Tomlin	.15	.08	.05
127	Gary Thomasson	.15	.08	.05
128	Tom Burgmeier	.15	.08	.05
129	Craig Reynolds	.15	.08	.05
130	Amos Otis	.15	.08	.05
131	Paul Mitchell	.15	.08	.05
132	Biff Pocoroba	.15	.08	.05
133	Jerry Turner	.15	.08	.05
134	Matt Keough	.15	.08	.05
135	Bill Buckner	.15	.08	.05
136	Dick Ruthven	.15	.08	.05
137	*John Castino*	.15	.08	.05
138	Ross Baumgarten	.15	.08	.05
139	*Dane Iorg*	.15	.08	.05
140	Rich Gossage	.25	.13	.08
141	Gary Alexander	.15	.08	.05
142	Phil Huffman	.15	.08	.05
143	Bruce Bochte	.15	.08	.05
144	Steve Comer	.15	.08	.05
145	Darrell Evans	.15	.08	.05
146	Bob Welch	.15	.08	.05
147	Terry Puhl	.15	.08	.05
148	Manny Sanguillen	.15	.08	.05
149	Tom Hume	.15	.08	.05
150	Jason Thompson	.15	.08	.05
151	Tom Hausman	.15	.08	.05
152	John Fulgham	.15	.08	.05
153	Tim Blackwell	.15	.08	.05
154	Lary Sorensen	.15	.08	.05
155	Jerry Remy	.15	.08	.05
156	Tony Brizzolara	.15	.08	.05
157	Willie Wilson	.15	.08	.05
158	Rob Picciolo	.15	.08	.05
159	Ken Clay	.15	.08	.05
160	Eddie Murray	3.00	1.50	.90
161	Larry Christenson	.15	.08	.05
162	Bob Randall	.15	.08	.05
163	Steve Swisher	.15	.08	.05
164a	Greg Pryor (No name.)	200.00	100.00	60.00
164b	Greg Pryor (Name in blue.)	.15	.08	.05
165	Omar Moreno	.15	.08	.05
166	Glenn Abbott	.15	.08	.05
167	Jack Clark	.15	.08	.05
168	Rick Waits	.15	.08	.05
169	Luis Gomez	.15	.08	.05
170	Burt Hooton	.15	.08	.05
171	Fernando Gonzalez	.15	.08	.05
172	Ron Hodges	.15	.08	.05
173	John Henry Johnson	.15	.08	.05
174	Ray Knight	.15	.08	.05
175	Rick Reuschel	.15	.08	.05
176	Champ Summers	.15	.08	.05
177	Dave Heaverlo	.15	.08	.05
178	Tim McCarver	.15	.08	.05
179	*Ron Davis*	.25	.13	.08
180	Warren Cromartie	.15	.08	.05
181	Moose Haas	.15	.08	.05
182	Ken Reitz	.15	.08	.05
183	Jim Anderson	.15	.08	.05
184	Steve Renko	.15	.08	.05
185	Hal McRae	.15	.08	.05
186	Junior Moore	.15	.08	.05
187	Alan Ashby	.15	.08	.05
188	Terry Crowley	.15	.08	.05
189	Kevin Kobel	.15	.08	.05
190	Buddy Bell	.15	.08	.05
191	Ted Martinez	.15	.08	.05
192	Braves Team (Bobby Cox)	.45	.25	.14
193	Dave Goltz	.15	.08	.05
194	Mike Easler	.15	.08	.05
195	John Montefusco	.15	.08	.05
196	Lance Parrish	.15	.08	.05

#	Player			
197	Byron McLaughlin	.15	.08	.05
198	Dell Alston	.15	.08	.05
199	Mike LaCoss	.15	.08	.05
200	Jim Rice	.30	.15	.09
201	Batting Leaders (Keith Hernandez, Fred Lynn)	.15	.08	.05
202	Home Run Leaders (Dave Kingman, Gorman Thomas)	.15	.08	.05
203	Runs Batted In Leaders (Don Baylor, Dave Winfield)	.35	.20	.11
204	Stolen Base Leaders (Omar Moreno, Willie Wilson)	.15	.08	.05
205	Victory Leaders (Mike Flanagan, Joe Niekro, Phil Niekro)	.25	.13	.08
206	Strikeout Leaders (J.R. Richard, Nolan Ryan)	3.50	1.75	1.00
207	ERA Leaders (Ron Guidry, J.R. Richard)	.25	.13	.08
208	Wayne Cage	.15	.08	.05
209	Von Joshua	.15	.08	.05
210	Steve Carlton	2.50	1.25	.70
211	Dave Skaggs	.15	.08	.05
212	Dave Roberts	.15	.08	.05
213	Mike Jorgensen	.15	.08	.05
214	Angels Team (Jim Fregosi)	.25	.13	.08
215	Sixto Lezcano	.15	.08	.05
216	Phil Mankowski	.15	.08	.05
217	Ed Halicki	.15	.08	.05
218	Jose Morales	.15	.08	.05
219	Steve Mingori	.15	.08	.05
220	Dave Concepcion	.15	.08	.05
221	Joe Cannon	.15	.08	.05
222	Ron Hassey	.25	.13	.08
223	Bob Sykes	.15	.08	.05
224	Willie Montanez	.15	.08	.05
225	Lou Piniella	.25	.13	.08
226	Bill Stein	.15	.08	.05
227	Len Barker	.15	.08	.05
228	Johnny Oates	.15	.08	.05
229	Jim Bibby	.15	.08	.05
230	Dave Winfield	2.50	1.25	.70
231	Steve McCatty	.15	.08	.05
232	Alan Trammell	.60	.30	.20
233	LaRue Washington	.15	.08	.05
234	Vern Ruhle	.15	.08	.05
235	Andre Dawson	1.00	.50	.30
236	Marc Hill	.15	.08	.05
237	Scott McGregor	.15	.08	.05
238	Rob Wilfong	.15	.08	.05
239	Don Aase	.15	.08	.05
240	Dave Kingman	.15	.08	.05
241	Checklist 122-242	.15	.08	.05
242	Lamar Johnson	.15	.08	.05
243	Jerry Augustine	.15	.08	.05
244	Cardinals Team (Ken Boyer)	.25	.13	.08
245	Phil Niekro	2.00	1.00	.60
246	Tim Foli	.15	.08	.05
247	Frank Riccelli	.15	.08	.05
248	Jamie Quirk	.15	.08	.05
249	Jim Clancy	.15	.08	.05
250	Jim Kaat	.15	.08	.05
251	Kip Young	.15	.08	.05
252	Ted Cox	.15	.08	.05
253	John Montague	.15	.08	.05
254	Paul Dade	.15	.08	.05
255	Dusty Baker	.15	.08	.05
256	Roger Erickson	.15	.08	.05
257	Larry Herndon	.15	.08	.05
258	Paul Moskau	.15	.08	.05
259	Mets Team (Joe Torre)	.60	.30	.20
260	Al Oliver	.20	.10	.06
261	Dave Chalk	.15	.08	.05
262	Benny Ayala	.15	.08	.05
263	Dave LaRoche	.15	.08	.05
264	Bill Robinson	.15	.08	.05
265	Robin Yount	2.50	1.25	.70
266	Bernie Carbo	.15	.08	.05
267	Dan Schatzeder	.15	.08	.05
268	Rafael Landestoy	.15	.08	.05
269	Dave Tobik	.15	.08	.05
270	Mike Schmidt	4.50	2.25	1.25
271	Dick Drago	.15	.08	.05
272	Ralph Garr	.15	.08	.05
273	Eduardo Rodriguez	.15	.08	.05
274	Dale Murphy	1.50	.70	.45
275	Jerry Koosman	.15	.08	.05
276	Tom Veryzer	.15	.08	.05
277	Rick Bosetti	.15	.08	.05
278	Jim Spencer	.15	.08	.05
279	Rob Andrews	.15	.08	.05
280	Gaylord Perry	2.00	1.00	.60
281	Paul Blair	.15	.08	.05
282	Mariners Team (Darrell Johnson)	.25	.13	.08
283	John Ellis	.15	.08	.05
284	Larry Murray	.15	.08	.05
285	Don Baylor	.25	.13	.08
286	Darold Knowles	.15	.08	.05
287	John Lowenstein	.15	.08	.05
288	Dave Rozema	.15	.08	.05
289	Bruce Bochy	.15	.08	.05
290	Steve Garvey	1.00	.50	.30
291	Randy Scarbery	.15	.08	.05
292	Dale Berra	.15	.08	.05
293	Elias Sosa	.15	.08	.05
294	Charlie Spikes	.15	.08	.05
295	Larry Gura	.15	.08	.05
296	Dave Rader	.15	.08	.05
297	Tim Johnson	.15	.08	.05
298	Ken Holtzman	.15	.08	.05
299	Steve Henderson	.15	.08	.05
300	Ron Guidry	.25	.13	.08
301	Mike Edwards	.15	.08	.05
302	Dodgers Team (Tom Lasorda)	.60	.30	.20
303	Bill Castro	.15	.08	.05
304	Butch Wynegar	.15	.08	.05
305	Randy Jones	.15	.08	.05
306	Denny Walling	.15	.08	.05
307	Rick Honeycutt	.15	.08	.05
308	Mike Hargrove	.15	.08	.05
309	Larry McWilliams	.15	.08	.05
310	Dave Parker	.15	.08	.05
311	Roger Metzger	.15	.08	.05
312	Mike Barlow	.15	.08	.05
313	Johnny Grubb	.15	.08	.05
314	Tim Stoddard	.15	.08	.05
315	Steve Kemp	.15	.08	.05
316	Bob Lacey	.15	.08	.05
317	Mike Anderson	.15	.08	.05
318	Jerry Reuss	.15	.08	.05
319	Chris Speier	.15	.08	.05
320	Dennis Eckersley	2.00	1.00	.60
321	Keith Hernandez	.15	.08	.05
322	Claudell Washington	.15	.08	.05
323	Mick Kelleher	.15	.08	.05
324	Tom Underwood	.15	.08	.05
325	Dan Driessen	.15	.08	.05
326	Bo McLaughlin	.15	.08	.05
327	Ray Fosse	.15	.08	.05
328	Twins Team (Gene Mauch)	.25	.13	.08
329	Bert Roberge	.15	.08	.05
330	Al Cowens	.15	.08	.05
331	Rich Hebner	.15	.08	.05
332	Enrique Romo	.15	.08	.05
333	Jim Norris	.15	.08	.05
334	Jim Beattie	.15	.08	.05
335	Willie McCovey	2.50	1.25	.70
336	George Medich	.15	.08	.05
337	Carney Lansford	.15	.08	.05
338	Johnny Wockenfuss	.15	.08	.05
339	John D'Acquisto	.15	.08	.05
340	Ken Singleton	.15	.08	.05
341	Jim Essian	.15	.08	.05
342	Odell Jones	.15	.08	.05
343	Mike Vail	.15	.08	.05
344	Randy Lerch	.15	.08	.05
345	Larry Parrish	.15	.08	.05
346	Buddy Solomon	.15	.08	.05
347	Harry Chappas	.15	.08	.05
348	Checklist 243-363	.15	.08	.05
349	Jack Brohamer	.15	.08	.05
350	George Hendrick	.15	.08	.05
351	Bob Davis	.15	.08	.05
352	Dan Briggs	.15	.08	.05
353	Andy Hassler	.15	.08	.05
354	Rick Auerbach	.15	.08	.05
355	Gary Matthews	.15	.08	.05
356	Padres Team (Jerry Coleman)	.25	.13	.08
357	Bob McClure	.15	.08	.05
358	Lou Whitaker	.25	.13	.08
359	Randy Moffitt	.15	.08	.05
360	Darrell Porter	.15	.08	.05
361	Wayne Garland	.15	.08	.05
362	Danny Goodwin	.15	.08	.05
363	Wayne Gross	.15	.08	.05
364	Ray Burris	.15	.08	.05
365	Bobby Murcer	.25	.13	.08
366	Rob Dressler	.15	.08	.05
367	Billy Smith	.15	.08	.05
368	Willie Aikens	.20	.10	.06
369	Jim Kern	.15	.08	.05
370	Cesar Cedeno	.15	.08	.05
371	Jack Morris	.15	.08	.05
372	Joel Youngblood	.15	.08	.05
373	Dan Petry	.20	.10	.06
374	Jim Gantner	.15	.08	.05
375	Ross Grimsley	.15	.08	.05
376	Gary Allenson	.15	.08	.05
377	Junior Kennedy	.15	.08	.05
378	Jerry Mumphrey	.15	.08	.05
379	Kevin Bell	.15	.08	.05
380	Garry Maddox	.15	.08	.05
381	Cubs Team (Preston Gomez)	.25	.13	.08
382	Dave Freisleben	.15	.08	.05
383	Ed Ott	.15	.08	.05
384	Joey McLaughlin	.15	.08	.05
385	Enos Cabell	.15	.08	.05
386	Darrell Jackson	.15	.08	.05
387a	Fred Stanley (Name in yellow.)	260.00	130.00	78.00
387b	Fred Stanley (Name in red.)	.15	.08	.05
388	Mike Paxton	.15	.08	.05
389	Pete LaCock	.15	.08	.05
390	Fergie Jenkins	2.00	1.00	.60
391	Tony Armas	.15	.08	.05
392	Milt Wilcox	.15	.08	.05
393	Ozzie Smith	8.00	4.00	2.00
394	Reggie Cleveland	.15	.08	.05
395	Ellis Valentine	.15	.08	.05
396	Dan Meyer	.15	.08	.05
397	Roy Thomas	.15	.08	.05
398	Barry Foote	.15	.08	.05
399	Mike Proly	.15	.08	.05
400	George Foster	.25	.13	.08
401	Pete Falcone	.15	.08	.05
402	Merv Rettenmund	.15	.08	.05
403	Pete Redfern	.15	.08	.05
404	Orioles Team (Earl Weaver)	.60	.30	.20
405	Dwight Evans	.15	.08	.05
406	Paul Molitor	2.50	1.25	.70
407	Tony Solaita	.15	.08	.05
408	Bill North	.15	.08	.05
409	Paul Splittorff	.15	.08	.05
410	Bobby Bonds	.15	.08	.05
411	Frank LaCorte	.15	.08	.05
412	Thad Bosley	.15	.08	.05
413	Allen Ripley	.15	.08	.05
414	George Scott	.15	.08	.05
415	Bill Atkinson	.15	.08	.05
416	Tom Brookens	.15	.08	.05
417	Craig Chamberlain	.15	.08	.05
418	Roger Freed	.15	.08	.05
419	Vic Correll	.15	.08	.05
420	Butch Hobson	.15	.08	.05
421	Doug Bird	.15	.08	.05
422	Larry Milbourne	.15	.08	.05
423	Dave Frost	.15	.08	.05
424	Yankees Team (Dick Howser)	.45	.25	.14
425	Mark Belanger	.15	.08	.05
426	Grant Jackson	.15	.08	.05
427	Tom Hutton	.15	.08	.05
428	Pat Zachry	.15	.08	.05
429	Duane Kuiper	.15	.08	.05
430	Larry Hisle	.15	.08	.05
431	Mike Krukow	.15	.08	.05
432	Willie Norwood	.15	.08	.05
433	Rich Gale	.15	.08	.05
434	Johnnie LeMaster	.15	.08	.05
435	Don Gullett	.15	.08	.05
436	Billy Almon	.15	.08	.05
437	Joe Niekro	.15	.08	.05
438	Dave Revering	.15	.08	.05
439	Mike Phillips	.15	.08	.05
440	Don Sutton	2.00	1.00	.60
441	Eric Soderholm	.15	.08	.05
442	Jorge Orta	.15	.08	.05
443	Mike Parrott	.15	.08	.05
444	Alvis Woods	.15	.08	.05
445	Mark Fidrych	.25	.13	.08
446	Duffy Dyer	.15	.08	.05
447	Nino Espinosa	.15	.08	.05
448	Jim Wohlford	.15	.08	.05
449	Doug Bair	.15	.08	.05
450	George Brett	6.00	3.00	1.50
451	Indians Team (Dave Garcia)	.25	.13	.08
452	Steve Dillard	.15	.08	.05
453	Mike Bacsik	.15	.08	.05
454	Tom Donohue	.15	.08	.05
455	Mike Torrez	.15	.08	.05
456	Frank Taveras	.15	.08	.05
457	Bert Blyleven	.15	.08	.05
458	Billy Sample	.15	.08	.05
459	Mickey Lolich	.15	.08	.05
460	Willie Randolph	.15	.08	.05
461	Dwayne Murphy	.15	.08	.05
462	Mike Sadek	.15	.08	.05
463	Jerry Royster	.15	.08	.05
464	John Denny	.15	.08	.05
465	Rick Monday	.15	.08	.05
466	Mike Squires	.15	.08	.05
467	Jesse Jefferson	.15	.08	.05
468	Aurelio Rodriguez	.15	.08	.05
469	Randy Niemann	.15	.08	.05
470	Bob Boone	.20	.10	.06
471	Hosken Powell	.15	.08	.05
472	Willie Hernandez	.15	.08	.05
473	Bump Wills	.15	.08	.05
474	Steve Busby	.15	.08	.05
475	Cesar Geronimo	.15	.08	.05
476	Bob Shirley	.15	.08	.05
477	Buck Martinez	.15	.08	.05
478	Gil Flores	.15	.08	.05
479	Expos Team (Dick Williams)	.25	.13	.08
480	Bob Watson	.15	.08	.05
481	Tom Paciorek	.15	.08	.05
482	Rickey Henderson	35.00	17.50	10.50
483	Bo Diaz	.15	.08	.05
484	Checklist 364-484	.15	.08	.05
485	Mickey Rivers	.15	.08	.05
486	Mike Tyson	.15	.08	.05
487	Wayne Nordhagen	.15	.08	.05
488	Roy Howell	.15	.08	.05
489	Preston Hanna	.15	.08	.05
490	Lee May	.15	.08	.05
491	Steve Mura	.15	.08	.05
492	Todd Cruz	.15	.08	.05
493	Jerry Martin	.15	.08	.05
494	Craig Minetto	.15	.08	.05
495	Bake McBride	.15	.08	.05
496	Silvio Martinez	.15	.08	.05
497	Jim Mason	.15	.08	.05
498	Danny Darwin	.15	.08	.05
499	Giants Team (Dave Bristol)	.25	.13	.08
500	Tom Seaver	3.00	1.50	.90
501	Rennie Stennett	.15	.08	.05
502	Rich Wortham	.15	.08	.05
503	Mike Cubbage	.15	.08	.05
504	Gene Garber	.15	.08	.05
505	Bert Campaneris	.15	.08	.05
506	Tom Buskey	.15	.08	.05
507	Leon Roberts	.15	.08	.05
508	U.L. Washington	.15	.08	.05
509	Ed Glynn	.15	.08	.05
510	Ron Cey	.15	.08	.05
511	Eric Wilkins	.15	.08	.05
512	Jose Cardenal	.15	.08	.05
513	Tom Dixon	.15	.08	.05
514	Steve Ontiveros	.15	.08	.05
515	Mike Caldwell	.15	.08	.05
516	Hector Cruz	.15	.08	.05
517	Don Stanhouse	.15	.08	.05
518	Nelson Norman	.15	.08	.05
519	Steve Nicosia	.15	.08	.05
520	Steve Rogers	.15	.08	.05
521	Ken Brett	.15	.08	.05
522	Jim Morrison	.15	.08	.05
523	Ken Henderson	.15	.08	.05
524	Jim Wright	.15	.08	.05
525	Clint Hurdle	.15	.08	.05
526	Phillies Team (Dallas Green)	.60	.30	.20
527	Doug Rau	.15	.08	.05
528	Adrian Devine	.15	.08	.05
529	Jim Barr	.15	.08	.05
530	Jim Sundberg	.15	.08	.05
531	Eric Rasmussen	.15	.08	.05
532	Willie Horton	.15	.08	.05
533	Checklist 485-605	.15	.08	.05
534	Andre Thornton	.15	.08	.05
535	Bob Forsch	.15	.08	.05
536	Lee Lacy	.15	.08	.05
537	Alex Trevino	.15	.08	.05
538	Joe Strain	.15	.08	.05
539	Rudy May	.15	.08	.05

540	Pete Rose	6.00	3.00	1.50
541	Miguel Dilone	.15	.08	.05
542	Joe Coleman	.15	.08	.05
543	Pat Kelly	.15	.08	.05
544	*Rick Sutcliffe*	2.00	1.00	.60
545	Jeff Burroughs	.15	.08	.05
546	Rick Langford	.15	.08	.05
547a	John Wathan	200.00	100.00	60.00
	(Name in yellow.)			
547b	John Wathan (Name in red.)	.15	.08	.05
548	Dave Rajsich	.15	.08	.05
549	Larry Wolfe	.15	.08	.05
550	Ken Griffey	.15	.08	.05
551	Pirates Team (Chuck Tanner)	.25	.13	.08
552	Bill Nahorodny	.15	.08	.05
553	Dick Davis	.15	.08	.05
554	Art Howe	.15	.08	.05
555	Ed Figueroa	.15	.08	.05
556	Joe Rudi	.15	.08	.05
557	Mark Lee	.15	.08	.05
558	Alfredo Griffin	.15	.08	.05
559	Dale Murray	.15	.08	.05
560	Dave Lopes	.15	.08	.05
561	Eddie Whitson	.15	.08	.05
562	Joe Wallis	.15	.08	.05
563	Will McEnaney	.15	.08	.05
564	Rick Manning	.15	.08	.05
565	Dennis Leonard	.15	.08	.05
566	Bud Harrelson	.15	.08	.05
567	Skip Lockwood	.15	.08	.05
568	*Gary Roenicke*	.15	.08	.05
569	Terry Kennedy	.15	.08	.05
570	Roy Smalley	.15	.08	.05
571	Joe Sambito	.15	.08	.05
572	Jerry Morales	.15	.08	.05
573	Kent Tekulve	.15	.08	.05
574	Scot Thompson	.15	.08	.05
575	Ken Kravec	.15	.08	.05
576	Jim Dwyer	.15	.08	.05
577	Blue Jays Team	.25	.13	.08
	(Bobby Mattick)			
578	Scott Sanderson	.15	.08	.05
579	Charlie Moore	.15	.08	.05
580	Nolan Ryan	15.00	7.50	3.75
581	Bob Bailor	.15	.08	.05
582	Brian Doyle	.15	.08	.05
583	Bob Stinson	.15	.08	.05
584	Kurt Bevacqua	.15	.08	.05
585	Al Hrabosky	.15	.08	.05
586	Mitchell Page	.15	.08	.05
587	Garry Templeton	.15	.08	.05
588	Greg Minton	.15	.08	.05
589	Chet Lemon	.15	.08	.05
590	Jim Palmer	2.50	1.25	.70
591	Rick Cerone	.15	.08	.05
592	Jon Matlack	.15	.08	.05
593	Jesus Alou	.15	.08	.05
594	Dick Tidrow	.15	.08	.05
595	Don Money	.15	.08	.05
596	Rick Matula	.15	.08	.05
597a	Tom Poquette	200.00	100.00	60.00
	(Name in yellow.)			
597b	Tom Poquette (Name in red.)	.15	.08	.05
598	Fred Kendall	.15	.08	.05
599	Mike Norris	.15	.08	.05
600	Reggie Jackson	4.00	2.00	1.25
601	Buddy Schultz	.15	.08	.05
602	Brian Downing	.15	.08	.05
603	Jack Billingham	.15	.08	.05
604	Glenn Adams	.15	.08	.05
605	Terry Forster	.15	.08	.05
606	Reds Team (John McNamara)	.25	.13	.08
607	Woodie Fryman	.15	.08	.05
608	Alan Bannister	.15	.08	.05
609	Ron Reed	.15	.08	.05
610	Willie Stargell	2.50	1.25	.70
611	Jerry Garvin	.15	.08	.05
612	Cliff Johnson	.15	.08	.05
613	Randy Stein	.15	.08	.05
614	John Hiller	.15	.08	.05
615	Doug DeCinces	.15	.08	.05
616	Gene Richards	.15	.08	.05
617	Joaquin Andujar	.15	.08	.05
618	Bob Montgomery	.15	.08	.05
619	Sergio Ferrer	.15	.08	.05
620	Richie Zisk	.15	.08	.05
621	Bob Grich	.15	.08	.05
622	Mario Soto	.15	.08	.05
623	Gorman Thomas	.15	.08	.05
624	Lerrin LaGrow	.15	.08	.05
625	Chris Chambliss	.15	.08	.05
626	Tigers Team	.75	.40	.25
	(Sparky Anderson)			
627	Pedro Borbon	.15	.08	.05
628	Doug Capilla	.15	.08	.05
629	Jim Todd	.15	.08	.05
630	Larry Bowa	.15	.08	.05
631	Mark Littell	.15	.08	.05
632	Barry Bonnell	.15	.08	.05
633	Bob Apodaca	.15	.08	.05
634	Glenn Borgmann	.15	.08	.05
635	John Candelaria	.15	.08	.05
636	Toby Harrah	.15	.08	.05
637	Joe Simpson	.15	.08	.05
638	*Mark Clear*	.15	.08	.05
639	Larry Biittner	.15	.08	.05
640	Mike Flanagan	.15	.08	.05
641	Ed Kranepool	.15	.08	.05
642	Ken Forsch	.15	.08	.05
643	John Mayberry	.15	.08	.05
644	Charlie Hough	.15	.08	.05
645	Rick Burleson	.15	.08	.05
646	Checklist 606-726	.25	.13	.08
647	Milt May	.15	.08	.05
648	Roy White	.15	.08	.05
649	Tom Griffin	.15	.08	.05
650	Joe Morgan	2.50	1.25	.70
651	Rollie Fingers	2.00	1.00	.60
652	Mario Mendoza	.15	.08	.05
653	Stan Bahnsen	.15	.08	.05
654	Bruce Boisclair	.15	.08	.05
655	Tug McGraw	.15	.08	.05
656	Larvell Blanks	.15	.08	.05
657	Dave Edwards	.15	.08	.05
658	Chris Knapp	.15	.08	.05
659	Brewers Team	.25	.13	.08
	(George Bamberger)			
660	Rusty Staub	.15	.08	.05
661	Orioles Future Stars	.15	.08	.05
	(Mark Corey, Dave Ford, Wayne Krenchicki)			
662	Red Sox Future Stars	.15	.08	.05
	(Joel Finch, Mike O'Berry, Chuck Rainey)			
663	Angels Future Stars	.25	.13	.08
	(*Ralph Botting, Bob Clark, Dickie Thon*)			
664	White Sox Future Stars	.15	.08	.05
	(*Mike Colbern, Guy Hoffman, Dewey Robinson*)			
665	Indians Future Stars	.15	.08	.05
	(Larry Andersen, Bobby Cuellar, Sandy Wihtol)			
666	Tigers Future Stars	.15	.08	.05
	(Mike Chris, Al Greene, Bruce Robbins)			
667	Royals Future Stars (*Renie Martin, Bill Paschall, Dan Quisenberry*)	1.00	.50	.30
668	Brewers Future Stars	.15	.08	.05
	(Danny Boitano, Willie Mueller, Lenn Sakata)			
669	Twins Future Stars (*Dan Graham, Rick Sofield, Gary Ward*)	.25	.13	.08
670	Yankees Future Stars	.15	.08	.05
	(Bobby Brown, Brad Gulden, Darryl Jones)			
671	A's Future Stars (*Derek Bryant, Brian Kingman, Mike Morgan*)	.50	.25	.15
672	Mariners Future Stars	.15	.08	.05
	(Charlie Beamon, Rodney Craig, Rafael Vasquez)			
673	Rangers Future Stars	.15	.08	.05
	(Brian Allard, Jerry Don Gleaton, Greg Mahlberg)			
674	Blue Jays Future Stars	.15	.08	.05
	Butch Edge, Pat Kelly, Ted Wilborn)			
675	Braves Future Stars	.15	.08	.05
	(Bruce Benedict, Larry Bradford, Eddie Miller)			
676	Cubs Future Stars	.15	.08	.05
	(Dave Geisel, Steve Macko, Karl Pagel)			
677	Reds Future Stars	.15	.08	.05
	(Art DeFreites, Frank Pastore, Harry Spilman)			
678	Astros Future Stars	.15	.08	.05
	(*Reggie Baldwin, Alan Knicely, Pete Ladd*)			
679	Dodgers Future Stars	.25	.13	.08
	(*Joe Beckwith, Mickey Hatcher, Dave Patterson*)			
680	Expos Future Stars	.15	.08	.05
	(*Tony Bernazard, Randy Miller, John Tamargo*)			
681	Mets Future Stars (*Dan Norman, Jesse Orosco, Mike Scott*)	1.00	.50	.30
682	Phillies Future Stars	.15	.08	.05
	(*Ramon Aviles, Dickie Noles, Kevin Saucier*)			
683	Pirates Future Stars	.15	.08	.05
	(Dorian Boyland, Alberto Lois, Harry Saferight)			
684	Cardinals Future Stars (*George Frazier, Tom Herr, Dan O'Brien*)	.30	.15	.09
685	Padres Future Stars	.15	.08	.05
	(Tim Flannery, Brian Greer, Jim Wilhelm)			
686	Giants Future Stars	.15	.08	.05
	(Greg Johnston, Dennis Littlejohn, Phil Nastu)			
687	Mike Heath	.15	.08	.05
688	Steve Stone	.15	.08	.05
689	Red Sox Team (Don Zimmer)	.25	.13	.08
690	Tommy John	.25	.13	.08
691	Ivan DeJesus	.15	.08	.05
692	Rawly Eastwick	.15	.08	.05
693	Craig Kusick	.15	.08	.05
694	Jim Rooker	.15	.08	.05
695	Reggie Smith	.15	.08	.05
696	Julio Gonzalez	.15	.08	.05
697	David Clyde	.15	.08	.05
698	Oscar Gamble	.15	.08	.05
699	Floyd Bannister	.15	.08	.05
700	Rod Carew	2.50	1.25	.70
701	*Ken Oberkfell*	.15	.08	.05
702	Ed Farmer	.15	.08	.05
703	Otto Velez	.15	.08	.05
704	Gene Tenace	.15	.08	.05
705	Freddie Patek	.15	.08	.05
706	Tippy Martinez	.15	.08	.05
707	Elliott Maddox	.15	.08	.05
708	Bob Tolan	.15	.08	.05
709	Pat Underwood	.15	.08	.05
710	Graig Nettles	.25	.13	.08
711	Bob Galasso	.15	.08	.05
712	Rodney Scott	.15	.08	.05
713	Terry Whitfield	.15	.08	.05
714	Fred Norman	.15	.08	.05
715	Sal Bando	.15	.08	.05
716	Lynn McGlothen	.15	.08	.05
717	Mickey Klutts	.15	.08	.05
718	Greg Gross	.15	.08	.05
719	Don Robinson	.15	.08	.05
720	Carl Yastrzemski	3.00	1.50	.90
721	Paul Hartzell	.15	.08	.05
722	Jose Cruz	.15	.08	.05
723	Shane Rawley	.15	.08	.05
724	Jerry White	.15	.08	.05
725	Rick Wise	.15	.08	.05
726	Steve Yeager	.15	.08	.05

1980 Topps Team Checklist Sheet

This uncut sheet of 26 1980 Topps team cards was available via a mail-in offer. The sheet was mailed with two folds and includes an offer to picture yourself on a baseball card. The sheet cards are printed on lighter card stock.

	NM	EX	VG
Uncut Sheet	15.00	7.50	4.50

1980 Topps N.Y. Yankees Proof

One of the most popular proof cards of the era is this N.Y. Yankees team photo card with an inset photo of manager Billy Martin, who was fired in October, 1979, after punching a marshmellow salesman. By the time the cards were issued, Martin's name and photo had been replaced by rookie manager Dick Howser. The card is blank-backed and usually shows evidence of having been handcut from a proof sheet.

	NM	EX	VG
N.Y. Yankees	650.00	320.00	195.00

1980 Topps(?) Stickers Prototypes

Anecdotal evidence connects these possible prototypes to Topps as a die-cut sticker issue that never materialized. The photos are taken from earlier covers of Sports Illustrated. Each pair measures 3-1/2" x 2-1/2" and has been stuck to a cardboard backing. It is not known whether this listing comprises the entirety of the samples. Because each pair is unique, no valuations are presented.

		NM	EX	VG
(1)	Johnny Bench, Maury Wills (Photo actually Bump Wills)			
(2)	Nino Espinosa, Ron Cey			
(3)	Dwight Evans, Carlton Fisk			
(4)	Don (Ron) Guidry, Dave Parker			
(5)	Reggie Jackson, J.R. Richard			

1980 Topps Superstar 5x7 Photos

In actuality, these cards measure 4-7/8" x 6-7/8". These were another Topps "test" issue that was bought out almost entirely by speculators. The 60 cards have a color photo on the front and a blue ink facsimile autograph. Backs have the player's name, team, position and card number. The issue was printed on different cardboard stocks, with the first on thick cardboard with a white back and the second on thinner cardboard with a gray back. Prices below are for the more common gray backs; white backs are valued 2.5X-3X the figures shown, except for triple-print cards (indicated by "3P" in checklist), which are valued at about 7.5X the gray-back price in the white-back version. The white backs were test marketed in three-card cello packs in selected geographical areas.

		NM	EX	VG
	Complete Set, Gray Backs (60):	10.00	5.00	3.00
	Complete Set, White Backs (60):	20.00	10.00	6.00
	Common Player, Gray Back:	.25	.13	.08
	Common Player, White Back:	.75	.40	.25
	Wax Box (48):	10.00		
1	Willie Stargell	1.00	.50	.30
2	Mike Schmidt (3P)	1.50	.70	.45
3	Johnny Bench	1.00	.50	.30
4	Jim Palmer	.75	.40	.25
5	Jim Rice	.50	.25	.15
6	Reggie Jackson (3P)	1.50	.70	.45
7	Ron Guidry	.45	.25	.14
8	Lee Mazzilli	.25	.13	.08
9	Don Baylor	.50	.25	.15
10	Fred Lynn	.25	.13	.08
11	Ken Singleton	.25	.13	.08
12	Rod Carew (3P)	.75	.40	.25
13	Steve Garvey (3P)	.50	.25	.15
14	George Brett (3P)	1.50	.70	.45
15	Tom Seaver	1.50	.70	.45
16	Dave Kingman	.25	.13	.08
17	Dave Parker (3P)	.25	.13	.08
18	Dave Winfield	1.00	.50	.30
19	Pete Rose	2.00	1.00	.60
20	Nolan Ryan	4.00	2.00	1.25
21	Graig Nettles	.25	.13	.08
22	Carl Yastrzemski	1.50	.70	.45
23	Tommy John	.40	.20	.12
24	George Foster	.25	.13	.08
25	J.R. Richard	.25	.13	.08
26	Keith Hernandez	.25	.13	.08
27	Bob Horner	.25	.13	.08
28	Eddie Murray	1.50	.70	.45
29	Steve Kemp	.25	.13	.08
30	Gorman Thomas	.25	.13	.08
31	Sixto Lezcano	.25	.13	.08
32	Bruce Sutter	1.00	.50	.30
33	Cecil Cooper	.25	.13	.08
34	Larry Bowa	.25	.13	.08
35	Al Oliver	.35	.20	.11
36	Ted Simmons	.25	.13	.08
37	Garry Templeton	.25	.13	.08
38	Jerry Koosman	.25	.13	.08
39	Darrell Porter	.25	.13	.08
40	Roy Smalley	.25	.13	.08
41	Craig Swan	.25	.13	.08
42	Jason Thompson	.25	.13	.08
43	Andre Thornton	.25	.13	.08
44	Rick Manning	.25	.13	.08
45	Kent Tekulve	.25	.13	.08
46	Phil Niekro	.75	.40	.25
47	Buddy Bell	.25	.13	.08
48	Randy Jones	.25	.13	.08
49	Brian Downing	.25	.13	.08
50	Amos Otis	.25	.13	.08
51	Rick Bosetti	.25	.13	.08
52	Gary Carter	.75	.40	.25
53	Larry Parrish	.25	.13	.08
54	Jack Clark	.25	.13	.08
55	Bruce Bochte	.25	.13	.08
56	Cesar Cedeno	.25	.13	.08
57	Chet Lemon	.25	.13	.08
58	Dave Revering	.25	.13	.08
59	Vida Blue	.25	.13	.08
60	Davey Lopes	.25	.13	.08

1980 Topps Test Coins

These silver-dollar size (1-3/8" diameter) metal coins appear to have been a Topps test issue. The coins have a player portrait at center on obverse. On reverse center is player personal data and a Topps copyright line. Coins have been seen in compositions resembling bronze, silver and gold. Some of the coins have a hole at top.

	NM	EX	VG
Rod Carew	450.00	225.00	150.00
Steve Garvey	450.00	225.00	150.00
Reggie Jackson	900.00	450.00	300.00

1953 Top Taste Bread Milwaukee Braves

STAR PLAYER
OF THE MILWAUKEE BRAVES
GEORGE CROWE

This series of black-and-white mini-posters (8-1/2" x 11-1/4") depicts members of the 1953 Braves holding loaves of bread. They were probably intended for grocery store window or bakery aisle display. Backs are blank. It's unknown how many players are in the set. See also, Pictsweet Milwaukee Braves.

		NM	EX	VG
	Common Player:	150.00	75.00	45.00
(1)	Lew Burdette	150.00	75.00	45.00
(2)	George Crowe	150.00	75.00	45.00
(3)	Andy Pafko	150.00	75.00	45.00
(4)	Bucky Walters	150.00	75.00	45.00

1976 Towne Club Discs

One of several regional sponsors of player disc sets in 1976 was the Towne Club Pop Centers chain. The discs are 3-3/8" diameter with a black-and-white player portrait photo in the center of the baseball design. A line of red stars is above, while the left and right panels feature one of several bright colors. Produced by Michael Schecter Associates under license from the Major League Baseball Players Association, the player photos have had uniform and cap logos removed. Backs are printed in red. The unnumbered checklist here is presented in alphabetical order.

		NM	EX	VG
	Complete Set (70):	50.00	25.00	15.00
	Common Player:	1.00	.50	.30
(1)	Henry Aaron	10.00	5.00	3.00
(2)	Johnny Bench	5.00	2.50	1.50
(3)	Vida Blue	1.00	.50	.30
(4)	Larry Bowa	1.00	.50	.30
(5)	Lou Brock	4.00	2.00	1.25
(6)	Jeff Burroughs	1.00	.50	.30
(7)	John Candelaria	1.00	.50	.30
(8)	Jose Cardenal	1.00	.50	.30
(9)	Rod Carew	4.00	2.00	1.25
(10)	Steve Carlton	4.00	2.00	1.25
(11)	Dave Cash	1.00	.50	.30
(12)	Cesar Cedeno	1.00	.50	.30
(13)	Ron Cey	1.00	.50	.30
(14)	Carlton Fisk	4.00	2.00	1.25
(15)	Tito Fuentes	1.00	.50	.30
(16)	Steve Garvey	3.00	1.50	.90
(17)	Ken Griffey	1.00	.50	.30
(18)	Don Gullett	1.00	.50	.30
(19)	Willie Horton	1.00	.50	.30
(20)	Al Hrabosky	1.00	.50	.30
(21)	Catfish Hunter	4.00	2.00	1.25
(22)	Reggie Jackson (A's)	7.50	3.75	2.25
(23)	Randy Jones	1.00	.50	.30
(24)	Jim Kaat	1.00	.50	.30
(25)	Don Kessinger	1.00	.50	.30
(26)	Dave Kingman	1.00	.50	.30
(27)	Jerry Koosman	1.00	.50	.30
(28)	Mickey Lolich	1.00	.50	.30
(29)	Greg Luzinski	1.00	.50	.30
(30)	Fred Lynn	1.00	.50	.30
(31)	Bill Madlock	1.00	.50	.30
(32)	Carlos May	1.00	.50	.30
(33)	John Mayberry	1.00	.50	.30
(34)	Bake McBride	1.00	.50	.30
(35)	Doc Medich	1.00	.50	.30
(36)	Andy Messersmith	1.00	.50	.30
(37)	Rick Monday	1.00	.50	.30
(38)	John Montefusco	1.00	.50	.30
(39)	Jerry Morales	1.00	.50	.30
(40)	Joe Morgan	4.00	2.00	1.25
(41)	Thurman Munson	5.00	2.50	1.50
(42)	Bobby Murcer	1.00	.50	.30
(43)	Al Oliver	1.00	.50	.30
(44)	Jim Palmer	4.00	2.00	1.25
(45)	Dave Parker	1.00	.50	.30
(46)	Tony Perez	4.00	2.00	1.25
(47)	Jerry Reuss	1.00	.50	.30
(48)	Brooks Robinson	5.00	2.50	1.50
(49)	Frank Robinson	5.00	2.50	1.50
(50)	Steve Rogers	1.00	.50	.30
(51)	Pete Rose	10.00	5.00	3.00

		NM	EX	VG
(52)	Nolan Ryan	20.00	10.00	6.00
(53)	Manny Sanguillen	1.00	.50	.30
(54)	Mike Schmidt	7.50	3.75	2.25
(55)	Tom Seaver	5.00	2.50	1.50
(56)	Ted Simmons	1.00	.50	.30
(57)	Reggie Smith	1.00	.50	.30
(58)	Willie Stargell	4.00	2.00	1.25
(59)	Rusty Staub	1.50	.70	.45
(60)	Rennie Stennett	1.00	.50	.30
(61)	Don Sutton	4.00	2.00	1.25
(62)	Andy Thornton	1.00	.50	.30
(63)	Luis Tiant	1.00	.50	.30
(64)	Joe Torre	2.50	1.25	.70
(65)	Mike Tyson	1.00	.50	.30
(66)	Bob Watson	1.00	.50	.30
(67)	Wilbur Wood	1.00	.50	.30
(68)	Jimmy Wynn	1.00	.50	.30
(69)	Carl Yastrzemski	6.00	3.00	1.75
(70)	Richie Zisk	1.00	.50	.30

1910 Toy Town Post Office

Rather than a card issuer, this enigmatic rubber-stamp has been found on the backs of dozens of 1910-era baseball cards. Measuring 1/2" in diameter the seal is in purple ink. At center is a barred circle with "TOY TOWN" above and "POST OFFICE" below. The stamp was part of a Milton Bradley post office toy set and has been seen on different types of cards that eventually made their way into the hobby. On low-grade cards, the stamp neither greatly adds nor detracts from the value of the card on which it is placed.

(See individual card issuers for base values.)

1965 Trade Bloc Minnesota Twins

These cards were produced as part of a baseball game which was marketed at Metropolitan Stadium for $1. The blank-back cards measure 2-1/4" x 3-1/2" and are printed in either blue or sepia tones. Besides Twins players and staff, the set includes cards of various team souvenir items as well as old Met Stadium. Besides the player photo, cards include a facsimile autograph, stats and personal data. The unnumbered cards are checklisted here in alphabetical order.

		NM	EX	VG
	Complete Set (52):	600.00	300.00	175.00
	Common Player:	15.00	7.50	4.50
	Common Non-player Card:	5.00	2.50	1.50
(1)	Bernard Allen	15.00	7.50	4.50
(2)	Bob Allison	20.00	10.00	6.00
(3)	Earl Battey	15.00	7.50	4.50
(4)	Dave Boswell	15.00	7.50	4.50
(5)	Gerald Fosnow	15.00	7.50	4.50
(6)	James Grant	15.00	7.50	4.50
(7)	Calvin Griffith	20.00	10.00	6.00
(8)	Jimmie Hall	15.00	7.50	4.50
(9)	Jim Kaat	25.00	12.50	7.50
(10)	Harmon Killebrew	60.00	30.00	18.00
(11)	Jerry Kindall	15.00	7.50	4.50
(12)	Johnny Klippstein	15.00	7.50	4.50
(13)	Frank Kostro	15.00	7.50	4.50
(14)	James Lemon	15.00	7.50	4.50
(15)	George "Doc" Lentz	15.00	7.50	4.50
(16)	Alfred Martin (Billy)	30.00	15.00	9.00
(17)	Sam Mele	15.00	7.50	4.50
(18)	Donald Mincher	15.00	7.50	4.50
(19)	Harold Naragon	15.00	7.50	4.50
(20)	Melvin Nelson	15.00	7.50	4.50
(21)	Joseph Nossek	15.00	7.50	4.50

		NM	EX	VG
(22)	Pedro Oliva (Tony)	40.00	20.00	12.00
(23)	Camilo Pascual	20.00	10.00	6.00
(24)	James Perry	15.00	7.50	4.50
(25)	Bill Pleis	15.00	7.50	4.50
(26)	Richard Rollins	15.00	7.50	4.50
(27)	John Sain	15.00	7.50	4.50
(28)	John Sevcik	15.00	7.50	4.50
(29)	Richard Stigman	15.00	7.50	4.50
(30)	Sandy Valdespino	15.00	7.50	4.50
(31)	Zoilo Versalles	25.00	12.50	7.50
(32)	Allan Worthington	15.00	7.50	4.50
(33)	Gerald Zimmerman	15.00	7.50	4.50
(34)	Metropolitan Stadium	10.00	5.00	3.00
(35)	L.A. Angels Logo	5.00	2.50	1.50
(36)	K.C. Athletics Logo	5.00	2.50	1.50
(37)	Cleveland Indians Logo	5.00	2.50	1.50
(38)	Baltimore Orioles Logo	5.00	2.50	1.50
(39)	Boston Red Sox Logo	5.00	2.50	1.50
(40)	Washington Senators Logo	5.00	2.50	1.50
(41)	Detroit Tigers Logo	5.00	2.50	1.50
(42)	Minnesota Twins Logo	5.00	2.50	1.50
(43)	Chicago White Sox Logo	5.00	2.50	1.50
(44)	N.Y. Yankees Logo	5.00	2.50	1.50
(45)	Twins Autographed Ball	5.00	2.50	1.50
(46)	Twins Autographed Bat	5.00	2.50	1.50
(47)	Twins Bobbin' Head Doll	5.00	2.50	1.50
(48)	Twins Cap	5.00	2.50	1.50
(49)	Twins Pennant	5.00	2.50	1.50
(50)	Twins Scorebook	5.00	2.50	1.50
(51)	Twins Warmup Jacket	5.00	2.50	1.50
(52)	Twins Yearbook	5.00	2.50	1.50

1964 Transfer-ette Chicago Cubs Iron-ons

This novelty item features artist-rendered portraits of Cubs players which were designed to be transferred to t-shirts, notebook covers or other items via an iron-on process. Each package contains three sheets of nine images; one each in blue, black and red. The sheets are about 8-3/8" x 10-3/4" with each player image about 2-1/2" x 2-3/4". According to the packaging, other teams were planned, along with larger two-color player portraits.

	NM	EX	VG
Complete Set:	50.00	25.00	15.00

BLACK SHEET
Ernie Banks
Dick Bertell
John Boccabella
Glen Hobbie
Calvin Koonce
Merritt Ranew
Andre Rodgers
Ron Santo
Jim Stewart
BLUE SHEET
Steve Boros
Lou Brock
Bob Buhl
Ellis Burton
Bill Cowan
Dick Ellsworth
Don Elston
Bob Kennedy
Jimmie Schaffer
RED SHEET
Tom Baker
Jim Brewer
Leo Burke
Larry Jackson
Don Landrum
Paul Toth
Jack Warner
Billy Williams
Chicago Cubs Logo

1964 Transfer-ette Chicago White Sox Iron-ons

This novelty item features artist-rendered portraits of White Sox players which were designed to be transferred to t-shirts, notebook covers or other items via an iron-on process. Each package contains three sheets of nine images; one each in blue, black and red. The sheets are about 8-3/8" x 10-3/4" with each player image about 2-1/2" x 2-3/4". According to the packaging, other teams were planned, along with larger two-color player portraits.

	NM	EX	VG
Complete Set:	40.00	20.00	12.00

BLACK SHEET

Jim Brosnan
Don Buford
John Buzhardt
Joe Cunningham
Jim Golden
Joel Horlen
Charlie Maxwell
Dave Nicholson
Gene Stephens
BLUE SHEET
Fritz Ackley
Frank Bauman (Baumann)
Camilo Carreon
Dave DeBusschere
Ed Fisher
Mike Joyce
J.C. Martin
Tom McCraw
Hoyt Wilhelm
RED SHEET
Ron Hansen
Ray Herbert
Mike Hershberger
Jim Landis
Gary Peters
Floyd Robinson
Pete Ward
Al Weis
White Sox Logo

1969 Transogram

These 2-1/2" x 3-1/2" cards were printed on the back of toy baseball player statue boxes. The cards feature a color photo of the player surrounded by a rounded white border. Below the photo is the player's name in red and his team and other personal details all printed in black. The overall background is yellow. The cards were designed to be cut off the box, but collectors prefer to find the box intact and, better still, with the statue inside. While the cards themselves are not numbered, there is a number on each box's end flap, which is the order in which the cards are checklisted here. Three-player boxes were also sold.

		NM	EX	VG
	CUT CARD OR STATUE			
(1)	Joe Azcue	12.50	6.25	3.75
(2)	Willie Horton	12.50	6.25	3.75
(3)	Luis Tiant	12.50	6.25	3.75
(4)	Denny McLain	12.50	6.25	3.75
(5)	Jose Cardenal	12.50	6.25	3.75
(6)	Al Kaline	30.00	15.00	9.00
(7)	Tony Oliva	15.00	7.50	4.50
(8)	Blue Moon Odom	12.50	6.25	3.75
(9)	Cesar Tovar	12.50	6.25	3.75
(10)	Rick Monday	12.50	6.25	3.75
(11)	Harmon Killebrew	25.00	12.50	7.50
(12)	Danny Cater	12.50	6.25	3.75
(13)	Brooks Robinson	35.00	17.50	10.00
(14)	Jim Fregosi	12.50	6.25	3.75
(15)	Dave McNally	12.50	6.25	3.75
(16)	Frank Robinson	35.00	17.50	10.00
(17)	Bobby Knoop	12.50	6.25	3.75
(18)	Rick Reichardt	12.50	6.25	3.75
(19)	Carl Yastrzemski	35.00	17.50	10.00
(20)	Pete Ward	12.50	6.25	3.75
(21)	Rico Petrocelli	12.50	6.25	3.75
(22)	Tommy John	15.00	7.50	4.50
(23)	Ken Harrelson	12.50	6.25	3.75
(24)	Luis Aparicio	25.00	12.50	7.50
(25)	Mike Epstein	12.50	6.25	3.75
(26)	Roy White	12.50	6.25	3.75
(27)	Camilo Pascual	12.50	6.25	3.75
(28)	Mel Stottlemyre	12.50	6.25	3.75
(29)	Frank Howard	15.00	7.50	4.50
(30)	Mickey Mantle	185.00	90.00	55.00
(31)	Lou Brock	25.00	12.50	7.50
(32)	Juan Marichal	25.00	12.50	7.50
(33)	Bob Gibson	25.00	12.50	7.50
(34)	Willie Mays	60.00	30.00	18.00
(35)	Tim McCarver	15.00	7.50	4.50
(36)	Willie McCovey	25.00	12.50	7.50
(37)	Don Wilson	12.50	6.25	3.75
(38)	Billy Williams	25.00	12.50	7.50
(39)	Dan Staub (Rusty)	15.00	7.50	4.50
(40)	Ernie Banks	45.00	22.50	13.50
(41)	Jim Wynn	12.50	6.25	3.75
(42)	Ron Santo	15.00	7.50	4.50
(43)	Tom Haller	12.50	6.25	3.75
(44)	Ron Swoboda	12.50	6.25	3.75
(45)	Willie Davis	12.50	6.25	3.75
(46)	Jerry Koosman	12.50	6.25	3.75
(47)	Jim Lefebvre	12.50	6.25	3.75
(48)	Tom Seaver	30.00	15.00	9.00
(49)	Joe Torre (Atlanta)	20.00	10.00	6.00
(50)	Tony Perez	25.00	12.50	7.50
(51)	Felipe Alou	12.50	6.25	3.75
(52)	Lee May	12.50	6.25	3.75

		NM	EX	VG
(53)	Hank Aaron	60.00	30.00	18.00
(54)	Pete Rose	60.00	30.00	18.00
(55)	Cookie Rojas	12.50	6.25	3.75
(56)	Roberto Clemente	60.00	30.00	18.00
(57)	Richie Allen	15.00	7.50	4.50
(58)	Matty Alou	12.50	6.25	3.75
(59)	Johnny Callison	12.50	6.25	3.75
(60)	Bill Mazeroski	25.00	12.50	7.50
	COMPLETE BOX W/STATUE			
(1)	Joe Azcue	170.00	85.00	50.00
(2)	Willie Horton	170.00	85.00	50.00
(3)	Luis Tiant	170.00	85.00	50.00
(4)	Denny McLain	170.00	85.00	50.00
(5)	Jose Cardenal	170.00	85.00	50.00
(6)	Al Kaline	350.00	175.00	105.00
(7)	Tony Oliva	200.00	100.00	60.00
(8)	Blue Moon Odom	170.00	85.00	50.00
(9)	Cesar Tovar	170.00	85.00	50.00
(10)	Rick Monday	170.00	85.00	50.00
(11)	Harmon Killebrew	400.00	200.00	120.00
(12)	Danny Cater	170.00	85.00	50.00
(13)	Brooks Robinson	500.00	250.00	150.00
(14)	Jim Fregosi	170.00	85.00	50.00
(15)	Dave McNally	170.00	85.00	50.00
(16)	Frank Robinson	500.00	250.00	150.00
(17)	Bobby Knoop	170.00	85.00	50.00
(18)	Rick Reichardt	170.00	85.00	50.00
(19)	Carl Yastrzemski	600.00	300.00	180.00
(20)	Pete Ward	170.00	85.00	50.00
(21)	Rico Petrocelli	170.00	85.00	50.00
(22)	Tommy John	240.00	120.00	72.50
(23)	Ken Harrelson	170.00	85.00	50.00
(24)	Luis Aparicio	350.00	175.00	105.00
(25)	Mike Epstein	170.00	85.00	50.00
(26)	Roy White	170.00	85.00	50.00
(27)	Camilo Pascual	170.00	85.00	50.00
(28)	Mel Stottlemyre	170.00	85.00	50.00
(29)	Frank Howard	200.00	100.00	60.00
(30)	Mickey Mantle	1,700	850.00	500.00
(31)	Lou Brock	350.00	175.00	105.00
(32)	Juan Marichal	350.00	175.00	105.00
(33)	Bob Gibson	350.00	175.00	105.00
(34)	Willie Mays	800.00	400.00	240.00
(35)	Tim McCarver	200.00	100.00	60.00
(36)	Willie McCovey	350.00	175.00	105.00
(37)	Don Wilson	170.00	85.00	50.00
(38)	Billy Williams	350.00	175.00	105.00
(39)	Dan Staub (Rusty)	240.00	120.00	72.50
(40)	Ernie Banks	700.00	350.00	210.00
(41)	Jim Wynn	170.00	85.00	50.00
(42)	Ron Santo	240.00	120.00	72.50
(43)	Tom Haller	170.00	85.00	50.00
(44)	Ron Swoboda	170.00	85.00	50.00
(45)	Willie Davis	170.00	85.00	50.00
(46)	Jerry Koosman	240.00	120.00	72.50
(47)	Jim Lefebvre	170.00	85.00	50.00
(48)	Tom Seaver	400.00	200.00	120.00
(49)	Joe Torre (Atlanta)	200.00	100.00	60.00
(50)	Tony Perez	350.00	175.00	105.00
(51)	Felipe Alou	200.00	100.00	60.00
(52)	Lee May	170.00	85.00	50.00
(53)	Hank Aaron	800.00	400.00	240.00
(54)	Pete Rose	800.00	400.00	240.00
(55)	Cookie Rojas	170.00	85.00	50.00
(56)	Roberto Clemente	900.00	450.00	270.00
(57)	Richie Allen	200.00	100.00	60.00
(58)	Matty Alou	170.00	85.00	50.00
(59)	Johnny Callison	170.00	85.00	50.00
(60)	Bill Mazeroski	350.00	175.00	105.00

1970 Transogram

The 1970 Transogram cards were found printed on boxes of three Transogram baseball player statues. The individual player cards are slightly larger than 1969's, at 2-9/16" x 3-1/2". The 30-card set has the same pictures as the 1969 set except for Joe Torre. All players in the '70 set were also in the '69 Transogram issue except for Reggie Jackson, Sam McDowell and Boog Powell. Each box contains a side panel with a series number and 1" x 1-1/4" portrait photos of the players in the series. Prices shown are for cards cut from the box.

	NM	EX	VG
Complete Set (30):	550.00	275.00	175.00
Complete Set, Boxes/Statues (10):	2,255	1,100	650.00
Common Player:	10.00	5.00	3.00

		NM	EX	VG
	Series 1 Boxed Set:	400.00	200.00	120.00
(1)	Pete Rose	50.00	25.00	15.00
(2)	Willie Mays	60.00	30.00	18.00
(3)	Cleon Jones	10.00	5.00	3.00
	Series 2 Boxed Set:	160.00	80.00	48.00
(4)	Ron Santo	15.00	7.50	4.50
(5)	Willie Davis	10.00	5.00	3.00
(6)	Willie McCovey	17.50	8.75	5.25
	Series 3 Boxed Set:	275.00	135.00	82.00
(7)	Juan Marichal	17.50	8.75	5.25
(8)	Joe Torre (St. Louis)	15.00	7.50	4.50
(9)	Ernie Banks	30.00	15.00	9.00
	Series 4 Boxed Set:	375.00	185.00	110.00
(10)	Hank Aaron	60.00	30.00	18.00
(11)	Jim Wynn	10.00	5.00	3.00
(12)	Tom Seaver	25.00	12.50	7.50
	Series 5 Boxed Set:	450.00	225.00	135.00
(13)	Bob Gibson	17.50	8.75	5.25
(14)	Roberto Clemente	100.00	50.00	30.00
(15)	Jerry Koosman	10.00	5.00	3.00
	Series 11 Boxed Set:	300.00	150.00	90.00
(16)	Denny McLain	12.50	6.25	3.75
(17)	Reggie Jackson	30.00	15.00	9.00
(18)	Boog Powell	15.00	7.50	4.50
	Series 12 Boxed Set:	175.00	87.00	52.00
(19)	Frank Robinson	25.00	12.50	7.50
(20)	Frank Howard	10.00	5.00	3.00
(21)	Rick Reichardt	10.00	5.00	3.00
	Series 13 Boxed Set:	225.00	110.00	67.00
(22)	Carl Yastrzemski	25.00	12.50	7.50
(23)	Tony Oliva	15.00	7.50	4.50
(24)	Mel Stottlemyre	10.00	5.00	3.00
	Series 14 Boxed Set:	180.00	90.00	54.00
(25)	Al Kaline	25.00	12.50	7.50
(26)	Jim Fregosi	10.00	5.00	3.00
(27)	Sam McDowell	10.00	5.00	3.00
	Series 15 Boxed Set:	180.00	90.00	54.00
(28)	Blue Moon Odom	10.00	5.00	3.00
(29)	Harmon Killebrew	25.00	12.50	7.50
(30)	Rico Petrocelli	10.00	5.00	3.00

1970 Transogram Mets

This Transogram set features members of the World Champion N.Y. Mets. Like the other 1970 Transograms, the issue was packaged in a three-statue cardboard box with cellophane front panel and cards printed on the back. Player cards are 2-9/16" x 3-1/2" and retain the basic format of Transogram cards of 1969-70: a color photo with player name in red and team, position and biographical details in black. Backs are blank. Values shown here are for cards cut from the box. Complete unopened boxes are worth 3-4X the figures shown.

		NM	EX	VG
	Complete Boxed Set (5):	1,400	700.00	425.00
	Complete Panel Set (5):	650.00	325.00	200.00
	Complete Card Set (15):	350.00	175.00	100.00
	Common Player:	12.50	6.25	3.75
	Series 21 Boxed Set	225.00	110.00	65.00
	Series 21 Uncut Box/Panel	125.00	65.00	35.00
(1)	Ed Kranepool	12.50	6.25	3.75
(2)	Al Weis	12.50	6.25	3.75
(3)	Tom Seaver	35.00	17.50	10.00
	Series 22 Boxed Set	125.00	65.00	35.00
	Series 22 Uncut Box/Panel	60.00	30.00	18.00
(4)	Ken Boswell	12.50	6.25	3.75
(5)	Jerry Koosman	12.50	6.25	3.75
(6)	Jerry Grote	12.50	6.25	3.75
	Series 23 Boxed Set	125.00	65.00	35.00
	Series 23 Uncut Box/Panel	60.00	30.00	18.00
(7)	Art Shamsky	12.50	6.25	3.75
(8)	Gary Gentry	12.50	6.25	3.75
(9)	Tommie Agee	12.50	6.25	3.75
	Series 24 Boxed Set	685.00	340.00	200.00
	Series 24 Uncut Box/Panel	350.00	175.00	100.00
(10)	Nolan Ryan	225.00	110.00	65.00
(11)	Tug McGraw	12.50	6.25	3.75
(12)	Cleon Jones	12.50	6.25	3.75
	Series 25 Boxed Set	150.00	75.00	45.00
	Series 25 Uncut Box/Panel	60.00	30.00	18.00
(13)	Ron Swoboda	12.50	6.25	3.75
(14)	Bud Harrelson	12.50	6.25	3.75
(15)	Donn Clendenon	12.50	6.25	3.75

1920s Otto Treulich & Son

This promotional photocard was issued, according to the blue rubber-stamped advertising on back, by Chicago clothier Otto Treulich & Son. Front of the approximately 2-3/4" x 3-1/2" card has a black-and-white studio portrait of Cubs pitcher Grover Cleveland Alexander, dressed to the nines (presumably in the haberdashery of the sponsor), and bearing a fac-simile autograph.

	NM	EX	VG
Grover Alexander	400.00	200.00	120.00

1909 T.T.T. Cigarettes (T204)

 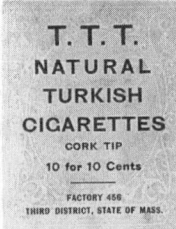

This is one of two brands of cigarette advertising found on the backs of the ornate, gold-trimmed T204 cards. The initials stand for T.T. Tinayens, the Boston firm which also produced Ramly cigarettes, more commonly found mentioned on the cards' backs. In recent years collectors have begun paying a premium as high as 4-5X for the T.T.T. versions.

Premium: 4-5X
(See checklist under Ramly Cigarettes listing.)

1888 Rafael Tuck & Sons Artistic Series Baseball

This series of die-cut color lithographed player figures does not represent actual players, but rather generic figures in late 19th Century uniforms labeled with the names of various major league teams of the era. The actual date of issue is unknown. The cardboard figures were issued in a sheet of 20 with duplicates. Individual figures vary in size with a typical piece about 1-1/2" wide and 2-3/4" high. Players are shown in batting, throwing and fielding poses. The set was lithographed in Germany and published in England by Rafael Tuck & Sons, a famous postcard publisher.

		NM	EX	VG
	Complete Set (10):	3,250	1,600	975.00
	Common Card:	350.00	175.00	105.00
(1)	Baltimore	350.00	175.00	105.00
(2)	Boston	350.00	175.00	105.00
(3)	Brooklyn	350.00	175.00	105.00
(4)	Chicago	350.00	175.00	105.00
(5)	Detroit	350.00	175.00	105.00
(6)	Indianapolis	350.00	175.00	105.00
(7)	New York	350.00	175.00	105.00
(8)	Philadelphia	350.00	175.00	105.00
(9)	Pittsburgh	350.00	175.00	105.00
(10)	St. Louis	350.00	175.00	105.00

1925 Turf Cigarettes

"Sports Records" is the name of a two-series, 50-card issue by Turf Cigarettes. The last card in the set depicts George Sisler (though not named) on the front in a color action scene. Black-and-white back of the card describes Sisler's batting prowess. Like other British tobacco cards of the era, size is 2-5/8" x 1-3/8".

		NM	EX	VG
50	Baseball (George Sisler)	90.00	45.00	25.00

1909-11 Ty Cobb Tobacco (T206)

 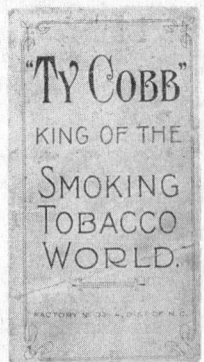

Much rarer than the famed Honus Wagner card from the related cigarette card series known collectively as T206, the Ty Cobb brand tobacco back was known in only about half a dozen collections until June 1997 when a find of five lower-grade specimens was auctioned. Because T206 was generally collected by front design, rather than back, through most of the hobby's history, it has only been in recent years that the value of the "value of the Ty Cobb-back" has begun to approach the other great rarities of the T206 series. The only front known with a Cobb tobacco back is the red-background portrait. Some of the greatest examples appear to have been hand-cut from a sheet. Cards measure nominally the same as T206, at about 1-7/16" x 2-5/8". Most, but not all, of the 11 known examples have a glossy coating on the front. Recent auction results of PSA and SGC graded examples are presented here.

	NM	EX	VG
SGC Fair	77,675		
SC Authentic	51,880		

1910-1911 T3 Turkey Red Cabinets

 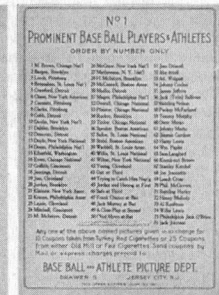

Turkey Red cabinet cards were obtained by mailing in coupons found in Turkey Red, Fez and Old Mill brand cigarettes. Turkey Reds measure 5-3/4" x 8", and feature full-color lithograph fronts with wide gray frames. Backs are known in three styles: 1) checklist with no ordering information, 2) checklist with ordering information, and, 3) with an illustrated ad for Turkey Red cigarettes. The checklist backs are found with both low- and high-number cards, the ad backs are only on cards #77-126. The series consists of 25 boxers and 100 baseball cards. Coupons issued in the cigarette boxes indicate the first 50 baseball player cards were produced for spring, 1910, delivery, with the 25 boxers produced later that year and the final 50 baseball players issued in 1911.

		NM	EX	VG
	Complete Set (130):	160,000	80,000	48,000
	Common Player:	1,500	600.00	360.00
	Turkey Red Ad Back: 1-1.5X			
1	Mordecai Brown	3,300	1,300	825.00
2	Bill Bergen	1,500	750.00	450.00
3	Tommy Leach	1,500	600.00	360.00
4	Roger Bresnahan	2,550	1,000	650.00
5	Sam Crawford	2,550	1,000	650.00
6	Hal Chase	1,700	700.00	425.00
7	Howie Camnitz	1,500	600.00	360.00
8	Fred Clarke	2,550	1,000	650.00
9	Ty Cobb	35,000	14,000	9,000
10	Art Devlin	1,500	600.00	360.00
11	Bill Dahlen	1,500	600.00	360.00
12	Wild Bill Donovan	1,500	600.00	360.00
13	Larry Doyle	1,500	600.00	360.00
14	Red Dooin	1,500	600.00	360.00
15	Kid Elberfeld	1,500	600.00	360.00
16	Johnny Evers	2,500	1,000	650.00
17	Clark Griffith	2,500	1,000	650.00
18	Hughie Jennings	2,500	1,000	650.00

		NM	EX	VG
19	Addie Joss	4,000	1,600	1,000
20	Tim Jordan	1,500	600.00	360.00
21	Red Kleinow	1,500	600.00	360.00
22	Harry Krause	1,500	600.00	360.00
23	Nap Lajoie	4,400	1,700	1,100
24	Mike Mitchell	1,500	600.00	360.00
25	Matty McIntyre	1,500	600.00	360.00
26	John McGraw	3,000	1,200	750.00
27	Christy Mathewson	16,000	6,000	4,000
28a	Harry McIntyre (Brooklyn)	1,500	600.00	360.00
28b	Harry McIntyre (Brooklyn and Chicago)	1,500	600.00	360.00
29	Amby McConnell	2,000	800.00	500.00
30	George Mullin	1,500	600.00	360.00
31	Sherry Magee	1,500	600.00	360.00
32	Orval Overall	1,500	600.00	360.00
33	Jake Pfeister	1,500	600.00	360.00
34	Nap Rucker	1,500	600.00	360.00
35	Joe Tinker	2,600	1,100	700.00
36	Tris Speaker	6,600	2,700	1,700
37	Slim Sallee	1,500	600.00	360.00
38	Jake Stahl	1,500	600.00	360.00
39	Rube Waddell	2,600	1,100	700.00
40	Vic Willis	2,600	1,100	700.00
41	Hooks Wiltse	1,500	600.00	360.00
42	Cy Young	10,000	4,000	2,500
43	Out At Third	1,600	600.00	400.00
44	Trying To Catch Him Napping	1,600	600.00	400.00
45	Jordan & Herzog At First	1,600	600.00	400.00
46	Safe At Third	1,600	600.00	400.00
47	Frank Chance	3,000	1,200	750.00
48	Jack Murray	1,500	600.00	360.00
49	A Close Play At Second	1,600	800.00	450.00
50	Chief Myers	1,500	600.00	360.00
77	Red Ames	1,500	600.00	360.00
78	Home Run Baker	2,600	1,100	700.00
79	George Bell	1,500	600.00	360.00
80	Chief Bender	2,600	1,100	700.00
81	Bob Bescher	1,500	600.00	360.00
82	Kitty Bransfield	1,500	600.00	360.00
83	Al Bridwell	1,500	600.00	360.00
84	George Browne	1,500	600.00	360.00
85	Bill Burns	1,500	600.00	360.00
86	Bill Carrigan	1,500	600.00	360.00
87	Eddie Collins	2,600	1,100	700.00
88	Harry Coveleski	1,500	600.00	360.00
89	Lou Criger	1,500	600.00	360.00
90a	Mickey Doolin (Doolan)	1,600	650.00	400.00
90b	Mickey Doolan (Name correct.)	2,600	1,000	650.00
91	Tom Downey	1,500	600.00	360.00
92	Jimmy Dygert	1,500	600.00	360.00
93	Art Fromme	1,500	600.00	360.00
94	George Gibson	1,500	600.00	360.00
95	Peaches Graham	1,500	600.00	360.00
96	Bob Groom	1,500	600.00	360.00
97	Dick Hoblitzell	1,500	600.00	360.00
98	Solly Hofman	1,500	600.00	360.00
99	Walter Johnson	16,000	6,500	4,000
100	Davy Jones	1,500	600.00	360.00
101	Wee Willie Keeler	2,600	1,100	650.00
102	Johnny Kling	1,500	600.00	360.00
103	Ed Konetchy	1,500	600.00	360.00
104	Ed Lennox	1,500	600.00	360.00
105	Hans Lobert	1,500	600.00	360.00
106	Harry Lord	1,500	600.00	360.00
107	Rube Manning	2,000	800.00	360.00
108	Fred Merkle	1,500	600.00	360.00
109	Pat Moran	1,500	600.00	360.00
110	George McBride	1,500	600.00	360.00
111	Harry Niles	1,500	600.00	360.00
112a	Dode Paskert (Cincinnati)	1,500	600.00	360.00
112b	Dode Paskert (Cincinnati and Philadelphia)	1,500	600.00	360.00
113	Bugs Raymond	1,500	600.00	360.00
114	Bob Rhoades (Rhoads)	12,000	5,000	3,000
115	Admiral Schlei	1,500	600.00	360.00
116	Boss Schmidt	1,500	600.00	360.00
117	Wildfire Schulte	1,500	600.00	360.00
118	Frank Smith	1,500	600.00	360.00
119	George Stone	1,500	600.00	360.00
120	Gabby Street	1,500	600.00	360.00
121	Billy Sullivan	1,500	600.00	360.00
122a	Fred Tenney (New York)	1,500	600.00	360.00
122b	Fred Tenney (New York and Boston)	1,500	600.00	360.00
123	Ira Thomas	1,500	600.00	360.00
124	Bobby Wallace	2,600	1,100	650.00
125	Ed Walsh	2,500	1,000	625.00
126	Owen Wilson	1,500	600.00	360.00

1911 T5 Pinkerton Cabinets

Because they are photographs affixed to a cardboard backing, the cards in the 1911 Pinkerton set are considered "true" cabinet cards. The Pinkerton cabinets are a rather obscure issue, and because of their original method of distribution, it would be virtually impossible to assemble a complete set today. It remains uncertain how many subjects exist in the set. Pinkerton, the parent of Red Man and other tobacco products, offered the cabinets in exchange for coupons found in cigarette packages. According to an original advertising sheet, some 376 different photos were available. A consumer could exchange 10 coupons for the card of his choice. The photos available included players from the 16 major league teams plus teams from the minor league American Association, Southern Michigan Association, and, probably, others. Pinkertons vary in both size and type of mount. The most desirable combination is a 3-3/8" x 5-1/2" photograph affixed to a thick cardboard mount measuring approximately 4-3/4" x 7-3/4". But original Pinkerton cabinets have also been found in different sizes and with less substantial backings. The most attractive mounts are embossed around the picture, but some Pinkertons have a white border surrounding the photograph. Prices listed are for cards with cardboard mounts. Cards with paper mounts are worth about 50-75 percent of listed prices. Some of the Pinkerton photos were reproduced in postcard size printed issues in later years; some with postcard style backs, some with scorecard backs and others are blank-backed (See 1911 Pinkerton).

		NM	EX	VG
Common Player:		1,000	500.00	315.00
Checklist Brochure:		625.00	315.00	190.00
Redemption Coupon:		500.00	250.00	150.00
Blank-Back Card: 5-10 Percent				
Postcard-Back: 10-15 Percent				
101	Jim Stephens	1,000	500.00	315.00
102	Bobby Wallace	2,500	1,250	750.00
103	Joe Lake	1,000	500.00	315.00
104	George Stone	1,000	500.00	315.00
105	Jack O'Connor	1,000	500.00	315.00
106	Bill Abstein	1,000	500.00	315.00
107	Rube Waddell	2,500	1,250	750.00
108	Roy Hartzell	1,000	500.00	315.00
109	Danny Hoffman	1,000	500.00	315.00
110	Dode Cris	1,000	500.00	315.00
111	Al Schweitzer	1,000	500.00	315.00
112	Art Griggs	1,000	500.00	315.00
113	Bill Bailey	1,000	500.00	315.00
114	Pat Newman	1,000	500.00	315.00
115	Harry Howell	1,000	500.00	315.00
117	Hobe Ferris	1,000	500.00	315.00
118	John McAleese	1,000	500.00	315.00
119	Ray Demmitt	1,000	500.00	315.00
120	Red Fisher	1,000	500.00	315.00
121	Frank Truesdale	1,000	500.00	315.00
122	Barney Pelty	1,000	500.00	315.00
123	Ed Killifer (Killefer)	1,000	500.00	315.00
151	Matty McIntyre	1,000	500.00	315.00
152	Jim Delahanty	1,000	500.00	315.00
153	Hughey Jennings	2,500	1,250	750.00
154	Ralph Works	1,000	500.00	315.00
155	George Moriarity (Moriarty)	1,000	500.00	315.00
156	Sam Crawford	2,500	1,250	750.00
157	Boss Schmidt	1,000	500.00	315.00
158	Owen Bush	1,000	500.00	315.00
159	Ty Cobb	20,000	10,000	6,000
160	Bill Donovan	1,000	500.00	315.00
161	Oscar Stanage	1,000	500.00	315.00
162	George Mullen (Mullin)	1,000	500.00	315.00
163	Davy Jones	1,000	500.00	315.00
164	Charley O'Leary	1,000	500.00	315.00
165	Tom Jones	1,000	500.00	315.00
166	Joe Casey	1,000	500.00	315.00
167	Ed Willetts (Willett)	1,000	500.00	315.00
168	Ed Lafeite (Lafitte)	1,000	500.00	315.00
169	Ty Cobb	20,000	4,530	2,720
170	Ty Cobb	20,000	4,530	2,720
201	John Evers	2,500	1,250	750.00
202	Mordecai Brown	2,500	1,250	750.00
203	King Cole	1,000	500.00	315.00
204	Johnny Cane	1,000	500.00	315.00
205	Heinie Zimmerman	1,000	500.00	315.00
206	Wildfire Schulte	1,000	500.00	315.00
207	Frank Chance	2,500	1,250	750.00
208	Joe Tinker	2,500	1,250	750.00
209	Orvall Overall	1,000	500.00	315.00
210	Jimmy Archer	1,000	500.00	315.00
211	Johnny Kling	1,000	500.00	315.00
212	Jimmy Sheckard	1,000	500.00	315.00
213	Harry McIntyre	1,000	500.00	315.00
214	Lew Richie	1,000	500.00	315.00
215	Ed Ruelbach	1,000	500.00	315.00
216	Artie Hoffman (Hofman)	1,000	500.00	315.00
217	Jake Pfeister	1,000	500.00	315.00
218	Harry Steinfeldt	1,000	500.00	315.00
219	Tom Needham	1,000	500.00	315.00
220	Ginger Beaumont	1,000	500.00	315.00
251	Christy Mathewson	10,000	2,815	1,690
252	Fred Merkle	1,000	500.00	315.00
253	Hooks Wiltsie	1,000	500.00	315.00
254	Art Devlin	1,000	500.00	315.00
255	Fred Snodgrass	1,000	500.00	315.00
256	Josh Devore	1,000	500.00	315.00
257	Red Murray	1,000	500.00	315.00
258	Cy Seymour	1,000	500.00	315.00
259	Rube Marquard	2,500	1,250	750.00
260	Larry Doyle	1,000	500.00	315.00
261	Bugs Raymond	1,000	500.00	315.00
262	Doc Crandall	1,000	500.00	315.00
263	Admiral Schlei	1,000	500.00	315.00
264	Chief Myers (Meyers)	1,000	500.00	315.00
265	Bill Dahlen	1,000	500.00	315.00
266	Beals Becker	1,000	500.00	315.00
267	Louis Drucke	1,000	500.00	315.00
301	Fred Luderus	1,000	500.00	315.00
302	John Titus	1,000	500.00	315.00
303	Red Dooin	1,000	500.00	315.00
304	Eddie Stack	1,000	500.00	315.00
305	Kitty Bransfield	1,000	500.00	315.00
306	Sherry Magee	1,000	500.00	315.00
307	Otto Knabe	1,000	500.00	315.00
308	Jimmy "Runt" Walsh	1,000	500.00	315.00
309	Earl Moore	1,000	500.00	315.00
310	Mickey Doolan	1,000	500.00	315.00
311	Ad Brennan	1,000	500.00	315.00
312	Bob Ewing	1,000	500.00	315.00
313	Lou Schettler	1,000	500.00	315.00
351	Joe Willis	1,000	500.00	315.00
352	Rube Ellis	1,000	500.00	315.00
353	Steve Evans	1,000	500.00	315.00
354	Miller Huggins	2,500	1,250	750.00
355	Arnold Hauser	1,000	500.00	315.00
356	Frank Corridon	1,000	500.00	315.00
357	Roger Bresnahan	2,500	1,250	750.00
358	Slim Sallee	1,000	500.00	315.00
359	Mike Mowrey	1,000	500.00	315.00
360	Ed Konetchy	1,000	500.00	315.00
361	Beckman	1,000	500.00	315.00
362	Rebel Oakes	1,000	500.00	315.00
363	Johnny Lush	1,000	500.00	315.00
364	Eddie Phelps	1,000	500.00	315.00
365	Robert Harmon	1,000	500.00	315.00
401	Lou (Pat) Moran	1,000	500.00	315.00
402	George McQuillian (McQuillan)	1,000	500.00	315.00
403	Johnny Bates	1,000	500.00	315.00
404	Eddie Grant	1,000	500.00	315.00
405	Tommy McMillan	1,000	500.00	315.00
406	Tommy Clark (Clarke)	1,000	500.00	315.00
407	Jack Rowan	1,000	500.00	315.00
408	Bob Bescher	1,000	500.00	315.00
409	Fred Beebe	1,000	500.00	315.00
410	Tom Downey	1,000	500.00	315.00
411	George Suggs	1,000	500.00	315.00
412	Hans Lobert	1,000	500.00	315.00
413	Jimmy Phelan	1,000	500.00	315.00
414	Dode Paskert	1,000	500.00	315.00
415	Ward Miller	1,000	500.00	315.00
416	Richard J. Egan	1,000	500.00	315.00
417	Art Fromme	1,000	500.00	315.00
418	Bill Burns	1,000	500.00	315.00
419	Clark Griffith	2,500	1,250	750.00
420	Dick Hoblitzell	1,000	500.00	315.00
421	Harry Gasper	1,000	500.00	315.00
422	Dave Altizer	1,000	500.00	315.00
423	Larry McLean	1,000	500.00	315.00
424	Mike Mitchell	1,000	500.00	315.00
451	John Hummel	1,000	500.00	315.00
452	Tony Smith	1,000	500.00	315.00
453	Bill Davidson	1,000	500.00	315.00
454	Ed Lennox	1,000	500.00	315.00
455	Zach Wheat	2,500	1,250	750.00
457	Elmer Knetzer	1,000	500.00	315.00
458	Rube Dessau	1,000	500.00	315.00
459	George Bell	1,000	500.00	315.00
460	Jake Daubert	1,000	500.00	315.00
461	Doc Scanlan	1,000	500.00	315.00
462	Nap Rucker	1,000	500.00	315.00
463	Cy Barger	1,000	500.00	315.00
464	Kaiser Wilhelm	1,000	500.00	315.00
465	Bill Bergen	1,000	500.00	315.00
466	Tex Erwin	1,000	500.00	315.00
501	Chas. Bender	2,500	1,250	750.00
502	John Coombs	1,000	500.00	315.00
503	Ed Plank	4,000	1,565	935.00
504	Amos Strunk	1,000	500.00	315.00
505	Connie Mack	2,500	1,250	750.00
506	Ira Thomas	1,000	500.00	315.00
507	Biscoe Lord (Briscoe)	1,000	500.00	315.00
508	Stuffy McInnis	1,000	500.00	315.00
509	Jimmy Dygert	1,000	500.00	315.00
510	Rube Oldring	1,000	500.00	315.00
511	Eddie Collins	2,500	1,250	750.00
512	Home Run Baker	3,000	1,500	900.00
513	Harry Krause	1,000	500.00	315.00
514	Harry Davis	1,000	500.00	315.00
515	Jack Barry	1,000	500.00	315.00
516	Jack Lapp	1,000	500.00	315.00
517	Cy Morgan	1,000	500.00	315.00
518	Danny Murphy	1,000	500.00	315.00
519	Topsy Hartsell	1,000	500.00	315.00
520	Paddy Livingston	1,000	500.00	315.00
521	P. Adkins	1,000	500.00	315.00
522	Eddie Collins	2,500	1,250	750.00
523	Paddy Livingston	1,000	500.00	315.00
551	Doc Gessler	1,000	500.00	315.00
552	Bill Cunningham	1,000	500.00	315.00
554	John Henry	1,000	500.00	315.00
555	Jack Lelivelt	1,000	500.00	315.00
556	Bobby Groome	1,000	500.00	315.00
557	Doc Ralston	1,000	500.00	315.00
558	Kid Elberfelt (Elberfeld)	1,000	500.00	315.00
559	Doc Reisling	1,000	500.00	315.00
560	Herman Schaefer	1,000	500.00	315.00
561	Walter Johnson	6,000	2,500	1,500
562	Dolly Gray	1,000	500.00	315.00
563	Wid Conroy	1,000	500.00	315.00
564	Charley Street	1,000	500.00	315.00
565	Bob Unglaub	1,000	500.00	315.00
566	Clyde Milan	1,000	500.00	315.00
567	George Browne	1,000	500.00	315.00
568	George McBride	1,000	500.00	315.00
569	Red Killifer (Killefer)	1,000	500.00	315.00
601	Addie Joss	2,500	1,250	750.00
602	Addie Joss	2,500	1,250	750.00
603	Napoleon Lajoie	2,500	1,250	750.00
604	Nig Clark (Clarke)	1,000	500.00	315.00
605	Cy Falkenberg	1,000	500.00	315.00
606	Harry Bemis	1,000	500.00	315.00
607	George Stovall	1,000	500.00	315.00
608	Fred Blanding	1,000	500.00	315.00
609	Elmer Koestner	1,000	500.00	315.00
610	Ted Easterly	1,000	500.00	315.00
611	Willie Mitchell	1,000	500.00	315.00
612	Hornhorst	1,000	500.00	315.00
613	Elmer Flick	2,500	1,250	750.00

614	Speck Harkness	1,000	500.00	315.00
615	Tuck Turner	1,000	500.00	315.00
616	Joe Jackson	50,000	10,000	6,000
617	Grover Land	1,000	500.00	315.00
618	Gladstone Graney	1,000	500.00	315.00
619	Dave Callahan	1,000	500.00	315.00
620	Ben DeMott	1,000	500.00	315.00
621	Neill Ball (Neal)	1,000	500.00	315.00
622	Dode Birmingham	1,000	500.00	315.00
623	George Kaler (Kahler)	1,000	500.00	315.00
624	Sid Smith	1,000	500.00	315.00
625	Bert Adams	1,000	500.00	315.00
626	Bill Bradley	1,000	500.00	315.00
627	Napoleon Lajoie	2,500	1,250	750.00
651	Bill Corrigan (Carrigan)	1,000	500.00	315.00
652	Joe Woods (Wood)	1,000	500.00	315.00
653	Heinie Wagner	1,000	500.00	315.00
654	Billy Purtell	1,000	500.00	315.00
655	Frank Smith	1,000	500.00	315.00
656	Harry Lord	1,000	500.00	315.00
657	Patsy Donovan	1,000	500.00	315.00
658	Duffy Lewis	1,000	500.00	315.00
659	Jack Kleinow	1,000	500.00	315.00
660	Ed Karger	1,000	500.00	315.00
661	Clyde Engle	1,000	500.00	315.00
662	Ben Hunt	1,000	500.00	315.00
663	Charlie Smith	1,000	500.00	315.00
664	Tris Speaker	3,000	1,155	695.00
665	Tom Madden	1,000	500.00	315.00
666	Larry Gardner	1,000	500.00	315.00
667	Harry Hooper	2,500	1,250	750.00
668	Marty McHale	1,000	500.00	315.00
669	Ray Collins	1,000	500.00	315.00
670	Jake Stahl	1,000	500.00	315.00
701	Dave Shean	1,000	500.00	315.00
702	Roy Miller	1,000	500.00	315.00
703	Fred Beck	1,000	500.00	315.00
704	Bill Collings (Collins)	1,000	500.00	315.00
705	Bill Sweeney	1,000	500.00	315.00
706	Buck Herzog	1,000	500.00	315.00
707	Bud Sharp (Sharpe)	1,000	500.00	315.00
708	Cliff Curtis	1,000	500.00	315.00
709	Al Mattern	1,000	500.00	315.00
710	Buster Brown	1,000	500.00	315.00
711	Bill Rariden	1,000	500.00	315.00
712	Grant	1,000	500.00	315.00
713	Ed Abbaticchio	1,000	500.00	315.00
714	Cecil Ferguson	1,000	500.00	315.00
715	Billy Burke	1,000	500.00	315.00
716	Sam Frock	1,000	500.00	315.00
717	Wilbur Goode (Good)	1,000	500.00	315.00
751	Charlie French	1,000	500.00	315.00
752	Patsy Dougherty	1,000	500.00	315.00
753	Shano Collins	1,000	500.00	315.00
754	Fred Parent	1,000	500.00	315.00
755	Willis Cole	1,000	500.00	315.00
756	Billy Sullivan	1,000	500.00	315.00
757	Rube Sutor (Suter)	1,000	500.00	315.00
758	Chick Gandil	2,315	1,155	695.00
759	Jim Scott	1,000	500.00	315.00
760	Ed Walsh	2,500	1,250	750.00
761	Gavvy Cravath	1,000	500.00	315.00
762	Bobby Messenger	1,000	500.00	315.00
763	Doc White	1,000	500.00	315.00
764	Rollie Zeider	1,000	500.00	315.00
765	Fred Payne	1,000	500.00	315.00
766	Lee Tannehill	1,000	500.00	315.00
767	Eddie Hahn	1,000	500.00	315.00
768	Hugh Duffy	2,500	1,250	750.00
769	Fred Olmstead	1,000	500.00	315.00
770	Lena Blackbourne (Blackburne)	1,000	500.00	315.00
771	Young "Cy" Young	1,000	500.00	315.00
801	Lew Brockett	1,000	500.00	315.00
802	Frank Laporte (LaPorte)	1,000	500.00	315.00
803	Bert Daniels	1,000	500.00	315.00
804	Walter Blair	1,000	500.00	315.00
805	Jack Knight	1,000	500.00	315.00
806	Jimmy Austin	1,000	500.00	315.00
807	Hal Chase	1,190	595.00	355.00
808	Birdie Cree	1,000	500.00	315.00
809	Jack Quinn	1,000	500.00	315.00
810	Walter Manning	1,000	500.00	315.00
811	Jack Warhop	1,000	500.00	315.00
812	Jeff Sweeney	1,000	500.00	315.00
813	Charley Hemphill	1,000	500.00	315.00
814	Harry Wolters	1,000	500.00	315.00
815	Tom Hughes	1,000	500.00	315.00
816	Earl Gardiner (Gardner)	1,000	500.00	315.00
851	John Flynn	1,000	500.00	315.00
852	Bill Powell	1,000	500.00	315.00
853	Honus Wagner	20,000	10,000	6,000
854	Bill Powell	1,000	500.00	315.00
855	Fred Clarke	2,500	1,250	750.00
856	Owen Wilson	1,000	500.00	315.00
857	George Gibson	1,000	500.00	315.00
858	Mike Simon	1,000	500.00	315.00
859	Tommy Leach	1,000	500.00	315.00
860	Lefty Leifeld (Leifield)	1,000	500.00	315.00
861	Nick Maddox	1,000	500.00	315.00
862	Dots Miller	1,000	500.00	315.00
863	Howard Camnitz	1,000	500.00	315.00
864	Deacon Phillippi (Phillippe)	1,000	500.00	315.00
865	Babe Adams	1,000	500.00	315.00
866	Ed Abbaticchio	1,000	500.00	315.00
867	Paddy O'Connor	1,000	500.00	315.00
868	Bobby Byrne	1,000	500.00	315.00
869	Vin Campbell	1,000	500.00	315.00
870	Ham Hyatt	1,000	500.00	315.00
871	Sam Leever	1,000	500.00	315.00
872	Hans Wagner	20,000	10,000	6,000
873	Hans Wagner	20,000	10,000	6,000
874	Bill McKecknie (McKechnie)	2,500	1,250	750.00
875	Kirby White	1,000	500.00	315.00
901	Jimmie Burke	1,000	500.00	315.00
902	Charlie Carr	1,000	500.00	315.00
903	Larry Cheney	1,000	500.00	315.00

904	Chet Chadbourne	1,000	500.00	315.00
905	Dan Howley	1,000	500.00	315.00
906	Jimmie Burke	1,000	500.00	315.00
907	Ray Mowe	1,000	500.00	315.00
908	Billy Milligan	1,000	500.00	315.00
909	Frank Oberlin	1,000	500.00	315.00
910	Ralph Glaze	1,000	500.00	315.00
911	O'Day	1,000	500.00	315.00
912	Kerns	1,000	500.00	315.00
913	Jim Duggan	1,000	500.00	315.00
914	Simmy Murch	1,000	500.00	315.00
915	Frank Delehanty	1,000	500.00	315.00
916	Craig	1,000	500.00	315.00
917	Jack Coffee (Coffey)	1,000	500.00	315.00
918	Lefty George	1,000	500.00	315.00
919	Otto Williams	1,000	500.00	315.00
920	M. Hayden	1,000	500.00	315.00
951	Joe Cantillion	1,000	500.00	315.00
952	Smith	1,000	500.00	315.00
953	Claud Rossman (Claude)	1,000	500.00	315.00
1001	Tony James	1,000	500.00	315.00
1002	Jack Powell	1,000	500.00	315.00
1003	Wm. J. Harbeau	1,000	500.00	315.00
1004	Homer Smoot	1,000	500.00	315.00
1051	Bill Friel	1,000	500.00	315.00
1052	Bill Friel	1,000	500.00	315.00
1053	Fred Odwell	1,000	500.00	315.00
1054	Alex Reilley	1,000	500.00	315.00
1055	Eugene Packard	1,000	500.00	315.00
1056	Irve Wrattan	1,000	500.00	315.00
1057	"Red" Nelson	1,000	500.00	315.00
1058	George Perring	1,000	500.00	315.00
1059	Glen Liebhardt	1,000	500.00	315.00
1060	Jimmie O'Rourke	1,000	500.00	315.00
1061	Fred Cook	1,000	500.00	315.00
1062	Charles Arbogast	1,000	500.00	315.00
1063	Jerry Downs	1,000	500.00	315.00
1064	"Bunk" Congalton	1,000	500.00	315.00
1065	Fred Carisch	1,000	500.00	315.00
1066	"Red" Sitton	1,000	500.00	315.00
1067	George Kaler (Kahler)	1,000	500.00	315.00
1068	Arthur Kruger	1,000	500.00	315.00
1102	Earl Yingling	1,000	500.00	315.00
1103	Jerry Freeman	1,800	500.00	315.00
1104	Harry Hinchman	1,000	500.00	315.00
1105	Jim Baskette (Toledo)	1,000	500.00	315.00
1106	Denny Sullivan	1,000	500.00	315.00
1107	Carl Robinson	1,000	500.00	315.00
1108	Bill Rodgers	1,000	500.00	315.00
1109	Hi West	1,000	500.00	315.00
1110	Billy Hallman	1,000	500.00	315.00
1111	Wm. Elwert	1,000	500.00	315.00
1112	Piano Legs Hickman	1,000	500.00	315.00
1113	Joe McCarthy	2,500	1,250	750.00
1114	Fred Abbott	1,000	500.00	315.00
1115	Jack Guilligan (Gilligan)	1,000	500.00	315.00
1510	Musser	1,000	500.00	315.00
1613	C. Winger	1,000	500.00	315.00

1911 T201 Mecca Double Folders

These cards found in packages of Mecca cigarettes feature one player when the card is open, and another when the card is folded; two players sharing the same pair of legs. Mecca Double Folders measure about 2-1/8" to 2-3/16" x 4-11/16". The pictures are color lithographs, the text is printed in black. The cards contain an innovation in the form of the first use of player statistics. The 50-card set contains 100 different players including a number of Hall of Famers. Examples authenticated and graded by major certification firms carry a much larger premium than most other cards of the era.

		NM	EX	VG
Complete Set (50):		25,000	7,000	2,650
Common Player:		385.00	85.00	30.00
(1)	William Abstein, John Butler	385.00	85.00	30.00
(2)	Frank Baker, Edward Collins	560.00	180.00	75.00
(3)	Harry Baker, Thomas Downie (Downey)	385.00	85.00	30.00
(4)	James Barrett, Grant McGlynn	385.00	85.00	30.00
(5)	John Barry, John Lapp	385.00	85.00	30.00
(6)	Charles Bender, Reuben Oldring	435.00	135.00	55.00
(7)	William Bergen, Zack Wheat	400.00	130.00	50.00
(8)	Walter Blair, Roy Hartzell	385.00	85.00	30.00
(9)	Roger Bresnahan, Miller Huggins	650.00	200.00	80.00

		NM	EX	VG
(10)	Albert Bridwell, Christy Matthewson (Mathewson)	1,200	375.00	150.00
(11)	Mordecai Brown, Arthur Hofman	425.00	140.00	55.00
(12)	Robert Byrne, Fred Clarke	400.00	115.00	45.00
(13)	Frank Chance, John Evers	600.00	200.00	80.00
(14)	Harold Chase, Edward Sweeney	400.00	100.00	40.00
(15)	Edward Cicotte, John Thoney	625.00	140.00	55.00
(16)	Thomas Clarke, Harry Gaspar	385.00	85.00	30.00
(17)	Ty Cobb, Sam Crawford	3,000	1,000	400.00
(18)	Leonard Cole, John Kling	385.00	85.00	30.00
(19)	John Coombs, Ira Thomas	385.00	85.00	30.00
(20)	Jake Daubert, Nap Rucker	385.00	85.00	30.00
(21)	Bill Donovan, Ralph Stroud	385.00	85.00	30.00
(22)	Charles Dooin, John Titus	385.00	85.00	30.00
(23)	Patsy Dougherty, Harry Lord	500.00	165.00	65.00
(24)	Jerry Downs, Fred Odwell	385.00	85.00	30.00
(25)	Larry Doyle, Chief Meyers	385.00	85.00	30.00
(26)	James Dygert, Cy Seymour	385.00	85.00	30.00
(27)	Norman Elberfeld, George McBride	385.00	85.00	30.00
(28)	Fred Falkenberg, Napoleon Lajoie	575.00	190.00	75.00
(29)	Edward Fitzpatrick, Ed Killian	385.00	85.00	30.00
(30)	Russell Ford, Otis Johnson	385.00	85.00	30.00
(31)	Edward Foster, Joseph Ward	385.00	85.00	30.00
(32)	Earl Gardner, Tris Speaker	600.00	200.00	80.00
(33)	George Gibson, Thomas Leach	385.00	85.00	30.00
(34)	George Graham, Al Mattern	385.00	85.00	30.00
(35)	Edward Grant, John McLean	385.00	85.00	30.00
(36)	Arnold Hauser, Ernest Lush	385.00	85.00	30.00
(37)	Charles Herzog, Roy Miller	385.00	85.00	30.00
(38)	Charles Hickman, Harry Hinchman	385.00	85.00	30.00
(39)	Hugh Jennings, Edgar Summers	425.00	140.00	55.00
(40)	Walter Johnson, Charles Street	1,200	400.00	160.00
(41)	Frank LaPorte, James Stephens	385.00	85.00	30.00
(42)	Joseph Lake, Robert Wallace	400.00	130.00	50.00
(43)	Albert Leifield, Mike Simon	385.00	85.00	30.00
(44)	John Lobert, Earl Moore	385.00	85.00	30.00
(45)	Arthur McCabe, Charles Starr	385.00	85.00	30.00
(46)	Lewis McCarty, Joseph McGinnity	400.00	130.00	60.00
(47)	Fred Merkle, George Wiltse	385.00	85.00	30.00
(48)	Frederick Payne, Edward Walsh	400.00	130.00	60.00
(49)	George Stovall, Terrence Turner	385.00	85.00	30.00
(50)	Otto Williams, Orville Woodruff	385.00	85.00	30.00

1912 T202 Hassan Triple Folders

Measuring about 5-1/4" x 2-1/4", Hassan cigarette cards carried the concept of multiple-player cards even further than the double-fold Mecca set of the previous year. Scored so that the player pictures on each end - which are full-color and very close to exact duplicates of T205 "Gold Borders" cards - can fold over the black-and-white action-photo center panel, the Hassan Triple Folder appears like a booklet when closed. The individual player panels are not necessarily related to the action scene. The Hassan Triple Folders feature player biographies on the back of the two individual cards with a description of the action on the back of the center panel. Values depend on the player featured in the center panel, as well as the players featured on the end cards. Backs can be found printed either in black (Factory 649) or red (Factory 30).

		NM	EX	VG
Complete Set (132):		175,000	45,000	20,000
Common Player:		600.00	175.00	55.00
(1)	A Close Play At The Home Plate (LaPorte, Wallace)	600.00	175.00	55.00
(2)	A Close Play At The Home Plate (Pelty, Wallace)	600.00	175.00	55.00
(3)	A Desperate Slide For Third (Cobb, O'Leary)	5,400	1,850	475.00
(4)	A Great Batsman (Barger, Bergen)	600.00	175.00	55.00
(5)	A Great Batsman (Bergen, Rucker)	600.00	175.00	55.00
(6)	Ambrose McConnell At Bat (Blair, Quinn)	600.00	175.00	55.00
(7)	A Wide Throw Saves Crawford (Mullin, Stanage)	600.00	175.00	55.00
(8)	Baker Gets His Man (Baker, Collins)	1,200	400.00	200.00

(9)	Birmingham Gets To Third (Johnson, Street)	1,250	450.00	175.00
(10)	Birmingham's Home Run (Birmingham, Turner)	600.00	175.00	55.00
(11)	Bush Just Misses Austin (Magee, Moran)	600.00	175.00	55.00
(12)	Carrigan Blocks His Man (Gaspar, McLean)	600.00	175.00	55.00
(13)	Carrigan Blocks His Man (Carrigan, Wagner)	600.00	175.00	55.00
(14)	Catching Him Napping (Bresnahan, Oakes)	600.00	175.00	55.00
(15)	Caught Asleep Off First (Bresnahan, Harmon)	600.00	175.00	55.00
(16)	Chance Beats Out A Hit (Chance, Foxen)	1,200	300.00	125.00
(17)	Chance Beats Out A Hit (Archer, McIntyre)	600.00	175.00	55.00
(18)	Chance Beats Out A Hit (Archer, Overall)	600.00	175.00	55.00
(19)	Chance Beats Out A Hit (Archer, Rowan)	600.00	175.00	55.00
(20)	Chance Beats Out A Hit (Chance, Shean)	1,100	350.00	200.00
(21)	Chase Dives Into Third (Chase, Wolter)	600.00	175.00	55.00
(22)	Chase Dives Into Third (Clarke, Gibson)	600.00	175.00	55.00
(23)	Chase Dives Into Third (Gibson, Phillippe)	600.00	175.00	55.00
(24)	Chase Gets Ball Too Late (Egan, Mitchell)	600.00	175.00	55.00
(25)	Chase Gets Ball Too Late (Chase, Wolter)	600.00	175.00	55.00
(26)	Chase Guarding First (Chase, Wolter)	600.00	175.00	55.00
(27)	Chase Guarding First (Clarke, Gibson)	600.00	175.00	55.00
(28)	Chase Guarding First (Gibson, Leifield)	600.00	175.00	55.00
(29)	Chase Ready For The Squeeze Play (Magee, Paskert)	600.00	175.00	55.00
(30)	Chase Safe At Third (Baker, Barry)	600.00	175.00	55.00
(31)	Chief Bender Waiting For A Good One (Bender, Thomas)	600.00	175.00	55.00
(32)	Clarke Hikes For Home (Bridwell, Kling)	600.00	175.00	55.00
(33)	Close At First (Ball, Stovall)	600.00	175.00	55.00
(34)	Close At The Plate (Payne, Walsh)	600.00	175.00	55.00
(35)	Close At The Plate (Payne, White)	600.00	175.00	55.00
(36)	Close At Third - Speaker (Speaker, Wood)	1,400	500.00	200.00
(37)	Close At Third - Wagner (Carrigan, Wagner)	600.00	175.00	55.00
(38)	Collins Easily Safe (Byrne, Clarke)	600.00	175.00	55.00
(39)	Collins Easily Safe (Baker, Collins)	600.00	175.00	55.00
(40)	Collins Easily Safe (Collins, Murphy)	600.00	175.00	55.00
(41)	Crawford About To Smash One (Stanage, Summers)	600.00	175.00	55.00
(42)	Cree Rolls Home (Daubert, Hummel)	600.00	175.00	55.00
(43)	Davy Jones' Great Slide (Delahanty, Jones)	600.00	175.00	55.00
(44)	Devlin Gets His Man (Devlin (Giants), Mathewson)	1,800	600.00	300.00
(45)	Devlin Gets His Man (Devlin (Rustlers), Mathewson)	3,500	1,200	500.00
(46)	Devlin Gets His Man (Fletcher, Mathewson)	1,900	700.00	300.00
(47)	Devlin Gets His Man (Mathewson, Meyers)	2,000	700.00	300.00
(48)	Donlin Out At First (Camnitz, Gibson)	600.00	175.00	55.00
(49)	Donlin Out At First (Doyle, Merkle)	600.00	175.00	55.00
(50)	Donlin Out At First (Leach, Wilson)	600.00	175.00	55.00
(51)	Donlin Out At First (Dooin, Magee)	600.00	175.00	55.00
(52)	Donlin Out At First (Gibson, Phillippe)	600.00	175.00	55.00
(53)	Dooin Gets His Man (Dooin, Doolan)	600.00	175.00	55.00
(54)	Dooin Gets His Man (Dooin, Lobert)	600.00	175.00	55.00
(55)	Dooin Gets His Man (Dooin, Titus)	600.00	175.00	55.00
(56)	Easy For Larry (Doyle, Merkle)	600.00	175.00	55.00
(57)	Elberfeld Beats The Throw (Elberfeld, Milan)	600.00	175.00	55.00
(58)	Elberfeld Gets His Man (Elberfeld, Milan)	600.00	175.00	55.00
(59)	Engle In A Close Play (Engle, Speaker)	1,300	400.00	200.00
(60)	Evers Makes A Safe Slide (Archer, Evers)	600.00	175.00	55.00
(61)	Evers Makes A Safe Slide (Chance, Evers)	1,700	600.00	300.00
(62)	Evers Makes A Safe Slide (Archer, Overall)	600.00	175.00	55.00
(63)	Evers Makes A Safe Slide (Archer, Reulbach)	600.00	175.00	55.00
(64)	Evers Makes A Safe Slide (Chance, Tinker)	3,000	1,000	400.00
(65)	Fast Work At Third (Cobb, O'Leary)	4,000	1,200	675.00
(66)	Ford Putting Over A Spitter (Ford, Vaughn)	600.00	175.00	55.00
(67)	Ford Putting Over A Spitter (Sweeney, Ford)	600.00	175.00	55.00

(68)	Good Play At Third (Cobb, Moriarity (Moriarty))	5,700	1,600	650.00
(69)	Grant Gets His Man (Grant, Hoblitzell)	600.00	175.00	55.00
(70)	Hal Chase Too Late (McConnell, McIntyre)	600.00	175.00	55.00
(71)	Hal Chase Too Late (McLean, Suggs)	600.00	175.00	55.00
(72)	Harry Lord At Third (Lennox, Tinker)	600.00	175.00	55.00
(73)	Hartzell Covering Third (Dahlen, Scanlan)	600.00	175.00	55.00
(74)	Hartsel Strikes Out (Gray, Groom)	600.00	175.00	55.00
(75)	Held At Third (Lord, Tannehill)	600.00	175.00	55.00
(76)	Jake Stahl Guarding First (Cicotte, Stahl)	1,300	500.00	200.00
(77)	Jim Delahanty At Bat (Delahanty, Jones)	600.00	175.00	55.00
(78)	Just Before The Battle (Ames, Meyers)	600.00	175.00	55.00
(79)	Just Before The Battle (Bresnahan, McGraw)	600.00	175.00	55.00
(80)	Just Before The Battle (Crandall, Meyers)	600.00	175.00	55.00
(81)	Just Before The Battle (Becker, Devore)	600.00	175.00	55.00
(82)	Just Before The Battle (Fletcher, Mathewson)	1,900	700.00	300.00
(83)	Just Before The Battle (Marquard, Meyers)	600.00	175.00	55.00
(84)	Just Before The Battle (Jennings, McGraw)	1,600	300.00	100.00
(85)	Just Before The Battle (Mathewson, Meyers)	1,300	500.00	200.00
(86)	Just Before The Battle (Murray, Snodgrass)	600.00	175.00	55.00
(87)	Just Before The Battle (Meyers, Wiltse)	600.00	175.00	55.00
(88)	Knight Catches A Runner (Johnson, Knight)	1,400	550.00	225.00
(89)	Lobert Almost Caught (Bridwell, Kling)	600.00	175.00	55.00
(90)	Lobert Almost Caught (Kling, Young)	1,950	450.00	225.00
(91)	Lobert Almost Caught (Kling, Mattern)	600.00	175.00	55.00
(92)	Lobert Almost Caught (Kling, Steinfeldt)	600.00	175.00	55.00
(93)	Lobert Gets Tenney (Dooin, Lobert)	600.00	175.00	55.00
(94)	Lord Catches His Man (Lord, Tannehil)	600.00	175.00	55.00
(95)	McConnell Caught (Needham, Richie)	600.00	175.00	55.00
(96)	McIntyre At Bat (McConnell, McIntyre)	600.00	175.00	55.00
(97)	Moriarty Spiked (Stanage, Willett)	600.00	175.00	55.00
(98)	Nearly Caught (Bates, Bescher)	600.00	175.00	55.00
(99)	Oldring Almost Home (Lord, Oldring)	600.00	175.00	55.00
(100)	Schaefer On First (McBride, Milan)	600.00	175.00	55.00
(101)	Schaefer Steals Second (Griffith, McBride)	600.00	175.00	55.00
(102)	Scoring From Second (Lord, Oldring)	600.00	175.00	55.00
(103)	Scrambling Back To First (Barger, Bergen)	600.00	175.00	55.00
(104)	Scrambling Back To First (Chase, Wolter)	600.00	175.00	55.00
(105)	Speaker Almost Caught (Clarke, Miller)	850.00	325.00	125.00
(106)	Speaker Rounding Third (Speaker, Wood)	1,400	500.00	300.00
(107)	Speaker Scores (Engle, Speaker)	1,400	500.00	200.00
(108)	Stahl Safe (Austin, Stovall)	600.00	175.00	55.00
(109)	Stone About To Swing (Schulte, Sheckard)	600.00	175.00	55.00
(110)	Sullivan Puts Up A High One (Evans, Huggins)	600.00	175.00	55.00
(111)	Sullivan Puts Up A High One (Gray, Groom)	600.00	175.00	55.00
(112)	Sweeney Gets Stahl (Ford, Vaughn)	600.00	175.00	55.00
(113)	Sweeney Gets Stahl (Ford, Sweeney)	600.00	175.00	55.00
(114)	Tenney Lands Safely (Latham, Raymond)	600.00	175.00	55.00
(115)	The Athletic Infield (Baker, Barry)	600.00	175.00	55.00
(116)	The Athletic Infield (Brown, Graham)	600.00	175.00	55.00
(117)	The Athletic Infield (Hauser, Konetchy)	600.00	175.00	55.00
(118)	The Athletic Infield (Krause, Thomas)	600.00	175.00	55.00
(119)	The Pinch Hitter (Egan, Hoblitzell)	600.00	175.00	55.00
(120)	The Scissors Slide (Birmingham, Turner)	600.00	175.00	55.00
(121)	Tom Jones At Bat (Fromme, McLean)	600.00	175.00	55.00
(122)	Tom Jones At Bat (Gaspar, McLean)	600.00	175.00	55.00
(123)	Too Late For Devlin (Ames, Meyers)	600.00	175.00	55.00
(124)	Too Late For Devlin (Crandall, Meyers)	600.00	175.00	55.00
(125)	Too Late For Devlin (Devlin (Giants), Mathewson)	2,000	700.00	300.00
(126)	Too Late For Devlin (Devlin (Rustlers), Mathewson)	3,900	1,400	600.00

(127)	Too Late For Devlin (Marquard, Meyers)	600.00	175.00	55.00
(128)	Too Late For Devlin (Meyers, Wiltse)	600.00	175.00	55.00
(129)	Ty Cobb Steals Third (Cobb, Jennings)	7,000	2,000	1,100
(130)	Ty Cobb Steals Third (Cobb, Moriarty)	5,400	1,850	850.00
(131)	Ty Cobb Steals Third (Austin, Stovall)	2,500	900.00	400.00
(132)	Wheat Strikes Out (Dahlen, Wheat)	1,300	500.00	200.00

1909 T204

(See 1909 Ramly Cigarettes, 1909 T.T.T. Cigarettes.)

1911 T205 Gold Border

Featuring distinctive gold-leaf borders, these cards were issued in a number of different cigarette brands. The cards nominally measure 1-7/16" x 2-5/8" although many cards, even though untrimmed or unaltered, measure somewhat less than those dimensions in length and/or width. American League cards feature a color lithograph of the player inside a stylized baseball diamond. National League cards have head-and-shoulders portraits on a plain background, plus the first-ever use of a facsimile autograph in a major card set. The 12 minor league players in the set feature three-quarter length portraits or action pictures in an elaborate frame of columns and other devices. Card backs of the major leaguers carry the player's full name (another first) and statistics. Card backs of the minor leaguers lack the statistics. The complete set price does not include the scarcer of the letter-suffixed variations. Values shown are for cards with the most common cigarette advertising on back: Piedmont and Sweet Caporal. Cards of other brands may carry a premium (see listings under brand name). The condition of the fragile gold leaf on the borders is an important grading consideration.

		NM	EX	VG
	Common Player:	500.00	80.00	25.00
(1)	Edward J. Abbaticchio	500.00	80.00	25.00
(2)	Doc Adkins	1,620	240.00	95.00
(3)	Leon K. Ames	500.00	80.00	25.00
(4)	Jas. P. Archer	500.00	80.00	25.00
(5)	Jimmy Austin	500.00	80.00	25.00
(6)	Bill Bailey	500.00	80.00	25.00
(7)	Home Run Baker	2,340	350.00	140.00
(8)	Neal Ball	500.00	80.00	25.00
(9)	E.B. Barger (Full "B" on cap.)	1,500	220.00	90.00
(10)	E.B. Barger (Partial "B" on cap.)	2,400	360.00	145.00
(11)	Jack Barry	500.00	80.00	25.00
(12)	Emil Batch	1,620	240.00	95.00
(13)	John W. Bates	500.00	80.00	25.00
(14)	Fred Beck	500.00	80.00	25.00
(15)	B. Becker	500.00	80.00	25.00
(16)	George G. Bell	500.00	80.00	25.00
(17)	Chas. Bender	2,100	315.00	120.00
(18)	William Bergen	500.00	80.00	25.00
(19)	Bob Bescher	500.00	80.00	25.00
(20)	Joe Birmingham	500.00	80.00	25.00
(21)	Lena Blackburne	500.00	80.00	25.00
(22)	William E. Bransfield	500.00	80.00	25.00
(23)	Roger P. Bresnahan (Mouth closed.)	1,680	250.00	105.00
(24)	Roger P. Bresnahan (Mouth open.)	3,420	510.00	210.00
(25)	A.H. Bridwell	500.00	80.00	25.00
(26)	Mordecai Brown	1,980	295.00	120.00
(27)	Robert Byrne	500.00	80.00	25.00
(28)	Hick Cady	1,620	240.00	95.00
(29)	H. Camnitz	500.00	80.00	25.00
(30)	Bill Carrigan	500.00	80.00	25.00
(31)	Frank J. Chance	2,280	345.00	140.00
(32a)	Hal Chase (Both ears show, gold diamond frame extends below shoulders.)	1,080	165.00	65.00
(32b)	Hal Chase (Both ears show, gold diamond frame ends at shoulders.)	1,620	240.00	95.00
(33)	Hal Chase (Only left ear shows.)	3,240	480.00	195.00
(34)	Ed Cicotte	2,580	390.00	150.00
(35)	Fred C. Clarke	1,500	220.00	90.00
(36)	Ty Cobb	13,200	3,750	1,080
(37)	Eddie Collins (Mouth closed.)	2,100	315.00	120.00
(38)	Eddie Collins (Mouth open.)	4,680	700.00	285.00
(39)	Jimmy Collins	2,580	390.00	155.00
(40)	Frank J. Corridon	500.00	80.00	25.00

#	Player	NM	EX	VG
(41a)	Otis Crandall ("t" not crossed in name)	1,020	150.00	60.00
(41b)	Otis Crandall ("t" crossed in name)	1,320	200.00	80.00
(42)	Lou Criger	500.00	80.00	25.00
(43)	W.F. Dahlen	2,200	400.00	175.00
(44)	Jake Daubert	500.00	10.00	25.00
(45)	Jim Delahanty	500.00	80.00	25.00
(46)	Arthur Devlin	500.00	80.00	25.00
(47)	Josh Devore	500.00	80.00	25.00
(48)	W.R. Dickson	500.00	80.00	25.00
(49)	Jiggs Donohue (Donahue)	2,880	435.00	175.00
(50)	Chas. S. Dooin	500.00	80.00	25.00
(51)	Michael J. Doolan	500.00	80.00	25.00
(52a)	Patsy Dougherty (Red sock for team emblem.)	2,500	500.00	200.00
(52b)	Patsy Dougherty (White sock for team emblem.)	1,000	400.00	100.00
(53)	Thomas Downey	500.00	80.00	25.00
(54)	Larry Doyle	500.00	80.00	25.00
(55)	Hugh Duffy	2,820	420.00	170.00
(56)	Jack Dunn	2,640	395.00	155.00
(57)	Jimmy Dygert	500.00	80.00	25.00
(58)	R. Egan	500.00	80.00	25.00
(59)	Kid Elberfeld	500.00	80.00	25.00
(60)	Clyde Engle	500.00	80.00	25.00
(61)	Louis Evans	500.00	80.00	25.00
(62)	John J. Evers	3,300	495.00	200.00
(63)	Robert Ewing	500.00	80.00	25.00
(64)	G.C. Ferguson	500.00	80.00	25.00
(65)	Ray Fisher	2,940	440.00	175.00
(66)	Arthur Fletcher	500.00	80.00	25.00
(67)	John A. Flynn	500.00	80.00	25.00
(68)	Russ Ford (Black cap.)	700.00	80.00	50.00
(69)	Russ Ford (White cap.)	2,220	330.00	135.00
(70)	Wm. A. Foxen	500.00	80.00	25.00
(71)	Jimmy Frick	1,620	240.00	100.00
(72)	Arthur Fromme	500.00	80.00	25.00
(73)	Earl Gardner	700.00	80.00	50.00
(74)	H.L. Gaspar	500.00	80.00	25.00
(75)	George Gibson	500.00	80.00	25.00
(76)	Wilbur Goode	500.00	80.00	25.00
(77)	George F. Graham (Rustlers)	500.00	80.00	25.00
(78)	George F. Graham (Cubs)	1,680	255.00	105.00
(79)	Edward L. Grant	2,400	360.00	145.00
(80a)	Dolly Gray (No stats on back.)	1,000	200.00	50.00
(80b)	Dolly Gray (Stats on back.)	4,800	720.00	290.00
(81)	Clark Griffith	1,800	270.00	110.00
(82)	Bob Groom	500.00	80.00	55.00
(83)	Charlie Hanford	1,620	240.00	100.00
(84)	Bob Harmon (Both ears show.)	500.00	80.00	25.00
(85)	Bob Harmon (Only left ear shows.)	2,520	380.00	150.00
(86)	Topsy Hartsel	500.00	80.00	25.00
(87)	Arnold J. Hauser	500.00	80.00	25.00
(88)	Charlie Hemphill	500.00	80.00	25.00
(89)	C.L. Herzog	500.00	80.00	25.00
(90a)	R. Hoblitzell (No stats on back.) (A PSA-graded EX-MT example was auctioned for $33,000 in 2005.)	500.00	21,600	9,900
(90b)	R. Hoblitzell ("Cin." after 2nd 1908 in stats.)	1,560	235.00	100.00
(90c)	R. Hoblitzel (Name incorrect, no "Cin." after 1908 in stats.)	3,420	510.00	210.00
(90d)	R. Hoblitzell (Name correct, no "Cin." after 1908 in stats.)	8,400	1,200	510.00
(91)	Danny Hoffman	500.00	80.00	25.00
(92)	Miller J. Huggins	1,920	290.00	115.00
(93)	John E. Hummel	500.00	80.00	25.00
(94)	Fred Jacklitsch	500.00	80.00	25.00
(95)	Hughie Jennings	1,440	215.00	85.00
(96)	Walter Johnson	8,400	1,320	510.00
(97)	D. Jones	500.00	80.00	25.00
(98)	Tom Jones	500.00	80.00	25.00
(99)	Addie Joss	9,000	1,500	700.00
(100)	Ed Karger	1,600	300.00	100.00
(101)	Ed Killian	500.00	80.00	25.00
(102)	Red Kleinow	1,560	235.00	90.00
(103)	John G. Kling	500.00	80.00	25.00
(104)	Jack Knight	500.00	80.00	25.00
(105)	Ed Konetchy	500.00	80.00	25.00
(106)	Harry Krause	500.00	80.00	25.00
(107)	Floyd M. Kroh	500.00	80.00	25.00
(108)	Frank LaPorte	500.00	80.00	25.00
(109)	Frank Lang (Lange)	500.00	80.00	25.00
(110a)	A. Latham (A. Latham on back.)	700.00	80.00	50.00
(110b)	A. Latham (W.A. Latham on back.)	1,600	300.00	50.00
(111)	Thomas W. Leach	500.00	80.00	25.00
(112)	Watty Lee	1,620	240.00	100.00
(113)	Sam Leever	500.00	80.00	25.00
(114a)	A. Leifield (Initial "A." on front.)	700.00	80.00	50.00
(114b)	A.P. Leifield (Initials "A.P." on front.)	1,600	300.00	50.00
(115)	Edgar Lennox	500.00	80.00	25.00
(116)	Paddy Livingston	500.00	80.00	25.00
(117)	John B. Lobert	500.00	80.00	25.00
(118)	Bris Lord (Athletics)	500.00	80.00	25.00
(119)	Harry Lord (White Sox)	500.00	80.00	25.00
(120)	Jno. C. Lush	500.00	80.00	25.00
(121)	Nick Maddox	500.00	80.00	25.00
(122)	Sherwood R. Magee	870.00	135.00	50.00
(123)	R.W. Marquard	2,280	345.00	140.00
(124)	C. Mathewson	8,820	1,320	495.00
(124a)	Christy Mathewson (1 loss variation only on Cycle backs.)	20,000	10,000	4,000
(125)	A.A. Mattern	500.00	80.00	25.00
(126)	Sport McAllister	1,620	240.00	100.00
(127)	George McBride	870.00	135.00	55.00
(128)	Amby McConnell	500.00	80.00	25.00
(129)	P.M. McElveen	500.00	80.00	25.00
(130)	J.J. McGraw	2,280	345.00	140.00
(131)	Harry McIntire (Cubs)	500.00	80.00	25.00
(132)	Matty McIntyre (White Sox)	500.00	80.00	25.00
(133)	M.A. McLean (Initials actually J.B.)	500.00	80.00	435.00
(134)	Fred Merkle	500.00	80.00	25.00
(135)	George Merritt	1,620	240.00	100.00
(136)	J.T. Meyers	500.00	80.00	25.00
(137)	Clyde Milan	500.00	80.00	25.00
(138)	J.D. Miller	500.00	80.00	25.00
(139)	M.F. Mitchell	500.00	80.00	25.00
(140a)	P.J. Moran (Stray line of type below stats.)	12,000	1,800	720.00
(140b)	P.J. Moran (No stray line.)	500.00	80.00	25.00
(141)	George Moriarty	500.00	80.00	25.00
(142)	George Mullin	500.00	80.00	25.00
(143)	Danny Murphy	500.00	80.00	25.00
(144)	Jack Murray	500.00	80.00	25.00
(145)	John Nee	1,620	240.00	100.00
(146)	Thomas J. Needham	500.00	80.00	25.00
(147)	Rebel Oakes	500.00	80.00	25.00
(148)	Rube Oldring	500.00	80.00	25.00
(149)	Charley O'Leary	500.00	80.00	25.00
(150)	Fred Olmstead	500.00	80.00	25.00
(151)	Orval Overall	500.00	80.00	25.00
(152)	Freddy Parent	500.00	80.00	25.00
(153)	George Paskert	500.00	80.00	25.00
(154)	Fred Payne	500.00	80.00	25.00
(155)	Barney Pelty	840.00	135.00	55.00
(156)	John Pfeister	500.00	80.00	25.00
(157)	Jimmy Phelan	1,620	240.00	100.00
(158)	E.J. Phelps	500.00	80.00	25.00
(159)	C. Phillippe	500.00	80.00	25.00
(160)	Jack Quinn	500.00	80.00	25.00
(161)	A.L. Raymond	1,600	400.00	200.00
(162)	E.M. Reulbach	500.00	80.00	25.00
(163)	Lewis Richie	500.00	80.00	25.00
(164)	John A. Rowan	3,000	500.00	200.00
(165)	George N. Rucker	500.00	80.00	25.00
(166)	W.D. Scanlan	2,940	440.00	175.00
(167)	Germany Schaefer	500.00	80.00	25.00
(168)	George Schlei	500.00	80.00	25.00
(169)	Boss Schmidt	500.00	80.00	25.00
(170)	F.M. Schulte	500.00	80.00	25.00
(171)	Jim Scott	500.00	80.00	25.00
(172)	B.H. Sharpe	500.00	80.00	25.00
(173)	David Shean (Rustlers)	500.00	80.00	25.00
(174)	David Shean (Cubs)	2,520	380.00	150.00
(175)	Jas. T. Sheckard	500.00	80.00	25.00
(176)	Hack Simmons	500.00	80.00	25.00
(177)	Tony Smith	500.00	80.00	25.00
(178)	Fred C. Snodgrass	500.00	80.00	25.00
(179)	Tris Speaker	5,190	780.00	315.00
(180)	Jake Stahl	1,140	170.00	75.00
(181)	Oscar Stanage	500.00	80.00	25.00
(182)	Harry Steinfeldt	500.00	80.00	25.00
(183)	George Stone	500.00	80.00	25.00
(184)	George Stovall	500.00	80.00	25.00
(185)	Gabby Street	500.00	80.00	25.00
(186)	George F. Suggs	3,000	500.00	200.00
(187)	Ed Summers	500.00	80.00	25.00
(188)	Jeff Sweeney	2,700	405.00	165.00
(189)	Lee Tannehill	500.00	80.00	25.00
(190)	Ira Thomas	500.00	80.00	25.00
(191)	Joe Tinker	2,160	330.00	135.00
(192)	John Titus	500.00	80.00	25.00
(193)	Terry Turner	2,640	395.00	155.00
(194)	James Vaughn	2,880	435.00	175.00
(195)	Charles Wagner	3,180	475.00	195.00
(196)	Bobby Wallace (With cap.)	1,770	270.00	110.00
(197a)	Bobby Wallace (No cap, one line of 1910 stats.)	18,000	2,700	1,080
(197b)	Bobby Wallace (No cap, two lines of 1910 stats.)	7,800	1,170	470.00
(198)	Ed Walsh	5,400	810.00	330.00
(199)	Z.D. Wheat	2,280	345.00	140.00
(200)	Doc White (White Sox)	500.00	80.00	25.00
(201)	Kirb. White (Pirates)	1,600	300.00	100.00
(202a)	Irvin K. Wilhelm ("suffered" in 18th line of bio. Very scarce, only found with Hassan back.)	9,000	3,000	2,000
(202b)	Irvin K. Wilhelm ("suffe ed" in 18th line of bio)	3,000	300.00	150.00
(203)	Ed Willett	500.00	80.00	25.00
(204)	J. Owen Wilson	500.00	80.00	25.00
(205)	George R. Wiltse (Both ears show.)	500.00	80.00	25.00
(206)	George R. Wiltse (Only right ear shows.)	2,580	390.00	155.00
(207)	Harry Wolter	500.00	80.00	25.00
(208)	Cy Young	11,100	1,650	665.00

1909-11 T206 White Border

The nearly 525 cards which make up the T206 set are the most popular of the early tobacco card issues. Players are depicted in color lithographs surrounded by a white border.

The player's last name on the 1-7/16" x 2-5/8" cards appears at the bottom with the city and league, when a city had more than one team. Backs contain an ad for one of 16 brands of cigarettes. There are 389 major leaguer cards and 134 minor leaguer cards in the set, but with front/back varieties the number of potentially different cards runs into the thousands. The set features many expensive cards including a number of pose and/or team variations. Values shown are for cards with the most common advertising on back: Piedmont and Sweet Caporal. Other backs carry a premium depending on scarcity (see listings under brand names). Several popularly collected printing errors have been included in the listings.

#	Player	NM	EX	VG
	Common Player:	400.00	100.00	50.00
(1)	Ed Abbaticchio (Blue sleeves.)	400.00	100.00	50.00
(2)	Ed Abbaticchio (Brown sleeves.)	400.00	100.00	50.00
(3)	Fred Abbott	400.00	100.00	50.00
(4)	Bill Abstein	400.00	100.00	50.00
(5)	Doc Adkins	400.00	100.00	50.00
(6)	Whitey Alperman	400.00	100.00	50.00
(7)	Red Ames (Hands at chest.)	800.00	200.00	75.00
(8)	Red Ames (Hands above head.)	400.00	100.00	50.00
(9)	Red Ames/Portrait	400.00	100.00	50.00
(10)	John Anderson	400.00	100.00	50.00
(11)	Frank Arellanes	400.00	100.00	50.00
(12)	Herman Armbruster	400.00	100.00	50.00
(13)	Harry Arndt	400.00	100.00	50.00
(14)	Jake Atz	400.00	100.00	50.00
(15)	Home Run Baker	1,700	350.00	175.00
(16)	Neal Ball (New York)	400.00	100.00	50.00
(17)	Neal Ball (Cleveland)	400.00	100.00	50.00
(18)	Jap Barbeau	400.00	100.00	50.00
(19)	Cy Barger	400.00	100.00	50.00
(20)	Jack Barry (Philadelphia)	400.00	100.00	50.00
(21)	Shad Barry (Milwaukee)	400.00	100.00	50.00
(22)	Jack Bastian	1,300	350.00	125.00
(23)	Emil Batch	400.00	100.00	50.00
(24)	Johnny Bates	400.00	100.00	50.00
(25)	Harry Bay	1,300	350.00	125.00
(26)	Ginger Beaumont	400.00	100.00	50.00
(27)	Fred Beck	400.00	100.00	50.00
(28)	Beals Becker	400.00	100.00	50.00
(29)	Jake Beckley	1,500	300.00	100.00
(30)	George Bell (Hands above head.)	400.00	100.00	50.00
(31)	George Bell (Pitching follow through.)	400.00	100.00	50.00
(32)	Chief Bender/Pitching (No trees in background.)	1,800	300.00	120.00
(33)	Chief Bender/Pitching (Trees in background.)	1,900	400.00	140.00
(34)	Chief Bender/Portrait	1,300	400.00	125.00
(35)	Bill Bergen/Btg	400.00	100.00	50.00
(36)	Bill Bergen/Catching	400.00	100.00	50.00
(37)	Heinie Berger	400.00	100.00	50.00
(38)	Bill Bernhard	1,300	400.00	125.00
(39)	Bob Bescher (Hands in air.)	400.00	100.00	50.00
(40)	Bob Bescher/Portrait	400.00	100.00	50.00
(41)	Joe Birmingham	900.00	200.00	100.00
(42)	Lena Blackburne	400.00	100.00	50.00
(43)	Jack Bliss	400.00	100.00	50.00
(44)	Frank Bowerman	400.00	100.00	50.00
(45)	Bill Bradley (Portrait)	400.00	100.00	50.00
(46)	Bill Bradley (With bat.)	400.00	100.00	50.00
(47)	Dave Brain	400.00	100.00	50.00
(48)	Kitty Bransfield	400.00	100.00	50.00
(49)	Roy Brashear	400.00	100.00	50.00
(50)	Ted Breitenstein	1,300	400.00	125.00
(51)	Roger Bresnahan/Portrait	1,700	300.00	100.00
(52)	Roger Bresnahan (With bat.)	1,350	300.00	100.00
(53)	Al Bridwell (Portrait, no cap.)	400.00	100.00	50.00
(54)	Al Bridwell (Portrait, with cap.)	400.00	100.00	50.00
(55a)	George Brown (Browne) (Chicago)	400.00	100.00	50.00
(55b)	George Brown (Browne) (Washington)	2,100	400.00	200.00
(56)	Mordecai Brown (Chicago on shirt.)	1,600	300.00	110.00
(57)	Mordecai Brown (Cubs on shirt.)	3,600	700.00	300.00
(58)	Mordecai Brown/Portrait	1,500	300.00	110.00
(59)	Al Burch/Btg	1,000	200.00	100.00
(60)	Al Burch/Fldg	400.00	100.00	50.00
(61)	Fred Burchell	400.00	100.00	50.00
(62)	Jimmy Burke	400.00	100.00	50.00
(63)	Bill Burns	400.00	100.00	50.00
(64)	Donie Bush	400.00	100.00	50.00
(65)	John Butler	400.00	100.00	50.00
(66)	Bobby Byrne	400.00	100.00	50.00
(67)	Howie Camnitz (Arm at side.)	400.00	100.00	50.00
(68)	Howie Camnitz (Arms folded.)	400.00	100.00	50.00
(69)	Howie Camnitz (Hands above head.)	400.00	100.00	50.00
(70)	Billy Campbell	400.00	100.00	50.00
(71)	Scoops Carey	1,300	400.00	125.00
(72)	Charley Carr	400.00	100.00	50.00
(73)	Bill Carrigan	400.00	100.00	50.00
(74)	Doc Casey	400.00	100.00	50.00
(75)	Peter Cassidy	400.00	100.00	50.00
(76)	Frank Chance/Btg	1,800	300.00	110.00
(77)	Frank Chance/Portrait (Red background.)	1,900	400.00	125.00
(78)	Frank Chance/Portrait (Yellow background.)	1,400	300.00	110.00
(79)	Bill Chappelle	400.00	100.00	50.00
(80)	Chappie Charles	400.00	100.00	50.00
(81)	Hal Chase (Holding trophy.)	800.00	200.00	100.00
(82)	Hal Chase/Portrait (Blue background.)	900.00	200.00	100.00
(83)	Hal Chase/Portrait (Pink background.)	1,000	200.00	100.00
(84)	Hal Chase/Throwing (Dark cap.)	1,000	200.00	100.00

(85)	Hal Chase/Throwiing (White cap.)	1,000	200.00	100.00
(86)	Jack Chesbro	1,900	300.00	125.00
(87)	Ed Cicotte	1,400	300.00	100.00
(88)	Bill Clancy (Clancey)	400.00	100.00	50.00
(89)	Josh Clark (Columbus) (Clarke)	400.00	100.00	50.00
(90)	Fred Clarke (Pittsburgh, holding bat.)	1,200	300.00	100.00
(91)	Fred Clarke/Portrait (Pittsburgh)	1,400	300.00	100.00
(92)	J.J. Clarke (Nig) (Cleveland)	400.00	100.00	50.00
(93)	Bill Clymer	400.00	100.00	50.00
(94)	Ty Cobb/Portrait (Green background.)	9,000	2,600	1,500
(95a)	Ty Cobb/Portrait (Red background.)	4,500	1,600	900.00
(95b)	Ty Cobb/Portrait (Red background, Ty Cobb brand back.)		120,000	72,000
(96)	Ty Cobb (Bat off shoulder.)	9,600	2,300	1,000
(97)	Ty Cobb (Bat on shoulder.)	9,300	1,900	1,000
(98)	Cad Coles	1,300	400.00	125.00
(99)	Eddie Collins (Philadelphia)	1,400	300.00	125.00
(100)	Jimmy Collins (Minneapolis)	1,300	200.00	100.00
(101)	Bunk Congalton	400.00	100.00	50.00
(102)	Wid Conroy/Fldg	400.00	100.00	50.00
(103)	Wid Conroy (With bat.)	400.00	100.00	50.00
(104)	Harry Covaleski (Coveleski)	400.00	100.00	50.00
(105)	Doc Crandall/Portrait (No cap.)	400.00	100.00	50.00
(106)	Doc Crandall/Portrait (With cap.)	400.00	100.00	50.00
(107)	Bill Cranston	1,300	400.00	125.00
(108)	Gavvy Cravath	400.00	100.00	50.00
(109)	Sam Crawford/Throwing	1,700	300.00	125.00
(110)	Sam Crawford (With bat.)	1,500	300.00	110.00
(111)	Birdie Cree	400.00	100.00	50.00
(112)	Lou Criger	400.00	100.00	50.00
(113)	Dode Criss	400.00	100.00	50.00
(114)	Monte Cross	400.00	100.00	50.00
(115a)	Bill Dahlen (Boston)	1,000	200.00	100.00
(115b)	Bill Dahlen (Brooklyn)	2,100	400.00	200.00
(116)	Paul Davidson	400.00	100.00	50.00
(117)	George Davis (Chicago)	1,600	300.00	100.00
(118)	Harry Davis (Philadelphia, Davis on front.)	400.00	100.00	50.00
(119)	Harry Davis (Philadelphia, H. Davis on front.)	400.00	100.00	50.00
(120)	Frank Delehanty (Delahanty) (Louisville)	400.00	100.00	50.00
(121)	Jim Delehanty (Delahanty) (Washington)	400.00	100.00	50.00
(122a)	Ray Demmitt (New York)	400.00	100.00	50.00
(122b)	Ray Demmitt (St. Louis)	42,000	13,000	6,500
(123)	Rube Dessau	400.00	100.00	50.00
(124)	Art Devlin	400.00	100.00	50.00
(125)	Josh Devore	400.00	100.00	50.00
(126)	Bill Dineen (Dinneen)	400.00	100.00	50.00
(127)	Mike Donlin/Fldg	800.00	200.00	100.00
(128)	Mike Donlin/Seated	800.00	200.00	100.00
(129)	Mike Donlin (With bat.)	400.00	100.00	50.00
(130)	Jiggs Donohue (Donahue)	400.00	100.00	50.00
(131)	Wild Bill Donovan/Portrait	400.00	100.00	50.00
(132)	Wild Bill Donovan/Throwing	400.00	100.00	50.00
(133)	Red Dooin	400.00	100.00	50.00
(134)	Mickey Doolan/Btg	400.00	100.00	50.00
(135)	Mickey Doolan/Fldg	400.00	100.00	50.00
(136)	Mickey Doolin (Doolan)	400.00	100.00	50.00
(137)	Gus Dorner	400.00	100.00	50.00
(138)	Patsy Dougherty (Arm in air.)	400.00	100.00	50.00
(139)	Patsy Dougherty/Portrait	400.00	100.00	50.00
(140)	Tom Downey/Btg	400.00	100.00	50.00
(141)	Tom Downey/Fldg	400.00	100.00	50.00
(142)	Jerry Downs	400.00	100.00	50.00
(143a)	Joe Doyle (N.Y. Nat'l., hands above head.)			72,000
(143b)	Joe Doyle (N.Y., hands above head.)	2,200	500.00	125.00
(144)	Larry Doyle/Portait (N.Y. Nat'l.)	400.00	100.00	50.00
(145)	Larry Doyle/Throwing (N.Y. Nat'l.)	400.00	100.00	50.00
(146)	Larry Doyle (N.Y. Nat'l., with bat.)	400.00	100.00	50.00
(147)	Jean Dubuc	400.00	100.00	50.00
(148)	Hugh Duffy	1,700	300.00	110.00
(149)	Jack Dunn (Baltimore)	400.00	100.00	50.00
(150)	Joe Dunn (Brooklyn)	400.00	100.00	50.00
(151)	Bull Durham	400.00	100.00	50.00
(152)	Jimmy Dygert	400.00	100.00	50.00
(153)	Ted Easterly	400.00	100.00	50.00
(154)	Dick Egan	400.00	100.00	50.00
(155a)	Kid Elberfeld (New York)	400.00	100.00	50.00
(155b)	Kid Elberfeld/Portrait (Washington)	6,600	1,200	500.00
(156)	Kid Elberfeld/Fldg (Washington)	400.00	100.00	50.00
(157)	Roy Ellam	1,300	400.00	125.00
(158)	Clyde Engle	400.00	100.00	50.00
(159)	Steve Evans	400.00	100.00	50.00
(160)	Johnny Evers/Portrait	3,000	600.00	200.00
(161)	Johnny Evers (With bat, Chicago on shirt.)	1,400	300.00	125.00
(162)	Johnny Evers (With bat, Cubs on shirt.)	1,900	400.00	150.00
(163)	Bob Ewing	400.00	100.00	50.00
(164)	Cecil Ferguson	400.00	100.00	50.00
(165)	Hobe Ferris	400.00	100.00	50.00
(166)	Lou Fiene/Portrait	400.00	100.00	50.00
(167)	Lou Fiene/Throwing	400.00	100.00	50.00
(168)	Steamer Flanagan	400.00	100.00	50.00
(169)	Art Fletcher	400.00	100.00	50.00
(170)	Elmer Flick	2,000	400.00	100.00
(171)	Russ Ford	400.00	100.00	50.00
(172)	Ed Foster	1,300	400.00	125.00
(173)	Jerry Freeman	400.00	100.00	50.00
(174)	John Frill	400.00	100.00	50.00
(175)	Charlie Fritz	1,300	400.00	125.00
(176)	Art Fromme	400.00	100.00	50.00
(177)	Chick Gandil	1,200	300.00	100.00
(178)	Bob Ganley	400.00	100.00	50.00
(179)	John Ganzel	400.00	100.00	50.00
(180)	Harry Gasper	400.00	100.00	50.00
(181)	Rube Geyer	400.00	100.00	50.00
(182)	George Gibson	400.00	100.00	50.00
(183)	Billy Gilbert	400.00	100.00	50.00
(184)	Wilbur Goode (Good)	400.00	100.00	50.00
(185)	Bill Graham (St. Louis)	400.00	100.00	50.00
(186)	Peaches Graham (Boston)	400.00	100.00	50.00
(187)	Dolly Gray	400.00	100.00	50.00
(188)	Ed Greminger	1,300	400.00	125.00
(189)	Clark Griffith/Btg	1,800	300.00	100.00
(190)	Clark Griffith/Portrait	1,600	300.00	100.00
(191)	Moose Grimshaw	400.00	100.00	50.00
(192)	Bob Groom	400.00	100.00	50.00
(193)	Tom Guiheen	1,300	400.00	125.00
(194)	Ed Hahn	400.00	100.00	50.00
(195)	Bob Hall	400.00	100.00	50.00
(196)	Bill Hallman	400.00	100.00	50.00
(197)	Jack Hannifan (Hannifin)	400.00	100.00	50.00
(198)	Bill Hart (Little Rock)	1,300	400.00	125.00
(199)	Jimmy Hart (Montgomery)	1,300	400.00	125.00
(200)	Topsy Hartsel	400.00	100.00	50.00
(201)	Jack Hayden	400.00	100.00	50.00
(202)	J. Ross Helm	1,300	400.00	125.00
(203)	Charlie Hemphill	400.00	100.00	50.00
(204)	Buck Herzog (Boston)	800.00	200.00	100.00
(205)	Buck Herzog (New York)	400.00	100.00	50.00
(206)	Gordon Hickman	1,300	400.00	125.00
(207)	Bill Hinchman (Cleveland)	400.00	100.00	50.00
(208)	Harry Hinchman (Toledo)	400.00	100.00	50.00
(209)	Dick Hoblitzell	400.00	100.00	50.00
(210)	Danny Hoffman (St. Louis)	400.00	100.00	50.00
(211)	Izzy Hoffman (Providence)	400.00	100.00	50.00
(212)	Solly Hofman	400.00	100.00	50.00
(213)	Bock Hooker	1,300	400.00	125.00
(214)	Del Howard (Chicago)	400.00	100.00	50.00
(215)	Ernie Howard (Savannah)	1,300	400.00	125.00
(216)	Harry Howell (Hand at waist.)	400.00	100.00	50.00
(217)	Harry Howell/Portrait	400.00	100.00	50.00
(218)	Miller Huggins (Hands at mouth.)	1,400	400.00	100.00
(219)	Miller Huggins/Portrait	1,200	200.00	100.00
(220)	Rudy Hulswitt	400.00	100.00	50.00
(221)	John Hummel	400.00	100.00	50.00
(222)	George Hunter	400.00	100.00	50.00
(223)	Frank Isbell	400.00	100.00	50.00
(224)	Fred Jacklitsch	400.00	100.00	50.00
(225)	Jimmy Jackson	400.00	100.00	50.00
(226)	Hughie Jennings (One hand showing.)	1,300	200.00	100.00
(227)	Hughie Jennings (Both hands showing.)	1,400	300.00	100.00
(228)	Hughie Jennings/Portrait	1,300	200.00	125.00
(229)	Walter Johnson (Hands at chest.)	5,400	1,000	400.00
(230)	Walter Johnson/Portrait	4,800	1,400	700.00
(231)	Fielder Jones (Chicago, hands at hips.)	400.00	100.00	50.00
(232)	Fielder Jones/Portrait (Chicago)	400.00	100.00	50.00
(233)	Davy Jones (Detroit)	400.00	100.00	50.00
(234)	Tom Jones (St. Louis)	400.00	100.00	50.00
(235)	Dutch Jordan (Atlanta)	1,300	400.00	125.00
(236)	Tim Jordan/Btg (Brooklyn)	400.00	100.00	50.00
(237)	Tim Jordan/Portrait (Brooklyn)	400.00	100.00	50.00
(238)	Addie Joss/Pitching	1,800	400.00	120.00
(239)	Addie Joss/Portrait	1,500	300.00	125.00
(240)	Ed Karger	400.00	100.00	50.00
(241)	Willie Keeler/Portrait	2,500	500.00	200.00
(242)	Willie Keeler (W/bat.)	2,500	500.00	200.00
(243)	Joe Kelley	1,300	200.00	100.00
(244)	J.F. Kiernan	1,300	400.00	125.00
(245)	Ed Killian/Pitching	400.00	100.00	50.00
(246)	Ed Killian/Portrait	400.00	100.00	50.00
(247)	Frank King	1,300	400.00	125.00
(248)	Rube Kisinger	400.00	100.00	50.00
(249a)	Red Kleinow (Boston)	2,100	400.00	200.00
(249b)	Red Kleinow/Catching (New York)	400.00	100.00	50.00
(250)	Red Kleinow (New York, with bat.)	400.00	100.00	50.00
(251)	Johnny Kling	400.00	100.00	50.00
(252)	Otto Knabe	400.00	100.00	50.00
(253)	Jack Knight/Portrait	400.00	100.00	50.00
(254)	Jack Knight (With bat.)	400.00	100.00	50.00
(255)	Ed Konetchy (Glove above head.)	400.00	100.00	50.00
(256)	Ed Konetchy (Glove near ground.)	400.00	100.00	50.00
(257)	Harry Krause/Pitching	400.00	100.00	50.00
(258)	Harry Krause/Portrait	400.00	100.00	50.00
(259)	Rube Kroh	400.00	100.00	50.00
(260)	Art Kruger (Krueger)	400.00	100.00	50.00
(261)	James Lafitte	1,300	400.00	125.00
(262)	Nap Lajoie/Portrait	3,600	700.00	300.00
(263)	Nap Lajoie/Throwing	2,900	500.00	200.00
(264)	Nap Lajoie (With bat.)	3,600	800.00	200.00
(265)	Joe Lake (New York)	400.00	100.00	50.00
(266)	Joe Lake (St. Louis, ball in hand.)	400.00	100.00	50.00
(267)	Joe Lake (St. Louis, no ball in hand.)	400.00	100.00	50.00
(268)	Frank LaPorte	400.00	100.00	50.00
(269)	Arlie Latham	400.00	100.00	50.00
(270)	Bill Lattimore	1,300	400.00	125.00
(271)	Jimmy Lavender	400.00	100.00	50.00
(272)	Tommy Leach (Bending over.)	400.00	100.00	50.00
(273)	Tommy Leach/Portrait	400.00	100.00	50.00
(274)	Lefty Leifield/Btg	400.00	100.00	50.00
(275)	Lefty Leifield/Pitching	400.00	100.00	50.00
(276)	Ed Lennox	400.00	100.00	50.00
(277)	Harry Lentz (Sentz)	1,300	400.00	125.00
(278)	Glenn Liebhardt	400.00	100.00	50.00
(279)	Vive Lindaman	400.00	100.00	50.00
(280)	Perry Lipe	1,300	400.00	125.00
(281)	Paddy Livingstone (Livingston)	400.00	100.00	50.00
(282)	Hans Lobert	400.00	100.00	50.00
(283)	Harry Lord	400.00	100.00	50.00
(284)	Harry Lumley	400.00	100.00	50.00
(285a)	Carl Lundgren (Chicago)	3,800	800.00	300.00
(285b)	Carl Lundgren (Kansas City)	400.00	100.00	50.00
(286)	Nick Maddox	400.00	100.00	50.00
(287a)	Sherry Magie (Magee) (Auction Results: May 08, Heritage SGC30 $13,145. May 08, Robert Edward PSA3 $17,000. May 08, Robert Edward PSA1 $6,500. Aug. 08, Mastro SGC20 $8,500. Jan. 09, eBay PSA 1.5 $7,096. Jan. 09, Sports cards plus PSA 2.5 $12,530.) Values shown represent recent auctions of examples graded by PSA, SGC or GAI. Purchase of ungraded specimens is not recommended. VG-EX - 21,250 / 19,720 VG - 15,000 GOOD - 12,000 FAIR - 3925 POOR - 4,500			
(287b)	Sherry Magee/Portrait	800.00	100.00	60.00
(288)	Sherry Magee (With bat.)	400.00	100.00	50.00
(289)	Bill Malarkey	400.00	100.00	50.00
(290)	Billy Maloney	400.00	100.00	50.00
(291)	George Manion	1,300	400.00	125.00
(292)	Rube Manning/Btg	400.00	100.00	50.00
(293)	Rube Manning/Pitching	400.00	100.00	50.00
(294)	Rube Marquard (Hands at thighs.)	1,600	300.00	100.00
(295)	Rube Marquard (Follow-through.)	1,600	300.00	100.00
(296)	Rube Marquard/Portrait	1,800	300.00	110.00
(297)	Doc Marshall	400.00	100.00	50.00
(298)	Christy Mathewson (Dark cap.)	2,700	1,000	300.00
(299)	Christy Mathewson/Portrait	5,200	1,100	450.00
(300)	Christy Mathewson (White cap.)	5,100	900.00	400.00
(301)	Al Mattern	400.00	100.00	50.00
(302)	John McAleese	400.00	100.00	50.00
(303)	George McBride	400.00	100.00	50.00
(304)	Pat McCauley	1,300	400.00	125.00
(305)	Moose McCormick	400.00	100.00	50.00
(306)	Pryor McElveen	400.00	100.00	50.00
(307)	Dan McGann	400.00	100.00	50.00
(308)	Jim McGinley	400.00	100.00	50.00
(309)	Iron Man McGinnity	1,400	200.00	100.00
(310)	Stoney McGlynn	400.00	100.00	50.00
(311)	John McGraw (Finger in air.)	2,100	400.00	200.00
(312)	John McGraw (Glove at hip.)	2,000	400.00	110.00
(313)	John McGraw/Portrait (No cap.)	1,700	300.00	110.00
(314)	John McGraw/Portrait (With cap.)	1,400	300.00	110.00
(315)	Harry McIntyre (Brooklyn)	400.00	100.00	50.00
(316)	Harry McIntyre (Brooklyn & Chicago)	400.00	100.00	50.00
(317)	Matty McIntyre (Detroit)	400.00	100.00	50.00
(318)	Larry McLean	400.00	100.00	50.00
(319)	George McQuillan (Ball in hand.)	400.00	100.00	50.00
(320)	George McQuillan (With bat.)	400.00	100.00	50.00
(321)	Fred Merkle/Portrait	400.00	100.00	60.00
(322)	Fred Merkle/Throwing	400.00	100.00	50.00
(323)	George Merritt	400.00	100.00	50.00
(324)	Chief Meyers	400.00	100.00	50.00
(325)	Clyde Milan	400.00	100.00	50.00
(326)	Dots Miller (Pittsburgh)	400.00	100.00	50.00
(327)	Molly Miller (Dallas)	1,300	400.00	125.00
(328)	Bill Milligan	400.00	100.00	50.00
(329)	Fred Mitchell (Toronto)	400.00	100.00	50.00
(330)	Mike Mitchell (Cincinnati)	400.00	100.00	50.00
(331)	Dan Moeller	400.00	100.00	50.00
(332)	Carlton Molesworth (Providence)	1,300	400.00	125.00
(333)	Herbie Moran (Providence)	400.00	100.00	50.00
(334)	Pat Moran (Chicago)	400.00	100.00	50.00
(335)	George Moriarty	400.00	100.00	50.00
(336)	Mike Mowrey	400.00	100.00	50.00
(337)	Dom Mullaney	1,300	400.00	125.00
(338)	George Mullen (Mullin)	400.00	100.00	50.00
(339)	George Mullen/Throwing	900.00	200.00	100.00
(340)	George Mullin (With bat.)	400.00	100.00	50.00
(341)	Danny Murphy/Btg	400.00	100.00	50.00
(342)	Danny Murphy/Throwing	900.00	200.00	100.00
(343)	Red Murray/Btg	400.00	100.00	50.00
(344)	Red Murray/Portrait	400.00	100.00	50.00
(345)	Chief Myers (Meyers)/Btg	400.00	100.00	50.00
(346)	Chief Myers (Meyers)/Fldg	400.00	100.00	50.00
(347)	Billy Nattress	400.00	100.00	50.00
(348)	Tom Needham	400.00	100.00	50.00
(349)	Simon Nicholls (Hands on knees.)	400.00	100.00	50.00
(350)	Simon Nichols (Nicholls)/Btg	400.00	100.00	50.00
(351)	Harry Niles	400.00	100.00	50.00
(352)	Rebel Oakes	400.00	100.00	50.00
(353)	Frank Oberlin	400.00	100.00	50.00
(354)	Peter O'Brien	400.00	100.00	50.00
(355a)	Bill O'Hara (New York)	400.00	100.00	50.00
(355b)	Bill O'Hara (St Louis. Recent Auctions: Apr. 08, Robert Edward SGC 20 $1,600. May 08, eBay PSA1 $1,650. July 08, Huggins & Scott SGC 20 $1,200. Oct. 08, Huggins & Scott PSA 4 mk $2,100. Jan. 09, Sports cards plus PSA 6 mc $5,035.)	42,000	13,000	6,500
(356)	Rube Oldring/Btg	400.00	100.00	50.00
(357)	Rube Oldring/Fldg	400.00	100.00	50.00
(358)	Charley O'Leary (Hands on knees.)	400.00	100.00	50.00
(359)	Charley O'Leary/Portrait	400.00	100.00	50.00
(360)	William J. O'Neil	400.00	100.00	50.00
(361)	Al Orth	1,300	400.00	125.00
(362)	William Otey	1,300	400.00	125.00
(363)	Orval Overall (Hand face level.)	400.00	100.00	50.00

(364)	Orval Overall (Hands waist level.)	400.00	100.00	50.00
(365)	Orval Overall/Portrait	400.00	100.00	50.00
(366)	Frank Owen	400.00	100.00	50.00
(367)	George Paige	1,300	400.00	125.00
(368)	Fred Parent	400.00	100.00	50.00
(369)	Dode Paskert	400.00	100.00	50.00
(370)	Jim Pastorius	400.00	100.00	50.00
(371)	Harry Pattee	900.00	200.00	100.00
(372)	Fred Payne	400.00	100.00	50.00
(373)	Barney Pelty (Horizontal photo.)	900.00	200.00	100.00
(374)	Barney Pelty (Vertical photo.)	400.00	100.00	50.00
(375)	Hub Perdue	1,300	400.00	125.00
(376)	George Perring	400.00	100.00	50.00
(377)	Arch Persons	1,300	400.00	125.00
(378)	Francis (Big Jeff) Pfeffer	400.00	100.00	50.00
(379)	Jake Pfeister (Pfiester)/Seated	400.00	100.00	50.00
(380)	Jake Pfeister (Pfiester)/Throwing	400.00	100.00	50.00
(381)	Jimmy Phelan	400.00	100.00	50.00
(382)	Eddie Phelps	400.00	100.00	50.00
(383)	Deacon Phillippe	400.00	100.00	50.00
(384)	Ollie Pickering	400.00	100.00	50.00
(385)	Eddie Plank (Auction results: May 08, Heritage SGC40, $77,675. June 08, Sports Cards Plus GAI3 $34,023. Aug 08, Mastro SGC "A" $17,000. Jan. 09, Sports Cards Plus PSA "A" $15,693. Feb. 09, Goodwin PSA 3 $52,638.) Values shown reflect recent auctions of examples graded by PSA, SGC or GAI. Purchase of ungraded specimens is not recommended. EX-MT - 100,000 VG - 60,000 GOOD - 35,000 POOR - 20,000			
(386)	Phil Poland	400.00	100.00	50.00
(387)	Jack Powell	900.00	200.00	100.00
(388)	Mike Powers	400.00	100.00	60.00
(389)	Billy Purtell	400.00	100.00	50.00
(390)	Ambrose Puttman (Puttmann)	400.00	100.00	50.00
(391)	Lee Quillen (Quillin)	400.00	100.00	50.00
(392)	Jack Quinn	400.00	100.00	50.00
(393)	Newt Randall	400.00	100.00	50.00
(394)	Bugs Raymond	400.00	100.00	50.00
(395)	Ed Reagan	1,300	400.00	125.00
(396)	Ed Reulbach (Glove showing.)	900.00	200.00	100.00
(397)	Ed Reulbach (No glove showing.)	400.00	100.00	50.00
(398)	Dutch Revelle	1,300	400.00	125.00
(399)	Bob Rhoades (Rhoads) (Hands at chest.)	400.00	100.00	50.00
(400)	Bob Rhoades (Rhoads) (Right arm extended.)	900.00	200.00	60.00
(401)	Charlie Rhodes	400.00	100.00	50.00
(402)	Claude Ritchey	400.00	100.00	50.00
(403)	Lou Ritter	400.00	100.00	50.00
(404)	Ike Rockenfeld	1,300	400.00	125.00
(405)	Claude Rossman	400.00	100.00	50.00
(406)	Nap Rucker/Portrait	400.00	100.00	50.00
(407)	Nap Rucker/Throwing	400.00	100.00	50.00
(408)	Dick Rudolph	400.00	100.00	50.00
(409)	Ray Ryan	1,300	400.00	125.00
(410)	Germany Schaefer (Detroit)	400.00	100.00	50.00
(411)	Germany Schaefer (Washington)	400.00	100.00	50.00
(412)	George Schirm	400.00	100.00	50.00
(413)	Larry Schlafly	400.00	100.00	50.00
(414)	Admiral Schlei/Btg	400.00	100.00	50.00
(415)	Admiral Schlei/Catching	400.00	100.00	50.00
(416)	Admiral Schlei/Portrait	400.00	100.00	50.00
(417)	Boss Schmidt/Portait	400.00	100.00	50.00
(418)	Boss Schmidt/Throwing	400.00	100.00	50.00
(419)	Ossee Schreck (Schreckengost)	780.00	140.00	55.00
(420)	Wildfire Schulte (Front view.)	1,000	100.00	60.00
(421)	Wildfire Schulte (Back view.)	400.00	100.00	50.00
(422)	Jim Scott	400.00	100.00	50.00
(423)	Charles Seitz	1,300	400.00	125.00
(424)	Cy Seymour/Btg	400.00	100.00	50.00
(425)	Cy Seymour/Portrait	400.00	100.00	50.00
(426)	Cy Seymour/Throwing	400.00	100.00	50.00
(427)	Spike Shannon	400.00	100.00	50.00
(428)	Bud Sharpe	400.00	100.00	50.00
(429)	Shag Shaughnessy	1,300	400.00	125.00
(430)	Al Shaw (St. Louis)	400.00	100.00	50.00
(431)	Hunky Shaw (Providence)	400.00	100.00	50.00
(432)	Jimmy Sheckard (Glove showing.)	400.00	100.00	50.00
(433)	Jimmy Sheckard (No glove showing.)	400.00	100.00	50.00
(434)	Bill Shipke	400.00	100.00	50.00
(435)	Jimmy Slagle	400.00	100.00	50.00
(436)	Carlos Smith (Shreveport)	1,300	400.00	125.00
(437)	Frank Smith (Chicago, F. Smith on front.)	400.00	100.00	50.00
(438a)	Frank Smith (Chicago, white cap.)	400.00	100.00	50.00
(438b)	Frank Smith (Chicago & Boston)	1,700	300.00	125.00
(439)	Happy Smith (Brooklyn)	400.00	100.00	50.00
(440)	Heinie Smith (Buffalo)	400.00	100.00	50.00
(441)	Sid Smith (Atlanta)	1,300	400.00	125.00
(442)	Fred Snodgrass/Btg	400.00	100.00	50.00
(443)	Fred Snodgrass/Catching	400.00	100.00	50.00
(444)	Bob Spade	400.00	100.00	50.00
(445)	Tris Speaker	4,500	800.00	325.00
(446)	Tubby Spencer	400.00	100.00	50.00
(447)	Jake Stahl (Glove shows.)	400.00	100.00	50.00
(448)	Jake Stahl (No glove shows.)	400.00	100.00	50.00
(449)	Oscar Stanage	400.00	100.00	50.00
(450)	Dolly Stark	1,300	400.00	125.00
(451)	Charlie Starr	400.00	100.00	50.00
(452)	Harry Steinfeldt/Portrait	400.00	100.00	50.00
(453)	Harry Steinfeldt (With bat.)	400.00	100.00	50.00
(454)	Jim Stephens	400.00	100.00	50.00
(455)	George Stone	400.00	100.00	50.00

(456)	George Stovall/Btg	400.00	100.00	50.00
(457)	George Stovall/Portrait	400.00	100.00	50.00
(458)	Sam Strang	400.00	100.00	50.00
(459)	Gabby Street/Catching	400.00	100.00	50.00
(460)	Gabby Street/Portrait	400.00	100.00	50.00
(461)	Billy Sullivan	400.00	100.00	50.00
(462)	Ed Summers	400.00	100.00	50.00
(463)	Bill Sweeney (Boston)	400.00	100.00	50.00
(464)	Jeff Sweeney (New York)	400.00	100.00	50.00
(465)	Jesse Tannehill (Washington)	400.00	100.00	50.00
(466)	Lee Tannehill (Chicago, L. Tannehill on front.)	400.00	100.00	50.00
(467)	Lee Tannehill (Chicago, Tannehill on front.)	400.00	100.00	50.00
(468)	Dummy Taylor	400.00	150.00	60.00
(469)	Fred Tenney	400.00	100.00	50.00
(470)	Tony Thebo	1,300	400.00	125.00
(471)	Jake Thielman	400.00	100.00	50.00
(472)	Ira Thomas	400.00	100.00	50.00
(473)	Woodie Thornton	1,300	400.00	125.00
(474)	Joe Tinker (Bat off shoulder.)	1,800	400.00	110.00
(475)	Joe Tinker (Bat on shoulder.)	1,700	300.00	110.00
(476)	Joe Tinker (Hands on knees.)	1,700	300.00	110.00
(477)	Joe Tinker/Portrait	1,800	400.00	125.00
(478)	John Titus	400.00	100.00	50.00
(479)	Terry Turner	400.00	100.00	50.00
(480)	Bob Unglaub	400.00	100.00	50.00
(481)	Juan Violat (Viola)	1,300	400.00	125.00
(482)	Rube Waddell/Portrait	1,800	300.00	125.00
(483)	Rube Waddell/Throwing	1,800	400.00	110.00
(484)	Heinie Wagner (Bat on left shoulder.)	400.00	100.00	50.00
(485)	Heinie Wagner (Bat on right shoulder.)	400.00	100.00	50.00
(486)	Honus Wagner (Some auction results: May 2008 Heritage Auctions, SGC10 $227,050. May 2008, Robert Edwards BVG1, $270,000. Aug. 2008 Mastro PSA 5 mc $1,620,000. Dec. 2008, Philip Weiss SGC40, $826,000.) Values shown refelct recent auctions of examples graded by PSA, SGC or GAI. Purchase of ungraded specimens is not recommended. NM-MT - 2,800,000 VG+ - 456,000 VG - 400,000 GOOD - 350,000 GOOD - 350,000 FAIR - 300,000 POOR - 270,000			
(487)	Bobby Wallace	1,500	300.00	100.00
(488)	Ed Walsh	2,300	400.00	200.00
(489)	Jack Warhop	400.00	100.00	50.00
(490)	Jake Weimer	400.00	100.00	50.00
(491)	James Westlake	1,300	400.00	125.00
(492)	Zack Wheat	1,500	300.00	140.00
(493)	Doc White/Pitching (Chicago)	400.00	100.00	50.00
(494)	Doc White/Portrait (Chicago)	400.00	100.00	50.00
(495)	Foley White (Houston)	1,300	400.00	125.00
(496)	Jack White (Buffalo)	400.00	100.00	50.00
(497)	Kaiser Wilhelm (Hands at chest.)	400.00	100.00	50.00
(498)	Kaiser Wilhelm (With bat.)	400.00	100.00	50.00
(499)	Ed Willett	400.00	100.00	50.00
(500)	Ed Willetts (Willett)	400.00	100.00	50.00
(501)	Jimmy Williams	400.00	100.00	50.00
(502)	Vic Willis/Portrait	1,700	400.00	100.00
(503)	Vic Willis/Throwing	1,700	300.00	100.00
(504)	Vic Willis (With bat.)	1,200	200.00	100.00
(505)	Owen Wilson	400.00	100.00	50.00
(506)	Hooks Wiltse/Pitching	400.00	100.00	50.00
(507)	Hooks Wiltse/Portrait (No cap.)	400.00	100.00	50.00
(508)	Hooks Wiltse/Portrait (With cap.)	400.00	100.00	50.00
(509)	Lucky Wright	400.00	100.00	50.00
(510)	Cy Young (Cleveland, glove shows.)	3,800	700.00	350.00
(511)	Cy Young (Cleveland, bare hand shows.)	4,400	800.00	375.00
(512)	Cy Young/Portrait (Cleveland)	8,700	1,600	700.00
(513)	Irv Young (Minneapolis)	400.00	100.00	50.00
(514)	Heinie Zimmerman	400.00	100.00	50.00

1909-11 T206 Errors

Because of the complexity of the lithographic process by which T206 cards were printed, a number of significant printing errors - missing colors, broken or missing type, etc. - are known. Early in hobby history some of these errors were collected alongside such true design variations as the "Magie" misspelling and Joe Doyle "N.Y. Nat'l." Because of the continued popularity of T206, some of these errors remain in

demand today and can command significant premium values. It should be noted, however, that not all similar errors within T206 bring such high prices; value seems dependent on the length of time the errors have been known in the hobby. Because of the ease with which various typographic elements - "S" in Snodgrass, "o" in Toronto, can be erased, many fakes of this type of error are known; collectors should be wary and consider having the cards professionally authenticated.

		NM	EX	VG
	Common Player (Missing one or more colors.)		250.00	150.00
	Common Player blank-back		400.00	240.00
(27)	Beck, no "B"s (Missing red ink.)		750.00	450.00
(28)	Becker, no "B" (Missing red ink.)		750.00	450.00
(95a)	Cobb, orange background (Missing red ink.)		1,500	900.00
(137)	Dopner (Three have been recently found, & authenticated: pricing pending sales)			
(164)	Ferguson, no "B" (Missing red ink.)		1,150	700.00
(279)	Lindaman, no "B" (Missing red ink.)		750.00	450.00
(286)	Maddox, Pittsburg (No team, name, city.)		3,000	1,800
(297)	Marshall, no "B" (Missing blue ink.)		1,000	600.00
(329)	Mitchell, "TORONT" (No last "O.")		1,000	600.00
(343)	Murray (Yellow background.)		750.00	450.00
(344)	Murry (Broken "A" in name, Lenox, Tolstoi, and Old Mill Back.")		6,500	2,100
(428)	Shappe, Newark (Should be Sharpe.)		1,600	1,000
(442)	nodgrass - batting (Should be Snodgrass; most of initial "S" missing.)		2,250	1,000
(443)	nodgrass - catching (All known examples, even those in grading company holders, are altered specimens with no collectible value.)			
(463)	Sweeney, no "B" (Missing magenta ink.)		2,600	2,700
(484)	Wagner, no "B" (Bat on left shoulder, missing magenta.)		1,250	750.00

1912 T207 Brown Background

Less popular and even less understood than their T205 and T206 antecedents from American Tobacco, the T207 "Brown Background" series shares the same approximately 1-7/16" x 2-5/8" format with the earlier T-cards. A chocolate background frames the rather drab player drawings, which rely on occasional bit of color on the uniform to break up the predominant earth tones. The cards have beige borders. A white strip below the picture has the player's last name, city and league. Unlike most other cards of its time, T207 has a glossy coating on front which over the years tends to crack and/or "craze" exacerbating the appaearance of creases and other signs of wear. Card backs have the player's full name, career summary and (usually) an ad for one of several brands of cigarettes. Red Cross brand backs are virtually impossible to find, while red Cycle advertising is noticeably scarcer than more common Broadleaf or "anonymous" (no-advertising) versions. Cards with Recruit Little Cigars advertising on back are the most common. There are a number of unaccountably scarce cards in the set, including a higher than usual number of obscure players.

		NM	EX	VG
Common Player:		225.00	110.00	70.00
Red Cycle Backs: 1.5X anonymous or Broadleaf backs.				
(1)	John B. Adams	1,760	615.00	355.00
(2)	Edward Ainsmith	225.00	110.00	70.00
(3)	Rafael Almeida	1,250	625.00	300.00
(4a)	James Austin (Insignia on shirt.)	440.00	155.00	90.00
(4b)	James Austin (No insignia on shirt.)	225.00	110.00	45.00
(5)	Neal Ball	225.00	110.00	70.00
(6)	Eros Barger	225.00	110.00	70.00
(7)	Jack Barry	250.00	90.00	50.00
(8)	Charles Bauman (Baumann)	1,250	625.00	300.00
(9)	Beals Becker	330.00	110.00	65.00

		NM	EX	VG
(10)	Chief (Albert) Bender	800.00	400.00	240.00
(11)	Joseph Benz	1,750	875.00	525.00
(12)	Robert Bescher	225.00	110.00	70.00
(13)	Joe Birmingham	1,250	625.00	300.00
(14)	Russell Blackburne	1,250	625.00	300.00
(15)	Fred Blanding	1,250	625.00	300.00
(16)	Jimmy Block	495.00	170.00	100.00
(17)	Ping Bodie	225.00	110.00	70.00
(18)	Hugh Bradley	225.00	110.00	70.00
(19)	Roger Bresnaham (Bresnahan)	1,200	600.00	350.00
(20)	J.F. Bushelman	1,250	625.00	300.00
(21)	Henry (Hank) Butcher	1,250	625.00	300.00
(22)	Robert M. Byrne	225.00	110.00	70.00
(23)	John James Callahan	225.00	110.00	70.00
(24)	Howard Camnitz	225.00	110.00	70.00
(25)	Max Carey	855.00	305.00	165.00
(26)	Bill Carrigan	225.00	110.00	70.00
(27)	George Chalmers	225.00	110.00	70.00
(28)	Frank Leroy Chance	715.00	250.00	145.00
(29)	Edward Cicotte	1,100	385.00	220.00
(30)	Tom Clarke	225.00	110.00	70.00
(31)	Leonard Cole	225.00	110.00	70.00
(32)	John Collins	305.00	105.00	60.00
(33)	Robert Coulson	225.00	110.00	70.00
(34)	Tex Covington	225.00	110.00	70.00
(35)	Otis Crandall	225.00	110.00	70.00
(36)	William Cunningham	1,100	550.00	325.00
(37)	Dave Danforth	250.00	95.00	50.00
(38)	Bert Daniels	440.00	155.00	90.00
(39)	John Daubert (Jake)	225.00	110.00	70.00
(40)	Harry Davis	250.00	90.00	50.00
(41)	Jim Delehanty	225.00	110.00	70.00
(42)	Claude Derrick	225.00	110.00	70.00
(43)	Arthur Devlin	250.00	95.00	50.00
(44)	Joshua Devore	225.00	110.00	70.00
(45)	Mike Donlin	7,750	3,875	2,325
(46)	Edward Donnelly	1,250	625.00	300.00
(47)	Charles Dooin	225.00	110.00	70.00
(48)	Tom Downey	880.00	310.00	175.00
(49)	Lawrence Doyle	440.00	155.00	90.00
(50)	Del Drake	385.00	135.00	75.00
(51)	Ted Easterly	225.00	110.00	70.00
(52)	George Ellis	660.00	230.00	135.00
(53)	Clyde Engle	360.00	125.00	70.00
(54)	R.E. Erwin	660.00	230.00	135.00
(55)	Louis Evans	225.00	110.00	70.00
(56)	John Ferry	225.00	110.00	70.00
(57a)	Ray Fisher (Blue cap.)	225.00	110.00	70.00
(57b)	Ray Fisher (White cap.)	300.00	150.00	75.00
(58)	Arthur Fletcher	225.00	110.00	70.00
(59)	Jacques Fournier	1,250	625.00	300.00
(60)	Arthur Fromme	250.00	90.00	50.00
(61)	Del Gainor	225.00	110.00	70.00
(62)	William Lawrence Gardner	330.00	110.00	65.00
(63)	Lefty George	440.00	220.00	110.00
(64)	Roy Golden	225.00	110.00	70.00
(65)	Harry Gowdy	225.00	110.00	70.00
(66)	George Graham	660.00	230.00	135.00
(67)	J.G. Graney	825.00	285.00	165.00
(68)	Vean Gregg	1,250	625.00	300.00
(69)	Casey Hageman	440.00	155.00	90.00
(70)	Charlie Hall	440.00	155.00	90.00
(71)	E.S. Hallinan	225.00	110.00	70.00
(72)	Earl Hamilton	225.00	110.00	70.00
(73)	Robert Harmon	225.00	110.00	70.00
(74)	Grover Hartley	440.00	155.00	90.00
(75)	Olaf Henriksen	230.00	110.00	60.00
(76)	John Henry	440.00	155.00	90.00
(77)	Charles Herzog	1,050	525.00	315.00
(78)	Robert Higgins	310.00	110.00	60.00
(79)	Chester Hoff	1,250	625.00	300.00
(80)	William Hogan	310.00	110.00	60.00
(81)	Harry Hooper	1,675	840.00	500.00
(82)	Ben Houser	1,250	625.00	300.00
(83)	Hamilton Hyatt	1,250	625.00	300.00
(84)	Walter Johnson	2,090	730.00	420.00
(85)	George Kaler	225.00	110.00	70.00
(86)	William Kelly	1,250	625.00	300.00
(87)	Jay Kirke	440.00	155.00	90.00
(88)	John Kling	715.00	250.00	145.00
(89)	Otto Knabe	225.00	110.00	70.00
(90)	Elmer Knetzer	225.00	110.00	70.00
(91)	Edward Konetchy	225.00	110.00	70.00
(92)	Harry Krause	225.00	110.00	70.00
(93)	"Red" Kuhn	1,250	625.00	300.00
(94)	Joseph Kutina	1,250	625.00	300.00
(95)	F.H. (Bill) Lange	1,250	625.00	300.00
(96)	Jack Lapp	225.00	110.00	70.00
(97)	W. Arlington Latham	225.00	110.00	70.00
(98)	Thomas W. Leach	225.00	110.00	70.00
(99)	Albert Leifield	225.00	110.00	70.00
(100)	Edgar Lennox	225.00	110.00	70.00
(101)	Duffy Lewis	495.00	170.00	100.00
(102a)	Irving Lewis (No emblem on sleeve.)	20,000	10,000	5,000
(102b)	Irving Lewis (Emblem on sleeve.)	10,450	5,000	3,000
(103)	Jack Lively	220.00	75.00	45.00
(104a)	Paddy Livingston ("A" on shirt.)	1,200	425.00	245.00
(104b)	Paddy Livingston (Big "C" on shirt.)	1,265	440.00	255.00
(104c)	Paddy Livingston (Small "C" on shirt.)	330.00	115.00	65.00
(105)	Briscoe Lord (Philadelphia)	440.00	155.00	90.00
(106)	Harry Lord (Chicago)	440.00	155.00	90.00
(107)	Louis Lowdermilk	10,450	3,660	2,090
(108)	Richard Marquard	605.00	210.00	120.00
(109)	Armando Marsans	770.00	270.00	155.00
(110)	George McBride	310.00	110.00	60.00
(111)	Alexander McCarthy	1,250	625.00	300.00
(112)	Edward McDonald	330.00	110.00	65.00
(113)	John J. McGraw	635.00	220.00	125.00
(114)	Harry McIntire	225.00	110.00	70.00
(115)	Matthew McIntyre	225.00	110.00	70.00
(116)	William McKechnie	2,000	1,000	500.00
(117)	Larry McLean	225.00	110.00	70.00

		NM	EX	VG
(118)	Clyde Milan	225.00	110.00	70.00
(119)	John B. Miller (Pittsburg)	225.00	110.00	70.00
(120)	Otto Miller (Brooklyn)	440.00	155.00	90.00
(121)	Roy Miller (Boston)	990.00	345.00	200.00
(122)	Ward Miller (Chicago)	8,000	4,000	2,000
(123)	Mike Mitchell (Cleveland, picture is Willie Mitchell.)	225.00	110.00	70.00
(124)	Mike Mitchell (Cincinnati)	330.00	110.00	65.00
(125)	Geo. Mogridge	1,500	750.00	375.00
(126)	Earl Moore	1,250	625.00	300.00
(127)	Patrick J. Moran	225.00	110.00	70.00
(128)	Cy Morgan (Philadelphia)	225.00	110.00	70.00
(129)	Ray Morgan (Washington)	225.00	110.00	70.00
(130)	George Moriarty	1,250	625.00	300.00
(131a)	George Mullin ("D" on cap.)	250.00	90.00	50.00
(131b)	George Mullin (No "D" on cap.)	745.00	260.00	150.00
(132)	Thomas Needham	330.00	110.00	65.00
(133)	Red Nelson	1,250	625.00	300.00
(134)	Herbert Northen (Hubbard)	310.00	110.00	60.00
(135)	Leslie Nunamaker	225.00	110.00	70.00
(136)	Rebel Oakes	225.00	110.00	70.00
(137)	Buck O'Brien	330.00	110.00	65.00
(138)	Rube Oldring	225.00	110.00	70.00
(139)	Ivan Olson	225.00	110.00	70.00
(140)	Martin J. O'Toole	225.00	110.00	70.00
(141)	George Paskart (Paskert)	225.00	110.00	70.00
(142)	Barney Pelty	2,000	1,250	500.00
(143)	Herbert Perdue	310.00	110.00	60.00
(144)	O.C. Peters	1,250	625.00	300.00
(145)	Arthur Phelan	1,250	625.00	300.00
(146)	Jack Quinn	440.00	155.00	90.00
(147)	Don Carlos Ragan	1,500	750.00	400.00
(148)	Arthur Rasmussen	1,500	750.00	400.00
(149)	Morris Rath	1,500	750.00	400.00
(150)	Edward Reulbach	330.00	115.00	65.00
(151)	Napoleon Rucker	440.00	155.00	90.00
(152)	J.B. Ryan	1,250	625.00	300.00
(153)	Victor Saier	2,300	810.00	470.00
(154)	William Scanlon	225.00	110.00	70.00
(155)	Germany Schaefer	225.00	110.00	70.00
(156)	Wilbur Schardt	225.00	110.00	70.00
(157)	Frank Schulte	225.00	110.00	70.00
(158)	Jim Scott	495.00	170.00	100.00
(159)	Henry Severoid (Severeid)	225.00	110.00	70.00
(160)	Mike Simon	225.00	110.00	70.00
(161)	Frank E. Smith (Cincinnati)	225.00	110.00	70.00
(162)	Wallace Smith (St. Louis)	225.00	110.00	70.00
(163)	Fred Snodgrass	225.00	110.00	70.00
(164)	Tristam Speaker	4,000	2,000	750.00
(165)	Harry Lee Spratt	225.00	110.00	70.00
(166)	Edward Stack	550.00	195.00	110.00
(167)	Oscar Stanage	225.00	110.00	70.00
(168)	William Steele	660.00	230.00	135.00
(169)	Harry Steinfeldt	440.00	155.00	90.00
(170)	George Stovall	225.00	110.00	70.00
(171)	Charles (Gabby) Street	250.00	90.00	50.00
(172)	Amos Strunk	225.00	110.00	70.00
(173)	William Sullivan	310.00	110.00	60.00
(174)	William J. Sweeney	1,250	625.00	300.00
(175)	Leeford Tannehill	225.00	110.00	70.00
(176)	C.D. Thomas	715.00	250.00	145.00
(177)	Joseph Tinker	880.00	310.00	175.00
(178)	Bert Tooley	225.00	110.00	70.00
(179)	Terence Turner (Terrence)	225.00	110.00	70.00
(180)	George Tyler	2,000	1,000	500.00
(181)	Jim Vaughn	385.00	135.00	75.00
(182)	Chas. (Heinie) Wagner	225.00	110.00	70.00
(183)	Ed (Dixie) Walker	225.00	110.00	70.00
(184)	Robert Wallace	1,250	625.00	300.00
(185)	John Warhop	225.00	110.00	70.00
(186)	George Weaver	5,225	1,815	1,045
(187)	Zach Wheat	880.00	310.00	175.00
(188)	G. Harris White	310.00	110.00	60.00
(189)	Ernest Wilie	275.00	95.00	55.00
(190)	Bob Williams	225.00	110.00	70.00
(191)	Arthur Wilson (New York)	250.00	90.00	50.00
(192)	Owen Wilson (Pittsburg)	1,250	625.00	300.00
(193)	George Wiltse	225.00	110.00	70.00
(194)	Ivey Wingo	385.00	135.00	75.00
(195)	Harry Wolverton	225.00	110.00	70.00
(196)	Joe Wood	2,640	925.00	530.00
(197)	Eugene Woodburn	880.00	310.00	175.00
(198)	Ralph Works	1,250	625.00	300.00
(199)	Stanley Yerkes	225.00	110.00	70.00
(200)	Rollie Zeider	330.00	110.00	65.00

1912 T227 Series Of Champions

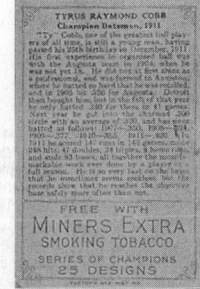

The 1912 "Series of Champions" card set issued by the "Honest Long Cut" and "Miners Extra" tobacco brands features several baseball stars among its 25 famous athletes of the day. Larger than a standard-size tobacco issue, each card in the "Champions" series measures 3-3/8" x 2-5/16". The back includes a relatively lengthy player biography, while the front features a lithograph of the player in action. Although the set includes only four baseball players, these attractive cards are popular among collectors because of the stature of the

four players selected. The "Champions" series holds additional significance because it includes the only known baseball cards issued under the "Miners Extra" brand name. The set carries the American Card Catalog designation of T227.

		NM	EX	VG
Complete Set (4):		22,500	10,000	5,500
Common Player:		3,600	1,620	900.00
(1)	"Home Run" Baker	3,600	1,620	900.00
(2)	"Chief" Bender	3,600	1,620	900.00
(3)	Ty Cobb	16,200	7,200	4,200
(4)	Rube Marquard	3,600	1,620	900.00

U

1906 Ullman Postcards

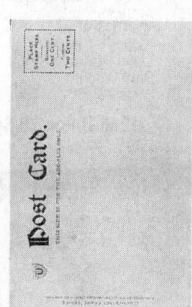

The designation of Giants' players as "World's Champions" dates this issue to 1906. The 3-1/2" x 5-1/2" cards have a black-and-white photo surrounded by a greenish or reddish-brown tone wooden-look frame with a plaque printed in the bottom border. Backs are printed in brown with typical postcard markings and include mention of "Ullman's 'Art Frame' Series." This checklist is likely not complete. The card of "Harry" (name actually Henry) Mathewson is the only known baseball card appearance of Christy's kid brother.

		NM	EX	VG
Common Player:		1,500	750.00	450.00
(1)	Leon Ames	1,500	750.00	450.00
(2)	Mike Donlin	1,500	750.00	450.00
(3)	George Ferguson	1,500	750.00	450.00
(4)	Matty Fitzgerald	1,500	750.00	450.00
(5)	Billy Gilbert	1,500	750.00	450.00
(6)	Christy Matthewson (Mathewson)	7,000	3,500	2,000
(7)	Harry (Henry) Mathewson	2,400	1,200	700.00
(8)	Dan McGann (McGann on 1st Base.)	1,500	750.00	450.00
(9)	"Iron Arm" McGinnity	2,000	1,000	600.00
(10)	Manager McGraw	3,000	1,500	900.00
(11)	Strang and Bowerman (Sammy Strang, Frank Bowerman)	1,800	900.00	500.00
(12)	Hooks Wiltse	1,500	750.00	450.00
(13)	1906 National League Champion Chicago, Cubs	2,500	1,250	750.00

1933 Uncle Jacks Candy

One of the lesser-known candy issues of the early 1930s was this New England regional set from Uncle Jacks, Inc., of Springfield, Mass., and Newport, R.I. The 1-7/8" x 2-7/8" blank-backed cards can be found printed in blue, red, purple or green duotone, and were sold in a see-through wax paper wrapper with a piece of candy and a coupon which could be redeemed (in quantities of 100) for a "league baseball" and a chance at a trip to the 1933 World Series. The set is among those listed in the American Card Catalog under the catchall number R317. The unnumbered cards are checklisted here alphabetically.

		NM	EX	VG
Complete Set (30):		80,000	40,000	24,000
Common Player:		1,300	650.00	400.00
(1)	Earl Averill	2,350	1,175	705.00
(2)	James L. Bottomley	2,350	1,175	705.00
(3)	Ed Brandt	1,300	650.00	400.00

		NM	EX	VG
(4)	Ben Chapman	1,300	650.00	400.00
(5)	Gordon Cochrane	2,350	1,175	705.00
(6)	Joe Cronin	2,350	1,175	705.00
(7)	Hazen Cuyler	2,350	1,175	705.00
(8)	George Earnshaw	1,300	650.00	400.00
(9)	Wesley Ferrell	1,300	650.00	400.00
(10)	Jimmie Foxx	4,500	2,200	1,350
(11)	Frank Frisch	2,350	1,175	705.00
(12)	Burleigh Grimes	2,350	1,175	705.00
(13)	"Lefty" Grove	3,375	1,700	1,000
(14)	"Wild Bill" Hallahan	1,300	650.00	400.00
(15)	Leo Hartnett	2,350	1,175	705.00
(16)	"Babe" Herman	1,300	650.00	400.00
(17)	Rogers Hornsby	3,375	1,700	1,000
(18)	Charles Klein	2,350	1,175	705.00
(19)	Tony Lazzeri	2,350	1,175	705.00
(20)	Fred Lindstrom	2,350	1,175	705.00
(21)	Ted Lyons	2,350	1,175	705.00
(22)	"Pepper" Martin	1,850	925.00	555.00
(23)	Herb Pennock	2,350	1,175	705.00
(24)	"Babe" Ruth ("King of Swat")	21,500	10,750	6,450
(25)	Al Simmons	2,350	1,175	705.00
(26)	"Bill" Terry	2,350	1,175	705.00
(27)	"Dazzy" Vance	2,350	1,175	705.00
(28)	Lloyd Waner	2,350	1,175	705.00
(29)	Paul Waner	2,350	1,175	705.00
(30)	Hack Wilson	2,350	1,175	705.00

1958 Union 76 Sports Club Booklets

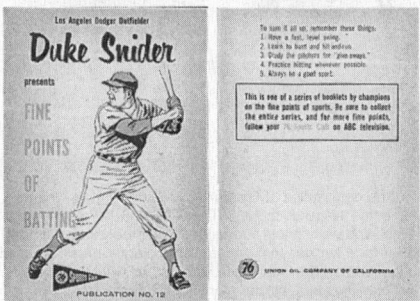

This series of sports instructional booklets was issued by Union Oil in conjunction with its Sports Club television program for youngsters. Besides seven baseball players, the series featured football, track, bowling, skiing, and other stars. The booklets are 12 pages and measure about 4" x 5-1/2". Fronts have a drawing of the player and are printed in Union Oil logo colors of orange and blue. The sports tips inside are well illustrated. Books are numbered on front.

		NM	EX	VG
	Complete (Baseball) Set (7):	160.00	80.00	45.00
	Common Player:	15.00	7.50	4.50
12	Duke Snider	35.00	17.50	10.50
14	Bob Lemon	20.00	10.00	6.00
15	Red Schoendienst	20.00	10.00	6.00
20	Bill Rigney	15.00	7.50	4.50
38	Jackie Jensen	15.00	7.50	4.50
39	Warren Spahn	25.00	12.50	7.50
41	Ernie Banks	35.00	17.50	10.50

1960 Union Oil Dodger Family Booklets

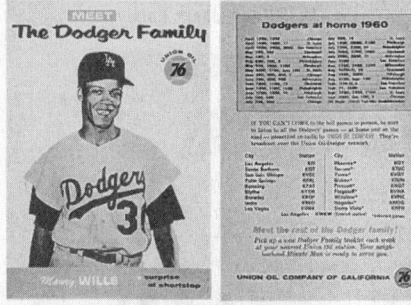

For its first major issue of Dodgers memorabilia, Union 76 gas stations in Southern California distributed a series of booklets profiling players and staff. Each 5-1/2" x 7-1/2" booklet has 16 black-and-white pages highlighted with red graphics. The covers have action poses with many other photos on the inside pages, along with a biography, personal information, career highlights, playing tips, etc. On back is a Dodgers schedule and Union 76 ad. The booklets were distributed on a one-per-week basis. They are listed here in alphabetical order.

		NM	EX	VG
	Complete Set (23):	150.00	75.00	45.00
	Common Player:	6.00	3.00	1.75
(1)	Walter Alston	7.50	3.75	2.25
(2)	Roger Craig	6.00	3.00	1.75
(3)	Tom Davis	7.50	3.75	2.25
(4)	Don Demeter	6.00	3.00	1.75
(5)	Don Drysdale	15.00	7.50	4.50
(6)	Chuck Essegian	6.00	3.00	1.75
(7)	Jim Gilliam	7.50	3.75	2.25
(8)	Gil Hodges	12.00	6.00	3.50
(9)	Frank Howard	7.50	3.75	2.25
(10)	Sandy Koufax	40.00	20.00	12.00
(11)	Norm Larker	6.00	3.00	1.75
(12)	Wally Moon	6.00	3.00	1.75
(13)	Charlie Neal	6.00	3.00	1.75
(14)	Johnny Podres	6.00	3.00	1.75
(15)	Ed Roebuck	6.00	3.00	1.75
(16)	John Roseboro	6.00	3.00	1.75
(17)	Larry Sherry	6.00	3.00	1.75
(18)	Norm Sherry	6.00	3.00	1.75
(19)	Duke Snider	15.00	7.50	4.50
(20)	Stan Williams	6.00	3.00	1.75
(21)	Maury Wills	7.50	3.75	2.25
(22)	Coaches (Joe Becker, Bobby Bragan, Greg Mulleavy, Pete Reiser)	6.00	3.00	1.75
(23)	Jerry Doggett, Vin Scully (Announcers)	6.00	3.00	1.75

1961 Union Oil Dodger Family Booklets

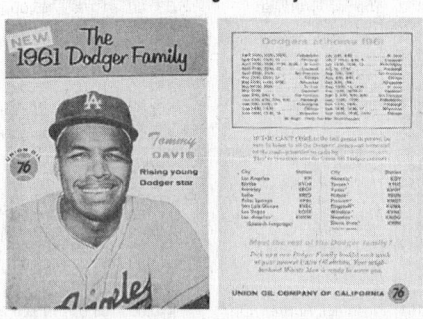

For a second consecutive year, Union 76 gas stations in Southern California distributed a series of booklets profiling team members and staff. The 5-1/2" x 7-1/2" booklets have 16 black-and-white pages highlighted with red graphics. The covers have large portraits while there are many photos on the inside pages, along with a biography, personal information, career highlights, playing tips, etc. On back is a Dodgers schedule and radio network information. The booklets were distributed on a one-per-week basis. They are listed here in alphabetical order.

		NM	EX	VG
	Complete Set (24):	175.00	85.00	50.00
	Common Player:	6.00	3.00	1.75
(1)	Walter Alston	7.50	3.75	2.25
(2)	Roger Craig	6.00	3.00	1.75
(3)	Tommy Davis	7.50	3.75	2.25
(4)	Willie Davis	7.50	3.75	2.25
(5)	Don Drysdale	15.00	7.50	4.50
(6)	Dick Farrell	6.00	3.00	1.75
(7)	Ron Fairly	6.00	3.00	1.75
(8)	Jim Gilliam	7.50	3.75	2.25
(9)	Gil Hodges	10.00	5.00	3.00
(10)	Frank Howard	7.50	3.75	2.25
(11)	Sandy Koufax	30.00	15.00	9.00
(12)	Norm Larker	6.00	3.00	1.75
(13)	Wally Moon	6.00	3.00	1.75
(14)	Charlie Neal	6.00	3.00	1.75
(15)	Ron Perranoski	6.00	3.00	1.75
(16)	Johnny Podres	6.00	3.00	1.75
(17)	John Roseboro	6.00	3.00	1.75
(18)	Larry Sherry	6.00	3.00	1.75
(19)	Norm Sherry	6.00	3.00	1.75
(20)	Duke Snider	15.00	7.50	4.50
(21)	Daryl Spencer	6.00	3.00	1.75
(22)	Stan Williams	6.00	3.00	1.75
(23)	Maury Wills	7.50	3.75	2.25
(24)	Jerry Doggett, Vin Scully (Announcers)	6.00	3.00	1.75

1962 Union Oil Dodgers Premium Pictures

 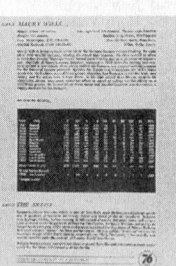

One of many premiums issued by Union Oil during the Dodgers' early years in Los Angeles, this set of player pictures is the most popular with collectors. The 8-1/2" x 11" pictures feature a large color pastel portrait of the player on front, along with a smaller action picture. The player's name is printed in the white border below. The artist's signature and a 1962 copyright are printed below the portrait. Backs are printed in black-and-white and include a career summary and complete minor and major league stats, a profile of sports artist Nicholas Volpe and an ad at bottom for Union Oil and its Union 76 brand of gasoline. The unnumbered pictures are checklisted here alphabetically. It was reported that 200,000 of each picture were produced.

		NM	EX	VG
	Complete Set (24):	225.00	115.00	70.00
	Common Player:	8.00	4.00	2.50
(1)	Larry Burright	8.00	4.00	2.50
(2)	Doug Camilli	8.00	4.00	2.50
(3)	Andy Carey	8.00	4.00	2.50
(4)	Tom Davis	10.00	5.00	3.00
(5)	Willie Davis	10.00	5.00	3.00
(6)	Don Drysdale	20.00	10.00	6.00
(7)	Ron Fairly	8.00	4.00	2.50
(8)	Jim Gilliam	10.00	5.00	3.00
(9)	Tim Harkness	8.00	4.00	2.50
(10)	Frank Howard	10.00	5.00	3.00
(11)	Sandy Koufax	40.00	20.00	12.00
(12)	Joe Moeller	8.00	4.00	2.50
(13)	Wally Moon	8.00	4.00	2.50
(14)	Ron Perranoski	8.00	4.00	2.50
(15)	Johnny Podres	8.00	4.00	2.50
(16)	Ed Roebuck	8.00	4.00	2.50
(17)	John Roseboro	8.00	4.00	2.50
(18)	Larry Sherry	8.00	4.00	2.50
(19)	Norm Sherry	8.00	4.00	2.50
(20)	Duke Snider	25.00	12.50	7.50
(21)	Daryl Spencer	8.00	4.00	2.50
(22)	Lee Walls	8.00	4.00	2.50
(23)	Stan Williams	8.00	4.00	2.50
(24)	Maury Wills	10.00	5.00	3.00

1964 Union Oil Dodgers Premium Pictures

 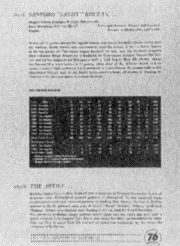

Paired pastel portraits, one in uniform and one in mufti, from sports artist Nicholas Volpe are featured on these large-format (8-1/2" x 11") premium pictures sponsored by Union Oil. The player's name is printed in the bottom border while the artist's signature is printed beneath the portraits. Backs are in black-and-white and feature personal data about the player and artist, complete minor and major league stats and Union Oil/Union 76 logos. The unnumbered pictures are checklisted here alphabetically.

		NM	EX	VG
	Complete Set (18):	165.00	80.00	50.00
	Common Player:	8.00	4.00	2.50
(1)	Tommy Davis	10.00	5.00	3.00
(2)	Willie Davis	10.00	5.00	3.00
(3)	Don Drysdale	20.00	10.00	6.00
(4)	Ron Fairly	8.00	4.00	2.50
(5)	Jim Gilliam	10.00	5.00	3.00
(6)	Frank Howard	10.00	5.00	3.00
(7)	Sandy Koufax	35.00	17.50	10.00
(8)	Bob Miller	8.00	4.00	2.50
(9)	Joe Moeller	8.00	4.00	2.50
(10)	Wally Moon	8.00	4.00	2.50
(11)	Phil Ortega	8.00	4.00	2.50
(12)	Wes Parker	8.00	4.00	2.50
(13)	Ron Perranoski	8.00	4.00	2.50
(14)	John Podres	8.00	4.00	2.50
(15)	John Roseboro	8.00	4.00	2.50
(16)	Dick Tracewski	8.00	4.00	2.50
(17)	Lee Walls	8.00	4.00	2.50
(18)	Maury Wills	10.00	5.00	3.00

1969 Union Oil Dodgers Premium Pictures

These 8-1/2" x 11" cards were given to fans attending week night "Player Portrait Night" promotional games. The premiums are similar in format to earlier and later sets sponsored by Union Oil and created by sports artist Nicholas Volpe. Fronts have pastel player portraits and action drawings against a black background. Backs are in black-and-white and have player biographies, stats and a career summary, along with a word about the artist and an ad for Union Oil/Union 76. The unnumbered pictures are checklisted here alphabetically.

		NM	EX	VG
	Complete Set (13):	120.00	60.00	35.00
	Common Player:	8.00	4.00	2.50
(1)	Walt Alston	10.00	5.00	3.00
(2)	Jim Brewer	8.00	4.00	2.50
(3)	Willie Davis	10.00	5.00	3.00
(4)	Don Drysdale	20.00	10.00	6.00
(5)	Ron Fairly	8.00	4.00	2.50
(6)	Tom Haller	8.00	4.00	2.50

		NM	EX	VG
(7)	Jim Lefebvre	8.00	4.00	2.50
(8)	Claude Osteen	8.00	4.00	2.50
(9)	Wes Parker	8.00	4.00	2.50
(10)	Paul Popovich	8.00	4.00	2.50
(11)	Bill Singer	8.00	4.00	2.50
(12)	Bill Sudakis	8.00	4.00	2.50
(13)	Don Sutton	13.50	6.75	4.00

1968 Uniroyal Keds Cincinnati Reds

These 2-1/2" x 3-3/4" cards are printed in blue duotone on thin paper. Blank backed, they were intended to be put into an accompanying album. These cards were issued between June 3-July 21 in four strips of five players. The remainder of the checklist is unknown.

		NM	EX	VG
Common Player:		40.00	20.00	12.00
(1)	Dave Bristol	40.00	20.00	12.00
(2)	Bob Johnson	40.00	20.00	12.00
(3)	Bob Lee	40.00	20.00	12.00
(4)	Jim Maloney	40.00	20.00	12.00
(5)	Lee May	40.00	20.00	12.00
(6)	Vada Pinson	50.00	25.00	15.00
(7)	Pete Rose	300.00	150.00	90.00

1979 United Press International

SPORTS NOSTALGIA

THEODORE SAMUEL WILLIAMS
(1918-)

"Ted" Williams was born in San Diego, California and during his career, he won six batting titles and hit 521 home runs. In 1946 he hit over .400, the last major league player to do so. He played for the Boston Red Sox (1939-42; 1946-60) and was elected to the Baseball Hall of Fame in 1966.

On September 28, 1960, Williams hit a 420-foot home run in the 8th inning during a game with Baltimore at Fenway Park. It was his 29th homer of the season and turned out to be Ted Williams' last 'at bat' in the majors before retiring.

UNITED PRESS INTERNATIONAL

Not widely circulated, and perhaps issued only as a prototype, these cards feature a tiny (2" x 2-1/4" clear vinyl record attached to the back. Overall, the card is 2-3/4" x 5" and has on front a black-and-white or color photo with a UPI credit line in the very wide white border at bottom. The back is headed either "Sports Nostalgia" or "Great Moments in Sports." Player identification and career highlights are printed on back. The vinyl mini-record could be played on an ancient electronic entertainment device known as a turntable. Similar card/records were produced for other sports and historical highlights.

		NM	EX	VG
Complete Set (9):		150.00	75.00	45.00
Common Player:		10.00	5.00	3.00
(1)	Hank Aaron (715th HR)	15.00	7.50	4.50
(2)	Joe DiMaggio (Hitting Streak Ends)	20.00	10.00	6.00
(3)	Lou Gehrig (Gehrig Day 7/4/39)	20.00	10.00	6.00
(4)	Mickey Mantle (Record HR)	25.00	12.50	7.50
(5)	Stan Musial (3,000th Hit)	15.00	7.50	4.50
(6)	Babe Ruth (Famous Home Run)	20.00	10.00	6.00
(7)	Gene Tenace (Record HR)	10.00	5.00	3.00
(8)	Bobby Thomson (Famous HR)	12.00	6.00	3.50
(9)	Ted Williams (Last At-Bat)	15.00	7.50	4.50

1932 Universal Pictures Babe Ruth Premium

See the Bambino Himself!

BABE RUTH

In a Home-Screen Baseball Story

"SLIDE BABE SLIDE"

at the

KEENEY THEATRE

SUNDAY, JUNE 19th—4 Days

NOTE (): Babe Ruth Invites Every Game Every Time Fan.

The Feature Picture is...

TALLULAH BANKHEAD

PAUL LUCAS · CHAS. BICKFORD · EUGENE PALLETTE

A woman—beautiful, desired and desiring, torn between passion and honor, wives and betrayal! Below the equator where backless bathing suits are quickly launched under secret skies

"THUNDER BELOW"

This 8" x 10" black-and-white photo was issued to promote what was advertised as a series of Babe Ruth shorts. The front pictures the movie star in a generic uniform with a facsimile autograph. On back is advertising for the theater bill. It is likely the pictures were distributed blank-backed, allowing local theaters to have their advertising added.

	NM	EX	VG
Babe Ruth	750.00	375.00	225.00

1925 Universal Toy & Novelty Brooklyn Dodgers (W504)

Printed on cheap paper in blue ink and intended to be cut apart into a team photo and 16 individual player cards, this set was originally issued on a 5-1/2" x 13" sheet. Single cut cards measure about 1-3/8" x 2-3/8", with the team picture about 5-1/2" x 3-1/2". Cards are blank-back. Cards are numbered in roughly alphabetical order beneath the photo, where the name, team, position and birth year are also printed.

		NM	EX	VG
Complete Sheet:		1,800	900.00	540.00
Complete Set, Singles (17):		1,200	600.00	360.00
Common Player:		50.00	25.00	15.00
101	Edward W. Brown	50.00	25.00	15.00
102	John H. De Berry	50.00	25.00	15.00
103	William L. Doak	50.00	25.00	15.00
104	Wm. C. Ehrhardt (First name Welton.)	50.00	25.00	15.00
105	J.F. Fournier	50.00	25.00	15.00
106	T.H. Griffith	50.00	25.00	15.00
107	Burleigh A. Grimes	100.00	50.00	30.00
108	C.P. Hargreaves	50.00	25.00	15.00
109	Andrew A. High	50.00	25.00	15.00
110	Andy. H. Johnston (First name Jimmy.)	50.00	25.00	15.00
111	John Mitchell	50.00	25.00	15.00
112	"Tiny" Osborne	50.00	25.00	15.00
113	Milton Stock	50.00	25.00	15.00
114	James W. Taylor	50.00	25.00	15.00
115	"Dazzy" Vance	100.00	50.00	30.00
116	Zack D. Wheat	100.00	50.00	30.00
---	Brooklyn National League Team Photo	550.00	275.00	165.00

1925 Universal Toy & Novelty New York Giants (W504)

Printed on thick cardboard and intended to be cut apart into a team photo and 16 individual player cards, this set was originally issued on a 5-1/2" x 13" sheet. Single cut cards measure about 1-3/8" x 2-3/8", with the team picture about 5" x 3-1/2". Cards are blank-back. Player cards are numbered beneath the photo, where the name, team, position and birth year are also printed.

		NM	EX	VG
Complete Sheet:		3,500	1,750	1,000
Complete Set (17):		3,000	1,500	900.00
Common Player:		125.00	60.00	35.00
133	Virgil Barnes	125.00	60.00	35.00
134	John N. Bentley	125.00	60.00	35.00
135	Frank Frisch	225.00	110.00	65.00
136	Harry Gowdy	125.00	60.00	35.00
137	Henry Groh	125.00	60.00	35.00
138	Travis Jackson	200.00	100.00	60.00
139	George Kelly	200.00	100.00	60.00
140	Emil Meusel	125.00	60.00	35.00
141	Hugh McQuillan	125.00	60.00	35.00
142	Arthur Nehf	125.00	60.00	35.00
143	Wilfred D. Ryan	125.00	60.00	35.00
144	Frank Snyder	125.00	60.00	35.00
145	Lewis R. Wilson	225.00	110.00	65.00
146	Ross Youngs	200.00	100.00	60.00
147	Hugh Jennings	200.00	100.00	60.00
148	John J. McGraw	200.00	100.00	60.00
---	New York National League Team Photo	400.00	200.00	120.00

1925 Universal Toy & Novelty N.Y. Yankees (W504)

Printed on thick cardboard and intended to be cut apart into a team photo and 16 individual player cards, this set was originally issued on a 5-1/2" x 13" sheet. Single cut cards measure about 1-3/8" x 2-3/8", with the team picture about 5" x 3-1/2". Cards are blank-back. Player cards are numbered in alphabetical order beneath the photo, where the name, team, position and birth year are also printed.

		NM	EX	VG
Complete Sheet:		4,000	2,000	1,200
Complete Set (17):		3,500	1,750	1,000
Common Player:		125.00	60.00	35.00
117	Bernard Bengough	125.00	60.00	35.00
118	Joseph Dugan	125.00	60.00	35.00
119	Waite Hoyt	200.00	100.00	60.00
120	Sam Jones	125.00	60.00	35.00
121	Robert Meusel	125.00	60.00	35.00
122	Walter C. Pipp	125.00	60.00	35.00
123	G.H. "Babe" Ruth	1,200	600.00	360.00
124	Wal. H. Schang	125.00	60.00	35.00
125	Robert J. Shawkey	125.00	60.00	35.00
126	Everett Scott	125.00	60.00	35.00
127	Urban Shocker	125.00	60.00	35.00
128	Aaron L. Ward	125.00	60.00	35.00
129	Lawton Witt	125.00	60.00	35.00
130	Carl Mays	140.00	70.00	42.00
131	Miller Huggins	200.00	100.00	60.00
132	Benj. Paschal	125.00	60.00	35.00
----	New York American League Team Photo	800.00	400.00	240.00

1925 Universal Toy & Novelty Washington Senators (W504)

Printed on thick cardboard and intended to be cut apart into a team photo and 16 individual player cards, this set was originally issued on a 5-1/2" x 13" sheet. Single cut cards measure about 1-3/8" x 2-3/8", with the team picture about 5" x 3-1/2". Cards are blank-back. Player cards are numbered beneath the photo, where the name, team, position and birth year are also printed.

		NM	EX	VG
Complete Sheet:				
Complete Set (17):				
Common Player:		50.00	25.00	15.00
149	Joe Judge	50.00	25.00	15.00
150	Wm. Hargrave	50.00	25.00	15.00
151	R. Peckinpaugh	50.00	25.00	15.00
152	O.L. Bluege	50.00	25.00	15.00
153	M.J. McNally	50.00	25.00	15.00
154	Sam Rice	200.00	100.00	60.00
155				
156				
157				
158				
159	Wm. Hargrave	50.00	25.00	15.00
160				
161				
162	Harold (Herold) Ruel	50.00	25.00	15.00
163				

| 164 | George Mogridge | 50.00 | 25.00 | 15.00 |
| --- | Washington American League Team Photo | 400.00 | 200.00 | 120.00 |

1933 U.S. Caramel (R328)

 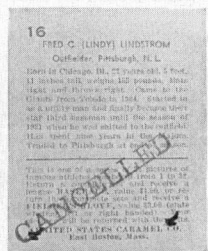

Produced by a Boston confectioner, this set is not limited to baseball, but is a set of 32 "Famous Athletes," of which 27 are baseball players. The 2-1/2" x 3" cards have a black-and-white picture on front with a red background and white border. Backs feature the player's name, position, team and league as well as a redemption ad and card number. The issue was among the last of the caramel card sets. The cards could be redeemed for a baseball and glove and were returned punch-cancelled and stamped. Card #16, short-printed to limit the number of prizes claimed, was first discovered in the late 1980s; only two examples are currently known.

		NM	EX	VG
Common Player:		750.00	370.00	220.00
1	Edward T. (Eddie) Collins	1,200	600.00	350.00
2	Paul (Big Poison) Waner	1,200	600.00	350.00
3	Robert T. (Bobby) Jones (golfer)	8,500	4,200	2,500
4	William (Bill) Terry	1,200	600.00	350.00
5	Earl B. Combs (Earle)	1,200	600.00	350.00
6	William (Bill) Dickey	1,200	600.00	350.00
7	Joseph (Joe) Cronin	1,200	600.00	350.00
8	Charles (Chick) Hafey	1,200	600.00	350.00
9	Gene Sarazen (golfer)	3,500	1,750	1,050
10	Walter (Rabbit) Maranville	1,200	600.00	350.00
11	Rogers (Rajah) Hornsby	3,250	1,600	975.00
12	Gordon (Mickey) Cochrane	1,200	600.00	350.00
13	Lloyd (Little Poison) Waner	1,200	600.00	350.00
14	Tyrus (Ty) Cobb	4,625	2,300	1,400
15	Eugene (Gene) Tunney (boxer)	1,200	600.00	350.00
16	Charles (Lindy) Lindstrom (2 known)			80,000
17	Al. Simmons	1,200	600.00	350.00
18	Anthony (Tony) Lazzeri	1,200	600.00	350.00
19	Walter (Wally) Berger	750.00	370.00	220.00
20	Charles (Large Charlie) Ruffing	1,200	600.00	350.00
21	Charles (Chuck) Klein	1,200	600.00	350.00
22	John (Jack) Dempsey (boxer)	1,850	925.00	555.00
23	James (Jimmy) Foxx	2,200	1,100	660.00
24	Frank J. (Lefty) O'Doul	875.00	440.00	260.00
25	Jack (Sailor Jack) Sharkey (boxer)	1,200	600.00	350.00
26	Henry (Lou) Gehrig	8,225	4,100	2,500
27	Robert (Lefty) Grove	2,050	1,025	615.00
28	Edward Brant (Brandt)	750.00	370.00	220.00
29	George Earnshaw	750.00	370.00	220.00
30	Frank (Frankie) Frisch	1,200	600.00	350.00
31	Vernon (Lefty) Gomez	1,200	600.00	350.00
32	George (Babe) Ruth	10,750	5,375	3,225

1973 U.S. Playing Card Ruth/Gehrig

These decks of playing cards were produced for sale by the Smithsonian Institution in Washington, D.C. The 2-1/4" x 3-1/2" cards were sold as a pair. Backs have colorized pictures of the Yankees greats; Ruth on an orange background and Gehrig on red.

	NM	EX	VG
Complete Set, Ruth (54):	25.00	12.50	7.50
Single Card, Ruth:	1.50	.75	.45
Complete Set, Gehrig (54):	15.00	7.50	4.50
Single Card, Gehrig:	.75	.40	.25

(A 50 percent premium attaches to a complete boxed pair of decks.)

1909-11 Uzit Cigarettes

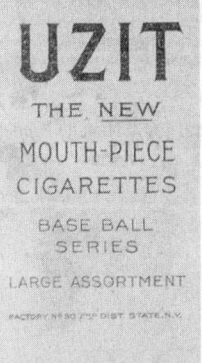

Uzit is generally accepted as the second scarcest back advertiser (after Drum) found on T206. The typographic back is printed in light blue ink.

PREMIUMS
Commons: 35-45X
Hall of Famers: 25-40X
(See T206 for checklist.)

1938-39 Val Decker Packing Co. Cincinnati Reds Postcards

(See 1937-39 Orcajo Cincinnati Reds postcards for checklist and values.)

1950s-70s Van Heusen Advisory Staff Photos

Not a great deal is known about the distribution of these 8" x 10" black-and-white player photos. It is likely the checklist here is not complete. The photos are bordered in white with the player name at bottom. In one of the lower corners is the logo of the clothing manufacturer. This issue is differentiated from the Phillies photos because of the action poses and multi-team composition of the known examples.

		NM	EX	VG
Common Player:		20.00	10.00	6.00
(1)	Ken Berry	20.00	10.00	6.00
(2)	Paul Blair	20.00	10.00	6.00
(3)	Curt Blefary	20.00	10.00	6.00
(4)	Jim Bouton	40.00	20.00	12.00
(5)	Johnny Callison (Phillies, bats on shoulder.)	30.00	15.00	9.00
(6)	Jerry Coleman/Throwing (Yankees)	25.00	12.50	7.50
(7)	Tommy Davis/Btg (Dodgers)	20.00	10.00	6.00
(8)	Dick Hall/Portrait (Phillies)	20.00	10.00	6.00
(9)	Bob Hendley (Braves, follow-through.)	20.00	10.00	6.00
(10)	Chuck Hinton	20.00	10.00	6.00
(11)	Dave Johnson	20.00	10.00	6.00
(12)	Don Lock (Phillies, upper body.)	20.00	10.00	6.00

(13)	Jim Palmer	60.00	30.00	18.00
(14)	Jim Piersall	25.00	12.50	7.50
(15)	Pedro Ramos	20.00	10.00	6.00
(16)	Cookie Rojas (Phillies, bat on shoulder.)	20.00	10.00	6.00
(17)	Bill Skowron (Dodgers, full-length.)	25.00	12.50	7.50
(18)	Tom Thresh	40.00	20.00	12.00
(19)	Billy Williams	60.00	30.00	18.00
(20)	Maury Wills/Btg (Dodgers)	25.00	12.50	7.50

1967 Van Heusen Phillies

Not a great deal is known about the distribution of these 8" x 10" black-and-white player portraits. It is possible the checklist here is not complete. The photos are bordered in white with the player name at bottom. At lower-right is the logo of the clothing manufacturer. This issue is differentiated from the Advisory Staff Photos because of the similitude of the portrait photos of the teammates.

		NM	EX	VG
Common Player:		20.00	10.00	6.00
(1)	Bo Belinsky	20.00	10.00	6.00
(2)	Jim Bunning	35.00	17.50	10.50
(3)	Wes Covington	20.00	10.00	6.00
(4)	Dick Ellsworth	20.00	10.00	6.00
(5)	Dick Groat	20.00	10.00	6.00
(6)	Cookie Rojas	20.00	10.00	6.00
(7)	Chris Short	20.00	10.00	6.00
(8)	Bill White	20.00	10.00	6.00

1912 Vassar Sweaters

Star players of the day are pictured wearing the sponsor's product over their uniforms in this issue of 4" x 6-3/4" black-and-white cards. Player names are in the white border at bottom. It is not known whether this checklist is complete.

		NM	EX	VG
Common Player:		1,900	950.00	600.00
(1)	Ty Cobb	7,500	3,750	2,250
(2)	Sam Crawford	2,600	1,300	800.00
(3)	Walter Johnson	4,200	2,100	1,250
(4)	Napoleon Lajoie	2,600	1,300	800.00
(5)	Smokey Joe Wood	1,900	950.00	600.00

1959 Venezuelan Topps

Beginning in 1959, Topps began marketing baseball cards in Venezuela, always a hotbed of baseball fandom. In most years, such as the debut set in 1959, the cards destined for the South American market represented a parallel of the first couple of series of Topps' regular U.S. issue. Print quality (usually lack of gloss on front) is the major difference between the two issues. Backs of some of the 1959 Venezuelan cards carry the credit line: "Impreso en Venezuela por Benco C.A., while some carry a Topps copyright line." A reality of the Venezuelan cards is that they tend to survive in low-grade condition due to the local custom of gluing cards into albums and scrapbooks. After its 1959 issue, Topps produced Venezuelan cards only in the even-numbered years, except for 1967, until the last of the sets was issued in 1968.

		NM	EX	VG
	Complete Set (196):	15,000	7,500	4,500
	Common Player:	45.00	18.00	11.00
1	Ford Frick	120.00	60.00	35.00
2	Eddie Yost	90.00	45.00	27.00
3	Don McMahon	90.00	45.00	27.00
4	Albie Pearson	90.00	45.00	27.00
5	Dick Donovan	90.00	45.00	27.00
6	Alex Grammas	90.00	45.00	27.00
7	Al Pilarcik	90.00	45.00	27.00
8	Phillies Team	150.00	75.00	45.00
9	Paul Giel	90.00	45.00	27.00
10	Mickey Mantle	4,000	2,000	1,200
11	Billy Hunter	90.00	45.00	27.00
12	Vern Law	90.00	45.00	27.00
13	Dick Gernert	90.00	45.00	27.00
14	Pete Whisenant	90.00	45.00	27.00
15	Dick Drott	90.00	45.00	27.00
16	Joe Pignatano	90.00	45.00	27.00
17	Danny's All-Stars (Ted Kluszewski, Danny Murtaugh, Frank Thomas)	100.00	50.00	30.00
18	Jack Urban	90.00	45.00	27.00
19	Ed Bressoud	90.00	45.00	27.00
20	Duke Snider	600.00	300.00	180.00
21	Connie Johnson	90.00	45.00	27.00
22	Al Smith	90.00	45.00	27.00
23	Murry Dickson	90.00	45.00	27.00
24	Red Wilson	90.00	45.00	27.00
25	Don Hoak	90.00	45.00	27.00
26	Chuck Stobbs	90.00	45.00	27.00
27	Andy Pafko	90.00	45.00	27.00
28	Red Worthington	90.00	45.00	27.00
29	Jim Bolger	90.00	45.00	27.00
30	Nellie Fox	300.00	150.00	90.00
31	Ken Lehman	90.00	45.00	27.00
32	Don Buddin	90.00	45.00	27.00
33	Ed Fitz Gerald	90.00	45.00	27.00
34	Pitchers Beware (Al Kaline, Charlie Maxwell)	225.00	112.50	67.50
35	Ted Kluszewski	150.00	75.00	45.00
36	Hank Aguirre	90.00	45.00	27.00
37	Gene Green	90.00	45.00	27.00
38	Morrie Martin	90.00	45.00	27.00
39	Ed Bouchee	90.00	45.00	27.00
40	Warren Spahn	300.00	150.00	90.00
41	Bob Martyn	90.00	45.00	27.00
42	Murray Wall	90.00	45.00	27.00
43	Steve Bilko	90.00	45.00	27.00
44	Vito Valentinetti	90.00	45.00	27.00
45	Andy Carey	90.00	45.00	27.00
46	Bill Henry	90.00	45.00	27.00
47	Jim Finigan	90.00	45.00	27.00
48	Orioles Team/Checklist 1-88	150.00	75.00	45.00
49	Bill Hall	90.00	45.00	27.00
50	Willie Mays	2,200	1,100	650.00
51	Rip Coleman	90.00	45.00	27.00
52	Coot Veal	90.00	45.00	27.00
53	Stan Williams	90.00	45.00	27.00
54	Mel Roach	90.00	45.00	27.00
55	Tom Brewer	90.00	45.00	27.00
56	Carl Sawatski	90.00	45.00	27.00
57	Al Cicotte	90.00	45.00	27.00
58	Eddie Miksis	90.00	45.00	27.00
59	Irv Noren	90.00	45.00	27.00
60	Bob Turley	90.00	45.00	27.00
61	Dick Brown	90.00	45.00	27.00
62	Tony Taylor	90.00	45.00	27.00
63	Jim Hearn	90.00	45.00	27.00
64	Joe DeMaestri	90.00	45.00	27.00
65	Frank Torre	90.00	45.00	27.00
66	Joe Ginsberg	90.00	45.00	27.00
67	Brooks Lawrence	90.00	45.00	27.00
68	Dick Schofield	90.00	45.00	27.00
69	Giants Team/Checklist 89-176	150.00	75.00	45.00
70	Harvey Kuenn	100.00	50.00	30.00
71	Don Bessent	90.00	45.00	27.00
72	Bill Renna	90.00	45.00	27.00
73	Ron Jackson	90.00	45.00	27.00
74	Directing the Power (Cookie Lavagetto, Jim Lemon, Roy Sievers)	90.00	45.00	27.00
75	Sam Jones	90.00	45.00	27.00
76	Bobby Richardson	100.00	50.00	30.00
77	John Goryl	90.00	45.00	27.00
78	Pedro Ramos	90.00	45.00	27.00
79	Harry Chiti	90.00	45.00	27.00
80	Minnie Minoso	110.00	55.00	32.50
81	Hal Jeffcoat	90.00	45.00	27.00
82	Bob Boyd	90.00	45.00	27.00
83	Bob Smith	90.00	45.00	27.00
84	Reno Bertoia	90.00	45.00	27.00
85	Harry Anderson	90.00	45.00	27.00
86	Bob Keegan	90.00	45.00	27.00
87	Danny O'Connell	90.00	45.00	27.00
88	Herb Score	90.00	45.00	27.00
89	Billy Gardner	90.00	45.00	27.00
90	Bill Skowron	110.00	55.00	32.50
91	Herb Moford	90.00	45.00	27.00
92	Dave Philley	90.00	45.00	27.00
93	Julio Becquer	90.00	45.00	27.00
94	White Sox Team	200.00	100.00	60.00
95	Carl Willey	90.00	45.00	27.00
96	Lou Berberet	90.00	45.00	27.00
97	Jerry Lynch	90.00	45.00	27.00
98	Arnie Portocarrero	90.00	45.00	27.00
99	Ted Kazanski	90.00	45.00	27.00
100	Bob Cerv	90.00	45.00	27.00
101	Alex Kellner	90.00	45.00	27.00
102	Felipe Alou	120.00	60.00	35.00
103	Billy Goodman	90.00	45.00	27.00
104	Del Rice	90.00	45.00	27.00
105	Lee Walls	90.00	45.00	27.00
106	Hal Woodeshick	90.00	45.00	27.00
107	Norm Larker	90.00	45.00	27.00
108	Zack Monroe	90.00	45.00	27.00
109	Bob Schmidt	90.00	45.00	27.00
110	George Witt	90.00	45.00	27.00
111	Redlegs Team/ Checklist 89-176	150.00	75.00	45.00
112	Billy Consolo	90.00	45.00	27.00
113	Taylor Phillips	90.00	45.00	27.00
114	Earl Battey	90.00	45.00	27.00
115	Mickey Vernon	90.00	45.00	27.00
116	Bob Allison	90.00	45.00	27.00
117	John Blanchard	90.00	45.00	27.00
118	John Buzhardt	90.00	45.00	27.00
119	John Callison	90.00	45.00	27.00
120	Chuck Coles	90.00	45.00	27.00
121	Bob Conley	90.00	45.00	27.00
122	Bennie Daniels	90.00	45.00	27.00
123	Don Dillard	90.00	45.00	27.00
124	Dan Dobbek	90.00	45.00	27.00
125	Ron Fairly	90.00	45.00	27.00
126	Eddie Haas	90.00	45.00	27.00
127	Kent Hadley	90.00	45.00	27.00
128	Bob Hartman	90.00	45.00	27.00
129	Frank Herrera	90.00	45.00	27.00
130	Lou Jackson	90.00	45.00	27.00
131	Deron Johnson	100.00	50.00	30.00
132	Don Lee	90.00	45.00	27.00
133	Bob Lillis	90.00	45.00	27.00
134	Jim McDaniel	90.00	45.00	27.00
135	Gene Oliver	90.00	45.00	27.00
136	Jim O'Toole	90.00	45.00	27.00
137	Dick Ricketts	90.00	45.00	27.00
138	John Romano	90.00	45.00	27.00
139	Ed Sadowski	90.00	45.00	27.00
140	Charlie Secrest	90.00	45.00	27.00
141	Joe Shipley	90.00	45.00	27.00
142	Dick Stigman	90.00	45.00	27.00
143	Willie Tasby	90.00	45.00	27.00
144	Jerry Walker	90.00	45.00	27.00
145	Dom Zanni	90.00	45.00	27.00
146	Jerry Zimmerman	90.00	45.00	27.00
147	Cubs' Clubbers (Ernie Banks, Dale Long, Walt Moryn)	275.00	135.00	82.50
148	Mike McCormick	90.00	45.00	27.00
149	Jim Bunning	275.00	135.00	82.50
150	Stan Musial	1,800	900.00	550.00
151	Bob Malkmus	90.00	45.00	27.00
152	Johnny Klippstein	90.00	45.00	27.00
153	Jim Marshall	90.00	45.00	27.00
154	Ray Herbert	90.00	45.00	27.00
155	Enos Slaughter	225.00	112.50	67.50
156	Ace Hurlers (Billy Pierce, Robin Roberts)	130.00	65.00	40.00
157	Felix Mantilla	90.00	45.00	27.00
158	Walt Dropo	90.00	45.00	27.00
159	Bob Shaw	90.00	45.00	27.00
160	Dick Groat	90.00	45.00	27.00
161	Frank Baumann	90.00	45.00	27.00
162	Bobby G. Smith	90.00	45.00	27.00
163	Sandy Koufax	2,800	1,400	840.00
164	Johnny Groth	90.00	45.00	27.00
165	Bill Bruton	90.00	45.00	27.00
166	Destruction Crew (Rocky Colavito, Larry Doby, Minnie Minoso)	350.00	175.00	105.00
167	Duke Maas	90.00	45.00	27.00
168	Carroll Hardy	90.00	45.00	27.00
169	Ted Abernathy	90.00	45.00	27.00
170	Gene Woodling	90.00	45.00	27.00
171	Willard Schmidt	90.00	45.00	27.00
172	A's Team/Checklist 177-242	150.00	75.00	45.00
173	Bill Monbouquette	90.00	45.00	27.00
174	Jim Pendleton	90.00	45.00	27.00
175	Dick Farrell	90.00	45.00	27.00
176	Preston Ward	90.00	45.00	27.00
177	Johnny Briggs	90.00	45.00	27.00
178	Ruben Amaro	90.00	45.00	27.00
179	Don Rudolph	90.00	45.00	27.00
180	Yogi Berra	750.00	370.00	220.00
181	Bob Porterfield	90.00	45.00	27.00
182	Milt Graff	90.00	45.00	27.00
183	Stu Miller	90.00	45.00	27.00
184	Harvey Haddix	90.00	45.00	27.00
185	Jim Busby	90.00	45.00	27.00
186	Mudcat Grant	90.00	45.00	27.00
187	Bubba Phillips	90.00	45.00	27.00
188	Juan Pizarro	90.00	45.00	27.00
189	Neil Chrisley	90.00	45.00	27.00
190	Bill Virdon	90.00	45.00	27.00
191	Russ Kemmerer	90.00	45.00	27.00
192	Charley Beamon	90.00	45.00	27.00
193	Sammy Taylor	90.00	45.00	27.00
194	Jim Brosnan	90.00	45.00	27.00
195	Rip Repulski	90.00	45.00	27.00
196	Billy Moran	90.00	45.00	27.00

1960 Venezuelan Topps

Unlike its 1959 issue, which had a printed-in-Venezuela notice on the backs, Topps' 1960 issue for that South American market is virtually identical, front and back, to the company's U.S. product, though a few cards do not carry the Topps copyright. The Venezuelan cards have less gloss on the front and the black ink on their backs is lighter. The Latin American version is a parallel of the first 198 cards from Topps' set. As usual with Latin American cards, low-grade examples are the norm due to the local collecting custom of pasting cards into albums and scrapbooks.

		NM	EX	VG
	Complete Set (198):	16,000	8,000	4,800
	Common Player:	80.00	40.00	25.00
1	Early Wynn	300.00	35.00	21.00
2	Roman Mejias	80.00	40.00	25.00
3	Joe Adcock	80.00	40.00	25.00
4	Bob Purkey	80.00	40.00	25.00
5	Wally Moon	80.00	40.00	25.00
6	Lou Berberet	80.00	40.00	25.00
7	Master and Mentor (Willie Mays, Bill Rigney)	350.00	175.00	120.00
8	Bud Daley	80.00	40.00	25.00
9	Faye Throneberry	80.00	40.00	25.00
10	Ernie Banks	600.00	300.00	180.00
11	Norm Siebern	80.00	40.00	25.00
12	Milt Pappas	80.00	40.00	25.00
13	Wally Post	80.00	40.00	25.00
14	Jim Grant	80.00	40.00	25.00
15	Pete Runnels	80.00	40.00	25.00
16	Ernie Broglio	80.00	40.00	25.00
17	Johnny Callison	80.00	40.00	25.00
18	Dodgers Team/Checklist 1-88	200.00	100.00	60.00
19	Felix Mantilla	80.00	40.00	25.00
20	Roy Face	80.00	40.00	25.00
21	Dutch Dotterer	80.00	40.00	25.00
22	Rocky Bridges	80.00	40.00	25.00
23	Eddie Fisher	80.00	40.00	25.00
24	Dick Gray	80.00	40.00	25.00
25	Roy Sievers	80.00	40.00	25.00
26	Wayne Terwilliger	80.00	40.00	25.00
27	Dick Drott	80.00	40.00	25.00
28	Brooks Robinson	450.00	225.00	135.00
29	Clem Labine	80.00	40.00	25.00
30	Tito Francona	80.00	40.00	25.00
31	Sammy Esposito	80.00	40.00	25.00
32	Sophomore Stalwarts (Jim O'Toole, Vada Pinson)	80.00	40.00	25.00
33	Tom Morgan	80.00	40.00	25.00
34	Sparky Anderson	225.00	120.00	70.00
35	Whitey Ford	350.00	175.00	120.00
36	Russ Nixon	80.00	40.00	25.00
37	Bill Bruton	80.00	40.00	25.00
38	Jerry Casale	80.00	40.00	25.00
39	Earl Averill	80.00	40.00	25.00
40	Joe Cunningham	80.00	40.00	25.00
41	Barry Latman	80.00	40.00	25.00
42	Hobie Landrith	80.00	40.00	25.00
43	Senators Team/Checklist 1-88	150.00	75.00	50.00
44	Bobby Locke	80.00	40.00	25.00
45	Roy McMillan	80.00	40.00	25.00
46	Jack Fisher	80.00	40.00	25.00
47	Don Zimmer	80.00	40.00	25.00
48	Hal Smith	80.00	40.00	25.00
49	Curt Raydon	80.00	40.00	25.00
50	Al Kaline	350.00	175.00	120.00
51	Jim Coates	80.00	40.00	25.00
52	Dave Philley	80.00	40.00	25.00
53	Jackie Brandt	80.00	40.00	25.00
54	Mike Fornieles	80.00	40.00	25.00
55	Bill Mazeroski	180.00	90.00	50.00
56	Steve Korcheck	80.00	40.00	25.00
57	Win-Savers (Turk Lown, Gerry Staley)	80.00	40.00	25.00
58	Gino Cimoli	80.00	40.00	25.00
59	Juan Pizarro	80.00	40.00	25.00
60	Gus Triandos	80.00	40.00	25.00
61	Eddie Kasko	80.00	40.00	25.00
62	Roger Craig	80.00	40.00	25.00
63	George Strickland	80.00	40.00	25.00
64	Jack Meyer	80.00	40.00	25.00
65	Elston Howard	90.00	45.00	30.00
66	Bob Trowbridge	80.00	40.00	25.00
67	Jose Pagan	80.00	40.00	25.00
68	Dave Hillman	80.00	40.00	25.00
69	Billy Goodman	80.00	40.00	25.00
70	Lou Burdette	80.00	40.00	25.00
71	Marty Keough	80.00	40.00	25.00
72	Tigers Team/Checklist 89-176	150.00	75.00	40.00
73	Bob Gibson	300.00	150.00	90.00
74	Walt Moryn	80.00	40.00	25.00
75	Vic Power	80.00	40.00	25.00
76	Bill Fischer	80.00	40.00	25.00
77	Hank Foiles	80.00	40.00	25.00
78	Bob Grim	80.00	40.00	25.00
79	Walt Dropo	80.00	40.00	25.00
80	Johnny Antonelli	80.00	40.00	25.00
81	Russ Snyder	80.00	40.00	25.00
82	Ruben Gomez	80.00	40.00	25.00
83	Tony Kubek	80.00	40.00	25.00
84	Hal Smith	80.00	40.00	25.00
85	Frank Lary	80.00	40.00	25.00
86	Dick Gernert	80.00	40.00	25.00
87	John Romonosky	80.00	40.00	25.00
88	John Roseboro	80.00	40.00	25.00
89	Hal Brown	80.00	40.00	25.00
90	Bobby Avila	80.00	40.00	25.00
91	Bennie Daniels	80.00	40.00	25.00
92	Whitey Herzog	200.00	100.00	60.00
93	Art Schult	80.00	40.00	25.00
94	Leo Kiely	80.00	40.00	25.00
95	Frank Thomas	80.00	40.00	25.00
96	Ralph Terry	80.00	40.00	25.00
97	Ted Lepcio	80.00	40.00	25.00
98	Gordon Jones	80.00	40.00	25.00
99	Lenny Green	80.00	40.00	25.00
100	Nellie Fox	180.00	90.00	50.00
101	Bob Miller	80.00	40.00	25.00
102	Kent Hadley	80.00	40.00	25.00
103	Dick Farrell	80.00	40.00	25.00
104	Dick Schofield	80.00	40.00	25.00
105	Larry Sherry	80.00	40.00	25.00
106	Billy Gardner	80.00	40.00	25.00
107	Carl Willey	80.00	40.00	25.00
108	Pete Daley	80.00	40.00	25.00
109	Cletis Boyer	80.00	40.00	25.00
110	Cal McLish	80.00	40.00	25.00
111	Vic Wertz	80.00	40.00	25.00

112	Jack Harshman	80.00	40.00	25.00
113	Bob Skinner	80.00	40.00	25.00
114	Ken Aspromonte	80.00	40.00	25.00
115	Fork and Knuckler (Roy Face, Hoyt Wilhelm)	90.00	45.00	25.00
116	Jim Rivera	80.00	40.00	25.00
117	Tom Borland	80.00	40.00	25.00
118	Bob Bruce	80.00	40.00	25.00
119	Chico Cardenas	80.00	40.00	25.00
120	Duke Carmel	80.00	40.00	25.00
121	Camilo Carreon	80.00	40.00	25.00
122	Don Dillard	80.00	40.00	25.00
123	Dan Dobbek	80.00	40.00	25.00
124	Jim Donohue	80.00	40.00	25.00
125	Dick Ellsworth	80.00	40.00	25.00
126	Chuck Estrada	80.00	40.00	25.00
127	Ronnie Hansen	80.00	40.00	25.00
128	Bill Harris	80.00	40.00	25.00
129	Bob Hartman	80.00	40.00	25.00
130	Frank Herrera	80.00	40.00	25.00
131	Ed Hobaugh	80.00	40.00	25.00
132	Frank Howard	100.00	50.00	30.00
133	Manuel Javier	80.00	40.00	25.00
134	Deron Johnson	90.00	45.00	25.00
135	Ken Johnson	80.00	40.00	25.00
136	Jim Kaat	120.00	60.00	40.50
137	Lou Klimchock	80.00	40.00	25.00
138	Art Mahaffey	80.00	40.00	25.00
139	Carl Mathias	80.00	40.00	25.00
140	Julio Navarro	80.00	40.00	25.00
141	Jim Proctor	80.00	40.00	25.00
142	Bill Short	80.00	40.00	25.00
143	Al Spangler	80.00	40.00	25.00
144	Al Stieglitz	80.00	40.00	25.00
145	Jim Umbricht	80.00	40.00	25.00
146	Ted Wieand	80.00	40.00	25.00
147	Bob Will	80.00	40.00	25.00
148	Carl Yastrzemski	3,500	1,750	1,000
149	Bob Nieman	80.00	40.00	25.00
150	Billy Pierce	80.00	40.00	25.00
151	Giants Team/ Checklist 177-264	150.00	75.00	40.00
152	Gail Harris	80.00	40.00	25.00
153	Bobby Thomson	80.00	40.00	25.00
154	Jim Davenport	80.00	40.00	25.00
155	Charlie Neal	80.00	40.00	25.00
156	Art Ceccarelli	80.00	40.00	25.00
157	Rocky Nelson	80.00	40.00	25.00
158	Wes Covington	80.00	40.00	25.00
159	Jim Piersall	90.00	45.00	25.00
160	Rival All-Stars (Ken Boyer, Mickey Mantle)	2,750	1,400	825.00
161	Ray Narleski	80.00	40.00	25.00
162	Sammy Taylor	80.00	40.00	25.00
163	Hector Lopez	80.00	40.00	25.00
164	Reds Team/Checklist 89-176	150.00	75.00	40.00
165	Jack Sanford	80.00	40.00	25.00
166	Chuck Essegian	80.00	40.00	25.00
167	Valmy Thomas	80.00	40.00	25.00
168	Alex Grammas	80.00	40.00	25.00
169	Jake Striker	80.00	40.00	25.00
170	Del Crandall	80.00	40.00	25.00
171	Johnny Groth	80.00	40.00	25.00
172	Willie Kirkland	80.00	40.00	25.00
173	Billy Martin	90.00	45.00	25.00
174	Indians Team/ Checklist 89-176	150.00	75.00	40.00
175	Pedro Ramos	80.00	40.00	25.00
176	Vada Pinson	90.00	45.00	25.00
177	Johnny Kucks	80.00	40.00	25.00
178	Woody Held	80.00	40.00	25.00
179	Rip Coleman	80.00	40.00	25.00
180	Harry Simpson	80.00	40.00	25.00
181	Billy Loes	80.00	40.00	25.00
182	Glen Hobbie	80.00	40.00	25.00
183	Eli Grba	80.00	40.00	25.00
184	Gary Geiger	80.00	40.00	25.00
185	Jim Owens	80.00	40.00	25.00
186	Dave Sisler	80.00	40.00	25.00
187	Jay Hook	80.00	40.00	25.00
188	Dick Williams	80.00	40.00	25.00
189	Don McMahon	80.00	40.00	25.00
190	Gene Woodling	80.00	40.00	25.00
191	Johnny Klippstein	80.00	40.00	25.00
192	Danny O'Connell	80.00	40.00	25.00
193	Dick Hyde	80.00	40.00	25.00
194	Bobby Gene Smith	80.00	40.00	25.00
195	Lindy McDaniel	80.00	40.00	25.00
196	Andy Carey	80.00	40.00	25.00
197	Ron Kline	80.00	40.00	25.00
198	Jerry Lynch	80.00	40.00	25.00

1962 Venezuelan Topps

For the first time in its short history of producing baseball cards for the Venezuelan market, Topps in 1962 reprinted virtually the entire back of each card in Spanish (except the League Leaders cards #51-60). The player personal data, the career summary and even the cartoon are En Espanol; only the stats are in English. There is no Topps credit or copyright line on the backs. Otherwise identical in format to the 1962 Topps North American issue, the Venezuelan set comprises the first 198 cards of the Topps issue, though cards #197 (Daryl Spencer) and 198 (Johnny Keane) have been replaced with two local Major Leaguers. Survivors of this issue tend to be in lower grades due to the common practice of gluing cards into albums or scrapbooks.

		NM	EX	VG
	Complete Set (198):	24,000	12,000	7,200
	Common Player:	90.00	45.00	30.0
1	Roger Maris	2,250	1,100	675.00
2	Jim Brosnan	90.00	45.00	30.0
3	Pete Runnels	90.00	45.00	30.0
4	John DeMerit	90.00	45.00	30.0
5	Sandy Koufax	1,200	600.00	400.00
6	Marv Breeding	90.00	45.00	30.0
7	Frank Thomas	90.00	45.00	30.0
8	Ray Herbert	90.00	45.00	30.0
9	Jim Davenport	90.00	45.00	30.0
10	Roberto Clemente	1,600	800.00	500.00
11	Tom Morgan	90.00	45.00	30.0
12	Harry Craft	90.00	45.00	30.0
13	Dick Howser	90.00	45.00	30.0
14	Bill White	90.00	45.00	30.0
15	Dick Donovan	90.00	45.00	30.0
16	Darrell Johnson	90.00	45.00	30.0
17	Johnny Callison	90.00	45.00	30.0
18	Managers' Dream (Mickey Mantle, Willie Mays)	4,500	2,250	1,200
19	Ray Washburn	90.00	45.00	30.0
20	Rocky Colavito	180.00	90.00	50.00
21	Jim Kaat	90.00	45.00	30.0
22	Checklist 1-88	90.00	45.00	30.0
23	Norm Larker	90.00	45.00	30.0
24	Tigers team	270.00	135.00	80.00
25	Ernie Banks	525.00	250.00	150.00
26	Chris Cannizzaro	90.00	45.00	30.0
27	Chuck Cottier	90.00	45.00	30.0
28	Minnie Minoso	125.00	60.00	40.00
29	Casey Stengel	375.00	200.00	125.00
30	Eddie Mathews	375.00	200.00	125.00
31	Tom Tresh	120.00	60.00	40.00
32	John Roseboro	90.00	45.00	30.00
33	Don Larsen	90.00	45.00	30.00
34	Johnny Temple	90.00	45.00	30.00
35	Don Schwall	90.00	45.00	30.00
36	Don Leppert	90.00	45.00	30.00
37	Tribe Hill Trio (Barry Latman, Jim Piersall, Dick Stigman)	90.00	45.00	30.00
38	Gene Stephens	90.00	45.00	30.00
39	Joe Koppe	90.00	45.00	30.00
40	Orlando Cepeda	200.00	100.00	60.00
41	Cliff Cook	90.00	45.00	30.00
42	Jim King	90.00	45.00	30.00
43	Dodgers team	375.00	200.00	125.00
44	Don Taussig	90.00	45.00	30.00
45	Brooks Robinson	600.00	300.00	180.00
46	Jack Baldschun	90.00	45.00	30.00
47	Bob Will	90.00	45.00	30.00
48	Ralph Terry	90.00	45.00	30.00
49	Hal Jones	90.00	45.00	30.00
50	Stan Musial	750.00	400.00	250.00
51	A.L. Batting Leaders (Norm Cash, Elston Howard, Al Kaline, Jim Piersall)	240.00	120.00	70.00
52	N.L. Batting Leaders (Ken Boyer, Roberto Clemente, Wally Moon, Vada Pinson)	700.00	350.00	200.00
53	A.L. Home Run Leaders (Jim Gentile, Harmon Killebrew, Mickey Mantle, Roger Maris)	1,200	600.00	400.00
54	N.L. Home Run Leaders (Orlando Cepeda, Willie Mays, Frank Robinson)	375.00	200.00	120.00
55	A.L. E.R.A. Leaders (Dick Donovan, Don Mossi, Milt Pappas, Bill Stafford)	90.00	45.00	30.00
56	N.L. E.R.A. Leaders (Mike McCormick, Jim O'Toole, Curt Simmons, Warren Spahn)	100.00	50.00	30.00
57	A.L. Win Leaders (Steve Barber, Jim Bunning, Whitey Ford, Frank Lary)	125.00	60.00	40.00
58	N.L. Win Leaders (Joe Jay, Jim O'Toole, Warren Spahn)	100.00	50.00	30.00
59	A.L. Strikeout Leaders (Jim Bunning, Whitey Ford, Camilo Pascual, Juan Pizzaro)	125.00	60.00	40.00
60	N.L. Strikeout Leaders (Don Drysdale, Sandy Koufax, Jim O'Toole, Stan Williams)	300.00	150.00	90.00
61	Cardinals Team	270.00	135.00	75.00
62	Steve Boros	90.00	45.00	30.00
63	Tony Cloninger	90.00	45.00	30.00
64	Russ Snyder	90.00	45.00	30.00
65	Bobby Richardson	120.00	60.00	40.00
66	Cuno Barragon (Barragan)	90.00	45.00	30.00
67	Harvey Haddix	90.00	45.00	30.00
68	Ken Hunt	90.00	45.00	30.00
69	Phil Ortega	90.00	45.00	30.00
70	Harmon Killebrew	375.00	200.00	120.00
71	Dick LeMay	90.00	45.00	30.00
72	Bob's Pupils (Steve Boros, Bob Scheffing, Jake Wood)	90.00	45.00	30.00
73	Nellie Fox	375.00	200.00	120.00
74	Bob Lillis	90.00	45.00	30.00
75	Milt Pappas	90.00	45.00	30.00
76	Howie Bedell	90.00	45.00	30.00
77	Tony Taylor	90.00	45.00	30.00
78	Gene Green	90.00	45.00	30.00
79	Ed Hobaugh	90.00	45.00	30.00
80	Vada Pinson	100.00	50.00	30.00
81	Jim Pagliaroni	90.00	45.00	30.00

82	Deron Johnson	90.00	45.00	30.00
83	Larry Jackson	90.00	45.00	30.00
84	Lenny Green	90.00	45.00	30.00
85	Gil Hodges	240.00	120.00	70.00
86	Donn Clendenon	90.00	45.00	30.00
87	Mike Roarke	90.00	45.00	30.00
88	Ralph Houk	90.00	45.00	30.00
89	Barney Schultz	90.00	45.00	30.00
90	Jim Piersall	90.00	45.00	30.00
91	J.C. Martin	90.00	45.00	30.00
92	Sam Jones	90.00	45.00	30.00
93	John Blanchard	90.00	45.00	30.00
94	Jay Hook	90.00	45.00	30.00
95	Don Hoak	90.00	45.00	30.00
96	Eli Grba	90.00	45.00	30.00
97	Tito Francona	90.00	45.00	30.00
98	Checklist 89-176	90.00	45.00	30.00
99	Boog Powell	225.00	120.00	70.00
100	Warren Spahn	375.00	180.00	120.00
101	Carroll Hardy	90.00	45.00	30.00
102	Al Schroll	90.00	45.00	30.00
103	Don Blasingame	90.00	45.00	30.00
104	Ted Savage	90.00	45.00	30.00
105	Don Mossi	90.00	45.00	30.00
106	Carl Sawatski	90.00	45.00	30.00
107	Mike McCormick	90.00	45.00	30.00
108	Willie Davis	90.00	45.00	30.00
109	Bob Shaw	90.00	45.00	30.00
110	Bill Skowron	100.00	50.00	30.00
111	Dallas Green	90.00	45.00	30.00
112	Hank Foiles	90.00	45.00	30.00
113	White Sox team	270.00	135.00	80.00
114	Howie Koplitz	90.00	45.00	30.00
115	Bob Skinner	90.00	45.00	30.00
116	Herb Score	90.00	45.00	30.00
117	Gary Geiger	90.00	45.00	30.00
118	Julian Javier	90.00	45.00	30.00
119	Danny Murphy	90.00	45.00	30.00
120	Bob Purkey	90.00	45.00	30.00
121	Billy Hitchcock	90.00	45.00	30.00
122	Norm Bass	90.00	45.00	30.00
123	Mike de la Hoz	90.00	45.00	30.00
124	Bill Pleis	90.00	45.00	30.00
125	Gene Woodling	90.00	45.00	30.00
126	Al Cicotte	90.00	45.00	30.00
127	Pride of the A's (Hank Bauer, Jerry Lumpe, Norm Siebern)	90.00	45.00	30.00
128	Art Fowler	90.00	45.00	30.00
129	Lee Walls	90.00	45.00	30.00
130	Frank Bolling	90.00	45.00	30.00
131	Pete Richert	90.00	45.00	30.00
132	Angels Team	270.00	135.00	80.00
133	Felipe Alou	125.00	65.00	40.00
134	Billy Hoeft	90.00	45.00	30.00
135	Babe as a Boy (Babe Ruth)	500.00	250.00	150.00
136	Babe Joins Yanks (Babe Ruth)	600.00	300.00	180.00
137	Babe and Mgr. Huggins (Babe Ruth)	500.00	250.00	150.00
138	The Famous Slugger (Babe Ruth)	600.00	300.00	180.00
139	Babe Hits 60 (Babe Ruth)	900.00	450.00	300.00
140	Gehrig and Ruth (Babe Ruth)	675.00	350.00	200.00
141	Twilight Years (Babe Ruth)	500.00	250.00	150.00
142	Coaching for the Dodgers (Babe Ruth)	500.00	250.00	150.00
143	Greatest Sports Hero (Babe Ruth)	500.00	250.00	150.00
144	Farewell Speech (Babe Ruth)	500.00	250.00	150.00
145	Barry Latman	90.00	45.00	30.00
146	Don Demeter	90.00	45.00	30.00
147	Bill Kunkel	90.00	45.00	30.00
148	Wally Post	90.00	45.00	30.00
149	Bob Duliba	90.00	45.00	30.00
150	Al Kaline	400.00	200.00	125.00
151	Johnny Klippstein	90.00	45.00	30.00
152	Mickey Vernon	90.00	45.00	30.00
153	Pumpsie Green	90.00	45.00	30.00
154	Lee Thomas	90.00	45.00	30.00
155	Stu Miller	90.00	45.00	30.00
156	Merritt Ranew	90.00	45.00	30.00
157	Wes Covington	90.00	45.00	30.00
158	Braves Team	270.00	135.00	80.00
159	Hal Reniff	90.00	45.00	30.00
160	Dick Stuart	90.00	45.00	30.00
161	Frank Baumann	90.00	45.00	30.00
162	Sammy Drake	90.00	45.00	30.00
163	Hot Corner Guardians (Cletis Boyer, Billy Gardner)	90.00	45.00	30.00
164	Hal Naragon	90.00	45.00	30.00
165	Jackie Brandt	90.00	45.00	30.00
166	Don Lee	90.00	45.00	30.00
167	Tim McCarver	400.00	200.00	125.00
168	Leo Posada	90.00	45.00	30.00
169	Bob Cerv	90.00	45.00	30.00
170	Ron Santo	120.00	60.00	40.00
171	Dave Sisler	90.00	45.00	30.00
172	Fred Hutchinson	90.00	45.00	30.00
173	Chico Fernandez	90.00	45.00	30.00
174	Carl Willey	90.00	45.00	30.00
175	Frank Howard	90.00	45.00	30.00
176	Eddie Yost	90.00	45.00	30.00
177	Bobby Shantz	90.00	45.00	30.00
178	Camilo Carreon	90.00	45.00	30.00
179	Tom Sturdivant	90.00	45.00	30.00
180	Bob Allison	90.00	45.00	30.00
181	Paul Brown	90.00	45.00	30.00
182	Bob Nieman	90.00	45.00	30.00
183	Roger Craig	90.00	45.00	30.00
184	Haywood Sullivan	90.00	45.00	30.00
185	Roland Sheldon	90.00	45.00	30.00
186	Mack Jones	90.00	45.00	30.00
187	Gene Conley	90.00	45.00	30.00
188	Chuck Hiller	90.00	45.00	30.00
189	Dick Hall	90.00	45.00	30.00
190	Wally Moon	90.00	45.00	30.00
191	Jim Brewer	90.00	45.00	30.00
192	Checklist 177-264	90.00	45.00	30.00
193	Eddie Kasko	90.00	45.00	30.00

		NM	EX	VG
194	Dean Chance	90.00	45.00	30.00
195	Joe Cunningham	90.00	45.00	30.00
196	Terry Fox	90.00	45.00	30.00
199	Elio Chacon	180.00	90.00	50.00
200	Luis Aparicio	750.00	375.00	225.00

1964 Venezuelan Topps

The first 370 cards of Topps' baseball set were issued in a parallel version for sale in Venezuela. Printed on thin cardboard with no front gloss, the cards are differentiated from the U.S. version by the use of a black border on back. Survivors of the issue are usually in low grade because of the common Latin American practice of collectors gluing the cards into the album that was made available. Venezuelan Topps cards were often cut up to 1/8" smaller than their U.S. counterparts.

		NM	EX	VG
	Complete Set (370):	20,000	10,000	6,000
	Common Player:	60.00	30.00	20.00
	Album:	600.00	300.00	180.00
1	N.L. E.R.A. Leaders (Dick Ellsworth, Bob Friend, Sandy Koufax)	180.00	90.00	50.00
2	A.L. E.R.A. Leaders (Camilo Pascual, Gary Peters, Juan Pizarro)	60.00	30.00	20.00
3	N.L. Pitching Leaders (Sandy Koufax, Jim Maloney, Juan Marichal, Warren Spahn)	120.00	60.00	40.00
4	A.L. Pitching Leaders (Jim Bouton, Whitey Ford, Camilo Pascual)	90.00	45.00	25.00
5	N.L. Strikeout Leaders (Don Drysdale, Sandy Koufax, Jim Maloney)	120.00	60.00	40.00
6	A.L. Strikeout Leaders (Jim Bunning, Camilo Pascual, Dick Stigman)	70.00	35.00	20.00
7	N.L. Batting Leaders (Hank Aaron, Roberto Clemente, Tommy Davis, Dick Groat)	200.00	100.00	60.00
8	A.L. Batting Leaders (Al Kaline, Rich Rollins, Carl Yastrzemski)	100.00	50.00	30.00
9	N.L. Home Run Leaders (Hank Aaron, Orlando Cepeda, Willie Mays, Willie McCovey)	150.00	75.00	40.00
10	A.L. Home Run Leaders (Bob Allison, Harmon Killebrew, Dick Stuart)	90.00	45.00	25.00
11	N.L. R.B.I. Leaders (Hank Aaron, Ken Boyer, Bill White)	100.00	50.00	30.00
12	A.L. R.B.I. Leaders (Al Kaline, Harmon Killebrew, Dick Stuart)	90.00	45.00	25.00
13	Hoyt Wilhelm	100.00	50.00	30.00
14	Dodgers Rookies (Dick Nen, Nick Willhite)	60.00	30.00	20.00
15	Zoilo Versalles	60.00	30.00	20.00
16	John Boozer	60.00	30.00	20.00
17	Willie Kirkland	60.00	30.00	20.00
18	Billy O'Dell	60.00	30.00	20.00
19	Don Wart	60.00	30.00	20.00
20	Bob Friend	60.00	30.00	20.00
21	Yogi Berra	200.00	100.00	60.00
22	Jerry Adair	60.00	30.00	20.00
23	Chris Zachary	60.00	30.00	20.00
24	Carl Sawatski	60.00	30.00	20.00
25	Bill Monbouquette	60.00	30.00	20.00
26	Gino Cimoli	60.00	30.00	20.00
27	Mets Team	125.00	60.00	40.00
28	Claude Osteen	60.00	30.00	20.00
29	Lou Brock	150.00	75.00	40.00
30	Ron Perranoski	60.00	30.00	20.00
31	Dave Nicholson	60.00	30.00	20.00
32	Dean Chance	60.00	30.00	20.00
33	Reds Rookies (Sammy Ellis, Mel Queen)	60.00	30.00	20.00
34	Jim Perry	60.00	30.00	20.00
35	Eddie Mathews	150.00	75.00	40.00
36	Hal Reniff	60.00	30.00	20.00
37	Smoky Burgess	60.00	30.00	20.00
38	Jim Wynn	60.00	30.00	20.00
39	Hank Aguirre	60.00	30.00	20.00
40	Dick Groat	60.00	30.00	20.00
41	Friendly Foes (Willie McCovey, Leon Wagner)	70.00	35.00	20.00
42	Moe Drabowsky	60.00	30.00	20.00
43	Roy Sievers	60.00	30.00	20.00
44	Duke Carmel	60.00	30.00	20.00
45	Milt Pappas	60.00	30.00	20.00
46	Ed Brinkman	60.00	30.00	20.00
47	Giants Rookies (Jesus Alou, Ron Herbel)	60.00	30.00	20.00
48	Bob Perry	60.00	30.00	20.00
49	Bill Henry	60.00	30.00	20.00
50	Mickey Mantle	3,600	1,800	1,000
51	Pete Richert	60.00	30.00	20.00
52	Chuck Hinton	60.00	30.00	20.00
53	Denis Menke	60.00	30.00	20.00
54	Sam Mele	60.00	30.00	20.00
55	Ernie Banks	150.00	75.00	40.00
56	Hal Brown	60.00	30.00	20.00
57	Tim Harkness	60.00	30.00	20.00
58	Don Demeter	60.00	30.00	20.00
59	Ernie Broglio	60.00	30.00	20.00
60	Frank Malzone	60.00	30.00	20.00
61	Angel Backstops (Bob Rodgers, Ed Sadowski)	60.00	30.00	20.00
62	Ted Savage	60.00	30.00	20.00
63	Johnny Orsino	60.00	30.00	20.00
64	Ted Abernathy	60.00	30.00	20.00
65	Felipe Alou	70.00	35.00	20.00
66	Eddie Fisher	60.00	30.00	20.00
67	Tigers Team	100.00	50.00	30.00
68	Willie Davis	60.00	30.00	20.00
69	Clete Boyer	70.00	35.00	20.00
70	Joe Torre	90.00	45.00	25.00
71	Jack Spring	60.00	30.00	20.00
72	Chico Cardenas	60.00	30.00	20.00
73	Jimmie Hall	60.00	30.00	20.00
74	Pirates Rookies (Tom Butters, Bob Priddy)	60.00	30.00	20.00
75	Wayne Causey	60.00	30.00	20.00
76	Checklist 1-88	60.00	30.00	20.00
77	Jerry Walker	60.00	30.00	20.00
78	Merritt Ranew	60.00	30.00	20.00
79	Bob Heffner	60.00	30.00	20.00
80	Vada Pinson	90.00	45.00	25.00
81	All-Star Vets (Nellie Fox, Harmon Killebrew)	100.00	50.00	30.00
82	Jim Davenport	60.00	30.00	20.00
83	Gus Triandos	60.00	30.00	20.00
84	Carl Willey	60.00	30.00	20.00
85	Pete Ward	60.00	30.00	20.00
86	Al Downing	60.00	30.00	20.00
87	Cardinals Team	200.00	100.00	60.00
88	John Roseboro	60.00	30.00	20.00
89	Boog Powell	70.00	35.00	20.00
90	Earl Battey	60.00	30.00	20.00
91	Bob Bailey	60.00	30.00	20.00
92	Steve Ridzik	60.00	30.00	20.00
93	Gary Geiger	60.00	30.00	20.00
94	Braves Rookies (Jim Britton, Larry Maxie)	60.00	30.00	20.00
95	George Altman	60.00	30.00	20.00
96	Bob Buhl	60.00	30.00	20.00
97	Jim Fregosi	60.00	30.00	20.00
98	Bill Bruton	60.00	30.00	20.00
99	Al Stanek	60.00	30.00	20.00
100	Elston Howard	70.00	35.00	20.00
101	Walt Alston	100.00	50.00	30.00
102	Checklist 89-176	60.00	30.00	20.00
103	Curt Flood	70.00	35.00	20.00
104	Art Mahaffey	60.00	30.00	20.00
105	Woody Held	60.00	30.00	20.00
106	Joe Nuxhall	60.00	30.00	20.00
107	White Sox Rookies (Bruce Howard, Frank Kreutzer)	60.00	30.00	20.00
108	John Wyatt	60.00	30.00	20.00
109	Rusty Staub	70.00	35.00	20.00
110	Albie Pearson	60.00	30.00	20.00
111	Don Elston	60.00	30.00	20.00
112	Bob Tillman	60.00	30.00	20.00
113	Grover Powell	60.00	30.00	20.00
114	Don Lock	60.00	30.00	20.00
115	Frank Bolling	60.00	30.00	20.00
116	Twins Rookies (Tony Oliva, Jay Ward)	90.00	45.00	25.00
117	Earl Francis	60.00	30.00	20.00
118	John Blanchard	60.00	30.00	20.00
119	Gary Kolb	60.00	30.00	20.00
120	Don Drysdale	150.00	75.00	40.00
121	Pete Runnels	60.00	30.00	20.00
122	Don McMahon	60.00	30.00	20.00
123	Jose Pagan	60.00	30.00	20.00
124	Orlando Pena	60.00	30.00	20.00
125	Pete Rose	900.00	450.00	275.00
126	Russ Snyder	60.00	30.00	20.00
127	Angels Rookies (Aubrey Gatewood, Dick Simpson)	60.00	30.00	20.00
128	Mickey Lolich	70.00	35.00	20.00
129	Amado Samuel	60.00	30.00	20.00
130	Gary Peters	60.00	30.00	20.00
131	Steve Boros	60.00	30.00	20.00
132	Braves Team	100.00	50.00	30.00
133	Jim Grant	60.00	30.00	20.00
134	Don Zimmer	60.00	30.00	20.00
135	Johnny Callison	60.00	30.00	20.00
136	World Series Game 1 (Koufax Strikes Out 15)	60.00	30.00	20.00
137	World Series Game 2 (Davis Sparks Rally)	60.00	30.00	20.00
138	World Series Game 3 (L.A. Takes 3rd Straight)	60.00	30.00	20.00
139	World Series Game 4 (Sealing Yanks' Doom)	60.00	30.00	20.00
140	World Series Summary (The Dodgers Celebrate)	60.00	30.00	20.00
141	Danny Murtaugh	60.00	30.00	20.00
142	John Bateman	60.00	30.00	20.00
143	Bubba Phillips	60.00	30.00	20.00
144	Al Worthington	60.00	30.00	20.00
145	Norm Siebern	60.00	30.00	20.00
146	Indians Rookies (Bob Chance, Tommy John)	100.00	50.00	30.00
147	Ray Sadecki	60.00	30.00	20.00
148	J.C. Martin	60.00	30.00	20.00
149	Paul Foytack	60.00	30.00	20.00
150	Willie Mays	750.00	375.00	220.00
151	Athletics Team	100.00	50.00	30.00
152	Denver Lemaster	60.00	30.00	20.00
153	Dick Williams	60.00	30.00	20.00
154	Dick Tracewski	60.00	30.00	20.00
155	Duke Snider	200.00	100.00	60.00
156	Bill Dailey	60.00	30.00	20.00
157	Gene Mauch	60.00	30.00	20.00
158	Ken Johnson	60.00	30.00	20.00
159	Charlie Dees	60.00	30.00	20.00
160	Ken Boyer	70.00	35.00	20.00
161	Dave McNally	60.00	30.00	20.00
162	Hitting Area (Vada Pinson, Dick Sisler)			
163	Donn Clendenon	60.00	30.00	20.00
164	Bud Daley	60.00	30.00	20.00
165	Jerry Lumpe	60.00	30.00	20.00
166	Marty Keough	60.00	30.00	20.00
167	Senators Rookies (Mike Brumley, Lou Piniella)	120.00	60.00	40.00
168	Al Weis	60.00	30.00	20.00
169	Del Crandall	60.00	30.00	20.00
170	Dick Radatz	60.00	30.00	20.00
171	Ty Cline	60.00	30.00	20.00
172	Indians Team	100.00	50.00	30.00
173	Ryne Duren	60.00	30.00	20.00
174	Doc Edwards	60.00	30.00	20.00
175	Billy Williams	100.00	50.00	30.00
176	Tracy Stallard	60.00	30.00	20.00
177	Harmon Killebrew	150.00	75.00	40.00
178	Hank Bauer	60.00	30.00	20.00
179	Carl Warwick	60.00	30.00	20.00
180	Tommy Davis	60.00	30.00	20.00
181	Dave Wickersham	60.00	30.00	20.00
182	Sox Sockers (Chuck Schilling, Carl Yastrzemski)	100.00	50.00	30.00
183	Ron Taylor	60.00	30.00	20.00
184	Al Luplow	60.00	30.00	20.00
185	Jim O'Toole	60.00	30.00	20.00
186	Roman Mejias	60.00	30.00	20.00
187	Ed Roebuck	60.00	30.00	20.00
188	Checklist 177-264	60.00	30.00	20.00
189	Bob Hendley	60.00	30.00	20.00
190	Bobby Richardson	70.00	35.00	20.00
191	Clay Dalrymple	60.00	30.00	20.00
192	Cubs Rookies (John Boccabella, Billy Cowan)	60.00	30.00	20.00
193	Jerry Lynch	60.00	30.00	20.00
194	John Goryl	60.00	30.00	20.00
195	Floyd Robinson	60.00	30.00	20.00
196	Jim Gentile	60.00	30.00	20.00
197	Frank Lary	60.00	30.00	20.00
198	Len Gabrielson	60.00	30.00	20.00
199	Joe Azcue	60.00	30.00	20.00
200	Sandy Koufax	600.00	300.00	180.00
201	Orioles Rookies (Sam Bowens, Wally Bunker)	60.00	30.00	20.00
202	Galen Cisco	60.00	30.00	20.00
203	John Kennedy	60.00	30.00	20.00
204	Matty Alou	60.00	30.00	20.00
205	Nellie Fox	125.00	65.00	40.00
206	Steve Hamilton	60.00	30.00	20.00
207	Fred Hutchinson	60.00	30.00	20.00
208	Wes Covington	60.00	30.00	20.00
209	Bob Allen	60.00	30.00	20.00
210	Carl Yastrzemski	200.00	100.00	60.00
211	Jim Coker	60.00	30.00	20.00
212	Pete Lovrich	60.00	30.00	20.00
213	Angels Team	100.00	50.00	30.00
214	Ken McMullen	60.00	30.00	20.00
215	Ray Herbert	60.00	30.00	20.00
216	Mike de la Hoz	60.00	30.00	20.00
217	Jim King	60.00	30.00	20.00
218	Hank Fischer	60.00	30.00	20.00
219	Young Aces (Jim Bouton, Al Downing)	70.00	35.00	20.00
220	Dick Ellsworth	60.00	30.00	20.00
221	Bob Saverine	60.00	30.00	20.00
222	Bill Pierce	60.00	30.00	20.00
223	George Banks	60.00	30.00	20.00
224	Tommie Sisk	60.00	30.00	20.00
225	Roger Maris	600.00	300.00	180.00
226	Colts Rookies (Gerald Grote, Larry Yellen)	60.00	30.00	20.00
227	Barry Latman	60.00	30.00	20.00
228	Felix Mantilla	60.00	30.00	20.00
229	Charley Lau	60.00	30.00	20.00
230	Brooks Robinson	220.00	110.00	70.00
231	Dick Calmus	60.00	30.00	20.00
232	Al Lopez	100.00	50.00	30.00
233	Hal Smith	60.00	30.00	20.00
234	Gary Bell	60.00	30.00	20.00
235	Ron Hunt	60.00	30.00	20.00
236	Bill Faul	60.00	30.00	20.00
237	Cubs Team	100.00	50.00	30.00
238	Roy McMillan	60.00	30.00	20.00
239	Herm Starrette	60.00	30.00	20.00
240	Bill White	60.00	30.00	20.00
241	Jim Owens	60.00	30.00	20.00
242	Harvey Kuenn	60.00	30.00	20.00
243	Phillies Rookies (Richie Allen, John Herrnstein)	100.00	50.00	30.00
244	Tony LaRussa	70.00	35.00	20.00
245	Dick Stigman	60.00	30.00	20.00
246	Manny Mota	60.00	30.00	20.00
247	Dave DeBusschere	60.00	30.00	20.00
248	Johnny Pesky	60.00	30.00	20.00
249	Doug Camilli	60.00	30.00	20.00
250	Al Kaline	220.00	110.00	70.00
251	Choo Choo Coleman	60.00	30.00	20.00
252	Ken Aspromonte	60.00	30.00	20.00
253	Wally Post	60.00	30.00	20.00
254	Don Hoak	60.00	30.00	20.00
255	Lee Thomas	60.00	30.00	20.00
256	Johnny Weekly	60.00	30.00	20.00
257	Giants Team	100.00	50.00	30.00
258	Garry Roggenburk	60.00	30.00	20.00
259	Harry Bright	60.00	30.00	20.00
260	Frank Robinson	200.00	100.00	60.00
261	Jim Hannan	60.00	30.00	20.00
262	Cardinals Rookies (Harry Fanok, Mike Shannon)	70.00	35.00	20.00
263	Chuck Estrada	60.00	30.00	20.00
264	Jim Landis	60.00	30.00	20.00

265	Jim Bunning	100.00	50.00	30.00
266	Gene Freese	60.00	30.00	20.00
267	Wilbur Wood	60.00	30.00	20.00
268	Bill's Got It	60.00	30.00	20.00
	(Danny Murtaugh, Bill Virdon)			
269	Ellis Burton	60.00	30.00	20.00
270	Rich Rollins	60.00	30.00	20.00
271	Bob Sadowski	60.00	30.00	20.00
272	Jake Wood	60.00	30.00	20.00
273	Mel Nelson	60.00	30.00	20.00
274	Checklist 265-352	60.00	30.00	20.00
275	John Tsitouris	60.00	30.00	20.00
276	Jose Tartabull	60.00	30.00	20.00
277	Ken Retzer	60.00	30.00	20.00
278	Bobby Shantz	60.00	30.00	20.00
279	Joe Koppe	60.00	30.00	20.00
280	Juan Marichal	125.00	65.00	40.00
281	Yankees Rookies	60.00	30.00	20.00
	(Jake Gibbs, Tom Metcalf)			
282	Bob Bruce	60.00	30.00	20.00
283	Tommy McCraw	60.00	30.00	20.00
284	Dick Schofield	60.00	30.00	20.00
285	Robin Roberts	125.00	65.00	40.00
286	Don Landrum	60.00	30.00	20.00
287	Red Sox Rookies	70.00	35.00	20.00
	(Tony Conigliaro, Bill Spanswick)			
288	Al Moran	60.00	30.00	20.00
289	Frank Funk	60.00	30.00	20.00
290	Bob Allison	60.00	30.00	20.00
291	Phil Ortega	60.00	30.00	20.00
292	Mike Roarke	60.00	30.00	20.00
293	Phillies Team	100.00	50.00	30.00
294	Ken Hunt	60.00	30.00	20.00
295	Roger Craig	60.00	30.00	20.00
296	Ed Kirkpatrick	60.00	30.00	20.00
297	Ken MacKenzie	60.00	30.00	20.00
298	Harry Craft	60.00	30.00	20.00
299	Bill Stafford	60.00	30.00	20.00
300	Hank Aaron	750.00	375.00	220.00
301	Larry Brown	60.00	30.00	20.00
302	Dan Pfister	60.00	30.00	20.00
303	Jim Campbell	60.00	30.00	20.00
304	Bob Johnson	60.00	30.00	20.00
305	Jack Lamabe	60.00	30.00	20.00
306	Giant Gunners (Orlando Cepeda, Willie Mays)	100.00	50.00	30.00
307	Joe Gibbon	60.00	30.00	20.00
308	Gene Stephens	60.00	30.00	20.00
309	Paul Toth	60.00	30.00	20.00
310	Jim Gilliam	60.00	30.00	20.00
311	Tom Brown	60.00	30.00	20.00
312	Tigers Rookies	60.00	30.00	20.00
	(Fritz Fisher, Fred Gladding)			
313	Chuck Hiller	60.00	30.00	20.00
314	Jerry Buchek	60.00	30.00	20.00
315	Bo Belinsky	60.00	30.00	20.00
316	Gene Oliver	60.00	30.00	20.00
317	Al Smith	60.00	30.00	20.00
318	Twins Team	100.00	50.00	30.00
319	Paul Brown	60.00	30.00	20.00
320	Rocky Colavito	100.00	50.00	30.00
321	Bob Lillis	60.00	30.00	20.00
322	George Brunet	60.00	30.00	20.00
323	John Buzhardt	60.00	30.00	20.00
324	Casey Stengel	100.00	50.00	30.00
325	Hector Lopez	60.00	30.00	20.00
326	Ron Brand	60.00	30.00	20.00
327	Don Blasingame	60.00	30.00	20.00
328	Bob Shaw	60.00	30.00	20.00
329	Russ Nixon	60.00	30.00	20.00
330	Tommy Harper	60.00	30.00	20.00
331	A.L. Bombers	1,200	600.00	400.00
	(Norm Cash, Al Kaline, Mickey Mantle, Roger Maris)			
332	Ray Washburn	60.00	30.00	20.00
333	Billy Moran	60.00	30.00	20.00
334	Lew Krausse	60.00	30.00	20.00
335	Don Mossi	60.00	30.00	20.00
336	Andre Rodgers	60.00	30.00	20.00
337	Dodgers Rookies	60.00	30.00	20.00
	(Al Ferrara, Jeff Torborg)			
338	Jack Kralick	60.00	30.00	20.00
339	Walt Bond	60.00	30.00	20.00
340	Joe Cunningham	60.00	30.00	20.00
341	Jim Roland	60.00	30.00	20.00
342	Willie Stargell	130.00	65.00	40.00
343	Senators Team	100.00	50.00	30.00
344	Phil Linz	60.00	30.00	20.00
345	Frank Thomas	60.00	30.00	20.00
346	Joe Jay	60.00	30.00	20.00
347	Bobby Wine	60.00	30.00	20.00
348	Ed Lopat	60.00	30.00	20.00
349	Art Fowler	60.00	30.00	20.00
350	Willie McCovey	150.00	75.00	40.00
351	Dan Schneider	60.00	30.00	20.00
352	Eddie Bressoud	60.00	30.00	20.00
353	Wally Moon	60.00	30.00	20.00
354	Dave Giusti	60.00	30.00	20.00
355	Vic Power	60.00	30.00	20.00
356	Reds Rookies	60.00	30.00	20.00
	(Bill McCool, Chico Ruiz)			
357	Charley James	60.00	30.00	20.00
358	Ron Kline	60.00	30.00	20.00
359	Jim Schaffer	60.00	30.00	20.00
360	Joe Pepitone	60.00	30.00	20.00
361	Jay Hook	60.00	30.00	20.00
362	Checklist 353-429	60.00	30.00	20.00
363	Dick McAuliffe	60.00	30.00	20.00
364	Joe Gaines	60.00	30.00	20.00
365	Cal McLish	60.00	30.00	20.00
366	Nelson Mathews	60.00	30.00	20.00
367	Fred Whitfield	60.00	30.00	20.00
368	White Sox Rookies	60.00	30.00	20.00
	(Fritz Ackley, Don Buford)			
369	Jerry Zimmerman	60.00	30.00	20.00
370	Hal Woodeshick	60.00	30.00	20.00

1966 Venezuelan Topps

The first 370 cards on Topps' 1966 baseball set were reprinted for sale in the Venezuelan market. Identical in design to the Topps cards, they have no Spanish on them. The South American version is printed on darker cardboard that has virtually no gloss on front and bright orange-pink highlights on back. Low-grade cards are the norm for this and other Venezuelan issues as it is common collector practice south of the border to mount cards in scrapbooks and albums. The Venezuelan cards are often found up to 1/8" smaller than their U.S. counterparts.

		NM	EX	VG
	Complete Set (370):	12,000	6,000	4,000
	Common Player:	45.00	25.00	15.00
1	Willie Mays	600.00	300.00	180.00
2	Ted Abernathy	45.00	25.00	15.00
3	Sam Mele	45.00	25.00	15.00
4	Ray Culp	45.00	25.00	15.00
5	Jim Fregosi	45.00	25.00	15.00
6	Chuck Schilling	45.00	25.00	15.00
7	Tracy Stallard	45.00	25.00	15.00
8	Floyd Robinson	45.00	25.00	15.00
9	Clete Boyer	45.00	25.00	15.00
10	Tony Cloninger	45.00	25.00	15.00
11	Senators Rookies	45.00	25.00	15.00
	(Brant Alyea, Pete Craig)			
12	John Tsitouris	45.00	25.00	15.00
13	Lou Johnson	45.00	25.00	15.00
14	Norm Siebern	45.00	25.00	15.00
15	Vern Law	45.00	25.00	15.00
16	Larry Brown	45.00	25.00	15.00
17	Johnny Stephenson	45.00	25.00	15.00
18	Roland Sheldon	45.00	25.00	15.00
19	Giants Team	120.00	60.00	40.00
20	Willie Horton	45.00	25.00	15.00
21	Don Nottebart	45.00	25.00	15.00
22	Joe Nossek	45.00	25.00	15.00
23	Jack Sanford	45.00	25.00	15.00
24	Don Kessinger	45.00	25.00	15.00
25	Pete Ward	45.00	25.00	15.00
26	Ray Sadecki	45.00	25.00	15.00
27	Orioles Rookies (Andy Etchebarren, Darold Knowles)	45.00	25.00	15.00
28	Phil Niekro	150.00	75.00	40.00
29	Mike Brumley	45.00	25.00	15.00
30	Pete Rose	560.00	280.00	160.00
31	Jack Cullen	45.00	25.00	15.00
32	Adolfo Phillips	45.00	25.00	15.00
33	Jim Pagliaroni	45.00	25.00	15.00
34	Checklist 1-88	45.00	25.00	15.00
35	Ron Swoboda	45.00	25.00	15.00
36	Catfish Hunter	150.00	75.00	40.00
37	Billy Herman	135.00	70.00	40.00
38	Ron Nischwitz	45.00	25.00	15.00
39	Ken Henderson	45.00	25.00	15.00
40	Jim Grant	45.00	25.00	15.00
41	Don LeJohn	45.00	25.00	15.00
42	Aubrey Gatewood	45.00	25.00	15.00
43	Don Landrum	45.00	25.00	15.00
44	Indians Rookies (Bill Davis, Tom Kelley)	45.00	25.00	15.00
45	Jim Gentile	45.00	25.00	15.00
46	Howie Koplitz	45.00	25.00	15.00
47	J.C. Martin	45.00	25.00	15.00
48	Paul Blair	45.00	25.00	15.00
49	Woody Woodward	45.00	25.00	15.00
50	Mickey Mantle	2,250	1,100	600.00
51	Gordon Richardson	45.00	25.00	15.00
52	Power Plus (Johnny Callison, Wes Covington)	45.00	25.00	15.00
53	Bob Duliba	45.00	25.00	15.00
54	Jose Pagan	45.00	25.00	15.00
55	Ken Harrelson	45.00	25.00	15.00
56	Sandy Valdespino	45.00	25.00	15.00
57	Jim Lefebvre	45.00	25.00	15.00
58	Dave Wickersham	45.00	25.00	15.00
59	Reds Team	120.00	60.00	40.00
60	Curt Flood	50.00	25.00	15.00
61	Bob Bolin	45.00	25.00	15.00
62	Merritt Ranew	45.00	25.00	15.00
63	Jim Stewart	45.00	25.00	15.00
64	Bob Bruce	45.00	25.00	15.00
65	Leon Wagner	45.00	25.00	15.00
66	Al Weis	45.00	25.00	15.00
67	Mets Rookies (Cleon Jones, Dick Selma)	50.00	25.00	15.00
68	Hal Reniff	45.00	25.00	15.00
69	Ken Hamlin	45.00	25.00	15.00
70	Carl Yastrzemski	225.00	120.00	75.00
71	Frank Carpin	45.00	25.00	15.00
72	Tony Perez	225.00	120.00	75.00
73	Jerry Zimmerman	45.00	25.00	15.00
74	Don Mossi	45.00	25.00	15.00
75	Tommy Davis	45.00	25.00	15.00
76	Red Schoendienst	135.00	65.00	40.00

77	Johnny Orsino	45.00	25.00	15.00
78	Frank Linzy	45.00	25.00	15.00
79	Joe Pepitone	45.00	25.00	15.00
80	Richie Allen	70.00	35.00	20.00
81	Ray Oyler	45.00	25.00	15.00
82	Bob Hendley	45.00	25.00	15.00
83	Albie Pearson	45.00	25.00	15.00
84	Braves Rookies (Jim Beauchamp, Dick Kelley)	45.00	25.00	15.00
85	Eddie Fisher	45.00	25.00	15.00
86	John Bateman	45.00	25.00	15.00
87	Dan Napoleon	45.00	25.00	15.00
88	Fred Whitfield	45.00	25.00	15.00
89	Ted Davidson	45.00	25.00	15.00
90	Luis Aparicio	375.00	190.00	120.00
91	Bob Uecker	70.00	35.00	20.00
92	Yankees Team	185.00	90.00	50.00
93	Jim Lonborg	45.00	25.00	15.00
94	Matty Alou	45.00	25.00	15.00
95	Pete Richert	45.00	25.00	15.00
96	Felipe Alou	70.00	35.00	20.00
97	Jim Merritt	45.00	25.00	15.00
98	Don Demeter	45.00	25.00	15.00
99	Buc Belters (Donn Clendenon, Willie Stargell)	90.00	45.00	25.00
100	Sandy Koufax	450.00	225.00	150.00
101	Checklist 89-176	45.00	25.00	15.00
102	Ed Kirkpatrick	45.00	25.00	15.00
103	Dick Groat	45.00	25.00	15.00
104	Alex Johnson	45.00	25.00	15.00
105	Milt Pappas	45.00	25.00	15.00
106	Rusty Staub	50.00	25.00	15.00
107	Athletics Rookies (Larry Stahl, Ron Tompkins)	45.00	25.00	15.00
108	Bobby Klaus	45.00	25.00	15.00
109	Ralph Terry	45.00	25.00	15.00
110	Ernie Banks	300.00	150.00	90.00
111	Gary Peters	45.00	25.00	15.00
112	Manny Mota	45.00	25.00	15.00
113	Hank Aguirre	45.00	25.00	15.00
114	Jim Gosger	45.00	25.00	15.00
115	Bill Henry	45.00	25.00	15.00
116	Walt Alston	135.00	70.00	40.00
117	Jake Gibbs	45.00	25.00	15.00
118	Mike McCormick	45.00	25.00	15.00
119	Art Shamsky	45.00	25.00	15.00
120	Harmon Killebrew	225.00	120.00	70.00
121	Ray Herbert	45.00	25.00	15.00
122	Joe Gaines	45.00	25.00	15.00
123	Pirates Rookies (Frank Bork, Jerry May)	45.00	25.00	15.00
124	Tug McGraw	45.00	25.00	15.00
125	Lou Brock	185.00	90.00	50.00
126	Jim Palmer	300.00	150.00	90.00
127	Ken Berry	45.00	25.00	15.00
128	Jim Landis	45.00	25.00	15.00
129	Jack Kralick	45.00	25.00	15.00
130	Joe Torre	70.00	35.00	20.00
131	Angels Team	120.00	60.00	40.00
132	Orlando Cepeda	150.00	75.00	40.00
133	Don McMahon	45.00	25.00	15.00
134	Wes Parker	45.00	25.00	15.00
135	Dave Morehead	45.00	25.00	15.00
136	Woody Held	45.00	25.00	15.00
137	Pat Corrales	45.00	25.00	15.00
138	Roger Repoz	45.00	25.00	15.00
139	Cubs Rookies (Byron Browne, Don Young)	45.00	25.00	15.00
140	Jim Maloney	45.00	25.00	15.00
141	Tom McCraw	45.00	25.00	15.00
142	Don Dennis	45.00	25.00	15.00
143	Jose Tartabull	45.00	25.00	15.00
144	Don Schwall	45.00	25.00	15.00
145	Bill Freehan	45.00	25.00	15.00
146	George Altman	45.00	25.00	15.00
147	Lum Harris	45.00	25.00	15.00
148	Bob Johnson	45.00	25.00	15.00
149	Dick Nen	45.00	25.00	15.00
150	Rocky Colavito	120.00	60.00	40.00
151	Gary Wagner	45.00	25.00	15.00
152	Frank Malzone	45.00	25.00	15.00
153	Rico Carty	45.00	25.00	15.00
154	Chuck Hiller	45.00	25.00	15.00
155	Marcelino Lopez	45.00	25.00	15.00
156	D P Combo (Hal Lanier, Dick Schofield)	45.00	25.00	15.00
157	Rene Lachemann	45.00	25.00	15.00
158	Jim Brewer	45.00	25.00	15.00
159	Chico Ruiz	45.00	25.00	15.00
160	Whitey Ford	225.00	120.00	70.00
161	Jerry Lumpe	45.00	25.00	15.00
162	Lee Maye	45.00	25.00	15.00
163	Tito Francona	45.00	25.00	15.00
164	White Sox Rookies (Tommie Agee, Marv Staehle)	45.00	25.00	15.00
165	Don Lock	45.00	25.00	15.00
166	Chris Krug	45.00	25.00	15.00
167	Boog Powell	70.00	35.00	20.00
168	Dan Osinski	45.00	25.00	15.00
169	Duke Sims	45.00	25.00	15.00
170	Cookie Rojas	45.00	25.00	15.00
171	Nick Willhite	45.00	25.00	15.00
172	Mets Team	225.00	120.00	70.00
173	Al Spangler	45.00	25.00	15.00
174	Ron Taylor	45.00	25.00	15.00
175	Bert Campaneris	70.00	35.00	20.00
176	Jim Davenport	45.00	25.00	15.00
177	Hector Lopez	45.00	25.00	15.00
178	Bob Tillman	45.00	25.00	15.00
179	Cardinals Rookies (Dennis Aust, Bob Tolan)	45.00	25.00	15.00
180	Vada Pinson	50.00	25.00	15.00
181	Al Worthington	45.00	25.00	15.00
182	Jerry Lynch	45.00	25.00	15.00
183	Checklist 177-264	45.00	25.00	15.00
184	Denis Menke	45.00	25.00	15.00
185	Bob Buhl	45.00	25.00	15.00
186	Ruben Amaro	45.00	25.00	15.00

187	Chuck Dressen	45.00	25.00	15.00
188	Al Luplow	45.00	25.00	15.00
189	John Roseboro	45.00	25.00	15.00
190	Jimmie Hall	45.00	25.00	15.00
191	Darrell Sutherland	45.00	25.00	15.00
192	Vic Power	45.00	25.00	15.00
193	Dave McNally	45.00	25.00	15.00
194	Senators Team	120.00	60.00	40.00
195	Joe Morgan	185.00	90.00	50.00
196	Don Pavletich	45.00	25.00	15.00
197	Sonny Siebert	45.00	25.00	15.00
198	Mickey Stanley	45.00	25.00	15.00
199	Chisox Clubbers	45.00	25.00	15.00
	(Floyd Robinson, Johnny Romano, Bill Skowron)			
200	Eddie Mathews	185.00	90.00	50.00
201	Jim Dickson	45.00	25.00	15.00
202	Clay Dalrymple	45.00	25.00	15.00
203	Jose Santiago	45.00	25.00	15.00
204	Cubs Team	135.00	70.00	40.00
205	Tom Tresh	45.00	25.00	15.00
206	Alvin Jackson	45.00	25.00	15.00
207	Frank Quilici	45.00	25.00	15.00
208	Bob Miller	45.00	25.00	15.00
209	Tigers Rookies	45.00	25.00	15.00
	(Fritz Fisher, John Hiller)			
210	Bill Mazeroski	120.00	60.00	40.00
211	Frank Kreutzer	45.00	25.00	15.00
212	Ed Kranepool	45.00	25.00	15.00
213	Fred Newman	45.00	25.00	15.00
214	Tommy Harper	45.00	25.00	15.00
215	N.L. Batting Leaders	450.00	225.00	150.00
	(Hank Aaron, Roberto Clemente, Willie Mays)			
216	A.L. Batting Leaders	225.00	120.00	70.00
	(Vic Davalillo, Tony Oliva, Carl Yastrzemski)			
217	N.L. Home Run Leaders	225.00	120.00	70.00
	(Willie Mays, Willie McCovey, Billy Williams)			
218	A.L. Home Run Leaders	90.00	45.00	25.00
	(Norm Cash, Tony Conigliaro, Willie Horton)			
219	N.L. RBI Leaders (Deron Johnson, Willie Mays, Frank Robinson)	135.00	70.00	40.00
220	A.L. RBI Leaders (Rocky Colavito, Willie Horton, Tony Oliva)	90.00	45.00	25.00
221	N.L. ERA Leaders (Sandy Koufax, Vern Law, Juan Marichal)	135.00	70.00	40.00
222	A.L. ERA Leaders (Eddie Fisher, Sam McDowell, Sonny Siebert)	50.00	25.00	15.00
223	N.L. Pitching Leaders (Tony Cloninger, Don Drysdale, Sandy Koufax)	135.00	70.00	40.00
224	A.L. Pitching Leaders (Jim Grant, Jim Kaat, Mel Stottlemyre)	45.00	25.00	15.00
225	N.L. Strikeout Leaders (Bob Gibson, Sandy Koufax, Bob Veale)	135.00	70.00	40.00
226	A.L. Strikeout Leaders (Mickey Lolich, Sam McDowell, Denny McLain, Sonny Siebert)	70.00	35.00	20.00
227	Russ Nixon	45.00	25.00	15.00
228	Larry Dierker	45.00	25.00	15.00
229	Hank Bauer	45.00	25.00	15.00
230	Johnny Callison	45.00	25.00	15.00
231	Floyd Weaver	45.00	25.00	15.00
232	Glenn Beckert	45.00	25.00	15.00
233	Dom Zanni	45.00	25.00	15.00
234	Yankees Rookies	50.00	25.00	15.00
	(Rich Beck, Roy White)			
235	Don Cardwell	45.00	25.00	15.00
236	Mike Hershberger	45.00	25.00	15.00
237	Billy O'Dell	45.00	25.00	15.00
238	Dodgers Team	150.00	75.00	40.00
239	Orlando Pena	45.00	25.00	15.00
240	Earl Battey	45.00	25.00	15.00
241	Dennis Ribant	45.00	25.00	15.00
242	Jesus Alou	45.00	25.00	15.00
243	Nelson Briles	45.00	25.00	15.00
244	Astros Rookies (Chuck Harrison, Sonny Jackson)	45.00	25.00	15.00
245	John Buzhardt	45.00	25.00	15.00
246	Ed Bailey	45.00	25.00	15.00
247	Carl Warwick	45.00	25.00	15.00
248	Pete Mikkelsen	45.00	25.00	15.00
249	Bill Rigney	45.00	25.00	15.00
250	Sam Ellis	45.00	25.00	15.00
251	Ed Brinkman	45.00	25.00	15.00
252	Denver Lemaster	45.00	25.00	15.00
253	Don Wert	45.00	25.00	15.00
254	Phillies Rookies (Fergie Jenkins, Bill Sorrell)	150.00	75.00	40.00
255	Willie Stargell	185.00	90.00	50.00
256	Lew Krausse	45.00	25.00	15.00
257	Jeff Torborg	45.00	25.00	15.00
258	Dave Giusti	45.00	25.00	15.00
259	Red Sox Team	120.00	60.00	40.00
260	Bob Shaw	45.00	25.00	15.00
261	Ron Hansen	45.00	25.00	15.00
262	Jack Hamilton	45.00	25.00	15.00
263	Tom Egan	45.00	25.00	15.00
264	Twins Rookies (Andy Kosco, Ted Uhlaender)	45.00	25.00	15.00
265	Stu Miller	45.00	25.00	15.00
266	Pedro Gonzalez	45.00	25.00	15.00
267	Joe Sparma	45.00	25.00	15.00
268	John Blanchard	45.00	25.00	15.00
269	Don Heffner	45.00	25.00	15.00
270	Claude Osteen	45.00	25.00	15.00

271	Hal Lanier	45.00	25.00	15.00
272	Jack Baldschun	45.00	25.00	15.00
273	Astro Aces (Bob Aspromonte, Rusty Staub)	45.00	25.00	15.00
274	Buster Narum	45.00	25.00	15.00
275	Tim McCarver	50.00	25.00	15.00
276	Jim Bouton	50.00	25.00	15.00
277	George Thomas	45.00	25.00	15.00
278	Calvin Koonce	45.00	25.00	15.00
279	Checklist 265-352	45.00	25.00	15.00
280	Bobby Knoop	45.00	25.00	15.00
281	Bruce Howard	45.00	25.00	15.00
282	Johnny Lewis	45.00	25.00	15.00
283	Jim Perry	45.00	25.00	15.00
284	Bobby Wine	45.00	25.00	15.00
285	Luis Tiant	70.00	35.00	20.00
286	Gary Geiger	45.00	25.00	15.00
287	Jack Aker	45.00	25.00	15.00
288	Dodgers Rookies	185.00	90.00	50.00
	(Bill Singer, Don Sutton)			
289	Larry Sherry	45.00	25.00	15.00
290	Ron Santo	70.00	35.00	20.00
291	Moe Drabowsky	45.00	25.00	15.00
292	Jim Coker	45.00	25.00	15.00
293	Mike Shannon	45.00	25.00	15.00
294	Steve Ridzik	45.00	25.00	15.00
295	Jim Hart	45.00	25.00	15.00
296	Johnny Keane	45.00	25.00	15.00
297	Jim Owens	45.00	25.00	15.00
298	Rico Petrocelli	45.00	25.00	15.00
299	Lou Burdette	45.00	25.00	15.00
300	Roberto Clemente	1,000	500.00	300.00
301	Greg Bollo	45.00	25.00	15.00
302	Ernie Bowman	45.00	25.00	15.00
303	Indians Team	120.00	60.00	40.00
304	John Herrnstein	45.00	25.00	15.00
305	Camilo Pascual	45.00	25.00	15.00
306	Ty Cline	45.00	25.00	15.00
307	Clay Carroll	45.00	25.00	15.00
308	Tom Haller	45.00	25.00	15.00
309	Diego Segui	45.00	25.00	15.00
310	Frank Robinson	185.00	90.00	50.00
311	Reds Rookies (Tommy Helms, Dick Simpson)	45.00	25.00	15.00
312	Bob Saverine	45.00	25.00	15.00
313	Chris Zachary	45.00	25.00	15.00
314	Hector Valle	45.00	25.00	15.00
315	Norm Cash	45.00	25.00	15.00
316	Jack Fisher	45.00	25.00	15.00
317	Dalton Jones	45.00	25.00	15.00
318	Harry Walker	45.00	25.00	15.00
319	Gene Freese	45.00	25.00	15.00
320	Bob Gibson	185.00	90.00	50.00
321	Rick Reichardt	45.00	25.00	15.00
322	Bill Faul	45.00	25.00	15.00
323	Ray Barker	45.00	25.00	15.00
324	John Boozer	45.00	25.00	15.00
325	Vic Davalillo	150.00	75.00	40.00
326	Braves Team	120.00	60.00	40.00
327	Bernie Allen	45.00	25.00	15.00
328	Jerry Grote	45.00	25.00	15.00
329	Pete Charton	45.00	25.00	15.00
330	Ron Fairly	45.00	25.00	15.00
331	Ron Herbel	45.00	25.00	15.00
332	Billy Bryan	45.00	25.00	15.00
333	Senators Rookies	45.00	25.00	15.00
	(Joe Coleman, Jim French)			
334	Marty Keough	45.00	25.00	15.00
335	Juan Pizarro	45.00	25.00	15.00
336	Gene Alley	45.00	25.00	15.00
337	Fred Gladding	45.00	25.00	15.00
338	Dal Maxvill	45.00	25.00	15.00
339	Del Crandall	45.00	25.00	15.00
340	Dean Chance	45.00	25.00	15.00
341	Wes Westrum	45.00	25.00	15.00
342	Bob Humphreys	45.00	25.00	15.00
343	Joe Christopher	45.00	25.00	15.00
344	Steve Blass	45.00	25.00	15.00
345	Bob Allison	45.00	25.00	15.00
346	Mike de la Hoz	45.00	25.00	15.00
347	Phil Regan	45.00	25.00	15.00
348	Orioles Team	185.00	90.00	45.00
349	Cap Peterson	45.00	25.00	15.00
350	Mel Stottlemyre	45.00	25.00	15.00
351	Fred Valentine	45.00	25.00	15.00
352	Bob Aspromonte	45.00	25.00	15.00
353	Al McBean	45.00	25.00	15.00
354	Smoky Burgess	45.00	25.00	15.00
355	Wade Blasingame	45.00	25.00	15.00
356	Red Sox Rookies (Owen Johnson, Ken Sanders)	45.00	25.00	15.00
357	Gerry Arrigo	45.00	25.00	15.00
358	Charlie Smith	45.00	25.00	15.00
359	Johnny Briggs	45.00	25.00	15.00
360	Ron Hunt	45.00	25.00	15.00
361	Tom Satriano	45.00	25.00	15.00
362	Gates Brown	45.00	25.00	15.00
363	Checklist 353-429	45.00	25.00	15.00
364	Nate Oliver	45.00	25.00	15.00
365	Roger Maris	300.00	150.00	90.00
366	Wayne Causey	45.00	25.00	15.00
367	Mel Nelson	45.00	25.00	15.00
368	Charlie Lau	45.00	25.00	15.00
369	Jim King	45.00	25.00	15.00
370	Chico Cardenas	45.00	25.00	15.00

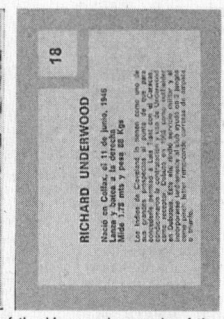

career summary. Like most of the Venezuelan cards of the era, these are crudely printed on cheap cardboard. Also like most Venezuelan cards, they are virtually impossible to find in any condition above Ex. Many are found with back damage due to having been glued into an album or scrapbook.

		NM	EX	VG
	Complete Set (138):	3,500	1,750	1,000
	Common Player:	20.00	10.00	6.00
1	Regino Otero	40.00	20.00	12.00
2	Alejandro Carrasquel	20.00	10.00	6.00
3	Pompeyo Davilillo	25.00	12.50	7.50
4	Gonzalo Marquez	20.00	10.00	6.00
5	Octavio (Cookie) Rojas	35.00	17.50	10.50
6	Teodoro Obregon	20.00	10.00	6.00
7	Paul Schaal	25.00	12.50	7.50
8	Juan Francia	20.00	10.00	6.00
9	Luis Tiant	60.00	30.00	18.00
10	Jose Tartabull	30.00	15.00	9.00
11	Vic Davalillo	25.00	12.50	7.50
12	Cesar Tovar	25.00	12.50	7.50
13	Ron Klimkowski	20.00	10.00	6.00
14	Diego Segui	35.00	17.50	10.50
15	Luis Penalver	20.00	10.00	6.00
16	Urbano Lugo	20.00	10.00	6.00
17	Aurelio Monteagudo	20.00	10.00	6.00
18	Richard Underwood	25.00	12.50	7.50
19	Nelson Castellanos	20.00	10.00	6.00
20	Manuel Mendible	20.00	10.00	6.00
21	Fidel Garcia	40.00	20.00	12.00
22	Luis Cordoba	20.00	10.00	6.00
23	Jesus Padron	20.00	10.00	6.00
24	Lorenzo Fernandez	20.00	10.00	6.00
25	Leopoldo Tovar	20.00	10.00	6.00
26	Carlos Loreto	20.00	10.00	6.00
27	Oswaldo Blanco	20.00	10.00	6.00
28	Sid (Syd) O'Brien	20.00	10.00	6.00
29	Cesar Gutierrez	20.00	10.00	6.00
30	Luis Garcia	20.00	10.00	6.00
31	Fred Klages	20.00	10.00	6.00
32	Isaias Chavez	20.00	10.00	6.00
33	Walter Williams	25.00	12.50	7.50
34	Jim Hicks	20.00	10.00	6.00
35	Gustavo Sposito	20.00	10.00	6.00
36	Cisco Carlos	20.00	10.00	6.00
37	Jim Mooring	20.00	10.00	6.00
38	Alonso Olivares	20.00	10.00	6.00
39	Graciliano Parra	20.00	10.00	6.00
40	Merritt Ranew	20.00	10.00	6.00
41	Everest Contramaestre	20.00	10.00	6.00
42	Orlando Reyes	20.00	10.00	6.00
43	Edicto Arteaga	20.00	10.00	6.00
44	Francisco Diaz	20.00	10.00	6.00
45	Victor Colina	20.00	10.00	6.00
46a	Ramon Diaz	20.00	10.00	6.00
46b	Francisco Diaz (Blue back.)	20.00	10.00	6.00
47	Luis E. Aparicio	185.00	90.00	55.00
48	Reynaldo Cordeiro	60.00	30.00	18.00
49	Luis Aparicio, Sr.	25.00	12.50	7.50
50	Ramon Webster	20.00	10.00	6.00
51	Remigio Hermoso	20.00	10.00	6.00
52	Miguel de la Hoz	20.00	10.00	6.00
53	Enzo Hernandez	20.00	10.00	6.00
54	Ed Watt	20.00	10.00	6.00
55	Angel Bravo	20.00	10.00	6.00
56	Marv (Merv) Rettenmund	25.00	12.50	7.50
57	Jose Herrera	20.00	10.00	6.00
58	Tom Fisher	20.00	10.00	6.00
59	Jim Weaver	20.00	10.00	6.00
60a	Juan Quintana	20.00	10.00	6.00
60b	Frank Fernandez (Blue back.)	20.00	10.00	6.00
61	Hector Urbano	20.00	10.00	6.00
62	Hector Brito (Blue back.)	20.00	10.00	6.00
63	Jesus Romero	20.00	10.00	6.00
64	Carlos A. Moreno	20.00	10.00	6.00
65	Nestor Mendible	20.00	10.00	6.00
66	Armando Ortiz	20.00	10.00	6.00
67	Graciano Ravelo	20.00	10.00	6.00
68	Paul Knechtges	20.00	10.00	6.00
69	Marcelino Lopez	25.00	12.50	7.50
70	Wilfredo Calvino	25.00	12.50	7.50
71	Jesus Avila	20.00	10.00	6.00
72	Carlos Pascual	45.00	22.00	13.50
73	Bob Burda	20.00	10.00	6.00
74	Elio Chacon	20.00	10.00	6.00
75	Jacinto Hernandez	20.00	10.00	6.00
76	Jose M. Tovar	20.00	10.00	6.00
77	Bill Whitby	20.00	10.00	6.00
78	Enrique Izquierdo	20.00	10.00	6.00
79	Hilario Valdespino	30.00	15.00	9.00
80	John Lewis	20.00	10.00	6.00
81	Hector Martinez	40.00	20.00	12.00
82	Rene Paredes	20.00	10.00	6.00
83	Danny Morris	20.00	10.00	6.00
84	Pedro Ramos	25.00	12.50	7.50
85	Jose Ramon Lopez	20.00	10.00	6.00
86	Jesus Rizales	20.00	10.00	6.00
87	Winston Acosta	20.00	10.00	6.00

1967 Venezuelan League

Three distinct series of baseball cards were issued in 1967 for sale in Venezuela, contiguously numbered. Cards #1-138 are players (including many future big leaguers) active in the country's Winter League. Cards are irregularly cut and somewhat smaller than the standard 2-1/2" x 3-1/2". Fronts have posed photos and a thin white border. The player name and position are at top in black, the team name is in large colored letters at bottom. Backs are printed horizontally in black on magenta with a few biographical bits and a one paragraph

#	Player	NM	EX	VG
88	Pablo Bello	20.00	10.00	6.00
89	David Concepcion	200.00	100.00	60.00
90	Manuel Garcia	20.00	10.00	6.00
91	Anibal Longa	20.00	10.00	6.00
92	Francisco Moscoso	20.00	10.00	6.00
93	Mel McGaha	20.00	10.00	6.00
94	Aquiles Gomez	20.00	10.00	6.00
95	Alfonso Carrasquel (Blue back.)	40.00	20.00	12.00
96	Tom Murray	20.00	10.00	6.00
97	Gustavo Gil	20.00	10.00	6.00
98	Damaso Blanco	20.00	10.00	6.00
99	Alberto Cambero	20.00	10.00	6.00
100	Don Bryant	20.00	10.00	6.00
101	George Culver	20.00	10.00	6.00
102	Teolindo Acosta	20.00	10.00	6.00
103	Aaron Pointer	20.00	10.00	6.00
104	Ed Kirkpatrick	20.00	10.00	6.00
105	Luis Rodriguez	20.00	10.00	6.00
106	Mike Daniel	20.00	10.00	6.00
107	Cecilio Prieto (Blue back.)	20.00	10.00	6.00
108	Juan Quiroz	20.00	10.00	6.00
108				
109	Juan Campos	20.00	10.00	6.00
110	Freddy Rivero	20.00	10.00	6.00
111	Dick LeMay	20.00	10.00	6.00
112	Raul Ortega	20.00	10.00	6.00
113	Bruno Estaba	20.00	10.00	6.00
114	Evangelista Nunez	20.00	10.00	6.00
115a	Robert Munoz	20.00	10.00	6.00
115b	Alfonso Carrasquel (Red back.)	40.00	20.00	12.00
116	Tony Castanos	20.00	10.00	6.00
117	Domingo Barboza	20.00	10.00	6.00
118	Lucio Celis	20.00	10.00	6.00
119	Carlos Santeliz	20.00	10.00	6.00
120	Barton Shirley	25.00	12.50	7.50
121	Neudo Morales	20.00	10.00	6.00
122	Robert Cox	100.00	50.00	30.00
123	Cruz Amaya (Blue back.)	20.00	10.00	6.00
124	Jim Campanis	75.00	37.50	22.00
125	Dave Roberts	20.00	10.00	6.00
126	Gerry Crider	20.00	10.00	6.00
127	Domingo Carrasquel	20.00	10.00	6.00
128	Leo Marentette	20.00	10.00	6.00
129	Frank Kreutzer	20.00	10.00	6.00
130	Jim Dickson	20.00	10.00	6.00
131	Bob Oliver	20.00	10.00	6.00
132	Jose Bracho	20.00	10.00	6.00
133a	Pablo Torrealba	20.00	10.00	6.00
133b	Pablo Torrealba (Different picture.)	20.00	10.00	6.00
134	Iran Paz	20.00	10.00	6.00
135	Eliecer Bueno	20.00	10.00	6.00
136	Claudio Urdaneta	20.00	10.00	6.00
137	Faustino Zabala	20.00	10.00	6.00
138	Dario Chirinos	20.00	10.00	6.00

1967 Venezuelan Retirado

 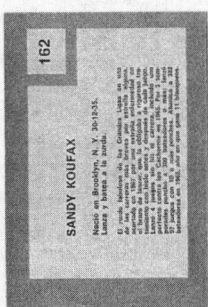

Three distinct series of baseball cards were issued in 1967 for sale in Venezuela, contiguously numbered. Cards #139-188 are former big league stars. The fronts of the roughly 2-1/2" x 3-1/2" Retirado cards have a blue background with the player's name in black at top and "RETIRADO" in red block letters at bottom. Player photos on the Retirado cards are sepia. Horizontal backs are printed in black on green with a bit of personal data and a career summary. Like most of the Venezuelan cards of the era, these are crudely printed on cheap cardboard. Also like most Venezuelan cards, they are virtually impossible to find in any condition above Ex. Many are found with back damage due to having been glued into an album or scrapbook.

#	Player	NM	EX	VG
Complete Set (50):		24,000	12,000	7,200
Common Player:		500.00	250.00	150.00
139	Walter Johnson	1,500	750.00	400.00
140	Bill Dickey	600.00	300.00	180.00
141	Lou Gehrig	3,500	1,750	1,000
142	Rogers Hornsby	600.00	300.00	180.00
143	Honus Wagner	1,300	750.00	450.00
144	Pie Traynor	500.00	250.00	150.00
145	Joe DiMaggio	3,700	1,850	1,200
146	Ty Cobb	2,700	1,350	750.00
147	Babe Ruth	4,800	2,400	1,500
148	Ted Williams	2,000	100.00	600.00
149	Mel Ott	500.00	250.00	150.00
150	Cy Young	750.00	375.00	200.00
151	Christy Mathewson	1,500	750.00	400.00
152	Warren Spahn	600.00	300.00	180.00
153	Mickey Cochrane	500.00	250.00	150.00
154	George Sisler	500.00	250.00	150.00
155	Jimmy Collins	500.00	250.00	150.00
156	Tris Speaker	600.00	300.00	180.00
157	Stan Musial	1,400	700.00	400.00
158	Luke Appling	500.00	250.00	150.00
159	Nap Lajoie	500.00	250.00	150.00
160a	Bill Terry	500.00	250.00	150.00
160b	Bob Feller	750.00	375.00	220.00
162	Sandy Koufax	1,600	800.00	500.00
163	Jimmie Foxx	600.00	300.00	180.00
164	Joe Cronin	500.00	250.00	150.00
165	Frankie Frisch	500.00	250.00	150.00
166	Paul Waner	500.00	250.00	150.00
167	Lloyd Waner	500.00	250.00	150.00
168	Lefty Grove	500.00	250.00	150.00
169	Bobby Doerr	500.00	250.00	150.00
170	Al Simmons	500.00	250.00	150.00
171	Grover Alexander	700.00	350.00	200.00
172	Carl Hubbell	500.00	250.00	150.00
173	Mordecai Brown	500.00	250.00	150.00
174	Ted Lyons	500.00	250.00	150.00
175	Johnny Vander Meer	500.00	250.00	150.00
176	Alex Carrasquel	600.00	300.00	180.00
177	Satchel Paige	1,200	600.00	400.00
178	Whitey Ford	1,000	500.00	300.00
179	Yogi Berra	1,000	500.00	300.00
180	Roy Campanella	900.00	450.00	300.00
181	Alfonso Carrasquel	750.00	375.00	220.00
182	Johnny Mize	500.00	250.00	150.00
183	Ted Kluszewski (Photo actually Gene Bearden.)	600.00	300.00	180.00
184	Jackie Robinson	1,500	750.00	400.00
185	Bobby Avila	500.00	250.00	150.00
186	Phil Rizzuto	600.00	300.00	180.00
187	Minnie Minoso	600.00	300.00	180.00
188	Connie Marrero	500.00	250.00	150.00

1967 Venezuelan Topps

 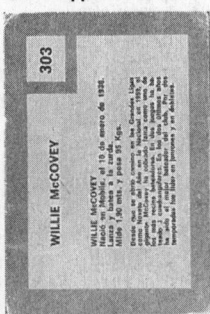

Cards numbered #189-338 in the 1967 Venezuelan issue feature then-current major leaguers. Card fronts are taken from Topps' 1967 baseball series, but are borderless, making them somewhat smaller than 2-1/2" x 3-1/2". Backs of the South American cards are horizontal and printed in black on blue and offer a few bits of personal data and a one-paragraph career summary. Like most Venezuelan cards of the era, these are crudely printed on cheap cardboard and seldom found in condition better than Ex. Many will show evidence on back of having been glued into an album or scrapbook.

#	Player	NM	EX	VG
Complete Set (150):		12,000	6,000	3,600
Common Player:		50.00	25.00	15.00
189	Luis Aparicio	225.00	120.00	75.00
190	Vic Davalillo	50.00	25.00	15.00
191	Cesar Tovar	50.00	25.00	15.00
192	Mickey Mantle	2,250	1,125	700.00
193	Carl Yastrzemski	150.00	75.00	40.00
194	Frank Robinson	150.00	75.00	40.00
195	Willie Horton	50.00	25.00	15.00
196	Gary Peters	50.00	25.00	15.00
197	Bert Campaneris	60.00	30.00	20.00
198	Norm Cash	50.00	25.00	15.00
199	Boog Powell	50.00	25.00	15.00
200	George Scott	50.00	25.00	15.00
201	Frank Howard	50.00	25.00	15.00
202	Rick Reichardt	50.00	25.00	15.00
203	Jose Cardenal	50.00	25.00	15.00
204	Rico Petrocelli	50.00	25.00	15.00
205	Lew Krausse	50.00	25.00	15.00
206	Harmon Killebrew	150.00	75.00	40.00
207	Leon Wagner	50.00	25.00	15.00
208	Joe Foy	50.00	25.00	15.00
209	Joe Pepitone	60.00	30.00	20.00
210	Al Kaline	150.00	75.00	40.00
211	Brooks Robinson	150.00	75.00	40.00
212	Bill Freehan	50.00	25.00	15.00
213	Jim Lonborg	50.00	25.00	15.00
214a	Ed Mathews	150.00	75.00	40.00
214b	Jim Bunning (Should be #174.)	135.00	65.00	40.00
215	Dick Green	50.00	25.00	15.00
216	Tom Tresh	60.00	30.00	20.00
217	Dean Chance	50.00	25.00	15.00
218	Paul Blair	50.00	25.00	15.00
219	Larry Brown	50.00	25.00	15.00
220	Fred Valentine	50.00	25.00	15.00
221	Al Downing	50.00	25.00	15.00
222	Earl Battey	50.00	25.00	15.00
223	Don Mincher	50.00	25.00	15.00
224	Tommie Agee	50.00	25.00	15.00
225	Jim McGlothlin	50.00	25.00	15.00
226	Zoilo Versalles	50.00	25.00	15.00
227	Curt Blefary	50.00	25.00	15.00
228	Joel Horlen	50.00	25.00	15.00
229	Stu Miller	50.00	25.00	15.00
230	Tony Oliva	60.00	30.00	20.00
231	Paul Casanova	50.00	25.00	15.00
232	Orlando Pena	50.00	25.00	15.00
233	Ron Hansen	50.00	25.00	15.00
234	Earl Wilson	50.00	25.00	15.00
235	Ken Boyer	60.00	30.00	20.00
236	Jim Kaat	50.00	25.00	15.00
237	Dalton Jones	50.00	25.00	15.00
238	Pete Ward	50.00	25.00	15.00
239	Mickey Lolich	50.00	25.00	15.00
240	Jose Santiago	50.00	25.00	15.00
241	Dick McAuliffe	50.00	25.00	15.00
242	Mel Stottlemyre	50.00	25.00	15.00
243	Camilo Pascual	50.00	25.00	15.00
244	Jim Fregosi	50.00	25.00	15.00
245	Tony Conigliaro	60.00	30.00	20.00
246	Sonny Siebert	50.00	25.00	15.00
247	Jim Perry	50.00	25.00	15.00
248	Dave McNally	50.00	25.00	15.00
249	Fred Whitfield	50.00	25.00	15.00
250	Ken Berry	50.00	25.00	15.00
251	Jim Grant	50.00	25.00	15.00
252	Hank Aguirre	50.00	25.00	15.00
253	Don Wert	50.00	25.00	15.00
254	Wally Bunker	50.00	25.00	15.00
255	Elston Howard	60.00	30.00	20.00
256	Dave Johnson	50.00	25.00	15.00
257	Hoyt Wilhelm	120.00	60.00	40.00
258	Don Buford	50.00	25.00	15.00
259	Sam McDowell	50.00	25.00	15.00
260	Bobby Knoop	50.00	25.00	15.00
261	Denny McLain	50.00	25.00	15.00
262	Steve Hargan	50.00	25.00	15.00
263	Jim Nash	50.00	25.00	15.00
264	Jerry Adair	50.00	25.00	15.00
265	Tony Gonzalez	50.00	25.00	15.00
266	Mike Shannon	50.00	25.00	15.00
267	Bob Gibson	135.00	65.00	40.00
268	John Roseboro	50.00	25.00	15.00
269	Bob Aspromonte	50.00	25.00	15.00
270	Pete Rose	375.00	200.00	120.00
271	Rico Carty	60.00	30.00	20.00
272	Juan Pizarro	50.00	25.00	15.00
273	Willie Mays	375.00	190.00	120.00
274	Jim Bunning	135.00	70.00	40.00
275	Ernie Banks	150.00	75.00	40.00
276	Curt Flood	60.00	30.00	20.00
277	Mack Jones	50.00	25.00	15.00
278	Roberto Clemente	675.00	340.00	180.00
279	Sammy Ellis	50.00	25.00	15.00
280	Willie Stargell	135.00	70.00	40.00
281	Felipe Alou	60.00	30.00	20.00
282	Ed Kranepool	50.00	25.00	15.00
283	Nelson Briles	50.00	25.00	15.00
284	Hank Aaron	375.00	190.00	120.00
285	Vada Pinson	60.00	30.00	20.00
286	Jim LeFebvre	50.00	25.00	15.00
287	Hal Lanier	50.00	25.00	15.00
288	Ron Swoboda	50.00	25.00	15.00
289	Mike McCormick	50.00	25.00	15.00
290	Lou Johnson	50.00	25.00	15.00
291	Orlando Cepeda	135.00	70.00	40.00
292	Rusty Staub	60.00	30.00	20.00
293	Manny Mota	50.00	25.00	15.00
294	Tommy Harper	50.00	25.00	15.00
295	Don Drysdale	135.00	70.00	40.00
296	Mel Queen	50.00	25.00	15.00
297	Red Schoendienst	120.00	60.00	40.00
298	Matty Alou	50.00	25.00	15.00
299	Johnny Callison	50.00	25.00	15.00
300	Juan Marichal	135.00	70.00	40.00
301	Al McBean	50.00	25.00	15.00
302	Claude Osteen	50.00	25.00	15.00
303	Willie McCovey	135.00	70.00	40.00
304	Jim Owens	50.00	25.00	15.00
305	Chico Ruiz	50.00	25.00	15.00
306	Ferguson Jenkins	135.00	70.00	40.00
307	Lou Brock	135.00	70.00	40.00
308	Joe Morgan	135.00	70.00	40.00
309	Ron Santo	75.00	40.00	25.00
310	Chico Cardenas	50.00	25.00	15.00
311	Richie Allen	70.00	35.00	20.00
312	Gaylord Perry	120.00	60.00	40.00
313	Bill Mazeroski	120.00	60.00	40.00
314	Tony Taylor	50.00	25.00	15.00
315	Tommy Helms	50.00	25.00	15.00
316	Jim Wynn	50.00	25.00	15.00
317	Don Sutton	120.00	60.00	40.00
318	Mike Cuellar	70.00	35.00	40.00
319	Willie Davis	50.00	25.00	15.00
320	Julian Javier	50.00	25.00	15.00
321	Maury Wills	50.00	25.00	15.00
322	Gene Alley	50.00	25.00	15.00
323	Ray Sadecki	50.00	25.00	15.00
324	Joe Torre	70.00	35.00	40.00
325	Jim Maloney	50.00	25.00	15.00
326	Jim Davenport	50.00	25.00	15.00
327	Tony Perez	135.00	70.00	40.00
328	Roger Maris	150.00	75.00	40.00
329	Chris Short	50.00	25.00	15.00
330	Jesus Alou	50.00	25.00	15.00
331	Darron Johnson	50.00	25.00	15.00
332	Tommy Davis	50.00	25.00	15.00
333	Bob Veale	50.00	25.00	15.00
334	Bill McCool	50.00	25.00	15.00
335	Jim Hart	50.00	25.00	15.00
336	Roy Face	50.00	25.00	15.00
337	Billy Williams	120.00	60.00	40.00
338	Dick Groat	50.00	25.00	15.00

1968 Venezuelan Topps

The first 370 cards of Topps' 1968 baseball card set were reproduced in South America for sale in Venezuela. Besides being rather crudely printed on cheaper, non-gloss cardboard, the cards are virtually identical to the Topps U.S. version. The only difference is a tiny line of yellow type on back which reads: "Hecho en Venezuela - C.A. Litoven." Like most 1960s Venezuelan issues, these cards are seldom found in condition better than Excellent, and often with evidence on back of having been glued into an album or scrapbook. Venezuelan Topps cards are often found cut slightly smaller than the U.S. version, up to 1/8".

1968 ROOKIE STARS — NOLAN RYAN • P — JERRY KOOSMAN • P — METS

1968 METS' ROOKIE STARS

#	Player	NM	EX	VG
	Complete Set (370):	37,500	19,000	11,500
	Common Player:	45.00	25.00	15.00
1	N.L. Batting Leaders (Matty Alou, Roberto Clemente, Tony Gonzalez)	120.00	60.00	40.00
2	A.L. Batting Leaders (Al Kaline, Frank Robinson, Carl Yastrzemski)	75.00	40.00	25.00
3	N.L. RBI Leaders (Hank Aaron, Orlando Cepeda, Roberto Clemente)	120.00	60.00	40.00
4	A.L. RBI Leaders (Harmon Killebrew, Frank Robinson, Carl Yastrzemski)	75.00	40.00	25.00
5	N.L. Home Run Leaders (Hank Aaron, Willie McCovey, Ron Santo, Jim Wynn)	90.00	45.00	25.00
6	A.L. Home Run Leaders (Frank Howard, Harmon Killebrew, Carl Yastrzemski)	75.00	40.00	25.00
7	N.L. ERA Leaders (Jim Bunning, Phil Niekro, Chris Short)	45.00	25.00	15.00
8	A.L. ERA Leaders (Joe Horlen, Gary Peters, Sonny Siebert)	45.00	25.00	15.00
9	N.L. Pitching Leaders (Jim Bunning, Fergie Jenkins, Mike McCormick, Claude Osteen)	45.00	25.00	15.00
10	A.L. Pitching Leaders (Dean Chance, Jim Lonborg, Earl Wilson)	45.00	25.00	15.00
11	N.L. Strikeout Leaders (Jim Bunning, Fergie Jenkins, Gaylord Perry)	45.00	25.00	15.00
12	A.L. Strikeout Leaders (Dean Chance, Jim Lonborg, Sam McDowell)	45.00	25.00	15.00
13	Chuck Hartenstein	45.00	25.00	15.00
14	Jerry McNertney	45.00	25.00	15.00
15	Ron Hunt	45.00	25.00	15.00
16	Indians Rookies (Lou Piniella, Richie Scheinblum)	60.00	30.00	20.00
17	Dick Hall	45.00	25.00	15.00
18	Mike Hershberger	45.00	25.00	15.00
19	Juan Pizarro	45.00	25.00	15.00
20	Brooks Robinson	180.00	90.00	50.00
21	Ron Davis	45.00	25.00	15.00
22	Pat Dobson	45.00	25.00	15.00
23	Chico Cardenas	45.00	25.00	15.00
24	Bobby Locke	45.00	25.00	15.00
25	Julian Javier	45.00	25.00	15.00
26	Darrell Brandon	45.00	25.00	15.00
27	Gil Hodges	75.00	40.00	25.00
28	Ted Uhlaender	45.00	25.00	15.00
29	Joe Verbanic	45.00	25.00	15.00
30	Joe Torre	60.00	30.00	20.00
31	Ed Stroud	45.00	25.00	15.00
32	Joe Gibbon	45.00	25.00	15.00
33	Pete Ward	45.00	25.00	15.00
34	Al Ferrara	45.00	25.00	15.00
35	Steve Hargan	45.00	25.00	15.00
36	Pirates Rookies (Bob Moose, Bob Robertson)	45.00	25.00	15.00
37	Billy Williams	120.00	60.00	40.00
38	Tony Pierce	45.00	25.00	15.00
39	Cookie Rojas	45.00	25.00	15.00
40	Denny McLain	60.00	30.00	20.00
41	Julio Gotay	45.00	25.00	15.00
42	Larry Haney	45.00	25.00	15.00
43	Gary Bell	45.00	25.00	15.00
44	Frank Kostro	45.00	25.00	15.00
45	Tom Seaver	180.00	90.00	50.00
46	Dave Ricketts	45.00	25.00	15.00
47	Ralph Houk	45.00	25.00	15.00
48	Ted Davidson	45.00	25.00	15.00
49	Ed Brinkman	45.00	25.00	15.00
50	Willie Mays	525.00	260.00	150.00
51	Bob Locker	45.00	25.00	15.00
52	Hawk Taylor	45.00	25.00	15.00
53	Gene Alley	45.00	25.00	15.00
54	Stan Williams	45.00	25.00	15.00
55	Felipe Alou	60.00	30.00	20.00
56	Orioles Rookies (Dave Leonhard, Dave May)	45.00	25.00	15.00
57	Dan Schneider	45.00	25.00	15.00
58	Eddie Mathews	180.00	90.00	50.00
59	Don Lock	45.00	25.00	15.00
60	Ken Holtzman	45.00	25.00	15.00
61	Reggie Smith	45.00	25.00	15.00
62	Chuck Dobson	45.00	25.00	15.00
63	Dick Kenworthy	45.00	25.00	15.00
64	Jim Merritt	45.00	25.00	15.00
65	John Roseboro	45.00	25.00	15.00
66	Casey Cox	45.00	25.00	15.00
67	Checklist 1-109 (Jim Kaat)	45.00	25.00	15.00
68	Ron Willis	45.00	25.00	15.00
69	Tom Tresh	45.00	25.00	15.00
70	Bob Veale	45.00	25.00	15.00
71	Vern Fuller	45.00	25.00	15.00
72	Tommy John	45.00	25.00	15.00
73	Jim Hart	45.00	25.00	15.00
74	Milt Pappas	45.00	25.00	15.00
75	Don Mincher	45.00	25.00	15.00
76	Braves Rookies (Jim Britton, Ron Reed)	45.00	25.00	15.00
77	Don Wilson	45.00	25.00	15.00
78	Jim Northrup	45.00	25.00	15.00
79	Ted Kubiak	45.00	25.00	15.00
80	Rod Carew	180.00	90.00	50.00
81	Larry Jackson	45.00	25.00	15.00
82	Sam Bowens	45.00	25.00	15.00
83	John Stephenson	45.00	25.00	15.00
84	Bob Tolan	45.00	25.00	15.00
85	Gaylord Perry	120.00	60.00	40.00
86	Willie Stargell	150.00	75.00	40.00
87	Dick Williams	45.00	25.00	15.00
88	Phil Regan	45.00	25.00	15.00
89	Jake Gibbs	45.00	25.00	15.00
90	Vada Pinson	60.00	30.00	20.00
91	Jim Ollom	45.00	25.00	15.00
92	Ed Kranepool	45.00	25.00	15.00
93	Tony Cloninger	45.00	25.00	15.00
94	Lee Maye	45.00	25.00	15.00
95	Bob Aspromonte	45.00	25.00	15.00
96	Senators Rookies (Frank Coggins, Dick Nold)	45.00	25.00	15.00
97	Tom Phoebus	45.00	25.00	15.00
98	Gary Sutherland	45.00	25.00	15.00
99	Rocky Colavito	75.00	40.00	25.00
100	Bob Gibson	135.00	70.00	40.00
101	Glenn Beckert	45.00	25.00	15.00
102	Jose Cardenal	45.00	25.00	15.00
103	Don Sutton	120.00	60.00	40.00
104	Dick Dietz	45.00	25.00	15.00
105	Al Downing	45.00	25.00	15.00
106	Dalton Jones	45.00	25.00	15.00
107	Checklist 110-196 (Juan Marichal)	45.00	25.00	15.00
108	Don Pavletich	45.00	25.00	15.00
109	Bert Campaneris	60.00	30.00	20.00
110	Hank Aaron	525.00	260.00	150.00
111	Rich Reese	45.00	25.00	15.00
112	Woody Fryman	45.00	25.00	15.00
113	Tigers Rookies (Tom Matchick, Daryl Patterson)	45.00	25.00	15.00
114	Ron Swoboda	45.00	25.00	15.00
115	Sam McDowell	45.00	25.00	15.00
116	Ken McMullen	45.00	25.00	15.00
117	Larry Jaster	45.00	25.00	15.00
118	Mark Belanger	45.00	25.00	15.00
119	Ted Savage	45.00	25.00	15.00
120	Mel Stottlemyre	45.00	25.00	15.00
121	Jimmie Hall	45.00	25.00	15.00
122	Gene Mauch	45.00	25.00	15.00
123	Jose Santiago	45.00	25.00	15.00
124	Nate Oliver	45.00	25.00	15.00
125	Joe Horlen	45.00	25.00	15.00
126	Bobby Etheridge	45.00	25.00	15.00
127	Paul Lindblad	45.00	25.00	15.00
128	Astros Rookies (Tom Dukes, Alonzo Harris)	45.00	25.00	15.00
129	Mickey Stanley	45.00	25.00	15.00
130	Tony Perez	135.00	70.00	40.00
131	Frank Bertaina	45.00	25.00	15.00
132	Bud Harrelson	45.00	25.00	15.00
133	Fred Whitfield	45.00	25.00	15.00
134	Pat Jarvis	45.00	25.00	15.00
135	Paul Blair	45.00	25.00	15.00
136	Randy Hundley	45.00	25.00	15.00
137	Twins Team	60.00	30.00	20.00
138	Ruben Amaro	45.00	25.00	15.00
139	Chris Short	45.00	25.00	15.00
140	Tony Conigliaro	60.00	30.00	20.00
141	Dal Maxvill	45.00	25.00	15.00
142	White Sox Rookies (Buddy Bradford, Bill Voss)	45.00	25.00	15.00
143	Pete Cimino	45.00	25.00	15.00
144	Joe Morgan	150.00	75.00	40.00
145	Don Drysdale	150.00	75.00	40.00
146	Sal Bando	45.00	25.00	15.00
147	Frank Linzy	45.00	25.00	15.00
148	Dave Bristol	45.00	25.00	15.00
149	Bob Saverine	45.00	25.00	15.00
150	Roberto Clemente	900.00	450.00	300.00
151	World Series Game 1 (Brock Socks 4 Hits in Opener)	45.00	25.00	15.00
152	World Series Game 2 (Yaz Smashes Two Homers)	60.00	30.00	20.00
153	World Series Game 3 (Briles Cools Off Boston)	45.00	25.00	15.00
154	World Series Game 4 (Gibson Hurls Shutout)	45.00	25.00	15.00
155	World Series Game 5 (Lonborg Wins Again)	45.00	25.00	15.00
156	World Series Game 6 (Petrocelli Socks Two Homers)	45.00	25.00	15.00
157	World Series Game 7 (St. Louis Wins It)	45.00	25.00	15.00
158	World Series Summary (The Cardinals Celebrate)	45.00	25.00	15.00
159	Don Kessinger	45.00	25.00	15.00
160	Earl Wilson	45.00	25.00	15.00
161	Norm Miller	45.00	25.00	15.00
162	Cardinals Rookies (Hal Gilson, Mike Torrez)	45.00	25.00	15.00
163	Gene Brabender	45.00	25.00	15.00
164	Ramon Webster	45.00	25.00	15.00
165	Tony Oliva	60.00	30.00	20.00
166	Claude Raymond	45.00	25.00	15.00
167	Elston Howard	75.00	40.00	25.00
168	Dodgers Team	75.00	40.00	25.00
169	Bob Bolin	45.00	25.00	15.00
170	Jim Fregosi	45.00	25.00	15.00
171	Don Nottebart	45.00	25.00	15.00
172	Walt Williams	45.00	25.00	15.00
173	John Boozer	45.00	25.00	15.00
174	Bob Tillman	45.00	25.00	15.00
175	Maury Wills	45.00	25.00	15.00
176	Bob Allen	45.00	25.00	15.00
177	Mets Rookies (*Jerry Koosman, Nolan Ryan*)	12,000	6,000	4,000
178	Don Wert	45.00	25.00	15.00
179	Bill Stoneman	45.00	25.00	15.00
180	Curt Flood	45.00	25.00	15.00
181	Jerry Zimmerman	45.00	25.00	15.00
182	Dave Giusti	45.00	25.00	15.00
183	Bob Kennedy	45.00	25.00	15.00
184	Lou Johnson	45.00	25.00	15.00
185	Tom Haller	45.00	25.00	15.00
186	Eddie Watt	45.00	25.00	15.00
187	Sonny Jackson	45.00	25.00	15.00
188	Cap Peterson	45.00	25.00	15.00
189	Bill Landis	45.00	25.00	15.00
190	Bill White	45.00	25.00	15.00
191	Dan Frisella	45.00	25.00	15.00
192	Checklist 197-283 (Carl Yastrzemski)	60.00	30.00	20.00
193	Jack Hamilton	45.00	25.00	15.00
194	Don Buford	45.00	25.00	15.00
195	Joe Pepitone	45.00	25.00	15.00
196	Gary Nolan	45.00	25.00	15.00
197	Larry Brown	45.00	25.00	15.00
198	Roy Face	45.00	25.00	15.00
199	A's Rookies (Darrell Osteen, Roberto Rodriquez)	45.00	25.00	15.00
200	Orlando Cepeda	120.00	60.00	40.00
201	Mike Marshall	45.00	25.00	15.00
202	Adolfo Phillips	45.00	25.00	15.00
203	Dick Kelley	45.00	25.00	15.00
204	Andy Etchebarren	45.00	25.00	15.00
205	Juan Marichal	135.00	70.00	40.00
206	Cal Ermer	45.00	25.00	15.00
207	Carroll Sembera	45.00	25.00	15.00
208	Willie Davis	45.00	25.00	15.00
209	Tim Cullen	45.00	25.00	15.00
210	Gary Peters	45.00	25.00	15.00
211	J.C. Martin	45.00	25.00	15.00
212	Dave Morehead	45.00	25.00	15.00
213	Chico Ruiz	45.00	25.00	15.00
214	Yankees Rookies (Stan Bahnsen, Frank Fernandez)	45.00	25.00	15.00
215	Jim Bunning	135.00	70.00	40.00
216	Bubba Morton	45.00	25.00	15.00
217	Turk Farrell	45.00	25.00	15.00
218	Ken Suarez	45.00	25.00	15.00
219	Rob Gardner	45.00	25.00	15.00
220	Harmon Killebrew	180.00	90.00	50.00
221	Braves Team	60.00	30.00	20.00
222	Jim Hardin	45.00	25.00	15.00
223	Ollie Brown	45.00	25.00	15.00
224	Jack Aker	45.00	25.00	15.00
225	Richie Allen	60.00	30.00	20.00
226	Jimmie Price	45.00	25.00	15.00
227	Joe Hoerner	45.00	25.00	15.00
228	Dodgers Rookies (Jack Billingham, Jim Fairey)	45.00	25.00	15.00
229	Fred Klages	45.00	25.00	15.00
230	Pete Rose	525.00	260.00	150.00
231	Dave Baldwin	45.00	25.00	15.00
232	Denis Menke	45.00	25.00	15.00
233	George Scott	45.00	25.00	15.00
234	Bill Monbouquette	45.00	25.00	15.00
235	Ron Santo	75.00	40.00	25.00
236	Tug McGraw	45.00	25.00	15.00
237	Alvin Dark	45.00	25.00	15.00
238	Tom Satriano	45.00	25.00	15.00
239	Bill Henry	45.00	25.00	15.00
240	Al Kaline	180.00	90.00	50.00
241	Felix Millan	45.00	25.00	15.00
242	Moe Drabowsky	45.00	25.00	15.00
243	Rich Rollins	45.00	25.00	15.00
244	John Donaldson	45.00	25.00	15.00
245	Tony Gonzalez	45.00	25.00	15.00
246	Fritz Peterson	45.00	25.00	15.00
247	Reds Rookies (Johnny Bench, Ron Tompkins)	600.00	300.00	180.00
248	Fred Valentine	45.00	25.00	15.00
249	Bill Singer	45.00	25.00	15.00
250	Carl Yastrzemski	200.00	100.00	60.00
251	Manny Sanguillen	60.00	30.00	20.00
252	Angels Team	60.00	30.00	20.00
253	Dick Hughes	45.00	25.00	15.00
254	Cleon Jones	45.00	25.00	15.00
255	Dean Chance	45.00	25.00	15.00
256	Norm Cash	60.00	30.00	20.00
257	Phil Niekro	120.00	60.00	40.00
258	Cubs Rookies (Jose Arcia, Bill Schlesinger)	45.00	25.00	15.00
259	Ken Boyer	45.00	25.00	15.00
260	Jim Wynn	45.00	25.00	15.00
261	Dave Duncan	45.00	25.00	15.00
262	Rick Wise	45.00	25.00	15.00
263	Horace Clarke	45.00	25.00	15.00
264	Ted Abernathy	45.00	25.00	15.00
265	Tommy Davis	45.00	25.00	15.00
266	Paul Popovich	45.00	25.00	15.00
267	Herman Franks	45.00	25.00	15.00
268	Bob Humphreys	45.00	25.00	15.00
269	Bob Tiefenauer	45.00	25.00	15.00
270	Matty Alou	45.00	25.00	15.00
271	Bobby Knoop	45.00	25.00	15.00
272	Ray Culp	45.00	25.00	15.00
273	Dave Johnson	45.00	25.00	15.00
274	Mike Cuellar	45.00	25.00	15.00
275	Tim McCarver	45.00	25.00	15.00
276	Jim Roland	45.00	25.00	15.00
277	Jerry Buchek	45.00	25.00	15.00
278	Checklist 284-370 (Orlando Cepeda)	45.00	25.00	15.00
279	Bill Hands	45.00	25.00	15.00
280	Mickey Mantle	3,000	1,500	900.00

#	Player	NM	EX	VG
281	Jim Campanis	45.00	25.00	15.00
282	Rick Monday	45.00	25.00	15.00
283	Mel Queen	45.00	25.00	15.00
284	John Briggs	45.00	25.00	15.00
285	Dick McAuliffe	45.00	25.00	15.00
286	Cecil Upshaw	45.00	25.00	15.00
287	White Sox Rookies (Mickey Abarbanel, Cisco Carlos)	45.00	25.00	15.00
288	Dave Wickersham	45.00	25.00	15.00
289	Woody Held	45.00	25.00	15.00
290	Willie McCovey	180.00	90.00	50.00
291	Dick Lines	45.00	25.00	15.00
292	Art Shamsky	45.00	25.00	15.00
293	Bruce Howard	45.00	25.00	15.00
294	Red Schoendienst	120.00	60.00	40.00
295	Sonny Siebert	45.00	25.00	15.00
296	Byron Browne	45.00	25.00	15.00
297	Russ Gibson	45.00	25.00	15.00
298	Jim Brewer	45.00	25.00	15.00
299	Gene Michael	45.00	25.00	15.00
300	Rusty Staub	60.00	30.00	20.00
301	Twins Rookies (George Mitterwald, Rick Renick)	45.00	25.00	15.00
302	Gerry Arrigo	45.00	25.00	15.00
303	Dick Green	45.00	25.00	15.00
304	Sandy Valdespino	45.00	25.00	15.00
305	Minnie Rojas	45.00	25.00	15.00
306	Mike Ryan	45.00	25.00	15.00
307	John Hiller	45.00	25.00	15.00
308	Pirates Team	75.00	40.00	25.00
309	Ken Henderson	45.00	25.00	15.00
310	Luis Aparicio	225.00	120.00	75.00
311	Jack Lamabe	45.00	25.00	15.00
312	Curt Blefary	45.00	25.00	15.00
313	Al Weis	45.00	25.00	15.00
314	Red Sox Rookies (Bill Rohr, George Spriggs)	45.00	25.00	15.00
315	Zoilo Versalles	45.00	25.00	15.00
316	Steve Barber	45.00	25.00	15.00
317	Ron Brand	45.00	25.00	15.00
318	Chico Salmon	45.00	25.00	15.00
319	George Culver	45.00	25.00	15.00
320	Frank Howard	60.00	30.00	20.00
321	Leo Durocher	75.00	40.00	25.00
322	Dave Boswell	45.00	25.00	15.00
323	Deron Johnson	45.00	25.00	15.00
324	Jim Nash	45.00	25.00	15.00
325	Manny Mota	45.00	25.00	15.00
326	Dennis Ribant	45.00	25.00	15.00
327	Tony Taylor	45.00	25.00	15.00
328	Angels Rookies (Chuck Vinson, Jim Weaver)	45.00	25.00	15.00
329	Duane Josephson	45.00	25.00	15.00
330	Roger Maris	180.00	90.00	50.00
331	Dan Osinski	45.00	25.00	15.00
332	Doug Rader	45.00	25.00	15.00
333	Ron Herbel	45.00	25.00	15.00
334	Orioles Team	75.00	40.00	25.00
335	Bob Allison	45.00	25.00	15.00
336	John Purdin	45.00	25.00	15.00
337	Bill Robinson	45.00	25.00	15.00
338	Bob Johnson	45.00	25.00	15.00
339	Rich Nye	45.00	25.00	15.00
340	Max Alvis	45.00	25.00	15.00
341	Jim Lemon	45.00	25.00	15.00
342	Ken Johnson	45.00	25.00	15.00
343	Jim Gosger	45.00	25.00	15.00
344	Donn Clendenon	45.00	25.00	15.00
345	Bob Hendley	45.00	25.00	15.00
346	Jerry Adair	45.00	25.00	15.00
347	George Brunet	45.00	25.00	15.00
348	Phillies Rookies (Larry Colton, Dick Thoenen)	45.00	25.00	15.00
349	Ed Spiezio	45.00	25.00	15.00
350	Hoyt Wilhelm	120.00	60.00	40.00
351	Bob Barton	45.00	25.00	15.00
352	Jackie Hernandez	45.00	25.00	15.00
353	Mack Jones	45.00	25.00	15.00
354	Pete Richert	45.00	25.00	15.00
355	Ernie Banks	200.00	100.00	60.00
356	Checklist 371-457 (Ken Holtzman)	45.00	25.00	15.00
357	Len Gabrielson	45.00	25.00	15.00
358	Mike Epstein	45.00	25.00	15.00
359	Joe Moeller	45.00	25.00	15.00
360	Willie Horton	45.00	25.00	15.00
361	Harmon Killebrew/AS	75.00	40.00	25.00
362	Orlando Cepeda/AS	60.00	30.00	20.00
363	Rod Carew/AS	75.00	40.00	25.00
364	Joe Morgan/AS	60.00	30.00	20.00
365	Brooks Robinson/AS	75.00	40.00	25.00
366	Ron Santo/AS	60.00	30.00	20.00
367	Jim Fregosi/AS	45.00	25.00	15.00
368	Gene Alley/AS	45.00	25.00	15.00
369	Carl Yastrzemski/AS	75.00	40.00	25.00
370	Hank Aaron/AS	375.00	190.00	120.00

1970 Ovenca Venezuelan League

After partial parallels of Topps cards were produced off and on between 1959 and 1968, Venezuelan collectors and fans were offered a completely home-brewed baseball card issue for the 1970-71 winter league season. Similar in quality (i.e., less substantial card stock) to earlier sets, these were printed by Sport Grafico for Ovenca, though neither entity is mentioned on the cards. Slightly larger than 2-1/2" x 3-1/2", cards have large color photos with color stripes above and below bearing player and team name and card number. Backs are printed in black on blue with lengthy comments about the player and his career. Gaps in this checklist will be filled as information comes to light.

#		NM	EX	VG
	Complete Set (300):	2,250	1,100	650.00
	Common Player:	20.00	10.00	6.00
	Album:	200.00	100.00	60.00
1	Cesar Gutierrez	20.00	10.00	6.00
2	Elio Chacon	20.00	10.00	6.00
3	Luis Rodriguez	20.00	10.00	6.00
4	David Concepcion	75.00	37.50	22.00
5	Roberto Munoz	20.00	10.00	6.00
6	Jesus Rizales	20.00	10.00	6.00
7	Virgilio Mata	20.00	10.00	6.00
8	Manuel Garcia	30.00	15.00	9.00
9	Cesar Garrido	20.00	10.00	6.00
10	Alejandro Tovar	20.00	10.00	6.00
11	William Salazar	20.00	10.00	6.00
12	Jose Lopez	20.00	10.00	6.00
13	Romulo Castillo	20.00	10.00	6.00
14	Victor Jimenez	20.00	10.00	6.00
15	Jose Saiz	20.00	10.00	6.00
16	Wilfredo Calvino	20.00	10.00	6.00
17	Jesus Avila	20.00	10.00	6.00
18	Cruz Rodriguez	20.00	10.00	6.00
19	Julio Bracho	20.00	10.00	6.00
20	David Concepcion, Cesar Gutierrez	25.00	12.50	7.50
21	Double Play (David Concepcion)	25.00	12.50	7.50
22	Tigres de Aragua Logo	10.00	5.00	3.00
23	Orlando Tavares	20.00	10.00	6.00
24	David Concepcion (In Action)	30.00	15.00	9.00
25	Aragua Action	10.00	5.00	3.00
26	Aragua Action	10.00	5.00	3.00
27	Cesar Gutierrez	20.00	10.00	6.00
28	Play at Home	10.00	5.00	3.00
29	Joe Foy	20.00	10.00	6.00
30	Dennis Paepke	20.00	10.00	6.00
31	Fred Norman	20.00	10.00	6.00
32	John Purdin	20.00	10.00	6.00
33	Steve Huntz	20.00	10.00	6.00
34	Claide (Clyde) Mashore	20.00	10.00	6.00
35	Steve Mingori	20.00	10.00	6.00
36	Jim Breazeale	20.00	10.00	6.00
37	Charles Day	20.00	10.00	6.00
38	Bob Stinson	20.00	10.00	6.00
39	Phil Hennigan	20.00	10.00	6.00
40	Aragua Checklist (Wilfredo Calvino)	25.00	12.50	7.50
41	Faustino Zabala	20.00	10.00	6.00
42	Pablo Torrealba	20.00	10.00	6.00
43	Erasmo Diaz	20.00	10.00	6.00
44	Sebastian Martinez	20.00	10.00	6.00
45	Neudo Morales	20.00	10.00	6.00
46	Iran Paz	20.00	10.00	6.00
47	Franklyn Moreno	20.00	10.00	6.00
48	Claudio Urdaneta	20.00	10.00	6.00
49	Dario Chirinos	20.00	10.00	6.00
50	Domingo Carrasquel	20.00	10.00	6.00
51	Enrique Gonzalez	20.00	10.00	6.00
52	Ednio Gonzalez	20.00	10.00	6.00
53	Humberto Donquis	20.00	10.00	6.00
54	Antonio Ruiz	20.00	10.00	6.00
55	Efrain Urquiola	20.00	10.00	6.00
56	Tony Pacheco	20.00	10.00	6.00
57	Lucio Celis	20.00	10.00	6.00
58	Domingo Barboza	20.00	10.00	6.00
59	Faustino Zabala, Neudo Morales	15.00	7.50	4.50
60	Lara Action	10.00	5.00	3.00
61	Tony Pacheco, Lucio Celis, Domingo Barboza	15.00	7.50	4.50
62	Lara Team Logo	10.00	5.00	3.00
63	Alexis Corro	20.00	10.00	6.00
64	Lara Rookies in Action	10.00	5.00	3.00
65	Lara Play at First	10.00	5.00	3.00
66	Lara Play at Home	10.00	5.00	3.00
67	Lara Action	10.00	5.00	3.00
68	Jim Shellenback	20.00	10.00	6.00
69	Scipio Spinks	20.00	10.00	6.00
70	Ken Forsch	20.00	10.00	6.00
71	Oscar Zamora	20.00	10.00	6.00
72	Ronald Cook	20.00	10.00	6.00
73	Jackie Brown	20.00	10.00	6.00
74	Orlando Martinez	20.00	10.00	6.00
75	Bobby Watson	25.00	12.50	7.50
76	Jose Martinez	20.00	10.00	6.00
77	Roger Metzger	20.00	10.00	6.00
78	Tommy Reynolds	20.00	10.00	6.00
79	Cleo James	20.00	10.00	6.00
80	Lara Checkist (Tony Pacheco)	10.00	5.00	3.00
81	Gustavo Gil	20.00	10.00	6.00
82	Jesus Aristimuno	20.00	10.00	6.00
83	Armando Ortiz	20.00	10.00	6.00
84	Orlando Reyes	20.00	10.00	6.00
85	Damaso Blanco	20.00	10.00	6.00
86				
87	Victor Colina	20.00	10.00	6.00
88	Nelson Cana	20.00	10.00	6.00
89	Francisco Diaz	20.00	10.00	6.00
90	Edito Arteaga	20.00	10.00	6.00
91	Concepcion Escalona	20.00	10.00	6.00
92	Gilberto Marcano	20.00	10.00	6.00
93	Luis A. Serrano	20.00	10.00	6.00
94				
95	Raul Ortega	20.00	10.00	6.00
96	Carlos Patato Pascual	20.00	10.00	6.00
97	Leopold Tovar	20.00	10.00	6.00
98	Manuel Gonzalez	20.00	10.00	6.00
99	Magallanes Action	10.00	5.00	3.00
100	Comienza el Partido	20.00	10.00	6.00
101	Magallanes Rookies	15.00	7.50	4.50
102				
103	Marcano en la Lomita	15.00	7.50	4.50
104	Magallanes Fans	10.00	5.00	3.00
105	Magallanes Action	10.00	5.00	3.00
106				
107	Hal King, Jim Holt, Clarence Gaston, Herman Hill	15.00	7.50	4.50
108	Magallanes Caribbean Champions	10.00	5.00	3.00
109				
110	Herman Hill	20.00	10.00	6.00
111	Jim Holt	20.00	10.00	6.00
112	Orlando Pena	20.00	10.00	6.00
113	Magallanes Action	10.00	5.00	3.00
114	Hal King	20.00	10.00	6.00
115	Jorge Lauzerique	20.00	10.00	6.00
116	Rigoberto Mendoza	20.00	10.00	6.00
117	Allan (Alan) Closter	20.00	10.00	6.00
118	Clarence Gaston	25.00	12.50	7.50
119	John Morris	20.00	10.00	6.00
120	Patato Pascual, Unknown	15.00	7.50	4.50
121	Victor Davalillo	20.00	10.00	6.00
122	Cesar Tovar	20.00	10.00	6.00
123	Gonzalo Marquez	20.00	10.00	6.00
124	Luis Penalver	20.00	10.00	6.00
125	Alberto Cambero	20.00	10.00	6.00
126	Urbano Lugo	20.00	10.00	6.00
127	Juan Campos	20.00	10.00	6.00
128	William Castillo	20.00	10.00	6.00
129	Nelson Garcia	20.00	10.00	6.00
130	Ramon Guanchez	20.00	10.00	6.00
131	Jesus Marcano Trillo	40.00	20.00	12.00
132	Manuel Mendible	20.00	10.00	6.00
133	Teodoro Obregon	20.00	10.00	6.00
134	Jesus Padron	20.00	10.00	6.00
135	Ulises Urrieta	20.00	10.00	6.00
136	Antonio "Loco" Torres	20.00	10.00	6.00
137	Leopoldo Posada	20.00	10.00	6.00
138	Pompeyo Davilillo	20.00	10.00	6.00
139	Alonso Olivares	20.00	10.00	6.00
140	Cesar Tovar/IA	15.00	7.50	4.50
141	Caracas Rookies in Action	15.00	7.50	4.50
142				
143	Andres Barrios	20.00	10.00	6.00
144	Heriberto Morillo	20.00	10.00	6.00
145	Angel Cordova	20.00	10.00	6.00
146	Freddy Rivero	20.00	10.00	6.00
147	Rafael Velasquez	20.00	10.00	6.00
148	Camilo Pascual	30.00	15.00	9.00
149	Cesar Tovar, Vic Davalillo	20.00	10.00	6.00
150	Luis Tiant	30.00	15.00	9.00
151	Roberto Musulungo Hernandez	20.00	10.00	6.00
152	Kurt Devecqua (Bevacqua)	30.00	15.00	9.00
153	Cookie Rojas	30.00	15.00	9.00
154	Larry Howard	20.00	10.00	6.00
155	Rick Scheinblum	20.00	10.00	6.00
156	Diego Segui	25.00	12.50	7.50
157	Gregory Conger	20.00	10.00	6.00
158	Richard Falker (Falkner)	20.00	10.00	6.00
159	Ed Sprague	20.00	10.00	6.00
160	Zulia Checklist (Pompeyo Davilillo)	15.00	7.50	4.50
161	Luis Aparicio	75.00	37.00	22.00
162	Teolindo Acosta	20.00	10.00	6.00
163	Gustavo Sposito	20.00	10.00	6.00
164	Juan Francia	20.00	10.00	6.00
165	Graciliano Parra	20.00	10.00	6.00
166	Simon Salaya	20.00	10.00	6.00
167	Nelson Castellanos	20.00	10.00	6.00
168	Edgar Urbina	20.00	10.00	6.00
169	Luis Gonzalez	20.00	10.00	6.00
170	Olinto Rojas	20.00	10.00	6.00
171	Everest Contramaestre	20.00	10.00	6.00
172	Juan Quiroz	20.00	10.00	6.00
173	Juan Quintana	20.00	10.00	6.00
174	Hugo Bello	20.00	10.00	6.00
175	Jesus Llamozas	20.00	10.00	6.00
176	Luis Aparicio (Manager)	45.00	22.00	13.50
177	Luis Aparicio, Sr.	25.00	12.50	7.50
178	Antonio Brinez	20.00	10.00	6.00
179	Carlos Dickson Bell	20.00	10.00	6.00
180	Alfonso Carrasquel	30.00	15.00	9.00
181	Zulia Action	10.00	5.00	3.00
182	Zulia Eagles Team Logo	20.00	10.00	6.00
183	Nidio Sirit	20.00	10.00	6.00
184	Zulia Action	10.00	5.00	3.00
185	Zulia Eagles Team Photo	10.00	5.00	3.00
186	Bobby Cox/IA	20.00	10.00	6.00
187	Zulia Play at Home	10.00	5.00	3.00
188	Alfonso Carrasquel, Luis Aparicio	25.00	12.50	7.50
189	Teolindo Acosta, Gustavo Sposito	15.00	7.50	4.50
190	Leonardo Cardenas	20.00	10.00	6.00
191	Bart Johnson	20.00	10.00	6.00
192	Jerry Crider	20.00	10.00	6.00
193	Getty Janesky (Gerry Janeski)	20.00	10.00	6.00
194	John Matias	20.00	10.00	6.00
195	Walter Williams	25.00	12.50	7.50
196	Steve Hovley	20.00	10.00	6.00
197	Frank Fernandez	20.00	10.00	6.00
198	John Donaldson	20.00	10.00	6.00
199	Donald Eddy	20.00	10.00	6.00
200	Zulia Checklist (Luis Aparicio)	30.00	15.00	9.00
201	Jose Herrera	20.00	10.00	6.00
202	Aurelio Monteagudo	20.00	10.00	6.00
203	Remigio Hermoso	20.00	10.00	6.00
204	Angel Bravo	20.00	10.00	6.00
205	Enzo Hernandez	20.00	10.00	6.00
206	Oswaldo Blanco	20.00	10.00	6.00

ARAGUA — 29

JOE FOY
Norteamericano - Lanza y batea a la derecha.

Estuvo anteriormente con los Medias Rojas de Boston de la Liga Americana. Los Metropolitanos de Nueva York, con serios problemas en la tercera base, adquirieron sus servicios a partir de la recien finalizada campaña de Grandes Ligas. Foy no rindió todo lo que de él se esperaba y el manager Hodges lo tuvo que alternar en la esquina caliente con Wayne Garret. Totalizó 239 a la ofensiva, producto de 75 imparables en 318 turnos, intervino en 98 juegos, anotó 39 carreras y remolcó 36, conectó 6 cuadrangulares y fue el tercer mejor estafador de su equipo con 22. Debido a su escaso rendimiento, fue enviado a las Menores al concluir la temporada. El próximo año deberá reportarse al club Triple "A".

207	Carlos Moreno	20.00	10.00	6.00
208	Adolfo Philips (Phillips)	20.00	10.00	6.00
209	Roberto Romero	20.00	10.00	6.00
210	Euclides Camejo	20.00	10.00	6.00
211	Oswaldo Troconis	20.00	10.00	6.00
212	Roberto Marcano	20.00	10.00	6.00
213	Victor Patino	20.00	10.00	6.00
214	Hector Urbano	20.00	10.00	6.00
215	Antonio Pipo Correa	20.00	10.00	6.00
216	Dave Garcia	25.00	12.50	7.50
217	Graciano Ravelo	20.00	10.00	6.00
218	Reinaldo Cordeiro	20.00	10.00	6.00
219	La Guaira Action	10.00	5.00	3.00
220	La Tropa Completa	20.00	10.00	6.00
221	Tomas Liscano Arias	20.00	10.00	6.00
222				
223	Jesus Romero	20.00	10.00	6.00
224	Julian Yanez	20.00	10.00	6.00
225	Enrique Gutierrez	20.00	10.00	6.00
226	Dionel Durand	20.00	10.00	6.00
227	Jose Gregorio Salas	20.00	10.00	6.00
228	Luis Camaleon Garcia	20.00	10.00	6.00
229	Alfredo Ortiz	20.00	10.00	6.00
230	Luis Contreras	20.00	10.00	6.00
231	Ed Spiezio	20.00	10.00	6.00
232	Paul Casanova	25.00	12.50	7.50
233	Mike Epstein	25.00	12.50	7.50
234	Casey Cox	20.00	10.00	6.00
235	Marcelino Lopez	20.00	10.00	6.00
236	Jerry Cram	20.00	10.00	6.00
237	Danny Coombs	20.00	10.00	6.00
238	Del Unser	20.00	10.00	6.00
239	Hector Brito	20.00	10.00	6.00
240	La Guaira Checklist	10.00	5.00	3.00
241	Larry Howard, Richie Scheinblum/IA	15.00	7.50	4.50
242	Ed Spiezio/IA	15.00	7.50	4.50
243	Clarence Gaston, Cesar Tovar/IA	15.00	7.50	4.50
244	Paul Casanova, Unknown	15.00	7.50	4.50
245	Vitico, Cesar Tovar	15.00	7.50	4.50
246	Pasion en el Juego	10.00	5.00	3.00
247	Luis Aparicio/IA	35.00	17.50	10.50
248	Angel Bravo/IA	15.00	7.50	4.50
249	Bobby Watson/IA	20.00	10.00	6.00
250	Alejandro "Palon" Carrasquel (Immortal)	25.00	12.50	7.50
251	Enrique Fonseca (Veteran)	20.00	10.00	6.00
252	Manuel Pollo Malpica (Immortal)	20.00	10.00	6.00
253	Emilio Cueche	20.00	10.00	6.00
254				
255	Felix "Tirahuequito" Machado (Veteran)			
256	Herberto Leal (Veteran)	20.00	10.00	6.00
257	Chucho Ramos (Veteran)	20.00	10.00	6.00
258	Julian Ladera (Veteran)	20.00	10.00	6.00
259	Carlos Ascanio (Immortal)	20.00	10.00	6.00
260	Jose Perez Colmenare (Immortal)	20.00	10.00	6.00
261	Isaias "Latigo" Chaves (Immortal)	20.00	10.00	6.00
262	Victor Garcia (Veteran)	20.00	10.00	6.00
263	Valentin Arevalo (Immortal)	20.00	10.00	6.00
264	Adolfredo Gonzalez (Veteran)	20.00	10.00	6.00
265	Hector Benitez Redondo (Veteran)	20.00	10.00	6.00
266	Ramon Fernandez (Veteran)	20.00	10.00	6.00
267	Guillermo Vento (Veteran)	20.00	10.00	6.00
268	Rafael Garcia Cedeno (Veteran)	20.00	10.00	6.00
269	Luis Oliveros (Veteran)	20.00	10.00	6.00
270	Luis Mono Zuloaga (Veteran)	20.00	10.00	6.00
271	Carlos Santeliz (Veteran)	20.00	10.00	6.00
272	Aureliano Patino	20.00	10.00	6.00
273	Rafael Olivares (Veteran)	20.00	10.00	6.00
274	Tarzan Contreras (Veteran)	20.00	10.00	6.00
275	Daniel Canonico	20.00	10.00	6.00
276	Babbino Fuenmayor (Veteran)	20.00	10.00	6.00
277	Rafael Galiz Tello (Veteran)	20.00	10.00	6.00
278	Pantaleon Espinoza	20.00	10.00	6.00
279	Miguel Sanabria (Veteran)	20.00	10.00	6.00
280				
281	Alfonso Carrasquel (Veteran)	40.00	20.00	12.00
282	Luis "Camaleon" Garcia (Veteran)	20.00	10.00	6.00
283	Balbino Inojosa (Veteran)	20.00	10.00	6.00
284	Humberto Popita Leal (Veteran)	20.00	10.00	6.00
285	Manuel Carrasquel (Veteran)	20.00	10.00	6.00
286	Ignacio Florez (Veteran)	20.00	10.00	6.00
287	Oscar Buzo Solorzino (Veteran)	20.00	10.00	6.00
288	Pelayo Chacon (Veteran)	20.00	10.00	6.00
289				
290	Micolas Berbesia (Veteran)	20.00	10.00	6.00
291	Julio Bracho (Veteran)	20.00	10.00	6.00
292	Dionisio Acosta (Veteran)	20.00	10.00	6.00
293	Gualberto Acosta (Veteran)	20.00	10.00	6.00
294	Winston Acosta (Veteran)	20.00	10.00	6.00
295	Jose Manuel Tovar (Veteran)	20.00	10.00	6.00
296	Carrao Bracho (Veteran)	20.00	10.00	6.00
297	Luis Romero Petit (Veteran)	20.00	10.00	6.00
298	Dalmiro Finol (Veteran)	20.00	10.00	6.00
299	Cerveceria Caracas Team Photo	20.00	10.00	6.00
300	Magallanes Campeones Nacionales Team	20.00	10.00	6.00

1972 Venezuelan Baseball Stamps

Utilizing most of the same photos as the 1972 Topps baseball cards, the 242 player stamps in this set feature only Major Leaguers, though with an overrepresentation of Hispanics, rather than the usual mix of U.S. and local talent. Stamps measure 2" x 2-9/16" and feature tombstone-shaped color

photos at center, surrounded by a green background. The only printing is the player name, team name (in Spanish) and stamp number, all in black. A white border surrounds the whole. Backs are blank as the stamps were meant to be mounted in an album. Because stamps are seldom seen in higher grade, only a VG price is presented here. Stamps in Good should be valued at 50 percent of the price shown, and stamps grading Fair at 25 percent.

		NM	EX	VG
	Complete Set (242):			4,900
	Common Player:			15.00
	Album:			150.00
1	Vic Davalillo			50.00
2	Doug Griffin			15.00
3	Rod Carew			150.00
4	Joel Horlen			15.00
5	Jim Fregosi			15.00
6	Rod Carew ("en acion" - In Action)			100.00
7	Billy Champion			15.00
8	Ron Hansen			15.00
9	Bobby Murcer			15.00
10	Nellie Briles			15.00
11	Fred Patek			15.00
12	Mike Epstein			15.00
13	Dave Marshall			15.00
14	Steve Hargan			15.00
15	Duane Josephson			15.00
16	Steve Garvey			22.50
17	Eddie Fisher			15.00
18	Jack Aker			15.00
19	Ron Brand			15.00
20	Del Rice			15.00
21	Ollie Brown			15.00
22	Jamie McAndrew			15.00
23	Willie Horton			15.00
24	Eddie Leon			15.00
25	Steve Hovley			15.00
26	Moe Drabowsky			15.00
27	Dick Selma			15.00
28	Jim Lyttle			15.00
29	Sal Bando			15.00
30	Bill Lee			15.00
31	Al Kaline			150.00
32	Mike Lum			15.00
33	Les Cain			15.00
34	Richie Hebner			15.00
35	Donn Clendenon			15.00
36	Ralph Houk			15.00
37	Luis Melendez			15.00
38	Jim Hickman			15.00
39	Manny Mota			15.00
40	Bob Locker			15.00
41	Ron Santo			20.00
42	Tony Cloninger			15.00
43	Joe Ferguson			15.00
44	Mike McCormick			15.00
45	Bobby Wine			15.00
46	Preston Gomez			15.00
47	Pat Corrales/IA			15.00
48	Hector Torres			15.00
49	Fritz Peterson			15.00
50	Jim Rooker			15.00
51	Chris Short			15.00
52	Juan Marichal/IA			22.50
53	Teddy Martinez			15.00
54	Ken Aspromonte			15.00
55	Bobby Bonds			15.00
56	Rich Robertson			15.00
57	Nate Colbert/IA			15.00
58	Jose Pagan/IA			15.00
59	Curt Blefary/IA			15.00
60	Bill Mazeroski			100.00
61	John Odom			15.00
62	George Stone			15.00
63	Lew Krausse			15.00
64	Bobby Knoop			15.00
65	Pete Rose/IA			225.00
66	Steve Luebber			15.00
67	Bill Voss			15.00
68	Chico Salmon			15.00
69	Ivan Murrell			15.00
70	Gil Garrido			15.00
71	Terry Crowley			15.00
72	Bill Russell			15.00
73	Steve Dunning			15.00
74	Ray Sadecki/IA			15.00
75	Al Gallagher/IA			15.00
76	Cesar Gutierrez			15.00
77	John Kennedy			15.00
78	Joe Hague			15.00
79	Bruce Del Canton			15.00
80	Ken Holtzman			15.00
81	Rico Carty			15.00
82	Roger Repoz			15.00
83	Fran Healy			15.00

84	Al Gallagher			15.00
85	Rich McKinney			15.00
86	Lowell Palmer			15.00
87	Jose Cardenal			15.00
88	Ed Kirkpatrick/IA			15.00
89	Steve Carlton			150.00
90	Gail Hopkins			15.00
91	Reggie Smith			15.00
92	Denny Riddleberger			15.00
93	Don Sutton			60.00
94	Bob Moose			15.00
95	Joe Decker			15.00
96	Bill Wilson			15.00
97	Mike Ferraro			15.00
98	Jack Hiatt			15.00
99	Bill Grabarkewitz			15.00
100	Larry Stahl			15.00
101	Jim Slaton			15.00
102	Jim Wynn			15.00
103	Phil Niekro			60.00
104	Danny Cater			15.00
105	Ray Sadecki			15.00
106	Jack Billingham			15.00
107	Dave Nelson			15.00
108	Rudy May			15.00
109	Don Money			15.00
110	Diego Segui			15.00
111	Jose Pagan			15.00
112	John Strohmayer			15.00
113	Wade Blasingame			15.00
114	Ken Wright			15.00
115	Ken Tatum			15.00
116	Mike Paul			15.00
117	Tom McCraw			15.00
118	Bob Gibson			125.00
119	Al Santorini			15.00
120	Leo Cardenas			15.00
121	Jimmy Stewart			15.00
122	Willie Crawford			15.00
123	Bob Aspromonte			15.00
124	Frank Duffy			15.00
125	Hal Lanier			15.00
126	Nate Colbert			15.00
127	Russ Gibson			15.00
128	Cesar Geronimo			15.00
129	Pat Kelly			15.00
130	Horacio Pina			15.00
131	Charlie Brinkman			15.00
132	Bill Virdon			15.00
133	Hal McRae			15.00
134	Tony Oliva/IA			25.00
135	Gonzalo Marquez			15.00
136	Willie Montanez			15.00
137	Dick Green			15.00
138	Jim Ray			15.00
139	Denis Menke			15.00
140	Fred Kendall			15.00
141	Vida Blue			15.00
142	Tom Grieve			15.00
143	Ed Kirkpatrick/IA			15.00
144	George Scott			15.00
145	Hal Breeden			15.00
146	Ken McMullen			15.00
147	Jim Perry/IA			15.00
148	Wayne Granger			15.00
149	Mike Hegan			15.00
150	Al Oliver			20.00
151	Frank Robinson/IA			100.00
152	Paul Blair			15.00
153	Phil Hennigan			15.00
154	Ron Stone			15.00
155	Gene Michael			15.00
156	Jerry McNertney			15.00
157	Marcelino Lopez			15.00
158	Dave May			15.00
159	Jim Hart			15.00
160	Joe Coleman			15.00
161	Rick Reichardt			15.00
162	Ed Brinkman			15.00
163	Dick McAuliffe			15.00
164	Paul Doyle			15.00
165	Terry Forster			15.00
166	Steve Hamilton			15.00
167	Mike Corkins			15.00
168	Dave Concepcion			75.00
169	Bill Sudakis			15.00
170	Juan Marichal			100.00
171	Harmon Killebrew			150.00
172	Luis Tiant			20.00
173	Ted Uhlaender			15.00
174	Tim Foli			15.00
175	Luis Aparicio/IA			200.00
176	Bert Campaneris			15.00
177	Charlie Sands			15.00
178	Darold Knowles			15.00
179	Jerry Koosman			15.00
180	Leo Cardenas/IA			15.00
181	Luis Alvarado			15.00
182	Graig Nettles			17.50
183	Walter Alston			20.00
184	Nolan Ryan			550.00
185	Ed Sprague			15.00
186	Rich Reese			15.00
187	Pete Rose			300.00
188	Bernie Allen			15.00
189	Lou Piniella			17.50
190	Jerry Reuss			15.00
191	Bob Pfeil			15.00
192	Bob Burda			15.00
193	Walt Williams			15.00
194	Dusty Baker			17.50
195	Rich Morales			15.00
196	Bill Stoneman			15.00
197	Hal King			15.00
198	Julian Javier			15.00
199	Dave Mason			15.00
200	Bob Veale			15.00
201	Jim Beauchamp			15.00

202	Ron Santo/IA	17.50
203	Tom Seaver	150.00
204	Jim Merritt	15.00
205	Jerry Koosman/IA	15.00
206	Dick Woodson	15.00
207	Wayne Simpson	15.00
208	Jose Laboy	15.00
209	Sam McDowell	15.00
210	Bob Bailey	15.00
211	Jim Fairey	15.00
212	Felipe Alou	25.00
213	Dave Concepcion/IA	50.00
214	Wilbur Wood/IA	15.00
215	Enzo Hernandez	15.00
216	Ron Reed	15.00
217	Stan Bahnsen	15.00
218	Ollie Brown/IA	15.00
219	Pat Jarvis	15.00
220	Tim Foli/IA	15.00
221	Denny McLain	15.00
222	Jerry Grote	15.00
223	Davey Johnson	15.00
224	John Odom/IA	15.00
225	Paul Casanova	15.00
226	George Culver	15.00
227	Pat Corrales	15.00
228	Jim Kaat	15.00
229	Archie Reynolds	15.00
230	Frank Reberger	15.00
231	Carl Yastrzemski	150.00
232	Jim Holt	15.00
233	Lenny Randle	15.00
234	Doug Griffin/IA	15.00
235	Doug Rader	15.00
236	Jesus Alou	15.00
237	Wilbur Wood/IA	15.00
238	Jim Kaat/IA	15.00
239	Fritz Peterson/IA	15.00
240	Dennis Leonard	15.00
241	Brooks Robinson	150.00
242	Felix Millan	15.00

1972 Venezuelan League Stickers

CARDENALES — 67 — LEW KRAUSSE

Issued in the winter league season of 1972-73, the Venezuelan League sticker set bears more than a passing similitude to the 1972 Topps baseball cards. The 2-1/2" x 3-1/2" stickers have tombstone-shaped photos framed in multi-colored borders with the team name at top and the player name in an oval cartouche at bottom. The sticker number is in a circle at top-right. Because they were intended to be mounted in an accompanying album, the backs are blank. Because so many of the stickers were once pasted into albums, and due to unfavorable climactic conditions, high-grade examples of Venezuelan stickers from the era are particularly scarce.

		NM	EX	VG
	Complete Set (249):			1,500
	Common Player:			20.00
	Album:			75.00
1	Dave Concepcion			30.00
2	Luis Rodriguez			25.00
3	Roberto Munoz			25.00
4	William Castillo			25.00
5	Jose Lopez			25.00
6	Armando Chacon			25.00
7	Juan Francia			25.00
8	Roric Harrison			25.00
9	Dave Concepcion, Escalona			30.00
10	Enrique Gutierrez			25.00
11	Luis Gonzalez			25.00
12	Jose Torres			25.00
13	William Salazar			25.00
14	Everest Contramaestre			25.00
15	Jesus Rizales			25.00
16	Ramon Velasquez			25.00
17	Rafael J. Velasquez			25.00
18	Jesus Loreto			25.00
19	Orlando Galindo			25.00
20	Jose Torres			25.00
21	Victor Jimenez			25.00
22	Hernan Silva			25.00
23	Leroy Stanton			25.00
24	Jesus Yanez			25.00
25	Orlando Tavares			25.00
26	Eddie Baez			25.00
27	Jim Frey			30.00
28	Eddie Watt			25.00
29	Aragua Team Logo			10.00
30	Carlos Orea			25.00
31	Rod Carew			75.00
32	Rod Carew, Enos Cabell			35.00
33	George Mitterwald			25.00
34	Enos Cabell			25.00
35	Eddy Baez			25.00
36	Teolindo Acosta			25.00
37	Ron Theobald			25.00

38	Milt Wilcox	30.00
39	Cesar Gutierrez	25.00
40	Ed Farmer	25.00
41	Dario Chirinos	25.00
42	Alberto Cambero	25.00
43	Eddy Diaz	25.00
44	Graciliano Parra	25.00
45	Bob Lee	25.00
46	Joe Keough	25.00
47	Dario Chirinos, Pablo Torrealba	25.00
48	Rafael Alvarez	25.00
49	Lucio Celis	25.00
50	Jose Martinez	25.00
51	Faustino Zabala	25.00
52	Jose Herrera	25.00
53	Monty Montgomery	25.00
54	Al Cowens	25.00
55	Lara Team	10.00
56	Luis Aparicio	60.00
57	Virgilio Mata	25.00
58	Franklin Moreno	25.00
59	Fidel Garcia	25.00
60	Victor Montilla	25.00
61	Bobby Mitchell	25.00
62	Pablo Torrealba	25.00
63	Joe Keough	25.00
64	Al Cowens	25.00
65	Dwight Evans	35.00
66	Rick Henninger	25.00
67	Lew Krausse	25.00
68	George Manz	25.00
69	John Lowenstein	25.00
70	Juan Quiroz	25.00
71	Sebastian Martinez	25.00
72	Claudio Urdaneta	25.00
73	Barry Raziano	25.00
74	Luis Aparicio	60.00
75	Lara Team Logo	10.00
76	Bobby Mitchell	25.00
77	Harold Hunter	25.00
78	Dick Pole	25.00
79	Carlos Davila	25.00
80	Enrique Gonzalez	25.00
81	Carlos Pascual	25.00
82	Edito Arteaga	25.00
83	William Fahey	25.00
84	Tomas Gonzalez	25.00
85	Rigoberto Mendoza	25.00
86	Rafael Jimenez	25.00
87	Jesus Aristimuno	25.00
88	Armando Ortiz	25.00
89	Bill Butler	25.00
90	Charles Day	25.00
91	Miguel Motolongo	25.00
92	Kurt Bavacqua (Bevacqua)	25.00
93	Esteban Padron	25.00
94	Angel Baez	25.00
95	Oscar Zamora	25.00
96	Manny Sarmiento	25.00
97	Nelson Canas	25.00
98	Victor Colina	25.00
99	Jerry Pirtle	25.00
100	Charles Day	25.00
101	Miguel Motolongo	25.00
102	Magallanes Group Photo	10.00
103	Jim Holt	25.00
104	Bob Darwin	25.00
105	Magallanes Team Logo	10.00
106	Oscar Del Busto	25.00
107	Jerry Jones	25.00
108	Eddie Leon	25.00
109	Armando Ortiz	25.00
110	Magallanes Team Photo	10.00
111	Magallanes Team Photo	10.00
112	Bob Darwin (Puzzle)	10.00
113	Bob Darwin	25.00
114	Rafael Cariel	25.00
115	Bob Darwin (Puzzle)	10.00
116	Bob Darwin (Puzzle)	10.00
117	Orlando Reyes	25.00
118	Edito Arteaga	25.00
119	Magallanes Roster (Carlos Pascual)	10.00
120	National Anthem	10.00
121	Barry Lersch	25.00
122	Elias Lugo	25.00
123	Simon Barreto	25.00
124	Manny Trillo	25.00
125	Joe Ferguson	25.00
126	Wilibaldo Quintana	25.00
127	Edgar Urbina	25.00
128	Nelson Garcia	25.00
129	Arguilio Freites	25.00
130	Carlos Rodriguez	25.00
131	Ozzie Virgil	25.00
132	Caracas Lions Team Logo	10.00
133	Virgilio Velasquez	25.00
134	Ed Sprague	25.00
135	Nelson Garcia	25.00
136	Jose Caldera	25.00
137	Antonio Armas	30.00
138	Dick Lange	25.00
139	Luis Sanz	25.00
140	Dave Lopez	25.00
141	Ulises Urrieta	25.00
142	Urbano Lugo	25.00
143	Bo Diaz	25.00
144	Andres Barrios	25.00
145	Victor Boll	25.00
146	Antonio Torres	25.00
147	Bert Campaneris	30.00
148	Carlos Alfonzo	25.00
149	Teodoro Obregon	25.00
150	Luis Penalver	25.00
151	Jose Ramon Jimenez	25.00
152	Cesar Tovar	25.00
153	Gonzalo Marquez	25.00

154	Dick Baney	25.00
155	Ed Armbrister	25.00
156	Ramon Webster	25.00
157	Francisco Navas	25.00
158	Hal McRae	25.00
159	Victor Davililo	25.00
160	Geoff Zahn	25.00
161	Jesus Camacaro	25.00
162	Ruiz, Parra	25.00
163	Posada, Dick Billings	25.00
164	Tom Grieve	25.00
165	Tom Grieve	25.00
166	Dick Billings	25.00
167	Peter Broberg	25.00
168	Victor Fainette	25.00
169	Cruz Rodriguez	25.00
170	Oscar Gamble	25.00
171	Olinto Rojas	25.00
172	Nelson Paiva	25.00
173	Jackie Brown	25.00
174	Gustavo Sposito	25.00
175	Levy Ochoa	25.00
176	Larry Bittner (Biittner)	25.00
177	William Kirkpatrick	25.00
178	Nevil Romero	25.00
179	Eduardo Benitez	25.00
180	Heriberto Lemus	25.00
181	Toby Harrah	25.00
182	Alfonzo Collazo	25.00
183	Jesus Reyes	25.00
184	Hely Boscan	25.00
185	Mike (Mickey) Scott	25.00
186	Roberto Bracho	25.00
187	Walter William (Williams)	25.00
188	Nevil Romero	25.00
189	Jose Alfaro	25.00
190	Leonel Carrion	25.00
191	Jesus Padron	25.00
192	Posada, Chico Carrasquel	25.00
193	Domingo Barboza	25.00
194	Eduardo Benitez	25.00
195	Nidio Sirit	25.00
196	Jose Carrao Bracho	25.00
197	Levi Ochoa	25.00
198	Hely Boscan	25.00
199	Victor Fainette, Leonel Carrion	25.00
200	Luis Rivas	25.00
201	Luis Tiant	25.00
202	Graciano Ravelo	25.00
203	Hector Artiles	25.00
204	Enzo Hernandez	25.00
205	Remigio Hermoso	25.00
206	Hector Brito	25.00
207	Victor Patino	25.00
208	Romualdo Blanco	25.00
209	Antonio Carrera	25.00
210	Euclides Camejo	25.00
211	Carlos Moreno	25.00
212	Oswaldo Blanco	25.00
213	Jorge Padron	25.00
214	Manuel Garcia	25.00
215	La Guaira Group Photo	10.00
216	La Guaira Group Photo	10.00
217	Jose Salas	25.00
218	Luis Sanchez	25.00
219	Raul Velarde	25.00
220	Al Bumbry	25.00
221	Group Photo	10.00
222	Ivan Murrell	25.00
223	Jose Cardenal	25.00
224	Group Photo	10.00
225	Group Photo	10.00
226	Angel Bravo	25.00
227	Tom Murphy	25.00
228	Hector Urbano	25.00
229	Camilo Pascual	25.00
230	Pat Kelly	25.00
231	Robert Marcano	25.00
232	Paul Casanova	25.00
233	Preston Gomez	25.00
234	La Guaira Team Logo	10.00
235	Ken Forsch	25.00
236	Luis Tiant (Puzzle)	10.00
237	Luis Tiant (Puzzle)	10.00
238	Dionel Durand	25.00
239	Luis Tiant (Puzzle)	10.00
240	Luis Tiant (Puzzle)	10.00
241	Jim Rooker (Puzzle)	10.00
242	Jim Rooker (Puzzle)	10.00
243	William Parker	25.00
244	Jim Rooker (Puzzle)	10.00
245	Jim Rooker (Puzzle)	10.00
246	Jose Herrera	25.00
247	Aurelio Monteagudo	25.00
248	Ivan Murrell	25.00
249	Roster (Preston Gomez)	10.00

1973 Venezuelan League Stickers

TIGRES — 29 — Milt Wilcox

These stickers were made for collection in an album and as such are typically found in low grade and/or with evidence of once having been so mounted. Several gaps in the reported checklist require further research. Many former and future Major Leaguers are included in the issue. The basic player stickers have color photos surrounded by a multi-color border with the team name at top and the player name at bottom. Stickers are about 2-1/2" x 3-1/2" and numbered on front. A colorful album to house the set was also issued.

		NM	EX	VG
Common Player:				20.00
Album:				75.00
1	Orlando Galindo			20.00
2	William Castillo			20.00
3	Everest Contramaestre			20.00
4	Luis Gonzalez			20.00
5	Jose Lopez			20.00
6	Cesar Orea			20.00
7	Luis H. Silva			20.00
8	Victor Jimenez			20.00
9	David Torres			20.00
10	Jose Torres			20.00
11	Ramon Velasquez			20.00
12	Jesus Avila			20.00
13	Carlos Loreto			20.00
14	Jesus Padron			20.00
15	Don Osborne			20.00
16	John Glass			20.00
17	Teolindo Acosta			20.00
18	Jim Todd			20.00
19	Roberto Munoz			20.00
20	Pete Lakock (LaCock)			20.00
21	Francisco Leandro			20.00
22	Jesus Rizales			20.00
23	Enos Cabell			25.00
24	Adrian Garret (Garrett)			20.00
25	Kurt Bavaqua (Bevacqua)			20.00
26	Jerry Moses			20.00
27	Jim Wiloughby (Willoughby)			20.00
28	Joel Youngblood			20.00
29	Milt Wilcox			25.00
30	Cesar Gutierrez			20.00
31	Efrain Urquiola			20.00
32	Carlos Pascual			20.00
33	Julio Bracho			20.00
34	Rafael Velasquez			20.00
35	Eddy Baez			20.00
36	Daniel Dubuc			20.00
37	Angel Leon			20.00
38	Angel Vargas			20.00
39	Motis Romero			20.00
40	Graciliano Parra			20.00
41	John Lowenstein			20.00
42	Nelson Garcia			20.00
43	Richard Burleson			25.00
44	Doug DeCinces			35.00
45	Eugene Martin			20.00
46	Jim Cox			20.00
47	Mike Adams			20.00
48	Richard Henninger			20.00
49	Sebastian Martinez			20.00
50	Lucio Celis			20.00
51	Alberto Cambero			20.00
52	Claudio Urdaneta			20.00
53	Victor Montilla			20.00
54	Pastor Perez			20.00
55	Enrique Gonzalez			20.00
56	Andres Barrios			20.00
57	Diego Herrera			20.00
58	Luis Aparicio			60.00
59	Teodoro Obregon			20.00
60	Dave Johnson			25.00
61	Roger Polanco			20.00
62	Ray Miller			20.00
63	Craig Caskey			20.00
64	David Wallace			20.00
65	Lara Team Logo			10.00
66	Herbert Hutson			20.00
67	Edgar Carusi			20.00
68	Luis Aponte			20.00
69	Joel Alcala			20.00
70	Dario Chirinos			20.00
71	Arnaldo Alvarado			20.00
72	Jose Bekis			20.00
73	Bill Moran			20.00
74	Steve McCartney			20.00
75	Lara Action			10.00
76	Rafael Alvarez			20.00
77	Juan Quiroz			20.00
78	Jim Rice			125.00
79	Ivan Murrel (Murrell)			20.00
80	James McKee			20.00
81	Rafael Cariel			20.00
82	George Theodore			20.00
83	Esteban Padron			20.00
84	Manuel Gonzalez			20.00
85	Edito Arteaga			20.00
86	Gus Gil			20.00
87	Oswaldo Olivares			20.00
88	Nelson Canas			20.00
89	Jesus Aristimuno			20.00
90	Orlando Reyes			20.00
91	Armando Ortiz			20.00
92	Gregorio Machado			20.00
93	Victor Colina			20.00
94	Alexis Ramirez			20.00
95	Jose Rios-Chiripa			20.00
96	Ed Napoleon			20.00
97	Bob Bailor			25.00
98	Dave Agustine (Augustine)			20.00
99	Bob Darwin			20.00
100	Gilberto Marcano			20.00
101	Jim Frey			25.00
102	Steve Braun			20.00
103	Don Hood			20.00
104	Mike Reinbach			20.00
105	Thomas Dettore			20.00
106	Wayne Garland			20.00
107	Mark Weens			20.00
108	Nelson Paiva			20.00
109	Manuel Sarmiento			20.00
110	Miguel Motolongo			20.00
111	Miguel Navas			20.00
112	Angel Baez			20.00
113	Raul Ortega			20.00
114	Humberto Montero			20.00
115	Tomas Gonzalez			20.00
116	Ruben Cabrera			20.00
117	Flores Bolivar			20.00
118	Felix Rodriguez			20.00
119	Ali Arape			20.00
120	Alexis Heredia			20.00
121	Arguilio Freites			20.00
122	Alfredo Ortiz			20.00
123	Simon Barreto			20.00
124	Urbano Lugo			20.00
125	Bo Diaz			20.00
126	Victor Boll			20.00
127	Jose Vinay Caldera			20.00
128	Leopoldo Tovar			20.00
129	Wilibaldo Quintana			20.00
130	Edgar Urbina			20.00
131	Ulises Urrieta			20.00
132	Antonio Torres			20.00
133	Luis Penalver			20.00
134	Heriberto Morillo			20.00
135	Tony Pacheco			20.00
136	Victor Davalillo			20.00
137	Jose Martinez			20.00
138	Jacinto Betancourt			20.00
139	Antonio Armas			40.00
140	Cesar Tovar			20.00
141	Jerry Johnson			20.00
142	Mike Anderson			20.00
143	Gonzalo Marquez			20.00
144	Peter Koegel			20.00
145	Pat Dobson			20.00
146	Craig Robinson			20.00
147	Luis Saez			20.00
148	Francisco Navas			20.00
149	Elias Lugo			20.00
150	Pablo Torrealba			20.00
151	Tom Grieve			20.00
152	Manny Trillo			40.00
153	Ed Sprague			20.00
154	Virgilio Velasquez			20.00
155	Dave Hamilton			20.00
156	Rafael Jimenez			20.00
157	Ubaldo Heredia			20.00
158	Rich Dempsey			30.00
159	Bill Parson (Parsons)			20.00
160	Caracas Leones			10.00
161	Gene Garber			25.00
162	Frank White			35.00
163	John Buck Martinez			20.00
164	Manuel Garcia			20.00
165	Jesus Padron			20.00
166	Oscar Gamble			25.00
167	Nelson Castellanos			20.00
168	Leo Posada			20.00
169	Eduardo Benitez			20.00
170	Luis Rivas			20.00
171	Alfonso Collazo			20.00
172	Levy Ochoa			20.00
173	Heriberto Lemus			20.00
174	Domingo Barboza			20.00
175	Jesus Reyes Barrios			20.00
176	Inal Fainete			20.00
177	Nidio Sirit			20.00
178	Nelson Paiva			20.00
179	Alfonso Carrasquel			35.00
180	Heli Boscan			20.00
181	Leonel Carrion			20.00
182	Jose Bracho			20.00
183	Gustavo Sposito			20.00
184	Iran Paz			20.00
185	Rich Reese			20.00
186	Al Cowans (Cowens)			25.00
187	Zulio Group Photo			10.00
188	Leo Posada, Alfonso Carrasquel			15.00
189	Octavio Rojas			20.00
190	Orlando Reyes			20.00
191	Mickey Scott			20.00
192	Harold King			20.00
193	Eduardo Acosta			20.00
194	Carlos Alfonso			20.00
195	Jose Lopez			20.00
196	Jerry Martin			20.00
197	Craig Kusick			20.00
198	Charles Murray			20.00
199	Alexis Corro			20.00
200	Jose Luis Alfaro			20.00
201	Juan Fco. Monasterio			20.00
202	Oscar Zamora			20.00
203	Ramon Moreno			20.00
204	Carlos Castillo			20.00
205	Ken Forsch			20.00
206	Leroy Stanton			20.00
207	Nevil Romero			20.00
208	Romualdo Blanco			20.00
209	Remigio Hermoso			20.00
210	Paul Casanova			20.00
211	Oswaldo Blanco			20.00
212	Oswaldo Troconis			20.00
213	Antonio Pipo Correa			20.00
214	Euclides Camejo			20.00
215	Dionel Duran			20.00
216	Hector Brito			20.00
217	Reinaldo Cordeiro			20.00
218	Jose Herrera			20.00
219	Hector Urbano			20.00
220	Jose Salas			20.00
221	Robert Marcano			20.00
222	Enzo Hernandez			20.00
223	Angel Bravo			20.00
224	Tomas Liscano			20.00
225	James Granford			20.00
226	Luis Salazar			20.00
227	Carlos Moreno			20.00
228	Manuel Malave			20.00
229	Al Bumbry			25.00
230	Luis Sanchez			20.00
231	Graziano Ravelo			20.00
232	La Guaira Tiburones Logo			10.00
233	John Jetter (Jeter)			20.00
234	Unknown			
235	Orlando Martinez			20.00
236	Tom Griffin			20.00
237	Lee Pitlock			20.00
238	Ray Burry			20.00
239	Preston Gomez			20.00
240	Aurelio Monteagudo			20.00
241	Carvajal/Bat Boy			20.00
242-	Unknown			
249				
250	Eduardo Benitez (a-t)			20.00
251	Ted (Tom) Heintzelman (b-t)			20.00
252	Ossie Virgil (c-t)			25.00
253	Alan Closter (d-t)			20.00
254	Carlos Avila (e-t)			20.00
255	David Concepcion (g-t)			40.00
256	Enrique Colina (h-t)			20.00
257	Damaso Blanco (a-n)			20.00
258	George Manz (a-c)			20.00
259	Peter MacKanin (b-c)			20.00
260	Neldy Castillo (c-c)			20.00
261	Leovanny Baez (a-z)			20.00
262	Mike Easler (b-z)			25.00
263	Peter Broberg (c-z)			20.00
264	Reggie Cleveland (d-z)			20.00
265	Stan Perzanowky (Perzanowski) (e-z)			20.00
266	Jerry Terrel (Terrell) (f-z)			20.00
267	Toby Harrah (h-z)			30.00
268	Franklyn Moreno (y-z)			20.00
269-	Unknown			
275				

1974 Venezuelan League Stickers

JOEL YOUNGBLOOD
OUTFIELD TIGRES

The 1974-75 winter league set of Venezuelan League stickers is a dead ringer for the 1968 Topps baseball cards. About 2-3/8" x 3-3/16", the stickers have photos framed in orange-mottled borders. The team name and position are in a circle at bottom, along with the player name in two colors. Because they were intended to be mounted in an accompanying album, the backs are blank. Because so many of the stickers were once pasted into albums, and due to unfavorable climactic conditions, high-grade examples of Venezuelan stickers from the era are particularly scarce.

		NM	EX	VG
Complete Set (275):				1,500
Common Player:				20.00
Album:				75.00
1	Arague Team Photo			10.00
2	Aragua Team Photo			10.00
3	Aragua Team Logo			10.00
4	Dave Concepcion			40.00
5	Ramon Velazquez			20.00
6	Carlos Orea			20.00
7	Francisco Leandro			20.00
8	Angel Hernandez			20.00
9	Armando Ortiz			20.00
10	Carlos Pascual			20.00
11	Argua Action			10.00
12	Milton Wilcox			25.00
13	Don Hood			20.00
14	Timothy Hosley			20.00
15	Teolindo Acosta			20.00
16	William Castillo			20.00
17	Aragua Action			10.00
18	Jesus Padron			20.00
19	Enos Cabell			25.00
20	Luis Silva			20.00
21	Aragua Action			10.00
22	Aragua Action			10.00
23	Joel Youngblood			25.00
24	Angel Vargas			20.00
25	Carlos Avila			20.00
26	Phil Gardner (Garner)			25.00
27	James Willoughby			20.00
28	Daniel Dubuc			20.00
29	Pancho			20.00
30	Aragua Action			10.00
31	Eastwick Rawlings (Rawly Eastwick)			25.00
32	David Torres			20.00

33	Robert Flynn	20.00
34	Duane Kuiper	25.00
35	Jesus Avila	20.00
36	Aragua Action	10.00
37	Aragua Action	10.00
38	Roberto Munoz	20.00
39	Eduardo Benitez	20.00
40	Aragua Action	.0010
41	Adrian Garret (Garrett)	20.00
42	Julio Bracho	20.00
43	Juan Quiroz	20.00
44	Angel Leon	20.00
45	Ossie Virgil	30.00
46	Lara Team Photo	10.00
47	Lara Team Photo	10.00
48	Lara Team Logo	10.00
49	Andres Barrios	20.00
50	Pastor Perez	20.00
51	Peter Koegel	20.00
52	Lara Action	10.00
53	Lowell Palmer	20.00
54	Alberto Cambero	20.00
55	Frank Snook	20.00
56	Steve McCartney	20.00
57	Lara Action	10.00
58	Dario Chirinos	20.00
59	Lara Action	10.00
60	Jim Cox	20.00
61	Terry Whitfield	20.00
62	Nelson Garcia	20.00
63	Lara Action	10.00
64	Sebastian Martinez	20.00
65	Lara Action	10.00
66	Rick Sawyer	20.00
67	Enrique Gonzalez	20.00
68	Tippy Martinez	30.00
69	Rafael Jimenez	20.00
70	Lara Action	10.00
71	Larvell Blanks	20.00
72	Franklin Tua	20.00
73	Craig Skok	20.00
74	Basilio Alvarado	20.00
75	Blas Arriechi	20.00
76	Dave Pagan	20.00
77	Roger Polanco	20.00
78	John Lowenstein	20.00
79	Francisco Leandro	20.00
80	Lucio Celis	20.00
81	Lara Action	10.00
82	Teodoro Obregon	20.00
83	Luis Aponte	20.00
84	Roberto Cox	40.00
85	Magallanes Team Photo	10.00
86	Magallanes Team Photo	10.00
87	Magallanes Team Logo	10.00
88	Oswaldo Olivares	20.00
89	Bob Bailor	25.00
90	Ali Arape	20.00
91	Jesus Aristimuno	20.00
92	Bob Andrews	20.00
93	Magallanes Action	10.00
94	Rick Stelmaszek	20.00
95	Damaso Blanco	20.00
96	Graciliano Parra	20.00
97	Merv Rettemund (Rettenmund)	25.00
98	Don Baylor	45.00
99	William Lister	20.00
100	Magallanes Action	10.00
101	Gregorio Machado	20.00
102	Doug Bair	20.00
103	Gilberto Marcano	20.00
104	Magallanes Action	10.00
105	Jim Sadowski	20.00
106	Miguel Nava	20.00
107	Ken (Kent) Tekulve	40.00
108	Wayne Garland	20.00
109	Magallanes Action	10.00
110	Alexis Ramirez	20.00
111	Dave Parker	60.00
112	Bob Veale	20.00
113	Manuel Sarmiento	20.00
114	Alberto Pedroza	20.00
115	Ruben Cabrera	20.00
116	Felix Rodriguez	20.00
117	Magallanes Action	10.00
118	Humberto Montero	20.00
119	Manuel Gonzalez	20.00
120	D. Flores	20.00
121	Jim Holt	20.00
122	Rafael Cariel	20.00
123	Magallanes Action	10.00
124	Deisi Bolivar	20.00
125	Edito Arteaga	20.00
126	Gustavo Gil	20.00
127	Larry Demeris (Demery)	20.00
128	Nelson Paiva	20.00
129	Steve Demeter	20.00
130	Caracas Leones Team Photo	10.00
131	Caracas Leones Team Photo	10.00
132	Caracas Leones Team Logo	10.00
133	Antonio Armas	40.00
134	Richard Dempsey	40.00
135	Toribio Garboza	20.00
136	Neldy Castillo	20.00
137	Ubaldo Heredia	20.00
138	Caracas Action	10.00
139	Jesus Marcano Trillo	40.00
140	Victor Albury	20.00
141	Uknown	20.00
142	Peter Broberg	20.00
143	Alfredo Ortiz	20.00
144	Leopoldo Tovar	20.00
145	Caracas Action	10.00
146	Tom Buskey	20.00
147	Virgilio Velasquez	20.00
148	Cesar Tovar	
149	Caracas Stadium	10.00
150	Don Stanhouse	20.00
151	Edgar Urbina	20.00
152	Pablo Torrealba	20.00
153	Jack Heidemann	20.00
154	Caracas Action	10.00
155	Luis Sanz	20.00
156	Gonzalo Marquez	20.00
157	Victor Davilillo	20.00
158	Bo Diaz	20.00
159	Caracas Action	10.00
160	Bill Butler	20.00
161	Elias Lugo	20.00
162	Tom Grieve	20.00
163	Caracas Action	10.00
164	Antonio Torres	20.00
165	Luis Penalver	20.00
166	Lenny Randle	20.00
167	Juan Gonzalez	20.00
168	Chuck Dobson	20.00
169	Urbano Lugo	20.00
170	Francisco Navas	20.00
171	Caracas Action	10.00
172	Jacinto Betancourt	20.00
173	Camilo Pascual	30.00
174	Frank White	30.00
175	Urbano Quintana	20.00
176	Jose Caldera	20.00
177	Caracas Action	10.00
178	Ulises Urrieta	20.00
179	Tomas Pacheco	20.00
180	La Guaira Tiburones Team Photo	10.00
181	La Guaira Tiburones Team Photo	10.00
182	La Guaira Tiburones Team Photo	10.00
183	Angel Bravo	20.00
184	Al Bumbry	25.00
185	Aurelio Monteagudo	20.00
186	Carlos Moreno	20.00
187	La Guaira Action	10.00
188	Hector Brito	20.00
189	Leroy Stanton	20.00
190	Romo Blanco	20.00
191	Marquina para Gorrias	10.00
192	Luis M. Sanchez	20.00
193	La Guaria Action	10.00
194	Jose Herrera	20.00
195	Victor Colina	20.00
196	Tiburones Team Bus	10.00
197	Jose Salas	20.00
198	La Guaira Action	10.00
199	Enzo Hernandez	20.00
200	Tomas Liscano	20.00
201	Paul Casanova	20.00
202	Machine	10.00
203	Graziano Ravelo	20.00
204	Ice Maker	10.00
205	Roland (Rowland) Office	20.00
206	Clubhouse	10.00
207	La Guaira Action	10.00
208	Dusty Baker	45.00
209	Replacements	10.00
210	Roric Harrison	20.00
211	Tom House	20.00
212	Jesus Aquino	20.00
213	Machine	10.00
214	La Guaira Action	10.00
215	Juan Monasterios	20.00
216	Angel Remigio Hermoso	20.00
217	Machine	10.00
218	Oswaldo Blanco	20.00
219	Infrared Light	10.00
220	Roberto Marcano	20.00
221	La Guaira Action	10.00
222	Jose Carvajal	20.00
223	Victor Patino	20.00
224	James Bird	20.00
225	La Guaira Action	10.00
226	Roland Sonny Jackson	25.00
227	Oscar Zamora	20.00
228	Antonio Pipo Correa	20.00
229	Manuel Malave	20.00
230	Nap Reyes	20.00
231	Zulia Aguilas Team Photo	10.00
232	Zluia Aguilas Team Photo	10.00
233	Zulia Aguilas Team Logo	10.00
234	Levy Ochoa	20.00
235	Billy Moran	20.00
236	Iran Paz	20.00
237	Alexis Corro	20.00
238	Zulia Action	10.00
239	Gus Sposito	20.00
240	Orlando Reyes	20.00
241	Carlos Alonso	20.00
242	Craig Kusick	20.00
243	Zulia Action	10.00
244	Domingo Barboza	20.00
245	Leonel Carrion	20.00
246	Jose Lopez	20.00
247	Bill Kirkpatrick	20.00
248	Alfonso Carrasquel	20.00
249	Richard Billings	20.00
250	Alfonzo Collazo	20.00
251	Orlando Ramirez	20.00
252	Ralph (Mickey) Scott	20.00
253	Luis Aparicio	60.00
254	Julio Bracho	20.00
255	Zulia Action	10.00
256	B. Jones	20.00
257	Heli Ramon Boscan	20.00
258	David Clyde	20.00
259	Cesar Gutierrez	20.00
260	Bob Randall	20.00
261	Jesus Reyes Barrios	20.00
262	Jose L. Alfaro	20.00
263	Claudio Urdaneta	20.00
264	Zulia Action	10.00
265	James Sundberg	30.00
266	Simon Barreto	20.00
267	Anthony Scott	20.00
268	Nidio Sirit	20.00
269	Zulia Action	10.00
270	Zulia Action	10.00
271	Leovanni Baez	20.00
272	Jefrey (Jeffrey) Terpko	20.00
273	Stan Perzanowski	20.00
274	Mike Easler	25.00
275	Jackie Moore	20.00

1976 Venezuelan League Stickers

The basic player stickers utizilize a design very similar to Topps' 1975 baseball cards, with player photos surrounded by a colorful border with the team name in large outline letters at top and the position is a baseball at bottom. Stickers are 2-3/8" x 3-3/16" and numbered on front. Like other Latin issues of the era, they are seldom available in high grade due to their intended useage and climactic conditions. Most of the stickers after #217 are specialty pieces with action photos, non-player subjects, multiple players, etc. A colorful album to house the set was also issued.

		NM	EX	VG
Complete Set (330):				2,000
Common Player:				20.00
Album:				75.00
1	Ossie Virgil			30.00
2	Patato Pascual			20.00
3	Jesus Avila			20.00
4	Raul Ortega			20.00
5	Dave Concepcion			40.00
6	Jesus Araujo			20.00
7	Preston Hanna			20.00
8	Victor Davilillo			20.00
9	Jesus Padron			20.00
10	Joseph Sdeb (Zdeb)			20.00
11	Alfredo Ortiz			20.00
12	Teolindo Acosta			20.00
13	Cesar Tovar			20.00
14	Craig Kusick			20.00
15	Angel Hernandez			20.00
16	Roberto Munoz			20.00
17	Fred Andrews			20.00
18	Rafael Alvarez			20.00
19	Luis Aparicio			50.00
20	Jeffrey Newman			20.00
21	Tommy Sant (Sandt)			20.00
22	Simon Barreto			20.00
23	Willie Norwood			20.00
24	Juan Quiroz			20.00
25	Douglas Capilla			20.00
26	William Butler			20.00
27	William Castillo			20.00
28	Robert Maneely			20.00
29	Peter Bromberg (Broberg)			20.00
30	Jesse Jefferson			20.00
31	Carlos Avila			20.00
32	Aragua Action			10.00
33	Aragua Action			10.00
34	Terry Whitfield			20.00
35	Aragua Action			10.00
36	Gary Lance			20.00
37	Robert Cox			40.00
38	Leo Posada			20.00
39	Lucio Celis			20.00
40	Enrique Gonzalez			20.00
41	Jose Musiu Lopez			20.00
42	Jose Sandoval			20.00
43	Victor Correll			20.00
44	Pedro Lobaton			20.00
45	Jim Norris			20.00
46	Luis Aponte			20.00
47	Orlando Gonzalez			20.00
48	Edguardo Benitez			20.00
49	George Zeber			20.00
50	Carlos Rodriguez			20.00
51	Graig (Craig) Robinson			20.00
52	Hernan Silva			20.00
53	Bob Oliver			20.00
54	Jose Herrera			20.00
55	Pete Mackanin			20.00
56	Roger Polanco			20.00
57	Lara Stadium			10.00
58	Arnaldo Alvarado			20.00
59	Ron Selak			20.00
60	Nelson Canas			20.00
61	John Sutton			20.00
62	Nelson Garcia			20.00
63	Victor Patino			20.00
64	Francisco Navas			20.00
65	Robert Polinsky			20.00
66	Franklin Tua			20.00
67	Oscar Zamora			20.00
68	David Torres			20.00

No.	Player	Price
69	Eddie Baez	20.00
70	Walter Williams	25.00
71	Cloyd Boyer	25.00
72	Carl (Garth?) Iorg	20.00
73	Pat Corrales	20.00
74	Alfonso Carrasquel	20.00
75	Antonio Torres	20.00
76	Camilo Pascual	30.00
77	Antonio Armas	40.00
78	Baudilio Diaz	20.00
79	Gary Beare	20.00
80	Steve Barr	20.00
81	Toribio Garboza	20.00
82	Mike Bassik (Bacsik)	20.00
83	Diego Segui	20.00
84	Jack Bastable	20.00
85	Ubaldo Heredia	20.00
86	Warren Cromartie	25.00
87	Elias Lugo	20.00
88	Mike (Mick) Kelleher	20.00
89	Marcano Trillo	40.00
90	Lenny Randle	20.00
91	Gonzalo Marquez	20.00
92	Jim Sadowski	20.00
93	Len Barker	25.00
94	Willi Quintana	20.00
95	Pablo Torrealba	20.00
96	Jim Hughes	20.00
97	Jose V. Caldera	20.00
98	Angel Vargas	20.00
99	Juan Gonzalez	20.00
100	Ulises Urrieta	20.00
101	Flores Bolivar	20.00
102	Robert Bowling	20.00
103	Rick Bladt	20.00
104	Luis Turner	20.00
105	Neldy Castillo	20.00
106	Adrian Garret (Garrett)	20.00
107	Bob Davis	20.00
108	La Guaira Action	10.00
109	Pompeyo Davalillo	20.00
110	Graciano Ravelo	20.00
111	Luis Lunar	20.00
112	Lester Morales	20.00
113	Enzo Hernandez	20.00
114	Aurelio Monteagudo	20.00
115	Angel Bravo	20.00
116	Carlos Moreno	20.00
117	Jose Cardenal	25.00
118	Rupert (Ruppert) Jones	20.00
119	Romo Blanco	20.00
120	Milton Ramirez	20.00
121	Antonio Correa	20.00
122	Clarence Gaston	25.00
123	Steve Lubber (Luebber)	20.00
124	Edwin Verhelst	20.00
125	Robert Johnson	20.00
126	Earl Bass	20.00
127	Jose Salas	20.00
128	Oswaldo Blanco	20.00
129	Steve Staag (Staggs)	20.00
130	Steve Patchin	20.00
131	Mike Kekish (Kekich)	20.00
132	Oswaldo Troconis	20.00
133	Dave May	20.00
134	Luis Salazar	20.00
135	Larry Gura	20.00
136	Rich Dauer	20.00
137	Pastor Perez	20.00
138	Paul Siebert	20.00
139	Luis M. Sanchez	20.00
140	Victor Colina	20.00
141	Adrian Devine	20.00
142	Robert Marcano	20.00
143	Juan Berenger (Berenguer)	25.00
144	Juan Monasterio	20.00
145	Donald Leppert	20.00
146	Gregorio Machado	20.00
147	Manuel Gonzalez	20.00
148	Wayne Granger	20.00
149	Remigio Hermoso	20.00
150	Rafael Cariel	20.00
151	Steve Dillard	20.00
152	Mitchell Page	20.00
153	Alexis Ramirez, Felix Rodriguez	15.00
154	Gary Wood	20.00
155	Ali Arape	20.00
156	Chris Batton	20.00
157	Gustavo Gil	20.00
158	Craig Reynolds	20.00
159	Jesus Aristimuno	20.00
160	Miguel Barreto	20.00
161	Alfonso Collazo	20.00
162	Steve Nicosia	20.00
163	Oswaldo Olivares	20.00
164	Robert Galasso	20.00
165	Alexis Ramirez	20.00
166	Craig Mitchell	20.00
167	Nelson Paiva	20.00
168	Ken Macha	20.00
169	Ruben Cabrera	20.00
170	Paul Reuschell (Reuschel)	20.00
171	Edito Arteaga	20.00
172	Olinto Rojas	20.00
173	Magallanes Action	10.00
174	Manny Sarmiento	20.00
175	Billy Moran	20.00
176	Eddie Watt	20.00
177	Michael Willis	20.00
178	Felix Rodriguez	20.00
179	James Easterly	20.00
180	Dave Parker	40.00
181	Luis Aparicio	50.00
182	Teodoro Obregon	20.00
183	Domingo Barboza	20.00
184	Not Issued, See #190	20.00
185	Gilberto Marcano	20.00
186	Jose Alfaro	20.00
187	Jesus Reyes	20.00
188	Mike (Mickey) Scott	20.00
189	Carl Frost	20.00
190a	Norman Shiera	20.00
190b	Orlando Pena (See #184.)	20.00
191	Orlando Reyes	20.00
192	Milt Wilcox	25.00
193	Andrew Dyes	20.00
194	J. Hernandez	20.00
195	Dario Chirinos	20.00
196	Greg Shanahan	20.00
197	Gustavo Sposito	20.00
198	Sebastian Martinez	20.00
199	Leonel Carrion	20.00
200	Dennis Lawallyn (Lewallyn)	20.00
201	Charky (Charlie) Moore	20.00
202	Steve Mallory	20.00
203	Gary Martz	20.00
204	Lamar Johnson	20.00
205	Tim Johnson	20.00
206	Levy Ochoa	20.00
207	Bill Dancy	20.00
208	Antonio Garcia	20.00
209	Nidio Sirit	20.00
210	Norman Shiera	20.00
211	Not Issued, See #221	20.00
212	Jesus Alfaro	20.00
213	Bobby Darwin	20.00
214	Zulia Action	10.00
215	Mike Seoane	20.00
216	Jim Gatner (Gantner)	20.00
217	Caracas Action	10.00
218	Caracas Action	10.00
219	Caracas Action	10.00
220	Caracas Action	10.00
221a	La Guaira Action	10.00
221b	Joe Chourio (See #211.)	20.00
222	Lara Action	10.00
223	Ulises Urrieta, Antonio Armas, Manny Trillo	20.00
224	Magallanes Dugout	10.00
225	Remigio Hermoso, Gustavo Gil	15.00
226	Caracas Action	10.00
227	Manny Trillo, Dave Concepcion	20.00
228	Zulia Action	10.00
229	Caracas Pizarra Scoreboard	10.00
230	La Guaira Action	10.00
231	Caracas Action	10.00
232	La Guaira Action	10.00
233	Zulia Action	10.00
234	Caracas Publico	10.00
235	Magallanes Action	10.00
236	Aragua Action	10.00
237	La Guaira Action	10.00
238	La Guaira Action	10.00
239	La Guaira Action	10.00
240	La Guaira Action	10.00
241	Manny Trillo, Jose Cardenal	20.00
242	Pompeyo Davilillo, Lacheman	15.00
243	La Guaira Action	10.00
244	La Guaira Action	10.00
245	Action	10.00
246	Zulia Action	10.00
247	Zulia Action	10.00
248	Tim Johnson	20.00
249	La Guaira Action	10.00
250	La Guaira Action	10.00
251	La Guaira Action	10.00
252	La Guaira Action	10.00
253	La Guaira Action	10.00
254	La Guaira Action	10.00
255	La Guaira Action	10.00
256	La Guaira Action	10.00
257	Caracas Action	10.00
258	La Guaira Action	10.00
259	Zulia Action	10.00
260	Caracas Action	10.00
261	Caracas Action	10.00
262	La Guaira Clubhouse	10.00
263	La Guaira Clubhouse	10.00
264	La Guaira Clubhouse	10.00
265	La Guaira Clubhouse	10.00
266	La Guaira Action	10.00
267	La Guaira Action	10.00
268	La Guaira Action	10.00
269	Panoramica	10.00
270	Zulia Action	10.00
271	Aragua Puzzle	10.00
272	Aragua Puzzle	10.00
273	Aragua Puzzle	10.00
274	Aragua Puzzle	10.00
275	Aragua Puzzle	10.00
276	Aragua Puzzle	10.00
277	Aragua Puzzle	10.00
278	Aragua Puzzle	10.00
279	Aragua Puzzle	10.00
280	Lara Puzzle	10.00
281	Lara Puzzle	10.00
282	Lara Puzzle	10.00
283	Lara Puzzle	10.00
284	Lara Puzzle	10.00
285	Lara Puzzle	10.00
286	Lara Puzzle	10.00
287	Lara Puzzle	10.00
288	Lara Puzzle	10.00
289	Caracas Puzzle	10.00
290	Caracas Puzzle	10.00
291	Caracas Puzzle	10.00
292	Caracas Puzzle	10.00
293	Caracas Puzzle	10.00
294	Caracas Puzzle	10.00
295	Caracas Puzzle	10.00
296	Caracas Puzzle	10.00
297	Caracas Puzzle	10.00
298	La Guaira Puzzle	10.00
299	La Guaira Puzzle	10.00
300	La Guaira Puzzle	10.00
301	La Guaira Puzzle	10.00
302	La Guaira Puzzle	10.00
303	La Guaira Puzzle	10.00
304	La Guaira Puzzle	10.00
305	La Guaira Puzzle	10.00
306	La Guaira Puzzle	10.00
307	Magallanes Puzzle	10.00
308	Magallanes Puzzle	10.00
309	Magallanes Puzzle	10.00
310	Magallanes Puzzle	10.00
311	Magallanes Puzzle	10.00
312	Magallanes Puzzle	10.00
313	Magallanes Puzzle	10.00
314	Magallanes Puzzle	10.00
315	Magallanes Puzzle	10.00
316	Zulia Puzzle	10.00
317	Zulia Puzzle	10.00
318	Zulia Puzzle	10.00
319	Zulia Puzzle	10.00
320	Zulia Puzzle	10.00
321	Zulia Puzzle	10.00
322	Zulia Puzzle	10.00
323	Zulia Puzzle	10.00
324	Zulia Puzzle	10.00
325	Magallanes Navagantes Logo	10.00
326	Aragua Tigres Logo	10.00
327	Caracas Leones Logo	10.00
328	Zulia Aguilas Logo	10.00
329	Lara Cardenales Logo	10.00
330	La Guaira Tiburones Logo	10.00

1977 Venezuelan Baseball Stickers

More than 400 pieces comprise this set of 2-3/8" x 3-1/8" blank-back stickers. The majority have color photos of winter league players with the team name, logo and position printed above, and the sticker number and name beneath the picture. There are many former and future Major League players in this group. A subset of some 50 stickers of American Major Leaguers is printed in reproduction of their 1977 Topps cards. Other stickers include group pictures, action photos, puzzle pieces, etc. The album issued to house the stickers has a player write-up in each space. Printed on very thin paper, and often removed from albums, these stickers are generally not found in condition above Very Good. For Good condition pieces, figure value at 50 percent of the prices shown here; stickers in Fair condition should be valued at 25 percent. Many of the stickers have player names misspelled.

	NM	EX	VG
Complete Set (402):	4,000		
Common Player:		15.00	
Album:			125.00
1	Aragua Tigers Logo		15.00
2	Ozzie Virgil Sr.		20.00
3	Jesus Avila		15.00
4	Raul Ortega		15.00
5	Simon Barreto		15.00
6	Gustavo Quiroz		15.00
7	Jerry Cram		15.00
8	Pat Cristelli		15.00
9	Preston Hanna		15.00
10	Angel Hernandez		15.00
11	John M'Callen		15.00
12	Randy Miller		15.00
13	Dale Murray		15.00
14	Mike Nagy		15.00
15	Stan Perzanowski		15.00
16	Juan Quiroz		15.00
17	Graciano Parra		15.00
18	Larry Cox		15.00
19	Lenn Sakata		15.00
20	Lester Straker		15.00
21	Nelson Torres		15.00
22	Carlos Avila		15.00
23	Orlando Galindo		15.00
24	Dave Wagner		15.00
25	Dave Concepcion		60.00
26	Alfredo Ortiz		15.00
27	Mike Lum, Dave Concepcion, Larry Parrish		15.00
28	Jesus Padron		15.00
29	Larry Parrish		15.00
30	Rob Picciolo		15.00
31	Luis Rivas		15.00
32	Bob Slater		15.00
33	Larry Murray		15.00
34	Dave Soderholm		15.00
35	Luis Benitez		15.00
36	Cesar Tovar, Victor Davalillo		20.00
37	Luis Bravo		15.00
38	William Castillo		15.00

No.	Name	Price
39	Terry Whitfield	15.00
40	Victor Davalillo	30.00
41	Mike Lum	15.00
42	Willie Norwood	15.00
43	Cesar Tovar	15.00
44	Joe Zdeb	15.00
45	Focion, Ozzie Virgil Sr.	15.00
46	Caracas Lions Logo	15.00
47	Felipe Alou	20.00
48	Alfonso Carrasquel (Chico)	35.00
49	Antonio Torres	15.00
50	Len Barker	15.00
51	Gary Beare	15.00
52	Cardell Camper	15.00
53	Juan Gonzalez	15.00
54	Paul Mirabella	15.00
55	Carney Lansford	15.00
56	Ubaldo Heredia	15.00
57	Elias Lugo	15.00
58	Oswaldo Troconis	15.00
59	Diego Segui	15.00
60	Lary Sorensen	15.00
61	Pablo Torrealba	15.00
62	Gustavo Bastardo	15.00
63	Luis Sanz	15.00
64	Steve Bowling	15.00
65	Tim Corcoran	15.00
66	Antonio Armas (Tony)	35.00
67	Toribio Garboza	15.00
68	Bob Molinaro	15.00
69	Willibaldo Quintana	15.00
70	Luis Turnes	15.00
71	Chuck Baker	15.00
72	Rob Belloir	15.00
73	Tom Brookens	15.00
74	Ron Hassey	15.00
75	Gonzalo Marquez	15.00
76	Bob Clark	15.00
77	Marcano Trillo (Manny)	30.00
78	Angel Vargas	15.00
79	Flores Bolivar	15.00
80	Baudilo Diaz (Bo)	15.00
81	Camilo Pascual	15.00
82	La Guaira Sharks Logo	15.00
83	Pompeyo Davalillo	17.50
84	Jose Martinez	15.00
85	Jim Willoughby	15.00
86	Romo Blanco	15.00
87	Mark Daly	15.00
88	Tom House	15.00
89	Danny Osborne	15.00
90	David Clyde	15.00
91	Luis Lunar	15.00
92	Randy McGilberry	15.00
93	Greg Minton	15.00
94	Aurelio Monteagudo	15.00
95	Carlos Moreno	15.00
96	Luis M. Sanchez	15.00
97	George Throop	15.00
98	Victor Colina	15.00
99	Edwin Verheist	15.00
100	John Wathan	15.00
101	Ruben Alcala	15.00
102	Ossie Blanco	15.00
103	Dave Cripe	15.00
104	Bob Marcano	15.00
105	Rudy Meoli	15.00
106	Pastor Perez	15.00
107	Milton Ramirez	15.00
108	Luis Salazar	15.00
109	Angel Bravo	15.00
110	Gene Clines	15.00
111	Jose Cardenal	15.00
112	Gabriel Ferrerc	15.00
113	Clint Hurdle	15.00
114	Juan Monasterio	15.00
115	Lester Morales	15.00
116	Carlos Hernandez	15.00
117	Nelo Lira	15.00
118	Raul Perez	15.00
119	Marcos Lunar	15.00
120	Franklin Moreno	15.00
121	Jerry Manuel	15.00
122	Ossie Blanco, Raul Perez	15.00
123	Tom McMillan	15.00
124	Roric Harrison	15.00
125	Tom Griffin	15.00
126	Juan Berenguer	15.00
127	Puzzle Piece (Reggie Jackson)	15.00
128	Puzzle Piece (Reggie Jackson)	15.00
129	Puzzle Piece (Reggie Jackson)	15.00
130	Puzzle Piece (Reggie Jackson)	15.00
131	Puzzle Piece (Reggie Jackson)	15.00
132	Puzzle Piece (Reggie Jackson)	15.00
133	Puzzle Piece (Reggie Jackson)	15.00
134	Puzzle Piece (Reggie Jackson)	15.00
135	Puzzle Piece (Reggie Jackson)	15.00
136	Reggie Jackson	325.00
137	Rod Carew	175.00
138	Dave Concepcion	90.00
139	Joe Morgan	125.00
140	Dave Parker	15.00
141	Carlton Fisk	125.00
142	Garry Maddox	15.00
143	George Foster	15.00
144	Fred Lynn	15.00
145	Lou Piniella	17.50
146	Mark Fidrych	175.00
147	Lou Brock	125.00
148	Mitchell Page	15.00
149	Sparky Lyle	15.00
150	Manny Sanguillen	15.00
151	Steve Carlton	125.00
152	Al Oliver	17.50
153	Davey Lopes	15.00
154	Johnny Bench	175.00
155	Richie Hebner	15.00
156	Cesar Cedeno	15.00
157	Manny Trillo	15.00
158	Nolan Ryan	1,500
159	Tom Seaver	175.00
160	Jim Palmer	125.00
161	Randy Jones	15.00
162	George Brett	325.00
163	Bill Madlock	15.00
164	Cesar Geronimo	15.00
165	Vida Blue	15.00
166	Tony Armas	.0035
167	Bill Campbell	15.00
168	Graig Nettles	15.00
169	Mike Schmidt	325.00
170	Willie Stargell	125.00
171	Ron Cey	15.00
172	Victor Davalillo	25.00
173	Pete Rose	375.00
174	Steve Yaeger	15.00
175	Frank Tanana	15.00
176	Carl Yastrzemski	175.00
177	Willie McCovey	125.00
178	Thurman Munson	125.00
179	Chris Chambliss	15.00
180	Bill Russell	15.00
181	Lara Cardinals Logo	15.00
182	Leo Posada	15.00
183	Lucio Celis	15.00
184	Enrique Gonzalez	15.00
185	Brian Abraham	15.00
186	Luis Aponte	15.00
187	Jose Lopez	15.00
188	Bobby Ramos	15.00
189	Tom Dixon	15.00
190	Gary Melson	15.00
191	Mark Budaska	15.00
192	Mark Fischlin	15.00
193	Garth Iorg	15.00
194	Mike Rowland	15.00
195	Dennis DeBarr	15.00
196	Gary Wilson	15.00
197	Dave McKay	15.00
198	Roberto Munoz	15.00
199	Roger Polanco	15.00
200	Pat Kelly	15.00
201	Hernan Silva	15.00
202	Francisco Navas	15.00
203	Pedro Lobaton	15.00
204	Pete Mackanin	15.00
205	Jose Caldera	15.00
206	Carlos Rodriguez (In Action)	15.00
207	Eddy Baez	15.00
208	Gary Metzeger	15.00
209	Rafael Sandoval	15.00
210	Arturo Sanchez	15.00
211	Franklin Tua	15.00
212	Teolindo Acosta	15.00
213	Arnaldo Alvarado	15.00
214	Orlando Gonzalez	15.00
215	Nelson Garcia	15.00
216	Terry Puhl	15.00
217	David Torres	15.00
218	Teolindo Acosta, Roberto Munoz	
219	Terry Puhl, Mark Budaska	15.00
220	Gary Gray	15.00
221	Gustavo Gil	15.00
222	Epi Guerrero	15.00
223	Bobby Ramos, Enrique Gonzalez	15.00
224	Rick Sawyer	15.00
225	S. Byre	15.00
226	Magallanes Navigators Logo	15.00
227	Alex Monchak	15.00
228	Manuel Gonzalez	15.00
229	Olinto Rojas	15.00
230	Gregorio Machado	15.00
231	Ali Arape	15.00
232	Miguel Barreto	15.00
233	Manny Sarmiento	15.00
234	Jesus Aristimuno, Alexis Ramirez, Felix Rodriguez	15.00
235	Ed Glynn	15.00
236	Luis Jiminez	15.00
237	Bob Adams	15.00
238	Edito Arteaga	15.00
239	Rafael Cariel	15.00
240	Eddie Solomon	15.00
241	Rick Williams	15.00
242	Miguel Nava	15.00
243	Rod Scurry	15.00
244	Mike Eduards (Edwards)	15.00
245	Earl Stephenson	15.00
246	Alfonso Collazo	15.00
247	Ruben Cabrera	15.00
248	Alfredo Torres	15.00
249	John Valle	15.00
250	Jesus Aristimuno	15.00
251	Joe Cannon	15.00
252	John Pacella	15.00
253	Oswaldo Olivares	15.00
254	Gary Hargis	15.00
255	Nelson Paiva	15.00
256	Bob Oliver	15.00
257	Alexis Ramirez	15.00
258	Larry Wolfe	15.00
259	Don Boyland (Doe)	15.00
260	Mark Wagner	15.00
261	Jim Wright	15.00
262	Mitchell Page	15.00
263	Felix Rodriguez	15.00
264	Willie Aaron	15.00
265	Justo Massaro	15.00
266	Norm Angelini	15.00
267	Fred Breining	15.00
268	Bill Sample	15.00
269	Than Smith	15.00
270	Harry Doris (Dorish)	15.00
271	Zulia Eagles Logo	15.00
272	Luis Aparicio	35.00
273	Toni Taylor (Tony)	15.00
274	Teodoro Obregon	15.00
275	Gilberto Marcano	15.00
276	Jose Alfaro	15.00
277	Danny Boitano	15.00
278	Jesus Reyes	15.00
279	Johel Chourio	15.00
280	Scott Sanderson	15.00
281	Charles Kiffin	15.00
282	Bill Dancy	15.00
283	Tim Johnson	15.00
284	Norman Shiera	15.00
285	Lonnie Smith	15.00
286	Manny Seoane	15.00
287	David Wallace	15.00
288	Lareu Whashington (LaRue Washington)	15.00
289	Danny Warthen	15.00
290	Sebastian Martinez	15.00
291	Warren Brusstar	15.00
292	Steven Waterburry (Waterbury)	15.00
293	Gustavo Sposito	15.00
294	Billy Connors	15.00
295	Bod Reece (Bob)	15.00
296	Al Velasquez	15.00
297	Jesus Alfaro	15.00
298	Todd Cruz	15.00
299	Efren Chourio	15.00
300	Tim Norrid	15.00
301	Leonel Carrion	15.00
302	Dario Chirinos	15.00
303	Bobby Darwin	15.00
304	Levy Ochoa	15.00
305	Orlando Reyez (Reyes)	15.00
306	Antonio Garcia	15.00
307	Fred Andrews	15.00
308	Domingo Barboza	15.00
309	Emilio Rodriguez	15.00
310	Roger Brown (Rogers "Bobby")	15.00
311	Nelson Munoz	15.00
312	Unknown	15.00
313	Greg Pryor	15.00
314	Early Espina	15.00
315	Leonel Carrion, Dario Chirinos	15.00
316	Luis Aparicio	25.00
317	Alfonso Carrasquel (Chico)	20.00
318	Dave Concepcion	20.00
319	Antonio Armas (Tony)	20.00
320	Marcano Trillo (Manny)	20.00
321	Pablo Torrealba	15.00
322	Manny Sarmiento	15.00
323	Baudilo Diaz (Bo)	15.00
324	Victor Davalillo	15.00
325	Puzzle Piece (Dave Parker)	15.00
326	Puzzle Piece (Dave Parker)	15.00
327	Puzzle Piece (Dave Parker)	15.00
328	Puzzle Piece (Dave Parker)	15.00
329	Puzzle Piece (Dave Parker)	15.00
330	Puzzle Piece (Dave Parker)	15.00
331	Puzzle Piece (Dave Parker)	15.00
332	Puzzle Piece (Dave Parker)	15.00
333	Puzzle Piece (Dave Parker)	15.00
334	Dave Parker	15.00
335	Steve Bowling	15.00
336	Jose Herrera	15.00
337	Mitchell Page	15.00
338	Enos Cabell	15.00
339	Orlando Reyes	15.00
340	Felix Rodriguez	15.00
341	Baudilo Diaz (Bo)	15.00
342	Gonzalo Marquez	15.00
343	Mike Kelleher	15.00
344	Juan Monasterio	15.00
345	Diego Segui	15.00
346	Steve Lueber (Luebber)	15.00
347	Mike Scott	15.00
348	Angel Bravo	15.00
349	Terry Whitfield	15.00
350	Bob Oliver	15.00
351	Tim Johnson (Johnson)	15.00
352	Gustavo Sposito	15.00
353	Jim Norris	15.00
354	Marcano Trillo (Manny)	20.00
355	Gary Woods	15.00
356	Felix Rodriguez	15.00
357	Dave May	15.00
358	Don Lepper (Leppert)	15.00
359	Magallanes Team Photo	15.00
360	Magallanes Team Photo	15.00
361	Action Photo	15.00
362	Action Photo	15.00
363	Antonio Torres, Leo Posada	15.00
364	Action Photo	15.00
365	Action Photo	15.00
366	Action Photo	15.00
367	Action Photo	15.00
368	Action Photo	15.00
369	Action Photo	15.00
370	Action Photo	15.00
371	Action Photo	15.00
372	Action Photo	15.00
373	Action Photo	15.00
374	Action Photo	15.00
375	Action Photo	15.00
376	Action Photo	15.00
377	Action Photo	15.00

#	Player	NM	EX	VG
378	Action Photo	15.00		
399	Action Photo (Misnumbered)	15.00		
380	Action Photo	15.00		
381	Action Photo	15.00		
382	Action Photo	15.00		
383	Action Photo	15.00		
384	Action Photo	15.00		
385	Action Photo	15.00		
386	Action Photo	15.00		
387	Action Photo	15.00		
388	Action Photo	15.00		
389	Antonio Torres, Franklin Parra	15.00		
390	Action Photo	15.00		
391	Angel Bravo, Luis Aparicio	20.00		
392	Action Photo	15.00		
393	Action Photo	15.00		
394	Action Photo	15.00		
395	Action Photo	15.00		
396	Action Photo	15.00		
397	Action Photo	15.00		
398	Action Photo	15.00		
399	Action Photo	15.00		
400	Action Photo	15.00		
401	Action Photo	15.00		
402	Tony Armas, Manny Trillo, Gonzalo Marquez	15.00		

1952 Victoria

(103) Raymond Dandridge
(103) Raymond Dandridge. — Posición: Infielder. Club: Marianao. Nació en Richmond, Virginia, hace 45 años. Mide 5'0''. Pesa 180 lbs. Batea y tira a la derecha. Uniforme: 28. Esta es su cuarta temporada con el Club Marianao. De 1935 a 1939 también jugó en Cuba con los teams de Santa Clara y Almendares. En el baseball organizado lleva cuatro años vistiendo la franela del Club Minneapolis, donde este verano bateó para .291, conectando 16 jonrones.

Obsequio de

COLECCIONES "VICTORIA"

Asista a los Juegos de Base Ball Profesional en el Stadium de La Habana

Estilo Comercial Registrado al No. 787 en el Ministerio de Comercio.

Produced during the 1952-53 Winter League season, these paper cards were formatted in the popular Latin American manner to be pasted into a colorful accompanying album. It is possible a principal venue for the set was the ballpark at Havana, since each card urges attendance at games there. The cards are printed on paper in a 2-1/8" x 3-1/8" size. Fronts have colorized photos with white borders, but no player identification. Backs are, of course, in Spanish and include a card number player personal data, career summary and a copyright notice. Besides local players, and former, current and future major league players, the set includes league umpires and broadcasters, etc. Names as presented in this checklist may not correspond exactly with those printed on card backs and may not be correct spellings of player names.

		NM	EX	VG
Complete Set (168):		13,000	6,500	3,500
Common Player:		90.00	45.00	30.00
Album:		700.00	350.00	200.00
1	Amado Maestri/Umpire	90.00	45.00	30.00
2	John Mullen/Umpire	90.00	45.00	30.00
3	Havana Stadium	90.00	45.00	30.00
4	Bernardino Rodriguez/Umpire	90.00	45.00	30.00
5	Raul Atan/Umpire	90.00	45.00	30.00
6	Cuco Conde/Broadcaster	90.00	45.00	30.00
7	Manolo de la Reguera/Broadcaster	90.00	45.00	30.00
8	Rafael (Felo) Ramirez/Broadcaster	120.00	60.00	40.00
9	Rafael Rubi/Broadcaster	90.00	45.00	30.00
10	Gabino Delgado/Broadcaster	90.00	45.00	30.00
11	Fernando Menendez/Broadcaster	90.00	45.00	30.00
12	Buck Canel/Broadcaster	100.00	50.00	30.00
13	Orlando Sanchez Diago/Broadcaster	90.00	45.00	30.00
14	Pedro Galiana/Broadcaster	90.00	45.00	30.00
15	Jess Losada/Broadcaster	90.00	45.00	30.00
16	Juan Ealo/Broadcaster	90.00	45.00	30.00
17	Rene Molina/Broadcaster	90.00	45.00	30.00
18	Miguel A. Ruiz/Broadcaster	90.00	45.00	30.00
19	Ruben Rodriguez/Broadcaster	90.00	45.00	30.00
20	Havana Lions Pennant	90.00	45.00	30.00
21	Miguel Gonzalez	120.00	60.00	40.00
22	Tomas (Pipo) de la Noval	90.00	45.00	30.00
23	Salvador Hernandez	90.00	45.00	30.00
24	Manuel Garcia	90.00	45.00	30.00
25	Edilio Alfaro	90.00	45.00	30.00
26	Julio Navarro	90.00	45.00	30.00
27	Richard Rand	90.00	45.00	30.00
28	Andres Fleitas	90.00	45.00	30.00
29	Isaac Seoane	90.00	45.00	30.00
30	Jimmie Kerrigan	90.00	45.00	30.00
31	Robert Alexander	90.00	45.00	30.00
32	Charles Sipples	90.00	45.00	30.00
33	Adrian Zabala	90.00	45.00	30.00
34	Rogelio Martinez	90.00	45.00	30.00
35	Carlos Pascual	120.00	60.00	40.00
36	Mario Picone	90.00	45.00	30.00
37	Eusebio Perez (Silverio)	90.00	45.00	30.00
38	Julio Moreno	90.00	45.00	30.00
39	Gilberto Torres	90.00	45.00	30.00
40	Bert Haas	90.00	45.00	30.00
41	Johnny Jorgensen	90.00	45.00	30.00
42	Lou Klein	90.00	45.00	30.00
43	Damon Phillips	90.00	45.00	30.00
44	Orlando Varona	90.00	45.00	30.00
45	Jorge Lopez	90.00	45.00	30.00
46	Pedro Formenthal	120.00	60.00	30.00
47	Robert Usher	90.00	45.00	30.00
48	Edmundo (Sandy) Amoros	120.00	60.00	40.00
49	Alejandro Crespo	100.00	50.00	30.00
50	Oscar Sardinas	90.00	45.00	30.00
51	Almendares Pennant	90.00	45.00	30.00
52	Robert Bragan	100.00	50.00	30.00
53	Clemente (Sungo) Carreras	90.00	45.00	30.00
54	Rodolfo Fernandez	90.00	45.00	30.00
55	Manuel Fernandez	90.00	45.00	30.00
56	Orlando Echevarria	90.00	45.00	30.00
57	Charles Thompson	90.00	45.00	30.00
58	Oscar Fernandez	90.00	45.00	30.00
59	Hal Erickson	90.00	45.00	30.00
60	Conrado Marrero	100.00	50.00	30.00
61	Agapito Mayor	90.00	45.00	30.00
62	Octavio Rubert	90.00	45.00	30.00
63	Edward Roebuck	90.00	45.00	30.00
64	Duke Markell	100.00	50.00	30.00
65	Rene Massip	90.00	45.00	30.00
66	Pedro Naranjo	90.00	45.00	30.00
67	Roque Contreras	90.00	45.00	30.00
68	Wayne McLeland	90.00	45.00	30.00
69	Frank Kellert	90.00	45.00	30.00
70	Forrest Jacobs	100.00	50.00	30.00
71	Hector Rodriguez	100.00	50.00	30.00
72	Willy Miranda	100.00	50.00	30.00
73	Roberto Ortiz	100.00	50.00	30.00
74	Frank Carswell	90.00	45.00	30.00
75	Asdrubal Baro	90.00	45.00	30.00
76	Paul Smith	90.00	45.00	30.00
77	Antonio Napoles	90.00	45.00	30.00
78	Francisco Campos	90.00	45.00	30.00
79	Angel Scull	90.00	45.00	30.00
80	Raymond Coleman	90.00	45.00	30.00
81	Gino Cimolli (Cimoli)	100.00	50.00	30.00
82	Amado Ibanez	90.00	45.00	30.00
83	Avelino Canizarez	90.00	45.00	30.00
84	Conrado Perez	90.00	45.00	30.00
85	Marianao Pennant	90.00	45.00	30.00
86	Fermin Guerra	100.00	50.00	30.00
87	Jose Maria Fernandez	100.00	50.00	30.00
88	Jose (Joe) Olivares	90.00	45.00	30.00
89	Ramon Carneado	90.00	45.00	30.00
90	Alejandro (Baby) Fernandez	90.00	45.00	30.00
91	Emilio Cabrera	90.00	45.00	30.00
92	Sandalio Consuegra	100.00	50.00	30.00
93	Tomas Fine	90.00	45.00	30.00
94	Miguel Fornieles	100.00	50.00	30.00
95	Camilo Pascual	120.00	60.00	40.00
96	Miguel Lopez	90.00	45.00	30.00
97	Clarence Iott	100.00	50.00	30.00
98	Dale Matthewson	90.00	45.00	30.00
99	Hampton Coleman	100.00	50.00	30.00
100	Terris McDuffie	120.00	60.00	40.00
101	Raul Sanchez	90.00	45.00	30.00
102	Lorenzo Cabrera	90.00	45.00	30.00
103	Ray Dandridge	1,600	800.00	500.00
104	Silvio Garcia	90.00	45.00	30.00
105	Carlos De Souza	90.00	45.00	30.00
106	Oreste (Minnie) Minoso	200.00	100.00	60.00
107	Sebastian Basso	90.00	45.00	30.00
108	William Wilson	90.00	45.00	30.00
109	Hank Workman	100.00	50.00	30.00
110	Fernando Pedroso	90.00	45.00	30.00
111	Juan Antonio Vistuer	90.00	45.00	30.00
112	Hiram Gonzalez	90.00	45.00	30.00
113	Julio Becquer	90.00	45.00	30.00
114	Stan Rojek	90.00	45.00	30.00
115	Ramiro (Cuco) Vasquez	90.00	45.00	30.00
116	Juan Izaguirre	90.00	45.00	30.00
117	Cienfuegos Pennant	90.00	45.00	30.00
118	Billy Herman	220.00	110.00	65.00
119	Oscar Rodriguez	90.00	45.00	30.00
120	Julio Rojo	90.00	45.00	30.00
121	Pedro Pages	90.00	45.00	30.00
122	Felix Masud	90.00	45.00	30.00
123	Rafael Noble	100.00	50.00	30.00
124	Mario Diaz	90.00	45.00	30.00
125	Luis Aloma	90.00	45.00	30.00
126	Santiago Ulrich	90.00	45.00	30.00
127	Armando Roche	90.00	45.00	30.00
128	Raul Lopez	90.00	45.00	30.00
129	Armando Suarez	90.00	45.00	30.00
130	Vincente Lopez	90.00	45.00	30.00
131	Ernesto Morillas	90.00	45.00	30.00
132	Alfredo Ibanez	90.00	45.00	30.00
133	Allen J. Gettel	90.00	45.00	30.00
134	Ken Lehman	90.00	45.00	30.00
135	Pat Mc Clothin (McGlothin)	100.00	50.00	30.00
136	Rogenio Otero	90.00	45.00	30.00
137	Felipe Montemayor	90.00	45.00	30.00
138	Jack Cassini	100.00	50.00	30.00
139	Donald Zimmer	120.00	60.00	40.00
140	Robert Wilson	90.00	45.00	30.00
141	Humberto Fernandez	90.00	45.00	30.00
142	Pedro Ballester	90.00	45.00	30.00
143	Walt Morin (Moryn)	100.00	50.00	30.00
144	Roberto Fernandez	90.00	45.00	30.00
145	Claro Duany	120.00	60.00	40.00
146	Pablo Garcia	90.00	45.00	30.00
147	James Pendleton	100.00	50.00	30.00
148	Oscar Sierra	90.00	45.00	30.00
149	Adolfo Luque	160.00	80.00	50.00
150	Cando Lopez	90.00	45.00	30.00
151	Joe Black	200.00	100.00	60.00
152	Napoleon Reyes	120.00	60.00	40.00
153	Rafael (Villa) Cabrera	90.00	45.00	30.00
154	Charles (Red) Barrett	100.00	50.00	30.00
155	Fred Martin	90.00	45.00	30.00
156	Isidoro Leon	90.00	45.00	30.00
157	John Rutherford	100.00	50.00	30.00
158	Max Lanier	100.00	50.00	30.00
159	Julio Ramos	90.00	45.00	30.00
160	Manuel Hidalgo	90.00	45.00	30.00
161	Wilfredo Calvino	90.00	45.00	30.00
162	Joe Nakamura	120.00	60.00	40.00
163	Martiniano Garay	90.00	45.00	30.00
164	Fernando Rodriguez	90.00	45.00	30.00
165	Anibal Navarrette	90.00	45.00	30.00
166	Rafael Rivas	90.00	45.00	30.00
167	Wilfredo Salas	90.00	45.00	30.00
168	Jocko Thompson	90.00	45.00	30.00

1908 Victor Publishing Cy Young

Eschewing booze, women and gambling made Cy Young famous, according to this postcard issued by an Ohio company near the end of the pitcher's career. The 3-1/2" x 5-1/2" card has a large black-and-white photographic portrait at center with maroon and black illustrations emblematic of typical ballplayers' vices in the corners. The divided-back is printed in black with typical postcard markings.

	NM	EX	VG
Cy Young	1,750	875.00	525.00

1915 Victory Tobacco (T214)

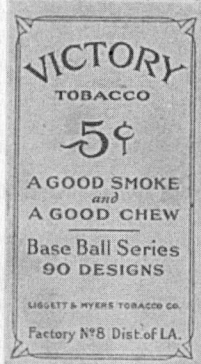

The T214 Victory set of 1915 is an obscure series of tobacco cards that is sometimes mistaken for the better-known T206 "White Border" set. The confusion is understandable because identical player poses were used for both sets. The Victory set can be easily identified, however, by the advertising for the Victory brand on the back of the cards. The set features players from the Federal League, both major leagues and at least one minor leaguer. While card backs advertise "90 Designs," fewer than 60 subjects have surfaced to date. The set had such limited distribution - apparently restricted to just the Louisiana area - and the cards are so rare that it may never be completely checklisted. Except for the advertising on the backs, the Victory cards are almost identical to the "Type 2" Coupon cards (T213), another obscure Louisiana tobacco set issued during the same period. Of the several tobacco sets issued in Louisana in the early part of the 20th Century, the T214 Victory cards are considered the most difficult to find. Gaps have been left in the numbering sequence to accommodate future additions.

		NM	EX	VG
Common Player:		8,000	4,000	2,400
(1)	Red Ames	7,200	2,880	1,440
(2)	Chief Bender	16,500	8,250	4,950
(3)	Roger Bresnahan	16,500	8,250	4,950
(4)	Al Bridwell	7,200	2,880	1,440
(5)	Howie Camnitz	7,200	2,880	1,440
(6)	Hal Chase/Portrait	18,000	9,000	5,500
(7)	Hal Chase/Throwing	18,000	9,000	5,500
(8)	Ty Cobb/Portrait (Red background.)	67,250	33,625	20,175
(9)	Doc Crandall	7,200	2,880	1,440
(10)	Birdie Cree	7,200	2,880	1,440
(11)	Josh Devore	7,200	2,880	1,440
(12)	Ray Demmitt	7,200	2,880	1,440
(13)	Mickey Doolan	7,200	2,880	1,440
(14)	Mike Donlin	7,200	2,880	1,440
(15)	Tom Downey	7,200	2,880	1,440
(16)	Larry Doyle	7,200	2,880	1,440
(17)	Kid Elberfeld	7,200	2,880	1,440
(18)	Johnny Evers	16,500	8,250	4,950
(19)	Russ Ford	7,200	2,880	1,440
(20)	Art Fromme	7,200	2,880	1,440
(21)	Chick Gandil	16,500	8,250	4,950

		NM	EX	VG
(22)	Rube Geyer	7,200	2,880	1,440
(23)	Clark Griffith	16,500	8,250	4,950
(24)	Bob Groom	7,200	2,880	1,440
(25)	Buck Herzog	7,200	2,880	1,440
(26)	Hughie Jennings	16,500	8,250	4,950
(27)	Walter Johnson (Hands at chest.)	25,000	12,500	7,500
(28)	Joe Kelley	16,500	8,250	4,950
(29)	Ed Konetchy	7,200	2,880	1,440
(30)	Nap Lajoie	20,000	10,000	6,000
(31)	Ed Lennox	7,200	2,880	1,440
(32)	Sherry Magee	7,200	2,880	1,440
(33)	Rube Marquard	16,500	8,250	4,950
(34)	John McGraw	16,500	8,250	4,950
(35)	George McQuillan	7,200	2,880	1,440
(36)	Chief Meyers/Catching	7,200	2,880	1,440
(37)	Chief Meyers/Portrait	7,200	2,880	1,440
(38)	George Mullin	7,200	2,880	1,440
(41)	Red Murray	7,200	2,880	1,440
(42)	Tom Needham	7,200	2,880	1,440
(43)	Rebel Oakes	7,200	2,880	1,440
(44)	Dode Paskert	7,200	2,880	1,440
(45)	Jack Quinn	7,200	2,880	1,440
(46)	Nap Rucker	7,200	2,880	1,440
(47)	Germany Schaefer	7,200	2,880	1,440
(48)	Wildfire Schulte	7,200	2,880	1,440
(49)	Frank Smith	7,200	2,880	1,440
(51)	Tris Speaker	22,500	11,250	6,750
(52)	George Stovall	7,200	2,880	1,440
(53)	Ed Summers	7,200	2,880	1,440
(54)	Bill Sweeney	7,200	2,880	1,440
(55)	Jeff Sweeney	7,200	2,880	1,440
(56)	Ira Thomas	7,200	2,880	1,440
(57)	Joe Tinker	16,500	8,250	4,950
(58)	Heinie Wagner	7,200	2,880	1,440
(59)	Zack Wheat	16,500	8,250	4,950
(60)	Kaiser Wilhelm	7,200	2,880	1,440
(61)	Hooks Wiltse	7,200	2,880	1,440

1929 Villa Theater Philadelphia A's

These cards were issued in conjunction with a World Series promotion by a Philadelphia movie house. Fronts of the black-and-white 3-5/8" x 5-3/4" cards have player portraits with the player identified by name and position in the lower-right corner of the bottom order. On back is an ambiguously worded message promising a team-autographed ball will be given away at the Saturday matinee. It is unknown whether the five players on this checklist represent the complete issue.

		NM	EX	VG
	Common Player:	125.00	65.00	40.00
(1)	Eddie Collins	250.00	125.00	75.00
(2)	Jimmy Dykes	125.00	65.00	40.00
(3)	George "Mule" Haas	125.00	65.00	40.00
(4)	Edmund "Bing" Miller	125.00	65.00	40.00
(5)	Rube Walberg	125.00	65.00	40.00

1886 Virginia Brights Black Stocking Nine (N48)

Issued during the late 1880s, though the attributed date is speculative, this series of cabinet-size (about 5" x 7-1/2") and super-size (7-1/2" x 132") blank-back cards was available by sending in coupons found in Allen & Ginter's Virginia Brights brand cigarettes. Fronts have a sepia photo of Rubenesque women in baseball uniforms posed before a painted ballpark backdrop. In the bottom border is "BLACK STOCKING NINE. ALLEN & GINTER'S / Virginia Brights Cigarettes. / Crop of 1884 / HAND MADE CROP OF 1884." The beveled edges of the cabinet mount were originally gilt-trimmed.

	NM	EX	VG
Common Card (Small):	2,400	1,200	700.00
Common Card (Large)	4,250	2,100	1,250

1887 Virginia Brights Polka Dot Nine

Issued during the late 1880s, though the attributed date is speculative, this series of cabinet-size (about 5" x 7-1/2") blank-back cards was available by sending in coupons found in Allen & Ginter's Virginia Brights brand cigarettes. Fronts have a sepia photo of women in baseball uniforms and polka-dot bandanas posed before a backdrop. In the top border of the yellow cardboard mount, printed in gold leaf, is "Virginia Brights / Cigarettes / CROP OF 1884." In a cartouche beneath the photo is "POLKA DOT NINE." Below that is "THE FULL SET OF THIS SERIES COMPRISES NINE DIFFERENT SUBJECTS. / REPRESENTING THE VARIOUS POSITIONS IN BASE BALL."

	NM	EX	VG
Common Card:	2,200	1,100	600.00

1888 Virginia Brights Girl Baseball Players

(See 1888 Allen & Ginter Girl Baseball Players.)

1888 Virginia Brights Black Stocking Nine

Issued during the late 1880s, this series of cabinet-size (about 5" x 7-1/2") blank-back cards was available by sending in coupons found in Allen & Ginter's Virginia Brights brand cigarettes. Fronts have a sepia photo of Rubenesque women in a baseball uniform posed before a painted ballpark backdrop. The picture is framed by a fancy design. In the border above is "Virginia Brights / Cigarettes / Crop of 1884." Below the photo is the series title "Black Stocking Nine" and "The Full Set of this Series Comprises Nine Different / Subjects Representing the Various Positions in Base-Ball."

	NM	EX	VG
Common Card:	2,400	1,200	725.00

1911-16 Virginia Extra Cigarettes (T216)

The T216 baseball card set, issued by several brands of the Peoples Tobacco Co., is the last of the Louisana cigarette sets and the most confusing. Apparently issued over a period of several years between 1911 and 1916, the set employs the same pictures as several contemporary caramel and bakery sets. Cards measure a nominal 1-1/2" x 2-5/8", thought reasonable allowance must be made in consideration of original cutting methodology. Positive identification can be made by the back of the cards. The Peoples Tobacco cards carry advertising for one of three brands of cigarettes: Kotton, Mino or Virginia Extra. The Kotton brand is the most common, while the Virginia Extra and Mino backs command a premium. T216 cards are found in two types; one has a glossy front finish, while a second scarcer type is printed on thin paper. The thin paper cards command an additional 15 percent premium. The cards represent players from the American, National and Federal Leagues.

		NM	EX	VG
	Common Player:	3,300	1,320	660.00
(1)	Jack Barry/Btg	3,300	1,320	660.00
(2)	Jack Barry/Fldg	3,300	1,320	660.00
(3)	Harry Bemis	3,300	1,320	660.00
(4a)	Chief Bender (Philadelphia, striped cap.)	8,800	3,520	1,760
(4b)	Chief Bender (Baltimore, striped cap.)	8,800	3,520	1,760
(5a)	Chief Bender (Philadelphia, white cap.)	8,800	3,520	1,760
(5b)	Chief Bender (Baltimore, white cap.)	8,800	3,520	1,760
(6)	Bill Bergen	3,300	1,320	660.00
(7a)	Bob Bescher (Cincinnati)	3,300	1,320	660.00
(7b)	Bob Bescher (St. Louis)	3,300	1,320	660.00
(8)	Roger Bresnahan	8,800	3,520	1,760
(9)	Al Bridwell (Batting)	3,300	1,320	660.00
(10a)	Al Bridwell/Sliding (New York)	3,300	1,320	660.00
(10b)	Al Bridwell/Sliding (St. Louis)	3,300	1,320	660.00
(11)	Donie Bush	3,300	1,320	660.00
(12)	Doc Casey	3,300	1,320	660.00
(13)	Frank Chance	8,800	3,520	1,760
(14a)	Hal Chase/Fldg (New York)	3,300	1,320	660.00
(14b)	Hal Chase/Fldg (Buffalo)	3,300	1,320	660.00
(15)	Hal Chase/Portrait	3,300	1,320	660.00
(16a)	Ty Cobb/Standing (Detroit Am.)	35,750	14,300	7,150
(16b)	Ty Cobb/Standing (Detroit Americans)	33,000	13,200	6,600
(17)	Ty Cobb/Btg (Detroit Americans)	33,000	13,200	6,600
(18a)	Eddie Collins (Phila. Am.)	8,800	3,520	1,760
(18b)	Eddie Collins (Phila. Amer.)	8,800	3,520	1,760
(19)	Eddie Collins (Chicago)	8,800	3,520	1,760
(20a)	Sam Crawford (Small print.)	8,800	3,520	1,760
(20b)	Sam Crawford (Large print.)	8,800	3,520	1,760
(21)	Harry Davis	3,300	1,320	660.00
(22)	Ray Demmitt	3,300	1,320	660.00
(23)	Art Devlin	3,300	1,320	660.00
(24a)	Wild Bill Donovan (Detroit)	3,300	1,320	660.00
(24b)	Wild Bill Donovan (New York)	3,300	1,320	660.00
(25a)	Red Dooin (Philadelphia)	3,300	1,320	660.00
(25b)	Red Dooin (Cincinnati)	3,300	1,320	660.00
(26a)	Mickey Doolan (Philadelphia)	3,300	1,320	660.00
(26b)	Mickey Doolan (Baltimore)	3,300	1,320	660.00
(27)	Patsy Dougherty	3,300	1,320	660.00
(28a)	Larry Doyle, Larry Doyle/Btg (N.Y. Nat'l.)	3,300	1,320	660.00
(28b)	Larry Doyle/Btg (New York Nat'l,.)	3,300	1,320	660.00
(29)	Larry Doyle/Throwing	3,300	1,320	660.00
(30)	Clyde Engle	3,300	1,320	660.00
(31a)	Johnny Evers (Chicago)	8,800	3,520	1,760
(31b)	Johnny Evers (Boston)	8,800	3,520	1,760
(32)	Art Fromme	3,300	1,320	660.00
(33a)	George Gibson (Pittsburg Nat'l, back view.)	3,300	1,320	660.00
(33b)	George Gibson (Pittsburgh Nat'l., back view.)	3,300	1,320	660.00
(34a)	George Gibson (Pittsburg Nat'l, front view.)	3,300	1,320	660.00
(34b)	George Gibson (Pittsburgh Nat'l., front view.)	3,300	1,320	660.00
(35a)	Topsy Hartsel (Phila. Am.)	3,300	1,320	660.00
(35b)	Topsy Hartsel (Phila. Amer.)	3,300	1,320	660.00
(36)	Roy Hartzell/Btg	3,300	1,320	660.00
(37)	Roy Hartzell/Catching	3,300	1,320	660.00
(38a)	Fred Jacklitsch (Philadelphia)	3,300	1,320	660.00
(38b)	Fred Jacklitsch (Baltimore)	3,300	1,320	660.00
(39a)	Hughie Jennings (Orange background.)	8,800	3,520	1,760
(39b)	Hughie Jennings (Red background.)	8,800	3,520	1,760
(40)	Red Kleinow	3,300	1,320	660.00
(41a)	Otto Knabe (Philadelphia)	3,300	1,320	660.00
(41b)	Otto Knabe (Baltimore)	3,300	1,320	660.00
(42)	Jack Knight	3,300	1,320	660.00
(43a)	Nap Lajoie/Fldg (Philadelphia)	13,750	5,500	2,750
(43b)	Nap Lajoie/Fldg (Cleveland)	13,750	5,500	2,750
(44)	Nap Lajoie/Portrait	13,750	5,500	2,750
(45a)	Hans Lobert (Cincinnati)	3,300	1,320	660.00
(45b)	Hans Lobert (New York)	3,300	1,320	660.00
(46)	Sherry Magee	3,300	1,320	660.00
(47)	Rube Marquard	8,800	3,520	1,760
(48a)	Christy Matthewson (Mathewson) (Large print.)	33,000	13,200	6,600
(48b)	Christy Matthewson (Mathewson) (Small print.)	33,000	13,200	6,600
(49a)	John McGraw (Large print.)	8,800	3,520	1,760
(49b)	John McGraw (Small print.)	8,800	3,520	1,760
(50)	Larry McLean	3,300	1,320	660.00
(51)	George McQuillan	3,300	1,320	660.00
(52)	Dots Miller	3,300	1,320	660.00
(53a)	Dots Miller/Fldg (Pittsburg)	3,300	1,320	660.00
(53b)	Dots Miller/Fldg (St. Louis)	3,300	1,320	660.00
(54a)	Danny Murphy (Philadelphia)	3,300	1,320	660.00
(54b)	Danny Murphy (Brooklyn)	3,300	1,320	660.00
(55)	Rebel Oakes	3,300	1,320	660.00
(56)	Bill O'Hara	3,300	1,320	660.00
(57)	Eddie Plank	8,800	3,520	1,760
(58a)	Germany Schaefer (Washington)	3,300	1,320	660.00
(58b)	Germany Schaefer (Newark)	3,300	1,320	660.00
(59)	Admiral Schlei	3,300	1,320	660.00
(60)	Boss Schmidt	3,300	1,320	660.00
(61)	Johnny Seigle	3,300	1,320	660.00
(62)	Dave Shean	3,300	1,320	660.00
(63)	Boss Smith (Schmidt)	3,300	1,320	660.00
(64)	Tris Speaker	16,500	6,600	3,300
(65)	Oscar Stanage	3,300	1,320	660.00
(66)	George Stovall	3,300	1,320	660.00
(67)	Jeff Sweeney	3,300	1,320	660.00
(68a)	Joe Tinker/Btg (Chicago Nat'l.)	8,800	3,520	1,760

(68b)	Joe Tinker/Btg (Chicago Feds.)	8,800	3,520	1,760
(69)	Joe Tinker/Portrait	8,800	3,520	1,760
(70a)	Honus Wagner/Btg (S.S.)	33,000	13,200	6,600
(70b)	Honus Wagner/Btg (2b.)	33,000	13,200	6,600
(71a)	Honus Wagner/Throwing (S.S.)	33,000	13,200	6,600
(71b)	Honus Wagner/Throwing (2b.)	33,000	13,200	6,600
(72)	Hooks Wiltse	3,300	1,320	660.00
(73)	Cy Young	22,000	8,800	4,400
(74a)	Heinie Zimmerman (2b.)	3,300	1,320	660.00
(74b)	Heinie Zimmerman (3b.)	3,300	1,320	660.00

1949 Vis-Ed Cleveland Indian Slide-Cards

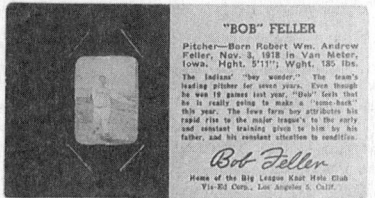

These unique novelties feature the members of the World Champion 1948 Cleveland Indians. The players are pictured on a single frame of 16mm film which has been inserted into slits cut on one end of the cardboard. The cardboard holders are dark blue and yellow, with blue printing. Fronts have player personal data, career highlights, the player's name in script and identification of the issuer. Backs have a list of "Magic Slides" which could be ordered for 33 cents each. It is likely that a slide-card exists for each of the players on that list, but only those which have been confirmed to date are check-listed here, in alphabetical order. Complete slide-cards measure 3-3/4" x 2". A plastic baseball-shaped viewer was sold with the slides.

		NM	EX	VG
Common Player:		75.00	37.00	22.00
(1)	Lou Boudreau	90.00	45.00	27.00
(2)	Larry Doby	100.00	50.00	30.00
(3)	Bob Feller	125.00	62.00	37.00
(4)	Joe Gordon	75.00	37.00	22.00
(5)	Jim Hegan	75.00	37.00	22.00
(6)	Ken Keltner	75.00	37.00	22.00

1949 Vis-Ed Cleveland Indian Magic Dials

Similar in concept to a Viewmaster, these hand-held "Magic Dial Big League Viewers" feature the members of the World Champion 1948 Cleveland Indians, plus Mickey Vernon, who joined the team in 1949, and, inexplicably, Pittsburgh Pirate Ralph Kiner. Each of the players is pictured on six single frames of 8 mm movie film (once in color, but now usually faded to sepia tones) mounted on a 2" cardboard circle within a red, white and blue 2-1/4" x 2" rectangular frame; the whole is held together by a metal rivet. The pictures can be viewed by turning the round cardboard dial. The dials came with a playing tips instructional pamphlet. Original price was 29 cents apiece.

		NM	EX	VG
Complete Set (15):		1,200	600.00	350.00
Common Player:		75.00	37.00	22.00
(1)	Gene Bearden	75.00	37.00	22.00
(2)	Lou Boudreau/Btg	125.00	62.00	37.00
(3)	Lou Boudreau (Double play.)	125.00	62.00	37.00
(4)	Lou Boudreau (Shortstop)	125.00	62.00	37.00
(5)	Larry Doby	125.00	62.00	37.00
(6)	Bob Feller	150.00	75.00	45.00
(7)	Joe Gordon (Double play.)	75.00	37.00	22.00
(8)	Joe Gordon (Second base.)	75.00	37.00	22.00
(9)	Jim Hegan	75.00	37.00	22.00
(10)	Ken Keltner	75.00	37.00	22.00
(11)	Ralph Kiner	125.00	62.00	37.00
(12)	Bob Lemon	125.00	62.00	37.00
(13)	Dale Mitchell	75.00	37.00	22.00
(14)	Satchel Paige	200.00	100.00	60.00
(15)	Mickey Vernon	75.00	37.00	22.00

1966 Volpe Tumblers

A number of teams co-operated in the production of baseball player 12-oz. thermal tumblers which were distributed at local gas stations for a small sum and/or a minimum fuel purchase. The plastic tumblers have artwork portraits and smaller action pictures by Nicholas Volpe and facsimile autographs on colorful backgrounds. The glasses are 5-1/4" tall and 3" in diameter at the rim.

		NM	EX	VG
Common Player:		20.00	10.00	6.00

CINCINNATI REDS
(1)	Chico Cardenas	20.00	10.00	6.00
(2)	Gordy Coleman	20.00	10.00	6.00
(3)	John Edwards	20.00	10.00	6.00
(4)	Sammy Ellis	20.00	10.00	6.00
(5)	Tommy Harper	20.00	10.00	6.00
(6)	Deron Johnson	20.00	10.00	6.00
(7)	Jim Maloney	20.00	10.00	6.00
(8)	Billy McCool	20.00	10.00	6.00
(9)	Joe Nuxhall	20.00	10.00	6.00
(10)	Jim O'Toole	20.00	10.00	6.00
(11)	Vada Pinson	30.00	15.00	9.00
(12)	Pete Rose	75.00	37.00	22.00

CLEVELAND INDIANS
(1)	Max Alvis	20.00	10.00	6.00
(2)	Joe Azcue	20.00	10.00	6.00
(3)	Larry Brown	20.00	10.00	6.00
(4)	Rocky Colavito	50.00	25.00	15.00
(5)	Vic Davalillo	20.00	10.00	6.00
(6)	Chuck Hinton	20.00	10.00	6.00
(7)	Dick Howser	20.00	10.00	6.00
(8)	Sam McDowell	20.00	10.00	6.00
(9)	Don McMahon	20.00	10.00	6.00
(10)	Sonny Siebert	20.00	10.00	6.00
(11)	Leon Wagner	20.00	10.00	6.00
(12)	Fred Whitfield	20.00	10.00	6.00

NEW YORK METS
(1)	Larry Bearnarth	20.00	10.00	6.00
(2)	Yogi Berra	50.00	25.00	15.00
(3)	Jack Fisher	20.00	10.00	6.00
(4)	Rob Gardner	20.00	10.00	6.00
(5)	Jim Hickman	20.00	10.00	6.00
(6)	Ron Hunt	20.00	10.00	6.00
(7)	Ed Kranepool	20.00	10.00	6.00
(8)	Johnny Lewis	20.00	10.00	6.00
(9)	Tug McGraw	20.00	10.00	6.00
(10)	Roy McMillan	20.00	10.00	6.00
(11)	Dick Stuart	20.00	10.00	6.00
(12)	Ron Swoboda	20.00	10.00	6.00

DETROIT TIGERS
(1)	Hank Aguirre	20.00	10.00	6.00
(2)	Norm Cash	30.00	15.00	9.00
(3)	Don Demeter	20.00	10.00	6.00
(4)	Bill Freehan	20.00	10.00	6.00
(5)	Willie Horton	20.00	10.00	6.00
(6)	Al Kaline	50.00	25.00	15.00
(7)	Mickey Lolich	20.00	10.00	6.00
(8)	Dick McAuliffe	20.00	10.00	6.00
(9)	Denny McLain	20.00	10.00	6.00
(10)	Joe Sparma	20.00	10.00	6.00
(11)	Don Wert	20.00	10.00	6.00
(12)	Dave Wickersham	20.00	10.00	6.00

LOS ANGELES DODGERS
(1)	Tommy Davis	20.00	10.00	6.00
(2)	Willie Davis	20.00	10.00	6.00
(3)	Don Drysdale	40.00	20.00	12.00
(4)	Ron Fairly	20.00	10.00	6.00
(5)	John Kennedy	20.00	10.00	6.00
(6)	Jim Lefebvre	20.00	10.00	6.00
(7)	Sandy Koufax	60.00	30.00	18.00
(8)	Claude Osteen	20.00	10.00	6.00
(9)	Wes Parker	20.00	10.00	6.00
(10)	Ron Perranoski	20.00	10.00	6.00
(11)	Johnny Roseboro	20.00	10.00	6.00
(12)	Maury Wills	20.00	10.00	6.00

1913 Voskamp's Coffee Pittsburgh Pirates

The 1913 Pittsburgh Pirates are featured in this set of cards given away in packages of coffee and tea and redeemable for seats at Pirates games. The 2-1/4" x 3-5/8" cards have black-and-white player photos on a plain white background, along with ID and a "Photo by Johnston" credit line. The black-and-white back has a checklist of the set and details of the ticket redemption program. Pose variations of the Hofman and O'Toole cards are reported to exist. The checklist for the unnumbered cards is presented here alphabetically. Because the set was issued just after the great tobacco card era, several of the Pirates in this set are not found on any other cards.

		NM	EX	VG
Common Player:		3,000	1,500	900.00
(1)	Babe Adams	3,000	1,500	900.00
(2)	Everitt Booe	3,000	1,500	900.00
(3)	Bobby Byrne	3,000	1,500	900.00
(4)	Howie Camnitz	3,000	1,500	900.00
(5)	Max Carey	3,000	1,500	900.00
(6)	Joe Conzelman	3,000	1,500	900.00
(7)	Jack Ferry	3,000	1,500	900.00
(8)	George Gibson	3,000	1,500	900.00
(9)	Claude Hendrix	3,000	1,500	900.00
(10)	Solly Hofman	3,000	1,500	900.00
(11)	Ham Hyatt	3,000	1,500	900.00
(12)	Bill Kelly	3,000	1,500	900.00
(13)	Ed Mensor (Existence not confirmed)			
(14)	Dots Miller	3,000	1,500	900.00
(15)	Marty O'Toole	3,000	1,500	900.00
(16)	Hank Robinson (Existence not confirmed)			
(17)	Mike Simon	3,000	1,500	900.00
(18)	Jim Viox	3,000	1,500	900.00
(19)	Honus Wagner	45,000	22,000	13,500
(20)	Owen Wilson	3,000	1,500	900.00

1910 Hans Wagner Cigars

Circa 1910 the Freeman Cigar Co. apparently envisioned marketing a product named for the Pirates star shortstop. While it appears the cigar was never actually produced, various packaging elements have survived in proof examples. Most pieces are embossed and have a color lithograph which features a portrait of Wagner against a ballgame background. "HANS WAGNER" is in red and gold above. Usually found in the bottom border is "Title & Design Registered by Freeman Cigar Co." Collectors must be aware that various modern fantasy pieces purporting to be of the same genre exist in the market.

	NM	EX	VG
Hans Wagner (7-1/4" x 6-1/2" box label)	15,000	7,500	4,500
Hans Wagner (4-1/2" octagonal label)	12,000	6,000	3,500
Hans Wagner (4-1/4" oval label)	15,000	7,500	4,500
Hans Wagner (3" cigar band)	1,600	800.00	480.00
Hans Wagner (Typographic box-side label.)	1,500	750.00	450.00
Hans Wagner (Typographic box-top label.)	7,500	3,750	2,250

1880s John M. Ward Fan

The specific date of production for this ornate hand fan is unknown. Some examples show on their back an advertisement for "C. Philpot" of Springfield, Maine. The central portion of the fan is a round piece of heavy cardboard, about 7-3/4" in diameter, that features a color lithographic portrait of Ward on a baseball background. Around the picture is a peach-colored ribbon. A wooden handle is attached on back.

	NM	EX	VG
John M. Ward	7,800	4,200	2,700

1934 Ward's Sporties Pins

The date of issue can only be approximated for this issue pf 1-1/4" diameter celluloid pin-back buttons. Ward's Sporties was evidently some kind of food product; at the center of each button is a black-and-white or blue-and-white portrait photo of a player with his name above and "Eats" below the picture. Printed around the photo portion in white on a red background is: "Good Sports Enjoy / WARD'S SPORTIES". Ward's bakeries issue several type of baseball cards and collectibles over the years, such as the 1947 Tip-Top bread cards. The checklist is in alphabetical order, and may not yet be complete.

		NM	EX	VG
Complete Set (8):		4,500	2,250	1,350
Common Player:		325.00	160.00	100.00
(1)	Dizzy Dean	1,000	500.00	300.00
(2)	Jimmy Dykes	325.00	160.00	100.00
(3)	Jimmie Foxx	1,000	500.00	300.00
(4)	Frank Frisch	650.00	325.00	195.00
(5)	Charlie Gehringer	650.00	325.00	195.00
(6)	Charlie Grimm	325.00	160.00	100.00
(7)	Schoolboy Rowe	325.00	160.00	100.00
(8)	Jimmie Wilson	325.00	160.00	100.00

1974 Pete Ward Clinic Photos

These black-and-white blank-back player pictures were issued in conjunction with a baseball clinic conducted by former major leaguer Pete Ward. The pictures of the clinic's instructors measure about 6" x 8".

		NM	EX	VG
Complete Set (6):		275.00	140.00	80.00
Common Player:		20.00	10.00	6.00
(1)	Mickey Mantle	150.00	75.00	45.00
(2)	Billy Martin	45.00	22.50	13.50
(3)	Pete Rose	100.00	50.00	30.00
(4)	Harry Walker	20.00	10.00	6.00
(5)	Pete Ward	20.00	10.00	6.00
(6)	Maury Wills	45.00	22.50	13.50

1916 Ware's

 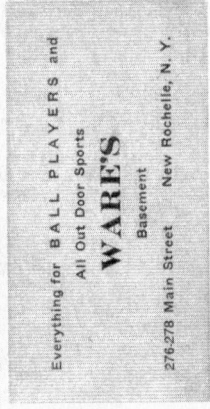

One of several regional advertisers to use this 200-card set as a promotional medium was this New Rochelle, N.Y., store's sporting goods department. The checklist and relative value information are listed under 1916 M101-4 Blank Backs. Collectors can expect to pay a significant premium for individual cards to enhance a type card or superstar card collection. The American Card Catalog listed these 1-5/8" x 3" black-and-white cards as H801-9.

PREMIUMS:
Common Players: 8-12X
Hall of Famers: 6-8X
(See 1916 M101-4 Blank Backs for checklist and base card values.)

1872 Warren Studio Boston Red Stockings Cabinets

 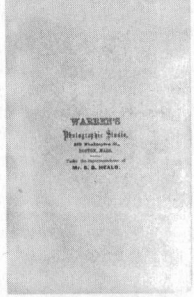

The champions from the premiere season of baseball's first professional league (some wearing their championship pins), are pictured on these cabinet cards. Members of the Boston Red Stockings were photographed in uniform at a local studio. The cards measure about 4-1/4" x 6-1/2" with sepia photos. In the bottom border is the name and address of the studio; information that is repeated on the otherwise blank back. Player identification is not found on the cards but can be deduced by studying contemporary team pictures.

		NM	EX	VG
Common Player:		6,500	3,000	2,000
(1)	Ross Barnes	9,000	4,000	2,500
(2)	Dave Birdsall	6,500	3,000	2,000
(3)	Charles Gould	6,500	3,000	2,000
(4)	Andy Leonard	6,500	3,000	2,000
(5)	Cal McVey	9,000	4,000	2,500
(6)	Fraley Rogers	6,500	3,000	2,000
(7)	John Ryan	6,500	3,000	2,000
(8)	Harry Schafer	6,500	3,000	2,000
(9)	Albert Spalding	42,000	9,000	5,400
(10)	George Wright	30,000	9,000	5,400
(11)	Harry Wright	30,000	9,000	5,400

1872-1874 Warren Studio Boston Red Stockings CDVs

The champions from the premiere season of baseball's first professional league (some wearing their championship pins), are pictured on these cartes de visites depict. Members of the Boston Red Stockings were photographed at a local studio, most of them being pictured in coat-and-tie with only Harry and George Wright in uniform. The cards measure about 2-1/2" x 4-1/4" with sepia photos bordered in white. In the bottom border is the name and address of the studio; information which is repeated on the otherwise blank back. Player identification is not found on the cards but can be deduced by studying contemporary team pictures.

		NM	EX	VG
Common Player:		4,500	3,000	2,000
(1)	Ross Barnes	4,500	3,000	2,000
(2)	Dave Birdsall	4,500	3,000	2,000
(3)	Charlie Gould	4,500	3,000	2,000
(4)	Andy Leonard	4,500	3,000	2,000
(5)	Cal McVey	4,500	3,000	2,000
(6)	Fraley Rogers	4,500	3,000	2,000
(7)	John Ryan	4,500	3,000	2,000
(8)	Harry Schafer	4,500	3,000	2,000
(9)	Albert Spalding	20,000	10,000	6,000
(10)	George Wright	15,000	7,500	4,500
(11)	George Wright (Uniform)	20,000	10,000	6,000
(12)	Harry Wright (Street clothes.)	15,000	7,500	4,500
(13)	Harry Wright (Uniform)	20,000	10,000	6,000

1874 Warren Studio Boston Red Stockings Cabinets

The champions from the National Association Boston Red Stockings were photographed in uniform at a local studio. The cards measure about 4-1/4" x 6-1/2" with sepia photos. In the bottom border is the name and address of the studio. Player identification is not found on the cards but can be deduced by studying contemporary team pictures.

		NM	EX	VG
Common Player:		5,500	2,750	1,650
(1)	Ross Barnes	8,250	2,750	1,650
(2)	Tommy Beals	6,600	2,750	1,650
(3)	George Hall	6,600	2,750	1,650
(4)	Andy Leonard	5,500	2,750	1,650
(5)	Cal McVey	8,250	2,750	1,650
(6)	Harry Schafer	6,600	2,750	1,650

1931 Washington Senators Picture Pack

This set of souvenir pictures offers player photos in a black-and-white, blank-back format of about 6-1/8" x 9-1/2". Each picture has a white border and a facsimile player autograph.

		NM	EX	VG
Complete Set (30):		800.00	400.00	240.00
Common Player:		25.00	12.50	7.50
(1)	Nick Altrock	35.00	17.50	10.50
(2)	Oswald Bluege	25.00	12.50	7.50
(3)	Cliff Bolton	25.00	12.50	7.50
(4)	Lloyd Brown	25.00	12.50	7.50
(5)	Robert Burke	25.00	12.50	7.50
(6)	Joe Cronin	50.00	25.00	15.00
(7)	Alvin Crowder	25.00	12.50	7.50
(8)	E.B. Eynon, Jr. (Secretary-Treasurer)	25.00	12.50	7.50
(9)	Charles Fischer	25.00	12.50	7.50
(10)	Edward Gharrity	25.00	12.50	7.50
(11)	Clark Griffith	45.00	22.00	13.50
(12)	Irving Hadley	25.00	12.50	7.50
(13)	William Hargrave	25.00	12.50	7.50
(14)	David Harris	25.00	12.50	7.50
(15)	Jack Hayes	25.00	12.50	7.50
(16)	Walter Johnson	125.00	62.00	37.00
(17)	Sam Jones	25.00	12.50	7.50
(18)	Baxter Jordan	25.00	12.50	7.50
(19)	Joe Judge	25.00	12.50	7.50
(20)	Joe Kuhel	25.00	12.50	7.50
(21)	Henry Manush	50.00	25.00	15.00
(22)	Fred Marberry	25.00	12.50	7.50
(23)	Mike Martin	25.00	12.50	7.50
(24)	Walter Masters	25.00	12.50	7.50
(25)	Charles Myer	25.00	12.50	7.50
(26)	Harry Rice	25.00	12.50	7.50
(27)	Sam Rice	25.00	12.50	7.50
(28)	Al Schacht	35.00	17.50	10.50
(29)	Roy Spencer	25.00	12.50	7.50
(30)	Sam West	25.00	12.50	7.50

1970 Washington Senators Traffic Safety

ERRORS IN BASEBALL COST GAMES

ERRORS IN TRAFFIC COST LIVES

PLAY IT SAFE!

EDDIE BRINKMAN
Short Stop
Washington Senators

D.C. DEPARTMENT OF MOTOR VEHICLES
Office of Traffic Safety

Distributed in 1970 by the Washington, D.C. Department of Motor Vehicles, this issue promoting traffic safety was one of the first police sets. Featuring black-and-white player photos, the cards measure 2-1/2" x 3-7/8" and have large borders surrounding the pictures. The player's name and position are below; the team name appears in smaller type at the bottom. The set can be found on either pink card stock, used for the original print run, or on bright yellow stock, used for two subsequent printings. Aurelio Rodriguez, who joined the team after the season began, is known only in yellow; all other players can be found in both yellow and pink. The pink varieties carry a higher value. The backs of the cards offer traffic safety tips.

		NM	EX	VG
Complete Set, Pink (10):		150.00	75.00	45.00
Common Player, Pink:		3.50	1.75	1.00
Complete Set, Yellow (11):		25.00	12.50	7.50
Common Player, Yellow:		2.50	1.25	.70
(1a)	Dick Bosman (Pink)	3.50	1.75	1.00
(1b)	Dick Bosman (Yellow)	2.50	1.25	.70
(2a)	Eddie Brinkman (Pink)	3.50	1.75	1.00
(2b)	Eddie Brinkman (Yellow)	2.50	1.25	.70
(3a)	Paul Casanova (Pink)	3.50	1.75	1.00
(3b)	Paul Casanova (Yellow)	2.50	1.25	.70
(4a)	Mike Epstein (Pink)	3.50	1.75	1.00
(4b)	Mike Epstein (Yellow)	2.50	1.25	.70
(5a)	Frank Howard (Pink)	10.00	5.00	3.00
(5b)	Frank Howard (Yellow)	7.50	3.75	2.25
(6a)	Darold Knowles (Pink)	3.50	1.75	1.00
(6b)	Darold Knowles (Yellow)	2.50	1.25	.70
(7a)	Lee Maye (Pink)	3.50	1.75	1.00
(7b)	Lee Maye (Yellow)	2.50	1.25	.70
(8a)	Dave Nelson (Pink)/SP	125.00	62.00	37.00
(8b)	Dave Nelson (Yellow)	2.50	1.25	.70
(9)	Aurelio Rodriguez (Yellow)/SP	5.00	2.50	1.50
(10a)	John Roseboro (Pink)	3.50	1.75	1.00
(10b)	John Roseboro (Yellow)	2.50	1.25	.70
(11a)	Ed Stroud (Pink)	3.50	1.75	1.00
(11b)	Ed Stroud (Yellow)	2.50	1.25	.70

1971 Washington Senators Traffic Safety

The 1971 Senators safety set was again issued by the Washington, D.C., Department of Motor Vehicles and was similar in design and size (2-1/2" x 3-7/8") to the previous year, except that it was printed on a pale yellow stock. The set, which features several new players, contains no scarce cards. The backs contain traffic safety messages.

A FAST BALL CAN GET
YOU "OUT" OF TROUBLE

A FAST CAR CAN GET
YOU "INTO" TROUBLE

PLAY IT SAFE!

D.C. DEPARTMENT OF MOTOR VEHICLES
Office of Traffic Safety

DENNY McLAIN
Pitcher
Washington Senators

	NM	EX	VG
Complete Set (10):	12.50	6.25	3.75
Uncut Sheet:	12.50	6.25	3.75
Common Player:	1.00	.50	.30
1) Dick Bosman	1.00	.50	.30
2) Paul Casanova	1.00	.50	.30
3) Tim Cullen	1.00	.50	.30
4) Joe Foy	1.00	.50	.30
5) Toby Harrah	1.00	.50	.30
6) Frank Howard	2.50	1.25	.70
7) Elliott Maddox	1.00	.50	.30
8) Tom McCraw	1.00	.50	.30
9) Denny McLain	3.00	1.50	.90
10) Don Wert	.60	.30	.20

1910 Washington Times

WALKER
WASHINGTON
WASHINGTON TIMES SERIES

Only American League players have so far been found in this issue by the Washington Times newspaper. The 2-9/16" x 3-9/16" cards have portrait or action photos of the players within a wide border. A white panel at bottom has the player name and team at left and "Washington Times Series" at right. All printing is in dark red. Backs are blank. The manner in which these cards were distributed is unknown, as is the extent of the checklist. The unnumbered cards are checklisted here in alphabetical order.

	NM	EX	VG
Common Player:	2,500	1,250	750.00
1) Ty Cobb	20,000	10,000	6,000
2) Eddie Collins	7,500	3,750	2,250
3) Wid Conroy	2,500	1,250	750.00
4) Sam Crawford	7,500	3,750	2,250
5) Harry Davis	2,500	1,250	750.00
6) Bob Groom	2,500	1,250	750.00
7) Nap Lajoie	7,500	3,750	2,250
8) George McBride	2,500	1,250	750.00
9) Clyde Milan	2,500	1,250	750.00
10) Frank Oberlin	2,500	1,250	750.00
11) Rube Oldring	2,500	1,250	750.00
12) Freddie Parent (Freddy)	2,500	1,250	750.00
13) Doc Reisling	2,500	1,250	750.00
14) Gabby Street	2,500	1,250	750.00
15) Lee Tannehill	2,500	1,250	750.00
16) Bob Unglaub	2,500	1,250	750.00
17) Dixie Walker	2,500	1,250	750.00
18) Ed. Walsh	7,500	3,750	2,250
19) Joe Wood	2,000	1,000	600.00
20) Cy Young	12,500	6,250	3,750

1951 WBKB "Lucky Fan" Chicago Cubs

This series of black-and-white player glossies appears to have been a promotional giveaway from WBKB radio or television station in conjunction with Ben Bey's "Lucky Fan" club contest. The 8-1/8" x 10" photos have a facsimile autograph on front. On back is a three-line rubber-stamped "COURTESY OF / BEN BEY "LUCKY FAN" / WBKB - CHICAGO." The checklist is arranged alphabetically.

	NM	EX	VG
Complete Set (28):	900.00	450.00	270.00
Common Player:	40.00	20.00	12.00
(1) Frank Baumholtz	40.00	20.00	12.00
(2) Bob Borkowski	40.00	20.00	12.00
(3) Smoky Burgess	50.00	25.00	15.00
(4) Phil Cavarretta	40.00	20.00	12.00
(5) Chuck Connors	100.00	50.00	30.00
(6) Jack Cusick	40.00	20.00	12.00
(7) Bruce Edwards	40.00	20.00	12.00
(8) Dee Fondy	40.00	20.00	12.00
(9) Joe Hatten	40.00	20.00	12.00
(10) Gene Hermanski	40.00	20.00	12.00
(11) Frank Hiller	40.00	20.00	12.00
(12) Ransom Jackson	40.00	20.00	12.00
(13) Hal Jeffcoat	40.00	20.00	12.00
(14) Bob Kelly	40.00	20.00	12.00
(15) Johnny Klippstein	40.00	20.00	12.00
(16) Dutch Leonard	40.00	20.00	12.00
(17) Turk Lown	40.00	20.00	12.00
(18) Cal McLish	40.00	20.00	12.00
(19) Eddie Miksis	40.00	20.00	12.00
(20) Paul Minner	40.00	20.00	12.00
(21) Mickey Owen	40.00	20.00	12.00
(22) Andy Pafko	50.00	25.00	15.00
(23) Bob Ramazotti	40.00	20.00	12.00
(24) Bob Rush	40.00	20.00	12.00
(25) Hank Sauer	40.00	20.00	12.00
(26) Bob Schultz	40.00	20.00	12.00
(27) Bill Serena	40.00	20.00	12.00
(28) Roy Smalley	45.00	22.00	13.50

1953 Weaver's Wafers Lincoln Chiefs

From the only two known cards, it is impossible to determine wheather this was a 1953 or a 1954 issue, since both players were on the Class A Western League farm club of the Boston Braves in both seasons. The fact that 1953 was the first year the team was a Braves' affiliate with the Chiefs nickname argues for that being the year of card issue. The 3-1/4" x 4-1/2" cards are printed in black-and-white on blank-back, thin cardboard stock. Besides a circled card number on front with the player name and position, there is advertising for the local potato chip company that issued the cards for KOLN radio, which broadcast the team's games. Staple holes at top of both known cards indicates they may have been stapled to bags of Weaver's chips.

	NM	EX	VG
VALUE UNDETERMINED			
9 Tom Neill			
17 Roger Wright			

1911-14 Weber Bakery (D304)

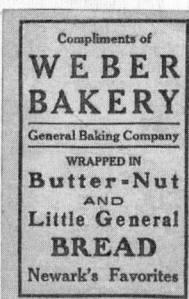

RUBE MARQUARD, N.Y. NATL.

Compliments of
WEBER BAKERY
General Baking Company
WRAPPED IN
Butter-Nut AND Little General
BREAD
Newark's Favorites

(See 1911-14 General Baking Co. for checklist and price information.)

1916 Weil Baking Co. (D329)

JOE JACKSON
L. F.—Chicago White Sox
87

THIS is one of a series of 200 action pictures of Major League Baseball Players, comprising Baseball's Hall of Fame.

H. Weil Baking Co.
4914 PRYTANIA STREET
NEW ORLEANS :: LA.

One of several issues by the New Orleans bakery, this 1-3/8" x 3" black-and-white set of 200 shares a checklist and relative values with the 1916 M101-4 Blank Backs set. Collectors can expect to pay a premium for a card with the Weil Baking ad on back to add to a type collection or superstar collection. The American Card Catalog lists this issue as D329.

	NM	EX	VG
Common Player:	250.00	125.00	75.00

		NM	EX	VG
1	Babe Adams	250.00	125.00	75.00
2	Sam Agnew	250.00	125.00	75.00
3	Eddie Ainsmith	250.00	125.00	75.00
4	Grover Alexander	1,100	550.00	325.00
5	Leon Ames	250.00	125.00	75.00
6	Jimmy Archer	250.00	125.00	75.00
7	Jimmy Austin	250.00	125.00	75.00
8	H.D. Baird	250.00	125.00	75.00
9	J. Franklin Baker	900.00	450.00	270.00
10	Dave Bancroft	900.00	450.00	270.00
11	Jack Barry	250.00	125.00	75.00
12	Zinn Beck	250.00	125.00	75.00
13	"Chief" Bender	900.00	450.00	270.00
14	Joe Benz	250.00	125.00	75.00
15	Bob Bescher	250.00	125.00	75.00
16	Al Betzel	250.00	125.00	75.00
17	Mordecai Brown	900.00	450.00	270.00
18	Eddie Burns	250.00	125.00	75.00
19	George Burns	250.00	125.00	75.00
20	Geo. J. Burns	250.00	125.00	75.00
21	Joe Bush	250.00	125.00	75.00
22	"Donie" Bush	250.00	125.00	75.00
23	Art Butler	250.00	125.00	75.00
24	Bobbie Byrne	250.00	125.00	75.00
25	Forrest Cady	250.00	125.00	75.00
26	Jimmy Callahan	250.00	125.00	75.00
27	Ray Caldwell	250.00	125.00	75.00
28	Max Carey	900.00	450.00	270.00
29	George Chalmers	250.00	125.00	75.00
30	Ray Chapman	250.00	125.00	75.00
31	Larry Cheney	250.00	125.00	75.00
32	Eddie Cicotte	1,250	625.00	375.00
33	Tom Clarke	250.00	125.00	75.00
34	Eddie Collins	900.00	450.00	270.00
35	"Shauno" Collins	250.00	125.00	75.00
36	Charles Comiskey	900.00	450.00	270.00
37	Joe Connolly	250.00	125.00	75.00
38	Ty Cobb	9,000	4,500	2,700
39	Harry Coveleskie (Coveleski)	250.00	125.00	75.00
40	Gavvy Cravath	250.00	125.00	75.00
41	Sam Crawford	900.00	450.00	270.00
42	Jean Dale	250.00	125.00	75.00
43	Jake Daubert	250.00	125.00	75.00
44	Charles Deal	250.00	125.00	75.00
45	Al Demaree	250.00	125.00	75.00
46	Josh Devore	250.00	125.00	75.00
47	William Doak	250.00	125.00	75.00
48	Bill Donovan	250.00	125.00	75.00
49	Charles Dooin	250.00	125.00	75.00
50	Mike Doolan	250.00	125.00	75.00
51	Larry Doyle	250.00	125.00	75.00
52	Jean Dubuc	250.00	125.00	75.00
53	Oscar Dugey	250.00	125.00	75.00
54	Johnny Evers	900.00	450.00	270.00
55	Urban Faber	900.00	450.00	270.00
56	"Hap" Felsch	2,500	1,250	750.00
57	Bill Fischer	250.00	125.00	75.00
58	Ray Fisher	250.00	125.00	75.00
59	Max Flack	250.00	125.00	75.00
60	Art Fletcher	250.00	125.00	75.00
61	Eddie Foster	250.00	125.00	75.00
62	Jacques Fournier	250.00	125.00	75.00
63	Del Gainer (Gainor)	250.00	125.00	75.00
64	"Chic" Gandil	900.00	450.00	270.00
65	Larry Gardner	250.00	125.00	75.00
66	Joe Gedeon	250.00	125.00	75.00
67	Gus Getz	250.00	125.00	75.00
68	Geo. Gibson	250.00	125.00	75.00
69	Wilbur Good	250.00	125.00	75.00
70	Hank Gowdy	250.00	125.00	75.00
71	John Graney	250.00	125.00	75.00
72	Clark Griffith	900.00	450.00	270.00
73	Tom Griffith	250.00	125.00	75.00
74	Heinie Groh	250.00	125.00	75.00
75	Earl Hamilton	250.00	125.00	75.00
76	Bob Harmon	250.00	125.00	75.00
77	Roy Hartzell	250.00	125.00	75.00
78	Claude Hendrix	250.00	125.00	75.00
79	Olaf Henriksen	250.00	125.00	75.00
80	John Henry	250.00	125.00	75.00
81	"Buck" Herzog	250.00	125.00	75.00
82	Hugh High	250.00	125.00	75.00
83	Dick Hoblitzell	250.00	125.00	75.00
84	Harry Hooper	900.00	450.00	270.00
85	Ivan Howard	250.00	125.00	75.00
86	Miller Huggins	900.00	450.00	270.00
87	Joe Jackson	32,500	16,250	975.00
88	William James	250.00	125.00	75.00
89	Harold Janvrin	250.00	125.00	75.00
90	Hugh Jennings	900.00	450.00	270.00
91	Walter Johnson	2,500	1,250	750.00
92	Fielder Jones	250.00	125.00	75.00
93	Joe Judge	250.00	125.00	75.00
94	Bennie Kauff	250.00	125.00	75.00
95	Wm. Killefer Jr.	250.00	125.00	75.00
96	Ed. Konetchy	250.00	125.00	75.00
97	Napoleon Lajoie	900.00	450.00	270.00
98	Jack Lapp	250.00	125.00	75.00
99	John Lavan	250.00	125.00	75.00
100	Jimmy Lavender	250.00	125.00	75.00
101	"Nemo" Leibold	250.00	125.00	75.00
102	H.B. Leonard	250.00	125.00	75.00
103	Duffy Lewis	175.00	100.00	50.00
104	Hans Lobert	250.00	125.00	75.00
105	Tom Long	250.00	125.00	75.00
106	Fred Luderus	250.00	125.00	75.00
107	Connie Mack	900.00	450.00	270.00
108	Lee Magee	250.00	125.00	75.00
109	Sherwood Magee	250.00	125.00	75.00
110	Al. Mamaux	250.00	125.00	75.00
111	Leslie Mann	250.00	125.00	75.00
112	"Rabbit" Maranville	900.00	450.00	270.00
113	Rube Marquard	900.00	450.00	270.00
114	J. Erskine Mayer	250.00	125.00	75.00
115	George McBride	250.00	125.00	75.00
116	John J. McGraw	900.00	450.00	270.00
117	Jack McInnis	250.00	125.00	75.00
118	Fred Merkle	250.00	125.00	75.00

#	Player	NM	EX	VG
119	Chief Meyers	250.00	125.00	75.00
120	Clyde Milan	250.00	125.00	75.00
121	John Miller	250.00	125.00	75.00
122	Otto Miller	250.00	125.00	75.00
123	Willie Mitchell	250.00	125.00	75.00
124	Fred Mollwitz	250.00	125.00	75.00
125	Pat Moran	250.00	125.00	75.00
126	Ray Morgan	250.00	125.00	75.00
127	Geo. Moriarty	250.00	125.00	75.00
128	Guy Morton	250.00	125.00	75.00
129	Mike Mowrey	250.00	125.00	75.00
130	Ed. Murphy	250.00	125.00	75.00
131	"Hy" Myers	250.00	125.00	75.00
132	J.A. Niehoff	250.00	125.00	75.00
133	Rube Oldring	250.00	125.00	75.00
134	Oliver O'Mara	250.00	125.00	75.00
135	Steve O'Neill	250.00	125.00	75.00
136	"Dode" Paskert	250.00	125.00	75.00
137	Roger Peckinpaugh	250.00	125.00	75.00
138	Walter Pipp	250.00	125.00	75.00
139	Derril Pratt (Derrill)	250.00	125.00	75.00
140	Pat Ragan	250.00	125.00	75.00
141	Bill Rariden	250.00	125.00	75.00
142	Eppa Rixey	900.00	450.00	270.00
143	Davey Robertson	250.00	125.00	75.00
144	Wilbert Robinson	900.00	450.00	270.00
145	Bob Roth	250.00	125.00	75.00
146	Ed. Roush	900.00	450.00	270.00
147	Clarence Rowland	250.00	125.00	75.00
148	"Nap" Rucker	250.00	125.00	75.00
149	Dick Rudolph	250.00	125.00	75.00
150	Reb Russell	250.00	125.00	75.00
151	Babe Ruth	45,000	22,000	13,500
152	Vic Saier	250.00	125.00	75.00
153	"Slim" Sallee	250.00	125.00	75.00
154	Ray Schalk	900.00	450.00	270.00
155	Walter Schang	250.00	125.00	75.00
156	Frank Schulte	250.00	125.00	75.00
157	Everett Scott	250.00	125.00	75.00
158	Jim Scott	250.00	125.00	75.00
159	Tom Seaton	250.00	125.00	75.00
160	Howard Shanks	250.00	125.00	75.00
161	Bob Shawkey	250.00	125.00	75.00
162	Ernie Shore	250.00	125.00	75.00
163	Burt Shotton	250.00	125.00	75.00
164	Geo. Sisler	900.00	450.00	270.00
165	J. Carlisle Smith	250.00	125.00	75.00
166	Fred Snodgrass	250.00	125.00	75.00
167	Geo. Stallings	250.00	125.00	75.00
168	Oscar Stanage	250.00	125.00	75.00
169	Charles Stengel	900.00	450.00	270.00
170	Milton Stock	250.00	125.00	75.00
171	Amos Strunk	250.00	125.00	75.00
172	Billy Sullivan	250.00	125.00	75.00
173	"Jeff" Tesreau	250.00	125.00	75.00
174	Joe Tinker	900.00	450.00	270.00
175	Fred Toney	250.00	125.00	75.00
176	Terry Turner	250.00	125.00	75.00
177	George Tyler	250.00	125.00	75.00
178	Jim Vaughn	250.00	125.00	75.00
179	Bob Veach	250.00	125.00	75.00
180	James Viox	250.00	125.00	75.00
181	Oscar Vitt	250.00	125.00	75.00
182	Hans Wagner	8,500	4,250	2,550
183	Clarence Walker	250.00	125.00	75.00
184	Ed. Walsh	900.00	450.00	270.00
185	W. Wambsganss (Photo actually Fritz Coumbe.)	250.00	125.00	75.00
186	Buck Weaver	1,750	875.00	525.00
187	Carl Weilman	250.00	125.00	75.00
188	Zach Wheat	900.00	450.00	270.00
189	Geo. Whitted	250.00	125.00	75.00
190	Fred Williams	250.00	125.00	75.00
191	Art Wilson	250.00	125.00	75.00
192	J. Owen Wilson	250.00	125.00	75.00
193	Ivy Wingo	250.00	125.00	75.00
194	"Mel" Wolfgang	250.00	125.00	75.00
195	Joe Wood	250.00	125.00	75.00
196	Steve Yerkes	250.00	125.00	75.00
197	"Pep" Young	250.00	125.00	75.00
198	Rollie Zeider	250.00	125.00	75.00
199	Heiny Zimmerman	250.00	125.00	75.00
200	Ed. Zwilling	250.00	125.00	75.00

1917 Weil Baking Co. (D328)

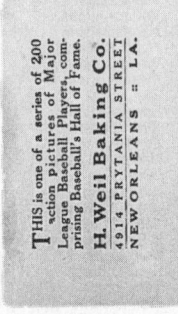

This set comprises one of several regional advertisers' use of the 200-card issue for promotional purposes. These cards are most often seen with the advertising of the Collins-McCarthy Candy Co. of San Francisco. Cards measure 2" x 3-1/4" and are printed in black-and-white. This set was listed as D328 in the American Card Catalog.

		NM	EX	VG
Common Player:		475.00	240.00	150.00
1	Sam Agnew	475.00	240.00	150.00

#	Player	NM	EX	VG
2	Grover Alexander	2,650	1,325	750.00
3	W.S. Alexander (W.E.)	475.00	240.00	150.00
4	Leon Ames	475.00	240.00	150.00
5	Fred Anderson	475.00	240.00	150.00
6	Ed Appleton	475.00	240.00	150.00
7	Jimmy Archer	475.00	240.00	150.00
8	Jimmy Austin	475.00	240.00	150.00
9	Jim Bagby	475.00	240.00	150.00
10	H.D. Baird	475.00	240.00	150.00
11	J. Franklin Baker	1,500	750.00	450.00
12	Dave Bancroft	1,500	750.00	450.00
13	Jack Barry	475.00	240.00	150.00
14	Joe Benz	475.00	240.00	150.00
15	Al Betzel	475.00	240.00	150.00
16	Ping Bodie	475.00	240.00	150.00
17	Joe Boehling	475.00	240.00	150.00
18	Eddie Burns	475.00	240.00	150.00
19	George Burns	475.00	240.00	150.00
20	Geo. J. Burns	475.00	240.00	150.00
21	Joe Bush	475.00	240.00	150.00
22	Owen Bush	475.00	240.00	150.00
23	Bobby Byrne	475.00	240.00	150.00
24	Forrest Cady	475.00	240.00	150.00
25	Max Carey	1,500	750.00	450.00
26	Ray Chapman	775.00	400.00	250.00
27	Larry Cheney	475.00	240.00	150.00
28	Eddie Cicotte	1,500	750.00	450.00
29	Tom Clarke	475.00	240.00	150.00
30	Ty Cobb	20,000	10,000	6,000
31	Eddie Collins	1,500	750.00	450.00
32	"Shauno" Collins (Shano)	475.00	240.00	150.00
33	Fred Coumbe	475.00	240.00	150.00
34	Harry Coveleskie (Coveleski)	475.00	240.00	150.00
35	Gavvy Cravath	475.00	240.00	150.00
36	Sam Crawford	1,500	750.00	450.00
37	Geo. Cutshaw	475.00	240.00	150.00
38	Jake Daubert	475.00	240.00	150.00
39	Geo. Dauss	475.00	240.00	150.00
40	Charles Deal	475.00	240.00	150.00
41	"Wheezer" Dell	475.00	240.00	150.00
42	William Doak	475.00	240.00	150.00
43	Bill Donovan	475.00	240.00	150.00
44	Larry Doyle	475.00	240.00	150.00
45	Johnny Evers	1,500	750.00	450.00
46	Urban Faber	1,500	750.00	450.00
47	"Hap" Felsch	3,300	1,650	1,000
48	Bill Fischer	475.00	240.00	150.00
49	Ray Fisher	475.00	240.00	150.00
50	Art Fletcher	475.00	240.00	150.00
51	Eddie Foster	475.00	240.00	150.00
52	Jacques Fournier	475.00	240.00	150.00
53	Del Gainer (Gainor)	475.00	240.00	150.00
54	Bert Gallia	475.00	240.00	150.00
55	"Chic" Gandil (Chick)	2,000	1,000	600.00
56	Larry Gardner	475.00	240.00	150.00
57	Joe Gedeon	475.00	240.00	150.00
58	Gus Getz	475.00	240.00	150.00
59	Frank Gilhooley	475.00	240.00	150.00
60	Wm. Gleason	475.00	240.00	150.00
61	M.A. Gonzales (Gonzalez)	475.00	240.00	150.00
62	Hank Gowdy	475.00	240.00	150.00
63	John Graney	475.00	240.00	150.00
64	Tom Griffith	475.00	240.00	150.00
65	Heinie Groh	475.00	240.00	150.00
66	Bob Groom	475.00	240.00	150.00
67	Louis Guisto	475.00	240.00	150.00
68	Earl Hamilton	475.00	240.00	150.00
69	Harry Harper	475.00	240.00	150.00
70	Grover Hartley	475.00	240.00	150.00
71	Harry Heilmann	1,500	750.00	450.00
72	Claude Hendrix	475.00	240.00	150.00
73	Olaf Henriksen	475.00	240.00	150.00
74	John Henry	475.00	240.00	150.00
75	"Buck" Herzog	475.00	240.00	150.00
76	Hugh High	475.00	240.00	150.00
77	Dick Hoblitzell	475.00	240.00	150.00
78	Walter Holke	475.00	240.00	150.00
79	Harry Hooper	1,500	750.00	450.00
80	Rogers Hornsby	2,650	1,325	750.00
81	Ivan Howard	475.00	240.00	150.00
82	Joe Jackson	55,000	27,500	16,500
83	Harold Janvrin	475.00	240.00	150.00
84	William James	475.00	240.00	150.00
85	C. Jamieson	475.00	240.00	150.00
86	Hugh Jennings	1,500	750.00	450.00
87	Walter Johnson	3,250	1,650	1,000
88	James Johnston	475.00	240.00	150.00
89	Fielder Jones	475.00	240.00	150.00
90	Joe Judge	475.00	240.00	150.00
91	Hans Lobert	475.00	240.00	150.00
92	Benny Kauff	475.00	240.00	150.00
93	Wm. Killefer Jr.	475.00	240.00	150.00
94	Ed. Konetchy	475.00	240.00	150.00
95	John Lavan	475.00	240.00	150.00
96	Jimmy Lavender	475.00	240.00	150.00
97	"Nemo" Leibold	475.00	240.00	150.00
98	H.B. Leonard	475.00	240.00	150.00
99	Duffy Lewis	475.00	240.00	150.00
100	Tom Long	475.00	240.00	150.00
101	Wm. Louden	475.00	240.00	150.00
102	Fred Luderus	475.00	240.00	150.00
103	Lee Magee	475.00	240.00	150.00
104	Sherwood Magee	475.00	240.00	150.00
105	Al Mamaux	475.00	240.00	150.00
106	Leslie Mann	475.00	240.00	150.00
107	"Rabbit" Maranville	1,500	750.00	450.00
108	Rube Marquard	1,500	750.00	450.00
109	Armando Marsans	475.00	240.00	150.00
110	J. Erskine Mayer	475.00	240.00	150.00
111	George McBride	475.00	240.00	150.00
112	Lew McCarty	475.00	240.00	150.00
113	John J. McGraw	1,500	750.00	450.00
114	Jack McInnis	475.00	240.00	150.00
115	Lee Meadows	475.00	240.00	150.00
116	Fred Merkle	475.00	240.00	150.00
117	"Chief" Meyers	475.00	240.00	150.00
118	Clyde Milan	475.00	240.00	150.00

#	Player	NM	EX	VG
119	Otto Miller	475.00	240.00	150.00
120	Clarence Mitchell	475.00	240.00	150.00
121	Ray Morgan	475.00	240.00	150.00
122	Guy Morton	475.00	240.00	150.00
123	"Mike" Mowrey	475.00	240.00	150.00
124	Elmer Myers	475.00	240.00	150.00
125	"Hy" Myers	475.00	240.00	150.00
126	A.E. Neale	750.00	375.00	225.00
127	Arthur Nehf	475.00	240.00	150.00
128	J.A. Niehoff	475.00	240.00	150.00
129	Steve O'Neill	475.00	240.00	150.00
130	"Dode" Paskert	475.00	240.00	150.00
131	Roger Peckinpaugh	475.00	240.00	150.00
132	"Pol" Perritt	475.00	240.00	150.00
133	"Jeff" Pfeffer	475.00	240.00	150.00
134	Walter Pipp	475.00	240.00	150.00
135	Derril Pratt (Derrill)	475.00	240.00	150.00
136	Bill Rariden	475.00	240.00	150.00
137	E.C. Rice	1,500	750.00	450.00
138	Wm. A. Ritter (Wm. H.)	475.00	240.00	150.00
139	Eppa Rixey	1,500	750.00	450.00
140	Davey Robertson	475.00	240.00	150.00
141	"Bob" Roth	475.00	240.00	150.00
142	Ed. Roush	1,500	750.00	450.00
143	Clarence Rowland	475.00	240.00	150.00
144	Dick Rudolph	475.00	240.00	150.00
145	William Rumler	475.00	240.00	150.00
146	Reb Russell	475.00	240.00	150.00
147	"Babe" Ruth	44,000	22,000	13,000
148	Vic Saier	475.00	240.00	150.00
149	"Slim" Sallee	475.00	240.00	150.00
150	Ray Schalk	1,500	750.00	450.00
151	Walter Schang	475.00	240.00	150.00
152	Frank Schulte	475.00	240.00	150.00
153	Ferd Schupp	475.00	240.00	150.00
154	Everett Scott	475.00	240.00	150.00
155	Hank Severeid	475.00	240.00	150.00
156	Howard Shanks	475.00	240.00	150.00
157	Bob Shawkey	475.00	240.00	150.00
158	Jas. Sheckard	475.00	240.00	150.00
159	Ernie Shore	475.00	240.00	150.00
160	C.H. Shorten	475.00	240.00	150.00
161	Burt Shotton	475.00	240.00	150.00
162	Geo. Sisler	1,500	750.00	450.00
163	Elmer Smith	475.00	240.00	150.00
164	J. Carlisle Smith	475.00	240.00	150.00
165	Fred Snodgrass	475.00	240.00	150.00
166	Tris Speaker	2,600	1,300	750.00
167	Oscar Stanage	475.00	240.00	150.00
168	Charles Stengel	1,500	750.00	450.00
169	Milton Stock	475.00	240.00	150.00
170	Amos Strunk	475.00	240.00	150.00
171	"Zeb" Terry	475.00	240.00	150.00
172	"Jeff" Tesreau	475.00	240.00	150.00
173	Chester Thomas	475.00	240.00	150.00
174	Fred Toney	475.00	240.00	150.00
175	Terry Turner	475.00	240.00	150.00
176	George Tyler	475.00	240.00	150.00
177	Jim Vaughn	475.00	240.00	150.00
178	Bob Veach	475.00	240.00	150.00
179	Oscar Vitt	475.00	240.00	150.00
180	Hans Wagner	15,000	7,500	4,500
181	Clarence Walker	475.00	240.00	150.00
182	Jim Walsh	475.00	240.00	150.00
183	Al Walters	475.00	240.00	150.00
184	W. Wambsganss	475.00	240.00	150.00
185	Buck Weaver	4,400	2,200	1,400
186	Carl Weilman	475.00	240.00	150.00
187	Zack Wheat	1,500	750.00	450.00
188	Geo. Whitted	475.00	240.00	150.00
189	Joe Wilhoit	475.00	240.00	150.00
190	Claude Williams	3,300	1,650	1,000
191	Fred Williams	475.00	240.00	150.00
192	Art Wilson	475.00	240.00	150.00
193	Lawton Witt	475.00	240.00	150.00
194	Joe Wood	1,000	500.00	300.00
195	William Wortman	475.00	240.00	150.00
196	Steve Yerkes	475.00	240.00	150.00
197	Earl Yingling	475.00	240.00	150.00
198	"Pep" (Ralph) Young	475.00	240.00	150.00
199	Rollie Zeider	475.00	240.00	150.00
200	Henry Zimmerman	475.00	240.00	150.00

1886 Welton Cigars N.Y. Giants (H812)

(See "1886 New York Base Ball Club" for checklist and values.)

1977 Wendy's Discs

Virtually identical in format to the several locally spo- sored disc sets of the previous year, these 3-3/8" diamet player discs were given away at participating stores in the fast-food hamburger chain. Discs once again feature black-and-white player portrait photos in the center of a baseball design. The left and right panels are in one of several bright colors. Licensed by the Players Association through Mike Schechter Associates, the player photos carry no uniform logos. Backs are printed in green. The unnumbered discs are checklisted here alphabetically.

		NM	EX	VG
Complete Set (70):		325.00	165.00	100.00
Common Player:		3.00	1.50	.90
(1)	Sal Bando	3.00	1.50	.90
(2)	Buddy Bell	3.00	1.50	.90
(3)	Johnny Bench	20.00	10.00	6.00
(4)	Larry Bowa	3.00	1.50	.90
(5)	Steve Braun	3.00	1.50	.90
(6)	George Brett	50.00	25.00	15.00
(7)	Lou Brock	12.50	6.25	3.75
(8)	Jeff Burroughs	3.00	1.50	.90
(9)	Bert Campaneris	3.00	1.50	.90
(10)	John Candelaria	3.00	1.50	.90
(11)	Jose Cardenal	3.00	1.50	.90
(12)	Rod Carew	12.50	6.25	3.75
(13)	Steve Carlton	12.50	6.25	3.75
(14)	Dave Cash	3.00	1.50	.90
(15)	Cesar Cedeno	3.00	1.50	.90
(16)	Ron Cey	3.00	1.50	.90
(17)	Dave Concepcion	3.00	1.50	.90
(18)	Dennis Eckersley	12.50	6.25	3.75
(19)	Mark Fidrych	6.00	3.00	1.75
q20)	Rollie Fingers	12.50	6.25	3.75
(21)	Carlton Fisk	12.50	6.25	3.75
(22)	George Foster	3.00	1.50	.90
(23)	Wayne Garland	3.00	1.50	.90
(24)	Ralph Garr	3.00	1.50	.90
(25)	Steve Garvey	4.50	2.25	1.25
(26)	Cesar Geronimo	3.00	1.50	.90
(27)	Bobby Grich	3.00	1.50	.90
(28)	Ken Griffey Sr.	3.00	1.50	.90
(29)	Don Gullett	3.00	1.50	.90
(30)	Mike Hargrove	3.00	1.50	.90
(31)	Al Hrabosky	3.00	1.50	.90
(32)	Jim Hunter	12.50	6.25	3.75
(33)	Reggie Jackson	45.00	22.50	13.50
(34)	Randy Jones	3.00	1.50	.90
(35)	Dave Kingman	3.00	1.50	.90
(36)	Jerry Koosman	3.00	1.50	.90
(37)	Dave LaRoche	3.00	1.50	.90
(38)	Greg Luzinski	3.00	1.50	.90
(39)	Fred Lynn	3.00	1.50	.90
(40)	Bill Madlock	3.00	1.50	.90
(41)	Rick Manning	3.00	1.50	.90
(42)	Jon Matlock	3.00	1.50	.90
(43)	John Mayberry	3.00	1.50	.90
(44)	Hal McRae	3.00	1.50	.90
(45)	Andy Messersmith	3.00	1.50	.90
(46)	Rick Monday	3.00	1.50	.90
(47)	John Montefusco	3.00	1.50	.90
(48)	Joe Morgan	12.50	6.25	3.75
(49)	Thurman Munson	12.50	6.25	3.75
(50)	Bobby Murcer	3.00	1.50	.90
(51)	Bill North	3.00	1.50	.90
(52)	Jim Palmer	12.50	6.25	3.75
(53)	Tony Perez	12.50	6.25	3.75
(54)	Jerry Reuss	3.00	1.50	.90
(55)	Brooks Robinson	15.00	7.50	4.50
(56)	Pete Rose	55.00	27.50	16.50
(57)	Joe Rudi	3.00	1.50	.90
(58)	Nolan Ryan	65.00	32.50	20.00
(59)	Manny Sanguillen	3.00	1.50	.90
(60)	Mike Schmidt	50.00	25.00	15.00
(61)	Tom Seaver	20.00	10.00	6.00
(62)	Bill Singer	3.00	1.50	.90
(63)	Willie Stargell	12.50	6.25	3.75
(64)	Rusty Staub	4.00	2.00	1.25
(65)	Luis Tiant	3.00	1.50	.90
(66)	Bob Watson	3.00	1.50	.90
(67)	Butch Wynegar	3.00	1.50	.90
(68)	Carl Yastrzemski	20.00	10.00	6.00
(69)	Robin Yount	12.50	6.25	3.75
(70)	Richie Zisk	3.00	1.50	.90

1963 Western Oil Minnesota Twins

 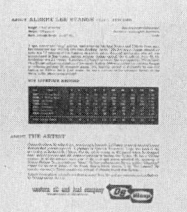

Issued by Mileage and DS gas stations, these 8-1/2" x 11" heavy paper portraits are the work of sports/entertainment artist Nicholas Volpe, who had done a similar series earlier for the Los Angeles Dodgers, and would do several more in the future for other baseball and NFL teams. The 1963 Twins issue features pastel portrait and action renderings against a black background on front. The player's name appears as a facsimile autograph in white on the painting and is printed in black in the white bottom border. Backs have biographical data and a career summary of the player at top. At center is a black box with complete major and minor league stats. At lower center is a biography of the artist, and, on most pictures, his portrait. The DS and Mileage logos of the Western Oil and Fuel Co. appear at bottom.

		NM	EX	VG
Complete Set (24):		150.00	75.00	45.00
Common Player:		10.00	5.00	3.00
(1)	Bernie Allen	10.00	5.00	3.00
(2)	Bob Allison	15.00	7.50	4.50
(3)	George Banks	10.00	5.00	3.00
(4)	Earl Battey	12.50	6.25	3.75
(5)	Bill Dailey	10.00	5.00	3.00
(6)	John Goryl	10.00	5.00	3.00
(7)	Lenny Green	10.00	5.00	3.00
(8)	Jimmie Hall	10.00	5.00	3.00
(9)	Jim Kaat	15.00	7.50	4.50
(10)	Harmon Killebrew	30.00	15.00	9.00
(11)	Sam Mele	10.00	5.00	3.00
(12)	Don Mincher	10.00	5.00	3.00
(13)	Ray Moore	10.00	5.00	3.00
(14)	Camilo Pascual	12.50	6.25	3.75
(15)	Jim Perry	10.00	5.00	3.00
(16)	Bill Pleis	10.00	5.00	3.00
(17)	Vic Power	12.00	6.00	3.50
(18)	Garry Roggenburk	10.00	5.00	3.00
(19)	Jim Roland	10.00	5.00	3.00
(20)	Rich Rollins	10.00	5.00	3.00
(21)	Lee Stange	10.00	5.00	3.00
(22)	Dick Stigman	10.00	5.00	3.00
(23)	Zoilo Versalles	12.50	6.25	3.75
(24)	Jerry Zimmerman	10.00	5.00	3.00

1964 Western Oil Minnesota Twins

Identical in format to the previous year's issue, the 1964 set of Twins pictures features the use of a second portrait of the player in civilian dress rather than an action picture. The 1964 issue also has background of pastel colors, rather than all-black, and, on back, an oval/arrow logo for Western brand gas, along with the Mileage and DS logos.

		NM	EX	VG
Complete Set (15):		120.00	60.00	35.00
Common Player:		10.00	5.00	3.00
(1)	Bernie Allen	10.00	5.00	3.00
(2)	Bob Allison	12.50	6.25	3.75
(3)	Earl Battey	12.50	6.25	3.75
(4)	Bill Dailey	10.00	5.00	3.00
(5)	Jimmie Hall	10.00	5.00	3.00
(6)	Jim Kaat	15.00	7.50	4.50
(7)	Harmon Killebrew	30.00	15.00	9.00
(8)	Don Mincher	10.00	5.00	3.00
(9)	Tony Oliva	25.00	12.50	7.50
(10)	Camilo Pascual	12.50	6.25	3.75
(11)	Bill Pleis	10.00	5.00	3.00
(12)	Jim Roland	10.00	5.00	3.00
(13)	Rich Rollins	10.00	5.00	3.00
(14)	Dick Stigman	10.00	5.00	3.00
(15)	Zoilo Versalles	12.50	6.25	3.75

1974 Weston Expos

This 10-card set features members of the Montreal Expos. Each full-color card measures 3-1/2" x 5-1/2" and includes a facsimile autograph in black ink with the player's name printed along the bottom. The backs are distinct because they are divided in half. The top of the card lists player data and 1973 statistics in English, while the bottom carries the same information in French. The cards are numbered according to the player's uniform number.

		NM	EX	VG
Complete Set (10):		10.00	5.00	3.00
Common Player:		1.50	.75	.45
3	Bob Bailey	1.50	.75	.45
8	Boots Day	1.50	.75	.45
12	John Boccabella	1.50	.75	.45
16	Mike Jorgensen	1.50	.75	.45
18	Steve Renko	1.50	.75	.45
19	Tim Foli	1.50	.75	.45
21	Ernie McAnally	1.50	.75	.45
26	Bill Stoneman	1.50	.75	.45
29	Ken Singleton	1.50	.75	.45
33	Ron Hunt	1.50	.75	.45

1888 WG1 Base Ball Playing Cards

This little-known set of playing cards featuring drawings of real baseball players in action poses was issued in 1888 and includes members of the eight National League teams of the day. Each club is represented by nine players - one at each position - making the set complete at 72 cards. The cards measure 2-1/2" x 3-1/2" and have a blue-on-blue lathework pattern on back. The cards were sold as a boxed set. They were designed to resemble a deck of regular playing cards, and the various positions were all assigned the same denomination (for example, all of the pitchers were kings, catchers were aces, etc.). There are no cards numbered either two, three, four or five; and rather than the typical hearts, clubs, diamonds and spades, each team represents a different "suit." The American Card Catalog designation is WG1.

		NM	EX	VG
Complete Set (72):		90,000	35,000	17,500
Common Player:		900.00	360.00	180.00
Box:		5,000	2,500	1,500
(1)	Ed Andrews	900.00	360.00	180.00
(2)	Cap Anson	6,250	2,500	1,250
(3)	Charles Bassett	900.00	360.00	180.00
(4)	Charles Bastian	900.00	360.00	180.00
(5)	Charles Bennett	900.00	360.00	180.00
(6)	Henry Boyle	900.00	360.00	180.00
(7)	Dan Brouthers	3,000	1,200	600.00
(8)	Tom Brown	900.00	360.00	180.00
(9)	Tom Burns	900.00	360.00	180.00
(10)	Fred Carroll	900.00	360.00	180.00
(11)	Dan Casey	900.00	360.00	180.00
(12)	John Clarkson	3,000	1,200	600.00
(13)	Jack Clements	900.00	360.00	180.00
(14)	John Coleman	900.00	360.00	180.00
(15)	Roger Connor	3,000	1,200	600.00
(16)	Abner Dalrymple	900.00	360.00	180.00
(17)	Jerry Denny	900.00	360.00	180.00
(18)	Jim Donelly	900.00	360.00	180.00
(19)	Fred Dunlap	900.00	360.00	180.00
(20)	Dude Esterbrook	900.00	360.00	180.00
(21)	Buck Ewing	3,000	1,200	600.00
(22)	Sid Farrar	900.00	360.00	180.00
(23)	Silver Flint	900.00	360.00	180.00
(24)	Jim Fogarty	900.00	360.00	180.00
(25)	Elmer Foster	900.00	360.00	180.00
(26)	Pud Galvin	3,000	1,200	600.00
(27)	Charlie Getzein (Getzien)	900.00	360.00	180.00
(28)	Jack Glasscock	900.00	360.00	180.00
(29)	George Gore	900.00	360.00	180.00
(30)	Ned Hanlon	3,000	1,200	600.00
(31)	Paul Hines	900.00	360.00	180.00
(32)	Joe Hornung	900.00	360.00	180.00
(33)	Dummy Hoy	1,350	550.00	275.00
(34)	Arthur Irwin (Philadelphia)	900.00	360.00	180.00
(35)	John Irwin (Washington)	900.00	360.00	180.00
(36)	Dick Johnston	900.00	360.00	180.00
(37)	Tim Keefe	3,000	1,200	600.00
(38)	King Kelly	4,250	1,700	850.00
(39)	Willie Kuehne	900.00	360.00	180.00
(40)	Connie Mack	3,250	1,300	650.00
(41)	Al Maul	900.00	360.00	180.00
(42)	Al Meyers (Myers) (Washington)	900.00	360.00	180.00
(43)	George Meyers (Myers) (Indianapolis)	900.00	360.00	180.00
(44)	John Morrill	900.00	360.00	180.00
(45)	Joseph Mulvey	900.00	360.00	180.00
(46)	Billy Nash	900.00	360.00	180.00
(47)	Billy O'Brien	900.00	360.00	180.00
(48)	Orator Jim O'Rourke	3,000	1,200	600.00
(49)	Bob Pettit	900.00	360.00	180.00
(50)	Fred Pfeffer	900.00	360.00	180.00
(51)	Danny Richardson (New York)	900.00	360.00	180.00
(52)	Hardy Richardson (Detroit)	900.00	360.00	180.00
(53)	Jack Rowe	900.00	360.00	180.00
(54)	Jimmy Ryan	900.00	360.00	180.00
(55)	Emmett Seery	900.00	360.00	180.00
(56)	George Shoch	900.00	360.00	180.00
(57)	Otto Shomberg (Schomberg)	900.00	360.00	180.00
(58)	Pap Smith	900.00	360.00	180.00
(59)	Marty Sullivan	900.00	360.00	180.00
(60)	Billy Sunday	3,000	1,200	600.00
(61)	Ezra Sutton	900.00	360.00	180.00
(62)	Sam Thompson	3,000	1,200	600.00
(63)	Mike Tiernan	900.00	360.00	180.00
(64)	Larry Twitchell	900.00	360.00	180.00
(65)	Rip Van Haltren	900.00	360.00	180.00
(66)	John Ward	3,000	1,200	600.00
(67)	Deacon White	900.00	360.00	180.00
(68)	Jim Whitney	900.00	360.00	180.00
(69)	Ned Williamson	900.00	360.00	180.00
(70)	Walt Wilmot	900.00	360.00	180.00
(71)	Medoc Wise	900.00	360.00	180.00
(72)	George Wood	900.00	360.00	180.00

1932 Wheaties Babe Ruth Flip Book

This novelty item measures about 1-3/4" x 2-1/2" and is stapled at the bottom. When properly thumbed, the individual black-and-white pages inside present a simulated moving picture, "Babe Ruth Shows You How to Hit a Home Run". The covers feature orange and blue artwork.

	NM	EX	VG
Babe Ruth	750.00	375.00	225.00

1933-1934 Wheaties

Sponsored by Wheaties via mail-in offers heard on baseball games on half a dozen radio stations, these black-and-white cards are blank-backed and feature posed action photo with facsimile autographs bordered in white. In a 3-1/4" x 5-3/8" format, they are similar in design to the later 1936 National Chicle "Fine Pens" (R313) and the Gold Medal Foods World Series (R313A) issue of 1934, though each of the photos found in this set are unique. To date, this likely incomplete checklist comprises on players from the Browns, Cardinals, Cubs, White Sox, Indians and the Des Moines Demons of the Western League.

		NM	EX	VG
Common Player:		275.00	135.00	80.00
(1)	Earl Averill	275.00	135.00	80.00
(2)	Geo. E. Blaeholder	45.00	22.50	13.50
(3)	Irving "Jack" Burns	45.00	22.50	13.50
(4)	Bruce Campbell	45.00	22.50	13.50
(5)	"Tex" Carleton	45.00	22.50	13.50
(6)	George Earnshaw	80.00	40.00	24.00
(7)	Red Faber	80.00	40.00	24.00
(8)	Fabian Gaffke	45.00	22.50	13.50
(9)	Odell Hale	180.00	90.00	55.00
(10)	Mel Harder	45.00	22.50	13.50
(11)	Roy Hudson	45.00	22.50	13.50
(12)	Chuck Klein	80.00	40.00	24.00
(13)	Jack Knott	45.00	22.50	13.50
(14)	Al Marchand	45.00	22.50	13.50
(15)	Ossie Orwoll	45.00	22.50	13.50
(16)	Al Simmons	80.00	40.00	24.00
(17)	Hal Trosky	45.00	22.50	13.50
(18)	Joe Vosmik	45.00	22.50	13.50
(19)	Bill Walker	45.00	22.50	13.50

1935 Wheaties - Series 1

This set of major leaguers (plus fictional sports hero Jack Armstrong) was issued on the back of Wheaties cereal boxes in 1935 and because of its design, is known as "Fancy Frame with Script Signature." The unnumbered cards measure 6" x 6-1/4" with frame, and 5" x 5-1/2" without the frame. The player photo is tinted blue, while the background is blue and orange. A facsimile autograph appears at the bottom of the photo. Illinois high school track star Herman "Jack" Waddlington posed for the photos of fictional Jack Armstrong "All-American Boy."

		NM	EX	VG
Complete Set (27):		3,000	1,500	900.00
Common Player:		50.00	25.00	15.50
(1)	Jack Armstrong/Btg	50.00	25.00	15.00
(2)	Jack Armstrong/Throwing	50.00	25.00	15.00
(3)	Wally Berger	50.00	25.00	15.00
(4)	Tommy Bridges	50.00	25.00	15.00
(5)	Mickey Cochrane (Black hat.)	90.00	45.00	27.00
(6)	Michey Cochrane (White hat.)	425.00	210.00	125.00
(7)	James "Rip" Collins	50.00	25.00	15.00
(8)	Dizzy Dean	325.00	160.00	97.00
(9)	Dizzy Dean, Paul Dean	250.00	125.00	75.00
(10)	Paul Dean	55.00	27.50	16.50
(11)	William Delancey	50.00	25.00	15.00
(12)	"Jimmie" Foxx	190.00	95.00	60.00
(13)	Frank Frisch	75.00	37.50	22.00
(14)	Lou Gehrig	475.00	235.00	140.00

		NM	EX	VG
(15)	Goose Goslin	75.00	37.50	22.00
(16)	Lefty Grove	125.00	65.00	35.00
(17)	Carl Hubbell	85.00	40.00	25.00
(18)	Travis C. Jackson	75.00	37.50	22.00
(19)	"Chuck" Klein	75.00	37.50	22.00
(20)	Gus Mancuso	50.00	25.00	15.00
(21)	Pepper Martin/Btg	55.00	27.00	16.50
(22)	Pepper Martin/Portrait	55.00	27.00	16.50
(23)	Joe Medwick	75.00	37.50	22.00
(24)	Melvin Ott	90.00	45.00	27.00
(25)	Harold Schumacher	50.00	25.00	15.00
(26)	Al Simmons	75.00	37.50	22.00
(27)	"Jo Jo" White	50.00	25.00	15.00

1936 Wheaties - Series 3

Consisting of 12 unnumbered cards, this set is similar in size (6" x 6-1/4" with frame) and design to the Wheaties of the previous year, but is known as "Fancy Frame with Printed Name and Data" because the cards also include a few printed words describing the player.

		NM	EX	VG
Complete Set (12):		1,600	800.00	475.00
Common Player:		45.00	22.00	13.50
(1)	Earl Averill	60.00	30.00	18.00
(2)	Mickey Cochrane	60.00	30.00	18.00
(3)	Jimmy Foxx	200.00	100.00	60.00
(4)	Lou Gehrig	750.00	375.00	225.00
(5)	Hank Greenberg	175.00	90.00	50.00
(6)	"Gabby" Hartnett	60.00	30.00	18.00
(7)	Carl Hubbell	65.00	32.50	20.00
(8)	"Pepper" Martin	50.00	25.00	15.00
(9)	Van L. Mungo	45.00	22.50	13.50
(10)	"Buck" Newsom	45.00	22.50	13.50
(11)	"Arky" Vaughan	60.00	30.00	18.00
(12)	Jimmy Wilson	45.00	22.50	13.50

1936 Wheaties - Series 4

This larger size (8-1/2" x 6") card also made up the back of a Wheaties box, and because of its distinctive border which featured drawings of small athletic figures, it is referred to as "Thin Orange Border/Figures in Border." Twelve major leaguers are pictured in the unnumbered set. The photos are enclosed in a 4" x 6-1/2" box. Below the photo is an endorsement for Wheaties, the "Breakfast of Champions," and a facsimile autograph.

		NM	EX	VG
Complete Set (12):		1,200	600.00	350.00
Common Player:		45.00	22.00	13.50
(1)	Curt Davis	45.00	22.50	13.50
(2)	Lou Gehrig	500.00	250.00	150.00
(3)	Charley Gehringer	75.00	37.50	22.00
(4)	Lefty Grove	165.00	85.00	50.00
(5)	Rollie Hemsley	45.00	22.50	13.50
(6)	Billy Herman	75.00	37.50	22.00
(7)	Joe Medwick	75.00	37.50	22.00
(8)	Mel Ott	80.00	40.00	25.00
(9)	Schoolboy Rowe	45.00	22.50	13.50
(10)	Arky Vaughan	75.00	37.50	22.00
(11)	Joe Vosmik	45.00	22.50	13.50
(12)	Lon Warneke	45.00	22.50	13.50

1936 Wheaties - Series 5

Often referred to as "How to Play Winning Baseball," this 12-card set features a large player photo surrounded by blue and white drawings that illustrate various playing tips. Different major leaguers offer advice on different aspects of the game. The cards again made up the back panel of a Wheaties box and measure 8-1/2" x 6-1/2". The cards are numbered

from 1 through 12, and it is now believed that each can be found with or without a small number "28" followed by a letter from "A" through "L."

		NM	EX	VG
Complete Set (12)		1,000	500.00	300.00
Common Player:		45.00	22.50	13.50
1	Lefty Gomez	85.00	45.00	25.00
2	Billy Herman	75.00	37.50	22.00
3	Luke Appling	75.00	37.50	22.00
4	Jimmie Foxx	90.00	45.00	27.00
5	Joe Medwick	75.00	37.50	22.00
6	Charles Gehringer	75.00	37.50	22.00
7a	Mel Ott (Tips in vertical sequence.)	95.00	45.00	25.00
7b	Mel Ott (Tips in two horizontal rows.)	95.00	45.00	25.00
8	Odell Hale	45.00	22.50	13.50
9	Bill Dickey	85.00	45.00	25.00
10	"Lefty" Grove	85.00	45.00	25.00
11	Carl Hubbell	80.00	40.00	25.00
12	Earl Averill	75.00	37.50	22.00

1936 Wheaties - Series UNC

These box-back cards were issued on single-serving packages of Wheaties that are marked, "Individual Service For Hotels Dining Cars Restaurants". The back panel measures about 2-3/4" x 4", and like many contemporary Wheaties box-back cards is printed in orange, white and blue. The player pictures and design of the single-serving box cards are similar to the central portions of the Wheaties cards cataloged as 1936 Series 4. Each of the five players known in the single-serving box series is also represented on Series 4, though it is not known whether the other eight players from Series 4 were also issued in the smaller size. Gaps have been left in the assigned numbers to accommodate future additions.

		NM	EX	VG
Common Player:		400.00	200.00	120.00
(2)	Lou Gehrig	2,000	1,000	600.00
(3)	Charley Gehringer	400.00	200.00	120.00
(4)	Lefty Grove	500.00	250.00	150.00
(7)	Joe Medwick	400.00	200.00	120.00
(8)	Mel Ott	500.00	250.00	150.00

1937 Wheaties - Series 6

Similar to the Series 5 set, this numbered, 12-card series is known as "How to Star in Baseball" and again includes a large player photo with small instructional drawings to illustrate playing tips. The cards measure 8-1/4" x 6" and include a facsimile autograph.

		NM	EX	VG
Complete Set (12):		1,000	500.00	300.00
Common Player:		35.00	17.50	10.00
1	Bill Dickey	75.00	37.50	22.00
2	Red Ruffing	60.00	30.00	18.00
3	Zeke Bonura	35.00	17.50	10.00
4	Charlie Gehringer	60.00	30.00	18.00
5	"Arky" Vaughn (Vaughan)	60.00	30.00	18.00
6	Carl Hubbell	60.00	30.00	18.00
7	John Lewis	35.00	17.50	10.00
8	Heinie Manush	60.00	30.00	18.00
9	"Lefty" Grove	75.00	37.50	22.00
10	Billy Herman	60.00	30.00	18.00
11	Joe DiMaggio	400.00	200.00	120.00
12	Joe Medwick	60.00	30.00	18.00

1937 Wheaties - Series 7

This set of 6" x 8-1/4" panels contains several different card designs. One style (picturing Lombardi, Travis and Mungo) has a white background with an orange border and a large orange circle behind the player. Another design (showing Bonura, DiMaggio and Bridges) has the player outlined against a bright orange background with a Wheaties endorsement along the bottom. A third format (picturing Moore, Radcliff and Martin) has a distinctive red, white and blue border. And a fourth design (featuring Trosky, Demaree and Vaughan) has a tilted picture against an orange background framed in blue and white. The set also includes four Pacific Coast League Players (#29M-29P). The cards are numbered with a small "29" followed by a letter from "A" through "P."

	NM	EX	VG
Complete Set (16):	1,200	600.00	350.00
Common Player:	45.00	22.50	13.50
29A "Zeke" Bonura	45.00	22.50	13.50
29B Cecil Travis	45.00	22.50	13.50
29C Frank Demaree	45.00	22.50	13.50
29D Joe Moore	45.00	22.50	13.50
29E Ernie Lombardi	60.00	30.00	18.00
29F John L. "Pepper" Martin	50.00	25.00	15.00
29G Harold Trosky	45.00	22.50	13.50
29H Raymond Radcliff	45.00	22.50	13.50
29I Joe DiMaggio	300.00	150.00	90.00
29J Tom Bridges	45.00	22.50	13.50
29K Van L. Mungo	45.00	22.50	13.50
29L "Arky" Vaughn (Vaughan)	60.00	30.00	18.00
29M Arnold Statz	100.00	50.00	30.00
29N Wes Schulmerich	100.00	50.00	30.00
29O Fred Mueller	100.00	50.00	30.00
29P Gene Lillard	100.00	50.00	30.00

1937 Wheaties - Series 8

Another series printed on the back of Wheaties boxes in 1937, the eight cards in this set are unnumbered and measure 8-1/2" x 6". There are several different designs, but in all of them the player photo is surrounded by speckles of color, causing this series to be known as the "Speckled Orange, White and Blue" series. A facsimile autograph is included, along with brief printed 1936 season statistics.

	NM	EX	VG
Complete Set (8):	1,300	650.00	400.00
Common Player:	120.00	60.00	36.00
Luke Appling	100.00	50.00	30.00
Earl Averill	100.00	50.00	30.00
Joe DiMaggio	450.00	225.00	135.00
Robert Feller	225.00	110.00	65.00
Chas. Gehringer	100.00	50.00	30.00
Lefty Grove	125.00	65.00	35.00
Carl Hubbell	125.00	65.00	35.00
Joe Medwick	100.00	50.00	30.00

1937 Wheaties - Series 9

This unnumbered set includes one player from each of the 16 major league teams and is generally referred to as the "Color Series." The cards measure 8-1/2" x 6" and were the back panels of Wheaties boxes. The player photos are shown inside or against large stars, circles, "V" shapes, rectangles and other geometric designs. A facsimile autograph and team designation are printed near the photo, while a Wheaties endorsement and a line of player stats appear along the bottom.

	NM	EX	VG
Complete Set (16):	1,600	800.00	480.00
Common Player:	50.00	25.00	15.00
(1) Zeke Bonura	50.00	25.00	15.00
(2) Tom Bridges	50.00	25.00	15.00
(3) Harland Clift (Harlond)	50.00	25.00	15.00
(4) Kiki Cuyler	75.00	37.50	22.50
(5) Joe DiMaggio	600.00	300.00	180.00
(6) Robert Feller	175.00	85.00	50.00
(7) Lefty Grove	100.00	50.00	30.00
(8) Billy Herman	75.00	37.50	22.50
(9) Carl Hubbell	90.00	45.00	27.50
(10) Buck Jordan	50.00	25.00	15.00
(11) "Pepper" Martin	60.00	30.00	18.00
(12) John Moore	50.00	25.00	15.00
(13) Wally Moses	50.00	25.00	15.00
(14) Van L. Mungo	50.00	25.00	15.00
(15) Cecil Travis	50.00	25.00	15.00
(16) Arky Vaughan	75.00	37.50	22.50

1937 Wheaties - Series 14

Much reduced in size (2-5/8" x 3-7/8"), these unnumbered cards made up the back panels of single-serving size Wheaties boxes. The player photo (which is sometimes identical to the photos used in the larger series) is set against an orange or white background. The player's name appears in large capital letters with his position and team in smaller capitals. A facsimile autograph and Wheaties endorsement are also included. Some cards are also found with the number "29" followed by a letter.

	NM	EX	VG
Complete Set (16):	5,000	2,500	1,500
Common Player:	200.00	100.00	60.00
(1) "Zeke" Bonura	200.00	100.00	60.00
(2) Tom Bridges	200.00	100.00	60.00
(3) Dolph Camilli	200.00	100.00	60.00
(4) Frank Demaree	200.00	100.00	60.00
(5) Joe DiMaggio	1,300	650.00	390.00
(6) Billy Herman	300.00	150.00	90.00
(7) Carl Hubbell	350.00	175.00	105.00
(8) Ernie Lombardi	300.00	150.00	90.00
(9) "Pepper" Martin	250.00	125.00	75.00
(10) Joe Moore	200.00	100.00	60.00
(11) Van Mungo	200.00	100.00	60.00
(12) Mel Ott	350.00	175.00	105.00
(13) Raymond Radcliff	200.00	100.00	60.00
(14) Cecil Travis	200.00	100.00	60.00
(15) Harold Trosky	200.00	100.00	60.00
(16a) "Arky" Vaughan (29L on card)	350.00	175.00	105.00
(16b) "Arky" Vaughan (No 29L on card.)	350.00	175.00	105.00

1938 Wheaties - Series 10

One player from each major league team is included in this 16-card set, referred to as the "Biggest Thrills in Baseball" series. Measuring 8-1/2" x 6", each numbered card was the back panel of a Wheaties box and pictures a player along with a printed description of his biggest thrill in baseball and facsimile autograph. All 16 cards in this series have also been found on paper stock.

	NM	EX	VG
Complete Set (16):	1,700	850.00	500.00
Common Player:	45.00	22.50	13.50
1 Bob Feller	160.00	80.00	45.00
2 Cecil Travis	45.00	22.50	13.50
3 Joe Medwick	65.00	32.50	20.00
4 Gerald Walker	45.00	22.50	13.50
5 Carl Hubbell	65.00	32.50	20.00
6 Bob Johnson	45.00	22.50	13.50
7 Beau Bell	45.00	22.50	13.50
8 Ernie Lombardi	65.00	32.50	20.00
9 Lefty Grove	80.00	40.00	24.00
10 Lou Fette	45.00	22.50	13.50
11 Joe DiMaggio	600.00	300.00	180.00
12 Pinky Whitney	45.00	22.50	13.50
13 Dizzy Dean	175.00	85.00	55.00
14 Charley Gehringer	65.00	32.50	20.00
15 Paul Waner	65.00	32.50	20.00
16 Dolf Camilli	45.00	22.50	13.50

1938 Wheaties - Series 11

Cards in this unnumbered, eight-card series measure 8-1/2" x 6" and show the players in street clothes either eating or getting ready to enjoy a bowl of Wheaties. Sometimes a waitress or other person also appears in the photo. The set is sometimes called the "Dress Clothes" or "Civies" series.

	NM	EX	VG
Complete Set (8):	750.00	375.00	225.00
Common Player:	60.00	30.00	18.00
(1) Lou Fette	60.00	30.00	18.00
(2) Jimmie Foxx	145.00	75.00	45.00
(3) Charlie Gehringer	115.00	55.00	35.00
(4) Lefty Grove	115.00	55.00	35.00
(5) Hank Greenberg, Roxie Lawson	115.00	55.00	35.00
(6) Lee Grissom, Ernie Lombardi	85.00	40.00	25.00
(7) Joe Medwick	85.00	40.00	25.00
(8) Lon Warneke	60.00	30.00	18.00

1938 Wheaties - Series 15

Another set of small (2-5/8" x 3-7/8") cards, the photos in this unnumbered series made up the back panels of single-serving size Wheaties boxes. The panels have orange, blue and white backgrounds. Some of the photos are the same as those used in the larger Wheaties panels.

	NM	EX	VG
Complete Set (11):	4,500	2,250	1,350
Common Player:	160.00	80.00	45.00
(1) "Zeke" Bonura	160.00	80.00	45.00
(2) Joe DiMaggio	1,300	650.00	390.00
(3) Charles Gehringer/Btg	400.00	200.00	120.00
(4) Chas. Gehringer/Leaping	400.00	200.00	120.00
(5) Hank Greenberg	500.00	250.00	150.00
(6) Lefty Grove	400.00	200.00	120.00
(7) Carl Hubbell	325.00	160.00	97.00
(8) John (Buddy) Lewis	160.00	80.00	45.00
(9) Heinie Manush	300.00	150.00	90.00
(10) Joe Medwick	300.00	150.00	90.00
(11) Arky Vaughan	300.00	150.00	90.00

1939 Wheaties - Series 12

The nine cards in this numbered series, known as the "Personal Pointers" series, measure 8-1/4" x 6" and feature an instructional format similar to earlier Wheaties issues. The cards feature a player photo along with printed tips on various aspects of hitting and pitching.

		NM	EX	VG
Complete Set (9):		1,500	750.00	450.00
Common Player:		100.00	50.00	30.00
1	Ernie Lombardi	160.00	80.00	45.00
2	Johnny Allen	100.00	50.00	30.00
3	Lefty Gomez	185.00	90.00	55.00
4	Bill Lee	100.00	50.00	30.00
5	Jimmie Foxx	250.00	125.00	75.00
6	Joe Medwick	160.00	80.00	45.00
7	Hank Greenberg	250.00	125.00	75.00
8	Mel Ott	185.00	90.00	55.00
9	Arky Vaughn (Vaughan)	160.00	80.00	45.00

1939 Wheaties - Series 13

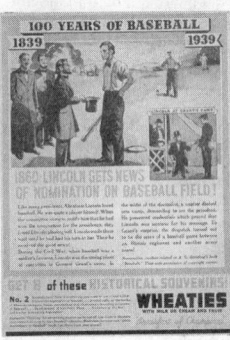

Issued in baseball's centennial year of 1939, this set of eight 6" x 6-3/4" cards commemorates "100 Years of Baseball." Each of the numbered panels illustrates a significant event in baseball history.

		NM	EX	VG
Complete Set (8):		650.00	325.00	200.00
Common Panel:		75.00	37.50	22.50
1	Design of First Diamond - 1838 (Abner Doubleday)	75.00	37.50	22.50
2	Gets News of Nomination on Field - 1860 (Abraham Lincoln)	125.00	62.50	37.50
3	Crowd Boos First Baseball Glove - 1869	75.00	37.50	22.50
4	Curve Ball Just an Illusion - 1877	75.00	37.50	22.50
5	Fencer's Mask is Pattern - 1877	75.00	37.50	22.50
6	Baseball Gets "All Dressed Up" - 1895	75.00	37.50	22.50
7	Modern Bludgeon Enters Game - 1895	75.00	37.50	22.50
8	"Casey at the Bat"	100.00	50.00	30.00

1940 Wheaties Champs of the USA

This set consists of 13 numbered panels (plus seven variations). Each pictures three athletes, including one, two or three baseball players; the others include football stars, golfers, skaters, racers, etc. The entire panel measures approximately 8-1/4" x 6", while the actual card measures approximately 6" square. Each athlete is pictured in what looks like a postage stamp with

a serrated edge. A brief biography appears alongside the "stamp." Some variations are known to exist among the first nine panels. The cards are numbered in the upper right corner.

		NM	EX	VG
Complete Set (20):		1,400	700.00	425.00
Common Panel:		50.00	25.00	15.00
1A	Bob Feller, Lynn Patrick, Charles "Red" Ruffing	135.00	67.00	40.00
1B	Leo Durocher, Lynn Patrick, Charles "Red" Ruffing	90.00	45.00	27.00
2A	Joe DiMaggio, Don Budge, Hank Greenberg	300.00	150.00	90.00
2B	Joe DiMaggio, Mel Ott, Ellsworth Vines	200.00	100.00	60.00
3	Bernie Bierman, Bill Dickey, Jimmie Foxx	125.00	62.00	37.00
4	Morris Arnovich, Capt R.K. Baker, Earl "Dutch" Clark	50.00	25.00	15.00
5	Madison (Matty) Bell, Ab Jenkins, Joe Medwick	50.00	25.00	15.00
6A	Ralph Guldahl, John Mize, Davey O'Brien	50.00	25.00	15.00
6B	Bob Feller, John Mize, Rudy York	90.00	45.00	27.00
6C	Ralph Guldahl, Gabby Hartnett, Davey O'Brien	50.00	25.00	15.00
7A	Joe Cronin, Cecil Isbell, Byron Nelson	50.00	25.00	15.00
7B	Joe Cronin, Hank Greenberg, Byron Nelson	75.00	37.00	22.00
7C	Paul Derringer, Cecil Isbell, Byron Nelson	50.00	25.00	15.00
8A	Ernie Lombardi, Jack Manders, George I. Myers	50.00	25.00	15.00
8B	Paul Derringer, Ernie Lombardi, George I. Myers	50.00	25.00	15.00
9	Bob Bartlett, Captain R.C. Hanson, Terrell Jacobs	50.00	25.00	15.00
10	Lowell "Red" Dawson, Billy Herman, Adele Inge	50.00	25.00	15.00
11	Dolph Camilli, Antoinette Concello, Wallace Wade	50.00	25.00	15.00
12	Luke Appling, Stanley Hack, Hugh McManus	50.00	25.00	15.00
13	Felix Adler, Hal Trosky, Mabel Vinson	50.00	25.00	15.00

1941 Wheaties Champs of the USA

This eight-card series is actually a continuation of the previous year's Wheaties set, and the format is identical. The set begins with number 14, starting where the 1940 set ended.

		NM	EX	VG
Complete Set (8):		800.00	400.00	240.00
Common Panel:		50.00	25.00	15.00
14	Felix Adler, Jimmie Foxx, Capt. R.G. Hanson	90.00	45.00	27.00
15	Bernie Bierman, Bob Feller, Jessie McLeod	90.00	45.00	27.00
16	Lowell "Red" Dawson, Hank Greenberg, J.W. Stoker	80.00	40.00	24.00
17	Antoinette Concello, Joe DiMaggio, Byron Nelson	300.00	150.00	90.00
18	Capt. R.L. Baker, Frank "Buck" McCormick, Harold "Pee Wee" Reese	90.00	45.00	27.00
19	William W. Robbins, Gene Sarazen, Gerald "Gee" Walker	50.00	25.00	15.00
20	Harry Danning, Barney McCosky, Bucky Walters	50.00	25.00	15.00
21	Joe "Flash" Gordon, Stan Hack, George I. Myers	50.00	25.00	15.00

1951 Wheaties

Printed as the backs of single-serving size boxes of Wheaties, the six-card 1951 set includes three baseball players and one football player, basketball player and golfer. Well-

trimmed cards measure 2-1/2" x 3-1/4". The cards feature blue line drawings of the athletes with a facsimile autograph and descriptive title below. There is a wide white border. A small hoard of complete sets of unused boxes made its way into the hobby in the early 1990s. Complete boxes should be priced at 1.5X the values shown here.

		NM	EX	VG
Complete Set (6):		650.00	325.00	195.00
Common Player:		85.00	42.00	25.00
(1)	Bob Feller (Baseball)	100.00	50.00	30.00
(2)	John Lujack (Football)	55.00	27.50	16.50
(3)	George Mikan (Basketball)	110.00	55.00	35.00
(4)	Stan Musial (Baseball)	150.00	75.00	45.00
(5)	Sam Snead (Golfer)	65.00	32.50	20.00
(6)	Ted Williams (Baseball)	200.00	100.00	60.00

1951 Wheaties Premium Photos

LARRY (YOGI) BERRA

Whether or not these 5" x 7" black-and-white, blank-back photos were ever issued at all, or only on a test basis is unknown. Despite being unmarked, they are reliably attributed to General Mills, possibly intended for use as a Wheaties premium. The photos found on several of the pictures are the same pictures used on the box-back Wheaties cards of 1952. The pictures appear in most cases to be re-uses of team-issued images from photo packs and the like. Player names are in the bottom border in capital letters. Each picture has a small alpha-numeric identifier in the lower-right corner. The scope of the issue is unknown as several letters from the sequence are missing. The letter shown in this checklist is preceded in each case by "A8491."

		NM	EX	VG
Complete Baseball Set (8):		4,000	2,000	1,200
Common Player:		100.00	50.00	30.00
A	Stan Musial	500.00	250.00	150.00
C	Richie Ashburn	180.00	90.00	50.00
D	Bob Feller	180.00	90.00	50.00
E	Al Rosen	100.00	50.00	30.00
F	Larry (Yogi) Berra	250.00	125.00	75.00
G	Mickey Mantle	2,400	1,200	720.00
H	Betty Schalow (Ice skater.)	25.00	12.00	7.50
J	Bob Lemon	100.00	50.00	30.00
K	Roy Campanella	225.00	120.00	75.00

1952 Wheaties

BOB FELLER
PITCHER, CLEVELAND INDIANS

These 2" x 2-3/4" cards appeared on the back of the popular cereal boxes. Actually, sports figures had been appearing on the backs of the boxes for many years, but in 1952, of the 30 athletes depicted, 10 were baseball players. That means there are 20 baseball cards, as each player appears in both a portrait and an action drawing. The cards have a blue line drawing on an orange background with a white border. The player's name, team, and position appear at the bottom. The cards have rounded corners, but are often found poorly cut from the boxes. This set was extensively counterfeited circa 2002, which had a chilling effect on values of cards not professionally graded by a major certification company.

		NM	EX	VG
Complete (Baseball) Set (20):		650.00	325.00	195.00
Common Player:		20.00	10.00	6.0
(1)	Larry "Yogi" Berra/Portrait	50.00	25.00	15.0
(2)	Larry "Yogi" Berra/Action	50.00	25.00	15.0
(3)	Roy Campanella/Portrait	50.00	25.00	15.0
(4)	Roy Campanella/Action	50.00	25.00	15.0
(5)	Bob Feller/Portrait	30.00	15.00	9.0
(6)	Bob Feller/Action	30.00	15.00	9.0
(7)	George Kell/Portrait	25.00	12.50	7.5
(8)	George Kell/Action	25.00	12.50	7.5

		NM	EX	VG
(9)	Ralph Kiner/Portrait	25.00	12.50	7.50
(10)	Ralph Kiner/Action	25.00	12.50	7.50
(11)	Bob Lemon/Portrait	25.00	12.50	7.50
(12)	Bob Lemon/Action	25.00	12.50	7.50
(13)	Stan Musial/Portrait	60.00	30.00	18.00
(14)	Stan Musial/Action	60.00	30.00	18.00
(15)	Phil Rizzuto/Portrait	30.00	15.00	9.00
(16)	Phil Rizzuto/Action	30.00	15.00	9.00
(17)	Elwin "Preacher" Roe/Portrait	20.00	10.00	6.00
(18)	Elwin "Preacher" Roe/Action	20.00	10.00	6.00
(19)	Ted Williams/Portrait	100.00	50.00	30.00
(20)	Ted Williams/Action	100.00	50.00	30.00

1952 Wheaties Tin Trays

This unique cereal box premium took the shape of a 4-7/8" x 5-1/8" tin tray which was glued to the back of Wheaties boxes. A cream-colored border surrounded the 3" x 4" color photo debossed at center. A black facsimile autograph appears across the photo. At top a small hole was punched for hanging the plaque. Backs were blank, and are often found with glue and paper residue on the gold-tone metal. Most of the plates have acquired numerous scratches and dings over the years, making true Near Mint examples very scarce. The unnumbered trays are checklisted alphabetically. A George Kell tray was long believed to exist but has never been verified.

		NM	EX	VG
Complete Set (4):		1,200	600.00	350.00
Common Player:		50.00	25.00	15.00
1)	Ralph Kiner	50.00	25.00	15.00
2)	Stan Musial	125.00	65.00	35.00
3)	Phil Rizzuto	60.00	30.00	18.00
4)	Jackie Robinson	1,100	550.00	330.00

1964 Wheaties Stamps

This General Mills' promotion included 50 player stamps and a 48-page orange album called "Wheaties Major League All-Star Baseball Player Stamp Album." The 2-1/2" x 2-3/4" stamps have a color player photo at center with a facsimile autograph and surrounded by a white border. Backs are blank. The unnumbered set is checklisted here in alphabetical order.

		NM	EX	VG
Complete Set (50):		500.00	250.00	150.00
Complete Set, In Album:		200.00	100.00	60.00
Complete Set, unused in Album		825.00	400.00	250.00
Common Player:		6.00	3.00	2.00
	Album:	60.00	30.00	20.00
1)	Hank Aaron	45.00	25.00	15.00
2)	Bob Allison	6.00	3.00	2.00
3)	Luis Aparicio	12.00	6.00	4.00
4)	Ed Bailey	6.00	3.00	2.00
5)	Steve Barber	6.00	3.00	2.00
6)	Earl Battey	6.00	3.00	2.00
7)	Jim Bouton	7.50	4.00	2.50
8)	Ken Boyer	7.50	4.00	2.50
9)	Jim Bunning	12.00	6.00	4.00
10)	Orlando Cepeda	15.00	7.50	4.00
11)	Roberto Clemente	70.00	35.00	20.00
12)	Ray Culp	6.00	3.00	2.00
13)	Tommy Davis	6.00	3.00	2.00
14)	John Edwards	6.00	3.00	2.00
15)	Whitey Ford	30.00	15.00	9.00
16)	Nellie Fox	15.00	7.50	4.00
17)	Bob Friend	6.00	3.00	2.00
18)	Jim Gilliam	7.50	4.00	2.50
19)	Jim Grant	6.00	3.00	2.00
20)	Dick Groat	6.00	3.00	2.00
21)	Elston Howard	7.50	4.00	2.50
22)	Larry Jackson	6.00	3.00	2.00
23)	Julian Javier	6.00	3.00	2.00
24)	Al Kaline	20.00	10.00	6.00
25)	Harmon Killebrew	20.00	10.00	6.00
26)	Don Leppert	6.00	3.00	2.00
27)	Frank Malzone	6.00	3.00	2.00
28)	Juan Marichal	12.00	6.00	4.00
29)	Willie Mays	45.00	25.00	15.00
30)	Ken McBride	6.00	3.00	2.00

		NM	EX	VG
(31)	Willie McCovey	15.00	7.50	4.00
(32)	Jim O'Toole	6.00	3.00	2.00
(33)	Albie Pearson	6.00	3.00	2.00
(34)	Joe Pepitone	7.50	4.00	2.50
(35)	Ron Perranoski	6.00	3.00	2.00
(36)	Juan Pizzaro	6.00	3.00	2.00
(37)	Dick Radatz	6.00	3.00	2.00
(38)	Bobby Richardson	9.00	4.50	3.00
(39)	Brooks Robinson	20.00	10.00	6.00
(40)	Ron Santo	9.00	4.50	3.00
(41)	Norm Siebern	6.00	3.00	2.00
(42)	Duke Snider	30.00	15.00	9.00
(43)	Warren Spahn	20.00	10.00	6.00
(44)	Joe Torre	9.00	4.50	3.00
(45)	Tom Tresh	7.50	4.00	2.50
(46)	Zoilo Versalles (Versalles)	6.00	3.00	2.00
(47)	Leon Wagner	6.00	3.00	2.00
(48)	Bill White	6.00	3.00	2.00
(49)	Hal Woodeshick	6.00	3.00	2.00
(50)	Carl Yastrzemski	30.00	15.00	9.00

1937 WHIO-Sy Burick Cincinnati Reds Postcards

(See 1937-39 Orcajo Cincinnati Reds postcards for checklist, values.)

1889 C.S. White & Co. Boston N.L.

(See 1889 Number 7 Cigars for checklist and value information.)

1921 White's Bakery Baltimore Orioles

This team set of the 1921 International League champions was advertised as being issued on a one-per-day basis in wrapped loaves of White's Big Tip-Top bread, a Baltimore product. Printed on thin card stock, the sepia-toned cards measure about 3-1/4" x 5-1/2". The unnumbered cards are checklisted here alphabetically, with gaps left in the assigned numbering to accomodate possible future additions. The team and card set included many former and future major leaguers, most notably Hall of Fame pitcher Lefty Grove.

		NM	EX	VG
Common Player:		2,400	1,200	725.00
(1)	James Aitcheson		2,400	1,200
(3)	Max Bishop		2,400	1,200
(5)	Rufus Clarke		2,400	1,200
(6)	Duck Davis		2,400	1,200
(7)	Jack Dunn		2,750	1,375
(8)	Ben Egan		2,400	1,200
(10)	Harry Frank		2,400	1,200
(11)	"Lefty" Groves (Grove)		30,000	15,000
(12)	Bill Holden		2,400	1,200
(13)	Merwin Jacobson		2,400	1,200
(14)	Wade Lefler		2,400	1,200
(15)	R. (Rudy) Kneisch		2,400	1,200
(16)	Otis Lawry		2,400	1,200
(17)	Jimmy Lyston		2,400	1,200
(18)	Fritz Maisel		2,400	1,200
(19)	Lefty Matthews		2,400	1,200
(20)	Jimmy Murphy		2,400	1,200
(21)	Jack Ogden		2,400	1,200
(22)	Jim Sullivan		2,400	1,200

1977 Wiffle Insert Discs

Similar in concept and format to the many contemporary MSA baseball player disc sets, the pieces inserted within Wiffle brand baseball, softball and bat boxes differ in that they are smaller, at 2-3/8" diameter, and feature a larger checklist. The discs feature black-and-white player portrait photos in the center of a baseball design. The left and right panels are in one of several bright colors. Licensed by the players' association through Mike Schechter Associates, the player photos carry no uniform logos. Backs are printed in black and orange. The unnumbered discs are checklisted here in alphabetical order.

		NM	EX	VG
Complete Set (80):		325.00	160.00	100.00
Common Player:		2.50	1.25	.70
(1)	Sal Bando	2.50	1.25	.70
(2)	Buddy Bell	2.50	1.25	.70
(3)	Johnny Bench	7.50	3.75	2.25
(4)	Vida Blue	2.50	1.25	.70
(5)	Bert Blyleven	3.00	1.50	.90
(6)	Bobby Bonds	2.50	1.25	.70
(7)	George Brett	12.00	6.00	3.50
(8)	Lou Brock	6.00	3.00	1.75
(9)	Bill Buckner	2.50	1.25	.70
(10)	Ray Burris	2.50	1.25	.70
(11)	Jeff Burroughs	2.50	1.25	.70
(12)	Bert Campaneris	2.50	1.25	.70
(13)	Rod Carew	6.00	3.00	1.75
(14)	Steve Carlton	6.00	3.00	1.75
(15)	Dave Cash	2.50	1.25	.70
(16)	Cesar Cedeno	2.50	1.25	.70
(17)	Ron Cey	2.50	1.25	.70
(18)	Chris Chambliss	2.50	1.25	.70
(19)	Dave Concepcion	2.50	1.25	.70
(20)	Dennis Eckersley	6.00	3.00	1.75
(21)	Mark Fidrych	3.50	1.75	1.00
(22)	Rollie Fingers	6.00	3.00	1.75
(23)	Carlton Fisk	6.00	3.00	1.75
(24)	George Foster	2.50	1.25	.70
(25)	Wayne Garland	2.50	1.25	.70
(26)	Ralph Garr	2.50	1.25	.70
(27)	Steve Garvey	5.00	2.50	1.50
(28)	Don Gullett	2.50	1.25	.70
(29)	Larry Hisle	2.50	1.25	.70
(30)	Al Hrabosky	2.50	1.25	.70
(31)	Catfish Hunter	6.00	3.00	1.75
(32)	Reggie Jackson	12.00	6.00	3.50
(33)	Randy Jones	2.50	1.25	.70
(34)	Dave Kingman	2.50	1.25	.70
(35)	Jerry Koosman	2.50	1.25	.70
(36)	Ed Kranepool	2.50	1.25	.70
(37)	Ron LeFlore	2.50	1.25	.70
(38)	Sixto Lezcano	2.50	1.25	.70
(39)	Davey Lopes	2.50	1.25	.70
(40)	Greg Luzinski	2.50	1.25	.70
(41)	Fred Lynn	2.50	1.25	.70
(42)	Garry Maddox	2.50	1.25	.70
(43)	Jon Matlock	2.50	1.25	.70
(44)	Gary Matthews	2.50	1.25	.70
(45)	Lee May	2.50	1.25	.70
(46)	John Mayberry	2.50	1.25	.70
(47)	Bake McBride	2.50	1.25	.70
(48)	Tug McGraw	2.50	1.25	.70
(49)	Hal McRae	2.50	1.25	.70
(50)	Andy Messersmith	2.50	1.25	.70
(51)	Randy Moffitt	2.50	1.25	.70
(52)	John Montefusco	2.50	1.25	.70
(53)	Joe Morgan	6.00	3.00	1.75
(54)	Thurman Munson	6.00	3.00	1.75
(55)	Graig Nettles	2.50	1.25	.70
(56)	Al Oliver	2.50	1.25	.70
(57)	Jorge Orta	2.50	1.25	.70
(58)	Jim Palmer	6.00	3.00	1.75
(59)	Dave Parker	6.00	3.00	1.75
(60)	Tony Perez	6.00	3.00	1.75
(61)	Gaylord Perry	6.00	3.00	1.75
(62)	Jim Rice	3.00	1.50	.90
(63)	Steve Rogers	2.50	1.25	.70
(64)	Pete Rose	15.00	7.50	4.50
(65)	Joe Rudi	2.50	1.25	.70
(66)	Nolan Ryan	30.00	15.00	9.00
(67)	Manny Sanguillen	2.50	1.25	.70
(68)	Mike Schmidt	12.00	6.00	3.50
(69)	Tom Seaver	7.50	3.75	2.25
(70)	Ted Simmons	2.50	1.25	.70
(71)	Reggie Smith	2.50	1.25	.70
(72)	Willie Stargell	6.00	3.00	1.75
(73)	Rusty Staub	2.50	1.25	.70
(74)	Frank Tanana	2.50	1.25	.70
(75)	Gene Tenace	2.50	1.25	.70
(76)	Luis Tiant	2.50	1.25	.70
(77)	Manny Trillo	2.50	1.25	.70
(78)	Bob Watson	2.50	1.25	.70
(79)	Carl Yastrzemski	7.50	3.75	2.25
(80)	Richie Zisk	2.50	1.25	.70

1978 Wiffle Box-Side Discs

Similar in concept and format to the many contemporary MSA baseball player disc sets, the pieces printed on the sides of Wiffle-brand baseball boxes differ in that they are smaller, at 2-3/8" diameter, and feature a larger checklist. The discs feature black-and-white player portrait photos in the center of a baseball design. The left and right panels are in one of several bright colors. Licensed by the players' association through Mike Schechter Associates, the player photos carry no uniform logos. Backs are printed in black and orange. The unnumbered discs are checklisted here alphabetically.

		NM	EX	VG
Complete Set (88):		325.00	160.00	100.00
Common Player:		2.50	1.25	.70
(1)	Sal Bando	2.50	1.25	.70
(2)	Buddy Bell	2.50	1.25	.70
(3)	Johnny Bench	7.50	3.75	2.25
(4)	Vida Blue	2.50	1.25	.70
(5)	Bert Blyleven	3.00	1.50	.90
(6)	Bobby Bonds	2.50	1.25	.70
(7)	George Brett	12.00	6.00	3.50
(8)	Lou Brock	6.00	3.00	1.75
(9)	Bill Buckner	2.50	1.25	.70
(10)	Ray Burris	2.50	1.25	.70
(11)	Jeff Burroughs	2.50	1.25	.70
(12)	Bert Campaneris	2.50	1.25	.70
(13)	John Candelaria	2.50	1.25	.70
(14)	Jose Cardenal	2.50	1.25	.70
(15)	Rod Carew	6.00	3.00	1.75
(16)	Steve Carlton	6.00	3.00	1.75
(17)	Dave Cash	2.50	1.25	.70
(18)	Cesar Cedeno	2.50	1.25	.70
(19)	Ron Cey	2.50	1.25	.70
(20)	Chris Chambliss	2.50	1.25	.70
(21)	Dave Concepcion	2.50	1.25	.70
(22)	Dennis Eckersley	6.00	3.00	1.75
(23)	Mark Fidrych	3.50	1.75	1.00
(24)	Rollie Fingers	6.00	3.00	1.75
(25)	Carlton Fisk	6.00	3.00	1.75
(26)	George Foster	2.50	1.25	.70
(27)	Wayne Garland	2.50	1.25	.70
(28)	Ralph Garr	2.50	1.25	.70
(29)	Steve Garvey	5.00	2.50	1.50
(30)	Don Gullett	2.50	1.25	.70
(31)	Larry Hisle	2.50	1.25	.70
(32)	Al Hrabosky	2.50	1.25	.70
(33)	Catfish Hunter	6.00	3.00	1.75
(34)	Reggie Jackson	12.00	6.00	3.50
(35)	Randy Jones	2.50	1.25	.70
(36)	Von Joshua	2.50	1.25	.70
(37)	Dave Kingman	2.50	1.25	.70
(38)	Jerry Koosman	2.50	1.25	.70
(39)	Ed Kranepool	2.50	1.25	.70
(40)	Ron LeFlore	2.50	1.25	.70
(41)	Sixto Lezcano	2.50	1.25	.70
(42)	Davey Lopes	2.50	1.25	.70
(43)	Greg Luzinski	2.50	1.25	.70
(44)	Fred Lynn	2.50	1.25	.70
(45)	Garry Maddox	2.50	1.25	.70
(46)	Jon Matlock	2.50	1.25	.70
(47)	Gary Matthews	2.50	1.25	.70
(48)	Lee May	2.50	1.25	.70
(49)	John Mayberry	2.50	1.25	.70
(50)	Bake McBride	2.50	1.25	.70
(51)	Tug McGraw	2.50	1.25	.70
(52)	Hal McRae	2.50	1.25	.70
(53)	Andy Messersmith	2.50	1.25	.70
(54)	Randy Moffitt	2.50	1.25	.70
(55)	John Montefusco	2.50	1.25	.70
(56)	Joe Morgan	6.00	3.00	1.75
(57)	Thurman Munson	6.00	3.00	1.75
(58)	Graig Nettles	2.50	1.25	.70
(59)	Bill North	2.50	1.25	.70
(60)	Al Oliver	2.50	1.25	.70
(61)	Jorge Orta	2.50	1.25	.70
(62)	Jim Palmer	6.00	3.00	1.75
(63)	Dave Parker	2.50	1.25	.70
(64)	Tony Perez	6.00	3.00	1.75
(65)	Gaylord Perry	6.00	3.00	1.75
(66)	Jim Rice	3.00	1.50	.90
(67)	Ellie Rodriguez	2.50	1.25	.70
(68)	Steve Rogers	2.50	1.25	.70
(69)	Pete Rose	15.00	7.50	4.50
(70)	Joe Rudi	2.50	1.25	.70
(71)	Nolan Ryan	30.00	15.00	9.00
(72)	Manny Sanguillen	2.50	1.25	.70
(73)	Mike Schmidt	12.00	6.00	3.50
(74)	Tom Seaver	7.50	3.75	2.25
(75)	Ted Simmons	2.50	1.25	.70
(76)	Reggie Smith	2.50	1.25	.70
(77)	Jim Spencer	2.50	1.25	.70
(78)	Willie Stargell	6.00	3.00	1.75
(79)	Rusty Staub	2.50	1.25	.70
(80)	Rennie Stennett	2.50	1.25	.70
(81)	Frank Tanana	2.50	1.25	.70
(82)	Gene Tenace	2.50	1.25	.70
(83)	Luis Tiant	2.50	1.25	.70
(84)	Manny Trillo	2.50	1.25	.70
(85)	Bob Watson	2.50	1.25	.70
(86)	Butch Wynegar	2.50	1.25	.70
(87)	Carl Yastrzemski	7.50	3.75	2.25
(88)	Richie Zisk	2.50	1.25	.70

1922 Willard's Chocolates Premium

Details on distribution of this 7-1/8" x 11-1/4" premium are unclear, likely involving some sort of wrapper or coupon redemp-

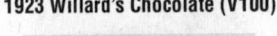

tion. The blank-back piece has a central photo of Babe Ruth in action. A facsimile autograph appears in a panel at bottom.

	NM	EX	VG
Babe Ruth	9,250	4,600	2,800

1923 Willard's Chocolate (V100)

Issued circa 1923, this set was produced by the Willard Chocolate Co. of Canada and features sepia-toned photographs on cards measuring about 2" x 3-1/4". The cards are blank-backed and feature the player's name in script on the front, along with a tiny credit line: "Photo by International." The set is complete at 180 cards and nearly one-fourth of the photos used in the set are identical to the better known E120 American Caramel set. The Willard set is identified as V100 in the American Card Catalog.

		NM	EX	VG
Common Player:		150.00	75.00	45.00
(1)	Chas. B. Adams	150.00	75.00	45.00
(2)	Grover C. Alexander	600.00	300.00	200.00
(3)	J.P. Austin	150.00	75.00	45.00
(4)	J.C. Bagby	150.00	75.00	45.00
(5)	J. Franklin Baker	450.00	225.00	140.00
(6)	David J. Bancroft	450.00	225.00	140.00
(7)	Turner Barber	150.00	75.00	45.00
(8)	Jesse L. Barnes	150.00	75.00	45.00
(9)	J.C. Bassler	150.00	75.00	45.00
(10)	L.A. Blue	150.00	75.00	45.00
(11)	Norman D. Boeckel	150.00	75.00	45.00
(12)	F.L. Brazil (Brazill)	150.00	75.00	45.00
(13)	G.H. Burns	150.00	75.00	45.00
(14)	Geo. J. Burns	150.00	75.00	45.00
(15)	Leon Cadore	150.00	75.00	45.00
(16)	Max G. Carey	450.00	225.00	140.00
(17)	Harold G. Carlson	150.00	75.00	45.00
(18)	Lloyd R Christenberry (Christenbury)	150.00	75.00	45.00
(19)	Vernon J. Clemons	150.00	75.00	45.00
(20)	T.R. Cobb	6,000	3,000	1,800
(21)	Bert Cole	150.00	75.00	45.00
(22)	John F. Collins	150.00	75.00	45.00
(23)	S. Coveleskie (Coveleski)	450.00	225.00	140.00
(24)	Walton E. Cruise	150.00	75.00	45.00
(25)	G.W. Cutshaw	150.00	75.00	45.00
(26)	Jacob E. Daubert	150.00	75.00	45.00
(27)	Geo. Dauss	150.00	75.00	45.00
(28)	F.T. Davis	150.00	75.00	45.00
(29)	Chas. A. Deal	150.00	75.00	45.00
(30)	William L. Doak	150.00	75.00	45.00
(31)	William E. Donovan	150.00	75.00	45.00
(32)	Hugh Duffy	450.00	225.00	140.00
(33)	J.A. Dugan	150.00	75.00	45.00
(34)	Louis B. Duncan	150.00	75.00	45.00
(35)	James Dykes	150.00	75.00	45.00
(36)	H.J. Ehmke	150.00	75.00	45.00
(37)	F.R. Ellerbe	150.00	75.00	45.00
(38)	E.G. Erickson	150.00	75.00	45.00
(39)	John J. Evers	450.00	225.00	140.00
(40)	U.C. Faber	450.00	225.00	140.00
(41)	B.A. Falk	150.00	75.00	45.00
(42)	Max Flack	150.00	75.00	45.00
(43)	Lee Fohl	150.00	75.00	45.00
(44)	Jacques F. Fournier	150.00	75.00	45.00
(45)	Frank F. Frisch	450.00	225.00	140.00
(46)	C.E. Galloway	150.00	75.00	45.00
(47)	W.C. Gardner	150.00	75.00	45.00
(48)	E.P. Gharrity	150.00	75.00	45.00
(49)	Geo. Gibson	150.00	75.00	45.00
(50)	Wm. Gleason	150.00	75.00	45.00
(51)	William Gleason	150.00	75.00	45.00

(52)	Henry M. Gowdy	150.00	75.00	45.00
(53)	I.M. Griffin	150.00	75.00	45.00
(54)	Tom Griffith	150.00	75.00	45.00
(55)	Burleigh A. Grimes	450.00	225.00	140.00
(56)	Charles J. Grimm	150.00	75.00	45.00
(57)	Jesse J. Haines	450.00	225.00	140.00
(58)	S.R. Harris	450.00	225.00	140.00
(59)	W.B. Harris	150.00	75.00	45.00
(60)	R.K. Hasty	150.00	75.00	45.00
(61)	H.E. Heilman (Heilmann)	450.00	225.00	140.00
(62)	Walter J. Henline	150.00	75.00	45.00
(63)	Walter L. Holke	150.00	75.00	45.00
(64)	Charles J. Hollocher	150.00	75.00	45.00
(65)	H.B. Hooper	450.00	225.00	140.00
(66)	Rogers Hornsby	600.00	300.00	180.00
(67)	W.C. Hoyt	450.00	225.00	140.00
(68)	Miller Huggins	450.00	225.00	140.00
(69)	W.C. Jacobsen (Jacobson)	150.00	75.00	45.00
(70)	C.D. Jamieson	150.00	75.00	45.00
(71)	Ernest Johnson	150.00	75.00	45.00
(72)	W.P. Johnson	1,150	575.00	350.00
(73)	James H. Johnston	150.00	75.00	45.00
(74)	R.W. Jones	150.00	75.00	45.00
(75)	Samuel Pond Jones	150.00	75.00	45.00
(76)	J.I. Judge	150.00	75.00	45.00
(77)	James W. Keenan	150.00	75.00	45.00
(78)	Geo. L. Kelly	450.00	225.00	140.00
(79)	Peter J. Kilduff	150.00	75.00	45.00
(80)	William Killefer	150.00	75.00	45.00
(81)	Lee King	150.00	75.00	45.00
(82)	Ray Kolp	150.00	75.00	45.00
(83)	John Lavan	150.00	75.00	45.00
(84)	H.L. Leibold	150.00	75.00	45.00
(85)	Connie Mack	450.00	225.00	140.00
(86)	J.W. Mails	150.00	75.00	45.00
(87)	Walter J. Maranville	450.00	225.00	140.00
(88)	Richard W. Marquard	450.00	225.00	140.00
(89)	C.W. Mays	150.00	75.00	45.00
(90)	Geo. F. McBride	150.00	75.00	45.00
(91)	H.M. McClellan	150.00	75.00	45.00
(92)	John J. McGraw	450.00	225.00	140.00
(93)	Austin B. McHenry	150.00	75.00	45.00
(94)	J. McInnis	150.00	75.00	45.00
(95)	Douglas McWeeney (McWeeny)	150.00	75.00	45.00
(96)	M. Menosky	150.00	75.00	45.00
(97)	Emil F. Meusel	150.00	75.00	45.00
(98)	R. Meusel	150.00	75.00	45.00
(99)	Henry W. Meyers	150.00	75.00	45.00
(100)	J.C. Milan	150.00	75.00	45.00
(101)	John K. Miljus	150.00	75.00	45.00
(102)	Edmund J. Miller	150.00	75.00	45.00
(103)	Elmer Miller	150.00	75.00	45.00
(104)	Otto L. Miller	150.00	75.00	45.00
(105)	Fred Mitchell	150.00	75.00	45.00
(106)	Geo. Mogridge	150.00	75.00	45.00
(107)	Patrick J. Moran	150.00	75.00	45.00
(108)	John D. Morrison	150.00	75.00	45.00
(109)	J.A. Mostil	150.00	75.00	45.00
(110)	Clarence F. Mueller	150.00	75.00	45.00
(111)	A. Earle Neale	150.00	75.00	45.00
(112)	Joseph Oeschger	150.00	75.00	45.00
(113)	Robert J. O'Farrell	150.00	75.00	45.00
(114)	J.C. Oldham	150.00	75.00	45.00
(115)	I.M. Olson	150.00	75.00	45.00
(116)	Geo. M. O'Neil	150.00	75.00	45.00
(117)	S.F. O'Neill	150.00	75.00	45.00
(118)	Frank J. Parkinson	150.00	75.00	45.00
(119)	Geo. H. Paskert	150.00	75.00	45.00
(120)	R.T. Peckinpaugh	150.00	75.00	45.00
(121)	H.J. Pennock	450.00	225.00	140.00
(122)	Ralph Perkins	150.00	75.00	45.00
(123)	Edw. J. Pfeffer	150.00	75.00	45.00
(124)	W.C. Pipp	150.00	75.00	45.00
(125)	Charles Elmer Ponder	150.00	75.00	45.00
(126)	Raymond R. Powell	150.00	75.00	45.00
(127)	D.B. Pratt	150.00	75.00	45.00
(128)	Joseph Rapp	150.00	75.00	45.00
(129)	John H. Rawlings	150.00	75.00	45.00
(130)	E.S. Rice (Should be E.C.)	450.00	225.00	140.00
(131)	Branch Rickey	525.00	275.00	160.00
(132)	James J. Ring	150.00	75.00	45.00
(133)	Eppa J. Rixey	450.00	225.00	140.00
(134)	Davis A. Robertson	150.00	75.00	45.00
(135)	Edwin Rommel	150.00	75.00	45.00
(136)	Edd J. Roush	450.00	225.00	140.00
(137)	Harold Ruel (Herold)	150.00	75.00	45.00
(138)	Allen Russell	150.00	75.00	45.00
(139)	G.H. Ruth	12,500	6,250	3,750
(140)	Wilfred D. Ryan	150.00	75.00	45.00
(141)	Henry F. Sallee	150.00	75.00	45.00
(142)	W.H. Schang	150.00	75.00	45.00
(143)	Raymond H. Schmandt	150.00	75.00	45.00
(144)	Everett Scott	150.00	75.00	45.00
(145)	Henry Severeid	150.00	75.00	45.00
(146)	Jos. W. Sewell	450.00	225.00	140.00
(147)	Howard S. Shanks	150.00	75.00	45.00
(148)	E.H. Sheely	150.00	75.00	45.00
(149)	Ralph Shinners	150.00	75.00	45.00
(150)	U.J. Shocker	150.00	75.00	45.00
(151)	G.H. Sisler	450.00	225.00	140.00
(152)	Earl L. Smith	150.00	75.00	45.00
(153)	Earl S. Smith	150.00	75.00	45.00
(154)	Geo. A. Smith	150.00	75.00	45.00
(155)	J.W. Smith	150.00	75.00	45.00
(156)	Tris E. Speaker	600.00	300.00	180.00
(157)	Arnold Staatz (Statz)	150.00	75.00	45.00
(158)	J.R. Stephenson	150.00	75.00	45.00
(159)	Milton J. Stock	150.00	75.00	45.00
(160)	John L. Sullivan	150.00	75.00	45.00
(161)	H.F. Tormahlen	150.00	75.00	45.00
(162)	Jas. A. Tierney	150.00	75.00	45.00
(163)	J.T. Tobin	150.00	75.00	45.00
(164)	Jas. L. Vaughn	150.00	75.00	45.00
(165)	R.H. Veach	150.00	75.00	45.00
(166)	C.W. Walker	150.00	75.00	45.00
(167)	A.L. Ward	150.00	75.00	45.00
(168)	Zack D. Wheat	450.00	225.00	140.00

(169)	George B. Whitted	150.00	75.00	45.00
(170)	Irvin K. Wilhelm	150.00	75.00	45.00
(171)	Roy H. Wilkinson	150.00	75.00	45.00
(172)	Fred C. Williams	150.00	75.00	45.00
(173)	K.R. Williams	150.00	75.00	45.00
(174)	Sam'l W. Wilson	150.00	75.00	45.00
(175)	Ivy B. Wingo	150.00	75.00	45.00
(176)	L.W. Witt	150.00	75.00	45.00
(177)	Joseph Wood	300.00	150.00	90.00
(178)	E. Yaryan	150.00	75.00	45.00
(179)	R.S. Young	150.00	75.00	45.00
(180)	Ross Young (Youngs)	450.00	225.00	140.00

1924 Willard's Chocolate Sports Champions (V122)

Three baseball players are featured among this 56-card Canadian set. The black-and-white cards are printed on thin paper measuring 1-3/8" x 3-3/8". Backs are blank. The set features male and female athletes from many different sports, with a distinct Canadian flavor. The candy company was headquartered in Toronto.

		NM	EX	VG
2	Eddie Collins	600.00	300.00	180.00
5	Babe Ruth	3,250	1,625	975.00
39	Ty Cobb	2,250	1,125	675.00

1911 Williams Baking Philadelphia A's (D359)

This Philadelphia Athletics team set is among the scarcest early 20th Century baking company issues. It commemorates the A's 1910 Championship season, and, except for pitcher Jack Coombs, the checklist includes nearly all key members of the club, including manager Connie Mack. The cards are the standard size for the era, 1-1/2" x 2-5/8". Fronts feature a player portrait set against a colored background. The player's name and the word "Athletics" appear at the bottom, while "World's Champions 1910" is printed along the top. Backs of the cards advertise the set as the "Athletics Series." Collectors should be aware that the same checklist was used for a similar Athletics set issued by Rochester Baking and Cullivan's Fireside tobacco (T208) and also that blank-backed versions are also known to exist, cataloged as E104 in the American Card Catalog.

		NM	EX	VG
	Complete Set (18):	85,000	35,000	17,000
	Common Player:	3,000	1,500	900.00
(1)	Home Run Baker	7,000	3,500	1,750
(2)	Jack Barry	3,000	1,500	900.00
(3)	Chief Bender	7,000	3,500	1,750
(4)	Eddie Collins	7,000	3,500	1,750
(5)	Harry Davis	6,000	3,000	1,500
(6)	Jimmy Dygert	3,000	1,500	900.00
(7)	Topsy Hartsel	3,000	1,500	900.00
(8)	Harry Krause	3,000	1,500	900.00
(9)	Jack Lapp	3,000	1,500	900.00
(10)	Paddy Livingston	3,000	1,500	900.00
(11)	Bris Lord	3,000	1,500	900.00

(12)	Connie Mack	14,000	7,900	4,575
(13)	Cy Morgan	3,000	1,500	900.00
(14)	Danny Murphy	6,000	3,000	1,500
(15)	Rube Oldring	3,000	1,500	900.00
(16)	Eddie Plank	14,000	7,900	4,575
(17)	Amos Strunk	3,000	1,500	900.00
(18a)	Ira Thomas (1910 at top)	3,000	1,500	900.00
(18b)	Ira Thomas (1910 at right)	3,000	1,500	900.00

1910 Williams Caramels (E103)

N. LAJOIE, 2d B., Cleveland
The Williams Caramel Co. Oxford, Pa.

This 30-card set issued by the Williams Caramel Co. of Oxford, Pa., in 1910 can be differentiated from other similar sets because it was printed on a thin paper stock rather than cardboard. Measuring approximately 1-3/4" x 2-5/8", each card features a player portrait set against a red background. The bottom of the card lists the player's last name, position and team; beneath that is the line, "The Williams Caramel Co. Oxford Pa." Nearly all of the photos in the set, which is designated E103 by the ACC, are identical to those in the M116 Sporting Life set.

		NM	EX	VG
	Complete Set (30):	160,000	80,000	48,000
	Common Player:	1,650	825.00	495.00
(1)	Chas. Bender	5,600	2,800	1,680
(2)	Roger Bresnahan	5,600	2,800	1,680
(3)	Mordecai Brown	5,600	2,800	1,680
(4)	Frank Chance	5,600	2,800	1,680
(5)	Hal Chase	3,750	1,875	1,125
(6)	Ty Cobb	45,000	18,000	9,000
(7)	Edward Collins	5,600	2,800	1,680
(8)	Sam Crawford	5,600	2,800	1,680
(9)	Harry Davis	1,650	825.00	495.00
(10)	Arthur Devlin	1,650	825.00	495.00
(11)	William Donovan	1,650	825.00	495.00
(12)	Chas. Dooin	1,650	825.00	495.00
(13)	L. Doyle	1,650	825.00	495.00
(14)	John Ewing	1,650	825.00	495.00
(15)	George Gibson	1,650	825.00	495.00
(16)	Hugh Jennings	5,600	2,800	1,680
(17)	David Jones	1,650	825.00	495.00
(18)	Tim Jordan	1,650	825.00	495.00
(19)	N. Lajoie	6,250	3,125	1,875
(20)	Thomas Leach	1,650	825.00	495.00
(21)	Harry Lord	1,650	825.00	495.00
(22)	Chris. Mathewson	18,000	7,200	3,600
(23)	John McLean	1,650	825.00	495.00
(24)	Geo. W. McQuillan	1,650	825.00	495.00
(25)	Pastorius	1,650	825.00	495.00
(26)	N. Rucker	1,650	825.00	495.00
(27)	Fred Tenny (Tenney)	1,650	825.00	495.00
(28)	Ira Thomas	1,650	825.00	495.00
(29)	Hans Wagner	36,000	14,400	7,200
(30)	Robert Wood	1,650	825.00	495.00

1889 E.R. Williams Card Game

This set of 52 playing cards came packed in its own box that advertised the set as the "Egerton R. Williams Popular Indoor Base Ball Game." Designed to look like a conventional deck of playing cards, the set included various players from the National League and the American Association. Although the set contains 52 cards (like a typical deck of playing cards) only 19 actually feature color drawings of players. Each of these cards pictures two different players (one at the top and a second at the bottom, separated by sepia-colored crossed bats in the middle), resulting in 38 different players. The remaining 33 cards in the deck are strictly game cards show-

ing a specific baseball play (such as "Batter Out on Fly" or "Two Base Hit," etc.). The cards have green-tinted backs and measure 2-7/16" x 3-1/2". Each one carries an 1889 copyright line by E.R. Williams.

	NM	EX	VG
Complete Boxed Set:	18,000	9,000	6,000
Common Player Card:	450.00	225.00	140.00
Common Game Action Card:	85.00	45.00	25.00
(1) Cap Anson, Buck Ewing	1,800	900.00	600.00
(2) Dan Brouthers, Arlie Latham	675.00	350.00	270.00
(3) Charles Buffinton, Bob Carruthers	450.00	225.00	140.00
(4) Hick Carpenter, Cliff Carroll	450.00	225.00	140.00
(5) Charles Comiskey, Roger Connor	900.00	450.00	270.00
(6) Pop Corkhill, Jim Fogarty	450.00	225.00	140.00
(7) John Clarkson, Tim Keefe	900.00	450.00	270.00
(8) Jerry Denny, Mike Tiernan	450.00	225.00	140.00
(9) Dave Foutz, King Kelly	1,650	825.00	500.00
(10) Pud Galvin, Dave Orr	675.00	350.00	270.00
(11) Jack Glasscock, Tommy Tucker	450.00	225.00	140.00
(12) Mike Griffin, Ed McKean	450.00	225.00	140.00
(13) Dummy Hoy, Long John Reilley (Reilly)	675.00	350.00	270.00
(14) Arthur Irwin, Ned Williamson	450.00	225.00	140.00
(15) Silver King, John Tener	675.00	350.00	270.00
(16) Al Myers, Cub Stricker	450.00	225.00	140.00
(17) Fred Pfeffer, Chicken Wolf	450.00	225.00	140.00
(18) Tom Ramsey, Gus Weyhing	450.00	225.00	140.00
(19) John Ward, Curt Welch	750.00	375.00	225.00

1961 J.B. Williams Co. Roger Maris Lithograph

ROGER MARIS

The maker of Lectric Shave and Aqua Velva offered fans a lithograph of Roger Maris hitting his 59th home run at Baltimore, Sept. 20, 1961. The 16" x 11" black-and-white print on parchment paper was available by mail for 25 cents and a box top from either of the shaving products. The artwork is by Robert Riger.

	NM	EX	VG
Roger Maris	200.00	100.00	60.00

1908 R.C. Williams Cy Young Postcard

Cy, Delivering the tosses.

A mature Cy Young, about age 42, is pictured on this postcard bearing the imprint of R.C. Williams. No other contemporary cards with this imprint have been reported.

	NM	EX	VG
Cy Young	800.00	400.00	240.00

1954 Wilson Franks

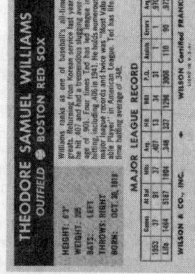

The 2-5/8" x 3-3/4" cards are among the most popular and scarcest baseball card sets issued with hot dogs during the 1950s. The cards feature color-added photos on the front along with a facsimile autograph and a package of frankfurters. Backs feature personal information, a career summary and 1953 and career statistics. Cards were packaged in direct contact with the meat, resulting in many exhibiting grease stains. Survival rates of the various players differ widely, probably based on the geography of initial distribution. A small hoard of roughly half the players was discovered in unissued condition in the late 1990s, temporarily influencing the market.

		NM	EX	VG
Complete Set (20):		35,000	17,500	10,500
Common Player:		1,100	550.00	325.00
Advertising Poster:		17,500	8,750	5,250
(1)	Roy Campanella	3,000	1,500	900.00
(2)	Del Ennis	1,100	550.00	325.00
(3)	Carl Erskine	1,100	550.00	325.00
(4)	Ferris Fain	1,100	550.00	325.00
(5)	Bob Feller	2,000	1,000	600.00
(6)	Nelson Fox	2,000	1,000	600.00
(7)	Johnny Groth	1,100	550.00	325.00
(8)	Stan Hack	1,100	440.00	220.00
(9)	Gil Hodges	2,750	1,100	550.00
(10)	Ray Jablonski	1,250	500.00	250.00
(11)	Harvey Kuenn	2,000	1,000	600.00
(12)	Roy McMillan	2,000	1,000	600.00
(13)	Andy Pafko	1,100	550.00	325.00
(14)	Paul Richards	1,600	800.00	475.00
(15)	Hank Sauer	1,600	800.00	475.00
(16)	Red Schoendienst	1,000	400.00	200.00
(17)	Enos Slaughter	1,600	800.00	475.00
(18)	Vern Stephens	1,100	550.00	325.00
(19)	Sammy White	1,100	550.00	325.00
(20)	Ted Williams	13,000	6,000	3,000

1961 Wilson Meats L.A.Dodgers/Angels

It is likely these 5-1/2" x 8-1/2" photos were prepared for promotional appearances by players on behalf of the meat company. The player name appears at the bottom of the photo and the sponsor's message appears at bottom, "Courtesy of WILSON & CO., Inc., Fine Meat Products." Backs are blank. The pictures are often found with player autographs, another indicator of their use at personal appearances.

		NM	EX	VG
(1)	Ron Fairly	50.00	25.00	15.00
(2)	Gil Hodges	75.00	37.00	22.00
(3)	Frank Howard	50.00	25.00	15.00
(4)	Ted Kluszewski	60.00	30.00	18.00

1950s-70s Wilson Advisory Staff Photos

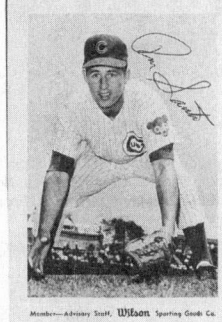

Advisory staff photos were a promotional item which debuted in the early 1950s, flourished in the 1960s and died in the early 1970s. Generally 8" x 10" (sometimes a little larger), these black-and-white (a few later were color) glossy photos picture players who had contracted with a major baseball equipment company to endorse and use their product. Usually the product - most often a glove - was prominently displayed in the photo. The pictures were often displayed in the windows of sporting goods stores or the walls of sports departments and were sometimes made available to customers. Because the companies tended to stick with players over the years, some photos were reissued, sometimes with and sometimes without a change of team, pose or style. The pho-

tos are checklisted here in alphabetical order. A pose description is given where known. It is unlikely this list is complete. Gaps have been left in the assigned numbering to accommodate future additions. In general, Wilson advisory staff photos feature the player name and a line of type indicating the player's status as an advisory staffer in the bottom border.

		NM	EX	VG
Common Player:		14.00	7.00	4.00
(1)	Bob Allison (Twins, full-length.)	20.00	10.00	6.00
(2)	Felipe Alou (Braves, neck-to-cap.)	25.00	12.50	7.50
(3)	Felipe Alou (Braves, upper body.)	25.00	12.50	7.50
(4)	Max Alvis (Indians, hands on knees.)	20.00	10.00	6.00
(5)	Max Alvis (Indians, upper body.)	20.00	10.00	6.00
(6)	Luis Aparicio/Fldg (White Sox, horizontal.)	50.00	25.00	15.00
(7)	Luis Aparicio (White Sox, fielding, full-length.)	40.00	20.00	12.00
(8)	Luis Aparicio (Orioles, full-length.)	50.00	25.00	15.00
(9)	Gerry Arrigo/ (Reds, full-length pitching.)	20.00	10.00	6.00
(10)	Ernie Banks/Btg	75.00	37.00	22.00
(11)	Ernie Banks/Fldg (Horizontal)	60.00	30.00	18.00
(12)	Glenn Beckert/Fldg (Cubs, ball in hand.)	25.00	12.50	7.50
(13)	Glenn Beckert/Fldg (Cubs, no ball.)	25.00	12.50	7.50
(14)	Paul Blair (Orioles, full-length.)	25.00	12.50	7.50
(15)	Don Blasingame (Cardinals, belt-up.)	20.00	10.00	6.00
(16)	Bob Bolin (Giants, pitching follow-through.)	20.00	10.00	6.00
(17)	Dave Boswell (Twins, full-length.)	20.00	10.00	6.00
(18)	Dave Boswell (Twins, waist-up, stretch position.)	20.00	10.00	6.00
(19)	Jackie Brandt (Orioles, full-length.)	20.00	10.00	6.00
(20)	Smoky Burgess (Pirates, sitting on step w/ three bats.)	20.00	10.00	6.00
(21)	Rico Carty/Btg (Milwaukee Braves)	20.00	10.00	6.00
(22)	Rico Carty (Milwaukee Braves, dugout step.)	20.00	10.00	6.00
(23)	Rico Carty/Btg (Atlanta Braves)	20.00	10.00	6.00
(24)	Paul Casanova (Senators, catching crouch.)	20.00	10.00	6.00
(25)	Norm Cash/Btg (Tigers, waist-up.)	25.00	12.50	7.50
(26)	Orlando Cepeda/Btg (Braves)	30.00	15.00	9.00
(27)	Orlando Cepeda (Cardinals, dugout step.)	25.00	12.50	7.50
(28)	Orlando Cepeda/Fldg (Cardinals)	25.00	12.50	7.50
(29)	Jim Davenport/Fldg (Giants)	20.00	10.00	6.00
(30)	Vic Davalillo (Indians, upper body.)	20.00	10.00	6.00
(31)	Willie Davis (Dodgers, full-length.)	20.00	10.00	6.00
(32)	Chuck Dobson (A's, full-length.)	20.00	10.00	6.00
(35)	"Moe" Drabowsky (Cubs, thighs-up.)	20.00	10.00	6.00
(36)	Don Drysdale (L.A. Dodgers, follow-through.)	25.00	12.50	7.50
(37)	Dick Ellsworth (Cubs, pitching follow-through.)	20.00	10.00	6.00
(38)	Dick Ellsworth (Phillies, full-length.)	20.00	10.00	6.00
(39)	Del Ennis/Kneeling (Cardinals)	20.00	10.00	6.00
(40)	Bob Feller/Seated (Glove on knee.)	120.00	60.00	36.00
(41)	Nellie Fox (White Sox, chest-up.)	35.00	17.50	10.50
(42)	Nellie Fox (White Sox, fielding grounder.)	50.00	25.00	15.00
(43)	Nelson Fox/Seated (White Sox)	50.00	25.00	15.00
(44)	Nelson Fox/Btg (Colt .45s)	50.00	25.00	15.00
(45)	Bill Freehan (Catching crouch.)	20.00	10.00	6.00
(46)	Bill Freehan (Two pictures.)	20.00	10.00	6.00
(47)	Phil Gagliano/Fldg (Cardinals, photo actually Ed Spiezio.)	25.00	12.50	7.50
(48)	Jim Gentile/Btg (Orioles, chest-up.)	20.00	10.00	6.00
(49)	Vernon "Lefty" Gomez (w/ glasses.)	25.00	12.50	7.50
(50)	Lefty Gomez (No glasses.)	25.00	12.50	7.50
(51)	Jim Hall/Fldg (Angels.)	25.00	12.50	7.50
(52a)	Don Hoak (Pirates, full-length, waist up.)	20.00	10.00	6.00
(52b)	Don Hoak (Pirates, waist up.)	20.00	10.00	6.00
(53)	Gil Hodges (L.A. Dodgers, belt-up batting.)	50.00	25.00	15.00
(54)	Willie Horton (Tigers, full-length.)	20.00	10.00	6.00
(55)	Bruce Howard (White Sox, pitching follow-through.)	20.00	10.00	6.00
(56)	Jim Hunter (K.C. A's, beginning wind-up.)	25.00	12.50	7.50
(57)	Jim Hunter (Oakland A's, full-length, photo actually Chuck Dobson.)	25.00	12.50	7.50
(58)	Mack Jones (Reds, full-length.)	20.00	10.00	6.00
(59)	Duane Josephson (White Sox, catching crouch.)	20.00	10.00	6.00
(61)	Jim Kaat (Twins, upper body.)	25.00	12.50	7.50
(62)	Al Kaline/Btg (Full-length)	75.00	37.00	22.00
(63)	Al Kaline/Btg (Upper body)	75.00	37.00	22.00
(64)	Al Kaline (Upper body, hands on knees.)	75.00	37.00	22.00
(65)	Al Kaline (Upper body.)	75.00	37.00	22.00
(66)	Al Kaline (Upper body, looking right.)	75.00	37.00	22.00
(67)	Harmon Killebrew/Btg (Twins, upper body.)	50.00	25.00	15.00
(68)	Harmon Killebrew/Btg (Twins, looking front.)	50.00	25.00	15.00
(69)	Harmon Killebrew (Twins, kneeling.)	50.00	25.00	15.00
(70)	Cal Koonce (Cubs, pitching follow-through.)	20.00	10.00	6.00
(71)	Harvey Kuenn/Btg (Tigers)	25.00	12.50	7.50
(72)	Harvey Kuenn (Tigers, upper body.)	25.00	12.50	7.50
(73)	Hal Lanier/Throwing (Giants)	20.00	10.00	6.00
(74)	Juan Marichal (Giants, upper body.)	25.00	12.50	7.50
(75)	Willie McCovey/Btg (Giants)	25.00	12.50	7.50
(76)	Sam McDowell (Indians, seated, no cap.)	25.00	12.50	7.50
(77)	Dennis McLain (Tigers, hands at chest.)	25.00	12.50	7.50
(78)	Roy McMillan/Btg (Braves)	20.00	10.00	6.00
(79)	Roy McMillan (Reds, belt-up.)	20.00	10.00	6.00
(81)	Denis Menke/Fldg (Braves)	20.00	10.00	6.00
(82)	Denis Menke (Braves, upper body.)	20.00	10.00	6.00
(83)	Don Mincher (Angels, full-length.)	20.00	10.00	6.00
(84)	Joe Morgan/Btg (Astros)	40.00	20.00	12.00
(85)	Joe Morgan/Fldg (Astros)	40.00	20.00	12.00
(86)	Jim Nash/Pitching (A's)	20.00	10.00	6.00
(87)	Rich Nye/Pitching (Cubs)	20.00	10.00	6.00
(88)	John Odom/Pitching (Kansas City A's.)	20.00	10.00	6.00
(89)	John Odom (Oakland A's, belt-up pose.)	20.00	10.00	6.00
(90)	John Orsino/Kneeling (Orioles)	20.00	10.00	6.00
(91)	Jim O'Toole (Reds, upper body, warm-up jacket.)	20.00	10.00	6.00
(92)	Jim O'Toole (White Sox, upper body.)	20.00	10.00	6.00
(93)	Ray Oyler/Fldg (Tigers)	20.00	10.00	6.00
(94)	Milt Pappas (Orioles, pitching, full-length.)	20.00	10.00	6.00
(95)	Milt Pappas (Orioles, pitching, knees-up.)	20.00	10.00	6.00
(96)	Don Pavletich (Reds, full-length.)	20.00	10.00	6.00
(97)	Don Pavletich/Squatting (Reds)	20.00	10.00	6.00
(98)	Albie Pearson (Angels, glove under left arm.)	20.00	10.00	6.00
(99)	Ron Perranoski (Dodgers, upper body.)	20.00	10.00	6.00
(100)	Ron Perranoski (Twins, belt-up from side.)	25.00	12.50	7.50
(101)	Ron Perranoski/Pitching (Twins,)	20.00	10.00	6.00
(102)	Gaylord Perry/Pitching (Giants)	25.00	12.50	7.50
(103)	Billy Pierce (White Sox, knees-up.)	25.00	12.50	7.50
(104)	Bob Purkey (Reds, waist-up.)	20.00	10.00	6.00
(105)	Doug Rader/Fldg (Astros)	20.00	10.00	6.00
(106)	Dick Rodatz (Radatz) (Red Sox, upper body.)	20.00	10.00	6.00
(107)	Dick Radatz (Red Sox, upper body.)	20.00	10.00	6.00
(108)	Pete Runnels (Red Sox, kneeling on deck.)	25.00	12.50	7.50
(109)	Ron Santo/Fldg (Cubs)	25.00	12.50	7.50
(110)	George Scott (Red Sox, upper body.)	20.00	10.00	6.00
(111)	Larry Sherry (Dodgers, full-length.)	20.00	10.00	6.00
(112)	Chris Short (Phillies, upper body.)	20.00	10.00	6.00
(113)	Hal Smith/Btg (Pirates)	25.00	12.50	7.50
(114)	Mickey Stanley (Tigers, full-length.)	20.00	10.00	6.00
(115)	Tony Taylor (Phillies, bat on shoulder.)	20.00	10.00	6.00
(116)	Frank Thomas (Pirates, waist-up.)	20.00	10.00	6.00
(117)	Frank Thomas/Btg (Cubs)	20.00	10.00	6.00
(119)	Jeff Torborg (Dodgers, holding mask.)	20.00	10.00	6.00
(121)	Al Weis (White Sox, ready to throw.)	20.00	10.00	6.00
(122)	Al Weis/Fldg (Mets)	20.00	10.00	6.00
(123)	Ted Williams/Btg	125.00	62.00	37.00
(125)	Bobby Wine (Phillies, ready to throw.)	20.00	10.00	6.00
(126)	Rick Wise (Phillies, upper body.)	20.00	10.00	6.00
(128)	Woody Woodward (Reds, belt-to-cap.)	25.00	12.50	7.50
(130)	Early Wynn (White Sox, full-length.)	25.00	12.50	7.50
(131)	Jim Wynn/Btg (Colt .45s, upper body.)	20.00	10.00	6.00

		NM	EX	VG
(132)	Jim Wynn/Btg (Astros, full-length.)	20.00	10.00	6.00
(133)	Don Zimmer (Cubs, waist-up batting.)	20.00	10.00	6.00

1955 Wilson Franks Baseball Books

A year after issuing its 20-card set of baseball cards as package inserts, Wilson Meats created a series of four Baseball Books ("for boys") and four Fun Books ("for girls") that were inserted into packages of Wilson Certified Franks. The comic-style books were 16 pages in a size of about 4-1/2" x 3-1/2", printed on low-grade paper. The front cover has a large comic book-style portrait of the player on a yellow background with a stylized baseball diamond. The inside pages have baseball tips presented in comic book illustrations.

		NM	EX	VG
	Complete Set (4):	500.00	250.00	150.00
	Common Player:	750.00	375.00	225.00
(1)	Pointers on Pitching (Bob Feller)			
(2)	Batting and Fielding Secrets (player unknown)			
(3)	Playing the Infield (Harvey Kuenn)	500.00	250.00	150.00
(4)	How to Catch (Sammy White)	500.00	250.00	150.00

1961 Wilson Advisory Staff Cards

Similar in format to the contemporary 8" x 10" photos, these 2-3/4" x 4" cards have black-and-white player poses on front, prominently displaying a Wilson glove. In the white bottom border is: "Member-Advisory Staff, Wilson Sporting Goods Co." A blue facsimile autograph is printed across the picture. Backs are blank. The checklist, presented here alphabetically, may not be complete.

		NM	EX	VG
	Common Player:	10.00	5.00	3.00
(1)	Dick Ellsworth	10.00	5.00	3.00
(2)	Don Hoak	12.00	6.00	3.50
(3)	Harvey Kuenn	12.00	6.00	3.50
(4)	Roy McMillan	10.00	5.00	3.00
(5)	Jim Piersall	12.00	6.00	3.50
(6)	Ron Santo	16.00	8.00	4.75

1977 Wilson Sporting Goods Mini-Posters

Though unmarked as such, these 6" x 9" cards are a promotion from Wilson. The blank-back cards have a color action photo with white borders and a facsimile autograph.

		NM	EX	VG
	Complete Set (10):	200.00	100.00	60.00
	Common Player:	10.00	5.00	3.00
(1)	Johnny Bench	35.00	17.50	10.50
(2)	George Brett	50.00	25.00	15.00
(3)	Rod Carew	30.00	15.00	9.00
(4)	Dave Concepcion	10.00	5.00	3.00
(5)	Steve Garvey	15.00	7.50	4.50
(6)	Reggie Jackson	40.00	20.00	12.00
(7)	Greg Luzinski	10.00	5.00	3.00
(8)	Pete Rose	75.00	37.00	22.00
(9)	Mike Schmidt	40.00	20.00	12.00
(10)	Tom Seaver	40.00	17.50	10.50

1955-1958 Don Wingfield Washington Nationals Postcards

This series of 3-1/2" x 5-1/2" black-and-white glossy postcards provided Nationals' players with a vehicle for accommodating fan requests. Player portraits or action poses are bordered in white with three (or in the case of Valdivielso, five) lines of type at bottom identifying the player, team and copyright holder. Most have "Photo Post Card" at top on back and "Devolite Peerless" in the stamp box. The unnumbered cards are checklisted here in alphabetical order.

JOSE VALDIVIELSO
WASHINGTON NATIONALS
Photo By – Don Wingfield
Griffith Stadium
Washington, D. C.

CHUCK STOBBS – WASHINGTON NATIONALS
Copyright 1955 – Don Wingfield
Griffith Stadium, Washington, D. C.

		NM	EX	VG
	Complete Set (12):	1,800	900.00	550.00
	Common Player:	150.00	75.00	45.00
(1)	Jim Busby	150.00	75.00	45.00
(2)	Chuck Dressen	150.00	75.00	45.00
(3)	Ed Fitz Gerald	150.00	75.00	45.00
(4)	Jim Lemon	175.00	85.00	55.00
(5)	Bob Porterfield	150.00	75.00	45.00
(6)	Pete Runnels	150.00	75.00	45.00
(7)	Roy Sievers	175.00	85.00	55.00
(8)	Chuck Stobbs	150.00	75.00	45.00
(9)	Dean Stone	150.00	75.00	45.00
(10)	Jose Valdivelso (Valdivielso)	175.00	85.00	55.00
(11)	Mickey Vernon	175.00	85.00	55.00
(12)	Ed Yost	150.00	75.00	45.00

1957-1959 Don Wingfield Photocards

These black-and-white glossy photocards are usually blank-back, evidently for use as in-person handouts, rather than by mail. In 3-1/2" size, the player photos are bordered in white with an especially wide white bottom border for affixing an autograph. Other than the autograph which may appear, the player is not identified on the card. Wingfield's name may appear in white letters in the lower-right corner of the photo, may be on a credit line on back or may not appear at all.

		NM	EX	VG
	Common Player:	50.00	25.00	15.00
(1)	Ted Abernathy	50.00	25.00	15.00
(2)	Bobby Allison	50.00	25.00	15.00
(3)	Tex Clevenger	50.00	25.00	15.00
(4)	Russ Kemmerer	50.00	25.00	15.00
(5)	Harmon Killebrew	100.00	50.00	30.00
(6)	Bob Usher	50.00	25.00	15.00
(7)	Hal Woodeshick	50.00	25.00	15.00

1960s Don Wingfield Postcards - B/W

A second type of player photo postcards was produced by Alexandria, Va., photographer Don Wingfield beginning around 1960. Also black-and-white, the 3-1/2" x 5-1/2" cards

have (usually) borderless poses on front with no extraneous graphics. Backs have standard postcard indicia plus (on most cards) the player name and team and a copyright line with Wingfield's name and address. At top on back is "Post Card," with "Place Stamp Here" in the postage box. Washington Senators players dominate the checklist which also includes stars of other teams. The autograph on the pictured card was added by the player after printing and is not part of the design. The currently known checklist is presented here alphabetically.

		NM	EX	VG
	Common Player:	50.00	25.00	15.00
(1)	Bob Allison	55.00	27.50	16.50
(2)	Ernie Banks	100.00	50.00	30.00
(3)	Earl Battey (Batting, chest to cap.)	50.00	25.00	15.00
(4)	Earl Battey (Kneeling w/bat.)	50.00	25.00	15.00
(5)	Norm Cash	60.00	30.00	18.00
(6)	Jim Coates	50.00	25.00	15.00
(7)	Rocky Colavito	60.00	30.00	18.00
(8)	Chuck Cottier	50.00	25.00	15.00
(9)	Bennie Daniels	50.00	25.00	15.00
(10)	Dan Dobbek	50.00	25.00	15.00
(11)	Nellie Fox	60.00	30.00	18.00
(12)	Jim Gentile	50.00	25.00	15.00
(13)	Gene Green	50.00	25.00	15.00
(14)	Steve Hamilton	50.00	25.00	15.00
(15)	Ken Hamlin	50.00	25.00	15.00
(16a)	Rudy Hernandez (Postcard back.)	50.00	25.00	15.00
(16b)	Rudy Hernandez (Restuarant ad on back.)	60.00	30.00	18.00
(17)	Ed Hobaugh	50.00	25.00	15.00
(18)	Elston Howard	60.00	30.00	18.00
(19)	Bob Johnson	50.00	25.00	15.00
(20)	Russ Kemmerer	50.00	25.00	15.00
(21)	Harmon Killebrew	100.00	50.00	30.00
(22)	Dale Long	50.00	25.00	15.00
(23)	Mickey Mantle	325.00	160.00	100.00
(24)	Roger Maris	200.00	100.00	60.00
(25)	Willie Mays	250.00	125.00	75.00
(26)	Stan Musial	200.00	100.00	60.00
(27)	Claude Osteen	50.00	25.00	15.00
(28)	Ken Retzer	50.00	25.00	15.00
(29)	Brooks Robinson	100.00	50.00	30.00
(30)	Don Rudolph	50.00	25.00	15.00
(31)	Bill Skowron	60.00	30.00	18.00
(32)	Dave Stenhouse	50.00	25.00	15.00
(33)	Jose Valdivielso	50.00	25.00	15.00
(34)	Gene Woodling	50.00	25.00	15.00
(35)	Bud Zipfel	50.00	25.00	15.00

1960s Don Wingfield Postcards - Color

Similar in format to the contemporary series of black-and-white player photo postcards, only a single player is known to have been issued in color by Alexandria, Va., photographer Don Wingfield. The card is 3-1/2" x 5-1/2" with standard postcard indicia on back.

		NM	EX	VG
C14711 Harmon Killebrew		110.00	55.00	33.00

1951-53 Wisconsin's Athletic Hall of Fame Postcards

ALOYSIUS H. (AL) SIMMONS

WISCONSIN'S ATHLETIC HALL OF FAME
THE ARENA
Milwaukee, Wisconsin

This set of black-and-white postcards reproduces the plaques of athletes in the state's Hall of Fame, as displayed in Milwaukee's Arena during the 1950s. Backs have typical postcard markings.

	NM	EX	VG
Complete Set (12):	150.00	75.00	45.00

Common Player:		10.00	5.00	3.00
(1)	Addie Joss	20.00	10.00	6.00
(2)	Alvin Kraenzlein (Track)	10.00	5.00	3.00
(3)	"Strangler" Lewis (Wrestling)	12.50	6.25	3.75
(4)	George McBride	10.00	5.00	3.00
(5)	Ralph Metcalfe (Track)	10.00	5.00	3.00
(6)	Ernie Nevers	20.00	10.00	6.00
(7)	"Kid" Nichols	20.00	10.00	6.00
(8)	"Pa" O'Dea (Football)	10.00	5.00	3.00
(9)	Dave Schreiner (Football)	10.00	5.00	3.00
(10)	Al Simmons	20.00	10.00	6.00
(11)	Billy Sullivan	12.50	6.25	3.75
(12)	Bob Zuppke (Basketball)	10.00	5.00	3.00

1922 Witmor Candy Co.

WALTER JOHNSON
P.—Washington Americans

Three types of Witmor issues are known, all following the format of the 1921-1922 W575-1 blank-back strip cards. Printed in black-and-white and measuring about 2" x 3-1/4", the three types are differentiated by the ads on the back for the San Francisco candy company. One type has the advertising in a vertical format. The other two types have horizontal advertising; the first line in one of those horizontal varieties ends with "the", the other has a first line that end with "of". Values of Witmor Candy cards carry a preium over the more common W575-1 versions. The extent to which the Witmors and W575-1s share a checklist, particularly the latter's variations, is unknown.

PREMIUMS:
Common Players: 3-4X
Hall of Famers: 3-4X
(See 1921-22 W575-1 for checklist and value information.)

1907 Wolverine News Co. Detroit Tigers

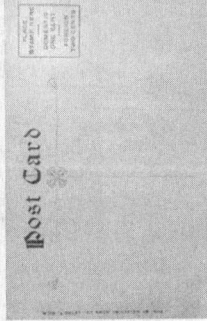

This series of postcards depicts members of the A.L. champ Tigers. The 3-5/16" x 5-5/16" black-and-white cards have poses or posed action photos on front, with a narrow white border at bottom carrying player identification. Backs are standard postcard format with a credit line to Wolverine News Co.

		NM	EX	VG
Complete Set (20):		24,000	12,000	7,200
Common Player:		200.00	100.00	60.00
(1)	Ty Cobb/Btg	9,000	4,500	2,700
(2)	Ty Cobb/Portrait	10,500	5,250	3,000
(3)	Bill Coughlin	200.00	100.00	60.00
(4)	Sam Crawford/Bunting	500.00	250.00	125.00
(5)	Sam Crawford (Chest-to-cap portrait.)	500.00	250.00	125.00
(6)	"Wild Bill" Donovan/Pitching	200.00	100.00	60.00
(7)	"Wild Bill" Donovan ("at the Water Wagon")	300.00	150.00	90.00
(8)	Jerry Downs	200.00	100.00	60.00
(9)	Hughie Jennings/Manager	500.00	250.00	150.00
(10)	Hughie Jennings (On the Coaching line.)	600.00	300.00	180.00
(11)	Davy Jones	200.00	100.00	60.00
(12)	Ed Killian	200.00	100.00	60.00
(13)	George Mullin	200.00	100.00	60.00
(14)	Charlie O'Leary	200.00	100.00	60.00
(15)	Fred Payne	200.00	100.00	60.00
(16)	Claude Rossman	200.00	100.00	60.00
(17)	Herman Schaefer	200.00	100.00	60.00
(18)	Herman Schaefer, Charley O'Leary	200.00	100.00	60.00
(19)	Charlie Schmidt	200.00	100.00	60.00
(20)	Eddie Siever	200.00	100.00	60.00

1886 J. Wood Studio N.Y. Giants Cabinets

Members of the 1886 N.Y. Giants were immportalized in this series of 4-1/4" x 6-7/8" studio cabinets. The sepia por-

traits are bordered in gold. The photos were likely available singly from the studio or as a complete set, with an advertising frontpiece and a 6-9/16" x 4-3/16" composite photo. It is interesting to note that on one version of the composite card, baseball caps were artificially added to the portraits. The photos became the basis for the same players' cards in several late 1880s card series.

		NM	EX	VG
Common Player:		10,000	5,000	3,000
(1)	Roger Connor	25,000	7,500	4,500
(2)	Larry Corcoran	10,000	5,000	3,000
(3)	Pat Deasley	10,000	5,000	3,000
(4)	Mike Dorgan	10,000	5,000	3,000
(5)	Dude Esterbrook	10,000	5,000	3,000
(6)	Buck Ewing	35,000	7,500	4,500
(7)	Joe Gerhardt	10,000	5,000	3,000
(8)	Pete Gillespie	10,000	5,000	3,000
(9)	Tim Keefe	25,000	7,500	4,500
(10)	Jim Mutrie	10,000	5,000	3,000
(11)	Jim O'Rourke	30,000	7,500	4,500
(12)	Danny Richardson	10,000	5,000	3,000
(13)	John Ward	30,000	7,500	4,500
(14)	Mickey Welch	25,000	7,500	4,500
(15)	N.Y. Giants Team Composite (No caps.)	25,000	10,000	6,000
(16)	N.Y. Giants Team Composite (With caps.)	25,000	10,000	6,000

1886 J. Wood Studio N.Y. Metropolitans Cabinets

Nattily attired in dress shirts and sporty dotted ties, members of the 1886 N.Y. Metropolitans of the American Association were immortalized in this series of 4-1/2" x 6-1/2" studio cabinets. The vignetted sepia portraits are framed in gold. The photos became the basis for the same players' cards in the "dotted tie" subset of the 1887 Old Judge cigarette card issue, indicating that more of the cabinet-size photos may yet be added to this checklist.

	NM	EX	VG
Common Player:	12,500	6,250	3,750
Jos. Crotty	12,500	6,250	3,750
E.L. Cushman	12,500	6,250	3,750
E.E. Foster	12,500	6,250	3,750
Al. Mays	12,500	6,250	3,750
Jas. Roseman	12,500	6,250	3,750

1921 Wool's American-Maid Bread

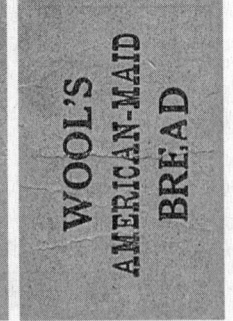

This seldom-seen variation of the W551 strip-card set appears to have been locally overprinted at an unknown location for use as a bread purchase premium. It is presumed the same checklist for W551 can be found with the Wool's back advertising. If ideally cut from the strip, the cards would measure 1-3/8" x 2-1/4". They feature color drawings and are unnumbered.

		NM	EX	VG
Complete Set (10):		6,000	3,000	1,800
Common Player:		160.00	80.00	48.00
(1)	Frank Baker	400.00	200.00	120.00
(2)	Dave Bancroft	400.00	200.00	120.00
(3)	Jess Barnes	250.00	125.00	75.00
(4)	Ty Cobb	2,000	1,000	600.00
(5)	Walter Johnson	750.00	375.00	225.00
(6)	Wally Pipp	300.00	150.00	90.00
(7)	Babe Ruth	2,500	1,250	750.00
(8)	George Sisler	400.00	200.00	120.00
(9)	Tris Speaker	600.00	300.00	180.00
(10)	Casey Stengel	450.00	225.00	135.00

1933 Worch Cigar

This set of unnumbered postcard-size (3-7/16" x 5-7/16") cards, utilizing photos from the Minneapolis Star and St. Paul Dispatch newspapers, was used as a promotion by Worch Cigar Co. of St. Paul, Minn. Although there is no advertising for Worch Cigars on the cards themselves, the cards were mailed in envelopes bearing the Worch name. The cards feature portrait or posed action photos. Player identification, which may be full name or last name, with or without team, may be found in several different styles, either printed on the background, or in a white or black box. Sometimes a photo credit is also present. Many pictures have the top of the background whited out.

		NM	EX	VG
Common Player:		175.00	90.00	55.00
(1)	Sparky Adams	175.00	90.00	55.00
(2)	Dale Alexander	175.00	90.00	55.00
(3)	Ivy Paul Andrews	175.00	90.00	55.00
(4a)	Earl Averill (Cleveland)	800.00	400.00	250.00
(4b)	Earl Averill (No team designation.)	800.00	400.00	250.00
(5)	Richard Bartell	175.00	90.00	55.00
(6)	Herman Bell	175.00	90.00	55.00
(7)	Walter Berger	175.00	90.00	55.00
(8)	Huck Betts	175.00	90.00	55.00
(9)	Max Bishop	175.00	90.00	55.00
(10)	Jim Bottomley	800.00	400.00	250.00
(11a)	Tom Bridges (Name and team in box.)	175.00	90.00	55.00
(11b)	Tom Bridges (No box.)	175.00	90.00	55.00
(12)	Clint Brown	175.00	90.00	55.00
(13a)	Donie Bush	175.00	90.00	55.00
(13b)	Donie Bush	175.00	90.00	55.00
(14a)	Max Carey (Brooklyn)	800.00	400.00	250.00
(14b)	Max Carey (No team designation.)	800.00	400.00	250.00
(15)	Tex Carlton	175.00	90.00	55.00
(16)	Ben Chapman	175.00	90.00	55.00
(17)	Chalmer Cissell	175.00	90.00	55.00
(18)	Mickey Cochrane	800.00	400.00	250.00
(19)	Ripper Collins	175.00	90.00	55.00
(20)	Earle Combs	800.00	400.00	250.00
(21)	Adam Comorosky	175.00	90.00	55.00
(22)	Estel Crabtree	175.00	90.00	55.00
(23)	Rodger Cramer (Roger)	175.00	90.00	55.00
(24)	Pat Crawford	175.00	90.00	55.00
(25)	Hugh Critz	175.00	90.00	55.00
(26a)	Joe Cronin (Name and team in box.)	800.00	400.00	250.00
(26b)	Joe Cronin (No box.)	800.00	400.00	250.00
(27)	Frank Crosetti	300.00	150.00	90.00
(28)	Alvin Crowder	175.00	90.00	55.00
(29a)	Tony Cuccinello (Photo background.)	175.00	90.00	55.00
(29b)	Tony Cuccinello (Blank background.)	175.00	90.00	55.00
(30)	KiKi Cuyler	800.00	400.00	250.00
(31)	Geo. Davis	175.00	90.00	55.00
(32)	Dizzy Dean	1,500	750.00	450.00
(33)	Wm. Dickey	900.00	450.00	270.00
(34)	Leo Durocher	800.00	400.00	250.00
(35)	James Dykes	175.00	90.00	55.00
(36)	George Earnshaw	175.00	90.00	55.00
(37)	Woody English	175.00	90.00	55.00
(38a)	Richard Ferrell (Name and team in box.)	800.00	400.00	250.00
(38b)	Richard Ferrell (No box.)	800.00	400.00	250.00
(39a)	Wesley Ferrell (Name and team in box.)	175.00	90.00	55.00
(39b)	Wesley Ferrell (No box.)	175.00	90.00	55.00
(40)	Fred Fitzsimmons	175.00	90.00	55.00
(41)	Lew Fonseca	175.00	90.00	55.00
(42)	Bob Fothergill	175.00	90.00	55.00
(43)	James Foxx	1,500	750.00	450.00
(44)	Fred Frankhouse	175.00	90.00	55.00
(45)	Frank Frisch	800.00	400.00	250.00
(46a)	Leon Gaslin (Name incorrect.)	800.00	400.00	250.00
(46b)	Leon Goslin (Name correct.)	800.00	400.00	250.00
(47)	Lou Gehrig	4,000	2,000	1,200
(48)	Charles Gehringer	800.00	400.00	250.00
(49)	George Gibson	175.00	90.00	55.00
(50)	Vernon Gomez	800.00	400.00	250.00
(51)	George Grantham	175.00	90.00	55.00
(52)	Grimes The Lord Of Burleigh (Burleigh Grimes)	800.00	400.00	250.00
(53)	Charlie Grimm	175.00	90.00	55.00
(54)	Robt. Grove	1,200	600.00	360.00
(55)	Frank Grube	175.00	90.00	55.00
(56)	Chic Hafey (Chick)	800.00	400.00	250.00
(57)	Jess Haines	800.00	400.00	250.00

(58)	Bill Hallahan	175.00	90.00	55.00
(59)	Mel Harder	175.00	90.00	55.00
(60)	Dave Harris	175.00	90.00	55.00
(61a)	Gabby Hartnett (Small projection.)	800.00	400.00	250.00
(61b)	Gabby Hartnett (Large projection.)	800.00	400.00	250.00
(62)	George Hass (Haas)	175.00	90.00	55.00
(63)	Ray Hayworth	175.00	90.00	55.00
(64)	Harvey Hendrick	175.00	90.00	55.00
(65)	Dutch Henry	175.00	90.00	55.00
(66)	"Babe" Herman	300.00	150.00	90.00
(67)	Bill Herman	800.00	400.00	250.00
(68)	Frank Higgins	175.00	90.00	55.00
(69)	Oral Hildebrand	175.00	90.00	55.00
(70)	"Shanty" Hogan	175.00	90.00	55.00
(71)	Roger Hornsby (Rogers)	1,200	600.00	360.00
(72)	Carl Hubbell	900.00	450.00	300.00
(73)	Travis Jackson	800.00	400.00	250.00
(74)	Hank Johnson	175.00	90.00	55.00
(75)	Syl Johnson	175.00	90.00	55.00
(76)	Smead Jolley	175.00	90.00	55.00
(77)	Wm. Kamm	175.00	90.00	55.00
(78)	Wes Kingdon	175.00	90.00	55.00
(79a)	Charles Klein (Philadelphia, N.L.)	800.00	400.00	250.00
(79b)	Charles Klein (Chicago, N.L.)	800.00	400.00	250.00
(80)	Jos. Kuhel	175.00	90.00	55.00
(81a)	Tony Lazzeri (Name and team in box.)	800.00	400.00	250.00
(81b)	Tony Lazzeri (No box.)	800.00	400.00	250.00
(82)	Sam Leslie	175.00	90.00	55.00
(83)	Ernie Lombardi	800.00	400.00	250.00
(84)	Al Lopez	800.00	400.00	2500.00
(85)	Red Lucas	175.00	90.00	55.00
(86)	Adolfo Luque	175.00	90.00	55.00
(87)	Ted Lyons	800.00	400.00	250.00
(88)	Connie Mack	800.00	400.00	250.00
(89)	Gus Mancuso	175.00	90.00	55.00
(90)	Henry Manush	800.00	400.00	250.00
(91)	Fred Marberry	175.00	90.00	55.00
(92)	Pepper Martin	400.00	200.00	125.00
(93)	Wm. McKechnie	800.00	400.00	250.00
(94)	Joe Medwick	800.00	400.00	250.00
(95)	Jim Mooney	175.00	90.00	55.00
(96)	Joe Moore	175.00	90.00	55.00
(97)	Joe Mowry	175.00	90.00	55.00
(98)	Van Mungo	175.00	90.00	55.00
(99)	Buddy Myer	175.00	90.00	55.00
(100)	"Lefty" O'Doul	400.00	200.00	120.00
(101)	Bob O'Farrell	175.00	90.00	55.00
(102)	Ernie Orsatti	175.00	90.00	55.00
(103)	Melvin Ott	900.00	450.00	300.00
(104)	Roy Parmelee	175.00	90.00	55.00
(105)	Homer Peel	175.00	90.00	55.00
(106)	George Pipgras	175.00	90.00	55.00
(107)	Harry Rice	175.00	90.00	55.00
(108)	Paul Richards	175.00	90.00	55.00
(109)	Eppa Rixey	800.00	400.00	250.00
(110)	Charles Ruffing	800.00	400.00	250.00
(111)	Jack Russell	175.00	90.00	55.00
(112)	Babe Ruth	6,000	3,000	1,800
(113)	"Blondy" Ryan	175.00	90.00	55.00
(114)	Wilfred Ryan	175.00	90.00	55.00
(115)	Fred Schulte	175.00	90.00	55.00
(116)	Hal Schumacher	175.00	90.00	55.00
(117a)	Luke Sewel (Sewell) (Name and team in box.)	175.00	90.00	55.00
(117b)	Luke Sewel (Sewell) (No box.)	175.00	90.00	55.00
(118)	Al Simmons	800.00	400.00	250.00
(119)	Ray Spencer	175.00	90.00	55.00
(120)	Casey Stengel	800.00	400.00	250.00
(121)	Riggs Stephenson	175.00	90.00	55.00
(122)	Walter Stewart	175.00	90.00	55.00
(123)	John Stone	175.00	90.00	55.00
(124)	Gabby Street	175.00	90.00	55.00
(125)	Gus Suhr	175.00	90.00	55.00
(126)	Evar Swanson	175.00	90.00	55.00
(127)	Dan Taylor	175.00	90.00	55.00
(128)	Bill Terry	800.00	400.00	250.00
(129)	Al Todd	175.00	90.00	55.00
(130)	Pie Traynor	800.00	400.00	250.00
(131)	William Urbanski	175.00	90.00	55.00
(132)	Dazzy Vance	800.00	400.00	250.00
(133)	Lloyd (Floyd) Vaughan	800.00	400.00	250.00
(134)	Johnny Vergez	175.00	90.00	55.00
(135)	George Walberg	175.00	90.00	55.00
(136)	Bill Walker	175.00	90.00	55.00
(137)	Gerald Walker	175.00	90.00	55.00
(138a)	Lloyd Waner (Photo background.)	800.00	400.00	250.00
(138b)	Lloyd Waner (Blank background.)	800.00	400.00	250.00
(139a)	Paul Waner (Photo background.)	800.00	400.00	250.00
(139b)	Paul Waner (Blank background, small projection.)	800.00	400.00	250.00
(139c)	Lloyd Waner (Blank background, large projection.)	800.00	400.00	250.00
(140)	Lon Warneke	175.00	90.00	55.00
(141)	George Watkins	175.00	90.00	55.00
(142)	Monte Weaver	175.00	90.00	55.00
(143)	Sam West	175.00	90.00	55.00
(144)	Earl Whitehill	175.00	90.00	55.00
(145)	Hack Wilson	800.00	400.00	250.00
(146)	Jimmy Wilson	175.00	90.00	55.00

1933 World Wide Gum (Canadian Goudey, V353)

Also known as "Canadian Goudeys," this 94-card set drew heavily on its U.S. contemporary. Card fronts are identical to the '33 Goudeys and the backs are nearly so. The first 52 cards in the set carry the same card numbers as their American counterparts, while cards #53-94 have different numbers than the U.S. version. Card backs can be found printed entirely in English, or in English and French; the former being somewhat scarcer. Cards measure approximately 2-3/8" x 2-7/8".

		NM	EX	VG
	Complete Set (94):	32,500	16,250	9,750
	Common Player:	100.00	50.00	30.00
1	Benny Bengough	600.00	60.00	35.00
2	Arthur (Dazzy) Vance	450.00	220.00	135.00
3	Hugh Critz	100.00	50.00	30.00
4	Henry (Heinie) Schuble	100.00	50.00	30.00
5	Floyd (Babe) Herman	125.00	62.50	37.50
6	Jimmy Dykes	100.00	50.00	30.00
7	Ted Lyons	450.00	220.00	135.00
8	Roy Johnson	100.00	50.00	30.00
9	Dave Harris	100.00	50.00	30.00
10	Glenn Myatt	100.00	50.00	30.00
11	Billy Rogell	100.00	50.00	30.00
12	George Pipgras	100.00	50.00	30.00
13	Lafayette Thompson	100.00	50.00	30.00
14	Henry Johnson	100.00	50.00	30.00
15	Victor Sorrell	100.00	50.00	30.00
16	George Blaeholder	100.00	50.00	30.00
17	Watson Clark	100.00	50.00	30.00
18	Herold (Muddy) Ruel	100.00	50.00	30.00
19	Bill Dickey	500.00	250.00	150.00
20	Bill Terry	450.00	220.00	135.00
21	Phil Collins	100.00	50.00	30.00
22	Harold (Pie) Traynor	450.00	220.00	135.00
23	Hazen (Ki-Ki) Cuyler	450.00	220.00	135.00
24	Horace Ford	100.00	50.00	30.00
25	Paul Waner	450.00	220.00	135.00
26	Chalmer Cissell	100.00	50.00	30.00
27	George Connally	100.00	50.00	30.00
28	Dick Bartell	100.00	50.00	30.00
29	Jimmy Foxx	800.00	400.00	240.00
30	Frank Hogan	100.00	50.00	30.00
31	Tony Lazzeri	450.00	220.00	135.00
32	John (Bud) Clancy	100.00	50.00	30.00
33	Ralph Kress	100.00	50.00	30.00
34	Bob O'Farrell	100.00	50.00	30.00
35	Al Simmons	450.00	220.00	135.00
36	Tommy Thevenow	100.00	50.00	30.00
37	Jimmy Wilson	100.00	50.00	30.00
38	Fred Brickell	100.00	50.00	30.00
39	Mark Koenig	100.00	50.00	30.00
40	Taylor Douthit	100.00	50.00	30.00
41	Gus Mancuso	100.00	50.00	30.00
42	Eddie Collins	450.00	220.00	135.00
43	Lew Fonseca	100.00	50.00	30.00
44	Jim Bottomley	450.00	220.00	135.00
45	Larry Benton	100.00	50.00	30.00
46	Ethan Allen	100.00	50.00	30.00
47	Henry "Heinie" Manush	450.00	220.00	135.00
48	Marty McManus	100.00	50.00	30.00
49	Frank Frisch	450.00	220.00	135.00
50	Ed Brandt	100.00	50.00	30.00
51	Charlie Grimm	100.00	50.00	30.00
52	Andy Cohen	100.00	50.00	30.00
53	Jack Quinn	100.00	50.00	30.00
54	Urban (Red) Faber	450.00	220.00	135.00
55	Lou Gehrig	3,000	1,500	900.00
56	John Welch	100.00	50.00	30.00
57	Bill Walker	100.00	50.00	30.00
58	Frank (Lefty) O'Doul	125.00	62.50	37.50
59	Edmund (Bing) Miller	100.00	50.00	30.00
60	Waite Hoyt	450.00	220.00	135.00
61	Max Bishop	100.00	50.00	30.00
62	"Pepper" Martin	90.00	40.00	22.50
63	Joe Cronin	450.00	220.00	135.00
64	Burleigh Grimes	450.00	220.00	135.00
65	Milton Gaston	100.00	50.00	30.00
66	George Grantham	100.00	50.00	30.00
67	Gus Bush	100.00	50.00	30.00
68	Willie Kamm	100.00	50.00	30.00
69	Gordon (Mickey) Cochrane	450.00	220.00	135.00
70	Adam Comorosky	100.00	50.00	30.00
71	Alvin Crowder	100.00	50.00	30.00
72	Willis Hudlin	100.00	50.00	30.00
73	Eddie Farrell	100.00	50.00	30.00
74	Leo Durocher	450.00	220.00	135.00
75	Walter Stewart	100.00	50.00	30.00
76	George Walberg	100.00	50.00	30.00
77	Glenn Wright	100.00	50.00	30.00
78	Charles (Buddy) Myer	100.00	50.00	30.00
79	James (Zack) Taylor	100.00	50.00	30.00
80	George Herman (Babe) Ruth	5,350	2,675	1,605
81	D'Arcy (Jake) Flowers	100.00	50.00	30.00
82	Ray Kolp	100.00	50.00	30.00
83	Oswald Bluege	100.00	50.00	30.00
84	Morris (Moe) Berg	600.00	275.00	150.00
85	Jimmy Foxx	400.00	180.00	100.00
86	Sam Byrd	100.00	50.00	30.00
87	Danny Mcfayden (McFayden)	100.00	50.00	30.00
88	Joe Judge	100.00	50.00	30.00
89	Joe Sewell	450.00	220.00	135.00
90	Lloyd Waner	450.00	220.00	135.00
91	Luke Sewell	100.00	50.00	30.00
92	Leo Mangum	100.00	50.00	30.00
93	George Herman (Babe) Ruth	5,250	2,625	1,575
94	Al Spohrer	100.00	50.00	30.00

1934 World Wide Gum (Canadian Goudey, V354)

Again a near-clone of the American issue, the '34 "Canadian Goudeys" feature the same number (96) and size (2-3/8"

x 2-7/8") of cards. Player selection is considerably different, however. Cards #1-48 feature the same front design as the '33 World Wide/Goudey sets. Cards #49-96 have the "Lou Gehrig says..." graphic on the front. Unlike the 1933 cards, backs are only found with bi-lingual text.

		NM	EX	VG
	Complete Set (96):	24,500	12,250	7,350
	Common Player:	90.00	45.00	27.00
1	Rogers Hornsby	900.00	400.00	250.00
2	Eddie Morgan	90.00	45.00	27.00
3	Valentine J. (Val) Picinich	90.00	45.00	27.00
4	Rabbit Maranville	350.00	175.00	105.00
5	Flint Rhem	90.00	45.00	27.00
6	Jim Elliott	90.00	45.00	27.00
7	Fred (Red) Lucas	90.00	45.00	27.00
8	Fred Marberry	90.00	45.00	27.00
9	Clifton Heathcote	90.00	45.00	27.00
10	Bernie Friberg	90.00	45.00	27.00
11	Elwood (Woody) English	90.00	45.00	27.00
12	Carl Reynolds	90.00	45.00	27.00
13	Ray Benge	90.00	45.00	27.00
14	Ben Cantwell	90.00	45.00	27.00
15	Irvin (Bump) Hadley	90.00	45.00	27.00
16	Herb Pennock	350.00	175.00	105.00
17	Fred Lindstrom	350.00	175.00	105.00
18	Edgar (Sam) Rice	350.00	175.00	105.00
19	Fred Frankhouse	90.00	45.00	27.00
20	Fred Fitzsimmons	90.00	45.00	27.00
21	Earl Coombs (Earle Combs)	350.00	175.00	105.00
22	George Uhle	90.00	45.00	27.00
23	Richard Coffman	90.00	45.00	27.00
24	Travis C. Jackson	350.00	175.00	105.00
25	Robert J. Burke	90.00	45.00	27.00
26	Randy Moore	90.00	45.00	27.00
27	John Henry (Heinie) Sand	90.00	45.00	27.00
28	George Herman (Babe) Ruth	4,200	2,000	1,600
29	Tris Speaker	425.00	212.50	127.50
30	Perce (Pat) Malone	90.00	45.00	27.00
31	Sam Jones	90.00	45.00	27.00
32	Eppa Rixey	350.00	175.00	105.00
33	Floyd (Pete) Scott	90.00	45.00	27.00
34	Pete Jablonowski	90.00	45.00	27.00
35	Clyde Manion	90.00	45.00	27.00
36	Dibrell Williams	90.00	45.00	27.00
37	Glenn Spencer	90.00	45.00	27.00
38	Ray Kremer	90.00	45.00	27.00
39	Phil Todt	90.00	45.00	27.00
40	Russell Rollings	90.00	45.00	27.00
41	Earl Clark	90.00	45.00	27.00
42	Jess Petty	90.00	45.00	27.00
43	Frank O'Rourke	90.00	45.00	27.00
44	Jesse Haines	350.00	175.00	105.00
45	Horace Lisenbee	90.00	45.00	27.00
46	Owen Carroll	90.00	45.00	27.00
47	Tom Zachary	90.00	45.00	27.00
48	Charlie Ruffing	350.00	175.00	105.00
49	Ray Benge	90.00	45.00	27.00
50	Elwood (Woody) English	90.00	45.00	27.00
51	Ben Chapman	90.00	45.00	27.00
52	Joe Kuhel	90.00	45.00	27.00
53	Bill Terry	350.00	175.00	105.00
54	Robert (Lefty) Grove	425.00	212.50	127.50
55	Jerome (Dizzy) Dean	450.00	220.00	140.00
56	Charles (Chuck) Klein	350.00	175.00	105.00
57	Charley Gehringer	350.00	175.00	105.00
58	Jimmy Foxx	525.00	262.50	157.50
59	Gordon (Mickey) Cochrane	350.00	175.00	105.00
60	Willie Kamm	90.00	45.00	27.00
61	Charlie Grimm	90.00	45.00	27.00
62	Ed Brandt	90.00	45.00	27.00
63	Tony Piet	90.00	45.00	27.00
64	Frank Frisch	350.00	175.00	105.00
65	Alvin Crowder	90.00	45.00	27.00
66	Frank Hogan	90.00	45.00	27.00
67	Paul Waner	350.00	175.00	105.00
68	Henry (Heinie) Manush	350.00	175.00	105.00
69	Leo Durocher	350.00	175.00	105.00
70	Floyd Vaughan	350.00	175.00	105.00
71	Carl Hubbell	425.00	212.50	127.50
72	Hugh Critz	90.00	45.00	27.00
73	John (Blondy) Ryan	90.00	45.00	27.00
74	Roger Cramer	90.00	45.00	27.00
75	Baxter Jordan	90.00	45.00	27.00
76	Ed Coleman	90.00	45.00	27.00
77	Julius Solters	90.00	45.00	27.00
78	Charles (Chick) Hafey	350.00	175.00	105.00
79	Larry French	90.00	45.00	27.00
80	Frank (Don) Hurst	90.00	45.00	27.00
81	Gerald Walker	90.00	45.00	27.00
82	Ernie Lombardi	350.00	175.00	105.00
83	Walter (Huck) Betts	90.00	45.00	27.00
84	Luke Appling	350.00	175.00	105.00
85	John Frederick	550.00	270.00	165.00
86	Fred Walker	90.00	45.00	27.00
87	Tom Bridges	90.00	45.00	27.00
88	Dick Porter	90.00	45.00	27.00
89	John Stone	90.00	45.00	27.00
90	James (Tex) Carleton	90.00	45.00	27.00
91	Joe Stripp	90.00	45.00	27.00
92	Lou Gehrig	3,400	1,700	1,020

		NM	EX	VG
93	George Earnshaw	90.00	45.00	27.00
94	Oscar Melillo	90.00	45.00	27.00
95	Oral Hildebrand	90.00	45.00	27.00
96	John Allen	90.00	45.00	27.00

1936 World Wide Gum (Canadian Goudey, V355)

No. 119
THOMAS N. OLIVER,
TORONTO LEAFS
Outfielder   Voltigeur

Born at Montgomery, Ala., January 15, 1904. Bats and throws right. A feed. Past, covers much ground. With Boston Red Sox and Phils in majors. With Baltimore in International one season. Can play third base as well as outfield.

Né à Montgomery, Ala., le 15 janvier, 1904. Decidée, à droit. Rapide, couvre beaucoup de terrain. Avec Boston Red Sox et Phils dans les Majeures. Avec Baltimore une saison dans l'Internationale. Quelque vecteur peut jouer au troisième but aussi.

BIG LEAGUE CHEWING GUM
World Wide Gum Co. Ltd. Granby, Que.
Printed in Canada.

No. 119 TOM OLIVER

This black and white Canadian set was issued by World Wide Gum in 1936. The cards measure approximately 2-1/2" x 2-7/8", and the set includes both portrait and action photos. The card number and player's name (appearing in all capital letters) are printed inside a white box below the photo.

		NM	EX	VG
Complete Set (135):		47,500	23,750	14,250
Common Player:		125.00	55.00	30.00
1	Jimmy Dykes	475.00	90.00	40.00
2	Paul Waner	400.00	200.00	120.00
3	Cy Blanton	125.00	55.00	30.00
4	Sam Leslie	125.00	55.00	30.00
5	Johnny Louis Vergez	125.00	55.00	30.00
6	Arky Vaughan	400.00	200.00	120.00
7	Bill Terry	400.00	200.00	120.00
8	Joe Moore	125.00	55.00	30.00
9	Gus Mancuso	125.00	55.00	30.00
10	Fred Marberry	125.00	55.00	30.00
11	George Selkirk	125.00	55.00	30.00
12	Spud Davis	125.00	55.00	30.00
13	Chuck Klein	400.00	200.00	120.00
14	Fred Fitzsimmons	125.00	55.00	30.00
15	Bill Delancey	125.00	55.00	30.00
16	Billy Herman	400.00	200.00	120.00
17	George Davis	125.00	55.00	30.00
18	Rip Collins	125.00	55.00	30.00
19	Dizzy Dean	650.00	325.00	195.00
20	Roy Parmelee	125.00	55.00	30.00
21	Vic Sorrell	125.00	55.00	30.00
22	Harry Danning	125.00	55.00	30.00
23	Hal Schumacher	125.00	55.00	30.00
24	Cy Perkins	125.00	55.00	30.00
25	Speedy Durocher	400.00	200.00	120.00
26	Glenn Myatt	125.00	55.00	30.00
27	Bob Seeds	125.00	55.00	30.00
28	Jimmy Ripple	125.00	55.00	30.00
29	Al Schacht	125.00	55.00	30.00
30	Pete Fox	125.00	55.00	30.00
31	Del Baker	125.00	55.00	30.00
32	Flea Clifton	125.00	55.00	30.00
33	Tommy Bridges	125.00	55.00	30.00
34	Bill Dickey	400.00	200.00	120.00
35	Wally Berger	125.00	55.00	30.00
36	Slick Castleman	125.00	55.00	30.00
37	Dick Bartell	125.00	55.00	30.00
38	Red Rolfe	125.00	55.00	30.00
39	Waite Hoyt	400.00	200.00	120.00
40	Wes Ferrell	125.00	55.00	30.00
41	Hank Greenberg	650.00	325.00	195.00
42	Charlie Gehringer	400.00	200.00	120.00
43	Goose Goslin	400.00	200.00	120.00
44	Schoolboy Rowe	125.00	55.00	30.00
45	Mickey Cochrane	400.00	200.00	120.00
46	Joe Cronin	400.00	200.00	120.00
47	Jimmie Foxx	650.00	325.00	195.00
48	Jerry Walker	125.00	55.00	30.00
49	Charlie Gelbert	125.00	55.00	30.00
50	Roy Hayworth (Ray)	125.00	55.00	30.00
51	Joe DiMaggio	22,500	11,000	4,000
52	Billy Rogell	125.00	55.00	30.00
53	Joe McCarthy	400.00	200.00	120.00
54	Phil Cavaretta (Cavarretta)	125.00	55.00	30.00
55	Kiki Cuyler	400.00	200.00	120.00
56	Lefty Gomez	400.00	200.00	120.00
57	Gabby Hartnett	400.00	200.00	120.00
58	Johnny Marcum	125.00	55.00	30.00
59	Burgess Whitehead	125.00	55.00	30.00
60	Whitey Whitehill	125.00	55.00	30.00
61	Buckey Walters	125.00	55.00	30.00
62	Luke Sewell	125.00	55.00	30.00
63	Joey Kuhel	125.00	55.00	30.00
64	Lou Finney	125.00	55.00	30.00
65	Fred Lindstrom	400.00	200.00	120.00
66	Paul Derringer	125.00	55.00	30.00
67	Steve O'Neil (O'Neill)	125.00	55.00	30.00
68	Mule Haas	125.00	55.00	30.00
69	Freck Owen	125.00	55.00	30.00
70	Wild Bill Hallahan	125.00	55.00	30.00
71	Bill Urbanski	125.00	55.00	30.00
72	Dan Taylor	125.00	55.00	30.00
73	Heinie Manush	400.00	200.00	120.00
74	Jo-Jo White	125.00	55.00	30.00
75	Mickey Medwick (Ducky)	400.00	200.00	120.00
76	Joe Vosmik	125.00	55.00	30.00
77	Al Simmons	250.00	125.00	75.00
78	Shag Shaughnessy	125.00	55.00	30.00
79	Harry Smythe	125.00	55.00	30.00
80	Benny Tate	125.00	55.00	30.00
81	Billy Rhiel	125.00	55.00	30.00
82	Lauri Myllykangas	125.00	55.00	30.00
83	Ben Sankey	125.00	55.00	30.00
84	Crip Polli	125.00	55.00	30.00
85	Jim Bottomley	400.00	200.00	120.00

		NM	EX	VG
86	William Clark	125.00	55.00	30.00
87	Ossie Bluege	125.00	55.00	30.00
88	Lefty Grove	400.00	200.00	120.00
89	Charlie Grimm	125.00	55.00	30.00
90	Ben Chapman	125.00	55.00	30.00
91	Frank Crosetti (Photo actually Sam Gibson)	125.00	60.00	30.00
92	John Pomorski	125.00	55.00	30.00
93	Jesse Haines	400.00	200.00	120.00
94	Chick Hafey	400.00	200.00	120.00
95	Tony Piet	125.00	55.00	30.00
96	Lou Gehrig	4,000	2,000	1,400
97	Bill Jurges	125.00	55.00	30.00
98	Smead Jolley	125.00	55.00	30.00
99	Jimmy Wilson	125.00	55.00	30.00
100	Lonnie Warneke	125.00	55.00	30.00
101	Lefty Tamulis	125.00	55.00	30.00
102	Charlie Ruffing	400.00	200.00	120.00
103	Earl Grace	125.00	55.00	30.00
104	Rox Lawson	125.00	55.00	30.00
105	Stan Hack	125.00	55.00	30.00
106	August Galan	125.00	55.00	30.00
107	Frank Frisch	400.00	200.00	120.00
108	Bill McKechnie	400.00	200.00	120.00
109	Bill Lee	125.00	55.00	30.00
110	Connie Mack	400.00	200.00	120.00
111	Frank Reiber	125.00	55.00	30.00
112	Zeke Bonura	125.00	55.00	30.00
113	Luke Appling	400.00	200.00	120.00
114	Monte Pearson	125.00	55.00	30.00
115	Bob O'Farrell	125.00	55.00	30.00
116	Marvin Duke	125.00	55.00	30.00
117	Paul Florence	125.00	55.00	30.00
118	John Berley	125.00	55.00	30.00
119	Tom Oliver	125.00	55.00	30.00
120	Norman Kies	125.00	55.00	30.00
121	Hal King	125.00	55.00	30.00
122	Tom Abernathy	125.00	55.00	30.00
123	Phil Hensick	125.00	55.00	30.00
124	Roy Schalk (Ray)	400.00	200.00	120.00
125	Paul Dunlap	125.00	55.00	30.00
126	Benny Bates	125.00	55.00	30.00
127	George Puccinelli	125.00	55.00	30.00
128	Stevie Stevenson	125.00	55.00	30.00
129	Rabbit Maranville	400.00	200.00	120.00
130	Bucky Harris	400.00	200.00	120.00
131	Al Lopez	400.00	200.00	120.00
132	Buddy Myer	125.00	55.00	30.00
133	Cliff Bolton	125.00	55.00	30.00
134	Estel Crabtree	125.00	55.00	30.00
135	Phil Weintraub	3,000	1,500	900.00

1939 World Wide Gum (Canadian Goudey, V351)

HOW TO SIGNAL

These premium pictures are analogous to the R303-A issue in the U.S. The 4" x 5-3/4" pictures were given away with the purchase of World Wide gum. The pictures are printed in sepia on cream-colored paper. Fronts have a bordered photo with facsimile autograph. Backs have a "How to . . ." baseball playing tip illustrated with drawings. Backs of the Canadian version differ from the U.S. pieces in the absence of a border line around the playing tip, and the use of a "Lithographed in Canada" notice at lower-right. The unnumbered pictures are checklisted here in alphabetical order.

		NM	EX	VG
Complete Set (25):		11,000	5,500	3,250
Common Player:		200.00	100.00	60.00
(1)	Morris Arnovich	200.00	100.00	60.00
(2)	Sam Bell	260.00	130.00	80.00
(3)	Zeke Bonura	200.00	100.00	60.00
(4)	Earl Caldwell	200.00	100.00	60.00
(5)	Flea Clifton	200.00	100.00	60.00
(6)	Frank Crosetti	280.00	140.00	80.00
(7)	Harry Danning	200.00	100.00	60.00
(8)	Dizzy Dean	500.00	250.00	150.00
(9)	Emile De Jonghe	260.00	130.00	80.00
(10)	Paul Derringer	200.00	100.00	60.00
(11)	Joe DiMaggio	2,100	1,050	650.00
(12)	Vince DiMaggio	200.00	100.00	60.00
(13)	Charlie Gehringer	450.00	225.00	150.00
(14)	Gene Hasson	260.00	130.00	80.00
(15)	Tommy Henrich	300.00	150.00	90.00
(16)	Fred Hutchinson	200.00	100.00	60.00
(17)	Phil Marchildon	200.00	100.00	60.00
(18)	Mike Meola	200.00	100.00	60.00
(19)	Arnold Moser	260.00	130.00	80.00
(20)	Frank Pytlak	200.00	100.00	60.00
(21)	Frank Reiber	200.00	100.00	60.00
(22)	Lee Rogers	200.00	100.00	60.00
(23)	Cecil Travis	200.00	100.00	60.00
(24)	Hal Trosky	200.00	100.00	60.00
(25)	Ted Williams	3,000	1,500	900.00

1975 WTMJ Milwaukee Brewers Broadcasters

To promote its schedule of radio and television broadcasts of Brewers baseball, WTMJ issued this set of broadcaster and schedule cards to potential sponsors. The standard 2-1/2" x 3-1/2" cards are printed in team colors of blue and gold. The on-air talent cards have portraits and facsimile autographs on front, with career summaries on back. The schedule cards have game-action photos on front along with the slogan, "Brewers 75: It's Gonna' Be A Whole New Ballgame!" The cards were distributed in a wax pack with gum.

		NM	EX	VG
Complete Set (7):		25.00	12.50	7.50
Common Card:		2.50	1.25	.70
1	Jim Irwin	4.00	2.00	1.25
2	Gary Bender	4.00	2.00	1.25
3	Bob Uecker	12.50	6.25	3.75
4	Merle Harmon	4.00	2.00	1.25
(5)	TV Schedule	2.50	1.25	.70
(6)	Radio Schedule, Part 1	2.50	1.25	.70
(7)	Radio Schedule, Part 2	2.50	1.25	.70

1910 W-UNC Strip Cards

MATHEWSON, N.Y.

Considerably earlier than most known strip cards, these pieces were cut from a notebook cover. The known players point to a 1910 issue date. Crudely printed on flimsy stock, the cards feature familiar colorized portraits of players on brightly colored backgrounds. The format is about 1-3/8" x 2-3/8" and some cards have evidence of a 1-16th" yellow strip around the outside of the black border. Player name and city are printed in the white border at bottom. Backs are blank. The unnumbered cards are listed here in alphabetical order, though the checklist may or may not be complete.

		NM	EX	VG
Common Player:		300.00	120.00	60.00
(1)	Babe Adams	300.00	120.00	60.00
(2)	Chief Bender	600.00	240.00	120.00
(3)	Roger Bresnahan	600.00	240.00	120.00
(4)	Donie Bush	300.00	120.00	60.00
(5)	Bobby Byrne	300.00	120.00	60.00
(6)	Bill Carrigan	300.00	120.00	60.00
(7)	Frank Chance	600.00	240.00	120.00
(8)	Hal Chase	450.00	180.00	90.00
(9)	Ty Cobb	3,750	1,875	1,100
(10)	Willis Cole	300.00	120.00	60.00
(11)	Eddie Collins	600.00	240.00	120.00
(12)	Jack Coombs	300.00	120.00	60.00
(13)	Sam Crawford	600.00	240.00	120.00
(14)	Johnny Evers	600.00	240.00	120.00
(15)	Solly Hoffman	300.00	120.00	60.00
(16)	Hughie Jennings	600.00	240.00	120.00
(17)	Walter Johnston (Johnson)	2,000	1,000	600.00
(18)	Johnny Kling	300.00	120.00	60.00
(19)	Ed Konetchy	300.00	120.00	60.00
(20)	Harry Lord	300.00	120.00	60.00
(21)	Sherry Magee	300.00	120.00	60.00
(22)	Christy Mathewson	2,200	1,100	650.00
(23)	Mike Mitchell	300.00	120.00	60.00
(24)	Tris Speaker	750.00	300.00	150.00
(25)	Oscar Stanage	300.00	120.00	60.00
(26)	Honus Wagner	3,500	1,750	1,050

1912 W-UNC Strip Cards

The attributed issue date is speculative, based on the limited known roster. In much the same size and format as W555, these small (photo image area is 1-3/8" x 1-1/2") blank-back cards appear to have been cut off a box or other packaging and may actually be candy cards. Black-and-white photos are framed in dark green with the player's last name in white capital letters below.

Common Player:	NM	EX	
(1) Bill Carrigan	2,000	800.00	400.00
(2) Tommy Leach	2,000	800.00	400.00
(3) Oscar Stanage	2,000	800.00	400.00
(4) Honus Wagner	7,500	3,000	1,500
(5) Cy Young	6,500	2,600	1,300

1915 W-UNC Strip Cards

Walter Johnson, Wash. Amer.

Utilizing many photos familiar to collectors from contemporary card sets, including pictures that were several years old at the time of issue, this appears to be a strip-card issue whose scarcity has caused it to elude cataloging efforts heretofore. Cards are printed in black-and-white, blank-backed and are nominally 1-3/4" x 2-3/4". Player or photo identification appears in the bottom border, or at right on horizontally formatted cards.

Common Player:	NM	EX	VG
(1) Ty Cobb	6,500	2,600	1,300
(2) Larry Doyle	500.00	200.00	100.00
(3) Johnny Evers	1,500	600.00	300.00
(4) Joe Jackson	16,000	6,400	3,200
(5) Walter Johnson	2,500	1,000	500.00
(6) Sherwood Magee	500.00	200.00	100.00
(7) Fred Maisel	500.00	200.00	100.00
(8) Walter (Rabbit) Maranville	1,500	600.00	300.00
(9) Rube Marquard	1,500	600.00	300.00
(10) Christy Mathewson	2,750	1,100	550.00
(11) Phila. Athletics, Champ.	750.00	300.00	150.00
(12) Ready for the Wallop (Honus Wagner, Roger Bresnahan)	1,500	600.00	300.00
(13) Nap Rucker	500.00	200.00	100.00
(14) Hans Wagner	3,500	1,400	700.00
(15) Joe Wood	600.00	240.00	120.00

1916-20 W-UNC "Big Head" Strip Cards

Given the known player content (perhaps not complete as listed here) and the fact that no team designations are printed on the cards, it is impossible to more accurately date this blank-back strip card issue. The 1-3/8" x 2-1/2" cards have color artwork of the players in full-body poses. The pictures are unusual in that the players' heads are out of proportion to the rest of the body. Whether the portraits were meant to be accurate portrayals is conjecture. Player names given here are as printed on the cards.

	NM	EX	VG
Complete Set (20):	16,000	6,400	3,200
Common Player:	500.00	350.00	150.00
(1) Jim Bagby	500.00	350.00	150.00
(2) Home Run Baker	800.00	475.00	300.00
(3) Dave Bancroft	800.00	475.00	300.00
(4) Ping Bodie	500.00	350.00	150.00
(5) Geo. Burns	500.00	350.00	150.00
(6) Leon Cadore	500.00	350.00	150.00
(7) Ty Cobb	4,000	2,500	1,250
(8) Larry Doyle	500.00	350.00	150.00
(9) Hinie Groh	500.00	350.00	150.00
(10) R. Hornsby	2,000	1,000	750.00
(11) Johnston (Walter Johnson)	1,500	850.00	500.00
(12) Joe Judge	500.00	350.00	150.00
(13) Eddy Konetchy	500.00	350.00	150.00
(14) Carl Mays	500.00	350.00	150.00

(15) Zeb Milan	500.00	350.00	150.00
(16) Sam Rice	800.00	475.00	300.00
(17) Babe Ruth	14,000	8,000	3,000
(18) Ray Schalk	800.00	475.00	300.00
(19) Wally Schang	500.00	350.00	150.00
(20) Geo. Sisler	1,500	850.00	500.00

1921 W-UNC Self-Developing Strip Cards

The technology of a self-developing photographic baseball card was popularized in the early 1930s by Ray-O-Print and again in the late late 1940s and early 1950s by Topps, but appears to have been pioneered circa 1921 by an unknown company which produced this series. Individual cards measure between 1-1/16" and 1-3/16" in width and 1-13/16" in depth. In black-and-white, they feature action poses on a dark background with the player name and team in white. A white border surrounds the picture. Backs are blank. The unnumbered cards are checklisted here alphabetically, though the list is probably incomplete.

Common Player:	NM	EX	VG
(1) Grover Alexander	450.00	180.00	90.00
(2) Ty Cobb	2,000	800.00	400.00
(3) Eddie Collins	300.00	120.00	60.00
(4) Jake Daubert	100.00	40.00	20.00
(5) Max Flack	250.00	100.00	50.00
(6) Max Flack	100.00	40.00	20.00
(7) "Roger (Rogers) Hornsby	350.00	140.00	70.00
(8) Doc Johnston	100.00	40.00	20.00
(9) Walter Johnston (Johnson)	900.00	360.00	180.00
(10) Bill Killifer (Killefer)	100.00	40.00	20.00
(11) Steve O'Neill	100.00	40.00	20.00
(12) Derrill Pratt	100.00	40.00	20.00
(13) "Babe" Ruth	3,500	1,400	700.00
(14) Wallie Schang	100.00	40.00	20.00

1929 W-UNC Playing Strip Cards (1)

Recent discoveries indicate that this issue was produced by Universal Toy & Novelty circa 1929. Likely printed on a sheet similar to other playing card/strip card sets of the era, the individual cards are about 1-1/2" x 2-1/2". The front has a crude black-and-white drawing of the player inside a suit-shaped design on a red (cubs and spades) or black (hearts and diamonds) background. Back is blank.

	NM	EX	VG
4C Walter Hoyt	250.00	125.00	75.00
6C Shanty Hogan	150.00	75.00	45.00
7S Doug McWeeny	150.00	75.00	45.00
5H Lou Gehrig	600.00	300.00	180.00
5D Babe Ruth	750.00	370.00	220.00

1920s W-UNC Playing Strip Cards (2)

Because only three players have thus far been checklisted from this set, it is not possible to more precisely date this issue. Likely printed on a sheet similar to other playing card/strip card sets of the era, the individual cards are about 1-1/2" x 2-1/2", printed in either red (hearts, diamonds) or black (clubs, spades), with a player photo at center. Backs are blank.

Values Undetermined
6C	Bob Meusel
9S	Tris Speaker
AD	Babe Ruth

1926 W-UNC Strip Cards

Ruth is the only baseball player known in this set of athletic, cinematic and historical subjects. The approximately 1-1/2" x 2-1/2" black-and-white, blue-and-white, or maroon-and-white blank-backed card identifies the player, position and team typographically within the photo and has the card number and name in the bottom border. The card has been seen with numbers 1, 52 and 71, as well as unnumbered.

		NM	EX	VG
1	Babe Ruth (Black-and-white.)	800.00	400.00	240.00
52	Babe Ruth (Blue duotone.)	800.00	400.00	240.00
71	Babe Ruth (Blue duotone.)	800.00	400.00	240.00
71	Babe Ruth (Maroon duotone.)	800.00	400.00	240.00
---	Babe Ruth (Unnumbered, maroon.)	1,100	550.00	330.00

1931 W-UNC Strip Cards

(14) ROBERT GROVE

This issue is virtually identical in format to the various 1928-1931 issues cataloged as W502, York Caramel, Yuengling Ice Cream, etc. The black-and-white, cards measure about 1-3/8" (give or take a 1/16") x 2-1/2". Player photos are bordered in white with the name printed in capital letters at bottom. At bottom-left is a card number in parentheses. This issue's checklist is identical to the 1931 W502. the only difference being these cards have blank backs.

		NM	EX	VG
Complete Set (60):		12,500	5,000	2,500
Common Player:		75.00	30.00	15.00
1	Muddy Ruel	75.00	30.00	15.00
2	John Grabowski	75.00	30.00	15.00
3	Mickey Cochrane	150.00	60.00	30.00
4	Bill Cissell	75.00	30.00	15.00
5	Carl Reynolds	75.00	30.00	15.00
6	Luke Sewell	75.00	30.00	15.00
7	Ted Lyons	150.00	60.00	30.00
8	Harvey Walker	75.00	30.00	15.00
9	Gerald Walker	75.00	30.00	15.00
10	Sam Byrd	75.00	30.00	15.00
11	Joe Vosmik	75.00	30.00	15.00
12	Dan MacFayden	75.00	30.00	15.00
13	William Dickey	150.00	60.00	30.00
14	Robert Grove	300.00	120.00	60.00
15	Al Simmons	150.00	60.00	30.00
16	Jimmy Foxx	300.00	120.00	60.00
17	Nick Altrock	75.00	30.00	15.00
18	Charlie Grimm	75.00	30.00	15.00
19	Bill Terry	150.00	60.00	30.00
20	Clifton Heathcote	75.00	30.00	15.00
21	Burleigh Grimes	150.00	60.00	30.00
22	Red Faber	150.00	60.00	30.00
23	Gabby Hartnett	150.00	60.00	30.00
24	Earl (Earle) Combs	150.00	60.00	30.00
25	Hack Wilson	150.00	60.00	30.00
26	Stanley Harris	150.00	60.00	30.00
27	John J. McGraw	150.00	60.00	30.00
28	Paul Waner	150.00	60.00	30.00
29	Babe Ruth	4,000	1,600	800.00
30	Herb Pennock	150.00	60.00	30.00
31	Joe Sewell	150.00	60.00	30.00
32	Lou Gehrig	2,000	800.00	400.00
33	Tony Lazzeri	150.00	60.00	30.00
34	Waite Hoyt	150.00	60.00	30.00
35	Glenn Wright	75.00	30.00	15.00
36	Leon (Goose) Goslin	150.00	60.00	30.00
37	Frank Frisch	150.00	60.00	30.00
38	George Uhle	75.00	30.00	15.00
39	Bob O'Farrell	75.00	30.00	15.00
40	Rogers Hornsby	200.00	80.00	40.00
41	"Pie" Traynor	150.00	60.00	30.00
42	Clarence Mitchell	75.00	30.00	15.00
43	Sherwood Smith	75.00	30.00	15.00
44	Miguel A. Gonzalez	75.00	30.00	15.00
45	Joe Judge	75.00	30.00	15.00
46	Eppa Rixey	150.00	60.00	30.00
47	Adolfo Luque	75.00	30.00	15.00
48	E.C. (Sam) Rice	150.00	60.00	30.00
49	Earl Sheely	75.00	30.00	15.00
50	Sam Jones	75.00	30.00	15.00
51	Bib A. Falk	75.00	30.00	15.00
52	Willie Kamm	75.00	30.00	15.00

53	Roger Peckinpaugh	75.00	30.00	15.00
54	Lester Bell	75.00	30.00	15.00
55	L. Waner	150.00	60.00	30.00
56	Eugene Hargrave	75.00	30.00	15.00
57	Harry Heilmann	150.00	60.00	30.00
58	Earl Smith	75.00	30.00	15.00
59	Dave Bancroft	150.00	60.00	30.00
60	George Kelly	150.00	60.00	30.00

1890 Wybrant Louisville Colonel Cabinets

The three members of the American Association championship team of 1890 are likely part of a larger series of cabinet cards in the standard 4-1/4" x 6-1/2" format with sepia toned player photos. The cards are the product of Frank Wybrant's t's studio in Louisville. This checklist is no doubt incomplete and gaps in the assigned numbering have been left for future additions..

		NM	EX	VG
	Common Player:	3,500	1,750	1,050
(6)	George Meakim	3,500	1,750	1,050
(9)	Farmer Weaver	3,500	1,750	1,050
(10)	Jimmy Wolf	3,500	1,750	1,050

1922 W501

TY COBB
Mgr.—Detroit Americans

This "strip card" set, known as W501 in the American Card Catalog, is closely connected to the more popular E121 American Caramel set of 1921 and 1922. Because they were handcut from strips, measurements are relative, with well-cut cards typically about 1-7/8" to 2" by about 3-3/8". The W501 cards are numbered in the upper-right corner and have the notation "G-4-22" in the upper-left corner, apparrently indicating the cards were issued in April of 1922.

		NM	EX	VG
	Complete Set (122):	37,500	19,000	11,500
	Common Player:	125.00	65.00	40.00
1	Ed Rounnel (Rommel)	125.00	65.00	40.00
2	Urban Shocker	125.00	65.00	40.00
3	Dixie Davis	125.00	65.00	40.00
4	George Sisler	450.00	225.00	140.00
5	Bob Veach	125.00	65.00	40.00
6	Harry Heilman (Heilmann)	450.00	225.00	140.00
7a	Ira Falgstead (Name incorrect.)	125.00	65.00	40.00
7b	Ira Flagstead (Name correct.)	125.00	65.00	40.00
8	Ty Cobb	4,700	2,350	1,400
9	Oscar Vitt	125.00	65.00	40.00
10	Muddy Ruel	125.00	65.00	40.00
11	Derrill Pratt	125.00	65.00	40.00
12	Ed Gharrity	125.00	65.00	40.00
13	Joe Judge	125.00	65.00	40.00
14	Sam Rice	450.00	225.00	140.00
15	Clyde Milan	125.00	65.00	40.00
16	Joe Sewell	450.00	225.00	140.00
17	Walter Johnson	1,125	575.00	350.00
18	Jack McInnis	125.00	65.00	40.00
19	Tris Speaker	575.00	300.00	160.00
20	Jim Bagby	125.00	65.00	40.00
21	Stanley Coveleskie (Coveleski)	450.00	225.00	140.00
22	Bill Wambsganss	125.00	65.00	40.00
23	Walter Mails	125.00	65.00	40.00
24	Larry Gardner	125.00	65.00	40.00
25	Aaron Ward	125.00	65.00	40.00
26	Miller Huggins	450.00	225.00	140.00
27	Wally Schang	125.00	65.00	40.00
28	Tom Rogers	125.00	65.00	40.00
29	Carl Mays	150.00	75.00	45.00
30	Everett Scott	125.00	65.00	40.00
31	Robert Shawkey	125.00	65.00	40.00
32	Waite Hoyt	450.00	225.00	140.00
33	Mike McNally	125.00	65.00	40.00
34	Joe Bush	125.00	65.00	40.00
35	Bob Meusel	125.00	65.00	40.00
36	Elmer Miller	125.00	65.00	40.00
37	Dick Kerr	125.00	65.00	40.00
38	Eddie Collins	450.00	225.00	140.00
39	Kid Gleason	125.00	65.00	40.00
40	Johnny Mostil	125.00	65.00	40.00
41	Bib Falk (Bibb)	125.00	65.00	40.00
42	Clarence Hodge	125.00	65.00	40.00
43	Ray Schalk	450.00	225.00	140.00
44	Amos Strunk	125.00	65.00	40.00
45	Eddie Mulligan	125.00	65.00	40.00
46	Earl Sheely	125.00	65.00	40.00
47	Harry Hooper	450.00	225.00	140.00
48	Urban Faber	450.00	225.00	140.00
49	Babe Ruth	7,500	3,750	2,250
50	Ivy B. Wingo	125.00	65.00	40.00
51	Earle Neale	150.00	75.00	45.00
52	Jake Daubert	125.00	65.00	40.00
53	Ed Roush	450.00	225.00	140.00
54	Eppa J. Rixey	450.00	225.00	140.00
55	Elwood Martin	125.00	65.00	40.00
56	Bill Killifer (Killefer)	125.00	65.00	40.00
57	Charles Hollocher	125.00	65.00	40.00
58	Zeb Terry	125.00	65.00	40.00
59	G.C. Alexander	750.00	375.00	225.00
60	Turner Barber	125.00	65.00	40.00
61	John Rawlings	125.00	65.00	40.00
62	Frank Frisch	450.00	225.00	140.00
63	Pat Shea	125.00	65.00	40.00
64	Dave Bancroft	450.00	225.00	140.00
65	Cecil Causey	125.00	65.00	40.00
66	Frank Snyder	125.00	65.00	40.00
67	Heinie Groh	125.00	65.00	40.00
68	Ross Young (Youngs)	450.00	225.00	140.00
69	Fred Toney	125.00	65.00	40.00
70	Arthur Nehf	125.00	65.00	40.00
71	Earl Smith	125.00	65.00	40.00
72	George Kelly	450.00	225.00	140.00
73	John J. McGraw	450.00	225.00	140.00
74	Phil Douglas	125.00	65.00	40.00
75	Bill Ryan	125.00	65.00	40.00
76	Jess Haines	450.00	225.00	140.00
77	Milt Stock	125.00	65.00	40.00
78	William Doak	125.00	65.00	40.00
79	George Toporcer	125.00	65.00	40.00
80	Wilbur Cooper	125.00	65.00	40.00
81	George Whitted	125.00	65.00	40.00
82	Chas. Grimm	125.00	65.00	40.00
83	Rabbit Maranville	450.00	225.00	140.00
84	Babe Adams	125.00	65.00	40.00
85	Carson Bigbee	125.00	65.00	40.00
86	Max Carey	450.00	225.00	140.00
87	Whitey Glazner	125.00	65.00	40.00
88	George Gibson	125.00	65.00	40.00
89	Bill Southworth	125.00	65.00	40.00
90	Hank Gowdy	125.00	65.00	40.00
91	Walter Holke	125.00	65.00	40.00
92	Joe Oeschger	125.00	65.00	40.00
93	Pete Kilduff	125.00	65.00	40.00
94	Hy Myers	125.00	65.00	40.00
95	Otto Miller	125.00	65.00	40.00
96	Wilbert Robinson	450.00	225.00	140.00
97	Zach Wheat	450.00	225.00	140.00
98	Walter Ruether	125.00	65.00	40.00
99	Curtis Walker	125.00	65.00	40.00
100	Fred Williams	125.00	65.00	40.00
101	Dave Danforth	125.00	65.00	40.00
102	Ed Rounnel (Rommel)	125.00	65.00	40.00
103	Carl Mays	150.00	75.00	45.00
104	Frank Frisch	450.00	225.00	140.00
105	Lou DeVormer	125.00	65.00	40.00
106	Tom Griffith	125.00	65.00	40.00
107	Harry Harper	125.00	65.00	40.00
108a	John Lavan	125.00	65.00	40.00
108b	John J. McGraw	450.00	225.00	140.00
109	Elmer Smith	125.00	65.00	40.00
110	George Dauss	125.00	65.00	40.00
111	Alexander Gaston	125.00	65.00	40.00
112	John Graney	125.00	65.00	40.00
113	Emil Muesel	125.00	65.00	40.00
114	Rogers Hornsby	575.00	300.00	180.00
115	Leslie Nunamaker	125.00	65.00	40.00
116	Steve O'Neill	125.00	65.00	40.00
117	Max Flack	125.00	65.00	40.00
118	Bill Southworth	125.00	65.00	40.00
119	Arthur Nehf	125.00	65.00	40.00
120	Chick Fewster	125.00	65.00	40.00

1928 W502

Issued in 1928, the manner of distribution for this set is unknown. Because some of the cards' backs indicate they were redeemable for prizes, they were most likely issued inside of a package of candy or similar product, or perhaps in an opaque envelope. The black-and-white cards measure about 1-3/8" x 2-1/2" and display the player's name at the bottom in capital letters preceded by a number in parentheses. The backs of the cards read either "One Bagger," "Three Bagger" or "Home Run." The listings here show two cards known to exist for numbers 38 and 40, which do not correspond to those numbers in 1931 W502. This raises the possibility there may have been a similar set issued in 1929 and/or 1930. The set carries the American Card Catalog designation W502.

		NM	EX	VG
	Complete Set (62):	13,500	5,400	2,700
	Common Player:	75.00	30.00	15.00
1	Burleigh Grimes	150.00	60.00	30.00
2	Walter Reuther (Ruether)	75.00	30.00	15.00
3	Joe Dugan	75.00	30.00	15.00
4	Red Faber	150.00	60.00	30.00
5	Gabby Hartnett	150.00	60.00	30.00
6	Babe Ruth	4,500	1,800	900.00
7	Bob Meusel	75.00	30.00	15.00
8	Herb Pennock	150.00	60.00	30.00
9	George Burns (Photo is George J., not George H. Burns.)	75.00	30.00	15.00
10	Joe Sewell	150.00	60.00	30.00
11	George Uhle	75.00	30.00	15.00
12	Bob O'Farrell	75.00	30.00	15.00
13	Rogers Hornsby	200.00	80.00	40.00
14	"Pie" Traynor	150.00	60.00	30.00
15	Clarence Mitchell	75.00	30.00	15.00
16	Eppa Jepha Rixey	150.00	60.00	30.00
17	Carl Mays	90.00	35.00	17.50
18	Adolfo Luque	75.00	30.00	15.00
19	Dave Bancroft	150.00	60.00	30.00
20	George Kelly	150.00	60.00	30.00
21	Earl Combs (Earle)	150.00	60.00	30.00
22	Harry Heilmann	150.00	60.00	30.00
23	Ray W. Schalk	150.00	60.00	30.00
24	Johnny Mostil	75.00	30.00	15.00
25	Hack Wilson (Photo actually Art Wilson.)	150.00	60.00	30.00
26	Lou Gehrig	1,750	700.00	350.00
27	Ty Cobb	1,750	700.00	350.00
28	Tris Speaker	200.00	80.00	40.00
29	Tony Lazzeri	150.00	60.00	30.00
30	Waite Hoyt	150.00	60.00	30.00
31	Sherwood Smith	75.00	30.00	15.00
32	Max Carey	150.00	60.00	30.00
33	Eugene Hargrave	75.00	30.00	15.00
34	Miguel L. Gonzales (Miguel A. Gonzalez)	75.00	30.00	15.00
35	Joe Judge	75.00	30.00	15.00
36	E.C. (Sam) Rice	150.00	60.00	30.00
37	Earl Sheely	75.00	30.00	15.00
38a	Sam Jones	75.00	30.00	15.00
38b	Emory E. Rigney	75.00	30.00	15.00
39	Bib A. Falk (Bibb)	75.00	30.00	15.00
40a	Nick Altrock	75.00	30.00	15.00
40b	Willie Kamm	75.00	30.00	15.00
41	Stanley Harris	150.00	60.00	30.00
42	John J. McGraw	150.00	60.00	30.00
43	Artie Nehf	75.00	30.00	15.00
44	Grover Alexander	250.00	100.00	50.00
45	Paul Waner	150.00	60.00	30.00
46	William H. Terry	150.00	60.00	30.00
47	Glenn Wright	75.00	30.00	15.00
48	Earl Smith	75.00	30.00	15.00
49	Leon (Goose) Goslin	150.00	60.00	30.00
50	Frank Frisch	150.00	60.00	30.00
51	Joe Harris	75.00	30.00	15.00
52	Fred (Cy) Williams	75.00	30.00	15.00
53	Eddie Roush	150.00	60.00	30.00
54	George Sisler	150.00	60.00	30.00
55	Ed Rommel	75.00	30.00	15.00
56	Rogers Peckinpaugh (Roger)	75.00	30.00	15.00
57	Stanley Coveleskie (Coveleski)	150.00	60.00	30.00
58	Lester Bell	75.00	30.00	15.00
59	Dave Bancroft	150.00	60.00	30.00
60	John P. McInnis	75.00	30.00	15.00

1931 W502

 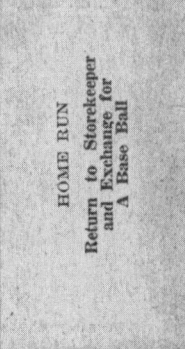

Issued in 1931, the manner of distribution for this set is unknown. Because some of the cards' backs indicate they were redeemable for prizes, they were most likely issued inside of a package of candy or similar product, or perhaps in an opaque envelope. The black-and-white cards measure about 1-3/8" x 2-1/2" and display the player's name at the bottom in capital letters preceded by a number in parentheses. The backs of the cards read either "One Bagger," "Three Bagger" or "Home Run." The set carries the American Card Catalog designation W502.

		NM	EX	VG
	Complete Set (60):	12,500	5,500	2,750
	Common Player:	90.00	35.00	17.50
1	Muddy Ruel	90.00	35.00	17.50
2	John Grabowski	90.00	35.00	17.50
3	Mickey Cochrane	150.00	60.00	30.00
4	Bill Cissell	90.00	35.00	17.50
5	Carl Reynolds	90.00	35.00	17.50
6	Luke Sewell	90.00	35.00	17.50
7	Ted Lyons	150.00	60.00	30.00
8	Harvey Walker	90.00	35.00	17.50
9	Gerald Walker	90.00	35.00	17.50
10	Sam Byrd	90.00	35.00	17.50

		NM	EX	VG
11	Joe Vosmik	90.00	35.00	17.50
12	Dan MacFayden	90.00	35.00	17.50
13	William Dickey	150.00	60.00	30.00
14	Robert Grove	250.00	100.00	50.00
15	Al Simmons	150.00	60.00	30.00
16	Jimmy Foxx	300.00	120.00	60.00
17	Nick Altrock	90.00	35.00	17.50
18	Charlie Grimm	90.00	35.00	17.50
19	Bill Terry	150.00	60.00	30.00
20	Clifton Heathcote	90.00	35.00	17.50
21	Burleigh Grimes	150.00	60.00	30.00
22	Red Faber	150.00	60.00	30.00
23	Gabby Hartnett	150.00	60.00	30.00
24	Earl (Earle) Combs	150.00	60.00	30.00
25	Hack Wilson	150.00	60.00	30.00
26	Stanley Harris	150.00	60.00	30.00
27	John J. McGraw	150.00	60.00	30.00
28	Paul Waner	150.00	60.00	30.00
29	Babe Ruth	4,500	1,800	900.00
30	Herb Pennock	150.00	60.00	30.00
31	Joe Sewell	150.00	60.00	30.00
32	Lou Gehrig	2,000	800.00	400.00
33	Tony Lazzeri	150.00	60.00	30.00
34	Waite Hoyt	150.00	60.00	30.00
35	Glenn Wright	90.00	35.00	17.50
36	Leon (Goose) Goslin	150.00	60.00	30.00
37	Frank Frisch	150.00	60.00	30.00
38	George Uhle	90.00	35.00	17.50
39	Bob O'Farrell	90.00	35.00	17.50
40	Rogers Hornsby	200.00	80.00	40.00
41	"Pie" Traynor	150.00	60.00	30.00
42	Clarence Mitchell	90.00	35.00	17.50
43	Sherwood Smith	90.00	35.00	17.50
44	Miguel A. Gonzalez	90.00	35.00	17.50
45	Joe Judge	90.00	35.00	17.50
46	Eppa Rixey	150.00	60.00	30.00
47	Adolfo Luque	90.00	35.00	17.50
48	E.C. (Sam) Rice	150.00	60.00	30.00
49	Earl Sheely	90.00	35.00	17.50
50	Sam Jones	90.00	35.00	17.50
51	Bib A. Falk	90.00	35.00	17.50
52	Willie Kamm	90.00	35.00	17.50
53	Roger Peckinpaugh	90.00	35.00	17.50
54	Lester Bell	90.00	35.00	17.50
55	L. Waner	150.00	60.00	30.00
56	Eugene Hargrave	90.00	35.00	17.50
57	Harry Heilmann	150.00	60.00	30.00
58	Earl Smith	90.00	35.00	17.50
59	Dave Bancroft	150.00	60.00	30.00
60	George Kelly	150.00	60.00	30.00

1922 W503

Issued circa 1923, this 64-card set of blank-backed cards, measuring 1-3/4" x 2-3/4", feature black and white player photos surrounded by a white border. The player's name and team appear on the card, along with a card number in either the left or right bottom corner. There is no indication of the set's producer, although it is believed the cards were issued with candy or gum. The set carries a W503 American Card Catalog designation.

		NM	EX	VG
	Complete Set (64):	40,000	16,000	8,000
	Common Player:	350.00	140.00	70.00
1	Joe Bush	350.00	140.00	70.00
2	Wally Schang	350.00	140.00	70.00
3	Dave Robertson	350.00	140.00	70.00
4	Wally Pipp	375.00	150.00	75.00
5	Bill Ryan	350.00	140.00	70.00
6	George Kelly	900.00	360.00	180.00
7	Frank Snyder	350.00	140.00	70.00
8	Jimmy O'Connell	350.00	140.00	70.00
9	Bill Cunningham	350.00	140.00	70.00
10	Norman McMillan	350.00	140.00	70.00
11	Waite Hoyt	900.00	360.00	180.00
12	Art Nehf	350.00	140.00	70.00
13	George Sisler	900.00	360.00	180.00
14	Al DeVormer	350.00	140.00	70.00
15	Casey Stengel	900.00	360.00	180.00
16	Ken Williams	350.00	140.00	70.00
17	Joe Dugan	350.00	140.00	70.00
18	"Irish" Meusel	350.00	140.00	70.00
19	Bob Meusel	350.00	140.00	70.00
20	Carl Mays	375.00	150.00	75.00
21	Frank Frisch	900.00	360.00	180.00
22	Jess Barnes	350.00	140.00	70.00
23	Walter Johnson	1,500	600.00	300.00
24	Claude Jonnard	350.00	140.00	70.00
25	Dave Bancroft	900.00	360.00	180.00
26	Johnny Rawlings	350.00	140.00	70.00

		NM	EX	VG
27	"Pep" Young	350.00	140.00	70.00
28	Earl Smith	350.00	140.00	70.00
29	Willie Kamm	350.00	140.00	70.00
30	Art Fletcher	350.00	140.00	70.00
31	"Kid" Gleason	350.00	140.00	70.00
32	"Babe" Ruth	12,000	4,800	2,400
33	Guy Morton	350.00	140.00	70.00
34	Heinie Groh	350.00	140.00	70.00
35	Leon Cadore	350.00	140.00	70.00
36	Joe Tobin	350.00	140.00	70.00
37	"Rube" Marquard	900.00	360.00	180.00
38	Grover Alexander	1,200	480.00	240.00
39	George Burns	350.00	140.00	70.00
40	Joe Oeschger	350.00	140.00	70.00
41	"Chick" Shorten	350.00	140.00	70.00
42	Roger Hornsby (Rogers)	1,100	440.00	220.00
43	Adolfo Luque	350.00	140.00	70.00
44	Zack Wheat	900.00	360.00	180.00
45	Herb Pruett (Hub)	350.00	140.00	70.00
46	Rabbit Maranville	900.00	360.00	180.00
47	Jimmy Ring	350.00	140.00	70.00
48	Sherrod Smith	350.00	140.00	70.00
49	Lea Meadows (Lee)	350.00	140.00	70.00
50	Aaron Ward	350.00	140.00	70.00
51	Herb Pennock	900.00	360.00	180.00
52	Carlson Bigbee (Carson)	350.00	140.00	70.00
53	Max Carey	900.00	360.00	180.00
54	Charles Robertson	350.00	140.00	70.00
55	Urban Shocker	350.00	140.00	70.00
56	Dutch Ruether	350.00	140.00	70.00
57	Jake Daubert	350.00	140.00	70.00
58	Louis Guisto	350.00	140.00	70.00
59	Ivy Wingo	350.00	140.00	70.00
60	Bill Pertica	350.00	140.00	70.00
61	Luke Sewell	350.00	140.00	70.00
62	Hank Gowdy	350.00	140.00	70.00
63	Jack Scott	350.00	140.00	70.00
64	Stan Coveleskie (Coveleski)	900.00	360.00	180.00

1926 W511

1. BABE RUTH

Ruth is the only baseball player known in this set of athletic, cinematic and historical subjects. The approximately 1-1/2" x 2-1/2" black-and-white, blue-and-white, or maroon-and-white blank-backed card identifies the player, position and team typographically within the photo and has the card number and name in the bottom border. The card has been seen with numbers 1, 52 and 71, as well as unnumbered.

		NM	EX	VG
1	Babe Ruth (Black-and-white.)	800.00	400.00	240.00
52	Babe Ruth (Blue duotone.)	800.00	400.00	240.00
71	Babe Ruth (Blue duotone.)	800.00	400.00	240.00
71	Babe Ruth (Maroon duotone.)	800.00	400.00	240.00
---	Babe Ruth (Unnumbered, maroon.)	1,100	550.00	330.00

1926-27 W512

3   "TY" COBB
Ex-Mgr. Detroit A.L.

One of the many "strip card" sets of the period, the W512 set was initially issued in 1926 and includes 10 baseball players among its 50 cards. Also featured are boxers, golfers, tennis players, aviators, movie stars and other celebrities. The 1-3/8" x 2-1/4" cards feature crude color drawings of the subjects with their names below. A card number appears in the lower-left corner. Baseball players lead off the set and are numbered from 1 to 10. Like most strip cards, they have blank backs. At least four of the baseball player cards have been found in a second type,

on which the team name is presented in a typewriter style font on the second line; these changes reflect player status as of 1927. Reprints of Ruth, Cobb, Johnson and Speaker are known.

		NM	EX	VG
	Common Player:	70.00	35.00	20.00
1	Dave Bancroft	100.00	50.00	20.00
2a	Grover Alexander (Cubs)	240.00	120.00	70.00
2b	Grover Alexander (Cardinals)	120.00	60.00	35.00
3a	"Ty" Cobb	400.00	200.00	125.00
3b	"Ty" Cobb (Ex-Mgr. Detroit A.L.)	450.00	225.00	140.00
4a	Tris Speaker	120.00	60.00	35.00
4b	Tris Speaker (Ex-Mgr. Cleveland A.L.)	120.00	60.00	35.00
5	Glen Wright (Glenn)	125.00	65.00	40.00
6	"Babe" Ruth	450.00	225.00	140.00
7a	Everett Scott (Yankees)	100.00	50.00	30.00
7b	Everett Scott (White Sox)	125.00	65.00	40.00
8a	Frank Frisch (Giants)	100.00	50.00	30.00
8b	Frank Frisch (Cardinals)	100.00	50.00	30.00
9a	Rogers Hornsby (Cardinals)	120.00	60.00	35.00
9b	Rogers Hornsby (Giants)	120.00	60.00	35.00
10	Dazzy Vance	100.00	50.00	30.00

1928 W513

69   Rube Benton
Giants Pitcher
New York National

This "strip card" set, issued in 1928 was actually a continuation of the W512 set issued two years earlier and is numbered starting with number 61 where the W512 set ended. The blank-backed cards measure 1-3/8" x 2-1/4" and display color drawings of the athletes, which include 14 boxers and the 26 baseball players listed here. The cards are numbered in the lower-left corner.

		NM	EX	VG
	Complete (Baseball) Set (26):	2,000	1,000	600.00
	Common Player:	65.00	35.00	20.00
61	Eddie Roush	100.00	50.00	30.00
62	Waite Hoyt	100.00	50.00	30.00
63	"Gink" Hendrick	65.00	35.00	20.00
64	"Jumbo" Elliott	65.00	35.00	20.00
65	John Miljus	65.00	35.00	20.00
66	Jumping Joe Dugan	65.00	35.00	20.00
67	Smiling Bill Terry	100.00	50.00	30.00
68	Herb Pennock	100.00	50.00	30.00
69	Rube Benton	65.00	35.00	20.00
70	Paul Waner	100.00	50.00	30.00
71	Adolfo Luque	65.00	35.00	20.00
72	Burleigh Grimes	100.00	50.00	30.00
73	Lloyd Waner	100.00	50.00	30.00
74	Hack Wilson	100.00	50.00	30.00
75	Hal Carlson	65.00	35.00	20.00
76	L. Grantham	65.00	35.00	20.00
77	Wilcey Moore (Wilcy)	65.00	35.00	20.00
78	Jess Haines	100.00	50.00	30.00
79	Tony Lazzeri	100.00	50.00	30.00
80	Al DeVormer	65.00	35.00	20.00
81	Joe Harris	65.00	35.00	20.00
82	Pie Traynor	100.00	50.00	30.00
83	Mark Koenig	65.00	35.00	20.00
84	Babe Herman	75.00	40.00	25.00
85	George Harper	65.00	35.00	20.00
86	Earl Coombs (Earle Combs)	100.00	50.00	30.00

1920-21 W514

LEFTY WILLIAMS
PITCHER
CHICAGO "WHITE SOX" A.L.

Consisting of 120 cards, the W514 set is the largest of the various "strip card" issues of its era. Issued between 1920-

1921, it is also one of the earliest and most widely-collected. The 1-3/8" x 2-1/2" cards feature color drawings of the players and display the card number in the lower-left corner. The player's name, position and team appear in the bottom border of the blank-backed cards. The set holds special interest for baseball historians because it includes seven of the eight Chicago "Black Sox" who were banned from baseball for their alleged role in throwing the 1919 World Series. The most famous of them, "Shoeless" Joe Jackson, makes his only strip card appearance in this set.

		NM	EX	VG
	Complete Set (124):	37,500	19,000	11,000
	Common Player:	100.00	50.00	30.00
1	Ira Flagstead	100.00	50.00	30.00
2	Babe Ruth	2,400	1,200	750.00
	(HOME RUN KING)			
3	Happy Felsch	1,500	750.00	450.00
4	Doc Lavan	100.00	50.00	30.00
5	Phil Douglas	100.00	50.00	30.00
6	Earle Neale	100.00	50.00	30.00
7	Leslie Nunamaker	100.00	50.00	30.00
8	Sam Jones	100.00	50.00	30.00
9	Claude Hendrix	100.00	50.00	30.00
10	Frank Schulte	100.00	50.00	30.00
11	Cactus Cravath	100.00	50.00	30.00
12	Pat Moran	100.00	50.00	30.00
13	Dick Rudolph	100.00	50.00	30.00
14	Arthur Fletcher	100.00	50.00	30.00
15	Joe Jackson	6,250	3,100	1,900
16	Bill Southworth	100.00	50.00	30.00
17	Ad Luque	100.00	50.00	30.00
18	Charlie Deal	100.00	50.00	30.00
19	Al Mamaux	100.00	50.00	30.00
20	Stuffy McInness (McInnis)	100.00	50.00	30.00
21a	Rabbit Maranville (Braves)	250.00	125.00	75.00
21b	Rabbit Maranville (Pirates)	250.00	125.00	75.00
22	Max Carey	250.00	125.00	75.00
23	Dick Kerr	100.00	50.00	30.00
24	George Burns	100.00	50.00	30.00
25	Eddie Collins	250.00	125.00	75.00
26	Steve O'Neil (O'Neill)	100.00	50.00	30.00
27	Bill Fisher	100.00	50.00	30.00
28	Rube Bressler	100.00	50.00	30.00
29	Bob Shawkey	100.00	50.00	30.00
30	Donie Bush	100.00	50.00	30.00
31	Chick Gandil	900.00	450.00	250.00
32	Ollie Zeider	100.00	50.00	30.00
33	Vean Gregg	100.00	50.00	30.00
34	Miller Huggins	250.00	125.00	75.00
35	Lefty Williams	1,000	500.00	300.00
36	Tub Spencer	100.00	50.00	30.00
37	Lew McCarty	100.00	50.00	30.00
38	Hod Eller	100.00	50.00	30.00
39	Joe Gedeon	100.00	50.00	30.00
40a	Dave Bancroft (Quakers)	250.00	125.00	75.00
40b	Dave Bancroft (Giants)	250.00	125.00	75.00
41	Clark Griffith	250.00	125.00	75.00
42	Wilbur Cooper	100.00	50.00	30.00
43	Ty Cobb	2,200	1,100	700.00
44	Roger Peckinpaugh	100.00	50.00	30.00
45	Nic Carter (Nick)	100.00	50.00	30.00
46	Heinie Groh	100.00	50.00	30.00
47a	Bob Roth (Indians)	100.00	50.00	30.00
47b	Bob Roth (Yankees)	100.00	50.00	30.00
48	Frank Davis	100.00	50.00	30.00
49	Leslie Mann	100.00	50.00	30.00
50	Fielder Jones	100.00	50.00	30.00
51	Bill Doak	100.00	50.00	30.00
52	John J. McGraw	250.00	125.00	75.00
53	Charles Hollocher	100.00	50.00	30.00
54	Babe Adams	100.00	50.00	30.00
55	Dode Paskert	100.00	50.00	30.00
56	Roger Hornsby (Rogers)	320.00	160.00	90.00
57	Max Rath	100.00	50.00	30.00
58	Jeff Pfeffer	100.00	50.00	30.00
59	Nick Cullop	100.00	50.00	30.00
60	Ray Schalk	250.00	125.00	75.00
61	Bill Jacobson	100.00	50.00	30.00
62	Nap Lajoie	280.00	140.00	80.00
63	George Gibson	100.00	50.00	30.00
64	Harry Hooper	250.00	125.00	75.00
65	Grover Alexander	375.00	190.00	120.00
66	Ping Bodie	100.00	50.00	30.00
67	Hank Gowdy	100.00	50.00	30.00
68	Jake Daubert	100.00	50.00	30.00
69	Red Faber	250.00	125.00	75.00
70	Ivan Olson	100.00	50.00	30.00
71	Pickles Dilhoefer	100.00	50.00	30.00
72	Christy Mathewson	1,100	550.00	325.00
73	Ira Wingo (Ivy)	100.00	50.00	30.00
74	Fred Merkle	100.00	50.00	30.00
75	Frank Baker	250.00	125.00	75.00
76	Bert Gallia	100.00	50.00	30.00
77	Milton Watson	100.00	50.00	30.00
78	Bert Shotten (Shotton)	100.00	50.00	30.00
79	Sam Rice	250.00	125.00	75.00
80	Dan Greiner	100.00	50.00	30.00
81	Larry Doyle	100.00	50.00	30.00
82	Eddie Cicotte	950.00	475.00	250.00
83	Hugo Bezdek	100.00	50.00	30.00
84	Wally Pipp	120.00	60.00	40.00
85	Eddie Rousch (Roush)	250.00	125.00	75.00
86	Slim Sallee	100.00	50.00	30.00
87	Bill Killifer (Killefer)	100.00	50.00	30.00
88	Bob Veach	100.00	50.00	30.00
89	Jim Burke	100.00	50.00	30.00
90	Everett Scott	100.00	50.00	30.00
91	Buck Weaver	1,400	700.00	420.00
92	George Whitted	100.00	50.00	30.00
93	Ed Konetchy	100.00	50.00	30.00
94	Walter Johnson	750.00	375.00	200.00
95	Sam Crawford	250.00	125.00	75.00
96	Fred Mitchell	100.00	50.00	30.00
97	Ira Thomas	100.00	50.00	30.00
98	Jimmy Ring	100.00	50.00	30.00
99	Wally Shange (Schang)	100.00	50.00	30.00
100	Benny Kauff	100.00	50.00	30.00
101	George Sisler	250.00	125.00	75.00
102	Tris Speaker	320.00	160.00	100.00
103	Carl Mays	120.00	60.00	40.00
104	Buck Herzog	100.00	50.00	30.00
105	Swede Risberg	3,500	1,750	1,100
106a	Hugh Jennings (Tigers)	250.00	125.00	75.00
106b	Hughie Jennings (Giants)	250.00	125.00	75.00
107	Pep Young	100.00	50.00	30.00
108	Walter Reuther (Ruether)	100.00	50.00	30.00
109	Joe Gharrity (Ed)	100.00	50.00	30.00
110	Zach Wheat	250.00	125.00	75.00
111	Jim Vaughn	100.00	50.00	30.00
112	Kid Gleason	100.00	50.00	30.00
113	Casey Stengel	250.00	125.00	75.00
114	Hal Chase	200.00	100.00	60.00
115	Oscar Stange (Stanage)	100.00	50.00	30.00
116	Larry Shean	100.00	50.00	30.00
117	Steve Pendergast	100.00	50.00	30.00
118	Larry Kopf	100.00	50.00	30.00
119	Charles (George) Whiteman	100.00	50.00	30.00
120	Jess Barnes	100.00	50.00	30.00

1923 W515-1

11. GEORGE SISLER
First Base
St. Louis Browns, A. L.

Cards in the 60-card "strip set" measure about 1-3/8" x 2-1/4" and feature color drawings. Backs are blank. The card number along with the player's name, position and team appear in the bottom border. Most cards also display a "U&U" copyright line, indicating that the photos on which the drawings were based were provided by Underwood & Underwood, a major news photo service of the day. The set has a heavy emphasis on New York players with 39 of the 60 cards depicting members of the Yankees, Dodgers or Giants. Babe Ruth appears on two cards and two other cards picture two players each.

		NM	EX	VG
	Complete Set (60):	8,000	3,200	1,600
	Common Player:	50.00	20.00	10.00
1	Bill Cunningham	50.00	20.00	10.00
2	Al Mamaux	50.00	20.00	10.00
3	"Babe" Ruth	1,600	650.00	325.00
4	Dave Bancroft	100.00	40.00	20.00
5	Ed Rommel	50.00	20.00	10.00
6	"Babe" Adams	50.00	20.00	10.00
7	Clarence Walker	50.00	20.00	10.00
8	Waite Hoyt	100.00	40.00	20.00
9	Bob Shawkey	50.00	20.00	10.00
10	"Ty" Cobb	750.00	300.00	150.00
11	George Sisler	100.00	40.00	20.00
12	Jack Bentley	50.00	20.00	10.00
13	Jim O'Connell	50.00	20.00	10.00
14	Frank Frisch	100.00	40.00	20.00
15	Frank Baker	100.00	40.00	20.00
16	Burleigh Grimes	100.00	40.00	20.00
17	Wally Schang	50.00	20.00	10.00
18	Harry Heilman (Heilmann)	100.00	40.00	20.00
19	Aaron Ward	50.00	20.00	10.00
20	Carl Mays	60.00	24.00	12.00
21	The Meusel Bros.	60.00	24.00	12.00
	(Bob Meusel, Irish Meusel)			
22	Arthur Nehf	50.00	20.00	10.00
23	Lee Meadows	50.00	20.00	10.00
24	"Casey" Stengel	100.00	40.00	20.00
25	Jack Scott	50.00	20.00	10.00
26	Kenneth Williams	50.00	20.00	10.00
27	Joe Bush	50.00	20.00	10.00
28	Tris Speaker	150.00	60.00	30.00
29	Ross Young (Youngs)	100.00	40.00	20.00
30	Joe Dugan	50.00	20.00	10.00
31	The Barnes Bros. (Jesse Barnes, Virgil Barnes)	60.00	24.00	12.00
32	George Kelly	100.00	40.00	20.00
33	Hugh McQuillen (McQuillan)	50.00	20.00	10.00
34	Hugh Jennings	100.00	40.00	20.00
35	Tom Griffith	50.00	20.00	10.00
36	Miller Huggins	100.00	40.00	20.00
37	"Whitey" Witt	50.00	20.00	10.00
38	Walter Johnson	400.00	160.00	80.00
39	"Wally" Pipp	50.00	20.00	10.00
40	"Dutch" Reuther (Ruether)	50.00	20.00	10.00
41	Jim Johnston	50.00	20.00	10.00
42	Willie Kamm	50.00	20.00	10.00
43	Sam Jones	50.00	20.00	10.00
44	Frank Snyder	50.00	20.00	10.00
45	John McGraw	100.00	40.00	20.00
46	Everett Scott	50.00	20.00	10.00
47	"Babe" Ruth	1,600	650.00	325.00
48	Urban Shocker	50.00	20.00	10.00
49	Grover Alexander	150.00	60.00	30.00
50	"Rabbit" Maranville	100.00	40.00	20.00

1923 W515-2

THE LITTLE

A near duplicate of the W515-1 set in every respect except size, the W515-2 strip cards are larger in format, at about 1-1/2" x 2-1/2". Placement of the U&U copyright also differs between some players' cards in each set. Cards may be found with letters in the top border from the title, "THE LITTLE WONDER PICTURE SERIES."

		NM	EX	VG
	Complete Set (60):	8,000	3,200	1,600
	Common Player:	50.00	25.00	15.00
1	Bill Cunningham	50.00	25.00	15.00
2	Al Mamaux	50.00	25.00	15.00
3	"Babe" Ruth	1,600	800.00	480.00
4	Dave Bancroft	100.00	50.00	30.00
5	Ed Rommel	50.00	25.00	15.00
6	"Babe" Adams	50.00	25.00	15.00
7	Clarence Walker	50.00	25.00	15.00
8	Waite Hoyt	100.00	50.00	30.00
9	Bob Shawkey	50.00	25.00	15.00
10	"Ty" Cobb	750.00	375.00	225.00
11	George Sisler	100.00	50.00	30.00
12	Jack Bentley	50.00	25.00	15.00
13	Jim O'Connell	50.00	25.00	15.00
14	Frank Frisch	100.00	50.00	30.00
15	Frank Baker	100.00	50.00	30.00
16	Burleigh Grimes	100.00	50.00	30.00
17	Wally Schang	50.00	25.00	15.00
18	Harry Heilman (Heilmann)	100.00	50.00	30.00
19	Aaron Ward	50.00	25.00	15.00
20	Carl Mays	60.00	30.00	18.00
21	The Meusel Bros.	60.00	30.00	18.00
	(Bob Meusel, Irish Meusel)			
22	Arthur Nehf	50.00	25.00	15.00
23	Lee Meadows	50.00	25.00	15.00
24	"Casey" Stengel	100.00	50.00	30.00
25	Jack Scott	50.00	25.00	15.00
26	Kenneth Williams	50.00	25.00	15.00
27	Joe Bush	50.00	25.00	15.00
28	Tris Speaker	150.00	75.00	45.00
29	Ross Young (Youngs)	100.00	50.00	30.00
30	Joe Dugan	50.00	25.00	15.00
31	The Barnes Bros.	60.00	30.00	18.00
	(Jesse Barnes, Virgil Barnes)			
32	George Kelly	100.00	50.00	30.00
33	Hugh McQuillen (McQuillan)	50.00	25.00	15.00
34	Hugh Jennings	100.00	50.00	30.00
35	Tom Griffith	50.00	25.00	15.00
36	Miller Huggins	100.00	50.00	30.00
37	"Whitey" Witt	50.00	25.00	15.00
38	Walter Johnson	400.00	200.00	120.00
39	"Wally" Pipp	50.00	25.00	15.00
40	"Dutch" Reuther (Ruether)	50.00	25.00	15.00
41	Jim Johnston	50.00	25.00	15.00
42	Willie Kamm	50.00	25.00	15.00
43	Sam Jones	50.00	25.00	15.00
44	Frank Snyder	50.00	25.00	15.00
45	John McGraw	100.00	50.00	30.00
46	Everett Scott	50.00	25.00	15.00
47	"Babe" Ruth	1,600	800.00	480.00
48	Urban Shocker	50.00	25.00	15.00
49	Grover Alexander	150.00	75.00	45.00
50	"Rabbit" Maranville	100.00	50.00	30.00
51	Ray Schalk	100.00	50.00	30.00
52	"Heinie" Groh	50.00	25.00	15.00
53	Wilbert Robinson	100.00	50.00	30.00
54	George Burns	50.00	25.00	15.00
55	Rogers Hornsby	150.00	75.00	45.00
56	Zack Wheat	100.00	50.00	30.00
57	Eddie Roush	100.00	50.00	30.00
58	Eddie Collins	100.00	50.00	30.00
59	Charlie Hollocher	50.00	25.00	15.00
60	Red Faber	100.00	50.00	30.00

The bottom section of W515-1 column:

51	Ray Schalk	100.00	40.00	20.00
52	"Heinie" Groh	50.00	20.00	10.00
53	Wilbert Robinson	100.00	40.00	20.00
54	George Burns	50.00	20.00	10.00
55	Rogers Hornsby	150.00	60.00	30.00
56	Zack Wheat	100.00	40.00	20.00
57	Eddie Roush	100.00	40.00	20.00
58	Eddie Collins	100.00	40.00	20.00
59	Charlie Hollocher	50.00	20.00	10.00
60	Red Faber	100.00	40.00	20.00

1920 W516-1

This "strip card" set consists of 30 cards featuring colored drawings - either portraits or full-length action poses. The blank-backed cards measure 1-1/2" x 2-1/2". The player's

LARRY DOYLE 13
2ND B. GIANTS

name, position and team appear beneath the picture in hand-printed style. To the right of the name is the card number. The set can be identified by an "IFS" or "IFC" copyright symbol, . representing International Feature Service/Company. Some cards can be found with part of a line of type at top that reads, "UNIVERSAL BASE BALL MATCHING CARDS."

		NM	EX	VG
Complete Set (30):		5,250	2,000	1,000
Common Player:		50.00	25.00	10.00
1	Babe Ruth	2,000	800.00	400.00
2	Heinie Groh	50.00	25.00	10.00
3	Ping Bodie	50.00	25.00	10.00
4	Ray Shalk (Schalk)	100.00	40.00	20.00
5	Tris Speaker	150.00	60.00	30.00
6	Ty Cobb	750.00	300.00	150.00
7	Roger Hornsby (Rogers)	150.00	60.00	30.00
8	Walter Johnson	300.00	120.00	60.00
9	Grover Alexander	150.00	60.00	30.00
10	George Burns	50.00	25.00	10.00
11	Jimmy Ring	50.00	25.00	10.00
12	Jess Barnes	50.00	25.00	10.00
13	Larry Doyle	50.00	25.00	10.00
14	Arty Fletcher	50.00	25.00	10.00
15	Dick Rudolph	50.00	25.00	10.00
16	Benny Kauf (Kauff)	50.00	25.00	10.00
17	Art Nehf	50.00	25.00	10.00
18	Babe Adams	50.00	25.00	10.00
19	Will Cooper	50.00	25.00	10.00
20	R. Peckinpaugh	50.00	25.00	10.00
21	Eddie Cicotte	100.00	40.00	20.00
22	Hank Gowdy	50.00	25.00	10.00
23	Eddie Collins	100.00	40.00	20.00
24	Christy Mathewson	400.00	160.00	80.00
25	Clyde Milan	50.00	25.00	10.00
26	M. Kelley (Should be G. Kelly.)	100.00	40.00	20.00
27	Ed Hooper (Harry)	100.00	40.00	20.00
28	Pep. Young	50.00	25.00	10.00
29	Eddie Rousch (Roush)	100.00	40.00	20.00
30	Geo. Bancroft (Dave)	100.00	40.00	20.00

1920 W516-1-2

TY COBB. 6
DETROIT OUTFIELD

This set is a re-issue of the W516-1-1 set, with several changes: The pictures are reverse images of W516-1-1, and are printed only in black, red and yellow. Well cut, the blank-back cards measure a nominal 1-1/2" x 2-3/8". The cards display a backwards "IFC" copyright symbol.

		NM	EX	VG
Complete Set (30):		5,250	2,000	1,000
Common Player:		50.00	25.00	10.00
1	Babe Ruth	2,000	1,000	600.00
2	Heinie Groh	50.00	25.00	10.00
3	Ping Bodie	50.00	25.00	10.00
4	Ray Shalk (Schalk)	100.00	40.00	20.00
5	Tris Speaker	150.00	60.00	30.00
6	Ty Cobb	750.00	300.00	150.00
7	Roger Hornsby (Rogers)	150.00	75.00	45.00
8	Walter Johnson	300.00	150.00	90.00
9	Grover Alexander	150.00	60.00	30.00
10	George Burns	50.00	25.00	10.00
11	Jimmy Ring	50.00	25.00	10.00

12	Jess Barnes	50.00	25.00	10.00
13	Larry Doyle	50.00	25.00	10.00
14	Arty Fletcher	50.00	25.00	10.00
15	Dick Rudolph	50.00	25.00	10.00
16	Benny Kauf (Kauff)	50.00	25.00	10.00
17	Art Nehf	50.00	25.00	10.00
18	Babe Adams	50.00	25.00	10.00
19	Will Cooper	50.00	25.00	10.00
20	R. Peckinpaugh	50.00	25.00	10.00
21	Eddie Cicotte	100.00	50.00	30.00
22	Hank Gowdy	50.00	25.00	10.00
23	Eddie Collins	100.00	40.00	20.00
24	Christy Mathewson	400.00	200.00	120.00
25	Clyde Milan	50.00	25.00	10.00
26	M. Kelley (Should be G. Kelly.)	100.00	40.00	20.00
27	Ed Hooper (Harry)	100.00	40.00	20.00
28	Pep. Young	50.00	25.00	10.00
29	Eddie Rousch (Roush)	100.00	40.00	20.00
30	Geo. Bancroft (Dave)	100.00	40.00	20.00

1921 W516-2-1

8 PING BODIE Outfielder 9 HEINIE GROH Third Base 10 BABE RUTH Outfielder

This set is essentially a re-issue of the W516-1 set, with several changes: The pictures are reverse images of W516-1, and are printed only in red and blue. Cards have been renumbered and have player identification in typeset serifed style. The blank-backed cards measure about 1-1/2" x 2-3/8". The cards display a backwards "IFC" copyright symbol.

		NM	EX	VG
Complete Set (30):		4,500	1,800	900.00
Common Player:		50.00	25.00	10.00
1	George Burns	50.00	25.00	10.00
2	Grover Alexander	150.00	60.00	30.00
3	Walter Johnson	250.00	100.00	50.00
4	Roger Hornsby (Rogers)	125.00	50.00	25.00
5	Ty Cobb	750.00	300.00	150.00
6	Tris Speaker	125.00	50.00	25.00
7	Ray Shalk (Schalk)	75.00	30.00	15.00
8	Ping Bodie	50.00	25.00	10.00
9	Heinie Groh	50.00	25.00	10.00
10	Babe Ruth	1,500	600.00	300.00
11	R. Peckinpaugh	50.00	25.00	10.00
12	Will. Cooper	50.00	25.00	10.00
13	Babe Adams	50.00	25.00	10.00
14	Art Nehf	50.00	25.00	10.00
15	Benny Kauf (Kauff)	50.00	25.00	10.00
16	Dick Rudolph	50.00	25.00	10.00
17	Arty. Fletcher	50.00	25.00	10.00
18	Larry Doyle	50.00	25.00	10.00
19	Jess Barnes	50.00	25.00	10.00
20	Jimmy Ring	50.00	25.00	10.00
21	George Bancroft (Dave)	75.00	30.00	15.00
22	Eddie Rousch (Roush)	75.00	30.00	15.00
23	Pep Young	50.00	25.00	10.00
24	Ed Hooper (Harry)	75.00	30.00	15.00
25	M. Kelley (Should be G. Kelly.)	75.00	30.00	15.00
26	Clyde Milan	50.00	25.00	10.00
27	Christy Mathewson	350.00	140.00	70.00
28	Eddie Collins	75.00	30.00	15.00
29	Hank Gowdy	50.00	25.00	10.00
30	Eddie Cicotte	125.00	50.00	25.00

1921 W516-2-2

BABE RUTH 10
YANKS PITCHER

This set is yet another variation in the W516 "family." In numbering it parallels W516-2-1, though the typography is in the same sans-serif font as W516-1. Like W516-2-1, the player pictures have been reversed. Well cut, the blank-backed cards measure a nominal 1-1/2" x 2-1/4". The cards display a backwards "IFC" copyright symbol in the picture portion.

		NM	EX	VG
Complete Set (30):		5,000	2,500	1,500
Common Player:		50.00	25.00	10.00

1	George Burns	50.00	25.00	10.00
2	Grover Alexander	150.00	75.00	45.00
3	Walter Johnson	300.00	150.00	90.00
4	Roger Hornsby (Rogers)	125.00	62.00	37.00
5	Ty Cobb	750.00	375.00	225.00
6	Tris Speaker	125.00	62.00	37.00
7	Ray Shalk (Schalk)	75.00	37.50	22.50
8	Ping Bodie	50.00	25.00	10.00
9	Heinie Groh	50.00	25.00	10.00
10	Babe Ruth	2,000	1,000	600.00
11	R. Peckinpaugh	50.00	25.00	10.00
12	Will. Cooper	50.00	25.00	10.00
13	Babe Adams	50.00	25.00	10.00
14	Art Nehf	50.00	25.00	10.00
15	Benny Kauf (Kauff)	50.00	25.00	10.00
16	Dick Rudolph	50.00	25.00	10.00
17	Arty. Fletcher	50.00	25.00	10.00
18	Larry Doyle	50.00	25.00	10.00
19	Jess Barnes	50.00	25.00	10.00
20	Jimmy Ring	50.00	25.00	10.00
21	George Bancroft (Dave)	75.00	37.50	22.50
22	Eddie Rousch (Roush)	75.00	37.50	22.50
23	Pep Young	50.00	25.00	10.00
24	Ed Hooper (Harry)	75.00	37.50	22.50
25	M. Kelley (Should be G. Kelly.)	75.00	37.50	22.50
26	Clyde Milan	50.00	25.00	10.00
27	Christy Mathewson	400.00	200.00	120.00
28	Eddie Collins	75.00	37.50	22.50
29	Hank Gowdy	50.00	25.00	10.00
30	Eddie Cicotte	100.00	50.00	30.00

1921 W516-2-3

19 JESS BARNES Pitcher

This issue shares a checklist with W516-2-1, and is likewise printed only in red and blue, with typography in a serifed typeface. Unlike W516-2-1, however, the images on these cards are not reversed, as can easily be ascertained by looking at the copyright symbol and letters.

		NM	EX	VG
Complete Set (30):		5,000	2,500	1,500
Common Player:				
1	George Burns	50.00	25.00	10.00
2	Grover Alexander	150.00	75.00	45.00
3	Walter Johnson	300.00	150.00	90.00
4	Roger Hornsby (Rogers)	125.00	62.00	37.00
5	Ty Cobb	750.00	375.00	225.00
6	Tris Speaker	125.00	62.00	37.00
7	Ray Shalk (Schalk)	75.00	30.00	15.00
8	Ping Bodie	50.00	25.00	10.00
9	Heinie Groh	50.00	25.00	10.00
10	Babe Ruth	2,000	1,000	600.00
11	R. Peckinpaugh	50.00	25.00	10.00
12	Will. Cooper	50.00	25.00	10.00
13	Babe Adams	50.00	25.00	10.00
14	Art Nehf	50.00	25.00	10.00
15	Benny Kauf (Kauff)	50.00	25.00	10.00
16	Dick Rudolph	50.00	25.00	10.00
17	Arty. Fletcher	50.00	25.00	10.00
18	Larry Doyle	50.00	25.00	10.00
19	Jess Barnes	50.00	25.00	10.00
20	Jimmy Ring	50.00	25.00	10.00
21	George Bancroft (Dave)	75.00	30.00	15.00
22	Eddie Rousch (Roush)	75.00	30.00	15.00
23	Pep Young	50.00	25.00	10.00
24	Ed Hooper (Harry)	75.00	30.00	15.00
25	M. Kelley (Should be G. Kelly.)	75.00	30.00	15.00
26	Clyde Milan	50.00	25.00	10.00
27	Christy Mathewson	400.00	200.00	120.00
28	Eddie Collins	75.00	30.00	15.00
29	Hank Gowdy	50.00	25.00	10.00
30	Eddie Cicotte	100.00	50.00	30.00

1931 W517

Ted Lyons

The 54-player W517 set is an issue of 3" x 4" cards generally found in a sepia color, though other colors are known. The cards feature a player photo as well as his name and team. The card number appears in a small circle on the front, while the backs are blank. The set is heavy in stars of the period including two Babe Ruths (#4 and 20). The cards were sold in vertical strips of three cards; some cards are found with baseball plays in a line at top. Complete set prices do not include variations. The set was reprinted in three-card-strip format in 1997, with "W-517" printed in the lower-left corner of the reprints.

		NM	EX	VG
	Complete Set (59):	15,000	7,500	4,400
	Common Player:	100.00	50.00	30.00
1	Earl Combs (Earle)	220.00	120.00	70.00
2	Pie Traynor	220.00	120.00	70.00
3	Eddie Rausch (Roush)	220.00	120.00	70.00
4	Babe Ruth (Throwing)	2,000	1,000	600.00
5a	Chalmer Cissell (Chicago)	100.00	50.00	30.00
5b	Chalmer Cissell (Cleveland)	100.00	50.00	30.00
6	Bill Sherdel	100.00	50.00	30.00
7	Bill Shore	100.00	50.00	30.00
8	Geo. Earnshaw	100.00	50.00	30.00
9	Bucky Harris	220.00	120.00	70.00
10	Charlie Klein	220.00	120.00	70.00
11a	Geo. Kelly (Reds)	100.00	50.00	30.00
11b	Geo. Kelly (Brooklyn)	175.00	90.00	50.00
12	Travis Jackson	220.00	120.00	70.00
13	Willie Kamm	100.00	50.00	30.00
14	Harry Heilman (Heilmann)	220.00	120.00	70.00
15	Grover Alexander	350.00	175.00	100.00
16	Frank Frisch	220.00	120.00	70.00
17	Jack Quinn	100.00	50.00	30.00
18	Cy Williams	100.00	50.00	30.00
19	Kiki Cuyler	220.00	120.00	70.00
20	Babe Ruth (Portrait)	2,400	1,200	750.00
21	Jimmie Foxx	475.00	250.00	150.00
22	Jimmy Dykes	100.00	50.00	30.00
23	Bill Terry	220.00	120.00	70.00
24	Freddy Lindstrom	220.00	120.00	70.00
25	Hughey Critz	100.00	50.00	30.00
26	Pete Donahue	100.00	50.00	30.00
27	Tony Lazzeri	220.00	120.00	70.00
28	Heine Manush (Heinie)	220.00	120.00	70.00
29a	Chick Hafey (Cardinals)	220.00	120.00	70.00
29b	Chick Hafey (Cincinnati)	220.00	120.00	70.00
30	Melvin Ott	275.00	140.00	80.00
31	Bing Miller	100.00	50.00	30.00
32	Geo. Haas	100.00	50.00	30.00
33a	Lefty O'Doul (Phillies)	125.00	65.00	40.00
33b	Lefty O'Doul (Brooklyn)	125.00	65.00	40.00
(34)	Paul Waner (No card number.)	220.00	120.00	70.00
34	Paul Waner (W/card number.)	220.00	120.00	70.00
35	Lou Gehrig	1,200	600.00	450.00
36	Dazzy Vance	220.00	120.00	70.00
37	Mickey Cochrane	220.00	120.00	70.00
38	Rogers Hornsby	300.00	150.00	90.00
39	Lefty Grove	260.00	130.00	80.00
40	Al Simmons	220.00	120.00	70.00
41	Rube Walberg	100.00	50.00	30.00
42	Hack Wilson	220.00	120.00	70.00
43	Art Shires	100.00	50.00	30.00
44	Sammy Hale	100.00	50.00	30.00
45	Ted Lyons	220.00	120.00	70.00
46	Joe Sewell	220.00	120.00	70.00
47	Goose Goslin	220.00	120.00	70.00
48	Lou Fonseca (Lew)	100.00	50.00	30.00
49	Bob Muesel (Meusel)	100.00	50.00	30.00
50	Lu Blue	100.00	50.00	30.00
51	Earl Averill	220.00	120.00	70.00
52	Eddy Collins (Eddie)	220.00	120.00	70.00
53	Joe Judge	100.00	50.00	30.00
54	Mickey Cochrane	220.00	120.00	70.00

1931 W517 Mini

Little is known about these smaller-format (1-3/4" x 2-3/4") versions of the W517 strip cards. They are identical in design to the more common 3" x 4" cards, although some, if not all, do not have the card number-in-circle found on regular W517s. Only 16 players from the larger-size W517 set are known in the mini version; some are seen with color variations.

		NM	EX	VG
	Complete Set (16):	7,250	3,600	2,200
	Common Player:	200.00	100.00	60.00
(1)	Mickey Cochrane	425.00	225.00	125.00
(2)	Eddy Collins (Eddie)	425.00	225.00	125.00
(3)	Hughey Critz	200.00	100.00	60.00
(4)	Pete Donahue	200.00	100.00	60.00
(5)	Lou Gehrig	2,000	1,000	600.00
(6)	Lefty Grove	475.00	240.00	135.00
(7)	Travis Jackson	425.00	225.00	125.00
(8)	Joe Judge	200.00	100.00	60.00
(9)	Willie Kamm	200.00	100.00	60.00
(10)	Geo. Kelly	200.00	100.00	60.00

(11)	Charlie Klein	425.00	225.00	125.00
(12)	Bing Miller	200.00	100.00	60.00
(13)	Lefty O'Doul	325.00	175.00	100.00
(14)	Art Shires	200.00	100.00	60.00
(15)	Dazzy Vance	425.00	225.00	125.00
(16)	Paul Waner	425.00	225.00	125.00

1920 W519 - Numbered 1

4 ERNIE KREUGER

Cards in this 20-card "strip set" measure 1-1/2" x 2-1/2" and feature player drawings set against a brightly colored background. A card number appears in the lower-left corner followed by the player's name, printed in capital letters. The player drawings are all posed portraits, except for Joe Murphy and Ernie Kreuger, who are shown catching. Like all strip cards, the cards were sold in strips and have blank backs. The date of issue may be approximate.

		NM	EX	VG
	Complete Set (20):	5,500	2,200	1,100
	Common Player:	100.00	40.00	20.00
1	Guy Morton	100.00	40.00	20.00
2	Rube Marquard	300.00	120.00	60.00
3	Gabby Cravath (Gavvy)	100.00	40.00	20.00
4	Ernie Krueger	100.00	40.00	20.00
5	Babe Ruth	2,400	960.00	480.00
6	George Sisler	300.00	120.00	60.00
7	Rube Benton	100.00	40.00	20.00
8	Jimmie Johnston	100.00	40.00	20.00
9	Wilbur Robinson (Wilbert)	300.00	120.00	60.00
10	Johnny Griffith	100.00	40.00	20.00
11	Frank Baker	300.00	120.00	60.00
12	Bob Veach	100.00	40.00	20.00
13	Jesse Barnes	100.00	40.00	20.00
14	Leon Cadore	100.00	40.00	20.00
15	Ray Schalk	300.00	120.00	60.00
16	Kid Gleasen (Gleason)	100.00	40.00	20.00
17	Joe Murphy	100.00	40.00	20.00
18	Frank Frisch	300.00	120.00	60.00
19	Eddie Collins	300.00	120.00	60.00
20	Wallie (Wally) Schang	100.00	40.00	20.00

1920 W519 - Numbered 2

20 BABE RUTH

A second type of numbered version of W519 exists on which the style of the card numbers differs as does, apparently, the numbering of the players. On Type 1 cards, the card number to the left of the player name is printed in the same heavy sans-serif style as the name. Type 2 cards have the number in a lighter typewriter-style font. While 10 Type 2 cards are currently confirmed to exist, it is expected the other 10 players from W519 were also issued.

		NM	EX	VG
12	Joe Murphy	100.00	40.00	20.00
12	Bobby Veach	100.00	40.00	20.00
13	Jesse Barnes	100.00	40.00	20.00
13	Frank Frisch	300.00	120.00	60.00
14	Eddie Collins	300.00	120.00	60.00
16	Guy Morton	100.00	40.00	20.00
17	Rube Marquard	300.00	120.00	60.00
19	Ernie Kreuger	100.00	40.00	20.00
20a	Babe Ruth	2,400	960.00	480.00
20b	Wallie Schange (Wally Schang)	100.00	40.00	20.00

1920 W519 - Unnumbered

EDDIE COLLINS

Cards in this 10-card set are identical in design and size (1-1/2" x 2-1/2") to the W519 Numbered set, except the player drawings are all set against a blue background and the cards are not numbered. With the lone exception of Eddie Ciotte, all of the subjects in the unnumbered set also appear in the numbered set.

		NM	EX	VG
	Complete Set (10):	4,000	2,000	1,200
	Common Player:	100.00	50.00	30.00
(1)	Eddie Cicotte	400.00	200.00	120.00
(2)	Eddie Collins	300.00	150.00	90.00
(3)	Gabby Cravath (Gavvy)	100.00	50.00	30.00
(4)	Frank Frisch	300.00	150.00	90.00
(5)	Kid Gleasen (Gleason)	100.00	50.00	30.00
(6)	Ernie Kreuger	100.00	50.00	30.00
(7)	Rube Marquard	300.00	150.00	90.00
(8)	Guy Morton	100.00	50.00	30.00
(9)	Joe Murphy	100.00	50.00	30.00
(10)	Babe Ruth	2,200	1,100	650.00

1920 W520

FLETCHER

Another "strip card" set issued circa 1920, cards in this set measure 1-3/8" x 2-1/4" and are numbered in the lower-right corner. The first nine cards in the set display portrait poses, while the rest are full-length action poses. Some of the poses in this set are the same as those in the W516 issue with the pictures reversed. The player's last name appears in the border beneath the picture. The cards are blank-backed.

		NM	EX	VG
	Complete Set (20):	4,000	1,600	800.00
	Common Player:	50.00	20.00	10.00
1	Dave Bancroft	150.00	60.00	30.00
2	Christy Mathewson	400.00	160.00	80.00
3	Larry Doyle	50.00	20.00	10.00
4	Jess Barnes	50.00	20.00	10.00
5	Art Fletcher	50.00	20.00	10.00
6	Wilbur Cooper	50.00	20.00	10.00
7	Mike Gonzales (Gonzalez)	50.00	20.00	10.00
8	Zach Wheat	150.00	60.00	30.00
9	Tris Speaker	200.00	80.00	40.00
10	Benny Kauff	50.00	20.00	10.00
11	Zach Wheat	150.00	60.00	30.00
12	Phil Douglas	50.00	20.00	10.00
13	Babe Ruth	2,000	800.00	400.00
14	Stan Koveleski (Coveleski)	150.00	60.00	30.00
15	Goldie Rapp	50.00	20.00	10.00
16	Pol Perritt	50.00	20.00	10.00
17	Otto Miller	50.00	20.00	10.00
18	George Kelly	150.00	60.00	30.00
19	Mike Gonzales (Gonzalez)	50.00	20.00	10.00
20	Les Nunamaker	50.00	20.00	10.00

1921 W521

This issue is closely related to the W519 Numbered set. In fact, it uses the same color drawings as that set with the pictures reversed, resulting in a mirror-image of the W519 cards. The player poses and the numbering system are identical, as are the various background colors. The W521 cards are blank-backed and were sold in strips.

10 JOHNNY GRIFFITH

	NM	EX	VG
Complete Set (20):	3,000	1,200	600.00
Common Player:	50.00	20.00	10.00
1 Guy Morton	50.00	20.00	10.00
2 Rube Marquard	150.00	60.00	30.00
3 Gabby Cravath (Gavvy)	50.00	20.00	10.00
4 Ernie Krueger	50.00	20.00	10.00
5 Babe Ruth	1,500	600.00	300.00
6 George Sisler	150.00	60.00	30.00
7 Rube Benton	50.00	20.00	10.00
8 Jimmie Johnston	50.00	20.00	10.00
9 Wilbur Robinson (Wilbert)	150.00	60.00	30.00
10 Johnny Griffith	50.00	20.00	10.00
11 Frank Baker	150.00	60.00	30.00
12 Bob Veach	50.00	20.00	10.00
13 Jesse Barnes	50.00	20.00	10.00
14 Leon Cadore	50.00	20.00	10.00
15 Ray Schalk	150.00	60.00	30.00
16 Kid Gleasen (Gleason)	50.00	20.00	10.00
17 Joe Murphy	50.00	20.00	10.00
18 Frank Frisch	150.00	60.00	30.00
19 Eddie Collins	150.00	60.00	30.00
20 Wallie (Wally) Schang	50.00	20.00	10.00

1920 W522

42 MIKE GONZALES

The 20 cards in this "strip card" set, issued circa 1920, are numbered from 31-50 and use the same players and drawings as the W520 set, issued about the same time. The cards measure 1-3/8" x 2-1/4" and are numbered in the lower left corner followed by the player's name. The cards have blank backs.

	NM	EX	VG
Complete Set (20):	5,000	2,000	1,000
Common Player:	75.00	30.00	15.00
31 Benny Kauf (Kauff)	75.00	30.00	15.00
32 Tris Speaker	300.00	120.00	60.00
33 Zach Wheat	225.00	90.00	45.00
34 Mike Gonzales (Gonzalez)	75.00	30.00	15.00
35 Wilbur Cooper	75.00	30.00	15.00
36 Art Fletcher	75.00	30.00	15.00
37 Jess Barnes	75.00	30.00	15.00
38 Larry Doyle	75.00	30.00	15.00
39 Christy Mathewson	900.00	360.00	180.00
40 Dave Bancroft	225.00	90.00	45.00
41 Les Nunamaker	75.00	30.00	15.00
42 Mike Gonzales (Gonzalez)	75.00	30.00	15.00
43 George Kelly	225.00	90.00	45.00
44 Otto Miller	75.00	30.00	15.00
45 Pol Perritt	75.00	30.00	15.00
46 Goldie Rapp	75.00	30.00	15.00
47 Stan Koveleski (Coveleski)	225.00	90.00	45.00
48 Babe Ruth	2,250	900.00	450.00
49 Phil Douglas	75.00	30.00	15.00
50 Zach Wheat	225.00	90.00	45.00

1921 W551

Another "strip set" issued circa 1920, these ten cards measure 1-3/8" x 2-1/4" and feature color drawings. The cards are unnumbered and blank-backed. Cards with typography in blue ink are modern reprints.

JESS BARNES
"GIANTS" N. L.

	NM	EX	VG
Complete Set (10):	2,000	800.00	400.00
Complete Set, Uncut Strip:	2,500	1,000	500.00
Common Player:	50.00	20.00	10.00
(1) Frank Baker	125.00	50.00	25.00
(2) Dave Bancroft	125.00	50.00	25.00
(3) Jess Barnes	50.00	20.00	10.00
(4) Ty Cobb	400.00	160.00	80.00
(5) Walter Johnson	175.00	70.00	35.00
(6) Wally Pipp	50.00	20.00	10.00
(7) Babe Ruth	1,100	450.00	225.00
(8) George Sisler	125.00	50.00	25.00
(9) Tris Speaker	150.00	60.00	30.00
(10) Casey Stengel	125.00	50.00	25.00

1929 W553

One of the more obscure strip card sets, and one of the last of the genre, this issue also is one of the most attractive. The set was issued by Marble Bubble Gum Novelties of Philadelphia, combining baseball players with movie stars. Player photos - the same pictures used in the contemporary Kashin Publications (R316) boxed set and anonymous W554 strip cards - are printed in either black on white or as duotones (blue, green and magenta seen thus far), with an ornate frame. Cards measure 1-3/4" x 2-3/4". There is a facsimile autograph on front and the player's team and league are also spelled out. Backs are blank. This checklist is probably incomplete. Gaps have been left in the assigned numbering for future additions.

	NM	EX	VG
Common Player:	100.00	50.00	30.00
(1) Lu Blue	100.00	50.00	30.00
(2) Mickey Cochrane	200.00	100.00	60.00
(4) Jimmie Foxx	300.00	150.00	90.00
(5) Frank Frisch	200.00	100.00	60.00
(6) Lou Gehrig	1,400	700.00	425.00
(7) Goose Goslin	200.00	100.00	60.00
(8) Burleigh Grimes	200.00	100.00	60.00
(9) Lefty Grove	250.00	125.00	75.00
(11) Rogers Hornsby	250.00	125.00	75.00
(13) Rabbit Maranville	200.00	100.00	60.00
(14) Bing Miller	100.00	50.00	30.00
(15) Lefty O'Doul	150.00	75.00	45.00
(16) Babe Ruth	1,700	850.00	510.00
(17) Al Simmons	200.00	100.00	60.00
(18) Pie Traynor	200.00	100.00	60.00

1930 W554

This unidentified set of black-and-white cards features most of the era's stars in action poses. A facsimile autograph appears on the front of each of the blank-back 5" x 7" pictures. Cards can be found either with and/or without player name and, sometimes, team spelled out in all-capital letters in the bottom white border, with the position in upper- and lower-case between. The unnumbered pictures are checklisted here in alphabetical order. A version of the issue has been seen with advertising for "Big Prize" on the back, printed in red. Another known back stamp is a round black ad for "A. Bonemery / ICE CREAM / CONFECTIONERY."

EDDIE ROMMEL—Pitcher PHILADELPHIA ATHLETICS

	NM	EX	VG
Complete Set (18):	3,500	1,400	700.00
Common Player:	60.00	25.00	12.50
(1) Gordon S. (Mickey) Cochrane	100.00	40.00	20.00
(2) Lewis A. Fonseca	60.00	25.00	12.50
(3) Jimmy Foxx	200.00	80.00	40.00
(4) Lou Gehrig	950.00	380.00	190.00
(5) Burleigh Grimes	100.00	40.00	20.00
(6) Robert M. Grove	125.00	50.00	25.00
(7) Waite Hoyt	100.00	40.00	20.00
(8) Joe Judge	60.00	25.00	12.50
(9) Charles (Chuck) Klein	100.00	40.00	20.00
(10) Douglas McWeeny	60.00	25.00	12.50
(11) Frank O'Doul	75.00	25.00	15.00
(12) Melvin Ott	125.00	50.00	25.00
(13) Herbert Pennock	100.00	40.00	20.00
(14) Eddie Rommel	60.00	25.00	12.50
(15) Babe Ruth	1,200	480.00	240.00
(16) Al Simmons	100.00	40.00	20.00
(17) Lloyd Waner	100.00	40.00	20.00
(18) Hack Wilson	125.00	50.00	25.00

1909-1910 W555

COBB, DETROIT AMER.

Designated as W555 in the American Card Catalog, the nearly square cards measure only 1-1/8" x 1-3-16" and feature a sepia-colored player photo. Sixty-six different cards have been discovered to date, but others may exist. A recent discovery indicates these cards were produced by Jay S. Meyer confectioners of Philly. The sets appear to be related to a series of contemporary candy cards (E93, E94, E97, and E98) because, with only two exceptions, the players and poses are the same. Recent discoveries also indicate the cards were issued four per box of Base Ball Snap Shots candy.

	NM	EX	VG
Complete Set (67):	25,000	10,000	5,000
Common Player:	125.00	50.00	25.00
(1) Red Ames	125.00	50.00	25.00
(2) Jimmy Austin	125.00	50.00	25.00
(3) Johnny Bates	125.00	50.00	25.00
(4) Chief Bender	375.00	150.00	75.00
(5) Bob Bescher	125.00	50.00	25.00
(6) Joe Birmingham	125.00	50.00	25.00
(7) Bill Bradley	125.00	50.00	25.00
(8) Kitty Bransfield	125.00	50.00	25.00
(9) Mordecai Brown	375.00	150.00	75.00
(10) Bobby Byrne	125.00	50.00	25.00
(11) Frank Chance	375.00	150.00	75.00
(12) Hal Chase	375.00	150.00	75.00
(13) Ed Cicotte	375.00	150.00	75.00
(14) Fred Clarke	375.00	150.00	75.00
(15) Ty Cobb	4,500	1,800	900.00
(16) Eddie Collins (Dark uniform.)	375.00	150.00	75.00
(17) Eddie Collins (Light uniform.)	375.00	150.00	75.00
(18) Harry Coveleskie (Coveleski)	125.00	50.00	25.00
(19) Sam Crawford	375.00	150.00	75.00
(20) Harry Davis	125.00	50.00	25.00
(21) Jim Delehanty (Delahanty)	125.00	50.00	25.00
(22) Art Devlin	125.00	50.00	25.00
(23) Josh Devore	125.00	50.00	25.00
(24) Wild Bill Donovan	125.00	50.00	25.00
(25) Red Dooin	125.00	50.00	25.00
(26) Mickey Doolan	125.00	50.00	25.00
(27) Bull Durham	125.00	50.00	25.00
(28) Jimmy Dygert	125.00	50.00	25.00
(29) Johnny Evers	375.00	150.00	75.00
(30) Russ Ford	125.00	50.00	25.00
(31) George Gibson	125.00	50.00	25.00
(32) Clark Griffith	375.00	150.00	75.00
(33) Topsy Hartsell (Hartsel)	125.00	50.00	25.00
(34) Bill Heinchman (Hinchman)	125.00	50.00	25.00
(35) Ira Hemphill	125.00	50.00	25.00
(36) Hughie Jennings	375.00	150.00	75.00
(37) Davy Jones	125.00	50.00	25.00
(38) Addie Joss	500.00	200.00	100.00
(39) Wee Willie Keeler	375.00	150.00	75.00
(40) Red Kleinow	125.00	50.00	25.00

		NM	EX	VG
(41)	Nap Lajoie	375.00	150.00	75.00
(42)	Joe Lake	125.00	50.00	25.00
(43)	Tommy Leach	125.00	50.00	25.00
(44)	Harry Lord	125.00	50.00	25.00
(45)	Sherry Magee	125.00	50.00	25.00
(46)	Christy Mathewson	2,000	800.00	400.00
(47)	Amby McConnell	125.00	50.00	25.00
(48)	John McGraw	375.00	150.00	75.00
(49)	Chief Meyers	125.00	50.00	25.00
(50)	Earl Moore	125.00	50.00	25.00
(51)	Mike Mowery	125.00	50.00	25.00
(52)	George Mullin	125.00	50.00	25.00
(53)	Red Murray	125.00	50.00	25.00
(54)	Nichols	125.00	50.00	25.00
(55)	Jim Pastorious (Pastorius)	125.00	50.00	25.00
(56)	Deacon Phillippi (Phillippe)	125.00	50.00	25.00
(57)	Eddie Plank	375.00	150.00	75.00
(58)	Fred Snodgrass	125.00	50.00	25.00
(59)	Harry Steinfeldt	125.00	50.00	25.00
(60)	Joe Tinker	375.00	150.00	75.00
(61)	Hippo Vaughn	125.00	50.00	25.00
(62)	Honus Wagner	2,500	1,000	500.00
(63)	Rube Waddell	375.00	150.00	75.00
(64)	Hooks Wiltse	125.00	50.00	25.00
(65)	Cy Young/Standing (Full name on front.)	1,500	600.00	300.00
(66)	Cy Young/Standing (Last name on front.)	1,500	600.00	300.00
(67)	Cy Young/Portrait	1,650	660.00	330.00

1927 W560

Although assigned a "W" number by the American Card Catalog, this is not a "strip card" issue in the same sense as most other "W" sets, although W560 cards are frequently found in uncut sheets of 16 cards. Cards measure a nominal 1-3/4" x 2-3/4" and are designed like a deck of playing cards, with the pictures on the various suits. The set includes aviators and other athletes in addition to baseball players. Cards can be found with designs printed in red or black, or less commonly with both and red and black on each card. Some players will also be found with different suit/value combinations.

		NM	EX	VG
Complete Set, Sheets (64):		3,250	1,625	975.00
Complete (Baseball) Set (49):		2,400	1,200	725.00
Common Player:		25.00	12.50	7.50
(1)	Vic Aldridge	25.00	12.50	7.50
(2)	Lester Bell	25.00	12.50	7.50
(3)	Larry Benton	25.00	12.50	7.50
(4)	Max Bishop	25.00	12.50	7.50
(5)	Del Bissonette	25.00	12.50	7.50
(6)	Jim Bottomley	45.00	22.50	13.50
(7)	Guy Bush	25.00	12.50	7.50
(8)	W. Clark	25.00	12.50	7.50
(9)	Andy Cohen	25.00	12.50	7.50
(10)	Mickey Cochrane	45.00	22.50	13.50
(11)	Hugh Critz	25.00	12.50	7.50
(12)	Kiki Cuyler	45.00	22.50	13.50
(13)	Taylor Douthit	25.00	12.50	7.50
(14)	Fred Fitzsimmons	25.00	12.50	7.50
(15)	Jim Foxx	110.00	55.00	35.00
(16)	Lou Gehrig	600.00	300.00	180.00
(17)	Goose Goslin	45.00	22.50	13.50
(18)	Sam Gray	25.00	12.50	7.50
(19)	Lefty Grove	60.00	30.00	18.00
(20)	Jesse Haines	45.00	22.50	13.50
(21)	Babe Herman	30.00	15.00	9.00
(22)	Roger Hornsby (Rogers)	60.00	30.00	18.00
(23)	Waite Hoyt	45.00	22.50	13.50
(24)	Henry Johnson	25.00	12.50	7.50
(25)	Walter Johnson	150.00	75.00	45.00
(26)	Willie Kamm	25.00	12.50	7.50
(27)	Remy Kremer	25.00	12.50	7.50
(28)	Fred Lindstrom	45.00	22.50	13.50
(29)	Fred Maguire	25.00	12.50	7.50
(30)	Fred Marberry	25.00	12.50	7.50
(31)	Johnny Mostil	25.00	12.50	7.50
(32)	Buddy Myer	25.00	12.50	7.50
(33)	Herb Pennock	45.00	22.50	13.50
(34)	George Pipgras	25.00	12.50	7.50
(35)	Flint Rhem	25.00	12.50	7.50
(36)	Babe Ruth	700.00	350.00	210.00
(37)	Luke Sewell	25.00	12.50	7.50
(38)	Willie Sherdel	25.00	12.50	7.50
(39)	Al Simmons	45.00	22.50	13.50
(40)	Thomas Thevenow	25.00	12.50	7.50
(41)	Fresco Thompson	25.00	12.50	7.50
(42)	George Uhle	25.00	12.50	7.50
(43)	Dazzy Vance	45.00	22.50	13.50
(44)	Rube Walberg	25.00	12.50	7.50
(45)	Lloyd Waner	45.00	22.50	13.50
(46)	Paul Waner	45.00	22.50	13.50
(47)	Fred "Cy" Williams	25.00	12.50	7.50
(48)	Jim Wilson	25.00	12.50	7.50
(49)	Glen Wright (Glenn)	25.00	12.50	7.50

1928 W565

Similar in concept to W560, the 50 cards comprising this set were printed on two 7" x 10-1/2" sheets of cheap cardboard, one in black-and-white and one in red-and-white, each with navy blue backs. Most of the cards in the issue are of movie stars, with a few boxers, ballplayers and other notables included. While most of the cards depict the person in the center of a playing card format, it is interesting to note that a full deck of cards cannot be made up by cutting the sheets. Individual cards are 1-1/4" x 2-1/8". Only the baseball players are listed here.

		NM	EX	VG
Complete Set, Sheets (50):		800.00	400.00	240.00
Common Player:		75.00	37.50	22.50
(1)	Lou Gehrig	300.00	150.00	90.00
(2)	Harry Heilmann	75.00	37.50	22.50
(3)	Tony Lazzeri	75.00	37.50	22.50
(4)	Al Simmons	75.00	37.50	22.50

1947 W571

(See 1947 Collectors & Traders Sport Star Subjects.)

1923 W572

These cards, designated as W572 by the American Card Catalog, measure 1-5/16" x 2-1/2" and are blank-backed. Fronts feature black-and-white or sepia player photos. The set is closely related to the popular E120 American Caramel set issued in 1922 and, with the exception of Ty Cobb, it uses the same photos. The cards were originally issued as strips of 10, with baseball players and boxers often mixed. They are found on either a white, slick stock or a dark, coarser cardboard. The player's name on the front of the cards appears in script. All cards have on front a copyright symbol and one of several alphabetical combinations indicating the source of the photo. The baseball players from the set are checklisted here in alphabetical order.

		NM	EX	VG
Complete (Baseball) Set (121):		19,000	9,500	5,700
Common Player:		75.00	40.00	25.00
(1)	Eddie Ainsmith	75.00	40.00	25.00
(2)	Vic Aldridge	75.00	40.00	25.00
(3)	Grover Alexander	375.00	195.00	220.00
(4)	Dave Bancroft	225.00	120.00	70.00
(5)	Walt Barbare	75.00	40.00	25.00
(6)	Jess Barnes	75.00	40.00	25.00
(7)	John Bassler	75.00	40.00	25.00
(8)	Lu Blue	75.00	40.00	25.00
(9)	Norman Boeckel	75.00	40.00	25.00
(10)	George Burns	75.00	40.00	25.00
(11)	Joe Bush	75.00	40.00	25.00
(12)	Leon Cadore	75.00	40.00	25.00
(13)	Virgil Cheevers (Cheeves)	75.00	40.00	25.00
(14)	Ty Cobb	2,000	1,000	600.00
(15)	Eddie Collins	225.00	120.00	70.00
(16)	John Collins	75.00	40.00	25.00
(17)	Wilbur Cooper	75.00	40.00	25.00
(18)	Stanley Coveleski	225.00	120.00	70.00
(19)	Walton Cruise	75.00	40.00	25.00
(20)	Dave Danforth	75.00	40.00	25.00
(21)	Jake Daubert	75.00	40.00	25.00
(22)	Hank DeBerry	75.00	40.00	25.00
(23)	Lou DeVormer	75.00	40.00	25.00
(24)	Bill Doak	75.00	40.00	25.00
(25)	Pete Donohue	75.00	40.00	25.00
(26)	Pat Duncan	75.00	40.00	25.00
(27)	Jimmy Dykes	75.00	40.00	25.00
(28)	Urban Faber	225.00	120.00	75.00
(29)	Bib Falk (Bibb)	75.00	40.00	25.00
(30)	Frank Frisch	225.00	120.00	70.00
(31)	C. Galloway	75.00	40.00	25.00
(32)	Ed Gharrity	75.00	40.00	25.00
(33)	Chas. Glazner	75.00	40.00	25.00
(34)	Hank Gowdy	75.00	40.00	25.00
(35)	Tom Griffith	75.00	40.00	25.00
(36)	Burleigh Grimes	225.00	120.00	70.00
(37)	Ray Grimes	75.00	40.00	25.00
(38)	Heinie Groh	75.00	40.00	25.00
(39)	Joe Harris	75.00	40.00	25.00
(40)	Stanley Harris	225.00	120.00	70.00
(41)	Joe Hauser	75.00	40.00	25.00
(42)	Harry Heilmann	225.00	120.00	70.00
(43)	Walter Henline	75.00	40.00	25.00
(44)	Chas. Hollocher	75.00	40.00	25.00
(45)	Harry Hooper	225.00	120.00	70.00
(46)	Rogers Hornsby	225.00	120.00	70.00
(47)	Waite Hoyt	225.00	120.00	70.00
(48)	Wilbur Hubbell	75.00	40.00	25.00
(49)	Wm. Jacobson	75.00	40.00	25.00
(50)	Chas. Jamieson	75.00	40.00	25.00
(51)	S. Johnson	75.00	40.00	25.00
(52)	Walter Johnson	750.00	375.00	225.00
(53)	Jimmy Johnston	75.00	40.00	25.00
(54)	Joe Judge	75.00	40.00	25.00
(55)	Geo. Kelly	225.00	120.00	70.00
(56)	Lee King	75.00	40.00	25.00
(57)	Larry Kopff (Kopf)	75.00	40.00	25.00
(58)	Geo. Leverette	75.00	40.00	25.00
(59)	Al Mamaux	75.00	40.00	25.00
(60)	"Rabbit" Maranville	225.00	120.00	70.00
(61)	"Rube" Marquard	225.00	120.00	70.00
(62)	Martin McManus	75.00	40.00	25.00
(63)	Lee Meadows	75.00	40.00	25.00
(64)	Mike Menosky	75.00	40.00	25.00
(65)	Bob Meusel	75.00	40.00	25.00
(66)	Emil Meusel	75.00	40.00	25.00
(67)	Geo. Mogridge	75.00	40.00	25.00
(68)	John Morrison	75.00	40.00	25.00
(69)	Johnny Mostil	75.00	40.00	25.00
(70)	Roliene Naylor	75.00	40.00	25.00
(71)	Art Nehf	75.00	40.00	25.00
(72)	Joe Oeschger	75.00	40.00	25.00
(73)	Bob O'Farrell	75.00	40.00	25.00
(74)	Steve O'Neill	75.00	40.00	25.00
(75)	Frank Parkinson	75.00	40.00	25.00
(76)	Ralph Perkins	75.00	40.00	25.00
(77)	H. Pillette	75.00	40.00	25.00
(78)	Ralph Pinelli	75.00	40.00	25.00
(79)	Wallie Pipp (Wally)	75.00	40.00	25.00
(80)	Ray Powell	75.00	40.00	25.00
(81)	Jack Quinn	75.00	40.00	25.00
(82)	Goldie Rapp	75.00	40.00	25.00
(83)	Walter Reuther (Ruether)	75.00	40.00	25.00
(84)	Sam Rice	225.00	120.00	70.00
(85)	Emory Rigney	75.00	40.00	25.00
(86)	Eppa Rixey	225.00	120.00	70.00
(87)	Ed Rommel	75.00	40.00	25.00
(88)	Eddie Roush	225.00	120.00	70.00
(89)	Babe Ruth	5,250	2,600	1,600
(90)	Ray Schalk	225.00	120.00	70.00
(91)	Wallie Schang (Wally)	75.00	40.00	25.00
(92)	Walter Schmidt	75.00	40.00	25.00
(93)	Joe Schultz	75.00	40.00	25.00
(94)	Hank Severeid	75.00	40.00	25.00
(95)	Joe Sewell	225.00	120.00	70.00
(96)	Bob Shawkey	75.00	40.00	25.00
(97)	Earl Sheely	75.00	40.00	25.00
(98)	Will Sherdel	75.00	40.00	25.00
(99)	Urban Shocker	75.00	40.00	25.00
(100)	George Sisler	225.00	120.00	70.00
(101)	Earl Smith	75.00	40.00	25.00
(102)	Elmer Smith	75.00	40.00	25.00
(103)	Jack Smith	75.00	40.00	25.00
(104)	Bill Southworth	75.00	40.00	25.00
(105)	Tris Speaker	225.00	120.00	70.00
(106)	Arnold Statz	75.00	40.00	25.00
(107)	Milton Stock	75.00	40.00	25.00
(108)	Jim Tierney	75.00	40.00	25.00
(109)	Harold Traynor	225.00	120.00	70.00
(110)	Geo. Uhle	75.00	40.00	25.00
(111)	Bob Veach	75.00	40.00	25.00
(112)	Clarence Walker	75.00	40.00	25.00
(113)	Curtis Walker	75.00	40.00	25.00
(114)	Bill Wambsganss	75.00	40.00	25.00
(115)	Aaron Ward	75.00	40.00	25.00
(116)	Zach Wheat	225.00	120.00	70.00
(117)	Fred Williams	75.00	40.00	25.00
(118)	Ken Williams	75.00	40.00	25.00
(119)	Ivy Wingo	75.00	40.00	25.00
(120)	Joe Wood	120.00	60.00	40.00
(121)	J.T. Zachary	75.00	40.00	25.00

1922 W573

These cards, identified as W573 in the American Card Catalog, are blank-backed, black-and-white versions of the popular E120 American Caramel set. These "strip cards," were sold in strips of 10 for a penny. The cards measure about 2-1/16" x 3-3/8", but allowances in width must be made because the cards were hand-cut from a horizontal strip. Some cards have been found with the advertising of various firms on back.

DAVE (BEAUTY) BANCROFT
SHORT STOP, NEW YORK NATIONALS

		NM	EX	VG
	Complete Set (240):	30,000	15,000	9,000
	Common Player:	100.00	50.00	30.00
(1)	Charles (Babe) Adams	100.00	50.00	30.00
(2)	Eddie Ainsmith	100.00	50.00	30.00
(3)	Vic Aldridge	100.00	50.00	30.00
(4)	Grover C. Alexander	400.00	200.00	120.00
(5)	Jim Bagby	100.00	50.00	30.00
(6)	Frank (Home Run) Baker	270.00	135.00	80.00
(7)	Dave (Beauty) Bancroft	270.00	135.00	80.00
(8)	Walt Barbare	100.00	50.00	30.00
(9)	Turner Barber	100.00	50.00	30.00
(10)	Jess Barnes	100.00	50.00	30.00
(11)	Clyde Barnhart	100.00	50.00	30.00
(12)	John Bassler	100.00	50.00	30.00
(13)	Will Bayne	100.00	50.00	30.00
(14)	Walter (Huck) Betts	100.00	50.00	30.00
(15)	Carson Bigbee	100.00	50.00	30.00
(16)	Lu Blue	100.00	50.00	30.00
(17)	Norman Boeckel	100.00	50.00	30.00
(18)	Sammy Bohne	100.00	50.00	30.00
(19)	George Burns	100.00	50.00	30.00
(20)	George Burns	100.00	50.00	30.00
(21)	"Bullet Joe" Bush	100.00	50.00	30.00
(22)	Leon Cadore	100.00	50.00	30.00
(23)	Marty Callaghan	100.00	50.00	30.00
(24)	Frank Calloway (Callaway)	100.00	50.00	30.00
(25)	Max Carey	270.00	135.00	80.00
(26)	Jimmy Caveney	100.00	50.00	30.00
(27)	Virgil Cheeves	100.00	50.00	30.00
(28)	Vern Clemons	100.00	50.00	30.00
(29)	Ty Cob (Cobb)	1,800	900.00	550.00
(30)	Bert Cole	100.00	50.00	30.00
(31)	Eddie Collins	270.00	135.00	80.00
(32)	John (Shano) Collins	100.00	50.00	30.00
(33)	T.P. (Pat) Collins	100.00	50.00	30.00
(34)	Wilbur Cooper	100.00	50.00	30.00
(35)	Harry Courtney	100.00	50.00	30.00
(36)	Stanley Coveleskie (Coveleski)	270.00	135.00	80.00
(37)	Elmer Cox	100.00	50.00	30.00
(38)	Sam Crane	100.00	50.00	30.00
(39)	Walton Cruise	100.00	50.00	30.00
(40)	Bill Cunningham	100.00	50.00	30.00
(41)	George Cutshaw	100.00	50.00	30.00
(42)	Dave Danforth	100.00	50.00	30.00
(43)	Jake Daubert	100.00	50.00	30.00
(44)	George Dauss	100.00	50.00	30.00
(45)	Frank (Dixie) Davis	100.00	50.00	30.00
(46)	Hank DeBerry	100.00	50.00	30.00
(47)	Albert Devormer (Lou DeVormer)	100.00	50.00	30.00
(48)	Bill Doak	100.00	50.00	30.00
(49)	Pete Donohue	100.00	50.00	30.00
(50)	"Shufflin" Phil Douglas	100.00	50.00	30.00
(51)	Joe Dugan	100.00	50.00	30.00
(52)	Louis (Pat) Duncan	100.00	50.00	30.00
(53)	Jimmy Dykes	100.00	50.00	30.00
(54)	Howard Ehmke	100.00	50.00	30.00
(55)	Frank Ellerbe	100.00	50.00	30.00
(56)	Urban (Red) Faber	270.00	135.00	80.00
(57)	Bib Falk (Bibb)	100.00	50.00	30.00
(58)	Dana Fillingim	100.00	50.00	30.00
(59)	Max Flack	100.00	50.00	30.00
(60)	Ira Flagstead	100.00	50.00	30.00
(61)	Art Fletcher	100.00	50.00	30.00
(62)	Horace Ford	100.00	50.00	30.00
(63)	Jack Fournier	100.00	50.00	30.00
(64)	Frank Frisch	270.00	135.00	80.00
(66)	Ollie Fuhrman	100.00	50.00	30.00
(66)	Clarance Galloway	100.00	50.00	30.00
(67)	Larry Gardner	100.00	50.00	30.00
(68)	Walter Gerber	100.00	50.00	30.00
(69)	Ed Gharrity	100.00	50.00	30.00
(70)	John Gillespie	100.00	50.00	30.00
(71)	Chas. (Whitey) Glazner	100.00	50.00	30.00
(72)	Johnny Gooch	100.00	50.00	30.00
(73)	Leon Goslin	270.00	135.00	80.00
(74)	Hank Gowdy	100.00	50.00	30.00
(75)	John Graney	100.00	50.00	30.00
(76)	Tom Griffith	100.00	50.00	30.00
(77)	Burleigh Grimes	270.00	135.00	80.00
(78)	Oscar Ray Grimes	100.00	50.00	30.00
(79)	Charlie Grimm	100.00	50.00	30.00
(80)	Heinie Groh	100.00	50.00	30.00
(81)	Jesse Haines	270.00	135.00	80.00
(82)	Earl Hamilton	100.00	50.00	30.00
(83)	Gene (Bubbles) Hargrave	100.00	50.00	30.00
(84)	Bryan Harris (Harriss)	100.00	50.00	30.00
(85)	Joe Harris	100.00	50.00	30.00

(86)	Stanley Harris	270.00	135.00	80.00
(87)	Chas. (Dowdy) Hartnett	270.00	135.00	80.00
(88)	Bob Hasty	100.00	50.00	30.00
(89)	Joe Hauser	140.00	70.00	45.00
(90)	Clif Heathcote	100.00	50.00	30.00
(91)	Harry Heilmann	270.00	135.00	80.00
(92)	Walter (Butch) Henline	100.00	50.00	30.00
(93)	Clarence (Shovel) Hodge	100.00	50.00	30.00
(94)	Walter Holke	100.00	50.00	30.00
(95)	Charles Hollocher	100.00	50.00	30.00
(96)	Harry Hooper	270.00	135.00	80.00
(97)	Rogers Hornsby	340.00	170.00	100.00
(98)	Waite Hoyt	270.00	135.00	80.00
(99)	Wilbur Hubbell (Wilbert)	100.00	50.00	30.00
(100)	Bernard (Bud) Hungling	100.00	50.00	30.00
(101)	Will Jacobson	100.00	50.00	30.00
(102)	Charlie Jamieson	100.00	50.00	30.00
(103)	Ernie Johnson	100.00	50.00	30.00
(104)	Sylvester Johnson	100.00	50.00	30.00
(105)	Walter Johnson	1,000	500.00	300.00
(106)	Jimmy Johnston	100.00	50.00	30.00
(107)	W.R. (Doc) Johnston	100.00	50.00	30.00
(108)	"Deacon" Sam Jones	100.00	50.00	30.00
(109)	Bob Jones	100.00	50.00	30.00
(110)	Percy Jones	100.00	50.00	30.00
(111)	Joe Judge	100.00	50.00	30.00
(112)	Ben Karr	100.00	50.00	30.00
(113)	Johnny Kelleher	100.00	50.00	30.00
(114)	George Kelly	270.00	135.00	80.00
(115)	Lee King	100.00	50.00	30.00
(116)	Wm (Larry) Kopff (Kopf)	100.00	50.00	30.00
(117)	Marty Krug	100.00	50.00	30.00
(118)	Johnny Lavan	100.00	50.00	30.00
(119)	Nemo Leibold	100.00	50.00	30.00
(120)	Roy Leslie	100.00	50.00	30.00
(121)	George Leverette (Leverett)	100.00	50.00	30.00
(122)	Adolfo Luque	100.00	50.00	30.00
(123)	Walter Mails	100.00	50.00	30.00
(124)	Al Mamaux	100.00	50.00	30.00
(125)	"Rabbit" Maranville	270.00	135.00	80.00
(126)	Cliff Markle	100.00	50.00	30.00
(127)	Richard (Rube) Marquard	270.00	135.00	80.00
(128)	Carl Mays	100.00	50.00	30.00
(129)	Hervey McClellan (Harvey)	100.00	50.00	30.00
(130)	Austin McHenry	100.00	50.00	30.00
(131)	"Stuffy" McInnis	100.00	50.00	30.00
(132)	Martin McManus	100.00	50.00	30.00
(133)	Mike McNally	100.00	50.00	30.00
(134)	Hugh McQuillan	100.00	50.00	30.00
(135)	Lee Meadows	100.00	50.00	30.00
(136)	Mike Menosky	100.00	50.00	30.00
(137)	Bob (Dutch) Meusel	100.00	50.00	30.00
(138)	Emil (Irish) Meusel	100.00	50.00	30.00
(139)	Clyde Milan	100.00	50.00	30.00
(140)	Edmund (Bing) Miller	100.00	50.00	30.00
(141)	Elmer Miller	100.00	50.00	30.00
(142)	Lawrence (Hack) Miller	100.00	50.00	30.00
(143)	Clarence Mitchell	100.00	50.00	30.00
(144)	George Mogridge	100.00	50.00	30.00
(145)	Roy Moore	100.00	50.00	30.00
(146)	John L. Mokan	100.00	50.00	30.00
(147)	John Morrison	100.00	50.00	30.00
(148)	Johnny Mostil	100.00	50.00	30.00
(149)	Elmer Myers	100.00	50.00	30.00
(150)	Hy Myers	100.00	50.00	30.00
(151)	Roliene Naylor (Roleine)	100.00	50.00	30.00
(152)	Earl "Greasy" Neale	100.00	50.00	30.00
(153)	Art Nehf	100.00	50.00	30.00
(154)	Les Nunamaker	100.00	50.00	30.00
(155)	Joe Oeschger	100.00	50.00	30.00
(156)	Bob O'Farrell	100.00	50.00	30.00
(157)	Ivan Olson	100.00	50.00	30.00
(158)	George O'Neil	100.00	50.00	30.00
(159)	Steve O'Neill	100.00	50.00	30.00
(160)	Frank Parkinson	100.00	50.00	30.00
(161)	Roger Peckinpaugh	100.00	50.00	30.00
(162)	Herb Pennock	270.00	135.00	80.00
(163)	Ralph (Cy) Perkins	100.00	50.00	30.00
(164)	Will Pertica	100.00	50.00	30.00
(165)	Jack Peters	100.00	50.00	30.00
(166)	Tom Phillips	100.00	50.00	30.00
(167)	Val Picinich	100.00	50.00	30.00
(168)	Herman Pillette	100.00	50.00	30.00
(169)	Ralph Pinelli	100.00	50.00	30.00
(170)	Wallie Pipp	100.00	50.00	30.00
(171)	Clark Pittenger (Clarke)	100.00	50.00	30.00
(172)	Raymond Powell	100.00	50.00	30.00
(173)	Derrill Pratt	100.00	50.00	30.00
(174)	Jack Quinn	100.00	50.00	30.00
(175)	Joe (Goldie) Rapp	100.00	50.00	30.00
(176)	John Rawlings	100.00	50.00	30.00
(177)	Walter (Dutch) Reuther (Ruether)	100.00	50.00	30.00
(178)	Sam Rice	270.00	135.00	80.00
(179)	Emory Rigney	100.00	50.00	30.00
(180)	Jimmy Ring	100.00	50.00	30.00
(181)	Eppa Rixey	270.00	135.00	80.00
(182)	Charles Robertson	100.00	50.00	30.00
(183)	Ed Rommel	100.00	50.00	30.00
(184)	Eddie Roush	270.00	135.00	80.00
(185)	Harold (Muddy) Ruel (Herold)	100.00	50.00	30.00
(186)	Babe Ruth	3,700	1,850	1,100
(187)	Ray Schalk	270.00	135.00	80.00
(188)	Wallie Schang	100.00	50.00	30.00
(189)	Ray Schmandt	100.00	50.00	30.00
(190)	Walter Schmidt	100.00	50.00	30.00
(191)	Joe Schultz	100.00	50.00	30.00
(192)	Everett Scott	100.00	50.00	30.00
(193)	Henry Severeid	100.00	50.00	30.00
(194)	Joe Sewell	270.00	135.00	80.00
(195)	Howard Shanks	100.00	50.00	30.00
(196)	Bob Shawkey	100.00	50.00	30.00
(197)	Earl Sheely	100.00	50.00	30.00
(198)	Will Sherdel	100.00	50.00	30.00
(199)	Ralph Shinners	100.00	50.00	30.00
(200)	Urban Shocker	100.00	50.00	30.00
(201)	Charles (Chick) Shorten	100.00	50.00	30.00
(202)	George Sisler	270.00	135.00	80.00

(203)	Earl Smith	100.00	50.00	30.00
(204)	Earl Smith	100.00	50.00	30.00
(205)	Elmer Smith	100.00	50.00	30.00
(206)	Jack Smith	100.00	50.00	30.00
(207)	Sherrod Smith	100.00	50.00	30.00
(208)	Colonel Snover	100.00	50.00	30.00
(209)	Frank Snyder	100.00	50.00	30.00
(210)	Al Sothoron	100.00	50.00	30.00
(211)	Bill Southworth	100.00	50.00	30.00
(212)	Tris Speaker	340.00	170.00	100.00
(213)	Arnold Statz	100.00	50.00	30.00
(214)	Milton Stock	100.00	50.00	30.00
(215)	Amos Strunk	100.00	50.00	30.00
(216)	Jim Tierney	100.00	50.00	30.00
(217)	John Tobin	100.00	50.00	30.00
(218)	Fred Toney	100.00	50.00	30.00
(219)	George Toporcer	100.00	50.00	30.00
(220)	Harold (Pie) Traynor	270.00	135.00	80.00
(221)	George Uhle	100.00	50.00	30.00
(222)	Elam Vangilder	100.00	50.00	30.00
(223)	Bob Veach	100.00	50.00	30.00
(224)	Clarence (Tillie) Walker	100.00	50.00	30.00
(225)	Curtis Walker	100.00	50.00	30.00
(226)	Al Walters	100.00	50.00	30.00
(227)	Bill Wambsganss	100.00	50.00	30.00
(228)	Aaron Ward	100.00	50.00	30.00
(229)	John Watson	100.00	50.00	30.00
(230)	Frank Welch	100.00	50.00	30.00
(231)	Zach Wheat	270.00	135.00	80.00
(232)	Fred (Cy) Williams	100.00	50.00	30.00
(233)	Kenneth Williams	100.00	50.00	30.00
(234)	Ivy Wingo	100.00	50.00	30.00
(235)	Joe Wood	100.00	50.00	30.00
(236)	Lawrence Woodall	100.00	50.00	30.00
(237)	Russell Wrightstone	100.00	50.00	30.00
(238)	Everett Yaryan	100.00	50.00	30.00
(239)	Ross Young (Youngs)	270.00	135.00	80.00
(240)	J.T. Zachary	100.00	50.00	30.00

1933 W574

WHITE SOX

Cards in this set measure an unusual 2-1/4" x 2-7/8". They are unnumbered and are listed here in alphabetical order. The black-and-white photos have a facsimile autograph and team name at bottom.

		NM	EX	VG
	Complete Set (29):	3,750	1,900	1,100
	Common Player:	75.00	40.00	25.00
(1)	Dale Alexander	75.00	40.00	25.00
(2)	Ivy Paul Andrews	75.00	40.00	25.00
(3)	Luke Appling	320.00	160.00	100.00
(4)	Earl Averill	320.00	160.00	100.00
(5)	George Blaeholder	75.00	40.00	25.00
(6)	Irving Burns	75.00	40.00	25.00
(7)	Pat Caraway	75.00	40.00	25.00
(8)	Chalmer Cissell	75.00	40.00	25.00
(9)	Harry Davis	75.00	40.00	25.00
(10)	Jimmy Dykes	75.00	40.00	25.00
(11)	George Earnshaw	75.00	40.00	25.00
(12)	Urban Faber	320.00	160.00	100.00
(13)	Lewis Fonseca	75.00	40.00	25.00
(14)	Jimmy Foxx	575.00	300.00	175.00
(15)	Victor Frasier	75.00	40.00	25.00
(16)	Robert Grove	450.00	225.00	150.00
(17)	Frank Grube	75.00	40.00	25.00
(18)	Irving Hadley	75.00	40.00	25.00
(19)	Willie Kamm	75.00	40.00	25.00
(20)	Bill Killefer	75.00	40.00	25.00
(21)	Ralph Kress	75.00	40.00	25.00
(22)	Fred Marberry	75.00	40.00	25.00
(23)	Roger Peckinpaugh	75.00	40.00	25.00
(24)	Frank Reiber	75.00	40.00	25.00
(25)	Carl Reynolds	75.00	40.00	25.00
(26)	Al Simmons	320.00	160.00	100.00
(27)	Joe Vosmik	75.00	40.00	25.00
(28)	Gerald Walker	75.00	40.00	25.00
(29)	Whitlow Wyatt	75.00	40.00	25.00

1921-1922 W575-1

The known variations indicate this set was issued over a period of time, likely encompassing more than one calendar year or baseball season. Designated as W575 in the American Card Catalog, these "strip cards" are essentially blank-backed versions of the contemporary American Caramel E121 set, though the checklists do not exactly correspond. Ideally cut cards in W575-1 measure 2" x 3-1/4" and are printed in black-and-white. It is almost impossible to distinguish W575-1 cards from the blank-backed Koester's Bread Yankees and Giants cards issued to commemorate the 1921 "Subway" World Series. This checklist may not be complete. Gaps have been left among the assigned numbers to accommodate future additions.

	NM	EX	VG
Common Player:	40.00	20.00	12.00

(1)	Chas. "Babe" Adams	40.00	20.00	12.00
(2)	G.C. Alexander	350.00	175.00	100.00
(3)	Grover Alexander	350.00	175.00	100.00
(4)	Jim Bagby	40.00	20.00	12.00
(5)	J. Franklin Baker	175.00	85.00	50.00
(6)	Frank Baker	175.00	85.00	50.00
(7)	Dave Bancroft/Btg	175.00	85.00	50.00
(8)	Dave Bancroft/Fldg	175.00	85.00	50.00
(9)	Turner Barber	40.00	20.00	12.00
(10)	Jesse Barnes	40.00	20.00	12.00
(11)	Howard Berry	40.00	20.00	12.00
(12)	L. Bigbee (Should be C.)	40.00	20.00	12.00
(13)	Ping Bodie	40.00	20.00	12.00
(14)	"Ed" Brown	40.00	20.00	12.00
(15)	George Burns	40.00	20.00	12.00
(16)	Geo. J. Burns	40.00	20.00	12.00
(17)	"Bullet Joe" Bush	40.00	20.00	12.00
(18)	Owen Bush	40.00	20.00	12.00
(19)	Max Carey/Btg	175.00	85.00	50.00
(20)	Max Carey (Hands on hips.)	175.00	85.00	50.00
(21)	Ty Cobb	2,000	1,000	600.00
(22)	Eddie Collins	175.00	85.00	50.00
(23)	"Rip" Collins	40.00	20.00	12.00
(24)	Stanley Coveleskie (Coveleski)	175.00	85.00	50.00
(25)	Bill Cunningham	40.00	20.00	12.00
(26a)	Jake Daubert (1B.)	40.00	20.00	12.00
(26b)	Jake Daubert (1st B.)	40.00	20.00	12.00
(28)	George Dauss	40.00	20.00	12.00
(29)	Dixie Davis	40.00	20.00	12.00
(30)	Charles Deal (Dark uniform.)	40.00	20.00	12.00
(31)	Charles Deal (Light uniform.)	40.00	20.00	12.00
(32)	Lou DeVormer (Photo actually Emil "Irish" Meusel)	40.00	20.00	12.00
(33)	William Doak	40.00	20.00	12.00
(34)	Bill Donovan/Pitching	40.00	20.00	12.00
(35)	Bill Donovan/Portrait	40.00	20.00	12.00
(36)	Phil Douglas	40.00	20.00	12.00
(37a)	Johnny Evers (Mgr.)	175.00	85.00	50.00
(37b)	Johnny Evers (Manager)	175.00	85.00	50.00
(39)	Urban Faber (Dark uniform.)	175.00	85.00	50.00
(40)	Urban Faber (White uniform.)	175.00	85.00	50.00
(42)	Bib Falk (Bibb)	40.00	20.00	12.00
(43)	Alex Ferguson	40.00	20.00	12.00
(44)	Wm. Fewster	40.00	20.00	12.00
(45)	Ira Flagstead	40.00	20.00	12.00
(46)	Art Fletcher	40.00	20.00	12.00
(47)	Eddie Foster	40.00	20.00	12.00
(48)	Frank Frisch	175.00	85.00	50.00
(49)	W.L. Gardner	40.00	20.00	12.00
(50)	Alexander Gaston	40.00	20.00	12.00
(51)	E.P. Gharrity	40.00	20.00	12.00
(52)	Chas. "Whitey" Glazner	40.00	20.00	12.00
(53)	"Kid" Gleason	40.00	20.00	12.00
(54)	"Mike" Gonzalez	40.00	20.00	12.00
(55)	Hank Gowdy	40.00	20.00	12.00
(56a)	John Graney (Util. o.f.)	40.00	20.00	12.00
(56b)	John Graney (O.F.)	40.00	20.00	12.00
(57)	Tom Griffith	40.00	20.00	12.00
(58)	Chas. Grimm	40.00	20.00	12.00
(59a)	Heinie Groh (Cincinnati)	40.00	20.00	12.00
(59b)	Heinie Groh (New York)	40.00	20.00	12.00
(62)	Jess Haines	175.00	85.00	50.00
(63)	Harry Harper	40.00	20.00	12.00
(64)	"Chicken" Hawks	40.00	20.00	12.00
(65)	Harry Heilman (Heilmann) (Holding bat.)	175.00	85.00	50.00
(66)	Harry Heilman (Heilmann) (Running)	175.00	85.00	50.00
(67)	John Henry	40.00	20.00	12.00
(68)	Clarence Hodge	40.00	20.00	12.00
(69)	Fred Hoffman	40.00	20.00	12.00
(70a)	Walter Holke/Portrait (1st B)	40.00	20.00	12.00
(70b)	Walter Holke/Portrait (1B)	40.00	20.00	12.00
(71)	Walter Holke/Throwing	40.00	20.00	12.00
(72a)	Charles Hollacher (Name incorrect.)	40.00	20.00	12.00
(72b)	Charles Hollocher (Name correct.)	40.00	20.00	12.00
(73)	Harry Hooper	175.00	85.00	50.00
(74a)	Rogers Hornsby (2nd B.)	250.00	125.00	75.00
(74b)	Rogers Hornsby (O.F.)	250.00	125.00	75.00
(75)	Waite Hoyt	175.00	85.00	50.00
(76)	Miller Huggins	175.00	85.00	50.00
(78)	Wm. C. Jacobson	40.00	20.00	12.00
(79)	Hugh Jennings	175.00	85.00	50.00
(80)	Walter Johnson (Arms at chest.)	500.00	250.00	150.00
(81)	Walter Johnson/Throwing	500.00	250.00	150.00
(82)	James Johnston	40.00	20.00	12.00
(84)	Joe Judge/Btg	40.00	20.00	12.00
(85)	Joe Judge/Fldg	40.00	20.00	12.00
(86a)	George Kelly (1st B.)	175.00	85.00	50.00
(86b)	George Kelly (1B.)	175.00	85.00	50.00
(88)	Dick Kerr	40.00	20.00	12.00
(89)	P.J. Kilduff	40.00	20.00	12.00
(90a)	Bill Killefer	40.00	20.00	12.00
(90b)	Bill Killefer (Killefer)	40.00	20.00	12.00
(92)	John Lavan	40.00	20.00	12.00
(93)	"Nemo" Leibold	40.00	20.00	12.00
(94)	Duffy Lewis	40.00	20.00	12.00
(95)	Walter Mails	40.00	20.00	12.00
(96)	Al. Mamaux	40.00	20.00	12.00
(97)	"Rabbit" Maranville	175.00	85.00	50.00
(98)	Elwood Martin	40.00	20.00	12.00
(99a)	Carl Mays (Name correct.)	40.00	20.00	12.00
(99b)	Carl May (Mays)	40.00	20.00	12.00
(100)	John McGraw (Mgr.)	175.00	85.00	50.00
(101)	John McGraw (Manager)	175.00	85.00	50.00
(102)	Jack McInnis	40.00	20.00	12.00
(103a)	M.J. McNally (3B.)	40.00	20.00	12.00
(103b)	M.J. McNally (3rd B.)	40.00	20.00	12.00
(104)	Lee Meadows	40.00	20.00	12.00
(105)	Emil Meusel	40.00	20.00	12.00
(106)	R. Meusel	40.00	20.00	12.00
(107)	Clyde Milan	40.00	20.00	12.00
(108)	Elmer Miller	40.00	20.00	12.00
(109)	Otto Miller	40.00	20.00	12.00

(110)	John Mitchell (S.S.)	40.00	20.00	12.00
(111)	John Mitchell (3rd B.)	40.00	20.00	12.00
(112)	Guy Morton	40.00	20.00	12.00
(113)	Johnny Mostil	40.00	20.00	12.00
(114)	Eddie Mulligan	40.00	20.00	12.00
(115)	Eddie Murphy	40.00	20.00	12.00
(116a)	"Hy" Myers (C.F./O.F.)	40.00	20.00	12.00
(116b)	Hy Myers (O.F.)	40.00	20.00	12.00
(117a)	A.E. Neale	75.00	37.50	22.50
(117b)	Earl Neale	75.00	37.00	22.00
(119)	Arthur Nehf	40.00	20.00	12.00
(120)	Joe Oeschger	40.00	20.00	12.00
(122)	Chas. O'Leary	40.00	20.00	12.00
(123)	Steve O'Neill	40.00	20.00	12.00
(124a)	Roger Peckinbaugh (Name incorrect.)	40.00	20.00	12.00
(124b)	Roger Peckinpaugh (Name correct.)	40.00	20.00	12.00
(125a)	Jeff Pfeffer (Brooklyn)	40.00	20.00	12.00
(125b)	Jeff Pfeffer (St. Louis)	40.00	20.00	12.00
(127)	William Piercy	40.00	20.00	12.00
(128)	Walter Pipp	40.00	20.00	12.00
(129)	D.B. Pratt	40.00	20.00	12.00
(130)	Jack Quinn	40.00	20.00	12.00
(131a)	John Rawlings (2nd B.)	40.00	20.00	12.00
(131b)	John Rawlings (2B.)	40.00	20.00	12.00
(133a)	E.S. Rice (Name incorrect.)	175.00	85.00	50.00
(133b)	E.C. Rice (Name correct.)	175.00	85.00	50.00
(134a)	Eppa Rixey	175.00	85.00	50.00
(134b)	Eppa Rixey, Jr.	175.00	85.00	50.00
(136)	Wilbert Robinson	175.00	85.00	50.00
(137)	Tom Rogers	40.00	20.00	12.00
(139)	Ed Rounnel (Rommel)	40.00	20.00	12.00
(140)	Robert Roth	40.00	20.00	12.00
(142a)	Ed Roush (O.F.)	175.00	85.00	50.00
(142b)	Ed Roush (C.F.)	175.00	85.00	50.00
(144)	"Muddy" Ruel	40.00	20.00	12.00
(145)	Walter Ruether	40.00	20.00	12.00
(146a)	"Babe" Ruth (R.F.)	3,500	1,750	1,000
(146b)	Babe Ruth (L.F.)	3,500	1,750	1,000
(147)	"Babe" Ruth (W/man, bird.)	3,500	1,750	1,000
(148a)	Bill Ryan	40.00	20.00	12.00
(148b)	"Bill" Ryan	40.00	20.00	12.00
(149a)	"Slim" Sallee (Ball in hand.)	40.00	20.00	12.00
(149b)	"Slim" Sallee (No ball in hand.)	40.00	20.00	12.00
(151)	Ray Schalk/Bunting	175.00	85.00	50.00
(152)	Ray Schalk/Cathcing	175.00	85.00	50.00
(153a)	Walter Schang	40.00	20.00	12.00
(153b)	Wally Schang	40.00	20.00	12.00
(154a)	Fred Schupp (Name incorrect.)	40.00	20.00	12.00
(154b)	Ferd Schupp (Name correct.)	40.00	20.00	12.00
(155a)	Everett Scott (Boston)	40.00	20.00	12.00
(155b)	Everett Scott (New York)	40.00	20.00	12.00
(157)	Hank Severeid	40.00	20.00	12.00
(159)	Robert Shawkey	40.00	20.00	12.00
(160a)	"Pat" Shea	40.00	20.00	12.00
(160b)	Pat Shea	40.00	20.00	12.00
(161)	Earl Sheely	40.00	20.00	12.00
(163)	Urban Shocker	40.00	20.00	12.00
(165)	George Sisler/Btg	175.00	85.00	50.00
(166)	George Sisler/Throwing	175.00	85.00	50.00
(168)	Earl Smith	40.00	20.00	12.00
(169)	Elmer Smith	40.00	20.00	12.00
(170)	J. Carlisle Smith	40.00	20.00	12.00
(171)	Frank Snyder	40.00	20.00	12.00
(172)	Bill Southworth	40.00	20.00	12.00
(173a)	Tris Speaker (Large projection.)	250.00	125.00	75.00
(173b)	Tris Speaker (Small projection.)	250.00	125.00	75.00
(175a)	Charles Stengel/Btg	175.00	85.00	50.00
(175b)	Charles Stengel/Portrait	175.00	85.00	50.00
(177)	Milton Stock	40.00	20.00	12.00
(178a)	Amos Strunk (C.F.)	40.00	20.00	12.00
(178b)	Amos Strunk (O.F.)	40.00	20.00	12.00
(180a)	Zeb Terry (Dark uniform, 2nd B.)	40.00	20.00	12.00
(180b)	Zeb Terry (Dark uniform, 2B.)	40.00	20.00	12.00
(181)	Zeb Terry (White uniform.)	40.00	20.00	12.00
(182)	Chester Thomas	40.00	20.00	12.00
(183)	Fred Toney (Both feet on ground.)	40.00	20.00	12.00
(184)	Fred Toney (One foot in air.)	40.00	20.00	12.00
(185)	George Toporcer	40.00	20.00	12.00
(186)	George Tyler	40.00	20.00	12.00
(187)	Jim Vaughn (Plain uniform.)	40.00	20.00	12.00
(188)	Jim Vaughn (Striped uniform.)	40.00	20.00	12.00
(189)	Bob Veach (Arm raised.)	40.00	20.00	12.00
(190)	Bob Veach (Arms folded.)	40.00	20.00	12.00
(191a)	Oscar Vitt (3rd B.)	40.00	20.00	12.00
(191b)	Oscar Vitt (3B.)	40.00	20.00	12.00
(192)	Curtis Walker	40.00	20.00	12.00
(193)	W. Wambsganss	40.00	20.00	12.00
(194)	Carl Weilman	40.00	20.00	12.00
(195)	Zach Wheat	175.00	85.00	50.00
(196)	George Whitted	40.00	20.00	12.00
(197)	Fred Williams	40.00	20.00	12.00
(198)	Ivy B. Wingo	40.00	20.00	12.00
(199)	Lawton Witt	40.00	20.00	12.00
(200)	Joe Wood	100.00	50.00	30.00
(202)	Pep Young	40.00	20.00	12.00
(203)	Ross Young (Youngs)	175.00	85.00	50.00

1922 W575-2

The blank-back, black-and-white cards in this set measure a nominal 2-1/8" x 3-3/8". Because of the design of the cards the set is sometimes called the "autograph on shoulder" series. Some cards have the player's position and team added to the name inscription. The cards were produced by Kromo Gravure Photo Co., Detroit, Mich., and sold as boxed set.

		NM	EX	VG
Complete Set (40):		13,500	6,750	4,000
Common Player:		100.00	50.00	30.00
(1)	Dave Bancroft	270.00	135.00	80.00
(2)	Johnnie Bassler	100.00	50.00	30.00
(3)	Joe Bush	100.00	50.00	30.00
(4)	Ty Cobb	2,700	1,350	800.00
(5)	Eddie Collins	270.00	135.00	80.00
(6)	Stan Coveleskie (Coveleski)	270.00	135.00	80.00
(7)	Jake Daubert	100.00	50.00	30.00
(8)	Joe Dugan	100.00	50.00	30.00
(9)	Red Faber	270.00	135.00	80.00
(10)	Frank Frisch	270.00	135.00	80.00
(11)	Walter H. Gerber	100.00	50.00	30.00
(12)	Harry Heilmann	270.00	135.00	80.00
(13)	Harry Hooper	270.00	135.00	80.00
(14)	Rogers Hornsby	400.00	200.00	120.00
(15)	Waite Hoyt	270.00	135.00	80.00
(16)	Joe Judge	100.00	50.00	30.00
(17)	Geo. Kelly	270.00	135.00	80.00
(18)	Rabbit Maranville	270.00	135.00	80.00
(19)	Rube Marquard	270.00	135.00	80.00
(20)	Guy Morton	100.00	50.00	30.00
(21)	Art Nehf	100.00	50.00	30.00
(22)	Derrill B. Pratt	100.00	50.00	30.00
(23)	Jimmy Ring	100.00	50.00	30.00
(24)	Eppa Rixey	270.00	135.00	80.00
(25)	Gene Robertson	100.00	50.00	30.00
(26)	Ed Rommell (Rommel)	100.00	50.00	30.00
(27)	Babe Ruth	5,000	2,500	1,500
(28)	Wally Schang	100.00	50.00	30.00
(29)	Everett Scott	100.00	50.00	30.00
(30)	Henry Severeid	100.00	50.00	30.00
(31)	Joe Sewell	270.00	135.00	80.00
(32)	Geo. Sisler	270.00	135.00	80.00
(33)	Tris Speaker	400.00	200.00	120.00
(34)	(Riggs) Stephenson	100.00	50.00	30.00
(35)	Zeb Terry	100.00	50.00	30.00
(36)	Bobbie Veach	100.00	50.00	30.00
(37)	Clarence Walker	100.00	50.00	30.00
(38)	Johnnie Walker	100.00	50.00	30.00
(39)	Zach Wheat	270.00	135.00	80.00
(40)	Kenneth Williams	100.00	50.00	30.00

1925-31 W590

Originally unlisted in the American Card Catalog, this strip-card set was given the number W590 in later editions. It is part of a larger set cataloged as W580 which includes movie stars, boxers and other athletes. These cards measure approximately 1-3/8" x 2-1/2". Fronts have black-and-white player photos with a white border. In the bottom border is the player name, position, city and league or team nickname. Some cards can be found with a "Former" designation before the position. Several variations are known in team designations, indicating the set was probably reissued at least once between 1927-31. Backs are blank. Only the baseball players are listed here, in alphabetical order.

		NM	EX	VG
Common Player:		75.00	37.00	22.00
(1a)	Grover C. Alexander (Chicago N.L.)	300.00	150.00	90.00
(1b)	Grover C. Alexander (House of David)	600.00	300.00	180.00
(2a)	Dave Bancroft (Boston N.L.)	150.00	75.00	45.00
(2b)	Dave Bancroft (New York N.L.)	150.00	75.00	45.00
(3a)	Jess Barnes ("Pitcher" Boston N.L.)	75.00	37.50	22.50
(3b)	Jess Barnes ("Former Pitcher" Boston N.L.)	75.00	37.50	22.50
(4)	Ray Blades (St. Louis Cardinals)	75.00	37.50	22.50
(5)	Pictbred Bluege (Ossie)(Third Baseman)	75.00	37.50	22.50
(6a)	George Bums (New York N.L.)	75.00	37.50	22.50
(6b)	George Burns (Philadelphia N.L.)	75.00	37.50	22.50
(7a)	George Burns (Cleveland A.L. - 1st Baseman)	75.00	37.50	22.50
(7b)	George Burns (Cleveland A.L. - Former 1st Baseman)	75.00	37.50	22.50
(8)	Max Carey (Pittsburg N.L.)	150.00	75.00	45.00
(9a)	Caveney (Jimmy)(Short Stop)	75.00	37.50	22.50
(9b)	Caveney (Jimmy) (Former Short Stop)	75.00	37.50	22.50
(10)	"Ty" Cobb	1,300	650.00	390.00
(11a)	Eddie Collins (Chicago White Sox)	175.00	85.00	50.00

		NM	EX	VG
(11b)	Eddie Collins (Philadelphia A.L.)	175.00	85.00	50.00
(12)	George Dauss (Former Pitcher - Detroit)	75.00	37.50	22.50
(13)	"Red" Faber	150.00	75.00	45.00
(14a)	Frankie Frisch (New York N.L.)	175.00	85.00	50.00
(14b)	Frank Frisch (St. Louis N.L.)	175.00	85.00	50.00
(15)	Lou Gehrig (1st Baseman)	1,125	560.00	335.00
(17a)	Hank Gowdy (Catcher)	75.00	37.50	22.50
(17b)	Hank Gowdy (Former Catcher)	75.00	37.50	22.50
(18)	Sam Gray	75.00	37.50	22.50
(19)	Charley Grimm (Chicago N.L.)	75.00	37.50	22.50
(20)	"Buckey" Harris (Manager, Washington A.L.)	150.00	75.00	45.00
(21a)	Rogers Hornsby (St. Louis N.L.)	200.00	100.00	60.00
(21b)	Rogers Hornsby (Boston N.L.)	200.00	100.00	60.00
(22)	Travis Jackson (Short Stop, New York N.L.)	150.00	75.00	45.00
(23)	Walter Johnson (Pitcher)	600.00	300.00	180.00
(24a)	George Kelly (New York N.L.)	150.00	75.00	45.00
(24b)	George Kelly (Chicago N.L.)	150.00	75.00	45.00
(25)	Fred Lindstrom	150.00	75.00	45.00
(26a)	Rabbit Maranville (Chicago N.L.)	150.00	75.00	45.00
(26b)	Rabbit Maranville (Boston N.L.)	150.00		45.00
(27)	Bob Meusel (Fielder, New York A.L.)	75.00	37.50	22.50
(28)	Jack Quinn	75.00	37.50	22.50
(29)	Eppa Rixey (Cincinnati N.L.)	150.00	75.00	45.00
(31)	Eddie Rommel	75.00	37.50	22.50
(32)	"Babe" Ruth (King of the Bat)	2,250	1,125	675.00
(33)	Heinie Sand	75.00	37.50	22.50
(34)	Geo. Sissler (Sisler)	150.00	75.00	45.00
(35)	Earl Smith	75.00	37.50	22.50
(36a)	Tris Speaker (Cleveland A.L.)	200.00	100.00	60.00
(36b)	Tris Speaker (Manager, Newark)	200.00	100.00	60.00
(37)	Roy Spencer	75.00	37.50	22.50
(38)	Milton Stock	75.00	37.50	22.50
(39a)	Phil Todt (Boston A.L.)	75.00	37.50	22.50
(39b)	Phil Todt (Philadelphia A.L.)	75.00	37.50	22.50
(40)	Dazzy Vance	150.00	75.00	45.00
(41)	Zach Wheat (Brooklyn N.L.)	150.00	75.00	45.00
(42a)	Kenneth Williams (St. Louis A.L.)	75.00	37.50	22.50
(42b)	Kenneth Williams (Boston A.L.)	75.00	37.50	22.50
(43a)	Ross Young (Youngs) (Right Fielder)	150.00	75.00	45.00
(43b)	Ross Young (Youngs) (Former Right Fielder)	150.00	75.00	45.00

1921 W9316

As crude as many of the strip cards of the era were, this issue was the worst. In the same blank-back format and size (about 1-1/2" x 2-1/2") as many contemporary strip cards, the set features 10 of the players from W519/W521. The artwork on these cards is very crudely done, almost child-like. The most striking feature about the pictures is the ruby red lips on the players. Unlisted in the American Card Catalog, this set was given the designation W9316 in John Stirling's Sports Card Catalog.

		NM	EX	VG
Complete Set (10):		2,000	800.00	400.00
Common Player:		175.00	70.00	35.00
1	Bob Veach	175.00	70.00	35.00
2	Frank Baker	275.00	110.00	55.00
3	Wilbur (Wilbert) Robinson	275.00	110.00	55.00
4	Johnny Griffith	175.00	70.00	35.00
5	Jimmie Johnston	175.00	70.00	35.00
6	Wallie Schange (Wally Schang)	175.00	70.00	35.00
7	Leon Cadore	175.00	70.00	35.00
8	George Sisler	275.00	110.00	55.00
9	Ray Schalk	275.00	110.00	55.00
10	Jesse Barnes	175.00	70.00	35.00

Y

1972 The Yawkey Red Sox

Boston Red Sox players of the 1930s are featured in this collectors' issue. The issue date given is only a guess. The 2-1/2" x 3-1/2" cards have black-and-white player photos with brown borders and black graphics. Backs are also in black-and-white with personal data, a career summary and a promotion for the Red Sox long-time charity, The Jimmy Fund. The unnumbered cards are listed here alphabetically.

		NM	EX	VG
Complete Set (45):		45.00	22.50	13.50
Common Player:		3.00	1.50	.90
(1)	Mel Almada	4.50	2.25	1.25
(2)	Morris "Moe" Berg	9.00	4.50	2.75
(3)	Max Bishop	3.00	1.50	.90
(4)	Doc Bowers	3.00	1.50	.90
(5)	Joe Cascarella	3.00	1.50	.90
(6)	Ben Chapman	3.00	1.50	.90
(7)	Bill Cissell	3.00	1.50	.90
(8)	Dusty Cooke	3.00	1.50	.90
(9)	Doc Cramer	3.00	1.50	.90
(10)	Joe Cronin	4.50	2.25	1.25
(11)	George Dickey	3.00	1.50	.90
(12)	Emerson Dickman	3.00	1.50	.90
(13)	Bobby Doerr	4.50	2.25	1.25
(14)	Rick Ferrell	4.50	2.25	1.25
(15)	Wes Ferrell	3.00	1.50	.90
(16)	Jimmie Foxx	7.50	3.75	2.25
(17)	Joe Gonzales	3.00	1.50	.90
(18)	Lefty Grove	6.00	3.00	1.75
(19)	Bucky Harris	4.50	2.25	1.25
(20)	Jim Henry	3.00	1.50	.90
(21)	Pinky Higgins	3.00	1.50	.90
(22)	Lefty Hockette	3.00	1.50	.90
(23)	Roy Johnson	3.00	1.50	.90
(24)	John Kroner	3.00	1.50	.90
(25)	Heinie Manush	4.50	2.25	1.25
(26)	Archie McKain	3.00	1.50	.90
(27)	Eric McNair	3.00	1.50	.90
(28)	Oscar Melillo	3.00	1.50	.90
(29)	Bing Miller	3.00	1.50	.90
(30)	Joe Mulligan	3.00	1.50	.90
(31)	Bobo Newsom	3.00	1.50	.90
(32)	Ted Olson	3.00	1.50	.90
(33)	Fritz Ostermueller	3.00	1.50	.90
(34)	George Pipgras	3.00	1.50	.90
(35)	Dusty Rhodes	3.00	1.50	.90
(36)	Walt Ripley	3.00	1.50	.90
(37)	Buck Rogers	3.00	1.50	.90
(38)	Jack Russell	3.00	1.50	.90
(39)	Tommy Thomas	3.00	1.50	.90
(40)	Hy Vandenberg	3.00	1.50	.90
(41)	Rube Walberg	3.00	1.50	.90
(42)	Johnny Welch	3.00	1.50	.90
(43)	Bill Werber	3.00	1.50	.90
(44)	Dib Williams	3.00	1.50	.90
(45)	Black Jack Wilson	3.00	1.50	.90

1959 Yoo-Hoo

Issued as a promotion for Yoo-Hoo chocolate flavored soft drink (it's a New York thing), this issue features five New York Yankees players. The black-and-white blank-backed cards measure 2-7/16" x 5-1/8", including a tab at the bottom which could be redeemed for various prizes. The top of the card features a posed spring training photo and includes a facsimile autograph and "Me for Yoo-Hoo" slogan. Prices shown here are for complete cards; cards without tabs would be valued at one-half of these figures. A Mickey Mantle advertising piece in larger size is often collected as an adjunct to the set, but no card of Mantle was issued. The Berra card is considerably scarcer than the others.

		NM	EX	VG
Complete Set, W/Tabs (5):		5,750	2,875	1,725
Complete Set, No Tabs (5):		1,350	675.00	415.00
Common Player, W/Tab:		800.00	400.00	240.00
Common Player, No Tab:				
WITH TAB				
(1)	Yogi Berra	1,200	600.00	360.00
(2)	Whitey Ford	1,200	600.00	360.00
(3)	Tony Kubek	800.00	400.00	240.00
(4)	Gil McDougald	800.00	400.00	240.00
(5)	Bill Skowron	800.00	400.00	240.00
NO TAB				
(1)	Yogi Berra	300.00	150.00	90.00
(2)	Whitey Ford	300.00	150.00	90.00
(3)	Tony Kubek	250.00	125.00	75.00
(4)	Gil McDougald	250.00	125.00	75.00
(5)	Bill Skowron	250.00	125.00	75.00

1959 Yoo-Hoo Mickey Mantle

In a different format than the other contemporary Yoo-Hoo Yankees cards, the manner of original distribution of this card is unclear. The 2-5/8" x 3-5/8" black-and-white card has a portrait photo and endorsement for the product on front. Back is blank.

	NM	EX	VG
Mickey Mantle	1,600	800.00	480.00

1959 Yoo-Hoo Bottle Caps

These lids for the chocolate soft drink feature black-and-white player portraits with the player name across the chest and "ME FOR" above with "YOO-HOO" below. Caps come in two styles, the older pry-off style and a later, larger, screw-top.

		NM	EX	VG
Common Player:		200.00	100.00	60.00
(1a)	Yogi Berra/Portrait	400.00	200.00	120.00
(1b)	Yogi Berra (Drinking Yoo-Hoo.)	400.00	200.00	120.00
(2a)	Whitey Ford (Cap straight.)	400.00	200.00	120.00
(2b)	Whitey Ford (Cap tilted.)	400.00	200.00	120.00
(3)	Tony Kubek	200.00	100.00	60.00
(4a)	Mickey Mantle (Large portrait.)	800.00	400.00	250.00
94b)	Mickey Mantle (Small portrait, name under YOO-HOO.)	800.00	400.00	250.00
(5)	Gil McDougald	200.00	100.00	60.00
(6)	Bobby Richardson (Screw top.)	200.00	100.00	60.00
(7)	Moose Skowron	200.00	100.00	60.00

1964 Yoo-Hoo Counter Sign

Seven N.Y. Yankees and Bill Skowron in a Senators' cap are pictured on this 11" x 14" easel-back counter display for the chocolate soft drink. Printed in brown, yellow and white, the sign has a hand holding a bottle in front of each player's portrait.

	NM	EX	VG
Yogi Berra, Whitey Ford, Elston Howard, Mickey Mantle, Joe Pepitone, Bobby Richardson, Moose Skowron, Tom Tresh	2,000	1,000	600.00

1927 York Caramels Type 1 (E210)

Issued in 1927 by the York Caramel Co. of York, Pa., these black-and-white cards are among the last of the caramel issues. Measuring 1-3/8" x 2-1/2", they are similar in appearance to earlier candy and tobacco cards. Fronts have the player's name in capital letters, with the number preceded by a number in parentheses. The back also lists the player's name in capital letters, along with a brief phrase describing him and the line, "This is one of a series of sixty of the most prominent stars in baseball." The bottom of the cards reads "York Caramel Co. York, Pa." The set includes several variations and is designated in the ACC as E210. It is closely related to the W502 set of the same year. Cards can be found on white or gray card stock. Type 1 cards can be differentiated from Type 2s by the orientation of the back printing. On Type 1 cards, the player name on back is at right when a normally-viewed front is turned over.

		NM	EX	VG
Complete Set (60):		40,000	16,000	8,000
Common Player:		250.00	100.00	50.00
1	Burleigh Grimes	500.00	200.00	100.00
2	Walter Reuther (Ruether)	500.00	200.00	100.00
3	Joe Duggan (Dugan)	250.00	100.00	50.00
4	Red Faber	500.00	200.00	100.00
5	Gabby Hartnett	500.00	200.00	100.00
6	Babe Ruth	15,000	4,800	2,400
7	Bob Meusel	250.00	100.00	50.00
8a	Herb Pennock (Team name on jersey.)	500.00	200.00	100.00
8b	Herb Pennock (No team name.)	250.00	100.00	50.00
9	George Burns	250.00	100.00	50.00
10	Joe Sewell	500.00	200.00	100.00
11	George Uhle	250.00	100.00	50.00
12a	Bob O'Farrel (O'Farrell) (Team name on jersey.)	250.00	100.00	50.00
12b	Bob O'Farrel (O'Farrell) (No team name.)	250.00	100.00	50.00
13	Rogers Hornsby	600.00	240.00	120.00
14	Pie Traynor	500.00	200.00	100.00
15	Clarence Mitchell	250.00	100.00	50.00
16	Eppa Jepha Rixey (Jeptha)	500.00	200.00	100.00
17	Carl Mays	250.00	100.00	50.00
18	Adolph Luque (Adolfo)	250.00	100.00	50.00
19	Dave Bancroft	500.00	200.00	100.00
20	George Kelly	500.00	200.00	100.00
21	Ira Flagstead	250.00	100.00	50.00
22	Harry Heilmann	500.00	200.00	100.00
23	Raymond W. Shalk (Schalk)	500.00	200.00	100.00
24	Johnny Mostil	250.00	100.00	50.00
25	Hack Wilson (Photo actually Art Wilson.)	500.00	200.00	100.00
26	Tom Zachary	250.00	100.00	50.00
27	Ty Cobb	6,500	2,600	1,300
28	Tris Speaker	600.00	240.00	120.00
29	Ralph Perkins	250.00	100.00	50.00
30	Jess Haines	500.00	200.00	100.00
31	Sherwood Smith (Photo actually Jack Coombs.)	250.00	100.00	50.00
32	Max Carey	500.00	200.00	100.00
33	Eugene Hargraves (Hargrave)	250.00	100.00	50.00
34	Miguel L. Gonzales (Miguel A. Gonzalez)	250.00	100.00	50.00
35a	Clifton Heathcot (Heathcote) (Team name on jersey.)	250.00	100.00	50.00
35b	Clifton Heathcot (Heathcote) (No team name.)	250.00	100.00	50.00
35c	Clifton Heathcote (Correct spelling.) (Team Name on jersey.)	250.00	100.00	50.00
36	E.C. (Sam) Rice	500.00	200.00	100.00
37	Earl Sheely	250.00	100.00	50.00
38a	Emory E. Rigney (Team name on jersey.)	250.00	100.00	50.00
38b	Emory E. Rigney (No team name.)	250.00	100.00	50.00
39	Bib A. Falk (Bibb)	250.00	100.00	50.00
40	Nick Altrock	250.00	100.00	50.00
41	Stanley Harris	500.00	200.00	100.00
42	John J. McGraw	500.00	200.00	100.00
43	Wilbert Robinson	500.00	200.00	100.00
44	Grover Alexander	750.00	300.00	150.00
45	Walter Johnson	1,000	400.00	200.00
46	William H. Terry (Photo actually Zeb Terry.)	500.00	200.00	100.00
47	Edward Collins	500.00	200.00	100.00
48	Marty McManus	250.00	100.00	50.00
49	Leon (Goose) Goslin	500.00	200.00	100.00
50	Frank Frisch	500.00	200.00	100.00
51	Jimmie Dykes	250.00	100.00	50.00
52	Fred (Cy) Williams	500.00	200.00	100.00
53	Eddie Roush	500.00	200.00	100.00
54	George Sisler	500.00	200.00	100.00
55	Ed Rommel	250.00	100.00	50.00
56a	Rogers Peckinpaugh (Roger) (Card number upside-down.)	250.00	100.00	50.00
56b	Rogers Peckinpaugh (Roger) (Card number corrected.)	250.00	100.00	50.00
57	Stanley Coveleskie (Coveleski)	500.00	200.00	100.00

		NM	EX	VG
58	Clarence Gallaway (Galloway)	250.00	100.00	50.00
59	Bob Shawkey	250.00	100.00	50.00
60	John P. McInnis	250.00	100.00	50.00

1927 York Caramels Type 2 (E210)

Type 2 York Caramels are in the same size and format as the Type 1 cards. They can be differentiated from Type 1 cards by the orientation of the back printing. On Type 2 cards, the player name appears at left when a normally-held card is turned over. Type 2 cards are all printed on white stock. Some players and photos were changed, and the descriptive lines about the players were changed on most cards.

		NM	EX	VG
	Complete Set (60):	45,000	18,000	9,000
	Common Player:	250.00	100.00	50.00
1	Burleigh Grimes	500.00	200.00	100.00
2	Walter Reuther (Ruether)	250.00	100.00	50.00
3	Joe Dugan	250.00	100.00	50.00
4	Red Faber	500.00	200.00	100.00
5	Gabby Hartnett	500.00	200.00	100.00
6	Babe Ruth	12,000	4,800	2,400
7	Bob Meusel	250.00	100.00	50.00
8	Herb Pennock (Profile)	500.00	200.00	100.00
9	George Burns	250.00	100.00	50.00
10	Joe Sewell	500.00	200.00	100.00
11	George Uhle	250.00	100.00	50.00
12	Bob O'Farrell	250.00	100.00	50.00
13	Rogers Hornsby	600.00	240.00	120.00
14	Pie Traynor	500.00	200.00	100.00
15	Clarence Mitchell	250.00	100.00	50.00
16	Eppa Rixey	500.00	200.00	100.00
17	Carl Mays	250.00	100.00	50.00
18	Adolfo Luque	250.00	100.00	50.00
19	Dave Bancroft	500.00	200.00	100.00
20	George Kelly	500.00	200.00	100.00
21	Earle Combs	500.00	200.00	100.00
22	Harry Heilmann	500.00	200.00	100.00
23	Ray W. Schalk	500.00	200.00	100.00
24	Johnny Mostil	250.00	100.00	50.00
25	Hack Wilson	500.00	200.00	100.00
26	Lou Gehrig	10,000	2,600	1,300
27	Ty Cobb	6,500	2,600	1,300
28	Tris Speaker	600.00	240.00	120.00
29	Tony Lazzeri	500.00	200.00	100.00
30	Waite Hoyt	500.00	200.00	100.00
31	Sherwood Smith (Photo actually Jack Coombs.)	250.00	100.00	50.00
32	Max Carey	500.00	200.00	100.00
33	Eugene Hargrave (Hargraves)	250.00	100.00	50.00
34	Miguel L. Gonzales (Miguel A. Gonzalez)	250.00	100.00	50.00
35	Joe Judge	250.00	100.00	50.00
36	E.C. (Sam) Rice	500.00	200.00	100.00
37	Earl Sheely	250.00	100.00	50.00
38	Sam Jones	250.00	100.00	50.00
39	Bib (Bibb) A. Falk	250.00	100.00	50.00
40	Willie Kamm	250.00	100.00	50.00
41	Stanley Harris	500.00	200.00	100.00
42	John J. McGraw	500.00	200.00	100.00
43	Artie Nehf	250.00	100.00	50.00
44	Grover Alexander	750.00	300.00	150.00
45	Paul Waner	500.00	200.00	100.00
46	William H. Terry (Photo actually Zeb Terry.)	500.00	200.00	100.00
47	Glenn Wright	250.00	100.00	50.00
48	Earl Smith	250.00	100.00	50.00
49	Leon (Goose) Goslin	500.00	200.00	100.00
50	Frank Frisch	500.00	200.00	100.00
51	Joe Harris	250.00	100.00	50.00
52	Fred (Cy) Williams	250.00	100.00	50.00
53	Eddie Roush	500.00	200.00	100.00
54	George Sisler	500.00	200.00	100.00
55	Ed Rommel	250.00	100.00	50.00
56	Rogers Peckinpaugh (Roger)	250.00	100.00	50.00
57	Stanley Coveleskie (Coveleski)	500.00	200.00	100.00
58	Lester Bell	250.00	100.00	50.00
59	L. Waner	500.00	200.00	100.00
60	John P. McInnis	250.00	100.00	50.00

1917 Youth's Companion Stamps

The date attributed is speculative. This set of poster-stamps was issued to promote a Boston-based weekly magazine. Although he is not named, the left-handed pitcher depicted in very Red Sox-like uniform on one of the color litho stamps evidently looks enough like Babe Ruth that collectors have been willing to pay hundreds of dollars for examples of this scarce issue. The 1-7/8" x 2-1/2" stamp is, of course, blank-backed and is part of a set which featured other sporting activities, hobbys and topics suitable for young readers.

	NM	EX	VG
(Babe Ruth?)	600.00	300.00	180.00

1928 Yuengling's Ice Cream (F50)

(28) TRIS SPEAKER

SAVE THESE PICTURES
One ice cream novelty will be given free for each picture of Babe Ruth
ALSO
One gallon of Yuengling's ice cream will be delivered free to the holder of a complete set of sixty different Baseball Stars, upon surrender of same to any Yuengling dealer. Babe Ruth may be saved for quarts of ice cream or a $5.00 skooter

Issued in 1928, the Yuengling's Ice Cream issue consists of 60 black-and-white cards measuring 1-3/8" x 2-1/2". The photos are similar to those used in the E210 and W502 sets. Other ice cream companies such as Harrington's and Tharp's produced nearly identical cards. Two types of cards are seen, though whether either or both can be found for all players is unknown. Besides typographical placement differences on front, the back of one type mentions a "$5.00 skooter" as a redemption, while the other type has no mention of the toy. Collectors could redeem an entire set of Yuengling's cards for a gallon of ice cream. Yuengling's, located in Pottsville, Pa., was a brewery that converted its product line to ice cream during Prohibition.

		NM	EX	VG
	Complete Set (60):	45,000	18,000	9,000
	Common Player:	250.00	100.00	50.00
1	Burleigh Grimes	500.00	200.00	100.00
2	Walter Reuther (Ruether)	250.00	100.00	50.00
3	Joe Dugan	250.00	100.00	50.00
4	Red Faber	500.00	200.00	100.00
5	Gabby Hartnett	500.00	200.00	100.00
6	Babe Ruth	12,000	4,800	2,400
7	Bob Meusel	250.00	100.00	50.00
8	Herb Pennock	500.00	200.00	100.00
9	George Burns	250.00	100.00	50.00
10	Joe Sewell	500.00	200.00	100.00
11	George Uhle	250.00	100.00	50.00
12	Bob O'Farrell	250.00	100.00	50.00
13	Rogers Hornsby	600.00	240.00	120.00
14	"Pie" Traynor	500.00	200.00	100.00
15	Clarence Mitchell	250.00	100.00	50.00
16	Eppa Jepha Rixey	500.00	200.00	100.00
17	Carl Mays	250.00	100.00	50.00
18	Adolfo Luque	250.00	100.00	50.00
19	Dave Bancroft	500.00	200.00	100.00
20	George Kelly	500.00	200.00	100.00
21	Earl (Earle) Combs	500.00	200.00	100.00
22	Harry Heilmann	500.00	200.00	100.00
23	Ray W. Schalk	500.00	200.00	100.00
24	Johnny Mostil	250.00	100.00	50.00
25	Hack Wilson	500.00	200.00	100.00
26	Lou Gehrig	6,500	2,600	1,300
27	Ty Cobb	6,500	2,600	1,300
28	Tris Speaker	600.00	240.00	120.00
29	Tony Lazzeri	500.00	200.00	100.00
30	Waite Hoyt	500.00	200.00	100.00
31	Sherwood Smith	250.00	100.00	50.00
32	Max Carey	500.00	200.00	100.00
33	Eugene Hargrave	250.00	100.00	50.00
34	Miguel L. Gonzales (Miguel A. Gonzalez)	250.00	100.00	50.00
35	Joe Judge	250.00	100.00	50.00
36	E.C. (Sam) Rice	500.00	200.00	100.00
37	Earl Sheely	250.00	100.00	50.00
38	Sam Jones	250.00	100.00	50.00
39	Bib (Bibb) A. Falk	250.00	100.00	50.00
40	Willie Kamm	250.00	100.00	50.00
41	Stanley Harris	500.00	200.00	100.00
42	John J. McGraw	500.00	200.00	100.00
43	Artie Nehf	250.00	100.00	50.00
44	Grover Alexander	750.00	300.00	150.00
45	Paul Waner	500.00	200.00	100.00
46	William H. Terry	500.00	200.00	100.00
47	Glenn Wright	250.00	100.00	50.00
48	Earl Smith	250.00	100.00	50.00
49	Leon (Goose) Goslin	500.00	200.00	100.00
50	Frank Frisch	500.00	200.00	100.00
51	Joe Harris	250.00	100.00	50.00
52	Fred (Cy) Williams	250.00	100.00	50.00
53	Eddie Roush	500.00	200.00	100.00
54	George Sisler	500.00	200.00	100.00
55	Ed. Rommel	250.00	100.00	50.00
56	Rogers Peckinpaugh (Roger)	250.00	100.00	50.00
57	Stanley Coveleskie (Coveleski)	500.00	200.00	100.00
58	Lester Bell	250.00	100.00	50.00
59	L. Waner	500.00	200.00	100.00
60	John P. McInnis	250.00	100.00	50.00

1888 Yum Yum Tobacco (N403)

An extremely rare series of tobacco cards, this set was issued in 1888 by August Beck & Co., Chicago. The cards vary slightly in size but average 1-3/8" x 2-3/4". They were distributed in packages of the company's Yum Yum smoking and chewing tobacco and are found in two distinct types: photographic portraits and full-length action drawings copied from photos used in the Old Judge sets of the same period. In both types, the player's name and position appear in capital letters below the photo, and the very bottom of the card states: "Smoke and Chew "Yum Yum" Tobacco. A. Beck & Co. Chicago, Ill." Players from all eight National League clubs, plus Brooklyn of the American Association, are included in the set. The checklist here has gaps left to accommodate future additions.

		NM	EX	VG
	Common Player:	9,000	5,000	3,000
(3)	Cap Anson/Portrait	45,000	22,500	13,500
(4)	Cap Anson/Btg	23,750	11,250	6,750
(7)	Lady Baldwin (Left arm extended.)	9,750	4,875	2,925
(11)	Dan Brouthers/Btg	18,000	9,000	5,400
(13)	Willard "California" Brown	9,750	4,875	2,925
(15)	Charles Buffington (Buffinton)	9,750	4,875	2,925
(17)	Tom Burns/Portrait	16,500	8,250	4,950
(18)	Tom Burns (With bat.)	9,750	4,875	2,925
(21)	John Clarkson/Portrait	30,000	15,000	9,000
(22)	John Clarkson (Throwing, arm back.)	18,000	9,000	5,400
(25)	John Coleman/Portrait	16,500	8,250	4,950
(27)	Roger Connor/Btg	18,000	9,000	5,400
(28)	Roger Connor/Portrait	30,000	15,000	9,000
(30)	Larry Corcoran/Portrait	16,500	8,250	4,950
(34)	Tom Daily (Daly)/Portrait (Photo actually Billy Sunday.)	17,250	8,625	5,175
(36)	Tom Deasley/Portrait	16,500	8,250	4,950
(39)	Mike Dorgan/Portrait	16,500	8,250	4,950
(40)	Dude Esterbrook/Portrait	16,500	8,250	4,950
(41)	Buck Ewing/Portrait	30,000	15,000	9,000
(42)	Buck Ewing (With bat.)	18,000	9,000	5,400
(45)	Silver Flint/Portrait	16,500	8,250	4,950
(47)	Jim Fogarty/Throwing	9,750	4,875	2,925
(49)	Pud Galvin (Ball in hands at chest.)	18,000	9,000	5,400
(51)	Joe Gerhardt	16,500	8,250	4,950
(53)	Charlie Getzein (Getzien)(Holding ball.)	9,750	4,875	2,925
(55)	Pete Gillespie/Portrait	16,500	8,250	4,950
(57)	Jack Glasscock	9,750	4,875	2,925
(59)	George Gore (Leaning on bat.)	9,750	4,875	2,925
(61)	Ed Greer/Portrait	16,500	8,250	4,950
(65)	Tim Keefe (Pitching)	18,000	9,000	5,400
(66)	Tim Keefe/Portrait	30,000	15,000	9,000
(67)	King Kelly/Btg	18,000	9,000	5,400
(68)	King Kelly (Photo, standing by urn.)	45,000	22,500	13,500
(70)	Gus Krock/Portrait	16,500	8,250	4,950
(72)	Connie Mack	18,000	9,000	5,400
(74)	Kid Madden (Ball in raised right hand.)	9,750	4,875	2,925
(76)	Doggie Miller (Leaning on bat.)	9,750	4,875	2,925
(78)	John Morrill (Leaning on bat.)	9,750	4,875	2,925
(80)	James Mutrie/Portrait	16,500	8,250	4,950
(82)	Billy Nash (Holding bat.)	9,750	4,875	2,925
(84)	Jim O'Rourke/Portrait	30,000	15,000	9,000
(85)	Jim O'Rourke (With bat.)	18,000	9,000	5,400
(87)	Fred Pfeffer (Bat on shoulder.)	9,750	4,875	2,925
(90)	Danny Richardson/Portrait	16,500	8,250	4,950
(92)	Chief Roseman/Portrait	16,500	8,250	4,950
(94)	Jimmy Ryan/Portrait	16,500	8,250	4,950
(95)	Jimmy Ryan/Throwing	9,750	4,875	2,925
(97)	Bill Sowders (Ball in hands at chest.)	9,750	4,875	2,925
(100)	Marty Sullivan/Portrait	16,500	8,250	4,950
(102)	Billy Sunday/Fldg	18,000	9,000	5,400
(103)	Billy Sunday/Portrait (Photo actually Mark Baldwin.)	18,000	9,000	5,400
(105)	Ezra Sutton/Btg	9,750	4,875	2,925
(110)	Mike Tiernan/Portrait	16,500	8,250	4,950
(111)	Mike Tiernan (With bat.)	9,750	4,875	2,925
(115)	Rip Van Haltren (Photo not Van Haltren.)	16,500	8,250	4,950
(119)	John Ward/Portrait	30,000	15,000	9,000
(123)	Mickey Welch (Ball in hands at chest.)	18,000	9,000	5,400
(124)	Mickey Welch/Portrait	30,000	15,000	9,000
(125)	Mickey Welch (Right arm extended.)	18,000	9,000	5,400
(129)	Jim Whitney/Throwing	9,750	4,875	2,925
(133)	George Wood/Throwing (Arm behind head.)	9,750	4,875	2,925

Z

1954-1955 Zipcards Baltimore Orioles

BALTIMORE

55-04
Zipcards

Tom Gastall

Given the homemade appearance of these cards, it must be surmised that they were an early collectors' issue. It is possible they date from as early as 1956, only a few years after the Orioles joined the American League. Cards are found in three formats. One type measures about 2" x 2-5/8" (all measurements are approximate due to the hand-cut nature of the cards) and is printed on thin yellow cardboard. They feature a chest-to-cap black-and-white circular player photo at center. A second type is about 2-3/4" x 3-5/8", black-and-white, with square portrait or posed action photos and "BALTIMORE" at top in what appears to be a picture of an embossed plastic Dymo label strip. The third type is also about 2-3/4" x 3-5/8" and is similar in design to the Dymo-lable format, except "Baltimore" is printed at top in a serifed italic typeface. All cards are blank-backed. Where known, the type of each card is indicated on this checklist by "RP" (round photo), "DL" (Dymo-label) or "SI" (serifed italic). It is possible this checklist is incomplete.

	NM	EX	VG
Common Player:	30.00	15.00	9.00
54-01 Jimmie Dykes	30.00	15.00	9.00
54-02 Tom Oliver	30.00	15.00	9.00
54-03 Frank Skaff	30.00	15.00	9.00
54-04 Eddie Waitkuss (Waitkus) (DL)	30.00	15.00	9.00
54-05 Chuck Diering (DL)	30.00	15.00	9.00
54-06 Chick Chakales (RP)	30.00	15.00	9.00
54-07 Marlin Stuart (RP)	30.00	15.00	9.00
54-08 Jim Brideweser (RP)	30.00	15.00	9.00
54-09 Chico Garcia (RP)	30.00	15.00	9.00
54-10 Jim Fridley (RP)	30.00	15.00	9.00
54-11 Billy O'Dell (DL)	30.00	15.00	9.00
54-12 Unknown			
54-13 Joe Durham (DL)	30.00	15.00	9.00
55-01 Wayne Causey (RP)	30.00	15.00	9.00
55-02 Jim Dyck	30.00	15.00	9.00
55-03 Hoot Evers (SI)	30.00	15.00	9.00
55-04 Tom Gastall (RP)	30.00	15.00	9.00
55-05 Bob Hale (RP)	30.00	15.00	9.00
55-06 Bob Kennedy (SI)	30.00	15.00	9.00
55-07 Don Leppert (SI)	30.00	15.00	9.00
55-08 Les Moss (SI)	30.00	15.00	9.00
55-09 Bob Nelson (RP)	30.00	15.00	9.00
55-10 Dave Philley (RP)	30.00	15.00	9.00
55-11 Unknown			
55-12 Unknown			
55-13 Art Schallock (RP)	30.00	15.00	9.00
55-14 Bobby Young (SI)	30.00	15.00	9.00
55-15 Unknown			
55-16 Lum Harris	30.00	15.00	9.00

1977 Zip'z Discs

Virtually identical in format to the several locally sponsored disc sets of the previous year, these 3-3/8" diameter player discs were given away at the sponsor's sundae bars around the cvountry. Some are found with a black rubber-stamp on back of the specific Zip's location. Discs once again feature black-and-white player portrait photos in the center of a baseball design. The left and right panels are in one of several bright colors. Licensed by the players' association through Mike Schechter Associates, the player photos carry no uniform logos. Backs are printed in reddish-orange. The unnumbered discs are checklisted here alphabetically.

	NM	EX	VG
Complete Set (70):	120.00	60.00	35.00
Common Player:	2.00	1.00	.60
(1) Sal Bando	2.00	1.00	.60
(2) Buddy Bell	2.00	1.00	.60
(3) Johnny Bench	7.50	3.75	2.25
(4) Larry Bowa	2.00	1.00	.60
(5) Steve Braun	2.00	1.00	.60
(6) George Brett	20.00	10.00	6.00
(7) Lou Brock	6.00	3.00	1.75
(8) Jeff Burroughs	2.00	1.00	.60
(9) Bert Campaneris	2.00	1.00	.60
(10) John Candelaria	2.00	1.00	.60
(11) Jose Cardenal	2.00	1.00	.60
(12) Rod Carew	6.00	3.00	1.75
(13) Steve Carlton	6.00	3.00	1.75
(14) Dave Cash	2.00	1.00	.60
(15) Cesar Cedeno	2.00	1.00	.60
(16) Ron Cey	2.00	1.00	.60
(17) Dave Concepcion	2.00	1.00	.60
(18) Dennis Eckersley	6.00	3.00	1.75
(19) Mark Fidrych	3.00	1.50	.90
(20) Rollie Fingers	6.00	3.00	1.75
(21) Carlton Fisk	6.00	3.00	1.75
(22) George Foster	2.00	1.00	.60
(23) Wayne Garland	2.00	1.00	.60
(24) Ralph Garr	2.00	1.00	.60
(25) Steve Garvey	5.00	2.50	1.50
(26) Cesar Geronimo	2.00	1.00	.60
(27) Bobby Grich	2.00	1.00	.60
(28) Ken Griffey Sr.	2.00	1.00	.60
(29) Don Gullett	2.00	1.00	.60
(30) Mike Hargrove	2.00	1.00	.60
(31) Al Hrabosky	2.00	1.00	.60
(32) Jim Hunter	6.00	3.00	1.75
(33) Reggie Jackson	15.00	7.50	4.50
(34) Randy Jones	2.00	1.00	.60
(35) Dave Kingman	2.00	1.00	.60
(36) Jerry Koosman	2.00	1.00	.60
(37) Dave LaRoche	2.00	1.00	.60
(38) Greg Luzinski	2.00	1.00	.60
(39) Fred Lynn	2.00	1.00	.60
(40) Bill Madlock	2.00	1.00	.60
(41) Rick Manning	2.00	1.00	.60
(42) Jon Matlock	2.00	1.00	.60
(43) John Mayberry	2.00	1.00	.60
(44) Hal McRae	2.00	1.00	.60
(45) Andy Messersmith	2.00	1.00	.60
(46) Rick Monday	2.00	1.00	.60
(47) John Montefusco	2.00	1.00	.60
(48) Joe Morgan	6.00	3.00	1.75
(49) Thurman Munson	5.00	2.50	1.50
(50) Bobby Murcer	2.00	1.00	.60
(51) Bill North	2.00	1.00	.60
(52) Jim Palmer	6.00	3.00	1.75
(53) Tony Perez	6.00	3.00	1.75
(54) Jerry Reuss	2.00	1.00	.60
(55) Brooks Robinson	7.50	3.75	2.25
(56) Pete Rose	25.00	12.50	7.50
(57) Joe Rudi	2.00	1.00	.60
(58) Nolan Ryan	35.00	17.50	10.00
(59) Manny Sanguillen	2.00	1.00	.60
(60) Mike Schmidt	15.00	7.50	4.50
(61) Tom Seaver	7.50	3.75	2.25
(62) Bill Singer	2.00	1.00	.60
(63) Willie Stargell	6.00	3.00	1.75
(64) Rusty Staub	2.00	1.00	.60
(65) Luis Tiant	2.00	1.00	.60
(66) Bob Watson	2.00	1.00	.60
(67) Butch Wynegar	2.00	1.00	.60
(68) Carl Yastrzemski	10.00	5.00	3.00
(69) Robin Yount	6.00	3.00	1.75
(70) Richie Zisk	2.00	1.00	.60

1950s Bill Zuber's Restaurant

These 3-1/2" x 5-1/2" black-and-white cards were produced as a promotional item for an Iowa restaurant owned by the former big league pitcher (1936-47). The semi-gloss front has a portrait and facsimile autograph. One type has an advertising message at left and the inscription, "Good Hitting." On back are printed Joe McCarthy's "Ten Commandments of Baseball." A second type has the inscription, "Sincerest Wishes," with a postcard-style back featuring an advertising message in the top-left corner.

	NM	EX	VG
(1) Bill Zuber	8.00	4.00	2.50
(Ten Commandments back.)			
(2) Bill Zuber (Postcard back.)	8.00	4.00	2.50

MODERN MAJOR LEAGUE (1981-2010)

The vast majority of cards and collectibles listed in this section were issued between 1981 and May 2010 and feature only major league players.

Because modern cards are generally not collected in lower grades, cards in this section carry only a Near Mint-to-Mint (NM/M) value quote. In general, post-1980 cards that grade Near Mint will retail at about 75 percent of the NM/M price, while Excellent condition cards bring about 40 percent. Cards in lesser condition are generally not considered collectible.

Values shown are for "raw" cards, that is, cards not authenticated, graded and encapsulated by an independent certification firm. Many cards that have been graded Mint, Gem Mint or Pristine by recognized major grading companies (SCD, SGC, BGS, GAI or PSA) will sell at a premium over the values quoted here. Because the standards and reputations of these companies vary widely, prices listed here cannot be correlated to values for "slabbed" cards

1991 Acme Reproductions Ryan-Seaver

This collectors' issue was produced in an edition of 10,000 in an over-size (4-1/4" x 3") format and style approximating a 1967 Topps card. The future Hall of Famers are pictured in their early days with the Mets. Facsimile autographs appear at the bottom of each photo. A total of 420 of the cards was authentically autographed by both players. Backs have a cartoon and biographical data on each player, plus a career summary up to 1967. Original issue price was $29, or $109 for the autographed card. Each came in a lucite holder with numbered certificate of authenticity. A 17-1/2" x 12-1/2" lithograph was produced in an edition of 3,000, with the first 1,000 autographed by each player. The litho sold for $219 autographed and $109 unsigned.

	NM/M
Nolan Ryan, Tom Seaver	10.00
Nolan Ryan, Tom Seaver/Auto.	200.00

1988 Action Packed

Action Packed released this test set in an effort to receive a license from Major League Baseball. The cards are styled like the Action Packed football card fronts. The flip sides are styled like Score baseball cards. The Ozzie Smith card is considered scarcer than the other five cards in the test set, while a hoard of Mattingly cards revealed in 1998 drove down the price of his card. Action Packed did not receive a license to produce baseball cards.

		NM/M
Complete Set (6):		45.00
Common Player:		6.00
(1)	Wade Boggs	12.50
(2)	Andre Dawson	7.50
(3)	Dwight Gooden	6.00
(4)	Carney Lansford	6.00
(5)	Don Mattingly	6.00
(6)	Ozzie Smith	30.00

1992 Action Packed Promos

This set was produced to preview Action Packed's All-Star Gallery card issue. The promo cards are identical in format to the regularly issued cards and use the same player photos. The only differences in the promos are found on the back, where the card number is missing from the lower-left corner and where a white "1992 Prototype" is overprinted on the gray background beneath the black career highlights. The promos were widely distributed at trade shows and to Action Packed's dealer network. The unnumbered promo cards are checklisted here alphabetically.

		NM/M
Complete Set (5):		6.00
Common Player:		1.00
(1)	Yogi Berra	1.50
(2)	Bob Gibson	1.00
(3)	Willie Mays	3.00
(4)	Warren Spahn	1.00
(5)	Willie Stargell	1.00

1992 Action Packed All-Star Gallery Series 1

Action Packed, makers of a high quality, embossed style football card for several years, entered the baseball card field in 1992 with its 84-card All-Star Gallery Series 1. The cards feature former baseball greats, with 72 of the 84 cards in color and the remaining in sepia tone. Each foil pack of seven cards reportedly contained at least one Hall of Famer, and the company also made special 24K gold leaf stamped cards of all of the HOFers that were randomly inserted in the packs.

		NM/M
Complete Set (84):		15.00
Common Player:		.10
Wax Pack:		.75
Wax Box (24):		12.50
1	Yogi Berra	.50
2	Lou Brock	.25
3	Bob Gibson	.25
4	Ferguson Jenkins	.25
5	Ralph Kiner	.25
6	Al Kaline	.40
7	Lou Boudreau	.25
8	Bobby Doerr	.25
9	Billy Herman	.25
10	Monte Irvin	.25
11	George Kell	.25
12	Robin Roberts	.25
13	Johnny Mize	.25
14	Willie Mays	1.00
15	Enos Slaughter	.25
16	Warren Spahn	.25
17	Willie Stargell	.25
18	Billy Williams	.25
19	Vernon Law	.10
20	Virgil Trucks	.10
21	Mel Parnell	.10
22	Wally Moon	.10
23	Gene Woodling	.10
24	Richie Ashburn	.25
25	Mark Fidrych	.25
26	Elroy Face	.10
27	Larry Doby	.25
28	Dick Groat	.10
29	Cesar Cedeno	.10
30	Bob Horner	.10
31	Bobby Richardson	.25
32	Bobby Murcer	.10
33	Gil McDougald	.10
34	Roy White	.10
35	Bill Skowron	.25
36	Mickey Lolich	.10
37	Minnie Minoso	.10
38	Billy Pierce	.10
39	Ron Santo	.25
40	Sal Bando	.10
41	Ralph Branca	.10
42	Bert Campaneris	.10
43	Joe Garagiola	.25
44	Vida Blue	.10
45	Frank Crosetti	.10
46	Luis Tiant	.10
47	Maury Wills	.10
48	Sam McDowell	.10
49	Jimmy Piersall	.10
50	Jim Lonborg	.10
51	Don Newcombe	.15
52	Bobby Thomson	.10
53	Wilbur Wood	.10
54	Carl Erskine	.10
55	Chris Chambliss	.10
56	Dave Kingman	.10
57	Ken Holtzman	.10
58	Bud Harrelson	.10
59	Clem Labine	.10
60	Tony Oliva	.10
61	George Foster	.10
62	Bobby Bonds	.10
63	Harvey Haddix	.10
64	Steve Garvey	.15
65	Rocky Colavito	.15
66	Orlando Cepeda	.25
67	Ed Lopat	.10
68	Al Oliver	.10
69	Bill Mazeroski	.25
70	Al Rosen	.10
71	Bob Grich	.10
72	Curt Flood	.10
73	Willie Horton	.10
74	Rico Carty	.10
75	Davey Johnson	.10
76	Don Kessinger	.10
77	Frank Thomas	.10
78	Bobby Shantz	.10
79	Herb Score	.10
80	Boog Powell	.15
81	Rusty Staub	.15
82	Bill Madlock	.10
83	Manny Mota	.10
84	Bill White	.10

1992 Action Packed Diamond Stars

The first 18 cards from Series 1 Action Packed ASG were produced in a gold-enhanced boxed-set version which included a diamond chip in 14-Karat gold setting. Each card was serially numbered from within an edition of 500.

		NM/M
Complete Set (18):		80.00
Common Player:		4.00
1G	Yogi Berra	7.50
2G	Lou Brock	4.00
3G	Bob Gibson	4.00
4G	Ferguson Jenkins	4.00
5G	Ralph Kiner	4.00
6G	Al Kaline	5.00
7G	Lou Boudreau	4.00
8G	Bobby Doerr	4.00
9G	Billy Herman	4.00
10G	Monte Irvin	4.00
11G	George Kell	4.00
12G	Robin Roberts	4.00
13G	Johnny Mize	4.00
14G	Willie Mays	12.50
15G	Enos Slaughter	4.00
16G	Warren Spahn	4.00
17G	Willie Stargell	4.00
18G	Billy Williams	4.00

1993 Action Packed All-Star Gallery Series 2

The Second Series of Action Packed All-Star Gallery was released in 1993, with cards numbered from 85 to 168. In a similar fashion to the First Series, Series Two features 52 cards in color, 31 in sepia tone and one as a colorized black and white. The series also includes two tongue-in-cheek cards - "Who's on First?" duo Bud Abbot and Lou Costello, and a card highlighting the TV and radio career of Bob Uecker.

		NM/M
Complete Set (84):		10.00
Common Player:		.10
Wax Pack (7):		1.00
Wax Box (24):		17.50
85	Cy Young	.15
86	Honus Wagner	.25
87	Christy Mathewson	.15
88	Ty Cobb	1.00
89	Eddie Collins	.10
90	Walter Johnson	.15
91	Tris Speaker	.15
92	Grover Alexander	.10
93	Edd Roush	.10
94	Babe Ruth	2.00
95	Rogers Hornsby	.15
96	Pie Traynor	.10
97	Lou Gehrig	1.00
98	Mickey Cochrane	.15
99	Lefty Grove	.10
100	Jimmie Foxx	.15
101	Tony Lazzeri	.10
102	Mel Ott	.10
103	Carl Hubbell	.10
104	Al Lopez	.10
105	Lefty Gomez	.10
106	Dizzy Dean	.15
107	Hank Greenberg	.10
108	Joe Medwick	.10
109	Arky Vaughan	.10
110	Bob Feller	.15
111	Hal Newhouser	.10
112	Early Wynn	.10
113	Bob Lemon	.10
114	Red Schoendienst	.10
115	Satchel Paige	.25
116	Whitey Ford	.15
117	Eddie Mathews	.15
118	Harmon Killebrew	.15
119	Roberto Clemente	1.50
120	Brooks Robinson	.15
121	Don Drysdale	.15
122	Luis Aparicio	.15
123	Willie McCovey	.15
124	Juan Marichal	.10
125	Gaylord Perry	.10
126	Catfish Hunter	.10
127	Jim Palmer	.15
128	Rod Carew	.15
129	Tom Seaver	.15
130	Rollie Fingers	.10
131	Joe Jackson	2.00
132	Pepper Martin	.10
133	Joe Gordon	.10
134	Marty Marion	.10
135	Allie Reynolds	.10
136	Johnny Sain	.10
137	Gil Hodges	.15
138	Ted Kluszewski	.15
139	Nellie Fox	.15
140	Billy Martin	.15
141	Smoky Burgess	.10
142	Lew Burdette	.10
143	Joe Black	.10
144	Don Larsen	.10
145	Ken Boyer	.10
146	Johnny Callison	.10
147	Norm Cash	.10
148	Keith Hernandez	.10
149	Jim Kaat	.10
150	Bill Freehan	.10
151	Joe Torre	.10
152	Bob Uecker	.15
153	Dave McNally	.10
154	Denny McLain	.10
155	Dick Allen	.10
156	Jimmy Wynn	.10
157	Tommy John	.10
158	Paul Blair	.10
159	Reggie Smith	.10
160	Jerry Koosman	.10
161	Thurman Munson	.15
162	Graig Nettles	.10
163	Ron Cey	.10
164	Cecil Cooper	.10
165	Dave Parker	.10
166	Jim Rice	.10
167	Kent Tekulve	.10
168	Who's on First? (Bud Abbott, Lou Costello)	.75

1992-93 Action Packed Gold

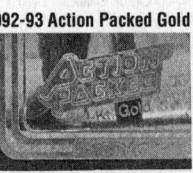

Essentially identical to the regular-issue Action Packed All-Star Gallery cards, these premium inserts are specially numbered with a "G" prefix and highlighted with 24-Karat gold detailing.

		NM/M
Complete Set (65):		175.00
Common Player:		2.50
Series 1		
1	Yogi Berra	4.00
2	Lou Brock	2.50
3	Bob Gibson	2.50
4	Ferguson Jenkins	2.50
5	Ralph Kiner	2.50
6	Al Kaline	3.50
7	Lou Boudreau	2.50
8	Bobby Doerr	2.50
9	Billy Herman	2.50
10	Monte Irvin	2.50
11	George Kell	2.50
12	Robin Roberts	2.50
13	Johnny Mize	2.50
14	Willie Mays	7.50
15	Enos Slaughter	2.50
16	Warren Spahn	2.50
17	Willie Stargell	2.50
18	Billy Williams	2.50
Series 2		
19	Cy Young	3.50
20	Honus Wagner	5.00
21	Christy Mathewson	3.50
22	Ty Cobb	6.00
23	Eddie Collins	2.50
24	Walter Johnson	3.50
25	Tris Speaker	3.50
26	Grover Alexander	3.25
27	Edd Roush	2.50
28	Babe Ruth	12.50
29	Rogers Hornsby	3.50
30	Pie Traynor	2.50
31	Lou Gehrig	10.00
32	Mickey Cochrane	3.25
33	Lefty Grove	3.25
34	Jimmie Foxx	3.50
35	Tony Lazzeri	2.50
36	Mel Ott	2.50
37	Carl Hubbell	2.50
38	Al Lopez	2.50
39	Lefty Gomez	2.50
40	Dizzy Dean	3.50
41	Hank Greenberg	3.50
42	Joe Medwick	2.50
43	Arky Vaughan	2.50
44	Bob Feller	3.50
45	Hal Newhouser	2.50
46	Early Wynn	2.50
47	Bob Lemon	2.50
48	Red Schoendienst	2.50
49	Satchel Paige	6.00
50	Whitey Ford	3.25
51	Eddie Mathews	3.25
52	Harmon Killebrew	3.25
53	Roberto Clemente	15.00
54	Brooks Robinson	3.25
55	Don Drysdale	3.25
56	Luis Aparicio	2.50
57	Willie McCovey	3.25
58	Juan Marichal	2.50
59	Gaylord Perry	2.50
60	Catfish Hunter	2.50
61	Jim Palmer	3.25
62	Rod Carew	3.25
63	Tom Seaver	3.25
64	Rollie Fingers	2.50

65	Who's on First? (Bud Abbott, Lou Costello)	3.50

1992 Action Packed 24-Kt. Gold

At least the first 18 cards in 1992 AP All-Star Gallery Series 1 were also issued in a full-coverage gold-foil version (as opposed to the gold-highlighted parallels). The cards are embossed front and back in gold-foil and numbered identically to the regular-issue cards. Each has a "24-Kt. Gold" imprint on front and is ink-jet serially numbered on back within an edition of 1,000.

		NM/M
Complete Set (18):		35.00
Common Player:		2.00
1	Yogi Berra	3.50
2	Lou Brock	2.50
3	Bob Gibson	2.50
4	Ferguson Jenkins	2.50
5	Ralph Kiner	2.50
6	Al Kaline	2.50
7	Lou Boudreau	2.00
8	Bobby Doerr	2.00
9	Billy Herman	2.00
10	Monte Irvin	2.00
11	George Kell	2.00
12	Robin Roberts	2.50
13	Johnny Mize	2.50
14	Willie Mays	7.50
15	Enos Slaughter	2.50
16	Warren Spahn	2.50
17	Willie Stargell	2.50
18	Billy Williams	2.50

1993 Action Packed Amoco/Coke

A special version of 18 of its All-Star Gallery cards was created by Action Packed for use as a premium by Amoco gas stations and Coca-Cola. Card fronts feature the same embossed color or sepia player photos with a heavily lacquered finish and gold-foil and black borders. Gray backs have biographical and career data, a few stats and sponsors' logos. Complete sets were available via a mail-in offer from Coke products. Most of these cards share card numbers and photos with AP's Series I ASG cards.

		NM/M
Complete Set (18):		4.00
Common Player:		.50
1	Yogi Berra	1.00
2	Lou Brock	.50
3	Bob Gibson	.50
4	Red Schoendienst	.50
5	Ralph Kiner	.50
6	Al Kaline	.75
7	Lou Boudreau	.50
8	Bobby Doerr	.50
9	Gaylord Perry	.50
10	Monte Irvin	.50
11	George Kell	.50
12	Robin Roberts	.60
13	Johnny Mize	.60
14	Willie Mays	2.00

15	Enos Slaughter	.50
16	Warren Spahn	.60
17	Willie Stargell	.60
18	Billy Williams	.50

1993 Action Packed 24-Kt. Gold

The first 46 cards of AP's All-Star Gallery Series II, along with the special Abbott & Costello card were produced in a limited gold edition as random pack inserts. Labeled "24-Kt. Gold" on front, the cards have the same format and design as the regular-issue, except the embossed front photo and incuse stats on back are on solid-gold foil. Each gold card carries a black ink-jetted serial number on back from within an edition of either 500 or 1,000.

		NM/M
Complete Set (47):		80.00
Common Player:		2.00
85	Cy Young	3.00
86	Honus Wagner	4.00
87	Christy Mathewson	4.00
88	Ty Cobb	6.00
89	Eddie Collins	2.00
90	Walter Johnson	4.00
91	Tris Speaker	2.00
92	Grover Alexander	2.00
93	Edd Roush	2.00
94	Babe Ruth	16.00
95	Rogers Hornsby	2.00
96	Pie Traynor	2.00
97	Lou Gehrig	10.00
98	Mickey Cochrane	2.00
99	Lefty Grove	2.00
100	Jimmie Foxx	3.00
101	Tony Lazzeri	2.00
102	Mel Ott	2.00
103	Carl Hubbell	2.00
104	Al Lopez	2.00
105	Lefty Gomez	2.00
106	Dizzy Dean	3.00
107	Hank Greenberg	3.00
108	Joe Medwick	2.00
109	Arky Vaughan	2.00
110	Bob Feller	3.00
111	Hal Newhouser	2.00
112	Early Wynn	2.00
113	Bob Lemon	2.00
114	Red Schoendienst	2.00
115	Satchel Paige	4.00
116	Whitey Ford	4.00
117	Eddie Mathews	2.00
118	Harmon Killebrew	2.00
119	Roberto Clemente	12.00
120	Brooks Robinson	2.00
121	Don Drysdale	2.00
122	Luis Aparicio	2.00
123	Willie McCovey	2.00
124	Juan Marichal	2.00
125	Gaylord Perry	2.00
126	Catfish Hunter	2.00
127	Jim Palmer	2.00
128	Rod Carew	2.00
129	Tom Seaver	2.00
130	Rollie Fingers	2.00
168	Who's on First? (Lou Costello, Bud Abbott)	3.00

1993 Action Packed Tom Seaver Prototypes

Tom Seaver's career was highlighted in this five-card promo set. Each card has an embossed front color photo surrounded by three gold pinstripes and a red border. Seaver's name is in red in a gold bar at bottom. Backs are printed in black and gold with a white undertype reading "1993 Prototype." Backs have biographical and career data, lifetime stats and a few sentences of career highlights. Cards have a "TS" prefix to the card number.

		NM/M
Complete Set (5):		8.00
Common Card:		2.00
1	The Franchise	2.00
2	Amazin' Mets	3.25
3	A Tearful Goodbye	2.00
4	Tom Terrific	2.00
5	Dazzling the Windy City	2.00

1983 Affiliated Food Rangers

This set, featuring the Texas Rangers, was issued as a promotion by the Affiliated Food Stores chain of Arlington, Texas. Complete sets were given to youngsters 13 and under at the September 3 Rangers game. Cards measure 2-3/8" x 3-1/2" and feature a full-color photo on the front. Also on the front, located inside a blue box, is the player's name, uniform number, and "1983 Rangers." Backs have a small player photo plus biographical and statistical information, along with the Affiliated logo and a brief promotional message. A total of 10,000 sets was reportedly printed. Cards are numbered by the players' uniform numbers in the checklist that follows.

		NM/M
Complete Set (28):		6.00
Common Player:		.25
1	Bill Stein	.25
2	Mike Richardt	.25
3	Wayne Tolleson	.25
5	Billy Sample	.25
6	Bobby Jones	.25
7	Bucky Dent	.35
8	Bobby Johnson	.25
9	Pete O'Brien	.25
10	Jim Sundberg	.25
11	Doug Rader	.25
12	Dave Hostetler	.25
14	Larry Biittner	.25
15	Larry Parrish	.25
17	Mickey Rivers	.30
21	Odell Jones	.25
24	Dave Schmidt	.25
25	Buddy Bell	.35
26	George Wright	.25
27	Frank Tanana	.25
29	John Butcher	.25
32	Jon Matlack	.25
40	Rick Honeycutt	.25
41	Dave Tobik	.25
46	Danny Darwin	.25
46	Jim Anderson	.25
48	Mike Smithson	.25
49	Charlie Hough	.30
---	Coaching Staff (Rich Donnelly, Glenn Ezell, Merv Rettenmund, Dick Such, Wayne Terwilliger)	.25

1990 Agfa Film

This "old-timers" set was distributed in three-card packs with the purchase of Agfa film. Produced by Michael Schecter Associates, whose logo appears on the back, the cards were not licensed by Major League Baseball, so team logos had to be eliminated from the photos. Cards have a white background with the film company's logos in the upper corners. Backs

---

are in black-and-white and have full major league regular season and post-season stats.

		NM/M
Complete Set (22):		7.50
Common Player:		.50
1	Willie Mays	2.00
2	Carl Yastrzemski	1.00
3	Harmon Killebrew	1.00
4	Joe Torre	.50
5	Al Kaline	1.00
6	Hank Aaron	2.00
7	Rod Carew	.75
8	Roberto Clemente	2.50
9	Luis Aparicio	.75
10	Roger Maris	1.00
11	Joe Morgan	.75
12	Maury Wills	.50
13	Brooks Robinson	.75
14	Tom Seaver	.75
15	Steve Carlton	.75
16	Whitey Ford	.75
17	Jim Palmer	.75
18	Rollie Fingers	.75
19	Bruce Sutter	.75
20	Willie McCovey	.75
21	Mike Schmidt	1.50
22	Yogi Berra	1.00

1990 All American Baseball Team

Produced by Mike Schecter Associates, this 24-card set includes many of the top players in the game. Team logos are airbrushed from the color photo on front, which is surrounded by a red, white and blue border and the MLB Players' Association logo. The backs are printed in blue on white stock, with a facsimile autograph appearing above the statistics.

		NM/M
Complete Set (24):		20.00
Common Player:		.50
1	George Brett	1.50
2	Mark McGwire	3.00
3	Wade Boggs	1.00
4	Cal Ripken, Jr.	4.00
5	Rickey Henderson	1.00
6	Dwight Gooden	.50
7	Bo Jackson	.75
8	Roger Clemens	1.50
9	Orel Hershiser	.50
10	Ozzie Smith	1.25
11	Don Mattingly	2.00
12	Kirby Puckett	1.25
13	Robin Yount	1.25
14	Tony Gwynn	1.25
15	Jose Canseco	.60
16	Nolan Ryan	4.00
17	Ken Griffey Jr.	2.50
18	Will Clark	.50
19	Ryne Sandberg	1.25
20	Kent Hrbek	.50
21	Carlton Fisk	1.00
22	Paul Molitor	1.00
23	Dave Winfield	1.00
24	Andre Dawson	.60

1987 Allstate Insurance

This six-card set was the second promotional series of baseball cards created by Allstate Insurance

---

graphic artist Ray Lending for internal use by the company. Modeled after the famous "Diamond Stars" from the 1930s, this set features full-color player portraits of legendary sluggers. "Life Grand Slam" (the promotion theme) is printed beneath the player portrait and the player's name appears in an upper corner. Black and white backs provide personal information, player profiles and career highlights; 15,000 sets of the cards were distributed, although only a few filtered into the collecting hobby. Cards measure 2-3/4" x 3-5/8" in size. Full-color 22" x 28" reproductions of the cards in this set were produced in poster format.

		NM/M
Complete Set (6):		75.00
Common Player:		10.00
(1)	Hank Aaron	12.00
(2)	Joe DiMaggio	15.00
(3)	Jimmie Foxx	10.00
(4)	Lou Gehrig	15.00
(5)	Babe Ruth	20.00
(6)	Ted Williams	15.00

1994 AMC Theaters S.F. Giants

This series of large-format (about 4-1/4" x 11"), blank-back photocards was sponsored by a Bay Area movie house chain. Cards have black-and-white action photos at center with player identification below. At top is a team logo, at bottom is a sponsor's logo. The unnumbered cards are checklisted here in alphabetical order.

		NM/M
Complete Set (33):		30.00
Common Player:		1.00
(1)	Dusty Baker	1.25
(2)	Rod Beck (Ready to pitch.)	1.00
(3)	Rod Beck (Piching follow through.)	1.00
(4)	Mike Benjamin	1.00
(5)	Todd Benzinger	1.00
(6)	Barry Bonds ('93 jersey)	9.00
(7)	Barry Bonds ('94 jersey)	9.00
(8)	Dave Burba	1.00
(9)	John Burkett	1.00
(10)	Mark Carreon	1.00
(11)	Royce Clayton	1.00
(12)	Steve Frey	1.00
(13)	Bryan Hickerson	1.00
(14)	Mike Jackson	1.00
(15)	Darren Lewis	1.00
(16)	Kirt Manwaring	1.00
(17)	Dave Martinez ('93 jersey)	1.00
(18)	Dave Martinez ('94 jersey)	1.00
(19)	Willie McGee	1.00
(20)	Rich Monteleone	1.00
(21)	John Patterson	1.00
(22)	Mark Portugal (Negative reversed, pitching lefty.)	1.00
(23)	Mark Portugal (Correct, pitching righty.)	1.00
(24)	Jeff Reed	1.00
(25)	Kevin Rogers/Standing	1.00
(26)	Kevin Rogers/Pitching	1.00
(27)	Steve Scarsone	1.00
(28)	Bill Swift	1.00
(29)	Robby Thompson ('93 jersey)	1.00
(30)	Robby Thompson ('94 jersey)	1.00
(31)	Salomon Torres	1.00
(32)	Matt Williams/Btg	1.50
(33)	Matt Williams/Fldg	1.50

1994 American Archives Origins of Baseball

This collectors' issue presents the history of baseball in America from 1744-1899. Sold in

---

box-set form only, the cards are in standard 2-1/2" x 3-1/2" format. Fronts feature sepia-toned photos and line-art on a black background. Backs have a lengthy narrative, also printed in sepia on black. Both sides are UV coated. Individual cards feature early players, team photos, game action scenes or other historical vignettes. The set was produced by American Archives.

		NM/M
Complete Set (101):		6.00
Common Card:		.10
1	Abner Doubleday	.10
2	Doubleday Field	.10
3	Rounders 1744	.10
4	Early Baseball 700 A.D.	.10
5	The Knickerbockers	.10
6	Alex Cartwright	.10
7	Baseball in the 1850s	.10
8	Social Clubs	.10
9	Brooklyn Eckfords	.10
10	New England Baseball	.10
11	Henry Chadwick	.10
12	Brooklyn Excelsiors	.10
13	Abraham Lincoln	.10
14	Andrew Johnson	.10
15	First Enclosed Park	.10
16	Brooklyn Atlantics	.10
17	James Creighton	.10
18	Baseball in the 1860s	.10
19	1869 Red Stockings	.10
20	Cincinnati Celebration	.10
21	Harry Wright	.10
22	Boston Ball Club 1872	.10
23	Arthur Cummings	.10
24	William Hulbert	.10
25	George Wright	.10
26	Albert Spalding	.10
27	Albert Bushong	.10
28	Bid McPhee	.10
29	James O'Rourke	.10
30	Pud Galvin	.10
31	Edwin Bligh	.10
32	William Purcell	.10
33	Roger Connor	.10
34	Cincinnati Ball Club 1882	.10
35	Peter Browning	.10
36	William Gleason	.10
37	Paul Hines	.10
38	Baseball in the 1880s	.10
39	Robert Carruthers	.10
40	New York Metropolitans	.10
41	St. George's Field	.10
42	Charles Radbourne	.10
43	George Andrews	.10
44	William Hoy	.10
45	Chicago Ball Club 1886	.10
46	Cap Anson	.10
47	John Clarkson	.10
48	Mike Kelly	.10
49	Buffalo Bisons 1887	.10
50	Moses Walker	.10
51	Detroit Ball Club 1887	.10
52	Little League	.10
53	Louisville Ball Club 1888	.10
54	John Farrell	.10
55	Walter Latham	.10
56	Fred Dunlap	.10
57	Tim Keefe	.10
58	Cincinnati Ball Club 1888	.10
59	1889 World Tour	.10
60	Dan Brouthers	.10
61	John M. Ward	.10
62	Albert Spalding	.10
63	The Baseball Cap	.10
64	Tom Esterbrook	.10
65	Mark Baldwin	.10
66	Tony Mullane	.10
67	John Glasscock	.10
68	Amos Rusie	.10
69	Jake Beckley	.10
70	Jimmy Collins	.10
71	Charles Comiskey	.10
72	Tom Connolly	.10
73	Mickey Welch	.10
74	Ed Delahanty	.10
75	Hugh Duffy	.10
76	Buck Ewing	.10
77	Clark Griffith	.10
78	Kid Nichols	.10
79	Billy Hamilton	.10
80	Ban Johnson	.10
81	Willie Keeler	.10
82	Bobby Wallace	.10

83	Napoleon Lajoie	.10
84	Connie Mack	.10
85	Fred Clarke	.10
86	Tommy McCarthy	.10
87	John McGraw	.10
88	Jesse Burkett	.10
89	Frank Chance	.10
90	Mordecai Brown	.10
91	New York Nationals	.10
92	Jack Chesbro	.10
93	Sam Thompson	.10
94	Boston v. New York 1891	.10
95	Rube Waddell	.10
96	Joel Kelley	.10
97	Addie Joss	.10
98	The Boston Beaneaters	.10
99	Baltimore Baseball Club	.10
100	The Game in 1899	.10
----	Bibliography	.10

1989 Ames 20/20 Club

This 33-card set was produced by Topps for the Ames toy store chain. As its name implies, the special boxed set highlights players who have recorded 20 home runs and 20 stolen bases in the same season. The glossy cards feature action or posed photos on the front with the player's name at the top and "Ames 20/20 Club" along the bottom. The Topps logo appears in the upper-right corner. Backs have lifetime stats, biographical data and career highlights.

		NM/M
Complete Set (33):		4.00
Common Player:		.10
1	Jesse Barfield	.10
2	Kevin Bass	.10
3	Don Baylor	.10
4	George Bell	.10
5	Barry Bonds	2.00
6	Phil Bradley	.10
7	Ellis Burks	.10
8	Jose Canseco	.25
9	Joe Carter	.10
10	Kal Daniels	.10
11	Eric Davis	.10
12	Mike Davis	.10
13	Andre Dawson	.25
14	Kirk Gibson	.10
15	Pedro Guerrero	.10
16	Rickey Henderson	.45
17	Bo Jackson	.25
18	Howard Johnson	.10
19	Jeffrey Leonard	.10
20	Kevin McReynolds	.10
21	Dale Murphy	.25
22	Dwayne Murphy	.10
23	Dave Parker	.10
24	Kirby Puckett	.60
25	Juan Samuel	.10
26	Ryne Sandberg	.60
27	Mike Schmidt	.75
28	Darryl Strawberry	.10
29	Alan Trammell	.10
30	Andy Van Slyke	.10
31	Devon White	.10
32	Dave Winfield	.45
33	Robin Yount	.45

1990 Ames All-Stars

This 33-card boxed set was the second annual issue produced by Topps for the Ames toy store chain. The cards measure 2-1/2" x 3-1/2" and have a high-gloss finish on front. The set's checklist comprises the active career leaders in runs produced per game. Backs have a green striped background and present player personal data and seasonal major league stats. Issue price for the set was $2.

		NM/M
Complete Set (33):		4.00
Common Player:		.10
1	Dave Winfield	.50
2	George Brett	.75
3	Jim Rice	.25
4	Dwight Evans	.10
5	Robin Yount	.50
6	Dave Parker	.10
7	Eddie Murray	.50
8	Keith Hernandez	.10
9	Andre Dawson	.25
10	Fred Lynn	.10
11	Dale Murphy	.35
12	Jack Clark	.10
13	Rickey Henderson	.50
14	Paul Molitor	.50
15	Cal Ripken	1.50
16	Wade Boggs	.60
17	Tim Raines	.10
18	Don Mattingly	.75
19	Kent Hrbek	.10
20	Kirk Gibson	.10
21	Julio Franco	.10
22	George Bell	.10
23	Darryl Strawberry	.10
24	Kirby Puckett	.60
25	Juan Samuel	.10
26	Alvin Davis	.10
27	Joe Carter	.10
28	Eric Davis	.10
29	Jose Canseco	.40
30	Wally Joyner	.10
31	Will Clark	.10
32	Ruben Sierra	.10
33	Danny Tartabull	.10

1999 Anaheim Angels Police

Sponsored by the Santa Ana district of the California Highway Patrol, five of the cards in this set feature players photographed with police officers. The 2-1/2" x 3-1/2" cards have borderless photos on two sides, with dark blue and gold stripes bearing player identification. The team and CHP logos are in opposite corners. Backs have a smaller version of the front photo along with player data, career information and a safety message.

		NM/M
Complete Set (10):		12.50
Common Player:		.50
1	Chuck Finley	.50
2	Shigetosi Hasegawa	.50
3	Gary DiSarcina	.50
4	Darin Erstad	2.00
5	Mo Vaughn	.50
6	Tim Salmon	
	(W/officers.)	1.00
7	Troy Percival	
	(W/officers.)	.50
8	Jim Edmonds	
	(W/officers.)	3.00
9	Troy Glaus	
	(W/officers.)	5.00
10	Santa Ana CHPs	.25

2000 Anaheim Angels Police

The California Highway Patrol sponsored this promotional set given away at an Angels game. Standard-size cards have color game-action photos which are borderless on top and right. At left and bottom are dark blue and gold stripes. A CHP badge logo appears in the lower-right. Backs have a monochrome version of the front photo, player

personal data and career information and a CHP Designated Driver logo at bottom. The back photos on Jim Edmonds' and Troy Percival's cards were switched.

		NM/M
Complete Set (10):		12.50
Common Player:		1.00
1	Chuck Finley	1.00
2	Shigetosi Hasegawa	1.00
3	Gary Disarcina	1.00
4	Darin Erstad	2.00
5	Mo Vaughn	1.00
6	Tim Salmon	2.00
7	Troy Percival	1.00
8	Jim Edmonds	2.00
9	Troy Glaus	4.00
10	CHP San Ana Area Police Officers	1.00

2000 APBA Super Stars Baseball

In the premiere edition of its board game for children, APBA included six player-image game pieces and 30 player cards, one from each team. The irregularly shaped game pieces are 1-11/16" at their widest point and 2-5/16" tall. The same player action picture appears on each side on a brightly colored background. The player cards are round-cornered, 2-1/2" x 3-1/2", with a game-action photo and green borders. The game's APBA Andy logo appears at lower-left. Backs have a few personal data and dice-throw results chart used to play the game. Player cards are unnumbered and listed here in alphabetical order. Retail price at time of issue was $19.95.

		NM/M
Complete Game:		10.00
Common Game Piece:		.50
Common Player Card:		.25
(1)	Barry Bonds	.75
(2)	Nomar Garciaparra	.45
(3)	Ken Griffey Jr.	.50
(4)	Mark McGwire	.60
(5)	Mike Piazza	.50
(6)	Alex Rodriguez	.60
(1)	Roberto Alomar	.30
(2)	Jeff Bagwell	.40
(3)	Barry Bonds	.75
(4)	Jeromy Burnitz	.25
(5)	Carlos Delgado	.35
(6)	Jermaine Dye	.25
(7)	Cliff Floyd	.25
(8)	Jason Giambi	.35
(9)	Juan Gonzalez	.30
(10)	Shawn Green	.30
(11)	Ken Griffey Jr.	.50
(12)	Vladimir Guerrero	.40
(13)	Tony Gwynn	.45
(14)	Todd Helton	.30
(15)	Derek Jeter	.75
(16)	Randy Johnson	.40
(17)	Chipper Jones	.45
(18)	Jason Kendall	.25
(19)	Matt Lawton	.25
(20)	Pedro Martinez	.40
(21)	Mark McGwire	.60
(22)	Mike Piazza	.50
(23)	Cal Ripken Jr.	.75
(24)	Alex Rodriguez	.60
(25)	Ivan Rodriguez	.30
(26)	Scott Rolen	.30
(27)	Sammy Sosa	.45
(28)	Frank Thomas	.35
(29)	Greg Vaughn	.25
(30)	Mo Vaughn	.25

1996 Arby's Cleveland Indians

These cards honor, according to the logo on front, "1995 Tribe Milestones." Fronts are bordered in black with the action photo vignetted in black. The player's milestone is printed in white on a red strip at bottom. Backs have a large baseball, bat and glove in the background with a

color portrait at top. A diamond shaped area at center has stats. Cello-wrapped cards were available one per week with a purchase.

		NM/M
Complete Set (8):		10.00
Common Player:		1.00
1	Eddie Murray (3,000th Hit)	3.00
2	Orel Hershiser (L.C.S. MVP in Both Leagues)	1.00
3	Manny Ramirez (Silver Slugger)	3.00
4	Jose Mesa (Saves Record)	1.00
5	Kenny Lofton (Gold Glove/Most Steals)	1.00
6	Omar Vizquel (3rd Straight Gold Glove)	1.00
7	Albert Belle (50/50 Season)	1.00
8	Carlos Baerga (.310+ Ave. Four Straight Years)	1.00

2004 Archway Seattle Mariners

This stadium give-away set was sponsored by Archway Cookies and produced by Upper Deck. Fronts have green and tan borders and game-action photos. Backs repeat the color scheme and include Major League stats and licensor logos.

		NM/M
Complete Set (16):		8.00
Common Player:		.25
1	Ichiro	6.00
2	Raul Ibanez	.25
3	Randy Winn	.25
4	John Olerud	.25
5	Bret Boone	.50
6	Rich Aurilia	.25
7	Scott Spiezio	.25
8	Dan Wilson	.25
9	Edgar Martinez	.50
10	Freddy Garcia	.25
11	Jamie Moyer	.25
12	Joel Pineiro	.50
13	Gil Meche	.25
14	Ryan Franklin	.25
15	Shigetoshi Hasegawa	.25
16	Eddie Guardado	.25

2003 Arizona Diamondbacks Can Kickers Club

The attributed date is speculative, since there is no copyright date on the cards. The method of

the cards' distrubtion is also unknown. These are high-tech chromium cards issued to support the team's anti-chewing tobacco program aimed at children. Fronts have color or colorized player photos with the player name at bottom. Backs are identical and feature a Peanuts cartoon, an anti-chew message and the club logo.

		NM/M
Complete Set (3):		10.00
Common Player:		2.00
(1)	Steve Finley	2.00
(2)	Joe Garagiola	3.00
(3)	Mark McGwire	6.00

2005 Arizona Republic Diamondbacks Deck

This stadium giveaway was sponsored by a local newspaper. Cards are 2-3/16" x 3-3/8" with rounded corners. Backs have a sponsor's logo. Each player appears four times in the deck, with an identical portrait photo on the same value card in each suit. Two Jokers complete the boxed set.

		NM/M
Complete Set (54):		10.00
Common Player:		.25
2	Koyie Hill	.25
3	Chad Tracy	.50
4	Craig Counsell	.25
5	Troy Glaus	.35
6	Royce Clayton	.25
7	Luis Gonzalez	.35
8	Jose Cruz, Jr.	.25
9	Shawn Green	.45
10	Brandon Webb	.35
J	Russ Ortiz	.25
Q	Mascot	.25
K	Bob Melvin	.25
A	Javier Vasquez	.35
JOKER	Mascot	.25
JOKER	Mascot	.25

1996 Arizona Lottery

To promote its Diamond Bucks scratch-off lottery game, the Arizona Lottery issued this three-card set of Hall of Fame players' cards. Fronts have black-and-white photos which have uniform logos airbrushed away. Borders are black. Backs are also in black-and-white, with player data and career highlights, along with the sponsors logos. Sets were given with the purchase of $5 in lottery tickets.

		NM/M
Complete Set (3):		7.50
Common Player:		2.00
(1)	Ernie Banks	4.00
(2)	Gaylord Perry	2.00
(3)	Brooks Robinson	3.00

2001 Armour Stars

The manner of distribution for this seven-card cello wrapped set is unknown. Produced by Playoff, the cards have game-action photos on front with red and black borders. A gold-foil Armour Stars logo is at bottom. Backs have a portrait photo, biographical data, 2000 and career stats and a trivia question about which condiments the player prefers on his hot dogs. All photos have had team logos removed.

		NM/M
Complete Set (7):		6.00
Common Player:		.50
1	Roberto Alomar	.50
2	Barry Bonds	2.00
3	Kevin Brown	.50
4	Roger Clemens	1.00
5	Greg Maddux	.75
6	Alex Rodriguez	1.50
7	Frank Thomas	.65

1997 AT&T Ambassadors of Baseball

Taking over for the tour previously sponsored by MCI, AT&T brought a visiting team of former major league ballplayers to overseas military bases in 1997, where they played base teams in exhibition games. Card fronts feature photos (with uniform logos airbrushed away) from the players' major league days, with AT&T and Ambassadors Tour logos. Backs have typical player data.

		NM/M
Complete Set (4):		30.00
Common Player:		6.00
(1)	Jesse Barfield	6.00
(2)	Darrell Evans	12.00
(3)	Al Hrabosky	6.00
(4)	Jerry Koosman	12.00

1981 Atlanta Braves Police

The first Atlanta Braves police set was a cooperative effort of the team, Hostess, Coca-Cola and the Atlanta Police Department. Card fronts feature full-color photos of

27 different Braves and manager Bobby Cox. Police and team logos are on the card backs. Card backs offer capsule biographies of the players, along with a tip for youngsters. The 2-5/8" x 4-1/8" cards are numbered by uniform number. Terry Harper (#19) appears to be somewhat scarcer than the other cards in the set. Reportedly, 33,000 sets were printed.

		NM/M
Complete Set (27):		10.00
Common Player:		.25
1	Jerry Royster	.25
3	Dale Murphy	3.00
4	Biff Pocoroba	.25
5	Bob Horner	.75
8	Bob Cox	.35
9	Luis Gomez	.25
13	Chris Chambliss	.25
15	Bill Nahorodny	.25
16	Rafael Ramirez	.25
17	Glenn Hubbard	.25
18	Claudell Washington	.25
19	Terry Harper (SP)	.75
20	Bruce Benedict	.25
24	John Montefusco	.25
25	Rufino Linares	.25
26	Gene Garber	.25
30	Brian Asselstine	.25
34	Larry Bradford	.25
35	Phil Niekro	1.50
37	Rick Camp	.25
39	Al Hrabosky	.25
40	Tommy Boggs	.25
42	Rick Mahler	.25
45	Ed Miller	.25
46	Gaylord Perry	1.50
49	Preston Hanna	.25
---	Hank Aaron	5.00

1982 Atlanta Braves Police

Dale Murphy (3)
Outfield

After their successful debut in 1981, the Atlanta Braves, the Atlanta Police Department, Coca-Cola and Hostess issued another card set in '82. This 30- card set is extremely close in format to the 1981 set and again measures 2-5/8" x 4-1/8". The full-color player photos are outstanding, and each card front also bears a statement marking the 1982 Braves' record-breaking 13-game win streak at the season's beginning. Card backs offer short biographies and "Tips from the Braves." Sponsors logos are also included. Reportedly, only 8,000 of these sets were printed.

		NM/M
Complete Set (30):		10.00
Common Player:		.25
1	Jerry Royster	.25
3	Dale Murphy	4.00
4	Biff Pocoroba	.25
6	Bob Horner	.50
9	Randy Johnson	.25
8	Bob Watson	.25
9	Joe Torre	1.00
10	Chris Chambliss	.25
15	Claudell Washington	.25
16	Rafael Ramirez	.25
17	Glenn Hubbard	.25
20	Bruce Benedict	.25
22	Brett Butler	.50
23	Tommie Aaron	.50
25	Rufino Linares	.25
26	Gene Garber	.25
27	Larry McWilliams	.25
34	Larry Whisenton	.25
32	Steve Bedrosian	.25
35	Phil Niekro	1.50
37	Rick Camp	.25
38	Joe Cowley	.25
39	Al Hrabosky	.25
42	Rick Mahler	.25
43	Bob Walk	.25
45	Bob Gibson	3.00
49	Preston Hanna	.25

52	Joe Pignatano	.25
53	Dal Maxvill	.25
54	Rube Walker	.25

1983 Atlanta Braves Police

Brett Butler (22)
Outfielder

An almost exact replica of their 1982 set, the 1983 Atlanta Braves police set includes 30 cards numbered by uniform. Sponsors Hostess, Coca-Cola and the Atlanta Police Department returned for the third year. The cards are again 2-5/8" x 4-1/8", with full-color photos and police and team logos on the card fronts. A statement noting the team's 1982 National League Western Division title in the upper right corner is the key difference on the card fronts. As in 1982, 8,000 sets were reportedly printed.

		NM/M
Complete Set (30):		6.00
Common Player:		.15
1	Jerry Royster	.15
3	Dale Murphy	3.00
4	Biff Pocoroba	.15
5	Bob Horner	.25
6	Randy G. Johnson	.15
8	Bob Watson	.15
9	Joe Torre	.50
10	Chris Chambliss	.15
11	Ken Smith	.15
15	Claudell Washington	.15
16	Rafael Ramirez	.15
17	Glenn Hubbard	.15
19	Terry Harper	.15
20	Bruce Benedict	.15
22	Brett Butler	.15
24	Larry Owen	.15
26	Gene Garber	.15
27	Pascual Perez	.15
29	Craig McMurtry	.15
32	Steve Bedrosian	.15
33	Pete Falcone	.15
35	Phil Niekro	1.00
36	Sonny Jackson	.15
37	Rick Camp	.15
46	Bob Gibson	2.00
49	Rick Behenna	.15
51	Terry Forster	.15
52	Joe Pignatano	.15
53	Dal Maxvill	.15
54	Rube Walker	.15

1984 Atlanta Braves Police

Bob Gibson (45)
Coach

A fourth annual effort by the Braves, the Atlanta Police Department, Coca-Cola and Hostess, this 30-card set continued to be printed in a 2-5/8" x 4-1/8" format, with full-color photos plus team and police logos on the card fronts. For the first time, the cards also have a large logo and date in the upper right corner. Hostess and Coke logos again are on the card backs, with brief player information and a safety tip. Two cards in the set (Pascual Perez and

Rafael Ramirez) were issued in Spanish. Cards were distributed two per week by Atlanta police officers. As in 1982 and 1983, a reported 8,000 sets were printed.

		NM/M
Complete Set (30):		8.00
Common Player:		.25
1	Jerry Royster	.25
3	Dale Murphy	3.00
5	Bob Horner	.40
6	Randy Johnson	.25
8	Bob Watson	.25
9	Joe Torre	.75
10	Chris Chambliss	.25
11	Mike Jorgensen	.25
15	Claudell Washington	.25
16	Rafael Ramirez	.25
17	Glenn Hubbard	.25
19	Terry Harper	.25
20	Bruce Benedict	.25
26	Alex Trevino	.25
26	Gene Garber	.25
27	Pascual Perez	.25
29	Gerald Perry	.25
29	Craig McMurtry	.25
31	Donnie Moore	.25
32	Steve Bedrosian	.25
33	Pete Falcone	.25
37	Rick Camp	.25
39	Len Barker	.25
42	Rick Mahler	.25
46	Bob Gibson	2.50
51	Terry Forster	.25
52	Joe Pignatano	.25
53	Dal Maxvill	.25
54	Rube Walker	.25
55	Luke Appling	2.00

1985 Atlanta Braves Police

Dale Murphy (3)
Outfielder

There are again 30 full-color cards in this fifth annual set. Hostess, Coca-Cola and the Atlanta Police Department joined the team as sponsors again for the 2-5/8" x 4-1/8" set. Card backs are similar to previous years, with the only difference on the fronts being a swap in position for the year and team logo. The cards are checklisted by uniform number.

		NM/M
Complete Set (30):		4.00
Common Player:		.25
2	Albert Hall	.25
3	Dale Murphy	3.00
5	Rick Cerone	.25
9	Bobby Wine	.25
10	Chris Chambliss	.25
11	Bob Horner	.45
14	Paul Runge	.25
15	Claudell Washington	.25
16	Rafael Ramirez	.25
17	Glenn Hubbard	.25
18	Paul Zuvella	.25
19	Terry Harper	.25
20	Bruce Benedict	.25
22	Eddie Haas	.25
24	Ken Oberkfell	.25
26	Gene Garber	.25
27	Pascual Perez	.25
28	Gerald Perry	.25
29	Craig McMurtry	.25
32	Steve Bedrosian	.25
33	Johnny Sain	.30
34	Zane Smith	.25
36	Brad Komminsk	.25
37	Rick Camp	.25
39	Len Barker	.25
42	Bruce Sutter	1.50
42	Rick Mahler	.25
51	Terry Forster	.25
52	Leo Mazzone	.25
53	Bobby Dews	.25

1986 Atlanta Braves Police

The Police Athletic League of Atlanta issued a 30-card full-color set featuring Braves players and personnel. Cards measure 2-5/8" x 4-1/8". Fronts include player photos with name, uniform number and position

Glenn Hubbard (17)
Second Base

below the photo. Backs offer the 100th Anniversary Coca-Cola logo, player information, statistics and a safety related tip. This was the sixth consecutive year that the Braves issued a safety set available from police officers in Atlanta.

		NM/M
Complete Set (30):		4.00
Common Player:		.25
2	Russ Nixon	.25
3	Dale Murphy	3.00
4	Bob Skinner	.25
5	Billy Sample	.25
7	Chuck Tanner	.25
8	Willie Stargell	1.50
9	Ozzie Virgil	.25
10	Chris Chambliss	.25
11	Bob Horner	.25
14	Andres Thomas	.25
15	Claudell Washington	.25
16	Rafael Ramirez	.25
17	Glenn Hubbard	.25
18	Omar Moreno	.25
19	Terry Harper	.25
20	Bruce Benedict	.25
23	Ted Simmons	.25
24	Ken Oberkfell	.25
26	Gene Garber	.25
29	Craig McMurtry	.25
30	Paul Assenmacher	.25
33	Johnny Sain	.25
34	Zane Smith	.25
38	Joe Johnson	.25
40	Bruce Sutter	2.00
42	Rick Mahler	.25
46	David Palmer	.25
48	Duane Ward	.25
49	Jeff Dedmon	.25
52	Al Monchak	.25

1987 Atlanta Braves Fire Safety

These fire safety cards were given out at several different Atlanta games, with about 25,000 sets in all being distributed. The 4" x 6" cards feature Braves players in an oval frame, bordered in red, white and blue. Only the player's last name is shown on front. Backs contain the player's name, position and personal data plus a Smokey Bear cartoon fire safety message.

		NM/M
Complete Set (27):		4.00
Common Player:		.25
1	Zane Smith	.25
2	Charlie Puleo	.25
3	Randy O'Neal	.25
4	David Palmer	.25
5	Rick Mahler	.25
6	Ed Olwine	.25
7	Jeff Dedmon	.25
8	Paul Assenmacher	.25
9	Gene Garber	.25
10	Jim Acker	.25
11	Bruce Benedict	.25
12	Ozzie Virgil	.25
13	Ted Simmons	.25
14	Dale Murphy	3.00

15	Graig Nettles	.35
16	Ken Oberkfell	.25
17	Gerald Perry	.25
18	Rafael Ramirez	.25
19	Ken Griffey	.25
20	Andres Thomas	.25
21	Glenn Hubbard	.25
22	Damaso Garcia	.25
23	Gary Roenicke	.25
24	Dion James	.25
25	Albert Hall	.25
26	Chuck Tanner	.25
---	Smokey Bear Logo Card/Checklist	.10

1986 Ault Foods Blue Jays Stickers

11 BELL

The Ault Foods Blue Jays set is comprised of 24 full-color stickers. Designed to be placed in a special album, the stickers measure 2" x 3" in size. The attractive album measures 9" x 12" and is printed on glossy stock. While the stickers carry no information except for the player's last name and uniform number, the 20-page album contains extensive personal and statistical information about each of the 24 players.

		NM/M
Complete Set (24):		12.50
Common Player:		.50
Album:		4.00
1	Tony Fernandez	1.00
5	Rance Mulliniks	.50
9	Damaso Garcia	.50
11	George Bell	1.50
12	Ernie Whitt	.50
13	Buck Martinez	.50
15	Lloyd Moseby	.50
17	Garth Iorg	.50
17	Kelly Gruber	.50
18	Jim Clancy	.50
22	Jimmy Key	1.00
23	Cecil Fielder	5.00
25	Steve Davis	.50
26	Willie Upshaw	.50
29	Jesse Barfield	.50
31	Jim Acker	.50
36	Doyle Alexander	.50
36	Bill Caudill	.50
37	Dave Stieb	1.00
39	Don Gordon	.50
44	Cliff Johnson	.50
46	Gary Lavelle	.50
50	Tom Henke	.50
53	Dennis Lamp	.50

1982 Authentic Sports Autographs Mickey Mantle Story

1968-Hits HR No. 529

This 72-card set chronicles the life of Mickey Mantle in contemporary photos, many from Mantle's own collection and many picturing him with such stars of the era as Maris, DiMaggio, Ted Williams, Mays, etc. A total of 20,000 sets were produced; 5,000 of them feature a genuine Mantle autograph on card #1 and 15,000 sets have no

autograph. Backs of cards from the autographed sets are printed in blue while the unautographed sets have backs printed in red. Issue price was $25 for the autographed set, $13 for the unsigned version.

		NM/M
Comp. Set, #1 Auto. (72):		200.00
Comp. Set, Unauto. (72):		45.00
Common Card:		1.00
1	Header card	1.00
2	Mickey & Merlyn 12/23/51	1.00
3	Spring Training 1951	1.50
4	Spring Training 1951	1.50
5	Mickey's Mom, Mickey & Merlyn	1.00
6	4/15/51 1st Homer in NY	1.00
7	1951 - DiMaggio, Mantle, Williams	1.50
8	1951- Mickey signs for 1952	1.00
9	Martin & Mickey Jr. 4/12/52	1.00
10	Brothers Roy and Ray	1.00
11	Spring Training 1952	1.00
12	1952- Bauer, Hopp, Mantle	1.50
13	1952 Season	1.00
14	Mantle & Martin 1952 Series	1.50
15	Billy & Mickey 1953	1.50
16	Knee Injury 1953	1.00
17	1953 - Before knee surgery	1.00
18	New business 1953	1.00
19	1953 World Series Power	1.00
20	1953 The long Home Run	1.50
21	1955 Hall of Fame Game	1.50
22	1955	1.00
23	1955 - Skowron, Rizzuto, Mantle	1.50
23	1954 - Jackie Robinson at 1st	1.00
25	1956 - Mickey with Ted Williams	1.50
25	1955 - Skowron, Berra, Mantle	1.00
27	1956 - Mickey safe at first	1.00
28	1956 World Series	1.00
29	1957 - Yogi, Whitey, Mickey	1.00
30	1957 - Roy Sievers with Mickey	1.00
31	1957 World Series	1.00
32	1957 Hitchcock Award	1.50
33	1957 - Mickey with Cardinal Spellman	1.00
34	1957 - Singing with Teresa Brewer	1.00
35	1957 - Brooks Robinson & Mickey	1.00
36	1958 World Series	1.00
37	1958 All Star Game with Banks	1.50
38	With Stengel 1959	1.00
39	1960 - With Roger Maris	1.50
40	1960 World Series	1.00
41	1961 All Star Game with Maris & Mays	1.00
42	Blanchard	1.50
43	1961 - with Maris & Mrs. Babe Ruth	1.50
44	1961 - Mickey Congratulates Maris	1.00
45	1961 - Maris & Mantle	1.00
46	400th Career HR 9/11/62	1.00
47	1962 World Series	1.50
48	1963 season	1.50
49	1963 World Series	1.50
50	1964 World Series	1.50
51	1964 - Pepitone, Ford, Mantle	1.50
52	1964 season	1.50
53	1965 Mickey's Day	1.50
54	1965 season	1.50
55	1966 - with Joe DiMaggio	1.50
56	Mantle family	1.00
57	1967 season	1.00
58	1968 - hits HR No. 529	1.50
59	1968 - Retirement	1.00
60	1968 - His farewell	1.50
61	Mickey's trophy room	1.00
62	1970 - Welcome back Coach	1.00
63	1973 - TV commercial	1.00
64	1974 visit	1.00
65	1974 visit	1.00
66	1974 Hall of Fame inductees	1.00
67	1979 Old Timers Game	1.00
68	1981 Old Timers Game	1.00
69	Family Day	1.00
70	The Mantle Swing	1.00
71	The Mantle Swing	1.00
72	The Mantle Swing	1.00

1983 Authentic Sports Autographs

1964 with the Giants

These collectors' issue sets of a dozen cards each present the careers of 11 Hall of Famers in pictures and words. Each 2-1/2" x 3-1/2" card has a black-and-white or color photo on front with a card title and red or green border graphics. Backs present a narrative of the player's career and some include a small portrait photo. Each set was made available in both an unautographed version and a version in which the No. 1 card was authentically autographed.

		NM/M
(1)	Hank Aaron Story	15.00
(1a)	Hank Aaron Story/Auto.	50.00
(2)	Yogi Berra Story	6.00
(2a)	Yogi Berra Story/Auto.	20.00
(3)	Joe DiMaggio Story	15.00
(3a)	Joe DiMaggio Story/Auto.	150.00
(4)	Bob Feller Story	7.50
(4a)	Bob Feller Story/Auto.	15.00
(5)	Juan Marichal Story	7.50
(5a)	Juan Marichal Story/Auto.	20.00
(6)	Willie Mays Story	10.00
(6a)	Willie Mays Story/Auto.	50.00
(7)	Johnny Mize Story	6.00
(7a)	Johnny Mize Story/Auto.	15.00
(8)	Brooks Robinson Story	6.00
(8a)	Brooks Robinson Story/Auto.	15.00
(9)	Frank Robinson Story	6.00
(9a)	Frank Robinson Story/Auto.	20.00
(10)	Duke Snider Story	6.00
(10a)	Duke Snider Story/Auto.	20.00
(11)	Warren Spahn Story	6.00
(11a)	Warren Spahn Story/Auto.	20.00

2005 Azteca Seattle Mariners Hispanic Heroes

#5 - tercera base

This set of M's Latino players was a stadium giveaway to 20,000 fans at the 3rd annual Latin American Beisbol Night, September 13 at Safeco Field.

		NM/M
Complete Set (9):		10.00
Common Player:		.50
1	Adrian Beltre	1.00
2	Yuniesky Betancourt	1.00
3	Eddie Guardado	.50
4	Felix Hernandez	5.00
5	Raul Ibanez	.50
6	Jose Lopez	1.00
7	Julio Mateo	.50
8	Joel Pineiro	.50
9	Yorvit Torrealba	.50

B

1998 Ball Park Detroit Tigers

Fans in attendance at the August 9 game at Tiger Stadium re-

ceived this team set sponsored by Ball Park franks, the stadium hot dog concessionairre. Cards are standard 2-1/2" x 3-1/2" format printed on light cardboard. Fronts have color posed or action photos with white borders. Player identification is in a strip at left. Backs have a light blue background, overprinted in dark blue with the player's personal data, stats and a 1997 season highlight, along with the sponsor's logo and a picture of a moving baseball.

		NM/M
Complete Set (26):		9.00
Common Player:		.50
01	Gabe Alvarez	.50
02	Matt Anderson	.50
03	Paul Bako	.50
04	Trey Beamon	.50
05	Buddy Bell	.50
06	Geronimo Berroa	.50
07	Doug Bochtler	.50
08	Doug Brocail	.50
09	Raul Casanova	.50
10	Frank Castillo	.50
11	Frank Catalanotto	.50
12	Tony Clark	.50
13	Dean Crow	.50
14	Deivi Cruz	.50
15	Damion Easley	.50
16	Bryce Florie	.50
17	Luis Gonzalez	2.50
18	Seth Greisinger	.50
19	Bobby Higginson	.75
20	Brian Hunter	.50
21	Todd Jones	.50
22	Brian Moehler	.50
23	Brian Powell	.50
24	Joe Randa	.50
25	Sean Runyan	.50
26	Justin Thompson	.50

1994 Baltimore Orioles Program Cards

Virtually the entire O's organization, major and minor leaguers, was included in this season-long promotion. One of 12 nine-card sheets was inserted into the team's programs, which sold for $3. A reported 17,000 sets were produced. The sheets are unperforated and measure 7-1/2" x 10-1/2". Fronts have color game-action or posed photos within an orange border. A team logo is at top-right. At bottom is a black strip with the player's number (if a major leaguer), name and position in white. Backs are printed in black and orange on white with biographical details and complete major and minor league stats. The unnumbered cards are checklisted here alphabetically.

		NM/M
Complete Set, Sheets (12):		25.00
Complete Set, Singles (108):		25.00
Common Player:		.25
(1)	Manny Alexander	.25
(2)	Brady Anderson	.25
(3)	Matt Anderson	.25

(4)	Harold Baines	.25
(5)	Myles Barnden	.25
(6)	Kimera Bartee	.25
(7)	Juan Bautista	.25
(8)	Armando Benitez	.25
(9)	Joe Borowski	.25
(10)	Brian Brewer	.25
(11)	Brandon Bridgers	.25
(12)	Cory Brown	.25
(13)	Damon Buford	.25
(14)	Philip Byrne	.25
(15)	Rocco Cafaro	.25
(16)	Paul Carey	.25
(17)	Carlos Chavez	.25
(18)	Eric Chavez	.25
(19)	Steve Chitren	.25
(20)	Mike Cook	.25
(21)	Shawn Curran	.25
(22)	Kevin Curtis	.25
(23)	Joey Dawley	.25
(24)	Jim Dedrick	.25
(25)	Cesar Devarez	.25
(26)	Mike Devereaux	.25
(27)	Brian DuBois	.25
(28)	Keith Eaddy	.25
(29)	Mark Eichhorn	.25
(30)	Scott Emerson	.25
(31)	Vaughn Eshelman	.25
(32)	Craig Faulkner	.25
(33)	Sid Fernandez	.25
(34)	Rick Forney	.25
(35)	Jim Foster	.25
(36)	Jesse Garcia	.25
(37)	Mike Garguilo	.25
(38)	Rich Gedman	.25
(39)	Leo Gomez	.25
(40)	Rene Gonzalez	.25
(41)	Curtis Goodwin	.25
(42)	Kris Gresham	.25
(43)	Shane Hale	.25
(44)	Jeffrey Hammonds	.25
(45)	Jimmy Haynes	.25
(46)	Chris Hoiles	.25
(47)	Tim Hullett	.25
(48)	Matt Jarvis	.25
(49)	Scott Klingenbeck	.25
(50)	Rick Krivda	.25
(51)	David Lamb	.25
(52)	Chris Lemp	.25
(53)	T.R. Lewis	.25
(54)	Brian Link	.25
(55)	John Lombardi	.25
(56)	Rob Lukachyk	.25
(57)	Calvin Maduro	.25
(58)	Barry Manuel	.25
(59)	Lincoln Martin	.25
(60)	Scott McClain	.25
(61)	Ben McDonald	.25
(62)	Kevin McGehee	.25
(63)	Mark McLemore	.25
(64)	Miguel Mejia	.25
(65)	Feliciano Mercedes	.25
(66)	Jose Millares	.25
(67)	Brent Miller	.25
(68)	Alan Mills	.25
(69)	Jamie Moyer	.25
(70)	Mike Mussina	1.50
(71)	Sherman Obando	.25
(72)	Alex Ochoa	.25
(73)	John O'Donoghue	.25
(74)	Mike Oquist	.25
(75)	Bo Ortiz	.25
(76)	Billy Owens	.25
(77)	Rafael Palmeiro	2.00
(78)	Dave Paveloff	.25
(79)	Brad Pennington	.25
(80)	Bill Percibel	.25
(81)	Jim Poole	.25
(82)	Jay Powell	.25
(83)	Arthur Rhodes	.25
(84)	Matt Riemer	.25
(85)	Cal Ripken Jr.	5.00
(86)	Kevin Ryan	.25
(87)	Chris Sabo	.25
(88)	Brian Sackinsky	.25
(89)	Francisco Saneaux	.25
(90)	Jason Satre	.25
(91)	David Segui	.25
(92)	Jose Serra	.25
(93)	Larry Shenk	.25
(94)	Lee Smith	.25
(95)	Lonnie Smith	.25
(96)	Mark Smith	.25
(97)	Garrett Stephenson	.25
(98)	Jeff Tackett	.25
(99)	Brad Tyler	.25
(100)	Pedro Ulises	.25
(101)	Jack Voight	.25
(102)	Jim Walker	.25
(103)	B.J. Waszgis	.25
(104)	Jim Wawruck	.25
(105)	Mel Wearing	.25
(106)	Mark Williamson	.25
(107)	Brian Wood	.25
(108)	Gregg Zaun	.25

1984 Baseball Cards Magazine Repli-Cards

DALE MURPHY
outfielder ATLANTA BRAVES

With its August 1984 issue, Baseball Cards Magazine pioneered the use of "repli-cards" to enhance feature articles and increase sales. The cards were printed on cardboard stock and stapled into the magazines. Most of the cards were done in the style of earlier popular card issues. though some featured original designs and others were reproductions of actual cards. Some of baseball's best artists' and photographers' work appears on the cards. The inclusion of repli-cards ceased after 1993 when abuses by other "publishers" caused baseball's licensors to threaten legal action. Values quoted are for single cards cut from the panel; complete panels or magazines command a premium. Cards are grouped by magazine issue and numbered with a month-designation.

		NM/M
Complete Set (3):		10.00
Aug.	Ted Williams (1953 Topps style)	4.50
Aug.	Dale Murphy (1953 Topps style)	3.50
Oct.	Mickey Mantle (1949 Bowman style)	6.00

1985 Baseball Cards Magazine Repli-Cards

CHUCK CONNORS
Chuck Connors

In three of its 1985 issues, Baseball Cards Magazine offered "repli-cards" to enhance feature articles and increase sales. The cards were printed on cardboard stock and stapled into the magazines. Original designs and reproductions of earlier cards were used. Values quoted are for single cards cut from the panel; complete panels or magazines command a premium. Cards are grouped by magazine issue and numbered with a month-designation.

		NM/M
Complete Set (6):		12.00
Common Player:		2.00
April	Chuck Connors (Original design.)	2.00
April	Chuck Connors (1952 Topps style.)	2.00
June	Pete Rose (Reproduction 1965 Topps.)	3.00
June	Fritz Ackley, Steve Carlton (Reproduction 1965 Topps.)	2.00
Oct.	Mickey Mantle (Reproduction 1955 Bowman #202.)	4.00
Oct.	Ernie Banks (Reproduction 1955 Bowman #242.)	2.00

1986 Baseball Cards Magazine Repli-Cards

In three of its 1986 issues, Baseball Cards Magazine offered "repli-cards" to enhance feature articles and increase sales. The cards were printed on cardboard stock and stapled into the magazines. Reproductions of existing cards and modern player cards done in the style of vintage issues were used.

4 1986 BBC MAGAZINE

Values quoted are for single cards cut from the panel; complete panels or magazines command a premium. Cards are grouped by magazine issue and numbered with a month-designation.

		NM/M
Complete Set (12):		12.00
Common Player:		.50
April	Vince Coleman (Kondritz Trading Cards sample.)	.50
April	Vince Coleman (Kondritz Trading Cards sample.)	.50
June	Stan Musial (Reproduction 1953 Bowman.)	2.00
June	Roy Campanella (Reproduction 1953 Bowman.)	1.00
June	Yogi Berra (Reproduction 1953 Bowman.)	1.50
Dec.	Don Mattingly (1951 Topps Red Back style)	3.00
Dec.	Wally Joyner (1951 Topps Red Back style)	.50
Dec.	Wade Boggs (1951 Topps All-Stars style)	1.50
Dec.	Dwight Gooden (1951 Topps All-Stars style)	.50
Dec.	George Brett (Reproduction 1981 Donruss proof.)	3.00
Dec.	Reggie Jackson (Reproduction 1981 Donruss proof.)	2.50
Dec.	Lou Piniella (Reproduction 1982 Fleer proof.)	.75

1987 Baseball Cards Magazine Repli-Cards

DOUBLE TROUBLE
McGWIRE AND DAVIS

In four of its 1987 issues, Baseball Cards Magazine offered "repli-cards" to enhance feature articles and increase sales. The cards were printed on cardboard stock and stapled into the magazines. Original designs and modern player cards done in the style of vintage issues were used. Values quoted are for single cards cut from the panel; complete panels or magazines command a premium. Cards are grouped by magazine issue and numbered with a month-designation.

		NM/M
Complete Set (10):		14.00
Common Player:		.40
April	Don Mattingly (1983 Donruss style)	5.00
April	Don Mattingly (1983 Topps style)	5.00
Sept.	Ozzie Canseco (Original "Future Stars" design.)	.40
Sept.	Patrick Lennon (Original "Future Stars" design.)	.40
Oct.	Eric Davis (1951 Bowman style)	.75
Oct.	Bo Jackson (1951 Bowman style)	.75
Oct.	Stan Musial (1951 Bowman style)	1.50
Dec.	Dale Murphy (1981 Fleer style)	1.50

Dec.	Tim Raines (1981 Fleer style)	.50
Dec.	Double Trouble (Eric Davis, Mark McGwire) (1981 Fleer style)	2.50

1988 Baseball Cards Magazine Repli-Cards

Mickey Mantle
OUTFIELD, NEW YORK YANKEES

In six of its 1988 issues, Baseball Cards Magazine offered "repli-cards" to enhance feature articles and increase sales. The cards were printed on cardboard stock and stapled into the magazines. Original designs, reproductions and modern player cards done in the style of vintage issues were used. Values quoted are for single cards cut from the panel; complete panels or magazines command a premium. Cards are grouped by magazine issue and numbered with a month-designation.

		NM/M
Complete Set (16):		27.50
Common Player:		.40
Feb.	Babe Ruth (1936 Diamond Stars style)	1.50
Feb.	Wade Boggs (1936 Diamond Stars style)	1.50
Feb.	Mark McGwire (1936 Diamond Stars style; available only via mail-in offer)	4.00
April	Ted Williams (1952 Topps style)	1.50
April	Ted Williams (Reproduction 1954 Bowman #66.)	2.50
June	Joey Meyer (Original design.)	.40
June	Sam Horn (Original design.)	.40
Aug.	Roger "Rocket" Clemens (1941 Play Ball style)	2.50
Aug.	Kirk Gibson (1941 Play Ball style)	.40
Aug.	Jack Clark (1941 Play Ball style)	.40
Oct.	Mickey Mantle (1956 Bowman proof style)	7.50
Oct.	Jackie Robinson (1952 Bowman style)	1.50
Oct.	Dave Winfield (1974 Topps "Washington" style)	1.25
Dec.	Mickey Mantle (Reproduction 1952 Bowman.)	2.50
Dec.	Mickey Mantle (Reproduction 1951 Bowman.)	4.50
Dec.	Mickey Mantle (Reproduction 1952 Topps.)	6.00

1989 Baseball Cards Magazine Repli-Cards

kirby puckett

MINNESOTA TWINS
OUTFIELD

Beginning with its January 1989 issue, Baseball Cards Magazine began issuing its repli-cards in panels of six cards per month, creating an annual set of 72 insert cards. Contemporary players were presented in the designs of classic Topps sets of the 1950s-1970s. In 1989 the magazine's cards were in the style of 1959 Topps. Besides the individual player's cards, specialty cards included "Rookie Stars of 1989" and multi-player feature cards.

		NM/M
Complete Set (72):		20.00
Common Player:		.15
1	Keith Hernandez	.15
2	Will Clark	.15
3	Andres Galarraga	.15
4	Mark McGwire	1.50
5	Don Mattingly	1.00
6	Ricky Jordan (Rookie Stars)	.15
7	Juan Samuel	.15
8	Julio Franco	.15
9	Harold Reynolds	.15
10	Gregg Jefferies (Rookie Stars)	.15
11	Ryne Sandberg	.75
12	Lou Whitaker	.15
13	Ozzie Smith	.75
14	Gary Sheffield (Rookie Stars)	.25
15	Alan Trammell	.15
16	Cal Ripken Jr.	2.00
17	Barry Larkin	.15
18	Tony Fernandez	.15
19	Mike Schmidt	1.00
20	Wade Boggs	.75
21	Gary Gaetti	.15
22	Chris Sabo (Rookie Stars)	.15
23	Paul Molitor	.60
24	Carney Lansford	.15
25	Dave Winfield	.60
26	Darryl Strawberry	.15
27	Tony Gwynn	.75
28	Darryl Hamilton	.15
29	Jose Canseco	.45
30	Andre Dawson	.25
31	Kirby Puckett	.75
32	Cameron Drew (Rookie Stars)	.15
33	Robin Yount	.60
34	Ellis Burks	.15
35	Eric Davis	.15
36	Joe Carter	.15
37	George Bell	.15
38	Kevin McReynolds	.15
39	Tim Raines	.15
40	Luis Medina (Rookie Stars)	.15
41	Mike Greenwell	.15
42	Kal Daniels	.15
43	Dwight Gooden	.15
44	Roger Clemens	1.00
45	Nolan Ryan	2.00
46	Erik Hanson	.15
47	Orel Hershiser	.15
48	Bret Saberhagen	.15
49	Jimmy Key	.15
50	Frank Viola	.15
51	Bruce Hurst	.15
52	Norm Charlton (Rookie Stars)	.15
53	Ted Higuera	.15
54	Mark Langston	.15
55	Damon Berryhill	.15
56	Carlton Fisk	.60
57	Terry Steinbach	.15
58	Sandy Alomar (Rookie Stars)	.15
59	Benito Santiago	.15
60	Bob Boone	.15
61	Jerome Walton (Rookie Stars)	.15
62	Jaime Navarro (Rookie Stars)	.15
63	Ken Griffey Jr. (Rookie Stars)	1.50
64	Jim Abbott (Rookie Stars)	.15
65	Junior Felix (Rookie Stars)	.15
66	Tom Gordon	.15
67	Power Plus (Kirby Puckett, Don Mattingly)	.65
68	Fence Busters (Julio Franco, Eric Davis, Ruben Sierra)	.15
69	N.L. Hitting Kings (Will Clark, Tony Gwynn)	.25
70	Keystone Combo (Ozzie Smith, Ryne Sandberg)	.50
71	Dinger Duo (Howard Johnson, Kevin Mitchell)	.15
72	Texas Heat (Nolan Ryan, Mike Scott)	.75

1990 Baseball Cards Magazine Repli-Cards

Beginning with its January 1989 issue, Baseball Cards Magazine began issuing its repli-cards in panels of six cards per month, creating an annual set of 72 insert cards. Contemporary players were presented in the designs of classic Topps sets of the 1950s-1970s. In 1990 the magazine's cards were in the style of 1969 Topps. Besides

the individual player's cards, there were a number of multi-player "Rookie Stars" cards.

		NM/M
Complete Set (72):		25.00
Common Player:		.15
1	Craig Biggio	.15
2	Kevin Mitchell	.15
3	Orel Hershiser	.15
4	Will Clark	.15
5	Eric Davis	.15
6	Tony Gwynn	.75
7	Mike Scott	.15
8	Barry Larkin	.15
9	John Smoltz	.15
10	Glenn Davis	.15
11	Roberto Alomar	.25
12	Rick Reuschel	.15
13	N.L. West Rookie Stars (Eric Anthony, Ed Whited)	.15
14	N.L. West Rookie Stars (Andy Benes, Steve Avery)	.15
15	N.L. West Rookie Stars (John Wetteland, Joe Oliver)	.15
16	Giants Rookie Stars (Randy McCament, Greg Litton)	.15
17	Dodgers Rookie Stars (Jose Offerman, Jose Vizcaino)	.15
18	Reds Rookie Stars (Scott Scudder, Rosario Rodriguez)	.15
19	Darryl Strawberry	.15
20	Von Hayes	.15
21	Dwight Smith	.15
22	Howard Johnson	.15
23	Pedro Guerrero	.15
24	Tim Raines	.15
25	Ozzie Smith	.75
26	Barry Bonds	2.00
27	Jerome Walton	.15
28	Ryne Sandberg	.75
29	Bobby Bonilla	.15
30	Mark Grace	.15
31	Cards Rookie Stars (Todd Zeile, Alex Cole)	.15
32	N.L. East Rookie Stars (Pat Combs, Dean Wilkins)	.15
33	N.L. East Rookie Stars (Steve Carter, Jeff Huson)	.15
34	Cubs Rookie Stars (Greg Smith, Derrick May)	.15
35	Expos Rookie Stars (Marquis Grissom, Larry Walker)	.45
36	Mets Rookie Stars (Wally Whitehurst, Blaine Beatty)	.15
37	Ken Griffey Jr.	1.50
38	Kirby Puckett	.75
39	Julio Franco	.15
40	Ruben Sierra	.15
41	Bo Jackson	.25
42	Jose Canseco	.35
43	Dennis Eckersley	.50
44	Bret Saberhagen	.15
45	Wally Joyner	.15
46	Carlton Fisk	.60
47	Nolan Ryan	2.00
48	Rickey Henderson	.60
49	White Sox Rookie Stars (Robin Ventura, Sammy Sosa)	7.50
50	A.L. West Rookie Stars (John Orton, Scott Radinsky)	.15
51	A.L. West Rookie Stars (Bobby Rose, Bob Hamelin)	.15
52	Rangers Rookie Stars (Monty Fariss, Juan Gonzalez)	.50
53	Mariners Rookie Stars (Tino Martinez, Roger Salkeld)	.15
54	Twins Rookie Stars (Terry Jorgensen, Paul Sorrento)	.15
55	Don Mattingly	1.00
56	Roger Clemens	1.00
57	Cal Ripken	2.00
58	Robin Yount	.60
59	Wade Boggs	.75
60	Fred McGriff	.15
61	Cecil Fielder	.15
62	Ellis Burks	.15
63	Sandy Alomar	.15
64	Alan Trammell	.15
65	Steve Sax	.15
66	Paul Molitor	.60
67	Brewers Rookie Stars (Bert Hefferman, Matias Carillo)	.15
68	A.L. East Rookie Stars (Ben McDonald, John Olerud)	.25
69	A.L. East Rookie Stars (Mark Whiten, Phil Clark)	.15
70	Yankees Rookie Stars (Jim Leyritz, Kevin Maas)	.15
71	Indians Rookie Stars (Mark Lewis, Carlos Baerga)	.15
72	Orioles Rookie Stars (David Segui, Chris Hoiles)	.15

1991 Baseball Cards Magazine Repli-Cards

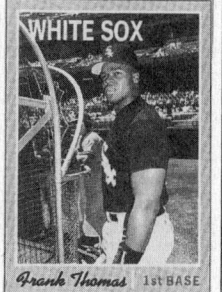

of-1st base

For the third year in 1991, Baseball Cards Magazine issued its repli-cards in panels of six cards per month, creating an annual set of 72 insert cards. Contemporary players were presented in the classic Topps design of 1966. Besides the individual players' cards, there are a number of multi-player feature cards and "Rookie Stars of 1991" multi-player cards, plus a 1952 Topps style card of Don Mattingly.

		NM/M
Complete Set (72):		18.00
Common Player:		.15
1	Eric Davis	.15
2	Cubs Rookie Stars (Lance Dickson, Hector Villanueva)	.15
3	Bobby Bonilla	.15
4	Len Dykstra	.15
5	John Franco	.15
6	Matt Williams	.15
7	Barry Bonds	2.00
8	Cards Rookie Stars (Geronimo Pena, Ray Lankford, Bernard Gilkey)	.15
9	Andre Dawson	.25
10	Dave Justice	.15
11	Triple Expos-ure (Larry Walker, Marquis Grissom, Delino DeShields)	.20
12	Howard Johnson	.15
13	Darryl Strawberry	.15
14	Astros Rookie Stars (Karl Rhodes, Andujar Cedeno, Mike Simms)	.15
15	Will Clark	.15
16	Barry Larkin	.15
17	Ramon Martinez	.15
18	Ron Gant	.15
19	Gregg Jefferies	.15
20	Giants Rookie Stars (Steve Decker, Steve Hosey, Mark Leonard)	.15
21	Todd Zeile	.15
22	Benito Santiago	.15
23	Eddie Murray	.60
24	Randy Myers	.15
25	Greg Maddux	.75
26	Phillies Rookie Stars (Mickey Morandini, Wes Chamberlain)	.15
27	Tim Wallach	.15
28	Dale Murphy	.25
29	Doug Drabek	.15
30	Kevin Mitchell	.15
31	Frank Viola	.15
32	Padres Rookie Stars (Rafael Valdez, Paul Faries)	.15
33	Hal Morris	.15
34	Pedro Guerrero	.15
35	Dwight Gooden	.15
36	Shawon Dunston	.15
37	Ken Griffey Jr.	1.00
38	Royals Rookie Stars (Sean Berry, Brian McRae)	.15
39	Roger Clemens	.85
40	Ellis Burks	.15
41	Robin Yount	.60
42	Frank Thomas	.60
43	Ruben Sierra	.15
44	Red Sox Rookie Stars (Mo Vaughn, Phil Plantier, Tim Naehring)	.15
45	Tim Raines	.15
46	Dave Parker	.15
47	Jose Canseco	.35
48	Glenn Davis	.15
49	Dave Winfield	.60
50	Chuck Knoblauch, Scott Leius, Willie Banks (Twins Rookie Stars)	.15
51	Joe Carter	.15
52	Cal Ripken	2.00
53	Carlton Fisk	.60
54	Julio Franco	.15
55	Don Mattingly	.85
56	Blue Jays Rookie Stars (Eddie Zosky, William Suero, Derek Bell)	.15
57	Sandy Alomar	.15
58	Juan Gonzalez	.30
59	Don Mattingly (1952 Topps style)	1.50
60	Mike Greenwell	.15
61	Chuck Finley	.15
62	Rangers Rookie Stars (Dean Palmer, Ivan Rodriguez, Gerald Alexander)	1.00
63	Scott Erickson	.15
64	Paul Molitor	.15
65	Triple Terrors (Cecil Fielder, Jose Canseco, Mark McGwire)	.60
66	Dennis Eckersley	.50
67	Brian Harper	.15
68	A.L. Rookie Stars (Bernie Williams, Wilson Alvarez) (No designation on front banner.)	.25
69	Robin Ventura	.15
70	Kirby Puckett	.75
71	Rafael Palmeiro	.15
72	Roberto Alomar	.25

1992 Baseball Cards Magazine Repli-Cards

Frank Thomas 1st BASE

The annual repli-card series inserted in Baseball Cards Magazine began in January with six-card panels each month. In May, panels were increased to eight cards and a UV coating was added to the front. Contemporary players were presented in the designs of classic Topps sets of the 1950s-1970s. In 1992 the magazine's cards were in the style of 1970 Topps. Besides the individual player's cards, specialty cards included "1992 Rookie Stars" multi-player and Team USA cards.

		NM/M
Complete Set (88):		20.00
Common Player:		.50
1	Eddie Murray	.50
2	Braves Rookie Stars (Ryan Klesko, Mark Wohlers)	.15
3	Barry Bonds	1.50
4	Will Clark	.15
5	Jose Canseco	.35
6	Ron Gant	.15
7	Ruben Sierra	.15
8	Reds Rookie Stars (Reggie Sanders, Mo Sanford)	.15
9	Terry Pendleton	.15
10	Hal Morris	.15
11	Kirby Puckett	.60
12	Paul Molitor	.50
13	Jack McDowell	.15
14	Dodgers Rookie Stars (Eric Karros, Tom Goodwin)	.15
15	Ramon Martinez	.15
16	Steve Avery	.15
17	Roger Clemens	.75
18	Jim Abbott	.15
19	Phil Plantier	.15
20	Giants Rookie Stars (Royce Clayton, Ted Wood)	.15
21	Frank Thomas	.50
22	Juan Gonzalez	.25
23	Felix Jose	.15
24	Chuck Knoblauch	.15
25	Tony Gwynn	.60
26	Julio Franco	.15
27	Greg Blosser	.15
	Frankie Rodriguez	.15
28	Wade Boggs	.60
29	Robin Ventura	.15
30	Shane Mack	.15
31	Roberto Alomar	.25
32	Don Mattingly	.75
33	Astros Rookie Stars (Ryan Bowen, Jeff Juden)	.15
34	Cal Ripken Jr.	1.50
35	Ozzie Smith	.60
36	Ken Griffey Jr.	1.00
37	Ivan Rodriguez	.40
38	Matt Williams	.15
39	Craig Biggio	.15
40	John Kruk	.15
41	George Brett	.75
42	Carlton Fisk	.50
43	Indians Rookie Stars (Kenny Lofton, Jim Thome)	.50
44	Andre Dawson	.25
45	Nolan Ryan	1.50
46	Robin Yount	.15
47	Ryne Sandberg	.60
48	Rickey Henderson	.50
49	Bobby Thigpen	.15
50	Dennis Eckersley	.40
51	Cards Rookie Stars (Brian Jordan, Dmitri Young)	.15
52	Jeff Reardon	.15
53	Bryan Harvey	.15
54	Tom Henke	.15
55	Lee Smith	.15
56	John Franco	.15
57	Cecil Fielder	.15
58	Darryl Strawberry	.15
59	Twins Rookie Stars (David McCarty, Scott Stahoviak)	.15
60	Mark McGwire	1.00
61	George Bell	.15
62	Fred McGriff	.15
63	Danny Tartabull	.15
64	Joe Carter	.15
65	Deion Sanders	.15
66	Roberto Alomar	.25
67	A.L. Rookie Stars (Eduardo Perez, Joe Vitiello, Bret Boone)	.15
68	Bip Roberts	.15
69	Ray Lankford	.15
70	Brady Anderson	.15
71	Tim Raines	.15
72	Marquis Grissom	.15
73	Dave Fleming	.15
74	Andy Benes	.15
75	Yankees Rookie Stars (Bob Wickman, Mark Hutton)	.15
76	Bill Swift	.15
77	Mike Mussina	.25
78	Donovan Osborne	.15
79	Juan Guzman	.15
80	Ken Brown	.15
81	Charles Johnson (USA)	.15
82	Jeffrey Hammonds (USA)	.15
83	Rick Helling (USA)	.15
84	Chris Wimmer (USA)	.15
85	Darren Dreifort (USA)	.15
86	Calvin Murray (USA)	.15
87	Phil Nevin (USA)	.15
88	B.J. Wallace (USA)	.15

1993 Baseball Cards/Sports Cards Magazine Repli-Cards

The annual repli-card series began in Baseball Cards Magazine in 1989 continued in 1993 with eight-card panels of UV-coated repli-cards stapled into each monthly issue. (Only seven cards were included in July; there are two #32 and no #40.) Contemporary players were presented in the design of the classic 1968 Topps set. Backs are printed in black, white and yellow and include an investment advisory about the player's cards. Besides the individual player's repli-cards, there is a group of "1993 Rookie Stars" multi-player cards. Effective with its May issue, the magazine's title was changed to Sports Cards, the copyright line on back reflecting that change.

		NM/M
Complete Set (95):		25.00
Common Player:		.15
1	Andy Van Slyke	.15
2	Ruben Sierra	.15
3	Carlos Baerga	.15
4	Gary Sheffield	.30
5	Chuck Knoblauch	.15
6	Danny Tartabull	.15
7	Angels Rookie Stars (Chad Curtis, Tim Salmon)	.45
8	Darren Daulton	.15
9	Deion Sanders	.20
10	Pat Listach	.15
11	Albert Belle	.15
12	Frank Thomas	.60
13	Dave Hollins	.15
14	Braves Rookie Stars (Javy Lopez, Mike Kelly)	.15
15	Travis Fryman	.15
16	Edgar Martinez	.15
17	Barry Bonds	1.50
18	Dennis Eckersley	.50
19	Brady Anderson	.15
20	Fred McGriff	.15
21	Paul Molitor	.60
22	Juan Gonzalez	.30
23	Dodgers Rookie Stars (Bill Ashley, Mike Piazza)	1.50
24	Larry Walker	.15
25	Dave Winfield	.60
26	Robin Yount	.15
27	George Brett	.85
28	Jack Morris	.15
29	Eddie Murray	.60
30	Nolan Ryan	1.50
31	Carlton Fisk	.60
32a	Dale Murphy	.30
32b	Jeff Bagwell	.60
33	Eric Karros	.15
34	Roberto Alomar	.25
35	Robin Ventura	.15
36	Delino DeShields	.15
37	Ken Griffey Jr.	1.00
38	Eric Anthony	.15
39	Marquis Grissom	.15
40	Cecil Fielder	.15
41	Mark McGwire	1.25
42	Ryne Sandberg	.75
43	Kirby Puckett	.75
44	Cal Ripken Jr.	1.50
45	David McCarty	.15
46	Joe Carter	.15
47	Dean Palmer	.15
48	Jack McDowell	.15
49	Roger Clemens	.85
50	Cal Eldred	.15
51	Tom Glavine	.25
52	Steve Avery	.15
53	Mike Mussina	.35
54	Brien Taylor	.15
55	Mark Grace	.15
56	Ray Lankford	.15
57	Shane Mack	.15
58	Terry Pendleton	.15
59	Tony Gwynn	.75
60	Rafael Palmeiro	.50
61	Will Clark	.15
62	Wil Cordero	.15
63	Cliff Floyd	.15
64	Aaron Sele	.15
65	Chipper Jones	.75
66	Frank Rodriguez	.15
67	Ryan Klesko	.15
68	Manny Ramirez	.60
69	Carlos Delgado	.30
70	Paul Shuey	.15
71	Barry Bonds	1.50
72	Andre Dawson	.30
73	Paul Molitor	.60
74	Greg Maddux	.75
75	Wade Boggs	.75
76	Bryan Harvey	.15
77	Andres Galarraga	.15
78	Gregg Jefferies	.15
79	Mike Piazza	1.00
80	J.T. Snow	.15
81	Ivan Rodriguez	.50
82	Derrick May	.15
83	Tim Salmon	.15
84	Greg Vaughn	.15
85	Kenny Lofton	.15
86	John Olerud	.15
87	Sammy Sosa	.75
88	Lee Smith	.15
89	Matt Williams	.15
90	Don Mattingly	.85
91	Willie Greene	.15
92	Jim Abbott	.15
93	Mo Vaughn	.15
94	Randy Johnson	.60

1990-92 Baseball Cards Presents Repli-Cards

JOHN OLERUD
John Olerud

Taking advantage of the boom in sports card collecting, Baseball Cards Magazine began a series of special newsstand magazine titles. Beginning with "Baseball Card Boom," dated February 1990, the series, officially known as "Baseball Cards Presents . . ." included baseball (and other sports) repli-cards in most of its issues through August 1992. Cards are listed here by issue in which they were inserted.

		NM/M
	Complete Set (61):	27.50
	Common Player:	.25
1	Don Mattingly	1.25
2	Dwight Gooden	.25
3	Jose Canseco	.35
4	Bo Jackson	.35
5	Ken Griffey Jr.	1.50
1	John Olerud	.25
2	Eric Anthony	.25
3	Greg Vaughn	.25
4	Todd Zeile	.25
5	Ben McDonald	.25
6	Deion Sanders (Mail-in offer only.)	.75
1	Mark Davis	.25
2	Bret Saberhagen	.25
3	Kirby Puckett	.65
4	Rickey Henderson	.25
5	Kevin Mitchell	.25
1	Cecil Fielder	.25
2	Rickey Henderson	.50
3	Barry Bonds	2.00
4	Ryne Sandberg	.65
5	Roger Clemens	1.00
1	Nolan Ryan	2.00
2	Eric Davis	.25
3	Ryne Sandberg	.65
4	Rickey Henderson	.50
5	Kevin Maas	.25
6	Dave Justice	.25
7	Jose Canseco	.35
8	Bo Jackson	.35
9	Roger Clemens	1.00
10	Ken Griffey Jr.	1.50
1	Babe Ruth (1936 Diamond Stars style)	1.00
1	Ted Williams (1952 Topps style)	.75
2	Rickey Henderson (1933 Goudey style)	.50
5	Roger Clemens (1941 Play Ball style)	1.00
325	Stan Musial (1951 Bowman style)	.65
11	Frank Thomas	.50
12	Dwight Gooden	.25
13	David Robinson/Basketball	.25
14	Will Clark	.25
15	Darryl Strawberry	.25
16	Kevin Mitchell	.25
17	Tony Gwynn	.65
18	Cal Ripken Jr.	2.00
19	Michael Jordan	1.50
20	Don Mattingly	1.25
1	Frank Thomas	.50
2	Scott Erickson	.25
3	Terry Pendleton	.25
4	Cal Ripken	2.00
5	Barry Bonds	2.00
1	Frank Thomas	.50
2	Jeff Bagwell	.50
3	Cecil Fielder	.25
4	Ken Griffey Jr.	1.50
5	Juan Gonzalez	.35
1	Ryne Sandberg	.65
2	Phil Plantier	.25
3	Barry Larkin	.25
4	Cecil Fielder	.25
5	Dave Justice	.25

1992 The Baseball Enquirer

This set of "Mystery Interview" cards parodies baseball players and baseball cards. The 2-1/2" x 3-1/2" cards have caricatures of well-known players on front, surrounded by a gray border and a blank white name box. A blue "Fun Stuff" trade-

mark is at bottom-right. Backs are printed in blue and black on white with a card number, another blank name box, issuer's trademarks and a mock interview with the player. Actual player names are not seen anywhere on the cards. Issued in 10-card polypacks at 49 cents, complete sets - 184,000 of them - were also issued at $5.

		NM/M
	Complete Set (64):	7.50
	Common Player:	.50
	Pack (10):	.25
	Box (36):	7.50
1	Bo Jackson	.65
2	Jose Canseco	.60
3	Mark Langston	.60
4	Billy Ripken	.60
5	David Justice	.50
6	Rob Deer	.50
7	Jack McDowell	.50
8	Cecil Fielder	.50
9	John Smoltz	.50
10	Will Clark	.50
11	Ken Caminiti	.50
12	Kent Hrbek	.50
13	Gregg Jefferies	.50
14	Bob Uecker	.75
15	Mike Greenwell	.50
16	No player	.05
17	Ken Griffey Jr.	2.00
18	Robin Yount	.75
19	Joe DiMaggio	2.00
20	Mackey Sasser	.50
21	Dave Stewart	.50
22	Barry Bonds	3.00
23	Don Zimmer	.50
24	Jack Morris	.50
25	George Brett	1.50
26	Tommy Lasorda	.50
27	Whitey Ford	.50
28	Bill Buckner	.50
29	Ozzie Smith	1.00
30	Stump Merrill	.50
31	Randy Johnson	.75
32	George Bell	.50
33	Johnny Bench	1.00
34	Rickey Henderson	.75
35	Jack Clark	.50
36	Jim Palmer	.50
37	Lenny Dykstra	.50
38	George Steinbrenner	.50
39	Dave Stieb	.50
40	Nolan Ryan	3.00
41	Chris Sabo	.50
42	Unidentified player	.50
43	Kirby Puckett	1.00
44	Lou Piniella	.50
45	Wade Boggs	1.00
46	Andre Dawson	.60
47	Roger Clemens	1.25
48	Pete Rose	2.00
49	David Cone	.50
50	Warren Cromartie	.50
51	Unidentified Umpire	.50
52	Phil Rizzuto	.50
53	Dan Gladden	.50
54	Mark Lemke	.50
55	Buck Rodgers	.50
56	Darryl Strawberry	.50
57	Rob Dibble	.50
58	Deion Sanders	.50
59	Tony Gwynn	1.00
60	Dale Murphy	.60
61	Albert Belle	.50
62	Don Mattingly	1.50
63	Andres Galarraga	.50
64	Babe Ruth	.75

1980-88 Baseball Immortals

One of the most popular of the "collectors' issues," this set is produced with the permission of Major League Baseball by Renata Galasso Inc. and TCMA. The set features players in the Baseball Hall of Fame and was first issued in 1980. For several years thereafter the set was updated to include new inductees. The cards measure 2-1/2" x 3-1/2" and have colorful borders. The card fronts include the player's name, po-

BASEBALL IMMORTALS / 1936 / OUTFIELDER BABE RUTH

sition and year of induction. The backs feature a short biography and a trivia question. The photos used are color; most players who were active before 1950 have colored black-and-white photos. The designation "first printing" appears on all cards issued in 1981 and after.

		NM/M
	Complete 1980 Set (173):	15.00
	Complete Set (199):	30.00
	Common Player:	.10
1	Babe Ruth	2.00
2	Ty Cobb	1.00
3	Walter Johnson	.20
4	Christy Mathewson	.20
5	Honus Wagner	.20
6	Morgan Bulkeley	.10
7	Ban Johnson	.10
8	Larry Lajoie	.10
9	Connie Mack	.10
10	John McGraw	.10
11	Tris Speaker	.10
12	George Wright	.10
13	Cy Young	.10
14	Grover Alexander	.10
15	Alexander Cartwright	.10
16	Henry Chadwick	.10
17	Cap Anson	.10
18	Eddie Collins	.10
19	Charles Comiskey	.10
20	Candy Cummings	.10
21	Buck Ewing	.10
22	Lou Gehrig	1.50
23	Willie Keeler	.10
24	Hoss Radbourne	.10
25	George Sisler	.10
26	Albert Spalding	.10
27	Rogers Hornsby	.10
28	Judge Landis	.10
29	Roger Bresnahan	.10
30	Dan Brouthers	.10
31	Fred Clarke	.10
32	James Collins	.10
33	Ed Delahanty	.10
34	Hugh Duffy	.10
35	Hughie Jennings	.10
36	Mike "King" Kelly	.10
37	James O'Rourke	.10
38	Wilbert Robinson	.10
39	Jesse Burkett	.10
40	Frank Chance	.10
41	Jack Chesbro	.10
42	John Evers	.10
43	Clark Griffith	.10
44	Thomas McCarthy	.10
45	Joe McGinnity	.10
46	Eddie Plank	.10
47	Joe Tinker	.10
48	Rube Waddell	.10
49	Ed Walsh	.10
50	Mickey Cochrane	.10
51	Frankie Frisch	.10
52	Lefty Grove	.10
53	Carl Hubbell	.10
54	Herb Pennock	.10
55	Pie Traynor	.10
56	Three Finger Brown	.10
57	Charlie Gehringer	.10
58	Kid Nichols	.10
59	Jimmie Foxx	.10
60	Mel Ott	.10
61	Harry Heilmann	.10
62	Paul Waner	.10
63	Ed Barrow	.10
64	Chief Bender	.10
65	Tom Connolly	.10
66	Dizzy Dean	.10
67	Bill Klem	.10
68	Al Simmons	.10
69	Bobby Wallace	.10
70	Harry Wright	.10
71	Bill Dickey	.10
72	Rabbit Maranville	.10
73	Bill Terry	.10
74	Home Run Baker	.10
75	Joe DiMaggio	2.00
76	Gabby Hartnett	.10
77	Ted Lyons	.10
78	Ray Schalk	.10
79	Dazzy Vance	.10
80	Joe Cronin	.10
81	Hank Greenberg	.10
82	Sam Crawford	.10
83	Joe McCarthy	.10
84	Zack Wheat	.10
85	Max Carey	.10
86	Billy Hamilton	.10
87	Bob Feller	.10
88	Bill McKechnie	.10
89	Jackie Robinson	1.00
90	Edd Roush	.10
91	John Clarkson	.10
92	Elmer Flick	.10
93	Sam Rice	.10
94	Eppa Rixey	.10
95	Luke Appling	.10
96	Red Faber	.10
97	Burleigh Grimes	.10
98	Miller Huggins	.10
99	Tim Keefe	.10
100	Heinie Manush	.10
101	John Ward	.10
102	Pud Galvin	.10
103	Casey Stengel	.10
104	Ted Williams	1.00
105	Branch Rickey	.10
106	Red Ruffing	.10
107	Lloyd Waner	.10
108	Kiki Cuyler	.10
109	Goose Goslin	.10
110	Joe (Ducky) Medwick	.10
111	Roy Campanella	.20
112	Stan Coveleski	.10
113	Waite Hoyt	.10
114	Stan Musial	.50
115	Lou Boudreau	.10
116	Earle Combs	.10
117	Ford Frick	.10
118	Jesse Haines	.10
119	Dave Bancroft	.10
120	Jake Beckley	.10
121	Chick Hafey	.10
122	Harry Hooper	.10
123	Joe Kelley	.10
124	Rube Marquard	.10
125	Satchel Paige	.50
126	George Weiss	.10
127	Yogi Berra	.20
128	Josh Gibson	.10
129	Lefty Gomez	.10
130	Will Harridge	.10
131	Sandy Koufax	1.00
132	Buck Leonard	.10
133	Early Wynn	.10
134	Ross Youngs	.10
135	Roberto Clemente	2.00
136	Billy Evans	.10
137	Monte Irvin	.10
138	George Kelly	.10
139	Warren Spahn	.10
140	Mickey Welch	.10
141	Cool Papa Bell	.10
142	Jim Bottomley	.10
143	Jocko Conlan	.10
144	Whitey Ford	.10
145	Mickey Mantle	5.00
146	Sam Thompson	.10
147	Earl Averill	.10
148	Bucky Harris	.10
149	Billy Herman	.10
150	Judy Johnson	.10
151	Ralph Kiner	.10
152	Oscar Charleston	.10
153	Roger Connor	.10
154	Cal Hubbard	.10
155	Bob Lemon	.10
156	Fred Lindstrom	.10
157	Robin Roberts	.10
158	Ernie Banks	.25
159	Martin Dihigo	.10
160	Pop Lloyd	.10
161	Al Lopez	.10
162	Amos Rusie	.10
163	Joe Sewell	.10
164	Addie Joss	.10
165	Larry MacPhail	.10
166	Eddie Mathews	.10
167	Warren Giles	.10
168	Willie Mays	1.00
169	Hack Wilson	.10
170	Duke Snider	.20
171	Al Kaline	.10
172	Chuck Klein	.10
173	Tom Yawkey	.10
174	Bob Gibson	.10
175	Rube Foster	.10
176	Johnny Mize	.10
177	Hank Aaron	1.00
178	Frank Robinson	.10
179	Happy Chandler	.10
180	Travis Jackson	.10
181	Brooks Robinson	.10
182	Juan Marichal	.10
183	George Kell	.10
184	Walter Alston	.10
185	Harmon Killebrew	.10
186	Luis Aparicio	.10
187	Don Drysdale	.10
188	Pee Wee Reese	.10
189	Rick Ferrell	.10
190	Willie McCovey	.10
191	Ernie Lombardi	.10
192	Bobby Doerr	.10
193	Arky Vaughan	.10
194	Enos Slaughter	.10
195	Lou Brock	.10
196	Hoyt Wilhelm	.10
197	Billy Williams	.10
198	"Catfish" Hunter	.10
199	Ray Dandridge	.10

1990 Baseball Wit

This 108-card set was released in two printings. The first printing fea-

Baseball Wit / 15   15

tured unnumbered cards and several errors. The second printing featured corrections and numbered cards. The set was available at several retail chains and feature trivia questions on the card backs. The set was dedicated to Little League baseball.

		NM/M
	Complete Set (108):	12.50
	Common Player:	.10
1	Orel Hershiser	.10
2	Tony Gwynn	.10
3	Mickey Mantle	2.50
4	Willie Stargell	.10
5	Don Baylor	.10
6	Hank Aaron	1.00
7	Don Larsen	.10
8	Lee Mazzilli	.10
9	Boog Powell	.10
10	Little League World Series	.10
11	Jose Canseco	.30
12	Mike Scott	.10
13	Bob Feller	.10
14	Ron Santo	.10
15	Mel Stottlemyre	.10
16	Shea Stadium	.10
17	Brooks Robinson	.25
18	Willie Mays	.30
19	Ernie Banks	.30
20	Keith Hernandez	.10
21	Bret Saberhagen	.10
22	Hall of Fame	.10
23	Luis Aparicio	.10
24	Yogi Berra	.30
25	Manny Mota	.10
26	Steve Garvey	.10
27	Bill Shea	.10
28	Fred Lynn	.10
29	Todd Worrell	.10
30	Roy Campanella	.30
31	Bob Gibson	.10
32	Gary Carter	.10
33	Jim Palmer	.25
34	Carl Yastrzemski	.25
35	Dwight Gooden	.10
36	Stan Musial	.50
37	Rickey Henderson	.25
38	Dale Murphy	.25
39	Mike Schmidt	.75
40	Gaylord Perry	.10
41	Ozzie Smith	.60
42	Reggie Jackson	.75
43	Steve Carlton	.25
44	Jim Perry	.10
45	Vince Coleman	.10
46	Tom Seaver	.25
47	Marty Marion	.10
48	Frank Robinson	.25
49	Joe DiMaggio	1.50
50	Ted Williams	1.00
51	Rollie Fingers	.10
52	Jackie Robinson	1.00
53	Victor Raschi	.10
54	Johnny Bench	.25
55	Nolan Ryan	1.50
56	Ty Cobb	1.00
57	Harry Steinfeldt	.10
58	James O'Rourke	.10
59	John McGraw	.10
60	Candy Cummings	.10
61	Jimmie Foxx	.10
62	Walter Johnson	.25
63	1903 World Series	.10
64	Satchel Paige	.40
65	Bobby Wallace	.10
66	Cap Anson	.10
67	Hugh Duffy	.10
68	Buck Ewing	.10
69	Bobo Holloman	.10
70	Ed Delehanty (Delahanty)	.10
71	Dizzy Dean	.10
72	Tris Speaker	.10
73	Lou Gehrig	1.50
74	Wee Willie Keeler	.10
75	Cal Hubbard	.10
76	Eddie Collins	.10
77	Chris Von Der Ahe	.10
78	Sam Crawford	.10
79	Cy Young	.25
80	Johnny Vander Meer	.10
81	Joey Jay	.10
82	Zack Wheat	.10
83	Jim Bottomley	.10
84	Honus Wagner	.30
85	Casey Stengel	.10
86	Babe Ruth	1.50
87	John Lindemuth	.10
88	Max Carey	.10
89	Mordecai Brown	.10
90	1869 Red Stockings	.10
91	Rube Marquard	.10
92	Horse Radbourne	.10
93	Hack Wilson	.10
94	Lefty Grove	.10
95	Carl Hubbell	.10
96	A.J. Cartwright	.10
97	Rogers Hornsby	.10
98	Ernest Thayer	.10
99	Connie Mack	.10
100	1939 Centennial Celebration	.10
101	Branch Rickey	.10
102	Dan Brouthers	.10
103	First Baseball Uniform	.10
104	Christy Mathewson	.25
105	Joe Nuxhall	.10
106	1939 Centennial Celebration	.10
107	President Taft	.10
108	Abner Doubleday	.10

1987 Baseball's All-Time Greats

Baseball's All-Time Greats / Playing Years 1955-1977 / BROOKS ROBINSON

Though the producer is not identified anywhere on the cards, this collectors' issue was created primarily for insertion in beginner's baseball card kits. One series of 50 cards was produced about 1987, a second series some years later. All cards have bright green or orange borders with a "window" at center in which players are pictured in either color or black-and-white photos, or artwork. The player's major league career span is in a tan oval towards bottom. Horizontal backs have a red strip at top with personal data and also include a career summary. The unnumbered cards are checklisted here in alphabetical order. Variations in photos and the presence or absence of team logos have been observed on some cards. Gaps have been left in the checklist to accommodate additions; "g" for green or "o" for orange borders is shown in parentheses where verified.

		NM/M
	Common Player:	.10
(1)	Henry Aaron	1.00
(2)	Joe Adcock	.10
(3)	Richie Allen	.10
(4)	Grover C. Alexander	.10
(5)	Luis Aparicio	.10
(6)	Luke Appling	.10
(7)	Ernie Banks	.25
(8)	Hank Bauer	.10
(9)	Johnny Bench	.15
(10)	"Yogi" Berra	.15
(11)	Lou Boudreau	.10
(12)	Lou Brock	.10
(13)	"Three Finger" Brown	.10
(14)	Jim Bunning	.10
(15)	Roy Campanella	.25
(16)	Rod Carew	.10
(17)	Orlando Cepeda	.10
(18)	Roberto Clemente	1.00
(19a)	Ty Cobb (g)	1.00
(19b)	Ty Cobb (o)	1.00
(20)	Mickey Cochrane	.10
(21)	Rocky Colavito	.10
(22)	Eddie Collins	.10
(23)	Sam Crawford	.10
(24)	Joe Cronin	.10
(25)	Alvin Dark	.10
(26)	Dizzy Dean	.10
(27)	Bill Dickey	.10
(28)	Joe DiMaggio	1.00
(29)	Larry Doby	.10
(30)	Don Drysdale	.10
(31)	Leo Durocher	.10
(32)	Carl Erskine	.10
(33)	Bob Feller	.10
(34)	Curt Flood	.10
(35a)	Whitey Ford (g) (Chest, cap logos.)	.10

(36)	Jimmie Foxx	.10
(37a)	Frankie Frisch (g) (Jersey logo.)	.10
(38)	Carl Furillo	.10
(39a)	Lou Gehrig (g)	1.25
(39b)	Lou Gehrig (g)	1.25
(40)	Charlie Gehringer	.10
(41)	Bob Gibson (g)	.25
(42)	Hank Greenberg	.10
(43)	"Lefty" Grove	.10
(44)	"Gabby" Hartnett	.10
(45)	Gil Hodges	.10
(46)	Rogers Hornsby	.10
(47)	Carl Hubbell	.10
(48)	Jim Hunter	.10
(49)	Monte Irvin	.10
(50)	Ferguson Jenkins	.10
(51)	Walter Johnson	.10
(52)	Jim Kaat	.10
(53)	George Kell	.10
(54)	Ralph Kiner	.10
(55)	Ted Kluszewski	.10
(56)	Don Larsen	.10
(57)	Bob Lemon	.10
(58)	Ernie Lombardi	.10
(59)	Eddie Lopat	.10
(62a)	Mickey Mantle (o) (Chest-up portrait.)	2.00
(63)	Juan Marichal	.10
(64)	Roger Maris	.50
(65)	Billy Martin	.10
(66)	Eddie Mathews	.10
(67)	Christy Mathewson	.25
(68)	Willie Mays	1.00
(69)	Bill Mazeroski	.10
(70)	Joe Morgan	.10
(71)	Thurman Munson	.10
(72)	Stan Musial	.50
(73)	Tony Oliva	.10
(74)	Mel Ott	.10
(75)	Jim Palmer	.10
(76)	Gaylord Perry	.10
(77)	Boog Powell	.10
(78)	Pee Wee Reese	.10
(79)	Robin Roberts	.10
(80a)	Brooks Robinson (g)(Baltimore jersey.)	.25
(81)	Frank Robinson (g)	.25
(82a)	Jackie Robinson (g)	1.00
(82b)	Jackie Robinson (o)	1.00
(83a)	Babe Ruth (g)	1.50
(83b)	Babe Ruth (o)	1.50
(84)	Tom Seaver	.10
(85)	Bobby Shantz	.10
(86)	Al Simmons	.10
(87)	George Sisler	.10
(88)	Enos Slaughter	.10
(89)	Duke Snider	.10
(92)	Warren Spahn (g)	.25
(92)	Tris Speaker	.10
(93)	Willie Stargell	.10
(94)	Bill Terry	.10
(95)	Bobby Thomson	.10
(96)	Pie Traynor	.10
(97)	Honus Wagner	.25
(98)	Ed Walsh	.10
(99)	Paul Waner	.10
(100)	Hoyt Wilhelm	.10
(101)	Billy Williams	.10
(102)	Ted Williams	1.00
(103)	Maury Wills	.10
(104)	Early Wynn	.10
(105)	Carl Yastrzemski	.25
(106)	Cy Young (o)	.25
(107)	Ross Youngs	.10

1988 Bazooka

This 22-card set from Topps marks the first Bazooka issue since 1971. Full-color player photos are bordered in white, with the player name printed on a red, white and blue bubble gum box in the lower right corner. Flip sides are also red, white and blue, printed vertically. A large, but faint, Bazooka logo backs the Topps baseball logo team name, card number, player's name and position, followed by batting records, personal information and brief career highlights. Cards were sold inside specially marked 59¢ and 79¢ Bazooka gum and candy boxes, one card per box.

		NM/M
Complete Set (22):		3.00
Common Player:		.10
1	George Bell	.10
2	Wade Boggs	.50
3	Jose Canseco	.25
4	Roger Clemens	.60
5	Vince Coleman	.10
6	Eric Davis	.10
7	Tony Fernandez	.10
8	Dwight Gooden	.10
9	Tony Gwynn	.50
10	Wally Joyner	.10
11	Don Mattingly	.60
12	Willie McGee	.10
13	Mark McGwire	.75
14	Kirby Puckett	.10
15	Tim Raines	.10
16	Dave Righetti	.10
17	Cal Ripken, Jr.	1.00
18	Juan Samuel	.10
19	Ryne Sandberg	.50
20	Benny Santiago	.10
21	Darryl Strawberry	.10
22	Todd Worrell	.10

1989 Bazooka

GREGG JEFFERIES

Topps produced this 22-card set in 1989 to be included (one card per box) in specially-marked boxes of its Bazooka brand bubblegum. The player photos have the words "Shining Star" along the top, while the player's name appears along the bottom of the card, along with the Topps Bazooka logo in the lower right corner. The cards are numbered alphabetically.

		NM/M
Complete Set (22):		3.00
Common Player:		.10
1	Tim Belcher	.10
2	Damon Berryhill	.10
3	Wade Boggs	.75
4	Jay Buhner	.10
5	Jose Canseco	.25
6	Vince Coleman	.10
7	Cecil Espy	.10
8	Dave Gallagher	.10
9	Ron Gant	.10
10	Kirk Gibson	.10
11	Paul Gibson	.10
12	Mark Grace	.10
13	Tony Gwynn	.75
14	Rickey Henderson	.50
15	Orel Hershiser	.10
16	Gregg Jefferies	.10
17	Ricky Jordan	.10
18	Chris Sabo	.10
19	Gary Sheffield	.40
20	Darryl Strawberry	.10
21	Frank Viola	.10
22	Walt Weiss	.10

1990 Bazooka

RICKEY HENDERSON

For the second consecutive year, Bazooka entitled its set "Shining Stars." Full-color action and posed player shots are featured on the card fronts. The flip sides feature player statistics in a style much like the cards from the previous two Bazooka issues. Unlike the past two releases, the cards are not num-

		NM/M
Complete Set (22):		3.00
Common Player:		.10
1	Kevin Mitchell	.10
2	Robin Yount	.40
3	Mark Davis	.10
4	Bret Saberhagen	.10
5	Fred McGriff	.10
6	Tony Gwynn	.50
7	Kirby Puckett	.50
8	Vince Coleman	.10
9	Rickey Henderson	.40
10	Ben McDonald	.10
11	Gregg Olson	.10
12	Todd Zeile	.10
13	Carlos Martinez	.10
14	Gregg Jefferies	.10
15	Craig Worthington	.10
16	Gary Sheffield	.25
17	Greg Briley	.10
18	Ken Griffey Jr.	1.50
19	Jerome Walton	.10
20	Bob Geren	.10
21	Tom Gordon	.10
22	Jim Abbott	.10

1991 Bazooka

GEORGE BRETT

For the third consecutive year Bazooka entitled its set "Shining Stars." The cards are styled like the 1990 issue, but include the Topps "40th Anniversary" logo. The 1991 issue is considered much scarcer than the previous releases. The cards measure 2-1/2" x 3-1/2" in size and 22 cards complete the set.

		NM/M
Complete Set (22):		5.00
Common Player:		.10
1	Barry Bonds	3.50
2	Rickey Henderson	.50
3	Bob Welch	.10
4	Doug Drabek	.10
5	Alex Fernandez	.10
6	Jose Offerman	.10
7	Frank Thomas	.10
8	Cecil Fielder	.10
9	Ryne Sandberg	.75
10	George Brett	1.00
11	Willie McGee	.10
12	Vince Coleman	.10
13	Hal Morris	.10
14	Delino DeShields	.10
15	Robin Ventura	.10
16	Jeff Russon	.10
17	Felix Jose	.10
18	Dave Justice	.10
19	Larry Walker	.10
20	Sandy Alomar, Jr.	.10
21	Kevin Appier	.10
22	Scott Radinsky	.10

1992 Bazooka

BILL BRUTON / WHITEY FORD / ED LOPAT / RICKEY HENDERSON

This set of 22 cards features miniature versions of the 1953 Topps Archives issue. The mini-cards are set against a blue background on front and back. Besides reproductions of issued 1953 Topps cards, these "Quadracards" include miniature versions of many of the

special cards created for the Archives set. Cards feature the Bazooka logo on back, and were distributed in boxes of that bubble gum.

		NM/M
Complete Set (22):		3.00
Common Player:		.10
1	Kevin Mitchell	.10
2	Robin Yount	.40
3	Mark Davis	.10
4	Bret Saberhagen	.10
5	Fred McGriff	.10
6	Tony Gwynn	.50
7	Kirby Puckett	.50
8	Vince Coleman	.10
9	Rickey Henderson	.40
10	Ben McDonald	.10
11	Gregg Olson	.10
12	Todd Zeile	.10
13	Carlos Martinez	.10
14	Gregg Jefferies	.10
15	Craig Worthington	.10
16	Gary Sheffield	.25
17	Greg Briley	.10
18	Ken Griffey Jr.	1.50
19	Jerome Walton	.10
20	Bob Geren	.10
21	Tom Gordon	.10
22	Jim Abbott	.10

		NM/M
Complete Tin-Box Set (22):		16.00
Complete Set (22):		8.00
Common Player:		.25
1	Joe Adcock, Bob Lemon, Willie Mays, Vic Wertz	1.50
2	Carl Furillo, Don Newcombe, Phil Rizzuto, Hank Sauer	.25
3	Ferris Fain, John Logan, Ed Mathews, Bobby Shantz	.25
4	Yogi Berra, Del Crandall, Howie Pollett, Gene Woodling	.25
5	Richie Ashburn, Leo Durocher, Allie Reynolds, Early Wynn	.25
6	Hank Aaron, Ray Boone, Luke Easter, Dick Williams	1.50
7	Ralph Branca, Bob Feller, Rogers Hornsby, Bobby Thomson	.25
8	Jim Gilliam, Billy Martin, Orestes Minoso, Hal Newhouser	.25
9	Smoky Burgess, John Mize, Preacher Roe, Warren Spahn	.25
10	Monte Irvin, Bobo Newsom, Duke Snider, Wes Westrum	.25
11	Carl Erskine, Jackie Jensen, George Kell, Al Schoendienst	.25
12	Bill Bruton, Whitey Ford, Ed Lopat, Mickey Vernon	.25
13	Joe Black, Lew Burdette, Johnny Pesky, Enos Slaughter	.25
14	Gus Bell, Mike Garcia, Mel Parnell, Jackie Robinson	1.25
15	Alvin Dark, Dick Groat, Pee Wee Reese, John Sain	.25
16	Gil Hodges, Sal Maglie, Wilmer Mizell, Billy Pierce	.45
17	Nellie Fox, Ralph Kiner, Ted Kluszewski, Eddie Stanky	.25
18	Ewell Blackwell, Vern Law, Satchell Paige, Jim Wilson	.45
19	Lou Boudreau, Roy Face, Harvey Haddix, Bill Rigney	.25
20	Roy Campanella, Walt Dropo, Harvey Kuenn, Al Rosen	.45
21	Joe Garagiola, Robin Roberts, Casey Stengel, Hoyt Wilhelm	.45
22	John Antonelli, Bob Friend, Dixie Walker, Ted Williams	1.00

1993 Bazooka Team USA

TODD HELTON / TEAM USA

The members of Team USA are featured on this boxed set. The 2-1/2" x 3-1/2" cards feature the same basic design as 1993 Topps baseball, except for a Bazooka gum logo in one of the upper corners. Both front and back feature posed player photos. Backs have a design simulating the U.S. flag and include amateur stats, biographical details and career highlights. The cards are virtually identical to the same players' cards in the 1993 Topps Traded set, with the addition of the Bazooka logo on front and the differences in card numbers. A special tin-boxed edition with 50 pieces of gum was produced in an edition reported as 750.

		NM/M
Complete Set (22):		100.00
Complete Tin Set (22):		150.00
Common Player:		.50
1	Terry Harvey	.50
2	Dante Powell	.50
3	Andy Barkett	.50
4	Steve Reich	.50
5	Charlie Nelson	.50
6	Todd Walker	1.00
7	Dustin Hermanson	1.00
8	Pat Clougherty	.50
9	Danny Graves	.50
10	Paul Wilson	.75
11	Todd Helton	90.00
12	Russ Johnson	.50
13	Darren Grass	.50
14	A.J. Hinch	.50
15	Mark Merila	.50
16	John Powell	.50
17	Bob Scafa	.50
18	Matt Beaumont	.50
19	Todd Dunn	.50
20	Mike Martin	.50
21	Carlton Loewer	.50
22	Bret Wagner	.50

1995 Bazooka

CALIFORNIA ANGELS

Topps returned to the beginner's level baseball card niche in 1995 by resurrecting its Bazooka brand name. The set was unabashedly aimed at the younger collector, offering five cards and a Bazooka Joe cartoon-wrapped chunk of bubblegum for 50 cents. Cards feature on their backs a "roulette" wheel design based on the player's 1994 stats, to be used to play a game of spinner baseball. A game instruction card and cardboard spinner was included in each pack. Limiting the set to 132 cards allowed for a concentration of established stars and hot youngsters. A 22-card Red Hot insert set is found at the rate of one card per six packs, on average. Factory sets offering the 132 base cards, five Red Hot inserts and 10 pieces of bubblegum were produced.

		NM/M
Complete Set (132):		3.00
Factory Set (132+5):		5.00
Common Player:		.05
Pack (5):		.30
Wax Box (36):		7.00
1	Greg Maddux	.50
2	Cal Ripken Jr.	1.00
3	Lee Smith	.05
4	Sammy Sosa	.50
5	Jason Bere	.05
6	Dave Justice	.05
7	Kevin Mitchell	.05
8	Ozzie Guillen	.05
9	Roger Clemens	.60
10	Mike Mussina	.30
11	Sandy Alomar	.05
12	Cecil Fielder	.05
13	Dennis Martinez	.05
14	Randy Myers	.05
15	Jay Buhner	.05
16	Ivan Rodriguez	.35
17	Mo Vaughn	.05
18	Ryan Klesko	.05
19	Chuck Finley	.05
20	Barry Bonds	1.00
21	Dennis Eckersley	.35
22	Kenny Lofton	.35
23	Rafael Palmeiro	.35
24	Mike Stanley	.05
25	Gregg Jefferies	.05
26	Robin Ventura	.05
27	Mark McGwire	.75
28	Ozzie Smith	.50
29	Troy Neel	.05
30	Tony Gwynn	.50
31	Ken Griffey Jr.	.65
32	Will Clark	.05
33	Craig Biggio	.05
34	Shawon Dunston	.05
35	Wilson Alvarez	.05
36	Bobby Bonilla	.05
37	Marquis Grissom	.05
38	Ben McDonald	.05
39	Delino DeShields	.05
40	Barry Larkin	.05
41	John Olerud	.05
42	Jose Canseco	.30
43	Greg Vaughn	.05
44	Gary Sheffield	.20
45	Paul O'Neill	.05
46	Bob Hamelin	.05
47	Don Mattingly	.60
48	John Franco	.05
49	Bret Boone	.05
50	Rick Aguilera	.05
51	Tim Wallach	.05
52	Roberto Kelly	.05
53	Danny Tartabull	.05
54	Randy Johnson	.40
55	Greg McMichael	.05
56	Bip Roberts	.05
57	David Cone	.05
58	Raul Mondesi	.05
59	Travis Fryman	.05
60	Jeff Conine	.05
61	Jeff Bagwell	.40
62	Rickey Henderson	.40
63	Fred McGriff	.05
64	Matt Williams	.05
65	Rick Wilkins	.05
66	Eric Karros	.05
67	Mel Rojas	.05
68	Juan Gonzalez	.20
69	Chuck Carr	.05
70	Moises Alou	.05
71	Mark Grace	.05
72	Alex Fernandez	.05
73	Rod Beck	.05
74	Ray Lankford	.05
75	Dean Palmer	.05
76	Joe Carter	.05
77	Mike Piazza	.65
78	Eddie Murray	.40
79	Dave Nilsson	.05
80	Brett Butler	.05
81	Roberto Alomar	.10
82	Jeff Kent	.05
83	Andres Galarraga	.05
84	Brady Anderson	.05
85	Jimmy Key	.05
86	Bret Saberhagen	.05
87	Chili Davis	.05
88	Jose Rijo	.05
89	Wade Boggs	.50
90	Len Dykstra	.05
91	Steve Howe	.05
92	Hal Morris	.05
93	Larry Walker	.05
94	Jeff Montgomery	.05
95	Wil Cordero	.05
96	Jay Bell	.05
97	Tom Glavine	.15
98	Chris Hoiles	.05
99	Steve Avery	.05
100	Ruben Sierra	.05
101	Mickey Tettleton	.05
102	Paul Molitor	.40
103	Carlos Baerga	.05
104	Walt Weiss	.05
105	Darren Daulton	.05
106	Jack McDowell	.05
107	Doug Drabek	.05
108	Mark Langston	.05
109	Manny Ramirez	.40
110	Kevin Appier	.05
111	Andy Benes	.05
112	Chuck Knoblauch	.05
113	Kirby Puckett	.50
114	Dante Bichette	.05
115	Deion Sanders	.10
116	Albert Belle	.05
117	Todd Zeile	.05
118	Devon White	.05
119	Tim Salmon	.05
120	Frank Thomas	.40
121	John Wetteland	.05
122	James Mouton	.05
123	Javy Lopez	.05
124	Carlos Delgado	.25
125	Cliff Floyd	.05
126	Alex Gonzalez	.05
127	Billy Ashley	.05
128	Rondell White	.05
129	Rico Brogna	.05
130	Melvin Nieves	.05
131	Jose Oliva	.05
132	J.R. Phillips	.05

Red Hot Inserts

TORONTO BLUE JAYS

Twenty-two of the game's biggest stars were chosen for inclusion in 1995 Baerga's only insert set - Red Hots. The chase cards are found at an average rate of one per six packs. Red Hots are identical to the players' cards in the regular set except that the background has been rendered in shades of red, and the player name printed in gold foil. Card numbers have an "RH" prefix.

		NM/M
Complete Set (22):		7.00
Common Player:		.15
1	Greg Maddux	1.00
2	Cal Ripken Jr.	2.00
3	Barry Bonds	2.00
4	Kenny Lofton	.15
5	Mike Piazza	1.50
6	Tony Gwynn	1.00
7	Ken Griffey Jr.	1.50
8	Barry Larkin	.15
9	Jose Canseco	.35
10	Paul O'Neill	.15
11	Randy Johnson	.75
12	David Cone	.15
13	Jeff Bagwell	.75
14	Matt Williams	.15
15	Mike Piazza	1.50
16	Roberto Alomar	.25
17	Jimmy Key	.15
18	Wade Boggs	1.00
19	Paul Molitor	.75
20	Carlos Baerga	.15
21	Albert Belle	.15
22	Frank Thomas	.75

1996 Bazooka

Topps' 1996 Bazooka set offers collectors interactive fun with its cards geared for a flipping game. Each front has an action photo of the player. The back contains one of five different Bazooka Joe characters, along with the Bazooka Ball game, the player's biographical data, and 1995 and career stats. Cards were available five per pack for 50 cents. The complete set was also offered in a factory set, packaged in an attractive gift box. As an exclusive bonus, one 1959 Bazooka Mickey Mantle reprint card is found in every factory set, along with 10 pieces of bubble gum.

		NM/M
Unopened Fact. Set (133):		9.00
Complete Set (132):		6.00
Common Player:		.05
Pack (5):		.40
Wax Box (36):		9.00
1	Ken Griffey Jr.	.75
2	J.T. Snow	.05
3	Rondell White	.05
4	Reggie Sanders	.05
5	Jeff Montgomery	.05
6	Mike Stanley	.05
7	Bernie Williams	.05
8	Mike Piazza	.75
9	Brian Hunter	.05
10	Len Dykstra	.05
11	Ray Lankford	.05
12	Kenny Lofton	.05
13	Robin Ventura	.05
14	Devon White	.05
15	Cal Ripken Jr.	1.50
16	Heathcliff Slocumb	.05
17	Ryan Klesko	.05
18	Terry Steinbach	.05
19	Travis Fryman	.05
20	Sammy Sosa	.50
21	Jim Thome	.35
22	Kenny Rogers	.05
23	Don Mattingly	.60
24	Kirby Puckett	.50
25	Matt Williams	.05
26	Larry Walker	.05
27	Tim Wakefield	.05
28	Greg Vaughn	.05
29	Denny Neagle	.05
30	Ken Caminiti	.05
31	Garret Anderson	.05
32	Brady Anderson	.05
33	Carlos Baerga	.05
34	Wade Boggs	.50
35	Roberto Alomar	.15
36	Eric Karros	.05
37	Jay Buhner	.05
38	Dante Bichette	.05
39	Darren Daulton	.05
40	Jeff Bagwell	.40
41	Jay Bell	.05
42	Dennis Eckersley	.35
43	Will Clark	.05
44	Tom Glavine	.20
45	Rick Aguilera	.05
46	Kevin Seitzer	.05
47	Bret Boone	.05
48	Mark Grace	.05
49	Ray Durham	.05
50	Rico Brogna	.05
51	Kevin Appier	.05
52	Moises Alou	.05
53	Jeff Conine	.05
54	Marty Cordova	.05
55	Jose Mesa	.05
56	Rod Beck	.05
57	Marquis Grissom	.05
58	David Cone	.05
59	Albert Belle	.05
60	Lee Smith	.05
61	Frank Thomas	.40
62	Roger Clemens	.60
63	Bobby Bonilla	.05
64	Paul Molitor	.40
65	Chuck Knoblauch	.05
66	Steve Finley	.05
67	Craig Biggio	.05
68	Ramon Martinez	.05
69	Jason Isringhausen	.05
70	Mark Wohlers	.05
71	Vinny Castilla	.05
72	Ron Gant	.05
73	Juan Gonzalez	.20
74	Mark McGwire	1.00
75	Jeff King	.05
76	Pedro Martinez	.40
77	Chad Curtis	.05
78	John Olerud	.05
79	Greg Maddux	.50
80	Derek Jeter	1.50
81	Mike Mussina	.25
82	Gregg Jefferies	.05
83	Jim Edmonds	.05
84	Carlos Perez	.05
85	Mo Vaughn	.05
86	Todd Hundley	.05
87	Roberto Hernandez	.05
88	Derek Bell	.05
89	Andres Galarraga	.05
90	Brian McRae	.05
91	Joe Carter	.05
92	Orlando Merced	.05
93	Cecil Fielder	.05
94	Dean Palmer	.05
95	Randy Johnson	.40
96	Chipper Jones	.50
97	Barry Larkin	.05
98	Hideo Nomo	.25
99	Gary Gaetti	.05
100	Edgar Martinez	.05
101	John Wetteland	.05
102	Rafael Palmeiro	.35
103	Chuck Finley	.05
104	Ivan Rodriguez	.35
105	Shawn Green	.10
106	Manny Ramirez	.40
107	Lance Johnson	.05
108	Jose Canseco	.20
109	Fred McGriff	.05
110	David Segui	.05
111	Tim Salmon	.05
112	Hal Morris	.05
113	Tino Martinez	.05
114	Bret Saberhagen	.05
115	Brian Jordan	.05
116	David Justice	.05
117	Jack McDowell	.05
118	Barry Bonds	1.50
119	Mark Langston	.05
120	John Valentin	.05
121	Raul Mondesi	.05
122	Quilvio Veras	.05
123	Randy Myers	.05
124	Tony Gwynn	.50
125	Johnny Damon	.20
126	Doug Drabek	.05
127	Bill Pulsipher	.05
128	Paul O'Neill	.05
129	Rickey Henderson	.40
130	Deion Sanders	.10
131	Orel Hershiser	.05
132	Gary Sheffield	.20

Mickey Mantle 1959 Reprint

Continuing its tribute to the late Mickey Mantle across all of its product lines, Topps produced a special reprint of the 1959 Bazooka Mantle card exclusively for inclusion in factory sets of its 1996 Bazooka cards. While the original '59 Mantle was printed in nearly 3" x 5" size on the bottom of gum boxes, the reprint is in the current 2-1/2" x 3-1/2" size.

Mickey Mantle 7.50

1992 Ben's Bakery Super Hitters Discs

Ben's Bakery, a small, eastern Canadian bakery, inserted promotional discs in its hot dog and hamburger buns in 1992. As in the case of 1991, which was the company's first year in the promotion, the 1992 set contained 20 different players, including many of the top stars in the country. Twenty of the game's top hitters, with a special emphasis on Blue Jays players, are featured in this regional issue by a small Eastern Canada bakery. The 2-3/4" diameter discs were packaged in the company's hot dog and hamburger buns. Fronts feature a color photo on which team logos have been airbrushed away. The bakery logo is flanked by a red "Super Hitters" in the white border at top. The player's name appears in white in an orange banner beneath the photo, with his team and position in blue at bottom. Backs are printed in black and include a few biographical details and 1991 stats, along with a card number and appropriate logos and copyright notices.

		NM/M
Complete Set (20):		15.00
Common Player:		.75
1	Cecil Fielder	.75
2	Joe Carter	.75
3	Roberto Alomar	1.00
4	Devon White	.75
5	Kelly Gruber	.75
6	Cal Ripken, Jr.	3.50
7	Kirby Puckett	2.00
8	Paul Molitor	1.50
9	Julio Franco	.75
10	Ken Griffey Jr.	3.00
11	Frank Thomas	1.50
12	Jose Canseco	1.25
13	Danny Tartabull	.75
14	Terry Pendleton	.75
15	Tony Gwynn	2.00
16	Howard Johnson	.75
17	Will Clark	.75
18	Barry Bonds	3.50
19	Ryne Sandberg	2.00
20	Bobby Bonilla	.75

1993 Ben's Bakery Super Pitchers Discs

An emphasis on Toronto's pitchers is noted in the checklist for this regional bakery issue. The 2-3/4" diameter discs were packed with hot dog and hamburger buns and follow a 1991 issue by the company featuring super hitters. A color player portrait at center has had the uniform logos airbrushed away. "Super Pitchers" in red flanks the bakery logo in the white border above the photo. The player's name appears in white in an orange banner beneath the photo, with his team and position in blue at bottom. Backs are printed in black and include minimal biographical data, a card number, 1992 stats and copyright information.

		NM/M
Complete Set (20):		10.00
Common Player:		.45
1	Dennis Eckersley	1.50
2	Chris Bosio	.45
3	Jack Morris	.45
4	Greg Maddux	2.50
5	Dennis Martinez	.45
6	Tom Glavine	.75
7	Doug Drabek	.45
8	John Smoltz	.45
9	Randy Myers	.45
10	Jack McDowell	.45
11	John Wetteland	.45
12	Roger Clemens	3.00
13	Mike Mussina	.75
14	Juan Guzman	.45
15	Jose Rijo	.45
16	Tom Henke	.45
17	Gregg Olson	.45
18	Jim Abbott	.45
19	Jimmy Key	.45
20	Rheal Cormier	.45

1987 David Berg Hot Dogs Cubs

Changing sponsors from Gatorade to David Berg Pure Beef Hot Dogs, the Chicago Cubs handed out a 26-card set of baseball cards to fans attending the July 29th game at Wrigley Field. The cards are printed in full-color on white stock and measure 2-7/8" x 4-1/4" in size. The set is numbered by the players' uniform numbers. The card backs contain player personal and statistical information, plus a full-color picture of a David Berg hot dog in a bun with all the garnishments. The set marked the sixth consecutive year the Cubs held a baseball card giveaway promotion.

		NM/M
Complete Set (26):		10.00
Common Player:		.40
1	Dave Martinez	.40
4	Gene Michael	.40
6	Keith Moreland	.40
7	Jody Davis	.40
8	Andre Dawson	1.00
10	Leon Durham	.40
11	Jim Sundberg	.40
12	Shawon Dunston	.40
19	Manny Trillo	.40
20	Bob Dernier	.40
21	Scott Sanderson	.40
22	Jerry Mumphrey	.40
23	Ryne Sandberg	5.00
24	Brian Dayett	.40
29	Chico Walker	.40
31	Greg Maddux	5.00
33	Frank DiPino	.40
34	Steve Trout	.40
36	Gary Matthews	.40
37	Ed Lynch	.40
39	Ron Davis	.40
40	Rick Sutcliffe	.40
46	Lee Smith	.40
47	Dickie Noles	.40
49	Jamie Moyer	.40
---	The Coaching Staff (Johnny Oates, Jim Snyder, Herm Starrette, John Vukovich, Billy Williams)	.40

1988 David Berg Hot Dogs Cubs

(17) MARK GRACE, IF

This oversized (2-7/8" x 4-1/2") set of 26 cards was distributed to fans at Wrigley Field on August 24th. The set includes cards for the manager and coaching staff, as well as players. Full-color action photos are framed in red and blue on a white background. The backs feature small black and white player close-ups, colorful team logos, statistics and sponsor logos (David Berg Hot Dogs and Venture Store Restaurants). The numbers in the following checklist refer to players' uniforms.

		NM/M
Complete Set (27):		17.50
Common Player:		.40
2	Vance Law	.40
4	Don Zimmer	.40
7	Jody Davis	.40
9	Andre Dawson	1.00
9	Damon Berryhill	.40
12	Shawon Dunston	.40
17	Mark Grace	1.00
18	Angel Salazar	.40
19	Manny Trillo	.40
21	Scott Sanderson	.40
22	Jerry Mumphrey	.40
23	Ryne Sandberg	4.00
24	Gary Varsho	.40
25	Rafael Palmeiro	2.50
28	Mitch Webster	.40
30	Darrin Jackson	.40
31	Greg Maddux	4.00
32	Calvin Schiraldi	.40
33	Frank DiPino	.40
37	Pat Perry	.40
40	Rick Sutcliffe	.40
41	Jeff Pico	.40
45	Al Nipper	.40
49	Jamie Moyer	.40
50	Les Lancaster	.40
54	Rich Gossage	.40
---	The Coaching Staff (Joe Altobelli, Chuck Cottier, Larry Cox, Jose Martinez, Dick Pole)	.40

1994 Big Apple 1969 Mets Discs

Big Apple Collector, Inc. released the "1969 World Champion Miracle Mets Commemorative Cap Sheet," which has likenesses of each of the 31 members of the squad captured in oil paintings by sports artist Ron Lewis. The player's likeness is centered in a 1-5/8" diameter round commemorative cap which is die cut but remains in place on the sheet. Each cap is gold foil accented, and each 11" x 14" sheet is produced in full color on 48-point card stock. The sheet has a suggested retail price of $39.95.

		NM/M
Complete Set (31):		12.00
Common Player:		.40
(1)	Gil Hodges	1.50
(2)	Rube Walker	.25
(3)	Yogi Berra	1.50
(4)	Joe Pignatano	.25
(5)	Ed Yost	.25
(6)	Tommie Agee	.25
(7)	Ken Boswell	.25
(8)	Don Cardwell	.25
(9)	Ed Charles	.25
(10)	Don Clendenon	.25
(11)	Jack DiLauro	.25
(12)	Duffy Dyer	.25
(13)	Wayne Garrett	.25
(14)	Rod Gaspar	.25
(15)	Gary Gentry	.25
(16)	Jerry Grote	.25
(17)	Bud Harrelson	.30
(18)	Cleon Jones	.25
(19)	Cal Koonce	.25
(20)	Jerry Koosman	.30
(21)	Ed Kranepool	.25
(22)	J.C. Martin	.25
(23)	Jim McAndrew	.25
(24)	Tug McGraw	.40
(25)	Bob Pfeil	.25
(26)	Nolan Ryan	4.00
(27)	Tom Seaver	2.00
(28)	Art Shamsky	.25
(29)	Ron Swoboda	.25
(30)	Ron Taylor	.25
(31)	Al Weis	.25

2001 The Big Book of Jewish Baseball

To promote its book on Jewish ballplayers, S.P.I. Books of Ft. Lee, N.J., issued a nine-card sheet. The sheet measures 8-1/2" x 12". At top on a purple background are nine cards which, if cut out on the yellow dotted lines, would each measure 2-11/16" x 3-3/8". Card #1 pictures the book's cover with its picture of Sandy Koufax. The other cards have color photos or colorized photos of some of the players featured in the book. Black-and-white backs have minimal player data and stats. At the bottom of the sheet is a coupon for ordering the book.

		NM/M
Sheet:		6.00
Complete Set (9):		6.00
Common Player:		.50
(1)	Book Cover (Sandy Koufax)	2.00
2	Lipman Pike	1.00
3	Moe Berg	1.00
4	Jesse Levis	.50
5	Harry Shuman	.50
6	Hank Greenberg	1.00
7	Harry Danning	.50
8	Cy Malis	.50
9	Hy Cohen	.50

1980s Big League Cards

Former major league pitcher and author Jim Bouton was a principal in the most successful of many "vanity" card manufacturers which sprang up in the 1980s and 1990s. For a price, anybody could send a picture to the New Jersey company and have it placed on a run of baseball cards. Persons could, and did, also send photos of ballplayers to create fantasy cards and at least several ballplayers who never appeared on cards contemporary with their careers had cards made up for themselves retroactively. Fronts have black, blue and red graphics. Backs are printed in blue on white with personal data, stats and other information provided by person ordering the cards. Unlike most other contemporary vanity cards, the Big League Cards are printed on thick quality similar to vintage baseball cards. There is no way to document the individual issue of these cards.

1986 Big League Chew

The 1986 Big League Chew set consists of 12 cards featuring the players who have hit 500 or more career home runs. The cards, which measure 2-1/2" x 3-1/2", were inserted in specially marked packages of Big League Chew, the shredded bubble gum developed by former major leaguer Jim Bouton. The set is entitled "Home Run Legends" and was available through a write-in offer on the package. Recent-day players in the set are shown in color photos, while the older sluggers are pictured in black and white.

		NM/M
Complete Set (12):		10.00
Common Player:		1.00
1	Hank Aaron	2.00
2	Babe Ruth	3.00
3	Willie Mays	2.00
4	Frank Robinson	1.00
5	Harmon Killebrew	1.00
6	Mickey Mantle	4.00
7	Jimmie Foxx	1.00
8	Ted Williams	2.00
9	Ernie Banks	1.00
10	Eddie Mathews	1.00
11	Mel Ott	1.00
12	500-HR Group Card	.50

1997 Big League Chew Alumni

Autographed cards of three Hall of Famers were available through a mail-in offer by Big League Chew shredded bubble gum. Cards could be obtained by sending in proofs of purchase from pouches with the players' photos on them. Each card comes with a certificate of authenticity from Major League Baseball Players Alumni, which licensed the issue. Because the cards are not licensed by Major League Baseball, uniform logos have been removed from the color photos. Cards have a green, orange and white color scheme on front and back and are standard 2-1/2" x 3-1/2". Backs include career highlights and lifetime stats.

		NM/M
Complete Set (3):		20.00
Common Player:		7.50
1	Juan Marichal	7.50
2	Brooks Robinson	7.50
3	Billy Williams	7.50

1982 Big League Collectibles Diamond Classics, Series 1

Attempting to recapture the flavor of vintage baseball cards, this collectors set presents former stars in a 2-1/2" x 3-3/4" format on thick white cardboard stock. Fronts have a painted player portrait in color with no other graphic elements. Backs are in black and blue and include in-depth biographical sketches and career stats. The edition was limited to 10,000 sets.

		NM/M
Complete Set (56):		30.00
Common Player:		.60
1	Joe DiMaggio	5.00
2	Enos Slaughter	.60
3	Smokey Joe Wood (Smoky)	.60
4	Roy Campanella	1.25
5	Charlie Gehringer	.60
6	Carl Hubbell	.60
7	Rogers Hornsby	.60
8	Arky Vaughan	.60
9	Al Simmons	.60
10	Wally Berger	.60
11	Sam Rice	.60
12	Dizzy Dean	.60
13	Babe Ruth	5.00
14	Frankie Frisch	.60
15	George Kell	.60
16	Pee Wee Reese	.60
17	Earl Averill	.60
18	Willie Mays	2.50
19	Frank Baker	.60
20	Hack Wilson	.60
21	Ted Williams	3.00
22	Chuck Klein	.60
23	Bill Dickey	.60
24	Johnny Mize	.60
25	Luke Appling	.60
26	Duke Snider	.60
27	Wahoo Sam Crawford	.60
28	Waite Hoyt	.60
29	Eddie Collins	.60
30	Warren Spahn	.60
31	Satchel Paige	1.25
32	Ernie Lombardi	.60
33	Dom DiMaggio	.60
34	Joe Garagiola	.60
35	Lou Gehrig	2.50
36	Burleigh Grimes	.60
37	Walter Johnson	.60
38	Bill Terry	.60
39	Ty Cobb	2.50
40	Pie Traynor	.60
41	Ted Lyons	.60
42	Richie Ashburn	.60
43	Lefty Grove	.60
44	Edd Roush	.60
45	Phil Rizzuto	.60
46	Stan Musial	2.00
47	Bob Feller	.60
48	Jackie Robinson	2.50
49	Hank Greenberg	1.25
50	Mel Ott	.60
51	Joe Cronin	.60
52	Lefty O'Doul	.60
53	Indian Bob Johnson	.60
54	Kiki Cuyler	.60
55	Mickey Mantle	7.50
---	Checklist	.10

1983 Big League Collectibles Diamond Classics, Series 2

A second series of cards featuring past greats was issued by Big League Collectibles in 1983. Again at 55 cards, the set featured painted portraits of the players on front, devoid of any other graphics. Backs are in red and black and include a lengthy career summary along with innovative stats and a few biographical bits. The 2-1/2" x 3-3/4" cards are printed on a heavy white cardboard stock. The series was produced in an edition of 10,000 sets.

		NM/M
Complete Set (56):		20.00
Common Player:		.60
56	Ernie Banks	1.50
57	Stan Coveleski	.60
58	Vince DiMaggio	.60
59	Sunny Jim Bottomley	.60
60	Sandy Koufax	4.00
61	Doc Cramer	.60
62	Ted Kluszewski	.60
63	Zeke Bonura	.60
64	Spud Davis	.60
65	Jackie Jensen	.60
66	Honus Wagner	.75
67	Brooks Robinson	1.25
68	Dazzy Vance	.60
69	George Uhle	.60
70	Juan Marichal	.60
71	Bobo Newsom	.60
72	Billy Herman	.60
73	Al Rosen	.60
74	Roberto Clemente	4.00
75	George Case	.60
76	Bill Nicholson	.60
77	Tommy Bridges	.60
78	Rabbit Maranville	.60
79	Bob Lemon	.60
80	Heinie Groh	.60
81	Tris Speaker	.60
82	Hank Aaron	4.00
83	Whitey Ford	1.25
84a	Guy Bush (Ernie Banks back.)	.60
84b	Guy Bush (Correct back.)	.60
85	Jimmie Foxx	.60
86	Marty Marion	.60
87a	Hal Newhouser (Charlie Grimm back.)	.60
87b	Hal Newhouser (Correct back.)	.60
88	George Kelley (Kelly)	.60
89	Harmon Killebrew	.60
90	Willie McCovey	.60
91	Mel Harder	.60
92	Vada Pinson	.60
93	Luis Aparicio	.60
94	Grover Alexander	.60
95	Joe Kuhel	.60
96	Casey Stengel	.60
97	Joe Sewell	.60
98	Red Lucas	.60
99	Luke Sewell	.60
100	Charlie Grimm	.60
101	Cecil Travis	.60
102	Travis Jackson	.60
103	Lou Boudreau	.60
104	Nap Rucker	.60
105	Chief Bender	.60
106	Riggs Stephenson	.60
107	Red Ruffing	.60
108	Robin Roberts	.60
109	Harland Clift (Harland)	.60
110	Ralph Kiner	.60
---	Checklist	.10

1983 Big League Collectibles Original All-Stars

Players in the first modern All-Star Game, staged in conjunction with the Chicago World's Fair in 1933, are featured in this collectors issue. The 2-1/2" x 3-3/4" cards feature pastel paintings of the players on front. A circled baseball at lower-left has player and set identification. Backs are printed in blue and black and include All-Star Game and overall 1933 season performance.

		NM/M
Complete Set (38):		20.00
Common Player:		.50
2	Connie Mack	.50
3	Alvin Crowder	.50
4	Lefty Gomez	.50
5	Jimmy Dykes	.50
6	Earl Averill	.50
7	Charlie Gehringer	.50
8	Lefty Grove	.50
9	Lou Gehrig	2.00
10	Al Simmons	.50
11	Ben Chapman	.50
12	Jimmie Foxx	.75
13	Oral Hildebrand	.50
14	Joe Cronin	.50
15	Bill Dickey	.50
16	Sam West	.50
17	Rick Ferrell	.50
18	Tony Lazzeri	.50
19	Wes Ferrell	.50
20	Babe Ruth	2.50
21	John McGraw	.50
22	Pepper Martin	.50
23	Woody English	.50
24	Paul Waner	.50
25	Lefty O'Doul	.50
26	Chuck Klein	.50
27	Tony Cuccinello	.50
28	Frankie Frisch	.50
29	Gabby Hartnett	.50
30	Carl Hubbell	.50
31	Chick Hafey	.50
32	Dick Bartell	.50
33	Bill Hallahan	.50
34	Hal Schumacher	.50
35	Lon Warneke	.50
36	Wally Berger	.50
37	Bill Terry	.50
38	Jimmy Wilson	.50
39	Pie Traynor	.50

1985 Big League Collectibles National Pastime 1930-1939

SYLVESTER W. JOHNSON Phi-N P

Major league baseball in the 1930s is chronicled in this boxed collectors set. In 2-1/8" x 3-1/8" format (the same size as the 1951-52 Bowmans), the cards feature painted player portraits on front with identification in the white border at bottom. Backs are in black and red on thick white cardboard stock and feature in-depth career summaries and unique stats. The edition was limited to 5,000 sets, with a serially numbered header card.

		NM/M
Complete Set (90):		45.00
Common Player:		.60
1	Header card	.10
2	William H. Walters	.60
3	Montgomery M. Pearson	.60
4	Stanley C. Hack	.60
5	Joseph E. Cronin	.60
6	Leo E. Durocher	.60
7	Max F. Bishop	.60
8	Frank O'Donnell Hurst	.60
9	W. Barney McCosky	.60
10	Remy P. Kremer	.60
11	Julius J. Solters	.60
12	Daniel K. MacFayden	.60
13	Gordon S. Cochrane	.60
14	Ethan N. Allen	.60
15	Luzerne A. Blue	.60
16	John R. Mize	.60
17	Joseph P. DiMaggio	3.50
18	George F. Grantham	.60
19	William E. Kamm	.60
20	Charles A. Root	.60
21	Morris Berg	2.00
22	Floyd C. Herman	.60
23	Henry E. Manush	.60
24	Adolf L. Camilli	.60
25	Rudolph P. York	.60
26	Truett B. Sewell	.60
27	Richard B. Ferrell	.60
28	Arthur C. Whitney	.60
29	Edmund J. Miller	.60
30	August R. Mancuso	.60
31	John B. Conlan	.60
32	Joseph M. Medwick	.60
33	John T. Allen	.60
34	John S. Vander Meer	.60
35	H. Earl Averill	.60
36	Taylor L. Douthit	.60
37	Charles S. Myer	.60
38	Van Lingle Mungo	.60
39	Smead P. Jolley	.60
40	C. Flint Rhem	.60
41	Leon A. Goslin	.60
42	Adam A. Comorosky	.60
43	Jack I. Burns	.60
44	Edward A. Brandt	.60
45	Robert L. Johnson	.60
46	Melvin T. Ott	.60
47	Monty F.P. Stratton	.60
48	Paul D. Dean	.60
49	H. Louis Gehrig	3.50
51	Frank A. McCormick	.60
52	J. Geoffrey Heath	.60
53	Charles L. Hartnett	.60
54	Oswald L. Bluege	.60
54	George H. Ruth	6.00
56	Robert P. Doerr	.60
56	Virgil L. Davis	.60
57	D. Dale Alexander	.60
58	James A. Tobin	.60
59	Joseph F. Vosmik	.60
60	Alfonso R. Lopez	.60
61	James E. Foxx	.60
62	Frederick L. Fitzsimmons	.60
63	Robert R. Fothergill	.60
64	Morton C. Cooper	.60
65	George A. Selkirk	.60
66	Burton E. Shotton	.60
67	Robert W.A. Feller	.60
68	Lawrence H. French	.60
69	Joseph I. Judge	.60
70	Clyde L. Sukeforth	.60
71	James R. Tabor	.60
72	Silas K. Johnson	.60
73	W. Earl Webb	.60
74	Charles F. Lucas	.60
75	Ralph Kress	.60
76	Charles D. Stengel	.60
77	George W. Haas	.60
78	Joe G. Moore	.60
79	Carl N. Reynolds	.60
80	James O. Carleton	.60
81	John J. Murphy	.60
82	Paul Derringer	.60
83	Harold A. Trosky, Sr.	.60
84	Fred C. Lindstrom	.60
85	Jack E. Russell	.60
86	Stanley G. Bordagaray	.60
87	Roy C. Johnson	.60
88	Sylvester W. Johnson	.60
89	Michael F. Higgins	.60
90	J. Floyd Vaughan	.60

1989 Bimbo Cookies Super Stars Discs

ROBERTO ALOMAR

A dozen Hispanic players are featured in this set of 2-3/4" diameter discs distributed in Puerto Rico in boxes of cookies. Color portrait photos at center have cap logos removed because the discs are licensed only by the players' union, not MLB; typical for issues from Michael Schechter Associates. The Bimbo bear logo is at top-center, with the player name in a yellow strip at bottom; team and position are in blue in the white border beneath that. Yellow stars, blue baseballs and red words "SUPER STARS" flank the player photo. Backs are printed in blue and have a few biographical details, 1988 and career stats, card number and appropriate logos.

		NM/M
Complete Set (12):		15.00
Common Player:		1.50
1	Carmelo Martinez	1.50
2	Candy Maldonado	1.50
3	Benito Santiago	1.50
4	Rey Quinones	1.50
5	Jose Oquendo	1.50
6	Ruben Sierra	1.50
7	Jose Lind	1.50
8	Juan Beniquez	1.50
9	Willie Hernandez	1.50
10	Juan Nieves	1.50
11	Jose Guzman	1.50
12	Roberto Alomar (Photo actually Sandy Alomar Jr.)	3.50

1991-1992 Bleachers Promos

To introduce its 1992 line-up of single-player 23-Karat gold trimmed card sets, Bleachers produced a series of promo cards. Fronts have color portraits of the players. Backs have another picture of the player and information about ordering and coming releases. The Nolan Ryan card, showing him winding up in a tuxedo, is known in several variations with different card show names stamped on front in gold, representing venues at which sample cards were given away.

		NM/M
Complete Set (3):		3.00
(1)	Ken Griffey Jr.	1.00
(2)	David Justice	.50
(3)	Nolan Ryan	2.00

1991 Bleachers Frank Thomas

This limited edition three-card set features 23-Karat gold cards. The photos feature Frank Thomas at different stages of his baseball career before the big leagues. Production was limited to 10,000 sets and 1,500 uncut strips. All are numbered and feature a gold facsimile autograph on the back.

		NM/M
Complete Set (3):		4.00
Common Card:		2.00
1	Frank Thomas (Auburn Tigers)	2.00
2	Frank Thomas (Sarasota White Sox)	2.00
3	Frank Thomas (Birmingham Barons)	2.00

1992 Bleachers Ken Griffey, Jr.

Young superstar Ken Griffey, Jr. is honored in this three-card set featuring him at different stages of his baseball career. The 23-Karat gold cards feature full-color photos and a facsimile autograph on the back. Production was limited to 10,000 cut sets and 1,500 uncut strips.

		NM/M
Complete Set (3):		10.00
Common Card:		3.00
1	Ken Griffey Jr. (Moeller High School)	4.00
2	Ken Griffey Jr. (Bellingham Mariners)	4.00
3	Ken Griffey Jr. (San Bernadino Spirit)	4.00

1992 Bleachers David Justice

Atlanta Brave slugger David Justice is the subject of this three card 23-Karat gold set. The cards depict Justice at different stages of his baseball career. Like the other Bleachers issues, production was limited to 10,000 cut card sets and 1,500 uncut strips.

		NM/M
Complete Set (3):		6.00
Common Card:		2.50
1	David Justice (Durham Bulls)	2.50
2	David Justice (Greenville Braves)	2.50
3	David Justice (Richmond Braves)	2.50

1992 Bleachers Nolan Ryan

Three stops along Ryan's minor league trail are recalled in this collectors issue. The 2-1/2" x 3-1/2" cards have photos of Ryan at center with different colored borders and trim on each card. "23KT," his name and team are gold-foil stamped on front. Backs have career information and highlights, along with a serial number from within an edition of 10,000. Cards with silver prismatic foil on front rather than gold were random inserts in sets. Three-card uncut strips were made available in an edition of 1,500.

		NM/M
Complete Set (3):		6.00
Common Card:		2.00
Silver-Foil:		2X
1	Nolan Ryan (Marion Mets)	2.00
2	Nolan Ryan (Greenville Mets)	2.00
3	Nolan Ryan (Jacksonville Suns)	2.00

1993 Bleachers Promos

To introduce its 1993 issues, Bleachers distributed large quantities of promo cards within the hobby to dealers and to the public at several large card shows. Most of the '93 promos can be found with several different show logos overprinted in gold foil on the front. All cards carry a 1993 copyright date on back, except the plain Ryan/tuxedo card, which has a 1992 date on back, but 1993 card-show indicia on front.

Original 23Kt Genuine Gold Border Cards & Holographic Prism Cards

		NM/M
Common Card:		1.00
(1)	Barry Bonds (Arizona State)	2.00
(2)	Ken Griffey Jr. (Moeller High School uniform.)	2.00
(3)	Nolan Ryan (Triple-exposure pitching.)	2.00
(4)	Nolan Ryan (Tuxedo, '92 copyright.)	2.00
(5)	Nolan Ryan (Tuxedo, gold background.)	2.00
(6)	Nolan Ryan (Tuxedo, silver speckled background.)	2.00
(7)	Nolan Ryan (Tuxedo, wavy silver background.)	2.00
(8)	Nolan Ryan (Western clothing.)	2.00
(9)	Nolan Ryan (W/glove and ball in Bleachers cap.)	2.00
(10)	Nolan Ryan (With Yellow Lab puppy.)	2.00
(11)	Ryne Sandberg (Three-sport high school photos.)	1.00

1993 Bleachers Barry Bonds

The pre-major league career of Barry Bonds is featured on this trio of collectors cards. Fronts have color photos of Bonds within a gold border. His name, team and the notation "23KT" are printed in gold foil. Backs have career data and highlights, along with a serial number. It was reported that 10,000 sets and 1,500 three-card strips were issued. Cards found with silver prismatic borders on front are random inserts in sets.

		NM/M
Complete Set (3):		9.00
Common Card:		4.00
Silver:		2X
1	Barry Bonds (Arizona State University)	4.00
2	Barry Bonds (Price Williams Pirates)	4.00
3	Barry Bonds (Hawaii Islanders)	4.00

1993 Bleachers Nolan Ryan

Nolan Ryan's career is recapped in this set of collectors issues. Fronts have prismatic foil borders around color or colorized

photos. Information on front is stamped in gold foil. Backs have a photo of a young Ryan along with career data and stats, and a serial number from within an announced edition of 10,000 sets and 1,500 three-card uncut strips.

		NM/M
Complete Set (6):		15.00
Common Card:		3.00
1	Nolan Ryan (Little League)	3.00
2	Nolan Ryan (High school.)	3.00
3	Nolan Ryan (Minor league highlights.)	3.00
4	Nolan Ryan (Minor league stats.)	3.00
5	Nolan Ryan (Strikeout record.)	3.00
6	Nolan Ryan (Career highlights.)	3.00

1993 Bleachers Nolan Ryan 23KT

"The Express" is pictured with each of his four major league teams in this collectors issue. Each 2-1/2" x 3-1/2" card has a color photo of Ryan at center with variously colored borders and gold-foil graphic highlights. Backs have his stats with that team, a facsimile autograph and a serial number from within an edition of 10,000 sets. Uncut strips were also issued, numbered to 1,500.

		NM/M
Complete Set (4):		15.00
Uncut Strip:		20.00
Common Card:		4.00
1	Nolan Ryan (Mets)	4.00
2	Nolan Ryan (Angels)	4.00
3	Nolan Ryan (Astros)	4.00
4	Nolan Ryan (Rangers)	4.00

1993 Bleachers Ryne Sandberg

Ryno's pre-major league career is featured on this trio of collectors cards. Fronts have color photos of Sandberg within a gold border. His name, team and the notation "23KT" are printed in gold foil. Backs have career data and highlights, along with a serial number. It was reported that 10,000 sets and 1,500 three-card, gold highlighted strips were issued. Cards found with silver prismatic borders on front are random inserts in sets.

		NM/M
Complete Set (3):		9.00
Common Card:		3.00
Gold Strip:		12.00
Silver:		3X
1	Ryne Sandberg (North Central H.S.)	3.00
2	Ryne Sandberg (Helena Phillies)	3.00
3	Ryne Sandberg (Reading Phillies)	3.00

1992 Blockbuster Video Pin/Cards

Given away at special promotional games, these combination collectibles feature a 2-3/4" x 4" card, beneath which is a perforated tab of 2-3/4" x 1-9/16". The card has a borderless photo with the player name and his uniform number. The tab has a sponsor's logo. Attached to the tab is an enameled pin, about 1-1/4" square, which has a representation of the player's jersey. The black-and-white back has a portrait photo, player biographical details

and career highlights. On back of the tab is a list of the Blockbuster locations participating in the promotion.

		NM/M
Common Player:		3.00
3	Jay Bell	3.00
6	Orlando Merced	3.00
15	Doug Drabek	3.00
24	Barry Bonds	15.00

1988 Blue Cross/Blue Shield Bob Uecker Reprint

Issued as a fund-raiser and sold for $3 to benefit Bob Uecker's Ride for the Arts bicycling event in 1988, this 2-1/2" x 3-1/2" card features on its front a reprint of Uecker's card from the 1963 Topps set. Back has history and details of the fund-raiser and the logos of Blue Cross and Blue Shield.

		NM/M
(1)	Bob Uecker	6.00

1987 Bluegrass State Games

Athletes with ties to Kentucky and public figures from the state are featured on this set issued in conjunction with the 1987 Bluegrass State Games. Fronts have color photos on a blue background with white borders. Beneath the photo are the logos of Champions Against Drugs and sponsors Coke and Valvoline. Backs have an anti-drug message from the pictured celebrity. Cards were handed out over the period May 25-October 19 by law enforcement officers. Only the baseball-related cards are listed here.

		NM/M
Complete Set (24):		50.00
Common Player:		.50
5	Doug Flynn	1.00

13	Pee Wee Reese	5.00
22	A.B. (Happy) Chandler	5.00

1987 Boardwalk and Baseball All Time Record Holders

This boxed set was a repackaging of the cards produced by Topps for Woolworth stores in 1985. Fronts have "framed" black-and-white or color photos with player identification in a "plaque" at bottom. Blue-on-orange backs have brief biographical data, a listing of the player's record and career highlights, and lifetime stats.

		NM/M
Common Player:		3.00
3	Jay Bell	3.00
6	Orlando Merced	3.00
15	Doug Drabek	3.00
24	Barry Bonds	15.00

1987 Boardwalk and Baseball Top Run Makers

Created by Topps for distribution at the Boardwalk and Baseball theme park near Orlando, Fla., the cards are standard size with a thin, pink border around a color action photo. The backs are printed in black and light red, with the Topps and B/B logos at the bottom. There are 33-cards in the "Top Run Makers" boxed set, all hitters. A checklist panel appears on the back panel of the box. A much scarcer version of each card can be found with no slash between the "B's" on front.

		NM/M
Complete Set (33):		4.00
Common Player:		.10
No Slash:		3X
1	Mike Schmidt	1.00
2	Eddie Murray	.45
3	Dale Murphy	.25
4	Dave Winfield	.45
5	Jim Rice	.25
6	Cecil Cooper	.10
7	Dwight Evans	.10
8	Rickey Henderson	.45
9	Robin Yount	.45
10	Andre Dawson	.25
11	Gary Carter	.45
12	Keith Hernandez	.10
13	George Brett	1.00
14	Bill Buckner	.10
15	Tony Armas	.10
16	Harold Baines	.10
17	Don Baylor	.10
18	Steve Garvey	.10
19	Lance Parrish	.10
20	Dave Parker	.10
21	Buddy Bell	.10
22	Cal Ripken, Jr.	1.50
23	Bob Horner	.10
24	Tim Raines	.10
25	Jack Clark	.10
26	Leon Durham	.10
27	Pedro Guerrero	.10
28	Kent Hrbek	.10
29	Kirk Gibson	.10
30	Ryne Sandberg	.60
31	Wade Boggs	.60
32	Don Mattingly	.75
33	Darryl Strawberry	.10

1987 Bohemian Hearth Bread Padres

Bohemian Hearth Bread of San Diego issued this Padres team set. Produced in conjunction with Mike Schechter Associates, the cards are 2-1/2" x 3-1/2". Fronts have a color portrait photo encompassed by a yellow border. The Bohemian Hearth logo is located in the upper-left corner. Card backs are printed in light brown on a cream stock and carry player personal and statistical information, along with a facsimile autograph.

		NM/M
Complete Set (22):		20.00
Common Player:		.50
1	Garry Templeton	.50
4	Jose Cora	.50
5	Randy Ready	.50
7	Steve Garvey	3.00
8	Kevin Mitchell	.50
9	John Kruk	.65
9	Benito Santiago	.75
10	Larry Bowa	.50
11	Tim Flannery	.50
14	Carmelo Martinez	.50
16	Marvell Wynne	.50
19	Tony Gwynn	15.00
21	James Steels	.50
22	Stan Jefferson	.50
30	Eric Show	.50
31	Ed Whitson	.50
34	Storm Davis	.50
37	Craig Lefferts	.50
40	Andy Hawkins	.50
41	Lance McCullers	.50
43	Dave Dravecky	.50
54	Rich Gossage	.50

1984 Borden's Reds Stickers

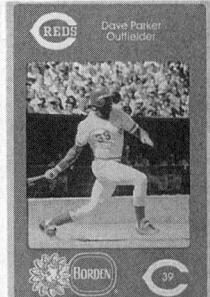

This regional set of eight Reds stickers was issued by Borden Dairy in the Cincinnati area in 1984. Originally issued in two perforated sheets of four stickers each, the individual stickers measure 2-1/2" x 3-7/8", while a full sheet measures 5-1/2" x 8". The colorful stickers feature a player photo surrounded by a bright red border with the Reds logo and the Borden logo in the corners. The backs display coupons for Borden dairy products. The set is numbered according to the players' uniform numbers.

		NM/M
Complete Panel (2):		8.00
Complete Singles (8):		8.00
Common Player:		5.00
PANEL (1)		5.00
2	Gary Redus	5.00
20	Eddie Milner	5.00
24	Tony Perez	5.00
46	Jeff Russell	5.00
PANEL (2)		
16	Ron Oester	5.00
36	Mario Soto	5.00
39	Dave Parker	5.00
44	Eric Davis	5.00

1983 Boston Herald SoxStamps

Current and former Red Sox stars are featured in this set of stamps issued by one of Boston's daily newspapers. Coupons in the paper could be redeemed for packets of stamps which could be mounted on a large (34" x 22") colorful wallchart. Persons completing the set could enter a contest for various prizes. Stamps #1-26 and 39-42 are in color and feature portrait photos of the '83 team. They measure 1" x 1-3/4". Stamps #27-38 and 43-50 are 1" x 1-1/8" and may have either color or black-and-white photos of current and former players. Values shown are for unused stamps.

		NM/M
Complete Set (50):		30.00
Common Player:		.50
Wallchart:		15.00
1	Jerry Remy	.50
2	Glenn Hoffman	.50
3	Luis Aponte	.50
4	Jim Rice	1.00
5	Mark Clear	.50
6	Reid Nichols	.50
7	Wade Boggs	5.00
8	Dennis Eckersley	2.00
9	Jeff Newman	.50
10	Bob Ojeda	.50
11	Ed Jurak	.50
12	Rick Miller	.50
13	Carl Yastrzemski	7.50
14	Mike Brown	.50
15	Bob Stanley	.50
16	John Tudor	.50
17	Gary Allenson	.50
18	Rich Gedman	.50
19	Tony Armas	.75
20	Doug Bird	.50
21	Bruce Hurst	.50
22	Dave Stapleton	.50
23	Dwight Evans	1.00
24	Julio Valdez	.50
25	John Henry Johnson	.50
26	Ralph Houk	.50
27	George Scott	.75
28	Bobby Doerr	.60
29	Frank Malzone	.50
30	Rico Petrocelli	.75
31	Carl Yastrzemski	5.00
32	Ted Williams	7.50
33	Dwight Evans	.75
34	Carlton Fisk	4.00
35	Dick Radatz	.50
36	Luis Tiant	.75
37	Mel Parnell	.50
38	Jim Rice	.75
39	Dennis Boyd	.60
40	Marty Barrett	.50
41	Brian Denman	.50
42	Steve Crawford	.50
43	Cy Young	.75
44	Jimmy Collins	.50
45	Tris Speaker	.75
46	Harry Hooper	.50
47	Lefty Grove	.60
48	Joe Cronin	.50
49	Jimmie Foxx	.75
50	Ted Williams	7.50

1982 Boston Red Sox Favorites

No issuer is identified on this collectors set, though some attribute it to the Boston Globe newspaper. The 2-1/2" x 3-1/2" cards are

black-and-white with rather wide white borders on front. There is no player identification on front. Backs are roughly in the style of 1955 Bowmans and have player identification, personal data, stats, career highlights and a trivia question.

		NM/M
Complete Set (128):		35.00
Common Player:		.25
1	Harry Agganis	2.00
2	Ken Aspromonte	.25
3	Bobby Avila	.25
4	Frank Baumann	.25
5	Lou Berberet	.25
6	Milt Bolling	.25
7	Lou Boudreau	.50
8	Ted Bowsfield	.25
9	Tom Brewer	.25
10	Don Buddin	.25
11	Jerry Casale	.25
12	Billy Consolo	.25
13	Pete Daley	.25
14	Ike Delock	.25
15	Dom DiMaggio	1.00
16	Bobby Doerr	.50
17	Walt Dropo	.50
18	Arnold Earley	.25
19	Hoot Evers	.25
20	Mike Fornieles	.25
21	Gary Geiger	.25
22	Don Gile	.25
23	Joe Ginsberg	.25
24	Billy Goodman	.25
25	Pumpsie Green	.35
26	Grady Hatten	.25
27	Mike Higgins	.25
28	Jackie Jensen	.50
29	George Kell	.50
30	Marty Keough	.25
31	Leo Kiely	.25
32	Ellis Kinder	.25
33	Billy Klaus	.25
34	Don Lenhardt	.25
35	Ted Lepcio	.25
36	Frank Malzone	.35
37	Gene Mauch	.35
38	Maury McDermott	.25
39	Bill Monbouquette	.25
40	Chet Nichols	.25
41	Willard Nixon	.25
42	Jim Pagliaroni	.25
43	Mel Parnell	.25
44	Johnny Pesky	.25
45	Jimmy Piersall	.25
46	Bob Porterfield	.25
47	Pete Runnels	.25
48	Dave Sisler	.25
49	Riverboat Smith	.25
50	Gene Stephens	.25
51	Vern Stephens	.25
52	Chuck Stobbs	.25
53	Dean Stone	.25
54	Frank Sullivan	.25
55	Haywood Sullivan	.25
56	Birdie Tebbetts	.25
57	Mickey Vernon	.35
58	Vic Wertz	.25
59	Sammy White	.25
60	Ted Williams	6.00
61	Ted Wills	.25
62	Earl Wilson	.25
63	Al Zarilla	.25
64	Norm Zauchin	.25
65	Ted Williams, Carl Yastrzemski	4.00
66	Jim Lonborg, George Scott, Dick Williams, Carl Yastrzemski	2.00
67	Billy Conigliaro, Tony Conigliaro	.75
68	Jerry Adair	.25
69	Mike Andrews	.25
70	Gary Bell	.25
71	Dennis Bennett	.25
72	Ed Bressoud	.25
73	Ken Brett	.25
74	Lu Clinton	.25
75	Tony Conigliaro	1.00
76	Billy Conigliaro	.25
77	Gene Conley	.25
78	Ray Culp	.25
79	Dick Ellsworth	.25
80	Joe Foy	.25
81	Russ Gibson	.25
82	Jim Gosger	.25
83	Lennie Green	.25
84	Ken Harrelson	.35
85	Tony Horton	.35
86	Elston Howard	.35
87	Dalton Jones	.25
88	Eddie Kasko	.25
89	Joe Lahoud	.25
90	Jack Lamabe	.25
91	Jim Lonborg	.50
92	Sparky Lyle	.50
93	Felix Mantilla	.25
94	Roman Mejias	.25
95	Don McMahon	.25
96	Dave Morehead	.25
97	Gerry Moses	.25
98	Mike Nagy	.25
99	Russ Nixon	.25
100	Gene Oliver	.25
101	Dan Osinski	.25
102	Rico Petrocelli	.50
103	Juan Pizzaro	.25
104	Dick Radatz	.35
105	Vicente Romo	.25
106	Mike Ryan	.25
107	Jose Santiago	.25
108	Chuck Schilling	.35
109	Dick Schofield	.25
110	Don Schwall	.25
111	George Scott	.35
112	Norm Siebern	.25
113	Sonny Seibert	.25
114	Reggie Smith	.35
115	Bill Spanswick	.25
116	Tracy Stallard	.25
117	Lee Stange	.25
118	Jerry Stephenson	.25
119	Dick Stuart	.25
120	Tom Sturdivant	.25
121	George Tartabull	.25
122	George Thomas	.25
123	Lee Thomas	.25
124	Bob Tillman	.25
125	Gary Waslewski	.25
126	Dick Williams	.25
127	John Wyatt	.25
128	Carl Yastrzemski	4.00

2001 Boston Red Sox 100 Seasons

This limited edition card set was issued by the team as part of its 100 seasons anniversary. One card was designated as a give-away at each of 16 home games during spring training. The first 4,000 fans at each game received that day's card. An additional 1,000 sets was reserved for team use. The 2-1/2" x 3-1/2" cards have sepia photos on front, along with a 100 seasons logo and the years the player was with the Red Sox. Backs have a Grapefruit League logo, a few career highlights and the logos of the sponsors, Aramark and gulfcoasting.com.

		NM/M
Complete Set (16):		25.00
Common Player:		1.00
1	Jimmy Collins	1.00
2	Cy Young	2.00
3	Tris Speaker	1.50
4	Babe Ruth	7.50
5	Lefty Grove	1.00
6	Joe Cronin	1.00
7	Jimmie Foxx	1.50
8	Bobby Doerr	1.00
9	Ted Williams	6.00
10	Dom DiMaggio	1.00
11	Johnny Pesky	1.00
12	Carl Yastrzemski	4.00
13	Carlton Fisk	3.00
14	Jim Rice	1.50
15	Nomar Garciaparra	4.50
16	Pedro Martinez	2.50

1993 Boston Red Sox Police

This police set was issued by the police department and local sponsors around the Red Sox spring training base in Florida. Card fronts have studio poses of the players. The Winter Haven P.D. and Police Athletic League logos are at

top, while the Red Sox logo, player ID and uniform number are beneath the portrait. Backs have a little personal data, some stats, a safety message and the names of sponsoring businesses.

		NM/M
Complete Set (28):		10.00
Common Player:		.50
1	Checklist	.10
2	Scott Bankhead	.50
3	Danny Darwin	.50
4	Andre Dawson	.75
5	Scott Fletcher	.50
6	Billy Hatcher	.50
7	Jack Clark	.50
8	Roger Clemens	5.00
9	Scott Cooper	.50
10	John Dopson	.50
11	Paul Quantrill	.50
12	Mike Greenwell	.50
13	Greg A. Harris	.50
14	Joe Hesketh	.50
15	Peter Hoy	.50
16	Daryl Irvine	.50
17	John Marzano	.50
18	Jeff McNeeley	.50
19	Tim Naehring	.50
20	Matt Young	.50
21	Jeff Plympton	.50
22	Bob Melvin	.50
23	Tony Pena	.50
24	Luis Rivera	.50
25	Scott Taylor	.50
26	John Valentin	.50
27	Mo Vaughn	.50
28	Frank Viola	.50

1987 Bowery Bank Joe DiMaggio

These cards were issued to promote the New York City bank's relationship with spokesman Joe DiMaggio. The 2-1/2" x 3-1/2" cards have a posed color photo on front. The back has biographical data, career highlights and stats printed in black and red.

	NM/M
Joe DiMaggio	17.50

1989 Bowman

Topps, which purchased Bowman in 1955, revived the brand name in 1989, issuing a 484-card set. The 2-1/2" x 3-3/4" cards are slightly taller than current standard. Fronts contain a full-color player photo, with facsimile autograph and the Bowman logo in an upper corner. Backs include a breakdown of the player's stats against each team in his league. A series of "Hot Rookie Stars" highlights the set. The cards were distributed in both wax packs and rack packs. Each pack included a special reproduction of a classic Bowman card with a sweepstakes on the back.

	NM/M
Unopened Fact. Set (484):	20.00
Complete Set (484):	15.00

Common Player:		.05
Wax Pack (12+1):		.75
Wax Box (36):		15.00
Rack Pack (40):		1.00
Rack Box (24):		20.00
1	Oswald Peraza	.05
2	Brian Holton	.05
3	Jose Bautista	.05
4	Pete Harnisch RC	.10
5	Dave Schmidt	.05
6	Gregg Olson	.05
7	Jeff Ballard	.05
8	Bob Melvin	.05
9	Cal Ripken, Jr.	.75
10	Randy Milligan	.05
11	Juan Bell RC	.05
12	Billy Ripken	.05
13	Jim Trabor	.05
14	Pete Stanicek	.05
15	Steve Finley RC	.25
16	Larry Sheets	.05
17	Phil Bradley	.05
18	Brady Anderson	.05
19	Lee Smith	.05
20	Tom Fischer	.05
21	Mike Boddicker	.05
22	Rob Murphy	.05
23	Wes Gardner	.05
24	John Dopson	.05
25	Bob Stanley	.05
26	Roger Clemens	.60
27	Rich Gedman	.05
28	Marty Barrett	.05
29	Luis Rivera	.05
30	Jody Reed	.05
31	Nick Esasky	.05
32	Wade Boggs	.50
33	Jim Rice	.05
34	Mike Greenwell	.05
35	Dwight Evans	.05
36	Ellis Burks	.05
37	Chuck Finley	.05
38	Kirk McCaskill	.05
39	Jim Abbott	.05
40	Bryan Harvey RC	.05
41	Bert Blyleven	.05
42	Mike Witt	.05
43	Bob McClure	.05
44	Bill Schroeder	.05
45	Lance Parrish	.05
46	Dick Schofield	.05
47	Wally Joyner	.05
48	Jack Howell	.05
49	Johnny Ray	.05
50	Chili Davis	.05
51	Tony Armas	.05
52	Claudell Washington	.05
53	Brian Downing	.05
54	Devon White	.05
55	Bobby Thigpen	.05
56	Bill Long	.05
57	Jerry Reuss	.05
58	Shawn Hillegas	.05
59	Melido Perez	.05
60	Jeff Bittiger	.05
61	Jack McDowell	.05
62	Carlton Fisk	.40
63	Steve Lyons	.05
64	Ozzie Guillen	.05
65	Robin Ventura	.05
66	Fred Manrique	.05
67	Dan Pasqua	.05
68	Ivan Calderon	.05
69	Ron Kittle	.05
70	Daryl Boston	.05
71	Dave Gallagher	.05
72	Harold Baines	.05
73	Charles Nagy RC	.15
74	John Farrell	.05
75	Kevin Wickander	.05
76	Greg Swindell	.05
77	Mike Walker	.05
78	Doug Jones	.05
79	Rich Yett	.05
80	Tom Candiotti	.05
81	Jesse Orosco	.05
82	Bud Black	.05
83	Andy Allanson	.05
84	Pete O'Brien	.05
85	Jerry Browne	.05
86	Brook Jacoby	.05
87	Mark Lewis RC	.05
88	Luis Aguayo	.05
89	Cory Snyder	.05
90	Oddibe McDowell	.05
91	Joe Carter	.05
92	Frank Tanana	.05
93	Jack Morris	.05
94	Doyle Alexander	.05
95	Steve Searcy	.05
96	Randy Bockus	.05
97	Jeff Robinson	.05
98	Mike Henneman	.05
99	Paul Gibson	.05
100	Frank Williams	.05
101	Matt Nokes	.05
102	Rico Brogna	.05
103	Lou Whitaker	.05
104	Al Pedrique	.05
105	Alan Trammell	.05
106	Chris Brown	.05
107	Pat Sheridan	.05
108	Gary Pettis	.05
109	Keith Moreland	.05
110	Mel Stottlemyre, Jr.	.05
111	Bret Saberhagen	.05
112	Floyd Bannister	.05
113	Jeff Montgomery	.05

114	Steve Farr	.05
115	Tom Gordon	.05
116	Charlie Leibrandt	.05
117	Mark Gubicza	.05
118	Mike MacFarlane	.05
119	Bob Boone	.05
120	Kurt Stillwell	.05
121	George Brett	.60
122	Frank White	.05
123	Kevin Seitzer	.05
124	Willie Wilson	.05
125	Pat Tabler	.05
126	Bo Jackson	.10
127	Hugh Walker	.05
128	Danny Tartabull	.05
129	Teddy Higuera	.05
130	Don August	.05
131	Juan Nieves	.05
132	Mike Birkbeck	.05
133	Dan Plesac	.05
134	Chris Bosio	.05
135	Bill Wegman	.05
136	Chuck Crim	.05
137	B.J. Surhoff	.05
138	Joey Meyer	.05
139	Dale Sveum	.05
140	Paul Molitor	.40
141	Jim Gantner	.05
142	Gary Sheffield RC	.75
143	Greg Brock	.05
144	Robin Yount	.40
145	Glenn Braggs	.05
146	Rob Deer	.05
147	Fred Toliver	.05
148	Jeff Reardon	.05
149	Allan Anderson	.05
150	Frank Viola	.05
151	Shane Rawley	.05
152	Juan Berenguer	.05
153	Johnny Ard	.05
154	Tim Laudner	.05
155	Brian Harper	.05
156	Al Newman	.05
157	Kent Hrbek	.05
158	Gary Gaetti	.05
159	Wally Backman	.05
160	Gene Larkin	.05
161	Greg Gagne	.05
162	Kirby Puckett	.05
163	Danny Gladden	.05
164	Randy Bush	.05
165	Dave LaPoint	.05
166	Andy Hawkins	.05
167	Dave Righetti	.05
168	Lance McCullers	.05
169	Jimmy Jones	.05
170	Al Leiter	.05
171	John Candelaria	.05
172	Don Slaught	.05
173	Jamie Quirk	.05
174	Rafael Santana	.05
175	Mike Pagliarulo	.05
176	Don Mattingly	.60
177	Ken Phelps	.05
178	Steve Sax	.05
179	Dave Winfield	.40
180	Stan Jefferson	.05
181	Rickey Henderson	.40
182	Bob Brower	.05
183	Roberto Kelly	.05
184	Curt Young	.05
185	Gene Nelson	.05
186	Bob Welch	.05
187	Rick Honeycutt	.05
188	Dave Stewart	.05
189	Mike Moore	.05
190	Dennis Eckersley	.35
191	Eric Plunk	.05
192	Storm Davis	.05
193	Terry Steinbach	.05
194	Ron Hassey	.05
195	Stan Royer	.05
196	Walt Weiss	.05
197	Mark McGwire	.65
198	Carney Lansford	.05
199	Glenn Hubbard	.05
200	Dave Henderson	.05
201	Jose Canseco	.30
202	Dave Parker	.05
203	Scott Bankhead	.05
204	Tom Niedenfuer	.05
205	Mark Langston	.05
206	Erik Hanson RC	.05
207	Mike Jackson	.05
208	Dave Valle	.05
209	Scott Bradley	.05
210	Harold Reynolds	.05
211	Tino Martinez	.05
212	Rich Renteria	.05
213	Rey Quinones	.05
214	Jim Presley	.05
215	Alvin Davis	.05
216	Edgar Martinez	.05
217	Darnell Coles	.05
218	Jeffrey Leonard	.05
219	Jay Buhner	.05
220	Ken Griffey Jr. RC	6.00
221	Drew Hall	.05
222	Bobby Witt	.05
223	Jamie Moyer	.05
224	Charlie Hough	.05
225	Nolan Ryan	.75
226	Jeff Russell	.05
227	Jim Sundberg	.05
228	Julio Franco	.05
229	Buddy Bell	.05
230	Scott Fletcher	.05
231	Jeff Kunkel	.05

232 Steve Buechele	.05	
233 Monty Fariss	.05	
234 Rick Leach	.05	
235 Ruben Sierra	.05	
236 Cecil Espy	.05	
237 Rafael Palmeiro	.35	
238 Pete Incaviglia	.05	
239 Dave Steib	.05	
240 Jeff Musselman	.05	
241 Mike Flanagan	.05	
242 Todd Stottlemyre	.05	
243 Jimmy Key	.05	
244 Tony Castillo	.05	
245 Alex Sanchez	.05	
246 Tom Henke	.05	
247 John Cerutti	.05	
248 Ernie Whitt	.05	
249 Bob Brenly	.05	
250 Rance Mulliniks	.05	
251 Kelly Gruber	.05	
252 Ed Sprague	.05	
253 Fred McGriff	.05	
254 Tony Fernandez	.05	
255 Tom Lawless	.05	
256 George Bell	.05	
257 Jesse Barfield	.05	
258 Sandy Alomar, Sr.	.05	
259 Ken Griffey	.05	
(With Ken Griffey Jr.)	.30	
260 Cal Ripken, Sr.	.05	
261 Mel Stottlemyre, Sr.	.05	
262 Zane Smith	.05	
263 Charlie Puleo	.05	
264 Derek Lilliquist	.05	
265 Paul Assenmacher	.05	
266 John Smoltz	.05	
267 Tom Glavine	.25	
268 Steve Avery RC	.05	
269 Pete Smith RC	.05	
270 Jody Davis	.05	
271 Bruce Benedict	.05	
272 Andres Thomas	.05	
273 Gerald Perry	.05	
274 Ron Gant	.05	
275 Darrell Evans	.05	
276 Dale Murphy	.25	
277 Dion James	.05	
278 Lonnie Smith	.05	
279 Geronimo Berroa	.05	
280 Steve Wilson	.05	
281 Rick Suctcliffe	.05	
282 Kevin Coffman	.05	
283 Mitch Williams	.05	
284 Greg Maddux	.50	
285 Paul Kilgus	.05	
286 Mike Harkey	.05	
287 Lloyd McClendon	.05	
288 Damon Berryhill	.05	
289 Ty Griffin	.05	
290 Ryne Sandberg	.50	
291 Mark Grace	.05	
292 Curt Wilkerson	.05	
293 Vance Law	.05	
294 Shawon Dunston	.05	
295 Jerome Walton	.05	
296 Mitch Webster	.05	
297 Dwight Smith	.05	
298 Andre Dawson	.25	
299 Jeff Sellers	.05	
300 Jose Rijo	.05	
301 John Franco	.05	
302 Rick Mahler	.05	
303 Ron Robinson	.05	
304 Danny Jackson	.05	
305 Rob Dibble	.05	
306 Tom Browning	.05	
307 Bo Diaz	.05	
308 Manny Trillo	.05	
309 Chris Sabo RC	.05	
310 Ron Oester	.05	
311 Barry Larkin	.05	
312 Todd Benzinger	.05	
313 Paul O'Neill	.05	
314 Kal Daniels	.05	
315 Joel Youngblood	.05	
316 Eric Davis	.05	
317 Dave Smith	.05	
318 Mark Portugal	.05	
319 Brian Meyer	.05	
320 Jim Deshaies	.05	
321 Juan Agosto	.05	
322 Mike Scott	.05	
323 Rick Rhoden	.05	
324 Jim Clancy	.05	
325 Larry Andersen	.05	
326 Alex Trevino	.05	
327 Alan Ashby	.05	
328 Craig Reynolds	.05	
329 Bill Doran	.05	
330 Rafael Ramirez	.05	
331 Glenn Davis	.05	
332 Willie Ansley RC	.05	
333 Gerald Young	.05	
334 Cameron Drew	.05	
335 Jay Howell	.05	
336 Tim Belcher	.05	
337 Fernando Valenzuela	.05	
338 Ricky Horton	.05	
339 Tim Leary	.05	
340 Bill Bene	.05	
341 Orel Hershiser	.05	
342 Mike Scioscia	.05	
343 Rick Dempsey	.05	
344 Willie Randolph	.05	
345 Alfredo Griffin	.05	
346 Eddie Murray	.40	
347 Mickey Hatcher	.05	
348 Mike Sharperson	.05	
349 John Shelby	.05	
350 Mike Marshall	.05	
351 Kirk Gibson	.05	
352 Mike Davis	.05	
353 Bryn Smith	.05	
354 Pascual Perez	.05	
355 Kevin Gross	.05	
356 Andy McGaffigan	.05	
357 Brian Holman	.05	
358 Dave Wainhouse	.05	
359 Denny Martinez	.05	
360 Tim Burke	.05	
361 Nelson Santovenia	.05	
362 Tim Wallach	.05	
363 Spike Owen	.05	
364 Rex Hudler	.05	
365 Andres Galarraga	.05	
366 Otis Nixon	.05	
367 Hubie Brooks	.05	
368 Mike Aldrete	.05	
369 Rock Raines	.05	
370 Dave Martinez	.05	
371 Bob Ojeda	.05	
372 Ron Darling	.05	
373 Wally Whitehurst	.05	
374 Randy Myers	.05	
375 David Cone	.05	
376 Dwight Gooden	.05	
377 Sid Fernandez	.05	
378 Dave Proctor	.05	
379 Gary Carter	.40	
380 Keith Miller	.05	
381 Gregg Jefferies	.05	
382 Tim Teufel	.05	
383 Kevin Elster	.05	
384 Dave Magadan	.05	
385 Keith Hernandez	.05	
386 Mookie Wilson	.05	
387 Darryl Strawberry	.05	
388 Kevin McReynolds	.05	
389 Mark Carreon	.05	
390 Jeff Parrett	.05	
391 Mike Maddux	.05	
392 Don Carman	.05	
393 Bruce Ruffin	.05	
394 Ken Howell	.05	
395 Steve Bedrosian	.05	
396 Floyd Youmans	.05	
397 Larry McWilliams	.05	
398 Pat Combs	.05	
399 Steve Lake	.05	
400 Dickie Thon	.05	
401 Ricky Jordan	.05	
402 Mike Schmidt	.60	
403 Tom Herr	.05	
404 Chris James	.05	
405 Juan Samuel	.05	
406 Von Hayes	.05	
407 Ron Jones	.05	
408 Curt Ford	.05	
409 Bob Walk	.05	
410 Jeff Robinson	.05	
411 Jim Gott	.05	
412 Scott Medvin	.05	
413 John Smiley	.05	
414 Bob Kipper	.05	
415 Brian Fisher	.05	
416 Doug Drabek	.05	
417 Mike Lavalliere	.05	
418 Ken Oberkfell	.05	
419 Sid Bream	.05	
420 Austin Manahan	.05	
421 Jose Lind	.05	
422 Bobby Bonilla	.05	
423 Glenn Wilson	.05	
424 Andy Van Slyke	.05	
425 Gary Redus	.05	
426 Barry Bonds	.75	
427 Don Heinkel	.05	
428 Ken Dayley	.05	
429 Todd Worrell	.05	
430 Brad DuVall	.05	
431 Jose DeLeon	.05	
432 Joe Magrane	.05	
433 John Ericks	.05	
434 Frank DiPino	.05	
435 Tony Pena	.05	
436 Ozzie Smith	.50	
437 Terry Pendleton	.05	
438 Jose Oquendo	.05	
439 Tim Jones	.05	
440 Pedro Guerrero	.05	
441 Milt Thompson	.05	
442 Willie McGee	.05	
443 Vince Coleman	.05	
444 Tom Brunansky	.05	
445 Walt Terrell	.05	
446 Eric Show	.05	
447 Mark Davis	.05	
448 Andy Benes RC	.10	
449 Eddie Whitson	.05	
450 Dennis Rasmussen	.05	
451 Bruce Hurst	.05	
452 Pat Clements	.05	
453 Benito Santiago	.05	
454 Sandy Alomar, Jr.	.05	
455 Garry Templeton	.05	
456 Jack Clark	.05	
457 Tim Flannery	.05	
458 Roberto Alomar	.25	
459 Camelo Martinez	.05	
460 John Kruk	.05	
461 Tony Gwynn	.50	
462 Jerald Clark	.05	
463 Don Robinson	.05	
464 Craig Lefferts	.05	
465 Kelly Downs	.05	
466 Rick Rueschel	.05	
467 Scott Garrelts	.05	
468 Wil Tejada	.05	
469 Kirt Manwaring	.05	
470 Terry Kennedy	.05	
471 Jose Uribe	.05	
472 Royce Clayton RC	.10	
473 Robby Thompson	.05	
474 Kevin Mitchell	.05	
475 Ernie Riles	.05	
476 Will Clark	.05	
477 Donnell Nixon	.05	
478 Candy Maldonado	.05	
479 Tracy Jones	.05	
480 Brett Butler	.05	
481 Checklist 1-121	.05	
482 Checklist 122-242	.05	
483 Checklist 243-363	.05	
484 Checklist 364-484	.05	

Tiffany

A special collectors' version of the revitalized Bowman cards was produced in 1989, differing from the regular-issue cards in the application of a high-gloss finish to the front and the use of a white cardboard stock. The "Tiffany" version (as the glossies are known to collectors), was sold only in complete boxed sets, with an estimated production of 6,000 sets.

	NM/M
Unopened Set (495):	165.00
Complete Set (495):	100.00
Common Player:	.25

Inserts

Bowman inserted sweepstakes cards in its 1989 packs. Each sweepstakes card reproduces a classic Bowman card on the front, with a prominent "REPRINT" notice. With one card in each pack, they are by no means scarce. A "Tiffany" version of the reprints was produced for inclusion in the factory set of 1989 Bowman cards. The glossy-front inserts are valued at 10X the standard version.

	NM/M
Complete Set (11):	3.50
Common Player:	.10
(1) Richie Ashburn	.10
(2) Yogi Berra	.10
(3) Whitey Ford	.10
(4) Gil Hodges	.10
(5) Mickey Mantle/1951	2.00
(6) Mickey Mantle/1953	1.50
(7) Willie Mays	.50
(8) Satchel Paige	.25
(9) Jackie Robinson	1.00
(10) Duke Snider	.10
(11) Ted Williams	1.00

1990 Bowman

Bowman followed its 1989 rebirth with a 528-card set in 1990. The 1990 cards follow the classic Bowman style featuring a full-color photo bordered in white. The Bowman logo appears in the upper-left corner. The player's team nickname and name appear on the bottom border of the card photo. Unlike the 1989 set, the 1990 cards are standard 2-1/2" x 3-1/2". Backs are horizontal and display the player's statistics against the teams in his league.

	NM/M
Unopened Factory Set (528):	20.00
Complete Set (528):	15.00
Common Player:	.05
Wax Pack (15):	.75
Wax Box (36):	15.00
Jumbo Pack (31):	1.00
Jumbo Box (24):	15.00
Rack Pack (39):	1.50
Rack Box (24):	20.00

1 Tommy Greene RC	.05	
2 Tom Glavine	.30	
3 Andy Nezelek	.05	
4 Mike Stanton	.05	
5 Rick Lueken	.05	
6 Kent Mercker	.05	
7 Derek Lilliquist	.05	
8 Charlie Liebrandt	.05	
9 Steve Avery	.05	
10 John Smoltz	.05	
11 Mark Lemke	.05	
12 Lonnie Smith	.05	
13 Oddibe McDowell	.05	
14 Tyler Houston RC	.05	
15 Jeff Blauser	.05	
16 Ernie Whitt	.05	
17 Alexis Infante	.05	
18 Jim Presley	.05	
19 Dale Murphy	.25	
20 Nick Esasky	.05	
21 Rick Sutcliffe	.05	
22 Mike Bielecki	.05	
23 Steve Wilson	.05	
24 Kevin Blankenship	.05	
25 Mitch Williams	.05	
26 Dean Wilkins	.05	
27 Greg Maddux	.50	
28 Mike Harkey	.05	
29 Mark Grace	.05	
30 Ryne Sandberg	.50	
31 Greg Smith	.05	
32 Dwight Smith	.05	
33 Damon Berryhill	.05	
34 Earl Cunningham	.05	
35 Jerome Walton	.05	
36 Lloyd McClendon	.05	
37 Ty Griffin	.05	
38 Shawon Dunston	.05	
39 Andre Dawson	.25	
40 Luis Salazar	.05	
41 Tim Layana	.05	
42 Rob Dibble	.05	
43 Tom Browning	.05	
44 Danny Jackson	.05	
45 Jose Rijo	.05	
46 Scott Scudder	.05	
47 Randy Myers	.05	
48 Brian Lane	.05	
49 Paul O'Neill	.05	
50 Barry Larkin	.05	
51 Reggie Jefferson	.05	
52 Jeff Branson	.05	
53 Chris Sabo	.05	
54 Joe Oliver	.05	
55 Todd Benzinger	.05	
56 Rolando Roomes	.05	
57 Hal Morris	.05	
58 Eric Davis	.05	
59 Scott Bryant	.05	
60 Ken Griffey	.05	
61 Darryl Kile RC	.05	
62 Dave Smith	.05	
63 Mark Portugal	.05	
64 Jeff Juden RC	.05	
65 Bill Gullickson	.05	
66 Danny Darwin	.05	
67 Larry Andersen	.05	
68 Jose Cano	.05	
69 Dan Schatzeder	.05	
70 Jim Deshaies	.05	
71 Mike Scott	.05	
72 Gerald Young	.05	
73 Ken Caminiti	.05	
74 Ken Oberkfell	.05	
75 Dave Rohde	.05	
76 Bill Doran	.05	
77 Andujar Cedeno	.05	
78 Craig Biggio	.05	
79 Karl Rhodes	.05	
80 Glenn Davis	.05	
81 Eric Anthony RC	.05	
82 John Wetteland	.05	
83 Jay Howell	.05	
84 Orel Hershiser	.05	
85 Tim Belcher	.05	
86 Kiki Jones	.05	
87 Mike Hartley	.05	
88 Ramon Martinez	.05	
89 Mike Scioscia	.05	
90 Willie Randolph	.05	
91 Juan Samuel	.05	
92 Jose Offerman RC	.05	
93 Dave Hansen	.05	
94 Jeff Hamilton	.05	
95 Alfredo Griffin	.05	
96 Tom Goodwin	.05	
97 Kirk Gibson	.05	
98 Jose Vizcaino	.05	
99 Kal Daniels	.05	
100 Hubie Brooks	.05	
101 Eddie Murray	.40	
102 Dennis Boyd	.05	
103 Tim Burke	.05	
104 Bill Sampen	.05	
105 Brett Gideon	.05	
106 Mark Gardner	.05	
107 Howard Farmer	.05	
108 Mel Rojas	.05	
109 Kevin Gross	.05	
110 Dave Schmidt	.05	
111 Denny Martinez	.05	
112 Jerry Goff	.05	
113 Andres Galarraga	.05	
114 Tim Welch	.05	
115 Marquis Grissom RC	.25	
116 Spike Owen	.05	
117 Larry Walker RC	1.00	
118 Rock Raines	.05	
119 Delino DeShields RC	.10	
120 Tom Foley	.05	
121 Dave Martinez	.05	
122 Frank Viola	.05	
123 Julio Valera	.05	
124 Alejandro Pena	.05	
125 David Cone	.05	
126 Dwight Gooden	.05	
127 Kevin Brown	.05	
128 John Franco	.05	
129 Terry Bross	.05	
130 Blaine Beatty	.05	
131 Sid Fernandez	.05	
132 Mike Marshall	.05	
133 Howard Johnson	.05	
134 Jaime Roseboro	.05	
135 Alan Zinter	.05	
136 Keith Miller	.05	
137 Kevin Elster	.05	
138 Kevin McReynolds	.05	
139 Barry Lyons	.05	
140 Gregg Jefferies	.05	
141 Darryl Strawberry	.05	
142 Todd Hundley RC	.10	
143 Scott Service	.05	
144 Chuck Malone	.05	
145 Steve Ontiveros	.05	
146 Roger McDowell	.05	
147 Ken Howell	.05	
148 Pat Combs	.05	
149 Jeff Parrett	.05	
150 Chuck McElroy	.05	
151 Jason Grimsley	.05	
152 Len Dykstra	.05	
153 Mickey Morandini	.05	
154 John Kruk	.05	
155 Dickie Thon	.05	
156 Ricky Jordan	.05	
157 Jeff Jackson	.05	
158 Darren Daulton	.05	
159 Tom Herr	.05	
160 Von Hayes	.05	
161 Dave Hollins RC	.05	
162 Carmelo Martinez	.05	
163 Bob Walk	.05	
164 Doug Drabek	.05	
165 Walt Terrell	.05	
166 Bill Landrum	.05	
167 Scott Ruskin	.05	
168 Bob Patterson	.05	
169 Bobby Bonilla	.05	
170 Jose Lind	.05	
171 Andy Van Slyke	.05	
172 Mike LaValliere	.05	
173 Willie Greene RC	.05	
174 Jay Bell	.05	
175 Sid Bream	.05	
176 Tom Prince	.05	
177 Wally Backman	.05	
178 Moises Alou RC	.25	
179 Steve Carter	.05	
180 Gary Redus	.05	
181 Barry Bonds	1.00	
182 Don Slaught	.05	
183 Joe Magrane	.05	
184 Bryn Smith	.05	
185 Todd Worrell	.05	
186 Jose Deleon	.05	
187 Frank DiPino	.05	
188 John Tudor	.05	
189 Howard Hilton	.05	
190 John Ericks	.05	
191 Ken Dayley	.05	
192 Ray Lankford RC	.10	
193 Todd Zeile	.05	
194 Willie McGee	.05	
195 Ozzie Smith	.50	
196 Milt Thompson	.05	
197 Terry Pendleton	.05	
198 Vince Coleman	.05	
199 Paul Coleman	.05	
200 Jose Oquendo	.05	
201 Pedro Guerrero	.05	
202 Tom Brunansky	.05	
203 Roger Smithberg	.05	
204 Eddie Whitson	.05	
205 Dennis Rasmussen	.05	
206 Craig Lefferts	.05	
207 Andy Benes	.05	
208 Bruce Hurst	.05	
209 Eric Show	.05	
210 Rafael Valdez	.05	
211 Joey Cora	.05	
212 Thomas Howard	.05	
213 Rob Nelson	.05	
214 Jack Clark	.05	
215 Garry Templeton	.05	
216 Fred Lynn	.05	
217 Tony Gwynn	.50	
218 Benny Santiago	.05	
219 Mike Pagliarulo	.05	
220 Joe Carter	.05	
221 Roberto Alomar	.25	
222 Bip Roberts	.05	
223 Rick Reuschel	.05	
224 Russ Swan	.05	
225 Eric Gunderson	.05	
226 Steve Bedrosian	.05	
227 Mike Remlinger	.05	
228 Scott Garrelts	.05	
229 Ernie Camacho	.05	
230 Andres Santana	.05	
231 Will Clark	.05	
232 Kevin Mitchell	.05	
233 Robby Thompson	.05	
234 Bill Bathe	.05	
235 Tony Perezchica	.05	
236 Gary Carter	.40	
237 Brett Butler	.05	
238 Matt Williams	.05	
239 Ernie Riles	.05	
240 Kevin Bass	.05	
241 Terry Kennedy	.05	
242 Steve Hosey RC	.05	
243 Ben McDonald RC	.15	
244 Jeff Ballard	.05	
245 Joe Price	.05	
246 Curt Schilling	.30	
247 Pete Harnisch	.05	
248 Mark Williamson	.05	
249 Gregg Olson	.05	
250 Chris Myers	.05	
251a David Segui	.05	
(No bio. data on back.)	3.50	
251b David Segui	.05	
(Bio. data on back.)	.05	
252 Joe Orsulak	.05	
253 Craig Worthington	.05	
254 Mickey Tettleton	.05	
255 Cal Ripken, Jr.	1.00	
256 Billy Ripken	.05	
257 Randy Milligan	.05	
258 Brady Anderson	.05	
259 Chris Hoiles RC	.05	
260 Mike Devereaux	.05	
261 Phil Bradley	.05	
262 Leo Gomez RC	.05	
263 Lee Smith	.05	
264 Mike Rochford	.05	
265 Jeff Reardon	.05	
266 Wes Gardner	.05	
267 Mike Boddicker	.05	
268 Roger Clemens	.60	
269 Rob Murphy	.05	
270 Mickey Pina	.05	
271 Tony Pena	.05	
272 Jody Reed	.05	
273 Kevin Romine	.05	
274 Mike Greenwell	.05	
275 Mo Vaughn RC	.60	
276 Danny Heep	.05	
277 Scott Cooper	.05	
278 Greg Blosser RC	.05	
279 Dwight Evans	.05	
280 Ellis Burks	.05	
281 Wade Boggs	.50	
282 Marty Barrett	.05	
283 Kirk McCaskill	.05	
284 Mark Langston	.05	
285 Bert Blyleven	.05	
286 Mike Fetters	.05	
287 Kyle Abbott	.05	
288 Jim Abbott	.05	
289 Chuck Finley	.05	
290 Gary DiSarcina	.05	
291 Dick Schofield	.05	
292 Devon White	.05	
293 Bobby Rose	.05	
294 Brian Downing	.05	
295 Lance Parrish	.05	
296 Jack Howell	.05	
297 Claudell Washington	.05	
298 John Orton	.05	
299 Wally Joyner	.05	
300 Lee Stevens	.05	
301 Chili Davis	.05	
302 Johnny Ray	.05	
303 Greg Hibbard	.05	
304 Eric King	.05	
305 Jack McDowell	.05	
306 Bobby Thigpen	.05	
307 Adam Peterson	.05	
308 Scott Radinsky RC	.05	
309 Wayne Edwards	.05	
310 Melido Perez	.05	
311 Robin Ventura	.05	
312 Sammy Sosa RC	2.00	
313 Dan Pasqua	.05	
314 Carlton Fisk	.40	
315 Ozzie Guillen	.05	
316 Ivan Calderon	.05	
317 Daryl Boston	.05	
318 Craig Grebeck	.05	
319 Scott Fletcher	.05	
320 Frank Thomas RC	3.00	
321 Steve Lyons	.05	
322 Carlos Martinez	.05	
323 Joe Skalski	.05	
324 Tom Candiotti	.05	
325 Greg Swindell	.05	
326 Steve Olin	.05	
327 Kevin Wickander	.05	
328 Doug Jones	.05	
329 Jeff Shaw	.05	
330 Kevin Bearse	.05	
331 Dion James	.05	
332 Jerry Browne	.05	

No	Player	Price
333	Albert Belle	.05
334	Felix Fermin	.05
335	Candy Maldonado	.05
336	Cory Snyder	.05
337	Sandy Alomar	.05
338	Mark Lewis	.05
339	Carlos Baerga RC	.10
340	Chris James	.05
341	Brook Jacoby	.05
342	Keith Hernandez	.05
343	Frank Tanana	.05
344	Scott Aldred	.05
345	Mike Henneman	.05
346	Steve Wapnick	.05
347	Greg Gohr	.05
348	Eric Stone	.05
349	Brian DuBois	.05
350	Kevin Ritz	.05
351	Rico Brogna	.05
352	Mike Heath	.05
353	Alan Trammell	.05
354	Chet Lemon	.05
355	Dave Bergman	.05
356	Lou Whitaker	.05
357	Cecil Fielder	.05
358	Milt Cuyler	.05
359	Tony Phillips	.05
360	Travis Fryman RC	.10
361	Ed Romero	.05
362	Lloyd Moseby	.05
363	Mark Gubicza	.05
364	Bret Saberhagen	.05
365	Tom Gordon	.05
366	Steve Farr	.05
367	Kevin Appier	.05
368	Storm Davis	.05
369	Mark Davis	.05
370	Jeff Montgomery	.05
371	Frank White	.05
372	Brent Mayne	.05
373	Bob Boone	.05
374	Jim Eisenreich	.05
375	Danny Tartabull	.05
376	Kurt Stillwell	.05
377	Bill Pecota	.05
378	Bo Jackson	.10
379	Bob Hamelin RC	.05
380	Kevin Seitzer	.05
381	Rey Palacios	.05
382	George Brett	.60
383	Gerald Perry	.05
384	Teddy Higuera	.05
385	Tom Filer	.05
386	Dan Plesac	.05
387	Cal Eldred RC	.05
388	Jaime Navarro	.05
389	Chris Bosio	.05
390	Randy Veres	.05
391	Gary Sheffield	.25
392	George Canale	.05
393	B.J. Surhoff	.05
394	Tim McIntosh	.05
395	Greg Brock	.05
396	Greg Vaughn	.05
397	Darryl Hamilton	.05
398	Dave Parker	.40
399	Paul Molitor	.40
400	Jim Gantner	.05
401	Rob Deer	.05
402	Billy Spiers	.05
403	Glenn Braggs	.05
404	Robin Yount	.40
405	Rick Aguilera	.05
406	Johnny Ard	.05
407	Kevin Tapani RC	.10
408	Park Pittman	.05
409	Allan Anderson	.05
410	Juan Berenguer	.05
411	Willie Banks	.05
412	Rich Yett	.05
413	Dave West	.05
414	Greg Gagne	.05
415	Chuck Knoblauch RC	.50
416	Randy Bush	.05
417	Gary Gaetti	.05
418	Kent Hrbek	.05
419	Al Newman	.05
420	Danny Gladden	.05
421	Paul Sorrento	.05
422	Derek Parks	.05
423	Scott Leius	.05
424	Kirby Puckett	.50
425	Willie Smith	.05
426	Dave Righetti	.05
427	Jeff Robinson	.05
428	Alan Mills	.05
429	Tim Leary	.05
430	Pascual Perez	.05
431	Alvaro Espinoza	.05
432	Dave Winfield	.40
433	Jesse Barfield	.05
434	Randy Velarde	.05
435	Rick Cerone	.05
436	Steve Balboni	.05
437	Mel Hall	.05
438	Bob Geren	.05
439	Bernie Williams RC	1.00
440	Kevin Maas RC	.05
441	Mike Blowers	.05
442	Steve Sax	.05
443	Don Mattingly	.60
444	Roberto Kelly	.05
445	Mike Moore	.05
446	Reggie Harris	.05
447	Scott Sanderson	.05
448	Dave Otto	.05
449	Dave Stewart	.05
450	Rick Honeycutt	.05
451	Dennis Eckersley	.35
452	Carney Lansford	.05
453	Scott Hemond	.05
454	Mark McGwire	.75
455	Felix Jose	.05
456	Terry Steinbach	.05
457	Rickey Henderson	.40
458	Dave Henderson	.05
459	Mike Gallego	.05
460	Jose Canseco	.30
461	Walt Weiss	.05
462	Ken Phelps	.05
463	Darren Lewis RC	.05
464	Ron Hassey	.05
465	Roger Salkeld RC	.05
466	Scott Bankhead	.05
467	Keith Comstock	.05
468	Randy Johnson	.40
469	Erik Hanson	.05
470	Mike Schooler	.05
471	Gary Eave	.05
472	Jeffrey Leonard	.05
473	Dave Valle	.05
474	Omar Vizquel	.05
475	Pete O'Brien	.05
476	Henry Cotto	.05
477	Jay Buhner	.05
478	Harold Reynolds	.05
479	Alvin Davis	.05
480	Darnell Coles	.05
481	Ken Griffey Jr.	.65
482	Greg Briley	.05
483	Scott Bradley	.05
484	Tino Martinez	.05
485	Jeff Russell	.05
486	Nolan Ryan	1.00
487	Robb Nen	.05
488	Kevin Brown	.05
489	Brian Bohanon	.05
490	Ruben Sierra	.05
491	Pete Incaviglia	.05
492	Juan Gonzalez RC	1.00
493	Steve Buechele	.05
494	Scott Coolbaugh	.05
495	Geno Petralli	.05
496	Rafael Palmeiro	.35
497	Julio Franco	.05
498	Gary Pettis	.05
499	Donald Harris	.05
500	Monty Fariss	.05
501	Harold Baines	.05
502	Cecil Espy	.05
503	Jack Daugherty	.05
504	Willie Blair	.05
505	Dave Steib	.05
506	Tom Henke	.05
507	John Cerutti	.05
508	Paul Kilgus	.05
509	Jimmy Key	.05
510	John Olerud RC	.75
511	Ed Sprague	.05
512	Manny Lee	.05
513	Fred McGriff	.05
514	Glenallen Hill	.05
515	George Bell	.05
516	Mookie Wilson	.05
517	Luis Sojo	.05
518	Nelson Liriano	.05
519	Kelly Gruber	.05
520	Greg Myers	.05
521	Pat Borders	.05
522	Junior Felix	.05
523	Eddie Zosky	.05
524	Tony Fernandez	.05
525	Checklist	.05
526	Checklist	.05
527	Checklist	.05
528	Checklist	.05

Tiffany

Reported production of fewer than 10,000 sets has created a significant premium for these glossy "Tiffany" versions of Bowman's 1990 baseball card set. The use of white cardboard stock and high-gloss front finish distinguishes these cards from regular-issue Bowmans.

	NM/M
Unopened Set (539):	200.00
Complete Set (539):	60.00
Common Player:	.25

Inserts

Bowman inserted sweepstakes cards in its 1990 packs, much like in 1989. This 11-card set features current players displayed in drawings by Craig Pursley.

	NM/M
Complete Set (11):	1.00
Common Player:	.05
(1) Will Clark	.05
(2) Mark Davis	.05
(3) Dwight Gooden	.05
(4) Bo Jackson	.10
(5) Don Mattingly	.40
(6) Kevin Mitchell	.05
(7) Gregg Olson	.05
(8) Nolan Ryan	.50
(9) Bret Saberhagen	.05
(10) Jerome Walton	.05
(11) Robin Yount	.25

1990 Bowman Lithographs

The paintings which were the basis for the sweepstakes insert cards in 1990 Bowman were also used in the creation of a set of 11" x 14" lithographs. The lithographs were offered as a prize in the sweepstakes or could be purchased from hobby dealers for a retail price in the $400-450 range.

	NM/M
Complete Set (11):	250.00
Common Player:	10.00
(1) Will Clark	10.00
(2) Mark Davis	10.00
(3) Dwight Gooden	10.00
(4) Bo Jackson	20.00
(5) Don Mattingly	50.00
(6) Kevin Mitchell	10.00
(7) Gregg Olson	10.00
(8) Nolan Ryan	100.00
(9) Bret Saberhagen	10.00
(10) Jerome Walton	10.00
(11) Robin Yount	25.00

1991 Bowman

The 1991 Bowman set features 704 cards compared to 528 cards in the 1990 issue. Bowman imitate the 1953 Bowman style. Special Rod Carew cards and gold foil-stamped cards are included. The set is numbered by teams. Like the 1989 and 1990 issues, the card backs feature a breakdown of performance against each other's team in the league.

	NM/M
Unopened Factory Set (704):	30.00
Complete Set (704):	20.00
Common Player:	.05
Wax Pack (14):	.75
Wax Box (36):	17.50
Cello Pack (29):	1.50
Cello Box (24):	25.00
1 Rod Carew-I	.10
2 Rod Carew-II	.10
3 Rod Carew-III	.10
4 Rod Carew-IV	.10
5 Rod Carew-V	.10
6 Willie Fraser	.05
7 John Olerud	.05

No	Player	Price
8	William Suero	.05
9	Roberto Alomar	.20
10	Todd Stottlemyre	.05
11	Joe Carter	.05
12	Steve Karsay RC	.10
13	Mark Whiten	.05
14	Pat Borders	.05
15	Mike Timlin	.05
16	Tom Henke	.05
17	Eddie Zosky	.05
18	Kelly Gruber	.05
19	Jimmy Key	.05
20	Jerry Schunk	.05
21	Manny Lee	.05
22	Dave Steib	.05
23	Pat Hentgen	.05
24	Glenallen Hill	.05
25	Rene Gonzales	.05
26	Ed Sprague	.05
27	Ken Dayley	.05
28	Pat Tabler	.05
29	Denis Boucher RC	.05
30	Devon White	.05
31	Dante Bichette	.05
32	Paul Molitor	.40
33	Greg Vaughn	.05
34	Dan Plesac	.05
35	Chris George	.05
36	Tim McIntosh	.05
37	Franklin Stubbs	.05
38	Bo Dodson	.05
39	Ron Robinson	.05
40	Ed Nunez	.05
41	Greg Brock	.05
42	Jaime Navarro	.05
43	Chris Bosio	.05
44	B.J. Surhoff	.05
45	Chris Johnson	.05
46	Willie Randolph	.05
47	Narciso Elvira	.05
48	Jim Gantner	.05
49	Kevin Brown	.05
50	Julio Machado	.05
51	Chuck Crim	.05
52	Gary Sheffield	.30
53	Angel Miranda	.05
54	Teddy Higuera	.05
55	Robin Yount	.40
56	Cal Eldred	.05
57	Sandy Alomar	.05
58	Greg Swindell	.05
59	Brook Jacoby	.05
60	Efrain Valdez	.05
61	Ever Magallanes	.05
62	Tom Candiotti	.05
63	Eric King	.05
64	Alex Cole	.05
65	Charles Nagy	.05
66	Mitch Webster	.05
67	Chris James	.05
68	Jim Thome RC	3.00
69	Carlos Baerga	.05
70	Mark Lewis	.05
71	Jerry Browne	.05
72	Jesse Orosco	.05
73	Mike Huff	.05
74	Jose Escobar	.05
75	Jeff Manto	.05
76	Turner Ward RC	.05
77	Doug Jones	.05
78	Bruce Egloff RC	.05
79	Tim Costo	.05
80	Beau Allred	.05
81	Albert Belle	.05
82	John Farrell	.05
83	Glenn Davis	.05
84	Joe Orsulak	.05
85	Mark Williamson	.05
86	Ben McDonald	.05
87	Billy Ripken	.05
88	Leo Gomez	.05
89	Bob Melvin	.05
90	Jeff Robinson	.05
91	Jose Mesa	.05
92	Gregg Olson	.05
93	Mike Devereaux	.05
94	Luis Mercedes	.05
95	Arthur Rhodes RC	.10
96	Juan Bell	.05
97	Mike Mussina RC	3.00
98	Jeff Ballard	.05
99	Chris Hoiles	.05
100	Brady Anderson	.05
101	Bob Milacki	.05
102	David Segui	.05
103	Dwight Evans	.05
104	Cal Ripken, Jr.	1.00
105	Mike Linskey	.05
106	Jeff Tackett RC	.05
107	Jeff Reardon	.05
108	Dana Kiecker	.05
109	Ellis Burks	.05
110	Dave Owen	.05
111	Danny Darwin	.05
112	Mo Vaughn	.05
113	Jeff McNeely	.05
114	Tom Bolton	.05
115	Greg Blosser	.05
116	Mike Greenwell	.05
117	Phil Plantier RC	.05
118	Roger Clemens	.60
119	John Marzano	.05
120	Jody Reed	.05
121	Scott Taylor	.05
122	Jack Clark	.05
123	Derek Livernois	.05
124	Tony Pena	.05
125	Tom Brunansky	.05
126	Carlos Quintana	.05
127	Tim Naehring	.05
128	Matt Young	.05
129	Wade Boggs	.50
130	Kevin Morton	.05
131	Pete Incaviglia	.05
132	Rob Deer	.05
133	Bill Gullickson	.05
134	Rico Brogna	.05
135	Lloyd Moseby	.05
136	Cecil Fielder	.05
137	Tony Phillips	.05
138	Mark Leiter	.05
139	John Cerutti	.05
140	Mickey Tettleton	.05
141	Milt Cuyler	.05
142	Greg Gohr	.05
143	Tony Bernazard	.05
144	Dan Gakeler	.05
145	Travis Fryman	.05
146	Dan Petry	.05
147	Scott Aldred	.05
148	John DeSilva	.05
149	Rusty Meacham	.05
150	Lou Whitaker	.05
151	Dave Haas	.05
152	Luis de los Santos	.05
153	Ivan Cruz	.05
154	Alan Trammell	.05
155	Pat Kelly RC	.05
156	Carl Everett RC	.25
157	Greg Cadaret	.05
158	Kevin Maas	.05
159	Jeff Johnson	.05
160	Willie Smith	.05
161	Gerald Williams	.05
162	Mike Humphreys	.05
163	Alvaro Espinoza	.05
164	Matt Nokes	.05
165	Wade Taylor	.05
166	Roberto Kelly	.05
167	John Habyan	.05
168	Steve Farr	.05
169	Jesse Barfield	.05
170	Steve Sax	.05
171	Jim Leyritz	.05
172	Robert Eenhoorn	.05
173	Bernie Williams	.05
174	Scott Lusader	.05
175	Torey Lovullo	.05
176	Chuck Cary	.05
177	Scott Sanderson	.05
178	Don Mattingly	.60
179	Mel Hall	.05
180	Juan Gonzalez	.30
181	Hensley Meulens	.05
182	Jose Offerman	.05
183	Jeff Bagwell RC	2.50
184	Jeff Conine RC	.25
185	Henry Rodriguez RC	.05
186	Jimmie Reese	.05
187	Kyle Abbott	.05
188	Lance Parrish	.05
189	Rafael Montalvo	.05
190	Floyd Bannister	.05
191	Dick Schofield	.05
192	Scott Lewis	.05
193	Jeff Robinson	.05
194	Kent Anderson	.05
195	Wally Joyner	.05
196	Chuck Finley	.05
197	Luis Sojo	.05
198	Jeff Richardson	.05
199	Dave Parker	.05
200	Jim Abbott	.05
201	Junior Felix	.05
202	Mark Langston	.05
203	Tim Salmon RC	1.00
204	Cliff Young	.05
205	Scott Bailes	.05
206	Bobby Rose	.05
207	Gary Gaetti	.05
208	Ruben Amaro	.05
209	Luis Polonia	.05
210	Dave Winfield	.40
211	Bryan Harvey	.05
212	Mike Moore	.05
213	Rickey Henderson	.40
214	Steve Chitren	.05
215	Bob Welch	.05
216	Terry Steinbach	.05
217	Ernie Riles	.05
218	Todd Van Poppel RC	.10
219	Mike Gallego	.05
220	Curt Young	.05
221	Todd Burns	.05
222	Vance Law	.05
223	Eric Show	.05
224	Don Peters RC	.05
225	Dave Stewart	.05
226	Dave Henderson	.05
227	Jose Canseco	.30
228	Walt Weiss	.05
229	Dann Howitt	.05
230	Willie Wilson	.05
231	Harold Baines	.05
232	Scott Hemond	.05
233	Joe Slusarski	.05
234	Mark McGwire	.75
235	Kirk Dressendorfer RC	.05
236	Craig Paquette RC	.05
237	Dennis Eckersley	.35
238	Dana Allison	.05
239	Scott Bradley	.05
240	Brian Holman	.05
241	Mike Schooler	.05
242	Rich Delucia	.05
243	Edgar Martinez	.05
244	Henry Cotto	.05
245	Omar Vizquel	.05
246a	Ken Griffey Jr.	.65
246b	Ken Griffey Sr. (Should be #255.)	.10
247	Jay Buhner	.05
248	Bill Krueger	.05
249	Dave Fleming RC	.05
250	Patrick Lennon RC	.05
251	Dave Valle	.05
252	Harold Reynolds	.05
253	Randy Johnson	.40
254	Scott Bankhead	.05
256	Greg Briley	.05
257	Tino Martinez	.05
258	Alvin Davis	.05
259	Pete O'Brien	.05
260	Erik Hanson	.05
261	Bret Boone	.50
262	Roger Salkeld	.05
263	Dave Burba	.05
264	Kerry Woodson RC	.05
265	Julio Franco	.05
266	Dan Peltier	.05
267	Jeff Russell	.05
268	Steve Buechele	.05
269	Donald Harris	.05
270	Robb Nen	.05
271	Rich Gossage	.05
272	Ivan Rodriguez RC	3.00
273	Jeff Huson	.05
274	Kevin Brown	.05
275	Dan Smith RC	.05
276	Gary Pettis	.05
277	Jack Daugherty	.05
278	Mike Jeffcoat	.05
279	Brad Arnsberg	.05
280	Nolan Ryan	1.00
281	Eric McCray	.05
282	Scott Chiamparino	.05
283	Ruben Sierra	.05
284	Geno Petralli	.05
285	Monty Fariss	.05
286	Rafael Palmeiro	.35
287	Bobby Witt	.05
288	Dean Palmer	.05
289	Tony Scruggs	.05
290	Kenny Rogers	.05
291	Bret Saberhagen	.05
292	Brian McRae RC	.05
293	Storm Davis	.05
294	Danny Tartabull	.05
295	David Howard	.05
296	Mike Boddicker	.05
297	Joel Johnston	.05
298	Tim Spehr	.05
299	Hector Wagner	.05
300	George Brett	.60
301	Mike Macfarlane	.05
302	Kirk Gibson	.05
303	Harvey Pulliam	.05
304	Jim Eisenreich	.05
305	Kevin Seitzer	.05
306	Mark Davis	.05
307	Kurt Stillwell	.05
308	Jeff Montgomery	.05
309	Kevin Appier	.05
310	Bob Hamelin	.05
311	Tom Gordon	.05
312	Kerwin Moore RC	.05
313	Hugh Walker	.05
314	Terry Shumpert	.05
315	Warren Cromartie	.05
316	Gary Thurman	.05
317	Steve Bedrosian	.05
318	Danny Gladden	.05
319	Jack Morris	.05
320	Kirby Puckett	.50
321	Kent Hrbek	.05
322	Kevin Tapani	.05
323	Denny Neagle	.05
324	Rich Garces	.05
325	Larry Casian	.05
326	Shane Mack	.05
327	Allan Anderson	.05
328	Junior Ortiz	.05
329	Paul Abbott RC	.05
330	Chuck Knoblauch	.05
331	Chili Davis	.05
332	Todd Ritchie RC	.05
333	Brian Harper	.05
334	Rick Aguilera	.05
335	Scott Erickson	.05
336	Pedro Munoz	.05
337	Scott Leius	.05
338	Greg Gagne	.05
339	Mike Pagliarulo	.05
340	Terry Leach	.05
341	Willie Banks	.05
342	Bobby Thigpen	.05
343	Roberto Hernandez RC	.10
344	Melido Perez	.05
345	Carlton Fisk	.40
346	Norberto Martin RC	.05
347	Johnny Ruffin RC	.05
348	Jeff Carter RC	.05
349	Lance Johnson	.05
350	Sammy Sosa	.50
351	Alex Fernandez	.05
352	Jack McDowell	.05
353	Bob Wickman	.05
354	Wilson Alvarez	.05
355	Charlie Hough	.05
356	Ozzie Guillen	.05
357	Cory Snyder	.05
358	Robin Ventura	.05
359	Scott Fletcher	.05
360	Cesar Bernhardt	.05

#	Player	Price
361	Dan Pasqua	.05
362	Tim Raines	.05
363	Brian Drahman	.05
364	Wayne Edwards	.05
365	Scott Radinsky	.05
366	Frank Thomas	.40
367	Cecil Fielder	.05
368	Julio Franco	.05
369	Kelly Gruber	.05
370	Alan Trammell	.05
371	Rickey Henderson	.30
372	Jose Canseco	.15
373	Ellis Burks	.05
374	Lance Parrish	.05
375	Dave Parker	.05
376	Eddie Murray	.30
377	Ryne Sandberg	.35
378	Matt Williams	.05
379	Barry Larkin	.05
380	Barry Bonds	.75
381	Bobby Bonilla	.05
382	Darryl Strawberry	.05
383	Benny Santiago	.05
384	Don Robinson	.05
385	Paul Coleman	.05
386	Milt Thompson	.05
387	Lee Smith	.05
388	Ray Lankford	.05
389	Tom Pagnozzi	.05
390	Ken Hill	.05
391	Jamie Moyer	.05
392	Greg Carmona RC	.05
393	John Ericks	.05
394	Bob Tewksbury	.05
395	Jose Oquendo	.05
396	Rheal Cormier	.05
397	Mike Milchin RC	.05
398	Ozzie Smith	.50
399	Aaron Holbert RC	.05
400	Jose DeLeon	.05
401	Felix Jose	.05
402	Juan Agosto	.05
403	Pedro Guerrero	.05
404	Todd Zeile	.05
405	Gerald Perry	.05
407	Bryn Smith	.05
408	Bernard Gilkey	.05
409	Rex Hudler	.05
410a	Ralph Branca, Bobby Thomson	.10
410b	Donovan Osborne	.05
411	Lance Dickson	.05
412	Danny Jackson	.05
413	Jerome Walton	.05
414	Sean Cheetham	.05
415	Joe Girardi	.05
416	Ryne Sandberg	.50
417	Mike Harkey	.05
418	George Bell	.05
419	Rick Wilkins RC	.05
420	Earl Cunningham	.05
421	Heathcliff Slocumb	.05
422	Mike Bielecki	.05
423	Jessie Hollins RC	.05
424	Shawon Dunston	.05
425	Dave Smith	.05
426	Greg Maddux	.50
427	Jose Vizcaino	.05
428	Luis Salazar	.05
429	Andre Dawson	.25
430	Rick Sutcliffe	.05
431	Paul Assenmacher	.05
432	Erik Pappas	.05
433	Mark Grace	.05
434	Denny Martinez	.05
435	Marquis Grissom	.05
436	Wil Cordero RC	.05
437	Tim Wallach	.05
438	Brian Barnes RC	.05
439	Barry Jones	.05
440	Ivan Calderon	.05
441	Stan Spencer RC	.05
442	Larry Walker	.05
443	Chris Haney RC	.05
444	Hector Rivera	.05
445	Delino DeShields	.05
446	Andres Galarraga	.05
447	Gilberto Reyes	.05
448	Willie Greene	.05
449	Greg Colbrunn	.05
450	Rondell White RC	.25
451	Steve Frey	.05
452	Shane Andrews RC	.10
453	Mike Fitzgerald	.05
454	Spike Owen	.05
455	Dave Martinez	.05
456	Dennis Boyd	.05
457	Eric Bullock	.05
458	Reid Cornelius RC	.05
459	Chris Nabholz	.05
460	David Cone	.05
461	Hubie Brooks	.05
462	Sid Fernandez	.05
463	Doug Simons RC	.05
464	Howard Johnson	.05
465	Chris Donnels	.05
466	Anthony Young	.05
467	Todd Hundley	.05
468	Rick Cerone	.05
469	Kevin Elster	.05
470	Wally Whitehurst	.05
471	Vince Coleman	.05
472	Dwight Gooden	.05
473	Charlie O'Brien	.05
474	Jeromy Burnitz RC	.50
475	John Franco	.05
476	Daryl Boston	.05
477	Frank Viola	.05

#	Player	Price
478	D.J. Dozier	.05
479	Kevin McReynolds	.05
480	Tom Herr	.05
481	Gregg Jefferies	.05
482	Pete Schourek	.05
483	Ron Darling	.05
484	Dave Magadan	.05
485	Andy Ashby RC	.05
486	Dale Murphy	.20
487	Von Hayes	.05
488	Kim Batiste RC	.05
489	Tony Longmire RC	.05
490	Wally Backman	.05
491	Jeff Jackson	.05
492	Mickey Morandini	.05
493	Darrel Akerfelds	.05
494	Ricky Jordan	.05
495	Randy Ready	.05
496	Darrin Fletcher	.05
497	Chuck Malone	.05
498	Pat Combs	.05
499	Dickie Thon	.05
500	Roger McDowell	.05
501	Len Dykstra	.05
502	Joe Boever	.05
503	John Kruk	.05
504	Terry Mulholland	.05
505	Wes Chamberlain	.05
506	Mike Lieberthal RC	.75
507	Darren Daulton	.05
508	Charlie Hayes	.05
509	John Smiley	.05
510	Gary Varsho	.05
511	Curt Wilkerson	.05
512	Orlando Merced RC	.05
513	Barry Bonds	1.00
514	Mike Lavalliere	.05
515	Doug Drabek	.05
516	Gary Redus	.05
517	William Pennyweather RC	.05
518	Randy Tomlin	.05
519	Mike Zimmerman RC	.05
520	Jeff King	.05
521	Kurt Miller RC	.05
522	Jay Bell	.05
523	Bill Landrum	.05
524	Zane Smith	.05
525	Bobby Bonilla	.05
526	Bob Walk	.05
527	Austin Manahan	.05
528	Joe Ausanio RC	.05
529	Andy Van Slyke	.05
530	Jose Lind	.05
531	Carlos Garcia RC	.05
532	Don Slaught	.05
533	Colin Powell	.25
534	Frank Bolick RC	.05
535	Gary Scott RC	.05
536	Nikco Riesgo	.05
537	Reggie Sanders RC	.25
538	Tim Howard RC	.05
539	Ryan Bowen RC	.05
540	Eric Anthony	.05
541	Jim Deshaies	.05
542	Tom Nevers	.05
543	Ken Caminiti	.05
544	Karl Rhodes	.05
545	Xavier Hernandez	.05
546	Mike Scott	.05
547	Jeff Juden	.05
548	Darryl Kile	.05
549	Willie Ansley	.05
550	Luis Gonzalez RC	1.00
551	Mike Simms RC	.05
552	Mark Portugal	.05
553	Jimmy Jones	.05
554	Jim Clancy	.05
555	Pete Harnisch	.05
556	Craig Biggio	.05
557	Eric Yelding	.05
558	Dave Rohde	.05
559	Casey Candaele	.05
560	Curt Schilling	.25
561	Steve Finley	.05
562	Javier Ortiz	.05
563	Andujar Cedeno	.05
564	Rafael Ramirez	.05
565	Kenny Lofton RC	.50
566	Steve Avery	.05
567	Lonnie Smith	.05
568	Kent Mercker	.05
569	Chipper Jones RC	6.00
570	Terry Pendleton	.05
571	Otis Nixon	.05
572	Juan Berenguer	.05
573	Charlie Leibrandt	.05
574	Dave Justice	.05
575	Keith Mitchell	.05
576	Tom Glavine	.25
577	Greg Olson	.05
578	Rafael Belliard	.05
579	Ben Rivera	.05
580	John Smoltz	.05
581	Tyler Houston	.05
582	Mark Wohlers	.05
583	Ron Gant	.05
584	Ramon Caraballo	.05
585	Sid Bream	.05
586	Jeff Treadway	.05
587	Javier Lopez RC	.75
588	Deion Sanders	.10
589	Mike Heath	.05
590	Ryan Klesko RC	.20
591	Bob Ojeda	.05
592	Alfredo Griffin	.05
593	Raul Mondesi RC	.25
594	Greg Smith	.05
595	Orel Hershiser	.05

#	Player	Price
596	Juan Samuel	.05
597	Brett Butler	.05
598	Gary Carter	.40
599	Stan Javier	.05
600	Kal Daniels	.05
601	Jamie McAndrew RC	.05
602	Mike Sharperson	.05
603	Jay Howell	.05
604	Eric Karros RC	.25
605	Tim Belcher	.05
606	Dan Opperman	.05
607	Lenny Harris	.05
608	Tom Goodwin	.05
609	Darryl Strawberry	.05
610	Ramon Martinez	.05
611	Kevin Gross	.05
612	Zakary Shinall	.05
613	Mike Scioscia	.05
614	Eddie Murray	.40
615	Ronnie Walden	.05
616	Will Clark	.05
617	Adam Hyzdu	.05
618	Matt Williams	.05
619	Don Robinson	.05
620	Jeff Brantley	.05
621	Greg Litton	.05
622	Steve Decker	.05
623	Robby Thompson	.05
624	Mark Leonard RC	.05
625	Kevin Bass	.05
626	Scott Garrelts	.05
627	Jose Uribe	.05
628	Eric Gunderson	.05
629	Steve Hosey	.05
630	Trevor Wilson	.05
631	Terry Kennedy	.05
632	Dave Righetti	.05
633	Kelly Downs	.05
634	Johnny Ard	.05
635	Eric Christopherson RC	.05
636	Kevin Mitchell	.05
637	John Burkett	.05
638	Kevin Rogers RC	.05
639	Bud Black	.05
640	Willie McGee	.05
641	Royce Clayton	.05
642	Tony Fernandez	.05
643	Ricky Bones	.05
644	Thomas Howard	.05
645	Dave Staton	.05
646	Jim Presley	.05
647	Tony Gwynn	.50
648	Marty Barrett	.05
649	Scott Coolbaugh	.05
650	Craig Lefferts	.05
651	Eddie Whitson	.05
652	Oscar Azocar	.05
653	Wes Gardner	.05
654	Bip Roberts	.05
655	Robbie Beckett RC	.05
656	Benny Santiago	.05
657	Greg W. Harris	.05
658	Jerald Clark	.05
659	Fred McGriff	.05
660	Larry Andersen	.05
661	Bruce Hurst	.05
662	Steve Martin	.05
663	Rafael Valdez	.05
664	Paul Faries RC	.05
665	Andy Benes	.05
666	Randy Myers	.05
667	Rob Dibble	.05
668	Glenn Sutko	.05
669	Glenn Braggs	.05
670	Billy Hatcher	.05
671	Joe Oliver	.05
672	Freddie Benavides	.05
673	Barry Larkin	.05
674	Chris Sabo	.05
675	Mariano Duncan	.05
676	Chris Jones RC	.05
677	Gino Minutelli RC	.05
678	Reggie Jefferson	.05
679	Jack Armstrong	.05
680	Chris Hammond	.05
681	Jose Rijo	.05
682	Bill Doran	.05
683	Terry Lee	.05
684	Tom Browning	.05
685	Paul O'Neill	.05
686	Eric Davis	.05
687	Dan Wilson RC	.05
688	Ted Power	.05
689	Tim Layana	.05
690	Norm Charlton	.05
691	Hal Morris	.05
692	Rickey Henderson	.35
693	Sam Militello RC	.05
694	Matt Mieske RC	.05
695	Paul Russo RC	.05
696	Domingo Mota RC	.05
697	Todd Guggiana RC	.05
698	Marc Newfield	.05
699	Checklist	.05
700	Checklist	.05
701	Checklist	.05
702	Checklist	.05
703	Checklist	.05
704	Checklist	.05

FRED McGRIFF

1992 Bowman

Topps introduced several changes with the release of its 1992 Bowman set. The 705-card set features 45 special insert cards stamped with gold foil. The cards are printed with a premium UV coated glossy card stock. Several players without major league experience are featured in the set. Included in this group are 1991 MVPs of the minor leagues and first round draft choices. Eighteen of the gold-foil enchanced cards have been identified as short-prints (designated SP in the listings), printed in quantities one-half the other foils.

	NM/M
Complete Set (705):	120.00
Common Player:	.10
Pack (15):	6.00
Wax Box (36):	160.00
Jumbo Pack (25):	8.00
Jumbo Box (36):	220.00

#	Player	Price
1	Ivan Rodriguez	1.25
2	Kirk McCaskill	.10
3	Scott Livingstone	.10
4	Salomon Torres RC	.50
5	Carlos Hernandez	.10
6	Dave Hollins	.10
7	Scott Fletcher	.10
8	Jorge Fabregas	.10
9	Andujar Cedeno	.10
10	Howard Johnson	.10
11	Trevor Hoffman RC	3.00
12	Roberto Kelly	.10
13	Gregg Jefferies	.10
14	Marquis Grissom	.10
15	Mike Ignasiak	.10
16	Jack Morris	.10
17	William Pennyweather	.10
18	Todd Stottlemyre	.10
19	Chito Martinez	.10
20	Roberto Alomar	.40
21	Sam Militello	.10
22	Hector Fajardo	.10
23	Paul Quantrill RC	.10
24	Chuck Knoblauch	.10
25	Reggie Jefferson	.10
26	Jeremy McGarity	.10
27	Jerome Walton	.10
28	Chipper Jones	15.00
29	Brian Barber RC	.10
30	Ron Darling	.10
31	Roberto Petagine RC	.10
32	Chuck Finley	.10
33	Edgar Martinez	.10
34	Napoleon Robinson	.10
35	Andy Van Slyke	.10
36	Bobby Thigpen	.10
37	Travis Fryman	.10
38	Eric Christopherson	.10
39	Terry Mulholland	.10
40	Darryl Strawberry	.10
41	Manny Alexander RC	.10
42	Tracey Sanders RC	.10
43	Pete Incaviglia	.10
44	Kim Batiste	.10
45	Frank Rodriguez	.10
46	Greg Swindell	.10
47	Delino DeShields	.10
48	John Ericks	.10
49	Franklin Stubbs	.10
50	Tony Gwynn	2.00
51	Clifton Garrett RC	.10
52	Mike Gardella	.10
53	Scott Erickson	.10
54	Gary Caballo	.10
55	Jose Oliva RC	.10
56	Brook Fordyce	.10
57	Mark Whiten	.10
58	Joe Slusarski	.10
59	J.R. Phillips RC	.10
60	Barry Bonds	4.00
61	Bob Milacki	.10
62	Keith Mitchell	.10
63	Angel Miranda	.10
64	Raul Mondesi	.10
65	Brian Koelling	.10
66	Brian McRae	.10
67	John Patterson	.10
68	John Wetteland	.10
69	Wilson Alvarez	.10
70	Wade Boggs	2.00
71	Darryl Ratliff	.10
72	Jeff Jackson	.10
73	Jeremy Hernandez	.10
74	Darryl Hamilton	.10
75	Rafael Belliard	.10
76	Ricky Trilcek	.10
77	Felipe Crespo RC	.10
78	Carney Lansford	.10
79	Ryan Long	.10
80	Kirby Puckett	2.00

#	Player	Price
81	Earl Cunningham	.10
82	Pedro Martinez	1.50
83	Scott Hatteberg	.10
84	Juan Gonzalez	.75
85	Robert Nutting	.10
86	Calvin Reese RC	.50
87	Dave Silvestri	.10
88	Scott Ruffcorn RC	.10
89	Rick Aguilera	.10
90	Cecil Fielder	.10
91	Kirk Dressendorfer	.10
92	Jerry DiPoto	.10
93	Mike Felder	.10
94	Craig Paquette	.10
95	Elvin Paulino	.10
96	Donovan Osborne	.10
97	Hubie Brooks	.10
98	Derek Lowe RC	4.00
99	David Zancanaro	.10
100	Ken Griffey Jr.	2.75
101	Todd Hundley	.10
102	Mike Trombley	.10
103	Ricky Gutierrez RC	.10
104	Braulio Castillo	.10
105	Craig Lefferts	.10
106	Rick Sutcliffe	.10
107	Dean Palmer	.10
108	Henry Rodriguez	.10
109	Mark Clark RC	.10
110	Kenny Lofton	.10
111	Mark Carreon	.10
112	J.T. Bruett RC	.10
113	Gerald Williams	.10
114	Frank Thomas	1.50
115	Kevin Reimer	.10
116	Sammy Sosa	2.00
117	Mickey Tettleton	.10
118	Reggie Sanders	.10
119	Trevor Wilson	.10
120	Cliff Brantley	.10
121	Spike Owen	.10
122	Jeff Montgomery	.10
123	Alex Sutherland	.10
124	Brien Taylor RC	.10
125	Brian Williams	.10
126	Kevin Seitzer	.10
127	Carlos Delgado RC	15.00
128	Gary Scott	.10
129	Scott Cooper	.10
130	Domingo Jean RC	.10
131	Pat Mahomes	.10
132	Mike Boddicker	.10
133	Roberto Hernandez	.10
134	Dave Valle	.10
135	Kurt Stillwell	.10
136	Brad Pennington RC	.10
137	Jermaine Swifton	.10
138	Ryan Hawblitzel	.10
139	Tito Navarro	.10
140	Sandy Alomar	.10
141	Todd Benzinger	.10
142	Danny Jackson	.10
143	Melvin Nieves	.25
144	Jim Campanis	.10
145	Luis Gonzalez	.10
146	Dave Doorneweerd	.10
147	Charlie Hayes	.10
148	Greg Maddux	2.00
149	Brian Harper	.10
150	Brent Miller	.10
151	Shawn Estes RC	.75
152	Mike Williams	.10
153	Charlie Hough	.10
154	Randy Myers	.10
155	Kevin Young RC	.10
156	Rick Wilkins	.10
157	Terry Schumpert	.10
158	Steve Karsay	.10
159	Gary DiSarcina	.10
160	Deion Sanders	.10
161	Tom Browning	.10
162	Dickie Thon	.10
163	Luis Mercedes	.10
164	Ricardo Ingram	.10
165	Tavo Alavarez RC	.10
166	Rickey Henderson	1.50
167	Jaime Navarro	.10
168	Billy Ashley RC	.10
169	Phil Dauphin	.10
170	Ivan Cruz	.10
171	Harold Baines	.10
172	Bryan Harvey	.10
173	Alex Cole	.10
174	Curtis Shaw	.10
175	Matt Williams	.10
176	Felix Jose	.10
177	Sam Horn	.10
178	Randy Johnson	1.50
179	Ivan Calderon	.10
180	Steve Avery	.10
181	William Suero	.10
182	Bill Swift	.10
183	Howard Battle RC	.10
184	Ruben Amaro	.10
185	Jim Abbott	.10
186	Mike Fitzgerald	.10
187	Bruce Hurst	.10
188	Jeff Juden	.10
189	Jeromy Burnitz	.10
190	Dave Burba	.10
191	Kevin Brown	.10
192	Patrick Lennon	.10
193	Jeffrey McNeely	.10
194	Wil Cordero	.10
195	Chili Davis	.10
196	Milt Cuyler	.10
197	Von Hayes	.10
198	Todd Revening RC	.10

#	Player	Price
199	Joel Johnson	.10
200	Jeff Bagwell	1.50
201	Alex Fernandez	.10
202	Todd Jones	.10
203	Charles Nagy	.10
204	Tim Raines	.10
205	Kevin Maas	.10
206	Julio Franco	.10
207	Randy Velarde	.10
208	Lance Johnson	.10
209	Scott Leius	.10
210	Derek Lee	.10
211	Joe Sondrini	.10
212	Royce Clayton	.10
213	Chris George	.10
214	Gary Sheffield	.75
215	Mark Gubicza	.10
216	Mike Moore	.10
217	Rick Huisman	.10
218	Jeff Russell	.10
219	D.J. Dozier	.10
220	Dave Martinez	.10
221	Al Newman	.10
222	Nolan Ryan	4.00
223	Teddy Higuera	.10
224	Damon Buford RC	.10
225	Ruben Sierra	.10
226	Tom Nevers	.10
227	Tommy Greene	.10
228	Nigel Wilson RC	.10
229	John DeSilva	.10
230	Bobby Witt	.10
231	Greg Cadaret	.10
232	John VanderWal	.10
233	Jack Clark	.10
234	Bill Doran	.10
235	Bobby Bonilla	.10
236	Steve Olin	.10
237	Derek Bell	.10
238	David Cone	.10
239	Victor Cole	.10
240	Rod Bolton	.10
241	Tom Pagnozzi	.10
242	Rob Dibble	.10
243	Michael Carter	.10
244	Don Peters	.10
245	Mike LaValliere	.10
246	Joe Perona	.10
247	Mitch Williams	.10
248	Jay Buhner	.10
249	Andy Benes	.10
250	Alex Ochoa RC	.10
251	Greg Blosser	.10
252	Jack Armstrong	.10
253	Juan Samuel	.10
254	Terry Pendleton	.10
255	Ramon Martinez	.10
256	Rico Brogna	.10
257	John Smiley	.10
258	Carl Everett	.10
259	Tim Salmon	.10
260	Will Clark	.10
261	Ugueth Urbina RC	.40
262	Jason Wood	.10
263	Dave Magadan	.10
264	Dante Bichette	.10
265	Jose DeLeon	.10
266	Mike Neill RC	.10
267	Paul O'Neill	.10
268	Anthony Young	.10
269	Greg Harris	.10
270	Todd Van Poppel	.10
271	Pete Castellano	.10
272	Tony Phillips	.10
273	Mike Gallego	.10
274	Steve Cooke RC	.10
275	Robin Ventura	.10
276	Kevin Mitchell	.10
277	Doug Linton	.10
278	Robert Eenhorn	.10
279	Gabe White RC	.10
280	Dave Stewart	.10
281	Mo Sanford	.10
282	Greg Perschke	.10
283	Kevin Flora	.10
284	Jeff Williams	.10
285	Keith Miller	.10
286	Andy Ashby	.10
287	Doug Dascenzo	.10
288	Eric Karros	.10
289	Glenn Murray RC	.10
290	Troy Percival RC	.10
291	Orlando Merced	.10
292	Peter Hoy	.10
293	Tony Fernandez	.10
294	Juan Guzman	.10
295	Jesse Barfield	.10
296	Sid Fernandez	.10
297	Scott Cepicky	.10
298	Garret Anderson RC	6.00
299	Cal Eldred	.10
300	Ryne Sandberg	2.00
301	Jim Gantner	.10
302	Mariano Rivera RC	25.00
303	Ron Lockett	.10
304	Jose Offerman	.10
305	Denny Martinez	.10
306	Luis Ortiz RC	.10
307	David Howard	.10
308	Russ Springer	.10
309	Chris Howard	.10
310	Kyle Abbott	.10
311	Aaron Sele RC	.10
312	Dave Justice	.10
313	Pete O'Brien	.10
314	Greg Hansell	.10
315	Dave Winfield	.10
316	Lance Dickson	.10

No.	Player	Price
317	Eric King	.10
318	Vaughn Eshelman	.10
319	Tim Belcher	.10
320	Andres Galarraga	.10
321	Scott Bullett	.10
322	Doug Strange	.10
323	Jerald Clark	.10
324	Dave Righetti	.10
325	Greg Hibbard	.10
326	Eric Dillman	.10
327	Shane Reynolds RC	.25
328	Chris Hammond	.10
329	Albert Belle	.10
330	Rich Becker RC	.10
331	Eddie Williams	.10
332	Donald Harris	.10
333	Dave Smith	.10
334	Steve Fireovid	.10
335	Steve Buechele	.10
336	Mike Schooler	.10
337	Kevin McReynolds	.10
338	Hensley Meulens	.10
339	Benji Gil RC	.10
340	Don Mattingly	2.50
341	Alvin Davis	.10
342	Alan Mills	.10
343	Kelly Downs	.10
344	Leo Gomez	.10
345	Tarrik Brock RC	.10
346	Ryan Turner	.10
347	John Smoltz	.10
348	Bill Sampen	.10
349	Paul Byrd	.10
350	Mike Bordick	.10
351	Jose Lind	.10
352	David Wells	.10
353	Barry Larkin	.10
354	Bruce Ruffin	.10
355	Luis Rivera	.10
356	Sid Bream	.10
357	Julian Vasquez	.10
358	Jason Bere RC	.10
359	Ben McDonald	.10
360	Scott Stahoviak	.10
361	Kirt Manwaring	.10
362	Jeff Johnson	.10
363	Rob Deer	.10
364	Tony Pena	.10
365	Melido Perez	.10
366	Clay Parker	.10
367	Dale Sveum	.10
368	Mike Scioscia	.10
369	Roger Salkeld	.10
370	Mike Stanley	.10
371	Jack McDowell	.10
372	Tim Wallach	.10
373	Billy Ripken	.10
374	Mike Christopher	.10
375	Paul Molitor	1.50
376	Dave Stieb	.10
377	Pedro Guerrero	.10
378	Russ Swan	.10
379	Bob Ojeda	.10
380	Donn Pall	.10
381	Eddie Zosky	.10
382	Darnell Coles	.10
383	Tom Smith	.10
384	Mark McGwire	3.00
385	Gary Carter	1.50
386	Rich Amaral	.10
387	Alan Embree	.10
388	Jonathan Hurst	.10
389	Bobby Jones RC	.10
390	Rico Rossy	.10
391	Dan Smith	.10
392	Terry Steinbach	.10
393	Jon Farrell	.10
394	Dave Anderson	.10
395	Benito Santiago	.10
396	Mark Wohlers	.10
397	Mo Vaughn	.10
398	Randy Kramer	.10
399	John Jaha RC	.10
400	Cal Ripken, Jr.	4.00
401	Ryan Bowen	.10
402	Tim McIntosh	.10
403	Bernard Gilkey	.10
404	Junior Felix	.10
405	Cris Colon	.10
406	Marc Newfield	.10
407	Bernie Williams	.10
408	Jay Howell	.10
409	Zane Smith	.10
410	Jeff Shaw	.10
411	Kerry Woodson	.10
412	Wes Chamberlain	.10
413	Dave Mlicki	.10
414	Benny Distefano	.10
415	Kevin Rogers	.10
416	Tim Naehring	.10
417	Clemente Nunez	.10
418	Luis Sojo	.10
419	Kevin Ritz	.10
420	Omar Oliveras	.10
421	Manuel Lee	.10
422	Julio Valera	.10
423	Omar Vizquel	.10
424	Darren Burton	.10
425	Mel Hall	.10
426	Dennis Powell	.10
427	Lee Stevens	.10
428	Glenn Davis	.10
429	Willie Greene	.10
430	Kevin Wickander	.10
431	Dennis Eckersley	1.25
432	Joe Orsulak	.10
433	Eddie Murray	1.50
434	Matt Stairs RC	.10
435	Wally Joyner	.10
436	Rondell White	.10
437	Rob Mauer	.10
438	Joe Redfield	.10
439	Mark Lewis	.10
440	Darren Daulton	.10
441	Mike Henneman	.10
442	John Cangelosi	.10
443	Vince Moore RC	.10
444	John Wehner	.10
445	Kent Hrbek	.10
446	Mark McLemore	.10
447	Bill Wegman	.10
448	Robby Thompson	.10
449	Mark Anthony	.10
450	Archi Cianfrocco	.10
451	Johnny Ruffin	.10
452	Javier Lopez	.10
453	Greg Gohr	.10
454	Tim Scott	.10
455	Stan Belinda	.10
456	Darrin Jackson	.10
457	Chris Gardner	.10
458	Esteban Beltre	.10
459	Phil Plantier	.10
460	Jim Thome	1.25
461	Mike Piazza RC	25.00
462	Matt Sinatro	.10
463	Scott Servais	.10
464	Brian Jordan RC	.75
465	Doug Drabek	.10
466	Carl Willis	.10
467	Bret Barbarie	.10
468	Hal Morris	.10
469	Steve Sax	.10
470	Jerry Willard	.10
471	Dan Wilson	.10
472	Chris Hoiles	.10
473	Rheal Cormier	.10
474	John Morris	.10
475	Jeff Reardon	.10
476	Mark Leiter	.10
477	Tom Gordon	.10
478	Kent Bottenfield RC	.10
479	Gene Larkin	.10
480	Dwight Gooden	.10
481	B.J. Surhoff	.10
482	Andy Stankiewicz	.10
483	Tino Martinez	.10
484	Craig Biggio	.10
485	Denny Neagle	.10
486	Rusty Meacham	.10
487	Kal Daniels	.10
488	Dave Henderson	.10
489	Tim Costo	.10
490	Doug Davis	.10
491	Frank Viola	.10
492	Cory Snyder	.10
493	Chris Martin	.10
494	Dion James	.10
495	Randy Tomlin	.10
496	Greg Vaughn	.10
497	Dennis Cook	.10
498	Rosario Rodriguez	.10
499	Dave Staton	.10
500	George Brett	2.50
501	Brian Barnes	.10
502	Butch Henry	.10
503	Harold Reynolds	.10
504	David Nied RC	.10
505	Lee Smith	.10
506	Steve Chitren	.10
507	Ken Hill	.10
508	Robbie Beckett	.10
509	Troy Afenir	.10
510	Kelly Gruber	.10
511	Bret Boone	.10
512	Jeff Branson	.10
513	Mike Jackson	.10
514	Pete Harnisch	.10
515	Chad Kreuter	.10
516	Joe Vitko	.10
517	Orel Hershiser	.10
518	John Doherty RC	.10
519	Jay Bell	.10
520	Mark Langston	.10
521	Dann Howitt	.10
522	Bobby Reed	.10
523	Roberto Munoz	.10
524	Todd Ritchie	.10
525	Bip Roberts	.10
526	Pat Listach RC	.10
527	Scott Brosius RC	.10
528	John Roper RC	.10
529	Phil Hiatt RC	.10
530	Denny Walling	.10
531	Carlos Baerga	.10
532	Manny Ramirez RC	25.00
533	Pat Clements	.10
534	Ron Gant	.10
535	Pat Kelly	.10
536	Billy Spiers	.10
537	Darren Reed	.10
538	Ken Caminiti	.10
539	Butch Huskey RC	.10
540	Matt Nokes	.10
541	John Kruk	.10
542	John Jaha/SP (Foil)	.40
543	Justin Thompson RC	.10
544	Steve Hosey	.10
545	Joe Kmak	.10
546	John Franco	.10
547	Devon White	.10
548	Elston Hansen/SP (Foil)	.40
549	Ryan Klesko	.10
550	Danny Tartabull	.10
551	Frank Thomas/SP (Foil)	1.50
552	Kevin Tapani	.10
553a	Willie Banks	.10
553b	Pat Clements	.10
554	B.J. Wallace RC/SP (Foil)	.40
555	Orlando Miller RC	.10
556	Mark Smith RC	.10
557	Tim Wallach (Foil)	.10
558	Bill Gullickson	.10
559	Derek Bell (Foil)	.10
560	Joe Randa (Foil)	.10
561	Frank Seminara	.10
562	Mark Gardner	.10
563	Rick Greene (Foil)	.10
564	Gary Gaetti	.10
565	Ozzie Guillen	.10
566	Charles Nagy (Foil)	.10
567	Mike Milchin	.10
568	Ben Shelton	.10
569	Chris Roberts (Foil)	.10
570	Ellis Burks	.10
571	Scott Scudder	.10
572	Jim Abbott (Foil)	.10
573	Joe Carter	.10
574	Steve Finley	.10
575	Jim Olander (Foil)	.10
576	Carlos Garcia	.10
577	Greg Olson	.10
578	Greg Swindell (Foil)	.10
579	Matt Williams (Foil)	.10
580	Mark Grace	.10
581	Howard House (Foil)	.10
582	Luis Polonia	.10
583	Erik Hanson	.10
584	Salomon Torres (Foil)	.10
585	Carlton Fisk	1.50
586	Bret Saberhagen	.10
587	Chad McDonnell RC (Foil)	.10
588	Jimmy Key	.10
589	Mike MacFarlane	.10
590	Barry Bonds (Foil)	3.50
591	Jamie McAndrew	.10
592	Shane Mack	.10
593	Kerwin Moore	.10
594	Joe Oliver	.10
595	Chris Sabo	.10
596	Alex Gonzalez RC	.50
597	Brett Butler	.10
598	Mark Hutton	.10
599	Andy Benes (Foil)	.10
600	Jose Canseco	.75
601	Darryl Kile	.10
602	Matt Stairs/SP (Foil)	.40
603	Rob Butler (Foil)	.10
604	Willie McGee	.10
605	Jack McDowell	.10
606	Tom Candiotti	.10
607	Ed Martel	.10
608	Matt Mieske (Foil)	.10
609	Darrin Fletcher	.10
610	Rafael Palmeiro	1.25
611	Bill Swift (Foil)	.10
612	Mike Mussina	.75
613	Vince Coleman	.10
614	Scott Cepicky (Foil)	.10
615	Mike Greenwell	.10
616	Kevin McGehee	.10
617	Jeffrey Hammonds (Foil)	.10
618	Scott Taylor	.10
619	Dave Otto	.10
620	Mark McGwire (Foil)	3.00
621	Kevin Tatar	.10
622	Steve Farr	.10
623	Ryan Klesko (Foil)	.10
624	Andre Dawson	.40
625	Tino Martinez/SP (Foil)	.50
626	Chad Curtis RC	.50
627	Mickey Morandini	.10
628	Gregg Olson/SP (Foil)	.40
629	Lou Whitaker	.10
630	Arthur Rhodes	.10
631	Brandon Wilson	.10
632	Lance Jennings RC	.10
633	Allen Watson RC	.10
634	Len Dykstra	.10
635	Joe Girardi	.10
636	Kiki Hernandez/SP (Foil)	.40
637	Mike Hampton RC	1.00
638	Al Osuna	.10
639	Kevin Appier	.10
640	Rick Helling/SP (Foil)	.40
641	Jody Reed	.10
642	Ray Lankford	.10
643	John Olerud	.10
644	Paul Molitor/SP (Foil)	1.50
645	Pat Borders	.10
646	Mike Morgan	.10
647	Larry Walker	.10
648	Pete Castellano/SP (Foil)	.40
649	Fred McGriff	.10
650	Walt Weiss	.10
651	Calvin Murray RC/SP (Foil)	.40
652	Dave Nilsson	.10
653	Greg Pirkl	.10
654	Robin Ventura/SP (Foil)	.40
655	Mark Portugal	.10
656	Roger McDowell	.10
657	Rick Hirtensteiner/SP (Foil)	.10
658	Glenallen Hill	.10
659	Greg Gagne	.10
660	Charles Johnson/SP (Foil)	.40
661	Brian Hunter	.10
662	Mark Lemke	.10
663	Tim Belcher/SP (Foil)	.40
664	Rich DeLucia	.10
665	Bob Walk	.10
666	Joe Carter/SP (Foil)	.40
667	Jose Guzman	.10
668	—	
669	Otis Nixon	.10
670	Phil Nevin (Foil)	.10
671	Eric Davis	.10
672	Damion Easley RC	.25
673	Will Clark (Foil)	.10
674	Mark Kiefer	.10
675	Ozzie Smith	2.00
676	Manny Ramirez (Foil)	15.00
677	Gregg Olson	.10
678	Cliff Floyd RC	1.00
679	Duane Singleton	.10
680	Jose Rijo	.10
681	Willie Randolph	.10
682	Michael Tucker RC (Foil)	.25
683	Darren Lewis	.10
684	Dale Murphy	.50
685	Mike Pagliarulo	.10
686	Paul Miller	.10
687	Mike Robertson	.10
688	Mike Devereaux	.10
689	Pedro Astacio	.10
690	Alan Trammell	.10
691	Roger Clemens	2.50
692	Bud Black	.10
693	Turk Wendell	.10
694	Barry Larkin/SP (Foil)	.75
695	Todd Zeile	.10
696	Pat Hentgen	.10
697	Eddie Taubensee RC	.10
698	Guillermo Vasquez	.10
699	Tom Glavine	.75
700	Robin Yount	1.50
701	Checklist	.10
702	Checklist	.10
703	Checklist	.10
704	Checklist	.10
705	Checklist	.10

1993 Bowman

CHIPPER JONES

Bowman's 708-card 1993 set once again features a premium UV-coated glossy stock. There are also 48 special insert cards, with gold foil stamping, randomly inserted one per pack or two per jumbo pack. The foil cards, numbered 339-374 and 693-704, feature top prospects and rookie-of-the-year candidates, as do several regular cards in the set. Cards are standard size.

	NM/M
Complete Set (708):	35.00
Common Player:	.10
Pack (15):	1.50
Wax Box (24):	35.00
Jumbo Pack (22):	2.50
Jumbo Box (20):	40.00

No.	Player	Price
1	Glenn Davis	.10
2	Hector Roa RC	.10
3	Ken Ryan RC	.10
4	Derek Wallace RC	.10
5	Jorge Fabregas	.10
6	Joe Oliver	.10
7	Brandon Wilson	.10
8	Mark Thompson RC	.10
9	Tracy Sanders	.10
10	Rich Renteria	.10
11	Lou Whitaker	.10
12	Brian Hunter RC	.10
13	Joe Vitiello	.10
14	Eric Karros	.10
15	Joe Kmak	.10
16	Tavo Alvarez	.10
17	Steve Dunn RC	.10
18	Tony Fernandez	.10
19	Melido Perez	.10
20	Mike Lieberthal	.10
21	Terry Steinbach	.10
22	Stan Belinda	.10
23	Jay Buhner	.10
24	Allen Watson	.10
25	Daryl Henderson RC	.10
26	Ray McDavid RC	.10
27	Shawn Green	.30
28	Bud Black	.10
29	Sherman Obando RC	.10
30	Mike Hostetler RC	.10
31	Nate Hinchey RC	.10
32	Randy Myers	.10
33	Brian Grebeck RC	.10
34	John Roper	.10
35	Larry Thomas	.10
36	Alex Cole	.10
37	Tom Kramer RC	.10
38	Matt Whisenant RC	.10
39	Chris Gomez RC	.10
40	Luis Gonzalez	.10
41	Kevin Appier	.10
42	Omar Daal RC	.10
43	Duane Singleton	.10
44	Bill Risley	.10
45	Pat Meares RC	.10
46	Butch Huskey	.10
47	Bobby Munoz	.10
48	Juan Bell	.10
49	Scott Lydy RC	.10
50	Dennis Moeller	.10
51	Marc Newfield	.10
52	Tripp Cromer RC	.10
53	Kurt Miller	.10
54	Jim Pena	.10
55	Juan Guzman	.10
56	Matt Williams	.10
57	Harold Reynolds	.10
58	Donnie Elliott RC	.10
59	Jon Shave RC	.10
60	Kevin Roberson RC	.10
61	Hilly Hathaway RC	.10
62	Jose Rijo	.10
63	Kerry Taylor RC	.10
64	Ryan Hawblitzel	.10
65	Glenallen Hill	.10
66	Ramon D. Martinez RC	.10
67	Travis Fryman	.10
68	Tom Nevers	.10
69	Phil Hiatt	.10
70	Tim Wallach	.10
71	B.J. Surhoff	.10
72	Rondell White	.10
73	Denny Hocking RC	.10
74	Mike Oquist RC	.10
75	Paul O'Neill	.10
76	Willie Banks	.10
77	Bob Welch	.10
78	Jose Sandoval RC	.10
79	Bill Haselman	.10
80	Rheal Cormier	.10
81	Dean Palmer	.10
82	Pat Gomez RC	.10
83	Steve Karsay	.10
84	Carl Hanselman RC	.10
85	T.R. Lewis RC	.10
86	Chipper Jones	2.00
87	Scott Hatteberg	.10
88	Greg Hibbard	.10
89	Lance Painter RC	.10
90	Chad Mottola RC	.10
91	Jason Bere	.10
92	Dante Bichette	.10
93	Sandy Alomar	.10
94	Carl Everett RC	.10
95	Danny Bautista RC	.10
96	Steve Finley	.10
97	David Cone	.10
98	Todd Hollandsworth	.10
99	Matt Mieske	.10
100	Larry Walker	.10
101	Shane Mack	.10
102	Aaron Ledesma RC	.10
103	Andy Pettitte RC	4.00
104	Kevin Stocker	.10
105	Mike Mobles	.10
106	Tony Menedez	.10
107	Derek Lowe	.10
108	Basil Shabazz	.10
109	Dan Smith	.10
110	Scott Sanders RC	.10
111	Todd Stottlemyre	.10
112	Benji Sikonton RC	.10
113	Rick Sutcliffe	.10
114	Lee Heath RC	.10
115	Jeff Russell	.10
116	Dave Stevens RC	.10
117	Mark Holzemer RC	.10
118	Tim Belcher	.10
119	Bobby Thigpen	.10
120	Roger Bailey RC	.10
121	Tony Mitchell RC	.10
122	Junior Felix	.10
123	Rich Robertson RC	.10
124	Andy Cook RC	.10
125	Brian Bevil RC	.10
126	Darryl Strawberry	.10
127	Cal Eldred	.10
128	Cliff Floyd	.10
129	Alan Newman	.10
130	Howard Johnson	.10
131	Jim Abbott	.10
132	Chad McConnell	.10
133	Miguel Jimenez RC	.10
134	Brett Backlund RC	.10
135	John Cummings RC	.10
136	Brian Barber	.10
137	Rafael Palmeiro	1.25
138	Tim Worrell RC	.10
139	Jose Pett RC	.10
140	Barry Bonds	4.00
141	Damon Buford	.10
142	Jeff Blauser	.10
143	Frankie Rodriguez	.10
144	Mike Morgan	.10
145	Gary DeSarcina	.10
146	Calvin Reese	.10
147	Johnny Ruffin	.10
148	David Nied	.10
149	Charles Nagy	.10
150	Mike Myers RC	.10
151	Kenny Carlyle RC	.10
152	Eric Anthony	.10
153	Jose Lind	.10
154	Pedro Martinez	1.50
155	Mark Kiefer	.10
156	Tim Laker RC	.10
157	Pat Mahomes	.10
158	Bobby Bonilla	.10
159	Domingo Jean	.10
160	Darren Daulton	.10
161	Mark McGwire	3.50
162	Jason Kendall RC	1.00
163	Desi Relaford	.10
164	Ozzie Canseco	.10
165	Rick Helling	.10
166	Steve Pegues RC	.10
167	Paul Molitor	1.50
168	Larry Carter RC	.10
169	Arthur Rhodes	.10
170	Damon Hollins RC	.10
171	Frank Viola	.10
172	Steve Trachsel RC	.25
173	J.T. Snow RC	.50
174	Keith Gordon RC	.10
175	Carlton Fisk	1.50
176	Jason Bates RC	.10
177	Mike Crosby RC	.10
178	Benny Santiago	.10
179	Mike Moore	.10
180	Jeff Juden	.10
181	Darren Burton	.10
182	Todd Williams RC	.10
183	John Jaha	.10
184	Mike Lansing RC	.50
185	Pedro Grifol RC	.10
186	Vince Coleman	.10
187	Pat Kelly	.10
188	Clemente Alvarez RC	.10
189	Ron Darling	.10
190	Orlando Merced	.10
191	Chris Bosio	.10
192	Steve Dixon RC	.10
193	Doug Dascenzo	.10
194	Ray Holbert RC	.10
195	Howard Battle	.10
196	Willie McGee	.10
197	John O'Donoghue RC	.10
198	Steve Avery	.10
199	Greg Blosser	.10
200	Ryne Sandberg	2.00
201	Joe Grahe	.10
202	Dan Wilson	.10
203	Domingo Martinez RC	.10
204	Andres Galarraga	.10
205	Jamie Taylor RC	.10
206	Darrell Whitmore RC	.10
207	Ben Blomdahl RC	.10
208	Doug Drabek	.10
209	Keith Miller	.10
210	Billy Ashley	.10
211	Mike Farrell RC	.10
212	John Wetteland	.10
213	Randy Tomlin	.10
214	Sid Fernandez	.10
215	Quilvio Veras RC	.10
216	Dave Hollins	.10
217	Mike Neill	.10
218	Andy Van Slyke	.10
219	Bret Boone	.10
220	Tom Pagnozzi	.10
221	Mike Welch RC	.10
222	Frank Seminara	.10
223	Ron Villone	.10
224	D.J. Thielen RC	.10
225	Cal Ripken, Jr.	4.00
226	Pedro Borbon RC	.10
227	Carlos Quintana	.10
228	Tommy Shields RC	.10
229	Tim Salmon	.10
230	John Smiley	.10
231	Ellis Burks	.10
232	Pedro Castellano	.10
233	Paul Byrd	.10
234	Bryan Harvey	.10
235	Scott Livingstone	.10
236	James Mouton RC	.10
237	Joe Randa	.10
238	Pedro Astacio	.10
239	Darryl Hamilton	.10
240	Joey Eischen RC	.10
241	Edgar Herrera RC	.10
242	Dwight Gooden	.10
243	Sam Militello	.10
244	Ron Blazier RC	.10
245	Ruben Sierra	.10
246	Al Martin	.10
247	Mike Felder	.10
248	Bob Tewksbury	.10
249	Craig Lefferts	.10
250	Luis Lopez	.10
251	Devon White	.10
252	Will Clark	.10
253	Mark Smith	.10
254	Terry Pendleton	.10
255	Aaron Sele	.10
256	Jose Viera RC	.10
257	Damion Easley	.10
258	Rod Lofton RC	.10
259	Chris Snopek RC	.10
260	Quinton McCracken RC	.10
261	Mike Matthews RC	.10
262	Hector Carrasco RC	.10
263	Rick Greene	.10
264	Chris Bolt RC	.10
265	George Brett	2.50
266	Rick Gorecki RC	.10
267	Francisco Gamez RC	.10
268	Marquis Grissom	.10
269	Kevin Tapani	.10
270	Ryan Thompson	.10
271	Gerald Williams	.10
272	Paul Fletcher RC	.10
273	Lance Blankenship	.10
274	Marty Pett RC	.10
275	Shawn Estes	.10

#	Player	Price
276	Rene Arocha RC	.10
277	Scott Evre RC	.10
278	Phil Plantier	.10
279	Paul Spoljaric RC	.10
280	Chris Gahbs	.10
281	Harold Baines	.10
282	Jose Oliva RC	.10
283	Matt Whiteside	.10
284	Brant Brown RC	.10
285	Russ Springer RC	.10
286	Chris Sabo	.10
287	Ozzie Guillen	.10
288	Marcus Moore RC	.10
289	Chad Ogea	.10
290	Walt Weiss	.10
291	Brian Edmondson	.10
292	Jimmy Gonzalez	.10
293	Danny Miceli RC	.10
294	Jose Offerman	.10
295	Greg Vaughn	.10
296	Frank Bolick	.10
297	Mike Maksudian RC	.10
298	John Franco	.10
299	Danny Tartabull	.10
300	Len Dykstra	.10
301	Bobby Witt	.10
302	Trey Beamon RC	.10
303	Tino Martinez	.10
304	Aaron Holbert	.10
305	Juan Gonzalez	.75
306	Billy Hall RC	.10
307	Duane Ward	.10
308	Rod Beck	.10
309	Jose Mercedes RC	.10
310	Otis Nixon	.10
311	Gettys Glaze RC	.10
312	Candy Maldonado	.10
313	Chad Curtis	.10
314	Tim Costo	.10
315	Mike Robertson	.10
316	Nigel Wilson	.10
317	Greg McMichael RC	.10
318	Scott Pose RC	.10
319	Ivan Cruz	.10
320	Greg Swindell	.10
321	Kevin McReynolds	.10
322	Tom Candiotti	.10
323	Bob Wishnevski RC	.10
324	Ken Hill	.10
325	Kirby Puckett	2.00
326	Tim Bogar RC	.10
327	Mariano Rivera	.30
328	Mitch Williams	.10
329	Craig Paquette	.10
330	Jay Bell	.10
331	Jose Martinez RC	.10
332	Rob Deer	.10
333	Brook Fordyce	.10
334	Matt Nokes	.10
335	Derek Lee	.10
336	Paul Ellis RC	.10
337	Desi Wilson RC	.10
338	Roberto Alomar	.30
339	Jim Tatum (Foil)	.10
340	J.T. Snow (Foil)	.10
341	Tim Salmon (Foil)	.10
342	Russ Davis RC (Foil)	.25
343	Javier Lopez (Foil)	.10
344	Troy O'Leary RC (Foil)	.10
345	Marty Cordova RC (Foil)	.60
346	Bubba Smith RC (Foil)	.10
347	Chipper Jones (Foil)	1.50
348	Jessie Hollins (Foil)	.10
349	Willie Greene (Foil)	.10
350	Mark Thompson (Foil)	.10
351	Nigel Wilson (Foil)	.10
352	Todd Jones (Foil)	.10
353	Raul Mondesi (Foil)	.10
354	Cliff Floyd (Foil)	.10
355	Bobby Jones (Foil)	.10
356	Kevin Stocker (Foil)	.10
357	Midre Cummings (Foil)	.10
358	Allen Watson (Foil)	.10
359	Ray McDavid (Foil)	.10
360	Steve Hosey (Foil)	.10
361	Brad Pennington (Foil)	.10
362	Frankie Rodriguez (Foil)	.10
363	Troy Percival (Foil)	.10
364	Jason Bere (Foil)	.10
365	Manny Ramirez (Foil)	.75
366	Justin Thompson (Foil)	.10
367	Joe Vitello (Foil)	.10
368	Tyrone Hill (Foil)	.10
369	David McCarty (Foil)	.10
370	Brien Taylor (Foil)	.10
371	Todd Van Poppel (Foil)	.10
372	Marc Newfield (Foil)	.10
373	Terrell Lowery RC (Foil)	.10
374	Alex Gonzalez (Foil)	.10
375	Ken Griffey Jr.	3.00
376	Donovan Osborne	.10
377	Ritchie Moody RC	.10
378	Shane Andrews	.10
379	Carlos Delgado	.65
380	Bill Swift	.10
381	Leo Gomez	.10
382	Ron Gant	.10
383	Scott Fletcher	.10
384	Matt Walbeck RC	.10
385	Chuck Finley	.10
386	Kevin Mitchell	.10
387	Wilson Alvarez	.10
388	John Burke RC	.10
389	Alan Embree	.10
390	Trevor Hoffman	.10
391	Alan Trammell	.10
392	Todd Jones	.10
393	Felix Jose	.10
394	Orel Hershiser	.10
395	Pat Listach	.10
396	Gabe White	.10
397	Dan Serafini RC	.10
398	Todd Hundley	.10
399	Wade Boggs	2.00
400	Tyler Green	.10
401	Mike Bordick	.10
402	Scott Bullett	.10
403	Lagrande Russell RC	.10
404	Ray Lankford	.10
405	Nolan Ryan	4.00
406	Robbie Beckett	.10
407	Brent Bowers RC	.10
408	Adell Davenport RC	.10
409	Brady Anderson	.10
410	Tom Glavine	.35
411	Doug Hecker RC	.10
412	Jose Guzman	.10
413	Luis Polonia	.10
414	Brian Williams	.10
415	Bo Jackson	.15
416	Eric Young	.10
417	Kenny Lofton	.10
418	Orestes Destrade	.10
419	Tony Phillips	.10
420	Jeff Bagwell	1.50
421	Hark Gardner	.10
422	Brett Butler	.10
423	Graeme Lloyd RC	.10
424	Delino DeShields	.10
425	Scott Erickson	.10
426	Jeff Kent	.10
427	Jimmy Key	.10
428	Mickey Morandini	.10
429	Marcos Arkas RC	.10
430	Don Slaught	.10
431	Randy Johnson	1.50
432	Omar Olivares	.10
433	Charlie Leibrandt	.10
434	Kurt Stillwell	.10
435	Scott Brow RC	.10
436	Robby Thompson	.10
437	Ben McDonald	.10
438	Deion Sanders	.10
439	Tony Pena	.10
440	Mark Grace	.10
441	Eduardo Perez	.10
442	Tim Pugh RC	.10
443	Scott Ruffcorn	.10
444	Jay Gainer RC	.10
445	Albert Belle	.10
446	Bret Barberie	.10
447	Justin Mashore	.10
448	Pete Harnisch	.10
449	Greg Gagne	.10
450	Eric Davis	.10
451	Dave Mlicki	.10
452	Moises Alou	.10
453	Rick Aguilera	.10
454	Eddie Murray	1.50
455	Bob Wickman	.10
456	Wes Chamberlain	.10
457	Brent Gates	.10
458	Paul Weber	.10
459	Mike Hampton	.10
460	Ozzie Smith	2.00
461	Tom Henke	.10
462	Ricky Gutuerrez	.10
463	Jack Morris	.10
464	Joel Chimelis RC	.10
465	Gregg Olson	.10
466	Javier Lopez	.10
467	Scott Cooper	.10
468	Willie Wilson	.10
469	Mark Langston	.10
470	Barry Larkin	.10
471	Rod Bolton	.10
472	Freddie Benavides	.10
473	Ken Ramos RC	.10
474	Chuck Carr	.10
475	Cecil Fielder	.10
476	Eddie Taubensee	.10
477	Chris Eddy RC	.10
478	Greg Hansell	.10
479	Kevin Reimer	.10
480	Denny Martinez	.10
481	Chuck Knoblauch	.10
482	Mike Draper	.10
483	Spike Owen	.10
484	Terry Mulholland	.10
485	Dennis Eckersley	1.25
486	Blas Minor	.10
487	Dave Fleming	.10
488	Dan Cholonsky RC	.10
489	Ivan Rodriguez	1.25
490	Gary Sheffield	.45
491	Ed Sprague	.10
492	Steve Hosey	.10
493	Jimmy Haynes RC	.10
494	John Smoltz	.10
495	Andre Dawson	.35
496	Rey Sanchez	.10
497	Ty Van Burkleo RC	.10
498	Bobby Ayala RC	.10
499	Tim Raines	.10
500	Charlie Hayes	.10
501	Paul Sorrento	.10
502	Richie Lewis RC	.10
503	Jason Pfaff RC	.10
504	Ken Caminiti	.10
505	Mike Macfarlane	.10
506	Jody Reed	.10
507	Bobby Hughes RC	.10
508	Wil Cordero	.10
509	George Tsanis RC	.10
510	Bret Saberhagen	.10
511	Derek Jeter RC	20.00
512	Gene Schall	.10
513	Curtis Shaw	.10
514	Steve Cooke	.10
515	Edgar Martinez	.10
516	Mike Milchin	.10
517	Billy Ripken	.10
518	Andy Benes	.10
519	Juan de la Rosa RC	.10
520	John Burkett	.10
521	Alex Ochoa	.10
522	Tony Tarasco RC	.10
523	Luis Ortiz	.10
524	Rick Williams	.10
525	Chris Turner RC	.10
526	Rob Dibble	.10
527	Jack McDowell	.10
528	Daryl Boston	.10
529	Bill Wertz	.10
530	Charlie Hough	.10
531	Sean Bergman	.10
532	Doug Jones	.10
533	Jeff Montgomery	.10
534	Roger Cedeno RC	.25
535	Robin Yount	1.50
536	Mo Vaughn	.10
537	Brian Harper	.10
538	Juan Castillo	.10
539	Steve Farr	.10
540	John Kruk	.10
541	Troy Neel	.10
542	Danny Clyburn RC	.10
543	Jim Converse RC	.10
544	Gregg Jefferies	.10
545	Jose Canseco	.40
546	Julio Bruno RC	.10
547	Rob Butler	.10
548	Royce Clayton	.10
549	Chris Hoiles	.10
550	Greg Maddux	2.00
551	Joe Ciccarella RC	.10
552	Ozzie Timmons	.10
553	Chili Davis	.10
554	Brian Koelling	.10
555	Frank Thomas	1.50
556	Vinny Castilla	.10
557	Reggie Jefferson	.10
558	Rob Natal	.10
559	Mike Henneman	.10
560	Craig Biggio	.10
561	Billy Brewer RC	.10
562	Dan Melendez	.10
563	Kenny Felder RC	.10
564	Miguel Batista RC	.10
565	Dave Winfield	1.50
566	Al Shirley	.10
567	Robert Eenhoorn	.10
568	Mike Williams	.10
569	Tanyon Sturtze RC	.10
570	Tim Wakefield	.10
571	Greg Pirkl	.10
572	Sean Lowe RC	.25
573	Terry Burows RC	.10
574	Kevin Higgins RC	.10
575	Joe Carter	.10
576	Kevin Rogers	.10
577	Manny Alexander	.10
578	Dave Justice	.10
579	Brian Conroy RC	.10
580	Jessie Hollins RC	.10
581	Ron Watson RC	.10
582	Bip Roberts	.10
583	Tom Urbani RC	.10
584	Jason Hutchins RC	.10
585	Carlos Baerga	.10
586	Jeff Mutis	.10
587	Justin Thompson	.10
588	Orlando Miller	.10
589	Brian McRae	.10
590	Ramon Martinez	.10
591	Dave Nilsson	.10
592	Jose Vidro RC	1.50
593	Rich Becker	.10
594	Preston Wilson RC	1.50
595	Don Mattingly	2.50
596	Tony Longmire	.10
597	Kevin Seitzer	.10
598	Midre Cummings RC	.10
599	Omar Vizquel	.10
600	Lee Smith	.10
601	David Hulse RC	.10
602	Darrell Sherman RC	.10
603	Alex Gonzalez	.10
604	Geronimo Pena	.10
605	Mike Devereaux	.10
606	Sterling Hitchcock RC	.25
607	Mike Greenwell	.10
608	Steve Buechele	.10
609	Troy Percival	.10
610	Bobby Kelly	.10
611	James Baldwin RC	.10
612	Jerald Clark	.10
613	Albie Lopez RC	.10
614	Dave Magadan	.10
615	Mickey Tettleton	.10
616	Sean Runyan RC	.10
617	Bob Hamelin	.10
618	Raul Mondesi	.10
619	Tyrone Hill	.10
620	Darrin Fletcher	.10
621	Mike Trombley	.10
622	Jeromy Burnitz	.10
623	Bernie Williams	.10
624	Mike Farmer RC	.10
625	Rickey Henderson	1.50
626	Carlos Garcia	.10
627	Jeff Darwin RC	.10
628	Todd Zeile	.10
629	Benji Gil	.10
630	Tony Gwynn	2.00
631	Aaron Small RC	.10
632	Joe Rosselli RC	.10
633	Mike Mussina	1.00
634	Ryan Klesko	.10
635	Roger Clemens	2.50
636	Sammy Sosa	2.00
637	Orlando Palmeiro RC	.10
638	Willie Greene	.10
639	George Bell	.10
640	Garvin Alston RC	.10
641	Pete Janicki RC	.10
642	Chris Sheff RC	.10
643	Felipe Lira RC	.10
644	Roberto Petagine RC	.10
645	Wally Joyner	.10
646	Mike Piazza	3.00
647	Jaime Navarro	.10
648	Jeff Hartsock RC	.10
649	David McCarty	.10
650	Bobby Jones	.10
651	Mark Hutton	.10
652	Kyle Abbott	.10
653	Steve Cox RC	.10
654	Jeff King	.10
655	Norm Charlton	.10
656	Mike Gulan RC	.10
657	Julio Franco	.10
658	Cameron Cairncross RC	.10
659	John Olerud	.10
660	Salomon Torres	.10
661	Brad Pennington	.10
662	Melvin Nieves	.10
663	Ivan Calderon	.10
664	Turk Wendell	.10
665	Chris Pritchett	.10
666	Reggie Sanders	.10
667	Robin Ventura	.10
668	Joe Girardi	.10
669	Manny Ramirez	1.50
670	Jeff Conine	.10
671	Greg Gohr	.10
672	Andujar Cedeno	.10
673	Les Norman RC	.10
674	Mike James RC	.10
675	Marshall Boze RC	.10
676	B.J. Wallace	.10
677	Kent Hrbek	.10
678	Jack Voight	.10
679	Brien Taylor	.10
680	Curt Schilling	.35
681	Todd Van Poppel	.10
682	Kevin Young	.10
683	Tommy Adams	.10
684	Bernard Gilkey	.10
685	Kevin Brown	.10
686	Fred McGriff	.10
687	Pat Borders	.10
688	Kirt Manwaring	.10
689	Sid Bream	.10
690	John Valentin	.10
691	Steve Olsen RC	.10
692	Roberto Mejia RC	.10
693	Carlos Delgado (Foil)	.50
694	Steve Gibralter RC (Foil)	.10
695	Gary Mota (Foil)	.10
696	Jose Malave RC (Foil)	.10
697	Larry Sutton RC (Foil)	.10
698	Dan Frye RC (Foil)	.10
699	Tim Clark RC (Foil)	.10
700	Brian Rupp RC (Foil)	.10
701	Felipe Alou, Moises Alou (Foil)	.10
702	Bobby Bonds, Barry Bonds (Foil)	1.00
703	Ken Griffey Sr., Ken Griffey Jr. (Foil)	1.00
704	Hal McRae, Brian McRae (Foil)	.10
705	Checklist 1	.10
706	Checklist 2	.10
707	Checklist 3	.10
708	Checklist 4	.10

1994 Bowman Previews

Bowman Preview cards were randomly inserted into Stadium Club 1994 Baseball Series II at a rate of one every 24 packs. This 10-card set featured several proven major league stars, as well as minor league players. Card number 10, James Mouton, is designed as a special MVP foil card.

		NM/M
Complete Set (10):		7.00

#	Player	Price
Common Player:		.50
1	Frank Thomas	1.50
2	Mike Piazza	3.00
3	Albert Belle	.50
4	Javier Lopez	.50
5	Cliff Floyd	.50
6	Alex Gonzalez	.50
7	Ricky Bottalico	.50
8	Tony Clark	.50
9	Mac Suzuki	.50
10	James Mouton (Foil)	.50

1994 Bowman

Bowman baseball for 1994 was a 682-card set issued all in one series, including a 52-card foil subset. There were 11 regular cards plus one foil card in each pack, with a suggested retail price of $2. The cards have a full-bleed design, with gold-foil stamping on every card. As in the past, the set includes numerous rookies and prospects, along with the game's biggest stars. The 52-card foil subset features 28 Top Prospects, with the player's team logo in the background; 17 Minor League MVPs, with a stadium in the background; and seven Diamonds in the Rough, with, you guessed it, a diamond as a backdrop.

		NM/M
Complete Set (682):		40.00
Common Player:		.10
Pack (12):		1.50
Wax Box (24):		30.00

#	Player	Price
1	Joe Carter	.10
2	Marcus Moore	.10
3	Doug Creek RC	.10
4	Pedro Martinez	1.50
5	Ken Griffey Jr.	3.00
6	Greg Swindell	.10
7	J.J. Johnson	.10
8	Homer Bush RC	.10
9	Arquimedez Pozo RC	.10
10	Bryan Harvey	.10
11	J.T. Snow	.10
12	Alan Benes RC	.10
13	Chad Kreuter	.10
14	Eric Karros	.10
15	Frank Thomas	1.50
16	Bret Saberhagen	.10
17	Terrell Lowery	.10
18	Rod Bolton	.10
19	Harold Baines	.10
20	Matt Walbeck	.10
21	Tom Glavine	.30
22	Todd Jones	.10
23	Alberto Castillo	.10
24	Ruben Sierra	.10
25	Don Mattingly	2.50
26	Mike Morgan	.10
27	Jim Musselwhite RC	.10
28	Matt Brunson RC	.10
29	Adam Meinershagen RC	.10
30	Joe Girardi	.10
31	Shane Halter	.10
32	Jose Paniagua RC	.10
33	Paul Perkins	.10
34	John Hudek RC	.10
35	Frank Viola	.10
36	David Lamb RC	.10
37	Marshall Boze	.10
38	Jorge Posada RC	6.00
39	Brian Anderson RC	.25
40	Mark Whiten	.10
41	Sean Bergman	.10
42	Jose Parra RC	.10
43	Mike Robertson	.10
44	Pete Walker RC	.10
45	Juan Gonzalez	.75
46	Cleveland Ladell RC	.10
47	Mark Smith	.10
48	Kevin Jarvis RC	.10
49	Amaury Telemaco RC	.10
50	Andy Van Slyke	.10
51	Rikkert Faneyte RC	.10
52	Curtis Shaw	.10
53	Matt Drews RC	.10
54	Wilson Alvarez	.10
55	Manny Ramirez	1.50
56	Bobby Munoz	.10
57	Ed Sprague	.10
58	Jamey Wright RC	.10
59	Jeff Montgomery	.10
60	Kirk Rueter	.10
61	Edgar Martinez	.10
62	Luis Gonzalez	.10
63	Tim Vanegmond RC	.10
64	Bip Roberts	.10
65	John Jaha	.10
66	Chuck Carr	.10
67	Chuck Finley	.10
68	Aaron Holbert	.10
69	Cecil Fielder	.10
70	Tom Engle RC	.10
71	Ron Karkovice	.10
72	Joe Orsulak	.10
73	Duff Brumley RC	.10
74	Craig Clayton RC	.10
75	Cal Ripken, Jr.	4.00
76	Brad Fullmer RC	.50
77	Tony Tarasco	.10
78	Terry Farrar RC	.10
79	Matt Williams	.10
80	Rickey Henderson	1.50
81	Terry Mulholland	.10
82	Sammy Sosa	2.00
83	Paul Sorrento	.10
84	Pete Incaviglia	.10
85	Darren Hall RC	.10
86	Scott Klingenbeck	.10
87	Dario Perez RC	.10
88	Ugueth Urbina	.10
89	Dave Vanhof RC	.10
90	Domingo Jean	.10
91	Otis Nixon	.10
92	Andres Berumen	.10
93	Jose Valentin	.10
94	Edgar Renteria RC	5.00
95	Chris Turner	.10
96	Ray Lankford	.10
97	Danny Bautista	.10
98	Chan Ho Park RC	1.00
99	Glenn DiSarcina RC	.10
100	Butch Huskey	.10
101	Ivan Rodriguez	1.00
102	Johnny Ruffin	.10
103	Alex Ochoa	.10
104	Torii Hunter RC	6.00
105	Ryan Klesko	.10
106	Jay Bell	.10
107	Kurt Peltzer RC	.10
108	Miguel Jimenez	.10
109	Russ Davis	.10
110	Derek Wallace	.10
111	Keith Lockhart RC	.10
112	Mike Lieberthal	.10
113	Dave Stewart	.10
114	Tom Schmidt	.10
115	Brian McRae	.10
116	Moises Alou	.10
117	Dave Fleming	.10
118	Jeff Bagwell	1.50
119	Luis Ortiz	.10
120	Tony Gwynn	2.00
121	Jaime Navarro	.10
122	Benny Santiago	.10
123	Darrel Whitmore	.10
124	John Mabry RC	.15
125	Mickey Tettleton	.10
126	Tom Candiotti	.10
127	Tim Raines	.10
128	Bobby Bonilla	.10
129	John Dettmer	.10
130	Hector Carrasco	.10
131	Chris Hoiles	.10
132	Rick Aguilera	.10
133	Dave Justice	.10
134	Esteban Loaiza RC	1.50
135	Barry Bonds	4.00
136	Bob Welch	.10
137	Mike Stanley	.10
138	Roberto Hernandez	.10
139	Sandy Alomar	.10
140	Darren Daulton	.10
141	Angel Martinez RC	.10
142	Howard Johnson	.10
143	Bob Hamelin	.10
144	J.J. Thobe RC	.10
145	Roger Salkeld	.10
146	Orlando Miller	.10
147	Dmitri Young	.10
148	Tim Hyers RC	.10
149	Mark Loretta RC	3.00
150	Chris Hammond	.10
151	Joel Moore RC	.10
152	Todd Zeile	.10
153	Wil Cordero	.10
154	Chris Smith	.10
155	James Baldwin	.10
156	Edgardo Alfonzo RC	1.00
157	Kym Ashworth RC	.10
158	Paul Bako RC	.10
159	Rick Krivda RC	.10
160	Pat Mahomes	.10
161	Damon Hollins	.10
162	Felix Martinez RC	.10
163	Jason Myers RC	.10
164	Izzy Molina RC	.10
165	Brien Taylor	.10
166	Kevin Orie RC	.10
167	Casey Whitten RC	.10
168	Tony Longmire	.10
169	John Olerud	.10
170	Mark Thompson	.10
171	Jorge Fabregas	.10
172	John Wetteland	.10
173	Dan Wilson	.10
174	Doug Drabek	.10
175	Jeffrey McNeely	.10
176	Melvin Nieves	.10

No.	Player	Price
177	Doug Glanville RC	.10
178	Javier De La Hoya RC	.10
179	Chad Curtis	.10
180	Brian Barber RC	.10
181	Mike Henneman	.10
182	Jose Offerman	.10
183	Robert Ellis RC	.10
184	John Franco	.10
185	Benji Gil	.10
186	Hal Morris	.10
187	Chris Sabo	.10
188	Blaise Ilsley RC	.10
189	Steve Avery	.10
190	Rick White RC	.10
191	Rod Beck	.10
(192)	Mark McGwire (No card number.)	3.00
193	Jim Abbott	.10
194	Randy Myers	.10
195	Kenny Lofton	.10
196	Mariano Duncan	.10
197	Lee Daniels RC	.10
198	Armando Reynoso	.10
199	Joe Randa	.10
200	Cliff Floyd	.10
201	Tim Harkrider RC	.10
202	Kevin Gallaher RC	.10
203	Scott Cooper	.10
204	Phil Stidham RC	.10
205	Jeff D'Amico RC	.25
206	Matt Whisenant	.10
207	De Shawn Warren	.10
208	Rene Arocha	.10
209	Tony Clark RC	.50
210	Jason Jacome RC	.10
211	Scott Christman RC	.10
212	Bill Pulsipher	.10
213	Dean Palmer	.10
214	Chad Mottola	.10
215	Manny Alexander	.10
216	Rich Becker	.10
217	Andre King RC	.10
218	Carlos Garcia	.10
219	Ron Pezzoni RC	.10
220	Steve Karsay	.10
221	Jose Musset RC	.10
222	Karl Rhodes	.10
223	Frank Cimorelli RC	.10
224	Kevin Jordan RC	.10
225	Duane Ward	.10
226	John Burke	.10
227	Mike MacFarlane	.10
228	Mike Lansing	.10
229	Chuck Knoblauch	.10
230	Ken Caminiti	.10
231	Gar Finnvold RC	.10
232	Derek Lee RC	12.00
233	Brady Anderson	.10
234	Vic Darensbourg RC	.10
235	Mark Langston	.10
236	T.J. Mathews RC	.10
237	Lou Whitaker	.10
238	Roger Cedeno	.10
239	Alex Fernandez	.10
240	Ryan Thompson	.10
241	Kerry Lacy RC	.10
242	Reggie Sanders	.10
243	Brad Pennington	.10
244	Bryan Eversgerd RC	.10
245	Greg Maddux	2.00
246	Jason Kendall	.10
247	J.R. Phillips	.10
248	Bobby Witt	.10
249	Paul O'Neill	.10
250	Ryne Sandberg	2.00
251	Charles Nagy	.10
252	Kevin Stocker	.10
253	Shawn Green	.30
254	Charlie Hayes	.10
255	Donnie Elliott	.10
256	Rob Fitzpatrick RC	.10
257	Tim Davis	.10
258	James Mouton	.10
259	Mike Greenwell	.10
260	Ray McDavid	.10
261	Mike Kelly	.10
262	Andy Larkin RC	.10
(263)	Marquis Riley (No card number.)	.10
264	Bob Tewksbury	.10
265	Brian Edmondson RC	.10
266	Eduardo Lantigua RC	.10
267	Brandon Wilson RC	.10
268	Mike Welch	.10
269	Tom Henke	.10
270	Calvin Reese	.10
271	Gregg Zaun RC	.10
272	Todd Ritchie	.10
273	Javier Lopez	.10
274	Kevin Young	.10
275	Kirt Manwaring	.10
276	Bill Taylor RC	.10
277	Robert Eenhoorn	.10
278	Jessie Hollins	.10
279	Julian Tavarez RC	.10
280	Gene Schall	.10
281	Paul Molitor	1.50
282	Neifi Perez RC	.10
283	Greg Gagne	.10
284	Marquis Grissom	.10
285	Randy Johnson	1.50
286	Pete Harnisch	.10
287	Joel Bennett RC	.10
288	Derek Bell	.10
289	Darryl Hamilton	.10
290	Gary Sheffield	.40
291	Eduardo Perez	.10
292	Basil Shabazz	.10
293	Eric Davis	.10
294	Pedro Astacio	.10
295	Robin Ventura	.10
296	Jeff Kent	.10
297	Rick Helling	.10
298	Joe Oliver	.10
299	Lee Smith	.10
300	Dave Winfield	1.50
301	Deion Sanders	.10
302	Ravelo Manzanillo RC	.10
303	Mark Portugal	.10
304	Brent Gates	.10
305	Wade Boggs	2.00
306	Rick Wilkins	.10
307	Carlos Baerga	.10
308	Curt Schilling	.35
309	Shannon Stewart	.10
310	Darren Holmes	.10
311	Robert Toth RC	.10
312	Gabe White	.10
313	Mac Suzuki RC	.10
314	Alvin Morman RC	.10
315	Mo Vaughn	.10
316	Bryce Florie RC	.10
317	Gabby Martinez RC	.10
318	Carl Everett	.10
319	Kerwin Moore	.10
320	Tom Pagnozzi	.10
321	Chris Gomez	.10
322	Todd Williams	.10
323	Pat Hentgen	.10
324	Kirk Presley RC	.10
325	Kevin Brown	.10
326	Jason Isringhausen RC	1.50
327	Rick Forney RC	.10
328	Carlos Pulido RC	.10
329	Terrell Wade RC	.10
330	Al Martin	.10
331	Dan Carlson RC	.10
332	Mark Acre RC	.10
333	Sterling Hitchcock	.10
334	Jon Ratliff RC	.10
335	Alex Ramirez RC	.10
336	Phil Geisler RC	.10
337	Eddie Zambrano RC (Foil)	.10
338	Jim Thome (Foil)	.60
339	James Mouton (Foil)	.10
340	Cliff Floyd (Foil)	.10
341	Carlos Delgado (Foil)	.40
342	Roberto Petagine (Foil)	.10
343	Tim Clark (Foil)	.10
344	Bubba Smith (Foil)	.10
345	Randy Curtis RC (Foil)	.10
346	Joe Biasucci RC (Foil)	.10
347	D.J. Boston RC (Foil)	.10
348	Ruben Rivera RC (Foil)	.75
349	Bryan Link RC (Foil)	.10
350	Mike Bell RC (Foil)	.25
351	Marty Watson RC (Foil)	.10
352	Jason Myers (Foil)	.10
353	Chipper Jones (Foil)	1.25
354	Brooks Kieschnick (Foil)	.10
355	Calvin Reese (Foil)	.10
356	John Burke (Foil)	.10
357	Kurt Miller (Foil)	.10
358	Orlando Miller (Foil)	.10
359	Todd Hollandsworth (Foil)	.10
360	Rondell White (Foil)	.10
361	Bill Pulsipher (Foil)	.10
362	Tyler Green (Foil)	.10
363	Midre Cummings (Foil)	.10
364	Brian Barber (Foil)	.10
365	Melvin Nieves (Foil)	.10
366	Salomon Torres (Foil)	.10
367	Alex Ochoa (Foil)	.10
368	Frank Rodriguez (Foil)	.10
369	Brian Anderson (Foil)	.10
370	James Baldwin (Foil)	.10
371	Manny Ramirez (Foil)	.75
372	Justin Thompson (Foil)	.10
373	Johnny Damon (Foil)	.50
374	Jeff D'Amico (Foil)	.10
375	Rich Becker (Foil)	.10
376	Derek Jeter (Foil)	3.00
377	Steve Karsay (Foil)	.10
378	Mac Suzuki (Foil)	.10
379	Benji Gil (Foil)	.10
380	Alex Gonzalez (Foil)	.10
381	Jason Bere (Foil)	.10
382	Brett Butler (Foil)	.10
383	Jeff Conine (Foil)	.10
384	Darren Daulton (Foil)	.10
385	Jeff Kent (Foil)	.10
386	Don Mattingly (Foil)	1.50
387	Mike Piazza (Foil)	2.00
388	Ryne Sandberg (Foil)	1.25
389	Rich Amaral	.10
390	Craig Biggio	.10
391	Jeff Suppan RC	.35
392	Andy Benes	.10
393	Cal Eldred	.10
394	Jeff Conine	.10
395	Tim Salmon	.10
396	Ray Suplee RC	.10
397	Tony Phillips	.10
398	Ramon Martinez	.10
399	Julio Franco	.10
400	Dwight Gooden	.10
401	Kevin Lomon RC	.10
402	Jose Rijo	.10
403	Mike Devereaux	.10
404	Mike Zolecki RC	.10
405	Fred McGriff	.10
406	Danny Clyburn	.10
407	Robby Thompson	.10
408	Terry Steinbach	.10
409	Luis Polonia	.10
410	Mark Grace	.10
411	Albert Belle	.10
412	John Kruk	.10
413	Scott Spiezio RC	.25
414	Ellis Burks	.10
415	Joe Vitiello	.10
416	Tim Costo	.10
417	Marc Newfield	.10
418	Oscar Henriquez RC	.10
419	Matt Perisho RC	.10
420	Julio Bruno	.10
421	Kenny Felder	.10
422	Tyler Green	.10
423	Jim Edmonds	.10
424	Ozzie Smith	2.00
425	Rich Greene	.10
426	Todd Hollandsworth	.10
427	Eddie Pearson RC	.10
428	Quilvio Veras	.10
429	Kenny Rogers	.10
430	Willie Greene	.10
431	Vaughn Eshelman	.10
432	Pat Meares	.10
433	Jermaine Dye RC	8.00
434	Steve Cooke	.10
435	Bill Swift	.10
436	Fausto Cruz RC	.10
437	Mark Hutton	.10
438	Brooks Kieschnick RC	.10
439	Yorkis Perez	.10
440	Len Dykstra	.10
441	Pat Borders	.10
442	Doug Walls RC	.10
443	Wally Joyner	.10
444	Ken Hill	.10
445	Eric Anthony	.10
446	Mitch Williams	.10
447	Cory Bailey RC	.10
448	Dave Staton	.10
449	Greg Vaughn	.10
450	Dave Magadan	.10
451	Chili Davis	.10
452	Gerald Santos RC	.10
453	Joe Perona	.10
454	Delino DeShields	.10
455	Jack McDowell	.10
456	Todd Hundley	.10
457	Ritchie Moody RC	.10
458	Bret Boone	.10
459	Ben McDonald	.10
460	Kirby Puckett	2.00
461	Gregg Olson	.10
462	Rich Aude RC	.10
463	John Burkett	.10
464	Troy Neel	.10
465	Jimmy Key	.10
466	Ozzie Timmons	.10
467	Eddie Murray	1.50
468	Mark Tranberg RC	.10
469	Alex Gonzalez	.10
470	David Nied	.10
471	Barry Larkin	.10
472	Brian Looney RC	.10
473	Shawn Estes	.10
474	A.J. Sager RC	.10
475	Roger Clemens	2.50
476	Vince Moore	.10
477	Scott Karl RC	.10
478	Kurt Miller	.10
479	Garret Anderson	.10
480	Allen Watson	.10
481	Jose Lima RC	.10
482	Rick Gorecki	.10
483	Jimmy Hurst RC	.10
484	Preston Wilson	.10
485	Will Clark	.10
486	Mike Ferry RC	.10
487	Curtis Goodwin RC	.10
488	Mike Myers	.10
489	Chipper Jones	2.00
490	Jeff King	.10
491	Bill Van Landingham RC	.10
492	Carlos Reyes RC	.10
493	Andy Pettitte	.10
494	Brant Brown	.10
495	Daron Kirkreit	.10
496	Ricky Bottalico RC	.25
497	Devon White	.10
498	Jason Johnson RC	.10
499	Vince Coleman	.10
500	Larry Walker	.10
501	Bobby Ayala	.10
502	Steve Finley	.10
503	Scott Fletcher	.10
504	Brad Ausmus	.10
505	Scott Talanoa RC	.10
506	Orestes Destrade	.10
507	Gary DiSarcina	.10
508	Willie Smith RC	.10
509	Alan Trammell	.10
510	Mike Piazza	3.00
511	Ozzie Guillen	.10
512	Jeromy Burnitz	.10
513	Darren Oliver	.10
514	Kevin Mitchell	.10
515	Rafael Palmeiro	1.00
516	David McCarty	.10
517	Jeff Blauser	.10
518	Trey Beamon	.10
519	Royce Clayton	.10
520	Dennis Eckersley	1.00
521	Bernie Williams	.10
522	Steve Buechele	.10
523	Denny Martinez	.10
524	Dave Hollins	.10
525	Joey Hamilton	.10
526	Andres Galarraga	.10
527	Jeff Granger	.10
528	Joey Eischen	.10
529	Desi Relaford	.10
530	Roberto Petagine	.10
531	Andre Dawson	.30
532	Ray Holbert	.10
533	Duane Singleton	.10
534	Kurt Abbott RC	.20
535	Bo Jackson	.10
536	Gregg Jefferies	.10
537	David Mysel	.10
538	Raul Mondesi	.10
539	Chris Snopek	.10
540	Brook Fordyce	.10
541	Ron Frazier RC	.10
542	Brian Koelling	.10
543	Jimmy Haynes	.10
544	Marty Cordova	.10
545	Jason Green RC	.10
546	Orlando Merced	.10
547	Lou Pote RC	.10
548	Todd Van Poppel	.10
549	Pat Kelly	.10
550	Turk Wendell	.10
551	Herb Perry RC	.10
552	Ryan Karp RC	.10
553	Juan Guzman	.10
554	Bryan Rekar RC	.10
555	Kevin Appier	.10
556	Chris Schwab RC	.10
557	Jay Buhner	.10
558	Andujar Cedeno	.10
559	Ryan McGuire RC	.10
560	Ricky Gutierrez	.10
561	Keith Kimsey RC	.10
562	Tim Clark	.10
563	Damion Easley	.10
564	Clint Davis RC	.10
565	Mike Moore	.10
566	Orel Hershiser	.10
567	Jason Bere	.10
568	Kevin McReynolds	.10
569	Leland Macon RC	.10
570	John Courtright RC	.10
571	Sid Fernandez	.10
572	Chad Roper	.10
573	Terry Pendleton	.10
574	Danny Miceli	.10
575	Joe Rosselli	.10
576	Mike Bordick	.10
577	Danny Tartabull	.10
578	Jose Guzman	.10
579	Omar Vizquel	.10
580	Tommy Greene	.10
581	Paul Spoljaric	.10
582	Walt Weiss	.10
583	Oscar Jimenez RC	.10
584	Rod Henderson	.10
585	Derek Lowe	.10
586	Richard Hidalgo RC	1.00
587	Shayne Bennett RC	.10
588	Tim Belk RC	.10
589	Matt Mieske	.10
590	Nigel Wilson	.10
591	Jeff Knox RC	.10
592	Bernard Gilkey	.10
593	David Cone	.10
594	Paul LoDuca RC	5.00
595	Scott Ruffcorn	.10
596	Chris Roberts	.10
597	Oscar Munoz RC	.10
598	Scott Sullivan RC	.10
599	Matt Jarvis RC	.10
600	Jose Canseco	.35
601	Tony Graffanino RC	.10
602	Don Slaught	.10
603	Brett King RC	.10
604	Jose Herrera RC	.10
605	Melido Perez	.10
606	Mike Hubbard RC	.10
607	Chad Ogea	.10
608	Wayne Gomes RC	.10
609	Roberto Alomar	.25
610	Angel Echevarria RC	.10
611	Jose Lind	.10
612	Darrin Fletcher	.10
613	Chris Bosio	.10
614	Darryl Kile	.10
615	Frank Rodriguez	.10
616	Phil Plantier	.10
617	Pat Listach	.10
618	Charlie Hough	.10
619	Ryan Hancock RC	.10
620	Darrel Deak RC	.10
621	Travis Fryman	.10
622	Brett Butler	.10
623	Lance Johnson	.10
624	Pete Smith	.10
625	James Hurst	.10
626	Roberto Kelly	.10
627	Mike Mussina	.50
628	Kevin Tapani	.10
629	John Smoltz	.10
630	Midre Cummings	.10
631	Salomon Torres	.10
632	Willie Adams RC	.10
633	Derek Jeter	4.00
634	Steve Trachsel	.10
635	Albie Lopez	.10
636	Jason Moler	.10
637	Carlos Delgado	.50
638	Roberto Mejia	.10
639	Darren Burton	.10
640	B.J. Wallace	.10
641	Brad Clontz RC	.10
642	Billy Wagner RC	1.00
643	Aaron Sele	.10
644	Cameron Cairncross RC	.10
645	Brian Harper	.10
(646)	Marc Valdes (No card number.)	.10
647	Mark Ratekin	.10
648	Terry Bradshaw RC	.10
649	Justin Thompson	.10
650	Mike Busch RC	.10
651	Joe Hall RC	.10
652	Bobby Jones	.10
653	Kelly Stinnett RC	.10
654	Rod Steph RC	.10
655	Jay Powell RC	.10
(656)	Keith Garagozzo RC (No card number.)	.10
657	Todd Dunn	.10
658	Charles Peterson RC	.10
659	Darren Lewis	.10
660	John Wasdin RC	.10
661	Tate Seefried RC	.10
662	Hector Trinidad RC	.10
663	John Carter RC	.10
664	Larry Mitchell	.10
665	David Catlett RC	.10
666	Dante Bichette	.10
667	Felix Jose	.10
668	Rondell White	.10
669	Tino Martinez	.10
670	Brian Hunter	.10
671	Jose Malave	.10
672	Archi Cianfrocco	.10
673	Mike Matheny RC	.15
674	Bret Barberie	.10
675	Andrew Lorraine RC	.10
676	Brian Jordan	.10
677	Tim Belcher	.10
678	Antonio Osuna RC	.10
679	Checklist I	.10
680	Checklist II	.10
681	Checklist III	.10
682	Checklist IV	.10

1994 Bowman Superstar Sampler

As an insert in 1994 Topps retail factory sets, three-card cello packs of "Superstar Sampler" cards were included. The packs contained special versions of the same player's 1994 Bowman, Finest and Stadium Club cards. Forty-five of the game's top stars are represented in the issue. The Bowman cards in this issue are identical to the cards in the regular set except for the appearance of a round "Topps Superstar Sampler" logo on back.

		NM/M
	Complete Set (45):	275.00
	Common Player:	2.00
1	Joe Carter	2.00
5	Ken Griffey Jr.	20.00
15	Frank Thomas	10.00
21	Tom Glavine	3.00
25	Don Mattingly	17.50
45	Juan Gonzalez	6.00
50	Andy Van Slyke	2.00
55	Manny Ramirez	10.00
69	Cecil Fielder	2.00
75	Cal Ripken Jr.	35.00
79	Matt Williams	2.00
118	Jeff Bagwell	10.00
120	Tony Gwynn	15.00
133	Dave Justice	2.00
135	Barry Bonds	35.00
140	Darren Daulton	2.00
169	John Olerud	2.00
200	Cliff Floyd	2.00
245	Greg Maddux	15.00
281	Paul Molitor	10.00
284	Marquis Grissom	2.00
285	Randy Johnson	2.00
290	Gary Sheffield	4.00
307	Carlos Baerga	2.00
315	Mo Vaughn	2.00
395	Tim Salmon	2.00
405	Fred McGriff	2.00
411	Mark Grace	2.00
411	Albert Belle	2.00
440	Len Dykstra	2.00
455	Jack McDowell	2.00
460	Kirby Puckett	15.00
471	Barry Larkin	2.00
475	Roger Clemens	17.50
500	Will Clark	2.00
500	Larry Walker	2.00
510	Mike Piazza	20.00
515	Rafael Palmeiro	9.00
526	Andres Galarraga	2.00
536	Gregg Jefferies	2.00
538	Raul Mondesi	2.00
600	Jose Canseco	6.00
609	Roberto Alomar	4.00

1994 Bowman's Best

The debut Bowman's Best consists of 90 red cards (largely veterans), 90 blue cards (rookies and young players) and 20 Mirror Images combining veteran and young stars by position. Utilizing Topps Finest technology, cards are full-color front and back with high-gloss surfaces. Cards were sold in eight-card foil packs with one Mirror Image card in each pack. A 200-card parallel version officially called "Special Effects," uses Topps refractor technology. Red and Blue sets each contain cards numbered 1-90, while the Mirror Image cards are numbered 91-110.

		NM/M
	Complete Set (200):	30.00
	Red Set (90):	10.00
	Blue Set (90):	20.00
	Common Player:	.15
	Pack (8):	1.50
	Wax Box (24):	30.00
1	Paul Molitor	1.50
2	Eddie Murray	1.50
3	Ozzie Smith	2.00
4	Rickey Henderson	1.50
5	Lee Smith	.15
6	Dave Winfield	1.50
7	Roberto Alomar	.30
8	Matt Williams	.15
9	Mark Grace	.15
10	Lance Johnson	.15
11	Darren Daulton	.15
12	Tom Glavine	.35
13	Gary Sheffield	.40
14	Rod Beck	.15
15	Fred McGriff	.15
16	Joe Carter	.15
17	Dante Bichette	.15
18	Danny Tartabull	.15
19	Juan Gonzalez	.75
20	Steve Avery	.15
21	John Wetteland	.15
22	Ben McDonald	.15
23	Jack McDowell	.15
24	Jose Canseco	.65
25	Tim Salmon	.15
26	Wilson Alvarez	.15
27	Gregg Jefferies	.15
28	John Burkett	.15
29	Greg Vaughn	.15
30	Robin Ventura	.15
31	Paul O'Neill	.15
32	Cecil Fielder	.15
33	Kevin Mitchell	.15
34	Jeff Conine	.15
35	Carlos Baerga	.15
36	Greg Maddux	2.00
37	Roger Clemens	2.25
38	Deion Sanders	.15
39	Delino DeShields	.15
40	Ken Griffey Jr.	2.50
41	Albert Belle	1.50
42	Wade Boggs	2.00
43	Andres Galarraga	.15
44	Aaron Sele	.15
45	Don Mattingly	2.25
46	David Cone	.15
47	Lenny Dykstra	.15
48	Brett Butler	.15
49	Bill Swift	.15
50	Bobby Bonilla	.15
51	Rafael Palmeiro	1.25
52	Moises Alou	.15
53	Jeff Bagwell	1.50
54	Mike Mussina	.15
55	Frank Thomas	1.50
56	Jose Rijo	.15
57	Ruben Sierra	.15
58	Randy Myers	.15
59	Barry Bonds	4.00
60	Jimmy Key	.15
61	Travis Fryman	.15
62	John Olerud	.15
63	David Justice	.15
64	Ray Lankford	.15
65	Bob Tewksbury	.15
66	Chuck Carr	.15
67	Jay Buhner	.15

#	Player	Price
68	Kenny Lofton	.15
69	Marquis Grissom	.15
70	Sammy Sosa	2.00
71	Cal Ripken Jr.	4.00
72	Ellis Burks	.15
73	Jeff Montgomery	.15
74	Julio Franco	.15
75	Kirby Puckett	2.00
76	Larry Walker	.15
77	Andy Van Slyke	.15
78	Tony Gwynn	2.00
79	Will Clark	.15
80	Mo Vaughn	.15
81	Mike Piazza	2.50
82	James Mouton	.15
83	Carlos Delgado	.60
84	Ryan Klesko	.15
85	Javy Lopez	.15
86	Raul Mondesi	.15
87	Cliff Floyd	.15
88	Manny Ramirez	1.50
89	Hector Carrasco	.15
90	Jeff Granger	.15
1	Chipper Jones	2.00
2	Derek Jeter	4.00
3	Bill Pulsipher	.15
4	James Baldwin	.15
5	Brooks Kieschnick RC	.50
6	Justin Thompson	.15
7	Midre Cummings	.15
8	Joey Hamilton	.15
9	Calvin Reese	.15
10	Brian Barber	.15
11	John Burke	.15
12	De Shawn Warren	.15
13	Edgardo Alfonzo RC	.75
14	Eddie Pearson RC	.15
15	Jimmy Haynes	.15
16	Danny Bautista	.15
17	Roger Cedeno	.15
18	Jon Lieber	.15
19	Billy Wagner RC	.75
20	Tate Seefried RC	.15
21	Chad Mottola	.15
22	Jose Malave	.15
23	Terrell Wade RC	.15
24	Shane Andrews	.15
25	Chan Ho Park RC	.75
26	Kirk Presley	.15
27	Robbie Beckett	.15
28	Orlando Miller	.15
29	Jorge Posada RC	8.00
30	Frank Rodriguez	.15
31	Brian Hunter	.15
32	Billy Ashley	.15
33	Rondell White	.15
34	John Roper	.15
35	Marc Valdes	.15
36	Scott Ruffcorn	.15
37	Rod Henderson	.15
38	Curt Goodwin	.15
39	Russ Davis	.15
40	Rick Gorecki	.15
41	Johnny Damon	.60
42	Roberto Petagine	.15
43	Chris Snopek	.15
44	Mark Acre	.15
45	Todd Hollandsworth	.15
46	Shawn Green	.35
47	John Carter	.15
48	Jim Pittsley	.15
49	John Wasdin RC	.15
50	D.J. Boston	.15
51	Tim Clark	.15
52	Alex Ochoa	.15
53	Chad Roper	.15
54	Mike Kelly	.15
55	Brad Fullmer RC	.50
56	Carl Everett	.15
57	Tim Belk RC	.15
58	Jimmy Hurst RC	.15
59	Mac Suzuki RC	.15
60	Michael Moore	.15
61	Alan Benes RC	.15
62	Tony Clark RC	1.00
63	Edgar Renteria RC	8.00
64	Trey Beamon	.15
65	LaTroy Hawkins RC	.15
66	Wayne Gomes RC	.15
67	Ray McDavid	.15
68	John Dettmer	.15
69	Willie Greene	.15
70	Dave Stevens	.15
71	Kevin Orie RC	.15
72	Chad Ogea	.15
73	Ben Van Ryn	.15
74	Kym Ashworth	.15
75	Dmitri Young	.15
76	Herb Perry	.15
77	Joey Eischen	.15
78	Arquimedez Pozo RC	.15
79	Ugueth Urbina	.15
80	Keith Williams	.15
81	John Frascatore RC	.15
82	Garey Ingram	.15
83	Aaron Small	.15
84	Olmedo Saenz RC	.15
85	Jesus Tavarez RC	.15
86	Jose Silva RC	.15
87	Gerald Witasick Jr. RC	.15
88	Jay Maldonado	.15
89	Keith Heberling	.15
90	Rusty Greer RC	.50
91	Frank Thomas, Kevin Young	.60
92	Fred McGriff, Brooks Kieschnick RC	.15
93	Matt Williams, Shane Andrews	.15
94	Cal Ripken Jr., Kevin Orie RC	1.50
95	Barry Larkin, Derek Jeter	1.50
96	Ken Griffey Jr., Johnny Damon	1.50
97	Barry Bonds, Rondell White	1.50
98	Albert Belle, Jimmy Hurst RC	.15
99	Raul Mondesi, Ruben Rivera RC	.15
100	Roger Clemens, Scott Ruffcorn	1.00
101	Greg Maddux, John Wasdin RC	.75
102	Tim Salmon, Chad Mottola	.15
103	Carlos Baerga, Arquimedez Pozo RC	.15
104	Mike Piazza, Bobby Hughes	1.00
105	Carlos Delgado, Melvin Nieves	.50
106	Javy Lopez, Jorge Posada RC	2.00
107	Manny Ramirez, Jose Malave	.65
108	Travis Fryman, Chipper Jones	.75
109	Steve Avery, Bill Pulsipher	.15
110	John Olerud, Shawn Green	.50

Refractors

This 200-card parallel set, officially titled "Special Effects," uses Topps' refractor technology. The refractors were packed at the rate of three per wax box of Bowman's Best, but are very difficult to differentiate from the regular high-tech cards.

Superstars: 8-10X
Stars: 4-8X

1995 Bowman

Large numbers of rookie cards and a lengthy run of etched-foil cards distinguishes the 1995 Bowman set. The set's basic cards share a design with a large color photo flanked at left by a severely horizontally compressed mirror image in green, and at bottom by a similar version in brown. Most of the bottom image is covered by the player's last name printed in silver (cards #1-220, rookies) or gold (cards #275-439, veterans) foil. A color team logo is in the lower-left corner of all cards, and the Bowman logo is in red foil at top. In between are the foil-etched subsets of "Minor League MVPs," "1st Impressions," and "Prime Prospects." Each of these cards, seeded one per regular pack and two per jumbo, has the player photo set against a background of textured color foil, with a prismatic silver border. Each of the foil cards can also be found in a gold-toned version, in a ratio of six silver to one gold. Backs of the rookies' cards have a portrait photo at right and a scouting report at left. Veterans' cards have either a scouting report for younger players, or a chart of stats versus each team played in 1994. Backs of all the foil cards have a scouting report.

	NM/M
Complete Set (439):	150.00
Common Player:	.10
Pack (10):	6.00
Wax Box (24):	125.00
Rack Pack (15):	5.00
Rack Box (24):	125.00

#	Player	Price
1	Billy Wagner	.10
2	Chris Widger	.10
3	Brent Bowers	.10
4	Bob Abreu RC	10.00
5	Lou Collier RC	.10
6	Juan Acevedo RC	.25
7	Jason Kelley RC	.10
8	Brian Sackinsky RC	.10
9	Scott Christman	.10
10	Damon Hollins	.10
11	Willis Otanez RC	.10
12	Jason Ryan RC	.10
13	Jason Giambi	.75
14	Andy Taulbee RC	.10
15	Mark Thompson	.10
16	Hugo Pivaral RC	.10
17	Brien Taylor	.10
18	Antonio Osuna	.10
19	Edgardo Alfonzo	.10
20	Carl Everett	.10
21	Matt Drews	.10
22	Bartolo Colon RC	4.00
23	Andruw Jones RC	8.00
24	Robert Person RC	.40
25	Derrek Lee	.75
26	John Ambrose RC	.10
27	Eric Knowles RC	.10
28	Chris Roberts	.10
29	Don Wengert	.10
30	Marcus Jensen RC	.10
31	Brian Barber	.10
32	Kevin Brown	.10
33	Benji Gil	.10
34	Mike Hubbard	.10
35	Bart Evans RC	.10
36	Enrique Wilson RC	.50
37	Brian Buchanan RC	.10
38	Ken Ray RC	.10
39	Micah Franklin RC	.10
40	Ricky Otero RC	.10
41	Jason Kendall	.10
42	Jimmy Hurst	.10
43	Jerry Wolak RC	.10
44	Jayson Peterson RC	.10
45	Allen Battle RC	.10
46	Scott Stahoviak	.10
47	Steve Schrenk RC	.10
48	Travis Miller RC	.25
49	Eddie Rios RC	.10
50	Mike Hampton	.10
51	Chad Frontera RC	.10
52	Tom Evans RC	.10
53	C.J. Nitkowski	.10
54	Clay Caruthers RC	.10
55	Shannon Stewart	.10
56	Jorge Posada	.50
57	Aaron Holbert	.10
58	Harry Berrios RC	.10
59	Steve Rodriguez	.10
60	Shane Andrews	.10
61	Will Cunnane RC	.10
62	Richard Hidalgo	.10
63	Bill Selby RC	.10
64	Jay Cranford RC	.10
65	Jeff Suppan	.10
66	Curtis Goodwin	.10
67	John Thomson RC	.10
68	Justin Thompson	.10
69	Troy Percival	.10
70	Matt Wagner RC	.10
71	Terry Bradshaw	.10
72	Greg Hansell	.10
73	John Burke	.10
74	Jeff D'Amico	.10
75	Ernie Young	.10
76	Jason Bates	.10
77	Chris Stynes	.10
78	Cade Gaspar RC	.10
79	Melvin Nieves	.10
80	Rick Gorecki	.10
81	Felix Rodriguez RC	.50
82	Ryan Hancock	.10
83	Chris Carpenter RC	6.00
84	Ray McDavid	.10
85	Chris Wimmer	.10
86	Doug Glanville	.10
87	DeShawn Warren	.10
88	Damian Moss RC	.50
89	Rafael Orellano RC	.10
90	Vladimir Guerrero RC	50.00
91	Raul Casanova RC	.40
92	Karim Garcia RC	.75
93	Bryce Florie	.10
94	Kevin Orie	.10
95	Ryan Nye RC	.10
96	Matt Sachse RC	.10
97	Ivan Arteaga RC	.10
98	Glenn Murray	.10
99	Stacy Hollins	.10
100	Jim Pittsley	.10
101	Craig Mattson RC	.10
102	Neifi Perez	.10
103	Keith Williams	.10
104	Roger Cedeno	.10
105	Tony Terry RC	.10
106	Jose Malave	.10
107	Joe Rosselli	.10
108	Kevin Jordan	.10
109	Sid Roberson RC	.10
110	Alan Embree	.10
111	Terrell Wade	.10
112	Bob Wolcott	.10
113	Carlos Perez RC	.10
114	Mike Bovee RC	.10
115	Tommy Davis RC	.10
116	Jeremey Kendall	.10
117	Rich Aude	.10
118	Rick Huisman	.10
119	Tim Belk	.10
120	Edgar Renteria	.25
121	Calvin Maduro RC	.10
122	Jerry Martin RC	.10
123	Ramon Fermin RC	.10
124	Kimera Bartee RC	.10
125	Mark Farris	.10
126	Frank Rodriguez	.10
127	Bobby Higginson RC	.50
128	Bret Wagner	.10
129	Edwin Diaz RC	.10
130	Jimmy Haynes	.10
131	Chris Weinke RC	.75
132	Damian Jackson RC	.10
133	Felix Martinez	.10
134	Edwin Hurtado RC	.25
135	Matt Raleigh RC	.10
136	Paul Wilson	.10
137	Ron Villone	.10
138	Eric Stuckenschneider RC	.10
139	Tate Seefried	.10
140	Rey Ordonez RC	.75
141	Eddie Pearson	.10
142	Kevin Gallaher	.10
143	Torii Hunter	.25
144	Daron Kirkreit	.10
145	Craig Wilson	.10
146	Ugueth Urbina	.10
147	Chris Snopek	.10
148	Kym Ashworth	.10
149	Wayne Gomes	.10
150	Mark Loretta	.10
151	Ramon Morel RC	.10
152	Trot Nixon	.20
153	Desi Relaford	.10
154	Scott Sullivan	.10
155	Marc Barcelo	.10
156	Willie Adams	.10
157	Derrick Gibson RC	.10
158	Brian Meadows RC	.10
159	Julian Tavarez	.10
160	Bryan Rekar	.10
161	Steve Gibralter	.10
162	Esteban Loaiza RC	.10
163	John Wasdin	.10
164	Kirk Presley	.10
165	Mariano Rivera	.50
166	Andy Larkin	.10
167	Sean Whiteside RC	.10
168	Matt Apana RC	.10
169	Shawn Senior RC	.10
170	Scott Gentile	.10
171	Quilvio Veras	.10
172	Elieser Marrero RC	1.00
173	Mendy Lopez RC	.10
174	Homer Bush	.10
175	Brian Stephenson RC	.10
176	Jon Nunnally RC	.10
177	Jose Herrera	.10
178	Corey Avrard RC	.10
179	David Bell	.10
180	Jason Isringhausen	.10
181	Jamey Wright	.10
182	Lonell Roberts RC	.10
183	Marty Cordova	.10
184	Amaury Telemaco	.10
185	John Mabry	.10
186	Andrew Vessel RC	.10
187	Jim Cole RC	.10
188	Marquis Riley	.10
189	Todd Dunn	.10
190	John Carter	.10
191	Donnie Sadler RC	.25
192	Mike Bell	.10
193	Chris Cumberland RC	.10
194	Jason Schmidt	.25
195	Matt Brunson	.10
196	James Baldwin	.10
197	Bill Simas RC	.10
198	Gus Gandarillas	.10
199	Mac Suzuki	.10
200	Rick Holifield RC	.10
201	Fernando Lunar RC	.10
202	Kevin Jarvis	.10
203	Everett Stull RC	.10
204	Steve Wojciechowski	.10
205	Shawn Estes	.10
206	Jermaine Dye	.10
207	Marc Kroon	.10
208	Peter Munro RC	.10
209	Pat Watkins	.10
210	Matt Smith	.10
211	Joe Vitiello	.10
212	Gerald Witasick Jr.	.10
213	Freddy Garcia RC	.10
214	Glenn Dishman RC	.10
215	Jay Canizaro RC	.10
216	Angel Martinez	.10
217	Yamil Benitez RC	.10
218	Fausto Macey RC	.10
219	Eric Owens	.10
220	Checklist	.10
221	Dwayne Hosey RC	.10
222	Brad Woodall RC (Minor League MVPs)	.25
223	Billy Ashley (Minor League MVPs)	.10
224	Mark Grudzielanek RC (Minor League MVPs)	2.00
225	Mark Johnson RC (Minor League MVPs)	.10
226	Tim Unroe RC (Minor League MVPs)	.10
227	Todd Greene (Minor League MVPs)	.10
228	Larry Sutton (Minor League MVPs)	.10
229	Derek Jeter (Minor League MVPs)	3.00
230	Sal Fasano RC (Minor League MVPs)	.10
231	Ruben Rivera (Minor League MVPs)	.10
232	Chris Truby RC (Minor League MVPs)	.10
233	John Donati (Minor League MVPs)	.10
234	Decomba Conner RC (Minor League MVPs)	.10
235	Sergio Nunez RC (Minor League MVPs)	.10
236	Ray Brown RC (Minor League MVPs)	.10
237	Juan Melo RC (Minor League MVPs)	.10
238	Hideo Nomo RC (First Impressions)	4.00
239	Jaime Bluma RC (First Impressions)	.10
240	Jay Payton RC (First Impressions)	1.50
241	Paul Konerko RC (First Impressions)	.75
242	Scott Elarton RC (First Impressions)	.50
243	Jeff Abbott RC (First Impressions)	.25
244	Jim Brower RC (First Impressions)	.10
245	Geoff Blum RC (First Impressions)	.40
246	Aaron Boone RC (First Impressions)	1.00
247	J.R. Phillips (Top Prospects)	.10
248	Alex Ochoa (Top Prospects)	.10
249	Nomar Garciaparra (Top Prospects)	5.00
250	Garret Anderson (Top Prospects)	.25
251	Ray Durham (Top Prospects)	.10
252	Paul Shuey (Top Prospects)	.10
253	Tony Clark (Top Prospects)	.10
254	Johnny Damon (Top Prospects)	1.00
255	Duane Singleton (Top Prospects)	.10
256	LaTroy Hawkins (Top Prospects)	.10
257	Andy Pettitte (Top Prospects)	.40
258	Ben Grieve (Top Prospects)	.10
259	Marc Newfield (Top Prospects)	.10
260	Terrell Lowery (Top Prospects)	.10
261	Shawn Green (Top Prospects)	.40
262	Chipper Jones (Top Prospects)	1.50
263	Brooks Kieschnick (Top Prospects)	.10
264	Calvin Reese (Top Prospects)	.10
265	Doug Million (Top Prospects)	.10
266	Marc Valdes (Top Prospects)	.10
267	Brian Hunter (Top Prospects)	.10
268	Todd Hollandsworth (Top Prospects)	.10
269	Rod Henderson (Top Prospects)	.10
270	Bill Pulsipher (Top Prospects)	.10
271	Scott Rolen RC (Top Prospects)	15.00
272	Trey Beamon (Top Prospects)	.10
273	Alan Benes (Top Prospects)	.10
274	Dustin Hermanson (Top Prospects)	.10
275	Ricky Bottalico	.10
276	Albert Belle	.10
277	Deion Sanders	.25
278	Matt Williams	.10
279	Jeff Bagwell	.75
280	Kirby Puckett	1.50
281	Dave Hollins	.10
282	Don Mattingly	1.50
283	Joey Hamilton	.10
284	Bobby Bonilla	.10
285	Moises Alou	.25
286	Tom Glavine	.25
287	Brett Butler	.10
288	Chris Hoiles	.10
289	Kenny Rogers	.10
290	Larry Walker	.25
291	Tim Raines	.10
292	Kevin Appier	.10
293	Roger Clemens	2.00
294a	Chuck Carr	.10
294b	Cliff Floyd (Should be #394.)	.10
295	Randy Myers	.10
296	Dave Nilsson	.10
297	Joe Carter	.10
298	Chuck Finley	.10
299	Ray Lankford	.10
300	Roberto Kelly	.10
301	Jon Lieber	.10
302	Travis Fryman	.10
303	Mark McGwire	1.50
304	Tony Gwynn	1.00
305	Kenny Lofton	.10
306	Mark Whiten	.10
307	Doug Drabek	.10
308	Terry Steinbach	.10
309	Ryan Klesko	.10
310	Mike Piazza	1.50
311	Ben McDonald	.10
312	Reggie Sanders	.10
313	Alex Fernandez	.10
314	Aaron Sele	.10
315	Gregg Jefferies	.10
316	Rickey Henderson	.75
317	Brian Anderson	.10
318	Jose Valentin	.10
319	Rod Beck	.10
320	Marquis Grissom	.10
321	Ken Griffey Jr.	2.00
322	Bret Saberhagen	.10
323	Juan Gonzalez	.50
324	Paul Molitor	.75
325	Gary Sheffield	.40
326	Darren Daulton	.10
327	Bill Swift	.10
328	Brian McRae	.10
329	Robin Ventura	.10
330	Lee Smith	.10
331	Fred McGriff	.20
332	Delino DeShields	.10
333	Edgar Martinez	.10
334	Mike Mussina	.50
335	Orlando Merced	.10
336	Carlos Baerga	.10
337	Wil Cordero	.10
338	Tom Pagnozzi	.10
339	Pat Hentgen	.10
340	Chad Curtis	.10
341	Darren Lewis	.10
342	Jeff Kent	.10
343	Bip Roberts	.10
344	Ivan Rodriguez	.50
345	Jeff Montgomery	.10
346	Hal Morris	.10
347	Danny Tartabull	.10
348	Raul Mondesi	.10
349	Ken Hill	.10
350	Pedro Martinez	1.00
351	Frank Thomas	.75
352	Manny Ramirez	1.00
353	Tim Salmon	.10
354	William Van Landingham	.10
355	Andres Galarraga	.10
356	Paul O'Neill	.10
357	Brady Anderson	.10
358	Ramon Martinez	.10
359	John Olerud	.10
360	Ruben Sierra	.10
361	Cal Eldred	.10
362	Jay Buhner	.10
363	Jay Bell	.10
364	Wally Joyner	.10
365	Chuck Knoblauch	.25
366	Len Dykstra	.10
367	John Wetteland	.10
368	Roberto Alomar	.25
369	Craig Biggio	.25
370	Ozzie Smith	1.50
371	Terry Pendleton	.10
372	Sammy Sosa	1.00
373	Carlos Garcia	.10
374	Jose Rijo	.10
375	Chris Gomez	.10
376	Barry Bonds	2.00
377	Steve Avery	.10
378	Rick Wilkins	.10
379	Pete Harnisch	.10
380	Dean Palmer	.10
381	Bob Hamelin	.10
382	Jason Bere	.10
383	Jimmy Key	.10
384	Dante Bichette	.10
385	Rafael Palmeiro	.50
386	David Justice	.10
387	Chili Davis	.10
388	Mike Greenwell	.10
389	Todd Zeile	.10
390	Jeff Conine	.10
391	Rick Aguilera	.10
392	Eddie Murray	.50
393	Mike Stanley	.10
395	Randy Johnson	1.00
396	David Nied	.10
397	Devon White	.10
398	Royce Clayton	.10
399	Andy Benes	.10
400	John Hudek	.10
401	Bobby Jones	.10
402	Eric Karros	.10
403	Will Clark	.25

#	Player	Price
404	Mark Langston	.10
405	Kevin Brown	.10
406	Greg Maddux	1.50
407	David Cone	.10
408	Wade Boggs	.75
409	Steve Trachsel	.10
410	Greg Vaughn	.10
411	Mo Vaughn	.10
412	Wilson Alvarez	.10
413	Cal Ripken Jr.	3.00
414	Rico Brogna	.10
415	Barry Larkin	.40
416	Cecil Fielder	.10
417	Jose Canseco	.50
418	Jack McDowell	.10
419	Mike Lieberthal	.10
420	Andrew Lorraine	.10
421	Rich Becker	.10
422	Tony Phillips	.10
423	Scott Ruffcorn	.10
424	Jeff Granger	.10
425	Greg Pirkl	.10
426	Dennis Eckersley	.50
427	Jose Lima	.10
428	Russ Davis	.10
429	Armando Benitez	.10
430	Alex Gonzalez	.10
431	Carlos Delgado	.75
432	Chan Ho Park	.10
433	Mickey Tettleton	.10
434	Dave Winfield	.75
435	John Burkett	.10
436	Orlando Miller	.10
437	Rondell White	.10
438	Jose Oliva	.10
439	Checklist	.10

Gold

The only chase cards in the '95 Bowman set are gold versions of the foil-etched "Minor League MVPs," "1st Impressions" and "Prime Prospects." The gold cards are found in every 6th (regular) or 12th (jumbo) pack, on average, in place of the silver versions.

	NM/M
Complete Set (54):	100.00
Common Player:	.50
Stars/RC's:	2.5X

1995 Bowman's Best

Actually made up of three sub-sets, all cards feature a player photo set against a silver foil background. The 90 veterans' cards have a broad gold-foil stripe in the background beneath the team logo; the 90 rookies cards have a similar stripe in tones of blue. All of those cards are printed in Topps' Finest technology. The 15 Mirror Image cards are in horizontal format, printed more conventionally on metallic foil, and have a rookie and veteran sharing the card. Backs of each card continue the color theme, have '94 and career stats and a highlight or two. Standard packaging was seven-card foil packs with inserts consisting of higher-tech parallel versions of the regular issue.

	NM/M
Complete Set (195):	200.00
Common Player:	.25

#	Player	Price
	Pack (7):	12.00
	Wax Box (24):	275.00
	Complete Set Red (90):	45.00
1	Randy Johnson	1.50
2	Joe Carter	.25
3	Chili Davis	.25
4	Moises Alou	.25
5	Gary Sheffield	.40
6	Kevin Appier	.25
7	Denny Neagle	.25
8	Ruben Sierra	.25
9	Darren Daulton	.25
10	Cal Ripken Jr.	4.00
11	Bobby Bonilla	.25
12	Manny Ramirez	1.50
13	Barry Bonds	4.00
14	Eric Karros	.25
15	Greg Maddux	2.00
16	Jeff Bagwell	1.50
17	Paul Molitor	1.50
18	Ray Lankford	.25
19	Mark Grace	.25
20	Kenny Lofton	.25
21	Tony Gwynn	2.00
22	Will Clark	.25
23	Roger Clemens	2.25
24	Dante Bichette	.25
25	Barry Larkin	.25
26	Wade Boggs	2.00
27	Kirby Puckett	2.00
28	Cecil Fielder	.25
29	Jose Canseco	.50
30	Juan Gonzalez	.75
31	David Cone	.25
32	Craig Biggio	.25
33	Tim Salmon	.25
34	David Justice	.25
35	Sammy Sosa	2.00
36	Mike Piazza	2.50
37	Carlos Baerga	.25
38	Jeff Conine	.25
39	Rafael Palmeiro	1.25
40	Bret Saberhagen	.25
41	Len Dykstra	.25
42	Mo Vaughn	.25
43	Wally Joyner	.25
44	Chuck Knoblauch	.25
45	Robin Ventura	.25
46	Don Mattingly	2.25
47	Dave Hollins	.25
48	Andy Benes	.25
49	Ken Griffey Jr.	2.50
50	Albert Belle	.25
51	Matt Williams	.25
52	Rondell White	.25
53	Raul Mondesi	.25
54	Brian Jordan	.25
55	Greg Vaughn	.25
56	Fred McGriff	.25
57	Roberto Alomar	.40
58	Dennis Eckersley	1.25
59	Lee Smith	.25
60	Eddie Murray	1.50
61	Kenny Rogers	.25
62	Ron Gant	.25
63	Larry Walker	.25
64	Chad Curtis	.25
65	Frank Thomas	1.50
66	Paul O'Neill	.25
67	Kevin Seitzer	.25
68	Marquis Grissom	.25
69	Mark McGwire	3.00
70	Travis Fryman	.25
71	Andres Galarraga	.25
72	Carlos Perez RC	.25
73	Tyler Green	.25
74	Marty Cordova	.25
75	Shawn Green	.40
76	Vaughn Eshelman	.25
77	John Mabry	.25
78	Jason Bates	.25
79	Jon Nunnally	.25
80	Ray Durham	.25
81	Edgardo Alfonzo	.25
82	Esteban Loaiza	.25
83	Hideo Nomo RC	10.00
84	Orlando Miller	.25
85	Alex Gonzalez	.25
86	Mark Grudzielanek RC	.65
87	Julian Tavarez	.25
88	Benji Gil	.25
89	Quilvio Veras	.25
90	Ricky Bottalico	.25
	Complete Set Blue (90):	150.00
1	Derek Jeter	3.00
2	Vladimir Guerrero RC	80.00
3	Bob Abreu RC	25.00
4	Chan Ho Park	.25
5	Paul Wilson	.25
6	Chad Ogea	.25
7	Andruw Jones RC	10.00
8	Brian Barber	.25
9	Andy Larkin	.25
10	Richie Sexson RC	6.00
11	Everett Stull RC	.25
12	Brooks Kieschnick	.25
13	Matt Murray	.25
14	John Wasdin	.25
15	Shannon Stewart	.25
16	Luis Ortiz	.25
17	Marc Kroon	.25
18	Todd Greene	.25
19	Juan Acevedo	.25
20	Tony Clark	.25
21	Jermaine Dye	.25
22	Derrek Lee	1.00
23	Pat Watkins	.25
24	Calvin Reese	.25

#	Player	Price
25	Ben Grieve	.25
26	Julio Santana RC	.25
27	Felix Rodriguez RC	.25
28	Paul Konerko	.50
29	Nomar Garciaparra	2.00
30	Pat Ahearne	.25
31	Jason Schmidt	.25
32	Billy Wagner	.25
33	Rey Ordonez RC	1.00
34	Curtis Goodwin	.25
35	Sergio Nunez RC	.25
36	Tim Belk	.25
37	Scott Elarton RC	1.00
38	Jason Isringhausen	.25
39	Trot Nixon	.35
40	Sid Roberson	.25
41	Ron Villone	.25
42	Ruben Rivera	.25
43	Rick Huisman	.25
44	Todd Hollandsworth	.25
45	Johnny Damon	1.00
46	Garret Anderson	.25
47	Jeff D'Amico	.25
48	Dustin Hermanson	.25
49	Juan Encarnacion RC	3.00
50	Andy Pettitte	.50
51	Chris Stynes	.25
52	Troy Percival	.25
53	LaTroy Hawkins	.25
54	Roger Cedeno	.25
55	Alan Benes	.25
56	Karim Garcia RC	1.50
57	Andrew Lorraine	.25
58	Gary Rath RC	.25
59	Bret Wagner	.25
60	Jeff Suppan	.25
61	Bill Pulsipher	.25
62	Jay Payton RC	3.00
63	Alex Ochoa	.25
64	Ugueth Urbina	.25
65	Armando Benitez	.25
66	George Arias	.25
67	Raul Casanova RC	.50
68	Matt Drews	.25
69	Jimmy Haynes	.25
70	Jimmy Hurst	.25
71	C.J. Nitkowski	.25
72	Tommy Davis RC	.25
73	Bartolo Colon RC	5.00
74	Chris Carpenter RC	10.00
75	Trey Beamon	.25
76	Bryan Rekar	.25
77	James Baldwin	.25
78	Marc Valdes	.25
79	Tom Fordham RC	.25
80	Marc Newfield	.25
81	Angel Martinez	.25
82	Brian Hunter	.25
83	Jose Herrera	.25
84	Glenn Dishman RC	.25
85	Jacob Cruz RC	.25
86	Paul Shuey	.25
87	Scott Rolen RC	25.00
88	Doug Million	.25
89	Desi Relaford	.25
90	Michael Tucker	.25
	Mirror Image:	.50
1	Ben Davis RC,	
	Ivan Rodriguez	1.00
2	Mark Redman RC,	
	Manny Ramirez	1.50
3	Reggie Taylor RC,	
	Deion Sanders	
	Ryan Jaroncyk,	
	Shawn Green	.50
5	Juan LeBron,	
	Juan Gonzalez	1.00
6	Toby McKnight,	
	Craig Biggio	.50
7	Michael Barrett RC,	
	Travis Fryman	1.00
8	Corey Jenkins, Mo Vaughn	.50
9	Ruben Rivera,	
	Frank Thomas	1.50
10	Curtis Goodwin,	
	Kenny Lofton	.50
11	Brian Hunter,	
	Tony Gwynn	1.75
12	Todd Greene,	
	Ken Griffey Jr.	2.50
	Karim Garcia,	
	Matt Williams	.75
14	Billy Wagner,	
	Randy Johnson	1.50
15	Pat Watkins,	
	Jeff Bagwell	1.50

Refractors

The large volume of silver foil in the background of the red and blue subsets in '95 Best make the Refractor technology much easier to see than in past issues. The chase cards, found one per six packs on average, also have a small "REFRACTOR" printed near the lower-left corner on back. The 15-card Mirror Image subset was not paralleled in Refractor technology, but in a process Topps calls "diffraction-foil" which creates a strong vertical-stripe rainbow effect in the background. Cards #72 (Carlos Perez) and 84 (Orlando Miller) can be found both with and without the "REFRACTOR" notice on back; neither version commands a premium.

	NM/M
Common Player:	1.00
Stars:	3-6X
Rookies:	2-3X

Refractors - Jumbo

These super-size versions of Bowman's Best Refractors were produced exclusively for inclusion as a one-per-box insert in retail boxes of the product distributed by ANCO to large retail chains. The 4-1/4" x 5-3/4" cards are identical in all ways except size to the regular refractors. The jumbo inserts were not produced in equal quantities, with the most popular players being printed in greater numbers.

	NM/M
Complete Set (10):	35.00
Common Player:	2.00
10	Cal Ripken Jr.	10.00
21	Greg Maddux	4.00
21	Tony Gwynn	4.00
35	Sammy Sosa	5.00
36	Mike Piazza	6.00
42	Mo Vaughn	2.00
49	Ken Griffey Jr.	6.00
50	Albert Belle	2.00
65	Frank Thomas	3.50
83	Hideo Nomo	3.00

1996 Bowman

KATSUHIRO MAEDA

In a "Guaranteed Value Program," Topps stated it would pay $100 for this set in 1999, if collectors mail in a request form (one per three packs), a $5 fee and the complete set in numerical order (only one per person). Every set redeemed was destroyed. The 385-card set has 110 veteran stars and 275 prospects. Backs of the prospects' cards provide a detailed scouting report. A "1st Bowman Card" gold-foil stamped logo was included on the card front for 156 players making their first appearance in a Bowman set. Insert sets include Bowman's Best Previews (along with Refractor and Atomic Refractor versions), a 1952

Mickey Mantle Bowman reprint (1 in 48 packs) and Minor League Player of the Year candidates. A 385-card parallel version of the entire base set was also produced on 18-point foilboard; seeded one per pack.

	NM/M
Complete Set (385):	50.00
Common Player:	.10
Foils:	1.5X
Pack (11):	2.00
Wax Box (24):	40.00
1	Cal Ripken Jr.	2.00
2	Ray Durham	.10
3	Ivan Rodriguez	.50
4	Fred McGriff	.10
5	Hideo Nomo	.50
6	Troy Percival	.20
7	Moises Alou	.10
8	Mike Stanley	.10
9	Jay Buhner	.10
10	Shawn Green	.25
11	Ryan Klesko	.10
12	Andres Galarraga	.10
13	Dean Palmer	.10
14	Jeff Conine	.10
15	Brian Hunter	.10
16	J.T. Snow	.10
17	Larry Walker	.10
18	Barry Larkin	.40
19	Alex Gonzalez	.10
20	Edgar Martinez	.10
21	Mo Vaughn	.10
22	Mark McGwire	1.50
23	Jose Canseco	.50
24	Jack McDowell	.10
25	Dante Bichette	.10
26	Wade Boggs	.50
27	Mike Piazza	1.00
28	Ray Lankford	.10
29	Craig Biggio	.25
30	Rafael Palmeiro	.50
31	Ron Gant	.10
32	Javy Lopez	.10
33	Brian Jordan	.10
34	Paul O'Neill	.10
35	Mark Grace	.25
36	Matt Williams	.20
37	Pedro Martinez	.75
38	Rickey Henderson	.50
39	Bobby Bonilla	.10
40	Todd Hollandsworth	.10
41	Jim Thome	.75
42	Gary Sheffield	.40
43	Tim Salmon	.10
44	Gregg Jefferies	.10
45	Roberto Alomar	.25
45p	Roberto Alomar	
	(Unmarked promo card,	
	fielding photo on front.)	3.00
46	Carlos Baerga	.10
47	Mark Grudzielanek	.10
48	Randy Johnson	.75
49	Tino Martinez	.25
50	Robin Ventura	.10
51	Ryne Sandberg	1.50
52	Jay Bell	.10
53	Jason Schmidt	.10
54	Frank Thomas	.75
55	Kenny Lofton	.10
56	Ariel Prieto	.10
57	David Cone	.10
58	Reggie Sanders	.10
59	Michael Tucker	.10
60	Vinny Castilla	.10
61	Lenny Dykstra	.10
62	Todd Hundley	.10
63	Brian McRae	.10
64	Dennis Eckersley	.40
65	Rondell White	.10
66	Eric Karros	.10
67	Greg Maddux	1.50
68	Kevin Appier	.10
69	Eddie Murray	.50
70	John Olerud	.10
71	Tony Gwynn	.75
72	David Justice	.10
73	Ken Caminiti	.10
74	Terry Steinbach	.10
75	Alan Benes	.10
76	Chipper Jones	1.00
77	Jeff Bagwell	.50
77p	Jeff Bagwell	
	(Unmarked promo card,	
	name in gold.)	6.00
78	Barry Bonds	2.00
79	Ken Griffey Jr.	1.50
80	Roger Cedeno	.10
81	Joe Carter	.10
82	Henry Rodriguez	.10
83	Jason Isringhausen	.10
84	Chuck Knoblauch	.10
85	Manny Ramirez	.75
86	Tom Glavine	.30
87	Jeffrey Hammonds	.10
88	Paul Molitor	.75
89	Roger Clemens	2.00
90	Greg Vaughn	.10
91	Marty Cordova	.10
92	Albert Belle	.40
93	Mike Mussina	.40
94	Garret Anderson	.10
95	Juan Gonzalez	.40
96	John Valentin	.10
97	Jason Giambi	.50
98	Kirby Puckett	1.50

#	Player	Price
99	Jim Edmonds	.25
100	Cecil Fielder	.10
101	Mike Aldrete	.10
102	Marquis Grissom	.10
103	Derek Bell	.10
104	Raul Mondesi	.10
105	Sammy Sosa	1.00
106	Travis Fryman	.10
107	Rico Brogna	.10
108	Will Clark	.25
109	Bernie Williams	.40
110	Brady Anderson	.10
111	Torii Hunter	.10
112	Derek Jeter	2.00
113	Mike Kusiewicz RC	.10
114	Scott Rolen	1.00
115	Ramon Castro	.10
116	Jose Guillen RC	2.50
117	Wade Walker	.10
118	Shawn Senior	.10
119	Onan Masaoka	.10
120	Marlon Anderson RC	.75
121	Katsuhiro Maeda RC	.25
122	Garrett Stephenson RC	.25
123	Butch Huskey	.10
124	D'Angelo Jimenez RC	.50
125	Tony Mounce RC	.20
126	Jay Canizaro	.10
127	Juan Melo	.10
128	Steve Gibralter	.10
129	Freddy Garcia	.10
130	Julio Santana	.10
131	Richard Hidalgo	.10
132	Jermaine Dye	.10
133	Willie Adams	.10
134	Everett Stull	.10
135	Ramon Morel	.10
136	Chan Ho Park	.10
137	Jamey Wright	.10
138	Luis Garcia RC	.10
139	Dan Serafini	.10
140	Ryan Dempster RC	.50
141	Tate Seefried	.10
142	Jimmy Hurst	.10
143	Travis Miller	.10
144	Curtis Goodwin	.10
145	Rocky Coppinger RC	.10
146	Enrique Wilson	.10
147	Jaime Bluma	.10
148	Andrew Vessel	.10
149	Damian Moss	.10
150	Shawn Gallagher RC	.10
151	Pat Watkins	.10
152	Jose Paniagua	.10
153	Danny Graves	.10
154	Bryon Gainey RC	.10
155	Steve Soderstrom	.10
156	Cliff Brumbaugh RC	.10
157	Eugene Kingsale RC	.10
158	Lou Collier	.10
159	Todd Walker	.10
160	Kris Detmers RC	.10
161	Josh Booty RC	.25
162	Greg Whiteman RC	.10
163	Damian Jackson	.10
164	Tony Clark	.10
165	Jeff D'Amico	.10
166	Johnny Damon	.50
167	Rafael Orellano	.10
168	Ruben Rivera	.10
169	Alex Ochoa	.10
170	Jay Powell	.10
171	Tom Evans	.10
172	Ron Villone	.10
173	Shawn Estes	.10
174	John Wasdin	.10
175	Bill Simas	.10
176	Kevin Brown	.10
177	Shannon Stewart	.10
178	Todd Greene	.10
179	Bob Wolcott	.10
180	Chris Snopek	.10
181	Nomar Garciaparra	1.00
182	Cameron Smith RC	.10
183	Matt Drews	.10
184	Jimmy Haynes	.10
185	Chris Carpenter	.25
186	Desi Relaford	.10
187	Ben Grieve	.10
188	Mike Bell	.10
189	Luis Castillo RC	.75
190	Ugueth Urbina	.10
191	Paul Wilson	.10
191p	Paul Wilson	
	(Unmarked promo card,	
	name in gold.)	1.00
192	Andruw Jones	.75
193	Wayne Gomes	.10
194	Craig Counsell RC	.75
195	Jim Cole	.10
196	Brooks Kieschnick	.10
197	Trey Beamon	.10
198	Marino Santana RC	.10
199	Bob Abreu	.25
200	Calvin Reese	.10
201	Dante Powell	.10
202	George Arias	.10
202p	George Arias	
	(Unmarked promo card,	
	name in gold.)	1.00
203	Jorge Velandia RC	.10
204	George Lombard RC	.10
205	Byron Browne RC	.10
206	John Frascatore	.10
207	Terry Adams	.10
208	Wilson Delgado RC	.10
209	Billy McMillon	.10
210	Jeff Abbott	.10

#	Player	
211	Trot Nixon	.10
212	Amaury Telemaco	.10
213	Scott Sullivan	.10
214	Justin Thompson	.10
215	Decomba Conner	.10
216	Ryan McGuire	.10
217	Matt Luke RC	.10
218	Doug Million	.10
219	Jason Dickson RC	.25
220	Ramon Hernandez RC	.50
221	Mark Bellhorn RC	.25
222	Eric Ludwick RC	.10
223	Luke Wilcox RC	.10
224	Marty Malloy RC	.10
225	Gary Coffee RC	.10
226	Wendell Magee RC	.10
227	Brett Tomko RC	.25
228	Derek Lowe	.10
229	Jose Rosado RC	.10
230	Steve Bourgeois RC	.10
231	Neil Weber RC	.10
232	Jeff Ware	.10
233	Edwin Diaz	.10
234	Greg Norton	.10
235	Aaron Boone	.10
236	Jeff Suppan	.10
237	Bret Wagner	.10
238	Elieser Marrero RC	.10
239	Will Cunnane RC	.10
240	Brian Barkley RC	.10
241	Jay Payton	.10
242	Marcus Jensen	.10
243	Ryan Nye	.10
244	Chad Mottola	.10
245	Scott McClain RC	.10
246	Jesse Ibarra RC	.10
247	Mike Darr RC	.10
248	Bobby Estalella RC	.50
249	Michael Barrett	.10
250	Jamie Lopiccolo RC	.10
251	Shane Spencer RC	.40
252	Ben Petrick RC	.50
253	Jason Bell RC	.10
254	Arnold Gooch RC	.10
255	T.J. Mathews	.10
256	Jason Ryan	.10
257	Pat Cline RC	.10
258	Rafael Carmona RC	.10
259	Carl Pavano RC	1.00
260	Ben Davis	.10
261	Matt Lawton RC	1.00
262	Kevin Sefcik RC	.10
263	Chris Fussell RC	.10
264	Mike Cameron RC	1.50
265	Marty Janzen RC	.10
266	Livan Hernandez RC	1.00
267	Raul Ibanez RC	1.50
268	Juan Encarnacion RC	.10
269	David Yocum RC	.10
270	Jonathan Johnson RC	.10
271	Reggie Taylor	.10
272	Danny Buxbaum RC	.10
273	Jacob Cruz	.10
274	Bobby Morris RC	.10
275	Andy Fox RC	.10
276	Greg Keagle	.10
277	Charles Peterson	.10
278	Derek Lee	.50
279	Bryant Nelson RC	.10
280	Antone Williamson	.10
281	Scott Elarton	.10
282	Shad Williams RC	.10
283	Rich Hunter RC	.10
284	Chris Sheff	.10
285	Derrick Gibson	.10
286	Felix Rodriguez	.10
287	Brian Banks RC	.10
288	Jason McDonald	.10
289	Glendon Rusch RC	.50
290	Gary Rath	.10
291	Peter Munro	.10
292	Tom Fordham	.10
293	Jason Kendall	.10
294	Russ Johnson	.10
295	Joe Long RC	.10
296	Robert Smith RC	.10
297	Jarrod Washburn RC	.75
298	Dave Coggin RC	.10
299	Jeff Yoder RC	.10
300	Jed Hansen RC	.10
301	Matt Morris RC	1.00
302	Josh Bishop RC	.10
303	Dustin Hermanson	.10
304	Mike Gulan	.10
305	Felipe Crespo	.10
306	Quinton McCracken RC	.10
307	Jim Bonnici RC	.10
308	Sal Fasano	.10
309	Gabe Alvarez RC	.10
310	Heath Murray RC	.10
311	Jose Valentin RC	.10
312	Bartolo Colon RC	.10
313	Olmedo Saenz	.10
314	Norm Hutchins RC	.10
315	Chris Holt	.10
316	David Doster RC	.10
317	Robert Person	.10
318	Donne Wall RC	.10
319	Adam Riggs RC	.10
320	Homer Bush	.10
321	Brad Rigby RC	.10
322	Lou Merloni RC	.25
323	Neifi Perez	.10
324	Chris Cumberland RC	.10
325	Alvie Shepherd RC	.10
326	Jarrod Patterson RC	.10
327	Ray Ricken RC	.10
328	Danny Klassen RC	.10
329	David Miller RC	.10
330	Chad Alexander RC	.10
331	Matt Beaumont	.10
332	Damon Hollins	.10
333	Todd Dunn	.10
334	Mike Sweeney RC	1.50
335	Richie Sexson	.40
336	Billy Wagner	.10
337	Ron Wright RC	.10
338	Paul Konerko	.25
339	Tommy Phelps RC	.10
340	Karim Garcia	.10
341	Mike Grace RC	.10
342	Russell Branyan RC	.40
343	Randy Winn RC	.50
344	A.J. Pierzynski RC	1.50
345	Mike Busby RC	.10
346	Matt Beech RC	.10
347	Jose Cepeda RC	.10
348	Brian Stephenson	.10
349	Rey Ordonez	.10
350	Rich Aurilia RC	1.00
351	Edgard Velazquez RC	.25
352	Raul Casanova	.10
353	Carlos Guillen RC	1.00
354	Bruce Aven RC	.10
355	Ryan Jones RC	.10
356	Derek Aucoin RC	.10
357	Brian Rose RC	.10
358	Richard Almanzar RC	.10
359	Fletcher Bates RC	.10
360	Russ Ortiz RC	.75
361	Wilton Guerrero RC	.10
362	Geoff Jenkins RC	1.00
363	Pete Janicki	.10
364	Yamil Benitez	.10
365	Aaron Holbert	.10
366	Tim Belk	.10
367	Terrell Wade	.10
368	Terrence Long	.10
369	Brad Fullmer	.10
370	Matt Wagner	.10
371	Craig Wilson	.10
372	Mark Loretta	.10
373	Eric Owens	.10
374	Vladimir Guerrero RC	1.00
375	Tommy Davis	.10
376	Donnie Sadler	.10
377	Edgar Renteria	.25
378	Todd Helton	.50
379	Ralph Milliard RC	.10
380	Darin Blood RC	.10
381	Shayne Bennett	.10
382	Mark Redman	.10
383	Felix Martinez	.10
384	Sean Watkins RC	.10
385	Oscar Henriquez	.10

Minor League Player of the Year

Fifteen prospects who were candidates for Minor League Player of the Year are featured in this 1996 Bowman baseball insert set. Cards were seeded one per every 12 packs.

		NM/M
	Complete Set (15):	12.50
	Common Player:	.50
1	Andruw Jones	4.00
2	Derrick Gibson	.50
3	Bob Abreu	.75
4	Todd Walker	.50
5	Jamey Wright	.50
6	Wes Helms	.50
7	Karim Garcia	.75
8	Bartolo Colon	2.00
9	Alex Ochoa	.50
10	Mike Sweeney	2.00
11	Ruben Rivera	.50
12	Gabe Alvarez	.50
13	Billy Wagner	.50
14	Vladimir Guerrero	4.00
15	Edgard Velazquez	.50

1952 Mickey Mantle Reprints

Reprints of Mickey Mantle's 1952 Bowman baseball card were created for insertion in Bowman and Bowman's Best products for 1996. The 2-1/2" x 3-1/2" card can be found in regular (gold seal on front), Finest, Finest Refractor and Atomic Refractor versions.

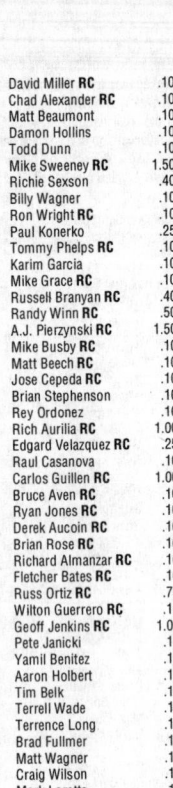

		NM/M
	Complete Set (4):	20.00
	Common Card:	2.50
20	Mickey Mantle/Reprint	2.50
20	Mickey Mantle/Finest	5.00
20	Mickey Mantle/Refractor	7.50
20	Mickey Mantle/ Atomic Refractor	10.00

1996 Bowman's Best Preview

These cards use Topps' Finest technology. The cards were seeded one per every 12 packs of 1996 Bowman baseball. Fifteen veterans and 15 prospects are featured in the set. Refractor versions are found one per 24 packs, with Atomic Refractors a 1:48 pick.

		NM/M
	Complete Set (30):	18.50
	Common Player:	.25
	Refractors:	1.5X
	Atomic Refractors:	2X
1	Chipper Jones	1.50
2	Alan Benes	.25
3	Brooks Kieshnick	.25
4	Barry Bonds	3.00
5	Rey Ordonez	.25
6	Tim Salmon	.25
7	Mike Piazza	2.00
8	Billy Wagner	.25
9	Andruw Jones	1.00
10	Tony Gwynn	1.50
11	Paul Wilson	.25
12	Calvin Reese	.25
13	Frank Thomas	1.00
14	Greg Maddux	1.50
15	Derek Jeter	3.00
16	Jeff Bagwell	1.00
17	Barry Larkin	.25
18	Todd Greene	.25
19	Ruben Rivera	.25
20	Richard Hidalgo	.25
21	Larry Walker	.25
22	Carlos Baerga	.25
23	Derrick Gibson	.25
24	Richie Sexson	.25
25	Mo Vaughn	.25
26	Hideo Nomo	.50
27	Nomar Garciaparra	1.50
28	Cal Ripken Jr.	3.00
29	Karim Garcia	.25
30	Ken Griffey Jr.	2.00

1996 Bowman's Best

Bowman's Best returns in its traditional format of 180 cards: 90 established stars and 90 up-and-coming prospects and rookies. Three types of insert sets are found in Bowman's Best: Mirror Image, Bowman's Best Cuts and the 1952 Bowman Mickey Mantle reprints. There are also parallel sets of Refractors and Atomic Refractors randomly seeded in packs. Refractors are found on average of one per 12 packs; Atomic Refractors are seeded one per 48 packs. Mirror Image Refractors are found one per 96 packs, while Mirror Image Atomic Refractors are seeded one per 192 packs. Refractor versions of the Mantle reprint are seeded one per every 96 packs; Atomic Refractor Mantle reprints are seeded in every 192nd pack.

		NM/M
	Complete Set (180):	30.00
	Common Player:	.25
	Refractors:	2X
	Atomics:	15X
	1952 Mickey Mantle:	2.50
	1952 Mantle Finest:	5.00
	1952 Mantle Refractor:	7.50
	1952 Mantle Atomic:	10.00
	Pack (6):	2.50
	Wax Box (24):	40.00
1	Hideo Nomo	.75
2	Edgar Martinez	.25
3	Cal Ripken Jr.	4.00
4	Wade Boggs	1.00
5	Cecil Fielder	.25
6	Albert Belle	.25
7	Chipper Jones	1.50
8	Ryne Sandberg	2.00
9	Tim Salmon	.25
10	Barry Bonds	3.00
11	Ken Caminiti	.25
12	Ron Gant	.25
13	Frank Thomas	1.00
14	Dante Bichette	.25
15	Jason Kendall	.25
16	Mo Vaughn	.25
17	Rey Ordonez	.25
18	Henry Rodriguez	.25
19	Ryan Klesko	.25
20	Jeff Bagwell	1.00
21	Randy Johnson	1.50
22	Jim Edmonds	.25
23	Kenny Lofton	.25
24	Andy Pettitte	.50
25	Brady Anderson	.25
26	Mike Piazza	2.50
27	Greg Vaughn	.25
28	Joe Carter	.25
29	Jason Giambi	1.00
30	Ivan Rodriguez	1.00
31	Jeff Conine	.25
32	Rafael Palmeiro	.75
33	Roger Clemens	3.00
34	Chuck Knoblauch	.25
35	Reggie Sanders	.25
36	Andres Galarraga	.25
37	Paul O'Neill	.25
38	Tony Gwynn	2.00
39	Paul Wilson	.25
40	Garret Anderson	.25
41	David Justice	.25
42	Eddie Murray	1.00
43	Mike Grace RC	.25
44	Marty Cordova	.25
45	Kevin Appier	.25
46	Raul Mondesi	.25
47	Jim Thome	1.00
48	Sammy Sosa	2.00
49	Craig Biggio	.50
50	Marquis Grissom	.25
51	Alan Benes	.25
52	Manny Ramirez	1.50
53	Gary Sheffield	.75
54	Mike Mussina	.50
55	Robin Ventura	.25
56	Johnny Damon	1.00
57	Jose Canseco	.75
58	Juan Gonzalez	.75
59	Tino Martinez	.25
60	Brian Hunter	.25
61	Fred McGriff	.25
62	Jay Buhner	.25
63	Carlos Delgado	.75
64	Moises Alou	.50
65	Roberto Alomar	.50
66	Barry Larkin	.50
67	Vinny Castilla	.25
68	Ray Durham	.25
69	Travis Fryman	.25
70	Jason Isringhausen	.25
71	Ken Griffey Jr.	2.50
72	John Smoltz	.25
73	Matt Williams	.25
74	Chan Ho Park	.25
75	Mark McGwire	2.50
76	Jeffrey Hammonds	.25
77	Will Clark	.25
78	Kirby Puckett	2.00
79	Derek Jeter	4.00
80	Derek Bell	.25
81	Eric Karros	.25
82	Lenny Dykstra	.25
83	Larry Walker	.50
84	Mark Grudzielanek	.25
85	Greg Maddux	2.50
86	Carlos Baerga	.25
87	Paul Molitor	1.00
88	John Valentin	.25
89	Mark Grace	.50
90	Ray Lankford	.25
91	Andruw Jones	1.50
92	Nomar Garciaparra	2.00
93	Alex Ochoa	.25
94	Derrick Gibson	.25
95	Jeff D'Amico	.25
96	Ruben Rivera	.25
97	Vladimir Guerrero	1.50
98	Calvin Reese	.25
99	Richard Hidalgo	.25
100	Bartolo Colon	.25
101	Karim Garcia	.25
102	Ben Davis	.25
103	Jay Powell	.25
104	Chris Snopek	.25
105	Glendon Rusch RC	1.00
106	Enrique Wilson	.25
107	Antonio Alfonseca RC	.75
108	Wilton Guerrero RC	.50
109	Jose Guillen	3.00
110	Miguel Mejia RC	.25
111	Jay Payton	.25
112	Scott Elarton	.25
113	Brooks Kieschnick	.25
114	Dustin Hermanson	.25
115	Roger Cedeno	.25
116	Matt Wagner	.25
117	Lee Daniels	.25
118	Ben Grieve	.25
119	Ugueth Urbina	.25
120	Danny Graves	.25
121	Dan Donato RC	.25
122	Matt Ruebel RC	.25
123	Mark Sievert RC	.25
124	Chris Stynes	.25
125	Jeff Abbott	.25
126	Rocky Coppinger RC	.25
127	Jermaine Dye	.25
128	Todd Greene	.25
129	Chris Carpenter	1.00
130	Edgar Renteria	.50
131	Matt Drews	.25
132	Edgard Velazquez RC	.50
133	Casey Whitten	.25
134	Ryan Jones RC	.25
135	Todd Walker	.25
136	Geoff Jenkins RC	2.00
137	Matt Morris RC	2.00
138	Richie Sexson	.75
139	Todd Dunwoody RC	.50
140	Gabe Alvarez RC	.25
141	J.J. Johnson	.25
142	Shannon Stewart	.25
143	Brad Fullmer	.25
144	Julio Santana	.25
145	Scott Rolen	1.00
146	Amaury Telemaco	.25
147	Trey Beamon	.25
148	Billy Wagner	.20
149	Todd Hollandsworth	.25
150	Doug Million	.25
151	Jose Valentin	.25
152	Wes Helms RC	.50
153	Jeff Suppan	.25
154	Luis Castillo	.50
155	Bob Abreu	.50
156	Paul Konerko	.50
157	Jamey Wright	.25
158	Eddie Pearson	.25
159	Jimmy Haynes	.25
160	Derrek Lee	.75
161	Damian Moss	.15
162	Carlos Guillen RC	2.00
163	Chris Fussell RC	.25
164	Mike Sweeney RC	3.00
165	Donnie Sadler	.15
166	Desi Relaford	.25
167	Steve Gibralter	.25
168	Neifi Perez	.25
169	Antone Williamson	.25
170	Marty Janzen RC	.25
171	Todd Helton	1.00
172	Raul Ibanez RC	2.00
173	Bill Selby	.25
174	Shane Monahan RC	.35
175	Robin Jennings RC	.25
176	Bobby Chouinard RC	.25
177	Einar Diaz	.25
178	Jason Thompson	.15
179	Rafael Medina RC	.25
180	Kevin Orie	.25

Cuts

Bowman's Best Cuts gave collectors the first die-cut chromium cards in a 15-card set of top stars. The cards were seeded one per 24 packs. Refractor versions are inserted on average of one per 48 packs; Atomic Refractor versions are found one per 96 packs.

Ken Griffey Jr.

		NM/M
	Complete Set (15):	15.00
	Common Player:	.50
	Refractors:	1.5X
	Atomic Refractors:	2X
1	Ken Griffey Jr.	2.50
2	Jason Isringhausen	.25
3	Derek Jeter	4.00
4	Andruw Jones	1.00
5	Chipper Jones	2.00
6	Ryan Klesko	.25
7	Raul Mondesi	.25
8	Hideo Nomo	.50
9	Mike Piazza	2.50
10	Manny Ramirez	.50
11	Cal Ripken Jr.	4.00
12	Ruben Rivera	.25
13	Tim Salmon	1.00
14	Frank Thomas	1.00
15	Jim Thome	.75

Mirror Image

Mirror Image inserts feature four top players at 10 different positions, pairing an American League veteran and a prospect on one side and a National League veteran and prospect on the other. These cards are seeded one per every 48 packs. Mirror Image Refractors (one in every 96 packs) and Mirror Image Atomic Refractors (one in every 192 packs) were also produced.

		NM/M
	Complete Set (10):	24.00
	Common Card:	1.50
	Refractors:	1.5X
	Atomics:	2X
1	Jeff Bagwell, Todd Helton, Frank Thomas, Richie Sexson	3.00
2	Craig Biggio, Luis Castillo, Roberto Alomar, Desi Relaford	1.50
3	Chipper Jones, Scott Rolen, Wade Boggs, George Arias	3.50
4	Barry Larkin, Neifi Perez, Cal Ripken Jr., Mark Bellhorn	6.00
5	Larry Walker, Karim Garcia, Albert Belle, Ruben Rivera	1.50
6	Barry Bonds, Andruw Jones, Kenny Lofton, Donnie Sadler	6.00
7	Tony Gwynn, Vladimir Guerrero, Ken Griffey Jr., Ben Grieve	4.50
8	Mike Piazza, Ben Davis, Ivan Rodriguez, Jose Valentin	4.50
9	Greg Maddux, Jamey Wright, Mike Mussina, Bartolo Colon	3.50
10	Tom Glavine, Billy Wagner, Randy Johnson, Jarrod Washburn	1.5

1997 Bowman Pre-Production

PP2 ATLANTA
HT: 6'1 WT: 185 BATS: RIGHT THROWS
BORN: 4-23-77, CURACAO, NETHERLANDS
SIGNED: BRAVES, 1991, AS FREE AGENT
SCOUTING

The format for 1997 Bowman's base set was previewed in this sample issue distributed to card dealers and the hobby press. The samples are virtually identical to the issued versions of the same players' cards, except they carry a "PP" prefix to the number on back.

	NM/M
Complete Set (4):	9.00
Common Player:	1.50
PP1 Jose Cruz, Jr.	1.50
PP2 Andruw Jones	2.00
PP3 Derek Jeter	4.50
PP4 Sammy Sosa	3.00

1997 Bowman

The 1997 Bowman set consists of 440 base cards, an increase of 55 cards from the '96 set. Fronts have a player photo within a red or blue frame with black borders. Backs feature another color photo, along with 1996 statistics broken down by opponent. Players making their first appearance in a Bowman set have a "1st Bowman Card" designation on the card. Prospects' cards have red foil on front; veterans have blue. Inserts include International parallels, Certified Autographs, Scout's Honor Roll and Bowman's Best Previews. Cards were sold in 10-card packs with a suggested retail price of $2.50. Topps offered collectors a $125 guarantee on the value of the set through the year 2000.

	NM/M
Complete Set (440):	50.00
Complete Series 1 (221):	25.00
Complete Series 2 (219):	25.00
Common Player:	.10
Series 1 Pack (10):	2.00
Series 1 Wax Box (24):	35.00
Series 2 Pack (10):	2.00
Series 2 Wax Box (24):	35.00
1 Derek Jeter	2.00
2 Edgar Renteria	.10
3 Chipper Jones	1.00
4 Hideo Nomo	.40
5 Tim Salmon	.25
6 Jason Giambi	.50
7 Robin Ventura	.10
8 Tony Clark	.10
9 Barry Larkin	.25
10 Paul Molitor	.75
11 Bernard Gilkey	.10
12 Jack McDowell	.10
13 Andy Benes	.10
14 Ryan Klesko	.10
15 Mark McGwire	1.50
16 Ken Griffey Jr.	1.50
17 Robb Nen	.10
18 Cal Ripken Jr.	2.00
19 John Valentin	.10
20 Ricky Bottalico	.10
21 Mike Lansing	.10
22 Ryne Sandberg	1.00
23 Carlos Delgado	.50
24 Craig Biggio	.25
25 Eric Karros	.10
26 Kevin Appier	.10
27 Mariano Rivera	.50
28 Vinny Castilla	.10
29 Juan Gonzalez	.40
30 Al Martin	.10
31 Jeff Cirillo	.10
32 Eddie Murray	.75
33 Ray Lankford	.10
34 Manny Ramirez	.75
35 Roberto Alomar	.25
36 Will Clark	.25
37 Chuck Knoblauch	.25
38 Harold Baines	.10
39 Trevor Hoffman	.10
40 Edgar Martinez	.10
41 Geronimo Berroa	.10
42 Rey Ordonez	.10
43 Mike Stanley	.10
44 Mike Mussina	.40
45 Kevin Brown	.10

46 Dennis Eckersley	.50
47 Henry Rodriguez	.10
48 Tino Martinez	.10
49 Eric Young	.10
50 Bret Boone	.10
51 Raul Mondesi	.10
52 Sammy Sosa	1.00
53 John Smoltz	.25
54 Billy Wagner	.10
55 Jeff D'Amico	.10
56 Ken Caminiti	.10
57 Jason Kendall	.10
58 Wade Boggs	.75
59 Andres Galarraga	.10
60 Jeff Brantley	.10
61 Mel Rojas	.10
62 Brian Hunter	.10
63 Bobby Bonilla	.10
64 Roger Clemens	1.50
65 Jeff Kent	.20
66 Matt Williams	.10
67 Albert Belle	.10
68 Jeff King	.10
69 John Wetteland	.10
70 Deion Sanders	.25
71 Bubba Trammell RC	.25
72 Felix Heredia RC	.25
73 Billy Koch RC	.25
74 Sidney Ponson RC	.25
75 Ricky Ledee RC	.25
76 Brett Tomko	.10
77 Braden Looper RC	.25
78 Damian Jackson	.10
79 Jason Dickson	.10
80 Chad Green RC	.10
81 R.A. Dickey RC	.10
82 Jeff Liefer	.10
83 Matt Wagner	.10
84 Richard Hidalgo	.10
85 Adam Riggs	.10
86 Robert Smith	.10
87 Chad Hermansen RC	.10
88 Felix Martinez	.10
89 J.J. Johnson	.10
90 Todd Dunwoody	.10
91 Katsuhiro Maeda	.25
92 Darin Erstad	.25
93 Elieser Marrero	.10
94 Bartolo Colon	.25
95 Chris Fussell	.10
96 Ugueth Urbina	.10
97 Josh Paul RC	.10
98 Jaime Bluma	.10
99 Seth Greisinger RC	.10
100 Jose Cruz RC	.25
101 Todd Dunn	.10
102 Joe Young RC	.10
103 Jonathan Johnson	.10
104 Justin Towle RC	.10
105 Brian Rose	.10
106 Jose Guillen	.10
107 Andruw Jones	.75
108 Mark Kotsay RC	1.00
109 Wilton Guerrero	.10
110 Jacob Cruz	.10
111 Mike Sweeney	.10
112 Julio Mosquera	.10
113 Matt Morris	.10
114 Wendell Magee	.10
115 John Thomson	.10
116 Javier Valentin RC	.10
117 Tom Fordham	.10
118 Ruben Rivera	.10
119 Mike Drumright RC	.10
120 Chris Holt	.10
121 Sean Maloney RC	.10
122 Michael Barrett	.10
123 Tony Saunders RC	.10
124 Kevin Brown	.10
125 Richard Almanzar	.10
126 Mark Redman	.10
127 Anthony Sanders RC	.10
128 Jeff Abbott	.10
129 Eugene Kingsale	.10
130 Paul Konerko	.40
131 Randall Simon RC	.25
132 Andy Larkin	.10
133 Rafael Medina	.10
134 Mendy Lopez	.10
135 Freddy Garcia	.10
136 Karim Garcia	.10
137 Larry Rodriguez RC	.10
138 Carlos Guillen	.10
139 Aaron Boone	.10
140 Donnie Sadler	.10
141 Brooks Kieschnick	.10
142 Everett Stull	.10
143 Everett Stull	.10
144 Enrique Wilson	.10
145 Milton Bradley RC	1.50
146 Kevin Orie	.10
147 Derek Wallace	.10
148 Russ Johnson	.10
149 Joe Lagarde RC	.10
150 Luis Castillo	.10
151 Jay Payton	.10
152 Joe Long	.10
153 Livan Hernandez	.10
154 Vladimir Nunez RC	.15
156a George Arias	.10
156b Calvin Reese	
(Should be #155.)	.10
157 Homer Bush	.10
159a Eric Milton RC	.50
159b Chris Carpenter	
(Should be #158.)	.50
160 Richie Sexson	.40
161 Carl Pavano	.10

162 Chris Gissell RC	.10
163 Mac Suzuki	.10
164 Pat Cline	.10
165 Ron Wright	.10
166 Dante Powell	.10
167 Mark Bellhorn	.10
168 George Lombard	.10
169 Pee Wee Lopez RC	.10
170 Paul Wilder RC	.10
171 Brad Fullmer	.10
172 Willie Martinez RC	.10
173 Dario Veras RC	.10
174 Dave Coggin	.10
175 Kris Benson RC	1.00
176 Torii Hunter	.25
177 D.T. Cromer RC	.10
178 Nelson Figueroa RC	.10
179 Hiram Bocachica RC	.15
180 Shane Monahan	.10
181 Jimmy Anderson RC	.10
182 Juan Melo	.10
183 Pablo Ortega RC	.10
184 Calvin Pickering RC	.50
185 Reggie Taylor	.10
186 Jeff Farnsworth RC	.10
187 Terrence Long	.10
188 Geoff Jenkins	.10
189 Steve Rain RC	.10
190 Nerio Rodriguez RC	.10
191 Derrick Gibson	.10
192 Darin Blood	.10
193 Ben Davis	.10
194 Adrian Beltre RC	2.00
195 Damian Sapp RC	.10
196 Kerry Wood RC	3.00
197 Nate Rolison RC	.10
198 Fernando Tatis RC	.25
199 Brad Penny RC	2.00
200 Jake Westbrook RC	.15
201 Edwin Diaz	.10
202 Joe Fontenot RC	.10
203 Matt Halloran RC	.10
204 Blake Stein RC	.10
205 Onan Masaoka	.10
206 Ben Petrick	.10
207 Matt Clement RC	1.00
208 Todd Greene	.10
209 Ray Ricken	.10
210 Eric Chavez RC	3.00
211 Edgard Velazquez	.10
212 Bruce Chen RC	.10
213 Danny Patterson RC	.10
214 Jeff Yoder	.10
215 Luis Ordaz RC	.10
216 Chris Widger	.10
217 Jason Brester	.10
218 Carlton Loewer	.10
219 Chris Reitsma RC	.10
220 Neifi Perez	.10
221 Hideki Irabu RC	.25
222 Ellis Burks	.10
223 Pedro Martinez	.75
224 Kenny Lofton	.10
225 Randy Johnson	.75
226 Terry Steinbach	.10
227 Bernie Williams	.25
228 Dean Palmer	.10
229 Alan Benes	.10
230 Marquis Grissom	.10
231 Gary Sheffield	.40
232 Curt Schilling	.40
233 Reggie Sanders	.10
234 Bobby Higginson	.10
235 Moises Alou	.20
236 Tom Glavine	.25
237 Mark Grace	.25
238 Ramon Martinez	.10
239 Rafael Palmeiro	.50
240 John Olerud	.10
241 Dante Bichette	.10
242 Greg Vaughn	.10
243 Jeff Bagwell	.75
244 Barry Bonds	2.00
245 Pat Hentgen	.10
246 Jim Thome	.50
247 Jermaine Allensworth	.10
248 Andy Pettitte	.25
249 Jay Bell	.10
250 John Jaha	.10
251 Jim Edmonds	.25
252 Ron Gant	.10
253 David Cone	.10
254 Jose Canseco	.40
255 Jay Buhner	.10
256 Greg Maddux	1.50
257 Brian McRae	.10
258 Lance Johnson	.10
259 Travis Fryman	.10
260 Paul O'Neill	.20
261 Ivan Rodriguez	.50
262 Gregg Jefferies	.10
263 Fred McGriff	.20
264 Derek Bell	.10
265 Jeff Conine	.10
266 Mike Piazza	1.50
267 Mark Grudzielanek	.10
268 Brady Anderson	.10
269 Marty Cordova	.10
270 Ray Durham	.10
271 Joe Carter	.10
272 Brian Jordan	.10
273 David Justice	.10
274 Tony Gwynn	1.00
275 Larry Walker	.10
276 Cecil Fielder	.10
277 Mo Vaughn	.50
278 Alex Fernandez	.10
279 Michael Tucker	.10

280 Jose Valentin	.10
281 Sandy Alomar	.10
282 Todd Hollandsworth	.10
283 Rico Brogna	.10
284 Rusty Greer	.10
285 Roberto Hernandez	.10
286 Hal Morris	.10
287 Johnny Damon	.75
288 Todd Hundley	.10
289 Rondell White	.10
290 Frank Thomas	.75
291 Don Denbow	.10
292 Derrek Lee	.50
293 Todd Walker	.10
294 Scott Rolen	.50
295 Wes Helms	.10
296 Bob Abreu	.25
297 John Patterson RC	1.50
298 Alex Gonzalez RC	.25
299 Grant Roberts RC	.25
300 Jeff Suppan RC	.10
301 Luke Wilcox	.10
302 Marlon Anderson	.10
303 Ray Brown	.10
304 Mike Caruso RC	.10
305 Sam Marsonek RC	.10
306 Brady Raggio RC	.10
307 Kevin McGlinchy RC	.25
308 Roy Halladay RC	3.00
309 Jeremi Gonzalez RC	.25
310 Aramis Ramirez RC	4.00
311 Dermal Brown RC	.10
312 Justin Thompson	.10
313 Jay Tessmer RC	.10
314 Mike Johnson	.10
315 Danny Clyburn	.10
316 Bruce Aven	.10
317 Keith Foulke RC	1.50
318 Jimmy Osting RC	.10
319 Valerio De Los Santos RC	.25
320 Shannon Stewart	.10
321 Willie Adams	.10
322 Larry Barnes	.10
323 Mark Johnson	.10
324 Chris Stowers RC	.10
325 Brandon Reed	.10
326 Randy Winn	.10
327 Steven Chavez	.10
328 Nomar Garciaparra	1.00
329 Jacque Jones RC	1.00
330 Chris Clemons	.10
331 Todd Helton	.50
332 Ryan Brannan RC	.10
333 Alex Sanchez RC	.25
334 Arnold Gooch	.10
335 Russell Branyan	.10
336 Daryle Ward	.10
337 John LeRoy RC	.10
338 Steve Cox	.10
339 Kevin Witt	.10
340 Norm Hutchins	.10
341 Gabby Martinez	.10
342 Kris Detmers	.10
343 Mike Villano RC	.10
344 Preston Wilson	.10
345 Jim Manias RC	.10
346 Deivi Cruz RC	.25
347 Donzell McDonald RC	.10
348 Rod Myers RC	.10
349 Shawn Chacon RC	.25
350 Elvin Hernandez RC	.10
351 Orlando Cabrera RC	1.00
352 Brian Banks	.10
353 Robbie Bell	.10
354 Brad Rigby	.10
355 Scott Elarton	.10
356 Kevin Sweeney RC	.10
357 Steve Soderstrom	.10
358 Ryan Nye	.10
359 Marlon Allen RC	.10
360 Donny Leon RC	.10
361 Garrett Neubart RC	.10
362 Abraham Nunez RC	.25
363 Adam Eaton RC	.50
364 Octavio Dotel RC	.40
365 Dean Crow RC	.10
366 Jason Baker RC	.10
367 Sean Casey	.10
368 Joe Lawrence RC	.10
369 Adam Johnson RC	.10
370 Scott Schoeneweis RC	.25
371 Gerald Witasick Jr.	.10
372 Ronnie Belliard RC	.25
373 Russ Ortiz	.10
374 Robert Stratton RC	.10
375 Bobby Estalella	.10
376 Corey Lee RC	.10
377 Carlos Beltran RC	.50
378 Mike Cameron	.10
379 Scott Randall RC	.10
380 Corey Erickson RC	.10
381 Jay Canizaro	.10
382 Kerry Robinson RC	.10
383 Todd Noel RC	.10
384 A.J. Zapp RC	.10
385 Jarrod Washburn RC	.10
386 Ben Grieve	.10
387 Javier Vazquez RC	1.50
388 Tony Graffanino	.10
389 Travis Lee RC	.50
390 DaRond Stovall	.10
391 Dennis Reyes RC	.25
392 Danny Buxbaum	.10
393 Marc Lewis RC	.10
394 Kelvim Escobar RC	.25
395 Danny Klassen	.10
396 Ken Cloude RC	.25
397 Gabe Alvarez	.10

398 Jaret Wright RC	.50
399 Raul Casanova	.10
400 Clayton Brunner RC	.10
401 Jason Marquis RC	.50
402 Marc Kroon	.10
403 Jamey Wright	.10
404 Matt Snyder RC	.10
405 Josh Garrett RC	.10
406 Juan Encarnacion	.10
407 Heath Murray	.10
408 Brett Herbison RC	.10
409 Brent Butler RC	.25
410 Danny Peoples RC	.25
411 Miguel Tejada RC	10.00
412 Damian Moss	.10
413 Jim Pittsley	.10
414 Dmitri Young	.10
415 Glendon Rusch	.10
416 Vladimir Guerrero	.75
417 Cole Liniak RC	.10
418 Ramon Hernandez RC	.10
419 Cliff Politte RC	.25
420 Mel Rosario RC	.10
421 Jorge Carrion RC	.10
422 John Barnes RC	.10
423 Chris Stowe RC	.10
424 Vernon Wells RC	4.00
425 Brett Caradonna RC	.10
426 Scott Hodges RC	.10
427 Jon Garland RC	1.50
428 Nathan Haynes RC	.25
429 Geoff Goetz RC	.10
430 Adam Kennedy RC	.50
431 T.J. Tucker RC	.10
432 Aaron Akin RC	.10
433 Jayson Werth RC	.50
434 Glenn Davis RC	.10
435 Mark Mangum RC	.10
436 Troy Cameron RC	.10
437 J.J. Davis RC	.10
438 Lance Berkman RC	8.00
439 Jason Standridge RC	.25
440 Jason Dellaero RC	.25
441 Hideki Irabu RC	.25

Certified Autographs

Ninety players signed autographs for inclusion in Series 1 and 2 packs. Each autograph card features a gold-foil Certified Autograph stamp on front and can be found in one of three versions: Blue, 1:96 packs; black, 1:503 packs and gold, 1:1,509 packs. Derek Jeter's card can also be found in a green-ink autographed version, inserted one per 1,928 packs. Card numbers have a "CA" prefix.

	NM/M
Common Blue:	2.00
Black:	1.5X
Gold:	4X
Derek Jeter Green:	1.5X
1 Jeff Abbott	2.00
2 Bob Abreu	40.00
3 Willie Adams	2.00
4 Brian Banks	2.00
5 Kris Benson	15.00
6 Darin Blood	2.00
7 Jaime Bluma	2.00
8 Kevin Brown	5.00
9 Ray Brown	2.00
10 Homer Bush	4.00
11 Mike Cameron	8.00
12 Jay Canizaro	3.00
13 Luis Castillo	5.00
14 Dave Coggin	2.00
15 Bartolo Colon	15.00
16 Rocky Coppinger	2.00
17 Jacob Cruz	2.00
18 Jose Cruz	8.00
19 Jeff D'Amico	5.00
20 Ben Davis	5.00
21 Mike Drumbright	5.00
22 Scott Elarton	5.00
23 Darin Erstad	10.00
24 Bobby Estalella	5.00
25 Joe Fontenot	4.00
26 Tom Fordham	2.00
27 Brad Fullmer	5.00
28 Chris Fussell	2.00
29 Karim Garcia	5.00
30 Kris Detmers	5.00
31 Todd Greene	5.00
32 Ben Grieve	5.00
33 Vladimir Guerrero	75.00

34 Jose Guillen	15.00
35 Roy Halladay	65.00
36 Wes Helms	5.00
37 Chad Hermansen	8.00
38 Richard Hidalgo	3.00
39 Todd Hollandsworth	3.00
40 Damian Jackson	3.00
41 Derek Jeter	120.00
42 Andruw Jones	20.00
43 Brooks Kieschnick	3.00
44 Eugene Kingsale	5.00
45 Paul Konerko	15.00
46 Marc Kroon	2.00
47 Derrek Lee	40.00
48 Travis Lee	5.00
49 Terrence Long	4.00
50 Curt Lyons	2.00
51 Elieser Marrero	3.00
52 Rafael Medina	3.00
53 Juan Melo	3.00
54 Shane Monahan	2.00
55 Julio Mosquera	2.00
56 Heath Murray	2.00
57 Ryan Nye	2.00
58 Kevin Orie	4.00
59 Russ Ortiz	5.00
60 Carl Pavano	30.00
61 Jay Payton	5.00
62 Neifi Perez	3.00
63 Sidney Ponson	10.00
64 Calvin Reese	8.00
65 Ray Ricken	3.00
66 Brad Rigby	3.00
67 Adam Riggs	3.00
68 Ruben Rivera	4.00
69 J.J. Johnson	2.00
70 Scott Rolen	40.00
71 Tony Saunders	3.00
72 Donnie Sadler	5.00
73 Richie Sexson	15.00
74 Scott Spiezio	6.00
75 Everett Stull	2.00
76 Mike Sweeney	15.00
77 Fernando Tatis	4.00
78 Miguel Tejada	80.00
79 Justin Thompson	5.00
80 Justin Towle	6.00
81 Billy Wagner	20.00
82 Todd Walker	5.00
83 Luke Wilcox	2.00
84 Paul Wilder	4.00
85 Enrique Wilson	5.00
86 Kerry Wood	60.00
87 Jamey Wright	5.00
88 Ron Wright	5.00
89 Dmitri Young	10.00
90 Nelson Figueroa	2.00

International

Inserted at the rate of one per pack, the International parallel set replaces the regular photo background on front and back with the flag of the player's native land. Card #441 from the regular-issue version does not exist as an International parallel.

	NM/M
Complete Set (440):	75.00
Complete Series 1 (221):	40.00
Complete Series 2 (219):	40.00
Common Player:	.25
Stars and Rookies:	1.5X

International Best

This Series 2 insert set features a flag design in the background of each card front depicting the player's country of origin. On back is another color photo, player personal data, a record of his best season and colored flags representing 14 nations which have sent players to the major leagues. One International Best card was inserted in every second series pack. Card numbers carry a "BBI" prefix. Refractor versions are a 1:48 parallel with Atomic Refractors found 1:96.

	NM/M
Complete Set (20):	20.00
Common Player:	.60
Refractors:	1.5X
Atomic Refractors:	2X

#	Player	Price
1	Frank Thomas	1.50
2	Ken Griffey Jr.	2.50
3	Juan Gonzalez	1.50
4	Bernie Williams	.60
5	Hideo Nomo	1.50
6	Sammy Sosa	3.50
7	Larry Walker	.60
8	Vinny Castilla	.60
9	Mariano Rivera	.75
10	Rafael Palmeiro	1.00
11	Nomar Garciaparra	3.50
12	Todd Walker	.60
13	Andruw Jones	1.50
14	Vladimir Guerrero	1.50
15	Ruben Rivera	.60
16	Bob Abreu	.75
17	Karim Garcia	.75
18	Katsuhiro Maeda	.60
19	Jose Cruz Jr.	1.00
20	Damian Moss	.60

Rookie of the Year Candidates

MARK KOTSAY

This 15-card insert was inserted in one per 12 packs of Bowman Series 2. Fronts feature a color shot of the player over a textured foil background, with the player's name across the bottom and the words "Rookie of the Year Favorites" across the top with the word "Rookie" in large script letters. Card numbers have a "ROY" prefix.

NM/M
#	Player	Price
	Complete Set (15):	9.00
	Common Player:	.50
1	Jeff Abbott	.50
2	Karim Garcia	.50
3	Todd Helton	2.50
4	Richard Hidalgo	.50
5	Geoff Jenkins	.50
6	Russ Johnson	.50
7	Paul Konerko	.75
8	Mark Kotsay	.50
9	Ricky Ledee	.50
10	Travis Lee	.75
11	Derrek Lee	1.50
12	Elieser Marrero	.50
13	Juan Melo	.50
14	Brian Rose	.50
15	Fernando Tatis	.50

Scout's Honor Roll

DARIN ERSTAD

This insert features 15 prospects deemed to have the most potential by Topps's scouts. Each card features a double-etched foil design and is inserted 1:12 packs.

NM/M
#	Player	Price
	Complete Set (15):	12.50
	Common Player:	.50
1	Dmitri Young	.50
2	Bob Abreu	.75
3	Vladimir Guerrero	2.00
4	Paul Konerko	.75
5	Kevin Orie	.50
6	Todd Walker	.50
7	Ben Grieve	1.00
8	Darin Erstad	1.00
9	Derrek Lee	.50
10	Jose Cruz	.50
11	Scott Rolen	1.00
12	Travis Lee	.75
13	Andruw Jones	2.00
14	Wilton Guerrero	.50
15	Nomar Garciaparra	2.50

1997 Bowman's Best Preview

NOMAR GARCIAPARRA

This 20-card set, featuring 10 veterans and 10 prospects, is a preview of the format used in the Bowman's Best product. Three different versions of the Preview cards were available: Regular (1:12 packs), Refractors (1:48) and Atomic Refractors (1:96).

NM/M
#	Player	Price
	Complete Set (20):	30.00
	Common Player:	.75
	Refractors:	1.5X
	Atomic Refractors:	2X
1	Frank Thomas	1.50
2	Ken Griffey Jr.	3.00
3	Barry Bonds	5.00
4	Derek Jeter	5.00
5	Chipper Jones	2.00
6	Mark McGwire	4.00
7	Cal Ripken Jr.	5.00
8	Kenny Lofton	.75
9	Gary Sheffield	.75
10	Jeff Bagwell	1.50
11	Wilton Guerrero	.75
12	Scott Rolen	1.00
13	Todd Walker	.75
14	Ruben Rivera	.75
15	Andruw Jones	1.50
16	Nomar Garciaparra	2.00
17	Vladimir Guerrero	1.50
18	Miguel Tejada	1.00
19	Bartolo Colon	.75
20	Katsuhiro Maeda	.75

1997 Bowman Chrome

DEREK JETER

Bowman Chrome was released in one 300-card series following the conclusion of the 1997 season. Four-card foil packs carried an SRP of $3. Each card reprints one of the regular Bowman set, utilizing chromium technology on front. Inserts include: International parallels, Rookie of the Year Favorites and Scout's Honor Roll.

NM/M
#	Player	Price
	Complete Set (300):	150.00
	Common Player:	.25
	Pack (3):	5.00
	Wax Box (24):	100.00
1	Derek Jeter	4.00
2	Chipper Jones	2.00
3	Hideo Nomo	.75
4	Tim Salmon	.25
5	Robin Ventura	.25
6	Tony Clark	.25
7	Barry Larkin	.50
8	Paul Molitor	1.00
9	Andy Benes	.25
10	Ryan Klesko	.25
11	Mark McGwire	3.00
12	Ken Griffey Jr.	2.50
13	Robb Nen	.25
14	Cal Ripken Jr.	4.00
15	John Valentin	.25
16	Ricky Bottalico	.25
17	Mike Lansing	.25
18	Ryne Sandberg	2.00
19	Carlos Delgado	1.00
20	Craig Biggio	.50
21	Eric Karros	.25
22	Kevin Appier	.25
23	Mariano Rivera	.75

#	Player	Price
24	Vinny Castilla	.25
25	Juan Gonzalez	.50
26	Al Martin	.25
27	Jeff Cirillo	.25
28	Ray Lankford	.25
29	Manny Ramirez	1.50
30	Roberto Alomar	.40
31	Will Clark	.25
32	Chuck Knoblauch	.25
33	Harold Baines	.25
34	Edgar Martinez	.25
35	Mike Mussina	.50
36	Kevin Brown	.25
37	Dennis Eckersley	.75
38	Tino Martinez	.25
39	Raul Mondesi	.25
40	Sammy Sosa	1.50
41	John Smoltz	.75
42	Billy Wagner	.25
43	Ken Caminiti	.25
44	Wade Boggs	1.50
45	Andres Galarraga	.25
46	Roger Clemens	3.00
47	Matt Williams	.25
48	Albert Belle	.25
49	Jeff King	.25
50	John Wetteland	.25
51	Deion Sanders	.50
52	Ellis Burks	.25
53	Pedro Martinez	1.50
54	Kenny Lofton	.25
55	Randy Johnson	1.50
56	Bernie Williams	.50
57	Marquis Grissom	.25
58	Gary Sheffield	.50
59	Curt Schilling	1.00
60	Reggie Sanders	.25
61	Bobby Higginson	.25
62	Moises Alou	.25
63	Tom Glavine	.50
64	Mark Grace	.50
65	Rafael Palmeiro	1.00
66	John Olerud	.25
67	Dante Bichette	.25
68	Jeff Bagwell	1.00
69	Barry Bonds	3.00
70	Pat Hentgen	.25
71	Jim Thome	.25
72	Andy Pettitte	.50
73	Jay Bell	.25
74	Jim Edmonds	.50
75	Ron Gant	.25
76	David Cone	.25
77	Jose Canseco	.75
78	Jay Buhner	.25
79	Greg Maddux	2.50
80	Lance Johnson	.25
81	Travis Fryman	.25
82	Paul O'Neill	.25
83	Ivan Rodriguez	1.00
84	Fred McGriff	.25
85	Mike Piazza	2.50
86	Brady Anderson	.25
87	Marty Cordova	.25
88	Joe Carter	.25
89	Brian Jordan	.25
90	David Justice	.25
91	Tony Gwynn	2.00
92	Larry Walker	.40
93	Mo Vaughn	.25
94	Sandy Alomar	.25
95	Rusty Greer	.25
96	Roberto Hernandez	.25
97	Hal Morris	.25
98	Todd Hundley	.25
99	Rondell White	.25
100	Frank Thomas	1.50
101	Bubba Trammell RC	.25
102	Sidney Ponson RC	1.50
103	Ricky Ledee RC	.50
104	Brett Tomko RC	.25
105	Braden Looper RC	.50
106	Jason Dickson	.25
107	Chad Green RC	.25
108	R.A. Dickey RC	.25
109	Jeff Liefer	.25
110	Richard Hidalgo	.25
111	Chad Hermansen RC	.50
112	Felix Martinez	.25
113	J.J. Johnson	.25
114	Todd Dunwoody	.25
115	Katsuhiro Maeda	.25
116	Darin Erstad	.25
117	Elieser Marrero	.25
118	Bartolo Colon	.25
119	Ugueth Urbina	.25
120	Jaime Bluma	.25
121	Seth Greisinger RC	.25
122	Jose Cruz Jr. RC	1.50
123	Todd Dunn	.25
124	Justin Towle RC	.25
125	Brian Rose	.25
126	Jose Guillen	.25
127	Andruw Jones	1.50
128	Mark Kotsay RC	2.50
129	Wilton Guerrero	.25
130	Jacob Cruz	.25
131	Mike Sweeney	.25
132	Matt Morris	.25
133	John Thomson	.25
134	Javier Valentin RC	.25
135	Mike Drumright RC	.25
136	Michael Barrett	.25
137	Tony Saunders RC	.25
138	Kevin Brown	.25
139	Anthony Sanders RC	.25
140	Jeff Abbott	.25
141	Eugene Kingsale	.25

#	Player	Price
142	Paul Konerko	.50
143	Randall Simon RC	.50
144	Freddy Garcia RC	.25
145	Karim Garcia	.25
146	Carlos Guillen	.25
147	Aaron Boone	.25
148	Donnie Sadler RC	.25
149	Brooks Kieschnick	.25
150	Scott Spiezio	.25
151	Kevin Orie	.25
152	Russ Johnson	.25
153	Livan Hernandez	.25
154	Vladimir Nunez RC	.75
155	Calvin Reese	.25
156	Chris Carpenter	.75
157	Eric Milton RC	1.50
158	Richie Sexson	.50
159	Carl Pavano	.25
160	Pat Cline	.25
161	Ron Wright	.25
162	Dante Powell	.25
163	Mark Bellhorn	.25
164	George Lombard	.25
165	Paul Wilder RC	.25
166	Brad Fullmer	.25
167	Kris Benson RC	2.00
168	Torii Hunter	.50
169	D.T. Cromer	.25
170	Nelson Figueroa RC	.50
171	Hiram Bocachica RC	.50
172	Shane Monahan	.25
173	Juan Melo	.25
174	Calvin Pickering RC	1.50
175	Reggie Taylor	.25
176	Geoff Jenkins	.25
177	Steve Rain RC	.25
178	Nerio Rodriguez	.25
179	Derrick Gibson	.25
180	Darin Blood	.25
181	Ben Davis	.25
182	Adrian Beltre RC	8.00
183	Kerry Wood RC	8.00
184	Nate Rolison	.25
185	Fernando Tatis RC	.50
186	Jake Westbrook RC	2.00
187	Edwin Diaz	.25
188	Joe Fontenot RC	.50
189	Matt Halloran RC	.25
190	Matt Clement RC	3.00
191	Todd Greene	.25
192	Eric Chavez RC	10.00
193	Edgard Velazquez	.25
194	Bruce Chen RC	.25
195	Jason Brester	.25
196	Chris Reitsma RC	.50
197	Neifi Perez	.25
198	Hideki Irabu RC	.50
199	Don Denbow RC	.25
200	Derrek Lee	.75
201	Todd Walker	.25
202	Scott Rolen	1.00
203	Wes Helms	.25
204	Bob Abreu	.50
205	John Patterson RC	2.00
206	Alex Gonzalez RC	.25
207	Grant Roberts RC	.50
208	Jeff Suppan	.25
209	Luke Wilcox	.25
210	Marlon Anderson	.25
211	Mike Caruso RC	.75
212	Roy Halladay RC	8.00
213	Jeremi Gonzalez RC	.25
214	Aramis Ramirez RC	10.00
215	Dermal Brown RC	.25
216	Justin Thompson	.25
217	Danny Clyburn	.25
218	Bruce Aven	.25
219	Keith Foulke RC	2.00
220	Shannon Stewart	.25
221	Larry Barnes	.25
222	Mark Johnson RC	.25
223	Randy Winn	.25
224	Nomar Garciaparra	2.00
225	Jacque Jones RC	4.00
226	Chris Clemons	.25
227	Todd Helton	1.00
228	Ryan Brannan RC	.25
229	Alex Sanchez RC	.50
230	Russell Branyan	.25
231	Daryle Ward	.25
232	Kevin Witt	.25
233	Gabby Martinez	.25
234	Preston Wilson	.25
235	Donzell McDonald RC	.25
236	Orlando Cabrera RC	5.00
237	Brian Banks	.25
238	Robbie Bell	.25
239	Brad Rigby	.25
240	Scott Elarton	.25
241	Donny Leon RC	.25
242	Abraham Nunez RC	1.00
243	Adam Eaton RC	2.00
244	Octavio Dotel RC	1.00
245	Sean Casey	.35
246	Joe Lawrence RC	.50
247	Adam Johnson RC	.25
248	Ronnie Belliard RC	1.00
249	Bobby Estalella	.25
250	Corey Lee RC	.25
251	Mike Cameron	.25
252	Kerry Robinson RC	.25
253	A.J. Zapp RC	.25
254	Jarrod Washburn	.25
255	Ben Grieve	.25
256	Javier Vazquez RC	3.00
257	Travis Lee RC	1.00
258	Dennis Reyes RC	.50
259	Danny Buxbaum	.25

#	Player	Price
260	Kelvim Escobar RC	1.00
261	Danny Klassen	.25
262	Ken Cloude RC	.50
263	Gabe Alvarez	.25
264	Clayton Brunner RC	.25
265	Jason Marquis RC	1.50
266	Jamey Wright	.25
267	Matt Snyder RC	.25
268	Josh Garrett RC	.25
269	Juan Encarnacion	.25
270	Heath Murray	.25
271	Brent Butler RC	1.00
272	Danny Peoples RC	.25
273	Miguel Tejada RC	20.00
274	Jim Pittsley	.25
275	Dmitri Young	.25
276	Vladimir Guerrero	1.50
277	Cole Liniak RC	.25
278	Ramon Hernandez	.25
279	Cliff Politte RC	.50
280	Mel Rosario RC	.25
281	Jorge Carrion RC	.25
282	John Barnes RC	.25
283	Chris Stowe RC	.25
284	Vernon Wells RC	15.00
285	Brett Caradonna RC	.25
286	Scott Hodges RC	.25
287	Jon Garland RC	4.00
288	Nathan Haynes RC	.50
289	Geoff Goetz RC	.50
290	Adam Kennedy RC	1.00
291	T.J. Tucker RC	.25
292	Aaron Akin RC	.25
293	Jayson Werth RC	2.50
294	Glenn Davis RC	.25
295	Mark Mangum RC	.25
296	Troy Cameron RC	.25
297	J.J. Davis RC	.25
298	Lance Berkman RC	30.00
299	Jason Standridge RC	.75
300	Jason Dellaero RC	.25

Refractors

All 300 cards in Bowman Chrome were reprinted in Refractor versions and inserted one per 12 packs. The cards are very similar to the base cards, but feature a refractive foil finish on front.

NM/M
Common Player:	1.00
Stars:	4X

International

Internationals paralleled all 300 cards in the base set with a flag from the player's native country in the background. These inserts were seeded one per four packs.

NM/M
Common Player:	1.00
Stars:	3X
Inserted 1:4	

International Refractors

Each International parallel card was also reprinted in a Refractor version. International Refractors were seeded one per 24 packs.

NM/M
Common Player:	2.00
Stars:	6X

ROY Candidates

MARK KOTSAY

This 15-card insert set features color action photos of 1998 Rookie of the Year candidates printed on chromium finish cards. Card backs are numbered with a "ROY" prefix and were inserted one per 24 packs of Bowman Chrome. Refractor versions are seeded one per 72 packs.

NM/M
#	Player	Price
	Complete Set (15):	9.00
	Common Player:	.50
	Refractors:	1.5X
1	Jeff Abbott	.50
2	Karim Garcia	.75
3	Todd Helton	2.50
4	Richard Hidalgo	.50
5	Geoff Jenkins	.50
6	Russ Johnson	.50
7	Paul Konerko	1.00

#	Player	Price
8	Mark Kotsay	.50
9	Ricky Ledee	.50
10	Travis Lee	.50
11	Derrek Lee	1.50
12	Elieser Marrero	.50
13	Juan Melo	.50
14	Brian Rose	.50
15	Fernando Tatis	.50

Scout's Honor Roll

TODD WALKER

This 15-card set features top prospects and rookies as selected by the Topps's scouts. These chromium cards are numbered with a "SHR" prefix and are inserted one per 12 packs, while Refractor versions are seeded one per 36 packs.

NM/M
#	Player	Price
	Complete Set (15):	12.00
	Common Player:	.50
	Refractors:	1.5X
1	Dmitri Young	.50
2	Bob Abreu	.75
3	Vladimir Guerrero	2.00
4	Paul Konerko	.75
5	Kevin Orie	.50
6	Todd Walker	.50
7	Ben Grieve	.50
8	Darin Erstad	1.00
9	Derrek Lee	.50
10	Jose Cruz, Jr.	.50
11	Scott Rolen	1.00
12	Travis Lee	.50
13	Andruw Jones	2.00
14	Wilton Guerrero	.50
15	Nomar Garciaparra	2.50

1997 Bowman's Best

DEION SANDERS

The 200-card base set is divided into a 100-card subset featuring current stars on a gold-chromium stock, and 100 cards of top prospects in silver chromium. Packs contain six cards and were issued with a suggested retail price of $5. Autographed cards of 10 different players were randomly inserted into packs, with each player signing regular, Refractor and Atomic Refractor versions of their cards. Bowman's Best Laser Cut and Mirror Image are the two other inserts, each with Refractor and Atomic Refractor editions.

NM/M
#	Player	Price
	Complete Set (200):	25.
	Common Player:	
	Star Refractors:	2.
	Star Atomics:	6.
	Pack (6):	2.
	Wax Box (24):	40.
1	Ken Griffey Jr.	
2	Cecil Fielder	
3	Albert Belle	
4	Todd Hundley	
5	Mike Piazza	
6	Matt Williams	
7	Mo Vaughn	
8	Ryne Sandberg	
9	Chipper Jones	
10	Edgar Martinez	
11	Kenny Lofton	
12	Ron Gant	
13	Moises Alou	

14	Pat Hentgen	.25
15	Steve Finley	.25
16	Mark Grace	.25
17	Jay Buhner	.25
18	Jeff Conine	.25
19	Jim Edmonds	.25
20	Todd Hollandsworth	.25
21	Andy Pettitte	.50
22	Jim Thome	.75
23	Eric Young	.25
24	Ray Lankford	.25
25	Marquis Grissom	.25
26	Tony Clark	.25
27	Jermaine Allensworth	.25
28	Ellis Burks	.25
29	Tony Gwynn	1.50
30	Barry Larkin	.25
31	John Olerud	.25
32	Mariano Rivera	.40
33	Paul Molitor	1.00
34	Ken Caminiti	.25
35	Gary Sheffield	.45
36	Al Martin	.25
37	John Valentin	.25
38	Frank Thomas	.75
39	John Jaha	.25
40	Greg Maddux	1.50
41	Alex Fernandez	.25
42	Dean Palmer	.25
43	Bernie Williams	.25
44	Deion Sanders	.25
45	Mark McGwire	2.00
46	Brian Jordan	.25
47	Bernard Gilkey	.25
48	Will Clark	.25
49	Kevin Appier	.25
50	Tom Glavine	.40
51	Chuck Knoblauch	.25
52	Rondell White	.25
53	Greg Vaughn	.25
54	Mike Mussina	.50
55	Brian McRae	.25
56	Chili Davis	.25
57	Wade Boggs	1.50
58	Jeff Bagwell	.75
59	Roberto Alomar	.35
60	Dennis Eckersley	.50
61	Ryan Klesko	.25
62	Manny Ramirez	1.00
63	John Wetteland	.25
64	Cal Ripken Jr.	2.00
65	Edgar Renteria	.25
66	Tino Martinez	.25
67	Larry Walker	.25
68	Gregg Jefferies	.25
69	Lance Johnson	.25
70	Carlos Delgado	.50
71	Craig Biggio	.25
72	Jose Canseco	.50
73	Barry Bonds	2.00
74	Juan Gonzalez	.50
75	Eric Karros	.25
76	Reggie Sanders	.25
77	Robin Ventura	.25
78	Hideo Nomo	.50
79	David Justice	.25
80	Vinny Castilla	.25
81	Travis Fryman	.25
82	Derek Jeter	2.00
83	Sammy Sosa	1.50
84	Ivan Rodriguez	.75
85	Rafael Palmeiro	.75
86	Roger Clemens	2.00
87	Jason Giambi	.50
88	Andres Galarraga	.25
89	Jermaine Dye	.25
90	Joe Carter	.25
91	Brady Anderson	.25
92	Derek Bell	.25
93	Randy Johnson	1.00
94	Fred McGriff	.25
95	John Smoltz	.25
96	Harold Baines	.25
97	Raul Mondesi	.25
98	Tim Salmon	.25
99	Carlos Baerga	.25
100	Dante Bichette	.25
101	Vladimir Guerrero	1.00
102	Richard Hidalgo	.25
103	Paul Konerko	.25
104	Alex Gonzalez RC	.50
105	Jason Dickson	.25
106	Jose Rosado	.25
107	Todd Walker	.25
108	Seth Greisinger RC	.40
109	Todd Helton	.75
110	Ben Davis	.25
111	Bartolo Colon	.25
112	Elieser Marrero	.25
113	Jeff D'Amico	.25
114	Miguel Tejada RC	8.00
115	Darin Erstad	.50
116	Kris Benson RC	1.00
117	Adrian Beltre RC	2.00
118	Neifi Perez	.25
119	Calvin Reese	.25
120	Carl Pavano	.25
121	Juan Melo	.25
122	Kevin McGlinchy RC	.50
123	Pat Cline	.25
124	Felix Heredia RC	.40
125	Aaron Boone	.25
126	Glendon Rusch	.25
127	Mike Cameron	.25
128	Justin Thompson	.25
129	Chad Hermansen RC	.25
130	Sidney Ponson RC	1.00
131	Willie Martinez RC	.25
132	Paul Wilder RC	.25
133	Geoff Jenkins	.25
134	Roy Halladay RC	2.00
135	Carlos Guillen	.25
136	Tony Batista	.25
137	Todd Greene	.25
138	Luis Castillo	.25
139	Jimmy Anderson RC	.25
140	Edgard Velazquez	.25
141	Chris Snopek	.25
142	Ruben Rivera	.25
143	Javier Valentin RC	.25
144	Brian Rose	.25
145	Fernando Tatis RC	.50
146	Dean Crow RC	.25
147	Karim Garcia	.25
148	Dante Powell	.25
149	Hideki Irabu	.40
150	Matt Morris	.25
151	Wes Helms	.25
152	Russ Johnson	.25
153	Jarrod Washburn	.25
154	Kerry Wood RC	4.00
155	Joe Fontenot RC	.25
156	Eugene Kingsale	.25
157	Terrence Long	.25
158	Calvin Maduro	.25
159	Jeff Suppan	.25
160	DaRond Stovall	.25
161	Mark Redman	.25
162	Ken Cloude RC	.25
163	Bobby Estalella	.25
164	Abraham Nunez RC	.75
165	Derrick Gibson	.25
166	Mike Drumright RC	.25
167	Katsuhiro Maeda	.25
168	Jeff Liefer	.25
169	Ben Grieve	.25
170	Bob Abreu	.25
171	Shannon Stewart	.25
172	Braden Looper RC	.40
173	Brant Brown	.25
174	Marlon Anderson	.25
175	Brad Fullmer	.25
176	Carlos Beltran	.25
177	Nomar Garciaparra	1.50
178	Derrek Lee	.75
179	Valerio De Los Santos RC	.25
180	Dmitri Young	.25
181	Jamey Wright	.25
182	Hiram Bocachica RC	.25
183	Wilton Guerrero	.25
184	Chris Carpenter	.25
185	Scott Spiezio	.25
186	Andruw Jones	1.00
187	Travis Lee RC	.75
188	Jose Cruz Jr. RC	1.00
189	Jose Guillen	.25
190	Jeff Abbott	.25
191	Ricky Ledee RC	.40
192	Mike Sweeney	.25
193	Donnie Sadler	.25
194	Scott Rolen	.75
195	Kevin Orie	.25
196	Jason Conti RC	.25
197	Mark Kotsay RC	.75
198	Eric Milton RC	1.00
199	Russell Branyan	.25
200	Alex Sanchez RC	.50

Autographs

Ten different players each signed 10 regular versions of their respective Bowman's Best cards (1:170 packs), 10 of their Bowman's Best Refractors (1:2,036 packs) and 10 of their Bowman's Best Atomic Refractors (1:6,107 packs). Each autograph card features a special Certified Autograph stamp on the front.

		NM/M
	Complete Set (10):	150.00
	Common Player:	5.00
	Refractors:	1.5X
	Atomics:	2X
29	Tony Gwynn	30.00
33	Paul Molitor	20.00
82	Derek Jeter	100.00
91	Brady Anderson	7.50
98	Tim Salmon	10.00
107	Todd Walker	5.00
183	Wilton Guerrero	5.00
185	Scott Spiezio	5.00
188	Jose Cruz Jr.	6.00
194	Scott Rolen	20.00

Cuts

Each of these 20-card inserts features a laser-cut pattern in the chromium stock. Backs have another color photo and list several of the player's career "Bests." Three different versions of each card are available: Regular (1:24 packs), Refractor (1:48) and Atomic Refractor (1:96). Cards are numbered with a "BC" prefix.

		NM/M
	Complete Set (20):	20.00
	Common Player:	.35
	Refractors:	1.5X
	Atomic Refractors:	2X
1	Derek Jeter	4.00
2	Chipper Jones	1.50
3	Frank Thomas	1.00
4	Cal Ripken Jr.	4.00
5	Mark McGwire	3.00
6	Ken Griffey Jr.	2.00
7	Jeff Bagwell	1.00
8	Mike Piazza	2.00
9	Ken Caminiti	.35
10	Albert Belle	.35
11	Jose Cruz Jr.	.35
12	Wilton Guerrero	.35
13	Darin Erstad	.50
14	Andruw Jones	1.00
15	Scott Rolen	.75
16	Jose Guillen	.35
17	Bob Abreu	.35
18	Vladimir Guerrero	1.00
19	Todd Walker	.35
20	Nomar Garciaparra	1.50

Mirror Image

This 10-card insert features four players on each double-sided card - two veterans and two rookies - utilizing Finest technology. Regular Mirror Image cards are found 1:48 packs, while Refractor versions are seeded 1:96 packs and Atomic Refractors are found 1:192 packs. Cards are numbered with an "MI" prefix.

		NM/M
	Complete Set (10):	35.00
	Common Card:	2.00
	Refractors:	1.5X
	Atomic Refractors:	2X
1	Nomar Garciaparra, Derek Jeter, Hiram Bocachica, Barry Larkin	7.50
2	Travis Lee, Frank Thomas, Derrek Lee, Jeff Bagwell	3.50
3	Kerry Wood, Greg Maddux, Kris Benson, John Smoltz	3.50
4	Kevin Brown, Ivan Rodriguez, Elieser Marrero, Mike Piazza	5.00
5	Jose Cruz Jr., Ken Griffey Jr., Andruw Jones, Barry Bonds	7.50
6	Jose Guillen, Juan Gonzalez, Richard Hidalgo, Gary Sheffield	2.00
7	Paul Konerko, Mark McGwire, Todd Helton, Rafael Palmeiro	6.00
8	Wilton Guerrero, Craig Biggio, Donnie Sadler, Chuck Knoblauch	2.00
9	Russell Branyan, Matt Williams, Adrian Beltre, Chipper Jones	3.50
10	Bob Abreu, Kenny Lofton, Vladimir Guerrero, Albert Belle	3.00

1997 Bowman's Best Jumbos

This large-format (4" x 5-5/8") version of 1997 Bowman's Best features 16 of the season's top stars and hottest rookies. Utilizing chromium, Refractor and Atomic Refractor technologies, the cards are identical in every way except size to the regular-issue Bowman's Best. The jumbos were sold only through Topps Stadium Club. Each of the sets consists of 12 chromium cards, plus three randomly packaged Refractors and one Atomic Refractor. About 900 sets were produced according to Topps sales literature, which breaks down to 700 regular cards, 170 Refractors and 60 Atomic Refractors of each player.

		NM/M
	Complete Set (16):	90.00
	Common Player:	4.50
	Refractor:	1.5X
	Atomic Refractor:	2X
1	Ken Griffey Jr.	7.50
5	Mike Piazza	7.50
9	Chipper Jones	6.00
11	Kenny Lofton	4.50
29	Tony Gwynn	6.00
33	Paul Molitor	5.00
38	Frank Thomas	5.00
45	Mark McGwire	9.00
64	Cal Ripken Jr.	12.00
73	Barry Bonds	12.00
82	Juan Gonzalez	4.50
82	Derek Jeter	12.00
101	Vladimir Guerrero	5.00
177	Nomar Garciaparra	6.00
186	Andruw Jones	5.00
188	Jose Cruz, Jr.	4.50

1998 Bowman

Bowman was a 441-card set released in a pair of 220-card series in 1998 (Orlando Hernandez, #221, was a late Series 1 addition.) Within each series are 150 prospects printed in a silver and blue design and 70 veterans printed in silver and red. Cards feature a Bowman seal, and in cases of a player's first Bowman card, a "Bowman Rookie Card" stamp is applied. The player's facsimile signature from his first contract runs down the side. The entire set was paralleled twice in Bowman International (one per pack) and Golden Anniversary (serially numbered to 50). Inserts in Series 1 include Autographs, Scout's Choice, and Japanese Rookies. Inserts in Series 2 include Autographs, 1999 Rookie of the Year Favorites, Minor League MVPs and Japanese Rookies.

		NM/M
	Complete Set (441):	40.00
	Series 1 (221):	20.00
	Series 2 (220):	20.00
	Common Player:	.10
	Internationals:	1.5X
	Inserted 1:1	
	Series 1 Pack (10):	2.00
	Series 1 Wax Box (24):	30.00
	Series 2 Pack (10):	1.50
	Series 2 Wax Box (24):	25.00
1	Nomar Garciaparra	1.50
2	Scott Rolen	.75
3	Andy Pettitte	.30
4	Ivan Rodriguez	.65
5	Mark McGwire	2.50
6	Jason Dickson	.10
7	Jose Cruz Jr.	.10
8	Jeff Kent	.10
9	Mike Mussina	.30
10	Jason Kendall	.10
11	Brett Tomko	.10
12	Jeff King	.10
13	Brad Radke	.10
14	Robin Ventura	.10
15	Jeff Bagwell	1.00
16	Greg Maddux	1.50
17	John Jaha	.10
18	Mike Piazza	2.00
19	Edgar Martinez	.10
20	David Justice	.10
21	Todd Hundley	.10
22	Tony Gwynn	1.50
23	Larry Walker	.10
24	Bernie Williams	.10
25	Edgar Renteria	.10
26	Rafael Palmeiro	.75
27	Tim Salmon	.10
28	Matt Morris	.10
29	Shawn Estes	.10
30	Vladimir Guerrero	1.00
31	Fernando Tatis	.10
32	Justin Thompson	.10
33	Ken Griffey Jr.	2.00
34	Edgardo Alfonzo	.10
35	Mo Vaughn	.10
36	Marty Cordova	.10
37	Craig Biggio	.10
38	Roger Clemens	1.75
39	Mark Grace	.10
40	Ken Caminiti	.10
41	Tony Womack	.10
42	Albert Belle	.10
43	Tino Martinez	.10
44	Sandy Alomar	.10
45	Jeff Cirillo	.10
46	Jason Giambi	.50
47	Darin Erstad	.25
48	Livan Hernandez	.10
49	Mark Grudzielanek	.10
50	Sammy Sosa	1.50
51	Curt Schilling	.30
52	Brian Hunter	.10
53	John Roskos RC	.10
54	Todd Walker	.10
55	Jose Guillen	.10
56	Jim Thome	.10
57	Tom Glavine	.30
58	Todd Greene	.10
59	Rondell White	.10
60	Roberto Alomar	.25
61	Tony Clark	.10
62	Vinny Castilla	.10
63	Barry Larkin	.10
64	Hideki Irabu	.10
65	Johnny Damon	.35
66	Juan Gonzalez	.50
67	John Olerud	.10
68	Gary Sheffield	.25
69	Raul Mondesi	.10
70	Chipper Jones	1.50
71	David Ortiz	.10
72	Warren Morris RC	.50
73	Alex Gonzalez	.10
74	Nick Bierbrodt	.10
75	Roy Halladay	.10
76	Danny Buxbaum	.10
77	Adam Kennedy	.10
78	Jared Sandberg RC	.75
79	Michael Barrett	.10
80	Gil Meche	.10
81	Jayson Werth	.10
82	Abraham Nunez	.10
83	Ben Petrick	.10
84	Brett Caradonna	.10
85	Mike Lowell RC	3.00
86	Clay Bruner RC	.10
87	John Curtice RC	.10
88	Bobby Estalella	.10
89	Juan Melo	.10
90	Arnold Gooch	.10
91	Kevin Millwood RC	1.00
92	Richie Sexson	.10
93	Orlando Cabrera	.10
94	Pat Cline	.10
95	Anthony Sanders	.10
96	Russ Johnson	.10
97	Ben Grieve	.10
98	Kevin McGlinchy	.10
99	Paul Wilder	.10
100	Russ Ortiz	.10
101	Ryan Jackson RC	.10
102	Heath Murray	.10
103	Brian Rose	.10
104	Ryan Radmanovich RC	.10
105	Ricky Ledee	.10
106	Jeff Wallace RC	.10
107	Ryan Minor RC	.10
108	Dennis Reyes	.10
109	James Manias RC	.10
110	Chris Carpenter	.10
111	Daryle Ward	.10
112	Vernon Wells	.10
113	Chad Green	.10
114	Mike Stoner RC	.10
115	Brad Fullmer	.10
116	Adam Eaton	.10
117	Jeff Liefer	.10
118	Corey Koskie RC	1.00
119	Todd Helton	.75
120	Jaime Jones RC	.10
121	Mel Rosario	.10
122	Geoff Goetz	.10
123	Adrian Beltre	.40
124	Jason Dellaero	.10
125	Gabe Kapler RC	.50
126	Scott Schoeneweis	.10
127	Ryan Brannan	.10
128	Aaron Akin	.10
129	Ryan Anderson RC	.25
130	Brad Penny	.10
131	Bruce Chen	.10
132	Eli Marrero	.10
133	Eric Chavez	.10
134	Troy Glaus RC	3.00
135	Troy Cameron	.10
136	Brian Sikorski RC	.10
137	Mike Kinkade RC	.10
138	Braden Looper	.10
139	Mark Mangum	.10
140	Danny Peoples	.10
141	J.J. Davis	.10
142	Ben Davis	.10
143	Jacque Jones	.10
144	Derrick Gibson	.10
145	Bronson Arroyo	.10
146	Cristian Guzman RC	.50
147	Jeff Abbott	.10
148	Mike Cuddyer RC	1.00
149	Jason Romano	.10
150	Shane Monahan	.10
151	Ntema Ndungidi RC	.10
152	Alex Sanchez	.10
153	Jack Cust RC	1.50
154	Brent Butler	.10
155	Ramon Hernandez	.10
156	Norm Hutchins	.10
157	Jason Marquis	.10
158	Jacob Cruz	.10
159	Rob Burger RC	.10
160	Eric Milton	.10
161	Preston Wilson	.10
162	Jason Fitzgerald RC	.10
163	Dan Serafini	.10
164	Peter Munro	.10
165	Trot Nixon	.10
166	Homer Bush	.10
167	Dermal Brown	.10
168	Chad Hermansen	.10
169	Julio Moreno	.10
170	John Roskos RC	.10
171	Grant Roberts	.10
172	Ken Cloude	.10
173	Jason Brester	.10
174	Jason Conti	.10
175	Jon Garland	.10
176	Robbie Bell	.10
177	Nathan Haynes	.10
178	Ramon Ortiz RC	.50
179	Shannon Stewart	.10
180	Pablo Ortega	.10
181	Jimmy Rollins RC	4.00
182	Sean Casey	.30
183	Ted Lilly RC	.25
184	Chris Enochs RC	.10
185	Magglio Ordonez RC	3.00
186	Mike Drumright	.10
187	Aaron Boone	.10
188	Matt Clement	.10
189	Todd Dunwoody	.10
190	Larry Rodriguez	.10
191	Todd Noel	.10
192	Geoff Jenkins	.10
193	George Lombard	.10
194	Lance Berkman	.10
195	Marcus McCain RC	.10
196	Ryan McGuire	.10
197	Jhensy Sandoval RC	.10
198	Corey Lee	.10
199	Mario Valdez	.10
200	Robert Fick RC	.20
201	Donnie Sadler	.10
202	Marc Kroon	.10
203	David Miller	.10
204	Jarrod Washburn	.10
205	Miguel Tejada	.30
206	Raul Ibanez	.10
207	John Patterson	.10
208	Calvin Pickering	.10
209	Felix Martinez	.10
210	Mark Redman	.10
211	Scott Elarton	.10
212	Jose Amado RC	.10
213	Kerry Wood	.40
214	Dante Powell	.10
215	Aramis Ramirez	.10
216	A.J. Hinch	.10
217	Dustin Carr RC	.10
218	Mark Kotsay	.10
219	Jason Standridge	.10
220	Luis Ordaz	.10
221	Orlando Hernandez RC	.50

222	Cal Ripken Jr.	3.00
223	Paul Molitor	1.00
224	Derek Jeter	3.00
225	Barry Bonds	3.00
226	Jim Edmonds	.10
227	John Smoltz	.10
228	Eric Karros	.10
229	Ray Lankford	.10
230	Rey Ordonez	.10
231	Kenny Lofton	.10
232	Alex Rodriguez	2.50
233	Dante Bichette	.10
234	Pedro Martinez	1.00
235	Carlos Delgado	.45
236	Rod Beck	.10
237	Matt Williams	.10
238	Charles Johnson	.10
239	Rico Brogna	.10
240	Frank Thomas	1.00
241	Paul O'Neill	.10
242	Jaret Wright	.10
243	Brant Brown	.10
244	Ryan Klesko	.10
245	Chuck Finley	.10
246	Derek Bell	.10
247	Delino DeShields	.10
248	Chan Ho Park	.10
249	Wade Boggs	1.50
250	Jay Buhner	.10
251	Butch Huskey	.10
252	Steve Finley	.10
253	Will Clark	.10
254	John Valentin	.10
255	Bobby Higginson	.10
256	Darryl Strawberry	.10
257	Randy Johnson	1.00
258	Al Martin	.10
259	Travis Fryman	.10
260	Fred McGriff	.10
261	Jose Valentin	.10
262	Andruw Jones	1.00
263	Kenny Rogers	.10
264	Moises Alou	.10
265	Denny Neagle	.10
266	Ugueth Urbina	.10
267	Derrek Lee	.45
268	Ellis Burks	.10
269	Mariano Rivera	.30
270	Dean Palmer	.10
271	Eddie Taubensee	.10
272	Brady Anderson	.10
273	Brian Giles	.10
274	Quinton McCracken	.10
275	Henry Rodriguez	.10
276	Andres Galarraga	.10
277	Jose Canseco	.45
278	David Segui	.10
279	Bret Saberhagen	.10
280	Kevin Brown	.10
281	Chuck Knoblauch	.10
282	Jeromy Burnitz	.10
283	Jay Bell	.10
284	Manny Ramirez	1.00
285	Rick Helling	.10
286	Francisco Cordova	.10
287	Bob Abreu	.20
288	J.T. Snow Jr.	.10
289	Hideo Nomo	.50
290	Brian Jordan	.10
291	Javy Lopez	.10
292	Travis Lee	.10
293	Russell Branyan	.10
294	Paul Konerko	.10
295	Masato Yoshii RC	.50
296	Kris Benson	.10
297	Juan Encarnacion	.10
298	Eric Milton	.10
299	Mike Caruso	.10
300	Ricardo Aramboles RC	.10
301	Bobby Smith	.10
302	Billy Koch	.10
303	Richard Hidalgo	.10
304	Justin Baughman RC	.10
305	Chris Gissell	.10
306	Donnie Bridges RC	.10
307	Nelson Lara RC	.10
308	Randy Wolf RC	1.00
309	Jason LaRue RC	.25
310	Jason Gooding RC	.10
311	Edgar Clemente RC	.10
312	Andrew Vessel	.10
313	Chris Reitsma	.10
314	Jesus Sanchez RC	.10
315	Buddy Carlyle RC	.10
316	Randy Winn	.10
317	Luis Rivera	.10
318	Marcus Thames RC	1.50
319	A.J. Pierzynski	.10
320	Scott Randall	.10
321	Damian Sapp	.10
322	Eddie Yarnell RC	.10
323	Luke Allen RC	.10
324	J.D. Smart	.10
325	Willie Martinez	.10
326	Alex Ramirez	.10
327	Eric DuBose RC	.10
328	Kevin Witt	.10
329	Dan McKinley RC	.10
330	Cliff Politte	.10
331	Vladimir Nunez	.10
332	John Halama RC	.25
333	Nerio Rodriguez	.10
334	Desi Relaford	.10
335	Robinson Checo	.10
336	John Nicholson	.10
337	Tom LaRosa RC	.10
338	Kevin Nicholson RC	.10
339	Javier Vazquez	.10

340	A.J. Zapp	.10
341	Tom Evans	.10
342	Kerry Robinson RC	.10
343	Gabe Gonzalez RC	.10
344	Ralph Milliard	.10
345	Enrique Wilson	.10
346	Elvin Hernandez	.10
347	Mike Lincoln RC	.10
348	Cesar King RC	.10
349	Cristian Guzman RC	1.00
350	Donzell McDonald	.10
351	Jim Parque RC	.25
352	Mike Saipe RC	.10
353	Carlos Febles RC	.40
354	Dernell Stenson RC	.25
355	Mark Osborne RC	.10
356	Odalis Perez RC	.40
357	Jason Dewey RC	.10
358	Joe Fontenot	.10
359	Jason Grilli RC	.10
360	Kevin Haverbusch RC	.25
361	Jay Yennaco RC	.10
362	Brian Buchanan	.10
363	John Barnes	.10
364	Chris Fussell	.10
365	Kevin Gibbs RC	.10
366	Joe Lawrence	.10
367	DaRond Stovall	.10
368	Brian Fuentes RC	.10
369	Jimmy Anderson	.10
370	Laril Gonzalez RC	.10
371	Scott Williamson RC	.40
372	Milton Bradley	.10
373	Jason Halper RC	.10
374	Brent Billingsley RC	.10
375	Joe DePastino RC	.10
376	Jake Westbrook	.10
377	Octavio Dotel	.10
378	Jason Williams RC	.10
379	Julio Ramirez RC	.10
380	Seth Greisinger	.10
381	Mike Judd RC	.10
382	Ben Ford RC	.10
383	Tom Bennett	.10
384	Adam Butler RC	.10
385	Wade Miller RC	.75
386	Kyle Peterson RC	.10
387	Tommy Peterman RC	.10
388	Onan Masaoka	.10
389	Jason Rakers RC	.10
390	Rafael Medina	.10
391	Luis Lopez	.10
392	Jeff Yoder	.10
393	Vance Wilson RC	.25
394	Fernando Seguignol RC	.25
395	Ron Wright	.10
396	Ruben Mateo RC	.40
397	Steve Lomasney RC	.25
398	Damian Jackson	.10
399	Mike Jerzembeck RC	.10
400	Luis Rivas RC	.25
401	Kevin Burford RC	.10
402	Glenn Davis	.10
403	Robert Luce RC	.10
404	Cole Liniak	.10
405	Matthew LeCroy RC	.20
406	Jeremy Giambi RC	.10
407	Shawn Chacon	.10
408	Dewayne Wise RC	.10
409	Steve Woodard	.25
410	Francisco Cordero RC	.25
411	Damon Minor RC	.20
412	Lou Collier	.10
413	Justin Towle	.10
414	Juan LeBron	.10
415	Michael Coleman	.10
416	Felix Rodriguez	.10
417	Paul Ah Yat RC	.10
418	Kevin Barker RC	.25
419	Brian Meadows	.10
420	Darnell McDonald RC	.20
421	Matt Kinney RC	.25
422	Mike Vavrek RC	.10
423	Courtney Duncan RC	.10
424	Kevin Millar RC	.50
425	Ruben Rivera	.10
426	Steve Shoemaker RC	.10
427	Dan Reichert RC	.10
428	Carlos Lee RC	2.00
429	Rod Barajas	.10
430	Pablo Ozuna RC	.20
431	Todd Belitz RC	.10
432	Sidney Ponson	.10
433	Steve Carver RC	.10
434	Esteban Yan	.10
435	Cedrick Bowers RC	.10
436	Marlon Anderson	.10
437	Carl Pavano	.10
438	Jae Weong Seo RC	.50
439	Jose Taveras RC	.10
440	Matt Anderson RC	.25
441	Darron Ingram RC	.10

Golden Anniversary

This 441-card parallel set celebrates Bowman's 50th anniversary with a gold, rather than black, facsimile autograph on each card. Golden Anniversary cards were inserted in both Series 1 (1:237) and Series 2 (1:194) packs and are sequentially numbered to 50.

	NM/M
Common Player:	4.00
Veteran Stars:	15-30X
Young Stars:	5-10X
Rookie Cards:	5-10X

International

All 441 cards in Bowman Series 1 and 2 are paralleled in an International version, with the player's native country highlighted. Background map designs and vital information were translated into the player's native language on these one per pack parallel cards.

	NM/M
Common Player:	.25
Stars:	1.5X
Inserted 1:1	

Autographs

Rookies and prospects are featured on the certified autograph cards found as '98 Bowman inserts. Each player signed cards in blue, silver and gold ink. The front of each autographed card bears a certification seal. Relative values in the current market come nowhere near reflecting those scarcities.

	NM/M
Common Player:	3.00
Inserted 1:149	
Silvers (1:992):	1.5-2.5X
Golds (1:2,976):	2-4X
1 Adrian Beltre	15.00
2 Brad Fullmer	5.00
3 Ricky Ledee	5.00
4 David Ortiz	35.00
5 Fernando Tatis	3.00
6 Kerry Wood	20.00
7 Mel Rosario	3.00
8 Cole Liniak	5.00
9 A.J. Hinch	3.00
10 Jhensy Sandoval	3.00
11 Jose Cruz Jr.	6.00
12 Richard Hidalgo	6.00
13 Geoff Jenkins	8.00
14 Carl Pavano	10.00
15 Richie Sexson	12.00
16 Tony Womack	5.00
17 Scott Rolen	20.00
18 Ryan Minor	5.00
19 Elieser Marrero	5.00
20 Jason Marquis	5.00
21 Mike Lowell	30.00
22 Todd Helton	20.00
23 Chad Green	3.00
24 Scott Elarton	3.00
25 Russell Branyan	5.00
26 Mike Drumright	3.00
27 Ben Grieve	5.00
28 Jacque Jones	8.00
29 Jared Sandberg	5.00
30 Grant Roberts	5.00
31 Mike Stoner	3.00
32 Brian Rose	3.00
33 Randy Winn	5.00
34 Justin Towle	3.00
35 Anthony Sanders	3.00
36 Rafael Medina	3.00
37 Corey Lee	3.00
38 Mike Kinkade	5.00
39 Norm Hutchins	3.00
40 Jason Brester	3.00
41 Ben Davis	5.00
42 Nomar Garciaparra	40.00
43 Jeff Liefer	3.00
44 Eric Milton	6.00
45 Preston Wilson	8.00
46 Miguel Tejada	30.00
47 Luis Ordaz	3.00
48 Travis Lee	5.00
49 Kris Benson	6.00
50 Jacob Cruz	3.00
51 Dermal Brown	5.00
52 Marc Kroon	3.00
53 Chad Hermansen	5.00
54 Roy Halladay	15.00
55 Eric Chavez	10.00
56 Jason Conti	3.00
57 Juan Encarnacion	5.00
58 Paul Wilder	3.00
59 Aramis Ramirez	15.00
60 Cliff Politte	3.00
61 Todd Dunwoody	3.00
62 Paul Konerko	10.00
63 Shane Monahan	3.00
64 Alex Sanchez	3.00
65 Jeff Abbott	3.00
66 John Patterson	3.00
67 Peter Munro	3.00
68 Jarrod Washburn	5.00
69 Derrek Lee	20.00
70 Ramon Hernandez	5.00

Japanese Rookies

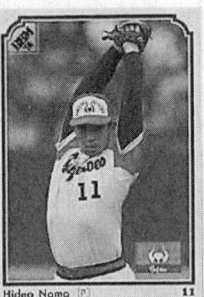

Bowman offered collectors a chance to receive original 1991 BBM-brand Japanese rookie cards of three players. Series 1 had rookie cards of Hideo Nomo and Shigetoshi Hasegawa inserted in one per 2,685 packs, while Series 2 offered Hideki Irabu seeded one per 4,411 packs. Card numbers have a "BBM" prefix.

	NM/M
Complete Set (3):	15.00
Common Player:	5.00
11 Hideo Nomo	10.00
17 Shigetoshi Hasegawa	5.00
Hideki Irabu	5.00

Minor League MVP

This 11-card insert set features players who are former Minor League MVPs who had graduated to the majors. Minor League MVPs are seeded one per 12 packs of Series 2 and are numbered with a "MVP" prefix.

	NM/M
Complete Set (11):	9.00
Common Player:	.50
1 Jeff Bagwell	1.00
2 Andres Galarraga	.50
3 Juan Gonzalez	1.50
4 Tony Gwynn	1.50
5 Vladimir Guerrero	1.00
6 Derek Jeter	3.00
7 Andruw Jones	1.00
8 Tino Martinez	.50
9 Manny Ramirez	1.00
10 Gary Sheffield	.60
11 Jim Thome	.65

Rookie of the Year Favorites

Rookie of the Year Favorites displays 10 players who had a legitimate shot at the 1999 ROY award in the opinion of the Bowman scouts. The insert was seeded one per 12 packs of Series 2 and numbered with an "ROY" prefix.

	NM/M
Complete Set (10):	6.00
Common Player:	.50
1 Adrian Beltre	.75
2 Troy Glaus	3.00
3 Chad Hermansen	.50
4 Matt Clement	.75
5 Eric Chavez	.75
6 Kris Benson	.50
7 Richie Sexson	.50
8 Randy Wolf	.50
9 Ryan Minor	.50
10 Alex Gonzalez	.50

Scout's Choice

This Series 1 insert has players with potential for Major League stardom. Fronts have action photos with gold-foil highlights. Backs have a portrait photo and an assessment of the player's skills in the traditional five areas of raw talent. Cards are numbered with an "SC" prefix.

	NM/M
Complete Set (21):	8.00
Common Player:	.25
Inserted 1:12	
1 Paul Konerko	.50
2 Richard Hidalgo	.25
3 Mark Kotsay	.25
4 Ben Grieve	.25
5 Chad Hermansen	.25
6 Matt Clement	.25
7 Brad Fullmer	.25
8 Eli Marrero	.25
9 Kerry Wood	1.50
10 Adrian Beltre	1.50
11 Ricky Ledee	.25
12 Travis Lee	.25
13 Abraham Nunez	.25
14 Ryan Anderson	.25
15 Dermal Brown	.25
16 Juan Encarnacion	.25
17 Aramis Ramirez	.25
18 Todd Helton	2.50
19 Kris Benson	.25
20 Russell Branyan	.25
21 Mike Stoner	.25

1998 Bowman Chrome

All 441 cards in Bowman 1 and 2 were reprinted with a chromium finish for Bowman Chrome. Chrome contains International and Golden Anniversary parallels, like Bowman. Internationals are seeded one per four packs, with Refractor versions every 24 packs. Golden Anniversary parallels are exclusive to hobby packs and inserted one per 164 packs and sequentially

numbered to 50 sets. Refractor versions are seeded one per 1,279 packs and numbered to just five sets. In addition, 50 Bowman Chrome Reprints were inserted with 25 in each series.

	NM/M
Complete Set (441):	100.00
Complete Series 1 (221):	60.00
Complete Series 2 (220):	50.00
Common Player:	.20
Series 1 Pack (4):	2.50
Series 2 Pack (4):	2.50
Series 1 Box (24):	45.00
Series 2 Box (24):	
1 Nomar Garciaparra	1.00
2 Scott Rolen	.75
3 Andy Pettitte	.40
4 Ivan Rodriguez	.75
5 Mark McGwire	2.50
6 Jason Dickson	.20
7 Jose Cruz Jr.	.20
8 Jeff Kent	.20
9 Mike Mussina	.50
10 Jason Kendall	.20
11 Brett Tomko	.20
12 Jeff King	.20
13 Brad Radke	.20
14 Robin Ventura	.20
15 Jeff Bagwell	1.00
16 Greg Maddux	1.50
17 John Jaha	.20
18 Mike Piazza	2.00
19 Edgar Martinez	.20
20 David Justice	.20
21 Todd Hundley	.20
22 Tony Gwynn	1.50
23 Larry Walker	.20
24 Bernie Williams	.20
25 Edgar Renteria	.20
26 Rafael Palmeiro	.75
27 Tim Salmon	.20
28 Matt Morris	.20
29 Shawn Estes	.20
30 Vladimir Guerrero	1.00
31 Fernando Tatis	.20
32 Justin Thompson	.20
33 Ken Griffey Jr.	2.00
34 Edgardo Alfonzo	.20
35 Mo Vaughn	.20
36 Marty Cordova	.20
37 Craig Biggio	.20
38 Roger Clemens	2.00
39 Mark Grace	.20
40 Ken Caminiti	.20
41 Tony Womack	.20
42 Albert Belle	.20
43 Tino Martinez	.20
44 Sandy Alomar	.20
45 Jeff Cirillo	.20
46 Jason Giambi	.50
47 Darin Erstad	.45
48 Livan Hernandez	.20
49 Mark Grudzielanek	.20
50 Sammy Sosa	1.50
51 Curt Schilling	.50
52 Brian Hunter	.20
53 Neifi Perez	.20
54 Todd Walker	.20
55 Jose Guillen	.20
56 Jim Thome	.40
57 Tom Glavine	.20
58 Todd Greene	.20
59 Rondell White	.20
60 Roberto Alomar	.35
61 Tony Clark	.20
62 Vinny Castilla	.20
63 Barry Larkin	.20
64 Hideki Irabu	.20
65 Johnny Damon	.60
66 Juan Gonzalez	.50
67 John Olerud	.20
68 Gary Sheffield	.45
69 Raul Mondesi	.20
70 Chipper Jones	1.50
71 David Ortiz	.20
72 Warren Morris RC	.50
73 Alex Gonzalez	.20
74 Nick Bierbrodt	.20
75 Roy Halladay	.20
76 Danny Buxbaum	.20
77 Adam Kennedy	.20
78 Jared Sandberg RC	.20
79 Michael Barrett	.20
80 Gil Meche	.20
81 Jayson Werth	.20
82 Abraham Nunez	.20

#	Player	Price
83	Ben Petrick	.20
84	Brett Caradonna	.20
85	Mike Lowell **RC**	6.00
86	Clay Bruner **RC**	.20
87	John Curtice **RC**	.20
88	Bobby Estalella	.20
89	Juan Melo	.20
90	Arnold Gooch	.20
91	Kevin Millwood **RC**	4.00
92	Richie Sexson	.20
93	Orlando Cabrera	.20
94	Pat Cline	.20
95	Anthony Sanders	.20
96	Russ Johnson	.20
97	Ben Grieve	.20
98	Kevin McGlinchy	.20
99	Paul Wilder	.20
100	Russ Ortiz	.20
101	Ryan Jackson **RC**	.50
102	Heath Murray	.20
103	Brian Rose	.20
104	Ryan Radmanovich **RC**	.20
105	Ricky Ledee	.20
106	Jeff Wallace **RC**	.20
107	Ryan Minor **RC**	.45
108	Dennis Reyes	.20
109	James Manias **RC**	.20
110	Chris Carpenter	.20
111	Daryle Ward	.20
112	Vernon Wells	.20
113	Chad Green	.20
114	Mike Stoner **RC**	.20
115	Brad Fullmer	.20
116	Adam Eaton	.20
117	Jeff Liefer	.20
118	Corey Koskie **RC**	1.50
119	Todd Helton	.75
120	Jaime Jones **RC**	.20
121	Mel Rosario	.20
122	Geoff Goetz	.20
123	Adrian Beltre	.40
124	Jason Dellaero	.20
125	Gabe Kapler **RC**	1.00
126	Scott Schoeneweis	.20
127	Ryan Brannan	.20
128	Aaron Akin	.20
129	Ryan Anderson **RC**	.50
130	Brad Penny	.20
131	Bruce Chen	.20
132	Eli Marrero	.20
133	Eric Chavez	.35
134	Troy Glaus **RC**	10.00
135	Troy Cameron	.20
136	Brian Sikorski **RC**	.20
137	Mike Kinkade **RC**	.50
138	Braden Looper	.20
139	Mark Mangum	.20
140	Danny Peoples	.20
141	J.J. Davis	.20
142	Ben Davis	.20
143	Jacque Jones	.20
144	Derrick Gibson	.20
145	Bronson Arroyo	.20
146	Luis De Los Santos **RC**	.20
147	Jeff Abbott	.20
148	Mike Cuddyer **RC**	1.50
149	Jason Romano	.20
150	Shane Monahan	.20
151	Ntema Ndungidi **RC**	.20
152	Alex Sanchez	.20
153	Jack Cust **RC**	5.00
154	Brent Butler	.20
155	Ramon Hernandez	.20
156	Norm Hutchins	.20
157	Jason Marquis	.20
158	Jacob Cruz	.20
159	Rob Burger **RC**	.20
160	Eric Milton	.20
161	Preston Wilson	.20
162	Jason Fitzgerald **RC**	.20
163	Dan Serafini	.20
164	Peter Munro	.20
165	Trot Nixon	.40
166	Homer Bush	.20
167	Dermal Brown	.20
168	Chad Hermansen	.20
169	Julio Moreno **RC**	.20
170	John Roskos **RC**	.20
171	Grant Roberts	.20
172	Ken Cloude	.20
173	Jason Brester	.20
174	Jason Conti	.20
175	Jon Garland	.20
176	Robbie Bell	.20
177	Nathan Haynes	.20
178	Ramon Ortiz **RC**	.50
179	Shannon Stewart	.20
180	Pablo Ortega	.20
181	Jimmy Rollins **RC**	10.00
182	Sean Casey	.45
183	Ted Lilly **RC**	.20
184	Chris Enochs **RC**	.20
185	Magglio Ordonez **RC**	3.00
186	Matt Wildright	.20
187	Aaron Boone	.20
188	Matt Clement	.20
189	Todd Dunwoody	.20
190	Larry Rodriguez	.20
191	Todd Noel	.20
192	Geoff Jenkins	.20
193	George Lombard	.20
194	Lance Berkman	.20
195	Marcus McCain **RC**	.20
196	Ryan McGuire	.20
197	Jhensy Sandoval **RC**	.20
198	Corey Lee	.20
199	Mario Valdez	.20
200	Robert Fick **RC**	.20

#	Player	Price
201	Donnie Sadler	.20
202	Marc Kroon	.20
203	David Miller	.20
204	Jarrod Washburn	.20
205	Miguel Tejada	.40
206	Raul Ibanez	.20
207	John Patterson	.20
208	Calvin Pickering	.20
209	Felix Martinez	.20
210	Mark Redman	.20
211	Scott Elarton	.20
212	Jose Amado **RC**	.20
213	Kerry Wood	.50
214	Dante Powell	.20
215	Aramis Ramirez	.20
216	A.J. Hinch	.20
217	Dustin Carr **RC**	.20
218	Mark Kotsay	.20
219	Jason Standridge	.20
220	Luis Ordaz	.20
221	Orlando Hernandez **RC**	3.00
222	Cal Ripken Jr.	3.00
223	Paul Molitor	1.00
224	Derek Jeter	3.00
225	Barry Bonds	3.00
226	Jim Edmonds	.20
227	John Smoltz	.20
228	Eric Karros	.20
229	Ray Lankford	.20
230	Rey Ordonez	.20
231	Kenny Lofton	.20
232	Alex Rodriguez	2.50
233	Dante Bichette	.20
234	Pedro Martinez	1.00
235	Carlos Delgado	.50
236	Rod Beck	.20
237	Matt Williams	.20
238	Charles Johnson	.20
239	Rico Brogna	.20
240	Frank Thomas	1.00
241	Paul O'Neill	.20
242	Jaret Wright	.20
243	Brant Brown	.20
244	Ryan Klesko	.20
245	Chuck Finley	.20
246	Derek Bell	.20
247	Delino DeShields	.20
248	Chan Ho Park	.20
249	Wade Boggs	1.50
250	Jay Buhner	.20
251	Butch Huskey	.20
252	Steve Finley	.20
253	Will Clark	.20
254	John Valentin	.20
255	Bobby Higginson	.20
256	Darryl Strawberry	.20
257	Randy Johnson	1.00
258	Al Martin	.20
259	Travis Fryman	.20
260	Fred McGriff	.20
261	Jose Valentin	.20
262	Andruw Jones	1.00
263	Kenny Rogers	.20
264	Moises Alou	.20
265	Denny Neagle	.20
266	Ugueth Urbina	.20
267	Derrek Lee	.50
268	Ellis Burks	.20
269	Mariano Rivera	.40
270	Dean Palmer	.20
271	Eddie Taubensee	.20
272	Brady Anderson	.20
273	Brian Giles	.20
274	Quinton McCracken	.20
275	Henry Rodriguez	.20
276	Andres Galarraga	.20
277	Jose Canseco	.40
278	David Segui	.20
279	Bret Saberhagen	.20
280	Kevin Brown	.20
281	Chuck Knoblauch	.20
282	Jeromy Burnitz	.20
283	Jay Bell	.20
284	Manny Ramirez	1.00
285	Rick Helling	.20
286	Francisco Cordova	.20
287	Bob Abreu	.30
288	J.T. Snow Jr.	.20
289	Hideo Nomo	.20
290	Brian Jordan	.20
291	Javy Lopez	.20
292	Aaron Akin **RC**	.20
293	Russell Branyan	.20
294	Paul Konerko	.20
295	Masato Yoshii **RC**	1.00
296	Kris Benson	.20
297	Juan Encarnacion	.20
298	Eric Milton	.20
299	Mike Caruso	.20
300	Ricardo Aramboles **RC**	.20
301	Bobby Smith	.20
302	Billy Koch	.20
303	Richard Hidalgo	.20
304	Justin Baughman **RC**	.20
305	Chris Gissell	.20
306	Donnie Bridges **RC**	.20
307	Nelson Lara **RC**	.20
308	Randy Wolf **RC**	1.00
309	Jason LaRue **RC**	.50
310	Jason Gooding **RC**	.20
311	Edgar Clemente **RC**	.20
312	Andrew Vessel	.20
313	Chris Reitsma	.20
314	Jesus Sanchez **RC**	.20
315	Buddy Carlyle **RC**	.20
316	Randy Winn	.20
317	Luis Rivera	.20
318	Marcus Thames **RC**	5.00

#	Player	Price
319	A.J. Pierzynski	.20
320	Scott Randall	.20
321	Damian Sapp	.20
322	Eddie Yarnell **RC**	.20
323	Luke Allen **RC**	.20
324	J.D. Smart	.20
325	Willie Martinez	.20
326	Alex Ramirez	.20
327	Eric DuBose **RC**	.20
328	Kevin Witt	.20
329	Dan McKinley **RC**	.20
330	Cliff Politte	.20
331	Vladimir Nunez	.20
332	John Halama **RC**	.50
333	Nerio Rodriguez	.20
334	Desi Relaford	.20
335	Robinson Checo	.20
336	John Nicholson	.20
337	Tom LaRosa **RC**	.20
338	Kevin Nicholson **RC**	.20
339	Javier Vazquez	.20
340	A.J. Zapp	.20
341	Tom Evans	.20
342	Kerry Robinson	.20
343	Gabe Gonzalez **RC**	.20
344	Ralph Milliard	.20
345	Enrique Wilson	.20
346	Elvin Hernandez	.20
347	Mike Lincoln **RC**	.35
348	Cesar King **RC**	.20
349	Cristian Guzman **RC**	.50
350	Donzell McDonald	.20
351	Jim Parque **RC**	.20
352	Mike Saipe **RC**	.20
353	Carlos Febles **RC**	.50
354	Dernell Stenson **RC**	.20
355	Mark Osborne **RC**	.20
356	Odalis Perez **RC**	2.00
357	Jason Dewey **RC**	.20
358	Joe Fontenot	.20
359	Jason Grilli **RC**	.40
360	Kevin Haverbusch **RC**	.20
361	Jay Yennaco **RC**	.20
362	Brian Buchanan	.20
363	John Barnes	.20
364	Chris Fussell	.20
365	Kevin Gibbs **RC**	.20
366	Joe Lawrence	.20
367	DaRond Stovall	.20
368	Brian Fuentes **RC**	.20
369	Jimmy Anderson	.20
370	Laril Gonzalez **RC**	.20
371	Scott Williamson **RC**	1.00
372	Milton Bradley	.20
373	Jason Halper **RC**	.20
374	Brent Billingsley **RC**	.20
375	Joe DePastino **RC**	.20
376	Jake Westbrook	.20
377	Octavio Dotel	.20
378	Jason Williams **RC**	.20
379	Julio Ramirez **RC**	.20
380	Seth Greisinger	.20
381	Mike Judd **RC**	.20
382	Ben Ford **RC**	.20
383	Tom Bennett **RC**	.20
384	Adam Butler **RC**	.20
385	Wade Miller **RC**	1.50
386	Kyle Peterson **RC**	.20
387	Tommy Peterman **RC**	.20
388	Onan Masaoka	.20
389	Jason Rakers **RC**	.20
390	Rafael Medina	.20
391	Luis Lopez	.20
392	Jeff Yoder	.20
393	Vance Wilson **RC**	.20
394	Fernando Seguignol **RC**	.35
395	Ron Wright	.20
396	Ruben Mateo **RC**	1.00
397	Steve Lomasney **RC**	.50
398	Damian Jackson	.20
399	Mike Jerzembeck **RC**	.20
400	Luis Rivas **RC**	.50
401	Kevin Burford **RC**	.20
402	Glenn Davis	.20
403	Robert Luce **RC**	.20
404	Cole Liniak	.20
405	Matthew LeCroy **RC**	.50
406	Jeremy Giambi **RC**	.20
407	Shawn Chacon	.20
408	Dewayne Wise **RC**	.20
409	Steve Woodard **RC**	.20
410	Francisco Cordero **RC**	.20
411	Damon Minor **RC**	.20
412	Lou Collier	.20
413	Justin Towle	.20
414	Juan LeBron	.20
415	Michael Coleman	.20
416	Felix Rodriguez	.20
417	Paul Ah Yat **RC**	.20
418	Kevin Barker **RC**	.20
419	Brian Meadows	.20
420	Darnell McDonald **RC**	.40
421	Matt Kinney **RC**	.40
422	Mike Vavrek **RC**	.20
423	Courtney Duncan **RC**	.20
424	Kevin Millar **RC**	1.50
425	Ruben Rivera	.20
426	Steve Shoemaker **RC**	.20
427	Dan Reichert **RC**	.20
428	Carlos Lee **RC**	6.00
429	Rod Barajas **RC**	.20
430	Pablo Ozuna **RC**	.50
431	Todd Belitz **RC**	.20
432	Sidney Ponson	.20
433	Steve Carver **RC**	.20
434	Esteban Yan **RC**	.20
435	Cedrick Bowers **RC**	.20
436	Marlon Anderson	.20

#	Player	Price
437	Carl Pavano	.20
438	Jae Weong Seo **RC**	1.00
439	Jose Taveras **RC**	.20
440	Matt Anderson **RC**	.50
441	Darron Ingram **RC**	.20

Refractors

Refractor versions for all 441 cards in Bowman Chrome Series 1 and 2 were created. The cards contained the word "Refractor" on the back in black letters directly under the card number.

	NM/M
Common Player:	2.00
Stars:	3X
Inserted 1:12	
Int'l Refractors:	6X
Inserted 1:24	

Golden Anniversary

Golden Anniversary parallels were printed for all 441 cards in Bowman Chrome. They are exclusive to hobby packs, seeded one per 164 packs and sequentially numbered to 50 sets. Refractor versions were also available, numbered to just five sets and inserted one per 1,279 packs.

	NM/M
Common Player:	5.00
Stars:	20X
Common Refractor:	20.00

International

All 441 cards throughout Bowman Chrome Series 1 and 2 were paralleled in International versions. Cards fronts have the regular background replaced by a map denoting the player's birthplace. Backs are written in the player's native language.

	NM/M
Common Player:	.50
Stars and Rookies:	1.5X
Inserted 1:4	

Reprints

Bowman Chrome Reprints showcase 50 of the most popular rookie cards to appear in the brand since 1948. The 25 odd-numbered cards are found in Series 1; the evens in Series 2. The Reprints are numbered with a "BC" prefix.

	NM/M
Complete Set (50):	20.00
Common Player:	.25
Inserted 1:12	
Refractors:	1.5X
Inserted 1:36	

#	Player	Price
1	Yogi Berra	.75
2	Jackie Robinson	2.00
3	Don Newcombe	.50
4	Satchel Paige	.50
5	Willie Mays	2.00
6	Gil McDougald	.25
7	Don Larsen	.25
8	Elston Howard	.25
9	Robin Ventura	.25
10	Brady Anderson	.25
11	Gary Sheffield	.50
12	Tino Martinez	.25

#	Player	Price
13	Ken Griffey Jr.	1.50
14	John Smoltz	.50
15	Sandy Alomar Jr.	.25
16	Larry Walker	.25
17	Todd Hundley	.25
18	Mo Vaughn	.25
19	Sammy Sosa	1.00
20	Frank Thomas	.50
21	Chuck Knoblauch	.25
22	Bernie Williams	.25
23	Juan Gonzalez	.50
24	Mike Mussina	.50
25	Jeff Bagwell	.50
26	Tim Salmon	.50
27	Ivan Rodriguez	.50
28	Kenny Lofton	.25
29	Chipper Jones	1.00
30	Javier Lopez	.25
31	Ryan Klesko	.25
32	Raul Mondesi	.25
33	Jim Thome	.25
34	Carlos Delgado	.25
35	Mike Piazza	1.00
36	Manny Ramirez	.50
37	Andy Pettitte	.50
38	Derek Jeter	2.00
39	Brad Fullmer	.25
40	Richard Hidalgo	.25
41	Tony Clark	.25
42	Andruw Jones	.25
43	Vladimir Guerrero	.75
44	Nomar Garciaparra	.75
45	Paul Konerko	.25
46	Ben Grieve	.25
47	Hideo Nomo	.25
48	Scott Rolen	.50
49	Jose Guillen	.25
50	Livan Hernandez	.25

1998 Bowman's Best

Bowman's Best was issued in a single 200-card series comprised of 100 prospects and 100 veterans. Prospects are shown on a silver background, while the veterans are showcased on gold. The set was paralleled twice: A Refractor version is seeded one per 20 packs and sequentially numbered to 400, while an Atomic Refractor version is a 1:82 find and numbered to 100 sets. Inserts include regular, Refractor and Atomic Refractor versions of: Autographs, Mirror Image and Performers.

	NM/M
Complete Set (200):	30.00
Common Player:	.25
Refractors:	8X
Production 400 Sets	
Atomic Refractors:	12X
Production 100 Sets	
Pack (6):	2.50
Wax Box (24):	35.00

#	Player	Price
1	Mark McGwire	2.00
2	Hideo Nomo	.50
3	Barry Bonds	3.00
4	Dante Bichette	.25
5	Chipper Jones	1.50
6	Frank Thomas	1.00
7	Kevin Brown	.25
8	Juan Gonzalez	.50
9	Jay Buhner	.25
10	Chuck Knoblauch	.25
11	Cal Ripken Jr.	3.00
12	Matt Williams	.25
13	Jim Edmonds	.25
14	Manny Ramirez	1.00
15	Tony Clark	.25
16	Mo Vaughn	.25
17	Bernie Williams	.25
18	Scott Rolen	.75
19	Gary Sheffield	.40
20	Albert Belle	.25
21	Mike Piazza	2.00
22	John Olerud	.25
23	Tony Gwynn	1.50
24	Jay Bell	.25
25	Jose Cruz Jr.	.25
26	Justin Thompson	.25
27	Ken Griffey Jr.	2.00
28	Sandy Alomar	.25
29	Mark Grudzielanek	.25
30	Mark Grace	.25
31	Ron Gant	.25

#	Player	Price
32	Javy Lopez	.25
33	Jeff Bagwell	1.00
34	Fred McGriff	.25
35	Rafael Palmeiro	.75
36	Vinny Castilla	.25
37	Andy Benes	.25
38	Pedro Martinez	1.00
39	Andy Pettitte	.40
40	Marty Cordova	.25
41	Rusty Greer	.25
42	Kevin Orie	.25
43	Chan Ho Park	.25
44	Ryan Klesko	.25
45	Alex Rodriguez	2.50
46	Travis Fryman	.25
47	Jeff King	.25
48	Roger Clemens	2.00
49	Darin Erstad	.50
50	Brady Anderson	.25
51	Jason Kendall	.25
52	John Valentin	.25
53	Ellis Burks	.25
54	Brian Hunter	.25
55	Paul O'Neill	.25
56	Ken Caminiti	.25
57	David Justice	.25
58	Eric Karros	.25
59	Pat Hentgen	.25
60	Greg Maddux	1.50
61	Craig Biggio	.25
62	Edgar Martinez	.25
63	Mike Mussina	.50
64	Larry Walker	.25
65	Tino Martinez	.25
66	Jim Thome	.60
67	Tom Glavine	.40
68	Raul Mondesi	.25
69	Marquis Grissom	.25
70	Randy Johnson	1.00
71	Steve Finley	.25
72	Jose Guillen	.25
73	Nomar Garciaparra	1.50
74	Wade Boggs	1.50
75	Bobby Higginson	.25
76	Robin Ventura	.25
77	Derek Jeter	3.00
78	Andruw Jones	1.00
79	Ray Lankford	.25
80	Vladimir Guerrero	1.00
81	Kenny Lofton	.25
82	Ivan Rodriguez	.75
83	Neifi Perez	.25
84	John Smoltz	.25
85	Tim Salmon	.25
86	Carlos Delgado	.25
87	Sammy Sosa	1.50
88	Jaret Wright	.25
89	Roberto Alomar	.40
90	Paul Molitor	1.00
91	Dean Palmer	.25
92	Barry Larkin	.25
93	Jason Giambi	.25
94	Curt Schilling	.40
95	Eric Young	.25
96	Denny Neagle	.25
97	Moises Alou	.25
98	Livan Hernandez	.25
99	Todd Hundley	.25
100	Andres Galarraga	.25
101	Travis Lee	.25
102	Lance Berkman	.25
103	Orlando Cabrera	.25
104	Mike Lowell **RC**	2.00
105	Ben Grieve	.25
106	Jae Weong Seo **RC**	.50
107	Richie Sexson	.50
108	Eli Marrero	.25
109	Aramis Ramirez	.25
110	Paul Konerko	.25
111	Carl Pavano	.25
112	Brad Fullmer	.25
113	Matt Clement	.25
114	Donzell McDonald	.25
115	Todd Helton	.75
116	Mike Caruso	.25
117	Donnie Sadler	.25
118	Bruce Chen	.25
119	Jarrod Washburn	.25
120	Adrian Beltre	.40
121	Ryan Jackson **RC**	.25
122	Kevin Millar **RC**	1.50
123	Corey Koskie **RC**	1.00
124	Dermal Brown	.25
125	Kerry Wood	.50
126	Juan Melo	.25
127	Ramon Hernandez	.25
128	Roy Halladay	.25
129	Ron Wright	.25
130	Darnell McDonald **RC**	.50
131	Odalis Perez **RC**	.75
132	Alex Cora **RC**	.25
133	Justin Towle	.25
134	Juan Encarnacion	.25
135	Brian Rose	.25
136	Russell Branyan	.25
137	Cesar King **RC**	.25
138	Ruben Rivera	.25
139	Ricky Ledee	.25
140	Vernon Wells	.25
141	Luis Rivas	.50
142	Brent Butler	.25
143	Karim Garcia	.25
144	George Lombard	.25
145	Masato Yoshii **RC**	.50
146	Braden Looper	.25
147	Alex Sanchez	.25
148	Kris Benson	.25
149	Mark Kotsay	.25

150	Richard Hidalgo	.25
151	Scott Elarton	.25
152	Ryan Minor RC	.25
153	Troy Glaus RC	5.00
154	Carlos Lee RC	2.00
155	Michael Coleman	.25
156	Jason Grilli RC	.50
157	Julio Ramirez RC	.50
158	Randy Wolf RC	.75
159	Ryan Brannan	.25
160	Edgar Clemente RC	.50
161	Miguel Tejada	.40
162	Chad Hermansen	.25
163	Ryan Anderson RC	.50
164	Ben Petrick	.25
165	Alex Gonzalez	.25
166	Ben Davis	.25
167	John Patterson	.25
168	Cliff Politte	.25
169	Randall Simon	.25
170	Javier Vazquez	.25
171	Kevin Witt	.25
172	Geoff Jenkins	.25
173	David Ortiz	.60
174	Derrick Gibson	.25
175	Abraham Nunez	.25
176	A.J. Hinch	.25
177	Ruben Mateo RC	.75
178	Magglio Ordonez RC	2.50
179	Todd Dunwoody	.25
180	Daryle Ward	.25
181	Mike Kinkade RC	.50
182	Willie Martinez	.25
183	Orlando Hernandez RC	1.50
184	Eric Milton	.25
185	Eric Chavez	.50
186	Damian Jackson	.25
187	Jim Parque RC	.50
188	Dan Reichert RC	.25
189	Mike Drumright	.25
190	Todd Walker	.25
191	Shane Monahan	.25
192	Derrek Lee	.65
193	Jeremy Giambi RC	.50
194	Dan McKinley RC	.25
195	Tony Armas RC	.75
196	Matt Anderson RC	.50
197	Jim Chamblee RC	.25
198	Francisco Cordero RC	.25
199	Calvin Pickering	.25
200	Reggie Taylor	.25

1998 Bowman's Best Refractors

Refractor versions for all 200 cards in Bowman's Best were available. Fronts featured a reflective finish, while backs were numbered to 400 and inserted one per 20 packs.

	NM/M
Common Player:	4.00
Stars:	8X
Production 400 Sets	

1998 Bowman's Best Atomic Refractors

Atomic Refractor versions were available for all 200 cards in Bowman's Best. The cards were printed in a prismatic foil on the front, sequentially numbered to 100 sets on the back and inserted one per 82 packs.

	NM/M
Common Player:	6.00
Stars:	12X
Production 100 Sets	

Autographs

This 10-card set offers autographs from five prospects and five veteran stars. Each card has on front the Topps "Certified Autograph Issue" logo for authentication.

		NM/M
Complete Set (10):		65.00
Common Player:		5.00
Inserted 1:180		
Refractors:		1.5X
Inserted 1:2,158		
Atomics:		2X
Inserted 1:6,437		
5	Chipper Jones	35.00
10	Chuck Knoblauch	5.00
15	Tony Clark	5.00
20	Albert Belle	8.00
25	Jose Cruz Jr.	5.00
105	Ben Grieve	5.00
110	Paul Konerko	15.00
115	Todd Helton	15.00
120	Adrian Beltre	15.00
125	Kerry Wood	20.00

Mirror Image Fusion

This 20-card die-cut insert features a veteran star on one side and a young player at the same position on the other. Regular versions are seeded one per 12 packs, while Refractors are found 1:809 packs and numbered within an edition of 100,

and Atomic Refractors are a 1:3,237 find numbered to 25. All have a "MI" prefix to the card number.

	NM/M
Complete Set (20):	35.00
Common Player (1:12):	.50
Refractor (1:809):	6X
Atomic Refractor (1:3,237):	12X
1	Frank Thomas, David Ortiz	2.00
2	Chuck Knoblauch, Enrique Wilson	.50
3	Nomar Garciaparra, Miguel Tejada	2.50
4	Alex Rodriguez, Mike Caruso	3.50
5	Cal Ripken Jr., Ryan Minor	4.50
6	Ken Griffey Jr., Ben Grieve	3.00
7	Juan Gonzalez, Juan Encarnacion	.75
8	Jose Cruz Jr., Ruben Mateo	.50
9	Randy Johnson, Ryan Anderson	1.50
10	Ivan Rodriguez, A.J. Hinch	1.25
11	Jeff Bagwell, Paul Konerko	1.50
12	Mark McGwire, Travis Lee	3.50
13	Craig Biggio, Chad Hermansen	.50
14	Mark Grudzielanek, Alex Gonzalez	.50
15	Chipper Jones, Adrian Beltre	2.50
16	Larry Walker, Mark Kotsay	.50
17	Tony Gwynn, Preston Wilson	2.50
18	Barry Bonds, Richard Hidalgo	4.50
19	Greg Maddux, Kerry Wood	2.50
20	Mike Piazza, Ben Petrick	3.00

Performers

Performers are 10 players who had the best minor league seasons in 1997. Regular versions were inserted one per six packs, while Refractors are seeded 1:809 and serially numbered to 200, and Atomic Refractors are 1:3,237 and numbered to 50 sets. All versions have card numbers with a "BP" prefix.

		NM/M
Complete Set (10):		4.00
Common Player:		.35
Refractor (1:309):		3X
Atomic Refractor (1:3,237):		5X
1	Ben Grieve	.35
2	Travis Lee	.35
3	Ryan Minor	.35
4	Todd Helton	2.00
5	Brad Fullmer	.35
6	Paul Konerko	.50
7	Adrian Beltre	.75
8	Richie Sexson	.35
9	Aramis Ramirez	.35
10	Russell Branyan	.35

1999 Bowman Pre-Production

Bowman's 1999 issue was introduced with this group of sample cards. Format is nearly identical to

the issued cards, except for the use of a "PP" prefix to the card number on back.

		NM/M
Complete Set (6):		4.00
Common Player:		.60
1	Andres Galarraga	.60
2	Raul Mondesi	.60
3	Vinny Castilla	.60
4	Corey Koskie	2.00
5	Octavio Dotel	.60
6	Dernell Stenson	.60

1999 Bowman

The set was issued in two 220-card series, each comprised of 70 veterans and 150 rookies and prospects. Rookie/prospect cards have blue metallic foil highlights; veteran cards are highlighted with red foil. On each card is the player's facsimile autograph, reproduced from their initial Topps contract.

		NM/M
Complete Set (440):		60.00
Complete Series 1 (220):		30.00
Complete Series 2 (220):		35.00
Common Player:		.10
Series 1 Pack (10):		2.00
Series 1 Box (24):		35.00
Series 2 Pack (10):		3.00
Series 2 Box (24):		50.00
1	Ben Grieve	.10
2	Kerry Wood	.40
3	Ruben Rivera	.10
4	Sandy Alomar	.10
5	Cal Ripken Jr.	2.00
6	Mark McGwire	1.75
7	Vladimir Guerrero	.75
8	Moises Alou	.10
9	Jim Edmonds	.10
10	Greg Maddux	1.00
11	Gary Sheffield	.40
12	John Valentin	.10
13	Chuck Knoblauch	.10
14	Tony Clark	.10
15	Rusty Greer	.10
16	Al Leiter	.10
17	Travis Lee	.10
18	Jose Cruz Jr.	.10
19	Pedro Martinez	.75
20	Paul O'Neill	.10
21	Todd Walker	.10
22	Vinny Castilla	.10
23	Barry Larkin	.10
24	Curt Schilling	.40
25	Jason Kendall	.10
26	Scott Erickson	.10
27	Andres Galarraga	.10
28	Jeff Shaw	.10
29	John Olerud	.10
30	Orlando Hernandez	.40
31	Larry Walker	.10
32	Andruw Jones	.75
33	Jeff Cirillo	.10
34	Barry Bonds	2.00
35	Manny Ramirez	.75
36	Mark Kotsay	.10
37	Ivan Rodriguez	.60
38	Jeff King	.10
39	Brian Hunter	.10
40	Ray Durham	.10
41	Bernie Williams	.10
42	Darin Erstad	.30
43	Chipper Jones	1.00

44	Pat Hentgen	.10
45	Eric Young	.10
46	Jaret Wright	.10
47	Juan Guzman	.10
48	Jorge Posada	.10
49	Bobby Higginson	.10
50	Jose Guillen	.10
51	Trevor Hoffman	.10
52	Ken Griffey Jr.	1.50
53	David Justice	.10
54	Matt Williams	.10
55	Eric Karros	.10
56	Derek Bell	.10
57	Ray Lankford	.10
58	Mariano Rivera	.25
59	Brett Tomko	.10
60	Mike Mussina	.40
61	Kenny Lofton	.25
62	Chuck Finley	.10
63	Alex Gonzalez	.10
64	Mark Grace	.10
65	Raul Mondesi	.10
66	David Cone	.10
67	Brad Fullmer	.10
68	Andy Benes	.10
69	John Smoltz	.10
70	Shane Reynolds	.10
71	Bruce Chen	.10
72	Adam Kennedy	.10
73	Jack Cust	.10
74	Matt Clement	.10
75	Derrick Gibson	.10
76	Darnell McDonald	.10
77	Adam Everett RC	.50
78	Ricardo Aramboles	.10
79	Mark Quinn RC	.25
80	Jason Rakers	.10
81	Seth Etherton RC	.35
82	Jeff Urban RC	.35
83	Manny Aybar	.10
84	Mike Nannini RC	.10
85	Onan Masaoka	.10
86	Rod Barajas	.10
87	Mike Frank	.10
88	Scott Randall	.10
89	Justin Bowles	.10
90	Chris Haas	.10
91	Arturo McDowell RC	.10
92	Matt Belisle RC	.35
93	Scott Elarton	.10
94	Vernon Wells	.10
95	Pat Cline	.10
96	Ryan Anderson	.10
97	Kevin Barker	.10
98	Ruben Mateo	.10
99	Robert Fick	.10
100	Corey Koskie	.10
101	Ricky Ledee	.10
102	Rick Elder RC	.25
103	Jack Cressend RC	.10
104	Joe Lawrence	.10
105	Mike Lincoln	.10
106	Kit Pellow RC	.35
107	Matt Burch RC	.25
108	Brent Butler	.10
109	Jason Dewey	.10
110	Cesar King	.10
111	Julio Ramirez	.10
112	Jake Westbrook	.10
113	Eric Valent RC	.35
114	Roosevelt Brown RC	.35
115	Choo Freeman RC	.35
116	Juan Melo	.10
117	Jason Grilli	.10
118	Jared Sandberg	.10
119	Glenn Davis	.10
120	David Riske RC	.25
121	Jacque Jones	.10
122	Corey Lee	.10
123	Michael Barrett	.10
124	Lariel Gonzalez	.10
125	Mitch Meluskey	.10
126	Freddy Garcia	.10
127	Tony Torcato RC	.25
128	Jeff Liefer	.10
129	Ntema Ndungidi	.10
130	Andy Brown RC	.35
131	Ryan Mills RC	.25
132	Andy Abad RC	.25
133	Carlos Febles	.10
134	Jason Tyner RC	.25
135	Mark Osborne	.10
136	Phil Norton RC	.25
137	Nathan Haynes	.10
138	Roy Halladay	.10
139	Juan Encarnacion	.10
140	Brad Penny	.10
141	Grant Roberts	.10
142	Aramis Ramirez	.10
143	Cristian Guzman	.25
144	Mamon Tucker RC	.25
145	Ryan Bradley	.10
146	Brian Simmons	.10
147	Dan Reichert	.10
148	Russ Branyon	.10
149	Victor Valencia RC	.25
150	Scott Schoeneweis	.25
151	Sean Spencer RC	.25
152	Odalis Perez	.10
153	Joe Fontenot	.10
154	Milton Bradley	.25
155	Josh McKinley RC	.25
156	Terrence Long	.25
157	Danny Klassen	.10
158	Paul Hoover RC	.25
159	Ron Belliard	.10
160	Armando Rios	.10
161	Ramon Hernandez	.10

162	Jason Conti	.10
163	Chad Hermansen	.10
164	Jason Standridge	.10
165	Jason Dellaero	.10
166	John Curtice	.10
167	Clayton Andrews RC	.10
168	Jeremy Giambi	.10
169	Alex Ramirez	.10
170	Gabe Molina RC	.10
171	Mario Encarnacion RC	.25
172	Mike Zywica RC	.25
173	Chip Ambres RC	.25
174	Trot Nixon	.25
175	Pat Burrell RC	2.00
176	Jeff Yoder	.10
177	Chris Jones RC	.25
178	Kevin Witt	.10
179	Keith Luuloa RC	.25
180	Billy Koch	.10
181	Damaso Marte RC	.10
182	Ryan Glynn RC	.25
183	Calvin Pickering	.10
184	Michael Cuddyer	.10
185	Nick Johnson RC	.75
186	Doug Mientkiewicz RC	1.00
187	Nate Cornejo RC	.35
188	Octavio Dotel	.10
189	Wes Helms	.10
190	Nelson Lara	.10
191	Chuck Abbott RC	.10
192	Tony Armas Jr.	.10
193	Gil Meche	.10
194	Ben Petrick	.10
195	Chris George RC	.25
196	Scott Hunter RC	.25
197	Ryan Brannan	.10
198	Amaury Garcia RC	.25
199	Chris Gissell	.10
200	Austin Kearns RC	1.50
201	Alex Gonzalez	.10
202	Wade Miller	.10
203	Scott Williamson	.10
204	Chris Enochs	.10
205	Fernando Seguignol	.10
206	Marlon Anderson	.10
207	Todd Sears RC	.25
208	Nate Bump RC	.25
209	J.M. Gold RC	.25
210	Matt LeCroy	.25
211	Alex Hernandez	.10
212	Luis Rivera	.10
213	Troy Cameron	.10
214	Alex Escobar RC	.50
215	Jason LaRue	.25
216	Kyle Peterson	.10
217	Brent Butler	.10
218	Dernell Stenson	.10
219	Adrian Beltre	.40
220	Daryle Ward	.25
----	Series 1 Checklist Folder	.25
221	Jim Thome	.60
222	Cliff Floyd	.10
223	Rickey Henderson	.75
224	Garret Anderson	.10
225	Ken Caminiti	.25
226	Bret Boone	.10
227	Jeromy Burnitz	.10
228	Steve Finley	.10
229	Miguel Tejada	.40
230	Greg Vaughn	.10
231	Jose Offerman	.10
232	Andy Ashby	.10
233	Albert Belle	.25
234	Fernando Tatis	.25
235	Todd Helton	.65
236	Sean Casey	.25
237	Brian Giles	.10
238	Andy Pettitte	.25
239	Fred McGriff	.10
240	Roberto Alomar	.30
241	Edgar Martinez	.10
242	Lee Stevens	.10
243	Shawn Green	.10
244	Ryan Klesko	.10
245	Sammy Sosa	1.00
246	Todd Hundley	.10
247	Shannon Stewart	.10
248	Randy Johnson	.75
249	Rondell White	.10
250	Mike Piazza	1.50
251	Craig Biggio	.25
252	David Wells	.10
253	Brian Jordan	.10
254	Edgar Renteria	.10
255	Bartolo Colon	.10
256	Frank Thomas	.75
257	Will Clark	.10
258	Dean Palmer	.10
259	Dmitri Young	.10
260	Scott Rolen	.60
261	Jeff Kent	.10
262	Dante Bichette	.10
263	Nomar Garciaparra	1.00
264	Tony Gwynn	1.00
265	Alex Rodriguez	1.75
266	Jose Canseco	.45
267	Jason Giambi	.40
268	Jeff Bagwell	.75
269	Carlos Delgado	.40
270	Tom Glavine	.25
271	Eric Davis	.10
272	Edgardo Alfonzo	.10
273	Tim Salmon	.10
274	Johnny Damon	.35
275	Rafael Palmeiro	.65
276	Denny Neagle	.10
277	Neifi Perez	.10
278	Roger Clemens	1.25

279	Brant Brown	.10
280	Kevin Brown	.10
281	Jay Bell	.10
282	Jay Buhner	.10
283	Matt Lawton	.10
284	Robin Ventura	.10
285	Juan Gonzalez	.35
286	Mo Vaughn	.10
287	Kevin Millwood	.10
288	Tino Martinez	.10
289	Justin Thompson	.10
290	Derek Jeter	2.00
291	Ben Davis	.10
292	Mike Lowell	.10
293	Joe Crede RC	.75
294	Micah Bowie RC	.10
295	Lance Berkman	.10
296	Jason Marquis	.25
297	Chad Green	.10
298	Dee Brown	.10
299	Jerry Hairston Jr.	.10
300	Gabe Kapler	.25
301	Brent Stentz RC	.25
302	Scott Mullen RC	.25
303	Brandon Reed	.10
304	Shea Hillenbrand RC	.50
305	J.D. Closser RC	.25
306	Gary Matthews Jr.	.25
307	Toby Hall RC	.25
308	Jason Phillips RC	.25
309	Jose Macias RC	.25
310	Jung Bong RC	.25
311	Ramon Soler RC	.25
312	Kelly Dransfeldt RC	.25
313	Carlos Hernandez RC	.25
314	Kevin Haverbusch	.10
315	Aaron Myette RC	.25
316	Chad Harville RC	.35
317	Kyle Farnsworth RC	.50
318	Travis Dawkins RC	.50
319	Willie Martinez	.10
320	Carlos Lee	.10
321	Carlos Pena RC	1.00
322	Peter Bergeron RC	.25
323	A.J. Burnett RC	.50
324	Bucky Jacobsen RC	.25
325	Mo Bruce RC	.25
326	Reggie Taylor	.10
327	Jackie Rexrode	.10
328	Alvin Morrow RC	.25
329	Carlos Beltran	.40
330	Eric Chavez	.25
331	John Patterson	.10
332	Jayson Werth	.10
333	Richie Sexson	.10
334	Randy Wolf	.10
335	Eli Marrero	.10
336	Paul LoDuca	.10
337	J.D. Smart RC	.10
338	Ryan Minor	.10
339	Kris Benson	.25
340	George Lombard	.10
341	Troy Glaus	.25
342	Eddie Yarnell	.10
343	Kip Wells RC	.50
344	C.C. Sabathia RC	2.00
345	Sean Burroughs RC	.50
346	Felipe Lopez RC	1.50
347	Ryan Rupe RC	.25
348	Orber Moreno RC	.25
349	Rafael Roque RC	.25
350	Alfonso Soriano RC	5.00
351	Pablo Ozuna	.10
352	Corey Patterson RC	1.00
353	Braden Looper	.10
354	Robbie Bell	.10
355	Mark Mulder RC	2.00
356	Angel Pena	.10
357	Kevin McGlinchy	.10
358	Michael Restovich RC	.35
359	Eric DuBose	.10
360	Geoff Jenkins	.10
361	Mark Harriger RC	.25
362	Junior Herndon RC	.25
363	Tim Raines Jr. RC	.25
364	Rafael Furcal RC	.75
365	Marcus Giles RC	1.00
366	Ted Lilly	.10
367	Jorge Toca RC	.10
368	David Kelton RC	.35
369	Adam Dunn RC	5.00
370	Guillermo Mota RC	.35
371	Brett Laxton RC	.35
372	Travis Harper RC	.25
373	Tom Davey RC	.25
374	Darren Blakely RC	.25
375	Tim Hudson RC	3.00
376	Jason Romano RC	.10
377	Dan Reichert	.10
378	Julio Lugo RC	.75
379	Jose Garcia RC	.25
380	Erubiel Durazo RC	.75
381	Jose Jimenez	.25
382	Chris Fussell	.10
383	Steve Lomasney	.25
384	Juan Pena RC	.25
385	Allen Levrault RC	.25
386	Juan Rivera RC	.25
387	Steve Colyer RC	.25
388	Joe Nathan RC	.25
389	Ron Walker RC	.25
390	Nick Bierbrodt	.10
391	Luke Prokopec RC	.25
392	Dave Roberts RC	.25
393	Mike Darr	.10
394	Abraham Nunez RC	.25
395	Giuseppe Chiaramonte RC	.25
396	Jermaine Van Buren RC	.10

397	Mike Kusiewicz	.10
398	Matt Wise RC	.25
399	Joe McEwing RC	.40
400	Matt Holliday RC	5.00
401	Willi Mo Pena RC	1.50
402	Ruben Quevedo RC	.25
403	Rob Ryan RC	.25
404	Freddy Garcia RC	1.00
405	Kevin Eberwein RC	.25
406	Jesus Colome RC	.25
407	Chris Singleton RC	.25
408	Bubba Crosby RC	.50
409	Jesus Cordero RC	.25
410	Donny Leon	.10
411	Goefrey Tomlinson RC	.25
412	Jeff Winchester RC	.25
413	Adam Piatt RC	.50
414	Robert Stratton	.10
415	T.J. Tucker	.10
416	Ryan Langerhans RC	.25
417	Anthony Shumaker RC	.25
418	Matt Miller RC	.25
419	Doug Clark RC	.25
420	Kory DeHaan RC	.25
421	David Eckstein RC	.75
422	Brian Cooper RC	.25
423	Brady Clark RC	.25
424	Chris Magruder RC	.25
425	Bobby Seay RC	.25
426	Aubrey Huff RC	1.00
427	Mike Jerzembeck	.10
428	Matt Blank RC	.25
429	Benny Agbayani RC	.25
430	Kevin Beirne RC	.25
431	Josh Hamilton RC	6.00
432	Josh Girdley RC	.25
433	Kyle Snyder RC	.25
434	Mike Paradis RC	.25
435	Jason Jennings RC	.25
436	David Walling RC	.25
437	Omar Ortiz RC	.25
438	Jay Gehrke RC	.25
439	Casey Burns RC	.25
440	Carl Crawford	2.50

Gold

Gold, rather than black, ink for the facsimile autograph, Bowman logo and player name on front, and serial number on back from within an edition of 99, designate these Gold cards. Stated odds of finding the Gold cards were one per 111 packs of Series 1, and 1:59 in Series 2.

NM/M
Common Player: 3.00
Gold Stars: 10X

International

International parallels are a one-per-pack insert. Fronts are printed in metallic silver on which the photo's background has been replaced with a scenic picture supposed to be indicative of the player's native land. That location is spelled out in the lower-left corner of the photo. Backs of the Internationals are printed in the player's native language.

NM/M
Common Player: .25
Int'l Stars: 1.5X

Autographs

Autographs were randomly inserted in Series 1 and 2 packs, with

each card bearing a Topps Certified Autograph seal on the front and numbered with a "BA" prefix on back. Levels of scarcity are color coded by the metallic-foil highlights on front: Golds are the most difficult to find at 1:1,941 Series 1 packs and 1:1,024 Series 2. Silvers are seeded 1:485 in Series 1, 1:256 Series 2. Blues are found at an average rate of 1:162 in first series and 1:85 in second series.

NM/M
Common Player: 3.00
Blues inserted 1:162 or 1:85
Silvers inserted 1:485 or 1:256
Golds inserted 1:1,954 or 1:1,024

1	Ruben Mateo/B	5.00
2	Troy Glaus/G	40.00
3	Ben Davis/G	8.00
4	Jayson Werth/B	5.00
5	Jerry Hairston Jr./S	4.00
6	Darnell McDonald/B	4.00
7	Calvin Pickering/S	8.00
8	Ryan Minor/S	4.00
9	Alex Escobar/B	5.00
10	Grant Roberts/B	5.00
11	Carlos Guillen/B	10.00
12	Ryan Anderson/S	6.00
13	Gil Meche/S	5.00
14	Russell Branyan/S	6.00
15	Alex Ramirez/S	5.00
16	Jason Rakers/S	5.00
17	Eddie Yarnall/B	5.00
18	Freddy Garcia/S	15.00
19	Jason Conti/B	3.00
20	Corey Koskie/B	5.00
21	Roosevelt Brown/B	5.00
22	Willie Martinez/B	3.00
23	Mike Jerzembeck/B	3.00
24	Lariel Gonzalez/B	3.00
25	Fernando Seguignol/B	3.00
26	Robert Fick/S	5.00
27	J.D. Smart/B	3.00
28	Ryan Mills/B	3.00
29	Chad Hermansen/G	5.00
30	Jason Grilli/B	5.00
31	Michael Cuddyer/B	5.00
32	Jacque Jones/S	10.00
33	Reggie Taylor/B	3.00
34	Richie Sexson/G	15.00
35	Michael Barrett/B	8.00
36	Paul LoDuca/B	5.00
37	Adrian Beltre/G	30.00
38	Peter Bergeron/B	4.00
39	Joe Fontenot/B	3.00
40	Randy Wolf/B	5.00
41	Nick Johnson/B	12.00
42	Ryan Bradley/B	4.00
43	Mike Lowell/B	15.00
44	Ricky Ledee/B	4.00
45	Mike Lincoln/S	4.00
46	Jeremy Giambi/B	5.00
47	Dermal Brown/B	5.00
48	Derrick Gibson/B	3.00
49	Scott Randall/B	5.00
50	Ben Petrick/S	5.00
51	Jason LaRue/B	3.00
52	Cole Liniak/B	3.00
53	John Curtice/B	3.00
54	Jackie Rexrode/B	3.00
55	John Patterson/B	4.00
56	Brad Penny/B	6.00
57	Jared Sandberg/B	6.00
58	Kerry Wood/G	25.00
59	Eli Marrero/B	3.00
60	Jason Marquis/B	8.00
61	George Lombard/S	3.00
62	Bruce Chen/S	3.00
63	Kevin Witt/S	4.00
64	Vernon Wells/B	15.00
65	Billy Koch/B	5.00
66	Roy Halladay/B	20.00
67	Nathan Haynes/B	5.00
68	Ben Grieve/B	8.00
69	Eric Chavez/G	10.00
70	Lance Berkman/B	12.00

1999 Bowman Early Risers

This insert set features 11 current baseball superstars who have already won a Rookie of the Year

award and who continue to excel. Cards have an "ER" prefix to the number on back.

NM/M
Complete Set (11): 8.00
Common Player: .25
Inserted 1:12

1	Mike Piazza	1.00
2	Cal Ripken Jr.	2.00
3	Jeff Bagwell	.50
4	Ben Grieve	.25
5	Kerry Wood	.40
6	Mark McGwire	1.50
7	Nomar Garciaparra	.75
8	Derek Jeter	2.00
9	Scott Rolen	.50
10	Jose Canseco	.45
11	Raul Mondesi	.25

Late Bloomers

This 10-card set features late-round picks from previous drafts who have emerged as bona fide stars. These inserts are numbered with an "LB" prefix.

NM/M
Complete Set (10): 4.00
Common Player: .25
Inserted 1:12

LB1	Mike Piazza	2.00
LB2	Jim Thome	.75
LB3	Larry Walker	.25
LB4	Vinny Castilla	.25
LB5	Andy Pettitte	.50
LB6	Jim Edmonds	.25
LB7	Kenny Lofton	.25
LB8	John Smoltz	.25
LB9	Mark Grace	.25
LB10	Trevor Hoffman	.25

Scout's Choice

Scout's Choice inserts were randomly inserted in Series 1 packs and feature a borderless, double-etched design. The 21-card set focuses on prospects who have potential to win a future Rookie of the Year award.

NM/M
Complete Set (21): 12.00
Common Player: .40
Inserted 1:12

SC1	Ruben Mateo	.40
SC2	Ryan Anderson	.40
SC3	Pat Burrell	3.00
SC4	Troy Glaus	4.00
SC5	Eric Chavez	1.00
SC6	Adrian Beltre	1.00
SC7	Bruce Chen	.40
SC8	Carlos Beltran	1.00
SC9	Alex Gonzalez	.40
SC10	Carlos Lee	.50
SC11	George Lombard	.40
SC12	Matt Clement	.40
SC13	Calvin Pickering	.40
SC14	Marlon Anderson	.40
SC15	Chad Hermansen	.40
SC16	Russell Branyan	.40
SC17	Jeremy Giambi	.40
SC18	Ricky Ledee	.40
SC19	John Patterson	.40
SC20	Roy Halladay	.75
SC21	Michael Barrett	.40

2000 Rookie of the Year

Randomly inserted in Series 2 packs, these cards have a borderless, double-etched foil design. The 10-card set focuses on players that have potential to win the 2000 Rookie of the Year award.

NM/M
Complete Set (10): 7.00
Common Player: .50
Inserted 1:12

1	Ryan Anderson	.50
2	Pat Burrell	2.50
3	A.J. Burnett	.50
4	Ruben Mateo	.50
5	Alex Escobar	.50
6	Pablo Ozuna	.50
7	Mark Mulder	1.00
8	Corey Patterson	1.00
9	George Lombard	.50
10	Nick Johnson	1.00

1999 Bowman Chrome

Bowman Chrome was released in two 220-card series as an upscale chromium parallel version of Bowman Baseball. Like Bowman, each series has 150 prospect cards with blue foil, while 70 veteran cards have red foil. Packs contain four cards with an original SRP of $3.

NM/M
Complete Set (440): 175.00
Complete Series 1 (220): 65.00
Complete Series 2 (220): 125.00
Common Player: .25
Series 1 Pack (4): 3.00
Series 1 Wax Box (24): 50.00
Series 2 Pack (4): 5.00
Series 2 Wax Box (24): 100.00

1	Ben Grieve	.25
2	Kerry Wood	.45
3	Ruben Rivera	.25
4	Sandy Alomar	.25
5	Cal Ripken Jr.	3.00
6	Mark McGwire	1.50
7	Vladimir Guerrero	1.00
8	Moises Alou	.25
9	Jim Edmonds	.25
10	Greg Maddux	1.50
11	Gary Sheffield	.50
12	John Valentin	.25
13	Chuck Knoblauch	.25
14	Tony Clark	.25
15	Rusty Greer	.25
16	Al Leiter	.25
17	Travis Lee	.25
18	Jose Cruz Jr.	.25
19	Pedro Martinez	1.00
20	Paul O'Neill	.25
21	Todd Walker	.25
22	Vinny Castilla	.25
23	Barry Larkin	.25
24	Curt Schilling	.40
25	Jason Kendall	.25
26	Scott Erickson	.25
27	Andres Galarraga	.25
28	Jeff Shaw	.25
29	John Olerud	.25
30	Orlando Hernandez	.40
31	Larry Walker	.25
32	Andruw Jones	.40
33	Jeff Cirillo	.25
34	Barry Bonds	3.00
35	Manny Ramirez	1.00
36	Mark Kotsay	.25
37	Ivan Rodriguez	.50
38	Jeff King	.25
39	Brian Hunter	.25
40	Ray Durham	.25
41	Bernie Williams	.25
42	Darin Erstad	.25
43	Chipper Jones	1.50
44	Pat Hentgen	.25
45	Eric Young	.25
46	Jaret Wright	.25
47	Juan Guzman	.25
48	Jorge Posada	.25
49	Bobby Higginson	.25
50	Jose Guillen	.25
51	Trevor Hoffman	.25
52	Ken Griffey Jr.	2.00
53	David Justice	.25
54	Matt Williams	.25
55	Eric Karros	.25
56	Derek Bell	.25
57	Ray Lankford	.25
58	Mariano Rivera	.40
59	Brett Tomko	.25
60	Mike Mussina	.50
61	Kenny Lofton	.25
62	Chuck Finley	.25
63	Alex Gonzalez	.25
64	Mark Grace	.25
65	Raul Mondesi	.25
66	David Cone	.25
67	Brad Fullmer	.25
68	Andy Benes	.25
69	John Smoltz	.25
70	Shane Reynolds	.25
71	Bruce Chen	.25
72	Adam Kennedy	.25
73	Jack Cust	.25
74	Matt Clement	.25
75	Derrick Gibson	.25
76	Darnell McDonald	.25
77	Adam Everett RC	.75
78	Ricardo Aramboles	.25
79	Mark Quinn RC	.50
80	Jason Rakers	.25
81	Seth Etherton RC	.50
82	Jeff Urban RC	.35
83	Manny Aybar	.25
84	Mike Nannini RC	.35
85	Onan Masaoka	.25
86	Rod Barajas	.25
87	Mike Frank	.25
88	Scott Randall	.25
89	Justin Bowles RC	.35
90	Chris Haas	.25
91	Arturo McDowell RC	.35
92	Matt Belisle RC	.50
93	Scott Elarton	.25
94	Vernon Wells	.25
95	Pat Cline	.25
96	Ryan Anderson	.25
97	Kevin Barker	.25
98	Ruben Mateo	.25
99	Robert Fick	.25
100	Corey Koskie	.25
101	Ricky Ledee	.25
102	Rick Elder RC	.35
103	Jack Cressend RC	.35
104	Joe Lawrence	.25
105	Mike Lincoln	.25
106	Kit Pellow RC	.50
107	Matt Burch RC	.35
108	Brent Butler	.25
109	Jason Dewey	.25
110	Cesar King	.25
111	Julio Ramirez	.25
112	Jake Westbrook	.25
113	Eric Valent RC	1.00
114	Roosevelt Brown RC	.25
115	Choo Freeman RC	1.50
116	Juan Melo	.25
117	Jason Grilli	.25
118	Jared Sandberg	.25
119	Glenn Davis	.25
120	David Riske RC	.35
121	Jacque Jones	.25
122	Corey Lee	.25
123	Michael Barrett	.25
124	Lariel Gonzalez	.25
125	Mitch Meluskey	.25
126	Freddy Garcia RC	.25
127	Tony Torcato RC	.25
128	Jeff Liefer	.25
129	Ntema Ndungidi	.25
130	Andy Brown RC	.50
131	Ryan Mills RC	.35
132	Andy Abad RC	.50
133	Carlos Febles	.25
134	Jason Tyner RC	.50
135	Mark Osborne	.25
136	Phil Norton RC	.35
137	Nathan Haynes	.25
138	Roy Halladay	.25
139	Juan Encarnacion	.25
140	Brad Penny	.25
141	Grant Roberts	.25
142	Aramis Ramirez	.25
143	Cristian Guzman	.25
144	Mamon Tucker RC	.35
145	Ryan Bradley	.25
146	Brian Simmons	.25
147	Dan Reichert	.25
148	Russ Branyon	.25
149	Victor Valencia RC	.35
150	Scott Schoeneweis	.25
151	Sean Spencer RC	.25
152	Odalis Perez	.25
153	Joe Fontenot	.25
154	Milton Bradley	.25
155	Josh McKinley RC	.35
156	Terrence Long	.25
157	Danny Klassen	.25
158	Paul Hoover RC	.35
159	Ron Belliard	.25
160	Armando Rios	.25
161	Ramon Hernandez	.25
162	Jason Conti	.25
163	Chad Hermansen	.25
164	Jason Standridge	.25
165	Jason Dellaero	.25
166	John Curtice	.25
167	Clayton Andrews RC	.35
168	Jeremy Giambi	.25
169	Alex Ramirez	.25
170	Gabe Molina RC	.25
171	Mario Encarnacion RC	.35
172	Mike Zywica RC	.35
173	Chip Ambres RC	.35
174	Trot Nixon	.25
175	Pat Burrell RC	10.00
176	Jeff Yoder	.25
177	Chris Jones RC	.35
178	Kevin Witt	.25
179	Keith Luuloa RC	.25
180	Billy Koch	.25
181	Damaso Marte RC	.35
182	Ryan Glynn RC	.35
183	Calvin Pickering	.25
184	Michael Cuddyer	.25
185	Nick Johnson RC	2.00
186	Doug Mientkiewicz RC	2.00
187	Nate Cornejo RC	1.00
188	Octavio Dotel	.25
189	Wes Helms	.25
190	Nelson Lara	.25
191	Chuck Abbott RC	.35
192	Tony Armas Jr.	.25
193	Gil Meche	.25
194	Ben Petrick	.25
195	Chris George RC	.35
196	Scott Hunter RC	.25
197	Ryan Brannan	.25
198	Amaury Garcia RC	.35
199	Chris Gissell	.25
200	Austin Kearns RC	2.00
201	Alex Gonzalez	.25
202	Wade Miller	.25
203	Scott Williamson	.25
204	Chris Enochs	.25
205	Fernando Seguignol	.25
206	Marlon Anderson	.25
207	Todd Sears RC	.35
208	Nate Bump RC	.25
209	J.M. Gold RC	.50
210	Matt LeCroy RC	.25
211	Alex Hernandez	.25
212	Luis Rivera	.25
213	Troy Cameron	.25
214	Alex Escobar RC	1.00
215	Jason LaRue	.25
216	Kyle Peterson	.25
217	Brent Butler	.25
218	Dernell Stenson	.25
219	Adrian Beltre	.40
220	Daryle Ward	.25
221	Jim Thome	.50
222	Cliff Floyd	.25
223	Rickey Henderson	1.00
224	Garret Anderson	.25
225	Ken Caminiti	.25
226	Bret Boone	.25
227	Jeromy Burnitz	.25
228	Steve Finley	.25
229	Miguel Tejada	.40
230	Greg Vaughn	.25
231	Jose Offerman	.25
232	Andy Ashby	.25
233	Albert Belle	.25
234	Fernando Tatis	.25
235	Todd Helton	.50
236	Sean Casey	.40
237	Brian Giles	.25
238	Andy Pettitte	.40
239	Fred McGriff	.25
240	Roberto Alomar	.40
241	Edgar Martinez	.25
242	Lee Stevens	.25
243	Shawn Green	.40
244	Ryan Klesko	.25
245	Sammy Sosa	1.00
246	Todd Hundley	.25
247	Shannon Stewart	.25
248	Randy Johnson	1.00

#	Player	Price
249	Rondell White	.25
250	Mike Piazza	2.00
251	Craig Biggio	.25
252	David Wells	.25
253	Brian Jordan	.25
254	Edgar Renteria	.25
255	Bartolo Colon	.25
256	Frank Thomas	1.00
257	Will Clark	.25
258	Dean Palmer	.25
259	Dmitri Young	.25
260	Scott Rolen	.50
261	Jeff Kent	.25
262	Dante Bichette	.25
263	Nomar Garciaparra	.50
264	Tony Gwynn	1.00
265	Alex Rodriguez	2.00
266	Jose Canseco	.50
267	Jason Giambi	.50
268	Jeff Bagwell	.50
269	Carlos Delgado	.50
270	Tom Glavine	.50
271	Eric Davis	.25
272	Edgardo Alfonzo	.25
273	Tim Salmon	.25
274	Johnny Damon	.50
275	Rafael Palmeiro	.50
276	Denny Neagle	.25
277	Neifi Perez	.25
278	Roger Clemens	1.50
279	Brant Brown	.25
280	Kevin Brown	.25
281	Jay Bell	.25
282	Jay Buhner	.25
283	Matt Lawton	.25
284	Robin Ventura	.25
285	Juan Gonzalez	.50
286	Mo Vaughn	.25
287	Kevin Millwood	.25
288	Tino Martinez	.25
289	Justin Thompson	.25
290	Derek Jeter	3.00
291	Ben Davis	.25
292	Mike Lowell	.25
293	Joe Crede RC	3.00
294	Micah Bowie RC	.50
295	Lance Berkman	.25
296	Jason Marquis	.25
297	Chad Green	.25
298	Dee Brown	.25
299	Jerry Hairston Jr.	.25
300	Gabe Kapler	.25
301	Brent Stentz RC	.35
302	Scott Mullen RC	.35
303	Brandon Reed	.25
304	Shea Hillenbrand RC	1.50
305	J.D. Closser RC	.50
306	Gary Matthews Jr.	.25
307	Toby Hall RC	.50
308	Jason Phillips RC	.35
309	Jose Macias RC	.50
310	Jung Bong RC	.35
311	Ramon Soler RC	.35
312	Kelly Dransfeldt RC	.50
313	Carlos Hernandez RC	.50
314	Kevin Haverbusch RC	.50
315	Aaron Myette RC	.50
316	Chad Harville RC	.50
317	Kyle Farnsworth RC	1.00
318	Travis Dawkins RC	.25
319	Willie Martinez RC	.25
320	Carlos Lee	.35
321	Carlos Pena RC	4.00
322	Peter Bergeron RC	.50
323	A.J. Burnett RC	4.00
324	Bucky Jacobsen RC	.50
325	Mo Bruce RC	.35
326	Reggie Taylor	.25
327	Jackie Rexrode	.25
328	Alvin Morrow RC	.25
329	Carlos Beltran	.50
330	Eric Chavez	.50
331	John Patterson	.25
332	Jayson Werth	.25
333	Richie Sexson	.25
334	Randy Wolf	.25
335	Eli Marrero	.25
336	Paul LoDuca	.25
337	J.D. Smart	.25
338	Ryan Minor	.25
339	Kris Benson	.25
340	George Lombard	.25
341	Troy Glaus	.50
342	Eddie Yarnell	.25
343	Kip Wells RC	1.00
344	C.C. Sabathia RC	8.00
345	Sean Burroughs RC	1.00
346	Felipe Lopez RC	4.00
347	Ryan Rupe RC	.50
348	Orber Moreno RC	.35
349	Rafael Roque RC	.35
350	Alfonso Soriano RC	20.00
351	Pablo Ozuna RC	.25
352	Corey Patterson RC	2.00
353	Braden Looper RC	.25
354	Robbie Bell	.25
355	Mark Mulder RC	2.00
356	Angel Pena	.25
357	Kevin McGlinchy RC	.25
358	Michael Restovich RC	1.00
359	Eric DuBose	.25
360	Geoff Jenkins	.25
361	Mark Harriger RC	.35
362	Junior Herndon RC	.35
363	Tim Raines Jr. RC	.35
364	Rafael Furcal RC	3.00
365	Marcus Giles RC	1.50
366	Ted Lilly	.25
367	Jorge Toca RC	.35
368	David Kelton RC	1.00
369	Adam Dunn RC	25.00
370	Guillermo Mota RC	.35
371	Brett Laxton RC	.35
372	Travis Harper RC	.35
373	Tom Davey RC	.35
374	Darren Blakely RC	.35
375	Tim Hudson RC	10.00
376	Jason Romano	.25
377	Dan Reichert	.25
378	Julio Lugo RC	.35
379	Jose Garcia RC	.35
380	Erubiel Durazo RC	1.00
381	Jose Jimenez	.25
382	Chris Fussell	.25
383	Steve Lomasney	.25
384	Juan Pena RC	.50
385	Allen Levrault RC	.35
386	Juan Rivera RC	.35
387	Steve Colyer RC	.35
388	Joe Nathan RC	1.50
389	Ron Walker RC	.35
390	Nick Bierbrodt	.25
391	Luke Prokopec RC	.35
392	Dave Roberts RC	.50
393	Mike Darr	.25
394	Abraham Nunez RC	1.00
395	Giuseppe Chiaramonte RC	.35
396	Jermaine Van Buren RC	.35
397	Mike Kusiewicz	.25
398	Matt Wise RC	.35
399	Joe McEwing RC	.50
400	Matt Holliday RC	20.00
401	Willi Mo Pena RC	4.00
402	Ruben Quevedo RC	.35
403	Rob Ryan RC	.35
404	Freddy Garcia RC	2.00
405	Kevin Eberwein RC	.35
406	Jesus Colome RC	.35
407	Chris Singleton RC	.35
408	Bubba Crosby RC	1.00
409	Jesus Cordero RC	.35
410	Donny Leon	.25
411	Goefrey Tomlinson RC	.35
412	Jeff Winchester RC	.35
413	Adam Piatt RC	.50
414	Robert Stratton	.25
415	T.J. Tucker	.25
416	Ryan Langerhans RC	1.00
417	Chris Wakeland RC	.35
418	Matt Miller RC	.35
419	Doug Clark RC	.35
420	Kory DeHaan RC	.35
421	David Eckstein RC	2.00
422	Brian Cooper RC	.35
423	Brady Clark RC	1.00
424	Chris Magruder RC	.35
425	Bobby Seay RC	.50
426	Aubrey Huff RC	5.00
427	Mike Jerzembeck RC	.35
428	Matt Blank RC	.35
429	Benny Agbayani RC	.35
430	Kevin Beirne RC	.35
431	Josh Hamilton RC	30.00
432	Josh Girdley RC	.35
433	Kyle Snyder RC	.35
434	Mike Paradis RC	.35
435	Jason Jennings RC	.75
436	David Walling RC	.35
437	Omar Ortiz RC	.35
438	Jay Gehrke RC	.35
439	Casey Burns RC	.35
440	Carl Crawford RC	12.00

Refractors

Refractor versions of all Bowman Chrome base cards and inserts were also created. Base card Refractors are found at the average rate of one per 12 packs. Scout's Choice Refractors are a 1:48 find; International Refractors (serially numbered within an edition of 100 each) are 1:76 and Diamond Aces Refractors are 1:84.

	NM/M
Common Player:	1.00
Refractor Stars:	5X

Gold

A gold, rather than black, facsimile signature differentiates this parallel from the base-card issue. At an average insertion rate of 1:12, the Series 1 Golds are twice as easy

JOSH McKINLEY

as the Series 2 (1:24). Conversely, a Refractor version which is limited to 25 serially numbered sets, is an easier pull in Series 2 (1:200) than in Series 1 (1:305).

	NM/M
Common Player, Series 1:	1.50
Common Player, Series 2:	2.00
Stars:	3X
Gold Refractors:	30X

International

BRUCE CHEN

Replacing the regular-card background with a scene from the player's native land gives this parallel issue an international flavor. For the geographically challenged, the place of birth is spelled out in the lower-left corner of the photo. In addition, the card backs are printed in the player's native language. Series 1 Internationals are found on the average of one per four packs, while the scarcer Series 2 Internationals are a 1:12 pick. Conversely, the Refractor version, individually numbered within an edition of 100 each is scarcer in Series 1 (1:76) than in Series 2 (1:50).

	NM/M
Common Player, Series 1:	.25
Common Player, Series 2:	.50
Stars:	1.5X
Common Refractor:	5.00
Refractors:	12X

Diamond Aces

DIAMOND ACES — PAT HENTGEN — BRUCE CHEN ATLANTA BRAVES

This 18-card set features nine emerging stars along with nine proven veterans. The cards have a prismatic look with "Diamond Aces" across the top. They are inserted in Series 1 packs. A parallel Refractor version is also randomly inserted.

	NM/M
Complete Set (18):	24.00
Common Player:	.50
Inserted 1:21	
Refractors:	1.5X
Inserted 1:84	
DA1 Troy Glaus	1.50
DA2 Eric Chavez	.75
DA3 Fernando Seguignol	.50
DA4 Ryan Anderson	.50
DA5 Ruben Mateo	.50
DA6 Carlos Beltran	1.00
DA7 Adrian Beltre	.75
DA8 Bruce Chen	.50
DA9 Pat Burrell	2.00
DA10 Mike Piazza	3.00
DA11 Ken Griffey Jr.	3.00
DA12 Chipper Jones	2.00
DA13 Derek Jeter	4.00
DA14 Mark McGwire	3.50
DA15 Nomar Garciaparra	2.00
DA16 Sammy Sosa	2.00
DA17 Juan Gonzalez	.75
DA18 Alex Rodriguez	3.50

Early Impact

The checklist of this Series 2 insert mixes a dozen youngsters - labeled "Early Impact" on front - who are already making a mark in the majors with eight veteran stars, whose cards are labeled "Lasting Impact." A Refractor version is a parallel.

	NM/M
Complete Set (20):	35.00
Common Player:	.75
Inserted 1:15	
Refractor:	1.5X
Inserted 1:75	
1 Alfonso Soriano	2.00
2 Pat Burrell	.75
3 Ruben Mateo	.75
4 A.J. Burnett	.75
5 Corey Patterson	1.00
6 Daryle Ward	.75
7 Eric Chavez	1.00
8 Troy Glaus	2.00
9 Sean Casey	1.00
10 Joe McEwing	.75
11 Gabe Kapler	.75
12 Michael Barrett	.75
13 Sammy Sosa	2.50
14 Alex Rodriguez	4.00
15 Mark McGwire	4.00
16 Derek Jeter	5.00
17 Nomar Garciaparra	2.50
18 Mike Piazza	3.00
19 Chipper Jones	2.50
20 Ken Griffey Jr.	3.00

Scout's Choice

This is a chromium parallel of the inserts found in Series 1 Bowman. The 21-card set showcases prospects that have potential to win a future Rookie of the Year award. Refractor parallels are also randomly inserted.

	NM/M
Complete Set (21):	20.00
Common Player:	.75
Inserted 1:12	
Refractors:	1.5X
Inserted 1:48	
SC1 Ruben Mateo	.75
SC2 Ryan Anderson	.75
SC3 Pat Burrell	3.00
SC4 Troy Glaus	4.00
SC5 Eric Chavez	4.00
SC6 Adrian Beltre	1.50
SC7 Bruce Chen	.75
SC8 Carlos Beltran	2.50
SC9 Alex Gonzalez	.75
SC10 Carlos Lee	1.00
SC11 George Lombard	.75
SC12 Matt Clement	.75
SC13 Calvin Pickering	.75
SC14 Marlon Anderson	.75
SC15 Chad Hermansen	.75
SC16 Russell Branyan	.75
SC17 Jeremy Giambi	.75
SC18 Ricky Ledee	.75
SC19 John Patterson	.75
SC20 Roy Halladay	1.00
SC21 Michael Barrett	.75

2000 Rookie of the Year

This is a chromium parallel of the inserts found in Series 2 Bowman. The 10-card set is inserted in Series 2 Chrome packs and showcases prospects that have potential to win the 2000 Rookie of the Year award. Refractor parallels are also randomly inserted.

	NM/M
Complete Set (10):	12.00
Common Player:	1.00
Inserted 1:20	
Refractors:	1.5-3X
Inserted 1:100	
1 Ryan Anderson	1.00
2 Pat Burrell	4.00
3 A.J. Burnett	1.00
4 Ruben Mateo	1.00
5 Alex Escobar	1.00
6 Pablo Ozuna	1.00
7 Mark Mulder	1.50
8 Corey Patterson	2.00
9 George Lombard	1.00
10 Nick Johnson	2.00

1999 Bowman's Best Pre-Production

LOPEZ

These cards were issued to draw interest to the '99 Bowman's Best issue. The promos are virtually identical to the issued version of each player's card except for the card number which is preceeded by a "PP" prefix.

	NM/M
Complete Set (3):	3.00
Common Player:	2.00
PP1 Javy Lopez	1.00
PP2 Marlon Anderson	1.00
PP3 J.M. Gold	1.00

1999 Bowman's Best

DARNELL STENSON

Bowman's Best consists of 200 cards printed on thick 27-point stock. Within the base set are 85 veteran stars printed on gold foil, 15 Best Performers on bronze foil, 50 Prospects on silver foil and 50 rookies on blue foil. The rookies are seeded one per pack. There are also two parallel versions: Refractors and Atomic Refractors. Refractors are inserted 1:15 packs and are sequentially numbered to 400, while Atomic Refractors are found 1:62 packs and are sequentially numbered to 100.

	NM/M
Complete Set (200):	30.00
Common Player:	.25
Pack (6):	2.00
Wax Box (24):	40.00
1 Chipper Jones	1.50
2 Brian Jordan	.25
3 David Justice	.25
4 Jason Kendall	.25
5 Mo Vaughn	.25
6 Jim Edmonds	.25
7 Wade Boggs	1.50
8 Jeremy Burnitz	.25
9 Todd Hundley	.25
10 Rondell White	.25
11 Cliff Floyd	.25
12 Sean Casey	.40
13 Bernie Williams	.25
14 Dante Bichette	.25
15 Greg Vaughn	.25
16 Andres Galarraga	.25
17 Ray Durham	.25
18 Jim Thome	.60
19 Gary Sheffield	.25
20 Frank Thomas	1.00
21 Orlando Hernandez	.35
22 Ivan Rodriguez	.75
23 Jose Cruz Jr.	.25
24 Jason Giambi	.50
25 Craig Biggio	.25
26 Kerry Wood	.45
27 Manny Ramirez	1.00
28 Curt Schilling	.45
29 Mike Mussina	.45
30 Tim Salmon	.25
31 Mike Piazza	2.00
32 Roberto Alomar	.40
33 Larry Walker	.25
34 Barry Larkin	.25
35 Nomar Garciaparra	1.50
36 Paul O'Neill	.25
37 Todd Walker	.25
38 Eric Karros	.25
39 Brad Fullmer	.25
40 John Olerud	.25
41 Todd Helton	.75
42 Raul Mondesi	.25
43 Jose Canseco	.50
44 Matt Williams	.25
45 Ray Lankford	.25
46 Carlos Delgado	.50
47 Darin Erstad	.50
48 Vladimir Guerrero	1.00
49 Robin Ventura	.25
50 Alex Rodriguez	2.50
51 Vinny Castilla	.25
52 Tony Clark	.25
53 Pedro Martinez	1.00
54 Rafael Palmeiro	.65
55 Scott Rolen	.65
56 Tino Martinez	.25
57 Tony Gwynn	1.50
58 Barry Bonds	3.00
59 Kenny Lofton	.25
60 Javy Lopez	.25
61 Mark Grace	.25
62 Travis Lee	.25
63 Kevin Brown	.25
64 Al Leiter	.25
65 Albert Belle	.25
66 Sammy Sosa	1.50
67 Greg Maddux	1.50
68 Mark Kotsay	.25
69 Dmitri Young	.25
70 Mark McGwire	2.50
71 Juan Gonzalez	.50
72 Andruw Jones	1.00
73 Derek Jeter	3.00
74 Randy Johnson	1.00
75 Cal Ripken Jr.	3.00
76 Shawn Green	.35
77 Moises Alou	.25
78 Tom Glavine	.45
79 Sandy Alomar	.25
80 Ken Griffey Jr.	2.00
81 Ryan Klesko	.25
82 Jeff Bagwell	1.00
83 Ben Grieve	.25
84 John Smoltz	.25
85 Roger Clemens	1.75
86 Ken Griffey Jr.	1.00
87 Roger Clemens	.85
88 Derek Jeter	1.50
89 Nomar Garciaparra	.75
90 Mark McGwire	1.25
91 Sammy Sosa	.75
92 Alex Rodriguez	1.25
93 Greg Maddux	.75
94 Vladimir Guerrero	1.00
95 Chipper Jones	.75
96 Kerry Wood	.30
97 Ben Grieve	.25
98 Tony Gwynn	.75
99 Juan Gonzalez	.30
100 Mike Piazza	1.00
101 Eric Chavez	.40
102 Billy Koch	.25
103 Dernell Stenson	.25
104 Marlon Anderson	.25
105 Ron Belliard	.25
106 Bruce Chen	.25
107 Carlos Beltran	.25
108 Chad Hermansen	.25
109 Ryan Anderson	.25
110 Michael Barrett	.25
111 Matt Clement	.25
112 Ben Davis	.25
113 Calvin Pickering	.25
114 Brad Penny	.25
115 Paul Konerko	.35
116 Alex Gonzalez	.25
117 George Lombard	.25
118 John Patterson	.25
119 Rob Bell	.25
120 Ruben Mateo	.25
121 Troy Glaus	.25
122 Ryan Bradley	.25
123 Carlos Lee	.25
124 Gabe Kapler	.25
125 Ramon Hernandez	.25
126 Carlos Febles	.25
127 Mitch Meluskey	.25
128 Michael Cuddyer	.25
129 Pablo Ozuna	.25
130 Jayson Werth	.25
131 Ricky Ledee	.25
132 Jeremy Giambi	.25
133 Danny Klassen	.25

#	Player	Price
134	Mark DeRosa	.25
135	Randy Wolf	.25
136	Roy Halladay	.35
137	Derrick Gibson	.25
138	Ben Petrick	.25
139	Warren Morris	.25
140	Lance Berkman	.25
141	Russell Branyan	.25
142	Adrian Beltre	.40
143	Juan Encarnacion	.25
144	Fernando Seguignol	.25
145	Corey Koskie	.25
146	Preston Wilson	.25
147	Homer Bush	.25
148	Daryle Ward	.25
149	Joe McEwing RC	.50
150	Peter Bergeron RC	.50
151	Pat Burrell RC	3.00
152	Choo Freeman RC	.50
153	Matt Belisle RC	.50
154	Carlos Pena RC	1.00
155	A.J. Burnett RC	.75
156	Doug Mientkiewicz RC	.75
157	Sean Burroughs RC	.50
158	Mike Zywica RC	.35
159	Corey Patterson RC	1.50
160	Austin Kearns RC	2.00
161	Chip Ambres RC	.35
162	Kelly Dransfeldt RC	.35
163	Mike Nannini RC	.35
164	Mark Mulder RC	2.00
165	Jason Tyner RC	.35
166	Bobby Seay RC	.50
167	Alex Escobar RC	.75
168	Nick Johnson RC	1.00
169	Alfonso Soriano RC	4.00
170	Clayton Andrews RC	.35
171	C.C. Sabathia RC	2.00
172	Matt Holliday RC	5.00
173	Brad Lidge RC	1.00
174	Kit Pellow RC	.50
175	J.M. Gold RC	.50
176	Roosevelt Brown RC	.50
177	Eric Valent RC	.50
178	Adam Everett RC	.75
179	Jorge Toca RC	.35
180	Matt Roney RC	.35
181	Andy Brown RC	.35
182	Phil Norton RC	.35
183	Mickey Lopez RC	.35
184	Chris George RC	.35
185	Arturo McDowell RC	.35
186	Jose Fernandez RC	.35
187	Seth Etherton RC	.50
188	Josh McKinley RC	.50
189	Nate Cornejo RC	.50
190	Giuseppe Chiaramonte RC	.35
191	Mamon Tucker RC	.35
192	Ryan Mills RC	.50
193	Chad Moeller RC	.50
194	Tony Torcato RC	.35
195	Jeff Winchester RC	.35
196	Rick Elder RC	.35
197	Matt Burch RC	.35
198	Jeff Urban RC	.35
199	Chris Jones RC	.35
200	Masao Kida RC	.50

Refractors

Inserted at an average rate of about one per 15 packs, Best Refractor's are so marked on the back in the card-number box at upper-right. Also found on back is a serial numbered stamped in gold-foil from within an edition of 400.

	NM/M
Complete Set (200):	250.00
Common Player:	1.00
Stars:	6X
Production 400 Sets	

Atomic Refractors

The vibrant refractive background on front announces these parallels which are found on average of about once per 62 packs. Backs identify the variation in the card-number box at upper-right and with a serial number from within an edition of 100 per card.

	NM/M
Common Player:	3.00
Stars:	12X
Production 100 Sets	

Franchise Best

Ten league leaders are featured in this insert set on three different technologies: Mach I, Mach II and Mach III. Mach I features die-cut Serillusion stock and is numbered to 3,000. Mach II features die-cut refractive styrene stock, numbered to 1,000; and, Mach III features die-cut polycarbonate stock and is limited to 500 numbered sets. All cards numbers have an "FB" prefix.

	NM/M
Complete Set (10):	15.00
Common Player:	.75
Production 3,000 Sets	
Mach II (1,000):	1.5X
Mach III (500):	2.5X
1 Mark McGwire	2.50
2 Ken Griffey Jr.	1.50
3 Sammy Sosa	1.25
4 Nomar Garciaparra	1.25
5 Alex Rodriguez	2.50
6 Derek Jeter	3.50
7 Mike Piazza	1.50
8 Frank Thomas	1.00
9 Chipper Jones	1.25
10 Juan Gonzalez	.75

Franchise Favorites

This six-card set features retired legends and current stars in three versions. Version A features a current star, Version B features a retired player and Version C pairs the current star with the retired player. Cards have an "FR" prefix to the number on back.

	NM/M
Complete Set (6):	12.00
Common Player:	.50
Inserted 1:75	
1A Derek Jeter	5.00
1B Don Mattingly	2.00
1C Derek Jeter, Don Mattingly	5.00
2A Scott Rolen	.50
2B Mike Schmidt	1.50
2C Scott Rolen, Mike Schmidt	

Franchise Favorites Autographs

This is a parallel autographed version of the regular Franchise Favorites inserts.

	NM/M
Common Player:	15.00
Version A & B 1:1,548	
Version C 1:6,191	
1A Derek Jeter	100.00
1B Don Mattingly	60.00
1C Derek Jeter, Don Mattingly	300.00
2A Scott Rolen	20.00
2B Mike Schmidt	50.00
2C Scott Rolen, Mike Schmidt	100.00

Future Foundations

Ten up-and-coming players are featured in this set that has the same technologies as the Franchise Best inserts and broken down the same way. The insert rates are 1:41 packs for Mach I, 1:124 for Mach II and 1:248 for Mach III.

	NM/M
Complete Set (10):	16.00
Common Player:	.75
Production 3,000 Sets	
Mach II (1,000):	1.5X
Mach III (500):	2.5X
1 Ruben Mateo	.75
2 Troy Glaus	4.00
3 Eric Chavez	1.50
4 Pat Burrell	4.00
5 Adrian Beltre	1.50
6 Ryan Anderson	.75
7 Alfonso Soriano	3.00
8 Brad Penny	.75
9 Derrick Gibson	.75
10 Bruce Chen	.75

Mirror Image

These inserts feature a veteran player on one side and a prospect on the other side for a total of 10 double-sided cards featuring 20 players. There are also parallel Refractor and Atomic Refractor versions.

	NM/M
Complete Set (10):	20.00
Common Player:	1.50
Inserted 1:24	
Refractors (1:96):	1.5X
Atomic Refractors (1:192):	2X
1 Alex Rodriguez, Alex Gonzalez	2.50
2 Ken Griffey Jr., Ruben Mateo	2.00
3 Derek Jeter, Alfonso Soriano	4.00
4 Sammy Sosa, Corey Patterson	1.50
5 Greg Maddux, Bruce Chen	1.50
6 Chipper Jones, Eric Chavez	1.50
7 Vladimir Guerrero, Carlos Beltran	1.50

		Price
8	Frank Thomas, Nick Johnson	1.50
9	Nomar Garciaparra, Pablo Ozuna	1.50
10	Mark McGwire, Pat Burrell	3.00

Rookie Locker Room Autographs

This five-card set features autographs of baseball's current hot prospects. Each card is branded with a "Topps Certified Autograph Issue" stamp.

	NM/M
Common Player:	4.00
Inserted 1:248	
1 Pat Burrell	15.00
2 Michael Barrett	5.00
3 Troy Glaus	10.00
4 Gabe Kapler	4.00
5 Eric Chavez	7.50

Rookie Locker Room Game-Worn Jerseys

This four-card set spotlights hot prospects and has a swatch of game-used jersey from the featured player embedded into the card.

	NM/M
Common Player:	3.00
Inserted 1:270	
1 Richie Sexson	5.00
2 Michael Barrett	3.00
3 Troy Glaus	8.00
4 Eric Chavez	5.00

Rookie Locker Room Game-Used Lumber

This six-card set features actual pieces of each player's game-used bat embedded into the cards.

	NM/M
Complete Set (6):	35.00
Common Player:	4.00
Inserted 1:258	
1 Pat Burrell	10.00
2 Michael Barrett	4.00
3 Troy Glaus	10.00
4 Gabe Kapler	4.00
5 Eric Chavez	7.50
6 Richie Sexson	5.00

Rookie of the Year

This set salutes 1998 AL and NL Rookie of Year award winners Kerry Wood and Ben Grieve. They are inserted 1:95 packs and are numbered with a ROY prefix. Ben Grieve also autographed some of the inserts which feature a "Topps Certified Autograph Issue" stamp. Autographs are seeded 1:1,241 packs.

	NM/M
Complete Set (2):	4.00
1 Ben Grieve	2.00
2 Kerry Wood	2.00
A1 Ben Grieve/Auto.	6.00

2000 Bowman

Released in one 440-card series. The card fronts are foil stamped to differentiate Veterans (gold foil)

from Rookies and Prospects (silver). All card fronts feature facsimile signatures from the players' original Topps contracts. All bona fide rookie cards also exhibit the "Bowman Rookie Card" stamped under the 2000 Bowman logo.

		NM/M
Complete Set (440):		65.00
Common Player:		.15
Common Rookie:		.25
Pack (10):		2.50
Box (24):		40.00
1	Vladimir Guerrero	.75
2	Chipper Jones	.75
3	Todd Walker	.15
4	Barry Larkin	.25
5	Bernie Williams	.40
6	Todd Helton	.50
7	Jermaine Dye	.15
8	Brian Giles	.15
9	Freddy Garcia	.15
10	Greg Vaughn	.15
11	Alex Gonzalez	.15
12	Luis Gonzalez	.25
13	Ron Belliard	.15
14	Ben Grieve	.15
15	Carlos Delgado	.50
16	Brian Jordan	.15
17	Fernando Tatis	.15
18	Ryan Rupe	.15
19	Miguel Tejada	.50
20	Mark Grace	.30
21	Kenny Lofton	.15
22	Eric Karros	.15
23	Cliff Floyd	.15
24	John Halama	.15
25	Cristian Guzman	.15
26	Scott Williamson	.15
27	Mike Lieberthal	.15
28	Tim Hudson	.40
29	Warren Morris	.15
30	Pedro Martinez	1.00
31	John Smoltz	.15
32	Ray Durham	.15
33	Chad Allen	.15
34	Tony Clark	.15
35	Tino Martinez	.25
36	J.T. Snow Jr.	.15
37	Kevin Brown	.25
38	Bartolo Colon	.15
39	Rey Ordonez	.15
40	Jeff Bagwell	.50
41	Ivan Rodriguez	.50
42	Eric Chavez	.25
43	Eric Milton	.15
44	Jose Canseco	.50
45	Shawn Green	.25
46	Rich Aurilia	.15
47	Roberto Alomar	.40
48	Brian Daubach	.15
49	Magglio Ordonez	.25
50	Derek Jeter	2.00
51	Kris Benson	.15
52	Albert Belle	.25
53	Rondell White	.15
54	Justin Thompson	.15
55	Nomar Garciaparra	.75
56	Chuck Finley	.15
57	Omar Vizquel	.15
58	Luis Castillo	.15
59	Richard Hidalgo	.15
60	Barry Bonds	2.00
61	Craig Biggio	.25
62	Doug Glanville	.15
63	Gabe Kapler	.15
64	Johnny Damon	.15
65	Pokey Reese	.15
66	Andy Pettitte	.25
67	B.J. Surhoff	.15
68	Richie Sexson	.40
69	Javy Lopez	.25
70	Raul Mondesi	.25
71	Darin Erstad	.25
72	Kevin Millwood	.15
73	Ricky Ledee	.15
74	John Olerud	.15
75	Sean Casey	.25
76	Carlos Febles	.15
77	Paul O'Neill	.25
78	Bob Abreu	.15
79	Neifi Perez	.15
80	Tony Gwynn	.75
81	Russ Ortiz	.15
82	Matt Williams	.15
83	Chris Carpenter	.15
84	Roger Cedeno	.15

#	Player	Price
85	Tim Salmon	.30
86	Billy Koch	.15
87	Jeromy Burnitz	.15
88	Edgardo Alfonzo	.15
89	Jay Bell	.15
90	Manny Ramirez	.75
91	Frank Thomas	.75
92	Mike Mussina	.50
93	J.D. Drew	.25
94	Adrian Beltre	.25
95	Alex Rodriguez	2.00
96	Larry Walker	.15
97	Juan Encarnacion	.15
98	Mike Sweeney	.15
99	Rusty Greer	.15
100	Randy Johnson	.75
101	Jose Vidro	.15
102	Preston Wilson	.15
103	Greg Maddux	1.50
104	Jason Giambi	.50
105	Cal Ripken Jr.	2.00
106	Carlos Beltran	.50
107	Vinny Castilla	.15
108	Mariano Rivera	.25
109	Mo Vaughn	.25
110	Rafael Palmeiro	.50
111	Shannon Stewart	.15
112	Mike Hampton	.15
113	Joe Nathan	.15
114	Ben Davis	.15
115	Andruw Jones	.25
116	Robin Ventura	.15
117	Damion Easley	.15
118	Jeff Cirillo	.15
119	Kerry Wood	.25
120	Scott Rolen	.75
121	Sammy Sosa	.75
122	Ken Griffey Jr.	1.50
123	Shane Reynolds	.15
124	Troy Glaus	.40
125	Tom Glavine	.35
126	Michael Barrett	.15
127	Al Leiter	.15
128	Jason Kendall	.15
129	Roger Clemens	1.00
130	Juan Gonzalez	.40
131	Corey Koskie	.15
132	Curt Schilling	.50
133	Mike Piazza	1.00
134	Gary Sheffield	.40
135	Jim Thome	.40
136	Orlando Hernandez	.25
137	Ray Lankford	.15
138	Geoff Jenkins	.15
139	Jose Lima	.15
140	Mark McGwire	1.50
141	Adam Piatt	.15
142	Pat Manning RC	.25
143	Marcos Castillo RC	.25
144	Lesli Brea RC	.25
145	Humberto Cota RC	.25
146	Ben Petrick	.15
147	Kip Wells	.15
148	Willi Mo Pena	.25
149	Chris Wakeland	.15
150	Brad Baker RC	.25
151	Robbie Morrison RC	.25
152	Reggie Taylor	.15
153	Brian Cole RC	.25
154	Peter Bergeron	.15
155	Roosevelt Brown	.15
156	Matt Cepicky RC	.25
157	Ramon Castro	.15
158	Brad Baisley RC	.25
159	Jeff Goldbach RC	.25
160	Mitch Meluskey	.15
161	Chad Harville	.15
162	Brian Cooper	.15
163	Marcus Giles	.15
164	Jim Morris	.50
165	Geoff Goetz	.15
166	Bobby Bradley RC	.25
167	Rob Bell	.15
168	Joe Crede	.15
169	Michael Restovich	.15
170	Quincy Foster RC	.25
171	Enrique Cruz RC	.25
172	Mark Quinn	.15
173	Nick Johnson	.15
174	Jeff Liefer	.15
175	Kevin Mench RC	.75
176	Steve Lomasney	.15
177	Jayson Werth	.15
178	Tim Drew	.15
179	Chip Ambres	.15
180	Ryan Anderson	.15
181	Matt Blank	.15
182	Giuseppe Chiaramonte	.15
183	Corey Myers RC	.25
184	Jeff Yoder	.15
185	Craig Dingman RC	.25
186	Jon Hamilton RC	.25
187	Toby Hall	.15
188	Russell Branyan	.15
189	Brian Falkenborg RC	.25
190	Aaron Harang RC	.75
191	Juan Pena	.15
192	Travis Thompson RC	.25
193	Alfonso Soriano	.50
194	Alejandro Diaz RC	.25
195	Carlos Pena	.15
196	Kevin Nicholson	.15
197	Mo Bruce	.15
198	C.C. Sabathia	.15
199	Carl Crawford	.15
200	Rafael Furcal	.25
201	Andrew Beinbrink RC	.25
202	Jimmy Osting	.15

203	Aaron McNeal RC	.25
204	Brett Laxton	.15
205	Chris George	.15
206	Felipe Lopez	.15
207	Ben Sheets RC	1.50
208	Mike Meyers RC	.40
209	Jason Conti	.15
210	Milton Bradley	.15
211	Chris Mears RC	.25
212	Carlos Hernandez RC	.50
213	Jason Romano	.15
214	Goefrey Tomlinson	.15
215	Jimmy Rollins	.40
216	Pablo Ozuna	.15
217	Steve Cox	.15
218	Terrence Long	.15
219	Jeff DaVanon RC	.40
220	Rick Ankiel	.25
221	Jason Standridge	.15
222	Tony Armas	.15
223	Jason Tyner	.15
224	Ramon Ortiz	.15
225	Daryle Ward	.15
226	Enger Veras RC	.25
227	Chris Jones RC	.25
228	Eric Cammack RC	.25
229	Ruben Mateo	.15
230	Ken Harvey RC	.50
231	Jake Westbrook	.15
232	Rob Purvis RC	.25
233	Choo Freeman	.15
234	Aramis Ramirez	.15
235	A.J. Burnett	.25
236	Kevin Barker	.15
237	Chance Caple RC	.25
238	Jarrod Washburn	.15
239	Lance Berkman	.15
240	Michael Wenner RC	.25
241	Alex Sanchez	.15
242	Jake Esteves RC	.25
243	Grant Roberts	.15
244	Mark Ellis RC	.50
245	Donny Leon	.15
246	David Eckstein	.15
247	Dicky Gonzalez RC	.25
248	John Patterson	.15
249	Chad Green	.15
250	Scot Shields RC	.25
251	Troy Cameron	.15
252	Jose Molina	.15
253	Rob Pugmire RC	.25
254	Rick Elder	.15
255	Sean Burroughs	.25
256	Josh Kalinowski RC	.25
257	Matt LeCroy	.15
258	Alex Graman RC	.50
259	Tomokazu Ohka RC	.50
260	Brady Clark	.15
261	Rico Washington RC	.25
262	Gary Matthews Jr.	.15
263	Matt Wise	.15
264	Keith Reed RC	.50
265	Santiago Ramirez RC	.25
266	Ben Broussard RC	.50
267	Ryan Langerhans	.15
268	Juan Rivera	.15
269	Shawn Gallagher	.15
270	Jorge Toca	.15
271	Brad Lidge	.15
272	Leo Estrella RC	.25
273	Ruben Quevedo	.15
274	Jack Cust	.15
275	T.J. Tucker	.15
276	Mike Colangelo	.15
277	Brian Schneider	.15
278	Calvin Murray	.15
279	Josh Girdley	.15
280	Mike Paradis	.15
281	Chad Hermansen	.15
282	Ty Howington RC	.50
283	Aaron Myette	.15
284	D'Angelo Jimenez	.15
285	Dernell Stenson	.15
286	Jerry Hairston Jr.	.15
287	Gary Majewski RC	.25
288	Derrin Ebert RC	.25
289	Steve Fish RC	.25
290	Carlos Hernandez	.15
291	Allen Levrault	.15
292	Sean McNally RC	.25
293	Randey Dorame RC	.25
294	Wes Anderson RC	.50
295	B.J. Ryan	.15
296	Alan Webb RC	.25
297	Brandon Inge RC	.75
298	David Walling	.15
299	Sun-Woo Kim RC	.40
300	Pat Burrell	.25
301	Rick Guttormson RC	.25
302	Gil Meche	.15
303	Carlos Zambrano RC	3.00
304	Eric Byrnes (Photo actually Bo Porter)	1.00
305	Robb Quinlan RC	.25
306	Jackie Rexrode	.15
307	Nate Bump	.15
308	Sean DePaula RC	.15
309	Matt Riley	.15
310	Ryan Minor	.15
311	J.J. Davis	.15
312	Randy Wolf	.15
313	Jason Jennings	.15
314	Scott Seabol RC	.25
315	Doug Davis	.15
316	Todd Moser RC	.25
317	Rob Ryan	.15
318	Bubba Crosby	.15
319	Lyle Overbay RC	1.00
320	Mario Encarnacion	.15
321	Francisco Rodriguez RC	2.00
322	Michael Cuddyer	.15
323	Eddie Yarnall	.15
324	Cesar Saba RC	.25
325	Travis Dawkins	.15
326	Alex Escobar	.15
327	Julio Zuleta RC	.40
328	Josh Hamilton	1.00
329	Nick Neugebauer RC	.25
330	Matt Belisle	.15
331	Kurt Ainsworth RC	.50
332	Tim Raines Jr.	.15
333	Eric Munson	.15
334	Donzell McDonald	.15
335	Larry Bigbie RC	.25
336	Matt Watson	.15
337	Aubrey Huff	.15
338	Julio Ramirez	.15
339	Jason Grabowski RC	.25
340	Jon Garland	.15
341	Austin Kearns	.25
342	Josh Pressley	.15
343	Miguel Olivo RC	.25
344	Julio Lugo	.15
345	Roberto Vaz	.15
346	Ramon Soler	.15
347	Brandon Phillips RC	2.00
348	Vince Faison RC	.25
349	Mike Venafro	.15
350	Rick Asadoorian RC	.25
351	B.J. Garbe RC	.25
352	Dan Reichert	.15
353	Jason Stumm RC	.25
354	Ruben Salazar RC	.15
355	Francisco Cordero	.15
356	Juan Guzman RC	.25
357	Mike Bacsik RC	.25
358	Jared Sandberg	.15
359	Rod Barajas	.15
360	Junior Brignac RC	.15
361	J.M. Gold	.15
362	Octavio Dotel	.15
363	David Kelton	.25
364	Scott Morgan RC	.25
365	Wascar Serrano RC	.15
366	Wilton Veras	.15
367	Eugene Kingsale	.15
368	Ted Lilly	.15
369	George Lombard	.15
370	Chris Haas	.15
371	Wilton Pena RC	.50
372	Vernon Wells	.15
373	Jason Royer RC	.25
374	Jeff Heaverlo RC	.25
375	Calvin Pickering	.15
376	Mike Lamb RC	.40
377	Kyle Snyder	.15
378	Javier Cardona RC	.25
379	Aaron Rowand RC	1.00
380	Dee Brown	.15
381	Brett Myers RC	1.00
382	Abraham Nunez	.20
383	Eric Valent	.15
384	Jody Gerut RC	.25
385	Adam Dunn	.50
386	Jay Gehrke	.15
387	Omar Ortiz	.15
388	Darnell McDonald	.15
389	Chad Alexander	.15
390	J.D. Closser	.15
391	Ben Christensen RC	.25
392	Adam Kennedy	.15
393	Nick Green RC	.25
394	Ramon Hernandez	.15
395	Roy Oswalt RC	4.00
396	Andy Tracy RC	.50
397	Eric Gagne	.25
398	Michael Tejera RC	.15
399	Adam Everett	.15
400	Corey Patterson	.75
401	Gary Knotts RC	.25
402	Ryan Christianson RC	.50
403	Eric Ireland RC	.15
404	Andrew Good RC	.25
405	Brad Penny	.15
406	Jason LaRue	.15
407	Kit Pellow	.15
408	Kevin Beirne	.15
409	Kelly Dransfield RC	.15
410	Jason Grilli	.15
411	Scott Downs RC	.25
412	Jesus Colome	.15
413	John Sneed RC	.15
414	Tony McKnight RC	.15
415	Luis Rivera	.15
416	Adam Eaton	.15
417	Mike MacDougal RC	.50
418	Mike Nannini	.15
419	Barry Zito RC	1.50
420	Dewayne Wise	.15
421	Jason Dellaero	.15
422	Chad Moeller	.15
423	Jason Marquis	.15
424	Tim Redding RC	.50
425	Mark Mulder	.50
426	Josh Paul	.15
427	Chris Enochs	.15
428	Wilfredo Rodriguez RC	.50
429	Kevin Witt	.15
430	Scott Sobkowiak RC	.25
431	McKay Christensen	.15
432	Jung Bong	.15
433	Keith Evans RC	.15
434	Garry Maddox Jr.	.15
435	Ramon Santiago RC	.50
436	Alex Cora	.15
437	Carlos Lee	.15
438	Jason Repko RC	.25
439	Matt Burch	.15
440	Shawn Sonnier RC	.25

Gold

Golds are a 440-card parallel to the base set and are highlighted by gold-stamped facsimile autographs on the card front. Golds are limited to 99 serial numbered sets.

Stars:	10-20X
Rookies:	4-8X
Production 99 Sets	

Retro/Future

These inserts are a parallel to the 440-card base set. The foiled card fronts have a horizontal format and a design reminiscent of the 1955 Bowman "television set" design. They were seeded one per pack.

	NM/M
Common Player:	.25
Stars:	2-3X
Rookies:	.75-2X
Inserted 1:1	

Autographs

Jose Vidro

This set consists of 40 players with card rarity differentiated by either a Blue, Silver or Gold foil Topps "Certified Autograph Issue" stamp. Card backs are numbered using the player initials and have a Topps serial numbered foil hologram to ensure the authenticity of the autograph.

		NM/M
Common Autograph:		5.00
Blue Inserted 1:144		
Silver 1:312		
Gold 1:1,604		
CA	Chip Ambres/B	5.00
RA	Rick Ankiel/G	25.00
CB	Carlos Beltran/G	40.00
LB	Lance Berkman/S	20.00
DB	Dee Brown/S	8.00
SB	Sean Burroughs/S	8.00
JDC	J.D. Closser/B	5.00
SC	Steve Cox/B	5.00
MC	Michael Cuddyer/S	10.00
JC	Jack Cust/S	15.00
SD	Scott Downs/S	10.00
JDD	J.D. Drew/G	25.00
AD	Adam Dunn/S	25.00
CF	Choo Freeman/B	5.00
RF	Rafael Furcal/S	15.00
AH	Aubrey Huff/B	8.00
JJ	Jason Jennings/B	8.00
NJ	Nick Johnson/S	10.00
AK	Austin Kearns/S	15.00
DK	David Kelton/B	5.00
RM	Ruben Mateo/B	15.00
MM	Mike Meyers/B	5.00
CP	Corey Patterson/S	15.00
BWP	Brad Penny/B	10.00
BP	Ben Petrick/G	10.00
AP	Adam Piatt/S	8.00
MQ	Mark Quinn/S	8.00
MR	Mike Restovich/B	5.00
MR	Matt Riley/S	8.00
JR	Jason Romano/B	5.00
BS	Ben Sheets/B	25.00
AS	Alfonso Soriano/G	40.00
EV	Eric Valent/B	5.00
JV	Jose Vidro/S	10.00
VW	Vernon Wells/G	20.00
SW	Scott Williamson/G	10.00
KJW	Kevin Witt/S	10.00
KLW	Kerry Wood/S	25.00
EY	Eddie Yarnall/G	10.00
JZ	Julio Zuleta/B	5.00

Bowman's Best Previews

This 10-card insert set is identical in design to 2000 Bowman's

DEREK JETER

Best. The card fronts have a Refractor like sheen and the card backs are numbered with a "BBP" prefix.

		NM/M
Complete Set (10):		15.00
Common Player:		.50
Inserted 1:18		
1	Derek Jeter	4.00
2	Ken Griffey Jr.	3.00
3	Nomar Garciaparra	2.00
4	Mike Piazza	2.00
5	Alex Rodriguez	4.00
6	Sammy Sosa	2.00
7	Mark McGwire	3.00
8	Pat Burrell	1.00
9	Josh Hamilton	1.00
10	Adam Piatt	.50

Early Indications

ALEX RODRIGUEZ

This 10-card set has a blue foiled card front with red foil stamping. Card backs are numbered with an "E" prefix.

		NM/M
Complete Set (10):		18.00
Common Player:		1.00
Inserted 1:24		
1	Nomar Garciaparra	1.00
2	Cal Ripken Jr.	4.00
3	Derek Jeter	4.00
4	Mark McGwire	2.50
5	Alex Rodriguez	3.00
6	Chipper Jones	1.50
7	Todd Helton	1.50
8	Vladimir Guerrero	1.50
9	Mike Piazza	1.50
10	Jose Canseco	1.00

Major Power

MAJOR POWER

ALEX RODRIGUEZ

This 10-card set spotlights the top home run hitters. Card fronts have a red border on a full foiled card front. These are numbered with an "MP" prefix on the card back.

		NM/M
Complete Set (10):		15.00
Common Player:		1.00
Inserted 1:24		
1	Mark McGwire	3.00
2	Chipper Jones	2.50
3	Alex Rodriguez	4.00
4	Sammy Sosa	2.50
5	Rafael Palmeiro	1.00
6	Ken Griffey Jr.	3.00
7	Nomar Garciaparra	1.50
8	Barry Bonds	4.00
9	Derek Jeter	5.00
10	Jeff Bagwell	1.00

Tool Time

RUBEN MATEO

This 20-card set focuses on the top minor league Prospects in five different categories: batting, power, speed, arm strength and defense. These are seeded 1:8 packs. Backs are numbered with a "TT" prefix.

		NM/M
Complete Set (20):		8.00
Common Player:		.40
Inserted 1:8		
1	Pat Burrell	1.00
2	Aaron Rowand	.40
3	Chris Wakeland	.40
4	Ruben Mateo	.40
5	Pat Burrell	.50
6	Adam Piatt	.50
7	Nick Johnson	.40
8	Jack Cust	.40
9	Rafael Furcal	.40
10	Julio Ramirez	.40
11	Travis Dawkins	.40
12	Corey Patterson	1.00
13	Ruben Mateo	.40
14	Jason Dellaero	.40
15	Sean Burroughs	.40
16	Ryan Langerhans	.40
17	D'Angelo Jimenez	.40
18	Corey Patterson	1.00
19	Troy Cameron	.40
20	Michael Cuddyer	.50

2000 Bowman Chrome

Mike Mussina

Released as a single series 440-card set, Bowman Chrome is identical in design to 2000 Bowman besides the Chromium finish on all cards. Foil highlights differentiate rookies and prospects (blue) from veterans (red). Three parallels to the base set are randomly seeded: Refractors, Retro/Future and Retro/Future Refractors.

		NM/M
Complete Set (440):		120.00
Common Player:		.25
Common Rookie:		.50
Pack (4):		2.50
Box (24):		50.00
1	Vladimir Guerrero	.75
2	Chipper Jones	1.00
3	Todd Walker	.25
4	Barry Larkin	.25
5	Bernie Williams	.50
6	Todd Helton	.75
7	Jermaine Dye	.25
8	Brian Giles	.25
9	Freddy Garcia	.25
10	Greg Vaughn	.25
11	Alex Gonzalez	.25
12	Luis Gonzalez	.25
13	Ron Belliard	.25
14	Ben Grieve	.25
15	Carlos Delgado	.75
16	Brian Jordan	.25
17	Fernando Tatis	.25
18	Ryan Rupe	.25
19	Miguel Tejada	.40
20	Mark Grace	.35
21	Kenny Lofton	.25
22	Eric Karros	.25
23	Cliff Floyd	.25
24	John Halama	.25
25	Cristian Guzman	.25
26	Scott Williamson	.25
27	Mike Lieberthal	.25
28	Tim Hudson	.40
29	Warren Morris	.25
30	Pedro Martinez	.75
31	John Smoltz	.25
32	Ray Durham	.25
33	Chad Allen	.25
34	Tony Clark	.25
35	Tino Martinez	.25
36	J.T. Snow Jr.	.25
37	Kevin Brown	.40
38	Bartolo Colon	.25
39	Rey Ordonez	.25
40	Jeff Bagwell	.50
41	Ivan Rodriguez	.50
42	Eric Chavez	.25
43	Eric Milton	.25
44	Jose Canseco	.50
45	Shawn Green	.25
46	Rich Aurilia	.25
47	Roberto Alomar	.50
48	Brian Daubach	.25
49	Magglio Ordonez	.50
50	Derek Jeter	2.00
51	Kris Benson	.25
52	Albert Belle	.25
53	Rondell White	.25
54	Justin Thompson	.25
55	Nomar Garciaparra	.50
56	Chuck Finley	.25
57	Omar Vizquel	.25
58	Luis Castillo	.25
59	Richard Hidalgo	.25
60	Barry Bonds	2.00
61	Craig Biggio	.25
62	Doug Glanville	.25
63	Gabe Kapler	.25
64	Johnny Damon	.40
65	Pokey Reese	.25
66	Andy Pettitte	.50
67	B.J. Surhoff	.25
68	Richie Sexson	.25
69	Javy Lopez	.25
70	Raul Mondesi	.25
71	Darin Erstad	.40
72	Kevin Millwood	.25
73	Ricky Ledee	.25
74	John Olerud	.25
75	Sean Casey	.25
76	Carlos Febles	.25
77	Paul O'Neill	.25
78	Bob Abreu	.25
79	Neifi Perez	.25
80	Tony Gwynn	1.00
81	Russ Ortiz	.25
82	Matt Williams	.25
83	Chris Carpenter	.25
84	Roger Cedeno	.25
85	Tim Salmon	.35
86	Billy Koch	.25
87	Jeromy Burnitz	.25
88	Edgardo Alfonzo	.25
89	Jay Bell	.15
90	Manny Ramirez	.75
91	Frank Thomas	.75
92	Mike Mussina	.50
93	J.D. Drew	.40
94	Adrian Beltre	.40
95	Alex Rodriguez	2.00
96	Larry Walker	.25
97	Juan Encarnacion	.25
98	Mike Sweeney	.25
99	Rusty Greer	.25
100	Randy Johnson	.75
101	Jose Vidro	.25
102	Preston Wilson	.25
103	Greg Maddux	1.50
104	Jason Giambi	.50
105	Cal Ripken Jr.	3.00
106	Carlos Beltran	.25
107	Vinny Castilla	.25
108	Mariano Rivera	.35
109	Mo Vaughn	.25
110	Rafael Palmeiro	.25
111	Shannon Stewart	.25
112	Mike Hampton	.25
113	Joe Nathan	.25
114	Ben Davis	.25
115	Andruw Jones	.50
116	Robin Ventura	.25
117	Damion Easley	.25
118	Jeff Cirillo	.25
119	Kerry Wood	.40
120	Scott Rolen	.50
121	Sammy Sosa	1.00
122	Ken Griffey Jr.	.75
123	Shane Reynolds	.25
124	Troy Glaus	.40
125	Tom Glavine	.50
126	Michael Barrett	.25
127	Al Leiter	.25
128	Jason Kendall	.25
129	Roger Clemens	1.50
130	Juan Gonzalez	.75
131	Corey Koskie	.25
132	Curt Schilling	.25
133	Mike Piazza	1.00
134	Gary Sheffield	.25
135	Jim Thome	.50
136	Orlando Hernandez	.25
137	Ray Lankford	.25
138	Geoff Jenkins	.25

#	Player	Price
139	Jose Lima	.25
140	Mark McGwire	1.50
141	Adam Piatt	.25
142	Pat Manning RC	.50
143	Marcos Castillo RC	.50
144	Lesli Brea RC	.50
145	Humberto Cota RC	.50
146	Ben Petrick	.25
147	Kip Wells	.25
148	Willi Mo Pena	.40
149	Chris Wakeland	.25
150	Brad Baker RC	.50
151	Robbie Morrison RC	.50
152	Reggie Taylor	.25
153	Matt Ginter RC	.50
154	Peter Bergeron	.25
155	Roosevelt Brown	.25
156	Matt Cepicky RC	.50
157	Ramon Castro	.25
158	Brad Baisley RC	.50
159	Jason Hart RC	1.00
160	Mitch Meluskey	.25
161	Chad Harville	.25
162	Brian Cooper	.25
163	Marcus Giles	.25
164	Jim Morris	.50
165	Geoff Goetz	.25
166	Bobby Bradley RC	.50
167	Rob Bell	.25
168	Joe Crede	.25
169	Michael Restovich	.50
170	Quincy Foster RC	.50
171	Enrique Cruz RC	.50
172	Mark Quinn	.25
173	Nick Johnson	.40
174	Jeff Liefer	.25
175	Kevin Mench RC	1.00
176	Steve Lomasney	.25
177	Jayson Werth	.25
178	Tim Drew	.25
179	Chip Ambres	.25
180	Ryan Anderson	.25
181	Matt Blank	.25
182	Giuseppe Chiaramonte	.25
183	Corey Myers RC	.25
184	Jeff Yoder	.25
185	Craig Dingman RC	.50
186	Jon Hamilton RC	.50
187	Toby Hall	.25
188	Russell Branyan	.25
189	Brian Falkenborg RC	.50
190	Aaron Harang	3.00
191	Juan Pena	.25
192	Chin-Hui Tsao RC	1.00
193	Alfonso Soriano	.75
194	Alejandro Diaz RC	.50
195	Carlos Pena	.25
196	Kevin Nicholson	.25
197	Mo Bruce	.25
198	C.C. Sabathia	.25
199	Carl Crawford	.25
200	Rafael Furcal	.25
201	Andrew Beinbrink RC	.50
202	Jimmy Osting	.25
203	Aaron McNeal RC	.50
204	Brett Laxton	.25
205	Chris George	.25
206	Felipe Lopez	.25
207	Ben Sheets RC	3.00
208	Mike Meyers RC	.50
209	Jason Conti	.25
210	Milton Bradley	.25
211	Chris Mears RC	.50
212	Carlos Hernandez RC	.50
213	Jason Romano	.25
214	Goefrey Tomlinson	.25
215	Jimmy Rollins	.75
216	Pablo Ozuna	.25
217	Steve Cox	.25
218	Terrence Long	.25
219	Jeff DaVanon RC	.50
220	Rick Ankiel	.75
221	Jason Standridge	.25
222	Tony Armas	.25
223	Jason Tyner	.25
224	Ramon Ortiz	.25
225	Daryle Ward	.25
226	Enger Veras RC	.50
227	Chris Jones RC	.50
228	Eric Cammack RC	.50
229	Ruben Mateo	.25
230	Ken Harvey RC	1.00
231	Jake Westbrook	.25
232	Rob Purvis RC	.50
233	Choo Freeman	.25
234	Aramis Ramirez	.25
235	A.J. Burnett	.25
236	Kevin Barker	.25
237	Chance Caple RC	.50
238	Jarrod Washburn	.25
239	Lance Berkman	.25
240	Michael Wenner RC	.50
241	Alex Sanchez	.25
242	Jake Esteves RC	.50
243	Grant Roberts	.25
244	Mark Ellis RC	.50
245	Donny Leon	.25
246	David Eckstein	.25
247	Dicky Gonzalez RC	.50
248	John Patterson	.25
249	Chad Green	.25
250	Scot Shields RC	.50
251	Troy Cameron	.25
252	Jose Molina	.25
253	Rob Pugmire RC	.50
254	Rick Elder	.25
255	Sean Burroughs	.50
256	Josh Kalinowski RC	.50
257	Matt LeCroy	.25
258	Alex Graman RC	.50
259	Juan Silvestre RC	.50
260	Brady Clark	.25
261	Rico Washington RC	.50
262	Gary Matthews Jr.	.25
263	Matt Wise	.25
264	Keith Reed RC	.50
265	Santiago Ramirez RC	.50
266	Ben Broussard RC	.50
267	Ryan Langerhans	.25
268	Juan Rivera	.25
269	Shawn Gallagher	.25
270	Jorge Toca	.25
271	Brad Lidge	.25
272	Leo Estrella RC	.50
273	Ruben Quevedo	.25
274	Jack Cust	.25
275	T.J. Tucker	.25
276	Mike Colangelo	.25
277	Brian Schneider	.25
278	Calvin Murray	.25
279	Josh Girdley	.25
280	Mike Paradis	.25
281	Chad Hermansen	.25
282	Ty Howington RC	.50
283	Aaron Myette	.25
284	D'Angelo Jimenez	.25
285	Dernell Stenson	.25
286	Jerry Hairston Jr.	.25
287	Gary Majewski RC	.50
288	Derrin Ebert RC	.50
289	Steve Fish RC	.50
290	Carlos Hernandez	.25
291	Allen Levrault	.25
292	Sean McNally RC	.50
293	Randey Dorame RC	.50
294	Wes Anderson RC	.50
295	B.J. Ryan	.25
296	Alan Webb RC	.50
297	Brandon Inge RC	1.50
298	David Walling	.25
299	Sun-Woo Kim RC	.500
300	Pat Burrell	.25
301	Rick Guttormson RC	.50
302	Gil Meche	.25
303	Carlos Zambrano RC	5.00
304	Eric Byrnes RC (Photo actually Bo Porter.)	1.00
305	Robb Quinlan RC	.50
306	Jackie Rexrode	.25
307	Nate Bump	.25
308	Sean DePaula RC	.50
309	Matt Riley	.25
310	Ryan Minor	.25
311	J.J. Davis	.25
312	Randy Wolf	.25
313	Jason Jennings	.25
314	Scott Seabol RC	.50
315	Doug Davis	.25
316	Todd Moser RC	.50
317	Rob Ryan	.25
318	Bubba Crosby	.25
319	Lyle Overbay RC	1.00
321	Francisco Rodriguez RC	5.00
322	Michael Cuddyer	.25
323	Eddie Yarnall	.25
324	Cesar Saba RC	.25
325	Travis Dawkins	.25
326	Alex Escobar	.25
327	Julio Zuleta RC	.50
328	Josh Hamilton	1.50
329	Carlos Urquiola RC	.50
330	Matt Belisle	.25
331	Kurt Ainsworth RC	.50
332	Tim Raines Jr.	.25
333	Eric Munson	.25
334	Donzell McDonald	.25
335	Larry Bigbie RC	.50
336	Matt Watson	.25
337	Aubrey Huff	.25
338	Julio Ramirez	.25
339	Jason Grabowski RC	.50
340	Jon Garland	.25
341	Austin Kearns	.50
342	Josh Pressley	.25
343	Miguel Olivo RC	.50
344	Julio Lugo	.25
345	Roberto Vaz	.25
346	Ramon Soler	.25
347	Brandon Phillips RC	4.00
348	Vince Faison RC	.50
349	Mike Venafro	.25
350	Rick Asadoorian RC	.50
351	B.J. Garbe RC	.50
352	Dan Reichert	.25
353	Jason Stumm RC	.50
354	Ruben Salazar RC	.50
355	Francisco Cordero	.25
356	Juan Guzman RC	.50
357	Mike Bacsik RC	.50
358	Jared Sandberg	.25
359	Rod Barajas	.25
360	Junior Brignac RC	.50
361	J.M. Gold	.25
362	Octavio Dotel	.25
363	David Kelton	.25
364	Scott Morgan RC	.50
365	Wascar Serrano RC	.50
366	Wilton Veras	.25
367	Eugene Kingsale	.25
368	Ted Lilly	.25
369	George Lombard	.25
370	Chris Haas	.25
371	Wilton Pena RC	.50
372	Vernon Wells	.25
373	Keith Ginter RC	.50
374	Jeff Heaverlo RC	.50
375	Calvin Pickering	.25
376	Mike Lamb RC	.50
377	Kyle Snyder	.25
378	Javier Cardona RC	.50
379	Aaron Rowand	1.50
380	Dee Brown	.25
381	Brett Myers RC	1.00
382	Abraham Nunez	.25
383	Eric Valent	.25
384	Jody Gerut RC	.50
385	Adam Dunn	.50
386	Jay Gehrke	.25
387	Omar Ortiz	.25
388	Darnell McDonald	.25
389	Chad Alexander	.25
390	J.D. Closser	.25
391	Ben Christensen RC	.50
392	Adam Kennedy	.25
393	Nick Green RC	.50
394	Ramon Hernandez	.25
395	Roy Oswalt RC	10.00
396	Andy Tracy RC	.75
397	Eric Gagne	.25
398	Michael Tejera RC	.50
399	Adam Everett	.25
400	Corey Patterson	.50
401	Gary Knotts RC	.50
402	Ryan Christianson RC	.50
403	Eric Ireland RC	.50
404	Andrew Good RC	.50
405	Brad Penny	.25
406	Jason LaRue	.25
407	Kit Pellow	.25
408	Kevin Beirne	.25
409	Kelly Dransfeldt	.25
410	Jason Grilli	.25
411	Scott Downs RC	.50
412	Jesus Colome	.25
413	John Sneed RC	.50
414	Tony McKnight RC	.50
415	Luis Rivera	.25
416	Adam Eaton	.25
417	Mike MacDougal RC	.50
418	Mike Nannini	.25
419	Barry Zito RC	3.00
420	Dewayne Wise	.25
421	Jason Dellaero	.25
422	Chad Moeller	.25
423	Jason Marquis	.25
424	Tim Redding	.50
425	Mark Mulder	.25
426	Josh Paul	.25
427	Chris Enochs	.25
428	Wilfredo Rodriguez RC	.50
429	Kevin Witt	.25
430	Scott Sobkowiak RC	.50
431	McKay Christensen	.25
432	Jung Bong	.25
433	Keith Evans RC	.50
434	Garry Maddox Jr.	.25
435	Ramon Santiago RC	.50
436	Alex Cora	.25
437	Carlos Lee	.25
438	Jason Repko RC	.50
439	Matt Burch	.25
440	Shawn Sonnier RC	.50

Rookies: .75X
Inserted 1:6
Refractors: 6-8X
Rookies: 1-30X
Inserted 1:60

Refractors

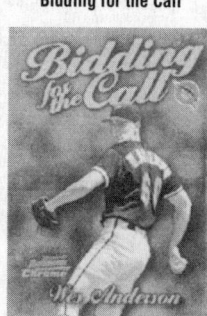

A parallel to the 440-card base set, these inserts have a mirror like sheen to them on the card front and are listed Refractor underneath the card number on the back. These were seeded 1:12 packs.

Stars: 4-8X
Rookies: 2-4X
Inserted 1:12

Retro/Future

This 440-card parallel to the base set is modeled after the 1955 Bowman "television set" design and are seeded 1:6 packs, with Refractors seeded 1:60 packs.

Stars: 1.5-3X

Bidding for the Call

Top minor league prospects are highlighted on a design with gold foil background on an all chromium finish. Card backs are numbered with a "BC" prefix. A Refractor parallel version was also produced.

		NM/M
Complete Set (15):		8.00
Common Player:		.50
Inserted 1:16		
Refractors:		2-4X
Inserted 1:160		
1	Adam Piatt	.50
2	Pat Burrell	1.00
3	Mark Mulder	.50
4	Nick Johnson	.50
5	Alfonso Soriano	2.00
6	Chin-Feng Chen	.50
7	Scott Sobkowiak	.50
8	Corey Patterson	.50
9	Jack Cust	.75
10	Sean Burroughs	.50
11	Josh Hamilton	2.00
12	Corey Myers	.50
13	Eric Munson	.50
14	Wes Anderson	.50
15	Lyle Overbay	.50

Meteoric Rise

This 10-card set spotlights players who all made their first All-Star team within their first two years. Card fronts have a futuristic background, with the player in an intergalactic setting. Card backs are numbered with a "MR" prefix. A Refractor parallel version also exists.

		NM/M
Complete Set (10):		15.00
Common Player:		1.00
Inserted 1:24		
Refractors:		2-4X
Inserted 1:240		
1	Nomar Garciaparra	1.50
2	Mark McGwire	3.00
3	Ken Griffey Jr.	3.00
4	Chipper Jones	2.50
5	Manny Ramirez	2.00
6	Mike Piazza	3.00
7	Cal Ripken Jr.	5.00
8	Ivan Rodriguez	2.00
9	Greg Maddux	3.00
10	Randy Johnson	2.00

Oversize

		NM/M
Complete Set (8):		8.00
Common Player:		.75
Inserted 1:Box		
1	Pat Burrell	2.00
2	Josh Hamilton	2.00
3	Rafael Furcal	2.00
4	Corey Patterson	1.50
5	A.J. Burnett	.75
6	Eric Munson	1.00
7	Nick Johnson	1.00
8	Alfonso Soriano	2.00

Rookie Class 2000

This set highlighted 10 prospects who were thought to contend for the 2000 Rookie of the Year awards. Backs are numbered with a "RC" prefix. A Refractor parallel version was also issued.

		NM/M
Complete Set (10):		6.00
Common Player:		.75
Inserted 1:24		
Refractors:		2-4X
Inserted 1:240		
1	Pat Burrell	2.00
2	Rick Ankiel	1.50
3	Ruben Mateo	.50
4	Vernon Wells	1.00
5	Mark Mulder	.50
6	A.J. Burnett	.75
7	Chad Hermansen	.50
8	Corey Patterson	.50
9	Rafael Furcal	1.00
10	Mike Lamb	.50

Teen Idols

This 15-card set highlights top teenagers who are predicted to emerge as major league standouts.

		NM/M
Complete Set (15):		10.00
Common Player:		.75
Inserted 1:16		
Refractors:		2-4X
Inserted 1:160		
1	Alex Rodriguez	5.00
2	Andruw Jones	.75
3	Juan Gonzalez	1.00
4	Ivan Rodriguez	1.00
5	Ken Griffey Jr.	3.00
6	Bobby Bradley	.50
7	Brett Myers	.50
8	C.C. Sabathia	1.50
9	Ty Howington	.50
10	Brandon Phillips	1.00
11	Rick Asadoorian	.50
12	Wily Pena	.50
13	Sean Burroughs	.50
14	Josh Hamilton	3.00
15	Rafael Furcal	1.00

2000 Bowman Draft Picks and Prospects

		NM/M
Complete Set (110):		40.00
Common Player:		.15
1	Pat Burrell	.25
2	Rafael Furcal	.25
3	Grant Roberts	.15
4	Barry Zito	.50
5	Julio Zuleta	.15
6	Mark Mulder	.25
7	Rob Bell	.15
8	Adam Piatt	.15
9	Mike Lamb	.15
10	Pablo Ozuna	.15
11	Jason Tyner	.15
12	Jason Marquis	.15
13	Eric Munson	.15
14	Seth Etherton	.15
15	Milton Bradley	.15
16	Nick Green	.15
17	Chin-Feng Chen RC	.50
18	Matt Boone RC	.25
19	Kevin Gregg RC	.50
20	Eddy Garabito RC	.25
21	Aaron Capista RC	.25
22	Esteban German RC	.25
23	Derek Thompson RC	.25
24	Phil Merrell RC	.25
25	Brian O'Connor RC	.25
26	Yamid Haad	.15
27	Hector Mercado RC	.25
28	Jason Woolf RC	.25
29	Eddie Furniss RC	.25
30	Cha Sueng Baek RC	.25
31	Colby Lewis RC	.75
32	Pasqual Coco RC	.25
33	Jorge Cantu RC	2.00
34	Erasmo Ramirez RC	.25
35	Bobby Kielty RC	.50
36	Joaquin Benoit RC	.50
37	Brian Esposito RC	.25
38	Michael Wenner	.15
39	Juan Rincon RC	.25
40	Yorvit Torrealba RC	.25
41	Chad Durham RC	.25
42	Jim Mann RC	.25
43	Shane Loux RC	.25
44	Luis Rivas	.15
45	Ken Chenard RC	.25
46	Mike Lockwood RC	.25
47	Yovanny Lara RC	.25
48	Bubba Carpenter RC	.25
49	Jeremy Griffiths RC	.25
50	John Stephens RC	.25
51	Pedro Feliz RC	.75
52	Kenny Kelly RC	.25
53	Neil Jenkins RC	.25
54	Mike Glendenning RC	.25
55	Bo Porter	.15
56	Eric Byrnes	.15
57	Tony Alvarez RC	.25
58	Kazuhiro Sasaki RC	.25
59	Chad Durbin RC	.25
60	Mike Bynum RC	.25
61	Travis Wilson RC	.25
62	Jose Leon	.25
63	Bill Ortega RC	.25
64	Geraldo Guzman RC	.25
65	Craig Anderson RC	.25
66	Carlos Silva RC	.50
67	Brad Thomas RC	.25
68	Chin-Hui Tsao RC	.25
69	Mark Buehrle RC	2.00
70	Juan Salas RC	.25
71	Denny Abreu RC	.25
72	Keith McDonald RC	.25
73	Chris Richard RC	.25
74	Tomas de la Rosa RC	.25
75	Vicente Padilla	.25
76	Justin Brunette RC	.25
77	Scott Linebrink RC	.25
78	Jeff Sparks RC	.25
79	Tike Redman RC	.25
80	John Lackey RC	1.50
81	Joe Strong RC	.25
82	Brian Tollberg RC	.25
83	Steve Sisco RC	.25
84	Chris Clapinski	.15
85	Augie Ojeda RC	.25
86	Adrian Gonzalez RC (Draft Picks)	3.00
87	Mike Stodolka RC (Draft Picks)	.25
88	Adam Johnson RC (Draft Picks)	.25
89	Matt Wheatland RC (Draft Picks)	.25
90	Corey Smith RC (Draft Picks)	.25
91	Rocco Baldelli RC (Draft Picks)	.75
92	Keith Bucktrot RC (Draft Picks)	.25
93	Adam Wainwright RC (Draft Picks)	2.00
94	Blaine Boyer RC (Draft Picks)	.25
95	Aaron Herr RC (Draft Picks)	.25
96	Scott Thorman RC (Draft Picks)	.50
97	Brian Digby RC (Draft Picks)	.25
98	Josh Shortslef RC (Draft Picks)	.25
99	Sean Smith RC (Draft Picks)	.25
100	Alex Cruz RC (Draft Picks)	.25
101	Marc Love RC (Draft Picks)	.25
102	Kevin Lee RC (Draft Picks)	.25
103	Victor Ramos RC (Draft Picks)	.25

#	Player	NM/M
104	Jason Kanoi RC (Draft Picks)	.25
105	Luis Escobar RC (Draft Picks)	.25
106	Tripper Johnson RC (Draft Picks)	.25
107	Phil Dumatrait RC (Draft Picks)	.25
108	Bryan Edwards RC (Draft Picks)	.25
109	Grady Sizemore RC (Draft Picks)	12.00
110	Thomas Mitchell RC (Draft Picks)	.25

Autograph

Pat Burrell

Common Autograph: 5.00 — NM/M
Inserted 1:Set

#	Player	NM/M
1	Pat Burrell	15.00
2	Rafael Furcal	15.00
3	Grant Roberts	5.00
4	Barry Zito	20.00
5	Julio Zuleta	5.00
6	Mark Mulder	10.00
7	Bob Bell	5.00
8	Adam Piatt	5.00
9	Mike Lamb	10.00
10	Pablo Ozuna	5.00
11	Jason Tyner	5.00
12	Jason Marquis	10.00
13	Eric Munson	6.00
14	Seth Etherton	5.00
15	Milton Bradley	12.00
17	Michael Wenner	5.00
18	Mike Glendenning	5.00
19	Tony Alvarez	5.00
20	Adrian Gonzalez	80.00
21	Corey Smith	10.00
22	Matt Wheatland	5.00
23	Adam Johnson	5.00
24	Mike Stodolka	5.00
25	Rocco Baldelli	15.00
26	Juan Rincon	5.00
27	Chad Durbin	5.00
28	Yorvit Torrealba	5.00
29	Nick Green	5.00
30	Derek Thompson	5.00
31	John Lackey	35.00
33	Kevin Gregg	8.00
35	Denny Abreu	5.00
36	Brian Tollberg	5.00
37	Yamid Haad	5.00
38	Grady Sizemore	100.00
39	Carlos Silva	12.00
40	Jorge Cantu	35.00
41	Bobby Kielty	5.00
42	Scott Thorman	8.00
43	Juan Salas	8.00
44	Phil Dumatrait	5.00
46	Mike Lockwood	5.00
47	Yovanny Lara	5.00
48	Tripper Johnson	5.00
49	Colby Lewis	10.00
50	Neil Jenkins	5.00
51	Keith Bucktrot	5.00
52	Eric Byrnes	10.00
53	Aaron Herr	5.00
54	Erasmo Ramirez	5.00
55	Chris Richard	5.00
57	Mike Bynum	5.00
58	Brian Esposito	5.00
59	Chris Clapinski	5.00
60	Augie Ojeda	5.00

2000 Bowman Chrome Draft Picks and Prospects

Jon Rauch

#	Player	NM/M
	Complete Set (110):	50.00
	Common Player:	.25
1	Pat Burrell	.50
2	Rafael Furcal	.50
3	Grant Roberts	.25
4	Barry Zito	2.00
5	Julio Zuleta	.50
6	Mark Mulder	.25
7	Rob Bell	.25
8	Adam Piatt	.50
9	Mike Lamb	.25
10	Pablo Ozuna	.25
11	Jason Tyner	.25
12	Jason Marquis	.25
13	Eric Munson	.25
14	Seth Etherton	.25
15	Milton Bradley	.25
16	Nick Green	.25
17	Chin-Feng Chen RC	.75
18	Matt Boone RC	.50
19	Kevin Gregg RC	.50
20	Eddy Garabito RC	.50
21	Aaron Capista RC	.50
22	Esteban German RC	.50
23	Derek Thompson RC	.50
24	Phil Merrell RC	.50
25	Brian O'Connor RC	.50
26	Yamid Haad	.25
27	Hector Mercado RC	.50
28	Jason Woolf RC	.50
29	Eddie Furniss RC	.50
30	Cha Sueng Baek RC	.50
31	Colby Lewis RC	.50
32	Pasqual Coco RC	.50
33	Jorge Cantu RC	3.00
34	Erasmo Ramirez RC	.50
35	Bobby Kielty RC	.50
36	Joaquin Benoit RC	.50
37	Brian Esposito RC	.50
38	Michael Wenner	.25
39	Juan Rincon RC	.50
40	Yorvit Torrealba RC	.50
41	Chad Durham RC	.50
42	Jim Mann RC	.50
43	Shane Loux RC	.50
44	Luis Rivas	.25
45	Ken Chenard RC	.50
46	Mike Lockwood RC	.50
47	Giovanni Lara RC	.50
48	Bubba Carpenter RC	.50
49	Ryan Dittfurth RC	.50
50	John Stephens RC	.50
51	Pedro Feliz RC	2.00
52	Kenny Kelly RC	.50
53	Neil Jenkins RC	.50
54	Mike Glendenning RC	.50
55	Bo Porter	.25
56	Eric Byrnes	.25
57	Tony Alvarez RC	.50
58	Kazuhiro Sasaki RC	.50
59	Chad Durbin RC	.50
60	Mike Bynum RC	.50
61	Travis Wilson RC	.50
62	Jose Leon RC	.50
63	Ryan Vogelsong RC	.50
64	Geraldo Guzman RC	.50
65	Craig Anderson RC	.50
66	Carlos Silva RC	.75
67	Brad Thomas RC	.50
68	Chin-Hui Tsao RC	1.00
69	Mark Buehrle RC	4.00
70	Juan Salas RC	.50
71	Denny Abreu RC	.50
72	Keith McDonald RC	.50
73	Chris Richard RC	.50
74	Tomas de la Rosa RC	.50
75	Vicente Padilla RC	.50
76	Justin Brunette RC	.50
77	Scott Linebrink RC	.50
78	Jeff Sparks RC	.50
79	Tike Redman RC	.50
80	John Lackey RC	2.50
81	Joe Strong RC	.50
82	Brian Tollberg RC	.50
83	Steve Sisco RC	.50
84	Chris Clapinski RC	.25
85	Augie Ojeda RC	.50
86	Adrian Gonzalez RC (Draft Picks)	8.00
87	Mike Stodolka RC (Draft Picks)	.50
88	Adam Johnson RC (Draft Picks)	.50
89	Matt Wheatland RC (Draft Picks)	.50
90	Corey Smith RC (Draft Picks)	.50
91	Rocco Baldelli RC (Draft Picks)	1.50
92	Keith Bucktrot RC (Draft Picks)	.50
93	Adam Wainwright RC (Draft Picks)	4.00
94	Blaine Boyer RC (Draft Picks)	.50
95	Aaron Herr RC (Draft Picks)	.50
96	Scott Thorman RC (Draft Picks)	1.00
97	Brian Digby RC (Draft Picks)	.50
98	Josh Shortslef RC (Draft Picks)	.50
99	Sean Smith RC (Draft Picks)	.50
100	Alex Cruz RC (Draft Picks)	.50
101	Marc Love RC (Draft Picks)	.50
102	Kevin Lee RC (Draft Picks)	.50
103	Timoniel Perez RC (Draft Picks)	.50
104	Alex Cabrera RC (Draft Picks)	.50
105	Shane Heams RC (Draft Picks)	.50
106	Tripper Johnson RC (Draft Picks)	.50
107	Brent Abernathy RC (Draft Picks)	.50
108	John Cotton RC (Draft Picks)	.50
109	Brad Wilkerson RC (Draft Picks)	1.00
110	Jon Rauch RC (Draft Picks)	.50

2000 Bowman's Best Pre-Production

Brett Myers

Three-card cello packs of promotional cards introduced the Bowman's Best issue for 2000. The cards are virtually identical to the regularly issued version except for the numbering on the back which includes a "PP" prefix.

#	Player	NM/M
	Complete Set (3):	6.00
	Common Player:	2.00
PP1	Larry Walker	2.00
PP2	Adam Dunn	2.00
PP3	Brett Myers	2.00

2000 Bowman's Best

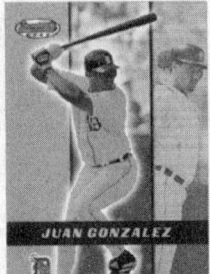

Juan Gonzalez

The base set consists of 200-cards on a mirror like sheen, reminiscent of Refractors. Veteran cards have gold highlights while rookies and prospects have blue highlights. There are three subsets: Best Performers (86-100), Prospects (101-150) and Rookies (151-200). Rookies are serially numbered to 2,999 on the card back and are randomly inserted on the average of 1:7 packs.

#	Player	NM/M
	Complete Set (200):	275.00
	Common Player:	.20
	Common Rookie (151-200):	5.00
	Production 2,999 Sets	
	Pack (4):	4.00
	Box (24):	75.00
1	Nomar Garciaparra	1.00
2	Chipper Jones	1.50
3	Damion Easley	.20
4	Bernie Williams	.40
5	Barry Bonds	3.00
6	Jermaine Dye	.20
7	John Olerud	.20
8	Mike Hampton	.20
9	Cal Ripken Jr.	3.00
10	Jeff Bagwell	.75
11	Troy Glaus	.50
12	J.D. Drew	.40
13	Jeromy Burnitz	.20
14	Carlos Delgado	.75
15	Shawn Green	.40
16	Kevin Millwood	.40
17	Rondell White	.20
18	Scott Rolen	.75
19	Jeff Cirillo	.20
20	Barry Larkin	.40
21	Brian Giles	.20
22	Roger Clemens	1.50
23	Manny Ramirez	1.00
24	Alex Gonzalez	.20
25	Mark Grace	.40
26	Fernando Tatis	.20
27	Randy Johnson	1.00
28	Roger Cedeno	.20
29	Brian Jordan	.20
30	Kevin Brown	.40
31	Greg Vaughn	.20
32	Roberto Alomar	.50
33	Larry Walker	.20
34	Rafael Palmeiro	.50
35	Curt Schilling	.50
36	Orlando Hernandez	.20
37	Todd Walker	.20
38	Juan Gonzalez	.50
39	Sean Casey	.25
40	Tony Gwynn	1.00
41	Albert Belle	.20
42	Gary Sheffield	.40
43	Michael Barrett	.20
44	Preston Wilson	.20
45	Jim Thome	.40
46	Shannon Stewart	.20
47	Mo Vaughn	.20
48	Ben Grieve	.20
49	Adrian Beltre	.40
50	Sammy Sosa	1.50
51	Bob Abreu	.40
52	Edgardo Alfonzo	.20
53	Carlos Febles	.20
54	Frank Thomas	1.00
55	Alex Rodriguez	2.50
56	Cliff Floyd	.20
57	Jose Canseco	.40
58	Erubiel Durazo	.20
59	Tim Hudson	.50
60	Craig Biggio	.20
61	Eric Karros	.20
62	Mike Mussina	.50
63	Robin Ventura	.20
64	Carlos Beltran	.75
65	Pedro Martinez	1.00
66	Gabe Kapler	.20
67	Jason Kendall	.20
68	Derek Jeter	3.00
69	Magglio Ordonez	.50
70	Mike Piazza	2.00
71	Mike Lieberthal	.20
72	Andres Galarraga	.20
73	Raul Mondesi	.20
74	Eric Chavez	.40
75	Greg Maddux	2.00
76	Matt Williams	.25
77	Kris Benson	.20
78	Ivan Rodriguez	.50
79	Pokey Reese	.20
80	Vladimir Guerrero	1.00
81	Mark McGwire	2.00
82	Vinny Castilla	.20
83	Todd Helton	1.00
84	Andruw Jones	.50
85	Ken Griffey Jr.	2.00
86	Mark McGwire (Best Performers)	1.00
87	Derek Jeter (Best Performers)	1.50
88	Chipper Jones (Best Performers)	.75
89	Nomar Garciaparra (Best Performers)	.50
90	Sammy Sosa (Best Performers)	.75
91	Cal Ripken Jr. (Best Performers)	1.50
92	Juan Gonzalez (Best Performers)	.50
93	Alex Rodriguez (Best Performers)	1.25
94	Barry Bonds (Best Performers)	1.50
95	Sean Casey (Best Performers)	.25
96	Vladimir Guerrero (Best Performers)	.50
97	Mike Piazza (Best Performers)	1.00
98	Shawn Green (Best Performers)	.25
99	Jeff Bagwell (Best Performers)	.50
100	Ken Griffey Jr. (Best Performers)	1.00
101	Rick Ankiel (Prospects)	.75
102	John Patterson (Prospects)	.20
103	David Walling (Prospects)	.20
104	Michael Restovich (Prospects)	.20
105	A.J. Burnett (Prospects)	.20
106	Matt Riley (Prospects)	.20
107	Chad Hermansen (Prospects)	.20
108	Choo Freeman (Prospects)	.20
109	Mark Quinn (Prospects)	.20
110	Corey Patterson (Prospects)	.40
111	Ramon Ortiz (Prospects)	.20
112	Vernon Wells (Prospects)	.40
113	Milton Bradley (Prospects)	.50
114	Travis Dawkins (Prospects)	.20
115	Sean Burroughs (Prospects)	.25
116	Willi Mo Pena (Prospects)	.40
117	Dee Brown (Prospects)	.20
118	C.C. Sabathia (Prospects)	1.50
119	Larry Bigbie RC (Prospects)	.20
120	Octavio Dotel (Prospects)	.20
121	Kip Wells (Prospects)	.20
122	Ben Petrick (Prospects)	.20
123	Mark Mulder (Prospects)	.40
124	Jason Standridge (Prospects)	.20
125	Adam Piatt (Prospects)	.20
126	Steve Lomasney (Prospects)	.20
127	Jayson Werth (Prospects)	1.50
128	Alex Escobar (Prospects)	.20
129	Ryan Anderson (Prospects)	.20
130	Adam Dunn (Prospects)	.50
131	Omar Ortiz (Prospects)	.20
132	Brad Penny (Prospects)	.20
133	Daryle Ward (Prospects)	.20
134	Eric Munson (Prospects)	.20
135	Nick Johnson (Prospects)	.50
136	Jason Jennings (Prospects)	.20
137	Tim Raines Jr. (Prospects)	.20
138	Ruben Mateo (Prospects)	.20
139	Jack Cust (Prospects)	.40
140	Rafael Furcal (Prospects)	.50
141	Eric Gagne (Prospects)	.40
142	Tony Armas (Prospects)	.20
143	Mike Paradis (Prospects)	.20
144	Chris George (Prospects)	.20
145	Alfonso Soriano (Prospects)	.75
146	Josh Hamilton (Prospects)	1.50
147	Michael Cuddyer (Prospects)	.40
148	Jay Gehrke (Prospects)	.20
149	Josh Girdley (Prospects)	.20
150	Pat Burrell (Prospects)	.75
151	Brett Myers RC	8.00
152	Scott Seabol RC	5.00
153	Keith Reed RC	5.00
154	Francisco Rodriguez RC	20.00
155	Barry Zito RC	20.00
156	Pat Manning RC	5.00
157	Ben Christensen RC	5.00
158	Corey Myers RC	5.00
159	Wascar Serrano RC	5.00
160	Wes Anderson RC	5.00
161	Andy Tracy RC	5.00
162	Cesar Saba RC	5.00
163	Mike Lamb RC	6.00
164	Bobby Bradley RC	5.00
165	Vince Faison RC	5.00
166	Ty Howington RC	8.00
167	Ken Harvey RC	5.00
168	Josh Kalinowski RC	5.00
169	Ruben Salazar RC	5.00
170	Aaron Rowand RC	8.00
171	Ramon Santiago RC	5.00
172	Scott Sobkowiak RC	5.00
173	Lyle Overbay RC	8.00
174	Rico Washington RC	5.00
175	Rick Asadoorian RC	5.00
176	Matt Ginter RC	5.00
177	Jason Stumm RC	5.00
178	B.J. Garbe RC	5.00
179	Mike MacDougal RC	5.00
180	Ryan Christianson RC	5.00
181	Kurt Ainsworth RC	5.00
182	Brad Baisley RC	5.00
183	Ben Broussard RC	5.00
184	Aaron McNeal RC	5.00
185	John Sneed RC	5.00
186	Junior Brignac RC	5.00
187	Chance Caple RC	5.00
188	Scott Downs RC	5.00
189	Matt Cepicky RC	5.00
190	Chin-Feng Chen RC	8.00
191	Johan Santana RC	90.00
192	Brad Baker RC	5.00
193	Jason Repko RC	5.00
194	Craig Dingman RC	5.00
195	Chris Wakeland RC	5.00
196	Rogelio Arias RC	5.00
197	Luis Matos RC	8.00
198	Robert Ramsay RC	5.00
199	Willie Bloomquist RC	8.00
200	Tony Pena Jr. RC	5.00

Bets

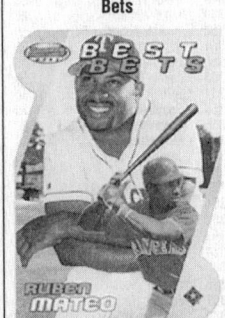

Ruben Mateo

This 10-card set highlighted prospects who had the best chance of making the big league. The upper left corner and bottom right corner are die-cut. A small action photo is superimposed over a larger background shot of the featured player. Backs are numbered with a "BBB" prefix.

#	Player	NM/M
	Complete Set (10):	10.00
	Common Player:	.75
	Inserted 1:15	
1	Pat Burrell	2.00
2	Alfonso Soriano	2.00
3	Corey Patterson	1.50
4	Eric Munson	.75
5	Sean Burroughs	1.00
6	Rafael Furcal	.75
7	Rick Ankiel	1.00
8	Nick Johnson	1.50
9	Ruben Mateo	.75
10	Josh Hamilton	1.00

Franchise Favorites

Two current players and two retired stars are featured in this six-card set. Card backs are numbered with a "FR" prefix.

#	Player	NM/M
	Complete Set (6):	15.00
	Common Player:	1.00
	Inserted 1:17	
1A	Sean Casey	1.00
1B	Johnny Bench	3.00
1C	Sean Casey, Johnny Bench	3.00
2A	Cal Ripken Jr.	5.00
2B	Brooks Robinson	2.00
2C	Cal Ripken Jr., Brooks Robinson	5.00

Franchise Favorites Autograph

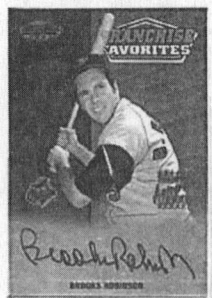

These autographs are seeded 1:1,291 packs, while the two dual autographed versions are inserted 1:5,153 packs.

#	Player	NM/M
	Common Player:	15.00
	Version A & B 1:1,291	
	Version C 1:5,153	
1A	Sean Casey	15.00
1B	Johnny Bench	50.00
1C	Sean Casey, Johnny Bench	100.00
2A	Cal Ripken Jr.	125.00
2B	Brooks Robinson	50.00
2C	Cal Ripken Jr., Brooks Robinson	250.00

Franchise 2000

Each of the 25-cards in this set have rounded corners on a holographic silver design. Backs are numbered with a "F" prefix.

		NM/M
	Complete Set (25):	60.00
	Common Player:	

Inserted 1:18

#	Player	NM/M
1	Cal Ripken Jr.	8.00
2	Nomar Garciaparra	6.00
3	Frank Thomas	2.00
4	Manny Ramirez	2.00
5	Juan Gonzalez	1.50
6	Carlos Beltran	2.00
7	Derek Jeter	8.00
8	Alex Rodriguez	6.00
9	Ben Grieve	1.00
10	Jose Canseco	1.50
11	Ivan Rodriguez	1.50
12	Mo Vaughn	1.00
13	Randy Johnson	3.00
14	Chipper Jones	4.00
15	Sammy Sosa	5.00
16	Ken Griffey Jr.	5.00
17	Larry Walker	1.00
18	Preston Wilson	1.00
19	Jeff Bagwell	2.00
20	Shawn Green	1.00
21	Vladimir Guerrero	2.00
22	Mike Piazza	5.00
23	Scott Rolen	2.00
24	Tony Gwynn	3.50
25	Barry Bonds	8.00

Locker Room Collection Autographs

Part of the Locker Room Collection, these autographs feature 19 players. Backs are numbered with a "LRCA" prefix.

		NM/M
Common Player:		8.00
Inserted 1:57		
1	Carlos Beltran	25.00
2	Rick Ankiel	20.00
3	Vernon Wells	12.00
4	Ruben Mateo	8.00
5	Ben Petrick	8.00
6	Adam Piatt	8.00
7	Eric Munson	8.00
8	Alfonso Soriano	40.00
9	Kerry Wood	15.00
10	Jack Cust	8.00
11	Rafael Furcal	15.00
12	Josh Hamilton	50.00
13	Brad Penny	8.00
14	Dee Brown	8.00
15	Milton Bradley	12.00
16	Ryan Anderson	8.00
17	John Patterson	8.00
18	Nick Johnson	10.00
19	Peter Bergeron	8.00

Locker Room Collection Jerseys

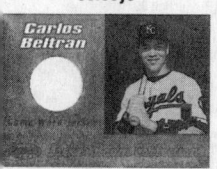

These inserts have a piece of game-worn jersey embedded into them and are numbered with a "LRCJ" prefix.

		NM/M
Common Player:		4.00
Inserted 1:206		
1	Carlos Beltran	12.00
2	Rick Ankiel	5.00
3	Adam Kennedy	4.00
4	Ben Petrick	4.00
5	Adam Piatt	4.00

Locker Room Collection Lumber

These inserts have a piece of game-used bat embedded into them. They are numbered with a "LRCL" prefix on the back.

		NM/M
Common Player:		5.00
Inserted 1:376		
1	Carlos Beltran	15.00
2	Rick Ankiel	5.00
3	Vernon Wells	10.00
4	Adam Kennedy	5.00
5	Ben Petrick	5.00
6	Eric Munson	5.00
7	Rafael Furcal	8.00
8	J.D. Drew	8.00
9	Pat Burrell	10.00

Rookie Signed Baseballs

Redemption inserts, redeemable for Rookie Signed Baseballs,

were randomly inserted. Signed baseball displays the Bowman "Rookie Autograph" logo and the Topps "Genuine Issue" sticker.

		NM/M
Complete Set (5):		75.00
Common Player:		15.00
Inserted 1:688		
1	Josh Hamilton	40.00
2	Rick Ankiel	20.00
3	Alfonso Soriano	50.00
4	Nick Johnson	30.00
5	Corey Patterson	20.00

Selections

This 15-card set is printed on a luminescent, die-cut design. The set features former Rookies of the Year and former No. 1 overall Draft Picks. These are seeded 1:30 packs. Backs are numbered with a "BBS" prefix.

		NM/M
Complete Set (15):		50.00
Common Player:		1.00
Inserted 1:30		
1	Alex Rodriguez	7.50
2	Ken Griffey Jr.	6.00
3	Pat Burrell	2.00
4	Mark McGwire	6.00
5	Derek Jeter	10.00
6	Nomar Garciaparra	3.00
7	Mike Piazza	6.00
8	Josh Hamilton	5.00
9	Cal Ripken Jr.	10.00
10	Jeff Bagwell	2.00
11	Chipper Jones	5.00
12	Jose Canseco	1.50
13	Carlos Beltran	3.00
14	Kerry Wood	2.00
15	Ben Grieve	1.00

Year By Year

This 10-card set highlights 10 duos who began their careers in the same year. They have a horizontal format on a mirror foiled card front. Backs are numbered with a "YY" prefix.

		NM/M
Complete Set (10):		25.00
Common Card:		1.50
Inserted 1:23		
1	Sammy Sosa, Ken Griffey Jr.	4.00
2	Nomar Garciaparra, Vladimir Guerrero	4.00
3	Alex Rodriguez, Jeff Cirillo	5.00
4	Mike Piazza, Pedro Martinez	4.00
5	Derek Jeter, Edgardo Alfonzo	6.00
6	Alfonso Soriano, Rick Ankiel	2.00
7	Mark McGwire, Barry Bonds	6.00
8	Juan Gonzalez, Larry Walker	1.50
9	Ivan Rodriguez, Jeff Bagwell	1.50
10	Shawn Green, Manny Ramirez	1.50

2001 Bowman

		NM/M
Complete Set (440):		140.00
Common Player:		.15
Common Rookie:		.25
Golds:		1-2X
Inserted 1:1		
Pack (10):		8.00
Box (24):		160.00
1	Jason Giambi	.40
2	Rafael Furcal	.25
3	Rick Ankiel	.25
4	Freddy Garcia	.15
5	Magglio Ordonez	.25
6	Bernie Williams	.40
7	Kenny Lofton	.15
8	Al Leiter	.15
9	Albert Belle	.15
10	Craig Biggio	.25
11	Mark Mulder	.15
12	Carlos Delgado	.25
13	Darin Erstad	.25
14	Richie Sexson	.15
15	Randy Johnson	.75
16	Greg Maddux	1.50
17	Cliff Floyd	.15
18	Mark Buehrle	.15
19	Chris Singleton	.15
20	Orlando Hernandez	.20
21	Javier Vazquez	.15
22	Jeff Kent	.25
23	Jim Thome	.50
24	John Olerud	.15
25	Jason Kendall	.15
26	Scott Rolen	.25
27	Tony Gwynn	.75
28	Edgardo Alfonzo	.15
29	Pokey Reese	.15
30	Todd Helton	.50
31	Mark Quinn	.15
32	Dan Tosca RC	.25
33	Dean Palmer	.15
34	Jacque Jones	.15
35	Ray Durham	.15
36	Rafael Palmeiro	.50
37	Carl Everett	.15
38	Ryan Dempster	.15
39	Randy Wolf	.15
40	Vladimir Guerrero	.75
41	Livan Hernandez	.15
42	Mo Vaughn	.25
43	Shannon Stewart	.15
44	Preston Wilson	.15
45	Jose Vidro	.15
46	Fred McGriff	.25
47	Kevin Brown	.15
48	Peter Bergeron	.15
49	Miguel Tejada	.50
50	Chipper Jones	.75
51	Edgar Martinez	.15
52	Tony Batista	.15
53	Jorge Posada	.40
54	Ricky Ledee	.15
55	Sammy Sosa	1.00
56	Steve Cox	.15
57	Tony Armas Jr.	.15
58	Gary Sheffield	.40
59	Bartolo Colon	.15
60	Pat Burrell	.40
61	Jay Payton	.15
62	Sean Casey	.25
63	Larry Walker	.25
64	Mike Mussina	.40
65	Nomar Garciaparra	.75
66	Darren Dreifort	.15
67	Richard Hidalgo	.15
68	Troy Glaus	.40
69	Ben Grieve	.15
70	Jim Edmonds	.25
71	Raul Mondesi	.15
72	Andruw Jones	.50
73	Luis Castillo	.15
74	Mike Sweeney	.15
75	Derek Jeter	2.00
76	Ruben Mateo	.15
77	Carlos Lee	.40
78	Cristian Guzman	.15
79	Mike Hampton	.25
80	J.D. Drew	.25
81	Matt Lawton	.15
82	Moises Alou	.25
83	Terrence Long	.15
84	Geoff Jenkins	.15
85	Manny Ramirez	.75
86	Johnny Damon	.50
87	Barry Larkin	.25
88	Pedro Martinez	.75
89	Juan Gonzalez	.40
90	Roger Clemens	2.00
91	Carlos Beltran	.50
92	Brad Radke	.15
93	Orlando Cabrera	.15
94	Roberto Alomar	.50
95	Barry Bonds	2.00
96	Tim Hudson	.25
97	Tom Glavine	.25
98	Jeromy Burnitz	.15
99	Adrian Beltre	.25
100	Mike Piazza	1.00
101	Kerry Wood	.40
102	Steve Finley	.15
103	Alex Cora	.15
104	Bob Abreu	.25
105	Neifi Perez	.15
106	Mark Redman	.15
107	Paul Konerko	.25
108	Jermaine Dye	.25
109	Brian Giles	.15
110	Ivan Rodriguez	.50
111	Vinny Castilla	.15
112	Adam Kennedy	.15
113	Eric Chavez	.25
114	Billy Koch	.15
115	Shawn Green	.25
116	Matt Williams	.15
117	Greg Vaughn	.15
118	Gabe Kapler	.15
119	Jeff Cirillo	.15
120	Frank Thomas	.50
121	David Justice	.25
122	Cal Ripken Jr.	3.00
123	Rich Aurilia	.15
124	Curt Schilling	.40
125	Barry Zito	.25
126	Brian Jordan	.15
127	Chan Ho Park	.25
128	J.T. Snow Jr.	.15
129	Kazuhiro Sasaki	.25
130	Alex Rodriguez	2.00
131	Mariano Rivera	.40
132	Eric Milton	.15
133	Andy Pettitte	.25
134	Scott Elarton	.15
135	Ken Griffey Jr.	1.50
136	Bengie Molina	.15
137	Jeff Bagwell	.50
138	Kevin Millwood	.15
139	Tino Martinez	.25
140	Mark McGwire	1.50
141	Larry Barnes	.15
142	John Buck RC	.25
143	Freddie Bynum RC	.15
144	Abraham Nunez	.15
145	Felix Diaz RC	.15
146	Horatio Estrada RC	.25
147	Ben Diggins	.15
148	Tsuyoshi Shinjo RC	.50
149	Rocco Baldelli	.25
150	Rod Barajas	.15
151	Luis Terrero	.15
152	Milton Bradley	.25
153	Kurt Ainsworth	.15
154	Russell Branyan	.15
155	Ryan Anderson	.15
156	Mitch Jones RC	.25
157	Alex Escobar	.25
158	Steve Bennett RC	.25
159	Ivanon Coffie	.15
160	Sean Burroughs	.15
161	Keith Bucktrot	.15
162	Tony Alvarez	.15
163	Joaquin Benoit	.15
164	Rick Asadoorian	.15
165	Ben Broussard	.25
166	Ryan Madson RC	1.50
167	Dee Brown	.15
168	Sergio Contreras RC	.25
169	John Barnes	.15
170	Ben Washburn RC	.50
171	Erick Almonte RC	.25
172	Shawn Fagan RC	.25
173	Gary Johnson RC	.25
174	Brady Clark	.15
175	Grant Roberts	.15
176	Tony Torcato	.15
177	Ramon Castro	.15
178	Esteban German	.15
179	Joe Hamer RC	.25
180	Nick Neugebauer	.25
181	Dernell Stenson	.15
182	Yhency Brazoban RC	.40
183	Aaron Myette	.15
184	Juan Sosa	.15
185	Brandon Inge	.15
186	Domingo Guante RC	.25
187	Adrian Brown	.15
188	Deivi Mendez RC	.25
189	Luis Matos	.15
190	Pedro Liriano RC	.50
191	Donnie Bridges	.15
192	Alex Cintron	.15
193	Jace Brewer	.15
194	Ron Davenport RC	.50
195	Jason Belcher RC	.25
196	Adrian Hernandez RC	.25
197	Bobby Kielty	.15
198	Reggie Griggs RC	.25
199	Reggie Abercrombie RC	1.00
200	Troy Farnsworth RC	.25
201	Matt Belisle	.15
202	Miguel Villilo RC	.50
203	Adam Everett	.15
204	John Lackey	.25
205	Pasqual Coco	.15
206	Adam Wainwright	.25
207	Matt White RC	.25
208	Chin-Feng Chen	.25
209	Jeff Andra RC	.25
210	Willie Bloomquist	.25
211	Wes Anderson	.15
212	Enrique Cruz	.15
213	Jerry Hairston Jr.	.15
214	Mike Bynum	.15
215	Brian Hitchcox RC	.25
216	Ryan Christianson	.15
217	J.J. Davis	.15
218	Jovanny Cedeno	.15
219	Elvin Nina	.15
220	Alex Graman	.15
221	Arturo McDowell	.15
222	Deivi Santos RC	.15
223	Jody Gerut	.15
224	Sun-Woo Kim	.15
225	Jimmy Rollins	.50
226	Pappy Ndungidi	.15
227	Ruben Salazar	.15
228	Josh Girdley	.15
229	Carl Crawford	.40
230	Luis Montanez	.50
231	Ramon Carvajal RC	.25
232	Matt Riley	.15
233	Ben Davis	.15
234	Jason Grabowski	.15
235	Chris George	.15
236	Hank Blalock RC	5.00
237	Roy Oswalt	.25
238	Eric Reynolds RC	.15
239	Brian Cole	.15
240	Denny Bautista RC	.75
241	Hector Garcia RC	.25
242	Joe Thurston RC	.50
243	Brad Cresse	.25
244	Corey Patterson	.25
245	Brett Evert RC	.25
246	Elpidio Guzman RC	.25
247	Vernon Wells	.25
248	Roberto Miniel RC	.25
249	Brian Bass RC	.50
250	Mark Burnett RC	.25
251	Juan Silvestre	.15
252	Pablo Ozuna	.15
253	Jayson Werth	.15
254	Russ Jacobsen RC	.15
255	Chad Hermansen	.15
256	Travis Hafner RC	3.00
257	Bradley Baker	.15
258	Gookie Dawkins	.15
259	Michael Cuddyer	.15
260	Mark Buehrle	.15
261	Ricardo Aramboles	.15
262	Esix Snead RC	.25
263	Wilson Betemit RC	.25
264	Albert Pujols RC	60.00
265	Joe Lawrence	.15
266	Ramon Ortiz	.15
267	Ben Sheets	.50
268	Luke Lockwood RC	.25
269	Toby Hall	.15
270	Jack Cust	.15
271	Pedro Feliz	.15
272	Noel Devarez RC	.15
273	Josh Beckett	.50
274	Alex Escobar	.15
275	Doug Gredvig RC	.15
276	Marcus Giles	.15
277	Jon Rauch	.25
278	Brian Schmitt RC	.25
279	Seung Song RC	.50
280	Kevin Mench	.15
281	Adam Eaton	.15
282	Shawn Sonnier	.15
283	Andy Van Hekken RC	.25
284	Aaron Rowand	.25
285	Tony Blanco RC	.50
286	Ryan Kohlmeier	.15
287	C.C. Sabathia	.40
288	Bubba Crosby	.15
289	Josh Hamilton	.75
290	Dee Haynes RC	.25
291	Jason Marquis	.15
292	Julio Zuleta	.15
293	Carlos Hernandez	.15
294	Matt LeCroy	.15
295	Andy Beal RC	.25
296	Carlos Pena	.25
297	Reggie Taylor	.15
298	Bob Keppel RC	.25
299	Miguel Cabrera (Photo actually Manuel Esquivia.)	.75
300	Ryan Franklin	.15
301	Brandon Phillips	.25
302	Victor Hall RC	.25
303	Tony Pena Jr.	.25
304	Jim Journell RC	.25
305	Cristian Guerrero	.25
306	Miguel Olivo	.25
307	Jin Ho Cho	.15
308	Choo Freeman	.25
309	Danny Borrell RC	.25
310	Doug Mientkiewicz	.15
311	Aaron Herr	.15
312	Keith Ginter	.15
313	Felipe Lopez	.25
314	Jeff Goldbach RC	.25
315	Travis Harper	.15
316	Paul LoDuca	.15
317	Joe Torres	.25
318	Eric Byrnes	.15
319	George Lombard	.15
320	David Krynzel	.25
321	Ben Christensen	.15
322	Aubrey Huff	.25
323	Lyle Overbay	.25
324	Sean McGowan	.15
325	Jeff Heaverlo	.15
326	Timo Perez	.15
327	Octavio Martinez RC	.25
328	Vince Faison	.15
329	David Parrish RC	.25
330	Bobby Bradley	.15
331	Jason Miller RC	.25
332	Corey Spencer RC	.25
333	Craig House	.15
334	Maxim St. Pierre RC	.25
335	Adam Johnson	.15
336	Joe Crede	.15
337	Greg Nash RC	.25
338	Chad Durbin	.15
339	Pat Magness RC	.25
340	Matt Wheatland	.15
341	Julio Lugo	.15
342	Grady Sizemore	.75
343	Adrian Gonzalez	.25
344	Tim Raines Jr.	.15
345	Rainier Olmedo RC	.25
346	Phil Dumatrait	.15
347	Brandon Mims RC	.25
348	Jason Jennings	.25
349	Phil Wilson RC	.25
350	Jason Hart	.25
351	Cesar Izturis	.15
352	Matt Butler RC	.25
353	David Kelton	.15
354	Luke Prokopec	.15
355	Corey Smith	.15
356	Joel Pineiro RC	.75
357	Ken Chenard	.15
358	Keith Reed	.15
359	David Walling	.15
360	Alexis Gomez RC	.50
361	Justin Morneau RC	10.00
362	Josh Fogg RC	.50
363	J.R. House	.15
364	Andy Tracy	.15
365	Kenny Kelly	.15
366	Aaron McNeal	.15
367	Nick Johnson	.15
368	Brian Esposito	.15
369	Charles Frazier RC	.25
370	Scott Heard	.15
371	Patrick Strange	.15
372	Mike Meyers	.15
373	Ryan Ludwick RC	5.00
374	Brad Wilkerson	.15
375	Allen Levrault	.15
376	Seth McClung RC	.40
377	Joe Nathan	.15
378	Rafael Soriano RC	.75
379	Chris Richard	.15
380	Xavier Nady	.15
381	Tike Redman	.15
382	Adam Dunn	.50
383	Jared Abruzzo RC	.25
384	Jason Richardson RC	.25
385	Matt Holliday	.50
386	Darwin Cubillian RC	.25
387	Mike Nannini	.15
388	Blake Williams RC	.25
389	Valentino Pascucci RC	.25
390	Jon Garland	.15
391	Josh Pressley	.15
392	Jose Ortiz	.15
393	Ryan Hannaman RC	.25
394	Steve Smyth RC	.25
395	John Patterson	.15
396	Chad Petty RC	.25
397	Jake Peavy RC	10.00
398	Onix Mercado RC	.25
399	Jason Romano	.25
400	Luis Torres RC	.25
401	Casey Fossum RC	.25
402	Eduardo Figueroa RC	.25
403	Bryan Barnowski RC	.25
404	Tim Redding	.25
405	Jason Standridge	.15
406	Marvin Seale RC	.25
407	Todd Moser RC	.15
408	Alex Gordon	.15
409	Steve Smitherman RC	.75
410	Ben Petrick	.15
411	Eric Munson	.15
412	Luis Rivas	.15
413	Matt Ginter	.15
414	Alfonso Soriano	.50
415	Rafael Boitel RC	.25
416	Dany Morban RC	.25
417	Justin Woodrowc RC	.25
418	Wilfredo Rodriguez	.15
419	Derrick Van Dusen RC	.25
420	Josh Spoerl RC	.15
421	J.C. Romero	.25
422	Juan Pierre	.15
423	Ed Rogers RC	.25
424	Tomokazu Ohka	.25
425	Ben Hendrickson RC	.25
426	Carlos Zambrano	.25
427	Brett Myers	.25
428	Scott Seabol	.15
429	Thomas Mitchell RC	.15
430	Jose Reyes RC	25.00
431	Kip Wells	.15
432	Willi Mo Pena	.25
433	Adam Pettyjohn RC	.25
434	Austin Kearns	.25
435	Rico Washington	.15
436	Doug Nickle RC	.25
437	Steve Lomasney	.15
438	Jason Jones RC	.25
439	Bobby Seay	.15
440	Justin Wayne RC	.50

Autographs

		NM/M
Common Autograph:		5.00
Inserted 1:74		
BB	Bryan Barnowski	5.00
WB	Wilson Betemit	15.00
JB	Jason Botts	5.00
SB	Sean Burroughs	5.00

FB	Freddie Bynum	5.00
ND	Noel Devarez	5.00
JD	Jose Diaz	5.00
BD	Ben Diggins	5.00
AE	Alex Escobar	5.00
RF	Rafael Furcal	15.00
AG	Adrian Gonzalez	20.00
AKG	Alex Gordon	5.00
AJG	Alex Graman	5.00
CG	Cristian Guerrero	5.00
TH	Travis Hafner	30.00
JH	Josh Hamilton	50.00
JWH	Jason Hart	5.00
JRH	J.R. House	5.00
RJ	Russ Jacobson	5.00
AJ	Adam Johnson	5.00
TJ	Tripper Johnson	5.00
DWK	David Kelton	5.00
DK	David Krynzel	5.00
PR	Pedro Liriano	5.00
SM	Sean McGowan	5.00
KM	Kevin Mench	5.00
LM	Luis Montanez	5.00
JM	Justin Morneau	75.00
LO	Lyle Overbay	10.00
ADP	Adam Piatt	5.00
JP	Josh Pressley	5.00
AP	Albert Pujols	500.00
BS	Ben Sheets	20.00
SDS	Steve Smyth	5.00
SS	Shawn Sonnier	5.00
SU	Sixto Urena	5.00
MV	Miguel Villilo	5.00
BW	Brad Wilkerson	10.00
BZ	Barry Zito	15.00

Autoproofs
Common Player:
Inserted 1:18,259H
Inserted 1:8,306HTA
Redemption Expired 4/30/03
Values Undetermined

Futures Game-Worn Jersey

NM/M
Common Player: 4.00
Inserted 1:82

KA	Kurt Ainsworth	4.00
CA	Craig Anderson	4.00
RA	Ryan Anderson	4.00
BB	Bobby Bradley	4.00
MB	Mike Bynum	4.00
RC	Ramon Castro	4.00
CC	Chin-Feng Chen	10.00
JC	Jack Cust	6.00
TD	Travis Dawkins	4.00
RD	Randey Dorame	4.00
AE	Alex Escobar	4.00
CG	Chris George	4.00
MG	Marcus Giles	4.00
JH	Josh Hamilton	20.00
CH	Carlos Hernandez	4.00
SK	Sun-Woo Kim	4.00
FL	Felipe Lopez	6.00
EM	Eric Munson	4.00
AM	Aaron Myette	4.00
NN	Ntema Ndungidi	4.00
TO	Tomokazu Ohka	4.00
RO	Ramon Ortiz	4.00
DCP	Corey Patterson	4.00
CP	Carlos Pena	8.00
BP	Ben Petrick	4.00
GR	Grant Roberts	4.00
JR	Jason Romano	4.00
BS	Ben Sheets	6.00
CT	Chin-Hui Tsao	10.00
VW	Vernon Wells	8.00
BW	Brad Wilkerson	4.00
TW	Travis Wilson	4.00
BZ	Barry Zito	4.00
JZ	Julio Zuleta	4.00

Futures Game Three-Piece Game-Used
NM/M
Common Player: 20.00

RC	Ramon Castro	20.00
CC	Chin-Feng Chen	80.00

JC	Jack Cust	20.00
TD	Travis Dawkins	20.00
AE	Alex Escobar	20.00
MG	Marcus Giles	20.00
JH	Josh Hamilton	40.00
FL	Felipe Lopez	20.00
EM	Eric Munson	25.00
NN	Ntema Ndungidi	20.00
DCP	Corey Patterson	20.00
CP	Carlos Pena	25.00
BP	Ben Petrick	20.00
JR	Jason Romano	20.00
VW	Vernon Wells	25.00
BW	Brad Wilkerson	20.00
TW	Travis Wilson	20.00
JZ	Julio Zuleta	20.00

Autographed Three-Piece Game-Used
No pricing due to scarcity.

Rookie of the Year Dual Jersey
NM/M
Inserted 1:2,202

ROYR	Kazuhiro Sasaki, Rafael Furcal	15.00

Rookie Reprints

NM/M
Complete Set (25): 50.00
Common Player: 1.50
Inserted 1:12

1	Yogi Berra	5.00
2	Ralph Kiner	2.50
3	Stan Musial	6.00
4	Warren Spahn	4.00
5	Roy Campanella	4.00
6	Bob Lemon	1.50
7	Robin Roberts	2.00
8	Duke Snider	4.00
9	Early Wynn	1.50
10	Richie Ashburn	1.50
11	Gil Hodges	2.00
12	Hank Bauer	2.00
13	Don Newcombe	1.50
14	Al Rosen	1.50
15	Willie Mays	8.00
16	Joe Garagiola	2.00
17	Whitey Ford	4.00
18	Lew Burdette	1.50
19	Gil McDougald	1.50
20	Minnie Minoso	1.50
21	Eddie Mathews	4.00
22	Harvey Kuenn	2.00
23	Don Larsen	3.00
24	Elston Howard	2.00
25	Don Zimmer	1.50

Autographed Rookie Reprints

NM/M
Common Autograph: 20.00
Inserted 1:2,467

1	Yogi Berra	70.00
2	Willie Mays	200.00
3	Stan Musial	100.00
4	Duke Snider	35.00
5	Warren Spahn	50.00
6	Ralph Kiner	25.00
7	Don Larsen	30.00
8	Don Zimmer	20.00
9	Minnie Minoso	20.00

Game-Used Bat Rookie Reprints

NM/M
Common Player: 10.00
Inserted 1:1,954

1	Willie Mays	60.00
2	Duke Snider	25.00
3	Minnie Minoso	10.00
4	Hank Bauer	10.00
5	Al Rosen	10.00

Autographed Game-Used Bat Rookie Reprints
Inserted 1:18,259
No pricing due to scarcity.

2001 Bowman Chrome

RAFAEL PALMEIRO • 1B
TEXAS RANGERS

NM/M
Common (1-110, 201-310): .25
Common Ref. (111-200, 311-330): 4.00
Inserted 1:4
Common Ref. Auto. (331-350): 25.00
Production 500
Pack (4): 15.00
Box (24): 350.00

1	Jason Giambi	.60
2	Rafael Furcal	.50
3	Bernie Williams	.50
4	Kenny Lofton	.25
5	Al Leiter	.25
6	Albert Belle	.25
7	Craig Biggio	.50
8	Mark Mulder	.40
9	Carlos Delgado	.75
10	Darin Erstad	.50
11	Richie Sexson	.40
12	Randy Johnson	1.00
13	Greg Maddux	1.50
14	Orlando Hernandez	.25
15	Javier Vazquez	.25
16	Jeff Kent	.50
17	Jim Thome	.50
18	John Olerud	.25
19	Jason Kendall	.25
20	Scott Rolen	.75
21	Tony Gwynn	1.00
22	Edgardo Alfonzo	.25
23	Pokey Reese	.25
24	Todd Helton	.75
25	Mark Quinn	.25
26	Dean Palmer	.25
27	Ray Durham	.25
28	Rafael Palmeiro	.75
29	Carl Everett	.25
30	Vladimir Guerrero	1.00
31	Livan Hernandez	.25
32	Preston Wilson	.25
33	Jose Vidro	.25
34	Fred McGriff	.25
35	Kevin Brown	.25
36	Miguel Tejada	.50
37	Chipper Jones	1.00
38	Edgar Martinez	.25
39	Tony Batista	.25
40	Jorge Posada	.50
41	Sammy Sosa	1.00
42	Gary Sheffield	.50
43	Bartolo Colon	.25
44	Pat Burrell	.50
45	Jay Payton	.25
46	Mike Mussina	.60
47	Nomar Garciaparra	.75
48	Darren Dreifort	.25
49	Richard Hidalgo	.25
50	Troy Glaus	.50
51	Ben Grieve	.25
52	Jim Edmonds	.40
53	Raul Mondesi	.25
54	Andruw Jones	.75
55	Mike Sweeney	.25
56	Derek Jeter	3.00
57	Ruben Mateo	.25
58	Cristian Guzman	.25
59	Mike Hampton	.25
60	J.D. Drew	.40
61	Matt Lawton	.25
62	Moises Alou	.40
63	Terrence Long	.25
64	Geoff Jenkins	.25
65	Manny Ramirez	1.00
66	Johnny Damon	.25
67	Pedro Martinez	1.00
68	Juan Gonzalez	.75
69	Roger Clemens	2.00
70	Carlos Beltran	.75
71	Roberto Alomar	.50
72	Barry Bonds	3.00
73	Tim Hudson	.50
74	Tom Glavine	.50
75	Jeromy Burnitz	.25
76	Adrian Beltre	.40
77	Mike Piazza	1.00
78	Kerry Wood	.40
79	Steve Finley	.25
80	Bobby Abreu	.40
81	Neifi Perez	.25
82	Mark Redman	.25
83	Paul Konerko	.40
84	Jermaine Dye	.25
85	Brian Giles	.25
86	Ivan Rodriguez	.75
87	Adam Kennedy	.25
88	Eric Chavez	.40
89	Billy Koch	.25
90	Shawn Green	.25
91	Matt Williams	.25
92	Greg Vaughn	.25
93	Jeff Cirillo	.25
94	Frank Thomas	.75
95	David Justice	.25
96	Cal Ripken Jr.	3.00
97	Curt Schilling	.75
98	Barry Zito	.40
99	Brian Jordan	.25
100	Chan Ho Park	.25
101	J.T. Snow Jr.	.25
102	Kazuhiro Sasaki	.25
103	Alex Rodriguez	2.50
104	Mariano Rivera	.25
105	Eric Milton	.25
106	Andy Pettitte	.50
107	Ken Griffey Jr.	2.00
108	Bengie Molina	.25
109	Jeff Bagwell	.75
110	Mark McGwire	2.00
111	Dan Tosca RC	4.00
112	Sergio Contreras RC	4.00
113	Mitch Jones RC	4.00
114	Ramon Carvajal RC	4.00
115	Ryan Madson RC	8.00
116	Hank Blalock RC	12.00
117	Ben Washburn RC	4.00
118	Erick Almonte RC	4.00
119	Shawn Fagan RC	4.00
120	Gary Johnson RC	4.00
121	Brett Evert RC	4.00
122	Joe Hamer RC	4.00
123	Yhency Brazoban RC	4.00
124	Domingo Guante RC	4.00
125	Deivi Mendez RC	4.00
126	Adrian Hernandez RC	4.00
127	Reggie Abercrombie RC	6.00
128	Steve Bennett RC	4.00
129	Matt White RC	4.00
130	Brian Hitchcox RC	4.00
131	Deivis Santos RC	4.00
132	Luis Montanez RC	4.00
133	Eric Reynolds RC	4.00
134	Denny Bautista RC	8.00
135	Hector Garcia RC	4.00
136	Joe Thurston RC	4.00
137	Tsuyoshi Shinjo RC	4.00
138	Elpidio Guzman RC	4.00
139	Brian Bass RC	4.00
140	Mark Burnett RC	4.00
141	Russ Jacobsen RC	4.00
142	Travis Hafner RC	15.00
143	Wilson Betemit RC	10.00
144	Luke Lockwood RC	4.00
145	Noel Devarez RC	4.00
146	Doug Gredvig RC	4.00
147	Seung Jun Song RC	4.00
148	Andy Van Hekken RC	4.00
149	Ryan Kohlmeier RC	4.00
150	Dee Haynes RC	4.00
151	Jim Journell RC	4.00
152	Chad Petty RC	4.00
153	Danny Borrell RC	4.00
154	David Krynzel RC	4.00
155	Octavio Martinez RC	4.00
156	David Parrish RC	4.00
157	Jason Miller RC	4.00
158	Corey Spencer RC	4.00
159	Maxim St. Pierre RC	4.00
160	Pat Magness RC	4.00
161	Rainier Olmedo RC	4.00
162	Brandon Mims RC	4.00
163	Phil Wilson RC	4.00
164	Jose Reyes RC	60.00
165	Matt Butler RC	4.00
166	Joel Pineiro RC	4.00
167	Ken Chenard	4.00
168	Alexis Gomez RC	4.00
169	Justin Morneau RC	60.00
170	Josh Fogg RC	4.00
171	Charles Frazier RC	4.00
172	Ryan Ludwick RC	25.00
173	Seth McClung RC	4.00
174	Justin Wayne RC	4.00
175	Rafael Soriano RC	6.00
176	Jared Abruzzo RC	4.00
177	Jason Richardson RC	4.00
178	Darwin Cubillan RC	4.00
179	Blake Williams RC	4.00
180	Valentino Pascucci RC	4.00
181	Ryan Hannaman RC	4.00
182	Steve Smyth RC	4.00
183	Jake Peavy RC	50.00
184	Onix Mercado RC	4.00
185	Luis Torres RC	4.00
186	Casey Fossum RC	4.00
187	Eduardo Figueroa RC	4.00
188	Bryan Barnowski RC	4.00
189	Jason Standridge RC	4.00
190	Marvin Seale RC	4.00
191	Steve Smitherman RC	4.00
192	Rafael Boitel RC	4.00
193	Dany Morban RC	4.00
194	Justin Woodrowc RC	4.00
195	Ed Rogers RC	4.00
196	Ben Hendrickson RC	4.00
197	Thomas Mitchell RC	4.00
198	Adam Pettyjohn RC	4.00
199	Doug Nickle RC	4.00
200	Jason Jones RC	4.00
201	Larry Barnes	.25
202	Ben Diggins	.25
203	Dee Brown	.25
204	Rocco Baldelli	.50
205	Luis Terrero	.25
206	Milton Bradley	.50
207	Kurt Ainsworth	.25
208	Sean Burroughs	.25
209	Rick Asadoorian	.25
210	Ramon Castro	.25
211	Nick Neugebauer	.25
212	Aaron Myette	.25
213	Luis Matos	.25
214	Donnie Bridges	.25
215	Alex Cintron	.25
216	Bobby Kielty	.25
217	Matt Belisle	.25
218	Adam Everett	.25
219	John Lackey	.25
220	Adam Wainwright	.75
221	Jerry Hairston Jr.	.25
222	Mike Bynum	.25
223	Ryan Christianson	.25
224	J.J. Davis	.25
225	Alex Graman	.25
226	Abraham Nunez	.25
227	Sun-Woo Kim	.25
228	Jimmy Rollins	1.00
229	Ruben Salazar	.25
230	Josh Girdley	.25
231	Carl Crawford	.50
232	Ben Davis	.25
233	Jason Grabowski	.25
234	Chris George	.25
235	Roy Oswalt	.75
236	Brian Cole	.25
237	Corey Patterson	.25
238	Vernon Wells	.50
239	Bradley Baker	.25
240	Gookie Dawkins	.25
241	Michael Cuddyer	.25
242	Ricardo Aramboles	.25
243	Ben Sheets	.50
244	Toby Hall	.25
245	Jack Cust	.25
246	Pedro Feliz	.25
247	Josh Beckett	.75
248	Alex Escobar	.25
249	Marcus Giles	.25
250	Jon Rauch	.25
251	Kevin Mench	.25
252	Shawn Sonnier	.25
253	Aaron Rowand	.50
254	C.C. Sabathia	.75
255	Bubba Crosby	.25
256	Josh Hamilton	1.00
257	Carlos Hernandez	.25
258	Carlos Pena	.50
259	Miguel Cabrera (Photo actually Manuel Esquivia.)	2.50
260	Brandon Phillips	.50
261	Tony Pena Jr.	.25
262	Cristian Guerrero	.25
263	Jin Ho Cho	.25
264	Aaron Herr	.25
265	Keith Ginter	.25
266	Felipe Lopez	.25
267	Travis Harper	.25
268	Joe Torres	.25
269	Eric Byrnes	.50
270	Ben Christensen	.25
271	Aubrey Huff	.25
272	Lyle Overbay	.25
273	Vince Faison	.25
274	Bobby Bradley	.25
275	Joe Crede	.25
276	Matt Wheatland	.25
277	Grady Sizemore	1.50
278	Adrian Gonzalez	.75
279	Timothy Raines Jr.	.25
280	Phil Dumatrait	.25
281	Jason Hart	.25
282	David Kelton	.25
283	David Walling	.25
284	J.R. House	.25
285	Kenny Kelly	.25
286	Aaron McNeal	.25
287	Nick Johnson	.25
288	Scott Heard	.25
289	Brad Wilkerson	.25
290	Allen Levrault	.25
291	Chris Richard	.25
292	Jared Sandberg	.25
293	Tike Redman	.25
294	Adam Dunn	.75
295	Josh Pressley	.25
296	Jose Ortiz	.25
297	Jason Romano	.25
298	Tim Redding	.25
299	Alex Gordon	.25
300	Ben Petrick	.25
301	Eric Munson	.25
302	Luis Rivas	.25
303	Matt Ginter	.25
304	Alfonso Soriano	.75
305	Wilfredo Rodriguez	.25
306	Brett Myers	.25
307	Scott Seabol	.25
308	Tony Alvarez	.25
309	Donzell McDonald	.25
310	Austin Kearns	.25
311	Will Ohman RC	4.00
312	Ryan Soules RC	4.00
313	Cody Ross RC	8.00
314	Bill Whitecotton RC	4.00
315	Mike Burns RC	4.00
316	Manuel Acosta RC	4.00
317	Lance Niekro RC	4.00
318	Travis Thompson RC	4.00
319	Zach Sorensen RC	4.00
320	Austin Evans RC	4.00
321	Brad Stiles RC	4.00
322	Joe Kennedy RC	4.00
323	Luke Martin RC	4.00
324	Juan Diaz RC	4.00
325	Pat Hallmark RC	4.00
326	Christian Parker RC	4.00
327	Ronny Corona RC	4.00
328	Jermaine Clark RC	4.00
329	Scott Dunn RC	4.00
330	Scott Chiasson RC	4.00
331	Greg Nash/Auto. RC	20.00
332	Brad Cresse/Auto.	25.00
333	John Buck/Auto. RC	40.00
334	Freddie Bynum/Auto. RC	25.00
335	Felix Diaz/Auto. RC	25.00
336	Jason Belcher/Auto. RC	25.00
337	Troy Farnsworth RC	25.00
338	Roberto Miniel RC	25.00
339	Esix Snead RC	25.00
340	Albert Pujols RC	3,000
341	Jeff Andra RC	25.00
342	Victor Hall RC	25.00
343	Pedro Liriano RC	25.00
344	Andy Beal RC	25.00
345	Bob Keppel RC	25.00
346	Brian Schmitt RC	25.00
347	Ron Davenport RC	25.00
348	Tony Blanco RC	25.00
349	Reggie Griggs RC	25.00
350	Derrick Van Dusen RC	25.00
351a	Ichiro Suzuki Eng. RC	80.00
351b	Ichiro Suzuki Japanese	80.00

Gold Refractors
Stars: 8-15X
Rookies: 1.5-3X
Production 99 Sets

BRIAN BASS • P
KANSAS CITY ROYALS

X-Fractors
RICHIE SEXSON • OF
MILWAUKEE BREWERS
Stars: 4-8X
Rookies: .75-1.5X
Inserted 1:23

Futures Game Memorabilia
NM/M
Common Player: 5.00
Inserted 1:460

KA	Kurt Ainsworth	8.00
CA	Craig Anderson	5.00
RA	Ryan Anderson	5.00
BB	Bobby Bradley	5.00
MB	Mike Bynum	5.00
RC	Ramon Castro	5.00
CC	Chin-Feng Chen	30.00
JC	Jack Cust	8.00
RD	Randey Dorame	5.00
AE	Alex Escobar	5.00
CG	Chris George	5.00
MG	Marcus Giles	5.00
JH	Josh Hamilton	20.00
CH	Carlos Hernandez	5.00
SK	Sun-Woo Kim	5.00
FL	Felipe Lopez	8.00
EM	Eric Munson	5.00
AM	Aaron Myette	5.00
NN	Ntema Ndungidi	5.00

TO	Tomokazu Ohka	5.00
DCP	Corey Patterson	8.00
CP	Carlos Pena	8.00
BP	Ben Petrick	5.00
JR	Jason Romano	5.00
BS	Ben Sheets	8.00
CT	Chin-Hui Tsao	40.00
BW	Brad Wilkerson	8.00
TW	Travis Wilson	5.00
BZ	Barry Zito	8.00
JZ	Julio Zuleta	5.00

Rookie Reprints

		NM/M
Complete Set (25):		50.00
Common Player:		2.00
Inserted 1:12		
Refractors:		2-3X
Production 299 Sets		
1	Yogi Berra	5.00
2	Ralph Kiner	3.00
3	Stan Musial	6.00
4	Warren Spahn	4.00
5	Roy Campanella	2.00
6	Bob Lemon	2.00
7	Robin Roberts	2.00
8	Duke Snider	4.00
9	Early Wynn	2.00
10	Richie Ashburn	3.00
11	Gil Hodges	3.00
12	Hank Bauer	2.00
13	Don Newcombe	2.00
14	Al Rosen	2.00
15	Willie Mays	8.00
16	Joe Garagiola	3.00
17	Whitey Ford	4.00
18	Lew Burdette	2.00
19	Gil McDougald	2.00
20	Minnie Minoso	2.00
21	Eddie Mathews	4.00
22	Harvey Kuenn	2.00
23	Don Larsen	3.00
24	Elston Howard	2.00
25	Don Zimmer	2.00

Rookie Reprint Relics

		NM/M
Common Player:		8.00
Inserted 1:244		
1	David Justice	8.00
2	Richie Sexson	8.00
3	Sean Casey	8.00
4	Mike Piazza	40.00
5	Carlos Delgado	8.00
6	Chipper Jones	25.00

2001 Bowman Draft Picks & Prospects

		NM/M
Complete Set (110):		45.00
Complete Factory Set (112):		50.00
Common Player:		.10
1	Alfredo Amezaga RC	.25
2	Andrew Good	.10
3	Kelly Johnson RC	1.50
4	Larry Bigbie	.10
5	Matt Thompson RC	.25
6	Wilton Chavez RC	.25
7	Joe Borchard RC	.25
8	David Espinosa	.10
9	Zach Day RC	.50
10	Brad Hawpe RC	2.50
11	Nate Cornejo	.10
12	Jim Kavourias RC	.25
13	Brad Lidge	.10
14	Angel Berroa RC	.25
15	Lamont Matthews RC	.25
16	Jose Garcia	.10
17	Grant Balfour RC	.25
18	Ron Chiavacci RC	.25
19	Jae Seo	.10
20	Juan Rivera	.10
21	D'Angelo Jimenez	.10
22	Aaron Harang	.10
23	Marlon Byrd RC	.75
24	Sean Burnett	.10
25	Josh Pearce RC	.25
26	Brandon Duckworth RC	.25
27	Jack Taschner RC	.25
28	Bo Robinson RC	.25
29	Brent Abernathy	.10
30	David Elder RC	.25
31	Scott Cassidy RC	.25
32	Dennis Tankersley RC	.40
33	Denny Stark	.10
34	Dave Williams RC	.25
35	Boof Bonser RC	.40
36	Kris Foster RC	.25
37	Neal Musser RC	.25
38	Shawn Chacon	.25
39	Mike Rivera RC	.25
40	Will Smith RC	.25
41	Morgan Ensberg RC	.50
42	Ken Harvey	.10
43	Ricardo Rodriguez RC	.25
44	Jose Mieses RC	.25
45	Luis Maza RC	.25
46	Julio Perez RC	.25
47	Billy Traber RC	.25
48	David Martinez RC	.25
49	Coco Crisp RC	1.00
50	Mario Ramos RC	.25
51	Matt Thornton RC	.25
52	Xavier Nady	.10
53	Ryan Vogelsong	.10
54	Jim Magrane RC	.25
55	Domingo Valdez RC	.25
56	Brent Butler	.10
57	Brian Tallet RC	.25
58	Brian Reith RC	.25
59	Mario Valenzuela RC	.25
60	Bobby Hill RC	.25
61	Rich Rundles RC	.25
62	Rick Elder	.10
63	J.D. Closser	.10
64	Scot Shields	.10
65	Miguel Olivo	.10
66	Stubby Clapp RC	.25
67	Jerome Williams RC	.25
68	Jason Lane RC	.50
69	Chase Utley RC	30.00
70	Erik Bedard RC	2.00
71	Alex Herrera RC	.20
72	Juan Cruz RC	.20
73	Billy Martin RC	.20
74	Ronnie Merrill RC	.20
75	Jason Kinchen RC	.20
76	Wilken Ruan RC	.20
77	Cody Ransom RC	.20
78	Bud Smith RC	.20
79	Wily Mo Pena	.10
80	Jeff Nettles RC	.20
81	Jamal Strong RC	.20
82	Bill Ortega	.10
83	Junior Zamora	.10
84	Ichiro Suzuki RC	8.00
85	Fernando Rodney RC	.20
86	Chris Smith RC	.20
87	John Van Benschoten RC	.50
88	Bobby Crosby RC	1.00
89	Kenny Baugh RC	.25
90	Jake Gautreau RC	.25
91	Gabe Gross RC	.50
92	Kris Honel RC	.40
93	Daniel Denham RC	.25
94	Aaron Heilman RC	.50
95	Irvin Guzman RC	1.00
96	Mike Jones RC	.50
97	John-Ford Griffin RC	.25
98	Macay McBride RC	.50
99	John Rheineckar RC	.50
100	Bronson Sardinha RC	.25
101	Jason Weintraub RC	.25
102	J.D. Martin RC	.25
103	Jayson Nix RC	.40
104	Noah Lowry RC	.50
105	Richard Lewis RC	.25
106	Brad Hennessey RC	.50
107	Jeff Mathis RC	.50
108	Jon Skaggs RC	.25
109	Justin Pope RC	.25
110	Josh Burrus RC	.25

Autographs

Thirteen players on the original checklist from Bowman were never issued.

		NM/M
Common Autograph:		5.00
Inserted 1:Set		
JA	Jared Abruzzo	.25
AA	Alfredo Amezaga	8.00
GA	Garrett Atkins	25.00
BB	Bobby Bradley	5.00
ANC	Antoine Cameron	5.00
ROC	Ramon Carvajal	5.00
RC	Ryan Church	15.00
AC	Alex Cintron	5.00
RD	Ryan Dittfurth	5.00
AE	Adam Everett	5.00
AF	Alex Fernandez	5.00
AG	Alexis Gomez	5.00
CG	Cristian Guerrero	5.00
BH	Beau Hale	5.00
SH	Scott Heard	5.00
AH	Aaron Herr	5.00
CI	Cesar Izturis	5.00
GJ	Gary Johnson	5.00
NJ	Nick Johnson	8.00
AK	Austin Kearns	10.00
JK	Joe Kennedy	5.00
JL	John Lackey	15.00
FL	Felipe Lopez	10.00
RI	Ryan Ludwick	50.00
RMM	Ryan Madson	10.00
TO	Tomo Ohka	5.00
RO	Roy Oswalt	20.00
CP	Christian Parra	5.00
BP	Brandon Phillips	15.00
JP	Joel Pineiro	10.00
NR	Nick Regilio	5.00
ER	Ed Rogers	5.00
SS	Scott Seabol	5.00
BS	Bud Smith	5.00
BJS	Brian Specht	5.00
JT	Joe Torres	5.00
JMW	Justin Wayne	5.00

Draft Pick Relics

		NM/M
Common Player:		4.00
One per factory set.		
CI	Cesar Izturis	4.00
GJ	Gary Johnson	4.00
NR	Nick Regilio	4.00
RC	Ryan Church	6.00
BJS	Brian Specht	4.00
JRH	J.R. House	4.00

Futures Game Relics

		NM/M
Common Player:		4.00
One per factory set.		
AA	Alfredo Amezaga	4.00
AD	Adam Dunn	10.00
AG	Adrian Gonzalez	10.00
AH	Alex Herrera	4.00
BM	Brett Myers	5.00
CD	Cody Ransom	4.00
CG	Chris George	4.00
CH	Carlos Hernandez	5.00
CU	Chase Utley	85.00
EB	Eric Bedard	15.00
GB	Grant Balfour	4.00
HB	Hank Blalock	10.00
JB	Joe Borchard	8.00
JC	Juan Cruz	5.00
JP	Josh Pearce	4.00
JR	Juan Rivera	4.00
LG	Luis Garcia	4.00
MC	Miguel Cabrera	10.00
MR	Mike Rivera	4.00
RR	Ricardo Rodriguez	4.00
SC	Scott Chiasson	4.00
SS	Seung Jun Song	5.00
TB	Toby Hall	4.00
WB	Wilson Betemit	4.00
WP	Wily Mo Pena	4.00
JAP	Juan Pena	4.00

2001 Bowman Heritage Promos

To introduce its Heritage issue, Topps produced this five-card promo set for distribution at the National Sports Collectors Convention in Cleveland, June 28 through July 1. The three Indians cards were available from the PSA booth, the Pujols card from the Beckett booth and the McGwire card from the SCD booth. Only 500 of each card were produced. Styled after the 1948 Bowman cards with black-and-white photos on front and gray cardboard backs, the promos are in the standard 2-1/2" x 3-1/2" size and were given away in a cello pack with a cello-wrapped piece of bubblegum.

		NM/M
Complete Set (5):		60.00
Common Player:		6.00
1	Roberto Alomar	6.00
2	Albert Pujols	50.00
3	C.C. Sabathia	6.00
4	Mark McGwire	12.50
5	Juan Gonzalez	6.00

2001 Bowman Heritage

		NM/M
Complete Set (440):		200.00
Common Player:		.15
Common (331-440):		1.00
Inserted 1:2		
Pack (10):		5.00
Box (24):		100.00
1	Chipper Jones	1.50
2	Pete Harnisch	.15
3	Brian Giles	.15
4	J.T. Snow	.15
5	Bartolo Colon	.15
6	Jorge Posada	.25
7	Shawn Green	.25
8	Derek Jeter	2.50
9	Benito Santiago	.15
10	Ramon Hernandez	.15
11	Bernie Williams	.40
12	Greg Maddux	1.50
13	Barry Bonds	2.00
14	Roger Clemens	1.50
15	Miguel Tejada	.50
16	Pedro Feliz	.15
17	Jim Edmonds	.25
18	Tom Glavine	.40
19	David Justice	.25
20	Rich Aurilia	.15
21	Jason Giambi	.50
22	Orlando Hernandez	.15
23	Shawn Estes	.15
24	Nelson Figueroa	.15
25	Terrence Long	.15
26	Mike Mussina	.50
27	Eric Davis	.15
28	Jimmy Rollins	.25
29	Andy Pettitte	.50
30	Shawon Dunston	.15
31	Tim Hudson	.40
32	Jeff Kent	.25
33	Scott Brosius	.15
34	Livan Hernandez	.15
35	Alfonso Soriano	1.00
36	Mark McGwire	1.50
37	Russ Ortiz	.15
38	Fernando Vina	.15
39	Ken Griffey Jr.	1.50
40	Edgar Renteria	.15
41	Kevin Brown	.15
42	Robb Nen	.15
43	Paul LoDuca	.25
44	Bobby Abreu	.25
45	Adam Dunn	.50
46	Osvaldo Fernandez	.15
47	Marvin Benard	.15
48	Mark Gardner	.15
49	Alex Rodriguez	2.00
50	Preston Wilson	.15
51	Roberto Alomar	.40
52	Ben Davis	.15
53	Derek Bell	.15
54	Ken Caminiti	.15
55	Barry Zito	.25
56	Scott Rolen	.75
57	Geoff Jenkins	.15
58	Mike Cameron	.15
59	Ben Grieve	.15
60	Chuck Knoblauch	.15
61	Matt Lawton	.15
62	Chan Ho Park	.15
63	Lance Berkman	.50
64	Carlos Beltran	.50
65	Dean Palmer	.15
66	Alex Gonzalez	.15
67	Larry Walker	.25
68	Magglio Ordonez	.50
69	Ellis Burks	.15
70	Mark Mulder	.50
71	Randy Johnson	.75
72	John Smoltz	.40
73	Jerry Hairston Jr.	.15
74	Pedro Martinez	.75
75	Fred McGriff	.25
76	Sean Casey	.25
77	C.C. Sabathia	.50
78	Todd Helton	.75
79	Brad Penny	.15
80	Mike Sweeney	.15
81	Billy Wagner	.15
82	Mark Buehrle	.15
83	Cristian Guzman	.15
84	Jose Vidro	.15
85	Pat Burrell	.40
86	Jermaine Dye	.25
87	Brandon Inge	.15
88	David Wells	.15
89	Mike Piazza	1.00
90	Jose Cabrera	.15
91	Cliff Floyd	.15
92	Matt Morris	.15
93	Raul Mondesi	.15
94	Joe Kennedy RC	.50
95	Jack Wilson RC	1.00
96	Andruw Jones	.40
97	Mariano Rivera	.50
98	Mike Hampton	.15
99	Roger Cedeno	.15
100	Jose Cruz	.15
101	Mike Lowell	.40
102	Pedro Astacio	.15
103	Joe Mays	.15
104	John Franco	.15
105	Tim Redding	.15
106	Sandy Alomar	.15
107	Bret Boone	.25
108	Josh Towers RC	.50
109	Matt Stairs	.15
110	Chris Truby	.15
111	Jeff Suppan	.15
112	J.C. Romero	.15
113	Felipe Lopez	.15
114	Ben Sheets	.40
115	Frank Thomas	.75
116	A.J. Burnett	.15
117	Tony Clark	.15
118	Mac Suzuki	.15
119	Brad Radke	.15
120	Jeff Shaw	.15
121	Nick Neugebauer	.15
122	Kenny Lofton	.15
123	Jacque Jones	.15
124	Brent Mayne	.15
125	Carlos Hernandez	.15
126	Shane Spencer	.15
127	John Lackey	.25
128	Sterling Hitchcock	.15
129	Darren Dreifort	.15
130	Rusty Greer	.15
131	Michael Cuddyer	.15
132	Tyler Houston	.15
133	Chin-Feng Chen	.15
134	Ken Harvey	.15
135	Marquis Grissom	.15
136	Russell Branyan	.15
137	Eric Karros	.15
138	Josh Beckett	.50
139	Todd Zeile	.15
140	Corey Koskie	.15
141	Steve Sparks	.15
142	Bobby Seay	.15
143	Tim Raines	.15
144	Julio Zuleta	.15
145	Jose Lima	.15
146	Dante Bichette	.15
147	Randy Keisler	.15
148	Brent Butler	.15
149	Antonio Alfonseca	.15
150	Bryan Rekar	.15
151	Jeffrey Hammonds	.15
152	Larry Bigbie	.15
153	Blake Stein	.15
154	Robin Ventura	.15
155	Rondell White	.15
156	Juan Silvestre	.15
157	Marcus Thames	.15
158	Sidney Ponson	.15
159	Juan Pena	.15
160	Charles Johnson	.15
161	Adam Everett	.15
162	Eric Munson	.15
163	Jason Isringhausen	.15
164	Brad Fullmer	.15
165	Miguel Olivo	.15
166	Fernando Tatis	.15
167	Freddy Garcia	.15
168	Tom Goodwin	.15
169	Armando Benitez	.15
170	Paul Konerko	.40
171	Jeff Cirillo	.15
172	Shane Reynolds	.15
173	Kevin Tapani	.15
174	Joe Crede	.25
175	Omar Infante RC	.50
176	Jake Peavy RC	5.00
177	Corey Patterson	.15
178	Alfredo Amezaga RC	.25
179	Jeromy Burnitz	.15
180	David Segui	.15
181	Marcus Giles	.15
182	Paul O'Neill	.25
183	John Olerud	.15
184	Andy Benes	.15
185	Brad Cresse RC	.25
186	Ricky Ledee	.15
187	Allen Levrault	.15
188	Royce Clayton	.15
189	Kelly Johnson RC	2.50
190	Quilvio Veras	.15
191	Mike Williams	.15
192	Jason Lane RC	1.00
193	Rick Helling	.15
194	Tim Wakefield	.15
195	James Baldwin	.15
196	Cody Ransom RC	.25
197	Bobby Kielty	.15
198	Bobby Jones	.15
199	Steve Cox	.15
200	Jamal Strong RC	.25
201	Steve Lomasney	.15
202	Bill Ortega	.15
203	Mike Matheny	.15
204	Jeff Randazzo RC	.25
205	Aubrey Huff	.15
206	Chuck Finley	.15
207	Denny Bautista RC	.50
208	Terry Mulholland	.15
209	Rey Ordonez	.15
210	Jason Belcher RC	.15
211	Orlando Cabrera	.15
212	Juan Encarnacion	.15
213	Dustin Hermanson	.15
214	Luis Rivas	.15
215	Mark Quinn	.15
216	Randy Velarde	.15
217	Billy Koch	.15
218	Ryan Rupe	.15
219	Keith Ginter	.15
220	Woody Williams	.15
221	Blake Williams RC	.25
222	Aaron Myette	.15
223	Joe Borchard RC	.50
224	Nate Cornejo	.15
225	Julian Tavarez	.15
226	Kevin Millwood	.15
227	Travis Hafner RC	2.00
228	Charles Nagy	.15
229	Mike Lieberthal	.15
230	Jeff Nelson	.15
231	Ryan Dempster	.15
232	Andres Galarraga	.15
233	Chad Durbin	.15
234	Timoniel Perez	.15
235	Troy O'Leary	.15
236	Kevin Young	.15
237	Gabe Kapler	.15
238	Juan Cruz RC	.50
239	Masato Yoshii	.15
240	Aramis Ramirez	.40
241	Matt Cooper RC	.15
242	Randy Flores RC	.25
243	Rafael Furcal	.15
244	David Eckstein	.15
245	Matt Clement	.15
246	Craig Biggio	.40
247	Rick Reed	.15
248	Jose Macias	.15
249	Alex Escobar	.15
250	Roberto Hernandez	.15
251	Andy Ashby	.15
252	Tony Armas	.15
253	Jamie Moyer	.15
254	Jason Tyner	.15
255	Ryan Ludwick RC	5.00
256	Jeff Conine	.15
257	Francisco Cordova	.15
258	Ted Lilly	.15
259	Joe Randa	.15
260	Jeff D'Amico	.15
261	Albie Lopez	.15
262	Kevin Appier	.15
263	Richard Hidalgo	.15
264	Omar Daal	.15
265	Ricky Gutierrez	.15
266	John Rocker	.15

267 Ray Lankford .15
268 Beau Hale RC .25
269 Tony Blanco RC .50
270 Derrek Lee .75
271 Jamey Wright .15
272 Alex Gordon .15
273 Jeff Weaver .15
274 Jaret Wright .15
275 Jose Hernandez .15
276 Bruce Chen .15
277 Todd Hollandsworth .15
278 Wade Miller .15
279 Luke Prokopec .15
280 Rafael Soriano RC .75
281 Damion Easley .15
282 Darren Oliver .15
283 Brandon Duckworth RC .25
284 Aaron Herr .15
285 Ray Durham .15
286 Adrian Hernandez RC .25
287 Ugueth Urbina .15
288 Scott Seabol .15
289 Lance Niekro RC .50
290 Trot Nixon .15
291 Adam Kennedy .15
292 Brian Schmitt RC .15
293 Grant Roberts .15
294 Benny Agbayani .15
295 Travis Lee .15
296 Erick Almonte RC .25
297 Jim Thome .15
298 Eric Young .15
299 Daniel Denham RC .25
300 Boof Bonser RC .75
301 Denny Neagle .15
302 Kenny Rogers .15
303 J.D. Closser .15
304 Chase Utley RC 20.00
305 Rey Sanchez .15
306 Sean McGowan .15
307 Justin Pope RC .25
308 Torii Hunter .40
309 B.J. Surhoff .15
310 Aaron Heilman RC .50
311 Gabe Gross RC .50
312 Lee Stevens .15
313 Todd Hundley .15
314 Macay McBride RC .50
315 Edgar Martinez .15
316 Omar Vizquel .15
317 Reggie Sanders .15
318 John-Ford Griffin RC .50
319 Tim Salmon (Photo actually Troy Glaus.) .50
320 Pokey Reese .15
321 Jay Payton .15
322 Doug Glanville .15
323 Greg Vaughn .15
324 Ruben Sierra .15
325 Kip Wells .15
326 Carl Everett .15
327 Garret Anderson .25
328 Jay Bell .15
329 Barry Larkin .25
330 Jeff Mathis RC .50
331 Adrian Gonzalez 2.00
332 Juan Rivera 1.00
333 Tony Alvarez 1.00
334 Xavier Nady 1.00
335 Josh Hamilton 3.00
336 Will Smith RC 1.00
337 Israel Alcantara 1.00
338 Chris George 1.00
339 Sean Burroughs 1.00
340 Jack Cust 1.00
341 Eric Byrnes 1.00
342 Carlos Pena 1.00
343 J.R. House 1.00
344 Carlos Silva 1.00
345 Mike Rivera RC 1.00
346 Adam Johnson 1.00
347 Scott Heard 1.00
348 Alex Cintron 1.00
349 Miguel Cabrera 3.00
350 Nick Johnson 1.00
351 Albert Pujols RC 50.00
352 Ichiro Suzuki RC 20.00
353 Carlos Delgado 1.50
354 Troy Glaus 1.50
355 Sammy Sosa 2.00
356 Ivan Rodriguez 2.00
357 Vladimir Guerrero 2.00
358 Manny Ramirez 2.00
359 Luis Gonzalez 1.00
360 Roy Oswalt 1.50
361 Moises Alou 1.50
362 Juan Gonzalez 1.50
363 Tony Gwynn 2.00
364 Hideo Nomo 1.00
365 Tsuyoshi Shinjo RC 1.00
366 Kazuhiro Sasaki 1.00
367 Cal Ripken Jr. 8.00
368 Rafael Palmeiro 2.00
369 J.D. Drew 1.00
370 Doug Mientkiewicz 1.00
371 Jeff Bagwell 2.00
372 Darin Erstad 1.00
373 Tom Gordon 1.00
374 Ben Petrick 1.00
375 Eric Milton 1.00
376 Nomar Garciaparra 2.00
377 Julio Lugo 1.00
378 Tino Martinez 1.50
379 Javier Vazquez 1.00
380 Jeremy Giambi 1.00
381 Marty Cordova 1.00
382 Adrian Beltre 1.50
383 John Burkett 1.00
384 Aaron Boone 1.00
385 Eric Chavez 1.00
386 Curt Schilling 2.00
387 Cory Lidle 1.00
388 Jason Schmidt 1.00
389 Johnny Damon 3.00
390 Steve Finley 1.00
391 Edgardo Alfonzo 1.00
392 Jose Valentin 1.00
393 Jose Canseco 1.50
394 Ryan Klesko 1.00
395 David Cone 1.00
396 Jason Kendall 1.00
397 Placido Polanco 1.00
398 Glendon Rusch 1.00
399 Aaron Sele 1.00
400 D'Angelo Jimenez 1.00
401 Mark Grace 1.50
402 Al Leiter 1.00
403 Brian Jordan 1.00
404 Phil Nevin 1.00
405 Brent Abernathy 1.00
406 Kerry Wood 1.50
407 Alex Gonzalez 1.00
408 Robert Fick 1.00
409 Dmitri Young 1.00
410 Wes Helms 1.00
411 Trevor Hoffman 1.00
412 Rickey Henderson 2.00
413 Bobby Higginson 1.00
414 Gary Sheffield 1.50
415 Darryl Kile 1.00
416 Richie Sexson 1.00
417 Frank Menechino 1.00
418 Javy Lopez 1.00
419 Carlos Lee 1.00
420 Jon Lieber 1.00
421 Hank Blalock RC 2.00
422 Marlon Byrd RC 2.50
423 Jason Kinchen RC 1.00
424 Morgan Ensberg RC 1.00
425 Greg "Toe" Nash RC 1.00
426 Dennis Tankersley RC 1.00
427 Joel Pineiro 1.00
428 Chris Smith RC 1.00
429 Jake Gautreau RC 1.00
430 John Van Benschoten RC 1.00
431 Travis Thompson 1.00
432 Orlando Hudson RC 3.00
433 Jerome Williams RC 1.00
434 Kevin Reese 1.00
435 Ed Rogers RC 1.00
436 Grant Balfour RC 1.00
437 Adam Pettyjohn RC 1.00
438 Hee Seop Choi RC 1.00
439 Justin Morneau RC 10.00
440 Mitch Jones RC 1.00

Autographs

NM/M
Common Player: 90.00
Inserted 1:44
BB Barry Bonds 180.00
RC Roger Clemens 100.00
AR Alex Rodriguez 100.00

Team Topps Legends Autographs

NM/M
Common Autograph: 30.00
Inserted 1:332
TT13F Warren Spahn/1965 40.00
TT21R Bob Feller/1952 30.00

1948 Bowman Reprints

NM/M
Complete Set (13): 10.00

Common Player: .75
Inserted 1:2
1 Ralph Kiner .75
2 Johnny Mize .75
3 Bobby Thomson .75
4 Yogi Berra 1.50
5 Phil Rizzuto 1.00
6 Bob Feller 1.00
7 Enos Slaughter .75
8 Stan Musial 2.00
9 Hank Sauer .75
10 Ferris Fain .75
11 Red Schoendienst .75
12 Allie Reynolds .75
13 Johnny Sain .75

1948 Bowman Reprint Autographs

NM/M
1 Warren Spahn 40.00
2 Bob Feller 40.00

1948 Reprint Relics

NM/M
Common Player: 8.00
Inserted 1:44
YB1 Yogi Berra 20.00
YB2 Yogi Berra 35.00
FF Ferris Fain 8.00
BF Bob Feller 12.00
RK Ralph Kiner 15.00
JM Johnny Mize 15.00
SM1 Stan Musial 30.00
PR Phil Rizzuto 15.00
HS Hank Sauer 8.00
RS Red Schoendienst 10.00
ES Enos Slaughter 10.00
BT Bobby Thomson 8.00

Chrome

Stars: 4-8X
SP's: 2-4X
Inserted 1:12

2001 Bowman's Best Pre-Production

The flashy new look for Bowman's Best in 2001 was debuted in this three-card sample set. Identical in format to the issued cards, they have textured foil printing on front and a matte back.

NM/M
Complete Set (3): 6.00
Common Player: 2.00
PP1 Todd Helton 3.00
PP2 Tim Hudson 2.00
PP3 Vernon Wells 2.00

2001 Bowman's Best

NM/M
Complete Set (200):
Common Player: .25
Common SP (151-200): 5.00
Production 2,999
Pack (5): 10.00
Box (24): 200.00
1 Vladimir Guerrero 1.00
2 Miguel Tejada .50
3 Geoff Jenkins .25
4 Jeff Bagwell .75
5 Todd Helton .75
6 Ken Griffey Jr. 2.00
7 Nomar Garciaparra .50
8 Chipper Jones 1.00
9 Darin Erstad .25
10 Frank Thomas 1.00
11 Jim Thome .50
12 Preston Wison .25
13 Kevin Brown .25
14 Derek Jeter 3.00
15 Scott Rolen .75
16 Ryan Klesko .25
17 Jeff Kent .40
18 Raul Mondesi .25
19 Greg Vaughn .25
20 Bernie Williams .40
21 Mike Piazza 1.00
22 Richard Hidalgo .25
23 Dean Palmer .25
24 Roberto Alomar .40
25 Sammy Sosa .75
26 Randy Johnson 1.00
27 Manny Ramirez 1.00
28 Roger Clemens 2.00
29 Terrence Long .25
30 Jason Kendall .25
31 Richie Sexson .40
32 David Wells .25
33 Andruw Jones .50
34 Pokey Reese .25
35 Juan Gonzalez .50
36 Carlos Beltran .75
37 Shawn Green .40
38 Mariano Rivera .50
39 John Olerud .40
40 Jim Edmonds .40
41 Andres Galarraga .25
42 Carlos Delgado .40
43 Kris Benson .25
44 Andy Pettitte .40
45 Jeff Cirillo .25
46 Magglio Ordonez .50
47 Tom Glavine .50
48 Garret Anderson .25
49 Cal Ripken Jr. 3.00
50 Pedro Martinez 1.00
51 Barry Bonds 3.00
52 Alex Rodriguez 2.50
53 Ben Grieve .25
54 Edgar Martinez .25
55 Jason Giambi .50
56 Jeromy Burnitz .25
57 Mike Mussina .50
58 Moises Alou .25
59 Sean Casey .40
60 Greg Maddux 2.00
61 Tim Hudson .25
62 Mark McGwire 1.50
63 Rafael Palmeiro .75
64 Tony Batista .25
65 Kazuhiro Sasaki .25
66 Jorge Posada .50
67 Johnny Damon 1.00
68 Brian Giles .25
69 Jose Vidro .25
70 Jermaine Dye .40
71 Craig Biggio .40
72 Larry Walker .40
73 Eric Chavez .25
74 David Segui .25
75 Tim Salmon .40
76 Javy Lopez .25
77 Paul Konerko .50
78 Barry Larkin .50
79 Mike Hampton .25
80 Bobby Higginson .25
81 Mark Mulder .40
82 Pat Burrell .40
83 Kerry Wood .50
84 J.T. Snow .25
85 Ivan Rodriguez .75
86 Edgardo Alfonzo .25
87 Orlando Hernandez .40
88 Gary Sheffield .50
89 Mike Sweeney .25
90 Carlos Lee .25
91 Rafael Furcal .50
92 Troy Glaus .50
93 Bartolo Colon .25
94 Cliff Floyd .25
95 Barry Zito .40
96 J.D. Drew .40
97 Eric Karros .25
98 Jose Valentin .25
99 Ellis Burks .25
100 David Justice .25
101 Larry Barnes .25
102 Rod Barajas .25
103 Tony Pena .25
104 Jerry Hairston Jr. .25
105 Keith Ginter .25
106 Corey Patterson .75
107 Aaron Rowand .40
108 Miguel Olivo .25
109 Gookie Dawkins .25
110 C.C. Sabathia .75
111 Ben Petrick .25
112 Eric Munson .25
113 Ramon Castro .25
114 Alex Escobar .25
115 Josh Hamilton 1.00
116 Jason Marquis .25
117 Ben Davis .25
118 Alex Cintron .25
119 Julio Zuleta .25
120 Ben Broussard .25
121 Adam Everett .25
122 Ramon Carvajal RC .75
123 Felipe Lopez .25
124 Alfonso Soriano 1.00
125 Jayson Werth .25
126 Donzell McDonald .25
127 Jason Hart .25
128 Joe Crede .50
129 Sean Burroughs .25
130 Jack Cust .25
131 Corey Smith .25
132 Adrian Gonzalez .25
133 J.R. House .25
134 Steve Lomasney .25
135 Tim Raines Jr. .25
136 Tony Alvarez .25
137 Doug Mientkiewicz .25
138 Rocco Baldelli .40
139 Jason Romano .25
140 Vernon Wells .50
141 Mike Bynum .25
142 Xavier Nady .25
143 Brad Wilkerson .25
144 Ben Diggins .25
145 Aubrey Huff .25
146 Eric Byrnes .25
147 Alex Gordon .40
148 Roy Oswalt .50
149 Brian Esposito .25
150 Scott Seabol .25
151 Erick Almonte RC 5.00
152 Gary Johnson RC 5.00
153 Pedro Liriano RC 5.00
154 Matt White RC 5.00
155 Luis Montanez RC 5.00
156 Brad Cresse RC 5.00
157 Wilson Betemit RC 6.00
158 Octavio Martinez RC 5.00
159 Adam Pettyjohn RC 5.00
160 Corey Spencer RC 5.00
161 Mark Burnett RC 5.00
162 Ichiro Suzuki RC 50.00
163 Alexis Gomez RC 5.00
164 Greg "Toe" Nash RC 5.00
165 Roberto Miniel RC 5.00
166 Justin Morneau RC 25.00
167 Ben Washburn RC 5.00
168 Bob Keppel RC 5.00
169 Deivi Mendez RC 5.00
170 Tsuyoshi Shinjo RC 5.00
171 Jared Abruzzo RC 5.00
172 Derrick Van Dusen RC 5.00
173 Hee Seop Choi RC 5.00
174 Albert Pujols RC 150.00
175 Travis Hafner RC 12.00
176 Ron Davenport RC 5.00
177 Luis Torres RC 5.00
178 Jake Peavy RC 25.00
179 Elvis Corporan RC 5.00
180 David Krynzel RC 5.00
181 Tony Blanco RC 5.00
182 Elpidio Guzman RC 5.00
183 Matt Butler RC 5.00
184 Joe Thurston RC 20.00
185 Andy Beal RC 5.00
186 Kevin Nulton RC 5.00
187 Sneideer Santos RC 5.00
188 Joe Dillon RC 5.00
189 Jeremy Blevins RC 5.00
190 Chris Amador RC 5.00
191 Mark Hendrickson RC 5.00
192 Willy Aybar RC 8.00
193 Antoine Cameron RC 5.00
194 Jonathan Johnson RC 5.00
195 Ryan Ketchner RC 5.00
196 Bjorn Ivy RC 5.00
197 Josh Kroeger RC 5.00
198 Ty Wigginton RC 8.00
199 Stubby Clapp RC 5.00
200 Jerrod Riggan RC 5.00

Autographs

NM/M
Common Player: 8.00
Inserted 1:95
SB Sean Burroughs 8.00
BC Brad Cresse 8.00
AG Adrian Gonzalez 20.00
JH Josh Hamilton 35.00
JRH J.R. House 8.00
TL Terrence Long 8.00
JR Jon Rauch 8.00

Exclusive Rookie Autographs

NM/M
Common Player: 5.00
Inserted 1:50
WA Willy Aybar 8.00
SC Stubby Clapp 5.00
BI Bjorn Ivy 5.00
JJ Jonathan Johnson 5.00
TW Ty Wigginton 10.00
JR Jerrod Riggan 5.00
SS Sneideer Santos 5.00
JB Jeremy Blevins 5.00
MH Mark Hendrickson 8.00

Franchise Favorites

NM/M
Complete Set (8): 30.00
Common Player: 1.50
Inserted 1:16
DM Don Mattingly 6.00
AR Alex Rodriguez 6.00
DE Darin Erstad 1.50
DW Dave Winfield 1.50
NR Nolan Ryan 2.00
RJ Reggie Jackson 2.00
MW Don Mattingly, Dave Winfield 4.00
RR Nolan Ryan, Alex Rodriguez 8.00
EJ Darin Erstad, Reggie Jackson 2.00

Franchise Favorites Autographs

NM/M
Common Player: 20.00

Inserted 1:556
Combo 1:4,436

DE	Darin Erstad	10.00
RJ	Reggie Jackson	40.00
EJ	Darin Erstad, Reggie Jackson	65.00
DM	Don Mattingly	60.00
MW	Don Mattingly, Dave Winfield	150.00
AR	Alex Rodriguez	90.00
NR	Nolan Ryan	80.00
RR	Nolan Ryan, Alex Rodriguez	300.00
DW	Dave Winfield	25.00

Franchise Favorites Relics

NM/M
Common Player: 5.00
Jersey 1:139
Pants 1:307
Combo Relic 1:1,114

JB	Jeff Bagwell	10.00
CB	Craig Biggio	6.00
BB	Craig Biggio, Jeff Bagwell	25.00
DE	Darin Erstad	5.00
RJ	Reggie Jackson	10.00
EJ	Reggie Jackson, Darin Erstad	25.00
DM	Don Mattingly	30.00
MW	Don Mattingly, Dave Winfield	65.00
AR	Alex Rodriguez	20.00
NR	Nolan Ryan	40.00
RR	Nolan Ryan, Alex Rodriguez	60.00
DW	Dave Winfield	8.00

Franchise Futures

NM/M
Complete Set (12): 15.00
Common Player: 1.00
Inserted 1:24

FF1	Josh Hamilton	2.50
FF2	Wes Helms	1.00
FF3	Alfonso Soriano	4.00
FF4	Nick Johnson	1.00
FF5	Jose Ortiz	1.00
FF6	Ben Sheets	1.50
FF7	Sean Burroughs	1.00
FF8	Ben Petrick	1.00
FF9	Corey Patterson	1.00
FF10	J.R. House	1.00
FF11	Alex Escobar	1.00
FF12	Travis Hafner	1.50

Game-Used Bats

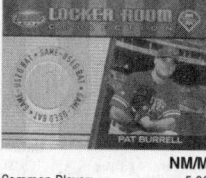

NM/M
Common Player: 5.00
Inserted 1:267

PB	Pat Burrell	10.00
SB	Sean Burroughs	5.00
AG	Adrian Gonzalez	10.00
EM	Eric Munson	5.00
CP	Corey Patterson	5.00

Game-Worn Jerseys

NM/M
Common Player: 5.00
Inserted 1:133

EC	Eric Chavez	5.00
MM	Mark Mulder	5.00
JP	Jay Payton	5.00
PR	Pokey Reese	5.00
PW	Preston Wilson	5.00

Impact Players

NM/M
Complete Set (20): 15.00
Common Player: .50
Inserted 1:7

IP1	Mark McGwire	3.00
IP2	Sammy Sosa	2.00
IP3	Manny Ramirez	1.00
IP4	Troy Glaus	1.00
IP5	Ken Griffey Jr.	2.00
IP6	Gary Sheffield	.75
IP7	Vladimir Guerrero	1.00
IP8	Carlos Delgado	.75
IP9	Jason Giambi	.75
IP10	Frank Thomas	1.50
IP11	Vernon Wells	.60
IP12	Carlos Pena	.50
IP13	Joe Crede	.50
IP14	Keith Ginter	.50
IP15	Aubrey Huff	.50
IP16	Brad Cresse	.50
IP17	Austin Kearns	.75
IP18	Nick Johnson	.50
IP19	Josh Hamilton	.50
IP20	Corey Patterson	.60

Rookie Fever

NM/M
Complete Set (10): 10.00
Common Player: .50
Inserted 1:10

RF1	Chipper Jones	2.00
RF2	Preston Wilson	.50
RF3	Todd Helton	1.00
RF4	Jay Payton	.50
RF5	Ivan Rodriguez	.75
RF6	Manny Ramirez	1.00
RF7	Derek Jeter	4.00
RF8	Orlando Hernandez	.50
RF9	Marcus Quinn	.50
RF10	Terrence Long	.50

Team Topps

NM/M
Common Player: 10.00
Overall odds 1:71.

13R	Warren Spahn/1952	40.00
37R	Tug McGraw/1965	10.00
48R	Bobby Richardson/1957	15.00
25R	Luis Tiant/1965 + Exchange	10.00
31R	Clete Boyer/1957	15.00
28R	Gil McDougald/1952	15.00
27R	Andy Pafko/1952	15.00
28R	Herb Score/1956	15.00
18R	Bob Gibson/1959	40.00

LUIS TIANT

29R	Moose Skowron/1954	15.00
37F	Tug McGraw/1985	10.00
28F	Herb Score/1962	15.00

2002 Bowman

CHRIS SNELLING

NM/M
Complete Set (440): 70.00
Common Player: .15
Common Rookie: .40
Pack (10): 4.50
Box (24): 90.00

#	Player	Price
1	Adam Dunn	.50
2	Derek Jeter	2.00
3	Alex Rodriguez	1.50
4	Miguel Tejada	.50
5	Nomar Garciaparra	.75
6	Toby Hall	.15
7	Brandon Duckworth	.15
8	Paul LoDuca	.15
9	Brian Giles	.15
10	C.C. Sabathia	.40
11	Curt Schilling	.75
12	Tsuyoshi Shinjo	.15
13	Ramon Hernandez	.15
14	Jose Cruz Jr.	.15
15	Albert Pujols	2.00
16	Joe Mays	.15
17	Javy Lopez	.15
18	J.T. Snow	.15
19	David Segui	.15
20	Jorge Posada	.40
21	Doug Mientkiewicz	.15
22	Jerry Hairston Jr.	.15
23	Bernie Williams	.40
24	Mike Sweeney	.15
25	Jason Giambi	.50
26	Ryan Dempster	.15
27	Ryan Klesko	.15
28	Mark Quinn	.15
29	Jeff Kent	.25
30	Eric Chavez	.25
31	Adrian Beltre	.25
32	Andruw Jones	.40
33	Alfonso Soriano	1.00
34	Aramis Ramirez	.40
35	Greg Maddux	1.50
36	Andy Pettitte	.50
37	Bartolo Colon	.15
38	Ben Sheets	.40
39	Bobby Higginson	.15
40	Ivan Rodriguez	.75
41	Brad Penny	.15
42	Carlos Lee	.25
43	Damion Easley	.15
44	Preston Wilson	.15
45	Jeff Bagwell	.50
46	Eric Milton	.15
47	Rafael Palmeiro	.50
48	Gary Sheffield	.40
49	J.D. Drew	.50
50	Jim Thome	.50
51	Ichiro Suzuki	1.50
52	Bud Smith	.15
53	Chan Ho Park	.15
54	D'Angelo Jimenez	.15
55	Ken Griffey Jr.	1.50
56	Wade Miller	.15
57	Vladimir Guerrero	.50
58	Troy Glaus	.40
59	Shawn Green	.25
60	Kerry Wood	.40
61	Jack Wilson	.15
62	Kevin Brown	.25
63	Marcus Giles	.15
64	Pat Burrell	.40
65	Larry Walker	.25
66	Sammy Sosa	.75
67	Raul Mondesi	.15
68	Tim Hudson	.25
69	Lance Berkman	.40
70	Mike Mussina	.40
71	Barry Zito	.25
72	Jimmy Rollins	.50
73	Barry Bonds	2.00
74	Craig Biggio	.40
75	Todd Helton	.50
76	Roger Clemens	1.50
77	Frank Catalanotto	.15
78	Josh Towers	.15
79	Roy Oswalt	.40
80	Chipper Jones	1.00
81	Cristian Guzman	.15
82	Darin Erstad	.25
83	Freddy Garcia	.15
84	Jason Tyner	.15
85	Carlos Delgado	.40
86	Jon Lieber	.15
87	Juan Pierre	.15
88	Matt Morris	.15
89	Phil Nevin	.25
90	Jim Edmonds	.25
91	Magglio Ordonez	.25
92	Mike Hampton	.15
93	Rafael Furcal	.15
94	Richie Sexson	.25
95	Luis Gonzalez	.25
96	Scott Rolen	.50
97	Tim Redding	.15
98	Moises Alou	.25
99	Jose Vidro	.15
100	Mike Piazza	1.00
101	Pedro Martinez	.75
102	Geoff Jenkins	.15
103	Johnny Damon	.75
104	Mike Cameron	.15
105	Randy Johnson	.75
106	David Eckstein	.15
107	Javier Vazquez	.15
108	Mark Mulder	.25
109	Robert Fick	.15
110	Roberto Alomar	.40
111	Wilson Betemit	.15
112	Chris Tritle RC	.15
113	Ed Rogers	.15
114	Juan Pena	.15
115	Josh Beckett	.50
116	Juan Cruz	.15
117	Noochie Varner RC	.15
118	Taylor Buchholz RC	.50
119	Mike Rivera	.15
120	Hank Blalock	.40
121	Hansel Izquierdo RC	.15
122	Orlando Hudson	.15
123	Bill Hall	.15
124	Jose Reyes	.75
125	Juan Rivera	.15
126	Eric Valent	.15
127	Scotty Layfield RC	.40
128	Austin Kearns	.40
129	Nic Jackson RC	.25
130	Chris Baker RC	.25
131	Chad Qualls RC	.40
132	Marcus Thames	.15
133	Nathan Haynes	.15
134	Brett Evert	.15
135	Joe Borchard	.15
136	Ryan Christianson	.15
137	Josh Hamilton	.50
138	Corey Patterson	.15
139	Travis Wilson	.15
140	Alex Escobar	.15
141	Alexis Gomez	.15
142	Nick Johnson	.15
143	Kenny Kelly	.15
144	Marlon Byrd	.15
145	Kory DeHaan	.15
146	Matt Belisle	.15
147	Carlos Hernandez	.15
148	Sean Burroughs	.15
149	Angel Berroa	.15
150	Aubrey Huff	.15
151	Travis Hafner	.40
152	Brandon Berger	.15
153	David Krynzel	.15
154	Ruben Salazar	.15
155	J.R. House	.15
156	Juan Silvestre	.15
157	Dewon Brazelton	.15
158	Jayson Werth	.15
159	Larry Barnes	.15
160	Elvis Pena	.15
161	Ruben Gotay RC	.40
162	Tommy Marx RC	.50
163	John Suomi RC	.40
164	Javier Colina	.15
165	Greg Sain RC	.40
166	Robert Cosby RC	.40
167	Angel Pagan RC	1.00
168	Ralph Santana RC	.40
169	Joe Orloski RC	.40
170	Shayne Wright RC	.40
171	Jay Caliguiri RC	.25
172	Greg Montalbano RC	.50
173	Rich Harden RC	2.00
174	Rich Thompson RC	.40
175	Fred Bastardo RC	.40
176	Alejandro Giron RC	.40
177	Jesus Medrano RC	.40
178	Kevin Deaton RC	.40
179	Mike Rosamond RC	.50
180	Jon Guzman RC	.40
181	Gerard Oakes RC	.40
182	Francisco Liriano RC	8.00
183	Matt Allegra RC	.50
184	Mike Snyder RC	.40
185	James Shanks RC	.40
186	Anderson Hernandez RC	.40
187	Dan Trumble RC	.40
188	Luis DePaula RC	.40
189	Randall Shelley RC	.40
190	Richard Lane RC	.40
191	Antwon Rollins RC	.50
192	Ryan Bukvich RC	.40
193	Derrick Lewis	.15
194	Eric Miller RC	.40
195	Justin Schuda RC	.40
196	Brian West RC	.40
197	Adam Roller RC	.40
198	Neal Frendling RC	.40
199	Jeremy Hill RC	.40
200	James Barrett RC	.40
201	Brett Kay RC	.50
202	Ryan Mottl RC	.40
203	Brad Nelson RC	.50
204	Juan Gonzalez	.25
205	Curtis Legendre RC	.40
206	Ronald Acuna RC	.40
207	Chris Flinn RC	.40
208	Nick Alvarez RC	.40
209	Jason Ellison RC	.40
210	Blake McGinley RC	.40
211	Dan Phillips RC	.50
212	Demetrius Heath RC	.40
213	Eric Bruntlett RC	.40
214	Joe Jiannetti RC	.40
215	Mike Hill RC	.40
216	Ricardo Cordova RC	.40
217	Mark Hamilton RC	.50
218	David Mattox RC	.40
219	Jose Morban RC	.40
220	Scott Wiggins RC	.50
221	Steve Green	.15
222	Brian Rogers	.15
223	Chin-Hui Tsao	.40
224	Kenny Baugh	.15
225	Nate Teut	.15
226	Josh Wilson RC	.15
227	Christian Parker	.15
228	Tim Raines Jr.	.15
229	Anastacio Martinez RC	.40
230	Richard Lewis	.15
231	Tim Kalita RC	.40
232	Edwin Almonte RC	.40
233	Hee Seop Choi	.25
234	Ty Howington	.15
235	Victor Alvarez RC	.40
236	Morgan Ensberg	.15
237	Jeff Austin RC	.40
238	Luis Terrero	.15
239	Adam Wainwright	.25
240	Clint Weibl RC	.40
241	Eric Cyr RC	.40
242	Marlyn Tisdale RC	.40
243	John VanBenschoten	.15
244	Ryan Raburn RC	.40
245	Miguel Cabrera	.75
246	Jung Bong	.15
247	Raul Chavez RC	.40
248	Erik Bedard	.25
249	Chris Snelling RC	.40
250	Joe Rogers RC	.40
251	Nate Field RC	.40
252	Matt Herges	.15
253	Matt Childers RC	.50
254	Erick Almonte	.15
255	Nick Neugebauer	.15
256	Ron Calloway RC	.40
257	Seung Jun Song	.15
258	Brandon Phillips	.25
259	Cole Barthel	.25
260	Jason Lane	.15
261	Jae Weong Seo	.15
262	Randy Flores	.15
263	Scott Chiasson	.15
264	Chase Utley	1.00
265	Tony Alvarez	.15
266	Ben Howard RC	.40
267	Nelson Castro RC	.40
268	Mark Lukasiewicz	.15
269	Eric Glaser RC	.40
270	Rob Henkel RC	.40
271	Jose Valverde RC	.40
272	Ricardo Rodriguez	.15
273	Chris Smith	.15
274	Mark Prior	1.50
275	Miguel Olivo	.15
276	Ben Broussard	.15
277	Zach Sorensen	.15
278	Brian Mallette RC	.40
279	Brad Wilkerson	.15
280	Carl Crawford	.25
281	Chone Figgins RC	1.00
282	Jimmy Alvarez RC	.40
283	Gavin Floyd	1.00
284	Josh Bonifay RC	.50
285	Garrett Guzman RC	.50
286	Blake Williams	.15
287	Matt Holliday	.50
288	Ryan Madson	.15
289	Luis Torres	.15
290	Jeff Verplancke RC	.40
291	Nate Espy RC	.40
292	Jeff Lincoln RC	.40
293	Ryan Snare RC	.40
294	Jose Ortiz	.15
295	Eric Munson	.15
296	Denny Bautista	.15
297	Willy Aybar	.15
298	Kelly Johnson	.15
299	Justin Morneau	.50
300	Derrick Van Dusen	.15
301	Chad Petty	.15
302	Mike Restovich	.15
303	Shawn Fagan	.15
304	Yurendell DeCaster RC	.40
305	Justin Wayne	.15
306	Mike Peeples RC	.40
307	Joel Guzman RC	.75
308	Ryan Vogelsong	.15
309	Jorge Padilla RC	.50
310	Grady Sizemore	.50
311	Joe Jester RC	.40
312	Jim Journell	.15
313	Bobby Seay	.15
314	Ryan Church RC	1.00
315	Grant Balfour	.15
316	Mitch Jones	.15
317	Travis Foley	.50
318	Bobby Crosby	.15
319	Adrian Gonzalez	.25
320	Ronnie Merrill	.15
321	Joel Pineiro	.15
322	John-Ford Griffin	.15
323	Brian Forystek RC	.40
324	Sean Douglass	.15
325	Manny Delcarmen RC	.40
326	Donnie Bridges	.15
327	Jim Kavourias	.15
328	Gabe Gross	.15
329	Greg "Toe" Nash	.15
330	Bill Ortega	.15
331	Joey Hammond RC	.40
332	Ramon Moreta RC	.40
333	Ron Davenport	.15
334	Brett Myers	.15
335	Carlos Pena	.15
336	Ezequiel Astacio RC	.40
337	Edwin Yan RC	.50
338	Josh Girdley	.15
339	Shaun Boyd	.15
340	Juan Rincon	.15
341	Chris Duffy RC	.50
342	Jason Kinchen	.15
343	Brad Thomas	.15
344	David Kelton	.15
345	Rafael Soriano	.15
346	Colin Young RC	.50
347	Eric Byrnes	.15
348	Chris Narveson RC	.50
349	John Rheinecker RC	.40
350	Mike Wilson RC	.40
351	Justin Sherrod RC	.50
352	Deivi Mendez	.15
353	Wily Mo Pena	.15
354	Brett Roneberg RC	.40
355	Trey Lunsford RC	.40
356	Jimmy Gobble RC	.40
357	Brent Butler	.15
358	Aaron Heilman	.15
359	Wilkin Ruan	.15
360	Brian Wolfe RC	.40
361	Cody Ransom	.15
362	Koyie Hill	.40
363	Scott Cassidy	.15
364	Tony Fontana RC	.50
365	Mark Teixeira	.50
366	Doug Sessions RC	.40
367	Victor Hall	.15
368	Josh Cisneros RC	.40
369	Kevin Mench	.15
370	Tike Redman	.15
371	Jeff Heaverlo	.15
372	Carlos Brackley RC	.40
373	Brad Hawpe	.50
374	Jesus Colome	.15
375	David Espinosa	.15
376	Jesse Foppert	.75
377	Ross Peeples RC	.40
378	Alexander Requena RC	.40
379	Joe Mauer	15.00
380	Carlos Silva	.15
381	David Wright	20.00
382	Craig Kuzmic RC	.50
383	Peter Zamora RC	.40
384	Matt Parker RC	.40
385	Ricardo Rodriguez	.15
386	Gary Cates Jr. RC	.40
387	Justin Reid RC	.50
388	Jake Mauer RC	.40
389	John-Ford Griffin	.15
390	Josh Barfield	.50
391	Luis Maza	.15
392	Henry Pichardo RC	.40
393	Michael Floyd RC	.40
394	Clint Nagreotte RC	.50
395	Jim Warden	.15
396	Mauricio Lara RC	.50
397	Alejandro Cadena RC	.40
398	Jonny Gomes RC	1.00
399	Jason Bulger RC	.40
400	Bobby Jenks RC	1.00
401	David Gil RC	.40
402	Joel Crump RC	.40
403	Kazuhisa Ishii RC	.50
404	So Taguchi RC	.40
405	Ryan Doumit RC	1.00
406	Macay McBride	.15
407	Brandon Claussen	.15
408	Chin-Feng Chen	.15
409	Josh Phelps	.25
410	Freddie Money RC	.40
411	Clifford Bartosh RC	.40
412	Josh Pearce	.15
413	Lyle Overbay	.15
414	Ryan Anderson	.15
415	Terrance Hill RC	.40
416	John Rodriguez RC	.40
417	Richard Stahl RC	.40
418	Brian Specht	.15
419	Chris Latham RC	.50
420	Carlos Cabrera RC	.40
421	Jose Bautista RC	.50
422	Kevin Frederick RC	.40

423	Jerome Williams	.50
424	Napoleon Calzado RC	.50
425	Benito Baez	.15
426	Xavier Nady	.15
427	Jason Botts RC	.40
428	Steve Bechler RC	.50
429	Reed Johnson RC	.50
430	Mark Outlaw RC	.40
431	Billy Sylvester	.15
432	Luke Lockwood	.15
433	Jake Peavy	.25
434	Alfredo Amezega	.15
435	Aaron Cook RC	.75
436	Josh Shaffer RC	.40
437	Dan Wright	.15
438	Ryan Gripp RC	.50
439	Alex Herrera	.15
440	Jason Bay RC	4.00

Gold

Stars: 1-2.5X
Rookies: 1-2X
Inserted 1:1

Uncirculated

		NM/M
Common Player:		4.00
Production 1,000 Sets		
112	Chris Tritle	6.00
113	Ed Rogers	4.00
114	Juan Pena	4.00
115	Josh Beckett	8.00
116	Juan Cruz	4.00
117	Noochie Varner	6.00
118	Taylor Buchholz	4.00
119	Mike Rivera	4.00
120	Hank Blalock	6.00
121	Hansel Izquierdo	4.00
122	Orlando Hudson	4.00
123	Bill Hall	4.00
124	Jose Reyes	8.00
125	Juan Rivera	4.00
126	Eric Valent	4.00
127	Scotty Layfield	4.00
128	Austin Kearns	600
129	Nic Jackson	4.00
130	Chris Baker	4.00
131	Chad Qualls	4.00

Autographs

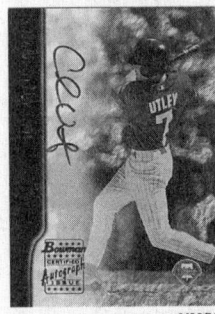

		NM/M
Common Autograph:		5.00
Inserted 1:37		
AA	Alfredo Amezega	5.00
GA	Garrett Atkins	8.00
JB	Josh Beckett	25.00
WB	Wilson Betemit	5.00
LB	Larry Bigbie	5.00
HB	Hank Blalock	8.00
TB	Tony Blanco	5.00
JAB	Jason Botts	5.00
MB	Marlon Byrd	10.00
BDC	Brian Cardwell	5.00
BC	Ben Christensen	5.00
BAC	Brandon Claussen	5.00
JD	Jeff Davanon	5.00
MD	Manny Delcarmen	8.00
RF	Randy Flores	5.00
RF	Ryan Franklin	5.00
KG	Keith Ginter	5.00
TH	Toby Hall	10.00
AH	Aubrey Huff	5.00
GJ	Gary Johnson	5.00
NJ	Nick Johnson	8.00
CK	Charles Kegley	5.00
JL	Jason Lane	8.00
NN	Nick Neugebauer	5.00
RO	Roy Oswalt	15.00
JP	Juan Pena	5.00
MP	Mark Prior	8.00
CR	Cody Ransom	5.00
JS	Juan Silvestre	5.00
TS	Terrmel Sledge	5.00
BS	Bud Smith	5.00
CS	Chris Smith	5.00
WS	Will Smith	5.00
BJS	Brian Specht	5.00
CT	Chris Tritle	5.00
CU	Chase Utley	200.00
DV	Domingo Valdez	5.00
NV	Noochie Varner	5.00
RV	Ryan Vogelsong	5.00
JLW	Jerome Williams	5.00
DW	Dan Wright	5.00

Autographed Futures Game Game-Used Base

		NM/M
Randomly Inserted		
TB	Toby Hall	15.00

Autographed Futures Game Game-Worn Jersey

Ryan Ludwick

		NM/M
Common Player:		15.00
Inserted 1:193		
WB	Wilson Betemit	15.00
CH	Carlos Hernandez	15.00
JRH	J.R. House	15.00
NJ	Nick Johnson	15.00
RL	Ryan Ludwick	30.00
CP	Carlos Pena	20.00
DT	Dennis Tankersley	15.00
JW	Jerome Williams	15.00

Game-Used Relics

Nate Cornejo

		NM/M
Common Player:		4.00
Inserted 1:165		
JA1	Jared Abruzzo	4.00
JA2	Jared Abruzzo	4.00
GA	Garrett Atkins	4.00
AB	Angel Berroa	4.00
AC	Antoine Cameron	4.00
RC	Ryan Church	4.00
ALC	Alex Cintron	4.00
NC	Nate Cornejo	4.00
RD	Ryan Dittfurth	4.00
AE	Adam Everett	4.00
AF1	Alex Fernandez	4.00
AF2	Alex Fernandez	4.00
AG	Alexis Gomez	4.00
CG	Cristian Guerrero	4.00
CI	Cesar Izturis	4.00
DJ	D'Angelo Jimenez	4.00
FJ	Forrest Johnson	4.00
AK	Austin Kearns	4.00
JL	Jason Lane	4.00
RM	Ryan Madson	4.00
NN	Nick Neugebauer	4.00
CP	Corey Patterson	4.00
RS	Ruben Salazar	4.00
RST	Richard Stahl	4.00
JS	Jamal Strong	4.00
CY	Colin Young	4.00

2002 Bowman Chrome

ICHIRO
OF-SEATTLE MARINERS

		NM/M
Complete Set (405):		.25
Common Player:		.25
Common SP:		3.00
Inserted 1:3		
Common Auto.(384-402,405)		10.00
Inserted 1:18		
Pack (4):		10.00
Box (18):		150.00
1	Adam Dunn	.50
2	Derek Jeter	3.00
3	Alex Rodriguez	2.50

4	Miguel Tejada	.50
5	Nomar Garciaparra	.75
6	Toby Hall	.25
7	Brandon Duckworth	.25
8	Paul LoDuca	.25
9	Brian Giles	.25
10	C.C. Sabathia	.50
11	Curt Schilling	.75
12	Tsuyoshi Shinjo	.25
13	Ramon Hernandez	.25
14	Jose Cruz Jr.	.25
15	Albert Pujols	3.00
16	Joe Mays	.25
17	Javy Lopez	.25
18	J.T. Snow	.25
19	David Segui	.25
20	Jorge Posada	.50
21	Doug Mientkiewicz	.25
22	Jerry Hairston Jr.	.25
23	Bernie Williams	.50
24	Mike Sweeney	.25
25	Jason Giambi	.75
26	Ryan Dempster	.25
27	Ryan Klesko	.25
28	Mark Quinn	.25
29	Jeff Kent	.25
30	Eric Chavez	.40
31	Adrian Beltre	.40
32	Andruw Jones	.50
33	Alfonso Soriano	1.00
34	Aramis Ramirez	.50
35	Greg Maddux	2.00
36	Andy Pettitte	.50
37	Bartolo Colon	.25
38	Ben Sheets	.40
39	Bobby Higginson	.25
40	Ivan Rodriguez	.50
41	Brad Penny	.25
42	Carlos Lee	.50
43	Damion Easley	.25
44	Preston Wilson	.25
45	Jeff Bagwell	.50
46	Eric Milton	.25
47	Rafael Palmeiro	.50
48	Gary Sheffield	.50
49	J.D. Drew	.40
50	Jim Thome	.75
51	Ichiro Suzuki	2.00
52	Bud Smith	.25
53	Chan Ho Park	.25
54	D'Angelo Jimenez	.25
55	Ken Griffey Jr.	2.00
56	Wade Miller	.25
57	Vladimir Guerrero	1.00
58	Troy Glaus	.50
59	Shawn Green	.40
60	Kerry Wood	.50
61	Jack Wilson	.25
62	Kevin Brown	.25
63	Marcus Giles	.25
64	Pat Burrell	.50
65	Larry Walker	.40
66	Sammy Sosa	1.00
67	Raul Mondesi	.25
68	Tim Hudson	.40
69	Lance Berkman	.50
70	Mike Mussina	.50
71	Barry Zito	.40
72	Jimmy Rollins	.75
73	Barry Bonds	3.00
74	Craig Biggio	.40
75	Todd Helton	.75
76	Roger Clemens	2.00
77	Frank Catalanotto	.25
78	Josh Towers	.25
79	Roy Oswalt	.40
80	Chipper Jones	1.50
81	Cristian Guzman	.25
82	Darin Erstad	.40
83	Freddy Garcia	.25
84	Jason Tyner	.25
85	Carlos Delgado	.50
86	Jon Lieber	.25
87	Juan Pierre	.25
88	Matt Morris	.25
89	Phil Nevin	.25
90	Jim Edmonds	.40
91	Magglio Ordonez	.40
92	Mike Hampton	.25
93	Rafael Furcal	.50
94	Richie Sexson	.40
95	Luis Gonzalez	.40
96	Scott Rolen	.50
97	Tim Redding	.25
98	Moises Alou	.40
99	Jose Vidro	.25
100	Mike Piazza	1.50
101	Pedro Martinez	1.00
102	Geoff Jenkins	.25
103	Johnny Damon	1.00
104	Mike Cameron	.25
105	Randy Johnson	1.00
106	David Eckstein	.25
107	Javier Vazquez	.25
108	Mark Mulder	.40
109	Robert Fick	.25
110	Roberto Alomar	.40
111	Wilson Betemit	.25
112	Chris Tritle/SP RC	4.00
113	Ed Rogers	.25
114	Juan Pena	.25
115	Josh Beckett	.50
116	Juan Cruz	.25
117	Noochie Varner/SP RC	5.00
118	Blake Williams	.25
119	Mike Rivera	.25
120	Hank Blalock	.40
121	Hansel Izquierdo/SP RC	4.00

122	Orlando Hudson	.25
123	Bill Hall	.25
124	Jose Reyes	1.00
125	Juan Rivera	.25
126	Eric Valent	.25
127	Scotty Layfield/SP RC	3.00
128	Austin Kearns	.25
129	Nic Jackson/SP RC	5.00
130	Scott Chiasson	.25
131	Chad Qualls/SP RC	4.00
132	Marcus Thames	.25
133	Nathan Haynes	.25
134	Joe Borchard	.25
135	Josh Hamilton	1.00
136	Corey Patterson	.25
137	Travis Wilson	.25
138	Alex Escobar	.25
139	Alexis Gomez	.25
140	Nick Johnson	.25
141	Marlon Byrd	.25
142	Kory DeHaan	.25
143	Carlos Hernandez	.25
144	Sean Burroughs	.25
145	Angel Berroa	.25
146	Aubrey Huff	.25
147	Travis Hafner	.50
148	Brandon Berger	.25
149	J.R. House	.25
150	Dewon Brazelton	.25
151	Jayson Werth	.25
152	Larry Barnes	.25
153	Ruben Gotay/SP RC	5.00
154	Tommy Marx/SP RC	3.00
155	John Suomi/SP RC	4.00
156	Javier Colina/SP	3.00
157	Greg Sain/SP	3.00
158	Robert Cosby/SP RC	4.00
159	Angel Pagan/SP RC	6.00
160	Ralph Santana RC	1.00
161	Joe Orloski RC	1.00
162	Shayne Wright/SP RC	3.00
163	Jay Caligiuri/SP RC	4.00
164	Greg Montalbano/SP RC	5.00
165	Rich Harden/SP RC	15.00
166	Rich Thompson/SP RC	3.00
167	Fred Bastardo/SP RC	3.00
168	Alejandro Giron/SP RC	3.00
169	Jesus Medrano/SP RC	3.00
170	Kevin Deaton/SP RC	4.00
171	Mike Rosamond RC	1.00
172	Jon Guzman/SP RC	3.00
173	Gerard Oakes/SP RC	4.00
174	Francisco Liriano/SP RC	30.00
175	Matt Allegra/SP RC	4.00
176	Mike Snyder/SP RC	4.00
177	James Shanks/SP RC	3.00
178	Anderson Hernandez/SP RC	4.00
179	Dan Trumble/SP RC	3.00
180	Luis DePaula/SP RC	4.00
181	Randall Shelley/SP RC	3.00
182	Richard Lane/SP RC	3.00
183	Antwon Rollins/SP RC	3.00
184	Ryan Bukvich/SP RC	4.00
185	Derrick Lewis/SP	3.00
186	Eric Miller/SP RC	3.00
187	Justin Schuda/SP RC	3.00
188	Brian West/SP RC	3.00
189	Brad Wilkerson/SP	.25
190	Neal Frendling/SP RC	3.00
191	Jeremy Hill/SP RC	3.00
192	James Barrett/SP RC	3.00
193	Brett Kay/SP RC	3.00
194	Ryan Mottl/SP RC	4.00
195	Brad Nelson/SP RC	3.00
196	Juan Gonzalez/SP	3.00
197	Curtis Legendre/SP RC	3.00
198	Ronald Acuna/SP RC	3.00
199	Chris Flinn/SP RC	3.00
200	Nick Alvarez/SP RC	3.00
201	Jason Ellison/SP RC	4.00
202	Blake McGinley/SP RC	3.00
203	Dan Phillips/SP RC	3.00
204	Demetrius Heath/SP RC	3.00
205	Eric Bruntlett/SP RC	3.00
206	Joe Jiannetti/SP RC	3.00
207	Mike Hill/SP RC	3.00
208	Ricardo Cordova/SP RC	3.00
209	Mark Hamilton/SP RC	3.00
210	David Mattox/SP RC	3.00
211	Jose Morban/SP RC	3.00
212	Scott Wiggins/SP RC	3.00
213	Steve Green	.25
214	Brian Rogers/SP	3.00
215	Kenny Baugh	.25
216	Anastacio Martinez/SP RC	3.00
217	Richard Lewis	.25
218	Tim Kalita/SP RC	3.00
219	Edwin Almonte/SP RC	3.00
220	Hee Seop Choi	.25
221	Ty Howington	.25
222	Victor Alvarez/SP RC	3.00
223	Morgan Ensberg	.25
224	Jeff Austin/SP RC	3.00
225	Clint Weibl/SP RC	4.00
226	Eric Cyr RC	1.00
227	Marlyn Tisdale/SP RC	3.00
228	John VanBenschoten	.25
229	Ruben Salazar	.25
230	Raul Chavez/SP RC	4.00
231	Brett Evert	.25
232	Joe Rogers/SP RC	3.00
233	Adam Wainwright	.50
234	Matt Herges	.25
235	Matt Childers/SP RC	4.00
236	Nick Neugebauer	.25

237	Carl Crawford	1.00
238	Seung Jun Song	.25
239	Randy Flores	.25
240	Jason Lane	.25
241	Chase Utley	4.00
242	Ben Howard/SP RC	3.00
243	Eric Glaser/SP RC	3.00
244	Josh Wilson RC	1.00
245	Jose Valverde/SP RC	4.00
246	Chris Smith	.25
247	Mark Prior	.50
248	Brian Mallette/SP RC	3.00
249	Chone Figgins/SP RC	8.00
250	Jimmy Alvarez/SP RC	3.00
251	Luis Terrero	.25
252	Josh Bonifay/SP RC	4.00
253	Garrett Guzman/SP RC	3.00
254	Jeff Verplancke/SP RC	3.00
255	Nate Espy/SP RC	4.00
256	Jeff Lincoln/SP RC	3.00
257	Ryan Snare/SP RC	4.00
258	Jose Ortiz	.25
259	Denny Bautista	.25
260	Willy Aybar	.25
261	Kelly Johnson	1.00
262	Shawn Fagan	.25
263	Yurendell DeCaster/SP RC	3.00
264	Mike Peeples/SP RC	3.00
265	Joel Guzman RC	3.00
266	Ryan Vogelsong	.25
267	Jorge Padilla/SP RC	3.00
268	Joe Jester/SP RC	3.00
269	Ryan Church/SP RC	6.00
270	Mitch Jones	.25
271	Travis Foley/SP	3.00
272	Bobby Crosby	.50
273	Adrian Gonzalez	.75
274	Ronnie Merrill	.25
275	Joel Pineiro	.25
276	John-Ford Griffin	.25
277	Brian Forystek/SP RC	3.00
278	Sean Douglass	.25
279	Manny Delcarmen/SP RC	4.00
280	Jim Kavourias/SP	3.00
281	Gabe Gross	.25
282	Bill Ortega	.25
283	Joey Hammond/SP RC	3.00
284	Brett Myers	.50
285	Carlos Pena	.50
286	Ezequiel Astacio/SP RC	3.00
287	Edwin Yan/SP RC	3.00
288	Chris Duffy/SP RC	4.00
289	Jason Kinchen	.25
290	Rafael Soriano	.25
291	Colin Young RC	.50
292	Eric Byrnes	.25
293	Chris Narveson/SP RC	5.00
294	John Rheinecker RC	.50
295	Mike Wilson/SP RC	4.00
296	Justin Sherrod/SP RC	4.00
297	Deivi Mendez	.25
298	Wily Mo Pena	.25
299	Brett Roneberg/SP RC	3.00
300	Trey Lunsford/SP RC	3.00
301	Christian Parker	.25
302	Brent Butler	.25
303	Aaron Heilman	.25
304	Wilkin Ruan	.25
305	Kenny Kelly	.25
306	Cody Ransom	.25
307	Koyie Hill/SP	3.00
308	Tony Fontana/SP RC	3.00
309	Mark Teixeira	2.00
310	Doug Sessions/SP RC	3.00
311	Josh Cisneros/SP RC	3.00
312	Carlos Brackley/SP RC	3.00
313	Tim Raines Jr.	.25
314	Ross Peeples/SP RC	4.00
315	Alexander Requena/SP RC	4.00
316	Chin-Hui Tsao	.25
317	Tony Alvarez	.25
318	Craig Kuzmic/SP RC	3.00
319	Peter Zamora/SP RC	3.00
320	Matt Parker/SP RC	3.00
321	Keith Ginter	.25
322	Gary Cates Jr./SP RC	3.00
323	Matt Belisle	.25
324	Ben Broussard	.25
325	Jake Mauer/auto RC	8.00
326	Dennis Tankersley	.25
327	Juan Silvestre	.25
327	Henry Pichardo/SP RC	3.00
328	Michael Floyd/SP RC	3.00
329	Clint Nageotte/SP RC	5.00
330	Raymond Cabrera/SP RC	4.00
331	Mauricio Lara/SP RC	3.00
332	Alejandro Cadena/SP RC	3.00
333	Jonny Gomes/SP RC	6.00
334	Jason Bulger/SP RC	4.00
335	Nate Teut	.25
336	David Gil/SP RC	3.00
337	Joel Crump/SP RC	3.00
338	Brandon Phillips	.50
339	Macay McBride	.50
340	Brandon Claussen	.50
341	Josh Phelps	.25
342	Freddie Money/SP RC	4.00
343	Clifford Bartosh/SP RC	3.00
344	Terrance Hill/SP RC	3.00
345	John Rodriguez/SP RC	4.00
346	Chris Latham/SP RC	3.00
347	Carlos Cabrera/SP RC	3.00
348	Jose Bautista/SP RC	3.00
349	Kevin Frederick/SP RC	3.00
350	Jerome Williams	.25
351	Napoleon Calzado/SP RC	3.00

352	Benito Baez/SP	3.00
353	Xavier Nady	.25
354	Jason Botts/SP RC	5.00
355	Steve Bechler/SP RC	4.00
356	Reed Johnson/SP RC	8.00
357	Mark Outlaw/SP RC	3.00
358	Jake Peavy	1.00
359	Josh Shaffer/SP RC	3.00
360	Dan Wright/SP	3.00
361	Ryan Gripp/SP RC	3.00
362	Nelson Castro/SP RC	3.00
363	Jason Bay/SP RC	15.00
364	Franklin German/SP RC	3.00
365	Corwin Malone/SP	3.00
366	Kelly Ramos/SP RC	3.00
367	John Ennis/SP RC	3.00
368	George Perez/SP	3.00
369	Rene Reyes/SP RC	3.00
370	Rolando Viera/SP RC	3.00
371	Earl Snyder/SP RC	4.00
372	Kyle Kane/SP	3.00
373	Mario Ramos/SP	3.00
374	Tyler Yates/SP	3.00
375	Jason Young/SP RC	5.00
376	Chris Bootcheck/SP RC	5.00
377	Jesus Cota/SP	3.00
378	Corky Miller/SP	3.00
379	Matt Erickson/SP RC	3.00
380	Justin Huber/SP RC	5.00
381	Felix Escalona/SP RC	3.00
382	Kevin Cash/SP RC	3.00
383	J.J. Putz/SP RC	4.00
384	Chris Snelling RC	8.00
385	David Wright RC	200.00
386	Brian Wolfe RC	10.00
387	Justin Reid RC	10.00
389	Ryan Raburn RC	10.00
390	Josh Barfield RC	10.00
391	Joe Mauer RC	180.00
392	Bobby Jenks RC	20.00
393	Rob Henkel RC	10.00
394	Jimmy Gobble RC	10.00
395	Jesse Foppert RC	10.00
396	Gavin Floyd RC	20.00
397	Nate Field RC	10.00
398	Ryan Doumit RC	25.00
399	Ron Calloway RC	10.00
400	Taylor Buchholz RC	10.00
401	Adam Roller RC	10.00
402	Cole Barthel	10.00
403	Kazuhisa Ishii/SP RC	5.00
404	So Taguchi/SP RC	4.00
405	Chris Baker RC	10.00

Refractors

ARAMIS RAMIREZ
3B-PITTSBURGH PIRATES

Star Refractors (1-220):	2-3X
SP Refractors:	.5-1.5X
Production 500	
X-Fractors (1-220):	3-5X
SP X-Fractors:	.75-2X
Production 250:	
Gold Refractors (1-220):	8-15X
SP Gold Refractors:	2-4X
Production 50	
Refractor Autos.	
(384-402,405)	.75-1.5X
Production 500	
X-Fractor Autos.:	.75-2X
Production 250	
Gold Autographs:	2-4X
Production 50	

Uncirculated

Cards:	1-30X
Production 350	
Autos. 10 cards of each player.	
No Pricing	

Ishii & Taguchi Autographs

	NM/M
Refractors:	.75-1.5X
Production 100	
X-Fractors:	2-4X
Production 50	
Golds: Production 10	
403	Kazuhisa Ishii	50.00
404	So Taguchi	25.00

Rookie Reprints

		NM/M
Complete Set (20):		25.00
Common Player:		1.00
Inserted 1:6		
Refractors:		1.5-2X
Inserted 1:18		
JB	Jeff Bagwell	1.50
BC	Bartolo Colon	1.00
CD	Carlos Delgado	1.00

JG	Juan Gonzalez	1.50
LG	Luis Gonzalez	1.00
KG	Ken Griffey Jr.	3.00
VG	Vladimir Guerrero	2.00
DJ	Derek Jeter	5.00
AJ	Andruw Jones	1.50
CJ	Chipper Jones	2.50
JK	Jason Kendall	1.00
MP	Mike Piazza	3.00
JP	Jorge Posada	1.00
IR	Ivan Rodriguez	1.00
SR	Scott Rolen	1.00
GS	Gary Sheffield	1.00
MS	Mike Sweeney	1.00
FT	Frank Thomas	1.50
LW	Larry Walker	1.00
BW	Bernie Williams	1.00

2002 Bowman Draft Picks & Prospects

NM/M
Complete Set (165): 35.00
Common Player: .15
Common RC: .25
Pack: (4 + 2 Chrome) 10.00
Box (24): 200.00

BDP1	Clint Everts RC	.50
BDP2	Fred Lewis RC	.75
BDP3	Jonathan Broxton RC	1.00
BDP4	Jason Anderson RC	.25
BDP5	Mike Eusebio RC	.25
BDP6	Zack Greinke RC	4.00
BDP7	Joe Blanton RC	1.00
BDP8	Sergio Santos RC	.50
BDP9	Jason Cooper RC	.50
BDP10	Delwyn Young RC	.50
BDP11	Jeremy Hermida RC	.75
BDP12	Dan Ortmeyer RC	.40
BDP13	Kevin Jepsen RC	.50
BDP14	Russ Adams RC	.50
BDP15	Mike Nixon RC	.40
BDP16	Nick Swisher RC	1.50
BDP17	Cole Hamels RC	8.00
BDP18	Brian Dopirak RC	.50
BDP19	James Loney RC	1.50
BDP20	Denard Span RC	2.00
BDP21	Billy Petrick RC	.25
BDP22	Jared Doyle RC	.25
BDP23	Jeff Francoeur RC	2.00
BDP24	Nick Bourgeois RC	.25
BDP25	Matt Cain RC	5.00
BDP26	John McCurdy RC	.40
BDP27	Mark Kiger RC	.15
BDP28	Bill Murphy RC	.40
BDP29	Matt Craig RC	.25
BDP30	Mike Megrew RC	.50
BDP31	Ben Crockett RC	.50
BDP32	Luke Hagerty RC	.50
BDP33	Matt Whitney RC	.50
BDP34	Dan Meyer RC	.50
BDP35	Jeremy Brown RC	.50
BDP36	Doug Johnson RC	.25
BDP37	Steve Obenchain RC	.25
BDP38	Matt Clanton RC	.40
BDP39	Mark Teahen RC	.75
BDP40	Thomas Carrow RC	.25
BDP41	Micah Schilling RC	.25
BDP42	Jason Pridie RC	.25
BDP43	Jason Pridie RC	.50
BDP44	Joey Votto RC	8.00
BDP45	Taber Lee RC	.50
BDP46	Adam Peterson RC	.25
BDP47	Adam Donachie RC	.40
BDP48	Josh Murray RC	.25
BDP49	Brent Clevlen RC	.50
BDP50	Chad Pleiness RC	.40
BDP51	Zach Hammes RC	.50
BDP52	Chris Snyder RC	.50
BDP53	Chris Smith	.25
BDP54	Justin Maureau RC	.25
BDP55	David Bush RC	.50
BDP56	Tim Gilhooly RC	.25
BDP57	Blair Barbier RC	.25
BDP58	Zach Segovia RC	.50
BDP59	Jeremy Reed RC	.50
BDP60	Matt Pender RC	.25
BDP61	Eric Thomas RC	.25
BDP62	Justin Jones RC	.50
BDP63	Brian Slocum RC	.40
BDP64	Larry Broadway RC	.50
BDP65	Bo Flowers RC	.25
BDP66	Scott White RC	.50
BDP67	Steve Stanley RC	.50
BDP68	Alex Merricks RC	.25
BDP69	Josh Womack RC	.40
BDP70	Dave Jensen RC	.25
BDP71	Curtis Granderson RC	5.00
BDP72	Pat Osborn RC	.40
BDP73	Nic Carter RC	.25
BDP74	Mitch Talbot RC	.50
BDP75	Don Murphy RC	.25
BDP76	Val Majewski RC	.50
BDP77	Javy Rodriguez RC	.25
BDP78	Fernando Pacheco RC	.40
BDP79	Steve Russell RC	.25
BDP80	Jon Slack RC	.25
BDP81	John Baker RC	.25
BDP82	Aaron Coonrod RC	.25
BDP83	Josh Johnson RC	2.50
BDP84	Jake Blalock RC	.50
BDP85	Alex Hart RC	.50
BDP86	Wes Bankston RC	.50
BDP87	Josh Rupe RC	.40
BDP88	Dan Cevette RC	.50
BDP89	Kiel Fisher RC	.50
BDP90	Alan Rick RC	.25
BDP91	Charlie Morton RC	.50
BDP92	Chad Spann RC	.50
BDP93	Kyle Boyer RC	.25
BDP94	Bob Malek RC	.25
BDP95	Ryan Rodriguez RC	.25
BDP96	Jordan Renz RC	.25
BDP97	Randy Frye RC	.25
BDP98	Rich Hill RC	.50
BDP99	B.J. Upton RC	3.00
BDP100	Dan Christensen RC	.50
BDP101	Casey Kotchman RC	.50
BDP102	Eric Good RC	.25
BDP103	Mike Fontenot RC	.75
BDP104	John Webb RC	.25
BDP105	Jason Dubois RC	.75
BDP106	Ryan Kibler RC	.25
BDP107	Jhonny Peralta RC	1.50
BDP108	Kirk Saarloos RC	.75
BDP109	Rhett Parrott RC	.25
BDP110	Jason Grove RC	.25
BDP111	Colt Griffin	.50
BDP112	Dallas McPherson RC	.50
BDP113	Oliver Perez RC	.75
BDP114	Marshall McDougall RC	.25
BDP115	Mike Wood RC	.40
BDP116	Scott Hairston	.75
BDP117	Jason Simontacchi RC	.50
BDP118	Taggert Bozied RC	.50
BDP119	Shelley Duncan RC	.75
BDP120	Dontrelle Willis RC	1.00
BDP121	Sean Burnett	.15
BDP122	Aaron Cook RC	.75
BPD123	Brett Evert	.15
BDP124	Jimmy Journell	.15
BDP125	Brett Myers	.15
BDP126	Brad Baker	.15
BDP127	Billy Traber	.50
BDP128	Adam Wainwright	.15
BDP129	Jason Young	.15
BDP130	John Buck	.15
BDP131	Kevin Cash RC	.25
BDP132	Jason Stokes RC	.50
BDP133	Drew Henson	.25
BDP134	Chad Tracy RC	.50
BDP135	Orlando Hudson	.15
BDP136	Brandon Phillips	.15
BDP137	Joe Borchard	.15
BDP138	Marlon Byrd	.15
BDP139	Carl Crawford	.25
BDP140	Michael Restovich	.15
BDP141	Corey Hart RC	1.50
BDP142	Edwin Almonte	.15
BDP143	Francis Beltran RC	.15
BDP144	Jorge De La Rosa RC	.75
BDP145	Gerardo Garcia RC	.25
BDP146	Franklyn German RC	.25
BDP147	Francisco Liriano	4.00
BDP148	Francisco Rodriguez	.50
BDP149	Ricardo Rodriguez	.15
BDP150	Seung Jun Song	.15
BDP151	John Stephens	.15
BDP152	Justin Huber RC	.50
BDP153	Victor Martinez	.50
BDP154	Hee Seop Choi	.15
BDP155	Justin Morneau	.50
BDP156	Miguel Cabrera	.75
BDP157	Victor Diaz RC	.50
BDP158	Jose Reyes	.50
BDP159	Omar Infante RC	.25
BDP160	Angel Berroa	.15
BDP161	Tony Alvarez	.15
BDP162	Shin-Soo Choo RC	1.50
BDP163	Wily Mo Pena	.15
BDP164	Andres Torres	.15
BDP165	Jose Lopez RC	2.00

Gold
Rookies: .75-1.5X
Inserted 1:1

Fabric of Future

NM/M
Common Player: 4.00
Inserted 1:55

EA	Edwin Almonte	4.00
TA	Tony Alvarez	4.00
FB	Francis Beltran	4.00
AB	Angel Berroa	4.00
SB	Sean Burnett	4.00
KC	Kevin Cash	4.00
HC	Hee Seop Choi	8.00
SC	Shin-Soo Choo	8.00
CC	Carl Crawford	8.00
JR	Jorge de la Rosa	4.00
VD	Victor Diaz	4.00
GG	Gerardo Garcia	4.00
FG	Franklyn German	4.00
CH	Corey Hart	5.00
DH	Drew Henson	5.00
JH	Justin Huber	4.00
JK	Josh Karp	4.00
FL	Francisco Liriano	10.00
JL	Jose Lopez	8.00
BM	Brett Meyers	4.00
WP	Wily Mo Pena	4.00
MR	Michael Restovich	4.00
JS	John Stephens	4.00
JS	Jason Stokes	4.00
AT	Andres Torres	4.00
BT	Billy Traber	4.00
CT	Chad Tracy	8.00
AW	Adam Wainwright	10.00

Freshman Fiber

NM/M
Common Player: 4.00
Bat inserted 1:605
Jersey 1:45

BA	Brent Abernathy	4.00
DB	Dewon Brazelton	4.00
MB	Marlon Byrd/Bat	4.00
TH	Toby Hall	4.00
JH	Josh Hamilton	10.00
AH	Aubrey Huff	6.00
AK	Austin Kearns/Bat	4.00
JK	Joe Kennedy	4.00
JS	Jared Sandberg	4.00
JWS	Jason Standridge	4.00
MT	Mark Teixeira/Bat	10.00
JV	John Van Benschoten	4.00

Signs of the Future

NM/M
Common Autograph: 5.00

EB	Erik Bedard	12.00
LB	Larry Bigbie	5.00
TB	Taylor Buchholz	5.00
DD	Daniel Denham	5.00
ME	Morgan Ensberg	8.00
MF	Mike Fontenot	8.00
KH	Kris Honel	5.00
BI	Brandon Inge	10.00
NJ	Nic Jackson	5.00
MJ	Mitch Jones	5.00
BK	Bob Keppel	5.00
TL	Todd Linden	8.00
JM	Jake Mauer	5.00
JEM	Justin Morneau	25.00
LN	Lance Niekro	5.00
CP	Christian Parra	5.00
BP	Brandon Phillips	15.00
JR	Juan Rivera	5.00
BS	Bud Smith	5.00
AT	Chad Tracy	10.00
JW	Jerome Williams	5.00

2002 Bowman Chrome Draft Picks & Prospects

NM/M
Complete Set (175): 275.00
Common Player: .25
Common RC: .50
1-165 Two Per Pack
Common Auto.(166-175): 10.00
Auto's Inserted 1:45

BDP1	Clint Everts RC	1.00
BDP2	Fred Lewis RC	.50
BDP3	Jonathan Broxton RC	2.00
BDP4	Jason Anderson RC	.50
BDP5	Mike Eusebio RC	.50
BDP6	Zack Greinke RC	12.00
BDP7	Joe Blanton RC	2.50
BDP8	Sergio Santos RC	.75
BDP9	Jason Cooper RC	.75
BDP10	Delwyn Young RC	1.00
BDP11	Jeremy Hermida RC	2.00
BDP12	Dan Ortmeyer RC	1.00
BDP13	Kevin Jepsen RC	1.00
BDP14	Russ Adams RC	1.00
BDP15	Mike Nixon RC	.50
BDP16	Nick Swisher RC	3.00
BDP17	Cole Hamels RC	25.00
BDP18	Brian Dopirak RC	2.00
BDP19	James Loney RC	4.00
BDP20	Denard Span RC	4.00
BDP21	Billy Petrick RC	.50
BDP22	Jared Doyle RC	.50
BDP23	Jeff Francoeur RC	8.00
BDP24	Nick Bourgeois RC	.50
BDP25	Matt Cain RC	15.00
BDP26	John McCurdy RC	1.00
BDP27	Mark Kiger RC	.50
BDP28	Bill Murphy RC	1.00
BDP29	Matt Craig RC	1.00
BDP30	Mike Megrew RC	1.00
BDP31	Ben Crockett RC	.50
BDP32	Luke Hagerty RC	1.00
BDP33	Matt Whitney RC	1.00
BDP34	Dan Meyer RC	1.50
BDP35	Jeremy Brown RC	.50
BDP36	Doug Johnson RC	.50
BDP37	Steve Obenchain RC	.50
BDP38	Matt Clanton RC	1.00
BDP39	Mark Teahen RC	1.50
BDP40	Thomas Carrow RC	.50
BDP41	Micah Schilling RC	1.00
BDP42	Blair Johnson RC	.50
BDP43	Jason Pridie RC	.50
BDP44	Joey Votto RC	20.00
BDP45	Taber Lee RC	.50
BDP46	Adam Peterson RC	.50
BDP47	Adam Donachie RC	1.00
BDP48	Josh Murray RC	.50
BDP49	Brent Clevlen RC	1.00
BDP50	Chad Pleiness RC	1.00
BDP51	Zach Hammes RC	1.00
BDP52	Chris Snyder RC	1.50
BDP53	Chris Smith	.50
BDP54	Justin Maureau RC	.50
BDP55	David Bush RC	1.00
BDP56	Tim Gilhooly RC	.50
BDP57	Blair Barbier RC	.50
BDP58	Zach Segovia RC	1.00
BDP59	Jeremy Reed RC	1.00
BDP60	Matt Pender RC	.50
BDP61	Eric Thomas RC	.50
BDP62	Justin Jones RC	1.00
BDP63	Brian Slocum RC	1.00
BDP64	Larry Broadway RC	1.50
BDP65	Bo Flowers RC	1.00
BDP66	Scott White RC	1.00
BDP67	Steve Stanley RC	.50
BDP68	Alex Merricks RC	.50
BDP69	Josh Womack RC	.50
BDP70	Dave Jensen RC	.50
BDP71	Curtis Granderson RC	15.00
BDP72	Pat Osborn RC	.75
BDP73	Nic Carter RC	.50
BDP74	Mitch Talbot RC	.50
BDP75	Don Murphy RC	.50
BDP76	Val Majewski RC	1.00
BDP77	Javy Rodriguez RC	.50
BDP78	Fernando Pacheco RC	.75
BDP79	Steve Russell RC	.50
BDP80	Jon Slack RC	.50
BDP81	John Baker RC	.50
BDP82	Aaron Coonrod RC	.50
BDP83	Josh Johnson RC	6.00
BDP84	Jake Blalock RC	1.00
BDP85	Alex Hart RC	1.00
BDP86	Wes Bankston RC	1.00
BDP87	Josh Rupe RC	1.00
BDP88	Dan Cevette RC	1.00
BDP89	Kiel Fisher RC	1.00
BDP90	Alan Rick RC	.50
BDP91	Charlie Morton RC	1.00
BDP92	Chad Spann RC	1.00
BDP93	Kyle Boyer RC	.50
BDP94	Bob Malek RC	.50
BDP95	Ryan Rodriguez RC	.50
BDP96	Jordan Renz RC	.50
BDP97	Randy Frye RC	.50
BDP98	Rich Hill RC	.75
BDP99	B.J. Upton RC	6.00
BDP100	Dan Christensen RC	1.00
BDP101	Casey Kotchman RC	1.50
BDP102	Eric Good RC	1.00
BDP103	Mike Fontenot RC	1.00
BDP104	John Webb RC	.50
BDP105	Jason Dubois RC	1.00
BDP106	Ryan Kibler RC	.50
BDP107	Jhonny Peralta RC	3.00
BDP108	Kirk Saarloos RC	1.50
BDP109	Rhett Parrott RC	.50
BDP110	Jason Grove RC	.50
BDP111	Colt Griffin RC	.50
BDP112	Dallas McPherson RC	.75
BDP113	Oliver Perez RC	1.50
BDP114	Marshall McDougall RC	.50
BDP115	Mike Wood RC	1.00
BDP116	Scott Hairston	.75
BDP117	Jason Simontacchi RC	1.00
BDP118	Taggert Bozied RC	.75
BDP119	Shelley Duncan RC	.75
BDP120	Dontrelle Willis RC	1.50
BDP121	Sean Burnett	.25
BDP122	Aaron Cook RC	1.50
BPD123	Brett Evert	.25
BDP124	Jimmy Journell	.25
BDP125	Brett Myers	.25
BDP126	Brad Baker	.25
BDP127	Billy Traber	.50
BDP128	Adam Wainwright	.50
BDP129	Jason Young	.50
BDP130	John Buck	.25
BDP131	Kevin Cash	.25
BDP132	Jason Stokes RC	.75
BDP133	Drew Henson	.50
BDP134	Chad Tracy RC	1.00
BDP135	Orlando Hudson	.50
BDP136	Brandon Phillips	.50
BDP137	Joe Borchard	.25
BDP138	Marlon Byrd	.25
BDP139	Carl Crawford	.50
BDP140	Michael Restovich	.25
BDP141	Corey Hart RC	4.00
BDP142	Edwin Almonte	.25
BDP143	Francis Beltran RC	1.00
BDP144	Jorge De La Rosa RC	1.50
BDP145	Gerardo Garcia RC	.50
BDP146	Franklyn German RC	.25
BDP147	Francisco Liriano	10.00
BDP148	Francisco Rodriguez	.50
BDP149	Ricardo Rodriguez	.50
BDP150	Seung Jun Song	.25
BDP151	John Stephens	.25
BDP152	Justin Huber	1.00
BDP153	Victor Martinez	.50
BDP154	Hee Seop Choi	.25
BDP155	Justin Morneau	.75
BDP156	Miguel Cabrera	2.00
BDP157	Victor Diaz RC	1.00
BDP158	Jose Reyes	1.00
BDP159	Omar Infante RC	.50
BDP160	Angel Berroa	.50
BDP161	Tony Alvarez	.25
BDP162	Shin-Soo Choo RC	5.00
BDP163	Wily Mo Pena	.50
BDP164	Andres Torres	.25
BDP165	Jose Lopez RC	5.00
BDP166	Scott Moore/Auto. RC	10.00
BDP167	Chris Gruler/Auto.	10.00
BDP168	Joe Saunders/ Auto. RC	15.00
BDP169	Jeff Francis/Auto.	10.00
BDP170	Royce Ring/Auto.	10.00
BDP171	Greg Miller/Auto.	10.00
BDP172	Brandon Weeden/ Auto. RC	10.00
BDP173	Drew Meyer/Auto. RC	10.00
BDP174	Khalil Greene/ Auto. RC	15.00
BDP175	Mark Schramek/ Auto. RC	10.00

Refractor
Cards 1-165: 2-4X
Rookies 1-175: 2-3X
1-165 Production 300 Sets
166-175 Inserted 1:154

Gold Refractor
Cards 1-165: 8-15X
Rookies 1-165: 5-10X
1-165 Production 50 Sets
166-175 No Pricing

X-Fractor
Cards 1-165: 2-5X
Rookies 1-165: 3-4X
Rookies 166-175: .75-1.5X
1-165 Production 150 Sets
166-175 Inserted 1:309

2002 Bowman Heritage

NM/M
Complete Set (440): 190.00
Common Player: .25
Common SP: 1.00
Inserted 1:2
Black Box Variations: 2-3X
Inserted 1:2
Pack (10): 3.00
Box (24): 60.00

1	Brent Abernathy	.25
2	Jermaine Dye	.25
3	James Shanks RC	.40
4	Chris Flinn RC	.40
5	Mike Peeples/SP RC	1.50
6	Gary Sheffield	.50
7	Livan Hernandez/SP	1.00
8	Jeff Austin RC	.40
9	Jeremy Giambi	.25
10	Adam Roller RC	.25
11	Sandy Alomar Jr/SP	1.00
12	Matt Williams/SP	1.00
13	Hee Seop Choi	.25
14	Jose Offerman	.25
15	Robin Ventura	.50
16	Craig Biggio	.50
17	David Wells	.40
18	Rob Henkel RC	.40
19	Edgar Martinez	.25
20	Matt Morris/SP	2.00
21	Jose Valentin	.25
22	Barry Bonds	2.50
23	Justin Schuda RC	.50
24	Josh Phelps	.50
25	John Rodriguez RC	.50
26	Angel Pagan RC	1.50
27	Aramis Ramirez	.50
28	Jack Wilson	.50
29	Roger Clemens	2.00
30	Kazuhisa Ishii RC	.75
31	Carlos Beltran	.75
32	Drew Henson/SP	1.50
33	Kevin Young/SP	.50
34	Juan Cruz	.25
35	Curtis Legendre RC	.40
36	Jose Morban RC	.50
37	Ricardo Cordova/SP RC	1.50
38	Adam Everett	.25
39	Mark Prior	.40
40	Jose Bautista RC	.75
41	Travis Foley	.25
42	Kerry Wood	.50
43	B.J. Surhoff	.25
44	Moises Alou	.40
45	Joey Hammond RC	.50
46	Eric Bruntlett RC	.50
47	Carlos Guillen	.50
48	Joe Crede	.40
49	Dan Phillips RC	.50
50	Jason LaRue	.25
51	Javy Lopez	.50
52	Larry Bigbie/SP	1.00
53	Chris Baker RC	.75
54	Marty Cordova	.25
55	C.C. Sabathia	.50
56	Mike Piazza	1.00
57	Brian Giles	.50
58	Mike Bordick/SP	1.00
59	Tyler Houston/SP	1.00
60	Gabe Kapler	.25
61	Ben Broussard	.25
62	Steve Finley/SP	1.50
63	Koyie Hill	.25
64	Jeff D'Amico	.25
65	Edwin Almonte	1.00
66a	Pedro J. Martinez	1.00
66b	Nomar Garciaparra (Same front and back as his #289 card.)	
67	Travis Fryman/SP	1.50
68	Brady Clark	.25
69	Reed Johnson/SP RC	.50
70	Mark Grace/SP	4.00
71	Tony Batista/SP	1.00
72	Roy Oswalt	.50
73	Pat Burrell	.50
74	Dennis Tankersley	.25
75	Ramon Ortiz	.25
76	Neal Frendling/SP RC	1.50
77	Omar Vizquel/SP	2.00
78	Hideo Nomo	.50
79	Orlando Hernandez/SP	1.50
80	Andy Pettitte	.50
81	Cole Barthel	.25
82	Bret Boone	.25
83	Alfonso Soriano	.50
84	Brandon Duckworth	.25
85	Ben Grieve	.25
86	Mike Rosamond/SP RC	1.50
87	Luke Prokopec	.25
88	Chone Figgins RC	2.00
89	Rick Ankiel/SP	2.00
90	David Eckstein	.25
91	Corey Koskie	.25
92	David Justice	.25
93	Jimmy Alvarez RC	.40
94	Jason Schmidt	.40
95	Reggie Sanders	.25
96	Victor Alvarez RC	.40
97	Brett Roneberg RC	.40
98	D'Angelo Jimenez	.25
99	Hank Blalock	.25
100	Juan Rivera	.25
101	Mark Buehrle/SP	1.50
102	Juan Uribe	.25
103	Royce Clayton/SP	1.00
104	Brett Kay RC	.40
105	John Olerud	.25
106	Richie Sexson	.25
107	Chipper Jones	1.00
108	Adam Dunn	.50
109	Tim Salmon/SP	1.50
110	Eric Karros	.25
111	Jose Vidro	.25
112	Jerry Hairston Jr.	.25
113	Anastacio Martinez RC	.50
114	Robert Fick/SP	1.50
115	Randy Johnson	

#	Player	Price
116	Trot Nixon/SP	2.00
117	Nick Bierbrodt/SP	1.00
118	Jim Edmonds	.40
119	Rafael Palmeiro	.50
120	Jose Macias	.25
121	Josh Beckett	.50
122	Sean Douglass	.25
123	Jeff Kent	.40
124	Tim Redding	.25
125	Xavier Nady	.25
126	Carl Everett	.25
127	Joe Randa	.25
128	Luke Hudson/SP	1.00
129	Eric Miller RC	.40
130	Melvin Mora	.25
131	Adrian Gonzalez	.25
132	Larry Walker/SP	1.50
133	Nic Jackson/SP RC	1.50
134	Mike Lowell/SP	1.50
135	Jim Thome	.50
136	Eric Milton	.25
137	Rich Thompson/SP RC	1.50
138	Placido Polanco/SP	1.00
139	Juan Pierre	.25
140	David Segui	.25
141	Chuck Finley	.25
142	Felipe Lopez	.25
143	Toby Hall	.25
144	Fred Bastardo RC	.25
145	Troy Glaus	.50
146	Todd Helton	.75
147	Ruben Gotay/SP RC	1.50
148	Darin Erstad	.40
149	Ryan Gripp/SP RC	1.50
150	Orlando Cabrera	.25
151	Jason Young RC	.50
152	Sterling Hitchcock/SP	1.00
153	Miguel Tejada	.75
154	Al Leiter	.25
155	Taylor Buchholz RC	.40
156	Juan Gonzalez	.40
157	Damion Easley	.25
158	Jimmy Gobble RC	1.00
159	Dennis Ulacia/SP	1.00
160	Shane Reynolds/SP	1.00
161	Javier Colina	.25
162	Frank Thomas	1.00
163	Chuck Knoblauch	.25
164	Sean Burroughs	.25
165	Greg Maddux	1.50
166	Jason Ellison RC	.50
167	Tony Womack	.25
168	Randall Shelley/SP RC	1.50
169	Jason Marquis	.25
170	Brian Jordan	.25
171	Darryl Kile	.25
172	Barry Zito	.40
173	Matt Allegra/SP RC	1.50
174	Ralph Santana/SP RC	1.50
175	Carlos Lee	.40
176	Richard Hidalgo/SP	1.00
177	Kevin Deaton RC	.50
178	Juan Encarnacion	.25
179	Mark Quinn	.25
180	Rafael Furcal	.40
181	Garret Anderson	.50
182	David Wright	15.00
183	Jose Reyes	.50
184	Mario Ramos/SP	1.00
185	J.D. Drew	.50
186	Juan Gonzalez	.25
187	Nick Neugebauer	.25
188	Alejandro Giron RC	.50
189	John Burkett	.25
190	Ben Sheets	.50
191	Vinny Castilla/SP	1.00
192	Cory Lidle	.25
193	Fernando Vina	.25
194	Russell Branyan/SP	1.00
195	Ben Davis	.25
196	Angel Berroa	.25
197	Alex Gonzalez	.25
198	Jared Sandberg	.25
199	Travis Lee/SP	1.00
200	Luis DePaula/SP RC	1.50
201	Ramon Hernandez/SP	1.00
202	Brandon Inge	.25
203	Aubrey Huff	.25
204	Mike Rivera	.25
205	Brad Nelson/SP	.50
206	Colt Griffin/SP	2.00
207	Joel Pineiro	.25
208	Adam Pettyjohn	.25
209	Mark Redman	.25
210	Roberto Alomar/SP	3.00
211	Denny Neagle	.25
212	Adam Kennedy	.25
213	Jason Arnold/SP	2.00
214	Jamie Moyer	.25
215	Aaron Boone	.25
216	Doug Glanville	.25
217	Nick Johnson/SP	1.00
218	Mike Cameron/SP	1.50
219	Tim Wakefield/SP	1.00
220	Todd Stottlemyre/SP	1.00
221	Mo Vaughn	.25
222	Vladimir Guerrero	.25
223	Bill Ortega	.25
224	Kevin Brown	.25
225	Peter Bergeron/SP	1.00
226	Shannon Stewart/SP	1.50
227	Eric Chavez	.50
228	Clint Weibl RC	.40
229	Todd Hollandsworth/SP	1.00
230	Jeff Bagwell	.50
231	Chad Qualls RC	.40
232	Ben Howard RC	1.00
233	Rondell White/SP	1.50

#	Player	Price
234	Fred McGriff	.20
235	Steve Cox/SP	1.00
236	Chris Tritle RC	1.50
237	Eric Valent	.25
238	Joe Mauer RC	8.00
239	Shawn Green	.40
240	Jimmy Rollins	.75
241	Edgar Renteria	.25
242	Edwin Yan RC	.40
243	Noochie Varner RC	.40
244	Kris Benson/SP	1.50
245	Mike Hampton	.25
246	So Taguchi/SP	1.00
247	Sammy Sosa	.75
248	Terrence Long	.25
249	Jason Bay RC	3.00
250	Kevin Millar/SP	1.00
251	Albert Pujols	2.50
252	Chris Latham RC	.40
253	Eric Byrnes	.25
254	Napoleon Calzado/SP RC	1.00
255	Bobby Higginson	.25
256	Ben Molina	.25
257	Torii Hunter/SP	3.00
258	Jason Giambi	.50
259	Bartolo Colon	.25
260	Benito Baez	.25
261	Ichiro Suzuki	2.00
262	Mike Sweeney	.25
263	Brian West RC	.40
264	Brad Penny	.25
265	Kevin Millwood/SP	2.00
266	Orlando Hudson	.25
267	Doug Mientkiewicz	.25
268	Luis Gonzalez/SP	1.50
269	Jay Caligiuri RC	.40
270	Nate Cornejo/SP	1.00
271	Lee Stevens	.25
272	Eric Hinske	.25
273	Antwon Rollins RC	.50
274	Bobby Jenks RC	1.00
275	Joe Mays	.25
276	Josh Shaffer RC	.40
277	Jonny Gomes RC	1.50
278	Bernie Williams	.50
279	Ed Rogers	.25
280	Carlos Delgado	.50
281	Raul Mondesi/SP	1.50
282	Jose Ortiz	.25
283	Cesar Izturis	.25
284	Ryan Dempster/SP	1.00
285	Brian Daubach	.25
286	Hansel Izquierdo RC	.40
287	Mike Lieberthal/SP	1.00
288	Marcus Thames	.25
289	Nomar Garciaparra	.50
290	Brad Fullmer	.25
291	Tino Martinez	.25
292	James Barrett RC	.40
293	Jacque Jones	.25
294	Nick Alvarez/SP RC	1.50
295	Jason Grove/SP RC	1.50
296	Mike Wilson/SP RC	1.50
297	J.T. Snow	.25
298	Cliff Floyd	.25
299	Todd Hundley/SP	1.00
300	Tony Clark/SP	1.00
301	Demetrius Heath RC	.40
302	Morgan Ensberg	.25
303	Cristian Guzman	.25
304	Frank Catalanotto	.25
305	Jeff Weaver	.25
306	Tim Hudson	.50
307	Scott Wiggins/SP RC	1.50
308	Shea Hillenbrand/SP	2.00
309	Todd Walker/SP	1.00
310	Tsuyoshi Shinjo	.25
311	Adrian Beltre	.25
312	Craig Kuzmic RC	.40
313	Paul Konerko	.40
314	Scott Hairston	1.50
315	Chan Ho Park	.25
316	Jorge Posada	.40
317	Chris Snelling RC	.75
318	Keith Foulke	.25
319	John Smoltz	.50
320	Ryan Church/SP RC	2.00
321	Mike Mussina	.75
322	Tony Armas Jr/SP	1.00
323	Craig Counsell	.25
324	Marcus Giles	.25
325	Greg Vaughn	.25
326	Curt Schilling	.75
327	Jeromy Burnitz	.25
328	Eric Byrnes	.25
329	Johnny Damon	.75
330	Michael Floyd/SP RC	1.50
331	Edgardo Alfonzo	.25
332	Jeremy Hill RC	.40
333	Josh Bonifay RC	.25
334	Byung-Hyun Kim	.25
335	Keith Ginter	.25
336	Ronald Acuna/SP RC	1.50
337	Mike Hill/SP RC	.40
338	Sean Casey	.25
339	Matt Anderson/SP	1.00
340	Dan Wright	.25
341	Ben Petrick	.25
342	Mike Sirotka/SP	1.00
343	Alex Rodriguez	2.50
344	Einar Diaz	.25
345	Derek Jeter	2.50
346	Jeff Conine	.25
347	Ray Durham/SP	1.00
348	Wilson Betemit/SP	1.00
349	Jeffrey Hammonds	.25
350	Dan Trumble/SP	.40
351	Phil Nevin/SP	1.50

#	Player	Price
352	A.J. Burnett	.25
353	Bill Mueller	.25
354	Charles Nagy	.25
355	Rusty Greer/SP	1.00
356	Jason Botts RC	.25
357	Magglio Ordonez	.50
358	Kevin Appier	.25
359	Brad Radke	.25
360	Chris George	.25
361	Chris Piersoll RC	.25
362	Ivan Rodriguez	.50
363	Jim Kavourias	.25
364	Rick Helling/SP	1.00
365	Dean Palmer	.25
366	Rich Aurilia/SP	1.00
367	Ryan Vogelsong	.25
368	Matt Lawton	.25
369	Wade Miller	.25
370	Dustin Hermanson	.25
371	Craig Wilson	.25
372	Todd Zeile/SP	1.00
373	Jon Guzman RC	.40
374	Ellis Burks	.25
375	Robert Cosby/SP RC	1.50
376	Jason Kendall	.25
377	Scott Rolen/SP	4.00
378	Andruw Jones	.50
379	Greg Sain RC	.40
380	Paul LoDuca	.25
381	Scotty Layfield RC	.40
382	Drew Henson	.50
383	Garrett Guzman RC	.40
384	Jack Cust	.25
385	Shayne Wright RC	.40
386	Derrek Lee	.75
387	Jesus Medrano RC	.40
388	Javier Vazquez	.25
389	Preston Wilson/SP	1.50
390	Gavin Floyd	1.50
391	Sidney Ponson/SP	1.00
392	Jose Hernandez	.25
393	Scott Erickson/SP	1.00
394	Jose Valverde RC	.40
395	Mark Hamilton/SP RC	1.50
396	Brad Cresse	.25
397	Danny Bautista	.25
398	Ray Lankford/SP	1.00
399	Miguel Batista/SP	1.00
400	Brent Butler	.25
401	Manny Delcarmen/SP RC	1.50
402	Kyle Farnsworth/SP	1.00
403	Freddy Garcia	.25
404	Joe Jiannetti RC	.40
405	Josh Barfield	.40
406	Corey Patterson	.25
407	Josh Towers	.25
408	Carlos Pena	.25
409	Jeff Cirillo	.25
410	Jon Lieber	.25
411	Woody Williams/SP	1.00
412	Richard Lane/SP RC	1.50
413	Alex Gonzalez	.25
414	Wilkin Ruan	.25
415	Geoff Jenkins	.25
416	Carlos Hernandez	.25
417	Matt Clement/SP	1.50
418	Jose Cruz Jr.	.25
419	Jake Mauer RC	.50
420	Matt Childers RC	.50
421	Tom Glavine/SP	2.50
422	Ken Griffey Jr.	2.00
423	Anderson Hernandez RC	.40
424	John Suomi RC	.40
425	Doug Sessions RC	.25
426	Jaret Wright	.25
427	Rolando Viera/SP RC	1.50
428	Aaron Sele	.25
429	Dmitri Young	.25
430	Ryan Klesko	.25
431	Kevin Tapani/SP	1.00
432	Joe Kennedy	.25
433	Austin Kearns	.40
434	Roger Cedeno	.25
435	Lance Berkman	.50
436	Frank Menechino	.25
437	Brett Myers	.25
438	Bobby Abreu	.50
439	Shawn Estes	.25

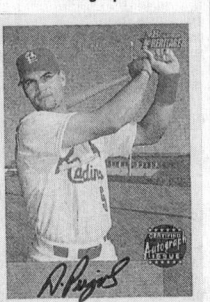

Autographs

	Player	NM/M
	Common Player:	8.00
	Inserted 1:45	
LB	Lance Berkman	25.00
HB	Hank Blalock	10.00
KG	Keith Ginter	8.00
TH	Toby Hall	8.00
DH	Drew Henson	8.00
KI	Kazuhisa Ishii	8.00
CI	Cesar Izturis	8.00
PL	Paul LoDuca	8.00
JM	Joe Mauer	75.00
RO	Roy Oswalt	15.00
MP	Mark Prior	10.00
AP	Albert Pujols	200.00
JR	Juan Rivera	8.00

1954 Bowman Reprints

		NM/M
	Complete Set (20):	40.00
	Common Player:	2.00
	Inserted 1:12	
RA	Richie Ashburn	2.00
YB	Yogi Berra	4.00
DC	Del Crandell	2.00
BF	Bob Feller	2.50
WF	Whitey Ford	4.00
NF	Nellie Fox	2.00
CL	Clem Labine	2.00
DL	Don Larsen	3.00
JL	Johnny Logan	2.00
WM	Willie Mays	6.00
GM	Gil McDougald	2.00
DM	Don Mueller	2.00
JP	Jimmy Piersall	2.00
AR	Allie Reynolds	2.00
PR	Phil Rizzuto	3.00
ES	Enos Slaughter	2.00
DS	Duke Snider	4.00
WW	Wes Westrum	2.00
HW	Hoyt Wilhelm	2.00
DW	Davey Williams	2.00

1954 Bowman Reprint Autographs

		NM/M
	Common Player:	10.00
	Inserted 1:118	
YB	Yogi Berra	50.00
DC	Del Crandell	15.00
CL	Clem Labine	15.00
JL	Johnny Logan	15.00
DM	Don Mueller	10.00
DW	Davey Williams	10.00

Team Topps Legends Autographs

	NM/M
Common Player:	8.00
Gil McDougald	10.00
Joe Pepitone	10.00
Bobby Richardson	10.00
Robin Roberts	15.00
Warren Spahn	40.00
Luis Tiant	10.00
Carl Yastrzemski	40.00

Chrome Refractor

	NM/M
Common Player:	2.00
Inserted 1:16	
Production 350 Sets	
Gold Refractors:	2-4X
Inserted 1:32	
Production 175 Sets	

Relics

DARIN ERSTAD

		NM/M
	Common Player:	4.00
	Inserted 1:47	
EA	Edgardo Alfonzo	4.00
JB	Josh Beckett	10.00
BB	Barry Bonds	20.00
EC	Eric Chavez	4.00
CD	Carlos Delgado	5.00

	Player	Price
JE	Jim Edmonds	4.00
DE	Darin Erstad	4.00
NG	Nomar Garciaparra	8.00
TG	Tony Gwynn	10.00
TH	Todd Helton	8.00
CJ	Chipper Jones	10.00
PK	Paul Konerko	8.00
GM	Greg Maddux	15.00
EM	Edgar Martinez	4.00
MP	Mike Piazza	10.00
MR	Albert Pujols	20.00
MR	Mariano Rivera	8.00
IR	Ivan Rodriguez	5.00
SR	Scott Rolen	10.00
TS	Tim Salmon	4.00
KS	Kazuhiro Sasaki	4.00
JS	John Smoltz	8.00
FT	Frank Thomas	8.00
JT	Jim Thome	4.00
LW	Larry Walker	4.00
PW	Preston Wilson	4.00

#	Player	Price
1	Edwin Almonte	2.00
2	Moises Alou	4.00
3	Benito Baez	2.00
4	Lance Berkman	5.00
5	Bret Boone	2.00
6	Taylor Buchholz	2.00
7	Pat Burrell	5.00
8	Sean Burroughs	2.00
9	Orlando Cabrera	2.00
10	Sean Casey	3.00
11	Matt Childers	2.00
12	Brady Clark	2.00
13	Roger Clemens	10.00
14	Marty Cordova	2.00
15	Craig Counsell	2.00
16	Juan Cruz	2.00
17	Jack Cust	3.00
18	Ben Davis	2.00
19	Sean Douglass	2.00
20	Brandon Duckworth	2.00
21	David Eckstein	3.00
22	Morgan Ensberg	2.00
23	Darin Erstad	3.00
24	Carl Everett	2.00
25	Nomar Garciaparra	5.00
26	Marcus Giles	2.00
27	Alex Gonzalez	2.00
28	Juan Gonzalez	2.00
29	Shawn Green	3.00
30	Cristian Guzman	2.00
31	Mike Hampton	3.00
32	Rob Henkel	2.00
33	Dave Wells	2.00
34	Brad Fullmer	2.00
35	Jeremy Giambi	2.00
36	Koyie Hill	2.00
37	Tim Hudson	4.00
38	Hansel Izquierdo	2.00
39	Geoff Jenkins	2.00
40	D'Angelo Jimenez	2.00
41	Andruw Jones	5.00
42	Brian Jordan	2.00
43	Jason Kendall	2.00
44	Ryan Klesko	2.00
45	Paul Konerko	4.00
46	Matt Lawton	2.00
47	Scotty Layfield	2.00
48	Paul LoDuca	2.00
49	Terrence Long	2.00
50	Pedro Martinez	8.00
51	Tino Martinez	2.00
52	Jake Mauer	2.00
53	Fred McGriff	4.00
54	Doug Mientkiewicz	2.00
55	Wade Miller	2.00
56	Melvin Mora	2.00
57	Mike Mussina	5.00
58	Hideo Nomo	4.00
59	Tomokazu Ohka	2.00
60	Magglio Ordonez	2.00
61	Rafael Palmeiro	5.00
62	Corey Patterson	3.00
63	Carlos Pena	5.00
64	Josh Phelps	2.00
65	Joel Pineiro	2.00
66	Luke Prokopec	2.00
67	Mark Quinn	2.00
68	Joe Randa	2.00
69	Tim Redding	2.00
70	Mark Redman	2.00
71	Jose Reyes	10.00
72	Juan Rivera	2.00
73	John Rodriguez	2.00
74	Antwon Rollins	2.00
75	C.C. Sabathia	5.00
76	Reggie Sanders	2.00
77	Curt Schilling	6.00
78	Jason Schmidt	3.00
79	David Segui	2.00
80	Richie Sexson	4.00
81	Doug Sessions	2.00
82	John Smoltz	5.00
83	Alfonso Soriano	6.00
84	Lee Stevens	2.00
85	Mike Sweeney	2.00
86	Dennis Tankersley	2.00
87	Marcus Thames	2.00
88	Frank Thomas	8.00
89	Josh Towers	2.00
90	Brent Abernathy	2.00
91	Eric Valent	2.00
92	Jose Valverde	2.00
93	Mo Vaughn	2.00
94	Robin Ventura	2.00
95	Jack Wilson	2.00
96	Dan Wright	2.00
97	Dmitri Young	2.00
98	Barry Zito	3.00

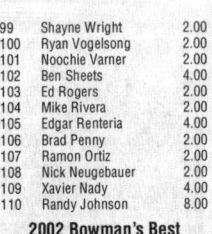

#	Player	Price
99	Shayne Wright	2.00
100	Ryan Vogelsong	2.00
101	Noochie Varner	2.00
102	Ben Sheets	4.00
103	Ed Rogers	2.00
104	Mike Rivera	2.00
105	Edgar Renteria	4.00
106	Brad Penny	2.00
107	Ramon Ortiz	2.00
108	Nick Neugebauer	2.00
109	Xavier Nady	4.00
110	Randy Johnson	8.00

2002 Bowman's Best

Casey Kotchman

AUTHENTIC GAME-USED BAT

	NM/M
Complete Set (181):	
Common Player:	.25
Common (91-181):	4.00
Inserted 1:Pack	
Blue (1-90):	1-2X
Production 300	
Red (1-90):	1-2X
Production 200	
Gold (1-90):	3-6X
Production 50	
Blue (91-181):	.75-1X
Production 500	
Red (91-181):	1-1.5X
Production 150	
Gold (91-181):	1-2X
Production 50	
Pack (5):	18.00
Box (10):	150.00

#	Player	Price
1	Josh Beckett	.75
2	Derek Jeter	3.00
3	Alex Rodriguez	3.00
4	Miguel Tejada	.75
5	Nomar Garciaparra	.75
6	Aramis Ramirez	.75
7	Jeremy Giambi	.50
8	Bernie Williams	.50
9	Juan Pierre	.50
10	Chipper Jones	2.00
11	Jimmy Rollins	.50
12	Alfonso Soriano	1.00
13	Daryle Ward	.25
14	Paul Konerko	.50
15	Tim Hudson	.50
16	Doug Mientkiewicz	.75
17	Todd Helton	.75
18	Moises Alou	.40
19	Juan Gonzalez	.50
20	Jorge Posada	.50
21	Jeff Kent	.50
22	Roger Clemens	1.50
23	Phil Nevin	.40
24	Brian Giles	.50
25	Carlos Delgado	.50
26	Jason Giambi	.50
27	Vladimir Guerrero	1.00
28	Cliff Floyd	.25
29	Shea Hillenbrand	.50
30	Ken Griffey Jr.	2.50
31	Mike Piazza	1.50
32	Carlos Pena	.40
33	Larry Walker	.50
34	Magglio Ordonez	.50
35	Mike Mussina	.50
36	Andruw Jones	.50
37	Mark Teixeira	.50
38	Curt Schilling	.50
39	Eric Chavez	.40
40	Bartolo Colon	.25
41	Eric Hinske	.25
42	Sean Burroughs	.25
43	Randy Johnson	1.00
44	Adam Dunn	1.00
45	Pedro Martinez	1.00
46	Garret Anderson	.25
47	Jim Thome	.75
48	Gary Sheffield	.75
49	Tsuyoshi Shinjo	.25
50	Albert Pujols	3.00
51	Ichiro Suzuki	.75
52	C.C. Sabathia	.75
53	Bobby Abreu	.50
54	Ivan Rodriguez	.50
55	J.D. Drew	.50
56	Jacque Jones	.25
57	Jason Kendall	.25
58	Javier Vazquez	.25
59	Jeff Bagwell	.50
60	Greg Maddux	.75
61	Jim Edmonds	.50
62	Austin Kearns	.25
63	Jose Vidro	.25
64	Kevin Brown	.25
65	Preston Wilson	.25

#	Player	Price
66	Sammy Sosa	.75
67	Lance Berkman	.75
68	Mark Mulder	.40
69	Marty Cordova	.25
70	Frank Thomas	.75
71	Mike Cameron	.25
72	Mike Sweeney	.25
73	Barry Bonds	2.00
74	Troy Glaus	.40
75	Barry Zito	.40
76	Pat Burrell	.50
77	Paul LoDuca	.25
78	Rafael Palmeiro	.50
79	Mark Prior	.40
80	Darin Erstad	.25
81	Richie Sexson	.40
82	Roberto Alomar	.25
83	Roy Oswalt	.50
84	Ryan Klesko	.25
85	Luis Gonzalez	.25
86	Scott Rolen	.50
87	Shannon Stewart	.25
88	Shawn Green	.40
89	Toby Hall	.25
90	Bret Boone	.40
91	Casey Kotchman/Bat	8.00
92	Jose Valverde/Auto. RC	8.00
93	Cole Barthel/Bat	4.00
94	Brad Nelson/Auto. RC	8.00
95	Mauricio Lara/Auto. RC	8.00
96	Ryan Gripp/Bat RC	8.00
97	Brian West/Auto. RC	8.00
98	Chris Piersoll/Auto. RC	8.00
99	Ryan Church/Auto. RC	10.00
100	Javier Colina/Auto.	8.00
101	Juan Gonzalez/Auto.	8.00
102	Benito Baez/Auto.	8.00
103	Mike Hill/Bat RC	4.00
104	Jason Grove/Auto. RC	8.00
105	Koyie Hill/Auto.	8.00
106	Mark Outlaw/Auto. RC	8.00
107	Jason Bay/Bat RC	15.00
108	Jorge Padilla/Auto. RC	8.00
109	Peter Zamora/Auto. RC	8.00
110	Joe Mauer/Auto. RC	150.00
111	Franklyn German/Auto. RC	8.00
112	Chris Flinn/Auto. RC	8.00
113	David Wright/Bat	40.00
114	Anastacio Martinez/Auto. RC	8.00
115	Nic Jackson/Bat RC	8.00
116	Rene Reyes/Auto. RC	8.00
117	Colin Young/Auto. RC	8.00
118	Joe Orloski/Auto. RC	8.00
119	Mike Wilson/Auto. RC	8.00
120	Rich Thompson/Auto. RC	8.00
121	Jake Mauer/Auto. RC	8.00
122	Mario Ramos/Auto.	8.00
123	Doug Sessions/Auto. RC	8.00
124	Doug DeVore/Bat RC	4.00
125	Travis Foley/Auto.	10.00
126	Chris Baker/Auto. RC	8.00
127	Michael Floyd/Auto. RC	8.00
128	Josh Barfield/Bat	5.00
129	Jose Bautista/Bat RC	8.00
130	Gavin Floyd/Auto.	12.00
131	Jason Botts/Bat RC	4.00
132	Clint Nageotte/Auto. RC	10.00
133	Jesus Cota/Auto.	10.00
134	Ron Calloway/Bat RC	4.00
135	Kevin Cash/Bat RC	4.00
136	Jonny Gomes/Auto. RC	10.00
137	Dennis Ulacia/Auto.	8.00
138	Ryan Snare/Auto. RC	8.00
139	Kevin Deaton/Auto. RC	8.00
140	Bobby Jenks/Auto. RC	12.00
141	Casey Kotchman/Auto.	12.00
142	Adam Walker/Auto. RC	8.00
143	Mike Gonzalez/Auto. RC	8.00
144	Ruben Gotay/Bat RC	5.00
145	Jason Grove/Bat RC	4.00
146	Freddy Sanchez/Auto. RC	15.00
147	Jason Arnold/Auto.	10.00
148	Scott Hairston/Auto.	10.00
149	Jason St. Clair/Auto. RC	8.00
150	Chris Tritle/Bat RC	4.00
151	Edwin Yan/Bat RC	4.00
152	Freddy Sanchez/Bat RC	10.00
153	Greg Sain/Bat RC	4.00
154	Yurendell DeCaster/Bat RC	5.00
155	Noochie Varner/Bat RC	5.00
156	Nelson Castro/Auto. RC	8.00
157	Randall Shelley/Bat RC	5.00
158	Reed Johnson/Bat RC	10.00
159	Ryan Raburn/Auto. RC	8.00
160	Jose Morban/Bat RC	5.00
161	Justin Schuda/Auto. RC	8.00
162	Henry Pichardo/Auto. RC	8.00
163	Josh Bard/Auto. RC	10.00
164	Josh Bonifay/Auto. RC	8.00
165	Brandon League/Auto. RC	8.00
166	Julio DePaula/Auto. RC	10.00
167	Todd Linden/Auto. RC	8.00
168	Francisco Liriano/Auto. RC	80.00
169	Chris Snelling/Auto. RC	8.00
170	Blake McGinley/Auto. RC	8.00
171	Cody McKay/Auto. RC	8.00
172	Jason Stanford/Auto. RC	8.00
173	Lenny Dinardo/Auto. RC	8.00
174	Greg Montalbano/Auto. RC	8.00
175	Earl Snyder/Auto. RC	8.00
176	Justin Huber/Auto. RC	10.00
177	Chris Narveson/Auto.	8.00
178	Jon Switzer/Auto.	8.00
179	Ronald Acuna/Auto. RC	8.00
180	Chris Duffy/Auto.	8.00
181	Kazuhisa Ishii/Bat RC	8.00

2003 Bowman

JOEY GOMES — OF

		NM/M
	Complete Set (330):	75.00
	Common Player:	.15
	Common Rookie:	.40
	Pack (10):	3.00
	Box (24):	60.00
1	Garret Anderson	.15
2	Derek Jeter	2.00
3	Gary Sheffield	.40
4	Matt Morris	.25
5	Derek Lowe	.15
6	Andy Van Hekken	.15
7	Sammy Sosa	.75
8	Ken Griffey Jr.	1.50
9	Omar Vizquel	.15
10	Jorge Posada	.40
11	Lance Berkman	.15
12	Mike Sweeney	.15
13	Adrian Beltre	.15
14	Richie Sexson	.25
15	A.J. Pierzynski	.15
16	Bartolo Colon	.15
17	Mike Mussina	.40
18	Paul Byrd	.15
19	Bobby Abreu	.40
20	Miguel Tejada	.15
21	Aramis Ramirez	.40
22	Edgardo Alfonzo	.15
23	Edgar Martinez	.25
24	Albert Pujols	2.00
25	Carl Crawford	.25
26	Eric Hinske	.15
27	Tim Salmon	.25
28	Luis Gonzalez	.25
29	Jay Gibbons	.15
30	John Smoltz	.15
31	Tim Wakefield	.15
32	Mark Prior	.50
33	Magglio Ordonez	.25
34	Adam Dunn	.25
35	Larry Walker	.25
36	Luis Castillo	.15
37	Wade Miller	.15
38	Carlos Beltran	.50
39	Odalis Perez	.15
40	Alex Sanchez	.15
41	Torii Hunter	.25
42	Cliff Floyd	.15
43	Andy Pettitte	.25
44	Francisco Rodriguez	.15
45	Eric Chavez	.40
46	Kevin Millwood	.25
47	Dennis Tankersley	.15
48	Hideo Nomo	.25
49	Freddy Garcia	.15
50	Randy Johnson	.75
51	Aubrey Huff	.25
52	Carlos Delgado	.40
53	Troy Glaus	.50
54	Junior Spivey	.15
55	Mike Hampton	.15
56	Sidney Ponson	.15
57	Aaron Boone	.15
58	Kerry Wood	.40
59	Willie Harris	.15
60	Nomar Garciaparra	.75
61	Todd Helton	.50
62	Mike Lowell	.40
63	Roy Oswalt	.40
64	Raul Ibanez	.15
65	Brian Jordan	.15
66	Geoff Jenkins	.15
67	Jermaine Dye	.15
68	Tom Glavine	.25
69	Bernie Williams	.40
70	Vladimir Guerrero	.75
71	Mark Mulder	.25
72	Jimmy Rollins	.40
73	Oliver Perez	.15
74	Rich Aurilia	.15
75	Joel Pineiro	.15
76	J.D. Drew	.25
77	Ivan Rodriguez	.50
78	Josh Phelps	.15
79	Darin Erstad	.40
80	Curt Schilling	.75
81	Paul LoDuca	.25
82	Marty Cordova	.15
83	Manny Ramirez	.75
84	Bobby Hill	.15
85	Paul Konerko	.40
86	Austin Kearns	.25
87	Jason Jennings	.15
88	Brad Penny	.15
89	Jeff Bagwell	.75
90	Shawn Green	.40
91	Jason Schmidt	.40
92	Doug Mientkiewicz	.15
93	Jose Vidro	.15
94	Bret Boone	.15
95	Jason Giambi	.40
96	Barry Zito	.40
97	Roy Halliday	.40
98	Pat Burrell	.40
99	Sean Burroughs	.15
100	Barry Bonds	2.00
101	Kazuhiro Sasaki	.15
102	Fernando Vina	.15
103	Chan Ho Park	.15
104	Andruw Jones	.75
105	Adam Kennedy	.15
106	Shea Hillenbrand	.15
107	Greg Maddux	1.50
108	Jim Edmonds	.40
109	Pedro J. Martinez	1.00
110	Moises Alou	.25
111	Jeff Weaver	.15
112	C.C. Sabathia	.15
113	Robert Fick	.15
114	A.J. Burnett	.15
115	Jeff Kent	.25
116	Kevin Brown	.15
117	Rafael Furcal	.25
118	Cristian Guzman	.15
119	Brad Wilkerson	.15
120	Mike Piazza	1.00
121	Alfonso Soriano	.75
122	Mark Ellis	.15
123	Vicente Padilla	.15
124	Eric Gagne	.15
125	Ryan Klesko	.15
126	Ichiro Suzuki	1.50
127	Tony Batista	.15
128	Roberto Alomar	.40
129	Alex Rodriguez	2.00
130	Jim Thome	.75
131	Jarrod Washburn	.15
132	Orlando Hudson	.15
133	Chipper Jones	1.50
134	Rodrigo Lopez	.15
135	Johnny Damon	.25
136	Matt Clement	.15
137	Frank Thomas	.75
138	Ellis Burks	.15
139	Carlos Pena	.15
140	Josh Beckett	.25
141	Joe Randa	.15
142	Brian Giles	.25
143	Kazuhisa Ishii	.15
144	Corey Koskie	.15
145	Orlando Cabrera	.15
146	Mark Buehrle	.25
147	Roger Clemens	1.50
148	Tim Hudson	.40
149	Randy Wolf	.15
150	Josh Fogg	.15
151	Phil Nevin	.15
152	John Olerud	.15
153	Scott Rolen	.75
154	Joe Kennedy	.15
155	Rafael Palmeiro	.50
156	Chad Hutchinson	.40
157	Quincy Carter	.15
158	Hee Seop Choi	.15
159	Joe Borchard	.15
160	Brandon Phillips	.15
161	Wily Mo Pena	.15
162	Victor Martinez	.15
163	Jason Stokes	.15
164	Ken Harvey	.15
165	Juan Rivera	.15
166	Jose Contreras RC	1.00
167	Dan Haren RC	1.00
168	Michel Hernandez RC	.50
169	Eider Torres RC	.50
170	Chris De La Cruz RC	.50
171	Ramon A. Martinez RC	.50
172	Mike Adams RC	.40
173	Justin Arneson RC	.50
174	Jamie Athas RC	.40
175	Dwaine Bacon RC	.40
176	Clint Barmes RC	.40
177	B.J. Barns RC	.40
178	Tyler Johnson RC	.50
179	Bobby Basham RC	.50
180	T.J. Bohn RC	.50
181	J.D. Durbin RC	.50
182	Brandon Bowe RC	.40
183	Craig Brazell RC	.50
184	Dusty Brown RC	.50
185	Brian Bruney RC	.50
186	Greg Bruso RC	.40
187	Jaime Bubela RC	.50
188	Bryan Bullington RC	.50
189	Brian Burgamy RC	.40
190	Eny Cabreja RC	.40
191	Daniel Cabrera RC	.50
192	Ryan Cameron RC	.40
193	Lance Caraccioli RC	.50
194	David Cash RC	.40
195	Bernie Castro RC	.40
196	Ismael Castro RC	.40
197	Daryl Clark RC	.50
198	Jeff Clark RC	.50
199	Chris Colton RC	.40
200	Dexter Cooper RC	.40
201	Callix Crabbe RC	.40
202	Chien-Ming Wang RC	3.00
203	Eric Crozier RC	.50
204	Nook Logan RC	.40
205	David DeJesus RC	.75
206	Matt DeMarco RC	.15
207	Chris Duncan RC	.75
208	Eric Eckenstahler RC	.40
209	Willie Eyre RC	.40
210	Evel Bastida-Martinez RC	.40
211	Chris Fallon RC	.75
212	Mike Flannery RC	.40
213	Mike O'Keefe RC	.40
214	Ben Francisco RC	1.00
215	Kason Gabbard RC	.50
216	Mike Gallo RC	.40
217	Jairo Garcia RC	.40
218	Angel Garcia RC	.40
219	Michael Garciaparra RC	.50
220	Joey Gomes RC	.40
221	Dusty Gomon RC	.40
222	Bryan Grace RC	.40
223	Tyson Graham RC	.40
224	Henry Guerrero RC	.40
225	Franklin Gutierrez RC	.50
226	Carlos Guzman RC	.40
227	Matthew Hagen RC	.50
228	Josh Hall RC	.50
229	Rob Hammock RC	.50
230	Brendan Harris RC	.75
231	Gary Harris RC	.40
232	Clay Hensley RC	.40
233	Michael Hinckley RC	.40
234	Luis Hodge RC	.40
235	Donnie Hood RC	.50
236	Travis Ishikawa RC	.50
237	Edwin Jackson RC	.50
238	Ardley Jansen RC	.50
239	Ferenc Jongejan RC	.40
240	Matt Kata RC	.50
241	Kazuhiro Takeoka RC	.40
242	Beau Kemp RC	.40
243	Il Kim RC	.50
244	Brennan King RC	.40
245	Cris Kroski RC	.40
246	Jason Kubel RC	1.50
247	Pete LaForest RC	.40
248	Wilfredo Ledezma RC	.40
249	Jeremy Bonderman RC	2.00
250	Gonzalo Lopez RC	.40
251	Brian Luderer RC	.50
252	Ruddy Lugo RC	.40
253	Wayne Lydon RC	.40
254	Mark Malaska RC	.40
255	Andy Marte RC	.40
256	Tyler Martin RC	.40
257	Branden Florence RC	.40
258	Aneudis Mateo RC	.40
259	Derell McCall RC	.40
260	Brian McCann RC	4.00
261	Mike McNutt RC	.40
262	Jacabo Meque RC	.40
263	Derek Michaelis RC	.50
264	Aaron Miles RC	.75
265	Jose Morales RC	.40
266	Dustin Moseley RC	.40
267	Adrian Myers RC	.40
268	Dan Neil RC	.40
269	Jon Nelson RC	.40
270	Mike Neu RC	.40
271	Leigh Neuage RC	.40
272	Weston O'Brien RC	.40
273	Trent Oeltjen RC	.40
274	Tim Olson RC	.50
275	David Pahucki RC	.40
276	Nathan Panther RC	.40
277	Arnie Munoz RC	.40
278	David Pember RC	.40
279	Jason Perry RC	.50
280	Matthew Peterson RC	.40
281	Ryan Shealy RC	1.00
282	Jorge Piedra RC	.40
283	Simon Pond RC	.40
284	Aaron Rakers RC	.40
285	Hanley Ramirez RC	5.00
286	Manuel Ramirez RC	.40
287	Kevin Randel RC	.50
288	Darrell Rasner RC	.50
289	Prentice Redman RC	.50
290	Eric Reed RC	.40
291	Wilton Reynolds RC	.40
292	Eric Riggs RC	.40
293	Carlos Rijo RC	.40
294	Raja Davis RC	.50
295	Aron Weston RC	.40
296	Arturo Rivas RC	.40
297	Kyle Roat RC	.40
298	Bubba Nelson RC	.50
299	Levi Robinson RC	.40
300	Ray Sadler RC	.50
301	Gary Schneidmiller RC	.40
302	Jon Schuerholz RC	.75
303	Corey Shafer RC	.40
304	Brian Shackelford RC	.40
305	Bill Simon RC	.40
306	Haj Turay RC	.40
307	Sean Smith RC	.40
308	Ryan Spataro RC	.40
309	Jemel Spearman RC	.50
310	Keith Stamler RC	.40
311	Luke Steidlmayer RC	.40
312	Adam Stern RC	.50
313	Jay Sitzman RC	.50
314	Thomari Story-Harden RC	.50
315	Terry Tiffee RC	.40
316	Nick Trzesniak RC	.40
317	Denny Tussen RC	.40
318	Scott Tyler RC	.40
319	Shane Victorino RC	2.00
320	Doug Waechter RC	.50
321	Brandon Watson RC	.50
322	Todd Wellemeyer RC	.50
323	Eli Whiteside RC	.50
324	Josh Willingham RC	1.00
325	Travis Wong RC	.50
326	Brian Wright RC	.40
327	Kevin Youkilis RC	4.00
328	Andy Sisco RC	.50
329	Dustin Yount RC	.50
330	Andrew Dominique RC	.40

Gold
Stars (1-165): 1-2X
Rookies (166-330): 1-2X
Inserted 1:1

Uncirculated
Stars (1-165): 3-5X
Rookies (166-330): 2-4X
Production 250 Sets

Future Fiber Relics

		NM/M
	Common Player:	4.00
RB	Rocco Baldelli	4.00
WB	Wilson Betemit	4.00
HB	Hank Blalock	6.00
JB	Jason Botts	4.00
SB	Sean Burroughs	4.00
KC	Kevin Cash	4.00
KD	Kory DeHaan	4.00
CD	Chris Duffy	4.00
PF	Pedro Feliz	5.00
AG	Adrian Gonzalez	6.00
JG	Jason Grove	4.00
JH	Josh Hamilton	10.00
NH	Nathan Haynes	4.00
DH	Drew Henson	4.00
AH	Aubrey Huff	4.00
RJ	Reed Johnson	4.00
AK	Austin Kearns	5.00
CK	Casey Kotchman	4.00
RK	Ryan Langerhans	4.00
JDM	Jake Mauer	4.00
JM	Joe Mauer	8.00
XN	Xavier Nady	5.00
MR	Michael Restovich	4.00
WR	Wilkin Ruan	4.00
FS	Freddy Sanchez	4.00
RS	Randall Shelley	5.00
BS	Bud Smith	4.00
ES	Esix Snead	4.00
ST	So Taguchi	4.00
JW	Justin Wayne	4.00
TW	Travis Wilson	4.00
DW	David Wright	15.00
EY	Edwin Yan	4.00

Futures Game Gear Relics

FUTURES GAME

		NM/M
	Common Player:	4.00
	Inserted 1:26	
EA	Edwin Almonte	4.00
TA	Tony Alvarez	4.00
BB	Brad Baker	4.00
FB	Francis Beltran	4.00
JEB	Joe Borchard	4.00
JB	John Buck	4.00
SB	Sean Burnett	4.00
MB	Marlon Byrd	4.00
MC	Miguel Cabrera	10.00
KC	Kevin Cash	4.00
HC	Hee Seop Choi	4.00
SC	Shin-Soo Choo	6.00
AC	Aaron Cook	5.00
CC	Carl Crawford	6.00
JDR	Jorge De La Rosa	4.00
VD	Victor Diaz	4.00
RD	Ryan Dittfurth	4.00
BE	Brett Evert	4.00
GG	Gerardo Garcia	4.00
BH	Bill Hall	4.00
CH	Corey Hart	6.00
DH	Drew Henson	4.00
JH	Justin Huber	4.00
OH	Orlando Hudson	4.00
OI	Omar Infante	4.00
JJ	Jimmy Journell	4.00
JK	Josh Karp	4.00
FL	Francisco Liriano	6.00
JL	Jose Lopez	4.00
VM	Victor Martinez	4.00
JM	Justin Morneau	10.00
BM	Brett Myers	5.00
LO	Lyle Overbay	4.00
WP	Wily Mo Pena	4.00
BP	Brandon Phillips	6.00
MR	Mike Restovich	4.00
JR	Jose Reyes	10.00
FR	Francisco Rodriguez	4.00
RR	Ricardo Rodriguez	4.00
SS	Seung Jun Song	4.00
JMS	John Stephens	4.00
JS	Jason Stokes	4.00
BT	Billy Traber	4.00
CT	Chad Tracey	4.00
AW	Adam Wainwright	8.00
JY	Jason Young	4.00

Futures Game MVP Autograph

		NM/M
	Complete Set (1):	
JR	Jose Reyes	40.00

ROY Dual Relic

		NM/M
	Inserted 1:765	
JH	Eric Hinske, Jason Jennings	10.00

Signs of the Future

DONALD LEVINSKI — P

		NM/M
	Common Autograph:	4.00
	Red Autographs:	1-2.5X
	Production 50 Sets	
JA	Jason Arnold	4.00
JB	John Buck	10.00
BB	Bryan Bullington	8.00
QC	Quincy Carter	8.00
NC	Nelson Castro	4.00
RC	Ryan Church	10.00
JC	Jesus Cota	4.00
JOG	Jonny Gomes	10.00
DG	Doug Gredvig	5.00
KG	Khalil Greene	5.00
ZG	Zack Greinke	40.00
JG	Jason Grove	5.00
JGU	Jeremy Guthrie	10.00
CH	Cole Hamels	80.00
JRH	Joel Hanrahan	4.00
CJH	Corey Hart	25.00
KH	Koyie Hill	5.00
CMH	Chad Hutchinson	10.00
BJ	Bobby Jenks	15.00
BK	Ben Kozlowski	5.00
BL	Brandon League	5.00
DL	Donald Levinski	8.00
FL	Fred Lewis	8.00
TL	Todd Linden	5.00
JL	James Loney	15.00
VM	Val Majewski	5.00
DHM	Dustin McGowan	5.00
CP	Chris Piersoll	5.00
HR	Hanley Ramirez	75.00
PR	Prentice Redman	5.00
JR	Jose Reyes	40.00
JSC	Jason St. Clair	5.00
FS	Freddy Sanchez	10.00
ZS	Zach Segovia	5.00
DS	Doug Sessions	5.00
BS	Brian Slocum	5.00
RS	Ryan Snare	5.00
MT	Mitch Talbot	5.00
AT	Andres Torres	5.00
AV	Andy Van Hekken	5.00
OV	Oscar Villarreal	5.00

Dual Signs of the Future Autograph

		NM/M
	Inserted 1:9,220	
CH	Quincy Carter, Chad Hutchinson	15.00

2003 Bowman Chrome

CRAIG BRAZELL — 1B

		NM/M
	Complete Set (351):	400.00
	Common Player:	.25
	Common Rookie:	.40
	Common RC Auto. (331-350):	10.00
	Pack (4):	7.00
	Box (18):	100.00
1	Garret Anderson	.25
2	Derek Jeter	3.00
3	Gary Sheffield	.50
4	Matt Morris	.35
5	Derek Lowe	.25
6	Andy Van Hekken	.25

#	Player	Price
7	Sammy Sosa	.75
8	Ken Griffey Jr.	2.00
9	Omar Vizquel	.40
10	Jorge Posada	.50
11	Lance Berkman	.50
12	Mike Sweeney	.25
13	Adrian Beltre	.50
14	Richie Sexson	.40
15	A.J. Pierzynski	.25
16	Bartolo Colon	.25
17	Mike Mussina	.75
18	Paul Byrd	.25
19	Bobby Abreu	.50
20	Miguel Tejada	.50
21	Aramis Ramirez	.50
22	Edgardo Alfonzo	.25
23	Edgar Martinez	.40
24	Albert Pujols	3.00
25	Carl Crawford	.40
26	Eric Hinske	.25
27	Tim Salmon	.40
28	Luis Gonzalez	.40
29	Jay Gibbons	.25
30	John Smoltz	.25
31	Tim Wakefield	.25
32	Mark Prior	.75
33	Magglio Ordonez	.40
34	Adam Dunn	.75
35	Larry Walker	.40
36	Luis Castillo	.25
37	Wade Miller	.25
38	Carlos Beltran	.75
39	Odalis Perez	.25
40	Alex Sanchez	.25
41	Torii Hunter	.50
42	Cliff Floyd	.25
43	Andy Pettitte	.50
44	Francisco Rodriguez	.25
45	Eric Chavez	.50
46	Kevin Millwood	.40
47	Dennis Tankersley	.25
48	Hideo Nomo	.50
49	Freddy Garcia	.25
50	Randy Johnson	.75
51	Aubrey Huff	.25
52	Carlos Delgado	.50
53	Troy Glaus	.50
54	Junior Spivey	.25
55	Mike Hampton	.25
56	Sidney Ponson	.25
57	Aaron Boone	.25
58	Kerry Wood	.50
59	Willie Harris	.25
60	Nomar Garciaparra	.50
61	Todd Helton	.75
62	Mike Lowell	.25
63	Roy Oswalt	.50
64	Raul Ibanez	.25
65	Brian Jordan	.25
66	Geoff Jenkins	.25
67	Jermaine Dye	.25
68	Tom Glavine	.50
69	Bernie Williams	.50
70	Vladimir Guerrero	1.00
71	Mark Mulder	.40
72	Jimmy Rollins	.50
73	Oliver Perez	.25
74	Rich Aurilia	.25
75	Joel Pineiro	.25
76	J.D. Drew	.40
77	Ivan Rodriguez	.50
78	Josh Phelps	.25
79	Darin Erstad	.40
80	Curt Schilling	1.00
81	Paul LoDuca	.25
82	Marty Cordova	.25
83	Manny Ramirez	1.00
84	Bobby Hill	.25
85	Paul Konerko	.50
86	Austin Kearns	.40
87	Jason Jennings	.25
88	Brad Penny	.25
89	Jeff Bagwell	.50
90	Shawn Green	.40
91	Jason Schmidt	.40
92	Doug Mientkiewicz	.25
93	Jose Vidro	.25
94	Bret Boone	.25
95	Jason Giambi	.50
96	Barry Zito	.50
97	Roy Halliday	.50
98	Pat Burrell	.50
99	Sean Burroughs	.25
100	Barry Bonds	3.00
101	Kazuhiro Sasaki	.25
102	Fernando Vina	.25
103	Chan Ho Park	.25
104	Andruw Jones	.50
105	Adam Kennedy	.25
106	Shea Hillenbrand	.25
107	Greg Maddux	2.00
108	Jim Edmonds	.40
109	Pedro J. Martinez	1.00
110	Moises Alou	.40
111	Jeff Weaver	.25
112	C.C. Sabathia	.25
113	Robert Fick	.25
114	A.J. Burnett	.25
115	Jeff Kent	.40
116	Kevin Brown	.25
117	Rafael Furcal	.25
118	Cristian Guzman	.25
119	Brad Wilkerson	.25
120	Mike Piazza	1.00
121	Alfonso Soriano	1.00
122	Mark Ellis	.25
123	Vicente Padilla	.25
124	Eric Gagne	.50

#	Player	Price
125	Ryan Klesko	.25
126	Ichiro Suzuki	2.00
127	Tony Batista	.25
128	Roberto Alomar	.50
129	Alex Rodriguez	2.50
130	Jim Thome	.50
131	Jarrod Washburn	.25
132	Orlando Hudson	.25
133	Chipper Jones	1.50
134	Rodrigo Lopez	.25
135	Johnny Damon	1.00
136	Matt Clement	.25
137	Frank Thomas	1.00
138	Ellis Burks	.25
139	Carlos Pena	.25
140	Josh Beckett	.50
141	Joe Randa	.25
142	Brian Giles	.25
143	Kazuhisa Ishii	.25
144	Corey Koskie	.25
145	Orlando Cabrera	.25
146	Mark Buehrle	.40
147	Roger Clemens	2.00
148	Tim Hudson	.25
149	Randy Wolf	.25
150	Josh Fogg	.25
151	Phil Nevin	.25
152	John Olerud	.25
153	Scott Rolen	.50
154	Joe Kennedy	.25
155	Rafael Palmeiro	.50
156	Chad Hutchinson	.50
157	Quincy Carter	.25
158	Hee Seop Choi	.40
159	Joe Borchard	.25
160	Brandon Phillips	.25
161	Wily Mo Pena	.25
162	Victor Martinez	.25
163	Jason Stokes	.25
164	Ken Harvey	.25
165	Juan Rivera	.25
166	Joe Valentine RC	1.00
167	Dan Haren	4.00
168	Michel Hernandez RC	1.00
169	Eider Torres RC	1.00
170	Chris De La Cruz RC	1.00
171	Ramon A. Martinez RC	1.00
172	Mike Adams RC	1.00
173	Justin Arneson RC	1.00
174	Jamie Athas RC	1.00
175	Dwaine Bacon RC	1.00
176	Clint Barmes RC	1.50
177	B.J. Barns RC	1.00
178	Tyler Johnson RC	1.00
179	Brandon Webb RC	8.00
180	T.J. Bohn RC	1.00
181	Ozzie Chavez RC	1.00
182	Brandon Bowe RC	1.00
183	Craig Brazell RC	1.00
184	Dusty Brown RC	1.00
185	Brian Bruney RC	1.00
186	Greg Bruso RC	1.00
187	Jaime Bubela RC	1.00
188	Matt Diaz RC	2.00
189	Brian Burgamy RC	1.00
190	Eny Cabreja RC	1.00
191	Daniel Cabrera RC	1.50
192	Ryan Cameron RC	1.00
193	Lance Caraccioli RC	1.00
194	David Cash RC	1.00
195	Bernie Castro RC	1.00
196	Ismael Castro RC	1.00
197	Cory Doyne RC	1.00
198	Jeff Clark RC	1.00
199	Chris Colton RC	1.00
200	Dexter Cooper RC	1.00
201	Callix Crabbe RC	1.00
202	Chien-Ming Wang RC	5.00
203	Eric Crozier RC	1.00
204	Nook Logan RC	1.00
205	David DeJesus RC	3.00
206	Matt DeMarco RC	1.00
207	Chris Duncan RC	2.00
208	Eric Eckenstahler RC	1.00
209	Willie Eyre RC	1.00
210	Evel Bastida-Martinez RC	1.00
211	Chris Fallon RC	1.00
212	Mike Flannery RC	1.00
213	Mike O'Keefe RC	1.00
214	Lew Ford RC	1.00
215	Kason Gabbard RC	1.00
216	Mike Gallo RC	1.00
217	Jairo Garcia RC	1.00
218	Angel Garcia RC	1.00
219	Michael Garciaparra RC	1.00
220	Jeremy Griffiths RC	1.00
221	Dusty Gomon RC	1.00
222	Bryan Grace RC	1.00
223	Tyson Graham RC	1.00
224	Henry Guerrero RC	1.00
225	Franklin Gutierrez RC	3.00
226	Carlos Guzman RC	1.00
227	Matthew Hagen RC	1.00
228	Josh Hall RC	1.00
229	Rob Hammock RC	1.00
230	Brendan Harris RC	1.50
231	Gary Harris RC	1.00
232	Clay Hensley RC	1.00
233	Michael Hinckley RC	1.00
234	Luis Hodge RC	1.00
235	Donnie Hood RC	1.00
236	Matt Hensley RC	1.00
237	Edwin Jackson RC	1.50
238	Ardley Jansen RC	1.00
239	Ferenc Jongejan RC	1.00
240	Matt Kata RC	1.00
241	Kazuhiro Takeoka RC	1.00
242	Charlie Manning RC	1.00

#	Player	Price
243	Il Kim RC	1.00
244	Brennan King RC	1.00
245	Cris Kroski RC	1.00
246	David Martinez RC	1.00
247	Pete LaForest RC	1.00
248	Wilfredo Ledezma RC	1.00
249	Jeremy Bonderman	2.00
250	Gonzalo Lopez RC	1.00
251	Brian Luderer RC	1.00
252	Ruddy Lugo RC	1.00
253	Wayne Lydon RC	1.00
254	Mark Malaska RC	1.00
255	Andy Marte RC	1.00
256	Tyler Martin RC	1.00
257	Branden Florence RC	1.00
258	Aneudis Mateo RC	1.00
259	Derell McCall RC	1.00
260	Elizardo Ramirez RC	1.00
261	Mike McNutt RC	1.00
262	Jacabo Meque RC	1.00
263	Derek Michaelis RC	1.00
264	Aaron Miles RC	2.00
265	Jose Morales RC	1.00
266	Dustin Moseley RC	1.00
267	Adrian Myers RC	1.00
268	Dan Neil RC	1.00
269	Jon Nelson RC	1.00
270	Mike Neu RC	1.00
271	Leigh Neuage RC	1.00
272	Weston O'Brien RC	1.00
273	Trent Oeltjen RC	1.00
274	Tim Olson RC	1.00
275	David Pahucki RC	1.00
276	Nathan Panther RC	1.00
277	Arnie Munoz RC	1.00
278	David Pember RC	1.00
279	Jason Perry RC	1.00
280	Matthew Peterson RC	1.00
281	Greg Aquino RC	1.00
282	Jorge Piedra RC	1.00
283	Simon Pond RC	1.00
284	Aaron Rakers RC	1.00
285	Felix Sanchez RC	1.00
286	Manuel Ramirez RC	1.00
287	Kevin Randel RC	1.00
288	Kelly Shoppach RC	2.00
289	Prentice Redman RC	1.00
290	Eric Reed RC	1.00
291	Wilton Reynolds RC	1.00
292	Eric Riggs RC	1.00
293	Carlos Rijo RC	1.00
294	Tyler Adamczyk RC	1.00
295	Jon-Mark Sprowl RC	1.00
296	Arturo Rivas RC	1.00
297	Kyle Roat RC	1.00
298	Bubba Nelson RC	1.00
299	Levi Robinson RC	1.00
300	Ray Sadler RC	1.00
301	Rylan Reed RC	1.00
302	Jon Schuerholz RC	1.00
303	Nobuaki Yoshida RC	1.00
304	Brian Shackelford RC	1.00
305	Bill Simon RC	1.00
306	Haj Turay RC	1.00
307	Sean Smith RC	1.00
308	Ryan Spataro RC	1.00
309	Jemel Spearman RC	1.00
310	Keith Stamler RC	1.00
311	Luke Steidlmayer RC	1.00
312	Adam Stern RC	1.00
313	Jay Sitzman RC	1.00
314	Mike Wodnicki RC	1.00
315	Terry Tiffee RC	1.00
316	Nick Trzesniak RC	1.00
317	Denny Tussen RC	1.00
318	Scott Tyler RC	1.00
319	Shane Victorino RC	6.00
320	Doug Waechter RC	1.00
321	Brandon Watson RC	1.00
322	Todd Wellemeyer RC	1.50
323	Eli Whiteside RC	1.00
324	Josh Willingham RC	3.00
325	Travis Wong RC	1.00
326	Brian Wright RC	1.00
327	Felix Pie RC	2.00
328	Andy Sisco RC	1.00
329	Dustin Yount RC	1.00
330	Andrew Dominique RC	1.00
331	Brian McCann	80.00
332	Jose Contreras RC	40.00
333	Corey Shafer RC	10.00
334	Hanley Ramirez RC	150.00
335	Ryan Shealy RC	10.00
336	Kevin Youkilis RC	50.00
337	Jason Kubel RC	20.00
338	Aron Weston RC	10.00
339	J.D. Durbin RC	10.00
340	Gary Schneidmiller RC	10.00
341	Travis Ishikawa RC	10.00
342	Ben Francisco RC	15.00
343	Bobby Basham RC	10.00
344	Joey Gomes RC	10.00
345	Beau Kemp RC	10.00
346	Thomari Story-Harden RC	10.00
347	Daryl Clark RC	10.00
348	Bryan Bullington RC	10.00
349	Rajai Davis RC	15.00
350	Darrell Rasner RC	10.00
351	Willie Mays	3.00

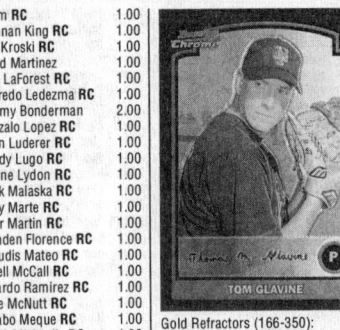

Gold Refractors (166-350): 2-3X
Production 170 Sets
Gold Refractors (331-350): 1-30X

Willie Mays Autograph
NM/M
Production 150
351AU Willie Mays 225.00

2003 Bowman Draft Picks & Prospects

		NM/M
Complete Set (165):		35.00
Common Player:		.15
Common Rookie:		.25
Pack (5 + 2 Chrome):		8.00
Box (24):		180.00
BDP1	Dontrelle Willis	.25
BDP2	Freddy Sanchez	.15
BDP3	Miguel Cabrera	.50
BDP4	Ryan Ludwick	.50
BDP5	Ty Wigginton	.15
BDP6	Mark Teixeira	.25
BDP7	Trey Hodges	.15
BDP8	Laynce Nix	.15
BDP9	Antonio Perez	.15
BDP10	Jody Gerut	.15
BDP11	Jae Weong Seo	.15
BDP12	Erick Almonte	.15
BDP13	Lyle Overbay	.15
BDP14	Billy Traber	.15
BDP15	Andres Torres	.15
BDP16	Jose Valverde	.15
BDP17	Aaron Heilman	.15
BDP18	Brandon Larson	.15
BDP19	Jung Bong	.15
BDP20	Jesse Foppert	.15
BDP21	Angel Berroa	.15
BDP22	Jeff DaVanon	.15
BDP23	Kurt Ainsworth	.15
BDP24	Brandon Claussen	.15
BDP25	Xavier Nady	.15
BDP26	Travis Hafner	.40
BDP27	Jerome Williams	.15
BDP28	Jose Reyes	.75
BDP29	Sergio Mitre RC	.25
BDP30	Bo Hart RC	.25
BDP31	Adam Miller RC	.50
BDP32	Brian Finch RC	.25
BDP33	Taylor Mattingly RC	.25
BDP34	Daric Barton RC	.75
BDP35	Chris Ray RC	.25
BDP36	Jarrod Saltalamacchia RC	1.00
BDP37	Dennis Dove RC	.25
BDP38	James Houser RC	.25
BDP39	Clinton King RC	.25
BDP40	Lou Palmisano RC	.25
BDP41	Dan Moore RC	.25
BDP42	Craig Stansberry RC	.25
BDP43	Jo Jo Reyes RC	.75
BDP44	Jake Stevens RC	.25
BDP45	Tom Gorzelanny RC	.75
BDP46	Brian Marshall RC	.25
BDP47	Scott Beerer RC	.25
BDP48	Javi Herrera RC	.25
BDP49	Steve Lerud RC	.25
BDP50	Josh Banks RC	.25
BDP51	Jonathan Papelbon RC	5.00
BDP52	Juan Valdes RC	.25
BDP53	Beau Vaghan RC	.25
BDP54	Matt Chico RC	.25
BDP55	Todd Jennings RC	.25
BDP56	Tony Gwynn Jr. RC	.50
BDP57	Matt Harrison RC	.25
BDP58	Aaron Mardsen RC	.25

BDP59	Casey Abrams RC	.25
BDP60	Cory Stuart RC	.25
BDP61	Mike Wagner RC	.25
BDP62	Jordan Pratt RC	.25
BDP63	Andre Randolph RC	.25
BDP64	Blake Balkcom RC	.25
BDP65	Josh Muecke RC	.25
BDP66	Jamie D'Antona RC	.25
BDP67	Cole Seifrig RC	.25
BDP68	Josh Anderson RC	.25
BDP69	Matt Lorenzo RC	.25
BDP70	Nate Spears RC	.25
BDP71	Chris Goodman RC	.25
BDP72	Brian McFall RC	.25
BDP73	Billy Hogan RC	.25
BDP74	Jamie Romak RC	.25
BDP75	Jeff Cook RC	.25
BDP76	Brooks McNiven RC	.25
BDP77	Xavier Paul RC	1.00
BDP78	Bob Zimmerman RC	.25
BDP79	Mickey Hall RC	.25
BDP80	Shaun Marcum RC	.50
BDP81	Matt Nachreiner RC	.25
BDP82	Chris Kinsey RC	.25
BDP83	Jonathan Fulton RC	.25
BDP84	Edgardo Baez RC	.25
BDP85	Robert Valido RC	.25
BDP86	Kenny Lewis RC	.25
BDP87	Trent Peterson RC	.25
BDP88	Johnny Woodard RC	.25
BDP89	Wes Littleton RC	.25
BDP90	Sean Rodriguez RC	.50
BDP91	Kyle Pearson RC	.25
BDP92	Josh Rainwater RC	.25
BDP93	Travis Schlichting RC	.25
BDP94	Tim Battle RC	.25
BDP95	Aaron Hill RC	.75
BDP96	Bob McCrory RC	.25
BDP97	Rick Guarno RC	.25
BDP98	Brandon Yarbrough RC	.25
BDP99	Peter Stonard RC	.25
BDP100	Darin Downs RC	.25
BDP101	Matt Bruback RC	.25
BDP102	Danny Garcia RC	.25
BDP103	Cory Stewart RC	.25
BDP104	Ferdin Tejeda RC	.25
BDP105	Kade Johnson RC	.25
BDP106	Andrew Brown RC	.25
BDP107	Aquilino Lopez RC	.25
BDP108	Stephen Randolph RC	.25
BDP109	Dave Matranga RC	.25
BDP110	Dustin McGowan RC	.50
BDP111	Juan Camacho RC	.25
BDP112	Cliff Lee	.50
BDP113	Jeff Duncan RC	.25
BDP114	C.J. Wilson	.25
BDP115	Brandon Roberson RC	.25
BDP116	David Corrente RC	.25
BDP117	Kevin Beavers RC	.25
BDP118	Anthony Webster RC	.25
BDP119	Oscar Villarreal RC	.25
BDP120	Hong-Chih Kuo RC	1.00
BDP121	Josh Barfield	.25
BDP122	Denny Bautista RC	.25
BDP123	Chris Burke RC	.25
BDP124	Robinson Cano RC	10.00
BDP125	Jose Castillo	.15
BDP126	Neal Cotts	.15
BDP127	Jorge De La Rosa	.15
BDP128	J.D. Durbin	.15
BDP129	Edwin Encarnacion	.50
BDP130	Gavin Floyd	.25
BDP131	Alexis Gomez	.15
BDP132	Edgar Gonzalez RC	.25
BDP133	Khalil Greene	.25
BDP134	Zack Greinke	.50
BDP135	Franklin Gutierrez	.15
BDP136	Rich Harden	.15
BDP137	J.J. Hardy	1.00
BDP138	Ryan Howard	20.00
BDP139	Justin Huber	.15
BDP140	David Kelton	.15
BDP141	David Krynzel	.15
BDP142	Pete LaForest	.15
BDP143	Adam LaRoche	.15
BDP144	Preston Larrison	.15
BDP145	John Maine RC	1.00
BDP146	Andy Marte	.15
BDP147	Jeff Mathis	.15
BDP148	Joe Mauer	.50
BDP149	Clint Nageotte	.15
BDP150	Chris Narveson	.15
BDP151	Ramon Nivar	.15
BDP152	Felix Pie	.75
BDP153	Guillermo Quiroz	.50
BDP154	Rene Reyes	.15
BDP155	Royce Ring	.15
BDP156	Alexis Rios	.75
BDP157	Grady Sizemore	.75
BDP158	Stephen Smitherman	.15
BDP159	Seung Jun Song	.15
BDP160	Scott Thorman	.15
BDP161	Chad Tracy	.25
BDP162	Chin-Hui Tsao	.15
BDP163	John Van Benschoten RC	.25
BDP164	Kevin Youkilis	1.00
BDP165	Chien-Ming Wang	1.00

Gold

Cards (1-165): 1-2X
Inserted 1:1

Fabric of Future

		NM/M
Common Player:		4.00
JB	Josh Barfield	4.00
RC	Robinson Cano	20.00
JD	J.D. Durbin	4.00
GF	Gavin Floyd	6.00
EG	Edgar Gonzalez	4.00
KG	Khalil Greene	4.00
ZG	Zack Greinke	10.00
FG	Franklin Gutierrez	4.00
RH	Rich Harden	4.00
RJH	Ryan Howard	30.00
JH	Justin Huber	4.00
AL	Adam LaRoche	6.00
AM	Andy Marte	4.00
JSM	Jeff Mathis	4.00
JM	Joe Mauer	12.00
CN	Chris Narveson	4.00
FP	Felix Pie	6.00
RR	Rene Reyes	4.00
RRR	Royce Ring	4.00
GS	Grady Sizemore	8.00

Prospect Premiums

		NM/M
Common Player:		4.00
RB	Rocco Baldelli	4.00
HB	Hank Blalock	4.00
CC	Carl Crawford	5.00
TH	Travis Hafner	6.00
BH	Brendan Harris	4.00
NH	Nathan Haynes	4.00
JM	Justin Morneau	8.00
CS	Chris Snelling	4.00
JT	Joe Thurston	4.00
CU	Chase Utley	12.00

Signs of the Future

		NM/M
Common Player:		5.00
JA	Jason Arnold	5.00
ZG	Zack Greinke	40.00
CS	Cory Stewart	5.00
DT	Dennis Tankersley	5.00
AT	Andres Torres	5.00

2003 Bowman Chrome Draft Picks & Prospects

		NM/M
Common Player:		.25
Common Rookie:		1.00
Common Rk Autograph (166-176):		10.00
BDP1	Dontrelle Willis	.25
BDP2	Freddy Sanchez	.25
BDP3	Miguel Cabrera	.75
BDP4	Ryan Ludwick	.25
BDP5	Ty Wigginton	.25
BDP6	Mark Teixeira	.25
BDP7	Trey Hodges	.25
BDP8	Laynce Nix	.25
BDP9	Antonio Perez	.25
BDP10	Jody Gerut	.25

Refractors

Stars (1-165, 351): 2-4X
Rookies (166-350): .5-1.5X
X-Fractors (1-165, 351): 3-6X
X-Fractors (166-350): 1-2X
Uncirc.Gold Refractors (1-165): 5-10X

BDP11	Jae Weong Seo	.25
BDP12	Erick Almonte	.25
BDP13	Lyle Overbay	.25
BDP14	Billy Traber	.25
BDP15	Andres Torres	.25
BDP16	Jose Valverde	.25
BDP17	Aaron Heilman	.25
BDP18	Brandon Larson	.25
BDP19	Jung Bong	.25
BDP20	Jesse Foppert	.25
BDP21	Angel Berroa	.25
BDP22	Jeff DaVanon	.25
BDP23	Kurt Ainsworth	.25
BDP24	Brandon Claussen	.25
BDP25	Xavier Nady	.25
BDP26	Travis Hafner	.50
BDP27	Jerome Williams	.25
BDP28	Jose Reyes	.75
BDP29	Sergio Mitre RC	1.00
BDP30	Bo Hart RC	1.00
BDP31	Adam Miller RC	1.50
BDP32	Brian Finch RC	.50
BDP33	Taylor Mattingly RC	1.00
BDP34	Daric Barton RC	1.50
BDP35	Chris Ray RC	1.00
BDP36	Jarrod Saltalamacchia RC	2.00
BDP37	Dennis Dove RC	1.00
BDP38	James Houser RC	1.00
BDP39	Clinton King RC	1.00
BDP40	Lou Palmisano RC	1.00
BDP41	Dan Moore RC	1.00
BDP42	Craig Stansberry RC	1.00
BDP43	Jo Jo Reyes RC	2.00
BDP44	Jake Stevens RC	1.00
BDP45	Tom Gorzelanny RC	1.50
BDP46	Brian Marshall RC	1.00
BDP47	Scott Beerer RC	1.00
BDP48	Javi Herrera RC	1.00
BDP49	Steve Lerud RC	1.00
BDP50	Josh Banks RC	1.50
BDP51	Jonathan Papelbon RC	5.00
BDP52	Juan Valdes RC	1.00
BDP53	Beau Vaghan RC	1.00
BDP54	Matt Chico RC	1.00
BDP55	Todd Jennings RC	1.00
BDP56	Tony Gwynn Jr. RC	1.00
BDP57	Matt Harrison RC	1.50
BDP58	Aaron Mardsen RC	1.00
BDP59	Casey Abrams RC	1.00
BDP60	Cory Stuart RC	1.00
BDP61	Mike Wagner RC	1.00
BDP62	Jordan Pratt RC	1.00
BDP63	Andre Randolph RC	1.00
BDP64	Blake Balkcom RC	1.00
BDP65	Josh Muecke RC	1.00
BDP66	Jamie D'Antona RC	1.00
BDP67	Cole Seifrig RC	1.00
BDP68	Josh Anderson RC	1.00
BDP69	Matt Lorenzo RC	1.00
BDP70	Nate Spears RC	1.00
BDP71	Chris Goodman RC	1.00
BDP72	Brian McFall RC	1.00
BDP73	Billy Hogan RC	1.00
BDP74	Jamie Romak RC	1.00
BDP75	Jeff Cook RC	1.00
BDP76	Brooks McNiven RC	1.00
BDP77	Xavier Paul RC	1.50
BDP78	Bob Zimmerman RC	1.00
BDP79	Mickey Hall RC	1.00
BDP80	Shaun Marcum RC	1.50
BDP81	Matt Nachreiner RC	1.00
BDP82	Chris Kinsey RC	1.00
BDP83	Jonathan Fulton RC	1.00
BDP84	Edgardo Baez RC	1.00
BDP85	Robert Valido RC	1.00
BDP86	Kenny Lewis RC	1.00
BDP87	Trent Peterson RC	1.00
BDP88	Johnny Woodard RC	1.00
BDP89	Wes Littleton RC	1.00
BDP90	Sean Rodriguez RC	1.00
BDP91	Kyle Pearson RC	1.00
BDP92	Josh Rainwater RC	1.00
BDP93	Travis Schlichting RC	1.00
BDP94	Tim Battle RC	1.00
BDP95	Aaron Hill RC	2.00
BDP96	Bob McCrory RC	1.00
BDP97	Rick Guarno RC	1.00
BDP98	Brandon Yarbrough RC	1.00
BDP99	Peter Stonard RC	1.00
BDP100	Darin Downs RC	1.00
BDP101	Matt Bruback RC	1.00
BDP102	Danny Garcia RC	1.00
BDP103	Cory Stewart RC	1.00
BDP104	Ferdin Tejeda RC	1.00
BDP105	Kade Johnson RC	1.00
BDP106	Andrew Brown RC	1.00
BDP107	Aquilino Lopez RC	1.00
BDP108	Stephen Randolph RC	1.00
BDP109	Dave Matranga RC	1.00
BDP110	Dustin McGowan RC	1.00
BDP111	Juan Camacho RC	1.00
BDP112	Cliff Lee	2.00
BDP113	Jeff Duncan RC	1.00
BDP114	C.J. Wilson	.50
BDP115	Brandon Roberson RC	1.00
BDP116	David Corrente RC	1.00
BDP117	Kevin Beavers RC	1.00
BDP118	Anthony Webster RC	1.00
BDP119	Oscar Villarreal RC	1.00
BDP120	Hong-Chih Kuo RC	2.00
BDP121	Josh Barfield	.15
BDP122	Denny Bautista	.15
BDP123	Chris Burke	1.00
BDP124	Robinson Cano RC	15.00
BDP125	Jose Castillo	.15
BDP126	Neal Cotts	.15

BDP127	Jorge De La Rosa	.15
BDP128	J.D. Durbin	.15
BDP129	Edwin Encarnacion	.50
BDP130	Gavin Floyd	.15
BDP131	Alexis Gomez	.15
BDP132	Edgar Gonzalez RC	.50
BDP133	Khalil Greene	.15
BDP134	Zack Greinke	.40
BDP135	Franklin Gutierrez	.50
BDP136	Rich Harden	.15
BDP137	J.J. Hardy	1.00
BDP138	Ryan Howard	35.00
BDP139	Justin Huber	.15
BDP140	David Kelton	.15
BDP141	David Krynzel	.15
BDP142	Pete LaForest	.15
BDP143	Adam LaRoche	.15
BDP144	Preston Larrison	.50
BDP145	John Maine RC	2.00
BDP146	Andy Marte	.15
BDP147	Jeff Mathis	.15
BDP148	Joe Mauer	1.00
BDP149	Clint Nageotte	.15
BDP150	Chris Narveson	.15
BDP151	Ramon Nivar RC	.15
BDP152	Felix Pie	1.00
BDP153	Guillermo Quiroz RC	1.00
BDP154	Rene Reyes	.15
BDP155	Royce Ring	.15
BDP156	Alexis Rios	1.50
BDP157	Grady Sizemore	1.00
BDP158	Stephen Smitherman	.15
BDP159	Seung Jun Song	.15
BDP160	Scott Thorman	.15
BDP161	Chad Tracy	.15
BDP162	Chin-Hui Tsao	.15
BDP163	John Van Benschoten RC	1.00
BDP164	Kevin Youkilis	5.00
BDP165	Chien-Ming Wang	15.00
BDP166	Chris Lubanski/ Auto.	15.00
BDP167	Ryan Harvey/Auto. RC	15.00
BDP168	Matt Murton/Auto. RC	10.00
BDP169	Jay Sborz/Auto. RC	10.00
BDP170	Brandon Wood/ Auto.	30.00
BDP171	Nick Markakis/ Auto.	60.00
BDP172	Rickie Weeks/ Auto.	20.00
BDP173	Eric Duncan/Auto.	15.00
BDP174	Chad Billingsley/ Auto.	40.00
BDP175	Ryan Wagner/ Auto. RC	10.00
BDP176	Delmon Young/ Auto. RC	30.00

Refractor

JOHN MAINE

Rookies (29-165):	2-4X
Inserted 1:11	
Autos. (166-176):	.75-1.5X
Inserted 1:196	

Gold Refractor

Rookies (29-165):	3-5X
Production 50 Sets	
Autos. (166-176):	No Pricing
Inserted 1:479	

X-Fractor

BROOKS McNIVEN

Rookies (29-165):	2-4X
Production 130 Sets	
Autos. (166-176):	.75-2X
Inserted 1:393	

2003 Bowman Heritage

MIGUEL CABRERA • Third Base • MARLINS

	NM/M
Complete Set (280):	60.00
Common Player:	.25
Cards 171-180 have three versions.	
Pack (8):	3.00
Box (24):	65.00

1	Jorge Posada	.50
2	Todd Helton	.75
3	Marcus Giles	.25
4	Eric Chavez	.25
5	Edgar Martinez	.25
6	Luis Gonzalez	.25
7	Corey Patterson	.25
8	Preston Wilson	.25
9	Ryan Klesko	.25
10	Randy Johnson	1.00
11	Eric Byrnes	.25
12	Carlos Lee	.40
13	Steve Finley	.25
14	A.J. Pierzynski	.25
15	Troy Glaus	.40
16	Darin Erstad	.40
17	Moises Alou	.40
18	Torii Hunter	.50
19	Marlon Byrd	.25
20	Mark Prior	.40
21	Shannon Stewart	.25
22	Craig Biggio	.40
23	Johnny Damon	.75
24	Robert Fick	.25
25	Jason Giambi	.75
26	Fernando Vina	.25
27	Aubrey Huff	.25
28	Benito Santiago	.25
29	Jay Gibbons	.25
30	Ken Griffey Jr.	2.00
31	Rocco Baldelli	.50
32	Pat Burrell	.50
33	A.J. Burnett	.25
34	Omar Vizquel	.25
35	Greg Maddux	1.50
36	Jae Weong Seo	.25
37	C.C. Sabathia	.25
38	Geoff Jenkins	.25
39	Ty Wigginton	.25
40	Jeff Kent	.40
41	Orlando Hudson	.25
42	Edgardo Alfonzo	.25
43	Greg Myers	.25
44	Melvin Mora	.25
45	Sammy Sosa	.75
46	Russ Ortiz	.25
47	Josh Beckett	.50
48	David Wells	.25
49	Woody Williams	.25
50	Alex Rodriguez	2.00
51	Randy Wolf	.25
52	Carlos Beltran	.75
53	Austin Kearns	.25
54	Trot Nixon	.25
55	Ivan Rodriguez	.50
56	Shea Hillenbrand	.25
57	Roberto Alomar	.40
58	John Olerud	.25
59	Michael Young	.25
60	Garret Anderson	.25
61	Mike Lieberthal	.25
62	Adam Dunn	.50
63	Raul Ibanez	.25
64	Kenny Lofton	.25
65	Ichiro Suzuki	1.50
66	Jarrod Washburn	.25
67	Shawn Chacon	.25
68	Alex Gonzalez	.25
69	Roy Halladay	.40
70	Vladimir Guerrero	1.00
71	Hee Seop Choi	.25
72	Brandon Phillips	.25
73	Ray Durham	.25
74	Mark Teixeira	.75
75	Hank Blalock	.25
76	Jerry Hairston Jr.	.25
77	Erubiel Durazo	.25
78	Frank Catalanotto	.25
79	Jacque Jones	.25
80	Bobby Abreu	.50
81	Mike Hampton	.25
82	Zach Day	.25
83	Jimmy Rollins	.75
84	Joel Pineiro	.25
85	Brett Myers	.25
86	Frank Thomas	1.00
87	Aramis Ramirez	.40
88	Paul LoDuca	.25
89	Bobby Higginson	.25
90	Brian Giles	.25
91	Jose Cruz Jr.	.25
92	Derek Lowe	.25
93	Mark Buehrle	.25
94	Wade Miller	.25
95	Derek Jeter	2.00
96	Bret Boone	.25
97	Tony Batista	.25
98	Sean Casey	.25
99	Eric Hinske	.25
100	Albert Pujols	2.00

101	Runelvys Hernandez	.25
102	Vernon Wells	.40
103	Kerry Wood	.40
104	Lance Berkman	.50
105	Alfonso Soriano	.75
106	Ken Harvey	.25
107	Bartolo Colon	.25
108	Andy Pettitte	.50
109	Rafael Furcal	.40
110	Dontrelle Willis	.25
111	Carl Crawford	.40
112	Scott Rolen	.50
113	Chipper Jones	1.00
114	Magglio Ordonez	.50
115	Bernie Williams	.50
116	Roy Oswalt	.50
117	Kevin Brown	.25
118	Cristian Guzman	.25
119	Kazuhisa Ishii	.25
120	Larry Walker	.40
121	Miguel Tejada	.50
122	Manny Ramirez	1.00
123	Mike Mussina	.50
124	Mike Lowell	.25
125	Barry Bonds	2.00
126	Aaron Boone	.25
127	Carlos Delgado	.50
128	Jose Vidro	.25
129	Brad Radke	.25
130	Rafael Palmeiro	.50
131	Mark Mulder	.25
132	Jason Schmidt	.25
133	Gary Sheffield	.50
134	Richie Sexson	.25
135	Barry Zito	.25
136	Tom Glavine	.40
137	Jim Edmonds	.40
138	Andruw Jones	.40
139	Pedro J. Martinez	1.00
140	Curt Schilling	.75
141	Joe Kennedy	.25
142	Nomar Garciaparra	.75
143	Vicente Padilla	.25
144	Kevin Millwood	.40
145	Shawn Green	.25
146	Jeff Bagwell	.50
147	Hideo Nomo	.25
148	Fred McGriff	.25
149	Matt Morris	.25
150	Roger Clemens	1.50
151	Damian Moss	.25
152	Orlando Cabrera	.25
153	Tim Hudson	.40
154	Mike Sweeney	.25
155	Jim Thome	.75
156	Rich Aurilia	.25
157	Mike Piazza	1.00
158	Edgar Renteria	.25
159	Javy Lopez	.25
160	Jamie Moyer	.25
161	Miguel Cabrera	.50
162	Adam Loewen RC	.50
163	Jose Reyes	.75
164	Zack Greinke	.25
165	Cole Hamels	.25
166	Jeremy Guthrie	.25
167	Victor Martinez	.40
168	Rich Harden	.25
169	Joe Mauer	.50
170	Khalil Greene	.25
171	Willie Mays	2.00
172	Phil Rizzuto	.50
173	Al Kaline	1.00
174	Warren Spahn	1.00
175	Jimmy Piersall	.50
176	Luis Aparicio	.50
177	Whitey Ford	1.00
178	Harmon Killebrew	1.00
179	Duke Snider	1.00
180	Bobby Richardson	.50
181	David Martinez	.25
182	Felix Pie RC	1.00
183	Kevin Correia RC	.50
184	Brandon Webb RC	3.00
185	Matt Diaz RC	.50
186	Lew Ford RC	.50
187	Jeremy Griffiths	.25
188	Matt Hensley RC	.75
189	Danny Garcia RC	.50
190	Elizardo Ramirez RC	.50
191	Greg Aquino RC	.50
192	Felix Sanchez RC	.50
193	Kelly Shoppach RC	.50
194	Bubba Nelson RC	.50
195	Mike O'Keefe RC	.50
196	Hanley Ramirez RC	8.00
197	Todd Wellemeyer RC	.75
198	Dustin Moseley RC	.50
199	Eric Crozier RC	.50
200	Ryan Shealy RC	1.00
201	Jeremy Bonderman	.75
202	Bo Hart RC	.75
203	Dusty Brown RC	.50
204	Rob Hammock RC	.50
205	Jorge Piedra RC	.50
206	Jason Kubel RC	1.50
207	Stephen Randolph RC	.50
208	Andy Sisco RC	.50
209	Matt Kata RC	.50
210	Robinson Cano RC	10.00
211	Ben Francisco RC	1.00
212	Arnie Munoz RC	.50
213	Ozzie Chavez RC	.50
214	Beau Kemp RC	.50
215	Travis Wong RC	.50
216	Brian McCann	5.00
217	Aquilino Lopez RC	.50
218	Bobby Basham RC	.50

219	Tim Olson RC	.50
220	Nathan Panther RC	.50
221	Wilfredo Ledezma RC	.50
222	Josh Willingham RC	1.00
223	David Cash RC	.50
224	Oscar Villarreal RC	.50
225	Jeff Duncan RC	.75
226	Dan Haren	2.00
227	Michel Hernandez RC	.50
228	Matt Murton RC	.50
229	Clay Hensley RC	.75
230	Tyler Johnson RC	.50
231	Tyler Martin RC	.50
232	J.D. Durbin RC	.50
233	Shane Victorino RC	2.50
234	Rajai Davis RC	1.00
235	Chien-Ming Wang RC	3.00
236	Travis Ishikawa RC	.50
237	Eric Eckenstahler	.25
238	Dustin McGowan RC	.50
239	Prentice Redman RC	.50
240	Haj Turay RC	.25
241	Matt DeMarco RC	.25
242	Lou Palmisano RC	.50
243	Eric Reed RC	.50
244	Willie Eyre RC	.50
245	Ferdin Tejeda RC	.50
246	Michael Garciaparra	.25
247	Michael Hinckley RC	.50
248	Branden Florence RC	.50
249	Trent Oeltjen RC	.50
250	Mike Neu RC	.50
251	Chris Lubanski RC	.50
252	Brandon Wood RC	1.00
253	Delmon Young RC	2.00
253	Delmon Young/ Auto. RC	25.00
254	Matt Harrison RC	.50
255	Chad Billingsley RC	3.00
256	Josh Anderson RC	.50
257	Brian McFall	.50
258	Ryan Wagner RC	.50
259	Billy Hogan RC	.50
260	Nate Spears RC	.50
261	Ryan Harvey RC	.75
262	Wes Littleton RC	.50
263	Xavier Paul RC	.75
264	Sean Rodriguez RC	.75
265	Brian Finch RC	.50
266	Josh Rainwater RC	.50
267	Brian Snyder RC	.50
268	Eric Duncan RC	.75
269	Rickie Weeks RC	1.50
270	Tim Battle RC	.50
271	Scott Beerer RC	.50
272	Aaron Hill RC	1.00
273	Casey Abrams RC	.50
274	Jonathan Fulton RC	.50
275	Todd Jennings RC	.50
276	Jordan Pratt RC	.50
277	Tom Gorzelanny RC	.75
278	Matt Lorenzo RC	.50
279	Jarrod Saltalamacchia RC	1.00
280	Mike Wagner RC	.50

Diamond Cuts

SCOTT ROLEN • Third Base • ST. LOUIS CARDINALS

	NM/M
Common Player:	4.00
Red:	1-2X
Production 56 Sets	

JA	Jeremy Affeldt	.25
MA	Moises Alou	5.00
TA	Tony Armas Jr.	4.00
JB	Jeff Bagwell	6.00
CB	Craig Biggio	6.00
HB	Hank Blalock	4.00
BB	Bret Boone	4.00
EC	Eric Chavez	4.00
JE	Jim Edmonds	6.00
JG	Jason Giambi	4.00
TG	Troy Glaus	6.00
MG	Mark Grace	4.00
VG	Vladimir Guerrero	4.00
CG	Cristian Guzman	4.00
TH	Todd Helton	6.00
RH	Rickey Henderson	12.00
JJ	Jason Jennings	4.00
AJ	Andruw Jones	4.00
CJ1	Chipper Jones/Jsy	8.00
CJ2	Chipper Jones/Bat	8.00
AK	Austin Kearns	4.00
PL	Paul LoDuca	4.00
JL	Javy Lopez	4.00
PM	Pedro J. Martinez	8.00
KM	Kevin Millwood	4.00
MM	Mark Mulder	4.00
BM	Brett Myers	4.00
HN	Hideo Nomo	8.00
RP1	Rafael Palmeiro/Jsy	8.00
RP2	Rafael Palmeiro/Bat	8.00
JLP	Josh Phelps	4.00
AP	Albert Pujols	15.00
JR	Jose Reyes	6.00
AR1	Alex Rodriguez/Jsy	10.00
AR2	Alex Rodriguez/Bat	10.00
SR1	Scott Rolen/Jsy	8.00

SR2	Scott Rolen/Bat	10.00
KI	Kazuhiro Sasaki	4.00
GS	Gary Sheffield	6.00
AS	Alfonso Soriano	8.00
SS1	Sammy Sosa/Jsy	10.00
SS2	Sammy Sosa/Bat	10.00
MS	Mike Sweeney	4.00
MT	Miguel Tejada	6.00
JV	Javier Vazquez	4.00
JW	Jarrod Washburn	4.00
VW	Vernon Wells	4.00
BW	Bernie Williams	6.00
KW	Kerry Wood	4.00
BZ	Barry Zito	6.00

Keith Olbermann Autograph

KEITH OLBERMANN

	NM/M
Inserted 1:1,421	
KO	Keith Olbermann	50.00

Signs of Greatness

	NM/M
Common Player:	6.00
Inserted 1:30	
Red Ink:	No Pricing
Production One Set	

CB	Chad Billingsley	25.00
RC	Robinson Cano	125.00
JD	Jeff Duncan	8.00
BF	Brian Finch	8.00
TG	Tom Gorzelanny	10.00
RH	Rich Harden	12.00
MM	Matt Murton	8.00
FP	Felix Pie	8.00
BS	Brian Snyder	8.00
RW	Rickie Weeks	15.00
DW	Dontrelle Willis	10.00
KY	Kevin Youkilis	25.00

2003 Bowman's Best

	NM/M
Complete Set:	
Common Player:	.50
Pack (5):	40.00
Box (10):	350.00

Veterans

GJA	Garret Anderson	.50
LB	Lance Berkman	.75
BLB	Barry Bonds	2.00
PB	Pat Burrell	.50
WRC	Roger Clemens	2.00
NG	Nomar Garciaparra	1.00
JGG	Jason Giambi	.75
BSG	Brian Giles	.50
SG	Shawn Green	.50
KG	Ken Griffey Jr.	2.50
VG	Vladimir Guerrero	1.00
TH	Todd Helton	1.00
TKH	Torii Hunter	.75

DJ	Derek Jeter	4.00
RJ	Randy Johnson	1.50
CJ	Chipper Jones	1.50
AK	Austin Kearns	.50
JFK	Jeff Kent	.50
GM	Greg Maddux	2.50
PM	Pedro J. Martinez	1.50
MOR	Magglio Ordonez	.50
MJP	Mike Piazza	1.50
MP	Mark Prior	1.00
AP	Albert Pujols	4.00
MR	Manny Ramirez	1.50
AR	Alex Rodriguez	3.00
CMS	Curt Schilling	1.50
AS	Alfonso Soriano	1.50
SS	Sammy Sosa	2.50
IS	Ichiro Suzuki	2.50
MS	Mike Sweeney	.50
MT	Miguel Tejada	1.00
JT	Jim Thome	1.00
LW	Larry Walker	.50
BZ	Barry Zito	.75

First-Year Players

JB	Jeremy Bonderman	1.50
TJB	T.J. Bohn	1.00
MB	Matt Bruback RC	1.00
BC	Bernie Castro RC	1.00
JC	Jose Contreras RC	1.50
MD	Matt Diaz RC	1.00
BJH	Bo Hart RC	1.00
RM	Ramon Martinez RC	1.00
MO	Mike O'Keefe RC	1.00
JMS	Jon-Mark Sprowl RC	1.00
TT	Terry Tiffee	1.00
HT	Haj Turay RC	1.00
SV	Shane Victorino RC	4.00
CW	Chien-Ming Wang RC	6.00
DY	Dustin Yount RC	1.00

First-Year Player Autographs

Common Auto.: 8.00
Inserted 1:1

TA	Tyler Adamczyk RC	8.00
GA	Greg Aquino RC	8.00
BWB	Bobby Basham RC	10.00
GB	Gregor Blanco RC	8.00
AB	Andrew Brown RC	8.00
BB	Bryan Bullington RC	8.00
RC	Ryan Cameron RC	8.00
DC	David Cash RC	8.00
OC	Ozzie Chavez RC	8.00
RD	Rajai Davis RC	12.00
CDC	Chris De La Cruz RC	8.00
MD	Matt Diaz RC	10.00
CAD	Carlos Duran RC	10.00
JDD	J.D. Durbin RC	8.00
WE	Willie Eyre RC	8.00
BF	Branden Florence RC	10.00
LF	Lew Ford RC	10.00
BLF	Ben Francisco RC	15.00
JG	Joey Gomes RC	10.00
JRG	Jeremy Griffiths RC	10.00
MNH	Matt Hagen RC	10.00
RWH	Robby Hammock RC	8.00
DH	Dan Haren RC	25.00
BH	Brendan Harris RC	10.00
MDH	Matt Hensley RC	8.00
MH	Michel Hernandez RC	10.00
MHI	Michael Hinckley RC	10.00
RH	Ryan Howard RC	250.00
TI	Travis Ishikawa RC	10.00
KJ	Kade Johnson RC	8.00
TJ	Tyler Johnson RC	10.00
MK	Matt Kata RC	10.00
BK	Beau Kemp RC	8.00
JK	Jason Bagwell RC	15.00
PL	Pete LaForest RC	10.00
WL	Wilfredo Ledezma RC	10.00
NL	Nook Logan RC	10.00
MDM	Mark Malaska RC	8.00
CM	Charlie Manning RC	10.00
DM	David Martinez	10.00
AM	Aneudis Mateo RC	8.00
BM	Brian McCann RC	50.00
DMM	Dustin McGowan RC	10.00
JM	Jose Morales	10.00
DAM	Dustin Moseley RC	10.00
TO	Tim Olson RC	10.00
FP	Felix Pie RC	15.00
ER	Elizardo Ramirez RC	10.00
HR	Hanley Ramirez RC	125.00
DR	Darrell Rasner	10.00
PR	Prentice Redman RC	8.00
FS	Felix Sanchez RC	10.00
GS	Gary Schneidmiller RC	8.00
CSS	Corey Shafer RC	10.00
RS	Ryan Shealy RC	10.00
KS	Kelly Shoppach RC	10.00
CS	Cory Stewart RC	10.00
TSH	Thomari Story-Harden RC	8.00
FT	Ferdin Tejeda RC	10.00
ET	Eider Torres RC	10.00
ST	Scott Tyler	10.00
JV	Joe Valentine RC	8.00
DW	Doug Waechter RC	10.00
AW	Aron Weston RC	8.00
JW	Josh Willingham RC	20.00
CJW	C.J. Wilson	8.00
KY	Kevin Youkilis RC	40.00
CW	Chien-Ming Wang RC	125.00

Blue

Blue Autographs: 1-1.5X
Inserted 1:32
Blue Base Card: 3-5X
Blue Rookies: 1-2X
Production 100

Red

Red Autographs: 2-4X
Inserted 1:63
Red Base Card: 4-8X
Red Rookies: 2-3X
Production 50

Double Play

NM/M
Common Card: 20.00
Inserted 1:55

EB	Elizardo Ramirez, Bryan Bullington	25.00
GK	Joey Gomes, Jason Kubel	50.00
SR	Felix Sanchez, Darrell Rasner	20.00
YS	Kevin Youkilis, Kelly Shoppach	40.00
HV	Dan Haren, Joe Valentine	25.00
GM	Jeremy Griffiths, David Martinez	20.00
HM	Michael Hinckley, Brian McCann	20.00
RS	Prentice Redman, Gary Schneidmiller	20.00
LL	Nook Logan, Wilfredo Ledezma	25.00
SB	Corey Shafer, Gregor Blanco	25.00

Triple Play

NM/M
Inserted 1:219

DRS	Rajai Davis, Hanley Ramirez, Ryan Shealy	85.00
BCS	Andrew Brown, David Cash, Cory Stewart	30.00

First-Year Player Relics

NM/M
Common Player: 5.00

RLD	Rajai Davis	8.00
JLF	Lew Ford	5.00
JGG	Joey Gomes	5.00
RJH	Ryan Howard	50.00
JJK	Jason Kubel	8.00
HRB	Hanley Ramirez	30.00
RNS	Ryan Shealy	5.00
KBS	Kelly Shoppach	8.00
KEY	Kevin Youkilis	12.00

2004 Bowman

NM/M
Complete Set (330): 70.00
Common Player: .15
Common Rookie: .50
Pack (10): 2.50
Box (24): 50.00

1	Garret Anderson	.15
2	Larry Walker	.25
3	Derek Jeter	2.00
4	Curt Schilling	.50
5	Carlos Zambrano	.40
6	Shawn Green	.25
7	Manny Ramirez	.75
8	Randy Johnson	.75
9	Jeremy Bonderman	.25
10	Alfonso Soriano	.75
11	Scott Rolen	.50
12	Kerry Wood	.25
13	Eric Gagne	.25
14	Ryan Klesko	.15
15	Kevin Millar	.15
16	Ty Wigginton	.15
17	David Ortiz	.75
18	Luis Castillo	.15
19	Bernie Williams	.40
20	Edgar Renteria	.25
21	Matt Kata	.15
22	Bartolo Colon	.25
23	Derek Lee	.50
24	Gary Sheffield	.40
25	Nomar Garciaparra	.75
26	Kevin Millwood	.25
27	Corey Patterson	.25
28	Carlos Beltran	.50
29	Mike Lieberthal	.15
30	Troy Glaus	.40
31	Preston Wilson	.15
32	Jorge Posada	.40
33	Bo Hart	.15
34	Mark Prior	.40
35	Hideo Nomo	.25
36	Jason Kendall	.15
37	Shea Hillenbrand	.15
38	Dmitri Young	.15
39	Aaron Boone	.15
40	Jim Edmonds	.40
41	Ryan Ludwick	.15
42	Brandon Webb	.25
43	Todd Helton	.50
44	Jacque Jones	.15
45	Xavier Nady	.15
46	Tim Salmon	.25
47	Kelvim Escobar	.15
48	Tony Batista	.15
49	Nick Johnson	.15
50	Jim Thome	.50
51	Casey Blake	.15
52	Trot Nixon	.25
53	Luis Gonzalez	.25
54	Dontrelle Willis	.25
55	Mike Mussina	.40
56	Carl Crawford	.25
57	Mark Buehrle	.25
58	Scott Podsednik	.25
59	Brian Giles	.15
60	Rafael Furcal	.25
61	Miguel Cabrera	.75
62	Rich Harden	.15
63	Mark Teixeira	.50
64	Frank Thomas	.75
65	Johan Santana	.50
66	Jason Schmidt	.25
67	Aramis Ramirez	.40
68	Jose Reyes	.75
69	Magglio Ordonez	.25
70	Mike Sweeney	.15
71	Eric Chavez	.25
72	Rocco Baldelli	.25
73	Sammy Sosa	.50
74	Javy Lopez	.15
75	Roy Oswalt	.25
76	Raul Ibanez	.15
77	Ivan Rodriguez	.50
78	Jerome Williams	.15
79	Carlos Lee	.25
80	Geoff Jenkins	.15
81	Sean Burroughs	.15
82	Marcus Giles	.15
83	Mike Lowell	.15
84	Barry Zito	.40
85	Aubrey Huff	.15
86	Esteban Loaiza	.15
87	Torii Hunter	.25
88	Phil Nevin	.15
89	Andruw Jones	.50
90	Josh Beckett	.40
91	Mark Mulder	.25
92	Hank Blalock	.25
93	Jason Phillips	.15
94	Russ Ortiz	.15
95	Juan Pierre	.25
96	Tom Glavine	.25
97	Gil Meche	.15
98	Ramon Ortiz	.15
99	Richie Sexson	.40
100	Albert Pujols	2.00
101	Javier Vazquez	.15
102	Johnny Damon	.50
103	Alex Rodriguez	1.50
104	Omar Vizquel	.25
105	Chipper Jones	.75
106	Lance Berkman	.40
107	Tim Hudson	.40
108	Carlos Delgado	.40
109	Austin Kearns	.25
110	Orlando Cabrera	.25
111	Edgar Martinez	.25
112	Melvin Mora	.15
113	Jeff Bagwell	.50
114	Marlon Byrd	.15
115	Vernon Wells	.25
116	C.C. Sabathia	.25
117	Cliff Floyd	.15
118	Ichiro Suzuki	1.00
119	Miguel Olivo	.15
120	Mike Piazza	.75
121	Adam Dunn	.40
122	Paul Lo Duca	.15
123	Brett Myers	.25
124	Michael Young	.25
125	Larry Bigbie	.15
126	Greg Maddux	1.00
127	Vladimir Guerrero	.50
128	Miguel Tejada	.40
129	Andy Pettitte	.40
130	Jose Cruz	.15
131	Ken Griffey Jr.	1.50
132	Shannon Stewart	.15
133	Joel Pineiro	.15
134	Luis Matos	.15
135	Jeff Kent	.25
136	Randy Wolf	.15
137	Chris Woodward	.15
138	Jody Gerut	.15
139	Jose Vidro	.15
140	Bret Boone	.15
141	Bill Mueller	.15
142	Angel Berroa	.15
143	Bobby Abreu	.25
144	Roy Halladay	.25
145	Delmon Young	.50
146	Jonny Gomes	.25
147	Rickie Weeks	.40
148	Edwin Jackson	.15
149	Neal Cotts	.15
150	Jason Bay	.25
151	Khalil Greene	.25
152	Joe Mauer	.40
153	Bobby Jenks	.15
154	Chin-Feng Chen	.15
154	Chin-Feng Chen/Jsy	10.00
155	Chien-Ming Wang	.75
155	Chien-Ming Wang/Jsy	10.00
156	Mickey Hall	.15
156	Mickey Hall/Jsy	5.00
157	James Houser	.15
157	James Houser/Jsy	5.00
158	Jay Sborz	.15
158	Jay Sborz/Jsy	5.00
159	Jonathan Fulton	.15
159	Jonathan Fulton/Jsy	5.00
160	Steve Lerud	.15
160	Steve Lerud/Jsy	5.00
161	Grady Sizemore	.15
161	Grady Sizemore/Auto.	25.00
162	Felix Pie	.15
162	Felix Pie/Auto.	10.00
163	Dustin McGowan	.15
163	Dustin McGowan/Auto.	8.00
164	Chris Lubanski	.15
164	Chris Lubanski/Jersey	5.00
165	Tom Gorzelanny	.15
165	Tom Gorzelanny/Auto.	10.00
166	Rudy Guillen RC	1.00
166	Rudy Guillen/auto RC	8.00
167	Bobby Brownlie RC	1.00
167	Bobby Brownlie/ Auto.	8.00
168	Conor Jackson	1.00
168	Conor Jackson/Auto.	10.00
169	Matt Moses	.50
169	Matt Moses/Auto.	8.00
170	Ervin Santana RC	1.50
170	Ervin Santana/Auto. RC	20.00
171	Merkin Valdez RC	.50
171	Merkin Valdez/Auto. RC	8.00
172	Erick Aybar RC	1.00
172	Erick Aybar/Auto. RC	10.00
173	Brad Sullivan	.50
173	Brad Sullivan/Auto.	10.00
174	David Aardsma	.50
174	David Aardsma/Auto.	10.00
175	Brad Snyder	.50
175	Brad Snyder/Auto.	10.00
176	Alberto Callaspo RC	.75
177	Brandon Medders RC	.50
178	Zach Miner RC	.50
179	Charlie Zink RC	.40
180	Adam Greenberg	.50
181	Kevin Howard RC	.50
182	Wanell Severino RC	.50
183	Kevin Kouzmanoff RC	1.00
184	Joel Zumaya RC	1.00
185	Skip Schumaker RC	.50
186	Nic Ungs RC	.50
187	Todd Self RC	.50
188	Brian Steffek RC	.50
189	Brock Peterson RC	.50
190	Greg Thissen RC	.50
191	Frank Brooks RC	.50
192	Estee Harris RC	.50
192	Estee Harris/Jsy RC	4.00
193	Chris Mabeus RC	.50
194	Daniel Giese RC	.50
195	Jared Wells RC	.50
196	Carlos Sosa RC	.50
197	Bobby Madritsch RC	.50
198	Calvin Hayes RC	.50
199	Omar Quintanilla RC	.50
200	Chris O'Riordan RC	.50
201	Tim Hutting RC	.50
202	Carlos Quentin RC	3.00
203	Brayan Pena RC	.50
204	Jeff Salazar RC	1.00
205	David Murphy	.75
206	Alberto Garcia RC	.50
207	Ramon Ramirez RC	.50
208	Luis Bolivar RC	.50
209	Rodney Choy Foo RC	.50
210	Kyle Sleeth	.50
211	Anthony Acevedo RC	.50
212	Chad Santos RC	.50
213	Jason Frasor RC	.50
214	Jesse Roman RC	.50
215	James Tomlin RC	.50
216	Josh Labandeira RC	.50
217	Joaquin Arias RC	.50
218	Don Sutton RC (Photo actually Nick Swisher.)	1.00
219	Danny Gonzalez RC	.50
220	Javier Guzman RC	.50
221	Anthony Lerew RC	.50
221	Anthony Lerew/Jsy RC	5.00
222	Jon Knott RC	.50
223	Jesse English RC	.50
224	Felix Hernandez RC	5.00
225	Travis Hanson RC	.50
226	Jesse Floyd RC	.50
227	Nick Gorneault RC	.50
228	Craig Ansman RC	.50
229	Wardell Starling RC	.50
230	Carl Loadenthal RC	.50
231	David Crouthers RC	.50
232	Harvey Garcia RC	.50
233	Casey Kopitzke RC	.50
234	Ricky Nolasco RC	1.00
235	Miguel Perez RC	.50
236	Ryan Mulhern RC	.50
237	Chris Aguila RC	.50
238	Brooks Conrad RC	.50
239	Damaso Espino RC	.50
240	Jereme Milons RC	.50
241	Luke Hughes RC	.50
242	Kory Casto RC	.50
243	Jose Valdez RC	.50
244	J.T. Stotts RC	.50
245	Lee Gwaltney RC	.50
246	Yoann Torrealba RC	.50
247	Omar Falcon RC	.50
248	Jon Coutlangus RC	.50
249	George Sherrill RC	.50
250	John Santor RC	.50
251	Tony Richie RC	.50
252	Kevin Richardson RC	.50
253	Tim Bittner RC	.50
254	Dustin Nippert RC	.75
255	Jose Capellan RC	.50
256	Donald Levinski RC	.50
257	Jerome Gamble RC	.50
258	Jeff Keppinger RC	1.00
259	Jason Szuminski RC	.50
260	Akinori Otsuka RC	.50
261	Ryan Budde RC	.50
262	Shingo Takatsu RC	.50
263	Jeffrey Allison	.40
264	Hector Gimenez RC	.50
265	Tim Frend RC	.50
266	Tom Farmer RC	.50
267	Shawn Hill RC	.50
268	Lastings Milledge	1.50
269	Scott Proctor RC	.50
270	Jorge Mejia RC	.50
271	Terry Jones RC	.50
272	Zach Duke RC	.75
273	Tim Stauffer RC	.50
274	Luke Anderson RC	.50
275	Hunter Brown RC	.50
276	Matt Lemanczyk RC	.50
277	Fernando Cortez RC	.50
278	Vince Perkins RC	.50
279	Tommy Murphy RC	.50
280	Mike Gosling	.50
281	Paul Bacot	.50
282	Matt Capps RC	.75
283	Juan Gutierrez RC	.50
284	Teodoro Encarnacion RC	.50
285	Juan Cedeno RC	.50
286	Matt Creighton RC	.50
287	Ryan Hankins RC	.50
288	Leo Nunez RC	.50
289	Dave Wallace RC	.50
290	Rob Tejeda RC	.50
291	Lincoln Holdzkom RC	.50
292	Jason Hirsh	1.00
293	Tydus Meadows RC	.50
294	Khalid Ballouli RC	.50
295	Benji DeQuin RC	.50
296	Tyler Davidson	1.00
297	Brent Colamarino RC	.50
298	Marcus McBeth RC	.50
299	Brad Eldred RC	.50
300	David Pauley RC	.50
301	Yadier Molina RC	2.50
302	Chris Shelton RC	.75
303	Travis Blackley RC	.50
304	Jon DeVries	.50
305	Sheldon Fulse RC	.50
306	Vito Chiaravalloti RC	.50
307	Warner Madrigal RC	.50
308	Reid Gorecki RC	.50
309	Sung Jung RC	.50
310	Peter Shier RC	.50
311	Michael Mooney RC	.50
312	Kenny Perez RC	.50
313	Mike Mallory RC	.50
314	Ben Himes RC	.50
315	Ivan Ochoa RC	.50
316	Donald Kelly RC	.50
317	Logan Kensing RC	.50
318	Kevin Davidson RC	.50
319	Brian Pilkington	.50
320	Alex Romero RC	.50
321	Chad Chop RC	.50
322	Dioner Navarro RC	.75
323	Casey Myers RC	.50
324	Mike Rouse	.50
325	Sergio Silva RC	.50
326	J.J. Furmaniak RC	.50
327	Brad Vericker RC	.50
328	Blake Hawksworth RC	1.00
329	Brock Jacobsen RC	.50
330	Alec Zumwalt RC	.50

Gold

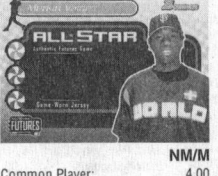

Stars: 1-2X
Rookies: 1-2X
Inserted 1:1

Uncirculated

Stars: 4-8X

Rookies: 3-5X
Production 245 Sets

1st Edition

NM/M
Stars: 3-5X
Rookies: 1-2X
HTA Exclusive
Pack (10): 4.00
Box (20): 75.00

Base of the Future Autographed Relic

NM/M
HTA Exclusive

GS	Grady Sizemore	30.00

Futures Game Gear

NM/M
Common Player: 4.00

DB	Denny Bautista	4.00
CB	Chris Burke	4.00
JC	Jose Castillo	4.00
NC	Neal Cotts	4.00
JD	Jorge De La Rosa	4.00
EE	Edwin Encarnacion	4.00
SH	Shawn Hill	4.00
EJ	Edwin Jackson	4.00
DK	David Kelton	4.00
DBK	David Krynzel	4.00
PL	Pete LaForest	4.00
JM	John Maine	4.00
CN	Clint Nageotte	4.00
RN	Ramon Nivar	4.00
GQ	Guillermo Quiroz	4.00
AR	Alexis Rios	8.00
ES	Ervin Santana	8.00
SS	Stephen Smitherman	8.00
SJS	Seung Jun Song	4.00
CT	Chad Tracy	4.00
ST	Scott Thorman	4.00
MV	Merkin Valdez	4.00
JV	John VanBenschoten	4.00
CW	Chien-Ming Wang	20.00
KY	Kevin Youkilis	10.00

Rookie of the Year Dual Relic

NM/M
Inserted 1:829

BW	Angel Berroa, Dontrelle Willis	15.00

Signs of Future

NM/M
Common Autograph: 8.00
Red Ink: No Pricing
Production 25 Sets

JB	Justin Backsmeyer	9.00
IC	Ismael Castro	9.00
BC	Brent Cleveln	9.00
ED	Eric Duncan	10.00
BF	Brian Finch	8.00
RH	Ryan Harvey	10.00
AH	Aaron Hill	10.00
JH	James Houser	8.00
TJ	Tyler Johnson	8.00
TL	Todd Linden	8.00
NM	Nick Markakis	25.00
BM	Brandon Medders	8.00
MM	Matt Murton	8.00
CS	Corey Shafer	8.00
GS	Grady Sizemore	30.00
BS	Brian Snyder	8.00
DS	Denard Span	20.00
JV	Joey Votto	8.00
BW	Brandon Wood	15.00

2004 Bowman Chrome

NM/M
Complete Set (350):
Common Player: .25
Common Rookie: .50
Common Rookie Auto. (331-350): 10.00
Inserted 1:18

FIRST Chrome YEAR
FELIX HERNANDEZ P

Pack (4):		5.00
Box (18):		80.00
1	Garret Anderson	.50
2	Larry Walker	.50
3	Derek Jeter	2.50
4	Curt Schilling	.75
5	Carlos Zambrano	.50
6	Shawn Green	.50
7	Manny Ramirez	1.00
8	Randy Johnson	1.00
9	Jeremy Bonderman	.50
10	Alfonso Soriano	1.00
11	Scott Rolen	1.00
12	Kerry Wood	.50
13	Eric Gagne	.50
14	Ryan Klesko	.25
15	Kevin Millar	.25
16	Ty Wigginton	.25
17	David Ortiz	1.50
18	Luis Castillo	.25
19	Bernie Williams	.50
20	Edgar Renteria	.50
21	Matt Kata	.25
22	Bartolo Colon	.50
23	Derrek Lee	.75
24	Gary Sheffield	.75
25	Nomar Garciaparra	.50
26	Kevin Millwood	.25
27	Corey Patterson	.50
28	Carlos Beltran	.75
29	Mike Lieberthal	.25
30	Troy Glaus	.50
31	Preston Wilson	.25
32	Jorge Posada	.50
33	Bo Hart	.25
34	Mark Prior	.75
35	Hideo Nomo	.50
36	Jason Kendall	.25
37	Roger Clemens	2.50
38	Dmitri Young	.25
39	Jason Giambi	.75
40	Jim Edmonds	.75
41	Ryan Ludwick	.25
42	Brandon Webb	.50
43	Todd Helton	.75
44	Jacque Jones	.25
45	Jamie Moyer	.25
46	Tim Salmon	.50
47	Kelvim Escobar	.25
48	Tony Batista	.25
49	Nick Johnson	.25
50	Jim Thome	1.00
51	Casey Blake	.25
52	Trot Nixon	.50
53	Luis Gonzalez	.50
54	Dontrelle Willis	.50
55	Mike Mussina	.50
56	Carl Crawford	.50
57	Mark Buehrle	.50
58	Scott Podsednik	.50
59	Brian Giles	.50
60	Rafael Furcal	.50
61	Miguel Cabrera	1.00
62	Rich Harden	.50
63	Mark Teixeira	.75
64	Frank Thomas	.75
65	Johan Santana	.75
66	Jason Schmidt	.50
67	Aramis Ramirez	.50
68	Jose Reyes	.75
69	Magglio Ordonez	.50
70	Mike Sweeney	.25
71	Eric Chavez	.50
72	Rocco Baldelli	.50
73	Sammy Sosa	.75
74	Javy Lopez	.25
75	Roy Oswalt	.50
76	Raul Ibanez	.25
77	Ivan Rodriguez	.75
78	Jerome Williams	.25
79	Carlos Lee	.50
80	Geoff Jenkins	.25
81	Sean Burroughs	.25
82	Marcus Giles	.25
83	Mike Lowell	.50
84	Barry Zito	.50
85	Aubrey Huff	.25
86	Esteban Loaiza	.25
87	Torii Hunter	.50
88	Phil Nevin	.25
89	Andruw Jones	.75
90	Josh Beckett	.50
91	Mark Mulder	.50
92	Hank Blalock	.50
93	Jason Phillips	.25
94	Russ Ortiz	.25
95	Juan Pierre	.25
96	Tom Glavine	.50

97	Gil Meche	.25
98	Ramon Ortiz	.25
99	Richie Sexson	.50
100	Albert Pujols	2.50
101	Javier Vazquez	.25
102	Johnny Damon	1.00
103	Alex Rodriguez	2.50
104	Omar Vizquel	.50
105	Chipper Jones	1.00
106	Lance Berkman	.50
107	Tim Hudson	.50
108	Carlos Delgado	.50
109	Austin Kearns	.40
110	Orlando Cabrera	.25
111	Edgar Martinez	.50
112	Melvin Mora	.25
113	Jeff Bagwell	.75
114	Marlon Byrd	.25
115	Vernon Wells	.50
116	C.C. Sabathia	.50
117	Cliff Floyd	.25
118	Ichiro Suzuki	2.00
119	Miguel Olivo	.25
120	Mike Piazza	1.00
121	Adam Dunn	.75
122	Paul Lo Duca	.25
123	Brett Myers	.25
124	Michael Young	.50
125	Sidney Ponson	.25
126	Greg Maddux	2.00
127	Vladimir Guerrero	1.00
128	Miguel Tejada	.50
129	Andy Pettitte	.50
130	Rafael Palmeiro	.75
131	Ken Griffey Jr.	2.00
132	Shannon Stewart	.25
133	Joel Pineiro	.25
134	Luis Matos	.25
135	Jeff Kent	.50
136	Randy Wolf	.25
137	Chris Woodward	.25
138	Jody Gerut	.25
139	Jose Vidro	.25
140	Bret Boone	.25
141	Bill Mueller	.25
142	Angel Berroa	.25
143	Bobby Abreu	.50
144	Roy Halladay	.50
145	Delmon Young	.50
146	Jonny Gomes	.50
147	Rickie Weeks	.50
148	Edwin Jackson	.25
149	Neal Cotts	.25
150	Jason Bay	.50
151	Khalil Greene	.50
152	Joe Mauer	.50
153	Bobby Jenks	.25
154	Chin-Feng Chen	.25
155	Chien-Ming Wang	.75
156	Mickey Hall	.25
157	James Houser	.25
158	Jay Sborz	.25
159	Jonathan Fulton	.25
160	Steve Lerud	.25
161	Grady Sizemore	.75
162	Felix Pie	.50
163	Dustin McGowan	.25
164	Chris Lubanski	.25
165	Tom Gorzelanny	.50
166	Rudy Guillen RC	1.00
167	Aarom Baldiris RC	.25
168	Conor Jackson	2.00
169	Matt Moses	1.00
170	Ervin Santana RC	4.00
171	Merkin Valdez RC	1.50
172	Erick Aybar RC	2.00
173	Brad Sullivan	1.00
174	Joey Gathright RC	1.00
175	Brad Snyder	1.00
176	Alberto Callaspo RC	3.00
177	Brandon Medders RC	1.00
178	Zach Miner	1.50
179	Charlie Zink RC	1.00
180	Adam Greenberg	1.50
181	Kevin Howard RC	1.00
182	Wanell Severino RC	1.00
183	Chin-Lung Hu RC	1.00
184	Joel Zumaya RC	2.50
185	Skip Schumaker RC	1.00
186	Nic Ungs RC	1.00
187	Todd Self RC	1.00
188	Brian Steffek RC	1.00
189	Brock Peterson RC	1.00
190	Greg Thissen RC	1.00
191	Frank Brooks RC	1.00
192	Scott Olsen RC	1.50
193	Chris Mabeus RC	1.00
194	Daniel Giese RC	1.00
195	Jared Wells RC	1.00
196	Carlos Sosa RC	1.00
197	Bobby Madritsch RC	1.00
198	Calvin Hayes RC	1.00
199	Omar Quintanilla RC	1.00
200	Chris O'Riordan RC	1.00
201	Tim Hutting RC	1.00
202	Carlos Quentin	8.00
203	Brayan Pena RC	1.00
204	Jeff Salazar RC	1.00
205	David Murphy	2.00
206	Alberto Garcia RC	1.00
207	Ramon Ramirez RC	1.00
208	Luis Bolivar RC	1.00
209	Rodney Choy Foo RC	1.00
210	Fausto Carmona RC	3.00
211	Anthony Acevedo RC	2.00
212	Chad Santos RC	1.00
213	Jason Frasor RC	1.00
214	Jesse Roman RC	1.00

215	James Tomlin RC	1.00
216	Josh Labandeira RC	1.00
217	Ryan Meaux RC	1.00
218	Don Sutton RC	1.00
219	Danny Gonzalez RC	1.00
220	Javier Guzman RC	1.00
221	Anthony Lerew RC	1.00
222	Jon Connolly RC	1.00
223	Jesse English RC	1.00
224	Hector Made RC	1.00
225	Travis Hanson	1.00
226	Jesse Floyd RC	1.00
227	Nick Gorneault RC	1.00
228	Craig Ansman RC	1.00
229	Paul McAnulty RC	1.00
230	Carl Loadenthal RC	1.00
231	David Crouthers RC	1.00
232	Harvey Garcia RC	1.00
233	Casey Kopitzke RC	1.00
234	Ricky Nolasco	3.00
235	Miguel Perez RC	1.00
236	Ryan Mulhern RC	1.00
237	Chris Aguila RC	1.00
238	Brooks Conrad RC	1.00
239	Damaso Espino RC	1.00
240	Jereme Milons RC	1.00
241	Luke Hughes RC	1.50
242	Kory Casto RC	1.00
243	Jose Valdez RC	1.00
244	J.T. Stotts	1.00
245	Lee Gwaltney RC	1.00
246	Yoann Torrealba RC	1.00
247	Omar Falcon RC	1.00
248	Jon Coutlangus RC	1.00
249	George Sherrill RC	1.00
250	John Santor RC	1.00
251	Tony Richie RC	1.00
252	Kevin Richardson RC	1.00
253	Tim Bittner RC	1.00
254	Chris Saenz RC	1.00
255	Jose Capellan RC	1.00
256	Donald Levinski	1.00
257	Jerome Gamble RC	1.00
258	Jeff Keppinger RC	2.00
259	Jason Szuminski RC	1.00
260	Akinori Otsuka RC	1.50
261	Ryan Budde RC	1.00
262	Marland Williams RC	1.00
263	Jeffrey Allison	1.00
264	Hector Gimenez RC	1.00
265	Tim Frend RC	1.00
266	Tom Farmer RC	1.00
267	Shawn Hill RC	1.00
268	Mike Huggins RC	1.00
269	Scott Proctor RC	1.50
270	Jorge Mejia RC	1.00
271	Terry Jones RC	1.00
272	Zach Duke RC	1.50
273	Jesse Crain	1.00
274	Luke Anderson RC	1.00
275	Hunter Brown RC	1.00
276	Matt Lemanczyk RC	1.00
277	Fernando Cortez RC	1.00
278	Vince Perkins RC	1.00
279	Tommy Murphy RC	1.00
280	Mike Gosling	1.00
281	Paul Bacot	1.00
282	Matt Capps RC	2.00
283	Juan Gutierrez RC	1.00
284	Teodoro Encarnacion RC	1.00
285	Chad Bentz RC	1.00
286	Kazuo Matsui RC	1.50
287	Ryan Hankins RC	1.00
288	Leo Nunez RC	1.00
289	Dave Wallace RC	1.00
290	Rob Tejeda RC	1.00
291	Paul Maholm RC	2.00
292	Casey Daigle RC	1.00
293	Tydus Meadows RC	1.00
294	Khalid Ballouli RC	1.00
295	Benji DeQuin RC	1.00
296	Tyler Davidson	1.00
297	Brent Colamarino RC	1.00
298	Marcus McBeth RC	1.00
299	Brad Eldred RC	1.00
300	David Pauley RC	1.00
301	Yadier Molina RC	5.00
302	Chris Shelton RC	1.00
303	Nyjer Morgan RC	2.00
304	Jon DeVries	1.00
305	Sheldon Fulse RC	1.00
306	Vito Chiaravalloti RC	1.00
307	Warner Madrigal RC	1.00
308	Reid Gorecki RC	1.00
309	Sung Jung RC	1.00
310	Peter Shier RC	1.00
311	Michael Mooney RC	1.00
312	Kenny Perez RC	1.00
313	Mike Mallory RC	1.00
314	Ben Himes RC	1.00
315	Ivan Ochoa RC	1.00
316	Donald Kelly RC	1.00
317	Tom Mastny RC	1.00
318	Kevin Davidson RC	1.00
319	Brian Pilkington RC	1.00
320	Alex Romero RC	1.00
321	Chad Chop RC	1.00
322	Kody Kirkland RC	1.00
323	Casey Myers RC	1.00
324	Mike Rouse RC	1.00
325	Sergio Silva RC	1.00
326	J.J. Furmaniak RC	1.00
327	Brad Vericker RC	1.00
328	Blake Hawksworth RC	1.00
329	Brock Jacobsen RC	1.00
330	Alec Zumwalt RC	1.00
331	Wardell Starling RC	10.00
332	Estee Harris RC	10.00

333	Kyle Sleeth	10.00
334	Dioner Navarro RC	15.00
335	Logan Kensing RC	10.00
336	Travis Blackley RC	10.00
337	Lincoln Holdzkom RC	10.00
338	Jason Hirsh	10.00
339	Juan Cedeno RC	10.00
340	Matt Creighton RC	10.00
341	Tim Stauffer	10.00
342	Shingo Takatsu RC	10.00
343	Lastings Milledge	20.00
344	Dustin Nippert RC	10.00
345	Felix Hernandez RC	100.00
346	Joaquin Arias RC	10.00
347	Kevin Kouzmanoff RC	20.00
348	Bobby Brownlie RC	10.00
349	David Aardsma RC	10.00
350	Jon Knott RC	10.00

Refractor

Stars (1-165):		2-4X
Rookies (166-330):		1-2X
Inserted 1:4		
Autograph (331-350):		1-2X
Inserted 1:100		

Gold Refractor

Stars (1-165):		4-8X
Rookies (166-330):		3-5X
Production 50		
Autograph (331-350):		No Pricing
Inserted 1:1,003		

X-Fractor

Chrome
LANCE BERKMAN OF

Stars (1-165):		3-5X
Rookies (166-330):		2-4X
Production 173		
Autograph (331-350):		No Pricing
Inserted 1:200		

Stars Of The Future

		NM/M
Inserted 1:600		
YSS	Delmon Young, Kyle Sleeth, Tim Stauffer	60.00
LHC	Chris Lubanski, Ryan Harvey, Chad Cordero	40.00
MHD	Nicholas Markakis, Aaron Hill, Eric Duncan	50.00

2004 Bowman Draft Picks & Prospects

FIRST Bowman YEAR
JOSE CAPELLAN P

		NM/M
Complete Set (1-165):		30.00
Common Player:		.15
Common Rookie:		.15
Pack (5 Bowman + 2 Chrome):		5.00
Box (24):		100.00
BDP1	Lyle Overbay	.25
BDP2	David Newhan	.15
BDP3	J.R. House	.15
BDP4	Chad Tracy	.15
BDP5	Humberto Quintero	.15
BDP6	David Bush	.15
BDP7	Scott Hairston	.15
BDP8	Mike Wood	.15
BDP9	Alexis Rios	.25
BDP10	Sean Burnett	.15
BDP11	Wilson Valdez	.15
BDP12	Lew Ford	.15
BDP13	Freddy Thon RC	.15
BDP14	Zack Greinke	.15
BDP15	Bucky Jacobsen	.25
BDP16	Kevin Youkilis	.25
BDP17	Grady Sizemore	.25
BDP18	Denny Bautista	.15
BDP19	David DeJesus	.15

BDP20	Casey Kotchman	.15
BDP21	David Kelton	.15
BDP22	Charles Thomas RC	.25
BDP23	Kazuhito Tadano RC	.50
BDP24	Justin Leone	.25
BDP25	Eduardo Villacis	.25
BDP26	Brian Dallimore RC	.25
BDP27	Nick Green	.25
BDP28	Sam McConnell	.25
BDP29	Brad Halsey RC	.25
BDP30	Roman Colon RC	.25
BDP31	Josh Fields	.75
BDP32	Cody Bunkelman	.50
BDP33	Jay Rainville RC	.75
BDP34	Richie Robnett RC	.75
BDP35	Jon Poterson RC	.75
BDP36	Huston Street RC	1.00
BDP37	Erick San Pedro RC	.25
BDP38	Cory Dunlap	.25
BDP39	Kurt Suzuki RC	.75
BDP40	Anthony Swarzak	.50
BDP41	Ian Desmond	1.00
BDP42	Chris Covington	.40
BDP43	Christian Garcia	.40
BDP44	Gaby Hernandez RC	1.00
BDP45	Steven Register	.25
BDP46	Eduardo Morlan	.25
BDP47	Collin Balester	.50
48	Nathan Phillips	.25
49	Dan Schwartzbauer	.25
50	Rafael Gonzalez	.25
51	K.C. Herren RC	.50
52	William Susdorf	.25
53	Rob Johnson	.25
54	Louis Marson	.50
55	Joe Koshansky RC	.50
56	Jamar Walton	.25
57	Mark Lowe	.75
58	Matt Macri RC	.75
59	Donny Lucy	.25
60	Mike Ferris	.50
61	Mike Nickeas	.25
62	Eric Hurley RC	.75
63	Scott Elbert RC	1.00
64	Blake DeWitt RC	.50
65	Danny Putnam RC	.50
66	J.P. Howell RC	.75
67	John Wiggins	.25
68	Justin Orenduff RC	.50
69	Ray Liotta RC	.75
70	Billy Buckner RC	.25
71	Eric Campbell RC	1.00
72	Olin Wick	.25
73	Sean Gamble	.40
74	Seth Smith	1.00
75	Wade Davis RC	1.00
76	Joe Jacobitz	.25
77	J.A. Happ	.50
78	Eric Ridener	.25
79	Matt Tuiasosopo RC	.75
80	Bradley Bergesen	.25
81	Javy Guerra	.40
82	Buck Shaw	.25
83	Paul Janish	.50
84	Sean Kazmar	.25
85	Josh Johnson RC	1.50
86	Angel Salome	.75
87	Jordan Parraz RC	.25
88	Kelvin Vazquez	.25
89	Grant Hansen	.25
90	Matt Fox RC	.50
91	Trevor Plouffe RC	1.00
92	Wes Whisler	.25
93	Curtis Thigpen	.50
94	Donnie Smith RC	.25
95	Luis Rivera	.40
96	Jesse Hoover	.25
97	Jason Vargas RC	1.00
98	Clary Carlsen	.25
99	Mark Robinson	.25
100	J.C. Holt RC	.40
101	Chad Blackwell	.25
102	Daryl Jones RC	.75
103	Jonathan Tierce	.25
104	Patrick Bryant	.25
105	Eddie Prasch	.40
106	Mitch Einertson RC	.75
107	Kyle Waldrop RC	.75
108	Jeff Marquez RC	.75
109	Zach Jackson RC	.50
110	Josh Wahpepah	.25
111	Adam Lind RC	1.50
112	Kyle Bloom	.25
113	Ben Harrison	.25
114	Taylor Tankersley RC	.75
115	Steven Jackson	.25
116	David Purcey RC	.50
117	Jacob McGee	1.50
118	Lucas Harrell RC	.25
119	Brandon Allen	.25
120	Van Pope	.50
121	Jeff Francis	.25
122	Joe Blanton	.25
123	Wilfredo Ledezma	.15
124	Bryan Bullington	.15
125	Jairo Garcia	.15
126	Matt Cain	.40
127	Arnie Munoz	.15
128	Clint Everts	.15
129	Jesus Cota	.15
130	Gavin Floyd	.15
131	Edwin Encarnacion	.15
132	Koyie Hill	.15
133	Ruben Gotay	.15
134	Jeff Mathis	.15
135	Andy Marte	.25
136	Dallas McPherson	.15
137	Justin Morneau	.40

138	Rickie Weeks	.25
139	Joel Guzman	.15
140	Shin-Soo Choo	.15
141	Yusmeiro Petit RC	1.00
142	Jorge Cortes	.25
143	Val Majewski	.15
144	Felix Pie	.25
145	Aaron Hill	.15
146	Jose Capellan	.25
147	Dioner Navarro RC	.50
148	Fausto Carmona RC	.50
149	Robinzon Diaz	.25
150	Felix Hernandez	2.00
151	Andres Blanco	.25
152	Jason Kubel	.15
153	Willy Taveras RC	.75
154	Merkin Valdez	.40
155	Robinson Cano	.25
156	Bill Murphy	.25
157	Chris Burke	.15
158	Kyle Sleeth	.25
159	B.J. Upton	.25
160	Tim Stauffer	.25
161	David Wright	1.00
162	Conor Jackson	.25
163	Brad Thompson RC	.25
164	Delmon Young	.40
165	Jeremy Reed	.15

Gold

FIRST Bowman YEAR
COLLIN BALESTER

Rookies:		.75-1.5X
Inserted 1:1		

Red

No Pricing	
Production One Set	

AFLAC All-Americans

Complete Set (40):		
Common Player:		

Printing Plates

No Pricing	
Production one for each color.	

Prospect Premiums

		NM/M
Common Player:		4.00
AB	Angel Berroa	4.00
KC	Kevin Cash	4.00
RH	Ryan Harvey	4.00
CJ	Conor Jackson	5.00
EJ	Edwin Jackson	4.00
LM	Lastings Milledge	10.00
DN	Dioner Navarro	4.00
CQ	Carlos Quentin	8.00
JR	Jeremy Reed	6.00
NS	Nick Swisher	6.00
BU	B.J. Upton	6.00
DY	Delmon Young	6.00

Signs of the Future

		NM/M
Common Player:		8.00
CC	Chad Cordero	8.00
JH	James Houser	8.00
AL	Adam Loewen	8.00
PM	Paul Maholm	10.00
TP	Tyler Pelland	8.00
TT	Terry Tiffee	8.00

2004 Bowman Chrome Draft Picks & Prospects

FIRST Chrome YEAR
PHILIP HUGHES

		NM/M
Complete Set (175):		
Common Player:		.25
Common Rookie:		.50
Common RC Auto. (166-175):		15.00
Inserted 1:60		

#	Player	Price
BDP1	Lyle Overbay	.50
BDP2	David Newhan	.25
BDP3	J.R. House	.25
BDP4	Chad Tracy	.25
BDP5	Humberto Quintero	.25
BDP6	David Bush	.25
BDP7	Scott Hairston	.25
BDP8	Mike Wood	.25
BDP9	Alexis Rios	.50
BDP10	Sean Burnett	.25
BDP11	Wilson Valdez	.25
BDP12	Lew Ford	.25
BDP13	Freddie Thon RC	1.00
BDP14	Zack Greinke	.40
BDP15	Bucky Jacobsen	.25
BDP16	Kevin Youkilis	.50
BDP17	Grady Sizemore	.75
BDP18	Denny Bautista	.25
BDP19	David DeJesus	.25
BDP20	Casey Kotchman	.25
BDP21	David Kelton	.25
BDP22	Charles Thomas RC	1.00
BDP23	Kazuhito Tadano RC	1.00
BDP24	Justin Leone RC	1.00
BDP25	Eduardo Villacis RC	1.00
BDP26	Brian Dallimore RC	1.00
BDP27	Nick Green RC	1.00
BDP28	Sam McConnell RC	1.00
BDP29	Brad Halsey RC	1.00
BDP30	Roman Colon RC	1.00
BDP31	Josh Fields RC	2.00
BDP32	Cody Bunkelman RC	1.00
BDP33	Jay Rainville RC	1.00
BDP34	Richie Robnett RC	1.00
BDP35	Huston Street RC	2.00
BDP36	Erick San Pedro RC	1.00
BDP37	Cory Dunlap RC	1.00
BDP38	Kurt Suzuki RC	3.00
BDP39	Anthony Swarzak RC	1.00
BDP40	Ian Desmond RC	3.00
BDP41	Chris Covington RC	1.00
BDP42	Christian Garcia RC	1.00
BDP43	Gaby Hernandez RC	3.00
BDP44	Steven Register RC	1.00
BDP45	Eduardo Morlan RC	1.00
BDP46	Collin Balester RC	1.00
BDP47	Nathan Phillips RC	1.00
BDP48	Dan Schwartzbauer RC	1.00
BDP49	Rafael Gonzalez RC	1.00
BDP50	K.C. Herren RC	1.00
BDP51	William Susdorf RC	1.00
BDP52	Rob Johnson RC	1.00
BDP53	Louis Marson RC	2.00
BDP54	Joe Koshansky RC	1.50
BDP55	Jamar Walton RC	1.00
BDP56	Mark Lowe RC	1.00
BDP57	Matt Macri RC	1.00
BDP58	Donny Lucy RC	1.00
BDP59	Mike Ferris RC	1.00
BDP60	Mike Nickeas RC	1.00
BDP61	Eric Hurley RC	3.00
BDP62	Scott Elbert RC	1.50
BDP63	Blake DeWitt RC	2.00
BDP64	Danny Putnam RC	1.50
BDP65	J.P. Howell RC	1.50
BDP66	John Wiggins RC	1.00
BDP67	Justin Orenduff RC	1.00
BDP68	Ray Liotta RC	1.00
BDP69	Billy Buckner RC	1.00
BDP70	Eric Campbell RC	3.00
BDP71	Olin Wick RC	1.00
BDP72	Sean Gamble RC	1.00
BDP73	Seth Smith RC	3.00
BDP74	Wade Davis RC	4.00
BDP75	Joe Jacobitz RC	1.00
BDP76	J.A. Happ RC	1.50
BDP77	Eric Ridener RC	1.00
BDP78	Matt Tuiasosopo RC	1.50
BDP79	Bradley Bergesen RC	1.00
BDP80	Javy Guerra RC	1.00
BDP81	Buck Shaw RC	1.50
BDP82	Paul Janish RC	1.00
BDP83	Sean Kazmar RC	1.00
BDP84	Josh Johnson RC	3.00
BDP85	Angel Salome RC	2.00
BDP86	Jordan Parraz RC	1.00
BDP87	Kelvin Vazquez RC	1.00
BDP88	Grant Hansen RC	1.00
BDP89	Matt Fox RC	1.00
BDP90	Trevor Plouffe RC	1.00
BDP91	Wes Whisler RC	1.00
BDP92	Curtis Thigpen RC	1.00
BDP93	Donnie Smith RC	1.00
BDP94	Luis Rivera RC	1.00
BDP95	Jesse Hoover RC	1.00
BDP96	Jason Vargas RC	1.00
BDP97	Clary Carlsen RC	1.00
BDP98	Mark Robinson RC	1.00
BDP99	J.C. Holt RC	1.00
BDP100	Chad Blackwell RC	1.00
BDP101	Daryl Jones RC	1.00
BDP102	Jonathan Tierce RC	1.00
BDP103	Patrick Bryant RC	1.00
BDP104	Eddie Prasch RC	1.00
BDP105	Mitch Einertson RC	1.50
BDP106	Kyle Waldrop RC	1.00
BDP107	Jeff Marquez RC	1.00
BDP108	Zach Jackson RC	1.00
BDP109	Josh Wahpepah RC	1.00
BDP110	Adam Lind RC	4.00
BDP111	Kyle Bloom RC	1.00
BDP112	Ben Harrison RC	1.00
BDP113	Taylor Tankersley RC	1.00
BDP114	Steven Jackson RC	1.00
BDP115	David Purcey RC	1.50
BDP116	Jacob McGee RC	1.00
BDP117	Lucas Harrell RC	1.00
BDP119	Brandon Allen RC	1.00
BDP120	Van Pope RC	1.00
BDP121	Jeff Francis	.25
BDP122	Joe Blanton	.25
BDP123	Wilfredo Ledezma	.25
BDP124	Bryan Bullington	.25
BDP125	Jairo Garcia	.25
BDP126	Matt Cain	.75
BDP127	Arnie Munoz	.25
BDP128	Clint Everts	.25
BDP129	Jesus Cota	.25
BDP130	Gavin Floyd	.25
BDP131	Edwin Encarnacion	.25
BDP132	Koyie Hill	.25
BDP133	Ruben Gotay	.25
BDP134	Jeff Mathis	.25
BDP135	Andy Marte	.50
BDP136	Dallas McPherson	.25
BDP137	Justin Morneau	.50
BDP138	Rickie Weeks	.40
BDP139	Joel Guzman	.25
BDP140	Shin-Soo Choo	.75
BDP141	Yusmeiro Petit RC	3.00
BDP142	Jorge Cortes RC	1.00
BDP143	Val Majewski	.25
BDP144	Felix Pie	.50
BDP145	Aaron Hill	.25
BDP146	Jose Capellan	.25
BDP147	Dioner Navarro RC	1.00
BDP148	Fausto Carmona RC	1.00
BDP149	Robinzon Diaz RC	1.00
BDP150	Felix Hernandez RC	5.00
BDP151	Andres Blanco RC	1.00
BDP152	Jason Kubel	.40
BDP153	Willy Taveras RC	1.50
BDP154	Merkin Valdez	1.00
BDP155	Robinson Cano	1.00
BDP156	Bill Murphy RC	.50
BDP157	Chris Burke	.25
BDP158	Kyle Sleeth	.75
BDP159	B.J. Upton	.75
BDP160	Tim Stauffer	1.00
BDP161	David Wright	2.50
BDP162	Conor Jackson	.50
BDP163	Brad Thompson	1.50
BDP164	Delmon Young	.50
BDP165	Jeremy Reed	.25
BDP166	Matt Bush RC	10.00
BDP167	Mark Rogers RC	10.00
BDP168	Thomas Diamond RC	10.00
BDP169	Greg Golson RC	10.00
BDP170	Homer Bailey RC	30.00
BDP171	Chris Lambert RC	10.00
BDP172	Neil Walker RC	15.00
BDP173	Bill Bray RC	10.00
BDP174	Phillip Hughes RC	85.00
BDP175	Gio Gonzalez RC	25.00

Refractor
Rookies: 2-4X
Inserted 1:11
Rookie Autos. (166-175): .75-1.5X
Inserted 1:204

Gold Refractor
Rookies: 10-20X
Production 50
Rookie Autos. (166-175): 3-5X
Inserted 1:2,045

X-Fractor

Rookies: 3-6X
Production 125
Rookie Autos. (166-175): 1-2X
Inserted 1:407

2004 Bowman Heritage

		NM/M
Complete Set (347):		
Common Player:		.15
Common SP:		
Common SP Rookie:		4.00
SP's inserted 1:3		
Pack (8):		4.00
Box (24):		80.00
1	Tom Glavine	.40
2	Mike Piazza/SP	8.00
3	Sidney Ponson	.15
4	Jerry Hairston Jr.	.15
5	Jermaine Dye	.25
6	Bobby Crosby	.15
7	Carlos Zambrano	.25
8	Moises Alou	.25
9	Alex Rodriguez/SP	10.00
10	Derek Jeter	2.00
11	Rafael Furcal	.25
12	J.D. Drew	.25
13	Joe Mauer/SP	4.00
14	Brad Radke	.15
15	Johnny Damon	.75
16	Derek Lowe	.15
17	Pat Burrell	.25
18	Mike Lieberthal	.15
19	Cliff Lee	.15
20	Ronnie Belliard	.15
21	Eric Gagne/SP	4.00
22	Brad Penny	.15
23	Al Kaline	.50
24	Mike Maroth	.15
25	Magglio Ordonez/SP	4.00
26	Mark Buehrle	.25
27	Jack Wilson	.15
28	Oliver Perez	.15
29	Al "Red" Schoendienst	.15
30	Yadier Molina RC	1.50
31	Ryan Freel	.15
32	Adam Dunn	.25
33	Paul Konerko	.40
34	Esteban Loaiza	.15
35	Ivan Rodriguez	.50
36	Carlos Guillen	.15
37	Adrian Beltre	.25
38	C.C. Sabathia	.25
39	Hideo Nomo	.40
40	Victor Martinez/SP	4.00
41	Bobby Abreu	.25
42	Randy Wolf	.15
43	Johnny Estrada	.15
44	Russ Ortiz	.15
45	Kenny Rogers	.15
46	Hank Blalock/SP	4.00
47	David Ortiz	1.00
48	Pedro Martinez/SP	6.00
49	Austin Kearns	.25
50	Ken Griffey Jr./SP	6.00
51	Mark Prior	.50
52	Kerry Wood	.40
53	Eric Chavez	.25
54	Tim Hudson	.25
55	Rafael Palmeiro/SP	4.00
56	Javy Lopez	.15
57	Jason Bay	.40
58	Craig Wilson	.15
59	Ed "Whitey" Ford	.50
60	Jason Giambi	.50
61	Scott Rolen/SP	4.00
62	Matt Morris	.15
63	Javier Vazquez	.15
64	Jim Thome	.50
65	Don Zimmer	.25
66	Shawn Green	.25
67	Don Larsen	.25
68	Gary Sheffield	.40
69	Jorge Posada	.50
70	Bernie Williams	.40
71	Chipper Jones	.75
72	Andruw Jones	.50
73	John Thomson	.15
74	Jim Edmonds	.40
75	Albert Pujols	2.00
76	Chris Carpenter	.50
77	Aubrey Huff/SP	4.00
78	Carl Crawford	.40
79	Victor Zambrano	.15
80	Alfonso Soriano/SP	5.00
81	Lance Berkman	.40
82	Mike Sweeney	.15
83	Ken Harvey	.15
84	Angel Berroa	.15
85	A.J. Burnett	.15
86	Mike Lowell	.15
87	Miguel Cabrera/SP	5.00
88	Preston Wilson	.15
89	Todd Helton/SP	.15
90	Larry Walker	.25
91	Vladimir Guerrero	.25
92	Garret Anderson	.15
93	Bartolo Colon	.15
94	Scott Hairston	.15
95	Richie Sexson/SP	4.00
96	Sean Casey	.15
97	Johnny Podres	.40
98	Andy Pettitte	.40
99	Roy Oswalt	.25
100	Roger Clemens/SP	8.00
101	Scott Podsednik	.25
102	Ben Sheets	.25
103	Lyle Overbay	.25
104	Nick Johnson/SP	4.00
105	Zach Day	.15
106	Jose Reyes	.75
107	Khalil Greene	.25
108	Sean Burroughs	.15
109	David Wells/SP	4.00
110	Jason Schmidt	.25
111	Neifi Perez	.15
112	Edgar Renteria	.15
113	Rich Aurilia	.15
114	Edgar Martinez	.15
115	Joel Pineiro	.15
116	Mark Teixeira	.40
117	Michael Young	.25
118	Ricardo Rodriguez	.15
119	Carlos Delgado	.50
120	Roy Halladay	.25
121	Jose Guillen	.15
122	Troy Glaus	.40
123	Shea Hillenbrand	.15
124	Luis Gonzalez	.25
125	Horacio Ramirez	.15
126	Melvin Mora	.15
127	Miguel Tejada/SP	4.00
128	Manny Ramirez	.75
129	Tim Wakefield	.15
130	Curt Schilling/SP	5.00
131	Aramis Ramirez	.40
132	Sammy Sosa/SP	4.00
133	Matt Clement	.15
134	Juan Uribe	.15
135	Dontrelle Willis	.25
136	Paul LoDuca	.15
137	Juan Pierre	.15
138	Kevin Brown	.15
139	Brian Giles, Marcus Giles	.15
140	Brian Giles	.15
141	Nomar Garciaparra/SP	4.00
142	Cesar Izturis	.15
143	Don Newcombe	.15
144	Craig Biggio	.25
145	Carlos Beltran	.50
146	Torii Hunter	.25
147	Livan Hernandez	.15
148	Cliff Floyd	.15
149	Barry Zito	.40
150	Mark Mulder	.25
151	Rocco Baldelli	.25
152	Bret Boone	.15
153	Jamie Moyer	.15
154	Ichiro Suzuki	1.50
155	Brett Myers	.15
156	Carl Pavano	.15
157	Josh Beckett	.25
158	Randy Johnson	.75
159	Trot Nixon	.15
160	Dmitri Young	.15
161	Jacque Jones	.15
162	Lew Ford	.15
163	Jose Vidro	.15
164	Mark Kotsay	.15
165	A.J. Pierzynski	.15
166	Dewon Brazelton	.15
167	Jeromy Burnitz	.15
168	Johan Santana	.50
169	Greg Maddux	1.00
170	Carl Erskine	.15
171	Robin Roberts	.15
172	Freddy Garcia	.15
173	Carlos Lee	.25
174	Jeff Bagwell	.40
175	Jeff Kent	.25
176	Kazuhisa Ishii	.15
177	Orlando Cabrera	.15
178	Shannon Stewart	.15
179	Mike Cameron	.15
180	Mike Mussina	.40
181	Frank Thomas	.75
182	Jaret Wright	.15
183	Alex Gonzalez/SP	4.00
184	Matt Lawton	.15
185	Derrek Lee	.50
186	Omar Vizquel	.15
187	Jeremy Bonderman	.25
188	Jake Westbrook	.15
189	Zack Greinke/SP	4.00
190	Chad Tracy	.15
191	Rondell White	.15
192	Alex Gonzalez	.15
193	Geoff Jenkins	.15
194	Ralph Kiner	.40
195	Al Leiter	.15
196	Kevin Millwood	.15
197	Jason Kendall	.15
198	Kris Benson	.15
199	Ryan Klesko	.15
200	Mark Loretta	.15
201	Richard Hidalgo	.15
202	Reed Johnson	.15
203	Luis Castillo	.15
204	Jon Zeringue/SP RC	4.00
205	Matt Bush RC	2.00
206	Kurt Suzuki/SP RC	4.00
207	Mark Rogers RC	2.00
208	Jason Vargas/SP RC	4.00
209	Homer Bailey RC	4.00
210	Ray Liotta/SP RC	4.00
211	Eric Campbell RC	2.00
212	Thomas Diamond RC	2.00
213	Gaby Hernandez/SP RC	6.00
214	Neil Walker RC	2.00
215	Bill Bray RC	1.00
216	Wade Davis/SP RC	6.00
217	David Purcey RC	1.00
218	Scott Elbert RC	2.00
219	Josh Fields RC	3.00
220	Josh Johnson/SP RC	4.00
221	Chris Lambert RC	2.00
222	Trevor Plouffe RC	3.00
223	Bruce Froemming	.15
224	Matt Macri/SP RC	4.00
225	Greg Golson RC	2.00
226	Phillip Hughes RC	7.00
227	Kyle Waldrop RC	2.00
228	Matt Tuiasosopo/SP RC	4.00
229	Richie Robnett RC	2.00
230	Taylor Tankersley RC	1.50
231	Blake DeWitt RC	2.00
232	Charlie Reliford	.15
233	Eric Hurley RC	1.00
234	Jordan Parraz/SP RC	4.00
235	J.P. Howell RC	1.00
236	Dana DeMuth	.15
237	Zach Jackson RC	.50
238	Justin Orenduff RC	1.00
239	Brad Thompson RC	1.00
240	J.C. Holt/SP RC	4.00
241	Matt Fox RC	1.00
242	Danny Putnam RC	1.00
243	Darryl Jones/SP RC	4.00
244	Jon Poterson RC	1.00
245	Gio Gonzalez RC	2.00
246	Lucas Harrell/SP RC	4.00
247	Jerry Crawford	.15
248	Jay Rainville RC	1.00
249	Donnie Smith/SP RC	4.00
250	Huston Street RC	2.00
251	Jeff Marquez RC	1.00
252	Reid Brignac RC	3.00
253	Yusmeiro Petit RC	1.00
254	K.C. Herren RC	1.00
255	Dale Scott	.15
256	Erick San Pedro RC	1.00
257	Ed Montague	.15
258	Billy Buckner RC	1.00
259	Mitch Einertson/SP RC	4.00
260	Aarom Baldiris RC	1.00
261	Conor Jackson	.25
262	Rick Reed	.15
263	Ervin Santana RC	3.00
264	Gerry Davis	.15
265	Merkin Valdez RC	1.00
266	Joey Gathright RC	1.00
267	Alberto Callaspo RC	1.00
268	Carlos Quentin/SP	6.00
269	Gary Darling	.15
270	Jeff Salazar/SP RC	4.00
271	Akinori Otsuka/SP RC	4.00
272	Joe Brinkman	.15
273	Omar Quintanilla RC	.50
274	Brian Runge	.15
275	Tom Mastny RC	.50
276	John Hirschbeck	.15
277	Warner Madrigal RC	.50
278	Joe West	.15
279	Paul Maholm RC	1.00
280	Larry Young	.15
281	Mike Reilly	.15
282	Kazuo Matsui/SP RC	4.00
283	Randy Marsh	.15
284	Frank Francisco RC	.50
285	Zach Duke RC	1.00
286	Tim McClelland	.15
287	Jesse Crain	.75
288	Hector Gimenez RC	.50
289	Marland Williams RC	.50
290	Brian Gorman	.15
291	Jose Capellan/SP RC	4.00
292	Tim Welke	.15
293	Javier Guzman RC	.50
294	Paul McAnulty RC	.50
295	Hector Made RC	.50
296	Jon Connolly RC	.50
297	Don Sutton RC	.50
298	Fausto Carmona RC	1.00
299	Ramon Ramirez RC	.50
300	Brad Snyder	1.00
301	Chin-Lung Hu RC	1.00
302	Rudy Guillen RC	.50
303	Matt Moses	1.00
304	Brad Halsey/SP RC	4.00
305	Erick Aybar RC	1.50
306	Brad Sullivan	1.00
307	Nick Gorneault RC	1.00
308	Craig Ansman RC	1.00
309	Ricky Nolasco	2.00
310	Luke Hughes RC	1.00
311	Danny Gonzalez RC	1.00
312	Josh Labandeira RC	.50
313	Donald Levinski	.50
314	Vince Perkins RC	.50
315	Tommy Murphy RC	.50
316	Chad Bentz RC	.50
317	Chris Shelton RC	.50
318	Nyjer Morgan/SP RC	4.00
319	Kody Kirkland RC	1.00
320	Blake Hawksworth RC	.50
321	Alex Romero RC	.50
322	Mike Gosling	.50
323	Ryan Budde	.50
324	Kevin Howard RC	.50
325	Wanell Macia RC	.50
326	Travis Blackley RC	.50
327	Kazuhito Tadano/SP RC	4.00
328	Shingo Takatsu RC	1.00
329	Joaquin Arias RC	.50
330	Juan Cedeno RC	.75
331	Bobby Brownlie RC	1.00
332	Lastings Milledge	2.00
333	Estee Harris RC	.75
334	Tim Stauffer/SP RC	4.00
335	Jon Knott	.50
336	David Aardsma	.50
337	Wardell Starling RC	.50
338	Dioner Navarro RC	1.00
339	Logan Kensing RC	.50
340	Jason Hirsh	1.50
341	Matt Creighton RC	.50
342	Felix Hernandez/SP RC	10.00
343	Kyle Sleeth	.50
344	Dustin Nippert RC	.50
345	Anthony Lerew RC	.50
346	Chris Saenz RC	.50
347	Steve Palermo	.15
348	Barry Bonds	20.00

Black & White
Stars: 2X
SP Stars: .5-1X
Rookies: 1-2X
SP Rookies: .5-.75X
Inserted 1:1

Mohagany
Stars: 15-25X
SP Stars: 3-4X
Rookies: 4-8X
SP Rookies: 3-5X
Production 25 Sets

Printing Plates
No Pricing
Production One Set

Commissioner's Cut
Production One

Signs of Authority

		NM/M
Common Autograph:		15.00
Inserted 1:49		
Red Ink:		1.5-2X
Production 55 Sets		
JB	Joe Brinkman	15.00
JC	Jerry Crawford	15.00
GDA	Gary Darling	15.00
GD	Gerry Davis	15.00
DD	Dana DeMuth	15.00
BF	Bruce Froemming	20.00
BG	Brian Gorman	15.00
JH	John Hirschbeck	15.00
RM	Randy Marsh	15.00
TM	Tim McClelland	15.00
EM	Ed Montague	15.00
SP	Steve Palermo	15.00
ER	Rick Reed	15.00
MR	Mike Reilly	15.00
CM	Charlie Reliford	15.00
BR	Brian Runge	15.00
DS	Dale Scott	20.00
TW	Tim Welke	15.00
JW	Joe West	20.00
LY	Larry Young	15.00

Signs of Glory

		NM/M
Common Autograph:		25.00
Inserted 1:246		
Red Ink:		2X
Production 55 Sets		
GK	George Kell	25.00
BK	Bob Kuzava	25.00
PR	Elwin "Preacher" Roe	30.00
BS	Bobby Shantz	25.00
MS	Bill "Moose" Skowron	30.00

Signs of Greatness

		NM/M
Common Autograph:		10.00
Inserted 1:57		
Red Ink:		2-4X
Production 55 Sets		
MB	Matt Bush	10.00
TD	Thomas Diamond	10.00
GG	Greg Golson	15.00
PH	Phillip Hughes	40.00
CL	Chris Lambert	10.00
JM	Jeff Marquez	10.00
TP	Trevor Plouffe	10.00
JR	Jay Rainville	10.00
MR	Mark Rogers	10.00
NW	Neil Walker	15.00

Threads of Greatness

		NM/M
Common Player:		4.00
Inserted 1:12		
Gold:		2-3X
Production 55 Sets		
MA	Moises Alou	5.00
JB	Jeff Bagwell	6.00
JB2	Jeff Bagwell	6.00
RB.	Rocco Baldelli	4.00
TB	Tony Batista	4.00
JB	Josh Beckett	4.00
JB2	Josh Beckett	4.00
AB	Adrian Beltre	4.00
AGB	Armando Benitez	4.00
LB	Lance Berkman	6.00
LB2	Lance Berkman	6.00
AMB	Angel Berroa	4.00
HB	Hank Blalock	4.00
HB2	Hank Blalock	4.00
WB3	Wade Boggs	8.00
BB	Bret Boone	4.00
BB2	Bret Boone	4.00
PB	Pat Burrell	4.00
MC	Miguel Cabrera	8.00
EC	Eric Chavez	4.00
EC2	Eric Chavez	4.00
RC	Roger Clemens	10.00
BC	Bobby Cox	4.00

JD	Johnny Damon	8.00
CE	Carl Everett	4.00
NG	Nomar Garciaparra	8.00
JG	Jason Giambi	5.00
JG2	Jason Giambi	5.00
JAG	Jason Gonzalez	5.00
RH	Roy Halladay	8.00
TH	Todd Helton	6.00
AJ	Andruw Jones	4.00
DJ	David Justice	4.00
PL	Paul LoDuca	4.00
JL	Javy Lopez	4.00
ML	Mike Lowell	4.00
JM	Joe Mauer	10.00
MCD	Mike McDougal	4.00
KM	Kevin Millwood	4.00
MM	Mark Mulder	4.00
MM2	Mark Mulder	4.00
HN	Hideo Nomo	4.00
JO	John Olerud	4.00
JO2	John Olerud	4.00
AEP	Andy Pettitte	4.00
MP	Mike Piazza	10.00
MP2	Mike Piazza	10.00
AP	Albert Pujols	15.00
AP2	Albert Pujols	15.00
MR	Manny Ramirez	8.00
MR2	Manny Ramirez	8.00
JR	Jose Reyes	10.00
AR	Alex Rodriguez	15.00
CS	C.C. Sabathia	8.00
JDS	Jason Schmidt	4.00
GS	Gary Sheffield	5.00
RS	Ruben Sierra	5.00
JS	John Smoltz	5.00
JS2	John Smoltz	6.00
AS	Alfonso Soriano	8.00
SS	Sammy Sosa	8.00
SS2	Sammy Sosa	8.00
SS3	Sammy Sosa	8.00
MS	Mike Sweeney	4.00
MCT	Mark Teixeira	6.00
MT	Miguel Tejada	5.00
MT2	Miguel Tejada	5.00
MT3	Miguel Tejada	5.00
FT	Frank Thomas	8.00
JT	Jim Thome	8.00
JT2	Jim Thome	8.00
OV	Omar Vizquel	4.00
JW	Jarrod Washburn	4.00
VW	Vernon Wells	5.00
BW	Bernie Williams	5.00
DW	Dontrelle Willis	5.00
KW	Kerry Wood	4.00
KW2	Kerry Wood	4.00
MY	Michael Young	4.00
BZ	Barry Zito	4.00

2004 Bowman Sterling

		NM/M
	Common Rookie:	5.00
	Pack (5):	60.00
	Box (6):	325.00
ABA	Aarom Baldiris RC	5.00
BBR	Bill Bray RC	5.00
RBR	Reid Brignac RC	10.00
BBU	Billy Buckner RC	5.00
JC	Jose Capellan RC	5.00
FC	Fausto Carmona RC	8.00
JCR	Jesse Crain RC	5.00
'D	Zach Duke RC	5.00
ME	Mitch Einertson RC	5.00
BE	Brad Eldred RC	5.00
MF	Mike Ferris RC	5.00
JFI	Josh Fields RC	6.00
MFO	Matt Fox RC	5.00
JG	Joey Gathright RC	5.00
GG	Greg Golson RC	5.00
GIG	Gio Gonzalez RC	5.00
FG	Freddy Guzman RC	5.00
GH	Gaby Hernandez RC	8.00
FH	Felix Hernandez RC	20.00
KCH	K.C. Herren RC	5.00
JH	Jesse Hoover RC	5.00
JPH	J.P. Howell RC	5.00
PH	Phillip Hughes RC	15.00
EH	Eric Hurley RC	5.00
CJ	Conor Jackson RC	5.00
ZJ	Zach Jackson RC	5.00
CLA	Chris Lambert RC	5.00
CH	Chin-Lung Hu RC	5.00
MMC	Matt Macri RC	5.00
HM	Hector Made RC	5.00
PGM	Paul Maholm RC	5.00
NM	Nyjer Morgan RC	6.00
CN	Chris Nelson RC	5.00

JO	Justin Orenduff RC	5.00
YP	Yusmeiro Petit RC	8.00
DPU	David Purcey RC	5.00
OQ	Omar Quintanilla RC	5.00
MRO	Mark Rogers RC	5.00
ESP	Erick San Pedro RC	5.00
NS	Nate Schierholtz RC	5.00
SSM	Seth Smith RC	8.00
KS	Kurt Suzuki RC	6.00
KT	Kazuhito Tadano RC	5.00
CT	Curtis Thigpen RC	5.00
BT	Brad Thompson RC	5.00
NW	Neil Walker RC	6.00
AWH	Anthony Whittington RC	5.00
MW	Marland Williams RC	5.00
JZ	Jon Zeringue RC	5.00

Rookie Relic Autographs

HB	Homer Bailey RC	20.00
BB	Brian Bixler RC	10.00
MB	Matt Bush RC	10.00
BD	Blake DeWitt RC	10.00
CG	Christian Garcia RC	10.00
SK	Scott Kazmir	20.00
JM	Jeff Marquez RC	10.00
SO	Scott Olsen RC	10.00
TP	Trevor Plouffe RC	10.00
DP	Danny Putnam RC	10.00
HS	Huston Street RC	15.00
TT	Taylor Tankersley RC	10.00
MT	Matt Tuiasosopo RC	10.00
KWA	Kyle Waldrop RC	10.00

Prospect Relic Autographs

RC	Robinson Cano	40.00
CC	Chad Cordero	10.00
DD	David DeJesus	10.00
RH	Ryan Harvey	15.00
CL	Chris Lubanski	10.00
FP	Felix Pie	10.00
BU	B.J. Upton	20.00
AW	Adam Wainwright	25.00
DW	David Wright	50.00
DY	Delmon Young	15.00

Rookie Autographs

CA	Chris Aguila RC	8.00
AC	Alberto Callaspo RC	15.00
HG	Hector Gimenez RC	10.00
BH	Blake Hawksworth RC	10.00
LH	Lincoln Holdzkom RC	10.00
RM	Ryan Meaux RC	8.00
MM	Matt Moses RC	10.00
VP	Vince Perkins RC	8.00
CQ	Carlos Quentin	30.00
JR	Jay Rainville RC	8.00
AR	Alex Romero RC	8.00
MR	Mike Rouse	8.00
JS	Jeremy Sowers RC	8.00
AZ	Alec Zumwalt RC	8.00

Relics: 5.00

MA	Moises Alou	5.00
JB	Jeff Bagwell	8.00
RB	Rocco Baldelli	5.00
CIB	Carlos Beltran	10.00
LB	Lance Berkman	5.00
AB	Angel Berroa	5.00
CB	Craig Biggio	5.00
HJB	Hank Blalock	5.00
MC	Miguel Cabrera	8.00
LC	Luis Castillo	5.00
HC	Hee Seop Choi	5.00
BC2	Bobby Crosby	5.00
JD	Johnny Damon	10.00
AD	Adam Dunn	8.00
JE	Johnny Estrada	5.00
EG	Eric Gagne	5.00
TG	Troy Glaus	5.00
TMG	Tom Glavine	8.00
VG	Vladimir Guerrero	10.00
TLH	Todd Helton	8.00
RJH	Richard Hidalgo	5.00
NJ	Nick Johnson	5.00
AJ	Andruw Jones	8.00
AK	Austin Kearns	5.00
JK	Jason Kendall	5.00
PL	Paul LoDuca	5.00
TM	Tino Martinez	5.00
MM	Mark Mulder	5.00
LN	Laynce Nix	5.00
RO	Russ Ortiz	5.00
RP	Rafael Palmeiro	6.00
MJP	Mike Piazza	10.00
JP	Juan Pierre	5.00
MP	Mark Prior	8.00
AP	Albert Pujols	20.00
ANR	Aramis Ramirez	5.00
MAR	Manny Ramirez	8.00
PR	Pokey Reese	5.00
AER	Alex Rodriguez	15.00
IR	Ivan Rodriguez	8.00
GS	Gary Sheffield	8.00
SS	Sammy Sosa	10.00
MCT	Mark Teixeira	6.00
MT1	Miguel Tejada/bat	8.00
MT2	Miguel Tejada/jsy	8.00
FT	Frank Thomas	10.00
BW	Bernie Williams	5.00
DWW	Dontrelle Willis	5.00
KW	Kerry Wood	5.00
MY	Michael Young	5.00

Refractors

Regular Rookies:	1.5-2X
Rookie Relic Autos.:	1-2X
Rookie Autos.:	1-2X
Prospect Relic Autos.:	1-2X
Relics:	1-2X
Production 199 Sets	

Black Refractors
No Pricing
Production 25 Sets

Red Refractor
No Pricing
Production One Set

Uncirculated

No Pricing
Production 16 Sets

Autographed Originals
Complete Set (51):
Common Player:

2004 Bowman's Best

NM/M

Complete Set:		
Common Player:		.25
Pack (5):		15.00
Box (5):		125.00

Veterans

GA	Garret Anderson	.25
CB	Carlos Beltran	.75
HB	Hank Blalock	.50
MTC	Miguel Cabrera	1.00
EC	Eric Chavez	.50
RC	Roger Clemens	2.50
CD	Carlos Delgado	.50
NAG	Nomar Garciaparra	1.00
JGG	Jason Giambi	.75
BG	Brian Giles	.25
VG	Vladimir Guerrero	1.00
TLH	Todd Helton	.75
RJ	Randy Johnson	1.00
LWJ	Chipper Jones	1.00
JLO	Javy Lopez	.25
MO	Magglio Ordonez	.25
LO	Lyle Overbay	.25
MJP	Mike Piazza	1.50
JP	Jorge Posada	.75
MWP	Mark Prior	.75
AP	Albert Pujols	3.00
MAR	Manny Ramirez	1.00
AER	Alex Rodriguez	2.50
IR	Ivan Rodriguez	.75
SR	Scott Rolen	1.00
CMS	Curt Schilling	1.00
JDS	Jason Schmidt	.50
RS	Richie Sexson	.50
AS	Alfonso Soriano	1.00
SS	Sammy Sosa	1.00
IS	Ichiro Suzuki	2.00
MT	Miguel Tejada	.50
JT	Jim Thome	.75
JAV	Jose Vidro	.25
MY	Michael Young	.25

First-Year Players

	Common Rookie	1.00
JJC	Jon Connolly RC	1.00
IR	Ivan Rodriguez RC	1.00
JRG	Joey Gathright RC	1.00
DG	Danny Gonzalez RC	1.00
NG	Nick Gorneault RC	1.00
MG	Mike Gosling	1.00
CH	Chin-Lung Hu RC	1.00
TJ	Terry Jones	1.00
AL	Anthony Lerew RC	1.00
HM	Hector Made RC	2.00
WM	Warner Madrigal RC	1.00
PMM	Paul McAnulty RC	1.00
AO	Akinori Otsuka RC	1.00
TS	Todd Self RC	1.00
KS	Kyle Sleeth	1.00
DS	Don Sutton RC	1.00

First-Year Player Autographs

	Common Autograph:	8.00
DA	David Aardsma	10.00
CMA	Craig Ansman RC	10.00

JA	Joaquin Arias RC	10.00
EA	Erick Aybar RC	15.00
BB	Bobby Brownlie RC	10.00
RB	Ryan Budde	10.00
KC	Kory Casto	10.00
JC	Juan Cedeno RC	10.00
VC	Vito Chiaravalloti RC	10.00
MDC	Matt Creighton RC	8.00
DC	David Crouthers	10.00
TD	Tyler Davidson	10.00
ZD	Zach Duke RC	10.00
JE	Jesse English RC	10.00
AG	Adam Greenberg	10.00
RG	Rudy Guillen RC	10.00
TOH	Travis Hanson	10.00
EH	Estee Harris RC	10.00
FH	Felix Hernandez RC	75.00
SH	Shawn Hill	10.00
JH	Jason Hirsh	10.00
LTH	Luke Hughes RC	10.00
CJ	Conor Jackson	15.00
LK	Logan Kensing RC	10.00
JK	Jon Knott RC	10.00
KK	Kevin Kouzmanoff	15.00
JL	Josh Labandeira RC	8.00
DL	Donald Levinski	10.00
PM	Paul Maholm RC	15.00
TRM	Tom Mastny RC	10.00
BEM	Brandon Medders RC	10.00
LM	Lastings Milledge	15.00
YM	Yadier Molina RC	25.00
DM	David Murphy	12.00
DN	Dioner Navarro	12.00
DDN	Dustin Nippert RC	10.00
RN	Ricky Nolasco	20.00
BP	Brayan Pena RC	8.00
QQ	Omar Quintanilla RC	10.00
RR	Ramon Ramirez RC	10.00
JS	Jeff Salazar RC	10.00
ES	Ervin Santana RC	20.00
BMS	Brad Snyder	15.00
WS	Wardell Starling RC	10.00
TJS	Tim Stauffer	10.00
BS	Brad Sullivan	10.00
JSZ	Jason Szuminski RC	10.00
RT	Rob Tejeda RC	10.00
NU	Nic Ungs RC	10.00
MV	Merkin Valdez	10.00
CZ	Charlie Zink RC	10.00

First-Year Player Relics

TB	Travis Blackley RC	5.00
KRK	Kody Kirkland RC	6.00
KM	Kazuo Matsui	6.00
KT	Kazuhito Tadano RC	6.00
ST	Shingo Takatsu RC	8.00

Green

Green Stars:	4-8X
Green Non-Auto. RC's:	1.5-3X
Production 100	
Green RC Autos.:	1-2X

Red

Red Stars:	No Pricing
Production 20	
Red Non-Auto. RC's:	No Pricing
Red RC Autos.:	No Pricing

Double Play Autographs
NM/M

	Common Duo:	20.00
	Inserted 1:33	
MH	Lastings Milledge, Estee Harris	40.00
QS	Omar Quintanilla, Brad Snyder	20.00
SC	Tim Stauffer, Vito Chiaravalloti	20.00
HJ	Travis Hanson, Conor Jackson	20.00
MN	Brandon Medders, Dustin Nippert	25.00
UK	Nic Ungs, Kevin Kouzmanoff	25.00
CC	Matt Creighton, David Crouthers	20.00
EN	Jesse English, Ricky Nolasco	20.00
SV	Ervin Santana, Merkin Valdez	30.00
SK	Jeff Salazar, Jon Knott	20.00

Triple Play Autographs
NM/M

	Common Trio:	30.00
	Inserted 1:109	
CBA	Juan Cedeno, Bobby Brownlie, Joaquin Arias	30.00
ALS	David Aardsma, Donald Levinski, Brad Sullivan	25.00
SSV	Tim Stauffer, Ervin Santana, Merkin Valdez	50.00

2005 Bowman
NM/M

Complete Set (330):	60.00
Common Player:	.15
Common Rookie:	.50
Pack (10):	3.00
Box (24):	60.00
1 Gavin Floyd	.15
2 Eric Chavez	.25
3 Miguel Tejada	.25
4 Dmitri Young	.15
5 Hank Blalock	.25
6 Kerry Wood	.25
7 Andy Pettitte	.40
8 Pat Burrell	.25
9 Johnny Estrada	.15
10 Frank Thomas	.50
11 Juan Pierre	.25
12 Tom Glavine	.40
13 Lyle Overbay	.25
14 Jim Edmonds	.40
15 Steve Finley	.15
16 Jermaine Dye	.25
17 Omar Vizquel	.15
18 Nick Johnson	.15
19 Brian Giles	.25
20 Justin Morneau	.25
21 Preston Wilson	.15
22 Wily Mo Pena	.15
23 Rafael Palmeiro	.50
24 Scott Kazmir	.25
25 Derek Jeter	2.00
26 Barry Zito	.25
27 Mike Lowell	.25
28 Jason Bay	.25
29 Ken Harvey	.15
30 Nomar Garciaparra	.50
31 Roy Halladay	.25
32 Todd Helton	.50
33 Mark Kotsay	.15
34 Jake Peavy	.40
35 David Wright	1.00
36 Dontrelle Willis	.40
37 Marcus Giles	.15
38 Chone Figgins	.15
39 Sidney Ponson	.15
40 Randy Johnson	.75
41 John Smoltz	.25
42 Kevin Millar	.15
43 Mark Teixeira	.50
44 Alex Rios	.25
45 Mike Piazza	1.00
46 Victor Martinez	.25
47 Jeff Bagwell	.50
48 Shawn Green	.25
49 Ivan Rodriguez	.50
50 Alex Rodriguez	1.50
51 Kazuo Matsui	.15
52 Mark Mulder	.40
53 Michael Young	.40
54 Javy Lopez	.15
55 Johnny Damon	.25
56 Jeff Francis	.15
57 Rich Harden	.25
58 Bobby Abreu	.40
59 Mark Loretta	.15
60 Gary Sheffield	.40
61 Jamie Moyer	.15
62 Garret Anderson	.25
63 Vernon Wells	.25
64 Orlando Cabrera	.15
65 Magglio Ordonez	.15
66 Ronnie Belliard	.15
67 Carlos Lee	.25
68 Carl Pavano	.25
69 Jon Lieber	.15
70 Aubrey Huff	.15
71 Rocco Baldelli	.25
72 Jason Schmidt	.25
73 Bernie Williams	.40
74 Hideki Matsui	1.00
75 Ken Griffey Jr.	1.50
76 Josh Beckett	.25
77 Mark Buehrle	.25
78 David Ortiz	.75
79 Luis Gonzalez	.25
80 Scott Rolen	.50
81 Joe Mauer	.50
82 Jose Reyes	.75
83 Adam Dunn	.50
84 Greg Maddux	1.00
85 Bartolo Colon	.25
86 Bret Boone	.25
87 Mike Mussina	.50
88 Ben Sheets	.40
89 Lance Berkman	.40
90 Miguel Cabrera	.75
91 C.C. Sabathia	.25
92 Mike Maroth	.15
93 Andruw Jones	.50
94 Jack Wilson	.15
95 Ichiro Suzuki	1.50
96 Geoff Jenkins	.15
97 Zack Greinke	.40
98 Jorge Posada	.40
99 Travis Hafner	.40
100 Barry Bonds	2.00
101 Aaron Rowand	.15
102 Aramis Ramirez	.40
103 Curt Schilling	.50
104 Melvin Mora	.15
105 Albert Pujols	2.00

106 Austin Kearns	.25
107 Shannon Stewart	.15
108 Carl Crawford	.40
109 Carlos Zambrano	.40
110 Roger Clemens	2.00
111 Javier Vazquez	.15
112 Randy Wolf	.15
113 Chipper Jones	.75
114 Larry Walker	.25
115 Alfonso Soriano	.75
116 Brad Wilkerson	.15
117 Bobby Crosby	.15
118 Jim Thome	.50
119 Oliver Perez	.25
120 Vladimir Guerrero	.50
121 Roy Oswalt	.40
122 Torii Hunter	.25
123 Rafael Furcal	.25
124 Luis Castillo	.15
125 Carlos Beltran	.50
126 Mike Sweeney	.15
127 Johan Santana	.50
128 Tim Hudson	.40
129 Troy Glaus	.40
130 Manny Ramirez	.75
131 Jeff Kent	.25
132 Jose Vidro	.15
133 Edgar Renteria	.15
134 Russ Ortiz	.15
135 Sammy Sosa	.75
136 Carlos Delgado	.40
137 Richie Sexson	.25
138 Pedro Martinez	.75
139 Adrian Beltre	.25
140 Mark Prior	.40
141 Omar Quintanilla	.15
142 Carlos Quentin	.25
143 Dan Johnson	.15
144 Jake Stevens	.15
145 Nate Schierholtz	.15
146 Neil Walker	.15
147 Bill Bray	.15
148 Taylor Tankersley	.15
149 Trevor Plouffe	.15
150 Felix Hernandez	.50
151 Phillip Hughes	.25
152 James Houser	.15
153 David Murphy	.25
154 Ervin Santana	.25
155 Anthony Whittington	.15
156 Chris Lambert	.15
157 Jeremy Sowers	.15
158 Gio Gonzalez	.25
159 Blake DeWitt	.25
160 Thomas Diamond	.15
161 Greg Golson	.15
162 David Aardsma	.15
163 Paul Maholm	.15
164 Mark Rogers	.15
165 Homer Bailey	.50
166 Chip Cannon RC	.50
167 Tony Giarratano RC	.50
168 Darren Fenster RC	.50
169 Elvys Quezada RC	.50
170 Glen Perkins RC	1.00
171 Ian Kinsler RC	5.00
172 Michael Bourn	1.00
173 Jeremy West RC	.50
174 Justin Verlander RC	3.00
175 Kevin West RC	.50
176 Luis Hernandez RC	.50
177 Matt Campbell RC	.50
178 Nate McLouth RC	1.00
179 Ryan Goleski RC	.50
180 Matt Lindstrom RC	.50
181 Matt DeSalvo RC	.50
182 Kole Strayhorn	.50
183 Jose Vaquedano RC	.50
184 James Jurries RC	.50
185 Ian Bladergroen RC	.50
186 Eric Nielsen RC	.50
187 Chris Vines RC	.50
188 Chris Denorfia RC	.50
189 Kevin Melillo RC	.50
190 Melky Cabrera RC	1.00
191 Ryan Sweeney RC	1.00
192 Sean Marshall RC	.50
193 Andy LaRoche RC	1.00
194 Tyler Pelland RC	.50
195 Mike Morse RC	.50
196 Wes Swackhamer RC	.50
197 Wade Robinson RC	.50
198 Dan Santin RC	.50
199 Steven Doetsch RC	.50
200 Shane Costa	.50
201 Scott Mathieson RC	.50
202 Ben Jones RC	.50
203 Michael Rogers RC	.50
204 Matt Rogelstad RC	.50
205 Luis Ramirez RC	.50
206 Landon Powell RC	.50
207 Erik Cordier RC	.50
208 Chris Seddon RC	.50
209 Chris Roberson RC	.50
210 Tom Oldham RC	.50
211 Dana Eveland RC	1.00
212 Cody Haerther RC	.50
213 Danny Core RC	.50
214 Craig Tatum RC	.50
215 Elliot Johnson RC	.50
216 Ender Chavez RC	.50
217 Errol Simonitsch RC	.50
218 Matt Van Der Bosch RC	.50
219 Eulogio de la Cruz RC	.50
220 C.J. Smith RC	.50
221 Adam Boeve RC	.50
222 Adam Harben RC	.50
223 Baltazar Lopez RC	.50

224	Russ Martin RC	1.50
225	Brian Bannister RC	1.00
226	Brian Miller RC	.50
227	Casey McGehee RC	1.00
228	Humberto Sanchez RC	1.00
229	Javon Moran RC	.50
230	Brandon McCarthy RC	.75
231	Danny Zell RC	.50
232	Jake Postlewait RC	.50
233	Juan Tejeda RC	.50
234	Keith Ramsey RC	.50
235	Lorenzo Scott RC	.50
236	Wladimir Balentien RC	1.00
237	Martin Prado RC	.50
238	Matt Albers RC	1.00
239	Brian Schweiger RC	.50
240	Brian Stavisky RC	.50
241	Pat Misch RC	.50
242	Pat Osborn RC	.50
243	Ryan Feierabend RC	.50
244	Shaun Marcum	.50
245	Kevin Collins RC	.50
246	Stuart Pomeranz RC	.50
247	Tetsu Yofu RC	.50
248	Hernan Iribarren RC	.75
249	Mike Spiegel RC	.50
250	Tony Arnerich RC	.50
251	Manny Parra RC	1.00
252	Drew Anderson RC	.50
253	T.J. Beam RC	.50
254	Pedro Lopez RC	.75
255	Andy Sides RC	.50
256	Bear Bay RC	.50
257	Bill McCarthy RC	.50
258	Daniel Haigwood RC	.50
259	Brian Sprout RC	.50
260	Bryan Triplett RC	.50
261	Steve Bondurant RC	.50
262	Darwinson Salazar RC	.50
263	David Shepard RC	.50
264	Johan Silva RC	.50
265	J.B. Thurmond RC	.50
266	Brandon Moorhead RC	.50
267	Kyle Nichols RC	.50
268	Jonathan Sanchez RC	1.00
269	Mike Esposito RC	.50
270	Erik Schindewolf RC	.50
271	Peeter Ramos RC	.50
272	Juan Senreiso RC	.50
273	Matthew Kemp RC	4.00
274	Vinny Rottino RC	.50
275	Micah Furtado RC	.50
276	George Kottaras RC	.75
277	Billy Butler RC	3.00
278	Buck Coats RC	.50
279	Ken Durost RC	.50
280	Nic Touchstone RC	.50
281	Jerry Owens RC	1.00
282	Stefan Bailie	.50
283	Jesse Gutierrez RC	.50
284	Chuck Tiffany RC	.50
285	Brendan Ryan RC	.50
286	Hayden Penn RC	.50
287	Shawn Bowman RC	.50
288	Alexander Smit RC	.50
289	Micah Schnurstein RC	.50
290	Jared Gothreaux RC	.50
291	Jair Jurrjens RC	1.50
292	Bobby Livingston RC	.50
293	Ryan Speier RC	.50
294	Zachary Parker RC	.50
295	Christian Colonel RC	.50
296	Scott Mitchinson RC	.50
297	Neil Wilson RC	.50
298	Chuck James RC	.50
299	Heath Totten RC	.50
300	Sean Tracey RC	.50
301	Ismael Ramirez RC	.50
302	Matt Brown RC	.50
303	Franklin Morales RC	1.00
304	Brandon Sing RC	.50
305	D.J. Houlton RC	.50
306	Jayce Tingler RC	.50
307	Mitchell Arnold RC	.50
308	Jim Burt RC	.50
309	Jason Motte RC	.50
310	David Gassner RC	.75
311	Andy Santana RC	.50
312	Kelvin Pichardo RC	.50
313	Carlos Carrasco RC	1.00
314	Willy Mota RC	.50
315	Frank Mata RC	.50
316	Carlos Gonzalez RC	2.00
317	Jeff Niemann RC	1.00
318	Chris Young RC	1.50
319	Billy Sadler	.50
320	Ricky Barrett	.50
321	Benjamin Harrison	.50
322	Steve Nelson RC	.50
323	Daryl Thompson RC	1.00
324	Philip Humber RC	1.00
325	Jeremy Harts RC	.50
326	Nick Masset RC	.50
327	Mike Rodriguez RC	.50
328	Mike Garber RC	.50
329	Kennard Bibbs RC	.50
330	Ryan Garko RC	1.00

Gold

Stars:	1-2X
Rookies:	1-2X
Inserted 1:1	

White

Stars:	3-6X
Rookies:	3-6X
Production 240 Sets	

1st Edition

		NM/M
Stars:		3-5X
Rookies:		1-2X
HTA Exclusive		
Pack (10):		3.50
Box (20):		60.00

A-Rod Throwbacks

		NM/M
Complete Set (4):		6.00
Common A-Rod:		2.00
94-AR-97-AR	Alex Rodriguez	2.00

A-Rod Throwbacks Autographs

		NM/M
Production 1-225		
96A-AR	Alex Rodriguez/99	150.00
97A-AR	Alex Rodriguez/225	150.00

A-Rod Throwbacks Relic

		NM/M
Quantity produced listed.		
96R-AR	Alex Rodriguez/99	20.00
97R-AR	Alex Rodriguez/800	15.00

Autographed Base Card Variations

			NM/M
Inserted 1:1,599			
141	Omar Quintanilla		8.00
142	Carlos Quentin		15.00
143	Dan Johnson		10.00
144	Jake Stevens		10.00
145	Nate Schierholtz		10.00
146	Neil Walker		15.00
147	Bill Bray		8.00
148	Taylor Tankersley		10.00
149	Trevor Plouffe		10.00
150	Felix Hernandez		30.00
151	Phillip Hughes		40.00
152	James Houser		10.00
153	David Murphy		10.00
154	Ervin Santana		15.00
155	Anthony Whittington		8.00
156	Chris Lambert		10.00
157	Jeremy Sowers		10.00
158	Gio Gonzalez		15.00
159	Blake DeWitt		15.00
160	Thomas Diamond		10.00
161	Greg Golson		10.00
162	David Aardsma		10.00
163	Paul Maholm		12.00
164	Mark Rogers		10.00
165	Homer Bailey		15.00

Dual Rookie of the Year Relic

		NM/M
Inserted 1:668		
ROY-BC	Jason Bay, Bobby Crosby	10.00

Futures Game Gear

		NM/M
JB	Joe Blanton	5.00
BB	Bryan Bullington	5.00
MC	Matt Cain	8.00
SC	Shin-Soo Choo	8.00
JCO	Jorge Cortes	5.00
JC	Jesus Cota	5.00
EE	Edwin Encarnacion	5.00
CE	Clint Everts	5.00
GF	Gavin Floyd	5.00
JF	Jeff Francis	5.00
JG	Jairo Garcia	5.00
RG	Ruben Gotay	5.00
JGU	Joel Guzman	5.00
AH	Aaron Hill	5.00
KH	Koyie Hill	5.00
WL	Wilfredo Ledezma	5.00
VM	Val Majewski	5.00
AMA	Andy Marte	5.00
JM	Jeff Mathis	5.00
DM	Dallas McPherson	5.00
JMO	Justin Morneau	8.00
AM	Arnie Munoz	5.00
YP	Yusmeiro Petit	5.00
FP	Felix Pie	5.00
RW	Rickie Weeks	6.00

Printing Plates

No Pricing
Production One Set

Relic Base Card Variations

		NM/M
Inserted 1:50		
2	Eric Chavez	5.00
5	Hank Blalock	8.00
23	Rafael Palmeiro	8.00
43	Mark Teixeira	8.00
49	Ivan Rodriguez	8.00
50	Alex Rodriguez	15.00
60	Gary Sheffield	8.00
65	Magglio Ordonez	5.00
78	David Ortiz	10.00
83	Adam Dunn	8.00
90	Miguel Cabrera	8.00
93	Andruw Jones	5.00
100	Barry Bonds	25.00
104	Melvin Mora	5.00
105	Albert Pujols	20.00
115	Alfonso Soriano	8.00
120	Vladimir Guerrero	8.00
125	Carlos Beltran	10.00
130	Manny Ramirez	8.00
135	Sammy Sosa	12.00

Signs of the Future

		NM/M
Common Auto.:		8.00
BB	Brian Bixler	10.00
MC	Melky Cabrera	12.00
RC	Robinson Cano	50.00
CC	Chad Cordero	10.00
BC	Bobby Crosby	8.00
BD	Blake DeWitt	10.00
CG	Christian Garcia	10.00
TG	Tom Gorzelanny	12.00
PH	Phillip Hughes	40.00
TH	Tim Hutting	10.00
SK	Scott Kazmir	15.00
AL	Adam Loewen	12.00
PM	Paul Maholm	12.00
DM	Dallas McPherson	10.00
SO	Scott Olson	10.00
TP	Trevor Plouffe	10.00
DP	Dan Putman	10.00
JR	Jay Rainville	10.00
RR	Richie Robnett	8.00
ES	Ervin Santana	15.00
JS	Jay Sborz	10.00
BMS	Brad Snyder	10.00
HS	Huston Street	20.00
BS	Brad Sullivan	10.00
TT	Taylor Tankersley	10.00
RW	Ryan Wagner	8.00
KW	Kyle Waldrop	10.00
AW	Anthony Whittington	10.00
DW	David Wright	65.00

Two of a Kind Autograph

No Pricing
Production 13

2005 Bowman Chrome

		NM/M
Complete Set (352):		
Common Player:		.25
Common Rookie:		1.00
Common RC Auto. (331-352):		10.00
Pack (4):		8.00
Box (18):		125.00
1	Gavin Floyd	.25
2	Eric Chavez	.50
3	Miguel Tejada	.75
4	Dmitri Young	.25
5	Hank Blalock	.50
6	Kerry Wood	.50
7	Andy Pettitte	.50
8	Pat Burrell	.50
9	Johnny Estrada	.25
10	Frank Thomas	.75
11	Juan Pierre	.25
12	Tom Glavine	.50
13	Lyle Overbay	.25
14	Jim Edmonds	.50
15	Steve Finley	.25
16	Jermaine Dye	.25
17	Omar Vizquel	.25
18	Nick Johnson	.25
19	Brian Giles	.25
20	Justin Morneau	.50
21	Preston Wilson	.25
22	Wily Mo Pena	.25
23	Rafael Palmeiro	.75
24	Scott Kazmir	.50
25	Derek Jeter	3.00
26	Barry Zito	.50
27	Mike Lowell	.25
28	Jason Bay	.50
29	Ken Harvey	.25
30	Nomar Garciaparra	1.00
31	Roy Halladay	.50
32	Todd Helton	.75
33	Mark Kotsay	.25
34	Jake Peavy	.50
35	David Wright	1.00
36	Dontrelle Willis	.50
37	Marcus Giles	.25
38	Chone Figgins	.25
39	Sidney Ponson	.25
40	Randy Johnson	1.00
41	John Smoltz	.50
42	Kevin Millar	.25
43	Mark Teixeira	.75
44	Alex Rios	.25
45	Mike Piazza	1.00
46	Victor Martinez	.50
47	Jeff Bagwell	.75
48	Shawn Green	.50
49	Ivan Rodriguez	.75
50	Alex Rodriguez	2.00
51	Kazuo Matsui	.25
52	Mark Mulder	.50
53	Michael Young	.50
54	Javy Lopez	.25
55	Johnny Damon	1.00
56	Jeff Francis	.25
57	Rich Harden	.50
58	Bobby Abreu	.50
59	Mark Loretta	.25
60	Gary Sheffield	.50
61	Jamie Moyer	.25
62	Garret Anderson	.50
63	Vernon Wells	.50
64	Orlando Cabrera	.25
65	Magglio Ordonez	.50
66	Ronnie Belliard	.25
67	Carlos Lee	.25
68	Carl Pavano	.25
69	Jon Lieber	.25
70	Aubrey Huff	.25
71	Rocco Baldelli	.25
72	Jason Schmidt	.25
73	Bernie Williams	.50
74	Hideki Matsui	2.00
75	Ken Griffey Jr.	2.00
76	Josh Beckett	.50
77	Mark Buehrle	.40
78	David Ortiz	1.00
79	Luis Gonzalez	.25
80	Scott Rolen	1.00
81	Joe Mauer	.75
82	Jose Reyes	.75
83	Adam Dunn	.75
84	Greg Maddux	2.00
85	Bartolo Colon	.40
86	Bret Boone	.25
87	Mike Mussina	.50
88	Ben Sheets	.50
89	Lance Berkman	.50
90	Miguel Cabrera	1.00
91	C.C. Sabathia	.25
92	Mike Maroth	.25
93	Andruw Jones	.50
94	Jack Wilson	.25
95	Ichiro Suzuki	2.00
96	Geoff Jenkins	.25
97	Zack Greinke	.25
98	Jorge Posada	.50
99	Travis Hafner	.50
100	Barry Bonds	3.00
101	Aaron Rowand	.25
102	Aramis Ramirez	.50
103	Curt Schilling	1.00
104	Melvin Mora	.25
105	Albert Pujols	3.00
106	Austin Kearns	.40
107	Shannon Stewart	.25
108	Carl Crawford	.50
109	Carlos Zambrano	.50
110	Roger Clemens	3.00
111	Javier Vazquez	.25
112	Randy Wolf	.25
113	Chipper Jones	1.00
114	Larry Walker	.50
115	Alfonso Soriano	1.00
116	Brad Wilkerson	.25
117	Bobby Crosby	.25
118	Jim Thome	.75
119	Oliver Perez	.25
120	Vladimir Guerrero	1.00
121	Roy Oswalt	.50
122	Torii Hunter	.40
123	Rafael Furcal	.25
124	Luis Castillo	.25
125	Carlos Beltran	.75
126	Mike Sweeney	.25
127	Johan Santana	.50
128	Tim Hudson	.50
129	Troy Glaus	.50
130	Manny Ramirez	1.00
131	Jeff Kent	.40
132	Jose Vidro	.25
133	Edgar Renteria	.40
134	Russ Ortiz	.25
135	Sammy Sosa	1.00
136	Carlos Delgado	.50
137	Richie Sexson	.50
138	Pedro Martinez	1.00
139	Adrian Beltre	.50
140	Mark Prior	.75
141	Omar Quintanilla	.25
142	Carlos Quentin	.25
143	Dan Johnson	.25
144	Jake Stevens	.25
145	Nate Schierholtz	.25
146	Neil Walker	.25
147	Bill Bray	.25
148	Taylor Tankersley	.25
149	Trevor Plouffe	.25
150	Felix Hernandez	1.00
151	Phillip Hughes	.50
152	James Houser	.25
153	David Murphy	.25
154	Ervin Santana	.25
155	Anthony Whittington	.25
156	Chris Lambert	.25
157	Jeremy Sowers	.25
158	Gio Gonzalez	.25
159	Blake DeWitt	.25
160	Thomas Diamond	.25
161	Greg Golson	.25
162	David Aardsma	.25
163	Paul Maholm	.25
164	Mark Rogers	.25
165	Homer Bailey	.50
166	Elvin Puello RC	1.00
167	Tony Giarratano RC	1.00
168	Darren Fenster RC	1.00
169	Elvys Quezada RC	1.00
170	Glen Perkins RC	1.50
171	Ian Kinsler RC	12.00
172	Adam Bostick RC	1.00
173	Jeremy West RC	1.50
174	Brett Harper RC	1.00
175	Kevin West RC	1.00
176	Luis Hernandez RC	1.00
177	Matt Campbell RC	1.00
178	Nate McLouth RC	2.00
179	Ryan Goleski RC	1.00
180	Matt Lindstrom RC	1.00
181	Matt DeSalvo RC	1.00
182	Kole Strayhorn RC	1.00
183	Jose Vaquedano RC	1.00
184	James Jurries RC	1.00
185	Ian Bladergroen RC	1.00
186	Kila Ka'aihue RC	2.00
187	Luke Scott RC	3.00
188	Chris Denorfia RC	1.00
189	Jai Miller RC	1.00
190	Melky Cabrera RC	2.50
191	Ryan Sweeney RC	1.50
192	Sean Marshall RC	1.50
193	Eric Abreu RC	1.50
194	Tyler Pelland RC	1.00
195	Cole Armstrong RC	1.00
196	John Hudgins RC	1.00
197	Wade Robinson RC	1.00
198	Dan Santin RC	1.00
199	Steven Doetsch RC	1.00
200	Shane Costa RC	1.00
201	Scott Mathieson RC	1.00
202	Ben Jones RC	1.00
203	Michael Rogers RC	1.00
204	Matt Rogelstad RC	1.00
205	Luis Ramirez RC	1.00
206	Landon Powell RC	1.00
207	Erik Cordier RC	1.00
208	Chris Seddon RC	1.00
209	Chris Roberson RC	1.00
210	Tom Oldham RC	1.00
211	Dana Eveland RC	1.00
212	Cody Haerther RC	1.00
213	Danny Core RC	1.00
214	Craig Tatum RC	1.00
215	Elliot Johnson RC	1.00
216	Ender Chavez RC	1.00
217	Errol Simonitsch RC	1.00
218	Matt Van Der Bosch RC	1.00
219	Eulogio de la Cruz RC	1.00
220	Drew Toussaint RC	1.00
221	Adam Boeve RC	1.00
222	Adam Harben RC	1.00
223	Baltazar Lopez RC	2.00
224	Russell Martin RC	2.00
225	Brian Bannister RC	2.00
226	Chris Walker RC	1.00
227	Casey McGehee RC	2.50
228	Humberto Sanchez RC	3.00
229	Javon Moran RC	1.00
230	Brandon McCarthy RC	1.00
231	Danny Zell RC	1.00
232	Kevin Barry RC	1.00
233	Juan Tejeda RC	1.00
234	Keith Ramsey RC	1.00
235	Lorenzo Scott RC	1.00
236	Jonathan Barratt RC	1.00
237	Martin Prado RC	2.50
238	Matt Albers RC	1.00
239	Brian Schweiger RC	1.00
240	Raul Tablado RC	1.00
241	Pat Misch RC	1.00
242	Pat Osborn RC	1.00
243	Ryan Feierabend RC	1.00
244	Shaun Marcum RC	1.00
245	Kevin Collins RC	1.00
246	Stuart Pomeranz RC	1.00
247	Tetsu Yofu RC	1.00
248	Hernan Iribarren RC	1.00
249	Michael Spidale RC	1.00
250	Tony Americh RC	1.00
251	Manny Parra RC	2.00
252	Drew Anderson RC	1.00
253	T.J. Beam RC	1.00
254	Claudio Arias RC	2.00
255	Andy Sides RC	1.00
256	Bear Bay RC	1.00
257	Bill McCarthy RC	1.00
258	Daniel Haigwood RC	1.00
259	Brian Sprout RC	1.00
260	Bryan Triplett RC	1.00
261	Steve Bondurant RC	1.00
262	Darwinson Salazar RC	1.00
263	David Shepard RC	1.00
264	Johan Silva RC	1.00
265	J.B. Thurmond RC	1.00
266	Brandon Moorhead RC	1.00
267	Kyle Nichols RC	1.00
268	Jonathan Sanchez RC	4.00
269	Mike Esposito RC	1.00
270	Erik Schindewolf RC	1.00
271	Peeter Ramos RC	1.00
272	Juan Senreiso RC	1.00
273	Travis Chick RC	1.00
274	Vinny Rottino RC	1.00
275	Micah Furtado RC	1.00
276	George Kottaras RC	1.50
277	Abel Gomez RC	1.00
278	Buck Coats RC	1.00
279	Ken Durost RC	1.00
280	Nick Touchstone RC	1.00
281	Jerry Owens RC	1.50
282	Stefan Bailie RC	1.00
283	Jesse Gutierrez RC	1.00
284	Chuck Tiffany RC	1.00
285	Brendan Ryan RC	1.00
286	Julio Pimentel RC	1.00
287	Shawn Bowman RC	1.00
288	Alexander Smit RC	1.00
289	Micah Schnurstein RC	1.00
290	Jared Gothreaux RC	1.00
291	Jair Jurrjens RC	3.00
292	Bobby Livingston RC	1.00
293	Ryan Speier RC	1.00
294	Zachary Parker RC	1.00
295	Christian Colonel RC	1.00
296	Scott Mitchinson RC	1.00
297	Neil Wilson RC	1.00
298	Chuck James RC	1.50
299	Heath Totten RC	1.00
300	Sean Tracey RC	1.00
301	Tadahito Iguchi RC	2.00
302	Matt Brown RC	1.00
303	Franklin Morales RC	2.00
304	Brandon Sing RC	1.00
305	D.J. Houlton RC	1.00
306	Jayce Tingler RC	1.00
307	Mitchell Arnold RC	1.00
308	Jim Burt RC	1.00
309	Jason Motte RC	1.00
310	David Gassner RC	1.00
311	Andy Santana RC	1.00
312	Kelvin Pichardo RC	1.00
313	Carlos Carrasco RC	3.00
314	Willy Mota RC	1.00
315	Frank Mata RC	1.00
316	Carlos Gonzalez RC	10.00
317	Jesse Floyd RC	1.00
318	Chris Young RC	4.00
319	Billy Sadler	1.00
320	Ricky Barrett RC	1.00
321	Benjamin Harrison RC	1.00
322	Steve Nelson RC	1.00
323	Daryl Thompson RC	2.00
324	Davis Romero RC	1.00
325	Jeremy Harts RC	1.00
326	Nick Masset RC	1.00
327	Thomas Pauly RC	1.00
328	Mike Garber RC	1.00

329	Kennard Bibbs RC	1.00
330	Colter Bean RC	1.00
331	Justin Verlander RC	50.00
332	Chip Cannon RC	20.00
333	Kevin Melillo RC	10.00
334	Jake Postlewait RC	10.00
335	Wes Swackhamer RC	10.00
336	Mike Rodriguez RC	10.00
337	Philip Humber RC	20.00
338	Jeff Niemann RC	20.00
339	Brian Miller RC	10.00
340	Chris Vines RC	10.00
341	Andy LaRoche RC	20.00
342	Michael Bourn	25.00
343	Eric Nielsen RC	10.00
344	Wladimir Balentien RC	25.00
345	Ismael Ramirez RC	10.00
346	Pedro Lopez RC	10.00
347	Shawn Bowman RC	10.00
348	Hayden Penn RC	10.00
349	Matthew Kemp RC	75.00
350	Brian Stavisky RC	10.00
351	C.J. Smith RC	10.00
352	Mike Morse RC	10.00
353	Billy Butler RC	50.00

Refractor
Stars (1-165): 2-4X
Rookies (166-330): 1-2X
Inserted 1:4
Autograph (331-353): 1-2X
Production 250 Sets

Blue Refractor
Stars (1-165): 3-5X
Rookies (166-330): 3-5X
Autograph (331-353): 1-2.5X
Production 150 Sets

Gold Refractor
Stars (1-165): 8-15X
Rookies (166-330): 15-25X
Autograph (331-353): 3-6X
Production 50 Sets

Red Refractor
No Pricing
Production 5 Sets

Superfractor
No Pricing
Production One Set

X-Fractor
Stars (1-165): 3-5X
Rookies (166-330): 2-5X
Autograph (331-353): 1-2.5X
Production 225 Sets

Printing Plates
No Pricing
Production one set per color.

A-Rod Throwback

NM/M
Complete Set (4): 6.00
Common A-Rod 2.00
Inserted 1:9
Refractor: 2-3X
Production 499 Sets
X-Fractor: 3-5X
Production 99 Sets
Superfractor: No Pricing
Production One Set
94AR-97AR Alex Rodriguez 2.00

A-Rod Throwback Autograph
NM/M
Quantity produced listed.
96AR Alex Rodriguez/50 160.00
97AR Alex Rodriguez/99 150.00

Two Of A Kind Autograph
No Pricing
Production 13

2005 Bowman Draft Picks & Prospects
NM/M
Complete Set (165): 30.00
Commmon Player: .15
Common Rookie .25
Pack (5 + 2 Chrome): 7.00
Box (24): 140.00

BDP1	Rickie Weeks	.15
BDP2	Kyle Davies	.15
BDP3	Garrett Atkins	.15
BDP4	Chien-Ming Wang	.50
BDP5	Dallas McPherson	.15
BDP6	Dan Johnson	.15
BDP7	Andy Sisco	.15
BDP8	Ryan Doumit	.15
BDP9	J.P. Howell	.15
BDP10	Tim Stauffer	.15
BDP11	Willy Taveras	.15
BDP12	Aaron Hill	.15
BDP13	Victor Diaz	.15
BDP14	Wilson Betemit	.15
BDP15	Ervin Santana	.15
BDP16	Mike Morse	.15
BDP17	Yadier Molina	.15
BDP18	Kelly Johnson	.15
BDP19	Clint Barmes	.15
BDP20	Robinson Cano	.40
BDP21	Brad Thompson	.15
BDP22	Jorge Cantu	.15
BDP23	Brad Halsey	.15
BDP24	Lance Niekro	.15
BDP25	D.J. Houlton	.15
BDP26	Ryan Church	.15
BDP27	Hayden Penn	.15
BDP28	Chris Young	.50
BDP29	Chad Orvella	.15
BDP30	Mark Teahen	.15
BDP31	Mark McCormick RC	.25
BDP32	Jay Bruce RC	10.00
BDP33	Beau Jones RC	.75
BDP34	Tyler Greene RC	.40
BDP35	Zach Ward RC	.75
BDP36	Josh Bell RC	.50
BDP37	Josh Wall RC	.50
BDP38	Nick Webber RC	.75
BDP39	Travis Buck RC	.75
BDP40	Kyle Winters RC	.25
BDP41	Mitch Boggs RC	.50
BDP42	Tommy Mendoza RC	.50
BDP43	Brad Corley RC	.40
BDP44	Drew Butera RC	.25
BDP45	Ryan Mount RC	.40
BDP46	Tyler Herron RC	.50
BDP47	Nick Weglarz RC	.75
BDP48	Brandon Erbe RC	.25
BDP49	Cody Allen RC	.25
BDP50	Eric Fowler RC	.25
BDP51	James Boone RC	.50
BDP52	Josh Flores RC	.25
BDP53	Brandon Monk RC	.50
BDP54	Kieron Pope RC	.40
BDP55	Kyle Cofield RC	.40
BDP56	Brent Lillibridge RC	.75
BDP57	Daryl Jones RC	.40
BDP58	Eli Iorg RC	.50
BDP59	Brett Hayes RC	.75
BDP60	Mike Durant RC	.75
BDP61	Michael Bowden RC	1.00
BDP62	Paul Kelly RC	.50
BDP63	Andrew McCutchen RC	2.50
BDP64	Travis Wood RC	.75
BDP65	Cesar Ramos RC	.25
BDP66	Chaz Roe RC	.40
BDP67	Matt Torra RC	.50
BDP68	Kevin Slowey RC	.75
BDP69	Trayvon Robinson RC	.40
BDP70	Reid Engel RC	.40
BDP71	Kris Harvey RC	.50
BDP72	Craig Italiano RC	.50
BDP73	Matt Maloney RC	1.00
BDP74	Sean West RC	1.00
BDP75	Henry Sanchez RC	.75
BDP76	Scott Blue RC	.25
BDP77	Jordan Schafer RC	1.50
BDP78	Chris Robinson RC	.25
BDP79	Chris Hobdy RC	.25
BDP80	Brandon Durden RC	.25
BDP81	Clay Buchholz RC	4.00
BDP82	Josh Geer RC	.25
BDP83	Sam LeCure RC	.25
BDP84	Justin Thomas RC	.25
BDP85	Brett Gardner RC	2.50
BDP86	Tommy Manzella RC	.25
BDP87	Matt Green RC	.25
BDP88	Yunel Escobar RC	.75
BDP89	Mike Costanzo RC	.75
BDP90	Nick Hundley RC	.25
BDP91	Zach Simons RC	.25
BDP92	Jacob Marceaux RC	.25
BDP93	Jed Lowrie RC	1.00
BDP94	Brandon Snyder RC	1.00
BDP95	Matt Goyen RC	.40
BDP96	Jon Egan RC	.40
BDP97	Drew Thompson RC	.40
BDP98	Bryan Anderson RC	1.00
BDP99	Clayton Richard RC	.25
BDP100	Jimmy Shull RC	.75
BDP101	Mark Pawelek RC	.75
BDP102	P.J. Phillips RC	.40
BDP103	John Drennen RC	.75
BDP104	Nolan Reimold RC	1.50
BDP105	Troy Tulowitzki RC	3.00
BDP106	Kevin Whelan RC	.25
BDP107	Wade Townsend RC	.25
BDP108	Micah Owings RC	.50
BDP109	Ryan Tucker RC	.40
BDP110	Jeff Clement RC	.75
BDP111	Josh Sullivan RC	.25
BDP112	Jeff Lyman RC	.25
BDP113	Brian Bogusevic RC	.75
BDP114	Trevor Bell RC	.50
BDP115	Brent Cox RC	.75
BDP116	Michael Billek RC	.25
BDP117	Garrett Olson RC	.50
BDP118	Steven Johnson RC	.25
BDP119	Chase Headley RC	1.50
BDP121	Daniel Carte RC	.50
BDP122	Francisco Liriano	.75
BDP123	Zach Jackson	.15
BDP124	Adam Loewen	.15
BDP125	Chris Lambert	.15
BDP126	Scott Mathieson RC	.25
BDP127	Paul Maholm	.15
BDP128	Fernando Nieve	.15
BDP129	Justin Verlander	.75
BDP130	Yusmeiro Petit	.40
BDP131	Joel Zumaya	.25
BDP132	Merkin Valdez	.15
BDP133	Ryan Garko RC	.75
BDP134	Edinson Volquez RC	3.00
BDP135	Russell Martin	.50
BDP136	Conor Jackson	.25
BDP137	Miguel Montero RC	.75
BDP138	Josh Barfield	.15
BDP139	Delmon Young	.75
BDP140	Andy LaRoche	.75
BDP141	William Bergolla	.15
BDP142	B.J. Upton	.15
BDP143	Hernan Iribarren RC	.25
BDP144	Brandon Wood	.40
BDP145	Jose Bautista	.15
BDP146	Edwin Encarnacion	.15
BDP147	Javier Herrera RC	.75
BDP148	Jeremy Hermida	.25
BDP149	Frank Diaz RC	.25
BDP150	Chris Young	.15
BDP151	Shin-Soo Choo	.15
BDP152	Kevin Thompson	.15
BDP153	Hanley Ramirez	.25
BDP154	Lastings Milledge	.25
BDP155	Luis Montanez	.15
BDP156	Justin Huber	.15
BDP157	Zachary Duke	.25
BDP158	Jeff Francoeur	.25
BDP159	Melky Cabrera	.50
BDP160	Bobby Jenks	.15
BDP161	Ian Snell	.15
BDP162	Fernando Cabrera	.15
BDP163	Troy Patton	.50
BDP164	Anthony Lerew	.15
BDP165	Nelson Cruz RC	2.00

White
Rookies: 3-5X
Production 225 Sets

Red
No Pricing
Production One Set

Base Relic Variations
NM/M
Common Player: 4.00

BDP121	Francisco Liriano	8.00
BDP122	Fausto Carmona	4.00
BDP123	Zach Jackson	4.00
BDP124	Adam Loewen	4.00
BDP125	Chris Lambert	4.00
BDP126	Scott Mathieson	4.00
BDP127	Paul Maholm	4.00
BDP128	Fernando Nieve	4.00
BDP129	Justin Verlander	8.00
BDP131	Joel Zumaya	6.00
BDP132	Merkin Valdez	4.00
BDP133	Ryan Garko	4.00
BDP134	Edinson Volquez	10.00
BDP135	Russell Martin	4.00
BDP136	Conor Jackson	4.00
BDP137	Miguel Montero	6.00
BDP138	Josh Barfield	4.00
BDP139	Delmon Young	4.00
BDP140	Andy LaRoche	4.00
BDP141	William Bergolla	4.00
BDP142	B.J. Upton	4.00
BDP143	Hernan Iribarren	4.00
BDP144	Brandon Wood	6.00
BDP145	Jose Bautista	4.00
BDP146	Edwin Encarnacion	4.00
BDP147	Javier Herrera	4.00
BDP148	Jeremy Hermida	4.00
BDP149	Frank Diaz	4.00
BDP150	Chris Young	4.00

Signs of the Future
NM/M
Common Player: 8.00

HB	Homer Bailey	20.00
BB	Bill Bray	8.00
JF	Jeff Frazier	8.00
GG	Greg Golson	8.00
AG	Angel Guzman	10.00
JH	Justin Hoyman	8.00
JJ	Justin Jones	8.00
DL	Donald Lucey	8.00
TL	Tyler Lumsden	8.00
DM	David Murphy	12.00
JP	Jonathan Poterson	8.00
DP	David Purcey	8.00
RR	Richie Robnett	8.00
JS	Jeremy Sowers	8.00

2005 Bowman Chrome Draft Picks & Prospects

NM/M
Complete Set (180):
Common Player: .25
Common Rookie: 1.00
Rk Auto. (166-180): 15.00

BDP1	Rickie Weeks	.40
BDP2	Kyle Davies	.25
BDP3	Garrett Atkins	.25
BDP4	Chien-Ming Wang	.75
BDP5	Dallas McPherson	.25
BDP6	Dan Johnson	.25
BDP7	Andy Sisco	.25
BDP8	Ryan Doumit	.25
BDP9	J.P. Howell	.25
BDP10	Tim Stauffer	.25
BDP11	Willy Taveras	.25
BDP12	Aaron Hill	.25
BDP13	Victor Diaz	.25
BDP14	Wilson Betemit	.25
BDP15	Ervin Santana	.25
BDP16	Mike Morse	.25
BDP17	Yadier Molina	.25
BDP18	Kelly Johnson	.25
BDP19	Clint Barmes	.25
BDP20	Robinson Cano	.75
BDP21	Brad Thompson	.25
BDP22	Jorge Cantu	.25
BDP23	Brad Halsey	.25
BDP24	Lance Niekro	.25
BDP25	D.J. Houlton	.25
BDP26	Ryan Church	.25
BDP27	Hayden Penn	.25
BDP28	Chris Young	1.00
BDP29	Chad Orvella	.50
BDP30	Mark Teahen	.50
BDP31	Mark McCormick RC	1.00
BDP32	Jay Bruce RC	20.00
BDP33	Beau Jones RC	1.00
BDP34	Tyler Greene RC	1.00
BDP35	Zach Ward RC	1.00
BDP36	Josh Bell RC	1.00
BDP37	Josh Wall RC	1.00
BDP38	Nick Webber RC	1.00
BDP39	Travis Buck RC	2.00
BDP40	Kyle Winters RC	1.00
BDP41	Mitch Boggs RC	1.00
BDP42	Tommy Mendoza RC	1.00
BDP43	Brad Corley RC	1.00
BDP44	Drew Butera RC	1.00
BDP45	Ryan Mount RC	1.00
BDP46	Tyler Herron RC	1.00
BDP47	Nick Weglarz RC	1.00
BDP48	Brandon Erbe RC	2.00
BDP49	Cody Allen RC	1.00
BDP50	Eric Fowler RC	1.00
BDP51	James Boone RC	1.00
BDP52	Josh Flores RC	2.00
BDP53	Brandon Monk RC	1.00
BDP54	Kieron Pope RC	1.00
BDP55	Kyle Cofield RC	1.00
BDP56	Brent Lillibridge RC	1.00
BDP57	Daryl Jones RC	1.00
BDP58	Eli Iorg RC	1.00
BDP59	Brett Hayes RC	1.00
BDP60	Mike Durant RC	1.00
BDP61	Michael Bowden RC	5.00
BDP62	Paul Kelly RC	1.00
BDP63	Andrew McCutchen RC	8.00
BDP64	Travis Wood RC	2.00
BDP65	Cesar Ramos RC	1.00
BDP66	Chaz Roe RC	1.00
BDP67	Matt Torra RC	1.00
BDP68	Kevin Slowey RC	3.00
BDP69	Trayvon Robinson RC	1.00
BDP70	Reid Engel RC	1.00
BDP71	Kris Harvey RC	1.00
BDP72	Craig Italiano RC	1.00
BDP73	Matt Maloney RC	1.00
BDP74	Sean West RC	1.00
BDP75	Henry Sanchez RC	1.00
BDP76	Scott Blue RC	1.00
BDP77	Jordan Schafer RC	3.00
BDP78	Chris Robinson RC	1.00
BDP79	Chris Hobdy RC	1.00
BDP80	Brandon Durden RC	1.00
BDP81	Clay Buchholz RC	15.00
BDP82	Josh Geer RC	1.00
BDP83	Sam LeCure RC	1.00
BDP84	Justin Thomas RC	1.00
BDP85	Brett Gardner RC	1.00
BDP86	Tommy Manzella RC	1.00
BDP87	Matt Green RC	1.00
BDP88	Yunel Escobar RC	3.00
BDP89	Mike Costanzo RC	1.00
BDP90	Nick Hundley RC	1.00
BDP91	Zach Simons RC	1.00
BDP92	Jacob Marceaux RC	1.00
BDP93	Jed Lowrie RC	2.50
BDP94	Brandon Snyder RC	1.00
BDP95	Matt Goyen RC	1.00
BDP96	Jon Egan RC	1.00
BDP97	Drew Thompson RC	1.00
BDP98	Bryan Anderson RC	1.00
BDP99	Clayton Richard RC	1.00
BDP100	Jimmy Shull RC	1.00
BDP101	Mark Pawelek RC	2.00
BDP102	P.J. Phillips RC	1.00
BDP103	John Drennen RC	1.00
BDP104	Nolan Reimold RC	2.00
BDP105	Troy Tulowitzki RC	8.00
BDP106	Kevin Whelan RC	1.00
BDP107	Wade Townsend RC	1.00
BDP108	Micah Owings RC	1.00
BDP109	Ryan Tucker RC	1.00
BDP110	Jeff Clement RC	1.00
BDP111	Josh Sullivan RC	1.00
BDP112	Jeff Lyman RC	1.00
BDP113	Brian Bogusevic RC	1.00
BDP114	Trevor Bell RC	1.00
BDP115	Brent Cox RC	1.00
BDP116	Michael Billek RC	1.00
BDP117	Garrett Olson RC	1.00
BDP118	Steven Johnson RC	1.00
BDP119	Chase Headley RC	4.00
BDP120	Daniel Carte RC	1.00
BDP121	Francisco Liriano	1.50
BDP122	Fausto Carmona	.25
BDP123	Zach Jackson	.25
BDP124	Adam Loewen	.25
BDP125	Chris Lambert	.25
BDP126	Scott Mathieson RC	1.00
BDP127	Paul Maholm	.25
BDP128	Fernando Nieve	.25
BDP129	Justin Verlander	3.00
BDP130	Yusmeiro Petit	.25
BDP131	Joel Zumaya	.50
BDP132	Merkin Valdez	.25
BDP133	Ryan Garko	2.00
BDP134	Edinson Volquez	8.00
BDP135	Russell Martin	.50
BDP136	Conor Jackson	.25
BDP137	Miguel Montero	2.00
BDP138	Josh Barfield	.25
BDP139	Delmon Young	.50
BDP140	Andy LaRoche	1.00
BDP141	William Bergolla	.25
BDP142	B.J. Upton	.25
BDP143	Hernan Iribarren	.50
BDP144	Brandon Wood	.50
BDP145	Jose Bautista	.25
BDP146	Edwin Encarnacion	.25
BDP147	Javier Herrera RC	1.00
BDP148	Jeremy Hermida	.50
BDP149	Frank Diaz RC	1.00
BDP150	Chris Young	.75
BDP151	Shin-Soo Choo	.25
BDP152	Kevin Thompson	.25
BDP153	Hanley Ramirez	1.00
BDP154	Lastings Milledge	.50
BDP155	Luis Montanez	.25
BDP156	Justin Huber	.25
BDP157	Zachary Duke	.25
BDP158	Jeff Francoeur	.50
BDP159	Melky Cabrera	.75
BDP160	Bobby Jenks	.25
BDP161	Ian Snell	.25
BDP162	Fernando Cabrera	.25
BDP163	Troy Patton	1.00
BDP164	Anthony Lerew	.25
BDP165	Nelson Cruz RC	5.00
BDP166	Stephen Drew RC	40.00
BDP167	Jered Weaver RC	40.00
BDP168	Ryan Braun RC	150.00
BDP169	John Mayberry Jr. RC	15.00
BDP170	Aaron Thompson RC	15.00
BDP171	Cesar Carrillo RC	15.00
BDP172	Jacoby Ellsbury RC	75.00
BDP173	Matt Garza RC	30.00
BDP174	Cliff Pennington RC	15.00
BDP175	Colby Rasmus RC	75.00
BDP176	Chris Volstad RC	15.00
BDP177	Ricky Romero RC	20.00
BDP178	Ryan Zimmerman RC	75.00
BDP179	C.J. Henry RC	10.00
BDP180	Eddy Martinez RC	10.00

Refractor
Rookies: 2-4X
Inserted 1:11
Rk Autos. (166-180): 1-1.5X
Production 500

Blue Refractor
Rookies: 4-6X
Rk Autos. (166-180): 1.5-3X
Production 150 Sets

Gold Refractor
Rookies: 8-15X
Rk Autos. (166-180): 4-6X
Production 50 Sets

Red Refractor
No Pricing
Production One Set

SuperFractor
No Pricing
Production One Set

X-Fractor
Rookies: 4-6X
Rk Autos. (166-180): 1-2X
Production 250 Sets

2005 Bowman Heritage

NM/M
Complete Set (349):
Common Player (1-300): .15
Common SP (301-349): 3.00
Inserted 1:3
Draft Pick Variations (325-349): 1-1.5X
One DPV pack per hobby box.
Pack (8): 4.00
Box (24): 85.00

1	Steven White RC	.75
2	Jorge Posada	.25
3	Brett Myers	.15
4	Pat Burrell	.25
5	Grady Sizemore	.50
6	Jeff Weaver	.15
7	Jeff Kent	.25
8	Mark Kotsay	.15
9	Nick Swisher	.25
10	Scott Rolen	.50
11	Matt Morris	.25
12	Luis Castillo	.15
13	Pedro Feliz	.15
14	Omar Vizquel	.25
15	Edgar Renteria	.15
16	David Wells	.15
17	Chad Cordero	.15
18	Brad Wilkerson	.15
19	Kelly Johnson	.15
20	Johnny Estrada	.15
21	Brian Roberts	.25
22	Jeromy Burnitz	.15
23	Magglio Ordonez	.25
24	Adam Dunn	.50
25	Randy Johnson	.75
26	Derek Jeter	2.00
27	Jon Lieber	.15
28	Jim Thome	.50
29	Ronnie Belliard	.15
30	Jake Westbrook	.15
31	Bengie Molina	.15
32	J.D. Drew	.25
33	Rich Harden	.25
34	David Eckstein	.15
35	Scott Podsednik	.25
36	Mark Buehrle	.15
37	Barry Bonds	1.00
38	Brian Schneider	.15
39	Tim Wakefield	.15
40	Craig Wilson	.15
41	Jose Vidro	.15
42	Jacque Jones	.15
43	Felix Hernandez	.50
44	Nomar Garciaparra	.75
45	Neifi Perez	.15
46	Brandon Inge	.15
47	Felipe Lopez	.15
48	Ken Griffey Jr.	1.50
49	Robinson Cano	.40
50	Jason Giambi	.50
51	Mike Lieberthal	.15
52	Bobby Abreu	.25
53	C.C. Sabathia	.25
54	Aaron Boone	.15
55	Milton Bradley	.15
56	Derek Lowe	.15
57	Barry Zito	.25
58	Jim Edmonds	.40
59	Jon Garland	.15
60	Tadahito Iguchi RC	1.00
61	Jason Schmidt	.25
62	David Ortiz	.75
63	Matt Lawton	.15
64	Zachary Duke	.25
65	Gary Sheffield	.40
66	Chipper Jones	.75
67	Sammy Sosa	.75
68	Rafael Palmeiro	.25
69	Carlos Zambrano	.25
70	Aramis Ramirez	.25
71	Chris Shelton	.15
72	Wily Mo Pena	.15
73	Mike Mussina	.50
74	Chien-Ming Wang	.50
75	Randy Wolf	.15
76	Jimmy Rollins	.25
77	Chase Utley	.50
78	Kevin Millwood	.15
79	Victor Martinez	.25
80	Morgan Ensberg	.15
81	Bartolo Colon	.15
82	Bobby Crosby	.15
83	Dan Johnson	.15
84	Danny Haren	.15

Base Set

#	Player	Price	#	Player	Price	#	Player	Price
85	Yadier Molina	.15	203	Hayden Penn RC	.50	321	Chris Young	5.00
86	Mark Mulder	.25	204	C.J. Smith RC	.25	322	Roy Oswalt	3.00
87	Russell Branyan	.15	205	Matt Albers RC	.25	323	Carlos Delgado	5.00
88	Lyle Overbay	.15	206	Jared Gothreaux RC	.25	324	Pedro Martinez	5.00
89	Edgardo Alfonzo	.15	207	Mike Rodriguez RC	.25	325	Jeff Clement RC	3.00
90	Mike Matheny	.15	208	Hernan Iribarren RC	.25	326	Jimmy Shull RC	3.00
91	J.T. Snow	.15	209	Manny Parra RC	1.00	327	Daniel Carte RC	4.00
92	Curt Schilling	.15	210	Kevin Collins RC	.50	328	Travis Buck RC	4.00
93	Oliver Perez	.15	211	Buck Coats RC	.50	329	Chris Volstad RC	5.00
94	Mark Redman	.15	212	Jeremy West RC	.25	330	Andrew McCutchen RC	8.00
95	Esteban Loaiza	.15	213	Ian Bladergroen RC	.25	331	Cliff Pennington RC	4.00
96	Livan Hernandez	.15	214	Chuck Tiffany RC	.25	332	John Mayberry Jr. RC	4.00
97	Ryan Church	.15	215	Andy LaRoche RC	1.00	333	C.J. Henry RC	4.00
98	Kyle Davies	.15	216	Frank Diaz RC	.25	334	Ricky Romero RC	5.00
99	Mike Hampton	.15	217	Jai Miller RC	.25	335	Aaron Thompson RC	5.00
100	Jeff Francoeur	.25	218	Tony Giarratano RC	.50	336	Cesar Carrillo RC	5.00
101	Javy Lopez	.15	219	Danny Zell RC	.25	337	Jacoby Ellsbury RC	15.00
102	Mark Prior	.75	220	Justin Verlander RC	5.00	338	Matt Garza RC	8.00
103	Kerry Wood	.15	221	Ryan Sweeney RC	1.00	339	Colby Rasmus RC	15.00
104	Carlos Guillen	.15	222	Brandon McCarthy RC	.50	340	Ryan Zimmerman RC	10.00
105	Dmitri Young	.15	223	Jerry Owens RC	.25	341	Ryan Braun RC	20.00
106	David Wright	1.00	224	Glen Perkins RC	.50	342	Brent Lillibridge RC	5.00
107	Cliff Floyd	.15	225	Kevin West RC	.25	343	Jay Bruce RC	10.00
108	Carlos Beltran	.50	226	Billy Butler RC	4.00	344	Matt Green RC	4.00
109	Melky Cabrera RC	2.00	227	Shane Costa RC	.50	345	Brent Cox RC	4.00
110	Carl Pavano	.15	228	Erik Schindewolf RC	.25	346	Jed Lowrie RC	4.00
111	Jamie Moyer	.15	229	Miguel Montero RC	1.00	347	Beau Jones RC	3.00
112	Joel Pineiro	.15	230	Stephen Drew RC	4.00	348	Eli Iorg RC	4.00
113	Adrian Beltre	.15	231	Matt DeSalvo RC	.25	349	Chaz Roe RC	4.00
114	Jhonny Peralta	.15	232	Ben Jones RC	.75			
115	Travis Hafner	.40	233	Bill McCarthy RC	.25			
116	Cesar Izturis	.15	234	Chuck James RC	.50			
117	Brad Penny	.15	235	Brandon Sing RC	.75			
118	Garret Anderson	.25	236	Andy Santana RC	.50			
119	Scott Kazmir	.15	237	Brendan Ryan RC	.50			
120	Aubrey Huff	.15	238	Wes Swackhamer RC	.50			
121	Larry Walker	.25	239	Jeff Niemann RC	1.00			
122	Albert Pujols	2.00	240	Ian Kinsler RC	.50			
123	Paul Konerko	.25	241	Micah Furtado RC	.50			
124	Frank Thomas	.50	242	Ryan Mount RC	.50			
125	Phil Nevin	.15	243	P.J. Phillips RC	.50			
126	Brian Giles	.15	244	Trevor Bell RC	.50			
127	Ramon Hernandez	.15	245	Jered Weaver RC	4.00			
128	Johnny Damon	.75	246	Eddy Martinez-Esteve RC	.75			
129	Trot Nixon	.15	247	Brian Bannister RC	.50			
130	Rocco Baldelli	.15	248	Philip Humber RC	1.00			
131	Carl Crawford	.25	249	Michael Rogers RC	.50			
132	Alfonso Soriano	.15	250	Landon Powell RC	.50			
133	Mark Teixeira	.50	251	Kennard Bibbs RC	.50			
134	Gustavo Chacin	.15	252	Nelson Cruz RC	3.00			
135	Vernon Wells	.25	253	Paul Kelly RC	.75			
136	Erik Bedard	.15	254	Kevin Slowey RC	2.00			
137	Daniel Cabrera	.15	255	Brandon Snyder RC	1.00			
138	Michael Barrett	.15	256	Nolan Reimold RC	1.00			
139	Greg Maddux	1.00	257	Brian Stavisky RC	.25			
140	Javier Vazquez	.15	258	Javier Herrera RC	1.00			
141	Chad Tracy	.15	259	Russell Martin RC	3.00			
142	Michael Young	.15	260	Matthew Kemp RC	3.00			
143	Kenny Rogers	.15	261	Wade Townsend RC	.75			
144	Mike Piazza	.75	262	Nick Touchstone RC	.50			
145	Jose Reyes	.40	263	Ryan Feierabend RC	.50			
146	Geoff Jenkins	.15	264	Bobby Livingston RC	.50			
147	Carlos Lee	.25	265	Wladimir Balentien RC	.75			
148	Brady Clark	.15	266	Keiichi Yabu RC	1.00			
149	Torii Hunter	.25	267	Craig Italiano RC	.50			
150	Johan Santana	.75	268	Ryan Goleski RC	.50			
151	Steve Finley	.15	269	Ryan Garko RC	1.00			
152	Darin Erstad	.25	270	Michael Bourn RC	.50			
153	Jake Peavy	.25	271	Scott Mathieson RC	.75			
154	Xavier Nady	.15	272	Scott Mitchinson RC	.50			
155	Ryan Klesko	.15	273	Tyler Greene RC	.75			
156	Ichiro Suzuki	1.50	274	Mark McCormick RC	.50			
157	Richie Sexson	.40	275	Daryl Jones RC	.50			
158	Raul Ibanez	.15	276	Travis Chick RC	.50			
159	Freddy Garcia	.15	277	Luis Hernandez RC	.25			
160	Brad Hawpe	.15	278	Steven Doetsch RC	.25			
161	Jeff Francis	.15	279	Chris Vines RC	.50			
162	Todd Helton	.40	280	Mike Costanzo RC	.50			
163	Clint Barmes	.15	281	Matt Maloney RC	.50			
164	Rodrigo Lopez	.15	282	Matt Goyen RC	.25			
165	Melvin Mora	.15	283	Jacob Marceaux RC	.25			
166	Brandon Webb	.15	284	David Gassner RC	.25			
167	Shawn Green	.25	285	Ricky Barrett RC	.25			
168	Moises Alou	.25	286	Jon Egan RC	.50			
169	Matt Clement	.25	287	Scott Blue RC	.25			
170	John Smoltz	.40	288	Steve Bondurant RC	.50			
171	Rafael Furcal	.25	289	Kevin Melillo RC	.50			
172	Jeff Bagwell	.25	290	Brad Corley RC	.50			
173	Roger Clemens	1.00	291	Brent Lillibridge RC	.50			
174	Dontrelle Willis	.40	292	Mike Morse RC	.25			
175	Paul LoDuca	.15	293	Justin Thomas RC	.50			
176	Zack Greinke	.15	294	Nick Webber RC	.25			
177	David DeJesus	.15	295	Mitch Boggs RC	.25			
178	Mike Sweeney	.15	296	Jeff Lyman RC	.50			
179	Ben Sheets	.25	297	Jordan Schafer RC	1.50			
180	Doug Davis	.15	298	Ismael Ramirez RC	.25			
181	Mike Cameron	.15	299	Chris Young RC	1.50			
182	Lance Berkman	.40	300	Brian Miller RC	.50			
183	Craig Biggio	.25	301	Jason Bay	4.00			
184	Shannon Stewart	.15	302	Tim Hudson	3.00			
185	Joe Mauer	.50	303	Miguel Tejada	4.00			
186	Justin Morneau	.15	304	Jeremy Bonderman	3.00			
187	Mike Maroth	.15	305	Alex Rodriguez	8.00			
188	Ivan Rodriguez	.50	306	Rickie Weeks	3.00			
189	Luis Gonzalez	.15	307	Manny Ramirez	6.00			
190	Troy Glaus	.25	308	Nick Johnson	3.00			
191	Adam Eaton	.15	309	Andruw Jones	3.00			
192	Khalil Greene	.25	310	Hideki Matsui	6.00			
193	Mike Lowell	.15	311	Jeremy Reed	5.00			
194	Miguel Cabrera	.75	312	Dallas McPherson	3.00			
195	Roy Halladay	.75	313	Vladimir Guerrero	5.00			
196	Ted Lilly	.15	314	Eric Chavez	3.00			
197	Alex Rios	.25	315	Chris Carpenter	4.00			
198	Josh Beckett	.25	316	Aaron Hill	3.00			
199	A.J. Burnett	.15	317	Derrek Lee	5.00			
200	Juan Pierre	.15	318	Mark Loretta	3.00			
201	Marcus Giles	.15	319	Garrett Atkins	3.00			
202	Craig Tatum RC	.50	320	Hank Blalock	3.00			

Mahogany

Stars (1-300): 1-2X
SP's (301-349): .5-1X
Inserted 1:1

Mini

Stars (1-300): 1-2X
SP's (301-349): .5-1X
Inserted 1:1

Red

No Pricing
Production One Set

Draft Pick Variation

NM/M
Variations (325-349): 1-1.5X base
One DPV pack per hobby box.

#	Player	Price
325	Jeff Clement	5.00
326	Jimmy Shull	5.00
327	Daniel Carte	5.00
328	Travis Buck	6.00
329	Chris Volstad	5.00
330	Andrew McCutchen	12.00
331	Cliff Pennington	7.00
332	John Mayberry Jr.	5.00
333	C.J. Henry	5.00
334	Ricky Romero	6.00
335	Aaron Thompson	6.00
336	Cesar Carrillo	6.00
337	Jacoby Ellsbury	15.00
338	Matt Garza	10.00
339	Colby Rasmus	15.00
340	Ryan Zimmerman	10.00
341	Ryan Braun	30.00
342	Brent Lillibridge	5.00
343	Jay Bruce	15.00
344	Matt Green	6.00
345	Brent Cox	6.00
346	Jed Lowrie	5.00
347	Beau Jones	6.00
348	Eli Iorg	6.00
349	Chaz Roe	6.00

Future Greatness

NM/M
Common Player: 4.00

Code	Player	Price
TB	Tony Blanco	4.00
JB	Joe Blanton	4.00
BB	Bryan Bullington	4.00
MC	Matt Cain	8.00
FC	Fausto Carmona	8.00
SC	Shin-Soo Choo	8.00
JC	Jorge Cortes	4.00
JCO	Jesus Cota	4.00
EE	Edwin Encarnacion	4.00
CE	Clint Everts	4.00
GF	Gavin Floyd	4.00
JF	Jeff Francis	4.00
JGA	Jairo Garcia	4.00
RG	Ruben Gotay	4.00
JG	Joel Guzman	4.00
AH	Aaron Hill	4.00
KH	Koyie Hill	4.00
JK	Jason Kubel	6.00
WL	Wilfredo Ledezma	4.00
VM	Val Majewski	4.00
AMA	Andy Marte	4.00
JMA	Jeff Mathis	4.00
DM	Dallas McPherson	4.00
JM	Justin Morneau	8.00
AM	Arnie Munoz	4.00
JP	Juan Perez	4.00
YP	Yusmeiro Petit	4.00
FP	Felix Pie	6.00
BT	Brad Thompson	4.00
RW	Rickie Weeks	6.00
DY	Delmon Young	6.00

Pieces of Greatness

NM/M
Common Player: 4.00

Code	Player	Price
JB	Josh Beckett	4.00
CB	Carlos Beltran	6.00
BB	Barry Bonds	20.00
MC	Miguel Cabrera	8.00
EC	Eric Chavez	4.00
RC	Roger Clemens	10.00
BC	Bobby Crosby	4.00
JD	Johnny Damon	8.00
CD	Carlos Delgado	6.00
AD	Adam Dunn	8.00
JG	Josh Gibson	15.00
TG	Troy Glaus	4.00
RH	Rich Harden	4.00
TH	Todd Helton	6.00
JK	Jeff Kent	4.00
PK	Paul Konerko	4.00
PM	Pedro Martinez	8.00
MMO	Melvin Mora	4.00
MM	Mark Mulder	4.00
BM	Brett Myers	4.00
AP	Albert Pujols	20.00
MR	Manny Ramirez	8.00
BR	Brian Roberts	4.00
AR	Alex Rodriguez	15.00
JS	John Smoltz	8.00
IS	Ichiro Suzuki	15.00
MT	Miguel Tejada	6.00
JT	Jim Thome	6.00
DW	Dontrelle Willis	6.00
DWR	David Wright	15.00
BZ	Barry Zito	4.00

Printing Plates

No Pricing
Production one set per color.

Signs of Greatness

NM/M
Common Player: 6.00

Code	Player	Price
RB	Ryan Braun	100.00
JB	Jay Bruce	40.00
PB	Patrick Bryant	6.00
MB	Matt Bush	6.00
TC	Travis Chick	6.00
TD	Thomas Diamond	8.00
SE	Scott Elbert	8.00
MG	Matt Green	8.00
AG	Angel Guzman	8.00
JH	J.P. Howell	8.00
PH	Philip Humber	10.00
ZJ	Zach Jackson	8.00
JJ	Jason Jaramillo	8.00
DJ	Dan Johnson	8.00
BL	Brent Lillibridge	8.00
DL	Donald Lucey	8.00
EM	Eddy Martinez-Esteve	8.00
JM	John Mayberry Jr.	8.00
AM	Andrew McCutchen	35.00
JP	Jonathan Papelbon	25.00
DP	David Purcey	8.00
RR	Ricky Romero	15.00
HS	Huston Street	20.00
CT	Curtis Thigpen	8.00
WW	Wes Whisler	8.00
JZ	Jon Zeringue	8.00
RZ	Ryan Zimmerman	25.00

51 Topps Heritage

NM/M
Common Player: 1.00

#	Player	Price
1	Adam Dunn	3.00
2	Zachary Duke	1.50
3	Alex Rodriguez	8.00
4	Vladimir Guerrero	3.00
5	Andruw Jones	2.00
6	Travis Chick	1.00
7	Alfonso Soriano	2.00
8	Scott Rolen	3.00
9	Brian Bannister	2.00
10	Randy Johnson	3.00
11	Barry Bonds	8.00
12	Pat Burrell	1.50
13	Barry Zito	1.50
14	Nomar Garciaparra	3.00
15	C.C. Sabathia	1.00
16	Miguel Tejada	2.00
17	Hideki Matsui	6.00
18	John Smoltz	2.00
19	Ken Griffey Jr.	5.00
20	Chris Carpenter	1.50
21	Ian Kinsler	1.50
22	Chuck Tiffany	1.50
23	Gary Sheffield	2.00
24	Mark Mulder	1.50
25	Ichiro Suzuki	5.00
26	Kerry Wood	1.50
27	Jose Reyes	1.00
28	Derrek Lee	2.00
29	Justin Verlander	2.00
30	Johnny Damon	3.00
31	Chris Volstad	1.00
32	Jeremy Bonderman	1.00
33	David Ortiz	3.00
34	Morgan Ensberg	1.00
35	Mark Buehrle	1.00
36	Chuck James	2.00
37	Miguel Cabrera	3.00
38	Magglio Ordonez	1.00
39	Michael Young	1.00
40	Carlos Beltran	2.00
41	Nick Johnson	1.00
42	Billy Butler	2.00
43	Brian Giles	1.00
44	Paul Konerko	1.50
45	Roy Oswalt	1.50
46	Bobby Abreu	1.50
47	Sammy Sosa	3.00
48	Aramis Ramirez	1.50
49	Torii Hunter	1.00
50	Aubrey Huff	1.00
51	Vernon Wells	1.50
52	Joe Mauer	1.50

51 Topps Heritage Red Back

NM/M
Common Player: 1.00

#	Player	Price
1	Andy LaRoche	3.00
2	Mike Piazza	4.00
3	Pedro Martinez	3.00
4	Wladimir Balentien	1.00
5	Tim Hudson	1.50
6	Richie Sexson	1.00
7	Carlos Delgado	1.00
8	Derek Jeter	8.00
9	Ryan Zimmerman	4.00
10	Mark Teixeira	2.00
11	David Wright	4.00
12	Jake Peavy	1.50
13	Jose Vidro	1.00
14	Jim Thome	2.00
15	Carlos Zambrano	1.50
16	Hank Blalock	1.50
17	Johan Santana	2.00
18	Cliff Pennington	1.00
19	Rafael Palmeiro	1.50
20	Curt Schilling	2.00
21	Brandon McCarthy	2.00
22	Stephen Drew	8.00
23	Jeff Niemann	2.00
24	Eric Chavez	1.00
25	Hernan Iribarren	1.00
26	Jered Weaver	2.00
27	Edgar Renteria	1.00
28	Travis Hafner	1.00
29	Frank Thomas	1.50
30	Brian Roberts	1.00
31	Anthony Reyes	1.00
32	Scott Kazmir	1.00
33	Carlos Lee	1.00
34	Jimmy Rollins	1.50
35	Garret Anderson	1.00
36	Jason Schmidt	1.00
37	Jon Garland	1.00
38	Dontrelle Willis	1.50
39	C.J. Henry	3.00
40	Greg Maddux	4.00
41	Todd Helton	2.00
42	Ivan Rodriguez	2.00
43	Chipper Jones	3.00
44	Rich Harden	1.00
45	Mark Prior	3.00
46	Roy Halladay	3.00
47	Albert Pujols	8.00
48	Roger Clemens	4.00
49	Andrew McCutchen	4.00
50	Scott Podsednik	1.50
51	Manny Ramirez	2.00
52	Carl Crawford	1.00
53	Jim Edmonds	1.50
54	Wily Mo Pena	1.00

51 Topps Heritage Blue Back

NM/M
Common Player: 1.00

#	Player	Price
1	Adam Dunn	3.00
2	Zachary Duke	1.50
3	Alex Rodriguez	8.00
4	Vladimir Guerrero	3.00
5	Andruw Jones	2.00
6	Travis Chick	2.00
7	Alfonso Soriano	2.00
8	Scott Rolen	3.00
9	Brian Bannister	2.00
10	Randy Johnson	3.00
11	Barry Bonds	8.00
12	Pat Burrell	1.50
13	Barry Zito	1.50
14	Nomar Garciaparra	1.00
15	C.C. Sabathia	1.00
16	Miguel Tejada	2.00
17	Hideki Matsui	6.00
18	John Smoltz	2.00
19	Ken Griffey Jr.	5.00
20	Chris Carpenter	1.50
21	Ian Kinsler	1.50
22	Chuck Tiffany	1.50
23	Gary Sheffield	2.00
24	Mark Mulder	1.50
25	Ichiro Suzuki	5.00
26	Kerry Wood	1.50
27	Jose Reyes	1.00
28	Derrek Lee	2.00
29	Justin Verlander	2.00
30	Johnny Damon	3.00
31	Chris Volstad	1.00
32	Jeremy Bonderman	1.00
33	David Ortiz	3.00
34	Morgan Ensberg	1.00
35	Mark Buehrle	1.00
36	Chuck James	2.00
37	Miguel Cabrera	3.00
38	Magglio Ordonez	1.00
39	Michael Young	1.00
40	Carlos Beltran	2.00
41	Nick Johnson	1.00
42	Billy Butler	2.00
43	Brian Giles	1.00
44	Paul Konerko	1.50
45	Roy Oswalt	1.50
46	Bobby Abreu	1.50
47	Sammy Sosa	3.00
48	Aramis Ramirez	1.50
49	Torii Hunter	1.00
50	Aubrey Huff	1.00
51	Vernon Wells	1.50
52	Joe Mauer	1.50

2005 Bowman Sterling

NM/M
Pack (5): 60.00
Box (6): 325.00

First Year Autographs

Code	Player	Price
MA	Matt Albers RC	10.00
RB	Ryan Braun RC	125.00
TC	Travis Chick RC	10.00
MG	Matt Green RC	10.00
CH	C.J. Henry RC	10.00
GK	George Kottaras RC	10.00
EM	Eddy Martinez-Esteve RC	10.00
JM	John Mayberry Jr. RC	10.00
GO	Garrett Olson RC	10.00
CP	Cliff Pennington RC	10.00
HS	Humberto Sanchez RC	15.00
BS	Brandon Sing RC	15.00
AT	Aaron Thompson RC	15.00
CV	Chris Volstad RC	10.00
SW	Steven White RC	10.00

Autographed First Year Relics

Code	Player	Price
TB	Trevor Bell RC	10.00
MB	Michael Bowden RC	25.00
JB	Jay Bruce RC	75.00
MC	Mike Conroy RC	15.00
BC	J. Brent Cox RC	15.00
JE	Jacoby Ellsbury RC	80.00
JG	Josh Geer RC	15.00
PH	Philip Humber RC	15.00
EI	Eli Iorg RC	15.00
BJ	Beau Jones RC	15.00
BL	Bobby Livingston RC	15.00
JL	Jed Lowrie RC	20.00
SM	Steve Marek RC	15.00
RM	Russell Martin RC	20.00
BM	Brandon McCarthy RC	15.00
AM	Andrew McCutchen	50.00
TM	Tyler Minges RC	15.00
JCN	John Nelson RC	15.00
JN	Jeff Niemann RC	20.00
JO	Justin Olson RC	10.00
CPP	Carmen Pignatiello RC	15.00
CR	Colby Rasmus RC	60.00
CRO	Chaz Roe RC	10.00
CS	C.J. Smith RC	10.00
RT	Raul Tablado RC	10.00
JV	Justin Verlander RC	60.00

Autographed Prospect Base Relics

Code	Player	Price
BB	Billy Buckner	15.00
SE	Scott Elbert	15.00
BE	Brad Eldred	15.00
JF	Josh Fields	15.00
AL	Adam Lind	15.00
CN	Chris Nelson	15.00
DP	Dustin Pedroia	65.00
CPP	Curtis Thigpen	10.00

First Year Base Cards

Code	Player	Price
BA	Brian Anderson	4.00
BRB	Brian Bogusevic RC	4.00
CBU	Clay Buchholz RC	30.00
TBU	Travis Buck RC	6.00
BBU	Billy Butler RC	12.00
CC	Cesar Carrillo RC	5.00
DC	Daniel Carte RC	6.00
JC	Jeff Clement RC	6.00
MCO	Mike Costanzo RC	4.00
BCR	Brad Corley RC	4.00
JDR	Jon Drennen RC	4.00
SD	Stephen Drew RC	10.00
JEG	Jon Egan RC	6.00
YE	Yunel Escobar RC	6.00
MGA	Matt Garza RC	10.00
TG	Tyler Greene RC	6.00
BH	Brett Hayes RC	4.00
CHE	Chase Headley RC	6.00
THE	Tyler Herron RC	5.00
NH	Nick Huntley RC	6.00
TI	Tadahito Iguchi RC	6.00
HI	Hernan Iribarren RC	4.00
CI	Craig Italiano RC	4.00
CJ	Chuck James RC	5.00
PK	Paul Kelly RC	4.00
ACL	Andy LaRoche RC	6.00
JLY	Jeff Lyman RC	4.00
MAM	Matt Maloney RC	4.00
JMA	Jacob Marceaux RC	4.00
MMC	Mark McCormick RC	6.00
RMO	Ryan Mount RC	6.00
PP	P.J. Phillips RC	4.00
CRA	Cesar Ramos RC	4.00
NR	Nolan Reimold RC	8.00
RR	Ricky Romero RC	6.00
HAS	Henry Sanchez RC	6.00
ZS	Zach Simons RC	4.00
KS	Kevin Slowey RC	6.00
BSN	Brandon Snyder RC	4.00
DT	Drew Thompson RC	4.00
CLT	Chuck Tiffany RC	6.00
MTO	Matt Torra RC	4.00
WT	Wade Townsend RC	4.00
TT	Troy Tulowitzki RC	12.00
JW	Josh Wall RC	6.00
JWE	Jered Weaver RC	

NW	Nick Webber **RC**	4.00
KW	Kevin Whelan **RC**	4.00
TW	Travis Wood **RC**	4.00
RZ	Ryan Zimmerman **RC**	20.00

Refractors

Rookies:	1.5-2X
Rookie Auto.:	1-2X
Rookie Relic Auto.:	1-2X
Production 199 Sets	

Black Refractors
No Pricing
Production 25 Sets

Red Refractor
No Pricing
Production One Set

MLB Logo Patch
No Pricing
Production One Set

Original Autographs

		NM/M
Production 1-160		
AJ4	Andruw Jones 02 B/122	25.00
AJ6	Andruw Jones 03 B/112	25.00
AJ8	Andruw Jones 04 B/71	25.00
DL1	Derrek Lee 95 B/27	25.00
DL2	Derrek Lee 96 B/29	25.00
DL5	Derrek Lee 98 B/22	25.00
DL6	Derrek Lee 04 B/92	25.00
DL7	Derrek Lee 04 BC/26	25.00
DW1	David Wright 04 BD/98	85.00
DW3	David Wright 05 B/139	85.00
GA1	Garret Anderson 04 BC/36	20.00
GA2	Garret Anderson 05 B/48	20.00
JR1	Jeremy Reed 04 BD/82	15.00
JR2	Jeremy Reed 04 BCD/48	20.00
MC2	Miguel Cabrera 02 BD/26	50.00
MC4	Miguel Cabrera 03 BD/27	50.00
MC5	Miguel Cabrera 03 BCD/25	50.00
MC6	Miguel Cabrera 04 B/127	25.00
MC7	Miguel Cabrera 04 BC/25	50.00
MC8	Miguel Cabrera 05 B/154	25.00
MC9	Miguel Cabrera 05 BC/25	50.00
MK3	Mark Kotsay 98 B/56	15.00
MK5	Mark Kotsay 99 B/75	15.00
MK7	Mark Kotsay 05 B/160	10.00
MK8	Mark Kotsay 05 BC/46	15.00
MY1	Michael Young 04 B/148	15.00
MY2	Michael Young 04 BC/64	15.00
MY3	Michael Young 05 B/92	15.00

Relics

		NM/M
Common Player:		4.00
Refractor:		1-1.5X
Production 199 Sets		
Black Refractor:		2-4X
Production 25 Sets		
JBE	Josh Beckett	4.00
RBE	Ronnie Belliard	4.00
CB	Carlos Beltran	6.00
HB	Hank Blalock	4.00
BLB	Barry Bonds	20.00
MCA	Miguel Cabrera	8.00
EC	Eric Chavez	4.00
JD	Johnny Damon	8.00
CD	Carlos Delgado	4.00
JPE	Jim Edmonds	6.00
RF	Rafael Furcal	4.00
JGI	Josh Gibson	15.00
MGI	Marcus Giles	4.00
KG	Khalil Greene	4.00
VG	Vladimir Guerrero	8.00
TLH	Todd Helton	6.00
THU	Tim Hudson	4.00
TH	Torii Hunter	4.00
LWJ	Chipper Jones	8.00
DL	Derrek Lee	6.00
PL	Paul LoDuca	4.00
GM	Greg Maddux	10.00
PM	Pedro Martinez	8.00
TM	Tino Martinez	4.00
VM	Victor Martinez	4.00

HM	Hideki Matsui	15.00
KM	Kevin Millar	4.00
BMU	Bill Mueller	4.00
MM	Mark Mulder	4.00
TN	Trot Nixon	4.00
DO	David Ortiz	10.00
MP	Mike Piazza	8.00
JP	Jorge Posada	6.00
MPR	Mark Prior	6.00
AP	Albert Pujols	20.00
ARA	Aramis Ramirez	4.00
MR	Manny Ramirez	8.00
AR	Alex Rodriguez	20.00
IR	Ivan Rodriguez	6.00
SR	Scott Rolen	8.00
CSU	Curt Schilling	6.00
GS	Gary Sheffield	6.00
JS	John Smoltz	6.00
AS	Alfonso Soriano	6.00
SS	Sammy Sosa	4.00
MTE	Mark Teixeira	8.00
MT	Miguel Tejada	4.00
DW	Dontrelle Willis	6.00
MY	Michael Young	4.00
BZ	Barry Zito	4.00

2005 Bowman's Best

		NM/M
Common Player:		.25
Common Rookie:		1.00
Common Rookie Auto. (101-143):		10.00
Production 974		
Pack (5):		14.00
Box (10):		120.00
1	Jose Vidro	.25
2	Adam Dunn	.50
3	Manny Ramirez	.75
4	Miguel Tejada	.50
5	Ken Griffey Jr.	1.00
6	Pedro Martinez	1.00
7	Alex Rodriguez	1.50
8	Ichiro Suzuki	1.50
9	Alfonso Soriano	.75
10	Brian Giles	.25
11	Roger Clemens	2.00
12	Todd Helton	.50
13	Ivan Rodriguez	.50
14	David Ortiz	.75
15	Sammy Sosa	1.00
16	Chipper Jones	.75
17	Mark Buehrle	.50
18	Miguel Cabrera	.75
19	Johan Santana	.75
20	Randy Johnson	.75
21	Jim Thome	.50
22	Vladimir Guerrero	.75
23	Dontrelle Willis	.50
24	Nomar Garciaparra	.75
25	Barry Bonds	2.00
26	Curt Schilling	.75
27	Carlos Beltran	.50
28	Albert Pujols	2.00
29	Mark Prior	.75
30	Derek Jeter	2.00
31	Ryan Garko **RC**	2.00
32	Eulogio de la Cruz **RC**	1.00
33	Luke Scott **RC**	2.00
34	Shane Costa **RC**	1.00
35	Casey McGehee **RC**	4.00
36	Jered Weaver **RC**	8.00
37	Kevin Melillo **RC**	1.00
38	D.J. Houlton **RC**	1.00
39	Brandon Moorhead **RC**	1.00
40	Jerry Owens **RC**	1.00
41	Elliot Johnson **RC**	1.50
42	Kevin West **RC**	1.00
43	Hernan Iribarren **RC**	1.00
44	Miguel Montero **RC**	4.00
45	Craig Tatum **RC**	1.00
46	Ryan Sweeney	2.00
47	Micah Furtado **RC**	1.00
48	Cody Haerther **RC**	1.00
49	Erik Abreu **RC**	1.00
50	Chuck Tiffany **RC**	2.00
51	Tadahito Iguchi **RC**	1.00
52	Frank Diaz **RC**	1.00
53	Errol Simonitsch **RC**	1.00
54	Wade Robinson **RC**	1.00
55	Adam Boeve **RC**	1.00
56	Steve Bondurant **RC**	1.00
57	Jason Motte **RC**	1.00
58	Juan Senreiso **RC**	1.00
59	Vinny Rottino **RC**	1.00
60	Jai Miller **RC**	1.00
61	Thomas Pauly **RC**	1.00
62	Tony Giarratano **RC**	1.00
63	Alexander Smit **RC**	1.00

64	Keiichi Yabu **RC**	1.00
65	Brian Bannister **RC**	1.50
66	Kennard Bibbs **RC**	1.00
67	Anthony Reyes **RC**	2.00
68	Tom Oldham **RC**	1.00
69	Benjamin Harrison **RC**	1.00
70	Daryl Thompson **RC**	2.00
71	Kevin Collins **RC**	1.00
72	Wes Swackhamer **RC**	1.00
73	Landon Powell **RC**	1.50
74	Matt Brown **RC**	1.00
75	Russell Martin **RC**	3.00
76	Nick Touchstone **RC**	1.00
77	Steven White **RC**	1.00
78	Ian Bladergroen **RC**	1.00
79	Sean Marshall **RC**	2.00
80	Nick Masset **RC**	1.00
81	Ryan Goleski **RC**	1.50
82	Matt Campbell **RC**	1.00
83	Manny Parra **RC**	2.00
84	Melky Cabrera **RC**	5.00
85	Ryan Feierabend **RC**	1.50
86	Nate McLouth **RC**	1.50
87	Glen Perkins **RC**	1.50
88	Kila Ka'aihue **RC**	2.50
89	Dana Eveland **RC**	1.50
90	Tyler Pelland **RC**	1.00
91	Matt Van Der Bosch **RC**	1.00
92	Andy Santana **RC**	1.00
93	Eric Nielsen **RC**	1.00
94	Brendan Ryan **RC**	1.00
95	Ian Kinsler **RC**	5.00
96	Matthew Kemp **RC**	8.00
97	Stephen Drew **RC**	10.00
98	Peeter Ramos **RC**	2.00
99	Chris Seddon **RC**	2.00
100	Chuck James **RC**	3.00
101	Travis Chick **RC**	10.00
102	Justin Verlander **RC**	60.00
103	Billy Butler **RC**	35.00
104	Chris Young **RC**	25.00
105	Jake Postlewait **RC**	10.00
106	C.J. Smith **RC**	10.00
107	Mike Rodriguez **RC**	10.00
108	Philip Humber **RC**	15.00
109	Jeff Niemann **RC**	20.00
110	Brian Miller **RC**	10.00
111	Chris Vines **RC**	10.00
112	Andy LaRoche **RC**	15.00
113	Mike Bourn **RC**	15.00
114	Wladimir Balentien **RC**	20.00
115	Ismael Ramirez **RC**	10.00
116	Hayden Penn **RC**	10.00
117	Pedro Lopez **RC**	10.00
118	Shawn Bowman **RC**	10.00
119	Chad Orvella **RC**	10.00
120	Sean Tracey **RC**	10.00
121	Bobby Livingston **RC**	10.00
122	Michael Rogers **RC**	10.00
123	Willy Mota **RC**	15.00
124	Brandon McCarthy **RC**	10.00
125	Mike Morse **RC**	10.00
126	Matt Lindstrom **RC**	10.00
127	Brian Stavisky **RC**	10.00
128	Rich Gardner **RC**	10.00
129	Scott Mitchinson **RC**	10.00
130	Billy McCarthy **RC**	10.00
131	Brandon Sing **RC**	12.00
132	Matt Albers **RC**	12.00
133	George Kottaras **RC**	15.00
134	Luis Hernandez **RC**	10.00
135	Humberto Sanchez **RC**	20.00
136	Buck Coats **RC**	12.00
137	Jonathan Barratt **RC**	10.00
138	Raul Tablado **RC**	12.00
139	Jake Mullinax **RC**	15.00
140	Edgar Varela **RC**	12.00
141	Ryan Garko **RC**	15.00
142	Nate McLouth **RC**	15.00
143	Shane Costa **RC**	15.00

Green Refractor

Stars:	2-3X
Rookies:	1-2X
Production 899	
Rookie Autos.	1-1.5X
Production 399	

Blue Refractor

Stars:	2-4X
Rookies:	1-2X
Production 499	
Rookie Autos.	1-1.5X
Production 299	

Red Refractor

Stars:	3-5X
Rookies:	2-3X
Rookie Autos.	1.5-2X
Production 199 Sets	

Silver Refractor

Stars:	4-6X
Rookies:	2-3X
Rookie Autos.	1.5-3X
Production 99 Sets	

Gold Refractor
No Pricing
Production 25 Sets

Printing Plates
No Pricing
Production one set for each color.

Printing Plates Autograph
No Pricing
Production one set for each color.

A-Rod Throwback

		NM/M
Production 100		
AR	Alex Rodriguez	150.00

A-Rod Throwback Autograph

		NM/M
Production 100		
AR	Alex Rodriguez	150.00

Bowman's Best Shortstops
Production 25

Mirror Image Spokesmen

Mirror Image Throwback

		NM/M
Production 50		
RR	Cal Ripken Jr., Alex Rodriguez	450.00

2006 Bowman

		NM/M
Complete Set (231):		
Common Player (1-200):		.15
Common RC (201-220):		.25
Common Auto. (219-231):		10.00
Pack (10):		3.00
Box (24):		60.00
1	Nick Swisher	.25
2	Ted Lilly	.15
3	John Smoltz	.25
4	Lyle Overbay	.15
5	Alfonso Soriano	.50
6	Javier Vazquez	.15
7	Ronnie Belliard	.15
8	Jose Reyes	.75
9	Brian Roberts	.25
10	Curt Schilling	.50
11	Adam Dunn	.50
12	Zack Greinke	.25
13	Carlos Guillen	.25
14	Jon Garland	.15
15	Robinson Cano	.50
16	Chris Burke	.15
17	Barry Zito	.25
18	Russ Adams	.15
19	Chris Capuano	.15
20	Scott Rolen	.50
21	Kerry Wood	.25
22	Scott Kazmir	.25
23	Brandon Webb	.25
24	Jeff Kent	.25
25	Albert Pujols	2.00
26	C.C. Sabathia	.25
27	Adrian Beltre	.25
28	Brad Wilkerson	.15
29	Randy Wolf	.15
30	Jason Bay	.25
31	Austin Kearns	.15
32	Clint Barmes	.15
33	Mike Sweeney	.25
34	Justin Verlander	.25
35	Justin Morneau	.25
36	Scott Podsednik	.25
37	Jason Giambi	.25
38	Steve Finley	.15
39	Morgan Ensberg	.25
40	Eric Chavez	.25
41	Roy Halladay	.25
42	Horacio Ramirez	.25
43	Ben Sheets	.25
44	Chris Carpenter	.40
45	Andruw Jones	.25
46	Carlos Zambrano	.25
47	Jonny Gomes	.25
48	Shawn Green	.15
49	Moises Alou	.15
50	Ichiro Suzuki	1.50
51	Juan Pierre	.15
52	Grady Sizemore	.40
53	Kazuo Matsui	.15
54	Jose Vidro	.15
55	Jake Peavy	.25
56	Dallas McPherson	.15
57	Ryan Howard	1.00
58	Zachary Duke	.15

59	Michael Young	.25
60	Todd Helton	.50
61	David DeJesus	.15
62	Ivan Rodriguez	.50
63	Johan Santana	.25
64	Danny Haren	.25
65	Derek Jeter	2.00
66	Greg Maddux	1.00
67	Jorge Cantu	.15
68	Conor Jackson (**RC**)	.25
69	Victor Martinez	.25
70	David Wright	1.00
71	Ryan Church	.25
72	Khalil Greene	.15
73	Jimmy Rollins	.50
74	Hank Blalock	.25
75	Pedro Martinez	.75
76	Jonathan Papelbon (**RC**)	1.00
77	Felipe Lopez	.15
78	Jeff Francis	.15
79	Andrew Sisco	.15
80	Hideki Matsui	1.00
81	Ken Griffey Jr.	1.50
82	Nomar Garciaparra	.75
83	Kevin Millwood	.25
84	Paul Konerko	.25
85	A.J. Burnett	.15
86	Mike Piazza	.75
87	Brian Giles	.15
88	Johnny Damon	.50
89	Jim Thome	.50
90	Roger Clemens	1.00
91	Aaron Rowand	.15
92	Rafael Furcal	.25
93	Gary Sheffield	.25
94	Mike Cameron	.15
95	Carlos Delgado	.25
96	Jorge Posada	.40
97	Denny Bautista	.15
98	Mike Maroth	.15
99	Brad Radke	.15
100	Alex Rodriguez	2.00
101	Freddy Garcia	.15
102	Oliver Perez	.15
103	Jon Lieber	.15
104	Melvin Mora	.25
105	Travis Hafner	.40
106	Matt Cain **RC**	1.00
107	Derek Lowe	.15
108	Luis Castillo	.15
109	Livan Hernandez	.15
110	Tadahito Iguchi	.25
111	Shawn Chacon	.15
112	Frank Thomas	.40
113	Josh Beckett	.40
114	Aubrey Huff	.25
115	Derrek Lee	.50
116	Chien-Ming Wang	.50
117	Joe Crede	.15
118	Torii Hunter	.25
119	J.D. Drew	.25
120	Troy Glaus	.40
121	Sean Casey	.25
122	Edgar Renteria	.25
123	Craig Wilson	.15
124	Adam Eaton	.15
125	Jeff Francoeur	.40
126	Bruce Chen	.15
127	Cliff Floyd	.15
128	Jeremy Reed	.15
129	Jake Westbrook	.15
130	Wily Mo Pena	.15
131	Toby Hall	.15
132	David Ortiz	.75
133	David Eckstein	.15
134	Brady Clark	.15
135	Marcus Giles	.15
136	Aaron Hill	.15
137	Mark Kotsay	.15
138	Carlos Lee	.40
139	Roy Oswalt	.40
140	Chone Figgins	.25
141	Mike Mussina	.50
142	Orlando Hernandez	.25
143	Magglio Ordonez	.25
144	Jim Edmonds	.40
145	Bobby Abreu	.25
146	Nick Johnson	.15
147	Carlos Beltran	.50
148	Jhonny Peralta	.25
149	Pedro Feliz	.15
150	Miguel Tejada	.50
151	Luis Gonzalez	.25
152	Carl Crawford	.25
153	Yadier Molina	.15
154	Rich Harden	.25
155	Tim Wakefield	.15
156	Rickie Weeks	.25
157	Johnny Estrada	.15
158	Gustavo Chacin	.15
159	Dan Johnson	.15
160	Willy Taveras	.15
161	Garret Anderson	.25
162	Randy Johnson	.75
163	Jermaine Dye	.25
164	Joe Mauer	.50
165	Ervin Santana	.25
166	Jeremy Bonderman	.15
167	Garrett Atkins	.15
168	Manny Ramirez	.75
169	Brad Eldred	.15
170	Chase Utley	.75
171	Mark Loretta	.15
172	Jose Vidro	.15
173	Tom Glavine	.40
174	Dontrelle Willis	.25
175	Mark Teixeira	.50
176	Felix Hernandez	.40

177	Cliff Lee	.25
178	Jason Schmidt	.25
179	Chad Tracy	.15
180	Rocco Baldelli	.15
181	Aramis Ramirez	.25
182	Andy Pettitte	.25
183	Mark Mulder	.25
184	Geoff Jenkins	.15
185	Chipper Jones	.75
186	Vernon Wells	.25
187	Bobby Crosby	.15
188	Lance Berkman	.40
189	Vladimir Guerrero	.75
190	Jose Capellan (**RC**)	.15
191	Brad Penny	.15
192	Jose Guillen	.15
193	Brett Myers	.25
194	Miguel Cabrera	.75
195	Bartolo Colon	.25
196	Craig Biggio	.25
197	Tim Hudson	.25
198	Mark Prior	.25
199	Mark Buehrle	.25
200	Barry Bonds	2.00
201	Anderson Hernandez (**RC**)	.25
202	Charlton Jimerson (**RC**)	.25
203	Jeremy Accardo **RC**	.50
204	Hanley Ramirez (**RC**)	1.00
205	Matt Capps (**RC**)	.50
206	John-Ford Griffin (**RC**)	.25
207	Chuck James (**RC**)	.25
208	Jaime Bubela (**RC**)	.25
209	Mark Woodyard (**RC**)	.25
210	Jason Botts (**RC**)	.25
211	Chris Demaria **RC**	.50
212	Miguel Perez (**RC**)	.25
213	Tom Gorzelanny (**RC**)	.50
214	Adam Wainwright (**RC**)	1.00
215	Ryan Garko (**RC**)	.25
216	Jason Bergmann **RC**	.50
217	J.J. Furmaniak (**RC**)	.25
218	Francisco Liriano (**RC**)	1.00
219	Kenji Johjima (**RC**)	1.00
219	Kenji Johjima/Auto. **RC**	20.00
220	Craig Hansen **RC**	1.50
220	Craig Hansen/Auto. **RC**	10.00
221	Ryan Zimmerman/ Auto. **RC**	30.00
222	Joey Devine/Auto. **RC**	10.00
223	Scott Olsen/Auto. (**RC**)	10.00
224	Darrell Rasner/Auto. **RC**	10.00
225	Craig Breslow/Auto. **RC**	10.00
226	Reggie Abercrombie/ Auto. (**RC**)	10.00
227	Dan Uggla/Auto. (**RC**)	25.00
228	Willie Eyre/Auto. (**RC**)	10.00
229	Joel Zumaya/Auto. (**RC**)	15.00
230	Ricky Nolasco/Auto. (**RC**)	20.00
231	Ian Kinsler/Auto. (**RC**)	30.00

White

Stars:	3-6X
Rookies (201-220):	3-6X
RC Auto. (219-231):	1-2X
Production 120 Sets	

Blue

Stars:	2-4X
Rookies (201-220):	2-4X
RC Auto. (219-231):	1-1.5X
Production 500 Sets	

Gold

Stars:	1-2X
Rookies (201-220):	1-2X
Inserted 1:1	

Red
No Pricing
Production One Set

Base of the Future

		NM/M
JH	Justin Huber	10.00

Prospects

		NM/M
Common Player:		.25
B1	Alex Gordon	1.00
B2	Jonathan George	.25
B3	Scott Walter	.25
B4	Brian Holliday	.25
B5	Ben Copeland	.50
B6	Bobby Wilson	.50
B7	Mayker Sandoval	.50
B8	Alejandro de Aza	.75
B9	David Munoz	.25
B10	Josh LeBlanc	.50

B11	Philippe Valiquette	.50
B12	Edwin Bellorin	.50
B13	Jason Quarles	.50
B14	Mark Trumbo	.75
B15	Steve Kelly	.25
B16	Jamie Hoffman	.25
B17	Joseph Bauserman	.25
B18	Nick Adenhart	1.00
B19	Mike Butia	.25
B20	Jon Weber	.25
B21	Luis Valdez	.50
B22	Rafael Rodriguez	.75
B23	Wyatt Toregas	.75
B24	John Vanden Berg	.25
B25	Mike Connolly	.25
B26	Mike O'Connor	1.00
B27	Garrett Mock	.25
B28	Bill Layman	.25
B29	Luis Pena	.25
B30	Billy Killian	.50
B31	Ross Ohlendorf	.25
B32	Mark Kaiser	.25
B33	Ryan Costello	.25
B34	Dale Thayer	.25
B35	Steve Garrabrants	.25
B36	Samuel Deduno	.25
B37	Juan Portes	1.00
B38	Javier Martinez	.25
B39	Clint Sammons	.25
B40	Andrew Kown	.75
B41	Matt Tolbert	.25
B42	Michael Ekstrom	.25
B43	Shawn Norris	.25
B44	Diory Hernandez	.25
B45	Chris Maples	.25
B46	Aaron Hathaway	.50
B47	Steven Baker	.25
B48	Greg Creek	.50
B49	Collin Mahoney	.25
B50	Corey Ragsdale	.50
B51	Ariel Nunez	.25
B52	Max Ramirez	1.00
B53	Eric Rodland	.50
B54	Dante Brinkley	.50
B55	Casey Craig	.50
B56	Ryan Spilborghs	1.00
B57	Fredy Deza	.25
B58	Jeff Frazier	.25
B59	Vince Cordova	.25
B60	Oswaldo Navarro	.75
B61	Jarod Rine	.25
B62	Jordan Tata	.75
B63	Ben Julianel	.50
B64	Yung-Chi Chen	1.00
B65	Carlos Torres	.50
B66	Juan Francia	.50
B67	Brett Smith	.50
B68	Francisco Leandro	.50
B69	Chris Turner	1.00
B70	Matt Joyce	1.00
B71	Jason Jones	.25
B72	Jose Diaz	.25
B73	Kevin Ool	.25
B74	Nate Bumstead	.25
B75	Omir Santos	.25
B76	Shawn Riggans	.25
B77	Ofilio Castro	.25
B78	Mike Rozier	.75
B79	Wilkin Ramirez	.75
B80	Yobal Duenas	.25
B81	Adam Bourassa	.50
B82	Tony Granadillo	.25
B83	Brad McCann	.50
B84	Dustin Majewski	.50
B85	Kelvin Jimenez	.25
B86	Mark Reed	1.00
B87	Asdrubal Cabrera	1.00
B88	James Barthmaier	.25
B89	Brandon Boggs	.50
B90	Raul Valdez	.25
B91	Jose Campusano	.50
B92	Henry Owens	.50
B93	Tug Hulett	.50
B94	Nate Gold	.25
B95	Lee Mitchell	.25
B96	John Hardy	.25
B97	Aaron Wideman	.25
B98	Brandon Roberts	.50
B99	Lou Santangelo	.25
B100	Kyle Kendrick	.75
B101	Michael Collins	.25
B102	Camilo Vazquez	.25
B103	Mark McLemore	.25
B104	Alexander Peralta	.25
B105	Josh Whitesell	.25
B106	Carlos Guevara	.25
B107	Michael Aubrey	.50
B108	Brandon Chaves	.25

B109	Leonard Davis	.25
B110	Kendry Morales	.75
B111	Koby Clemens	10.00
B112	Lance Broadway	10.00
B113	Cameron Maybin	40.00
B114	Mike Aviles	20.00
B115	Kyle Blanks	30.00
B116	Chris Dickerson	10.00
B117	Sean Gallagher	15.00
B118	Jamar Hill	10.00
B119	Garrett Mock	10.00
B120	Kendry Morales	25.00
B121	Russel Rohlicek	10.00
B122	Clete Thomas	15.00
B123	Josh Kinney	10.00
B124	Justin Huber	10.00

Prospects White

White:		4-6X
White Autos.:		1.5-2X
Production 120 Sets		

Prospects Blue

Blue:		2-3X
Blue Autos.:		1.5X
Production 500 Sets		

Prospects Gold

Gold:		1-1.5X
Inserted 1:1		

Chrome Prospects

		NM/M
Common Prospect:		.50
BC1	Alex Gordon	2.50
BC2	Jonathan George	.50
BC3	Scott Walter	.50
BC4	Brian Holliday	.50
BC5	Ben Copeland	1.00
BC6	Bobby Wilson	1.50
BC7	Mayker Sandoval	1.50
BC8	Alejandro de Aza	1.00
BC9	David Munoz	.75
BC10	Josh LeBlanc	1.00
BC11	Philippe Valiquette	1.00
BC12	Edwin Bellorin	1.00
BC13	Jason Quarles	1.00
BC14	Mark Trumbo	1.00
BC15	Steve Kelly	.75
BC16	Jamie Hoffman	.75
BC17	Joseph Bauserman	1.00
BC18	Nick Adenhart	2.00
BC19	Mike Butia	.75
BC20	Jon Weber	.75
BC21	Luis Valdez	1.00
BC22	Rafael Rodriguez	1.00
BC23	Wyatt Toregas	1.00
BC24	John Vanden Berg	.75
BC25	Mike Connolly	.75
BC26	Mike O'Connor	1.50
BC27	Garrett Mock	.75
BC28	Bill Layman	.75
BC29	Luis Pena	.75
BC30	Billy Killian	1.00
BC31	Ross Ohlendorf	.50
BC32	Mark Kaiser	.75
BC33	Ryan Costello	.75
BC34	Dale Thayer	.50
BC35	Steve Garrabrants	.75
BC36	Samuel Deduno	.75
BC37	Juan Portes	1.00
BC38	Javier Martinez	.75
BC39	Clint Sammons	1.00
BC40	Andrew Kown	1.50
BC41	Matt Tolbert	.75
BC42	Michael Ekstrom	.75
BC43	Shawn Norris	.75
BC44	Diory Hernandez	.75
BC45	Chris Maples	.75
BC46	Aaron Hathaway	1.00
BC47	Steven Baker	.75
BC48	Greg Creek	1.00
BC49	Collin Mahoney	.75
BC50	Corey Ragsdale	1.50
BC51	Ariel Nunez	.50
BC52	Max Ramirez	2.00
BC53	Eric Rodland	1.00
BC54	Dante Brinkley	1.00
BC55	Casey Craig	1.00
BC56	Ryan Spilborghs	2.50
BC57	Fredy Deza	.75
BC58	Jeff Frazier	.50
BC59	Vince Cordova	.50
BC60	Oswaldo Navarro	1.00
BC61	Jarod Rine	.75
BC62	Jordan Tata	1.50
BC63	Ben Julianel	1.00
BC64	Yung-Chi Chen	2.00

BC65	Carlos Torres	1.50
BC66	Juan Francia	1.50
BC67	Brett Smith	1.00
BC68	Francisco Leandro	1.00
BC69	Chris Turner	2.00
BC70	Matt Joyce	2.00
BC71	Jason Jones	1.00
BC72	Jose Diaz	.50
BC73	Kevin Ool	.75
BC74	Nate Bumstead	1.00
BC75	Omir Santos	1.00
BC76	Shawn Riggans	1.00
BC77	Ofilio Castro	.50
BC78	Mike Rozier	1.50
BC79	Wilkin Ramirez	2.00
BC80	Yobal Duenas	1.00
BC81	Adam Bourassa	1.00
BC82	Tony Granadillo	1.00
BC83	Brad McCann	2.00
BC84	Dustin Majewski	1.00
BC85	Kelvin Jimenez	.50
BC86	Mark Reed	1.00
BC87	Asdrubal Cabrera	2.00
BC88	James Barthmaier	1.00
BC89	Brandon Boggs	1.00
BC90	Raul Valdez	.50
BC91	Jose Campusano	1.50
BC92	Henry Owens	1.00
BC93	Tug Hulett	1.00
BC94	Nate Gold	1.00
BC95	Lee Mitchell	1.00
BC96	John Hardy	.75
BC97	Aaron Wideman	.75
BC98	Brandon Roberts	1.50
BC99	Lou Santangelo	.50
BC100	Kyle Kendrick	2.50
BC101	Michael Collins	2.00
BC102	Camilo Vazquez	.75
BC103	Mark McLemore	.50
BC104	Alexander Peralta	.75
BC105	Josh Whitesell	1.00
BC106	Carlos Guevara	.50
BC107	Michael Aubrey	1.50
BC108	Brandon Chaves	1.00
BC109	Leonard Davis	1.00
BC110	Kendry Morales	2.50

Chrome Prospects Refractor

Refractor (1-110):	2-4X
Production 500 Sets	

Chrome Prospects X-Fractor

X-Fractor (1-110):	3-6X
Production 250 Sets	

Chrome Prospects Red Refractor

No Pricing	
Production Five Sets	

Chrome Prospects Gold Refractor

Gold Refractor (1-110):	8-15X
Production 50 Sets	

Chrome Prospects Blue Refractor

Blue Refractor (1-110):	4-6X
Production 150 Sets	

Chrome Prospects Orange Refractor

No Pricing	
Production 25 Sets	

Signs of the Future

		NM/M
Common Auto.:		10.00
BB	Brian Bogusevic	10.00
MB	Michael Bowden	15.00
RB	Ryan Braun	50.00
TB	Travis Buck	15.00
JC	Jeff Clement	10.00
BC	Ben Copeland	10.00
MC	Mike Costanzo	10.00
TC	Trevor Crowe	10.00
JD	John Drennen	10.00
JE	Jacoby Ellsbury	50.00
YE	Yunel Escobar	20.00
JM	John Mayberry Jr.	10.00
GO	Garrett Olson	10.00
CR	Cesar Ramos	10.00
RR	Ricky Romero	10.00
HS	Henry Sanchez	10.00
DS	Denard Span	20.00
AT	Aaron Thompson	15.00
RT	Ryan Tucker	10.00
TT	Troy Tulowitzki	25.00
SW	Sean West	10.00

2006 Bowman Chrome

		NM/M
Complete Set (224):		
Common Player:		.25
Common Rookie (201-220):		.50
Pack (4):		9.00
Box (18):		150.00
1	Nick Swisher	.25
2	Ted Lilly	.25
3	John Smoltz	.75
4	Lyle Overbay	.25
5	Alfonso Soriano	.75
6	Javier Vazquez	.25
7	Ronnie Belliard	.25
8	Jose Reyes	.75
9	Brian Roberts	.50
10	Curt Schilling	.75

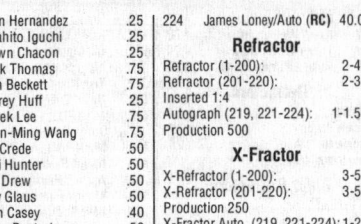

11	Adam Dunn	.75
12	Zack Greinke	.50
13	Carlos Guillen	.50
14	Jon Garland	.25
15	Robinson Cano	.50
16	Chris Burke	.25
17	Barry Zito	.50
18	Russ Adams	.25
19	Chris Capuano	.25
20	Scott Rolen	.75
21	Kerry Wood	.50
22	Scott Kazmir	.50
23	Brandon Webb	.75
24	Jeff Kent	.40
25	Albert Pujols	2.50
26	C.C. Sabathia	.50
27	Adrian Beltre	.50
28	Brad Wilkerson	.25
29	Randy Wolf	.25
30	Jason Bay	.50
31	Austin Kearns	.25
32	Clint Barmes	.25
33	Mike Sweeney	.25
34	Kevin Youkilis	.50
35	Justin Morneau	.25
36	Scott Podsednik	.25
37	Jason Giambi	.75
38	Steve Finley	.25
39	Morgan Ensberg	.25
40	Eric Chavez	.25
41	Roy Halladay	.50
42	Horacio Ramirez	.25
43	Ben Sheets	.40
44	Chris Carpenter	.50
45	Andruw Jones	.75
46	Carlos Zambrano	.50
47	Jonny Gomes	.25
48	Shawn Green	.40
49	Moises Alou	.40
50	Ichiro Suzuki	1.50
51	Juan Pierre	.25
52	Grady Sizemore	.50
53	Kazuo Matsui	.25
54	Jose Vidro	.25
55	Jake Peavy	.50
56	Dallas McPherson	.25
57	Ryan Howard	2.00
58	Zachary Duke	.25
59	Michael Young	.50
60	Todd Helton	.75
61	David DeJesus	.25
62	Ivan Rodriguez	.75
63	Johan Santana	.75
64	Danny Haren	.50
65	Derek Jeter	2.50
66	Greg Maddux	1.50
67	Jorge Cantu	.25
68	J.J. Hardy	.50
69	Victor Martinez	.50
70	David Wright	1.50
71	Ryan Church	.25
72	Khalil Greene	.25
73	Jimmy Rollins	.75
74	Hank Blalock	.40
75	Pedro Martinez	1.00
76	Chris Shelton	.25
77	Felipe Lopez	.25
78	Jeff Francis	.25
79	Andrew Sisco	.25
80	Hideki Matsui	1.50
81	Ken Griffey Jr.	1.50
82	Nomar Garciaparra	.50
83	Kevin Millwood	.50
84	Paul Konerko	.50
85	A.J. Burnett	.50
86	Mike Piazza	1.00
87	Brian Giles	.40
88	Johnny Damon	1.00
89	Jim Thome	.75
90	Roger Clemens	2.50
91	Aaron Rowand	.25
92	Rafael Furcal	.50
93	Gary Sheffield	.50
94	Mike Cameron	.25
95	Carlos Delgado	.50
96	Jorge Posada	.50
97	Denny Bautista	.25
98	Mike Maroth	.25
99	Brad Radke	.25
100	Alex Rodriguez	2.50
101	Freddy Garcia	.25
102	Oliver Perez	.25
103	Jon Lieber	.25
104	Melvin Mora	.25
105	Travis Hafner	.50
106	Alex Rios	.25
107	Derek Lowe	.25
108	Luis Castillo	.25

109	Livan Hernandez	.25
110	Tadahito Iguchi	.25
111	Shawn Chacon	.25
112	Frank Thomas	.75
113	Josh Beckett	.75
114	Aubrey Huff	.25
115	Derrek Lee	.75
116	Chien-Ming Wang	.75
117	Joe Crede	.50
118	Torii Hunter	.50
119	J.D. Drew	.50
120	Troy Glaus	.50
121	Sean Casey	.40
122	Edgar Renteria	.50
123	Craig Wilson	.25
124	Adam Eaton	.25
125	Jeff Francoeur	.75
126	Bruce Chen	.25
127	Cliff Floyd	.25
128	Jeremy Reed	.25
129	Jake Westbrook	.25
130	Wily Mo Pena	.25
131	Toby Hall	.25
132	David Ortiz	1.00
133	David Eckstein	.25
134	Brady Clark	.25
135	Marcus Giles	.25
136	Aaron Hill	.25
137	Mark Kotsay	.25
138	Carlos Lee	.25
139	Roy Oswalt	.50
140	Chone Figgins	.50
141	Mike Mussina	.75
142	Orlando Hernandez	.25
143	Magglio Ordonez	.50
144	Jim Edmonds	.50
145	Bobby Abreu	.50
146	Nick Johnson	.25
147	Carlos Beltran	.75
148	Jhonny Peralta	.25
149	Pedro Feliz	.25
150	Miguel Tejada	.50
151	Luis Gonzalez	.40
152	Carl Crawford	.50
153	Yadier Molina	.50
154	Rich Harden	.50
155	Tim Wakefield	.50
156	Rickie Weeks	.50
157	Johnny Estrada	.25
158	Gustavo Chacin	.25
159	Dan Johnson	.25
160	Willy Taveras	.25
161	Garret Anderson	.40
162	Randy Johnson	1.00
163	Jermaine Dye	.50
164	Joe Mauer	.75
165	Ervin Santana	.50
166	Jeremy Bonderman	.50
167	Garrett Atkins	.50
168	Manny Ramirez	1.00
169	Brad Eldred	.50
170	Chase Utley	.75
171	Mark Loretta	.25
172	John Patterson	.50
173	Tom Glavine	.50
174	Dontrelle Willis	.50
175	Mark Teixeira	.50
176	Felix Hernandez	.50
177	Cliff Lee	.25
178	Jason Schmidt	.40
179	Chad Tracy	.25
180	Rocco Baldelli	.25
181	Aramis Ramirez	.50
182	Andy Pettitte	.50
183	Mark Mulder	.25
184	Geoff Jenkins	.25
185	Chipper Jones	.75
186	Vernon Wells	.50
187	Bobby Crosby	.25
188	Lance Berkman	.50
189	Vladimir Guerrero	.75
190	Coco Crisp	.25
191	Brad Penny	.25
192	Jose Guillen	.25
193	Brett Myers	.25
194	Miguel Cabrera	.75
195	Bartolo Colon	.25
196	Craig Biggio	.40
197	Tim Hudson	.50
198	Mark Prior	.50
199	Mark Buehrle	.40
200	Barry Bonds	2.50
201	Anderson Hernandez (RC)	.50
202	Jose Capellan (RC)	.50
203	Jeremy Accardo (RC)	.50
204	Hanley Ramirez (RC)	2.50
205	Matt Capps (RC)	.50
206	Jonathan Papelbon (RC)	1.50
207	Chuck James (RC)	.50
208	Matt Cain (RC)	.50
209	Cole Hamels (RC)	1.50
210	Jason Botts (RC)	.50
211	Lastings Milledge (RC)	.50
212	Conor Jackson (RC)	.75
213	Yusmeiro Petit (RC)	.50
214	Alay Soler RC	.50
215	Willy Aybar (RC)	.50
216	Adam Loewen (RC)	.50
217	Justin Verlander (RC)	2.00
218	Francisco Liriano (RC)	3.00
219	Kenji Johjima RC	3.00
219	Kenji Johjima/Auto. RC	15.00
220	Craig Hansen RC	2.00
221	Prince Fielder/Auto. (RC)	65.00
222	Josh Barfield/Auto. (RC)	10.00
223	Fausto Carmona/Auto. (RC)	15.00
224	James Loney/Auto (RC)	40.00

Refractor

Refractor (1-200):	2-4X
Refractor (201-220):	2-3X
Inserted 1:4	
Autograph (219, 221-224):	1-1.5X
Production 500	

X-Fractor

X-Fractor (1-200):	3-5X
X-Fractor (201-220):	3-5X
Production 250	
X-Fractor Auto. (219, 221-224):	1-2X
Production 225	

Blue Refractor

Blue Refractor (1-200):	3-6X
Blue Refractor (201-220):	4-6X
Production 150	
Blue Ref. Auto. (219, 221-224):	1-2.5X
Production 150	

Gold Refractor

Gold Refractor (1-200):	8-15X
Gold Refractor (201-220):	8-15X
Production 50	
Gold Ref Auto. (219, 221-224):	3-5X
Production 50	

Orange Refractor

Orange Refractor (1-200):	15-25X
Orange Refractor (201-220):	15-25X
Production 25	
Orange Ref. Auto. (221-224):	No Pricing
Production 25	

Red Refractor

No Pricing
Production Five Sets

Super Fractor

No Pricing
Production One Set

Printing Plates

No Pricing
Production One Set

Bowman Chrome Prospects

		NM/M
Common Prospect:		.50
BC111	Koby Clemens	1.00
BC112	Lance Broadway	1.50
BC113	Cameron Maybin	6.00
BC114	Mike Aviles	2.50
BC115	Kyle Blanks	3.00
BC116	Chris Dickerson	1.00
BC117	Sean Gallagher	2.00
BC118	Jamar Hill	1.00
BC119	Garrett Mock	.75
BC120	Russel Rohlicek	1.00
BC121	Clete Thomas	1.00
BC122	Elvis Andrus	6.00
BC123	Brandon Moss	1.00
BC124	Mark Holliman	1.50
BC125	Jose Tabata	6.00
BC126	Corey Wimberly	2.00
BC127	Bobby Wilson	1.00
BC128	Edward Mujica	1.50
BC129	Hunter Pence	4.00
BC130	Adam Heether	.50
BC131	Andy Wilson	.50
BC132	Radhames Liz	2.00
BC133	Garrett Patterson	.50
BC134	Carlos Gomez	3.00
BC135	Jared Lansford	1.00
BC136	Jose Arredondo	1.00
BC137	Renee Cortez	1.00
BC138	Francisco Rosario	1.00
BC139	Brian Stokes	.50
BC140	Will Thompson	1.00
BC141	Ernesto Frieri	1.00
BC142	Jose Mijares	1.00
BC143	Jeremy Slayden	1.00
BC144	Brandon Fahey	1.00
BC145	Jason Windsor	1.50
BC146	Shawn Nottingham	1.00
BC147	Dallas Trahern	1.00
BC148	Jon Niese	1.50
BC149	A.J. Shappi	.50
BC150	Jordan Pals	.50
BC151	Tim Moss	.50
BC152	Stephen Marek	1.00
BC153	Mat Gamel	4.00
BC154	Sean Henn	.50
BC155	Matt Guillory	.50

BC156	Brandon Jones	4.00
BC157	Gary Galvez	1.00
BC158	Shane Lindsay	1.50
BC159	Jesus Reina	.50
BC160	Lorenzo Cain	3.00
BC161	Chris Britton	1.00
BC162	Yovani Gallardo	4.00
BC163	Matt Walker	1.00
BC164	Shaun Cumberland	1.00
BC165	Ryan Patterson	1.00
BC166	Michael Hollimon	1.00
BC167	Eude Brito	.50
BC168	John Bowker	1.50
BC169	James Avery	.50
BC170	John Bannister	.50
BC171	Juan Ciriaco	.50
BC172	Manuel Corpas	1.00
BC173	Leo Rosales	.50
BC174	Tim Kennelly	.50
BC175	Adam Russell	.50
BC176	Jeremy Hellickson	5.00
BC177	Ryan Klosterman	1.00
BC178	Evan Meek	1.00
BC179	Steve Murphy	2.00
BC180	Scott Feldman	.50
BC181	Pablo Sandoval	1.50
BC182	Dexter Fowler	2.00
BC183	Jairo Cuevas	1.00
BC184	Andrew Pinckney	1.00
BC185	Marino Salas	.50
BC186	Justin Christian	1.00
BC187	Ching-Lung Lo	1.00
BC188	Randy Roth	1.00
BC189	Andrew Sonnanstine	1.00
BC190	Josh Outman	1.00
BC191	Yuber A. Rodriguez	1.00
BC192	Hainley Statia	2.00
BC193	Kevin Estrada	1.50
BC194	Jeff Karstens	1.50
BC195	Corey Coles	1.00
BC196	Gustavo Espinoza	1.00
BC197	Brian Horwitz	.50
BC198	Landon Jacobsen	1.00
BC199	Ben Krosschell	1.00
BC200	Jason Jaramillo	1.00
BC201	Josh Wilson	1.00
BC202	Jason Ray	1.00
BC203	Brent Dlugach	1.00
BC204	Cesar Jimenez	1.00
BC205	Eric Haberer	.50
BC206	Felipe Paulino	.50
BC207	Alcides Escobar	4.00
BC208	Jose Ascanio	1.00
BC209	Yoel Hernandez	1.00
BC210	Geoff Vandel	1.50
BC211	Travis Denker	1.50
BC212	Ramon Alvarado	1.50
BC213	Welinson Baez	1.50
BC214	Chris Kolkhorst	.50
BC215	Emiliano Fruto	.50
BC216	Luis Cota	1.00
BC217	Mark Worrell	1.50
BC218	Cla Meredith	1.50
BC219	Emmanuel Garcia	1.50
BC220	B.J. Szymanski	1.00
BC221	Alex Gordon/Auto.	15.00
BC222	Mark Pawelek/Auto.	15.00
BC223	Justin Upton/Auto.	120.00
BC224	Sean West/Auto.	15.00
BC225	Tyler Greene/Auto.	15.00
BC226	Josh Kinney/Auto.	15.00
BC227	Pedro Lopez/Auto.	10.00
BC228	Troy Patton Auto.	15.00
BC229	Chris Iannetta/Auto.	15.00
BC230	Jared Wells/Auto.	10.00
BC231	Brandon Wood/Auto.	15.00
BC232	Josh Geer/Auto.	15.00
BC233	Cesar Carrillo/Auto.	15.00
BC234	Franklin Gutierrez/Auto.	15.00
BC235	Matt Garza/Auto.	20.00
BC236	Eli Iorg/Auto.	15.00
BC237	Trevor Bell/Auto.	10.00
BC238	Jeff Lyman/Auto.	10.00
BC239	Jon Lester/Auto.	50.00
BC240	Kevin Morales/Auto.	30.00
BC241	J. Brent Cox/Auto.	10.00
BC242	Jose Bautista/Auto.	20.00
BC243	Josh Sullivan/Auto.	10.00
BC244	Brandon Snyder/Auto.	10.00
BC245	Elvin Puello/Auto.	10.00
BC246	Henry Sanchez/Auto.	10.00
BC247	Jacob Marceaux/Auto.	10.00

Prospects Refractors
Refractor (111-220): 2-4X
Refractor Auto. (221-247): 1-1.5X
Production 500 Sets

Prospects X-Fractors
X-Refractor (111-220): 3-5X
Production 250
X-Refractor Auto. (221-247): 1-2X
Production 225

Prospects Blue Refractors
Blue Refractor (111-220): 4-6X
Blue Refractor Auto. (221-247): 1-2.5X
Production 150 Sets

Prospects Gold Refractors
Gold Refractor (111-220): 8-15X
Gold Refractor Auto. (221-247): 3-5X
Production 50 Sets

Prospects Orange Refractors
Orange Refractor (111-220): 15-25X
Orange Refractor Auto. (221-247): 4-6X
Production 25 Sets

Prospects Red Refractors
No Pricing
Production Five Sets

Prospects Super Fractors
No Pricing
Production One Set

2006 Bowman Chrome Draft
NM/M
Complete Set (55): 25.00
Common Player: .50

1	Matt Kemp (RC)	4.00
2	Taylor Tankersley (RC)	.50
3	Michael Napoli (RC)	1.00
4	Brian Bannister (RC)	.50
5	Melky Cabrera (RC)	.50
6	Bill Bray (RC)	.50
7	Brian Anderson (RC)	.50
8	Jered Weaver (RC)	2.00
9	Chris Duncan (RC)	.50
10	Boof Bonser (RC)	.50
11	Mike Rouse (RC)	.50
12	David Pauley (RC)	.50
13	Russell Martin (RC)	1.00
14	Jeremy Sowers (RC)	.50
15	Kevin Reese (RC)	.50
16	John Rheinecker (RC)	.50
17	Tommy Murphy (RC)	.50
18	Sean Marshall (RC)	1.00
19	Jason Kubel (RC)	1.00
20	Chad Billingsley (RC)	1.50
21	Kendry Morales (RC)	1.50
22	Jon Lester (RC)	4.00
23	Brandon Fahey RC	.50
24	Josh Johnson (RC)	1.00
25	Kevin Frandsen (RC)	.50
26	Casey Janssen RC	.50
27	Scott Thorman (RC)	.75
28	Scott Mathieson (RC)	.50
29	Jeremy Hermida (RC)	.50
30	Dustin Nippert (RC)	.50
31	Kevin Thompson (RC)	.50
32	Bobby Livingston (RC)	.50
33	Travis Ishikawa (RC)	.50
34	Jeff Mathis (RC)	.50
35	Charlie Haeger RC	1.00
36	Josh Willingham (RC)	.50
37	Taylor Buchholz (RC)	.50
38	Joel Guzman (RC)	.50
39	Zach Jackson RC	.50
40	Howie Kendrick (RC)	1.00
41	T.J. Beam (RC)	1.00
42	Ty Taubenheim RC	1.00
43	Erick Aybar (RC)	.50
44	Anibal Sanchez (RC)	1.00
45	Mike Pelfrey RC	5.00
46	Shawn Hill (RC)	.50
47	Chris Roberson (RC)	.50
48	Carlos Villanueva RC	.50
49	Andre Ethier (RC)	2.50
50	Anthony Reyes (RC)	1.00
51	Franklin Gutierrez (RC)	.50
52	Angel Guzman (RC)	.50
53	Michael O'Connor RC	.50
54	James Shields (RC)	3.00
55	Nate McLouth (RC)	.50

SuperFractor
No Pricing
Production One Set

Red Refractor
No Pricing
Production Five Sets

Orange Refractor
Orange Refractor (1-55): 15-25X
Production 25 Sets

Gold Refractor
Gold Refractor (1-55): 8-15X
Production 50 Sets

Blue Refractor
Blue Refractor (1-55): 4-8X
Production 199 Sets

X-Fractor
X-Fractor (1-55): 3-6X
Production 299 Sets

Refractor
Refractor (1-55): 2-4X

Draft Picks
NM/M
Complete Set (90):
Common Draft Pick (1-65): 1.00
Common (66-90): 20.00

1	Tyler Colvin	8.00
2	Chris Marrero	5.00
3	Hank Conger	3.00
4	Chris Parmelee	3.00
5	Jason Place	3.00
6	Billy Rowell	5.00
7	Travis Snider	10.00
8	Colton Willems	3.00
9	Chase Fontaine	2.00
10	Jon Jay	2.00
11	Wade LeBlanc	1.50
12	Justin Masterson	4.00
13	Gary Daley	1.50

14	Justin Edwards	1.00
15	Charlie Yarbrough	1.50
16	Cyle Hankerd	3.00
17	Zach McAllister	2.00
18	Tyler Robertson	1.00
19	Joe Smith	1.00
20	Nate Culp	1.00
21	John Holdzkom	1.00
22	Patrick Bresnehan	1.00
23	Chad Lee	1.00
24	Ryan Morris	1.00
25	D'Arby Myers	1.50
26	Garrett Olson	1.00
27	Jon Still	1.00
28	Brandon Rice	1.00
29	Chris Davis	2.50
30	Zack Daeges	1.50
31	Bobby Henson	1.50
32	George Kontos	1.50
33	Jermaine Mitchell	1.50
34	Adam Coe	1.50
35	Dustin Richardson	1.50
36	Allen Craig	1.00
37	Austin McClune	1.50
38	Doug Fister	1.00
39	Corey Madden	1.00
40	Justin Jacobs	1.50
41	Jim Negrych	1.00
42	Tyler Norrick	1.50
43	Adam Davis	1.00
44	Brett Logan	1.00
45	Brian Omogrosso	1.00
46	Kyle Drabek	4.00
47	Jamie Ortiz	2.00
48	Alex Presley	1.00
49	Terrance Warren	1.50
50	David Christensen	2.00
51	Helder Velazquez	2.00
52	Matt McBride	1.50
53	Quintin Berry	2.00
54	Michael Eisenberg	1.00
55	Dan Garcia	1.00
56	Scott Cousins	1.00
57	Sean Land	1.00
58	Kristopher Medlen	3.00
59	Tyler Reves	1.50
60	John Shelby	1.50
61	Jordan Newton	1.50
62	Ricky Orta	1.00
63	Jason Donald	1.50
64	David Huff	1.50
65	Brett Sinkbeil	1.00
66	Evan Longoria/Auto.	200.00
67	Cody Johnson/Auto.	15.00
68	Kris Johnson/Auto.	15.00
69	Kasey Kiker/Auto.	15.00
70	Ronny Bourquin/Auto.	10.00
71	Adrian Cardenas/Auto.	20.00
72	Matt Antonelli/Auto.	10.00
73	Brooks Brown/Auto.	15.00
74	Steven Evarts/Auto.	15.00
75	Joshua Butler/Auto.	15.00
76	Chad Huffman/Auto.	15.00
77	Steven Wright/Auto.	15.00
78	Cory Rasmus/Auto.	15.00
79	Brad Furnish/Auto.	10.00
80	Andrew Carpenter/Auto.	10.00
81	Dustin Evans/Auto.	10.00
82	Tommy Hickman/Auto.	15.00
83	Matt Long/Auto.	15.00
84	Clayton Kershaw/Auto.	60.00
85	Kyle McCulloch/Auto.	15.00
86	Pedro Beato/Auto.	15.00
87	Kyler Burke/Auto.	15.00
88	Stephen Englund/Auto.	15.00
89	Michael Felix/Auto.	15.00
90	Sean Watson/Auto.	15.00

Draft Picks X-Fractor
X-Fractor (1-65): 3-6X
Production 299 Sets
X-Fractor Auto. (66-90): 1-2X
Production 225 Sets

Draft Picks Refractor
Refractor (1-65): 2-4X
Refractor Auto. (66-90): 1-1.5X
Production 500 for #'s 66-90

Draft Picks SuperFractor
No Pricing
Production One Set

Draft Picks Red Refractor
No Pricing
Production Five Sets

Draft Picks Orange Refractor
Orange Refractor (1-65): 15-25X
Production 25 Sets
Orange Auto. (66-90): No Pricing
Production 25 Sets

Draft Picks Gold Refractor
Gold Refractor (1-65): 8-15X
Production 50 Sets
Gold Auto. (66-90): 3-5X
Production 50 Sets

Draft Picks Blue Refractor
Blue Refractor (1-65): 4-8X
Production 199 Sets
Blue Auto. (66-90): 1-2.5X
Production 150 Sets

Future's Game Prospects
NM/M
Complete Set (45): 20.00
Common Player: .50

1	Nick Adenhart	1.00
2	Joel Guzman	.50
3	Ryan Braun	.50
4	Carlos Carrasco	.50
5	Neil Walker	.50
6	Pablo Sandoval	2.00
7	Gio Gonzalez	.50
8	Joey Votto	1.00
9	Luis Cruz	.50
10	Nolan Reimold	.50
11	Juan Salas	.50
12	Josh Fields	.50
13	Yovani Gallardo	1.00
14	Radhames Liz	.50
15	Eric Patterson	.50
16	Cameron Maybin	1.50
17	Edgar Martinez	.50
18	Hunter Pence	1.00
19	Phillip Hughes	2.00
20	Trent Oeltjen	.50
21	Nick Pereira	.50
22	Wladimir Balentien	.50
23	Stephen Drew	1.50
24	Davis Romero	.50
25	Joe Koshansky	.50
26	Chin-Lung Hu	1.00
27	Jason Hirsh	1.00
28	Jose Tabata	1.00
29	Eric Hurley	.50
30	Yung-Chi Chen	1.00
31	Howie Kendrick	1.00
32	Humberto Sanchez	1.00
33	Alex Gordon	.75
34	Yunel Escobar	.50
35	Travis Buck	.75
36	Billy Butler	1.00
37	Homer Bailey	.50
38	George Kottaras	.50
39	Kurt Suzuki	.50
40	Joaquin Arias	.50
41	Matt Lindstrom	.50
42	Sean Smith	.50
43	Carlos Gonzalez	1.00
44	Jaime Garcia	3.00
45	Jose Garcia	1.00

Future's Game Red Refractor
No Pricing
Production Five Sets

Future's Game Orange Refractor
Orange (1-45): 15-30X
Production 25 Sets

Future's Game Gold Refractor
Gold (1-45): 8-15X
Production 50 Sets

Future's Game Blue Refractor
Blue (1-45): 4-8X
Production 199 Sets

Future's Game X-Fractor
X-Fractor (1-45): 3-6X
Production 299 Sets

Future's Game Refractor
Refractor (1-45): 2-4X

Head of the Class Dual Auto.
NM/M
Production 174
Refractor: 1-1.5X
Production 50
Gold Refractor: No Pricing
Production 25
RU Alex Rodriguez, Justin Upton 150.00

2006 Bowman Draft
NM/M
Complete Set (55): 10.00
Common Player: .25
Pack (5 + 2 Chrome): 5.00
Box (24): 100.00

1	Matthew Kemp (RC)	1.50
2	Taylor Tankersley (RC)	.25
3	Michael Napoli RC	.50
4	Brian Bannister (RC)	.25
5	Melky Cabrera (RC)	.25
6	Bill Bray (RC)	.25
7	Brian Anderson (RC)	.25
8	Jered Weaver (RC)	.75
9	Chris Duncan (RC)	.25
10	Boof Bonser (RC)	.50
11	Mike Rouse (RC)	.25
12	David Pauley (RC)	.25
13	Russell Martin (RC)	.25
14	Jeremy Sowers (RC)	.25
15	Kevin Reese (RC)	.25
16	John Rheinecker (RC)	.25
17	Tommy Murphy (RC)	.25
18	Sean Marshall (RC)	.25
19	Jason Kubel (RC)	.25
20	Chad Billingsley (RC)	.75
21	Kendry Morales (RC)	1.00
22	Jon Lester (RC)	1.50
23	Brandon Fahey RC	.25
24	Josh Johnson (RC)	.25
25	Kevin Frandsen (RC)	.25
26	Casey Janssen RC	.25
27	Scott Thorman (RC)	.25
28	Scott Mathieson (RC)	.25
29	Jeremy Hermida (RC)	.25
30	Dustin Nippert (RC)	.25
31	Kevin Thompson (RC)	.25
32	Bobby Livingston (RC)	.25
33	Travis Ishikawa (RC)	.25
34	Jeff Mathis (RC)	.25
35	Charlie Haeger RC	.50
36	Josh Willingham (RC)	.25
37	Taylor Buchholz (RC)	.25
38	Joel Guzman (RC)	.25
39	Zach Jackson (RC)	.25
40	Howie Kendrick (RC)	.50
41	T.J. Beam (RC)	.25
42	Ty Taubenheim RC	.50
43	Erick Aybar (RC)	.25
44	Anibal Sanchez (RC)	.25
45	Mike Pelfrey RC	2.00
46	Shawn Hill (RC)	.25
47	Chris Roberson (RC)	.25
48	Carlos Villanueva RC	.25
49	Andre Ethier (RC)	1.00
50	Anthony Reyes (RC)	.25
51	Franklin Gutierrez (RC)	.25
52	Angel Guzman (RC)	.25
53	Michael O'Connor RC	.25
54	James Shields RC	.50
55	Nate McLouth (RC)	.25

Printing Plates
No Pricing
Production one set per color.

Red
No Pricing
Production One Set

White
White (1-55): 2-5X
Production 225 Sets

Gold
Gold (1-55): 1-2X
Inserted 1:1

Draft Picks
NM/M
Complete Set (65): 20.00
Common Draft Pick (1-65): .50

1	Tyler Colvin	2.50
2	Chris Marrero	1.50
3	Hank Conger	1.00
4	Chris Parmelee	1.00
5	Jason Place	1.00
6	Billy Rowell	1.00
7	Travis Snider	3.00
8	Colton Willems	.75
9	Chase Fontaine	.50
10	Jon Jay	.50
11	Wade LeBlanc	1.00
12	Justin Masterson	1.50
13	Gary Daley	.50
14	Justin Edwards	.50
15	Charlie Yarbrough	.50
16	Cyle Hankerd	1.00
17	Zach McAllister	.50
18	Tyler Robertson	.50
19	Joe Smith	.50
20	Nate Culp	.50
21	John Holdzkom	.50
22	Patrick Bresnehan	.50
23	Chad Lee	.50
24	Ryan Morris	.50
25	D'Arby Myers	.75
26	Garrett Olson	.75
27	Jon Still	.50
28	Brandon Rice	.50
29	Chris Davis	.75
30	Zack Daeges	.50
31	Bobby Henson	.50
32	George Kontos	.50
33	Jermaine Mitchell	.75
34	Adam Coe	.50
35	Dustin Richardson	.50
36	Allen Craig	.50
37	Austin McClune	.50
38	Doug Fister	.50
39	Corey Madden	.50
40	Justin Jacobs	.50
41	Jim Negrych	.50
42	Tyler Norrick	.50
43	Adam Davis	.50
44	Brett Logan	.50
45	Brian Omogrosso	.50
46	Kyle Drabek	1.00
47	Jamie Ortiz	.50
48	Alex Presley	.50
49	Terrance Warren	.50
50	David Christensen	.50
51	Helder Velazquez	.50
52	Matt McBride	.50
53	Quintin Berry	.50
54	Michael Eisenberg	.50
55	Dan Garcia	.50
56	Scott Cousins	.50
57	Sean Land	.50
58	Kristopher Medlen	1.00
59	Tyler Reves	.50
60	John Shelby	.50
61	Jordan Newton	.50
62	Ricky Orta	.50
63	Jason Donald	.50
64	David Huff	.50
65	Brett Sinkbeil	.50

Future's Game Prospects
NM/M
Complete Set (45): 10.00
Common Player: .25

1	Nick Adenhart	.50
2	Joel Guzman	.25
3	Ryan Braun	.25
4	Carlos Carrasco	.25
5	Neil Walker	.25
6	Pablo Sandoval	1.00
7	Gio Gonzalez	.25
8	Joey Votto	1.00
9	Luis Cruz	.25
10	Nolan Reimold	.25
11	Juan Salas	.25
12	Josh Fields	.50
13	Yovani Gallardo	.50
14	Radhames Liz	.25
15	Eric Patterson	.25
16	Cameron Maybin	1.00
17	Edgar Martinez	.50
18	Hunter Pence	.50
19	Phillip Hughes	.75
20	Trent Oeltjen	.25
21	Nick Pereira	.25
22	Wladimir Balentien	.50
23	Stephen Drew	.50
24	Davis Romero	.25
25	Joe Koshansky	.25
26	Chin-Lung Hu	.25
27	Jason Hirsh	.25
28	Jose Tabata	.75
29	Eric Hurley	.25
30	Yung-Chi Chen	.75
31	Howie Kendrick	.50
32	Humberto Sanchez	.50
33	Alex Gordon	.50
34	Yunel Escobar	.25
35	Travis Buck	.50
36	Billy Butler	.50
37	Homer Bailey	.50
38	George Kottaras	.25
39	Kurt Suzuki	.50
40	Joaquin Arias	.25
41	Matt Lindstrom	.25
42	Sean Smith	.25
43	Carlos Gonzalez	.50
44	Jaime Garcia	1.50
45	Jose Garcia	.50

Future's Game Prospects Relics
NM/M
Common Player: 4.00

1	Nick Adenhart	8.00
2	Joel Guzman	4.00
3	Ryan Braun	15.00
4	Carlos Carrasco	4.00
5	Neil Walker	4.00
6	Pablo Sandoval	8.00
7	Gio Gonzalez	4.00
8	Joey Votto	8.00
9	Luis Cruz	4.00
10	Nolan Reimold	6.00
11	Juan Salas	4.00
12	Josh Fields	8.00
13	Yovani Gallardo	8.00
14	Radhames Liz	4.00
15	Eric Patterson	4.00

16	Cameron Maybin	8.00
17	Edgar Martinez	4.00
18	Hunter Pence	6.00
19	Phillip Hughes	10.00
20	Trent Oeltjen	4.00
21	Nick Pereira	4.00
22	Wladimir Balentien	5.00
23	Stephen Drew	8.00
24	Davis Romero	4.00
25	Joe Koshansky	4.00
26	Chin-Lung Hu	8.00
27	Jason Hirsh	4.00
28	Jose Tabata	8.00
29	Eric Hurley	4.00
30	Yung-Chi Chen	50.00
31	Howie Kendrick	6.00
32	Humberto Sanchez	4.00
33	Alex Gordon	6.00
34	Yunel Escobar	8.00
35	Travis Buck	6.00
36	Billy Butler	8.00
37	Homer Bailey	8.00
38	George Kottaras	4.00
39	Kurt Suzuki	6.00
40	Joaquin Arias	4.00
41	Matt Lindstrom	4.00
42	Sean Smith	4.00
43	Carlos Gonzalez	8.00
44	Jaime Garcia	15.00
45	Jose Garcia	4.00

Signs of the Future

		NM/M
	Common Autograph:	6.00
BS	Brandon Snyder	8.00
KC	Koby Clemens	10.00
AG	Alex Gordon	15.00
CI	Chris Iannetta	8.00
MO	Micah Owings	8.00
JC	Jeff Clement	8.00
CR	Clayton Richard	8.00
TB	Travis Buck	12.00
BJ	Beau Jones	12.00
DJ	Daryl Jones	10.00
CDR	Chaz Roe	8.00
JM	Jacob Marceaux	8.00
CTI	Craig Italiano	8.00
JB	Jay Bruce	40.00
WT	Wade Townsend	8.00
MM	Mark McCormick	8.00
HS	Henry Sanchez	6.00
MC	Mike Costanzo	8.00
CRA	Cesar Ramos	8.00

2006 Bowman Heritage

		NM/M
Complete Set (300):		
Common Player (1-200):		.15
Common SP (even #'s 202-300):	3.00	
Inserted 1:3		
Pack (8):		3.00
Box (24):		60.00
1	David Wright	1.00
2	Andruw Jones	.25
3	Ryan Howard	1.50
4	Jason Bay	.40
5	Paul Konerko	.40
6	Jake Peavy	.25
7	Todd Jones	.15
8	Troy Glaus	.25
9	Rocco Baldelli	.15
10	Rafael Furcal	.25
11	Freddy Sanchez	.25
12	Jermaine Dye	.25
13	A.J. Burnett	.15
14	Michael Cuddyer	.15
15	Barry Zito	.25
16	Chipper Jones	.75
17	Paul LoDuca	.15
18	Mark Mulder	.15
19	Raul Ibanez	.15
20	Carlos Delgado	.40
21	Marcus Giles	.15
22	Danny Haren	.25
23	Justin Morneau	.40
24	Livan Hernandez	.15
25	Ken Griffey Jr.	1.50
26	Aaron Hill	.15
27	Tadahito Iguchi	.15
28	Nate Robertson	.15
29	Kevin Millwood	.15
30	Jim Thome	.40
31	Aubrey Huff	.15
32	Dontrelle Willis	.25
33	Khalil Greene	.25
34	Doug Davis	.15
35	Ivan Rodriguez	.50
36	Rickie Weeks	.25

37	Jhonny Peralta	.25
38	Yadier Molina	.15
39	Eric Chavez	.25
40	Alfonso Soriano	.75
41	Pat Burrell	.25
42	B.J. Ryan	.15
43	Carl Crawford	.25
44	Preston Wilson	.15
45	Jorge Posada	.40
46	Carlos Zambrano	.25
47	Mark Teahen	.15
48	Nick Johnson	.15
49	Mark Kotsay	.15
50	Derek Jeter	2.00
51	Moises Alou	.15
52	Ryan Freel	.15
53	Shannon Stewart	.15
54	Casey Blake	.15
55	Edgar Renteria	.25
56	Frank Thomas	.50
57	Ty Wigginton	.15
58	Jeff Kent	.25
59	Chien-Ming Wang	.50
60	Josh Beckett	.50
61	Chase Utley	.75
62	Gary Matthews	.15
63	Torii Hunter	.25
64	Bobby Jenks	.15
65	Wilson Betemit	.15
66	Jeremy Bonderman	.25
67	Scott Rolen	.75
68	Brad Penny	.15
69	Jacque Jones	.15
70	Jose Reyes	.75
71	Brian Roberts	.25
72	John Smoltz	.25
73	Johnny Estrada	.15
74	Ronnie Belliard	.15
75	Vladimir Guerrero	.75
76	A.J. Pierzynski	.15
77	Garrett Atkins	.40
78	Adam LaRoche	.15
79	Mark Loretta	.15
80	Todd Helton	.50
81	Jose Vidro	.15
82	Carlos Guillen	.25
83	Michael Barrett	.15
84	Lyle Overbay	.15
85	Travis Hafner	.25
86	Shea Hillenbrand	.15
87	Julio Lugo	.15
88	Tim Hudson	.25
89	Scott Podsednik	.15
90	Roy Halladay	.25
91	Bartolo Colon	.15
92	Ryan Langerhans	.15
93	Tom Glavine	.40
94	Ken Rogers	.15
95	Robinson Cano	.75
96	Mark Prior	.25
97	Jason Schmidt	.25
98	Bengie Molina	.15
99	Jon Lieber	.15
100	Alex Rodriguez	2.00
101	Scott Kazmir	.25
102	Jeff Francoeur	.50
103	Chris Carpenter	.40
104	Juan Uribe	.15
105	Mariano Rivera	.40
106	Rich Harden	.25
107	Jack Wilson	.15
108	Austin Kearns	.15
109	Marcus Thames	.15
110	Miguel Tejada	.25
111	Chone Figgins	.25
112	Bronson Arroyo	.15
113	Chad Cordero	.25
114	Bill Hall	.15
115	Curt Schilling	.50
116	David Eckstein	.15
117	Ramon Hernandez	.15
118	Eric Byrnes	.25
119	Clint Barmes	.15
120	Bobby Abreu	.25
121	Joe Crede	.15
122	Derek Lowe	.15
123	Jason Marquis	.15
124	Erik Bedard	.25
125	Derek Lee	.50
126	Brian McCann	.40
127	Magglio Ordonez	.25
128	Ben Sheets	.15
129	Brandon Inge	.15
130	Miguel Cabrera	.75
131	Jim Edmonds	.25
132	John Lackey	.40
133	Kevin Mench	.15
134	Adrian Beltre	.25
135	Curtis Granderson	.50
136	Shawn Green	.25
137	Jose Contreras	.15
138	Joe Nathan	.15
139	Bobby Crosby	.25
140	Johnny Damon	.50
141	Brad Hawpe	.15
142	Brandon Phillips	.40
143	Victor Martinez	.40
144	Jimmy Rollins	.75
145	Corey Patterson	.15
146	Grady Sizemore	.50
147	Placido Polanco	.15
148	Mike Lowell	.15
149	Francisco Rodriguez	.15
150	Ichiro Suzuki	1.50
151	Kris Benson	.15
152	Scott Hatteberg	.15
153	Akinori Otsuka	.15
154	Cesar Izturis	.15

155	Roger Clemens	2.00
156	Kerry Wood	.25
157	Tom Gordon	.15
158	Sean Casey	.15
159	Jose Lopez	.15
160	Orlando Hernandez	.15
161	Aramis Ramirez	.40
162	J.D. Drew	.25
163	David DeJesus	.15
164	Craig Biggio	.25
165	Brad Myers	.15
166	C.C. Sabathia	.40
167	Zachary Duke	.15
168	Luis Castillo	.15
169	Hideki Matsui	1.00
170	Brian Giles	.15
171	Coco Crisp	.15
172	Richie Sexson	.25
173	Nomar Garciaparra	.25
174	Roy Oswalt	.25
175	David Ortiz	.75
176	Matt Morris	.15
177	Felipe Lopez	.15
178	Garret Anderson	.15
179	Kevin Youkilis	.25
180	Alex Rios	.40
181	John Garland	.15
182	Luis Gonzalez	.15
183	Cliff Floyd	.15
184	Juan Encarnacion	.15
185	Nick Swisher	.25
186	Mike Cameron	.15
187	Jose Castillo	.15
188	Ray Durham	.15
189	Jorge Cantu	.15
190	Andy Pettitte	.25
191	Chad Tracy	.15
192	Adrian Gonzalez	.40
193	Jose Valentin	.15
194	Mark Buehrle	.25
195	Huston Street	.15
196	Chris Capuano	.15
197	Aaron Rowand	.15
198	Billy Wagner	.15
199	Orlando Cabrera	.25
200	Albert Pujols	2.00
201	Dan Uggla (RC)	1.00
202	Alay Soler RC	3.00
203	Matt Kemp (RC)	2.50
204	Michael Napoli RC	3.00
205	Joel Zumaya (RC)	1.00
206	Mike Pelfrey RC	5.00
207	Ian Kinsler (RC)	.50
208	Josh Willingham (RC)	3.00
209	Erick Aybar (RC)	3.00
210	Willie Eyre (RC)	3.00
211	Kendry Morales (RC)	5.00
212	Scott Thorman (RC)	3.00
213	Hanley Ramirez (RC)	1.00
214	Boof Bonser (RC)	3.00
215	Anthony Reyes (RC)	.50
216	Justin Huber (RC)	3.00
217	Yusmeiro Petit (RC)	.50
218	Jason Bartlett (RC)	4.00
219	Shin-Soo Choo RC	2.00
220	Francisco Liriano (RC)	5.00
221	Craig Hansen (RC)	.50
222	Ricky Nolasco (RC)	.50
223	Adam Loewen (RC)	.50
224	Scott Olsen (RC)	3.00
225	Cole Hamels (RC)	1.50
226	Martin Prado (RC)	4.00
227	James Loney (RC)	1.50
228	Kevin Thompson (RC)	3.00
229	Adam Jones (RC)	1.50
230	Josh Johnson (RC)	4.00
231	Anderson Hernandez(RC)	.40
232	Tony Gwynn Jr. (RC)	3.00
233	Casey Janssen (RC)	.50
234	Taylor Tankersley (RC)	3.00
235	Mike Thompson RC	
236	Jeremy Sowers (RC)	3.00
237	Anibal Sanchez (RC)	.50
238	Adam Wainwright (RC)	8.00
239	Rich Hill (RC)	.50
240	Russell Martin (RC)	4.00
241	Joe Inglett RC	
242	Tony Pena (RC)	3.00
243	Joshua Sharpless RC	.50
244	Darrell Rasner (RC)	3.00
245	Joe Saunders (RC)	.50
246	Jon Lester (RC)	8.00
247	Jeremy Hermida (RC)	.50
248	Chad Billingsley (RC)	4.00
249	Bobby Livingston (RC)	.50
250	Justin Verlander RC	6.00
251	Mickey Mantle	10.00
252	Hank Blalock	3.00
253	Manny Ramirez	1.00
254	Mike Mussina	5.00
255	Greg Maddux	2.00
256	Jason Giambi	4.00
257	Mark Teixeira	.75
258	Carlos Beltran	4.00
259	Matt Holliday	5.00
260	Pedro Martinez	5.00
261	Joe Mauer	1.00
262	Melvin Mora	3.00
263	Mike Piazza	1.50
264	B.J. Upton	4.00
265	Vernon Wells	.75
266	Gary Sheffield	4.00
267	Randy Johnson	1.00
268	Ryan Zimmerman	4.00
269	Lance Berkman	.75
270	Johan Santana	5.00
271	Carlos Lee	.50
272	Brandon Webb	3.00
273	Adam Dunn	.75
274	Michael Young	

275	Barry Bonds	2.00
276	Jonathan Papelbon (RC)	4.00
277	Howie Kendrick (RC)	
278	Melky Cabrera (RC)	3.00
279	Jered Weaver (RC)	5.00
280	Josh Barfield (RC)	3.00
281	Chuck James (RC)	
282	Lastings Milledge (RC)	4.00
283	Nick Markakis (RC)	1.00
284	Jose Capellan (RC)	
285	Prince Fielder (RC)	3.00
286	Jason Botts (RC)	3.00
287	Eliezer Alfonzo RC	.50
288	Sean Marshall (RC)	3.00
289	Ryan Garko (RC)	.75
290	Stephen Drew (RC)	5.00
291	Joel Guzman (RC)	
292	Hong-Chih Kuo (RC)	3.00
293	Zach Miner (RC)	
294	Angel Guzman (RC)	
295	Andre Ethier (RC)	1.50
296	Fausto Carmona (RC)	3.00
297	Ronny Paulino (RC)	.75
298	Matt Cain (RC)	6.00
299	Carlos Quentin (RC)	.75
300	Kenji Johjima RC	4.00

Mini

Mini (1-300):	1-2X
Inserted 1:1	

Foil

Foil (1-300):	1-2X
Foil (301-350):	.5-1X
Inserted 1:1	

Black

No Pricing	
Production One Set	

Printing Plates

No Pricing	
Production One Set	

Signs of Greatness

		NM/M
	Common Autograph:	8.00
	White:	No Pricing
	Production Five Sets	
	Black:	No Pricing
	Production One Set	
BB	Brian Bogusevic	10.00
LB	Lance Broadway	10.00
KC	Koby Clemens	12.00
JCL	Jeff Clement	10.00
JC	Jesus Cota	8.00
TC	Trevor Crowe	15.00
JD	John Drennen	8.00
SG	Sean Gallagher	12.00
AG	Alex Gordon	15.00
JH	Justin Huber	8.00
CI	Craig Italiano	8.00
SL	Sam LeCure	8.00
MM	Matt Maloney	8.00
CM	Cameron Maybin	10.00
JS	Jarrod Saltalamacchia	40.00
BS	Brandon Snyder	10.00
ST	Steve Tolleson	8.00
WT	Wade Townsend	8.00
RT	Ryan Tucker	8.00
JU	Justin Upton	60.00
KW	Kevin Whelan	10.00
BW	Brandon Wood	15.00

Pieces of Greatness

		NM/M
	Common Player:	5.00
	Inserted 1:12	
	White:	1.5-3X
	Production 49 Sets	
	Black:	No Pricing
	Production One Set	

PIECES OF GREATNESS
AUTHENTIC GAME-WORN JERSEY

LB	Lance Berkman	6.00
CB	Craig Biggio	8.00
HB	Hank Blalock	5.00
BB	Barry Bonds	15.00
MB	Milton Bradley	5.00
RC	Robinson Cano	20.00
AD	Adam Dunn	5.00
JD	Jermaine Dye	5.00
DE	David Eckstein	8.00
EE	Edwin Encarnacion	5.00
ME	Morgan Ensberg	5.00
CF	Cliff Floyd	5.00
JF	Jeff Francoeur	6.00
RF	Rafael Furcal	5.00
VG	Vladimir Guerrero	8.00
THE	Todd Helton	6.00
RH	Ryan Howard	25.00
TH	Torii Hunter	5.00
AJ	Andruw Jones	5.00
AJ2	Andruw Jones	5.00
CJ	Chipper Jones	8.00
CJ2	Chipper Jones	8.00
NJ	Nick Johnson	5.00
JK	Jeff Kent	5.00
AL	Adam LaRoche	5.00
DL	Derek Lee	5.00
JL	Javy Lopez	5.00
ML	Mike Lowell	5.00
GM	Greg Maddux	10.00
VM	Victor Martinez	5.00
XN	Xavier Nady	5.00
MO	Magglio Ordonez	5.00
DO	David Ortiz	8.00
AJP	A.J. Pierzynski	5.00
SP	Scott Podsednik	60.00
AP	Albert Pujols	25.00
AP2	Albert Pujols	25.00
ARA	Aramis Ramirez	5.00
MR	Manny Ramirez	8.00
BR	Brian Roberts	5.00
AR	Alex Rodriguez	15.00
CS	Curt Schilling	8.00
GS	Gary Sheffield	5.00
NS	Nick Swisher	5.00
JT	Jim Thome	6.00
CU	Chase Utley	8.00
BW	Brad Wilkerson	5.00
DW	Dontrelle Willis	5.00
MY	Michael Young	5.00
BZ	Barry Zito	5.00

Prospects

		NM/M
	Common Prospect:	.50
	Inserted 2:Pack	
	Black:	No Pricing
	Production One Set	
BHP1	Justin Upton	6.00
BHP2	Koby Clemens	1.00
BHP3	Lance Broadway	1.00
BHP4	Cameron Maybin	2.00
BHP5	Garrett Mock	1.00
BHP6	Alex Gordon	1.50
BHP7	Ben Copeland	1.00
BHP8	Nick Adenhart	1.00
BHP9	Yung-Chi Chen	2.00
BHP10	Tim Moss	.50
BHP11	Francisco Leandro	1.00
BHP12	Brad McCann	1.00
BHP13	Dallas Trahern	1.00
BHP14	Dustin Majewski	1.00
BHP15	James Barthmaier	1.00
BHP16	Nate Gold	1.00
BHP17	John Hardy	.50
BHP18	Mark McLemore	1.00
BHP19	Michael Aubrey	1.00
BHP20	Mark Holliman	1.00
BHP21	Bobby Wilson	1.00
BHP22	Radhames Liz	1.00
BHP23	Jose Tabata	2.00
BHP24	Jared Lansford	.50
BHP25	Brent Dlugach	.50
BHP26	Steve Garrabrants	.50
BHP27	Eric Haberer	1.00
BHP28	Chris Dickerson	.50
BHP29	Welinson Baez	1.00
BHP30	Chris Kolkhorst	.50
BHP31	Brandon Moss	1.00
BHP32	Corey Wimberly	.50
BHP33	Ryan Patterson	1.00
BHP34	Michael Hollimon	1.00
BHP35	John Bannister	1.00
BHP36	Pablo Sandoval	2.00
BHP37	Dexter Fowler	1.00
BHP38	Elvis Andrus	4.00
BHP39	Jason Windsor	1.00
BHP40	B.J. Szymanski	1.00
BHP41	Yovani Gallardo	2.00
BHP42	John Bowker	1.50
BHP43	Justin Christian	1.00

BHP44	Andrew Sonnanstine	.75
BHP45	Jeremy Slayden	.50
BHP46	Brandon Jones	.50
BHP47	Travis Denker	1.00
BHP48	Emmanuel Garcia	1.00
BHP49	Landon Jacobsen	1.00
BHP50	Kevin Estrada	1.00
BHP51	Ross Ohlendorf	.50
BHP52	Wyatt Toregas	.50
BHP53	Andrew Kown	1.00
BHP54	Steve Kelly	.50
BHP55	Mike Butia	.50
BHP56	Mike Connolly	1.00
BHP57	Brian Horwitz	1.00
BHP58	Dale Thayer	.50
BHP59	Diory Hernandez	1.00
BHP60	Samuel Deduno	1.00
BHP61	Jamie Hoffman	1.00
BHP62	Matt Tolbert	1.00
BHP63	Michael Ekstrom	1.00
BHP64	Chris Maples	1.00
BHP65	Adam Coe	1.00
BHP66	Max Ramirez	1.50
BHP67	Evan MacLane	1.00
BHP68	Jose Campusano	.50
BHP69	Lou Santangelo	1.00
BHP70	Shawn Riggans	1.00
BHP71	Kyle Kendrick	.75
BHP72	Oswaldo Navarro	1.00
BHP73	Eric Rodland	1.00
BHP74	Omir Santos	1.00
BHP75	Kyle McCulloch	.50
BHP76	Evan Longoria	6.00
BHP77	Adrian Cardenas	1.00
BHP78	Steven Wright	.50
BHP79	Andrew Carpenter	1.00
BHP80	Dustin Evans	1.50
BHP81	Chad Tracy	.50
BHP82	Matthew Sulentic	2.00
BHP83	Adam Ottavino	1.00
BHP84	Matt Long	.50
BHP85	Clayton Kershaw	4.00
BHP86	Matt Antonelli	1.00
BHP87	Chris Parmelee	1.00
BHP88	Billy Rowell	1.00
BHP89	Chase Fontaine	1.00
BHP90	Chris Murrero	1.00
BHP91	Jamie Ortiz	1.00
BHP92	Sean Watson	1.00
BHP93	Brooks Brown	1.00
BHP94	Brad Furnish	1.00
BHP95	Chad Huffman	1.00
BHP96	Pedro Beato	1.50
BHP97	Kyler Burke	1.00
BHP98	Stephen Englund	1.00
BHP99	Tyler Norrick	.50
BHP100	Brent Sinkbeil	.50

Draft Pick Variations

		NM/M
	One five card pack per box.	
BHP76	Evan Longoria	8.00
BHP77	Adrian Cardenas	1.00
BHP78	Steven Wright	1.00
BHP79	Andrew Carpenter	1.00
BHP80	Dustin Evans	2.00
BHP81	Chad Tracy	1.00
BHP82	Matthew Sulentic	4.00
BHP83	Adam Ottavino	2.00
BHP84	Matt Long	1.00
BHP85	Clayton Kershaw	5.00
BHP86	Matt Antonelli	1.00
BHP87	Chris Parmelee	2.00
BHP88	Billy Rowell	1.00
BHP89	Chase Fontaine	1.00
BHP90	Chris Murrero	2.00
BHP91	Jamie Ortiz	1.00
BHP92	Sean Watson	1.00
BHP93	Brooks Brown	1.00
BHP94	Brad Furnish	3.00
BHP95	Chad Huffman	3.00
BHP96	Pedro Beato	3.00
BHP97	Kyler Burke	1.00
BHP98	Stephen Englund	1.00
BHP99	Tyler Norrick	1.00
BHP100	Brent Sinkbeil	1.00

2006 Bowman Originals

		NM/M
Complete Set (55):		50.00
Common Player (1-35):		1.00
Common Player (36-55):		5.00
Pack (7):		50.00
Box (6):		250.00
1	David Wright	3.00
2	Derek Jeter	5.00
3	Eric Chavez	
4	Ken Griffey Jr.	4.00
5	Albert Pujols	5.00
6	Ryan Howard	5.00

#	Player	Price
7	Joe Mauer	1.50
8	Andruw Jones	1.50
9	Nomar Garciaparra	2.00
10	Michael Young	1.00
11	Miguel Tejada	1.50
12	Alfonso Soriano	2.00
13	Alex Rodriguez	5.00
14	Paul Konerko	1.50
15	Carl Crawford	1.00
16	Nick Johnson	1.00
17	Jim Thome	1.50
18	Ivan Rodriguez	1.50
19	Chipper Jones	2.00
20	Pedro Martinez	2.00
21	Carlos Delgado	1.50
22	Roger Clemens	5.00
23	Mark Teixeira	1.50
24	Manny Ramirez	2.00
25	Barry Bonds	5.00
26	Vernon Wells	1.00
27	Vladimir Guerrero	2.00
28	Miguel Cabrera	2.00
29	Victor Martinez	1.00
30	Derrek Lee	1.50
31	Carlos Lee	1.00
32	Ichiro Suzuki	3.00
33	Johan Santana	1.50
34	David Ortiz	2.00
35	Jason Bay	1.50
36	Kendry Morales (RC)	3.00
37	Nick Markakis (RC)	4.00
38	Conor Jackson (RC)	2.00
39	Justin Verlander (RC)	5.00
40	Ryan Zimmerman (RC)	5.00
41	Jeremy Hermida (RC)	2.00
42	Dan Uggla (RC)	3.00
43	Matt Kemp (RC)	4.00
44	Lastings Milledge (RC)	3.00
45	Kenji Johjima RC	2.00
46	Ian Kinsler (RC)	3.00
47	Hanley Ramirez RC	6.00
48	Melky Cabrera (RC)	2.00
49	Willy Aybar (RC)	2.00
50	Jonathan Papelbon (RC)	3.00
51	Prince Fielder (RC)	5.00
52	Cole Hamels (RC)	5.00
53	Josh Barfield (RC)	2.00
54	Alay Soler RC	2.00
55	Russell Martin (RC)	2.00

Blue
Blue (1-55): 2-3X
Production 249 Sets

Black

Black (1-55): 3-5X
Production 99 Sets

Red
No Pricing
Production One Set

Printing Plates
No Pricing
Production one set per color.

Buyback Autographs

Card	NM/M
Adam Loewen/68	15.00
Adam Loewen/719	10.00
Adam Loewen/198	15.00
Adrian Gonzalez/976	25.00
Albert Pujols/44	250.00
Albert Pujols/50	250.00
Alex Gordon/49	40.00
Alex Gordon/32	40.00
Andrew McCutchen/391	40.00
Andrew McCutchen/33	60.00
Andrew McCutchen/561	35.00
Andruw Jones/34	30.00
Andruw Jones/22	30.00
Andruw Jones/24	30.00
Andruw Jones/28	30.00
Andruw Jones/48	20.00
Andy LaRoche/109	20.00
Andy LaRoche/60	20.00
Andy LaRoche/66	20.00
Andy LaRoche/734	15.00
Alex Rodriguez/21	150.00
Alex Rodriguez/22	150.00
B.J. Upton/58	30.00
B.J. Upton/136	25.00
B.J. Upton/667	20.00
B.J. Upton/120	25.00
Beau Jones/576	15.00
Beau Jones/63	30.00
Beau Jones/339	20.00
Beau Jones/323	30.00
Billy Buckner/99	15.00
Billy Buckner/432	10.00
Billy Buckner/182	10.00
Billy Buckner/33	20.00
Billy Wagner/56	30.00
Billy Wagner/47	30.00
Billy Wagner/64	25.00
Billy Wagner/90	20.00
Billy Wagner/99	20.00
Billy Wagner/37	30.00
Billy Wagner/38	30.00
Brandon Phillips/46	15.00
Brandon Phillips/26	20.00
Brandon Phillips/67	10.00
Brandon Phillips/28	20.00
Brandon Phillips/32	15.00
Brandon Phillips/140	15.00
Brandon Phillips/35	15.00
Brandon Phillips/335	10.00
Brandon Phillips/257	10.00
Brandon Snyder/461	15.00
Brandon Wood/20	15.00
Brandon Wood/100	20.00
Brandon Wood/627	15.00
Brandon Wood/239	20.00
Brent Cox/240	15.00
Brent Cox/66	20.00
Brent Cox/688	15.00
Carl Crawford/37	25.00
Carl Crawford/40	25.00
Carl Crawford/20	30.00
Carl Crawford/30	25.00
Carl Crawford/71	20.00
Carl Crawford/71	20.00
Carl Crawford/334	15.00
Carl Crawford/279	15.00
Carlos Silva/996	10.00
Cesar Ramos/25	25.00
Cesar Ramos/76	25.00
Cesar Ramos/161	15.00
Cesar Ramos/732	10.00
Chase Utley/23	100.00
Chase Utley/150	75.00
Chase Utley/303	75.00
Chase Utley/23	80.00
Chaz Roe/73	15.00
Chaz Roe/774	10.00
Chaz Roe/132	10.00
Chien-Ming Wang/25	200.00
Chien-Ming Wang/25	250.00
Chien-Ming Wang/25	200.00
Chien-Ming Wang/25	250.00
Chipper Jones/20	85.00
Chipper Jones/20	85.00
Chipper Jones/20	85.00
Chipper Jones/20	85.00
Chipper Jones/20	85.00
Chris Young/70	20.00
Chris Young/772	20.00
Chris Young/146	20.00
Chris Young/211	20.00
Chris Young/44	75.00
Chris Young/88	40.00
Chris Young/81	40.00
Chris Young/558	25.00
Clint Barmes/61	20.00
Clint Barmes/113	15.00
Clint Barmes/375	15.00
Clint Barmes/430	10.00
Conor Jackson/70	15.00
Conor Jackson/78	20.00
Conor Jackson/457	10.00
Conor Jackson/360	10.00
Craig Italiano/160	15.00
Craig Italiano/658	10.00
Craig Italiano/163	15.00
Dan Johnson/276	15.00
Dan Johnson/575	15.00
Dan Johnson/101	15.00
Dan Johnson/29	10.00
David Wright/543	60.00
David Wright/264	120.00
David Wright/45	70.00
David Wright/64	70.00
Derrek Lee/61	25.00
Dontrelle Willis/147	15.00
Dontrelle Willis/55	20.00
Dontrelle Willis/525	15.00
Dontrelle Willis/79	15.00
Dontrelle Willis/78	20.00
Dontrelle Willis/24	15.00
Dontrelle Willis/36	15.00
Eli Iorg/167	15.00
Eli Iorg/151	15.00
Eli Iorg/672	15.00
Eric Chavez/34	20.00
Eric Chavez/301	15.00
Eric Chavez/25	15.00
Eric Chavez/70	15.00
Eric Chavez/62	15.00
Ervin Santana/369	15.00
Ervin Santana/544	15.00
Ervin Santana/51	20.00
Ervin Santana/109	20.00
Ervin Santana/76	20.00
Ervin Santana/67	20.00
Ervin Santana/62	50.00
Fausto Carmona/131	10.00
Fausto Carmona/56	15.00
Fausto Carmona/263	15.00
Francisco Cordero/64	10.00
Francisco Cordero/87	10.00
Francisco Cordero/49	10.00
Francisco Cordero/138	10.00
Francisco Cordero/140	10.00
Francisco Liriano/142	35.00
Francisco Liriano/63	40.00
Francisco Liriano/47	35.00
Francisco Liriano/222	10.00
Francisco Liriano/350	25.00
Francisco Liriano/212	65.00
Garrett Atkins/121	15.00
Garrett Atkins/27	20.00
Garrett Atkins/209	15.00
Garrett Atkins/581	15.00
Garrett Atkins/38	15.00
Hanley Ramirez/435	40.00
Hanley Ramirez/98	50.00
Hanley Ramirez/466	40.00
Jason Bay/24	30.00
Jason Bay/298	20.00
Jason Bay/50	25.00
Jason Bay/58	25.00
Jason Bay/70	25.00
Jason Botts/29	15.00
Jason Botts/31	15.00
Jason Botts/269	10.00
Jason Botts/46	15.00
Jason Botts/59	15.00
Jason Botts/577	10.00
Jason Kubel/232	15.00
Jason Kubel/127	15.00
Jason Kubel/25	25.00
Jason Kubel/77	20.00
Jason Marquis/944	8.00
Jason Marquis/26	15.00
Jay Bruce/66	125.00
Jay Bruce/434	50.00
Jed Lowrie/123	15.00
Jed Lowrie/141	15.00
Jed Lowrie/716	15.00
Jeff Mathis/127	15.00
Jeff Mathis/185	15.00
Jeff Mathis/97	15.00
Jerome Williams/292	8.00
Jerome Williams/48	10.00
Jerome Williams/45	10.00
Jerome Williams/97	8.00
Joel Guzman/274	15.00
Joel Guzman/54	10.00
Joel Guzman/53	10.00
Joel Zumaya/233	15.00
Joel Zumaya/57	15.00
Joel Zumaya/96	25.00
Joel Zumaya/582	15.00
Joel Zumaya/163	15.00
John Drennen/78	10.00
John Drennen/387	10.00
John Van Benschoten/51	15.00
John Van Benschoten/24	20.00
John Van Benschoten/130	15.00
John Van Benschoten/272	10.00
Jonny Gomes/341	15.00
Jonny Gomes/27	40.00
Jonny Gomes/175	15.00
Jonny Gomes/363	10.00
Josh Barfield/158	15.00
Josh Barfield/557	10.00
Josh Barfield/178	15.00
Josh Geer/343	10.00
Josh Geer/138	10.00
Justin Huber/32	15.00
Justin Huber/99	15.00
Justin Huber/572	10.00
Justin Huber/212	10.00
Justin Huber/26	20.00
Justin Huber/37	15.00
Justin Upton/1000	80.00
Kevin Gregg/988	10.00
Lastings Milledge/166	20.00
Lastings Milledge/166	20.00
Lastings Milledge/632	15.00
Mark Mulder/20	10.00
Mark Mulder/20	10.00
Mark Mulder/20	10.00
Mark Mulder/20	10.00
Mark Mulder/20	10.00
Matt Cain/36	40.00
Matt Cain/389	20.00
Matt Maloney/350	15.00
Matt Maloney/50	40.00
Matt Maloney/20	40.00
Matt Maloney/60	30.00
Matt Torra/456	15.00
Matt Torra/37	20.00
Melky Cabrera/163	20.00
Melky Cabrera/191	20.00
Melky Cabrera/60	20.00
Melky Cabrera/24	30.00
Melky Cabrera/95	20.00
Merkin Valdez/41	15.00
Merkin Valdez/325	8.00
Merkin Valdez/70	15.00
Merkin Valdez/66	15.00
Micah Owings/138	15.00
Micah Owings/648	10.00
Michael Bowden/27	20.00
Michael Bowden/24	20.00
Michael Bowden/449	15.00
Miguel Cabrera/70	40.00
Miguel Cabrera/70	40.00
Miguel Cabrera/69	40.00
Miguel Cabrera/98	40.00
Miguel Cabrera/63	40.00
Miguel Cabrera/130	50.00
Mike Costanzo/466	15.00
Mike Lamb/993	10.00
Morgan Ensberg/74	15.00
Morgan Ensberg/334	10.00
Morgan Ensberg/64	15.00
Nick Swisher/342	15.00
Nick Swisher/73	20.00
Nick Swisher/31	30.00
Nolan Reimold/41	30.00
Nolan Reimold/419	15.00
Nolan Reimold/30	40.00
Rich Harden/87	15.00
Rich Harden/82	15.00
Rich Harden/70	15.00
Rich Harden/68	10.00
Rich Harden/68	15.00
Ricky Nolasco/52	25.00
Ricky Nolasco/256	20.00
Ricky Nolasco/148	25.00
Robinson Cano/90	60.00
Robinson Cano/72	60.00
Robinson Cano/101	60.00
Robinson Cano/222	50.00
Roy Oswalt/96	25.00
Roy Oswalt/42	30.00
Roy Oswalt/61	30.00
Roy Oswalt/63	40.00
Roy Oswalt/25	50.00
Roy Oswalt/199	25.00
Russell Martin/33	20.00
Russell Martin/96	15.00
Russell Martin/577	15.00
Russell Martin/252	15.00
Ryan Howard/50	350.00
Scott Elbert/99	30.00
Scott Elbert/330	25.00
Scott Elbert/60	30.00
Scott Kazmir/99	15.00
Scott Kazmir/36	15.00
Scott Kazmir/153	10.00
Scott Kazmir/26	15.00
Scott Kazmir/661	12.00
Scott Mathieson/472	8.00
Scott Mathieson/108	20.00
Scott Mathieson/25	20.00
Scott Thorman/980	10.00
Sean West/394	15.00
Sean West/70	20.00
Shaun Marcum/133	15.00
Shaun Marcum/26	20.00
Shaun Marcum/138	20.00
Shaun Marcum/153	20.00
Shaun Marcum/33	25.00
Travis Buck/60	20.00
Travis Buck/44	30.00
Travis Buck/747	10.00
Travis Hafner/114	20.00
Travis Hafner/96	20.00
Travis Hafner/386	20.00
Travis Hafner/45	25.00
Travis Hafner/280	20.00
Trevor Bell/146	15.00
Trevor Bell/28	15.00
Trevor Bell/689	15.00
Troy Patton/211	15.00
Troy Patton/510	20.00
Troy Patton/736	15.00
Vernon Wells/52	25.00
Vernon Wells/100	25.00
Vernon Wells/25	40.00
Vernon Wells/96	25.00
Vernon Wells/68	25.00
Vernon Wells/56	25.00
Vernon Wells/40	40.00
Vernon Wells/29	40.00
Vernon Wells/426	20.00
Vladimir Guerrero/21	80.00
Vladimir Guerrero/45	60.00
Vladimir Guerrero/20	80.00
Wade Townsend/423	15.00
Wade Townsend/53	20.00
Wily Mo Pena/79	20.00
Wily Mo Pena/70	20.00
Wily Mo Pena/69	20.00
Wily Mo Pena/134	20.00
Wily Mo Pena/62	20.00
Xavier Nady/105	20.00
Xavier Nady/72	20.00
Xavier Nady/192	15.00
Xavier Nady/213	15.00
Xavier Nady/294	15.00
Xavier Nady/41	20.00
Yunel Escobar/69	30.00
Yunel Escobar/395	20.00
Yusmeiro Petit/68	20.00
Yusmeiro Petit/102	20.00
Yusmeiro Petit/160	20.00
Yusmeiro Petit/630	15.00

Prospects

	NM/M
Common Player:	2.00
Blue:	1.5-2X
Production 249 Sets	
Black:	2-4X

DEXTER FOWLER

Production 99 Sets

Red:	No Pricing
Production One Set	

#	Player	Price
1	Cameron Maybin	5.00
2	Koby Clemens	2.00
3	Lance Broadway	2.00
4	Chris Dickerson	2.00
5	Garrett Mock	2.00
6	Ben Copeland	2.00
7	Nick Adenhart	2.00
8	Brad McCann	3.00
9	Dustin Majewski	2.00
10	Jimmy Barthmaier	2.00
11	Michael Aubrey	2.00
12	Evan Longoria	12.00
13	Clayton Kershaw	8.00
14	Juan Francia	2.00
15	Elvis Andrus	8.00
16	Mark Trumbo	2.00
17	Shawn Riggans	2.00
18	Asdrubal Cabrera	3.00
19	Mark McLemore	2.00
20	Radhames Liz	2.00
21	Mat Gamel	5.00
22	Wilkin Ramirez	2.00
23	Jared Lansford	2.00
24	Hunter Pence	4.00
25	Justin Upton	10.00
26	Brent Dlugach	2.00
27	B.J. Szymanski	2.00
28	Stephen Marek	2.00
29	Shaun Cumberland	2.00
30	Yovani Gallardo	4.00
31	Will Venable	2.00
32	A.J. Shappi	2.00
33	Dallas Trahern	2.00
34	Jason Jaramillo	2.00
35	Jose Tabata	5.00
36	Jose Campusano	2.00
37	Ryan Patterson	2.00
38	Andrew Pinckney	2.00
39	Dexter Fowler	2.00
40	Cody Johnson	3.00
41	Steve Murphy	2.00
42	Mark Reed	2.00
43	Chris Iannetta	2.00
44	Michael Hollimon	2.00
45	Omir Santos	2.00
46	Diory Hernandez	2.00
47	Matt Tolbert	2.00
48	Jeff Frazier	2.00
49	Max Ramirez	3.00
50	Alex Gordon	4.00
51	Steve Garrabrants	2.00
52	Steven Baker	2.00
53	Ryan Klosterman	2.00
54	Michael Collins	2.00
55	Corey Wimberly	2.00

2006 Bowman Sterling

FIELDER

	NM/M
Common Relic:	5.00
Pack (5):	60.00
Box (6):	300.00
CB Carlos Beltran	8.00
CB2 Carlos Beltran	8.00
LB Lance Berkman	5.00
HB Hank Blalock	5.00
BLB Barry Bonds	20.00
MC Miguel Cabrera	10.00
MC2 Miguel Cabrera	10.00
RC Robinson Cano	15.00
CC Chris Carpenter	8.00
EC Eric Chavez	5.00
JDD Johnny Damon	8.00
AD Adam Dunn	5.00
ME Morgan Ensberg	5.00
VG Vladimir Guerrero	10.00
JRH Rich Harden	5.00
TH Todd Helton	8.00
RH Ryan Howard	25.00
AJ Andruw Jones	8.00
LWJ Chipper Jones	8.00
PK Paul Konerko	8.00
MCM Mickey Mantle	80.00
PM Pedro Martinez	8.00
HM Hideki Matsui	20.00
MM Mark Mulder	5.00

Abbr	Player	Price
DO	David Ortiz	10.00
MJP	Mike Piazza	10.00
AP	Albert Pujols	25.00
AP2	Albert Pujols	25.00
AR	Aramis Ramirez	8.00
MR	Manny Ramirez	10.00
MR2	Manny Ramirez	10.00
BR	Brian Roberts	5.00
AER	Alex Rodriguez	20.00
IR	Ivan Rodriguez	8.00
SR	Scott Rolen	8.00
JAS	Johan Santana	8.00
CS	Curt Schilling	8.00
GS	Grady Sizemore	8.00
APS	Alfonso Soriano	10.00
IS	Ichiro Suzuki	25.00
MCT	Mark Teixeira	8.00
MT	Miguel Tejada	8.00
JHT	Jim Thome	8.00
DWW	Dontrelle Willis	8.00
DW	David Wright	20.00

Common Rookie: 4.00

Abbr	Player	Price
BA	Brian Anderson (RC)	4.00
WA	Willy Aybar (RC)	4.00
BB	Brian Bannister (RC)	4.00
CRB	Chad Billingsley (RC)	10.00
BON	Boof Bonser (RC)	4.00
MCC	Melky Cabrera (RC)	6.00
JD	Joey Devine RC	4.00
SD	Stephen Drew (RC)	10.00
KF	Kevin Frandsen (RC)	4.00
RK	Ryan Garko (RC)	4.00
DG	David Gassner (RC)	4.00
EG	Enrique Gonzalez (RC)	4.00
FG	Franklin Gutierrez (RC)	4.00
TGJ	Tony Gwynn Jr. (RC)	6.00
CRH	Craig Hansen (RC)	4.00
CJ	Conor Jackson (RC)	4.00
CHJ	Chuck James (RC)	4.00
CJJ	Casey Janssen RC	4.00
KJ	Kenji Johjima RC	4.00
JJ	Josh Johnson (RC)	8.00
JK	Jeff Karstens RC	4.00
MK	Matt Kemp (RC)	8.00
HK	Howie Kendrick (RC)	8.00
FL	Francisco Liriano (RC)	10.00
JL	James Loney (RC)	8.00
NM	Nick Markakis (RC)	8.00
RM	Russell Martin (RC)	4.00
SM	Scott Mathieson (RC)	4.00
JM	Jeff Mathis (RC)	4.00
KM	Kendry Morales (RC)	4.00
SO	Scott Olsen (RC)	4.00
JP	Jonathan Papelbon (RC)	6.00
DP	David Pauley (RC)	4.00
MPP	Mike Pelfrey RC	10.00
HP	Hayden Penn (RC)	4.00
CQ	Carlos Quentin (RC)	4.00
HR	Hanley Ramirez (RC)	10.00
AS	Anibal Sanchez (RC)	4.00
JS	James Shields RC	4.00
MS	Matt Smith (RC)	4.00
ALS	Alay Soler RC	4.00
JBS	Jeremy Sowers (RC)	4.00
TT	Taylor Tankersley (RC)	4.00
JTA	Jordan Tata RC	6.00
DU	Dan Uggla (RC)	6.00
JV	Justin Verlander (RC)	10.00
JW	Jered Weaver (RC)	8.00
RZ	Ryan Zimmerman (RC)	10.00
BZ	Benjamin Zobrist (RC)	6.00
JZ	Joel Zumaya (RC)	4.00

Common Rookie Autograph:

Abbr	Player	Price
JLB	Josh Barfield (RC)	10.00
JCB	Jason Botts (RC)	10.00
AE	Andre Ethier (RC)	30.00
JI	Joe Inglett RC	15.00
IK	Ian Kinsler (RC)	30.00
LM	Lastings Milledge (RC)	15.00
ZM	Zach Miner (RC)	10.00
RN	Ricky Nolasco (RC)	20.00

Common Rookie Relic Auto.:

Abbr	Player	Price
JB	Jason Bulger (RC)	10.00
PF	Prince Fielder (RC)	50.00
CI	Chris Iannetta (RC)	15.00
CH	Cole Hamels (RC)	40.00
HK	Howie Kendrick (RC)	15.00
JTL	Jon Lester (RC)	40.00
BL	Bobby Livingston (RC)	10.00
MN	Erik Naposki RC	10.00
RP	Ronny Paulino (RC)	10.00
YP	Yusmeiro Petit (RC)	15.00
MP	Martin Prado (RC)	20.00
ALR	Anthony Reyes (RC)	15.00
JT	Jack Taschner (RC)	10.00
ST	Scott Thorman (RC)	10.00

Refractors

Rookies:	1.5-2X
Rookie Auto.:	1-2X
Rookie Relic Auto.:	1-2X

Relics:		1-2X
Prospects:		1.5-2X
Prospect Auto.:		1-2X
Production 199 Sets		

Black Refractors
No Pricing
Production 25 Sets

Printing Plates
No Pricing
Production One Set

Red Refractors
No Pricing
Production One Set

Gold Refractors
No Pricing
Production 10 Sets

Prospect Autographs

		NM/M
BA	Brandon Allen	8.00
MAA	Matt Antonelli	15.00
MA	Mike Aviles	25.00
PB	Pedro Beato	10.00
RB	Ronny Bourquin	10.00
BB	Brooks Brown	10.00
TB	Travis Buck	15.00
KB	Kyler Burke	10.00
JBU	Joshua Butler	10.00
AC	Adrian Cardenas	25.00
KC	Koby Clemens	15.00
JC	Jeff Clement	10.00
TC	Tyler Colvin	40.00
HC	Hank Conger	20.00
TC	Trevor Crowe	10.00
CD	Chris Dickerson	10.00
KD	Kyle Drabek	15.00
DE	Dustin Evans	10.00
SE	Steven Evarts	15.00
MF	Michael Felix	10.00
BF	Brad Furnish	10.00
AG	Alex Gordon	20.00
DH	Daniel Haigwood	10.00
BH	Brett Hayes	10.00
CH	Chase Headley	25.00
LH	Luke Hochevar	20.00
DHU	David Huff	15.00
CHH	Chad Huffman	15.00
JJ	Jeremy Jeffress	15.00
CJ	Cody Johnson	15.00
KJ	Kris Johnson	15.00
CK	Clayton Kershaw	40.00
KK	Kasey Kiker	10.00
EL	Evan Longoria	125.00
PL	Pedro Lopez	8.00
CM	Cameron Maybin	35.00
MM	Mark McCormick	10.00
KM	Kyle McCulloch	10.00
GM	Garrett Mock	10.00
BM	Brandon Moss	15.00
JN	Jason Neighborgall	10.00
AO	Adam Ottavino	10.00
MO	Micah Owings	10.00
CP	Chris Parmelee	10.00
TP	Troy Patton	10.00
EP	Elvin Puello	10.00
CR	Cory Rasmus	10.00
JR	Joshua Rodriguez	10.00
BR	Billy Rowell	20.00
JS	Jarrod Saltalamacchia	15.00
BSI	Brett Sinkbeil	10.00
BS	Brandon Snyder	10.00
WT	Wade Townsend	10.00
CT	Chad Tracy	10.00
JU	Justin Upton	75.00
SWA	Sean Watson	10.00
JW	Johnny Whittleman	15.00
CW	Colten Willems	15.00
BW	Brandon Wood	20.00
SW	Steven Wright	10.00

Prospect

		NM/M
NA	Nick Adenhart	5.00
EA	Elvis Andrus	12.00
MRA	Michael Aubrey	5.00
JRB	Jimmy Barthmaier	5.00
AJC	Asdrubal Cabrera	6.00
JAC	Jose Campusano	5.00
YC	Yung-Chi Chen	15.00
ADC	Adam Coe	5.00
MC	Michael Collins	5.00
BC	Ben Copeland	5.00
SC	Shaun Cumberland	5.00
CD	Chris Dickerson	5.00
BD	Brent Dlugach	5.00
DF	Dexter Fowler	6.00
JF	Juan Francia	5.00
JKF	Jeff Frazier	5.00
YG	Yovani Gallardo	8.00
MG	Mat Gamel	15.00
SGG	Steve Garrabrants	5.00
DIH	Diory Hernandez	5.00
MH	Michael Hollimon	5.00
JJ	Jason Jaramillo	5.00
BJ	Brandon Jones	5.00
RK	Ryan Klosterman	5.00
JTL	Jared Lansford	5.00
RL	Radhames Liz	5.00
EM	Evan MacLane	5.00
DM	Dustin Majewski	6.00
SM	Stephen Marek	5.00
BWM	Brad McCann	5.00
MSM	Mark McLemore	5.00
GLM	Garrett Mock	5.00
SMM	Steve Murphy	5.00
ON	Oswaldo Navarro	5.00
RP	Ryan Patterson	6.00
HP	Hunter Pence	6.00
AP	Andrew Pinckney	5.00
MRR	Max Ramirez	6.00
WR	Wilkin Ramirez	5.00
MR	Mark Reed	5.00
SR	Shawn Riggans	5.00
OS	Omir Santos	5.00
AS	A.J. Shappi	5.00
BJS	B.J. Szymanski	5.00
JT	Jose Tabata	10.00
CMT	Matt Tolbert	8.00
DT	Dallas Trahern	5.00
MT	Mark Trumbo	6.00
WV	Will Venable	5.00
CW	Corey Wimberly	5.00

2007 Bowman

	NM/M
Complete Set (237):	
Common Player:	.15
Common RC (201-220):	.25
Common RC Auto.:	10.00
Pack (10):	3.00
Box (24):	55.00
1 Hanley Ramirez	.50
2 Justin Verlander	.50
3 Ryan Zimmerman	.40
4 Jered Weaver	.25
5 Stephen Drew	.50
6 Jonathan Papelbon	.50
7 Melky Cabrera	.25
8 Francisco Liriano	.25
9 Prince Fielder	.75
10 Dan Uggla	.25
11 Jeremy Sowers	.15
12 Carlos Quentin	.15
13 Chuck James	.15
14 Andre Ethier	.25
15 Cole Hamels	.50
16 Kenji Johjima	.25
17 Chad Bilingsley	.25
18 Ian Kinsler	.25
19 Jason Hirsh	.15
20 Nicholas Markakis	.25
21 Jeremy Hermida	.15
22 Ryan Shealy	.15
23 Scott Olsen	.15
24 Russell Martin	.40
25 Conor Jackson	.25
26 Erik Bedard	.40
27 Brian McCann	.25
28 Michael Barrett	.15
29 Brandon Phillips	.40
30 Garrett Atkins	.25
31 Freddy Garcia	.15
32 Mark Loretta	.15
33 Craig Biggio	.25
34 Jeremy Bonderman	.25
35 Johan Santana	.75
36 Jorge Posada	.40
37 Brian Bannister	.15
38 Carlos Delgado	.50
39 Gary Mathews Jr.	.15
40 Mike Cameron	.15
41 Adrian Beltre	.25
42 Freddy Sanchez	.15
43 Austin Kearns	.15
44 Mark Buehrle	.15
45 Miguel Cabrera	.75
46 Josh Beckett	.50
47 Chone Figgins	.25
48 Edgar Renteria	.25
49 Derek Lowe	.15
50 Ryan Howard	1.50
51 Shawn Green	.15
52 Jason Giambi	.50
53 Ervin Santana	.15
54 Jack Wilson	.15
55 Roy Oswalt	.50
56 Danny Haren	.25
57 Jose Vidro	.15
58 Kevin Millwood	.15
59 Jim Edmonds	.25
60 Carl Crawford	.50
61 Randy Wolf	.15
62 Paul LoDuca	.15
63 Johnny Estrada	.15
64 Brian Roberts	.25
65 Manny Ramirez	.75
66 Jose Contreras	.15
67 Josh Barfield	.15
68 Juan Pierre	.15
69 David DeJesus	.15
70 Gary Sheffield	.40
71 Jon Lieber	.15
72 Randy Johnson	.75
73 Rickie Weeks	.25
74 Brian Giles	.15
75 Ichiro Suzuki	1.00
76 Nick Swisher	.25
77 Justin Morneau	.50
78 Scott Kazmir	.25
79 Lyle Overbay	.15
80 Alfonso Soriano	.75
81 Brandon Webb	.25
82 Joe Crede	.15
83 Corey Patterson	.15
84 Kenny Rogers	.15
85 Ken Griffey Jr.	1.50
86 Cliff Lee	.15
87 Mike Lowell	.25
88 Marcus Giles	.15
89 Orlando Cabrera	.25
90 Derek Jeter	2.00
91 Josh Johnson	.15
92 Carlos Guillen	.15
93 Bill Hall	.25
94 Michael Cuddyer	.15
95 Miguel Tejada	.25
96 Todd Helton	.50
97 C.C. Sabathia	.25
98 Tadahito Iguchi	.15
99 Jose Reyes	.75
100 David Wright	1.00
101 Barry Zito	.25
102 Jake Peavy	.25
103 Richie Sexson	.40
104 A.J. Burnett	.15
105 Eric Chavez	.25
106 Jorge Cantu	.15
107 Grady Sizemore	.50
108 Bronson Arroyo	.15
109 Mike Mussina	.40
110 Magglio Ordonez	.25
111 Anibal Sanchez	.15
112 Jeff Francoeur	.40
113 Kevin Youkilis	.40
114 Aubrey Huff	.15
115 Carlos Zambrano	.25
116 Mark Teahen	.15
117 Carlos Silva	.15
118 Pedro Martinez	.50
119 Hideki Matsui	.75
120 Mike Piazza	.75
121 Jason Schmidt	.25
122 Greg Maddux	1.50
123 Joe Blanton	.15
124 Chris Carpenter	.25
125 David Ortiz	.75
126 Alex Rios	.25
127 Nick Johnson	.15
128 Carlos Lee	.25
129 Pat Burrell	.25
130 Ben Sheets	.25
131 Kazuo Matsui	.15
132 Adam Dunn	.50
133 Jermaine Dye	.25
134 Curt Schilling	.75
135 Chad Tracy	.15
136 Vladimir Guerrero	.75
137 Melvin Mora	.15
138 John Smoltz	.25
139 Craig Monroe	.15
140 Dontrelle Willis	.25
141 Jeff Francis	.15
142 Chipper Jones	.75
143 Frank Thomas	.50
144 Brett Myers	.15
145 Xavier Nady	.15
146 Robinson Cano	.40
147 Jeff Kent	.25
148 Scott Rolen	.25
149 Roy Halladay	.50
150 Joe Mauer	.50
151 Bobby Abreu	.25
152 Matt Cain	.25
153 Hank Blalock	.15
154 Chris Capuano	.15
155 Jake Westbrook	.15
156 Javier Vazquez	.15
157 Garret Anderson	.15
158 Aramis Ramirez	.40
159 Mark Kotsay	.15
160 Matthew Kemp	.25
161 Adrian Gonzalez	.25
162 Felix Hernandez	.25
163 David Eckstein	.15
164 Curtis Granderson	.40
165 Paul Konerko	.25
166 Orlando Hudson	.15
167 Tim Hudson	.25
168 J.D. Drew	.25
169 Chien-Ming Wang	.50
170 Jimmy Rollins	.25
171 Matt Morris	.15
172 Raul Ibanez	.15
173 Mark Teixeira	.40
174 Ted Lilly	.15
175 Albert Pujols	2.00
176 Carlos Beltran	.50
177 Lance Berkman	.40
178 Ivan Rodriguez	.50
179 Torii Hunter	.25
180 Johnny Damon	.50
181 Chase Utley	.75
182 Jason Bay	.40
183 Jeff Weaver	.15
184 Troy Glaus	.25
185 Rocco Baldelli	.15
186 Rafael Furcal	.25
187 Jim Thome	.50
188 Travis Hafner	.40
189 Matt Holliday	.50
190 Andruw Jones	.50
191 Ramon Hernandez	.15
192 Victor Martinez	.25
193 Aaron Hill	.15
194 Michael Young	.25
195 Vernon Wells	.25
196 Mark Mulder	.15
197 Derrek Lee	.50
198 Tom Glavine	.25
199 Chris Young	.25
200 Alex Rodriguez	2.00
201 Delmon Young (RC)	.50
202 Alexi Casilla RC	.25
203 Shawn Riggans (RC)	.25
204 Jeff Baker (RC)	.50
205 Hector Gimenez (RC)	.25
206 Ubaldo Jimenez (RC)	2.50
207 Adam Lind (RC)	.50
208 Joaquin Arias (RC)	.25
209 David Murphy (RC)	.25
210 Daisuke Matsuzaka RC	3.00
211 Jerry Owens (RC)	.25
212 Ryan Sweeney (RC)	.25
213 Kei Igawa RC	.75
214 Fred Lewis (RC)	.50
215 Philip Humber (RC)	.25
216 Kevin Hooper (RC)	.25
217 Jeff Fiorentino (RC)	.25
218 Michael Bourn (RC)	.50
219 Hideki Okajima RC	1.00
219 Hideki Okajima/Auto. RC	20.00
220 Josh Fields (RC)	.50
221 Andrew Miller/Auto. RC	15.00
222 Troy Tulowitzki/Auto. (RC)	25.00
223 Ryan Braun/Auto. RC	15.00
224 Oswaldo Navarro/Auto. RC	10.00
225 Philip Humber/Auto. RC	15.00
226 Mitch Maier/Auto. (RC)	15.00
227 Jerry Owens/Auto. (RC)	15.00
228 Mike Rabelo/Auto. RC	20.00
229 Delwyn Young/Auto. RC	10.00
230 Miguel Montero/Auto. RC	15.00
231 Akinori Iwamura/Auto. RC	20.00
232 Matt Lindstrom/Auto. (RC)	10.00
233 Josh Hamilton/Auto. (RC)	40.00
235 Elijah Dukes/Auto. RC	10.00
236 Sean Henn/Auto. (RC)	10.00
237 Barry Bonds	2.00

Blue
Blue:	2-4X
Blue RC Auto.:	1X
Production 500 Sets	

Gold
Gold (1-220): 1-2X
Inserted 1:1

Orange
Orange:	3-6X
Orange RC Auto.:	1-1.5X
Production 250 Sets	

Red
No Pricing
Production One Set

Printing Plates
No Pricing
Production one set per color.

Alex Rodriguez Road to 500

	NM/M
Common Rodriguez:	2.00
Inserted 2:Box	
Autograph:	No Pricing
Production One Set	

Chrome Prospects

	NM/M
Complete Set (110):	50.00
Common Player:	.50
Inserted 2:Hobby Pack	
1 Cooper Brannon	1.00
2 Jason Taylor	1.50
3 Shawn O'Malley	1.00
4 Robert Alcombrack	1.00
5 Dellin Betances	2.00
6 Jeremy Papelbon	1.00
7 Adam Carr	1.00
8 Matthew Clarkson	.50
9 Darin McDonald	1.00
10 Brandon Rice	1.00
11 Matthew Sweeney	1.50
12 Scott Deal	1.00
13 Brennan Boesch	1.00
14 Scott Taylor	1.00
15 Michael Brantley	2.00
16 Yahmed Yema	1.00
17 Brandon Morrow	1.00
18 Cole Garner	1.00
19 Erik Lis	1.50
20 Lucas French	1.00
21 Aaron Cunningham	2.00
22 Ryan Schreppel	1.00
23 Kevin Russo	1.00
24 Yohan Pino	1.00
25 Michael Sullivan	.50
26 Trey Shields	.50
27 Danny Matienzo	1.00
28 Chuck Lofgren	2.00
29 Gerrit Simpson	.50
30 David Haehnel	.50
31 Marvin Lowrance	.50
32 Kevin Ardoin	.50
33 Edwin Maysonet	.50
34 Derek Griffith	.50
35 Sam Fuld	1.00
36 Chase Wright	1.50
37 Brandon Roberts	.50
38 Kyle Aselton	.50
39 Steven Sollmann	1.00
40 Michael Devaney	1.00
41 Charlie Fermaint	.50
42 Jesse Litsch	1.50
43 Bryan Hansen	.50
44 Ramon Garcia	.50
45 John Otness	1.50
46 Trey Hearne	.50
47 Habelito Hernandez	.50
48 Edgar Garcia	1.50
49 Seth Fortenberry	.50
50 Reid Brignac	2.00
51 Derek Rodriguez	.50
52 Ervin Alcantara	1.00
53 Tom Hottovy	1.00
54 Jesus Flores	1.00
55 Matt Palmer	.50
56 Brian Henderson	.50
57 John Gragg	.50
58 Jay Garthwaite	1.00
59 Esmerling Vasquez	.50
60 Gilberto Mejia	.50
61 Aaron Jensen	.50
62 Cedric Brooks	.50
63 Brandon Mann	.50
64 Myron Leslie	1.00
65 Ray Aguilar	.50
66 Jesus Guzman	2.00
67 Sean Thompson	.50
68 Jarrett Hoffpauir	1.00
69 Matt Goodson	.50
70 Neal Musser	.50
71 Tony Abreu	2.00
72 Tony Peguero	.50
73 Michael Bertram	1.00
74 Randy Wells	.50
75 Bradley Davis	.50
76 Jay Sawatski	1.00
77 Vic Buttler	.50
78 Jose Oyervidez	.50
79 Doug Deeds	1.00
80 Daniel Dement	.50
81 Spike Lundberg	.50
82 Ricardo Nanita	.50
83 Brad Knox	1.00
84 Will Venable	1.50
85 Greg Smith	1.50
86 Pedro Powell	1.00
87 Gabriel Medina	1.00
88 Duke Sardinha	.50
89 Mike Madsen	1.50
90 Rayner Bautista	.50
91 T.J. Nall	.50
92 Neil Sellers	1.00
93 Andrew Dobies	.50
94 Leo Daigle	.50
95 Brian Duensing	1.50
96 Vincent Blue	.50
97 Fernando Rodriguez	1.00
98 Derin McMains	1.00
99 Adam Bass	.50
100 Justin Ruggiano	1.50
101 Jared Burton	1.00
102 Mike Parisi	1.00
103 Aaron Peel	1.00
104 Evan Englebrook	1.00
105 Sendy Vasquez	1.00
106 Desmond Jennings	4.00
107 Clay Harris	1.00
108 Cody Strait	1.00
109 Ryan Mullins	1.00
110 Ryan Webb	1.00

Chrome Prospects Refractor
Refractor (1-110): 2-4X
Production 500 Sets

Chrome Prospects Blue Refractor
Blue Refractor (1-110): 4-8X
Production 150 Sets

Chrome Prospects Gold Refractor
Gold Refractor (1-110): 10-20X
Production 50 Sets

Chrome Prospects Orange Refractor
Orange Refractor (1-110): No Pricing
Production 25 Sets

Chrome Prospects Red Refractor
Red Refractor (1-110): No Pricing
Production Five Sets

Chrome Prospects SuperFractor
Superfractor (1-110): No Pricing
Production One Set

Chrome Prospects X-Fractor
X-Fractor (1-110): 3-6X
Production 275 Sets

Prospects

	NM/M
Complete Set (135):	
Common Player (1-110):	.25
Common Auto. (111-135):	10.00
1 Cooper Brannon	.25
2 Jason Taylor	.75
3 Shawn O'Malley	.25
4 Robert Alcombrack	.25
5 Dellin Betances	1.00
6 Jeremy Papelbon	.25
7 Adam Carr	.25
8 Matthew Clarkson	.25
9 Darin McDonald	.25
10 Brandon Rice	.25
11 Matthew Sweeney	.50
12 Scott Deal	.25
13 Brennan Boesch	.25
14 Scott Taylor	.25
15 Michael Brantley	.25
16 Yahmed Yema	.25
17 Brandon Morrow	.25
18 Cole Garner	.25
19 Erik Lis	.25
20 Lucas French	.25
21 Aaron Cunningham	.25
22 Ryan Schreppel	.25
23 Kevin Russo	.25
24 Yohan Pino	.25
25 Michael Sullivan	.25

#	Player	Price
26	Trey Shields	.25
27	Danny Matienzo	.25
28	Chuck Lofgren	.50
29	Gerrit Simpson	.25
30	David Haehnel	.25
31	Marvin Lowrance	.25
32	Kevin Ardoin	.25
33	Edwin Maysonet	.25
34	Derek Griffith	.25
35	Sam Fuld	.25
36	Chase Wright	.50
37	Brandon Roberts	.25
38	Kyle Aselton	.25
39	Steven Sollmann	.25
40	Michael Devaney	.25
41	Charlie Fermaint	.25
42	Jesse Litsch	.50
43	Bryan Hansen	.25
44	Ramon Garcia	.25
45	John Otness	.50
46	Trey Hearne	.25
47	Habelito Hernandez	.25
48	Edgar Garcia	.50
49	Seth Fortenberry	.25
50	Reid Brignac	.50
51	Derek Rodriguez	.25
52	Ervin Alcantara	.25
53	Tom Hottovy	.25
54	Jesus Flores	.25
55	Matt Palmer	.25
56	Brian Henderson	.25
57	John Gragg	.25
58	Jay Garthwaite	.25
59	Esmerling Vasquez	.25
60	Gilberto Mejia	.25
61	Aaron Jensen	.25
62	Cedric Brooks	.25
63	Brandon Mann	.25
64	Myron Leslie	.25
65	Ray Aguilar	.25
66	Jesus Guzman	.50
67	Sean Thompson	.25
68	Jarrett Hoffpauir	.25
69	Matt Goodson	.25
70	Neal Musser	.25
71	Tony Abreu	1.50
72	Tony Peguero	.25
73	Michael Bertram	.25
74	Randy Wells	.75
75	Bradley Davis	.25
76	Jay Sawatski	.25
77	Vic Buttler	.25
78	Jose Oyervidez	.25
79	Doug Deeds	.25
80	Daniel Dement	.25
81	Spike Lundberg	.25
82	Ricardo Nanita	.25
83	Brad Knox	.25
84	Will Venable	.25
85	Greg Smith	.50
86	Pedro Powell	.25
87	Gabriel Medina	.25
88	Duke Sardinha	.25
89	Mike Madsen	.25
90	Rayner Bautista	.25
91	T.J. Nall	.25
92	Neil Sellers	.25
93	Andrew Dobies	.25
94	Leo Daigle	.25
95	Brian Duensing	.50
96	Vincent Blue	.25
97	Fernando Rodriguez	.25
98	Derin McMains	.25
99	Adam Bass	.25
100	Justin Ruggiano	.25
101	Jared Burton	.25
102	Mike Parisi	.25
103	Aaron Peel	.25
104	Evan Englebrook	.25
105	Sendy Vasquez	.25
106	Desmond Jennings	1.50
107	Clay Harris	.25
108	Cody Strait	.25
109	Ryan Mullins	.25
110	Ryan Webb	.25
111	Kyle Drabek	15.00
112	Evan Longoria	50.00
113	Tyler Colvin	25.00
114	Matt Long	10.00
115	Jeremy Jeffress	10.00
116	Kasey Kiker	10.00
117	Hank Conger	10.00
118	Cody Johnson	10.00
119	David Huff	10.00
120	Tommy Hickman	10.00
121	Chris Parmelee	10.00
122	Dustin Evans	10.00
123	Brett Sinkbeil	10.00
124	Andrew Carpenter	15.00
125	Colton Willems	10.00
126	Matt Antonelli	15.00
127	Marcus Sanders	10.00
128	Joshua Rodriguez	15.00
129	Keith Weiser	10.00
130	Chad Tracy	15.00
131	Matthew Sulentic	15.00
132	Adam Ottavino	10.00
133	Jarrod Saltalamacchia	15.00
134	Kyle Blanks	20.00
135	Brad Eldred	10.00

Prospects Blue
Blue (1-110): 2-4X
Blue RC Auto. (111-135): 1X
Production 500 Sets

Prospects Gold
Gold (1-110): 1-2X

Inserted 1:1

Prospects Orange
Orange (1-110): 3-6X
Orange RC Auto. (111-135): 1-1.5X
Production 250 Sets

Prospects Red
No Pricing
Production One Set

Prospects Orange
Orange (1-110): 3-5X
Production 250 Sets

Signs of the Future

		NM/M
	Common Auto:	10.00
KD	Kyle Drabek	15.00
DB	Dellin Betances	40.00
JBC	J. Brent Cox	15.00
JD	John Drennen	10.00
DS	Denard Span	15.00
KC	Koby Clemens	10.00
EH	Estee Harris	10.00
MN	Mike Neu	10.00
RO	Ross Ohlendorf	15.00
CG	Chris Getz	10.00
AR	Adam Russell	15.00
JC	Jesus Cota	10.00
JB	John Baker	10.00
BM	Brandon Moss	10.00
CS	Chad Santos	10.00
KS	Kurt Suzuki	15.00
JJ	Jair Jurrjens	20.00
MA	Mike Aviles	10.00
TT	Taylor Teagarden	10.00
SK	Shane Komine	10.00
ME	Mike Edwards	10.00
MM	Matthew Merricks	10.00
JDA	Jamie D'Antona	10.00
JBB	John Bowker	15.00
CR	Chris Robinson	10.00
JW	Jared Wells	10.00
BF	Ben Fritz	10.00
BB	Brian Bixler	10.00
CM	Christopher McConnell	10.00
JCB	Jordan Brown	15.00
FP	Felix Pie	20.00
ER	Eric Reed	10.00
AM	Andrew McCutchen	25.00
MR	Michael Rogers	10.00
RB	Reid Brignac	20.00
RG	Rich Gardner	10.00
SG	Sean Gallagher	10.00
CJS	Chris Seddon	10.00

2007 Bowman Chrome

#	Player	NM/M
	Common Player:	.25
	Common RC:	.50
	Pack (4):	6.00
	Box (18):	95.00
1	Hanley Ramirez	.75
2	Justin Verlander	.75
3	Ryan Zimmerman	.50
4	Jered Weaver	.50
5	Stephen Drew	.40
6	Jonathan Papelbon	.50
7	Melky Cabrera	.50
8	Francisco Liriano	.25
9	Prince Fielder	1.00
10	Dan Uggla	.50
11	Jeremy Sowers	.25
12	Carlos Quentin	.25
13	Chuck James	.25
14	Andre Ethier	.50
15	Cole Hamels	.50
16	Kenji Johjima	.25
17	Chad Billingsley	.50
18	Ian Kinsler	.50
19	Jason Hirsh	.25
20	Nicholas Markakis	.50
21	Jeremy Hermida	.25
22	Ryan Shealy	.25
23	Scott Olsen	.25
24	Russell Martin	.50
25	Conor Jackson	.25
26	Erik Bedard	.50
27	Brian McCann	.50
28	Michael Barrett	.25
29	Brandon Phillips	.50
30	Garrett Atkins	.50
31	Freddy Garcia	.25
32	Mark Loretta	.25
33	Craig Biggio	.50
34	Jeremy Bonderman	.50
35	Johan Santana	.75
36	Jorge Posada	.50
37	Victor Martinez	.50
38	Carlos Delgado	.50
39	Gary Matthews	.50
40	Mike Cameron	.25
41	Adrian Beltre	.25
42	Freddy Sanchez	.25
43	Austin Kearns	.25
44	Mark Buehrle	.25
45	Miguel Cabrera	1.00
46	Josh Beckett	.75
47	Chone Figgins	.25
48	Edgar Renteria	.25
49	Derek Lowe	.25
50	Ryan Howard	2.00
51	Shawn Green	.25
52	Jason Giambi	.25
53	Ervin Santana	.25
54	Aaron Hill	.25
55	Roy Oswalt	.50
56	Danny Haren	.40
57	Jose Vidro	.25
58	Kevin Millwood	.25
59	Jim Edmonds	.25
60	Carl Crawford	.50
61	Randy Wolf	.25
62	Paul LoDuca	.25
63	Johnny Estrada	.25
64	Brian Roberts	.50
65	Manny Ramirez	1.00
66	Jose Contreras	.25
67	Josh Barfield	.25
68	Juan Pierre	.25
69	David DeJesus	.25
70	Gary Sheffield	.75
71	Michael Young	.50
72	Randy Johnson	.75
73	Rickie Weeks	.40
74	Brian Giles	.25
75	Ichiro Suzuki	1.50
76	Nick Swisher	.50
77	Justin Morneau	.75
78	Scott Kazmir	.25
79	Lyle Overbay	.25
80	Alfonso Soriano	1.00
81	Brandon Webb	.50
82	Joe Crede	.25
83	Corey Patterson	.25
84	Kenny Rogers	.25
85	Ken Griffey Jr.	2.00
86	Cliff Lee	.25
87	Mike Lowell	.25
88	Marcus Giles	.25
89	Orlando Cabrera	.50
90	Derek Jeter	2.50
91	Ramon Hernandez	.25
92	Carlos Guillen	.25
93	Bill Hall	.25
94	Michael Cuddyer	.25
95	Miguel Tejada	.75
96	Todd Helton	.75
97	C.C. Sabathia	.50
98	Tadahito Iguchi	.25
99	Jose Reyes	1.00
100	David Wright	1.00
101	Barry Zito	.50
102	Jake Peavy	.50
103	Richie Sexson	.25
104	A.J. Burnett	.25
105	Eric Chavez	.25
106	Vernon Wells	.50
107	Grady Sizemore	.75
108	Bronson Arroyo	.25
109	Mike Mussina	.50
110	Magglio Ordonez	.50
111	Anibal Sanchez	.25
112	Jeff Francoeur	.50
113	Kevin Youkilis	.25
114	Aubrey Huff	.25
115	Carlos Zambrano	.50
116	Mark Teahen	.25
117	Mark Mulder	.50
118	Pedro Martinez	1.00
119	Hideki Matsui	1.50
120	Mike Piazza	1.00
121	Jason Schmidt	.25
122	Greg Maddux	2.00
123	Joe Blanton	.25
124	Chris Carpenter	.75
125	David Ortiz	1.00
126	Alex Rios	.40
127	Nick Johnson	.25
128	Carlos Lee	.50
129	Pat Burrell	.50
130	Ben Sheets	.50
131	Derrek Lee	.50
132	Adam Dunn	.50
133	Jermaine Dye	.40
134	Curt Schilling	.75
135	Chad Tracy	.25
136	Vladimir Guerrero	1.00
137	Melvin Mora	.25
138	John Smoltz	.50
139	Craig Monroe	.25
140	Dontrelle Willis	.50
141	Jeff Francis	.25
142	Chipper Jones	1.00
143	Frank Thomas	1.00
144	Brett Myers	.25
145	Tom Glavine	.75
146	Robinson Cano	.75
147	Jeff Kent	.50
148	Scott Rolen	.75
149	Roy Halladay	.50
150	Joe Mauer	.50
151	Bobby Abreu	.50
152	Matt Cain	.50
153	Hank Blalock	.50
154	Chris Young	.50
155	Jake Westbrook	.25
156	Javier Vazquez	.25
157	Garret Anderson	.50
158	Aramis Ramirez	.50
159	Mark Kotsay	.25
160	Matthew Kemp	.50
161	Adrian Gonzalez	.50
162	Felix Hernandez	.50
163	David Eckstein	.25
164	Curtis Granderson	.50
165	Paul Konerko	.50
166	Alex Rodriguez	2.50
167	Tim Hudson	.50
168	J.D. Drew	.25
169	Chien-Ming Wang	1.00
170	Jimmy Rollins	.75
171	Matt Morris	.25
172	Raul Ibanez	.25
173	Mark Teixeira	.75
174	Ted Lilly	.25
175	Albert Pujols	2.50
176	Carlos Beltran	1.00
177	Lance Berkman	.50
178	Ivan Rodriguez	.75
179	Torii Hunter	.50
180	Johnny Damon	.75
181	Chase Utley	1.00
182	Jason Bay	.50
183	Jeff Weaver	.25
184	Troy Glaus	.50
185	Rocco Baldelli	.25
186	Rafael Furcal	.50
187	Jim Thome	.75
188	Travis Hafner	.50
189	Matt Holliday	.50
190	Andruw Jones	.50
191	Andrew Miller RC	1.00
192	Ryan Braun RC	.50
193	Oswaldo Navarro RC	.50
194	Mike Rabelo RC	.50
195	Delwyn Young (RC)	.50
196	Miguel Montero (RC)	.75
197	Matt Lindstrom (RC)	.50
198	Josh Hamilton (RC)	2.50
199	Elijah Dukes RC	.50
200	Sean Henn (RC)	.50
201	Delmon Young (RC)	.75
202	Alexi Casilla RC	.50
203	Hunter Pence (RC)	1.50
204	Jeff Baker (RC)	.50
205	Hector Gimenez (RC)	.50
206	Ubaldo Jimenez (RC)	3.00
207	Adam Lind (RC)	1.00
208	Joaquin Arias (RC)	.75
209	David Murphy (RC)	.50
210	Daisuke Matsuzaka RC	4.00
211	Jerry Owens (RC)	.50
212	Ryan Sweeney (RC)	.50
213	Kei Igawa (RC)	.75
214	Mitch Maier RC	.50
215	Philip Humber (RC)	.50
216	Troy Tulowitzki (RC)	2.50
217	Tim Lincecum RC	10.00
218	Michael Bourn (RC)	1.00
219	Hideki Okajima RC	1.00
220	Josh Fields (RC)	.50

Refractors
Refractor (1-190): 2-4X
Refractor (191-220): 1.5-2X
Inserted 4:Box

Blue Refractor
Blue Refractor (1-190): 4-6X
Blue Refractor RC (191-220): 3-5X
Production 150 Sets

Gold Refractor
Gold Refractor (1-190): 10-15X
Gold Refractor RC (191-220): 8-15X
Production 50 Sets

Orange Refractor
Orange Refractor (1-190): 10-20X
Orange Refractor RC (191-220): 10-20X
Production 25 Sets

Red Refractor
Production Five Sets

Super-Fractor
Production One Set

X-Fractor
X-Fractor (1-190): 3-5X
X-Fractor RC (191-220): 2-4X
Production 250 Sets

Printing Plates
Production One Set

Chrome Prospects

CHAMBERLAIN

		NM/M
	Common Player:	.50
	Common RC: (221-256):	10.00
BC1	Cooper Brannon	1.00
BC2	Jason Taylor	1.00
BC3	Shawn O'Malley	.50
BC4	Robert Alcombrack	.50
BC5	Dellin Betances	4.00
BC6	Jeremy Papelbon	.50
BC7	Adam Carr	.50
BC8	Matthew Clarkson	.50
BC9	Darin McDonald	.50
BC10	Brandon Rice	.50
BC11	Matthew Sweeney	1.50
BC12	Scott Deal	.50
BC13	Brennan Boesch	.50
BC14	Scott Taylor	.50
BC15	Michael Brantley	1.00
BC16	Yahmed Yema	.50
BC17	Brandon Morrow	.50
BC18	Cole Garner	.50
BC19	Erik Lis	1.00
BC20	Lucas French	.50
BC21	Aaron Cunningham	2.00
BC22	Ryan Schreppel	.50
BC23	Kevin Russo	.50
BC24	Yohan Pino	1.00
BC25	Michael Sullivan	.50
BC26	Trey Shields	1.00
BC27	Danny Matienzo	.50
BC28	Chuck Lofgren	.50
BC29	Gerrit Simpson	.50
BC30	David Haehnel	.50
BC31	Marvin Lowrance	.50
BC32	Kevin Ardoin	.50
BC33	Edwin Maysonet	.50
BC34	Derek Griffith	.50
BC35	Sam Fuld	1.00
BC36	Chase Wright	2.00
BC37	Brandon Roberts	.50
BC38	Kyle Aselton	.50
BC39	Steven Sollmann	.50
BC40	Michael Devaney	.50
BC41	Charlie Fermaint	.50
BC42	Jesse Litsch	1.00
BC43	Bryan Hansen	.50
BC44	Ramon Garcia	1.00
BC45	John Otness	.50
BC46	Trey Hearne	.50
BC47	Habelito Hernandez	.50
BC48	Edgar Garcia	.50
BC49	Seth Fortenberry	.50
BC50	Reid Brignac	1.00
BC51	Derek Rodriguez	.50
BC52	Ervin Alcantara	.50
BC53	Tom Hottovy	.50
BC54	Jesus Flores	1.00
BC55	Matt Palmer	.50
BC56	Brian Henderson	.50
BC57	John Gragg	.50
BC58	Jay Garthwaite	.50
BC59	Esmerling Vasquez	1.00
BC60	Gilberto Mejia	.50
BC61	Aaron Jensen	.50
BC62	Cedric Brooks	1.00
BC63	Brandon Mann	.50
BC64	Myron Leslie	.50
BC65	Ray Aguilar	.50
BC66	Jesus Guzman	2.00
BC67	Sean Thompson	.50
BC68	Jarrett Hoffpauir	1.00
BC69	Matt Goodson	.50
BC70	Neal Musser	.50
BC71	Tony Abreu	1.50
BC72	Tony Peguero	1.00
BC73	Michael Bertram	.50
BC74	Randy Wells	.50
BC75	Bradley Davis	.50
BC76	Jay Sawatski	.50
BC77	Vic Buttler	1.00
BC78	Jose Oyervidez	.50
BC79	Doug Deeds	1.00
BC80	Daniel Dement	.50
BC81	Spike Lundberg	.50
BC82	Ricardo Nanita	1.00
BC83	Brad Knox	1.00
BC84	Will Venable	1.00
BC85	Greg Smith	.50
BC86	Pedro Powell	.50
BC87	Gabriel Medina	.50
BC88	Duke Sardinha	.50
BC89	Mike Madsen	.50
BC90	Rayner Bautista	.50
BC91	T.J. Nall	.50
BC92	Neil Sellers	.50
BC93	Andrew Dobies	.50
BC94	Leo Daigle	.50
BC95	Brian Duensing	2.00
BC96	Vincent Blue	.50
BC97	Fernando Rodriguez	.50
BC98	Derin McMains	.50
BC99	Adam Bass	.50
BC100	Justin Ruggiano	1.00
BC101	Jared Burton	.50
BC102	Mike Parisi	.50
BC103	Aaron Peel	1.00
BC104	Evan Englebrook	.50
BC105	Sendy Vasquez	.50
BC106	Desmond Jennings	4.00
BC107	Clay Harris	1.00
BC108	Cody Strait	.50
BC109	Ryan Mullins	.50
BC110	Ryan Webb	.50
BC111	Mike Carp	1.00
BC112	Greg Porter	.50
BC113	Joe Ness	.50
BC114	Matt Camp	.50
BC115	Carlos Fisher	.50
BC116	Bryan Bass	.50
BC117	Jeff Baisley	.50
BC118	Blake Badenhop	1.00
BC119	Grant Psomas	.50
BC120	Eric Young Jr.	1.00
BC121	Henry Rodriguez	.50
BC122	Carlos Fernandez	.50
BC123	Chris Errecart	.50
BC124	Brandon Hynick	1.50
BC125	Jose Constanza	.50
BC126	Steve Delabar	.50
BC127	Raul Barron	.50
BC128	Nick DeBarr	.50
BC129	Reegie Corona	1.00
BC130	Thomas Fairchild	.50
BC131	Bryan Byrne	.50
BC132	Kurt Mertins	.50
BC133	Erik Averill	.50
BC134	Matt Young	.50
BC135	Ryan Rogowski	.50
BC136	Andrew Bailey	1.50
BC137	Jonathan Van Every	.50
BC138	Scott Shoemaker	.50
BC139	Steve Singleton	.50
BC140	Mitch Atkins	.50
BC141	Robert Rohrbaugh	1.00
BC142	Ole Sheldon	.50
BC143	Adam Ricks	.50
BC144	Daniel Mayora	1.50
BC145	Johnny Cueto	8.00
BC146	Jim Fasano	.50
BC147	Jared Goedert	1.50
BC148	Jonathan Ash	.50
BC149	Derek Miller	.50
BC150	Juan Miranda	1.50
BC151	J.R. Mathes	.50
BC152	Craig Cooper	.50
BC153	Drew Locke	.50
BC154	Michael MacDonald	.50
BC155	Ryan Norwood	.50
BC156	Tony Butler	1.50
BC157	Pat Dobson	.50
BC158	Cody Ehlers	.50
BC159	Dan Fournier	.50
BC160	Joe Gaetti	.50
BC161	Mark Wagner	1.50
BC162	Tommy Hanson	6.00
BC163	Sharlon Schoop	.50
BC164	Woods Fines	.50
BC165	Chad Boyd	.50
BC166	Kala Kaaihu	3.00
BC167	Chris Salamida	1.00
BC168	Brendan Katin	1.00
BC169	Terrance Blunt	.50
BC170	Tobi Stoner	1.00
BC171	Phil Coke	.50
BC172	O.D. Gonzalez	.50
BC173	Christopher Cody	.50
BC174	Cedric Hunter	2.00
BC175	Whit Robbins	.50
BC176	Chris Begg	.50
BC177	Nathan Southard	.50
BC178	Dan Brauer	.50
BC179	Jared Keel	.50
BC180	Chance Douglass	1.00
BC181	Daniel Murphy	1.00
BC182	Anthony Hatch	.50
BC183	Justin Byler	.50
BC184	Scott Lewis	.50
BC185	Andrew Fie	.50
BC186	Chorye Spoone	1.00
BC187	Cole Bruce	.50
BC188	Adam Cowart	1.00
BC189	Chris Nowak	.50
BC190	Gorkys Hernandez	3.00
BC191	Devin Ivany	.50
BC192	Jordan Smith	.50
BC193	Philip Britton	.50
BC194	Cole Gillespie	1.00
BC195	Brett Anderson	2.50
BC196	Joe Mather	1.00
BC197	Eddie Degerman	.50
BC198	Ronald Prettyman	.50
BC199	Patrick Reilly	.50
BC200	Tyler Clippard	1.00
BC201	Nick Van Stratten	.50
BC202	Todd Redmond	.50
BC203	Michael Martinez	.50
BC204	Alberto Bastardo	.75
BC205	Vasili Spanos	.50
BC206	Shane Benson	.50
BC207	Brent Johnson	.50
BC208	Brett Campbell	.50
BC209	Dustin Martin	.50
BC210	Chris Carter	2.00
BC211	Alfred Joseph	.50
BC212	Carlos Leon	.50
BC213	Gabriel Sanchez	1.00
BC214	Carlos Corporan	.50
BC215	Emerson Frostad	.50
BC216	Karl Gelinas	.50
BC217	Ryan Finan	.50
BC218	Noe Rodriguez	.50
BC219	Archie Gilbert	.50
BC220	Jeff Locke	2.00
BC221	Fernando Martinez/Auto.	40.00
BC222	Jeremy Papelbon/Auto.	15.00
BC223	Ryan Adams/Auto.	10.00
BC224	Chris Perez/Auto.	10.00
BC225	J.R. Towles/Auto.	15.00
BC226	Tommy Mendoza/Auto.	15.00
BC227	Jeff Samardzija/Auto.	15.00
BC228	Sergio Perez/Auto.	15.00
BC229	Justin Reed/Auto.	15.00
BC230	Luke Hochevar/Auto.	15.00
BC231	Ivan DeJesus/Auto.	15.00
'C232	Kevin Mulvey/Auto.	15.00
BC233	Chris Coghlan/Auto.	20.00
BC234	Trevor Cahill/Auto.	25.00
BC235	Peter Bourjos/Auto.	10.00
BC236	Joba Chamberlain/Auto.	50.00
BC237	Josh Rodriguez/Auto.	15.00
BC238	Tim Lincecum/Auto.	175.00
BC239	Chris Perez/Auto.	15.00
BC240	Greg Reynolds/Auto.	15.00
BC241	Wes Hodges/Auto.	15.00
BC242	Chad Reineke/Auto.	15.00
BC243	Emmanuel Burriss/Auto.	15.00
BC244	Henry Sosa/Auto.	15.00
BC245	Cesar Nicolas/Auto.	15.00
BC246	Yung II Jung/Auto.	15.00

BC247	Eric Patterson/Auto.	15.00
BC248	Hunter Pence/Auto.	25.00
BC249	Dellin Betances/Auto.	15.00
BC250	Will Venable/Auto.	20.00
BC251	Zach McAllister/Auto.	10.00
BC252	Mark Hamilton/Auto.	10.00
BC253	Paul Estrada/Auto.	15.00
BC254	Brad Lincoln/Auto.	15.00
BC255	Cedric Hunter/Auto.	20.00
BC256	Chad Rodgers/Auto.	15.00

Chrome Prospects Refractor
Refractor (1-200):	3-5X
Refractor (201-256):	1-1.5X
Production 500 Sets	

Chrome Prospects Blue Refractor
Blue Refractor (1-200):	5-10X
Blue Refractor Auto. (201-256):	1.5-2.5X
Production 150 Sets	

Chrome Prospects Gold Refractor
Gold Refractor (1-200):	15-25X
Gold Refractor Auto.(201-256):	3-5X
Production 50 Sets	

Chrome Prospects Orange Refractor
Orange Refractor (1-200):	No Pricing
Orange Refract Auto. (201-256):	No Pricing
Production 25 Sets	

Chrome Prospects Red Refractor
No Pricing	
Production Five Sets	

Chrome Prospects X-Fractor
X-Fractor (1-200):	4-8X
Production 250 Sets	
X-Fractor Auto. (201-256):	1-2X
Production 225 Sets	

2007 Bowman Draft

		NM/M
Complete Set (54):		15.00
Common RC:		.25
Hobby Pack (7):		4.00
Hobby Box (24):		80.00
1	Travis Buck (RC)	.25
2	Matt Chico (RC)	.25
3	Justin Upton RC	2.50
4	Chase Wright RC	.25
5	Kevin Kouzmanoff (RC)	.25
6	John Danks RC	.25
7	Alejandro De Aza RC	.25
8	Jamie Vermilyea RC	.25
9	Jesus Flores RC	.25
10	Glen Perkins (RC)	.25
11	Tim Lincecum RC	3.00
12	Cameron Maybin RC	1.00
13	Brandon Morrow RC	.25
14	Mike Rabelo RC	.25
15	Alex Gordon RC	.75
16	Zack Segovia (RC)	.25
17	Jon Knott (RC)	.25
18	Joba Chamberlain RC	1.50
19	Danny Putnam (RC)	.25
20	Matt DeSalvo (RC)	.25
21	Fred Lewis (RC)	.25
22	Sean Gallagher (RC)	.25
23	Brandon Wood (RC)	.25
24	Dennis Dove (RC)	.25
25	Hunter Pence (RC)	1.00
26	Jarrod Saltalamacchia (RC)	.25
27	Ben Francisco (RC)	.25
28	Doug Slaten RC	.25
29	Tony Abreu RC	.25
30	Billy Butler (RC)	.50
31	Jesse Litsch RC	.25
32	Nate Schierholtz (RC)	.25
33	Jared Burton RC	.25
34	Matt Brown RC	.25
35	Dallas Braden RC	.25
36	Carlos Gomez RC	.25
37	Brian Stokes (RC)	.25
38	Kory Casto (RC)	.25
39	Mark McLemore (RC)	.25
40	Andy LaRoche (RC)	.50
41	Tyler Clippard (RC)	.25
42	Curtis Thigpen (RC)	.25
43	Yunel Escobar (RC)	.50
44	Andrew Sonnanstine RC	.25

45	Felix Pie (RC)	.25
46	Homer Bailey (RC)	.50
47	Kyle Kendrick RC	.25
48	Angel Sanchez RC	.25
49	Phil Hughes (RC)	2.50
50	Ryan Braun (RC)	1.50
51	Kevin Slowey (RC)	.25
52	Brendan Ryan (RC)	.25
53	Yovani Gallardo RC	.50
54	Mark Reynolds RC	.25
237	Barry Bonds	1.00

Blue
Blue:	2-4X
Production 399 Sets	

Gold

Gold:	1-2X
Inserted 1:1	

Red
Production One Set

Printing Plates
No Pricing
Production one set per color.

A-Rod Road to 500
	NM/M
Common A-Rod (426-450):	2.00
Inserted 2:Box	
Autographs:	No Pricing
Production One Set	

Draft Picks
		NM/M
Complete Set (65):		15.00
Common Draft Pick:		.25
1	Cody Crowell	.25
2	Karl Bolt	.25
3	Corey Brown	.25
4	Tyler Mach	.25
5	Trevor Pippin	.25
6	Ed Easley	.25
7	Cory Luebke	.25
8	Darin Mastroianni	.25
9	Ryan Zink	.25
10	Brandon Hamilton	.50
11	Kyle Lotzkar	.50
12	Freddie Freeman	1.50
13	Nicholas Barnese	.25
14	Travis d'Arnaud	.25
15	Eric Eiland	.25
16	John Ely	.25
17	Oliver Marmol	.25
18	Eric Sogard	.25
19	Lars Davis	.25
20	Sam Runion	.50
21	Austin Gallagher	.50
22	Matt West	.50
23	Derek Norris	.25
24	Taylor Holiday	.25
25	Dustin Biell	.25
26	Julio Borbon	.50
27	Brant Rustich	.25
28	Andrew Lambo	1.00
29	Corey Kluber	.25
30	Justin Jackson	.50
31	Scott Carroll	.25
32	Danny Rams	.25
33	Thomas Eager	.25
34	Matt Dominguez	1.00
35	Steven Souza	.50
36	Craig Heyer	.25
37	Michael Taylor	1.00
38	Drew Bowman	.25
39	Frank Gailey	.25
40	Jeremy Hefner	.25
41	Reynaldo Navarro	.50
42	Daniel Descalso	.50
43	Leroy Hunt	.25
44	Jason Kiley	.25
45	Ryan Pope	.50
46	Josh Horton	.25
47	Jason Monti	.25
48	Richard Lucas	.50
49	Jonathan Lucroy	.50
50	Sean Doolittle	.75
51	Mike McDade	.50
52	Charlie Culberson	.50
53	Michael Moustakas	5.00
54	Jason Heyward	10.00
55	David Price	2.50
56	Brad Mills	.25
57	John Tolisano	.25
58	Jarrod Parker	.75
59	Wendell Fairley	1.00
60	Gary Gattis	.25
61	Madison Bumgarner	2.00

62	Danny Payne	.25
63	Jake Smolinski	.25
64	Matt LaPorta	1.50
65	Jackson Williams	.25

Draft Picks Blue
Blue:	2-4X
Production 399 Sets	

Draft Picks Gold
Gold:	1-2X
Inserted 1:1	

Draft Picks Red
No Pricing
Production One Set

Draft Picks Printing Plates
Production one set per color.

Future's Game Prospects

		NM/M
Complete Set (66-110):		8.00
Common Prospect:		.25
66	Pedro Beato	.25
67	Collin Balester	.25
68	Carlos Carrasco	.25
69	Clay Buchholz	.50
70	Emiliano Fruto	.25
71	Joba Chamberlain	1.00
72	Deolis Guerra	.25
73	Kevin Mulvey	.25
74	Franklin Morales	.25
75	Luke Hochevar	.50
76	Henry Sosa	.25
77	Clayton Kershaw	.75
78	Rich Thompson	.25
79	Chuck Lofgren	.25
80	Rick Vanden Hurk	.25
81	Mike Madsen	.25
82	Robinzon Diaz	.25
83	Jeff Niemann	.50
84	Max Ramirez	.25
85	Geovany Soto	.50
86	Elvis Andrus	.50
87	Bryan Anderson	.25
88	German Duran	.25
89	J.R. Towles	.50
90	Alcides Escobar	.50
91	Brian Bocock	.25
92	Chin-Lung Hu	.25
93	Adrian Cardenas	.25
94	Freddy Sandoval	.25
95	Chris Coghlan	.50
96	Craig Stansberry	.25
97	Brent Lillibridge	.25
98	Joey Votto	.50
99	Evan Longoria	1.00
100	Wladimir Balentien	.25
101	Johnny Whittleman	.25
102	Gorkys Hernandez	.25
103	Jay Bruce	1.00
104	Matt Tolbert	.25
105	Jacoby Ellsbury	1.00
106	Mike Saunders	.50
107	Cameron Maybin	1.00
108	Carlos Gonzalez	.50
109	Colby Rasmus	.50
110	Justin Upton	2.00

Future's Game Prospects Blue
Blue:	2-4X
Production 399 Sets	

Future's Game Prospects Gold
Gold:	1-2X
Inserted 1:1	

Future's Game Prospects Red
No Pricing
Production One Set

Future's Game Prospect Printing Plate
Production one set per color.

Future's Game Prospects Jersey
		NM/M
Complete Player:		5.00
68	Carlos Carrasco	5.00
69	Clay Buchholz	12.00
71	Joba Chamberlain	10.00
73	Kevin Mulvey	5.00
74	Franklin Morales	5.00

75	Luke Hochevar	5.00
78	Rich Thompson	5.00
83	Jeff Niemann	8.00
84	Max Ramirez	5.00
89	J.R. Towles	5.00
95	Chris Coghlan	8.00
96	Craig Stansberry	5.00
97	Brent Lillibridge	5.00
98	Joey Votto	12.00
102	Gorkys Hernandez	8.00
105	Jacoby Ellsbury	25.00
106	Mike Saunders	8.00
107	Cameron Maybin	8.00
108	Carlos Gonzalez	8.00
110	Justin Upton	15.00

Head of the Class Dual Autograph
		NM/M
Production 174 Sets		
Refractor:		1-1.5X
Production 50 Sets		
Gold Refractor:		No Pricing
Production 25 Sets		
SuperFractor:		No Pricing
Production One Set		
GH	Jonathan Gilmore, Jason Heyward	100.00
HP	Luke Hochevar, David Price	50.00

Signs of the Future
		NM/M
Common Auto.:		10.00
HC	Hank Conger	10.00
AL	Anthony Lerew	10.00
BA	Brandon Allen	10.00
CM	Casey McGehee	20.00
PH	Philip Humber	10.00
CMM	Carlos Marmol	20.00
RD	Ryan Delaughter	10.00
AM	Adam Miller	15.00
CD	Chris Dickerson	10.00
CMC	Chris McConnell	15.00
JK	John Koronka	10.00
JR	John Rheinecker	10.00
JV	Jonathan Van Every	15.00
TC	Trevor Crowe	15.00
FM	Fernando Martinez	25.00
JGA	Jaime Garcia	25.00

2007 Bowman Chrome Draft

		NM/M
Complete Set (54):		25.00
Common RC:		.50
1	Travis Buck (RC)	.50
2	Matt Chico (RC)	.50
3	Justin Upton RC	3.00
4	Chase Wright RC	1.00
5	Kevin Kouzmanoff (RC)	.50
6	John Danks RC	.50
7	Alejandro De Aza RC	.50
8	Jamie Vermilyea RC	.50
9	Jesus Flores RC	.50
10	Glen Perkins (RC)	.50
11	Tim Lincecum RC	6.00
12	Cameron Maybin RC	2.00
13	Brandon Morrow RC	.50
14	Mike Rabelo RC	.50
15	Alex Gordon RC	1.00
16	Zack Segovia (RC)	.50
17	Jon Knott (RC)	.50
18	Joba Chamberlain RC	2.00
19	Danny Putnam (RC)	.50
20	Matt DeSalvo (RC)	.50
21	Fred Lewis (RC)	.50
22	Sean Gallagher (RC)	.50
23	Brandon Wood (RC)	.50
24	Dennis Dove (RC)	.50
25	Hunter Pence (RC)	1.50
26	Jarrod Saltalamacchia (RC)	.50
27	Ben Francisco (RC)	.50
28	Doug Slaten RC	.50
29	Tony Abreu RC	.50
30	Billy Butler (RC)	1.00
31	Jesse Litsch RC	.50
32	Nate Schierholtz (RC)	.50
33	Jared Burton RC	.50
34	Matt Brown RC	.50
35	Dallas Braden RC	1.50
36	Carlos Gomez RC	.50
37	Brian Stokes (RC)	.50
38	Kory Casto (RC)	.50
39	Mark McLemore (RC)	.50
40	Andy LaRoche (RC)	1.00
41	Tyler Clippard (RC)	.50
42	Curtis Thigpen (RC)	.50

43	Yunel Escobar (RC)	.50
44	Andrew Sonnanstine RC	.50
45	Felix Pie (RC)	.50
46	Homer Bailey (RC)	1.00
47	Kyle Kendrick RC	.50
48	Angel Sanchez RC	.50
49	Phil Hughes (RC)	4.00
50	Ryan Braun (RC)	3.00
51	Kevin Slowey (RC)	.50
52	Brendan Ryan (RC)	.50
53	Yovani Gallardo (RC)	.50
54	Mark Reynolds RC	.50
237	Barry Bonds	2.00

Refractor
Refractor:	2-3X
Inserted 1:11	

Blue Refractor
Blue Refractor:	3-5X
Production 199 Sets	

Gold Refractor
Gold Refractor:	8-15X
Production 50 Sets	

Orange Refractor
Orange Refractor:	No Pricing
Production 25 Sets	

Red Refractor
No Pricing
Production Five Sets

SuperFractor
No Pricing
Production One Set

X-Fractor
X-Fractor:	3-4X
Production 299 Sets	

Draft Picks

		NM/M
Common Draft Pick (1-65):		.50
Common DP Auto. (111-140):		15.00
1	Cody Crowell	.75
2	Karl Bolt	.50
3	Corey Brown	.50
4	Tyler Mach	.50
5	Trevor Pippin	.50
6	Ed Easley	.50
7	Cory Luebke	.50
8	Darin Mastroianni	.50
9	Ryan Zink	.75
10	Brandon Hamilton	1.00
11	Kyle Lotzkar	1.00
12	Freddie Freeman	4.00
13	Nicholas Barnese	1.50
14	Travis d'Arnaud	.75
15	Eric Eiland	1.00
16	John Ely	.50
17	Oliver Marmol	.50
18	Eric Sogard	.50
19	Lars Davis	.50
20	Sam Runion	1.50
21	Austin Gallagher	1.50
22	Matt West	1.50
23	Derek Norris	.75
24	Taylor Holiday	.50
25	Dustin Biell	.50
26	Julio Borbon	1.00
27	Brant Rustich	.50
28	Andrew Lambo	3.00
29	Corey Kluber	.50
30	Justin Jackson	1.50
31	Scott Carroll	.50
32	Danny Rams	.75
33	Thomas Eager	.50
34	Matt Dominguez	3.00
35	Steven Souza	1.00
36	Craig Heyer	.50
37	Michael Taylor	3.00
38	Drew Bowman	.50
39	Frank Gailey	.50
40	Jeremy Hefner	.50
41	Reynaldo Navarro	.75
42	Daniel Descalso	1.00
43	Leroy Hunt	.50
44	Jason Kiley	.50
45	Ryan Pope	1.50
46	Josh Horton	.75
47	Jason Monti	.50
48	Richard Lucas	.50
49	Jonathan Lucroy	1.50
50	Sean Doolittle	2.50
51	Mike McDade	.50
52	Charlie Culberson	1.50
53	Michael Moustakas	4.00

54	Jason Heyward	25.00
55	David Price	6.00
56	Brad Mills	.50
57	John Tolisano	1.00
58	Jarrod Parker	2.00
59	Wendell Fairley	3.00
60	Gary Gattis	1.50
61	Madison Bumgarner	5.00
62	Danny Payne	1.50
63	Jake Smolinski	1.50
64	Matt LaPorta	3.00
65	Jackson Williams	.50
111	Daniel Moskos	15.00
112	Ross Detwiler	25.00
113	Tim Alderson	25.00
114	Beau Mills	25.00
115	Devin Mesoraco	20.00
116	Kyle Lotzkar	20.00
117	Blake Beavan	20.00
118	Peter Kozma	20.00
119	Chris Withrow	20.00
120	Cory Luebke	20.00
121	Nick Schmidt	20.00
122	Michael Main	25.00
123	Aaron Poreda	20.00
124	James Simmons	15.00
125	Ben Revere	25.00
126	Joe Savery	20.00
127	Jonathan Gilmore	20.00
128	Todd Frazier	25.00
129	Matt Mangini	15.00
130	Casey Weathers	15.00
131	Nick Noonan	20.00
132	Kellen Kulbacki	20.00
133	Michael Burgess	30.00
134	Nick Hagadone	20.00
135	Clayton Mortensen	15.00
136	Justin Jackson	15.00
137	Ed Easley	15.00
138	Corey Brown	20.00
139	Danny Payne	15.00
140	Travis d'Arnaud	15.00

Draft Picks Blue Refractor
Blue Refract.(1-65):	6-12X
Production 199	
Blue Refr. Auto. (111-140):	2-3X
Production 150 Sets	

Draft Picks Gold Refractor
Gold Refract.(1-65):	20-30X
Gold Refr. Auto. (111-140):	4-8X
Production 50 Sets	

Draft Picks Orange Refractor
No Pricing
Production 25 Sets

Draft Picks Printing Plate
No Pricing
Production one set per color.

Draft Picks Red Refractor
No Pricing
Production Five Sets

Draft Picks Refractor
Refractor (1-65):	2-4X
Inserted 1:11	
Refractor Auto. (111-140):	1-1.5X
Production 500 for autos.	

Draft Picks X-Fractor
X-Fractor (1-65):	4-8X
Production 299	
X-Fractor Auto. (111-140):	1-2X
Production 225	

Draft Picks SuperFractor
No Pricing
Production One Set

Future's Game Prospects Base
		NM/M
Common Player:		8.00
Production 135 Sets		.50
86	Elvis Andrus	12.00
87	Bryan Anderson	8.00
88	German Duran	8.00
89	J.R. Towles	10.00
91	Brian Bocock	8.00
92	Chin-Lung Hu	15.00
93	Adrian Cardenas	10.00
94	Freddy Sandoval	8.00
95	Chris Coghlan	12.00
97	Brent Lillibridge	8.00
98	Joey Votto	15.00
99	Evan Longoria	20.00
101	Johnny Whittleman	8.00
102	Gorkys Hernandez	8.00
103	Jay Bruce	20.00
105	Jacoby Ellsbury	15.00
106	Mike Saunders	10.00
108	Carlos Gonzalez	8.00
109	Colby Rasmus	15.00
110	Justin Upton	20.00

Future's Game Blue Refractor
Blue Refractor:	3-5X
Production 199 Sets	

Future's Game Gold Refractor
Gold Refractor:	8-15X
Production 50 Sets	

Future's Game Orange Refractor
No Pricing
Production 25 Sets

Future's Game Red Refractor
No Pricing
Production Five Sets

Future's Game Refractor
Refractor: 2-3X
Inserted 1:11

Future's Game Superfractor
No Pricing
Production One Set

Future's Game X-Fractor
X-Fractor: 3-4X
Production 299 Sets

Future's Game Prospects
		NM/M
Complete Set (66-110):		15.00
Common Prospect:		.50
66	Pedro Beato	.50
67	Collin Balester	.50
68	Carlos Carrasco	.50
69	Clay Buchholz	1.00
70	Emiliano Fruto	.50
71	Joba Chamberlain	2.00
72	Deolis Guerra	.50
73	Kevin Mulvey	.50
74	Franklin Morales	.50
75	Luke Hochevar	1.00
76	Henry Sosa	.50
77	Clayton Kershaw	1.00
78	Rich Thompson	.50
79	Chuck Lofgren	.50
80	Rick Vanden Hurk	.50
81	Mike Madsen	.50
82	Robinzon Diaz	.50
83	Jeff Niemann	1.00
84	Max Ramirez	.50
85	Geovany Soto	1.00
86	Elvis Andrus	2.00
87	Bryan Anderson	.50
88	German Duran	.50
89	J.R. Towles	.50
90	Alcides Escobar	.75
91	Brian Bocock	.50
92	Chin-Lung Hu	.50
93	Adrian Cardenas	.50
94	Freddy Sandoval	.50
95	Chris Coghlan	1.00
96	Craig Stansberry	.50
97	Brent Lillibridge	.50
98	Joey Votto	1.50
99	Evan Longoria	3.00
100	Wladimir Balentien	.50
101	Johnny Whittleman	.50
102	Gorkys Hernandez	.50
103	Jay Bruce	2.00
104	Matt Tolbert	.50
105	Jacoby Ellsbury	2.50
106	Mike Saunders	1.50
107	Cameron Maybin	2.00
108	Carlos Gonzalez	1.00
109	Colby Rasmus	1.00
110	Justin Upton	2.00

Future's Game Prospects Patch
		NM/M
Common Player:		15.00
Production 99 Sets		
66	Pedro Beato	15.00
67	Collin Balester	15.00
68	Carlos Carrasco	15.00
69	Clay Buchholz	25.00
70	Emiliano Fruto	15.00
71	Joba Chamberlain	40.00
72	Deolis Guerra	20.00
73	Kevin Mulvey	15.00
74	Franklin Morales	15.00
75	Luke Hochevar	15.00
76	Henry Sosa	15.00
77	Clayton Kershaw	25.00
78	Rich Thompson	15.00
79	Chuck Lofgren	20.00
80	Rick Vanden Hurk	20.00
81	Mike Madsen	15.00
82	Robinzon Diaz	15.00
83	Jeff Niemann	20.00
84	Max Ramirez	15.00
85	Geovany Soto	25.00
86	Elvis Andrus	35.00
87	Bryan Anderson	20.00
88	German Duran	25.00
89	J.R. Towles	25.00
90	Alcides Escobar	20.00
91	Brian Bocock	15.00
92	Chin-Lung Hu	40.00
93	Adrian Cardenas	20.00
94	Freddy Sandoval	15.00
95	Chris Coghlan	15.00
96	Craig Stansberry	15.00
97	Brent Lillibridge	15.00
98	Joey Votto	30.00
99	Evan Longoria	40.00
100	Wladimir Balentien	15.00
101	Johnny Whittleman	15.00
102	Gorkys Hernandez	15.00
103	Jay Bruce	40.00
104	Matt Tolbert	20.00
105	Jacoby Ellsbury	40.00
106	Mike Saunders	20.00
107	Cameron Maybin	25.00
108	Carlos Gonzalez	25.00
109	Colby Rasmus	30.00
110	Justin Upton	40.00

2007 Bowman Heritage

		NM/M
Complete Set (251):		
Common Player (1-200):		.25
Common RC (201-251):		.50
Common SP:		3.00
Inserted 1:3		
SP's don't have auto on front.		
Pack (8):		3.00
Box (24):		60.00
1	Jeff Francoeur	.50
2	Jered Weaver	.40
3	Derrek Lee	.40
4	Todd Helton	.50
5	Shawn Hill	.25
6	Ivan Rodriguez	.50
7	Mickey Mantle	5.00
8	Ramon Hernandez	.25
9	Randy Johnson	.75
10	Jermaine Dye	.25
11	Brian Roberts	.40
12	Hank Blalock	.25
13	Chien-Ming Wang	.75
14	Mike Lowell	.50
15	Brandon Webb	.50
16	Kelly Johnson	.25
17	Nick Johnson	.25
18	Zach Duke	.25
19	Aaron Hill	.25
20	Miguel Tejada	.50
21	Mark Buehrle	.40
22	Michael Young	.50
23	Carlos Delgado	.50
24	Anibal Sanchez	.25
25	Vladimir Guerrero	.75
26	Russell Martin	.40
27	Lance Berkman	.40
28	Bobby Crosby	.25
29	Javier Vazquez	.25
30	Manny Ramirez	.75
31	Rich Hill	.25
32	Mike Sweeney	.25
33	Jeff Kent	.40
34	Noah Lowry	.25
35	Alfonso Soriano	.75
36	Paul LoDuca	.25
37	J.D. Drew	.25
38	C.C. Sabathia	.40
39	Craig Biggio	.40
40	Adam Dunn	.50
41	Josh Beckett	.50
42	Carlos Guillen	.25
43	Jeff Francis	.25
44	Orlando Hudson	.25
45	Grady Sizemore	.40
46	Jason Jennings	.25
47	Mark Teixeira	.40
48	Freddy Garcia	.25
49	Adrian Gonzalez	.40
50	Albert Pujols	2.00
51	Tom Glavine	.50
52	J.J. Hardy	.40
53	Bobby Abreu	.40
54	Bartolo Colon	.25
55	Garrett Atkins	.40
56	Moises Alou	.25
57	Cliff Lee	.25
58	Mike Cuddyer	.25
59	Brandon Phillips	.40
60	Jeremy Bonderman	.40
61	Rickie Weeks	.40
62	Chris Carpenter	.50
63	Frank Thomas	.75
64	Victor Martinez	.40
65	Dontrelle Willis	.40
66	Jim Thome	.50
67	Aaron Rowand	.25
68	Andy Pettitte	.50
69	Brian McCann	.40
70	Roger Clemens	2.00
71	Gary Matthews	.25
72	Bronson Arroyo	.25
73	Jeremy Hermida	.25
74	Eric Chavez	.40
75	David Ortiz	.75
76	Stephen Drew	.50
77	Ronnie Belliard	.25
78	James Shields	.50
79	Richie Sexson	.40
80	Johan Santana	.75
81	Orlando Cabrera	.25
82	Aramis Ramirez	.50
83	Greg Maddux	1.00
84	Reggie Sanders	.25
85	Carlos Zambrano	.25
86	Bengie Molina	.25
87	David DeJesus	.25
88	Adam Wainwright	.40
89	Conor Jackson	.25
90	David Wright	1.00
91	Ryan Garko	.25
92	Bill Hall	.25
93	Marcus Giles	.25
94	Kenny Rogers	.25
95	Joe Mauer	.40
96	Hanley Ramirez	.75
97	Brian Giles	.25
98	Danny Haren	.25
99	Robinson Cano	.50
100	Ryan Howard	1.00
101	Andruw Jones	.40
102	Aaron Harang	.25
103	Hideki Matsui	1.50
104	Nick Swisher	.40
105	Pedro Martinez	.75
106	Felipe Lopez	.25
107	Erik Bedard	.50
108	Rafael Furcal	.40
109	Curt Schilling	.50
110	Jose Reyes	.75
111	Adam LaRoche	.40
112	Mike Mussina	.50
113	Melvin Mora	.25
114	Zack Greinke	.25
115	Justin Morneau	.75
116	Ervin Santana	.25
117	Ken Griffey Jr.	1.50
118	David Eckstein	.25
119	Jamie Moyer	.25
120	Jorge Posada	.40
121	Justin Verlander	.50
122	Sammy Sosa	.75
123	Jason Schmidt	.25
124	Josh Willingham	.25
125	Roy Oswalt	.50
126	Travis Hafner	.40
127	John Maine	.25
128	Willy Taveras	.25
129	Magglio Ordonez	.50
130	Barry Zito	.40
131	Prince Fielder	1.00
132	Michael Barrett	.25
133	Livan Hernandez	.25
134	Troy Glaus	.40
135	Rocco Baldelli	.40
136	Jason Giambi	.50
137	Austin Kearns	.25
138	Dan Uggla	.40
139	Pat Burrell	.40
140	Carlos Beltran	.50
141	Carlos Quentin	.25
142	Johnny Estrada	.25
143	Torii Hunter	.40
144	Carlos Lee	.50
145	Mike Piazza	.75
146	Mark Teahen	.25
147	Juan Pierre	.40
148	Paul Konerko	.50
149	Freddy Sanchez	.25
150	Derek Jeter	2.00
151	Orlando Hernandez	.25
152	Raul Ibanez	.25
153	John Smoltz	.50
154	Scott Rolen	.50
155	Jimmy Rollins	.50
156	A.J. Burnett	.25
157	Jason Varitek	.25
158	Ben Sheets	.40
159	Matt Cain	.40
160	Carl Crawford	.40
161	Jeff Suppan	.25
162	Tadahito Iguchi	.25
163	Kevin Millwood	.25
164	Chris Duncan	.25
165	Rich Harden	.25
166	Joe Crede	.25
167	Chipper Jones	.75
168	Gary Sheffield	.50
169	Cole Hamels	.50
170	Jason Bay	.40
171	Jhonny Peralta	.40
172	Aubrey Huff	.25
173	Xavier Nady	.25
174	Kazuo Matsui	.25
175	Vernon Wells	.50
176	Johnny Damon	.40
177	Jim Edmonds	.40
178	Jose Vidro	.25
179	Garret Anderson	.25
180	Alex Rios	.40
181	Ichiro Suzuki	1.50
181	Ichiro Suzuki/SP	6.00
182	Jake Peavy	.50
182	Jake Peavy/SP	4.00
183	Ian Kinsler	.50
183	Ian Kinsler/SP	3.00
184	Tom Gorzelanny	.25
184	Tom Gorzelanny/SP	3.00
185	Miguel Cabrera	.75
185	Miguel Cabrera/SP	5.00
186	Scott Kazmir	.40
186	Scott Kazmir/SP	3.00
187	Matt Holliday	.50
187	Matt Holliday/SP	3.00
188	Roy Halladay	.50
188	Roy Halladay/SP	3.00
189	Ryan Zimmerman	.50
189	Ryan Zimmerman/SP	3.00
190	Alex Rodriguez	2.00
190	Alex Rodriguez/SP	8.00
191	Kenji Johjima	.25
191	Kenji Johjima/SP	3.00
192	Gil Meche	.25
192	Gil Meche/SP	3.00
193	Chase Utley	.75
193	Chase Utley/SP	5.00
194	Jeremy Sowers	.25
194	Jeremy Sowers/SP	3.00
195	John Lackey	.25
195	John Lackey/SP	3.00
196	Nick Markakis	.50
196	Nick Markakis/SP	4.00
197	Tim Hudson	.40
197	Tim Hudson/SP	3.00
198	B.J. Upton	.50
198	B.J. Upton/SP	5.00
199	Felix Hernandez	.50
199	Felix Hernandez/SP	4.00
200	Barry Bonds	2.00
200	Barry Bonds/SP	8.00
201	Jarrod Saltalamacchia (RC)	.50
202	Tim Lincecum RC	6.00
203	Kory Casto (RC)	.50
204	Sean Henn (RC)	.50
205	Hector Gimenez (RC)	.50
206	Homer Bailey (RC)	1.00
207	Yunel Escobar (RC)	.50
208	Matt Lindstrom (RC)	.50
209	Tyler Clippard (RC)	.50
210	Joe Smith RC	.50
211	Tim Abreu RC	.50
212	Billy Butler (RC)	1.00
213	Gustavo Molina (RC)	.50
214	Brian Stokes (RC)	.50
215	Kevin Slowey (RC)	.50
216	Curtis Thigpen (RC)	.50
217	Carlos Gomez RC	1.00
218	Rick Vanden Hurk RC	.50
219	Michael Bourn (RC)	.50
220	Jeff Baker (RC)	.50
221	Andy LaRoche (RC)	1.00
222	Andrew Sonnanstine RC	.50
223	Chase Wright (RC)	.50
224	Mark Reynolds RC	2.00
225	Matt Chico (RC)	.50
226	Hunter Pence (RC)	1.00
226	Hunter Pence/SP	4.00
227	John Danks (RC)	.50
227	John Danks/SP	3.00
228	Elijah Dukes RC	.50
228	Elijah Dukes/SP	3.00
229	Kei Igawa RC	1.00
229	Kei Igawa/SP	3.00
230	Felix Pie (RC)	.75
230	Felix Pie/SP	3.00
231	Jesus Flores (RC)	.50
231	Jesus Flores/SP	3.00
232	Dallas Braden RC	.50
232	Dallas Braden/SP	3.00
233	Akinori Iwamura RC	1.00
233	Akinori Iwamura/SP	3.00
234	Ryan Braun (RC)	2.50
234	Ryan Braun/SP	8.00
235	Alex Gordon RC	1.00
235	Alex Gordon/SP	4.00
236	Micah Owings (RC)	.50
236	Micah Owings/SP	3.00
237	Kevin Kouzmanoff (RC)	.75
237	Kevin Kouzmanoff/SP	3.00
238	Glen Perkins (RC)	.50
238	Glen Perkins/SP	3.00
239	Danny Putnam (RC)	.50
239	Danny Putnam/SP	3.00
240	Phil Hughes (RC)	.50
240	Phil Hughes/SP	8.00
241	Ryan Sweeney (RC)	.50
241	Ryan Sweeney/SP	3.00
242	Josh Hamilton (RC)	1.50
242	Josh Hamilton/SP	6.00
243	Hideki Okajima RC	1.00
243	Hideki Okajima/SP	3.00
244	Adam Lind (RC)	1.00
244	Adam Lind/SP	3.00
245	Travis Buck (RC)	.50
245	Travis Buck/SP	3.00
246	Miguel Montero (RC)	.50
246	Miguel Montero/SP	3.00
247	Brandon Morrow RC	1.00
247	Brandon Morrow/SP	3.00
248	Troy Tulowitzki (RC)	2.00
248	Troy Tulowitzki/SP	6.00
249	Delmon Young (RC)	1.00
249	Delmon Young/SP	3.00
250	Daisuke Matsuzaka RC	4.00
250	Daisuke Matsuzaka/SP	10.00
251	Joba Chamberlain RC	5.00

Red
Production One Set

Black
Black: 10-15X
Black SP's: 3-5X
Production 52 Sets

Printing Plates
Production one set per color.

Rainbow
Rainbow: 1-2X

Rainbow SP's: .5-1X
Inserted 1:1

A-Rod Road to 500
		NM/M
Common A-Rod (351-375):		2.00
Inserted 2:Box		
Autograph:		No Pricing
Production One Set		

Box Topper

		NM/M
Common Player:		3.00
Inserted 1:Box		
1	Alex Rodriguez	10.00
2	Barry Bonds	10.00
3	Ryan Howard	6.00
4	David Wright	6.00
5	Ichiro Suzuki	6.00
6	Hideki Matsui	6.00
7	Mickey Mantle	15.00
8	Manny Ramirez	4.00
9	David Ortiz	4.00
10	Vladimir Guerrero	4.00
11	Jose Reyes	5.00
12	Albert Pujols	10.00
13	Alfonso Soriano	3.00
14	Matt Holliday	3.00
15	Miguel Cabrera	3.00
16	Phil Hughes	8.00
17	Daisuke Matsuzaka	10.00
18	Delmon Young	4.00
19	Troy Tulowitzki	5.00
20	Felix Pie	3.00
21	Alex Gordon	4.00
22	Hunter Pence	5.00
23	Akinori Iwamura	3.00
24	Josh Hamilton	4.00
25	Kei Igawa	3.00

Mickey Mantle Shortprints
		NM/M
Complete Set (5):		40.00
Common Mantle:		10.00
Black:		3-6X
Production 52 Sets		
Red:		No Pricing
Production One Set		
1-5	Mickey Mantle	10.00

Pieces of Greatness

		NM/M
Common Player:		4.00
Black:		2-3X
Production 52 Sets		
Red:		No Pricing
RB	Rocco Baldelli	6.00
LB	Lance Berkman	6.00
CB	Craig Biggio	6.00
JB	Jeremy Bonderman	4.00
BB	Barry Bonds	20.00
MC	Miguel Cabrera	8.00
RC	Robinson Cano	8.00
RC2	Robinson Cano	8.00
EC	Eric Chavez	4.00
BC	Bobby Crosby	4.00
JD	Johnny Damon	8.00
JDD	J.D. Drew	8.00
AD	Adam Dunn	6.00
JE	Juan Encarnacion	4.00
DE	Darin Erstad	4.00
AE	Andre Ethier	4.00
JF	Jeff Francoeur	6.00
JFR	Jeff Francis	4.00
RF	Rafael Furcal	4.00
BG	Brian Giles	4.00
AG	Alex Gonzalez	4.00
LG	Luis Gonzalez	4.00
SG	Shawn Green	4.00
VG	Vladimir Guerrero	8.00
CH	Cole Hamels	10.00
RH	Rich Harden	4.00
TH	Todd Helton	8.00
TH2	Todd Helton	8.00
THU	Tim Hudson	6.00
TI	Tadahito Iguchi	4.00
AJ	Andruw Jones	6.00
JK	Jeff Kent	4.00
PK	Paul Konerko	6.00
PK2	Paul Konerko	6.00
CK	Corey Koskie	4.00
AL	Adam LaRoche	4.00
BL	Brad Lidge	4.00
ML	Mike Lowell	4.00
GM	Greg Maddux	10.00
HM	Hideki Matsui	15.00
JM	Joe Mauer	6.00
YM	Yadier Molina	4.00
MM	Mark Mulder	4.00
TN	Trot Nixon	4.00
MO	Magglio Ordonez	4.00
DO	David Ortiz	8.00
DO2	David Ortiz	8.00
CP	Corey Patterson	4.00
MP	Mike Piazza	8.00
AR	Aramis Ramirez	8.00
MR	Manny Ramirez	8.00
MR2	Manny Ramirez	8.00
JR	Jose Reyes	8.00
ARO	Alex Rodriguez	15.00
IR	Ivan Rodriguez	6.00
CS	Curt Schilling	8.00
GS	Gary Sheffield	8.00
GSI	Grady Sizemore	8.00
NS	Nick Swisher	8.00
MT	Mark Teixeira	8.00
MTE	Miguel Tejada	8.00
FT	Frank Thomas	8.00
CU	Chase Utley	8.00
TW	Tim Wakefield	8.00
DW	Dontrelle Willis	8.00
DWR	David Wright	10.00
BZ	Barry Zito	4.00
CBE	Carlos Beltran	8.00
CT	Chad Tracy	4.00

Prospects

		NM/M
Common Prospect:		.50
Inserted 2:Pack		
Black:		10-15X
Production 52 Sets		
Red:		No Pricing
Production One Set		
1	Thomas Fairchild	.50
2	Peter Bourjos	1.00
3	Brett Campbell	.50
4	Cesar Nicolas	.50
5	Kala Kaaihu	1.00
6	Zach McAllister	1.00
7	Chad Reineke	.50
8	Anthony Hatch	.50
9	Cedric Hunter	1.00
10	Chris Carter	1.50
11	Tommy Hanson	5.00
12	Dellin Betances	.50
13	John Otness	.50
14	Derin McMains	.50
15	Greg Reynolds	.50
16	Jonathan Van Every	.50
17	Eddie Degerman	.50
18	Cody Strait	.50
19	Noe Rodriguez	.50
20	Young-Il Jung	.50
21	Reegie Corona	1.00
22	Carlos Corporan	.50
23	Chance Douglass	.50
24	Leo Daigle	.50
25	Jeff Samardzija	2.00
26	Mark Wagner	.50
27	Chuck Lofgren	1.00
28	Bryan Byrne	.50
29	Daniel Mayora	1.00
30	Gorkys Hernandez	2.00
31	Joshua Rodriguez	.50
32	Brad Knox	.50
33	Scott Lewis	.50
34	Joe Gaetti	.50
35	Mike Saunders	.50
36	Brendan Katin	.50

37	Brennan Boesch	.50
38	Jay Garthwaite	.50
39	Michael Devaney	.50
40	J.R. Towles	1.50
41	Joe Ness	1.00
42	Michael Martinez	1.00
43	Justin Byler	1.00
44	Chris Coghlan	1.00
45	Eric Young Jr.	1.00
46	J.R. Mathes	1.00
47	Ivan DeJesus Jr.	.50
48	Woods Fines	.50
49	Andrew Fie	.50
50	Luke Hochevar	2.00
51	Will Venable	.50
52	Todd Redmond	.50
53	Matthew Sweeney	.50
54	Trevor Cahill	3.00
55	Mike Carp	.50
56	Henry Sosa	.50
57	Emerson Frostad	.50
58	Jeremy Jeffress	1.00
59	Whit Robbins	.50
60	Joba Chamberlain	3.00
61	Raul Barron	.50
62	Aaron Cunningham	1.00
63	Greg Smith	1.00
64	Jeff Baisley	.50
65	Vic Buttler	.50
66	Steve Singleton	.50
67	Josh Papelbon	1.00
68	Ryan Finan	.50
69	Deolis Guerra	1.50
70	Vasili Spanos	1.00
71	Patrick Reilly	1.00
72	Tom Hottovy	1.00
73	Daniel Murphy	1.00
74	Matt Young	1.00
75	Brian Bocock	1.00
76	Chris Salamida	.50
77	Nathan Southard	.50
78	Brandon Hynick	.50
79	Chris Nowak	.50
80	Reid Brignac	1.00
81	Cole Garner	.50
82	Nick Van Stratten	1.00
83	Jeremy Papelbon	1.00
84	Jarrett Hoffpauir	.50
85	Kevin Mulvey	.50
86	Matt Miller	.50
87	Devin Ivany	1.00
88	Marcus Sanders	.50
89	Michael MacDonald	.50
90	Gabriel Sanchez	.50
91	Ryan Norwood	.50
92	Jim Fasano	.50
93	Ryan Adams	.50
94	Evan Englebrook	.50
95	Juan Miranda	2.00
96	Greg Porter	.50
97	Shane Benson	.50
98	Sam Fuld	1.00
99	Cooper Brannon	.50
100	Fernando Martinez	4.00

Signs of Greatness
NM/M

Common Autograph:		8.00
Black:		1.5-2X
Production 52 Sets		
Red:		No Pricing
Production One Set		
DW	David Wright	75.00
CJ	Chipper Jones	60.00
CC	Carl Crawford	15.00
CH	Cole Hamels	30.00
JH	J.P. Howell	8.00
BJ	Blake Johnson	15.00
JP	Jorge Posada	35.00
NR	Nolan Reimold	15.00
CA	Carlos Arroyo	15.00
JB	John Buck	15.00
JC	Jorge Cantu	8.00
GM	Garrett Mock	10.00
AO	Adam Ottavino	15.00
RD	Rajai Davis	10.00
MM	Matt Maloney	10.00
WJB	Joe Benson	15.00
JCB	Jordan Brown	15.00
TG	Tony Giarratano	8.00
GG	Glenn Gibson	15.00
EJ	Elliot Johnson	10.00
JM	Jeff Manship	15.00
SS	Scott Sizemore	15.00
MT	Mike Thompson	15.00
SE	Stephen Englund	10.00
AF	Andrew Fie	15.00
SJ	Seth Johnston	10.00
SK	Sean Kazmar	10.00
JL	Jeff Locke	20.00
SP	Steve Pearce	20.00
CS	Chorye Spoone	10.00
WCS	Cody Strait	10.00
JT	J.R. Towles	15.00
JW	Johnny Whittleman	15.00

2007 Bowman's Best
NM/M

Common Player (1-33):		.75
Common Auto. (23-51):		15.00
Common RC (52-81):		4.00
Production 799		
Common RC Auto.(71-99):		10.00
Pack (5):		20.00
Box (15):		240.00
1	Jose Reyes	2.00
2	Derek Jeter	4.00
3	Vladimir Guerrero	1.50

Jose Reyes — New York Mets — SS

4	Ichiro Suzuki	3.00
5	Jason Bay	.75
6	Joe Mauer	.75
7	Alfonso Soriano	1.50
8	David Ortiz	1.50
9	Andruw Jones	.75
10	Roger Clemens	3.00
11	Grady Sizemore	1.50
12	Magglio Ordonez	.75
13	Carl Crawford	.75
14	Chase Utley	1.50
15	Mark Teixeira	1.00
16	Ryan Zimmerman	1.00
17	Ken Griffey Jr.	3.00
18	Derrek Lee	1.00
19	Barry Bonds	4.00
20	Chipper Jones	1.50
21	Vernon Wells	.75
22	Manny Ramirez	1.50
23	Alex Rodriguez	4.00
23	Alex Rodriguez/Auto.	150.00
24	Ryan Howard	2.50
24	Ryan Howard/Auto.	75.00
25	Tom Glavine	1.00
25	Tom Glavine/Auto.	60.00
26	Gary Sheffield	1.00
26	Gary Sheffield/Auto.	25.00
27	Miguel Cabrera	1.50
27	Miguel Cabrera/Auto.	30.00
28	Robinson Cano	1.00
28	Robinson Cano/Auto.	30.00
29	David Wright	2.00
29	David Wright/Auto.	40.00
30	Jim Thome	1.00
30	Jim Thome/Auto.	30.00
31	Albert Pujols	4.00
31	Albert Pujols/Auto.	175.00
32	Jorge Posada	.75
33	Brian McCann	.75
33	Brian McCann/Auto.	35.00
34	Josh Barfield/Auto.	10.00
35	Melky Cabrera/Auto.	15.00
36	Bill Hall/Auto.	15.00
37	Cole Hamels/Auto.	30.00
38	Adam LaRoche/Auto.	15.00
39	Matt Holliday/Auto.	30.00
40	Jeremy Hermida/Auto.	10.00
41	Jonathan Papelbon/Auto.	
42	Hanley Ramirez/Auto.	35.00
43	Justin Verlander/Auto.	30.00
44	Andre Ethier/Auto.	25.00
46	Erik Bedard/Auto.	20.00
47	Freddy Sanchez/Auto.	15.00
48	Adrian Gonzalez/Auto.	15.00
49	Russell Martin/Auto.	15.00
50	B.J. Upton/Auto.	15.00
51	Prince Fielder/Auto.	30.00
52	Tony Abreu RC	4.00
53	Ben Francisco (RC)	4.00
54	Billy Butler (RC)	4.00
55	Phil Hughes (RC)	15.00
56	Josh Fields (RC)	4.00
57	Carlos Gomez (RC)	4.00
58	Akinori Iwamura RC	4.00
59	Matt Brown RC	4.00
60	Jesus Flores RC	4.00
61	Mike Fontenot (RC)	4.00
62	Ryan Feierabend (RC)	4.00
63	Miguel Montero (RC)	4.00
64	Daisuke Matsuzaka RC	10.00
64	Daisuke Matsuzaka/Jsy RC	15.00
65	Kei Igawa RC	4.00
66	Shawn Riggans (RC)	4.00
67	Masumi Kuwata RC	6.00
68	Kevin Slowey (RC)	4.00
69	Josh Hamilton (RC)	8.00
70	Curtis Thigpen (RC)	4.00
71	Justin Upton RC	12.00
71	Justin Upton/Auto. RC	75.00
72	Delmon Young (RC)	6.00
72	Delmon Young/Auto. (RC)	15.00
73	Brandon Wood (RC)	6.00
73	Brandon Wood/Auto. (RC)	15.00
74	Felix Pie (RC)	6.00
74	Felix Pie/Auto. (RC)	15.00
75	Alex Gordon RC	6.00
75	Alex Gordon/Auto. RC	15.00
76	Mark Reynolds RC	6.00
76	Mark Reynolds/Auto. RC	30.00
77	Tyler Clippard (RC)	5.00
77	Tyler Clippard/Auto. (RC)	15.00
78	Adam Lind (RC)	6.00
78	Adam Lind/Auto. (RC)	20.00
79	Hunter Pence (RC)	6.00
79	Hunter Pence/Auto. (RC)	20.00
81	Jarrod Saltalamacchia (RC)	4.00
81	Jarrod Saltalamacchia/Auto. (RC)	12.00
82	Kevin Kouzmanoff/Auto. RC	
83	Glen Perkins/Auto. (RC)	10.00
84	Michael Bourn/Auto. RC	10.00
85	Andrew Miller/Auto. RC	15.00
86	Fred Lewis/Auto. (RC)	15.00
88	Joba Chamberlain/Auto. RC	40.00
89	Hideki Okajima/Auto. RC	20.00
90	Troy Tulowitzki/Auto. (RC)	25.00
91	Ryan Sweeney/Auto. RC	10.00
92	Matt Lindstrom/Auto. RC	10.00
93	Tim Lincecum/Auto. RC	100.00
94	Homer Bailey/Auto. RC	20.00
95	Matt DeSalvo/Auto. RC	15.00
96	Alejandro De Aza/Auto. RC	
97	Ryan Braun/Auto. (RC)	50.00
99	Andy LaRoche (RC)	15.00

Prospects

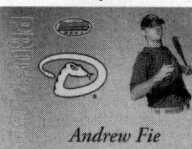

Andrew Fie

NM/M

Common Player (1-40):		4.00
Production 499		
Common Auto. (37-60):		10.00
1	Greg Smith	10.00
2	J.R. Towles	6.00
3	Jeff Locke	10.00
4	Henry Sosa	6.00
5	Ivan DeJesus Jr.	8.00
6	Brad Lincoln	6.00
7	Josh Papelbon	8.00
8	Mark Hamilton	6.00
9	Sam Fuld	8.00
10	Thomas Fairchild	4.00
11	Chris Carter	6.00
12	Chuck Lofgren	4.00
13	Joe Gaetti	4.00
14	Zach McAllister	4.00
15	Cole Gillespie	10.00
16	Jeremy Papelbon	6.00
17	Mike Carp	4.00
18	Cody Strait	4.00
19	Gorkys Hernandez	8.00
20	Andrew Fie	4.00
21	Erik Lis	4.00
22	Chance Douglass	4.00
23	Vasili Spanos	4.00
24	Desmond Jennings	10.00
25	Vic Buttler	4.00
26	Cedric Hunter	4.00
27	Emerson Frostad	4.00
28	Michael Devaney	6.00
29	Eric Young Jr.	4.00
30	Evan Englebrook	4.00
31	Aaron Cunningham	6.00
32	Dellin Betances	10.00
33	Mike Saunders	6.00
34	Deolis Guerra	8.00
35	Brian Bocock	8.00
36	Rich Thompson	6.00
37	Greg Reynolds	4.00
37	Greg Reynolds/Auto.	10.00
38	Jeff Samardzija	5.00
38	Jeff Samardzija/Auto.	15.00
39	Evan Longoria	8.00
39	Evan Longoria/Auto.	60.00
40	Luke Hochevar	8.00
40	Luke Hochevar/Auto.	15.00
41	James Avery/Auto.	8.00
42	Joe Mather/Auto.	15.00
43	Hank Conger/Auto.	15.00
44	Adam Miller/Auto.	15.00
45	Clayton Kershaw/Auto.	40.00
46	Adam Ottavino/Auto.	15.00
47	Jason Place/Auto.	20.00
48	Billy Rowell/Auto.	12.00
49	Brett Sinkbeil/Auto.	10.00
50	Colton Willems/Auto.	15.00
51	Cameron Maybin/Auto.	25.00
52	Jeremy Jeffress/Auto.	15.00
53	Fernando Martinez/Auto.	30.00
54	Chris Marrero/Auto.	20.00
55	Kyle McCulloch/Auto.	15.00
56	Chris Parmelee/Auto.	15.00
57	Emmanuel Burris/Auto.	15.00
58	Chris Coghlan/Auto.	20.00
59	Chris Perez/Auto.	10.00
60	David Huff/Auto.	10.00

Green
NM/M

Green (1-33):	2-4X
Green RC (52-99):	1-2X
Production 249	

Blue
NM/M

Blue (1-33):	3-5X
Blue Auto.(23-51):	1-1.5X
Blue RC (52-81):	1-2X
Blue RC Auto. (71-99):	1-1.5X
Matsuzaka Blue Jersey	40.00
Production 99 Sets	

Gold
NM/M

Gold (1-33):	4-6X
Gold Auto. (23-51):	1-2X
Gold RC (52-81):	2-4X
Gold RC Auto. (71-99):	1-2X
Matsuzaka Gold Jersey	60.00
Production 50 Sets	

Red
No Pricing
Production One Set

Printing Plates
Production one set per color.

Prospects Blue
NM/M

Blue (1-40):	1-2X
Blue Auto. (37-60):	1-1.5X
Production 99 Sets	

Prospects Green
NM/M

Green (1-40):	1-1.5X
Production 249 Sets	

Prospects Gold
NM/M

Gold (1-40):	2-3X
Gold Auto. (37-60):	1.5-3X
Production 50 Sets	

Prospects Red
Production One Set

Barry Bonds 756
NM/M

Inserted 1:20		
BB756	Barry Bonds	8.00

AROD 500
NM/M

Inserted 1:20		
AR500	Alex Rodriguez	8.00

A-Rod Road to 500
NM/M

Common A-Rod (401-425):	15.00
Autographs:	No Pricing
Production One Set	

2007 Bowman Sterling

TIM LINCECUM

NM/M

Common RC:		3.00
Common RC Auto.:		10.00
Pack (5):		55.00
Box (6):		300.00
AAL	Adam Lind (RC)	3.00
AG	Alex Gordon RC	3.00
AI	Akinori Iwamura RC	3.00
AL	Andy LaRoche (RC)	3.00
AM	Andrew Miller RC	3.00
AS	Andrew Sonnanstine RC	3.00
BB	Billy Butler (RC)	5.00
BF	Ben Francisco (RC)	3.00
BS	Brian Stokes (RC)	3.00
BW	Brandon Wood (RC)	4.00
CG	Carlos Gomez (RC)	3.00
CH	Chase Headley/Auto. (RC)	15.00
CM	Cameron Maybin/Auto. RC	20.00
CT	Curtis Thigpen (RC)	3.00
DM	Daisuke Matsuzaka RC	6.00
DMM	David Murphy (RC)	3.00
DP	Danny Putnam (RC)	3.00
DY	Delmon Young (RC)	3.00
FL	Fred Lewis (RC)	3.00
FP	Felix Pie/Auto. (RC)	15.00
GO	Garrett Olson (RC)	3.00
GP	Glen Perkins/Auto. (RC)	10.00
HB	Homer Bailey/Auto. (RC)	15.00
HG	Hector Gimenez (RC)	3.00
HO	Hideki Okajima (RC)	5.00
HP	Hunter Pence (RC)	3.00
JB	Jeff Baker (RC)	3.00
JC1	Joba Chamberlain RC	15.00
JC2	Joba Chamberlain/Auto. RC	40.00
JD	John Danks/Auto. (RC)	15.00
JDF	Josh Fields (RC)	3.00
JE	Jacoby Ellsbury (RC)	
JF	Jesus Flores RC	4.00
JH	Josh Hamilton/Auto. (RC)	50.00
JL	Jesse Litsch/Auto. RC	10.00
JQF	Jake Fox RC	4.00
JR	Jo Jo Reyes (RC)	4.00
JS	Jarrod Saltalamacchia/Auto. RC	15.00
JU	Justin Upton RC	8.00
KI	Kei Igawa RC	3.00
KK	Kevin Kouzmanoff (RC)	3.00
KKS	Kurt Suzuki/Auto. RC	10.00
KRK	Kyle Kendrick/Auto. RC	15.00
KS	Kevin Slowey/Auto. RC	15.00
MB	Michael Bourn (RC)	3.00
MC	Matt Chico/Auto. (RC)	10.00
MF	Mike Fontenot (RC)	4.00
MK	Masumi Kuwata RC	4.00
MM	Miguel Montero (RC)	3.00
MO	Micah Owings (RC)	3.00
MP	Manny Parra (RC)	3.00
MR	Mark Reynolds RC	5.00
MSM	Mark McLemore (RC)	3.00
NG	Nick Gorneault/Auto. (RC)	10.00
NS	Nate Schierholtz/Auto. (RC)	10.00
PH	Phil Hughes (RC)	8.00
PH	Phil Hughes/Auto. (RC)	40.00
RB	Ryan Braun/Auto. (RC)	40.00
RS	Ryan Sweeney (RC)	3.00
RV	Rick Vanden Hurk RC	4.00
SD	Shelley Duncan (RC)	4.00
SG	Sean Gallagher (RC)	4.00
TA	Tony Abreu RC	3.00
TB	Travis Buck (RC)	3.00
TC	Tyler Clippard (RC)	3.00
TL	Tim Lincecum/Auto. RC	125.00
TM	Travis Metcalf RC	4.00
UJ	Ubaldo Jimenez RC	10.00
YE	Yunel Escobar (RC)	3.00
YG	Yovani Gallardo/Auto. (RC)	20.00
Common Memorabilia:		4.00
AER	Alex Rodriguez	20.00
AJ	Andruw Jones	6.00
AP	Albert Pujols	15.00
AR	Alex Rios	6.00
AS	Alfonso Soriano	6.00
BLB	Barry Bonds	15.00
BP	Brad Penny	4.00
BR	Brian Roberts	4.00
BU	B.J. Upton	6.00
BW	Brandon Webb	6.00
CAB	Craig Biggio	6.00
CAG	Carlos Guillen	6.00
CH	Cole Hamels	6.00
CL	Carlos Lee	6.00
CMS	Curt Schilling	4.00
DDY	Dmitri Young	4.00
DO	David Ortiz	7.00
DW	David Wright	10.00
DWW	Dontrelle Willis	4.00
EC	Eric Chavez	4.00
IS	Ichiro Suzuki	20.00
JAV	Jason Varitek	6.00
JBR	Jose Reyes	10.00
JE	Jim Edmonds	4.00
JS	Johan Santana	10.00
JV	Justin Verlander	10.00
LB	Lance Berkman	6.00
MAR	Manny Ramirez	8.00
MC	Melky Cabrera	4.00
MCT	Mark Teixeira	8.00
MH	Matt Holliday	6.00
MJO	Magglio Ordonez	6.00
MM	Mickey Mantle	80.00
MT	Miguel Tejada	6.00
MY	Michael Young	6.00
OC	Orlando Cabrera	4.00
PF	Prince Fielder	10.00
RB	Rocco Baldelli	4.00
RC	Roger Clemens	15.00
RJC	Robinson Cano	6.00
RJH	Ryan Howard	15.00
RZ	Ryan Zimmerman	8.00
SK	Scott Kazmir	6.00
TH	Tim Hudson	6.00
TLH	Todd Helton	6.00
TW	Tim Wakefield	4.00
VG	Vladimir Guerrero	8.00

Refractors

JESUS FLORES

RC's:	1-2X
RC Auto.:	1-2X
Relics:	1-2X

Black Refractors
No Pricing
Production 25 Sets

Red Refractors
Production One Set

Printing Plates
Production one set per color.

Dual Autographs
NM/M

Common Dual Auto.:		20.00
Refractors:		1-1.5X
Production 199 Sets		
Black Refractor:		No Pricing
Production 25 Sets		
Red Refractors:		No Pricing
Production One Set		
BV	Jay Bruce, Joey Votto	75.00
CH	Shin-Soo Choo, Chin-Lung Hu	30.00
GM	Deolis Guerra, Fernando Martinez	40.00
HC	Phil Hughes, Joba Chamberlain	100.00
HP	Luke Hochevar, David Price	40.00
LC	Evan Longoria, Carl Crawford	50.00
MM	John Maine, Lastings Milledge	20.00
PB	Hunter Pence, Ryan Braun	50.00
PP	Jeremy Papelbon, Josh Papelbon	25.00
PS	Felix Pie, Jeff Samardzija	25.00

Prospects

MIKE CARP

NM/M

Common Prospect:		3.00
Common Prospect Auto.:		8.00
AC	Adrian Cardenas/Jsy/Auto.	10.00
AF	Andrew Fie	3.00
ALC	Aaron Cunningham	5.00
AP	Aaron Poreda/Auto.	15.00
BB	Brian Bocock/Jsy/Auto.	15.00
BB	Blake Beavan/Auto.	15.00
BEL	Brad Lincoln	3.00
BH	Brandon Hamilton	3.00
BHB	Burke Badenhop	3.00
BL	Bryan LaHair/Auto.	8.00
BM	Brandon MaGee/Auto.	15.00
BMI	Beau Mills/Auto.	15.00
BR	Ben Revere/Auto.	15.00
BWH	Brandon Hynick	5.00
CB	Collin Balester/Jsy/Auto.	10.00
CC	Chris Carter	8.00
CD	Chance Douglass	3.00
CG	Cole Gillespie/Auto.	15.00
CH	Chin-Lung Hu/Jsy/Auto.	20.00
CH	Cedric Hunter	3.00
CK	Clayton Kershaw/Jsy/Auto.	40.00
CL	Chuck Lofgren/Jsy/Auto.	15.00
CM	Clayton Mortensen/Auto.	10.00
CN	Chris Nowak	3.00
CR	Colby Rasmus/Jsy/Auto.	30.00
CS	Cody Strait	15.00
CW	Chris Withrow/Auto.	15.00
CWW	Casey Weathers/Auto.	10.00
DB	Daniel Bard/Auto.	20.00
DBE	Dellin Betances	8.00
DG	Deolis Guerra/Jsy/Auto.	20.00
DI	Devin Ivany	3.00
DJ	Desmond Jennings	5.00
DL	Drew Locke	3.00
DM	Daniel Moskos/Auto.	15.00
DME	Devin Mesoraco/Auto.	15.00
DMM	Derek Miller	3.00
DPP	David Price/Auto.	60.00
DS	James Simmons/Auto.	3.00
EE	Ed Easley	3.00
EL	Evan Longoria/Auto.	80.00
EL	Erik Lis/Auto.	10.00
EM	Emerson Frostad	3.00
EY	Eric Young Jr.	3.00
FF	Freddie Freeman	
GD	German Duran/Jsy/Auto.	15.00
GH	Gorkys Hernandez	6.00

GP	Greg Porter	3.00
GR	Greg Reynolds	3.00
GS	Greg Smith	3.00
HS	Henry Sosa/Jsy/Auto.	15.00
ID	Ivan DeJesus	4.00
IS	Ian Stewart/Jsy/Auto.	25.00
JA	J.P. Arencibia/Auto.	15.00
JAA	James Avery/Auto.	8.00
JB	Jay Bruce Jersey/Auto.	40.00
JB	Joe Benson/Auto.	15.00
JBO	Julio Borbon/Auto.	15.00
JG	Jonathan Gilmore/Auto.	15.00
JGA	Joe Gaetti	3.00
JGO	Jared Goedert	3.00
JH	Jason Heyward/Auto.	165.00
JJ	Justin Jackson	3.00
JL	Jeff Locke	8.00
JM	Joe Mather	5.00
JO	Josh Outman/Auto.	10.00
JP	Jason Place	3.00
JPA	Jeremy Papelbon	5.00
JPP	Josh Papelbon	5.00
JS	Joe Savery/Auto.	15.00
JS	Jeff Samardzija	5.00
JSM	Jake Smolinski	5.00
JT	J.R. Towles	6.00
JV	Joey Votto/Jsy/Auto.	30.00
JV	Josh Vitters/Auto.	25.00
JVE	Johnny Van Every	3.00
JW	Johnny Whittleman/Jsy/Auto.	10.00
KA	Kevin Ahrens/Auto.	15.00
KK	Kellen Kulbacki/Auto.	15.00
KK	Kala Kaaihu	6.00
MB	Michael Burgess/Auto.	25.00
MBB	Madison Bumgarner/Auto.	40.00
MC	Mike Carp	3.00
MCA	Mitch Canham/Auto.	10.00
MD	Mike Daniel/Auto.	3.00
MDE	Michael Devaney	3.00
MDO	Matt Dominguez/Auto.	20.00
MH	Mark Hamilton	3.00
MIM	Michael Main/Auto.	15.00
MLP	Matt LaPorta/Auto.	25.00
MM	Mike Madsen/Jsy/Auto.	10.00
MM	Matt McBride/Auto.	15.00
MMG	Matt Mangini/Auto.	15.00
MP	Mike Parisi/Auto.	10.00
MS	Mike Saunders	6.00
MY	Matt Young	3.00
NH	Nick Hagadone/Auto.	20.00
NN	Nick Noonan/Auto.	10.00
NS	Nick Schmidt/Auto.	10.00
OS	Ole Sheldon	3.00
PB	Pedro Beato/Jsy/Auto.	10.00
PK	Peter Kozma/Auto.	15.00
RD	Ross Detwiler/Auto.	20.00
RM	Ryan Mount/Auto.	8.00
RT	Rich Thompson	3.00
SF	Sam Fuld	6.00
SP	Steve Pearce/Jsy/Auto.	20.00
TA	Tim Alderson/Auto.	15.00
TF	Todd Frazier/Auto.	20.00
TF	Thomas Fairchild	3.00
TM	Tommy Manzella/Auto.	8.00
TS	Travis Snider/Auto.	40.00
TW	Ty Weeden/Auto.	15.00
VB	Vic Buttler	3.00
VS	Vasili Spanos	3.00
WF	Wendell Fairley/Auto.	15.00
WT	Wade Townsend/Auto.	8.00
ZM	Zach McAllister	3.00

Prospects Refractors
Prospects: 1-2X
Autos: 1-2X
Production 199 Sets

Prospects Black Refractors
No Pricing
Production 25 Sets

Prospects Red Refractors
Production One Set

A-Rod Road to 500
NM/M
Common A-Rod (450-475): 10.00
Autographs: No Pricing
Production One Set

2008 Bowman

NM/M
Common Player (1-200): .15
Common RC (201-220): .25

Common RC Auto.(221-230): 10.00
Pack (10): 3.00
Box (24): 65.00

1	Ryan Braun	.75
2	David DeJesus	.15
3	Brandon Phillips	.40
4	Mark Teixeira	.40
5	Daisuke Matsuzaka	.75
6	Justin Upton	.50
7	Jered Weaver	.25
8	Todd Helton	.50
9	Cameron Maybin	.25
10	Erik Bedard	.25
11	Jason Bay	.25
12	Cole Hamels	.40
13	Bobby Abreu	.25
14	Carlos Zambrano	.40
15	Vladimir Guerrero	.75
16	Joe Blanton	.15
17	Bengie Molina	.15
18	Paul Maholm	.15
19	Adrian Gonzalez	.25
20	Brandon Webb	.50
21	Carl Crawford	.25
22	A.J. Burnett	.25
23	Dmitri Young	.15
24	Jeremy Hermida	.15
25	C.C. Sabathia	.50
26	Adam Dunn	.50
27	Matt Garza	.15
28	Adrian Beltre	.25
29	Kevin Millwood	.15
30	Manny Ramirez	.75
31	Javier Vazquez	.15
32	Carlos Delgado	.40
33	Jason Schmidt	.15
34	Torii Hunter	.40
35	Ivan Rodriguez	.50
36	Nick Markakis	.40
37	Gil Meche	.15
38	Garrett Atkins	.25
39	Fausto Carmona	.25
40	Joe Mauer	.75
41	Tom Glavine	.50
42	Hideki Matsui	1.00
43	Scott Rolen	.50
44	Tim Lincecum	.40
45	Prince Fielder	.75
46	Ted Lilly	.15
47	Frank Thomas	.50
48	Tom Gorzelanny	.15
49	Lance Berkman	.50
50	David Ortiz	.75
51	Dontrelle Willis	.15
52	Travis Hafner	.25
53	Aaron Harang	.25
54	Chris Young	.25
55	Vernon Wells	.25
56	Francisco Liriano	.25
57	Eric Chavez	.15
58	Phil Hughes	.40
59	Melvin Mora	.15
60	Johan Santana	.75
61	Brian McCann	.25
62	Pat Burrell	.25
63	Chris Carpenter	.25
64	Brian Giles	.15
65	Jose Reyes	.75
66	Hanley Ramirez	.75
67	Ubaldo Jimenez	.40
68	Felix Pie	.15
69	Jeremy Bonderman	.25
70	Jimmy Rollins	.50
71	Miguel Tejada	.50
72	Derek Lowe	.25
73	Alex Gordon	.40
74	John Maine	.25
75	Alfonso Soriano	.50
76	Richie Sexson	.25
77	Ben Sheets	.25
78	Hunter Pence	.40
79	Magglio Ordonez	.25
80	Josh Beckett	.25
81	Victor Martinez	.25
82	Mark Buehrle	.25
83	Jason Varitek	.40
84	Chien-Ming Wang	.50
85	Ken Griffey Jr.	1.50
86	Billy Butler	.15
87	Brad Penny	.15
88	Carlos Beltran	.50
89	Curt Schilling	.50
90	Jorge Posada	.40
91	Andruw Jones	.25
92	Bobby Crosby	.15
93	Freddy Sanchez	.15
94	Barry Zito	.15
95	Miguel Cabrera	.75
96	B.J. Upton	.25
97	Matt Cain	.25
98	Lyle Overbay	.15
99	Austin Kearns	.15
100	Alex Rodriguez	2.00
101	Rich Harden	.15
102	Justin Morneau	.40
103	Oliver Perez	.15
104	Gary Matthews	.15
105	Matt Holliday	.40
106	Justin Verlander	.40
107	Orlando Cabrera	.25
108	Rich Hill	.15
109	Tim Hudson	.25
110	Ryan Zimmerman	.50
111	Roy Oswalt	.40
112	Nick Swisher	.25
113	Raul Ibanez	.15
114	Kelly Johnson	.15
115	Alex Rios	.25
116	John Lackey	.25
117	Robinson Cano	.25
118	Michael Young	.25
119	Jeff Francis	.25
120	Grady Sizemore	.50
121	Mike Lowell	.25
122	Aramis Ramirez	.40
123	Stephen Drew	.25
124	Yovani Gallardo	.25
125	Chase Utley	.75
126	Dan Haren	.25
127	Jose Vidro	.15
128	Ronnie Belliard	.15
129	Yunel Escobar	.15
130	Greg Maddux	1.50
131	Garret Anderson	.15
132	Aubrey Huff	.15
133	Paul Konerko	.25
134	Dan Uggla	.25
135	Roy Halladay	.25
136	Andre Ethier	.15
137	Orlando Hernandez	.15
138	Troy Tulowitzki	.40
139	Carlos Guillen	.15
140	Scott Kazmir	.25
141	Aaron Rowand	.15
142	Jim Edmonds	.15
143	Jermaine Dye	.15
144	Orlando Hudson	.15
145	Derek Lee	.15
146	Travis Buck	.15
147	Zack Greinke	.25
148	Jeff Kent	.15
149	John Smoltz	.50
150	David Wright	1.00
151	Joba Chamberlain	.50
152	Adam LaRoche	.25
153	Kevin Youkilis	.25
154	Troy Glaus	.25
155	Nick Johnson	.15
156	J.J. Hardy	.15
157	Felix Hernandez	.40
158	Khalil Greene	.15
159	Gary Sheffield	.25
160	Albert Pujols	2.00
161	Chuck James	.15
162	Rocco Baldelli	.15
163	Eric Byrnes	.25
164	Brad Hawpe	.25
165	Delmon Young	.25
166	Chris Young	.25
167	Brian Roberts	.25
168	Russell Martin	.40
169	Hank Blalock	.15
170	Yadier Molina	.15
171	Jeremy Guthrie	.15
172	Chipper Jones	.75
173	Johnny Damon	.25
174	Ryan Garko	.15
175	Jake Peavy	.50
176	Chone Figgins	.25
177	Edgar Renteria	.25
178	Jim Thome	.50
179	Carlos Pena	.25
180	Corey Patterson	.15
181	Dustin Pedroia	.25
182	Brett Myers	.25
183	Josh Hamilton	.50
184	Randy Johnson	.50
185	Ichiro Suzuki	1.50
186	Aaron Hill	.15
187	Jarrod Saltalamacchia	.15
188	Mike Cuddyer	.15
189	Jeff Francoeur	.40
190	Derek Jeter	2.00
191	Curtis Granderson	.50
192	James Loney	.25
193	Brian Bannister	.15
194	Carlos Lee	.40
195	Pedro Martinez	.50
196	Asdrubal Cabrera	.15
197	Kenji Johjima	.25
198	Bartolo Colon	.15
199	Jacoby Ellsbury	.50
200	Ryan Howard	.75
201	Radhames Liz RC	.50
202	Justin Ruggiano RC	.50
203	Lance Broadway RC	.50
204	Joey Votto (RC)	2.00
205	Billy Buckner (RC)	.25
206	Joe Koshansky (RC)	.25
207	Ross Detwiler RC	.50
208	Chin-Lung Hu (RC)	.50
209	Luke Hochevar (RC)	.75
210	Jeff Clement (RC)	.50
211	Troy Patton (RC)	.50
212	Hiroki Kuroda RC	1.00
213	Emilio Bonifacio RC	.50
214	Andres Galarraga RC	1.00
215	Josh Anderson (RC)	.50
216	Nick Blackburn RC	.75
217	Seth Smith (RC)	.75
218	Jonathan Meloan RC	.50
219	Alberto Gonzalez (RC)	.50
220	Josh Banks (RC)	.50
221	Clay Buchholz/Auto. (RC)	25.00
222	Nyjer Morgan/Auto. (RC)	12.00
223	Brandon Jones/Auto. RC	10.00
224	Sam Fuld/Auto. RC	10.00
225	Daric Barton/Auto. RC	10.00
226	Chris Seddon/Auto. (RC)	10.00
227	J.R. Towles/Auto. RC	10.00
228	Steve Pearce/Auto. RC	12.00
229	Ross Ohlendorf/Auto. RC	10.00
230	Clint Sammons/Auto. (RC)	10.00

Red
Production One Set

Orange
Orange (1-220): 3-6X
Orange Auto. (221-230): 1-1.5X
Production 250 Sets

Blue
Blue (1-220): 2-4X
Blue Auto. (221-230): 1X
Production 500 Sets

Gold

Gold (1-220): 1-2X
Inserted 1:1

Prospects

NM/M
Complete Set (110): 25.00
Common Prospect: .25
Inserted 2:Pack

BP1	Max Sapp	.50
BP2	Jamie Richmond	.50
BP3	Darren Ford	.25
BP4	Sergio Romo	.25
BP5	Jacob Butler	.25
BP6	Glenn Gibson	.25
BP7	Tom Hagan	.25
BP8	Michael McCormick	.25
BP9	Gregorio Petit	.25
BP10	Bobby Parnell	.25
BP11	Jeff Kindel	.25
BP12	Anthony Claggett	.25
BP13	Chris Frey	.25
BP14	Jonah Nickerson	.25
BP15	Anthony Martinez	.25
BP16	Rusty Ryal	.25
BP17	Justin Berg	.25
BP18	Gerardo Parra	.25
BP19	Wesley Wright	.25
BP20	Stephen Chapman	.25
BP21	Chance Chapman	.25
BP22	Brett Pill	.25
BP23	Zach Phillips	.25
BP24	John Raynor	.25
BP25	Danny Duffy	.25
BP26	Brian Finegan	.25
BP27	Jonathan Venters	.50
BP28	Steve Tolleson	.25
BP29	Ben Jukich	.25
BP30	Matt Weston	.25
BP31	Kyle Mura	.25
BP32	Luke Hetherington	.25
BP33	Michael Daniel	.25
BP34	Jake Renshaw	.25
BP35	Greg Halman	1.00
BP36	Ryan Khoury	.25
BP37	Ryan Ouellette	.25
BP38	Mike Brantley	.25
BP39	Eric Brown	.25
BP40	Jose Duarte	.25
BP41	Eli Tintor	.25
BP42	Kent Sakamoto	.25
BP43	Luke Montz	.25
BP44	Alex Cobb	.25
BP45	Mike McKenry	.25
BP46	Javier Castillo	.25
BP47	Jeff Stevens	.25
BP48	Greg Burns	.25
BP49	Blake Johnson	.25
BP50	Austin Jackson	2.50
BP51	Anthony Recker	.25
BP52	Luis Durango	.25
BP53	Engel Beltre	1.00
BP54	Seth Bynum	.25
BP55	Ryan Strieby	.25
BP56	Iggy Suarez	.25
BP57	Ryan Morris	.25
BP58	Scott Van Slyke	.25
BP59	Tyler Kolodny	.50
BP60	Joseph Martinez	.25
BP61	Aaron Mathews	.25
BP62	Phillip Cuadrado	.25
BP63	Alex Liddi	.25
BP64	Alex Burnett	.25
BP65	Brian Barton	.50
BP66	David Welch	.25
BP67	Kyle Reynolds	.25
BP68	Francisco Hernandez	.25
BP69	Logan Morrison	1.50
BP70	Ronald Ramirez	.25
BP71	Brad Miller	.25
BP72	Braedyn Pruitt	.50
BP73	Jason Fernandez	.25
BP74	Joseph Mahoney	.25
BP75	Quentin Davis	.25
BP76	P.J. Walters	.75
BP77	Jordan Czarniecki	.25
BP78	Jonathan Mota	.50
BP79	Michael Hernandez	.25
BP80	James Guerrero	.25
BP81	Chris Johnson	.25
BP82	Daniel Cortes	.50
BP83	Sal Sanchez	.25
BP84	Sean Henry	.25
BP85	Caleb Gindl	.75
BP86	Tommy Everidge	.25
BP87	Matt Rizzotti	.25
BP88	Luis Munoz	.25
BP89	Matt Klimas	.25
BP90	Angel Reyes	.25
BP91	Sean Danielson	.25
BP92	Omar Poveda	.25
BP93	Mario Lisson	.25
BP94	Brian Mathews	.25
BP95	Matt Buschmann	.25
BP96	Greg Thomson	.25
BP97	Matt Inouye	.25
BP98	Aneury Rodriguez	.25
BP99	Bradley Harman	.25
BP100	Aaron Bates	.50
BP101	Graham Taylor	.25
BP102	Kenny Holmberg	.25
BP103	Greg Dowling	.25
BP104	Ronnie Ray	.25
BP105	Mike Wlodarczyk	.25
BP106	Jose Martinez	.25
BP107	Jason Stephens	.50
BP108	Will Rhymes	.25
BP109	Joey Side	.25
BP110	Brandon Waring	1.50

Prospects Red
Production One Set

Prospects Blue
Blue (1-110): 2-4X
Production 500 Sets

Prospects Gold
Gold (1-110): 1-2X
Inserted 1:3

Chrome Prospects

NM/M
Common Prospect (1-110): .50
Inserted 2:Pack
Common Auto. (111-130): 10.00

BCP1	Max Sapp	1.00
BCP2	Jamie Richmond	.50
BCP3	Darren Ford	.50
BCP4	Sergio Romo	.50
BCP5	Jacob Butler	.50
BCP6	Glenn Gibson	.50
BCP7	Tom Hagan	.50
BCP8	Michael McCormick	.50
BCP9	Gregorio Petit	.50
BCP10	Bobby Parnell	1.00
BCP11	Jeff Kindel	.50
BCP12	Anthony Claggett	1.00
BCP13	Chris Frey	.50
BCP14	Jonah Nickerson	.50
BCP15	Anthony Martinez	.50
BCP16	Rusty Ryal	.50
BCP17	Justin Berg	.50
BCP18	Gerardo Parra	1.50
BCP19	Wesley Wright	.50
BCP20	Stephen Chapman	.50
BCP21	Chance Chapman	.50
BCP22	Brett Pill	.50
BCP23	Zach Phillips	.50
BCP24	John Raynor	1.50
BCP25	Danny Duffy	2.00
BCP26	Brian Finegan	.50
BCP27	Jonathan Venters	1.00
BCP28	Steve Tolleson	1.00
BCP29	Ben Jukich	.50
BCP30	Matt Weston	.50
BCP31	Kyle Mura	.50
BCP32	Luke Hetherington	.50
BCP33	Michael Daniel	1.00
BCP34	Jake Renshaw	.50
BCP35	Greg Halman	2.50
BCP36	Ryan Khoury	.50
BCP37	Ryan Ouellette	1.00
BCP38	Mike Brantley	.50
BCP39	Eric Brown	.50
BCP40	Jose Duarte	.50
BCP41	Eli Tintor	1.00
BCP42	Kent Sakamoto	.50
BCP43	Luke Montz	1.50
BCP44	Alex Cobb	.50
BCP45	Mike McKenry	.50
BCP46	Javier Castillo	.50
BCP47	Jeff Stevens	.50
BCP48	Greg Burns	.50
BCP49	Blake Johnson	.50
BCP50	Austin Jackson	5.00
BCP51	Anthony Recker	.50
BCP52	Luis Durango	.50
BCP53	Engel Beltre	3.00
BCP54	Seth Bynum	.50
BCP55	Ryan Strieby	.50
BCP56	Iggy Suarez	1.00
BCP57	Ryan Morris	.50
BCP58	Scott Van Slyke	.50
BCP59	Tyler Kolodny	1.50
BCP60	Joseph Martinez	.50
BCP61	Aaron Mathews	.50
BCP62	Phillip Cuadrado	.50
BCP63	Alex Liddi	.50
BCP64	Alex Burnett	.50
BCP65	Brian Barton	1.00
BCP66	David Welch	.50
BCP67	Kyle Reynolds	.50
BCP68	Francisco Hernandez	.50
BCP69	Logan Morrison	4.00
BCP70	Ronald Ramirez	.50
BCP71	Brad Miller	.50
BCP72	Braedyn Pruitt	1.00
BCP73	Jason Fernandez	.50
BCP74	Joseph Mahoney	1.00
BCP75	Quentin Davis	.50
BCP76	P.J. Walters	1.50
BCP77	Jordan Czarniecki	.50
BCP78	Jonathan Mota	1.00
BCP79	Michael Hernandez	.50
BCP80	James Guerrero	.50
BCP81	Chris Johnson	.50
BCP82	Daniel Cortes	1.50
BCP83	Sal Sanchez	.50
BCP84	Sean Henry	.50
BCP85	Caleb Gindl	1.50
BCP86	Tommy Everidge	.50
BCP87	Matt Rizzotti	.50
BCP88	Luis Munoz	.50
BCP89	Matt Klimas	.50
BCP90	Angel Reyes	1.00
BCP91	Sean Danielson	.50
BCP92	Omar Poveda	.50
BCP93	Mario Lisson	.50
BCP94	Brian Mathews	.50
BCP95	Matt Buschmann	.50
BCP96	Greg Thomson	.50
BCP97	Matt Inouye	.50
BCP98	Aneury Rodriguez	.50
BCP99	Bradley Harman	.50
BCP100	Aaron Bates	1.00
BCP101	Graham Taylor	.50
BCP102	Kenny Holmberg	.50
BCP103	Greg Dowling	.50
BCP104	Ronnie Ray	.50
BCP105	Mike Wlodarczyk	.50
BCP106	Jose Martinez	.50
BCP107	Jason Stephens	1.00
BCP108	Will Rhymes	.50
BCP109	Joey Side	.50
BCP110	Brandon Waring	5.00
BCP111	David Price/Auto.	65.00
BCP112	Michael Moustakas/Auto.	40.00
BCP113	Matt LaPorta/Auto.	25.00
BCP114	Wendell Fairley/Auto.	20.00
BCP115	Josh Vitters/Auto.	40.00
BCP116	Jonathan Bachanov/Auto.	20.00
BCP117	Edward Kunz/Auto.	15.00
BCP118	Matt Dominguez/Auto.	20.00
BCP119	Kyle Lotzkar/Auto.	15.00
BCP120	Madison Bumgarner/Auto.	40.00
BCP121	Jason Heyward/Auto.	160.00
BCP122	Julio Borbon/Auto.	15.00
BCP123	Josh Smoker/Auto.	15.00
BCP124	Jarrod Parker/Auto.	15.00
BCP125	Kevin Ahrens/Auto.	15.00
BCP126	J.P. Arencibia/Auto.	15.00
BCP127	Josh Bell/Auto.	15.00
BCP128	Scott Cousins/Auto.	15.00
BCP129	Brandon Hynick/Auto.	15.00
BCP130	Alan Johnson/Auto.	10.00

Chrome Prospects Red Refractor
No Pricing
Production Five Sets

Chrome Prospects Orange Refractor

No Pricing
Production 25 Sets

Chrome Prospects SuperFractor

Production One Set

Chrome Prospects Gold Refractor

Gold (1-110):	15-25X
Gold Autos. (111-130):	4-6X
Production 50 Sets	

Chrome Prospects Blue Refractor

Blue (1-110):	5-10X
Blue Autos. (111-130):	2-3X
Production 150 Sets	

Chrome Prospects X-Fractor

X-Fractor (1-110):	4-8X
Production 275	
X-Fractor Autos. (111-130):	1-2X
Auto. Production 250	

Chrome Prospects Refractor

Refractor (1-110):	3-5X
Production 599	
Refractor Auto. (111-130):	1-1.5X
Auto. Production 500	

Scouts Autographs

		NM/M
Common Auto.:		5.00
BF	Bob Fontaine Jr.	5.00
TD	Tony DeMacio	5.00
MR	Mike Rizzo	5.00
JD	Jon Deeble	5.00
TC	Ty Coslow	5.00
TCU	Tom Couston	5.00
RA	Ralph Avila	5.00
LW	Leon Wurth	5.00
JL	Jerry Lafferty	5.00
CB	Chris Bourjos	5.00
BS	Bowman Scout	10.00
AS	Alex Smith	5.00
TK	Tim Kelly	5.00
DJ	Dave Jennings	5.00
JC	Jerome Cochran	5.00
DO	Dan Ontiveros	5.00
DL	Don Lyle	5.00
JH	Josue Herrera	5.00
JM	Joe Mason	5.00
BB	Bill Buck	5.00
BE	Bob Engle	5.00

2008 Bowman Chrome

		NM/M
Common Player (1-190):		.25
Common RC (191-220):		.50
Pack (4):		4.00
Box (18):		60.00
1	Ryan Braun	.75
2	David DeJesus	.25
3	Brandon Phillips	.25
4	Mark Teixeira	.50
5	Daisuke Matsuzaka	.75
6	Justin Upton	.50
7	Jered Weaver	.25
8	Todd Helton	.50
9	Adam Jones	.40
10	Erik Bedard	.40
11	Jason Bay	.40
12	Cole Hamels	.50
13	Bobby Abreu	.50
14	Carlos Zambrano	.50
15	Vladimir Guerrero	.75
16	Joe Blanton	.25
17	Paul Maholm	.25
18	Adrian Gonzalez	.40
19	Brandon Webb	.50
20	Carl Crawford	.50
21	A.J. Burnett	.25
22	Dmitri Young	.25
23	Jeremy Hermida	.25
24	C.C. Sabathia	.50
25	Adam Dunn	.50
26	Matt Garza	.25
27	Adrian Beltre	.25
28	Kevin Millwood	.25
29	Manny Ramirez	.75
30	Javier Vazquez	.25
31	Carlos Delgado	.50
32	Torii Hunter	.40
33	Ivan Rodriguez	.50

34	Nick Markakis	.50
35	Gil Meche	.25
36	Garrett Atkins	.40
37	Fausto Carmona	.25
38	Joe Mauer	.50
39	Tom Glavine	.50
40	Hideki Matsui	.75
41	Scott Rolen	.40
42	Tim Lincecum	.50
43	Prince Fielder	.50
44	Kazuo Matsui	.25
45	Tom Gorzelanny	.25
46	Lance Berkman	.50
47	David Ortiz	.75
48	Dontrelle Willis	.25
49	Travis Hafner	.25
50	Aaron Harang	.25
51	Chris Young	.40
52	Vernon Wells	.40
53	Francisco Liriano	.40
54	Eric Chavez	.25
55	Phil Hughes	.50
56	Melvin Mora	.25
57	Johan Santana	.75
58	Brian McCann	.40
59	Pat Burrell	.50
60	Chris Carpenter	.25
61	Brian Giles	.25
62	Jose Reyes	.75
63	Hanley Ramirez	.75
64	Ubaldo Jimenez	.75
65	Felix Pie	.25
66	Jeremy Bonderman	.25
67	Jimmy Rollins	.50
68	Miguel Tejada	.40
69	Derek Lowe	.25
70	Alex Gordon	.40
71	John Maine	.25
72	Alfonso Soriano	.75
73	Ben Sheets	.40
74	Hunter Pence	.50
75	Magglio Ordonez	.40
76	Josh Beckett	.50
77	Victor Martinez	.40
78	Mark Buehrle	.25
79	Jason Varitek	.40
80	Chien-Ming Wang	.50
81	Ken Griffey Jr.	1.50
82	Billy Butler	.25
83	Brad Penny	.25
84	Carlos Beltran	.50
85	Curt Schilling	.50
86	Jorge Posada	.40
87	Andruw Jones	.40
88	Bobby Crosby	.25
89	Freddy Sanchez	.25
90	Barry Zito	.25
91	Miguel Cabrera	.75
92	B.J. Upton	.40
93	Matt Cain	.40
94	Lyle Overbay	.25
95	Austin Kearns	.25
96	Alex Rodriguez	2.50
97	Rich Harden	.40
98	Justin Morneau	.50
99	Oliver Perez	.25
100	Gary Matthews Jr.	.25
101	Matt Holliday	.50
102	Justin Verlander	.40
103	Orlando Cabrera	.25
104	Rich Hill	.25
105	Tim Hudson	.40
106	Ryan Zimmerman	.40
107	Roy Oswalt	.40
108	Nick Swisher	.40
109	Raul Ibanez	.25
110	Kelly Johnson	.25
111	Alex Rios	.50
112	John Lackey	.25
113	Robinson Cano	.50
114	Michael Young	.40
115	Jeff Francis	.25
116	Grady Sizemore	.75
117	Mike Lowell	.40
118	Aramis Ramirez	.40
119	Stephen Drew	.40
120	Yovani Gallardo	.40
121	Chase Utley	.75
122	Dan Haren	.40
123	Yunel Escobar	.25
124	Greg Maddux	1.50
125	Garret Anderson	.25
126	Aubrey Huff	.25
127	Paul Konerko	.40
128	Dan Uggla	.40
129	Roy Halladay	.40
130	Andre Ethier	.25
131	Orlando Hernandez	.25
132	Troy Tulowitzki	.40
133	Carlos Guillen	.25
134	Scott Kazmir	.40
135	Aaron Rowand	.25
136	Jim Edmonds	.25
137	Jermaine Dye	.40
138	Orlando Hudson	.25
139	Derek Lee	.50
140	Travis Buck	.25
141	Zack Greinke	.25
142	Jeff Kent	.40
143	John Smoltz	.50
144	David Wright	1.00
145	Joba Chamberlain	.75
146	Adam LaRoche	.25
147	Kevin Youkilis	.50
148	Troy Glaus	.40
149	Nick Johnson	.25
150	J.J. Hardy	.40
151	Felix Hernandez	.40

152	Gary Sheffield	.40
153	Albert Pujols	2.50
154	Chuck James	.25
155	Kosuke Fukudome RC	3.00
156	Eric Byrnes	.25
157	Brad Hawpe	.25
158	Delmon Young	.25
159	Brian Roberts	.25
160	Russell Martin	.40
161	Hank Blalock	.25
162	Yadier Molina	.25
163	Jeremy Guthrie	.25
164	Chipper Jones	1.00
165	Johnny Damon	.50
166	Ryan Garko	.25
167	Jake Peavy	.50
168	Chone Figgins	.40
169	Edgar Renteria	.25
170	Jim Thome	.50
171	Carlos Pena	.40
172	Dustin Pedroia	.50
173	Brett Myers	.25
174	Josh Hamilton	.75
175	Randy Johnson	.75
176	Ichiro Suzuki	1.50
177	Aaron Hill	.25
178	Corey Hart	.25
179	Jarrod Saltalamacchia	.25
180	Jeff Francoeur	.25
181	Derek Jeter	2.50
182	Curtis Granderson	.50
183	James Loney	.25
184	Brian Bannister	.25
185	Carlos Lee	.50
186	Pedro Martinez	.50
187	Asdrubal Cabrera	.25
188	Kenji Johjima	.25
189	Jacoby Ellsbury	.50
190	Ryan Howard	.75
191	Sean Rodriguez (RC)	.50
192	Justin Ruggiano RC	1.00
193	Jed Lowrie (RC)	1.00
194	Joey Votto (RC)	3.00
195	Denard Span (RC)	2.00
196	Bradley Harman RC	1.00
197	Jeff Niemann (RC)	1.00
198	Chin-Lung Hu (RC)	1.00
199	Luke Hochevar RC	1.00
200	German Duran RC	.50
201	Troy Patton (RC)	.50
202	Hiroki Kuroda RC	1.00
203	David Purcey (RC)	.50
204	Armando Galarraga RC	3.00
205	John Bowker (RC)	.50
206	Nick Blackburn RC	1.50
207	Hernan Iribarren (RC)	.50
208	Greg Smith RC	.50
209	Alberto Gonzalez (RC)	1.00
210	Justin Masterson (RC)	1.00
211	Brian Barton RC	.50
212	Robinzon Diaz (RC)	.50
213	Clete Thomas RC	1.00
214	Kazuo Fukumori RC	1.00
215	Jayson Nix (RC)	.50
216	Evan Longoria RC	6.00
217	Johnny Cueto RC	2.50
218	Matt Tolbert RC	1.00
219	Masahide Kobayashi RC	1.00
220	Callix Crabbe (RC)	.50

Refractor

Refractor (1-190):	2-4X
RC (191-220):	1.5-2X

X-Fractor

X-Fractor (1-190):	3-5X
RC (191-220):	2-4X
Production 250 Sets	

Blue Refractor

Blue Refractor (1-190):	4-6X
RC (191-220):	3-5X
Production 150 Sets	

Gold Refractor

Gold Refractor (1-190):	10-15X
RC (191-220):	8-15X
Production 50 Sets	

Orange Refractor

Orange Refractor (1-190):	10-20X
RC (191-220):	10-20X
Production 25 Sets	

Red Refractor

No Pricing
Production 5 Sets

Super-Fractor

Production One Set

Chrome Prospects

		NM/M
Common Prospect (131-240):		.50
Common Prospect Auto. (241-285):		10.00
131	Zhenwang Zhang	1.00
132	Chris Nash	.50
133	Sergio Morales	.50
134	Carlos Santana	3.00
135	Carlos Monasterios	.50
136	Quincy Latimore	.50
137	Yamaico Navarro	1.50
138	Ryan Mullins	.50
139	Collin DeLome	.50
140	Hector Correa	.50
141	Mitch Canham	1.00
142	Robert Fish	.50
143	Ryan Royster	.50

144	Eric Barrett	1.00
145	Deibinson Romero	1.00
146	Jeff Gerbe	.50
147	Lucas Duda	.50
148	Bryan Morris	1.00
149	Andrew Romine	.50
150	Glenn Gibson	.50
151	Dan Brezeale	.50
152	Shairon Martis	1.00
153	Helder Velazquez	.50
154	Alan Farina	.50
155	Brandon Barnes	.50
156	Waldis Joaquin	.50
157	Luis De La Cruz	.50
158	Yunesky Sanchez	.50
159	Mitch Hilligoss	1.00
160	Vin Mazzaro	1.00
161	Marcus Davis	.50
162	Tony Barnette	.50
163	Joe Benson	1.00
164	Jake Arrieta	1.50
165	Alfredo Silverio	.50
166	Duane Below	.50
167	Kai Liu	1.00
168	Zach Britton	.50
169	Jaime Pedroza	.50
170	Frank Herrmann	.50
171	Justin Turner	1.00
172	Jeff Manship	.50
173	Paul Winterling	.50
174	Nathan Vineyard	1.00
175	Jason Delaney	.50
176	Ivan Nova	.50
177	Esmailyn Gonzalez	1.00
178	Brett Cecil	1.00
179	Jose Martinez	1.50
180	Brad Peacock	.50
181	Justin Snyder	1.00
182	Steve Garrison	1.00
183	Joe Mahoney	.50
184	Graham Godfrey	.50
185	Larry Williams	.50
186	Jeremy Haynes	.50
187	Brent Brewer	.50
188	Jhoulys Chacin	3.00
189	Nevin Ashley	.50
190	Justin Cassel	.50
191	Jon Jay	.50
192	Chris Huseby	1.00
193	D.J. Jones	1.00
194	David Bromberg	.50
195	Juan Francisco	2.50
196	Zach Jevne	.50
197	Darwin Barney	.50
198	Jose Ortegano	.50
199	Dominic Brown	2.50
200	Kyle Ginley	.50
201	David Wood	.50
202	Jhonny Nunez	.50
203	Carlos Rivero	1.50
204	Anthony Varvaro	.50
205	Christian Lopez	.50
206	Travis Banwart	.50
207	Rhyne Hughes	1.00
208	Heath Rollins	.50
209	Zack Cozart	1.00
210	Mike Dunn	1.00
211	Chris Pettit	.50
212	Dan Berlind	.50
213	Ernesto Mejia	1.50
214	Hector Rondon	.50
215	Jose Vallejo	.50
216	Kyle Schmidt	.50
217	Bubba Bell	1.00
218	Charlie Furbush	.50
219	Pedro Baez	1.50
220	Brandon MaGee	.50
221	Clint Robinson	1.00
222	Fabio Castillo	1.00
223	Brad Emaus	.50
224	Mike DeJesus	.50
225	Brandon Laird	.50
226	R.J. Seidel	1.00
227	Agustin Murillo	.50
228	Trevor Reckling	2.00
229	Hector Gomez	1.50
230	Jordan Norberto	.50
231	Steve Hill	.50
232	Hassan Pena	.50
233	Justin Henry	1.00
234	Chase Lirette	.50
235	Christian Marrero	.50
236	Will Kline	.50
237	Johan Limonta	.50
238	Duke Welker	.50
239	Jeudy Valdez	.50
240	Elvin Ramirez	.50
241	Josh Kreuzer/Auto.	15.00

242	Ryan Zink/Auto.	20.00
243	Matt Harrison/Auto.	20.00
244	Dustin Richardson/ Auto.	15.00
245	Fautino de los Santos/ Auto.	15.00
246	Austin Jackson/Auto.	50.00
247	Jordan Schafer/Auto.	20.00
248	Daryl Thompson/Auto.	15.00
249	Lars Anderson/Auto.	40.00
250	Tim Bascom/Auto.	15.00
251	Brandon Hicks/Auto.	15.00
252	David Kopp/Auto.	10.00
253	Dan Lehmann/Auto.	10.00
254	Jordan Zimmerman/ Auto.	20.00
255	Cale Iorg/Auto	15.00
256	Austin Romine/Auto.	20.00
257	Chaz Roe/Auto.	10.00
258	Danny Rams/Auto.	15.00
259	Daniel Bard/Auto.	20.00
260	Engel Beltre/Auto.	20.00
261	Michael Watt/Auto.	15.00
262	Brennan Boesch/Auto.	15.00
263	Matt Latos/Auto.	25.00
264	John Jaso/Auto.	15.00
265	Adrian Alaniz/Auto.	20.00
266	Matt Green/Auto.	15.00
267	Andrew Lambo/Auto.	20.00
268	Michael McCardell/ Auto.	20.00
269	Chris Valaika/Auto.	20.00
270	Cole Rohrbough/Auto.	20.00
271	Andrew Brackman/ Auto.	20.00
272	Bud Norris/Auto.	15.00
273	Ryan Kalish/Auto.	20.00
274	Jake McGee/Auto.	15.00
275	Aaron Cunningham/ Auto.	20.00
276	Mitch Boggs/Auto	15.00
277	Bradley Suttle/Auto.	15.00
278	Henry Rodriguez/Auto	15.00
279	Mario Lisson/Auto.	15.00
280	Ludovicus Van Mil/ Auto.	15.00
281	Angel Villalona/Auto.	25.00
282	Mark Melancon/Auto.	20.00
283	Brian Dinkelman/Auto.	15.00
284	Daniel McCutchen/Auto.	15.00
285	Rene Tosoni/Auto.	15.00

Chrome Prospects Refractor

Refractor (131-240):	3-5X
Refractor Auto. (241-285):	1-1.5X
Production 500 Sets	

Chrome Prospects X-Fractor

X-fractor (131-240):	4-8X
X-fractor Auto. (241-285):	1-1.5X
Production 250 Sets	

Chrome Prospects Blue Refractor

Blue (131-240):	6-12X
Blue Auto. (241-285):	1-2X
Production 150 Sets	

Chrome Prospects Gold Refractor

Gold (131-240):	15-25X
Gold Auto. (241-285):	3-5X
Production 50 Sets	

Chrome Prospects Orange Refractor

Orange (131-240):	No Pricing
Orange Auto. (241-285):	No Pricing
Production 25 Sets	

Chrome Prospects Red Refractor

Red (131-240):	No Pricing
Red Auto. (241-285):	No Pricing
Production 5 Sets	

Chrome Prospects Super-Fractor

Production One Set

Head of the Class

		NM/M
Refractor:		1-1.5X
Production 99 Sets		
Gold Refactor:		2-2.5X
Production 50 Sets		
FL	Prince Fielder, Matt LaPorta	75.00
LP	Evan Longoria, David Price/350	125.00
CH	Joba Chamberlain, Phil Hughes/350	75.00

2008 Bowman Chrome Draft

		NM/M
Complete Set (55):		20.00
Common Player:		.50
1	Nick Adenhart (RC)	.50
2	Michael Aubrey RC	1.00
3	Mike Aviles RC	1.00
4	Burke Badenhop RC	.50
5	Wladimir Balentien (RC)	.50
6	Collin Balester (RC)	.50
6	Collin Balester/Auto.	8.00
7	Josh Banks (RC)	.50
8	Wes Bankston (RC)	.50
9	Joey Votto (RC)	2.50

10	Mitch Boggs (RC)	.50
11	Jay Bruce (RC)	2.00
12	Chris Carter (RC)	1.00
13	Justin Christian RC	1.00
14	Chris Davis RC	1.00
15	Blake DeWitt (RC)	1.00
15	Blake DeWitt Auto	15.00
16	Nick Evans RC	.50
17	Jaime Garcia RC	2.00
18	Brett Gardner (RC)	1.00
19	Carlos Gonzalez (RC)	.75
20	Matt Harrison (RC)	.50
21	Micah Hoffpauir RC	.50
22	Nick Hundley (RC)	.50
23	Eric Hurley (RC)	.50
24	Elliot Johnson (RC)	.50
25	Matt Joyce (RC)	1.00
26	Clayton Kershaw RC	2.00
26	Clayton Kershaw/Auto.	25.00
27	Evan Longoria (RC)	.50
27	Evan Longoria/Auto.	75.00
28	Matt Macri (RC)	.75
29	Chris Perez RC	.75
30	Max Ramirez RC	.50
31	Greg Reynolds (RC)	.50
32	Brooks Conrad (RC)	.50
33	Max Scherzer RC	1.50
34	Daryl Thompson (RC)	.50
35	Taylor Teagarden RC	.75
36	Rich Thompson RC	.50
37	Ryan Tucker (RC)	.50
38	Jonathan Van Every RC	.50
39	Chris Volstad (RC)	.75
39	Chris Volstad/Auto.	15.00
40	Michael Hollimon RC	.50
41	Brad Ziegler RC	1.50
42	Jamie D'Antona (RC)	.50
43	Clayton Richard (RC)	.50
44	Edgar Gonzalez (RC)	.50
45	Bryan LaHair RC	.50
46	Warner Madrigal (RC)	.50
47	Reid Brignac (RC)	.75
48	David Robertson RC	.50
49	Nick Stavinoha RC	1.00
50	Jai Miller (RC)	.50
51	Charlie Morton (RC)	.50
52	Brandon Boggs (RC)	.50
53	Joe Mather RC	1.00
54	Gregorio Petit RC	.50
55	Jeff Samardzija RC	1.00

Blue Refractors

Blue:	4-6X
Production 99 Sets	

Gold Refractors

Gold:	6-12X
Gold Auto.:	2-3X
Production 50 Sets	

Refractors

Refractor:	2-3X
Refractor Auto.:	1-1.5X
Auto. Production 99	

Orange Refractors

Orange:	No Pricing
Production 25 Sets	

Red Refractors

Production One Set

X-Fractors

ANDREW LIEBEL

X-Fractors 2-4X
Production 199 Sets

Printing Plates

No Pricing
Production one set per color.

Prospects

JUSTIN BRISTOW

	NM/M
Common Player (1-110):	.50
Common Auto. (111-128):	10.00
Refractor:	2-4X
Refractor Auto.:	1-1.25X
Auto. Production 500	
Blue Refractor:	5-10X
Production 99	
Blue Refrac. Auto.:	1-2.5X
Production 150	
Gold Refractor:	20-30X
Gold Ref. Auto.:	4-6X
Production 50 Sets	
Orange Refractor:	No Pricing
Production 25 Sets	
X-Fractor:	4-6X
Production 199	
X-Fractor Auto.:	1-1.5X
Production 225	
SuperFractor:	No Pricing
Production One Set	

1 Rick Porcello 2.50
2 Braeden Schlehuber .50
3 Kenny Wilson .50
4 Jeff Lanning .50
5 Kevin Dubler .50
6 Eric Campbell 1.00
7 Tyler Chatwood .50
8 Tyreace House 1.00
9 Adrian Nieto 1.00
10 Robbie Grossman 1.00
11 Jordan Danks 1.50
12 Jay Austin 1.00
13 Ryan Perry 1.00
14 Ryan Chaffee 1.00
15 Niko Vasquez 1.50
16 Shane Dyer .50
17 Benji Gonzalez .50
18 Miles Reagan .50
19 Anthony Ferrara .50
20 Markus Brisker .50
21 Justin Bristow .50
22 Richard Bleier 1.00
23 Jeremy Beckham 1.00
24 Xavier Avery 1.00
25 Christian Vazquez .50
26 Nick Romero .50
27 Trey Watten .50
28 Brett Jacobson .50
29 Tyler Sample .50
30 T.J. Steele 1.00
31 Christian Friedrich 1.50
32 Graham Hicks 1.00
33 Shane Peterson 1.00
34 Brett Hunter .50
35 Tim Federowicz .50
36 Isaac Galloway 1.00
37 Logan Schafer .50
38 Paul Demny .50
39 Clayton Shunick .50
40 Andrew Liebel .50
41 Brandon Crawford .50
42 Blake Tekotte 1.00
43 Jason Corder .50
44 Bryan Shaw .50
45 Edgar Olmos .50
46 Dusty Coleman .50
47 Johnny Giavotella .50
48 Tyson Ross 1.00
49 Brent Morel .50
50 Dennis Raben 1.00
51 Jake Odorizzi 1.50
52 Ryne White .50
53 Devaris Strange-Gordon .50
54 Tim Murphy .50
55 Jake Jefferies .50
56 Anthony Capra .50
57 Kyle Weiland 1.50
58 Anthony Bass 1.00
59 Scott Green .50
60 Zeke Spruill 1.50
61 L.J. Hoes 1.00
62 Tyler Cline .50
63 Matt Cerda .50
64 Bobby Lanigan .50
65 Mike Sheridan .50
66 Carlos Carrasco .50
67 Nate Schierholtz .50
68 Jesus Delgado .50
69 Andrew McCutchen 1.00
70 Shairon Martis .50
71 Matt LaPorta 1.00
72 Eddie Morlan .50
73 Greg Golson .50
74 Julio Pimentel .50
75 Dexter Fowler 1.00
76 Henry Rodriguez .50
77 Cliff Pennington 1.00
78 Hector Rondon .50
79 Wes Hodges .50
80 Polin Trinidad .50
81 Chris Getz .50
82 Welington Castillo .50
83 Mat Gamel 1.50
84 Pablo Sandoval .50
85 Jason Donald .50
86 Jesus Montero 1.00
87 Jamie D'Antona .50
88 Wil Inman .50
89 Elvis Andrus 1.50
90 Taylor Teagarden .75
91 Scott Campbell .50
92 Jake Arrieta .50
93 Juan Francisco .50
94 Lou Marson .50
95 Luke Hughes .50
96 Bryan Anderson .50
97 Ramiro Pena .50
98 Jesse Todd .50
99 Gorkys Hernandez .50
100 Casey Weathers .50
101 Fernando Martinez 1.00
102 Clayton Richard .50
103 Gerardo Parra .50
104 Kevin Pucetas 1.00
105 Wilkin Ramirez .50
106 Ryan Mattheus 1.00
107 Angel Villalona 1.50
108 Brett Anderson 1.00
109 Chris Valaika 1.00
110 Trevor Cahill 1.00
111 Wilmer Flores/Auto. 25.00
112 Lonnie Chisenhall/Auto. 15.00
113 Carlos Gutierrez/Auto. 15.00
114 Derek Holland/Auto. 25.00
115 Mike Stanton/Auto. 125.00
116 Ike Davis/Auto. 50.00
117 Anthony Hewitt/Auto. 15.00
118 Gordon Beckham/Auto. 50.00
119 Dan Schlereth/Auto. 10.00
120 Zach Collier/Auto. 20.00
121 Evan Frederickson/Auto. 10.00
122 Mike Montgomery/Auto. 15.00
123 Cody Adams/Auto. 10.00
124 Brad Hand/Auto. 10.00
125 Josh Reddick/Auto. 15.00
126 Michel Inoa/Auto. 30.00
127 Jesus Montero/Auto. 50.00
128 Buster Posey/Auto. 80.00

2008 Bowman Draft

	NM/M
Complete Set (55):	15.00
Common Player:	.25
Pack (5 + 2 Chrome):	3.00
Box (24):	60.00

1 Nick Adenhart (RC) .50
2 Michael Aubrey RC .50
3 Mike Aviles RC .50
4 Burke Badenhop RC .25
5 Wladimir Balentien (RC) .25
6 Collin Balester (RC) .25
7 Josh Banks (RC) .25
8 Wes Bankston (RC) .25
9 Joey Votto (RC) 1.00
10 Mitch Boggs (RC) .25
11 Jay Bruce (RC) 1.00
12 Chris Carter (RC) .50
13 Justin Christian RC .50
14 Chris Davis RC .75
15 Blake DeWitt (RC) .75
16 Nick Evans RC .25
17 Jaime Garcia RC 1.00
18 Brett Gardner (RC) .50
19 Carlos Gonzalez (RC) .50
20 Matt Harrison (RC) .25
21 Micah Hoffpauir RC .25
22 Nick Hundley (RC) .25
23 Eric Hurley (RC) .25
24 Elliot Johnson (RC) .25
25 Matt Joyce (RC) .25
26 Clayton Kershaw RC 1.00
27 Evan Longoria RC 3.00
28 Matt Macri (RC) .25
29 Chris Perez RC .50
30 Max Ramirez RC .25
31 Greg Reynolds (RC) .25
32 Brooks Conrad (RC) .25
33 Max Scherzer RC .75
34 Daryl Thompson (RC) .25
35 Taylor Teagarden RC .50
36 Rich Thompson RC .25
37 Ryan Tucker (RC) .25
38 Jonathan Van Every RC .25
39 Chris Volstad (RC) .25
40 Michael Hollimon RC .25
41 Brad Ziegler RC .75
42 Jamie D'Antona (RC) .25
43 Clayton Richard (RC) .25
44 Edgar Gonzalez (RC) .25
45 Bryan LaHair RC .25
46 Warner Madrigal (RC) .25
47 Reid Brignac (RC) .50
48 David Robertson (RC) .50
49 Nick Stavinoha RC .25
50 Jai Miller (RC) .25
51 Charlie Morton (RC) .25
52 Brandon Boggs (RC) .25
53 Joe Mather RC .50
54 Gregorio Petit RC .50
55 Jeff Samardzija RC .75

Blue

Blue 2-3X
Production 399 Sets

Gold

Gold: 1-2X
Inserted 1:1

Printing Plates

No Pricing
Production one set per color.

AFLAC Autographs

	NM/M
Common Auto.	15.00
Inserted 1:215 Hobby	

AF Anthony Ferrara 15.00
AN Adrian Nieto 15.00
BB Blake Beavan 30.00
DB Drake Britton 20.00
DR Danny Rams 15.00
FF Freddie Freeman 75.00
IG Isaac Galloway 35.00
JG Jon Gilmore 20.00
JH Jason Heyward 475.00
JS Josh Smoker 25.00
JT John Tolisano 15.00
JV Josh Vitters 60.00
MB Madison Bumgarner 85.00
MM Michael Main 30.00
NN Nick Noonan 35.00
PD Paul Demny 15.00
QM Quinton Miller 20.00
RP Rick Porcello 100.00
TA Tim Alderson 50.00
XA Xavier Avery 30.00

Prospects

JEREMY BECKHAM

	NM/M
Complete Set (110):	20.00
Common Player:	.25
Blue:	3-4X
Production 399 Sets	
Gold:	1-2X
Inserted 1:1	
Red:	No Pricing
Production One Set	

1 Rick Porcello 2.00
2 Braeden Schlehuber .25
3 Kenny Wilson .25
4 Jeff Lanning .25
5 Kevin Dubler .25
6 Eric Campbell .50
7 Tyler Chatwood .25
8 Tyreace House .25
9 Adrian Nieto .50
10 Robbie Grossman .50
11 Jordan Danks .50
12 Jay Austin .50
13 Ryan Perry .25
14 Ryan Chaffee .25
15 Niko Vasquez .75
16 Shane Dyer .25
17 Benji Gonzalez .25
18 Miles Reagan .25
19 Anthony Ferrara .25
20 Markus Brisker .25
21 Justin Bristow .25
22 Richard Bleier .50
23 Jeremy Beckham .25
24 Xavier Avery .50
25 Christian Vazquez .50
26 Nick Romero .25
27 Trey Watten .25
28 Brett Jacobson .25
29 Tyler Sample .25
30 T.J. Steele .75
31 Christian Friedrich .75
32 Graham Hicks .50
33 Shane Peterson .50
34 Brett Hunter .50
35 Tim Federowicz .50
36 Isaac Galloway .50
37 Logan Schafer .50
38 Paul Demny .25
39 Clayton Shunick .25
40 Andrew Liebel .25
41 Brandon Crawford .50
42 Blake Tekotte .50
43 Jason Corder .25
44 Bryan Shaw .25
45 Edgar Olmos .25
46 Dusty Coleman .25
47 Johnny Giavotella .25
48 Tyson Ross .25
49 Brent Morel .25
50 Dennis Raben .25
51 Jake Odorizzi .75
52 Ryne White .25
53 Devaris Strange-Gordon .25
54 Tim Murphy .25
55 Jake Jefferies .25
56 Anthony Capra .25
57 Kyle Weiland .75
58 Anthony Bass .50
59 Scott Green .25
60 Zeke Spruill .75
61 L.J. Hoes .50
62 Tyler Cline .25
63 Matt Cerda .25
64 Bobby Lanigan .25
65 Mike Sheridan .25
66 Carlos Carrasco .25
67 Nate Schierholtz .25
68 Jesus Delgado .25
69 Andrew McCutchen .50
70 Shairon Martis .25
71 Matt LaPorta .75
72 Eddie Morlan .25
73 Greg Golson .25
74 Julio Pimentel .25
75 Dexter Fowler .50
76 Henry Rodriguez .25
77 Cliff Pennington .50
78 Hector Rondon .25
79 Wes Hodges .25
80 Polin Trinidad .25
81 Chris Getz .25
82 Welington Castillo .25
83 Mat Gamel .75
84 Pablo Sandoval .75
85 Jason Donald .25
86 Jesus Montero .50
87 Jamie D'Antona .25
88 Wil Inman .25
89 Elvis Andrus .50
90 Taylor Teagarden .50
91 Scott Campbell .25
92 Jake Arrieta .25
93 Juan Francisco .25
94 Lou Marson .25
95 Luke Hughes .25
96 Bryan Anderson .25
97 Ramiro Pena .25
98 Jesse Todd .25
99 Gorkys Hernandez .25
100 Casey Weathers .25
101 Fernando Martinez .50
102 Clayton Richard .25
103 Gerardo Parra .25
104 Kevin Pucetas .50
105 Wilkin Ramirez .25
106 Ryan Mattheus .50
107 Angel Villalona .75
108 Brett Anderson .25
109 Chris Valaika .50
110 Trevor Cahill .50

Prospects Jerseys

	NM/M
Retail Exclusive	

70 Shairon Martis 8.00
71 Matt LaPorta 8.00
73 Eddie Morlan 5.00
74 Julio Pimentel 5.00
75 Dexter Fowler 5.00
77 Cliff Pennington 5.00
80 Polin Trinidad 10.00
82 Welington Castillo 5.00
87 Jamie D'Antona 5.00
88 Wil Inman 8.00
93 Juan Francisco 8.00
94 Lou Marson 8.00
96 Bryan Anderson 8.00
97 Ramiro Pena 8.00
102 Clayton Richard 5.00
103 Gerardo Parra 8.00

Signs of the Future

	NM/M
Retail Exclusive	

DM Daniel Murphy 20.00
TS Travis Snider 25.00
KD Kyle Drabek 10.00
BS Brad Salmon 8.00
EM Evan MacLane 8.00
OS Oswaldo Sosa 10.00
GK George Kontos 15.00
BP Billy Petrick 8.00
CW Corey Wimberly 8.00

2008 Bowman Sterling

JOEY VOTTO — CINCINNATI REDS

	NM/M
Common RC:	3.00
Common RC Auto.:	10.00
Pack (5):	50.00
Box (6):	250.00

LH Luke Hochevar RC 5.00
DB Daric Barton (RC) 3.00
NA Nick Adenhart (RC) 3.00
EH Eric Hurley (RC) 3.00
CK Clayton Kershaw RC 15.00
CK Clayton Kershaw/399 Variation 15.00
DP David Purcey (RC) 8.00
RT Ryan Tucker (RC) 3.00
JV Joey Votto (RC) 10.00
JV J. Votto/399 Variation 10.00
JBC Jeff Clement (RC) 3.00
MA Michael Aubrey RC 5.00
MT Matt Tolbert RC 5.00
JCO Johnny Cueto RC 8.00
HI Hernan Iribarren (RC) 3.00
MK Masahide Kobayashi RC 6.00
JL Jed Lowrie RC 6.00
JL Jed Lowrie/399 Variation 6.00
JT J.R. Towles RC 4.00
JB Josh Banks (RC) 3.00
CG Carlos Gonzalez (RC) 8.00
CG Carlos Gonzalez/399 Variation 8.00
BH Brian Horwitz (RC) 5.00
SR Sean Rodriguez (RC) 5.00
KF Kosuke Fukudome RC 6.00
KF Kosuke Fukudome/399 Variation 8.00
CLH Chin-Lung Hu (RC) 4.00
WB Wladimir Balentien (RC) 4.00
JN Jeff Niemann (RC) 3.00
JAB Jay Bruce RC 10.00
JAB Jay Bruce/399 Variation 10.00
BJ Brandon Jones RC 6.00
NB Nick Blackburn (RC) 5.00
CB Clay Buchholz (RC) 5.00
GD German Duran (RC) 3.00
RL Radhames Liz RC 3.00
HK Hiroki Kuroda RC 8.00
HK Hiroki Kuroda/399 Variation 3.00
MRR Max Ramirez RC 3.00
MRR Max Ramirez/399 Variation 5.00
NLS Nick Stavinoha RC 3.00
JM Jai Miller RC 3.00
MJ Matt Joyce RC 3.00
GB Gregor Blanco (RC) 5.00
CC Chris Carter (RC) 5.00
CM Charlie Morton (RC) 3.00
CP Cliff Pennington (RC) 4.00
CP Cliff Pennington/399 Variation 5.00
JC Justin Christian RC 3.00
GR Greg Reynolds (RC) 3.00
JS Jeff Samardzija RC 6.00
JS Jeff Samardzija/399 Variation 8.00

	NM/M
Retail Exclusive	

BG Brett Gardner (RC) 8.00
RB Reid Brignac (RC) 3.00
NH Nick Hundley (RC) 5.00
CR Clayton Richard (RC) 5.00
BZ Brad Ziegler RC 5.00
NE Nick Evans RC 5.00
CD Chris Davis RC 5.00
GS Greg Smith/Auto. 8.00
EL Evan Longoria/Auto. RC 60.00
ES Seth Smith/Auto. 8.00
BJB Brian Bixler/Auto. RC 10.00

AG Armando Galarraga/ Auto. RC 20.00
JR Justin Ruggiano/ Auto. RC 10.00
CP Chris Perez/Auto. RC 10.00
ARU Adam Russell/ Auto. RC 10.00
CG Chris Getz/Auto. RC 10.00
TT Taylor Teagarden/ Auto. RC 15.00

Refractors

RC's: 1-2X
RC Autos.: 1-1.5X
Production 199 Sets

Gold Refractors

Gold RC's: 2-3X
Gold Autos.: 2-3X
Production 50 Sets

Black Refractors

No Pricing
Production 25 Sets

Red Refractors

No Pricing
Production One Set

Printing Plates

Production one set per color.

Dual Autographs

	NM/M
Production 325 Sets	
Refractor:	1-1.2X
Production 99 Sets	
Gold Refractor:	1-1.5X
Production 50 Sets	
Black Refractor:	2-2.5X
Production 25 Sets	

PB Buster Posey, Gordon Beckham 60.00
RS Alex Rios, Travis Snider 35.00
MM Jesus Montero, Mark Melancon 40.00
LS Evan Longoria, Geovany Soto 80.00

Prospects

AUSTIN JACKSON

	NM/M
Common Prospect:	3.00
Refractors:	1-2X
Refractor Auto.:	1-1.5X
Production 199 Sets	
Gold Refractor:	2-4X
Gold Ref. Auto.:	2-3X
Production 50 Sets	
Black Refractor:	No Pricing
Production 25 Sets	

JB Jonathan Bachanov 3.00
YS Yunesky Sanchez 3.00
RR Rusty Ryal 3.00
GP Gerardo Parra 3.00
BH Brandon Hicks 5.00
ZB Zach Britton 3.00
BB Bubba Bell 5.00
RK Ryan Kalish 5.00
MI Matt Inouye 3.00
CV Chris Valaika 5.00
BW Brandon Waring 5.00
RM Ryan Morris 5.00
JC Jhoulys Chacin 5.00
JC Jordan Czarniecki 3.00
AR Aneury Rodriguez 3.00
CI Cale Iorg 5.00
LM Logan Morrison 8.00
GT Graham Taylor 5.00
CJ Chris Johnson 5.00
CD Daniel Cortes 5.00
DD Danny Duffy 10.00
MW Michael Watt 5.00
MB Mike Brantley 5.00
ST Steve Tolleson 3.00
RT Rene Tosoni 5.00
EK Edward Kunz 5.00
JS Justin Snyder 5.00
AJ Austin Jackson 15.00
AB Andrew Brackman 8.00
FS Fautino De Los Santos 4.00
MR Matt Rizzotti 4.00
TH Tom Hagan 5.00
MC Mitch Canham 5.00
RP Rick Porcello 15.00
JJ Jon Jay 5.00
JM Jake McGee 3.00
AC Alex Cobb 5.00
EB Engel Beltre 5.00
BC Brett Cecil 8.00

Code	Player	Price
AM	Aaron Mathews	3.00
SM	Shairon Martis	5.00
JZ	Jordan Zimmerman	4.00
AA	Adrian Alaniz	5.00
JSM	Josh Smoker	5.00
MD	Michael Daniel	3.00
XA	Xavier Avery	6.00
NV	Niko Vasquez	8.00
NR	Nick Romero	3.00
KW	Kenny Wilson	3.00
BS	Braeden Schlehuber	3.00
MM	Mark Melancon/Auto.	15.00
LA	Lars Anderson/Auto.	30.00
CT	Chris Tillman/Auto.	30.00
JL	Jeff Locke/Auto.	10.00
VM	Vin Mazzaro/Auto.	15.00
CGU	Carlos Gutierrez/Auto.	15.00
IDA	Ike Davis/Auto.	40.00
AH	Anthony Hewitt/Auto.	15.00
LL	Lance Lynn/Auto.	10.00
BHA	Brad Hand/Auto.	10.00
JLI	Josh Lindblom/Auto.	10.00
JK	Jason Knapp/Auto.	15.00
AMO	Adam Moore/Auto.	15.00
GB	Gordon Beckham/Auto.	40.00
DH	David Hernandez/Auto.	15.00
TF	Tim Fedroff/Auto.	15.00
EH	Eric Hacker/Auto.	15.00
CSA	Carlos Santana/Auto.	40.00
BP	Buster Posey/Auto.	50.00
AC	Andrew Cashner/Auto.	15.00
LC	Lonnie Chisenhall/Auto.	15.00
DS	Dan Schlereth/Auto.	10.00
PT	Polin Trinidad/Auto.	10.00
QM	Quinton Miller/Auto.	10.00
JR	Javier Rodriguez/Auto.	10.00
CB	Charlie Blackmon/Auto.	10.00
KK	Kala Kaaihue/Auto.	10.00
GH	Greg Halman/Auto.	35.00
EA	Elvis Andrus/Jsy/Auto.	20.00
JD	Jason Donald/Jsy/Auto.	20.00
JA	Jake Arrieta/Jsy/Auto.	20.00
GGH	Gorkys Hernandez/Jsy/Auto.	15.00
JM	Jesus Montero/Jsy/Auto.	35.00
FM	Fernando Martinez/Jsy/Auto.	20.00
CC	Carlos Carrasco/Jsy/Auto.	15.00

Relics

RUSS MARTIN — LOS ANGELES DODGERS

		NM/M
	Common Relic:	5.00
	Refractor:	1-1.5X
	Production 199 Sets	
	Gold Refractor:	2-3X
	Production 50 Sets	
	Black Refractor:	No Pricing
	Production 25 Sets	
MM	Mickey Mantle	60.00
AP	Albert Pujols	15.00
TL	Tim Lincecum	15.00
JC	Joba Chamberlain	6.00
MH	Matt Holliday	5.00
RM	Russell Martin	5.00
DY	Delmon Young	5.00
JU	Justin Upton	8.00
VG	Vladimir Guerrero	8.00
MC	Miguel Cabrera	8.00
BM	Brian McCann	5.00
DM	Daisuke Matsuzaka	12.00
VM	Victor Martinez	5.00
HR	Hanley Ramirez	8.00
HP	Hunter Pence	6.00
RB	Ryan Braun	12.00
AR	Alex Rodriguez	15.00
CW	Chien-Ming Wang	10.00
CH	Cole Hamels	8.00
RH	Ryan Howard	8.00
JR	Jimmy Rollins	8.00
GS	Geovany Soto	8.00
DW	David Wright	10.00
NM	Nick Markakis	8.00
JE	Jacoby Ellsbury	10.00
MT	Mark Teixeira	6.00
CJ	Chipper Jones	8.00
EV	Edinson Volquez	5.00
CU	Chase Utley	8.00
IS	Ichiro Suzuki	15.00
JH	Josh Hamilton	15.00
DO	David Ortiz	8.00
MR	Manny Ramirez	8.00
PF	Prince Fielder	8.00
JR	Jose Reyes	8.00
CC	Carl Crawford	5.00

2009 Bowman

JONATHON NIESE

	NM/M
Complete Set (220):	
Common Player:	.15
Hobby Pack (10):	3.00
Hobby Box (24):	65.00
1 David Wright	1.00
2 Albert Pujols	2.00
3 Alex Rodriguez	1.50
4 Chase Utley	.75
5 Chien-Ming Wang	.25
6 Jimmy Rollins	.50
7 Ken Griffey Jr.	1.50
8 Manny Ramirez	.75
9 Chipper Jones	.75
10 Ichiro Suzuki	1.00
11 Justin Morneau	.50
12 Hanley Ramirez	.75
13 Cliff Lee	.25
14 Ryan Howard	1.00
15 Ian Kinsler	.50
16 Jose Reyes	.75
17 Ted Lilly	.15
18 Miguel Cabrera	.75
19 Nate McLouth	.15
20 Josh Beckett	.50
21 John Lackey	.25
22 David Ortiz	.75
23 Carlos Lee	.40
24 Adam Dunn	.40
25 B.J. Upton	.25
26 Curtis Granderson	.25
27 David DeJesus	.15
28 C.C. Sabathia	.75
29 Russell Martin	.25
30 Torii Hunter	.25
31 Rich Harden	.15
32 Johnny Damon	.50
33 Cristian Guzman	.15
34 Grady Sizemore	.75
35 Jorge Posada	.40
36 Placido Polanco	.15
37 Ryan Ludwick	.25
38 Dustin Pedroia	.75
39 Matt Garza	.25
40 Prince Fielder	.75
41 Rick Ankiel	.25
42 Jonathan Sanchez	.15
43 Erik Bedard	.15
44 Ryan Braun	1.00
45 Ervin Santana	.25
46 Brian Roberts	.25
47 Mike Jacobs	.15
48 Phil Hughes	.15
49 Justin Masterson	.25
50 Felix Hernandez	.50
51 Stephen Drew	.25
52 Bobby Abreu	.40
53 Jay Bruce	.50
54 Josh Hamilton	.75
55 Garrett Atkins	.25
56 Jacoby Ellsbury	.50
57 Johan Santana	.25
58 James Shields	.25
59 Armando Galarraga	.15
60 Carlos Pena	.40
61 Matt Kemp	.50
62 Joey Votto	.50
63 Raul Ibanez	.25
64 Casey Kotchman	.15
65 Hunter Pence	.25
66 Daniel Murphy	.15
67 Carlos Beltran	.25
68 Evan Longoria	1.00
69 Daisuke Matsuzaka	.50
70 Cole Hamels	.50
71 Robinson Cano	.40
72 Clayton Kershaw	.75
73 Kenji Johjima	.15
74 Kazuo Matsui	.15
75 Jayson Werth	.25
76 Brian McCann	.25
77 Barry Zito	.15
78 Glen Perkins	.15
79 Jeff Francoeur	.25
80 Derek Jeter	2.00
81 Ryan Doumit	.15
82 Dan Haren	.25
83 Justin Duchscherer	.15
84 Marlon Byrd	.15
85 Derek Lowe	.15
86 Pat Burrell	.15
87 Jair Jurrjens	.15
88 Zack Greinke	.25
89 Jon Lester	.25
90 Justin Verlander	.25
91 Jorge Cantu	.15
92 John Maine	.15
93 Brad Hawpe	.15
94 Mike Aviles	.15
95 Victor Martinez	.25
96 Ryan Dempster	.15
97 Miguel Tejada	.25
98 Joe Mauer	.40
99 Scott Olsen	.15
100 Tim Lincecum	1.00
101 Francisco Liriano	.40
102 Chris Iannetta	.15
103 Jamie Moyer	.15
104 Milton Bradley	.15
105 John Lannan	.15
106 Yovani Gallardo	.40
107 Xavier Nady	.15
108 Jermaine Dye	.25
109 Dioner Navarro	.15
110 Joba Chamberlain	.40
111 Nelson Cruz	.25
112 Johnny Cueto	.25
113 Adam LaRoche	.15
114 Aaron Rowand	.15
115 Jason Bay	.25
116 Aaron Cook	.15
117 Mark Teixeira	.50
118 Magglio Ordonez	.25
119 Rafael Furcal	.15
120 Mark Buehrle	.15
121 Alexi Casilla	.15
122 Scott Kazmir	.25
123 Nick Swisher	.15
124 Carlos Gomez	.15
125 Javier Vazquez	.15
126 Paul Konerko	.25
127 Ronnie Belliard	.15
128 Pat Neshek	.15
129 Josh Johnson	.15
130 Carlos Zambrano	.25
131 Chris Davis	.50
132 Bobby Crosby	.15
133 Alex Gordon	.25
134 Chris Young	.15
135 Carlos Delgado	.40
136 Adam Wainwright	.25
137 Justin Upton	.50
138 Tim Hudson	.15
139 J.D. Drew	.25
140 Adam Lind	.25
141 Mike Lowell	.25
142 Lance Berkman	.40
143 J.J. Hardy	.25
144 A.J. Burnett	.15
145 Jake Peavy	.50
146 Blake DeWitt	.25
147 Matt Holliday	.40
148 Carl Crawford	.25
149 Andre Ethier	.25
150 Howie Kendrick	.15
151 Ryan Zimmerman	.50
152 Troy Tulowitzki	.25
153 Brett Myers	.15
154 Chris Young	.15
155 Jered Weaver	.25
156 Jeff Clement	.15
157 Alex Rios	.25
158 Shane Victorino	.25
159 Jeremy Hermida	.15
160 James Loney	.25
161 Michael Young	.25
162 Aramis Ramirez	.25
163 Geovany Soto	.40
164 Aubrey Huff	.15
165 Delmon Young	.15
166 Vernon Wells	.25
167 Chone Figgins	.25
168 Carlos Quentin	.50
169 Chad Billingsley	.40
170 Matt Cain	.40
171 Derek Lee	.25
172 A.J. Pierzynski	.15
173 Collin Balester	.15
174 Greg Smith	.15
175 Alfonso Soriano	.50
176 Adrian Gonzalez	.50
177 George Sherrill	.15
178 Nick Markakis	.50
179 Brandon Webb	.50
180 Vladimir Guerrero	.75
181 Roy Oswalt	.40
182 Adam Jones	.40
183 Edinson Volquez	.25
184 Yunel Escobar	.15
185 Joe Saunders	.15
186 Yadier Molina	.15
187 Kevin Youkilis	.50
188 Dan Uggla	.25
189 Kosuke Fukudome	.25
190 Matt Antonelli RC	.75
191 Jeff Baisley RC	.15
192 Jason Bourgeois (RC)	.50
193 Michael Bowden (RC)	.50
194 Andrew Carpenter (RC)	.50
195 Phil Coke RC	.50
196 Aaron Cunningham RC	.50
197 Alcides Escobar RC	.50
198 Dexter Fowler (RC)	.50
199 Mat Gamel RC	1.00
200 Josh Geer (RC)	.50
201 Greg Golson (RC)	.50
202 John Jaso RC	.50
203 Kila Ka'aihue (RC)	.50
204 George Kottaras RC	.50
205 Lou Marson RC	1.00
206 Shairon Martis RC	.75
207 Juan Miranda RC	.50
208 Luke Montz RC	.50
209 Jon Niese RC	.50
210 Bobby Parnell (RC)	.50
211 Fernando Perez (RC)	.50
212 David Price RC	2.50
214 Angel Salome (RC)	.50
215 Gaby Sanchez RC	.50
216 Freddy Sandoval (RC)	.50
217 Travis Snider RC	1.00
218 Will Venable RC	.50
219 Edwin Maysonet RC	.50
220 Josh Outman RC	.50
221 Luke Montz/Auto.	10.00
222 Kila Ka'aihue/Auto.	15.00
223 Conor Gillaspie/Auto. RC	15.00
224 Aaron Cunningham/Auto.	15.00
225 Mat Gamel/Auto.	30.00
226 Matt Antonelli/Auto.	10.00
227 Robert Parnell/Auto.	15.00
228 Jose Mijares/Auto. RC	15.00
229 Josh Geer/Auto.	10.00
230 Shairon Martis/Auto.	15.00

Blue
Blue (1-220): 2-4X
Blue (221-230): 1X
Production 500 Sets

Gold

MIGUEL CABRERA

Gold (1-220): 1-2X
Inserted 1:1

Orange
Orange (1-220): 3-6X
Orange Auto. (221-230): 1-1.25X
Production 250 Sets.

Red
Production One Set

Printing Plates
Production one set per color.

Prospects

NEFTALI FELIZ

	NM/M
Common Prospect:	.25
1 Neftali Feliz	1.00
2 Oscar Tejeda	.50
3 Greg Veloz	.50
4 Julio Teheran	1.00
5 Michael Almanzar	.75
6 Stolmy Pimentel	.75
7 Matt Moore	.75
8 Jericho Jones	.50
9 Kelvin de la Cruz	.50
10 Jose Ceda	.50
11 Jesse Darcy	.25
12 Kenny Gilbert	.50
13 Will Smith	.50
14 Sam Freeman	.50
15 Adam Reifer	.50
16 Ehire Adrianza	1.00
17 Michael Pineda	.75
18 Jordan Walden	.50
19 Angel Morales	.50
20 Neil Ramirez	.75
21 Kyeong Kang	.75
22 Luis Jimenez	.50
23 Tyler Flowers	1.00
24 Petey Paramore	.50
25 Jeremy Hamilton	.25
26 Tyler Yockey	.50
27 Sawyer Carroll	.75
28 Jeremy Farrell	.50
29 Tyson Brummett	.50
30 Alex Buchholz	.50
31 Luis Sumoza	.50
32 Jonathan Waltenbury	.50
33 Edgar Osuna	.50
34 Curt Smith	.50
35 Evan Bigley	.50
36 Miguel Fermin	.50
37 Ben Lasater	.75
38 David Freese	1.00
39 Jon Kibler	.25
40 Cristian Beltre	.25
41 Alfredo Figaro	.50
42 Marc Rzepczynski	.50
43 Joshua Collmenter	.50
44 Adam Mills	.25
45 Wilson Ramos	.50
46 Esmil Rogers	.50
47 Jon Mark Owings	.50
48 Chris Johnson	.50
49 Abraham Almonte	.50
50 Patrick Ryan	.50
51 Yefri Carvajal	.75
52 Ruben Tejada	.50
53 Edilio Colina	.50
54 Wilber Bucardo	.25
55 Nelson Perez	.50
56 Andrew Rundle	.50
57 Anthony Ortega	.25
58 Wilin Rosario	.50
59 Parker Frazier	.75
60 Kyle Farrell	.50
61 Erik Komatsu	.75
62 Michael Stutes	.50
63 David Genao	.25
64 Jack Cawley	.25
65 Jacob Goldberg	.25
66 Jarred Bogany	.25
67 Jason McEachern	.50
68 Matt Rigoli	.25
69 Jose Duran	.50
70 Justin Greene	1.00
71 Nino Leyja	.50
72 Michael Swinson	.50
73 Miguel Flores	.25
74 Nick Buss	.50
75 Brett Oberholtzer	.50
76 Pat McAnaney	.50
77 Sean Conner	.50
78 Ryan Verdugo	.50
79 Will Atwood	.25
80 Tommy Johnson	.50
81 Rene Garcia	.25
82 Robert Brooks	.50
83 Seth Garrison	.25
84 Steve Upchurch	.50
85 Zach Moore	.50
86 Derrick Phillips	.25
87 Dominic De La Osa	.25
88 Jose Barajas	.25
89 Bryan Petersen	.25
90 Mike Cisco	.25

Prospects Blue
Blue: 2-4X
Production 500 Sets

Prospects Gold
Gold: 1-2.5X

Prospects Orange

RYAN VERDUGO

Orange: 4-6X
Production 250 Sets

Prospects Autographs

		NM/M
	Common Auto.	15.00
DG	Deolis Guerra	15.00
GB	Gordon Beckham	25.00
BP	Buster Posey	35.00
AH	Anthony Hewitt	15.00
TD	Travis D'Arnaud	15.00
RK	Ryan Kalish	15.00
GK	George Kontos	15.00
NG	Nick Gorneault	15.00
JK	Jason Knapp	20.00
BH	Brad Hand	15.00

Prospects Chrome

TYLER FLOWERS

	NM/M
Common Chrome Prospect:	.50
Refractor:	3-5X
Production 599	
Refractor Auto.:	1-1.25X
Production 500 Sets	
X-Fractor:	4-8X
Production 299	
X-Fractor Auto.:	1-1.5X
Production 250	
Blue Refractor:	8-12X
Blue Refractor Auto.:	1-2X
Production 150	
Gold Refractor:	15-25X
Gold Refr. Auto.:	2-4X
Production 50 Sets	
Orange Refractor:	No Pricing
Production 25 Sets	
Red Refractor:	No Pricing
Production 5 Sets	
SuperFractor:	One set produced.
1 Neftali Feliz	2.50
2 Oscar Tejeda	1.00
3 Greg Veloz	1.00
4 Julio Teheran	2.00
5 Michael Almanzar	1.50
6 Stolmy Pimentel	1.50
7 Matt Moore	1.00
8 Jericho Jones	1.00
9 Kelvin de la Cruz	1.00
10 Jose Ceda	1.00
11 Jesse Darcy	.50
12 Kenny Gilbert	1.00
13 Will Smith	1.00
14 Sam Freeman	1.00
15 Adam Reifer	1.00
16 Ehire Adrianza	2.00
17 Michael Pineda	1.00
18 Jordan Walden	1.00
19 Angel Morales	1.00
20 Neil Ramirez	1.50
21 Kyeong Kang	1.50
22 Luis Jimenez	1.00
23 Tyler Flowers	2.00
24 Petey Paramore	1.00
25 Jeremy Hamilton	.50
26 Tyler Yockey	1.00
27 Sawyer Carroll	1.50
28 Jeremy Farrell	1.00
29 Tyson Brummett	1.00
30 Alex Buchholz	1.00
31 Luis Sumoza	1.00
32 Jonathan Waltenbury	1.00
33 Edgar Osuna	1.00
34 Curt Smith	1.00
35 Evan Bigley	.50
36 Miguel Fermin	1.00
37 Ben Lasater	1.50
38 David Freese	1.50
39 Jon Kibler	.50
40 Cristian Beltre	.50
41 Alfredo Figaro	1.00
42 Marc Rzepczynski	1.00
43 Joshua Collmenter	1.00
44 Adam Mills	.50
45 Wilson Ramos	1.00
46 Esmil Rogers	1.00
47 Jon Mark Owings	1.00
48 Chris Johnson	1.00
49 Abraham Almonte	1.00
50 Patrick Ryan	1.00
51 Yefri Carvajal	1.50
52 Ruben Tejada	1.00
53 Edilio Colina	1.00
54 Wilber Bucardo	.50
55 Nelson Perez	1.00
56 Andrew Rundle	1.00
57 Anthony Ortega	1.00
58 Wilin Rosario	1.00
59 Parker Frazier	1.50
60 Kyle Farrell	.50
61 Erik Komatsu	1.50
62 Michael Stutes	1.00
63 David Genao	.50
64 Jack Cawley	.50
65 Jacob Goldberg	.50
66 Jarred Bogany	.50
67 Jason McEachern	.50
68 Matt Rigoli	.50
69 Jose Duran	1.00
70 Justin Greene	2.00
71 Nino Leyja	1.00
72 Michael Swinson	1.00
73 Miguel Flores	.50
74 Nick Buss	1.00
75 Brett Oberholtzer	1.00
76 Pat McAnaney	1.00
77 Sean Conner	1.00
78 Ryan Verdugo	1.00
79 Will Atwood	.5
80 Tommy Johnson	.5
81 Rene Garcia	.5
82 Robert Brooks	.5
83 Seth Garrison	.5
84 Steve Upchurch	.5
85 Zach Moore	.5
86 Derrick Phillips	.5
87 Dominic De La Osa	.5
88 Jose Barajas	.5
89 Bryan Petersen	.5
90 Mike Cisco	.5
111 Beamer Weems/Auto.	15.0
112 Logan Morrison/Auto.	15.0
113 Greg Halman/Auto.	30.0
114 Logan Forsythe/Auto.	20.0
115 Lance Lynn/Auto.	20.0
116 Javier Rodriguez/Auto.	20.0
117 Josh Lindblom/Auto.	20.0
118 Blake Tekotte/Auto.	20.0

#	Player	Price
119	Johnny Giavotella/Auto.	15.00
120	Jason Knapp/Auto.	20.00
121	Charlie Blackmon/Auto.	20.00
122	David Hernandez/Auto.	15.00
123	Adam Moore/Auto.	20.00
124	Bobby Lanigan/Auto.	15.00
125	Jay Austin/Auto.	20.00
126	Quinton Miller/Auto.	15.00
127	Eric Sogard/Auto.	15.00

WBC

YU DARVISH

NM/M

Common Player: .50

#	Player	Price
BW1	Yu Darvish	2.50
BW2	Phillippe Aumont	1.00
BW3	Concepcion Rodriguez	.50
BW4	Michel Enriquez	1.00
BW5	Yulieski Gourriel	.50
BW6	Shinnosuke Abe	.50
BW7	Gift Ngoepe	.50
BW8	Dylan Lindsay	.50
BW9	Nick Weglarz	.50
BW10	Mitch Dening	.50
BW11	Justin Erasmus	.50
BW12	Aroldis Chapman	1.50
BW13	Alex Liddi	1.00
BW14	Alexander Smit	.50
BW15	Juan Carlos Sulbaran	.50
BW16	Cheng-Min Peng	1.00
BW17	Chenhao Li	.50
BW18	Tao Bu	.50
BW19	Greg Halman	1.00
BW20	Fu-Te Ni	.50

WBC Chrome

YULIESKI GOURRIEL

NM/M

Common Player: .50
#'s 21-60 found in Bowman Chrome
Refractor: 3-5X
Production 599 Sets
X-Fractor: 4-8X
Production 299 Sets
(21-60) Production 250
Blue Refractor: 8-12X
Production 150 Sets
Gold Refractor: 15-25X
Production 50 Sets
Orange Refractor: No Pricing
Production 25 Sets
Red Refractor: No Pricing
Production 5 Sets
SuperFractor 1 of 1's exist

#	Player	Price
1	Yu Darvish	5.00
2	Phillippe Aumont	2.00
3	Concepcion Rodriguez	1.00
4	Michel Enriquez	2.00
5	Yulieski Gourriel	1.00
6	Shinnosuke Abe	1.00
7	Gift Ngoepe	1.00
8	Dylan Lindsay	1.00
9	Nick Weglarz	1.00
10	Mitch Dening	1.00
11	Justin Erasmus	1.00
12	Aroldis Chapman	3.00
13	Alex Liddi	2.00
14	Alexander Smit	1.00
15	Juan Carlos Sulbaran	1.00
16	Cheng-Min Peng	2.00
17	Chenhao Li	1.00
18	Tao Bu	1.00
19	Greg Halman	1.00
20	Fu-Te Ni	1.00
21	Norichika Aoki	1.50
22	Hisashi Iwakuma	1.00
23	Tae Kyun Kim	1.00
24	Dae Ho Lee	1.00
25	Wang Chao	.50
26	Yi-Chuan Lin	.50
27	James Beresford	.50
28	Shuichi Murata	1.50
29	Hung-Wen Chen	.50
30	Masahiro Tanaka	2.00
31	Kao Kuo-Ching	.50
32	Po Yu Lin	.50
33	Yolexis Ulacia	.50
34	Kwang-Hyun Kim	1.00
35	Kenley Jansen	.50
36	Luis Durango	.50
37	Ray Chang	.50
38	Hein Robb	.50
39	Kyuji Fujikawa	1.00
40	Ruben Tejada	.50
41	Hector Olivera	.50
42	Bryan Engelhardt	.50
43	Dennis Neuman	.50
44	Vladimir Garcia	.50
45	Michihiro Ogasawara	1.00
46	Yen-Wen Kuo	.50
47	Takahiro Mahara	.50
48	Hiroyuki Nakajima	1.50
49	Yoennis Cespedes	1.00
50	Alfredo Despaigne	.50
51	Suk Min-Yoon	.50
52	Chih-Hsien Chiang	.50
53	Hyun-Soo Kim	.50
54	Chih-Kang Kao	.50
55	Frederick Cepeda	1.00
56	Yi-Feng Kuo	.50
57	Toshiya Sugiuchi	.50
58	Shunsuke Watanabe	1.00
59	Max Ramirez	.50
60	Bradley Harman	.50

2009 Bowman Chrome

NM/M

Common Player: .25
Common RC: 1.00
Hobby Pack (4): 4.00
Hobby Box (18): 60.00

#	Player	Price
1	David Wright	1.00
2	Albert Pujols	2.50
3	Alex Rodriguez	2.00
4	Chase Utley	1.00
5	Chien-Ming Wang	.75
6	Jimmy Rollins	.75
7	Ken Griffey Jr.	1.50
8	Manny Ramirez	1.00
9	Chipper Jones	1.00
10	Ichiro Suzuki	1.50
11	Justin Morneau	.50
12	Hanley Ramirez	.75
13	Cliff Lee	.50
14	Ryan Howard	1.50
15	Ian Kinsler	.75
16	Jose Reyes	1.00
17	Ted Lilly	.25
18	Miguel Cabrera	.75
19	Nate McLouth	.50
20	Josh Beckett	.75
21	John Lackey	.50
22	David Ortiz	.75
23	Carlos Lee	.50
24	Adam Dunn	.50
25	B.J. Upton	.50
26	Curtis Granderson	.75
27	David DeJesus	.25
28	C.C. Sabathia	.75
29	Russell Martin	.50
30	Torii Hunter	.50
31	Rich Harden	.25
32	Johnny Damon	.50
33	Cristian Guzman	.25
34	Grady Sizemore	.75
35	Jorge Posada	.50
36	Placido Polanco	.50
37	Ryan Ludwick	.50
38	Dustin Pedroia	1.00
39	Matt Garza	.25
40	Prince Fielder	1.00
41	Rick Ankiel	.50
42	David Huff RC	1.00
43	Erik Bedard	.25
44	Ryan Braun	1.00
45	Ervin Santana	.25
46	Brian Roberts	.50
47	Mike Jacobs	.25
48	Phil Hughes	.50
49	Justin Masterson	.25
50	Felix Hernandez	.50
51	Stephen Drew	.50
52	Bobby Abreu	.50
53	Jay Bruce	.50
54	Josh Hamilton	.75
55	Garrett Atkins	.25
56	Jacoby Ellsbury	.75
57	Johan Santana	.75
58	James Shields	.50
59	Sergio Escalona RC	2.00
60	Carlos Pena	.50
61	Matt Kemp	1.00
62	Joey Votto	.75
63	Raul Ibanez	.50
64	Casey Kotchman	.25
65	Hunter Pence	.50
66	Daniel Murphy RC	3.00
67	Carlos Beltran	.50
68	Evan Longoria	1.50
69	Daisuke Matsuzaka	1.00
70	Cole Hamels	.75
71	Robinson Cano	.50
72	Clayton Kershaw	.75
73	Kenji Johjima	.25
74	Kazuo Matsui	.50
75	Jayson Werth	.50
76	Brian McCann	.50
77	Barry Zito	.25
78	Glen Perkins	.25
79	Jeff Francoeur	.25
80	Derek Jeter	2.50
81	Ryan Doumit	.25
82	Dan Haren	.50
83	Justin Duchscherer	.25
84	Marlon Byrd	.25
85	Derek Lowe	.25
86	Pat Burrell	.50
87	Jair Jurrjens	.50
88	Zack Greinke	.75
89	Jon Lester	.50
90	Justin Verlander	.50
91	Jorge Cantu	.25
92	John Maine	.25
93	Brad Hawpe	.25
94	Mike Aviles	.25
95	Victor Martinez	.25
96	Ryan Dempster	.25
97	Miguel Tejada	.25
98	Joe Mauer	.75
99	Scott Olsen	.25
100	Tim Lincecum	1.00
101	Francisco Liriano	.25
102	Chris Iannetta	.25
103	Greg Burke RC	1.00
104	Milton Bradley	.25
105	John Lannan	.25
106	Yovani Gallardo	.25
107	Luke French (RC)	1.00
108	Jermaine Dye	.25
109	Dioner Navarro	.25
110	Joba Chamberlain	1.00
111	Nelson Cruz	.50
112	Johnny Cueto	.50
113	Adam LaRoche	.25
114	Aaron Rowand	.25
115	Jason Bay	.25
116	Roy Halladay	.50
117	Mark Teixeira	.75
118	Gavin Floyd	.25
119	Magglio Ordonez	.50
120	Rafael Furcal	.50
121	Mark Buehrle	.25
122	Alexi Casilla	.25
123	Scott Kazmir	.25
124	Nick Swisher	.50
125	Carlos Gomez	.25
126	Javier Vazquez	.25
127	Paul Konerko	.25
128	Nolan Reimold (RC)	1.50
129	Gerardo Parra RC	2.00
130	Josh Johnson	.25
131	Carlos Zambrano	.25
132	Chris Davis	.50
133	Bobby Crosby	.25
134	Alex Gordon	.50
135	Chris Young	.25
136	Carlos Delgado	.25
137	Adam Wainwright	.50
138	Justin Upton	.50
139	Chris Coghlan RC	3.00
140	J.D. Drew	.25
141	Adam Lind	.50
142	Mike Lowell	.50
143	Lance Berkman	.50
144	J.J. Hardy	.25
145	A.J. Burnett	.50
146	Jake Peavy	.50
147	Xavier Paul RC	1.00
148	Matt Holliday	.50
149	Carl Crawford	.50
150	Andre Ethier	.50
151	Howie Kendrick	.50
152	Ryan Zimmerman	.50
153	Troy Tulowitzki	.50
154	Brett Myers	.25
155	Chris Young	.50
156	Jered Weaver	.50
157	Jeff Clement	.25
158	Alex Rios	.25
159	Shane Victorino	.25
160	Jeremy Hermida	.25
161	James Loney	.25
162	Michael Young	.50
163	Aramis Ramirez	.50
164	Geovany Soto	.50
165	Aubrey Huff	.25
166	Rick Porcello RC	5.00
167	Vernon Wells	.25
168	Chone Figgins	.25
169	Carlos Quentin	.50
170	Chad Billingsley	.50
171	Matt Cain	.50
172	Derek Lee	.50
173	A.J. Pierzynski	.25
174	Daniel Bard RC	1.00
175	Bobby Scales RC	1.50
176	Alfonso Soriano	.50
177	Adrian Gonzalez	.75
178	Andrew McCutchen (RC)	3.00
179	Nick Markakis	.50
180	Brandon Webb	.50
181	Vladimir Guerrero	.75
182	Roy Oswalt	.50
183	Adam Jones	.50
184	Edinson Volquez	.25
185	Gordon Beckham RC	6.00
186	Joe Saunders	.25
187	Yadier Molina	.25
188	Kevin Youkilis	.75
189	Dan Uggla	.25
190	Kosuke Fukudome	.50
191	Matt LaPorta RC	2.50
192	Trevor Cahill RC	1.50
193	Derek Holland RC	3.00
194	Michael Bowden (RC)	2.00
195	Andrew Carpenter RC	1.50
196	Phil Coke RC	.50
197	Graham Taylor RC	2.00
198	Alcides Escobar RC	2.00
199	Dexter Fowler (RC)	2.00
200	Mat Gamel RC	3.00
201	Jordan Zimmermann RC	3.00
202	Greg Golson (RC)	1.00
203	Andrew Bailey RC	1.50
204	David Hernandez RC	.50
205	George Kottaras (RC)	1.00
206	Lou Marson (RC)	1.00
207	Shairon Martis RC	1.50
208	Juan Miranda RC	1.50
209	Tyler Greene (RC)	1.00
210	Jon Niese RC	1.50
211	Bobby Parnell RC	1.50
212	Colby Rasmus (RC)	2.00
213	David Price RC	5.00
214	Angel Salome (RC)	1.00
215	Gaby Sanchez RC	1.00
216	Freddy Sandoval (RC)	1.00
217	Travis Snider RC	3.00
218	Will Venable RC	1.50
219	Brett Anderson RC	3.00
220	Josh Outman RC	1.50

Refractors
Refractor: 2-3X
Refractor RC: 1-1.5X
Inserted 1:4

Blue Refractors
Blue: 4-6X
Blue RC: 3-4X
Production 150 Sets

Gold Refractors
Gold: 8-12X
Gold RC: 4-6X
Production 50 Sets

Orange Refractors
Orange: 10-20X
Orange RC: No Pricing
Production 25 Sets

Red Refractors
No Pricing
Production 5 Sets

SuperFractor
Production One Set

X-Fractors
X-Fractor: 3-4X
X-Fractor RC: 1-2.5X
Production 250 Sets

Printing Plates
Production one set per color.

Prospects

TOMMY HANSON

NM/M

Common Prospect: .50
Common Auto.: 10.00
Autos 1:34 Hobby
Refractor: 3-5X
Refractor Auto: 1-1.25X
Production 500 Sets
Blue Refractor: 8-12X
Blue Ref. Auto: 1-2.5X
Production 150 Sets
Gold Refractor: 15-25X
Gold Ref. Auto: 3-5X
Production 50 Sets
Orange Refractor: No Pricing
Production 25 Sets
Red Refractor: No Pricing
Production 5 Sets
X-Fractor: 4-8X
X-Fractor Auto.: 1-1.5X
Production 250 Sets
SuperFractor 1 of 1's exist.

#	Player	Price
91	Rinku Singh/Auto.	15.00
92	Dinesh Kumar Patel/Auto.	15.00
93	Matt Miller/Auto.	10.00
94	Pat Venditte/Auto.	25.00
95	Zach Putnam/Auto.	15.00
96	Robbie Grossman/Auto.	12.00
97	Tommy Hanson/Auto.	50.00
98	Matt Mitchell/Auto.	12.00
99	Graham Hicks/Auto.	12.00
100	Chris Marrero/Auto.	15.00
101	Freddie Freeman/Auto.	30.00
102	Chris Johnson/Auto.	12.00
103	Edgar Olmos/Auto.	15.00
104	Argenis Diaz/Auto.	12.00
105	Brett Anderson/Auto.	15.00
106	Juan Carlos Sulbaran/Auto.	15.00
107	Cody Scarpetta/Auto.	15.00
108	Carlos Santana/Auto.	40.00
109	Brad Emaus/Auto.	12.00
110	Dayan Viciedo/Auto.	30.00
111	Tim Federowicz/Auto.	12.00
112	Allen Craig/Auto.	15.00
113	Kyle Weiland/Auto.	15.00
114	Connor Graham/Auto.	10.00
128	Efrain Nieves	.75
129	Kam Mickolio	.50
130	Terrell Alliman	.50
131	J.R. Higley	.75
132	Rashun Dixon	1.00
133	Brian Baisley	.50
134	Tim Collins	.50
135	Kyle Greenwalt	1.00
136	C.J. Lee	.50
137	Hector Correa	.50
138	Wily Peralta	.50
139	Bryan Price	.50
140	Jarrod Holloway	.50
141	Alfredo Silverio	.50
142	Brad Dydalewicz	.50
143	Alexander Torres	.50
144	Chris Hicks	.50
145	Andy Parrino	.50
146	Casey McGehee (RC)	.50
147	Chris Schwinden	.50
148	Matt Kennelly	.50
149	Freddy Galvis	.50
150	Mauricio Robles	1.00
151	Kevin Eichhorn	.50
152	Danny Hudson	1.50
153	Carlos Martinez	.50
154	Danny Carroll	.50
155	Maikel Cleto	.50
156	Mike Affronti	.50
157	Mike Pontius	.50
158	Richard Castillo	.50
159	Jon Redding	.50
160	Aaron King	.50
161	Mark Hallberg	.50
162	Chris Luck	1.00
163	Wilmer Font	1.50
164	Chad Lundahl	.50
165	Isaias Asencio	.50
166	Denny Almonte	.75
167	Carmen Angelini	.50
168	Paul Clemens	.50
169	Federico Hernandez	.50
170	Mario Martinez	1.00
171	Bryan Shaw	.50
172	Bryan Augenstein	.50
173	Santos Rodriguez	.50
174	Delvi Cid	.75
175	Todd Doolittle	.50
176	Rossmel Perez	.50
177	Philippe Valiquette	.50
178	Julian Sampson	.50
179	Eric Farris	.50
180	Taylor Harbin	.50
181	Clayton Cook	.50
182	Jovan Rosa	.50
183	Starlin Castro	10.00
184	Brock Huntzinger	.50
185	Jack McGeary	.50
186	Moises Sierra	.50
187	Luis Exposito	1.00
188	Danny Farquhar	.50
189	Layton Hiller	.50
190	Michael Harrington	.50
191	Nate Tenbrink	.50
192	Jason Rook	.50
193	Ryan Kulik	.50
194	Kunnil Gomez	.50
195	Brad James	.50
196	John Anderson	.50
197	Pernell Halliman	.50

2009 Bowman Draft

TOMMY HANSON

Complete Set (55): 15.00
Common Player: .25
Pack (7): 3.00
Box (24): 65.00

#	Player	Price
BDP1	Tommy Hanson RC	2.00
BDP2	Jeff Manship RC	.25
BDP3	Trevor Bell (RC)	.25
BDP4	Trevor Cahill RC	.75
BDP5	Trent Oeltjen (RC)	.25
BDP6	Kevin Mulvey RC	.25
BDP7	Wyatt Toregas RC	.25
BDP8	Rusty Ryal RC	.25
BDP9	Mike Carp (RC)	.25
BDP10	Jorge Padilla (RC)	.25
BDP11	J.D. Martin (RC)	.25
BDP12	Dusty Ryan RC	.25
BDP13	Alex Avila RC	.50
BDP14	Brandon Allen (RC)	.25
BDP15	Tommy Everidge (RC)	.50
BDP16	Bud Norris RC	.25
BDP17	Neftali Feliz RC	.50
BDP18	Mat Latos RC	.50
BDP19	Ryan Perry RC	.25
BDP20	Craig Tatum (RC)	.50
BDP21	Chris Tillman RC	.50
BDP22	Jhoulys Chacin RC	.50
BDP23	Michael Saunders RC	.50
BDP24	Jeff Stevens RC	.25
BDP25	Luis Valdez RC	.25
BDP26	Robert Manuel RC	.25
BDP27	Ryan Webb (RC)	.25
BDP28	Marc Rzepczynski RC	.50
BDP29	Travis Schlichting (RC)	.25
BDP30	Barbaro Canizares RC	.25
BDP31	Brad Mills RC	.25
BDP32	Dusty Brown (RC)	.50
BDP33	Tim Wood RC	.25
BDP34	Drew Sutton RC	.25
BDP35	Jarrett Hoffpauir RC	.25
BDP36	Jose Lobaton RC	.25
BDP37	Aaron Bates RC	.25
BDP38	Clayton Mortensen RC	.25
BDP39	Ryan Sadowski RC	.25
BDP40	Fu-Te Ni RC	.25
BDP41	Casey McGehee (RC)	.50
BDP42	Omir Santos RC	.25
BDP43	Brent Leach RC	.25
BDP44	Diory Hernandez RC	.25
BDP45	Wilkin Castillo RC	.25
BDP46	Trevor Crowe RC	.50
BDP47	Sean West (RC)	.25
BDP48	Clayton Richard (RC)	.25
BDP49	Julio Borbon RC	.75
BDP50	Kyle Blanks RC	.50
BDP51	Jeff Gray RC	.25
BDP52	Gio Gonzalez (RC)	.50
BDP53	Vin Mazzaro RC	.25
BDP54	Josh Reddick RC	.75
BDP55	Fernando Martinez RC	.25

Blue
Blue: 2-4X
Production 399 Sets

Gold
Gold: 1-2X
Inserted 1:1

Red
Production One Set
Printing Plates
Production one set per color.

ALFAC Autographs
Common Auto.:
Inserted 1:238

#	Player	Price
1	Brooks Pounders	20.00
2	Jiovanni Mier	30.00
3	Max Stassi	50.00
4	Zack Wheeler	70.00
5	Neil Ramirez	15.00
6	Robert Stock	30.00
7	Sequoyah Stonecipher	25.00
8	Donovan Tate	100.00
9	Tyler Matzek	50.00
10	D.J. Lemahieu	30.00
11	David Nick	25.00
12	Matthew Davidson	25.00
13	Wesley Freeman	15.00

Prospects
Complete Set (75): 20.00
Common Player: .25
Blue: 2-4X
Production 399 Sets
Gold: 1-2X
Inserted 1:1
Red 1 of 1's exist

#	Player	Price
BDPP1	Tanner Bushue	.75
BDPP2	Billy Hamilton	.75
BDPP3	Enrique Hernandez	.50
BDPP4	Virgil Hill	.50
BDPP5	Josh Hodges	.75
BDPP6	Christopher Lovett	.25
BDPP7	Michael Belfiore	.25
BDPP8	Jobduan Morales	.25
BDPP9	Anthony Morris	.25
BDPP10	Telvin Nash	.75
BDPP11	Brooks Pounders	.75
BDPP12	Kyle Rose	.50
BDPP13	Seth Schwindenhammer	.75
BDPP14	Patrick Lehman	.75
BDPP15	Mathew Weaver	.75
BDPP16	Brian Dozier	.50
BDPP17	Sequoyah Stonecipher	.75
BDPP18	Shannon Wilkerson	.50
BDPP19	Jerry Sullivan	.50
BDPP20	Jamie Johnson	.25
BDPP21	Kent Matthes	.50
BDPP22	Ben Paulsen	.25
BDPP23	Matthew Davidson	.75
BDPP24	Benjamin Carlson	.25
BDPP25	Brock Holt	.75
BDPP26	Ben Orloff	.25
BDPP27	D.J. LeMahieu	.75
BDPP28	Erik Castro	.75
BDPP29	James Jones	.75
BDPP30	Cory Burns	.25
BDPP31	Chris Wade	.25
BDPP32	Jaff Decker	1.50
BDPP33	Naoya Washiya	.50
BDPP34	Brandt Walker	.50

BDPP35	Jordan Henry	.75
BDPP36	Austin Adams	.50
BDPP37	Andrew Bellatti	.75
BDPP38	Paul Applebee	.75
BDPP39	Robert Stock	1.50
BDPP40	Michael Flacco	.25
BDPP41	Jonathan Meyer	.25
BDPP42	Cody Rogers	1.00
BDPP43	Matt Heidenreich	.50
BDPP44	David Holmberg	.75
BDPP45	Mycal Jones	.50
BDPP46	David Hale	.75
BDPP47	Dusty Odenbach	.25
BDPP48	Robert Hefflinger	.25
BDPP49	Buddy Baumann	.25
BDPP50	Thomas Berryhill	.25
BDPP51	Darrell Ceciliani	.25
BDPP52	Derek McCallum	.50
BDPP53	Taylor Freeman	.50
BDPP54	Tyler Townsend	.75
BDPP55	Tobias Streich	.75
BDPP56	Ryan Jackson	.75
BDPP57	Chris Herrmann	.75
BDPP58	Robert Shields	.50
BDPP59	Devin Fuller	.25
BDPP60	Brad Stillings	.25
BDPP61	Ryan Goins	.50
BDPP62	Chase Austin	.50
BDPP63	Brett Nommensen	.50
BDPP64	Egan Smith	.75
BDPP65	Daniel Mahoney	.25
BDPP66	Darin Gorski	.25
BDPP67	Dustin Dickerson	.50
BDPP68	Victor Black	.75
BDPP69	Dallas Keuchel	.75
BDPP70	Nate Baker	.25
BDPP71	David Nick	.75
BDPP72	Brian Moran	.25
BDPP73	Mark Fleury	.25
BDPP74	Brett Wallach	.75
BDPP75	Adam Buschini	.50

WBC Prospects

Complete Set (35):		15.00
Common Player:		.25
Blue:		2-4X
Production 399 Sets		
Gold:		1-2X
Inserted 1:1		
Red 1 of 1's exist		
BDPW1	Ichiro Suzuki	1.50
BDPW2	Yu Darvish	1.50
BDPW3	Phillippe Aumont	.75
BDPW4	Derek Jeter	2.00
BDPW5	Dustin Pedroia	1.00
BDPW6	Earl Agnoly	.25
BDPW7	Jose Reyes	.75
BDPW8	Michel Enriquez	.25
BDPW9	David Ortiz	.50
BDPW10	Chunhua Dong	.50
BDPW11	Munenori Kawasaki	1.00
BDPW12	Arquimedes Nieto	.25
BDPW13	Bernie Williams	.50
BDPW14	Pedro Lazo	.25
BDPW15	Jing-Chao Wang	.75
BDPW16	Chris Barnwell	.25
BDPW17	Elmer Dessens	.25
BDPW18	Russell Martin	.50
BDPW19	Luca Panerati	.25
BDPW20	Adam Dunn	.50
BDPW21	Andy Gonzalez	.25
BDPW22	Daisuke Matsuzaka	1.00
BDPW23	Daniel Berg	.25
BDPW24	Aroldis Chapman	2.50
BDPW25	Justin Morneau	.50
BDPW26	Miguel Cabrera	.75
BDPW27	Magglio Ordonez	.25
BDPW28	Shawn Bowman	.25
BDPW29	Robbie Cordemans	.50
BDPW30	Paolo Espino	.50
BDPW31	Chipper Jones	1.00
BDPW32	Frederick Cepeda	.25
BDPW33	Ubaldo Jimenez	.25
BDPW34	Seiichi Uchikawa	.50
BDPW35	Norichika Aoki	.75

Bowman Chrome Draft

Mat Latos

Complete Set (55):		25.00
Common Player:		.50
Blue Refractor:		3-5X
Production 99 Sets		
Gold Refractor:		6-10X
Production 50 Sets		
Orange Refractor:		No Pricing
Production 25 Sets		
Red Refractor:		No Pricing
Production 5 Sets		
Refractors:		1-2X
Inserted 1:11		
X-Fractors:		2-4X
Production 199 Sets		
BDP1	Tommy Hanson RC	4.00
BDP2	Jeff Manship RC	.50
BDP3	Trevor Bell (RC)	.50
BDP4	Trevor Cahill RC	1.00
BDP5	Trent Oeltjen (RC)	.50
BDP6	Wyatt Toregas RC	.50
BDP7	Kevin Mulvey RC	.50
BDP8	Rusty Ryal (RC)	.50
BDP9	Mike Carp (RC)	.50
BDP10	Jorge Padilla (RC)	.50
BDP11	J.D. Martin (RC)	.50
BDP12	Dusty Ryan (RC)	.50
BDP13	Alex Avila RC	1.25
BDP14	Brandon Allen (RC)	.50
BDP15	Tommy Everidge (RC)	.50
BDP16	Bud Norris RC	.50
BDP17	Neftali Feliz RC	1.50
BDP18	Mat Latos RC	.50
BDP19	Ryan Perry RC	1.50
BDP20	Craig Tatum (RC)	.50
BDP21	Chris Tillman RC	1.00
BDP22	Jhoulys Chacin RC	.75
BDP23	Michael Saunders RC	1.00
BDP24	Jeff Stevens RC	.50
BDP25	Luis Valdez RC	.50
BDP26	Robert Manuel RC	.50
BDP27	Ryan Webb (RC)	.50
BDP28	Marc Rzepczynski RC	1.00
BDP29	Travis Schlichting (RC)	1.00
BDP30	Barbaro Canizares RC	.50
BDP31	Brad Mills RC	.50
BDP32	Dusty Brown (RC)	.50
BDP33	Tim Wood RC	.50
BDP34	Drew Sutton RC	1.00
BDP35	Jarrett Hoffpauir RC	.50
BDP36	Jose Lobaton RC	.50
BDP37	Aaron Bates RC	.50
BDP38	Clayton Mortensen RC	.50
BDP39	Ryan Sadowski RC	.50
BDP40	Fu-Te Ni RC	1.00
BDP41	Casey McGehee (RC)	.50
BDP42	Omir Santos RC	.50
BDP43	Brent Leach RC	.75
BDP44	Diory Hernandez RC	.50
BDP45	Wilkin Castillo RC	.50
BDP46	Trevor Crowe RC	.50
BDP47	Sean West (RC)	.50
BDP48	Clayton Richard (RC)	.50
BDP49	Julio Borbon RC	1.00
BDP50	Kyle Blanks RC	1.00
BDP51	Jeff Gray RC	.50
BDP52	Gio Gonzalez (RC)	.50
BDP53	Vin Mazzaro RC	.50
BDP54	Josh Reddick RC	1.00
BDP55	Fernando Martinez RC	1.50

Chrome Prospects

Common Player (1-75):		.50
Common Auto. (76-97):		10.00
Blue Refractor (1-75):		4-8X
Production 99		
Blue Refractor Auto.:		1-2X
Production 150		
Gold Refractor (1-75):		8-12X
Production 50		
Gold Refractor Auto.:		2-4X
Production 50		
Orange Refractor:		No Pricing
Production 25 Sets		
Red Refractor:		No Pricing
Production 5 Sets		
Refractor (1-75):		2-4X
Inserted 1:11		
Refractor Auto.:		1-1.2X
Production 500		
SuperFractor 1 of 1's exist		
X-Fractors:		3-5X
Production 199		
X-Fractor Auto.:		1-1.5X
Production 225		
BDPP1	Tanner Bushue	1.00
BDPP2	Billy Hamilton	1.00
BDPP3	Enrique Hernandez	.50
BDPP4	Virgil Hill	.50
BDPP5	Josh Hodges	1.00
BDPP6	Christopher Lovett	.50
BDPP7	Michael Belfiore	.50
BDPP8	Jobduan Morales	.75
BDPP9	Anthony Morris	.50
BDPP10	Telvin Nash	1.00
BDPP11	Brooks Pounders	1.50
BDPP12	Kyle Rose	.50
BDPP13	Seth Schwindenhammer	1.00
BDPP14	Patrick Lehman	1.00
BDPP15	Mathew Weaver	.50
BDPP16	Brian Dozier	.50
BDPP17	Sequoyah Stonecipher	1.00
BDPP18	Shannon Wilkerson	.50
BDPP19	Jerry Sullivan	.50
BDPP20	Jamie Johnson	.50
BDPP21	Kent Matthes	.50
BDPP22	Ben Paulsen	.50
BDPP223	Matthew Davidson	1.00

BDPP24	Benjamin Carlson	.50
BDPP25	Brock Holt	1.00
BDPP26	Ben Orloff	.75
BDPP27	D.J. LeMahieu	1.00
BDPP28	Erik Castro	1.00
BDPP29	James Jones	1.00
BDPP30	Cory Burns	.75
BDPP31	Chris Wade	.75
BDPP32	Jaff Decker	2.50
BDPP33	Naoya Washiya	.75
BDPP34	Brandt Walker	.75
BDPP35	Jordan Henry	1.00
BDPP36	Austin Adams	.75
BDPP37	Andrew Bellatti	1.00
BDPP38	Paul Applebee	1.25
BDPP39	Robert Stock	2.50
BDPP40	Michael Flacco	.75
BDPP41	Jonathan Meyer	.75
BDPP42	Cody Rogers	1.00
BDPP43	Matt Heidenreich	.75
BDPP44	David Holmberg	1.00
BDPP45	Mycal Jones	.75
BDPP46	David Hale	.75
BDPP47	Dusty Odenbach	.50
BDPP48	Robert Hefflinger	.50
BDPP49	Buddy Baumann	.50
BDPP50	Thomas Berryhill	.50
BDPP51	Darrell Ceciliani	.50
BDPP52	Derek McCallum	.50
BDPP53	Taylor Freeman	.50
BDPP54	Tyler Townsend	1.00
BDPP55	Tobias Streich	1.00
BDPP56	Ryan Jackson	.75
BDPP57	Chris Herrmann	1.00
BDPP58	Robert Shields	.50
BDPP59	Devin Fuller	.75
BDPP60	Brad Stillings	.50
BDPP61	Ryan Goins	.50
BDPP62	Chase Austin	.50
BDPP63	Brett Nommensen	.75
BDPP64	Egan Smith	.75
BDPP65	Daniel Mahoney	.75
BDPP66	Darin Gorski	.50
BDPP67	Dustin Dickerson	.75
BDPP68	Victor Black	1.00
BDPP69	Dallas Keuchel	1.00
BDPP70	Nate Baker	.75
BDPP71	David Nick	1.00
BDPP72	Brian Moran	.50
BDPP73	Mark Fleury	.50
BDPP74	Brett Wallach	1.00
BDPP75	Adam Buschini	.50
BDPP76	Tony Sanchez/Auto.	20.00
BDPP77	Eric Arnett/Auto.	15.00
BDPP78	Tim Wheeler/Auto.	15.00
BDPP79	Matt Hobgood/Auto.	25.00
BDPP80	Matt Bashore/Auto.	15.00
BDPP81	Randal Grichuk/ Auto.	20.00
BDPP82	A.J. Pollock/Auto.	15.00
BDPP83	Reymond Fuentes/ Auto.	20.00
BDPP84	Jiovanni Mier/Auto.	15.00
BDPP85	Steve Matz/Auto.	15.00
BDPP86	Zack Wheeler/Auto.	25.00
BDPP87	Mike Minor/Auto.	20.00
BDPP88	Jared Mitchell/Auto.	25.00
BDPP89	Mike Trout/Auto.	50.00
BDPP90	Alex White/Auto.	15.00
BDPP91	Bobby Borchering/ Auto.	15.00
BDPP92	Chad James/Auto.	10.00
BDPP93	Tyler Matzek/Auto.	25.00
BDPP94	Max Stassi/Auto.	25.00
BDPP95	Drew Storen/Auto.	15.00
BDPP96	Brad Boxberger/ Auto.	10.00
BDPP97	Mike Leake/Auto.	30.00

Chrome WBC Prospects

Complete Set (35):		20.00
Common Player:		.50
Blue Refractors:		4-6X
Production 99 Sets		
Gold Refractor:		6-10X
Production 50 Sets		
Orange Refractors:		No Pricing
Production 25 Sets		
Red Refractor:		No Pricing
Production 5 Sets		
Refractor:		2-3X
Inserted 1:11		
SuperFractor 1 of 1's exist		
X-Fractors:		2-4X
Production 199 Sets		
BDPW1	Ichiro Suzuki	2.00
BDPW2	Yu Darvish	2.50
BDPW3	Phillippe Aumont	1.50
BDPW4	Derek Jeter	4.00
BDPW5	Dustin Pedroia	1.50
BDPW6	Earl Agnoly	.50
BDPW7	Jose Reyes	.50
BDPW8	Michel Enriquez	.50
BDPW9	David Ortiz	1.00
BDPW10	Chunhua Dong	1.00
BDPW11	Munenori Kawasaki	1.50
BDPW12	Arquimedes Nieto	.50
BDPW13	Bernie Williams	1.00
BDPW14	Pedro Lazo	.50
BDPW15	Jing-Chao Wang	.50
BDPW16	Chris Barnwell	.50
BDPW17	Elmer Dessens	.50
BDPW18	Russell Martin	1.00
BDPW19	Luca Panerati	.50
BDPW20	Adam Dunn	.75
BDPW21	Andy Gonzalez	.50
BDPW22	Daisuke Matsuzaka	1.50
BDPW23	Daniel Berg	.50
BDPW24	Aroldis Chapman	3.00
BDPW25	Justin Morneau	.75
BDPW26	Miguel Cabrera	1.00
BDPW27	Magglio Ordonez	.50
BDPW28	Shawn Bowman	.50
BDPW29	Robbie Cordemans	.50
BDPW30	Paolo Espino	.50
BDPW31	Chipper Jones	1.50
BDPW32	Frederick Cepeda	.75
BDPW33	Ubaldo Jimenez	.50
BDPW34	Seiichi Uchikawa	.75
BDPW35	Norichika Aoki	1.00

2009 Bowman Sterling

Rick Porcello — Detroit Tigers

Common RC:		2.50
Pack (5):		40.00
Box (6):		225.00
AA	Alex Avila RC	4.00
AB	Antonio Bastardo/ Auto.	8.00
AB	Andrew Bailey RC	5.00
AC	Andrew Carpenter RC	4.00
AM	Andrew McCutchen (RC) RC	8.00
BD	Brian Duensing RC	4.00
BN	Brad Nelson (RC)	2.50
BS	Bobby Scales RC	4.00
CC	Chris Coghlan RC	5.00
CM	Casey McGehee/ Auto.	12.00
CR	Colby Rasmus RC	4.00
CT	Chris Tillman/Auto. RC	10.00
DB	Daniel Bard RC	2.50
DF	Dexter Fowler (RC)	3.00
DH	David Hernandez RC	2.50
DP	David Price RC	5.00
DS	Daniel Schlereth/ Auto. RC	8.00
EC	Everth Cabrera RC	4.00
EY	Eric Young Jr. RC	2.50
FC	Francisco Cervelli RC	5.00
FM	Fernando Martinez RC	5.00
FN	Fu-Te Ni RC	4.00
GB	Gordon Beckham/ Auto. RC	40.00
GG	Greg Golson (RC)	2.50
GK	George Kottaras RC	2.50
GP	Gerardo Parra RC	4.00
JB	Julio Borbon RC	4.00
JC	Jhoulys Chacin RC	4.00
JH	Jarrett HoffpAutoir (RC)	2.50
JH	Justin Masterson/ Auto. (RC)	10.00
JM	Juan Miranda RC	4.00
JS	Jordan Schafer (RC)	4.00
JZ	Jordan Zimmermann RC	2.50
KB	Kyle Blanks RC	4.00
KK	Kenshin Kawakimi RC	4.00
KU	Koji Uehara RC	5.00
MG	Mat Gamel RC	5.00
ML	Mat Latos RC	3.00
MM	Mark Melancon RC	5.00
MS	Michael Saunders RC	4.00
MT	Matt Tuiasosopo (RC)	2.50
NR	Nolan Reimold/Auto.	15.00
NR	Nolan Reimold (RC)	2.50
RP	Ryan Perry/Auto. RC	10.00
RP	Rick Porcello RC	6.00
SR	Shane Robinson RC	2.50
TC	Trevor Crowe RC	2.50
TG	Tyler Greene (RC)	2.50
TH	Tommy Hanson/ Auto. RC	50.00
TS	Travis Snider RC	5.00
WR	Wilkin Ramirez RC	2.50
WV	Will Venable RC	2.50
ABB	Aaron Bates RC	2.50
CTT	Carlos Torres RC	2.50
DFR	David Freese RC	2.50
DHE	Diory Hernandez RC	2.50
DHO	Derek Holland RC	4.00
JHO	Jamie Hoffmann RC	2.50
JMA	John Mayberry Jr. (RC)	2.50

Printing Plates

Production one set per color.		
Black Refractors:		No Pricing
Production 25 Sets		

Gold Refractors

Gold:		2-4X
Production 50 Sets		

Refractors

Refractors:		1-1.5X
Refractor Auto.:		1.2X
Production 199 Sets		

Red Refractors

Production One Set		
Dual Autographs		
Inserted 1:8		
Refractor:		1.25X
Production 199		
Black Refractor:		2-2.5X
Production 25 Sets		
Gold Refractor:		1-2X
Production 50 Sets		
Red 1 of 1's exist		
BPFC	Carlos Santana Michael Stanton	25.00
BPGB	Buster Posey Gordon Beckham	50.00
CTDH	Chris Tillman David Hernandez	15.00
JKZC	Logan Morrison Michael Stanton	15.00
JMFD	Jennry Mejia Felix Doubront	15.00
NRJR	Nolan Reimold Greg Golson	15.00
RPCI	Ryan Perry Cale Lorg	15.00

Prospects

Common Player:		2.00
Common Auto.:		20.00
Black Refractor:		No Pricing
Production 25 Sets		
Gold Refractor:		2-4X
Gold Refractor Auto.:		1-2X
Production 50 Sets		
Refractors:		1.25X
Production 199 Sets		
Red 1 of 1's exist		
AA	Abraham Almonte	2.00
AB	Alex Buchholz	3.00
AF	Alfredo Figaro	2.00
AM	Adam Mills	2.00
AO	Anthony Ortega	2.00
AP	A.J. Pollock/Auto.	15.00
AR	Andrew Rundle	3.00
AS	Alfredo Silverio	2.00
AW	Alex White/Auto.	12.00
BB	Bobby Borchering/ Auto.	15.00
BB	Brian Baisley	2.00
BO	Brett Oberholtzer	3.00
BP	Bryan Petersen	2.00
CA	Carmen Angelini	2.00
CH	Chris Heisey/Auto.	15.00
CJ	Chad Jenkins/Auto.	10.00
CL	C.J. Lee	2.00
CM	Carlos Martinez	3.00
DA	Denny Almonte	3.00
DH	Daniel Hudson/Auto.	15.00
DP	Dinesh Patel/Auto.	8.00
DS	Drew Storen/Auto.	8.00
DV	Dayan Viciedo/Auto.	20.00
EA	Eric Arnett/Auto.	10.00
EA	Ehire Adrianza	4.00
EC	Edilio Colina	3.00
EK	Erik Komatsu	3.00
FG	Freddy Galvis	3.00
GV	Greg Veloz	2.00
JC	Jose Ceda	2.00
JG	Justin Greene	3.00
JM	Jared Mitchell/Auto.	25.00
JR	Jovan Rosa	2.00
JT	Julio Teheran	5.00
JW	Jordan Walden	3.00
KK	Kyeong Kang	3.00
LE	Luis Exposito	3.00
LJ	Luis Jimenez	3.00
LS	Luis Sumoza	2.00
MA	Michael Almanzar	5.00
MC	Michael Cisco	3.00
MH	Matt Hobgood/Auto.	15.00
ML	Mike Leake/Auto.	15.00
MM	Matthew Moore	5.00
MM	Mike Minor/Auto.	12.00
MP	Michael Pineda	5.00
MS	Michael Swinson	3.00
MT	Mike Trout/Auto.	15.00
NB	Nick Buss	2.00
NP	Nelson Perez	3.00
NR	Neil Ramirez	3.00
OT	Oscar Tejeda	5.00
PP	Petey Paramore	3.00
PV	Pat Venditte/Auto.	15.00
RD	Rashun Dixon	5.00
RF	Reymond Fuentes/ Auto.	15.00
RG	Robbie Grossman/ Auto.	8.00
RS	Rinku Singh/Auto.	8.00
RT	Ruben Tejada	2.00
SC	Scott Campbell/Auto.	8.00
SP	Stolmy Pimentel	3.00
SW	Christopher Schwinden	2.00
TF	Tyler Flowers	5.00
TM	Tyler Matzek/Auto.	20.00
TS	Tony Sanchez/Auto.	15.00
TW	Tim Wheeler/Auto.	10.00
TY	Tyler Yockey	3.00
WF	Wilmer Font	3.00
WR	Wilin Rosario	3.00
WS	Will Smith	3.00
ZW	Zack Wheeler/Auto.	20.00
CJA	Chad James/Auto.	10.00
CLU	Chad Lundahl	2.00
JMM	Jiovanni Mier/Auto.	12.00
JMO	Jon Mark Owings	2.00
MAF	Michael Affronti	2.00
RGR	Randal Grichuk/Auto.	15.00
TME	Tommy Mendonca/ Auto.	15.00

WBC Relics

Common Jersey:		5.00
Black Refractors:		2.5X
Production 25 Sets		
Blue Refractor:		1.25X
Production 125 Sets		
Gold Refractor:		1-2X
Production 50 Sets		
Refractor:		1.25X
Production 199 Sets		
Red 1 of 1's exist		
AC	Aroldis Chapman	20.00
AM	Alexander Mayeta	5.00
AO	Adam Ottavino	5.00
AS	Alexander Smit	5.00
BW	Bernie Williams	5.00
CL	Chenhao Li	5.00
CR	Concepcion Rodriguez	5.00
DL	Dae Ho Lee	8.00
DN	Drew Naylor	5.00
EG	Edgar Gonzalez	8.00
FC	Frederick Cepeda	5.00
FF	Fei Feng	8.00
FN	Fu-Te Ni	8.00
GH	Greg Halman	5.00
HC	Hung-Wen Chen	5.00
HO	Hein Robb	5.00
HR	Hanley Ramirez	8.00
IS	Ichiro Suzuki	40.00
JC	Johnny Cueto	5.00
JE	Justin Erasmus	5.00
JL	Jae Woo Lee	5.00
JS	Juancarlos Sulbaran	5.00
KF	Kosuke Fukudome	8.00
KK	Kwang-Hyun Kim	10.00
KL	Kai Liu	5.00
LH	Luke Hughes	5.00
LR	Luis Rodriguez	5.00
MC	Miguel Cabrera	8.00
MD	Mitchell Dening	8.00
ME	Michel Enriquez	5.00
MT	Miguel Tejada	8.00
NA	Norichika Aoki	15.00
NP	Nick Punto	5.00
NW	Nick Weglarz	8.00
PA	Phillipe Aumont	8.00
PK	Po-Hsuan Keng	8.00
PM	Pedro Martinez	8.00
RM	Russell Martin	8.00
SA	Shinnosuke Abe	5.00
SC	Shin-Soo Choo	10.00
TK	Tae Kyun Kim	8.00
XZ	Xiaotian Zhang	8.00
YC	Yoennis Cespedes	8.00
YD	Yu Darvish	20.00
YG	Yulieski Gourriel	8.00
HRR	Hyun-Jin Ryu	10.00
JCC	Jorge Cantu	5.00
JLL	Jin Young Lee	10.00
LHH	Liam Hendriks	5.00

2010 Bowman

Complete Set (220):		30.00
Common Player:		.25
Common RC (191-220):		.25
Hobby Pack (10):		4.00
Hobby Box (24):		90.00
1	Ryan Braun	1.00
2	Kevin Youkilis	.50
3	Jay Bruce	.50
4	Will Venable	.25
5	Zack Greinke	.50
6	Adrian Gonzalez	.50
7	Carl Crawford	.50
8	Scott Baker	.25
9	Matt Kemp	.75
10	Stephen Drew	.25
11	Jair Jurrjens	.25
12	Jose Reyes	.50
13	Josh Hamilton	.50
14	Carlos Pena	.25
15	Ubaldo Jimenez	.25
16	Jason Kubel	.25
17	Josh Beckett	.25
18	Martin Prado	.25
19	Jake Peavy	.25
20	Shin-Soo Choo	.25
21	Luke Hochever	.25
22	Alcides Escobar	.25
23	Brandon Webb	.25
24	Raul Ibanez	.25
25	Ryan Zimmerman	.50
26	Jeff Niemann	.25
27	Adam Dunn	.50
28	Matt Cain	.50
29	Robinson Cano	.50
30	Andre Ethier	.50
31	Jhoulys Chacin	.25
32	Mark Buehrle	.25
33	Magglio Ordonez	.40
34	Michael Cuddyer	.25
35	Andrew Bailey	.25
36	Akinori Iwamura	.25
37	Brian Roberts	.40
38	Howie Kendrick	.25
39	Derek Holland	.40
40	Ken Griffey Jr.	1.00
41	A.J. Burnett	.50
42	Scott Rolen	.25
43	Kenshin Kawakami	.25
44	Carlos Lee	.40
45	Chris Carpenter	.25
46	Adam Lind	.25
47	Jered Weaver	.25
48	Chris Coghlan	.25
49	Clayton Kershaw	.75
50	Prince Fielder	.50
51	Freddy Sanchez	.25

Base Set (continued)

#	Player	Price
52	CC Sabathia	.50
53	Jayson Werth	.50
54	David Price	.75
55	Matt Holliday	.50
56	Brett Anderson	.25
57	Alexei Ramirez	.40
58	Johnny Cueto	.25
59	Bobby Abreu	.40
60	Ian Kinsler	.40
61	Ricky Romero	.25
62	Cristian Guzman	.25
63	Ryan Doumit	.25
64	Mat Latos	.25
65	Andrew McCutchen	.50
66	John Maine	.25
67	Kurt Suzuki	.25
68	Carlos Beltran	.40
69	Chad Billingsley	.40
70	Nick Markakis	.40
71	Yovani Gallardo	.40
72	Dexter Fowler	.25
73	David Ortiz	.50
74	Kosuke Fukudome	.25
75	Daisuke Matsuzaka	.50
76	Michael Young	.25
77	Rajai Davis	.25
78	Yadier Molina	.50
79	Francisco Liriano	.50
80	Evan Longoria	1.00
81	Trevor Cahill	.25
82	Aramis Ramirez	.40
83	Jimmy Rollins	.50
84	Russell Martin	.25
85	Dan Haren	.40
86	Billy Butler	.40
87	James Shields	.40
88	Dan Uggla	.40
89	Wandy Rodriguez	.25
90	Chase Utley	.75
91	Ryan Dempster	.25
92	Ben Zobrist	.25
93	Jeff Francoeur	.25
94	Koji Uehara	.25
95	Victor Martinez	.40
96	Tim Hudson	.40
97	Carlos Gonzalez	.40
98	David DeJesus	.25
99	Brad Hawpe	.40
100	Justin Upton	.50
101	Jorge Posada	.50
102	Cole Hamels	.50
103	Elvis Andrus	.50
104	Adam Wainwright	.50
105	Alfonso Soriano	.40
106	James Loney	.40
107	Vernon Wells	.40
108	Lance Berkman	.40
109	Matt Garza	.40
110	Gordon Beckham	.50
111	Torii Hunter	.50
112	Brandon Phillips	.40
113	Nelson Cruz	.50
114	Chris Tillman	.25
115	Miguel Cabrera	.50
116	Kevin Slowey	.25
117	Shane Victorino	.50
118	Paul Maholm	.25
119	Kyle Blanks	.25
120	Johan Santana	.50
121	Nate McLouth	.25
122	Kazuo Matsui	.25
123	Troy Tulowitzki	.50
124	Jon Lester	.50
125	Chipper Jones	.75
126	Clay Buchholz	.40
127	Todd Helton	.40
128	Alex Gordon	.25
129	Derrek Lee	.40
130	Justin Morneau	.50
131	Michael Bourn	.25
132	B.J. Upton	.40
133	Jose Lopez	.25
134	Justin Verlander	.75
135	Hunter Pence	.40
136	Daniel Murphy	.25
137	Delmon Young	.25
138	Carlos Quentin	.40
139	Edinson Volquez	.25
140	Dustin Pedroia	.75
141	Justin Masterson	.25
142	Josh Willingham	.25
143	Miguel Montero	.25
144	Alex Rios	.40
145	David Wright	.75
146	Curtis Granderson	.50
147	Rich Harden	.50
148	Hideki Matsui	.50
149	Edwin Jackson	.25
150	Miguel Tejada	.40
151	John Lackey	.50
152	Vladimir Guerrero	.50
153	Max Scherzer	.50
154	Jason Bay	.40
155	Javier Vasquez	.40
156	Johnny Damon	.50
157	Cliff Lee	.50
158	Chone Figgins	.25
159	Kevin Millwood	.25
160	Roy Halladay	.75
161	Alex Rodriguez	1.50
162	Pablo Sandoval	.50
163	Ryan Howard	1.00
164	Rick Porcello	.50
165	Hanley Ramirez	.50
166	Brian McCann	.50
167	Kendry Morales	.40
168	Josh Johnson	.40
169	Joe Mauer	.75
170	Grady Sizemore	.50
171	J.A. Happ	.40
172	Ichiro Suzuki	1.00
173	Aaron Hill	.25
174	Mark Teixeira	.50
175	Tim Lincecum	1.00
176	Denard Span	.25
177	Roy Oswalt	.40
178	Manny Ramirez	.50
179	Jorge De La Rosa	.25
180	Joey Votto	.75
181	Neftali Feliz	.40
182	Yunel Escobar	.25
183	Carlos Zambrano	.40
184	Erick Aybar	.25
185	Albert Pujols	2.00
186	Felix Hernandez	.50
187	Adam Jones	.40
188	Jacoby Ellsbury	.75
189	Mark Reynolds	.40
190	Derek Jeter	2.00
191	John Raynor RC	.50
192	Carlos Monasterios RC	.50
193	Kanekoa Texeira RC	.50
194	David Herndon RC	.50
195	Ruben Tejada RC	.50
196	Mike Leake RC	2.50
197	Jenrry Mejia RC	1.00
198	Austin Jackson RC	3.00
199	Scott Sizemore RC	1.00
200	Jason Heyward RC	5.00
201	Neil Walker (RC)	.50
202	Tommy Manzella RC	.75
203	Wade Davis RC	.75
204	Eric Young Jr. (RC)	.50
205	Luis Durango RC	.50
206	Madison Bumgarner RC	1.50
207	Brent Dlugach (RC)	.50
208	Buster Posey RC	3.00
209	Henry Rodriguez RC	.50
210	Tyler Flowers RC	.75
211	Michael Dunn RC	.50
212	Drew Stubbs RC	.75
213	Brandon Allen (RC)	.75
214	Daniel McCutchen RC	.50
215	Juan Francisco RC	.50
216	Eric Hacker RC	.50
217	Michael Brantley RC	.50
218	Dustin Richardson RC	.50
219	Josh Thole RC	.50
220	Daniel Hudson RC	.50

Blue
Blue (1-190): 2-4X
Blue RC (191-220): 1-2X
Production 520 Sets

Gold
Gold (1-220): 1-2X
Inserted 1:1

Orange
Orange (1-190): 3-5X
Orange RC (191-220): 2-3X
Production 250 Sets

Red
Production One Set

Printing Plates
Production one set per color.

1992 Bowman Throwbacks

Common Player: .50
Inserted 1:2

#	Player	Price
1	Jimmy Rollins	.75
2	Ryan Zimmerman	.75
3	Alex Rodriguez	2.50
4	Andrew McCutchen	1.00
5	Mark Reynolds	.50
6	Jason Bay	.75
7	Hideki Matsui	1.00
8	Carlos Beltran	.50
9	Justin Morneau	.75
10	Matt Cain	.75
11	Russell Martin	.50
12	Alfonso Soriano	.50
13	Joe Mauer	1.00
14	Troy Tulowitzki	1.00
15	Miguel Tejada	.50
16	Adrian Gonzalez	.75
17	Carlos Zambrano	.50
18	Hunter Pence	.50
19	Torii Hunter	.75
20	Michael Young	.50
21	Pablo Sandoval	1.00
22	Manny Ramirez	1.00
23	Jose Reyes	.75
24	Carl Crawford	.75
25	CC Sabathia	.75
26	Josh Beckett	.75
27	Dan Uggla	.50
28	Josh Johnson	.75
29	Raul Ibanez	.50
30	Grady Sizemore	.75
31	Nate McLouth	.50
32	Robinson Cano	.75
33	Carlos Lee	.50
34	Jorge Posada	.75
35	B.J. Upton	.50
36	Ubaldo Jimenez	1.00
37	Ryan Braun	1.50
38	Aaron Hill	.50
39	Rick Porcello	.75
40	Nick Markakis	.75
41	Felix Hernandez	.75
42	Matt Holliday	.75
43	Prince Fielder	1.00
44	Yadier Molina	.75
45	Justin Upton	1.00
46	Carlos Pena	.75
47	Miguel Cabrera	.75
48	Dan Haren	.50
49	Cliff Lee	.75
50	Victor Martinez	.50
51	Josh Hamilton	1.00
52	Evan Longoria	2.00
53	Johan Santana	1.00
54	Ryan Howard	1.50
55	Jon Lester	1.00
56	Mark Buehrle	.50
57	Lance Berkman	.50
58	Roy Oswalt	.50
59	Dustin Pedroia	1.00
60	Daisuke Matsuzaka	.75
61	Joey Votto	.75
62	Ken Griffey Jr.	1.50
63	Jacoby Ellsbury	1.00
64	David Wright	3.00
65	Derek Jeter	3.00
66	Chase Utley	1.50
67	Mark Teixeira	1.00
68	Justin Verlander	1.00
69	Kendry Morales	.75
70	Adam Jones	.75
71	Vladimir Guerrero	.75
72	Albert Pujols	3.00
73	Roy Halladay	1.00
74	Matt Kemp	.75
75	Kevin Youkilis	.75
76	Jake Peavy	.75
77	Hanley Ramirez	1.00
78	Ian Kinsler	.75
79	Ichiro Suzuki	1.50
80	Curtis Granderson	.75
81	Gordon Beckham	.75
82	Jayson Werth	.75
83	Brandon Webb	.75
84	Adam Dunn	.75
85	David Ortiz	.75
86	Cole Hamels	1.00
87	Brian McCann	.75
88	Zack Greinke	1.00
89	Tim Lincecum	2.00
90	Andre Ethier	.75
91	Matt Garza	.50
92	Billy Butler	.50
93	Yovani Gallardo	.75
94	Chone Figgins	.50
95	Yunel Escobar	.50
96	Alexei Ramirez	.50
97	Clayton Kershaw	.75
98	Chris Coghlan	.50
99	Denard Span	.50
100	A.J. Burnett	.75
101	Ivan Rodriguez	.50
102	Chipper Jones	1.00
103	Carlos Delgado	.50
104	Gary Sheffield	.50
105	Garret Anderson	.50
106	Mariano Rivera	1.00
107	John Smoltz	.75
108	Omar Vizquel	.50
109	Jim Thome	.75
110	Manny Ramirez	1.00

Bowman Chrome RC Autos.

Common Auto.: 8.00
Refractor: 1-1.5X
Production 500
Blue Refractor: 1-2X
Production 250 Sets
Gold Refractor: 3-5X
Production 50 Sets
Superfractor 1 of 1's exist

#	Player	Price
198	Austin Jackson	20.00
199	Scott Sizemore	15.00
200	Jason Heyward	85.00
209	Henry Rodriguez	8.00
211	Michael Dunn	10.00
212	Drew Stubbs	15.00
213	Brandon Allen	10.00
214	Daniel McCutchen	10.00
215	Juan Francisco	10.00
216	Eric Hacker	10.00
217	Michael Brantley	10.00
218	Dustin Richardson	10.00
219	Josh Thole	10.00
220	Daniel Hudson	10.00

Chrome 18U USA Baseball

Common Card: 1.50
Refractor: 1-2X
Production 777 Sets
Blue Refractor: 3-4X
Production 250 Sets
Gold Refractor: 8-12X
Production 50 Sets
Orange Refractor: 10-15X
Production 25 Sets
Red Refractor: No Pricing
Production 5 Sets

#	Player	Price
1	Cody Buckel	2.00
2	Nick Castellanos	3.00
3	Garin Cecchini	2.00
4	Sean Coyle	2.00
5	Nicky Delmonico	1.50
6	Kevin Gausman	2.00
7	Cory Hahn	1.50
8	Bryce Harper	35.00
9	Kevin Keyes	2.00
10	Manny Machado	6.00
11	Connor Mason	1.50
12	Ladson Montgomery	1.50
13	Phillip Pfeifer	2.00
14	Brian Ragira	2.00
15	Robbie Ray	1.50
16	Kyle Ryan	1.50
17	Jameson Taillon	5.00
18	A.J. Vanegas	2.00
19	Karsten Whitson	3.00
20	Tony Wolters	2.00

Chrome Prospects

Common Chrome Prospect: .50
Refractor: 2-3X
Production 777 Sets
Blue Refractor: 4-6X
Production 250 Sets
Gold Refractor: 10-15X
Production 50 Sets
Orange Refractor: 15-20X
Production 25 Sets
Red Refractor: No Pricing
Production 5 Sets
Refractor Auto.: 1-1.5X
Production 500 Sets
Blue Refractor Auto.: 3-4X
Production 150 Sets
Gold Refractor Auto.: 4-8X
Production 50 Sets
Orange Refractor Auto.: 6-10X
Production 25 Sets

#	Player	Price
1	Stephen Strasburg	40.00
2	Melky Mesa	.50
3	Cole McCurry	.50
4	Tyler Henley	.50
5	Andrew Cashner	1.50
6	Konrad Schmidt	.50
7	Jean Segura	.50
8	Jon Gaston	.50
9	Nick Santomauro	.50
10	Aroldis Chapman	4.00
11	Logan Watkins	1.00
12	Bo Bowman	.50
13	Jeff Antigua	.50
14	Matt Adams	.50
15	Joseph Cruz	.50
16	Sebastian Valle	1.00
17	Stefan Gartrell	.50
18	Pedro Ciriaco	.50
19	Tyson Gillies	1.50
20	Casey Crosby	2.00
21	Luis Exposito	.50
22	Welington Dotel	.50
23	Alexander Torres	.50
24	Byron Wiley	.50
25	Pedro Florimon	.50
26	Cody Satterwhite	.50
27	Craig Clark	.50
28	Jason Christian	.50
29	Tommy Mendonca	1.00
30	Ryan Dent	.50
31	Jhan Marinez	.50
32	Eric Niesen	1.00
33	Gustavo Nunez	.50
34	Scott Shaw	.50
35	Welinton Ramirez	.50
36	Trevor May	2.00
37	Mitch Moreland	1.00
38	Nick Czyz	.50
39	Edinson Rincon	1.00
40	Domingo Santana	2.50
41	Carson Blair	.50
42	Rashun Dixon	.50
43	Alexander Colome	2.00
44	Allan Dykstra	.50
45	J.J. Hoover	.50
46	Abner Abreu	1.00
47	Daniel Nava	1.00
48	Simon Castro	2.00
49	Brian Baisley	.50
50	Tony Delmonico	.50
51	Chase D'Arnaud	.50
52	Sheng-An Sun	.50
53	Leandro Castro	1.00
54	Charlie Leesman	.50
55	Caleb Joseph	1.00
56	Rolando Gomez	.50
57	John Lamb	1.50
58	Adam Wilk	.50
59	Randall Delgado	1.50
60	Neil Medchill	1.00
61	Josh Donaldson	.50
62	Zach Gentile	.50
63	Kiel Roling	.50
64	Wes Freeman	.50
65	Brian Pellegrini	.50
66	Kyle Jensen	.50
67	Evan Anundsen	.50
68	Hak-Ju Lee	1.50
69	C.J. Retherford	.50
70	Dillon Gee	1.00
71	Bo Greenwell	.50
72	Matt Tucker	.50
73	Joe Serafin	.50
74	Matt Brown	.50
75	Alexis Oliveras	.50
76	James Beresford	.50
77	Steve Lombardozzi	.50
78	Curtis Petersen	.50
79	Eric Farris	.50
80	Yen-Wen Kuo	.50
81	Caleb Brewer	.50
82	Jacob Elmore	.50
83	Jared Clark	.50
84	Yowill Espinal	.50
85	Jae-Hoon Ha	.50
86	Michael Wing	.50
87	Wilmer Font	1.00
88	Jake Kahaulelio	.50
89	Dustin Ackley	2.00
89	Dustin Ackley/Auto.	40.00
90	Donavan Tate	2.00
90	Donavan Tate/Auto.	30.00
91	Nolan Arenado	1.00
91	Nolan Arenado/Auto.	20.00
92	Rex Brothers	.50
92	Rex Brothers/Auto.	10.00
93	Brett Jackson	1.50
93	Brett Jackson/Auto.	25.00
94	Chad Jenkins	.50
94	Chad Jenkins/Auto.	10.00
95	Slade Heathcott	1.00
95	Slade Heathcott/Auto.	25.00
96	J.R. Murphy	1.00
96	J.R. Murphy/Auto.	15.00
97	Patrick Schuster	.50
97	Patrick Schuster/Auto.	10.00
98	Alexia Amarista	1.00
98	Alexia Amarista/Auto.	15.00
99	Thomas Neal	1.00
99	Thomas Neal/Auto.	20.00
100	Starlin Castro	3.00
100	Starlin Castro/Auto.	50.00
101	Anthony Rizzo	1.00
101	Anthony Rizzo/Auto.	20.00
102	Felix Doubront	1.00
102	Felix Doubront/Auto.	15.00
103	Nick Franklin	1.00
103	Nick Franklin/Auto.	20.00
104	Anthony Gose	1.00
104	Anthony Gose/Auto.	10.00
105	Julio Teheran	1.50
105	Julio Teheran/Auto.	30.00
106	Grant Green	1.00
106	Grant Green/Auto.	15.00
107	David Lough	1.00
107	David Lough/Auto.	10.00
108	Jose Iglesias	2.00
108	Jose Iglesias/Auto.	30.00
109	Jaff Decker	1.00
109	Jaff Decker/Auto.	20.00
110	D.J. LeMahieu	1.00
110	D.J. LeMahieu/Auto.	15.00
111	Craig Clark/Auto.	8.00
112	Jefry Marte/Auto.	15.00
113	Josh Donaldson/Auto.	8.00
114	Steven Hensley/Auto.	15.00
115	James Darnell/Auto.	12.00
116	Kirk Nieuwenhuis/Auto.	12.00
117	Wil Myers/Auto.	20.00
118	Bryan Mitchell/Auto.	10.00
119	Martin Perez/Auto.	25.00

Chrome USA Baseball

Common Player: 1.50
Refractor: 1-2X
Production 777 Sets
Blue Refractor: 3-5X
Production 250 Sets
Gold Refractor: 10-15X
Production 50 Sets
Orange Refractor: 12-20X
Production 25 Sets
Red Refractor: No Pricing
Production 5 Sets

#	Player	Price
1	Trevor Bauer	1.50
2	Chad Bettis	1.50
3	Bryce Brentz	4.00
4	Michael Choice	3.00
5	Gerrit Cole	3.00
6	Christian Colon	2.50
7	Blake Forsythe	1.50
8	Yasmani Grandal	2.50
9	Sonny Gray	2.00
10	Rick Hague	1.50
11	Tyler Holt	1.50
12	Casey McGrew	1.50
13	Brad Miller	1.50
14	Matt Newman	1.50
15	Nick Pepitone	1.50
16	Drew Pomeranz	3.00
17	T.J. Walz	2.00
18	Cody Wheeler	2.00
19	Andy Wilkins	1.50
20	Asher Wojciechowski	2.00
21	Kolten Wong	1.50
22	Tony Zych	1.50

Expectations

Common Duo: .50
Inserted 1:3

#	Player 1	Player 2	Price
1	Jorge Posada	Jesus Montero	.50
2	Ryan Howard	Domonic Brown	1.00
3	Hanley Ramirez	Mike Stanton	1.00
4	Chipper Jones	Freddie Freeman	1.00
5	Tim Lincecum	Stephen Strasburg	6.00
6	Jose Reyes	Wilmer Flores	.75
7	David Wright	Ike Davis	2.50
8	Alfonso Soriano	Starlin Castro	1.00
9	Jay Bruce	Todd Frazier	.75
10	Ryan Braun	Mat Gamel	1.50
11	Jon Lester	Madison Bumgarner	1.50
12	Ubaldo Jimenez	Tyler Matzek	1.50
13	Joe Mauer	Buster Posey	4.00
14	Carl Crawford	Desmond Jennings	2.00
15	Evan Longoria	Alex Liddi	1.50
16	Andrew McCutchen	Jose Tabata	1.00
18	Aramis Ramirez	Josh Vitters	5.00
19	Ryan Zimmerman	Ian Desmond	1.00
20	Alex Gordon	Mike Moustakas	1.00
21	Adam Dunn	Chris Marrero	.75
22	Mike Napoli	Hank Conger	1.00
23	Pablo Sandoval	Thomas Neal	
24	Carlos Quentin	Tyler Flowers	.50
25	Victor Martinez	Carlos Santana	2.00
26	Carlos Zambrano	Andrew Cashner	.75
27	Jose Lopez	Dustin Ackley	2.00
28	Rich Harden	Neftali Feliz	
29	Johnny Damon	Slade Heathcott	
30	Kevin Youkilis	Lars Anderson	1.50
31	Dan Haren	Jarrod Parker	1.00
32	Matt Kemp	Jared Mitchell	
33	Will Venable	Donavan Tate	
34	Andre Ethier	Andrew Lambo	
35	Brian McCann	Tony Sanchez	1.00
36	Josh Beckett	Chris Withrow	1.00
37	Matt Cain	Zack Wheeler	.50
38	Johnny Cueto	Jenrry Mejia	
39	David Price	Jake McGee	1.00
40	Matt Garza	Jeremy Hellickson	.75
41	Nick Markakis	Josh Bell	.50
42	Ivan Rodriguez	Derek Norris	.50
43	Elvis Andrus	Jiovanni Mier	1.00
44	Mark Reynolds	Bobby Borchering	.50
45	Prince Fielder	Chris Carter	1.50
46	Grady Sizemore	Jordan Brown	.50
47	Stephen Drew	Pedro Ciriaco	.50
48	Chad Billingsley	John Ely	.50
49	Justin Morneau	Christopher Parmelee	1.00
50	Roy Halladay	Kyle Drabek	1.00

Futures Game Triple Relic

Common Triple Jersey: 8.00
Production 99 Sets

#	Player	Price
AE	Alcides Escobar	10.00
AL	Alex Liddi	10.00
BC	Barbaro Canizares	8.00
BL	Brad Lincoln	10.00
CC	Chris Carter	15.00
CH	Chris Heisey	20.00
CS	Carlos Santana	20.00
CT	Chris Tillman	10.00
DD	Danny Duffy	15.00
DJ	Daryl Jones	8.00
DV	Dayan Viciedo	10.00
EY	Eric Young Jr.	8.00
FS	Francisco Samuel	10.00
JC	Jhoulys Chacin	8.00
JH	Jason Heyward	80.00
JM	Jesus Montero	15.00
JP	Jarrod Parker	20.00
JV	Josh Vitters	15.00
KD	Kyle Drabek	15.00
KK	Kyeong Kang	8.00
LD	Luis Durango	15.00
LS	Leyson Septimo	8.00
MB	Madison Bumgarner	15.00
ML	Mat Latos	10.00
MS	Mike Stanton	35.00
NF	Neftali Feliz	15.00
NW	Nick Weglarz	15.00
PB	Pedro Baez	8.00
RT	Rene Tosoni	10.00
SC	Starlin Castro	30.00
SS	Scott Sizemore	10.00
TF	Tyler Flowers	8.00
TG	Tyson Gillies	15.00
TR	Trevor Reckling	15.00
WF	Wilmer Flores	15.00
YF	Yohan Flande	10.00
DJE	Desmond Jennings	15.00

Prospect Autographs

Common Auto.:
No Pricing

Prospects

Complete Set (110):		35.00
Common Prospect:		.25
Blue:		2-3X
Production 520 Sets		
Orange:		3-5X
Production 250 Sets		
Red:		No Pricing
Production 5 Sets		
1	Stephen Strasburg	20.00
1	Stephen Strasburg/	
	Auto.	500.00
2	Melky Mesa	.25
3	Cole McCurry	.25
4	Tyler Henley	.25
5	Andrew Cashner	.75
6	Konrad Schmidt	.25
7	Jean Segura	.25
8	Jon Gaston	.25
9	Nick Santomauro	.25
10	Aroldis Chapman	2.00
11	Logan Watkins	.50
12	Bo Bowman	.50
13	Jeff Antigua	.25
14	Matt Adams	.25
15	Joseph Cruz	.25
16	Sebastian Valle	.50
17	Stefan Gartrell	.25
18	Pedro Ciriaco	.25
19	Tyson Gillies	.75
20	Casey Crosby	1.00
21	Luis Exposito	.25
22	Welington Dotel	.25
23	Alexander Torres	.25
24	Byron Wiley	.25
25	Pedro Florimon	.25
26	Cody Satterwhite	.25
27	Craig Clark	.25
28	Jason Christian	.25
29	Tommy Mendonca	.50
30	Ryan Dent	.25
31	Jhan Marinez	.25
32	Eric Niesen	.25
33	Gustavo Nunez	.25
34	Scott Shaw	.25
35	Welinton Ramirez	.25
36	Trevor May	1.00
37	Mitch Moreland	.50
38	Nick Czyz	.25
39	Edinson Rincon	.50
40	Domingo Santana	1.50
41	Carson Blair	.25
42	Rashun Dixon	.25
43	Alexander Colome	1.00
44	Allan Dykstra	.25
45	J.J. Hoover	.25
46	Abner Abreu	.50
47	Daniel Nava	.50
48	Simon Castro	1.00
49	Brian Baisley	.25
50	Tony Delmonico	.50
51	Chase D'Arnaud	.50
52	Sheng-An Kuo	.50
53	Leandro Castro	.50
54	Charlie Leesman	.25
55	Caleb Joseph	.25
56	Rolando Gomez	.25
57	John Lamb	.75
58	Adam Wilk	.25
59	Randall Delgado	.50
60	Neil Medchill	.50
61	Josh Donaldson	.25
62	Zach Gentile	.25
63	Kiel Roling	.25
64	Wes Freeman	.25
65	Brian Pellegrini	.25
66	Kyle Jensen	.25
67	Evan Anundsen	.25
68	Hak-Ju Lee	.75
69	C.J. Retherford	.25
70	Dillon Gee	.50
71	Bo Greenwell	.50
72	Matt Tucker	.25
73	Joe Serafin	.25
74	Matt Brown	.25
75	Alexis Oliveras	.25
76	James Beresford	.25
77	Steve Lombardozzi	.25
78	Curtis Petersen	.25
79	Eric Farris	.25
80	Yen-Wen Kuo	.25
81	Caleb Brewer	.25
82	Jacob Elmore	.25
83	Jared Clark	.25
84	Yowill Espinal	.25
85	Jae-Hoon Ha	.25
86	Michael Wing	.25
87	Wilmer Font	.50
88	Jake Kahaulelio	.25
89	Dustin Ackley	1.00
90	Donavan Tate	1.00
91	Nolan Arenado	.50
92	Rex Brothers	.50
93	Brett Jackson	.75
94	Chad Jenkins	.25
95	Slade Heathcott	.50
96	J.R. Murphy	.50
97	Patrick Schuster	.25
98	Alexia Amarista	.25
99	Thomas Neal	.25
100	Starlin Castro	1.50
101	Anthony Rizzo	.50
102	Felix Doubront	.50
103	Nick Franklin	.50
104	Anthony Gose	.25
105	Julio Teheran	.75
106	Grant Green	.50
107	David Lough	.25
108	Jose Iglesias	1.00
109	Jaff Decker	.50
110	D.J. LeMahieu	.50

Topps 100 Prospects

Common 100 Prospect:		.50
Inserted 1:2		
TP1	Stephen Strasburg	10.00
TP2	Aroldis Chapman	1.00
TP3	Jason Heyward	3.00
TP4	Jesus Montero	.50
TP5	Mike Stanton	2.00
TP6	Mike Moustakas	.50
TP7	Kyle Drabek	1.00
TP8	Tyler Matzek	1.00
TP9	Austin Jackson	1.00
TP10	Starlin Castro	2.00
TP11	Todd Frazier	1.00
TP12	Carlos Santana	1.00
TP13	Josh Vitters	1.50
TP14	Neftali Feliz	.75
TP15	Tyler Flowers	.50
TP16	Alcides Escobar	.75
TP17	Ike Davis	2.00
TP18	Domonic Brown	1.00
TP19	Donavan Tate	1.50
TP20	Buster Posey	1.50
TP21	Dustin Ackley	2.00
TP22	Desmond Jennings	1.00
TP23	Brandon Allen	.50
TP24	Freddie Freeman	1.00
TP25	Jake Arrieta	1.00
TP26	Bobby Borchering	2.00
TP27	Logan Morrison	1.00
TP28	Christian Friederich	.50
TP29	Wilmer Flores	1.00
TP30	Austin Romine	.50
TP31	Tony Sanchez	1.00
TP32	Madison Bumgarner	.50
TP33	Mike Montgomery	1.00
TP34	Andrew Lambo	.50
TP35	Derek Norris	.50
TP36	Chris Withrow	.50
TP37	Thomas Neal	.50
TP38	Trevor Reckling	.50
TP39	Andrew Cashner	.50
TP40	Daniel Hudson	.50
TP41	Jiovanni Mier	.50
TP42	Grant Green	.50
TP43	Jeremy Hellickson	1.00
TP44	Felix Doubront	.50
TP45	Martin Perez	1.00
TP46	Jenrry Mejia	1.00
TP47	Adrian Cardenas	.50
TP48	Ivan DeJesus Jr.	.50
TP49	Nolan Arenado	.50
TP50	Slade Heathcott	1.00
TP51	Ian Desmond	1.00
TP52	Michael Taylor	.50
TP53	Jaime Garcia	1.00
TP54	Jose Tabata	.50
TP55	Josh Bell	.50
TP56	Jarrod Parker	.50
TP57	Matt Dominguez	.50
TP58	Koby Clemens	.50
TP59	Angel Morales	2.00
TP60	Juan Francisco	.50
TP61	John Ely	1.00
TP62	Brett Jackson	2.00
TP63	Chad Jenkins	1.00
TP64	Jose Iglesias	.50
TP65	Logan Forsythe	.50
TP66	Alex Liddi	1.50
TP67	Eric Arnett	2.00
TP68	Wilkin Ramirez	.50
TP69	Lars Anderson	.50
TP70	Jared Mitchell	.50
TP71	Mike Leake	.50
TP72	D.J. LeMahieu	1.00
TP73	Chris Marrero	1.00
TP74	Matt Moore	1.00
TP75	Jordan Brown	.50
TP76	Christopher Parmelee	1.00
TP77	Ryan Kalish	1.00
TP78	A.J. Pollock	1.00
TP79	Alex White	2.00
TP80	Scott Sizemore	.50
TP81	Jay Austin	.50
TP82	Zach McAllister	.50
TP83	Max Stassi	1.50
TP84	Robert Stock	2.50
TP85	Jake McGee	1.00
TP86	Zack Wheeler	1.00
TP87	Chase D'Arnaud	.50
TP88	Danny Duffy	.50
TP89	Josh Lindblom	.50
TP90	Anthony Gose	1.00
TP91	Simon Castro	.50
TP92	Chris Carter	.50
TP93	Matt Hobgood	1.00
TP94	Ben Revere	.50
TP95	Mat Gamel	.50
TP96	Anthony Hewitt	.50
TP97	Julio Teheran	.50
TP98	Josh Reddick	.50
TP99	Hank Conger	.50
TP100	Jordan Walden	.50

1992-2004 Boy Scouts of America Atlanta Braves

In 1992 the Atlanta-area Boy Scouts of America began a "Collector's Edition" series of commemorative baseball cards featuring Braves players. The 2-1/2" x 3-1/2" cards

have a variety of designs with color photos, usually game-action. Red, white and blue backs have player information and stats and logos of the team, sponsor(s), and/or BSA.

		NM/M
Complete Set (13):		50.00
Common Player:		2.00
(1)	Jeff Treadway/1992	3.00
(2)	Dale Murphy/1993	15.00
(3)	Deion Sanders/1994	8.00
(4)	Gregory McMichael/	
	1995	3.00
(5)	Ryan Klesko/1996	5.00
(6)	Jeff Blauser/1997	3.00
(7)	Greg Maddux/1998	12.00
(8)	John Rocker/1999	5.00
(9)	John Smoltz/2000	3.00
(10)	Tom Glavine/2001	3.00
(11)	Kevin Millwood/2002)	2.00
(12)	Marcus Giles/2003	2.00
(13)	Russ Ortiz/2004	2.00

1998 Bryan Braves Team Photo Set

After a one-year absence and a change of stadium hot dog vendors, the Braves again distributed a team photo foldout in 1998. The 10-5/8" x 31-3/8" three-panel perforated sheet has a large team photo and individual 2-1/8" x 3-1/8" cards of 35 players and staff. The player cards have a portrait photo on a background of brown baseballs and faded red "A"s. The player name is in gold at the bottom; his position vertically in a blue strip at left. A red Bryan logo is at top-left. Backs are in red, white and blue with biographical and career notes and stats. The unnumbered cards are checklisted here alpabetically.

		NM/M
Complete Foldout Set:		8.00
Common Player:		.10
(1)	Danny Bautista	.10
(2)	Jim Beacuhamp	.10
(3)	Rafael Belliard	.10
(4)	Adam Butler	.10
(5)	Norm Charlton	.10
(6)	Greg Colbrunn	.10
(7)	Pat Corrales	.10
(8)	Bobby Cox	.10
(9)	Bobby Dews	.10
(10)	Frank Fultz	.10
(11)	Andres Galarraga	.10
(12)	Tom Glavine	1.00
(13)	Tony Graffanino	.10
(14)	Ozzie Guillen	.10
(15)	Andruw Jones	1.50
(16)	Chipper Jones	3.00
(17)	Clarence Jones	.10
(18)	Ryan Klesko	.10
(19)	Kerry Ligtenberg	.10
(20)	Keith Lockhart	.10
(21)	Javy Lopez	.10
(22)	Greg Maddux	2.00
(23)	Dennis Martinez	.10
(24)	Leo Mazzone	.10
(25)	Kevin Millwood	.50
(26)	Denny Neagle	.10
(27)	Eddie Perez	.10
(28)	John Rocker	.10
(29)	Rudy Seanez	.10
(30)	John Smoltz	1.00
(31)	Russ Springer	.10
(32)	Michael Tucker	.10
(33)	Walt Weiss	.10
(34)	Gerald Williams	.10
(35)	Ned Yost	.10
(36)	Team Photo	.50

1999 Bryan Braves

These Tuesday-night homestand give-away cards were sponsored by the team's hot dog vendor and given away three players at a time to children only. Completion of a set is thus a challenge. The cards of Hernandez, Mulholland and Myers were late-season additions and differ from the rest of the set in that the player names in gold vertically at left are in upper- and lower-case type, while most cards have the name in all-caps. The 2-1/2" x 3-1/2" cards have player portraits bordered in blue at left and bottom. The position is in gold at bottom; the uniform number in gold at top. A red Bryan logo is at lower-left. Black, white and blue backs have minimal player vitae and full professional stats. The unnumbered cards are checklisted here in alphabetical order.

		NM/M
Complete Set (30):		32.50
Common Player:		1.00
(1)	Don Baylor	1.00
(2)	Bret Boone	1.00
(3)	Pat Corrales	1.00
(4)	Bobby Cox	1.00
(5)	Bobby Dews	1.00
(6)	Tom Glavine	1.50
(7)	Ozzie Guillen	1.00
(8)	Jose Hernandez	1.00
(9)	Glenn Hubbard	1.00
(10)	Brian Hunter	1.00
(11)	Andruw Jones	2.50
(12)	Chipper Jones	4.00
(13)	Brian Jordan	1.00
(14)	Ryan Klesko	1.00
(15)	Keith Lockhart	1.00
(16)	Javy Lopez	1.00
(17)	Greg Maddux	3.00
(18)	Leo Mazzone	1.00
(19)	Kevin Millwood	1.00
(20)	Terry Mulholland	1.00
(21)	Greg Myers	1.00
(22)	Otis Nixon	1.00
(23)	Eddie Perez	1.00
(24)	Odalis Perez	1.00
(25)	Mike Remlinger	1.00
(26)	John Rocker	1.00
(27)	Rudy Seanez	1.00
(28)	John Smoltz	1.50
(29)	Walt Weiss	1.00
(30)	Ned Yost	1.00

1999 Bryan Braves Team Photo Set

Children visiting Turner Field for a late-season game received this foldout sponsored by the team's hot dog vendor. The 10-5/8" x 31-3/8" three-panel perforated sheet has a large team photo and individual 2-1/8" x 3-1/8" cards of 35 players and staff. The player cards have a portrait photo on a baseball background. The player name and position are at left. A large red Bryan logo is at top-right. Backs are in red, white and black with biographical and career notes and stats. The unnumbered cards are checklisted here alphabetically.

		NM/M
Complete Foldout Set:		8.00
Common Player:		.10
(1)	Don Baylor	.10
(2)	Bret Boone	.25
(3)	Bruce Chen	.10
(4)	Pat Corrales	.10
(5)	Bobby Cox	.10
(6)	Bobby Dews	.10
(7)	Frank Fultz	.10
(8)	Tom Glavine	.10
(9)	Ozzie Guillen	.10
(10)	Jose Hernandez	.10
(11)	Glenn Hubbard	.10
(12)	Brian Hunter	.10
(13)	Andruw Jones	1.50
(14)	Chipper Jones	3.00
(15)	Brian Jordan	.10
(16)	Ryan Klesko	.10
(17)	Keith Lockhart	.10
(18)	Javy Lopez	.10
(19)	Greg Maddux	2.00
(20)	Leo Mazzone	.10
(21)	Kevin McGlinchy	.10
(22)	Kevin Millwood	.50
(23)	Terry Mulholland	.10
(24)	Greg Myers	.10
(25)	Otis Nixon	.10
(26)	Eddie Perez	.10
(27)	Mike Remlinger	.10
(28)	John Rocker	.10
(29)	Rudy Seanez	.10
(30)	Randall Simon	.10
(31)	John Smoltz	1.00
(32)	Russ Springer	.10
(33)	Walt Weiss	.10
(34)	Gerald Williams	.10
(35)	Ned Yost	.10
(36)	Team Photo	.50

2000 Bryan Braves

For the first time since the Braves hot dog concessionaires began issuing annual stadium give-away card sets in 1989, the number of Tuesday home games in 2000 dictated that some players be issued in more than one variation to allow for three cards to be given away each date. The 2-1/2" x 3-1/2" cards have game-action photos vignetted with blue borders. The player's full name and position are in red at left, and his last name in white at right. His uniform number is at top. A red Bryan logo is at bottom. Black, white and blue backs have a few bits of personal data and complete minor and major league stats. The unnumbered cards are checklisted here alphabetically.

		NM/M
Complete Set (39):		45.00
Common Player:		1.00
(1)	Andy Ashby	1.00
(2)	Bobby Bonilla	1.00
(3)	John Burkett	1.00
(4)	Pat Corrales	1.00
(5)	Bobby Cox	1.00
(6)	Bobby Dews	1.00
(7)	Rafael Furcal	1.50
(8)	Andres Galarraga/Btg	1.00
(9)	Andres Galarraga/Fldg	1.00
(10)	Tom Glavine	2.00
(11)	Glenn Hubbard	1.00
(12)	Andruw Jones	
	(Batting stance.)	2.50

2000 Bryan Braves Team Photo Set

Children visiting Turner Field for a late-season game received this foldout sponsored by the team's hot dog vendor. The 10-5/8" x 31-3/8" three-panel perforated sheet has a large team photo and individual 2-1/8" x 3-1/8" cards of 35 players and staff. The staff cards have a portrait photo on a blue background. The player cards have game-action photos. All cards are bordered in brown with a nameplate design at bottom with identification and a Bryan logo. Backs are in red, white and black with biographical and career notes and stats. The unnumbered cards are checklisted here alphabetically.

		NM/M
Complete Foldout Set:		8.00
Common Player:		.10
(1)	Andy Ashby	.10
(2)	Bobby Bonilla	.10
(3)	John Burkett	.10
(4)	Bobby Cox	.10
(5)	Pat Corrales	.10
(6)	Bobby Dews	.10
(7)	Frank Fultz	.10
(8)	Rafael Furcal	.75
(9)	Andres Galarraga	.10
(10)	Tom Glavine	1.00
(11)	Glenn Hubbard	1.00
(12)	Andruw Jones	1.00
(13)	Chipper Jones	3.00
(14)	Brian Jordan	.10
(15)	Wally Joyner	.10
(16)	Kerry Ligtenberg	.10
(17)	Keith Lockhart	.10
(18)	Javy Lopez	.10
(19)	Greg Maddux	1.50
(20)	Leo Mazzone	.10
(21)	Kevin McGlinchy	.10
(22)	Kevin Millwood	.10
(23)	Terry Mulholland	.10
(24)	Eddie Perez	.10
(25)	Odalis Perez	.10
(26)	Mike Remlinger	.10
(27)	Merv Rettenmund	.10
(28)	John Rocker	.10
(29)	Reggie Sanders	.10
(30)	Rudy Seanez	.10
(31)	John Smoltz	1.00
(32)	B.J. Surhoff	.10
(33)	Quilvio Veras	.10
(34)	Walt Weiss	.10
(35)	Ned Yost	.10

(13)	Andruw Jones	
	(Follow-through.)	2.50
(14)	Chipper Jones	
	(Back turned.)	4.00
(15)	Chipper Jones/Fldg	4.00
(16)	Brian Jordan/Btg	1.00
(17)	Brian Jordan/Portrait	1.00
(18)	Wally Joyner	1.00
(19)	Kerry Ligtenberg	1.00
(20)	Keith Lockhart	1.00
(21)	Javy Lopez/Btg	1.00
(22)	Javy Lopez/Catching	1.00
(23)	Greg Maddux	3.00
(24)	Leo Mazzone	1.00
(25)	Kevin McGlinchy	1.00
(26)	Kevin Millwood	1.00
(27)	Terry Mulholland	1.00
(28)	Eddie Perez	1.00
(29)	Odalis Perez	1.00
(30)	Mike Remlinger	1.00
(31)	Merv Rettenmund	1.00
(32)	John Rocker	1.00
(33)	Reggie Sanders	1.00
(34)	Rudy Seanez	1.00
(35)	John Smoltz	2.00
(36)	B.J. Surhoff	1.00
(37)	Quilvio Veras	1.00
(38)	Walt Weiss	1.00
(39)	Ned Yost	1.00

2001 Bryan Braves

Three cards were given out at each Tuesday home game to children 12 and under from this set sponsored by Turner Field's hot dog vendor. The 2-1/2" x 3-1/2" cards have game-action photos with a team logo at top, a sponsor's logo at bottom, a trio of ghost-image baseballs at left and the player name and position at right. Black, white and blue backs have minimal player personal data and complete pro stats. The unnumbered cards are checklisted here in alphabetical order. Due to the manner of their distribution, assembly of a complete set is difficult.

		NM/M
Complete Set (29):		30.00
Common Player:		1.00
(1)	Rico Brogna	1.00
(2)	John Burkett	1.00
(3)	Jose Cabrera	1.00
(4)	Ken Caminiti	1.00
(5)	Bobby Cox	1.00
(6)	Mark DeRosa	1.00
(7)	Bobby Dews	1.00
(8)	Rafael Furcal	1.50
(9)	Marcus Giles	1.00
(10)	Tom Glavine	2.00
(11)	Wes Helms	1.00
(12)	Andruw Jones	2.50
(13)	Chipper Jones	4.00
(14)	Brian Jordan	1.00
(15)	Kerry Ligtenberg	1.00
(16)	Keith Lockhart	1.00
(17)	George Lombard	1.00
(18)	Javy Lopez	1.00
(19)	Greg Maddux	3.00
(20)	Jason Marquis	1.00
(21)	Dave Martinez	1.00
(22)	Leo Mazzone	1.00
(23)	Kevin Millwood	1.50
(24)	Odalis Perez	1.00
(25)	Mike Remlinger	1.00
(26)	John Rocker	2.00
(27)	John Smoltz	2.00
(28)	B.J. Surhoff	1.00
(29)	Quilvio Veras	1.00

2001 Bryan Braves Team Photo Set

Children visiting Turner Field for a late-season game received this foldout sponsored by the team's hot dog vendor. The 10-5/8" x 31-3/8" three-panel perforated sheet has a large team photo and individual 2-1/8" x 3-1/8" cards of 35 players and staff. The staff cards have a portrait photo; the player cards have game-action photos. All photos are in the "sweet spot" on baseball background with name and position in red at left and a large Bryan logo at lower-right. Backs are red, white and black with biographical and career notes and

		NM/M
Complete Foldout Set:		8.00
Common Player:		.10
(1)	Henry Blanco	.10
(2)	Darren Bragg	.10
(3)	Vinny Castilla	.10
(4)	Pat Corrales	.10
(5)	Bobby Cox	.10
(6)	Mark DeRosa	.10
(7)	Bobby Dews	.10
(8)	Julio Franco	.10
(9)	Matt Franco	.10
(10)	Frank Fultz	.10
(11)	Rafael Furcal	.10
(12)	Jesse Garcia	.10
(13)	Marcus Giles	.10
(14)	Tom Glavine	1.00
(15)	Chris Hammond	.10
(16)	Wes Helms	.10
(17)	Darren Holmes	.10
(18)	Glenn Hubbard	.10
(19)	Andruw Jones	1.00
(20)	Chipper Jones	3.00
(21)	Kerry Ligtenberg	.10
(22)	Keith Lockhart	.10
(23)	Albie Lopez	.10
(24)	Javy Lopez	.10
(25)	Greg Maddux	2.00
(26)	Jason Marquis	.10
(27)	Leo Mazzone	.10

stats on a ghost image of the front photo. The unnumbered cards are checklisted here alpabetically.

		NM/M
(28)	Kevin Millwood	.35
(29)	Damian Moss	.25
(30)	Terry Pendleton	.10
(31)	Mike Remlinger	.10
(32)	Gary Sheffield	.35
(33)	John Smoltz	1.00
(34)	Tim Spooneybarger	.10
(35)	Ned Yost	.10
(36)	Team Photo	.50

1982 Builders Emporium Los Angeles Dodgers

Shoppers at this chain of building supply stores in Southern California were able to receive one of this seven-card set with each visit. Cards are printed in black-and-white in 11" x 8-1/2" format with blank backs. Fronts of the player cards have both portrait and action photos, the manager's card has only a portrait. Team and sponsors' logos are at bottom-right. The unnumbered cards are checklisted here in alphabetical order.

		NM/M
Complete Set (7):		35.00
Common Player:		6.00
(1)	Dusty Baker	6.00
(2)	Ron Cey	6.00
(3)	Steve Garvey	9.00
(4)	Pedro Guerrero	6.00
(5)	Tommy Lasorda	6.00
(6)	Jerry Reuss	6.00
(7)	Steve Sax	6.00

1982 Burger King Braves

A set consisting of 27 "Collector Lids" featuring the Atlanta Braves was issued by Burger King restaurants in 1982. The plastic lids, 3-5/8" in diameter, were placed on a special Coca-Cola cup which listed the scores of the Braves' season-opening 13-game win streak. A black-and-white photo plus the player's name, position, height, weight, and 1981 statistics are found on the lid front. The unnumbered, blank-backed lids also contain logos for Burger King, Coca-Cola, and the Major League Baseball Players Association.

		NM/M
Complete Set (27):		20.00
Common Player:		1.00
(1)	Steve Bedrosian	1.00
(2)	Bruce Benedict	1.00
(3)	Tommy Boggs	1.00
(4)	Brett Butler	1.50
(5)	Rick Camp	1.00
(6)	Chris Chambliss	1.00
(7)	Ken Dayley	1.00
(8)	Gene Garber	1.00
(9)	Preston Hanna	1.00
(10)	Terry Harper	1.00
(11)	Bob Horner	1.50
(12)	Al Hrabosky	1.00
(13)	Glenn Hubbard	1.00
(14)	Randy Johnson	1.00
(15)	Rufino Linares	1.00
(16)	Rick Mahler	1.00
(17)	Larry McWilliams	1.00
(18)	Dale Murphy	12.50
(19)	Phil Niekro	3.00
(20)	Biff Pocoroba	1.00
(21)	Rafael Ramirez	1.00
(22)	Jerry Royster	1.00
(23)	Ken Smith	1.00
(24)	Bob Walk	1.00
(25)	Claudell Washington	1.00
(26)	Bob Watson	1.00
(27)	Larry Whisenton	1.00

1982 Burger King Indians

This set was sponsored by WUAB-TV and Burger Kings in the Cleveland vicinity. The cards' green borders encompass a large yellow area which contains a black-and-white photo plus a baseball tip. Manager Dave Garcia and his coaches provide the baseball hints. The cards, which measure 3" x 5", are unnumbered and blank-backed.

		NM/M
Complete Set (12):		7.00
Common Player:		.75
(1)	Dave Garcia (Be In The Game)	.75
(2)	Dave Garcia (Sportsmanship)	.75
(3)	Johnny Goryl (Rounding The Bases)	.75
(4)	Johnny Goryl (3rd Base Running)	.75
(5)	Tom McCraw (Follow Thru)	.75
(6)	Tom McCraw (Selecting A Bat)	.75
(7)	Tom McCraw (Watch The Ball)	.75
(8)	Mel Queen (Master One Pitch)	.75
(9)	Mel Queen (Warm Up)	.75
(10)	Dennis Sommers (Get Down On A Ground Ball)	.75
(11)	Dennis Sommers (Protect Your Fingers)	.75
(12)	Dennis Sommers (Tagging First Base)	.75

1986 Burger King

Burger King restaurants in the Pennsylvania and New Jersey areas issued a set entitled "All-Pro Series." Cards were issued with the purchase of a Whopper sandwich and came in folded panels of two cards each, along with a coupon card. Fronts feature a color photo and identification plus the Burger King logo. Due to a lack of MLB licensing, team insignias on the players' uniforms were airbrushed away. Backs are in black-and-white and contain brief biographical and statistical information.

		NM/M
Complete Panel Set (10):		3.00
Complete Singles Set (20):		3.00
Common Panel:		.25
Common Single Player:		.05
PANEL (1)		.40
1	Tony Pena	.05
2	Dave Winfield	.20
PANEL (2)		1.00
3	Fernando Valenzuela	.05
4	Pete Rose	.45
PANEL (3)		1.00
5	Mike Schmidt	.40
6	Steve Carlton	.20

1982 Burger King

1987 Burger King

The 1987 "All-Pro 2nd Edition Series" set was part of a giveaway promotion at participating Burger King restaurants. The set is comprised of 20 players on ten different panels, each with a three-card panel (includes a coupon card) measuring 7-5/8" x 3-1/2". Fronts feature a full-color photo and Burger King logo surrounded by a blue stars-and-stripes border. Backs are black-and-white with a brief biography and 1986/Career statistics. The set was produced by Mike Schecter Associates and, as with many MSA issues, all team insignias were airbrushed away.

		NM/M
Complete Panel Set (10):		3.00
Complete Singles Set (20):		3.00
Common Panel:		.30
Common Single Player:		.05
PANEL 1		.75
1	Wade Boggs	.40
2	Gary Carter	.30
PANEL (2)		.75
3	Will Clark	.05
4	Roger Clemens	.50
PANEL (3)		.40
5	Steve Garvey	.20
6	Ron Darling	.05
PANEL (4)		.30
7	Pedro Guerrero	.05
8	Von Hayes	.05
PANEL (5)		.40
9	Rickey Henderson	.30
10	Keith Hernandez	.05
PANEL (6)		.30
11	Wally Joyner	.05
12	Mike Krukow	.05
PANEL (7)		1.00
13	Don Mattingly	.50
14	Ozzie Smith	.40
PANEL (8)		.30
15	Tony Pena	.05
16	Jim Rice	.20
PANEL (9)		1.00
17	Ryne Sandberg	.40
18	Mike Schmidt	.50
PANEL (10)		.30
19	Darryl Strawberry	.05
20	Fernando Valenzuela	.05

1994 Burger King Cal Ripken Jr.

Although the cards themselves do not indicate it, this issue was co-sponsored by Burger King and Coke, and distributed in BK restaurants in the Baltimore-Washington area. Cards were available in three-card packs for 25 cents with the purchase of a Coke product. Each pack contains two regular cards and a gold card. Each of the nine cards could be found in a regular and gold version. Cards feature color photos with a semi-circular black border at top or left. "Score

"94" appears in orange in one of the upper corners, along with an Orioles logo. Cal Ripken, Jr.'s name appears at the bottom. On the gold premium version, there is a gold-foil circle around the Orioles logo and Ripken's name appears in gold, rather than white. Backs have a smaller color photo, again meeting at a semi-circular edge with the black border at left and bottom. In the black are another Score logo, a card number, an Orioles logo, a headline and a few career details and/or stats. Cards are UV coated on each side. Several hundred of the cards were personally autographed by Ripken and distributed in a drawing.

		NM/M
Complete Set (9):		5.00
Complete Set, Gold (9):		9.00
Common Card:		.75
Common Card, Gold:		1.25
Autographed Card:		185.00
1	Double Honors	.75
1a	Double Honors/Gold	1.25
2	Perennial All-Star	.75
2a	Perennial All-Star/Gold	1.25
3	Peerless Power	.75
3a	Peerless Power/Gold	1.25
4	Fitness Fan	.75
4a	Fitness Fan/Gold	1.25
5	Prime Concerns	.75
5a	Prime Concerns/Gold	1.25
6	Home Run Club	.75
6a	Home Run Club/Gold	1.25
7	The Iron Man	.75
7a	The Iron Man/Gold	1.25
8	Heavy Hitter	.75
8a	Heavy Hitter/Gold	1.25
9	Gold Glover	.75
9a	Gold Glover/Gold	1.25

1997 Burger King Cal Ripken Jr.

Three years after its 1994 tribute, Burger King in 1997 created an eight-card set honoring the future Hall of Famer. Participating BK outlets in Maryland, the District of Columbia, Delaware, Pennsylvania, Virginia and West Virginia offered the cards for 99¢ with a meal purchase or $1.15 without. Each card was produced in two forms: with and without a gold holographic foil facsimile autograph and "1 of 10,000" notation. The 2-1/2" x 3-1/2" cards have action photos of Ripken on front with muted backgrounds. His name, uniform number and team logo also appear. Backs, numbered "X/8" have another color photo with ghosted background and a paragraph of a career highlight. Autographed cards were part of a prize structure explained on information cards accompanying the Ripken card in each pack.

		NM/M
Complete Set (8):		5.00
Complete Gold Set (8):		10.00
Common Card:		1.00
Common Gold Card:		2.00
Autographed Card:		185.00
1-8	Cal Ripken Jr.	1.00
--	Autograph Information Card	.25

1999 Burger King N.Y. Yankees

Members of the World Champion 1998 N.Y. Yankees are featured on this three-sheet set of cards sold by metropolitan New York Burger King restaurants in April-May, 1999. The 12-1/2" x 10-1/2" perforated sheets each include nine standard-size cards. Fronts feature action photos with the Yankees and Fleer logos. Backs have the same photo along with season and career stats and highlights, printed on a ghosted background of a Yankees pinstriped jersey. The Fleer and team logos appear on back, as do those of the players' union and the restaurant chain. On the sheet along with the player cards are a checklist, team schedule, mention of the BK Cancer Foundation of New York and a kids' club offer.

		NM/M
Complete Sheet Set (3):		7.50
Complete Singles Set (27):		7.50
Common Player:		.25
SHEET 1		6.00
1	Derek Jeter	4.00
2	Paul O'Neill	.25
3	Scott Brosius	.25
4	Mariano Rivera	.50
5	Chuck Knoblauch	.25
6	Graeme Lloyd	.25
7	Joe Girardi	.25
8	Orlando Hernandez	.25
9	Tim Raines	.25
SHEET 2		3.50
10	Bernie Williams	.45
11	Tino Martinez	.25
12	Andy Pettitte	.40
13	Hideki Irabu	.25
14	Ramiro Mendoza	.25
15	Jeff Nelson	.25
16	Homer Bush	.25
17	Darren Holmes	.25
18	Yankees Championship History	.25
SHEET 3		3.50
19	David Cone	.25
20	David Wells	.25
21	Chili Davis	.25
22	Darryl Strawberry	.25
23	Ricky Ledee	.25
24	Jorge Posada	.25
25	Luis Sojo	.25
26	Chad Curtis	.25
27	Mike Stanton	.25

C

1989 Cadaco All-Star Baseball Discs

This set of player discs was sold with and intended for use in a board game. Fronts of the 3-1/2" diameter position players' discs have a yellow border sectioned with numbers from 1 to 14, indicating that player's likelihood of performing a specific baseball result based on career stats. At center is a color player

photo from which the uniform details have been airbrushed. Logos of the game's producer and the Major League Players Association flank the portrait. The player's name, team and position are below the photo. Backs have up to five years of recent stats and lifetime totals, along with a few biographical data. Several of the discs have player names misspelled. Each disc can be found either with or without the team name and league on back. Four error discs from the initial print run (with team, league on back) were corrected. The unnumbered discs are checklisted alphabetically.

		NM/M
Complete Set (63):		20.00
Common Player:		.25
(1)	Harold Baines	.25
(2)	Wade Boggs	2.00
(3)	Bobby Bonilla	.25
(4)	George Brett	2.50
(5)	Jose Canseco	1.00
(6)	Gary Carter	1.50
(7)	Joe Carter	.25
(8)	Will Clark	.25
(9a)	Rodger Clemens (First name misspelled.)	3.00
(9b)	Roger Clemens (Corrected)	3.00
(10)	Vince Coleman	.25
(11)	David Cone	.25
(12)	Alvin Davis	.25
(13)	Eric Davis	.25
(14)	Glenn Davis	.25
(15)	Andre Dawson	.65
(16)	Shawon Dunston	.25
(17)	Dennis Eckersley	.60
(18)	Carlton Fisk	1.50
(19)	Scott Fletcher	.25
(20a)	John Frannko (Last name misspelled.)	.35
(20b)	John Franco (Corrected)	.25
(21)	Julio Franko (Franco)	.25
(22)	Gary Gaetti	.25
(23)	Andres Galarraga	.25
(24)	Kirk Gibson	.25
(25)	Mike Greenwell	.25
(26)	Mark Gubicza	.25
(27)	Pedro Guerrero	.25
(28)	Tony Gwynn	2.00
(29)	Rickey Henderson	1.50
(30)	Orel Hershiser	.25
(31)	Kent Hrbek	.25
(32)	Danny Jackson	.25
(33a)	Barry Larkin (Wrong photo.)	.65
(33b)	Barry Larkin (Corrected)	.25
(34)	Greg Maddux	2.00
(35)	Don Mattingly	2.50
(36a)	Mark McGwire (Last name misspelled.)	4.50
(36b)	Mark McGwire (Corrected)	4.50
(37)	Fred McGriff	.25
(38)	Paul Molitor	1.50
(39)	Tony Pena	.25
(40)	Gerald Perry	.25
(41)	Dan Plesac	.25
(42)	Kirby Puckett	2.00
(43)	Johnny Ray	.25
(44)	Jeff Reardon	.25
(45)	Cal Ripken, Jr.	4.50
(46)	Babe Ruth	3.50
(47)	Nolan Ryan	4.50
(48)	Juan Samuel	.25
(49)	Ryne Sandberg	2.00
(50)	Benito Santiago	.25
(51)	Steve Sax	.25
(52)	Mike Schmidt	2.25
(53)	Kevin Seitzer	.25
(54)	Ozzie Smith	2.00
(55)	Terry Steinbach	.25
(56)	Dave Stewart	.25
(57)	Darryl Strawberry	.25
(58)	Andres Thomas	.25
(59)	Alan Trammell (Trammell)	.25
(60)	Andy Van Slyke	.25
(61)	Frank Viola	.25
(62)	Dave Winfield	1.50
(63)	Todd Worrell	.25

1990 Cadaco All-Star Baseball Discs

This set of player discs was sold with and intended for use in a board game. Fronts of the 3-1/2"

diameter position players' discs have a border sectioned with numbers from 1 to 14, indicating that player's likelihood of performing a specific baseball result based on career stats. At center is a color player photo from which the uniform details have been airbrushed. Logos of the game's producer and the Major League Players Association flank the portrait. The player's name, team and position are below the photo. Backs have up to five years of recent stats and lifetime totals, along with a few biographical data. A handful of the game's past greats were included among the contemporary players which make up the bulk of the disc set. The unnumbered discs are checklisted alphabetically.

		NM/M
Complete Set (63):		20.00
Common Player:		.25
(1)	Harold Baines	.25
(2)	Damon Berryhill	.25
(3)	Craig Biggio	.25
(4)	Wade Boggs	2.00
(5)	Bobby Bonilla	.25
(6)	Jose Canseco	1.00
(7)	Will Clark	.25
(8)	Roger Clemens	2.50
(9)	Roberto Clemente	4.00
(10)	Ty Cobb	2.50
(11)	Vince Coleman	.25
(12)	Eric Davis	.25
(13)	Glenn Davis	.25
(14)	Andre Dawson	.65
(15)	Shawon Dunston	.25
(16)	Tony Fernandez	.25
(17)	Carlton Fisk	1.50
(18)	Julio Franco	.25
(19)	Gary Gaetti	.25
(20)	Lou Gehrig	4.00
(21)	Kirk Gibson	.25
(22)	Mark Grace	.25
(23)	Ken Griffey Jr.	3.00
(24)	Pedro Guerrero	.25
(25)	Tony Gwynn	2.00
(26)	Rickey Henderson	1.50
(27)	Orel Hershiser	.25
(28)	Bo Jackson	.60
(29)	Howard Johnson	.25
(30)	Carney Lansford	.25
(31)	Barry Larkin	.25
(32)	Greg Maddux	2.00
(33)	Don Mattingly	2.50
(34)	Fred McGriff	.25
(35)	Mark McGwire	3.50
(36)	Kevin Mitchell	.25
(37)	Tony Pena	.25
(38)	Kirby Puckett	2.00
(39)	Willie Randolph	.25
(40)	Cal Ripken Jr.	4.50
(41)	Babe Ruth	4.00
(42)	Nolan Ryan	4.50
(43)	Bret Saberhagen	.25
(44)	Chris Sabo	.25
(45)	Ryne Sandberg	2.00
(46)	Benito Santiago	.25
(47)	Steve Sax	.25
(48)	Mike Scott	.25
(49)	Kevin Seitzer	.25
(50)	Ruben Sierra	.25
(51)	Ozzie Smith	2.00
(52)	Terry Steinbach	.25
(53)	Dave Stewart	.25
(54)	Mickey Tettleton	.25
(55)	Robby Thompson	.25
(56)	Alan Trammell	.25
(57)	Jose Uribe	.25
(58)	Andy Van Slyke	.25
(59)	Honus Wagner	1.50
(60)	Jerome Walton	.25
(61)	Lou Whitaker	.25
(62)	Matt Williams	.25
(63)	Robin Yount	1.50

1991 Cadaco All-Star Baseball Discs

This set of player discs was sold with and intended for use in a board game. Fronts of the 3-1/2" diameter discs have a yellow border sectioned with numbers from 1 to 14, indicating that player's likelihood of performing a specific baseball result based on career

stats. At center is a color player photo from which the uniform details have been airbrushed. Logos of the game's producer and the Major League Players Association flank the portrait. The player's name, team and position are below the photo. Backs have up to five years of recent stats and lifetime totals, along with a few biographical data. The unnumbered discs are checklisted alphabetically.

		NM/M
Complete Set (62):		20.00
Common Player:		.25
(1)	Kevin Appier	.25
(2)	Carlos Baerga	.25
(3)	Harold Baines	.25
(4)	Derek Bell	.25
(5)	George Bell	.25
(6)	Jay Bell	.25
(7)	Mike Boddicker	.25
(8)	Wade Boggs	2.00
(9)	Hubie Brooks	.25
(10)	Jose Canseco	.75
(11)	Roger Clemens	2.50
(12)	Roberto Clemente	4.00
(13)	Ty Cobb	2.50
(14)	Alex Cole	.25
(15)	Jeff Conine	.25
(16)	Andre Dawson	.65
(17)	Shawon Dunston	.25
(18)	Lenny Dykstra	.25
(19)	Carlton Fisk	1.50
(20)	Darrin Fletcher	.25
(21)	Gary Gaetti	.25
(22)	Greg Gagne	.25
(23)	Mike Gallego	.25
(24)	Lou Gehrig	4.00
(25)	Kirk Gibson	.25
(26)	Tom Glavine	.50
(27)	Mark Grace	.25
(28)	Ken Griffey Jr.	3.00
(29)	Tony Gwynn	2.00
(30)	Charlie Hayes	.25
(31)	Rickey Henderson	1.50
(32)	Orel Hershiser	.25
(33)	Bo Jackson	.50
(34)	Howard Johnson	.25
(35)	Randy Johnson	1.50
(36)	Ricky Jordan	.25
(37)	David Justice	.25
(38)	Ray Lankford	.25
(39)	Ramon Martinez	.25
(40)	Don Mattingly	2.50
(41)	Mark McGwire	3.50
(42)	Brian McRae	.25
(43)	Joe Oliver	.25
(44)	Tony Pena	.25
(45)	Kirby Puckett	2.00
(46)	Cal Ripken Jr.	4.50
(47)	Babe Ruth	4.00
(48)	Nolan Ryan	4.50
(49)	Bret Saberhagen	.25
(50)	Chris Sabo	.25
(51)	Ryne Sandberg	2.00
(52)	Benito Santiago	.25
(53)	Steve Sax	.25
(54)	Gary Sheffield	.75
(55)	Ozzie Smith	2.00
(56)	Dave Stewart	.25
(57)	Darryl Strawberry	.25
(58)	Frank Thomas	1.50
(59)	Robin Ventura	.25
(60)	Hector Villanueva	.25
(61)	Honus Wagner	1.50
(62)	Lou Whitaker	.25

1993 Cadaco All-Star Baseball Discs

This set of player discs was sold with and intended for use in a board game. Fronts of the 3-1/2" diameter discs have a yellow border sectioned with numbers from 1 to 14, indicating that player's likelihood of performing a specific baseball result based on career stats. At center is a color player photo from which the uniform details have been airbrushed. Logos of the game's producer and the Major League Baseball Players Association flank the portrait. The player's name, team and position are below the photo. Backs have up to five years of recent stats and lifetime

		NM/M
Complete Set (62):		20.00
Common Player:		.25
(1)	Roberto Alomar	.35
(2)	Harold Baines	.25
(3)	Craig Biggio	.25
(4)	Wade Boggs	2.00
(5)	Barry Bonds	4.50
(6)	Bobby Bonilla	.25
(7)	Jose Canseco	.75
(8)	Will Clark	.25
(9)	Roger Clemens	2.50
(10)	Roberto Clemente	4.00
(11)	Ty Cobb	2.50
(12)	Vince Coleman	.25
(13)	Eric Davis	.25
(14)	Glenn Davis	.25
(15)	Andre Dawson	.65
(16)	Delino DeShields	.25
(17)	Shawon Dunston	.25
(18)	Tony Fernandez	.25
(19)	Cecil Fielder	.25
(20)	Carlton Fisk	1.50
(21)	Julio Franco	.25
(22)	Gary Gaetti	.25
(23)	Lou Gehrig	3.00
(24)	Kirk Gibson	.25
(25)_	Mark Grace	.25
(26)	Ken Griffey Jr.	3.00
(27)	Kelly Gruber	.25
(28)	Tony Gwynn	2.00
(29)	Rickey Henderson	1.50
(30)	Orel Hershiser	.25
(31)	David Justice	.25
(32)	Bo Jackson	.50
(33)	Howard Johnson	.25
(34)	Barry Larkin	.25
(35)	Ramon Martinez	.25
(36)	Don Mattingly	2.50
(37)	Fred McGriff	.25
(38)	Mark McGwire	3.50
(39)	Kevin Mitchell	.25
(40)	Kevin Mitchell	.25
(41)	Tony Pena	.25
(42)	Kirby Puckett	2.00
(43)	Cal Ripken Jr.	4.50
(44)	Babe Ruth	4.00
(45)	Nolan Ryan	4.50
(46)	Bret Saberhagen	.25
(47)	Chris Sabo	.25
(48)	Ryne Sandberg	2.00
(49)	Benito Santiago	.25
(50)	Steve Sax	.25
(51)	Gary Sheffield	.75
(52)	Ruben Sierra	.25
(53)	Ozzie Smith	2.00
(54)	Terry Steinbach	.25
(55)	Dave Stewart	.25
(56)	Mickey Tettleton	.25
(57)	Alan Trammell	.25
(58)	Jose Uribe	.25
(59)	Honus Wagner	1.50
(60)	Lou Whitaker	.25
(61)	Matt Williams	.25
(62)	Robin Yount	1.50

			NM/M
	(11)	Larry Herndon	.50
	(12)	Chet Lemon	.50
	(13)	Aurelio Lopez	.50
	(14)	Jack Morris	1.00
	(15)	Lance Parrish	1.00
	(16)	Dan Petry	.50
	(17)	Bill Scherrer	.50
	(18)	Alan Trammell	2.50
	(19)	Lou Whitaker	1.50
	(20)	Milt Wilcox	.50

1986 Cain's Potato Chips Tigers

For the second year in a row, player discs of the Detroit Tigers were found in boxes of Cain's Potato Chips sold in the Detroit area. Twenty discs make up the set which is branded as a "1986 Annual Collectors' Edition." Discs, measuring 2-3/4" in diameter, have fronts which contain a color photo plus the player's name, team and position. The Cain's logo and the Major League Baseball Players Association's logo also appear. The backs, which display black print on white stock, contain player information plus the card number.

		NM/M
Complete Set (20):		7.50
Common Player:		.50
1	Tom Brookens	.50
2	Willie Hernandez	.50
3	Dave Bergman	.50
4	Lou Whitaker	1.25
5	Dave LaPoint	.50
6	Lance Parrish	.75
7	Randy O'Neal	.50
8	Nelson Simmons	.50
9	Larry Herndon	.50
10	Doug Flynn	.50
11	Jack Morris	.75
12	Dan Petry	.50
13	Walt Terrell	.50
14	Chet Lemon	.50
15	Frank Tanana	.50
16	Kirk Gibson	.75
17	Darrell Evans	.75
18	Dave Collins	.50
19	John Grubb	.50
20	Alan Trammell	2.00

1987 Cain's Potato Chips Tigers

Player discs of the Detroit Tigers were inserted in boxes of Cain's Potato Chips for the third consecutive year. The 1987 edition is made up of cards each measuring 2-3/4" in diameter. The discs, which were packaged in a cellophane wrapper, feature a full-color photo surrounded by an orange border. Backs are printed in red on white stock. The set was produced by Mike Schechter and Associates.

		NM/M
Complete Set (20):		12.5
Common Player:		.50
1	Tom Brookens	.50
2	Darnell Coles	.50
3	Mike Heath	.50
4	Dave Bergman	.50
5	Dwight Lowry	.50
6	Darrell Evans	1.0
7	Alan Trammell	2.5
8	Lou Whitaker	1.7
9	Kirk Gibson	.8
10	Chet Lemon	.5
11	Larry Herndon	.8
12	John Grubb	.5
13	Willie Hernandez	.8

1985 Cain's Potato Chips Tigers

This set commemorating the 1984 World Champion Tigers was issued in bags of Cain's Potato Chips in the Michigan area in 1985. The yellow-bordered, unnumbered cards measure 2-3/4" in diameter and feature full-color oval photos inside a diamond. The word "Cain's" appears in the upper left corner, while the player's name appears in the lower left with his position directly below the photo. The words "1984 World Champions" are printed in the upper right corner. Backs include 1984 statistics.

		NM/M
Complete Set (20):		10.00
Common Player:		.50
(1)	Doug Bair	.50
(2)	Juan Berenguer	.50
(3)	Dave Bergman	.50
(4)	Tom Brookens	.50
(5)	Marty Castillo	.50
(6)	Darrell Evans	1.00
(7)	Barbaro Garbey	.50
(8)	Kirk Gibson	1.00
(9)	John Grubb	.50
(10)	Willie Hernandez	.50

14	Jack Morris	1.00
15	Dan Petry	.60
16	Walt Terrell	.60
17	Mark Thurmond	.60
18	Pat Sheridan	.60
19	Eric King	.60
20	Frank Tanana	.60

1984 California Angels Fire Safety

This 32-card set was distributed at a June home game to fans 14 and under. Cards measure 2-1/2" x 3-1/2". Fronts have full-color action photos along a portrait of Smokey the Bear and U.S. and California Forest Service logos commemorating Smokey's 40th birthday. Black-and-white backs have minimal player data and stats and a tip for preventing forest fires.

		NM/M
Complete Set (32):		4.00
Common Player:		.25
(1)	Don Aase	.25
(2)	Juan Beniquez	.25
(3)	Bob Boone	.45
(4)	Rick Burleson	.25
(5)	Rod Carew	1.50
(6)	John Curtis	.25
(7)	Doug DeCinces	.25
(8)	Brian Downing	.25
(9)	Ken Forsch	.25
(10)	Bobby Grich	.25
(11)	Reggie Jackson	2.00
(12)	Ron Jackson	.25
(13)	Tommy John	.50
(14)	Curt Kaufman	.25
(15)	Bruce Kison	.25
(16)	Frank LaCorte	.25
(17)	Fred Lynn	.45
(18)	John McNamara	.25
(19)	Jerry Narron	.25
(20)	Gary Pettis	.25
(21)	Robert Picciolo	.25
(22)	Ron Romanick	.25
(23)	Luis Sanchez	.25
(24)	Dick Schofield	.25
(25)	Daryl Sconiers	.25
(26)	Jim Slaton	.25
(27)	Ellis Valentine	.25
(28)	Robert Wilfong	.25
(29)	Mike Witt	.25
(30)	Geoff Zahn	.25
---	Forestry Dept. Logo Card	.10
---	Smokey Logo Card	.10

1985 California Angels Fire Safety

This full-color set of large-format cards was given to fans attending the July 14 game at Anaheim Stadium. Fronts feature player photos with their last name at the top above the picture. In the bottom border are a portrait of Smokey the Bear, and logos of the Angels, California Forestry Service and U.S. Forestry Service. Cards measure 4-1/4" x 6". On back,

printed in black-and-white, are personal data, a few stats and a wildfire safety tip.

		NM/M
Complete Set (24):		5.00
Common Player:		.25
1	Mike Witt	.25
2	Reggie Jackson	1.50
3	Bob Boone	.45
4	Mike Brown	.25
5	Rod Carew	1.00
6	Doug DeCinces	.25
7	Brian Downing	.25
8	Ken Forsch	.25
9	Gary Pettis	.25
10	Jerry Narron	.25
11	Ron Romanick	.25
12	Bobby Grich	.25
13	Dick Schofield	.25
14	Juan Beniquez	.25
15	Geoff Zahn	.25
16	Luis Sanchez	.25
17	Jim Slaton	.25
18	Doug Corbett	.25
19	Ruppert Jones	.25
20	Rob Wilfong	.25
21	Donnie Moore	.25
22	Pat Clements	.25
23	Tommy John	.50
24	Gene Mauch	.25

1986 California Angels Fire Safety

The Angels, in conjuction with the U.S. and California Forestry Services, issued this set promoting Wildfire Prevention. Cards measure 4-1/4" x 6" and offer a full-color front with the player's picture in an oval frame. Backs have player stats with a drawing and fire safety tip. The sets were given out August 9 at the game in Anaheim Stadium.

		NM/M
Complete Set (24):		5.00
Common Player:		.25
1	Mike Witt	.25
2	Reggie Jackson	1.50
3	Bob Boone	.40
4	Don Sutton	1.00
5	Kirk McCaskill	.25
6	Doug DeCinces	.25
7	Brian Downing	.25
8	Doug Corbett	.25
9	Gary Pettis	.25
10	Jerry Narron	.25
11	Ron Romanick	.25
12	Bobby Grich	.25
13	Dick Schofield	.25
14	George Hendrick	.25
15	Rick Burleson	.25
16	John Candelaria	.25
17	Jim Slaton	.25
18	Darrell Miller	.25
19	Ruppert Jones	.25
20	Rob Wilfong	.25
21	Donnie Moore	.25
22	Wally Joyner	1.00
23	Terry Forster	.25
24	Gene Mauch	.25

1987 California Angels Fire Safety

The U.S. Forestry Service distributed this set to 25,000 fans in attendance at Anaheim Stadium on August 1. The full-color cards measure 4" x 6". Fronts carry a design of baseballs and bats framing the player photo. Only the player's last name is given. At bottom is a Smokey Bear portrait and team logo. Backs contain the player's name, position and personal data along with a Smokey Bear cartoon fire prevention tip and sponsors' logos.

		NM/M
Complete Set (24):		5.00
Common Player:		.25
1	Mike Witt	.25
2	Reggie Jackson	1.50
3	Bob Boone	.45
4	Mike Brown	.25
5	Rod Carew	1.00
6	Doug DeCinces	.25
7	Brian Downing	.25
8	Ken Forsch	.25
9	Gary Pettis	.25
10	Jerry Narron	.25
11	Ron Romanick	.25
12	Bobby Grich	.25
13	Dick Schofield	.25
14	Juan Beniquez	.25
15	Geoff Zahn	.25
16	Luis Sanchez	.25
17	Jim Slaton	.25
18	Doug Corbett	.25
19	Ruppert Jones	.25
20	Rob Wilfong	.25
21	Donnie Moore	.25
22	Pat Clements	.25
23	Tommy John	.50
24	Gene Mauch	.25

1988 California Angels Fire Safety

These borderless full-color cards (2-1/2" x 3-1/2") are highlighted by a thin white outline on front. The player name, team logo and a Smokey Bear picture logo appear in the photo's lower-right corner. Backs are black-and-white and include personal information and a large cartoon fire prevention tip. Part of the U.S. Forest Service fire prevention campaign, the cards were distributed in three separate in-stadium giveaways during August and September games.

		NM/M
Complete Set (25):		4.50
Common Player:		.25
1	Cookie Rojas	.25
2	Johnny Ray	.25
3	Jack Howell	.25
4	Mike Witt	.25
5	Tony Armas	.25
6	Gus Polidor	.25
7	DeWayne Buice	.25
8	Dan Petry	.25
9	Bob Boone	.50
10	Chili Davis	.25
11	Greg Minton	.25
12	Kirk McCaskill	.25
13	Devon White	.25
14	Willie Fraser	.25
15	Chuck Finley	.25
16	Dick Schofield	.25
17	Wally Joyner	.50
18	Brian Downing	.25
19	Stewart Cliburn	.25
20	Donnie Moore	.25
21	Bryan Harvey	.25
22	Mark McLemore	.25
23	Butch Wynegar	.25
24	George Hendrick	.25
---	Team Logo/Checklist	.10

1989 California Angels All-Stars Fire Safety

The U.S. Forest Service, in conjunction with the California Angels, issued this all-time team set. The 2-1/2" x 3-1/2" cards have a silver border with the player photo outlined in red. Beneath the photo a banner across homeplate reads "Angels All-Stars," along with the player's name and position, which are flanked by Smokey Bear on the left and the Angels 1989 All-Star Game logo on the right. Card backs highlight the player's career with the Angels and include an illustrated fire prevention tip.

		NM/M
Complete Set (20):		6.00
Common Player:		.25
1	Bill Rigney	.25
2	Dean Chance	.40
3	Jim Fregosi	.25
4	Bobby Knoop	.25
5	Don Mincher	.25
6	Clyde Wright	.25
7	Nolan Ryan	4.00
8	Frank Robinson	1.00
9	Frank Tanana	1.00
10	Rod Carew	1.00
11	Bobby Grich	.25
12	Brian Downing	.25
13	Don Baylor	.25
14	Fred Lynn	.35
15	Reggie Jackson	1.50
16	Doug DeCinces	.25
17	Bob Boone	.35
18	Wally Joyner	.50
19	Mike Witt	.25
20	Johnny Ray	.25

1990 California Angels Fire Safety

This set was released by the U.S. Forestry Service in conjunction with the California Angels. The sets were distributed at the May 27 home game. The 2-1/2" x 3-1/2" cards feature full-color action photos surrounded by metallic silver borders. Team and Smokey Bear logos appear on front. Backs contain player data and a cartoon Smokey Bear message urging the prevention of forest fires.

		NM/M
Complete Set (20):		5.00
Common Player:		.25
1	Jim Abbott	.25
2	Bert Blyleven	.50
3	Chili Davis	.25
4	Brian Downing	.25
5	Chuck Finley	.25
6	Willie Fraser	.25
7	Bryan Harvey	.25
8	Jack Howell	.25
9	Wally Joyner	.50
10	Mark Langston	.25
11	Kirk McCaskill	.25
12	Mark McLemore	.25
13	Lance Parrish	.25
14	Johnny Ray	.25
15	Dick Schofield	.25
16	Mike Witt	.25
17	Claudell Washington	.25
18	Devon White	.25
19	Scott Bailes	.25
20	Bob McClure	.25

1991 California Angels Fire Safety

This set was sponsored by the California Department of Forestry. Front of the 2-1/2" x 3-1/2" cards features gray borders surrounding full-color action photos. The flip sides feature a fire safety cartoon and biographical information, along with sponsor logos, printed in blue and red on white.

		NM/M
Complete Set (20):		6.00
Common Player:		.25
1	Luis Polonia	.25
2	Junior Felix	.25
3	Dave Winfield	2.00
4	Dave Parker	.25
5	Lance Parrish	.25
6	Wally Joyner	.35
7	Jim Abbott	.45
8	Mark Langston	.25
9	Dick Schofield	.25
10	Kirk McCaskill	.25
11	Jack Howell	.25
12	Donnie Hill	.25
13	Gary Gaetti	.25
14	Chuck Finley	.25
15	Luis Sojo	.25
16	Mark Eichhorn	.25
17	Bryan Harvey	.25
18	Jeff Robinson	.25
19	Scott Lewis	.25
20	John Orton	.25

1992 California Angels Police

This safety set was sponsored by Carl's Jr. fast food restaurants and distributed by the Orange County Sheriff's Dept. Single cards were distributed to children over the course of the season and complete sets were handed out at the Angels' September 19 game. Fronts have color player action photos on a star-studded red, white and blue border. Backs have a small black-and-white portrait photo, stats, career highlights, an anti-drug message and sponsors' logos.

		NM/M
Complete Set (18):		8.00
Common Player:		.50
1	Jim Abbott	.60
2	Gene Autry	1.00
3	Bert Blyleven	.75
4	Hubie Brooks	.50
5	Chad Curtis	.50
6	Alvin Davis	.50
7	Gary DiSarcina	.50
8	Junior Felix	.50
9	Chuck Finley	.50
10	Gary Gaetti	.50
11	Rene Gonzalez	.50
12	Von Hayes	.50
13	Carl Karcher	.50
14	Mark Langston	.50
15	Luis Polonia	.50
16	Bobby Rose	.50
17	Lee Stevens	.50
18	Happy Star (Mascot)	.50

1993 California Angels Police

Sponsored by the Carl's Jr. hamburger restaurant chain and distributed through the California Chiefs & Sheriffs Assn., it was reported that 20,000-25,000 sets were produced. The 2-1/2" x 3-1/2" cards have a player action photo on front. Backs are printed in blue

and black and include a portrait photo, career highlights, stats and an anti-drug message.

J.T. Snow
First Base

		NM/M
Complete Set (21):		16.00
Common Player:		.50
1	Gene Autry	1.00
2	Carl Karcher	.50
3	Buck Rodgers	.50
4	Rod Carew	3.50
5	Kelly Gruber	.50
6	Chili Davis	.50
7	Chad Curtis	.50
8	Mark Langston	.50
9	Scott Sanderson	.50
10	J.T. Snow	2.00
11	Rene Gonzalez	.50
12	Jimmie Reese	.50
13	Damion Easley	.50
14	Julio Valera	.50
15	Luis Polonia	.50
16	John Orton	.50
17	Gary DiSarcina	.50
18	Greg Myers	.50
19	Chuck Finley	.50
20	Tim Salmon	2.50
21	Happy Star (Mascot)	.50

1995 California Angels Police

The California Highway Patrol sponsored this safety set to coincide with the Angels 35th anniversary. Cards have action photos bordered in gray and dark blue. The team's anniversary logo and CHP logo appear in opposite corners. Black-and-white backs have a few bit of player data and a safety tip.

		NM/M
Complete Set (16):		20.00
Common Player:		1.00
1	Tim Salmon	2.00
2	Chuck Finley	1.00
3	Mark Langston	1.00
4	Gary Disarcina	1.00
5	Damion Easley	1.00
6	Spike Owen	1.00
7	Troy Percival	1.00
8	Chili Davis	1.00
9	Jim Edmonds	2.00
10	Rex Hudler	1.00
11	Greg Myers	1.00
12	Brian Anderson	1.00
13	J.T. Snow	1.50
14	Tony Phillips	1.00
15	Lee Smith	1.50
16	Marcel Lachemann, Don Watkins (Chief, CHP)	1.00

2004 California Angels Card Deck

This stadium giveaway was sponsored by Coast Plaza Doctors Hospital and Redio Disney. Cards are 2-1/4" x 3-7/16" with rounded corners. Red backs have team and sponsors' logos. Each player appears four times in the deck, with an identical portrait photo on the same value card in each suit. Two Rally Monkey jokers complete the boxed set.

		NM/M
Complete Set (54):		10.00
Common Player:		.25
2	Adam Kennedy	.25
3	Garret Anderson	.25
4	Bartolo Colon	.25
5	David Eckstein	.25
6	Jose Guillen	.35
7	Darin Erstad	.25
8	Kelvim Escobar	.25
9	Tim Salmon	.25
10	Bengie Molina	.25
J	Troy Percival	.25
Q	Troy Glaus	.40
K	Vladimir Guerrero	.50
A	Mike Scioscia	.25
Joker	Rally Monkey	.25

1992-93 Canadian Card News Repli-Cards

Krause Publications short-lived attempt to service the Canadian card collecting market with a newsstand magazine included the use of repli-card panels of five in each of the magazine's five issues. The cards feature a mix of hockey players, CFL stars and Blue Jays and Expos. Only the baseball players are listed here.

		NM/M
Complete (Baseball) Set (12):		6.50
Common Player:		.50
2	Kelly Gruber	.50
3	Roberto Alomar	.75
5	Larry Walker, Marquis Grissom, Delino DeShields	.50
8	Dave Winfield	2.00
14	Ken Hill	.50
16	Jimmy Key	.50
17	Pat Borders	.50
21	Joe Carter	.50
22	Larry Walker	.75
23	Delino DeShields	.50
24	Derek Bell	.50
25	Wil Cordero	.50

1996 Canadian Club Classic Stars of the Game

A promotion for Canadian Club's Classic 12 whisky offered a series of autographed Hall of Famer

cards. One card was included in a special folder attached to bottles. An offer sheet inside gave details for ordering other cards for $5 each plus proof of purchase. Also in the bottle-hanger was a certificate of authenticity for the enclosed signed card. In standard 2-1/2" x 3-1/2" format, cards feature vintage color player photos on which uniform logos have been deleted. Cards have a black border, are highlighted in gold foil and have an authentic autograph on front. Backs have career stats and summary. Cards #1-4 were labeled as Series I, cards #5-6 are Series II.

		NM/M
Complete Set (6):		60.00
Common Player:		6.00
1	Brooks Robinson	12.00
2	Billy Williams	6.00
3	Willie Stargell	13.50
4	Ernie Banks	17.50
5	Frank Robinson	15.00
6	Rollie Fingers	6.00

2000 CaP Cure Home Run Challenge

As part of its fund-raising "Home Run Challenge" promotion June 15-20, 2000, the Association for the Cure of Cancer of the Prostate issued a nine-card perforated sheet of 2-1/2" x 3-1/2" cards. Fronts have an action photo with black borders. At top-left is the CaP Cure logo, at lower-right is the MLBPA logo. Backs have messages promoting the cause, along with contact information for the organization.

		NM/M
Complete Sheet:		20.00
Complete Set (9):		20.00
Common Player:		2.00
(1)	Jason Giambi	2.00
(2)	Ken Griffey Jr.	3.00
(3)	Tony Gwynn	2.50
(4)	Derek Jeter	5.00
(5)	Mark McGwire	4.00
(6)	Alex Rodriguez	4.00
(7)	Sammy Sosa	2.50
(8)	Robin Ventura	1.00
(9)	Header Card	.25

2001 CaP Cure Home Run Challenge

As part of its fund-raising "Home Run Challenge" promotion, the Association for the Cure of Cancer of the Prostate issued a nine-card perforated sheet of 2-1/2" x 3-1/2" cards. Each card has two fronts, with each side having an action photo which is borderless at top, bottom and right. The CaP Cure logo is at lower-right, the player name and uniform number in a colored strip at right and the MLB Players Choice logo at top-left. The association phone number is at left.

The center card on the sheet offers a contest to win autographed baseballs, utilizing the individual serial number on the back.

		NM/M
Complete Sheet:		15.00
Common Card:		1.50
(1)	Jeff Bagwell, Carlos Delgado	1.50
(2)	Jay Bell, Alex Rodriguez	3.00
(3)	Nomar Garciaparra, Sammy Sosa	2.00
(4)	Jason Giambi, Mark McGwire	2.50
(5)	Ken Griffey Jr., Robin Ventura	2.25
(6)	Tony Gwynn, Ivan Rodriguez	2.00
(7)	Derek Jeter, Mike Sweeney	3.00
(8)	Chipper Jones, Jim Thome	2.00
(9)	Contest Card	.25

2002 CaP Cure Home Run Challenge

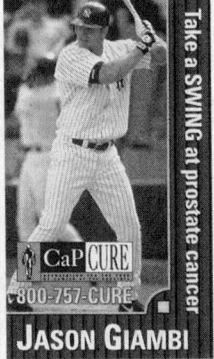

In its third season, the Association for the Cure of Cancer of the Prostate reduced the number of cards to four and the size of the cards to 1-5/8" x 2-3/4". Cards have action photos on front, which are repeated in ghost-image form on back. A Q-and-A about prostate cancer is presented on back.

		NM/M
Complete Set (4):		8.00
Common Player:		1.50
(1)	Derek Jeter	3.50
(2)	Jason Giambi	1.50
(3)	Ken Griffey Jr.	2.50
(4)	Sammy Sosa	2.00

1994 Capital Cards 1969 Mets Postcards

Capital Cards, produced a 32-card postcard set of members of the 1969 World Champion New York Mets from Ron Lewis paintings, limited to 25,000 sets. Capital Cards also produced 5,000 uncut sheets that were individually numbered and carried a suggested retail price of $99.95. The boxed postcard set retailed for $39.95. The cards could also be purchased with autographs.

		NM/M
Complete Set (32):		15.00
Common Player:		.35
Uncut Sheet:		15.00
1	Logo Card	.35
2	Gil Hodges	2.00
3	Rube Walker	.35
4	Yogi Berra	2.00
5	Joe Pignatano	.35
6	Ed Yost	.35
7	Tommie Agee	.35
8	Ken Boswell	.35
9	Don Cardwell	.35
10	Ed Charles	.35
11	Donn Clendenon	.35
12	Jack DiLauro	.35
13	Duffy Dyer	.35
14	Wayne Garrett	.35
15	Rod Gaspar	.35
16	Gary Gentry	.35
17	Jerry Grote	.35
18	Bud Harrelson	.50
19	Cleon Jones	.35
20	Cal Koonce	.35
21	Jerry Koosman	.50
22	Ed Kranepool	.35
23	J.C. Martin	.35
24	Jim McAndrew	.35
25	Tug McGraw	.50
26	Bob Pfeil	.35
27	Nolan Ryan	6.00
28	Tom Seaver	3.00
29	Art Shamsky	.35
30	Ron Swoboda	.35
31	Ron Taylor	.35
32	Al Weis	.35

1989 Cap'n Crunch

This 22-card set was produced by Topps for Cap'n Crunch cereal boxes. Two cards and a stick of gum were included in each cereal box while the offer was active. The fronts of these 2-1/2" x 3-1/2" cards feature red, white and blue borders. The card backs are horizontal and feature lifetime statistics. The set was not offered in any complete set deal.

		NM/M
Complete Set (22):		5.00
Common Player:		.10
1	Jose Canseco	.40
2	Kirk Gibson	.10
3	Orel Hershiser	.10
4	Frank Viola	.10
5	Tony Gwynn	.65
6	Cal Ripken	1.50
7	Darryl Strawberry	.10
8	Don Mattingly	.75
9	George Brett	.75
10	Andre Dawson	.25
11	Dale Murphy	.25
12	Alan Trammell	.10
13	Eric Davis	.10
14	Jack Clark	.10
15	Eddie Murray	.50
16	Mike Schmidt	.75
17	Dwight Gooden	.10
18	Roger Clemens	.75
19	Will Clark	.10
20	Kirby Puckett	.65
21	Robin Yount	.50
22	Mark McGwire	1.00

1995 Cardtoons

Just about everything related to baseball comes in for the jab in this set of parody cards. Players, teams, attitudes, owners, mascots, Hall of Famers, announcers and the business of baseball are all panned. Besides a base set of 95 cards, there are several insert issues and send-away prizes. Cards are stan-

dard 2-1/2" x 3-1/2" with easily identifiable caricatures on front and sophomoric humor on the back. The cards make a point of stating they are parodies and not licensed either by the players or Major League Baseball. While they carry a 1993 copyright date, the cards were not issued until 1995.

		NM/M
Complete Set (95):		10.00
Common Card:		.25
1	Hey Abbott	.25
2	Robin Adventura	.25
3	Roberto Alamode	.30
4	Don Battingly	1.25
5	Cow Belle	.25
6	Jay Bellhop	.25
7	Fowl Boggs	1.00
8	Treasury Bonds	2.50
9	True Brett	1.25
10	Wild Pitch Mitch	.25
11	Balou's Brothers (Felipe Balou, Moises Balou)	.25
12	Charlie Bustle	2.00
13	Brett Butter	.25
14	Rambo Canseco	.40
15	Roberto Cementie	2.50
16	Roger Clemency	1.25
17	Will Clock	.25
18	David Clone	.25
19	Tom Clowning	.25
20	Mr. Club	1.00
21	Joe Crater	.25
22	Doolin' Daulton	.25
23	Chili Dog Davis	.25
24	Doug Drawback	.25
25	Dennis Excellency	.65
26	Silly Fanatic	.25
27	Wand Gonzalez	.40
28	Amazing Grace	.25
29	Tom Grapevine	.25
30	Marquis Gruesome	.25
31	Homerin' Hank	2.00
32	Kevin Happier	.25
33	Pete Harness	.25
34	Charlie Haze	.25
35	Egotisticky Henderson	.75
36	Sayanora Infielder	.25
37	Snoozin' Ted & Tarzan Jane	.25
38	Cloud Johnson	.75
39	Sandy K-Fax	2.00
40	The Say What Kid	2.00
41	Tommy Lasagna	.25
42	Greg Maddogs	1.00
43	Stamp the Man	1.00
44	Mark McBash	2.00
45	Fred McGruff	.25
46	Mount Mick	3.00
47	Pat Moustache	.25
48	Ozzie Myth	1.00
49	Bob Nukesbury	.25
50	Reggie October	1.00
51	Doctor OK	.25
52	Rafael Palmist	.65
53	Lose Piniella	.25
54	Vince Poleman	.25
55	Charlie Puff	.25
56	Rob Quibble	.25
57	Darryl Razzberry	.25
58	Cal Ripkenwinkle	2.50
59	Budge Rodriguez	.65
60	Ryne Sandbox	1.00
61	Steve Saxophone	.25
62	Harry Scary	.25
63	Scary Sheffield	.45
64	Ruben Siesta	.25
65	Dennis Smartinez	.25
66	Lee Smite	.25
67	Ken Spiffey Jr.	1.50
68	Nails Spikestra	.25
69	The Splendid Spinner	2.00
70	Toad Stottlemyre	.25
71	Raging Tartabull	.25
72	Robbery Thompson	.25
73	Alan Trampoline	.25
74	Monster Truk	.25
75	Shawon Tungsten	.25
76	Tony Twynn	1.00
77	Andy Van Tyke	.25
78	Derrick Ventriloquist	.25
79	Frank Violin	.25
80	Rap Winfielder	.75
81	Robinhood Yount	.75
82	Swift Justice	.25
83	Brat Saberhagen	.25
84	Mike Pizazz	1.50
85	Andres Colorado	.25
86	Money Bagswell	.25
87	Video Nomo	.40
88	Out of the Park	.25
89	Tim Wallet	.25
90	Checklist	.10
91	Greenback Jack	.25
92	Mighty Matt Power Hitter	.25
93	Frankenthomas	.75
94	Neon Peon Slanders	.35
95	Just Air Jordan	2.50
---	Replacement Card No. 1 (Redeemable for "Cardtoons Annual Awards" set with payment of $26.95.)	.10
---	Replacement Card No. 2 (Redeemable for Cardtoons binder and plastic sheets with payment of $18.95.)	.13
---	Replacement card No. 3 (Redeemable for Cardtoons phone card set of four with payment of $39.95.)	.13

1995 Cardtoons Awards Replacement Set

This set was available via a mail-in offer for $26.95.

		NM/M
Complete Set (8):		6.25
Common Card:		1.00
R1	No Ball Peace Prize	1.00
R2	Forrest Grump	1.00
R3	Most Virtous Player	1.00
R4	Golden Glove Award	1.00
R5	Comdown Player of the Year	1.00
R6	Corkville Slugger	1.00
R7	Can't Get No Relief	1.00
R8	1994 World Series Champ	1.00

1995 Cardtoons Big Bang Bucks

This insert set lampoons baseball's top 20 salaried players. Fronts resemble U.S. currency overprinted with gold foil in denominations of five, six and seven million. A player caricature portrait is in color at center of the 3-1/2" x 2-1/2" card. Backs give the player's salary history and rationale for his being overpaid. A statement on back says the cards are intended to be a parody and that they are not licensed by MLB or the Players Union. The cards are numbered with the "BB" prefix.

		NM/M
Complete Set (20):		20.00
Common Card:		1.00
1	Treasury Bonds	4.00
2	Sayanora Infielder	1.00
3	Cal Ripkenwinkle	4.00
4	Bobby Bonus	1.00
5	Joe Crater	1.00
6	Kirby Plunkit	1.00
7	David Clone	1.00
8	Ken Spiffey Jr.	3.00
9	Ruben Siesta	1.00
10	Greg Maddogs	2.00
11	Mark McBash	3.50
12	Rafael Palmist	1.50
13	Roberto Alamode	1.00
14	Greenback Jack	1.00
15	Raging Tartabull	1.00
16	Jimmy Kiwi	1.00
17	Roger Clemency	2.25
18	Rambo Canseco	1.25
19	Tom Grapevine	1.00
20	John Smileyface	1.00

1995 Cardtoons Field of Greed Puzzle Set

These nine-cards are inserts which form a "Field of Greed" picture when the individual cards are aligned. Fronts have 1/9th of the cartoon puzzle, backs have a history of baseball's recent labor problems. Cards have an "FOG" prefix to their number.

		NM/M
Complete Set (9):		1.50
Common Card:		.25

		NM/M
1	1972 Strike	.25
2	1973 Lockout	.25
3	1976 Lockout	.25
4	1980 Strike	.25
5	1981 Strike	.25
6	1985 Strike	.25
7	1990 Lockout	.25
8	1994 Strike	.25
9	Future Problems	.25

1995 Cardtoons Grand Slam Foils

This insert set utilizes foil printing technology to give a high-tech look to the caricatures of major leaguers. Fronts have cartoon parodies of the players, backs attempt to be humorous. A note on back says the cards are not licensed by either the players or Major League Baseball. Cards are numbered with a "F" prefix.

	NM/M
Complete Set (10):	12.00
Common Player:	1.00
Bo Action	1.50
Andre Awesome	1.25
Bobby Bonus	1.00
Steve Bravery	1.00
Carlton Fist	2.00
E.T. McGee	1.00
Kirby Plunkitt	4.00
Jose Rheostat	1.00
Sir Noble Ryan	6.00
Day-Glo Sabo	1.00

1995 Cardtoons Politics in Baseball

This insert set takes a poke at the perceived problems of baseball during the 1994-95 strike. Fronts have cartoons, backs have pointed commentary. Cards are numbered with the "S" prefix.

	NM/M
Complete Set (11):	3.00
Common Card:	.15
Pledge of Allegiance	.15
The Wave	.15
Slick Willie	1.50
Umpires Convention	.15
The Slide	.15
SH-H-H-H-H-H	.15

7	Throwing Out the First Contract	.15
8	Babe Rush	1.00
9	Hot Prospect	.15
10	Let's Play Ball	.15
11	Role Model	.15

1992 Carl's Jr. Padres

For the fifth consecutive year the San Diego Padres issued a card set in conjunction with the Jr. Padres program. Carl's Jr., a fast food chain, began sponsoring the set in 1991. The set contains 25 cards and was available in either nine-card perforated sheets or precut. At 2-9/16" x 3-9/16" the cards are slightly larger than current standard. Player photos feature an All-Star Game logo in the lower-right corner. On the white border, the player's name and position are printed in dark blue beneath the photo. The team name is in light brown above the photo. On back, the player's stats, career highlights and biographical data are printed in dark blue. The unnumbered cards are checklisted here in alphabetical order.

		NM/M
Complete Set (25):		6.00
Common Player:		.25
(1)	Larry Anderson	.25
(2)	Oscar Azocar	.25
(3)	Andy Benes	.25
(4)	Dann Bilardello	.25
(5)	Jerald Clark	.25
(6)	Tony Fernandez	.25
(7)	Tony Gwynn	4.00
(8)	Greg Harris	.25
(9)	Bruce Hurst	.25
(10)	Darrin Jackson	.25
(11)	Craig Lefferts	.25
(12)	Mike Maddux	.25
(13)	Fred McGriff	.25
(14)	Jose Melendez	.25
(15)	Randy Myers	.25
(16)	Greg Riddoch	.25
(17)	Rich Rodriguez	.25
(18)	Benito Santiago	.25
(19)	Gary Sheffield	.50
(20)	Craig Shipley	.25
(21)	Kurt Stillwell	.25
(22)	Tim Teufel	.25
(23)	Kevin Ward	.25
(24)	Ed Whitson	.25
(25)	All-Star Logo	.25

2003 Carl's Jr. San Diego Padres

Marking the team's 35th anniversary, the fast-food chain sponsored a card giveaway at Qualcomm on September 6. A baker's dozen past and current Padres stars are featured in the set, in several designs in 2-1/2" x 3-1/2" format on thin cardboard. Fronts have game-action color photos. On a two-toned blue background on back stats for the player's tenure with the Pads, printed in white, along with team and

sponsor logos are presented. The unnumbered cards are listed here in alphabetical order.

		NM/M
Complete Set (13):		8.00
Common Player:		.25
(1)	Roberto Alomar	.40
(2)	Bruce Bochy	.25
(3)	Kevin Brown	.25
(4)	Ken Caminiti	.25
(5)	Steve Finley	.25
(6)	Steve Garvey	.50
(7)	Tony Gwynn	3.00
(8)	Trevor Hoffman	.25
(9)	Randy Jones	.25
(10)	Gaylord Perry	.50
(11)	Benito Santiago	.25
(12)	Ozzie Smith	3.00
(13)	Dave Winfield	2.00

1992 Carlson Travel 1982 Brewers

The team's American League Championship season of 1982 was commemorated a decade later with this card set given away at a Brewers promotional date. The cards were sponsored by Carlson Travel and United Airlines, whose logos appear on the front of the cards, along with Channel 6 television, whose logo is on the back. Fronts feature game-action photos of the '82 Brewers, borderless at top and sides. Beneath the photo is a thin gold stripe, then a blue stripe with the player's name and position in white. A red, white and blue 1982 World Series logo appears in the lower-left corner. Backs are printed in blue, and include 1982 stats and a summary of the player's season. Player cards are numbered by uniform number in the upper-left.

		NM/M
Complete Set (31):		12.00
Common Player:		.25
4	Paul Molitor	5.00
5	Ned Yost	.25
7	Don Money	.25
10	Bob McClure	.25
11	Ed Romero	.25
13	Roy Howell	.25
15	Cecil Cooper	.25
16	Marshall Edwards	.25
17	Jim Gantner	.25
19	Robin Yount	5.00
20	Gorman Thomas	.25
21	Don Sutton	1.00
22	Charlie Moore	.25
23	Ted Simmons	.25
24	Ben Oglivie	.25
27	Pete Ladd	.25
29	Mark Brouhard	.25
30	Moose Haas	.25
32	Harvey Kuenn	.25
33	Doc Medich	.25
34	Rollie Fingers	1.00
41	Jim Slaton	.25
46	Jerry Augustine	.25
47	Dwight Bernard	.25
48	Mike Caldwell	.25
50	Pete Vuckovich	.25
---	Coaches (Pat Dobson, Larry Haney, Ron Hansen, Cal McLish, Harry Warner)	.25
---	Team Card	.25
---	Bernie Brewer (Mascot)	.25
---	Post-season Rally	.25
---	$50 Travel Coupon	.25

1985 CBS Radio Game of the Week

To promote its Game of the Week radio broadcasts, CBS issued a six-card set picturing network announcers, including Hall of Famer Johnny Bench. The cards, standard 2-1/2" x 3-1/2" format, were sent to CBS affiliate stations only. Fronts

of the full-color cards picture the announcers in CBS Radio Sports baseball-style uniforms.

		NM/M
Complete Set (6):		55.00
Common Player:		3.00
(1)	Johnny Bench	35.00
(2)	Brent Musburger	15.00
(3)	Lindsey Nelson	7.50
(4)	John Rooney	3.00
(5)	Dick Stockton	4.50
(6)	Bill White	7.50

1986 CBS Radio Game of the Week

For the second consecutive year, CBS Radio Sports issued a five-card set featuring announcers used by the network for the Game of the Week and post-season broadcasts. The cards, packaged in a custom-designed wax wrapper, were sent to CBS radio affiliates as a promotion. The color cards measure 2-1/2" x 3-1/2".

		NM/M
Complete Set (5):		35.00
Common Player:		3.00
(1)	Sparky Anderson	15.00
(2)	Jack Buck	10.00
(3)	Howard David	3.00
(4)	Ernie Harwell	10.00
(5)	Ted Robinson	3.00

1987 Champion Phillies

This four card set is interesting in that the players are not identified on the card fronts or backs. The full-color cards, which measure 2-3/4" x 4-5/16", were produced by the Champion Spark Plug Co. as part of a contest held at participating Big A, Car Quest and Pep Boys auto parts stores. Entrants were advised to return the scratch-off coupon portion of the card for a chance to win a Blackbird Racer. Each card contains a scratch-off portion which may have contained an instant prize.

Each card can be found with either a Big A, Car Quest or Pep Boys logo in the lower left corner on the card front. The contest was also sponsored in part by the Philadelphia Phillies and radio station WIP.

		NM/M
Complete Set (4):		15.00
Common Player:		1.00
(1)	Von Hayes (Glove on knee.)	1.00
(2)	Steve Jeltz (#30 on uniform.)	1.00
(3)	Juan Samuel (Laying on base.)	1.00
(4)	Mike Schmidt (Making throw.)	12.00

1981 Champions of American Sport

From June 1981, through June 1982, Phillip Morris and Miller Beer sponsored a traveling exhibition of sporting art and artifacts from The National Portrait Gallery and the Smithsonian Institution. In conjunction with the exhibitions in Washington, D.C., Chicago, Los Angeles and New York, an 18-card souvenir set was issued featuring many of the top athletes featured in the exhibits. The set was released in the form of an 8" x 11"-page booklet. Inside were two sheets of nine cards each. The perforated cards could be separated into individual cards of 2-1/2" x 3-3/4" dimensions. Fronts featured colored photos or artwork, backs had quotes about the athlete and stats. The unnumbered cards are checklisted here alphabetically.

		NM/M
Complete Set, Booklet:		60.00
Complete Set, Singles (18):		40.00
Common Player:		2.00
(1)	Muhammad Ali	6.00
(2)	Arthur Ashe	2.00
(3)	Peggy Fleming	2.00
(4)	A.J. Foyt	2.00
(5)	Eric Heiden	2.00
(6)	Bobby Hull	4.00
(7)	Sandy Koufax	6.00
(8)	Joe Louis	3.00
(9)	Bob Mathias	2.00
(10)	Willie Mays	6.00
(11)	Joe Namath	5.00
(12)	Jack Nicklaus	5.00
(13)	Knute Rockne	2.00
(14)	Bill Russell	5.00
(15)	Jim Ryun	2.00
(16)	Willie Shoemaker	2.00
(17)	Casey Stengel	2.00
(18)	Johnny Unitas	2.00

1988 Chef Boyardee

This uncut sheet features 12 each American and National League players. Color player portraits are printed beneath a red, white and blue

"1988 1st Annual Collector's Edition" header. The player name, team and position appear beneath his photo. Card backs are printed in blue on red and include biographical information, stats and career highlights. The set was produced by American Home Food Products for distribution via a mail-in offer involving proofs of purchase from the company's Chef Boyardee products. Photos, licensed only by the Players Union, have had uniform logos airbrushed off.

		NM/M
Complete Set, Sheet:		6.00
Complete Set, Singles (24):		6.00
Common Player:		.10
1	Mark McGwire	1.00
2	Eric Davis	.10
3	Jack Morris	.10
4	George Bell	.10
5	Ozzie Smith	.60
6	Tony Gwynn	.60
7	Cal Ripken, Jr.	1.50
8	Todd Worrell	.10
9	Larry Parrish	.10
10	Gary Carter	.50
11	Ryne Sandberg	.60
12	Keith Hernandez	.60
13	Kirby Puckett	.60
14	Mike Schmidt	.75
15	Frank Viola	.10
16	Don Mattingly	.75
17	Dale Murphy	.25
18a	Andre Dawson (1987 team is Expos)	.25
18b	Andre Dawson (1987 team is Cubs)	.25
19	Mike Scott	.10
20	Rickey Henderson	.50
21	Jim Rice	.10
22	Wade Boggs	.60
23	Roger Clemens	.75
24	Fernando Valenzuela	.10

1996 Chevrolet/Geo Pirates Team Sheet

Western Pennsylvania Chevy/Geo dealers sponsored this issue of a team card set given away at the May 12 game vs. the Giants. The individual 2-1/4" x 3-1/4" cards are perforated for removal from the sheet. Individual cards have a color player photo at center with team name and '96 logo at top in a red stripe and the player name and Chev logo at bottom in an orange stripe. Backs are in black-and-white. The cards are checklisted here in alphabetical order.

		NM/M
Complete Set, Uncut Sheet:		9.00
Complete Set, Singles (30):		7.00
Common Player:		.25
(1)	Jay Bell	.25
(2)	Cam Bonifay	.25
(3)	Jacob Brumfield	.25
(4)	Jason Christiansen	.25
(5)	Dave Clark	.25
(6)	Steve Cooke	.25
(7)	Francisco Cordova	.25
(8)	Danny Darwin	.25
(9)	John Ericks	.25
(10)	Carlos Garcia	.25
(11)	Lee Hancock	.25
(12)	Charlie Hayes	.25
(13)	Mark Johnson	.25
(14)	Jason Kendall	.75
(15)	Jim Leyland	.25
(16)	Jeff King	.25
(17)	Mike Kingery	.25
(18)	Nelson Liriano	.25
(19)	Jon Lieber	.25
(20)	Al Martin	.25
(21)	Orlando Merced	.25
(22)	Dan Miceli	.25
(23)	Denny Neagle	.25
(24)	Keith Osik	.25
(25)	Steve Parris	.25

(26)	Dan Plesac	.25
(27)	Zane Smith	.25
(28)	Paul Wagner	.25
(29)	John Wehner	.25
(30)	Pirate Parrot (Mascot)	.25

1992 Chevron Giants Hall of Fame Pins

Willie Mays

This series of card/pin combinations was distributed by Chevron gas stations honoring San Francisco Giants enshrined in baseball's Hall of Fame. Fronts of the 2-1/2" x 5" cards have a color player photo in an oval frame with an orange border. The player name and team logo are in a large white strip at bottom. Black-and-white backs have a small player portrait photo, some personal data, career highlights and pictures of the pins in the set. An enameled pin, about 1-1/8" x 1-1/4", with a representation of the player in action, is attached at the bottom of the card.

		NM/M
Complete Set (3):		15.00
Common Player:		4.00
24	Willie Mays	7.50
36	Gaylord Perry	4.00
44	Willie McCovey	4.00

2004 Chevron Clean Outta' Here

This premium set was regionally marketed with customers receiving a one-card pack with each $8 fuel purchase. Fronts have game-action photos and a Chevron "Clean Outta' Here" logo. Red, white and blue backs have stats, player data and career highlights. Printed on thin cardboard, the cards were produced by Upper Deck.

		NM/M
Complete Set (12):		3.00
Common Player:		.25
1	Andruw Jones	.50
2	Hank Blalock	.35
3	Jeff Bagwell	.50
4	Vladimir Guerrero	.50
5	Shawn Green	.35
6	Mike Lowell	.25
7	Aubrey Huff	.25
8	Richie Sexson	.25
9	Brian Giles	.25
10	Bret Boone	.25
11	A.J. Pierzynski	.25
12	Eric Chavez	.25

1985 Chicago Cubs Playing Cards

A regular 52-card deck plus two jokers comprise this set produced by long-time Cubs broadcaster Jack Brickhouse, whose photo and trademark phrase "Hey Hey!" are featured on the back of each card. Card fronts have a black-and-white photo with player(s) names and a date beneath. Traditional suit and value marking of a playing card deck are included in the corners of the 2-1/2" x 3-1/2" round-cornered cards. The cards are arranged in roughly chronological order.

		NM/M
Complete Set (54):		10.00
Common Player:		.25
AH	Jack Brickhouse	.25
2H	1876 Champions	
	(Team composite photo.)	.25
3H	Cap Anson	.25
4H	Joe Tinker, Johnny Evers,	
	Frank Chance,	
	Harry Steinfeldt	2.00
5H	Ed Reulbach	.25
6H	Mordecai Brown	.25
7H	Jim Vaughn	.25
8H	Joe McCarthy	.25
9H	Jimmy Cooney	.25
10H	Rogers Hornsby	.50
JH	Hack Wilson	.50
QH	"Homers Row" (Hack Wilson,	
	Babe Ruth, Lou Gehrig)	.50
KH	Babe Ruth	
	("Called the Shot")	4.00
AC	Lon Warneke	.25
2C	Augie Galan	.25
3C	1935 Pennant Winning Cubs	
	(Team photo.)	.25
4C	Dizzy Dean	.50
5C	Gabby Hartnett	.25
6C	Billy Herman	.25
7C	Charlie Root	.25
8C	Charlie Grimm	.25
9C	Andy Pafko	.25
10C	Stan Hack	.25
JC	Phil Cavarretta	.25
QC	National League Champs	
	1945 (Team photo.)	.25
KC	Bill Nicholson	.25
KD	Hank Sauer	.25
QD	Ernie Banks	4.00
JD	Sam Jones	.25
10D	Dale Long	.30
9D	Lou Boudreau	.25
8D	Don Cardwell	.25
7D	Ken Hubbs	.50
6D	Billy Williams	.30
5D	1969 Cubs - The Team	
	That Almost Made It	
	(Composite photo.)	.25
4D	Ken Holtzman	.25
3D	Ron Santo	.25
2D	Fergie Jenkins	.40
AD	Burt Hooten (Hooton)	.25
KS	Milt Pappas	.25
QS	Rick Reuschel	.25
JS	Bill Madlock	.25
10S	Dallas Green	.25
9S	Jody Davis	.25
8S	Rick Sutcliffe	.25
7S	Jim Frey	.25
6S	Ryne Sandberg	4.00
5S	Eastern Division Champs	
	1984 (Team photo.)	.25
4S	Bob Dernier	.25
3S	Gary Matthews	.25
2S	Keith Moreland	.25
AS	Leon Durham	.25
Joker	Ron Cey	.25
Joker	Hey! and Holy Cow!	
	(Jack Brickhouse,	
	Harry Caray.)	.25

1988 Chicago Cubs Fire Safety

This set of four oversize (approximately 3-7/8" x 5-1/2") cards was produced on a single perforated sheet for distribution to fans

as part of a U.S. Forest Service fire prevention campaign. Card fronts feature color player photos framed with vertical blue and pink borders and the player's name in light blue at bottom. Team and Smokey logos flank the name while the team name is printed in red above the photo. Backs have a bit of player biography and a large cartoon fire safety message.

		NM/M
Complete Set (4):		7.00
Common Card:		1.00
1	Vance Law	
	(With Smokey.)	2.00
2	Vance Law/Fldg	2.00
3	Vance Law/Btg	2.00
4	Smokey Bear	1.00

1992 Chicago White Sox 1917 Team Issue Reprints

FRED McMULLEN
THIRD BASE

Card dealer Greg Manning, who purchased the unique original set of 1917 White Sox team-issue cards in 1991 issued a collectors' reprint set a year later. The reprints are in 2" x 3" format, slightly larger than the originals. The cards of the banned "Black Sox" have had a black frame added around the picture and have career information and 1919 stats on back. The other cards have blank backs. A second, colorized card of Joe Jackson was added to the reprint set. The unnumbered cards are checklisted here in alphabetical order.

		NM/M
Complete Set (26):		9.00
Common Player:		.25
(1)	Joe Benz	.25
(2)	Eddie Cicotte	1.00
(3)	Eddie Collins	.25
(4)	Shano Collins	.25
(5)	Charles Comiskey	.25
(6)	Dave Danforth	.25
(7)	Red Faber	.25
(8)	Happy Felsch	.50
(9)	Chick Gandil	1.00
(10)	Kid Gleason	.25
(11)	Joe Jackson	
	(Black-and-white.)	3.00
(11)	Joe Jackson (Colorized)	3.00
(12)	Joe Jenkins	.25
(13)	Ted Jourdan	.25
(14)	Nemo Leibold	.25
(15)	Byrd Lynn	.25
(16)	Fred McMullin	.50
(17)	Eddie Murphy	.25
(18)	Swede Risberg	.50
(19)	Pants Rowland	.25
(20)	Reb Russell	.25
(21)	Ray Schalk	.25
(22)	James Scott	.25
(23)	Buck Weaver	1.00
(24)	Lefty Williams	.50
(25)	Mellie Wolfgang	.25

2005 Chicago White Sox Carlton Fisk

This oversize (8-1/2" x 11") card was a Comiskey Park stadium giveaway on August 7 when the Hall of Famer's uniform number was retired by the White Sox. Sponsored by Nike, the back of the card has personal data and career stats.

	NM/M
Carlton Fisk	7.50

1994 Churchs Chicken Hometown Stars

Produced by Pinnacle Brands for distribution in the fried chicken restaurant chain, the cards were distributed in packs of four with the purchase of a nine-piece family meal or were sold separately for 69 cents. Each foil pack contained three regular cards and one card with gold foil instead of regular printing on the player's name and "Hometown Stars." Every fourth pack contains one of 10 "Show Stoppers" Dufex-process chase cards. In standard 2-1/2" x 3-1/2", the cards featured full-bleed front action photos with the Churchs logo at lower-left and the player's name at lower-right. "Hometown Stars" is printed vertically at top-left. Backs have a portrait photo at left, a career summary and 1993 and career stats. Because the cards were licensed by the Major League Baseball Players Association, but not Major League Baseball, both the front and the back photos on each card have had the uniform logos airbrushed away.

		NM/M
Complete Set (28):		7.00
Complete Set (Gold) (28):		15.00
Common Player:		.10
Common Player (Gold):		.25
1	Brian McRae	.10
1a	Brian McRae/Gold	.25
2	Dwight Gooden	.10
2a	Dwight Gooden/Gold	.25
3	Ruben Sierra	.10
3a	Ruben Sierra/Gold	.25
4	Greg Maddux	1.00
4a	Greg Maddux/Gold	1.50
5	Kirby Puckett	1.00
5a	Kirby Puckett/Gold	1.50
6	Jeff Bagwell	.75
6a	Jeff Bagwell/Gold	1.00
7	Cal Ripken, Jr.	1.50
7a	Cal Ripken, Jr./Gold	2.50
8	Lenny Dykstra	.10
8a	Lenny Dykstra/Gold	.25
9	Tim Salmon	.10
9a	Tim Salmon/Gold	.25
10	Matt Williams	.10
10a	Matt Williams/Gold	.25
11	Roberto Alomar	.30
11a	Roberto Alomar/Gold	.45
12	Barry Larkin	.10
12a	Barry Larkin/Gold	.25
13	Roger Clemens	1.00

13a	Roger Clemens/Gold	1.75
14	Mike Piazza	1.25
14a	Mike Piazza/Gold	2.00
15	Travis Fryman	.10
15a	Travis Fryman/Gold	.25
16	Ryne Sandberg	1.00
16a	Ryne Sandberg/Gold	1.50
17	Robin Ventura	.10
17a	Robin Ventura/Gold	.25
18	Gary Sheffield	.35
18a	Gary Sheffield/Gold	.50
19	Carlos Baerga	.10
19a	Carlos Baerga/Gold	.25
20	Jay Bell	.10
20a	Jay Bell (Gold)	.25
21	Edgar Martinez	.10
21a	Edgar Martinez/Gold	.25
22	Phil Plantier	.10
22a	Phil Plantier/Gold	.25
23	Danny Tartabull	.10
23a	Danny Tartabull/Gold	.25
24	Marquis Grissom	.10
24a	Marquis Grissom/Gold	.25
25	Robin Yount	.75
25a	Robin Yount/Gold	1.00
26	Ozzie Smith	1.00
26a	Ozzie Smith/Gold	1.50
27	Ivan Rodriguez	.60
27a	Ivan Rodriguez/Gold	.75
28	Dante Bichette	.10
28a	Dante Bichette/Gold	.25

1994 Churchs Chicken Show Stoppers

Ten of baseball's top home-run hitters are featured in this insert set. Found approximately once every four packs in the four-card packs distributed by the fried chicken chain, the cards were produced by Pinnacle Brands using its foil-printing Dufex process. A player action photo is depicted inside a home-plate shaped frame at right. "Show Stoppers" is printed vertically at left in red and yellow tones. The background merges from green at left to purple at right, with the player's name in black in a yellow-to-red rainbow effect box beneath the photo. The Churchs logo is at bottom-left. On back is a portrait photo in a light blue box. There is a description of the player's home run prowess along with gold boxes showing his 1993 homers, slugging percentage and at bat/home run ratio. The border mirrors the front's green-to-purple effect. Because the cards are not licensed by Major League Baseball, the uniform logos have been removed from both the front and back photos.

		NM/M
Complete Set (10):		7.50
Common Player:		.50
1	Juan Gonzalez	.75
2	Barry Bonds	2.50
3	Ken Griffey Jr.	2.00
4	David Justice	.50
5	Frank Thomas	1.50
6	Fred McGriff	.50
7	Albert Belle	.50
8	Joe Carter	.50
9	Cecil Fielder	.50
10	Mickey Tettleton	.50

1998 CHW San Francisco Giants

At four special Senior Citizens Days at 3Com Park Giants home games, cards of four Hall of Famers were given away. The promotion was sponsored by Catholic Healthcare West, whose logo and name appear at top-left on the cards' fronts. Fronts combine vintage action photos and recent portrait shots and include a fac-

willie mays

simile autograph. Backs provide a tip for healthy living and the phone numbers of various health care providers.

		NM/M
Complete Set (4):		20.00
Common Player:		4.00
(1)	Orlando Cepeda	4.00
(2)	Juan Marichal	4.00
(3)	Willie Mays	12.00
(4)	Willie McCovey	4.00

1982 Cincinnati Reds Yearbook Cards

Clint Hurdle
Outfielder

In 1982 the Reds began a series of yearbook inserts consisting of two nine-card sheets. The 16-3/4" x 10-7/8" sheet contains 18 perforated 2-5/8" x 3-3/4" cards. Fronts have color photos with red graphics and a white border. Backs are in black-and-white and include complete major and minor league stats. The cards are checklisted here by uniform number.

		NM/M
Complete Set, Sheet:		7.50
Complete Set, Singles (18):		6.00
Common Player:		.25
3	John McNamara	.25
5	Johnny Bench	3.00
13	Dave Concepcion	.25
16	Ron Oester	.25
21	Paul Householder	.25
22	Dan Driessen	.25
28	Cesar Cedeno	.25
29	Alex Trevino	.25
30	Clint Hurdle	.25
35	Frank Pastore	.25
36	Mario Soto	.25
38	Bruce Berenyi	.25
41	Tom Seaver	2.00
47	Tom Hume	.25
49	Joe Price	.25
51	Mike LaCoss	.25
---	Best in Baseball	.25
---	Riverfront Stadium	.25

1983 Cincinnati Reds Yearbook Cards

JOHNNY BENCH
INFIELDER

This 16-3/4" x 10-7/8" cardboard sheet was stapled into the Reds 1983 yearbook. The sheet contains 18 2-5/8" x 3-3/4" cards perforated for removal. Fronts have color game-action photos with red graphics. Backs are in black-and-white and include complete career stats. Cards are checklisted here by uniform number.

		NM/M
	Complete Set, Sheet:	6.00
	Complete Set, Singles (18):	5.00
	Common Player:	.25
	Gary Redus	.25
5	Johnny Bench	3.00
	Russ Nixon	.25
13	Dave Concepcion	.25
16	Ron Oester	.25
20	Eddie Milner	.25
21	Paul Householder	.25
	Dan Driessen	.25
	Charlie Puleo	.25
	Cesar Cedeno	.25
29	Alex Trevino	.25
	Rich Gale	.25
35	Frank Pastore	.25
36	Mario Soto	.25
	Bruce Berenyi	.25
47	Tom Hume	.25
49	Joe Price	.25
---	Riverfront Stadium	.25

1984 Cincinnati Reds Yearbook Cards

Once again in 1984 the Reds inserted a 16-3/4" x 11" cardboard panel into their yearbook. The sheet contains 18 cards, 2-5/8" x 3-3/4", perforated for removal. Fronts have color photos with a large red frame and white borders. Backs are in black-and-white with complete major and minor league stats. Cards are checklisted here by uniform number.

		NM/M
	Complete Set, Sheet:	5.00
	Complete Set, Singles (18):	3.00
	Common Player:	.25
	Gary Redus	.25
	Vern Rapp	.25
1	Dann Bilardello	.25
2	Nick Esasky	.25
3	Dave Concepcion	.25
6	Ron Oester	.25
	Eddie Milner	.25
	Dan Driessen	.25
	Tony Perez	1.00
	Duane Walker	.25
	Bill Scherrer	.25
	Frank Pastore	.25
	Mario Soto	.25
	Bruce Berenyi	.25
	Dave Parker	.35
	Tom Hume	.25
	Joe Price	.25
	Bob Howsam (President)	.25

1985 Cincinnati Reds Yearbook Cards

Once again in 1985 the Reds inserted a 16-3/4" x 11" cardboard panel into their yearbook. The sheet contains 18 cards, 2-5/8" x 3-3/4", perforated for removal. Fronts have color photos with red and white graphics. Backs are in black-and-white with complete major and minor league stats. Cards are checklisted here alphabetically.

		NM/M
	Complete Sheet:	6.00
	Complete Set (18):	5.00
	Common Player:	.25
	Cesar Cedeno	.25
	Dave Concepcion	.25
	Eric Davis	.75
	Nick Esasky	.25
	Tom Foley	.25
	John Franco	.25
	Brad Gulden	.25
	Wayne Krenchicki	.25
	Eddie Milner	.25
	Ron Oester	.25
	Dave Parker	.25
	Ted Power	.25

(13)	Joe Price	.25
(14)	Pete Rose	3.00
(15)	Jeff Russell	.25
(16)	Mario Soto	.25
(17)	Jay Tibbs	.25
(18)	Duane Walker	.25

2003 Cincinnati Reds Scratch-Offs

The first 10,000 fans entering the newly opened Great American Ball Park for a trio of promotional dates received a special scratch-off card. The card has a game-action borderless photo on front. At top left is the sponsor's (Klosterman or Kroger) logo, with a silver box beneath. Scratching off the box revealed whether the fan won one of 500 player-autographed balls which were given away that day. The team's 2003 logo is at bottom-right. The back has the same logos, along with a career summary and an ink-jetted serial number.

		NM/M
	Complete Set (3):	4.00
	Common Player:	1.00
(1)	Johnny Bench	2.00
(2)	Aaron Boone	1.00
(3)	Adam Dunn	1.50

1996 Circa

This hobby-exclusive product was limited to 2,000 sequentially numbered cases. The regular-issue set has 196 player cards, including 10 top prospects and four prospects. Circa also has a 200-card parallel set called Rave which is limited to 150 sets. Each Rave card is sequentially numbered from 1-150. Two other insert sets were also produced - Access and Boss.

		NM/M
	Complete Set (200):	15.00
	Common Player:	.10
	Raves:	30X
	Pack (8):	1.50
	Wax Box (24):	25.00
1	Roberto Alomar	.25
2	Brady Anderson	.10
3	Rocky Coppinger RC	.10
4	Eddie Murray	.75
5	Mike Mussina	.35
6	Randy Myers	.10
7	Rafael Palmeiro	.65
8	Cal Ripken Jr.	2.00
9	Jose Canseco	.50
10	Roger Clemens	1.00
11	Mike Greenwell	.10
12	Tim Naehring	.10
13	John Valentin	.10
14	Mo Vaughn	.50
15	Tim Wakefield	.10
16	Jim Abbott	.10
17	Garret Anderson	.10
18	Jim Edmonds	.10
19	Darin Erstad RC	2.00
20	Chuck Finley	.10
21	Troy Percival	.10
22	Tim Salmon	.10
23	J.T. Snow	.10
24	Wilson Alvarez	.10
25	Harold Baines	.10
26	Ray Durham	.10
27	Alex Fernandez	.10
28	Tony Phillips	.10
29	Frank Thomas	.75
30	Robin Ventura	.10
31	Sandy Alomar Jr.	.10
32	Albert Belle	.10
33	Kenny Lofton	.10
34	Dennis Martinez	.10
35	Jose Mesa	.10
36	Charles Nagy	.10
37	Manny Ramirez	.75
37p	Manny Ramirez/OPS	2.00
38	Jim Thome	.60
39	Travis Fryman	.10
40	Bob Higginson	.10
41	Melvin Nieves	.10
42	Alan Trammell	.10
43	Kevin Appier	.10
44	Johnny Damon	.30
45	Keith Lockhart	.10
46	Jeff Montgomery	.10
47	Joe Randa	.10
48	Bip Roberts	.10
49	Ricky Bones	.10
50	Jeff Cirillo	.10
51	Marc Newfield	.10
52	Dave Nilsson	.10
53	Kevin Seitzer	.10
54	Ron Coomer	.10
55	Marty Cordova	.10
56	Roberto Kelly	.10
57	Chuck Knoblauch	.10
58	Paul Molitor	.75
59	Kirby Puckett	1.00
60	Scott Stahoviak	.10
61	Wade Boggs	1.00
62	David Cone	.10
63	Cecil Fielder	.10
64	Dwight Gooden	.10
65	Derek Jeter	2.00
66	Tino Martinez	.10
67	Paul O'Neill	.10
68	Andy Pettitte	.35
69	Ruben Rivera	.10
70	Bernie Williams	.10
71	Geronimo Berroa	.10
72	Jason Giambi	.45
73	Mark McGwire	1.50
74	Terry Steinbach	.10
75	Todd Van Poppel	.10
76	Jay Buhner	.10
77	Norm Charlton	.10
78	Ken Griffey Jr.	1.25
79	Randy Johnson	.75
80	Edgar Martinez	.10
81	Alex Rodriguez	1.50
82	Paul Sorrento	.10
83	Dan Wilson	.10
84	Will Clark	.10
85	Kevin Elster	.10
86	Juan Gonzalez	.40
87	Rusty Greer	.10
88	Ken Hill	.10
89	Mark McLemore	.10
90	Dean Palmer	.10
91	Roger Pavlik	.10
92	Ivan Rodriguez	.65
93	Joe Carter	.10
94	Carlos Delgado	.35
95	Juan Guzman	.10
96	John Olerud	.10
97	Ed Sprague	.10
98	Jermaine Dye	.10
99	Tom Glavine	.30
100	Marquis Grissom	.10
101	Andruw Jones	.75
102	Chipper Jones	1.00
103	David Justice	.10
104	Ryan Klesko	.10
105	Greg Maddux	1.00
106	Fred McGriff	.10
107	John Smoltz	.10
108	Brant Brown	.10
109	Mark Grace	.10
110	Brian McRae	.10
111	Ryne Sandberg	1.00
112	Sammy Sosa	1.00
113	Steve Trachsel	.10
114	Bret Boone	.10
115	Eric Davis	.10
116	Steve Gibralter	.10
117	Barry Larkin	.10
118	Reggie Sanders	.10
119	John Smiley	.10
120	Dante Bichette	.10
121	Ellis Burks	.10
122	Vinny Castilla	.10
123	Andres Galarraga	.10
124	Larry Walker	.10
125	Eric Young	.10
126	Kevin Brown	.10
127	Greg Colbrunn	.10
128	Jeff Conine	.10
129	Charles Johnson	.10
130	Al Leiter	.10
131	Gary Sheffield	.50
132	Devon White	.10
133	Jeff Bagwell	.75
134	Derek Bell	.10
135	Craig Biggio	.10
136	Doug Drabek	.10
137	Brian Hunter	.10
138	Darryl Kile	.10
139	Shane Reynolds	.10
140	Brett Butler	.10
141	Eric Karros	.10
142	Ramon Martinez	.10
143	Raul Mondesi	.10
144	Hideo Nomo	.40
145	Chan Ho Park	.10
146	Mike Piazza	1.25
147	Moises Alou	.10
148	Yamil Benitez	.10
149	Mark Grudzielanek	.10
150	Pedro Martinez	.75
151	Henry Rodriguez	.10
152	David Segui	.10
153	Rondell White	.10
154	Carlos Baerga	.10
155	John Franco	.10
156	Bernard Gilkey	.10
157	Todd Hundley	.10
158	Jason Isringhausen	.10
159	Lance Johnson	.10
160	Alex Ochoa	.10
161	Rey Ordonez	.10
162	Paul Wilson	.10
163	Ron Blazier	.10
164	Ricky Bottalico	.10
165	Jim Eisenreich	.10
166	Pete Incaviglia	.10
167	Mickey Morandini	.10
168	Ricky Otero	.10
169	Curt Schilling	.25
170	Jay Bell	.10
171	Charlie Hayes	.10
172	Jason Kendall	.10
173	Jeff King	.10
174	Al Martin	.10
175	Alan Benes	.10
176	Royce Clayton	.10
177	Brian Jordan	.10
178	Ray Lankford	.10
179	John Mabry	.10
180	Willie McGee	.10
181	Ozzie Smith	1.00
182	Todd Stottlemyre	.10
183	Andy Ashby	.10
184	Ken Caminiti	.10
185	Steve Finley	.10
186	Tony Gwynn	1.00
187	Rickey Henderson	.75
188	Wally Joyner	.10
189	Fernando Valenzuela	.10
190	Greg Vaughn	.10
191	Rod Beck	.10
192	Barry Bonds	2.00
193	Shawon Dunston	.10
194	Chris Singleton	.10
195	Robby Thompson	.10
196	Matt Williams	.10
197	Checklist (Barry Bonds)	.75
198	Checklist (Ken Griffey Jr.)	.65
199	Checklist (Cal Ripken Jr.)	.75
200	Checklist (Frank Thomas)	.40

Rave

Rainbow metallic foil highlights on front and a serial number on back from within an edition of 150 of each card differentiate this parallel issue from the Circa base cards. Announced insertion rate for Raves was one per 60 packs.

	NM/M
Common Player:	2.00
Stars:	30X

Access

This 1996 Fleer Circa insert set highlights 30 players on a three-panel foldout design that includes multiple photographs, personal information and statistics. The cards were seeded about one every 12 packs.

		NM/M
	Complete Set (30):	50.00
	Common Player:	.60
1	Cal Ripken Jr.	6.00
2	Mo Vaughn	.60
3	Tim Salmon	.75
4	Frank Thomas	2.00
5	Albert Belle	.75
6	Kenny Lofton	.60
7	Manny Ramirez	2.00
8	Paul Molitor	2.00
9	Kirby Puckett	3.00
10	Paul O'Neill	.60
11	Mark McGwire	5.00
12	Ken Griffey Jr.	4.00
13	Randy Johnson	2.00
14	Greg Maddux	3.00
15	John Smoltz	.60
16	Sammy Sosa	4.00
17	Barry Larkin	.60
18	Gary Sheffield	1.00
19	Jeff Bagwell	2.00
20	Hideo Nomo	2.00
21	Mike Piazza	4.00
22	Moises Alou	.60
23	Henry Rodriguez	.60
24	Rey Ordonez	.60
25	Jay Bell	.60
26	Ozzie Smith	3.00
27	Tony Gwynn	3.00
28	Rickey Henderson	2.00
29	Barry Bonds	6.00
30	Matt Williams	.60
30p	Matt Williams/OPS	1.00

Boss

This insert set showcases the game's top stars on an embossed design. Cards were seeded one per six packs.

		NM/M
	Complete Set (50):	50.00
	Common Player:	.45
1	Roberto Alomar	1.00
2	Cal Ripken Jr.	5.00
2p	Cal Ripken Jr./OPS	3.00
3	Jose Canseco	1.50
4	Mo Vaughn	.45
5	Tim Salmon	.60
6	Frank Thomas	2.00
7	Robin Ventura	.45
8	Albert Belle	.60
9	Kenny Lofton	.45
10	Manny Ramirez	2.00
11	Dave Nilsson	.45
12	Chuck Knoblauch	.45
13	Paul Molitor	2.00
14	Kirby Puckett	3.00
15	Wade Boggs	3.00
16	Dwight Gooden	.45
17	Paul O'Neill	.45
18	Mark McGwire	4.00
19	Jay Buhner	.45
20	Ken Griffey Jr.	3.50
21	Randy Johnson	2.00
22	Will Clark	.60
23	Juan Gonzalez	2.00
24	Joe Carter	.45
25	Tom Glavine	.45
26	Ryan Klesko	.45
27	Greg Maddux	3.00
28	John Smoltz	.45
29	Ryne Sandberg	3.00
30	Sammy Sosa	3.50
31	Barry Larkin	.45
32	Reggie Sanders	.45
33	Dante Bichette	.45
34	Andres Galarraga	.45
35	Charles Johnson	.45
36	Gary Sheffield	1.50
37	Jeff Bagwell	2.00
38	Hideo Nomo	2.00
39	Mike Piazza	3.50
40	Moises Alou	.45
41	Henry Rodriguez	.45
42	Rey Ordonez	.45
43	Ricky Otero	.45
44	Jay Bell	.45
45	Royce Clayton	.45
46	Ozzie Smith	3.00
47	Tony Gwynn	3.00
48	Rickey Henderson	2.00
49	Barry Bonds	5.00
50	Matt Williams	.45

1997 Circa

Circa baseball returned for the second year in 1997, with a 400-card set, including 393 player cards and seven checklists. Cards feature action photos on a dynamic graphic arts background, and arrived in eight-card packs. The set was paralleled in a Rave insert and was accompanied by five inserts: Boss, Fast Track, Icons, Limited Access and Rave Reviews.

		NM/M
	Complete Set (400):	15.00
	Common Player:	.10
	Pack (8):	1.00
	Retail Wax Box (18):	15.00
	Hobby Wax Box (36):	30.00
1	Kenny Lofton	.10
2	Ray Durham	.10
3	Mariano Rivera	.20
4	Jon Lieber	.10
5	Tim Salmon	.10
6	Mark Grudzielanek	.10
7	Neifi Perez	.10
8	Cal Ripken Jr.	3.00
9	John Olerud	.10
10	Edgar Renteria	.10
11	Jose Rosado	.10
12	Mickey Morandini	.10
13	Orlando Miller	.10
14	Ben McDonald	.10
15	Hideo Nomo	.40
16	Fred McGriff	.10
17	Sean Berry	.10
18	Roger Pavlik	.10
19	Aaron Sele	.10
20	Joey Hamilton	.10
21	Roger Clemens	1.25
22	Jose Herrera	.10
23	Ryne Sandberg	1.00
24	Ken Griffey Jr.	1.50
25	Barry Bonds	3.00
26	Dan Naulty	.10
27	Wade Boggs	1.00
28	Ray Lankford	.10
29	Rico Brogna	.10
30	Wally Joyner	.10
31	F.P. Santangelo	.10
32	Vinny Castilla	.10
33	Eddie Murray	.75
34	Kevin Elster	.10
35	Mike Macfarlane	.10
36	Jeff Kent	.10
37	Orlando Merced	.10
38	Jason Isringhausen	.10
39	Chad Ogea	.10
40	Greg Gagne	.10
41	Curt Lyons	.10
42	Mo Vaughn	.10
43	Rusty Greer	.10
44	Shane Reynolds	.10
45	Frank Thomas	.75
46	Chris Hoiles	.10
47	Scott Sanders	.10
48	Mark Lemke	.10
49	Fernando Vina	.10
50	Mark McGwire	2.00
51	Bernie Williams	.10
52	Bobby Higginson	.10
53	Kevin Tapani	.10
54	Rich Becker	.10
55	Felix Heredia RC	.30
56	Delino DeShields	.10
57	Rick Wilkins	.10
58	Edgardo Alfonzo	.10
59	Brett Butler	.10
60	Ed Sprague	.10
61	Joe Randa	.10
62	Ugueth Urbina	.10
63	Todd Greene	.10
64	Devon White	.10
65	Bruce Ruffin	.10
66	Mark Gardner	.10
67	Omar Vizquel	.10
68	Luis Gonzalez	.10
69	Tom Glavine	.25
70	Cal Eldred	.10
71	William Van Landingham	.10

72 Jay Buhner	.10
73 James Baldwin	.10
74 Robin Jennings	.10
75 Terry Steinbach	.10
76 Billy Taylor	.10
77 Armando Benitez	.10
78 Joe Girardi	.10
79 Jay Bell	.10
80 Damon Buford	.10
81 Deion Sanders	.15
82 Bill Haselman	.10
83 John Flaherty	.10
84 Todd Stottlemyre	.10
85 J.T. Snow	.10
86 Felipe Lira	.10
87 Steve Avery	.10
88 Trey Beamon	.10
89 Alex Gonzalez	.10
90 Mark Clark	.10
91 Shane Andrews	.10
92 Randy Myers	.10
93 Gary Gaetti	.10
94 Jeff Blauser	.10
95 Tony Batista	.10
96 Todd Worrell	.10
97 Jim Edmonds	.10
98 Eric Young	.10
99 Roberto Kelly	.10
100 Alex Rodriguez	2.00
100p Alex Rodriguez/OPS	2.00
101 Julio Franco	.10
102 Jeff Bagwell	.75
103 Bobby Witt	.10
104 Tino Martinez	.10
105 Shannon Stewart	.10
106 Brian Banks	.10
107 Eddie Taubensee	.10
108 Terry Mulholland	.10
109 Lyle Mouton	.10
110 Jeff Conine	.10
111 Johnny Damon	.30
112 Quilvio Veras	.10
113 Wilton Guerrero	.10
114 Dmitri Young	.10
115 Garret Anderson	.10
116 Bill Pulsipher	.10
117 Jacob Brumfield	.10
118 Mike Lansing	.10
119 Jose Canseco	.50
120 Mike Bordick	.10
121 Kevin Stocker	.10
122 Frank Rodriguez	.10
123 Mike Cameron	.10
124 Tony Womack RC	.25
125 Bret Boone	.10
126 Moises Alou	.10
127 Tim Naehring	.10
128 Brant Brown	.10
129 Todd Zeile	.10
130 Dave Nilsson	.10
131 Donne Wall	.10
132 Jose Mesa	.10
133 Mark McLemore	.10
134 Mike Stanton	.10
135 Dan Wilson	.10
136 Jose Offerman	.10
137 David Justice	.10
138 Kirt Manwaring	.10
139 Raul Casanova	.10
140 Ron Coomer	.10
141 Dave Hollins	.10
142 Shawn Estes	.10
143 Darren Daulton	.10
144 Turk Wendell	.10
145 Darrin Fletcher	.10
146 Marquis Grissom	.10
147 Andy Benes	.10
148 Nomar Garciaparra	1.00
149 Andy Pettitte	.30
150 Tony Gwynn	1.00
151 Robb Nen	.10
152 Kevin Seitzer	.10
153 Ariel Prieto	.10
154 Scott Karl	.10
155 Carlos Baerga	.10
156 Wilson Alvarez	.10
157 Thomas Howard	.10
158 Kevin Appier	.10
159 Russ Davis	.10
160 Justin Thompson	.10
161 Pete Schourek	.10
162 John Burkett	.10
163 Roberto Alomar	.25
164 Darren Holmes	.10
165 Travis Miller	.10
166 Mark Langston	.10
167 Juan Guzman	.10
168 Pedro Astacio	.10
169 Mark Johnson	.10
170 Mark Leiter	.10
171 Heathcliff Slocumb	.10
172 Dante Bichette	.10
173 Brian Giles RC	1.00
174 Paul Wilson	.10
175 Eric Davis	.10
176 Charles Johnson	.10
177 Willie Greene	.10
178 Geronimo Berroa	.10
179 Mariano Duncan	.10
180 Robert Person	.10
181 David Segui	.10
182 Ozzie Guillen	.10
183 Osvaldo Fernandez	.10
184 Dean Palmer	.10
185 Bob Wickman	.10
186 Eric Karros	.10
187 Travis Fryman	.10
188 Andy Ashby	.10

189 Scott Stahoviak	.10
190 Norm Charlton	.10
191 Craig Paquette	.10
192 John Smoltz	.10
193 Orel Hershiser	.10
194 Glenallen Hill	.10
195 George Arias	.10
196 Brian Jordan	.10
197 Greg Vaughn	.10
198 Rafael Palmeiro	.60
199 Darryl Kile	.10
200 Derek Jeter	3.00
201 Jose Vizcaino	.10
202 Rick Aguilera	.10
203 Jason Schmidt	.10
204 Trot Nixon	.10
205 Tom Pagnozzi	.10
206 Mark Wohlers	.10
207 Lance Johnson	.10
208 Carlos Delgado	.40
209 Cliff Floyd	.10
210 Kent Mercker	.10
211 Matt Mieske	.10
212 Ismael Valdes	.10
213 Shawon Dunston	.10
214 Melvin Nieves	.10
215 Tony Phillips	.10
216 Scott Spiezio	.10
217 Michael Tucker	.10
218 Matt Williams	.10
219 Ricky Otero	.10
220 Kevin Ritz	.10
221 Darryl Strawberry	.10
222 Troy Percival	.10
223 Eugene Kingsale	.10
224 Julian Tavarez	.10
225 Jermaine Dye	.10
226 Jason Kendall	.10
227 Sterling Hitchcock	.10
228 Jeff Cirillo	.10
229 Roberto Hernandez	.10
230 Ricky Bottalico	.10
231 Bobby Bonilla	.10
232 Edgar Martinez	.10
233 John Valentin	.10
234 Ellis Burks	.10
235 Benito Santiago	.10
236 Terrell Wade	.10
237 Armando Reynoso	.10
238 Danny Graves	.10
239 Ken Hill	.10
240 Dennis Eckersley	.65
241 Darin Erstad	.25
242 Lee Smith	.10
243 Cecil Fielder	.10
244 Tony Clark	.10
245 Scott Erickson	.10
246 Bob Abreu	.10
247 Ruben Sierra	.10
248 Chili Davis	.10
249 Darryl Hamilton	.10
250 Albert Belle	.10
251 Todd Hollandsworth	.10
252 Terry Adams	.10
253 Rey Ordonez	.10
254 Steve Finley	.10
255 Jose Valentin	.10
256 Royce Clayton	.10
257 Sandy Alomar	.10
258 Mike Lieberthal	.10
259 Ivan Rodriguez	.65
260 Rod Beck	.10
261 Ron Karkovice	.10
262 Mark Gubicza	.10
263 Chris Holt	.10
264 Jaime Bluma	.10
265 Francisco Cordova	.10
266 Javy Lopez	.10
267 Reggie Jefferson	.10
268 Kevin Brown	.10
269 Scott Brosius	.10
270 Dwight Gooden	.10
271 Marty Cordova	.10
272 Jeff Brantley	.10
273 Joe Carter	.10
274 Todd Jones	.10
275 Sammy Sosa	1.00
276 Randy Johnson	.75
277 B.J. Surhoff	.10
278 Chan Ho Park	.10
279 Jamey Wright	.10
280 Manny Ramirez	.75
281 John Franco	.10
282 Tim Worrell	.10
283 Scott Rolen	.60
284 Reggie Sanders	.10
285 Mike Fetters	.10
286 Tim Wakefield	.10
287 Trevor Hoffman	.10
288 Donovan Osborne	.10
289 Phil Nevin	.10
290 Jermaine Allensworth	.10
291 Rocky Coppinger	.10
292 Tim Raines	.10
293 Henry Rodriguez	.10
294 Paul Sorrento	.10
295 Tom Goodwin	.10
296 Raul Mondesi	.10
297 Allen Watson	.10
298 Derek Bell	.10
299 Gary Sheffield	.45
300 Paul Molitor	.75
301 Shawn Green	.15
302 Darren Oliver	.10
303 Jack McDowell	.10
304 Denny Neagle	.10
305 Doug Drabek	.10
306 Mel Rojas	.10

307 Andres Galarraga	.10
308 Alex Ochoa	.10
309 Gary DiSarcina	.10
310 Ron Gant	.10
311 Gregg Jefferies	.10
312 Ruben Rivera	.10
313 Vladimir Guerrero	.75
314 Willie Adams	.10
315 Bip Roberts	.10
316 Mark Grace	.10
317 Bernard Gilkey	.10
318 Marc Newfield	.10
319 Al Leiter	.10
320 Otis Nixon	.10
321 Tom Candiotti	.10
322 Mike Stanley	.10
323 Jeff Fassero	.10
324 Billy Wagner	.10
325 Todd Walker	.10
326 Chad Curtis	.10
327 Quinton McCracken	.10
328 Will Clark	.10
329 Andruw Jones	.75
330 Robin Ventura	.10
331 Curtis Pride	.10
332 Barry Larkin	.10
333 Jimmy Key	.10
334 David Wells	.10
335 Mike Holtz	.10
336 Paul Wagner	.10
337 Greg Maddux	1.00
338 Curt Schilling	.35
339 Steve Trachsel	.10
340 John Wetteland	.10
341 Rickey Henderson	.75
342 Ernie Young	.10
343 Harold Baines	.10
344 Bobby Jones	.10
345 Jeff D'Amico	.10
346 John Mabry	.10
347 Pedro Martinez	.75
348 Mark Lewis	.10
349 Dan Miceli	.10
350 Chuck Knoblauch	.10
351 John Smiley	.10
352 Brady Anderson	.10
353 Jim Leyritz	.10
354 Al Martin	.10
355 Pat Hentgen	.10
356 Mike Piazza	1.50
357 Charles Nagy	.10
358 Luis Castillo	.10
359 Paul O'Neill	.10
360 Steve Reed	.10
361 Tom Gordon	.10
362 Craig Biggio	.10
363 Jeff Montgomery	.10
364 Jamie Moyer	.10
365 Ryan Klesko	.10
366 Todd Hundley	.10
367 Bobby Estalella	.10
368 Jason Giambi	.50
369 Brian Hunter	.10
370 Ramon Martinez	.10
371 Carlos Garcia	.10
372 Hal Morris	.10
373 Juan Gonzalez	.40
374 Brian McRae	.10
375 Mike Mussina	.40
376 John Ericks	.10
377 Larry Walker	.10
378 Chris Gomez	.10
379 John Jaha	.10
380 Rondell White	.10
381 Chipper Jones	1.00
382 David Cone	.10
383 Alan Benes	.10
384 Troy O'Leary	.10
385 Ken Caminiti	.10
386 Jeff King	.10
387 Mike Hampton	.10
388 Jaime Navarro	.10
389 Brad Radke	.10
390 Joey Cora	.10
391 Jim Thome	.60
392 Alex Fernandez	.10
393 Chuck Finley	.10
394 Andruw Jones Checklist	.35
395 Ken Griffey Jr. Checklist	.60
396 Frank Thomas Checklist	.35
397 Alex Rodriguez Checklist	.75
398 Cal Ripken Jr. Checklist	1.00
399 Mike Piazza Checklist	.60
400 Greg Maddux Checklist	.45

In its second year, Circa Rave parallel inserts were limited to inclusion only in hobby packs at the stated. rate of one card per "30 to 40" packs. Raves are distinguished from regular-edition Circa cards by the use of purple metallic foil for the brand name and player identification on front. Rave backs carry a silver-foil serial number detailing its position within a production of 150 for each card.

	NM/M
Common Player:	3.00
Stars/Rookies:	10-15X

Boss

Boss was Circa's most common insert series. Twenty embossed cards were seeded one per six packs, displaying some of baseball's best players. A Super Boss parallel insert features metallic-foil background and graphics on front, and is inserted at a rate of one per 36 packs.

		NM/M
Complete Set (20):		10.00
Common Player:		.15
Super Boss:		2X
1	Jeff Bagwell	.60
2	Albert Belle	.15
3	Barry Bonds	2.00
4	Ken Caminiti	.15
5	Juan Gonzalez	.30
6	Ken Griffey Jr.	1.00
7	Tony Gwynn	.75
8	Derek Jeter	2.00
9	Andruw Jones	.60
10	Chipper Jones	.75
11	Greg Maddux	.75
12	Mark McGwire	1.50
13	Mike Piazza	1.00
14	Manny Ramirez	.60
15	Cal Ripken Jr.	2.00
16	Alex Rodriguez	1.50
17	John Smoltz	.15
18	Frank Thomas	.60
19	Mo Vaughn	.15
20	Bernie Williams	.15

Emerald Autograph Redemption Cards

These box-topper cards were a hobby exclusive redeemable until May 31, 1998, for autographed special cards of six young stars. Fronts have a green-foil enhanced player action photo. Backs provide details of the redemption program.

		NM/M
Complete Set (6):		6.50
Common Player:		.50
(1)	Darin Erstad	1.25
(2)	Todd Hollandsworth	.50
(3)	Alex Ochoa	.50
(4)	Alex Rodriguez	6.00
(5)	Scott Rolen	1.50
(6)	Todd Walker	.50

Rave

Emerald Autographs

Special green-foil enhanced cards of six top young stars were available via a mail-in redemption. The cards feature authentic player signatures on front and an embossed authentication seal. Backs are identical to the regular card of each featured player.

	NM/M
Complete Set (6):	100.00
Common Player:	6.00
100 Alex Rodriguez	75.00
241 Darin Erstad	9.00
251 Todd Hollandsworth	6.00
283 Scott Rolen	12.00
308 Alex Ochoa	6.00
325 Todd Walker	6.00

Fast Track

Fast Track highlights 10 top rookies and young stars on a flocked background simulating grass. Cards were inserted every 24 packs.

		NM/M
Complete Set (10):		12.00
Common Player:		.50
1	Vladimir Guerrero	1.50
2	Todd Hollandsworth	.50
3	Derek Jeter	4.00
4	Andruw Jones	1.50
5	Chipper Jones	2.50
6	Andy Pettitte	1.00
7	Mariano Rivera	.75
8	Alex Rodriguez	3.00
9	Scott Rolen	1.25
10	Todd Walker	.50

Icons

Twelve of baseball's top sluggers were displayed on 100-percent holofoil cards in Icons. Icons were found at a rate of one per 36 packs.

		NM/M
Complete Set (12):		25.00
Common Player:		.50
1	Juan Gonzalez	.75
2	Ken Griffey Jr.	3.00
3	Tony Gwynn	2.00
4	Derek Jeter	5.00
5	Chipper Jones	2.00
6	Greg Maddux	2.00
7	Mark McGwire	4.00
8	Mike Piazza	3.00
9	Cal Ripken Jr.	5.00
10	Alex Rodriguez	4.00
11	Frank Thomas	1.50
12	Matt Williams	.50

Limited Access

Limited Access was a retail-only insert found every 18 packs. Cards feature an in-depth, statistical analysis including the player's favorite hit and each pitcher's least favorite hitter to face. Limited Access is formatted as a die-cut, bi-fold design resembling a book.

		NM/M
Complete Set (15):		30.00
Common Player:		1.25
1	Jeff Bagwell	2.00
2	Albert Belle	1.25
3	Barry Bonds	2.00
4	Juan Gonzalez	1.50
5	Ken Griffey Jr.	3.25
6	Tony Gwynn	2.50
7	Derek Jeter	5.00
8	Chipper Jones	2.50
9	Greg Maddux	2.50
10	Mark McGwire	4.00
11	Mike Piazza	3.50
12	Cal Ripken Jr.	5.00
13	Alex Rodriguez	4.00
14	Frank Thomas	2.00
15	Mo Vaughn	1.25

Rave Reviews

Hitters that continually put up great numbers were selected for Rave Reviews. The insert was found every 288 packs and was printed on 100-percent holofoil.

		NM/M
Complete Set (12):		75.00
Common Player:		3.00
1	Albert Belle	3.00
2	Barry Bonds	12.00
3	Juan Gonzalez	3.00
4	Ken Griffey Jr.	7.50
5	Tony Gwynn	6.00
6	Greg Maddux	6.00
7	Mark McGwire	9.00
8	Eddie Murray	4.00
9	Mike Piazza	7.50
10	Cal Ripken Jr.	12.00
11	Alex Rodriguez	9.00
12	Frank Thomas	4.50

1998 Circa Thunder

Circa Thunder was issued as one series of 300 cards, sold in packs of eight for $1.59. The set marked SkyBox's brand transition from Circa to Thunder so the cards are labeled with both names. Inserts include: Rave and Super Rave parallels, Boss, Fast Track, Quick Strike, Limited Access, Rave Review and Thunder Boomers.

		NM/M
Complete Set (300):		10.00
Common Player:		.10
Pack (8):		1.00
Wax Box (36):		20.00
1	Ben Grieve	.10
2	Derek Jeter	2.50
3	Alex Rodriguez	2.00
4	Paul Molitor	.75
5	Nomar Garciaparra	1.00
6	Fred McGriff	.10
7	Kenny Lofton	.10
8a	Cal Ripken Jr.	2.50
8b	Marquis Grissom (Should be #280.)	.10
8s	Cal Ripken Jr. ("PROMOTIONAL SAMPLE" on back.)	2.50
9	Matt Williams	.10
10	Chipper Jones	1.00
11	Barry Larkin	.10
12	Steve Finley	.10
13	Billy Wagner	.10
14	Rico Brogna	.10
15	Tim Salmon	.10
16	Hideo Nomo	.40
17	Tony Clark	.10
18	Jason Kendall	.10
19	Juan Gonzalez	.40
20	Jeromy Burnitz	.10
21	Roger Clemens	1.25
22	Mark Grace	.10
23	Robin Ventura	.10
24	Manny Ramirez	.75
25	Mark McGwire	2.00
26	Gary Sheffield	.50
27	Vladimir Guerrero	.75
28	Butch Huskey	.10
29	Cecil Fielder	.10
30	Roderick Myers	.10
31	Greg Maddux	1.00
32	Bill Mueller	.10
33	Larry Walker	.10
34	Henry Rodriguez	.10
35	Mike Mussina	.35
36	Ricky Ledee	.10
37	Bobby Bonilla	.10
38	Curt Schilling	.35
39	Luis Gonzalez	.10
40	Troy Percival	.10
41	Eric Milton	.10
42	Mo Vaughn	.10
43	Raul Mondesi	.10
44	Kenny Rogers	.10
45	Frank Thomas	.75
46	Jose Canseco	.50
47	Tom Glavine	.35
48	Rich Butler RC	.10
49	Jay Buhner	.10
50	Jose Cruz Jr.	.10
51	Bernie Williams	.10
52	Doug Glanville	.10
53	Travis Fryman	.10
54	Rey Ordonez	.10
55	Jeff Conine	.10
56	Trevor Hoffman	.10
57	Kirk Rueter	.10
58	Ron Gant	.10
59	Carl Everett	.10
60	Joe Carter	.10
61	Livan Hernandez	.10
62	John Jaha	.10
63	Ivan Rodriguez	.65
64	Willie Blair	.10
65	Todd Helton	.65
66	Kevin Young	.10
67	Mike Caruso	.10
68	Steve Trachsel	.10
69	Marty Cordova	.10
70	Alex Fernandez	.10
71	Eric Karros	.10
72	Reggie Sanders	.10
73	Russ Davis	.10
74	Roberto Hernandez	.10
75	Barry Bonds	2.50
76	Alex Gonzalez	.10
77	Roberto Alomar	.25
78	Troy O'Leary	.10
79	Bernard Gilkey	.10
80	Ismael Valdes	.10
81	Travis Lee	.10
82	Brant Brown	.10
83	Gary DiSarcina	.10
84	Joe Randa	.10
85	Jaret Wright	.10
86	Quilvio Veras	.10
87	Rickey Henderson	.75
88	Randall Simon	.10
89	Mariano Rivera	.25
90	Ugueth Urbina	.10
91	Fernando Vina	.10
92	Alan Benes	.10
93	Dante Bichette	.10
94	Karim Garcia	.10
95	A.J. Hinch	.10

96	Shane Reynolds	.10
97	Kevin Stocker	.10
98	John Wetteland	.10
99	Terry Steinbach	.10
100	Ken Griffey Jr.	1.50
101	Mike Cameron	.10
102	Damion Easley	.10
103	Randy Myers	.10
104	Jason Schmidt	.10
105	Jeff King	.10
106	Gregg Jefferies	.10
107	Sean Casey	.15
108	Mark Kotsay	.10
109	Brad Fullmer	.10
110	Wilson Alvarez	.10
111	Sandy Alomar Jr.	.10
112	Walt Weiss	.10
113	Doug Jones	.10
114	Andy Benes	.10
115	Paul O'Neill	.10
116	Dennis Eckersley	.65
117	Todd Greene	.10
118	Bobby Jones	.10
119	Darrin Fletcher	.10
120	Eric Young	.10
121	Jeffrey Hammonds	.10
122	Mickey Morandini	.10
123	Chuck Knoblauch	.10
124	Moises Alou	.10
125	Miguel Tejada	.15
126	Brian Anderson	.10
127	Edgar Renteria	.10
128	Mike Lansing	.10
129	Quinton McCracken	.10
130	Ray Lankford	.10
131	Andy Ashby	.10
132	Kelvim Escobar	.10
133	Mike Lowell RC	.75
134	Randy Johnson	.75
135	Andres Galarraga	.10
136	Armando Benitez	.10
137	Rusty Greer	.10
138	Jose Guillen	.10
139	Paul Konerko	.15
140	Edgardo Alfonzo	.10
141	Jim Leyritz	.10
142	Mark Clark	.10
143	Brian Johnson	.10
144	Scott Rolen	.60
145	David Cone	.10
146	Jeff Shaw	.10
147	Shannon Stewart	.10
148	Brian Hunter	.10
149	Garret Anderson	.10
150	Jeff Bagwell	.75
151	James Baldwin	.10
152	Devon White	.10
153	Jim Thome	.60
154	Wally Joyner	.10
155	Mark Wohlers	.10
156	Jeff Cirillo	.10
157	Jason Giambi	.60
158	Royce Clayton	.10
159	Dennis Reyes	.10
160	Raul Casanova	.10
161	Pedro Astacio	.10
162	Todd Dunwoody	.10
163	Sammy Sosa	1.00
164	Todd Hundley	.10
165	Wade Boggs	1.00
166	Robb Nen	.10
167	Dan Wilson	.10
168	Hideki Irabu	.10
169	B.J. Surhoff	.10
170	Carlos Delgado	.40
171	Fernando Tatis	.10
172	Bob Abreu	.15
173	David Ortiz	.50
174	Tony Womack	.10
175	Magglio Ordonez RC	1.00
176	Aaron Boone	.10
177	Brian Giles	.10
178	Kevin Appier	.10
179	Chuck Finley	.10
180	Brian Rose	.10
181	Ryan Klesko	.10
182	Mike Stanley	.10
183	Dave Nilsson	.10
184	Carlos Perez	.10
185	Jeff Blauser	.10
186	Richard Hidalgo	.10
187	Charles Johnson	.10
188	Vinny Castilla	.10
189	Joey Hamilton	.10
190	Bubba Trammell	.10
191	Eli Marrero	.10
192	Scott Erickson	.10
193	Pat Hentgen	.10
194	Jorge Fabregas	.10
195	Tino Martinez	.10
196	Bobby Higginson	.10
197	Dave Hollins	.10
198	Rolando Arrojo RC	.25
199	Joey Cora	.10
200	Mike Piazza	1.50
201	Reggie Jefferson	.10
202	John Smoltz	.10
203	Bobby Smith	.10
204	Tom Goodwin	.10
205	Omar Vizquel	.10
206	John Olerud	.10
207	Matt Stairs	.10
208	Bobby Estalella	.10
209	Miguel Cairo	.10
210	Shawn Green	.20
211	Jon Nunnally	.10
212	Al Leiter	.10
213	Matt Lawton	.10

214	Brady Anderson	.10
215	Jeff Kent	.10
216	Ray Durham	.10
217	Al Martin	.10
218	Jeff D'Amico	.10
219	Kevin Tapani	.10
220	Jim Edmonds	.10
221	Jose Vizcaino	.10
222	Jay Bell	.10
223	Ken Caminiti	.10
224	Craig Biggio	.10
225	Bartolo Colon	.10
226	Neifi Perez	.10
227	Delino DeShields	.10
228	Javier Lopez	.10
229	David Wells	.10
230	Brad Rigby	.10
231	John Franco	.10
232	Michael Coleman	.10
233	Edgar Martinez	.10
234	Francisco Cordova	.10
235	Johnny Damon	.30
236	Deivi Cruz	.10
237	J.T. Snow	.10
238	Enrique Wilson	.10
239	Rondell White	.10
240	Aaron Sele	.10
241	Tony Saunders	.10
242	Ricky Bottalico	.10
243	Cliff Floyd	.10
244	Chili Davis	.10
245	Brian McRae	.10
246	Brad Radke	.10
247	Chan Ho Park	.10
248	Lance Johnson	.10
249	Rafael Palmeiro	.65
250	Tony Gwynn	1.00
251	Denny Neagle	.10
252	Dean Palmer	.10
253	Jose Valentin	.10
254	Matt Morris	.10
255	Ellis Burks	.10
256	Jeff Suppan	.10
257	Jimmy Key	.10
258	Justin Thompson	.10
259	Brett Tomko	.10
260	Mark Grudzielanek	.10
261	Mike Hampton	.10
262	Jeff Fassero	.10
263	Charles Nagy	.10
264	Pedro Martinez	.75
265	Todd Zeile	.10
266	Will Clark	.10
267	Abraham Nunez	.10
268	Dave Martinez	.10
269	Jason Dickson	.10
270	Eric Davis	.10
271	Kevin Orie	.10
272	Derek Lee	.50
273	Andruw Jones	.75
274	Juan Encarnacion	.10
275	Carlos Baerga	.10
276	Andy Pettitte	.35
277	Brent Brede	.10
278	Paul Sorrento	.10
279	Mike Lieberthal	.10
280	(Not issued, see #8)	
281	Darin Erstad	.25
282	Willie Greene	.10
283	Derek Bell	.10
284	Scott Spiezio	.10
285	David Segui	.10
286	Albert Belle	.10
287	Ramon Martinez	.10
288	Jeremi Gonzalez	.10
289	Shawn Estes	.10
290	Ron Coomer	.10
291	John Valentin	.10
292	Kevin Brown	.10
293	Michael Tucker	.10
294	Brian Jordan	.10
295	Darryl Kile	.10
296	David Justice	.10
297	Jose Cruz Jr. Checklist	.10
298	Alex Rodriguez Checklist	1.00
299	Ken Griffey Jr. Checklist	.75
300	Frank Thomas Checklist	.65

Rave

Rave parallels each card in Circa Thunder except for the four checklist cards. A special silver sparkling foil is used on the player's name and the Thunder logo on front. This 296-card set was in-

serted approximately one per 36 packs and sequentially numbered to 150 sets on the back.

	NM/M
Common Player:	2.00
Stars:	15X

Super Rave

Only 25 Super Rave parallel sets were printed and they were inserted approximately one per 216 packs. The set contains 296 player cards (no checklist cards). Fronts are identified by sparkling gold foil on the player's name and the Thunder logo, with sequential numbering on the back to 25.

	NM/M
Common Player:	6.00
Stars:	40X

Boss

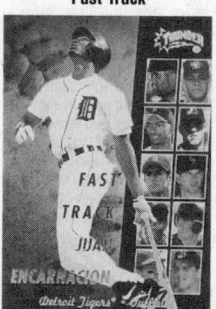

This insert set has cards embossed with the player's last name in large letters across the top.

		NM/M
Complete Set (20):		10.00
Common Player:		.25
Inserted 1:6		
1B	Jeff Bagwell	.75
2B	Barry Bonds	2.00
3B	Roger Clemens	1.00
4B	Jose Cruz Jr.	.25
5B	Nomar Garciaparra	1.00
6B	Juan Gonzalez	.40
7B	Ken Griffey Jr.	1.25
8B	Tony Gwynn	1.00
9B	Derek Jeter	2.00
10B	Chipper Jones	1.00
11B	Travis Lee	.25
12B	Greg Maddux	1.00
13B	Pedro Martinez	.75
14B	Mark McGwire	1.50
15B	Mike Piazza	1.25
16B	Cal Ripken Jr.	2.00
17B	Alex Rodriguez	1.50
18B	Scott Rolen	.50
19B	Frank Thomas	.75
20B	Larry Walker	.25

Fast Track

This 10-card insert showcases some of the top young stars in baseball. Fronts picture the player over a closeup of a gold foil baseball on the left. The right side has smaller head shots of all 10 players with the featured player's head in gold foil.

		NM/M
Complete Set (10):		8.00
Common Player:		.25
Inserted 1:24		
1FT	Jose Cruz Jr.	.25
2FT	Juan Encarnacion	.25
3FT	Brad Fullmer	.25
4FT	Nomar Garciaparra	4.00
5FT	Todd Helton	2.50
6FT	Livan Hernandez	.25
7FT	Travis Lee	.25
8FT	Neifi Perez	.25
9FT	Scott Rolen	1.50
10FT	Jaret Wright	.25

Limited Access

These retail-exclusive insert cards are bi-fold and die-cut with foil stamping on front. The theme of the insert was to provide an in-depth statistical scouting analysis of each player.

		NM/M
Complete Set (15):		17.50
Common Player:		.50
Inserted 1:18		
1LA	Jeff Bagwell	1.25
2LA	Roger Clemens	1.75
3LA	Jose Cruz Jr.	.50
4LA	Nomar Garciaparra	1.50
5LA	Juan Gonzalez	1.00
6LA	Ken Griffey Jr.	2.00
7LA	Tony Gwynn	1.50
8LA	Derek Jeter	3.00
9LA	Greg Maddux	1.50
10LA	Pedro Martinez	1.25
11LA	Mark McGwire	2.50
12LA	Mike Piazza	2.00
13LA	Alex Rodriguez	2.50
14LA	Frank Thomas	1.25
15LA	Larry Walker	.50

Quick Strike

This insert pictures players over a colorful die-cut foil-board front.

		NM/M
Complete Set (12):		20.00
Common Player:		.50
Inserted 1:36		
1QS	Jeff Bagwell	2.00
2QS	Roger Clemens	2.75
3QS	Jose Cruz Jr.	.50
4QS	Nomar Garciaparra	2.50
5QS	Ken Griffey Jr.	3.00
6QS	Greg Maddux	2.50
7QS	Pedro Martinez	2.00
8QS	Mark McGwire	4.00
9QS	Mike Piazza	3.00
10QS	Alex Rodriguez	4.00
11QS	Frank Thomas	2.00
12QS	Larry Walker	.50

Rave Reviews

Rave Reviews cards are die-cut in a horizontal design with bronze foil etching and the image of a ballfield in the background.

		NM/M
Complete Set (15):		100.00
Common Player:		2.00
Inserted 1:288		
1RR	Jeff Bagwell	5.00
2RR	Barry Bonds	15.00
3RR	Roger Clemens	7.50
4RR	Jose Cruz Jr.	2.00
5RR	Nomar Garciaparra	6.00
6RR	Juan Gonzalez	3.50
7RR	Ken Griffey Jr.	10.00
8RR	Tony Gwynn	6.00
9RR	Derek Jeter	15.00
10RR	Greg Maddux	6.00
11RR	Mark McGwire	12.50
12RR	Mike Piazza	10.00
13RR	Alex Rodriguez	12.50
14RR	Frank Thomas	5.00
15RR	Larry Walker	1.50

Thunder Boomers

Thunder Boomers feature top power hitters imposed over a see-through cloud-like plastic center with the imagery of a wooden fence with a large hole blasted through the middle of it.

		NM/M
Complete Set (12):		50.00
Common Player:		1.50
Inserted 1:96		
1TB	Jeff Bagwell	6.00
2TB	Barry Bonds	1.50
3TB	Jay Buhner	1.50
4TB	Andres Galarraga	1.50
5TB	Juan Gonzalez	3.00
6TB	Ken Griffey Jr.	7.50
7TB	Tino Martinez	1.50
8TB	Mark McGwire	9.00
9TB	Mike Piazza	7.50
10TB	Frank Thomas	6.00
11TB	Jim Thome	4.50
12TB	Larry Walker	1.50

1985 Circle K

Produced by Topps for Circle K stores, this set is titled "Baseball All Time Home Run Kings." The 2-1/2" x 3-1/2" cards are numbered on the back according to the player's position on the all-time career home run list. Joe DiMaggio, who ranked 31st, was not included in the set. Glossy card fronts generally feature a color photo, although black-and-whites were utilized for a few of the homer kings who played before 1960. Backs have blue and red print on white stock and contain the player's career batting statistics. The set was issued in a specially designed box.

		NM/M
Complete Set (33):		5.00
Common Player:		.10
1	Hank Aaron	1.25
2	Babe Ruth	2.00
3	Willie Mays	1.25
4	Frank Robinson	.15
5	Harmon Killebrew	.15
6	Mickey Mantle	2.50
7	Jimmie Foxx	.15
8	Willie McCovey	.15
9	Ted Williams	1.25
10	Ernie Banks	.30
11	Eddie Mathews	.15
12	Mel Ott	.15
13	Reggie Jackson	.60
14	Lou Gehrig	1.25
15	Stan Musial	.25
16	Willie Stargell	.15
17	Carl Yastrzemski	.25
18	Billy Williams	.15
19	Mike Schmidt	.60
20	Duke Snider	.30
21	Al Kaline	.25
22	Johnny Bench	.25

23	Frank Howard	.15
24	Orlando Cepeda	.15
25	Norm Cash	.15
26	Dave Kingman	.15
27	Rocky Colavito	.15
28	Tony Perez	.15
29	Gil Hodges	.30
30	Ralph Kiner	.15
32	Johnny Mize	.15
33	Yogi Berra	.30
34	Lee May	.15

1993 City Pride Roberto Clemente

Roberto Clemente

To assist in the building of the statue of Roberto Clemente which was unveiled at Three Rivers Stadium during All-Star festivities in 1994, Pittsburgh's City Pride bakery contributed a portion of sales proceeds from a special run of bread loaves featuring Roberto Clemente cards. The cards came in a special plastic pouch within the bread wrapper to protect them from stains. The wrapper itself included a portrait of Clemente and details of the statue project. The 2-1/2" x 3-1/2" cards featured sepia-toned or color photos of Clemente inside black and gold borders. A color team logo appears in the lower-right corner with his name in an orange stripe at the bottom of the photo. Backs are in black-and-white and contain a narrative of Clemente's career, with one card containing his lifetime stats. The unnumbered cards are checklisted here in chronological order.

		NM/M
Complete Set (6):		6.00
Common Card:		1.50
(1)	Roberto Clemente/Btg (1934-1958, sepia photo)	1.50
(2)	Roberto Clemente/Btg (1960-1966, color photo)	1.50
(3)	Roberto Clemente (1971-1972, running to first base)	1.50
(4)	Roberto Clemente/Portrait (1972-1973)	1.50
(5)	Roberto Clemente (Fielding records, kneeling with one bat.)	1.50
(6)	Roberto Clemente (Batting record, kneeling with five bats.)	1.50

1993 Clark Candy Reggie Jackson

The reintroduction of the "Reggie" candy bar by the Clark company was accompanied by a three-card set highlighting his career produced by Upper Deck. One card was found in each candy bar. Cards have a color photo of Jackson on front, on which uniform logos have been removed. Backs have an equipment montage and a paragraph about the slugger. Clark

and UD logos appear on front, with an UD hologram on back. A limited number (200) of autographed cards were randomly inserted.

		NM/M
Complete Set (3):		3.00
Common Player:		1.00
Autographed Card:		75.00
C1	Reggie Jackson (Hall of Fame, 1993)	1.00
C2	Reggie Jackson (Mr. October, 1977)	1.00
C3	Reggie Jackson (A.L. MVP, 1973)	1.00

1987 Classic Major League Baseball Game

Pete Rose

The "Classic Major League Baseball Board Game" set consists of 100 full-color cards used to play the game in which participants answer trivia questions found on the card backs. Cards measure 2-1/2" x 3-1/2" and are printed on semi-gloss stock. Backs carry the player's career stats besides the trivia questions. The game was produced by Game Time, Ltd. of Marietta, Ga., and sold for $19.95 in most retail outlets. In 1991-92 the set was selling for $200 or more, with the Bo Jackson card advertised as high as $80.

		NM/M
Complete Boxed Set:		25.00
Complete Set (100):		20.00
Common Player:		.05
1	Pete Rose	2.00
2	Len Dykstra	.05
3	Darryl Strawberry	.05
4	Keith Hernandez	.05
5	Gary Carter	.65
6	Wally Joyner	.05
7	Andres Thomas	.05
8	Pat Dodson	.05
9	Kirk Gibson	.05
10	Don Mattingly	1.00
11	Dave Winfield	.65
12	Rickey Henderson	.65
13	Dan Pasqua	.05
14	Don Baylor	.05
15	Bo Jackson	2.50
16	Pete Incaviglia	.05
17	Kevin Bass	.05
18	Barry Larkin	.05
19	Dave Magadan	.05
20	Steve Sax	.05
21	Eric Davis	.05
22	Mike Pagliarulo	.05
23	Fred Lynn	.05
24	Reggie Jackson	1.00
25	Larry Parrish	.05
26	Tony Gwynn	.75
27	Steve Garvey	.20
28	Glenn Davis	.05
29	Tim Raines	.05
30	Vince Coleman	.05
31	Willie McGee	.05
32	Ozzie Smith	.75
33	Dave Parker	.05
34	Tony Pena	.05
35	Ryne Sandberg	.75
36	Brett Butler	.05
37	Dale Murphy	.25
38	Bob Horner	.05
39	Pedro Guerrero	.05
40	Brook Jacoby	.05
41	Carlton Fisk	.65
42	Harold Baines	.05
43	Rob Deer	.05
44	Robin Yount	.65
45	Paul Molitor	.65
46	Jose Canseco	.50
47	George Brett	1.00
48	Jim Presley	.05
49	Rich Gedman	.05
50	Lance Parrish	.05
51	Eddie Murray	.65
52	Cal Ripken, Jr.	3.00
53	Kent Hrbek	.05
54	Gary Gaetti	.05
55	Kirby Puckett	.75
56	George Bell	.05
57	Tony Fernandez	.05
58	Jesse Barfield	.05

59	Jim Rice	.25
60	Wade Boggs	.75
61	Marty Barrett	.05
62	Mike Schmidt	1.00
63	Von Hayes	.05
64	Jeff Leonard	.05
65	Chris Brown	.05
66	Dave Smith	.05
67	Mike Krukow	.05
68	Ron Guidry	.05
69	Rob Woodward (Photo actually Pat Dodson.)	
70	Rob Murphy	.05
71	Andres Galarraga	.05
72	Dwight Gooden	.05
73	Bob Ojeda	.05
74	Sid Fernandez	.05
75	Jesse Orosco	.05
76	Roger McDowell	.05
77	John Tutor (Tudor)	.05
78	Tom Browning	.05
79	Rick Aguilera	.05
80	Lance McCullers	.05
81	Mike Scott	.05
82	Nolan Ryan	3.00
83	Bruce Hurst	.05
84	Roger Clemens	1.00
85	Oil Can Boyd	.05
86	Dave Righetti	.05
87	Dennis Rasmussen	.05
88	Bret Saberhagen (Saberhagen)	.05
89	Mark Langston	.05
90	Jack Morris	.05
91	Fernando Valenzuela	.05
92	Orel Hershiser	.05
93	Rick Honeycutt	.05
94	Jeff Reardon	.05
95	John Habyan	.05
96	Goose Gossage	.05
97	Todd Worrell	.05
98	Floyd Youmans	.05
99	Don Aase	.05
100	John Franco	.05

1987 Classic Travel Update (Yellow)

B.J. Surhoff

Game Time, Ltd. of Marietta, Ga., issued as an update to its Classic Baseball Board Game a 50-card set entitled "Travel Edition." Cards measure 2-1/2" x 3-1/2" in the same format as the first release, except with yellow, rather than green, borders. Numbered from 101 to 150, the "Travel Edition," besides updating player trades and showcasing rookies, offers several highlights from the 1987 season. All new trivia questions are found on the card backs. It was reported that about 50,000 of the set's 150,000 press run was mistakenly printed with green, rather than yellow backs; the green-back errors sell for a premium.

		NM/M
Complete Set (50):		15.00
Common Player:		.05
Green-backs:		1.5X
101	Mike Schmidt	.75
102	Eric Davis	.05
103	Pete Rose	1.50
104	Don Mattingly	.75
105	Wade Boggs	.60
106	Dale Murphy	.20
107	Glenn Davis	.05
108	Wally Joyner	.05
109	Bo Jackson	.15
110	Cory Snyder	.05
111	Jim Lindeman	.05
112	Kirby Puckett	.60
113	Barry Bonds	10.00
114	Roger Clemens	.75
115	Oddibe McDowell	.05
116	Bret Saberhagen	.05
117	Joe Magrane	.05
118	Scott Fletcher	.05
119	Mark McLemore	.05
120	Who Me? (Joe Niekro)	.25
121	Mark McGwire	2.00
122	Darryl Strawberry	.05
123	Mike Scott	.05
124	Andre Dawson	.20
125	Jose Canseco	.50

126	Kevin McReynolds	.05
127	Joe Carter	.05
128	Casey Candaele	.05
129	Matt Nokes	.05
130	Kal Daniels	.05
131	Pete Incaviglia	.05
132	Benito Santiago	.05
133	Barry Larkin	.05
134	Gary Pettis	.05
135	B.J. Surhoff	.05
136	Juan Nieves	.05
137	Jim Deshaies	.05
138	Pete O'Brien	.05
139	Kevin Seitzer	.05
140	Devon White	.05
141	Rob Deer	.05
142	Kurt Stillwell	.05
143	Edwin Correa	.05
144	Dion James	.05
145	Danny Tartabull	.05
146	Jerry Browne	.05
147	Ted Higuera	.05
148	Jack Clark	.05
149	Ruben Sierra	.05
150	Mark McGwire, Eric Davis	.60

1988 Classic Travel Update 1 (Red)

Phil Niekro

This set was produced for use with the travel edition of Game Time's Classic Baseball Board Game. Special cards in the set include a McGwire/Mattingly, an instruction card with McGwire/Canseco and three different cards featuring Phil Niekro (in different uniforms). Update I card fronts have red borders, a yellow Classic logo in the upper-left corner and a black and beige name banner beneath the photo. Backs are printed in red and pink on white and include the player name, personal info, major league records, a baseball question and space for the player autograph. Classic card series sold via hobby dealers and retail toy stores nationwide. Game Time Ltd., the set's producer, was purchased by Scoreboard of Cherry Hill, N.J. in 1988.

		NM/M
Complete Set (50):		4.00
Common Player:		.05
151	Don Mattingly, Mark McGwire	.45
152	Don Mattingly	.65
153	Mark McGwire	1.00
154	Eric Davis	.05
155	Wade Boggs	.50
156	Dale Murphy	.15
157	Andre Dawson	.15
158	Roger Clemens	.65
159	Kevin Seitzer	.05
160	Benito Santiago	.05
161	Kal Daniels	.05
162	John Kruk	.05
163	Bill Ripken	.05
164	Kirby Puckett	.50
165	Jose Canseco	.30
166	Matt Nokes	.05
167	Mike Schmidt	.60
168	Tim Raines	.05
169	Ryne Sandberg	.50
170	Dave Winfield	.40
171	Dwight Gooden	.05
172	Bret Saberhagen	.05
173	Willie McGee	.05
174	Jack Morris	.05
175	Jeff Leonard	.05
176	Cal Ripken, Jr.	1.50
177	Pete Incaviglia	.05
178	Devon White	.05
179	Nolan Ryan	1.50
180	Ruben Sierra	.05
181	Todd Worrell	.05
182	Glenn Davis	.05
183	Frank Viola	.05
184	Cory Snyder	.05
185	Tracy Jones	.05
186	Terry Steinbach	.05
187	Julio Franco	.05
188	Larry Sheets	.05
189	John Marzano	.05
190	Kevin Elster	.05
191	Vincente Palacios	.05

192	Kent Hrbek	.05
193	Eric Bell	.05
194	Kelly Downs	.05
195	Jose Lind	.05
196	Dave Stewart	.05
197	Jose Canseco, Mark McGwire	.45
198	Phil Niekro	.10
199	Phil Niekro	.10
200	Phil Niekro	.10

1988 Classic Travel Update 2 (Blue)

Darryl Strawberry

This set was produced for use with the travel edition of Game Time's Classic Baseball Board Game. Fronts have blue borders, a yellow Classic logo in the upper-left corner and a black and beige name banner beneath the photo. Backs are printed in blue on white and include the player name, personal info, major league records, a baseball question and space for the player autograph. Classic card series are sold via hobby dealers and retail toy stores nationwide. Game Time Ltd., the set's producer, was purchased by Scoreboard of Cherry Hill, N.J. in 1988.

		NM/M
Complete Set (50):		4.00
Common Player:		.05
201	Dale Murphy, Eric Davis	.10
202	B.J. Surhoff	.05
203	John Kruk	.05
204	Sam Horn	.05
205	Jack Clark	.05
206	Wally Joyner	.05
207	Matt Nokes	.05
208	Bo Jackson	.10
209	Darryl Strawberry	.05
210	Ozzie Smith	.60
211	Don Mattingly	.75
212	Mark McGwire	1.50
213	Eric Davis	.05
214	Wade Boggs	.05
215	Dale Murphy	.25
216	Andre Dawson	.25
217	Roger Clemens	.75
218	Kevin Seitzer	.05
219	Benito Santiago	.05
220	Tony Gwynn	.60
221	Mike Scott	.05
222	Steve Bedrosian	.05
223	Vince Coleman	.05
224	Rick Sutcliffe	.05
225	Will Clark	.05
226	Pete Rose	1.00
227	Mike Greenwell	.05
228	Ken Caminiti	.05
229	Ellis Burks	.05
230	Dave Magadan	.05
231	Alan Trammell	.05
232	Paul Molitor	.50
233	Gary Gaetti	.05
234	Rickey Henderson	.50
235	Danny Tartabull	.05
236	Bobby Bonilla	.05
237	Mike Dunne	.05
238	Al Leiter	.05
239	John Farrell	.05
240	Joe Magrane	.05
241	Mike Henneman	.05
242	George Bell	.05
243	Gregg Jefferies	.10
244	Jay Buhner	.05
245	Todd Benzinger	.05
246	Matt Williams	.05
(247)	Don Mattingly, Mark McGwire (No card number on back.)	.50
248	George Brett	.50
249	Jimmy Key	.05
250	Mark Langston	.05

1989 Classic

This 100-card set was released by The Score Board to accompany trivia board games. Fronts have a wide border which graduates from pink at the top to blue at the bottom. Card backs are printed in blue. The flip

David Cone

side includes personal information, and major league record in a boxed area. Another boxed area below the record presents five trivia questions. The lower border on back provides an autograph space. The Classic card series was sold by retail stores and hobby dealers nationwide.

		NM/M
Complete Set (100):		6.00
Common Player:		.05
1	Orel Hershiser	.05
2	Wade Boggs	.50
3	Jose Canseco	.30
4	Mark McGwire	1.00
5	Don Mattingly	.60
6	Gregg Jefferies	.05
7	Dwight Gooden	.05
8	Darryl Strawberry	.05
9	Eric Davis	.05
10	Joey Meyer	.05
11	Joe Carter	.05
12	Paul Molitor	.40
13	Mark Grace	.05
14	Kurt Stillwell	.05
15	Kirby Puckett	.50
16	Keith Miller	.05
17	Glenn Davis	.05
18	Will Clark	.05
19	Cory Snyder	.05
20	Jose Lind	.05
21	Andres Thomas	.05
22	Dave Smith	.05
23	Mike Scott	.05
24	Kevin McReynolds	.05
25	B.J. Surhoff	.05
26	Mackey Sasser	.05
27	Chad Kreuter	.05
28	Hal Morris	.05
29	Wally Joyner	.05
30	Tony Gwynn	.50
31	Kevin Mitchell	.05
32	Dave Winfield	.40
33	Billy Bean	.05
34	Steve Bedrosian	.05
35	Ron Gant	.05
36	Len Dykstra	.05
37	Andre Dawson	.25
38	Brett Butler	.05
39	Rob Deer	.05
40	Tommy John	.05
41	Gary Gaetti	.05
42	Tim Raines	.05
43	George Bell	.05
44	Dwight Evans	.05
45	Denny Martinez	.05
46	Andres Galarraga	.05
47	George Brett	.60
48	Mike Schmidt	.60
49	Dave Steib	.05
50	Rickey Henderson	.40
51	Craig Biggio	.05
52	Mark Lemke	.05
53	Chris Sabo	.05
54	Jeff Treadway	.05
55	Kent Hrbek	.05
56	Cal Ripken, Jr.	1.50
57	Tim Belcher	.05
58	Ozzie Smith	.50
59	Keith Hernandez	.05
60	Pedro Guerrero	.05
61	Greg Swindell	.05
62	Bret Saberhagen	.05
63	John Tudor	.05
64	Gary Carter	.40
65	Kevin Seitzer	.05
66	Jesse Barfield	.05
67	Luis Medina	.05
68	Walt Weiss	.05
69	Terry Steinbach	.05
70	Barry Larkin	.05
71	Pete Rose	.75
72	Luis Salazar	.05
73	Benito Santiago	.05
74	Kal Daniels	.05
75	Kevin Elster	.05
76	Rob Dibble	.05
77	Bobby Witt	.05
78	Steve Searcy	.05
79	Sandy Alomar (Photo is Roberto Alomar.)	.05
80	Chili Davis	.05
81	Alvin Davis	.05
82	Charlie Leibrandt	.05
83	Robin Yount	.40
84	Mark Carreon	.05

85	Pascual Perez	.05
86	Dennis Rasmussen	.05
87	Ernie Riles	.05
88	Melido Perez	.05
89	Doug Jones	.05
90	Dennis Eckersley	.35
91	Bob Welch	.05
92	Bob Milacki	.05
93	Jeff Robinson	.05
94	Mike Henneman	.05
95	Randy Johnson	1.00
96	Ron Jones	.05
97	Jack Armstrong	.05
98	Willie McGee	.05
99	Ryne Sandberg	.50
100	David Cone, Danny Jackson	.05

1989 Classic Travel Update 1 (Orange)

Roberto Alomar

Sold only as a 50-card complete set under the official name of "Travel Update I," these cards are identical in format to the 1989 Classic 100-card set with the exception that the borders are orange at the top, graduating to maroon at the bottom. Backs are maroon.

		NM/M
Complete Set (50):		5.00
Common Player:		.05
101	Gary Sheffield	.25
102	Wade Boggs	.50
103	Jose Canseco	.30
104	Mark McGwire	1.00
105	Orel Hershiser	.05
106	Don Mattingly	.60
107	Dwight Gooden	.05
108	Darryl Strawberry	.05
109	Eric Davis	.05
110	Bam Bam Meulens	.05
111	Andy Van Slyke	.05
112	Al Leiter	.05
113	Matt Nokes	.05
114	Mike Krukow	.05
115	Tony Fernandez	.05
116	Fred McGriff	.05
117	Barry Bonds	1.50
118	Gerald Perry	.05
119	Roger Clemens	.60
120	Kirk Gibson	.05
121	Greg Maddux	.50
122	Bo Jackson	.10
123	Danny Jackson	.05
124	Dale Murphy	.20
125	David Cone	.05
126	Tom Browning	.05
127	Roberto Alomar	.25
128	Alan Trammell	.05
129	Ricky Jordan	.05
130	Ramon Martinez	.05
131	Ken Griffey Jr.	3.00
132	Gregg Olson	.05
133	Carlos Quintana	.05
134	Dave West	.05
135	Cameron Drew	.05
136	Ted Higuera	.05
137	Sil Campusano	.05
138	Mark Gubicza	.05
139	Mike Boddicker	.05
140	Paul Gibson	.05
141	Jose Rijo	.05
142	John Costello	.05
143	Cecil Espy	.05
144	Frank Viola	.05
145	Erik Hanson	.05
146	Juan Samuel	.05
147	Harold Reynolds	.05
148	Joe Magrane	.05
149	Mike Greenwell	.05
150	Darryl Strawberry, Will Clark	.05

1989 Classic Travel Update 2 (Purple)

Numbered from 151-200, this set features rookies and traded players with their new teams. The cards are purple and gray and were sold as part of a board game with baseball trivia questions.

		NM/M
Complete Set (50):		5.00
Common Player:		.05
151	Jim Abbott	

Jerome Walton

152	Ellis Burks	.05
153	Mike Schmidt	.75
154	Gregg Jefferies	.05
155	Mark Grace	.05
156	Jerome Walton	.05
157	Bo Jackson	.10
158	Jack Clark	.05
159	Tom Glavine	.20
160	Eddie Murray	.45
161	John Dopson	.05
162	Ruben Sierra	.05
163	Rafael Palmeiro	.40
164	Nolan Ryan	1.50
165	Barry Larkin	.05
166	Tommy Herr	.05
167	Roberto Kelly	.05
168	Glenn Davis	.05
169	Glenn Braggs	.05
170	Juan Bell	.05
171	Todd Burns	.05
172	Derek Lilliquist	.05
173	Orel Hershiser	.05
174	John Smoltz	.05
175	Ozzie Guillen, Ellis Burks	.05
176	Kirby Puckett	.60
177	Robin Ventura	.05
178	Allan Anderson	.05
179	Steve Sax	.05
180	Will Clark	.05
181	Mike Devereaux	.05
182	Tom Gordon	.05
183	Rob Murphy	.05
184	Pete O'Brien	.05
185	Cris Carpenter	.05
186	Tom Brunansky	.05
187	Bob Boone	.05
188	Lou Whitaker	.05
189	Dwight Gooden	.05
190	Mark McGwire	1.00
191	John Smiley	.05
192	Tommy Gregg	.05
193	Ken Griffey Jr.	3.00
194	Bruce Hurst	.05
195	Greg Swindell	.05
196	Nelson Liriano	.05
197	Randy Myers	.05
198	Kevin Mitchell	.05
199	Dante Bichette	.05
200	Deion Sanders	.10

1990 Classic

Ozzie Smith

Classic baseball returned in 1990 with a 150-card set. Cards have a blue border on front, with splashes of pink. The cards were again sold as part of a baseball trivia game.

		NM/M
Complete Set (150):		4.00
Common Player:		.05
1	Nolan Ryan	1.00
2	Bo Jackson	.10
3	Gregg Olson	.05
4	Tom Gordon	.05
5	Robin Ventura	.05
6	Will Clark	.05
7	Ruben Sierra	.05
8	Mark Grace	.05
9	Luis de los Santos	.05
10	Bernie Williams	.05
11	Eric Davis	.05
12	Carney Lansford	.05
13	John Smoltz	.05
14	Gary Sheffield	.20
15	Kent Merker	.05
16	Don Mattingly	.60
17	Tony Gwynn	.50
18	Ozzie Smith	.50
19	Fred McGriff	.05
20	Ken Griffey Jr.	.65

21a	Deion Sanders ("Prime Time")	.30
21b	Deion Sanders (Deion "Prime Time" Sanders)	.15
22	Jose Canseco	.25
23	Mitch Williams	.05
24	Cal Ripken, Jr.	1.00
25	Bob Geren	.05
26	Wade Boggs	.05
27	Ryne Sandberg	.50
28	Kirby Puckett	.50
29	Mike Scott	.05
30	Dwight Smith	.05
31	Craig Worthington	.05
32	Ricky Jordan	.05
33	Darryl Strawberry	.05
34	Jerome Walton	.05
35	John Olerud	.05
36	Tom Glavine	.15
37	Rickey Henderson	.30
38	Rolando Roomes	.05
39	Mickey Tettleton	.05
40	Jim Abbott	.05
41	Dave Righetti	.05
42	Mike LaValliere	.05
43	Rob Dibble	.05
44	Pete Harnisch	.05
45	Jose Offerman	.05
46	Walt Weiss	.05
47	Mike Greenwell	.05
48	Barry Larkin	.05
49	Dave Gallagher	.05
50	Junior Felix	.05
51	Roger Clemens	.60
52	Lonnie Smith	.05
53	Jerry Browne	.05
54	Greg Briley	.05
55	Delino DeShields	.05
56	Carmelo Martinez	.05
57	Craig Biggio	.05
58	Dwight Gooden	.05
59a	Bo, Ruben, Mark (Bo Jackson, Ruben Sierra, Mark McGwire)	.25
59b	A.L. Fence Busters (Bo Jackson, Ruben Sierra, Mark McGwire)	.15
60	Greg Vaughn	.05
61	Roberto Alomar	.20
62	Steve Bedrosian	.05
63	Devon White	.05
64	Kevin Mitchell	.05
65	Marquis Grissom	.05
66	Brian Holman	.05
67	Julio Franco	.05
68	Dave West	.05
69	Harold Baines	.05
70	Eric Anthony	.05
71	Glenn Davis	.05
72	Mark Langston	.05
73	Matt Williams	.05
74	Rafael Palmeiro	.05
75	Pete Rose, Jr.	.25
76	Ramon Martinez	.05
77	Dwight Evans	.05
78	Mackey Sasser	.05
79	Mike Schooler	.05
80	Dennis Cook	.05
81	Orel Hershiser	.05
82	Barry Bonds	1.00
83	Geronimo Berroa	.05
84	George Bell	.05
85	Andre Dawson	.25
86	John Franco	.05
87a	Clark/Gwynn (Will Clark, Tony Gwynn)	.25
87b	N.L. Hit Kings (Will Clark, Tony Gwynn)	.15
88	Glenallen Hill	.05
89	Jeff Ballard	.05
90	Todd Zeile	.05
91	Frank Viola	.05
92	Ozzie Guillen	.05
93	Jeff Leonard	.05
94	Dave Smith	.05
95	Dave Parker	.05
96	Jose Gonzalez	.05
97	Dave Steib	.05
98	Charlie Hayes	.05
99	Jesse Barfield	.05
100	Joey Belle	.15
101	Jeff Reardon	.05
102	Bruce Hurst	.05
103	Luis Medina	.05
104	Mike Moore	.05
105	Vince Coleman	.05
106	Alan Trammell	.05
107	Randy Myers	.05
108	Frank Tanana	.05
109	Craig Lefferts	.05
110	John Wetteland	.05
111	Chris Gwynn	.05
112	Mark Carreon	.05
113	Von Hayes	.05
114	Doug Jones	.05
115	Andres Galarraga	.05
116	Carlton Fisk	.30
117	Paul O'Neill	.05
118	Tim Raines	.05
119	Tom Brunansky	.05
120	Andy Benes	.05
121	Mark Portugal	.05
122	Willie Randolph	.05
123	Jeff Blauser	.05
124	Don August	.05
125	Chuck Cary	.05
126	John Smiley	.05
127	Terry Mullholland	.05

128	Harold Reynolds	.05
129	Hubie Brooks	.05
130	Ben McDonald	.05
131	Kevin Ritz	.05
132	Luis Quinones	.05
133a	Bam Bam Meulens (Last name incorrect.)	.25
133b	Bam Bam Meulens (Last name correct.)	.05
134	Bill Spiers	.05
135	Andy Hawkins	.05
136	Alvin Davis	.05
137	Lee Smith	.05
138	Joe Carter	.05
139	Bret Saberhagen	.05
140	Sammy Sosa	1.00
141	Matt Nokes	.05
142	Bert Blyleven	.05
143	Bobby Bonilla	.05
144	Howard Johnson	.05
145	Joe Magrane	.05
146	Pedro Guerrero	.05
147	Robin Yount	.30
148	Dan Gladden	.05
149	Steve Sax	.05
150a	Clark/Mitchell (Will Clark, Kevin Mitchell)	.05
150b	Bay Bombers (Will Clark, Kevin Mitchell)	.25

1990 Classic Series 2

Juan Gonzalez

As in previous years, Classic released a 50-card second series set for use with its trivia board game. Unlike earlier update sets, the 1990 Series II set is numbered 1-50 with a "T" designation accompanying the card number. Cards measure 2-1/2" x 3-1/2" and share the format of the original 1990 Classic cards; Series II cards have pink borders with blue highlights. The cards were issued only in complete set form.

		NM/M
Complete Set (50):		3.00
Common Player:		.05
1	Gregg Jefferies	.05
2	Steve Adkins	.05
3	Sandy Alomar, Jr.	.05
4	Steve Avery	.05
5	Mike Blowers	.05
6	George Brett	.75
7	Tom Browning	.05
8	Ellis Burks	.05
9	Joe Carter	.05
10	Jerald Clark	.05
11	"Hot Corners" (Matt Williams, Will Clark)	.10
12	Pat Combs	.05
13	Scott Cooper	.05
14	Mark Davis	.05
15	Storm Davis	.05
16	Larry Walker	.05
17	Brian DuBois	.05
18	Len Dykstra	.05
19	John Franco	.05
20	Kirk Gibson	.05
21	Juan Gonzalez	.20
22	Tommy Greene	.05
23	Kent Hrbek	.05
24	Mike Huff	.05
25	Bo Jackson	.10
26	Nolan Knows Bo (Bo Jackson, Nolan Ryan)	1.50
27	Roberto Kelly	.05
28	Mark Langston	.05
29	Ray Lankford	.05
30	Kevin Maas	.05
31	Julio Machado	.05
32	Greg Maddux	.60
33	Mark McGwire	1.00
34	Paul Molitor	.40
35	Hal Morris	.05
36	Dale Murphy	.05
37	Eddie Murray	.40
38	Jaime Navarro	.05
39	Dean Palmer	.05
40	Derek Parks	.05
41	Bobby Rose	.05
42	Wally Joyner	.05
43	Chris Sabo	.05
44	Benito Santiago	.05
45	Mike Stanton	.05
46	Terry Steinbach	.05

47	Dave Stewart	.05
48	Greg Swindell	.05
49	Jose Vizcaino	.05
---	"Royal Flush" (Bret Saberhagen, Mark Davis)	

1990 Classic Series 3

Scott Coolbaugh

Classic's third series of 1990 features the same format as the previous two releases. Series 3 borders are yellow with blue accents. The cards have trivia questions on back and are numbered 1T-100T. No card 51T or 57T exists. Two cards in the set are unnumbered. Like other Classic issues, the cards are designed for use with the trivia board game and were sold only as complete sets.

		NM/M
Complete Set (100):		4.00
Common Player:		.05
1	Ken Griffey Jr.	.75
2	John Tudor	.05
3	John Kruk	.05
4	Mark Gardner	.05
5	Scott Radinsky	.05
6	John Burkett	.05
7	Will Clark	.05
8	Gary Carter	.40
9	Ted Higuera	.05
10	Dave Parker	.05
11	Dante Bichette	.05
12	Don Mattingly	.60
13	Greg Harris	.05
14	David Hollins	.05
15	Matt Nokes	.05
16	Kevin Tapani	.05
17	Shane Mack	.05
18	Randy Myers	.05
19	Greg Olson	.05
20	Shawn Abner	.05
21	Jim Presley	.05
22	Randy Johnson	.40
23	Edgar Martinez	.05
24	Scott Coolbaugh	.05
25	Jeff Treadway	.05
26	Joe Klink	.05
27	Rickey Henderson	.40
28	Sam Horn	.05
29	Kurt Stillwell	.05
30	Andy Van Slyke	.05
31	Willie Banks	.05
32	Jose Canseco	.35
33	Felix Jose	.05
34	Candy Maldonado	.05
35	Carlos Baerga	.05
36	Keith Hernandez	.05
37	Frank Viola	.05
38	Pete O'Brien	.05
39	Pat Borders	.05
40	Mike Heath	.05
41	Kevin Brown	.05
42	Chris Bosio	.05
43	Shawn Boskie	.05
44	Carlos Quintana	.05
45	Juan Samuel	.05
46	Tim Layana	.05
47	Mike Harkey	.05
48	Gerald Perry	.05
49	Mike Witt	.05
50	Joe Orsulak	.05
52	Willie Blair	.05
53	Gene Larkin	.05
54	Jody Reed	.05
55	Jeff Reardon	.05
56	Kevin McReynolds	.05
57	Eric Yelding	.05
58	Fred Lynn	.05
59	Jim Leyritz	.05
60	John Orton	.05
61	Mike Lieberthal	.05
62	Mike Hartley	.05
63	Kal Daniels	.05
64	Terry Shumpert	.05
65	Sil Campusano	.05
66	Tony Pena	.05
67	Barry Bonds	1.00
68	Oddibe McDowell	.05
69	Kelly Gruber	.05
70	Willie Randolph	.05
71	Rick Parker	.05
72	Bobby Bonilla	.05
73	Jack Armstrong	.05
74	Hubie Brooks	.05
75	Hubie Brooks	.05

76	Sandy Alomar, Jr.	.05
77	Ruben Sierra	.05
78	Erik Hanson	.05
79	Tony Phillips	.05
80	Rondell White	.05
81	Bobby Thigpen	.05
82	Ron Walden	.05
83	Don Peters	.05
84	#6 (Nolan Ryan)	1.00
85	Lance Dickson	.05
86	Ryne Sandberg	.60
87	Eric Christopherson	.05
88	Shane Andrews	.05
89	Marc Newfield	.05
90	Adam Hyzdu	.05
91	"Texas Heat" (Nolan Ryan, Reid Ryan)	1.00
92	Chipper Jones	.75
93	Frank Thomas	.75
94	Cecil Fielder	.05
95	Delino DeShields	.05
96	John Olerud	.05
97	Dave Justice	.05
98	Joe Oliver	.05
99	Alex Fernandez	.05
100	Todd Hundley	.05
---	Mike Marshall (Game instructions on back.)	.05
---	4 in 1 (Frank Viola, Nolan/Reid Ryan, Chipper Jones, Don Mattingly)	.50

1991 Classic

Top rookies and draft picks highlight this set from Classic. The cards come with a trivia board game and accessories. Fronts have fading blue borders with a touch of red. A blank-back "4-in-1" micro-player card is included with each game set.

		NM/M
Complete Set (99):		4.00
Common Player:		.05
1	John Olerud	.05
2	Tino Martinez	.05
3	Ken Griffey Jr.	.65
4	Jeromy Burnitz	.05
5	Ron Gant	.05
6	Mike Benjamin	.05
7	Steve Decker	.05
8	Matt Williams	.05
9	Rafael Novoa	.05
10	Kevin Mitchell	.05
11	Dave Justice	.05
12	Leo Gomez	.05
13	Chris Hoiles	.05
14	Ben McDonald	.05
15	David Segui	.05
16	Anthony Telford	.05
17	Mike Mussina	.30
18	Roger Clemens	.60
19	Wade Boggs	.50
20	Tim Naehring	.05
21	Joe Carter	.05
22	Phil Plantier	.05
23	Rob Dibble	.05
24	Mo Vaughn	.05
25	Lee Stevens	.05
26	Chris Sabo	.05
27	Mark Grace	.05
28	Derrick May	.05
29	Ryne Sandberg	.50
30	Matt Stark	.05
31	Bobby Thigpen	.05
32	Frank Thomas	.40
33	Don Mattingly	.60
34	Eric Davis	.05
35	Reggie Jefferson	.05
36	Alex Cole	.05
37	Mark Lewis	.05
38	Tim Costo	.05
39	Sandy Alomar, Jr.	.05
40	Travis Fryman	.05
41	Cecil Fielder	.05
42	Milt Cuyler	.05
43	Andujar Cedeno	.05
44	Danny Darwin	.05
45	Randy Henis	.05
46	George Brett	.60
47	Jeff Conine	.05
48	Bo Jackson	.10
49	Brian McRae	.05
50	Brent Mayne	.05
51	Eddie Murray	.40

52	Ramon Martinez	.05
53	Jim Neidlinger	.05
54	Jim Poole	.05
55	Tim McIntosh	.05
56	Randy Veres	.05
57	Kirby Puckett	.50
58	Todd Ritchie	.05
59	Rich Garces	.05
60	Moises Alou	.05
61	Delino DeShields	.05
62	Oscar Azocar	.05
63	Kevin Maas	.05
64	Alan Mills	.05
65	John Franco	.05
66	Chris Jelic	.05
67	Dave Magadan	.05
68	Darryl Strawberry	.05
69	Hensley Meulens	.05
70	Juan Gonzalez	.20
71	Reggie Harris	.05
72	Rickey Henderson	.40
73	Mark McGwire	.75
74	Willie McGee	.05
75	Todd Van Poppel	.05
76	Bob Welch	.05
77	"Future Aces" (Todd Van Poppel, Don Peters, David Zancanaro, Kirk Dressendorfer)	.05
78	Lenny Dykstra	.05
79	Mickey Morandini	.05
80	Wes Chamberlain	.05
81	Barry Bonds	1.00
82	Doug Drabek	.05
83	Randy Tomlin	.05
84	Scott Chiamparino	.05
85	Rafael Palmeiro	.35
86	Nolan Ryan	1.00
87	Bobby Witt	.05
88	Fred McGriff	.05
89	Dave Steib	.05
90	Ed Sprague	.05
91	Vince Coleman	.05
92	Rod Brewer	.05
93	Bernard Gilkey	.05
94	Roberto Alomar	.20
95	Chuck Finley	.05
96	Dale Murphy	.20
97	Jose Rijo	.05
98	Hal Morris	.05
99	"Friendly Foes" (Dwight Gooden, Darryl Strawberry)	.25
----	John Olerud, Dwight Gooden, Jose Canseco, Darryl Strawberry	.10

1991 Classic Series 2

Tim Raines

Classic released a 100-card second series in 1991. Cards feature the same format as the first series, with the exception of border color; Series II features maroon borders. The cards are designed for trivia game use. Series II includes several players with new teams and top rookies. Special Four-In-One, 300 Game Winner and Strikeout Kings cards are included with each set.

NM/M
Complete Set (100): 4.50
Common Player: .05

1	Ken Griffey Jr.	.75
2	Wilfredo Cordero	.05
3	Cal Ripken, Jr.	1.00
4	D.J. Dozier	.05
5	Darrin Fletcher	.05
6	Glenn Davis	.05
7	Alex Fernandez	.05
8	Cory Snyder	.05
9	Tim Raines	.05
10	Greg Swindell	.05
11	Mark Lewis	.05
12	Rico Brogna	.05
13	Gary Sheffield	.30
14	Paul Molitor	.50
15	Kent Hrbek	.05
16	Scott Erickson	.05
17	Steve Sax	.05
18	Dennis Eckersley	.40
19	Jose Canseco	.30
20	Kirk Dressendorfer	.05
21	Ken Griffey Sr.	.05
22	Erik Hanson	.05
23	Dan Peltier	.05

24	John Olerud	.05
25	Eddie Zosky	.05
26	Steve Avery	.05
27	John Smoltz	.05
28	Frank Thomas	.50
29	Jerome Walton	.05
30	George Bell	.05
31	Jose Rijo	.05
32	Randy Myers	.05
33	Barry Larkin	.05
34	Eric Anthony	.05
35	Dave Hansen	.05
36	Eric Karros	.05
37	Jose Offerman	.05
38	Marquis Grissom	.05
39	Dwight Gooden	.05
40	Gregg Jefferies	.05
41	Pat Combs	.05
42	Todd Zeile	.05
43	Benito Santiago	.05
44	Dave Staton	.05
45	Tony Fernandez	.05
46	Fred McGriff	.05
47	Jeff Brantley	.05
48	Junior Felix	.05
49	Jack Morris	.05
50	Chris George	.05
51	Henry Rodriguez	.05
52	Paul Marak	.05
53	Ryan Klesko	.05
54	Darren Lewis	.05
55	Lance Dickson	.05
56	Anthony Young	.05
57	Willie Banks	.05
58	Mike Bordick	.05
59	Roger Salkeld	.05
60	Steve Karsay	.05
61	Bernie Williams	.05
62	Mickey Tettleton	.05
63	Dave Justice	.05
64	Steve Decker	.05
65	Roger Clemens	.65
66	Phil Plantier	.05
67	Ryne Sandberg	.60
68	Sandy Alomar, Jr.	.05
69	Cecil Fielder	.05
70	George Brett	.65
71	Delino DeShields	.05
72	Dave Magadan	.05
73	Darryl Strawberry	.05
74	Juan Gonzalez	.25
75	Rickey Henderson	.50
76	Willie McGee	.05
77	Todd Van Poppel	.05
78	Barry Bonds	1.00
79	Doug Drabek	.05
80	Nolan Ryan (300 games)	1.00
81	Roberto Alomar	.20
82	Ivan Rodriguez	.50
83	Dan Opperman	.05
84	Jeff Bagwell	.50
85	Braulio Castillo	.05
86	Doug Simons	.05
87	Wade Taylor	.05
88	Gary Scott	.05
89	Dave Stewart	.05
90	Mike Simms	.05
91	Luis Gonzalez	.05
92	Bobby Bonilla	.05
93	Tony Gwynn	.60
94	Will Clark	.05
95	Rich Rowland	.05
96	Alan Trammell	.05
97	"Strikeout Kings" (Nolan Ryan, Roger Clemens)	.50
98	Joe Carter	.05
99	Jack Clark	.05
100	Four-In-One	.20

1991 Classic Series 3

Tim Salmon

Green borders highlight Classic's third series of cards for 1991. The set includes a gameboard and player cards featuring trivia questions on the back. Statistics and biographical information are also found on back.

NM/M
Complete Set (100): 4.50
Common Player: .05

1	Jim Abbott	.05
2	Craig Biggio	.05
3	Wade Boggs	.45
4	Bobby Bonilla	.05
5	Ivan Calderon	.05
6	Jose Canseco	.25
7	Andy Benes	.05
8	Wes Chamberlain	.05
9	Will Clark	.05
10	Royce Clayton	.05
11	Gerald Alexander	.05
12	Chili Davis	.05
13	Eric Davis	.05
14	Andre Dawson	.25
15	Rob Dibble	.05
16	Chris Donnels	.05
17	Scott Erickson	.05
18	Monty Fariss	.05
19	Ruben Amaro Jr.	.05
20	Chuck Finley	.05
21	Carlton Fisk	.35
22	Carlos Baerga	.05
23	Ron Gant	.05
24	Dave Justice, Ron Gant	.05
25	Mike Gardiner	.05
26	Tom Glavine	.15
27	Joe Grahe	.05
28	Derek Bell	.05
29	Mike Greenwell	.05
30	Ken Griffey Jr.	.75
31	Leo Gomez	.05
32	Tom Goodwin	.05
33	Tony Gwynn	.45
34	Mel Hall	.05
35	Brian Harper	.05
36	Dave Henderson	.05
37	Albert Belle	.05
38	Orel Hershiser	.05
39	Brian Hunter	.05
40	Howard Johnson	.05
41	Felix Jose	.05
42	Wally Joyner	.05
43	Jeff Juden	.05
44	Pat Kelly	.05
45	Jimmy Key	.05
46	Chuck Knoblauch	.05
47	John Kruk	.05
48	Ray Lankford	.05
49	Ced Landrum	.05
50	Scott Livingstone	.05
51	Kevin Maas	.05
52	Greg Maddux	.45
53	Dennis Martinez	.05
54	Edgar Martinez	.05
55	Pedro Martinez	.50
56	Don Mattingly	.50
57	Orlando Merced	.05
58	Keith Mitchell	.05
59	Kevin Mitchell	.05
60	Paul Molitor	.35
61	Jack Morris	.05
62	Hal Morris	.05
63	Kevin Morton	.05
64	Pedro Munoz	.05
65	Eddie Murray	.35
66	Jack McDowell	.05
67	Jeff McNeely	.05
68	Brian McRae	.05
69	Kevin McReynolds	.05
70	Gregg Olson	.05
71	Rafael Palmeiro	.30
72	Dean Palmer	.05
73	Tony Phillips	.05
74	Kirby Puckett	.45
75	Carlos Quintana	.05
76	Pat Rice	.05
77	Cal Ripken, Jr.	1.00
78	Ivan Rodriguez	.30
79	Nolan Ryan	1.00
80	Bret Saberhagen	.05
81	Tim Salmon	.05
82	Juan Samuel	.05
83	Ruben Sierra	.05
84	Heathcliff Slocumb	.05
85	Joe Slusarski	.05
86	John Smiley	.05
87	Dave Smith	.05
88	Ed Sprague	.05
89	Todd Stottlemyre	.05
90	Mike Timlin	.05
91	Greg Vaughn	.05
92	Frank Viola	.05
93	John Wehner	.05
94	Devon White	.05
95	Matt Williams	.05
96	Rick Wilkins	.05
97	Bernie Williams	.05
98	Starter & Stopper (Goose Gossage, Nolan Ryan)	.20
99	Gerald Williams	.05
----	4-in-1 (Bobby Bonilla, Will Clark, Cal Ripken Jr., Scott Erickson)	.25

1991 Classic Collector's Edition

The Classic Collector's edition made its debut in 1991. This package includes a board game, trivia baseball player cards, a baseball tips booklet and a certificate of authenticity, all packaged in a collector's edition box. Each box is individually and sequentially numbered on the outside, with a reported 100,000 available.

NM/M
Complete Set (200): 7.50
Common Player: .05

Cal Ripken, Jr.

1	Frank Viola	.05
2	Tim Wallach	.05
3	Lou Whitaker	.05
4	Brett Butler	.05
5	Jim Abbott	.05
6	Jack Armstrong	.05
7	Craig Biggio	.05
8	Brian Barnes	.05
9	Dennis "Oil Can" Boyd	.05
10	Tom Browning	.05
11	Tom Brunansky	.05
12	Ellis Burks	.05
13	Harold Baines	.05
14	Kal Daniels	.05
15	Mark Davis	.05
16	Storm Davis	.05
17	Tom Glavine	.25
18	Mike Greenwell	.05
19	Kelly Gruber	.05
20	Mark Gubicza	.05
21	Pedro Guerrero	.05
22	Mike Harkey	.05
23	Orel Hershiser	.05
24	Ted Higuera	.05
25	Von Hayes	.05
26	Andre Dawson	.25
27	Shawon Dunston	.05
28	Roberto Kelly	.05
29	Joe Magrane	.05
30	Dennis Martinez	.05
31	Kevin McReynolds	.05
32	Matt Nokes	.05
33	Dan Plesac	.05
34	Dave Parker	.05
35	Randy Johnson	.40
36	Bret Saberhagen	.05
37	Mackey Sasser	.05
38	Mike Scott	.05
39	Ozzie Smith	.50
40	Kevin Seitzer	.05
41	Ruben Sierra	.05
42	Kevin Tapani	.05
43	Danny Tartabull	.05
44	Robby Thompson	.05
45	Andy Van Slyke	.05
46	Greg Vaughn	.05
47	Harold Reynolds	.05
48	Will Clark	.05
49	Gary Gaetti	.05
50	Joe Grahe	.05
51	Carlton Fisk	.40
52	Robin Ventura	.05
53	Ozzie Guillen	.05
54	Tom Candiotti	.05
55	Doug Jones	.05
56	Eric King	.05
57	Kirk Gibson	.05
58	Tim Costo	.05
59	Robin Yount	.40
60	Sammy Sosa	.50
61	Jesse Barfield	.05
62	Marc Newfield	.05
63	Jimmy Key	.05
64	Felix Jose	.05
65	Mark Whiten	.05
66	Tommy Greene	.05
67	Kent Mercker	.05
68	Greg Maddux	.50
69	Danny Jackson	.05
70	Reggie Sanders	.05
71	Eric Yelding	.05
72	Karl Rhodes	.05
73	Fernando Valenzuela	.05
74	Chris Nabholz	.05
75	Andres Galarraga	.05
76	Howard Johnson	.05
77	Hubie Brooks	.05
78	Terry Mulholland	.05
79	Paul Molitor	.40
80	Roger McDowell	.05
81	Darren Daulton	.05
82	Zane Smith	.05
83	Ray Lankford	.05
84	Bruce Hurst	.05
85	Andy Benes	.05
86	John Burkett	.05
87	Dave Righetti	.05
88	Steve Karsay	.05
89	D.J. Dozier	.05
90	Jeff Bagwell	.40
91	Joe Carter	.05
92	Wes Chamberlain	.05
93	Vince Coleman	.05
94	Pat Combs	.05
95	Jerome Walton	.05
96	Jeff Conine	.05
97	Alan Trammell	.05
98	Don Mattingly	.55

99	Ramon Martinez	.05
100	Dave Magadan	.05
101	Greg Swindell	.05
102	Dave Stewart	.05
103	Gary Sheffield	.30
104	George Bell	.05
105	Mark Grace	.05
106	Steve Sax	.05
107	Ryne Sandberg	.50
108	Chris Sabo	.05
109	Jose Rijo	.05
110	Cal Ripken, Jr.	1.00
111	Kirby Puckett	.50
112	Eddie Murray	.40
113	Roberto Alomar	.20
114	Randy Myers	.05
115	Rafael Palmeiro	.35
116	John Olerud	.05
117	Gregg Jefferies	.05
118	Kent Hrbek	.05
119	Marquis Grissom	.05
120	Ken Griffey Jr.	.60
121	Dwight Gooden	.05
122	Juan Gonzalez	.20
123	Ron Gant	.05
124	Travis Fryman	.05
125	John Franco	.05
126	Dennis Eckersley	.35
127	Cecil Fielder	.05
128	Phil Plantier	.05
129	Kevin Mitchell	.05
130	Kevin Maas	.05
131	Mark McGwire	.75
132	Ben McDonald	.05
133	Lenny Dykstra	.05
134	Delino DeShields	.05
135	Jose Canseco	.30
136	Eric Davis	.05
137	George Brett	.55
138	Steve Avery	.05
139	Eric Anthony	.05
140	Bobby Thigpen	.05
141	Ken Griffey Sr.	.05
142	Barry Larkin	.05
143	Jeff Brantley	.05
144	Bobby Bonilla	.05
145	Jose Offerman	.05
146	Mike Mussina	.30
147	Erik Hanson	.05
148	Dale Murphy	.15
149	Roger Clemens	.55
150	Tino Martinez	.05
151	Todd Van Poppel	.05
152	Mo Vaughn	.05
153	Derrick May	.05
154	Jack Clark	.05
155	Dave Hansen	.05
156	Tony Gwynn	.50
157	Brian McRae	.05
158	Matt Williams	.05
159	Kirk Dressendorfer	.05
160	Scott Erickson	.05
161	Tony Fernandez	.05
162	Willie McGee	.05
163	Fred McGriff	.05
164	Leo Gomez	.05
165	Bernard Gilkey	.05
166	Bobby Witt	.05
167	Doug Drabek	.05
168	Rob Dibble	.05
169	Glenn Davis	.05
170	Danny Darwin	.05
171	Eric Karros	.05
172	Eddie Zosky	.05
173	Todd Zeile	.05
174	Tim Raines	.05
175	Benito Santiago	.05
176	Dan Peltier	.05
177	Darryl Strawberry	.05
178	Hal Morris	.05
179	Hensley Meulens	.05
180	John Smoltz	.05
181	Frank Thomas	.40
182	Dave Staton	.05
183	Scott Chiamparino	.05
184	Alex Fernandez	.05
185	Mark Lewis	.05
186	Bo Jackson	.10
187	Mickey Morandini (Photo actually Darren Daulton.)	.05
188	Cory Snyder	.05
189	Rickey Henderson	.40
190	Junior Felix	.05
191	Milt Cuyler	.05
192	Wade Boggs	.50
193	"Justice Prevails" (David Justice)	.05
194	Sandy Alomar, Jr.	.05
195	Barry Bonds	1.00
196	Nolan Ryan	1.00
197	Rico Brogna	.05
198	Steve Decker	.05
199	Bob Welch	.05
200	Andujar Cedeno	.05

1991 Classic/American Collectables Nolan Ryan

This set of Nolan Ryan highlights was produced by Classic for American Collectables and sold as a limited-edition issue. The cards feature color photos of Ryan bordered in a garish green and yellow design. Backs have personal data and stats printed in black on green, along with a color MLB logo.

Nolan Ryan
Mets '66 - '71

NM/M
Complete Set (10): 7.50
Common Card: 1.00

1	Nolan Ryan (Mets '66-'71)	1.00
2	Nolan Ryan (Angels '72-'79)	1.00
3	Nolan Ryan (Astros '80-'88)	1.00
4	Nolan Ryan (Rangers '89-'90)	1.00
5	Nolan Ryan (5000 K's)	1.00
6	Nolan Ryan (6th No-No)	1.00
7	Nolan Ryan (Angels '72-'79)	1.00
8	Nolan Ryan (Astros '80-'88)	1.00
9	Nolan Ryan (Rangers '89-'90)	1.00
10	Nolan Ryan (300 Wins)	1.00

1992 Classic Series 1

CHITO MARTINEZ

Classic introduced an innovative design with the release of its 1992 set. Fronts feature full-color photos bordered in white, while backs feature statistics, biographical information and trivia questions accented by a fading stadium shot. The cards were released with a gameboard and are numbered on back with a "T" prefix.

NM/M
Complete Set (100): 4.50
Common Player: .05

1	Jim Abbott	.05
2	Kyle Abbott	.05
3	Scott Aldred	.05
4	Roberto Alomar	.20
5	Wilson Alvarez	.05
6	Andy Ashby	.05
7	Steve Avery	.05
8	Jeff Bagwell	.40
9	Bret Barberie	.05
10	Kim Batiste	.05
11	Derek Bell	.05
12	Jay Bell	.05
13	Albert Belle	.05
14	Andy Benes	.05
15	Sean Berry	.05
16	Barry Bonds	1.00
17	Ryan Bowen	.05
18	Trifecta (Alejandro Pena, Mark Wohlers, Kent Mercker)	.05
19	Scott Brosius	.05
20	Jay Buhner	.05
21	David Burba	.05
22	Jose Canseco	.35
23	Andujar Cedeno	.05
24	Will Clark	.05
25	Royce Clayton	.05
26	Roger Clemens	.50
27	David Cone	.05
28	Scott Cooper	.05
29	Chris Cron	.05
30	Len Dykstra	.05
31	Cal Eldred	.05
32	Hector Fajardo	.05
33	Cecil Fielder	.05
34	Dave Fleming	.05
35	Steve Foster	.05
36	Julio Franco	.05
37	Carlos Garcia	.05
38	Tom Glavine	.05
39	Tom Goodwin	.05

40	Ken Griffey Jr.	.65
41	Chris Haney	.05
42	Bryan Harvey	.05
43	Rickey Henderson	.40
44	Carlos Hernandez	.05
45	Roberto Hernandez	.05
46	Brook Jacoby	.05
47	Howard Johnson	.05
48	Pat Kelly	.05
49	Darryl Kile	.05
50	Chuck Knoblauch	.05
51	Ray Lankford	.05
52	Mark Leiter	.05
53	Darren Lewis	.05
54	Scott Livingstone	.05
55	Shane Mack	.05
56	Chito Martinez	.05
57	Dennis Martinez	.05
58	Don Mattingly	.50
59	Paul McClellan	.05
60	Chuck McElroy	.05
61	Fred McGriff	.05
62	Orlando Merced	.05
63	Luis Mercedes	.05
64	Kevin Mitchell	.05
65	Hal Morris	.05
66	Jack Morris	.05
67	Mike Mussina	.30
68	Denny Neagle	.05
69	Tom Pagnozzi	.05
70	Terry Pendleton	.05
71	Phil Plantier	.05
72	Kirby Puckett	.45
73	Carlos Quintana	.05
74	Willie Randolph	.05
75	Arthur Rhodes	.05
76	Cal Ripken	1.00
77	Ivan Rodriguez	.35
78	Nolan Ryan	1.00
79	Ryne Sandberg	.45
80	Deion Sanders	.10
81	Reggie Sanders	.05
82	Mo Sanford	.05
83	Terry Shumpert	.05
84	Tim Spehr	.05
85	Lee Stevens	.05
86	Darryl Strawberry	.05
87	Kevin Tapani	.05
88	Danny Tartabull	.05
89	Frank Thomas	.40
90	Jim Thome	.30
91	Todd Van Poppel	.05
92	Andy Van Slyke	.05
93	John Wehner	.05
94	John Wetteland	.05
95	Devon White	.05
96	Brian Williams	.05
97	Mark Wohlers	.05
98	Robin Yount	.40
99	Eddie Zosky	.05
--	4-in-1 (Barry Bonds, Roger Clemens, Steve Avery, Nolan Ryan)	.50

1992 Classic Series 2

The 100-cards in Classic's 1992 Series II came packaged with a gameboard and spinner. In a completely different format from Classic's other '92 issues, Series II features player photos bordered at left and right with red or blue color bars which fade toward top and bottom. Backs have biographical data, previous-year and career statistics and five trivia questions, along with a color representation of the team's uniform. Cards, except the 4-In-1, are numbered with a "T" prefix.

		NM/M
Complete Set (100):		4.50
Common Player:		.05
1	Jim Abbott	.05
2	Jeff Bagwell	.40
3	Jose Canseco	.30
4	Julio Valera	.05
5	Scott Brosius	.05
6	Mark Langston	.05
7	Andy Stankiewicz	.05
8	Gary DiSarcina	.05
9	Pete Harnisch	.05
10	Mark McGwire	.75
11	Ricky Bones	.05
12	Steve Avery	.05

13	Deion Sanders	.10
14	Mike Mussina	.25
15	Dave Justice	.05
16	Pat Hentgen	.05
17	Tom Glavine	.20
18	Juan Guzman	.05
19	Ron Gant	.05
20	Kelly Gruber	.05
21	Eric Karros	.05
22	Derrick May	.05
23	Dave Hansen	.05
24	Andre Dawson	.25
25	Eric Davis	.05
26	Ozzie Smith	.45
27	Sammy Sosa	.45
28	Lee Smith	.05
29	Ryne Sandberg	.45
30	Robin Yount	.40
31	Matt Williams	.05
32	John Vander Wal	.05
33	Bill Swift	.05
34	Delino DeShields	.05
35	Royce Clayton	.05
36	Moises Alou	.05
37	Will Clark	.05
38	Darryl Strawberry	.05
39	Larry Walker	.05
40	Ramon Martinez	.05
41	Howard Johnson	.05
42	Tino Martinez	.05
43	Dwight Gooden	.05
44	Ken Griffey Jr.	.60
45	David Cone	.05
46	Kenny Lofton	.05
47	Bobby Bonilla	.05
48	Carlos Baerga	.05
49	Don Mattingly	.50
50	Sandy Alomar, Jr.	.05
51	Lenny Dykstra	.05
52	Tony Gwynn	.45
53	Felix Jose	.05
54	Rick Sutcliffe	.05
55	Wes Chamberlain	.05
56	Cal Ripken, Jr.	1.00
57	Kyle Abbott	.05
58	Leo Gomez	.05
59	Gary Sheffield	.20
60	Anthony Young	.05
61	Roger Clemens	.50
62	Rafael Palmeiro	.35
63	Wade Boggs	.45
64	Andy Van Slyke	.05
65	Ruben Sierra	.05
66	Denny Neagle	.05
67	Nolan Ryan	1.00
68	Doug Drabek	.05
69	Ivan Rodriguez	.35
70	Barry Bonds	1.00
71	Chuck Knoblauch	.05
72	Reggie Sanders	.05
73	Cecil Fielder	.05
74	Barry Larkin	.05
75	Scott Aldred	.05
76	Rob Dibble	.05
77	Brian McRae	.05
78	Tim Belcher	.05
79	George Brett	.50
80	Frank Viola	.05
81	Roberto Kelly	.05
82	Jack McDowell	.05
83	Mel Hall	.05
84	Esteban Beltre	.05
85	Robin Ventura	.05
86	George Bell	.05
87	Frank Thomas	.40
88	John Smiley	.05
89	Bobby Thigpen	.05
90	Kirby Puckett	.45
91	Kevin Mitchell	.05
92	Peter Hoy	.05
93	Russ Springer	.05
94	Donovan Osborne	.05
95	Dave Silvestri	.05
96	Chad Curtis	.05
97	Pat Mahomes	.05
98	Danny Tartabull	.05
99	John Doherty	.05
---	4-in-1 (Ryne Sandberg, Mike Mussina, Reggie Sanders, Jose Canseco)	.25

1992 Classic Collector's Edition

The second annual 200-card "Collector's Edition" set was packaged with a gameboard, spinner,

generic player pieces, a mechanical scoreboard and a book of tips from star players. The UV-coated card fronts feature color player photos against a deep purple border. Backs have a few biographical details, previous season and career stats, plus five trivia questions in case anyone actually wanted to play the game.

		NM/M
Complete Set (200):		9.00
Common Player:		.05
1	Chuck Finley	.05
2	Craig Biggio	.05
3	Luis Gonzalez	.05
4	Pete Harnisch	.05
5	Jeff Juden	.05
6	Harold Baines	.05
7	Kirk Dressendorfer	.05
8	Dennis Eckersley	.35
9	Dave Henderson	.05
10	Dave Stewart	.05
11	Joe Carter	.05
12	Juan Guzman	.05
13	Dave Stieb	.05
14	Todd Stottlemyre	.05
15	Ron Gant	.05
16	Brian Hunter	.05
17	Dave Justice	.05
18	John Smoltz	.05
19	Mike Stanton	.05
20	Chris George	.05
21	Paul Molitor	.40
22	Omar Olivares	.05
23	Lee Smith	.05
24	Ozzie Smith	.50
25	Todd Zeile	.05
26	George Bell	.05
27	Andre Dawson	.25
28	Shawon Dunston	.05
29	Mark Grace	.05
30	Greg Maddux	.50
31	Dave Smith	.25
32	Brett Butler	.05
33	Orel Hershiser	.05
34	Eric Karros	.05
35	Ramon Martinez	.05
36	Jose Offerman	.05
37	Juan Samuel	.05
38	Delino DeShields	.05
39	Marquis Grissom	.05
40	Tim Wallach	.05
41	Eric Gunderson	.05
42	Willie McGee	.05
43	Dave Righetti	.05
44	Robby Thompson	.05
45	Matt Williams	.05
46	Sandy Alomar, Jr.	.05
47	Reggie Jefferson	.05
48	Mark Lewis	.05
49	Robin Ventura	.05
50	Tino Martinez	.05
51	Roberto Kelly	.05
52	Vince Coleman	.05
53	Dwight Gooden	.05
54	Todd Hundley	.05
55	Kevin Maas	.05
56	Wade Taylor	.05
57	Bryan Harvey	.05
58	Leo Gomez	.05
59	Ben McDonald	.05
60	Ricky Bones	.05
61	Tony Gwynn	.50
62	Benito Santiago	.05
63	Wes Chamberlain	.05
64	Tommy Greene	.05
65	Dale Murphy	.15
66	Steve Buechele	.05
67	Doug Drabek	.05
68	Joe Grahe	.05
69	Rafael Palmeiro	.35
70	Wade Boggs	.50
71	Ellis Burks	.05
72	Mike Greenwell	.05
73	Mo Vaughn	.05
74	Derek Bell	.05
75	Rob Dibble	.05
76	Barry Larkin	.05
77	Jose Rijo	.05
78	Doug Henry	.05
79	Chris Sabo	.05
80	Pedro Guerrero	.05
81	George Brett	.60
82	Tom Gordon	.05
83	Mark Gubicza	.05
84	Mark Whiten	.05
85	Brian McRae	.05
86	Danny Jackson	.05
87	Milt Cuyler	.05
88	Travis Fryman	.05
89	Mickey Tettleton	.05
90	Alan Trammell	.05
91	Lou Whitaker	.05
92	Chili Davis	.05
93	Scott Erickson	.05
94	Kent Hrbek	.05
95	Alex Fernandez	.05
96	Carlton Fisk	.40
97	Ramon Garcia	.05
98	Ozzie Guillen	.05
99	Tim Raines	.05
100	Bobby Thigpen	.05
101	Kirby Puckett	.50
102	Bernie Williams	.05

103	Dave Hansen	.05
104	Kevin Tapani	.05
105	Don Mattingly	.60
106	Frank Thomas	.40
107	Monty Fariss	.05
108	Bo Jackson	.10
109	Jim Abbott	.05
110	Jose Canseco	.25
111	Phil Plantier	.05
112	Brian Williams	.05
113	Mark Langston	.05
114	Wilson Alvarez	.05
115	Roberto Hernandez	.05
116	Darryl Kile	.05
117	Ryan Bowen	.05
118	Rickey Henderson	.40
119	Mark McGwire	1.00
120	Devon White	.05
121	Roberto Alomar	.20
122	Kelly Gruber	.05
123	Eddie Zosky	.05
124	Tom Glavine	.25
125	Kal Daniels	.05
126	Cal Eldred	.05
127	Deion Sanders	.05
128	Robin Yount	.40
129	Cecil Fielder	.05
130	Ray Lankford	.05
131	Ryne Sandberg	.50
132	Darryl Strawberry	.05
133	Chris Haney	.05
134	Dennis Martinez	.05
135	Bryan Hickerson	.05
136	Will Clark	.05
137	Hal Morris	.05
138	Charles Nagy	.05
139	Jim Thome	.35
140	Albert Belle	.05
141	Reggie Sanders	.05
142	Scott Cooper	.05
143	David Cone	.05
144	Anthony Young	.05
145	Howard Johnson	.05
146	Arthur Rhodes	.05
147	Scott Aldred	.05
148	Mike Mussina	.25
149	Fred McGriff	.05
150	Andy Benes	.05
151	Ruben Sierra	.05
152	Len Dykstra	.05
153	Andy Van Slyke	.05
154	Orlando Merced	.05
155	Barry Bonds	1.50
156	John Smiley	.05
157	Julio Franco	.05
158	Juan Gonzalez	.20
159	Ivan Rodriguez	.35
160	Willie Banks	.05
161	Eric Davis	.05
162	Eddie Murray	.40
163	Dave Fleming	.05
164	Wally Joyner	.05
165	Kevin Mitchell	.05
166	Ed Taubensee	.05
167	Danny Tartabull	.05
168	Ken Hill	.05
169	Willie Randolph	.05
170	Kevin McReynolds	.05
171	Gregg Jefferies	.05
172	Patrick Lennon	.05
173	Luis Mercedes	.05
174	Glenn Davis	.05
175	Bret Saberhagen	.05
176	Bobby Bonilla	.05
177	Kenny Lofton	.05
178	Jose Lind	.05
179	Royce Clayton	.05
180	Scott Scudder	.05
181	Chuck Knoblauch	.05
182	Terry Pendleton	.05
183	Nolan Ryan	1.50
184	Rob Maurer	.05
185	Brian Bohanon	.05
186	Ken Griffey Jr.	.75
187	Jeff Bagwell	.40
188	Steve Avery	.05
189	Roger Clemens	.60
190	Cal Ripken, Jr.	1.50
191	Kim Batiste	.05
192	Bip Roberts	.05
193	Greg Swindell	.05
194	Dave Winfield	.40
195	Steve Sax	.05
196	Frank Viola	.05
197	Mo Sanford	.05
198	Kyle Abbott	.05
199	Jack Morris	.05
200	Andy Ashby	.05

1993 Classic

A 100-card travel edition of Classic's baseball trivia cards was produced for 1993. Cards feature game-action player photos with dark blue borders. Backs have previous season and career stats along with five trivia questions. Card numbers have a "T" prefix.

		NM/M
Complete Set (100):		4.00
Common Player:		.05
1	Jim Abbott	.05
2	Roberto Alomar	.20
3	Moises Alou	.05
4	Brady Anderson	.05
5	Eric Anthony	.05

David Justice OF

6	Alex Arias	.05
7	Pedro Astacio	.05
8	Steve Avery	.05
9	Carlos Baerga	.05
10	Jeff Bagwell	.40
11	George Bell	.05
12	Albert Belle	.05
13	Craig Biggio	.05
14	Barry Bonds	1.00
15	Bobby Bonilla	.05
16	Mike Bordick	.05
17	George Brett	.55
18	Jose Canseco	.30
19	Joe Carter	.05
20	Royce Clayton	.05
21	Roger Clemens	.55
22	Greg Colbrunn	.05
23	David Cone	.05
24	Darren Daulton	.05
25	Delino DeShields	.05
26	Rob Dibble	.05
27	Dennis Eckersley	.35
28	Cal Eldred	.05
29	Scott Erickson	.05
30	Junior Felix	.05
31	Tony Fernandez	.05
32	Cecil Fielder	.05
33	Steve Finley	.05
34	Dave Fleming	.05
35	Travis Fryman	.05
36	Tom Glavine	.25
37	Juan Gonzalez	.20
38	Ken Griffey Jr.	.60
39	Marquis Grissom	.05
40	Juan Guzman	.05
41	Tony Gwynn	.50
42	Rickey Henderson	.40
43	Felix Jose	.05
44	Wally Joyner	.05
45	David Justice	.05
46	Eric Karros	.05
47	Roberto Kelly	.05
48	Ryan Klesko	.05
49	Chuck Knoblauch	.05
50	John Kruk	.05
51	Ray Lankford	.05
52	Barry Larkin	.05
53	Pat Listach	.05
54	Kenny Lofton	.05
55	Shane Mack	.05
56	Greg Maddux	.50
57	Dave Magadan	.05
58	Edgar Martinez	.05
59	Don Mattingly	.55
60	Ben McDonald	.05
61	Jack McDowell	.05
62	Fred McGriff	.05
63	Mark McGwire	.75
64	Kevin McReynolds	.05
65	Sam Militello	.05
66	Paul Molitor	.40
67	Jeff Montgomery	.05
68	Jack Morris	.05
69	Eddie Murray	.40
70	Mike Mussina	.30
71	Otis Nixon	.05
72	Donovan Osborne	.05
73	Terry Pendleton	.05
74	Mike Piazza	.60
75	Kirby Puckett	.50
76	Cal Ripken, Jr.	1.00
77	Bip Roberts	.05
78	Ivan Rodriguez	.35
79	Nolan Ryan	1.00
80	Ryne Sandberg	.50
81	Deion Sanders	.10
82	Reggie Sanders	.05
83	Frank Seminara	.05
84	Gary Sheffield	.30
85	Ruben Sierra	.05
86	John Smiley	.05
87	Lee Smith	.05
88	Ozzie Smith	.50
89	John Smoltz	.05
90	Danny Tartabull	.05
91	Bob Tewksbury	.05
92	Frank Thomas	.40
93	Andy Van Slyke	.05
94	Mo Vaughn	.05
95	Robin Ventura	.05
96	Tim Wakefield	.05
97	Larry Walker	.05
98	Dave Winfield	.40
99	Robin Yount	.40
---	4-in-1 (Mark McGwire, Sam Militello, Ryan Klesko, Greg Maddux)	.50

1996 Classic/Metallic Impressions Nolan Ryan

Nolan Ryan's career is traced in this set of 2-5/8" x 3-5/8" embossed metal cards produced for Classic by Metallic Impressions. The center of each card's front is a raised color photo which continues in muted tones of yellow and orange to the edges. The Classic and The Metal Edge logos are embossed, as well. Horizontal backs are identical in design with a color portrait of Ryan at left and a paragraph describing a highlight or milestone at right. Classic and Cooperstown Collection logos are in opposite corners. Each of 14,950 sets was sold with a numbered certificate of authenticity in an embossed lithographed metal box.

		NM/M
Complete Boxed Set (10):		7.50
Single Card:		1.00
1	Nolan Ryan (Career ends with Rangers.)	1.00
2	Nolan Ryan (1970s, California Angels.)	1.00
3	Nolan Ryan (Major League debut.)	1.00
4	Nolan Ryan (Over-40 no-hitters.)	1.00
5	Nolan Ryan (Rangers no-hitters.)	1.00
6	Nolan Ryan (Mets trade Ryan.)	1.00
7	Nolan Ryan (Joins Astros.)	1.00
8	Nolan Ryan (Career records.)	1.00
9	Nolan Ryan (Lean years in Houston.)	1.00
10	Nolan Ryan ("Ryan Express" returns to A.L.)	1.00

1989 Cleveland Indians Team Issue

(28) Cory Snyder, OF

The Cleveland Indians released this oversized (2-3/4" x 4-1/2") set in 1989. Cards feature a full-color player photo on front with the "Tribe" logo in the upper left corner. Card backs include major and minor league statistics and a facsimile autograph.

		NM/M
Complete Set (28):		6.00
Common Player:		.25
(1)	Doc Edwards	.25
(2)	Joel Skinner	.25
(3)	Andy Allanson	.25
(4)	Tom Candiotti	.25
(5)	Doug Jones	.25
(6)	Keith Atherton	.25
(7)	Rich Yett	.25
(8)	John Farrell	.25
(9)	Rod Nichols	.25
(10)	Joe Skalski	.25
(11)	Pete O'Brien	.25
(12)	Jerry Browne	.25
(13)	Brook Jacoby	.25
(14)	Felix Fermin	.25
(15)	Bud Black	.25

		NM/M
(16)	Brad Havens	.25
(17)	Greg Swindell	.25
(18)	Scott Bailes	.25
(19)	Jesse Orosco	.25
(20)	Oddibe McDowell	.25
(21)	Joe Carter	.50
(22)	Cory Snyder	.25
(23)	Louie Medina	.25
(24)	Dave Clark	.25
(25)	Brad Komminsk	.25
(26)	Luis Aguayo	.25
(27)	Pat Keedy	.25
(28)	Tribe Coaches	.25

1990 Cleveland Indians Team Issue

(17) Keith Hernandez, 1B

The Cleveland Indians released this oversized (2-7/8" x 4-1/4") set in 1990. Cards feature a full-color portrait photo on front with the "Tribe" logo in the top-left corner. Player name, uniform number and position are in the bottom border. Backs are blank.

		NM/M
Complete Set (46):		12.00
Common Player:		.25
(1)	Beau Allred	.25
(2)	Sandy Alomar Jr.	.50
(3)	Carlos Baerga	.25
(4)	Kevin Bearse	.25
(5)	Joey (Albert) Belle	2.00
(6)	Bud Black	.25
(7)	Tom Brookens	.25
(8)	Jerry Browne	.25
(9)	Tom Candiotti	.25
(10)	Colin Charland	.25
(11)	Rich Dauer	.25
(12)	John Farrell	.25
(13)	Felix Fermin	.25
(14)	Cecilio Guante	.25
(15)	Mike Hargrove	.35
(16)	Keith Hernandez	.40
(17)	Luis Isaac	.25
(18)	Brook Jacoby	.25
(19)	Chris James	.25
(20)	Dion James	.25
(21)	Doug Jones	.25
(22)	Carl Kelipuleole	.25
(23)	Tom Lampkin	.25
(24)	Tom Magrann	.25
(25)	Candy Maldonado	.25
(26)	Jeff Manto	.25
(27)	John McNamara	.25
(28)	Jose Morales	.25
(29)	Rod Nichols	.25
(30)	Al Nipper	.25
(31)	Steve Olin	.25
(32)	Jesse Orosco	.25
(33)	Doug Robertson	.25
(34)	Rudy Seanez	.25
(35)	Jeff Shaw	.25
(36)	Doug Sisk	.25
(37)	Joe Skalski	.25
(38)	Joel Skinner	.25
(39)	Cory Snyder	.25
(40)	Greg Swindell	.25
(41)	Sergio Valdez	.25
(42)	Mike Walker	.25
(43)	Mitch Webster	.25
(44)	Kevin Wickander	.25
(45)	Mark Wiley	.25
(46)	Billy Williams	.25

1993 Cleveland Indians Team Issue

Albert Belle

Only the mascot's card carries the logo of the television station which sponsored this team set. In 2-1/2" x 3-1/2" format printed on thin cardboard, the fronts feature color game-action photos with borders of red, white and blue. The player's uniform number appears in the lower-left corner. Backs are in black-and-white with major league career stats and a log commemorating the team's 61 years at Municipal Stadium. The set is checklisted here alphabetically.

		NM/M
Complete Set (34):		12.00
Common Player:		.25
(1)	Sandy Alomar Jr.	.50
(2)	Carlos Baerga	.25
(3)	Albert Belle	1.00
(4)	Mike Bielecki	.25
(5)	Mike Christopher	.25
(6)	Mark Clark	.25
(7)	Dennis Cook	.25
(8)	Alvaro Espinoza	.25
(9)	Felix Fermin	.25
(10)	Mike Hargrove	.25
(11)	Glenallen Hill	.25
(12)	Thomas Howard	.25
(13)	Reggie Jefferson	.25
(14)	Wayne Kirby	.25
(15)	Tom Kramer	.25
(16)	Mark Lewis	.25
(17)	Derek Lilliquist	.25
(18)	Kenny Lofton	.35
(19)	Carlos Martinez	.25
(20)	Jose Mesa	.25
(21)	Jeff Mutis	.25
(22)	Charles Nagy	.25
(23)	Bob Ojeda	.25
(24)	Junior Ortiz	.25
(25)	Eric Plunk	.25
(26)	Ted Power	.25
(27)	Scott Scudder	.25
(28)	Joel Skinner	.25
(29)	Paul Sorrento	.25
(30)	Jim Thome	2.00
(31)	Jeff Treadway	.25
(32)	Kevin Wickander	.25
(33)	Indians Coaches (Rick Adair, Ken Bolke, Dom Chiti, Ron Clark, Jose Morales, Dave Nelson, Jeff Newman)	.25
(34)	Slider (Mascot)	.25

2005 Cloverdale Meats Seattle Mariners

Ryan Franklin

Cloverdale Mets sponsored a kids' trading card stadium giveaway on June 16, distributing 27-card packs to fans 14 and under. Each pack contained 20 different cards and seven duplicates to trade in an effort to complete the set. Fronts of the 2-1/2" x 3-1/2" cards have game-action photos. Full-color backs have a portrait photo, player data and trivia, and team and sponsor's logos.

		NM/M
Complete Set (27):		10.00
Common Player:		.35
1	Mike Hargrove	.35
2	Adrian Beltre	.75
3	Willie Bloomquist	.35
4	Bret Boone	.35
5	Ryan Franklin	.35
6	Eddie Guardado	.35
7	Shigetoshi Hasegawa	.35
8	Raul Ibanez	.35
9	Bobby Madritsch	.35
10	Julio Mateo	.35
11	Gil Meche	.35
12	Jamie Moyer	.35
13	Jeff Nelson	.35
14	Miguel Olivo	.35
15	Joel Pineiro	.35
16	J.J. Putz	.35
17	Jeremy Reed	.75
18	Pokey Reese	.35
19	Aaron Sele	.35
20	Richie Sexson	.35
21	Scott Spiezio	.35
22	Ichiro Suzuki	3.00
23	Matt Thornton	.35
24	Wilson Valdez	.35
25	Ron Villone	.35
26	Dan Wilson	.35
27	Randy Winn	.35

1992 Clovis Police Department Mark's Moments

MARK McGWIRE

Highlights of Mark McGwire's career to that point are shown and/or described in this set of police cards from the Clovis, Calif., P.D. Cards have color photos framed in gold with green borders. The city seal is at upper-left, the Oakland description of a "Moment," a safety tip, the description of the "Moment" on front, a safety tip, the logo of the Clovis P.D., another team logo and sponsors' credits.

	NM/M
Complete Set (24):	35.00
Common Card:	1.50

1981 Coca-Cola

JOHNNY BENCH

In 1981 Topps produced for Coca-Cola 12-card sets for 11 American and National League teams. The sets include 11 player cards and one unnumbered header card. The 2-1/2" x 3-1/2" cards are identical in format to the 1981 Topps regular issue with an added Coca-Cola logo. Backs differ from the '81 Topps regular set in that they are numbered 1-11 and carry the Coca-Cola trademark and copyright line. The header cards contain an offer for 132-card uncut sheets of 1981 Topps baseball cards. Some New York Yankees' cards were prepared, but never issued; to date, only three of the players are known.

		NM/M
Complete Set (No Yankees) (132):		20.00
Common Player:		.10
Boston Red Sox Team Set		3.00
1	Tom Burgmeier	.10
2	Dennis Eckersley	.35
3	Dwight Evans	.20
4	Bob Stanley	.10
5	Glenn Hoffman	.10
6	Carney Lansford	.10
7	Frank Tanana	.10
8	Tony Perez	.75
9	Jim Rice	.50
10	Dave Stapleton	.10
11	Carl Yastrzemski	2.00
----	Red Sox Header Card	.05
Chicago Cubs Team Set		1.25
1	Tim Blackwell	.10
2	Bill Buckner	.20
3	Ivan DeJesus	.10
4	Leon Durham	.10
5	Steve Henderson	.10
6	Mike Krukow	.10
7	Ken Reitz	.10
8	Rick Reuschel	.10
9	Scot Thompson	.10
10	Dick Tidrow	.10
11	Mike Tyson	.10
----	Cubs Header Card	.05
Chicago White Sox Team Set		1.00
1	Britt Burns	.10
2	Todd Cruz	.10
3	Rich Dotson	.10
4	Jim Essian	.10
5	Ed Farmer	.10
6	Lamar Johnson	.10
7	Ron LeFlore	.10
8	Chet Lemon	.10
9	Bob Molinaro	.10
10	Jim Morrison	.10
11	Wayne Nordhagen	.10
----	White Sox Header Card	.05
Cincinnati Reds Team Set		3.50
1	Johnny Bench	2.75
2	Dave Collins	.10
3	Dave Concepcion	.10
4	Dan Driessen	.10
5	George Foster	.20
6	Ken Griffey	.20
7	Tom Hume	.10
8	Ray Knight	.20
9	Ron Oester	.10
10	Tom Seaver	1.75
11	Mario Soto	.10
----	Reds Header Card	.05
Detroit Tigers Team Set		2.25
1	Champ Summers	.10
2	Al Cowens	.10
3	Rich Hebner	.10
4	Steve Kemp	.10
5	Aurelio Lopez	.10
6	Jack Morris	.35
7	Lance Parrish	.35
8	Johnny Wockenfuss	.10
9	Alan Trammell	.75
10	Lou Whitaker	.35
11	Kirk Gibson	.35
----	Tigers Header Card	.05
Houston Astros Team Set		5.00
1a	Alan Ashby	.10
1b	Nolan Ryan	25.00
2	Cesar Cedeno	.10
3	Jose Cruz	.10
4	Art Howe	.10
5	Rafael Landestoy	.10
6	Joe Niekro	.20
7	Terry Puhl	.10
8	J.R. Richard	.20
9	Nolan Ryan	4.00
10	Joe Sambito	.10
11	Don Sutton	.75
----	Astros Header Card	.05
Kansas City Royals Team Set		3.00
1	Willie Aikens	.10
2	George Brett	2.00
3	Larry Gura	.10
4	Dennis Leonard	.10
5	Hal McRae	.20
6	Amos Otis	.10
7	Dan Quisenberry	.10
8	U.L. Washington	.10
9	John Wathan	.10
10	Frank White	.10
11	Willie Wilson	.20
----	Royals Header Card	.05
New York Mets Team Set		1.25
1	Neil Allen	.10
2	Doug Flynn	.10
3	Dave Kingman	.35
4	Randy Jones	.10
5	Pat Zachry	.10
6	Lee Mazzilli	.10
7	Rusty Staub	.20
8	Craig Swan	.10
9	Frank Taveras	.10
10	Alex Trevino	.10
11	Joel Youngblood	.10
----	Mets Header Card	.05
New York Yankees Team Set		75.00
1	Rich Gossage	15.00
2	Reggie Jackson	60.00
3	Rick Cerone	12.50
----	Yankees Header Card	.05
Philadelphia Phillies Team Set		6.00
1	Bob Boone	.35
2	Larry Bowa	.20
3	Steve Carlton	1.25
4	Greg Luzinski	.10
5	Garry Maddox	.10
6	Bake McBride	.10
7	Tug McGraw	.20
8	Pete Rose	2.75
9	Mike Schmidt	2.75
10	Lonnie Smith	.10
11	Manny Trillo	.10
----	Phillies Header Card	.05
Pittsburgh Pirates Team Set		3.00
1	Jim Bibby	.10
2	John Candelaria	.10
3	Mike Easler	.10
4	Tim Foli	.10
5	Phil Garner	.10
6	Bill Madlock	.20
7	Omar Moreno	.10
8	Ed Ott	.10
9	Dave Parker	.30
10	Willie Stargell	2.00
11	Kent Tekulve	.10
----	Pirates Header Card	.05
St. Louis Cardinals Team Set		1.25
1	Bob Forsch	.10
2	George Hendrick	.10
3	Keith Hernandez	.20
4	Tom Herr	.10
5	Sixto Lezcano	.10
6	Ken Oberkfell	.10
7	Darrell Porter	.10
8	Tony Scott	.10
9	Lary Sorensen	.10
10	Bruce Sutter	.50
11	Garry Templeton	.10
----	Cardinals Header Card	.05

1981 Coca-Cola Brigham's Red Sox Ad Signs

These 6" x 17-1/2" blank-back cardboard ad pieces were designed to be folded into a countertop tent card, identical on each side. The color player photos on the ad pieces are different than those found on the issued cards.

		NM/M
Complete Set (11):		35.00
Common Player:		2.00
(1)	Tom Burgmeier	2.00
(2)	Dennis Eckersley	4.00
(3)	Dwight Evans	3.00
(4)	Bob Stanley	2.00
(5)	Glenn Hoffman	2.00
(6)	Carney Lansford	2.00
(7)	Frank Tanana	2.00
(8)	Tony Perez	6.00
(9)	Jim Rice	8.00
(10)	Dave Stapleton	2.00
(11)	Carl Yastrzemski	15.00

1982 Coca-Cola Brigham's Red Sox

CARL YASTRZEMSKI

Coca-Cola, in conjunction with Brigham's Ice Cream stores, issued a 23-card set in the Boston area featuring Red Sox players. The Topps-produced cards are 2-1/2" x 3-1/2", are identical in format to the regular 1982 Topps set but contain the Coca-Cola and Brigham's logos in the corners. The cards were distributed in three-card cello packs, including an unnumbered header card.

		NM/M
Complete Set (23):		5.00
Common Player:		.25
1	Gary Allenson	.25
2	Tom Burgmeier	.25
3	Mark Clear	.25
4	Steve Crawford	.25
5	Dennis Eckersley	1.50
6	Dwight Evans	.35
7	Rich Gedman	.25
8	Garry Hancock	.25
9	Glen Hoffman (Glenn)	.25
10	Carney Lansford	.25
11	Rick Miller	.25
12	Reid Nichols	.25
13	Bob Ojeda	.25
14	Tony Perez	1.50
15	Chuck Rainey	.25
16	Jerry Remy	.25
17	Jim Rice	1.00
18	Bob Stanley	.25
19	Dave Stapleton	.25
20	Mike Torrez	.25
21	John Tudor	.25
22	Carl Yastrzemski	3.00
----	Header Card	.10

1982 Coca-Cola Reds

Produced by Topps for Coca-Cola, the set consists of 23 cards featuring the Cincinnati Reds and was distributed in the Cincinnati area. The cards, which are 2-1/2" x 3-1/2" in size, are identical in design to the regular 1982 Topps set but have a Coca-Cola logo on the front and red backs. An unnumbered header card is included in the set.

		NM/M
Complete Set (23):		3.00
Common Player:		.25
1	Johnny Bench	2.00
2	Bruce Berenyi	.25
3	Larry Biittner	.25
4	Cesar Cedeno	.25
5	Dave Concepcion	.35
6	Dan Driessen	.25
7	Greg Harris	.25
8	Paul Householder	.25
9	Tom Hume	.25
10	Clint Hurdle	.25
11	Jim Kern	.25
12	Wayne Krenchicki	.25
13	Rafael Landestoy	.25
14	Charlie Leibrandt	.25
15	Mike O'Berry	.25
16	Ron Oester	.25
17	Frank Pastore	.25
18	Joe Price	.25
19	Tom Seaver	1.00
20	Mario Soto	.25
21	Alex Trevino	.25
22	Mike Vail	.25
----	Header Card	.05

1985 Coca-Cola Dodgers Photocards

The first of two annual player photocard sets sponsored by Coke, these 3-1/2" x 5-1/2" cards feature color player action photos on front surrounded by a white border. Below the photo is a 1985 copyright notice, the player's name is at bottom. Backs have a Coca-Cola logo in the lower-right corner, and may be found both with and without a printed message. The unnumbered cards are checklisted here in alphabetical order.

		NM/M
Complete Set (34):		15.00
Common Player:		.50
(1)	Joe Amalfitano	.50
(2)	Dave Anderson	.50
(3)	Bob Bailor	.50
(4)	Monty Basgall	.50
(5)	Tom Brennan	.50

(6)	Greg Brock	.50
(7)	Bobby Castillo	.50
(8)	Mark Cresse	.50
(9)	Carlos Diaz	.50
(10)	Mariano Duncan	.60
(11)	Pedro Guerrero	.50
(12)	Orel Hershiser	2.00
(13)	Rick Honeycutt	.50
(14)	Steve Howe	.60
(15)	Ken Howell	.50
(16)	Jay Johnstone	.50
(17)	Ken Landreaux	.50
(18)	Tommy Lasorda	.75
(19)	Candy Maldonado	.50
(20)	Mike Marshall	.50
(21)	Manny Mota	.50
(22)	Tom Niedenfuer	.50
(23)	Al Oliver	.60
(24)	Alejandro Pena	.50
(25)	Ron Perranoski	.50
(26)	Jerry Reuss	.50
(27)	R.J. Reynolds	.50
(28)	Bill Russell	.50
(29)	Steve Sax	.50
(30)	Mike Scioscia	.50
(31)	Fernando Valenzuela	.75
(32)	Bob Welch	.50
(33)	Terry Whitfield	.50
(34)	Steve Yeager	.50

1985 Coca-Cola Pirates

13 Steve Kemp OF

A companion set to the cards issued in the 1985 Pirates yearbook, this set was given away to the first 10,000 youngsters attending May 18 and July 13 home games. The card of Kent Tekulve was withdrawn after his trade to the Phillies, making it quite scarce. The 2-1/2" x 3-1/2" cards have a color photo at center, surrounded by black and gold borders. A white panel at bottom has the player's name, position and uniform number. Backs are in black-and-white and feature complete major and minor league stats, plus the Cameron/Coca-Cola sponsors' logos.

		NM/M
Complete Set (29) (No Tekulve.):		12.00
Complete Set (30)(W/Tekulve.):		20.00
Common Player:		.50
3	Jim Morrison	.50
2	Johnny Ray	.50
5	Bill Madlock	1.00
6	Tony Pena	.60
9	Chuck Tanner	.50
10	Tim Foli	.50
11	Joe Orsulak	.50
12	Bill Almon	.50
13	Steve Kemp	.50
14	George Hendrick	.50
16	Lee Mazzilli	.50
17	Jerry Dybzinski	.50
19	Rod Scurry	.50
22	Lee Tunnell	.50
25	Jose DeLeon	.50
27	Kent Tekulve	7.50
28	Sixto Lezcano	.50
29	Rick Rhoden	.50
30	Jason Thompson	.50
34	Mike Bielecki	.50
35	Al Holland	.50
36	Marvell Wynne	.50
37	Rafael Belliard	.50
44	Don Robinson	.50
45	John Candelaria	.50
47	Cecilio Guante	.50
49	Larry McWilliams	.50
51	Doug Frobel	.50
---	Pirates Coaches	.50

1985 Coca-Cola White Sox

Featuring past and present White Sox players, the cards in this set were given out on Tuesday night home games. The 2-5/8" x 4-1/8" cards contain a color photo of a current Sox member. A red box at the bottom of the card carries the team logo, player name, uniform number and position, plus a small oval por-

trait of a past Sox player. Backs contain the Coca-Cola logo and lifetime stats for the current and past player. The set is listed here by the player's uniform number with the last three cards being unnumbered. Complete sets were available through a fan club offer found in White Sox programs.

		NM/M
Complete Set (30):		7.50
Common Player:		.25
0	Oscar Gamble, Zeke Bonura	.25
1	Scott Fletcher, Luke Appling	.60
3	Harold Baines, Bill Melton	.75
5	Luis Salazar, Chico Carrasquel	.25
7	Marc Hill, Sherman Lollar	.25
8	Daryl Boston, Jim Landis	.25
10	Tony LaRussa, Al Lopez	.25
12	Julio Cruz, Nellie Fox	1.50
13	Ozzie Guillen, Luis Aparicio	2.00
17	Jerry Hairston Sr., Smoky Burgess	.50
20	Joe DeSa, Carlos May	.25
22	Joel Skinner, J.C. Martin	.25
23	Rudy Law, Bill Skowron	.50
24	Floyd Bannister, Red Faber	.25
29	Greg Walker, Dick Allen	1.00
30	Gene Nelson, Early Wynn	.75
32	Tim Hulett, Pete Ward	.25
37	Richard Dotson, Ed Walsh	.25
37	Dan Spillner, Thornton Lee	.25
40	Britt Burns, Gary Peters	.25
41	Tom Seaver, Ted Lyons	2.00
42	Ron Kittle, Minnie Minoso	1.00
43	Bob James, Hoyt Wilhelm	.25
---	Tom Paciorek, Eddie Collins	.25
46	Tim Lollar, Billy Pierce	.25
50	Juan Agosto, Wilbur Wood	.25
72	Carlton Fisk, Ray Schalk	1.50
---	Comiskey Park	.50
---	Ribbie & Roobarb (Mascots)	.25
---	Nancy Faust (Organist)	.25

1986 Coca-Cola Dodgers Photocards

©1986 L.A. Dodgers   All Rights Reserved
Dave Anderson

For a second year Coke sponsored this set of 3-1/2" x 5-1/2" color cards. Fronts feature an action photo with white borders. Beneath the photo is a 1986 copyright line; the player's name is at bottom. Backs have a red Coca-Cola logo in the lower-right corner, and can be found either otherwise blank or with a message to fans from the pictured player, along with a facsimile autograph. The unnumbered cards are checklisted here alphabetically.

		NM/M
Complete Set (34):		15.00
Common Player:		.50
(1)	Joe Amalfitano	.50
(2)	Dave Anderson	.50
(3)	Monty Basgall	.50
(4)	Greg Brock	.50
(5)	Enos Cabell	.50
(6)	Cesar Cedeno	.50
(7)	Mark Cresse	.50
(8)	Carlos Diaz	.50
(9)	Mariano Duncan	.50
(10)	Pedro Guerrero	.50
(11)	Orel Hershiser	1.00
(12)	Ben Hines	.50
(13)	Rick Honeycutt	.50
(14)	Ken Howell	.50
(15)	Ken Landreaux	.50
(16)	Tom Lasorda	.75
(17)	Bill Madlock	.50
(18)	Mike Marshall	.50
(19)	Len Matuszek	.50
(20)	Manny Mota	.50
(21)	Tom Niedenfuer	.50
(22)	Alejandro Pena	.50
(23)	Ron Perranoski	.50
(24)	Dennis Powell	.50
(25)	Jerry Reuss	.50
(26)	Bill Russell	.50
(27)	Steve Sax	.50
(28)	Mike Scioscia	.50
(29)	Franklin Stubbs	.50
(30)	Alex Trevino	.50
(31)	Fernando Valenzuela	.75
(32)	Ed Vande Berg	.50
(33)	Bob Welch	.50
(34)	Terry Whitfield	.50

1986 Coca-Cola White Sox

FLOYD BANNISTER P/19

For the second year in a row, Coca-Cola, in conjunction with the Chicago White Sox, issued a 30-card set. As in 1985, cards were given out at the park on Tuesday night games. Full sets were available through a fan club offer found in the White Sox program. The 2-5/8" x 4-1/8" cards feature 25 players plus other team personnel. Fronts have a color photo (a game-action shot in most instances) and a white bar at the bottom. A black and white bat with "SOX" shown on the barrel is located within the white bar, along with the player's name, position and uniform number. The white and gray backs with black print include the Coca-Cola trademark. Lifetime statistics are shown on all player cards, but there is no personal information such as height, weight or age. The non-player cards are blank-backed save for the name and logo at the top. The cards in the checklist that follows are numbered by the players' uniform numbers, with the last five cards of the set being unnumbered.

		NM/M
Complete Set (30):		12.00
Common Player:		.25
1	Wayne Tolleson	.25
3	Harold Baines	.75
7	Marc Hill	.25
8	Daryl Boston	.25
12	Julio Cruz	.25
13	Ozzie Guillen	.50
17	Jerry Hairston Sr.	.25
19	Floyd Bannister	.25
20	Reid Nichols	.25
22	Joel Skinner	.25
24	Dave Schmidt	.25
29	Bobby Bonilla	1.00
29	Greg Walker	.25
30	Gene Nelson	.25
32	Tim Hulett	.25
33	Neil Allen	.25
34	Richard Dotson	.25
40	Joe Cowley	.25
42	Tom Seaver	3.00
42	Ron Kittle	.35
43	Bob James	.25
44	John Cangelosi	.25
50	Juan Agosto	.25
52	Joel Davis	.25
72	Carlton Fisk	3.00
---	Ribbie & Roobarb (Mascots)	.25
---	Nancy Faust (Organist)	.25
---	Ken "Hawk" Harrelson	.35
---	Tony LaRussa	.25
---	Minnie Minoso	1.50

1987 Coca-Cola Tigers

★★★ 1987 ★★★ COLLECTORS' EDITION
DETROIT TIGERS
Pat Sheridan   OUTFIELD

Coca-Cola and S. Abraham & Sons, Inc. issued a set of 18 baseball cards featuring members of the Detroit Tigers. The set is comprised of six four-part folding panels. Each panel includes three player cards (each 2-1/2" x 3-1/2") and one team logo card. A bright yellow border surrounds the full-color photo. The backs are designed on a vertical format and contain personal data and career statistics. The set was produced by Mike Schecter and Associates.

		NM/M
Complete Panel Set (6):		4.00
Complete Singles Set (18):		2.00
Common Panel:		.50
Common Player:		.05
Panel		.85
1	Kirk Gibson	.30
2	Larry Herndon	.05
3	Walt Terrell	.05
Panel		1.50
4	Alan Trammell	.05
5	Frank Tanana	.05
6	Pat Sheridan	.05
Panel		.85
7	Jack Morris	.30
8	Mike Heath	.05
9	Dave Bergman	.05
Panel		.50
10	Chet Lemon	.05
11	Dwight Lowry	.05
12	Dan Petry	.05
Panel		.85
13	Darrell Evans	.05
14	Darnell Coles	.05
15	Willie Hernandez	.05
Panel		1.00
16	Lou Whitaker	.25
17	Tom Brookens	.05
18	John Grubb	.05

1987 Coca-Cola White Sox

Chicago
3 Harold Baines, OF

The Chicago White Sox Fan Club, in conjunction with Coca-Cola, offered members a set of 30 trading cards. For the $10 membership fee, fans received the set plus additional fan club gifts and privileges. The cards, 2-5/8" x 4", feature full-color photos inside a blue and red border. Backs include the player's name, position, uniform number and statistics, plus the Coca-Cola logo. Cards are checklisted here by uniform number.

		NM/M
Complete Set (30):		7.50
Common Player:		.25
1	Jerry Royster	.25
3	Harold Baines	.50
5	Ron Karkovice	.25
8	Daryl Boston	.25
10	Fred Manrique	.25
12	Steve Lyons	.25
13	Ozzie Guillen	.50
14	Russ Morman	.25
15	Donnie Hill	.25
16	Jim Fregosi	.25
17	Jerry Hairston Sr.	.25
19	Floyd Bannister	.25
21	Gary Redus	.25
22	Ivan Calderon	.25
25	Ron Hassey	.25
26	Jose DeLeon	.25
29	Greg Walker	.25
32	Tim Hulett	.25
33	Neil Allen	.25
34	Rich Dotson	.25
36	Ray Searage	.25
37	Bobby Thigpen	.25
40	Jim Winn	.25
43	Bob James	.25
50	Joel McKeon	.25
52	Joel Davis	.25
72	Carlton Fisk	3.00
---	Ribbie & Roobarb (Mascots)	.25
---	Nancy Faust (Organist)	.25
---	Minnie Minoso	.75

1988 Coca-Cola Padres

LARRY BOWA
PADRES
#10 Manager

A 20-card set sponsored by Coca-Cola was designed as part of the San Diego Padres Junior Fan Club promotion for 1988. This set was distributed as a nine-card starter sheet, with 11 additional single cards handed out during various home games. The standard-size cards feature full-color player photos framed by a black and orange border. The player's name is printed above the photo; uniform number and position appear at lower-right. A large Padres logo curves upward from the lower-left corner. Backs are brown on white and include the Padres logo at upper-left opposite the player's name and personal information. Career highlights and 1987 stats appear in the center of the card back above the Coca-Cola and Junior Padres Fan Club logos.

		NM/M
Complete Set (21):		20.00
Common Player:		.50
Panel		
1	Garry Templeton	.60
3	Randy Ready	.50
10	Larry Bowa	.60
19	Tim Flannery	.50
35	Chris Brown	.50
45	Jimmy Jones	.50
48	Mark Davis	.50
55	Mark Grant	.50
----	20th Anniversary Logo Card	.10
Singles		
7	Keith Moreland	1.00
8	John Kruk	2.00
15	Benito Santiago	2.00
17	Carmelo Martinez	1.00
15	Jack McKeon	1.00
19	Tony Gwynn	6.00
22	Stan Jefferson	1.00
27	Mark Parent	1.00
30	Eric Show	1.00
31	Ed Whitson	1.00
41	Lance McCullers	1.00
51	Greg Booker	1.00

1988 Coca-Cola White Sox

Part of a fan club membership package, this unnumbered 30-card set features full-color photos of 27 players, the team mascot, team organist and Comis-

key Park. Cards have a bright red border, with team logo in the photo's lower-left corner. The player name fills the bottom border. Backs are printed in black on gray and white and include player name, personal info and career summary. The set was included in the $10 membership package, with a portion of the cost going to the ChiSox Kids Charity.

		NM/M
Complete Set (30):		5.00
Common Player:		.25
(1)	Harold Baines	.50
(2)	Daryl Boston	.25
(3)	Ivan Calderon	.25
(4)	John Davis	.25
(5)	Jim Fregosi	.25
(6)	Carlton Fisk	2.50
(7)	Ozzie Guillen	.50
(8)	Donnie Hill	.25
(9)	Rick Horton	.25
(10)	Lance Johnson	.25
(11)	Dave LaPoint	.25
(12)	Bill Long	.25
(13)	Steve Lyons	.25
(14)	Jack McDowell	.30
(15)	Fred Manrique	.25
(16)	Minnie Minoso	.75
(17)	Dan Pasqua	.25
(18)	John Pawlowski	.25
(19)	Melido Perez	.25
(20)	Billy Pierce	.25
(21)	Gary Redus	.25
(22)	Jerry Reuss	.25
(23)	Mark Salas	.25
(24)	Jose Segura	.25
(25)	Bobby Thigpen	.25
(26)	Greg Walker	.25
(27)	Kenny Williams	.25
(28)	Nancy Faust (Organist)	.25
(29)	Ribbie & Roobarb (Mascots)	
(30)	Comiskey Park	.40

1989 Coca-Cola Padres

#25 First Base
JACK CLARK

This 20-card set is part of the Junior Padres Fan Club membership package. Members receive a nine-card starter set printed on one large perforated sheet. Additional cards are distributed to kids at specially designated games (free admission for kids). Fronts feature an orange-and-brown double border, with a bright orange Padres logo printed at lower-left. Uniform number and position are printed diagonally across the upper-left corner, with the player's name in large block letters along the bottom border.

		NM/M
Complete Set (21):		26.00
Common Player:		.50
Panel		
1	Garry Templeton	.60
5	Randy Ready	.50
12	Roberto Alomar	4.50
44	Carmelo Martinez	.50
15	Jack McKeon	.50
30	Eric Show	.50
31	Ed Whitson	.50

43 Dennis Rasmussen .50
---- Logo Card .10
Singles
6 Luis Salazar 1.00
9 Benito Santiago 1.00
10 Leon Roberts 1.00
11 Tim Flannery 1.00
18 Chris James 1.00
19 Tony Gwynn 8.00
25 Jack Clark 1.00
27 Mark Parent 1.00
35 Walt Terrell 1.00
47 Bruce Hurst 1.00
48 Mark Davis 1.00
55 Mark Grant 1.00

1989 Coca-Cola White Sox

Steve Lyons • 2B

For the fifth straight year, Coca-Cola sponsored a set of cards featuring the Chicago White Sox. The 30-card set was distributed to fans attending a special promotional game at Comiskey Park and was also available by mail to members of the ChiSox fan club. Card fronts feature blue borders with red and white graphics and a pair of crossed bats. Horizontal backs include player biographies, personal data and the Coca-Cola logo. Cards measure 2-5/8" x 3-1/2".

NM/M
Complete Set (30): 5.00
Common Player: .20
1 New Comiskey Park/1991 .40
2 Comiskey Park .40
3 Jeff Torborg .20
4 Coaching staff (Dave LaRoche, Terry Bevington, Walt Hriniak, Sammy Ellis, Glenn Rosenbaum, Ron Clark) .20
5 Harold Baines .45
6 Daryl Boston .20
7 Ivan Calderon .20
8 Carlton Fisk 2.50
9 Dave Gallagher .20
10 Ozzie Guillen .50
11 Shawn Hillegas .20
12 Barry Jones .20
13 Ron Karkovice .20
14 Eric King .20
15 Ron Kittle .20
16 Bill Long .20
17 Steve Lyons .20
18 Donn Pall .20
19 Dan Pasqua .20
20 Ken Patterson .20
21 Melido Perez .20
22 Jerry Reuss .20
23 Billy Jo Robidoux .20
24 Steve Rosenberg .20
25 Jeff Schaefer .20
26 Bobby Thigpen .20
27 Greg Walker .20
28 Eddie Williams .20
29 Nancy Faust (Organist) .20
30 Minnie Minoso .75

1990 Coca-Cola Padres

TONY GWYNN

This set was designed for members of the Junior Padres Club sponsored by Coca-Cola. Each member received an eight-card panel and then received two different single cards at every Jun-ior Padres Club game attended. Card fronts feature full-color photos with the Padres logo in the upper-right corner of the card. Backs feature statistics, career highlights and a red Coca-Cola logo. The cards are numbered by the player's uniform number.

NM/M
Complete Set (21): 16.00
Common Player: .35
Panel
10 Bip Roberts .35
15 Jack McKeon .35
30 Eric Show .35
31 Ed Whitson .35
40 Andy Benes .75
43 Dennis Rasmussen .35
55 Mark Grant .35
---- Logo Card .35
Singles
1 Garry Templeton .50
8 Fred Lynn .75
9 Benito Santiago 1.00
11 Craig Lefferts .50
12 Roberto Alomar 4.00
13 Mike Pagliarulo .50
17 Joe Carter 1.00
19 Tony Gwynn 6.00
25 Jack Clark .50
27 Mark Parent .50
38 Calvin Schiraldi .50
46 Greg Harris .50
47 Bruce Hurst .50

1990 Coca-Cola Garry Templeton

Coca-Cola, Vons stores and the Padres joined forces to release this special pin/baseball card collectible in honor of Garry Templeton becoming the club's all-time leader in games played. The card front features a full-color photo of Templeton and displays "Most Games Played" and "The Captain" in orange at the top of the photo. "Templeton" appears vertically in white along the left border. The Coca-Cola and Padre logos also appear on the card front. The bottom of the card features a perforated edge where the pin is attached as an extension of the card. The card back is printed in black and white and displays biographical information, career highlights and career statistics.

NM/M
Card/Pin Combination: 1.50
(1) Most Games Played Card (Garry Templeton) .50
(2) Most Games Played Pin (Garry Templeton) 1.00

1990 Coca-Cola Tigers

(9) LARRY SHEETS Outfielder

Once again utilizing the larger 2-7/8" x 4-1/4" format, this set was jointly sponsored by Coke and Kroger grocery stores and distributed at the July 14 game. Cards feature color action photos on front, surrounded by green borders. Backs have a black-and-white portrait photo, the appropriate logos and complete minor and major league stats. The player's uniform number appears in the upper-left corner.

NM/M
Complete Set (28): 6.00
Common Player: .15
(1) Sparky Anderson .50
(2) Dave Bergman .15
(3) Brian DuBois .15
(4) Cecil Fielder .25
(5) Paul Gibson .15
(6) Jerry D. Gleaton .15
(7) Mike Heath .15
(8) Mike Henneman .15
(9) Tracy Jones .15
(10) Chet Lemon .15
(11) Urbano Lugo .15
(12) Jack Morris .20
(13) Lloyd Moseby .15
(14) Matt Nokes .15
(15) Edwin Nunez .15
(16) Dan Petry .15
(17) Tony Phillips .25
(18) Kevin Ritz .15
(19) Jeff Robinson .15
(20) Ed Romero .15
(21) Mark Salas .15
(22) Larry Sheets .15
(23) Frank Tanana .15
(24) Alan Trammell .75
(25) Gary Ward .15
(26) Lou Whitaker .40
(27) Ken Williams .15
(28) Coaches (Billy Consolo, Alex Grammas, Billy Muffett, Vada Pinson, Dick Tracewski) .15

1990 Coca-Cola White Sox

TOP PROSPECT • FRANK THOMAS

An attractive "Comiskey Park 1910-1990" logo is featured on the front of each card in this set. Fronts also feature full-color photos with a thin white inner border. The cards are numbered according to uniform number, with the exception of four special cards including Top Prospect Frank Thomas. Horizontal card backs feature black print on white and gray stock; 1989 statistics and career highlights are provided. The 1990 set marks the sixth straight year that Coca-Cola sponsored a White Sox set.

NM/M
Complete Set (30): 80.00
Common Player: .25
1 Lance Johnson .25
7 Scott Fletcher .25
10 Jeff Torborg .25
12 Steve Lyons .25
13 Ozzie Guillen .50
14 Craig Grebeck .25
17 Dave Gallagher .25
20 Ron Karkovice .25
22 Ivan Calderon .25
23 Robin Ventura 1.00
24 Carlos Martinez .25
25 Sammy Sosa 65.00
27 Greg Hibbard .25
29 Jack McDowell .25
30 Donn Pall .25
31 Scott Radinsky .25
32 Melido Perez .25
34 Ken Patterson .25
36 Eric King .25
37 Bobby Thigpen .25
42 Ron Kittle .25
44 Dan Pasqua .25
45 Wayne Edwards .25
50 Barry Jones .25
52 Jerry Kutzler .25
72 Carlton Fisk 5.00
--- Top Prospect (Frank Thomas) 15.00
--- White Sox Manager, Coaches (Jeff Torborg) .25
--- Captains (Ozzie Guillen, Carlton Fisk) 1.00
--- Rookies (Wayne Edwards, Craig Greback, Jerry Kutzler, Scott Radinsky, Robin Ventura) .35

1991 Coca-Cola Don Mattingly

Don Mattingly

Though sponsored by Coca-Cola, the manner of distribution of this issue is unclear. The "Mattingly's 23" logo on each side of the card suggests a connection to his Evansville, Ind., restaurant. Fronts of the 2-1/2" x 3-1/2" cards have photos in black-and-white or color, or artwork. The border is white with blue pinstripes. The year of the picture is at top of the photo and there is a Coke logo at bottom. Backs are printed in red and blue and contain career highlights and stats, along with a card number and logos.

NM/M
Complete Set (15): 10.00
Common Card: 1.00
1 Don Mattingly/1978 1.00
2 Don Mattingly/1979 1.00
3 Don Mattingly/1980 1.00
4 Don Mattingly/1981 1.00
5 Don Mattingly/1982 1.00
6 Don Mattingly/1983 1.00
7 Don Mattingly/'83-'84 1.00
8 Don Mattingly/1984 1.00
9 Don Mattingly/1985 1.00
10 Don Mattingly/1986 1.00
11 Don Mattingly/1987 1.00
12 Don Mattingly/1990 1.00
13 Don Mattingly/1991 (Photo) 1.00
14 Don Mattingly/1991 (Artwork) 1.00
15 Don Mattingly/1991 (Coca-Cola logo.) 1.00

1991 Coca-Cola Tigers

(1) MICKEY TETTLETON-C ... 20

This set was sponsored by Coca-Cola and Kroger, whose logos appear on the red, white and blue backs. The oversize (2-7/8" x 4-1/4") cards feature game-action or portrait color photos on front along with the player's name vertically printed on the right border and the Tigers logo in the lower-left corner. Backs are printed horizontally and feature complete minor and major league statistics. The set is numbered according to uniform number, which appears in an orange triangle on front.

NM/M
Complete Set (28): 7.00
Common Player: .35
1 Lou Whitaker .75
2 Alan Trammell 1.00
4 Tony Phillips .35
10 Andy Allanson .35
11 Sparky Anderson .75
14 Dave Bergman .35
18 Lloyd Moseby .35
19 Jerry Don Gleaton .35
20 Mickey Tettleton .35
22 Milt Cuyler .35
23 Mark Leiter .35
24 Travis Fryman .35
25 John Shelby .35
26 Frank Tanana .35
27 Mark Salas .35
29 Pete Incaviglia .35
31 Kevin Ritz .35
35 Walt Terrell .35
36 Bill Gullickson .35
39 Mike Henneman .35
42 Mike Dalton .35
44 Rob Deer .35
45 Cecil Fielder .35
46 Dan Petry .35
47 Paul Gibson .35
49 Steve Searcy .35
55 John Cerutti .35
--- Tigers Coaches (Billy Consolo, Jim Davenport, Alex Grammas, Billy Muffett, Vada Pinson, Dick Tracewski) .35

1992 Coca-Cola Nolan Ryan Career Series

This 26-card set was produced by Donruss in conjunction with Coca-Cola to honor Nolan Ryan's 26 major league seasons. One Nolan Ryan card was packaged with three regular 1992 Donruss cards in special 12-packs of Coke. Complete sets, in a black, red and gold box, were available through a mail-in offer. The 2-1/2" x 3-1/2" cards have a full-color photo on front, framed by a gold border. Ryan's name is printed in gold toward the bottom, above a blue bar which presents a team and year. The Coke logo is at upper right. On back there are details of Ryan's performance in the indicated year, the card number, and team and Coke logos. An 18" x 12" color poster picturing the cards and a photo of a Ryan-autographed ball was issued as a point-of-purchase display.

NM/M
Complete Set (26): 7.50
Common Card: .50
Display Poster: 15.00
1 1966 Breaking In .50
2 1968 Record-Setting Rookie .50
3 1969 World Champions .50
4 1970 Growing Pains .50
5 1971 Traded .50
6 1972 Fitted for a Halo .50
7 1973 First Two No-Nos and a Record .50
8 1974 No-Hitter No. 3/ Another K Record .50
9 1975 Tying Koufax .50
10 1976 Back on Track .50
11 1977 Carrying the Load .50
12 1978 A Year of Injuries .50
13 1979 California Farewell .50
14 1980 Coming Home .50
15 1981 A Gusher in Houston .50
16 1982 Mounting 'Em Up .50
17 1983 Passing the Big Train .50
18 1984 Misleading Signs of Age .50
19 1985 Another Milestone/ A New Contract .50
20 1986 The Elbow Flares Up Again .50
21 1987 Another ERA/ Strikeout Crown at 40 .50
22 1988 Leaving Home Again .50
23 1989 5,000 Strikeouts .50
24 1990 Win No. 300, No-Hitter No. 6 .50
25 1991 No-Hitter No. 7 .50
26 1992 Man of Records .50

1992 Coca-Cola Tigers

(1) Lou Whitaker IF

This set of large-format (2-7/8" x 4-1/4") cards features central photos of the Bengals in action. Dark blue stripes at top and bottom have the team name in white, while the player name, uniform number and position are printed in black on an orange stripe directly beneath the photo. A color team logo in the upper-right completes the front design. Backs have complete major and minor league stats, a few personal data and color logos of Coke and the Kroger grocery chain.

NM/M
Complete Set (28): 5.00
Common Player: .15
1 Lou Whitaker .35
2 Alan Trammell .75
4 Tony Phillips .15
7 Scott Livingstone .15
9 Skeeter Barnes .15
11 Sparky Anderson .50
14 Dave Bergman .15
15 Mark Carreon .15
19 Gary Pettis .15
19 Chad Kreuter .15
20 Mickey Tettleton .15
22 Milt Cuyler .15
23 Mark Leiter .15
24 Travis Fryman .15
26 Frank Tanana .15
27 Kurt Knudsen .15
28 Rob Deer .15
31 Kevin Ritz .15
32 Dan Gladden .15
35 Walt Terrell .15
36 Bill Gullickson .15
39 Mike Henneman .15
43 Mike Munoz .15
44 John Doherty .15
45 Cecil Fielder .25
46 John Kiely .15
48 Les Lancaster .15
--- Tigers Coaches (Billy Consolo, Gene Roof, Larry Herndon, Dick Tracewksi, Billy Muffett, Dan Whitmer) .15

1992 Coca-Cola/Hardees Major League Line-Up Discs

This set of 3" diameter "Major League Line-Up" cardboard discs was a regional give-away sponsored by Coca-Cola and distributed by Hardee's restaurants. The glossy discs have player photos at center with position and uniform numbers at the sides. Backs are in black-and-white with a few stats and career highlights and various logos. A checklist disc was also distributed.

NM/M
Complete Set (24): 12.00
Common Player: .50
1 Roger Clemens 2.50
2 Sandy Alomar Jr. 1.25
3 Rafael Palmeiro 1.25
4 Roberto Alomar .50
5 Kelly Gruber .50
6 Ozzie Guillen .50
7 Devon White .50
8 David Henderson .50
9 Robin Yount 1.50
10 Chili Davis .50

11	Chuck Knoblauch	.50
12	Paul Molitor	1.50
13	Tom Glavine	.75
14	Benito Santiago	.50
15	Hal Morris	.50
16	Delino DeShields	.50
17	Matt Williams	.50
18	Ozzie Smith	2.00
19	Andy Van Slyke	.50
20	Andre Dawson	.75
21	Ron Gant	.50
22	Jeff Bagwell	1.50
23	Terry Pendleton	.50
24	Brett Butler	.50

1993 Coca-Cola Commanders of the Hill

Coca-Cola and Topps teamed up to print a 30-card Commanders of the Hill set in 1993. The cards were available in five-card packages with soft-drink purchases on military bases at base exchange food court concessions. The set was divided into three areas: Cy Young Winners, Strikeout Leaders and Team ERA Leaders, with the National League player's names in yellow on a red background and the American League in red on yellow.

		NM/M
Complete Set (30):		5.00
Common Player:		.10
1	Dennis Eckersley	.50
2	Mike Mussina	.40
3	Roger Clemens	1.00
4	Jim Abbott	.10
5	Jack McDowell	.10
6	Charles Nagy	.10
7	Bill Gullickson	.10
8	Kevin Appier	.10
9	Bill Wegman	.10
10	John Smiley	.10
11	Melido Perez	.10
12	Dave Stewart	.10
13	Dave Fleming	.10
14	Kevin Brown	.10
15	Juan Guzman	.10
16	Randy Johnson	.60
17	Greg Maddux	.75
18	Tom Glavine	.35
19	Greg Maddux	.75
20	Jose Rijo	.10
21	Pete Harnisch	.10
22	Tom Candiotti	.10
23	Denny Martinez	.10
24	Sid Fernandez	.10
25	Curt Schilling	.35
26	Doug Drabek	.10
27	Bob Tewksbury	.10
28	Andy Benes	.10
29	Bill Swift	.10
30	John Smoltz	.10

1995 Coca-Cola Minnesota Twins POGs

Over the course of three games in July 1995, the Twins issued a three-sheet series of POGs, 15,000 at each game. The souvenir measures about 10-1/4" x 9-1/2" and features a large color game photo, around and above which are POGs, about 1-1/8" diameter, of players, coaches and sponsors. The POGs are die-cut for removal from the sheets. Each sheet has 11 players or coaches, and each has the same four sponsors' POGs.

Fronts have player portrait photos while backs have a repeating Coca-Cola logo. The POGs are unnumbered and listed here alphabetically by sheet. The players are not identified on the POGs themselves.

		NM/M
Complete Set, Sheets (3):		12.00
Complete Set, Singles (33):		9.00
Common Player:		.25
Series 1, July 1		**4.00**
(1)	Rick Aguilera	.25
(2)	Rich Becker	.25
(3)	Marty Cordova	.25
(4)	Terry Crowley	.25
(5)	Eddie Guardado	.25
(6)	Jeff Reboulet	.25
(7)	Rich Robertson	.25
(8)	Scott Stahoviak	.25
(9)	Dick Such	.25
(10)	Kevin Tapani	.25
(11)	Matt Walbeck	.25
Series 2, July 17		**3.00**
(12)	Alex Cole	.25
(13)	Scott Erickson	.25
(14)	Ron Gardenhire	.25
(15)	Chip Hale	.25
(16)	Chuck Knoblauch	.25
(17)	Scott Leius	.25
(18)	Pat Mahomes	.25
(19)	Pedro Munoz	.25
(20)	Erik Schullstrom	.25
(21)	Dave Stevens	.25
(22)	Scott Ullger	.25
Series 3, July 28		**5.00**
(23)	Jerald Clark	.25
(24)	Mark Guthrie	.25
(25)	Tom Kelly	.25
(26)	Kevin Maas	.25
(27)	Pat Meares	.25
(28)	Matt Merullo	.25
(29)	Kirby Puckett	3.50
(30)	Brad Radke	.25
(31)	Rick Stelmaszek	.25
(32)	Mike Trombley	.25
(33)	Jerry White	.25
---	Coca-Cola	.05
---	Fox 29 TV	.05
---	Minnesota Twins Logo	.10
---	Nestle	.05

1995 Coca-Cola Pittsburgh Pirates POGs

To celebrate the 25th anniversary of Three Rivers Stadium, Coca-Cola and the Pirates issued a set of POGs marking the 25 greatest baseball moments at the stadium. The POGs were issued nine apiece on heavy 6" x 8" cardboard panels. Individual POGs measure about 1-3/4" diameter and are perforated at the edge so they can be removed from the panel. Most fronts have a border of team-color orange and black, with central photos in black-and-white or color. Backs of #1-8 have a green Fruitopia ad; backs of #10-18 have an ad for Sprite in green, while #9, 19-25 have a red Coca-Cola ad on back.

		NM/M
Complete Set Panels (3):		15.00
Complete Set Singles (27):		9.00
Common POG:		.25
1	1994 All-Star Game (All-Star logo)	.25
2	Roberto Clemente (3,000th Hit)	2.00
3	Roberto Clemente (Uniform #21 retired.)	2.00
4	Pirates Win 1979 N.L. Pennant (We Are Family logo)	.25
5	John Candelaria (No-Hitss Dodgers)	.25
6	Willie Stargell (Uniform #8 retired.)	.50
7	Mike Schmidt (500th Home Run)	.75
8	Kent Tekulve (First Game, 7/16/70)	.25
--	Coke/Fruitopia Logos	.05
9	First World Series Night Game	.25
10	Nellie Briles (1971 World Series 2-Hitter)	.25

11	Pirates Win 1971 N.L. Pennant	.25
12	Pirates Clinch N.L. East, 1979	.25
13	Pirates Clinch N.L. East, 1992 (Jim Leyland)	.25
14	Bob Gibson (No-Hits Pirates 8/14/71)	.40
15	1979 World Series Game 5 (Jim Rooker)	.25
16	Pirates Clinch N.L. East, 1971	.25
17	Beat Braves in NLCS Game 5, 1992	.25
18	John Milner (Grand Slam Beats Phillis 8/5/79)	.25
19	Barry Bonds (11th Inning HR Beats St. Louis 8/12/91)	.75
20	Jeff King (5 Runs in 9th to Beat Dodgers, 5/28/90)	.25
21	Danny Murtaugh (Murtaugh, Joe L. Brown Retire)	.25
22	"Gunner" Returns to Broadcast Booth	.25
23	Sweep Phillies in 9/29/78 Doubleheader	.25
24	Jim Leyland (Makes Pittsburgh Debut)	.25
25	1974 All-Star Game (Program)	.25
---	Coke Logos	.05

1995 Coca-Cola/Publix Florida Marlins

Coca-Cola and the Publix grocery store chain sponsored this team set issue. Fronts of the standard-size (2-1/2" x 3-1/2") cards have color player action photos on a large background of the team logo. Backs have a color portrait photo and stats. Cards are checklisted here by uniform number.

		NM/M
Complete Set (27):		7.50
Common Player:		.50
3	Quilvio Veras	.50
4	Greg Colbrunn	.50
6	Tommy Gregg	.50
7	Kurt Abbott	.50
8	Andre Dawson	2.50
9	Terry Pendleton	.50
10	Gary Sheffield	2.50
11	Chris Hammond	.50
14	Jerry Browne	.50
15	Marcel Lacheman	.50
17	Darrell Whitmore	.50
21	Chuck Carr	.50
23	Charles Johnson	.50
26	Alex Arias	.50
28	Mark Gardner	.50
29	Mario Diaz	.50
31	Robb Nen	.50
34	John Burkett	.50
34	Bryan Harvey	.50
39	David Weathers	.50
42	Jeremy Hernandez	.50
48	Pat Rapp	.50
51	Terry Mathews	.50
52	Randy Veres	.50
58	Yorkis Perez	.50
---	Coaches	.50
---	Billy the Marlin (Mascot)	.50

1996 Coca-Cola/Kroger Nolan Ryan Card/Pin

Culminating activities during Nolan Ryan Appreciation Week at Arlington, September 12-15, fans attending the September 15 game, during which Ryan's uniform number was retired by the Rangers, received a baseball card/pin combination sponsored by Coca-Cola and Kroger grocers. The giveaway is a 2-1/2" x 5-1/2" cardboard panel. At top is a 2-1/2" x 3-7/8" card separated by perforations from the bottom panel on which the 1-1/8" x 1-1/2" enameled jersey pin is affixed. The front has a spring training game-action color photo of Ryan. The back is in

black-and-white with a career summary, sponsor' logos and a picture of the pin.

	NM/M
Card/Pin Combination:	7.00

1998 Coca-Cola Chipper Jones

This 2-1/2" x 3-1/2" card was an Atlanta-area exclusive. The front shows the Braves' star enjoying a Coke. On back is a coupon for a free 20-oz. Coca-Cola.

	NM/M
Chipper Jones	10.00

2002 Coca-Cola S.F. Giants

A dozen of the most popular Giants are pictured in game-action photos on the fronts of these regionally issued cards. Two-card cello packs were inserted in each specially marked 24-can case of Coke, making acquisition of the set an expensive proposition. The glossy fronts have red borders with Coca-Cola and team logos in the lower corners. Backs have a portrait photo, a few bits of personal data and stats, and a host of appropriate logos.

		NM/M
Complete Set (12):		20.00
Common Player:		1.00
1	Jeff Kent	1.00
2	Rich Aurilia	1.00
3	J.T. Snow	1.00
4	Marvin Benard	1.00
5	Pedro Feliz	1.00
6	Shawon Dunston	1.00
7	Robb Nen	1.00
8	Felix Rodriguez	1.00

9	Russ Ortiz	1.00
10	Kirk Reuter	1.00
11	Livan Hernandez	1.00
12	Barry Bonds	12.00

1989 Barry Colla Postcards

In 1989 California baseball photographer Barry Colla began a series of player postcard sets. Each set contains eight postcards of the player and was sold in a white paper envelope with the team logo. The postcards are identical in format, measuring 3-1/2" x 5-1/2". Fronts feature borderless color photos on high-gloss stock. Backs are printed in black-and-white and feature a team logo at center. The player's name, uniform number, team and position are printed in the upper-left. A card number appears at top-center.

		NM/M
1-8	Will Clark	3.00
1-8	Jose Canseco	4.00
1-8	Andre Dawson	4.00
1-8	Mike Greenwell	3.00
1-8	Don Mattingly	5.00
1-8	Mark McGwire	6.00
1-8	Kevin Mitchell	3.00
1-8	Ozzie Smith	4.50

1990 Barry Colla Promos

Each of the 12-card single-player sets produced by photographer Barry Colla in 1990 was preceded by a promo card. The promos feature the same borderless color photography as the issued cards. Backs have information on date and size of the limited-edition issues and ordering information printed in black and white. Checklist of the unnumbered cards is presented here in alphabetical order.

		NM/M
Complete Set (4):		6.00
Common Player:		1.00
(1)	Jose Canseco	2.00
(2)	Will Clark	1.00
(3)	Kevin Maas	1.00
(4)	Don Mattingly	3.00

1990 Barry Colla

In 1990 baseball photographer Barry Colla began production of a series of single-player card sets. In standard 2-1/2" x 3-1/2" size, the cards featured high-gloss borderless photos on front, with no extraneous graphics. Backs feature stats, career notes, personal data and team logos. The 12-card sets were sold in small decorative cardboard boxes. Production figures are noted in parentheses.

		NM/M
1-12	Jose Canseco (20,000)	3.00

1-12	Will Clark (15,000)	2.00
1-12	Kevin Maas (7,500)	2.00
1-12	Don Mattingly (15,000)	7.50

1990 Barry Colla Postcards

Barry Colla continued his series of single-player postcard sets 1990. The basic format continued unchanged. The 3-1/2" x 5-1/2" card feature borderless color game-action and posed photos on high-gloss stock. Black-and-white backs feature a team logo at center, a card number at top and, in the upper-left, the player's name, uniform number, team and position. Sets were sold in white paper envelopes with color team logos on the front.

		NM/M
1-8	Mark Grace	3.00

1991 Barry Colla Promos

Each of the eight 12-card single-player sets produced by California photographer Barry Colla in 1991 was preceded by the issue of a promo card. Identical in format, the promos feature high quality borderless photos on glossy stock. Backs are printed in black-and-white and include information on the size and release date of the limited-edition set, along with ordering information and appropriate logos. The checklist of the unnumbered promo cards is presented here alphabetically.

		NM/M
Complete Set (10):		12.00
Common Player:		1.00
(1a)	Roberto Alomar	1.00
(1b)	Roberto Alomar (French)	1.50
(2)	Barry Bonds	4.00
(3a)	Joe Carter	1.00
(3b)	Joe Carter (French)	1.00
(4)	Dwight Gooden	1.00
(5)	Ken Griffey Jr.	3.00
(6)	Dave Justice	1.00
(7)	Ryne Sandberg	2.50
(8)	Darryl Strawberry	1.00

1991 Barry Colla

In 1991 baseball photographer Barry Colla continued production of a series of single-player card sets. In standard 2-1/2" x 3-1/2" size, the cards featured high-gloss borderless photos on front, with no extraneous graphics. Backs feature stats, career notes, personal data and team logos. The 12-card sets were sold in small decorative cardboard boxes. Production figures are noted in parentheses.

		NM/M
1-12	Roberto Alomar/7,500	2.00
1-12	Barry Bonds/7,500	12.00
1-12	Joe Carter/7,500	1.50
1-12	Dwight Gooden/15,000	1.50
1-12	Ken Griffey Jr./15,000	6.00
1-12	David Justice/15,000	1.50
1-12	Ryne Sandberg/15,000	4.00
1-12	Darryl Strawberry/15,000	1.50

1991 Barry Colla Postcards

Only one single-player postcard set was produced by Barry Colla in 1991: Ryne Sandberg. The eight-card set, like the 1989-90 issues, features full-color game-action and posed photos presented on a borderless, high-gloss 3-1/2" x 5-1/2" format. Back design was changed for the 1991 issue. The team logo now appears in the upper-left corner with the player's name at top and his uniform number, team and position beneath. Sets were sold in a white paper envelope featuring a color Cubs logo.

		NM/M
1-8	Ryne Sandberg	5.00

1992 Barry Colla Promos

Each of the seven card sets produced by California photographer Barry Colla in 1992 was preceded by a promo card. In standard 2-1/2" x 3-1/2" size, the promos follow the format of the regular-issue cards with a borderless color photo on high-gloss stock. All of the card backs are printed in black-and-white and feature ordering information about the sets, expected release date and issue size and appropriate logos. Some promo cards feature checklists of all existing Colla Collection card sets. The unnumbered promo cards are checklisted here alphabetically.

		NM/M
Complete Set (7):		7.50
Common Player:		1.00
(1)	All-Star Set (Juan Guzman)	1.00
(2)	Steve Avery	1.00
(3)	Jeff Bagwell	1.50
(4)	Tony Gwynn	1.50
(5)	Mark McGwire	2.00
(6)	Frank Thomas	1.50
(7)	Nolan Ryan	2.50

1992 Barry Colla

In 1992 photographer Barry Colla continued production of a series of single-player card sets. In standard 2-1/2" x 3-1/2" size, the cards featured high-gloss borderless photos on front, with no extraneous graphics. Backs feature stats, career notes, personal data, team logos and/or a cartoon. Card #1 in each set was serially numbered on the back. The 12-card sets were sold in small decorative cardboard boxes. Production figures are noted in parentheses. One in every 125 Mark McGwire sets contained an autographed card numbered from an edition of 200, but since the cards are not otherwise marked, caution should be exercised in paying a significant premium for such a set.

		NM/M
1-12	Steve Avery/7,500	2.00
1-12	Jeff Bagwell/25,000	4.00
1-12	Tony Gwynn/7,500	6.00
1-12	Mark McGwire/15,000	6.00
1-12	Mark McGwire (Autographed edition).	300.00
1-12	Nolan Ryan/25,000	6.00
1-12	Frank Thomas/25,000	4.00

1992 Barry Colla All-Stars

The 1992 Colla All-Star set consists of 24 players from the All-Star game in San Diego that year, packaged in a collector's box. Limited to 25,000 sets, the first card in each set is numbered and collectors had the opportunity to win numbered and autographed Roberto Alomar cards. Two hundred autographed Frank Thomas cards were also created for use as a premium, but he did not play in the 1992 All-Star Game due to injury.

		NM/M
Complete Set (24):		7.00
Common Player:		.25
1	Mark McGwire	1.50
2	Will Clark	.25
3	Roberto Alomar	.35
3a	Roberto Alomar (Autographed)	10.00
4	Ryne Sandberg	1.00

5	Cal Ripken, Jr.	2.00
6	Ozzie Smith	1.00
7	Wade Boggs	1.00
8	Terry Pendleton	.25
9	Kirby Puckett	1.00
10	Chuck Knoblauch	.25
11	Ken Griffey Jr.	1.25
12	Joe Carter	.25
13	Sandy Alomar, Jr.	.25
14	Benito Santiago	.25
15	Mike Mussina	.35
16	Fred McGriff	.25
17	Dennis Eckersley	.75
18	Tony Gwynn	1.00
19	Roger Clemens	1.00
20	Gary Sheffield	.35
21	Jose Canseco	.35
22	Barry Bonds	2.00
23	Ivan Rodriguez	.75
24	Tony Fernandez	.25
---	Frank Thomas/Auto.	25.00

1992 Barry Colla Postcards

KEN GRIFFEY, JR.

Only one single-player postcard set was produced by Barry Colla in 1992: Ivan Rodriguez. The four-card set, like the 1989-91 issues, features full-color game-action and posed photos presented on a borderless, high-gloss 3-1/2" x 5-1/2" format. Besides the I-Rod set, Colla also produced at least one one-card "set," apparently on special order. These cards are in the same format as his other issues and are individually serially numbered on back from within an edition of 4,000.

		NM/M
1-4	Ivan Rodriguez	4.00
6492	Ken Griffey Jr.	6.00

1993 Barry Colla All-Stars

MATT WILLIAMS THIRD BASE

For the second year in 1993 California photographer Barry Colla produced a 24-card All-Star set commemorating the game played in Baltimore on July 13. The specially boxed collector's edition includes an unnumbered All-Star logo/checklist card. Cards feature black borders on the UV-coated front, featuring game-action or posed photos. Team logos are centered beneath the photo, with the player's name and position in white at bottom. Backs are also bordered in black and include another player color photo, league and All-Star logos and information and stats on prior All-Star Game appearances.

		NM/M
Complete Set (25):		4.00
Common Player:		.15
1	Roberto Alomar	.30
2	Barry Bonds	.75
3	Ken Griffey Jr.	.50
4	John Kruk	.15
5	Kirby Puckett	.45
6	Darren Daulton	.15

7	Wade Boggs	.45
8	Matt Williams	.15
9	Cal Ripken, Jr.	.75
10	Ryne Sandberg	.45
11	Ivan Rodriguez	.30
12	Andy Van Slyke	.15
13	John Olerud	.15
14	Tom Glavine	.25
15	Juan Gonzalez	.30
16	David Justice	.15
17	Mike Mussina	.25
18	Tony Gwynn	.45
19	Joe Carter	.15
20	Barry Larkin	.15
21	Brian Harper	.15
22	Ozzie Smith	.45
23	Mark McGwire	.60
24	Mike Piazza	.50
---	Checklist	.05

1993 Barry Colla Postcards

Following a one-year layoff, Barry Colla continued his single-player, eight-card postcard series in 1993 with a pair of sets. Like the earlier issues, the cards are 3-1/2" x 5-1/2" and feature high-gloss fronts with borderless game-action and posed photos. Black-and-white backs have a more traditional postcard format than earlier issues. The sets were sold in white paper envelopes with color team logos on front. A version of each set was made with an embossed gold-foil team logo on front; they are valued about 5X the regular issue.

		NM/M
1-8	Mike Piazza	3.50
1-8	Cal Ripken Jr.	6.00

1994 Collector's Choice Promos

Upper Deck used a pair of promo cards to preview its new 1994 Collector's Choice brand. Ken Griffey Jr. was featured on the promos, though the photos differ from those which appear on his regular-issue card, as does the card number. "For Promotional Use Only" is printed diagonally in black on both the front and back of the regular-size card. The 5" x 7-3/8" promo card uses the same front photo as the smaller promo and has advertising on the back describing the Collector's Choice issue.

		NM/M
50	Ken Griffey Jr.	5.00
---	Ken Griffey Jr. (Jumbo)	5.00

1994 Collector's Choice

This base-brand set, released in two series, was more widely available than the regular 1994 Upper Deck issue. Cards feature UD production staples such as UV coating and hologram and have large photos with a narrow pin-stripe border. Backs have stats and a color photo. Series 1 has 320 cards and subsets titled Rookie Class, Draft Picks and Top Performers. Series 2 subsets are Up Close and Personal, Future Foundation and Rookie Class. Each of the set's player cards can also be found with either a gold- (1 in 36 packs) or silver-foil replica-autograph card; one silver-signature card appears in every pack. Factory sets include five randomly selected gold-signature cards.

	NM/M
Unopened Fact. Set (675):	25.00
Complete Set (670):	20.00
Common Player:	.05
Silver Signature:	2.5X
Gold Signature:	15X
Series 1 Pack (12):	.35
Series 1 Box (36):	8.00
Series 2 Pack (12):	.75
Series 2 Box (36):	17.50
1 Rich Becker RC	.05
2 Greg Blosser	.05
3 Midre Cummings	.05
4 Carlos Delgado	.30
5 Steve Dreyer RC	.05
6 Carl Everett RC	.50
7 Cliff Floyd	.05
8 Alex Gonzalez	.05
9 Shawn Green	.10
10 Butch Huskey	.05
11 Mark Hutton	.05
12 Miguel Jimenez	.05
13 Steve Karsay	.05
14 Marc Newfield	.05
15 Luis Ortiz	.05
16 Manny Ramirez	.60
17 Johnny Ruffin	.05
18 Scott Stahoviak RC	.05
19 Salomon Torres	.05
20 Gabe White RC	.10
21 Brian Anderson RC	.05
22 Wayne Gomes RC	.05
23 Jeff Granger	.05
24 Steve Soderstrom RC	.05
25 Trot Nixon RC	.50
26 Kirk Presley RC	.05
27 Matt Brunson RC	.05
28 Brooks Kieschnick RC	.05
29 Billy Wagner RC	.50
30 Matt Drews RC	.05
31 Kurt Abbott RC	.05
32 Luis Alicea	.05
33 Roberto Alomar	.20
34 Sandy Alomar Jr.	.05
35 Moises Alou	.05
36 Wilson Alvarez	.05
37 Rich Amaral	.05
38 Eric Anthony	.05
39 Luis Aquino	.05
40 Jack Armstrong	.05
41 Rene Arocha	.05
42 Rich Aude RC	.05
43 Brad Ausmus	.05
44 Steve Avery	.05
45 Bob Ayrault	.05
46 Willie Banks	.05
47 Bret Barberie	.05
48 Kim Batiste	.05
49 Rod Beck	.05
50 Jason Bere	.05
51 Sean Berry	.05
52 Dante Bichette	.05
53 Jeff Blauser	.05
54 Mike Blowers	.05
55 Tim Bogar	.05
56 Tom Bolton	.05
57 Ricky Bones	.05
58 Bobby Bonilla	.05
59 Bret Boone	.05
60 Pat Borders	.05
61 Mike Bordick	.05
62 Daryl Boston	.05
63 Ryan Bowen	.05
64 Jeff Branson	.05
65 George Brett	.85
66 Steve Buechele	.05
67 Dave Burba	.05
68 John Burkett	.05
69 Jeromy Burnitz	.05
70 Brett Butler	.05

71 Rob Butler	.05
72 Ken Caminiti	.05
73 Cris Carpenter	.05
74 Vinny Castilla	.05
75 Andujar Cedeno	.05
76 Wes Chamberlain	.05
77 Archi Cianfrocco	.05
78 Dave Clark	.05
79 Jerald Clark	.05
80 Royce Clayton	.05
81 David Cone	.05
82 Jeff Conine	.05
83 Steve Cooke	.05
84 Scott Cooper	.05
85 Joey Cora	.05
86 Tim Costa	.05
87 Chad Curtis	.05
88 Ron Darling	.05
89 Danny Darwin	.05
90 Rob Deer	.05
91 Jim Deshaies	.05
92 Delino DeShields	.05
93 Rob Dibble	.05
94 Gary DiSarcina	.05
95 Doug Drabek	.05
96 Scott Erickson	.05
97 Rikkert Faneyte RC	.05
98 Jeff Fassero	.05
99 Alex Fernandez	.05
100 Cecil Fielder	.05
101 Dave Fleming	.05
102 Darrin Fletcher	.05
103 Scott Fletcher	.05
104 Mike Gallego	.05
105 Carlos Garcia	.05
106 Jeff Gardner	.05
107 Brent Gates	.05
108 Benji Gil	.05
109 Bernard Gilkey	.05
110 Chris Gomez	.05
111 Luis Gonzalez	.05
112 Tom Gordon	.05
113 Jim Gott	.05
114 Mark Grace	.05
115 Tommy Greene	.05
116 Willie Greene	.05
117 Ken Griffey Jr.	1.00
118 Bill Gullickson	.05
119 Ricky Gutierrez	.05
120 Juan Guzman	.05
121 Chris Gwynn	.05
122 Tony Gwynn	.75
123 Jeffrey Hammonds	.05
124 Erik Hanson	.05
125 Gene Harris	.05
126 Greg Harris	.05
127 Bryan Harvey	.05
128 Billy Hatcher	.05
129 Hilly Hathaway	.05
130 Charlie Hayes	.05
131 Rickey Henderson	.60
132 Mike Henneman	.05
133 Pat Hentgen	.05
134 Roberto Hernandez	.05
135 Orel Hershiser	.05
136 Phil Hiatt	.05
137 Glenallen Hill	.05
138 Ken Hill	.05
139 Eric Hillman	.05
140 Chris Hoiles	.05
141 Dave Hollins	.05
142 David Hulse	.05
143 Todd Hundley	.05
144 Pete Incaviglia	.05
145 Danny Jackson	.05
146 John Jaha	.05
147 Domingo Jean	.05
148 Gregg Jefferies	.05
149 Reggie Jefferson	.05
150 Lance Johnson	.05
151 Bobby Jones	.05
152 Chipper Jones	.75
153 Todd Jones	.05
154 Brian Jordan	.05
155 Wally Joyner	.05
156 Dave Justice	.05
157 Ron Karkovice	.05
158 Eric Karros	.05
159 Jeff Kent	.05
160 Jimmy Key	.05
161 Mark Kiefer	.05
162 Darryl Kile	.05
163 Jeff King	.05
164 Wayne Kirby	.05
165 Ryan Klesko	.05
166 Chuck Knoblauch	.05
167 Chad Kreuter	.05
168 John Kruk	.05
169 Mark Langston	.05
170 Mike Lansing	.05
171 Barry Larkin	.05
172 Manuel Lee	.05
173 Phil Leftwich RC	.05
174 Darren Lewis	.05
175 Derek Lilliquist	.05
176 Jose Lind	.05
177 Albie Lopez	.05
178 Javier Lopez	.05
179 Torey Lovullo	.05
180 Scott Lydy	.05
181 Mike Macfarlane	.05
182 Shane Mack	.05
183 Greg Maddux	.05
184 Dave Magadan	.05
185 Joe Magrane	.05
186 Kirt Manwaring	.05
187 Al Martin	.05
188 Pedro A. Martinez RC	.05

No.	Player	Price
189	Pedro Martinez	.60
190	Ramon Martinez	.05
191	Tino Martinez	.05
192	Don Mattingly	.85
193	Derrick May	.05
194	David McCarty	.05
195	Ben McDonald	.05
196	Roger McDowell	.05
197	Fred McGriff	.05
198	Mark McLemore	.05
199	Greg McMichael	.05
200	Jeff McNeely	.05
201	Brian McRae	.05
202	Pat Meares	.05
203	Roberto Mejia	.05
204	Orlando Merced	.05
205	Jose Mesa	.05
206	Blas Minor	.05
207	Angel Miranda	.05
208	Paul Molitor	.60
209	Raul Mondesi	.05
210	Jeff Montgomery	.05
211	Mickey Morandini	.05
212	Mike Morgan	.05
213	Jamie Moyer	.05
214	Bobby Munoz	.05
215	Troy Neel	.05
216	Dave Nilsson	.05
217	John O'Donoghue	.05
218	Paul O'Neill	.05
219	Jose Offerman	.05
220	Joe Oliver	.05
221	Greg Olson	.05
222	Donovan Osborne	.05
223	Jayhawk Owens	.05
224	Mike Pagliarulo	.05
225	Craig Paquette	.05
226	Roger Pavlik	.05
227	Brad Pennington	.05
228	Eduardo Perez	.05
229	Mike Perez	.05
230	Tony Phillips	.05
231	Hipolito Pichardo	.05
232	Phil Plantier	.05
233	Curtis Pride RC	.05
234	Tim Pugh	.05
235	Scott Radinsky	.05
236	Pat Rapp	.05
237	Kevin Reimer	.05
238	Armando Reynoso	.05
239	Jose Rijo	.05
240	Cal Ripken, Jr.	2.00
241	Kevin Roberson	.05
242	Kenny Rogers	.05
243	Kevin Rogers	.05
244	Mel Rojas	.05
245	John Roper	.05
246	Kirk Rueter	.05
247	Scott Ruffcorn	.05
248	Ken Ryan	.05
249	Nolan Ryan	2.00
250	Bret Saberhagen	.05
251	Tim Salmon	.05
252	Reggie Sanders	.05
253	Curt Schilling	.20
254	David Segui	.05
255	Aaron Sele	.05
256	Scott Servais	.05
257	Gary Sheffield	.30
258	Ruben Sierra	.05
259	Don Slaught	.05
260	Lee Smith	.05
261	Cory Snyder	.05
262	Paul Sorrento	.05
263	Sammy Sosa	.75
264	Bill Spiers	.05
265	Mike Stanley	.05
266	Dave Staton	.05
267	Terry Steinbach	.05
268	Kevin Stocker	.05
269	Todd Stottlemyre	.05
270	Doug Strange	.05
271	Bill Swift	.05
272	Kevin Tapani	.05
273	Tony Tarasco	.05
274	Julian Tavarez RC	.05
275	Mickey Tettleton	.05
276	Ryan Thompson	.05
277	Chris Turner	.05
278	John Valentin	.05
279	Todd Van Poppel	.05
280	Andy Van Slyke	.05
281	Mo Vaughn	.05
282	Robin Ventura	.05
283	Frank Viola	.05
284	Jose Vizcaino	.05
285	Omar Vizquel	.05
286	Larry Walker	.05
287	Duane Ware	.05
288	Allen Watson	.05
289	Bill Wegman	.05
290	Turk Wendell	.05
291	Lou Whitaker	.05
292	Devon White	.05
293	Rondell White	.05
294	Mark Whiten	.05
295	Darrell Whitmore	.05
296	Bob Wickman	.05
297	Rick Wilkins	.05
298	Bernie Williams	.05
299	Matt Williams	.05
300	Woody Williams	.05
301	Nigel Wilson	.05
302	Dave Winfield	.60
303	Anthony Young	.05
304	Eric Young	.05
305	Todd Zeile	.05
306	Jack McDowell, John Burkett, Tom Glavine/TP	.05
307	Randy Johnson/TP	.25
308	Randy Myers/TP	.05
309	Jack McDowell/TP	.05
310	Mike Piazza/TP	.40
311	Barry Bonds/TP	.60
312	Andres Galarraga/TP	.05
313	Juan Gonzalez, Barry Bonds/TP	.45
314	Albert Belle/TP	.05
315	Kenny Lofton/TP	.05
316	Checklist 1-64 (Barry Bonds)	.50
317	Checklist 65-128 (Ken Griffey Jr.)	.35
318	Checklist 129-192 (Mike Piazza)	.35
319	Checklist 193-256 (Kirby Puckett)	.25
320	Checklist 257-320 (Nolan Ryan)	.50
321	Checklist 321-370 (Roberto Alomar)	.10
322	Checklist 371-420 (Roger Clemens)	.30
323	Checklist 421-470 (Juan Gonzalez)	.10
324	Checklist 471-520 (Ken Griffey Jr.)	.35
325	Checklist 521-570 (David Justice)	.05
326	Checklist 571-620 (John Kruk)	.05
327	Checklist 621-670 (Frank Thomas)	.20
328	Angels Checklist (Tim Salmon)	.05
329	Astros Checklist (Jeff Bagwell)	.20
330	Athletics Checklist (Mark McGwire)	.45
331	Blue Jays Checklist (Roberto Alomar)	.10
332	Braves Checklist (David Justice)	.05
333	Brewers Checklist (Pat Listach)	.05
334	Cardinals Checklist (Ozzie Smith)	.25
335	Cubs Checklist (Ryne Sandberg)	.25
336	Dodgers Checklist (Mike Piazza)	.35
337	Expos Checklist (Cliff Floyd)	.05
338	Giants Checklist (Barry Bonds)	.50
339	Indians Checklist (Albert Belle)	.05
340	Mariners Checklist (Ken Griffey Jr.)	.35
341	Marlins Checklist (Gary Sheffield)	.10
342	Mets Checklist (Dwight Gooden)	.05
343	Orioles Checklist (Cal Ripken, Jr.)	.50
344	Padres Checklist (Tony Gwynn)	.25
345	Phillies Checklist (Lenny Dykstra)	.05
346	Pirates Checklists (Andy Van Slyke)	.05
347	Rangers Checklist (Juan Gonzalez)	.10
348	Red Sox Checklist (Roger Clemens)	.30
349	Reds Checklist (Barry Larkin)	.05
350	Rockies Checklist (Andres Galarraga)	.05
351	Royals Checklist (Kevin Appier)	.05
352	Tigers Checklist (Cecil Fielder)	.05
353	Twins Checklist (Kirby Puckett)	.25
354	White Sox Checklist (Frank Thomas)	.20
355	Yankees Checklist (Don Mattingly)	.30
356	Bo Jackson	.10
357	Randy Johnson	.60
358	Darren Daulton	.05
359	Charlie Hough	.05
360	Andres Galarraga	.05
361	Mike Felder	.05
362	Chris Hammond	.05
363	Shawon Dunston	.05
364	Junior Felix	.05
365	Ray Lankford	.05
366	Darryl Strawberry	.05
367	Dave Magadan	.05
368	Gregg Olson	.05
369	Len Dykstra	.05
370	Darrin Jackson	.05
371	Dave Stewart	.05
372	Terry Pendleton	.05
373	Arthur Rhodes	.05
374	Benito Santiago	.05
375	Travis Fryman	.05
376	Scott Brosius	.05
377	Stan Belinda	.05
378	Derek Parks	.05
379	Kevin Seitzer	.05
380	Wade Boggs	.75
381	Wally Whitehurst	.05
382	Scott Leius	.05
383	Danny Tartabull	.05
384	Harold Reynolds	.05
385	Tim Raines	.05
386	Darryl Hamilton	.05
387	Felix Fermin	.05
388	Jim Eisenreich	.05
389	Kurt Abbott	.05
390	Kevin Appier	.05
391	Chris Bosio	.05
392	Randy Tomlin	.05
393	Bob Hamelin	.05
394	Kevin Gross	.05
395	Wil Cordero	.05
396	Joe Girardi	.05
397	Orestes Destrade	.05
398	Chris Haney	.05
399	Xavier Hernandez	.05
400	Mike Piazza	1.00
401	Alex Arias	.05
402	Tom Candiotti	.05
403	Kirk Gibson	.05
404	Chuck Carr	.05
405	Brady Anderson	.05
406	Greg Gagne	.05
407	Bruce Ruffin	.05
408	Scott Hemond	.05
409	Keith Miller	.05
410	John Wetteland	.05
411	Eric Anthony	.05
412	Andre Dawson	.25
413	Doug Henry	.05
414	John Franco	.05
415	Julio Franco	.05
416	Dave Hansen	.05
417	Mike Harkey	.05
418	Jack Armstrong	.05
419	Joe Orsulak	.05
420	John Smoltz	.05
421	Scott Livingstone	.05
422	Darren Holmes	.05
423	Ed Sprague	.05
424	Jay Buhner	.05
425	Kirby Puckett	.75
426	Phil Clark	.05
427	Anthony Young	.05
428	Reggie Jefferson	.05
429	Mariano Duncan	.05
430	Tom Glavine	.20
431	Dave Henderson	.05
432	Melido Perez	.05
433	Paul Wagner	.05
434	Tim Worrell	.05
435	Ozzie Guillen	.05
436	Mike Butcher	.05
437	Jim Deshaies	.05
438	Kevin Young	.05
439	Tom Browning	.05
440	Mike Greenwell	.05
441	Mike Stanton	.05
442	John Doherty	.05
443	John Dopson	.05
444	Carlos Baerga	.05
445	Jack McDowell	.05
446	Kent Mercker	.05
447	Ricky Jordan	.05
448	Jerry Browne	.05
449	Fernando Vina	.05
450	Jim Abbott	.05
451	Teddy Higuera	.05
452	Tim Naehring	.05
453	Jim Leyritz	.05
454	Frank Castillo	.05
455	Joe Carter	.05
456	Craig Biggio	.05
457	Geronimo Pena	.05
458	Alejandro Pena	.05
459	Mike Moore	.05
460	Randy Myers	.05
461	Greg Myers	.05
462	Greg Hibbard	.05
463	Jose Guzman	.05
464	Tom Pagnozzi	.05
465	Marquis Grissom	.05
466	Tim Wallach	.05
467	Joe Grahe	.05
468	Bob Tewksbury	.05
469	B.J. Surhoff	.05
470	Kevin Mitchell	.05
471	Bobby Witt	.05
472	Milt Thompson	.05
473	John Smiley	.05
474	Alan Trammell	.05
475	Mike Mussina	.30
476	Rick Aguilera	.05
477	Jose Valentin	.05
478	Harold Baines	.05
479	Bip Roberts	.05
480	Edgar Martinez	.05
481	Rheal Cormier	.05
482	Hal Morris	.05
483	Pat Kelly	.05
484	Roberto Kelly	.05
485	Chris Sabo	.05
486	Kent Hrbek	.05
487	Scott Kamieniecki	.05
488	Walt Weiss	.05
489	Karl Rhodes	.05
490	Derek Bell	.05
491	Chili Davis	.05
492	Brian Harper	.05
493	Felix Jose	.05
494	Trevor Hoffman	.05
495	Dennis Eckersley	.50
496	Pedro Astacio	.05
497	Jay Bell	.05
498	Randy Velarde	.05
499	David Wells	.05
500	Frank Thomas	.60
501	Mark Lemke	.05
502	Mike Devereaux	.05
503	Chuck McElroy	.05
504	Luis Polonia	.05
505	Damion Easley	.05
506	Greg A. Harris	.05
507	Chris James	.05
508	Terry Mulholland	.05
509	Pete Smith	.05
510	Rickey Henderson	.60
511	Sid Fernandez	.05
512	Al Leiter	.05
513	Doug Jones	.05
514	Steve Farr	.05
515	Chuck Finley	.05
516	Bobby Thigpen	.05
517	Jim Edmonds	.05
518	Graeme Lloyd	.05
519	Dwight Gooden	.05
520	Pat Listach	.05
521	Kevin Bass	.05
522	Willie Banks	.05
523	Steve Finley	.05
524	Delino DeShields	.05
525	Mark McGwire	1.50
526	Greg Swindell	.05
527	Chris Nabholz	.05
528	Scott Sanders	.05
529	David Segui	.05
530	Howard Johnson	.05
531	Jaime Navarro	.05
532	Jose Vizcaino	.05
533	Mark Lewis	.05
534	Pete Harnisch	.05
535	Robby Thompson	.05
536	Marcus Moore	.05
537	Kevin Brown	.05
538	Mark Clark	.05
539	Sterling Hitchcock	.05
540	Will Clark	.05
541	Denis Boucher	.05
542	Jack Morris	.05
543	Pedro Munoz	.05
544	Bret Boone	.05
545	Ozzie Smith	.75
546	Dennis Martinez	.05
547	Dan Wilson	.05
548	Rick Sutcliffe	.05
549	Kevin McReynolds	.05
550	Roger Clemens	.85
551	Todd Benzinger	.05
552	Bill Haselman	.05
553	Bobby Munoz	.05
554	Ellis Burks	.05
555	Ryne Sandberg	.75
556	Lee Smith	.05
557	Danny Bautista	.05
558	Rey Sanchez	.05
559	Norm Charlton	.05
560	Jose Canseco	.35
561	Tim Belcher	.05
562	Denny Neagle	.05
563	Eric Davis	.05
564	Jody Reed	.05
565	Kenny Lofton	.05
566	Gary Gaetti	.05
567	Todd Worrell	.05
568	Mark Portugal	.05
569	Dick Schofield	.05
570	Andy Benes	.05
571	Zane Smith	.05
572	Bobby Ayala	.05
573	Chip Hale	.05
574	Bob Welch	.05
575	Deion Sanders	.10
576	Dave Nied	.05
577	Pat Mahomes	.05
578	Charles Nagy	.05
579	Otis Nixon	.05
580	Dean Palmer	.05
581	Roberto Petagine	.05
582	Dwight Smith	.05
583	Jeff Russell	.05
584	Mark Dewey	.05
585	Greg Vaughn	.05
586	Brian Hunter	.05
587	Willie McGee	.05
588	Pedro J. Martinez	.60
589	Roger Salkeld	.05
590	Jeff Bagwell	.60
591	Spike Owen	.05
592	Jeff Reardon	.05
593	Erik Pappas	.05
594	Brian Williams	.05
595	Eddie Murray	.60
596	Henry Rodriguez	.05
597	Erik Hanson	.05
598	Stan Javier	.05
599	Mitch Williams	.05
600	John Olerud	.05
601	Vince Coleman	.05
602	Damon Berryhill	.05
603	Tom Brunansky	.05
604	Robb Nen	.05
605	Rafael Palmeiro	.50
606	Cal Eldred	.05
607	Jeff Brantley	.05
608	Alan Mills	.05
609	Jeff Nelson	.05
610	Barry Bonds	2.00
611	Carlos Pulido RC	.05
612	Tim Hyers RC	.05
613	Steve Howe	.05
614	Brian Turang RC	.05
615	Leo Gomez	.05
616	Jesse Orosco	.05
617	Dan Pasqua	.05
618	Marvin Freeman	.05
619	Tony Fernandez	.05
620	Albert Belle	.05
621	Eddie Taubensee	.05
622	Mike Jackson	.05
623	Jose Bautista	.05
624	Jim Thome	.40
625	Ivan Rodriguez	.50
626	Ben Rivera	.05
627	Dave Valle	.05
628	Tom Henke	.05
629	Omar Vizquel	.05
630	Juan Gonzalez	.30
631	Roberto Alomar (Up Close)	.10
632	Barry Bonds (Up Close)	.60
633	Juan Gonzalez (Up Close)	.15
634	Ken Griffey Jr. (Up Close)	.50
635	Michael Jordan (Up Close)	1.50
636	Dave Justice (Up Close)	.05
637	Mike Piazza (Up Close)	.05
638	Kirby Puckett (Up Close)	.25
639	Tim Salmon (Up Close)	.05
640	Frank Thomas (Up Close)	.35
641	Alan Benes RC/FF	.05
642	Johnny Damon/FF	.35
643	Brad Fullmer RC/FF	.25
644	Derek Jeter/FF	2.00
645	Derrek Lee RC/FF	.75
646	Alex Ochoa/FF	.05
647	Alex Rodriguez RC/FF	6.00
648	Jose Silva RC/FF	.05
649	Terrell Wade RC/FF	.05
650	Preston Wilson/FF	.05
651	Shane Andrews (Rookie Class)	.15
652	James Baldwin (Rookie Class)	.05
653	Ricky Bottalico RC (Rookie Class)	.10
654	Tavo Alvarez (Rookie Class)	.05
655	Donnie Elliott (Rookie Class)	.05
656	Joey Eischen (Rookie Class)	.05
657	Jason Giambi (Rookie Class)	.50
658	Todd Hollandsworth (Rookie Class)	.05
659	Brian Hunter (Rookie Class)	.05
660	Charles Johnson (Rookie Class)	.05
661	Michael Jordan RC (Rookie Class)	3.00
662	Jeff Juden (Rookie Class)	.05
663	Kelly Mouton (Rookie Class)	.05
664	James Mouton (Rookie Class)	.05
665	Ray Holbert (Rookie Class)	.05
666	Pokey Reese (Rookie Class)	.05
667	Ruben Santana RC (Rookie Class)	.05
668	Paul Spoljaric (Rookie Class)	.05
669	Luis Lopez (Rookie Class)	.05
670	Matt Walbeck (Rookie Class)	.05

1994 Collector's Choice Gold Signature

A super-scarce parallel set of the premiere-issue Collector's Choice in 1994 was the gold-signature version produced on average of only once per 36 foil packs. In addition to a gold-foil facsimile signature on the card front, this edition features gold-colored borders on the regular player cards.

	NM/M
Common Player:	2.00
Stars:	15X

Home Run All-Stars

Among the most attractive of the 1994 chase cards, the perceived high production (over a million sets according to stated odds of winning) of this set keeps it affordable. Sets were available by a mail-in offer to persons who found a winner card in Series 1 foil packs (about one per box). Cards feature a combination of brick-bordered hologram and color player photo on front, along with a gold-foil facsimile autograph. On back the brick border is repeated, as is the photo on the hologram, though this time in full color. There is a stadium photo in the background, over which is printed a description of the player's home run prowess. A numbering error resulted in two cards numbered HA4 and no card with the HA5 number.

		NM/M
Complete Set (8):		4.00
Common Player:		.25
1HA	Juan Gonzalez	.50
2HA	Ken Griffey Jr.	1.50
3HA	Barry Bonds	2.50
4HAa	Bobby Bonilla	.25
4HAb	Cecil Fielder	.25
6HA	Albert Belle	.25
7HA	David Justice	.25
8HA	Mike Piazza	1.50

1994 Collector's Choice Silver Signature

Each of the cards in the debut edition of Upper Deck's Collector's Choice brand was also issued in a parallel edition bearing a facsimile silver-foil signature on front. The silver-signature cards were inserted at a one-per-pack rate in the set's foil packs, and proportionately in other types of packaging.

		NM/M
Common Player:		.15
Stars:		2.5X
647	Alex Rodriguez (White Letters. Some A-Rod Silver Signature parallels were mistakenly printed on base cards with his name and other details on front and back printed in white, rather than gray.)	100.00

1994 Collector's Choice Team vs. Team Scratchoff

Team vs. Team scratch-offs are a 15-card set, with one game card being inserted into every pack of Collector's Choice 1994 baseball. Each card allowed two persons to play a nine-inning baseball game. Game cards also double as a prize card in the "You Crash The Deck" contest.

		NM/M
Complete Set (15):		4.50
Common Card:		.25
1	Blue Jays-White Sox (Roberto Alomar, Frank Thomas)	.30

1994 Collector's Choice Team vs. Team Scratchoff

No.	Player	Value
2	Phillies-Braves (Lenny Dykstra, David Justice)	.25
3	Mariners-Rangers (Ken Griffey Jr., Juan Gonzalez)	.50
4	Dodgers-Giants (Mike Piazza, Barry Bonds)	.75
5	Red Sox-Yankees (Roger Clemens, Don Mattingly)	.45
6	Reds-Astros (Barry Larkin, Jeff Bagwell)	.25
7	Orioles-Tigers (Cal Ripken Jr., Cecil Fielder)	.75
8	Cubs-Cardinals (Ryne Sandberg, Ozzie Smith)	.35
9	Athletics-Angels (Mark McGwire, Tim Salmon)	.60
10	Pirates-Expos (Andy Van Slyke, Cliff Floyd)	.25
11	Brewers-Indians (Pat Listach, Albert Belle)	.25
12	Rockies-Padres (Andres Galarraga, Tony Gwynn)	.35
13	Twins-Royals (Kirby Puckett, Brian McRae)	.35
14	Mets-Marlins (Dwight Gooden, Gary Sheffield)	.25
15	N.L. All-Stars-A.L. All-Stars (Barry Bonds, Ken Griffey Jr.)	.75

1995 Collector's Choice

Issued in a single series, Upper Deck's base-brand baseball series features a number of sub-sets within the main body of the issue, as well as several insert sets. Basic cards feature large photos on front and back, with the back having full major league stats. The set opens with a 27-card Rookie Class subset featuring front photos on which the background has been rendered in hot pink tones. Backs have a lime-green box with a scouting report on the player and a box featuring 1994 minor and major league stats. The next 18 cards are Future Foundation cards which have the prospects pictured with a poster-ized background on front, with backs similar to the Rookie Class cards. Career finale cards of five retired superstars follow, then a run of Best of the '90s cards honoring record-setting achieve-ments, followed by cards depict-ing major award winners of the previous season. Each of the last three named subsets features bor-derless color photos on front, with backs similar to the regular cards. Immediately preceding the regular cards, which are arranged in team-set order, is a five-card What's the Call? subset featuring cartoon rep-resentations of the players. A set of five checklist cards marking ca-reer highlights ends the set.

	NM/M
Unopened Fact. Set (545):	17.50
Complete Set (530):	12.50
Common Player:	.05
Silver Stars:	2X
Gold Stars:	6X
Pack (12):	1.00
Wax Box (36):	20.00

No.	Player	Value
1	Charles Johnson (Rookie Class)	.05
2	Scott Ruffcorn (Rookie Class)	.05
3	Ray Durham (Rookie Class)	.05
4	Armando Benitez (Rookie Class)	.05
5	Alex Rodriguez (Rookie Class)	1.25
6	Julian Tavarez (Rookie Class)	.05
7	Chad Ogea (Rookie Class)	.05
8	Quilvio Veras (Rookie Class)	.05
9	Phil Nevin (Rookie Class)	.05
10	Michael Tucker (Rookie Class)	.05
11	Mark Thompson (Rookie Class)	.05
12	Rod Henderson (Rookie Class)	.05
13	Andrew Lorraine (Rookie Class)	.05
14	Joe Randa (Rookie Class)	.05
15	Derek Jeter (Rookie Class)	1.50
16	Tony Clark (Rookie Class)	.05
17	Juan Castillo (Rookie Class)	.05
18	Mark Acre (Rookie Class)	.05
19	Orlando Miller (Rookie Class)	.05
20	Paul Wilson (Rookie Class)	.05
21	John Mabry (Rookie Class)	.05
22	Garey Ingram (Rookie Class)	.05
23	Garret Anderson (Rookie Class)	.05
24	Dave Stevens (Rookie Class)	.05
25	Dustin Hermanson (Rookie Class)	.05
26	Paul Shuey (Rookie Class)	.05
27	J.R. Phillips (Rookie Class)	.05
28	Ruben Rivera/FF	.05
29	Nomar Garciaparra/FF	.75
30	John Wasdin/FF	.05
31	Jim Pittsley/FF	.05
32	Scott Elarton RC/FF	.15
33	Raul Casanova RC/FF	.05
34	Todd Greene/FF	.05
35	Bill Pulsipher/FF	.05
36	Trey Beamon/FF	.05
37	Curtis Goodwin/FF	.05
38	Doug Million/FF	.05
39	Karim Garcia RC/FF	1.00
40	Ben Grieve/FF	.05
41	Mark Farris/FF	.05
42	Juan Acevedo RC/FF	.05
43	C.J. Nitkowski/FF	.05
44	Travis Miller RC/FF	.10
45	Reid Ryan/FF	.10
46	Nolan Ryan	1.50
47	Robin Yount	.50
48	Ryne Sandberg	.75
49	George Brett	.85
50	Mike Schmidt	.85
51	Cecil Fielder (Best of the 90's)	.05
52	Nolan Ryan (Best of the 90's)	.75
53	Rickey Henderson (Best of the 90's)	.20
54	George Brett, Robin Yount, Dave Winfield (Best of the 90's)	.25
55	Sid Bream (Best of the 90's)	.05
56	Carlos Baerga (Best of the 90's)	.05
57	Lee Smith (Best of the 90's)	.05
58	Mark Whiten (Best of the 90's)	.05
59	Joe Carter (Best of the 90's)	.05
60	Barry Bonds (Best of the 90's)	.75
61	Tony Gwynn (Best of the 90's)	.40
62	Ken Griffey Jr. (Best of the 90's)	.50
63	Greg Maddux (Best of the 90's)	.40
64	Frank Thomas (Best of the 90's)	.35
65	Dennis Martinez, Kenny Rogers (Best of the 90's)	.05
66	David Cone (Cy Young)	.05
67	Greg Maddux (Cy Young)	.75
68	Jimmy Key (Most Victories)	.05
69	Fred McGriff (All-Star MVP)	.05
70	Ken Griffey Jr. (HR Champ)	1.00
71	Matt Williams (HR Champ)	.05
72	Paul O'Neill (Batting Title)	.05
73	Tony Gwynn (Batting Title)	.40
74	Randy Johnson (Ks Leader)	.60
75	Frank Thomas (MVP)	.60
76	Jeff Bagwell (MVP)	.60
77	Kirby Puckett (RBI leader)	.75
78	Bob Hamelin (ROY)	.05
79	Raul Mondesi (ROY)	.05
80	Mike Piazza (All-Star)	1.00
81	Kenny Lofton (SB Leader)	.05
82	Barry Bonds (Gold Glove)	1.50
83	Albert Belle/AS	.05
84	Juan Gonzalez (HR Champ)	.30
85	Cal Ripken Jr. (2,000 Straight Games)	1.50
86	Barry Bonds (What's the Call?)	.75
87	Mike Piazza (What's the Call?)	.60
88	Ken Griffey Jr. (What's the Call?)	.50
89	Frank Thomas (What's the Call?)	.35
90	Juan Gonzalez (What's the Call?)	.10
91	Jorge Fabregas	.05
92	J.T. Snow	.05
93	Spike Owen	.05
94	Eduardo Perez	.05
95	Bo Jackson	.10
96	Damion Easley	.05
97	Gary DiSarcina	.05
98	Jim Edmonds	.05
99	Chad Curtis	.05
100	Tim Salmon	.05
101	Chili Davis	.05
102	Chuck Finley	.05
103	Mark Langston	.05
104	Brian Anderson	.05
105	Lee Smith	.05
106	Phil Leftwich	.05
107	Chris Donnels	.05
108	John Hudek	.05
109	Craig Biggio	.05
110	Luis Gonzalez	.05
111	Brian L. Hunter	.05
112	James Mouton	.05
113	Scott Servais	.05
114	Tony Eusebio	.05
115	Derek Bell	.05
116	Doug Drabek	.05
117	Shane Reynolds	.05
118	Darryl Kile	.05
119	Greg Swindell	.05
120	Phil Plantier	.05
121	Todd Jones	.05
122	Steve Ontiveros	.05
123	Bobby Witt	.05
124	Brent Gates	.05
125	Rickey Henderson	.60
126	Scott Brosius	.05
127	Mike Bordick	.05
128	Fausto Cruz	.05
129	Stan Javier	.05
130	Mark McGwire	1.25
131	Geronimo Berroa	.05
132	Terry Steinbach	.05
133	Steve Karsay	.05
134	Dennis Eckersley	.50
135	Ruben Sierra	.05
136	Ron Darling	.05
137	Todd Van Poppel	.05
138	Alex Gonzalez	.05
139	John Olerud	.05
140	Roberto Alomar	.20
141	Darren Hall	.05
142	Ed Sprague	.05
143	Devon White	.05
144	Shawn Green	.20
145	Paul Molitor	.60
146	Pat Borders	.05
147	Carlos Delgado	.35
148	Juan Guzman	.05
149	Pat Hentgen	.05
150	Joe Carter	.05
151	Dave Stewart	.05
152	Todd Stottlemyre	.05
153	Dick Schofield	.05
154	Chipper Jones	.75
155	Ryan Klesko	.20
156	Dave Justice	.05
157	Mike Kelly	.05
158	Roberto Kelly	.05
159	Tony Tarasco	.05
160	Javier Lopez	.05
161	Steve Avery	.05
162	Greg McMichael	.05
163	Kent Mercker	.05
164	Mark Lemke	.05
165	Tom Glavine	.20
166	Jose Oliva	.05
167	John Smoltz	.05
168	Jeff Blauser	.05
169	Troy O'Leary	.05
170	Greg Vaughn	.05
171	Jody Reed	.05
172	Kevin Seitzer	.05
173	Jeff Cirillo	.05
174	B.J. Surhoff	.05
175	Cal Eldred	.05
176	Jose Valentin	.05
177	Turner Ward	.05
178	Darryl Hamilton	.05
179	Pat Listach	.05
180	Matt Mieske	.05
181	Brian Harper	.05
182	Dave Nilsson	.05
183	Mike Fetters	.05
184	John Jaha	.05
185	Ricky Bones	.05
186	Geronimo Pena	.05
187	Bob Tewksbury	.05
188	Todd Zeile	.05
189	Danny Jackson	.05
190	Ray Lankford	.05
191	Bernard Gilkey	.05
192	Brian Jordan	.05
193	Tom Pagnozzi	.05
194	Rick Sutcliffe	.05
195	Mark Whiten	.05
196	Tom Henke	.05
197	Rene Arocha	.05
198	Allen Watson	.05
199	Mike Perez	.05
200	Ozzie Smith	.75
201	Anthony Young	.05
202	Rey Sanchez	.05
203	Steve Buechele	.05
204	Shawon Dunston	.05
205	Mark Grace	.05
206	Glenallen Hill	.05
207	Eddie Zambrano	.05
208	Rick Wilkins	.05
209	Derrick May	.05
210	Sammy Sosa	.75
211	Kevin Roberson	.05
212	Steve Trachsel	.05
213	Willie Banks	.05
214	Kevin Foster	.05
215	Randy Myers	.05
216	Mike Morgan	.05
217	Rafael Bournigal	.05
218	Delino DeShields	.05
219	Tim Wallach	.05
220	Eric Karros	.05
221	Jose Offerman	.05
222	Tom Candiotti	.05
223	Ismael Valdes	.05
224	Henry Rodriguez	.05
225	Billy Ashley	.05
226	Darren Dreifort	.05
227	Ramon Martinez	.05
228	Pedro Astacio	.05
229	Orel Hershiser	.05
230	Brett Butler	.05
231	Todd Hollandsworth	.05
232	Chan Ho Park	.05
233	Mike Lansing	.05
234	Sean Berry	.05
235	Rondell White	.05
236	Ken Hill	.05
237	Marquis Grissom	.05
238	Larry Walker	.05
239	John Wetteland	.05
240	Cliff Floyd	.05
241	Joey Eischen	.05
242	Lou Frazier	.05
243	Darrin Fletcher	.05
244	Pedro J. Martinez	.60
245	Wil Cordero	.05
246	Jeff Fassero	.05
247	Butch Henry	.05
248	Mel Rojas	.05
249	Kirk Rueter	.05
250	Moises Alou	.05
251	Rod Beck	.05
252	John Patterson	.05
253	Robby Thompson	.05
254	Royce Clayton	.05
255	William Van Landingham	.05
256	Darren Lewis	.05
257	Kirt Manwaring	.05
258	Mark Portugal	.05
259	Bill Swift	.05
260	Rikkert Faneyte	.05
261	Mike Jackson	.05
262	Todd Benzinger	.05
263	Bud Black	.05
264	Salomon Torres	.05
265	Eddie Murray	.60
266	Mark Clark	.05
267	Paul Sorrento	.05
268	Jim Thome	.45
269	Omar Vizquel	.05
270	Carlos Baerga	.05
271	Jeff Russell	.05
272	Herbert Perry	.05
273	Sandy Alomar Jr.	.05
274	Dennis Martinez	.05
275	Manny Ramirez	.60
276	Wayne Kirby	.05
277	Charles Nagy	.05
278	Albie Lopez	.05
279	Jeromy Burnitz	.05
280	Dave Winfield	.60
281	Tim Davis	.05
282	Marc Newfield	.05
283	Tino Martinez	.05
284	Mike Blowers	.05
285	Goose Gossage	.05
286	Luis Sojo	.05
287	Edgar Martinez	.05
288	Rich Amaral	.05
289	Felix Fermin	.05
290	Jay Buhner	.05
291	Dan Wilson	.05
292	Bobby Ayala	.05
293	Dave Fleming	.05
294	Greg Pirkl	.05
295	Reggie Jefferson	.05
296	Greg Hibbard	.05
297	Yorkis Perez	.05
298	Kurt Miller	.05
299	Chuck Carr	.05
300	Gary Sheffield	.30
301	Jerry Browne	.05
302	Dave Magadan	.05
303	Kurt Abbott	.05
304	Pat Rapp	.05
305	Jeff Conine	.05
306	Benito Santiago	.05
307	Dave Weathers	.05
308	Robb Nen	.05
309	Chris Hammond	.05
310	Bryan Harvey	.05
311	Charlie Hough	.05
312	Greg Colbrunn	.05
313	David Segui	.05
314	Rico Brogna	.05
315	Jeff Kent	.05
316	Jose Vizcaino	.05
317	Jim Lindeman	.05
318	Carl Everett	.05
319	Ryan Thompson	.05
320	Bobby Bonilla	.05
321	Joe Orsulak	.05
322	Pete Harnisch	.05
323	Doug Linton	.05
324	Todd Hundley	.05
325	Bret Saberhagen	.05
326	Kelly Stinnett	.05
327	Jason Jacome	.05
328	Bobby Jones	.05
329	John Franco	.05
330	Rafael Palmeiro	.50
331	Chris Hoiles	.05
332	Leo Gomez	.05
333	Chris Sabo	.05
334	Brady Anderson	.05
335	Jeffrey Hammonds	.05
336	Dwight Smith	.05
337	Jack Voigt	.05
338	Harold Baines	.05
339	Ben McDonald	.05
340	Mike Mussina	.30
341	Bret Barberie	.05
342	Jamie Moyer	.05
343	Mike Oquist	.05
344	Sid Fernandez	.05
345	Eddie Williams	.05
346	Joey Hamilton	.05
347	Brian Williams	.05
348	Luis Lopez	.05
349	Steve Finley	.05
350	Andy Benes	.05
351	Andujar Cedeno	.05
352	Bip Roberts	.05
353	Ray McDavid	.05
354	Ken Caminiti	.05
355	Trevor Hoffman	.05
356	Mel Nieves	.05
357	Brad Ausmus	.05
358	Andy Ashby	.05
359	Scott Sanders	.05
360	Gregg Jefferies	.05
361	Mariano Duncan	.05
362	Dave Hollins	.05
363	Kevin Stocker	.05
364	Fernando Valenzuela	.05
365	Lenny Dykstra	.05
366	Jim Eisenreich	.05
367	Ricky Jordan	.05
368	Doug Jones	.05
369	Ricky Jordan	.05
370	Darren Daulton	.05
371	Mike Lieberthal	.05
372	Bobby Munoz	.05
373	John Kruk	.05
374	Curt Schilling	.20
375	Orlando Merced	.05
376	Carlos Garcia	.05
377	Lance Parrish	.05
378	Steve Cooke	.05
379	Jeff King	.05
380	Jay Bell	.05
381	Al Martin	.05
382	Paul Wagner	.05
383	Rick White	.05
384	Midre Cummings	.05
385	Jon Lieber	.05
386	Dave Clark	.05
387	Don Slaught	.05
388	Denny Neagle	.05
389	Zane Smith	.05
390	Andy Van Slyke	.05
391	Ivan Rodriguez	.50
392	David Hulse	.05
393	John Burkett	.05
394	Kevin Brown	.05
395	Dean Palmer	.05
396	Otis Nixon	.05
397	Rick Helling	.05
398	Kenny Rogers	.05
399	Darren Oliver	.05
400	Will Clark	.05
401	Jeff Frye	.05
402	Kevin Gross	.05
403	John Dettmer	.05
404	Manny Lee	.05
405	Rusty Greer	.05
406	Aaron Sele	.05
407	Carlos Rodriguez	.05
408	Scott Cooper	.05
409	John Valentin	.05
410	Roger Clemens	.85
411	Mike Greenwell	.05
412	Tim Vanegmond	.05
413	Tom Brunansky	.05
414	Steve Farr	.05
415	Jose Canseco	.35
416	Joe Hesketh	.05
417	Ken Ryan	.05
418	Tim Naehring	.05
419	Frank Viola	.05
420	Andre Dawson	.25
421	Mo Vaughn	.05
422	Jeff Brantley	.05
423	Pete Schourek	.05
424	Hal Morris	.05
425	Deion Sanders	.10
426	Brian L. Hunter	.05
427	Bret Boone	.05
428	Willie Greene	.05
429	Ron Gant	.05
430	Barry Larkin	.05
431	Reggie Sanders	.05
432	Eddie Taubensee	.05
433	Jack Morris	.05
434	Jose Rijo	.05
435	Johnny Ruffin	.05
436	John Smiley	.05
437	John Roper	.05
438	David Nied	.05
439	Roberto Mejia	.05
440	Andres Galarraga	.05
441	Mike Kingery	.05
442	Curt Leskanic	.05
443	Walt Weiss	.05
444	Marvin Freeman	.05
445	Charlie Hayes	.05
446	Eric Young	.05
447	Ellis Burks	.05
448	Joe Girardi	.05
449	Lance Painter	.05
450	Dante Bichette	.05
451	Bruce Ruffin	.05
452	Jeff Granger	.05
453	Wally Joyner	.05
454	Jose Lind	.05
455	Jeff Montgomery	.05
456	Gary Gaetti	.05
457	Greg Gagne	.05
458	Vince Coleman	.05
459	Mike Macfarlane	.05
460	Brian McRae	.05
461	Tom Gordon	.05
462	Kevin Appier	.05
463	Billy Brewer	.05
464	Mark Gubicza	.05
465	Travis Fryman	.05
466	Danny Bautista	.05
467	Sean Bergman	.05
468	Mike Henneman	.05
469	Mike Moore	.05
470	Cecil Fielder	.05
471	Alan Trammell	.05
472	Kirk Gibson	.05
473	Tony Phillips	.05
474	Mickey Tettleton	.05
475	Lou Whitaker	.05
476	Chris Gomez	.05
477	John Doherty	.05
478	Greg Gohr	.05
479	Bill Gullickson	.05
480	Rick Aguilera	.05
481	Matt Walbeck	.05
482	Kevin Tapani	.05
483	Scott Erickson	.05
484	Steve Dunn	.05
485	David McCarty	.05
486	Scott Leius	.05
487	Pat Meares	.05
488	Jeff Reboulet	.05
489	Pedro Munoz	.05
490	Chuck Knoblauch	.05
491	Rich Becker	.05
492	Alex Cole	.05
493	Pat Mahomes	.05
494	Ozzie Guillen	.05
495	Tim Raines	.05
496	Kirk McCaskill	.05
497	Olmedo Saenz	.05
498	Scott Sanderson	.05
499	Lance Johnson	.05
500	Michael Jordan	1.50
501	Warren Newson	.05
502	Ron Karkovice	.05
503	Wilson Alvarez	.05
504	Jason Bere	.05
505	Robin Ventura	.05
506	Alex Fernandez	.05
507	Roberto Hernandez	.05
508	Norberto Martin	.05
509	Bob Wickman	.05
510	Don Mattingly	.85
511	Melido Perez	.05
512	Pat Kelly	.05
513	Randy Velarde	.05
514	Tony Fernandez	.05
515	Jack McDowell	.05
516	Luis Polonia	.05
517	Bernie Williams	.05
518	Danny Tartabull	.05
519	Mike Stanley	.05
520	Wade Boggs	.75
521	Jim Leyritz	.05
522	Steve Howe	.05
523	Scott Kamieniecki	.05
524	Russ Davis	.05
525	Jim Abbott	.05
526	Checklist 1-106 (Eddie Murray)	.05
527	Checklist 107-212 (Alex Rodriguez)	.20
528	Checklist 213-318 (Jeff Bagwell)	.20
529	Checklist 319-424 (Joe Carter)	.05
530	Checklist 425-530 (Fred McGriff)	.05
---	National Packtime Offer Card	

Silver Signature

A silver-foil facsimile autograph added to the card front is the only difference between these chase cards and regular-issue Collector's Choice cards. The silver-signature inserts are found one per pack in regular foil packs, and two per pack in retail jumbo packs.

	NM/M
Common Player:	.10
Stars:	2X

Gold Signature

The top-of-the-line chase card in 1995 Collector's Choice is the Gold Signature parallel set. Each of the 530 cards in the set was created in a special gold version that was found on average only one per box of foil packs. Other than the addition of a gold-foil facsimile autograph on front, the cards are identical to regular-issue Collector's Choice.

	NM/M
Common Player:	.50
Stars:	6X

1995 Collector's Choice Trade Cards

A series of five mail-in redemption cards was included as inserts into UD Collector's Choice, at the rate of approximately one per 11 packs. The cards could be sent in with $2 to receive 11 Collector's Choice Update cards, as specified on the front of the card. The trade offer expired on Feb. 1, 1996. Cards are numbered with the "TC" prefix.

	NM/M
Complete Set (5):	1.00
Common Player:	.25
1	Larry Walker (#531-541)	.25
2	David Cone (#542-552)	.25
3	Marquis Grissom (#553-563)	.25
4	Terry Pendleton (#564-574)	.25
5	Fernando Valenzuela (#575-585)	.25

1995 Collector's Choice Redemption Cards

These update cards were available only via a mail-in offer involving trade cards found in foil packs. Each trade card was redeemable for a specific 11-card set of players shown in their new uniforms as a result of rookie call-ups, trades and free agent signings. The cards are in the same format as the regular 1995 Collector's Choice issue. The update redemption cards are numbered by team nickname from Angels through Yankees, the numbers running contiguously from the body of the CC set.

	NM/M
Complete Set (55):	2.50
Common Player:	.10
531	Tony Phillips	.10
532	Dave Magadan	.10
533	Mike Gallego	.10
534	Dave Stewart	.10
535	Todd Stottlemyre	.10
536	David Cone	.10
537	Marquis Grissom	.10
538	Derrick May	.10
539	Joe Oliver	.10
540	Scott Cooper	.10
541	Ken Hill	.10
542	Howard Johnson	.10
543	Brian McRae	.10
544	Jaime Navarro	.10
545	Ozzie Timmons	.10
546	Roberto Kelly	.10
547	Hideo Nomo	1.50
548	Shane Andrews	.10
549	Mark Grudzielanek	.10
550	Carlos Perez	.10
551	Henry Rodriguez	.10
552	Tony Tarasco	.10
553	Glenallen Hill	.10
554	Terry Mulholland	.10
555	Orel Hershiser	.10
556	Darren Bragg	.10
557	John Burkett	.10
558	Bobby Witt	.10
559	Terry Pendleton	.10
560	Andre Dawson	.50
561	Brett Butler	.10
562	Kevin Brown	.10
563	Doug Jones	.10
564	Andy Van Slyke	.10
565	Jody Reed	.10
566	Fernando Valenzuela	.10
567	Charlie Hayes	.10
568	Benji Gil	.10
569	Mark McLemore	.10
570	Mickey Tettleton	.10
571	Bob Tewksbury	.10
572	Rheal Cormier	.10
573	Vaughn Eshelman	.10
574	Mike Macfarlane	.10
575	Mark Whiten	.10
576	Benito Santiago	.10
577	Jason Bates	.10
578	Bill Swift	.10
579	Larry Walker	.10
580	Chad Curtis	.10
581	Bobby Higginson	.10
582	Marty Cordova	.10
583	Mike Devereaux	.10
584	John Kruk	.10
585	John Wetteland	.10

1995 Collector's Choice Crash the Game

These insert cards gave collectors a reason to follow box scores around the major leagues between June 18-October 1. Each of 20 noted home run hitters can be found with three different dates foil-stamped on the card front. If the player hit a home run on that day, the card could be redeemed for a set of 20 special prize cards. Stated odds of finding a You Crash the Game card were one in five packs. Most of the inserts are sil-

ver-foil enhanced, with about one in eight being found with gold foil. Winning cards are much scarcer than the others since they had to be mailed in for redemption.

	NM/M
Complete Set, Silver (20):	5.00
Common Player, Silver:	.15
Complete Set, Gold (20):	12.00
Common Player, Gold:	.35
CG1	Jeff Bagwell (July 30)	.25
CG1	Jeff Bagwell (Aug. 13)	.25
CG1	Jeff Bagwell (Sept. 28)	.25
CG2	Albert Belle (June 18)	.15
CG2	Albert Belle (Aug. 26)	.15
CG2	Albert Belle (Sept. 20)	.15
CG3	Barry Bonds (June 28)	1.00
CG3	Barry Bonds (July 9)	1.00
CG3	Barry Bonds (Sept. 6)	1.00
CG4	Jose Canseco (June 30)(Winner)	1.00
CG4	Jose Canseco (July 30)(Winner)	1.00
CG4	Jose Canseco (Sept. 3)	.35
CG5	Joe Carter (July 14)	.15
CG5	Joe Carter (Aug. 9)	.15
CG5	Joe Carter (Sept. 23)	.15
CG6	Cecil Fielder (July 4)	.15
CG6	Cecil Fielder (Aug. 2)	.15
CG6	Cecil Fielder (Oct. 1)	.15
CG7	Juan Gonzalez (June 29)	.30
CG7	Juan Gonzalez (Aug. 13)	.30
CG7	Juan Gonzalez (Sept. 3)(Winner)	1.00
CG8	Ken Griffey Jr. (July 2)	.60
CG8	Ken Griffey Jr. (Aug. 24)(Winner)	2.50
CG8	Ken Griffey Jr. (Sept. 15)	.60
CG9	Bob Hamelin (July 23)	.15
CG9	Bob Hamelin (Aug. 1)	.15
CG9	Bob Hamelin (Sept. 29)	.15
CG10	David Justice (June 24)	.15
CG10	David Justice (July 25)	.15
CG10	David Justice (Oct. 1)	.15
CG11	Ryan Klesko (July 13)	.15
CG11	Ryan Klesko (Aug. 20)	.15
CG11	Ryan Klesko (Sept. 10)	.15
CG12	Fred McGriff (Aug. 25)	.15
CG12	Fred McGriff (Sept. 8)	.15
CG12	Fred McGriff (Sept. 24)	.15
CG13	Mark McGwire (July 23)	.75
CG13	Mark McGwire (Aug. 3)(Winner)	3.00
CG13	Mark McGwire (Sept. 27)	.75
CG14	Raul Mondesi (July 27)(Winner)	.75
CG14	Raul Mondesi (Aug. 13)	.15
CG14	Raul Mondesi (Sept. 15)(Winner)	.75
CG15	Mike Piazza (July 23)(Winner)	2.00
CG15	Mike Piazza (Aug. 27)(Winner)	2.00
CG15	Mike Piazza (Sept. 19)	.60
CG16	Manny Ramirez (June 21)	.35
CG16	Manny Ramirez (Aug. 13)	.35
CG16	Manny Ramirez (Aug. 26)	.35
CG17	Alex Rodriguez (Sept. 10)	.75
CG17	Alex Rodriguez (Sept. 18)	.75
CG17	Alex Rodriguez (Sept. 24)	.75
CG18	Gary Sheffield (July 5)	.30
CG18	Gary Sheffield (Aug. 13)	.30
CG18	Gary Sheffield (Sept. 4)(Winner)	2.00
CG19	Frank Thomas (July 26)	.50
CG19	Frank Thomas (Aug. 17)	.50
CG19	Frank Thomas (Sept. 23)	.50
CG20	Matt Williams (July 29)	.15
CG20	Matt Williams (Aug. 12)	.15
CG20	Matt Williams (Sept. 19)	.15

1995 Collector's Choice Crash the Game

	NM/M
CG6	Cecil Fielder (July 4)	.35
CG6	Cecil Fielder (Aug. 2)	.35
CG6	Cecil Fielder (Oct. 1)	.35
CG7	Juan Gonzalez (June 29)	.45
CG7	Juan Gonzalez (Aug. 13)	.45
CG7	Juan Gonzalez (Sept. 3)(Winner)	1.50
CG8	Ken Griffey Jr. (July 2)	1.50
CG8	Ken Griffey Jr. (Aug. 24)(Winner)	3.00
CG8	Ken Griffey Jr. (Sept. 15)	1.50
CG9	Bob Hamelin (July 23)	.35
CG9	Bob Hamelin (Aug. 1)	.35
CG9	Bob Hamelin (Sept. 29)	.35
CG10	David Justice (June 24)	.35
CG10	David Justice (July 25)	.35
CG10	David Justice (Sept. 17)	.35
CG11	Ryan Klesko (July 13)	.35
CG11	Ryan Klesko (Aug. 20)	.35
CG11	Ryan Klesko (Sept. 10)	.35
CG12	Fred McGriff (Aug. 25)	.35
CG12	Fred McGriff (Sept. 8)	.35
CG12	Fred McGriff (Sept. 24)	.35
CG13	Mark McGwire (July 23)	2.00
CG13	Mark McGwire (Aug. 3)(Winner)	4.00
CG13	Mark McGwire (Sept. 27)	2.00
CG14	Raul Mondesi (July 27)(Winner)	1.25
CG14	Raul Mondesi (Aug. 13)	.45
CG14	Raul Mondesi (Sept. 15)(Winner)	1.25
CG15	Mike Piazza (July 23)(Winner)	3.00
CG15	Mike Piazza (Aug. 27)(Winner)	3.00
CG15	Mike Piazza (Sept. 19)	1.00
CG16	Manny Ramirez (June 21)	.75
CG16	Manny Ramirez (Aug. 13)	.75
CG16	Manny Ramirez (Aug. 26)	.75
CG17	Alex Rodriguez (Sept. 10)	1.00
CG17	Alex Rodriguez (Sept. 18)	1.00
CG17	Alex Rodriguez (Sept. 24)	1.00
CG18	Gary Sheffield (July 5)	.75
CG18	Gary Sheffield (Aug. 13)	.75
CG18	Gary Sheffield (Sept. 4)(Winner)	2.00
CG19	Frank Thomas (July 26)	.65
CG19	Frank Thomas (Aug. 17)	.65
CG19	Frank Thomas (Sept. 23)	.65
CG20	Matt Williams (July 29)	.45
CG20	Matt Williams (Aug. 12)	.45
CG20	Matt Williams (Sept. 19)	.45

1995 Collector's Choice Crash Winners

These 20-card sets were awarded to collectors who redeemed "You Crash the Game" winners cards. A silver-foil enhanced set was sent to winners with silver redemption cards, a gold version was sent to gold winners. A $3 redemption fee was required. Fronts are similar to the game cards, except for the foil printing down the left side in the place of the game date. Instead of redemption rules on the back of award cards there are career highlights at left and a panel at right with the names of the players in the set.

	NM/M
Complete Set, Silver (20):	6.00
Complete Set, Gold (20):	25.00
Common Player, Silver:	.25
Common Player, Gold:	1.00
CR1	Jeff Bagwell	.60
CR2	Albert Belle	.35
CR3	Barry Bonds	2.50
CR4	Jose Canseco	.50
CR5	Joe Carter	.25
CR6	Cecil Fielder	.25
CR7	Juan Gonzalez	.50
CR8	Ken Griffey Jr.	1.50
CR9	Bob Hamelin	.25
CR10	Dave Justice	.25
CR11	Ryan Klesko	.25
CR12	Fred McGriff	.25
CR13	Mark McGwire	2.00
CR14	Raul Mondesi	.25
CR15	Mike Piazza	1.50
CR16	Manny Ramirez	.60
CR17	Alex Rodriguez	2.00
CR18	Gary Sheffield	.50
CR19	Frank Thomas	2.00
CR20	Matt Williams	.25
CR1	Jeff Bagwell	2.00
CR2	Albert Belle	1.00
CR3	Barry Bonds	4.00
CR4	Jose Canseco	1.50
CR5	Joe Carter	1.00
CR6	Cecil Fielder	1.00
CR7	Juan Gonzalez	1.50
CR8	Ken Griffey Jr.	3.00
CR9	Bob Hamelin	1.00
CR10	Dave Justice	1.00
CR11	Ryan Klesko	1.00
CR12	Fred McGriff	1.00
CR13	Mark McGwire	3.00
CR14	Raul Mondesi	1.00
CR15	Mike Piazza	3.00
CR16	Manny Ramirez	2.00
CR17	Alex Rodriguez	3.50
CR18	Gary Sheffield	1.00
CR19	Frank Thomas	2.00
CR20	Matt Williams	1.00

1995 Collector's Choice Michael Jordan Jumbo

A limited edition of 10,000 of these 3" x 5" cards was produced for direct sales to consumers. The card is in the format of the 1995 Collector's Choice Rookie Class subset and includes a silver foil facsimile of Jordan's autograph on front. Back includes a serial number in the lower-right corner.

	NM/M
661	Michael Jordan	15.00

1995 Collector's Choice Ichiro Suzuki

This card was part of a set produced by Upper Deck's Collector's Choice brand in conjunction with a series of NBA games held in Japan. The cards were made for various members of the media, sports dignitaries, etc., to be used as personal business cards. Cards are in standard 2-1/2" x 3-1/2" format.

	NM/M
59	Ichiro Suzuki	1,000

1995 Collector's Choice/SE

The first Upper Deck baseball card issue for 1995 was this 265-card set which uses blue borders and a blue foil "Special Edition" trapezoidal logo to impart a premium look. The set opens with a Rookie Class subset of 25 cards on which the background has been rendered in orange hues. A series of six Record Pace cards, horizontal with blue and yellow backgrounds, immediately precedes the regular cards. Base cards in the set are arranged in team-alpha order. Front and back have large color photos, while backs offer complete major league stats. Interspersed within the teams are special cards with borderless front designs honoring players who won significant awards in the 1994 season. Another subset, Stat Leaders, pictures various players in a silver dollar-sized circle at the center of the card and lists the 1994 leaders in that category on the back. A dozen-card Fantasy Team subset near the end of the set lists the top-rated players at each position, picturing one of them on front, with a giant blue baseball. The set closes with five checklists honoring career highlights from the '94 season.

	NM/M
Complete Set (265):	17.50
Common Player:	.05
Silver Stars:	1.5X
Gold Stars:	8X
Pack (12):	1.25
Wax Box (36):	25.00
1	Alex Rodriguez	1.50
2	Derek Jeter	2.00
3	Dustin Hermanson	.05
4	Bill Pulsipher	.05
5	Terrell Wade	.05
6	Darren Dreifort	.05
7	LaTroy Hawkins	.05
8	Alex Ochoa	.05
9	Paul Wilson	.05
10	Ernie Young	.05
11	Alan Benes	.05
12	Garret Anderson	.05
13	Armando Benitez	.05
14	Robert Perez	.05
15	Herbert Perry	.05
16	Jose Silva	.05
17	Orlando Miller	.05
18	Russ Davis	.05
19	Jason Isringhausen	.05
20	Ray McDavid	.05
21	Duane Singleton	.05
22	Paul Shuey	.05
23	Steve Dunn	.05
24	Mike Lieberthal	.05
25	Chan Ho Park	.05
26	Ken Griffey Jr. (Record Pace)	.65
27	Tony Gwynn (Record Pace)	.40
28	Chuck Knoblauch (Record Pace)	.05
29	Frank Thomas (Record Pace)	.35
30	Matt Williams (Record Pace)	.05
31	Chili Davis	.05
32	Chad Curtis	.05
33	Brian Anderson	.05
34	Chuck Finley	.05
35	Tim Salmon	.10
36	Bo Jackson	.10
37	Doug Drabek	.05
38	Craig Biggio	.05
39	Ken Caminiti	.05
40	Jeff Bagwell	.65
41	Darryl Kile	.05
42	John Hudek	.05
43	Brian L. Hunter	.05
44	Dennis Eckersley	.05
45	Mark McGwire	1.50
46	Brent Gates	.05
47	Steve Karsay	.05
48	Rickey Henderson	.65
49	Terry Steinbach	.05
50	Ruben Sierra	.05
51	Roberto Alomar	.25
52	Carlos Delgado	.05
53	Alex Gonzalez	.05
54	Joe Carter	.25
55	Paul Molitor	.65
56	Juan Guzman	.05
57	John Olerud	.25
58	Shawn Green	.25
59	Tom Glavine	.25
60	Greg Maddux	.75
61	Roberto Kelly	.05
62	Ryan Klesko	.05
63	Javier Lopez	.05
64	Jose Oliva	.05
65	Fred McGriff	.05

#	Player	Price
66	Steve Avery	.05
67	Dave Justice	.05
68	Ricky Bones	.05
69	Cal Eldred	.05
70	Greg Vaughn	.05
71	Dave Nilsson	.05
72	Jose Valentin	.05
73	Matt Mieske	.05
74	Todd Zeile	.05
75	Ozzie Smith	.75
76	Bernard Gilkey	.05
77	Ray Lankford	.05
78	Bob Tewksbury	.05
79	Mark Whiten	.05
80	Gregg Jefferies	.05
81	Randy Myers	.05
82	Shawon Dunston	.05
83	Mark Grace	.25
84	Derrick May	.05
85	Sammy Sosa	.75
86	Steve Trachsel	.05
87	Brett Butler	.05
88	Delino DeShields	.05
89	Orel Hershiser	.05
90	Mike Piazza	1.00
91	Todd Hollandsworth	.05
92	Eric Karros	.05
93	Ramon Martinez	.05
94	Tim Wallach	.05
95	Raul Mondesi	.05
96	Larry Walker	.05
97	Wil Cordero	.05
98	Marquis Grissom	.05
99	Ken Hill	.05
100	Cliff Floyd	.05
101	Pedro J. Martinez	.65
102	John Wetteland	.05
103	Rondell White	.05
104	Moises Alou	.05
105	Barry Bonds	2.00
106	Darren Lewis	.05
107	Mark Portugal	.05
108	Matt Williams	.05
109	William Van Landingham	.05
110	Bill Swift	.05
111	Robby Thompson	.05
112	Rod Beck	.05
113	Darryl Strawberry	.05
114	Jim Thome	.50
115	Dave Winfield	.65
116	Eddie Murray	.65
117	Manny Ramirez	.75
118	Carlos Baerga	.25
119	Kenny Lofton	.05
120	Albert Belle	.05
121	Mark Clark	.05
122	Dennis Martinez	.05
123	Randy Johnson	.65
124	Jay Buhner	.05
125	Ken Griffey Jr.	1.00
125a	Ken Griffey Jr./OPS	1.50
126	Rich Gossage	.05
127	Tino Martinez	.05
128	Reggie Jefferson	.05
129	Edgar Martinez	.05
130	Gary Sheffield	.30
131	Pat Rapp	.05
132	Bret Barberie	.05
133	Chuck Carr	.05
134	Jeff Conine	.05
135	Charles Johnson	.05
136	Benito Santiago	.05
137	Matt Williams (Stat Leaders)	.05
138	Jeff Bagwell (Stat Leaders)	.35
139	Kenny Lofton (Stat Leaders)	.05
140	Tony Gwynn (Stat Leaders)	.40
141	Jimmy Key (Stat Leaders)	.05
142	Greg Maddux (Stat Leaders)	.40
143	Randy Johnson (Stat Leaders)	.25
144	Lee Smith (Stat Leaders)	.05
145	Bobby Bonilla	.05
146	Jason Jacome	.05
147	Jeff Kent	.05
148	Ryan Thompson	.05
149	Bobby Jones	.05
150	Bret Saberhagen	.05
151	John Franco	.05
152	Lee Smith	.05
153	Rafael Palmeiro	.60
154	Brady Anderson	.05
155	Cal Ripken Jr.	2.00
156	Jeffrey Hammonds	.05
157	Mike Mussina	.35
158	Chris Hoiles	.05
159	Ben McDonald	.05
160	Tony Gwynn	.75
161	Joey Hamilton	.05
162	Andy Benes	.05
163	Trevor Hoffman	.05
164	Phil Plantier	.05
165	Derek Bell	.05
166	Bip Roberts	.05
167	Eddie Williams	.05
168	Fernando Valenzuela	.05
169	Mariano Duncan	.05
170	Lenny Dykstra	.05
171	Darren Daulton	.05
172	Danny Jackson	.05
173	Bobby Munoz	.05
174	Doug Jones	.05
175	Jay Bell	.05
176	Zane Smith	.05
177	Jon Lieber	.05
178	Carlos Garcia	.05
179	Orlando Merced	.05
180	Andy Van Slyke	.05
181	Rick Helling	.05
182	Rusty Greer	.05
183	Kenny Rogers	.05
184	Will Clark	.05
185	Jose Canseco	.05
186	Juan Gonzalez	.35
187	Dean Palmer	.05
188	Ivan Rodriguez	.60
189	John Valentin	.05
190	Roger Clemens	.85
191	Aaron Sele	.05
192	Scott Cooper	.05
193	Mike Greenwell	.05
194	Mo Vaughn	.25
195	Andre Dawson	.05
196	Ron Gant	.05
197	Jose Rijo	.05
198	Bret Boone	.05
199	Deion Sanders	.10
200	Barry Larkin	.05
201	Hal Morris	.05
202	Reggie Sanders	.05
203	Kevin Mitchell	.05
204	Marvin Freeman	.05
205	Andres Galarraga	.05
206	Walt Weiss	.05
207	Charlie Hayes	.05
208	David Nied	.05
209	Dante Bichette	.05
210	David Cone	.05
211	Jeff Montgomery	.05
212	Felix Jose	.05
213	Mike Macfarlane	.05
214	Wally Joyner	.05
215	Bob Hamelin	.05
216	Brian McRae	.05
217	Kirk Gibson	.05
218	Lou Whitaker	.05
219	Chris Gomez	.05
220	Cecil Fielder	.05
221	Mickey Tettleton	.05
222	Travis Fryman	.05
223	Tony Phillips	.05
224	Rick Aguilera	.05
225	Scott Erickson	.05
226	Chuck Knoblauch	.05
227	Kent Hrbek	.05
228	Shane Mack	.05
229	Kevin Tapani	.05
230	Kirby Puckett	.75
231	Julio Franco	.05
232	Jack McDowell	.05
233	Jason Bere	.05
234	Alex Fernandez	.05
235	Frank Thomas	.65
236	Ozzie Guillen	.05
237	Robin Ventura	.05
238	Michael Jordan	2.00
239	Wilson Alvarez	.05
240	Don Mattingly	.85
241	Jim Abbott	.05
242	Jim Leyritz	.05
243	Paul O'Neill	.05
244	Melido Perez	.05
245	Wade Boggs	.75
246	Mike Stanley	.05
247	Danny Tartabull	.05
248	Jimmy Key	.05
249	Greg Maddux (Fantasy Team)	.40
250	Randy Johnson (Fantasy Team)	.20
251	Bret Saberhagen (Fantasy Team)	.05
252	John Wetteland (Fantasy Team)	.05
253	Mike Piazza (Fantasy Team)	.50
254	Jeff Bagwell (Fantasy Team)	.35
255	Craig Biggio (Fantasy Team)	.05
256	Matt Williams (Fantasy Team)	.05
257	Wil Cordero (Fantasy Team)	.05
258	Kenny Lofton (Fantasy Team)	.05
259	Barry Bonds (Fantasy Team)	.75
260	Dante Bichette (Fantasy Team)	.05
261	Checklist 1-53 (Ken Griffey Jr.)	.35
262	Checklist 54-106 (Goose Gossage)	.05
263	Checklist 107-159 (Cal Ripken Jr.)	.45
264	Checklist 160-212 (Kenny Rogers)	.05
265	Checklist 213-265 (John Valentin)	.05

Silver

The cards in this parallel edition feature the addition of a silver-foil facsimile autograph on the card front. Also, the blue SE logo and card borders have been replaced with silver on the chase cards, which are found on average of one per pack.

Common Player: .15
Stars: 1.5X

Gold

Each of the cards in the SE issue can be found in a premium chase card version which replaces the blue border and SE logo with gold, and adds a gold-foil facsimile autograph to the front of the card. The gold-version SE inserts are found on average of one per 36 packs.

NM/M
Common Player: 1.00
Stars: 8X

1996 Collector's Choice Promo

To introduce its base-brand set, Upper Deck issued a promotional sample card of Ken Griffey, Jr. Numbered 100 (he's #310 in the issued set), the back is overprinted "For Promotional Use Only".

NM/M
100 Ken Griffey Jr. 4.00

1996 Collector's Choice

The third year for Collector's Choice includes 730 cards in two series with packs formatted in retail and hobby versions. The 280 regular player cards are joined by subsets of Rookie Class, International Flavor, Traditional Threads, Fantasy Team, Stat Leaders, Season Highlights, First Class, Arizona Fall League, Awards and Checklists. Packs feature a number of different insert sets including silver and gold signature parallel sets, interactive "You Make the Play" cards, four cards from the cross-brand Cal Ripken Collection and three postseason trade cards redeemable for 10-card sets recalling the League Championships and World Series. An additional 30 cards (#761-790) featuring traded players in their new uniforms was issued only in factory sets.

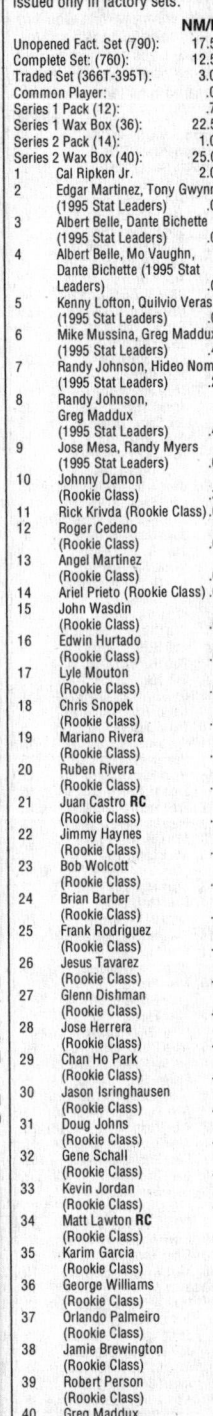

NM/M
Unopened Fact. Set (790): 17.50
Complete Set: (760): 12.50
Traded Set (366T-395T): 3.00
Common Player: .05
Series 1 Pack (12): .75
Series 1 Wax Box (36): 22.50
Series 2 Pack (14): 1.00
Series 2 Wax Box (40): 25.00

#	Player	Price
1	Cal Ripken Jr.	2.00
2	Edgar Martinez, Tony Gwynn (1995 Stat Leaders)	.05
3	Albert Belle, Dante Bichette (1995 Stat Leaders)	.05
4	Albert Belle, Mo Vaughn, Dante Bichette (1995 Stat Leaders)	.05
5	Kenny Lofton, Quilvio Veras (1995 Stat Leaders)	.05
6	Mike Mussina, Greg Maddux (1995 Stat Leaders)	.40
7	Randy Johnson, Hideo Nomo (1995 Stat Leaders)	.25
8	Randy Johnson, Greg Maddux (1995 Stat Leaders)	.40
9	Jose Mesa, Randy Myers (1995 Stat Leaders)	.05
10	Johnny Damon (Rookie Class)	.35
11	Rick Krivda (Rookie Class)	.05
12	Roger Cedeno (Rookie Class)	.05
13	Angel Martinez (Rookie Class)	.05
14	Ariel Prieto (Rookie Class)	.05
15	John Wasdin (Rookie Class)	.05
16	Edwin Hurtado (Rookie Class)	.05
17	Lyle Mouton (Rookie Class)	.05
18	Chris Snopek (Rookie Class)	.05
19	Mariano Rivera (Rookie Class)	.15
20	Ruben Rivera (Rookie Class)	.05
21	Juan Castro RC (Rookie Class)	.05
22	Jimmy Haynes (Rookie Class)	.05
23	Bob Wolcott (Rookie Class)	.05
24	Brian Barber (Rookie Class)	.05
25	Frank Rodriguez (Rookie Class)	.05
26	Jesus Tavarez (Rookie Class)	.05
27	Glenn Dishman (Rookie Class)	.05
28	Jose Herrera (Rookie Class)	.05
29	Chan Ho Park (Rookie Class)	.05
30	Jason Isringhausen (Rookie Class)	.05
31	Doug Johns (Rookie Class)	.05
32	Gene Schall (Rookie Class)	.05
33	Kevin Jordan (Rookie Class)	.05
34	Matt Lawton RC (Rookie Class)	.10
35	Karim Garcia (Rookie Class)	.05
36	George Williams (Rookie Class)	.05
37	Orlando Palmeiro (Rookie Class)	.05
38	Jamie Brewington (Rookie Class)	.05
39	Robert Person (Rookie Class)	.05
40	Greg Maddux	.75
41	Marquis Grissom	.05
42	Chipper Jones	.75
43	David Justice	.05
44	Mark Lemke	.05
45	Fred McGriff	.05
46	Javy Lopez	.05
47	Mark Wohlers	.05
48	Jason Schmidt	.05
49	John Smoltz	.05
50	Curtis Goodwin	.05
51	Gregg Zaun	.05
52	Armando Benitez	.05
53	Manny Alexander	.05
54	Chris Hoiles	.05
55	Harold Baines	.05
56	Ben McDonald	.05
57	Scott Erickson	.05
58	Jeff Manto	.05
59	Luis Alicea	.05
60	Roger Clemens	.85
61	Rheal Cormier	.05
62	Vaughn Eshelman	.05
63	Zane Smith	.05
64	Mike Macfarlane	.05
65	Erik Hanson	.05
66	Tim Naehring	.05
67	Lee Tinsley	.05
68	Troy O'Leary	.05
69	Garret Anderson	.05
70	Chili Davis	.05
71	Jim Edmonds	.05
72	Troy Percival	.05
73	Mark Langston	.05
74	Spike Owen	.05
75	Tim Salmon	.05
76	Brian Anderson	.05
77	Lee Smith	.05
78	Jim Abbott	.05
79	Jim Bullinger	.05
80	Mark Grace	.05
81	Todd Zeile	.05
82	Kevin Foster	.05
83	Howard Johnson	.05
84	Brian McRae	.05
85	Randy Myers	.05
86	Jaime Navarro	.05
87	Luis Gonzalez	.05
88	Ozzie Timmons	.05
89	Wilson Alvarez	.05
90	Frank Thomas	.60
91	James Baldwin	.05
92	Ray Durham	.05
93	Alex Fernandez	.05
94	Ozzie Guillen	.05
95	Tim Raines	.05
96	Roberto Hernandez	.05
97	Lance Johnson	.05
98	John Kruk	.05
99	Mark Portugal	.05
100	Don Mattingly (Traditional Threads)	.65
101	Jose Canseco (Traditional Threads)	.15
102	Raul Mondesi (Traditional Threads)	.05
103	Cecil Fielder (Traditional Threads)	.05
104	Ozzie Smith (Traditional Threads)	.40
105	Frank Thomas (Traditional Threads)	.45
106	Sammy Sosa (Traditional Threads)	.50
107	Fred McGriff (Traditional Threads)	.05
108	Barry Bonds (Traditional Threads)	1.00
109	Thomas Howard	.05
110	Ron Gant	.05
111	Eddie Taubensee	.05
112	Hal Morris	.05
113	Jose Rijo	.05
114	Pete Schourek	.05
115	Reggie Sanders	.05
116	Benito Santiago	.05
117	Jeff Brantley	.05
118	Julian Tavarez	.05
119	Carlos Baerga	.05
120	Jim Thome	.40
121	Jose Mesa	.05
122	Dennis Martinez	.05
123	Dave Winfield	.60
124	Eddie Murray	.60
125	Manny Ramirez	.05
126	Paul Sorrento	.05
127	Kenny Lofton	.60
128	Eric Young	.05
129	Jason Bates	.05
130	Bret Saberhagen	.05
131	Andres Galarraga	.05
132	Joe Girardi	.05
133	John Vander Wal	.05
134	David Nied	.05
135	Dante Bichette	.05
136	Vinny Castilla	.05
137	Kevin Ritz	.05
138	Felipe Lira	.05
139	Joe Boever	.05
140	Cecil Fielder	.05
141	John Flaherty	.05
142	Kirk Gibson	.05
143	Brian Maxcy	.05
144	Lou Whitaker	.05
145	Alan Trammell	.05
146	Bobby Higginson	.05
147	Chad Curtis	.05
148	Quilvio Veras	.05
149	Jerry Browne	.05
150	Andre Dawson	.25
151	Robb Nen	.05
152	Greg Colbrunn	.05
153	Chris Hammond	.05
154	Kurt Abbott	.05
155	Charles Johnson	.05
156	Terry Pendleton	.05
157	Dave Weathers	.05
158	Mike Hampton	.05
159	Craig Biggio	.05
160	Jeff Bagwell	.60
161	Brian L. Hunter	.05
162	Mike Henneman	.05
163	Dave Magadan	.05
164	Shane Reynolds	.05
165	Derek Bell	.05
166	Orlando Miller	.05
167	James Mouton	.05
168	Melvin Bunch	.05
169	Tom Gordon	.05
170	Kevin Appier	.05
171	Tom Goodwin	.05
172	Greg Gagne	.05
173	Gary Gaetti	.05
174	Jeff Montgomery	.05
175	Jon Nunnally	.05
176	Michael Tucker	.05
177	Joe Vitiello	.05
178	Billy Ashley	.05
179	Tom Candiotti	.05
180	Hideo Nomo	.30
181	Chad Fonville	.05
182	Todd Hollandsworth	.05
183	Eric Karros	.05
184	Roberto Kelly	.05
185	Mike Piazza	1.00
186	Ramon Martinez	.05
187	Tim Wallach	.05
188	Jeff Cirillo	.05
189	Sid Roberson	.05
190	Kevin Seitzer	.05
191	Mike Fetters	.05
192	Steve Sparks	.05
193	Matt Mieske	.05
194	Joe Oliver	.05
195	B.J. Surhoff	.05
196	Alberto Reyes	.05
197	Fernando Vina	.05
198	LaTroy Hawkins	.05
199	Marty Cordova	.05
200	Kirby Puckett	.75
201	Brad Radke	.05
202	Pedro Munoz	.05
203	Scott Klingenbeck	.05
204	Pat Meares	.05
205	Chuck Knoblauch	.05
206	Scott Stahoviak	.05
207	Dave Stevens	.05
208	Shane Andrews	.05
209	Moises Alou	.05
210	David Segui	.05
211	Cliff Floyd	.05
212	Carlos Perez	.05
213	Mark Grudzielanek	.05
214	Butch Henry	.05
215	Rondell White	.05
216	Mel Rojas	.05
217	Ugueth Urbina	.05
218	Edgardo Alfonzo	.05
219	Carl Everett	.05
220	John Franco	.05
221	Todd Hundley	.05
222	Bobby Jones	.05
223	Bill Pulsipher	.05
224	Rico Brogna	.05
225	Jeff Kent	.05
226	Chris Jones	.05
227	Butch Huskey	.05
228	Robert Eenhoorn	.05
229	Sterling Hitchcock	.05
230	Wade Boggs	.75
231	Derek Jeter	2.00
232	Tony Fernandez	.05
233	Jack McDowell	.05
234	Andy Pettitte	.35
235	David Cone	.05
236	Mike Stanley	.05
237	Don Mattingly	.85
238	Geronimo Berroa	.05
239	Scott Brosius	.05
240	Rickey Henderson	.60
241	Terry Steinbach	.05
242	Mike Gallego	.05
243	Jason Giambi	.40
244	Steve Ontiveros	.05
245	Dennis Eckersley	.50
246	Dave Stewart	.05
247	Don Wengert	.05
248	Paul Quantrill	.05
249	Ricky Bottalico	.05
250	Kevin Stocker	.05
251	Lenny Dykstra	.05
252	Tony Longmire	.05
253	Tyler Green	.05
254	Mike Mimbs	.05
255	Charlie Hayes	.05
256	Mickey Morandini	.05
257	Heathcliff Slocumb	.05
258	Jeff King	.05
259	Midre Cummings	.05
260	Mark Johnson	.05
261	Freddy Garcia	.05
262	Jon Lieber	.05
263	Esteban Loaiza	.05
264	Danny Miceli	.05
265	Orlando Merced	.05
266	Denny Neagle	.05
267	Steve Parris	.05
268	Fantasy Team '95 (Greg Maddux)	.35
269	Fantasy Team '95 (Randy Johnson)	.20
270	Fantasy Team '95 (Hideo Nomo)	.15
271	Fantasy Team '95 (Jose Mesa)	.05
272	Fantasy Team '95 (Mike Piazza)	.05

#	Name	Value
273	Fantasy Team '95 (Mo Vaughn)	.05
274	Fantasy Team '95 (Craig Biggio)	.05
275	Fantasy Team '95 (Edgar Martinez)	.05
276	Fantasy Team '95 (Barry Larkin)	.05
277	Fantasy Team '95 (Sammy Sosa)	.50
278	Fantasy Team '95 (Dante Bichette)	.05
279	Fantasy Team '95 (Albert Belle)	.05
280	Ozzie Smith	.75
281	Mark Sweeney	.05
282	Terry Bradshaw	.05
283	Allen Battle	.05
284	Danny Jackson	.05
285	Tom Henke	.05
286	Scott Cooper	.05
287	Tripp Cromer	.05
288	Bernard Gilkey	.05
289	Brian Jordan	.05
290	Tony Gwynn	.75
291	Brad Ausmus	.05
292	Bryce Florie	.05
293	Andres Berumen	.05
294	Ken Caminiti	.05
295	Bip Roberts	.05
296	Trevor Hoffman	.05
297	Roberto Petagine	.05
298	Jody Reed	.05
299	Fernando Valenzuela	.05
300	Barry Bonds	2.00
301	Mark Leiter	.05
302	Mark Carreon	.05
303	Royce Clayton	.05
304	Kirt Manwaring	.05
305	Glenallen Hill	.05
306	Deion Sanders	.10
307	Joe Rosselli	.05
308	Robby Thompson	.05
309	William Van Landingham	.05
310	Ken Griffey Jr.	1.00
311	Bobby Ayala	.05
312	Joey Cora	.05
313	Mike Blowers	.05
314	Darren Bragg	.05
315	Randy Johnson	.60
316	Alex Rodriguez	1.50
317	Andy Benes	.05
318	Tino Martinez	.05
319	Dan Wilson	.05
320	Will Clark	.05
321	Jeff Frye	.05
322	Benji Gil	.05
323	Rick Helling	.05
324	Mark McLemore	.05
325	Dave Nilsson (International Flavor)	.05
326	Larry Walker (International Flavor)	.05
327	Jose Canseco (International Flavor)	.15
328	Raul Mondesi (International Flavor)	.05
329	Manny Ramirez (International Flavor)	.30
330	Robert Eenhoorn (International Flavor)	.05
331	Chili Davis (International Flavor)	.05
332	Hideo Nomo (International Flavor)	.15
333	Benji Gil (International Flavor)	.05
334	Fernando Valenzuela (International Flavor)	.05
335	Dennis Martinez (International Flavor)	.05
336	Roberto Kelly (International Flavor)	.05
337	Carlos Baerga (International Flavor)	.05
338	Juan Gonzalez (International Flavor)	.15
339	Roberto Alomar (International Flavor)	.10
340	Chan Ho Park (International Flavor)	.05
341	Andres Galarraga (International Flavor)	.05
342	Midre Cummings (International Flavor)	.05
343	Otis Nixon	.05
344	Jeff Russell	.05
345	Ivan Rodriguez	.50
346	Mickey Tettleton	.05
347	Bob Tewksbury	.05
348	Domingo Cedeno	.05
349	Lance Parrish	.05
350	Joe Carter	.05
351	Devon White	.05
352	Carlos Delgado	.35
353	Alex Gonzalez	.05
354	Darren Hall	.05
355	Paul Molitor	.60
356	Al Leiter	.05
357	Randy Knorr	.05
358	Checklist 1-46 (12-player Astros-Padres trade)	.05
359	Checklist 47-92 (Hideo Nomo)	.15
360	Checklist 93-138 (Ramon Martinez)	.05
361	Checklist 139-184 (Robin Ventura)	.05
362	Checklist 185-230 (Cal Ripken Jr.)	.30
363	Checklist 231-275 (Ken Caminiti)	.05
364	Checklist 276-320 (Eddie Murray)	.20
365	Checklist 321-365 (Randy Johnson)	.15
366	A.L. Divisional Series (Tony Pena)	.10
367	A.L. Divisional Series (Jim Thome)	.25
368	A.L. Divisional Series (Don Mattingly)	.60
369	A.L. Divisional Series (Jim Leyritz)	.10
370	A.L. Divisional Series (Ken Griffey Jr.)	.60
371	A.L. Divisional Series (Edgar Martinez)	.10
372	N.L. Divisional Series (Pete Schourek)	.10
373	N.L. Divisional Series (Mark Lewis)	.10
374	N.L. Divisonal Series (Chipper Jones)	.50
375	N.L. Divisional Series (Fred McGriff)	.10
376	N.L. Championship Series (Javy Lopez)	.10
377	N.L. Championship Series (Fred McGriff)	.10
378	N.L. Championship Series (Charlie O'Brien)	.10
379	N.L. Championship Series (Mike Devereaux)	.10
380	N.L. Championship Series (Mark Wohlers)	.10
381	A.L. Championship Series (Bob Wolcott)	.10
382	A.L. Championship Series (Manny Ramirez)	.25
383	A.L. Championship Series (Jay Buhner)	.10
384	A.L. Championship Series (Orel Hershiser)	.10
385	A.L. Championship Series (Kenny Lofton)	.10
386	World Series (Greg Maddux)	.50
387	World Series (Javy Lopez)	.10
388	World Series (Kenny Lofton)	.10
389	World Series (Eddie Murray)	.10
390	World Series (Luis Polonia)	.10
391	World Series (Pedro Borbon)	.10
392	World Series (Jim Thome)	.25
393	World Series (Orel Hershiser)	.10
394	World Series (David Justice)	.10
395	World Series (Tom Glavine)	.10
396	Braves Team Checklist (Greg Maddux)	.25
397	Mets Team Checklist (Brett Butler)	.05
398	Phillies Team Checklist (Darren Daulton)	.05
399	Marlins Team Checklist (Gary Sheffield)	.05
400	Expos Team Checklist (Moises Alou)	.05
401	Reds Team Checklist (Barry Larkin)	.05
402	Astros Team Checklist (Jeff Bagwell)	.20
403	Cubs Team Checklist (Sammy Sosa)	.35
404	Cardinals Team Checklist (Ozzie Smith)	.25
405	Pirates Team Checklist (Jeff King)	.05
406	Dodgers Team Checklist (Mike Piazza)	.50
407	Rockies Team Checklist (Dante Bichette)	.05
408	Padres Team Checklist (Tony Gwynn)	.25
409	Giants Team Checklist (Barry Bonds)	.45
410	Indians Team Checklist (Kenny Lofton)	.05
411	Royals Team Checklist (Jon Nunnally)	.05
412	White Sox Team Checklist (Frank Thomas)	.20
413	Brewers Team Checklist (Greg Vaughn)	.05
414	Twins Team Checklist (Paul Molitor)	.05
415	Mariners Team Checklist (Ken Griffey Jr.)	.35
416	Angels Team Checklist (Jim Edmonds)	.05
417	Rangers Team Checklist (Juan Gonzalez)	.15
418	Athletics Team Checklist (Mark McGwire)	.75
419	Red Sox Team Checklist (Roger Clemens)	.15
420	Yankees Team Checklist (Wade Boggs)	.35
421	Orioles Team Checklist (Cal Ripken Jr.)	.40
422	Tigers Team Checklist (Cecil Fielder)	.05
423	Blue Jays Team Checklist (Joe Carter)	.05
424	Osvaldo Fernandez RC (Rookie Class)	.15
425	Billy Wagner (Rookie Class)	.05
426	George Arias (Rookie Class)	.05
427	Mendy Lopez (Rookie Class)	.05
428	Jeff Suppan (Rookie Class)	.05
429	Rey Ordonez (Rookie Class)	.05
430	Brooks Kieschnick (Rookie Class)	.05
431	Raul Ibanez RC (Rookie Class)	.05
432	Livan Hernandez RC (Rookie Class)	.20
433	Shannon Stewart (Rookie Class)	.05
434	Steve Cox (Rookie Class)	.05
435	Trey Beamon (Rookie Class)	.05
436	Sergio Nunez (Rookie Class)	.05
437	Jermaine Dye (Rookie Class)	.05
438	Mike Sweeney RC (Rookie Class)	.45
439	Richard Hidalgo (Rookie Class)	.05
440	Todd Greene (Rookie Class)	.05
441	Robert Smith RC (Rookie Class)	.05
442	Rafael Orellano (Rookie Class)	.05
443	Wilton Guerrero RC (Rookie Class)	.05
444	David Doster RC (Rookie Class)	.05
445	Jason Kendall (Rookie Class)	.05
446	Edgar Renteria (Rookie Class)	.05
447	Scott Spiezio (Rookie Class)	.05
448	Jay Canizaro (Rookie Class)	.05
449	Enrique Wilson (Rookie Class)	.05
450	Bob Abreu (Rookie Class)	.10
451	Dwight Smith	.05
452	Jeff Blauser	.05
453	Steve Avery	.05
454	Brad Clontz	.05
455	Tom Glavine	.20
456	Mike Mordecai	.05
457	Rafael Belliard	.05
458	Greg McMichael	.05
459	Pedro Borbon	.05
460	Ryan Klesko	.05
461	Terrell Wade	.05
462	Brady Anderson	.05
463	Roberto Alomar	.20
464	Bobby Bonilla	.05
465	Mike Mussina	.40
466	Cesar Devarez RC	.05
467	Jeffrey Hammonds	.05
468	Mike Devereaux	.05
469	B.J. Surhoff	.05
470	Rafael Palmeiro	.50
471	John Valentin	.05
472	Mike Greenwell	.05
473	Dwayne Hosey	.05
474	Tim Wakefield	.05
475	Jose Canseco	.35
476	Aaron Sele	.05
477	Stan Belinda	.05
478	Mike Stanley	.05
479	Jamie Moyer	.05
480	Mo Vaughn	.35
481	Randy Velarde	.05
482	Gary DiSarcina	.05
483	Jorge Fabregas	.05
484	Rex Hudler	.05
485	Chuck Finley	.05
486	Tim Wallach	.05
487	Eduardo Perez	.05
488	Scott Sanderson	.05
489	J.T. Snow	.05
490	Sammy Sosa	.75
491	Terry Adams	.05
492	Matt Franco	.05
493	Scott Servais	.05
494	Frank Castillo	.05
495	Ryne Sandberg	.75
496	Rey Sanchez	.05
497	Steve Trachsel	.05
498	Jose Hernandez	.05
499	Dave Martinez	.05
500	Babe Ruth (First Class)	1.00
501	Ty Cobb (First Class)	.50
502	Walter Johnson (First Class)	.10
503	Christy Mathewson (First Class)	.10
504	Honus Wagner (First Class)	.10
505	Robin Ventura	.05
506	Jason Bere	.05
507	Mike Cameron RC	.05
508	Ron Karkovice	.05
509	Matt Karchner	.05
510	Harold Baines	.05
511	Kirk McCaskill	.05
512	Larry Thomas	.05
513	Danny Tartabull	.05
514	Steve Gibralter	.05
515	Bret Boone	.05
516	Jeff Branson	.05
517	Kevin Jarvis	.05
518	Xavier Hernandez	.05
519	Eric Owens	.05
520	Barry Larkin	.05
521	Dave Burba	.05
522	John Smiley	.05
523	Paul Assenmacher	.05
524	Chad Ogea	.05
525	Orel Hershiser	.05
526	Alan Embree	.05
527	Tony Pena	.05
528	Omar Vizquel	.05
529	Mark Clark	.05
530	Albert Belle	.05
531	Charles Nagy	.05
532	Herbert Perry	.05
533	Darren Holmes	.05
534	Ellis Burks	.05
535	Bill Swift	.05
536	Armando Reynoso	.05
537	Curtis Leskanic	.05
538	Quinton McCracken	.05
539	Steve Reed	.05
540	Larry Walker	.05
541	Walt Weiss	.05
542	Bryan Rekar	.05
543	Tony Clark	.05
544	Steve Rodriguez	.05
545	C.J. Nitkowski	.05
546	Todd Steverson	.05
547	Jose Lima	.05
548	Phil Nevin	.05
549	Chris Gomez	.05
550	Travis Fryman	.05
551	Mark Lewis	.05
552	Alex Arias	.05
553	Marc Valdes	.05
554	Kevin Brown	.05
555	Jeff Conine	.05
556	John Burkett	.05
557	Devon White	.05
558	Pat Rapp	.05
559	Jay Powell	.05
560	Gary Sheffield	.30
561	Jim Dougherty	.05
562	Todd Jones	.05
563	Tony Eusebio	.05
564	Darryl Kile	.05
565	Doug Drabek	.05
566	Mike Simms	.05
567	Derrick May	.05
568	Donne Wall RC	.05
569	Greg Swindell	.05
570	Jim Pittsley	.05
571	Bob Hamelin	.05
572	Mark Gubicza	.05
573	Chris Haney	.05
574	Keith Lockhart	.05
575	Mike Macfarlane	.05
576	Les Norman	.05
577	Joe Randa	.05
578	Chris Stynes	.05
579	Greg Gagne	.05
580	Raul Mondesi	.05
581	Delino DeShields	.05
582	Pedro Astacio	.05
583	Antonio Osuna	.05
584	Brett Butler	.05
585	Todd Worrell	.05
586	Mike Blowers	.05
587	Felix Rodriguez	.05
588	Ismael Valdes	.05
589	Ricky Bones	.05
590	Greg Vaughn	.05
591	Mark Loretta	.05
592	Cal Eldred	.05
593	Chuck Carr	.05
594	Dave Nilsson	.05
595	John Jaha	.05
596	Scott Karl	.05
597	Pat Listach	.05
598	Jose Valentin RC	.05
599	Mike Trombley	.05
600	Paul Molitor	.60
601	Dave Hollins	.05
602	Ron Coomer	.05
603	Matt Walbeck	.05
604	Roberto Kelly	.05
605	Rick Aguilera	.05
606	Pat Mahomes	.05
607	Jeff Reboulet	.05
608	Rich Becker	.05
609	Tim Scott	.05
610	Pedro J. Martinez	.60
611	Kirk Rueter	.05
612	Tavo Alvarez	.05
613	Yamil Benitez	.05
614	Darrin Fletcher	.05
615	Mike Lansing	.05
616	Henry Rodriguez	.05
617	Tony Tarasco	.05
618	Alex Ochoa	.05
619	Tim Bogar	.05
620	Bernard Gilkey	.05
621	Dave Mlicki	.05
622	Brent Mayne	.05
623	Ryan Thompson	.05
624	Pete Harnisch	.05
625	Lance Johnson	.05
626	Jose Vizcaino	.05
627	Doug Henry	.05
628	Scott Kamieniecki	.05
629	Jim Leyritz	.05
630	Ruben Sierra	.05
631	Pat Kelly	.05
632	Joe Girardi	.05
633	John Wetteland	.05
634	Melido Perez	.05
635	Paul O'Neill	.05
636	Jorge Posada	.05
637	Bernie Williams	.05
638	Mark Acre	.05
639	Mike Bordick	.05
640	Mark McGwire	1.50
641	Fausto Cruz	.05
642	Ernie Young	.05
643	Todd Van Poppel	.05
644	Craig Paquette	.05
645	Brent Gates	.05
646	Pedro Munoz	.05
647	Andrew Lorraine	.05
648	Sid Fernandez	.05
649	Jim Eisenreich	.05
650	Johnny Damon (Arizona Fall League)	.30
651	Dustin Hermanson (Arizona Fall League)	.05
652	Joe Randa (Arizona Fall League)	.05
653	Michael Tucker (Arizona Fall League)	.05
654	Alan Benes (Arizona Fall League)	.05
655	Chad Fonville (Arizona Fall League)	.05
656	David Bell (Arizona Fall League)	.05
657	Jon Nunnally (Arizona Fall League)	.05
658	Chan Ho Park (Arizona Fall League)	.05
659	LaTroy Hawkins (Arizona Fall League)	.05
660	Jamie Brewington (Arizona Fall League)	.05
661	Quinton McCracken (Arizona Fall League)	.05
662	Tim Unroe (Arizona Fall League)	.05
663	Jeff Ware (Arizona Fall League)	.05
664	Todd Greene (Arizona Fall League)	.05
665	Andrew Lorraine (Arizona Fall League)	.05
666	Ernie Young (Arizona Fall League)	.05
667	Toby Borland	.05
668	Lenny Webster	.05
669	Benito Santiago	.05
670	Gregg Jefferies	.05
671	Darren Daulton	.05
672	Curt Schilling	.25
673	Mark Whiten	.05
674	Todd Zeile	.05
675	Jay Bell	.05
676	Paul Wagner	.05
677	Dave Clark	.05
678	Nelson Liriano	.05
679	Ramon Morel	.05
680	Charlie Hayes	.05
681	Angelo Encarnacion	.05
682	Al Martin	.05
683	Jacob Brumfield	.05
684	Mike Kingery	.05
685	Carlos Garcia	.05
686	Tom Pagnozzi	.05
687	David Bell	.05
688	Todd Stottlemyre	.05
689	Jose Oliva	.05
690	Ray Lankford	.05
691	Mike Morgan	.05
692	John Frascatore	.05
693	John Mabry	.05
694	Mark Petkovsek	.05
695	Alan Benes	.05
696	Steve Finley	.05
697	Marc Newfield	.05
698	Andy Ashby	.05
699	Marc Kroon	.05
700	Wally Joyner	.05
701	Joey Hamilton	.05
702	Dustin Hermanson	.05
703	Scott Sanders	.05
704	Marty Cordova (Award Win.-ROY)	.05
705	Hideo Nomo (Award Win.-ROY)	.15
706	Mo Vaughn (Award Win.-MVP)	.05
707	Barry Larkin (Award Win.-MVP)	.05
708	Randy Johnson (Award Win.-CY)	.20
709	Greg Maddux (Award Win.-CY)	.35
710	Mark McGwire (Award-Comeback)	.75
711	Ron Gant (Award-Comeback)	.05
712	Andujar Cedeno	.05
713	Brian Johnson	.05
714	J.R. Phillips	.05
715	Rod Beck	.05
716	Sergio Valdez	.05
717	Marvin Benard RC	.25
718	Steve Scarsone	.05
719	Rich Aurilia RC	.10
720	Matt Williams	.05
721	John Patterson	.05
722	Shawn Estes	.05
723	Russ Davis	.05
724	Rich Amaral	.05
725	Edgar Martinez	.05
726	Norm Charlton	.05
727	Paul Sorrento	.05
728	Luis Sojo	.05
729	Arquimedez Pozo	.05
730	Jay Buhner	.05
731	Chris Bosio	.05
732	Chris Widger	.05
733	Kevin Gross	.05
734	Darren Oliver	.05
735	Dean Palmer	.05
736	Matt Whiteside	.05
737	Luis Ortiz	.05
738	Roger Pavlik	.05
739	Damon Buford	.05
740	Juan Gonzalez	.30
741	Rusty Greer	.05
742	Lou Frazier	.05
743	Pat Hentgen	.05
744	Tomas Perez	.05
745	Juan Guzman	.05
746	Otis Nixon	.05
747	Robert Perez	.05
748	Ed Sprague	.05
749	Tony Castillo	.05
750	John Olerud	.05
751	Shawn Green	.10
752	Jeff Ware	.05
753	Checklist 396-441/Blake St. Bombers (Dante Bichette, Larry Walker, Andres Galarraga, Vinny Castilla)	.05
754	Checklist 442-487 (Greg Maddux)	.25
755	Checklist 488-533 (Marty Cordova)	.05
756	Checklist 534-579 (Ozzie Smith)	.35
757	Checklist 580-625 (John Vander Wal)	.05
758	Checklist 626-670 (Andres Galarraga)	.05
759	Checklist 671-715 (Frank Thomas)	.20
760	Checklist 716-760 (Tony Gwynn)	.25
761	Randy Myers	.05
762	Kent Mercker	.10
763	David Wells	.05
764	Tom Gordon	.10
765	Wil Cordero	.10
766	Dave Magadan	.10
767	Doug Jones	.10
768	Kevin Tapani	.10
769	Curtis Goodwin	.10
770	Julio Franco	.10
771	Jack McDowell	.10
772	Al Leiter	.10
773	Sean Berry	.10
774	Bip Roberts	.10
775	Jose Offerman	.10
776	Ben McDonald	.10
777	Dan Serafini	.10
778	Ryan McGuire	.10
779	Tim Raines	.10
780	Tino Martinez	.10
781	Kenny Rogers	.10
782	Bob Tewksbury	.10
783	Rickey Henderson	.60
784	Ron Gant	.10
785	Gary Gaetti	.10
786	Andy Benes	.10
787	Royce Clayton	.10
788	Darryl Hamilton	.10
789	Ken Hill	.10
790	Erik Hanson	.10

Silver Signature

A silver border instead of white, and a facsimile autograph in silver ink on the card front differentiate these parallel insert cards from the regular-issue Collector's Choice. The inserts are seeded at the rate of one per pack.

NM/M

Common Player: .10
Stars: 1.5X

Gold Signature

This insert set parallels each card in the regular Collector's Choice set. Found on average of one per 35 packs, the cards are nearly identical to the regular version except for the presence of a facsimile autograph in gold ink on the front and gold, instead of white, borders.

	NM/M
Common Player:	1.00
Stars:	10X

1996 Collector's Choice A Cut Above

This 10-card set highlights the career of Ken Griffey Jr. The front has a color photo with "The Griffey Years" printed in the left border and a title in the right border. Die-cut gold-foil tops have "A CUT ABOVE" in black. Backs have a portrait photo on a marbled border and a narrative. This set was inserted one per six-card Wal-Mart exclusive pack.

	NM/M
Complete Set (10):	8.00
Common Card:	1.00
CA1 Ken Griffey Jr. (Teenage Rookie)	1.00
CA2 Ken Griffey Jr. (Great Defense)	1.00
CA3 Ken Griffey Jr. (Fun-Loving)	1.00
CA4 Ken Griffey Jr. (All-Star Games)	1.00
CA5 Ken Griffey Jr. ('93 Season)	1.00
CA6 Ken Griffey Jr. ('94 HR Records)	1.00
CA7 Ken Griffey Jr. ('94 Season)	1.00
CA8 Ken Griffey Jr. ('95 Season)	1.00
CA9 Ken Griffey Jr. ('95 Postseason)	1.00
CA10 Ken Griffey Jr. ('96: A Look Ahead)	1.00

Crash the Game

For a second season, UD continued its interactive chase card series, "You Crash the Game." At a ratio of about one per five packs for a silver version and one per 49 packs for a gold version, cards of the game's top sluggers could be found bearing one of three date ranges representing a three- or four-game series in which that player was scheduled to play during the 1996 season. If the player hit a home run during the series shown on the card, the card could be redeemed (for $1.75) by mail for a "Super Premium" wood-and-plastic card of the

player. Both silver and gold Crash cards feature silver and red prismatic foil behind the player action photo. Silver versions have the Crash logo, series dates and player ID in silver foil on front; those details are in gold foil on the gold cards. Backs have contest rules printed on a gray (silver) or yellow (gold) background. Card numbers are preceded by a "CG" prefix. Cards were redeemable only until Nov. 25, 1996. Winning cards are indicated with an asterisk; they would be in shorter supply than those which could not be redeemed.

	NM/M
Complete Set (90):	75.00
Common Silver Player:	.50
Golds:	2X
1a Chipper Jones (July 11-14*)	2.50
1b Chipper Jones (Aug. 27-29*)	2.50
1c Chipper Jones (Sept. 19-23)	1.50
2a Fred McGriff (July 1-3)	.50
2b Fred McGriff (Aug. 30-Sept. 1)	.50
2c Fred McGriff (Sept. 10-12*)	1.00
3a Rafael Palmeiro (July 4-7*)	1.75
3b Rafael Palmeiro (Aug. 29-Sept. 1)	.75
3c Rafael Palmeiro (Sept. 26-29)	.75
4a Cal Ripken Jr. (June 27-30)	2.50
4b Cal Ripken Jr. (July 25-28*)	5.00
4c Cal Ripken Jr. (Sept. 2-4)	2.50
5a Jose Canseco (June 27-30)	.50
5b Jose Canseco (July 11-14*)	1.50
5c Jose Canseco (Aug. 23-25)	.65
6a Mo Vaughn (June 21-23*)	1.00
6b Mo Vaughn (July 18-21*)	1.00
6c Mo Vaughn (Sept. 20-22)	.50
7a Jim Edmonds (July 18-21*)	1.00
7b Jim Edmonds (Aug. 16-18*)	1.00
7c Jim Edmonds (Sept. 20-22)	.50
8a Tim Salmon (June 20-23)	.50
8b Tim Salmon (July 30-Aug. 1)	.50
8c Tim Salmon (Sept. 9-12)	.50
9a Sammy Sosa (July 4-7*)	2.50
9b Sammy Sosa (Aug. 1-4*)	2.50
9c Sammy Sosa (Sept. 2-4)	1.50
10a Frank Thomas (June 27-30)	
10b Frank Thomas (July 4-7)	1.00
10c Frank Thomas (Sept. 2-4*)	2.00
11a Albert Belle (June 25-26)	.50
11b Albert Belle (Aug. 2-5*)	1.00
11c Albert Belle (Sept. 6-8)	.50
12a Manny Ramirez (July 18-21*)	2.00
12b Manny Ramirez (Aug. 26-28)	1.00
12c Manny Ramirez (Sept. 9-12*)	2.00
13a Jim Thome (June 27-30)	.75
13b Jim Thome (July 4-7*)	1.25
13c Jim Thome (Sept. 23-25)	.75
14a Dante Bichette (July 11-14*)	1.00
14b Dante Bichette (Aug. 9-11)	.50
14c Dante Bichette (Sept. 9-12)	.50
15a Vinny Castilla (July 1-3)	
15b Vinny Castilla (Aug. 23-25*)	1.00
15c Vinny Castilla (Sept. 13-15*)	1.00
16a Larry Walker (June 24-26)	.50
16b Larry Walker (July 18-21)	.50
16c Larry Walker (Sept. 27-29)	.50
17a Cecil Fielder (June 27-30)	.50
17b Cecil Fielder (July 30-Aug. 1*)	1.00
17c Cecil Fielder (Sept. 17-19*)	1.00
18a Gary Sheffield (July 4-7)	.65
18b Gary Sheffield (Aug. 2-4)	.65
18c Gary Sheffield (Sept. 5-8*)	1.50
19a Jeff Bagwell (July 4-7*)	2.00
19b Jeff Bagwell (Aug. 16-18)	1.00
19c Jeff Bagwell (Sept. 13-15)	1.00
20a Eric Karros (July 4-7*)	1.00
20b Eric Karros (Aug. 13-15*)	1.00
20c Eric Karros (Sept. 16-18)	1.00
21a Mike Piazza (June 27-30*)	3.00
21b Mike Piazza (July 26-28)	1.75
21c Mike Piazza (Sept. 12-15*)	3.00
22a Ken Caminiti (July 11-14*)	1.00
22b Ken Caminiti (Aug. 16-18*)	1.00
22c Ken Caminiti (Sept. 19-22*)	1.00
23a Barry Bonds (June 27-30*)	5.00
23b Barry Bonds (July 22-24)	2.50
23c Barry Bonds (Sept. 24-26)	2.50
24a Matt Williams (July 11-14*)	1.00
24b Matt Williams (Aug. 19-21)	.50
24c Matt Williams (Sept. 27-29)	.50
25a Jay Buhner (June 20-23)	.50
25b Jay Buhner (July 25-28)	.50
25c Jay Buhner (Aug. 29-Sept. 1*)	1.00
26a Ken Griffey Jr. (July 18-21*)	3.00
26b Ken Griffey Jr. (Aug. 16-18*)	3.00
26c Ken Griffey Jr. (Sept. 20-22*)	3.00
27a Ron Gant (June 24-27*)	1.00
27b Ron Gant (July 11-14*)	1.00
27c Ron Gant (Sept. 27-29*)	1.00
28a Juan Gonzalez (June 28-30*)	1.25
28b Juan Gonzalez (July 15-17*)	1.25
28c Juan Gonzalez (Aug. 6-8)	1.25
29a Mickey Tettleton (July 4-7*)	1.00
29b Mickey Tettleton (Aug. 6-8)	.50
29c Mickey Tettleton (Sept. 6-8*)	1.00
30a Joe Carter (June 25-27)	.50
30b Joe Carter (Aug. 5-8)	.50
30c Joe Carter (Aug. 23-25)	.50

1996 Collector's Choice Crash Winners

Collectors who held "You Crash The Game" insert cards with date ranges on which the pictured player hit a home run could redeem them (for $1.75 per card) for a premium card of that player. The redemption cards have a layer of clear plastic bonded to a wood-laminate front. Within a starburst cutout at center is the player photo with a red background. Cards have a Crash/ Game logo in the lower-right corner, in either silver or gold, depending on which winning card was submitted for exchange. Backs have 1995 and career stats along with licensing and copyright data. There were no winning cards of Tim Salmon, Larry Walker or Joe Carter.

	NM/M
Complete Set (27):	35.00
Common Player:	1.00
Golds:	2X
CR1 Chipper Jones	2.50
CR2 Fred McGriff	1.00
CR3 Rafael Palmeiro	1.75
CR4 Cal Ripken Jr.	4.00
CR5 Jose Canseco	1.50
CR6 Mo Vaughn	1.00
CR7 Jim Edmonds	1.00
CR9 Sammy Sosa	2.50
CR10 Frank Thomas	2.00
CR11 Albert Belle	1.00
CR12 Manny Ramirez	2.00
CR13 Jim Thome	1.50
CR14 Dante Bichette	1.00
CR15 Vinny Castilla	1.00
CR17 Cecil Fielder	1.00
CR18 Gary Sheffield	1.50
CR19 Jeff Bagwell	2.00
CR20 Eric Karros	1.00
CR21 Mike Piazza	3.00
CR22 Ken Caminiti	1.00
CR23 Barry Bonds	4.00
CR24 Matt Williams	1.00
CR25 Jay Buhner	1.00
CR26 Ken Griffey Jr.	3.00
CR27 Ron Gant	1.00
CR28 Juan Gonzalez	1.50
CR29 Mickey Tettleton	1.00

Nomo Scrapbook

The five-card, regular-sized set was randomly inserted in 1996 Collector's Choice baseball. Fronts depict the Dodgers pitcher in action with his name in atypical lowercase type up the right border. Backs feature in-depth text below Nomo's name. A version featuring Japanese text was issued in Japan.

	NM/M
Complete Set (5):	10.00
Common Card:	2.00
Japanese:	3X
1-5 Hideo Nomo	2.00

Ripken Collection

The 23-card, regular-sized Cal Ripken Collection was randomly inserted in various Upper Deck baseball releases in 1996. Cards #1-4 were found in Series 1 Collector's Choice; cards 5-8 were found in Upper Deck Series 1; cards 9-12 in Collector's Choice Series 2; cards 13-17 in Upper Deck Series 2; cards 18-22 in SP baseball and the header card in Collector's Choice.

	NM/M
Complete Set (1-4, 9-12)	15.00
Common Card:	2.50
Header Card:	2.00

1996 Collector's Choice Cal Ripken Jr. Jumbo

This 5" x 3-1/2" card is a virtual parallel to the #1 card in the multi-brand Ripken set which was issued to mark his career to the point of his 2,131st consecutive game. This version, however, was sold only through a television shopping program. The front has a silver facsimile autograph. On back is a "Limited Edition" seal and a serial number within an edition of 21,310.

	NM/M
1 Cal Ripken Jr.	5.00

1996 Collector's Choice You Make the Play

This insert series of interactive game cards was packaged with Series 1 Collector's Choice. Each player's card can be found with one of two play outcomes printed thereon, which are then used to play a baseball card game utilizing a playing field and scorecard found on box bottoms. Regular versions of the cards are seeded one per pack, while gold-signature versions are found one per 36 packs.

	NM/M
Complete Set (45):	60.00
Common Player:	.50
Gold:	4X
1a Kevin Appier (Strike out.)	.50
1b Kevin Appier (Pick off.)	.50
2a Carlos Baerga (Home run.)	.50
2b Carlos Baerga (Ground out.)	.50
3a Jeff Bagwell (Walk)	1.00
3b Jeff Bagwell (Strike out.)	1.00
4a Jay Bell (Sacrifice)	.50
4b Jay Bell (Walk)	.50
5a Albert Belle (Fly out.)	.50
5b Albert Belle (Home run.)	.50
6a Craig Biggio (Walk)	.50
6b Craig Biggio (Strike out.)	.50
7a Wade Boggs (Single)	1.50
7b Wade Boggs (Ground out.)	1.50
8a Barry Bonds (Strike out.)	3.00
8b Barry Bonds (Reach on error.)	3.00
9a Bobby Bonilla (Walk)	.50
9b Bobby Bonilla (Strike out.)	.50
10a Jose Canseco (Single)	.75
10b Jose Canseco (Double)	.75
11a Joe Carter (Double)	.50
11b Joe Carter (Fly out.)	.50
12a Darren Daulton (Ground out.)	.50
12b Darren Daulton (Catcher's interference.)	.50
13a Cecil Fielder (Stolen base.)	.50
13b Cecil Fielder (Home run.)	.50
14a Ron Gant (Home run.)	.50
14b Ron Gant (Fly out.)	.50
15a Juan Gonzalez (Double)	.65
15b Juan Gonzalez (Fly out.)	.65
16a Ken Griffey Jr. (Home run.)	2.00
16b Ken Griffey Jr. (Hit by pitch.)	2.00
17a Tony Gwynn (Single)	1.50
17b Tony Gwynn (Ground out.)	1.50
18a Randy Johnson (Strike out.)	1.00
18b Randy Johnson (K-Reach on wild pitch.)	1.00
19a Chipper Jones (Walk)	1.50
19b Chipper Jones (Strike out.)	1.50
20a Barry Larkin (Ground out.)	.50
20b Barry Larkin (Stolen base.)	.50
21a Kenny Lofton (Triple)	1.50
21b Kenny Lofton (Stolen base.)	.50
22a Greg Maddux (Single)	1.50
22b Greg Maddux (Strike out.)	1.50
23a Don Mattingly (Fly out.)	1.75
23b Don Mattingly (Double)	1.75
24a Fred McGriff (Double)	.50
24b Fred McGriff (Home run.)	.50
25a Mark McGwire (Strike out.)	2.50
25b Mark McGwire (Home run.)	2.50
26a Paul Molitor (Ground out.)	1.00
26b Paul Molitor (Single)	1.00
27a Raul Mondesi (Single)	.50
27b Raul Mondesi (Fly out.)	.50
28a Eddie Murray (Sacrifice fly.)	1.00
28b Eddie Murray (Ground out.)	1.00
29a Hideo Nomo (Strike out.)	.65
29b Hideo Nomo (Balk)	.50
30a Jon Nunnally (Single)	.50
30b Jon Nunnally (Error)	.50
31a Mike Piazza (Strike out.)	2.00
31b Mike Piazza (Single)	2.00
32a Kirby Puckett (Walk)	1.50
32b Kirby Puckett (Ground out.)	1.50
33a Cal Ripken Jr. (Home run.)	3.00
33b Cal Ripken Jr. (Double)	3.00
34a Alex Rodriguez (Strike out.)	2.50
34b Alex Rodriguez (Triple)	2.50
35a Tim Salmon (Sacrifice fly.)	.50
35b Tim Salmon (Strike out.)	.50
36a Gary Sheffield (Fly out.)	.65
36b Gary Sheffield (Single)	.65
37a Lee Smith (Strike out.)	.50
37b Lee Smith (Pick off of lead runner.)	.50
38a Ozzie Smith (Ground out.)	1.50
38b Ozzie Smith (Single)	1.50
39a Sammy Sosa (Stolen base.)	1.50
39b Sammy Sosa (Single)	1.50
40a Frank Thomas (Walk)	1.00
40b Frank Thomas (Home run.)	1.00
41a Greg Vaughn (Sacrifice fly.)	.50
41b Greg Vaughn (Strike out.)	.50
42a Mo Vaughn (Hit by pitch.)	.50
42b Mo Vaughn (Stolen base.)	.50
43a Larry Walker (Strike out.)	.50
43b Larry Walker (Walk)	.50
44a Rondell White (Triple)	.50
44b Rondell White (Fly out.)	.50
45a Matt Williams (Home run.)	.50
45b Matt Williams (Single)	.50

1997 Collector's Choice

The 506-card, standard-size set contains five subsets: Rookie Class (1-27), Leaders (56-63), Postseason (218-224), Ken Griffey Jr. Checklists (244-249) and Griffey Hot List (325-334). Insert sets are: All-Star Connection, Big Shots, Stick'Ums, Premier Power, Clearly Dominant, The Big Show, Toast of the Town and New Frontier. Basic card fronts feature a color action shot with the player's name appearing on the bottom edge. The team logo is located in the lower-left corner and each card features a white border. Backs contain another action shot on the upper half with biography, and career/season stats. The cards were issued in 12-card packs retailing for 99 cents. A factory set was issued that includes 10 Premier Power jumbo cards.

	NM/M
Factory Set (516):	16.00
Complete Set (506):	12.00
Common Player:	.05
Pack (12):	1.00
Wax Box (36):	20.00
1 Andruw Jones (Rookie Class)	1.00
2 Rocky Coppinger (Rookie Class)	.05
3 Jeff D'Amico (Rookie Class)	.05
4 Dmitri Young (Rookie Class)	.05
5 Darin Erstad (Rookie Class)	.75
6 Jermaine Allensworth (Rookie Class)	.05
7 Damian Jackson (Rookie Class)	.05
8 Bill Mueller (Rookie Class)	.05
9 Jacob Cruz (Rookie Class)	.05
10 Vladimir Guerrero (Rookie Class)	1.00
11 Marty Janzen (Rookie Class)	.05
12 Kevin L. Brown (Rookie Class)	.05
13 Willie Adams (Rookie Class)	.05
14 Wendell Magee (Rookie Class)	.05

15 Scott Rolen (Rookie Class) .65
16 Matt Beech (Rookie Class) .05
17 Neifi Perez (Rookie Class) .05
18 Jamey Wright (Rookie Class) .05
19 Jose Paniagua (Rookie Class) .05
20 Todd Walker (Rookie Class) .05
21 Justin Thompson (Rookie Class) .05
22 Robin Jennings (Rookie Class) .05
23 Dario Veras RC (Rookie Class) .05
24 Brian Lesher (Rookie Class) .05
25 Nomar Garciaparra (Rookie Class) 1.25
26 Luis Castillo (Rookie Class) .05
27 Brian Giles RC (Rookie Class) .75
28 Jermaine Dye .05
29 Terrell Wade .05
30 Fred McGriff .05
31 Marquis Grissom .05
32 Ryan Klesko .05
33 Javier Lopez .05
34 Mark Wohlers .05
35 Tom Glavine .25
36 Denny Neagle .05
37 Scott Erickson .05
38 Chris Hoiles .05
39 Roberto Alomar .25
40 Eddie Murray .75
41 Cal Ripken Jr. 2.00
42 Randy Myers .05
43 B.J. Surhoff .05
44 Rick Krivda .05
45 Jose Canseco .50
46 Heathcliff Slocumb .05
47 Jeff Suppan .05
48 Tom Gordon .05
49 Aaron Sele .05
50 Mo Vaughn .05
51 Darren Bragg .05
52 Wil Cordero .05
53 Scott Bullett .05
54 Terry Adams .05
55 Jackie Robinson .35
56 Tony Gwynn, Alex Rodriguez (Batting Leaders) .35
57 Andres Galarraga, Mark McGwire (Homer Leaders) .05
58 Andres Galarraga, Albert Belle (RBI Leaders) .05
59 Eric Young, Kenny Lofton (SB Leaders) .05
60 John Smoltz, Andy Pettitte (Victory Leaders) .05
61 John Smoltz, Roger Clemens (Strikout Leaders) .20
62 Kevin Brown, Juan Guzman (ERA Leaders) .05
63 John Wetteland, Todd Worrell, Jeff Brantley (Save Leaders) .05
64 Scott Servais .05
65 Sammy Sosa 1.00
66 Ryne Sandberg 1.00
67 Frank Castillo .05
68 Rey Sanchez .05
69 Steve Trachsel .05
70 Robin Ventura .05
71 Wilson Alvarez .05
72 Tony Phillips .05
73 Lyle Mouton .05
74 Mike Cameron .05
75 Harold Baines .05
76 Albert Belle .75
77 Chris Snopek .05
78 Reggie Sanders .05
79 Jeff Brantley .05
80 Barry Larkin .05
81 Kevin Jarvis .05
82 John Smiley .05
83 Pete Schourek .05
84 Thomas Howard .05
85 Lee Smith .05
86 Omar Vizquel .05
87 Julio Franco .05
88 Orel Hershiser .05
89 Charles Nagy .05
90 Matt Williams .05
91 Dennis Martinez .05
92 Jose Mesa .05
93 Sandy Alomar Jr. .05
94 Jim Thome .50
95 Vinny Castilla .05
96 Armando Reynoso .05
97 Kevin Ritz .05
98 Larry Walker .25
99 Eric Young .05
100 Dante Bichette .05
101 Quinton McCracken .05
102 John Vander Wal .05
103 Phil Nevin .05
104 Tony Clark .05
105 Alan Trammell .25
106 Felipe Lira .05
107 Curtis Pride .05
108 Bobby Higginson .05
109 Mark Lewis .05
110 Travis Fryman .05
111 Al Leiter .05

112 Devon White .05
113 Jeff Conine .05
114 Charles Johnson .05
115 Andre Dawson .25
116 Edgar Renteria .05
117 Robb Nen .05
118 Kevin Brown .05
119 Derek Bell .05
120 Bob Abreu .10
121 Mike Hampton .05
122 Todd Jones .05
123 Billy Wagner .05
124 Shane Reynolds .05
125 Jeff Bagwell .75
126 Brian L. Hunter .05
127 Jeff Montgomery .05
128 Rod Myers RC .05
129 Tim Belcher .05
130 Kevin Appier .05
131 Mike Sweeney .05
132 Craig Paquette .05
133 Joe Randa .05
134 Michael Tucker .05
135 Raul Mondesi .05
136 Tim Wallach .05
137 Brett Butler .05
138 Karim Garcia .10
139 Todd Hollandsworth .05
140 Eric Karros .05
141 Hideo Nomo .40
142 Ismael Valdes .05
143 Cal Eldred .05
144 Scott Karl .05
145 Matt Mieske .05
146 Mike Fetters .05
147 Mark Loretta .05
148 Fernando Vina .05
149 Jeff Cirillo .05
150 Dave Nilsson .05
151 Kirby Puckett 1.00
152 Rich Becker .05
153 Chuck Knoblauch .65
154 Marty Cordova .05
155 Paul Molitor .75
156 Rick Aguilera .05
157 Pat Meares .05
158 Frank Rodriguez .05
159 David Segui .05
160 Henry Rodriguez .05
161 Shane Andrews .05
162 Pedro J. Martinez .75
163 Mark Grudzielanek .05
164 Mike Lansing .05
165 Rondell White .05
166 Ugueth Urbina .05
167 Rey Ordonez .05
168 Robert Person .05
169 Carlos Baerga .05
170 Bernard Gilkey .05
171 John Franco .05
172 Pete Harnisch .05
173 Butch Huskey .05
174 Paul Wilson .05
175 Bernie Williams .05
176 Dwight Gooden .05
177 Wade Boggs 1.00
178 Ruben Rivera .05
179 Jim Leyritz .05
180 Derek Jeter 2.00
181 Tino Martinez .05
182 Tim Raines .05
183 Scott Brosius .05
184 Jason Giambi .60
185 Geronimo Berroa .05
186 Ariel Prieto .05
187 Scott Spiezio .05
188 John Wasdin .05
189 Ernie Young .05
190 Mark McGwire 1.50
191 Jim Eisenreich .05
192 Ricky Bottalico .05
193 Darren Daulton .05
194 David Doster .05
195 Gregg Jefferies .05
196 Lenny Dykstra .05
197 Curt Schilling .20
198 Todd Stottlemyre .05
199 Willie McGee .05
200 Ozzie Smith 1.00
201 Dennis Eckersley .65
202 Ray Lankford .05
203 John Mabry .05
204 Alan Benes .05
205 Ron Gant .05
206 Archi Cianfrocco .05
207 Fernando Valenzuela .05
208 Greg Vaughn .05
209 Steve Finley .05
210 Tony Gwynn 1.00
211 Rickey Henderson .75
212 Trevor Hoffman .05
213 Jason Thompson .05
214 Osvaldo Fernandez .05
215 Glenallen Hill .05
216 William Van Landingham .05
217 Marvin Benard .05
218 Juan Gonzalez (Postseason) .10
219 Roberto Alomar (Postseason) .05
220 Brian Jordan (Postseason) .05
221 John Smoltz (Postseason) .05
222 Javy Lopez (Postseason) .05
223 Bernie Williams (Postseason) .05
224 Jim Leyritz, John Wetteland (Postseason) .05
225 Barry Bonds 2.00

226 Rich Aurilia .05
227 Jay Canizaro .05
228 Dan Wilson .05
229 Bob Wolcott .05
230 Ken Griffey Jr. 1.25
231 Sterling Hitchcock .05
232 Edgar Martinez .05
233 Joey Cora .05
234 Norm Charlton .05
235 Alex Rodriguez 1.50
236 Bobby Witt .05
237 Darren Oliver .05
238 Kevin Elster .05
239 Rusty Greer .05
240 Juan Gonzalez .40
241 Will Clark .05
242 Dean Palmer .05
243 Ivan Rodriguez .25
244 Checklist (Ken Griffey Jr.) .25
245 Checklist (Ken Griffey Jr.) .25
246 Checklist (Ken Griffey Jr.) .25
247 Checklist (Ken Griffey Jr.) .25
248 Checklist (Ken Griffey Jr.) .25
249 Checklist (Ken Griffey Jr.) .25
250 Eddie Murray .75
251 Troy Percival .05
252 Garret Anderson .05
253 Allen Watson .05
254 Jason Dickson .05
255 Jim Edmonds .05
256 Chuck Finley .05
257 Randy Velarde .05
258 Shigetosi Hasegawa .05
259 Todd Greene .05
260 Tim Salmon .05
261 Mark Langston .05
262 Dave Hollins .05
263 Gary DiSarcina .05
264 Kenny Lofton .05
265 John Smoltz .05
266 Greg Maddux 1.00
267 Jeff Blauser .05
268 Alan Embree .05
269 Mark Lemke .05
270 Chipper Jones 1.00
271 Mike Mussina .65
272 Rafael Palmeiro .65
273 Jimmy Key .05
274 Mike Bordick .05
275 Brady Anderson .05
276 Eric Davis .05
277 Jeffrey Hammonds .05
278 Reggie Jefferson .05
279 Tim Naehring .05
280 John Valentin .05
281 Troy O'Leary .05
282 Shane Mack .05
283 Mike Stanley .05
284 Tim Wakefield .05
285 Brian McRae .05
286 Brooks Kieschnick .05
287 Shawon Dunston .05
288 Kevin Foster .05
289 Mel Rojas .05
290 Mark Grace .05
291 Brant Brown .05
292 Amaury Telemaco .05
293 Dave Martinez .05
294 Jaime Navarro .05
295 Ray Durham .05
296 Ozzie Guillen .05
297 Roberto Hernandez .05
298 Ron Karkovice .05
299 James Baldwin .05
300 Frank Thomas .75
301 Eddie Taubensee .05
302 Bret Boone .05
303 Willie Greene .05
304 Dave Burba .05
305 Deion Sanders .10
306 Reggie Sanders .05
307 Hal Morris .05
308 Pokey Reese .05
309 Tony Fernandez .05
310 Manny Ramirez .75
311 Chad Ogea .05
312 Jack McDowell .05
313 Kevin Mitchell .05
314 Chad Curtis .05
315 Steve Kline .05
316 Kevin Seitzer .05
317 Kirt Manwaring .05
318 Bill Swift .05
319 Ellis Burks .05
320 Andres Galarraga .05
321 Bruce Ruffin .05
322 Mark Thompson .05
323 Walt Weiss .05
324 Todd Jones .05
325 Andruw Jones (Griffey Hot List) .50
326 Chipper Jones (Griffey Hot List) .75
327 Mo Vaughn (Griffey Hot List) .05
328 Frank Thomas (Griffey Hot List) .50
329 Albert Belle (Griffey Hot List) .10
330 Mark McGwire (Griffey Hot List) 1.00
331 Derek Jeter (Griffey Hot List) 1.50
332 Alex Rodriguez (Griffey Hot List) 1.00
333 Jay Buhner (Griffey Hot List) .05

334 Ken Griffey Jr. (Griffey Hot List) .75
335 Brian L. Hunter .05
336 Brian Johnson .05
337 Omar Olivares .05
338 Deivi Cruz RC .05
339 Damion Easley .05
340 Melvin Nieves .05
341 Moises Alou .05
342 Jim Eisenreich .05
343 Mark Hutton .05
344 Alex Fernandez .05
345 Gary Sheffield .35
346 Pat Rapp .05
347 Brad Ausmus .05
348 Sean Berry .05
349 Darryl Kile .05
350 Craig Biggio .05
351 Chris Holt .05
352 Luis Gonzalez .05
353 Pat Listach .05
354 Jose Rosado .05
355 Mike Macfarlane .05
356 Tom Goodwin .05
357 Chris Haney .05
358 Chili Davis .05
359 Jose Offerman .05
360 Johnny Damon .30
361 Bip Roberts .05
362 Ramon Martinez .05
363 Pedro Astacio .05
364 Todd Zeile .05
365 Mike Piazza 1.25
366 Greg Gagne .05
367 Chan Ho Park .05
368 Wilton Guerrero .05
369 Todd Worrell .05
370 John Jaha .05
371 Steve Sparks .05
372 Mike Matheny .05
373 Marc Newfield .05
374 Jeromy Burnitz .05
375 Jose Valentin .05
376 Ben McDonald .05
377 Roberto Kelly .05
378 Bob Tewksbury .05
379 Ron Coomer .05
380 Brad Radke .05
381 Matt Lawton .05
382 Dan Naulty .05
383 Scott Stahoviak .05
384 Matt Wagner .05
385 Jim Bullinger .05
386 Carlos Perez .05
387 Darrin Fletcher .05
388 Chris Widger .05
389 F.P. Santangelo .05
390 Lee Smith .05
391 Bobby Jones .05
392 Jim Olerud .05
393 Mark Clark .05
394 Jason Isringhausen .05
395 Todd Hundley .05
396 Lance Johnson .05
397 Edgardo Alfonzo .05
398 Alex Ochoa .05
399 Darryl Strawberry .05
400 David Cone .05
401 Paul O'Neill .05
402 Joe Girardi .05
403 Charlie Hayes .05
404 Andy Pettitte .25
405 Mariano Rivera .25
406 Mariano Duncan .05
407 Kenny Rogers .05
408 Cecil Fielder .05
409 George Williams .05
410 Jose Canseco .35
411 Tony Batista .05
412 Steve Karsay .05
413 Dave Telgheder .05
414 Billy Taylor .05
415 Mickey Morandini .05
416 Calvin Maduro .05
417 Mark Leiter .05
418 Kevin Stocker .05
419 Mike Lieberthal .05
420 Rico Brogna .05
421 Mark Portugal .05
422 Rex Hudler .05
423 Mark Johnson .05
424 Esteban Loiaza .05
425 Lou Collier .05
426 Kevin Elster .05
427 Francisco Cordova .05
428 Marc Wilkins .05
429 Joe Randa .05
430 Jason Kendall .05
431 Jon Lieber .05
432 Steve Cooke .05
433 Emil Brown RC .05
434 Tony Womack RC .25
435 Al Martin .05
436 Jason Schmidt .05
437 Andy Benes .05
438 Delino DeShields .05
439 Royce Clayton .05
440 Brian Jordan .05
441 Donovan Osborne .05
442 Gary Gaetti .05
443 Tom Pagnozzi .05
444 Joey Hamilton .05
445 Wally Joyner .05
446 John Flaherty .05
447 Chris Gomez .05
448 Sterling Hitchcock .05
449 Andy Ashby .05
450 Ken Caminiti .05

451 Tim Worrell .05
452 Jose Vizcaino .05
453 Rod Beck .05
454 Wilson Delgado .05
455 Darryl Hamilton .05
456 Mark Lewis .05
457 Mark Gardner .05
458 Rick Wilkins .05
459 Scott Sanders .05
460 Kevin Orie .05
461 Glendon Rusch .05
462 Juan Melo .05
463 Richie Sexson .05
464 Bartolo Colon .05
465 Jose Guillen .05
466 Heath Murray .05
467 Aaron Boone .05
468 Bubba Trammell RC .05
469 Jeff Abbott .05
470 Derrick Gibson .05
471 Matt Morris .05
472 Ryan Jones .05
473 Pat Cline .05
474 Adam Riggs .05
475 Jay Payton .05
476 Derrek Lee .50
477 Elieser Marrero .05
478 Lee Tinsley .05
479 Jamie Moyer .05
480 Jay Buhner .05
481 Bob Wells .05
482 Jeff Fassero .05
483 Paul Sorrento .05
484 Russ Davis .05
485 Randy Johnson .75
486 Roger Pavlik .05
487 Damon Buford .05
488 Julio Santana .05
489 Mark McLemore .05
490 Mickey Tettleton .05
491 Ken Hill .05
492 Benji Gil .05
493 Ed Sprague .05
494 Mike Timlin .05
495 Pat Hentgen .05
496 Orlando Merced .05
497 Carlos Garcia .05
498 Carlos Delgado .35
499 Juan Guzman .05
500 Roger Clemens 1.00
501 Erik Hanson .05
502 Otis Nixon .05
503 Shawn Green .10
504 Charlie O'Brien .05
505 Joe Carter .05
506 Alex Gonzalez .05

31 Mark Grudzielanek .10
32 Sammy Sosa .60
33 Steve Finley .10
34 Gary Sheffield .25
35 Todd Hundley .10
36 Greg Maddux .60
37 Mo Vaughn .10
38 Eric Young .10
39 Vinny Castilla .10
40 Derek Jeter 1.50
41 Lance Johnson .10
42 Ellis Burks .10
43 Dante Bichette .10
44 Javy Lopez .10
45 Hideo Nomo .25

Big Shots

This 20-card insert depicts the game's top stars in unique photos. Cards were inserted 1:12 packs. Gold Signature Editions, featuring a gold foil-stamped fac-simile autograph, were inserted 1:144 packs. Fronts are highlight-ed in silver foil. Backs repeat a por-tion of the front photo, have a pic-ture of the photographer and his comments about the picture.

	NM/M
Complete Set (19):	15.00
Common Player:	.25
Gold Signature Edition:	2X
1 Ken Griffey Jr.	2.00
2 Nomar Garciaparra	1.50
3 Brian Jordan	.25
4 Scott Rolen	2.50
5 Alex Rodriguez	2.50
6 Larry Walker	.25
7 Mariano Rivera	.35
8 Cal Ripken Jr.	3.00
9 Deion Sanders	.25
10 Frank Thomas	1.00
11 Dean Palmer	.25
12 Ken Caminiti	.25
13 Derek Jeter	3.00
14 Barry Bonds	3.00
15 Chipper Jones	1.50
16 Mo Vaughn	.25
17 Jay Buhner	.25
18 Mike Piazza	2.00
19 Tony Gwynn	1.50

All-Star Connection

This 45-card insert from Series 2 highlights All-Star caliber players. Cards feature a large starburst pat-tern on a metallic-foil background behind the player's photo. They were inserted one per pack.

	NM/M
Complete Set (45):	10.00
Common Player:	.10
1 Mark McGwire	1.00
2 Chuck Knoblauch	.10
3 Jim Thome	.35
4 Alex Rodriguez	1.00
5 Ken Griffey Jr.	.75
6 Brady Anderson	.10
7 Albert Belle	.50
8 Ivan Rodriguez	.40
9 Pat Hentgen	.10
10 Frank Thomas	.50
11 Roberto Alomar	.25
12 Robin Ventura	.10
13 Cal Ripken Jr.	1.50
14 Juan Gonzalez	.50
15 Manny Ramirez	.50
16 Bernie Williams	.25
17 Terry Steinbach	.10
18 Andy Pettitte	.25
19 Jeff Bagwell	.50
20 Craig Biggio	.10
21 Ken Caminiti	.10
22 Barry Larkin	.10
23 Tony Gwynn	.50
24 Barry Bonds	1.50
25 Kenny Lofton	.10
26 Mike Piazza	.75
27 John Smoltz	.10
28 Andres Galarraga	.10
29 Ryne Sandberg	.60
30 Chipper Jones	.75

Big Show

The 45-card, regular-sized set was inserted one per pack of Series 1. Backs feature player comments written by ESPN SportsCenter hosts Keith Olbermann and Dan Patrick, whose portraits appear both front and back. On front, print-ed on metallic foil, is an action shot of the player, with his name printed along the left border of the horizon-tal cards. The cards are numbered "X/45." A parallel set to this chase-card series carries a gold-foil "World Headquarters Edition" seal at lower-right and was a 1:35 insert.

	NM/M
Complete Set (45):	7.00
Common Player:	.10
World Headquarters:	8X
1 Greg Maddux	.50
2 Chipper Jones	.50
3 Andruw Jones	.40
4 John Smoltz	.10
5 Cal Ripken Jr.	1.00
6 Roberto Alomar	.25
7 Rafael Palmeiro	.35
8 Eddie Murray	.40
9 Jose Canseco	.30
10 Roger Clemens	.55
11 Mo Vaughn	.25
12 Jim Edmonds	.10

13	Tim Salmon	.10
14	Sammy Sosa	.50
15	Albert Belle	.10
16	Frank Thomas	.40
17	Barry Larkin	.10
18	Kenny Lofton	.10
19	Manny Ramirez	.40
20	Matt Williams	.10
21	Dante Bichette	.10
22	Gary Sheffield	.30
23	Craig Biggio	.10
24	Jeff Bagwell	.40
25	Todd Hollandsworth	.10
26	Raul Mondesi	.10
27	Hideo Nomo	.25
28	Mike Piazza	.60
29	Paul Molitor	.40
30	Kirby Puckett	.50
31	Rondell White	.10
32	Rey Ordonez	.10
33	Paul Wilson	.10
34	Derek Jeter	1.00
35	Andy Pettitte	.25
36	Mark McGwire	.75
37	Jason Kendall	.10
38	Ozzie Smith	.50
39	Tony Gwynn	.50
40	Barry Bonds	1.00
41	Alex Rodriguez	.75
42	Jay Buhner	.10
43	Ken Griffey Jr.	.60
44	Randy Johnson	.40
45	Juan Gonzalez	.25

1997 Collector's Choice Big Show World Headquarters

The 45-card chase set in Series 2 is also found in a special parallel version which carries a "World Headquarters Edition" gold-foil seal on front at the lower-right.

	NM/M
Complete Set (45):	50.00
Common Player:	1.50
Stars:	8X

Clearly Dominant

The five-card, regular-sized set features Seattle outfielder Ken Griffey Jr. on each card and was inserted every 144 packs of 1997 Collector's Choice baseball.

	NM/M
Complete Set (5):	16.00
Common Card:	4.00
CD1-CD5 Ken Griffey Jr.	4.00

1997 Collector's Choice Clearly Dominant Jumbos

Each of the five Ken Griffey Jr. cards from the Collector's Choice insert set was also produced in a special retail-only 5" x 3-1/2" jumbo version. The supersize Clearly Dominant cards were packaged in a special collectors' kit which also included a Griffey stand-up figure and eight packs of CC cards, retailing for about $15. The cards could also be purchased as a complete set for $10. Cards are numbered with a "CD" prefix.

	NM/M
Complete Set (5):	10.00
Common Card:	2.00
1-5 Ken Griffey Jr.	2.00

1997 Collector's Choice Hot List Jumbos

These 5" x 7" versions of the "Ken Griffey Jr.'s Hot List" subset from Series 2 are an exclusive box-

topper in certain retail packaging of Collector's Choice. Other than size, the jumbos are identical to the regular Hot List cards, including foil background printing on front.

	NM/M
Complete Set (10):	15.00
Common Player:	.50
325 Andruw Jones	1.50
326 Chipper Jones	2.00
327 Mo Vaughn	.50
328 Frank Thomas	1.50
329 Albert Belle	.50
330 Mark McGwire	3.00
331 Derek Jeter	4.00
332 Alex Rodriguez	3.00
333 Jay Buhner	.50
334 Ken Griffey Jr.	2.50

New Frontier

This is a 40-card Series 2 insert highlighting anticipated interleague matchups. Cards were designed with each player's action photo superimposed on a metallic-foil background depicting half of a ballfield. Pairs could then be displayed side-by-side. Cards were inserted 1:69 packs. They are numbered and carry a "NF" prefix.

		NM/M
Complete Set (40):		75.00
Common Player:		1.00
1	Alex Rodriguez	5.00
2	Tony Gwynn	3.00
3	Jose Canseco	1.25
4	Hideo Nomo	1.25
5	Mark McGwire	5.00
6	Barry Bonds	6.00
7	Juan Gonzalez	1.25
8	Ken Caminiti	1.00
9	Tim Salmon	1.00
10	Mike Piazza	4.00
11	Ken Griffey Jr.	4.00
12	Andres Galarraga	1.00
13	Jay Buhner	1.00
14	Dante Bichette	1.00
15	Frank Thomas	2.00
16	Ryne Sandberg	3.00
17	Roger Clemens	3.50
18	Andruw Jones	2.00
19	Jim Thome	1.50
20	Sammy Sosa	3.00
21	David Justice	1.00
22	Deion Sanders	1.00
23	Todd Walker	1.00
24	Kevin Orie	1.00
25	Albert Belle	1.00
26	Jeff Bagwell	2.00
27	Manny Ramirez	1.00
28	Brian Jordan	1.00
29	Derek Jeter	6.00
30	Chipper Jones	3.00
31	Mo Vaughn	1.00
32	Gary Sheffield	1.50
33	Carlos Delgado	1.50
34	Vladimir Guerrero	1.50
35	Cal Ripken Jr.	6.00
36	Greg Maddux	3.00
37	Cecil Fielder	1.00
38	Todd Hundley	1.00
39	Mike Mussina	1.25
40	Scott Rolen	1.50

Premier Power

The 20-card, regular-sized set was included one per 15 packs of Series 1. Fronts feature an ac-

tion photo with the "Premier Power" logo in silver foil in the lower half and "spotlights" aiming out toward the sides. The bottom portion of the card is transparent red. Backs are bordered in red with the same card front shot appearing in black-and-white above a brief description and "Power Facts." The cards are numbered with a "PP" prefix. A parallel gold-foil version was available every 69 packs.

		NM/M
Complete Set (20):		20.00
Common Player:		.40
Gold:		2X
1	Mark McGwire	3.00
2	Brady Anderson	.40
3	Ken Griffey Jr.	2.50
4	Albert Belle	.40
5	Juan Gonzalez	.60
6	Andres Galarraga	.40
7	Jay Buhner	.40
8	Mo Vaughn	.40
9	Barry Bonds	3.50
10	Gary Sheffield	.75
11	Todd Hundley	.40
12	Frank Thomas	1.50
13	Sammy Sosa	2.00
14	Ken Caminiti	.40
15	Vinny Castilla	.40
16	Ellis Burks	.40
17	Rafael Palmeiro	1.00
18	Alex Rodriguez	3.00
19	Mike Piazza	2.50
20	Eddie Murray	1.50

1997 Collector's Choice Premier Power Jumbo

Each factory set of 1997 Collector's Choice included 10 supersize (3" x 5") versions of the Premier Power inserts. Besides the size, the jumbos differ from the insert version in the addition of a metallic facsimile autograph on front.

		NM/M
Complete Set (20):		15.00
Common Player:		.50
1	Mark McGwire	2.50
2	Brady Anderson	.50
3	Ken Griffey Jr.	2.00
4	Albert Belle	.50
5	Juan Gonzalez	.75
6	Andres Galarraga	.50
7	Jay Buhner	.50
8	Mo Vaughn	.50
9	Barry Bonds	3.00
10	Gary Sheffield	.65
11	Todd Hundley	.50
12	Frank Thomas	1.00
13	Sammy Sosa	1.50
14	Ken Caminiti	.50
15	Vinny Castilla	.50
16	Ellis Burks	.50
17	Rafael Palmeiro	.75
18	Alex Rodriguez	2.50
19	Mike Piazza	2.00
20	Eddie Murray	1.50

Stick'Ums

The 30-piece 2-1/2" x 3-1/2" sticker set was inserted one per three packs of Series 1 Collector's Choice. Fronts feature a bright background color and include five different peel-off stickers: An action shot of the player, a pennant in team colors featuring the player's name, a team logo, an Upper Deck Collector's Choice logo and a "Super Action Stick'Ums" decal. Backs feature the player checklist in black ink over a gray background. An unnumbered version of the stickers (without Smith and Puckett) was sold in a special retail-only package.

		NM/M
Complete Set (30):		5.00
Common Player:		.05
1	Ozzie Smith	.50
2	Andruw Jones	.40
3	Alex Rodriguez	.75
4	Paul Molitor	.40
5	Jeff Bagwell	.40
6	Manny Ramirez	.40
7	Kenny Lofton	.05
8	Albert Belle	.05
9	Jay Buhner	.05
10	Chipper Jones	.50
11	Barry Larkin	.05
12	Dante Bichette	.05
13	Mike Piazza	.60
14	Andres Galarraga	.05
15	Barry Bonds	1.00
16	Brady Anderson	.05
17	Gary Sheffield	.20
18	Jim Thome	.35
19	Tony Gwynn	.50
20	Cal Ripken Jr.	1.00
21	Sammy Sosa	.50
22	Juan Gonzalez	.20
23	Greg Maddux	.50
24	Ken Griffey Jr.	.60
25	Mark McGwire	.75
26	Kirby Puckett	.50
27	Mo Vaughn	.05
28	Vladimir Guerrero	.40
29	Ken Caminiti	.05
30	Frank Thomas	.40

Toast of the Town

This 30-card Series 2 insert features top stars on foil-enhanced cards. Odds of finding one are 1:35 packs. Cards are numbered with a "T" prefix.

		NM/M
Complete Set (30):		40.00
Common Player:		.30
1	Andruw Jones	2.00
2	Chipper Jones	2.50
3	Greg Maddux	2.50
4	John Smoltz	.30
5	Kenny Lofton	.30
6	Brady Anderson	.30
7	Cal Ripken Jr.	6.00
8	Mo Vaughn	.30
9	Sammy Sosa	2.50
10	Albert Belle	.30
11	Frank Thomas	2.00
12	Barry Larkin	.30
13	Manny Ramirez	2.00
14	Jeff Bagwell	2.00
15	Mike Piazza	4.00
16	Paul Molitor	2.00
17	Vladimir Guerrero	2.00
18	Todd Hundley	.30
19	Derek Jeter	6.00
20	Andy Pettitte	.45
21	Bernie Williams	.30
22	Mark McGwire	5.00
23	Scott Rolen	1.00
24	Ken Caminiti	.30
25	Tony Gwynn	2.50
26	Barry Bonds	6.00
27	Ken Griffey Jr.	4.00
28	Alex Rodriguez	5.00
29	Juan Gonzalez	.75
30	Roger Clemens	3.00

1997 Collector's Choice Update

This update set was offered via a mail-in redemption offer. Traded players in their new uniforms and

1997 rookies are the focus of the set. Fronts are color photos which are borderless at top and sides. Beneath each photo the player's name and team logo appear in a red (A.L.) or blue (N.L.) baseball design. Backs have another photo, major and minor league career stats and a trivia question. Cards are numbered with a "U" prefix.

		NM/M
Complete Set (30):		2.00
Common Player:		.10
1	Jim Leyritz	.10
2	Matt Perisho	.10
3	Michael Tucker	.10
4	Mike Johnson	.10
5	Jaime Navarro	.10
6	Doug Drabek	.10
7	Terry Mulholland	.10
8	Brett Tomko	.10
9	Marquis Grissom	.10
10	David Justice	.10
11	Brian Moehler	.10
12	Bobby Bonilla	.10
13	Todd Dunwoody	.10
14	Tony Saunders	.10
15	Jay Bell	.10
16	Jeff King	.10
17	Terry Steinbach	.10
18	Steve Bieser	.10
19	Takashi Kashiwada RC	.10
20	Hideki Irabu	.10
21	Damon Mashore	.10
22	Quilvio Veras	.10
23	Will Cunnane	.10
24	Jeff Kent	.50
25	J.T. Snow	.10
26	Dante Powell	.10
27	Jose Cruz Jr.	.10
28	John Burkett	.10
29	John Wetteland	.10
30	Benito Santiago	.10

You Crash the Game

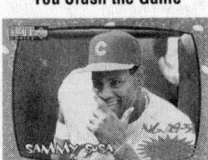

A 30-player interactive set found in Series 2 packs features the game's top home run hitters. Cards were inserted 1:5 packs. Fronts feature a red-foil Crash logo and a range of game dates. Those holding cards of players who homered in that span could (for $2 per card handling fee) redeem them for high-tech versions. Instant winner cards (seeded 1:721) were redeemable for complete 30-card upgrade sets. Winning cards are marked with an asterisk; theoretically they would be scarcer than losing cards because many were redeemed. The contest cards expired on Sept. 8, 1997. Cards are numbered with a "CG" prefix.

	NM/M
Complete Set (90):	65.00
Common Player:	.25
July 28-30	.25
August 8-11	.25
Sept. 19-21	.25
August 15-17	1.00
August 29-31	1.00
Sept. 12-14	1.00
August 22-24*	1.50
Sept. 1-3	.75
Sept. 19-22	.75
July 31-Aug. 3*	.75
Sept. 4-7	.25
Sept. 19-22	.25
July 29-30	.60
Aug. 29-31	.60
Sept. 26-28	.60
August 8-10*	4.00
Sept. 1-3*	4.00
Sept. 11-14	2.00
August 14-17	.25
August 29-31*	.50
Sept. 23-25*	.25
August 1-3*	2.00
August 29-31	1.00
Sept. 19-21*	2.00
August 7-10	.25
Sept. 11-14	.25
Sept. 19-21*	.50
August 29-31	.75
Sept. 1-3	.25
Sept. 23-25*	1.50
August 12-14*	1.50
August 29-31	.75
Sept. 11-14*	1.50
July 28-30	1.00
August 15-18*	1.00
Sept. 19-22	.50
August 4-5	.50
Sept. 1-3*	.50
Sept. 23-25	.50
July 24-27*	1.50
August 28-29	.25
Sept. 26-28*	.25
August 12-13	.25
Sept. 4-7*	.50
Sept. 19-21	.50
August 8-10*	.50
August 30-31	.50
Sept. 12-14	.75
August 1-3*	.75
Sept. 12-14*	.75
Sept. 9-10	.75
Sept. 19-22*	1.50
Sept. 23-25*	1.50
August 1-3	.25
August 15-17	.25
Sept. 25-28*	.50
August 11-12	.25
Sept. 5-8*	2.50
Sept. 19-21*	2.50
August 22-24	.75
August 29-31	.75
Sept. 19-22	.75
August 29-31	.75
Sept. 4-7	.25
Sept. 26-28*	.25
August 22-24	.35
Sept. 12-14	.35
Sept. 26-28	.35
July 31-Aug. 3	1.50
August 30-31	1.50
Sept. 19-22*	3.00
August 8-10	.25
Sept. 4-7	.25
Sept. 17-18*	.50
August 5-7	2.00
Sept. 4-7*	4.00
Sept. 23-24*	2.00
August 7-10	.25
August 28-29	.25
Sept. 1-3	.25
August 22-24*	1.25
August 28-29	1.25
Sept. 19-22*	2.50
July 29-31	1.50
August 30-31	1.50
Sept. 12-15	1.50
August 11-13*	.25
August 30-31	.40
Sept. 19-21*	.75

You Crash the Game Winners

These are the prize cards from CC's interactive "You Crash the Game" cards in Series 2. Persons who redeemed a Crash card with the correct date(s) on which the pictured player homered received (for a $2 handling fee) this high-end version of the Crash card. The redemption cards have the same basic design as the contest cards, but use different player photos with fronts printed on metallic-foil stock, and a team logo in place of the Crash foil logo. Where the contest cards have game rules on back, the redemption cards have another photo of the player and career highlights. Complete redemption sets were available upon redeeming an instant winner card, found on average of one per 721 packs. Because some cards were only available in complete redemption sets (marked with an "SP" here), and others might have been available for more than one date range, some cards will be scarcer than others.

	NM/M
Complete Set (30):	55.00
Common Player:	.50
CG1 Ryan Klesko/SP	1.25
CG2 Chipper Jones/SP	12.00
CG3 Andruw Jones	.75
CG4 Brady Anderson	.50
CG5 Rafael Palmeiro/SP	2.50
CG6 Cal Ripken Jr.	10.00
CG7 Mo Vaughn	.50
CG8 Sammy Sosa	3.00
CG9 Albert Belle	.50
CG10 Frank Thomas	1.00
CG11 Manny Ramirez	.75
CG12 Jim Thome	.65
CG13 Matt Williams	.50
CG14 Dante Bichette	.50
CG15 Vinny Castilla	.50
CG16 Andres Galarraga	.50
CG17 Gary Sheffield	.65
CG18 Jeff Bagwell	.75
CG19 Eric Karros	.50
CG20 Mike Piazza	2.50
CG21 Vladimir Guerrero/SP	3.00
CG22 Cecil Fielder/SP	1.25
CG23 Jose Canseco/SP	2.00
CG24 Mark McGwire	7.50
CG25 Ken Caminiti	.50
CG26 Barry Bonds	10.00
CG27 Jay Buhner/SP	1.25
CG28 Ken Griffey Jr.	2.50
CG29 Alex Rodriguez/SP	9.00
CG30 Juan Gonzalez	.60

You Crash/Game Instant Winner

Found on average of one per 721 packs, these Instant Winner cards could be redeemed (with a $2 handling fee) for a complete set of You Crash the Game exchange cards - the only way eight of the Crash winner cards could be obtained. These special cards have a red foil "instant winner!" logo on front and a congratulatory message on back, along with instructions for redemption prior to the Dec. 8, 1997, deadline.

	NM/M
Complete Set (30):	300.00
Common Player:	2.00

1997 Collector's Choice Team Sets

A special version of Collector's Choice cards for several popular major league teams was produced in two retail packages by Upper Deck. In one version, blister packs containing 13 player cards and a metallic-foil team logo/checklist card was sold for a suggested retail price of $1.99. The second version, exclusive to Wal-Mart, is a hard plastic blister pack containing two cello-wrapped packages. One holds a random assortment of 15 Series 1 Collector's Choice cards. The other has 13 player cards and a foil logo/checklist card for a specific team. The team-set cards are identical to the regular-issue cards, from either Series 1 or Series 2, except each of the team-set cards has a number on back which differs from the

regular edition. Packaged with the Wal-Mart version is a 3-1/2" x 5" "Home Team Heroes" card, listed seperately.

	NM/M
Common Player:	.10
Atlanta Braves Team Set:	3.00
AB Team Logo/Checklist	.10
AB1 Andruw Jones	.60
AB2 Kenny Lofton	.10
AB3 Fred McGriff	.10
AB4 Michael Tucker	.10
AB5 Ryan Klesko	.10
AB6 Javy Lopez	.10
AB7 Mark Wohlers	.10
AB8 Tom Glavine	.25
AB9 Denny Neagle	.10
AB10 Chipper Jones	.75
AB11 Jeff Blauser	.10
AB12 Greg Maddux	.75
AB13 John Smoltz	.10
Baltimore Orioles Team Set:	2.00
BO Team Logo/Checklist	.10
BO1 Rocky Coppinger	.10
BO2 Scott Erickson	.10
BO3 Chris Hoiles	.10
BO4 Roberto Alomar	.30
BO5 Cal Ripken Jr.	1.50
BO6 Randy Myers	.10
BO7 B.J. Surhoff	.10
BO8 Mike Mussina	.40
BO9 Rafael Palmeiro	.50
BO10 Jimmy Key	.10
BO11 Mike Bordick	.10
BO12 Brady Anderson	.10
BO13 Eric Davis	.10
Chicago White Sox Team Set:	2.50
CW Team Logo/Checklist	.10
CW1 Robin Ventura	.10
CW2 Wilson Alvarez	.10
CW3 Tony Phillips	.10
CW4 Lyle Mouton	.10
CW5 James Baldwin	.10
CW6 Harold Baines	.10
CW7 Albert Belle	.10
CW8 Chris Snopek	.10
CW9 Ray Durham	.10
CW10 Frank Thomas	.60
CW11 Ozzie Guillen	.10
CW12 Roberto Hernandez	.10
CW13 Jaime Navarro	.10
Cleveland Indians Team Set:	1.50
CI Team Logo/Checklist	.10
CI1 Brian Giles	.10
CI2 Omar Vizquel	.10
CI3 Julio Franco	.10
CI4 Orel Hershiser	.10
CI5 Charles Nagy	.10
CI6 Matt Williams	.10
CI7 Jose Mesa	.10
CI8 Sandy Alomar	.10
CI9 Jim Thome	.50
CI10 David Justice	.10
CI11 Marquis Grissom	.10
CI12 Chad Ogea	.10
CI13 Manny Ramirez	.60
Colorado Rockies Team Set:	1.25
CR Team Logo/Checklist	.10
CR1 Dante Bichette	.10
CR2 Vinny Castilla	.10
CR3 Kevin Ritz	.10
CR4 Larry Walker	.10
CR5 Eric Young	.10
CR6 Quinton McCracken	.10
CR7 John Vander Wal	.10
CR8 Jamey Wright	.10
CR9 Mark Thompson	.10
CR10 Andres Galarraga	.10
CR11 Ellis Burks	.10
CR12 Kirt Manwaring	.10
CR13 Walt Weiss	.10
Florida Marlins Team Set:	2.00
FM Team Logo/Checklist	.10
FM1 Luis Castillo	.10
FM2 Al Leiter	.10
FM3 Devon White	.10
FM4 Jeff Conine	.10
FM5 Charles Johnson	.10
FM6 Edgar Renteria	.10
FM7 Robb Nen	.10
FM8 Kevin Brown	.10
FM9 Gary Sheffield	.45
FM10 Alex Fernandez	.10
FM11 Pat Rapp	.10
FM12 Moises Alou	.10
FM13 Bobby Bonilla	.10
L.A. Dodgers Team Set:	3.00
LA Team Logo/Checklist	.10
LA1 Raul Mondesi	.10
LA2 Brett Butler	.10
LA3 Todd Hollandsworth	.10
LA4 Eric Karros	.10
LA5 Hideo Nomo	.30
LA6 Ismael Valdes	.10
LA7 Wilton Guerrero	.10
LA8 Ramon Martinez	.10
LA9 Greg Gagne	.10
LA10 Mike Piazza	1.00
LA11 Chan Ho Park	.10
LA12 Todd Worrell	.10
LA13 Todd Zeile	.10
New York Yankees Team Set:	3.00
NY Team Logo/Checklist	.10
NY1 Bernie Williams	.10
NY2 Dwight Gooden	.10
NY3 Wade Boggs	.75

NY4	Ruben Rivera	.10
NY5	Derek Jeter	1.50
NY6	Tino Martinez	.10
NY7	Tim Raines	.10
NY8	Joe Girardi	.10
NY9	Charlie Hayes	.10
NY10	Andy Pettitte	.30
NY11	Cecil Fielder	.10
NY12	Paul O'Neill	.10
NY13	David Cone	.10
Seattle Mariners Team Set:		3.00
SM	Team Logo/Checklist	.10
SM1	Dan Wilson	.10
SM2	Ken Griffey Jr.	1.00
SM3	Edgar Martinez	.10
SM4	Joey Cora	.10
SM5	Norm Charlton	.10
SM6	Alex Rodriguez	1.25
SM7	Randy Johnson	.60
SM8	Paul Sorrento	.10
SM9	Jamie Moyer	.10
SM10	Jay Buhner	.10
SM11	Russ Davis	.10
SM12	Jeff Fassero	.10
SM13	Bob Wells	.10
Texas Rangers Team Set:		3.00
TR	Team Logo/Checklist	.10
TR1	Bobby Witt	.10
TR2	Darren Oliver	.10
TR3	Rusty Greer	.10
TR4	Juan Gonzalez	.30
TR5	Will Clark	.10
TR6	Dean Palmer	.10
TR7	Ivan Rodriguez	.50
TR8	John Wetteland	.10
TR9	Mark McLemore	.10
TR10	John Burkett	.10
TR11	Benji Gil	.10
TR12	Ken Hill	.10
TR13	Mickey Tettleton	.10

1998 Collector's Choice

The 530-card Collectors Choice set was issued in two 265-card series. Series 1 features 197 regular cards, five checklists and four subsets: Cover Story features 18 of the league's top stars, Rookie Class has 27 young players, the nine-card Top of the Charts subset honors 1997's statistical leaders and Masked Marauders is a nine-card subset. Inserts in Series 1 are Super Action Stick-Ums, Evolution Revolution and StarQuest. Series 2 has 233 regular cards, five checklist cards, an 18-card Rookie Class subset and the nine-card Golden Jubilee subset. Inserts in Series 2 include Mini Bobbing Head Cards, You Crash the Game and StarQuest. Factory sets include a random assortment of 10 StarQuest cards.

	NM/M
Unopened Fact. Set (540):	15.00
Complete Set (530):	10.00
Common Player:	.05
Pack (14):	1.00
Wax Box (36):	15.00
1 Nomar Garciaparra (Cover Glory)	.50
2 Roger Clemens (Cover Glory)	.50
3 Larry Walker (Cover Glory)	.50
4 Mike Piazza (Cover Glory)	.60
5 Mark McGwire (Cover Glory)	.75
6 Tony Gwynn (Cover Glory)	.45
7 Jose Cruz Jr. (Cover Glory)	.05
8 Frank Thomas (Cover Glory)	.40
9 Tino Martinez (Cover Glory)	.05
10 Ken Griffey Jr. (Cover Glory)	.60
11 Barry Bonds (Cover Glory)	.85
12 Scott Rolen (Cover Glory)	.30
13 Randy Johnson (Cover Glory)	.15
14 Ryne Sandberg (Cover Glory)	.35

15	Eddie Murray	
	(Cover Glory)	.15
16	Kevin Brown (Cover Glory)	.05
17	Greg Maddux	
	(Cover Glory)	.35
18	Sandy Alomar Jr.	
	(Cover Glory)	.05
19	Checklist (Ken Griffey Jr., Adam Riggs)	.40
20	Checklist (Nomar Garciaparra, Charlie O'Brien)	.10
21	Checklist (Ben Grieve, Ken Griffey Jr., Larry Walker, Mark McGwire)	.50
22	Checklist (Mark McGwire, Cal Ripken Jr.)	.50
23	Checklist (Tino Martinez)	.05
24	Jason Dickson	.05
25	Darin Erstad	.25
26	Todd Greene	.05
27	Chuck Finley	.05
28	Garret Anderson	.05
29	Dave Hollins	.05
30	Rickey Henderson	.60
31	John Smoltz	.05
32	Michael Tucker	.05
33	Jeff Blauser	.05
34	Javier Lopez	.05
35	Andruw Jones	.60
36	Denny Neagle	.05
37	Randall Simon	.05
38	Mark Wohlers	.05
39	Harold Baines	.05
40	Cal Ripken Jr.	1.50
41	Mike Bordick	.05
42	Jimmy Key	.05
43	Armando Benitez	.05
44	Scott Erickson	.05
45	Eric Davis	.05
46	Bret Saberhagen	.05
47	Darren Bragg	.05
48	Steve Avery	.05
49	Jeff Frye	.05
50	Aaron Sele	.05
51	Scott Hatteberg	.05
52	Tom Gordon	.05
53	Kevin Orie	.05
54	Kevin Foster	.05
55	Ryne Sandberg	.75
56	Doug Glanville	.05
57	Tyler Houston	.05
58	Steve Trachsel	.05
59	Mark Grace	.05
60	Frank Thomas	.60
61	Scott Eyre RC	.05
62	Jeff Abbott	.05
63	Chris Clemons	.05
64	Jorge Fabregas	.05
65	Robin Ventura	.05
66	Matt Karchner	.05
67	Jon Nunnally	.05
68	Aaron Boone	.05
69	Pokey Reese	.05
70	Deion Sanders	.10
71	Jeff Shaw	.05
72	Eduardo Perez	.05
73	Brett Tomko	.05
74	Bartolo Colon	.05
75	Manny Ramirez	.60
76	Jose Mesa	.05
77	Brian Giles	.05
78	Richie Sexson	.05
79	Orel Hershiser	.05
80	Matt Williams	.05
81	Walt Weiss	.05
82	Jerry DiPoto	.05
83	Quinton McCracken	.05
84	Neifi Perez	.05
85	Vinny Castilla	.05
86	Ellis Burks	.05
87	John Thomson	.05
88	Willie Blair	.05
89	Bob Hamelin	.05
90	Tony Clark	.05
91	Todd Jones	.05
92	Deivi Cruz	.05
93	Frank Catalanotto RC	.15
94	Justin Thompson	.05
95	Gary Sheffield	.25
96	Kevin Brown	.05
97	Charles Johnson	.05
98	Bobby Bonilla	.05
99	Livan Hernandez	.05
100	Paul Konerko (Rookie Class)	.10
101	Craig Counsell (Rookie Class)	.05
102	Magglio Ordonez RC (Rookie Class)	1.00
103	Garrett Stephenson (Rookie Class)	.05
104	Ken Cloude (Rookie Class)	.05
105	Miguel Tejada (Rookie Class)	.05
106	Juan Encarnacion (Rookie Class)	.05
107	Dennis Reyes (Rookie Class)	.05
108	Orlando Cabrera (Rookie Class)	.05
109	Kelvim Escobar (Rookie Class)	.05
110	Ben Grieve (Rookie Class)	.05
111	Brian Rose (Rookie Class)	.05
112	Fernando Tatis (Rookie Class)	.05
113	Tom Evans (Rookie Class)	.05

114	Tom Fordham (Rookie Class)	.05
115	Mark Kotsay (Rookie Class)	.05
116	Mario Valdez (Rookie Class)	.05
117	Jeremi Gonzalez (Rookie Class)	.05
118	Todd Dunwoody (Rookie Class)	.05
119	Javier Valentin (Rookie Class)	.05
120	Todd Helton (Rookie Class)	.50
121	Jason Varitek (Rookie Class)	.10
122	Chris Carpenter (Rookie Class)	.05
123	Kevin Millwood RC (Rookie Class)	.75
124	Brad Fullmer (Rookie Class)	.05
125	Jaret Wright (Rookie Class)	.05
126	Brad Rigby (Rookie Class)	.05
127	Edgar Renteria	.05
128	Robb Nen	.05
129	Tony Pena	.05
130	Craig Biggio	.05
131	Brad Ausmus	.05
132	Shane Reynolds	.05
133	Mike Hampton	.05
134	Billy Wagner	.05
135	Richard Hidalgo	.05
136	Jose Rosado	.05
137	Yamil Benitez	.05
138	Felix Martinez	.05
139	Jeff King	.05
140	Jose Offerman	.05
141	Joe Vitiello	.05
142	Tim Belcher	.05
143	Brett Butler	.05
144	Greg Gagne	.05
145	Mike Piazza	1.00
146	Ramon Martinez	.05
147	Raul Mondesi	.05
148	Adam Riggs	.05
149	Eddie Murray	.50
150	Jeff Cirillo	.05
151	Scott Karl	.05
152	Mike Fetters	.05
153	Dave Nilsson	.05
154	Antone Williamson	.05
155	Jeff D'Amico	.05
156	Jose Valentin	.05
157	Brad Radke	.05
158	Torii Hunter	.05
159	Chuck Knoblauch	.05
160	Paul Molitor	.60
161	Travis Miller	.05
162	Rich Robertson	.05
163	Ron Coomer	.05
164	Mark Grudzielanek	.05
165	Lee Smith	.05
166	Vladimir Guerrero	.60
167	Dustin Hermanson	.05
168	Ugueth Urbina	.05
169	F.P. Santangelo	.05
170	Rondell White	.05
171	Bobby Jones	.05
172	Edgardo Alfonzo	.05
173	John Franco	.05
174	Carlos Baerga	.05
175	Butch Huskey	.05
176	Rey Ordonez	.05
177	Matt Franco	.05
178	Dwight Gooden	.05
179	Chad Curtis	.05
180	Tino Martinez	.05
181	Charlie O'Brien (Masked Marauders)	.05
182	Sandy Alomar Jr. (Masked Marauders)	.05
183	Raul Casanova (Masked Marauders)	.05
184	Jim Leyritz (Masked Marauders)	.05
185	Mike Piazza (Masked Marauders)	.60
186	Ivan Rodriguez (Masked Marauders)	.25
187	Charles Johnson (Masked Marauders)	.05
188	Brad Ausmus (Masked Marauders)	.05
189	Brian Johnson (Masked Marauders)	.05
190	Wade Boggs	.75
191	David Wells	.05
192	Tim Raines	.05
193	Ramiro Mendoza	.05
194	Willie Adams	.05
195	Matt Stairs	.05
196	Jason McDonald	.05
197	Dave Magadan	.05
198	Mark Bellhorn	.05
199	Ariel Prieto	.05
200	Jose Canseco	.35
201	Bobby Estalella	.05
202	Tony Barron RC	.05
203	Midre Cummings	.05
204	Ricky Bottalico	.05
205	Mike Grace	.05
206	Rico Brogna	.05
207	Mickey Morandini	.05
208	Lou Collier	.05
209	Kevin Polcovich RC	.05
210	Kevin Young	.05

211	Jose Guillen	.05
212	Esteban Loaiza	.05
213	Marc Wilkins	.05
214	Jason Schmidt	.05
215	Gary Gaetti	.05
216	Fernando Valenzuela	.05
217	Willie McGee	.05
218	Alan Benes	.05
219	Eli Marrero	.05
220	Mark McGwire	1.25
221	Matt Morris	.05
222	Trevor Hoffman	.05
223	Will Cunnane	.05
224	Joey Hamilton	.05
225	Ken Caminiti	.05
226	Derrek Lee	.05
227	Mark Sweeney	.05
228	Carlos Hernandez	.05
229	Brian Johnson	.05
230	Jeff Kent	.05
231	Kirk Rueter	.05
232	Bill Mueller	.05
233	Dante Powell	.05
234	J.T. Snow	.05
235	Shawn Estes	.05
236	Dennis Martinez	.05
237	Jamie Moyer	.05
238	Dan Wilson	.05
239	Joey Cora	.05
240	Ken Griffey Jr.	1.00
241	Paul Sorrento	.05
242	Jay Buhner	.05
243	Hanley Frias RC	.05
244	John Burkett	.05
245	Juan Gonzalez	.30
246	Rick Helling	.05
247	Darren Oliver	.05
248	Mickey Tettleton	.05
249	Ivan Rodriguez	.45
250	Joe Carter	.05
251	Pat Hentgen	.05
252	Marty Janzen	.05
253	Frank Thomas, Tony Gwynn (Top of the Charts)	.25
254	Mark McGwire, Ken Griffey Jr., Larry Walker (Top of the Charts)	.50
255	Ken Griffey Jr., Andres Galarraga (Top of the Charts)	.40
256	Brian Hunter, Tony Womack (Top of the Charts)	.05
257	Roger Clemens, Denny Neagle (Top of the Charts)	.10
258	Roger Clemens, Curt Schilling (Top of the Charts)	.30
259	Roger Clemens, Pedro J. Martinez (Top of the Charts)	.25
260	Randy Myers, Jeff Shaw (Top of the Charts)	.05
261	Nomar Garciaparra, Scott Rolen (Top of the Charts)	.25
262	Charlie O'Brien	.05
263	Shannon Stewart	.05
264	Robert Person	.05
265	Carlos Delgado	.25
266	Checklist (Matt Williams, Travis Lee)	.05
267	Checklist (Nomar Garciaparra, Cal Ripken Jr.)	.50
268	Checklist (Mark McGwire, Mike Piazza)	.50
269	Checklist (Tony Gwynn, Ken Griffey Jr.)	.40
270	Checklist (Fred McGriff, Jose Cruz Jr.)	.05
271	Andruw Jones (Golden Jubilee)	.25
272	Alex Rodriguez (Golden Jubilee)	.65
273	Juan Gonzalez (Golden Jubilee)	.15
274	Nomar Garciaparra (Golden Jubilee)	.25
275	Ken Griffey Jr. (Golden Jubilee)	
276	Tino Martinez (Golden Jubilee)	
277	Roger Clemens (Golden Jubilee)	.40
278	Barry Bonds (Golden Jubilee)	.85
279	Mike Piazza (Golden Jubilee)	.60
280	Tim Salmon (Golden Jubilee)	
281	Gary DiSarcina	.05
282	Cecil Fielder	.05
283	Ken Hill	.05
284	Troy Percival	.05
285	Jim Edmonds	.05
286	Allen Watson	.05
287	Brian Anderson	.05
288	Jay Bell	.05
289	Jorge Fabregas	.05
290	Devon White	.05
291	Jeff Suppan	.05
292	Jeff Suppan	.05
293	Tony Batista	.05
294	Brent Brede	.05
295	Andy Benes	.05
296	Felix Rodriguez	.05
297	Karim Garcia	.05
298	Omar Daal	.05
299	Andy Stankiewicz	.05

#	Player	Price
300	Matt Williams	.05
301	Willie Blair	.05
302	Ryan Klesko	.05
303	Tom Glavine	.25
304	Walt Weiss	.05
305	Greg Maddux	.75
306	Chipper Jones	.75
307	Keith Lockhart	.05
308	Andres Galarraga	.05
309	Chris Hoiles	.05
310	Roberto Alomar	.25
311	Joe Carter	.05
312	Doug Drabek	.05
313	Jeffrey Hammonds	.05
314	Rafael Palmeiro	.40
315	Mike Mussina	.40
316	Brady Anderson	.05
317	B.J. Surhoff	.05
318	Dennis Eckersley	.45
319	Jim Leyritz	.05
320	Mo Vaughn	.25
321	Nomar Garciaparra	.75
322	Reggie Jefferson	.05
323	Tim Naehring	.05
324	Troy O'Leary	.05
325	Pedro J. Martinez	.50
326	John Valentin	.05
327	Mark Clark	.05
328	Rod Beck	.05
329	Mickey Morandini	.05
330	Sammy Sosa	.75
331	Jeff Blauser	.05
332	Lance Johnson	.05
333	Scott Servais	.05
334	Kevin Tapani	.05
335	Henry Rodriguez	.05
336	Jaime Navarro	.05
337	Benji Gil	.05
338	James Baldwin	.05
339	Mike Cameron	.05
340	Ray Durham	.05
341	Chris Snopek	.05
342	Eddie Taubensee	.05
343	Bret Boone	.05
344	Willie Greene	.05
345	Barry Larkin	.05
346	Chris Stynes	.05
347	Pete Harnisch	.05
348	Dave Burba	.05
349	Sandy Alomar Jr.	.05
350	Kenny Lofton	.05
351	Geronimo Berroa	.05
352	Omar Vizquel	.05
353	Travis Fryman	.05
354	Dwight Gooden	.05
355	Jim Thome	.40
356	David Justice	.05
357	Charles Nagy	.05
358	Chad Ogea	.05
359	Pedro Astacio	.05
360	Larry Walker	.05
361	Mike Lansing	.05
362	Kirt Manwaring	.05
363	Dante Bichette	.05
364	Jamey Wright	.05
365	Darryl Kile	.05
366	Luis Gonzalez	.05
367	Joe Randa	.05
368	Raul Casanova	.05
369	Damion Easley	.05
370	Brian L. Hunter	.05
371	Bobby Higginson	.05
372	Brian Moehler	.05
373	Scott Sanders	.05
374	Jim Eisenreich	.05
375	Derrek Lee	.35
376	Jay Powell	.05
377	Cliff Floyd	.05
378	Alex Fernandez	.05
379	Felix Heredia	.05
380	Jeff Bagwell	.60
381	Bill Spiers	.05
382	Chris Holt	.05
383	Carl Everett	.05
384	Derek Bell	.05
385	Moises Alou	.05
386	Ramon Garcia	.05
387	Mike Sweeney	.05
388	Glendon Rusch	.05
389	Kevin Appier	.05
390	Dean Palmer	.05
391	Jeff Conine	.05
392	Johnny Damon	.25
393	Jose Vizcaino	.05
394	Todd Hollandsworth	.05
395	Eric Karros	.05
396	Todd Zeile	.05
397	Chan Ho Park	.05
398	Ismael Valdes	.05
399	Eric Young	.05
400	Hideo Nomo	.25
401	Mark Loretta	.05
402	Doug Jones	.05
403	Jeromy Burnitz	.05
404	John Jaha	.05
405	Marquis Grissom	.05
406	Mike Matheny	.05
407	Todd Walker	.05
408	Marty Cordova	.05
409	Matt Lawton	.05
410	Terry Steinbach	.05
411	Pat Meares	.05
412	Rick Aguilera	.05
413	Otis Nixon	.05
414	Derrick May	.05
415	Carl Pavano (Rookie Class)	.05
416	A.J. Hinch (Rookie Class)	.05

#	Player	Price
417	David Dellucci RC (Rookie Class)	.10
418	Bruce Chen (Rookie Class)	.05
419	Darron Ingram RC (Rookie Class)	.05
420	Sean Casey (Rookie Class)	.20
421	Mark L. Johnson (Rookie Class)	.05
422	Gabe Alvarez (Rookie Class)	.05
423	Alex Gonzalez (Rookie Class)	.05
424	Daryle Ward (Rookie Class)	.05
425	Russell Branyan (Rookie Class)	.05
426	Mike Caruso (Rookie Class)	.05
427	Mike Kinkade RC (Rookie Class)	.20
428	Ramon Hernandez (Rookie Class)	.05
429	Matt Clement (Rookie Class)	.05
430	Travis Lee (Rookie Class)	.05
431	Shane Monahan (Rookie Class)	.05
432	Rich Butler RC (Rookie Class)	.05
433	Chris Widger	.05
434	Jose Vidro	.05
435	Carlos Perez	.05
436	Ryan McGuire	.05
437	Brian McRae	.05
438	Al Leiter	.05
439	Rich Becker	.05
440	Todd Hundley	.05
441	Dave Mlicki	.05
442	Bernard Gilkey	.05
443	John Olerud	.05
444	Paul O'Neill	.05
445	Andy Pettitte	.30
446	David Cone	.05
447	Chili Davis	.05
448	Bernie Williams	.05
449	Joe Girardi	.05
450	Derek Jeter	1.50
451	Mariano Rivera	.20
452	George Williams	.05
453	Kenny Rogers	.05
454	Tom Candiotti	.05
455	Rickey Henderson	.60
456	Jason Giambi	.40
457	Scott Spiezio	.05
458	Doug Glanville	.05
459	Desi Relaford	.05
460	Curt Schilling	.20
461	Bob Abreu	.10
462	Gregg Jefferies	.05
463	Scott Rolen	.40
464	Mike Lieberthal	.05
465	Tony Womack	.05
466	Jermaine Allensworth	.05
467	Francisco Cordova	.05
468	Jon Lieber	.05
469	Al Martin	.05
470	Jason Kendall	.05
471	Todd Stottlemyre	.05
472	Royce Clayton	.05
473	Brian Jordan	.05
474	John Mabry	.05
475	Ray Lankford	.05
476	Delino DeShields	.05
477	Ron Gant	.05
478	Mark Langston	.05
479	Steve Finley	.05
480	Tony Gwynn	.75
481	Andy Ashby	.05
482	Wally Joyner	.05
483	Greg Vaughn	.05
484	Sterling Hitchcock	.05
485	J. Kevin Brown	.05
486	Orel Hershiser	.05
487	Charlie Hayes	.05
488	Darryl Hamilton	.05
489	Mark Gardner	.05
490	Barry Bonds	1.50
491	Robb Nen	.05
492	Kirk Rueter	.05
493	Randy Johnson	.50
494	Jeff Fassero	.05
495	Alex Rodriguez	1.25
496	David Segui	.05
497	Rich Amaral	.05
498	Russ Davis	.05
499	Bubba Trammell	.05
500	Wade Boggs	.75
501	Roberto Hernandez	.05
502	Dave Martinez	.05
503	Dennis Springer	.05
504	Paul Sorrento	.05
505	Wilson Alvarez	.05
506	Mike Kelly	.05
507	Albie Lopez	.05
508	Tony Saunders	.05
509	John Flaherty	.05
510	Fred McGriff	.05
511	Quinton McCracken	.05
512	Terrell Wade	.05
513	Kevin Stocker	.05
514	Kevin Elster	.05
515	Will Clark	.05
516	Bobby Witt	.05
517	Tom Goodwin	.05
518	Aaron Sele	.05
519	Lee Stevens	.05
520	Rusty Greer	.05

#	Player	Price
521	John Wetteland	.05
522	Darrin Fletcher	.05
523	Jose Canseco	.35
524	Randy Myers	.05
525	Jose Cruz Jr.	.05
526	Shawn Green	.15
527	Tony Fernandez	.05
528	Alex Gonzalez	.05
529	Ed Sprague	.05
530	Roger Clemens	.85

1998 Collector's Choice Cover Glory 5x7

		NM/M
Complete Set (10):		10.00
Common Player:		1.00
1	Nomar Garciaparra	1.50
2	Roger Clemens	2.00
3	Larry Walker	1.00
4	Mike Piazza	2.50
5	Mark McGwire	3.00
6	Tony Gwynn	1.50
7	Jose Cruz Jr.	1.00
8	Frank Thomas	1.25
9	Tino Martinez	1.00
10	Ken Griffey Jr.	2.50

Evolution Revolution

This 28-card insert features one player from each Major League team. The fronts picture the team jersey and open to reveal the player's top 1997 accomplishment. Evolution Revolution was inserted in Series 1 packs. Cards are numbered with an "ER" prefix.

		NM/M
Complete Set (28):		36.00
Common Player:		.40
Inserted 1:13		
1	Tim Salmon	.40
2	Greg Maddux	2.50
3	Cal Ripken Jr.	6.00
4	Mo Vaughn	.40
5	Sammy Sosa	2.50
6	Frank Thomas	1.50
7	Barry Larkin	.40
8	Jim Thome	.65
9	Larry Walker	.40
10	Travis Fryman	.40
11	Gary Sheffield	.65
12	Jeff Bagwell	1.50
13	Johnny Damon	.65
14	Mike Piazza	4.00
15	Jeff Cirillo	.40
16	Paul Molitor	1.50
17	Vladimir Guerrero	1.50
18	Todd Hundley	.40
19	Tino Martinez	.40
20	Jose Canseco	.65
21	Scott Rolen	.75
22	Al Martin	.40
23	Mark McGwire	5.00
24	Tony Gwynn	2.50
25	Barry Bonds	6.00
26	Ken Griffey Jr.	4.00
27	Juan Gonzalez	.75
28	Roger Clemens	3.00

1998 Collector's Choice Golden Jubilee Jumbos

The Golden Jubilee subset cards from Series 2 C.C. were reproduced in 4X (5" x 7") size as one-per-box inserts in special versions of retail packaging.

		NM/M
Complete Set (10):		15.00
Common Player:		1.00
306	Chipper Jones	2.00
321	Nomar Garciaparra	2.00
360	Larry Walker	1.00
450	Derek Jeter	4.00
463	Scott Rolen	1.25
480	Tony Gwynn	2.00
490	Barry Bonds	4.00

MIKE PIAZZA Catcher

	NM/M
Complete Set (9):	17.50
Common Player:	1.00
271	Andruw Jones	1.50
272	Alex Rodriguez	4.00
273	Juan Gonzalez	1.00
274	Nomar Garciaparra	2.00
275	Ken Griffey Jr.	3.00
276	Tino Martinez	1.00
277	Roger Clemens	2.00
278	Barry Bonds	5.00
279	Mike Piazza	3.00

1998 Collector's Choice Jumbos (3.5x5)

These double-size versions of various Series 1 cards were available one per special blister pack of Collector's Choice sold in retail chains.

		NM/M
Complete Set (15):		17.50
Common Player:		1.00
35	Andruw Jones	1.50
40	Cal Ripken Jr.	3.00
55	Ryne Sandberg	1.75
95	Frank Thomas	1.50
97	Gary Sheffield	1.25
145	Charles Johnson	1.00
145	Mike Piazza	2.00
160	Paul Molitor	1.50
180	Tino Martinez	1.00
220	Mark McGwire	2.50
225	Ken Caminiti	1.00
240	Ken Griffey Jr.	2.00
242	Jay Buhner	1.00
245	Juan Gonzalez	1.25
249	Ivan Rodriguez	1.25

1998 Collector's Choice Jumbos (5x7)

These super-size (5" x 7") cards were one-per-box inserts in Series 2 retail packaging. Besides being four times the size of a normal card, the 5x7s are identical to the regular versions.

Mini Bobbing Heads

The cards in this 30-card insert series can be punched out and assembled into a stand-up figure with a removable bobbing head. They are a Series 2 insert.

		NM/M
Complete Set (30):		20.00
Common Player:		.25
Inserted 1:3		
1	Tim Salmon	.25
2	Travis Lee	.25
3	Matt Williams	.25
4	Chipper Jones	1.00
5	Greg Maddux	1.00
6	Cal Ripken Jr.	2.50
7	Nomar Garciaparra	1.00
8	Mo Vaughn	.25
9	Sammy Sosa	1.00
10	Frank Thomas	.75
11	Kenny Lofton	.25
12	Jaret Wright	.25
13	Larry Walker	.25
14	Tony Clark	.25
15	Edgar Renteria	.25
16	Jeff Bagwell	.75
17	Mike Piazza	1.50
18	Vladimir Guerrero	.75
19	Derek Jeter	2.50
20	Ben Grieve	.25
21	Scott Rolen	.50
22	Mark McGwire	2.00
23	Tony Gwynn	1.00
24	Barry Bonds	2.50
25	Ken Griffey Jr.	1.50
26	Alex Rodriguez	2.00
27	Fred McGriff	.25
28	Juan Gonzalez	.40
29	Roger Clemens	1.25
30	Jose Cruz Jr.	.25

Rookie Class: Prime Choice

This 18-card set is a parallel of the Rookie Class subset. Each card is foil-stamped with the words "Prime Choice Reserve." This hobby-only set is sequentially numbered to 500 and was inserted in Series 2 packs.

		NM/M
Complete Set (18):		30.00
Common Player:		2.00
415	Carl Pavano	2.00
416	A.J. Hinch	2.00
417	David Dellucci	2.00
418	Bruce Chen	2.00
419	Darron Ingram	2.00
420	Sean Casey	5.00
421	Mark L. Johnson	2.00
422	Gabe Alvarez	2.00
423	Alex Gonzalez	2.00
424	Daryle Ward	2.00
425	Russell Branyan	2.00
426	Mike Caruso	2.00
427	Mike Kinkade	2.00
428	Ramon Hernandez	2.00
429	Matt Clement	2.00
430	Travis Lee	2.50
431	Shane Monahan	2.00
432	Rich Butler	2.00

StarQuest - Series 1

The StarQuest insert in Series 1 consists of 90 cards within four tiers. The tiers are designated by the number of stars found on front, the more the better: Special Delivery (#1-45, one star), Students of the Game (two stars, #46-65),

	NM/M
495	Alex Rodriguez	3.00
525	Jose Cruz Jr.	1.00
530	Roger Clemens	2.50

Super Powers (three stars, #66-80) and Super Star Domain (four stars, #81-90). All cards are numbered with a "SQ" prefix.

		NM/M
Complete Set (90):		185.00
Common Special Delivery (1-45):		.25
Inserted 1:1		
Common Student of the Game (46-65):		.75
Inserted 1:21		
Common Super Power (66-80):		2.00
Inserted 1:71		
Common Superstar Domain (81-90):		3.00
Inserted 1:145		
1	Nomar Garciaparra	1.50
2	Scott Rolen	.75
3	Jason Dickson	.25
4	Jaret Wright	.25
5	Kevin Orie	.25
6	Jose Guillen	.25
7	Matt Morris	.25
8	Mike Cameron	.25
9	Kevin Polcovich	.25
10	Jose Cruz Jr.	.25
11	Miguel Tejada	.40
12	Fernando Tatis	.25
13	Todd Helton	.65
14	Ken Cloude	.25
15	Ben Grieve	.25
16	Dante Powell	.25
17	Bubba Trammell	.25
18	Juan Encarnacion	.25
19	Derrek Lee	.50
20	Paul Konerko	.35
21	Richard Hidalgo	.25
22	Denny Neagle	.25
23	David Justice	.25
24	Pedro J. Martinez	1.00
25	Greg Maddux	1.50
26	Edgar Martinez	.25
27	Cal Ripken Jr.	2.50
28	Tim Salmon	.25
29	Shawn Estes	.25
30	Ken Griffey Jr.	2.00
31	Brad Radke	.25
32	Andy Pettitte	.50
33	Curt Schilling	.40
34	Raul Mondesi	.25
35	Alex Rodriguez	2.25
36	Jeff Kent	.25
37	Jeff Bagwell	.50
38	Juan Gonzalez	.50
39	Barry Bonds	2.50
40	Mark McGwire	2.00
41	Frank Thomas	1.00
42	Ray Lankford	.25
43	Tony Gwynn	1.50
44	Mike Piazza	1.75
45	Tino Martinez	.25
46	Nomar Garciaparra	3.00
47	Paul Molitor	1.50
48	Chuck Knoblauch	.75
49	Rusty Greer	.75
50	Cal Ripken Jr.	6.00
51	Roberto Alomar	1.00
52	Scott Rolen	1.00
53	Derek Jeter	6.00
54	Mark Grace	.75
55	Randy Johnson	1.50
56	Craig Biggio	.75
57	Kenny Lofton	.75
58	Eddie Murray	1.50
59	Ryne Sandberg	2.00
60	Rickey Henderson	1.50
61	Darin Erstad	.75
62	Jim Edmonds	.75
63	Ken Caminiti	.75
64	Ivan Rodriguez	1.25
65	Tony Gwynn	2.00
66	Tony Clark	2.00
67	Andres Galarraga	2.00
68	Rafael Palmeiro	3.00
69	Manny Ramirez	6.00
70	Albert Belle	2.00
71	Jay Buhner	2.00
72	Mo Vaughn	2.00
73	Barry Bonds	15.00
74	Chipper Jones	7.50
75	Jeff Bagwell	6.00
76	Jim Thome	3.00
77	Sammy Sosa	7.50
78	Todd Hundley	2.00
79	Matt Williams	2.00
80	Vinny Castilla	2.00
81	Jose Cruz Jr.	3.00

82	Frank Thomas	7.50
83	Juan Gonzalez	4.00
84	Mike Piazza	15.00
85	Alex Rodriguez	20.00
86	Larry Walker	3.00
87	Tino Martinez	3.00
88	Greg Maddux	12.50
89	Mark McGwire	20.00
90	Ken Griffey Jr.	15.00

StarQuest - Series 2

The 30-card StarQuest insert was included in Series 2 packs. The insert has four parallel tiers - Single, Double, Triple and Home Run - designated by the number of baseball diamond icons on the card front. Single cards were inserted 1:1, Doubles 1:21, Triples 1:71 and Home Runs are sequentially numbered to 100. The second series SQ cards feature a front design with the letters "QSUTEASRT" in color blocks vertically at left.

	NM/M
Complete Set (30):	17.50
Common Player:	.25
Singles 1:1	
Doubles 1:21	2X
Triples 1:71	6X
Home Runs:	15X

1	Ken Griffey Jr.	1.25
2	Jose Cruz Jr.	.25
3	Cal Ripken Jr.	2.00
4	Roger Clemens	1.00
5	Frank Thomas	.75
6	Derek Jeter	2.00
7	Alex Rodriguez	1.50
8	Andruw Jones	.75
9	Vladimir Guerrero	.75
10	Mark McGwire	1.50
11	Kenny Lofton	.25
12	Pedro J. Martinez	.75
13	Greg Maddux	1.00
14	Larry Walker	.25
15	Barry Bonds	2.00
16	Chipper Jones	1.00
17	Jeff Bagwell	.75
18	Juan Gonzalez	.50
19	Tony Gwynn	1.00
20	Mike Piazza	1.25
21	Tino Martinez	.25
22	Mo Vaughn	.20
23	Ben Grieve	.25
24	Scott Rolen	.60
25	Nomar Garciaparra	1.00
26	Paul Konerko	.35
27	Jaret Wright	.25
28	Gary Sheffield	.50
29	Travis Lee	.25
30	Todd Helton	.65

1998 Collector's Choice StarQuest Super Powers Jumbos

This enlarged (3-1/2" x 5") version of the StarQuest Super Powers cards from Series 1 were a retail-only variation found one per blister pack of specially marked Collector's Choice product.

	NM/M
Complete Set (10):	17.50

Common Player:		1.00
SQ67	Andres Galarraga	1.00
SQ68	Rafael Palmeiro	2.00
SQ69	Manny Ramirez	2.50
SQ70	Albert Belle	1.00
SQ71	Jay Buhner	1.00
SQ72	Mo Vaughn	1.00
SQ73	Barry Bonds	5.00
SQ74	Chipper Jones	3.00
SQ75	Jeff Bagwell	2.50
SQ76	Jim Thome	1.50

Stickums

This 30-card insert was seeded 1:3 Series 1 packs. The stickers can be peeled off the card and reused.

	NM/M
Complete Set (30):	7.00
Common Player:	.10
Inserted 1:3	

1	Andruw Jones	.35
2	Chipper Jones	.50
3	Cal Ripken Jr.	1.00
4	Nomar Garciaparra	.45
5	Mo Vaughn	.10
6	Ryne Sandberg	.45
7	Sammy Sosa	.45
8	Frank Thomas	.35
9	Albert Belle	.10
10	Jim Thome	.35
11	Manny Ramirez	.35
12	Larry Walker	.10
13	Gary Sheffield	.20
14	Jeff Bagwell	.35
15	Mike Piazza	.60
16	Paul Molitor	.35
17	Pedro J. Martinez	.35
18	Todd Hundley	.10
19	Derek Jeter	1.00
20	Tino Martinez	.10
21	Curt Schilling	.25
22	Mark McGwire	.75
23	Tony Gwynn	.45
24	Barry Bonds	1.00
25	Ken Griffey Jr.	.60
26	Alex Rodriguez	.75
27	Juan Gonzalez	.30
28	Ivan Rodriguez	.30
29	Roger Clemens	.50
30	Jose Cruz Jr.	.10

You Crash the Game

These 90 game cards were inserted one per five Series 2 packs. Each card features a player and a list of dates. If the pictured player hit a home run on one of those days, collectors with the card could mail it in for a graphically enhanced prize version. Instant Winner cards of each player were also inserted at the rate of 1:721 and could be exchanged for the complete 30-card prize set. Deadline for exchange of all winning cards was Dec. 1, 1998. Winning cards are designated here with an asterisk and can be expected to be somewhat scarcer than non-winning dates.

	NM/M
Complete Set (90):	75.00
Common Player:	.50
Instant Winner:	8X
Inserted 1:5	

CG1	Ken Griffey Jr. (June 26-28*)	1.50
CG1	Ken Griffey Jr. (July 7)	1.25
CG1	Ken Griffey Jr. (Sept. 21-24*)	3.00
CG2	Travis Lee (July 27-30)	.50
CG2	Travis Lee (Aug. 27-30)	.50
CG2	Travis Lee (Sept. 17-20)	.50
CG3	Larry Walker (July 17-19)	.50

CG3	Larry Walker (Aug. 27-30*)	1.00
CG3	Larry Walker (Sept. 25-27*)	1.00
CG4	Tony Clark (July 9-12*)	1.00
CG4	Tony Clark (June 30-July 2)	.50
CG4	Tony Clark (Sept. 4-6)	.50
CG5	Cal Ripken Jr. (June 22-25*)	4.00
CG5	Cal Ripken Jr. (July 2)	2.00
CG5	Cal Ripken Jr. (Sept. 4-6)	2.00
CG6	Tim Salmon (June 22-25)	.50
CG6	Tim Salmon (Aug. 28-30)	.50
CG6	Tim Salmon (Sept. 14-15)	.50
CG7	Vinny Castilla (June 30-July 2*)	1.00
CG7	Vinny Castilla (Aug. 27-30*)	1.00
CG7	Vinny Castilla (Sept. 7-10*)	1.00
CG8	Fred McGriff (June 22-25)	.50
CG8	Fred McGriff (July 3-5)	.50
CG8	Fred McGriff (Sept. 18-20*)	1.00
CG9	Matt Williams (July 17-29)	.50
CG9	Matt Williams (Sept. 14-16*)	1.00
CG9	Matt Williams (Sept. 18-20)	.50
CG10	Mark McGwire (July 7)	1.50
CG10	Mark McGwire (July 24-26*)	3.50
CG10	Mark McGwire (Aug. 18-19*)	3.50
CG11	Albert Belle (July 3-5)	.50
CG11	Albert Belle (Aug. 21-23*)	1.00
CG11	Albert Belle (Sept. 11-13)	.50
CG12	Jay Buhner (July 9-12*)	1.00
CG12	Jay Buhner (Aug. 6-9)	.50
CG12	Jay Buhner (Sept. 25-27)	.50
CG13	Vladimir Guerrero (June 22-25)	.75
CG13	Vladimir Guerrero (Aug. 10-12*)	1.50
CG13	Vladimir Guerrero (Sept. 14-16*)	1.50
CG14	Andruw Jones (July 16-19*)	1.50
CG14	Andruw Jones (Aug. 27-30*)	1.50
CG14	Andruw Jones (Sept. 17-20)	.75
CG15	Nomar Garciaparra (July 9-12)	1.00
CG15	Nomar Garciaparra (Aug. 13-16*)	2.50
CG15	Nomar Garciaparra (Sept. 24-27)	1.50
CG16	Ken Caminiti (June 26-28*)	1.00
CG16	Ken Caminiti (July 13-15*)	1.00
CG16	Ken Caminiti (Sept. 10-13)	.50
CG17	Sammy Sosa (July 9-12*)	2.50
CG17	Sammy Sosa (Aug. 27-30*)	2.50
CG17	Sammy Sosa (Sept. 18-20)	1.00
CG18	Ben Grieve (June 30-July 2*)	1.00
CG18	Ben Grieve (Aug. 14-16)	.50
CG18	Ben Grieve (Sept. 24-27)	.50
CG19	Mo Vaughn (July 7)	.50
CG19	Mo Vaughn (Sept. 7-9)	.50
CG19	Mo Vaughn (Sept. 24-27*)	1.00
CG20	Frank Thomas (July 7)	.75
CG20	Frank Thomas (July 17-19*)	1.50
CG20	Frank Thomas (Sept. 4-6)	.75
CG21	Manny Ramirez (July 9-12)	.75
CG21	Manny Ramirez (Aug. 13-16*)	1.50
CG21	Manny Ramirez (Sept. 18-20*)	1.50
CG22	Jeff Bagwell (July 7)	.50
CG22	Jeff Bagwell (Aug. 28-30*)	1.50
CG22	Jeff Bagwell (Sept. 4-6*)	1.50
CG23	Jose Cruz Jr. (July 9-12)	.50
CG23	Jose Cruz Jr. (Aug. 13-16)	.50
CG23	Jose Cruz Jr. (Sept. 18-20)	.50
CG24	Alex Rodriguez (July 7*)	3.50
CG24	Alex Rodriguez (Aug. 6-9*)	3.50
CG24	Alex Rodriguez (Sept. 21-23*)	3.50
CG25	Mike Piazza (June 22-25*)	3.00
CG25	Mike Piazza (July 7)	1.25
CG25	Mike Piazza (Sept. 10-13*)	3.00
CG26	Tino Martinez (June 26-28*)	1.00
CG26	Tino Martinez (July 9-12)	.50
CG26	Tino Martinez (Aug. 13-16)	.50
CG27	Chipper Jones (July 3-5)	1.00
CG27	Chipper Jones (Aug. 27-30)	1.00

CG27	Chipper Jones (Sept. 17-20)	1.00
CG28	Juan Gonzalez (July 7)	.60
CG28	Juan Gonzalez (Aug. 6-9*)	1.25
CG28	Juan Gonzalez (Sept. 11-13*)	1.25
CG29	Jim Thome (June 22-23)	.60
CG29	Jim Thome (July 23-26*)	1.25
CG29	Jim Thome (Sept. 24-27)	.60
CG30	Barry Bonds (July 7*)	4.00
CG30	Barry Bonds (Sept. 4-6)	2.00
CG30	Barry Bonds (Sept. 18-20*)	4.00

1998 Collector's Choice You Crash the Game Winners

Collectors who redeemed winning "Crash" cards prior to the Dec. 1, 1998 deadline received an upgraded version of that player's card. Similar in format, the winners' cards have an action photo on front (different than the game card), with a metallic foil background. Instead of dates in the three circles at bottom are the letters "W I N." Backs have a career summary and stats, instead of the redemption instructions found on the game cards. The cards are numbered with a "CG" prefix. Cards of players who didn't homer during their designated dates were available only by redeeming a scarce (1:721 packs) Instant Win card. They are indicated here by "SP."

	NM/M
Complete Set (30):	9.00
Common Player:	.25

CG1	Ken Griffey Jr.	1.00
CG2	Travis Lee (SP)	.75
CG3	Larry Walker	.25
CG4	Tony Clark	.25
CG5	Cal Ripken Jr.	1.50
CG6	Tim Salmon/SP	.60
CG7	Vinny Castilla	.25
CG8	Fred McGriff	.25
CG9	Matt Williams	.25
CG10	Mark McGwire	1.25
CG11	Albert Belle	.25
CG12	Jay Buhner	.25
CG13	Vladimir Guerrero	.50
CG14	Andruw Jones	.50
CG15	Nomar Garciaparra	.75
CG16	Ken Caminiti	.25
CG17	Sammy Sosa	.75
CG18	Ben Grieve	.25
CG19	Mo Vaughn	.25
CG20	Frank Thomas	.50
CG21	Manny Ramirez	.50
CG22	Jeff Bagwell	.50
CG23	Jose Cruz Jr./SP	.60
CG24	Alex Rodriguez	1.25
CG25	Mike Piazza	1.00
CG26	Tino Martinez	.25
CG27	Chipper Jones/SP	1.50
CG28	Juan Gonzalez	.35
CG29	Jim Thome	.35
CG30	Barry Bonds	1.50

You Crash/Game Instant Winner

Found on average of one per 721 packs, these Instant Winner cards could be redeemed (with a $2 handling fee) for a complete set of You Crash the Game exchange cards - the only way Crash winner cards of Travis Lee, Jose Cruz Jr. and Chipper Jones could be obtained. These special cards have an instant winner logo on front in place of game dates, and a congratulatory message on back along with instructions for redemption prior to the Dec. 1, 1998 deadline.

	NM/M
Complete Set (30):	250.00
Common Player:	4.00

1995 Collector's Edge Ball Park Franks Baseball Legends

"Baseball Legends" Yogi Berra and Brooks Robinson are featured in this hot dog promotional set. Sunday newspapers on March 5 featured a coupon used to obtain the pair of autographed cards for

eight proofs-of-purchase, or $2.50 with four UPCs or $5 with two UPCs. Cards have color photos, with uniform logos removed, and marbled borders. An authentic autograph is across the front of the card. Backs have a portrait photo and career summary. Each card was accompanied by a card-like certificate of authenticity.

	NM/M
Complete Set (2):	20.00
(1)	Yogi Berra	16.00
(2)	Frank Robinson	8.00

1993 Colorado Fever Rockies

In its inaugural issue, a fan magazine titled "Colorado Fever" issued a sheet of nine baseball cards in both its "Regional" and "Metro" editions. Stapled into the center of the magazine is an 8-3/8" x 11" cardboard insert. One panel has nine Rockies cards which are not perforated and would measure about 2-5/8" x 3-5/8" if cut from the sheet. Cards from the Metro edition feature players in uniform; most of the cards from the Regional edition show the players in street clothes. It is not known whether future editions of the announced twice-annual magazine were ever published or if they contained baseball card inserts.

	NM/M
Complete Set (18):	8.00
Common Player:	.50

1M	David Nied	.50
2M	Charlie Hayes	.50
3M	Andy Ashby	.50
4M	Joe Girardi	.50
5M	Don Baylor	.60
6M	Andres Galarraga	.50
7M	Jim Tatum	.50
8M	Vinny Castilla	.50
9M	Dante Bichette	.50
1R	Alex Cole	.50
2R	Don Baylor	.60
3R	Dante Bichette	.50
4R	Jeff Parrett	.50
5R	David Nied	.50
6R	Butch Henry	.50
7R	Andres Galarraga	.50
8R	Daryl Boston	.50
9R	Joe Girardi	.50

1994 Colorado Rockies Police

The Rockies' premiere police set is an oversized (2-5/8" x 4") effort with posed and action player photos on a yellow and purple background on front. Team logo and name are above the photo, while ID and uniform number are beneath the photo. Backs are printed in purple with a few bits of personal data and stats, a safety

message and sponsors' logos. The cards are checklisted here in alphabetical order.

	NM/M
Complete Set (27):	6.00
Common Player:	.50

(1)	Don Baylor	.75
(2)	Dante Bichette	.75
(3)	Willie Blair	.50
(4)	Kent Bottenfield	.50
(5)	Ellis Burks	.50
(6)	Vinny Castilla	.50
(7)	Marvin Freeman	.50
(8)	Andres Galarraga	.75
(9)	Andres Galarraga (Batting champion.)	.75
(10)	Joe Girardi	.50
(11)	Mike Harkey	.50
(12)	Greg Harris	.50
(13)	Charlie Hayes	.50
(14)	Darren Holmes	.50
(15)	Howard Johnson	.50
(16)	Nelson Liriano	.50
(17)	Roberto Mejia	.50
(18)	Mike Munoz	.50
(19)	David Nied	.50
(20)	Steve Reed	.50
(21)	Armando Reynoso	.50
(22)	Bruce Ruffin	.50
(23)	Danny Sheaffer	.50
(24)	Darrell Sherman	.50
(25)	Walt Weiss	.50
(26)	Eric Young	.50
(27)	Rockies Coaches (Larry Bearnarth, Dwight Evans, Gene Glynn, Ron Hassey, Bill Plummer, Don Zimmer)	.50

1995 Colorado Rockies Police

Castilla • 1995

With only a dozen players included, this is one of the smallest safety sets of the genre. The 2-5/8" x 4" cards have color player action photos on front, bordered in black with the team logo in the lower-right corner. The player's last name and year appear in orange in the upper-right. Backs are in black-and-white and include a safety message or cartoon, and a few biographical data and stats. Cards are checklisted by uniform number.

	NM/M
Complete Set (12):	5.00
Common Player:	.50

6	Jason Bates	.50
7	Joe Girardi	.50
9	Vinny Castilla	.50
10	Dante Bichette	.50
12	Mike Kingery	.50
14	Andres Galarraga	.75
20	Bill Swift	.50
21	Eric Young	.50
22	Walt Weiss	.50
25	Don Baylor	.75
26	Ellis Burks	.50
33	Larry Walker	1.50

1996 Colorado Rockies Police

Painter • 28

The Rockies third annual safety set is the team's largest, at 27 cards. The set's format is 2-5/8" x 4" and is sponsored by Kansas City Life Insurance. Fronts have game-action photos, with the team logo, player last name and uniform number at bottom. Backs are printed in purple and feature a safety-message cartoon. The set was initially distributed to fans attending an April game. The set is checklisted here by uniform number. A Spanish-language version of the set was also issued.

		NM/M
Complete Set (27):		5.00
Common Player:		.25
Spanish:		2X
1	Trenidad Hubbard	.25
3	Quinton McCracken	.25
6	Jason Bates	.25
9	Vinny Castilla	.25
10	Dante Bichette	.25
14	Andres Galarraga	.50
16	Curtis Leskanic	.25
18	Bruce Ruffin	.25
20	Bill Swift	.25
21	Eric Young	.25
22	Walt Weiss	.25
23	Bryan Rekar	.25
25	Don Baylor	.35
26	Ellis Burks	.25
28	Lance Painter	.25
30	Kevin Ritz	.25
31	Bret Saberhagen	.35
32	Mark Thompson	.25
33	Larry Walker	1.00
34	Jayhawk Owens	.25
35	John Vander Wal	.25
38	Roger Bailey	.25
39	Steve Reed	.25
40	Darren Holmes	.25
42	Armando Reynoso	.25
43	Mike Munoz	.25
44	Marvin Freeman	.25

1997 Colorado Rockies Police

In conjunction with the Colorado Association of Chiefs of Police, the Rockies handed out this safety set at a designated home game early in the season. It is the team's fourth annual safety set. The 2-1/2" x 3-1/2" cards feature game-action photos on front surrounded by a white border. The team logo is at upper-left; player identification is in purple and gray stripes diagonally at bottom. Backs are in black-and-white and have some player personal data, a career-best stat lines and a safety message. Cards are numbered by uniform number in a baseball at upper-right.

		NM/M
Complete Set (12):		5.00
Common Player:		.60
3	Quinton McCracken	.60
8	Kirt Manwaring	.60
9	Vinny Castilla	.60
10	Dante Bichette	.75
14	Andres Galarraga	.75
20	Bill Swift	.60
21	Eric Young	.60
22	Walt Weiss	.60
25	Don Baylor	.75
26	Ellis Burks	.60
33	Larry Walker	1.50
00	Dinger (Mascot)	.60

1998 Colorado Rockies Police

Children attending a May 31 promotional game at Coors Field received this set of Rockies cards. Game-action color photos are featured on front, borderless at top, bottom and left. At right is a vertical gray stripe with the player's name and position; team logo and name are at bottom. On back is a

player portrait photo, identification, biographical details, an inspirational message and logos of the sponsoring organizations.

		NM/M
Complete Set (12):		6.00
Common Player:		.35
3	Mike Lansing	.50
4	Jeffrey Hammonds	.50
5	Neifi Perez	.50
7	Jeff Cirillo	.50
8	Brent Mayne	.50
17	Todd Helton	3.00
24	Tom Goodwin	.50
25	Buddy Bell	.50
30	Rolando Arrojo	.50
33	Larry Walker	1.50
00	Dinger (Mascot)	.50
---	Coors Field	.75

1999 Colorado Rockies Police

Children attending a promotional game at Coors Field received this set of Rockies cards. Borderless game-action color photos are featured on front. At right is a vertical strip with the team name; the player name and position are at bottom. On back is a player portrait photo, identification, biographical details, a safety message and logos of the sponsoring organizations.

		NM/M
Complete Set (12):		6.00
Common Player:		1.00
(1)	Dante Bichette	1.00
(2)	Vinny Castilla	1.00
(3)	Dinger (Mascot)	1.00
(4)	Jerry DiPoto	1.00
(5)	Darryl Hamilton	1.00
(6)	Todd Helton	2.50
(7)	Darryl Kile	1.00
(8)	Mike Lansing	1.00
(9)	Jim Leyland	1.00
(10)	Kirt Manwaring	1.00
(11)	Neifi Perez	1.00
(12)	Larry Walker	1.50

2000 Colorado Rockies Police

Children attending a May 28 promotional game at Coors Field received this set of Rockies cards. Borderless game-action color photos are featured on front. On

back is a player portrait photo, identification, biographical details, an inspirational message and a credit line for the Colorado Association of Chiefs of Police.

		NM/M
Complete Set (12):		6.00
Common Player:		.75
3	Mike Lansing	.75
4	Jeffrey Hammonds	.75
5	Neifi Perez	.75
7	Jeff Cirillo	.75
8	Brent Mayne	.75
17	Todd Helton	3.00
24	Tom Goodwin	.75
25	Buddy Bell	.75
30	Rolando Arrojo	.75
33	Larry Walker	1.50
00	Dinger (Mascot)	.75

2002 Colorado Rockies Police

The Rockies hot dog vendor sponsored this stadium give-away safety set featuring the manager and 11 popular players. The 2-1/2" x 3-1/2" cards have game-action photos vignetted on front with white borders. A 10-year team anniversary logo is lower-left. Horizontal backs have a portrait photo in the top-right corner and a ghosted image of the front photo at left, which is overprinted with player data, 2001 stats, career highlights and a safety or inspirational message in English or Spanish. The sponsor and team logos are at right.

		NM/M
Complete Set (12):		6.00
Common Player:		.50
3	Jose Ortiz	.50
8	Juan Uribe	.50
9	Juan Pierre	1.50
10	Mike Hampton	.50
12	Todd Zeile	.50
13	Clint Hurdle	.50
15	Denny Neagle	.50
17	Todd Helton	2.50
27	Todd Hollandsworth	.50
29	Gary Bennett	.50
33	Larry Walker	1.00
00	Dinger (Mascot)	.50

2005 Comcast Oakland A's

Sponsored by Comcast, 15,000 of these team sets were given away at the September 24 game. Fronts have a gold border. Green-and-gold backs have player personal data.

		NM/M
Complete Set (32):		10.00
Common Player:		.25
(1)	Team Photo/Checklist	.25
2	Ken Macha	.25
3	Eric Chavez	.75
4	Barry Zito	.75
5	Mark Kotsay	.25
6	Rich Harden	.75
7	Jason Kendall	.25
8	Bobby Crosby	1.00
9	Jay Payton	.25

10	Scott Hatteberg	.25
11	Huston Street	1.00
12	Mark Ellis	.25
13	Dan Haren	.75
14	Nick Swisher	.75
15	Joe Blanton	.75
16	Marco Scutaro	.25
17	Kirk Saarloos	.25
18	Dan Johnson	.75
19	Kiko Calero	.25
20	Bobby Kielty	.25
21	Justin Duchscherer	.25
22	Adam Melhuse	.25
23	Ricardo Rincon	.25
24	Joe Kennedy	.25
25	Keiichi Yabu	.25
26	Erubiel Durazo	.25
27	Juan Cruz	.25
28	Keith Ginter	.25
29	Octavio Dotel	.25
30	Charles Thomas	.25
31	Jay Witaskic	.25
32	Coaching Staff (Brad Fischer, Bob Geren, Dave Hudgens, Rene Lachemann, Curt Young, Ron Washington)	.25

1995 Comic Images National Pastime Promo

This unnumbered card was issued to promote Comic Images' set of baseball history cards. The 2-1/2" x 3-1/2" card has a familiar color photo of company spokesman Phil Rizzuto on front, done up in chromium technology and with the Yankees team logos removed from the uniform. The back advertises the forthcoming card set.

	NM/M
Phil Rizzuto	3.00

1995 Comic Images The National Pastime

This set is principally made up of 19th Century baseball images done up in 20th Century chromium card technology to detail the history of baseball from the 1860s through the 1950s. As might be expected, there was little positive reaction from collectors. Photos of old baseball collectibles, including a few vintage baseball cards are scattered throughout the set as are a few actual player photos. Hall of Famer Phil Rizzuto was tapped to promote the issue, but his name was misspelled on the cards' box. A number of special inserts including Rizzuto autographed cards were part of the issue.

		NM/M
Complete Set (90):		8.00
Common Card:		.10
Autographed Rizzuto Card:		35.00
MagnaChrome Rizzuto		
Career Card (6):		2.00
MagnaChrome Diamond		
Cover (3):		1.00
Medallion Card:		2.00

Six-card Case-Topper Sheet:		6.00
1	Sportsman's Park	.10
2	Harper's Weekly, August, 1913	.10
3	Shibe Park	.10
4	Polo Grounds Print	.10
5	Forbes Field	.10
6	Hall of Fame (Phil Rizzuto)	.25
7	League Park	.10
8	Highlander Park	.10
9	South Side Park	.10
10	Catchers' Mitt	.10
11	Baseball Trophy	.10
12	Baseball Plate	.10
13	Bisque Figure	.10
14	Beanbag	.10
15	Tobacco Carved Figure	.10
16	Sunday Magazine	.10
17	Street & Smith Sport	.10
18	Collier's	.10
19	Bluebook	.10
20	Chadwick's	.10
21	Harper's Weekly	.10
22	American Magazine	.10
23	Crazy Baseball Stories	.10
24	New York Giants, 1892	.10
25	Cincinnati American Association, 1882	.10
26	Chicago White Stockings, 1885	.10
27	Baltimore Blues, 1890	.10
28	Chicago & All-Americans, 1889	.10
29	Philadelphia Baseball Team, 1910	.10
30	1887 Goodwin & Co. Champions	.25
31	John McGraw	.15
32	Home Run (1885 trade card)	.10
33	Lorillard Chicago BBC	.10
34	Boston BBC	.10
35	Out at First (Trade card.)	.10
36	"Coffee Cards"	.10
37	Uncut Sheet - Detail	.10
38	Tobin Lithographers	.10
39	Uncut Sheet - Die Cut	.10
40	Patsy Dougherty (T207)	.10
41	A Regular Corker (1885 trade card)	.10
42	Barker's Advertising Book	.10
43	Toledo BBC Tobacco Poster	.10
44	Shredded Wheat Advertisement	.10
45	BVD Advertisement	.10
46	Police Gazette Poster	.10
47	Japanese Poster	.10
48	Safe Hit Vegetable Crate Label	.10
49	Slide, Kelly, Slide Poster	.10
50	Peck & Snyder Hat Advertisement	.10
51	Reach Gloves Catalog	.10
52	New York Giants Scorecard	.10
53	Game Card	.10
54	Wright & Ditson Guide	.10
55	1933 All-Star Game Program	.10
56	Stadium Scene	.10
57	Currier & Ives Print	.10
58	Scorecard Artwork	.10
59	Folk Art	.10
60	Batter (Wrong front, belongs to #73.)	.10
61	Cartoon	.10
62	Teddy Roosevelt Cartoon	.10
63	Uncle Sam Cartoon	.10
64	Casey at the Bat	.15
65	Seymour Church Print	.10
66	Valentine Card	.10
67	Pinup Book	.10
68	Uncle Sam WWI Sheet Music	.10
69	Baseball Sheet Music	.10
70	Saturday Globe	.10
71	Ft. Wayne Woman Player	.15
72	Spalding Baseball Guide	.10
73	Rally Day Postcard (Wrong front, belongs to #60.)	.10
74	Spalding Advertisement Die Cut	.10
75	Our Baseball Club Cover	.10
76	Jake Beckley	.15
77	Cap Anson (Allen & Ginter album page)	.25
78	St. Louis Player	.10
79	Sam Thompson (Scrap's Die Cut)	.15
80	Bobby Wallace (Turkey Red cabinet)	.15
81	Fogarty & McGuire (Jim Fogarty, Deacon McGuire (1887 Kalamazoo Bats detail)	.15
82	Yank Robinson (1887 die-cut game card)	.15
83	Charles Comiskey (1887 Scrap's tobacco die-cut)	.15
84	Picked Off! (Action photo.)	.10
85	Error (Action photo.)	.10
86	Third Base (Action photo.)	.10
87	Safe at Home (Action photo.)	.10
88	Baseball Action (Action photo.)	.10
89	Great Fielding (Action photo.)	.10
90	Checklist	.10

1991 Conlon Collection Prototypes

The cards which previewed the debut set of Conlon Collection cards in the 1990s can generally be identified by the lack of Major League Baseball logo and Curtis Management copyright information on back. Except for the colorized Babe Ruth card, they are not otherwise marked as prototypes. While most of the 1991 Conlon prototypes were distributed in relatively small quantities, reportedly 2,940, the colorized Ty Cobbs was an edition of 60,000 and the colorized Babe Ruth card was produced for the 12th National Sports Collectors Convention in Anaheim, Calif., to the tune of 225,000 cards.

		NM/M
Complete Set (6):		9.00
Common Player:		2.00
13	Ty Cobb (Colorized edition of 60,000.)	4.50
34	Dizzy Dean	2.00
111	Lou Gehrig	3.50
145	Babe Ruth	4.50
145	Babe Ruth (Colorized, edition of 225,000.)	3.00
250	Ty Cobb	3.00

1991 Conlon Collection

This 330-card set features the photography of Charles Martin Conlon, who was active from before 1910 through the early 1940s. Black-and-white photos are set against black borders on the UV-coated card fronts. Megacards worked with The Sporting News (owners of the Conlon photos) to release the set. Several subsets are featured such as Hall of Famers, 1927 New York Yankees, MVPs and more. The backs feature statistics and career highlights and can be found either with or without the MLB logo.

		NM/M
Complete Factory Set (330):		13.50
Factory Set w/Auto. Feller:		16.00
Complete Set (330):		9.00
Common Player:		.10
Wax Pack (18):		.50
Wax Box (36):		15.00
1	Rogers Hornsby	.25
2	James E. Foxx	.25
3	Jay H. Dean	.25
4	Walter J.V. Maranville	.10
5	Paul G. Waner	.10
6	Lloyd J. Waner	.10
7	Melvin T. Ott	.15
8	John P. Wagner	.25
9	Walter P. Johnson	.25
10	Carl O. Hubbell	.15
11	Frank F. Frisch	.15
12	Hazen S. Cuyler	.15

No	Player	Price
13	Charles H. Ruffing	.10
14	Henry B. Greenberg	.15
15	John J. Evers	.10
16	Hugh A. Jennings	.10
17	David J. Bancroft	.10
18	Joseph M. Medwick	.10
19	Theodore A. Lyons	.10
20	Charles A. Bender	.10
21	Edward T. Collins	.10
22	James L. Bottomley	.10
23	Robert M. Grove	.15
24	Max Carey	.10
25	Burleigh A. Grimes	.10
26	Ross M. Youngs	.10
27	Ernest N. Lombardi	.10
28	Joseph V. McCarthy	.10
29	Lewis R. Wilson	.10
30	Charles H. Klein	.10
31	Howard E. Averill Sr.	.10
32	Grover C. Alexander	.15
33	Charles J. Hafey	.10
34	William B. McKechnie	.10
35	Robert W.A. Feller	.15
36	Harold J. Traynor	.10
37	Charles D. Stengel	.15
38	Joseph F. Vaughan	.10
39	Eppa Rixey	.10
40	Joseph W. Sewell	.10
41	Urban C. Faber	.10
42	Travis C. Jackson	.10
43	Jesse J. Haines	.10
44	Tristram E. Speaker	.25
45	Cornelius Mack	.10
46	Cornelius Mack	.10
47	Cornelius Mack	.10
48	Raymond W. Schalk	.10
49	Aloysius H. Simmons	.10
50	Joseph E. Cronin	.10
51	Gordon S. Cochrane	.10
52	Harry E. Heilmann	.10
53	John R. Mize	.15
54	Edgar C. Rice	.10
55	Edd J. Roush	.10
56	Enos B. Slaughter	.10
57	Christopher Mathewson	.25
58	Fred C. Lindstrom	.10
59	Charles L. Hartnett	.10
60	George L. Kelly	.10
61	Stanley R. Harris	.10
62	Leon A. Goslin	.10
63	Henry E. Manush	.10
64	William H. Terry	.10
65	John J. McGraw	.10
66	George H. Sisler	.10
67	Vernon L. Gomez	.10
68	Joseph I. Judge	.10
69	Thomas J. Thevenow	.10
70	Charles M. Gelbert	.10
71	Minter C. Hayes	.10
72	Robert R. Fothergill	.10
73	Adam A. Comorosky	.10
74	Earl S. Smith	.10
75	Samuel D. Gray	.10
76	Peter W. Appleton	.10
77	Eugene Moore Jr.	.10
78	Arndt L. Jorgens	.10
79	William H. Knickerbocker	.10
80	Carl N. Reynolds	.10
81	Oscar D. Melillo	.10
82	John H. Burnett	.10
83	Alvin J. Powell	.10
84	John J. Murphy	.10
85	Leroy E. Parmelee	.10
86	James A. Ripple	.10
87	Gerald H. Walker	.10
88	George L. Earnshaw	.10
89	William H. Southworth	.10
90	Wallace Moses	.10
91	George E. Walberg	.10
92	James J. Dykes	.10
93	Charles H. Root	.10
94	John W. Cooney	.10
95	Charles J. Grimm	.10
96	Robert L. Johnson	.10
97	John W. Scott	.10
98	Raymond A. Radcliff	.10
99	Frederick R. Ostermueller	.10
100	Julian V. Wera	.10
101	Miller J. Huggins	.10
102	Raymond A. Morehart	.10
103	Bernard O. Bengough	.10
104	Walter H. Ruether	.10
105	Earle B. Combs	.10
106	Myles L. Thomas	.10
107	Benjamin E. Paschal	.10
108	Cedric M. Durst	.10
109	William W. Moore	.10
110	George H. Ruth	1.00
111	Louis H. Gehrig	.50
112	Joseph A. Dugan	.10
113	Anthony M. Lazzeri	.10
114	Urban J. Shocker	.10
115	Waite C. Hoyt	.10
116	Charles T. O'Leary	.10
117	Arthur Fletcher	.10
118	Tharon L. Collins	.10
119	Joseph O. Giard	.10
120	Herbert J. Pennock	.10
121	Michael Gazella	.10
122	Robert W. Meusel	.10
123	George W. Pipgras	.10
124	John P. Grabowski	.10
125	Mark A. Koenig	.10
126	Stanley C. Hack	.10
127	Earl O. Whitehill	.10
128	William C. Lee	.10
129	Frank O. Mancuso	.10
130	Francis R. Blades	.10
131	John I. Burns	.10
132	Clinton H. Brown	.10
133	William J. Dietrich	.10
134	Darrell E. Blanton	.10
135	Harry B. Hooper	.10
136	Charles H. Shorten	.10
137	Clarence W. Walker	.10
138	George Foster	.10
139	John J. Barry	.10
140	Samuel J. Pones	.10
141	Ernest G. Shore	.10
142	Hubert B. Leonard	.10
143	Herbert J. Pennock	.10
144	Harold C. Janvrin	.10
145	George H. Ruth	1.00
146	George E. Lewis	.10
147	William L. Gardner	.10
148	Richard C. Hoblitzel	.10
149	Lewis E. Scott	.10
150	Carl W. Mays	.10
151	John A. Niehoff	.10
152	Burton E. Shotton	.10
153	Leon K. Ames	.10
154	Fred Williams	.10
155	William W. Hinchman	.10
156	James R. Shawkey	.10
157	Walter C. Pipp	.10
158	George J. Burns	.10
159	Robert H. Veach	.10
160	Harold H. Chase	.10
161	Thomas L. Hughes	.10
162	Derrill B. Pratt	.10
163	Henry K. Groh	.10
164	Zachariah D. Wheat	.10
165	Francis J. O'Doul	.10
166	William E. Kamm	.10
167	Paul G. Waner	.10
168	Fred C. Snodgrass	.10
169	Floyd C. Herman	.10
170	Albert H. Bridwell	.10
171	John T. Meyers	.10
172	John B. Lobert	.10
173	Raymond B. Bressler	.10
174	Samuel P. Jones	.10
175	Robert A. O'Farrell	.10
176	George Toporcer	.10
177	George E. McNeely	.10
178	John H. Knott	.10
179	Clarence F. Mueller	.10
180	Thomas J.D. Bridges	.10
181	Lloyd A. Brown	.10
182	Lawrence J. Benton	.10
183	Max F. Bishop	.10
184	Morris Berg	.20
185	Ralph F. Perkins	.10
186	Stephen F. O'Neill	.10
187	Glenn C. Myatt	.10
188	Joseph A. Kuhel	.10
189	Martin J. McManus	.10
190	Charles F. Lucas	.10
191	John P. McInnis	.10
192	Edmund J. Miller	.10
193	James L. Sewell	.10
194	William H. Sherdel	.10
195	Harold J. Rhyne	.10
196	Guy T. Bush	.10
197	Ervin Fox	.10
198	Wesley C. Ferrell	.10
199	Roy C. Johnson	.10
200	William Wambsganss	.10
201	George H. Burns	.10
202	Clarence E. Mitchell	.10
203	Cornelius Ball	.10
204	John H. Neun	.10
205	Homer W. Summa	.10
206	Ernest K. Padgett	.10
207	Walter H. Holke	.10
208	Forrest G. Wright	.10
209	Henry M. Gowdy	.10
210	James W. Taylor	.10
211	Benjamin C. Cantwell	.10
212	Joseph F. Demaree	.10
213	Samuel P. Derringer	.10
214	William A. Hallahan	.10
215	Daniel K. MacFayden	.10
216	Harry F. Rice	.10
217	Robert Eldridge Smith	.10
218	Jackson R. Stephenson	.10
219	Perce L. Malone	.10
220	Henry B. Tate	.10
221	Joseph F. Vosmik	.10
222	George A. Watkins	.10
223	James Wilson	.10
224	George E. Uhle	.10
225	Melvin T. Ott	.15
226	Nicholas Altrock	.10
227	Charles H. Ruffing	.10
228	Joseph V.L. Krakauskas	.10
229	Walter A. Berger	.10
230	Norman L. Newsom	.10
231	Lonnie Warneke	.10
232	Frank E. Snyder	.10
233	Myril O. Hoag	.10
234	Baldomero M. Almada	.10
235	Ivy B. Wingo	.10
236	James P. Austin	.10
237	Henry J. Bonura	.10
238	Russell G. Wrightstone	.10
239	Alfred C. Todd	.10
240	Harold B. Warstler	.10
241	Samuel F. West	.10
242	Arthur C. Reinhart	.10
243	Walter C. Stewart	.10
244	John B. Gooch	.10
245	Eugene F. Hargrave	.10
246	George W. Harper	.10
247	George W. Connally	.10
248	Edgar G. Braxton	.10
249	Walter H. Schang	.10
250	Tyrus R. Cobb	.50
251	Rogers Hornsby	.15
252	Richard W. Marquard	.10
253	Carl O. Hubbell	.15
254	Joe Wood	.10
255	Robert M. Grove	.15
256	Lynwood T. Rowe	.10
257	Alvin F. Crowder	.10
258	Walter P. Johnson	.15
259	Charles J. Hafey	.10
260	Frederick L. Fitzsimmons	.10
261	William E. Webb	.10
262	Earle B. Combs	.10
263	Edward J. Konetchy	.10
264	Taylor L. Douthit	.10
265	Lloyd J. Waner	.10
266	Gordon S. Cochrane	.10
267	John O. Wilson	.10
268	Harold J. Traynor	.10
269	Virgil L. Davis	.10
270	Henry E. Manush	.10
271	Michael F. Higgins	.10
272	Adrian Joss	.10
273	Edward Augustine Walsh	.10
274	Johnny L.R. Martin	.10
275	Joseph W. Sewell	.10
276	Hubert B. Leonard	.10
277	Clifford C. Cravath	.10
278	Oral C. Hildebrand	.10
279	Remy P. Kremer	.10
280	Frank A. Pytlak	.10
281	Samuel D. Byrd	.10
282	Curtis B. Davis	.10
283	Lewis A. Fonseca	.10
284	Herold D. Ruel	.10
285	Julius J. Solters	.10
286	Fred W. Schulte	.10
287	John P. Quinn	.10
288	Arthur C. Whitney	.10
289	Jonathon T. Stone	.10
290	Hugh M. Critz	.10
291	Ira J. Flagstead	.10
292	George P. Grantham	.10
293	Samuel D. Hale	.10
294	James F. Hogan	.10
295	Oswald L. Bluege	.10
296	Debs Garms	.10
297	Augistaf B. Friberg	.10
298	Edward A. Brandt	.10
299	Ralston B. Hemsley	.10
300	Charles H. Klein	.10
301	Morton C. Cooper	.10
302	James L. Bottomley	.10
303	James E. Foxx	.15
304	Frank Schulte	.10
305	Frank F. Frisch	.15
306	Frank A. McCormick	.10
307	Jacob E. Daubert	.10
308	Roger T. Peckinpaugh	.10
309	George H. Burns	.10
310	Louis H. Gehrig	.50
311	Aloysius H. Simmons	.10
312	Edward T. Collins	.10
313	Charles L. Hartnett	.10
314	Joseph E. Cronin	.10
315	Paul G. Waner	.10
316	Robert A. O'Farrell	.10
317	Lawrence J. Doyle	.10
318	Lynford H. Lary	.10
319	Frank S. May	.10
320	Roy H. Spencer	.10
321	Samuel R. Coffman	.10
322	Peter J. Donohue	.10
323	George W. Haas	.10
324	Edward S. Farrell	.10
325	Charles F. Rhem	.10
326	Frederick Marberry	.10
327	Charles Martin Conlon	.10
328	Checklist 1-110	.10
329	Checklist 111-220	.10
330	Checklist 221-330	.10

1992 Conlon Collection

ALLEN SOTHORON
ST. LOUIS BROWNS - PITCHER 1917

Conlon set. Each of the 1992 cards has a gray "PROTOTYPE" over-printed diagonally on the back.

	NM/M
Complete set (6):	9.00
Common Player:	.50
14 Joe Jackson (Colorized, edition of 60,000.)	3.00
331 Christy Mathewson	1.50
400 Joe Jackson	2.50
450 Hughie Jennings	.50
500 Ty Cobb	2.00
520 Goose Goslin	.10

In their second season, the 330 cards of the Conlon Collection were numbered consecutively where the 1991 premiere issue ended. Cards 331-660 also maintained the high-gloss black-and-white format of the previous year. Many subsets within the issue carry special designations on the card fronts. Subsets included no-hitters, Triple Crown winners, "Great Stories," nicknames and more.

	NM/M
Factory Set (330):	25.00
Complete Set (330):	15.00
Common Player:	.10
Wax Pack:	.50
Wax Box (36):	15.00

No	Player	Price
331	Christopher Mathewson	.15
332	George L. Wiltse	.10
333	George N. Rucker	.10
334	Leon K. Ames	.10
335	Charles A. Bender	.10
336	Joe Wood	.10
337	Edward Augustine Walsh	.10
338	George J. Mullin	.10
339	Earl A. Hamilton	.10
340	Charles M Tesreau	.10
341	James Scott	.10
342	Richard W. Marquard	.10
343	Claude R. Hendrix	.15
344	James S. Lavender	.10
345	Leslie A. Bush	.10
346	Hubert B. Leonard	.10
347	Fred A. Toney	.10
348	James L. Vaughn	.10
349	Ernest G. Koob	.10
350	Robert Groom	.10
351	Ernest G. Shore	.10
352	Horace O. Eller	.10
353	Walter P. Johnson	.15
354	Charles C. Robertson	.10
355	Jesse L. Barnes	.10
356	Samuel P. Jones	.10
357	Howard J. Ehmke	.10
358	Jesse J. Haines	.10
359	Theodore A. Lyons	.10
360	Carl O. Hubbell	.15
361	Wesley C. Ferrell	.10
362	Robert J. Burke	.10
363	Paul D. Dean	.10
364	Norman L. Newsom	.10
365	Lloyd V. Kennedy	.10
366	William J. Dietrich	.10
367	John S. Vander Meer	.10
368	John S. Vander Meer	.10
369	Montgomery M. Pearson	.10
370	Robert W.A. Feller	.15
371	Lonnie Warneke	.10
372	James A. Tobin	.10
373	Earl A. Moore	.10
374	William H. Dineen	.10
375	Malcolm W. Eason	.10
376	George A. Mogridge	.10
377	Clarence A. Vance	.10
378	James O. Carleton	.10
379	Clyde M. Shoun	.10
380	Franklin W. Hayes	.10
381	Benjamin R. Frey	.10
382	Henry W. Johnson	.10
383	Ralph Kress	.10
384	John T. Allen	.10
385	Harold A. Trosky Sr.	.10
386	Eugene F. Robertson	.10
387	Lemuel F. Young	.10
388	George A. Selkirk	.10
389	Edwin L. Wells	.10
390	James D. Weaver	.10
391	George McQuinn	.10
392	John B. Lobert	.10
393	Ernest E. Swanson	.10
394	Ernest A. Nevers	.10
395	James J. Levey	.10
396	Hugo F. Bezdek	.10
397	Walter E. French	.10
398	Charles F. Berry	.10
399	Franklin T. Grube	.10
400	Charles W. Dressen	.10
401	Alfred E. Neale	.10
402	Henry A. Vick	.10
403	James F. Thorpe	.50
404	Walter J. Gilbert	.10
405	John L. Urban	.10
406	Everett V. Purdy	.10
407	Albert O. Wright	.10
408	William M. Urbanski	.10
409	Charles W. Fischer	.10
410	John R. Warner	.10
411	Charles W. Cissell	.10
412	Mervin D.J. Shea	.10
413	Adolfo Luque	.10
414	John L. Bassler	.10
415	Arvel O. Hale	.10
416	Lawrence R. French	.10
417	William C. Walker	.10
418	Allen L. Cooke	.10
419	Philip J. Todt	.10
420	Ivy P. Andrews	.10
421	William J. Herman	.10
422	Tristram E. Speaker	.15
423	Aloysius H. Simmons	.10
424	Lewis R. Wilson	.10
425	Tyrus R. Cobb	.40
426	George H. Ruth	.10
427	Ernest N. Lombardi	.10
428	Jay H. Dean	.15
429	Lloyd J. Waner	.10
430	Henry B. Greenberg	.15
431	Robert M. Grove	.10
432	Gordon S. Cochrane	.10
433	Burleigh A. Grimes	.10
434	Harold J. Traynor	.10
435	John R. Mize	.15
436	Edgar C. Rice	.10
437	Leon A. Goslin	.10
438	Charles H. Klein	.10
439	Cornelius Mack	.10
440	James L. Bottomley	.10
441	Jackson R. Stephenson	.10
442	Kenneth Williams	.10
443	Charles B. Adams	.10
444	Joseph J. Jackson	.50
445	Harold Newhouser	.10
446	Wesley C. Ferrell	.10
447	Francis J. O'Doul	.10
448	Walter H. Schang	.10
449	Sherwood R. Magee	.10
450	Michael J. Donlin	.10
451	Roger M. Cramer	.10
452	Richard W. Bartell	.10
453	Earle T. Mack	.10
454	Walter G. Brown	.10
455	John A. Heving	.10
456	Percy L. Jones	.10
457	Theodore Blankenship	.10
458	Abraham H. Wingo	.10
459	Roger P. Bresnahan	.10
460	William J. Klem	.10
461	Charles L. Gehringer	.10
462	Stanley A. Coveleski	.10
463	Edward S. Plank	.10
464	Clark C.F. Griffith	.10
465	Herbert J. Pennock	.10
466	Earle B. Combs	.10
467	Robert P. Doerr	.10
468	Waite C. Hoyt	.10
469	Thomas H. Connolly	.10
470	Harry B. Hooper	.10
471	Richard B. Ferrell	.10
472	William G. Evans	.10
473	William J. Herman	.10
474	William M. Dickey	.10
475	Lucius B. Appling	.15
476	Ralph A. Pinelli	.10
477	Donald E. McNair	.10
478	John F. Blake	.10
479	Valentine J. Picinich	.10
480	Fred A. Heimach	.10
481	John G. Graney	.10
482	Ewell A. Russell	.10
483	Urban C. Faber	.10
484	Benjamin M. Kauff	.10
485	Clarence L. Rowland	.10
486	Robert H. Veach	.10
487	James C. Bagby	.10
488	William D. Perritt	.10
489	Charles L. Herzog	.10
490	Arthur Fletcher	.10
491	Walter H. Holke	.10
492	Arthur N. Nehf	.10
493	Lafayette F. Thompson	.10
494	James D. Welsh	.10
495	Oscar J. Vitt	.10
496	Owen T. Carroll	.10
497	James K. O'Dea	.10
498	Fredrick M. Frankhouse	.10
499	Jewel W. Ens	.10
500	Morris Arnovich	.10
501	Walter Gerber	.10
502	George W. Davis	.10
503	Charles S. Myer	.10
504	Samuel A. Leslie	.10
505	Walter C. Bolton	.10
506	Fred Walker	.10
507	John W. Smith	.10
508	Irving D. Hadley	.10
509	Clyde E. Crouse	.10
510	Joseph C. Glenn	.10
511	Clyde E. Kimsey	.10
512	Louis K. Finney	.10
513	Alfred V. Lawson	.10
514	Charles P. Fullis	.10
515	Earl H. Sheely	.10
516	George Gibson	.10
517	John J. Broaca	.10
518	Bibb A. Falk	.10
519	Frank O. Hurst	.10
520	Grover A. Hartley	.10
521	Donald H. Heffner	.10
522	Harvey L. Hendrick	.10
523	Allen S. Sothoron	.10
524	Anthony F. Piet	.10
525	Tyrus R. Cobb	.40
526	James E. Foxx	.15
527	Rogers Hornsby	.15
528	Napoleon LaJoie	.15
529	Louis H. Gehrig	.40
530	Henry Zimmerman	.10
531	Charles H. Klein	.10
532	Hugh Duffy	.10
533	Robert M. Grove	.15
534	Grover C. Alexander	.15
535	Amos W. Rusie	.10
536	Vernon L. Gomez	.10
537	William H. Walters	.10
538	Urban J. Hodapp	.10
539	Bruce D. Campbell	.10
540	Horace M. Lisenbee	.10
541	John F. Fournier	.10
542	James R. Tabor	.10
543	John H. Burnett	.10
544	Roy A. Hartzell	.10
545	Walter P. Gautreau	.10
546	Emil O. Yde	.10
547	Robert L. Johnson	.10
548	Joseph J. Hauser	.10
549	Edward M. Reulbach	.10
550	Baldomero M. Almada	.10
551	Gordon S. Cochrane	.10
552	Carl O. Hubbell	.15
553	Charles L. Gehringer	.10
554	Aloysius H. Simmons	.10
555	Mordecai P.C. Brown	.10
556	Hugh A. Jennings	.10
557	Norman A. Elberfeld	.10
558	Charles D. Stengel	.10
559	Alexander Schacht	.10
560	James E. Foxx	.15
561	George L. Kelly	.10
562	Lloyd J. Waner	.10
563	Paul G. Waner	.10
564	Walter P. Johnson	.10
565	John Franklin Baker	.10
566	Roy J. Hughes	.10
567	Lewis S. Riggs	.10
568	John H. Whitehead	.10
569	Elam R. Vangilder	.10
570	William A. Zitzmann	.10
571	Walter J. Schmidt	.10
572	John A. Tavener	.10
573	Joseph E. Genewich	.10
574	John A. Marcum	.10
575	Fred Hofmann	.10
576	Robert A. Rolfe	.10
577	Victor G. Sorrell	.10
578	Floyd J. Scott	.10
579	Alphonse Thomas	.10
580	Alfred J. Smith	.10
581	John J. Henline	.10
582	Edward T. Collins	.10
583	Earle B. Combs	.10
584	John J. McGraw	.10
585	Lewis R. Wilson	.10
586	Charles L. Hartnett	.10
587	Hazen S. Cuyler	.10
588	William H. Terry	.10
589	Joseph V. McCarthy	.10
590	Henry B. Greenberg	.15
591	Tristram E. Speaker	.10
592	William B. McKechnie	.10
593	Stanley R. Harris	.10
594	Herbert J. Pennock	.10
595	George H. Sisler	.10
596	Fred C. Lindstrom	.10
597	Howard E. Averill Sr.	.10
598	David J. Bancroft	.10
599	Cornelius Mack	.10
600	Joseph E. Cronin	.10
601	Kenneth L. Ash	.10
602	Alfred R. Spohrer	.10
603	Lee R. Mahaffey	.10
604	James F. O'Rourke	.10
605	Ulysses S.G. Stoner	.10
606	Frank H. Gabler	.10
607	Thomas F. Padden	.10
608	Charles A. Shires	.10
609	Sherrod M. Smith	.10
610	Philip Weintraub	.10
611	Russell Van Atta	.10
612	Joyner C. White	.10
613	Clifford G. Melton	.10
614	James J. Ring	.10
615	John H. Sand	.10
616	David D. Alexander	.10
617	Kent Greenfield	.10
618	Edwin H. Dyer	.10
619	William H. Sherdel	.10
620	Hubert M. Lanier	.10
621	Robert A. O'Farrell	.10
622	Rogers Hornsby	.15
623	William A. Beckman	.10
624	Morton C. Cooper	.10
625	William P. Delancey	.10
626	Martin W. Marion	.10
627	William H. Southworth	.10
628	John R. Mize	.15
629	Joseph M. Medwick	.10

1992 Conlon Collection Prototypes

JOE JACKSON
CLEVELAND INDIANS - OUTFIELD 1913

Along with the 1991 Babe Ruth prototype card, these five cards were distributed at the Ana-heim National Sports Collectors Convention in 1991. The an-nounced distribution was 20,000 of each card except the Joe Jackson, which had a press run of 67,000. Except for card 331, all the proto-types have different numbers than the same card in the regular-issue

630	Grover C. Alexander	.15
631	Paul D. Dean	.10
632	Herman S. Bell	.10
633	William W. Cooper	.10
634	Frank F. Frisch	.10
635	Jay H. Dean	.15
636	Donald J. Gutteridge	.10
637	Johnny L.R. Martin	.10
638	Edward J. Konetchy	.10
639	William A. Hallahan	.10
640	Lonnie Warneke	.10
641	Terry B. Moore	.10
642	Enos B. Slaughter	.10
643	Clarence F. Mueller	.10
644	George Toporcer	.10
645	James L. Bottomley	.10
646	Francis R. Blades	.10
647	Jesse J. Haines	.10
648	Andrew A. High	.10
649	Miller J. Huggins	.10
650	Ernesto R. Orsatti	.10
651	Lester R. Bell	.10
652	Charles E. Street	.10
653	Walter H. Roettger	.10
654	Sylvester W. Johnson	.10
655	Miguel A. Gonzalez	.10
656	James A. Collins	.10
657	Charles J. Hafey	.10
658	Checklist 331-440	.10
659	Checklist 441-550	.10
660	Checklist 551-660	.10

1992-94 Conlon Collection Gold

FRANKIE FRISCH
NATIONAL LEAGUE - 2ND BASE 1933

Four of the heroes of the inaugural All-Star Game of 1933 were featured in a pop-up ad in the program for the 1992 Game in San Diego. One card was inserted into each of the programs printed for distribution at the game and by mail order. Each card was reported printed in an edition of 34,000. Cards are similar in format to the regular Conlon Collection issues except for the gold-foil border around the player photo on front and the use of a "G" suffix to the card number. A banner at top front reads, "Game of the Century." On back is a summary of the player's 1933 All-Star performance and his stats. Gold editions of other Conlon cards were also issued in several different venues in 1993-94. Six cards (#665-880) were included in 1992 Conlon factory sets in editions of up to 90,000. The Johnson-Ryan gold card was available only in packaging sold in Eckerd stores, while the 1994 Cobb gold card was only available at Toys R Us. Cards are numbered with a "G" suffix.

		NM/M
Complete Set (12):		50.00
Common Player:		2.00
661	Bill Terry	2.00
662	Lefty Gomez	2.00
663	Babe Ruth	12.00
664	Frankie Frisch	2.00
665	Carl Hubbell	2.00
667	Charlie Gehringer (Edition of 20,000.)	4.00
730	Luke Appling (Edition of 20,000.)	4.00
770	Tommy Henrich	2.00
820	John McGraw	2.00
880	Gabby Hartnett	2.00
934	Walter Johnson, Nolan Ryan (Edition of 100,000.)	12.00
1000	Ty Cobb (Edition of 100,000.)	6.00

1992 Conlon Collection 13th National

These samples of the 1993 Conlon Collection series were distributed at the National Sports Collectors Convention in Atlanta in 1992. Other than the Joe Jackson

card, they carry the same numbers as the regularly issued versions. Designs are also identical except for the overprint on back in outline letters, "13TH NATIONAL."

		NM/M
Complete Set (4):		4.00
Common Player:		.50
14	Joe Jackson	1.00
663	George H. Ruth	2.00
775	John T. Meyers	.50
800	James L. Vaughn	.50

1993 Conlon Collection Prototypes

RED FABER
CHICAGO WHITE SOX - PITCHER 1932

The cards in this issue were produced to preview the basic set and various subsets of the 1993 Conlon Collection issue. Cards are similar to the regular-issue set with the exception that the word "PROTOTYPE" is printed in gray diagonally on back. Production of most of the black-and-white cards was 60,000, though Gomez and Frisch were limited to 10,000 apiece. Three of the cards can be found with "All Star FanFest" notations on back, having been distributed as samples there.

		NM/M
Complete Set (8):		3.00
Common Player:		1.00
661	Bill Terry	1.00
661	Bill Terry (All Star FanFest)	2.00
662	Lefty Gomez	1.00
663	Babe Ruth	6.00
664	Frankie Frisch	1.00
710	Red Faber	1.00
710	Red Faber (All Star FanFest)	2.00
775	Chief Meyers	1.00
800	Hugh Vaughn	1.00
888	Babe Ruth (Colorized, edition of 52,000.)	5.00
905	Lena Blackburne	1.00
905	Lena Blackbourne (All Star FanFest)	2.00
934	Walter Johnson, Nolan Ryan (Colorized edition of 52,000.)	4.00

1993 Conlon Collection

WALTER JOHNSON
HURLER OF THE UNSEEN FASTBALL 1927

The third annual Conlon Collection issue of 330 cards is numbered 661-990, a continuation of the series produced in 1991-92. The format of black-and-white photos produced 50-90 years ago by Charles Martin Conlon and surrounded by a wide black border and UV coating was continued. As with earlier issues, card backs contain brief biographical data, a few stats and well-written career highlights. The 1993 set also featured many subsets arranged by topic, such as spitballers, native Americans, players who overcame handicaps, etc. One subset com-

pared Nolan Ryan with star pitchers in baseball history and included a fantasy photo of Ryan shaking hands in the dugout with Walter Johnson (card #934).

		NM/M
Complete Set in Commemorative Tin:		20.00
Complete Set (330):		15.00
Common Player:		.10
Wax Pack:		.50
Wax Box (36):		15.00
661	William H. Terry	.10
662	Vernon L. Gomez	.10
663	George H. Ruth	.50
664	Frank F. Frisch	.10
665	Carl O. Hubbell	.10
666	Aloysius H. Simmons	.10
667	Charles L. Gehringer	.15
668	Howard E. Averill Sr.	.15
669	Robert M. Grove	.15
670	Harold J. Traynor	.15
671	Charles H. Klein	.15
672	Paul G. Waner	.10
673	Louis H. Gehrig	.40
674	Richard B. Ferrell	.10
675	Charles L. Hartnett	.10
676	Joseph E. Cronin	.10
677	Charles J. Hafey	.10
678	James J. Dykes	.10
679	Samuel F. West	.10
680	Johnny L.R. Martin	.10
681	Francis J. O'Doul	.10
682	Alvin F. Crowder	.10
683	James Wilson	.10
684	Richard W. Bartell	.10
685	William A. Hallahan	.10
686	Walter A. Berger	.10
687	Lonnie Warneke	.10
688	William B. Chapman	.10
689	Elwood G. English	.10
690	James H. Reese	.10
691	Roscoe A. Holm	.10
692	Charles D. Jamieson	.10
693	Jonathan T.W. Zachary	.10
694	John C. Ryan	.10
695	Earl J. Adams	.10
696	William E. Hunnefield	.10
697	Henry L. Meadows	.10
698	Thomas F. Carey	.10
699	John W. Rawlings	.10
700	Kenneth E. Holloway	.10
701	Lance C. Richbourg	.10
702	Raymond L. Fisher	.10
703	Edward Augustine Walsh	.10
704	Richard Rudolph	.10
705	Raymond B. Caldwell	.10
706	Burleigh A. Grimes	.10
707	Stanley A. Coveleski	.10
708	George A. Hildebrand	.10
709	John P. Quinn	.10
710	Urban C. Faber	.10
711	Urban J. Shocker	.10
712	Hubert B. Leonard	.10
713	Louis L. Koupal	.10
714	James C. Wasdell	.10
715	John H. Lindell	.10
716	Don W. Padgett	.10
717	Nelson T. Potter	.10
718	Lynwood T. Rowe	.10
719	David C. Danforth	.10
720	Claude W. Passeau	.10
721	Harry L. Kelley	.10
722	John T. Allen	.10
723	Thomas J.D. Bridges	.10
724	William C. Lee	.10
725	Fredrick M. Frankhouse	.10
726	John J. McCarthy	.10
727	Glen D. Russell	.10
728	Emory E. Rigney	.10
729	Howard S. Shanks	.10
730	Lucius B. Appling	.10
731	William J. Byron	.10
732	Earle B. Combs	.10
733	Henry B. Greenberg	.15
734	Walter W. Beck	.10
735	Hollis J. Thurston	.10
736	Lewis R. Wilson	.10
737	William A. McGowan	.10
738	Henry J. Bonura	.10
739	Thomas C. Baker	.10
740	William C. Jacobson	.10
741	Hazen S. Cuyler	.10
742	George F. Blaeholder	.10
743	Wilson D. Miles	.10
744	Lee E. Handley	.10
745	John F. Collins	.10
746	Wilfred P. Ryan	.10
747	Aaron L. Ward	.10
748	Montgomery M. Pearson	.10
749	Jacob W. Early	.10
750	William F. Atwood	.10
751	Mark A. Koenig	.10
752	John A. Hassett	.10
753	David J. Jones	.10
754	John P. Wagner	.25
755	William M. Dickey	.15
756	Albert M. Butcher	.10
757	Waite C. Hoyt	.10
758	Walter P. Johnson	.15
759	Howard J. Ehmke	.10
760	Norman L. Newsom	.10
761	Anthony M. Lazzeri	.10
762	Anthony M. Lazzeri	.10
763	Spurgeon F. Chandler	.10
764	Walter K. Higbe	.10

765	Paul R. Richards	.10
766	Rogers Hornsby	.15
767	Joseph F. Vosmik	.10
768	Jesse J. Haines	.10
769	William H. Walters	.10
770	Thomas D. Henrich	.10
771	James E. Thorpe	.40
772	Euel W. Moore	.10
773	Rudolph P. York	.10
774	Charles A. Bender	.10
775	John T. Meyers	.10
776	Robert L. Johnson	.10
777	Roy C. Johnson	.10
778	Richard T. Porter	.10
779	Ethan N. Allen	.10
780	Harry F. Sallee	.10
781	Roy C. Bell	.10
782	Arnold J. Statz	.10
783	Frank J. Henry	.10
784	Charles L. Woodall	.10
785	Philip E. Collins	.10
786	Joseph W. Sewell	.10
787	William J. Herman	.10
788	Rueben H. Oldring	.10
789	William H. Walker	.10
790	Joseph C. Schultz	.10
791	Fred E. Maguire	.10
792	Claude W. Willoughby	.10
793	James A. Ferguson	.10
794	John D. Morrison	.10
795	Tristram E. Speaker	.15
796	Tyrus R. Cobb	.40
797	Max Carey	.10
798	George H. Sisler	.10
799	Charles J. Hollocher	.10
800	James L. Vaughn	.10
801	Samuel P. Jones	.10
802	Harry B. Hooper	.10
803	Clifford C. Cravath	.10
804	Walter P. Johnson	.15
805	Jacob E. Daubert	.10
806	Jesse C. Milan	.10
807	Hugh A. McQuillan	.10
808	George F. Brickell	.10
809	Joseph V. Stripp	.10
810	Urban J. Hodapp	.10
811	John L. Vergez	.10
812	Linus R. Frey	.10
813	William W. Regan	.10
814	Norman R. Young	.10
815	Charles C. Robertson	.10
816	Walter F. Judnich	.10
817	Joseph B. Tinker	.15
818	John Evers	.15
819	Frank L. Chance	.15
820	John J. McGraw	.10
821	Charles J. Grimm	.10
822	Ted Lyons	.10
823	Joe McCarthy	.10
824	Connie Mack	.10
825	George Gibson	.10
826	Steve O'Neill	.10
827	Tristram E. Speaker	.15
828	William F. Carrigan	.10
829	Charles D. Stengel	.15
830	Miller J. Huggins	.10
831	William B. McKechnie	.10
832	Charles W. Dressen	.10
833	Charles E. Street	.10
834	Melvin T. Ott	.15
835	Frank F. Frisch	.10
836	George H. Sisler	.10
837	Napoleon LaJoie	.15
838	Tyrus R. Cobb	.40
839	William H. Southworth	.10
840	Clark C.F. Griffith	.10
841	William H. Terry	.10
842	Rogers Hornsby	.15
843	Joseph E. Cronin	.10
844	Alfonso R. Lopez	.10
845	Stanley R. Harris	.10
846	Wilbert Robinson	.10
847	Hugh A. Jennings	.10
848	James J. Dykes	.10
849	Roy J. Cullenbine	.10
850	Graham E. Moore	.10
851	John H. Rothrock	.10
852	William H. Lamar	.10
853	Monte Weaver	.10
854	Ival R. Goodman	.10
855	Henry L. Severeid	.10
856	Fred G. Haney	.10
857	Joseph B. Shaute	.10
858	Smead P. Jolley	.10
859	Edwin D. Williams	.10
860	Bernard O. Bengough	.10
861	Richard B. Ferrell	.10
862	Robert A. O'Farrell	.10
863	Virgil L. Davis	.10
864	Franklin W. Hayes	.10
865	Herold D. Ruel	.10
866	Gordon S. Cochrane	.10
867	John Kling	.10
868	Ivy B. Wingo	.10
869	William M. Dickey	.15
870	Frank E. Snyder	.10
871	Roger P. Bresnahan	.10
872	Walter H. Schang	.10
873	Alfonso R. Lopez	.10
874	James Wilson	.10
875	Valentine J. Picinich	.10
876	Stephen F. O'Neill	.10
877	Ernest N. Lombardi	.10
878	John L. Bassler	.10
879	Raymond W. Schalk	.10
880	Charles L. Hartnett	.10
881	Bruce D. Campbell	.10
882	Charles H. Ruffing	.10

883	Mordecai P.C. Brown	.10
884	Peter J. Archer	.10
885	David E. Keefe	.10
886	Nathan H. Andrews	.10
887	Edgar C. Rice	.10
888	George H. Ruth	.50
889	Charles J. Hafey	.10
890	Oscar D. Melillo	.10
891	Joe Wood	.10
892	John J. Evers	.10
893	George Toporcer	.10
894	Myril O. Hoag	.10
895	Robert G. Weiland	.10
896	Joseph A. Marty	.10
897	Sherwood R. Magee	.10
898	Daniel T. Taylor	.10
899	William E. Kamm	.10
900	Samuel J.T. Sheckard	.10
901	Sylvester W. Johnson	.10
902	Stephen R. Sundra	.10
903	Roger M. Cramer	.10
904	Hubert S. Pruett	.10
905	Russell A. Blackburne	.10
906	Eppa Rixey	.10
907	Leon A. Goslin	.10
908	George L. Kelly	.10
909	James L. Bottomley	.10
910	Christopher Mathewson	.15
911	Anthony M. Lazzeri	.10
912	John A. Mostil	.10
913	Robert P. Doerr	.10
914	Walter J.V. Maranville	.10
915	Harry E. Heilmann	.10
916	Rodrick J. Wallace	.10
917	James E. Foxx	.15
918	John R. Mize	.10
919	John N. Bentley	.10
920	Alexander Schacht	.10
921	Parke E. Coleman	.10
922	George H. Paskert	.10
923	Horace H. Ford	.10
924	Randolph E. Moore	.10
925	Milburn J. Shoffner	.10
926	Richard W. Siebert	.10
927	Anthony C. Kaufmann	.10
928	Jay H. Dean, Nolan Ryan	.25
929	Clarence A. Vance, Nolan Ryan	.25
930	Robert M. Grove, Nolan Ryan	.25
931	George E. Waddell, Nolan Ryan	.25
932	Grover C. Alexander, Nolan Ryan	.25
933	Robert W.A. Feller, Nolan Ryan	.25
934	Walter P. Johnson, Nolan Ryan	.50
935	Theodore A. Lyons, Nolan Ryan	.25
936	James C. Bagby	.10
937	Joseph Sugden	.10
938	Robert E. Grace	.10
939	John G. Heath	.10
940	Kenneth Williams	.10
941	Marvin J. Owen	.10
942	Cyril R. Weatherly	.10
943	Edward C. Morgan	.10
944	John C. Rizzo	.10
945	Archie R. McKain	.10
946	Robert M. Garbark	.10
947	John B. Osborn	.10
948	John S. Podgajny	.10
949	Joseph P. Evans	.10
950	George A. Rensa	.10
951	John H. Humphries	.10
952	Merritt P. Cain	.10
953	Roy E. Hansen	.10
954	John A. Niggeling	.10
955	Harold J. Wiltse	.10
956	Alejandro A.A.E. Carrasquel	.10
957	George A. Grant	.10
958	Philip W. Weinert	.10
959	Ervin B. Brame	.10
960	Raymond J. Harrell	.10
961	Edward K. Linke	.10
962	Samuel B. Gibson	.10
963	John C. Watwood	.10
964	James T. Prothro	.10
965	Julio G. Bonetti	.10
966	Howard R. Mills	.10
967	Clarence E. Galloway	.10
968	Harold J. Kelleher	.10
969	Elon C. Hogsett	.10
970	Edward B. Heusser	.10
971	Edward J. Baecht	.10
972	Otto H. Saltzgaver	.10
973	Leroy G. Herrmann	.10
974	Beveric B. Bean	.10
975	Harry Seibold	.10
976	Howard V. Keen	.10
977	William J. Barrett	.10
978	Patrick H. McNulty	.10
979	George E. Turbeville	.10
980	Edward D. Phillips	.10
981	Garland M. Buckeye	.10
982	Victor P. Frasier	.10
983	John G. Rhodes	.10
984	Emile D. Barnes	.10
985	James C. Edwards	.10
986	Herschel E. Bennett	.10
987	Carmen P. Hill	.10
988	Checklist 661-770	.10
989	Checklist 771-880	.10
990	Checklist 881-990	.10

1993-95 Conlon Collection Color

BOB FELLER
CLEVELAND INDIANS - PITCHER 1938

The cards in this set were previously released in black-and-white in regular 1991-94 Conlon sets. Cards 1-12 were issued as bonus cards in Megacards accessory items; 250,000 of each were produced. Cards 13-20 were randomly inserted in 1993 Conlon counter and blister packs; 100,000 of those were produced. Cards 21-22, in an edition of 75,000, were only available through a send-away offer. Card 23 was available exclusively as an insert in the 7th Edition SCD Baseball Card Price Guide, in an edition of 60,000. Cards 24-39 were issued in 1994. Numbers 24-28 were random inserts printed to the number of 84,000 apiece. Cards 29-30 were a send-away premium; #31-33 were hobby foil inserts. All were issued in quantities of 12,000. Cards 34-37 - 48,000 of each - are a Toys R Us exclusive insert. Cards 38-39 were special-offer premiums. A special printing of 24,000 of #28 were issued with a "Conlon Collection Day" overprint on back and were distributed at the Sept. 11, 1994, St. Louis Cardinals game.

		NM/M
Complete Set (47):		100.00
Common Player:		2.00
1	Sunny Jim Bottomley	2.00
2	Lefty Grove	5.00
3	Lou Gehrig	10.00
4	Babe Ruth	10.00
5	Casey Stengel	2.00
6	Rube Marquard	2.00
7	Walter Johnson	5.00
8	Lou Gehrig	5.00
9	Christy Mathewson	5.00
10	Ty Cobb	5.00
11	Mel Ott	2.00
12	Carl Hubbell	2.00
13	Al Simmons	2.00
14	Connie Mack	2.00
15	Grover C. Alexander	2.00
16	Jimmie Foxx	3.00
17	Lloyd Waner	2.00
18	Tris Speaker	4.00
19	Dizzy Dean	3.00
20	Rogers Hornsby	3.00
21	Shoeless Joe Jackson	7.50
22	Jim Thorpe	7.50
23	Bob Feller	8.00
24	Hal Newhouser	2.00
25	Hughie Jennings	2.00
26	Red Faber	2.00
27	Enos Slaughter	2.00
28	Johnny Mize	2.00
28CCD	Johnny Mize	4.00
29	Pie Traynor	2.00
30	Walter Johnson, Nolan Ryan	4.00
31	Lou Gehrig	2.00
32	Benny Bengough	2.00
33	Babe Ruth	2.00
34	Charlie Gehringer	2.00
35	Babe Ruth	2.00
36	Bill Dickey	2.00
37	Mordecai Brown	2.00
38	Ray Schalk	4.00
39	Home Run Baker	5.00
40	Frank Frisch	2.00
41	Hack Wilson	2.00
42	Ty Cobb	6.00
43	Honus Wagner	4.00
44	John McGraw	2.00
45	Reds vs. Giants	4.00
46	Indians vs. Yanks	3.00
47	Babe Ruth	12.00

1993 Conlon Collection Master Series

"The Best There Was" was the subtitle on this portfolio of oversized (10" x 8") cards produced from the photos of Charles

Martin Conlon. On the high-gloss card fronts, a wide black border surrounds the black-and-white photo, with a gold-foil pinstripe border between the two. The player's name appears in gold at the bottom. Backs are printed in black-and-white and feature a large player portrait, complete major league stats and a career summary. A serial numbered certificate placing the set within an edition of 25,000 was included with the set; a deluxe portfolio album to house the collection was available for $10.

		NM/M
Complete Set (9):		15.00
Common Card:		1.50
1	Title card	.50
2	Babe Ruth	6.00
3	Lou Gehrig, Walter Johnson	4.00
4	Honus Wagner	3.00
5	Mickey Cochrane	1.50
6	Tris Speaker	1.50
7	Ty Cobb	4.00
8	Rogers Hornsby	1.50
9	Pie Traynor	1.50

1993 Conlon Collection Color Masters

Some of the premier photography of Charles Martin Conlon was computer color-enhanced and placed on these oversized (10" x 8") cards in a special edition of 25,000. High-gloss fronts feature the colorized photos separated by a thin white pinstripe from the dark blue background. Backs are printed in black and blue on white and feature a career summary or other historical data, along with a description of the front photo. A serially numbered certificate of authenticity accompanied the set and could be redeemed, along with $10, for a deluxe portfolio to house the collection.

		NM/M
Complete Set (9):		15.00
Common Player:		1.50
1	Title Card	.50
2	Napoleon Lajoie	1.50
3	Walter Johnson, Nolan Ryan (Fantasy photo.)	6.00
4	Action at Hilltop Park	.50
5	Babe Ruth	6.00
6	Frank Baker	1.50
7	John McGraw	1.50
8	John McGraw, Wilbert Robinson, Christy Mathewson	1.50
9	Hughie Jennings	1.50

1994 Conlon Collection Prototypes

A large gray "PROTOTYPE" overprint on back identifies these cards as sample of the fourth annual edition of Conlon Collection cards by Megacards. Cards carry the same number as issued versions. It was reported that 26,000 prototypes were issued of Martin, Traynor, Hubbell, Klem and Koenig; while 52,000 each were issued of Jackson and the Deans.

		NM/M
Complete Set (8):		8.00
Common Player		1.00
991	Pepper Martin	1.00
1030	Joe Jackson	3.00
1050	Pie Traynor	1.00
1105	Carl Hubbell	1.00
1140	Lefty Grove	1.00

1170	Dizzy Dean, Paul Dean	1.50
1190	Bill Klem	1.00
1230	Mark Koenig	1.00

1994 Conlon Collection

DAFFY & DIZZY DEAN

The production of "old-timers" cards based on the baseball photography of Charles M. Conlon from the 1910s through the 1930s continued into a fourth year in 1994 with another 330-card series, numbered 991-1320. Once again the format of previous years was continued. Subsets included the 1919 Chicago White Sox, major league brothers and action photos.

		NM/M
Complete Set in Commemorative Tin:		40.00
Complete Set (330):		30.00
Common Player:		.10
Wax Box (36):		40.00
991	Johnny L.R. Martin	.10
992	Joseph W. Sewell	.10
993	Edd J. Roush	.10
994	Richard B. Ferrell	.10
995	John J. Broaca	.10
996	James L. Sewell	.10
997	Burleigh A. Grimes	.10
998	Lewis R. Wilson	.10
999	Robert M. Grove	.40
1000	Tyrus R. Cobb	.45
1001	John J. McGraw	.10
1002	Edward S. Plank	.10
1003	Samuel P. Jones	.10
1004	James L. Bottomley	.10
1005	Henry B. Greenberg	.15
1006	Lloyd J. Waner	.10
1007	William W. Moore	.10
1008	Lucius B. Appling	.10
1009	Harold Newhouser	.10
1010	Alfonso R. Lopez	.10
1011	Tyrus R. Cobb	.40
1012	Charles A. Nichols	.10
1013	Edward Augustine Walsh	.10
1014	Hugh Duffy	.10
1015	Richard W. Marquard	.10
1016	Adrian Joss	.10
1017	Rodrick J. Wallace	.10
1018	William H. Keeler	.10
1019	Jacob E. Daubert	.10
1020	Harry F. Sallee	.10
1021	Adolfo Luque	.10
1022	Ivy B. Wingo	.10
1023	Edd J. Roush	.10
1024	William A. Rariden	.10
1025	Sherwood R. Magee	.10
1026	Louis B. Duncan	.10
1027	Horace O. Eller	.10
1028	Alfred E. Neale	.10
1029	George D. Weaver	.10
1030	Joseph J. Jackson	.50
1031	Arnold Gandil	.10
1032	Charles A. Risberg	.10
1033	Raymond W. Schalk	.10
1034	Edward V. Cicotte	.10
1035	William H. James	.10
1036	Harry L. Leibold	.10
1037	Richard H. Kerr	.10
1038	William J. Gleason	.10
1039	Frederick W. McMullin (Middle initial actually "D.")	.10
1040	Edward T. Collins	.10
1041	Sox Pitchers (Lefty Williams, Bill James, Ed Cicotte, Dicky Kerr)	.10
1042	Sox Outfielders (Nemo Leibold, Happy Felsch, Shano Collins)	.10
1043	Kenneth F. Keltner	.10
1044	Charles F. Berry	.10
1045	Walter J. Lutzke	.10
1046	John C. Schulte	.10
1047	John V. Welch	.10
1048	Jack E. Russell	.10
1049	John J. Murray	.10
1050	Harold J. Traynor	.10
1051	Michael J. Donlin	.10
1052	Charles L. Hartnett	.10
1053	Anthony M. Lazzeri	.10
1054	Lawrence H. Miller	.10
1055	Clarence A. Vance	.10
1056	Williams F. Carrigan	.10
1057	John J. Murphy	.10
1058	Clifton E Heathcote	.10

1059	Joseph A. Dugan	.10
1060	Walter J.V. Maranville	.10
1061	Thomas D. Henrich	.10
1062	Leroy E. Parmelee	.10
1063	Vernon L. Gomez	.10
1064	Ernest N. Lombardi	.10
1065	David J. Bancroft	.10
1066	William B. McKechnie	.10
1067	John A. Hassett	.10
1068	Spurgeon F. Chandler	.10
1069	Roy J. Hughes	.10
1070	George A. Dauss	.10
1071	Joseph J. Hauser	.10
1072	Virgil L. Davis	.10
1073	Albert M. Butcher	.10
1074	Louis P. Chiozza	.10
1075	Center Field Bleachers	.10
1076	Charles L. Gehringer	.10
1077	Henry E. Manush	.10
1078	Charles H. Ruffing	.10
1079	Melvin L. Harder	.10
1080	George H. Ruth	.50
1081	William B. Chapman	.10
1082	Louis H. Gehrig	.40
1083	James E. Foxx	.15
1084	Aloysius H. Simmons	.10
1085	Joseph E. Cronin	.10
1086	William M. Dickey	.15
1087	Gordon S. Cochrane	.10
1088	Vernon L. Gomez	.10
1089	Howard E. Averill Sr.	.10
1090	Samuel F. West	.10
1091	Frank F. Frisch	.10
1092	William J. Herman	.10
1093	Harold J. Traynor	.10
1094	Joseph M. Medwick	.10
1095	Charles H. Klein	.10
1096	Hazen S. Cuyler	.10
1097	Melvin T. Ott	.15
1098	Walter T. Berger	.10
1099	Paul G. Waner	.10
1100	William H. Terry	.10
1101	Travis C. Jackson	.10
1102	Joseph F. Vaughan	.10
1103	Charles L. Hartnett	.10
1104	Alfonso R. Lopez	.10
1105	Carl O. Hubbell	.15
1106	Lonnie Warneke	.10
1107	Van L. Mungo	.10
1108	Johnny J.R. Martin	.10
1109	Jay H. Dean	.15
1110	Fredrick M. Frankhouse	.10
1111	Giulaedeau Spink Heydler	.10
1112	JG Taylor Spink/ Mrs. Spink	.10
1113	Hirchman, Keller	.10
1114	Victor E. Aldridge	.10
1115	Michael F. Higgins	.10
1116	Harold G. Carlson	.10
1117	Frederick L. Fitzsimmons	.10
1118	William H. Walters	.10
1119	Nicholas Altrock	.10
1120	Charles W. Dressen	.10
1121	Mark A. Koenig	.10
1122	Charles L. Gehringer	.10
1123	Lloyd V. Kennedy	.10
1124	Harlond B. Clift	.10
1125	Ernest G. Phelps	.10
1126	John R. Mize	.15
1127	Harold H. Schumacher	.10
1128	Ethan N. Allen	.10
1129	William A. Wambsganss	.10
1130	Frederick Leach	.10
1131	John W. Clancy	.10
1132	John F. Stewart	.10
1133	Wilbur L. Brubaker	.10
1134	Leslie Mann	.10
1135	Howard J. Ehmke	.10
1136	Aloysius H. Simmons	.10
1137	George L. Earnshaw	.10
1138	George W. Haas	.10
1139	Edmund J. Miller	.10
1140	Robert M. Grove	.15
1141	John P. Boley	.10
1142	Edward T. Collins Sr.	.10
1143	Walter E. French	.10
1144	Donald E. McNair	.10
1145	William D. Shores	.10
1146	Gordon S. Cochrane	.10
1147	Homer W. Summa	.10
1148	John P. Quinn	.10
1149	Max F. Bishop	.10
1150	James J. Dykes	.10
1151	George E. Walberg	.10
1152	James E. Foxx	.15
1153	George H. Burns	.10
1154	Roger M. Cramer	.10
1155	Samuel D. Hale	.10
1156	Edwin A. Rommel	.10
1157	Ralph F. Perkins	.10
1158	James J. Cronin	.10
1159	Cornelius Mack	.10
1160	Raymond C. Kolp	.10
1161	Clyde J. Manion	.10
1162	Franklin T. Grube	.10
1163	Stephen A. Swetonic	.10
1164	Joseph B. Tinker	.10
1165	John J. Evers	.15
1166	Frank L. Chance	.15
1167	Emerson Dickman	.10
1168	John T. Tobin	.10
1169	Wesley C. Ferrell	.10
1170	Jay H. Dean	.15
1171	Tony & Al Cuccinello (Tony Cuccinello, Al Cuccinello)	.10
1172	Harry Coveleski, Stan Coveleski	.10

1173	Bob Johnson, Roy Johnson	.10
1174	Andy & Hugh High	.10
1175	Joe Sewell, Luke Sewell	.10
1176	Joe Heving, John Heving	.10
1177	Ab & Ivy Wingo	.10
1178	Wade Killefer, Bill Killefer	.10
1179	Bubbles Hargrave, Pinky Hargrave	.10
1180	Paul Waner, Lloyd Waner	.10
1181	John S. Vander Meer	.10
1182	Joe G. Moore	.10
1183	Robert J. Burke	.10
1184	John F. Moore	.10
1185	John J. Egan	.10
1186	Thomas H. Connolly	.10
1187	Frank H. O'Loughlin	.10
1188	John E. Reardon	.10
1189	Charles B. Moran	.10
1190	William J. Klem	.10
1191	Albert D. Stark	.10
1192	Albert L. Orth	.10
1193	William E. Bransfield	.10
1194	Roy Van Graflan	.10
1195	Eugene F. Hart	.10
1196	John B. Conlan	.10
1197	Ralph A. Pinelli	.10
1198	John F. Sheridan	.10
1199	Richard F. Nallin	.10
1200	William H. Dineen	.10
1201	Henry F. O'Day	.10
1202	Charles Rigler	.10
1203	Robert D. Emslie	.10
1204	Charles H. Pfirman	.10
1205	Harry C. Geisel	.10
1206	Ernest C. Quigley	.10
1207	Emmett T. Ormsby	.10
1208	George A. Hildebrand	.10
1209	George J. Moriarty	.10
1210	William G. Evans	.10
1211	Clarence B. Owens	.10
1212	William A. McGowan	.10
1213	Walter K. Higbe	.10
1214	Taylor L. Douthit	.10
1215	Delmar D. Baker	.10
1216	Albert W. Demaree	.10
1217	Cornelius Mack	.10
1218	Napoleon Lajoie	.15
1219	John P. Wagner	.25
1220	Christopher Mathewson	.15
1221	Samuel E. Crawford	.10
1222	Tristram E. Speaker	.15
1223	Grover C. Alexander	.10
1224	Joseph E. Bowman	.10
1225	John D. Rigney	.10
1226	William E. Webb	.10
1227	Lloyd A. Moore	.10
1228	Bruce D. Campbell	.10
1229	Luzerne A. Blue	.10
1230	Mark A. Koenig	.10
1231	Walter H. Schang	.10
1232	Max Carey	.10
1233	Frank F. Frisch	.10
1234	Owen J. Bush	.10
1235	Goerge S. Davis	.10
1236	William G. Rogell	.10
1237	James A. Collins	.10
1238	Mauricel L. Burrus	.10
1239	Ernest E. Swanson	.10
1240	Elwood G. English	.10
1241	Joseph Harris	.10
1242	Harry H. McCurdy	.10
1243	Richard W. Bartell	.10
1244	Rupert L. Thompson	.10
1245	Charles B. Adams	.10
1246	Arthur N. Nehf	.10
1247	John G. Graney	.10
1248	Theodore A. Lyons	.10
1249	Louis H. Gehrig	.40
1250	Michael F. Welch	.10
1251	Urban C. Faber	.10
1252	Joseph J. McGinnity	.10
1253	Rogers Hornsby	.15
1254	Melvin T. Ott	.15
1255	Walter P. Johnson	.15
1256	Edgar C. Rice	.10
1257	James A. Tobin	.10
1258	Roger T. Peckinpaugh	.10
1259	George T. Stovall	.10
1260	Fredrick C. Merkle	.10
1261	Harry W. Collins	.10
1262	Henry C. Lind	.10
1263	George N. Rucker	.10
1264	Hollis J. Thurston	.10
1265	Alexander Metzler	.10
1266	Charles Martin Conlon	.10
1267	McCarty Gets Magee (Lew McCarty, Lee Magee)	.10
1268	Sliding Home	.10
1269	Kauff Safe at 3rd (Benny Kauff)	.10
1270	Groh Out at 3rd (Heine Groh)	.10
1271	Mollwitz Out at the Plate (Fred Mollwitz)	.10
1272	Burns Safe at Home	.10
1273	Lee Magee Out Stealing 3rd (Lee Magee)	.10
1274	Killefer Out at Plate (Bill Killefer)	.10
1275	John M. Warhop	.10
1276	Emil J. Leonard	.10
1277	Alvin F. Crowder	.10
1278	Chester P. Laabs	.10
1279	Leslie A. Bush	.10
1280	Raymond B. Bressler	.10
1281	Robet M. Brown	.10
1282	Bernard Deviveiros	.10

1283	Leslie W. Tietje	.10
1284	Charles Devens	.10
1285	Elliott A. Bigelow	.10
1286	John O. Dickshot	.10
1287	Charles L. Chatham	.10
1288	Walter E. Beall	.10
1289	Richard D. Attreau	.10
1290	Anthony V. Brief	.10
1291	James J. Gleason	.10
1292	Walter D. Shaner	.10
1293	Clifford R. Crawford	.10
1294	Manuel Salvo	.10
1295	Calvin L. Dorsett	.10
1296	Russell D. Peters	.10
1297	John D. Couch	.10
1298	Frank W. Ulrich	.10
1299	James M. Bivin	.10
1300	Paul E. Strand	.10
1301	John Y. Lanning	.10
1302	William R. Brenzel	.10
1303	Don Songer	.10
1304	Emil H. Levsen	.10
1305	Otto A. Bluege	.10
1306	Fabian S. Gaffke	.10
1307	Maurice J. Archdeacon	.10
1308	James B. Chaplin	.10
1309	Lawrence J. Rosenthal	.10
1310	William M. Bagwell	.10
1311	Ralph F. Dawson	.10
1312	John P.J. Sturm	.10
1313	Haskell C. Billings	.10
1314	Vernon S. Wilshere	.10
1315	Robert A. Asbjornson	.10
1316	Henry J. Steinbacher	.10
1317	Stanwood F. Baumgartner	.10
1318	Checklist 991-1100	.10
1319	Checklist 1101-1210	.10
1320	Checklist 1211-1320	.10

1994 Conlon Collection Burgundy

A parallel version of the 1994 Conlon series with burgundy, rather than black, borders was issued as a one-per-pack insert.

		NM/M
Complete Set (330):		30.00
Common Player:		.50

1995 Conlon Collection Prototypes

LOU GEHRIG
NEW YORK YANKEES – 1ST BASE   1935

Megacards issued this 10-card series of prototypes to introduce its basic series for 1995. Cards are similar to the issued versions except that they lack the gold-foil enhancements on front and have different card numbers on some of the card backs. Cards have "PROMOTIONAL" printed diagonally on the back. Prototypes are listed here alphabetically.

		NM/M
Complete Set (10):		12.00
Common Player:		2.00
(1)	Lou Boudreau	2.00
(2)	Ray Chapman	2.00
(3)	Charles Comiskey	2.00
(4)	Bill Dickey	2.00
(5)	Bob Feller	2.00
(6)	Lou Gehrig	3.00
(7)	Charles L. Hartnett	2.00
(8)	Walter J.V. Maranville	2.00
(9)	Babe Ruth	2.00
(10)	Tris Speaker	2.00

1995 Conlon Collection

ANDY COHEN
NEW YORK GIANTS – 2ND BASE   1926

Gold-foil enhanced printing was a first for the Conlon Collection in 1995. For the first time, each regular card in the issue featured gold frames around the black-and-white photos, and a gold Conlon Collection seal at lower-right. Background for the 1995 cards is in dark green, with typography in white. Backs are black-and-white and feature an in-depth descriptive vignette. In its fifth year, numbers for Conlon Collection cards continued from previous years, beginning at #1321. The first series, cards 1321-1430, were issued in February, a second series, #1431-1540, was announced for August release but was never issued. A special Babe Ruth 100th birthday anniversary card was included with the issue, bearing a combined Topps/Conlon Collection logo and paralleling card #3 in the 1995 Topps issue. Conlon cards for 1995 were issued in plastic clam-shell packaging of 22, 55 or 110 cards. Once again, many of the cards in the set were grouped into themes such as "Baseball Goes to War," "Nicknames" and "Beating the Odds."

		NM/M
Complete Set, Commemorative Tin:		100.00
Complete Set (111):		80.00
Common Player:		1.00
1321	Grover Alexander	1.00
1322	Christy Mathewson	1.50
1323	Eddie Grant	1.00
1324	Gabby Street	1.00
1325	Hank Gowdy	1.00
1326	Jack Bentley	1.00
1327	Eppa Rixey	1.00
1328	Bob Shawkey	1.00
1329	Rabbit Maranville	1.00
1330	Casey Stengel	1.00
1331	Herb Pennock	1.00
1332	Eddie Collins	1.00
1333	Buddy Hassett	1.00
1334	Andy Cohen	1.00
1335	Hank Greenberg	1.50
1336	Andy High	1.00
1337	Bob Feller	1.00
1338	George Earnshaw	1.00
1339	Jack Knott	1.00
1340	Larry French	1.00
1341	Skippy Roberge	1.00
1342	Boze Berger	1.00
1343	Bill Posedel	1.00
1344	Kirby Higbe	1.00
1345	Bob Neighbors	1.00
1346	Hugh Mulcahy	1.00
1347	Harry Walker	1.00
1348	Buddy Lewis	1.00
1349	Cecil Travis	1.00
1350	Moe Berg	2.00
1351	Nixey Callahan	1.00
1352	Heinie Peitz	1.00
1353	Doc White	1.00
1354	Smokey Joe Wood	1.00
1355	Larry Gardner	1.00
1356	Steve O'Neill	1.00
1357	Tris Speaker	1.00
1358	Bill Wambsganss	1.00
1359	Geo. H. Burns	1.00
1360	Charlie Jamieson	1.00
1361	Les Nunamaker	1.00
1362	Stan Coveleski	1.00
1363	Joe Sewell	1.00
1364	Jim Bagby	1.00
1365	Duster Mails	1.00
1366	Jack Graney	1.00
1367	Elmer Smith	1.00
1368	Tommy Leach	1.00
1369	Russ Ford	1.00
1370	Harry Wolter	1.00
1371	Dazzy Vance	1.00
1372	Germany Schaefer	1.00
1373	Elbie Fletcher	1.00
1374	Clark Griffith	1.00
1375	Al Simmons	1.00
1376	Billy Jurges	1.00
1377	Earl Averill	1.00
1378	Bill Klem	1.00
1379	Armando Marsans	1.00
1380	Mike Gonzalez	1.00
1381	Jacques Fournier	1.00
1382	Ol' Stubblebeard (Burleigh Grimes)	1.00
1383	Freshest Man on Earth (Arlie Latham)	1.00
1384	Cracker (Ray Schalk)	1.00
1385	Goose (Goose Goslin)	1.00
1386	Unser Choe (Joe Hauser)	1.00
1387	The People's Cherce (Dixie Walker)	1.00
1388	The Crab (Jesse Burkett)	1.00
1389	Mountain Music (Cliff Melton)	1.00
1390	Gee (Gee Walker)	1.00
1391	Tony Cuccinello	1.00

1392	Vern Kennedy	1.00
1393	Tuck Stainback	1.00
1394	Ed Barrow	1.00
1395	Ford Frick	1.00
1396	Ban Johnson	1.00
1397	Charles Comiskey	1.00
1398	Jacob Ruppert	1.00
1399	Branch Rickey	1.00
1400	Jack Kieran	1.00
1401	Mike Ryba	1.00
1402	Stan Spence	1.00
1403	Red Barrett	1.00
1404	Gabby Hartnett	1.00
1405	Babe Ruth	3.00
1406	Fred Merkle	1.00
1407	Claude Passeau	1.00
1408	Smokey Joe Wood	1.00
1409	Cliff Heathcote	1.00
1410	Walt Cruise	1.00
1411	Cookie Lavagetto	1.00
1412	Tony Lazzari	1.00
1413	Atley Donald	1.00
1414	Ken Raffensberger	1.00
1415	Dizzy Trout	1.00
1416	Augie Galan	1.00
1417	Monty Stratton	1.00
1418	Claude Passeau	1.00
1419	Oscar Grimes Jr.	1.00
1420	Rollie Hemsley	1.00
1421	Lou Gehrig	2.00
1422	Tom Sunkel	1.00
1423	Tris Speaker	1.00
1424	Chick Fewster	1.00
1425	Lou Boudreau	1.00
1426	Hank Leiber	1.00
1427	Eddie Mayo	1.00
1428	Charley Gelbert	1.00
1429	Jackie Hayes	1.00
1430	Checklist 1321-1430	1.00
3C	Babe Ruth (100th Birthday)	4.00

1995 Conlon Collection In the Zone

An eight-card set comparing Ken Griffey Jr. with superstars of the past was randomly inserted into 1995 Conlon Collection packs. Fronts feature a colorized background photo of the player with whom Griffey is being compared. A smaller color photo of Griffey is in the foreground. An "In the Zone" logo is at lower-left. Backs share a background photo of Griffey and have a black-and-white portrait of the comparison player in the upper-left. Narrative describes how the two players compare. A card number is at upper-right in the Zone logo. Megacard and Cooperstown Collection logos are at bottom. The first six cards of the series coould be found in Conlon Collection packs, cards 7 and 8 were available only through a mail-in offer for $2 plus five proofs-of-purchase. The print run was announced as no more than 50,000 sets.

		NM/M
Complete Set (8):		12.00
Common Card:		2.00
1	Ken Griffey Jr., Babe Ruth	3.50
2	Ken Griffey Jr., Lou Gehrig	4.00
3	Ken Griffey Jr., Ty Cobb	3.00
4	Ken Griffey Jr., Jimmie Foxx	2.00
5	Ken Griffey Jr., Mel Ott	2.00
6	Ken Griffey Jr., Joe Jackson	3.00
7	Ken Griffey Jr., Tris Speaker	2.00
8	Ken Griffey Jr., Jim Bottomley	2.00

1979-83 Coral-Lee Postcards

A number of baseball subjects were among a series of sports postcards published by Coral-Lee of California. Two formats are seen,

---

standard postcard size of 3-1/2" x 5-1/2", and a larger 4" x 6" style seen on cards numbered 14 or higher. The standard-size cards have borderless color portrait photos on front, with no identification. Postcard style backs have the player's id, along with publisher, printer and copyright information in black-and-white. Most are dated. The larger cards have action photos on front, with backs similar to the smaller type. This list may not be complete as far as baseball-related cards within the series.

		NM/M
Common Player:		
1	Pete Rose	3.00
2	Davey Lopes	.25
3	Dave Winfield	1.50
4	Billy Martin	1.00
5	George Steinbrenner, Billy Martin, Reggie Jackson, Thurman Munson	1.50
6	Reggie Jackson	1.50
7	Bruce Kison	.25
8	Bobby Grich	.25
9	Rod Carew	.50
10	Tommy John	.25
11	Dick Howser	.25
12	George Brett	1.00
13	Brooks Robinson	1.50
14-C	Cal Ripken Jr.	2.00
15-C	Carl Yastrzemski	1.00
16-C	Joe Morgan	.50
18-C	Graig Nettles	.25
69	Willie Mays, Ronald Reagan, Edward Stack	1.00
81	Fernando Valenzuela, Jose Lopez Portillo	1.00

1988-93 Costacos Brothers Ad Cards

During the hey-day of sports hero personality posters in the late 1980s and early 1990s, one of the industry's major players, Costacos Brothers, issued a series of 4" x 6" cards to advertise their poster offerings. Card fronts duplicate the issued poster, while backs contain an ad for the poster company. Players in many sports were included in the series but only the baseball players are listed here.

		NM/M
Complete Set (31):		125.00
Common Player:		4.00
(1)	Barry Bonds (License to Thrill)	10.00
(2)	Bobby Bonilla (Bobby Bo)	4.00
(3)	Will Clark (Thriller)	4.00
(4)	Will Clark (Willpower)	4.00
(5)	Roger Clemens (The Rocket)	8.00
(6)	Darren Daulton (D-Day)	4.00
(7)	Glenn Davis (The Big Bopper)	4.00

---

(8)	Andre Dawson (Class for All Seasons) (w/Jordan, Payton)	4.00
(9)	Lenny Dykstra (Nails)	4.00
(10)	Dennis Eckersley (Cy of Relief)	5.00
(11)	Andres Galarraga (The Big Cat)	4.00
(12)	Kirk Gibson (Big Game Hunter)	4.00
(13)	Dwight Gooden (Doc)	4.00
(14)	Tom Gordon (Flash)	4.00
(15)	Mike Greenwell (Gator Tough)	4.00
(16)	Ken Griffey Sr., Ken Griffey Jr. (The Next Generation)	8.00
(17)	Ken Griffey Jr. (In Jr. We Trust)	9.00
(18)	Derek Jeter (Jeter Airways)	9.00
(19)	Howard Johnson (HoJo)	4.00
(20)	Eric Karros (The Artful Dodger)	4.00
(21)	Barry Larkin (Red Hot)	4.00
(22)	Don Mattingly (The Man With The Golden Glove)	7.50
(23)	Fred McGriff (Blue Thunder)	4.00
(24)	Kevin Mitchell (Bat Man)	4.00
(25)	Kirby Puckett (The Wrecking Ball)	7.50
(26)	Tim Raines (Steal Wheels)	4.00
(27)	Harold Reynolds (Turning Point)	4.00
(28)	Benito Santiago (Thou Shalt Not Steal!)	4.00
(29)	Steve Sax (Sax Appeal)	4.00
(30)	Darryl Strawberry (Straw-Some)	4.00
(31)	Greg Swindell, Pete Harnisch, Doug Drabek (Shooting Stars)	4.00

1991 Country Hearth Mariners

This 29-card set was inserted in loaves of bread and also given away at a Mariner home game. The card fronts feature full-color glossy photos, while the flip sides feature statistics.

		NM/M
Complete Set (29):		15.00
Common Player:		.50
1	Jim Lefebvre	.50
2	Jeff Schaefer	.50
3	Harold Reynolds	.75
4	Greg Briley	.50
5	Scott Bradley	.50
6	Dave Valle	.50
7	Edgar Martinez	1.00
8	Pete O'Brien	.50
9	Omar Vizquel	1.00
10	Tino Martinez	1.00
11	Scott Bankhead	.50
12	Bill Swift	.50
13	Jay Buhner	1.00
14	Alvin Davis	.50
15	Ken Griffey, Jr.	10.00
16	Tracy Jones	.50
17	Brent Knackert	.50
18	Henry Cotto	.50
19	Ken Griffey Sr.	.50
20	Keith Comstock	.50
21	Brian Holman	.50
22	Russ Swan	.50
23	Mike Jackson	.50
24	Erik Hanson	.50
25	Mike Schooler	.50
26	Randy Johnson	3.00
27	Rich DeLucia	.50
28	The Griffeys (Ken Griffey Jr., Ken Griffey Sr.)	2.00
29	Mascot	.50

1993 Country Time Brooks Robinson

Sponsored by Country Time drink mix, this set honors the career of the Orioles' Hall of Fame third baseman. The 2-1/2" x 3-5/8" cards feature color and colorized action photos with pale yellow frames, black diamond and textured green backgrounds and red and black borders. "Country Time Legends" and MLB logos appear in one of the bottom corners. Backs are printed in black, green and yellow and have a few sentences about some phase of Robinson's career. The cards are not numbered.

		NM/M
Complete Set (8):		7.00
Common Card:		1.00
(1)	Title Card	.25
(2)	Brooks Robinson/Btg (Back view.)	1.00
(3)	Brooks Robinson/Btg (Front view.)	1.00
(4)	Brooks Robinson/Btg (Horizontal.)	1.00
(5)	Brooks Robinson/Fldg (Horizontal white jersey.)	1.00
(6)	Brooks Robinson/Fldg (Horizontal orange jersey.)	1.00
(7)	Brooks Robinson/Fldg (Vertical.)	1.00
(8)	Brooks Robinson (Saluting crowd.)	1.00

1982 Cracker Jack

The Topps-produced 1982 Cracker Jack set was issued to promote the first "Old Timers Baseball Classic," held in Washington, D.C. The set was issued in two sheets of eight player cards, plus an advertising card located in the center. Individual cards are 2-1/2" x 3-1/2", with the complete sheets measuring 7-1/2" x 10-1/2". Cards #1-8 feature American League players with #9-16 being former National League stars. Fronts feature a full-color photo inside a Cracker Jack border. Backs contain the sponsor's logo plus a short player biography and his lifetime pitching or batting record. Complete sheets were available through a write-in offer.

		NM/M
Complete Panel Set (2):		12.00
Complete Singles Set (17):		10.00
Common Single Player:		.50
A.L. Panel		6.00
1	Larry Doby	.50
2	Bob Feller	.50
3	Whitey Ford	.50
4	Al Kaline	.50
5	Harmon Killebrew	.50
6	Mickey Mantle	5.00
7	Tony Oliva	.50
8	Brooks Robinson	.50
---	Advertising Card	.05
N.L. Panel		4.00
9	Hank Aaron	2.00
10	Ernie Banks	.50
11	Ralph Kiner	.50
12	Eddie Mathews	.50
13	Willie Mays	2.00
14	Robin Roberts	.50
15	Duke Snider	.50
16	Warren Spahn	.50
---	Advertising Card	.05

1991 Cracker Jack Topps 1st Series

In their first issue in almost 10 years, Cracker Jack inserted miniature cards (1-1/4" x 1-3/4") as the toy surprise in packages of the famous snack. The company produced two 36-card series, portraying many of

---

the top stars in the game. Card fronts are identical to the corresponding regular-issue Topps cards, but the backs are significantly different because of the small amount of space available for statistics. The Cracker Jack sailor logo appears on the bright red backs, along with copyright information listing Borden, Cracker Jack's parent company. These are sometimes found on 2-1/2" x 3-1/2" cards bearing four different of the minicards; these were cut from sheets illegally removed from the printer.

		NM/M
Complete Set (36):		10.00
Common Player:		.25
1	Nolan Ryan	3.00
2	Paul Molitor	.60
3	Tim Raines	.25
4	Frank Viola	.25
5	Sandy Alomar Jr.	.25
6	Ryne Sandberg	.75
7	Don Mattingly	1.00
8	Pedro Guerrero	.25
9	Jose Rijo	.25
10	Jose Canseco	.40
11	Dave Parker	.25
12	Doug Drabek	.25
13	Cal Ripken	3.00
14	Dave Justice	.25
15	George Brett	1.00
16	Eric Davis	.25
17	Mark Langston	.25
18	Rickey Henderson	.60
19	Barry Bonds	3.00
20	Kevin Maas	.25
21	Len Dykstra	.25
22	Roger Clemens	1.00
23	Robin Yount	.60
24	Mark Grace	.25
25	Bo Jackson	.40
26	Tony Gwynn	.75
27	Mark McGwire	2.00
28	Dwight Gooden	.25
29	Wade Boggs	.75
30	Kevin Mitchell	.25
31	Cecil Fielder	.25
32	Bobby Thigpen	.25
33	Benito Santiago	.25
34	Kirby Puckett	.75
35	Will Clark	.25
36	Ken Griffey Jr.	1.50

1991 Cracker Jack Topps 2nd Series

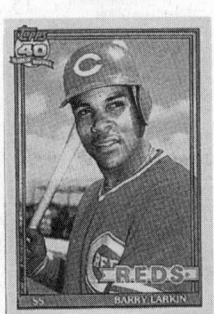

A second series of 36 micro cards was found in Cracker Jack boxes later in the 1991 season. Again numbered from 1-18, the 1-1/4" x 1-3/4" cards carry a "2nd Series" designation on the back above the card number. Like the first series, these cards replicate the front of the 1991 Topps issue and have modified back design which includes the "Sailor Jack" logo of the candy company. Four-card panels, believed to have been cut from sheets illegally removed from the printer, are known.

		NM/M
Complete Set (36):		5.00
Common Player:		.35
1	Eddie Murray	.75
2	Carlton Fisk	.75
3	Eric Anthony	.40
4	Kelly Gruber	.40
5	Von Hayes	.40
6	Ben McDonald	.40
7	Andre Dawson	.60
8	Ellis Burks	.40
9	Matt Williams	.40
10	Dave Stewart	.40
11	Barry Larkin	.40
12	Chuck Finley	.40
13	Shane Andrews	.40
14	Bret Saberhagen	.40
15	Bobby Bonilla	.40
16	Roberto Kelly	.40
17	Orel Hershiser	.40
18	Ruben Sierra	.40
19	Ron Gant	.40
20	Frank Thomas	1.00
21	Tim Wallach	.40
22	Gregg Olson	.40
23	Shawon Dunston	.40
24	Kent Hrbek	.40
25	Ramon Martinez	.40
26	Alan Trammell	.40
27	Ozzie Smith	2.00
28	Bob Welch	.40
29	Chris Sabo	.40
30	Steve Sax	.40
31	Bip Roberts	.40
32	Dave Steib	.40
33	Howard Johnson	.40
34	Mike Greenwell	.40
35	Delino DeShields	.40
36	Alex Fernandez	.40

1992 Cracker Jack Donruss Series 1

In 1992, Cracker Jack turned to Donruss to produce the cards for the surprise in their packages. The first series of micro cards (1-1/4" x 1-3/4") was numbered 1-36 and features many top players. Card fronts are identical to the regular-issue '92 Donruss, but the backs have a different format and much less information because of the tiny space available. The backs have a blue border, with some spot red printing and the Cracker Jack sailor logo in the lower-left corner.

		NM/M
Complete Set (36):		20.00
Common Player:		.50
Album:		10.00
1	Dennis Eckersley	1.00
2	Jeff Bagwell	1.25
3	Jim Abbott	.50
4	Steve Avery	.50
5	Kelly Gruber	.50
6	Ozzie Smith	1.50
7	Lance Dickson	.50
8	Robin Yount	1.25
9	Brett Butler	.50
10	Sandy Alomar Jr.	.50
11	Travis Fryman	.50
12	Ken Griffey Jr.	2.00
13	Cal Ripken	4.00
14	Will Clark	.50
15	Nolan Ryan	4.00
16	Tony Gwynn	1.50
17	Roger Clemens	1.75
18	Wes Chamberlain	.50
19	Barry Larkin	.50
20	Brian McRae	.50
21	Marquis Grissom	.50
22	Cecil Fielder	.50
23	Dwight Gooden	.50
24	Chuck Knoblauch	.50
25	Jose Canseco	.65
26	Terry Pendleton	.50
27	Ivan Rodriguez	1.00
28	Ryne Sandberg	1.50
29	Kent Hrbek	.50
30	Ramon Martinez	.50
31	Todd Zeile	.50
32	Hal Morris	.50
33	Robin Ventura	.50
34	Doug Drabek	.50
35	Frank Thomas	1.25
36	Don Mattingly	1.75

1992 Cracker Jack Donruss Series 2

The Second Series of the 1992 Crack Jack Donruss set is almost identical to the first series, with the only change being different players and red border on the back instead of blue. The micro cards are numbered 1-36, just as in the first series.

		NM/M
Complete Set (36):		15.00
Common Player:		.50
1	Craig Biggio	.50
2	Tom Glavine	.65

3	David Justice	.50
5	Lee Smith	.50
6	Mark Grace	.50
7	George Bell	.50
8	Darryl Strawberry	.50
9	Eric Davis	.50
10	Ivan Calderon	.50
11	Royce Clayton	.50
12	Matt Williams	.50
13	Fred McGriff	.50
14	Len Dykstra	.50
15	Barry Bonds	3.00
16	Reggie Sanders	.50
17	Chris Sabo	.50
18	Howard Johnson	.50
19	Bobby Bonilla	.50
20	Rickey Henderson	.75
21	Mark Langston	.50
22	Joe Carter	.50
23	Paul Molitor	.75
24	Glenallen Hill	.50
25	Edgar Martinez	.50
26	Gregg Olson	.50
27	Ruben Sierra	.50
28	Julio Franco	.50
29	Phil Plantier	.50
30	Wade Boggs	1.00
31	George Brett	1.25
32	Alan Trammell	.50
33	Kirby Puckett	1.00
34	Scott Erickson	.50
35	Matt Nokes	.50
36	Danny Tartabull	.50
	Jack McDowell	.50

1993 Cracker Jack Anniversary

In 1993, as part of the company's 100th anniversary celebration, Cracker Jack issued a 24-card set of mini replicas of its famous 1915 cards. The cards, 1-1/4" x 1-3/4", were included in specially-marked packages of the famous snack. The set features Hall of Famers such as Cobb, Mathewson, Walter Johnson and others, plus the Joe Jackson card. A red plastic album, with color pictures of the replicas inside, was also available.

		NM/M
Complete Set (24):		10.00
Common Player:		.50
Album:		5.00
1	Ty Cobb	1.50
2	Joe Jackson	3.00
3	Honus Wagner	1.00
4	Christy Mathewson	.75
5	Walter Johnson	.75
6	Tris Speaker	.50
7	Grover Alexander	.50
8	Nap Lajoie	.50
9	Rube Marquard	.50
10	Connie Mack	.50
11	Johnny Evers	.50
12	Branch Rickey	.50
13	Fred Clarke	.50
14	Harry Hooper	.50
15	Zack Wheat	.50
16	Joe Tinker	.50
17	Eddie Collins	.50
18	Mordecai Brown	.50
19	Eddie Plank	.50
20	Rabbit Maranville	.50
21	John McGraw	.50
22	Miller Huggins	.50
23	Ed Walsh	.50
24	Leslie Bush	.50

1997 Cracker Jack All Stars

After an hiatus of three years, Cracker Jack resumed the use of baseball cards as premiums in 1997 with a 20-card All Stars set. Like the other CJ issues of the 1990s, this set features miniature (1-5/16" x 1-3/4") cards. Cards feature player action photos on front along with a Cracker Jack All Stars logo. Photos have uniform logos removed as the set is licensed only by the Players Association and not Major League Baseball. Backs are printed in red and blue with Cracker Jack and MLBPA logos, a few stats and personal data. Cards were also distributed as prizes in various promotional contests conducted by American Sports Classics, which inserted a logo card within the regular Cracker Jack prize wrapping.

		NM/M
Complete Set (20):		15.00
Common Player:		.50
1	Jeff Bagwell	1.00
2	Chuck Knoblauch	.50
3	Cal Ripken Jr.	3.00
4	Chipper Jones	1.50
5	Derek Jeter	3.00
6	Barry Larkin	.50
7	Bernie Williams	.50
8	Barry Bonds	3.00
9	Kenny Lofton	.50
10	Gary Sheffield	.65
11	Sammy Sosa	1.50
12	Paul Molitor	1.00
13	Andres Galarraga	.50
14	Ivan Rodriguez	.75
15	Mike Piazza	2.00
16	Andy Pettitte	.65
17	Tom Glavine	.65
18	Albert Belle	.50
19	Mark McGwire	2.50
20	Mo Vaughn	.50
Album:		2.00

1999 Cracker Jack Mac Stickers

In conjunction with its season-long promotion with Rawlings in which various Big Mac equipment items were given away, individual boxes of the snack could be found bearing one of 10 different McGwire stickers. The 1-1/2" x 2-1/8" stickers each include some type of interactive play element. Values shown are for opened, but complete, prize booklets. The color photos of McGwire on the stickers have had uniform logos removed.

	NM/M
Complete Set (10):	5.00
Common Sticker:	.50

1999 Cracker Jack Mark McGwire Home Run Record

One of several premiums which were part of a Rawlings promotion in boxes of Cracker Jack and related mail-in offers, this card marks McGwire's 70-HR season of 1998. The front is optical-variable, offering an image of McGwire in his home run-followthrough and, with a change in viewing angle, tipping his helmet to the crowd. Back has the date and distance of each of his 1998 homers, along with Rawling and Cracker Jack logos. The card is in standard 2-1/2" x 3-1/2" format.

	NM/M
Mark McGwire	10.00

1999 Cracker Jack Mark McGwire Spinners

"Home Run Around" is the name given to these spinner discs found as prizes in Cracker Jack boxes. The 1-5/8" plastic discs have a "magic motion" picture of McGwire on front with a large "70." Around the front rim are segments with other numbers. Instructions on back are to spin the disc and stop it to see if the player can hit more homers than McGwire. A raised spot at center allow the disc to be spun. While the Rawlings logo appears on front and back, Cardinals uniform logos have been deleted from the photos.

	NM/M
Complete Set (5):	10.00
Common Disc:	2.00

2002 Cracker Jack All-Stars

After skipping four years, Cracker Jack resumed the use of baseball cards as premiums in 2002 with a 30-card All-Stars set produced by Topps. Like the CJ issues of the 1990s, this set features miniature (1-5/8" x 2-1/8") cards with player action photos on front along with a Cracker Jack All-Stars logo. The checklist shows one player from each team. Backs are printed in color with Cracker Jack, Topps and MLB/MLBPA logos, a few stats and personal data. Complete sets in a customer holder were available by mail for $9.99.

		NM/M
Complete Set (30):		12.00
Common Player:		.25
1	Roger Clemens	.75
2	Pedro Martinez	.50
3	Carlos Delgado	.25
4	Jeff Conine	.25
5	Greg Vaughn	.25
6	Jim Thome	.40
7	Brad Radke	.25
8	Frank Thomas	.50
9	Steve Sparks	.25
10	Carlos Beltran	.35
11	Ichiro	2.00
12	Mark Mulder	.25
13	Troy Glaus	.45
14	Alex Rodriguez	1.50
15	Chipper Jones	.65
16	Bobby Abreu	.25
17	Mike Piazza	1.00
18	Cliff Floyd	.25
19	Vladimir Guerrero	.50
20	Jeff Bagwell	.25
21	Albert Pujols	1.50
22	Sammy Sosa	.65
23	Richie Sexson	.25
24	Sean Casey	.25
25	Brian Giles	.25
26	Randy Johnson	.50
27	Barry Bonds	2.00
28	Kevin Brown	.25
29	Phil Nevin	.25
30	Todd Helton	.40

2003 Cracker Jack All-Stars

The baseball cards inserted in boxes of Cracker Jack for 2003 were an entirely new format, printed on round-cornered 1-5/8" x 1-5/8" plastic squares. The printing is formatted to give the cards a diamond shape. Fronts have a player portrait in the upper half with personal data below. Team and sponsor logos also appear. Backs have team and sponsor logos, along with those of the licensors. The unnumbered cards are checklisted here alphabetically. Besides product insertion, the complete set was available by mail, along with a color 10-1/2" x 21" poster in which the cards could be displayed, for about $12.

		NM/M
Complete Set (32):		12.00
Common Player:		.50
Poster:		5.00
(1)	Roberto Alomar	.60
(2)	Jeff Bagwell	.75
(3)	Tony Batista	.50
(4)	Carlos Beltran	.60
(5)	Bret Boone	.50
(6)	Ellis Burks	.50
(7)	A.J. Burnett	.50
(8)	Pat Burrell	.50
(9)	Sean Casey	.50
(10)	Carlos Delgado	.65
(11)	Damion Easley	.50
(12)	Jason Giambi	.65
(13)	Brian Giles	.50
(14)	Troy Glaus	.65
(15)	Shawn Green	.60
(16)	Ben Grieve	.50
(17)	Vladimir Guerrero	.75
(18)	Todd Helton	.65
(19)	Torii Hunter	.50
(20)	Randy Johnson	.75
(21)	Chipper Jones	1.00
(22)	Ryan Klesko	.50
(23)	Paul Konerko	.60
(24)	Pedro Martinez	.75
(25)	Mark Mulder	.50
(26)	Robb Nen	.50
(27)	Rafael Palmeiro	.65
(28)	Albert Pujols	2.00
(29)	Ben Sheets	.50
(30)	Sammy Sosa	1.00
(31)	All-Star Game Logo	.15
(32)	Cracker Jack Logo	.15

2004 Cracker Jack Baseball History

Illustrations of great moments in baseball history are reproduced in this set of Cracker Jack prize inserts. When opened,

each 2" x 2-1/2" prize wrapper has the illustration on one side and narrative on the other. If detached and folded, the illustration reveals the answer to a trivia question.

		NM/M
Complete Set (10):		10.00
Common Player:		.50
(1)	Aaron Hits #715 (Hank Aaron)	1.00
(2)	Back to Back (Johnny Vander Meer)	1.00
(3)	Jackie Robinson	1.00
(4)	Joe DiMaggio - The Streak	1.00
(5)	Larsen's Perfect Game (Don Larsen)	.50
(6)	Pete Gray	.25
(7)	Roberto Clemente	2.00
(8)	Ruth's Called Shot (Babe Ruth)	2.00
(9)	Shot Heard Round the World (Bobby Thomson)	.50
(10)	The Catch (Willie Mays)	1.00

2005 Cracker Jack Ballpark Legends

A set of 10 small booklets featuring past stars was produced for inclusion in 99-cent packages of Cracker Jack. The prize was in the form of a small (about 1-1/2" x 2-1/8") booklet about the individual player, with a baseball card in the center. The booklet has a career summary and checklist. The card is a heavily retouched photo with uniform details removed, "BALLPARK LEGENDS" at top and the player name between stars at bottom. Backs have biographical data, career highlights and lifetime stats.

Complete Set, Booklets (10):
Common Player Booklet:
Unattached Cards: 50 Percent

1980-83 Cramer Baseball Legends

Consecutively numbered, this set was issued over a period of four years by Cramer Sports Promotions, the forerunner of today's Pacific card company. Sold in wax packs and measuring the standard 2-1/2" x 3-1/2", the cards have a sepia-toned photo on front with a black frame. In the background is a weathered wooden slat design with the player's name on a hanging board beneath. The borders are dull yellow. Backs are printed in brown and include a few personal data, career stats and a career summary. Cards 1-30 were issued in 1980; #31-60 in 1981; #61-90 in 1982 and #90-124 in 1983. Cards #121-124 were issued on the 1983 wax box.

		NM/M
Complete Set (124):		45.00
Complete Set (120):		
Common Player:		.25
1980		
1	Babe Ruth	3.00
2	Heinie Manush	.25
3	Rabbit Maranville	.25
4	Earl Averill	.25
5	Joe DiMaggio	2.00
6	Mickey Mantle	3.00
7	Hank Aaron	1.50
8	Stan Musial	1.25
9	Bill Terry	.25
10	Sandy Koufax	1.50
11	Ernie Lombardi	.25
12	Dizzy Dean	.25
13	Lou Gehrig	2.00
14	Walter Alston	.25
15a	Jackie Robinson/Portrait	4.00
15b	Jackie Robinson/Btg	1.00
16	Jimmie Foxx	.25
17	Billy Southworth	.25
18	Honus Wagner	.50
19	Duke Snider	.25
20	Rogers Hornsby	.25
21	Paul Waner	.25
22	Luke Appling	.25
23	Billy Herman	.25
24	Lloyd Waner	.25
25	Fred Hutchinson	.25
26	Eddie Collins	.25
27	Lefty Grove	.25
28	Chuck Connors	.25
29	Lefty O'Doul	.25
30	Hank Greenberg	.25
1981		
31	Ty Cobb	2.50
32	Enos Slaughter	.25
33	Ernie Banks	.45
34	Christy Mathewson	.35
35	Mel Ott	.25
36	Pie Traynor	.25
37	Clark Griffith	.25
38	Mickey Cochrane	.25
39	Joe Cronin	.25
40	Leo Durocher	.25
41	Frank Baker	.25
42	Joe Tinker	.25
43	John McGraw	.25
44	Bill Dickey	.25
45	Walter Johnson	.35
46	Frankie Frisch	.25
47	Casey Stengel	.25
48	Willie Mays	2.00
49	Johnny Mize	.25
50	Roberto Clemente	4.00
51	Burleigh Grimes	.25
52	Pee Wee Reese	.25
53	Bob Feller	.25
54	Brooks Robinson	.25
55	Sam Crawford	.25
56	Robin Roberts	.25
57	Warren Spahn	.25
58	Joe McCarthy	.25
59	Jocko Conlan	.25
60	Satchel Paige	.75
1982		
61	Ted Williams	3.00
62	George Kelly	.25
63	Gil Hodges	.25
64	Jim Bottomley	.25
65	Al Kaline	.25
66	Harvey Kuenn	.25
67	Yogi Berra	.25
68	Nellie Fox	.25
69	Harmon Killebrew	.25
70	Edd Roush	.25
71	Mordecai Brown	.25
72	Gabby Hartnett	.25
73	Early Wynn	.25
74	Nap Lajoie	.25
75	Charlie Grimm	.25
76	Joe Garagiola	.25
77	Ted Lyons	.25
78	Mickey Vernon	.25
79	Lou Bourdreau	.25
80	Al Dark	.25
81	Ralph Kiner	.25
82	Phil Rizzuto	.25
83	Stan Hack	.25
84	Frank Chance	.25
85	Ray Schalk	.25
86	Bill McKechnie	.25
87	Travis Jackson	.25
88	Pete Reiser	.25
89	Carl Hubbell	.25
90	Roy Campanella	.25
1983		
91	Cy Young	.25
92	Kiki Cuyler	.25
93	Chief Bender	.25
94	Richie Ashburn	.25
95	Riggs Stephenson	.25
96	Minnie Minoso	.25
97	Hack Wilson	.25
98	Al Lopez	.25
99	Willie Keeler	.25
100	Fred Lindstrom	.25
101	Roger Maris	.25
102	Roger Bresnahan	.25
103	Monty Stratton	.25
104	Goose Goslin	.25
105	Earle Combs	.25

#	Player	Price
106	Pepper Martin	.25
107	Joe Jackson	3.00
108	George Sisler	.25
109	Red Ruffing	.25
110	Johnny Vander Meer	.25
111	Herb Pennock	.25
112	Chuck Klein	.25
113	Paul Derringer	.25
114	Addie Joss	.25
115	Bobby Thomson	.25
116	Chick Hafey	.25
117	Lefty Gomez	.25
118	George Kell	.25
119	Al Simmons	.25
120	Bob Lemon	.25
121	Hoyt Wilhelm	1.00
122	Arky Vaughan	1.00
123	Frank Robinson	1.50
124	Grover Alexander	1.50

1991 Crown/Coke Orioles

Claiming to include every player for the modern (1954-1991) Baltimore Orioles, this 501-card set was issued in four series. The first three series contain 120 cards each in a format of a dozen perforated cards on each of 10 sheets. Those series were given away at May 17, June 28 and August 11 home games. The fourth series, 12 sheets of 12 cards each, including three blank cards, was available only at participating Crown gas stations, which also sold the first three series following the give-away days at the ballpark. Cards measure 2-1/2" x 3-3/16" and are perforated on two, three or four sides, depending on their position on the sheet. All players are featured in sepia-toned head shots, virtually all in Orioles' uniform. Around the photos are borders of, successively, green, orange, black and white. The player's name and position appear in a black banner above the photo. In the lower-left corner is a 1954-1991 Memorial Stadium "Season to Remember" logo. That logo is repeated at bottom-center of the black-and-white backs, flanked by the logos of Coca-Cola and Crown. A card number appears in the lower-right. Most cards were numbered alphabetically. Backs include stats for the player's major league career and time with the Orioles.

		NM/M
Complete Set (501):		30.00
Common Player:		.15
1	Don Aase	.15
2	Cal Abrams	.15
3	Jerry Adair	.15
4	Bobby Adams	.15
5	Mike Adamson	.15
6	Jay Aldrich	.15
7	Bob Alexander	.15
8	Doyle Alexander	.15
9	Brady Anderson	.40
10	John Anderson	.15
11	Mike Anderson	.15
12	Luis Aparicio	1.25
13	Tony Arnold	.15
14	Bobby Avila	.15
15	Benny Ayala	.15
16	Bob Bailor	.15
17	Frank Baker	.15
18	Jeff Ballard	.15
19	George Bamberger	.15
20	Steve Barber	.15
21	Ray "Buddy" Barker	.15
22	Ed Barnowski	.15
23	Jose Bautista	.15
24	Don Baylor	.40
25	Charlie Beamon	.15
26	Fred Beene	.15
27	Mark Belanger	.15
28	Eric Bell	.15
29	Juan Bell	.15
30	Juan Beniquez	.15
31	Neil Berry	.15
32	Frank Bertaina	.15
33	Fred Besana	.15
34	Vern Bickford	.15
35	Babe Birrer	.15
36	Paul Blair	.15
37	Curt Blefary	.15
38	Mike Blyzka	.15
39	Mike Boddicker	.15
40	Juan Bonilla	.15
41	Bob Bonner	.15
42	Dan Boone	.15
43	Rich Bordi	.15
44	Dave Boswell	.15
45	Sam Bowens	.15
46	Bob Boyd	.15
47	Gene Brabender	.15
48	Phil Bradley	.15
49	Jackie Brandt	.15
50	Marv Breeding	.15
51	Jim Brideweser	.15
52	Nellie Briles	.15
53	Dick Brown	.15
54	Hal Brown	.15
55	Larry Brown	.15
56	Mark Brown	.15
57	Marty Brown	.15
58	George Brunet	.15
59	Don Buford	.25
60	Al Bumbry	.15
61	Wally Bunker	.15
62	Leo Burke	.15
63	Rick Burleson	.15
64	Pete Burnside	.15
65	Jim Busby	.15
66	John Buzhardt	.15
67	Harry Byrd	.15
68	Enos Cabell	.15
69	Chico Carrasquel	.15
70	Camilo Carreon	.15
71	Foster Castleman	.15
72	Wayne Causey	.15
73	Art Ceccarelli	.15
74	Bob Chakales	.15
75	Tony Chevez	.15
76	Tom Chism	.15
77	Gino Cimoli	.15
78	Gil Coan	.15
79	Rich Coggins	.15
80	Joe Coleman	.15
81	Rip Coleman	.15
82	Fritz Connally	.15
83	Sandy Consuegra	.15
84	Doug Corbett	.15
85	Mark Corey	.15
86	Clint Courtney	.15
87	Billy Cox	.15
88	Dave Criscione	.15
89	Terry Crowley	.15
90	Todd Cruz	.15
91	Mike Cuellar	.30
92	Angie Dagres	.15
93	Clay Dalrymple	.15
94	Rich Dauer	.15
95	Jerry DaVanon	.15
96	Butch Davis	.15
97	Storm Davis	.15
98	Tommy Davis	.15
99	Doug DeCinces	.25
100	Luis DeLeon	.15
101	Ike Delock	.15
102	Rick Dempsey	.15
103	Mike Devereaux	.15
104	Chuck Diering	.15
105	Gordon Dillard	.15
106	Bill Dillman	.15
107	Mike Dimmel	.15
108	Ken Dixon	.15
109	Pat Dobson	.15
110	Tom Dodd	.15
111	Harry Dorish	.15
112	Moe Drabowsky	.15
113	Dick Drago	.15
114	Walt Dropo	.15
115	Tom Dukes	.15
116	Dave Duncan	.15
117	Ryne Duren	.15
118	Joe Durham	.15
119	Jim Dwyer	.15
120	Jim Dyck	.15
121	Mike Epstein	.15
122	Chuck Essegian	.15
123	Chuck Estrada	.15
124	Andy Etchebarren	.15
125	Hoot Evers	.15
126	Ed Farmer	.15
127	Chico Fernandez	.15
128	Don Ferrarese	.15
129	Jim Finigan	.15
130	Steve Finley	.15
131	Mike Fiore	.15
132	Eddie Fisher	.15
133	Jack Fisher	.15
134	Tom Fisher	.15
135	Mike Flanagan	.15
136	John Flinn	.15
137	Bobby Floyd	.15
138	Hank Foiles	.15
139	Dan Ford	.15
140	Dave Ford	.15
141	Mike Fornieles	.15
142	Howie Fox	.15
143	Tito Francona	.15
144	Joe Frazier	.15
145	Roger Freed	.15
146	Jim Fridley	.15
147	Jim Fuller	.15
148	Joe Gaines	.15
149	Vinicio "Chico" Garcia	.15
150	Kiko Garcia	.15
151	Billy Gardner	.15
152	Wayne Garland	.15
153	Tommy Gastall	.15
154	Jim Gentile	.25
155	Ken Gerhart	.15
156	Paul Gilliford	.15
157	Joe Ginsberg	.15
158	Leo Gomez	.15
159	Rene Gonzales	.15
160	Billy Goodman	.15
161	Dan Graham	.15
162	Ted Gray	.15
163	Gene Green	.15
164	Lenny Green	.15
165	Bobby Grich	.30
166	Mike Griffin	.15
167	Ross Grimsley	.15
168	Wayne Gross	.15
169	Glenn Gulliver	.15
170	Jackie Gutierrez	.15
171	John Habyan	.15
172	Harvey Haddix	.15
173	Bob Hale	.15
174	Dick Hall	.15
175	Bert Hamric	.15
176	Larry Haney	.15
177	Ron Hansen	.15
178	Jim Hardin	.15
179	Larry Harlow	.15
180	Pete Harnisch	.15
181	Tommy Harper	.15
182	Bob Harrison	.15
183	Roric Harrison	.15
184	Jack Harshman	.15
185	Mike Hart	.15
186	Paul Hartzell	.15
187	Grady Hatton	.15
188	Brad Havens	.15
189	Drungo Hazewood	.15
190	Jehosie Heard	.15
191	Mel Held	.15
192	Woodie Held	.15
193	Ellie Hendricks	.25
194	Leo Hernandez	.15
195	Whitey Herzog	.15
196	Kevin Hickey	.15
197	Billy Hoeft	.15
198	Chris Hoiles	.15
199	Fred Holdsworth	.15
200	Brian Holton	.15
201	Ken Holtzman	.15
202	Don Hood	.15
203	Sam Horn	.15
204	Art Houtteman	.15
205	Bruce Howard	.15
206	Rex Hudler	.15
207	Phil Huffman	.15
208	Keith Hughes	.15
209	Mark Huismann	.15
210	Tim Hulett	.15
211	Billy Hunter	.15
212	Dave Huppert	.15
213	Jim Hutto	.15
214	Dick Hyde	.15
215	Grant Jackson	.15
216	Lou Jackson	.15
217	Reggie Jackson	5.00
218	Ron Jackson	.15
219	Jesse Jefferson	.15
220	Stan Jefferson	.15
221	Bob Johnson	.15
222	Connie Johnson	.15
223	Darrell Johnson	.15
224	Dave Johnson	.15
225	Davey Johnson	.25
226	David Johnson	.15
227	Don Johnson	.15
228	Ernie Johnson	.15
229	Gordon Jones	.15
230	Ricky Jones	.15
231	O'Dell Jones	.15
232	Sam Jones	.15
233	George Kell	.75
234	Frank Kellert	.15
235	Pat Kelly	.15
236	Bob Kennedy	.15
237	Terry Kennedy	.15
238	Joe Kerrigan	.15
239	Mike Kinnunen	.15
240	Willie Kirkland	.15
241	Ron Kittle	.15
242	Billy Klaus	.15
243	Ray Knight	.25
244	Darold Knowles	.15
245	Dick Kokos	.15
246	Brad Komminsk	.15
247	Dave Koslo	.15
248	Wayne Krenchicki	.15
249	Lou Kretlow	.15
250	Dick Kryhoski	.15
251	Bob Kuzava	.15
252	Lee Lacy	.15
253	Hobie Landrith	.15
254	Tito Landrum	.15
255	Don Larsen	.25
256	Charlie Lau	.25
257	Jim Lehew	.15
258	Ken Lehman	.15
259	Don Lenhardt	.15
260	Dave Leonhard	.15
261	Don Leppert	.15
262	Dick Littlefield	.15
263	Charlie Locke	.15
264	Whitey Lockman	.15
265	Billy Loes	.15
266	Ed Lopat	.15
267	Carlos Lopez	.15
268	Marcelino Lopez	.15
269	John Lowenstein	.15
270	Steve Luebber	.15
271	Dick Luebke	.15
272	Fred Lynn	.45
273	Bobby Mabe	.15
274	Elliott Maddox	.15
275	Hank Majeski	.15
276	Roger Marquis	.15
277	Freddie Marsh	.15
278	Jim Marshall	.15
279	Morrie Martin	.15
280	Dennis Martinez	.25
281	Tippy Martinez	.25
282	Tom Matchick	.15
283	Charlie Maxwell	.15
284	Dave May	.15
285	Lee May	.15
286	Rudy May	.15
287	Mike McCormick	.15
288	Ben McDonald	.15
289	Jim McDonald	.15
290	Scott McGregor	.25
291	Mickey McGuire	.15
292	Jeff McKnight	.15
293	Dave McNally	.25
294	Sam Mele	.15
295	Francisco Melendez	.15
296	Bob Melvin	.15
297	Jose Mesa	.15
298	Eddie Miksis	.15
299	Bob Milacki	.15
300	Bill Miller	.15
301	Dyar Miller	.15
302	John Miller	.15
303	Randy Miller	.15
304	Stu Miller	.15
305	Randy Milligan	.15
306	Paul Mirabella	.15
307	Willy Miranda	.15
308	John Mitchell	.15
309	Paul Mitchell	.15
310	Ron Moeller	.15
311	Bob Molinaro	.15
312	Ray Moore	.15
313	Andres Mora	.15
314	Jose Morales	.15
315	Keith Moreland	.15
316	Mike Morgan	.15
317	Dan Morogiello	.15
318	John Morris	.15
319	Les Moss	.15
320	Curt Motton	.15
321	Eddie Murray	1.50
322	Ray Murray	.15
323	Tony Muser	.15
324	Buster Narum	.15
325	Bob Nelson	.15
326	Roger Nelson	.15
327	Carl Nichols	.15
328	Dave Nicholson	.15
329	Tom Niedenfuer	.15
330	Bob Nieman	.15
331	Donell Nixon	.15
332	Joe Nolan	.15
333	Dickie Noles	.15
334	Tim Nordbrook	.15
335	Jim Northrup	.15
336	Jack O'Connor	.15
337	Billy O'Dell	.15
338	John O'Donoghue	.15
339	Tom O'Malley	.15
340	Johnny Oates	.15
341	Chuck Oertel	.15
342	Bob Oliver	.15
343	Gregg Olson	.15
344	John Orsino	.15
345	Joe Orsulak	.15
346	John Pacella	.15
347	Dave Pagan	.15
348	Erv Palica	.15
349	Jim Palmer	1.50
350	John Papa	.15
351	Milt Pappas	.15
352	Al Pardo	.15
353	Kelly Paris	.15
354	Mike Parrott	.15
355	Tom Patton	.15
356	Albie Pearson	.15
357	Orlando Pena	.15
358	Oswaldo Peraza	.15
359	Buddy Peterson	.15
360	Dave Philley	.15
361	Tom Phoebus	.15
362	Al Pilarcik	.15
363	Duane Pillette	.15
364	Lou Piniella	.25
365	Dave Pope	.15
366	Arnie Portocarrero	.15
367	Boog Powell	1.00
368	Johnny Powers	.15
369	Carl Powis	.15
370	Joe Price	.15
371	Jim Pyburn	.15
372	Art Quirk	.15
373	Jamie Quirk	.15
374	Allan Ramirez	.15
375	Floyd Rayford	.15
376	Mike Reinbach	.15
377	Merv Rettenmund	.15
378	Bob Reynolds	.15
379	Del Rice	.15
380	Pete Richert	.15
381	Jeff Rineer	.15
382	Bill Ripken	.15
383	Cal Ripken	9.00
384	Robin Roberts	1.25
385	Brooks Robinson	4.00
386	Earl Robinson	.15
387	Eddie Robinson	.15
388	Frank Robinson	3.00
389	Sergio Robles	.15
390	Aurelio Rodriguez	.15
391	Vic Rodriguez	.15
392	Gary Roenicke	.15
393	Saul Rogovin	.15
394	Wade Rowdon	.15
395	Ken Rowe	.15
396	Willie Royster	.15
397	Vic Roznovsky	.15
398	Ken Rudolph	.15
399	Lenn Sakata	.15
400	Chico Salmon	.15
401	Orlando Sanchez	.15
402	Bob Saverine	.15
403	Art Schallock	.15
404	Bill Scherrer	.15
405	Curt Schilling	.75
406	Dave Schmidt	.15
407	Johnny Schmitz	.15
408	Jeff Schneider	.15
409	Rick Schu	.15
410	Mickey Scott	.15
411	Kal Segrist	.15
412	David Segui	.15
413	Al Severinsen	.15
414	Larry Sheets	.15
415	John Shelby	.15
416	Barry Shetrone	.15
417	Tom Shopay	.15
418	Bill Short	.15
419	Norm Siebern	.15
420	Nelson Simmons	.15
421	Ken Singleton	.25
422	Doug Sisk	.15
423	Dave Skaggs	.15
424	Lou Sleater	.15
425	Al Smith	.15
426	Billy Smith	.15
427	Hal Smith	.15
428	"Texas" Mike Smith	.15
429	Nate Smith	.15
430	Nate Snell	.15
431	Russ Snyder	.15
432	Don Stanhouse	.15
433	Pete Stanicek	.15
434	Herm Starrette	.15
435	John Stefero	.15
436	Gene Stephens	.15
437	Vern Stephens	.15
438	Earl Stephenson	.15
439	Sammy Stewart	.15
440	Royle Stillman	.15
441	Wes Stock	.15
442	Tim Stoddard	.15
443	Dean Stone	.15
444	Jeff Stone	.15
445	Steve Stone	.25
446	Marlin Stuart	.15
447	Gordie Sundin	.15
448	Bill Swaggerty	.15
449	Willie Tasby	.15
450	Joe Taylor	.15
451	Dorn Taylor	.15
452	Anthony Telford	.15
453	Johnny Temple	.15
454	Mickey Tettleton	.15
455	Valmy Thomas	.15
456	Bobby Thomson	.25
457	Marv Thorneberry	.15
458	Mark Thurmond	.15
459	Jay Tibbs	.15
460	Mike Torrez	.15
461	Jim Traber	.15
462	Gus Triandos	.15
463	Paul "Dizzy" Trout	.15
464	Bob Turley	.15
465	Tom Underwood	.15
466	Fred Valentine	.15
467	Dave Van Gorder	.15
468	Dave Vineyard	.15
469	Ozzie Virgil	.15
470	Eddie Waitkus	.15
471	Greg Walker	.15
472	Jerry Walker	.15
473	Pete Ward	.15
474	Carl Warwick	.15
475	Ron Washington	.15
476	Eddie Watt	.15
477	Don Welchel	.15
478	George Werley	.15
479	Vic Wertz	.15
480	Wally Westlake	.15
481	Mickey Weston	.15
482	Alan Wiggins	.15
483	Bill Wight	.15
484	Hoyt Wilhelm	.50
485	Dallas Williams	.15
486	Dick Williams	.15
487	Earl Williams	.15
488	Mark Williamson	.15
489	Jim Wilson	.15
490	Gene Woodling	.15
491	Craig Worthington	.15
492	Bobby Young	.15
493	Mike Young	.15
494	Frank Zupo	.15
495	George Zuverink	.15
496	Glenn Davis	.15
497	Dwight Evans	.25
498	Dave Gallagher	.15
499	Paul Kilgus	.15
500	Jeff Robinson	.15
501	Ernie Whitt	.15

on a white background on front; backs have black-and-white stats, logos, and career highlights. Cal Ripken, Jr. and Tippy Martinez were the only active players portrayed in the set. Suggested retail price at issue was $4 per series; about $2 with a gasoline purchase. A collector's album could also be purchased.

		NM/M
Complete Set (12):		20.00
Common Player:		1.00
SET 1		10.00
(1)	Frank Robinson	3.00
(2)	Brooks Robinson	4.00
(3)	Jim Palmer	3.00
(4)	Rick Dempsey	1.00
SET 2		12.00
(5)	Cal Ripken Jr.	10.00
(6)	Tippy Martinez	1.00
(7)	Bobby Grich	1.00
(8)	Earl Weaver	1.00
SET 3		4.00
(9)	Boog Powell	1.50
(10)	Paul Blair	1.00
(11)	Terry Crowley	1.00
(12)	Ken Singleton	1.00

1998 CyberAction

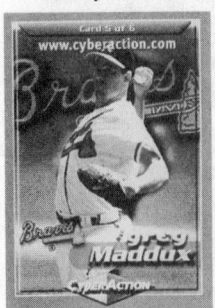

During the 1998 National Sports Collectors Convention in Chicago, CyberAction gave away samples of this product. The cards are printed on flimsy cardboard in standard 2-1/2" x 3-1/2" format. Fronts have a blue-bordered action photo at center. In the background is a large team logo. The firm's website address is at top; its logo at bottom. Backs have details on winning a World Series trip.

		NM/M
Complete Set (6):		11.00
Common Player:		1.50
1	Ken Griffey Jr.	2.25
2	Mark McGwire	2.50
3	Barry Bonds	3.00
4	Derek Jeter	2.00
5	Greg Maddux	2.00
6	Larry Walker	1.50

1992 Crown Orioles Action Standups

Crown Petroleum released a set of standup cards in 1992 of 12 Oriole greats, most retired, that was sold at service stations in three series. The 4-1/4" x 9" cards have color photos

1992 Dairy Queen Team USA

In 1992, in conjunction with the Dairy Queen Team USA Sundae-in-a-Helmet promotion, customers received a four-card pack of Team USA cards, part of a 33-card set manufactured by Topps for the company. Included in the set are Team USA players from the 1984 and 1988 Olympics, many of whom have gone on to major league stardom. The set also has 15 Team USA Prospects, a 1988 Gold Medal team celebration card and a card of 1992 coach Ron Fraser. Fronts feature each player in their Team USA uniform and the backs include statistics from amateur, Team USA and pro-

		NM/M
13	Andy Benes/1988	.25
14	Joe Slusarski/1988	.25
15	Ed Sprague/1988	.25
16	Bret Barberie/1988	.25
17	Gold Medal/1988	.25
18	Jeff Granger/1992	.25
19	John Dettmer/1992	.25
20	Todd Greene/1992	.25
21	Jeffrey Hammonds/1992	.25
22	Dan Melendez/1992	.25
23	Kennie Steenstra/1992	.25
24	Todd Johnson/1992	.25
25	Chris Roberts/1992	.25
26	Steve Rodriguez/1992	.25
27	Charles Johnson/1992	.25
28	Chris Wimmer/1992	.25
29	Tony Phillips/1992	.25
30	Craig Wilson/1992	.25
31	Jason Giambi/1992	6.00
32	Paul Shuey/1992	.25
33	Ron Fraser/1992 (Coach)	.25

1993 Dairy Queen Magic Mariner Moments Pin/Cards

		NM/M
	Complete Set (4):	10.00
	Common Player:	2.00
1	Randy Johnson ('92 AL K King)	3.25
2	Edgar Martinez ('92 AL Batting Champ)	2.00
3	Chris Bosio (No-Hitter)	2.00
4	Ken Griffey Jr. ('92 All-Star MVP)	4.00

1994 Dairy Queen Ken Griffey, Jr.

Distributed by Dairy Queen stores in the Pacific Northwest, this set was issued in two different versions, with green borders and with gold borders. All cards feature a "Ken Griffey Jr. Golden Moments" logo in the upper-left corner. His name and the DQ logo appear at the bottom. Backs have another photo of Griffey along with a description of the career highlight depicted on front, sponsors' logos and a card number. Values shown here are for green-bordered cards; gold-bordered cards sell for about twice those figures.

		NM/M
	Complete Set (10):	7.50
	Common Player:	.75
	Gold:	2X
1	Ken Griffey Jr. ("The Spider Man Catch")	.75
2	Ken Griffey Jr. ("Back to Back Homeruns")	.75
3	Ken Griffey Jr. (Hit .327 in 1991)	.75
4	Ken Griffey Jr. (1992 All-Star MVP)	.75
5	Ken Griffey Jr. ("Dialing Long Distance")	.75
6	Ken Griffey Jr. ("8 Straight Homeruns")	.75
7	Ken Griffey Jr. (4-Time Golden Glove Winner)	.75
8	Ken Griffey Jr. (45 Homeruns in 1993)	.75
9	Ken Griffey Jr. (Major League Career Hitting Record)	.75
10	Ken Griffey Jr. ("Looking to 1994")	.75

Danbury Mint 22 Kt. Gold Cooperstown Collection

A series of embossed 22kt. gold-foil cards was offered by the private mint beginning in 1996. Each month two cards were sent to subscribers. The standard-size cards have a player picture on front with team logo and player identification at bottom. Backs have career stats. Each card was sealed in acrylic. An album for the set has identification labels with name in both printed and facsimile autograph form. Only persons who completed Set 1 were allowed to purchase subsequent sets. While each card is numbered, they are checklisted here alphabetically within series. Because the Babe Ruth card was used as a free promotional give-away, it is more common than the others. Some players' team identification and stats were changed from year-to-year.

		NM/M
	Complete Set (200):	750.00
	Common Player (1-50):	5.00
	Common Player (51-100):	6.00
	Common Player (101-150):	7.50
	Common Player (151-200):	7.50
(1)	Richie Allen	4.00
(2)	Paul Blair	3.00
(3)	Vida Blue	4.00
(4)	Bert Blyleven	3.00
(5)	Roy Campanella	6.00
(6)	Bert Campaneris	3.00
(7)	Gary Carter	4.00
(8)	Cesar Cedeno	3.00
(9)	Orlando Cepeda	4.00
(10)	Ty Cobb	7.50
(11)	Mickey Cochrane	3.00
(12)	Eddie Collins	3.00
(13)	Dizzy Dean	5.00
(14)	Bob Feller	4.00
(15)	George Foster	3.00
(16)	Steve Garvey	3.00
(17)	Lou Gehrig	7.50

		NM/M
(18)	Lefty Gomez	3.00
(19)	Gil Hodges	4.00
(20)	Carl Hubbell	3.00
(21)	Walter Johnson	5.00
(22)	Jim Kaat	3.00
(23)	Don Kessinger	3.00
(24)	Harmon Killebrew	4.00
(25)	Jerry Koosman	3.00
(26)	Mickey Lolich	3.00
(27)	Sparky Lyle	3.00
(28)	Fred Lynn	3.00
(29)	Bill Mazeroski	4.00
(30)	Minnie Minoso	3.00
(31)	Johnny Mize	3.00
(32)	Thurman Munson	5.00
(33)	Graig Nettles	3.00
(34)	Phil Niekro	3.00
(35)	Tony Oliva	3.00
(36)	Al Oliver	3.00
(37)	Satchel Paige	7.50
(38)	Jim Palmer	3.00
(39)	Herb Pennock	3.00
(40)	Tony Perez	3.00
(41)	Boog Powell	3.00
(42)	Brooks Robinson	4.00
(43)	Babe Ruth	2.50
(44)	Duke Snider	3.00
(45)	Tris Speaker	3.00
(46)	Willie Stargell	3.00
(47)	Luis Tiant	3.00
(48)	Honus Wagner	5.00
(49)	Maury Wills	3.00
(50)	Cy Young	5.00
(51)	Grover Alexander	6.00
(52)	Sandy Alomar Jr.	6.00
(53)	Jeff Bagwell	9.00
(54)	Dusty Baker	6.00
(55)	Albert Belle	6.00
(56)	Wade Boggs	10.00
(57)	Barry Bonds	17.50
(58)	Joe Carter	6.00
(59)	Will Clark	6.00
(60)	Roger Clemens	12.00
(61)	Dwight Evans	6.00
(62)	Jim Fregosi	6.00
(63)	Andres Galarraga	6.00
(64)	Bob Gibson	6.00
(65)	Ken Griffey Jr.	13.50
(66)	Tony Gwynn	10.00
(67)	Rogers Hornsby	6.00
(68)	Catfish Hunter	6.00
(69)	Joe Jackson	17.50
(70)	Ferguson Jenkins	6.00
(71)	Derek Jeter	17.50
(72)	Randy Johnson	9.00
(73)	Jimmy Key	6.00
(74)	Ralph Kiner	6.00
(75)	Don Larsen	6.00
(76)	Greg Maddux	10.00
(77)	Juan Marichal	6.00
(78)	Eddie Mathews	7.50
(79)	Christy Mathewson	9.00
(80)	Fred McGriff	6.00
(81)	Mark McGwire	15.00
(82)	Dave McNally	6.00
(83)	Bobby Murcer	6.00
(84)	Dale Murphy	7.50
(85)	Gaylord Perry	6.00
(86)	Rico Petrocelli	6.00
(87)	Andy Pettitte	7.50
(88)	Mike Piazza	13.50
(89)	Cal Ripken Jr.	17.50
(90)	Alex Rodriguez	15.00
(91)	Joe Rudi	6.00
(92)	Ron Santo	6.00
(93)	Gary Sheffield	6.00
(94)	John Smoltz	6.00
(95)	Sammy Sosa	10.00
(96)	Warren Spahn	6.00
(97)	Billy Williams	6.00
(98)	Bobby Thomson	6.00
(99)	Mo Vaughn	6.00
(100)	Hoyt Wilhelm	6.00
(101)	Brady Anderson	7.50
(102)	Luis Aparicio	7.50
(103)	Kevin Appier	7.50
(104)	Richie Ashburn	9.00
(105)	Lou Boudreau	7.50
(106)	Lou Brock	7.50
(107)	Kevin Brown	7.50
(108)	Jim Bunning	7.50
(109)	Jose Canseco	9.00
(110)	David Cone	7.50
(111)	Rollie Fingers	7.50
(112)	Chuck Finley	7.50
(113)	Curt Flood	7.50
(114)	Jimmie Foxx	10.00
(115)	Nomar Garciaparra	12.00
(116)	Tom Glavine	7.50
(117)	Juan Gonzalez	7.50
(118)	Luis Gonzalez	7.50
(119)	Mark Grace	7.50
(120)	Shawn Green	7.50
(121)	Burleigh Grimes	7.50
(122)	Lefty Grove	7.50
(123)	Al Hrabosky	7.50
(124)	Chipper Jones	12.00
(125)	Al Kaline	9.00
(126)	Tony Lazzeri	7.50
(127)	Bill Lee	7.50
(128)	Jose Lima	7.50
(129)	Bill Madlock	7.50
(130)	Roger Maris	9.00
(131)	Pedro Martinez	10.00
(132)	Tino Martinez	7.50
(133)	Tug McGraw	7.50
(134)	Kevin Millwood	7.50
(135)	Joe Morgan	7.50

		NM/M
(136)	Charles Nagy	7.50
(137)	Mel Ott	7.50
(138)	Rafael Palmeiro	7.50
(139)	Manny Ramirez	9.00
(140)	Jim Rice	7.50
(141)	Ivan Rodriguez	7.50
(142)	Edd Roush	7.50
(143)	Manny Sanguillen	7.50
(144)	Curt Schilling	7.50
(145)	Ron Swoboda	7.50
(146)	Greg Vaughn	7.50
(147)	Larry Walker	7.50
(148)	Zack Wheat	7.50
(149)	Bernie Williams	7.50
(150)	Jim Wynn	7.50
(151)	Bobby Abreu	7.50
(152)	Roberto Alomar	7.50
(153)	Moises Alou	7.50
(154)	Carlos Beltran	7.50
(155)	Armando Benitez	7.50
(156)	Lance Berkman	7.50
(157)	Bret Boone	7.50
(158)	Ellis Burks	7.50
(159)	Sean Casey	7.50
(160)	Carlos Delgado	10.00
(161)	J.D. Drew	10.00
(162)	Jim Edmonds	7.50
(163)	Cliff Floyd	7.50
(164)	Freddy Garcia	7.50
(165)	Jason Giambi	10.00
(166)	Brian Giles	7.50
(167)	Troy Glaus	7.50
(168)	Vladimir Guerrero	12.50
(169)	Mike Hampton	7.50
(170)	Todd Helton	10.00
(171)	Trevor Hoffman	7.50
(172)	Tim Hudson	10.00
(173)	Andruw Jones	12.50
(174)	Jeff Kent	7.50
(175)	Ryan Klesko	7.50
(176)	Al Leiter	7.50
(177)	Edgar Martinez	7.50
(178)	Raul Mondesi	7.50
(179)	Matt Morris	7.50
(180)	Jamie Moyer	7.50
(181)	Mark Mulder	7.50
(182)	Mike Mussina	9.00
(183)	Robb Nen	7.50
(184)	Phil Nevin	7.50
(185)	John Olerud	7.50
(186)	Magglio Ordonez	7.50
(187)	Roy Oswalt	7.50
(188)	Chan Ho Park	7.50
(189)	Troy Percival	7.50
(190)	Albert Pujols	15.00
(191)	Brad Radke	7.50
(192)	Mariano Rivera	7.50
(193)	Kazuhiro Sasaki	7.50
(194)	Jeff Shaw	7.50
(195)	Alfonso Soriano	9.00
(196)	Frank Thomas	12.50
(197)	Jim Thome	7.50
(198)	Billy Wagner	7.50
(199)	Kerry Wood	9.00
(200)	Barry Zito	9.00

1991 Jimmy Dean

Baseball cards were inserted into packages of Jimmy Dean sausages in 1991. The complete set consists of 25 star players' cards. Red and yellow borders surround color player photos on the card fronts. No team logos appear on the cards. The card backs feature statistics, biographical information and a facsimile autograph. The set is entitled the "Signature Edition." An uncut sheet was also available via special offer.

		NM/M
	Complete Set (25):	5.00
	Common Player:	.15
	Uncut Sheet:	6.00
1	Will Clark	.15
2	Ken Griffey Jr.	.75
3	Dale Murphy	.25
4	Barry Bonds	1.00
5	Darryl Strawberry	.15
6	Ryne Sandberg	.50
7	Gary Sheffield	.25
8	Sandy Alomar, Jr.	.15
9	Frank Thomas	.45
10	Barry Larkin	.15
11	Kirby Puckett	.45
12	George Brett	.60

		NM/M
13	Kevin Mitchell	.15
14	Dave Justice	.15
15	Cal Ripken, Jr.	1.00
16	Craig Biggio	.15
17	Rickey Henderson	.45
18	Roger Clemens	.60
19	Jose Canseco	.25
20	Ozzie Smith	.50
21	Cecil Fielder	.15
22	Dave Winfield	.45
23	Kevin Maas	.15
24	Nolan Ryan	1.00
25	Dwight Gooden	.15

1992 Jimmy Dean

For the second year in a row, baseball cards were inserted into packages of Jimmy Dean sausage in 1992. Featuring 18 star players, the set portrays the player's name on a vertical panel at the left of the card, along with his team name and position. The Jimmy Dean logo appears in the lower-right corner. Major League team logos have been eliminated from the photos.

		NM/M
	Complete Set (18):	5.00
	Common Player:	.15
1	Jim Abbott	.15
2	Barry Bonds	1.50
3	Jeff Bagwell	.45
4	Frank Thomas	.45
5	Steve Avery	.15
6	Chris Sabo	.15
7	Will Clark	.15
8	Don Mattingly	.60
9	Darryl Strawberry	.15
10	Roger Clemens	.60
11	Ken Griffey Jr.	1.00
12	Chuck Knoblauch	.15
13	Tony Gwynn	.50
14	Juan Gonzalez	.30
15	Cecil Fielder	.15
16	Bobby Bonilla	.15
17	Wes Chamberlain	.15
18	Ryne Sandberg	.50

1992 Jimmy Dean Living Legends

Approximately 100,000 of these six-card sets were made available via a mail-in offer for $1 and proofs of purchase from the company's breakfast meats. Color photos on front have had uniform logos removed and are overprinted with a gold-foil facsimile autograph. Other gold foil highlights the player, team and sponsor names on front. Backs are printed in black and yellow and include a few biographical details, career highlights and summary statistics.

		NM/M
	Complete Set (6):	8.00
	Common Player:	1.00
1	George Brett	2.00
2	Carlton Fisk	1.00
3	Ozzie Smith	1.50
4	Robin Yount	1.00
5	Cal Ripken, Jr.	3.00
6	Nolan Ryan	3.00

1992 Jimmy Dean Rookie Stars

Nine of 1992's hottest rookies were featured in this set issued as inserts into various Jimmy Dean meat products. Cards feature full-bleed photos on which uniform logos have been airbrushed away. A 1992 Rookie Star logo appears at upper-left, atop a black vertical strip containing the player's name, team and position. A white strip at bottom has the Jimmy Dean logo. On back, personal data and minor and major league stats are featured in a center panel, surrounded by a light blue border.

		NM/M
	Complete Set (9):	3.00
	Common Player:	.50
1	Andy Stankiewicz	.50
2	Pat Listach	.50
3	Brian Jordan	.50
4	Eric Karros	.50
5	Reggie Sanders	.50
6	Dave Fleming	.50
7	Donovan Osborne	.50
8	Kenny Lofton	.50
9	Moises Alou	.50

1993 Jimmy Dean

Issued in the company's meat products and via a mail-in offer, this set, once again features player photos on which the uniform logos have been airbrushed away, due to lack of a license from Major League Baseball. A pair of horizontal color bars in one of the lower corners contains a Jimmy Dean logo and the player's name. Backs have a line drawing portrait of the player, along with stats, personal data and logos:

		NM/M
	Complete Set (28):	6.00
	Common Player:	.15
1	Frank Thomas	.50
2	Barry Larkin	.15
3	Cal Ripken, Jr.	1.25
4	Andy Van Slyke	.15
5	Darren Daulton	.15
6	Don Mattingly	.65
7	Roger Clemens	.65
8	Juan Gonzalez	.35
9	Mark Langston	.15
10	Barry Bonds	1.25
11	Ken Griffey Jr.	.75
12	Cecil Fielder	.15
13	Kirby Puckett	.60
14	Tom Glavine	.25
15	George Brett	.65
16	Nolan Ryan	1.25
17	Eddie Murray	.50
18	Gary Sheffield	.35
19	Doug Drabek	.15
20	Ray Lankford	.15
21	Benito Santiago	.15
22	Mark McGwire	1.00
23	Kenny Lofton	.15
24	Eric Karros	.15
25	Ryne Sandberg	.50
26	Charlie Hayes	.15

27	Mike Mussina	.25
28	Pat Listach	.15

1993 Jimmy Dean Rookie Cards

Jimmy Dean Foods issued a Rookie Stars baseball card set in 1993. The nine-card set features promising rookies, with players highlighted against a marblized background with color photos on both sides of the cards. The cards were distributed randomly in three-card sets in specially-marked packages of Jimmy Dean products.

		NM/M
Complete Set (9):		3.00
Common Player:		.10
(1)	Rich Amaral	.10
(2)	Vinny Castilla	.15
(3)	Jeff Conine	.25
(4)	Brent Gates	.10
(5)	Wayne Kirby	.10
(6)	Mike Lansing	.25
(7)	David Nied	.10
(8)	Mike Piazza	2.00
(9)	Tim Salmon	.75

1995 Jimmy Dean All Time Greats

Six Hall of Famers are featured in this promotion for the country singer's breakfast meats. Besides inclusion of regular cards in food packages, a send-away deal offered autographed cards of three of the players for proofs of purchase and $7 apiece. Cards feature action photos on which team uniform logos have been removed; while the cards are licensed by the Major League Baseball Players Alumni, they are not sanctioned by MLB. A large "1995 All Time Greats Collectors Set" logo appears in the upper-right corner on front, while the Jimmy Dean logo and player name are in the lower-left. Full color backs offer a career summary and lifetime stats, along with a ghost image of the front photo.

		NM/M
Complete Set (6):		5.00
Common Player:		.50
1	Rod Carew	1.00
2	Jim "Catfish" Hunter	.50
2a	Jim "Catfish" Hunter/Auto.	15.00
3	Al Kaline	1.50
3a	Al Kaline/Auto.	8.00
4	Mike Schmidt	1.50
5	Billy Williams	.50
5a	Billy Williams/Auto.	8.00
6	Carl Yastrzemski	1.50

1997 Jimmy Dean Great Moments

These two-card sets were available via a mail-in offer for $12.95 apiece plus proofs of pur-

chase. Each set consists of an autographed "Great Moments in Baseball" card with an action photo and a "Great Baseball Stadiums" card featuring a player photo set against the stadium background. All pictures are sepia toned with uniform logos removed. Cards have player or stadium information on the backs and came with a certificate of authenticity.

		NM/M
Complete Set (4):		35.00
(1)	Yogi Berra/Auto.	20.00
(2)	Yogi Berra (Yankee Stadium)	5.00
(3)	Brooks Robinson/Auto.	10.00
(4)	Brooks Robinson (Memorial Stadium)	3.00

1984 Decathlon Negro League Baseball Stars

According to contemporary advertising, this set was produced in conjunction with the Negro Baseball Hall of History in Kentucky, to a total of 2,000 sets and 300 uncut sheets. The cards and checklist are identical to the 1986 issue by Larry Fritsch Cards, which purchased rights to the set, except for the copyright line at bottom on back.

		NM/M
Complete Set (119):		35.00
Common Player:		.30
Stars:		3X

1985 Decathlon Ultimate Baseball Card Set

Originally intended to be a six-series, 90-card issue, this collectors' set was cut short after the first series. The large-format (4" x 5-5/8") cards feature front color artwork by former Topps artist Gerry Dvorak. The portraits are surrounded by a white border. Black-and-white backs have a career capsule. Announced as an edition of 10,000 sets, original issue price was about $11.

		NM/M
Complete Set (15):		20.00
Common Player:		1.00
1	Ty Cobb	3.00
2	Honus Wagner	3.00
3	Babe Ruth	5.00
4	Lou Gehrig	4.00
5	Frank Baker	1.00
6	Casey Stengel	1.00
7	Moses Walker	1.00
8	Cy Young	1.00

9	Joe DiMaggio	4.00
10	John McGraw	1.00
11	Josh Gibson	1.00
12	Johnny Mize	1.00
13	Walter Johnson	1.00
14	Walter Alston	1.00
15	Enos Slaughter	1.00

1993 Dempster's Blue Jays

One of several Canadian baseball card issues marking the 1992 World Series victory of the Toronto Blue Jays, the Dempster's stores set is a 25-card issue in standard 2-1/2" x 3-1/2", UV-coatd on both sides. Fronts have a large dark blue border with white horizontal white pinstripes. An action photo is at center, with the player's name and position below. The Jays World Championship logo and Players Association logo are at top; the sponsor's logo at lower-right. A baseball at bottom center has the card number. Backs feature a large portrait photo at top, against a dark blue background. Color bars carry the player's '92 and career stats. A facsimile autograph appears beneath the team logo at right.

		NM/M
Complete Set (25):		6.50
Common Player:		.25
1	Juan Guzman	.25
2	Roberto Alomar	.75
3	Danny Cox	.25
4	Paul Molitor	4.00
5	Todd Stottlemyre	.25
6	Joe Carter	.50
7	Jack Morris	.35
8	Ed Sprague	.25
9	Turner Ward	.25
10	John Olerud	.75
11	Duane Ward	.25
12	Alfredo Griffin	.25
13	Cito Gaston	.25
14	Dave Stewart	.25
15	Mark Eichhorn	.25
16	Darnell Coles	.25
17	Randy Knorr	.25
18	Al Leiter	.25
19	Pat Hentgen	.25
20	Devon White	.25
21	Pat Borders	.25
22	Darrin Jackson	.25
23	Dick Schofield	.25
24	Luis Sojo	.25
25	Mike Timlin	.25

1991 Denny's Grand Slam

This 26-card set was produced by Upper Deck and features one player from each Major League team. One hologram card was distributed with the purchase of a Grand Slam meal. The cards are numbered on the front and are 3-D. The card backs describe grand slams hit by the featured player.

		NM/M
Complete Set (26):		12.50
Common Player:		.50

1	Ellis Burks	.50
2	Cecil Fielder	.50
3	Will Clark	.50
4	Eric Davis	.50
5	Dave Parker	.50
6	Kelly Gruber	.50
7	Kent Hrbek	.50
8	Don Mattingly	1.50
9	Brook Jacoby	.50
10	Mark McGwire	2.00
11	Howard Johnson	.50
12	Tim Wallach	.50
13	Ricky Jordan	.50
14	Andre Dawson	.75
15	Eddie Murray	1.00
16	Danny Tartabull	.50
17	Bobby Bonilla	.50
18	Benito Santiago	.50
19	Alvin Davis	.50
20	Cal Ripken	2.50
21	Ruben Sierra	.50
22	Pedro Guerrero	.50
23	Wally Joyner	.50
24	Craig Biggio	.50
25	Dave Justice	.50
26	Tim Raines	.50

1992 Denny's Grand Slam

The second year of the Denny's Gland Slam promotion featured one power hitter from each major league team, portrayed on a hologram in front of a scene from his team's city. As in the first year, the cards were produced by Upper Deck and given away, one at a time, with a Denny's purchase during the middle of the summer. An album with plastic pages holding four cards each was also available.

		NM/M
Complete Set (26):		7.50
Common Player:		.25
Album:		3.00
1	Marquis Grissom	.25
2	Ken Caminiti	.25
3	Fred McGriff	.25
4	Felix Jose	.25
5	Jack Clark	.25
6	Albert Belle	.25
7	Sid Bream	.25
8	Robin Ventura	.25
9	Cal Ripken, Jr.	2.00
10	Ryne Sandberg	1.00
11	Paul O'Neill	.25
12	Luis Polonia	.25
13	Cecil Fielder	.25
14	Kal Daniels	.25
15	Brian McRae	.25
16	Howard Johnson	.25
17	Greg Vaughn	.25
18	Dale Murphy	.60
19	Kent Hrbek	.25
20	Barry Bonds	2.00
21	Matt Nokes	.25
22	Jose Canseco	.50
23	Jay Buhner	.25
24	Will Clark	.25
25	Ruben Sierra	.25
26	Joe Carter	.25

1993 Denny's Grand Slam

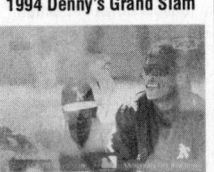

The 1993 Denny's Grand Slam set expanded to 28 cards with the addition of the Florida and

Colorado expansion teams. The featured color photos of one grand slam slugger for each team superimposed over a hologram background. The reverse of each card gives anecdotes about the player's grand slams along with his career total. The cards were distributed at participating Denny's restaurants during mid-summer.

		NM/M
Complete Set (28):		7.50
Common Player:		.25
1	Chili Davis	.25
2	Eric Anthony	.25
3	Rickey Henderson	.60
4	Joe Carter	.25
5	Terry Pendleton	.25
6	Robin Yount	.60
7	Ray Lankford	.25
8	Ryne Sandberg	.75
9	Darryl Strawberry	.25
10	Marquis Grissom	.25
11	Will Clark	.25
12	Albert Belle	.25
13	Edgar Martinez	.25
14	Benito Santiago	.25
15	Eddie Murray	.60
16	Cal Ripken, Jr.	2.00
17	Gary Sheffield	.45
18	Dave Hollins	.25
19	Andy Van Slyke	.25
20	Juan Gonzalez	.45
21	John Valentin	.25
22	Joe Oliver	.25
23	Dante Bichette	.25
24	Wally Joyner	.25
25	Cecil Fielder	.25
26	Kirby Puckett	.75
27	Robin Ventura	.25
28	Danny Tartabull	.25

1994 Denny's Grand Slam

For its fourth annual hologram card promotion, Denny's chose a horizontal format with portrait and action photos of one player from each major league team. Designated the "Anniversary Edition," the set features the 125th year logo at bottom center, with the player's name at left; Upper Deck and Denny's logos are at top. On back the same two photos are conventionally printed along with a brief player biography, appropriate logos and copyright notices. The cards are numbered alphabetically. Cards were available with certain menu items from July 1 through Aug. 31. Each restaurant received one special boxed set for use as a contest prize. These sets include a special Reggie Jackson "Route to Cooperstown" hologram card; the edition was limited to about 1,500.

		NM/M
Complete Set (28 / No Jackson): 7.50		
Common Player:		.25
1	Jim Abbott	.25
2	Roberto Alomar	.35
3	Kevin Appier	.25
4	Jeff Bagwell	.60
5	Albert Belle	.25
6	Barry Bonds	2.00
7	Bobby Bonilla	.25
8	Lenny Dykstra	.25
9	Cal Eldred	.25
10	Cecil Fielder	.25
11	Andres Galarraga	.25
12	Juan Gonzalez	.40
13	Ken Griffey Jr.	1.00
14	Tony Gwynn	.60
15	Rickey Henderson	.60
16	Kent Hrbek	.25
17	David Justice	.25
18	Mike Piazza	1.50
19	Jose Rijo	.25
20	Cal Ripken, Jr.	2.00
21	Tim Salmon	.25
22	Ryne Sandberg	.75
23	Gary Sheffield	.25
24	Ozzie Smith	.75
25	Frank Thomas	.60
26	Andy Van Slyke	.25
27	Mo Vaughn	.25
28	Larry Walker	.25
---	Reggie Jackson	60.00

1995 Denny's Classic Hits

For the fifth consecutive year, this August 1-September 30 promotion offered a hologram baseball card with the purchase of selected items from the restaurant's "Classic Hits" menu. The cards were produced for Denny's by Upper Deck and combine photographic and holographic images of the player on the horizontal-format front. Backs have another color photo, career highlights, and past-season/lifetime stats. Each Major League team is represented in the set by one player card. According to advertisements for the promotion, a total of 8,000,000 cards was produced - about 286,000 of each player.

		NM/M
Complete Set (28)		6.00
Common Player:		.15
1	Roberto Alomar	.30
2	Moises Alou	.15
3	Jeff Bagwell	.35
4	Albert Belle	.15
5	Jason Bere	.15
6	Roger Clemens	.60
7	Darren Daulton	.15
8	Cecil Fielder	.15
9	Andres Galarraga	.15
10	Juan Gonzalez	.35
11	Ken Griffey Jr.	.75
12	Tony Gwynn	.50
13	Barry Larkin	.15
14	Greg Maddux	.50
15	Don Mattingly	.50
16	Mark McGwire	1.00
17	Orlando Merced	.15
18	Jeff Montgomery	.15
19	Rafael Palmeiro	.35
20	Mike Piazza	1.00
21	Kirby Puckett	.50
22	Bret Saberhagen	.15
23	Tim Salmon	.30
24	Gary Sheffield	.15
25	Ozzie Smith	.50
26	Sammy Sosa	.50
27	Greg Vaughn	.15
28	Matt Williams	.15

1996 Denny's Instant Replay Holograms

Pinnacle, in its first year as supplier for Denny's annual baseball card promotion, attempted breakthrough technology that didn't quite hit the mark. The hologram portion of the card front was supposed to show as much as four seconds of on-field action, but unless viewed at exactly the right distance and angle, and under exacting light requirements, the action is little more than a silver-foil streak. Card fronts also included a color player photo. Another color photo appears on the back, along with a description of the action on front for those who couldn't master the "Full Motion" hologram. Cards were sold in single-card foil packs for 49 cents (limit two) with a qualifying purchase. Besides the hologram card, each pack includes a card explaining "How To View a Full Motion Hologram." Besides the regular cards, two "Grand Slam" chase sets were issued along with instant winner cards for complete card sets or trips to the World Series. Stated odds on the chase cards would indicate about 750,000 of each regular card were produced. One player from each team is represented in the checklist.

		NM/M
Complete Set (28):		5.00
Common Player:		.15
1	Greg Maddux	.50
2	Cal Ripken Jr.	1.00
3	Frank Thomas	.45
4	Albert Belle	.15
5	Mo Vaughn	.15
6	Jeff Bagwell	.45
7	Jay Buhner	.15
8	Barry Bonds	1.00
9	Ryne Sandberg	.50
10	Hideo Nomo	.35
11	Kirby Puckett	.50
12	Gary Sheffield	.30
13	Barry Larkin	.15
14	Wade Boggs	.15
15	Tony Gwynn	.50
16	Tim Salmon	.15
17	Jason Isringhausen	.15
18	Cecil Fielder	.15
19	Dante Bichette	.15
20	Ozzie Smith	.50
21	Ivan Rodriguez	.35
22	Kevin Appier	.15
23	Joe Carter	.15
24	Moises Alou	.15
25	Mark McGwire	.75
26	Kevin Seitzer	.15
27	Darren Daulton	.15
28	Jay Bell	.15

1996 Denny's Grand Slam

Exploding fireworks in the background are an allegory for the firepower brought to the plate by the sluggers featured in this chase set from Denny's annual baseball card promotion. A Grand Slam card is randomly substituted for the standard hologram card about once every 56 packs.

		NM/M
Complete Set (10):		13.50
Common Player:		1.00
1	Cal Ripken Jr.	2.50
2	Frank Thomas	1.50
3	Mike Piazza	2.25
4	Tony Gwynn	2.00
5	Sammy Sosa	2.00
6	Barry Bonds	2.50
7	Jeff Bagwell	1.50
8	Albert Belle	1.00
9	Mo Vaughn	1.00
10	Kirby Puckett	2.00

1996 Denny's Grand Slam Artist's Proofs

A specially marked Artist's Proof version of the Grand Slam chase cards are substituted for the standard hologram card in about every 360 packs, according to stated odds.

		NM/M
Complete Set (10):		50.00
Common Player:		2.00
1	Cal Ripken Jr.	10.00
2	Frank Thomas	5.00
3	Mike Piazza	7.50
4	Tony Gwynn	6.00
5	Sammy Sosa	6.00
6	Barry Bonds	10.00
7	Jeff Bagwell	5.00
8	Albert Belle	2.00
9	Mo Vaughn	2.00
10	Kirby Puckett	6.00

1997 Denny's 3-D Holograms

Denny's seventh annual baseball card issue was produced by Pinnacle and showcases two popular card technologies. Fronts of the 3-1/2" x 2-1/2" horizontal cards feature a deep 3D look. Backs have a player portrait hologram at the right. A partial baseball at left is the background for player data and stats along with sponsor and licensor logos. Cards were distributed one per pack for 59

cents from June 26-September 3, with 10 cents from the sale of each card donated to children's charities. The set features one player from each major league team, plus a Jackie Robinson tribute card.

		NM/M
Complete Set (29):		8.00
Common Player:		.20
1	Tim Salmon	.20
2	Rafael Palmeiro	.45
3	Mo Vaughn	.50
4	Frank Thomas	.50
5	David Justice	.20
6	Travis Fryman	.20
7	Johnny Damon	.35
8	John Jaha	.20
9	Chuck Knoblauch	.20
10	Mark McGwire	1.00
11	Alex Rodriguez	1.00
12	Juan Gonzalez	.35
13	Roger Clemens	.65
14	Derek Jeter	1.50
15	Andruw Jones	.50
16	Sammy Sosa	.60
17	Barry Larkin	.20
18	Dante Bichette	.20
19	Jeff Bagwell	.50
20	Mike Piazza	.75
21	Gary Sheffield	.35
22	Vladimir Guerrero	.50
23	Todd Hundley	.20
24	Jason Kendall	.20
25	Ray Lankford	.20
26	Ken Caminiti	.20
27	Barry Bonds	1.50
28	Scott Rolen	.40
29	Jackie Robinson (50th Anniversary Commemorative)	1.50

1997 Denny's Larry Doby

In the same format as the restaurant chain's regular set of 1997, this card honors the first black player to appear in the American League. The card was available only at the All-Star FanFest and All-Star Game in Cleveland in early July. Fronts have a black-and-white 3-D image; backs have a color hologram at right and a 50th anniversary logo at upper-left. Personal data, career highlights and stats are included, as well as appropriate logos.

		NM/M
		6.00
1	Larry Doby	6.00

1981 Detroit News Tigers Centennial

The 100th anniversary of professional baseball in Detroit was marked by "The Detroit News" with the issue of this set honoring "The Boys of Summer." The 2-1/2" x 3-1/2" cards have black-and-white photos on front, over a mock sports page. Cards can be found either with or without a red border on front, though the relative scarcity of each version is not known. Black-and-white backs have player data, career summary and stats, or a description of the front photo/highlight.

		NM/M
Complete Set (135):		30.00
Common Player:		.25

1	Detroit Boys of Summer	
2	100th Anniversary	.25
3	Charles W. Bennett	.25
4	Mickey Cochrane	.25
5	Harry Heilmann	.25
6	Walter O. Briggs	.25
7	Mark Fidrych	.75
8	1887 Tigers	.25
9	Tiger Stadium	.25
10	Rudy York	.25
11	George Kell	.25
12	Steve O'Neill	.25
13	John Hiller	.25
14	1934 Tigers	.25
15	Charlie Gehringer	.45
16	Denny McLain	.60
17	Billy Rogell	.25
18	Ty Cobb	5.00
19	Sparky Anderson	.60
20	Davy Jones	.25
21	Kirk Gibson	.45
22	Pat Mullin	.25
23	1972 Tigers	.25
24	What a Night	.25
25	"Doc" Cramer	.25
26	Mickey Stanley	.25
27	Johnny Lipon	.25
28	Jo Jo White	.25
29	Recreation Park	.25
30	Wild Bill Donovan	.25
31	Ray Oyler	.25
32	Earl Whitehill	.25
33	Billy Hoeft	.25
34	Johnny Groth	.25
35	Hughie Jennings	.25
36	Mayo Smith	.25
37	Bennett Park	.25
38	Tigers Win	.25
39	Donie Bush	.25
40	Harry Coveleski	.25
41	Paul Richards	.25
42	Jonathan Stone	.25
43	Bill Swift	.25
44	Roy Cullenbine	.25
45	Hoot Evers	.25
46	Tigers Win Series	.25
47	Art Houtteman	.25
48	Aurelio Rodriguez	.25
49	Fred Hutchinson	.25
50	Don Mossi	.25
51	Gehrig's Streak Ends in Detroit (Lou Gehrig)	2.50
52	Earl Wilson	.25
53	Jim Northrup	.25
54	1907 Tigers	.25
55	Greenberg's Two Homers Ties Ruth (Hank Greenberg)	.45
56	Mickey Lolich	.45
57	Tommy Bridges	.25
58	Al Benton	.25
59	Del Baker	.25
60	Lou Whitaker	.45
61	Navin Field	.25
62	1945 Tigers	.25
63	Ernie Harwell	.25
64	League Champs	.25
65	Bobo Newsom	.25
66	Don Wert	.25
67	Ed Summers	.25
68	Billy Martin	.45
69	Alan Trammell	1.50
70	Dale Alexander	.25
71	Ed Brinkman	.25
72	Right Man in Right Place Wins (Ted Williams)	2.00
73	Bill Freehan	.25
74	Norm Cash	.60
75	George Dauss	.25
76	Aurelio Lopez	.25
77	Charlie Maxwell	.25
78	Ed Barrow	.25
79	Willie Horton	.25
80	Denny Sets Record (Denny McLain)	.45
81	Dan Brouthers	.25
82	John E. Fetzer	.25
83	Heinie Manush	.25
84	1935 Tigers	.25
85	Ray Boone	.25
86	Bob Fothergill	.25
87	Steve Kemp	.25
88	Ed Killian	.25
89	Giebell is Ineligible (Floyd Giebell)	.25
90	Pinky Higgins	.25
91	Lance Parrish	.25
92	Eldon Auker	.25
93	Birdie Tebbetts	.25
94	Schoolboy Rowe	.25
95	McLain Wins 30th (Denny McLain)	.45
96	1909 Tigers	.25
97	Harvey Kuenn	.40
98	Jim Bunning	.60
99	1940 Tigers	.25
100	Rocky Colavito	2.50
101	Kaline Enters Hall of Fame (Al Kaline)	1.00
102	Billy Bruton	.25
103	Germany Schaefer	.25
104	Frank Bolling	.25
105	Briggs Stadium	.25
106	Bucky Harris	.25
107	Gates Brown	.25
108	Martin Made the Difference (Billy Martin)	.25
109	1908 Tigers	.25
	"Gee" Walker	.25

110	Pete Fox	.25
111	Virgil Trucks	.25
112	1968 Tigers	1.50
113	Dizzy Trout	.25
114	Barney McCosky	.25
115	Lu Blue	.25
116	Hal Newhouser	.25
117	Tigers are Home for Series	.25
118	Bobby Veach	.25
119	George Mullins (Mullin)	.25
120	Reggie's Super Homer (Reggie Jackson)	.60
121	Sam Crawford	.25
122	Hank Aguirre	.25
123	Vic Wertz	.25
124	Goose Goslin	.25
125	Frank Lary	.25
126	Joe Coleman	.25
127	Ed Katalinas	.25
128	Jack Morris	.25
129	3 Time AL Leaders	.25
130	James A. Campbell	.25
131	Ted Gray	.25
132	Al Kaline	5.00
133	Hank Greenberg	2.50
134	Dick McAuliffe	.25
135	Ozzie Virgil	.25

1988 Detroit Tigers Police

LOU WHITAKER 2B
B-L, T-R, HT: 5'11", WT: 160, BORN: 5-12-57

This unnumbered issue, sponsored by the Michigan State Police features 13 players and manager Sparky Anderson in full-color standard-size (2-1/2" x 3-1/2") cards. Player photos are framed by a blue border, with the Detroit logo upper left and a large name block that lists the player's name, position batting/throwing preference, height, weight and birthday beneath the photo. The backs carry an anti-drug or anti-crime message.

		NM/M
Complete Set (14):		7.00
Common Player:		.50
(1)	Doyle Alexander	.50
(2)	Sparky Anderson	1.00
(3)	Dave Bergman	.50
(4)	Tom Brookens	.50
(5)	Darrell Evans	.60
(6)	Larry Herndon	.50
(7)	Chet Lemon	.50
(8)	Jack Morris	.60
(9)	Matt Nokes	.50
(10)	Jeff Robinson	.50
(11)	Frank Tanana	.50
(12)	Walt Terrell	.50
(13)	Alan Trammell	1.00
(14)	Lou Whitaker	.75

1989 Detroit Tigers Police

(21) GUILLERMO HERNANDEZ—P
B-L, T-L, HT: 6'2", WT: 185, BORN: 11-14-54

This unnumbered issue, distributed and sponsored by the Michigan State Police Department features 14 full-color 2-1/2" x 3-1/2" cards. Player photos are framed by a blue and orange border, with the team logo in the upper left and biographical information below the photo. The card backs feature anti-drug or anti-crime messages.

		NM/M
Complete Set (14):		4.00
Common Player:		.25
(1)	Doyle Alexander	.25

(2)	Sparky Anderson	.75
(3)	Dave Bergman	.25
(4)	Mike Henneman	.25
(5)	Guillermo Hernandez	.25
(6)	Chet Lemon	.25
(7)	Fred Lynn	.25
(8)	Jack Morris	.35
(9)	Matt Nokes	.25
(10)	Jeff Robinson	.25
(11)	Pat Sheridan	.25
(12)	Frank Tanana	.25
(13)	Alan Trammell	.75
(14)	Lou Whitaker	.50

1991 Detroit Tigers Police

One of the scarcer safety issues is this Tigers team issue. Cards have a color player action photo on front with orange and blue team-color graphics. Backs have a safety message and the logos of sponsors HSP and Team Michigan, along with the Michigan State Police. The unnumbered cards are checklisted here alphabetically.

		NM/M
Complete Set (14):		7.00
Common Player:		.50
(1)	Sparky Anderson	.75
(2)	Dave Bergman	.50
(3)	Cecil Fielder	.75
(4)	Travis Fryman	.50
(5)	Paul Gibson	.50
(6)	Jerry Don Gleaton	.50
(7)	Lloyd Moseby	.50
(8)	Dan Petry	.50
(9)	Tony Phillips	.50
(10)	Mark Salas	.50
(11)	John Shelby	.50
(12)	Frank Tanana	.50
(13)	Alan Trammell	.75
(14)	Lou Whitaker	.75

1993 DiamondMarks Prototypes

In the same format as the regular-issue DiamondMark cards, these promos were produced to preview the concept for dealers and collectors. The promo cards feature different photos than those used on the issued version. The unnumbered cards are listed here alphabetically. On the back of the promos, the phrase "1993 PROTOTYPE" appears vertically at left.

		NM/M
Complete Set (8):		40.00
Common Player:		3.00
(1)	Roberto Alomar	4.00
(2)	Will Clark	3.00
(3)	Dennis Eckersley	5.00
(4)	Juan Gonzalez	4.00
(5)	Ken Griffey Jr.	10.00
(6)	Kirby Puckett	7.50
(7)	Ryne Sandberg	6.00
(8)	Frank Thomas	6.00

1993 DiamondMarks

While they look like baseball cards and were sold in foil packs like baseball cards, DiamondMarks were licensed as book marks. Issued by Barry Colla Productions, the 2-1/2" x 5" cards feature Barry Colla's trademark high-quality player photos on front and back. The UV-coated fronts feature black borders with the player's name in white above the photo and a color team logo beneath. Backs, also bordered in black, feature two color player photos in an

ROBERTO ALOMAR
BLUE JAYS

open book design. There is a portrait photo on the left and a head-and-shoulders reproduction of the front photo at right. A bookmark with team logo is incorporated in the design. The 120-card set is unnumbered and is arranged in the checklist below alphabetically within league and team.

		NM/M
Complete Set (120):		12.00
Common Player:		.15
Wax Box (48):		20.00
Atlanta Braves		
(1)	Steve Avery	.15
(2)	Ron Gant	.15
(3)	Tom Glavine	.35
(4)	David Justice	.15
(5)	Terry Pendleton	.15
(6)	Deion Sanders	.25
(7)	John Smoltz	.15
Chicago Cubs		
(8)	Mark Grace	.15
(9)	Randy Myers	.15
(10)	Ryne Sandberg	.75
(11)	Jose Vizcaino	.15
Cincinnati Reds		
(12)	Bobby Kelly	.15
(13)	Barry Larkin	.15
(14)	Kevin Mitchell	.15
(15)	Jose Rijo	.15
(16)	Reggie Sanders	.15
Colorado Rockies		
(17)	Dante Bichette	.15
(18)	Daryl Boston	.15
(19)	Andres Galarraga	.15
(20)	Charlie Hayes	.15
Florida Marlins		
(21)	Orestes Destrade	.15
(22)	Benito Santiago	.15
(23)	Gary Sheffield	.35
(24)	Walt Weiss	.15
Houston Astros		
(25)	Jeff Bagwell	.60
(26)	Craig Biggio	.15
(27)	Ken Caminiti	.15
(28)	Luis Gonzalez	.15
Los Angeles Dodgers		
(29)	Brett Butler	.15
(30)	Eric Davis	.15
(31)	Orel Hershiser	.15
(32)	Eric Karros	.15
(33)	Ramon Martinez	.15
(34)	Mike Piazza	1.50
(35)	Darryl Strawberry	.15
Montreal Expos		
(36)	Moises Alou	.15
(37)	Delino DeShields	.15
(38)	Marquis Grissom	.15
(39)	Dennis Martinez	.15
(40)	Larry Walker	.15
New York Mets		
(41)	Bobby Bonilla	.15
(42)	Dwight Gooden	.15
(43)	Howard Johnson	.15
(44)	Eddie Murray	.60
Philadelphia Phillies		
(45)	Darren Daulton	.15
(46)	Lenny Dykstra	.15
(47)	Dave Hollins	.15
(48)	John Kruk	.15
Pittsburgh Pirates		
(49)	Jay Bell	.15
(50)	Al Martin	.15
(51)	Orlando Merced	.15
(52)	Andy Van Slyke	.15
St. Louis Cardinals		
(53)	Gregg Jefferies	.15
(54)	Tom Pagnozzi	.15
(55)	Ozzie Smith	.75
(56)	Todd Zeile	.15
San Diego Padres		
(57)	Derek Bell	.15
(58)	Tony Gwynn	.75
(59)	Fred McGriff	.35
San Francisco Giants		
(60)	Barry Bonds	2.00

(61) John Burkett .15
(62) Will Clark .15
(63) Matt Williams .15

Baltimore Orioles
(64) Brady Anderson .15
(65) Mike Mussina .30
(66) Cal Ripken, Jr. 2.00

Boston Red Sox
(67) Roger Clemens 1.00
(68) Andre Dawson .30
(69) Mike Greenwell .15
(70) Mo Vaughn .15

Detroit Tigers
(71) Cecil Fielder .15
(72) Tony Phillips .15
(73) Mickey Tettleton .15
(74) Alan Trammell .15

Cleveland Indians
(75) Sandy Alomar Jr. .15
(76) Carlos Baerga .15
(77) Albert Belle .15
(78) Kenny Lofton .15

Chicago White Sox
(79) Bo Jackson .25
(80) Frank Thomas .60
(81) Robin Ventura .15

California Angels
(82) Chad Curtis .15
(83) Gary DiSarcina .15
(84) Tim Salmon .15
(85) J.T. Snow .15

Kansas City Royals
(86) George Brett 1.00
(87) Wally Joyner .15
(88) Mike MacFarlane .15
(89) Brian McRae .15

Milwaukee Brewers
(90) Darryl Hamilton .15
(91) Pat Listach .15
(92) B.J. Surhoff .15
(93) Robin Yount .60

Minnesota Twins
(94) Kent Hrbek .15
(95) Chuck Knoblauch .15
(96) Kirby Puckett .75
(97) Dave Winfield .60

New York Yankees
(98) Wade Boggs .75
(99) Don Mattingly 1.00
(100) Danny Tartabull .15

Oakland Athletics
(101) Dennis Eckersley .50
(102) Rickey Henderson .60
(103) Mark McGwire 1.50
(104) Ruben Sierra .15
(105) Terry Steinbach .15

Seattle Mariners
(106) Ken Griffey Jr. 1.50
(107) Edgar Martinez .15
(108) Pete O'Brien .15
(109) David Valle .15

Texas Rangers
(110) Jose Canseco .35
(111) Juan Gonzalez .35
(112) Ivan Rodriguez .50
(113) Nolan Ryan 2.00

Toronto Blue Jays
(114) Roberto Alomar .30
(115) Pat Borders .15
(116) Joe Carter .15
(117) Juan Guzman .15
(118) Paul Molitor .60
(119) John Olerud .15
(120) Dave Stewart .15

1993 DiamondMarks Inserts

KEN GRIFFEY, JR.

Randomly inserted into packs of DiamondMarks cards at the rate of one per 48-pack carton was a series of eight cards featuring the baseball artwork of Terry Smith. The inserts are the same 2-1/2" x 5" size as the regular issue and carry on with the basic black bordered design, though the inserts are UV-coated both front and back. Beneath the fantasy-design player art on the front is the player's name. On back the open book design is seen again, with a short player pro-

file on the left and a Barry Colla photo portrait on the right, along with the appropriate team logo.

sions of each card in the set have a red rubber-stamped ad on back.

nally sold at $19.95. Promo ver-

	NM/M
Complete Set (8):	50.00
Common Player:	5.00
(1) Roberto Alomar	6.00
(2) Barry Bonds	15.00
(3) Ken Griffey Jr.	10.00
(4) David Justice	5.00
(5) John Olerud	5.00
(6) Nolan Ryan	15.00
(7) Frank Thomas	7.50
(8) Robin Yount	7.50

1981 Diamond Stars Extension Set

BENNY FREY

About 1980 an uncut sheet of artwork apparently intended for use in the original Diamond Stars series (1934-36) was discovered. The art was used to create a collectors' issue "extension" set by Den's Collectors Den of Maryland. The new cards were printed in the same 2-3/8" x 2-7/8" format as the 1930s issue with the player name on front. Backs are printed in blue with a career summary, biographical details and a 1981 copyright line. The set was sold in a heavy paper wrapper patterned after the original.

	NM/M
Complete Set (12):	5.00
Uncut Sheet:	25.00
Common Player:	.25
109 Benny Frey	.25
110 Pete Fox	.25
111 Phil Cavarretta	.35
112 Leon Goslin	.50
113 Mel Harder	.35
114 Roger Cramer	.35
115 Gene Moore	.25
116 Rip Collins	.35
117 Linus Frey	.25
118 Vernon Gomez	1.00
119 Jim Bottomley, Rogers Hornsby	1.50
120 Lon Warneke	.25

1993 Diamond Stars Extension Set

In the style of the 1934-36 Diamond Stars bubblegum cards from National Chicle Co., this collectors' issue features colorful painting of players from the mid-1930s. Cards measure about 2-3/8" x 2-7/8" with white borders on front with no player identification or other graphics. The artwork is by D'August Roth Martin. Backs have player id, personal data and a career summary purporting to have been written by Travis Lake in Aug., 1936, the man who wrote the backs for the original cards. A copyright line at bottom identifies the "Extended Edition" as a 1993 issue of "The Chicle Fantasy Co." According to the set's producer, 4,166 were printed with 1,936 cut into hand-numbered sets which were origi-

Complete Set, Uncut Sheet:	15.00
Complete Set (36):	10.00
Common Player:	.25
121 Moe Berg	2.00
122 Harlond Clift	.25
123 Joe Cronin	.50
124 Dizzy Dean	.50
125 Paul Dean	.50
126 Joe DiMaggio	3.00
127 Leo Durocher	.50
128 Bob Feller	1.00
129 Carl Fisher	.25
130 Lou Gehrig	2.00
131 Bump Hadley	.25
132 Jesse Haines	.25
133 Bad News Hale	.25
134 Gabby Hartnett	.25
135 Babe Herman	.25
136 Billy Herman	.25
137 Waite Hoyt	.25
138 Bob Johnson	.25
139 Chuck Klein	.50
140 Mike Kreevich	.25
141 Fred Lindstrom	.25
142 Connie Mack	.50
143 Joe McCarthy	.25
144 Bill McKechnie	.25
145 Johnny Mize	.60
146 Johnny Moore	.25
147 Hugh Mulcahy	.25
148 Buck Newsom	.25
149 Al Smith	.25
150 Casey Stengel	1.00
151 Arky Vaughan	.25
152 Gee Walker	.25
153 Kenesaw M. Landis	.25
Cool Papa Bell	.25
Josh Gibson	.50
Satchel Paige	1.00
Title Card	.10

1992 Diet Pepsi Collector Series

Dwight Gooden

This Canadian issue includes 30 top stars, with a slight emphasis on the two Canadian teams. Because the set is licensed only by the players' association, and not Major League Baseball, all photos had team logos eliminated. Fronts feature action photo with Diet Pepsi logos in a strip below. Backs have a portrait photo, recent stats and a facsimile autograph. Card number 5 of Tom Glavine can be found showing him pitching right-handed (error) or left-handed (right). Cards are UV coated on both sides. A poster picturing all 30 cards was also issued. Cards were issued in three-card packs.

	NM/M
Complete Set (30):	7.00
Poster:	7.50
Common Player:	.15
1 Roger Clemens	.60
2 Dwight Gooden	.15
3 Tom Henke	.15
4 Dennis Martinez	.15
5a Tom Glavine (Pitching right-handed.)	.25
5b Tom Glavine (Pitching left-handed.)	.75
6 Jack Morris	.15
7 Dennis Eckersley	.35
8 Jeff Reardon	.15
9 Bryan Harvey	.15
10 Sandy Alomar Jr.	.15
11 Carlton Fisk	.40
12 Gary Carter	.40
13 Cecil Fielder	.15
14 Will Clark	.40
15 Roberto Alomar	.30
16 Ryne Sandberg	.50
17 Cal Ripken Jr.	1.50
18 Barry Larkin	.15
19 Ozzie Smith	.50
20 Kelly Gruber	.15
21 Wade Boggs	.50

22 Tim Wallach	.15
23 Howard Johnson	.15
24 Jose Canseco	.30
25 Joe Carter	.15
26 Ken Griffey Jr.	.65
27 Kirby Puckett	.50
28 Rickey Henderson	.40
29 Barry Bonds	1.50
30 Dave Winfield	.40

2002 Disabled American Veterans

Ben SHEETS

In conjunction with its "DAV at the Ballpark" program, the vets' service organization and many Major League teams had special promotions during the 2002 season. Baseball cards featuring one or more members of the home team were distributed to fans. Cards share a format of standard 2-1/2" x 3-1/2" size with glossy coating on both sides. Fronts have action pictures against a ghosted image of the home ballpark. A small portrait photo also appears, along with team and DAV logos and a card number. Backs have information about the DAV and contact data. This checklist is not complete.

	NM/M
Common Player:	1.00
2 Ben Sheets	1.00
5 Trevor Hoffman	1.00
12 Steve Cox	1.00
13 Jay Gibbons	1.00
14 Rusty Greer	1.00
15 Danny Graves	1.00
16 Todd Helton	1.50
17 Eddie Guardado	1.00
20 Kazuhiro Sasaki	1.00
21 Ichiro Suzuki	2.50
22 Mike Cameron, Mark McLemore	1.00
23 Mike Scioscia	1.00

2003 Disabled American Veterans

Richie SEXSON

In conjunction with its "DAV at the Ballpark" program, the vets' service organization and several Major League teams had special promotions during the 2003 season. Baseball cards featuring one or more members of the home team were distributed to fans. Cards share a format of standard 2-1/2" x 3-1/2" size with glossy coating on both sides. Fronts have action pictures against a ghosted image of the home ballpark. A team and DAV logo also appear, along with uniform and "Limited Edition" card numbers. Backs have information about the DAV and contact data. This checklist is not complete.

	NM/M
Common Player:	1.00
3 Richie Sexson	1.00
9 Rocco Baldelli	1.50

12 Edgar Martinez	1.00
23 Preston Wilson	1.00
26 Adam Dunn	1.00

2004 Disabled American Veterans

In conjunction with its "DAV at the Ballpark" program, the vets' service organization and several Major League teams had special promotions during the 2004 season. Baseball cards featuring one or more members of the home team were distributed to fans. Cards share a format of standard 2-1/2" x 3-1/2" size with glossy coating on both sides. Fronts have a large portrait photo and smaller action photo. A team logo and uniform number are at top, at bottom is "Limited Edition" and a card number. Backs have information about the DAV and contact data.

	NM/M
Complete Set (42):	30.00
Common Player:	1.00
1 Robby Hammock	1.00
2 Austin Kearns	2.00
3 Larry Bigbie	1.00
4 Wes Helms	1.00
5 Scott Podsednik	2.00
6 Ben Sheets	1.00
7 Brian Giles	1.00
8 Joel Pineiro	1.50
9 Dan Wilson	1.00
10 Ron Gardenhire	1.00
11 Eddie Guardado	1.00
12 Raul Ibanez	1.00
13 Hank Blalock	4.00
14 Mark Teixeira	2.00
15 Michael Young	1.00
16 Danys Baez	1.00
17 Jose Cruz Jr.	1.00
18 Robert Fick	1.00
19 Toby Hall	1.00
20 Tino Martinez	1.00
21 Mike Maroth	1.00
22 Lou Piniella	1.00
23 Damian Rolls	1.00
24 Doug Waechter	1.00
25 Victor Zambrano	1.00
26 Don Zimmer	1.00
27 J.D. Drew	3.00
28 Horacio Ramirez	1.00
29 Jeff Kent	1.00
30 John Thomson	1.00
31 John Estrada	1.00
32 Rafael Furcal	1.00
33 John Smoltz	1.00
34 Chipper Jones	5.00
35 Marcus Giles	1.00
36 Andruw Jones	4.00
37 Josh Beckett	2.00
38 Miguel Cabrera	1.50
39 Hee Seop Choi	1.00
40 Brad Penny	1.00
41 Juan Pierre	1.50
42 Dontrelle Willis	1.00

2005 Disabled American Veterans

ICHIRO SUZUKI

These cards were issued by vets' service organization and several Major League teams in special promotions during the 2005 season. Baseball cards featuring one or more members of the home team were distributed to fans. Cards share a format of standard 2-1/2" x 3-1/2" size with glossy coating on both sides. Fronts have an action photo on a ball-and-glove

background with team logo. At bottom is "Limited Edition" and a card number. Backs have information about the DAV and contact data.

Common Player:

1988 Domino's Pizza Tigers

Denny McLain

Domino's Pizza produced a 28-card set commemorating the 20th anniversary of the 1968 World Champion Detroit Tigers. The cards were given away at an Old Timers Game at Tiger Stadium in 1988. The cards, which measure 2-1/2" x 3-1/2", feature black and white photos semi-surrounded by a two-stripe band. The stripes on the card's left side are the same color (red and light blue) as the Domino's Pizza logo in the upper corner. The stripes on the card's right side match the colors of the Tigers logo (red and dark blue). The backs of all the cards (except for Ernie Harwell) contain a brief summary of the Tigers' 1968 season. Located at the bottom on the card backs are the players' major league records through 1968 plus their 1968 World Series statistics.

	NM/M
Complete Set (29):	8.00
Common Player:	.25
(1) Gates Brown	.25
(2) Norm Cash	1.00
(3) Wayne Comer	.25
(4) Pat Dobson	.25
(5) Bill Freehan	.60
(6) John Hiller	.25
(7) Ernie Harwell (Announcer)	.40
(8) Willie Horton	.40
(9a) Al Kaline/Btg	3.00
(9b) Al Kaline (In outfield.)	3.00
(10) Fred Lasher	.25
(11) Mickey Lolich	.75
(12) Tom Matchick	.25
(13) Ed Mathews	1.25
(14) Dick McAuliff (McAuliffe)	.75
(15) Denny McLain	.75
(16) Don McMahon	.25
(17) Jim Northrup	.25
(18) Ray Oyler	.25
(19) Daryl Patterson	.25
(20) Jim Price	.25
(21) Joe Sparma	.25
(22) Mickey Stanley	.25
(23) Dick Tracewski	.25
(24) Jon Warden	.25
(25) Don Wert	.25
(26) Earl Wilson	.25
(27) Header Card	.05
(28) Coupon Card	.05

1980 Donruss Prototypes

When it became apparent that Topps' monopoly on baseball card production was going to be ended by the courts, Memphis-based Donruss began work to produce a bubblegum card set for 1981. As part of its research, Donruss created a three-card prototype panel in three different sizes to test collector preference. Two of the prototypes have player pictures, the third does not. Backs are blank.

	NM/M
Small Panel (About 6" x 2-3/4"):	75.00
Regular Panel (About 7-1/2" x 3-1/2"):	75.00
Large Panel (About 10-1/2" x 4-3/4".):	75.00
George Brett (2" x 2-3/4")	35.00
George Brett (2-1/2" x 3-1/2")	35.00
George Brett (3-1/2" x 4-3/4")	30.00
Reggie Jackson (2" x 2-3/4")	35.00
Reggie Jackson (2-1/2" x 3-1/2")	35.00
Reggie Jackson (3-1/2" x 4-3/4")	30.00
No Player Pictured (2" x 2-3/4")	7.50
No Player Pictured (2-1/2" x 3-1/2")	5.00
No Player Pictured (2-1/2" x 3-1/2")	5.00

1981 Donruss Promo Sheet

Rookie sensation Joe Charbonneau was the featured attraction when this sample sheet was issued to introduce Donruss' debut baseball card issue. The 10" x 7" sheet is comprised of eight of the cards which appeared in the set.

	NM/M
Complete Sheet:	35.00

1981 Donruss

TOM SEAVER PITCHER — Reds

The Donruss Co. of Memphis, Tenn., produced its premiere baseball card issue in 1981 with a set that consisted of 600 numbered cards and five unnumbered checklists. The cards, which measure 2-1/2" x 3-1/2", are printed on thin stock. The card fronts contain the Donruss logo plus the year of issue. The card backs are designed on a vertical format and have black print on red and white. The set, entitled "First Edition Collector Series," contains nearly 40 variations, those being first-printing errors that were corrected in a subsequent print run. The cards were sold in wax packs with bubblegum. The complete set price does not include the higher priced variations.

	NM/M
Complete Set (605):	25.00
Uncut Sheet Set (5):	65.00
Common Player:	.10
Wax Pack (18):	2.00
Wax Box (36):	60.00

1 Ozzie Smith 2.00
2 Rollie Fingers 1.00
3 Rick Wise .10
4 Gene Richards .10
5 Alan Trammell .60
6 Tom Brookens .10
7a Duffy Dyer (1980 Avg. .185) .25
7b Duffy Dyer (1980 Avg. 185) .10
8 Mark Fidrych .15
9 Dave Rozema .10
10 Ricky Peters .10

11 Mike Schmidt 3.00
12 Willie Stargell 1.25
13 Tim Foli .10
14 Manny Sanguillen .10
15 Grant Jackson .10
16 Eddie Solomon .10
17 Omar Moreno .10
18 Joe Morgan 1.25
19 Rafael Landestoy .10
20 Bruce Bochy .10
21 Joe Sambito .10
22 Manny Trillo .10
23a Dave Smith RC (Incomplete box around stats.) .10
23b Dave Smith RC (Complete box around stats.) .15
24 Terry Puhl .10
25 Bump Wills .10
26a John Ellis (Danny Walton photo - with bat.) .30
26b John Ellis (John Ellis photo - with glove.) .10
27 Jim Kern .10
28 Richie Zisk .10
29 John Mayberry .10
30 Bob Davis .10
31 Jackson Todd .10
32 Al Woods .10
33 Steve Carlton 1.50
34 Lee Mazzilli .10
35 John Stearns .10
36 Roy Jackson .10
37 Mike Scott .10
38 Lamar Johnson .10
39 Kevin Bell .10
40 Ed Farmer .10
41 Ross Baumgarten .10
42 Leo Sutherland .10
43 Dan Meyer .10
44 Ron Reed .10
45 Mario Mendoza .10
46 Rick Honeycutt .10
47 Glenn Abbott .10
48 Leon Roberts .10
49 Rod Carew 1.50
50 Bert Campaneris .10
51a Tom Donahue (Incorrect spelling.) .25
51b Tom Donohue (Donohue on front.) .10
52 Dave Frost .10
53 Ed Halicki .10
54 Dan Ford .10
55 Garry Maddox .10
56a Steve Garvey (Surpassed 25 HR.) 1.25
56b Steve Garvey (Surpassed 21 HR.) .60
57 Bill Russell .10
58 Don Sutton 1.00
59 Reggie Smith .10
60 Rick Monday .10
61 Ray Knight .10
62 Johnny Bench 1.50
63 Mario Soto .10
64 Doug Bair .10
65 George Foster .10
66 Jeff Burroughs .10
67 Keith Hernandez .10
68 Tom Herr .10
69 Bob Forsch .10
70 John Fulgham .10
71a Bobby Bonds (Lifetime HR 986.) .35
71b Bobby Bonds (Lifetime HR 326.) .15
72a Rennie Stennett ("...breaking broke leg..." on back) .25
72b Rennie Stennett ("...breaking leg..." on back) .10
73 Joe Strain .10
74 Ed Whitson .10
75 Tom Griffin .10
76 Bill North .10
77 Gene Garber .10
78 Mike Hargrove .10
79 Dave Rosello .10
80 Ron Hassey .10
81 Sid Monge .10
82a Joe Charbonneau RC ("For some reason, Phillies..." on back.) 2.00
82b Joe Charbonneau RC ("Phillies..." on back.) .25
83 Cecil Cooper .10
84 Sal Bando .10
85 Moose Haas .10
86 Mike Caldwell .10
87a Larry Hisle ("...Twins with 28 RBI." on back.) .25
87b Larry Hisle ("...Twins with 28 HR" on back.) .10
88 Luis Gomez .10
89 Larry Parrish .10
90 Gary Carter 1.25
91 Bill Gullickson RC .15
92 Fred Norman .10
93 Tommy Hutton .10
94 Carl Yastrzemski 1.50
95 Glenn Hoffman .10
96 Dennis Eckersley 1.25
97a Tom Burgmeier (Throws: Right) .25
97b Tom Burgmeier (Throws: Left) .10
98 Win Remmerswaal .10
99 Bob Horner .10
100 George Brett 3.00

101 Dave Chalk .10
102 Dennis Leonard .10
103 Renie Martin .10
104 Amos Otis .15
105 Graig Nettles .15
106 Eric Soderholm .10
107 Tommy John .10
108 Tom Underwood .10
109 Lou Piniella .10
110 Mickey Klutts .10
111 Bobby Murcer .10
112 Eddie Murray 1.50
113 Rick Dempsey .10
114 Scott McGregor .10
115 Ken Singleton .10
116 Gary Roenicke .10
117 Dave Revering .10
118 Mike Norris .10
119 Rickey Henderson 2.00
120 Mike Heath .10
121 Dave Cash .10
122 Randy Jones .10
123 Eric Rasmussen .10
124 Jerry Mumphrey .10
125 Richie Hebner .10
126 Mark Wagner .10
127 Jack Morris .10
128 Dan Petry .10
129 Bruce Robbins .10
130 Champ Summers .10
131a Pete Rose ("See card 251" on back.) 2.00
131b Pete Rose ("See card 371" on back.) 2.00
132 Willie Stargell 1.25
133 Ed Ott .10
134 Jim Bibby .10
135 Bert Blyleven .10
136 Dave Parker .10
137 Bill Robinson .10
138 Enos Cabell .10
139 Dave Bergman .10
140 J.R. Richard .10
141 Ken Forsch .10
142 Larry Bowa .10
143 Frank LaCorte (Photo actually Randy Niemann.) .10
144 Dennis Walling .10
145 Buddy Bell .10
146 Fergie Jenkins 1.00
147 Danny Darwin .10
148 John Grubb .10
149 Alfredo Griffin .10
150 Jerry Garvin .10
151 Paul Mirabella RC .10
152 Rick Bosetti .10
153 Dick Ruthven .10
154 Frank Taveras .10
155 Craig Swan .10
156 Jeff Reardon RC 1.00
157 Steve Henderson .10
158 Jim Morrison .10
159 Glenn Borgmann .10
160 Lamarr Hoyt (LaMarr) RC .10
161 Rich Wortham .10
162 Thad Bosley .10
163 Julio Cruz .10
164a Del Unser (No 3B in stat heads.) .25
164b Del Unser (3B in stat heads) .10
165 Jim Anderson .10
166 Jim Beattie .10
167 Shane Rawley .10
168 Joe Simpson .10
169 Rod Carew 1.50
170 Fred Patek .10
171 Frank Tanana .10
172 Alfredo Martinez .10
173 Chris Knapp .10
174 Joe Rudi .10
175 Greg Luzinski .10
176 Steve Garvey .60
177 Joe Ferguson .10
178 Bob Welch .10
179 Dusty Baker .10
180 Rudy Law .10
181 Dave Concepcion .10
182 Johnny Bench 1.50
183 Mike LaCoss .10
184 Ken Griffey .10
185 Dave Collins .10
186 Brian Asselstine .10
187 Garry Templeton .10
188 Mike Phillips .10
189 Pete Vukovich .10
190 John Urrea .10
191 Tony Scott .10
192 Darrell Evans .10
193 Milt May .10
194 Bob Knepper .10
195 Randy Moffitt .10
196 Larry Herndon .10
197 Rick Camp .10
198 Andre Thornton .10
199 Tom Veryzer .10
200 Gary Alexander .10
201 Rick Waits .10
202 Rick Manning .10
203 Paul Molitor 1.25
204 Jim Gantner .10
205 Paul Mitchell .10
206 Reggie Cleveland .10
207 Sixto Lezcano .10
208 Bruce Benedict .10
209 Rodney Scott .10
210 John Tamargo .10
211 Bill Lee .10

212 Andre Dawson .75
213 Rowland Office .10
214 Carl Yastrzemski 1.50
215 Jerry Remy .10
216 Mike Torrez .10
217 Skip Lockwood .10
218 Fred Lynn .10
219 Chris Chambliss .10
220 Willie Aikens .10
221 John Wathan .10
222 Dan Quisenberry .10
223 Willie Wilson .10
224 Clint Hurdle .10
225 Bob Watson .10
226 Jim Spencer .10
227 Ron Guidry .15
228 Reggie Jackson 2.00
229 Oscar Gamble .10
230 Jeff Cox .10
231 Luis Tiant .10
232 Rich Dauer .10
233 Dan Graham .10
234 Mike Flanagan .10
235 John Lowenstein .10
236 Benny Ayala .10
237 Wayne Gross .10
238 Rick Langford .10
239 Tony Armas .10
240a Bob Lacy (Incorrect spelling.) .25
240b Bob Lacey (Correct spelling.) .10
241 Gene Tenace .10
242 Bob Shirley .10
243 Gary Lucas .10
244 Jerry Turner .10
245 John Wockenfuss .10
246 Stan Papi .10
247 Milt Wilcox .10
248 Dan Schatzeder .10
249 Steve Kemp .10
250 Jim Lentine .10
251 Pete Rose 2.00
252 Bill Madlock .10
253 Dale Berra .10
254 Kent Tekulve .10
255 Enrique Romo .10
256 Mike Easler .10
257 Chuck Tanner .10
258 Art Howe .10
259 Alan Ashby .10
260 Nolan Ryan 5.00
261a Vern Ruhle (Ken Forsch photo - head shot.) .25
261b Vern Ruhle (Vern Ruhle photo - waist to head shot.) .10
262 Bob Boone .10
263 Cesar Cedeno .10
264 Jeff Leonard .10
265 Pat Putnam .10
266 Jon Matlack .10
267 Dave Rajsich .10
268 Billy Sample .10
269 Damaso Garcia RC .10
270 Tom Buskey .10
271 Joey McLaughlin .10
272 Barry Bonnell .10
273 Tug McGraw .10
274 Mike Jorgensen .10
275 Pat Zachry .10
276 Neil Allen .10
277 Joel Youngblood .10
278 Greg Pryor .10
279a Britt Burns RC .10
280 Rich Dotson RC .25
281 Chet Lemon .10
282 Rusty Kuntz .10
283 Ted Cox .10
284 Sparky Lyle .10
285 Larry Cox .10
286 Floyd Bannister .10
287 Byron McLaughlin .10
288 Rodney Craig .10
289 Bobby Grich .10
290 Dickie Thon .10
291 Mark Clear .10
292 Dave Lemanczyk .10
293 Jason Thompson .10
294 Rick Miller .10
295 Lonnie Smith .10
296 Ron Cey .10
297 Steve Yeager .10
298 Bobby Castillo .10
299 Manny Mota .10
300 Jay Johnstone .10
301 Dan Driessen .10
302 Joe Nolan .10
303 Paul Householder .10
304 Harry Spilman .10
305 Cesar Geronimo .10
306a Gary Mathews (Mathews on front.) .35
306b Gary Matthews (Matthews on front.) .10
307 Ken Reitz .10
308 Ted Simmons .10
309 John Littlefield .10
310 George Frazier .10
311 Dane Iorg .10
312 Mike Ivie .10
313 Dennis Littlejohn .10
314 Gary LaVelle (Lavelle) .10
315 Jack Clark .10
316 Jim Wohlford .10
317 Rick Matula .10
318 Toby Harrah .10
319a Dwane Kuiper (Dwane on front.) .25

319b Duane Kuiper (Duane on front.) .10
320 Len Barker .10
321 Victor Cruz .10
322 Dell Alston .10
323 Robin Yount 1.25
324 Charlie Moore .10
325 Lary Sorensen .10
326a Gorman Thomas ("...30-HR mark 4th..." on back) .25
326b Gorman Thomas ("...30-HR mark 3rd..." on back) .10
327 Bob Rodgers .10
328 Phil Niekro 1.00
329 Chris Speier .10
330a Steve Rodgers (Rodgers on front.) .25
330b Steve Rogers (Rogers on front.) .10
331 Woodie Fryman .10
332 Warren Cromartie .10
333 Jerry White .10
334 Tony Perez 1.25
335 Carlton Fisk 1.25
336 Dick Drago .10
337 Steve Renko .10
338 Jim Rice .75
339 Jerry Royster .10
340 Frank White .10
341 Jamie Quirk .10
342a Paul Spittorff (Spittorff on front.) .25
342b Paul Splittorff (Splittorff on front.) .10
343 Marty Pattin .10
344 Pete LaCock .10
345 Willie Randolph .10
346 Rick Cerone .10
347 Rich Gossage .10
348 Reggie Jackson 2.00
349 Ruppert Jones .10
350 Dave McKay .10
351 Yogi Berra .50
352 Doug Decinces (DeCinces) .10
353 Jim Palmer 1.25
354 Tippy Martinez .10
355 Al Bumbry .10
356 Earl Weaver .50
357a Bob Picciolo (Bob on front.) .25
357b Rob Picciolo (Rob on front.) .10
358 Matt Keough .10
359 Dwayne Murphy .10
360 Brian Kingman .10
361 Bill Fahey .10
362 Steve Mura .10
363 Dennis Kinney .10
364 Dave Winfield 1.25
365 Lou Whitaker .10
366 Lance Parrish .10
367 Tim Corcoran .10
368 Pat Underwood .10
369 Al Cowens .10
370 Sparky Anderson .50
371 Pete Rose 3.00
372 Phil Garner .10
373 Steve Nicosia .10
374 John Candelaria .10
375 Don Robinson .10
376 Lee Lacy .10
377 John Milner .10
378 Craig Reynolds .10
379a Luis Pujois (Pujois on front.) .25
379b Luis Pujols (Pujols on front.) .10
380 Joe Niekro .10
381 Joaquin Andujar .10
382 Keith Moreland RC .15
383 Jose Cruz .10
384 Bill Virdon .10
385 Jim Sundberg .10
386 Doc Medich .10
387 Al Oliver .10
388 Jim Norris .10
389 Bob Bailor .10
390 Ernie Whitt .10
391 Otto Velez .10
392 Roy Howell .10
393 Bob Walk RC .10
394 Doug Flynn .10
395 Pete Falcone .10
396 Tom Hausman .10
397 Elliott Maddox .10
398 Mike Squires .10
399 Marvis Foley .10
400 Steve Trout .10
401 Wayne Nordhagen .10
402 Tony Larussa (LaRussa) .10
403 Bruce Bochte .10
404 Bake McBride .10
405 Jerry Narron .10
406 Rob Dressler .10
407 Dave Heaverlo .10
408 Tom Paciorek .10
409 Carney Lansford .10
410 Brian Downing .10
411 Don Aase .10
412 Jim Barr .10
413 Don Baylor .10
414 Jim Fregosi .10
415 Dallas Green .10
416 Dave Lopes .10
417 Jerry Reuss .10
418 Rick Sutcliffe .10
419 Derrel Thomas .10

420 Tommy LaSorda (Lasorda.) .50
421 Charlie Leibrandt RC .25
422 Tom Seaver 1.50
423 Ron Oester .10
424 Junior Kennedy .10
425 Tom Seaver 1.50
426 Bobby Cox .10
427 Leon Durham RC .20
428 Terry Kennedy .10
429 Silvio Martinez .10
430 George Hendrick .10
431 Red Schoendienst .50
432 John LeMaster .10
433 Vida Blue .10
434 John Montefusco .10
435 Terry Whitfield .10
436 Dave Bristol .10
437 Dale Murphy .75
438 Jerry Dybzinski .10
439 Jorge Orta .10
440 Wayne Garland .10
441 Miguel Dilone .10
442 Dave Garcia .10
443 Don Money .10
444a Buck Martinez (Photo reversed.) .35
444b Buck Martinez (Photo correct.) .10
445 Jerry Augustine .10
446 Ben Oglivie .10
447 Jim Slaton .10
448 Doyle Alexander .10
449 Tony Bernazard .10
450 Scott Sanderson .10
451 Dave Palmer .10
452 Stan Bahnsen .10
453 Dick Williams .10
454 Rick Burleson .10
455 Gary Allenson .10
456 Bob Stanley .10
457a John Tudor RC (Lifetime W/L 9.7.) .40
457b John Tudor RC (Lifetime W/L 9-7.) .20
458 Dwight Evans .10
459 Glenn Hubbard .10
460 U L Washington .10
461 Larry Gura .10
462 Rich Gale .10
463 Hal McRae .10
464 Jim Frey .10
465 Bucky Dent .10
466 Dennis Werth .10
467 Ron Davis .10
468 Reggie Jackson 2.50
469 Bobby Brown .10
470 Mike Davis RC .10
471 Gaylord Perry 1.25
472 Mark Belanger .10
473 Jim Palmer 1.25
474 Sammy Stewart .10
475 Tim Stoddard .10
476 Steve Stone .10
477 Jeff Newman .10
478 Steve McCatty .10
479 Billy Martin .10
480 Mitchell Page .10
481 Steve Carlton (CY) .40
482 Bill Buckner .10
483a Ivan DeJesus (Lifetime hits 702.) .25
483b Ivan DeJesus (Lifetime hits 642.) .10
484 Cliff Johnson .10
485 Lenny Randle .10
486 Larry Milbourne .10
487 Roy Smalley .10
488 John Castino .10
489 Ron Jackson .10
490a Dave Roberts (1980 highlights begins "Showed pop...") .25
490b Dave Roberts (1980 highlights begins "Declared himself...") .10
491 George Brett (MVP) 1.50
492 Mike Cubbage .10
493 Rob Wilfong .10
494 Danny Goodwin .10
495 Jose Morales .10
496 Mickey Rivers .10
497 Mike Edwards .10
498 Mike Sadek .10
499 Lenn Sakata .10
500 Gene Michael .10
501 Dave Roberts .10
502 Steve Dillard .10
503 Jim Essian .10
504 Rance Mulliniks .10
505 Darrell Porter .10
506 Joe Torre .50
507 Terry Crowley .10
508 Bill Travers .10
509 Nelson Norman .10
510 Bob McClure .10
511 Steve Howe RC .15
512 Dave Rader .10
513 Mick Kelleher .10
514 Kiko Garcia .10
515 Larry Biittner .10
516a Willie Norwood (1980 highlights begins "Spent most...") .25
516b Willie Norwood (1980 highlights begins "Traded in...") .10
517 Bo Diaz .10

#	Player	Price
518	Juan Beniquez	.10
519	Scot Thompson	.10
520	Jim Tracy	.10
521	Carlos Lezcano	.10
522	Joe Amalfitano	.10
523	Preston Hanna	.10
524a	Ray Burris (1980 highlights begins "Went on...")	.25
524b	Ray Burris (1980 highlights begins "Drafted by...")	.10
525	Broderick Perkins	.10
526	Mickey Hatcher	.10
527	John Goryl	.10
528	Dick Davis	.10
529	Butch Wynegar	.10
530	Sal Butera	.10
531	Jerry Koosman	.10
532a	Jeff (Geoff) Zahn (1980 highlights begins "Was 2nd in...")	.25
532b	Jeff (Geoff) Zahn (1980 highlights begins "Signed a 3 year ...")	.10
533	Dennis Martinez	.10
534	Gary Thomasson	.10
535	Steve Macko	.15
536	Jim Kaat	.15
537	Best Hitters (George Brett, Rod Carew)	1.50
538	Tim Raines RC	3.00
539	Keith Smith	.10
540	Ken Macha	.10
541	Burt Hooton	.10
542	Butch Hobson	.10
543	Bill Stein	.10
544	Dave Stapleton	.10
545	Bob Pate	.10
546	Doug Corbett	.10
547	Darrell Jackson	.10
548	Pete Redfern	.10
549	Roger Erickson	.10
550	Al Hrabosky	.10
551	Dick Tidrow	.10
552	Dave Ford	.10
553	Dave Kingman	.10
554a	Mike Vail (1980 highlights begins "After...")	.25
554b	Mike Vail (1980 highlights begins "Traded...")	.10
555a	Jerry Martin (1980 highlights begins "Overcame...")	.25
555b	Jerry Martin (1980 highlights begins "Traded...")	.10
556a	Jesus Figueroa (1980 highlights begins "Had...")	.25
556b	Jesus Figueroa (1980 highlights begins "Traded...")	.10
557	Don Stanhouse	.10
558	Barry Foote	.10
559	Tim Blackwell	.10
560	Bruce Sutter	1.25
561	Rick Reuschel	.10
562	Lynn McGlothen	.10
563a	Bob Owchinko (1980 highlights begins "Traded...")	.25
563b	Bob Owchinko (1980 highlights begins "Involved...")	.10
564	John Verhoeven	.10
565	Ken Landreaux	.10
566a	Glen Adams (Glen on front.)	.25
566b	Glenn Adams (Glenn on front.)	.10
567	Hosken Powell	.10
568	Dick Noles	.10
569	Danny Ainge RC	2.00
570	Bobby Mattick	.10
571	Joe LeFebvre (Lefebvre)	.10
572	Bobby Clark	.10
573	Dennis Lamp	.10
574	Randy Lerch	.10
575	Mookie Wilson RC	.30
576	Ron LeFlore	.10
577	Jim Dwyer	.10
578	Bill Castro	.10
579	Greg Minton	.10
580	Mark Littell	.10
581	Andy Hassler	.10
582	Dave Stieb	.10
583	Ken Oberkfell	.10
584	Larry Bradford	.10
585	Fred Stanley	.10
586	Bill Caudill	.10
587	Doug Capilla	.10
588	George Riley	.10
589	Willie Hernandez	.10
590	Mike Schmidt (MVP)	1.50
591	Steve Stone (Cy Young 1980)	.10
592	Rick Sofield	.10
593	Bombo Rivera	.10
594	Gary Ward	.10
595a	Dave Edwards (1980 highlights begins "Sidelined...")	.25
595b	Dave Edwards (1980 highlights begins "Traded...")	.10
596	Mike Proly	.10
597	Tommy Boggs	.10
598	Greg Gross	.10
599	Elias Sosa	.10
600	Pat Kelly	.10
----	Checklist 1-120 (51 Tom Donohue)	.25
----	Checklist 1-120 (51 Tom Donahue)	.10
----	Checklist 121-240	.10
----	Checklist 241-360 (306 Gary Mathews)	.25
----	Checklist 241-360 (306 Gary Matthews)	.10
----	Checklist 361-480 (379 Luis Pujois)	.25
----	Checklist 361-480 (379 Luis Pujols)	.10
----	Checklist 481-600 (566 Glen Adams)	.25
----	Checklist 481-600 (566 Glenn Adams)	.10

1982 Donruss

Using card stock thicker than the previous year, Donruss issued a 660-card set which includes 653 numbered cards and seven un-numbered checklists. The cards were sold with puzzle pieces rather than gum as a result of a lawsuit by Topps. The puzzle pieces (three pieces on one card per pack) feature Babe Ruth. The first 26 cards of the set, entitled Diamond Kings, showcase the artwork of Dick Perez. Card fronts display the Donruss logo and the year of issue. Backs have black and blue ink on white stock and include the player's career highlights. The complete set price does not include the higher priced variations.

	NM/M
Unopened Fact. Set (660):	50.00
Complete Set (660):	45.00
Complete Set, Uncut Sheets (5):	175.00
Common Player:	.10
Babe Ruth Puzzle:	1.00
Wax Pack (15):	2.50
Wax Box (36):	80.00

#	Player	Price
1	Pete Rose (Diamond King)	4.00
2	Gary Carter (DK)	1.25
3	Steve Garvey (DK)	.45
4	Vida Blue (DK)	.10
5a	Alan Trammel (DK) (Last name incorrect.)	1.00
5b	Alan Trammell (DK)(Corrected)	.30
6	Len Barker (DK)	.10
7	Dwight Evans (DK)	.15
8	Rod Carew (DK)	1.25
9	George Hendrick (DK)	.10
10	Phil Niekro (DK)	1.00
11	Richie Zisk (DK)	.10
12	Dave Parker (DK)	.25
13	Nolan Ryan (DK)	5.00
14	Ivan DeJesus (DK)	.10
15	George Brett (DK)	2.00
16	Tom Seaver (DK)	1.25
17	Dave Kingman (DK)	.15
18	Dave Winfield (DK)	1.25
19	Mike Norris (DK)	.10
20	Carlton Fisk (DK)	1.25
21	Ozzie Smith (DK)	1.50
22	Roy Smalley (DK)	.10
23	Buddy Bell (DK)	.10
24	Ken Singleton (DK)	.10
25	John Mayberry (DK)	.10
26	Gorman Thomas (DK)	.10
27	Earl Weaver	.50
28	Rollie Fingers	1.00
29	Sparky Anderson	.50
30	Dennis Eckersley	1.25
31	Dave Winfield	1.25
32	Burt Hooton	.10
33	Rick Waits	.10
34	George Brett	2.00
35	Steve McCatty	.10
36	Steve Rogers	.10
37	Bill Stein	.10
38	Steve Renko	.10
39	Mike Squires	.10
40	George Hendrick	.10
41	Bob Knepper	.10
42	Steve Carlton	1.25
43	Larry Biittner	.10
44	Chris Welsh	.10
45	Steve Nicosia	.10
46	Jack Clark	.10
47	Chris Chambliss	.10
48	Ivan DeJesus	.10
49	Lee Mazzilli	.10
50	Julio Cruz	.10
51	Pete Redfern	.10
52	Dave Stieb	.10
53	Doug Corbett	.10
54	George Bell RC	.50
55	Joe Simpson	.10
56	Rusty Staub	.10
57	Hector Cruz	.10
58	Claudell Washington RC	.10
59	Enrique Romo	.10
60	Gary Lavelle	.10
61	Tim Flannery	.10
62	Joe Nolan	.10
63	Larry Bowa	.10
64	Sixto Lezcano	.10
65	Joe Sambito	.10
66	Bruce Kison	.10
67	Wayne Nordhagen	.10
68	Woodie Fryman	.10
69	Billy Sample	.10
70	Amos Otis	.10
71	Matt Keough	.10
72	Toby Harrah	.10
73	Dave Righetti RC	.30
74	Carl Yastrzemski	1.50
75	Bob Welch	.10
76a	Alan Trammel (Last name misspelled.)	1.00
76b	Alan Trammell (Corrected)	.10
77	Rick Dempsey	.10
78	Paul Molitor	1.25
79	Dennis Martinez	.10
80	Jim Slaton	.10
81	Champ Summers	.10
82	Carney Lansford	.10
83	Barry Foote	.10
84	Steve Garvey	.45
85	Rick Manning	.10
86	John Wathan	.10
87	Brian Kingman	.10
88	Andre Dawson	.50
89	Jim Kern	.10
90	Bobby Grich	.10
91	Bob Forsch	.10
92	Art Howe	.10
93	Marty Bystrom	.10
94	Ozzie Smith	1.50
95	Dave Parker	.10
96	Doyle Alexander	.10
97	Al Hrabosky	.10
98	Frank Taveras	.10
99	Tim Blackwell	.10
100	Floyd Bannister	.10
101	Alfredo Griffin	.10
102	Dave Engle	.10
103	Mario Soto	.10
104	Ross Baumgarten	.10
105	Ken Singleton	.10
106	Ted Simmons	.10
107	Jack Morris	.25
108	Bob Watson	.10
109	Dwight Evans	.10
110	Tom Lasorda	.50
111	Bert Blyleven	.10
112	Dan Quisenberry	.10
113	Rickey Henderson	1.25
114	Gary Carter	1.25
115	Brian Downing	.10
116	Al Oliver	.10
117	LaMarr Hoyt	.10
118	Cesar Cedeno	.10
119	Keith Moreland	.10
120	Bob Shirley	.10
121	Terry Kennedy	.10
122	Frank Pastore	.10
123	Gene Garber	.10
124	Tony Pena RC	.10
125	Allen Ripley	.10
126	Randy Martz	.10
127	Richie Zisk	.10
128	Mike Scott	.10
129	Lloyd Moseby	.10
130	Rob Wilfong	.10
131	Tim Stoddard	.10
132	Gorman Thomas	.10
133	Dan Petry	.10
134	Bob Stanley	.10
135	Lou Piniella	.15
136	Pedro Guerrero	.10
137	Len Barker	.10
138	Richard Gale	.10
139	Wayne Gross	.10
140	Tim Wallach RC	.50
141	Gene Mauch	.10
142	Doc Medich	.10
143	Tony Bernazard	.10
144	Bill Virdon	.10
145	John Littlefield	.10
146	Dave Bergman	.10
147	Dick Davis	.10
148	Tom Seaver	1.50
149	Matt Sinatro	.10
150	Chuck Tanner	.10
151	Leon Durham	.10
152	Gene Tenace	.10
153	Al Bumbry	.10
154	Mark Brouhard	.10
155	Rick Peters	.10
156	Jerry Remy	.10
157	Rick Reuschel	.10
158	Steve Howe	.10
159	Alan Bannister	.10
160	U L Washington	.10
161	Rick Langford	.10
162	Bill Gullickson	.10
163	Mark Wagner	.10
164	Geoff Zahn	.10
165	Ron LeFlore	.10
166	Dane Iorg	.10
167	Joe Niekro	.10
168	Pete Rose	3.00
169	Dave Collins	.10
170	Rick Wise	.10
171	Jim Bibby	.10
172	Larry Herndon	.10
173	Bob Horner	.10
174	Steve Dillard	.10
175	Mookie Wilson	.10
176	Dan Meyer	.10
177	Fernando Arroyo	.10
178	Jackson Todd	.10
179	Darrell Jackson	.10
180	Al Woods	.10
181	Jim Anderson	.10
182	Dave Kingman	.10
183	Steve Henderson	.10
184	Brian Asselstine	.10
185	Rod Scurry	.10
186	Fred Breining	.10
187	Danny Boone	.10
188	Junior Kennedy	.10
189	Sparky Lyle	.10
190	Whitey Herzog	.10
191	Dave Smith	.10
192	Ed Ott	.10
193	Greg Luzinski	.10
194	Bill Lee	.10
195	Don Zimmer	.10
196	Hal McRae	.10
197	Mike Norris	.10
198	Duane Kuiper	.10
199	Rick Cerone	.10
200	Jim Rice	.45
201	Steve Yeager	.10
202	Tom Brookens	.10
203	Jose Morales	.10
204	Roy Howell	.10
205	Tippy Martinez	.10
206	Moose Haas	.10
207	Al Cowens	.10
208	Dave Stapleton	.10
209	Bucky Dent	.10
210	Ron Cey	.10
211	Jorge Orta	.10
212	Jamie Quirk	.10
213	Jeff Jones	.10
214	Tim Raines	.25
215	Jon Matlack	.10
216	Rod Carew	1.50
217	Jim Kaat	.15
218	Joe Pittman	.10
219	Larry Christenson	.10
220	Juan Bonilla	.10
221	Mike Easler	.10
222	Vida Blue	.10
223	Rick Camp	.10
224	Mike Jorgensen	.10
225	Jody Davis RC	.10
226	Mike Parrott	.10
227	Jim Clancy	.10
228	Hosken Powell	.10
229	Tom Hume	.10
230	Britt Burns	.10
231	Jim Palmer	1.25
232	Bob Rodgers	.10
233	Milt Wilcox	.10
234	Dave Revering	.10
235	Mike Torrez	.10
236	Robert Castillo	.10
237	Von Hayes RC	.25
238	Renie Martin	.10
239	Dwayne Murphy	.10
240	Rodney Scott	.10
241	Fred Patek	.10
242	Mickey Rivers	.10
243	Steve Trout	.10
244	Jose Cruz	.10
245	Manny Trillo	.10
246	Lary Sorensen	.10
247	Dave Edwards	.10
248	Dan Driessen	.10
249	Tommy Boggs	.10
250	Dale Berra	.10
251	Ed Whitson	.10
252	Lee Smith RC	4.00
253	Tom Paciorek	.10
254	Pat Zachry	.10
255	Luis Leal	.10
256	John Castino	.10
257	Rich Dauer	.10
258	Cecil Cooper	.10
259	Dave Rozema	.10
260	John Tudor	.10
261	Jerry Mumphrey	.10
262	Jay Johnstone	.10
263	Bo Diaz	.10
264	Dennis Leonard	.10
265	Jim Spencer	.10
266	John Milner	.10
267	Don Aase	.10
268	Jim Sundberg	.10
269	Lamar Johnson	.10
270	Frank LaCorte	.10
271	Barry Evans	.10
272	Enos Cabell	.10
273	Del Unser	.10
274	George Foster	.10
275	Brett Butler RC	.50
276	Lee Lacy	.10
277	Ken Reitz	.10
278	Keith Hernandez	.10
279	Doug DeCinces	.10
280	Charlie Moore	.10
281	Lance Parrish	.10
282	Ralph Houk	.10
283	Rich Gossage	.10
284	Jerry Reuss	.10
285	Mike Stanton	.10
286	Frank White	.10
287	Bob Owchinko	.10
288	Scott Sanderson	.10
289	Bump Wills	.10
290	Dave Frost	.10
291	Chet Lemon	.10
292	Tito Landrum	.10
293	Vern Ruhle	.10
294	Mike Schmidt	2.00
295	Sam Mejias	.10
296	Gary Lucas	.10
297	John Candelaria	.10
298	Jerry Martin	.10
299	Dale Murphy	.50
300	Mike Lum	.10
301	Tom Hausman	.10
302	Glenn Abbott	.10
303	Roger Erickson	.10
304	Otto Velez	.10
305	Danny Goodwin	.10
306	John Mayberry	.10
307	Lenny Randle	.10
308	Bob Bailor	.10
309	Jerry Morales	.10
310	Rufino Linares	.10
311	Kent Tekulve	.10
312	Joe Morgan	1.25
313	John Urrea	.10
314	Paul Householder	.10
315	Garry Maddox	.10
316	Mike Ramsey	.10
317	Alan Ashby	.10
318	Bob Clark	.10
319	Tony LaRussa	.15
320	Charlie Lea	.10
321	Danny Darwin	.10
322	Cesar Geronimo	.10
323	Tom Underwood	.10
324	Andre Thornton	.10
325	Rudy May	.10
326	Frank Tanana	.10
327	Davey Lopes	.10
328	Richie Hebner	.10
329	Mike Flanagan	.10
330	Mike Caldwell	.10
331	Scott McGregor	.10
332	Jerry Augustine	.10
333	Stan Papi	.10
334	Rick Miller	.10
335	Graig Nettles	.15
336	Dusty Baker	.10
337	Dave Garcia	.10
338	Larry Gura	.10
339	Cliff Johnson	.10
340	Warren Cromartie	.10
341	Steve Comer	.10
342	Rick Burleson	.10
343	John Martin	.10
344	Craig Reynolds	.10
345	Mike Proly	.10
346	Ruppert Jones	.10
347	Omar Moreno	.10
348	Greg Minton	.10
349	Rick Mahler RC	.10
350	Alex Trevino	.10
351	Mike Krukow	.10
352a	Shane Rawley (Jim Anderson photo - shaking hands.)	.50
352b	Shane Rawley (Correct photo - kneeling.)	.15
353	Garth Iorg	.10
354	Pete Mackanin	.10
355	Paul Moskau	.10
356	Richard Dotson	.10
357	Steve Stone	.10
358	Larry Hisle	.10
359	Aurelio Lopez	.10
360	Oscar Gamble	.10
361	Tom Burgmeier	.10
362	Terry Forster	.10
363	Joe Charboneau	.25
364	Ken Brett	.10
365	Tony Armas	.10
366	Chris Speier	.10
367	Fred Lynn	.10
368	Buddy Bell	.10
369	Jim Essian	.10
370	Terry Puhl	.10
371	Greg Gross	.10
372	Bruce Sutter	1.25
373	Joe Lefebvre	.10
374	Ray Knight	.10
375	Bruce Benedict	.10
376	Tim Foli	.10
377	Al Holland	.10
378	Ken Kravec	.10
379	Jeff Burroughs	.10
380	Pete Falcone	.10
381	Ernie Whitt	.10
382	Brad Havens	.10
383	Terry Crowley	.10
384	Don Money	.10
385	Dan Schatzeder	.10
386	Gary Allenson	.10
387	Yogi Berra	.50
388	Ken Landreaux	.10
389	Mike Hargrove	.10
390	Darryl Motley	.10
391	Dave McKay	.10
392	Stan Bahnsen	.10
393	Ken Forsch	.10
394	Mario Mendoza	.10
395	Jim Morrison	.10
396	Mike Ivie	.10
397	Broderick Perkins	.10
398	Darrell Evans	.10
399	Ron Reed	.10
400	Johnny Bench	1.50
401	Steve Bedrosian RC	.20
402	Bill Robinson	.10
403	Bill Buckner	.10
404	Ken Oberkfell	.10
405	Cal Ripken, Jr. RC	40.00
406	Jim Gantner	.10
407	Kirk Gibson	.10
408	Tony Perez	1.00
409	Tommy John	.10
410	Dave Stewart RC	2.50
411	Dan Spillner	.10
412	Willie Aikens	.10
413	Mike Heath	.10
414	Ray Burris	.10
415	Leon Roberts	.10
416	Mike Witt RC	.15
417	Bobby Molinaro	.10
418	Steve Braun	.10
419	Nolan Ryan	4.00
420	Tug McGraw	.10
421	Dave Concepcion	.10
422a	Juan Eichelberger (Gary Lucas photo - white player.)	.50
422b	Juan Eichelberger (Correct photo - black player.)	.10
423	Rick Rhoden	.10
424	Frank Robinson	.50
425	Eddie Miller	.10
426	Bill Caudill	.10
427	Doug Flynn	.10
428	Larry Anderson (Andersen)	.10
429	Al Williams	.10
430	Jerry Garvin	.10
431	Glenn Adams	.10
432	Barry Bonnell	.10
433	Jerry Narron	.10
434	John Stearns	.10
435	Mike Tyson	.10
436	Glenn Hubbard	.10
437	Eddie Solomon	.10
438	Jeff Leonard	.10
439	Randy Bass	.10
440	Mike LaCoss	.10
441	Gary Matthews	.10
442	Mark Littell	.10
443	Don Sutton	1.00
444	John Harris	.10
445	Vada Pinson	.10
446	Elias Sosa	.10
447	Charlie Hough	.10
448	Willie Wilson	.10
449	Fred Stanley	.10
450	Tom Veryzer	.10
451	Ron Davis	.10
452	Mark Clear	.10
453	Bill Russell	.10
454	Lou Whitaker	.10
455	Dan Graham	.10
456	Reggie Cleveland	.10
457	Sammy Stewart	.10
458	Pete Vuckovich	.10
459	John Wockenfuss	.10
460	Glenn Hoffman	.10
461	Willie Randolph	.10
462	Fernando Valenzuela	.10
463	Ron Hassey	.10
464	Paul Splittorff	.10
465	Rob Picciolo	.10
466	Larry Parrish	.10
467	Johnny Grubb	.10
468	Dan Ford	.10
469	Silvio Martinez	.10
470	Kiko Garcia	.10
471	Bob Boone	.10
472	Luis Salazar	.10
473	Randy Niemann	.10
474	Tom Griffin	.10
475	Phil Niekro	1.00
476	Hubie Brooks RC	.10
477	Dick Tidrow	.10
478	Jim Beattie	.10
479	Damaso Garcia	.10
480	Mickey Hatcher	.10
481	Joe Price	.10
482	Ed Farmer	.10
483	Eddie Murray	1.25
484	Ben Oglivie	.10
485	Kevin Saucier	.10
486	Bobby Murcer	.10
487	Bill Campbell	.10
488	Reggie Smith	.10
489	Wayne Garland	.10
490	Jim Wright	.10
491	Billy Martin	.10
492	Jim Fanning	.10
493	Don Baylor	.10
494	Rick Honeycutt	.10
495	Carlton Fisk	1.25
496	Denny Walling	.10
497	Bake McBride	.10
498	Darrell Porter	.10
499	Gene Richards	.10
500	Ron Oester	.10
501	Ken Dayley RC	.10
502	Jason Thompson	.10
503	Milt May	.10
504	Doug Bird	.10
505	Bruce Bochte	.10
506	Neil Allen	.10

#	Player	Price
507	Joey McLaughlin	.10
508	Butch Wynegar	.10
509	Gary Roenicke	.10
510	Robin Yount	1.25
511	Dave Tobik	.10
512	Rich Gedman RC	.15
513	Gene Nelson RC	.10
514	Rick Monday	.10
515	Miguel Dilone	.10
516	Clint Hurdle	.10
517	Jeff Newman	.10
518	Grant Jackson	.10
519	Andy Hassler	.10
520	Pat Putnam	.10
521	Greg Pryor	.10
522	Tony Scott	.10
523	Steve Mura	.10
524	Johnnie LeMaster	.10
525	Dick Ruthven	.10
526	John McNamara	.10
527	Larry McWilliams	.10
528	Johnny Ray RC	.15
529	Pat Tabler RC	.15
530	Tom Herr	.10
531a	San Diego Chicken (W/trademark symbol.)	.75
531b	San Diego Chicken (No trademark symbol.)	.50
532	Sal Butera	.10
533	Mike Griffin	.10
534	Kelvin Moore	.10
535	Reggie Jackson	2.00
536	Ed Romero	.10
537	Derrel Thomas	.10
538	Mike O'Berry	.10
539	Jack O'Connor	.10
540	Bob Ojeda RC	.25
541	Roy Lee Jackson	.10
542	Lynn Jones	.10
543	Gaylord Perry	1.00
544a	Phil Garner (Photo reversed.)	.50
544b	Phil Garner (Photo correct.)	.10
545	Garry Templeton	.10
546	Rafael Ramirez	.10
547	Jeff Reardon	.10
548	Ron Guidry	.10
549	Tim Laudner RC	.15
550	John Henry Johnson	.10
551	Chris Bando	.10
552	Bobby Brown	.10
553	Larry Bradford	.10
554	Scott Fletcher RC	.20
555	Jerry Royster	.10
556	Shooty Babbitt	.10
557	Kent Hrbek RC	2.00
558	Yankee Winners (Ron Guidry, Tommy John)	.15
559	Mark Bomback	.10
560	Julio Valdez	.10
561	Buck Martinez	.10
562	Mike Marshall RC	.15
563	Rennie Stennett	.10
564	Steve Crawford	.10
565	Bob Babcock	.10
566	Johnny Podres	.10
567	Paul Serna	.10
568	Harold Baines	1.00
569	Dave LaRoche	.10
570	Lee May	.10
571	Gary Ward	.10
572	John Denny	.10
573	Roy Smalley	.10
574	Bob Brenly RC	.20
575	Bronx Bombers (Reggie Jackson, Dave Winfield)	1.50
576	Luis Pujols	.10
577	Butch Hobson	.10
578	Harvey Kuenn	.10
579	Cal Ripken, Sr.	.10
580	Juan Berenguer	.10
581	Benny Ayala	.10
582	Vance Law	.10
583	Rick Leach RC	.10
584	George Frazier	.10
585	Phillies Finest (Pete Rose, Mike Schmidt)	1.00
586	Joe Rudi	.10
587	Juan Beniquez	.10
588	Luis DeLeon RC	.10
589	Craig Swan	.10
590	Dave Chalk	.10
591	Billy Gardner	.10
592	Sal Bando	.10
593	Bert Campaneris	.10
594	Steve Kemp	.10
595a	Randy Lerch (Braves)	.25
595b	Randy Lerch (Brewers)	.10
596	Bryan Clark	.10
597	Dave Ford	.10
598	Mike Scioscia	.10
599	John Lowenstein	.10
600	Rene Lachmann (Lachemann)	.10
601	Mick Kelleher	.10
602	Ron Jackson	.10
603	Jerry Koosman	.10
604	Dave Goltz	.10
605	Ellis Valentine	.10
606	Lonnie Smith	.10
607	Joaquin Andujar	.10
608	Garry Hancock	.10
609	Jerry Turner	.10
610	Bob Bonner	.10
611	Jim Dwyer	.10
612	Terry Bulling	.10
613	Joel Youngblood	.10
614	Larry Milbourne	.10
615	Phil Roof (Photo actually Gene Roof.)	.10
616	Keith Drumright	.10
617	Dave Rosello	.10
618	Rickey Keeton	.10
619	Dennis Lamp	.10
620	Sid Monge	.10
621	Jerry White	.10
622	Luis Aguayo RC	.10
623	Jamie Easterly	.10
624	Steve Sax RC	.50
625	Dave Roberts	.10
626	Rick Bosetti	.10
627	Terry Francona RC	.50
628	Pride of the Reds (Johnny Bench, Tom Seaver)	1.00
629	Paul Mirabella	.10
630	Rance Mulliniks	.10
631	Kevin Hickey	.10
632	Reid Nichols	.10
633	Dave Geisel	.10
634	Ken Griffey	.10
635	Bob Lemon	.15
636	Orlando Sanchez	.10
637	Bill Almon	.10
638	Danny Ainge	1.00
639	Willie Stargell	1.25
640	Bob Sykes	.10
641	Ed Lynch	.10
642	John Ellis	.10
643	Fergie Jenkins	1.00
644	Lenn Sakata	.10
645	Julio Gonzales	.10
646	Jesse Orosco	.10
647	Jerry Dybzinski	.10
648	Tommy Davis	.10
649	Ron Gardenhire	.10
650	Felipe Alou	.10
651	Harvey Haddix	.10
652	Willie Upshaw	.10
653	Bill Madlock	.10
----	Checklist 1-26 DK (5 Trammell)	.25
----	Checklist 1-26 DK (5 Trammell)	.10
----	Checklist 27-130	.10
----	Checklist 131-234	.10
----	Checklist 235-338	.10
----	Checklist 339-442	.10
----	Checklist 443-544	.10
----	Checklist 545-653	.10

1982-89 Donruss Puzzle Promo Sheets

Part of the advertising materials which Donruss issued each year was a series of approximately 8" x 10-7/8" color glossy sheets picturing the Dick Perez art which appear on the Diamond Kings puzzle pieces inserted into card packs.

		NM/M
Complete Set (10):		20.00
Common Player:		2.50
(1)	Babe Ruth (1982)	2.50
(2)	Ty Cobb (1983)	2.50
(3)	Mickey Mantle (1983)	2.50
(4)	Duke Snider (1984)	2.50
(5)	Ted Williams (1984)	2.50
(6)	Lou Gehrig (1985)	2.50
(7)	Hank Aaron (1986)	2.50
(8)	Roberto Clemente (1987)	2.50
(9)	Stan Musial (1988)	2.50
(10)	Warren Spahn (1989)	2.50

1983 Donruss Promo Sheet

To debut its 1983 card design for dealers, Donruss prepared this eight-card sheet, including one Diamond Stars card. Card fronts are identical to the issued versions. Backs of most cards differ in the Career Highlights write-up. The sheet measures 10" x 7".

	NM/M
Uncut Sheet:	10.00

1983 Donruss

The 1983 Donruss set consists of 653 numbered cards plus seven unnumbered checklists. The 2-1/2" x 3-1/2" cards were issued with puzzle pieces (three pieces on one card per pack) that feature Ty Cobb. The first 26 cards in the set were once again the Diamond Kings series. The card fronts display the Donruss logo and the year of issue. The card backs have black print on yellow and white and include statistics, career highlights, and the player's contract status. (DK) in the checklist below indicates cards which belong to the Diamond Kings series.

		NM/M
Unopened Fact. Set (660):		50.00
Complete Set (660):		40.00
Common Player:		.10
Ty Cobb Puzzle:		2.50
Wax Pack (15):		2.50
Wax Box (36):		80.00

#	Player	Price
1	Fernando Valenzuela (DK)	.15
2	Rollie Fingers (DK)	.75
3	Reggie Jackson (DK)	2.50
4	Jim Palmer (DK)	1.00
5	Jack Morris (DK)	.15
6	George Foster (DK)	.15
7	Jim Sundberg (DK)	.10
8	Willie Stargell (DK)	1.00
9	Dave Stieb (DK)	.15
10	Joe Niekro (DK)	.15
11	Rickey Henderson (DK)	1.25
12	Dale Murphy (DK)	.50
13	Toby Harrah (DK)	.10
14	Bill Buckner (DK)	.15
15	Willie Wilson (DK)	.10
16	Steve Carlton (DK)	1.25
17	Ron Guidry (DK)	.15
18	Steve Rogers (DK)	.10
19	Kent Hrbek (DK)	.25
20	Keith Hernandez (DK)	.20
21	Floyd Bannister (DK)	.10
22	Johnny Bench (DK)	2.00
23	Britt Burns (DK)	.10
24	Joe Morgan (DK)	1.25
25	Carl Yastrzemski (DK)	2.00
26	Terry Kennedy (DK)	.10
27	Gary Roenicke	.10
28	Dwight Bernard	.10
29	Pat Underwood	.10
30	Gary Allenson	.10
31	Ron Guidry	.10
32	Burt Hooton	.10
33	Chris Bando	.10
34	Vida Blue	.10
35	Rickey Henderson	1.25
36	Ray Burris	.10
37	John Butcher	.10
38	Don Aase	.10
39	Jerry Koosman	.10
40	Bruce Sutter	1.00
41	Jose Cruz	.10
42	Pete Rose	3.00
43	Cesar Cedeno	.10
44	Floyd Chiffer	.10
45	Larry McWilliams	.10
46	Alan Fowlkes	.10
47	Dale Murphy	.50
48	Doug Bird	.10
49	Hubie Brooks	.10
50	Floyd Bannister	.10
51	Jack O'Connor	.10
52	Steve Senteney	.10
53	Gary Gaetti RC	1.00
54	Damaso Garcia	.10
55	Gene Nelson	.10
56	Mookie Wilson	.10
57	Allen Ripley	.10
58	Bob Horner	.10
59	Tony Pena	.10
60	Gary Lavelle	.10
61	Tim Lollar	.10
62	Frank Pastore	.10
63	Garry Maddox	.10
64	Bob Forsch	.10
65	Harry Spilman	.10
66	Geoff Zahn	.10
67	Salome Barojas	.10
68	David Palmer	.10
69	Charlie Hough	.10
70	Dan Quisenberry	.10
71	Tony Armas	.10
72	Rick Sutcliffe	.10
73	Steve Balboni	.10
74	Jerry Remy	.10
75	Mike Scioscia	.10
76	John Wockenfuss	.10
77	Jim Palmer	1.00
78	Rollie Fingers	.75
79	Joe Nolan	.10
80	Pete Vuckovich	.10
81	Rick Leach	.10
82	Rick Miller	.10
83	Graig Nettles	.15
84	Ron Cey	.10
85	Miguel Dilone	.10
86	John Wathan	.10
87	Kelvin Moore	.10
88a	Byrn Smith (First name incorrect.)	.35
88b	Bryn Smith (First name correct.)	.10
89	Dave Hostetler	.10
90	Rod Carew	1.50
91	Lonnie Smith	.10
92	Bob Knepper	.10
93	Marty Bystrom	.10
94	Chris Welsh	.10
95	Jason Thompson	.10
96	Tom O'Malley	.10
97	Phil Niekro	.75
98	Neil Allen	.10
99	Bill Buckner	.10
100	Ed Vande Berg RC	.10
101	Jim Clancy	.10
102	Robert Castillo	.10
103	Bruce Berenyi	.10
104	Carlton Fisk	1.25
105	Mike Flanagan	.10
106	Cecil Cooper	.10
107	Jack Morris	.10
108	Mike Morgan	.10
109	Luis Aponte	.10
110	Pedro Guerrero	.10
111	Len Barker	.10
112	Willie Wilson	.10
113	Dave Beard	.10
114	Mike Gates	.10
115	Reggie Jackson	2.50
116	George Wright	.10
117	Vance Law	.10
118	Nolan Ryan	4.00
119	Mike Krukow	.10
120	Ozzie Smith	2.00
121	Broderick Perkins	.10
122	Tom Seaver	1.50
123	Chris Chambliss	.10
124	Chuck Tanner	.10
125	Johnnie LeMaster	.10
126	Mel Hall RC	.15
127	Bruce Bochte	.10
128	Charlie Puleo RC	.10
129	Luis Leal	.10
130	John Pacella	.10
131	Glenn Gulliver	.10
132	Don Money	.10
133	Dave Rozema	.10
134	Bruce Hurst	.10
135	Rudy May	.10
136	Tom LaSorda (Lasorda)	.40
137	Dan Spillner (Photo actually Ed Whitson.)	.10
138	Jerry Martin	.10
139	Mike Norris	.10
140	Al Oliver	.10
141	Daryl Sconiers	.10
142	Lamar Johnson	.10
143	Harold Baines	.10
144	Alan Ashby	.10
145	Garry Templeton	.10
146	Al Holland	.10
147	Bo Diaz	.10
148	Dave Concepcion	.10
149	Rick Camp	.10
150	Jim Morrison	.10
151	Randy Martz	.10
152	Keith Hernandez	.10
153	John Lowenstein	.10
154	Mike Caldwell	.10
155	Milt Wilcox	.10
156	Rich Gedman	.10
157	Rich Gossage	.20
158	Jerry Reuss	.10
159	Rufino Linares	.10
160	Larry Gura	.10
161	Dwayne Murphy	.10
162	Woodie Fryman	.10
163	Steve Comer	.10
164	Ken Forsch	.10
165	Dennis Lamp	.10
166	David Green	.10
167	Terry Puhl	.10
168	Mike Schmidt	2.50
169	Eddie Milner RC	.10
170	John Curtis	.10
171	Don Robinson	.10
172	Richard Gale	.10
173	Steve Bedrosian	.10
174	Willie Hernandez	.10
175	Ron Gardenhire	.10
176	Jim Beattie	.10
177	Tim Laudner	.10
178	Buck Martinez	.10
179	Kent Hrbek	.10
180	Alfredo Griffin	.10
181	Larry Andersen	.10
182	Pete Falcone	.10
183	Jody Davis	.10
184	Glenn Hubbard	.10
185	Dale Berra	.10
186	Greg Minton	.10
187	Gary Lucas	.10
188	Dave Van Gorder	.10
189	Bob Dernier	.10
190	Willie McGee RC	1.50
191	Dickie Thon	.10
192	Bob Boone	.10
193	Britt Burns	.10
194	Jeff Reardon	.10
195	Jon Matlack	.10
196	Don Slaught RC	.15
197	Fred Stanley	.10
198	Rick Manning	.10
199	Dave Righetti	.10
200	Dave Stapleton	.10
201	Steve Yeager	.10
202	Enos Cabell	.10
203	Sammy Stewart	.10
204	Moose Haas	.10
205	Lenn Sakata	.10
206	Charlie Moore	.10
207	Alan Trammell	.15
208	Jim Rice	.40
209	Roy Smalley	.10
210	Bill Russell	.10
211	Andre Thornton	.10
212	Willie Aikens	.10
213	Dave McKay	.10
214	Tim Blackwell	.10
215	Buddy Bell	.10
216	Doug DeCinces	.10
217	Tom Herr	.10
218	Frank LaCorte	.10
219	Steve Carlton	1.25
220	Terry Kennedy	.10
221	Mike Easler	.10
222	Jack Clark	.10
223	Gene Garber	.10
224	Scott Holman	.10
225	Mike Proly	.10
226	Terry Bulling	.10
227	Jerry Garvin	.10
228	Ron Davis	.10
229	Tom Hume	.10
230	Marc Hill	.10
231	Dennis Martinez	.10
232	Jim Gantner	.10
233	Larry Pashnick	.10
234	Dave Collins	.10
235	Tom Burgmeier	.10
236	Ken Landreaux	.10
237	John Denny	.10
238	Hal McRae	.10
239	Matt Keough	.10
240	Doug Flynn	.10
241	Fred Lynn	.10
242	Billy Sample	.10
243	Tom Paciorek	.10
244	Joe Sambito	.10
245	Sid Monge	.10
246	Ken Oberkfell	.10
247	Joe Pittman (Photo actually Juan Eichelberger.)	.10
248	Mario Soto	.10
249	Claudell Washington	.10
250	Rick Rhoden	.10
251	Darrell Evans	.10
252	Steve Henderson	.10
253	Manny Castillo	.10
254	Craig Swan	.10
255	Joey McLaughlin	.10
256	Pete Redfern	.10
257	Ken Singleton	.10
258	Robin Yount	1.25
259	Elias Sosa	.10
260	Bob Ojeda	.10
261	Bobby Murcer	.10
262	Candy Maldonado RC	.10
263	Rick Waits	.10
264	Greg Pryor	.10
265	Bob Owchinko	.10
266	Chris Speier	.10
267	Bruce Kison	.10
268	Mark Wagner	.10
269	Steve Kemp	.10
270	Phil Garner	.10
271	Gene Richards	.10
272	Renie Martin	.10
273	Dave Roberts	.10
274	Dan Driessen	.10
275	Rufino Linares	.10
276	Lee Lacy	.10
277	Ryne Sandberg RC	12.00
278	Darrell Porter	.10
279	Cal Ripken, Jr.	4.00
280	Jamie Easterly	.10
281	Bill Fahey	.10
282	Glenn Hoffman	.10
283	Willie Randolph	.10
284	Fernando Valenzuela	.10
285	Alan Bannister	.10
286	Paul Splittorff	.10
287	Joe Rudi	.10
288	Bill Gullickson	.10
289	Danny Darwin	.10
290	Andy Hassler	.10
291	Ernesto Escarrega	.10
292	Steve Mura	.10
293	Tony Scott	.10
294	Manny Trillo	.10
295	Greg Harris	.10
296	Luis DeLeon	.10
297	Kent Tekulve	.10
298	Atlee Hammaker	.10
299	Bruce Benedict	.10
300	Fergie Jenkins	.75
301	Dave Kingman	.10
302	Bill Caudill	.10
303	John Castino	.10
304	Ernie Whitt	.10
305	Randy S. Johnson	.10
306	Garth Iorg	.10
307	Gaylord Perry	.75
308	Ed Lynch	.10
309	Keith Moreland	.10
310	Rafael Ramirez	.10
311	Bill Madlock	.10
312	Milt May	.10
313	John Montefusco	.10
314	Wayne Krenchicki	.10
315	George Vukovich	.10
316	Joaquin Andujar	.10
317	Craig Reynolds	.10
318	Rick Burleson	.10
319	Richard Dotson	.10
320	Steve Rogers	.10
321	Dave Schmidt	.10
322	Bud Black RC	.15
323	Jeff Burroughs	.10
324	Von Hayes	.10
325	Butch Wynegar	.10
326	Carl Yastrzemski	1.50
327	Ron Roenicke	.10
328	Howard Johnson RC	1.00
329	Rick Dempsey	.10
330a	Jim Slaton (One yellow box on back.)	.25
330b	Jim Slaton (Two yellow boxes on back.)	.10
331	Benny Ayala	.10
332	Ted Simmons	.10
333	Lou Whitaker	.10
334	Chuck Rainey	.10
335	Lou Piniella	.15
336	Steve Sax	.10
337	Toby Harrah	.10
338	George Brett	2.50
339	Davey Lopes	.10
340	Gary Carter	1.25
341	John Grubb	.10
342	Tim Foli	.10
343	Jim Kaat	.15
344	Mike LaCoss	.10
345	Larry Christenson	.10
346	Juan Bonilla	.10
347	Omar Moreno	.10
348	Chili Davis	.10
349	Tommy Boggs	.10
350	Rusty Staub	.15
351	Bump Wills	.10
352	Rick Sweet	.10
353	Jim Gott RC	.10
354	Terry Felton	.10
355	Jim Kern	.10
356	Bill Almon	.10
357	Tippy Martinez	.10
358	Roy Howell	.10
359	Dan Petry	.10
360	Jerry Mumphrey	.10
361	Mark Clear	.10
362	Mike Marshall	.10
363	Lary Sorensen	.10
364	Amos Otis	.10
365	Rick Langford	.10
366	Brad Mills	.10
367	Brian Downing	.10
368	Mike Richardt	.10
369	Aurelio Rodriguez	.10
370	Dave Smith	.10
371	Tug McGraw	.10
372	Doug Bair	.10
373	Ruppert Jones	.10
374	Alex Trevino	.10
375	Ken Dayley	.10
376	Rod Scurry	.10
377	Bob Brenly	.10
378	Scot Thompson	.10
379	Julio Cruz	.10
380	John Stearns	.10
381	Dale Murray	.10
382	Frank Viola RC	1.50
383	Al Bumbry	.10
384	Ben Oglivie	.10
385	Dave Tobik	.10
386	Bob Stanley	.10
387	Andre Robertson	.10
388	Jorge Orta	.10
*389	Ed Whitson	.10
390	Don Hood	.10
391	Tom Underwood	.10
392	Tim Wallach	.10
393	Steve Renko	.10
394	Mickey Rivers	.10
395	Greg Luzinski	.10
396	Art Howe	.10
397	Alan Wiggins	.10
398	Jim Barr	.10
399	Ivan DeJesus	.10
400	Tom Lawless RC	.10
401	Bob Walk	.10
402	Jimmy Smith	.10
403	Lee Smith	.20
404	George Hendrick	.10
405	Eddie Murray	1.25
406	Marshall Edwards	.10
407	Lance Parrish	.10
408	Carney Lansford	.10
409	Dave Winfield	1.25

410	Bob Welch	.10
411	Larry Milbourne	.10
412	Dennis Leonard	.10
413	Dan Meyer	.10
414	Charlie Lea	.10
415	Rick Honeycutt	.10
416	Mike Witt	.10
417	Steve Trout	.10
418	Glenn Brummer	.10
419	Denny Walling	.10
420	Gary Matthews	.10
421	Charlie Liebrandt (Leibrandt)	.10
422	Juan Eichelberger	.10
423	Matt Guante (Cecilio) RC	.10
424	Bill Laskey	.10
425	Jerry Royster	.10
426	Dickie Noles	.10
427	George Foster	.10
428	Mike Moore RC	.25
429	Gary Ward	.10
430	Barry Bonnell	.10
431	Ron Washington	.10
432	Rance Mulliniks	.10
433	Mike Stanton	.10
434	Jesse Orosco	.10
435	Larry Bowa	.10
436	Biff Pocoroba	.10
437	Johnny Ray	.10
438	Joe Morgan	1.25
439	Eric Show RC	.15
440	Larry Biittner	.10
441	Greg Gross	.10
442	Gene Tenace	.10
443	Danny Heep	.10
444	Bobby Clark	.10
445	Kevin Hickey	.10
446	Scott Sanderson	.10
447	Frank Tanana	.10
448	Cesar Geronimo	.10
449	Jimmy Sexton	.10
450	Mike Hargrove	.10
451	Doyle Alexander	.10
452	Dwight Evans	.10
453	Terry Forster	.10
454	Tom Brookens	.10
455	Rich Dauer	.10
456	Rob Picciolo	.10
457	Terry Crowley	.10
458	Ned Yost	.10
459	Kirk Gibson	.10
460	Reid Nichols	.10
461	Oscar Gamble	.10
462	Dusty Baker	.10
463	Jack Perconte	.10
464	Frank White	.10
465	Mickey Klutts	.10
466	Warren Cromartie	.10
467	Larry Parrish	.10
468	Bobby Grich	.10
469	Dane Iorg	.10
470	Joe Niekro	.10
471	Ed Farmer	.10
472	Tim Flannery	.10
473	Dave Parker	.10
474	Jeff Leonard	.10
475	Al Hrabosky	.10
476	Ron Hodges	.10
477	Leon Durham	.10
478	Jim Essian	.10
479	Roy Lee Jackson	.10
480	Brad Havens	.10
481	Joe Price	.10
482	Tony Bernazard	.10
483	Scott McGregor	.10
484	Paul Molitor	1.25
485	Mike Ivie	.10
486	Ken Griffey	.10
487	Dennis Eckersley	1.00
488	Steve Garvey	.40
489	Mike Fischlin	.10
490	U.L. Washington	.10
491	Steve McCatty	.10
492	Roy Johnson	.10
493	Don Baylor	.10
494	Bobby Johnson	.10
495	Mike Squires	.10
496	Bert Roberge	.10
497	Dick Ruthven	.10
498	Tito Landrum	.10
499	Sixto Lezcano	.10
500	Johnny Bench	1.50
501	Larry Whisenton	.10
502	Manny Sarmiento	.10
503	Fred Breining	.10
504	Bill Campbell	.10
505	Todd Cruz	.10
506	Bob Bailor	.10
507	Dave Stieb	.10
508	Al Williams	.10
509	Dan Ford	.10
510	Gorman Thomas	.10
511	Chet Lemon	.10
512	Mike Torrez	.10
513	Shane Rawley	.10
514	Mark Belanger	.10
515	Rodney Craig	.10
516	Onix Concepcion	.10
517	Mike Heath	.10
518	Andre Dawson	.50
519	Luis Sanchez	.10
520	Terry Bogener	.10
521	Rudy Law	.10
522	Ray Knight	.10
523	Joe Lefebvre	.10
524	Jim Wohlford	.10
525	Julio Franco RC	2.00
526	Ron Oester	.10
527	Rick Mahler	.10
528	Steve Nicosia	.10
529	Junior Kennedy	.10
530a	Whitey Herzog (One yellow box on back.)	.25
530b	Whitey Herzog (Two yellow boxes on back.)	.15
531a	Don Sutton (Blue frame.)	.75
531b	Don Sutton (Green frame.)	.75
532	Mark Brouhard	.10
533a	Sparky Anderson (One yellow box on back.)	.50
533b	Sparky Anderson (Two yellow boxes on back.)	.50
534	Roger LaFrancois	.10
535	George Frazier	.10
536	Tom Niedenfuer	.10
537	Ed Glynn	.10
538	Lee May	.10
539	Bob Kearney	.10
540	Tim Raines	.10
541	Paul Mirabella	.10
542	Luis Tiant	.10
543	Ron LeFlore	.10
544	Dave LaPoint RC	.15
545	Randy Moffitt	.10
546	Luis Aguayo	.10
547	Brad Lesley	.10
548	Luis Salazar	.10
549	John Candelaria	.10
550	Dave Bergman	.10
551	Bob Watson	.10
552	Pat Tabler	.10
553	Brent Gaff	.10
554	Al Cowens	.10
555	Tom Brunansky	.10
556	Lloyd Moseby	.10
557a	Pascual Perez (Twins)	.25
557b	Pascual Perez (Braves)	.10
558	Willie Upshaw	.10
559	Richie Zisk	.10
560	Pat Zachry	.10
561	Jay Johnstone	.10
562	Carlos Diaz	.10
563	John Tudor	.10
564	Frank Robinson	.50
565	Dave Edwards	.10
566	Paul Householder	.10
567	Ron Reed	.10
568	Mike Ramsey	.10
569	Kiko Garcia	.10
570	Tommy John	.10
571	Tony LaRussa	.10
572	Joel Youngblood	.10
573	Wayne Tolleson RC	.10
574	Keith Creel	.10
575	Billy Martin	.10
576	Jerry Dybzinski	.10
577	Rick Cerone	.10
578	Tony Perez	1.00
579	Greg Brock RC	.10
580	Glen Wilson (Glenn)	.10
581	Tim Stoddard	.10
582	Bob McClure	.10
583	Jim Dwyer	.10
584	Ed Romero	.10
585	Larry Herndon	.10
586	Wade Boggs RC	10.00
587	Jay Howell	.10
588	Dave Stewart	.10
589	Bert Blyleven	.10
590	Dick Howser	.10
591	Wayne Gross	.10
592	Terry Francona	.10
593	Don Werner	.10
594	Bill Stein	.10
595	Jesse Barfield	.10
596	Bobby Molinaro	.10
597	Mike Vail	.10
598	Tony Gwynn RC	12.00
599	Gary Rajsich	.10
600	Jerry Ujdur	.10
601	Cliff Johnson	.10
602	Jerry White	.10
603	Bryan Clark	.10
604	Joe Ferguson	.10
605	Guy Sularz	.10
606a	Ozzie Virgil (Green frame around photo.)	.25
606b	Ozzie Virgil (Orange frame around photo.)	.10
607	Terry Harper	.10
608	Harvey Kuenn	.10
609	Jim Sundberg	.10
610	Willie Stargell	1.25
611	Reggie Smith	.10
612	Rob Wilfong	.10
613	Niekro Brothers (Joe Niekro, Phil Niekro)	.25
614	Lee Elia	.10
615	Mickey Hatcher	.10
616	Jerry Hairston Sr.	.10
617	John Martin	.10
618	Wally Backman	.10
619	Storm Davis RC	.15
620	Alan Knicely	.10
621	John Stuper	.10
622	Matt Sinatro	.10
623	Gene Petralli RC	.10
624	Duane Walker	.10
625	Dick Williams	.10
626	Pat Corrales	.10
627	Vern Ruhle	.10
628	Joe Torre	.10
629	Anthony Johnson	.10
630	Steve Howe	.10
631	Gary Woods	.10
632	Lamarr Hoyt (LaMarr)	.10
633	Steve Swisher	.10
634	Terry Leach	.10
635	Jeff Newman	.10
636	Brett Butler	.10
637	Gary Gray	.10
638	Lee Mazzilli	.10
639a	Ron Jackson (A's)	2.50
639b	Ron Jackson (Angels - green frame around photo.)	.25
639c	Ron Jackson (Angels - red frame around photo.)	.15
640	Juan Beniquez	.10
641	Dave Rucker	.10
642	Luis Pujols	.10
643	Rick Monday	.10
644	Hosken Powell	.10
645	San Diego Chicken	.20
646	Dave Engle	.10
647	Dick Davis	.10
648	MVP's (Vida Blue, Joe Morgan, Frank Robinson)	.15
649	Al Chambers	.10
650	Jesus Vega	.10
651	Jeff Jones	.10
652	Marvis Foley	.10
653	Ty Cobb (puzzle)	.10
----	DK checklist (Dick Perez) (No word "Checklist" on back.)	.25
----	DK Checklist (Dick Perez) (Word "Checklist" on back.)	.10
----	Checklist 27-130	.10
----	Checklist 131-234	.10
----	Checklist 235-338	.10
----	Checklist 339-442	.10
----	Checklist 443-546	.10
----	Checklist 547-653	.10

1983 Donruss Action All-Stars Promo Sheet

To introduce its series of large-format star cards, Donruss issued this sample sheet with four players on a 10" x 7" format.

	NM/M
Complete Sheet:	15.00

1983 Donruss Action All-Stars

Eddie Murray

The cards in this 60-card set are designed on a horizontal format and contain a large close-up photo of the player on the left and a smaller action photo on the right. The 5" x 3-1/2" cards have deep red borders and contain the Donruss logo and the year of issue. Backs are printed in black on red and white and contain statistical and biographical information. The cards were sold with puzzle pieces (three pieces on one card per pack) that feature Mickey Mantle.

	NM/M
Complete Set (60):	6.00
Common Player:	.05
Mickey Mantle Puzzle:	6.00
Cello Pack (3):	.35
Cello Box (36):	15.00

1	Eddie Murray	.30
2	Dwight Evans	.05
3a	Reggie Jackson (Red covers part of statistics on back.)	.50
3b	Reggie Jackson (Red does not cover any statistics on back.)	.50
4	Greg Luzinski	.05
5	Larry Herndon	.05
6	Al Oliver	.05
7	Bill Buckner	.05
8	Jason Thompson	.05
9	Andre Dawson	.20
10	Greg Minton	.05
11	Terry Kennedy	.05
12	Phil Niekro	.25
13	Willie Wilson	.05
14	Johnny Bench	.45
15	Ron Guidry	.05
16	Hal McRae	.05
17	Damaso Garcia	.05
18	Gary Ward	.05
19	Cecil Cooper	.05
20	Keith Hernandez	.05
21	Ron Cey	.05
22	Rickey Henderson	.30
23	Nolan Ryan	2.00
24	Steve Carlton	.30
25	John Stearns	.05
26	Jim Sundberg	.05
27	Joaquin Andujar	.05
28	Gaylord Perry	.25
29	Jack Clark	.05
30	Bill Madlock	.05
31	Pete Rose	1.00
32	Mookie Wilson	.05
33	Rollie Fingers	.25
34	Lonnie Smith	.05
35	Tony Pena	.05
36	Dave Winfield	.30
37	Tim Lollar	.05
38	Rod Carew	.30
39	Toby Harrah	.05
40	Buddy Bell	.05
41	Bruce Sutter	.25
42	George Brett	.75
43	Carlton Fisk	.30
44	Carl Yastrzemski	.45
45	Dale Murphy	.20
46	Bob Horner	.05
47	Dave Concepcion	.05
48	Dave Stieb	.05
49	Kent Hrbek	.05
50	Lance Parrish	.05
51	Joe Niekro	.05
52	Cal Ripken, Jr.	2.00
53	Fernando Valenzuela	.05
54	Rickie Zisk	.05
55	Leon Durham	.05
56	Robin Yount	.30
57	Mike Schmidt	.75
58	Gary Carter	.30
59	Fred Lynn	.05
60	Checklist	.05

1983 Donruss Hall of Fame Heroes Promo Sheet

To introduce its series of former star Perez-Steele art cards, Donruss issued this sample sheet which reproduces four of the cards in a 5" x 7" format.

	NM/M
Complete Sheet:	10.00

1983 Donruss Hall of Fame Heroes

HALL OF FAME HEROES — Bob Lemon

The artwork of Dick Perez is featured in the 44-card Hall of Fame Heroes set issued in 1983. The 2-1/2" x 3-1/2" cards were available in wax packs that contained eight cards plus a Mickey Mantle puzzle piece card (three pieces on one card). Backs display red and blue print on white stock and contain a short biographical sketch.

	NM/M
Complete Set (44):	5.00
Common Player:	.10
Mickey Mantle Puzzle:	6.00
Wax Pack (8):	.75
Wax Box (36):	15.00

1	Ty Cobb	.75
2	Walter Johnson	.15
3	Christy Mathewson	.15
4	Josh Gibson	.15
5	Honus Wagner	.35
6	Jackie Robinson	.75
7	Mickey Mantle	2.00
8	Luke Appling	.15
9	Ted Williams	.75
10	Johnny Mize	.10
11	Satchel Paige	.35
12	Lou Boudreau	.10
13	Jimmie Foxx	.10
14	Duke Snider	.25
15	Monte Irvin	.10
16	Hank Greenberg	.25
17	Roberto Clemente	1.00
18	Al Kaline	.15
19	Frank Robinson	.15
20	Joe Cronin	.10
21	Burleigh Grimes	.10
22	The Waner Brothers (Lloyd Waner, Paul Waner)	.10
23	Grover Alexander	.10
24	Yogi Berra	.25
25	James Bell	.15
26	Bill Dickey	.15
27	Cy Young	.15
28	Charlie Gehringer	.10
29	Dizzy Dean	.15
30	Bob Lemon	.10
31	Red Ruffing	.10
32	Stan Musial	.60
33	Carl Hubbell	.10
34	Hank Aaron	.75
35	John McGraw	.10
36	Bob Feller	.15
37	Casey Stengel	.10
38	Ralph Kiner	.10
39	Roy Campanella	.25
40	Mel Ott	.10
41	Robin Roberts	.10
42	Early Wynn	.10
43	Mickey Mantle Puzzle Card	.25
--	Checklist	.05

1984 Donruss Promo Sheet

The front designs of nine 1984 Donruss baseball cards were printed on this glossy paper sheet to introduce the company's design for 1994. The 7-1/2" x 10-1/2" sheets are blank-backed. Players are listed here alphabetically.

	NM/M
Complete Sheet:	15.00

1984 Donruss

JOE NIEKRO P

The 1984 Donruss set consists of 651 numbered cards, seven unnumbered checklists and two "Living Legends" cards (designated A and B). The A and B cards were issued only in wax packs and were not available to hobby dealers purchasing factory sets. The card fronts differ in style from the previous years, however the Donruss logo and year of issue are still included. Backs have black print on green and white and are identical in format to the preceding year. The 2-1/2" x 3-1/2" cards were issued in packs with three pieces of a 63-piece puzzle of Duke Snider. The complete set price in the checklist that follows does not include the higher priced variations. Cards marked with (DK) or (RR) in the checklist refer to the Diamond Kings and Rated Rookies subsets. Each of the Diamond Kings cards and the DK checklist can be found in two varieties. The more common has Frank Steele's name misspelled "Steel" in the credit line at the bottom-right corner on the back. The error was later corrected.

	NM/M
Unopened Fact. Set (658):	150.00
Complete Set (660):	75.00
Common Player:	.15
Duke Snider Puzzle:	2.00
Wax Pack (15):	4.50
Wax Box (36):	150.00
Rack Pack (45):	15.00

A	Living Legends (Rollie Fingers, Gaylord Perry)	1.50
B	Living Legends (Johnny Bench, Carl Yastrzemski)	4.00
1a	Robin Yount (DK) (Steel)	2.50
1b	Robin Yount (DK) (Steele)	3.00
2a	Dave Concepcion (DK) (Steel)	.25
2b	Dave Concepcion (DK) (Steele)	.35
3a	Dwayne Murphy (DK) (Steel)	.25
3b	Dwayne Murphy (DK) (Steele)	.35
4a	John Castino (DK) (Steel)	.35
4b	John Castino (DK) (Steele)	.35
5a	Leon Durham (DK) (Steel)	.25
5b	Leon Durham (DK) (Steele)	.35
6a	Rusty Staub (DK) (Steel)	.35
6b	Rusty Staub (DK) (Steele)	.45
7a	Jack Clark (DK) (Steel)	.25
7b	Jack Clark (DK) (Steele)	.35
8a	Dave Dravecky (DK) (Steel)	.25
8b	Dave Dravecky (DK) (Steele)	.35
9a	Al Oliver (DK) (Steel)	.35
9b	Al Oliver (DK) (Steele)	.50
10a	Dave Righetti (DK) (Steel)	.35
10b	Dave Righetti (DK) (Steele)	.35
11a	Hal McRae (DK) (Steel)	.25
11b	Hal McRae (DK) (Steele)	.25
12a	Ray Knight (DK) (Steel)	.25
12b	Ray Knight (DK) (Steele)	.35
13a	Bruce Sutter (DK) (Steel)	2.50
13b	Bruce Sutter (DK) (Steele)	3.00
14a	Bob Horner (DK) (Steel)	.25
14b	Bob Horner (DK) (Steele)	.25
15a	Lance Parrish ((DK) (Steel)	.25
15b	Lance Parrish (DK) (Steele)	.35
16a	Matt Young (DK) (Steel)	.25
16b	Matt Young (DK) (Steele)	.35
17a	Fred Lynn (DK) (Steel)	.25
17b	Fred Lynn (DK) (Steele)	.25
18a	Ron Kittle (DK) (Steel)	.25
18b	Ron Kittle (DK) (Steele)	.25
19a	Jim Clancy (DK) (Steel)	.25
19b	Jim Clancy (DK) (Steele)	.25
20a	Bill Madlock (DK) (Steel)	.25
20b	Bill Madlock (DK) (Steele)	.25
21a	Larry Parrish (DK) (Steel)	.25
21b	Larry Parrish (DK) (Steele)	.35
22a	Eddie Murray (DK) (Steel)	2.50
22b	Eddie Murray (DK) (Steele)	3.00
23a	Mike Schmidt (DK) (Steel)	3.00
23b	Mike Schmidt (DK) (Steele)	4.00
24a	Pedro Guerrero (DK) (Steel)	.35
24b	Pedro Guerrero (DK) (Steele)	.35
25a	Andre Thornton (DK) (Steel)	.25
25b	Andre Thornton (DK) (Steele)	.35
26a	Wade Boggs (DK) (Steel)	3.00
26b	Wade Boggs (DK) (Steele)	3.00
27	Joel Skinner RC (RR)	.15
28	Tom Dunbar (RR)	.15
29a	Mike Stenhouse (RR) (no number on back)	1.00
29b	Mike Stenhouse (RR) (29 on back)	1.00
30a	Ron Darling RC (RR) (no number on back)	1.50
30b	Ron Darling RC (RR) (30 on back)	2.50
31	Dion James RC (RR)	.15
32	Tony Fernandez RC (RR)	2.00
33	Angel Salazar (RR)	.15
34	Kevin McReynolds RC (RR)	.15
35	Dick Schofield RC (RR)	.20

#	Player	Price		#	Player	Price		#	Player	Price		#	Player	Price		#	Player	Price		#	Player	Price
36	Brad Komminsk RC (RR)	.15		154	Alan Bannister	.15		272	Dave Rozema	.15		390	Randy Moffitt	.15		508	Marvell Wynne RC	.15		625	Runnin' Reds (David Green, Willie McGee, Lonnie Smith, Ozzie Smith)	.75
37	Tim Teufel RC (RR)	.25		155	Willie Aikens	.15		273	Dave Stapleton	.15		391	Ron Washington	.15		509	Mike Krukow	.15		626	Rudy May	.15
38	Doug Frobel (RR)	.15		156	Jeff Burroughs	.15		274	Lou Piniella	.25		392	Gary Roenicke	.15		510	Dick Ruthven	.15		627	Matt Keough	.15
39	Greg Gagne RC (RR)	1.00		157	Bryan Little	.15		275	Jose Morales	.15		393	Tom Candiotti RC	.75		511	Al Cowens	.15		628	Jose DeLeon RC	.15
40	Mike Fuentes (RR)	.15		158	Bob Boone	.15		276	Brod Perkins	.15		394	Larry Pashnick	.15		512	Cliff Johnson	.15		629	Jim Essian	.15
41	Joe Carter RC (RR)	8.00		159	Dave Hostetler	.15		277	Butch Davis	.15		395	Dwight Evans	.15		513	Randy Bush RC	.15		630	Darnell Coles RC	.15
42	Mike Brown (RR)	.15		160	Jerry Dybzinski	.15		278	Tony Phillips	.15		396	Goose Gossage	.25		*514	Sammy Stewart	.15		631	Mike Warren	.15
43	Mike Jeffcoat (RR)	.15		161	Mike Madden	.15		279	Jeff Reardon	.15		397	Derrel Thomas	.15		515	Bill Schroeder RC	.15		632	Del Crandall	.15
44	Sid Fernandez RC (RR)	2.00		162	Luis DeLeon	.15		280	Ken Forsch	.15		398	Juan Eichelberger	.15		516	Aurelio Lopez	.15		633	Dennis Martinez	.15
45	Brian Dayett (RR)	.15		163	Willie Hernandez	.15		281	Pete O'Brien RC	.15		399	Leon Roberts	.15		517	Mike Brown	.15		634	Mike Moore	.15
46	Chris Smith (RR)	.15		164	Frank Pastore	.15		282	Tom Paciorek	.15		400	Davey Lopes	.15		518	Graig Nettles	.25		635	Lary Sorensen	.15
47	Eddie Murray	3.00		165	Rick Camp	.15		283	Frank LaCorte	.15		401	Bill Gullickson	.15		519	Dave Sax	.15		636	Ricky Nelson	.15
48	Robin Yount	3.00		166	Lee Mazzilli	.15		284	Tim Lollar	.15		402	Geoff Zahn	.15		520	Gerry Willard	.15		637	Omar Moreno	.15
49	Lance Parrish	.15		167	Scot Thompson	.15		285	Greg Gross	.15		403	Billy Sample	.15		521	Paul Splittorff	.15		638	Charlie Hough	.15
50	Jim Rice	1.00		168	Bob Forsch	.15		286	Alex Trevino	.15		404	Mike Squires	.15		522	Tom Burgmeier	.15		639	Dennis Eckersley	2.50
51	Dave Winfield	3.00		169	Mike Flanagan	.15		287	Gene Garber	.15		405	Craig Reynolds	.15		523	Chris Speier	.15		640	Walt Terrell RC	.15
52	Fernando Valenzuela	.15		170	Rick Manning	.15		288	Dave Parker	.15		406	Eric Show	.15		524	Bobby Clark	.15		641	Denny Walling	.15
53	George Brett	5.00		171	Chet Lemon	.15		289	Lee Smith	.25		407	John Denny	.15		525	George Wright	.15		642	Dave Anderson RC	.15
54	Rickey Henderson	3.00		172	Jerry Remy	.15		290	Dave LaPoint	.15		408	Dann Bilardello	.15		526	Dennis Lamp	.15		643	Jose Oquendo RC	.15
55	Gary Carter	3.00		173	Ron Guidry	.20		291	John Shelby RC	.15		409	Bruce Benedict	.15		527	Tony Scott	.15		644	Bob Stanley	.15
56	Buddy Bell	.15		174	Pedro Guerrero	.15		292	Charlie Moore	.15		410	Kent Tekulve	.15		528	Ed Whitson	.15		645	Dave Geisel	.15
57	Reggie Jackson	5.00		175	Willie Wilson	.15		293	Alan Trammell	.15		411	Mel Hall	.15		529	Ron Reed	.15		646	Scott Garrelts RC	.15
58	Harold Baines	.15		176	Carney Lansford	.15		294	Tony Armas	.15		412	John Stuper	.15		530	Charlie Puleo	.15		647	Gary Pettis RC	.15
59	Ozzie Smith	4.00		177	Al Oliver	.15		295	Shane Rawley	.15		413	Rick Dempsey	.15		531	Jerry Royster	.15		648	Duke Snider Puzzle Card	.15
60	Nolan Ryan	8.00		178	Jim Sundberg	.15		296	Greg Brock	.15		414	Don Sutton	1.50		532	Don Robinson	.15		649	Johnnie LeMaster	.15
61	Pete Rose	7.50		179	Bobby Grich	.15		297	Hal McRae	.15		415	Jack Morris	.15		533	Steve Trout	.15		650	Dave Collins	.15
62	Ron Oester	.15		180	Richard Dotson	.15		298	Mike Davis	.15		416	John Tudor	.15		534	Bruce Sutter	2.50		651	San Diego Chicken	.25
63	Steve Garvey	.75		181	Joaquin Andujar	.15		299	Tim Raines	.15		417	Willie Randolph	.15		535	Bob Horner	.15		----	Checklist 1-26 DK (Perez-Steel on back.)	.15
64	Jason Thompson	.15		182	Jose Cruz	.15		300	Bucky Dent	.15		418	Jerry Reuss	.15		536	Pat Tabler	.15		----	Checklist 1-26 DK (Perez-Steele on back.)	.15
65	Jack Clark	.15		183	Mike Schmidt	5.00		301	Tommy John	.25		419	Don Slaught	.15		537	Chris Chambliss	.15		----	Checklist 27-130	.15
66	Dale Murphy	1.50		184	Gary Redus RC	.25		302	Carlton Fisk	3.00		420	Steve McCatty	.15		538	Bob Ojeda	.15		----	Checklist 131-234	.15
67	Leon Durham	.15		185	Garry Templeton	.15		303	Darrell Porter	.15		421	Tim Wallach	.15		539	Alan Ashby	.15		----	Checklist 235-338	.15
68	Darryl Strawberry	2.00		186	Tony Pena	.15		304	Dickie Thon	.15		422	Larry Parrish	.15		540	Jay Johnstone	.15		----	Checklist 339-442	.15
69	Richie Zisk	.15		187	Greg Minton	.15		305	Garry Maddox	.15		423	Brian Downing	.15		541	Bob Dernier	.15		----	Checklist 443-546	.15
70	Kent Hrbek	.15		188	Phil Niekro	1.50		306	Cesar Cedeno	.15		424	Britt Burns	.15		542	Brook Jacoby RC	.15		----	Checklist 547-651	.15
71	Dave Stieb	.15		189	Fergie Jenkins	1.50		307	Gary Lucas	.15		425	David Green	.15		543	U.L. Washington	.15				
72	Ken Schrom	.15		190	Mookie Wilson	.15		308	Johnny Ray	.15		426	Jerry Mumphrey	.15		544	Danny Darwin	.15				
73	George Bell	.15		191	Jim Beattie	.15		309	Andy McGaffigan	.15		427	Ivan DeJesus	.15		545	Kiko Garcia	.15				
74	John Moses	.15		192	Gary Ward	.15		310	Claudell Washington	.15		428	Mario Soto	.15		546	Vance Law	.15				
75	Ed Lynch	.15		193	Jesse Barfield	.15		311	Ryne Sandberg	5.00		429	Gene Richards	.15		547	Tug McGraw	.15				
76	Chuck Rainey	.15		194	Pete Filson	.15		312	George Foster	.15		430	Dale Berra	.15		548	Dave Smith	.15				
77	Biff Pocoroba	.15		195	Roy Lee Jackson	.15		313	Spike Owen RC	.25		431	Darrell Evans	.15		549	Len Matuszek	.15				
78	Cecilio Guante	.15		196	Rick Sweet	.15		314	Gary Gaetti	.15		432	Glenn Hubbard	.15		550	Tom Hume	.15				
79	Jim Barr	.15		197	Jesse Orosco	.15		315	Willie Upshaw	.15		433	Jody Davis	.15		551	Dave Dravecky	.15				
80	Kurt Bevacqua	.15		198	Steve Lake RC	.15		316	Al Williams	.15		434	Danny Heep	.15		552	Rick Rhoden	.15				
81	Tom Foley	.15		199	Ken Dayley	.15		317	Jorge Orta	.15		435	Ed Nunez RC	.15		553	Duane Kuiper	.15				
82	Joe Lefebvre	.15		200	Manny Sarmiento	.15		318	Orlando Mercado	.15		436	Bobby Castillo	.15		554	Rusty Staub	.20				
83	Andy Van Slyke RC	2.00		201	Mark Davis	.15		319	Junior Ortiz RC	.15		437	Ernie Whitt	.15		555	Bill Campbell	.15				
84	Bob Lillis	.15		202	Tim Flannery	.15		320	Mike Proly	.15		438	Scott Ullger	.15		556	Mike Torrez	.15				
85	Rick Adams	.15		203	Bill Scherrer	.15		321	Randy S. Johnson	.15		439	Doyle Alexander	.15		557	Dave Henderson	.15				
86	Jerry Hairston Sr.	.15		204	Al Holland	.15		322	Jim Morrison	.15		440	Domingo Ramos	.15		558	Len Whitehouse	.15				
87	Bob James	.15		205	David Von Ohlen	.15		323	Max Venable	.15		441	Craig Swan	.15		559	Barry Bonnell	.15				
88	Joe Altobelli	.15		206	Mike LaCoss	.15		324	Tony Gwynn	5.00		442	Warren Brusstar	.15		560	Rick Lysander	.15				
89	Ed Romero	.15		207	Juan Beniquez	.15		325	Duane Walker	.15		443	Len Barker	.15		561	Garth Iorg	.15				
90	John Grubb	.15		208	Juan Agosto RC	.15		326	Ozzie Virgil	.15		444	Mike Easler	.15		562	Bryan Clark	.15				
91	John Henry Johnson	.15		209	Bobby Ramos	.15		327	Jeff Lahti	.15		445	Renie Martin	.15		563	Brian Giles	.15				
92	Juan Espino	.15		210	Al Bumbry	.15		328	Bill Dawley RC	.15		446	Dennis Rasmussen RC	.25		564	Vern Ruhle	.15				
93	Candy Maldonado	.15		211	Mark Brouhard	.15		329	Rob Wilfong	.15		447	Ted Power	.15		565	Steve Bedrosian	.15				
94	Andre Thornton	.15		212	Howard Bailey	.15		330	Marc Hill	.15		448	Charlie Hudson RC	.15		566	Larry McWilliams	.15				
95	Onix Concepcion	.15		213	Bruce Hurst	.15		331	Ray Burris	.15		449	Danny Cox RC	.15		567	Jeff Leonard	.15				
96	Don Hill RC	.15		214	Bob Shirley	.15		332	Allan Ramirez	.15		450	Kevin Bass	.15		568	Alan Wiggins	.15				
97	Andre Dawson	1.50		215	Pat Zachry	.15		333	Chuck Porter	.15		451	Daryl Sconiers	.15		569	Jeff Russell RC	.15				
98	Frank Tanana	.15		216	Julio Franco	.98		334	Wayne Krenchicki	.15		452	Scott Fletcher	.15		570	Salome Barojas	.15				
99	Curt Wilkerson RC	.15		217	Mike Armstrong	.15		335	Gary Allenson	.15		453	Bryn Smith	.15		571	Dane Iorg	.15				
100	Larry Gura	.15		218	Dave Beard	.15		336	Bob Meacham RC	.15		454	Jim Dwyer	.15		572	Bob Knepper	.15				
101	Dwayne Murphy	.15		219	Steve Rogers	.15		337	Joe Beckwith	.15		455	Rob Picciolo	.15		573	Gary Lavelle	.15				
102	Tom Brennan	.15		220	John Butcher	.15		338	Rick Sutcliffe	.15		456	Enos Cabell	.15		574	Gorman Thomas	.15				
103	Dave Righetti	.15		221	Mike Smithson RC	.15		339	Mark Huismann RC	.15		457	Dennis Boyd RC	.20		575	Manny Trillo	.15				
104	Steve Sax	.15		222	Frank White	.15		340	Tim Conroy RC	.15		458	Butch Wynegar	.15		576	Jim Palmer	3.00				
105	Dan Petry	.15		223	Mike Heath	.15		341	Scot Sanderson	.15		459	Burt Hooton	.15		577	Dale Murray	.15				
106	Cal Ripken, Jr.	8.00		224	Chris Bando	.15		342	Larry Biittner	.15		460	Ron Hassey	.15		578	Tom Brookens	.15				
107	Paul Molitor	3.00		225	Roy Smalley	.15		343	Dave Stewart	.15		461	Danny Jackson RC	.15		579	Rich Gedman	.15				
108	Fred Lynn	.15		226	Dusty Baker	.15		344	Darryl Motley	.15		462	Bob Kearney	.15		580	Bill Doran RC	.25				
109	Neil Allen	.15		227	Lou Whitaker	.15		345	Chris Codiroli RC	.15		463	Terry Francona	.15		581	Steve Yeager	.15				
110	Joe Niekro	.15		228	John Lowenstein	.15		346	Rick Behenna	.15		464	Wayne Tolleson	.15		582	Dan Spillner	.15				
111	Steve Carlton	3.00		229	Ben Oglivie	.15		347	Andre Robertson	.15		465	Mickey Rivers	.15		583	Dan Quisenberry	.15				
112	Terry Kennedy	.15		230	Doug DeCinces	.15		348	Mike Marshall	.15		466	John Wathan	.15		584	Rance Mulliniks	.15				
113	Bill Madlock	.15		231	Lonnie Smith	.15		349	Larry Herndon	.15		467	Bill Almon	.15		585	Storm Davis	.15				
114	Chili Davis	.15		232	Ray Knight	.15		350	Rich Dauer	.15		468	George Vukovich	.15		586	George Schmidt	.15				
115	Jim Gantner	.15		233	Gary Matthews	.15		351	Cecil Cooper	.15		469	Steve Kemp	.15		587	Bill Russell	.15				
116	Tom Seaver	4.00		234	Juan Bonilla	.15		352	Rod Carew	3.00		470	Ken Landreaux	.15		588	Pat Sheridan RC	.15				
117	Bill Buckner	.15		235	Rod Scurry	.15		353	Willie McGee	.15		471	Milt Wilcox	.15		589	Rafael Ramirez	.15				
118	Bill Caudill	.15		236	Atlee Hammaker	.15		354	Phil Garner	.15		472	Tippy Martinez	.15		590	Bud Anderson	.15				
119	Jim Clancy	.15		237	Mike Caldwell	.15		355	Joe Morgan	3.00		473	Ted Simmons	.15		591	George Frazier	.15				
120	John Castino	.15		238	Keith Hernandez	.15		356	Luis Salazar	.15		474	Tim Foli	.15		592	Lee Tunnell RC	.15				
121	Dave Concepcion	.15		239	Larry Bowa	.15		357	John Candelaria	.15		475	George Hendrick	.15		593	Kirk Gibson	.15				
122	Greg Luzinski	.15		240	Tony Bernazard	.15		358	Bill Laskey	.15		476	Terry Puhl	.15		594	Scott McGregor	.15				
123	Mike Boddicker	.15		241	Damaso Garcia	.15		359	Bob McClure	.15		477	Von Hayes	.15		595	Bob Bailor	.15				
124	Pete Ladd	.15		242	Tom Brunansky	.15		360	Dave Kingman	.15		478	Bobby Brown	.15		596	Tom Herr	.15				
125	Juan Berenguer	.15		243	Dan Driessen	.15		361	Ron Cey	.15		479	Lee Lacy	.15		597	Luis Sanchez	.15				
126	John Montefusco	.15		244	Ron Kittle	.15		362	Matt Young RC	.15		480	Joel Youngblood	.15		598	Dave Engle	.15				
127	Ed Jurak	.15		245	Tim Stoddard	.15		363	Lloyd Moseby	.15		481	Jim Slaton	.15		599	Craig McMurtry RC	.15				
128	Tom Niedenfuer	.15		246	Bob L. Gibson	.15		364	Frank Viola	.15		482	Mike Fitzgerald RC	.15		600	Tom O'Malley	.15				
129	Bert Blyleven	.25		247	Marty Castillo	.15		365	Eddie Milner	.15		483	Keith Moreland	.15		601	Nick Esasky RC	.15				
130	Bud Black	.15		248	Don Mattingly RC	25.00		366	Floyd Bannister	.15		484	Ron Roenicke	.15		602	Ron Hodges	.15				
131	Gorman Heimueller	.15		249	Jeff Newman	.15		367	Dan Ford	.15		485	Luis Leal	.15		603	Ed Vande Berg	.15				
132	Dan Schatzeder	.15		250	Alejandro Pena RC	.15		368	Moose Haas	.15		486	Bryan Oelkers	.15		604	Alfredo Griffin	.15				
133	Ron Jackson	.15		251	Toby Harrah	.15		369	Doug Bair	.15		487	Bruce Berenyi	.15		605	Glenn Hoffman	.15				
134	Tom Henke RC	1.00		252	Cesar Geronimo	.15		370	Ray Fontenot RC	.15		488	LaMarr Hoyt	.15		606	Hubie Brooks	.15				
135	Kevin Hickey	.15		253	Tom Underwood	.15		371	Luis Aponte	.15		489	Joe Nolan	.15		607	Richard Barnes (Photo actually Neal Heaton.)	.15				
136	Mike Scott	.15		254	Doug Flynn	.15		372	Jack Fimple	.15		490	Marshall Edwards	.15		608	Greg Walker RC	.15				
137	Bo Diaz	.15		255	Andy Hassler	.15		373	Neal Heaton RC	.15		491	Mike Laga RC	.15		609	Ken Singleton	.15				
138	Glenn Brummer	.15		256	Odell Jones	.15		374	Greg Pryor	.15		492	Rick Cerone	.15		610	Mark Clear	.15				
139	Sid Monge	.15		257	Rudy Law	.15		375	Wayne Gross	.15		493	Mike Miller (Rick)	.15		611	Buck Martinez	.15				
140	Rich Gale	.15		258	Harry Spilman	.15		376	Charlie Lea	.15		494	Rick Honeycutt	.15		612	Ken Griffey	.20				
141	Brett Butler	.15		259	Marty Bystrom	.15		377	Steve Lubratich	.15		495	Mike Hargrove	.15		613	Reid Nichols	.15				
142	Brian Harper	.15		260	Dave Rucker	.15		378	Jon Matlack	.15		496	Joe Simpson	.15		614	Doug Sisk RC	.15				
143	John Rabb	.15		261	Ruppert Jones	.15		379	Julio Cruz	.15		497	Keith Atherton RC	.15		615	Bob Brenly	.15				
144	Gary Woods	.15		262	Jeff Jones	.15		380	John Mizerock	.15		498	Chris Welsh	.15		616	Joey McLaughlin	.15				
145	Pat Putnam	.15		263	Gerald Perry RC	.15		381	Kevin Gross RC	.15		499	Bruce Kison	.15		617	Glenn Wilson	.15				
146	Jim Acker RC	.15		264	Gene Tenace	.15		382	Mike Ramsey	.15		500	Bob Johnson	.15		618	Bob Stoddard	.15				
147	Mickey Hatcher	.15		265	Brad Wellman	.15		383	Doug Gwosdz	.15		501	Jerry Koosman	.15		619	Len Sakata (Lenn)	.15				
148	Todd Cruz	.15		266	Dickie Noles	.15		384	Kelly Paris	.15		502	Frank DiPino	.15		620	Mike Young RC	.15				
149	Tom Tellmann	.15		267	Jamie Allen	.15		385	Pete Falcone	.15		503	Tony Perez	2.00		621	John Stefero	.15				
150	John Wockenfuss	.15		268	Jim Gott	.15		386	Milt May	.15		504	Ken Oberkfell	.15		622	Carmelo Martinez RC	.15				
151	Wade Boggs	5.00		269	Ron Davis	.15		387	Fred Breining	.15		505	Mark Thurmond RC	.15		623	Dave Bergman	.15				
152	Don Baylor	.15		270	Benny Ayala	.15		388	Craig Lefferts RC	.25		506	Joe Price	.15		624						
153	Bob Welch	.15		271	Ned Yost	.15		389	Steve Henderson	.15		507	Pascual Perez	.15								

1984 Donruss Action All-Stars

Full-color photos on the card fronts and backs make the 1984 Donruss Action All-Stars set somewhat unusual. Fronts contain a large action photo plus the Donruss logo and year of issue inside a deep gold border. The top half of the backs features a close-up photo with the bottom portion containing biographical and statistical information. The 3-1/2" x 5" cards were sold with Ted Williams puzzle pieces.

	NM/M
Complete Set (60):	4.00
Common Player:	.05
Ted Williams Puzzle:	2.50
Cello Pack (5):	.75
Cello Box (36):	12.50
1 Gary Lavelle	.05
2 Willie McGee	.05
3 Tony Pena	.05
4 Lou Whitaker	.05
5 Robin Yount	.40
6 Doug DeCinces	.05
7 John Castino	.05
8 Terry Kennedy	.05
9 Rickey Henderson	.40
10 Bob Horner	.05
11 Harold Baines	.05
12 Buddy Bell	.05
13 Fernando Valenzuela	.05
14 Nolan Ryan	1.00
15 Andre Thornton	.05
16 Gary Redus	.05
17 Pedro Guerrero	.05
18 Andre Dawson	.25
19 Dave Stieb	.05
20 Cal Ripken, Jr.	1.00
21 Ken Singleton	.05
22 Wade Boggs	.50
23 Keith Hernandez	.05
24 Steve Carlton	.40
25 Hal McRae	.05
26 John Lowenstein	.05
27 Fred Lynn	.05
28 Bill Buckner	.05
29 Chris Chambliss	.05
30 Richie Zisk	.05
31 Jack Clark	.05
32 George Hendrick	.05
33 Bill Madlock	.05
34 Lance Parrish	.05

1984 Donruss Action All-Stars (continued)

#	Player	Price
35	Paul Molitor	.40
36	Reggie Jackson	.60
37	Kent Hrbek	.05
38	Steve Garvey	.15
39	Carney Lansford	.05
40	Dale Murphy	.15
41	Greg Luzinski	.05
42	Larry Parrish	.05
43	Ryne Sandberg	.50
44	Dickie Thon	.05
45	Bert Blyleven	.05
46	Ron Oester	.05
47	Dusty Baker	.05
48	Steve Rogers	.05
49	Jim Clancy	.05
50	Eddie Murray	.40
51	Ron Guidry	.05
52	Jim Rice	.20
53	Tom Seaver	.40
54	Pete Rose	.75
55	George Brett	.60
56	Dan Quisenberry	.05
57	Mike Schmidt	.60
58	Ted Simmons	.05
59	Dave Righetti	.05
60	Checklist	.05

1984 Donruss Champions

The Champions set includes ten Hall of Famers, 49 current players and a numbered checklist. Hall of Famers' cards (called Grand Champions) feature the artwork of Dick Perez, while cards of the current players (called Champions) are color photos. All cards measure 3-1/2" x 5". The Grand Champions represent hallmarks of excellence in various statistical categories, while the Champions are the leaders among then-active players in each category. The cards were issued with Duke Snider puzzle pieces.

NM/M

Complete Set (60): 4.00
Common Player: .10
Duke Snider Puzzle: 2.00
Pack (5):
Box (36): 12.50

#	Player	Price
1	Babe Ruth	1.25
2	George Foster	.10
3	Dave Kingman	.10
4	Jim Rice	.25
5	Gorman Thomas	.10
6	Ben Oglivie	.10
7	Jeff Burroughs	.10
8	Hank Aaron	.75
9	Reggie Jackson	.60
10	Carl Yastrzemski	.50
11	Mike Schmidt	.60
12	Graig Nettles	.10
13	Greg Luzinski	.10
14	Ted Williams	.75
15	George Brett	.60
16	Wade Boggs	.50
17	Hal McRae	.10
18	Bill Buckner	.10
19	Eddie Murray	.35
20	Rogers Hornsby	.10
21	Rod Carew	.35
22	Bill Madlock	.10
23	Lonnie Smith	.10
24	Cecil Cooper	.10
25	Ken Griffey	.10
26	Ty Cobb	.60
27	Pete Rose	.75
28	Rusty Staub	.10
29	Tony Perez	.15
30	Al Oliver	.10
31	Cy Young	.25
32	Gaylord Perry	.15
33	Ferguson Jenkins	.15
34	Phil Niekro	.15
35	Jim Palmer	.15
36	Tommy John	.10
37	Walter Johnson	.25
38	Steve Carlton	.15
39	Nolan Ryan	1.25
40	Tom Seaver	.35
41	Don Sutton	.15
42	Bert Blyleven	.15
43	Frank Robinson	.35
44	Joe Morgan	.35
45	Rollie Fingers	.15
46	Keith Hernandez	.10
47	Robin Yount	.35
48	Cal Ripken, Jr.	1.25
49	Dale Murphy	.15
50	Mickey Mantle	1.50
51	Johnny Bench	.50
52	Carlton Fisk	.35
53	Tug McGraw	.10
54	Paul Molitor	.35
55	Carl Hubbell	.10
56	Steve Garvey	.15
57	Dave Parker	.35
58	Gary Carter	.35
59	Fred Lynn	.10
60	Checklist	.05

1985 Donruss Promo Sheet

To introduce its design for 1985, Donruss distributed this 8-1/2" x 11" paper sample sheet to dealers. The blank-back sheet has examples of nine Donruss cards from the '85 set. Players are listed here in alphabetical order.

NM/M

Complete Sheet: 8.00

1985 Donruss

The black-bordered 1985 Donruss set includes 653 numbered cards and seven unnumbered checklists. Displaying the artwork of Dick Perez for the fourth consecutive year, cards #1-26 feature the Diamond Kings series. Donruss, reacting to the hobby craze over rookie cards, included a Rated Rookies subset (cards #27-46). The cards, in standard 2-1/2" x 3-1/2", were issued with a Lou Gehrig puzzle. Backs repeat the front of previous years with black print on yellow and white. The complete set price does not include the higher priced variations. (DK) and (RR) refer to the Diamond Kings and Rated Rookies subsets.

NM/M

Unopened Fact. Set (660): 75.00
Complete Set (660): 50.00
Common Player: .10
Lou Gehrig Puzzle: 3.00
Wax Pack (15): 4.00
Wax Box (36): 120.00
Rack Pack (45): 7.00

#	Player	Price
1	Ryne Sandberg (DK)	2.50
2	Doug DeCinces (DK)	.10
3	Rich Dotson (DK)	.10
4	Bert Blyleven (DK)	.25
5	Lou Whitaker (DK)	.10
6	Dan Quisenberry (DK)	.10
7	Don Mattingly (DK)	4.00
8	Carney Lansford (DK)	.10
9	Frank Tanana (DK)	.10
10	Willie Upshaw (DK)	.10
11	Claudell Washington (DK)	.10
12	Mike Marshall (DK)	.10
13	Joaquin Andujar (DK)	.10
14	Cal Ripken, Jr. (DK)	6.00
15	Jim Rice (DK)	.75
16	Don Sutton (DK)	1.00
17	Frank Viola (DK)	.10
18	Alvin Davis (DK)	.10
19	Mario Soto (DK)	.10
20	Jose Cruz (DK)	.10
21	Charlie Lea (DK)	.10
22	Jesse Orosco (DK)	.10
23	Juan Samuel (DK)	.10
24	Tony Pena (DK)	.10
25	Tony Gwynn (DK)	2.50
26	Bob Brenly (DK)	.10
27	Danny Tartabull RC (RR)	1.50
28	Mike Bielecki RC (RR)	.10
29	Steve Lyons RC (RR)	.25
30	Jeff Reed RC (RR)	.10
31	Tony Brewer (RR)	.10
32	John Morris RC (RR)	.10
33	Daryl Boston RC (RR)	.15
34	Alfonso Pulido (RR)	.10
35	Steve Kiefer (RR)	.10
36	Larry Sheets RC (RR)	.10
37	Scott Bradley RC (RR)	.10
38	Calvin Schiraldi RC (RR)	.10
39	Shawon Dunston RC (RR)	1.50
40	Charlie Mitchell (RR)	.10
41	Billy Hatcher (RR)	.15
42	Russ Stephans (RR)	.10
43	Alejandro Sanchez (RR)	.10
44	Steve Jeltz RC (RR)	.10
45	Jim Traber RC (RR)	.10
46	Doug Loman (RR)	.10
47	Eddie Murray	2.00
48	Robin Yount	2.00
49	Lance Parrish	.10
50	Jim Rice	.75
51	Dave Winfield	2.00
52	Fernando Valenzuela	.10
53	George Brett	3.00
54	Dave Kingman	.10
55	Gary Carter	2.00
56	Buddy Bell	.10
57	Reggie Jackson	3.00
58	Harold Baines	.10
59	Ozzie Smith	2.00
60	Nolan Ryan	6.00
61	Mike Schmidt	3.00
62	Dave Parker	.10
63	Tony Gwynn	2.50
64	Tony Pena	.10
65	Jack Clark	.10
66	Dale Murphy	.60
67	Ryne Sandberg	2.50
68	Keith Hernandez	.10
69	Alvin Davis	.10
70	Kent Hrbek	.10
71	Willie Upshaw	.10
72	Dave Engle	.10
73	Alfredo Griffin	.10
74a	Jack Perconte (Last line of highlights begins "Batted .346...")	.10
74b	Jack Perconte (Last line of highlights begins "Led the ...")	.15
75	Jesse Orosco	.10
76	Jody Davis	.10
77	Bob Horner	.10
78	Larry McWilliams	.10
79	Joel Youngblood	.10
80	Alan Wiggins	.10
81	Ron Oester	.10
82	Ozzie Virgil	.10
83	Ricky Horton RC	.10
84	Bill Doran	.10
85	Rod Carew	2.00
86	LaMarr Hoyt	.10
87	Tim Wallach	.10
88	Mike Flanagan	.10
89	Jim Sundberg	.10
90	Chet Lemon	.10
91	Bob Stanley	.10
92	Willie Randolph	.10
93	Bill Russell	.10
94	Julio Franco	.10
95	Dan Quisenberry	.10
96	Bill Caudill	.10
97	Bill Gullickson	.10
98	Danny Darwin	.10
99	Curtis Wilkerson	.10
100	Bud Black	.10
101	Tony Phillips	.10
102	Tony Bernazard	.10
103	Jay Howell	.10
104	Burt Hooton	.10
105	Milt Wilcox	.10
106	Rich Dauer	.10
107	Don Sutton	1.00
108	Mike Witt	.10
109	Bruce Sutter	1.50
110	Enos Cabell	.10
111	John Denny	.10
112	Dave Dravecky	.10
113	Marvell Wynne	.10
114	Johnnie LeMaster	.10
115	Chuck Porter	.10
116	John Gibbons	.10
117	Keith Moreland	.10
118	Darnell Coles	.10
119	Dennis Lamp	.10
120	Ron Davis	.10
121	Nick Esasky	.10
122	Vance Law	.10
123	Gary Roenicke	.10
124	Bill Schroeder	.10
125	Dave Rozema	.10
126	Bobby Meacham	.10
127	Marty Barrett	.10
128	R.J. Reynolds RC	.15
129	Ernie Camacho	.10
130	Jorge Orta	.10
131	Lary Sorensen	.10
132	Terry Francona	.10
133	Fred Lynn	.10
134	Bobby Jones	.10
135	Jerry Hairston Sr.	.10
136	Kevin Bass	.10
137	Garry Maddox	.10
138	Dave LaPoint	.10
139	Kevin McReynolds	.10
140	Wayne Krenchicki	.10
141	Rafael Ramirez	.10
142	Rod Scurry	.10
143	Greg Minton	.10
144	Tim Stoddard	.10
145	Steve Henderson	.10
146	George Bell	.10
147	Dave Meier	.10
148	Sammy Stewart	.10
149	Mark Brouhard	.10
150	Larry Herndon	.10
151	Oil Can Boyd	.10
152	Brian Dayett	.10
153	Tom Niedenfuer	.10
154	Brook Jacoby	.10
155	Onix Concepcion	.10
156	Tim Conroy	.10
157	Joe Hesketh RC	.15
158	Brian Downing	.10
159	Tommy Dunbar	.10
160	Marc Hill	.10
161	Phil Garner	.10
162	Jerry Davis	.10
163	Bill Campbell	.10
164	John Franco RC	1.50
165	Len Barker	.10
166	Benny Distefano RC	.10
167	George Frazier	.10
168	Tito Landrum	.10
169	Cal Ripken, Jr.	6.00
170	Cecil Cooper	.10
171	Alan Trammell	.10
172	Wade Boggs	2.50
173	Don Baylor	.10
174	Pedro Guerrero	.10
175	Frank White	.10
176	Rickey Henderson	2.00
177	Charlie Lea	.10
178	Pete O'Brien	.10
179	Doug DeCinces	.10
180	Ron Kittle	.10
181	George Hendrick	.10
182	Joe Niekro	.10
183	Juan Samuel	.10
184	Mario Soto	.10
185	Goose Gossage	.15
186	Johnny Ray	.10
187	Bob Brenly	.10
188	Craig McMurtry	.10
189	Leon Durham	.10
190	Dwight Gooden	.25
191	Barry Bonnell	.10
192	Tim Teufel	.10
193	Dave Stieb	.10
194	Mickey Hatcher	.10
195	Jesse Barfield	.10
196	Al Cowens	.10
197	Hubie Brooks	.10
198	Steve Trout	.10
199	Glenn Hubbard	.10
200	Bill Madlock	.10
201	Jeff Robinson RC	.10
202	Eric Show	.10
203	Dave Concepcion	.10
204	Ivan DeJesus	.10
205	Neil Allen	.10
206	Jerry Mumphrey	.10
207	Mike Brown	.10
208	Carlton Fisk	2.00
209	Bryn Smith	.10
210	Tippy Martinez	.10
211	Dion James	.10
212	Willie Hernandez	.10
213	Mike Easler	.10
214	Ron Guidry	.10
215	Rick Honeycutt	.10
216	Brett Butler	.10
217	Larry Gura	.10
218	Ray Burris	.10
219	Steve Rogers	.10
220	Frank Tanana	.10
221	Ned Yost	.10
222	Bret Saberhagen	.25
223	Mike Davis	.10
224	Bert Blyleven	.15
225	Steve Kemp	.10
226	Jerry Reuss	.10
227	Darrell Evans	.10
228	Wayne Gross	.10
229	Jim Gantner	.10
230	Bob Boone	.10
231	Lonnie Smith	.10
232	Frank DiPino	.10
233	Jerry Koosman	.10
234	Graig Nettles	.15
235	John Tudor	.10
236	John Rabb	.10
237	Rick Manning	.10
238	Mike Fitzgerald	.10
239	Gary Matthews	.10
240	Jim Presley RC	.10
241	Dave Collins	.10
242	Gary Gaetti	.10
243	Dann Bilardello	.10
244	Rudy Law	.10
245	John Lowenstein	.10
246	Tom Tellmann	.10
247	Howard Johnson	.10
248	Ray Fontenot	.10
249	Tony Armas	.10
250	Candy Maldonado	.10
251	Mike Jeffcoat RC	.10
252	Dane Iorg	.10
253	Bruce Bochte	.10
254	Pete Rose	5.00
255	Don Aase	.10
256	George Wright	.10
257	Britt Burns	.10
258	Mike Scott	.10
259	Len Matuszek	.10
260	Dave Rucker	.10
261	Craig Lefferts	.10
262	Jay Tibbs RC	.10
263	Bruce Benedict	.10
264	Don Robinson	.10
265	Gary Lavelle	.10
266	Scott Sanderson	.10
267	Matt Young	.10
268	Ernie Whitt	.10
269	Houston Jimenez	.10
270	Ken Dixon RC	.10
271	Peter Ladd	.10
272	Juan Berenguer	.10
273	Roger Clemens	25.00
274	Rick Cerone	.10
275	Dave Anderson	.10
276	George Vukovich	.10
277	Greg Pryor	.10
278	Mike Warren	.10
279	Bob James	.10
280	Bobby Grich	.10
281	Mike Mason RC	.10
282	Ron Reed	.10
283	Alan Ashby	.10
284	Mark Thurmond	.10
285	Joe Lefebvre	.10
286	Ted Power	.10
287	Chris Chambliss	.10
288	Lee Tunnell	.10
289	Rich Bordi	.10
290	Glenn Brummer	.10
291	Mike Boddicker	.10
292	Rollie Fingers	1.00
293	Lou Whitaker	.10
294	Dwight Evans	.10
295	Don Mattingly	5.00
296	Mike Marshall	.10
297	Willie Wilson	.10
298	Mike Heath	.10
299	Tim Raines	.10
300	Larry Parrish	.10
301	Geoff Zahn	.10
302	Rich Dotson	.10
303	David Green	.10
304	Jose Cruz	.10
305	Steve Carlton	2.00
306	Gary Redus	.10
307	Steve Garvey	.40
308	Jose DeLeon	.10
309	Randy Lerch	.10
310	Claudell Washington	.10
311	Lee Smith	.25
312	Darryl Strawberry	.10
313	Jim Beattie	.10
314	John Butcher	.10
315	Damaso Garcia	.10
316	Mike Smithson	.10
317	Luis Leal	.10
318	Ken Phelps	.10
319	Wally Backman	.10
320	Ron Cey	.10
321	Brad Komminsk	.10
322	Jason Thompson	.10
323	Frank Williams RC	.10
324	Tim Lollar	.10
325	Eric Davis RC	1.50
326	Von Hayes	.10
327	Andy Van Slyke	.10
328	Craig Reynolds	.10
329	Dick Schofield	.10
330	Scott Fletcher	.10
331	Jeff Reardon	.10
332	Rick Dempsey	.10
333	Ben Oglivie	.10
334	Dan Petry	.10
335	Jackie Gutierrez	.10
336	Dave Righetti	.10
337	Alejandro Pena	.10
338	Mel Hall	.10
339	Pat Sheridan	.10
340	Keith Atherton	.10
341	David Palmer	.10
342	Gary Ward	.10
343	Dave Stewart	.10
344	Mark Gubicza RC	.50
345	Carney Lansford	.10
346	Jerry Willard	.10
347	Ken Griffey	.10
348	Franklin Stubbs RC	.10
349	Aurelio Lopez	.10
350	Al Bumbry	.10
351	Charlie Moore	.10
352	Luis Sanchez	.10
353	Darrell Porter	.10
354	Bill Dawley	.10
355	Charlie Hudson	.10
356	Garry Templeton	.10
357	Cecilio Guante	.10
358	Jeff Leonard	.10
359	Paul Molitor	2.00
360	Ron Gardenhire	.10
361	Larry Bowa	.10
362	Bob Kearney	.10
363	Garth Iorg	.10
364	Tom Brunansky	.10
365	Brad Gulden	.10
366	Greg Walker	.10
367	Mike Young	.10
368	Rick Waits	.10
369	Doug Bair	.10
370	Bob Shirley	.10
371	Bob Ojeda	.10
372	Bob Welch	.10
373	Neal Heaton	.10
374	Danny Jackson (Photo actually Steve Farr.)	.10
375	Donnie Hill	.10
376	Mike Stenhouse	.10
377	Bruce Kison	.10
378	Wayne Tolleson	.10
379	Floyd Bannister	.10
380	Vern Ruhle	.10
381	Tim Corcoran	.10
382	Kurt Kepshire	.10
383	Bobby Brown	.10
384	Dave Van Gorder	.10
385	Rick Mahler	.10
386	Lee Mazzilli	.10
387	Bill Laskey	.10
388	Thad Bosley	.10
389	Al Chambers	.10
390	Tony Fernandez	.10
391	Ron Washington	.10
392	Bill Swaggerty	.10
393	Bob L. Gibson	.10
394	Marty Castillo	.10
395	Steve Crawford	.10
396	Clay Christiansen	.10
397	Bob Bailor	.10
398	Mike Hargrove	.10
399	Charlie Leibrandt	.10
400	Tom Burgmeier	.10
401	Razor Shines	.10
402	Rob Wilfong	.10
403	Tom Henke	.10
404	Al Jones	.10
405	Mike LaCoss	.10
406	Luis DeLeon	.10
407	Greg Gross	.10
408	Tom Hume	.10
409	Rick Camp	.10
410	Milt May	.10
411	Henry Cotto RC	.10
412	Dave Von Ohlen	.10
413	Scott McGregor	.10
414	Ted Simmons	.10
415	Jack Morris	.10
416	Bill Buckner	.10
417	Butch Wynegar	.10
418	Steve Sax	.10
419	Steve Balboni	.10
420	Dwayne Murphy	.10
421	Andre Dawson	.65
422	Charlie Hough	.10
423	Tommy John	.15
424a	Tom Seaver (Floyd Bannister photo, left-hander.)	2.00
424b	Tom Seaver (Correct photo.)	7.50
425	Tom Herr	.10
426	Terry Puhl	.10
427	Al Holland	.10
428	Eddie Milner	.10
429	Terry Kennedy	.10
430	John Candelaria	.10
431	Manny Trillo	.10
432	Ken Oberkfell	.10
433	Rick Sutcliffe	.10
434	Ron Darling	.10
435	Spike Owen	.10
436	Frank Viola	.10
437	Lloyd Moseby	.10
438	Kirby Puckett	8.00
439	Jim Clancy	.10
440	Mike Moore	.10
441	Doug Sisk	.10
442	Dennis Eckersley	1.50
443	Gerald Perry	.10
444	Dale Berra	.10
445	Dusty Baker	.10
446	Ed Whitson	.10
447	Cesar Cedeno	.10
448	Rick Schu RC	.10
449	Joaquin Andujar	.10
450	Mark Bailey RC	.10
451	Ron Romanick RC	.10
452	Julio Cruz	.10
453	Miguel Dilone	.10
454	Storm Davis	.10
455	Jaime Cocanower	.10
456	Barbaro Garbey	.10
457	Rich Gedman	.10
458	Phil Niekro	1.00
459	Mike Scioscia	.10
460	Pat Tabler	.10
461	Darryl Motley	.10
462	Chris Codoroli (Codiroli)	.10
463	Doug Flynn	.10
464	Billy Sample	.10
465	Mickey Rivers	.10
466	John Wathan	.10
467	Bill Krueger	.10
468	Andre Thornton	.10
469	Rex Hudler	.10
470	Sid Bream RC	.25
471	Kirk Gibson	.10
472	John Shelby	.10
473	Moose Haas	.10
474	Doug Corbett	.10
475	Willie McGee	.10
476	Bob Knepper	.10
477	Kevin Gross	.10
478	Carmelo Martinez	.10
479	Kent Tekulve	.10
480	Chili Davis	.10
481	Bobby Clark	.10

482	Mookie Wilson	.10
483	Dave Owen	.10
484	Ed Nunez	.10
485	Rance Mulliniks	.10
486	Ken Schrom	.10
487	Jeff Russell	.10
488	Tom Paciorek	.10
489	Dan Ford	.10
490	Mike Caldwell	.10
491	Scottie Earl	.10
492	Jose Rijo	.10
493	Bruce Hurst	.10
494	Ken Landreaux	.10
495	Mike Fischlin	.10
496	Don Slaught	.10
497	Steve McCatty	.10
498	Gary Lucas	.10
499	Gary Pettis	.10
500	Marvis Foley	.10
501	Mike Squires	.10
502	Jim Pankovits RC	.10
503	Luis Aguayo	.10
504	Ralph Citarella	.10
505	Bruce Bochy	.10
506	Bob Owchinko	.10
507	Pascual Perez	.10
508	Lee Lacy	.10
509	Atlee Hammaker	.10
510	Bob Dernier	.10
511	Ed Vande Berg	.10
512	Cliff Johnson	.10
513	Len Whitehouse	.10
514	Dennis Martinez	.30
515	Ed Romero	.10
516	Rusty Kuntz	.10
517	Rick Miller	.10
518	Dennis Rasmussen	.10
519	Steve Yeager	.10
520	Chris Bando	.10
521	U.L. Washington	.10
522	Curt Young RC	.10
523	Angel Salazar	.10
524	Curt Kaufman	.10
525	Odell Jones	.10
526	Juan Agosto	.10
527	Denny Walling	.10
528	Andy Hawkins	.10
529	Sixto Lezcano	.10
530	Skeeter Barnes	.10
531	Randy S. Johnson	.10
532	Jim Morrison	.10
533	Warren Brusstar	.10
534a	Jeff Pendleton RC (Error)	1.00
534b	Terry Pendleton RC (Correct)	4.50
535	Vic Rodriguez	.10
536	Bob McClure	.10
537	Dave Bergman	.10
538	Mark Clear	.10
539	Mike Pagliarulo RC	.25
540	Terry Whitfield	.10
541	Joe Beckwith	.10
542	Jeff Burroughs	.10
543	Dan Schatzeder	.10
544	Donnie Scott	.10
545	Jim Slaton	.10
546	Greg Luzinski	.10
547	Mark Salas RC	.10
548	Dave Smith	.10
549	John Wockenfuss	.10
550	Frank Pastore	.10
551	Tim Flannery	.10
552	Rick Rhoden	.10
553	Mark Davis	.10
554	Jeff Dedmon RC	.15
555	Gary Woods	.10
556	Danny Heep	.10
557	Mark Langston	.10
558	Darrell Brown	.10
559	Jimmy Key	.10
560	Rick Lysander	.10
561	Doyle Alexander	.10
562	Mike Stanton	.10
563	Sid Fernandez	.10
564	Richie Hebner	.10
565	Alex Trevino	.10
566	Brian Harper	.10
567	Dan Gladden RC	.25
568	Luis Salazar	.10
569	Tom Foley	.10
570	Larry Andersen	.10
571	Danny Cox	.10
572	Joe Sambito	.10
573	Juan Beniquez	.10
574	Joel Skinner	.10
575	Randy St. Claire RC	.10
576	Floyd Rayford	.10
577	Roy Howell	.10
578	John Grubb	.10
579	Ed Jurak	.10
580	John Montefusco	.10
581	Orel Hershiser RC	3.00
582	Tom Waddell RC	.10
583	Mark Huismann	.10
584	Joe Morgan	2.00
585	Jim Wohlford	.10
586	Dave Schmidt	.10
587	Jeff Kunkel RC	.10
588	Hal McRae	.10
589	Bill Almon	.10
590	Carmen Castillo	.10
591	Omar Moreno	.10
592	Ken Howell RC	.10
593	Tom Brookens	.10
594	Joe Nolan	.10
595	Willie Lozado	.10
596	Tom Nieto RC	.10
597	Walt Terrell	.10
598	Al Oliver	.10

599	Shane Rawley	.10
600	Denny Gonzalez RC	.10
601	Mark Grant RC	.10
602	Mike Armstrong	.10
603	George Foster	.10
604	Davey Lopes	.10
605	Salome Barojas	.10
606	Roy Lee Jackson	.10
607	Pete Filson	.10
608	Duane Walker	.10
609	Glenn Wilson	.10
610	Rafael Santana RC	.10
611	Roy Smith	.10
612	Ruppert Jones	.10
613	Joe Cowley	.10
614	Al Nipper RC (Photo actually Mike Brown.)	.15
615	Gene Nelson	.10
616	Joe Carter	.10
617	Ray Knight	.10
618	Chuck Rainey	.10
619	Dan Driessen	.10
620	Daryl Sconiers	.10
621	Bill Stein	.10
622	Roy Smalley	.10
623	Ed Lynch	.10
624	Jeff Stone RC	.10
625	Bruce Berenyi	.10
626	Kelvin Chapman	.10
627	Joe Price	.10
628	Steve Bedrosian	.10
629	Vic Mata	.10
630	Mike Krukow	.10
631	Phil Bradley RC	.15
632	Jim Gott	.10
633	Randy Bush	.10
634	Tom Browning RC	.25
635	Lou Gehrig Puzzle Card	.10
636	Reid Nichols	.10
637	Dan Pasqua RC	.25
638	German Rivera	.10
639	Don Schulze RC	.10
640a	Mike Jones (Last line of highlights begins "Was 11- 7...")	.10
640b	Mike Jones (Last line of highlights begins "Spent some ...")	.15
641	Pete Rose	4.00
642	Wade Rowdon RC	.10
643	Jerry Narron	.10
644	Darrell Miller RC	.10
645	Tim Hulett RC	.10
646	Andy McGaffigan	.10
647	Kurt Bevacqua	.10
648	John Russell RC	.10
649	Ron Robinson RC	.10
650	Donnie Moore	.10
651a	Two for the Title (Don Mattingly, Dave Winfield) (Yellow letters.)	3.00
651b	Two for the Title (Don Mattingly, Dave Winfield) (White letters.)	4.50
652	Tim Laudner	.10
653	Steve Farr RC	.10
----	Checklist 1-26 DK	.10
----	Checklist 27-130	.10
----	Checklist 131-234	.10
----	Checklist 235-338	.10
----	Checklist 339-442	.10
----	Checklist 443-546	.10
----	Checklist 547-653	.10

1985 Donruss Box Panels

In 1985, Donruss placed on the bottoms of its wax pack boxes a four-card panel which included three player cards and a Lou Gehrig puzzle card. The player cards, numbered PC1 through PC3, have backs identical to the regular 1985 Donruss issue. The card fronts are identical in design to the regular issue, but carry different photos.

		NM/M
Complete Panel:		2.50
Complete Singles Set (4):		2.50
Common Player:		.10
PC1	Dwight Gooden	.25
PC2	Ryne Sandberg	2.50
PC3	Ron Kittle	.10
---	Lou Gehrig (Puzzle card.)	.10

1985 Donruss Action All-Stars

In 1985, Donruss issued an Action All-Stars set for the third consecutive year. Card fronts fea-

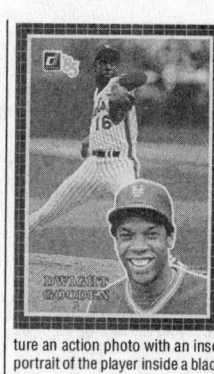

-ture an action photo with an inset portrait of the player inside a black border with grey boxes through it. The card backs have black print on blue and white and include statistical and biographical information. The cards were issued with a Lou Gehrig puzzle.

		NM/M
Complete Set (60):		4.00
Common Player:		.05
Lou Gehrig Puzzle:		3.00
Cello Pack (3):		.50
Cello Box (36):		9.00
1	Tim Raines	.05
2	Jim Gantner	.05
3	Mario Soto	.05
4	Spike Owen	.05
5	Lloyd Moseby	.05
6	Damaso Garcia	.05
7	Cal Ripken, Jr.	1.00
8	Dan Quisenberry	.05
9	Eddie Murray	.50
10	Tony Pena	.05
11	Buddy Bell	.05
12	Dave Winfield	.50
13	Ron Kittle	.05
14	Rich Gossage	.05
15	Dwight Evans	.05
16	Al Davis	.05
17	Mike Schmidt	.75
18	Pascual Perez	.05
19	Tony Gwynn	.60
20	Nolan Ryan	1.00
21	Robin Yount	.50
22	Mike Marshall	.05
23	Brett Butler	.05
24	Ryne Sandberg	.60
25	Dale Murphy	.20
26	George Brett	.75
27	Jim Rice	.25
28	Ozzie Smith	.60
29	Larry Parrish	.05
30	Jack Clark	.05
31	Manny Trillo	.05
32	Dave Kingman	.05
33	Geoff Zahn	.05
34	Pedro Guerrero	.05
35	Dave Parker	.05
36	Rollie Fingers	.35
37	Fernando Valenzuela	.05
38	Wade Boggs	.60
39	Reggie Jackson	.75
40	Kent Hrbek	.05
41	Keith Hernandez	.05
42	Lou Whitaker	.05
43	Tom Herr	.05
44	Alan Trammell	.05
45	Butch Wynegar	.05
46	Leon Durham	.05
47	Dwight Gooden	.20
48	Don Mattingly	.75
49	Phil Niekro	.25
50	Johnny Ray	.05
51	Doug DeCinces	.05
52	Willie Upshaw	.05
53	Lance Parrish	.05
54	Jody Davis	.05
55	Steve Carlton	.50
56	Juan Samuel	.05
57	Gary Carter	.50
58	Harold Baines	.05
59	Eric Show	.05
60	Checklist	.04

1985 Donruss Diamond Kings Supers

RYNE SANDBERG

The 1985 Donruss Diamond Kings Supers are enlarged versions of the Diamond Kings cards in the regular 1985 Donruss set. The cards measure 4-15/16" x 6-3/4". The Diamond Kings series features the artwork of Dick Perez. Twenty-eight cards make up the Super set - 26 DK cards, an unnumbered checklist, and an unnumbered Dick Perez card. The back of the Perez card contains a brief history of Dick Perez and the Perez-Steele Galleries. The set could be obtained through a mail-in offer found on wax pack wrappers.

		NM/M
Complete Set (28):		5.00
Common Player:		.10
1	Ryne Sandberg	1.00
2	Doug DeCinces	.10
3	Richard Dotson	.10
4	Bert Blyleven	.10
5	Lou Whitaker	.10
6	Dan Quisenberry	.10
7	Don Mattingly	1.50
8	Carney Lansford	.10
9	Frank Tanana	.10
10	Willie Upshaw	.10
11	Claudell Washington	.10
12	Mike Marshall	.10
13	Joaquin Andujar	.10
14	Cal Ripken, Jr.	2.00
15	Jim Rice	.25
16	Don Sutton	.10
17	Frank Viola	.10
18	Alvin Davis	.10
19	Mario Soto	.10
20	Jose Cruz	.10
21	Charlie Lea	.10
22	Jesse Orosco	.10
23	Juan Samuel	.10
24	Tony Pena	.10
25-	Tony Gwynn	1.00
26	Bob Brenly	.10
	Checklist	.03
	Dick Perez (DK artist)	.10

1985 Donruss Highlights

PETE ROSE TY-BREAKING HIT — Highlights

Designed in the style of the regular 1985 Donruss set, this issue features the Player of the Month in the major leagues plus highlight cards of special baseball events and milestones of the 1985 season. Fifty-six cards, including an unnumbered checklist, comprise the set which was available only through hobby dealers. The cards measure 2-1/2" x 3-1/2" and have glossy fronts. The last two cards in the set feature Donruss' picks for the A.L. and N.L. Rookies of the Year. The set was issued in a specially designed box.

		NM/M
Complete Set (56):		3.00
Common Player:		.05
1	Sets Opening Day Record (Tom Seaver)	.10
2	Establishes A.L. Save Mark (Rollie Fingers)	.05
3	A.L. Player of the Month - April (Mike Davis)	.05
4	A.L. Pitcher of the Month - April (Charlie Leibrandt)	.05
5	N.L. Player of the Month - April (Dale Murphy)	.10
6	N.L. Pitcher of the Month - April (Fernando Valenzuela)	.05
7	N.L. Shortstop Record (Larry Bowa)	.05
8	Joins Reds 2000 Hit Club (Dave Concepcion)	.05
9	Eldest Grand Slammer (Tony Perez)	.05
10	N.L. Career Run Leader (Pete Rose)	.50
11	A.L. Player of the Month - May (George Brett)	.25

12	A.L. Pitcher of the Month - May (Dave Stieb)	.05
13	N.L. Player of the Month - May (Dave Parker)	.05
14	N.L. Pitcher of the Month - May (Andy Hawkins)	.05
15	Records 11th Straight Win (Andy Hawkins)	.05
16	Two Homers In First Inning (Von Hayes)	.05
17	A.L. Player of the Month - June (Rickey Henderson)	.15
18	A.L. Pitcher of the Month - June (Jay Howell)	.05
19	N.L. Player of the Month - June (Pedro Guerrero)	.05
20	N.L. Pitcher of the Month - June (John Tudor)	.05
21	Marathon Game Iron Men (Gary Carter, Keith Hernandez)	.05
22	Records 4000th K (Nolan Ryan)	.05
23	All-Star Game MVP (LaMarr Hoyt)	.05
24	1st Ranger To Hit For Cycle (Oddibe McDowell)	.05
25	A.L. Player of the Month - July (George Brett)	.25
26	A.L. Pitcher of the Month - July (Bret Saberhagen)	.05
27	N.L. Player of the Month - July (Keith Hernandez)	.05
28	N.L. Pitcher of the Month - July (Fernando Valenzuela)	.05
29	Record Setting Base Stealers (Vince Coleman, Willie McGee)	.05
30	Notches 300th Career Win (Tom Seaver)	.10
31	Strokes 3000th Hit (Rod Carew)	.10
32	Establishes Met Record (Dwight Gooden)	.05
33	Achieves Strikeout Milestone (Dwight Gooden)	.05
34	Explodes For 9 RBI (Eddie Murray)	.05
35	A.L. Career Hbp Leader (Don Baylor)	.05
36	A.L. Player of the Month - August (Don Mattingly)	.50
37	A.L. Pitcher of the Month - August (Dave Righetti)	.05
38	N.L. Player of the Month - August (Willie McGee)	.05
39	N.L. Pitcher of the Month - August (Shane Rawley)	.05
40	Ty-Breaking Hit (Pete Rose)	.50
41	Hits 3 HRs, Drives In 8 Runs (Andre Dawson)	.05
42	Sets Yankee Theft Mark (Rickey Henderson)	.15
43	20 Wins In Rookie Season (Tom Browning)	.05
44	Yankee Milestone For Hits (Don Mattingly)	.50
45	A.L. Player of the Month - September (Don Mattingly)	.50
46	A.L. Pitcher of the Month - September (Charlie Leibrandt)	.05
47	N.L. Player of the Month - September (Gary Carter)	.05
48	N.L. Pitcher of the Month - September (Dwight Gooden)	.05
49	Major League Record Setter (Wade Boggs)	.25
50	Hurls Shutout For 300th Win (Phil Niekro)	.05
51	Venerable HR King (Darrell Evans)	.05
52	N.L. Switch-hitting Record (Willie McGee)	.05
53	Equals DiMaggio Feat (Dave Winfield)	.05
54	Donruss N.L. Rookie of the Year (Vince Coleman)	.10
55	Donruss A.L. Rookie of the Year (Ozzie Guillen)	.10
	Checklist	.05

1985 Donruss Sluggers of The Hall of Fame

In much the same manner as the 1959-71 Bazooka cards were issued, this eight-player set consists of cards printed on the bottom panel of a box of bubble gum. When cut off the box, cards measure 3-1/2" x 6-1/2", with blank backs. Players are pictured on the cards in paintings done by Dick Perez. Cards were issued on blue Color Bubbles brand boxes and on red Super Bubble boxes, each numbered on a tab at top or bottom; this checklist is arranged by the number on the card front.

		NM/M
Complete Set (8):		6.00

Common Player:		.30
1	Babe Ruth	2.00
2	Ted Williams	1.00
3	Lou Gehrig	1.00
4	Johnny Mize	.30
5	Stan Musial	.60
6	Mickey Mantle	2.50
7	Hank Aaron	.75
8	Frank Robinson	.45

1986 Donruss

BILL BUCKNER

In 1986, Donruss issued a 660-card set which included 653 numbered cards and seven unnumbered checklists. The 2-1/2" x 3-1/2" cards have fronts that feature blue borders and backs that have black print on blue and white. For the fifth year in a row, the first 26 cards in the set are Diamond Kings. The Rated Rookies subset (#27-46) appears once again. The cards were distributed with a Hank Aaron puzzle. The complete set price does not include the higher priced variations. In the checklist that follows, (DK) and (RR) refer to the Diamond Kings and Rated Rookies series.

		NM/M
Unopened Factory Set (660):		35.00
Complete Set (660):		30.00
Common Player:		.05
Hank Aaron Puzzle:		3.00
Wax Pack (15):		1.25
Wax Box (36):		35.00
Rack Pack (45):		2.50
1	Kirk Gibson (DK)	.15
2	Goose Gossage (DK)	.15
3	Willie McGee (DK)	.05
4	George Bell (DK)	.05
5	Tony Armas (DK)	.05
6	Chili Davis (DK)	.05
7	Cecil Cooper (DK)	.05
8	Mike Boddicker (DK)	.05
9	Davey Lopes (DK)	.05
10	Bill Doran (DK)	.05
11	Bret Saberhagen (DK)	.10
12	Brett Butler (DK)	.05
13	Harold Baines (DK)	.15
14	Mike Davis (DK)	.05
15	Tony Perez (DK)	1.00
16	Willie Randolph (DK)	.05
17	Bob Boone (DK)	.05
18	Orel Hershiser (DK)	.10
19	Johnny Ray (DK)	.05
20	Gary Ward (DK)	.05
21	Rick Mahler (DK)	.05
22	Phil Bradley (DK)	.05
23	Jerry Koosman (DK)	.10
24	Tom Brunansky (DK)	.05
25	Andre Dawson (DK)	.50
26	Dwight Gooden (DK)	.10
27	Kal Daniels RC (RR)	.15
28	Fred McGriff RC (RR)	4.00
29	Cory Snyder RC (RR)	.10
30	Jose Guzman RC (RR)	.05
31	Ty Gainey RC (RR)	.05
32	Johnny Abrego RC (RR)	.05
33a	Andres Galarraga RC (RR)(Accent mark over e of Andres on back.)	2.00
33b	Andres Galarraga RC (RR) (No accent mark.))	2.00
34	Dave Shipanoff RC (RR)	.05
35	Mark McLemore RC (RR)	.50
36	Marty Clary RC (RR)	.05
37	Paul O'Neill RC (RR)	2.00
38	Danny Tartabull RC (RR)	.05
39	Jose Canseco RC (RR)	6.00
40	Juan Nieves RC (RR)	.05
41	Lance McCullers RC (RR)	.05
42	Rick Surhoff RC (RR)	.05
43	Todd Worrell RC (RR)	.25
44	Bob Kipper (RR)	.05
45	John Habyan RC (RR)	.05
46	Mike Woodard RC (RR)	.05
47	Mike Boddicker	.05
48	Robin Yount	1.50
49	Lou Whitaker	.05
50	Dennis Boyd	.05
51	Rickey Henderson	1.50
52	Mike Marshall	.05
53	George Brett	2.50
54	Dave Kingman	.05

#	Player	Price
55	Hubie Brooks	.05
56	Oddibe McDowell RC	.15
57	Doug DeCinces	.05
58	Britt Burns	.05
59	Ozzie Smith	2.00
60	Jose Cruz	.05
61	Mike Schmidt	2.50
62	Pete Rose	3.00
63	Steve Garvey	.40
64	Tony Pena	.05
65	Chili Davis	.05
66	Dale Murphy	.40
67	Ryne Sandberg	2.00
68	Gary Carter	1.50
69	Alvin Davis	.05
70	Kent Hrbek	.05
71	George Bell	.05
72	Kirby Puckett	2.00
73	Lloyd Moseby	.05
74	Bob Kearney	.05
75	Dwight Gooden	.05
76	Gary Matthews	.05
77	Rick Mahler	.05
78	Benny Distefano	.05
79	Jeff Leonard	.05
80	Kevin McReynolds	.05
81	Ron Oester	.05
82	John Russell	.05
83	Tommy Herr	.05
84	Jerry Mumphrey	.05
85	Ron Romanick	.05
86	Daryl Boston	.05
87	Andre Dawson	.50
88	Eddie Murray	1.50
89	Dion James	.05
90	Chet Lemon	.05
91	Bob Stanley	.05
92	Willie Randolph	.05
93	Mike Scioscia	.05
94	Tom Waddell	.05
95	Danny Jackson	.05
96	Mike Davis	.05
97	Mike Fitzgerald	.05
98	Gary Ward	.05
99	Pete O'Brien	.05
100	Bret Saberhagen	.05
101	Alfredo Griffin	.05
102	Brett Butler	.05
103	Ron Guidry	.15
104	Jerry Reuss	.05
105	Jack Morris	.05
106	Rick Dempsey	.05
107	Ray Burris	.05
108	Brian Downing	.05
109	Willie McGee	.05
110	Bill Doran	.05
111	Kent Tekulve	.05
112	Tony Gwynn	2.00
113	Marvell Wynne	.05
114	David Green	.05
115	Jim Gantner	.05
116	George Foster	.05
117	Steve Trout	.05
118	Mark Langston	.05
119	Tony Fernandez	.05
120	John Butcher	.05
121	Ron Robinson	.05
122	Dan Spillner	.05
123	Mike Young	.05
124	Paul Molitor	1.50
125	Kirk Gibson	.05
126	Ken Griffey	.05
127	Tony Armas	.05
128	Mariano Duncan RC	.15
129	Pat Tabler (Mr. Clutch)	.05
130	Frank White	.05
131	Carney Lansford	.05
132	Vance Law	.05
133	Dick Schofield	.05
134	Wayne Tolleson	.05
135	Greg Walker	.05
136	Denny Walling	.05
137	Ozzie Virgil	.05
138	Ricky Horton	.05
139	LaMarr Hoyt	.05
140	Wayne Krenchicki	.05
141	Glenn Hubbard	.05
142	Cecilio Guante	.05
143	Mike Krukow	.05
144	Lee Smith	.15
145	Edwin Nunez	.05
146	Dave Stieb	.05
147	Mike Smithson	.05
148	Ken Dixon	.05
149	Danny Darwin	.05
150	Chris Pittaro	.05
151	Bill Buckner	.05
152	Mike Pagliarulo	.05
153	Bill Russell	.05
154	Brook Jacoby	.05
155	Pat Sheridan	.05
156	Mike Gallego RC	.05
157	Jim Wohlford	.05
158	Gary Pettis	.05
159	Toby Harrah	.05
160	Richard Dotson	.05
161	Bob Knepper	.05
162	Dave Dravecky	.05
163	Greg Gross	.05
164	Eric Davis	.50
165	Gerald Perry	.05
166	Rick Rhoden	.05
167	Keith Moreland	.05
168	Jack Clark	.05
169	Storm Davis	.05
170	Cecil Cooper	.05
171	Alan Trammell	.05
172	Roger Clemens	2.50
173	Don Mattingly	2.50
174	Pedro Guerrero	.05
175	Willie Wilson	.05
176	Dwayne Murphy	.05
177	Tim Raines	.05
178	Larry Parrish	.05
179	Mike Witt	.05
180	Harold Baines	.05
181	Vince Coleman RC	.35
182	Jeff Heathcock RC	.05
183	Steve Carlton	1.50
184	Mario Soto	.05
185	Goose Gossage	.10
186	Johnny Ray	.05
187	Dan Gladden	.05
188	Bob Horner	.05
189	Rick Sutcliffe	.05
190	Keith Hernandez	.05
191	Phil Bradley	.05
192	Tom Brunansky	.05
193	Jesse Barfield	.05
194	Frank Viola	.05
195	Willie Upshaw	.05
196	Jim Beattie	.05
197	Darryl Strawberry	.05
198	Ron Cey	.05
199	Steve Bedrosian	.05
200	Steve Kemp	.05
201	Manny Trillo	.05
202	Garry Templeton	.05
203	Dave Parker	.05
204	John Denny	.05
205	Terry Pendleton	.05
206	Terry Puhl	.05
207	Bobby Grich	.05
208	Ozzie Guillen RC	2.00
209	Jeff Reardon	.05
210	Cal Ripken, Jr.	3.00
211	Bill Schroeder	.05
212	Dan Petry	.05
213	Jim Rice	.50
214	Dave Righetti	.05
215	Fernando Valenzuela	.05
216	Julio Franco	.05
217	Darryl Motley	.05
218	Dave Collins	.05
219	Tim Wallach	.05
220	George Wright	.05
221	Tommy Dunbar	.05
222	Steve Balboni	.05
223	Jay Howell	.05
224	Joe Carter	.05
225	Ed Whitson	.05
226	Orel Hershiser	.05
227	Willie Hernandez	.05
228	Lee Lacy	.05
229	Rollie Fingers	1.00
230	Bob Boone	.05
231	Joaquin Andujar	.05
232	Craig Reynolds	.05
233	Shane Rawley	.05
234	Eric Show	.05
235	Jose DeLeon	.05
236	Jose Uribe RC	.05
237	Moose Haas	.05
238	Wally Backman	.05
239	Dennis Eckersley	1.25
240	Mike Moore	.05
241	Damaso Garcia	.05
242	Tim Teufel	.05
243	Dave Concepcion	.05
244	Floyd Bannister	.05
245	Fred Lynn	.05
246	Charlie Moore	.05
247	Walt Terrell	.05
248	Dave Winfield	1.50
249	Dwight Evans	.05
250	Dennis Powell RC	.05
251	Andre Thornton	.05
252	Onix Concepcion	.05
253	Mike Heath	.05
254a	David Palmer (2B on front)	.05
254b	David Palmer (P on front)	.15
255	Donnie Moore	.05
256	Curtis Wilkerson	.05
257	Julio Cruz	.05
258	Nolan Ryan	3.00
259	Jeff Stone	.05
260a	John Tudor (1981 Games is .18)	.05
260b	John Tudor (1981 Games is 18)	.15
261	Mark Thurmond	.05
262	Jay Tibbs	.05
263	Rafael Ramirez	.05
264	Larry McWilliams	.05
265	Mark Davis	.05
266	Bob Dernier	.05
267	Matt Young	.05
268	Jim Clancy	.05
269	Mickey Hatcher	.05
270	Sammy Stewart	.05
271	Bob L. Gibson	.05
272	Nelson Simmons	.05
273	Rich Gedman	.05
274	Butch Wynegar	.05
275	Ken Howell	.05
276	Mel Hall	.05
277	Jim Sundberg	.05
278	Chris Codiroli	.05
279	Herman Winningham RC	.05
280	Rod Carew	1.50
281	Don Slaught	.05
282	Scott Fletcher	.05
283	Bill Dawley	.05
284	Andy Hawkins	.05
285	Glenn Wilson	.05
286	Nick Esasky	.05
287	Claudell Washington	.05
288	Lee Mazzilli	.05
289	Jody Davis	.05
290	Darrell Porter	.05
291	Scott McGregor	.05
292	Ted Simmons	.05
293	Aurelio Lopez	.05
294	Marty Barrett	.05
295	Dale Berra	.05
296	Greg Brock	.05
297	Charlie Leibrandt	.05
298	Bill Krueger	.05
299	Bryn Smith	.05
300	Burt Hooton	.05
301	Stu Cliburn RC	.05
302	Luis Salazar	.05
303	Ken Dayley	.05
304	Frank DiPino	.05
305	Von Hayes	.05
306a	Gary Redus (1983 2B is .20)	.05
306b	Gary Redus (1983 2B is 20)	.15
307	Craig Lefferts	.05
308	Sam Khalifa	.05
309	Scott Garrelts	.05
310	Rick Cerone	.05
311	Shawon Dunston	.05
312	Howard Johnson	.05
313	Jim Presley	.05
314	Gary Gaetti	.05
315	Luis Leal	.05
316	Mark Salas	.05
317	Bill Caudill	.05
318	Dave Henderson	.05
319	Rafael Santana	.05
320	Leon Durham	.05
321	Bruce Sutter	1.25
322	Jason Thompson	.05
323	Bob Brenly	.05
324	Carmelo Martinez	.05
325	Eddie Milner	.05
326	Juan Samuel	.05
327	Tom Nieto	.05
328	Dave Smith	.05
329	Urbano Lugo RC	.05
330	Joel Skinner	.05
331	Bill Gullickson	.05
332	Floyd Rayford	.05
333	Ben Oglivie	.05
334	Lance Parrish	.05
335	Jackie Gutierrez	.05
336	Dennis Rasmussen	.05
337	Terry Whitfield	.05
338	Neal Heaton	.05
339	Jorge Orta	.05
340	Donnie Hill	.05
341	Joe Hesketh	.05
342	Charlie Hough	.05
343	Dave Rozema	.05
344	Greg Pryor	.05
345	Mickey Tettleton	.05
346	George Vukovich	.05
347	Don Baylor	.05
348	Carlos Diaz	.05
349	Barbaro Garbey	.05
350	Larry Sheets	.05
351	Ted Higuera RC	.10
352	Juan Beniquez	.05
353	Bob Forsch	.05
354	Mark Bailey	.05
355	Larry Andersen	.05
356	Terry Kennedy	.05
357	Don Robinson	.05
358	Jim Gott	.05
359	Earnest Riles RC	.05
360	John Christensen RC	.05
361	Ray Fontenot	.05
362	Spike Owen	.05
363	Jim Acker	.05
364a	Ron Davis (Last line in highlights ends with "...inMay.")	.05
364b	Ron Davis (Last line in highlights ends with "...relievers (9).")	.15
365	Tom Hume	.05
366	Carlton Fisk	1.50
367	Nate Snell	.05
368	Rick Manning	.05
369	Darrell Evans	.05
370	Ron Hassey	.05
371	Wade Boggs	2.00
372	Rick Honeycutt	.05
373	Chris Bando	.05
374	Bud Black	.05
375	Steve Henderson	.05
376	Charlie Lea	.05
377	Reggie Jackson	2.50
378	Dave Schmidt	.05
379	Bob James	.05
380	Glenn Davis	.05
381	Tim Corcoran	.05
382	Danny Cox	.05
383	Tim Flannery	.05
384	Tom Browning	.05
385	Rick Camp	.05
386	Jim Morrison	.05
387	Dave LaPoint	.05
388	Davey Lopes	.05
389	Al Cowens	.05
390	Doyle Alexander	.05
391	Tim Laudner	.05
392	Don Aase	.05
393	Jaime Cocanower	.05
394	Randy O'Neal	.05
395	Mike Easler	.05
396	Scott Bradley	.05
397	Tom Niedenfuer	.05
398	Jerry Willard	.05
399	Lonnie Smith	.05
400	Bruce Bochte	.05
401	Terry Francona	.05
402	Jim Slaton	.05
403	Bill Stein	.05
404	Tim Hulett	.05
405	Alan Ashby	.05
406	Tim Stoddard	.05
407	Garry Maddox	.05
408	Ted Power	.05
409	Len Barker	.05
410	Denny Gonzalez	.05
411	George Frazier	.05
412	Andy Van Slyke	.05
413	Jim Dwyer	.05
414	Paul Householder	.05
415	Alejandro Sanchez	.05
416	Steve Crawford	.05
417	Dan Pasqua	.05
418	Enos Cabell	.05
419	Mike Jones	.05
420	Steve Kiefer	.05
421	Tim Burke RC	.05
422	Mike Mason	.05
423	Ruppert Jones	.05
424	Jerry Hairston Sr.	.05
425	Tito Landrum	.05
426	Jeff Calhoun	.05
427	Don Carman RC	.05
428	Tony Perez	1.00
429	Jerry Davis	.05
430	Bob Walk	.05
431	Brad Wellman	.05
432	Terry Forster	.05
433	Billy Hatcher	.05
434	Clint Hurdle	.05
435	Ivan Calderon RC	.05
436	Pete Filson	.05
437	Tom Henke	.05
438	Dave Engle	.05
439	Tom Filer	.05
440	Gorman Thomas	.05
441	Rick Aguilera RC	.25
442	Scott Sanderson	.05
443	Jeff Dedmon	.05
444	Joe Orsulak RC	.10
445	Atlee Hammaker	.05
446	Jerry Royster	.05
447	Buddy Bell	.05
448	Dave Rucker	.05
449	Ivan DeJesus	.05
450	Jim Pankovits	.05
451	Jerry Narron	.05
452	Bryan Little	.05
453	Gary Lucas	.05
454	Dennis Martinez	.05
455	Ed Romero	.05
456	Bob Melvin RC	.05
457	Glenn Hoffman	.05
458	Bob Shirley	.05
459	Bob Welch	.05
460	Carmen Castillo	.05
461	Dave Leeper	.05
462	Tim Birtsas RC	.05
463	Randy St. Claire	.05
464	Chris Welsh	.05
465	Greg Harris	.05
466	Lynn Jones	.05
467	Dusty Baker	.05
468	Roy Smith	.05
469	Andre Robertson	.05
470	Ken Landreaux	.05
471	Dave Bergman	.05
472	Gary Roenicke	.05
473	Pete Vuckovich	.05
474	Kirk McCaskill RC	.10
475	Jeff Lahti	.05
476	Mike Scott	.05
477	Darren Daulton RC	1.50
478	Graig Nettles	.15
479	Bill Almon	.05
480	Greg Minton	.05
481	Randy Ready	.05
482	Len Dykstra RC	1.50
483	Thad Bosley	.05
484	Harold Reynolds RC	1.00
485	Al Oliver	.05
486	Roy Smalley	.05
487	John Franco	.05
488	Juan Agosto	.05
489	Al Pardo	.05
490	Bill Wegman RC	.05
491	Frank Tanana	.05
492	Brian Fisher RC	.05
493	Mark Clear	.05
494	Len Matuszek	.05
495	Ramon Romero	.05
496	John Wathan	.05
497	Rob Picciolo	.05
498	U.L. Washington	.05
499	John Candelaria	.05
500	Duane Walker	.05
501	Gene Nelson	.05
502	John Mizerock	.05
503	Luis Aguayo	.05
504	Kurt Kepshire	.05
505	Ed Wojna	.05
506	Joe Price	.05
507	Milt Thompson RC	.05
508	Junior Ortiz	.05
509	Vida Blue	.05
510	Steve Engel	.05
511	Karl Best	.05
512	Cecil Fielder RC	2.00
513	Frank Eufemia	.05
514	Tippy Martinez	.05
515	Billy Robidoux RC	.05
516	Bill Scherrer	.05
517	Bruce Hurst	.05
518	Rich Bordi	.05
519	Steve Yeager	.05
520	Tony Bernazard	.05
521	Hal McRae	.05
522	Jose Rijo	.05
523	Mitch Webster RC	.05
524	Jack Howell RC	.05
525	Alan Bannister	.05
526	Ron Kittle	.05
527	Phil Garner	.05
528	Kurt Bevacqua	.05
529	Kevin Gross	.05
530	Bo Diaz	.05
531	Ken Oberkfell	.05
532	Rick Reuschel	.05
533	Ron Meridith	.05
534	Steve Braun	.05
535	Wayne Gross	.05
536	Ray Searage	.05
537	Tom Brookens	.05
538	Al Nipper	.05
539	Billy Sample	.05
540	Steve Sax	.05
541	Dan Quisenberry	.05
542	Tony Phillips	.05
543	Floyd Youmans RC	.05
544	Steve Buechele RC	.05
545	Craig Gerber	.05
546	Joe DeSa	.05
547	Brian Harper	.05
548	Kevin Bass	.05
549	Tom Foley	.05
550	Dave Van Gorder	.05
551	Bruce Bochy	.05
552	R.J. Reynolds	.05
553	Chris Brown RC	.05
554	Bruce Benedict	.05
555	Warren Brusstar	.05
556	Danny Heep	.05
557	Darnell Coles	.05
558	Greg Gagne	.05
559	Ernie Whitt	.05
560	Ron Washington	.05
561	Jimmy Key	.05
562	Billy Swift	.05
563	Ron Darling	.05
564	Dick Ruthven	.05
565	Zane Smith	.05
566	Sid Bream	.05
567a	Joel Youngblood (P on front)	.05
567b	Joel Youngblood (IF on front)	.15
568	Mario Ramirez	.05
569	Tom Runnells	.05
570	Rick Schu	.05
571	Bill Campbell	.05
572	Dickie Thon	.05
573	Al Holland	.05
574	Reid Nichols	.05
575	Bert Roberge	.05
576	Mike Flanagan	.05
577	Tim Leary	.05
578	Mike Laga	.05
579	Steve Lyons	.05
580	Phil Niekro	1.00
581	Gilberto Reyes	.05
582	Jamie Easterly	.05
583	Mark Gubicza	.05
584	Stan Javier RC	.15
585	Bill Laskey	.05
586	Jeff Russell	.05
587	Dickie Noles	.05
588	Steve Farr	.05
589	Steve Ontiveros RC	.05
590	Mike Hargrove	.05
591	Marty Bystrom	.05
592	Franklin Stubbs	.05
593	Larry Herndon	.05
594	Bill Swaggerty	.05
595	Carlos Ponce	.05
596	Pat Perry RC	.05
597	Ray Knight	.05
598	Steve Lombardozzi RC	.05
599	Brad Havens	.05
600	Pat Clements RC	.05
601	Joe Niekro	.05
602	Hank Aaron Puzzle Card	.05
603	Dwayne Henry RC	.05
604	Mookie Wilson	.05
605	Buddy Biancalana	.05
606	Rance Mulliniks	.05
607	Alan Wiggins	.05
608	Joe Cowley	.05
609a	Tom Seaver (Green stripes around name.)	1.50
609b	Tom Seaver (Yellow stripes around name.)	2.00
610	Neil Allen	.05
611	Don Sutton	1.00
612	Fred Toliver RC	.05
613	Jay Baller	.05
614	Marc Sullivan	.05
615	John Grubb	.05
616	Bruce Kison	.05
617	Bill Madlock	.05
618	Chris Chambliss	.05
619	Dave Stewart	.05
620	Tim Lollar	.05
621	Gary Lavelle	.05
622	Charles Hudson	.05
623	Joel Davis RC	.05
624	Joe Johnson RC	.05
625	Sid Fernandez	.05
626	Dennis Lamp	.05
627	Terry Harper	.05
628	Jack Lazorko	.05
629	Roger McDowell RC	.05
630	Mark Funderburk	.05
631	Ed Lynch	.05
632	Rudy Law	.05
633	Roger Mason RC	.05
634	Mike Felder RC	.05
635	Ken Schrom	.05
636	Bob Ojeda	.05
637	Ed Vande Berg	.05
638	Bobby Meacham	.05
639	Cliff Johnson	.05
640	Garth Iorg	.05
641	Dan Driessen	.05
642	Mike Brown	.05
643	John Shelby	.05
644	Pete Rose (RB)	.50
645	Knuckle Brothers (Joe Niekro, Phil Niekro)	.25
646	Jesse Orosco	.05
647	Billy Beane RC	.05
648	Cesar Cedeno	.05
649	Bert Blyleven	.15
650	Max Venable	.05
651	Fleet Feet (Vince Coleman, Willie McGee)	.25
652	Calvin Schiraldi	.05
653	King of Kings (Pete Rose)	3.00
----	Checklist 1-26 DK	.05
----	Checklist 27-130 (45 is Beane)	.05
----	Checklist 27-130 (45 is Habyan)	.05
----	Checklist 131-234	.05
----	Checklist 235-338	.05
----	Checklist 339-442	.05
----	Checklist 443-546	.05
----	Checklist 547-653	.05

1986 Donruss Box Panels

For the second year in a row, Donruss placed baseball cards on the bottom of its wax and cello pack boxes. The cards, printed four to a panel, are standard 2-1/2" x 3-1/2". With numbering that begins where Donruss left off in 1985, cards PC4 through PC6 were found on boxes of regular Donruss issue wax packs. Cards PC7 through PC9 were found on boxes of the 1986 All- Star/Pop-up packs. An unnumbered Hank Aaron puzzle card was included on each box.

	NM/M
Complete Panel Set (2):	3.00
Complete Singles Set (8):	3.00
Common Single Player:	.15
Panel	.50
PC4 Kirk Gibson	.15
PC5 Willie Hernandez	.15
PC6 Doug DeCinces	.15
--- Aaron Puzzle Card	.05
Panel	2.00
PC7 Wade Boggs	1.50
PC8 Lee Smith	.20
PC9 Cecil Cooper	.15
--- Aaron Puzzle Card	.05

1986 Donruss All-Stars

Issued in conjunction with the 1986 Donruss Pop-Ups set, the All-Stars consist of 60 cards in 3-1/2" x 5" format. Fifty-nine players involved in the 1985 All-Star game plus an unnumbered checklist comprise the set. Card fronts have the same blue border found on the regular 1986 Donruss issue. Retail packs included one Pop-up card, three All-Stars cards and one Hank Aaron puzzle-piece card.

	NM/M
Complete Set (60):	6.00
Common Player:	.05
Hank Aaron puzzle:	3.00
Cello Pack (3):	.50
Cello Box (36):	6.00
1 Tony Gwynn	.50
2 Tommy Herr	.05
3 Steve Garvey	.20
4 Dale Murphy	.20
5 Darryl Strawberry	.05
6 Graig Nettles	.05
7 Terry Kennedy	.05
8 Ozzie Smith	.50
9 LaMarr Hoyt	.05
10 Rickey Henderson	.35
11 Lou Whitaker	.05
12 George Brett	.75
13 Eddie Murray	.40
14 Cal Ripken, Jr.	1.50
15 Dave Winfield	.40
16 Jim Rice	.25
17 Carlton Fisk	.40
18 Jack Morris	.05
19 Jose Cruz	.05
20 Tim Raines	.05
21 Nolan Ryan	1.50
22 Tony Pena	.05
23 Jack Clark	.05
24 Dave Parker	.05
25 Tim Wallach	.05
26 Ozzie Virgil	.05
27 Fernando Valenzuela	.05
28 Dwight Gooden	.05
29 Glenn Wilson	.05
30 Garry Templeton	.05
31 Goose Gossage	.05
32 Ryne Sandberg	.50
33 Jeff Reardon	.05
34 Pete Rose	1.00
35 Scott Garrelts	.05
36 Willie McGee	.05
37 Ron Darling	.05
38 Dick Williams	.05
39 Paul Molitor	.40
40 Damaso Garcia	.05
41 Phil Bradley	.05
42 Dan Petry	.05
43 Willie Hernandez	.05
44 Tom Brunansky	.05
45 Alan Trammell	.05
46 Donnie Moore	.05
47 Wade Boggs	.50
48 Ernie Whitt	.05
49 Harold Baines	.05
50 Don Mattingly	.75
51 Gary Ward	.05
52 Bert Blyleven	.05
53 Jimmy Key	.05
54 Cecil Cooper	.05
55 Dave Stieb	.05
56 Rich Gedman	.05
57 Jay Howell	.05
58 Sparky Anderson	.05
59 Minneapolis Metrodome	.05
Checklist	.03

1986 Donruss Diamond Kings Supers

BRET SABERHAGEN

Donruss produced a set of large-format Diamond Kings in 1986 for the second year in a row. The 4-11/16" x 6-3/4" cards are enlarged versions of the 26 Diamond Kings cards found in the regular 1986 Donruss set, plus an unnumbered checklist and an unnumbered Pete Rose "King of Kings" card.

	NM/M
Complete Set (28):	6.00
Common Player:	.25

1 Kirk Gibson	.25
2 Goose Gossage	.25
3 Willie McGee	.25
4 George Bell	.25
5 Tony Armas	.25
6 Chili Davis	.25
7 Cecil Cooper	.25
8 Mike Boddicker	.25
9 Davey Lopes	.25
10 Bill Doran	.25
11 Bret Saberhagen	.25
12 Brett Butler	.25
13 Harold Baines	.25
14 Mike Davis	.25
15 Tony Perez	.75
16 Willie Randolph	.25
17 Orel Hershiser	.25
18 Johnny Ray	.25
19 Gary Ward	.25
20 Rick Mahler	.25
21 Phil Bradley	.25
22 Jerry Koosman	.25
23 Tom Brunansky	.25
24 Andre Dawson	.50
25 Dwight Gooden	.25
26 Checklist	.05
King of Kings (Pete Rose)	4.00

1986 Donruss Highlights

Donruss, for the second year in a row, issued a 56-card highlights set featuring cards of each league's Player of the Month plus significant events of the 1986 season. The cards, 2-1/2" x 3-1/2", are similar in design to the regular 1986 Donruss set but have a gold border instead of blue. A yellow "Highlights" logo appears in the lower-left corner of each card front. Backs are designed on a vertical format and feature black print on a yellow background. As in 1985, the set includes Donruss' picks for the Rookies of the Year. A new feature was three cards honoring the 1986 Hall of Fame inductees. The set, available only through hobby dealers, was issued in a specially designed box. Each card can also be found with the word "Highlights" in the logo in white, a much scarcer variation that sometimes attracts significant premiums from single-player specialist collectors.

	NM/M
Complete Set (56):	3.00
Common Player:	.05
White "Highlights":	20X

1 Homers In First At-Bat (Will Clark)	.05
2 Oakland Milestone For Strikeouts (Jose Rijo)	.05
3 Royals' All-Time Hit Man (George Brett)	.50
4 Phillies RBI Leader (Mike Schmidt)	.50
5 KKKKKKKKKKKKKKKKKKKK (Roger Clemens)	.50
6 A.L. Pitcher of the Month-April (Roger Clemens)	.50
7 A.L. Player of the Month-April (Kirby Puckett)	.25
8 N.L. Pitcher of the Month-April (Dwight Gooden)	.05
9 N.L. Player of the Month-April (Johnny Ray)	.05
10 Eclipses Mantle HR Record (Reggie Jackson)	.50
11 First Five Hit Game of Career (Wade Boggs)	.25
12 A.L. Pitcher of the Month-May (Don Aase)	.05
13 A.L. Player of the Month-May (Wade Boggs)	.50
14 N.L. Pitcher of the Month-May (Jeff Reardon)	.05
15 N.L. Player of the Month-May (Hubie Brooks)	.05
16 Notches 300th Career Win (Don Sutton)	.05
17 Starts Season 14-0 (Roger Clemens)	.50
18 A.L. Pitcher of the Month-June (Roger Clemens)	.50
19 A.L. Player of the Month-June (Kent Hrbek)	.05
20 N.L. Pitcher of the Month-June (Rick Rhoden)	.05
21 N.L. Player of the Month-June (Kevin Bass)	.05
22 Blasts 4 HRS in 1 Game (Bob Horner)	.05
23 Starting All Star Rookie (Wally Joyner)	.05
24 Starts 3rd Straight All Star Game (Darryl Strawberry)	.05
25 Ties All Star Game Record (Fernando Valenzuela)	.05
26 All Star Game MVP (Roger Clemens)	.50
27 A.L. Pitcher of the Month-July (Jack Morris)	.05
28 A.L. Player of the Month-July (Scott Fletcher)	.05
29 N.L. Pitcher of the Month-July (Todd Worrell)	.05
30 N.L. Player of the Month-July (Eric Davis)	.05
31 Records 3000th Strikeout (Bert Blyleven)	.05
32 1986 Hall of Fame Inductee (Bobby Doerr)	.05
33 1986 Hall of Fame Inductee (Ernie Lombardi)	.05
34 1986 Hall of Fame Inductee (Willie McCovey)	.25
35 Notches 4000th K (Steve Carlton)	.25
36 Surpasses DiMaggio Record (Mike Schmidt)	.50
37 Records 3rd "Quadruple Double" (Juan Samuel)	.05
38 A.L. Pitcher of the Month-August (Mike Witt)	.05
39 A.L. Player of the Month-August (Doug DeCinces)	.05
40 N.L. Pitcher of the Month-August (Bill Gullickson)	.05
41 N.L. Player of the Month-August (Dale Murphy)	.15
42 Sets Tribe Offensive Record (Joe Carter)	.05
43 Longest HR In Royals Stadium (Bo Jackson)	.15
44 Majors 1st No-Hitter In 2 Years (Joe Cowley)	.05
45 Sets M.L. Strikeout Record (Jim Deshaies)	.05
46 No Hitter Clinches Division (Mike Scott)	.05
47 A.L. Pitcher of the Month-September (Bruce Hurst)	.05
48 A.L. Player of the Month-September (Don Mattingly)	.50
49 N.L. Pitcher of the Month-September (Mike Krukow)	.05
50 N.L. Player of the Month-September (Steve Sax)	.05
51 A.L. Record For Steals By A Rookie (John Cangelosi)	.05
52 Shatters M.L. Save Mark (Dave Righetti)	.05
53 Yankee Record For Hits & Doubles (Don Mattingly)	.05
54 Donruss N.L. Rookie of the Year (Todd Worrell)	.05
55 Donruss A.L. Rookie of the Year (Jose Canseco)	.50
56 Highlight Checklist	.05

1986 Donruss Pop-Ups

Issued in conjunction with the 1986 Donruss All-Stars set, the Pop-Ups (18 unnumbered cards) feature the 1985 All-Star Game starting lineups. The cards, 2-1/2" x 5", are die-cut and fold out to form a three-dimensional stand-up card. The background for the cards is the Minneapolis Metrodome, site of the 1985 All-Star Game. Retail packs included one Pop-Up card, three All-Star cards and one Hank Aaron puzzle card.

	NM/M
Complete Set (18):	4.00
Common Player:	.05
Hank Aaron Puzzle:	3.00
Cello Pack (3):	.50
Cello Box (36):	6.00
(1) George Brett	.75
(2) Carlton Fisk	.40
(3) Steve Garvey	.20
(4) Tony Gwynn	.50
(5) Rickey Henderson	.40
(6) Tommy Herr	.05
(7) LaMarr Hoyt	.05
(8) Terry Kennedy	.05
(9) Jack Morris	.05
(10) Dale Murphy	.25
(11) Eddie Murray	.25
(12) Graig Nettles	.05
(13) Jim Rice	.25
(14) Cal Ripken, Jr.	1.00
(15) Ozzie Smith	.50
(16) Darryl Strawberry	.05
(17) Lou Whitaker	.05
(18) Dave Winfield	.40

Rookies

Entitled "The Rookies," this 56-card set includes the top 55 rookies of 1986 plus an unnumbered checklist. The cards are similar in format to the 1986 Donruss regular issue, except that the borders are green rather than blue. Several of the rookies who had cards in the regular 1986 Donruss set appear again in "The Rookies" set. The sets, which were only available through hobby dealers, came in a specially designed box.

	NM/M
Unopened Set (56):	35.00
Opened Set (56):	30.00
Common Player:	.05
1 Wally Joyner RC	.50
2 Tracy Jones	.05
3 Allan Anderson	.05
4 Ed Correa	.05
5 Reggie Williams	.05
6 Charlie Kerfeld	.05
7 Andres Galarraga	.15
8 Bob Tewksbury	.05
9 Al Newman	.05
10 Andres Thomas	.05
11 Barry Bonds RC	25.00
12 Juan Nieves	.05
13 Mark Eichhorn	.05
14 Dan Plesac	.05
15 Cory Snyder	.05
16 Kelly Gruber	.05
17 Kevin Mitchell RC	.25
18 Steve Lombardozzi	.05
19 Mitch Williams	.05
20 John Cerutti	.05
21 Todd Worrell	.05
22 Jose Canseco	2.00
23 Pete Incaviglia RC	.15
24 Jose Guzman	.05
25 Scott Bailes	.05
26 Greg Mathews	.05
27 Eric King	.05
28 Paul Assenmacher	.05
29 Jeff Sellers	.05
30 Bobby Bonilla RC	.25
31 Doug Drabek RC	.25
32 Will Clark RC	1.00
33 Bip Roberts	.05
34 Jim Deshaies	.05
35 Mike LaValliere	.05
36 Scott Bankhead	.05
37 Dale Sveum	.05
38 Bo Jackson	2.00
39 Rob Thompson	.05
40 Eric Plunk	.05
41 Bill Bathe	.05
42 John Kruk RC	.25
43 Andy Allanson	.05
44 Mark Portugal	.05
45 Danny Tartabull	.05
46 Bob Kipper	.05
47 Gene Walter	.05
48 Rey Quinonez	.05
49 Bobby Witt	.05
50 Bill Mooneyham	.05
51 John Cangelosi	.05
52 Ruben Sierra RC	.05
53 Rob Woodward	.05
54 Ed Hearn	.05
55 Joel McKeon	.05
56 Checklist 1-56	.05

1987 Donruss

LANCE McCULLERS P

The 1987 Donruss set consists of 660 numbered cards, each measuring 2-1/2" x 3-1/2". Color photos are surrounded by a bold black border separated by two narrow bands of yellow which enclose a brown area filled with baseballs. The player's name, team and team logo appear on the card fronts along with the words "Donruss '87." The card backs are designed on a horizontal format and contain black print on a yellow and white background. The backs are very similar to those in previous years' sets. Backs of cards issued in wax and rack packs face to the left when turned over, while those issued in factory sets face to the right. Cards checklisted with a (DK) suffix are Diamond Kings; cards with an (RR) suffix are Rated Rookies.

	NM/M
Unopened Fact. Set (660):	40.00
Complete Set (660):	30.00
Common Player:	.05
Roberto Clemente Puzzle:	2.50
Wax Pack (15):	1.25
Wax Box (36):	35.00
Rack Pack (45):	3.00
Jumbo Rack (75):	4.00
1 Wally Joyner (DK)	.25
2 Roger Clemens (DK)	1.00
3 Dale Murphy (DK)	.25
4 Darryl Strawberry (DK)	.05
5 Ozzie Smith (DK)	.75
6 Jose Canseco (DK)	.40
7 Charlie Hough (DK)	.05
8 Brook Jacoby (DK)	.05
9 Fred Lynn (DK)	.05
10 Rick Rhoden (DK)	.05
11 Chris Brown (DK)	.05
12 Von Hayes (DK)	.05
13 Jack Morris (DK)	.10
14a Kevin McReynolds (DK) (No yellow stripe on back.)	.25
14b Kevin McReynolds (DK) (Yellow stripe on back.)	.25
15 George Brett (DK)	1.00
16 Ted Higuera (DK)	.05
17 Hubie Brooks (DK)	.05
18 Mike Scott (DK)	.05
19 Kirby Puckett (DK)	.75
20 Dave Winfield (DK)	.60
21 Lloyd Moseby (DK)	.05
22a Eric Davis (DK) (No yellow stripe on back.)	.25
22b Eric Davis (DK) (Yellow stripe on back.)	.15
23 Jim Presley (DK)	.05
24 Keith Moreland (DK)	.05
25a Greg Walker (DK) (No yellow stripe on back.)	.05
25b Greg Walker (DK) (Yellow stripe on back.)	.05
26 Steve Sax (DK)	.10
27 Checklist 1-27	.05
28 B.J. Surhoff RC (RR)	.05
29 Randy Myers RC (RR)	.50
30 Ken Gerhart RC (RR)	.05
31 Benito Santiago (RR)	.15
32 Greg Swindell RC (RR)	.15
33 Mike Birkbeck RC (RR)	.05
34 Terry Steinbach RC (RR)	.25
35 Bo Jackson (RR)	1.50
36 Greg Maddux RC (RR)	8.00
37 Jim Lindeman RC (RR)	.05
38 Devon White RC (RR)	.75
39 Eric Bell RC (RR)	.05
40 Will Fraser RC (RR)	.05
41 Jerry Browne RC (RR)	.05
42 Chris James RC (RR)	.05
43 Rafael Palmeiro RC (RR)	4.00
44 Pat Dodson RC (RR)	.05
45 Duane Ward RC (RR)	.10
46 Mark McGwire (RR)	6.00
47 Bruce Fields RC (RR) (Photo actually Darnell Coles.)	.10
48 Eddie Murray	.60
49 Ted Higuera	.05
50 Kirk Gibson	.05
51 Oil Can Boyd	.05
52 Don Mattingly	1.00
53 Pedro Guerrero	.05
54 George Brett	1.00
55 Jose Rijo	.05
56 Tim Raines	.05
57 Ed Correa RC	.05
58 Mike Witt	.05
59 Greg Walker	.05
60 Ozzie Smith	.75
61 Glenn Davis	.05
62 Glenn Wilson	.05
63 Tom Browning	.05
64 Tony Gwynn	.75
65 R.J. Reynolds	.05
66 Will Clark	.25
67 Ozzie Virgil	.05
68 Rick Sutcliffe	.05
69 Gary Carter	.60
70 Mike Moore	.05
71 Bert Blyleven	.10
72 Tony Fernandez	.05
73 Kent Hrbek	.05
74 Lloyd Moseby	.05
75 Alvin Davis	.05
76 Keith Hernandez	.05
77 Ryne Sandberg	.75
78 Dale Murphy	.40
79 Sid Bream	.05
80 Chris Brown	.05
81 Steve Garvey	.05
82 Mario Soto	.05
83 Shane Rawley	.05
84 Willie McGee	.05
85 Jose Cruz	.05
86 Brian Downing	.05
87 Ozzie Guillen	.05
88 Hubie Brooks	.05
89 Cal Ripken, Jr.	2.50
90 Juan Nieves	.05
91 Lance Parrish	.05
92 Jim Rice	.25
93 Ron Guidry	.10
94 Fernando Valenzuela	.05
95 Andy Allanson RC	.05
96 Willie Wilson	.05
97 Jose Canseco	.40
98 Jeff Reardon	.05
99 Bobby Witt RC	.20
100 Checklist 28-133	.05
101 Jose Guzman	.05
102 Steve Balboni	.05
103 Tony Phillips	.05
104 Brook Jacoby	.05
105 Dave Winfield	.60
106 Orel Hershiser	.05
107 Lou Whitaker	.05
108 Fred Lynn	.05
109 Bill Wegman	.05
110 Donnie Moore	.05
111 Jack Clark	.05
112 Bob Knepper	.05
113 Von Hayes	.05
114 Bip Roberts RC	.25
115 Tony Pena	.05
116 Scott Garrelts	.05
117 Paul Molitor	.60
118 Darryl Strawberry	.05
119 Shawon Dunston	.05
120 Jim Presley	.05
121 Jesse Barfield	.05
122 Gary Gaetti	.05
123 Kurt Stillwell RC	.10
124 Joel Davis	.05
125 Mike Boddicker	.05
126 Robin Yount	.60
127 Alan Trammell	.05
128 Dave Righetti	.05
129 Dwight Evans	.05
130 Mike Scioscia	.05
131 Julio Franco	.05
132 Bret Saberhagen	.05
133 Mike Davis	.05
134 Joe Hesketh	.05
135 Wally Joyner	.05
136 Don Slaught	.05
137 Daryl Boston	.05
138 Nolan Ryan	2.50
139 Mike Schmidt	1.00
140 Tommy Herr	.05
141 Garry Templeton	.05
142 Kal Daniels	.05
143 Billy Sample	.05
144 Johnny Ray	.05
145 Rob Thompson RC	.05
146 Bob Dernier	.05
147 Danny Tartabull	.05
148 Ernie Whitt	.05
149 Kirby Puckett	.75
150 Mike Young	.05
151 Ernest Riles	.05
152 Frank Tanana	.05
153 Rich Gedman	.05
154 Willie Randolph	.05
155a Bill Madlock (Name in brown band.)	.10

#	Player	Price
155b	Bill Madlock (Name in red band.)	.25
156a	Joe Carter (Name in brown band.)	.10
156b	Joe Carter (Name in red band.)	.25
157	Danny Jackson	.05
158	Carney Lansford	.05
159	Bryn Smith	.05
160	Gary Pettis	.05
161	Oddibe McDowell	.05
162	John Cangelosi RC	.10
163	Mike Scott	.05
164	Eric Show	.05
165	Juan Samuel	.05
166	Nick Esasky	.05
167	Zane Smith	.05
168	Mike Brown	.05
169	Keith Moreland	.05
170	John Tudor	.05
171	Ken Dixon	.05
172	Jim Gantner	.05
173	Jack Morris	.05
174	Bruce Hurst	.05
175	Dennis Rasmussen	.05
176	Mike Marshall	.05
177	Dan Quisenberry	.05
178	Eric Plunk	.05
179	Tim Wallach	.05
180	Steve Buechele	.05
181	Don Sutton	.50
182	Dave Schmidt	.05
183	Terry Pendleton	.05
184	Jim Deshaies RC	.05
185	Steve Bedrosian	.05
186	Pete Rose	2.00
187	Dave Dravecky	.05
188	Rick Reuschel	.05
189	Dan Gladden	.05
190	Rick Mahler	.05
191	Thad Bosley	.05
192	Ron Darling	.05
193	Matt Young	.05
194	Tom Brunansky	.05
195	Dave Stieb	.05
196	Frank Viola	.05
197	Tom Henke	.05
198	Karl Best	.05
199	Dwight Gooden	.05
200	Checklist 134-239	.05
201	Steve Trout	.05
202	Rafael Ramirez	.05
203	Bob Walk	.05
204	Roger Mason	.05
205	Terry Kennedy	.05
206	Ron Oester	.05
207	John Russell	.05
208	Greg Mathews RC	.05
209	Charlie Kerfeld	.05
210	Reggie Jackson	1.00
211	Floyd Bannister	.05
212	Vance Law	.05
213	Rich Bordi	.05
214	Dan Plesac RC	.10
215	Dave Collins	.05
216	Bob Stanley	.05
217	Joe Niekro	.05
218	Tom Niedenfuer	.05
219	Brett Butler	.05
220	Charlie Leibrandt	.05
221	Steve Ontiveros	.05
222	Tim Burke	.05
223	Curtis Wilkerson	.05
224	Pete Incaviglia RC	.10
225	Lonnie Smith	.05
226	Chris Codiroli	.05
227	Scott Bailes RC	.05
228	Rickey Henderson	.60
229	Ken Howell	.05
230	Darnell Coles	.05
231	Don Aase	.05
232	Tim Leary	.05
233	Bob Boone	.05
234	Ricky Horton	.05
235	Mark Bailey	.05
236	Kevin Gross	.05
237	Lance McCullers	.05
238	Cecilio Guante	.05
239	Bob Melvin	.05
240	Billy Jo Robidoux	.05
241	Roger McDowell	.05
242	Leon Durham	.05
243	Ed Nunez	.05
244	Jimmy Key	.05
245	Mike Smithson	.05
246	Bo Diaz	.05
247	Carlton Fisk	.60
248	Larry Sheets	.05
249	Juan Castillo RC	.05
250	Eric King RC	.05
251	Doug Drabek	.05
252	Wade Boggs	.75
253	Mariano Duncan	.05
254	Pat Tabler	.05
255	Frank White	.05
256	Alfredo Griffin	.05
257	Floyd Youmans	.05
258	Rob Wilfong	.05
259	Pete O'Brien	.05
260	Tim Hulett	.05
261	Dickie Thon	.05
262	Darren Daulton	.05
263	Vince Coleman	.05
264	Andy Hawkins	.05
265	Eric Davis	.05
266	Andres Thomas RC	.05
267	Mike Diaz RC	.05
268	Chili Davis	.05
269	Jody Davis	.05
270	Phil Bradley	.05
271	George Bell	.05
272	Keith Atherton	.05
273	Storm Davis	.05
274	Rob Deer	.05
275	Walt Terrell	.05
276	Roger Clemens	1.00
277	Mike Easler	.05
278	Steve Sax	.05
279	Andre Thornton	.05
280	Jim Sundberg	.05
281	Bill Bathe	.05
282	Jay Tibbs	.05
283	Dick Schofield	.05
284	Mike Mason	.05
285	Jerry Hairston Sr.	.05
286	Bill Doran	.05
287	Tim Flannery	.05
288	Gary Redus	.05
289	John Franco	.05
290	Paul Assenmacher RC	.10
291	Joe Orsulak	.05
292	Lee Smith	.10
293	Mike Laga	.05
294	Rick Dempsey	.05
295	Mike Felder	.05
296	Tom Brookens	.05
297	Al Nipper	.05
298	Mike Pagliarulo	.05
299	Franklin Stubbs	.05
300	Checklist 240-345	.05
301	Steve Farr	.05
302	Bill Mooneyham RC	.05
303	Andres Galarraga	.05
304	Scott Fletcher	.05
305	Jack Howell	.05
306	Russ Morman RC	.05
307	Todd Worrell	.05
308	Dave Smith	.05
309	Jeff Stone	.05
310	Ron Robinson	.05
311	Bruce Bochy	.05
312	Jim Winn	.05
313	Mark Davis	.05
314	Jeff Dedmon	.05
315	Jamie Moyer RC	.10
316	Wally Backman	.05
317	Ken Phelps	.05
318	Steve Lombardozzi	.05
319	Marc Mulliniks	.05
320	Tim Laudner	.05
321	Mark Eichhorn RC	.10
322	Lee Guetterman RC	.05
323	Sid Fernandez	.05
324	Jerry Mumphrey	.05
325	David Palmer	.05
326	Bill Almon	.05
327	Candy Maldonado	.05
328	John Kruk	.05
329	John Denny	.05
330	Milt Thompson	.05
331	Mike LaValliere RC	.10
332	Alan Ashby	.05
333	Doug Corbett	.05
334	Ron Karkovice RC	.05
335	Mitch Webster	.05
336	Lee Lacy	.05
337	Glenn Braggs RC	.05
338	Dwight Lowry	.05
339	Don Baylor	.05
340	Brian Fisher	.05
341	Reggie Williams RC	.05
342	Tom Candiotti	.05
343	Rudy Law	.05
344	Curt Young	.05
345	Mike Fitzgerald	.05
346	Ruben Sierra	.60
347	Mitch Williams RC	.25
348	Jorge Orta	.05
349	Mickey Tettleton	.05
350	Ernie Camacho	.05
351	Ron Kittle	.05
352	Ken Landreaux	.05
353	Chet Lemon	.05
354	John Shelby	.05
355	Mark Clear	.05
356	Doug DeCinces	.05
357	Ken Dayley	.05
358	Phil Garner	.05
359	Steve Jeltz	.05
360	Ed Whitson	.05
361	Barry Bonds	10.00
362	Vida Blue	.05
363	Cecil Cooper	.05
364	Bob Ojeda	.05
365	Dennis Eckersley	.50
366	Mike Morgan	.05
367	Willie Upshaw	.05
368	Allan Anderson RC	.05
369	Bill Gullickson	.05
370	Bobby Thigpen RC	.10
371	Juan Beniquez	.05
372	Charlie Moore	.05
373	Dan Petry	.05
374	Rod Scurry	.05
375	Tom Seaver	.75
376	Ed Vande Berg	.05
377	Tony Bernazard	.05
378	Greg Pryor	.05
379	Dwayne Murphy	.05
380	Andy McGaffigan	.05
381	Kirk McCaskill	.05
382	Greg Harris	.05
383	Rich Dotson	.05
384	Craig Reynolds	.05
385	Greg Gross	.05
386	Tito Landrum	.05
387	Craig Lefferts	.05
388	Dave Parker	.05
389	Bob Horner	.05
390	Pat Clements	.05
391	Jeff Leonard	.05
392	Chris Speier	.05
393	John Moses	.05
394	Garth Iorg	.05
395	Greg Gagne	.05
396	Nate Snell	.05
397	Bryan Clutterbuck RC	.05
398	Darrell Evans	.05
399	Steve Crawford	.05
400	Checklist 346-451	.05
401	Phil Lombardi RC	.05
402	Rick Honeycutt	.05
403	Ken Schrom	.05
404	Bud Black	.05
405	Donnie Hill	.05
406	Wayne Krenchicki	.05
407	Chuck Finley RC	.35
408	Toby Harrah	.05
409	Steve Lyons	.05
410	Kevin Bass	.05
411	Marvell Wynne	.05
412	Ron Roenicke	.05
413	Tracy Jones RC	.05
414	Gene Garber	.05
415	Mike Bielecki	.05
416	Frank DiPino	.05
417	Andy Van Slyke	.05
418	Jim Dwyer	.05
419	Ben Oglivie	.05
420	Dave Bergman	.05
421	Joe Sambito	.05
422	Bob Tewksbury RC	.30
423	Len Matuszek	.05
424	Mike Kingery RC	.05
425	Dave Kingman	.05
426	Al Newman RC	.05
427	Gary Ward	.05
428	Ruppert Jones	.05
429	Harold Baines	.05
430	Pat Perry	.05
431	Terry Puhl	.05
432	Don Carman	.05
433	Eddie Milner	.05
434	LaMarr Hoyt	.05
435	Rick Rhoden	.05
436	Jose Uribe	.05
437	Ken Oberkfell	.05
438	Ron Davis	.05
439	Jesse Orosco	.05
440	Scott Bradley	.05
441	Randy Bush	.05
442	John Cerutti RC	.05
443	Roy Smalley	.05
444	Kelly Gruber	.05
445	Bob Kearney	.05
446	Ed Hearn RC	.05
447	Scott Sanderson	.05
448	Bruce Benedict	.05
449	Junior Ortiz	.05
450	Mike Aldrete RC	.05
451	Kevin McReynolds	.05
452	Rob Murphy RC	.05
453	Kent Tekulve	.05
454	Curt Ford	.05
455	Davey Lopes	.05
456	Bobby Grich	.05
457	Jose DeLeon	.05
458	Andre Dawson	.35
459	Mike Flanagan	.05
460	Joey Meyer RC	.05
461	Chuck Cary RC	.05
462	Bill Buckner	.05
463	Bob Shirley	.05
464	Jeff Hamilton RC	.05
465	Phil Niekro	.50
466	Mark Gubicza	.05
467	Jerry Willard	.05
468	Bob Sebra RC	.05
469	Larry Parrish	.05
470	Charlie Hough	.05
471	Hal McRae	.05
472	Dave Leiper RC	.05
473	Mel Hall	.05
474	Dan Pasqua	.05
475	Bob Welch	.05
476	Johnny Grubb	.05
477	Jim Traber	.05
478	Chris Bosio RC	.05
479	Mark McLemore	.05
480	John Morris	.05
481	Billy Hatcher	.05
482	Dan Schatzeder	.05
483	Rich Gossage	.10
484	Jim Morrison	.05
485	Bob Brenly	.05
486	Bill Schroeder	.05
487	Mookie Wilson	.05
488	Dave Martinez RC	.10
489	Harold Reynolds	.05
490	Jeff Hearron	.05
491	Mickey Hatcher	.05
492	Barry Larkin RC	2.00
493	Bob James	.05
494	John Habyan	.05
495	Jim Adduci RC	.05
496	Mike Heath	.05
497	Tim Stoddard	.05
498	Tony Armas	.05
499	Dennis Powell	.05
500	Checklist 452-557	.05
501	Chris Bando	.05
502	David Cone RC	2.00
503	Jay Howell	.05
504	Tom Foley	.05
505	Ray Chadwick RC	.05
506	Mike Loynd RC	.05
507	Neil Allen	.05
508	Danny Darwin	.05
509	Rick Schu	.05
510	Jose Oquendo	.05
511	Gene Walter	.05
512	Terry McGriff RC	.05
513	Ken Griffey	.05
514	Benny Distefano	.05
515	Terry Mulholland RC	.25
516	Ed Lynch	.05
517	Bill Swift	.05
518	Manny Lee	.05
519	Andre David	.05
520	Scott McGregor	.05
521	Rick Manning	.05
522	Willie Hernandez	.05
523	Marty Barrett	.05
524	Wayne Tolleson	.05
525	Jose Gonzalez RC	.05
526	Cory Snyder	.05
527	Buddy Biancalana	.05
528	Moose Haas	.05
529	Wilfredo Tejada RC	.05
530	Stu Cliburn	.05
531	Dale Mohorcic RC	.05
532	Ron Hassey	.05
533	Ty Gainey	.05
534	Jerry Royster	.05
535	Mike Maddux RC	.05
536	Ted Power	.05
537	Ted Simmons	.05
538	Rafael Belliard RC	.05
539	Chico Walker	.05
540	Bob Forsch	.05
541	John Stefero	.05
542	Dale Sveum RC	.05
543	Mark Thurmond	.05
544	Jeff Sellers RC	.05
545	Joel Skinner	.05
546	Alex Trevino	.05
547	Randy Kutcher RC	.05
548	Joaquin Andujar	.05
549	Casey Candaele RC	.10
550	Jeff Russell	.05
551	John Candelaria	.05
552	Joe Cowley	.05
553	Danny Cox	.05
554	Denny Walling	.05
555	Bruce Ruffin RC	.10
556	Buddy Bell	.05
557	Jimmy Jones RC	.05
558	Bobby Bonilla	.05
559	Jeff Robinson	.05
560	Ed Olwine	.05
561	Glenallen Hill RC	.25
562	Lee Mazzilli	.05
563	Mike Brown	.05
564	George Frazier	.05
565	Mike Sharperson RC	.10
566	Mark Portugal RC	.05
567	Rick Leach	.05
568	Mark Langston	.05
569	Rafael Santana	.05
570	Manny Trillo	.05
571	Cliff Speck	.05
572	Bob Kipper	.05
573	Kelly Downs RC	.05
574	Randy Asadoor RC	.05
575	Dave Magadan RC	.25
576	Marvin Freeman RC	.05
577	Jeff Lahti	.05
578	Jeff Calhoun	.05
579	Gus Polidor	.05
580	Gene Nelson	.05
581	Tim Teufel	.05
582	Odell Jones	.05
583	Mark Ryal	.05
584	Randy O'Neal	.05
585	Mike Greenwell RC	.50
586	Ray Knight	.05
587	Ralph Bryant RC	.05
588	Carmen Castillo	.05
589	Ed Wojna	.05
590	Stan Javier	.05
591	Jeff Musselman RC	.05
592	Mike Stanley RC	.05
593	Darrell Porter	.05
594	Drew Hall RC	.05
595	Rob Nelson RC	.05
596	Bryan Oelkers	.05
597	Scott Nielsen RC	.05
598	Brian Holton RC	.05
599	Kevin Mitchell RC	.50
600	Checklist 558-660	.05
601	Jackie Gutierrez	.05
602	Barry Jones RC	.05
603	Jerry Narron	.05
604	Steve Lake	.05
605	Jim Pankovits	.05
606	Ed Romero	.05
607	Dave LaPoint	.05
608	Don Robinson	.05
609	Mike Krukow	.05
610	Dave Valle RC	.05
611	Len Dykstra	.05
612	Roberto Clemente Puzzle Card	.25
613	Mike Trujillo	.05
614	Damaso Garcia	.05
615	Neal Heaton	.05
616	Juan Berenguer	.05
617	Steve Carlton	.75
618	Gary Lucas	.05
619	Geno Petralli	.05
620	Rick Aguilera	.05
621	Fred McGriff	.05
622	Dave Henderson	.05
623	Dave Clark RC	.05
624	Angel Salazar	.05
625	Randy Hunt	.05
626	John Gibbons	.05
627	Kevin Brown RC	2.00
628	Bill Dawley	.05
629	Aurelio Lopez	.05
630	Charlie Hudson	.05
631	Ray Soff	.05
632	Ray Hayward RC	.05
633	Spike Owen	.05
634	Glenn Hubbard	.05
635	Kevin Elster RC	.10
636	Mike LaCoss	.05
637	Dwayne Henry	.05
638	Rey Quinones RC	.05
639	Jim Clancy	.05
640	Larry Andersen	.05
641	Calvin Schiraldi	.05
642	Stan Jefferson RC	.05
643	Marc Sullivan	.05
644	Mark Grant	.05
645	Cliff Johnson	.05
646	Howard Johnson	.05
647	Dave Sax	.05
648	Dave Stewart	.05
649	Danny Heep	.05
650	Joe Johnson	.05
651	Bob Brower RC	.05
652	Rob Woodward	.05
653	John Mizerock	.05
654	Tim Pyznarski RC	.05
655	Luis Aquino RC	.05
656	Mickey Brantley	.05
657	Doyle Alexander	.05
658	Sammy Stewart	.05
659	Jim Acker	.05
660	Pete Ladd	.05

Issued in conjunction with the Donruss Pop-Ups set for the second consecutive year, the 1987 Donruss All-Stars consist of 59 players (plus a checklist) who were selected to the 1986 All-Star Game. Measuring 3-1/2" x 5" in size, the card fronts feature black borders and American or National League logos. Included on back are the player's career highlights and All-Star Game statistics. Retail packs included one Pop-Up card, three All-Star cards and one Roberto Clemente puzzle card.

	NM/M
Complete Set (60):	4.00
Common Player:	.05
Roberto Clemente Puzzle:	2.50
Wax Pack:	.35
Wax Box (48):	5.00
1 Wally Joyner	.40
2 Dave Winfield	.40
3 Lou Whitaker	.05
4 Kirby Puckett	.50
5 Cal Ripken, Jr.	1.00
6 Rickey Henderson	.50
7 Wade Boggs	.65
8 Roger Clemens	.65
9 Lance Parrish	.05
10 Dick Howser	.05
11 Keith Hernandez	.05
12 Darryl Strawberry	.05
13 Ryne Sandberg	.25
14 Dale Murphy	.25
15 Ozzie Smith	.50
16 Tony Gwynn	.50
17 Mike Schmidt	.65
18 Dwight Gooden	.25
19 Gary Carter	.40
20 Whitey Herzog	.05
21 Jose Canseco	.25
22 John Franco	.05
23 Jesse Barfield	.05
24 Rick Rhoden	.05
25 Harold Baines	.05
26 Sid Fernandez	.05
27 George Brett	.65
28 Steve Sax	.05
29 Jim Presley	.05
30 Dave Smith	.05
31 Eddie Murray	.40
32 Mike Scott	.05
33 Don Mattingly	.65
34 Dave Parker	.05
35 Tony Fernandez	.05
36 Tim Raines	.05
37 Brook Jacoby	.05
38 Chili Davis	.05
39 Rich Gedman	.05
40 Kevin Bass	.05
41 Frank White	.05
42 Glenn Davis	.05
43 Willie Hernandez	.05
44 Chris Brown	.05
45 Jim Rice	.05
46 Tony Pena	.05
47 Don Aase	.05
48 Hubie Brooks	.05
49 Charlie Hough	.05
50 Jody Davis	.05
51 Mike Witt	.05
52 Jeff Reardon	.05
53 Ken Schrom	.05
54 Fernando Valenzuela	.05
55 Dave Righetti	.05
56 Shane Rawley	.05
57 Ted Higuera	.05
58 Mike Krukow	.05
59 Lloyd Moseby	.05
60 Checklist	.05

1987 Donruss Box Panels

Continuing with an idea they initiated in 1985, Donruss once again placed baseball cards on the bottoms of their retail boxes. The cards, which are 2-1/2" x 3-1/2" in size, come four to a panel with each panel containing an unnumbered Roberto Clemente puzzle card. With numbering that begins where Donruss left off in 1986, cards PC 10 through PC 12 were found on boxes of Donruss regular issue wax packs. Cards PC 13 through PC 15 were located on boxes of the 1987 All-Star/Pop-Up packs.

		NM/M
Complete Panel Set (2):		4.00
Complete Singles Set (8):		4.00
Common Single Player:		.15
Panel		1.50
10	Dale Murphy	.40
11	Jeff Reardon	.15
12	Jose Canseco	.60
----	Roberto Clemente Puzzle Card	.15
Panel		3.00
13	Mike Scott	.15
14	Roger Clemens	2.00
15	Mike Krukow	.15
----	Roberto Clemente Puzzle Card	.15

1987 Donruss All-Stars

1987 Donruss Diamond Kings Supers

For a third season, Donrus produced a set of enlarged Dia-mond Kings, measuring 4-11/16" 6-3/4". The 28-cards feature the artwork of Dick Perez, and contai 26 player cards, a checklist and Roberto Clemente puzzle card. Th set was available through a mail-i offer for $9.50 plus three wrappers

		NM/M
Complete Set (28):		5.00
Common Player:		.15
1	Wally Joyner	.15
2	Roger Clemens	1.50
3	Dale Murphy	.30
4	Darryl Strawberry	.15
5	Ozzie Smith	1.00
6	Jose Canseco	.30
7	Charlie Hough	.15
8	Brook Jacoby	.15
9	Fred Lynn	.15
10	Rick Rhoden	.15
11	Chris Brown	.15
12	Von Hayes	.15
13	Jack Morris	.15
14	Kevin McReynolds	.15
15	George Brett	1.50
16	Ted Higuera	.15
17	Hubie Brooks	.15
18	Mike Scott	.15
19	Kirby Puckett	1.00
20	Dave Winfield	.60
21	Lloyd Moseby	.15
22	Eric Davis	.15
23	Jim Presley	.15
24	Keith Moreland	.15
25	Greg Walker	.15
26	Steve Sax	.15
27	Checklist	.05
---	Roberto Clemente Puzzle Card	.50

1987 Donruss Highlights

For a third consecutive year, Donruss produced a 56-card set which highlighted the special events of the 1987 baseball season. The 2-1/2" x 3-1/2" cards have a front design similar to the regular 1987 Donruss set. A blue border and the "Highlights" logo are the significant differences. The backs feature black print on a white background and include the date the event took place plus the particulars. As in the past, the set includes Donruss's picks for the A.L. and N.L. Rookies of the Year. The set was issued in a specially designed box and was available only through hobby dealers.

		NM/M
Complete Set (56):		3.00
Common Player:		.05
1	First No-Hitter For Brewers (Juan Nieves)	.05
2	Hits 500th Homer (Mike Schmidt)	.35
3	N.L. Player of the Month - April (Eric Davis)	.05
4	N.L. Pitcher of the Month - April (Sid Fernandez)	.05
5	A.L. Player of the Month - April (Brian Downing)	.05
6	A.L. Pitcher of the Month - April (Bret Saberhagen)	.05
7	Free Agent Holdout Returns (Tim Raines)	.05
8	N.L. Player of the Month - May (Eric Davis)	.05
9	N.L. Pitcher of the Month - May (Steve Bedrosian)	.05
10	A.L. Player of the Month - May (Larry Parrish)	.05
11	A.L. Pitcher of the Month - May (Jim Clancy)	.05
12	N.L. Player of the Month - June (Tony Gwynn)	.25
13	N.L. Pitcher of the Month - June (Orel Hershiser)	.05
14	A.L. Player of the Month - June (Wade Boggs)	.25
15	A.L. Pitcher of the Month - June (Steve Ontiveros)	.05
16	All Star Game Hero (Tim Raines)	.05
17	Consecutive Game Homer Streak (Don Mattingly)	.35
18	1987 Hall of Fame Inductee (Jim "Catfish" Hunter)	.10
19	1987 Hall of Fame Inductee (Ray Dandridge)	.10
20	1987 Hall of Fame Inductee (Billy Williams)	.10
21	N.L. Player of the Month - July (Bo Diaz)	.05
22	N.L. Pitcher of the Month - July (Floyd Youmans)	.05
23	A.L. Player of the Month - July (Don Mattingly)	.35
24	A.L. Pitcher of the Month - July (Frank Viola)	.05
25	Strikes Out 4 Batters In 1 Inning (Bobby Witt)	.05
26	Ties A.L. 9-Inning Game Hit Mark (Kevin Seitzer)	.05
27	Sets Rookie Home Run Record (Mark McGwire)	.50
28	Sets Cubs' 1st Year Homer Mark (Andre Dawson)	.05
29	Hits In 39 Straight Games (Paul Molitor)	.15
30	Record Weekend (Kirby Puckett)	.25
31	N.L. Player of the Month - August (Andre Dawson)	.05
32	N.L. Pitcher of the Month - August (Doug Drabek)	.05
33	A.L. Player of the Month - August (Dwight Evans)	.05
34	A.L. Pitcher of the Month - August (Mark Langston)	.05
35	100 RBI In 1st 2 Major League Seasons (Wally Joyner)	.25
36	100 SB In 1st 3 Major League Seasons (Vince Coleman)	.05
37	Orioles' All Time Homer King (Eddie Murray)	.15
38	Ends Consecutive Innings Streak (Cal Ripken)	.10
39	Blue Jays Hit Record 10 Homers In 1 Game (Rob Ducey, Fred McGriff, Ernie Whitt)	.05
40	Equal A's RBI Marks (Jose Canseco, Mark McGwire)	.35
41	Sets All-Time Catching Record (Bob Boone)	.05
42	Sets Mets' One-Season HR Mark (Darryl Strawberry)	.05
43	N.L.'s All-Time Switch Hit HR King (Howard Johnson)	.05
44	Five Straight 200-Hit Seasons (Wade Boggs)	.25
45	Eclipses Rookie Game Hitting Streak (Benito Santiago)	.05
46	Eclipses Jackson's A's HR Record (Mark McGwire)	.05
47	13th Rookie To Collect 200 Hits (Kevin Seitzer)	.05
48	Sets Slam Record (Don Mattingly)	.35
49	N.L. Player of the Month - September (Darryl Strawberry)	.05
50	N.L. Pitcher of the Month - September (Pascual Perez)	.05
51	A.L. Player of the Month - September (Alan Trammell)	.05
52	A.L. Pitcher of the Month - September (Doyle Alexander)	.05
53	Strikeout King - Again (Nolan Ryan)	.50
54	Donruss A.L. Rookie of the Year (Mark McGwire)	.50
55	Donruss N.L. Rookie of the Year (Benito Santiago)	.05
56	Highlight Checklist	.05

1987 Donruss Opening Day

REGGIE JACKSON DH

The Donruss Opening Day set includes all players in major league baseball's starting lineups on the opening day of the 1987 baseball season. Cards in the 272-piece set measure 2-1/2" x 3-1/2" and have a glossy coating. The fronts are identical in design to the regular Donruss set, but new photos were utilized along with maroon borders as opposed to black. The backs carry black printing on white and yellow and offer a brief player biography plus the player's career statistics. The set was packaged in a sturdy 15" by 5" by 2" box with a clear acetate lid.

		NM/M
Unopened Fact. Set (272):		25.00
Complete Set (272):		12.00
Common Player:		.10
1	Doug DeCinces	.10
2	Mike Witt	.10
3	George Hendrick	.10
4	Dick Schofield	.10
5	Devon White	.10
6	Butch Wynegar	.10
7	Wally Joyner	.10
8	Mark McLemore	.10
9	Brian Downing	.10
10	Gary Pettis	.10
11	Bill Doran	.10
12	Phil Garner	.10
13	Jose Cruz	.10
14	Kevin Bass	.10
15	Mike Scott	.10
16	Glenn Davis	.10
17	Alan Ashby	.10
18	Billy Hatcher	.10
19	Craig Reynolds	.10
20	Carney Lansford	.10
21	Mike Davis	.10
22	Reggie Jackson	.75
23	Mickey Tettleton	.10
24	Jose Canseco	.35
25	Rob Nelson	.10
26	Tony Phillips	.10
27	Dwayne Murphy	.10
28	Alfredo Griffin	.10
29	Curt Young	.10
30	Willie Upshaw	.10
31	Mike Sharperson	.10
32	Rance Mulliniks	.10
33	Ernie Whitt	.10
34	Jesse Barfield	.10
35	Tony Fernandez	.10
36	Lloyd Moseby	.10
37	Jimmy Key	.10
38	Fred McGriff	.10
39	George Bell	.10
40	Dale Murphy	.25
41	Rick Mahler	.10
42	Ken Griffey	.10
43	Andres Thomas	.10
44	Dion James	.10
45	Ozzie Virgil	.10
46	Ken Oberkfell	.10
47	Gary Roenicke	.10
48	Glenn Hubbard	.10
49	Bill Schroeder	.10
50	Greg Brock	.10
51	Billy Jo Robidoux	.10
52	Glenn Braggs	.10
53	Jim Gantner	.10
54	Paul Molitor	.50
55	Dale Sveum	.10
56	Ted Higuera	.10
57	Rob Deer	.10
58	Robin Yount	.50
59	Jim Lindeman	.10
60	Vince Coleman	.10
61	Tommy Herr	.10
62	Terry Pendleton	.10
63	John Tudor	.10
64	Tony Pena	.10
65	Ozzie Smith	.60
66	Tito Landrum	.10
67	Jack Clark	.10
68	Bob Dernier	.10
69	Rick Sutcliffe	.10
70	Andre Dawson	.30
71	Keith Moreland	.10
72	Jody Davis	.10
73	Brian Dayett	.10
74	Leon Durham	.10
75	Ryne Sandberg	.60
76	Shawon Dunston	.10
77	Mike Marshall	.10
78	Bill Madlock	.10
79	Orel Hershiser	.10
80	Mike Ramsey	.10
81	Ken Landreaux	.10
82	Mike Scioscia	.10
83	Franklin Stubbs	.10
84	Mariano Duncan	.10
85	Steve Sax	.10
86	Mitch Webster	.10
87	Reid Nichols	.10
88	Tim Wallach	.10
89	Floyd Youmans	.10
90	Andres Galarraga	.10
91	Hubie Brooks	.10
92	Jeff Reed	.10
93	Alonzo Powell	.10
94	Vance Law	.10
95	Bob Brenly	.10
96	Will Clark	.10
97	Chili Davis	.10
98	Mike Krukow	.10
99	Jose Uribe	.10
100	Chris Brown	.10
101	Rob Thompson	.10
102	Candy Maldonado	.10
103	Jeff Leonard	.10
104	Tom Candiotti	.10
105	Chris Bando	.10
106	Cory Snyder	.10
107	Pat Tabler	.10
108	Andre Thornton	.10
109	Joe Carter	.10
110	Tony Bernazard	.10
111	Julio Franco	.10
112	Brook Jacoby	.10
113	Brett Butler	.10
114	Donnell Nixon	.10
115	Alvin Davis	.10
116	Mark Langston	.10
117	Harold Reynolds	.10
118	Ken Phelps	.10
119	Mike Kingery	.10
120	Dave Valle	.10
121	Rey Quinones	.10
122	Phil Bradley	.10
123	Jim Presley	.10
124	Keith Hernandez	.10
125	Kevin McReynolds	.10
126	Rafael Santana	.10
127	Bob Ojeda	.10
128	Darryl Strawberry	.10
129	Mookie Wilson	.10
130	Gary Carter	.50
131	Tim Teufel	.10
132	Howard Johnson	.10
133	Cal Ripken, Jr.	2.00
134	Rick Burleson	.10
135	Fred Lynn	.10
136	Eddie Murray	.10
137	Ray Knight	.10
138	Alan Wiggins	.10
139	John Shelby	.10
140	Mike Boddicker	.10
141	Ken Gerhart	.10
142	Terry Kennedy	.10
143	Steve Garvey	.25
144	Marvell Wynne	.10
145	Kevin Mitchell	.10
146	Tony Gwynn	.60
147	Joey Cora	.10
148	Benito Santiago	.10
149	Eric Show	.10
150	Garry Templeton	.10
151	Carmelo Martinez	.10
152	Von Hayes	.10
153	Lance Parrish	.10
154	Milt Thompson	.10
155	Mike Easler	.10
156	Juan Samuel	.10
157	Steve Jeltz	.10
158	Glenn Wilson	.10
159	Shane Rawley	.10
160	Mike Schmidt	.75
161	Andy Van Slyke	.10
162	Johnny Ray	.10
163a	Barry Bonds (Dark jersey, photo actually Johnny Ray.)	600.00
163b	Barry Bonds (White jersey, correct photo.)	9.00
164	Junior Ortiz	.10
165	Rafael Belliard	.10
166	Bob Patterson	.10
167	Bobby Bonilla	.10
168	Sid Bream	.10
169	Jim Morrison	.10
170	Jerry Browne	.10
171	Scott Fletcher	.10
172	Ruben Sierra	.10
173	Larry Parrish	.10
174	Pete O'Brien	.10
175	Pete Incaviglia	.10
176	Don Slaught	.10
177	Oddibe McDowell	.10
178	Charlie Hough	.10
179	Steve Buechele	.10
180	Bob Stanley	.10
181	Wade Boggs	.60
182	Jim Rice	.30
183	Bill Buckner	.10
184	Dwight Evans	.10
185	Spike Owen	.10
186	Don Baylor	.10
187	Marc Sullivan	.10
188	Marty Barrett	.10
189	Dave Henderson	.10
190	Bo Diaz	.10
191	Barry Larkin	.10
192	Kal Daniels	.10
193	Terry Francona	.10
194	Tom Browning	.10
195	Ron Oester	.10
196	Buddy Bell	.10
197	Eric Davis	.10
198	Dave Parker	.10
199	Dave Balboni	.10
200	Danny Tartabull	.10
201	Ed Hearn	.10
202	Buddy Biancalana	.10
203	Danny Jackson	.10
204	Frank White	.10
205	Bo Jackson	.25
206	George Brett	.75
207	Kevin Seitzer	.10
208	Willie Wilson	.10
209	Orlando Mercado	.10
210	Darrell Evans	.10
211	Larry Herndon	.10
212	Jack Morris	.10
213	Chet Lemon	.10
214	Mike Heath	.10
215	Darnell Coles	.10
216	Alan Trammell	.10
217	Terry Harper	.10
218	Lou Whitaker	.10
219	Gary Gaetti	.10
220	Tom Nieto	.10
221	Kirby Puckett	.60
222	Tom Brunansky	.10
223	Greg Gagne	.10
224	Dan Gladden	.10
225	Mark Davidson	.10
226	Bert Blyleven	.10
227	Steve Lombardozzi	.10
228	Kent Hrbek	.10
229	Gary Redus	.10
230	Ivan Calderon	.10
231	Tim Hulett	.10
232	Carlton Fisk	.50
233	Greg Walker	.10
234	Ron Karkovice	.10
235	Ozzie Guillen	.10
236	Harold Baines	.10
237	Donnie Hill	.10
238	Rich Dotson	.10
239	Mike Pagliarulo	.10
240	Joel Skinner	.10
241	Don Mattingly	.75
242	Gary Ward	.10
243	Dave Winfield	.50
244	Dan Pasqua	.10
245	Wayne Tolleson	.10
246	Willie Randolph	.10
247	Dennis Rasmussen	.10
248	Rickey Henderson	.50
249	Angels Checklist	.05
250	Astros Checklist	.05
251	Athletics Checklist	.05
252	Blue Jays Checklist	.05
253	Braves Checklist	.05
254	Brewers Checklist	.05
255	Cardinals Checklist	.05
256	Dodgers Checklist	.05
257	Expos Checklist	.05
258	Giants Checklist	.05
259	Indians Checklist	.05
260	Mariners Checklist	.05
261	Orioles Checklist	.05
262	Padres Checklist	.05
263	Phillies Checklist	.05
264	Pirates Checklist	.05
265	Rangers Checklist	.05
266	Red Sox Checklist	.05
267	Reds Checklist	.05
268	Royals Checklist	.05
269	Tigers Checklist	.05
270	Twins Checklist	.05
271	White Sox/Cubs Checklist	.05
272	Yankees/Mets Checklist	.05

1987 Donruss Pop-Ups

DICK HOWSER MANAGER · AL

For the second straight year, Donruss released in conjunction with its All-Stars issue a set of cards designed to fold out to form a three-dimensional stand-up card. Consisting of 20 cards, as opposed to the previous year's 18, the 1987 Donruss Pop-Ups set contains players selected to the 1986 All-Star Game. Background for the 2-1/2" x 5" cards is the Houston Astrodome, site of the 1986 mid-summer classic. Retail packs included one Pop-Up card, three All-Star cards and one Roberto Clemente puzzle card.

		NM/M
Complete Set (20):		3.00
Common Player:		.10
Roberto Clemente Puzzle:		2.50
Wax Pack:		.35
Wax Box (48):		5.00
(1)	Wade Boggs	.50
(2)	Gary Carter	.40
(3)	Roger Clemens	.60
(4)	Dwight Gooden	.50
(5)	Tony Gwynn	.50
(6)	Rickey Henderson	.40
(7)	Keith Hernandez	.25
(8)	Whitey Herzog	.10
(9)	Dick Howser	.10
(10)	Wally Joyner	.50
(11)	Lance Parrish	.10
(12)	Lance Parrish	.10
(13)	Kirby Puckett	.75
(14)	Cal Ripken, Jr.	.75
(15)	Ryne Sandberg	.50
(16)	Mike Schmidt	.60
(17)	Ozzie Smith	.50
(18)	Darryl Strawberry	.10
(19)	Lou Whitaker	.10
(20)	Dave Winfield	.40

Rookies

KEVIN SEITZER 3B

As they did in 1986, Donruss issued a 56-card set highlighting the major leagues' most promising rookies. The cards are standard 2-1/2" x 3-1/2" and are identical in design to the regular Donruss issue. The card fronts have green borders as opposed to the black found in the regular issue and carry the words "The Rookies" in the lower-left portion of the card. The set came housed in a specially designed box and was available only through hobby dealers.

		NM/M
Unopened Fact. Set (56):		15.00
Complete Set (56):		10.00
Common Player:		.05
1	Mark McGwire	6.00
2	Eric Bell	.05
3	Mark Williamson	.05
4	Mike Greenwell	.05
5	Ellis Burks	.05
6	DeWayne Buice	.05
7	Mark Mclemore (McLemore)	.05
8	Devon White	.05
9	Willie Fraser	.05
10	Lester Lancaster	.05
11	Ken Williams	.05
12	Matt Nokes	.05
13	Jeff Robinson	.05
14	Bo Jackson	.25
15	Kevin Seitzer	.05
16	Billy Ripken	.05
17	B.J. Surhoff	.05
18	Chuck Crim	.05
19	Mike Birbeck	.05
20	Chris Bosio	.05
21	Les Straker	.05
22	Mark Davidson	.05
23	Gene Larkin	.05
24	Ken Gerhart	.05
25	Luis Polonia	.05
26	Terry Steinbach	.05
27	Mickey Brantley	.05
28	Mike Stanley	.05
29	Jerry Browne	.05
30	Todd Benzinger	.05
31	Fred McGriff	.25
32	Mike Henneman	.05
33	Casey Candaele	.05
34	Dave Magadan	.05
35	David Cone	.05
36	Mike Jackson	.05
37	John Mitchell	.05
38	Mike Dunne	.05
39	John Smiley	.05
40	Joe Magrane	.05
41	Jim Lindeman	.05
42	Shane Mack	.05
43	Stan Jefferson	.05
44	Benito Santiago	.05
45	Matt Williams RC	1.50
46	Dave Meads	.05
47	Rafael Palmeiro	4.00
48	Bill Long	.05
49	Bob Brower	.05
50	James Steels	.05
51	Paul Noce	.05
52	Greg Maddux	5.00
53	Jeff Musselman	.05
54	Brian Holton	.05
55	Chuck Jackson	.05
56	Checklist 1-56	.03

1988 Donruss Promo Sheet

The full effect of the 1988 Donruss border design of black, blue and red geometric patterns was previewed on this promo sheet. Printed on glossy paper with blank-back, eight logical cards (all pitchers) and a Diamond King are showcased on the 7-1/2" x 10-1/2" sheet.

NM/M
Uncut Sheet: 7.50

1988 Donruss

Darryl Strawberry OF

The 1988 Donruss set consists of 660 cards, each measuring 2-1/2" x 3-1/2". Fronts feature a full-color photo surrounded by a colorful border - alternating stripes of black, red, black, blue, black, blue, black, red and black (in that order) - separated by soft-focus edges and airbrushed fades. The player's name and position appear in a red band at the bottom of the card. The Donruss logo is situated in the upper-left corner, while the team logo is located in the lower-right. For the seventh consecutive season, Donruss included a subset of "Diamond Kings" cards (#1-27) in the issue. And for the fifth straight year, Donruss incorporated the popular "Rated Rookies" (card #28-47) with the set. Twenty-six of the cards between #603-660 were short-printed to accommodate the printing of the 26 MVP insert cards.

	NM/M
Unopened Fact. Set (660):	10.00
Complete Set (660):	8.00
Common Player:	.05
Stan Musial Puzzle:	1.00
Wax Pack (15):	.40
Wax Box (36):	10.00
Cello Pack (36):	.75
Cello Box (24):	12.00
Rack Pack (45):	.75

No.	Player	Price
1	Mark McGwire (DK)	.75
2	Tim Raines (DK)	.05
3	Benito Santiago (DK)	.05
4	Alan Trammell (DK)	.05
5	Danny Tartabull (DK)	.05
6	Ron Darling (DK)	.05
7	Paul Molitor (DK)	.40
8	Devon White (DK)	.05
9	Andre Dawson (DK)	.25
10	Julio Franco (DK)	.05
11	Scott Fletcher (DK)	.05
12	Tony Fernandez (DK)	.05
13	Shane Rawley (DK)	.05
14	Kal Daniels (DK)	.05
15	Jack Clark (DK)	.05
16	Dwight Evans (DK)	.05
17	Tommy John (DK)	.05
18	Andy Van Slyke (DK)	.05
19	Gary Gaetti (DK)	.05
20	Mark Langston (DK)	.05
21	Will Clark (DK)	.05
22	Glenn Hubbard (DK)	.05
23	Billy Hatcher (DK)	.05
24	Bob Welch (DK)	.05
25	Ivan Calderon (DK)	.05
26	Cal Ripken, Jr. (DK)	1.00
27	Checklist 1-27	.05
28	Mackey Sasser RC (RR)	.05
29	Jeff Treadway RC (RR)	.05
30	Mike Campbell RC (RR)	.05
31	Lance Johnson RC (RR)	.15
32	Nelson Liriano RC (RR)	.05
33	Shawn Abner (RR)	.05
34	Roberto Alomar RC (RR)	1.00
35	Shawn Hillegas RC (RR)	.05
36	Joey Meyer (RR)	.05
37	Kevin Elster (RR)	.05
38	Jose Lind RC (RR)	.05
39	Kirt Manwaring RC (RR)	.05
40	Mark Grace RC (RR)	.50
41	Jody Reed RC (RR)	.10
42	John Farrell RC (RR)	.05
43	Al Leiter RC (RR)	.20
44	Gary Thurman RC (RR)	.05
45	Vicente Palacios RC (RR)	.05
46	Eddie Williams RC (RR)	.05
47	Jack McDowell RC (RR)	.20
48	Ken Dixon	.05
49	Mike Birkbeck	.05
50	Eric King	.05
51	Roger Clemens	.60
52	Pat Clements	.05
53	Fernando Valenzuela	.05
54	Mark Gubicza	.05
55	Jay Howell	.05
56	Floyd Youmans	.05
57	Ed Correa	.05
58	DeWayne Buice RC	.05
59	Jose DeLeon	.05
60	Danny Cox	.05
61	Nolan Ryan	1.00
62	Steve Bedrosian	.05
63	Tom Browning	.05
64	Mark Davis	.05
65	R.J. Reynolds	.05
66	Kevin Mitchell	.05
67	Ken Oberkfell	.05
68	Rick Sutcliffe	.05
69	Dwight Gooden	.05
70	Scott Bankhead	.05
71	Bert Blyleven	.10
72	Jimmy Key	.05
73	Les Straker RC	.05
74	Jim Clancy	.05
75	Mike Moore	.05
76	Ron Darling	.05
77	Ed Lynch	.05
78	Dale Murphy	.20
79	Doug Drabek	.05
80	Scott Garrelts	.05
81	Ed Whitson	.05
82	Rob Murphy	.05
83	Shane Rawley	.05
84	Greg Mathews	.05
85	Jim Deshaies	.05
86	Mike Witt	.05
87	Donnie Hill	.05
88	Jeff Reed	.05
89	Mike Boddicker	.05
90	Ted Higuera	.05
91	Walt Terrell	.05
92	Bob Stanley	.05
93	Dave Righetti	.05
94	Orel Hershiser	.05
95	Chris Bando	.05
96	Bret Saberhagen	.05
97	Curt Young	.05
98	Tim Burke	.05
99	Charlie Hough	.05
100a	Checklist 28-137	.05
100b	Checklist 28-133	.05
101	Bobby Witt	.05
102	George Brett	.60
103	Mickey Tettleton	.05
104	Scott Bailes	.05
105	Mike Pagliarulo	.05
106	Mike Scioscia	.05
107	Tom Brookens	.05
108	Ray Knight	.05
109	Dan Plesac	.05
110	Wally Joyner	.05
111	Bob Forsch	.05
112	Mike Scott	.05
113	Kevin Gross	.05
114	Benito Santiago	.05
115	Bob Kipper	.05
116	Mike Krukow	.05
117	Chris Bosio	.05
118	Sid Fernandez	.05
119	Jody Davis	.05
120	Mike Morgan	.05
121	Mark Eichhorn	.05
122	Jeff Reardon	.05
123	John Franco	.05
124	Richard Dotson	.05
125	Eric Bell	.05
126	Juan Nieves	.05
127	Jack Morris	.05
128	Rick Rhoden	.05
129	Rich Gedman	.05
130	Ken Howell	.05
131	Brook Jacoby	.05
132	Danny Jackson	.05
133	Gene Nelson	.05
134	Neal Heaton	.05
135	Willie Fraser	.05
136	Jose Guzman	.05
137	Ozzie Guillen	.05
138	Bob Knepper	.05
139	Mike Jackson RC	.05
140	Joe Magrane RC	.05
141	Jimmy Jones	.05
142	Ted Power	.05
143	Ozzie Virgil	.05
144	Felix Fermin RC	.05
145	Kelly Downs	.05
146	Shawon Dunston	.05
147	Scott Bradley	.05
148	Dave Stieb	.05
149	Frank Viola	.05
150	Terry Kennedy	.05
151	Bill Wegman	.05
152	Matt Nokes RC	.10
153	Wade Boggs	.50
154	Wayne Tolleson	.05
155	Mariano Duncan	.05
156	Julio Franco	.05
157	Charlie Leibrandt	.05
158	Terry Steinbach	.05
159	Mike Fitzgerald	.05
160	Jack Lazorko	.05
161	Mitch Williams	.05
162	Greg Walker	.05
163	Alan Ashby	.05
164	Tony Gwynn	.50
165	Bruce Ruffin	.05
166	Ron Robinson	.05
167	Zane Smith	.05
168	Junior Ortiz	.05
169	Jamie Moyer	.05
170	Tony Pena	.05
171	Cal Ripken, Jr.	1.00
172	B.J. Surhoff	.05
173	Lou Whitaker	.05
174	Ellis Burks RC	.20
175	Ron Guidry	.10
176	Steve Sax	.05
177	Danny Tartabull	.05
178	Carney Lansford	.05
179	Casey Candaele	.05
180	Scott Fletcher	.05
181	Mark McLemore	.05
182	Ivan Calderon	.05
183	Jack Clark	.05
184	Glenn Davis	.05
185	Luis Aguayo	.05
186	Bo Diaz	.05
187	Stan Jefferson	.05
188	Sid Bream	.05
189	Bob Brenly	.05
190	Dion James	.05
191	Leon Durham	.05
192	Jesse Orosco	.05
193	Alvin Davis	.05
194	Gary Gaetti	.05
195	Fred McGriff	.05
196	Steve Lombardozzi	.05
197	Rance Mulliniks	.05
198	Rey Quinones	.05
199	Gary Carter	.40
200a	Checklist 138-247	.05
200b	Checklist 134-239	.05
201	Keith Moreland	.05
202	Ken Griffey	.05
203	Tommy Gregg RC	.05
204	Will Clark	.05
205	John Kruk	.05
206	Buddy Bell	.05
207	Von Hayes	.05
208	Tommy Herr	.05
209	Craig Reynolds	.05
210	Gary Pettis	.05
211	Harold Baines	.05
212	Vance Law	.05
213	Ken Gerhart	.05
214	Jim Gantner	.05
215	Chet Lemon	.05
216	Dwight Evans	.05
217	Don Mattingly	.60
218	Franklin Stubbs	.05
219	Pat Tabler	.05
220	Bo Jackson	.10
221	Tony Phillips	.05
222	Tim Wallach	.05
223	Ruben Sierra	.05
224	Steve Buechele	.05
225	Frank White	.05
226	Alfredo Griffin	.05
227	Greg Swindell	.05
228	Willie Randolph	.05
229	Mike Marshall	.05
230	Alan Trammell	.05
231	Eddie Murray	.40
232	Dale Sveum	.05
233	Dick Schofield	.05
234	Jose Oquendo	.05
235	Bill Doran	.05
236	Milt Thompson	.05
237	Marvell Wynne	.05
238	Bobby Bonilla	.05
239	Chris Speier	.05
240	Glenn Braggs	.05
241	Wally Backman	.05
242	Ryne Sandberg	.50
243	Phil Bradley	.05
244	Kelly Gruber	.05
245	Tom Brunansky	.05
246	Ron Oester	.05
247	Bobby Thigpen	.05
248	Fred Lynn	.05
249	Paul Molitor	.40
250	Darrell Evans	.05
251	Gary Ward	.05
252	Bruce Hurst	.05
253	Bob Welch	.05
254	Joe Carter	.05
255	Willie Wilson	.05
256	Mark McGwire	.75
257	Mitch Webster	.05
258	Brian Downing	.05
259	Mike Stanley	.05
260	Carlton Fisk	.40
261	Billy Hatcher	.05
262	Glenn Wilson	.05
263	Ozzie Smith	.50
264	Randy Ready	.05
265	Kurt Stillwell	.05
266	David Palmer	.05
267	Mike Diaz	.05
268	Rob Thompson	.05
269	Andre Dawson	.25
270	Lee Guetterman	.05
271	Willie Upshaw	.05
272	Randy Bush	.05
273	Larry Sheets	.05
274	Rob Deer	.05
275	Kirk Gibson	.05
276	Marty Barrett	.05
277	Rickey Henderson	.40
278	Pedro Guerrero	.05
279	Brett Butler	.05
280	Kevin Seitzer	.05
281	Mike Davis	.05
282	Andres Galarraga	.05
283	Devon White	.05
284	Pete O'Brien	.05
285	Jerry Hairston Sr.	.05
286	Kevin Bass	.05
287	Carmelo Martinez	.05
288	Juan Samuel	.05
289	Kal Daniels	.05
290	Albert Hall	.05
291	Andy Van Slyke	.05
292	Lee Smith	.10
293	Vince Coleman	.05
294	Tom Niedenfuer	.05
295	Robin Yount	.40
296	Jeff Robinson RC	.05
297	Todd Benzinger RC	.10
298	Dave Winfield	.40
299	Mickey Hatcher	.05
300a	Checklist 248-357	.05
300b	Checklist 240-345	.05
301	Bud Black	.05
302	Jose Canseco	.25
303	Tom Foley	.05
304	Pete Incaviglia	.05
305	Bob Boone	.05
306	Bill Long RC	.05
307	Willie McGee	.05
308	Ken Caminiti RC	.20
309	Darren Daulton	.05
310	Tracy Jones	.05
311	Greg Booker	.05
312	Mike LaValliere	.05
313	Chili Davis	.05
314	Glenn Hubbard	.05
315	Paul Noce RC	.05
316	Keith Hernandez	.05
317	Mark Langston	.05
318	Keith Atherton	.05
319	Tony Fernandez	.05
320	Kent Hrbek	.05
321	John Cerutti	.05
322	Mike Kingery	.05
323	Dave Magadan	.05
324	Rafael Palmeiro	.35
325	Jeff Dedmon	.05
326	Barry Bonds	1.00
327	Jeffrey Leonard	.05
328	Tim Flannery	.05
329	Dave Concepcion	.05
330	Mike Schmidt	.60
331	Bill Dawley	.05
332	Larry Andersen	.05
333	Jack Howell	.05
334	Ken Williams RC	.05
335	Bryn Smith	.05
336	Billy Ripken RC	.10
337	Greg Brock	.05
338	Mike Heath	.05
339	Mike Greenwell	.05
340	Claudell Washington	.05
341	Jose Gonzalez	.05
342	Mel Hall	.05
343	Jim Eisenreich	.05
344	Tony Bernazard	.05
345	Tim Raines	.05
346	Bob Brower	.05
347	Larry Parrish	.05
348	Thad Bosley	.05
349	Dennis Eckersley	.35
350	Cory Snyder	.05
351	Rick Cerone	.05
352	John Shelby	.05
353	Larry Herndon	.05
354	John Habyan	.05
355	Chuck Crim RC	.05
356	Gus Polidor	.05
357	Ken Dayley	.05
358	Danny Darwin	.05
359	Lance Parrish	.05
360	James Steels RC	.05
361	Al Pedrique RC	.05
362	Mike Aldrete	.05
363	Juan Castillo	.05
364	Len Dykstra	.05
365	Luis Quinones	.05
366	Jim Presley	.05
367	Lloyd Moseby	.05
368	Kirby Puckett	.50
369	Eric Davis	.05
370	Gary Redus	.05
371	Dave Schmidt	.05
372	Mark Clear	.05
373	Dave Bergman	.05
374	Charles Hudson	.05
375	Calvin Schiraldi	.05
376	Alex Trevino	.05
377	Tom Candiotti	.05
378	Steve Farr	.05
379	Mike Gallego	.05
380	Andy McGaffigan	.05
381	Kirk McCaskill	.05
382	Oddibe McDowell	.05
383	Floyd Bannister	.05
384	Denny Walling	.05
385	Don Carman	.05
386	Todd Worrell	.05
387	Eric Show	.05
388	Dave Parker	.05
389	Rick Mahler	.05
390	Mike Dunne	.10
391	Candy Maldonado	.05
392	Bob Dernier	.05
393	Dave Valle	.05
394	Ernie Whitt	.05
395	Juan Berenguer	.05
396	Mike Young	.05
397	Mike Felder	.05
398	Willie Hernandez	.05
399	Jim Rice	.25
400a	Checklist 358-467	.05
400b	Checklist 346-451	.05
401	Tommy John	.10
402	Brian Holton	.05
403	Carmen Castillo	.05
404	Jamie Quirk	.05
405	Dwayne Murphy	.05
406	Jeff Parrett RC	.05
407	Don Sutton	.35
408	Jerry Browne	.05
409	Jim Winn	.05
410	Dave Smith	.05
411	Shane Mack RC	.05
412	Greg Gross	.05
413	Nick Esasky	.05
414	Damaso Garcia	.05
415	Brian Fisher	.05
416	Brian Dayett	.05
417	Curt Ford	.05
418	Mark Williamson RC	.05
419	Bill Schroeder	.05
420	Mike Henneman RC	.10
421	John Marzano RC	.05
422	Ron Kittle	.05
423	Matt Young	.05
424	Steve Balboni	.05
425	Luis Polonia RC	.05
426	Randy St. Claire	.05
427	Greg Harris	.05
428	Johnny Ray	.05
429	Ray Searage	.05
430	Ricky Horton	.05
431	Gerald Young RC	.05
432	Rick Schu	.05
433	Paul O'Neill	.05
434	Rich Gossage	.10
435	John Cangelosi	.05
436	Mike LaCoss	.05
437	Gerald Perry	.05
438	Dave Martinez	.05
439	Darryl Strawberry	.05
440	John Moses	.05
441	Greg Gagne	.05
442	Jesse Barfield	.05
443	George Frazier	.05
444	Garth Iorg	.05
445	Ed Nunez	.05
446	Rick Aguilera	.05
447	Jerry Mumphrey	.05
448	Rafael Ramirez	.05
449	John Smiley RC	.10
450	Atlee Hammaker	.05
451	Lance McCullers	.05
452	Guy Hoffman	.05
453	Chris James	.05
454	Terry Pendleton	.05
455	Dave Meads RC	.05
456	Bill Buckner	.05
457	John Pawlowski RC	.05
458	Bob Sebra	.05
459	Jim Dwyer	.05
460	Jay Aldrich RC	.05
461	Frank Tanana	.05
462	Oil Can Boyd	.05
463	Dan Pasqua	.05
464	Tim Crews RC	.10
465	Andy Allanson	.05
466	Bill Pecota RC	.05
467	Steve Ontiveros	.05
468	Hubie Brooks	.05
469	Paul Kilgus RC	.05
470	Dale Mohorcic	.05
471	Dan Quisenberry	.05
472	Dave Stewart	.05
473	Dave Clark	.05
474	Joel Skinner	.05
475	Dave Anderson	.05
476	Dan Petry	.05
477	Carl Nichols RC	.05
478	Ernest Riles	.05
479	George Hendrick	.05
480	John Morris	.05
481	Manny Hernandez RC	.05
482	Jeff Stone	.05
483	Chris Brown	.05
484	Mike Bielecki	.05
485	Dave Dravecky	.05
486	Rick Manning	.05
487	Bill Almon	.05
488	Jim Sundberg	.05
489	Ken Phelps	.05
490	Tom Henke	.05
491	Dan Gladden	.05
492	Barry Larkin	.05
493	Fred Manrique RC	.05
494	Mike Griffin	.05
495	Mark Knudson RC	.05
496	Bill Madlock	.05
497	Tim Stoddard	.05
498	Sam Horn RC	.05
499	Tracy Woodson RC	.05
500a	Checklist 468-577	.05
500b	Checklist 452-557	.05
501	Ken Schrom	.05
502	Angel Salazar	.05
503	Eric Plunk	.05
504	Joe Hesketh	.05
505	Greg Minton	.05
506	Geno Petralli	.05
507	Bob James	.05
508	Robbie Wine RC	.05
509	Jeff Calhoun	.05
510	Steve Lake	.05
511	Mark Grant	.05
512	Frank Williams	.05
513	Jeff Blauser RC	.10
514	Bob Walk	.05
515	Craig Lefferts	.05
516	Manny Trillo	.05
517	Jerry Reed	.05
518	Rick Leach	.05
519	Mark Davidson RC	.05
520	Jeff Ballard RC	.05
521	Dave Stapleton RC	.05
522	Pat Sheridan	.05
523	Al Nipper	.05
524	Steve Trout	.05
525	Jeff Hamilton	.05
526	Tommy Hinzo RC	.05
527	Lonnie Smith	.05
528	Greg Cadaret RC	.05
529	Rob McClure (Bob)	.05
530	Chuck Finley	.05
531	Jeff Russell	.05
532	Steve Lyons	.05
533	Terry Puhl	.05
534	Eric Nolte RC	.05
535	Kent Tekulve	.05
536	Pat Pacillo RC	.05
537	Charlie Puleo	.05
538	Tom Prince RC	.05
539	Greg Maddux	.50
540	Jim Lindeman	.05
541	Pete Stanicek RC	.05
542	Steve Kiefer	.05
543	Jim Morrison	.05
544	Spike Owen	.05
545	Jay Buhner RC	.50
546	Mike Devereaux RC	.10
547	Jerry Don Gleaton	.05
548	Jose Rijo	.05
549	Dennis Martinez	.05
550	Mike Loynd	.05
551	Darrell Miller	.05
552	Dave LaPoint	.05
553	John Tudor	.05
554	Rocky Childress RC	.05
555	Wally Ritchie RC	.05
556	Terry McGriff	.05
557	Dave Leiper	.05
558	Jeff Robinson	.05
559	Jose Uribe	.05
560	Ted Simmons	.05
561	Lester Lancaster RC	.10
562	Keith Miller RC	.05
563	Harold Reynolds	.05
564	Gene Larkin RC	.05
565	Cecil Fielder	.05
566	Roy Smalley	.05
567	Duane Ward	.05
568	Bill Wilkinson RC	.05
569	Howard Johnson	.05
570	Frank DiPino	.05
571	Pete Smith RC	.05
572	Darnell Coles	.05
573	Don Robinson	.05
574	Rob Nelson	.05
575	Dennis Rasmussen	.05
576	Steve Jeltz (Photo actually Juan Samuel.)	
577	Tom Pagnozzi RC	.05
578	Ty Gainey	.05
579	Gary Lucas	.05
580	Ron Hassey	.05
581	Herm Winningham	.05
582	Rene Gonzales RC	.05
583	Brad Komminsk	.05
584	Doyle Alexander	.05
585	Jeff Sellers	.05
586	Bill Gullickson	.05
587	Tim Belcher	.05
588	Doug Jones RC	.05
589	Melido Perez RC	.05
590	Rick Honeycutt	.05
591	Pascual Perez	.05
592	Curt Wilkerson	.05
593	Steve Howe	.05
594	John Davis RC	.05
595	Storm Davis	.05
596	Sammy Stewart	.05
597	Neil Allen	.05
598	Alejandro Pena	.05
599	Mark Thurmond	.05
600a	Checklist 578-BC26	.05
600b	Checklist 558-660	.05
601	Jose Mesa RC	.10
602	Don August RC	.05
603	Terry Leach/SP	.05
604	Tom Newell RC	.05
605	Randall Byers RC/SP	.10
606	Jim Gott	.05
607	Harry Spilman	.05
608	John Candelaria	.05
609	Mike Brumley RC	.05
610	Mickey Brantley	.05
611	Jose Nunez RC/SP	.10
612	Tom Nieto	.05
613	Rick Reuschel	.05
614	Lee Mazzilli/SP	.05
615	Scott Lusader RC	.05
616	Bobby Meacham	.05
617	Kevin McReynolds/SP	.05
618	Gene Garber	.05
619	Barry Lyons RC/SP	.05

620	Randy Myers	.05
621	Donnie Moore	.05
622	Domingo Ramos	.05
623	Ed Romero	.05
624	Greg Myers RC	.10
625	Ripken Baseball Family (Billy Ripken, Cal Ripken, Jr., Cal Ripken, Sr.)	.40
626	Pat Perry	.05
627	Andres Thomas/SP	.10
628	Matt Williams/SP	.15
629	Dave Hengel RC	.05
630	Jeff Musselman/SP	.10
631	Tim Laudner	.05
632	Bob Ojeda/SP	.10
633	Rafael Santana	.05
634	Wes Gardner/SP	.05
635	Roberto Kelly RC/SP	.15
636	Mike Flanagan/SP	.10
637	Jay Bell RC	.35
638	Bob Melvin	.05
639	Damon Berryhill RC	.05
640	David Wells RC/SP	.40
641	Stan Musial Puzzle Card	.05
642	Doug Sisk	.05
643	Keith Hughes RC	.05
644	Tom Glavine RC	1.00
645	Al Newman	.05
646	Scott Sanderson	.05
647	Scott Terry	.05
648	Tim Teufel/SP	.10
649	Garry Templeton/SP	.10
650	Manny Lee/SP	.10
651	Roger McDowell/SP	.10
652	Mookie Wilson/SP	.10
653	David Cone/SP	.10
654	Ron Gant RC/SP	.20
655	Joe Price/SP	.10
656	George Bell/SP	.10
657	Gregg Jefferies RC/SP	.25
658	Todd Stottlemyre RC/SP	.25
659	Geronimo Berroa RC/SP	.20
660	Jerry Royster/SP	.10

1988 Donruss MVP

This 26-card set of standard-size player cards replaced the Donruss box-bottom cards in 1988. The bonus cards (numbered BC1 - BC26) were randomly inserted in Donruss wax or rack packs. Cards feature the company's choice of Most Valuable Player for each major league team and are titled "Donruss MVP." The MVP cards were not included in the factory-collated sets. Fronts carry the same basic red-blue-black border design as the 1988 Donruss basic issue. Backs are the same as the regular issue, except for the numbering system.

		NM/M
Complete Set (26):		3.00
Common Player:		.10
1	Cal Ripken, Jr.	1.00
2	Eric Davis	.10
3	Paul Molitor	.40
4	Mike Schmidt	.60
5	Ivan Calderon	.10
6	Tony Gwynn	.50
7	Wade Boggs	.50
8	Andy Van Slyke	.10
9	Joe Carter	.10
10	Andre Dawson	.25
11	Alan Trammell	.10
12	Mike Scott	.10
13	Wally Joyner	.10
14	Dale Murphy	.20
15	Kirby Puckett	.50
16	Pedro Guerrero	.10
17	Kevin Seitzer	.10
18	Tim Raines	.10
19	George Bell	.10
20	Darryl Strawberry	.10
21	Don Mattingly	.60
22	Ozzie Smith	.50
23	Mark McGwire	.75
24	Will Clark	.10
25	Alvin Davis	.05
26	Ruben Sierra	.10

1988 Donruss All-Stars

For the third consecutive year, this set of 64 cards was marketed in conjunction with Donruss

Caption: Keith Hernandez 1B

Pop-Ups. The 1988 issue included a major change - the cards were reduced in size from 3-1/2" x 5" to a standard 2-1/2" x 3-1/2". The set features players from the 1987 All-Star Game starting lineup. Card fronts feature full-color photos, framed in blue, black and white, with a Donruss logo at upper-left. Player name and position appear in a red banner below the photo, along with the appropriate National or American League logo. Backs include player stats and All-Star Game record. In 1988, All-Stars cards were distributed in individual packages containing three All-Stars, one Pop-Up and three Stan Musial puzzle pieces.

		NM/M
Complete Set (64):		5.00
Common Player:		.05
Stan Musial Puzzle:		1.00
Wax Pack:		.50
Wax Box (48):		10.00
1	Don Mattingly	.60
2	Dave Winfield	.40
3	Willie Randolph	.05
4	Rickey Henderson	.40
5	Cal Ripken, Jr.	1.00
6	George Bell	.05
7	Wade Boggs	.50
8	Bret Saberhagen	.05
9	Terry Kennedy	.05
10	John McNamara	.05
11	Jay Howell	.05
12	Harold Baines	.05
13	Harold Reynolds	.05
14	Bruce Hurst	.05
15	Kirby Puckett	.50
16	Matt Nokes	.05
17	Pat Tabler	.05
18	Dan Plesac	.05
19	Mark McGwire	.75
20	Mike Witt	.05
21	Larry Parrish	.05
22	Alan Trammell	.05
23	Dwight Evans	.05
24	Jack Morris	.05
25	Tony Fernandez	.05
26	Mark Langston	.05
27	Kevin Seitzer	.05
28	Tom Henke	.05
29	Dave Righetti	.05
30	Oakland Coliseum	.05
31	Wade Boggs (Top Vote Getter)	.25
32	Checklist 1-32	.05
33	Jack Clark	.05
34	Darryl Strawberry	.50
35	Ryne Sandberg	.50
36	Andre Dawson	.05
37	Ozzie Smith	.50
38	Eric Davis	.05
39	Mike Schmidt	.60
40	Mike Scott	.05
41	Gary Carter	.40
42	Davey Johnson	.05
43	Rick Sutcliffe	.05
44	Willie McGee	.05
45	Hubie Brooks	.05
46	Dale Murphy	.20
47	Bo Diaz	.05
48	Pedro Guerrero	.05
49	Keith Hernandez	.05
50	Ozzie Virgil	.05
51	Tony Gwynn	.50
52	Rick Reuschel	.05
53	John Franco	.05
54	Jeffrey Leonard	.05
55	Juan Samuel	.05
56	Orel Hershiser	.05
57	Tim Raines	.05
58	Sid Fernandez	.05
59	Tim Wallach	.05
60	Lee Smith	.05
61	Steve Bedrosian	.05
62	Tim Raines (MVP)	.05
63	Ozzie Smith (Top Vote Getter)	.25
64	Checklist 33-64	.05

1988 Donruss Baseball's Best

The design of this 336-card set is similar to the regular 1988 Donruss issue with the exception

of the borders which are orange, instead of blue. Player photos on the glossy front are framed by the Donruss logo upper-left, team logo lower-right and a bright red and white player name that spans the bottom margin. Backs are black and white, framed by a yellow border, and include personal information, year-by-year stats and major league totals. This set was packaged in a bright red cardboard box containing six individually shrink-wrapped packs of 56 cards. Donruss marketed the set via retail chain outlets with a suggested retail price of $21.95.

		NM/M
Complete Set (336):		10.00
Common Player:		.05
1	Don Mattingly	.75
2	Ron Gant	.05
3	Bob Boone	.05
4	Mark Grace	.15
5	Andy Allanson	.05
6	Kal Daniels	.05
7	Floyd Bannister	.05
8	Alan Ashby	.05
9	Marty Barrett	.05
10	Tim Belcher	.05
11	Harold Baines	.05
12	Hubie Brooks	.05
13	Doyle Alexander	.05
14	Gary Carter	.50
15	Glenn Braggs	.05
16	Steve Bedrosian	.05
17	Barry Bonds	1.50
18	Bert Blyleven	.10
19	Tom Brunansky	.05
20	John Candelaria	.05
21	Shawn Abner	.05
22	Jose Canseco	.30
23	Brett Butler	.05
24	Scott Bradley	.05
25	Ivan Calderon	.05
26	Rich Gossage	.05
27	Brian Downing	.05
28	Jim Rice	.25
29	Dion James	.05
30	Terry Kennedy	.05
31	George Bell	.05
32	Scott Fletcher	.05
33	Bobby Bonilla	.05
34	Tim Burke	.05
35	Darrell Evans	.05
36	Mike Davis	.05
37	Shawon Dunston	.05
38	Kevin Bass	.05
39	George Brett	.75
40	David Cone	.05
41	Ron Darling	.05
42	Roberto Alomar	.60
43	Dennis Eckersley	.40
44	Vince Coleman	.05
45	Sid Bream	.05
46	Gary Gaetti	.05
47	Phil Bradley	.05
48	Jim Clancy	.05
49	Jack Clark	.05
50	Mike Krukow	.05
51	Henry Cotto	.05
52	Rich Dotson	.05
53	Jim Gantner	.05
54	John Franco	.05
55	Pete Incaviglia	.05
56	Joe Carter	.05
57	Roger Clemens	.75
58	Gerald Perry	.05
59	Jack Howell	.05
60	Vance Law	.05
61	Jay Bell	.05
62	Eric Davis	.05
63	Gene Garber	.05
64	Glenn Davis	.05
65	Wade Boggs	.60
66	Kirk Gibson	.05
67	Carlton Fisk	.50
68	Casey Candaele	.05
69	Mike Heath	.05
70	Kevin Elster	.05
71	Greg Brock	.05
72	Don Carman	.05
73	Doug Drabek	.05
74	Greg Gagne	.05

75	Danny Cox	.05
76	Rickey Henderson	.50
77	Chris Brown	.05
78	Terry Steinbach	.05
79	Will Clark	.05
80	Mickey Brantley	.05
81	Ozzie Guillen	.05
82	Greg Maddux	.60
83	Kirk McCaskill	.05
84	Dwight Evans	.05
85	Ozzie Virgil	.05
86	Mike Morgan	.05
87	Tony Fernandez	.05
88	Jose Guzman	.05
89	Mike Dunne	.05
90	Andres Galarraga	.05
91	Mike Henneman	.05
92	Alfredo Griffin	.05
93	Rafael Palmeiro	.40
94	Jim Deshaies	.05
95	Mark Gubicza	.05
96	Dwight Gooden	.05
97	Howard Johnson	.05
98	Mark Davis	.05
99	Dave Stewart	.05
100	Joe Magrane	.05
101	Brian Fisher	.05
102	Kent Hrbek	.05
103	Kevin Gross	.05
104	Tom Henke	.05
105	Mike Pagliarulo	.05
106	Kelly Downs	.05
107	Alvin Davis	.05
108	Willie Randolph	.05
109	Rob Deer	.05
110	Bo Diaz	.05
111	Paul Kilgus	.05
112	Tom Candiotti	.05
113	Dale Murphy	.20
114	Rick Mahler	.05
115	Wally Joyner	.05
116	Ryne Sandberg	.60
117	John Farrell	.05
118	Nick Esasky	.05
119	Bo Jackson	.10
120	Bill Doran	.05
121	Ellis Burks	.05
122	Pedro Guerrero	.05
123	Dave LaPoint	.05
124	Neal Heaton	.05
125	Willie Hernandez	.05
126	Roger McDowell	.05
127	Ted Higuera	.05
128	Von Hayes	.05
129	Mike LaValliere	.05
130	Dan Gladden	.05
131	Willie McGee	.05
132	Al Leiter	.05
133	Mark Grant	.05
134	Bob Welch	.05
135	Dave Dravecky	.05
136	Mark Langston	.05
137	Dan Pasqua	.05
138	Rick Sutcliffe	.05
139	Dan Petry	.05
140	Rich Gedman	.05
141	Ken Griffey	.05
142	Eddie Murray	.50
143	Jimmy Key	.05
144	Dale Mohorcic	.05
145	Jose Lind	.05
146	Dennis Martinez	.05
147	Chet Lemon	.05
148	Orel Hershiser	.05
149	Dave Martinez	.05
150	Billy Hatcher	.05
151	Charlie Leibrandt	.05
152	Keith Hernandez	.05
153	Kevin McReynolds	.05
154	Tony Gwynn	.60
155	Stan Javier	.05
156	Tony Pena	.05
157	Andy Van Slyke	.05
158	Gene Larkin	.05
159	Chris James	.05
160	Fred McGriff	.60
161	Rick Rhoden	.05
162	Scott Garrelts	.05
163	Mike Campbell	.05
164	Dave Righetti	.05
165	Paul Molitor	.50
166	Danny Jackson	.05
167	Pete O'Brien	.05
168	Julio Franco	.05
169	Mark McGwire	1.00
170	Zane Smith	.05
171	Johnny Ray	.05
172	Lester Lancaster	.05
173	Mel Hall	.05
174	Tracy Jones	.05
175	Kevin Seitzer	.05
176	Bob Knepper	.05
177	Mike Greenwell	.05
178	Mike Marshall	.05
179	Melido Perez	.05
180	Tim Raines	.05
181	Jack Morris	.05
182	Darryl Strawberry	.05
183	Robin Yount	.50
184	Lance Parrish	.05
185	Darnell Coles	.05
186	Kirby Puckett	.60
187	Terry Pendleton	.05
188	Don Slaught	.05
189	Jimmy Jones	.05
190	Dave Parker	.05
191	Mike Aldrete	.05
192	Mike Moore	.05

193	Greg Walker	.05
194	Calvin Schiraldi	.05
195	Dick Schofield	.05
196	Jody Reed	.05
197	Pete Smith	.05
198	Cal Ripken, Jr.	1.50
199	Lloyd Moseby	.05
200	Ruben Sierra	.05
201	R.J. Reynolds	.05
202	Bryn Smith	.05
203	Gary Pettis	.05
204	Steve Sax	.05
205	Frank DiPino	.05
206	Mike Scott	.05
207	Kurt Stillwell	.05
208	Mookie Wilson	.05
209	Lee Mazzilli	.05
210	Lance McCullers	.05
211	Rick Honeycutt	.05
212	John Tudor	.05
213	Jim Gott	.05
214	Frank Viola	.05
215	Juan Samuel	.05
216	Jesse Barfield	.05
217	Claudell Washington	.05
218	Rick Reuschel	.05
219	Jim Presley	.05
220	Tommy John	.05
221	Dan Plesac	.05
222	Barry Larkin	.05
223	Mike Stanley	.05
224	Cory Snyder	.05
225	Andre Dawson	.25
226	Ken Oberkfell	.05
227	Devon White	.05
228	Jamie Moyer	.05
229	Brook Jacoby	.05
230	Rob Murphy	.05
231	Bret Saberhagen	.05
232	Nolan Ryan	1.50
233	Bruce Hurst	.05
234	Jesse Orosco	.05
235	Bobby Thigpen	.05
236	Pascual Perez	.05
237	Matt Nokes	.05
238	Bob Ojeda	.05
239	Joey Meyer	.05
240	Shane Rawley	.05
241	Jeff Robinson	.05
242	Jeff Reardon	.05
243	Ozzie Smith	.60
244	Dave Winfield	.50
245	John Kruk	.05
246	Carney Lansford	.05
247	Candy Maldonado	.05
248	Ken Phelps	.05
249	Ken Williams	.05
250	Al Nipper	.05
251	Mark McLemore	.05
252	Lee Smith	.05
253	Albert Hall	.05
254	Billy Ripken	.05
255	Kelly Gruber	.05
256	Charlie Hough	.05
257	John Smiley	.05
258	Tim Wallach	.05
259	Frank Tanana	.05
260	Mike Scioscia	.05
261	Damon Berryhill	.05
262	Dave Smith	.05
263	Willie Wilson	.05
264	Len Dykstra	.05
265	Randy Myers	.05
266	Keith Moreland	.05
267	Eric Plunk	.05
268	Todd Worrell	.05
269	Bob Walk	.05
270	Keith Atherton	.05
271	Mike Schmidt	.75
272	Mike Flanagan	.05
273	Rafael Santana	.05
274	Rob Thompson	.05
275	Rey Quinones	.05
276	Cecilio Guante	.05
277	B.J. Surhoff	.05
278	Chris Sabo	.05
279	Mitch Williams	.05
280	Greg Swindell	.05
281	Alan Trammell	.05
282	Storm Davis	.05
283	Chuck Finley	.05
284	Dave Stieb	.05
285	Scott Bailes	.05
286	Larry Sheets	.05
287	Danny Tartabull	.05
288	Checklist	.05
289	Todd Benzinger	.05
290	John Shelby	.05
291	Steve Lyons	.05
292	Mitch Webster	.05
293	Walt Terrell	.05
294	Pete Stanicek	.05
295	Chris Bosio	.05
296	Milt Thompson	.05
297	Fred Lynn	.05
298	Juan Berenguer	.05
299	Ken Dayley	.05
300	Joel Skinner	.05
301	Benito Santiago	.05
302	Ron Hassey	.05
303	Jose Uribe	.05
304	Harold Reynolds	.05
305	Dale Sveum	.05
306	Glenn Wilson	.05
307	Mike Witt	.05
308	Ron Robinson	.05
309	Denny Walling	.05
310	Joe Orsulak	.05

311	David Wells	.05
312	Steve Buechele	.05
313	Jose Oquendo	.05
314	Floyd Youmans	.05
315	Lou Whitaker	.05
316	Fernando Valenzuela	.05
317	Mike Boddicker	.05
318	Gerald Young	.05
319	Frank White	.05
320	Bill Wegman	.05
321	Tom Niedenfuer	.05
322	Ed Whitson	.05
323	Curt Young	.05
324	Greg Mathews	.05
325	Doug Jones	.05
326	Tommy Herr	.05
327	Kent Tekulve	.05
328	Rance Mulliniks	.05
329	Checklist	.05
330	Craig Lefferts	.05
331	Franklin Stubbs	.05
332	Rick Cerone	.05
333	Dave Schmidt	.05
334	Larry Parrish	.05
335	Tom Browning	.05
336	Checklist	.05

1988 Donruss Diamond Kings Supers

Caption: TOMMY JOHN

This 28-card set (including the checklist) marks the fourth edition of Donruss' super-size (5" x 7") set. These cards are exact duplicates of the 1988 Diamond Kings that feature player portraits by Dick Perez. A 12-piece Stan Musial puzzle was also included with the purchase of the super-size set which was marketed via a mail-in offer printed on Donruss wrappers.

		NM/M
Complete Set (28):		5.00
Common Player:		.10
1	Mark McGwire	2.00
2	Tim Raines	.10
3	Benito Santiago	.10
4	Alan Trammell	.10
5	Danny Tartabull	.10
6	Ron Darling	.10
7	Paul Molitor	1.00
8	Devon White	.10
9	Andre Dawson	.25
10	Julio Franco	.10
11	Scott Fletcher	.10
12	Tony Fernandez	.10
13	Shane Rawley	.10
14	Kal Daniels	.10
15	Jack Clark	.10
16	Dwight Evans	.10
17	Tommy John	.15
18	Andy Van Slyke	.10
19	Gary Gaetti	.10
20	Mark Langston	.10
21	Will Clark	.10
22	Glenn Hubbard	.10
23	Billy Hatcher	.10
24	Bob Welch	.10
25	Ivan Calderon	.10
26	Cal Ripken, Jr.	3.00
27	Checklist	.05
641	Stan Musial Puzzle Card	.10

1988 Donruss Pop-Ups

Caption: WADE BOGGS RED SOX - 3B

Donruss' 1988 Pop-Up cards were reduced to the standard 2-1/2 x 3-1/2". The set includes 20 cards that fold out so that the upper portion of the player stands upright, giving a three-dimensional effect. Pop-Ups feature players from the All-Star Game starting lineup. Fronts have the player's name, team and position printed in black on a yellow banner near the bottom. As in previous issues, backs contain only the player's name, league and position and a Leaf copyright. Pop-Ups were distributed in individual packages containing one Pop-Up, five Stan Musial puzzle pieces and three All-Star cards.

	NM/M
Complete Set (20):	4.00
Common Player:	.05
Stan Musial Puzzle:	1.00
Wax Pack:	.50
Wax Box (48):	10.00
(1) George Bell	.05
(2) Wade Boggs	.50
(3) Gary Carter	.40
(4) Jack Clark	.05
(5) Eric Davis	.05
(6) Andre Dawson	.25
(7) Rickey Henderson	.40
(8) Davey Johnson	.05
(9) Don Mattingly	.65
(10) Terry Kennedy	.05
(11) John McNamara	.05
(12) Willie Randolph	.05
(13) Cal Ripken, Jr.	1.00
(14) Bret Saberhagen	.05
(15) Ryne Sandberg	.50
(16) Mike Schmidt	.65
(17) Mike Scott	.05
(18) Ozzie Smith	.50
(19) Darryl Strawberry	.05
(20) Dave Winfield	.40

Rookies

For the third consecutive year, Donruss issued a 56-card boxed set highlighting current rookies. The complete set includes a checklist and a 15-piece Stan Musial Diamond Kings puzzle. As in previous years, the set is similar to the company's basic issue, with the exception of the logo and border color. Card fronts feature red, green and black-striped borders, with a red-and-white player name printed in the lower-left corner beneath the photo. "The Rookies" logo is printed in red, white and black in the lower-right corner. Backs are printed in black on bright aqua and include personal data, recent performance stats and major league totals, as well as 1984-88 minor league stats. The cards are the standard 2-1/2" x 3-1/2".

	NM/M
Complete Set (56):	4.00
Common Player:	.05
1 Mark Grace	.25
2 Mike Campbell	.05
3 Todd Frowirth RC	.05
4 Dave Stapleton	.05
5 Shawn Abner	.05
6 Jose Cecena RC	.05
7 Dave Gallagher RC	.05
8 Mark Parent RC	.05
9 Cecil Espy RC	.05
10 Pete Smith	.05
11 Jay Buhner	.25
12 Pat Borders RC	.05
13 Doug Jennings RC	.05
14 Brady Anderson RC	1.00
15 Pete Stanicek	.05
16 Roberto Kelly	.05
17 Jeff Treadway	.05
18 Walt Weiss RC	.05
19 Paul Gibson RC	.05
20 Tim Crews	.05
21 Melido Perez	.05
22 Steve Peters RC	.05
23 Craig Worthington RC	.05
24 John Trautwein RC	.05
25 DeWayne Vaughn RC	.05
26 David Wells	.15
27 Al Leiter	.15
28 Tim Belcher	.05
29 Johnny Paredes RC	.05
30 Chris Sabo RC	.05
31 Damon Berryhill	.05
32 Randy Milligan	.05
33 Gary Thurman	.05
34 Kevin Elster	.05
35 Roberto Alomar	1.50
36 Edgar Martinez RC (Photo actually Edwin Nunez.)	1.50
37 Todd Stottlemyre	.15
38 Joey Meyer	.05
39 Carl Nichols	.05
40 Jack McDowell	.05
41 Jose Bautista RC	.05
42 Sil Campusano RC	.05
43 John Dopson RC	.05
44 Jody Reed	.05
45 Darrin Jackson RC	.05
46 Mike Capel RC	.05
47 Ron Gant	.50
48 John Davis	.05
49 Kevin Coffman RC	.05
50 Cris Carpenter RC	.05
51 Mackey Sasser	.05
52 Luis Alicea RC	.05
53 Bryan Harvey RC	.05
54 Steve Ellsworth RC	.05
55 Mike Macfarlane RC	.05
56 Checklist 1-56	.05

1988 Donruss Team Books

Three pages of nine cards each and a Stan Musial puzzle highlight these special team collection books. The cards feature the same design as the regular 1988 Donruss cards, but contain a 1988 copyright date instead of 1987 like the regular set. The cards are numbered like the regular issue with the exception of new cards of traded players and rookies produced especially for the team collection books. Books are commonly found complete with the cards and puzzle. The puzzle pieces are perforated for removal, but the card sheets are not.

	NM/M
Complete Set, Books (5):	12.00
Common Player:	.05
Boston Red Sox Team Book:	3.00
NEW Brady Anderson	.50
NEW Rick Cerone	.05
NEW Steve Ellsworth	.05
NEW Dennis Lamp	.05
NEW Kevin Romine	.05
NEW Lee Smith	.25
NEW Mike Smithson	.05
NEW John Trautwein	.05
41 Jody Reed	.05
51 Roger Clemens	.75
92 Bob Stanley	.05
129 Rich Gedman	.05
153 Wade Boggs	.65
174 Ellis Burks	.05
216 Dwight Evans	.05
252 Bruce Hurst	.05
276 Marty Barrett	.05
297 Todd Benzinger	.05
339 Mike Greenwell	.05
399 Jim Rice	.25
421 John Marzano	.05
462 Oil Can Boyd	.05
498 Sam Horn	.05
544 Spike Owen	.05
585 Jeff Sellers	.05
623 Ed Romero	.05
634 Wes Gardner	.05
Chicago Cubs Team Book:	3.00
NEW Mike Bielecki	.05
NEW Rich Gossage	.25
NEW Drew Hall	.05
NEW Darrin Jackson	.05
NEW Vance Law	.05
NEW Al Nipper	.05
NEW Angel Salazar	.05
NEW Calvin Schiraldi	.05
40 Mark Grace	.50
68 Rick Sutcliffe	.05
119 Jody Davis	.05
146 Shawon Dunston	.05
169 Jamie Moyer	.05
191 Leon Durham	.05
242 Ryne Sandberg	.65
269 Andre Dawson	.25
315 Paul Noce	.05
324 Rafael Palmeiro	.40
438 Dave Martinez	.05
447 Jerry Mumphrey	.05
488 Jim Sundberg	.05
516 Manny Trillo	.05
539 Greg Maddux	.65
561 Les Lancaster	.05
570 Frank DiPino	.05
639 Damon Berryhill	.05
646 Scott Sanderson	.05
N.Y. Mets Team Book:	3.00
NEW Jeff Innis	.05
NEW Mackey Sasser	.05
NEW Gene Walter	.05
37 Kevin Elster	.05
69 Dwight Gooden	.05
76 Ron Darling	.05
118 Sid Fernandez	.05
199 Gary Carter	.50
241 Wally Backman	.05
316 Keith Hernandez	.05
323 Dave Magadan	.05
364 Len Dykstra	.05
439 Darryl Strawberry	.05
446 Rick Aguilera	.05
562 Keith Miller	.05
569 Howard Johnson	.05
603 Terry Leach	.05
614 Lee Mazzilli	.05
617 Kevin McReynolds	.05
619 Barry Lyons	.05
620 Randy Myers	.05
632 Bob Ojeda	.05
648 Tim Teufel	.05
651 Roger McDowell	.05
652 Mookie Wilson	.05
653 David Cone	.05
657 Gregg Jefferies	.35
N.Y. Yankees Team Book:	3.00
NEW John Candelaria	.05
NEW Jack Clark	.05
NEW Jose Cruz	.05
NEW Richard Dotson	.05
NEW Cecilio Guante	.05
NEW Lee Guetterman	.05
NEW Rafael Santana	.05
NEW Steve Shields	.05
NEW Don Slaught	.15
43 Al Leiter	.05
93 Dave Righetti	.05
105 Mike Pagliarulo	.05
128 Rick Rhoden	.05
175 Ron Guidry	.10
217 Don Mattingly	.75
228 Willie Randolph	.05
251 Gary Ward	.05
277 Rickey Henderson	.50
278 Dave Winfield	.50
340 Claudell Washington	.05
374 Charles Hudson	.05
401 Tommy John	.10
474 Joel Skinner	.05
497 Tim Stoddard	.05
545 Jay Buhner	.10
616 Bobby Meacham	.05
635 Roberto Kelly	.05
Oakland A's Team Book:	3.00
NEW Don Baylor	.25
NEW Ron Hassey	.05
NEW Dave Henderson	.05
NEW Glenn Hubbard	.05
NEW Stan Javier	.05
NEW Doug Jennings	.05
NEW Ed Jurak	.05
NEW Dave Parker	.15
NEW Walt Weiss	.15
NEW Bob Welch	.05
NEW Matt Young	.05
97 Curt Young	.05
133 Gene Nelson	.05
158 Terry Steinbach	.05
178 Carney Lansford	.05
221 Tony Phillips	.05
256 Mark McGwire	1.00
302 Jose Canseco	.30
349 Dennis Eckersley	.40
379 Mike Gallego	.05
425 Luis Polonia	.05
467 Steve Ontiveros	.05
472 Dave Stewart	.05
503 Eric Plunk	.05
528 Greg Cadaret	.05
590 Rick Honeycutt	.05
595 Storm Davis	.05

1989 Donruss Promo Sheet

To introduce its card design for 1989, Donruss produced this sheet. Printed on semi-gloss paper, the 7-1/2" x 10-1/2" blank-back sheet has images of seven regular cards, a Diamond King and an MVP.

	NM/M
Complete Sheet:	10.00

1989 Donruss

Fred McGriff 1B

This basic annual issue consists of 660 2-1/2" x 3-1/2" cards, including 26 Diamond Kings (DK) portrait cards and 20 Rated Rookies (RR) cards. Top and bottom borders of the cards are printed in a variety of colors that fade from dark to light. A white-lettered player name is printed across the top margin. The team logo appears upper-right and the Donruss logo lower-left. A black outer stripe varnish gives faintly visible filmstrip texture to the border. Backs are in orange and black, similar to the 1988 design, with personal info, recent stats and major league totals. Team logo sticker cards (22 total) and Warren Spahn puzzle cards (63 total) are included in individual wax packs of cards. Each regular player card can be found with a back variation in the header line above the stats: i.e., "*De-notes" or "*Denotes*." Neither version carries a premium.

	NM/M
Unopened Fact. Set (660):	17.50
Complete Set (660):	15.00
Common Player:	.05
Warren Spahn Puzzle:	.50
Wax Pack (15):	.75
Wax Box (36):	15.00
Cello Pack (32):	1.00
Cello Box (24):	15.00
Rack Pack (45):	.75
1 Mike Greenwell (DK)	.05
2 Bobby Bonilla (DK)	.05
3 Pete Incaviglia (DK)	.05
4 Chris Sabo (DK)	.05
5 Robin Yount (DK)	.40
6 Tony Gwynn (DK)	.50
7 Carlton Fisk (DK)	.40
8 Cory Snyder (DK)	.05
9 David Cone (DK)	.05
10 Kevin Seitzer (DK)	.05
11 Rick Reuschel (DK)	.05
12 Johnny Ray (DK)	.05
13 Dave Schmidt (DK)	.05
14 Andres Galarraga (DK)	.05
15 Kirk Gibson (DK)	.05
16 Fred McGriff (DK)	.15
17 Mark Grace (DK)	.15
18 Jeff Robinson (DK)	.05
19 Vince Coleman (DK)	.05
20 Dave Henderson (DK)	.05
21 Harold Reynolds (DK)	.05
22 Gerald Perry (DK)	.05
23 Frank Viola (DK)	.05
24 Steve Bedrosian (DK)	.05
25 Glenn Davis (DK)	.05
26 Don Mattingly (DK)	.60
27 Checklist 1-27	.05
28 Sandy Alomar, Jr. RC (RR)	.35
29 Steve Searcy RC (RR)	.05
30 Cameron Drew RC (RR)	.05
31 Gary Sheffield RC (RR)	1.00
32 Erik Hanson RC (RR)	.05
33 Ken Griffey Jr. RC (RR)	6.00
34 Greg Harris RC (RR)	.05
35 Gregg Jefferies (RR)	.05
36 Luis Medina RC (RR)	.05
37 Carlos Quintana RC (RR)	.05
38 Felix Jose RC (RR)	.05
39 Cris Carpenter RC (RR)	.05
40 Ron Jones RC (RR)	.05
41 Dave West RC (RR)	.05
42 Randy Johnson RC (RR)	3.00
43 Mike Harkey RC (RR)	.05
44 Pete Harnisch RC (RR)	.10
45 Tom Gordon RC (RR)	.25
46 Gregg Olson RC (RR)	.10
47 Alex Sanchez RC (RR)	.05
48 Ruben Sierra	.35
49 Rafael Palmeiro	.35
50 Ron Gant	.35
51 Cal Ripken, Jr.	1.00
52 Wally Joyner	.05
53 Gary Carter	.40
54 Andy Van Slyke	.05
55 Robin Yount	.40
56 Pete Incaviglia	.05
57 Greg Brock	.05
58 Melido Perez	.05
59 Craig Lefferts	.05
60 Gary Pettis	.05
61 Danny Tartabull	.05
62 Guillermo Hernandez	.05
63 Ozzie Smith	.50
64 Gary Gaetti	.05
65 Mark Davis	.05
66 Lee Smith	.05
67 Dennis Eckersley	.35
68 Wade Boggs	.50
69 Mike Scott	.05
70 Fred McGriff	.05
71 Tom Browning	.05
72 Claudell Washington	.05
73 Mel Hall	.05
74 Don Mattingly	.60
75 Steve Bedrosian	.05
76 Juan Samuel	.05
77 Mike Scioscia	.05
78 Dave Righetti	.05
79 Alfredo Griffin	.05
80 Eric Davis	.05
81 Juan Berenguer	.05
82 Todd Worrell	.05
83 Joe Carter	.05
84 Steve Sax	.05
85 Frank White	.05
86 John Kruk	.05
87 Rance Mulliniks	.05
88 Alan Ashby	.05
89 Charlie Leibrandt	.05
90 Frank Tanana	.05
91 Jose Canseco	.25
92 Barry Bonds	1.00
93 Harold Reynolds	.05
94 Mark McLemore	.05
95 Mark McGwire	.75
96 Eddie Murray	.40
97 Tim Raines	.05
98 Rob Thompson	.05
99 Kevin McReynolds	.05
100 Checklist 28-137	.05
101 Carlton Fisk	.40
102 Dave Martinez	.05
103 Glenn Braggs	.05
104 Dale Murphy	.15
105 Ryne Sandberg	.50
106 Dennis Martinez	.05
107 Pete O'Brien	.05
108 Dick Schofield	.05
109 Henry Cotto	.05
110 Mike Marshall	.05
111 Keith Moreland	.05
112 Tom Brunansky	.05
113 Kelly Gruber	.05
114 Brook Jacoby	.05
115 Keith Brown RC	.05
116 Matt Nokes	.05
117 Keith Hernandez	.05
118 Bob Forsch	.05
119 Bert Blyleven	.10
120 Willie Wilson	.05
121 Tommy Gregg	.05
122 Jim Rice	.25
123 Bob Knepper	.05
124 Danny Jackson	.05
125 Eric Plunk	.05
126 Brian Fisher	.05
127 Mike Pagliarulo	.05
128 Tony Gwynn	.50
129 Lance McCullers	.05
130 Andres Galarraga	.05
131 Jose Uribe	.05
132 Kirk Gibson	.05
133 David Palmer	.05
134 R.J. Reynolds	.05
135 Greg Walker	.05
136 Kirk McCaskill	.05
137 Shawon Dunston	.05
138 Andy Allanson	.05
139 Rob Murphy	.05
140 Mike Aldrete	.05
141 Terry Kennedy	.05
142 Scott Fletcher	.05
143 Steve Balboni	.05
144 Bret Saberhagen	.05
145 Ozzie Virgil	.05
146 Dale Sveum	.05
147 Darryl Strawberry	.05
148 Harold Baines	.05
149 George Bell	.05
150 Dave Parker	.05
151 Bobby Bonilla	.05
152 Mookie Wilson	.05
153 Ted Power	.05
154 Nolan Ryan	1.00
155 Jeff Reardon	.05
156 Tim Wallach	.05
157 Jamie Moyer	.05
158 Rich Gossage	.10
159 Dave Winfield	.40
160 Von Hayes	.05
161 Willie McGee	.05
162 Rich Gedman	.05
163 Tony Pena	.05
164 Mike Morgan	.05
165 Charlie Hough	.05
166 Mike Stanley	.05
167 Andre Dawson	.20
168 Joe Boever	.05
169 Pete Stanicek	.05
170 Bob Boone	.05
171 Ron Darling	.05
172 Bob Walk	.05
173 Rob Deer	.05
174 Steve Buechele	.05
175 Ted Higuera	.05
176 Ozzie Guillen	.05
177 Candy Maldonado	.05
178 Doyle Alexander	.05
179 Mark Gubicza	.05
180 Alan Trammell	.05
181 Vince Coleman	.05
182 Kirby Puckett	.50
183 Chris Brown	.05
184 Marty Barrett	.05
185 Stan Javier	.05
186 Mike Greenwell	.05
187 Billy Hatcher	.05
188 Jimmy Key	.05
189 Nick Esasky	.05
190 Don Slaught	.05
191 Cory Snyder	.05
192 John Candelaria	.05
193 Mike Schmidt	.60
194 Kevin Gross	.05
195 John Tudor	.05
196 Neil Allen	.05
197 Orel Hershiser	.05
198 Kal Daniels	.05
199 Kent Hrbek	.05
200 Checklist 138-247	.05
201 Joe Magrane	.05
202 Scott Bailes	.05
203 Tim Belcher	.05
204 George Brett	.60
205 Benito Santiago	.05
206 Tony Fernandez	.05
207 Gerald Young	.05
208 Bo Jackson	.10
209 Chet Lemon	.05
210 Storm Davis	.05
211 Doug Drabek	.05
212 Mickey Brantley (Photo actually Nelson Simmons.)	.05
213 Devon White	.05
214 Dave Stewart	.05
215 Dave Schmidt	.05
216 Bryn Smith	.05
217 Brett Butler	.05
218 Bob Ojeda	.05
219 Steve Rosenberg RC	.05
220 Hubie Brooks	.05
221 B.J. Surhoff	.05
222 Rick Mahler	.05
223 Rick Sutcliffe	.05
224 Neal Heaton	.05
225 Mitch Williams	.05
226 Chuck Finley	.05
227 Mark Langston	.05
228 Jesse Orosco	.05
229 Ed Whitson	.05
230 Terry Pendleton	.05
231 Lloyd Moseby	.05
232 Greg Swindell	.05
233 John Franco	.05
234 Jack Morris	.05
235 Howard Johnson	.05
236 Glenn Davis	.05
237 Frank Viola	.05
238 Kevin Seitzer	.05
239 Gerald Perry	.05
240 Dwight Evans	.05
241 Jim Deshaies	.05
242 Bo Diaz	.05
243 Carney Lansford	.05
244 Mike LaValliere	.05
245 Rickey Henderson	.40
246 Roberto Alomar	.20
247 Jimmy Jones	.05
248 Pascual Perez	.05
249 Will Clark	.05
250 Fernando Valenzuela	.05
251 Shane Rawley	.05
252 Sid Bream	.05
253 Steve Lyons	.05
254 Brian Downing	.05
255 Mark Grace	.05
256 Tom Candiotti	.05
257 Barry Larkin	.05
258 Mike Krukow	.05
259 Billy Ripken	.05
260 Cecilio Guante	.05
261 Scott Bradley	.05
262 Floyd Bannister	.05
263 Pete Smith	.05
264 Jim Gantner	.05
265 Roger McDowell	.05
266 Bobby Thigpen	.05
267 Jim Clancy	.05

#	Player	Price
268	Terry Steinbach	.05
269	Mike Dunne	.05
270	Dwight Gooden	.05
271	Mike Heath	.05
272	Dave Smith	.05
273	Keith Atherton	.05
274	Tim Burke	.05
275	Damon Berryhill	.05
276	Vance Law	.05
277	Rich Dotson	.05
278	Lance Parrish	.05
279	Dennis Walling	.05
280	Roger Clemens	.60
281	Greg Mathews	.05
282	Tom Niedenfuer	.05
283	Paul Kilgus	.05
284	Jose Guzman	.05
285	Calvin Schiraldi	.05
286	Charlie Puleo	.05
287	Joe Orsulak	.05
288	Jack Howell	.05
289	Kevin Elster	.05
290	Jose Lind	.05
291	Paul Molitor	.40
292	Cecil Espy	.05
293	Bill Wegman	.05
294	Dan Pasqua	.05
295	Scott Garrelts	.05
296	Walt Terrell	.05
297	Ed Hearn	.05
298	Lou Whitaker	.05
299	Ken Dayley	.05
300	Checklist 248-357	.05
301	Tommy Herr	.05
302	Mike Brumley	.05
303	Ellis Burks	.05
304	Curt Young	.05
305	Jody Reed	.05
306	Bill Doran	.05
307	David Wells	.05
308	Ron Robinson	.05
309	Rafael Santana	.05
310	Julio Franco	.05
311	Jack Clark	.05
312	Chris James	.05
313	Milt Thompson	.05
314	John Shelby	.05
315	Mike Davis	.05
316	Chris Sabo RC	.15
317	Greg Gagne	.05
318	Jose Oquendo	.05
319	John Farrell	.05
320	Franklin Stubbs	.05
321	Kurt Stillwell	.05
322	Shawn Abner	.05
323	Mike Flanagan	.05
324	Kevin Bass	.05
325	Pat Tabler	.05
326	Mike Henneman	.05
327	Rick Honeycutt	.05
328	John Smiley	.05
329	Rey Quinones	.05
330	Johnny Ray	.05
331	Bob Welch	.05
332	Larry Sheets	.05
333	Jeff Parrett	.05
334	Rick Reuschel	.05
335	Randy Myers	.05
336	Ken Williams	.05
337	Andy McGaffigan	.05
338	Joey Meyer	.05
339	Dion James	.05
340	Les Lancaster	.05
341	Tom Foley	.05
342	Geno Petralli	.05
343	Dan Petry	.05
344	Alvin Davis	.05
345	Mickey Hatcher	.05
346	Marvell Wynne	.05
347	Danny Cox	.05
348	Dave Stieb	.05
349	Jay Bell	.05
350	Jeff Treadway	.05
351	Luis Salazar	.05
352	Len Dykstra	.05
353	Juan Agosto	.05
354	Gene Larkin	.05
355	Steve Farr	.05
356	Paul Assenmacher	.05
357	Todd Benzinger	.05
358	Larry Andersen	.05
359	Paul O'Neill	.05
360	Ron Hassey	.05
361	Jim Gott	.05
362	Ken Phelps	.05
363	Tim Flannery	.05
364	Randy Ready	.05
365	Nelson Santovenia RC	.05
366	Kelly Downs	.05
367	Danny Heep	.05
368	Phil Bradley	.05
369	Jeff Robinson	.05
370	Ivan Calderon	.05
371	Mike Witt	.05
372	Greg Maddux	.50
373	Carmen Castillo	.05
374	Jose Rijo	.05
375	Joe Price	.05
376	R.C. Gonzalez	.05
377	Oddibe McDowell	.05
378	Jim Presley	.05
379	Brad Wellman	.05
380	Tom Glavine	.20
381	Dan Plesac	.05
382	Wally Backman	.05
383	Dave Gallagher RC	.05
384	Tom Henke	.05
386	Luis Polonia	.05
387	Junior Ortiz	.05
388	David Cone	.05
389	Dave Bergman	.05
390	Danny Darwin	.05
391	Dan Gladden	.05
392	John Dopson RC	.05
393	Frank DiPino	.05
394	Al Nipper	.05
395	Willie Randolph	.05
396	Don Carman	.05
397	Scott Terry	.05
398	Rick Cerone	.05
399	Tom Pagnozzi	.05
400	Checklist 358-467	.05
401	Mickey Tettleton	.05
402	Curtis Wilkerson	.05
403	Jeff Russell	.05
404	Pat Perry	.05
405	Jose Alvarez RC	.05
406	Rick Schu	.05
407	Sherman Corbett RC	.05
408	Dave Magadan	.05
409	Bob Kipper	.05
410	Don August	.05
411	Bob Brower	.05
412	Chris Bosio	.05
413	Jerry Reuss	.05
414	Atlee Hammaker	.05
415	Jim Walewander	.05
416	Mike Macfarlane RC	.10
417	Pat Sheridan	.05
418	Pedro Guerrero	.05
419	Allan Anderson	.05
420	Mark Parent RC	.05
421	Bob Stanley	.05
422	Mike Gallego	.05
423	Bruce Hurst	.05
424	Dave Meads	.05
425	Jesse Barfield	.05
426	Rob Dibble RC	.15
427	Joel Skinner	.05
428	Ron Kittle	.05
429	Rick Rhoden	.05
430	Bob Dernier	.05
431	Steve Jeltz	.05
432	Rick Dempsey	.05
433	Roberto Kelly	.05
434	Dave Anderson	.05
435	Herm Winningham	.05
436	Al Newman	.05
437	Jose DeLeon	.05
438	Doug Jones	.05
439	Brian Holton	.05
440	Jeff Montgomery	.05
441	Dickie Thon	.05
442	Cecil Fielder	.05
443	John Fishel RC	.05
444	Jerry Don Gleaton	.05
445	Paul Gibson RC	.05
446	Walt Weiss	.05
447	Glenn Wilson	.05
448	Mike Moore	.05
449	Chili Davis	.05
450	Dave Henderson	.05
451	Jose Bautista RC	.05
452	Rex Hudler	.05
453	Bob Brenly	.05
454	Mackey Sasser	.05
455	Daryl Boston	.05
456	Mike Fitzgerald	.05
457	Jeffery Leonard	.05
458	Bruce Sutter	.35
459	Mitch Webster	.05
460	Joe Hesketh	.05
461	Bobby Witt	.05
462	Stew Cliburn	.05
463	Scott Bankhead	.05
464	Ramon Martinez RC	.05
465	Dave Leiper	.05
466	Luis Alicea RC	.05
467	John Cerutti	.05
468	Ron Washington	.05
469	Jeff Reed	.05
470	Jeff Robinson	.05
471	Sid Fernandez	.05
472	Terry Puhl	.05
473	Charlie Lea	.05
474	Israel Sanchez RC	.05
475	Bruce Benedict	.05
476	Oil Can Boyd	.05
477	Craig Reynolds	.05
478	Frank Williams	.05
479	Greg Cadaret	.05
480	Randy Kramer RC	.05
481	Dave Eiland RC	.05
482	Eric Show	.05
483	Garry Templeton	.05
484	Wallace Johnson	.05
485	Kevin Mitchell	.05
486	Tim Crews	.05
487	Mike Maddux	.05
488	Dave LaPoint	.05
489	Fred Manrique	.05
490	Greg Minton	.05
491	Doug Dascenzo RC	.05
492	Willie Upshaw	.05
493	Jack Armstrong RC	.05
494	Kirt Manwaring	.05
495	Jeff Ballard	.05
496	Jeff Kunkel	.05
497	Mike Campbell	.05
498	Gary Thurman	.05
499	Zane Smith	.05
500	Checklist 468-577	.05
501	Mike Birkbeck	.05
502	Terry Leach	.05
503	Shawn Hillegas	.05
504	Manny Lee	.05
505	Doug Jennings RC	.05
506	Ken Oberkfell	.05
507	Tim Teufel	.05
508	Tom Brookens	.05
509	Rafael Ramirez	.05
510	Fred Toliver	.05
511	Brian Holman RC	.05
512	Mike Bielecki	.05
513	Jeff Pico RC	.05
514	Charles Hudson	.05
515	Bruce Ruffin	.05
516	Larry McWilliams	.05
517	Jeff Sellers	.05
518	John Costello RC	.05
519	Brady Anderson	.05
520	Craig McMurtry	.05
521	Ray Hayward	.05
522	Drew Hall	.05
523	Mark Lemke RC	.05
524	Oswald Peraza RC	.05
525	Bryan Harvey RC	.05
526	Rick Aguilera	.05
527	Tom Prince	.05
528	Mark Clear	.05
529	Jerry Browne	.05
530	Juan Castillo	.05
531	Jack McDowell RC	.05
532	Chris Speier	.05
533	Darrell Evans	.05
534	Luis Aquino	.05
535	Eric King	.05
536	Ken Hill RC	.05
537	Randy Bush	.05
538	Shane Mack	.05
539	Tom Bolton	.05
540	Gene Nelson	.05
541	Wes Gardner	.05
542	Ken Caminiti	.05
543	Duane Ward	.05
544	Norm Charlton RC	.10
545	Hal Morris RC	.25
546	Rich Yett	.05
547	Hensley Meulens RC	.10
548	Greg Harris	.05
549	Darren Daulton	.05
550	Jeff Hamilton	.05
551	Luis Aguayo	.05
552	Tim Leary	.05
553	Ron Oester	.05
554	Steve Lombardozzi	.05
555	Tim Jones RC	.05
556	Bud Black	.05
557	Alejandro Pena	.05
558	Jose DeJesus RC	.05
559	Dennis Rasmussen	.05
560	Pat Borders RC	.25
561	Craig Biggio	.05
562	Luis de los Santos RC	.05
563	Fred Lynn	.05
564	Todd Burns RC	.05
565	Felix Fermin	.05
566	Darnell Coles	.05
567	Willie Fraser	.05
568	Glenn Hubbard	.05
569	Craig Worthington RC	.05
570	Johnny Paredes RC	.05
571	Don Robinson	.05
572	Barry Lyons	.05
573	Bill Long	.05
574	Tracy Jones	.05
575	Juan Nieves	.05
576	Andres Thomas	.05
577	Rolando Roomes RC	.05
578	Luis Rivera	.05
579	Chad Kreuter RC	.10
580	Tony Armas	.05
581	Jay Buhner	.05
582	Ricky Horton	.05
583	Andy Hawkins	.05
584	Sil Campusano RC	.05
585	Dave Clark	.05
586	Van Snider RC	.05
587	Todd Frohwirth	.05
588	Warren Spahn Puzzle Card	.05
589	William Brennan RC	.05
590	German Gonzalez RC	.05
591	Ernie Whitt	.05
592	Jeff Blauser	.05
593	Spike Owen	.05
594	Matt Williams	.05
595	Lloyd McClendon	.05
596	Steve Ontiveros	.05
597	Scott Medvin RC	.05
598	Hipolito Pena RC	.05
599	Jerald Clark RC	.05
600a	Checklist 578-BC26 (#635 is Kurt Schilling)	.10
600b	Checklist 578-BC26 (#635 is Curt Schilling)	.05
619	Adam Peterson	.05
620	Todd Stottlemyre	.05
621	Lance Blankenship RC	.05
622	Miguel Garcia RC	.05
623	Keith Miller	.05
624	Ricky Jordan RC	.05
625	Ernest Riles	.05
626	John Moses	.05
627	Nelson Liriano	.05
628	Mike Smithson	.05
629	Scott Sanderson	.05
630	Dale Mohorcic	.05
631	Marvin Freeman	.05
632	Mike Young	.05
633	Dennis Lamp	.05
634	Dante Bichette RC	.25
635	Curt Schilling RC	3.00
636	Scott May RC	.05
637	Mike Schooler RC	.05
638	Rick Leach	.05
639	Tom Lampkin RC	.05
640	Brian Meyer RC	.05
641	Brian Harper	.05
642	John Smoltz	.05
643	Jose Canseco (40/40)	.15
644	Bill Schroeder	.05
645	Edgar Martinez	.10
646	Dennis Cook RC	.05
647	Barry Jones	.05
648	Orel Hershiser (59 and Counting)	.05
649	Rod Nichols RC	.05
650	Jody Davis	.05
651	Bob Milacki RC	.05
652	Mike Jackson	.05
653	Derek Lilliquist RC	.05
654	Paul Mirabella	.05
655	Mike Diaz	.05
656	Jeff Musselman	.05
657	Jerry Reed	.05
658	Kevin Blankenship RC	.05
659	Wayne Tolleson	.05
660	Eric Hetzel RC	.05

1989 Donruss Grand Slammers

One card from this 12-card set was included in each Donruss cello pack. The complete insert set was included in factory sets. The featured players all hit grand slams in 1988. The 2-1/2" x 3-1/2" cards feature full color action photos. Backs tell the story of the player's grand slam. As many as five border-color variations on the front of each card have been discovered, but the prices are not affected.

		NM/M
Complete Set (12):		2.00
Common Player:		.25
1	Jose Canseco	.35
2	Mike Marshall	.25
3	Walt Weiss	.25
4	Kevin McReynolds	.25
5	Mike Greenwell	.25
6	Dave Winfield	.50
7	Mark McGwire	1.50
8	Keith Hernandez	.25
9	Franklin Stubbs	.25
10	Danny Tartabull	.25
11	Jesse Barfield	.25
12	Ellis Burks	.25

1989 Donruss Blue Chip Cards

		NM/M
Complete Set (12):		1,200
Common Player:		60.00
1	Jose Canseco	125.00
2	Mike Marshall	60.00
3	Walt Weiss	60.00
4	Kevin McReynolds	60.00
5	Mike Greenwell	60.00
6	Dave Winfield	150.00
7	Mark McGwire	400.00
8	Keith Hernandez	75.00
9	Franklin Stubbs	60.00
10	Danny Tartabull	60.00
11	Jesse Barfield	60.00
12	Kevin Brown	60.00

1989 Donruss MVP

This set, numbered BC1-BC26, was randomly inserted in Donruss wax packs, but not in-cluded in factory sets or other card packs. Players highlighted were selected by Donruss, one player per team. MVP cards feature a variation of the design in the basic Donruss issue, with multi-color upper and lower borders and black side borders. The "MVP" designation in large, bright letters serves as a backdrop for the full-color player photo. The cards measure 2-1/2" x 3-1/2".

		NM/M
Complete Set (26):		2.00
Common Player:		.05
1	Kirby Puckett	.40
2	Mike Scott	.05
3	Joe Carter	.05
4	Orel Hershiser	.05
5	Jose Canseco	.25
6	Darryl Strawberry	.05
7	George Brett	.50
8	Andre Dawson	.20
9	Paul Molitor	.30
10	Andy Van Slyke	.05
11	Dave Winfield	.30
12	Kevin Gross	.05
13	Mike Greenwell	.05
14	Ozzie Smith	.40
15	Cal Ripken	1.00
16	Andres Galarraga	.05
17	Alan Trammell	.05
18	Kal Daniels	.05
19	Fred McGriff	.05
20	Tony Gwynn	.40
21	Wally Joyner	.05
22	Will Clark	.05
23	Ozzie Guillen	.05
24	Gerald Perry	.05
25	Alvin Davis	.05
26	Ruben Sierra	.05

1989 Donruss All-Stars

For the fourth consecutive year Donruss featured a 64-card set with players from the 1988 All-Star Game. The card fronts include a red-to-gold fade or gold-to-red fade border and blue vertical side borders. The top border features the player's name and position along with the "Donruss 89" logo. Each full-color player photo is highlighted by a thin white line and includes a league logo in the lower right corner. Card backs reveal an orange-gold border and black and white printing. The player's ID and personal information is displayed with a gold star on both sides. The star in the left corner includes the card number. 1988 All-Star game statistics and run totals follow along with a career highlights feature surrounded by the team, All-Star Game MLB, MLBPA, and Leaf Inc. logos. The All-Stars were distributed in wax packages containing five All-Stars, one Pop-Up, and one three-piece Warren Spahn puzzle card.

		NM/M
Complete Set (64):		4.00
Common Player:		.10
Warren Spahn Puzzle:		.50
Wax Pack (5+1):		.30
Wax Box (48):		10.00
1	Mark McGwire	.75
2	Jose Canseco	.25
3	Paul Molitor	.40
4	Rickey Henderson	.40
5	Cal Ripken, Jr.	1.00
6	Dave Winfield	.40
7	Wade Boggs	.50
8	Frank Viola	.10
9	Terry Steinbach	.10
10	Tom Kelly	.10
11	George Brett	.65
12	Doyle Alexander	.10
13	Gary Gaetti	.10
14	Roger Clemens	.65
15	Mike Greenwell	.10
16	Dennis Eckersley	.40
17	Carney Lansford	.10
18	Mark Gubicza	.10
19	Tim Laudner	.10
20	Doug Jones	.10
21	Don Mattingly	.65
22	Dan Plesac	.10
23	Kirby Puckett	.50
24	Jeff Reardon	.10
25	Johnny Ray	.10
26	Jeff Russell	.10
27	Harold Reynolds	.10
28	Dave Stieb	.10
29	Kurt Stillwell	.10
30	Jose Canseco	.25
31	Terry Steinbach	.10
32	A.L. Checklist	.10
33	Will Clark	.10
34	Darryl Strawberry	.10
35	Ryne Sandberg	.50
36	Andre Dawson	.50
37	Ozzie Smith	.50
38	Vince Coleman	.10
39	Bobby Bonilla	.10
40	Dwight Gooden	.10
41	Gary Carter	.40
42	Whitey Herzog	.10
43	Shawon Dunston	.10
44	David Cone	.10
45	Andres Galarraga	.10
46	Mark Davis	.10
47	Barry Larkin	.10
48	Kevin Gross	.10
49	Vance Law	.10
50	Orel Hershiser	.10
51	Willie McGee	.10
52	Danny Jackson	.10
53	Rafael Palmeiro	.35
54	Bob Knepper	.10
55	Lance Parrish	.10
56	Greg Maddux	.50
57	Gerald Perry	.10
58	Bob Walk	.10
59	Chris Sabo	.10
60	Todd Worrell	.10
61	Andy Van Slyke	.10
62	Ozzie Smith	.50
63	Riverfront Stadium	.10
64	N.L. Checklist	.05

1989 Donruss Baseball's Best

For the second consecutive year, Donruss issued a "Baseball's Best" set in 1989 to highlight the game's top players. The special 336-card set was packaged in a special box and was sold at various retail chains nationwide following the conclusion of the 1989 baseball season. The cards are styled after the regular 1989 Donruss set with green borders and a glossy finish. The set included a Warren Spahn puzzle.

		NM/M
Unopened Set (336):		30.00
Complete Set (336):		25.00
Common Player:		.05
1	Don Mattingly	.75
2	Tom Glavine	.25
3	Bert Blyleven	.10
4	Andre Dawson	.25
5	Pete O'Brien	.05
6	Eric Davis	.05
7	George Brett	.75
8	Glenn Davis	.05

No.	Player	Price
9	Ellis Burks	.05
10	Kirk Gibson	.05
11	Carlton Fisk	.50
12	Andres Galarraga	.05
13	Alan Trammell	.05
14	Dwight Gooden	.05
15	Paul Molitor	.50
16	Roger McDowell	.05
17	Doug Drabek	.05
18	Kent Hrbek	.05
19	Vince Coleman	.05
20	Steve Sax	.05
21	Roberto Alomar	.20
22	Carney Lansford	.05
23	Will Clark	.05
24	Alvin Davis	.05
25	Bobby Thigpen	.05
26	Ryne Sandberg	.60
27	Devon White	.05
28	Mike Greenwell	.05
29	Dale Murphy	.20
30	Jeff Ballard	.05
31	Kelly Gruber	.05
32	Julio Franco	.05
33	Bobby Bonilla	.05
34	Tim Wallach	.05
35	Lou Whitaker	.05
36	Jay Howell	.05
37	Greg Maddux	.60
38	Bill Doran	.05
39	Danny Tartabull	.05
40	Darryl Strawberry	.05
41	Ron Darling	.05
42	Tony Gwynn	.60
43	Mark McGwire	1.00
44	Ozzie Smith	.60
45	Andy Van Slyke	.05
46	Juan Berenguer	.05
47	Von Hayes	.05
48	Tony Fernandez	.05
49	Eric Plunk	.05
50	Ernest Riles	.05
51	Harold Reynolds	.05
52	Andy Hawkins	.05
53	Robin Yount	.50
54	Danny Jackson	.05
55	Nolan Ryan	1.50
56	Joe Carter	.05
57	Jose Canseco	.35
58	Jody Davis	.05
59	Lance Parrish	.05
60	Mitch Williams	.05
61	Brook Jacoby	.05
62	Tom Browning	.05
63	Kurt Stillwell	.05
64	Rafael Ramirez	.05
65	Roger Clemens	.75
66	Mike Scioscia	.05
67	Dave Gallagher	.05
68	Mark Langston	.05
69	Chet Lemon	.05
70	Kevin McReynolds	.05
71	Rob Deer	.05
72	Tommy Herr	.05
73	Barry Bonds	1.50
74	Frank Viola	.05
75	Pedro Guerrero	.05
76	Dave Righetti	.05
77	Bruce Hurst	.05
78	Rickey Henderson	.50
79	Robby Thompson	.05
80	Randy Johnson	6.00
81	Harold Baines	.05
82	Calvin Schiraldi	.05
83	Kirk McCaskill	.05
84	Lee Smith	.05
85	John Smoltz	1.00
86	Mickey Tettleton	.05
87	Jimmy Key	.05
88	Rafael Palmeiro	.45
89	Sid Bream	.05
90	Dennis Martinez	.05
91	Frank Tanana	.05
92	Eddie Murray	.50
93	Shawon Dunston	.05
94	Mike Scott	.05
95	Bret Saberhagen	.05
96	David Cone	.05
97	Kevin Elster	.05
98	Jack Clark	.05
99	Dave Stewart	.05
100	Jose Oquendo	.05
101	Jose Lind	.05
102	Gary Gaetti	.05
103	Ricky Jordan	.05
104	Fred McGriff	.05
105	Don Slaught	.05
106	Jose Uribe	.05
107	Jeffrey Leonard	.05
108	Lee Guetterman	.05
109	Chris Bosio	.05
110	Barry Larkin	.05
111	Ruben Sierra	.05
112	Greg Swindell	.05
113	Gary Sheffield	1.00
114	Lonnie Smith	.05
115	Chili Davis	.05
116	Damon Berryhill	.05
117	Tom Candiotti	.05
118	Kal Daniels	.05
119	Mark Gubicza	.05
120	Jim Deshaies	.05
121	Dwight Evans	.05
122	Mike Morgan	.05
123	Dan Pasqua	.05
124	Bryn Smith	.05
125	Doyle Alexander	.05
126	Howard Johnson	.05
127	Chuck Crim	.05
128	Darren Daulton	.05
129	Jeff Robinson	.05
130	Kirby Puckett	.60
131	Joe Magrane	.05
132	Jesse Barfield	.05
133	Mark Davis (Photo actually Dave Leiper.)	.05
134	Dennis Eckersley	.45
135	Mike Krukow	.05
136	Jay Buhner	.05
137	Ozzie Guillen	.05
138	Rick Sutcliffe	.05
139	Wally Joyner	.05
140	Wade Boggs	.60
141	Jeff Treadway	.05
142	Cal Ripken	1.50
143	Dave Steib	.05
144	Pete Incaviglia	.05
145	Bob Walk	.05
146	Nelson Santovenia	.05
147	Mike Heath	.05
148	Willie Randolph	.05
149	Paul Kilgus	.05
150	Billy Hatcher	.05
151	Steve Farr	.05
152	Gregg Jefferies	.05
153	Randy Myers	.05
154	Garry Templeton	.05
155	Walt Weiss	.05
156	Terry Pendleton	.05
157	John Smiley	.05
158	Greg Gagne	.05
159	Lenny Dykstra	.05
160	Nelson Liriano	.05
161	Alvaro Espinoza	.05
162	Rick Reuschel	.05
163	Omar Vizquel	.05
164	Clay Parker	.05
165	Dan Plesac	.05
166	John Franco	.05
167	Scott Fletcher	.05
168	Cory Snyder	.05
169	Bo Jackson	.10
170	Tommy Gregg	.05
171	Jim Abbott	.05
172	Jerome Walton	.05
173	Doug Jones	.05
174	Todd Benzinger	.05
175	Frank White	.05
176	Craig Biggio	.50
177	John Dopson	.05
178	Alfredo Griffin	.05
179	Melido Perez	.05
180	Tim Burke	.05
181	Matt Nokes	.05
182	Gary Carter	.50
183	Ted Higuera	.05
184	Ken Howell	.05
185	Rey Quinones	.05
186	Wally Backman	.05
187	Tom Brunansky	.05
188	Steve Balboni	.05
189	Marvell Wynne	.05
190	Dave Henderson	.05
191	Don Robinson	.05
192	Ken Griffey Jr.	9.00
193	Ivan Calderon	.05
194	Mike Bielecki	.05
195	Johnny Ray	.05
196	Rob Murphy	.05
197	Andres Thomas	.05
198	Phil Bradley	.05
199	Junior Felix	.05
200	Jeff Russell	.05
201	Mike LaValliere	.05
202	Kevin Gross	.05
203	Keith Moreland	.05
204	Mike Marshall	.05
205	Dwight Smith	.05
206	Jim Clancy	.05
207	Kevin Seitzer	.05
208	Keith Hernandez	.05
209	Bob Ojeda	.05
210	Ed Whitson	.05
211	Tony Phillips	.05
212	Milt Thompson	.05
213	Randy Kramer	.05
214	Randy Bush	.05
215	Randy Ready	.05
216	Duane Ward	.05
217	Jimmy Jones	.05
218	Scott Garrelts	.05
219	Scott Bankhead	.05
220	Lance McCullers	.05
221	B.J. Surhoff	.05
222	Chris Sabo	.05
223	Steve Buechele	.05
224	Joel Skinner	.05
225	Orel Hershiser	.05
226	Derek Lilliquist	.05
227	Claudell Washington	.05
228	Lloyd McClendon	.05
229	Felix Fermin	.05
230	Paul O'Neill	.05
231	Charlie Leibrandt	.05
232	Dave Smith	.05
233	Bob Stanley	.05
234	Tim Belcher	.05
235	Eric King	.05
236	Spike Owen	.05
237	Mike Henneman	.05
238	Juan Samuel	.05
239	Greg Brock	.05
240	John Kruk	.05
241	Glenn Wilson	.05
242	Jeff Reardon	.05
243	Todd Worrell	.05
244	Dave LaPoint	.05
245	Walt Terrell	.05
246	Mike Moore	.05
247	Kelly Downs	.05
248	Dave Valle	.05
249	Ron Kittle	.05
250	Steve Wilson	.05
251	Dick Schofield	.05
252	Marty Barrett	.05
253	Dion James	.05
254	Bob Milacki	.05
255	Ernie Whitt	.05
256	Kevin Brown	.05
257	R.J. Reynolds	.05
258	Tim Raines	.05
259	Frank Williams	.05
260	Jose Gonzalez	.05
261	Mitch Webster	.05
262	Ken Caminiti	.05
263	Bob Boone	.05
264	Dave Magadan	.05
265	Rick Aguilera	.05
266	Chris James	.05
267	Bob Welch	.05
268	Ken Dayley	.05
269	Junior Ortiz	.05
270	Allan Anderson	.05
271	Steve Jeltz	.05
272	George Bell	.05
273	Roberto Kelly	.05
274	Brett Butler	.05
275	Mike Schooler	.05
276	Ken Phelps	.05
277	Glenn Braggs	.05
278	Jose Rijo	.05
279	Bobby Witt	.05
280	Jerry Browne	.05
281	Kevin Mitchell	.05
282	Craig Worthington	.05
283	Greg Minton	.05
284	Nick Esasky	.05
285	John Farrell	.05
286	Rick Mahler	.05
287	Tom Gordon	.05
288	Gerald Young	.05
289	Jody Reed	.05
290	Jeff Hamilton	.05
291	Gerald Perry	.05
292	Hubie Brooks	.05
293	Bo Diaz	.05
294	Terry Puhl	.05
295	Jim Gantner	.05
296	Jeff Parrett	.05
297	Mike Boddicker	.05
298	Dan Gladden	.05
299	Tony Pena	.05
300	Checklist	.05
301	Tom Henke	.05
302	Pascual Perez	.05
303	Steve Bedrosian	.05
304	Ken Hill	.05
305	Jerry Reuss	.05
306	Jim Eisenreich	.05
307	Jack Howell	.05
308	Rick Cerone	.05
309	Tim Leary	.05
310	Joe Orsulak	.05
311	Jim Dwyer	.05
312	Geno Petralli	.05
313	Rick Honeycutt	.05
314	Tom Foley	.05
315	Kenny Rogers	.05
316	Mike Flanagan	.05
317	Bryan Harvey	.05
318	Billy Ripken	.05
319	Jeff Montgomery	.05
320	Erik Hanson	.05
321	Brian Downing	.05
322	Gregg Olson	.05
323	Terry Steinbach	.05
324	Sammy Sosa	12.00
325	Gene Harris	.05
326	Mike Devereaux	.05
327	Dennis Cook	.05
328	David Wells	.05
329	Checklist	.05
330	Kirt Manwaring	.05
331	Jim Presley	.05
332	Checklist	.05
333	Chuck Finley	.05
334	Rob Dibble	.05
335	Cecil Espy	.05
336	Dave Parker	.05

(continuation of Diamond King Supers listing)

No.	Player	Price
12	Johnny Ray	.25
13	Dave Schmidt	.25
14	Andres Galarraga	.25
15	Kirk Gibson	.25
16	Fred McGriff	.25
17	Mark Grace	.25
18	Jeff Robinson	.25
19	Vince Coleman	.25
20	Dave Henderson	.25
21	Harold Reynolds	.25
22	Gerald Perry	.25
23	Frank Viola	.25
24	Steve Bedrosian	.25
25	Glenn Davis	.25
26	Don Mattingly	2.00
27	Checklist	.05

1989 Donruss Pop-Ups

This set features the 18 starters from the 1988 Major League All-Star game. The cards are designed with a perforated outline so each player can be popped up to stand upright. The flip side features a red, white, and blue "Cincinnati Reds All-Star Game" logo at the top, a league designation, and the player's name and position. The lower portion displays instructions for creating the base of the Pop-Up. The Pop-Ups were marketed in packs with five All-Star cards and Warren Spahn puzzle-piece cards.

	NM/M
Complete Set (20):	2.00
Common Player:	.10
Warren Spahn Puzzle:	.50
Wax Pack (5+1):	.30
Wax Box (48):	10.00
(1) Mark McGwire	.45
(2) Jose Canseco	.20
(3) Paul Molitor	.25
(4) Rickey Henderson	.25
(5) Cal Ripken, Jr.	.50
(6) Dave Winfield	.25
(7) Wade Boggs	.35
(8) Frank Viola	.10
(9) Terry Steinbach	.10
(10) Tom Kelly	.10
(11) Will Clark	.25
(12) Darryl Strawberry	.10
(13) Ryne Sandberg	.35
(14) Andre Dawson	.10
(15) Ozzie Smith	.35
(16) Vince Coleman	.10
(17) Bobby Bonilla	.10
(18) Dwight Gooden	.10
(19) Gary Carter	.25
(20) Whitey Herzog	.10

Rookies

For the fourth straight year, Donruss issued a 56-card "Rookies" set in 1989. As in previous years, the set is similar in design to the regular Donruss set, except for a new "The Rookies" logo and a green and black border.

	NM/M
Complete Set (56):	8.00
Common Player:	.05
1 Gary Sheffield	.75
2 Gregg Jefferies	.05

1989 Donruss Diamond King Supers

Once again for 1989, collectors could acquire a 4-3/4" x 6-3/4" version of the Diamond King subset via a wrapper mail-in offer. Other than size, cards are identical to the DKs in the regular issue.

	NM/M
Complete Set (27):	5.00
Common Player:	.25
1 Mike Greenwell	.25
2 Bobby Bonilla	.25
3 Pete Incaviglia	.25
4 Chris Sabo	.25
5 Robin Yount	1.00
6 Tony Gwynn	1.50
7 Carlton Fisk	1.00
8 Cory Snyder	.25
9 David Cone	.25
10 Kevin Seitzer	.25
11 Rick Reuschel	.25

No.	Player	Price
3	Ken Griffey Jr.	5.00
5	Tom Gordon	.05
5	Billy Spiers	.05
7	Deion Sanders RC	.50
7	Donn Pall	.05
9	Steve Carter	.05
9	Francisco Oliveras	.05
10	Steve Wilson	.05
12	Bob Geren	.05
12	Tony Castillo	.05
13	Kenny Rogers	.05
14	Carlos Martinez	.05
15	Edgar Martinez	.05
16	Jim Abbott	.05
17	Torey Lovullo	.05
18	Mark Carreon	.05
19	Geronimo Berroa	.05
20	Luis Medina	.05
21	Sandy Alomar, Jr.	.05
22	Bob Milacki	.05
23	Joe Girardi RC	.10
24	German Gonzalez	.05
25	Craig Worthington	.05
26	Jerome Walton	.05
27	Gary Wayne	.05
28	Tim Jones	.05
29	Dante Bichette	.05
30	Alexis Infante	.05
31	Ken Hill	.05
32	Dwight Smith	.05
33	Luis de los Santos	.05
34	Eric Yelding	.05
35	Gregg Olson	.05
36	Phil Stephenson	.05
37	Ken Patterson	.05
38	Rick Wrona	.05
39	Mike Brumley	.05
40	Cris Carpenter	.05
41	Jeff Brantley	.05
42	Ron Jones	.05
43	Randy Johnson	2.00
44	Kevin Brown	.05
45	Ramon Martinez	.05
46	Greg Harris	.05
47	Steve Finley	.05
48	Randy Kramer	.05
49	Erik Hanson	.05
50	Matt Merullo	.05
51	Mike Devereaux	.05
52	Clay Parker	.05
53	Omar Vizquel	.05
54	Derek Lilliquist	.05
55	Junior Felix	.05
56	Checklist	.05

1989 Donruss Traded

Donruss issued its first "Traded" set in 1989, releasing a 56-card boxed set designed in the same style as the regular 1989 Donruss set. The set included a Stan Musial puzzle card and a checklist.

	NM/M
Complete Set (56):	2.00
Common Player:	.05
1 Jeffrey Leonard	.05
2 Jack Clark	.05
3 Kevin Gross	.05
4 Tommy Herr	.05
5 Bob Boone	.05
6 Rafael Palmeiro	.30
7 John Dopson	.05
8 Willie Randolph	.05
9 Chris Brown	.05
10 Wally Backman	.05
11 Steve Ontiveros	.05
12 Eddie Murray	.45
13 Lance McCullers	.05
14 Spike Owen	.05
15 Rob Murphy	.05
16 Pete O'Brien	.05
17 Ken Williams	.05
18 Nick Esasky	.05
19 Nolan Ryan	1.50
20 Brian Holton	.05
21 Mike Moore	.05
22 Joel Skinner	.05
23 Steve Sax	.05
24 Rick Mahler	.05
25 Mike Aldrete	.05
26 Jesse Orosco	.05
27 Dave LaPoint	.05
28 Walt Terrell	.05
29 Eddie Williams	.05
30 Mike Devereaux	.05
31 Julio Franco	.05

No.	Player	Price
32	Jim Clancy	.05
33	Felix Fermin	.05
34	Curtis Wilkerson	.05
35	Bert Blyleven	.05
36	Mel Hall	.05
37	Eric King	.05
38	Mitch Williams	.05
39	Jamie Moyer	.05
40	Rick Rhoden	.05
41	Phil Bradley	.05
42	Paul Kilgus	.05
43	Milt Thompson	.05
44	Jerry Browne	.05
45	Bruce Hurst	.05
46	Claudell Washington	.05
47	Todd Benzinger	.05
48	Steve Balboni	.05
49	Oddibe McDowell	.05
50	Charles Hudson	.05
51	Ron Kittle	.05
52	Andy Hawkins	.05
53	Tom Brookens	.05
54	Tom Niedenfuer	.05
55	Jeff Parrett	.05
56	Checklist	.05

1990 Donruss Previews

1990 PREVIEW CARDS
No. 10 of 12
JEROME WALTON
OUTFIELDER
CAREER HIGHLIGHTS

To introduce its 1990 baseball issue, Donruss sent two preview cards from a set of 12 to each member of its dealers' network. Though the photos are different than those used on the issued versions, the front format was the same. Backs are printed in black on white and contain career highlights, but no stats. Issued at the dawn of the "promo card" craze, and succeeding the relatively valueless sample sheets used by most companies in earlier years, little value was attached to these preview cards initially. Today they are among the scarcest of the early-1990s promos.

	NM/M
Complete Set (12):	85.00
Common Player:	3.00
1 Todd Zeile	3.00
2 Ben McDonald	3.00
3 Bo Jackson	7.50
4 Will Clark	3.00
5 Dave Stewart	3.00
6 Kevin Mitchell	3.00
7 Nolan Ryan	50.00
8 Howard Johnson	3.00
9 Tony Gwynn	25.00
10 Jerome Walton	3.00
11 Wade Boggs	25.00
12 Kirby Puckett	25.00

1990 Donruss

Donruss marked its 10th anniversary in the baseball card hobby with a 715-card set in 1990, up from previous 660-card sets. The standard-size cards feature bright red borders with the player's name in script at the top. The set includes 26 "Diamond Kings" (DK) in the checklist, 20 "Rated Rookies" (RR) and a Carl Yastrzemski puzzle. Each All-Star card back has two variations. The more common has the stats box headed "All-Star Performance." Slightly scarcer versions say "Recent Major League Performance," and are worth about twice the value of the correct version.

	NM/M
Unopened Factory Set (716):	10.00
Complete Set (716):	7.50
Common Player:	
Carl Yastrzemski Puzzle:	1.00
Wax Pack (16):	.50
Wax Box (36):	10.00
Rack Pack (48):	1.00
Blister Rack (78):	1.50

No.	Player	NM/M
1	Bo Jackson (Diamond King)	.15
2	Steve Sax (DK)	.05
3a	Ruben Sierra (DK) (No vertical black line at top-right on back.)	.25
3b	Ruben Sierra (DK) (Vertical line at top-right on back.)	.10
4	Ken Griffey Jr. (DK)	.65
5	Mickey Tettleton (DK)	.05
6	Dave Stewart (DK)	.05
7	Jim Deshaies (DK)	.05
8	John Smoltz (DK)	.05
9	Mike Bielecki (DK)	.05
10a	Brian Downing (DK) (Reversed negative.))	.25
10b	Brian Downing (DK) (Corrected)	.05
11	Kevin Mitchell (DK)	.05
12	Kelly Gruber (DK)	.05
13	Joe Magrane (DK)	.05
14	John Franco (DK)	.05
15	Ozzie Guillen (DK)	.05
16	Lou Whitaker (DK)	.05
17	John Smiley (DK)	.05
18	Howard Johnson (DK)	.05
19	Willie Randolph (DK)	.05
20	Chris Bosio (DK)	.05
21	Tommy Herr (DK)	.05
22	Dan Gladden (DK)	.05
23	Ellis Burks (DK)	.05
24	Pete O'Brien (DK)	.05
25	Bryn Smith (DK)	.05
26	Ed Whitson (DK)	.05
27	Checklist 1-27	
28	Robin Ventura (Rated Rookie)	.05
29	Todd Zeile RC (RR)	.15
30	Sandy Alomar, Jr. (RR)	.05
31	Kent Mercker RC (RR)	.10
32	Ben McDonald RC (RR)	.25
33a	Juan Gonzalez (Reversed negative.) RC (RR)	2.00
33b	Juan Gonzalez RC (RR) (Corrected)	1.50
34	Eric Anthony RC (RR)	.05
35	Mike Fetters RC (RR)	.05
36	Marquis Grissom RC (RR)	.50
37	Greg Vaughn RC (RR)	.25
38	Brian Dubois (RR)	.05
39	Steve Avery RC (RR)	.10
40	Mark Gardner RC (RR)	.05
41	Andy Benes (RR)	.05
42	Delino DeShields RC (RR)	.15
43	Scott Coolbaugh RC (RR)	.05
44	Pat Combs RC (RR)	.10
45	Alex Sanchez RC (RR)	.05
46	Kelly Mann RC (RR)	.05
47	Julio Machado RC (RR)	.05
48	Pete Incaviglia	.05
49	Shawon Dunston	.05
50	Jeff Treadway	.05
51	Jeff Ballard	.05
52	Claudell Washington	.05
53	Juan Samuel	.05
54	John Smiley	.05
55	Rob Deer	.05
56	Geno Petralli	.05
57	Chris Bosio	.05
58	Carlton Fisk	.40
59	Kirt Manwaring	.05
60	Chet Lemon	.05
61	Bo Jackson	.10
62	Doyle Alexander	.05
63	Pedro Guerrero	.05
64	Allan Anderson	.05
65	Greg Harris	.05
66	Mike Greenwell	.05
67	Walt Weiss	.05
68	Wade Boggs	.50
69	Jim Clancy	.05
70	Junior Felix RC	.05
71	Barry Larkin	.05
72	Dave LaPoint	.05
73	Joel Skinner	.05
74	Jesse Barfield	.05
75	Tommy Herr	.05
76	Ricky Jordan	.05
77	Eddie Murray	.40
78	Steve Sax	.05
79	Tim Belcher	.05
80	Danny Jackson	.05
81	Kent Hrbek	.05
82	Milt Thompson	.05
83	Brook Jacoby	.05
84	Mike Marshall	.05
85	Kevin Seitzer	.05
86	Tony Gwynn	.50
87	Dave Steib	.05
88	Dave Smith	.05
89	Bret Saberhagen	.05
90	Alan Trammell	.05
91	Tony Phillips	.05
92	Doug Drabek	.05
93	Jeffrey Leonard	.05
94	Wally Joyner	.05
95	Carney Lansford	.05
96	Cal Ripken, Jr.	1.00
97	Andres Galarraga	.05
98	Kevin Mitchell	.05
99	Howard Johnson	.05
100a	Checklist 28-129	
100b	Checklist 28-125	.05
101	Melido Perez	.05
102	Spike Owen	.05
103	Paul Molitor	.40
104	Geronimo Berroa	.05
105	Ryne Sandberg	.50
106	Bryn Smith	.05
107	Steve Buechele	.05
108	Jim Abbott	.05
109	Alvin Davis	.05
110	Lee Smith	.05
111	Roberto Alomar	.20
112	Rick Reuschel	.05
113a	Kelly Gruber (Born 2/22.)	.05
113b	Kelly Gruber (Born 2/26.)	.20
114	Joe Carter	.05
115	Jose Rijo	.05
116	Greg Minton	.05
117	Bob Ojeda	.05
118	Glenn Davis	.05
119	Jeff Reardon	.05
120	Kurt Stillwell	.05
121	John Smoltz	.05
122	Dwight Evans	.05
123	Eric Yelding	.05
124	John Franco	.05
125	Jose Canseco	.20
126	Barry Bonds	1.00
127	Lee Guetterman	.05
128	Jack Clark	.05
129	Dave Valle	.05
130	Hubie Brooks	.05
131	Ernest Riles	.05
132	Mike Morgan	.05
133	Steve Jeltz	.05
134	Jeff Robinson	.05
135	Ozzie Guillen	.05
136	Chili Davis	.05
137	Mitch Webster	.05
138	Jerry Browne	.05
139	Bo Diaz	.05
140	Robby Thompson	.05
141	Craig Worthington	.05
142	Julio Franco	.05
143	Brian Holman	.05
144	George Brett	.60
145	Tom Glavine	.20
146	Robin Yount	.40
147	Gary Carter	.40
148	Ron Kittle	.05
149	Tony Fernandez	.05
150	Dave Stewart	.05
151	Gary Gaetti	.05
152	Kevin Elster	.05
153	Gerald Perry	.05
154	Jesse Orosco	.05
155	Wally Backman	.05
156	Dennis Martinez	.05
157	Rick Sutcliffe	.05
158	Greg Maddux	.50
159	Andy Hawkins	.05
160	John Kruk	.05
161	Jose Oquendo	.05
162	John Dopson	.05
163	Joe Magrane	.05
164	Billy Ripken	.05
165	Fred Manrique	.05
166	Nolan Ryan	1.00
167	Damon Berryhill	.05
168	Dale Murphy	.20
169	Mickey Tettleton	.05
170a	Kirk McCaskill (Born 4/19.)	.05
170b	Kirk McCaskill (Born 4/9.)	.10
171	Dwight Gooden	.05
172	Jose Lind	.05
173	B.J. Surhoff	.05
174	Ruben Sierra	.05
175	Dan Plesac	.05
176	Dan Pasqua	.05
177	Kelly Downs	.05
178	Matt Nokes	.05
179	Luis Aquino	.05
180	Frank Tanana	.05
181	Tony Pena	.05
182	Dan Gladden	.05
183	Bruce Hurst	.05
184	Roger Clemens	.60
185	Mark McGwire	.75
186	Rob Murphy	.05
187	Jim Deshaies	.05
188	Fred McGriff	.05
189	Rob Dibble	.05
190	Don Mattingly	.60
191	Felix Fermin	.05
192	Roberto Kelly	.05
193	Dennis Cook	.05
194	Darren Daulton	.05
195	Alfredo Griffin	.05
196	Eric Plunk	.05
197	Orel Hershiser	.05
198	Paul O'Neill	.05
199	Randy Bush	.05
200a	Checklist 130-231	.05
200b	Checklist 126-223	.05
201	Ozzie Smith	.50
202	Pete O'Brien	.05
203	Jay Howell	.05
204	Mark Gubicza	.05
205	Ed Whitson	.05
206	George Bell	.05
207	Mike Scott	.05
208	Charlie Leibrandt	.05
209	Mike Heath	.05
210	Dennis Eckersley	.35
211	Mike LaValliere	.05
212	Darnell Coles	.05
213	Lance Parrish	.05
214	Mike Moore	.05
215	Steve Finley RC	.20
216	Tim Raines	.05
217a	Scott Garrelts (Born 10/20.)	.05
217b	Scott Garrelts (Born 10/30.)	.10
218	Kevin McReynolds	.05
219	Dave Gallagher	.05
220	Tim Wallach	.05
221	Chuck Crim	.05
222	Lonnie Smith	.05
223	Andre Dawson	.20
224	Nelson Santovenia	.05
225	Rafael Palmeiro	.35
226	Devon White	.05
227	Harold Reynolds	.05
228	Ellis Burks	.05
229	Mark Parent	.05
230	Will Clark	.05
231	Jimmy Key	.05
232	John Farrell	.05
233	Eric Davis	.05
234	Johnny Ray	.05
235	Darryl Strawberry	.05
236	Bill Doran	.05
237	Greg Gagne	.05
238	Jim Eisenreich	.05
239	Tommy Gregg	.05
240	Marty Barrett	.05
241	Rafael Ramirez	.05
242	Chris Sabo	.05
243	Dave Henderson	.05
244	Andy Van Slyke	.05
245	Alvaro Espinoza	.05
246	Garry Templeton	.05
247	Gene Harris	.05
248	Kevin Gross	.05
249	Brett Butler	.05
250	Willie Randolph	.05
251	Roger McDowell	.05
252	Rafael Belliard	.05
253	Steve Rosenberg	.05
254	Jack Howell	.05
255	Marvell Wynne	.05
256	Tom Candiotti	.05
257	Todd Benzinger	.05
258	Don Robinson	.05
259	Phil Bradley	.05
260	Cecil Espy	.05
261	Scott Bankhead	.05
262	Frank White	.05
263	Andres Thomas	.05
264	Glenn Braggs	.05
265	David Cone	.05
266	Bobby Thigpen	.05
267	Nelson Liriano	.05
268	Terry Steinbach	.05
269	Kirby Puckett	.50
270	Gregg Jefferies	.05
271	Jeff Blauser	.05
272	Cory Snyder	.05
273	Roy Smith	.05
274	Tom Foley	.05
275	Mitch Williams	.05
276	Paul Kilgus	.05
277	Don Slaught	.05
278	Von Hayes	.05
279	Vince Coleman	.05
280	Mike Boddicker	.05
281	Ken Dayley	.05
282	Mike Devereaux	.05
283	Kenny Rogers RC	.05
284	Jeff Russell	.05
285	Jerome Walton RC	.10
286	Derek Lilliquist	.05
287	Joe Orsulak	.05
288	Dick Schofield	.05
289	Ron Darling	.05
290	Bobby Bonilla	.05
291	Jim Gantner	.05
292	Bobby Witt	.05
293	Greg Brock	.05
294	Ivan Calderon	.05
295	Steve Bedrosian	.05
296	Mike Henneman	.05
297	Tom Gordon	.05
298	Lou Whitaker	.05
299	Terry Pendleton	.05
300a	Checklist 232-333	.05
300b	Checklist 224-321	.05
301	Juan Berenguer	.05
302	Mark Davis	.05
303	Nick Esasky	.05
304	Rickey Henderson	.40
305	Rick Cerone	.05
306	Craig Biggio	.05
307	Duane Ward	.05
308	Tom Browning	.05
309	Walt Terrell	.05
310	Greg Swindell	.05
311	Dave Righetti	.05
312	Mike Maddux	.05
313	Len Dykstra	.05
314	Jose Gonzalez	.05
315	Steve Balboni	.05
316	Mike Scioscia	.05
317	Ron Oester	.05
318	Gary Wayne RC	.05
319	Todd Worrell	.05
320	Doug Jones	.05
321	Jeff Hamilton	.05
322	Danny Tartabull	.05
323	Chris James	.05
324	Mike Flanagan	.05
325	Gerald Young	.05
326	Bob Boone	.05
327	Frank Williams	.05
328	Dave Parker	.05
329	Sid Bream	.05
330	Mike Schooler	.05
331	Bert Blyleven	.10
332	Bob Welch	.05
333	Bob Milacki	.05
334	Tim Burke	.05
335	Jose Uribe	.05
336	Randy Myers	.05
337	Eric King	.05
338	Mark Langston	.05
339	Ted Higuera	.05
340	Oddibe McDowell	.05
341	Lloyd McClendon	.05
342	Pascual Perez	.05
343	Kevin Brown	.05
344	Chuck Finley	.05
345	Erik Hanson	.05
346	Rich Gedman	.05
347	Bip Roberts	.05
348	Matt Williams	.05
349	Tom Henke	.05
350	Brad Komminsk	.05
351	Jeff Reed	.05
352	Brian Downing	.05
353	Frank Viola	.05
354	Terry Puhl	.05
355	Brian Harper	.05
356	Steve Farr	.05
357	Joe Boever	.05
358	Danny Heep	.05
359	Larry Andersen	.05
360	Rolando Roomes	.05
361	Mike Gallego	.05
362	Bob Kipper	.05
363	Clay Parker	.05
364	Mike Pagliarulo	.05
365	Ken Griffey Jr.	.65
366	Rex Hudler	.05
367	Pat Sheridan	.05
368a	Kirk Gibson (May 25 birthdate.)	.05
368b	Kirk Gibson (May 28 birthdate.)	.05
369	Jeff Parrett	.05
370	Bob Walk	.05
371	Ken Patterson	.05
372	Bryan Harvey	.05
373	Mike Bielecki	.05
374	Tom Magrann RC	.05
375	Rick Mahler	.05
376	Craig Lefferts	.05
377	Gregg Olson	.05
378	Jamie Moyer	.05
379	Randy Johnson	.40
380	Jeff Montgomery	.05
381	Marty Clary	.05
382	Bill Spiers RC	.05
383	Dave Magadan	.05
384	Greg Hibbard RC	.05
385	Ernie Whitt	.05
386	Rick Honeycutt	.05
387	Dave West	.05
388	Keith Hernandez	.05
389	Jose Alvarez	.05
390	Albert Belle	.05
391	Rick Aguilera	.05
392	Mike Fitzgerald	.05
393	Dwight Smith RC	.05
394	Steve Wilson RC	.05
395	Bob Geren RC	.05
396	Randy Ready	.05
397	Ken Hill	.05
398	Jody Reed	.05
399	Tom Brunansky	.05
400a	Checklist 334-435	.05
400b	Checklist 322-419	.05
401	Rene Gonzales	.05
402	Harold Baines	.05
403	Cecilio Guante	.05
404	Joe Girardi	.05
405a	Sergio Valdez RC (Black line crosses S in Sergio.)	.10
405b	Sergio Valdez (Corrected)	.05
406	Mark Williamson	.05
407	Glenn Hoffman	.05
408	Jeff Innis RC	.05
409	Randy Kramer	.05
410	Charlie O'Brien	.05
411	Charlie Hough	.05
412	Gus Polidor	.05
413	Trevor Wilson	.05
414	Kevin Ritz RC	.05
415	Gary Thurman	.05
416	Jeff Robinson	.05
417	Scott Terry	.05
418	Tim Laudner	.05
419	Dennis Rasmussen	.05
420	Luis Rivera	.05
421	Jim Corsi	.05
422	Eric Hetzel	.05
423	Ken Caminiti	.05
424	David Wells	.05
425	Norm Charlton	.05
426	Deion Sanders	.05
427	Dion James	.05
428	Chuck Cary	.05
429	Ken Howell	.05
430	Rod Nichols	.05
431	Steve Lake	.05
432	Kal Daniels	.05
433	Lance McCullers	.05
434	Lenny Harris	.05
435	Scott Scudder RC	.05
436	Gene Larkin	.05
437	Dan Quisenberry	.05
438	Steve Olin RC	.05
439	Mickey Hatcher	.05
440	Willie Wilson	.05
441	Mark Grant	.05
442	Mookie Wilson	.05
443	Alex Trevino	.05
444	Pat Tabler	.05
445	Dave Bergman	.05
446	Todd Burns	.05
447	R.J. Reynolds	.05
448	Jay Buhner	.05
449	Lee Stevens RC	.05
450	Ron Hassey	.05
451	Bob Melvin	.05
452	Dave Martinez	.05
453	Greg Litton RC	.05
454	Mark Carreon	.05
455	Scott Fletcher	.05
456	Otis Nixon	.05
457	Tony Fossas RC	.05
458	John Russell	.05
459	Paul Assenmacher	.05
460	Zane Smith	.05
461	Jack Daugherty RC	.05
462	Rich Monteleone RC	.05
463	Greg Briley	.05
464	Mike Smithson	.05
465	Benito Santiago	.05
466	Jeff Brantley RC	.05
467	Jose Nunez	.05
468	Scott Bailes	.05
469	Ken Griffey	.05
470	Bob McClure	.05
471	Mackey Sasser	.05
472	Glenn Wilson	.05
473	Kevin Tapani RC	.10
474	Bill Buckner	.05
475	Ron Gant	.05
476	Kevin Romine	.05
477	Juan Agosto	.05
478	Herm Winningham	.05
479	Storm Davis	.05
480	Jeff King	.05
481	Kevin Mmahat RC	.05
482	Carmelo Martinez	.05
483	Omar Vizquel	.05
484	Jim Dwyer	.05
485	Bob Knepper	.05
486	Dave Anderson	.05
487	Ron Jones	.05
488	Jay Bell	.05
489	Sammy Sosa RC	3.00
490	Kent Anderson	.05
491	Domingo Ramos	.05
492	Dave Clark	.05
493	Tim Birtsas	.05
494	Ken Oberkfell	.05
495	Larry Sheets	.05
496	Jeff Kunkel	.05
497	Jim Presley	.05
498	Mike Macfarlane	.05
499	Pete Smith	.05
500a	Checklist 436-537	.05
500b	Checklist 420-517	.05
501	Gary Sheffield	.20
502	Terry Bross RC	.05
503	Jerry Kutzler RC	.05
504	Lloyd Moseby	.05
505	Curt Young	.05
506	Al Newman	.05
507	Keith Miller	.05
508	Mike Stanton RC	.20
509	Rich Yett	.05
510	Tim Drummond RC	.05
511	Joe Hesketh	.05
512	Rick Wrona RC	.05
513	Luis Salazar	.05
514	Hal Morris	.05
515	Terry Mullholland	.05
516	John Morris	.05
517	Carlos Quintana	.05
518	Frank DiPino	.05
519	Randy Milligan	.05
520	Chad Kreuter	.05
521	Mike Jeffcoat	.05
522	Mike Harkey	.05
523a	Andy Nezelek (Born 1985.)	.05
523b	Andy Nezelek (Born 1965.)	.05
524	Dave Schmidt	.05
525	Tony Armas	.05
526	Barry Lyons	.05
527	Rick Reed RC	.05
528	Jerry Reuss	.05
529	Dean Palmer RC	.10
530	Jeff Peterek RC	.05
531	Carlos Martinez RC	.05
532	Atlee Hammaker	.05
533	Mike Brumley	.05
534	Terry Leach	.05
535	Doug Strange RC	.05
536	Jose DeLeon	.05
537	Shane Rawley	.05
538	Joey Cora	.05
539	Eric Hetzel	.05
540	Gene Nelson	.05
541	Wes Gardner	.05
542	Mark Portugal	.05
543	Al Leiter	.05
544	Jack Armstrong	.05
545	Greg Cadaret	.05
546	Rod Nichols	.05
547	Luis Polonia	.05
548	Charlie Hayes	.05
549	Dickie Thon	.05
550	Tim Crews	.05
551	Dave Winfield	.40
552	Mike Davis	.05
553	Ron Robinson	.05
554	Carmen Castillo	.05
555	John Costello	.05
556	Bud Black	.05
557	Rick Dempsey	.05
558	Jim Acker	.05
559	Eric Show	.05
560	Pat Borders	.05
561	Danny Darwin	.05
562	Rick Luecken RC	.05
563	Edwin Nunez	.05
564	Felix Jose	.05
565	John Cangelosi	.05
566	Billy Swift	.05
567	Bill Schroeder	.05
568	Stan Javier	.05
569	Jim Traber	.05
570	Wallace Johnson	.05
571	Donell Nixon	.05
572	Sid Fernandez	.05
573	Lance Johnson	.05
574	Andy McGaffigan	.05
575	Mark Knudson	.05
576	Tommy Greene RC	.05
577	Mark Grace	.05
578	Larry Walker RC	1.00
579	Mike Stanley	.05
580	Mike Witt	.05
581	Scott Bradley	.05
582	Greg Harris	.05
583a	Kevin Hickey (Black stripe over top of "K" vertical stroke.)	.05
583b	Kevin Hickey (Black stripe under "K.")	.05
584	Lee Mazzilli	.05
585	Jeff Pico	.05
586	Joe Oliver RC	.05
587	Willie Fraser	.05
588	Puzzle card (Carl Yastrzemski)	.05
589	Kevin Bass	.05
590	John Moses	.05
591	Tom Pagnozzi	.05
592	Tony Castillo RC	.05
593	Jerald Clark	.05
594	Dan Schatzeder	.05
595	Luis Quinones	.05
596	Pete Harnisch	.05
597	Gary Redus	.05
598	Mel Hall	.05
599	Rick Schu	.05
600a	Checklist 538-639	.05
600b	Checklist 518-617	.05
601	Mike Kingery	.05
602	Terry Kennedy	.05
603	Mike Sharperson	.05
604	Don Carman	.05
605	Jim Gott	.05
606	Donn Pall	.05
607	Rance Mulliniks	.05
608	Curt Wilkerson	.05
609	Mike Felder	.05
610	Guillermo Hernandez	.05
611	Candy Maldonado	.05
612	Mark Thurmond	.05
613	Rick Leach	.05
614	Jerry Reed	.05
615	Franklin Stubbs	.05
616	Billy Hatcher	.05
617	Don August	.05
618	Tim Teufel	.05
619	Shawn Hillegas	.05
620	Manny Lee	.05
621	Gary Ward	.05
622	Mark Guthrie RC	.05
623	Jeff Musselman	.05
624	Mark Lemke	.05
625	Fernando Valenzuela	.05
626	Paul Sorrento RC	.05
627	Glenallen Hill	.05
628	Les Lancaster	.05
629	Vance Law	.05
630	Randy Velarde	.05
631	Todd Frohwirth	.05
632	Willie McGee	.05
633	Oil Can Boyd	.05
634	Cris Carpenter	.05
635	Brian Holton	.05
636	Tracy Jones	.05
637	Terry Steinbach/AS	.05
638	Brady Anderson	.05
639a	Jack Morris (Black line crosses J of Jack.)	.10
639b	Jack Morris (Corrected)	.05
640	Jaime Navarro RC	.05
641	Darrin Jackson	.05
642	Mike Dyer RC	.05
643	Mike Schmidt	.60
644	Henry Cotto	.05
645	John Cerutti	.05
646	Francisco Cabrera RC	.05
647	Scott Sanderson	.05
648	Brian Meyer	.05
649	Ray Searage	.05
650	Bo Jackson/AS	.25
651	Steve Lyons	.05
652	Mike LaCoss	.05
653	Ted Power	.05
654	Howard Johnson/AS	.05
655	Mauro Gozzo RC	.05
656	Mike Blowers RC	.05
657	Paul Gibson	.05
658	Neal Heaton	.05
659a	Nolan Ryan 5,000 K's (King of Kings (#665) back.)	1.50

659b Nolan Ryan 5,000 K's (Correct back.) .60
660a Harold Baines/AS (Black line through star on front, Recent Major League Performance on back.) .25
660b Harold Baines/AS (Black line through star on front, All-Star Game Performance on back.) .25
660c Harold Baines/AS (Black line behind star on front, Recent Major League Performance on back.) .25
660d Harold Baines/AS (Black line behind star on front, All-Star Game Performance on back.) .10
661 Gary Pettis .05
662 Clint Zavaras RC .05
663 Rick Reuschel/AS .05
664 Alejandro Pena .05
665a Nolan Ryan (King of Kings) (5,000 K's (#659) back.) 1.50
665b Nolan Ryan (King of Kings) (Correct back.) 1.00
665c Nolan Ryan (King of Kings) (No number on back.) 1.00
666 Ricky Horton .05
667 Curt Schilling .05
668 Bill Landrum .05
669 Todd Stottlemyre .05
670 Tim Leary .05
671 John Wetteland RC .25
672 Calvin Schiraldi .05
673 Ruben Sierra/AS .05
674 Pedro Guerrero/AS .05
675 Ken Phelps .05
676 Cal Ripken/AS .50
677 Denny Walling .05
678 Goose Gossage .05
679 Gary Mielke RC .05
680 Bill Bathe .05
681 Tom Lawless .05
682 Xavier Hernandez RC .05
683 Kirby Puckett/AS .25
684 Mariano Duncan .05
685 Ramon Martinez .05
686 Tim Jones .05
687 Tom Filer .05
688 Steve Lombardozzi .05
689 Bernie Williams RC 1.00
690 Chip Hale RC .05
691 Beau Allred RC .05
692 Ryne Sandberg/AS .25
693 Jeff Huson RC .05
694 Curt Ford .05
695 Eric Davis (AS) .05
696 Scott Lusader .05
697 Mark McGwire (AS) .40
698 Steve Cummings RC .05
699 George Canale RC .05
700a Checklist 640-715/ BC1-BC26 .05
700b Checklist 640-716/ BC1-BC26 .05
700c Checklist 618-716 .05
701 Julio Franco/AS .05
702 Dave Johnson RC .05
703 Dave Stewart/AS .05
704 Dave Justice RC .50
705 Tony Gwynn/AS .25
706 Greg Myers .05
707 Will Clark/AS .05
708 Benito Santiago/AS .05
709 Larry McWilliams .05
710 Ozzie Smith/AS .25
711 John Olerud RC .50
712 Wade Boggs/AS .25
713 Gary Eave RC .05
714 Bob Tewksbury .05
715 Kevin Mitchell/AS .05
716 A. Bartlett Giamatti .25

1990 Donruss Grand Slammers

For the second consecutive year Donruss produced a set in honor of players who hit grand slams in the previous season. The cards are styled after the 1990 Donruss regular issue. The cards were inserted in 1990 Donruss factory sets, and one card per cello pack. Each card can be found with blue borders or with blue and green borders, and with or without the split black stripe near the right end on back.

	NM/M
Complete Set (12):	2.00
Common Player:	.10
1 Matt Williams	.10
2 Jeffrey Leonard	.10
3 Chris James	.10
4 Mark McGwire	1.50
5 Dwight Evans	.10
6 Will Clark	.10
7 Mike Scioscia	.10
8 Todd Benzinger	.10
9 Fred McGriff	.10
10 Kevin Bass	.10
11 Jack Clark	.10
12 Bo Jackson	.25

1990 Donruss MVP

This special 26-card set includes one player from each Major League team. Numbered BC-1 (the "BC" stands for "Bonus Card") through BC-26, the cards from this set were randomly packed in 1990 Donruss wax packs and were not available in factory sets or other types of packaging. The red-bordered cards are similar in design to the regular 1990 Donruss set, except the player photos are set against a special background made up of the "MVP" logo.

	NM/M
Complete Set (26):	1.25
Common Player:	.10
1 Bo Jackson	.20
2 Howard Johnson	.10
3 Dave Stewart	.10
4 Tony Gwynn	.35
5 Orel Hershiser	.10
6 Pedro Guerrero	.10
7 Tim Raines	.10
8 Kirby Puckett	.35
9 Alvin Davis	.10
10 Ryne Sandberg	.35
11 Kevin Mitchell	.10
12a John Smoltz (Photo of Tom Glavine.)	1.50
12b John Smoltz (Corrected)	.30
13 George Bell	.10
14 Julio Franco	.10
15 Paul Molitor	.25
16 Bobby Bonilla	.10
17 Mike Greenwell	.10
18 Cal Ripken	.50
19 Carlton Fisk	.25
20 Chili Davis	.10
21 Glenn Davis	.10
22 Steve Sax	.10
23 Eric Davis	.10
24 Greg Swindell	.10
25 Von Hayes	.10
26 Alan Trammell	.10

1990 Donruss Aqueous Test

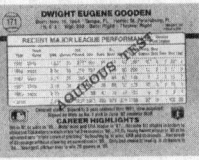

Little is known about this mystery issue which few hobbyists had ever heard of prior to 1999. The cards appear in all major respects to be regular 1990 Donruss cards, but on back have the words "AQUEOUS TEST" printed. The test cards also lack the period after "INC" in the copyright line at upper-right. Approximately 2,000-2,500 cards in total are known, with only part of the '90 checklist represented in the test issue. As few as one specimen each are known for some cards, while a half-dozen or more of others are recorded. Because of limited supply, prices can be volatile depending on the activity of single-player specialist collectors at any given time. It is possible the checklist here is not complete. The cards may have been produced to test a semi-gloss coating known in the printing trade as aqueous.

	NM/M
Common Player:	5.00
1 Bo Jackson/DK	17.50
3 Ruben Sierra/DK	5.00
6 Dave Stewart/DK	6.50
8 Mike Bielecki/DK	5.00
9 Mike Bielecki/DK	5.00
16 Lou Whitaker/DK	5.00
19 Howard Johnson/DK	5.00
22 Dan Gladden/DK	5.00
28 Pete O'Brien/DK	5.00
28 Robin Ventura (Rated Rookie)	15.00
29 Todd Zeile (Rated Rookie)	15.00
30 Sandy Alomar Jr. (Rated Rookie)	15.00
31 Kent Mercker (Rated Rookie)	5.00
32 Ben McDonald (Rated Rookie)	7.50
33 Juan Gonzalez (Rated Rookie) (Reversed negatives.)	75.00
34 Eric Anthony (Rated Rookie)	5.00
35 Mike Fetters (Rated Rookie)	5.00
48 Pete Incaviglia	5.00
51 Jeff Ballard	5.00
52 Claudell Washington	5.00
55 Rob Deer	5.00
56 Geno Petralli	5.00
57 Chris Bosio	5.00
60 Chet Lemon	5.00
61 Bo Jackson	25.00
63 Pedro Guerrero	5.00
64 Allan Anderson	5.00
65 Greg Harris	5.00
66 Mike Greenwell	5.00
68 Wade Boggs	60.00
70 Junior Felix	5.00
71 Barry Larkin	5.00
72 Dave LaPoint	5.00
74 Jesse Barfield	5.00
77 Eddie Murray	45.00
78 Steve Sax	5.00
79 Tim Belcher	5.00
80 Danny Jackson	5.00
82 Kent Hrbek	5.00
83 Brook Jacoby	5.00
84 Mike Marshall	5.00
85 Kevin Seitzer	5.00
86 Tony Gwynn	60.00
87 Dave Steib	5.00
89 Bret Saberhagen	5.00
90 Alan Trammell	5.00
91 Tony Phillips	5.00
93 Jeff Leonard	5.00
94 Wally Joyner	5.00
95 Carney Lansford	5.00
96 Cal Ripken Jr.	100.00
97 Andres Galarraga	5.00
99 Kevin Mitchell	5.00
100 Checklist 28-129	2.50
102 Spike Owen	5.00
103 Paul Molitor	45.00
105 Ryne Sandberg	60.00
106 Steve Buechele	5.00
108 Jim Abbott	35.00
109 Alvin Davis	5.00
110 Lee Smith	5.00
111 Roberto Alomar	15.00
112 Rick Reuschel	5.00
113 Kelly Gruber	5.00
116 Joe Carter	5.00
115 Jose Rijo	5.00
117 Bobby Ojeda	5.00
118 Glenn Davis	5.00
119 Jeff Reardon	5.00
120 Kurt Stillwell	5.00
122 Dwight Evans	5.00
124 John Franco	5.00
125 Jose Canseco	35.00
126 Barry Bonds	100.00
127 Lee Guetterman	5.00
128 Jack Clark	5.00
129 Dave Valle	5.00
132 Mike Morgan	5.00
133 Steve Jeltz	5.00
134 Jeff Robinson	5.00
139 Bo Diaz	5.00
140 Robby Thompson	5.00
141 Craig Worthington	5.00
144 George Brett	75.00
145 Tom Glavine	15.00
146 Robin Yount	45.00
147 Gary Carter	45.00
148 Ron Kittle	5.00
149 Tony Fernandez	5.00
150 Dave Stewart	5.00
151 Gary Gaetti	5.00
154 Jesse Orosco	5.00
155 Wally Backman	5.00
156 Dennis Martinez	5.00
157 Rick Sutcliffe	6.50
158 Greg Maddux	60.00
160 John Kruk	5.00
162 John Dopson	5.00
164 Billy Ripken	5.00
165 Fred Manrique	5.00
166 Nolan Ryan	100.00
167 Damon Berryhill	5.00
168 Dale Murphy	35.00
169 Mickey Tettleton	5.00
170 Kirk McCaskill	5.00
171 Dwight Gooden	5.00
172 Jose Lind	5.00
173 B.J. Surhoff	5.00
174 Ruben Sierra	5.00
175 Dan Plesac	5.00
176 Dan Pasqua	5.00
177 Kelly Downs	5.00
178 Matt Nokes	5.00
179 Luis Aquino	5.00
180 Frank Tanana	5.00
181 Tony Pena	5.00
182 Dan Gladden	5.00
183 Bruce Hurst	5.00
184 Roger Clemens	75.00
185 Mark McGwire	85.00
186 Rob Murphy	5.00
187 Jim Deshaies	5.00
188 Fred McGriff	5.00
189 Rob Dibble	5.00
190 Don Mattingly	75.00
191 Felix Fermin	5.00
192 Roberto Kelly	5.00
193 Dennis Cook	5.00
194 Darren Daulton	5.00
195 Alfredo Griffin	5.00
196 Eric Plunk	5.00
197 Orel Hershiser	5.00
198 Paul O'Neill	5.00
199 Randy Bush	5.00
201 Ozzie Smith	60.00
202 Pete O'Brien	5.00
203 Jay Howell	5.00
204 Mark Gubicza	5.00
205 Ed Whitson	5.00
206 George Bell	5.00
207 Mike Scott	5.00
208 Charlie Leibrandt	5.00
209 Mike Heath	5.00
210 Dennis Eckersley	45.00
211 Mike LaValliere	5.00
212 Darnell Coles	5.00
213 Lance Parrish	5.00
214 Mike Moore	5.00
215 Steve Finley	5.00
216 Tim Raines	5.00
217 Scott Garrelts	5.00
218 Kevin McReynolds	5.00
219 Dave Gallagher	5.00
220 Tim Wallach	5.00
221 Chuck Crim	5.00
222 Lonnie Smith	5.00
223 Andre Dawson	15.00
224 Nelson Santovenia	5.00
225 Rafael Palmeiro	45.00
226 Devon White	5.00
227 Harold Reynolds	6.50
228 Ellis Burks	5.00
229 Mark Parent	5.00
230 Will Clark	6.50
231 Jimmy Key	5.00
232 John Farrell	5.00
233 Eric Davis	5.00
234 Johnny Ray	5.00
235 Darryl Strawberry	5.00
236 Bill Doran	5.00
237 Greg Gagne	5.00
238 Jim Eisenreich	5.00
239 Tommy Gregg	5.00
240 Marty Barrett	5.00
241 Rafael Ramirez	5.00
242 Chris Sabo	5.00
243 Dave Henderson	5.00
244 Andy Van Slyke	5.00
245 Alvaro Espinoza	5.00
246 Garry Templeton	5.00
247 Gene Harris	5.00
248 Kevin Gross	5.00
249 Brett Butler	5.00
250 Willie Randolph	5.00
251 Roger McDowell	5.00
252 Rafael Belliard	5.00
253 Steve Rosenberg	5.00
254 Jack Howell	5.00
255 Marvell Wynne	5.00
256 Tom Candiotti	5.00
257 Todd Benzinger	5.00
258 Don Robinson	5.00
259 Phil Bradley	5.00
260 Cecil Espy	5.00
261 Scott Bankhead	5.00
262 Frank White	5.00
263 Andre Thomas	5.00
264 Glenn Braggs	5.00
265 David Cone	5.00
266 Bobby Thigpen	5.00
267 Nelson Liriano	5.00
268 Terry Steinbach	5.00
269 Kirby Puckett	60.00
270 Gregg Jefferies	5.00
271 Jeff Blauser	5.00
272 Cory Snyder	5.00
273 Roy Smith	5.00
274 Tom Foley	5.00
275 Mitch Williams	5.00
276 Paul Kilgus	5.00
277 Don Slaught	5.00
278 Von Hayes	5.00
279 Vince Coleman	5.00
280 Mike Boddicker	5.00
281 Ken Dayley	5.00
282 Mike Devereaux	5.00
283 Kenny Rogers	5.00
BC-1 Bo Jackson (MVP)	15.00
BC-2 Howard Johnson (MVP)	5.00
BC-3 Dave Stewart (MVP)	5.00
BC-4 Tony Gwynn (MVP)	45.00
BC-5 Orel Hershiser (MVP)	5.00
BC-6 Pedro Guerrero (MVP)	5.00
BC-7 Tim Raines (MVP)	6.50
BC-8 Kirby Puckett (MVP)	45.00
BC-9 Alvin Davis (MVP)	5.00

1990 Donruss Blue/White Test Issue

Relatively few examples of this test printing have found their way into the hobby. The cards are "two-headed" with the fronts of two different cards printed back-to-back. The cards use the same photos found on the issued versions and differ only in the border colors. Each card can be found with one side bordered in blue and the other bordered in white. The blue side of the card has a glossier finish than the white. The number of different players' cards which can be found in this version is unknown.

1990 Donruss Best A.L.

This 144-card set features the top players of the American League. The 2-1/2" x 3-1/2" cards feature the same front design as the regular Donruss set, exception with blue borders instead of red. Backs feature a yellow frame with complete statistics and biographical information provided. This marks the first year that Donruss divided its baseball-best issue into two sets designated by league.

	NM/M
Complete Set (144):	10.00
Common Player:	.05
1 Ken Griffey Jr.	1.00
2 Bob Milacki	.05
3 Mike Boddicker	.05
4 Bert Blyleven	.05
5 Carlton Fisk	.50
6 Greg Swindell	.05
7 Alan Trammell	.05
8 Mark Davis	.05
9 Chris Bosio	.05
10 Gary Gaetti	.05
11 Matt Nokes	.05
12 Dennis Eckersley	.45
13 Kevin Brown	.05
14 Tom Henke	.05
15 Mickey Tettleton	.05
16 Jody Reed	.05
17 Mark Langston	.05
18 Melido Perez	.05
19 John Farrell	.05
20 Tony Phillips	.05
21 Bret Saberhagen	.05
22 Robin Yount	.50
23 Kirby Puckett	.60
24 Steve Sax	.05
25 Dave Stewart	.05
26 Alvin Davis	.05
27 Geno Petralli	.05
28 Mookie Wilson	.05
29 Jeff Ballard	.05
30 Ellis Burks	.05
31 Wally Joyner	.05
32 Bobby Thigpen	.05
33 Keith Hernandez	.05
34 Jack Morris	.05
35 George Brett	.75
36 Dan Plesac	.05
37 Brian Harper	.05
38 Don Mattingly	.75
39 Dave Henderson	.05
40 Scott Bankhead	.05
41 Rafael Palmeiro	.45
42 Jimmy Key	.05
43 Gregg Olson	.05
44 Tony Pena	.05
45 Jack Howell	.05
46 Eric King	.05
47 Cory Snyder	.05
48 Frank Tanana	.05
49 Nolan Ryan	2.00
50 Bob Boone	.05
51 Dave Parker	.05
52 Allan Anderson	.05
53 Tim Leary	.05
54 Mark McGwire	1.50
55 Dave Valle	.05
56 Fred McGriff	.05
57 Cal Ripken	2.00
58 Roger Clemens	.75
59 Lance Parrish	.05
60 Robin Ventura	.05
61 Doug Jones	.05
62 Lloyd Moseby	.05
63 Bo Jackson	.15
64 Paul Molitor	.05
65 Kent Hrbek	.05
66 Mel Hall	.05
67 Bob Welch	.05
68 Erik Hanson	.05
69 Harold Baines	.05
70 Junior Felix	.05
71 Craig Worthington	.05
72 Jeff Reardon	.05
73 Johnny Ray	.05
74 Ozzie Guillen	.05
75 Brook Jacoby	.05
76 Chet Lemon	.05
77 Mark Gubicza	.05
78 B.J. Surhoff	.05
79 Rick Aguilera	.05
80 Pascual Perez	.05
81 Jose Canseco	.30
82 Mike Schooler	.05
83 Jeff Huson	.05
84 Kelly Gruber	.05
85 Randy Milligan	.05
86 Wade Boggs	.60
87 Dave Winfield	.50
88 Scott Fletcher	.05
89 Tom Candiotti	.05
90 Mike Heath	.05
91 Kevin Seitzer	.05
92 Ted Higuera	.05
93 Kevin Tapani	.05
94 Roberto Kelly	.05
95 Walt Weiss	.05
96 Checklist	.05
97 Sandy Alomar	.05
98 Pete O'Brien	.05
99 Jeff Russell	.05
100 John Olerud	.05
101 Pete Harnisch	.05
102 Dwight Evans	.05
103 Chuck Finley	.05
104 Sammy Sosa	6.00
105 Mike Henneman	.05
106 Kurt Stillwell	.05
107 Greg Vaughn	.05
108 Dan Gladden	.05
109 Jesse Barfield	.05
110 Willie Randolph	.05
111 Randy Johnson	.50
112 Julio Franco	.05
113 Tony Fernandez	.05
114 Ben McDonald	.05
115 Mike Greenwell	.05
116 Luis Polonia	.05
117 Carney Lansford	.05
118 Bud Black	.05
119 Lou Whitaker	.05
120 Jim Eisenreich	.05
121 Gary Sheffield	.20
122 Shane Mack	.05
123 Alvaro Espinoza	.05
124 Rickey Henderson	.50
125 Jeffrey Leonard	.05
126 Gary Pettis	.05
127 Dave Steib	.05
128 Danny Tartabull	.05
129 Joe Orsulak	.05
130 Tom Brunansky	.05
131 Dick Schofield	.05
132 Candy Maldonado	.05
133 Cecil Fielder	.05
134 Terry Shumpert	.05
135 Greg Gagne	.05
136 Dave Righetti	.05
137 Terry Steinbach	.05
138 Harold Reynolds	.05
139 George Bell	.05
140 Carlos Quintana	.05
141 Ivan Calderon	.05
142 Greg Brock	.05
143 Ruben Sierra	.05
144 Checklist	.05

1990 Donruss Best N.L.

This 144-card set features the top players in the National League for 1990. The 2-1/2" x 3-1/2" cards feature the same design as the regular 1990 Donruss cards, except they have blue, rather than red borders. Traded players are featured with their new teams. This set, along with the A.L. Best set, was available at select retail stores and within the hobby.

		NM/M
Complete Set (144):		7.50
Common Player:		.05
1	Eric Davis	.05
2	Tom Glavine	.20
3	Mike Bielecki	.05
4	Jim Deshaies	.05
5	Mike Scioscia	.05
6	Spike Owen	.05
7	Dwight Gooden	.05
8	Ricky Jordan	.05
9	Doug Drabek	.05
10	Bryn Smith	.05
11	Tony Gwynn	.75
12	John Burkett	.05
13	Nick Esasky	.05
14	Greg Maddux	.75
15	Joe Oliver	.05
16	Mike Scott	.05
17	Tim Belcher	.05
18	Kevin Gross	.05
19	Howard Johnson	.05
20	Darren Daulton	.05
21	John Smiley	.05
22	Ken Dayley	.05
23	Craig Lefferts	.05
24	Will Clark	.05
25	Greg Olson	.05
26	Ryne Sandberg	.75
27	Tom Browning	.05
28	Eric Anthony	.05
29	Juan Samuel	.05
30	Dennis Martinez	.05
31	Kevin Elster	.05
32	Tom Herr	.05
33	Sid Bream	.05
34	Terry Pendleton	.05
35	Kevin Bass	.05
36	Roberto Alomar	.20
37	Jim Presley	.05
38	Les Lancaster	.05
39	Paul O'Neill	.05
40	Dave Smith	.05
41	Kirk Gibson	.05
42	Tim Burke	.05
43	David Cone	.05
44	Ken Howell	.05
45	Barry Bonds	6.00
46	Joe Magrane	.05
47	Andy Benes	.05
48	Gary Carter	.50
49	Pat Combs	.05
50	John Smoltz	.05
51	Mark Grace	.05
52	Barry Larkin	.05
53	Danny Darwin	.05
54	Orel Hershiser	.05
55	Tim Wallach	.05
56	Dave Magadan	.05
57	Roger McDowell	.05
58	Bill Landrum	.05
59	Jose DeLeon	.05
60	Bip Roberts	.05
61	Matt Williams	.05
62	Dale Murphy	.20
63	Dwight Smith	.05
64	Chris Sabo	.05
65	Glenn Davis	.05
66	Jay Howell	.05
67	Andres Galarraga	.05
68	Frank Viola	.05
69	John Kruk	.05
70	Bobby Bonilla	.05
71	Todd Zeile	.05
72	Joe Carter	.05
73	Robby Thompson	.05
74	Jeff Blauser	.05
75	Mitch Williams	.05
76	Rob Dibble	.05
77	Rafael Ramirez	.05
78	Eddie Murray	.50
79	Dave Martinez	.05
80	Darryl Strawberry	.05
81	Dickie Thon	.05
82	Jose Lind	.05
83	Ozzie Smith	.75
84	Bruce Hurst	.05
85	Kevin Mitchell	.05

86	Lonnie Smith	.05
87	Joe Girardi	.05
88	Randy Myers	.05
89	Craig Biggio	.05
90	Fernando Valenzuela	.05
91	Larry Walker	.05
92	John Franco	.05
93	Dennis Cook	.05
94	Bob Walk	.05
95	Pedro Guerrero	.05
96	Checklist	.05
97	Andre Dawson	.25
98	Ed Whitson	.05
99	Steve Bedrosian	.05
100	Oddibe McDowell	.05
101	Todd Benzinger	.05
102	Bill Doran	.05
103	Alfredo Griffin	.05
104	Tim Raines	.05
105	Sid Fernandez	.05
106	Charlie Hayes	.05
107	Mike LaValliere	.05
108	Jose Oquendo	.05
109	Jack Clark	.05
110	Scott Garrelts	.05
111	Ron Gant	.05
112	Shawon Dunston	.05
113	Mariano Duncan	.05
114	Eric Yelding	.05
115	Hubie Brooks	.05
116	Delino DeShields	.05
117	Gregg Jefferies	.05
118	Len Dykstra	.05
119	Andy Van Slyke	.05
120	Lee Smith	.05
121	Benito Santiago	.05
122	Jose Uribe	.05
123	Jeff Treadway	.05
124	Jerome Walton	.05
125	Billy Hatcher	.05
126	Ken Caminiti	.05
127	Kal Daniels	.05
128	Marquis Grissom	.05
129	Kevin McReynolds	.05
130	Wally Backman	.05
131	Willie McGee	.05
132	Terry Kennedy	.05
133	Garry Templeton	.05
134	Lloyd McClendon	.05
135	Daryl Boston	.05
136	Jay Bell	.05
137	Mike Pagliarulo	.05
138	Vince Coleman	.05
139	Brett Butler	.05
140	Von Hayes	.05
141	Ramon Martinez	.05
142	Jack Armstrong	.05
143	Franklin Stubbs	.05
144	Checklist	.05

1990 Donruss Diamond Kings Supers

Donruss made this set available through a mail-in offer. Three wrappers, $10 and $2 for postage were necessary to obtain this set. The cards are exactly the same design as the regular Donruss Diamond Kings except they measure approximately 5" x 6-3/4" in size. The artwork of Dick Perez is featured.

		NM/M
Complete Set (26):		5.00
Common Player:		.10
1	Bo Jackson	.25
2	Steve Sax	.10
3	Ruben Sierra	.10
4	Ken Griffey Jr.	4.00
5	Mickey Tettleton	.10
6	Dave Stewart	.10
7	Jim Deshaies	.10
8	John Smoltz	.10
9	Mike Bielecki	.10
10	Brian Downing	.10
11	Kevin Mitchell	.10
12	Kelly Gruber	.10
13	Joe Magrane	.10
14	John Franco	.10
15	Ozzie Guillen	.10
16	Lou Whitaker	.10
17	John Smiley	.10
18	Howard Johnson	.10
19	Willie Randolph	.10
20	Chris Bosio	.10
21	Tommy Herr	.10
22	Dan Gladden	.10
23	Ellis Burks	.10
24	Pete O'Brien	.10
25	Bryn Smith	.10
26	Ed Whitson	.10

1990 Donruss Learning Series

Cards from this 55-card set were released as part of an educational package available to schools. The cards are styled like the regular-issue 1990 Donruss cards, but feature a special "learning series" logo on the front. The backs feature career highlights, statistics and card numbers. The cards were not released directly to the hobby.

		NM/M
Complete Set (56):		1.00
Common Player:		.05
1	Sandy Alomar	.05
2	John Olerud	.40
3	Pat Combs	.05

		NM/M
Complete Set (55):		25.00
Common Player:		.10
1	George Brett (DK)	3.00
2	Kevin Mitchell	.10
3	Andy Van Slyke	.10
4	Benito Santiago	.10
5	Gary Carter	1.00
6	Jose Canseco	.50
7	Rickey Henderson	1.00
8	Ken Griffey Jr.	4.00
9	Ozzie Smith	2.00
10	Dwight Gooden	.10
11	Ryne Sandberg (DK)	2.00
12	Don Mattingly	2.50
13	Ozzie Guillen	.10
14	Dave Righetti	.10
15	Rick Dempsey	.10
16	Tom Herr	.10
17	Julio Franco	.10
18	Von Hayes	.10
19	Cal Ripken	6.00
20	Alan Trammell	.10
21	Wade Boggs	2.00
22	Glenn Davis	.10
23	Will Clark	.10
24	Nolan Ryan	6.00
25	George Bell	.10
26	Cecil Fielder	.10
27	Gregg Olson	.10
28	Tim Wallach	.10
29	Ron Darling	.10
30	Kelly Gruber	.10
31	Shawn Boskie	.10
32	Mike Greenwell	.10
33	Dave Parker	.10
34	Joe Magrane	.10
35	Dave Stewart	.10
36	Kent Hrbek	.10
37	Robin Yount	1.00
38	Bo Jackson	.15
39	Fernando Valenzuela	.10
40	Sandy Alomar, Jr.	.10
41	Lance Parrish	.10
42	Candy Maldonado	.10
43	Mike LaValliere	.10
44	Jim Abbott	.10
45	Edgar Martinez	.10
46	Kirby Puckett	2.00
47	Delino DeShields	.10
48	Tony Gwynn	2.00
49	Carlton Fisk	1.00
50	Mike Scott	.10
51	Barry Larkin	.10
52	Andre Dawson	.35
53	Tom Glavine	.50
54	Tom Browning	.10
55	Checklist	.05

1991 Donruss Previews

Once again in late 1990 Donruss distributed individual cards from a 12-card preview issue to its dealer network as an introduction to its 1991 issue. Like the previous year's preview cards, the '91 samples utilized the format which would follow on the regular-issue cards, but the photos were different. This has helped create demand for these cards from superstar collectors. Backs are printed in black-and-white and have little more than a player name, card number and MLB logos.

		NM/M
Complete Set (12):		135.00
Common Player:		2.50
1	Dave Justice	2.50
2	Doug Drabek	2.50
3	Scott Chiamparino	2.50
4	Ken Griffey Jr.	35.00
5	Bob Welch	2.50
6	Tino Martinez	2.50
7	Nolan Ryan	45.00
8	Dwight Gooden	2.50
9	Ryne Sandberg	17.50
10	Barry Bonds	45.00
11	Jose Canseco	7.50
12	Eddie Murray	12.00

1991 Donruss

Donruss used a two-series format in 1991. The first series was released in December 1990, and the second in February 1991. The 1991 design is somewhat reminiscent of the 1986 set, with blue borders on Series I cards; green on Se-

Rookies

For the fifth straight year, Donruss issued a 56-card "Rookies" set in 1990. As in previous years, the set is similar in design to the regular Donruss set, except for a new "The Rookies" logo and green borders instead of red. The set is packaged in a special box and includes a Carl Yastrzemski puzzle card.

4	Brian Dubois	.05
5	Felix Jose	.05
6	Delino DeShields	.05
7	Mike Stanton	.05
8	Mike Munoz	.05
9	Craig Grebeck	.05
10	Joe Kraemer	.05
11	Jeff Huson	.05
12	Bill Sampen	.05
13	Brian Bohanon	.05
14	Dave Justice	.40
15	Robin Ventura	.05
16	Greg Vaughn	.05
17	Wayne Edwards	.05
18	Shawn Boskie	.05
19	Carlos Baerga RC	.20
20	Mark Gardner	.05
21	Kevin Appier	.05
22	Mike Harkey	.05
23	Tim Layana	.05
24	Glenallen Hill	.05
25	Jerry Kutzler	.05
26	Mike Blowers	.05
27	Scott Ruskin	.05
28	Dana Kiecker	.05
29	Willie Blair	.05
30	Ben McDonald	.05
31	Todd Zeile	.05
32	Scott Coolbaugh	.05
33	Xavier Hernandez	.05
34	Mike Hartley	.05
35	Kevin Wickander	.05
36	Kevin Wickander	.05
37	Carlos Hernandez	.05
38	Brian Traxler	.05
39	Marty Brown	.05
40	Scott Radinsky	.05
41	Julio Machado	.05
42	Steve Avery	.05
43	Mark Lemke	.05
44	Alan Mills	.05
45	Marquis Grissom	.05
46	Greg Olson	.05
47	Dave Hollins	.05
48	Jerald Clark	.05
49	Eric Anthony	.05
50	Tim Drummond	.05
51	John Burkett	.05
52	Brent Knackert	.05
53	Jeff Shaw	.05
54	John Orton	.05
55	Terry Shumpert	.05
56	Checklist	.05

ries II. Limited edition cards including an autographed Ryne Sandberg card (5,000) were randomly inserted in wax packs. Other features of the set include 40 Rated Rookies, (RR) in the checklist, Legends and Elite insert series, and another Diamond King (DK) subset. Cards were distributed in packs with Willie Stargell puzzle pieces.

		NM/M
Factory Set w/Previews (788):		12.00
Factory Collector's Set (792):		12.00
Complete Set (770):		8.00
Common Player:		.05
Willie Stargell Puzzle:		.50
Series 1 or 2 Pack (15):		.50
Series 1 or 2 Wax Box (36):		12.50
1	Dave Steib/DK	.05
2	Craig Biggio/DK	.05
3	Cecil Fielder/DK	.05
4	Barry Bonds/DK	1.00
5	Barry Larkin/DK	.05
6	Dave Parker/DK	.05
7	Len Dykstra/DK	.05
8	Bobby Thigpen/DK	.05
9	Roger Clemens/DK	.60
10	Ron Gant/DK	.05
11	Delino DeShields/DK	.05
12	Roberto Alomar/DK	.20
13	Sandy Alomar/DK	.05
14	Ryne Sandberg/DK	.50
15	Ramon Martinez/DK	.05
16	Edgar Martinez/DK	.05
17	Dave Magadan/DK	.05
18	Matt Williams/DK	.05
19	Rafael Palmeiro/DK	.40
20	Bob Welch/DK	.05
21	Dave Righetti/DK	.05
22	Brian Harper/DK	.05
23	Gregg Olson/DK	.05
24	Kurt Stillwell/DK	.05
25	Pedro Guerrero/DK	.05
26	Chuck Finley/DK	.05
27	Diamond King checklist	.05
28	Tino Martinez (Rated Rookie)	.05
29	Mark Lewis (RR)	.05
30	Bernard Gilkey RC (RR)	.10
31	Hensley Meulens (RR)	.05
32	Derek Bell RC (RR)	.30
33	Jose Offerman (RR)	.05
34	Terry Bross (RR)	.05
35	Leo Gomez RC (RR)	.05
36	Derrick May (RR)	.05
37	Kevin Morton RC (RR)	.05
38	Moises Alou (RR)	.05
39	Julio Valera RC (RR)	.05
40	Milt Cuyler (RR)	.05
41	Phil Plantier RC (RR)	.10
42	Scott Chiamparino RC (RR)	
43	Ray Lankford RC (RR)	.20
44	Mickey Morandini RC (RR)	
		.10
45	Dave Hansen (RR)	.05
46	Kevin Belcher RC (RR)	.05
47	Darrin Fletcher (RR)	.05
48	Steve Sax/AS	.05
49	Ken Griffey Jr./AS	.30
50a	Jose Canseco/AS (A's in stat line on back.)	.10
50b	Jose Canseco/AS (AL in stat line on back.)	.25
51	Sandy Alomar/AS	.05
52	Cal Ripken, Jr./AS	.50
53	Rickey Henderson/AS	.20
54	Bob Welch/AS	.05
55	Wade Boggs/AS	.25
56	Mark McGwire/AS	.50
57a	Jack McDowell (Career Games 30)	.05
57b	Jack McDowell (Career Games 63)	.25
58	Jose Lind	.05
59	Alex Fernandez	.05
60	Pat Combs	.05
61	Mike Walker RC	.05
62	Juan Samuel	.05
63	Mike Blowers	.05
64	Mark Guthrie	.05
65	Mark Salas	.05
66	Tim Jones	.05
67	Tim Leary	.05
68	Andres Galarraga	.05
69	Bob Milacki	.05

70	Tim Belcher	.05
71	Todd Zeile	.05
72	Jerome Walton	.05
73	Kevin Seitzer	.05
74	Jerald Clark	.05
75	John Smoltz	.05
76	Mike Henneman	.05
77	Ken Griffey Jr.	.65
78	Jim Abbott	.05
79	Gregg Jefferies	.05
80	Kevin Reimer	.05
81	Roger Clemens	.60
82	Mike Fitzgerald	.05
83	Bruce Hurst	.05
84	Eric Davis	.05
85	Paul Molitor	.40
86	Will Clark	.05
87	Mike Bielecki	.05
88	Bret Saberhagen	.05
89	Nolan Ryan	1.00
90	Bobby Thigpen	.05
91	Dickie Thon	.05
92	Duane Ward	.05
93	Luis Polonia	.05
94	Terry Kennedy	.05
95	Kent Hrbek	.05
96	Danny Jackson	.05
97	Sid Fernandez	.05
98	Jimmy Key	.05
99	Franklin Stubbs	.05
100	Checklist 28-103	.05
101	R.J. Reynolds	.05
102	Dave Stewart	.05
103	Dan Pasqua	.05
104	Dan Plesac	.05
105	Mark McGwire	.75
106	John Farrell	.05
107	Don Mattingly	.60
108	Carlton Fisk	.40
109	Ken Oberkfell	.05
110	Darrel Akerfelds	.05
111	Gregg Olson	.05
112	Mike Scioscia	.05
113	Bryn Smith	.05
114	Bob Geren	.05
115	Tom Candiotti	.05
116	Kevin Tapani	.05
117	Jeff Treadway	.05
118	Alan Trammell	.05
119	Pete O'Brien	.05
120	Joel Skinner	.05
121	Mike LaValliere	.05
122	Dwight Evans	.05
123	Jody Reed	.05
124	Lee Guetterman	.05
125	Tim Burke	.05
126	Dave Johnson	.05
127	Fernando Valenzuela	.05
128	Jose DeLeon	.05
129	Andre Dawson	.20
130	Gerald Perry	.05
131	Greg Harris	.05
132	Tom Glavine	.25
133	Lance McCullers	.05
134	Randy Johnson	.40
135	Lance Parrish	.05
136	Mackey Sasser	.05
137	Geno Petralli	.05
138	Dennis Lamp	.05
139	Dennis Martinez	.05
140	Mike Pagliarulo	.05
141	Hal Morris	.05
142	Dave Parker	.05
143	Brett Butler	.05
144	Paul Assenmacher	.05
145	Mark Gubicza	.05
146	Charlie Hough	.05
147	Sammy Sosa	.50
148	Randy Ready	.05
149	Kelly Gruber	.05
150	Devon White	.05
151	Gary Carter	.40
152	Gene Larkin	.05
153	Chris Sabo	.05
154	David Cone	.05
155	Todd Stottlemyre	.05
156	Glenn Wilson	.05
157	Bob Walk	.05
158	Mike Gallego	.05
159	Greg Hibbard	.05
160	Chris Bosio	.05
161	Mike Moore	.05
162	Jerry Browne	.05
163	Steve Sax	.05
164	Melido Perez	.05
165	Danny Darwin	.05
166	Roger McDowell	.05
167	Bill Ripken	.05
168	Mike Sharperson	.05
169	Lee Smith	.05
170	Matt Nokes	.05
171	Jesse Orosco	.05
172	Rick Aguilera	.05
173	Jim Presley	.05
174	Lou Whitaker	.05
175	Harold Reynolds	.05
176	Brook Jacoby	.05
177	Wally Backman	.05
178	Wade Boggs	.50
179	Chuck Cary	.05
180	Tom Foley	.05
181	Pete Harnisch	.05
182	Mike Morgan	.05
183	Bob Tewksbury	.05
184	Joe Girardi	.05
185	Storm Davis	.05
186	Ed Whitson	.05
187	Steve Avery	.05

#	Player	Price
188	Lloyd Moseby	.05
189	Scott Bankhead	.05
190	Mark Langston	.05
191	Kevin McReynolds	.05
192	Julio Franco	.05
193	John Dopson	.05
194	Oil Can Boyd	.05
195	Bip Roberts	.05
196	Billy Hatcher	.05
197	Edgar Diaz	.05
198	Greg Litton	.05
199	Mark Grace	.05
200	Checklist 104-179	.05
201	George Brett	.60
202	Jeff Russell	.05
203	Ivan Calderon	.05
204	Ken Howell	.05
205	Tom Henke	.05
206	Bryan Harvey	.05
207	Steve Bedrosian	.05
208	Al Newman	.05
209	Randy Myers	.05
210	Daryl Boston	.05
211	Manny Lee	.05
212	Dave Smith	.05
213	Don Slaught	.05
214	Walt Weiss	.05
215	Donn Pall	.05
216	Jamie Navarro	.05
217	Willie Randolph	.05
218	Rudy Seanez	.05
219	Jim Leyritz RC	.15
220	Ron Karkovice	.05
221	Ken Caminiti	.05
222a	Von Hayes (Traded players' first names included in How Acquired on back.)	.05
222b	Von Hayes (No first names.)	.05
223	Cal Ripken, Jr.	1.00
224	Lenny Harris	.05
225	Milt Thompson	.05
226	Alvaro Espinoza	.05
227	Chris James	.05
228	Dan Gladden	.05
229	Jeff Blauser	.05
230	Mike Heath	.05
231	Omar Vizquel	.05
232	Doug Jones	.05
233	Jeff King	.05
234	Luis Rivera	.05
235	Ellis Burks	.05
236	Greg Cadaret	.05
237	Dave Martinez	.05
238	Mark Williamson	.05
239	Stan Javier	.05
240	Ozzie Smith	.50
241	Shawn Boskie RC	.05
242	Tom Gordon	.05
243	Tony Gwynn	.50
244	Tommy Gregg	.05
245	Jeff Robinson	.05
246	Keith Comstock	.05
247	Jack Howell	.05
248	Keith Miller	.05
249	Bobby Witt	.05
250	Rob Murphy	.05
251	Spike Owen	.05
252	Garry Templeton	.05
253	Glenn Braggs	.05
254	Ron Robinson	.05
255	Kevin Mitchell	.05
256	Les Lancaster	.05
257	Mel Stottlemyre RC	.10
258	Kenny Rogers	.05
259	Lance Johnson	.05
260	John Kruk	.05
261	Fred McGriff	.05
262	Dick Schofield	.05
263	Trevor Wilson	.05
264	David West	.05
265	Scott Scudder	.05
266	Dwight Gooden	.05
267	Willie Blair RC	.05
268	Mark Portugal	.05
269	Doug Drabek	.05
270	Dennis Eckersley	.35
271	Eric King	.05
272	Robin Yount	.40
273	Carney Lansford	.05
274	Carlos Baerga	.05
275	Dave Righetti	.05
276	Scott Fletcher	.05
277	Eric Yelding	.05
278	Charlie Hayes	.05
279	Jeff Ballard	.05
280	Orel Hershiser	.05
281	Jose Oquendo	.05
282	Mike Witt	.05
283	Mitch Webster	.05
284	Greg Gagne	.05
285	Greg Olson RC	.05
286	Tony Phillips	.05
287	Scott Bradley	.05
288	Cory Snyder	.05
289	Jay Bell	.05
290	Kevin Romine	.05
291	Jeff Robinson	.05
292	Steve Frey	.05
293	Craig Worthington	.05
294	Tim Crews	.05
295	Joe Magrane	.05
296	Hector Villanueva RC	.05
297	Terry Shumpert RC	.05
298	Joe Carter	.05
299	Kent Mercker	.05
300	Checklist 180-255	.05
301	Chet Lemon	.05

#	Player	Price
302	Mike Schooler	.05
303	Dante Bichette	.05
304	Kevin Elster	.05
305	Jeff Huson	.05
306	Greg Harris	.05
307	Marquis Grissom	.05
308	Calvin Schiraldi	.05
309	Mariano Duncan	.05
310	Bill Spiers	.05
311	Scott Garrelts	.05
312	Mitch Williams	.05
313	Mike Macfarlane	.05
314	Kevin Brown	.05
315	Robin Ventura	.05
316	Darren Daulton	.05
317	Pat Borders	.05
318	Mark Eichhorn	.05
319	Jeff Brantley	.05
320	Shane Mack	.05
321	Rob Dibble	.05
322	John Franco	.05
323	Junior Felix	.05
324	Casey Candaele	.05
325	Bobby Bonilla	.05
326	Dave Henderson	.05
327	Wayne Edwards	.05
328	Mark Knudson	.05
329	Terry Steinbach	.05
330	Colby Ward	.05
331	Oscar Azocar RC	.05
332	Scott Radinsky RC	.10
333	Eric Anthony	.05
334	Steve Lake	.05
335	Bob Melvin	.05
336	Kal Daniels	.05
337	Tom Pagnozzi	.05
338	Alan Mills RC	.05
339	Steve Olin	.05
340	Juan Berenguer	.05
341	Francisco Cabrera	.05
342	Dave Bergman	.05
343	Henry Cotto	.05
344	Sergio Valdez	.05
345	Bob Patterson	.05
346	John Marzano	.05
347	Dana Kiecker RC	.05
348	Dion James	.05
349	Hubie Brooks	.05
350	Bill Landrum	.05
351	Bill Sampen RC	.05
352	Greg Briley	.05
353	Paul Gibson	.05
354	Dave Eiland	.05
355	Steve Finley	.05
356	Bob Boone	.05
357	Steve Buechele	.05
358	Chris Hoiles	.05
359	Larry Walker	.05
360	Frank DiPino	.05
361	Mark Grant	.05
362	Dave Magadan	.05
363	Robby Thompson	.05
364	Lonnie Smith	.05
365	Steve Farr	.05
366	Dave Valle	.05
367	Tim Naehring RC	.05
368	Jim Acker	.05
369	Jeff Reardon	.05
370	Tim Teufel	.05
371	Juan Gonzalez	.20
372	Luis Salazar	.05
373	Rick Honeycutt	.05
374	Greg Maddux	.50
375	Jose Uribe	.05
376	Donnie Hill	.05
377	Don Carman	.05
378	Craig Grebeck RC	.05
379	Willie Fraser	.05
380	Glenallen Hill	.05
381	Joe Oliver	.05
382	Randy Bush	.05
383	Alex Cole	.05
384	Norm Charlton	.05
385	Gene Nelson	.05
386a	Checklist 256-331 (Blue Borders)	.05
386b	Checklist 256-331 (Green Borders)	.05
387	Rickey Henderson (MVP)	.20
388	Lance Parrish (MVP)	.05
389	Fred McGriff (MVP)	.05
390	Dave Parker (MVP)	.05
391	Candy Maldonado (MVP)	.05
392	Ken Griffey Jr. (MVP)	.50
393	Gregg Olson (MVP)	.05
394	Rafael Palmeiro (MVP)	.20
395	Roger Clemens (MVP)	.30
396	George Brett (MVP)	.30
397	Cecil Fielder (MVP)	.30
398	Brian Harper (MVP)	.05
399	Bobby Thigpen (MVP)	.05
400	Roberto Kelly (MVP)	.05
401	Danny Darwin (MVP)	.05
402	Dave Justice (MVP)	.05
403	Lee Smith (MVP)	.05
404	Ryne Sandberg (MVP)	.20
405	Eddie Murray (MVP)	.20
406	Tim Wallach (MVP)	.05
407	Kevin Mitchell (MVP)	.05
408	Darryl Strawberry (MVP)	.05
409	Joe Carter (MVP)	.05
410	Len Dykstra (MVP)	.05
411	Doug Drabek (MVP)	.05
412	Chris Sabo (MVP)	.05
413	Paul Marak RC (RR)	.05
414	Tim McIntosh RC (RR)	.05
415	Brian Barnes RC (RR)	.05
416	Eric Gunderson RC (RR)	.05

#	Player	Price
417	Mike Gardiner RC (RR)	.05
418	Steve Carter (RR)	.05
419	Gerald Alexander RC (RR)	.05
420	Rich Garces RC (RR)	.05
421	Chuck Knoblauch RC (RR)	.50
422	Scott Aldred RC (RR)	.05
423	Wes Chamberlain RC (RR)	.05
424	Lance Dickson RC (RR)	.05
425	Greg Colbrunn RC (RR)	.10
426	Rich Delucia RC (RR)	.05
427	Jeff Conine RC (RR)	.50
428	Steve Decker RC (RR)	.05
429	Turner Ward RC (RR)	.05
430	Mo Vaughn (RR)	.05
431	Steve Chitren (RR)	.05
432	Mike Benjamin (RR)	.05
433	Ryne Sandberg/AS	.25
434	Len Dykstra/AS	.05
435	Andre Dawson/AS	.15
436	Mike Scioscia/AS	.05
437	Ozzie Smith/AS	.25
438	Kevin Mitchell/AS	.05
439	Jack Armstrong/AS	.05
440	Chris Sabo/AS	.05
441	Will Clark/AS	.05
442	Mel Hall	.05
443	Mark Gardner	.05
444	Mike Devereaux	.05
445	Kirk Gibson	.05
446	Terry Pendleton	.05
447	Mike Harkey	.05
448	Jim Eisenreich	.05
449	Benito Santiago	.05
450	Oddibe McDowell	.05
451	Cecil Fielder	.05
452	Ken Griffey Sr.	.05
453	Bert Blyleven	.10
454	Howard Johnson	.05
455	Monty Farris	.05
456	Tony Pena	.05
457	Tim Raines	.05
458	Dennis Rasmussen	.05
459	Luis Quinones	.05
460	B.J. Surhoff	.05
461	Ernest Riles	.05
462	Rick Sutcliffe	.05
463	Danny Tartabull	.05
464	Pete Incaviglia	.05
465	Carlos Martinez	.05
466	Ricky Jordan	.05
467	John Cerutti	.05
468	Dave Winfield	.40
469	Francisco Oliveras	.05
470	Roy Smith	.05
471	Barry Larkin	.05
472	Ron Darling	.05
473	David Wells	.05
474	Glenn Davis	.05
475	Neal Heaton	.05
476	Ron Hassey	.05
477	Frank Thomas	.40
478	Greg Vaughn	.05
479	Todd Burns	.05
480	Candy Maldonado	.05
481	Dave LaPoint	.05
482	Alvin Davis	.05
483	Mike Scott	.05
484	Dale Murphy	.20
485	Ben McDonald	.05
486	Jay Howell	.05
487	Vince Coleman	.05
488	Alfredo Griffin	.05
489	Sandy Alomar	.05
490	Kirby Puckett	.50
491	Andres Thomas	.05
492	Jack Morris	.05
493	Matt Young	.05
494	Greg Myers	.05
495	Barry Bonds	1.00
496	Scott Cooper	.05
497	Dan Schatzeder	.05
498	Jesse Barfield	.05
499	Jerry Goff	.05
500	Checklist 332-408	.05
501	Anthony Telford RC	.05
502	Eddie Murray	.40
503	Omar Olivares RC	.05
504	Ryne Sandberg	.50
505	Jeff Montgomery	.05
506	Mark Parent	.05
507	Ron Gant	.05
508	Frank Tanana	.05
509	Jay Buhner	.05
510	Max Venable	.05
511	Wally Whitehurst	.05
512	Gary Pettis	.05
513	Tom Brunansky	.05
514	Tim Wallach	.05
515	Craig Lefferts	.05
516	Tim Layana RC	.05
517	Darryl Hamilton	.05
518	Rick Reuschel	.05
519	Steve Wilson	.05
520	Kurt Stillwell	.05
521	Rafael Palmeiro	.30
522	Ken Patterson	.05
523	Len Dykstra	.05
524	Tony Fernandez	.05
525	Kent Anderson	.05
526	Mark Leonard RC	.05
527	Allan Anderson	.05
528	Tom Browning	.05
529	Frank Viola	.05
530	John Olerud	.05
531	Juan Agosto	.05
532	Zane Smith	.05
533	Scott Sanderson	.05
534	Barry Jones	.05

#	Player	Price
535	Mike Felder	.05
536	Jose Canseco	.20
537	Felix Fermin	.05
538	Roberto Kelly	.05
539	Brian Holman	.05
540	Mark Davidson	.05
541	Terry Mulholland	.05
542	Randy Milligan	.05
543	Jose Gonzalez	.05
544	Craig Wilson RC	.05
545	Mike Hartley	.05
546	Greg Swindell	.05
547	Gary Gaetti	.05
548	Dave Justice	.05
549	Steve Searcy	.05
550	Erik Hanson	.05
551	Dave Stieb	.05
552	Andy Van Slyke	.05
553	Mike Greenwell	.05
554	Kevin Maas	.05
555	Delino Deshields	.05
556	Curt Schilling	.20
557	Ramon Martinez	.05
558	Pedro Guerrero	.05
559	Dwight Smith	.05
560	Mark Davis	.05
561	Shawn Abner	.05
562	Charlie Leibrandt	.05
563	John Shelby	.05
564	Bill Swift	.05
565	Mike Fetters	.05
566	Alejandro Pena	.05
567	Ruben Sierra	.05
568	Carlos Quintana	.05
569	Kevin Gross	.05
570	Derek Lilliquist	.05
571	Jack Armstrong	.05
572	Greg Brock	.05
573	Mike Kingery	.05
574	Greg Smith	.05
575	Brian McRae RC	.10
576	Jack Daugherty	.05
577	Ozzie Guillen	.05
578	Joe Boever	.05
579	Luis Sojo	.05
580	Chili Davis	.05
581	Don Robinson	.05
582	Brian Harper	.05
583	Paul O'Neill	.05
584	Bob Ojeda	.05
585	Mookie Wilson	.05
586	Rafael Ramirez	.05
587	Gary Redus	.05
588	Jamie Quirk	.05
589	Shawn Hilligas	.05
590	Tom Edens RC	.05
591	Joe Klink	.05
592	Charles Nagy	.05
593	Eric Plunk	.05
594	Tracy Jones	.05
595	Craig Biggio	.05
596	Jose DeJesus	.05
597	Mickey Tettleton	.05
598	Chris Gwynn	.05
599	Rex Hudler	.05
600	Checklist 409-506	.05
601	Jim Gott	.05
602	Jeff Manto	.05
603	Nelson Liriano	.05
604	Mark Lemke	.05
605	Clay Parker	.05
606	Edgar Martinez	.05
607	Mark Whiten RC	.10
608	Ted Power	.05
609	Tom Bolton	.05
610	Tom Herr	.05
611	Andy Hawkins	.05
612	Scott Ruskin	.05
613	Ron Kittle	.05
614	John Wetteland	.05
615	Mike Perez RC	.05
616	Dave Clark	.05
617	Brent Mayne	.05
618	Jack Clark	.05
619	Marvin Freeman	.05
620	Edwin Nunez	.05
621	Russ Swan	.05
622	Johnny Ray	.05
623	Charlie O'Brien	.05
624	Joe Bitker RC	.05
625	Mike Marshall	.05
626	Otis Nixon	.05
627	Andy Benes	.05
628	Ron Oester	.05
629	Ted Higuera	.05
630	Kevin Bass	.05
631	Damon Berryhill	.05
632	Bo Jackson	.10
633	Brad Arnsberg	.05
634	Jerry Willard	.05
635	Tommy Greene	.05
636	Bob MacDonald RC	.05
637	Kirk McCaskill	.05
638	John Burkett	.05
639	Paul Abbott RC	.05
640	Todd Benzinger	.05
641	Todd Hundley	.05
642	George Bell	.05
643	Javier Ortiz RC	.05
644	Sid Bream	.05
645	Bob Welch	.05
646	Phil Bradley	.05
647	Bill Krueger	.05
648	Rickey Henderson	.40
649	Kevin Wickander	.05
650	Steve Balboni	.05
651	Gene Harris	.05
652	Jim Deshaies	.05
653	Jason Grimsley	.05
654	Joe Orsulak	.05

#	Player	Price
655	Jimmy Poole RC	.05
656	Felix Jose	.05
657	Dennis Cook	.05
658	Tom Brookens	.05
659	Junior Ortiz	.05
660	Jeff Parrett	.05
661	Jerry Don Gleaton	.05
662	Brent Knackert	.05
663	Rance Mulliniks	.05
664	John Smiley	.05
665	Larry Andersen	.05
666	Willie McGee	.05
667	Chris Nabholz RC	.05
668	Brady Anderson	.05
669	Darren Holmes RC	.10
670	Ken Hill	.05
671	Gary Varsho	.05
672	Bill Pecota	.05
673	Fred Lynn	.05
674	Kevin D. Brown	.05
675	Dan Petry	.05
676	Mike Jackson	.05
677	Wally Joyner	.05
678	Danny Jackson	.05
679	Bill Haselman RC	.05
680	Mike Boddicker	.05
681	Mel Rojas RC	.05
682	Roberto Alomar	.20
683	Dave Justice (R.O.Y.)	.05
684	Chuck Crim	.05
685a	Matt Williams (Last line of Career Highlights ends, "most DP's in.")	.05
685b	Matt Williams (Last line ends "8/24-27/87.")	.25
686	Shawon Dunston	.05
687	Jeff Schulz RC	.05
688	John Barfield RC	.05
689	Gerald Young	.05
690	Luis Gonzalez RC	.75
691	Frank Wills	.05
692	Chuck Finley	.05
693	Sandy Alomar (R.O.Y.)	.05
694	Tim Drummond	.05
695	Herm Winningham	.05
696	Darryl Strawberry	.05
697	Al Leiter	.05
698	Karl Rhodes RC	.05
699	Stan Belinda	.05
700	Checklist 507-604	.05
701	Lance Blankenship	.05
702	Willie Stargell (Puzzle Card)	.05
703	Jim Gantner	.05
704	Reggie Harris RC	.05
705	Rob Ducey	.05
706	Tim Hulett	.05
707	Atlee Hammaker	.05
708	Xavier Hernandez	.05
709	Chuck McElroy	.05
710	John Mitchell	.05
711	Carlos Hernandez	.05
712	Geronimo Pena	.05
713	Jim Neidlinger RC	.05
714	John Orton	.05
715	Terry Leach	.05
716	Mike Stanton	.05
717	Walt Terrell	.05
718	Luis Aquino	.05
719	Bud Black	.05
720	Bob Kipper	.05
721	Jeff Gray RC	.05
722	Jose Rijo	.05
723	Curt Young	.05
724	Jose Vizcaino	.05
725	Randy Tomlin RC	.05
726	Junior Noboa	.05
727	Bob Welch (Award Winner)	.05
728	Gary Ward	.05
729	Rob Deer	.05
730	David Segui RC	.05
731	Mark Carreon	.05
732	Vicente Palacios	.05
733	Sam Horn	.05
734	Howard Farmer RC	.05
735	Ken Dayley	.05
736	Kelly Mann	.05
737	Joe Grahe RC	.05
738	Kelly Downs	.05
739	Jimmy Kremers RC	.05
740	Kevin Appier	.05
741	Jeff Reed	.05
742	Jose Rijo (World Series)	.05
743	Dave Rohde RC	.05
744	Dr. Dirt/Mr. Clean (Len Dykstra, Dale Murphy)	.10
745	Paul Sorrento	.05
746	Thomas Howard	.05
747	Matt Stark RC	.05
748	Harold Baines	.05
749	Doug Dascenzo	.05
750	Doug Drabek (Award Winner)	.05
751	Gary Sheffield	.20
752	Terry Lee RC	.05
753	Jim Vatcher RC	.05
754	Lee Stevens	.05
755	Randy Veres	.05
756	Bill Doran	.05
757	Gary Wayne	.05
758	Pedro Munoz RC	.05
759	Chris Hammond	.05
760	Checklist 605-702	.05
761	Rickey Henderson (MVP)	.20
762	Barry Bonds (MVP)	.50

#	Player	Price
763	Billy Hatcher (World Series)	.05
764	Julio Machado	.05
765	Jose Mesa	.05
766	Willie Randolph (World Series)	.05
767	Scott Erickson RC	.10
768	Travis Fryman	.05
769	Rich Rodriguez RC	.05
770	Checklist 703-770; BC1-BC22	.05

Elite

Donruss released a series of special inserts in 1991. Ten thousand of each Elite card was released, while 7,500 Legend cards and 5,000 Signature cards were issued. Cards were inserted in wax packs and feature marble borders. The Legend card features a Dick Perez drawing. Each card is designated with a serial number on the back.

		NM/M
Complete Set (10):		250.00
Common Player:		15.00
1	Barry Bonds	60.00
2	George Brett	40.00
3	Jose Canseco	25.00
4	Andre Dawson	15.00
5	Doug Drabek	7.50
6	Cecil Fielder	7.50
7	Rickey Henderson	25.00
8	Matt Williams	7.50
---	Nolan Ryan (Legend)	65.00
---	Ryne Sandberg (Signature)	100.00

1991 Donruss Grand Slammers

This set features players who hit grand slams in 1990. The cards are styled after the 1991 Donruss regular-issue cards. The featured player is showcased with a star in the background. The set was included in factory sets and randomly in jumbo packs.

		NM/M
Complete Set (14):		2.00
Common Player:		.10
1	Joe Carter	.10
2	Bobby Bonilla	.10
3	Kal Daniels	.10
4	Jose Canseco	.30
5	Barry Bonds	1.00
6	Jay Buhner	.10
7	Cecil Fielder	.10
8	Matt Williams	.10
9	Andres Galarraga	.10
10	Luis Polonia	.10
11	Mark McGwire	.75
12	Ron Karkovice	.10
13	Darryl Strawberry	.10
14	Mike Greenwell	.10

1991 Donruss Highlights

These inserts feature highlights from the 1990 season. Cards have a "BC" (Bonus Card) prefix to the number and are styled after the 1991 regular-issue Donruss cards. Cards 1-10 feature

George Brett — 3 DECADE CHAMP

blue borders due to their release with Series 1 cards. Cards 11-22 feature green borders and were released with Series 2 cards. A highlight logo appears on the front of the card. Each highlight is explained in depth on the card back.

		NM/M
Complete Set (22):		3.00
Common Player:		.10
1	Mark Langston, Mike Witt (No-Hit Mariners)	.10
2	Randy Johnson (No-Hits Tigers)	.25
3	Nolan Ryan (No-Hits A's)	.50
4	Dave Stewart (No-Hits Blue Jays)	.10
5	Cecil Fielder (50 Homer Club)	.10
6	Carlton Fisk (Record Home Run)	.20
7	Ryne Sandberg (Sets Fielding Records)	.25
8	Gary Carter (Breaks Catching Mark)	.20
9	Mark McGwire (Home Run Milestone)	.45
10	Bo Jackson (4 Consecutive HRs)	.15
11	Fernando Valenzuela (No-Hits Cardinals)	.10
12a	Andy Hawkins (PITCHER)	2.50
12b	Andy Hawkins (No-Hits White Sox)	.10
13	Melido Perez (No-Hits Yankees)	.10
14	Terry Mulholland (No-Hits Giants)	.10
15	Nolan Ryan (300th Win)	.50
16	Delino DeShields (4 Hits In Debut)	.10
17	Cal Ripken (Errorless Games)	.50
18	Eddie Murray (Switch Hit Homers)	.20
19	George Brett (3 Decade Champ)	.30
20	Bobby Thigpen (Shatters Save Mark)	.10
21	Dave Stieb (No-Hits Indians)	.10
22	Willie McGee (NL Batting Champ)	.10

1991 Donruss Diamond Kings Supers

Donruss made this set available through a mail-in offer. Three wrappers, $12 and postage were necessary to obtain this set. The cards are exactly the same design as the regular Donruss Diamond Kings except they measure approximately 5" x 6-3/4" in size. The artwork of Dick Perez is featured.

		NM/M
Complete Set (26):		8.00
Common Player:		.25
1	Dave Steib	.25
2	Craig Biggio	.25
3	Cecil Fielder	.25
4	Barry Bonds	4.50
5	Barry Larkin	.25
6	Dave Parker	.25
7	Len Dykstra	.25
8	Bobby Thigpen	.25
9	Roger Clemens	2.50
10	Ron Gant	.25
11	Delino DeShields	.25
12	Roberto Alomar	.40
13	Sandy Alomar	.25
14	Ryne Sandberg	1.50
15	Ramon Martinez	.25
16	Edgar Martinez	.25
17	Dave Magadan	.25
18	Matt Williams	.25
19	Rafael Palmeiro	1.00
20	Bob Welch	.25
21	Dave Righetti	.25
22	Brian Harper	.25
23	Gregg Olson	.25
24	Kurt Stillwell	.25
25	Pedro Guerrero	.25
26	Chuck Finley	.25

Rookies

Brian Hunter — FIRST BASE

Red borders highlight the 1991 Donruss Rookies cards. This set marks the sixth year that Donruss produced such an issue. As in past years, "The Rookies" logo appears on the card fronts. The set is packaged in a special box and includes a Willie Stargell puzzle card.

		NM/M
Complete Set (56):		4.00
Common Player:		.05
1	Pat Kelly	.05
2	Rich DeLucia	.05
3	Wes Chamberlain	.05
4	Scott Leius	.05
5	Darryl Kile	.05
6	Milt Cuyler	.05
7	Todd Van Poppel	.05
8	Ray Lankford	.05
9	Brian Hunter	.05
10	Tony Perezchica	.05
11	Ced Landrum	.05
12	Dave Burba	.05
13	Ramon Garcia	.05
14	Ed Sprague	.05
15	Warren Newson	.05
16	Paul Faries	.05
17	Luis Gonzalez	.15
18	Charles Nagy	.05
19	Chris Hammond	.05
20	Frank Castillo	.05
21	Pedro Munoz	.05
22	Orlando Merced	.05
23	Jose Melendez	.05
24	Kirk Dressendorfer	.05
25	Heathcliff Slocumb	.05
26	Doug Simons	.05
27	Mike Timlin	.05
28	Jeff Fassero	.05
29	Mark Leiter	.05
30	Jeff Bagwell RC	2.50
31	Brian McRae	.05
32	Mark Whiten	.05
33	Ivan Rodriguez RC	1.50
34	Wade Taylor	.05
35	Darren Lewis	.05
36	Mo Vaughn	.25
37	Mike Remlinger	.05
38	Rick Wilkins	.05
39	Chuck Knoblauch	.25
40	Kevin Morton	.05
41	Carlos Rodriguez	.05
42	Mark Lewis	.05
43	Brent Mayne	.05
44	Chris Haney	.05
45	Denis Boucher	.05
46	Mike Gardiner	.05
47	Jeff Johnson	.05
48	Dean Palmer	.25
49	Chuck McElroy	.05
50	Chris Jones	.05
51	Scott Kamieniecki	.05
52	Al Osuna	.05
53	Rusty Meacham	.05
54	Chito Martinez	.05
55	Reggie Jefferson	.05
56	Checklist	.05

1992 Donruss Previews

Ryan Klesko — BRAVES • FIRST BASE

Four-card cello packs distributed to members of the Donruss dealers' network previewed the forthcoming 1992 baseball card issue. The preview cards have the same format, front and back photos as their counterparts in the regular set. Only the card number, the security underprinting, "Donruss Preview Card," and the stats, complete only through 1990, differ.

		NM/M
Complete Set (12):		25.00
Common Player:		.50
1	Wade Boggs	2.50
2	Barry Bonds	7.50
3	Will Clark	.50
4	Andre Dawson	.75
5	Dennis Eckersley	1.50
6	Robin Ventura	.50
7	Ken Griffey Jr.	4.00
8	Kelly Gruber	.50
9	Ryan Klesko (Rated Rookie)	
10	Cal Ripken, Jr.	7.50
11	Nolan Ryan (Highlight)	7.50
12	Todd Van Poppel	.50

1992 Donruss

John Kruk — PHILLIES • FIRST BASE

For the second consecutive year, Donruss released its card set in two series. The 1992 cards feature improved stock, an anti-counterfeit feature and include both front and back photos. Once again Rated Rookies and All-Stars are included in the set. Special highlight cards also can be found in the 1992 Donruss set. Production was reduced in 1992 compared to 1988-1991. Retail factory sets include four 1992 Leaf preview cards.

		NM/M
Unopened Retail Set (788):		15.00
Unopened Hobby Set (784):		12.50
Unopened "Coca-Cola" Set (784):		25.00
Complete Set (784):		12.00
Common Player:		.05
Rod Carew Puzzle:		.50
Series 1 or 2 Pack (15):		.50
Series 1 or 2 Wax Box (36):		15.00
Blister Rack (92):		1.50
1	Mark Wohlers/RR RC	.05
2	Wil Cordero/RR	.05
3	Kyle Abbott/RR RC	.05
4	Dave Nilsson/RR RC	.05
5	Kenny Lofton/RR	.15
6	Luis Mercedes/RR RC	.05
7	Roger Salkeld/RR RC	.05
8	Eddie Zosky/RR	.05
9	Todd Van Poppel/RR RC	.10
10	Frank Seminara/RR RC	.05
11	Andy Ashby/RR RC	.10
12	Reggie Jefferson/RR	.05
13	Ryan Klesko/RR RC	.05
14	Carlos Garcia/RR RC	.10
15	John Ramos/RR RC	.05
16	Eric Karros/RR	.05
17	Pat Lennon/RR RC	.05
18	Eddie Taubensee/RR RC	.05
19	Roberto Hernandez/RR RC	.05
20	D.J. Dozier/RR	.05
21	Dave Henderson/AS	.05
22	Cal Ripken, Jr./AS	.50
23	Wade Boggs/AS	.25
24	Ken Griffey Jr./AS	.35
25	Jack Morris/AS	.05
26	Danny Tartabull/AS	.05
27	Cecil Fielder/AS	.05
28	Roberto Alomar/AS	.10
29	Sandy Alomar/AS	.05
30	Rickey Henderson/AS	.25
31	Ken Hill	.05
32	John Habyan	.05
33	Otis Nixon (Highlight)	.05
34	Tim Wallach	.05
35	Cal Ripken, Jr.	1.00
36	Gary Carter	.35
37	Juan Agosto	.05
38	Doug Dascenzo	.05
39	Kirk Gibson	.05
40	Benito Santiago	.05
41	Otis Nixon	.05
42	Andy Allanson	.05
43	Brian Holman	.05
44	Dick Schofield	.05
45	Dave Magadan	.05
46	Rafael Palmeiro	.35
47	Jody Reed	.05
48	Ivan Calderon	.05
49	Greg Harris	.05
50	Chris Sabo	.05
51	Paul Molitor	.35
52	Robby Thompson	.05
53	Dave Smith	.05
54	Mark Davis	.05
55	Kevin Brown	.05
56	Donn Pall	.05
57	Len Dykstra	.05
58	Roberto Alomar	.15
59	Jeff Robinson	.05
60	Willie McGee	.05
61	Jay Buhner	.05
62	Mike Pagliarulo	.05
63	Paul O'Neill	.05
64	Hubie Brooks	.05
65	Kelly Gruber	.05
66	Ken Caminiti	.05
67	Gary Redus	.05
68	Harold Baines	.05
69	Charlie Hough	.05
70	B.J. Surhoff	.05
71	Walt Weiss	.05
72	Shawn Hillegas	.05
73	Roberto Kelly	.05
74	Jeff Ballard	.05
75	Craig Biggio	.05
76	Pat Combs	.05
77	Jeff Robinson	.05
78	Tim Belcher	.05
79	Cris Carpenter	.05
80	Checklist 1-79	.05
81	Steve Avery	.05
82	Chris James	.05
83	Brian Harper	.05
84	Charlie Leibrandt	.05
85	Mickey Tettleton	.05
86	Pete O'Brien	.05
87	Danny Darwin	.05
88	Bob Walk	.05
89	Jeff Reardon	.05
90	Bobby Rose	.05
91	Danny Jackson	.05
92	John Morris	.05
93	Bud Black	.05
94	Tommy Greene (Highlight)	.05
95	Rick Aguilera	.05
96	Gary Gaetti	.05
97	David Cone	.05
98	John Olerud	.05
99	Joel Skinner	.05
100	Jay Bell	.05
101	Bob Milacki	.05
102	Norm Charlton	.05
103	Chuck Crim	.05
104	Terry Steinbach	.05
105	Juan Samuel	.05
106	Steve Howe	.05
107	Rafael Belliard	.05
108	Joey Cora	.05
109	Tommy Greene	.05
110	Gregg Olson	.05
111	Frank Tanana	.05
112	Lee Smith	.05
113	Greg Harris	.05
114	Dwayne Henry	.05
115	Chili Davis	.05
116	Kent Mercker	.05
117	Brian Barnes	.05
118	Rich DeLucia	.05
119	Andre Dawson	.20
120	Carlos Baerga	.05
121	Mike LaValliere	.05
122	Jeff Gray	.05
123	Bruce Hurst	.05
124	Alvin Davis	.05
125	John Candelaria	.05
126	Matt Nokes	.05
127	George Bell	.05
128	Bret Saberhagen	.05
129	Jeff Russell	.05
130	Jim Abbott	.05
131	Bill Gullickson	.05
132	Todd Zeile	.05
133	Dave Winfield	.35
134	Wally Whitehurst	.05
135	Matt Williams	.05
136	Tom Browning	.05
137	Marquis Grissom	.05
138	Erik Hanson	.05
139	Rob Dibble	.05
140	Don August	.05
141	Tom Henke	.05
142	Dan Pasqua	.05
143	George Brett	.60
144	Jerald Clark	.05
145	Robin Ventura	.05
146	Dale Murphy	.20
147	Dennis Eckersley	.30
148	Eric Yelding	.05
149	Mario Diaz	.05
150	Casey Candaele	.05
151	Steve Olin	.05
152	Luis Salazar	.05
153	Kevin Maas	.05
154	Nolan Ryan (Highlight)	.50
155	Barry Jones	.05
156	Chris Hoiles	.05
157	Bobby Ojeda	.05
158	Pedro Guerrero	.05
159	Paul Assenmacher	.05
160	Checklist 80-157	.05
161	Mike Macfarlane	.05
162	Craig Lefferts	.05
163	Brian Hunter RC	.05
164	Alan Trammell	.05
165	Ken Griffey Jr.	.65
166	Lance Parrish	.05
167	Brian Downing	.05
168	John Barfield	.05
169	Jack Clark	.05
170	Chris Nabholz	.05
171	Tim Teufel	.05
172	Chris Hammond	.05
173	Robin Yount	.35
174	Dave Righetti	.05
175	Joe Girardi	.05
176	Mike Boddicker	.05
177	Dean Palmer	.05
178	Greg Hibbard	.05
179	Randy Ready	.05
180	Devon White	.05
181	Mark Eichhorn	.05
182	Mike Felder	.05
183	Joe Klink	.05
184	Steve Bedrosian	.05
185	Barry Larkin	.05
186	John Franco	.05
187	Ed Sprague RC	.05
188	Mark Portugal	.05
189	Jose Lind	.05
190	Bob Welch	.05
191	Alex Fernandez	.05
192	Gary Sheffield	.20
193	Rickey Henderson	.35
194	Rod Nichols	.05
195	Scott Kamieniecki RC	.05
196	Mike Flanagan	.05
197	Steve Finley	.05
198	Darren Daulton	.05
199	Leo Gomez	.05
200	Mike Morgan	.05
201	Bob Tewksbury	.05
202	Sid Bream	.05
203	Sandy Alomar	.05
204	Greg Gagne	.05
205	Juan Berenguer	.05
206	Cecil Fielder	.05
207	Randy Johnson	.35
208	Tony Pena	.05
209	Doug Drabek	.05
210	Wade Boggs	.45
211	Bryan Harvey	.05
212	Jose Vizcaino	.05
213	Alonzo Powell RC	.05
214	Will Clark	.05
215	Rickey Henderson (Highlight)	.20
216	Jack Morris	.05
217	Junior Felix	.05
218	Vince Coleman	.05
219	Jimmy Key	.05
220	Alex Cole	.05
221	Bill Landrum	.05
222	Randy Milligan	.05
223	Jose Rijo	.05
224	Greg Vaughn	.05
225	Dave Stewart	.05
226	Lenny Harris	.05
227	Scott Sanderson	.05
228	Jeff Blauser	.05
229	Ozzie Guillen	.05
230	John Kruk	.05
231	Bob Melvin	.05
232	Milt Cuyler	.05
233	Felix Jose	.05
234	Ellis Burks	.05
235	Pete Harnisch	.05
236	Kevin Tapani	.05
237	Terry Pendleton	.05
238	Mark Gardner	.05
239	Harold Reynolds	.05
240	Checklist 158-237	.05
241	Mike Harkey	.05
242	Felix Fermin	.05
243	Barry Bonds	1.00
244	Roger Clemens	.60
245	Dennis Rasmussen	.05
246	Jose DeLeon	.05
247	Orel Hershiser	.05
248	Mel Hall	.05
249	Rick Wilkins RC	.05
250	Tom Gordon	.05
251	Kevin Reimer	.05
252	Luis Polonia	.05
253	Mike Henneman	.05
254	Tom Pagnozzi	.05
255	Chuck Finley	.05
256	Mackey Sasser	.05
257	John Burkett	.05
258	Hal Morris	.05
259	Larry Walker	.05
260	Billy Swift	.05
261	Joe Oliver	.05
262	Julio Machado	.05
263	Todd Stottlemyre	.05
264	Matt Merullo	.05
265	Brent Mayne	.05
266	Thomas Howard	.05
267	Lance Johnson	.05
268	Terry Mulholland	.05
269	Rick Honeycutt	.05
270	Luis Gonzalez	.05
271	Jose Guzman	.05
272	Jimmy Jones	.05
273	Mark Lewis	.05
274	Rene Gonzales	.05
275	Jeff Johnson RC	.05
276	Dennis Martinez (Highlight)	.05
277	Delino DeShields	.05
278	Sam Horn	.05
279	Kevin Gross	.05
280	Jose Oquendo	.05
281	Mark Grace	.05
282	Mark Gubicza	.05
283	Fred McGriff	.05
284	Ron Gant	.05
285	Lou Whitaker	.05
286	Edgar Martinez	.05
287	Ron Tingley	.05
288	Kevin McReynolds	.05
289	Ivan Rodriguez	.30
290	Mike Gardiner	.05
291	Chris Haney RC	.05
292	Darrin Jackson	.05
293	Bill Doran	.05
294	Ted Higuera	.05
295	Jeff Brantley	.05
296	Les Lancaster	.05
297	Jim Eisenreich	.05
298	Ruben Sierra	.05
299	Scott Radinsky	.05
300	Jose DeJesus	.05
301	Mike Timlin RC	.05
302	Luis Sojo	.05
303	Kelly Downs	.05
304	Scott Bankhead	.05
305	Pedro Munoz	.05
306	Scott Scudder	.05
307	Kevin Elster	.05
308	Duane Ward	.05
309	Darryl Kile RC	.10
310	Orlando Merced	.05
311	Dave Henderson	.05
312	Tim Raines	.05
313	Mark Lee RC	.05
314	Mike Gallego	.05
315	Charles Nagy	.05
316	Jesse Barfield	.05
317	Todd Frohwirth	.05
318	Al Osuna	.05
319	Darrin Fletcher	.05
320	Checklist 238-316	.05
321	David Segui	.05
322	Stan Javier	.05
323	Bryn Smith	.05
324	Jeff Treadway	.05
325	Mark Whiten	.05
326	Kent Hrbek	.05
327	Dave Justice	.05
328	Tony Phillips	.05
329	Rob Murphy	.05
330	Kevin Morton	.05
331	John Smiley	.05
332	Luis Rivera	.05
333	Wally Joyner	.05
334	Heathcliff Slocumb RC	.05
335	Rick Cerone	.05
336	Mike Remlinger RC	.05
337	Mike Moore	.05
338	Lloyd McClendon	.05
339	Al Newman	.05
340	Kirk McCaskill	.05
341	Howard Johnson	.05
342	Greg Myers	.05
343	Kal Daniels	.05
344	Bernie Williams	.05
345	Shane Mack	.05
346	Gary Thurman	.05
347	Dante Bichette	.05
348	Mark McGwire	.75
349	Travis Fryman	.05
350	Ray Lankford	.05
351	Mike Jeffcoat	.05
352	Jack McDowell	.05
353	Mitch Williams	.05
354	Mike Devereaux	.05
355	Andres Galarraga	.05
356	Henry Cotto	.05
357	Scott Bailes	.05
358	Jeff Bagwell	.35
359	Scott Leius	.05
360	Zane Smith	.05
361	Bill Pecota	.05
362	Tony Fernandez	.05
363	Glenn Braggs	.05
364	Bill Spiers	.05
365	Vicente Palacios	.05
366	Tim Burke	.05
367	Randy Tomlin	.05
368	Kenny Rogers	.05
369	Brett Butler	.05
370	Pat Kelly	.05
371	Bip Roberts	.05
372	Gregg Jefferies	.05
373	Kevin Bass	.05
374	Ron Karkovice	.05
375	Paul Gibson	.05
376	Bernard Gilkey	.05
377	Dave Gallagher	.05
378	Bill Wegman	.05
379	Pat Borders	.05
380	Ed Whitson	.05
381	Gilberto Reyes	.05
382	Russ Swan	.05
383	Andy Van Slyke	.05
384	Wes Chamberlain	.05
385	Steve Chitren	.05
386	Greg Olson	.05
387	Brian McRae	.05
388	Rich Rodriguez	.05
389	Steve Decker	.05
390	Chuck Knoblauch	.05
391	Bobby Witt	.05
392	Eddie Murray	.35
393	Juan Gonzalez	.20
394	Scott Ruskin	.05
395	Jay Howell	.05
396	Checklist 317-396	.05
397	Royce Clayton/RR	.05
398	John Jaha/RR RC	.05

No.	Player	Price
399	Dan Wilson/RR	.05
400	Archie Corbin/RR RC	.05
401	Barry Manuel/RR RC	.05
402	Kim Batiste/RR	.05
403	Pat Mahomes/RR RC	.05
404	Dave Fleming/RR	.05
405	Jeff Juden/RR	.05
406	Jim Thome/RR	.40
407	Sam Militello/RR	.05
408	Jeff Nelson/RR RC	.05
409	Anthony Young/RR	.05
410	Tino Martinez/RR	.05
411	Jeff Mutis/RR	.05
412	Rey Sanchez/RR RC	.05
413	Chris Gardner/RR RC	.05
414	John Vander Wal/RR RC	.10
415	Reggie Sanders/RR	.05
416	Brian Williams/RR RC	.05
417	Mo Sanford/RR	.05
418	David Weathers/RR RC	.05
419	Hector Fajardo/RR RC	.05
420	Steve Foster/RR	.05
421	Lance Dickson/RR	.05
422	Andre Dawson/AS	.15
423	Ozzie Smith/AS	.25
424	Chris Sabo/AS	.05
425	Tony Gwynn/AS	.25
426	Tom Glavine/AS	.05
427	Bobby Bonilla/AS	.05
428	Will Clark/AS	.05
429	Ryne Sandberg/AS	.25
430	Benito Santiago/AS	.05
431	Ivan Calderon/AS	.05
432	Ozzie Smith	.45
433	Tim Leary	.05
434	Bret Saberhagen (Highlight)	.05
435	Mel Rojas	.05
436	Ben McDonald	.05
437	Tim Crews	.05
438	Rex Hudler	.05
439	Chico Walker	.05
440	Kurt Stillwell	.05
441	Tony Gwynn	.45
442	John Smoltz	.05
443	Lloyd Moseby	.05
444	Mike Schooler	.05
445	Joe Grahe	.05
446	Dwight Gooden	.05
447	Oil Can Boyd	.05
448	John Marzano	.05
449	Bret Barberie	.05
450	Mike Maddux	.05
451	Jeff Reed	.05
452	Dale Sveum	.05
453	Jose Uribe	.05
454	Bob Scanlan	.05
455	Kevin Appier	.05
456	Jeff Huson	.05
457	Ken Patterson	.05
458	Ricky Jordan	.05
459	Tom Candiotti	.05
460	Lee Stevens	.05
461	Rod Beck RC	.10
462	Dave Valle	.05
463	Scott Erickson	.05
464	Chris Jones	.05
465	Mark Carreon	.05
466	Rob Ducey	.05
467	Jim Corsi	.05
468	Jeff King	.05
469	Curt Young	.05
470	Bo Jackson	.15
471	Chris Bosio	.05
472	Jamie Quirk	.05
473	Jesse Orosco	.05
474	Alvaro Espinoza	.05
475	Joe Orsulak	.05
476	Checklist 397-477	.05
477	Gerald Young	.05
478	Wally Backman	.05
479	Juan Bell	.05
480	Mike Scioscia	.05
481	Omar Olivares	.05
482	Francisco Cabrera	.05
483	Greg Swindell	.05
484	Terry Leach	.05
485	Tommy Gregg	.05
486	Scott Aldred	.05
487	Greg Briley	.05
488	Phil Plantier	.05
489	Curtis Wilkerson	.05
490	Tom Brunansky	.05
491	Mike Fetters	.05
492	Frank Castillo	.05
493	Joe Boever	.05
494	Kirt Manwaring	.05
495	Wilson Alvarez (Highlight)	.05
496	Gene Larkin	.05
497	Gary DiSarcina	.05
498	Frank Viola	.05
499	Manuel Lee	.05
500	Albert Belle	.05
501	Stan Belinda	.05
502	Dwight Evans	.05
503	Eric Davis	.05
504	Darren Holmes	.05
505	Mike Bordick	.05
506	Dave Hansen	.05
507	Lee Guetterman	.05
508	Keith Mitchell RC	.05
509	Melido Perez	.05
510	Dickie Thon	.05
511	Mark Williamson	.05
512	Mark Salas	.05
513	Milt Thompson	.05
514	Mo Vaughn	.05
515	Jim Deshaies	.05
516	Rich Garces	.05
517	Lonnie Smith	.05
518	Spike Owen	.05
519	Tracy Jones	.05
520	Greg Maddux	.45
521	Carlos Martinez	.05
522	Neal Heaton	.05
523	Mike Greenwell	.05
524	Andy Benes	.05
525	Jeff Schaefer	.05
526	Mike Sharperson	.05
527	Wade Taylor	.05
528	Jerome Walton	.05
529	Storm Davis	.05
530	Jose Hernandez RC	.05
531	Mark Langston	.05
532	Rob Deer	.05
533	Geronimo Pena	.05
534	Juan Guzman RC	.10
535	Pete Schourek	.05
536	Todd Benzinger	.05
537	Billy Hatcher	.05
538	Tom Foley	.05
539	Dave Cochrane	.05
540	Mariano Duncan	.05
541	Edwin Nunez	.05
542	Rance Mulliniks	.05
543	Carlton Fisk	.35
544	Luis Aquino	.05
545	Ricky Bones	.05
546	Craig Grebeck	.05
547	Charlie Hayes	.05
548	Jose Canseco	.25
549	Andujar Cedeno	.05
550	Geno Petralli	.05
551	Javier Ortiz	.05
552	Rudy Seanez	.05
553	Rich Gedman	.05
554	Eric Plunk	.05
555	Nolan Ryan, Rich Gossage (Highlight)	.25
556	Checklist 478-555	.05
557	Greg Colbrunn	.05
558	Chito Martinez RC	.05
559	Darryl Strawberry	.05
560	Luis Alicea	.05
561	Dwight Smith	.05
562	Terry Shumpert	.05
563	Jim Vatcher	.05
564	Deion Sanders	.10
565	Walt Terrell	.05
566	Dave Burba	.05
567	Dave Howard	.05
568	Todd Hundley	.05
569	Jack Daugherty	.05
570	Scott Cooper	.05
571	Bill Sampen	.05
572	Jose Melendez	.05
573	Freddie Benavides	.05
574	Jim Gantner	.05
575	Trevor Wilson	.05
576	Ryne Sandberg	.45
577	Kevin Seitzer	.05
578	Gerald Alexander	.05
579	Mike Huff	.05
580	Von Hayes	.05
581	Derek Bell	.05
582	Mike Stanley	.05
583	Kevin Mitchell	.05
584	Mike Jackson	.05
585	Dan Gladden	.05
586	Ted Power	.05
587	Jeff Innis	.05
588	Bob MacDonald	.05
589	Jose Tolentino RC	.05
590	Bob Patterson	.05
591	Scott Brosius RC	.10
592	Frank Thomas	.35
593	Darryl Hamilton	.05
594	Kirk Dressendorfer	.05
595	Jeff Shaw	.05
596	Don Mattingly	.60
597	Glenn Davis	.05
598	Andy Mota	.05
599	Jason Grimsley	.05
600	Jimmy Poole	.05
601	Jim Gott	.05
602	Stan Royer	.05
603	Marvin Freeman	.05
604	Denis Boucher	.05
605	Denny Neagle	.05
606	Mark Lemke	.05
607	Jerry Don Gleaton	.05
608	Brent Knackert	.05
609	Carlos Quintana	.05
610	Bobby Bonilla	.05
611	Joe Hesketh	.05
612	Daryl Boston	.05
613	Shawon Dunston	.05
614	Danny Cox	.05
615	Darren Lewis	.05
616	Alejandro Pena, Kent Mercker, Mark Wohlers (Highlight)	.05
617	Kirby Puckett	.45
618	Franklin Stubbs	.05
619	Chris Donnels	.05
620	David Wells	.05
621	Mike Aldrete	.05
622	Bob Kipper	.05
623	Anthony Telford	.05
624	Randy Myers	.05
625	Willie Randolph	.05
626	Joe Slusarski	.05
627	John Wetteland	.05
628	Greg Cadaret	.05
629	Tom Glavine	.20
630	Wilson Alvarez	.05
631	Wally Ritchie	.05
632	Mike Mussina	.25
633	Mark Leiter	.05
634	Gerald Perry	.05
635	Matt Young	.05
636	Checklist 556-635	.05
637	Scott Hemond	.05
638	David West	.05
639	Jim Clancy	.05
640	Doug Piatt	.05
641	Omar Vizquel	.05
642	Rick Sutcliffe	.05
643	Glenallen Hill	.05
644	Gary Varsho	.05
645	Tony Fossas	.05
646	Jack Howell	.05
647	Jim Campanis RC	.05
648	Chris Gwynn	.05
649	Jim Leyritz	.05
650	Chuck McElroy	.05
651	Sean Berry	.05
652	Donald Harris	.05
653	Don Slaught	.05
654	Rusty Meacham RC	.05
655	Scott Terry	.05
656	Ramon Martinez	.05
657	Keith Miller	.05
658	Ramon Garcia	.05
659	Milt Hill RC	.05
660	Steve Frey	.05
661	Bob McClure	.05
662	Ced Landrum RC	.05
663	Doug Henry RC	.05
664	Candy Maldonado	.05
665	Carl Willis	.05
666	Jeff Montgomery	.05
667	Craig Shipley RC	.05
668	Warren Newson RC	.05
669	Mickey Morandini	.05
670	Brook Jacoby	.05
671	Ryan Bowen RC	.05
672	Bill Krueger	.05
673	Rob Mallicoat	.05
674	Doug Jones	.05
675	Scott Livingstone	.05
676	Danny Tartabull	.05
677	Joe Carter (Highlight)	.05
678	Cecil Espy	.05
679	Randy Velarde	.05
680	Bruce Ruffin	.05
681	Ted Wood RC	.05
682	Dan Plesac	.05
683	Eric Bullock	.05
684	Junior Ortiz	.05
685	Dave Hollins	.05
686	Dennis Martinez	.05
687	Larry Andersen	.05
688	Doug Simons	.05
689	Tim Spehr RC	.05
690	Calvin Jones RC	.05
691	Mark Guthrie	.05
692	Alfredo Griffin	.05
693	Joe Carter	.05
694	Terry Mathews RC	.05
695	Pascual Perez	.05
696	Gene Nelson	.05
697	Gerald Williams	.05
698	Chris Cron RC	.05
699	Steve Buechele	.05
700	Paul McClellan	.05
701	Jim Lindeman	.05
702	Francisco Oliveras	.05
703	Rob Maurer RC	.05
704	Pat Hentgen RC	.15
705	Jaime Navarro	.05
706	Mike Magnante RC	.05
707	Nolan Ryan	1.00
708	Bobby Thigpen	.05
709	John Cerutti	.05
710	Steve Wilson	.05
711	Hensley Meulens	.05
712	Rheal Cormier RC	.05
713	Scott Bradley	.05
714	Mitch Webster	.05
715	Roger Mason	.05
716	Checklist 636-716	.05
717	Jeff Fassero RC	.05
718	Cal Eldred	.05
719	Sid Fernandez	.05
720	Bob Zupcic RC	.05
721	Jose Offerman	.05
722	Cliff Brantley RC	.05
723	Ron Darling	.05
724	Dave Stieb	.05
725	Hector Villanueva	.05
726	Mike Hartley	.05
727	Arthur Rhodes RC	.05
728	Randy Bush	.05
729	Steve Sax	.05
730	Dave Otto	.05
731	John Wehner RC	.05
732	Dave Martinez	.05
733	Ruben Amaro RC	.05
734	Billy Ripken	.05
735	Steve Farr	.05
736	Shawn Abner	.05
737	Gil Heredia RC	.05
738	Ron Jones	.05
739	Tony Castillo	.05
740	Sammy Sosa	.45
741	Julio Franco	.05
742	Tim Naehring	.05
743	Steve Wapnick RC	.05
744	Craig Wilson	.05
745	Darrin Chapin RC	.05
746	Chris George RC	.05
747	Mike Simms	.05
748	Rosario Rodriguez	.05
749	Skeeter Barnes	.05
750	Roger McDowell	.05
751	Dann Howitt	.05
752	Paul Sorrento	.05
753	Braulio Castillo RC	.05
754	Yorkis Perez RC	.05
755	Willie Fraser	.05
756	Jeremy Hernandez RC	.05
757	Curt Schilling	.20
758	Steve Lyons	.05
759	Dave Anderson	.05
760	Willie Banks	.05
761	Mark Leonard	.05
762	Jack Armstrong	.05
763	Scott Servais	.05
764	Ray Stephens	.05
765	Junior Noboa	.05
766	Jim Olander RC	.05
767	Joe Magrane	.05
768	Lance Blankenship	.05
769	Mike Humphreys RC	.05
770	Jarvis Brown RC	.05
771	Damon Berryhill	.05
772	Alejandro Pena	.05
773	Jose Mesa	.05
774	Gary Cooper RC	.05
775	Carney Lansford	.05
776	Mike Bielecki	.05
777	Charlie O'Brien	.05
778	Carlos Hernandez	.05
779	Howard Farmer	.05
780	Mike Stanton	.05
781	Reggie Harris	.05
782	Xavier Hernandez	.05
783	Bryan Hickerson RC	.05
784	Checklist 717-BC8	.05

1992 Donruss Bonus Cards

The eight bonus cards were randomly inserted in 1992 foil packs and are numbered with a "BC" prefix. Both leagues' MVPs, Cy Young and Rookie of the Year award winners are featured, as are logo cards for the expansion Colorado Rockies and Florida Marlins. Cards are standard size in a format similar to the regular issue.

		NM/M
Complete Set (8):		5.00
Common Player:		.25
1	Cal Ripken, Jr. (MVP)	2.50
2	Terry Pendleton (MVP)	.25
3	Roger Clemens (Cy Young)	2.00
4	Tom Glavine (Cy Young)	.40
5	Chuck Knoblauch (Rookie of the Year)	.25
6	Jeff Bagwell (Rookie of the Year)	1.50
7	Colorado Rockies	.25
8	Florida Marlins	.25

Diamond Kings

Donruss changed its Diamond Kings style and distribution in 1992. The cards still feature the art of Dick Perez, but quality was improved from past years. The cards were randomly inserted in foil packs. One player from each team is featured. Card numbers have a "DK" prefix.

		NM/M
Complete Set (27):		17.50
Common Player:		.40
1	Paul Molitor	.50
2	Will Clark	.50
3	Joe Carter	.50
4	Julio Franco	.50
5	Cal Ripken, Jr.	6.00
6	Dave Justice	.50
7	George Bell	.50
8	Frank Thomas	2.00
9	Wade Boggs	4.00
10	Scott Sanderson	.50
11	Jeff Bagwell	2.00
12	John Kruk	.50
13	Felix Jose	.50
14	Harold Baines	.50
15	Dwight Gooden	.50
16	Brian McRae	.50
17	Jay Bell	.50
18	Brett Butler	.50
19	Hal Morris	.50
20	Mark Langston	.50
21	Scott Erickson	.50
22	Randy Johnson	2.00
23	Greg Swindell	.50
24	Dennis Martinez	.50
25	Tony Phillips	.50
26	Fred McGriff	.50
27	Checklist	.10

1992 Donruss Diamond Kings Supers

Produced in very limited numbers, possibly as a prototype for use in a sales presentation to a major retail chain, these 4-7/8" x 6-3/4" cards are identical in virtually everything but size to the regular 1992 DK inserts. Both front and back feature a high-gloss finish.

		NM/M
Complete Set (27):		900.00
Common Player:		15.00
1	Paul Molitor	95.00
2	Will Clark	15.00
3	Joe Carter	15.00
4	Julio Franco	15.00
5	Cal Ripken, Jr.	335.00
6	Dave Justice	15.00
7	George Bell	15.00
8	Frank Thomas	100.00
9	Wade Boggs	125.00
10	Scott Sanderson	15.00
11	Jeff Bagwell	95.00
12	John Kruk	15.00
13	Felix Jose	15.00
14	Harold Baines	15.00
15	Dwight Gooden	15.00
16	Brian McRae	15.00
17	Jay Bell	15.00
18	Brett Butler	15.00
19	Hal Morris	15.00
20	Mark Langston	15.00
21	Scott Erickson	15.00
22	Randy Johnson	75.00
23	Greg Swindell	15.00
24	Dennis Martinez	15.00
25	Tony Phillips	15.00
26	Fred McGriff	15.00
27	Checklist (Dick Perez)	5.00

Elite

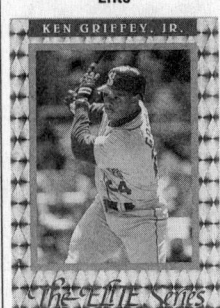

Donruss continued its Elite series in 1992 by inserting cards in foil packs. Each card was released in the same quantity as the 1991 inserts - 10,000 Elite, 7,500 Legend and 5,000 Signature. The Elite cards, now featuring a prismatic border, are numbered as a continuation of the 1991 issue.

		NM/M
Complete Set (12):		300.00
Common Player:		7.50
9	Wade Boggs	15.00
10	Joe Carter	7.50
11	Will Clark	7.50
12	Dwight Gooden	7.50
13	Ken Griffey Jr.	30.00
14	Tony Gwynn	15.00
15	Howard Johnson	7.50
16	Terry Pendleton	7.50
17	Kirby Puckett	15.00
18	Frank Thomas	15.00
---	Rickey Henderson (Legend)	20.00
---	Cal Ripken, Jr. (Signature)	250.00

Rookies

Donruss increased the size of its Rookies set in 1992 to include 132 cards. In the past the cards were released only in boxed set form, but the 1992 cards were available in packs. Special "Phenoms" cards were randomly inserted into Rookies packs. The Phenoms cards feature black borders, while the Rookies cards are styled after the regular 1992 Donruss issue. The cards are numbered alphabetically.

		NM/M
Complete Set (132):		6.00
Common Player:		.05
Pack (12):		.50
Wax Box (36):		10.00
1	Kyle Abbott	.05
2	Troy Afenir	.05
3	Rich Amaral	.05
4	Ruben Amaro	.05
5	Billy Ashley	.05
6	Pedro Astacio	.05
7	Jim Austin	.05
8	Robert Ayrault	.05
9	Kevin Baez	.05
10	Esteban Beltre	.05
11	Brian Bohanon	.05
12	Kent Bottenfield	.05
13	Jeff Branson	.05
14	Brad Brink	.05
15	John Briscoe	.05
16	Doug Brocail	.05
17	Rico Brogna	.05
18	J.T. Bruett	.05
19	Jacob Brumfield	.05
20	Jim Bullinger	.05
21	Kevin Campbell	.05
22	Pedro Castellano	.05
23	Mike Christopher	.05
24	Archi Cianfrocco	.05
25	Mark Clark	.05
26	Craig Colbert	.05
27	Victor Cole	.05
28	Steve Cooke	.05
29	Tim Costo	.05
30	Chad Curtis	.05
31	Doug Davis	.05
32	Gary DiSarcina	.05
33	John Doherty	.05
34	Mike Draper	.05
35	Monty Fariss	.05
36	Bien Figueroa	.05
37	John Flaherty	.05
38	Tim Fortugno	.05
39	Eric Fox	.05
40	Jeff Frye RC	.05
41	Ramon Garcia	.05
42	Brent Gates	.05
43	Tom Goodwin	.05
44	Buddy Groom	.05
45	Jeff Grotewold	.05
46	Juan Guerrero	.05
47	Johnny Guzman	.05
48	Shawn Hare	.05
49	Ryan Hawblitzel	.05
50	Bert Heffernan	.05
51	Butch Henry	.05
52	Cesar Hernandez	.05

#	Player	Price
53	Vince Horsman	.05
54	Steve Hosey	.05
55	Pat Howell	.05
56	Peter Hoy	.05
57	Jon Hurst	.05
58	Mark Hutton	.05
59	Shawn Jeter	.05
60	Joel Johnston	.05
61	Jeff Kent	1.00
62	Kurt Knudsen	.05
63	Kevin Koslofski	.05
64	Danny Leon	.05
65	Jesse Levis	.05
66	Tom Marsh	.05
67	Ed Martel	.05
68	Al Martin	.05
69	Pedro Martinez	2.00
70	Derrick May	.05
71	Matt Maysey	.05
72	Russ McGinnis	.05
73	Tim McIntosh	.05
74	Jim McNamara	.05
75	Jeff McNeely	.05
76	Rusty Meacham	.05
77	Tony Melendez	.05
78	Henry Mercedes	.05
79	Paul Miller	.05
80	Joe Millette	.05
81	Blas Minor	.05
82	Dennis Moeller	.05
83	Raul Mondesi	.25
84	Rob Natal	.05
85	Troy Neel	.05
86	David Nied	.05
87	Jerry Nielsen	.05
88	Donovan Osborne	.05
89	John Patterson	.05
90	Roger Pavlik	.05
91	Dan Peltier	.05
92	Jim Pena	.05
93	William Pennyfeather	.05
94	Mike Perez	.05
95	Hipolito Pichardo	.05
96	Greg Pirkl	.05
97	Harvey Pulliam	.05
98	Manny Ramirez RC	3.00
99	Pat Rapp	.05
100	Jeff Reboulet	.05
101	Darren Reed	.05
102	Shane Reynolds	.05
103	Bill Risley	.05
104	Ben Rivera	.05
105	Henry Rodriguez	.05
106	Rico Rossy	.05
107	Johnny Ruffin	.05
108	Steve Scarsone	.05
109	Tim Scott	.05
110	Steve Shifflett	.05
111	Dave Silvestri	.05
112	Matt Stairs	.05
113	William Suero	.05
114	Jeff Tackett	.05
115	Eddie Taubensee	.05
116	Rick Trlicek	.05
117	Scooter Tucker	.05
118	Shane Turner	.05
119	Julio Valera	.05
120	Paul Wagner	.05
121	Tim Wakefield	.05
122	Mike Walker	.05
123	Bruce Walton	.05
124	Lenny Webster	.05
125	Bob Wickman	.05
126	Mike Williams	.05
127	Kerry Woodson	.05
128	Eric Young	.05
129	Kevin Young	.05
130	Pete Young	.05
131	Checklist	.05
132	Checklist	.05

Rookie Phenoms

The first 12 cards in this insert set were available in Donruss Rookies foil packs. Cards 13-20 were found randomly packed in jumbo packs. Predominantly black on both front and back, the borders are highlighted with gold. A gold-foil "Phenoms" appears at top front.

		NM/M
Complete Set (20):		12.50
Common Player:		.25
1	Moises Alou	.25
2	Bret Boone	.50
3	Jeff Conine	.25

#	Player	Price
4	Dave Fleming	.25
5	Tyler Green	.25
6	Eric Karros	.25
7	Pat Listach	.25
8	Kenny Lofton	.25
9	Mike Piazza	-10.00
10	Tim Salmon	.50
11	Andy Stankiewicz	.25
12	Dan Walters	.25
13	Ramon Caraballo	.25
14	Brian Jordan	.25
15	Ryan Klesko	.25
16	Sam Militello	.25
17	Frank Seminara	.25
18	Salomon Torres	.25
19	John Valentin	.25
20	Wil Cordero	.25

Update

RICK SUTCLIFFE ORIOLES - PITCHER

Each retail factory set of 1992 Donruss cards contained a cellowrapped four-card selection from this 22-card Update set. The cards feature the same basic format as the regular '92 Donruss, except they carry a "U" prefix to the card number on back. The cards feature rookies, highlights and traded players from the 1992 season.

		NM/M
Complete Set (22):		15.00
Common Player:		.50
1	Pat Listach/RR	.50
2	Andy Stankiewicz/RR	.50
3	Brian Jordan/RR	.50
4	Dan Walters/RR	.50
5	Chad Curtis/RR	.50
6	Kenny Lofton/RR	1.50
7	Mark McGwire (Highlight)	8.00
8	Eddie Murray (Highlight)	1.00
9	Jeff Reardon (Highlight)	.50
10	Frank Viola	.50
11	Gary Sheffield	.75
12	George Bell	.50
13	Rick Sutcliffe	.50
14	Wally Joyner	.50
15	Kevin Seitzer	.50
16	Bill Krueger	.50
17	Danny Tartabull	.50
18	Dave Winfield	2.00
19	Gary Carter	1.50
20	Bobby Bonilla	.50
21	Cory Snyder	.50
22	Bill Swift	.50

1992 Donruss/Durivage Montreal Expos

SPIKE OWEN Shortstop

Green borders and posed portrait photos are featured in this custom-published team set which Donruss produced for the Quebec bakery Durivage. Bilingual backs have personal data, recent major league stats and appropriate logos on a gray pinstriped background. Roster changes are reflected in the assignment of the same number to different players in several cases.

		NM/M
Complete Set (26):		50.00
Common Player:		2.00
Album:		5.00
1	Bret Barberie	2.00

#	Player	Price
2a	Chris Haney	2.00
2b	Brian Barnes	2.00
3a	Bill Sampen	2.00
3b	Phil Bradley	2.00
4	Ivan Calderon	2.00
5	Gary Carter	10.00
6	Delino DeShields	2.00
7	Jeff Fassero	2.00
8	Darrin Fletcher	2.00
9	Mark Gardner	2.00
10	Marquis Grissom	2.00
11	Ken Hill	2.00
12	Dennis Martinez	2.00
13	Chris Nabholz	2.00
14	Spike Owen	2.00
15a	Tom Runnells	2.00
15b	Felipe Alou	3.00
16a	John Vander Wal	2.00
16b	Matt Stairs	2.00
17a	Bill Landrum	2.00
17b	Dave Wainhouse	2.00
18	Larry Walker	10.00
19	Tim Wallach	2.00
20	John Wetteland	2.00
---	Checklist	1.00

1993 Donruss Previews

ROGER CLEMENS RHP

Twenty-two of the game's biggest stars were selected for inclusion in the preview version of Donruss' 1993 baseball card set. The previews follow the same basic format of the regular-issue 1993 except for the addition of the word "PREVIEW" above the card number in the home plate on back. Front photos are different between the preview and issued versions.

		NM/M
Complete Set (22):		60.00
Common Player:		1.50
1	Tom Glavine	2.00
2	Ryne Sandberg	5.00
3	Barry Larkin	1.50
4	Jeff Bagwell	4.00
5	Eric Karros	1.50
6	Larry Walker	1.50
7	Eddie Murray	4.00
8	Darren Daulton	1.50
9	Andy Van Slyke	1.50
10	Gary Sheffield	2.00
11	Will Clark	1.50
12	Cal Ripken Jr.	9.00
13	Roger Clemens	6.00
14	Frank Thomas	4.00
15	Cecil Fielder	1.50
16	George Brett	6.00
17	Robin Yount	4.00
18	Don Mattingly	6.00
19	Dennis Eckersley	3.50
20	Ken Griffey Jr.	7.50
21	Jose Canseco	2.50
22	Roberto Alomar	2.00

1993 Donruss

ROBERTO ALOMAR 2B

Rated Rookies and a randomly inserted Diamond Kings subset once again are featured in the 1993 Donruss set. Series I of the set includes 396 cards. Card fronts feature white borders surrounding a full-color player photo. The flip sides feature an additional photo, biographical information and ca-

---

reer statistics. The cards are numbered on the back and the card's series is given with the number. The cards are UV coated. Series II contains a subset of players labeled with an "Expansion Draft" headline over their Marlins or Rockies team logo on front, even though the player photos are in the uniform of their previous team.

		NM/M
Complete Set (792):		10.00
Common Player:		.05
Series 1 or 2 Pack (14):		.50
Series 1 or 2 Box (36):		10.00
1	Craig Lefferts	.05
2	Kent Mercker	.05
3	Phil Plantier	.05
4	Alex Arias RC	.05
5	Julio Valera	.05
6	Dan Wilson	.05
7	Frank Thomas	.50
8	Eric Anthony	.05
9	Derek Lilliquist	.05
10	Rafael Bournigal RC	.05
11	Manny Alexander RC (Rated Rookie)	.05
12	Bret Barberie	.05
13	Mickey Tettleton	.05
14	Anthony Young	.05
15	Tim Spehr	.05
16	Bob Ayrault RC	.05
17	Bill Wegman	.05
18	Jay Bell	.05
19	Rick Aguilera	.05
20	Todd Zeile	.05
21	Steve Farr	.05
22	Andy Benes	.05
23	Lance Blankenship	.05
24	Ted Wood	.05
25	Omar Vizquel	.05
26	Steve Avery	.05
27	Brian Bohanon	.05
28	Rick Wilkins	.05
29	Devon White	.05
30	Bobby Ayala RC	.05
31	Leo Gomez	.05
32	Mike Simms	.05
33	Ellis Burks	.05
34	Steve Wilson	.05
35	Jim Abbott	.05
36	Tim Wallach	.05
37	Wilson Alvarez	.05
38	Daryl Boston	.05
39	Sandy Alomar, Jr.	.05
40	Mitch Williams	.05
41	Rico Brogna	.05
42	Gary Varsho	.05
43	Kevin Appier	.05
44	Eric Wedge/RR	.05
45	Dante Bichette	.05
46	Jose Oquendo	.05
47	Mike Trombley RC	.05
48	Dan Walters	.05
49	Gerald Williams	.05
50	Bud Black	.05
51	Bobby Witt	.05
52	Mark Davis	.05
53	Shawn Barton RC	.05
54	Paul Assenmacher	.05
55	Kevin Reimer	.05
56	Billy Ashley/RR RC	.05
57	Eddie Zosky	.05
58	Chris Sabo	.05
59	Billy Ripken	.05
60	Scooter Tucker RC	.05
61	Tim Wakefield/RR RC	.10
62	Mitch Webster	.05
63	Jack Clark	.05
64	Mark Gardner	.05
65	Lee Stevens	.05
66	Todd Hundley	.05
67	Bobby Thigpen	.05
68	Dave Hollins	.05
69	Jack Armstrong	.05
70	Alex Cole	.05
71	Mark Carreon	.05
72	Todd Worrell	.05
73	Steve Shifflett RC	.05
74	Jerald Clark	.05
75	Paul Molitor	.50
76	Larry Carter RC	.05
77	Rich Rowland	.05
78	Damon Berryhill	.05
79	Willie Banks	.05
80	Hector Villanueva	.05
81	Mike Gallego	.05
82	Tim Belcher	.05
83	Mike Bordick	.05
84	Craig Biggio	.05
85	Lance Parrish	.05
86	Brett Butler	.05
87	Mike Timlin	.05
88	Brian Barnes	.05
89	Brady Anderson	.05
90	D.J. Dozier	.05
91	Frank Viola	.05
92	Darren Daulton	.05
93	Chad Curtis	.05
94	Zane Smith	.05
95	George Bell	.05
96	Rex Hudler	.05
97	Mark Whiten	.05
98	Tim Teufel	.05
99	Kevin Ritz	.05

#	Player	Price
100	Jeff Brantley	.05
101	Jeff Conine	.05
102	Vinny Castilla	.05
103	Greg Vaughn	.05
104	Steve Buechele	.05
105	Darren Reed	.05
106	Bip Roberts	.05
107	John Habyan	.05
108	Scott Servais	.05
109	Walt Weiss	.05
110	J.T. Snow/RR	.50
111	Jay Buhner	.05
112	Darryl Strawberry	.05
113	Roger Pavlik RC	.05
114	Chris Nabholz	.05
115	Pat Borders	.05
116	Pat Howell RC	.05
117	Gregg Olson	.05
118	Curt Schilling	.25
119	Roger Clemens	.65
120	Victor Cole	.05
121	Gary DiSarcina	.05
122	Checklist 1-80	.05
123	Steve Sax	.05
124	Chuck Carr	.05
125	Mark Lewis	.05
126	Tony Gwynn	.60
127	Travis Fryman	.05
128	Dave Burba	.05
129	Wally Joyner	.05
130	John Smoltz	.05
131	Cal Eldred	.05
132	Checklist 81-159	.05
133	Arthur Rhodes	.05
134	Jeff Blauser	.05
135	Scott Cooper	.05
136	Doug Strange	.05
137	Luis Sojo	.05
138	Jeff Branson RC	.05
139	Alex Fernandez	.05
140	Ken Caminiti	.05
141	Charles Nagy	.05
142	Tom Candiotti	.05
143	Willie Green/RR	.05
144	John Vander Wal	.05
145	Kurt Knudsen RC	.05
146	John Franco	.05
147	Eddie Pierce RC	.05
148	Kim Batiste	.05
149	Darren Holmes	.05
150	Steve Cooke RC	.05
151	Terry Jorgensen	.05
152	Mark Clark RC	.05
153	Randy Velarde	.05
154	Greg Harris	.05
155	Kevin Campbell RC	.05
156	John Burkett	.05
157	Kevin Mitchell	.05
158	Deion Sanders	.05
159	Jose Canseco	.25
160	Jeff Hartsock RC	.05
161	Tom Quinlan RC	.05
162	Tim Pugh RC	.05
163	Glenn Davis	.05
164	Shane Reynolds RC	.10
165	Jody Reed	.05
166	Mike Sharperson	.05
167	Scott Lewis	.05
168	Dennis Martinez	.05
169	Scott Radinsky	.05
170	Dave Gallagher	.05
171	Jim Thome	.45
172	Terry Mulholland	.05
173	Milt Cuyler	.05
174	Bob Patterson	.05
175	Jeff Montgomery	.05
176	Tim Salmon/RR	1.
177	Franklin Stubbs	.05
178	Donovan Osborne	.05
179	Jeff Reboulet RC	.05
180	Jeremy Hernandez	.05
181	Charlie Hayes	.05
182	Matt Williams	.05
183	Mike Raczka	.05
184	Francisco Cabrera	.05
185	Rich DeLucia	.05
186	Sammy Sosa	.60
187	Ivan Rodriguez	.45
188	Bret Boone/RR	.15
189	Juan Guzman	.05
190	Tom Browning	.05
191	Randy Milligan	.05
192	Steve Finley	.05
193	John Patterson/RR	.05
194	Kip Gross	.05
195	Tony Fossas	.05
196	Ivan Calderon	.05
197	Junior Felix	.05
198	Pete Schourek	.05
199	Craig Grebeck	.05
200	Juan Bell	.05
201	Guillermo Hill	.05
202	Danny Jackson	.05
203	John Kiely	.05
204	Bob Tewksbury	.05
205	Kevin Koslofski RC	.05
206	Craig Shipley	.05
207	John Jaha	.05
208	Royce Clayton	.05
209	Mike Piazza/RR	2.00
210	Ron Gant	.05
211	Scott Erickson	.05
212	Doug Dascenzo	.05
213	Andy Stankiewicz	.05
214	Geronimo Berroa	.05
215	Dennis Eckersley	.05
216	Al Osuna	.05
217	Tino Martinez	.05

#	Player	Price
218	Henry Rodriguez RC	.05
219	Ed Sprague	.05
220	Ken Hill	.05
221	Chito Martinez	.05
222	Bret Saberhagen	.05
223	Mike Greenwell	.05
224	Mickey Morandini	.05
225	Chuck Finley	.05
226	Denny Neagle	.05
227	Kirk McCaskill	.05
228	Rheal Cormier	.05
229	Paul Sorrento	.05
230	Darrin Jackson	.05
231	Rob Deer	.05
232	Bill Swift	.05
233	Kevin McReynolds	.05
234	Terry Pendleton	.05
235	Dave Nilsson	.05
236	Chuck McElroy	.05
237	Derek Parks	.05
238	Norm Charlton	.05
239	Matt Nokes	.05
240	Juan Guerrero RC	.05
241	Jeff Parrett	.05
242	Ryan Thompson/RR	.05
243	Dave Fleming	.05
244	Dave Hansen	.05
245	Monty Fariss	.05
246	Archi Cianfrocco RC	.05
247	Pat Hentgen	.05
248	Bill Pecota	.05
249	Ben McDonald	.05
250	Cliff Brantley	.05
251	John Valentin RC	.05
252	Jeff King	.05
253	Reggie Williams RC	.05
254	Checklist 160-238	.05
255	Ozzie Guillen	.05
256	Mike Perez	.05
257	Thomas Howard	.05
258	Kurt Stillwell	.05
259	Mike Henneman	.05
260	Steve Decker	.05
261	Brent Mayne	.05
262	Otis Nixon	.05
263	Mark Keifer RC	.05
264	Checklist 239-317	.05
265	Richie Lewis RC	.05
266	Pat Gomez RC	.05
267	Scott Taylor RC	.05
268	Shawon Dunston	.05
269	Greg Myers	.05
270	Tim Costo	.05
271	Greg Hibbard	.05
272	Pete Harnisch	.05
273	Dave Mlicki RC	.05
274	Orel Hershiser	.05
275	Sean Berry/RR	.05
276	Doug Simons	.05
277	John Doherty RC	.05
278	Eddie Murray	.50
279	Chris Haney	.05
280	Stan Javier	.05
281	Jaime Navarro	.05
282	Orlando Merced	.05
283	Kent Hrbek	.05
284	Bernard Gilkey	.05
285	Russ Springer	.05
286	Mike Maddux	.05
287	Eric Fox RC	.05
288	Mark Leonard	.05
289	Tim Leary	.05
290	Brian Hunter	.05
291	Donald Harris	.05
292	Bob Scanlan	.05
293	Turner Ward	.05
294	Hal Morris	.05
295	Jimmy Poole	.05
296	Doug Jones	.05
297	Tony Pena	.05
298	Ramon Martinez	.05
299	Tim Fortugno RC	.05
300	Marquis Grissom	.05
301	Lance Johnson	.05
302	Jeff Kent RC	1.00
303	Reggie Jefferson	.05
304	Wes Chamberlain	.05
305	Shawn Hare RC	.05
306	Mike LaValliere	.05
307	Gregg Jefferies	.05
308	Troy Neel/RR RC	.05
309	Pat Listach	.05
310	Geronimo Pena	.05
311	Pedro Munoz	.05
312	Guillermo Velasquez RC	.05
313	Roberto Kelly	.05
314	Mike Jackson	.05
315	Rickey Henderson	.50
316	Mark Lemke	.05
317	Erik Hanson	.05
318	Derrick May	.05
319	Geno Petralli	.05
320	Melvin Nieves/RR	.05
321	Doug Linton RC	.05
322	Rob Dibble	.05
323	Chris Hoiles	.05
324	Jimmy Jones	.05
325	Dave Staton/RR	.05
326	Pedro Martinez	.05
327	Paul Quantrill RC	.05
328	Greg Colbrunn	.05
329	Hilly Hathaway RC	.05
330	Jeff Innis	.05
331	Ron Karkovice	.05
332	Keith Shepherd RC	.05
333	Alan Embree RC	.05
334	Paul Wagner RC	.05
335	Dave Haas RC	.05

#	Player	Price
336	Ozzie Canseco	.05
337	Bill Sampen	.05
338	Rich Rodriguez	.05
339	Dean Palmer	.05
340	Greg Litton	.05
341	Jim Tatum/RR	.05
342	Todd Haney RC	.05
343	Larry Casian	.05
344	Ryne Sandberg	.60
345	Sterling Hitchcock RC	.10
346	Chris Hammond	.05
347	Vince Horsman RC	.05
348	Butch Henry RC	.05
349	Dann Howitt	.05
350	Roger McDowell	.05
351	Jack Morris	.05
352	Bill Krueger	.05
353	Cris Colon RC	.05
354	Joe Vitko RC	.05
355	Willie McGee	.05
356	Jay Baller	.05
357	Pat Mahomes	.05
358	Roger Mason	.05
359	Jerry Nielsen RC	.05
360	Tom Pagnozzi	.05
361	Kevin Baez RC	.05
362	Tim Scott RC	.05
363	Domingo Martinez RC	.05
364	Kirt Manwaring	.05
365	Rafael Palmeiro	.45
366	Ray Lankford	.05
367	Tim McIntosh	.05
368	Jessie Hollins RC	.05
369	Scott Leius	.05
370	Bill Doran	.05
371	Sam Militello RC	.05
372	Ryan Bowen	.05
373	Dave Henderson	.05
374	Dan Smith/RR	.05
375	Steve Reed RC	.05
376	Jose Offerman	.05
377	Kevin Brown	.05
378	Darrin Fletcher	.05
379	Duane Ward	.05
380	Wayne Kirby/RR	.05
381	Steve Scarsone RC	.05
382	Mariano Duncan	.05
383	Ken Ryan RC	.05
384	Lloyd McClendon	.05
385	Brian Holman	.05
386	Braulio Castillo	.05
387	Danny Leon RC	.05
388	Omar Olivares	.05
389	Kevin Wickander	.05
390	Fred McGriff	.05
391	Phil Clark	.05
392	Darren Lewis	.05
393	Phil Hiatt RC	.10
394	Mike Morgan	.05
395	Shane Mack	.05
396	Checklist 318-396	.05
397	David Segui	.05
398	Rafael Belliard	.05
399	Tim Naehring	.05
400	Frank Castillo	.05
401	Joe Grahe	.05
402	Reggie Sanders	.05
403	Roberto Hernandez	.05
404	Luis Gonzalez	.05
405	Carlos Baerga	.05
406	Carlos Hernandez	.05
407	Pedro Astacio/RR	.05
408	Mel Rojas	.05
409	Scott Livingstone	.05
410	Chico Walker	.05
411	Brian McRae	.05
412	Ben Rivera	.05
413	Ricky Bones	.05
414	Andy Van Slyke	.05
415	Chuck Knoblauch	.05
416	Luis Alicea	.05
417	Bob Wickman	.05
418	Doug Brocail	.05
419	Scott Brosius	.05
420	Rod Beck	.05
421	Edgar Martinez	.05
422	Ryan Klesko	.05
423	Nolan Ryan	1.50
424	Rey Sanchez	.05
425	Roberto Alomar	.20
426	Barry Larkin	.05
427	Mike Mussina	.30
428	Jeff Bagwell	.50
429	Mo Vaughn	.05
430	Eric Karros	.05
431	John Orton	.05
432	Wil Cordero	.05
433	Jack McDowell	.05
434	Howard Johnson	.05
435	Albert Belle	.05
436	John Kruk	.05
437	Skeeter Barnes	.05
438	Don Slaught	.05
439	Rusty Meacham	.05
440	Tim Laker/RR	.05
441	Robin Yount	.50
442	Brian Jordan	.05
443	Kevin Tapani	.05
444	Gary Sheffield	.25
445	Rich Monteleone	.05
446	Will Clark	.05
447	Jerry Browne	.05
448	Jeff Treadway	.05
449	Mike Schooler	.05
450	Mike Harkey	.05
451	Julio Franco	.05
452	Kevin Young/RR	.05
453	Kelly Gruber	.05
454	Jose Rijo	.05
455	Mike Devereaux	.05
456	Andujar Cedeno	.05
457	Damion Easley/RR	.05
458	Kevin Gross	.05
459	Matt Young	.05
460	Matt Stairs	.05
461	Luis Polonia	.05
462	Dwight Gooden	.05
463	Warren Newson	.05
464	Jose DeLeon	.05
465	Jose Mesa	.05
466	Danny Cox	.05
467	Dan Gladden	.05
468	Gerald Perry	.05
469	Mike Boddicker	.05
470	Jeff Gardner	.05
471	Doug Henry	.05
472	Mike Benajmin	.05
473	Dan Peltier/RR	.05
474	Mike Stanton	.05
475	John Smiley	.05
476	Dwight Smith	.05
477	Jim Leyritz	.05
478	Dwayne Henry	.05
479	Mark McGwire	1.00
480	Pete Incaviglia	.05
481	Dave Cochrane	.05
482	Eric Davis	.05
483	John Olerud	.05
484	Ken Bottenfield	.05
485	Mark McLemore	.05
486	Dave Magadan	.05
487	John Marzano	.05
488	Ruben Amaro	.05
489	Rob Ducey	.05
490	Stan Belinda	.05
491	Dan Pasqua	.05
492	Joe Magrane	.05
493	Brook Jacoby	.05
494	Gene Harris	.05
495	Mark Leiter	.05
496	Bryan Hickerson	.05
497	Tom Gordon	.05
498	Pete Smith	.05
499	Chris Bosio	.05
500	Shawn Boskie	.05
501	Dave West	.05
502	Milt Hill	.05
503	Pat Kelly	.05
504	Joe Boever	.05
505	Terry Steinbach	.05
506	Butch Huskey/RR	.05
507	David Valle	.05
508	Mike Scioscia	.05
509	Kenny Rogers	.05
510	Moises Alou	.05
511	David Wells	.05
512	Mackey Sasser	.05
513	Todd Frohwirth	.05
514	Ricky Jordan	.05
515	Mike Gardiner	.05
516	Gary Redus	.05
517	Gary Gaetti	.05
518	Checklist 397-476	.05
519	Carlton Fisk	.50
520	Ozzie Smith	.60
521	Rod Nichols	.05
522	Benito Santiago	.05
523	Bill Gullickson	.05
524	Robby Thompson	.05
525	Mike Macfarlane	.05
526	Sid Bream	.05
527	Darryl Hamilton	.05
528	Checklist 477-555	.05
529	Jeff Tackett	.05
530	Greg Olson	.05
531	Bob Zupcic	.05
532	Mark Grace	.25
533	Steve Frey	.05
534	Dave Martinez	.05
535	Robin Ventura	.05
536	Casey Candaele	.05
537	Kenny Lofton	.05
538	Jay Howell	.05
539	Fernando Ramsey/RR	.05
540	Larry Walker	.05
541	Cecil Fielder	.05
542	Lee Guetterman	.05
543	Keith Miller	.05
544	Len Dykstra	.05
545	B.J. Surhoff	.05
546	Bob Walk	.05
547	Brian Harper	.05
548	Lee Smith	.05
549	Danny Tartabull	.05
550	Frank Seminara	.05
551	Henry Mercedes	.05
552	Dave Righetti	.05
553	Ken Griffey Jr.	.75
554	Tom Glavine	.25
555	Juan Gonzalez	.25
556	Jim Bullinger	.05
557	Derek Bell	.05
558	Cesar Hernandez	.05
559	Cal Ripken, Jr.	1.50
560	Eddie Taubensee	.05
561	John Flaherty	.05
562	Todd Benzinger	.05
563	Hubie Brooks	.05
564	Delino DeShields	.05
565	Tim Raines	.05
566	Sid Fernandez	.05
567	Steve Olin	.05
568	Tommy Greene	.05
569	Buddy Groom	.05
570	Randy Tomlin	.05
571	Hipolito Pichardo	.05
572	Rene Arocha/RR	.05
573	Mike Fetters	.05
574	Felix Jose	.05
575	Gene Larkin	.05
576	Bruce Hurst	.05
577	Bernie Williams	.05
578	Trevor Wilson	.05
579	Bob Welch	.05
580	Dave Justice	.05
581	Randy Johnson	.50
582	Jose Vizcaino	.05
583	Jeff Huson	.05
584	Rob Maurer/RR	.05
585	Todd Stottlemyre	.05
586	Joe Oliver	.05
587	Bob Milacki	.05
588	Rob Murphy	.05
589	Greg Pirkl/RR	.05
590	Lenny Harris	.05
591	Luis Rivera	.05
592	John Wetteland	.05
593	Mark Langston	.05
594	Bobby Bonilla	.05
595	Esteban Beltre	.05
596	Mike Hartley	.05
597	Felix Fermin	.05
598	Carlos Garcia	.05
599	Frank Tanana	.05
600	Pedro Guerrero	.05
601	Terry Shumpert	.05
602	Wally Whitehurst	.05
603	Kevin Seitzer	.05
604	Chris James	.05
605	Greg Gohr/RR	.05
606	Mark Wohlers	.05
607	Kirby Puckett	.60
608	Greg Maddux	.60
609	Don Mattingly	.65
610	Greg Cadaret	.05
611	Dave Stewart	.05
612	Mark Portugal	.05
613	Pete O'Brien	.05
614	Bobby Ojeda	.05
615	Joe Carter	.05
616	Pete Young	.05
617	Sam Horn	.05
618	Vince Coleman	.05
619	Wade Boggs	.60
620	Todd Pratt RC	.05
621	Ron Tingley	.05
622	Doug Drabek	.05
623	Scott Hemond	.05
624	Tim Jones	.05
625	Dennis Cook	.05
626	Jose Melendez	.05
627	Mike Munoz	.05
628	Jim Pena	.05
629	Gary Thurman	.05
630	Charlie Leibrandt	.05
631	Scott Fletcher	.05
632	Andre Dawson	.25
633	Greg Gagne	.05
634	Greg Swindell	.05
635	Kevin Maas	.05
636	Xavier Hernandez	.05
637	Ruben Sierra	.05
638	Dimitri Young/RR	.05
639	Harold Reynolds	.05
640	Tom Goodwin	.05
641	Todd Burns	.05
642	Jeff Fassero	.05
643	Dave Winfield	.50
644	Willie Randolph	.05
645	Luis Mercedes	.05
646	Dale Murphy	.20
647	Danny Darwin	.05
648	Dennis Moeller	.05
649	Chuck Crim	.05
650	Checklist 556-634	.05
651	Shawn Abner	.05
652	Tracy Woodson	.05
653	Scott Scudder	.05
654	Tom Lampkin	.05
655	Alan Trammell	.05
656	Cory Snyder	.05
657	Chris Gwynn	.05
658	Lonnie Smith	.05
659	Jim Austin	.05
660	Checklist 635-713	.05
661	Tim Hulett	.05
662	Marvin Freeman	.05
663	Greg Harris	.05
664	Heathcliff Slocumb	.05
665	Mike Butcher	.05
666	Steve Foster	.05
667	Donn Pall	.05
668	Darryl Kile	.05
669	Jesse Levis	.05
670	Jim Gott	.05
671	Mark Hutton RC	.05
672	Brian Drahman	.05
673	Chad Kreuter	.05
674	Tony Fernandez	.05
675	Jose Lind	.05
676	Kyle Abbott	.05
677	Dan Plesac	.05
678	Barry Bonds	1.50
679	Chili Davis	.05
680	Stan Royer	.05
681	Scott Kamienicki	.05
682	Carlos Martinez	.05
683	Mike Moore	.05
684	Candy Maldanado	.05
685	Jeff Nelson	.05
686	Lou Whitaker	.05
687	Jose Guzman	.05
688	Manuel Lee	.05
689	Bob MacDonald	.05
690	Scott Bankhead	.05
691	Alan Mills	.05
692	Brian Williams	.05
693	Tom Brunansky	.05
694	Lenny Webster	.05
695	Greg Briley	.05
696	Paul O'Neill	.05
697	Joey Cora	.05
698	Charlie O'Brien	.05
699	Junior Ortiz	.05
700	Ron Darling	.05
701	Tony Phillips	.05
702	William Pennyfeather	.05
703	Mark Gubicza	.05
704	Steve Hosey/RR	.05
705	Henry Cotto	.05
706	David Hulse RC	.05
707	Mike Pagliarulo	.05
708	Dave Stieb	.05
709	Melido Perez	.05
710	Jimmy Key	.05
711	Jeff Russell	.05
712	David Cone	.05
713	Russ Swan	.05
714	Mark Guthrie	.05
715	Checklist 714-792	.05
716	Al Martin/RR	.05
717	Randy Knorr	.05
718	Mike Stanley	.05
719	Rick Sutcliffe	.05
720	Terry Leach	.05
721	Chipper Jones/RR	1.00
722	Jim Eisenreich	.05
723	Tom Henke	.05
724	Jeff Frye	.05
725	Harold Baines	.05
726	Scott Sanderson	.05
727	Tom Foley	.05
728	Bryan Harvey/ED	.05
729	Tom Edens	.05
730	Eric Young/ED	.05
731	Dave Weathers/ED	.05
732	Spike Owen	.05
733	Scott Aldred/ED	.05
734	Cris Carpenter/ED	.05
735	Dion James	.05
736	Joe Girardi/ED	.05
737	Nigel Wilson/ED	.05
738	Scott Chiamparino/ED	.05
739	Jeff Reardon	.05
740	Willie Blair/ED	.05
741	Jim Corsi/ED	.05
742	Ken Patterson	.05
743	Andy Ashby/ED	.05
744	Rob Natal/ED	.05
745	Kevin Bass	.05
746	Freddie Benavides/ED	.05
747	Chris Donnels/ED	.05
748	Kerry Woodson RC	.05
749	Calvin Jones/ED	.05
750	Gary Scott	.05
751	Joe Orsulak	.05
752	Armando Reynoso/ED	.05
753	Monty Fariss/ED	.05
754	Billy Hatcher	.05
755	Denis Boucher/ED	.05
756	Walt Weiss	.05
757	Mike Fitzgerald	.05
758	Rudy Seanez	.05
759	Bret Barberie/ED	.05
760	Mo Sanford/ED	.05
761	Pedro Castellano/ED RC	.05
762	Chuck Carr/ED	.05
763	Steve Howe	.05
764	Andres Galarraga	.05
765	Jeff Conine/ED	.05
766	Ted Power	.05
767	Butch Henry/ED	.05
768	Steve Decker/ED	.05
769	Storm Davis	.05
770	Vinny Castilla/ED	.05
771	Junior Felix/ED	.05
772	Walt Terrell	.05
773	Brad Ausmus/ED	.05
774	Jamie McAndrew/ED	.05
775	Milt Thompson	.05
776	Charlie Hayes/ED	.05
777	Jack Armstrong/ED	.05
778	Dennis Rasmussen	.05
779	Darren Holmes/ED	.05
780	Alex Arias RC	.05
781	Randy Bush	.05
782	Javier Lopez/RR	.05
783	Dante Bichette	.05
784	John Johnstone/ED	.05
785	Rene Gonzales	.05
786	Alex Cole/ED	.05
787	Jeromy Burnitz/RR	.05
788	Michael Huff	.05
789	Anthony Telford/ED	.05
790	Jerald Clark/ED	.05
791	Joel Johnston	.05
792	David Nied/RR	.05

#	Player	Price
2	Ryne Sandberg	3.00
3	Roger Clemens	3.50
4	Kirby Puckett	3.00
5	Bill Swift	.25
6	Larry Walker	.25
7	Juan Gonzalez	.75
8	Wally Joyner	.25
9	Andy Van Slyke	.25
10	Robin Ventura	.25
11	Bip Roberts	.25
12	Roberto Kelly	.25
13	Carlos Baerga	.25
14	Orel Hershiser	.25
15	Cecil Fielder	.25
16	Robin Yount	1.50
17	Darren Daulton	.25
18	Mark McGwire	4.00
19	Tom Glavine	.75
20	Roberto Alomar	.50
21	Gary Sheffield	.75
22	Bob Tewksbury	.25
23	Brady Anderson	.25
24	Craig Biggio	.25
25	Eddie Murray	1.50
26	Luis Polonia	.25
27	Nigel Wilson	.25
28	David Nied	.25
29	Pat Listach	.25
30	Eric Karros	.25
31	Checklist	.05

Elite

Continuing the card numbering from the 1992 Elite set, the Elite '93 inserts utilized a silver-foil prismatic front border with blue back printing. Each card is serial numbered as one of 10,000; this identified production number helping to make the Elites among the more valuable of insert cards.

		NM/M
Complete Set (20):		150.00
Common Player:		10.00
19	Fred McGriff	10.00
20	Ryne Sandberg	20.00
21	Eddie Murray	15.00
22	Paul Molitor	15.00
23	Barry Larkin	10.00
24	Don Mattingly	25.00
25	Dennis Eckersley	15.00
26	Roberto Alomar	12.50
27	Edgar Martinez	10.00
28	Gary Sheffield	12.50
29	Darren Daulton	10.00
30	Larry Walker	10.00
31	Barry Bonds	30.00
32	Andy Van Slyke	10.00
33	Mark McGwire	25.00
34	Cecil Fielder	10.00
35	Dave Winfield	15.00
36	Juan Gonzalez	12.50
---	Robin Yount (Legend)	17.50
---	Will Clark (Signature)	40.00

1993 Donruss Elite Supers

A Wal-Mart exclusive, Donruss produced 3-1/2" x 5" versions of its 1993 Elite inserts, added Nolan Ryan and Frank Thomas and a new card of Barry Bonds in his Giants uniform and packaged them one per shrink-wrapped box with Series 1 Donruss left-overs. Each super-size card features a

Diamond Kings

The traditional Donruss Diamond Kings cards were again used as an insert in Series 2 and Series 2 foil packs in 1993. The first 15 cards were found in Series 1 packs, while cards 16-31 were available in the second series packs.

		NM/M
Complete Set (31):		17.50
Common Player:		.25
1	Ken Griffey Jr.	4.00

color player photo and silver-foil prismatic borders on front. Backs are printed in blue and include a serial number identifying each of the cards from an edition of 5,000.

		NM/M
Complete Set (20):		150.00
Common Player:		5.00
1	Fred McGriff	5.00
2	Ryne Sandberg	17.50
3	Eddie Murray	10.00
4	Paul Molitor	10.00
5	Barry Larkin	5.00
6	Don Mattingly	20.00
7	Dennis Eckersley	10.00
8	Roberto Alomar	6.50
9	Edgar Martinez	5.00
10	Gary Sheffield	6.50
11	Darren Daulton	5.00
12	Larry Walker	5.00
13	Barry Bonds	25.00
14	Andy Van Slyke	5.00
15	Mark McGwire	25.00
16	Cecil Fielder	5.00
17	Dave Winfield	10.00
18	Juan Gonzalez	7.50
19	Frank Thomas	15.00
20	Nolan Ryan	40.00

Long Ball Leaders

Carrying a prefix of "LL" before the card number, these inserts were released in Series 1 (#1-9) and Series 2 (#10-18) jumbo packs, detailing mammoth home runs of the previous season.

		NM/M
Complete Set (18):		5.00
Common Player:		.10
1	Rob Deer	.10
2	Fred McGriff	.10
3	Albert Belle	.10
4	Mark McGwire	2.00
5	Dave Justice	.25
6	Jose Canseco	.25
7	Kent Hrbek	.10
8	Roberto Alomar	.10
9	Ken Griffey Jr.	1.50
10	Frank Thomas	.50
11	Darryl Strawberry	.10
12	Felix Jose	.10
13	Cecil Fielder	.10
14	Juan Gonzalez	.20
15	Ryne Sandberg	.75
16	Gary Sheffield	.20
17	Jeff Bagwell	.50
18	Larry Walker	.10

MVPs

This set was inserted in jumbo packs of both Series 1 and Series 2. Cards carry a MVP prefix to the card number.

		NM/M
Complete Set (26):		10.00
Common Player:		.10
1	Luis Polonia	.10
2	Frank Thomas	.60
3	George Brett	.75
4	Paul Molitor	.10
5	Don Mattingly	.60
6	Roberto Alomar	.25
7	Terry Pendleton	.10
8	Eric Karros	.10

9	Larry Walker	.10
10	Eddie Murray	.60
11	Darren Daulton	.10
12	Ray Lankford	.10
13	Will Clark	.10
14	Cal Ripken, Jr.	2.00
15	Roger Clemens	.75
16	Carlos Baerga	.10
17	Cecil Fielder	.10
18	Kirby Puckett	.65
19	Mark McGwire	1.50
20	Ken Griffey Jr.	1.25
21	Juan Gonzalez	.30
22	Ryne Sandberg	.65
23	Bip Roberts	.10
24	Jeff Bagwell	.60
25	Barry Bonds	2.00
26	Gary Sheffield	.25

Spirit of the Game

Series 1 and Series 2 foil and jumbo packs could be found with these cards randomly inserted. Several multi-player cards are included in the set. Card numbers bear an SG prefix.

		NM/M
Complete Set (20):		5.00
Common Player:		.25
1	Turning Two (Dave Winfield, Mike Bordick)	.35
2	Play at the Plate (David Justice)	.25
3	In There (Roberto Alomar)	.30
4	Pumped (Dennis Eckersley)	.60
5	Dynamic Duo (Juan Gonzalez, Jose Canseco)	.50
6	Gone (Frank Thomas, George Bell)	.60
7	Safe or Out? (Wade Boggs)	.75
8	The Thrill (Will Clark)	.30
9	Safe at Home (Damon Berryhill, Bip Roberts, Glenn Braggs)	.25
10	Thirty X 31 (Cecil Fielder, Mickey Tettleton, Rob Deer)	.25
11	Bag Bandit (Kenny Lofton)	.25
12	Back to Back (Fred McGriff, Gary Sheffield)	.30
13	Range Rovers (Greg Gagne, Barry Larkin)	.25
14	The Ball Stops Here (Ryne Sandberg)	.75
15	Over the Top (Carlos Baerga, Gary Gaetti)	.25
16	At the Wall (Danny Tartabull)	.25
17	Head First (Brady Anderson)	.25
18	Big Hurt (Frank Thomas)	.65
19	No-Hitter (Kevin Gross)	.25
20	3,000 (Robin Yount)	.65

1993 Donruss Elite Dominators

Created as a premium to move left-over boxes of its 1993 product on a home shopping network at $100 apiece, this special edition was produced in standard 2-1/2" x 3-1/2" size in a format similar to the 1991-93 Donruss Elite

chase cards. Cards feature green prismatic borders, liberal use of foil stamping, etc. Only 5,000 of each card were produced, and each card is serially numbered on the back. Half of the cards of Nolan Ryan, Juan Gonzalez, Don Mattingly and Paul Molitor were personally autographed by the player.

		NM/M
Complete Set (20):		135.00
Common Player:		3.00
1	Ryne Sandberg	10.00
2	Fred McGriff	3.00
3	Greg Maddux	10.00
4	Ron Gant	3.00
5	Dave Justice	3.00
6	Don Mattingly	12.00
7	Tim Salmon	3.00
8	Mike Piazza	12.00
9	John Olerud	3.00
10	Nolan Ryan	20.00
11	Juan Gonzalez	5.00
12	Ken Griffey Jr.	12.00
13	Frank Thomas	7.50
14	Tom Glavine	4.50
15	George Brett	12.00
16	Barry Bonds	20.00
17	Albert Belle	3.00
18	Paul Molitor	7.50
19	Cal Ripken, Jr.	20.00
20	Roberto Alomar	5.00
Autographed Cards:		
6	Don Mattingly	35.00
10	Nolan Ryan	65.00
11	Juan Gonzalez	20.00
18	Paul Molitor	20.00

1993 Donruss Masters of the Game

Donruss issued a series of "Masters of the Game" art cards that were available only at Wal-Mart stores. The oversized cards (3-1/2" x 5") feature the artwork of Dick Perez, creator of the Diamond Kings for the same company. The cards came issued one to a pack, along with a foil pack of 1993 Donruss cards for a retail price of about $3.

		NM/M
Complete Set (16):		15.00
Common Player:		1.00
1	Frank Thomas	1.50
2	Nolan Ryan	3.00
3	Gary Sheffield	1.25
4	Fred McGriff	1.00
5	Ryne Sandberg	1.75
6	Cal Ripken, Jr.	3.00
7	Jose Canseco	1.25
8	Ken Griffey Jr.	2.50
9	Will Clark	1.00
10	Roberto Alomar	1.00
11	Juan Gonzalez	1.25
12	David Justice	1.00
13	Kirby Puckett	1.75
14	Barry Bonds	3.00
15	Robin Yount	1.50
16	Deion Sanders	1.00

1993 Donruss 1992 Blue Jays Commemorative Set

Issued only as a special gold-boxed set, this series commemorates the Toronto Blue Jays 1992 World Championship. Each player on the Jays '92 roster has a card. There are also special cards recalling each game of the Series and a SkyDome card. The World Series highlights cards have a bunting design at top and a gold-foil World Series logo on front. Player cards feature borderless photos; a Blue Jays "Commemorative Set" logo is at lower-left. Backs have a player photo at top and a stat box at bottom with season, career and 1992 LCS and World Series numbers.

		NM/M
Complete Set (54):		5.00
Common Card:		.15
1	Checklist/Logo Card	.15
2	Roberto Alomar	.45
3	Derek Bell	.15
4	Pat Borders	.15
5	Joe Carter	.45
6	Alfredo Griffin	.15
7	Kelly Gruber	.15
8	Manuel Lee	.15
9	Candy Maldonado	.15
10	John Olerud	.45
11	Ed Sprague	.15
12	Pat Tabler	.15
13	Devon White	.15
14	Dave Winfield	1.00
15	David Cone	.25
16	Mark Eichhorn	.15
17	Juan Guzman	.15
18	Tom Henke	.15
19	Jimmy Key	.15
20	Jack Morris	.25
21	Todd Stottlemyre	.15
22	Mike Timlin	.15
23	Duane Ward	.15
24	David Wells	.40
25	Randy Knorr	.15
26	Rance Mulliniks	.15
27	Tom Quinlan	.15
28	Cito Gaston	.15
29	Dave Steib	.15
30	Ken Dayley	.15
31	Turner Ward	.15
32	Eddie Zosky	.15
33	Pat Hentgen	.15
34	Al Leiter	.15
35	Doug Linton	.15
36	Bob MacDonald	.15
37	Rick Trlicek	.15
38	Domingo Martinez	.15
39	Mike Maksudian	.15
40	Rob Ducey	.15
41	Jeff Kent	.60
42	Greg Myers	.15
43	Dave Weathers	.15
44	Skydome	.15
45	Trophy Presentation (Jim Kaat, Cito Gaston, Paul Beeston, Bobby Brown)	.15
World Series Highlights		
1WS	Series Opener (Blue Jays vs. Braves)	.10
2WS	Game 1 - Carter Homers in 4th	.25
3WS	Homer	.10
4WS	Game 3 - Maldonado Drives in Game-Winner	.10
5WS	Game 4 - Key's Win Puts Jays Up 3-1	.10
6WS	Game 5 - Olerud Scores Both Jays Runs	.10
7WS	Game 6 - Winfield's Double in 11th Wins	.25
8WS	Pat Border Series MVP	.10
9WS	World Champs Celebration	.10

1994 Donruss Promotional Samples

To introduce both its regular 1994 issue and the "Special Edition" gold cards, Donruss produced this 12-card promo set for

distribution to its dealer network. The promos are virtually identical in format to the regular cards except for the large gray diagonal overprint "PROMOTIONAL SAMPLE" on both front and back. Card numbers also differ on the promos.

		NM/M
Complete Set (12):		10.00
Common Player:		.50
1	Barry Bonds	2.00
2	Darren Daulton	.50
3	John Olerud	.50
4	Frank Thomas	1.00
5	Mike Piazza	1.50
6	Tim Salmon	.50
7	Ken Griffey Jr.	1.50
8	Fred McGriff	.50
9	Don Mattingly	1.25
10	Gary Sheffield	.75
Special Edition Gold:		
1G	Barry Bonds (Special Edition Gold)	2.50
4G	Frank Thomas (Special Edition Gold)	1.00

1994 Donruss

Donruss released its 1994 set in two 330-card series. Each series also includes, 50 Special Edition gold cards and several insert sets. Regular cards have full-bleed photos and are UV coated and foil stamped. Special Edition cards are gold-foil stamped on both sides and are included in each pack. Insert sets titled Spirit of the Game and Decade Dominators were produced in regular and super (3-1/2 x 5") formats. Other inserts were MVPs and Long Ball Leaders in regular size and super-size Award Winners. An Elite series of cards, continuing from previous years with #37-48, was also issued as inserts. A 10th Anniversary insert set features 10 popular 1984 Donruss cards in gold-foil enhanced reprint versions.

		NM/M
Complete Set (660):		15.00
Common Player:		.05
Series 1 or 2 Pack (13):		.50
Series 1 or 2 Box (36):		12.50
1	Nolan Ryan (Career Salute 27 Years.)	1.00
2	Mike Piazza	1.00
3	Moises Alou	.05
4	Ken Griffey Jr.	1.00
5	Gary Sheffield	.25
6	Roberto Alomar	.20
7	John Kruk	.05
8	Gregg Olson	.05
9	Gregg Jefferies	.05
10	Tony Gwynn	.65
11	Chad Curtis	.05
12	Craig Biggio	.05
13	John Burkett	.05
14	Carlos Baerga	.05
15	Robin Yount	.60
16	Dennis Eckersley	.50
17	Dwight Gooden	.05
18	Ryne Sandberg	.65
19	Rickey Henderson	.60
20	Jack McDowell	.05
21	Jay Bell	.05
22	Kevin Brown	.05
23	Robin Ventura	.05
24	Paul Molitor	.60
25	Dave Justice	.05
26	Rafael Palmeiro	.50
27	Cecil Fielder	.05

28	Chuck Knoblauch	.05
29	Dave Hollins	.05
30	Jimmy Key	.05
31	Mark Langston	.05
32	Darryl Kile	.05
33	Ruben Sierra	.05
34	Ron Gant	.05
35	Ozzie Smith	.65
36	Wade Boggs	.65
37	Marquis Grissom	.05
38	Will Clark	.05
39	Kenny Lofton	.05
40	Cal Ripken, Jr.	2.00
41	Steve Avery	.05
42	Mo Vaughn	.05
43	Brian McRae	.05
44	Mickey Tettleton	.05
45	Barry Larkin	.05
46	Charlie Hayes	.05
47	Kevin Appier	.05
48	Robby Thompson	.05
49	Juan Gonzalez	.30
50	Paul O'Neill	.05
51	Marcos Armas	.05
52	Mike Butcher	.05
53	Ken Caminiti	.05
54	Pat Borders	.05
55	Pedro Munoz	.05
56	Tim Belcher	.05
57	Paul Assenmacher	.05
58	Damon Berryhill	.05
59	Ricky Bones	.05
60	Rene Arocha	.05
61	Shawn Boskie	.05
62	Pedro Astacio	.05
63	Frank Bolick	.05
64	Bud Black	.05
65	Sandy Alomar, Jr.	.05
66	Rich Amaral	.05
67	Luis Aquino	.05
68	Kevin Baez	.05
69	Mike Devereaux	.05
70	Andy Ashby	.05
71	Larry Andersen	.05
72	Steve Cooke	.05
73	Mario Daiz	.05
74	Rob Deer	.05
75	Bobby Ayala	.05
76	Freddie Benavides	.05
77	Stan Belinda	.05
78	John Doherty	.05
79	Willie Banks	.05
80	Spike Owen	.05
81	Mike Bordick	.05
82	Chili Davis	.05
83	Luis Gonzalez	.05
84	Ed Sprague	.05
85	Jeff Reboulet	.05
86	Jason Bere	.05
87	Mark Hutton	.05
88	Jeff Blauser	.05
89	Cal Eldred	.05
90	Bernard Gilkey	.05
91	Frank Castillo	.05
92	Jim Gott	.05
93	Greg Colbrunn	.05
94	Jeff Brantley	.05
95	Jeremy Hernandez	.05
96	Norm Charlton	.05
97	Alex Arias	.05
98	John Franco	.05
99	Chris Hoiles	.05
100	Brad Ausmus	.05
101	Wes Chamberlain	.05
102	Mark Dewey	.05
103	Benji Gil/RR	.05
104	John Dopson	.05
105	John Smiley	.05
106	David Nied	.05
107	George Brett (Career Salute 21 Years.)	.75
108	Kirk Gibson	.05
109	Larry Casian	.05
110	Checklist (Ryne Sandberg 2,000 Hits)	.25
111	Brent Gates	.05
112	Damion Easley	.05
113	Pete Harnisch	.05
114	Danny Cox	.05
115	Kevin Tapani	.05
116	Roberto Hernandez	.05
117	Domingo Jean	.05
118	Sid Bream	.05
119	Doug Henry	.05
120	Omar Olivares	.05
121	Mike Harkey	.05
122	Carlos Hernandez	.05
123	Jeff Fassero	.05
124	Dave Burba	.05
125	Wayne Kirby	.05
126	John Cummings	.05
127	Bret Barberie	.05
128	Todd Hundley	.05
129	Tim Hulett	.05
130	Phil Clark	.05
131	Danny Jackson	.05
132	Tom Foley	.05
133	Donald Harris	.05
134	Scott Fletcher	.05
135	Johnny Ruffin/RR	.05
136	Jerald Clark	.05
137	Billy Brewer	.05
138	Dan Gladden	.05
139	Eddie Guardado	.05
140	Checklist (Cal Ripken, Jr. 2,000 Hits)	.35
141	Scott Hemond	.05
142	Steve Frey	.05

143	Xavier Hernandez	.05
144	Mark Eichhorn	.05
145	Ellis Burks	.05
146	Jim Leyritz	.05
147	Mark Lemke	.05
148	Pat Listach	.05
149	Donovan Osborne	.05
150	Glenallen Hill	.05
151	Orel Hershiser	.05
152	Darrin Fletcher	.05
153	Royce Clayton	.05
154	Derek Lilliquist	.05
155	Mike Felder	.05
156	Jeff Conine	.05
157	Ryan Thompson	.05
158	Ben McDonald	.05
159	Ricky Gutierrez	.05
160	Terry Mulholland	.05
161	Carlos Garcia	.05
162	Tom Henke	.05
163	Mike Greenwell	.05
164	Thomas Howard	.05
165	Joe Girardi	.05
166	Hubie Brooks	.05
167	Greg Gohr	.05
168	Chip Hale	.05
169	Rick Honeycutt	.05
170	Hilly Hathaway	.05
171	Todd Jones	.05
172	Tony Fernandez	.05
173	Bo Jackson	.10
174	Bobby Munoz	.05
175	Greg McMichael	.05
176	Graeme Lloyd	.05
177	Tom Pagnozzi	.05
178	Derrick May	.05
179	Pedro Martinez	.60
180	Ken Hill	.05
181	Bryan Hickerson	.05
182	Jose Mesa	.05
183	Dave Fleming	.05
184	Henry Cotto	.05
185	Jeff Kent	.05
186	Mark McLemore	.05
187	Trevor Hoffman	.05
188	Todd Pratt	.05
189	Blas Minor	.05
190	Charlie Leibrandt	.05
191	Tony Pena	.05
192	Larry Luebbers **RC**	.05
193	Greg Harris	.05
194	David Cone	.05
195	Bill Gullickson	.05
196	Brian Harper	.05
197	Steve Karsay/RR	.05
198	Greg Myers	.05
199	Mark Portugal	.05
200	Pat Hentgen	.05
201	Mike La Valliere	.05
202	Mike Stanley	.05
203	Kent Mercker	.05
204	Dave Nilsson	.05
205	Erik Pappas	.05
206	Mike Morgan	.05
207	Roger McDowell	.05
208	Mike Lansing	.05
209	Kirt Manwaring	.05
210	Randy Milligan	.05
211	Erik Hanson	.05
212	Orestes Destrade	.05
213	Mike Maddux	.05
214	Alan Mills	.05
215	Tim Mauser	.05
216	Ben Rivera	.05
217	Don Slaught	.05
218	Bob Patterson	.05
219	Carlos Quintana	.05
220	Checklist (Tim Raines 2,000 Hits)	.05
221	Hal Morris	.05
222	Darren Holmes	.05
223	Chris Gwynn	.05
224	Chad Kreuter	.05
225	Mike Hartley	.05
226	Scott Lydy	.05
227	Eduardo Perez	.05
228	Greg Swindell	.05
229	Al Leiter	.05
230	Scott Radinsky	.05
231	Bob Wickman	.05
232	Otis Nixon	.05
233	Kevin Reimer	.05
234	Geronimo Pena	.05
235	Kevin Roberson/RR	.05
236	Jody Reed	.05
237	Kirk Rueter/RR	.05
238	Willie McGee	.05
239	Charles Nagy	.05
240	Tim Leary	.05
241	Carl Everett	.05
242	Charlie O'Brien	.05
243	Mike Pagliarulo	.05
244	Kerry Taylor	.05
245	Kevin Stocker	.05
246	Joel Johnston	.05
247	Geno Petralli	.05
248	Jeff Russell	.05
249	Joe Oliver	.05
250	Robert Mejia	.05
251	Chris Haney	.05
252	Bill Krueger	.05
253	Shane Mack	.05
254	Terry Steinbach	.05
255	Luis Polonia	.05
256	Eddie Taubensee	.05
257	Dave Stewart	.05
258	Tim Raines	.05
259	Bernie Williams	.05

No.	Player	Price
260	John Smoltz	.05
261	Kevin Seitzer	.05
262	Bob Tewksbury	.05
263	Bob Scanlan	.05
264	Henry Rodriguez	.05
265	Tim Scott	.05
266	Scott Sanderson	.05
267	Eric Plunk	.05
268	Edgar Martinez	.05
269	Charlie Hough	.05
270	Joe Orsulak	.05
271	Harold Reynolds	.05
272	Tim Teufel	.05
273	Bobby Thigpen	.05
274	Randy Tomlin	.05
275	Gary Redus	.05
276	Ken Ryan	.05
277	Tim Pugh	.05
278	Jayhawk Owens	.05
279	Phil Hiatt/RR	.05
280	Alan Trammell	.05
281	Dave McCarty/RR	.05
282	Bob Welch	.05
283	J.T. Snow	.05
284	Brian Williams	.05
285	Devon White	.05
286	Steve Sax	.05
287	Tony Tarasco	.05
288	Bill Spiers	.05
289	Allen Watson	.05
290	Checklist (Rickey Henderson 2,000 Hits)	.05
291	Joe Vizcaino	.05
292	Darryl Strawberry	.05
293	John Wetteland	.05
294	Bill Swift	.05
295	Jeff Treadway	.05
296	Tino Martinez	.05
297	Richie Lewis	.05
298	Bret Saberhagen	.05
299	Arthur Rhodes	.05
300	Guillermo Velasquez	.05
301	Milt Thompson	.05
302	Doug Strange	.05
303	Aaron Sele	.05
304	Bip Roberts	.05
305	Bruce Ruffin	.05
306	Jose Lind	.05
307	David Wells	.05
308	Bobby Witt	.05
309	Mark Wohlers	.05
310	B.J. Surhoff	.05
311	Mark Whiten	.05
312	Turk Wendell	.05
313	Raul Mondesi	.05
314	Brian Turang RC	.05
315	Chris Hammond	.05
316	Tim Bogar	.05
317	Brad Pennington	.05
318	Tim Worrell	.05
319	Mitch Williams	.05
320	Rondell White/RR	.05
321	Frank Viola	.05
322	Manny Ramirez/RR	.75
323	Gary Wayne	.05
324	Mike Macfarlane	.05
325	Russ Springer	.05
326	Tim Wallach	.05
327	Salomon Torres/RR	.05
328	Omar Vizquel	.05
329	Andy Tomberlin RC	.05
330	Chris Sabo	.05
331	Mike Mussina	.30
332	Andy Benes	.05
333	Darren Daulton	.05
334	Orlando Merced	.05
335	Mark McGwire	1.50
336	Dave Winfield	.60
337	Sammy Sosa	.65
338	Eric Karros	.05
339	Greg Vaughn	.05
340	Don Mattingly	.75
341	Frank Thomas	.60
342	Fred McGriff	.05
343	Kirby Puckett	.65
344	Roberto Kelly	.05
345	Wally Joyner	.05
346	Andres Galarraga	.05
347	Bobby Bonilla	.05
348	Benito Santiago	.05
349	Barry Bonds	2.00
350	Delino DeShields	.05
351	Albert Belle	.05
352	Randy Johnson	.60
353	Tim Salmon	.05
354	John Olerud	.05
355	Dean Palmer	.05
356	Roger Clemens	.75
357	Jim Abbott	.05
358	Mark Grace	.05
359	Ozzie Guillen	.05
360	Lou Whitaker	.05
361	Jose Rijo	.05
362	Jeff Montgomery	.05
363	Chuck Finley	.05
364	Tom Glavine	.25
365	Jeff Bagwell	.60
366	Joe Carter	.05
367	Ray Lankford	.05
368	Ramon Martinez	.05
369	Jay Buhner	.05
370	Matt Williams	.05
371	Larry Walker	.30
372	Jose Canseco	.05
373	Len Dykstra	.05
374	Bryan Harvey	.05
375	Andy Van Slyke	.05
376	Ivan Rodriguez	.50
377	Kevin Mitchell	.05
378	Travis Fryman	.05
379	Duane Ward	.05
380	Greg Maddux	.65
381	Scott Servais	.05
382	Greg Olson	.05
383	Rey Sanchez	.05
384	Tom Kramer	.05
385	David Valle	.05
386	Eddie Murray	.60
387	Kevin Higgins	.05
388	Dan Wilson	.05
389	Todd Frohwirth	.05
390	Gerald Williams	.05
391	Hipolito Pichardo	.05
392	Pat Meares	.05
393	Luis Lopez	.05
394	Ricky Jordan	.05
395	Bob Walk	.05
396	Sid Fernandez	.05
397	Todd Worrell	.05
398	Darryl Hamilton	.05
399	Randy Myers	.05
400	Rod Brewer	.05
401	Lance Blankenship	.05
402	Steve Finley	.05
403	Phil Leftwich RC	.05
404	Juan Guzman	.05
405	Anthony Young	.05
406	Jeff Gardner	.05
407	Ryan Bowen	.05
408	Fernando Valenzuela	.05
409	David West	.05
410	Kenny Rogers	.05
411	Bob Zupcic	.05
412	Eric Young	.05
413	Bret Boone	.05
414	Danny Tartabull	.05
415	Bob MacDonald	.05
416	Ron Karkovice	.05
417	Scott Cooper	.05
418	Dante Bichette	.05
419	Tripp Cromer	.05
420	Billy Ashley	.05
421	Roger Smithberg	.05
422	Dennis Martinez	.05
423	Mike Blowers	.05
424	Darren Lewis	.05
425	Junior Ortiz	.05
426	Butch Huskey	.05
427	Jimmy Poole	.05
428	Walt Weiss	.05
429	Scott Bankhead	.05
430	Deion Sanders	.65
431	Scott Bullett	.05
432	Jeff Huson	.05
433	Tyler Green	.05
434	Billy Hatcher	.05
435	Bob Hamelin	.05
436	Reggie Sanders	.05
437	Scott Erickson	.05
438	Steve Reed	.05
439	Randy Velarde	.05
440	Checklist (Tony Gwynn 2,000 Hits)	.15
441	Terry Leach	.05
442	Danny Bautista	.05
443	Kent Hrbek	.05
444	Rick Wilkins	.05
445	Tony Phillips	.05
446	Dion James	.05
447	Joey Cora	.05
448	Andre Dawson	.15
449	Pedro Castellano	.05
450	Tom Gordon	.05
451	Rob Dibble	.05
452	Ron Darling	.05
453	Chipper Jones	.65
454	Joe Grahe	.05
455	Domingo Cedeno	.05
456	Tom Edens	.05
457	Mitch Webster	.05
458	Jose Bautista	.05
459	Troy O'Leary	.05
460	Todd Zeile	.05
461	Sean Berry	.05
462	Brad Holman RC	.05
463	Dave Martinez	.05
464	Mark Lewis	.05
465	Paul Carey	.05
466	Jack Armstrong	.05
467	David Telgheder	.05
468	Gene Harris	.05
469	Danny Darwin	.05
470	Kim Batiste	.05
471	Tim Wakefield	.05
472	Craig Lefferts	.05
473	Jacob Brumfield	.05
474	Lance Painter	.05
475	Milt Cuyler	.05
476	Melido Perez	.05
477	Derek Parks	.05
478	Gary DiSarcina	.05
479	Steve Bedrosian	.05
480	Eric Anthony	.05
481	Julio Franco	.05
482	Tommy Greene	.05
483	Pat Kelly	.05
484	Nate Minchey/RR	.05
485	William Pennyfeather	.05
486	Harold Baines	.05
487	Howard Johnson	.05
488	Angel Miranda	.05
489	Scott Sanders	.05
490	Shawon Dunston	.05
491	Mel Rojas	.05
492	Jeff Nelson	.05
493	Archi Cianfrocco	.05
494	Al Martin	.05
495	Mike Gallego	.05
496	Mike Henneman	.05
497	Armando Reynoso	.05
498	Mickey Morandini	.05
499	Rick Renteria	.05
500	Rick Sutcliffe	.05
501	Bobby Jones/RR	.05
502	Gary Gaetti	.05
503	Rick Aguilera	.05
504	Todd Stottlemyre	.05
505	Mike Mohler	.05
506	Mike Stanton	.05
507	Jose Guzman	.05
508	Kevin Rogers	.05
509	Chuck Carr	.05
510	Chris Jones	.05
511	Brent Mayne	.05
512	Greg Harris	.05
513	Dave Henderson	.05
514	Eric Hillman	.05
515	Dan Peltier	.05
516	Craig Shipley	.05
517	John Valentin	.05
518	Wilson Alvarez	.05
519	Andujar Cedeno	.05
520	Troy Neel	.05
521	Tom Candiotti	.05
522	Matt Mieske	.05
523	Jim Thome	.50
524	Lou Frazier	.05
525	Mike Jackson	.05
526	Pedro Martinez	.05
527	Roger Pavlik	.05
528	Kent Bottenfield	.05
529	Felix Jose	.05
530	Mark Guthrie	.05
531	Steve Farr	.05
532	Craig Paquette	.05
533	Doug Jones	.05
534	Luis Alicea	.05
535	Cory Snyder	.05
536	Paul Sorrento	.05
537	Nigel Wilson	.05
538	Jeff King	.05
539	Willie Green	.05
540	Kirk McCaskill	.05
541	Al Osuna	.05
542	Greg Hibbard	.05
543	Brett Butler	.05
544	Jose Valentin	.05
545	Wil Cordero	.05
546	Chris Bosio	.05
547	Jamie Moyer	.05
548	Jim Eisenreich	.05
549	Vinny Castilla	.05
550	Checklist (Dave Winfield 3,000 Hits)	.05
551	John Roper	.05
552	Lance Johnson	.05
553	Scott Kamienicki	.05
554	Mike Moore	.05
555	Steve Buechele	.05
556	Terry Pendleton	.05
557	Todd Van Poppel	.05
558	Rob Butler	.05
559	Zane Smith	.05
560	David Hulse	.05
561	Tim Costo	.05
562	John Habyan	.05
563	Terry Jorgensen	.05
564	Matt Nokes	.05
565	Kevin McReynolds	.05
566	Phil Plantier	.05
567	Chris Turner	.05
568	Carlos Delgado	.40
569	John Jaha	.05
570	Dwight Smith	.05
571	John Vander Wal	.05
572	Trevor Wilson	.05
573	Felix Fermin	.05
574	Marc Newfield/RR	.05
575	Jeromy Burnitz	.05
576	Leo Gomez	.05
577	Curt Schilling	.25
578	Kevin Young	.05
579	Jerry Spradlin RC	.05
580	Curt Leskanic	.05
581	Carl Willis	.05
582	Alex Fernandez	.05
583	Mark Holzemer	.05
584	Domingo Martinez	.05
585	Pete Smith	.05
586	Brian Jordan	.05
587	Kevin Gross	.05
588	J.R. Phillips/RR	.05
589	Chris Nabholz	.05
590	Bill Wertz	.05
591	Derek Bell	.05
592	Brady Anderson	.05
593	Matt Turner	.05
594	Pete Incaviglia	.05
595	Greg Gagne	.05
596	John Flaherty	.05
597	Scott Livingstone	.05
598	Rod Bolton	.05
599	Mike Perez	.05
600	Checklist (Roger Clemens 2,000 Strikeouts)	.25
601	Tony Castillo	.05
602	Henry Mercedes	.05
603	Mike Fetters	.05
604	Rod Beck	.05
605	Damon Buford	.05
606	Matt Whiteside	.05
607	Shawn Green	.25
608	Midre Cummings/RR	.05
609	Jeff McNeeley	.05
610	Danny Sheaffer	.05
611	Paul Wagner	.05
612	Torey Lovullo	.05
613	Javier Lopez	.05
614	Mariano Duncan	.05
615	Doug Brocail	.05
616	Dave Hansen	.05
617	Ryan Klesko	.05
618	Eric Davis	.05
619	Scott Ruffcorn/RR	.05
620	Mike Trombley	.05
621	Jaime Navarro	.05
622	Rheal Cormier	.05
623	Jose Offerman	.05
624	David Segui	.05
625	Robb Nen/RR	.05
626	Dave Gallagher	.05
627	Julian Tavarez RC	.05
628	Chris Gomez	.05
629	Jeffrey Hammonds/RR	.05
630	Scott Brosius	.05
631	Willie Blair	.05
632	Doug Drabek	.05
633	Bill Wegman	.05
634	Jeff McKnight	.05
635	Rich Rodriguez	.05
636	Steve Trachsel	.05
637	Buddy Groom	.05
638	Sterling Hitchcock	.05
639	Chuck McElroy	.05
640	Rene Gonzales	.05
641	Dan Plesac	.05
642	Jeff Branson	.05
643	Darrell Whitmore	.05
644	Paul Quantrill	.05
645	Rich Rowland	.05
646	Curtis Pride RC	.05
647	Erik Plantenberg	.05
648	Albie Lopez	.05
649	Rich Batchelor RC	.05
650	Lee Smith	.05
651	Cliff Floyd	.05
652	Pete Schourek	.05
653	Reggie Jefferson	.05
654	Bill Haselman	.05
655	Steve Hosey	.05
656	Mark Clark	.05
657	Mark Davis	.05
658	Dave Magadan	.05
659	Candy Maldonado	.05
660	Checklist (Mark Langston 2,000 Strikeouts)	.05

Special Edition - Gold

In 1994 Donruss added a Special Edition subset of 100 of the game's top players. Fifty cards each were included one or two per pack in all types of Donruss' Series 1 and 2 packaging. The cards use the same photos and format as the regular-issue version, but have special gold-foil stamping on front in the area of the team logo and player name, and on back in a "Special Edition" number box in the upper-left corner.

	NM/M
Complete Set (100):	7.50
Common Player:	.10
1 Nolan Ryan	1.50
2 Mike Piazza	1.00
3 Moises Alou	.10
4 Ken Griffey Jr.	1.00
5 Gary Sheffield	.20
6 Roberto Alomar	.20
7 John Kruk	.10
8 Gregg Olson	.10
9 Gregg Jefferies	.10
10 Tony Gwynn	.65
11 Chad Curtis	.10
12 Craig Biggio	.10
13 John Burkett	.10
14 Carlos Baerga	.10
15 Robin Yount	.60
16 Dennis Eckersley	.10
17 Dwight Gooden	.10
18 Ryne Sandberg	.65
19 Rickey Henderson	.60
20 Jack McDowell	.10
21 Jay Bell	.10
22 Kevin Brown	.10
23 Robin Ventura	.10
24 Paul Molitor	.60
25 David Justice	.10
26 Rafael Palmeiro	.50
27 Cecil Fielder	.10
28 Chuck Knoblauch	.10
29 Dave Hollins	.10
30 Jimmy Key	.10
31 Mark Langston	.10
32 Darryl Kile	.10
33 Ruben Sierra	.10
34 Ron Gant	.10
35 Ozzie Smith	.65
36 Wade Boggs	.65
37 Marquis Grissom	.10
38 Will Clark	.10
39 Kenny Lofton	.10
40 Cal Ripken, Jr.	1.50
41 Steve Avery	.10
42 Mo Vaughn	.10
43 Brian McRae	.10
44 Mickey Tettleton	.10
45 Barry Larkin	.10
46 Charlie Hayes	.10
47 Kevin Appier	.10
48 Robby Thompson	.10
49 Juan Gonzalez	.30
50 Paul O'Neill	.10
51 Mike Mussina	.40
52 Andy Benes	.10
53 Darren Daulton	.10
54 Orlando Merced	.10
55 Mark McGwire	1.25
56 Dave Winfield	.60
57 Sammy Sosa	.65
58 Eric Karros	.10
59 Greg Vaughn	.10
60 Don Mattingly	.75
61 Frank Thomas	.60
62 Fred McGriff	.10
63 Kirby Puckett	.65
64 Roberto Kelly	.10
65 Wally Joyner	.10
66 Andres Galarraga	.10
67 Bobby Bonilla	.10
68 Benito Santiago	.10
69 Barry Bonds	1.50
70 Delino DeShields	.10
71 Albert Belle	.10
72 Randy Johnson	.60
73 Tim Salmon	.10
74 John Olerud	.10
75 Dean Palmer	.10
76 Roger Clemens	.75
77 Jim Abbott	.10
78 Mark Grace	.10
79 Ozzie Guillen	.10
80 Lou Whitaker	.10
81 Jose Rijo	.10
82 Jeff Montgomery	.10
83 Chuck Finley	.10
84 Tom Glavine	.10
85 Jeff Bagwell	.60
86 Joe Carter	.10
87 Ray Lankford	.10
88 Ramon Martinez	.10
89 Jay Buhner	.10
90 Matt Williams	.10
91 Larry Walker	.10
92 Jose Canseco	.25
93 Len Dykstra	.10
94 Bryan Harvey	.10
95 Andy Van Slyke	.10
96 Ivan Rodriguez	.50
97 Kevin Mitchell	.10
98 Travis Fryman	.10
99 Duane Ward	.10
100 Greg Maddux	.65

Anniversary-1984

RICKEY HENDERSON OF

This set commemorates and features 10 of the most popular cards from Donruss' 1984 set. The cards, inserted in Series I hobby foil packs only, are "holographically enhanced" with foil stamping and UV coating.

	NM/M
Complete Set (10):	20.00
Common Player:	1.00
1 Joe Carter	1.00
2 Robin Yount	1.50
3 George Brett	2.50
4 Rickey Henderson	1.50
5 Nolan Ryan	6.00
6 Cal Ripken, Jr.	6.00
7 Wade Boggs	2.50
8 Don Mattingly	2.50
9 Ryne Sandberg	2.00
10 Tony Gwynn	2.00

1994 Donruss Award Winners Supers

Major award winners of the 1993 season are honored in this super-size (3-1/2" x 5") insert set. One card was packaged in each box of U.S. jumbo packs and in each Canadian foil-pack box. On a gold-tone background, the card backs have another player photo, a description of his award winning performance and a white strip with a serial number identifying the card's place in an edition of 10,000.

	NM/M
Complete Set (10):	25.00
Common Player:	1.25
1 Barry Bonds (N.L. MVP)	5.00
2 Greg Maddux (N.L. Cy Young)	2.50
3 Mike Piazza (N.L. ROY)	3.50
4 Barry Bonds (N.L. HR Champ)	2.50
5 Kirby Puckett (All-Star MVP)	2.50
6 Frank Thomas (A.L. MVP)	2.00
7 Jack McDowell (A.L. Cy Young)	1.25
8 Tim Salmon (A.L. ROY)	1.25
9 Juan Gonzalez (A.L. HR Champ)	1.50
10 Paul Molitor (World Series MVP)	2.00

Decade Dominators

CECIL FIELDER HOMERUNS

Donruss selected 10 top home run hitters (Series I) and 10 RBI leaders of the 1990s for this insert set. Cards were issued in all types of Series I and II packs. Full-bleed UV-coated cards were gold-foil enhanced on the front. Backs featured another full-color player photo and charted information on his 1990s home run or RBI output and ranking.

	NM/M
Complete Set (20):	15.00
Common Player:	.35
Series 1	
1 Cecil Fielder	.35
2 Barry Bonds	2.50
3 Fred McGriff	.35
4 Matt Williams	.35
5 Joe Carter	.35
6 Juan Gonzalez	.40
7 Jose Canseco	.35
8 Ron Gant	.35
9 Ken Griffey Jr.	1.50
10 Mark McGwire	2.00
Series 2	
1 Tony Gwynn	1.00
2 Frank Thomas	.75
3 Paul Molitor	.35
4 Edgar Martinez	.35
5 Kirby Puckett	.35
6 Ken Griffey, Jr.	1.50
7 Barry Bonds	2.50
8 Willie McGee	.35
9 Len Dykstra	.35
10 John Kruk	.35

1994 Donruss Decade Dominators Supers

Super-size (3-1/2" x 5") versions of the 1994 Donruss Decade Dominators insert cards were produced as a premium, one card being packaged in a paper checklist envelope in each hobby box of Donruss foil packs. The supers are identical in format to the regular-size cards with the exception of a white serial number strip on the back, identifying each card's position in an edition of 10,000.

		NM/M
Complete Set (20):		25.00
Common Player:		1.00
Series 1		
1	Cecil Fielder	1.00
2	Barry Bonds	2.50
3	Fred McGriff	1.00
4	Matt Williams	1.00
5	Joe Carter	1.00
6	Juan Gonzalez	1.00
7	Jose Canseco	1.25
8	Ron Gant	1.00
9	Ken Griffey Jr.	2.00
10	Mark McGwire	2.00
Series 2		
1	Tony Gwynn	2.00
2	Frank Thomas	1.50
3	Paul Molitor	1.50
4	Edgar Martinez	1.00
5	Kirby Puckett	2.00
6	Ken Griffey, Jr.	2.25
7	Barry Bonds	2.50
8	Willie McGee	1.00
9	Lenny Dykstra	2.00
10	John Kruk	.25

Diamond Kings

The artwork of Dick Perez is again featured on this insert set included in foil packs. Player art is set against garish color backgrounds with a red-and-silver "Diamond Kings" foil logo above, and the player's name in script at bottom. Backs are printed in red on pale yellow and feature a 1993 season summary. Cards have a DK preface to the number. Cards #1-14 and #29, Dave Winfield, were included in Series 1 packs; cards #15-28 are found in Series 2, along with the checklist card (#30), featuring a Dick Perez self-portrait.

		NM/M
Complete Set (30):		12.00
Common Player:		.25
1	Barry Bonds	2.50
2	Mo Vaughn	.25
3	Steve Avery	.25
4	Tim Salmon	.25
5	Rick Wilkins	.25
6	Brian Harper	.25
7	Andres Galarraga	.25
8	Albert Belle	.25
9	John Kruk	.25
10	Ivan Rodriguez	.75
11	Tony Gwynn	1.25
12	Brian McRae	.25

13	Bobby Bonilla	.25
14	Ken Griffey Jr.	2.00
15	Mike Piazza	2.00
16	Don Mattingly	1.50
17	Barry Larkin	.25
18	Ruben Sierra	.25
19	Orlando Merced	.25
20	Greg Vaughn	.25
21	Gregg Jefferies	.25
22	Cecil Fielder	.25
23	Moises Alou	.25
24	John Olerud	.25
25	Gary Sheffield	.25
26	Mike Mussina	.60
27	Jeff Bagwell	1.00
28	Frank Thomas	1.00
29	Dave Winfield	
	(King of Kings)	1.00
30	Dick Perez (Checklist)	.25

1994 Donruss Diamond Kings Supers

Each retail box of 1994 Donruss foil packs contains one super-size (4-7/8" x 6-13/16") version of the Diamond Kings inserts. Series 1 boxes offer cards #1-14, while #15-28 are found in Series 2 boxes. A 29th card, honoring Dave Winfield, was also produced. Super DKs are identical in format to the regular-size inserts, with the exception of a white serial number strip on the back which identifies the card within an edition of 10,000.

		NM/M
Complete Set (29):		70.00
Common Player:		2.00
1	Barry Bonds	7.50
2	Mo Vaughn	2.00
3	Steve Avery	2.00
4	Tim Salmon	2.00
5	Rick Wilkins	2.00
6	Brian Harper	2.00
7	Andres Galarraga	2.00
8	Albert Belle	2.00
9	John Kruk	2.00
10	Ivan Rodriguez	3.50
11	Tony Gwynn	5.00
12	Brian McRae	2.00
13	Bobby Bonilla	2.00
14	Ken Griffey Jr.	6.50
15	Mike Piazza	6.50
16	Don Mattingly	6.00
17	Barry Larkin	2.00
18	Ruben Sierra	2.00
19	Orlando Merced	2.00
20	Greg Vaughn	2.00
21	Gregg Jefferies	2.00
22	Cecil Fielder	2.00
23	Moises Alou	2.00
24	John Olerud	2.00
25	Gary Sheffield	3.00
26	Mike Mussina	3.00
27	Jeff Bagwell	4.00
28	Frank Thomas	4.00
29	Dave Winfield	
	(King of Kings)	4.00

Elite

Donruss continued its popular Elite Series with 12 more players in 1994. The cards, numbered #37-48, were inserted in foil packs only. The cards feature the player

in a diamond on the front; the back offers an opinion of why the player is considered an elite and is serially numbered to 10,000.

		NM/M
Complete Set (12):		50.00
Common Player:		4.00
37	Frank Thomas	6.00
38	Tony Gwynn	7.50
39	Tim Salmon	4.00
40	Albert Belle	4.00
41	John Kruk	4.00
42	Juan Gonzalez	5.00
43	John Olerud	4.00
44	Barry Bonds	12.00
45	Ken Griffey Jr.	9.00
46	Mike Piazza	9.00
47	Jack McDowell	4.00
48	Andres Galarraga	4.00

Long Ball Leaders

The "Tale of the Tape" for the 1993 season is chronicled in this Series II hobby-only foil-pack insert. Silver prismatic foil highlights the typography on the front of the card which includes the "Long Ball Leaders" logos (complete with embossed baseball), the player's last name and the distance of his blast. Cards backs have another player photo superimposed on the venue in which the home run was hit. The distance is repeated in silver over the ballpark photo. In a wide silver box at bottom is data about the home run.

		NM/M
Complete Set (10):		6.00
Common Player:		.30
1	Cecil Fielder	.30
2	Dean Palmer	.30
3	Andres Galarraga	.30
4	Bo Jackson	.40
5	Ken Griffey Jr.	1.50
6	Dave Justice	.30
7	Mike Piazza	1.50
8	Frank Thomas	1.00
9	Barry Bonds	3.00
10	Juan Gonzalez	.50

MVPs

These inserts were included in 1994 jumbo packs only. The fronts have a large metallic blue MVP logo, beneath which is a red stripe with the player's name and position in white. Backs have a portrait photo, stats for 1993 and a summary of why the player was selected as team MVP.

		NM/M
Complete Set (28):		20.00
Common Player:		.25
1	Dave Justice	.25
2	Mark Grace	.25
3	Jose Rijo	.25
4	Andres Galarraga	.25
5	Bryan Harvey	.25
6	Jeff Bagwell	1.00
7	Mike Piazza	2.50
8	Moises Alou	.25

9	Bobby Bonilla	.25
10	Len Dykstra	.25
11	Jeff King	.25
12	Gregg Jefferies	.25
13	Tony Gwynn	1.50
14	Barry Bonds	4.00
15	Cal Ripken, Jr.	4.00
16	Mo Vaughn	.25
17	Tim Salmon	.25
18	Frank Thomas	1.00
19	Albert Belle	.25
20	Cecil Fielder	.25
21	Wally Joyner	.25
22	Greg Vaughn	.25
23	Kirby Puckett	1.50
24	Don Mattingly	2.00
25	Ruben Sierra	.25
26	Ken Griffey Jr.	2.50
27	Juan Gonzalez	.50
28	John Olerud	.25

Spirit of the Game

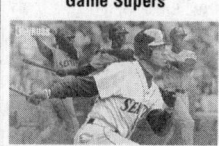

Ten players are featured in this insert set, packaged exclusively in retail boxes. Horizontal in format, fronts feature a color player action photo set against a gold-tone background which has the appearance of a multiple-exposure photo. On back a player portrait photo is set against a backdrop of red, white and blue bunting. There is a short previous-season write-up at right. Cards #1-5 were included with Series I, cards 6-10 were in Series II packs.

		NM/M
Complete Set (10):		10.00
Common Player:		.70
1	John Olerud	.50
2	Barry Bonds	2.50
3	Ken Griffey Jr.	2.00
4	Mike Piazza	2.00
5	Juan Gonzalez	.60
6	Frank Thomas	1.00
7	Tim Salmon	.50
8	Dave Justice	.50
9	Don Mattingly	1.50
10	Len Dykstra	.50

1994 Donruss Spirit of the Game Supers

Virtually identical in format to the regular-size "Spirit of the Game" cards, these 3-1/2" x 5" versions have gold-foil, rather than holographic printing on the front, and have a serial number on back identifying it from an edition of 10,000. One super card was inserted in each specially designated retail box.

		NM/M
Complete Set (10):		20.00
Common Player:		1.50
1	John Olerud	1.50
2	Barry Bonds	4.00
3	Ken Griffey Jr.	3.50
4	Mike Piazza	3.50
5	Juan Gonzalez	2.00
6	Frank Thomas	2.50
7	Tim Salmon	1.50
8	Dave Justice	1.50
9	Don Mattingly	3.00
10	Len Dykstra	1.50

1995 Donruss Samples

The cards in this preview release of Donruss' 1995 baseball issue are virtually identical to the issued versions of the same players' cards except for slight picture cropping differences. They are unmarked as to sample status.

		NM/M
Complete Set (7):		10.00
Common Player:		1.00
5	Mike Piazza	2.00
8	Barry Bonds	3.00
20	Jeff Bagwell	1.50
42	Juan Gonzalez	1.00
55	Don Mattingly	2.00
275	Frank Thomas	1.50
331	Greg Maddux	1.50

1995 Donruss

A pair of player photos on the front of each card and silver-foil highlights are featured on the 1995 Donruss set. Besides the main action photo on front, each card has a second photo in a home plate frame at lower-left. A silver-foil ribbon beneath has the player's team and name embossed. Above the small photo is the player's position, with a half-circle of stars over all; both elements in silver foil. Completing the silver-foil highlights is the Donruss logo at upper-left. Full-bleed backs have yet another action photo at center, with a large team logo at left and five years' worth of stats plus career numbers at bottom. Donruss was issued in retail and hobby 12-card packs, magazine distributor packs of 16 and jumbo packs of 20 cards. New to Donruss in 1995 were Super Packs. These were packs that contained complete insert sets and were seeded every 90 packs.

		NM/M
Complete Set (550):		20.00
Common Player:		.05
Press Proofs:		15X
Series 1 or 2 Pack (12):		.75
Series 1 or 2 Wax Box (36):		20.00
1	Dave Justice	.05
2	Rene Arocha	.05
3	Sandy Alomar Jr.	.05
4	Luis Lopez	.05
5	Mike Piazza	1.50
6	Bobby Jones	.05
7	Damion Easley	.05
8	Barry Bonds	2.50
9	Mike Mussina	.40
10	Kevin Seitzer	.05
11	John Smiley	.05
12	W. Van Landingham	.05
13	Ron Darling	.05
14	Walt Weiss	.05
15	Mike Lansing	.05
16	Allen Watson	.05
17	Aaron Sele	.05
18	Randy Johnson	.65
19	Dean Palmer	.05
20	Jeff Bagwell	.65
21	Curt Schilling	.05
22	Darrell Whitmore	.05
23	Steve Trachsel	.05
24	Dan Wilson	.05
25	Steve Finley	.05
26	Bret Boone	.05
27	Charles Johnson	.05
28	Mike Stanton	.05
29	Ismael Valdes	.05
30	Salomon Torres	.05
31	Eric Anthony	.05
32	Spike Owen	.05
33	Joey Cora	.05
34	Robert Eenhoorn	.05
35	Rick White	.05
36	Omar Vizquel	.05
37	Carlos Delgado	.45
38	Eddie Williams	.05
39	Shawon Dunston	.05
40	Darrin Fletcher	.05
41	Leo Gomez	.05
42	Juan Gonzalez	.40
43	Luis Alicea	.05
44	Ken Ryan	.05
45	Lou Whitaker	.05
46	Mike Blowers	.05
47	Willie Blair	.05
48	Todd Van Poppel	.05
49	Roberto Alomar	.25
50	Ozzie Smith	.75
51	Sterling Hitchcock	.05
52	Mo Vaughn	.40
53	Rick Aguilera	.05
54	Kent Mercker	.05
55	Don Mattingly	1.00
56	Bob Scanlan	.05
57	Wilson Alvarez	.05
58	Jose Mesa	.05
59	Scott Kamieniecki	.05
60	Todd Jones	.05

61	John Kruk	.05
62	Mike Stanley	.05
63	Tino Martinez	.05
64	Eddie Zambrano	.05
65	Todd Hundley	.05
66	Jamie Moyer	.05
67	Rich Amaral	.05
68	Jose Valentin	.05
69	Alex Gonzalez	.05
70	Kurt Abbott	.05
71	Delino DeShields	.05
72	Brian Anderson	.05
73	John Vander Wal	.05
74	Turner Ward	.05
75	Tim Raines	.05
76	Mark Acre	.05
77	Jose Offerman	.05
78	Jimmy Key	.05
79	Mark Whiten	.05
80	Mark Gubicza	.05
81	Darren Hall	.05
82	Travis Fryman	.05
83	Cal Ripken, Jr.	2.50
84	Geronimo Berroa	.05
85	Bret Barberie	.05
86	Andy Ashby	.05
87	Steve Avery	.05
88	Rich Becker	.05
89	John Valentin	.05
90	Glenallen Hill	.05
91	Carlos Garcia	.05
92	Dennis Martinez	.05
93	Pat Kelly	.05
94	Orlando Miller	.05
95	Felix Jose	.05
96	Mike Kingery	.05
97	Jeff Kent	.05
98	Pete Incaviglia	.05
99	Chad Curtis	.05
100	Thomas Howard	.05
101	Hector Carrasco	.05
102	Tom Pagnozzi	.05
103	Danny Tartabull	.05
104	Donnie Elliott	.05
105	Danny Jackson	.05
106	Steve Dunn	.05
107	Roger Salkeld	.05
108	Jeff King	.05
109	Cecil Fielder	.05
110	Checklist	.05
111	Denny Neagle	.05
112	Troy Neel	.05
113	Rod Beck	.05
114	Alex Rodriguez	2.00
115	Joey Eischen	.05
116	Tom Candiotti	.05
117	Ray McDavid	.05
118	Vince Coleman	.05
119	Pete Harnisch	.05
120	David Nied	.05
121	Pat Rapp	.05
122	Sammy Sosa	.75
123	Steve Reed	.05
124	Jose Oliva	.05
125	Rick Bottalico	.05
126	Jose DeLeon	.05
127	Pat Hentgen	.05
128	Will Clark	.05
129	Mark Dewey	.05
130	Greg Vaughn	.05
131	Darren Dreifort	.05
132	Ed Sprague	.05
133	Lee Smith	.05
134	Charles Nagy	.05
135	Phil Plantier	.05
136	Jason Jacome	.05
137	Jose Lima	.05
138	J.R. Phillips	.05
139	J.T. Snow	.05
140	Mike Huff	.05
141	Billy Brewer	.05
142	Jeromy Burnitz	.05
143	Ricky Bones	.05
144	Carlos Rodriguez	.05
145	Luis Gonzalez	.05
146	Mark Lemke	.05
147	Al Martin	.05
148	Mike Bordick	.05
149	Robb Nen	.05
150	Wil Cordero	.05
151	Edgar Martinez	.05
152	Gerald Williams	.05
153	Esteban Beltre	.05
154	Mike Moore	.05
155	Mark Langston	.05
156	Mark Clark	.05
157	Bobby Ayala	.05
158	Rick Wilkins	.05
159	Bobby Munoz	.05
160	Checklist	.05
161	Scott Erickson	.05
162	Paul Molitor	.65
163	Jon Lieber	.05
164	Jason Grimsley	.05
165	Norberto Martin	.05
166	Javier Lopez	.05
167	Brian McRae	.05
168	Gary Sheffield	.40
169	Marcus Moore	.05
170	John Hudek	.05
171	Kelly Stinett	.05
172	Chris Gomez	.05
173	Rey Sanchez	.05
174	Juan Guzman	.05
175	Chan Ho Park	.05
176	Terry Shumpert	.05
177	Steve Ontiveros	.05
178	Brad Ausmus	.05

#	Player	Price
179	Tim Davis	.05
180	Billy Ashley	.05
181	Vinny Castilla	.05
182	Bill Spiers	.05
183	Randy Knorr	.05
184	Brian Hunter	.05
185	Pat Meares	.05
186	Steve Buechele	.05
187	Kirt Manwaring	.05
188	Tim Naehring	.05
189	Matt Mieske	.07
190	Josias Manzanillo	.05
191	Greg McMichael	.05
192	Chuck Carr	.05
193	Midre Cummings	.05
194	Darryl Strawberry	.05
195	Greg Gagne	.05
196	Steve Cooke	.05
197	Woody Williams	.05
198	Ron Karkovice	.05
199	Phil Leftwich	.05
200	Jim Thome	.50
201	Brady Anderson	.05
202	Pedro Martinez	.65
203	Steve Karsay	.05
204	Reggie Sanders	.05
205	Bill Risley	.05
206	Jay Bell	.05
207	Kevin Brown	.05
208	Tim Scott	.05
209	Len Dykstra	.05
210	Willie Greene	.05
211	Jim Eisenreich	.05
212	Cliff Floyd	.05
213	Otis Nixon	.05
214	Eduardo Perez	.05
215	Manuel Lee	.05
216	Armando Benitez RC	.10
217	Dave McCarty	.05
218	Scott Livingstone	.05
219	Chad Kreuter	.05
220	Checklist	.05
221	Brian Jordan	.05
222	Matt Whiteside	.05
223	Jim Edmonds	.05
224	Tony Gwynn	.75
225	Jose Lind	.05
226	Marvin Freeman	.05
227	Ken Hill	.05
228	David Hulse	.05
229	Joe Hesketh	.05
230	Roberto Petagine	.05
231	Jeffrey Hammonds	.05
232	John Jaha	.05
233	John Burkett	.05
234	Hal Morris	.05
235	Tony Castillo	.05
236	Ryan Bowen	.05
237	Wayne Kirby	.05
238	Brent Mayne	.05
239	Jim Bullinger	.05
240	Mike Lieberthal	.05
241	Barry Larkin	.05
242	David Segui	.05
243	Jose Bautista	.05
244	Hector Fajardo	.05
245	Orel Hershiser	.05
246	James Mouton	.05
247	Scott Leius	.05
248	Tom Glavine	.25
249	Danny Bautista	.05
250	Jose Mercedes	.05
251	Marquis Grissom	.05
252	Charlie Hayes	.05
253	Ryan Klesko	.05
254	Vicente Palacios	.05
255	Matias Carillo	.05
256	Gary DiSarcina	.05
257	Kirk Gibson	.05
258	Garey Ingram	.05
259	Alex Fernandez	.05
260	John Mabry	.05
261	Chris Howard	.05
262	Miguel Jimenez	.05
263	Heath Slocumb	.05
264	Albert Belle	.05
265	Dave Clark	.05
266	Joe Orsulak	.05
267	Joey Hamilton	.05
268	Mark Portugal	.05
269	Kevin Tapani	.05
270	Sid Fernandez	.05
271	Steve Dreyer	.05
272	Denny Hocking	.05
273	Troy O'Leary	.05
274	Milt Cuyler	.05
275	Frank Thomas	.65
276	Jorge Fabregas	.05
277	Mike Gallego	.05
278	Mickey Morandini	.05
279	Roberto Hernandez	.05
280	Henry Rodriguez	.05
281	Garret Anderson	.05
282	Bob Wickman	.05
283	Gar Finnvold	.05
284	Paul O'Neill	.05
285	Royce Clayton	.05
286	Chuck Knoblauch	.05
287	Johnny Ruffin	.05
288	Dave Nilsson	.05
289	David Cone	.05
290	Chuck McElroy	.05
291	Kevin Stocker	.05
292	Jose Rijo	.05
293	Sean Berry	.05
294	Ozzie Guillen	.05
295	Chris Hoiles	.05
296	Kevin Foster	.05

#	Player	Price
297	Jeff Frye	.05
298	Lance Johnson	.05
299	Mike Kelly	.05
300	Ellis Burks	.05
301	Roberto Kelly	.05
302	Dante Bichette	.05
303	Alvaro Espinoza	.05
304	Alex Cole	.05
305	Rickey Henderson	.65
306	Dave Weathers	.05
307	Shane Reynolds	.05
308	Bobby Bonilla	.05
309	Junior Felix	.05
310	Jeff Fassero	.05
311	Darren Lewis	.05
312	John Doherty	.05
313	Scott Servais	.05
314	Rick Helling	.05
315	Pedro Martinez	.65
316	Wes Chamberlain	.05
317	Bryan Eversgerd	.05
318	Trevor Hoffman	.05
319	John Patterson	.05
320	Matt Walbeck	.05
321	Jeff Montgomery	.05
322	Mel Rojas	.05
323	Eddie Taubensee	.05
324	Ray Lankford	.05
325	Jose Vizcaino	.05
326	Carlos Baerga	.05
327	Jack Voigt	.05
328	Julio Franco	.05
329	Brent Gates	.05
330	Checklist	.05
331	Greg Maddux	.75
332	Jason Bere	.05
333	Bill Wegman	.05
334	Tuffy Rhodes	.05
335	Kevin Young	.05
336	Andy Benes	.05
337	Pedro Astacio	.05
338	Reggie Jefferson	.05
339	Tim Belcher	.05
340	Ken Griffey Jr.	1.50
341	Mariano Duncan	.05
342	Andres Galarraga	.05
343	Rondell White	.05
344	Cory Bailey	.05
345	Bryan Harvey	.05
346	John Franco	.05
347	Greg Swindell	.05
348	David West	.05
349	Fred McGriff	.05
350	Jose Canseco	.35
351	Orlando Merced	.05
352	Rheal Cormier	.05
353	Carlos Pulido	.05
354	Terry Steinbach	.05
355	Wade Boggs	.05
356	B.J. Surhoff	.05
357	Rafael Palmeiro	.60
358	Anthony Young	.05
359	Tom Brunansky	.05
360	Todd Stottlemyre	.05
361	Chris Turner	.05
362	Joe Boever	.05
363	Jeff Blauser	.05
364	Derek Bell	.05
365	Matt Williams	.05
366	Jeremy Hernandez	.05
367	Joe Girardi	.05
368	Mike Devereaux	.05
369	Jim Abbott	.05
370	Manny Ramirez	.65
371	Kenny Lofton	.05
372	Mark Smith	.05
373	Dave Fleming	.05
374	Dave Stewart	.05
375	Roger Pavlik	.05
376	Hipolito Pichardo	.05
377	Bill Taylor	.05
378	Robin Ventura	.05
379	Bernard Gilkey	.05
380	Kirby Puckett	.75
381	Steve Howe	.05
382	Devon White	.05
383	Roberto Mejia	.05
384	Darrin Jackson	.05
385	Mike Morgan	.05
386	Rusty Meacham	.05
387	Bill Swift	.05
388	Lou Frazier	.05
389	Andy Van Slyke	.05
390	Brett Butler	.05
391	Bobby Witt	.05
392	Jeff Conine	.05
393	Tim Hyers	.05
394	Terry Pendleton	.05
395	Ricky Jordan	.05
396	Eric Plunk	.05
397	Melido Perez	.05
398	Darryl Kile	.05
399	Mark McLemore	.05
400	Greg Harris	.05
401	Jim Leyritz	.05
402	Doug Strange	.05
403	Tim Salmon	.05
404	Terry Mulholland	.05
405	Robby Thompson	.05
406	Ruben Sierra	.05
407	Tony Phillips	.05
408	Moises Alou	.05
409	Felix Fermin	.05
410	Pat Listach	.05
411	Kevin Bass	.05
412	Ben McDonald	.05
413	Scott Cooper	.05
414	Jody Reed	.05

#	Player	Price
415	Deion Sanders	.05
416	Ricky Gutierrez	.05
417	Gregg Jefferies	.05
418	Jack McDowell	.05
419	Al Leiter	.05
420	Tony Longmire	.05
421	Paul Wagner	.05
422	Geronimo Pena	.05
423	Ivan Rodriguez	.60
424	Kevin Gross	.05
425	Kirk McCaskill	.05
426	Greg Myers	.05
427	Roger Clemens	1.00
428	Chris Hammond	.05
429	Randy Myers	.05
430	Roger Mason	.05
431	Bret Saberhagen	.05
432	Jeff Reboulet	.05
433	John Olerud	.05
434	Bill Gullickson	.05
435	Eddie Murray	.65
436	Pedro Munoz	.05
437	Charlie O'Brien	.05
438	Jeff Nelson	.05
439	Mike Macfarlane	.05
440	Checklist	.05
441	Derrick May	.05
442	John Roper	.05
443	Darryl Hamilton	.05
444	Dan Miceli	.05
445	Tony Eusebio	.05
446	Jerry Browne	.05
447	Wally Joyner	.05
448	Brian Harper	.05
449	Scott Fletcher	.05
450	Bip Roberts	.05
451	Pete Smith	.05
452	Chili Davis	.05
453	Dave Hollins	.05
454	Tony Pena	.05
455	Butch Henry	.05
456	Craig Biggio	.05
457	Zane Smith	.05
458	Ryan Thompson	.05
459	Mike Jackson	.05
460	Mark McGwire	2.00
461	John Smoltz	.05
462	Steve Scarsone	.05
463	Greg Colbrunn	.05
464	Shawn Green	.25
465	David Wells	.05
466	Jose Hernandez	.05
467	Chip Hale	.05
468	Tony Tarasco	.05
469	Kevin Mitchell	.05
470	Billy Hatcher	.05
471	Jay Buhner	.05
472	Ken Caminiti	.05
473	Tom Henke	.05
474	Todd Worrell	.05
475	Mark Eichhorn	.05
476	Bruce Ruffin	.05
477	Chuck Finley	.05
478	Marc Newfield	.05
479	Paul Shuey	.05
480	Bob Tewksbury	.05
481	Ramon Martinez	.05
482	Melvin Nieves	.05
483	Todd Zeile	.05
484	Benito Santiago	.05
485	Stan Javier	.05
486	Kirk Rueter	.05
487	Andre Dawson	.25
488	Eric Karros	.05
489	Dave Magadan	.05
490	Checklist	.05
491	Randy Velarde	.05
492	Larry Walker	.05
493	Cris Carpenter	.05
494	Tom Gordon	.05
495	Dave Burba	.05
496	Darren Bragg	.05
497	Darren Daulton	.05
498	Don Slaught	.05
499	Pat Borders	.05
500	Lenny Harris	.05
501	Joe Ausanio	.05
502	Alan Trammell	.05
503	Mike Fetters	.05
504	Scott Ruffcorn	.05
505	Rich Rowland	.05
506	Juan Samuel	.05
507	Bo Jackson	.10
508	Jeff Branson	.05
509	Bernie Williams	.05
510	Paul Sorrento	.05
511	Dennis Eckersley	.60
512	Pat Mahomes	.05
513	Rusty Greer	.05
514	Luis Polonia	.05
515	Willie Banks	.05
516	John Wetteland	.05
517	Mike LaValliere	.05
518	Tommy Greene	.05
519	Mark Grace	.05
520	Bob Hamelin	.05
521	Scott Sanderson	.05
522	Joe Carter	.05
523	Jeff Brantley	.05
524	Andrew Lorraine	.05
525	Rico Brogna	.05
526	Shane Mack	.05
527	Mark Wohlers	.05
528	Scott Sanders	.05
529	Chris Bosio	.05
530	Andujar Cedeno	.05
531	Kenny Rogers	.05
532	Doug Drabek	.05

#	Player	Price
533	Curt Leskanic	.05
534	Craig Shipley	.05
535	Craig Grebeck	.05
536	Cal Eldred	.05
537	Mickey Tettleton	.05
538	Harold Baines	.05
539	Tim Wallach	.05
540	Damon Buford	.05
541	Lenny Webster	.05
542	Kevin Appier	.05
543	Raul Mondesi	.05
544	Eric Young	.05
545	Russ Davis	.05
546	Mike Benjamin	.05
547	Mike Greenwell	.05
548	Scott Brosius	.05
549	Brian Dorsett	.05
550	Checklist	.05

Press Proofs

Designated as Press Proofs, the first 2,000 cards of each player in the '95 Donruss set were enhanced with gold, rather than silver, foil and inserted into packs at an average rate of one per 20 packs.

	NM/M
Complete Set (550):	150.00
Common Player:	1.00
Stars:	15X

All-Stars

Exclusive to Wal-Mart jumbo packs were Donruss All-Stars. Nine cards featuring American Leaguers were inserted into Series 1, while nine National League All-Stars were inserted into Series 2 jumbos.

		NM/M
Complete Set (18):		26.00
Common Player:		.40
AL1	Jimmy Key	.40
AL2	Ivan Rodriguez	1.25
AL3	Frank Thomas	1.50
AL4	Roberto Alomar	.60
AL5	Wade Boggs	2.00
AL6	Cal Ripken, Jr.	4.50
AL7	Joe Carter	.40
AL8	Ken Griffey Jr.	3.00
AL9	Kirby Puckett	2.00
NL1	Greg Maddux	2.00
NL2	Mike Piazza	3.00
NL3	Gregg Jefferies	.40
NL4	Mariano Duncan	.40
NL5	Matt Williams	.40
NL6	Ozzie Smith	2.00
NL7	Barry Bonds	4.50
NL8	Tony Gwynn	2.00
NL9	Dave Justice	2.00

Bomb Squad

Bomb Squad features the top six home run hitters in each league on double-sided cards. These cards were only inserted into Se-

ries I retail and magazine distributor packs at a rate of one per 24 retail packs and one per 16 magazine distributor packs.

		NM/M
Complete Set (6):		3.00
Common Player:		.50
1	Ken Griffey Jr., Matt Williams	1.00
2	Frank Thomas, Jeff Bagwell	.75
3	Albert Belle, Barry Bonds	1.50
4	Jose Canseco, Fred McGriff	.60
5	Cecil Fielder, Andres Galarraga	.50
6	Joe Carter, Kevin Mitchell	.50

Diamond Kings

Continuing a tradition begun in 1982, artist Dick Perez painted a series of 28 water colors to produce insert cards of the game's best; 14 in each series. A portrait of the player appears on a party-colored background, with Diamond Kings in gold across the top. DKs were inserted in Series 1 and 2 packs at a rate of one per 10.

		NM/M
Complete Set (29):		35.00
Common Player:		.75
1	Frank Thomas	3.00
2	Jeff Bagwell	3.00
3	Chili Davis	.75
4	Dante Bichette	.75
5	Ruben Sierra	.75
6	Jeff Conine	.75
7	Paul O'Neill	.75
8	Bobby Bonilla	.75
9	Joe Carter	.75
10	Moises Alou	.75
11	Kenny Lofton	.75
12	Matt Williams	.75
13	Kevin Seitzer	.75
14	Sammy Sosa	3.50
15	Scott Cooper	.75
16	Raul Mondesi	.75
17	Will Clark	.75
18	Lenny Dykstra	.75
19	Kirby Puckett	3.50
20	Hal Morris	.75
21	Travis Fryman	.75
22	Greg Maddux	2.50
23	Rafael Palmeiro	.75
24	Tony Gwynn	3.50
25	David Cone	.75
26	Al Martin	.75
27	Ken Griffey Jr.	5.00
28	Gregg Jefferies	.75
29	Checklist	.10

Dominators

Dominators is a nine-card chase set inserted into hobby packs of Series II Donruss baseball at a rate of one per 24 packs. These acetate cards feature three of the top players at each position on a horizontal format.

		NM/M
Complete Set (9):		7.50
Common Player:		.50
1	David Cone, Mike Mussina, Greg Maddux	1.00
2	Ivan Rodriguez, Mike Piazza, Darren Daulton	2.00
3	Fred McGriff, Frank Thomas, Jeff Bagwell	1.50
4	Roberto Alomar, Carlos Baerga, Craig Biggio	.75

5	Robin Ventura, Travis Fryman, Matt Williams	.50
6	Cal Ripken Jr., Barry Larkin, Wil Cordero	2.50
7	Albert Belle, Barry Bonds, Moises Alou	2.50
8	Ken Griffey Jr., Kenny Lofton, Marquis Grissom	2.00
9	Kirby Puckett, Paul O'Neill, Tony Gwynn	2.00

Elite

Another Donruss insert tradition continues with the fifth annual presentation of the Elite series. Each of the 12 cards (six each Series 1 and 2) is produced in a numbered edition of 10,000 and inserted into all types of packaging at the rate of one per 210 packs.

	NM/M
Complete Set (12):	100.00
Common Player:	6.00
49 Jeff Bagwell	12.00
50 Paul O'Neill	6.00
51 Greg Maddux	15.00
52 Mike Piazza	17.50
53 Matt Williams	6.00
54 Ken Griffey Jr.	17.50
55 Frank Thomas	12.00
56 Barry Bonds	20.00
57 Kirby Puckett	15.00
58 Fred McGriff	6.00
59 Jose Canseco	9.00
60 Albert Belle	6.00

Long Ball Leaders

Exclusive to Series 1 hobby packs, these cards feature the top long-distance home runs of 1994 in an eye-popping holographic foil presentation. Stated odds of picking one from a hobby pack are one in 24.

		NM/M
Complete Set (8):		7.50
Common Player:		.50
1	Frank Thomas	1.50
2	Fred McGriff	1.50
3	Ken Griffey Jr.	2.00
4	Matt Williams	1.00
5	Mike Piazza	2.00
6	Jose Canseco	.75
7	Barry Bonds	2.50
8	Jeff Bagwell	1.50

Mound Marvels

Mound Marvels is an eight-card insert set containing some of the best pitchers in baseball. Cards were inserted into one per 18 retail and magazine packs of Donruss Series II. Each card features a two-way mirror that allows collectors to see the players' face through the mirror.

	NM/M
Complete Set (8):	7.50
Common Player:	1.00
1 Greg Maddux	4.00
2 David Cone	1.00
3 Mike Mussina	2.00
4 Bret Saberhagen	1.00
5 Jimmy Key	1.00
6 Doug Drabek	1.00
7 Randy Johnson	3.00
8 Jason Bere	1.00

1995 Donruss/Top of the Order Card Game

In one of the earliest efforts to wed the play factor and collectibility that had made various fantasy card games so successful in 1994-95, Donruss created the interactive Top of the Order baseball card game. Printed on playing card stock with rounded corners and semi-gloss surface, the player cards feature color action photos and all manners of game-action indicators. Backs of each card are printed primarily in green with Donruss logos. Cards were sold in several types of packaging, including 80- and 160-card boxed sets, and 12-card foil "booster" packs. Stars' cards were printed in lesser quantities than those of journeyman players, resulting in values higher than would be the case based on player popularity alone if all cards were printed in equal quantities. The unnumbered cards are checklisted here in alphabetical order within team and league.

	NM/M
Complete Set (360):	125.00
Common Player:	.10
Starter Deck (80):	6.00
Starter Deck (160):	12.00
Wax Pack (12):	1.00
Wax Box (36):	20.00
(1) Brady Anderson	.10
(2) Harold Baines	.10
(3) Bret Barberie	.10
(4) Armando Benitez	.10
(5) Bobby Bonilla	.10
(6) Scott Erickson	.10
(7) Leo Gomez	.10
(8) Curtis Goodwin	.10
(9) Jeffrey Hammonds	.10
(10) Chris Hoiles	.10
(11) Doug Jones	.10
(12) Ben McDonald	.10
(13) Mike Mussina	1.50
(14) Rafael Palmeiro	2.50
(15) Cal Ripken Jr.	10.00
(16) Rick Aguilera	.10
(17) Luis Alicea	.10
(18) Jose Canseco	1.50
(19) Roger Clemens	5.00
(20) Mike Greenwell	.10
(21) Erik Hanson	.10
(22) Mike Macfarlane	.10
(23) Tim Naehring	.10
(24) Troy O'Leary	.10
(25) Ken Ryan	.10
(26) Aaron Sele	.10
(27) Lee Tinsley	.10
(28) John Valentin	.10
(29) Mo Vaughn	.10
(30) Jim Abbott	.10
(31) Mike Butcher	.10
(32) Chili Davis	.10
(33) Gary DiSarcina	.10
(34) Damion Easley	.10
(35) Jim Edmonds	.10
(36) Chuck Finley	.10
(37) Mark Langston	.10
(38) Greg Myers	.10
(39) Spike Owen	.10
(40) Troy Percival	.10
(41) Tony Phillips	.10
(42) Tim Salmon	.10
(43) Lee Smith	.10
(44) J.T. Snow	.10
(45) Jason Bere	.10
(46) Mike Devereaux	.10
(47) Ray Durham	.10
(48) Alex Fernandez	.10
(49) Ozzie Guillen	.10
(50) Roberto Hernandez	.10
(51) Lance Johnson	.10
(52) Ron Karkovice	.10
(53) Tim Raines	.10
(54) Frank Thomas	3.00
(55) Robin Ventura	.10
(56) Sandy Alomar Jr.	.10
(57) Carlos Baerga	.10
(58) Albert Belle	.10
(59) Kenny Lofton	.10
(60) Dennis Martinez	.10
(61) Jose Mesa	.10
(62) Eddie Murray	3.00
(63) Charles Nagy	.10
(64) Tony Pena	.10
(65) Eric Plunk	.10
(66) Manny Ramirez	3.00
(67) Paul Sorrento	.10
(68) Jim Thome	2.00
(69) Omar Vizquel	.10
(70) Danny Bautista	.10
(71) Joe Boever	.10
(72) Chad Curtis	.10
(73) Cecil Fielder	.10
(74) John Flaherty	.10
(75) Travis Fryman	.10
(76) Kirk Gibson	.10
(77) Chris Gomez	.10
(78) Mike Henneman	.10
(79) Bob Higginson	.10
(80) Alan Trammell	.10
(81) Lou Whitaker	.10
(82) Kevin Appier	.10
(83) Billy Brewer	.10
(84) Vince Coleman	.10
(85) Gary Gaetti	.10
(86) Greg Gagne	.10
(87) Tom Goodwin	.10
(88) Tom Gordon	.10
(89) Mark Gubicza	.10
(90) Bob Hamelin	.10
(91) Phil Hiatt	.10
(92) Wally Joyner	.10
(93) Brent Mayne	.10
(94) Jeff Montgomery	.10
(95) Ricky Bones	.10
(96) Mike Fetters	.10
(97) Darryl Hamilton	.10
(98) Pat Listach	.10
(99) Matt Mieske	.10
(100) Dave Nilsson	.10
(101) Joe Oliver	.10
(102) Kevin Seitzer	.10
(103) B.J. Surhoff	.10
(104) Jose Valentin	.10
(105) Greg Vaughn	.10
(106) Bill Wegman	.10
(107) Alex Cole	.10
(108) Marty Cordova	.10
(109) Chuck Knoblauch	.10
(110) Scott Leius	.10
(111) Pat Meares	.10
(112) Pedro Munoz	.10
(113) Kirby Puckett	4.00
(114) Scott Stahoviak	.10
(115) Mike Trombley	.10
(116) Matt Walbeck	.10
(117) Wade Boggs	4.00
(118) David Cone	.10
(119) Tony Fernandez	.10
(120) Don Mattingly	5.00
(121) Jack McDowell	.10
(122) Paul O'Neill	.10
(123) Melido Perez	.10
(124) Luis Polonia	.10
(125) Ruben Sierra	.10
(126) Mike Stanley	.10
(127) Randy Velarde	.10
(128) John Wetteland	.10
(129) Bob Wickman	.10
(130) Bernie Williams	.10
(131) Gerald Williams	.10
(132) Geronimo Berroa	.10
(133) Mike Bordick	.10
(134) Scott Brosius	.10
(135) Dennis Eckersley	.10
(136) Brent Gates	.10
(137) Rickey Henderson	3.00
(138) Stan Javier	.10
(139) Mark McGwire	8.00
(140) Steve Ontiveros	.10
(141) Terry Steinbach	.10
(142) Todd Stottlemyre	.10
(143) Danny Tartabull	.10
(144) Bobby Ayala	.10
(145) Andy Benes	.10
(146) Mike Blowers	.10
(147) Jay Buhner	.10
(148) Joey Cora	.10
(149) Alex Diaz	.10
(150) Ken Griffey Jr.	6.00
(151) Randy Johnson	3.00
(152) Edgar Martinez	.10
(153) Tino Martinez	.10
(154) Bill Risley	.10
(155) Alex Rodriguez	8.00
(156) Dan Wilson	.10
(157) Will Clark	.10
(158) Jeff Frye	.10
(159) Benji Gil	.10
(160) Juan Gonzalez	1.50
(161) Rusty Greer	.10
(162) Mark McLemore	.10
(163) Otis Nixon	.10
(164) Dean Palmer	.10
(165) Ivan Rodriguez	2.50
(166) Kenny Rogers	.10
(167) Jeff Russell	.10
(168) Mickey Tettleton	.10
(169) Bob Tewksbury	.10
(170) Bobby Witt	.10
(171) Roberto Alomar	.30
(172) Joe Carter	.10
(173) Alex Gonzalez	.10
(174) Candy Maldonado	.10
(175) Paul Molitor	3.00
(176) John Olerud	.10
(177) Lance Parrish	.10
(178) Ed Sprague	.10
(179) Devon White	.10
(180) Woody Williams	.10
(181) Steve Avery	.10
(182) Jeff Blauser	.10
(183) Tom Glavine	.50
(184) Marquis Grissom	.10
(185) Chipper Jones	4.00
(186) Dave Justice	.10
(187) Ryan Klesko	.10
(188) Mark Lemke	.10
(189) Javier Lopez	.10
(190) Greg Maddux	4.00
(191) Fred McGriff	.10
(192) Greg McMichael	.10
(193) John Smoltz	.10
(194) Mark Wohlers	.10
(195) Jim Bullinger	.10
(196) Shawon Dunston	.10
(197) Kevin Foster	.10
(198) Luis Gonzalez	.10
(199) Mark Grace	.10
(200) Brian McRae	.10
(201) Randy Myers	.10
(202) Jaime Navarro	.10
(203) Rey Sanchez	.10
(204) Scott Servais	.10
(205) Sammy Sosa	4.00
(206) Steve Trachsel	.10
(207) Todd Zeile	.10
(208) Bret Boone	.10
(209) Jeff Branson	.10
(210) Jeff Brantley	.10
(211) Hector Carrasco	.10
(212) Ron Gant	.10
(213) Lenny Harris	.10
(214) Barry Larkin	.10
(215) Darren Lewis	.10
(216) Hal Morris	.10
(217) Mark Portugal	.10
(218) Jose Rijo	.10
(219) Reggie Sanders	.10
(220) Pete Schourek	.10
(221) John Smiley	.10
(222) Eddie Taubensee	.10
(223) Dave Wells	.10
(224) Jason Bates	.10
(225) Dante Bichette	.10
(226) Vinny Castilla	.10
(227) Andres Galarraga	.10
(228) Joe Girardi	.10
(229) Mike Kingery	.10
(230) Steve Reed	.10
(231) Bruce Ruffin	.10
(232) Bret Saberhagen	.10
(233) Bill Swift	.10
(234) Larry Walker	.10
(235) Walt Weiss	.10
(236) Eric Young	.10
(237) Kurt Abbott	.10
(238) John Burkett	.10
(239) Chuck Carr	.10
(240) Greg Colbrunn	.10
(241) Jeff Conine	.10
(242) Andre Dawson	.35
(243) Chris Hammond	.10
(244) Charles Johnson	.10
(245) Robb Nen	.10
(246) Terry Pendleton	.10
(247) Gary Sheffield	.50
(248) Quilvio Veras	.10
(249) Jeff Bagwell	3.00
(250) Derek Bell	.10
(251) Craig Biggio	.10
(252) Doug Drabek	.10
(253) Tony Eusebio	.10
(254) John Hudek	.10
(255) Brian Hunter	.10
(256) Todd Jones	.10
(257) Dave Magadan	.10
(258) Orlando Miller	.10
(259) James Mouton	.10
(260) Shane Reynolds	.10
(261) Greg Swindell	.10
(262) Billy Ashley	.10
(263) Tom Candiotti	.10
(264) Delino DeShields	.10
(265) Eric Karros	.10
(266) Roberto Kelly	.10
(267) Ramon Martinez	.10
(268) Raul Mondesi	.10
(269) Hideo Nomo	1.50
(270) Jose Offerman	.10
(271) Mike Piazza	6.00
(272) Kevin Tapani	.10
(273) Ismael Valdes	.10
(274) Tim Wallach	.10
(275) Todd Worrell	.10
(276) Moises Alou	.10
(277) Sean Berry	.10
(278) Wil Cordero	.10
(279) Jeff Fassero	.10
(280) Darrin Fletcher	.10
(281) Mike Lansing	.10
(282) Pedro J. Martinez	3.00
(283) Carlos Perez	.10
(284) Mel Rojas	.10
(285) Tim Scott	.10
(286) David Segui	.10
(287) Tony Tarasco	.10
(288) Rondell White	.10
(289) Rico Brogna	.10
(290) Brett Butler	.10
(291) John Franco	.10
(292) Pete Harnisch	.10
(293) Todd Hundley	.10
(294) Bobby Jones	.10
(295) Jeff Kent	.10
(296) Joe Orsulak	.10
(297) Ryan Thompson	.10
(298) Jose Vizcaino	.10
(299) Ricky Bottalico	.10
(300) Darren Daulton	.10
(301) Mariano Duncan	.10
(302) Lenny Dykstra	.10
(303) Jim Eisenreich	.10
(304) Tyler Green	.10
(305) Charlie Hayes	.10
(306) Dave Hollins	.10
(307) Gregg Jefferies	.10
(308) Mickey Morandini	.10
(309) Curt Schilling	.50
(310) Heathcliff Slocumb	.10
(311) Kevin Stocker	.10
(312) Jay Bell	.10
(313) Jacob Brumfield	.10
(314) Dave Clark	.10
(315) Carlos Garcia	.10
(316) Mark Johnson	.10
(317) Jeff King	.10
(318) Nelson Liriano	.10
(319) Al Martin	.10
(320) Orlando Merced	.10
(321) Dan Miceli	.10
(322) Denny Neagle	.10
(323) Mark Parent	.10
(324) Dan Plesac	.10
(325) Scott Cooper	.10
(326) Bernard Gilkey	.10
(327) Tom Henke	.10
(328) Ken Hill	.10
(329) Danny Jackson	.10
(330) Brian Jordan	.10
(331) Ray Lankford	.10
(332) John Mabry	.10
(333) Jose Oquendo	.10
(334) Tom Pagnozzi	.10
(335) Ozzie Smith	4.00
(336) Andy Ashby	.10
(337) Brad Ausmus	.10
(338) Ken Caminiti	.10
(339) Andujar Cedeno	.10
(340) Steve Finley	.10
(341) Tony Gwynn	4.00
(342) Joey Hamilton	.10
(343) Trevor Hoffman	.10
(344) Jody Reed	.10
(345) Bip Roberts	.10
(346) Eddie Williams	.10
(347) Rod Beck	.10
(348) Mike Benjamin	.10
(349) Barry Bonds	10.00
(350) Royce Clayton	.10
(351) Glenallen Hill	.10
(352) Kirt Manwaring	.10
(353) Terry Mulholland	.10
(354) John Patterson	.10
(355) J.R. Phillips	.10
(356) Deion Sanders	.25
(357) Steve Scarsone	.10
(358) Robby Thompson	.10
(359) William VanLandingham	.10
(360) Matt Williams	.10

1996 Donruss Samples

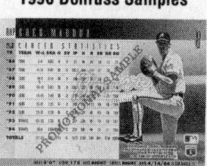

To introduce its 1996 series to dealers and the hobby press, Donruss issued an eight-card sample set. Identical in format to the issued version, the samples are numbered differently from the same players' cards in the regular issue (except #1, Frank Thomas). The samples also differ in that they lack 1995 stats on back, may have slightly different wording in the career highlights, and have printed on front and back a diagonal gray "PROMOTIONAL SAMPLE."

	NM/M
Complete Set (8):	9.00
Common Player:	1.00
1 Frank Thomas	1.00
2 Barry Bonds	2.50
3 Hideo Nomo	1.00
4 Ken Griffey Jr.	1.50
5 Cal Ripken Jr.	2.50
6 Manny Ramirez	1.00
7 Mike Piazza	1.50
8 Greg Maddux	1.25

1996 Donruss

DANTE BICHETTE

A clean, borderless look marks the 1996 Donruss regular-issue cards. Besides the player name in white inside a fading team-color stripe at top-right, the only graphic enhancement on front is a 7/8" square foil box at bottom-center with the company and team name, team logo, player position and uniform number. The foil box is enhanced with team colors, which are carried over to the horizontal backs. Backs also feature a color action photo, a large gray team logo, stats and career highlights. Basic packaging was 12-card foil packs with a suggested retail price of $1.79. Several types of insert cards were offered, each at a virtually unprecedented rate of scarcity. The set was issued in two series; Series 1 with 330 cards, Series 2 with 220 cards.

	NM/M
Complete Set (550):	20.00
Complete Series 1 (330):	12.00
Complete Series 2 (220):	10.00
Common Player:	.05
Press Proofs:	7X
Series 1 Pack (12):	1.00
Series 1 Wax Box (36):	20.00
Series 2 Pack (12):	1.00
Series 2 Wax Box (18):	12.50
1 Frank Thomas	1.00
2 Jason Bates	.05
3 Steve Sparks	.05
4 Scott Servais	.05
5 Angelo Encarnacion	.05
6 Scott Sanders	.05
7 Billy Ashley	.05
8 Alex Rodriguez	2.00
9 Sean Bergman	.05
10 Brad Radke	.05
11 Andy Van Slyke	.05
12 Joe Girardi	.05
13 Mark Grudzielanek	.05
14 Rick Aguilera	.05
15 Randy Veres	.05
16 Tim Bogar	.05
17 Dave Veres	.05
18 Kevin Stocker	.05
19 Marquis Grissom	.05
20 Will Clark	.05
21 Jay Bell	.05
22 Allen Battle	.05
23 Frank Rodriguez	.05
24 Terry Steinbach	.05
25 Gerald Williams	.05
26 Sid Roberson	.05
27 Gregg Zaun	.05
28 Ozzie Timmons	.05
29 Vaughn Eshelman	.05
30 Ed Sprague	.05
31 Gary DiSarcina	.05
32 Joe Boever	.05
33 Steve Avery	.05
34 Brad Ausmus	.05
35 Kirt Manwaring	.05
36 Gary Sheffield	.25
37 Jason Bere	.05
38 Jeff Manto	.05
39 David Cone	.05
40 Manny Ramirez	1.00
41 Sandy Alomar	.05
42 Curtis Goodwin/RR	.05
43 Tino Martinez	.05
44 Woody Williams	.05
45 Dean Palmer	.05
46 Hipolito Pichardo	.05
47 Jason Giambi	.60
48 Lance Johnson	.05
49 Bernard Gilkey	.05
50 Kirby Puckett	1.25
51 Tony Fernandez	.05
52 Alex Gonzalez	.05
53 Bret Saberhagen	.05
54 Lyle Mouton/RR	.05
55 Brian McRae	.05
56 Mark Gubicza	.05
57 Sergio Valdez	.05
58 Darrin Fletcher	.05
59 Steve Parris	.05
60 Johnny Damon/RR	.35
61 Rickey Henderson	1.00
62 Darrell Whitmore	.05
63 Roberto Petagine	.05
64 Trenidad Hubbard	.05
65 Heathcliff Slocumb	.05
66 Steve Finley	.05
67 Mariano Rivera	.25
68 Brian Hunter	.05
69 Jamie Moyer	.05
70 Ellis Burks	.05
71 Pat Kelly	.05
72 Mickey Tettleton	.05
73 Garret Anderson	.05
74 Andy Pettitte/RR	.75
75 Glenallen Hill	.05
76 Brent Gates	.05
77 Lou Whitaker	.05
78 David Segui	.05
79 Dan Wilson	.05
80 Pat Listach	.05
81 Jeff Bagwell	1.00
82 Ben McDonald	.05
83 John Valentin	.05
84 John Jaha	.05
85 Pete Schourek	.05
86 Bryce Florie	.05
87 Brian Jordan	.05
88 Ron Karkovice	.05
89 Al Leiter	.05
90 Tony Longmire	.05
91 Nelson Liriano	.05
92 David Bell	.05
93 Kevin Gross	.05
94 Tom Candiotti	.05
95 Dave Martinez	.05
96 Greg Myers	.05
97 Rheal Cormier	.05
98 Chris Hammond	.05
99 Randy Myers	.05
100 Bill Pulsipher/RR	.05
101 Jason Isringhausen/RR	.05
102 Dave Stevens	.05
103 Roberto Alomar	.20
104 Bob Higginson/RR	.05
105 Eddie Murray	1.00
106 Matt Walbeck	.05
107 Mark Wohlers	.05
108 Jeff Nelson	.05
109 Tom Goodwin	.05
110 Checklist 1-83 Cal Ripken Jr. (2,131 Consecutive Games)	1.25
111 Rey Sanchez	.05
112 Hector Carrasco	.05
113 B.J. Surhoff	.05
114 Dan Miceli	.05
115 Dean Hartgraves	.05
116 John Burkett	.05
117 Gary Gaetti	.05
118 Ricky Bones	.05
119 Mike Macfarlane	.05
120 Bip Roberts	.05
121 Dave Mlicki	.05
122 Chili Davis	.05
123 Mark Whiten	.05
124 Herbert Perry	.05
125 Butch Henry	.05
126 Derek Bell	.05
127 Al Martin	.05
128 John Franco	.05
129 William Van Landingham	.05
130 Mike Bordick	.05
131 Mike Mordecai	.05
132 Robby Thompson	.05
133 Greg Colbrunn	.05
134 Domingo Cedeno	.05
135 Chad Curtis	.05
136 Jose Hernandez	.05
137 Scott Klingenbeck	.05
138 Ryan Klesko	.05
139 John Smiley	.05
140 Charlie Hayes	.05
141 Jay Buhner	.05
142 Doug Drabek	.05
143 Roger Pavlik	.05
144 Todd Worrell	.05
145 Cal Ripken Jr.	2.50
146 Steve Reed	.05
147 Chuck Finley	.05
148 Mike Blowers	.05
149 Orel Hershiser	.05
150 Allen Watson	.05
151 Ramon Martinez	.05
152 Melvin Nieves	.05
153 Tripp Cromer	.05
154 Yorkis Perez	.05
155 Stan Javier	.05
156 Mel Rojas	.05
157 Aaron Sele	.05
158 Eric Karros	.05
159 Robb Nen	.05
160 Raul Mondesi	.05
161 John Wetteland	.05
162 Tim Scott	.05
163 Kenny Rogers	.05
164 Melvin Bunch	.05
165 Rod Beck	.05
166 Andy Benes	.05
167 Lenny Dykstra	.05
168 Orlando Merced	.05
169 Tomas Perez	.05
170 Xavier Hernandez	.05
171 Ruben Sierra	.05

No	Player	Price
172	Alan Trammell	.05
173	Mike Fetters	.05
174	Wilson Alvarez	.05
175	Erik Hanson	.05
176	Travis Fryman	.05
177	Jim Abbott	.05
178	Bret Boone	.05
179	Sterling Hitchcock	.05
180	Pat Mahomes	.05
181	Mark Acre	.05
182	Charles Nagy	.05
183	Rusty Greer	.05
184	Mike Stanley	.05
185	Jim Bullinger	.05
186	Shane Andrews	.05
187	Brian Keyser	.05
188	Tyler Green	.05
189	Mark Grace	.05
190	Bob Hamelin	.05
191	Luis Ortiz	.05
192	Joe Carter	.05
193	Eddie Taubensee	.05
194	Brian Anderson	.05
195	Edgardo Alfonzo	.05
196	Pedro Munoz	.05
197	David Justice	.05
198	Trevor Hoffman	.05
199	Bobby Ayala	.05
200	Tony Eusebio	.05
201	Jeff Russell	.05
202	Mike Hampton	.05
203	Walt Weiss	.05
204	Joey Hamilton	.05
205	Roberto Hernandez	.05
206	Greg Vaughn	.05
207	Felipe Lira	.05
208	Harold Baines	.05
209	Tim Wallach	.05
210	Manny Alexander	.05
211	Tim Laker	.05
212	Chris Haney	.05
213	Brian Maxcy	.05
214	Eric Young	.05
215	Darryl Strawberry	.05
216	Barry Bonds	2.50
217	Tim Naehring	.05
218	Scott Brosius	.05
219	Reggie Sanders	.05
220	Checklist 84-166 Eddie Murray (3,000 Career Hits)	.35
221	Luis Alicea	.05
222	Albert Belle	.05
223	Benji Gil	.05
224	Dante Bichette	.05
225	Bobby Bonilla	.05
226	Todd Stottlemyre	.05
227	Jim Edmonds	.05
228	Todd Jones	.05
229	Shawn Green	.25
230	Javy Lopez	.05
231	Ariel Prieto	.05
232	Tony Phillips	.05
233	James Mouton	.05
234	Jose Oquendo	.05
235	Royce Clayton	.05
236	Chuck Carr	.05
237	Doug Jones	.05
238	Mark Mclemore (McLemore)	.05
239	Bill Swift	.05
240	Scott Leius	.05
241	Russ Davis	.05
242	Ray Durham/RR	.05
243	Matt Mieske	.05
244	Brent Mayne	.05
245	Thomas Howard	.05
246	Troy O'Leary	.05
247	Jacob Brumfield	.05
248	Mickey Morandini	.05
249	Todd Hundley	.05
250	Chris Bosio	.05
251	Omar Vizquel	.05
252	Mike Lansing	.05
253	John Mabry	.05
254	Mike Perez	.05
255	Delino DeShields	.05
256	Wil Cordero	.05
257	Mike James	.05
258	Todd Van Poppel	.05
259	Joey Cora	.05
260	Andre Dawson	.25
261	Jerry DiPoto	.05
262	Rick Krivda	.05
263	Glenn Dishman	.05
264	Mike Mimbs	.05
265	John Ericks	.05
266	Jose Canseco	.35
267	Jeff Branson	.05
268	Curt Leskanic	.05
269	Jon Nunnally	.05
270	Scott Stahoviak	.05
271	Jeff Montgomery	.05
272	Hal Morris	.05
273	Esteban Loaiza	.05
274	Rico Brogna	.05
275	Dave Winfield	1.00
276	J.R. Phillips	.05
277	Todd Zeile	.05
278	Tom Pagnozzi	.05
279	Mark Lemke	.05
280	Dave Magadan	.05
281	Greg McMichael	.05
282	Mike Morgan	.05
283	Moises Alou	.05
284	Dennis Martinez	.05
285	Jeff Kent	.05
286	Mark Johnson	.05
287	Darren Lewis	.05
288	Brad Clontz	.05
289	Chad Fonville/RR	.05
290	Paul Sorrento	.05
291	Lee Smith	.05
292	Tom Glavine	.25
293	Antonio Osuna	.05
294	Kevin Foster	.05
295	Sandy Martinez RC	.05
296	Mark Leiter	.05
297	Julian Tavarez	.05
298	Mike Kelly	.05
299	Joe Oliver	.05
300	John Flaherty	.05
301	Don Mattingly	1.50
302	Pat Meares	.05
303	John Doherty	.05
304	Joe Vitiello	.05
305	Vinny Castilla	.05
306	Jeff Brantley	.05
307	Mike Greenwell	.05
308	Midre Cummings	.05
309	Curt Schilling	.25
310	Ken Caminiti	.05
311	Scott Erickson	.05
312	Carl Everett	.05
313	Charles Johnson	.05
314	Alex Diaz	.05
315	Jose Mesa	.05
316	Mark Carreon	.05
317	Carlos Perez/RR	.05
318	Ismael Valdes	.05
319	Frank Castillo	.05
320	Tom Henke	.05
321	Spike Owen	.05
322	Joe Orsulak	.05
323	Paul Menhart	.05
324	Pedro Borbon	.05
325	Checklist 167-249 Paul Molitor (1,000 Career RBI)	.35
326	Jeff Cirillo	.05
327	Edwin Hurtado	.05
328	Orlando Miller	.05
329	Steve Ontiveros	.05
330	Checklist 250-330 Kirby Puckett (1,000 Career RBI)	.75
331	Scott Bullett	.05
332	Andres Galarraga	.05
333	Cal Eldred	.05
334	Sammy Sosa	1.25
335	Don Slaught	.05
336	Jody Reed	.05
337	Roger Cedeno	.05
338	Ken Griffey Jr.	1.75
339	Todd Hollandsworth	.05
340	Mike Trombley	.05
341	Gregg Jefferies	.05
342	Larry Walker	.05
343	Pedro Martinez	.05
344	Dwayne Hosey	.05
345	Terry Pendleton	.05
346	Pete Harnisch	.05
347	Tony Castillo	.05
348	Paul Quantrill	.05
349	Fred McGriff	.05
350	Ivan Rodriguez	.65
351	Butch Huskey	.05
352	Ozzie Smith	1.25
353	Marty Cordova	.05
354	John Wasdin	.05
355	Wade Boggs	1.25
356	Dave Nilsson	.05
357	Rafael Palmeiro	.65
358	Luis Gonzalez	.05
359	Reggie Jefferson	.05
360	Carlos Delgado	.60
361	Orlando Palmeiro	.05
362	Chris Gomez	.05
363	John Smoltz	.05
364	Marc Newfield	.05
365	Matt Williams	.05
366	Jesus Tavarez	.05
367	Bruce Ruffin	.05
368	Sean Berry	.05
369	Randy Velarde	.05
370	Tony Pena	.05
371	Jim Thome	.60
372	Jeffrey Hammonds	.05
373	Bob Wolcott	.05
374	Juan Guzman	.05
375	Juan Gonzalez	.50
376	Michael Tucker	.05
377	Doug Johns	.05
378	Mike Cameron RC	.75
379	Ray Lankford	.05
380	Jose Parra	.05
381	Jimmy Key	.05
382	John Olerud	.05
383	Kevin Ritz	.05
384	Tim Raines	.05
385	Rich Amaral	.05
386	Keith Lockhart	.05
387	Steve Scarsone	.05
388	Cliff Floyd	.05
389	Rich Aude	.05
390	Hideo Nomo	.50
391	Geronimo Berroa	.05
392	Pat Rapp	.05
393	Dustin Hermanson	.05
394	Greg Maddux	1.25
395	Darren Daulton	.05
396	Kenny Lofton	.05
397	Ruben Rivera	.05
398	Billy Wagner	.05
399	Kevin Brown	.05
400	Mike Kingery	.05
401	Bernie Williams	.05
402	Otis Nixon	.05
403	Damion Easley	.05
404	Paul O'Neill	.05
405	Deion Sanders	.05
406	Dennis Eckersley	1.00
407	Tony Clark	.05
408	Rondell White	.05
409	Luis Sojo	.05
410	David Hulse	.05
411	Shane Reynolds	.05
412	Chris Hoiles	.05
413	Lee Tinsley	.05
414	Scott Karl	.05
415	Ron Gant	.05
416	Brian Johnson	.05
417	Jose Oliva	.05
418	Jack McDowell	.05
419	Paul Molitor	1.00
420	Ricky Bottalico	.05
421	Paul Wagner	.05
422	Terry Bradshaw	.05
423	Bob Tewksbury	.05
424	Mike Piazza	1.75
425	Luis Andujar RC	.05
426	Mark Langston	.05
427	Stan Belinda	.05
428	Kurt Abbott	.05
429	Shawon Dunston	.05
430	Bobby Jones	.05
431	Jose Vizcaino	.05
432	Matt Lawton RC	.05
433	Pat Hentgen	.05
434	Cecil Fielder	.05
435	Carlos Baerga	.05
436	Rich Becker	.05
437	Chipper Jones	1.25
438	Bill Risley	.05
439	Kevin Appier	.05
440	Checklist	.05
441	Jaime Navarro	.05
442	Barry Larkin	.05
443	Jose Valentin RC	.05
444	Bryan Rekar	.05
445	Rick Wilkins	.05
446	Quilvio Veras	.05
447	Greg Gagne	.05
448	Mark Kiefer	.05
449	Bobby Witt	.05
450	Andy Ashby	.05
451	Alex Ochoa	.05
452	Jorge Fabregas	.05
453	Gene Schall	.05
454	Ken Hill	.05
455	Tony Tarasco	.05
456	Donnie Wall	.05
457	Carlos Garcia	.05
458	Ryan Thompson	.05
459	Marvin Benard RC	.05
460	Jose Herrera	.05
461	Jeff Blauser	.05
462	Chris Hook	.05
463	Jeff Conine	.05
464	Devon White	.05
465	Danny Bautista	.05
466	Steve Trachsel	.05
467	C.J. Nitkowski	.05
468	Mike Devereaux	.05
469	David Wells	.05
470	Jim Eisenreich	.05
471	Edgar Martinez	.05
472	Craig Biggio	.05
473	Jeff Frye	.05
474	Karim Garcia	.05
475	Jimmy Haynes	.05
476	Darren Holmes	.05
477	Tim Salmon	.05
478	Randy Johnson	1.00
479	Eric Plunk	.05
480	Scott Cooper	.05
481	Chan Ho Park	.05
482	Ray McDavid	.05
483	Mark Petkovsek	.05
484	Greg Swindell	.05
485	George Williams	.05
486	Yamil Benitez	.05
487	Tim Wakefield	.05
488	Kevin Tapani	.05
489	Derrick May	.05
490	Checklist (Ken Griffey Jr.)	1.00
491	Derek Jeter	2.50
492	Jeff Fassero	.05
493	Benito Santiago	.05
494	Tom Gordon	.05
495	Jamie Brewington	.05
496	Vince Coleman	.05
497	Kevin Jordan	.05
498	Jeff King	.05
499	Mike Simms	.05
500	Jose Rijo	.05
501	Denny Neagle	.05
502	Jose Lima	.05
503	Kevin Seitzer	.05
504	Alex Fernandez	.05
505	Mo Vaughn	.05
506	Phil Nevin	.05
507	J.T. Snow	.05
508	Andujar Cedeno	.05
509	Ozzie Guillen	.05
510	Mark Clark	.05
511	Mark McGwire	2.00
512	Jeff Reboulet	.05
513	Armando Benitez	.05
514	LaTroy Hawkins	.05
515	Brett Butler	.05
516	Tavo Alvarez	.05
517	Chris Snopek	.05
518	Mike Mussina	.50
519	Darryl Kile	.05
520	Wally Joyner	.05
521	Willie McGee	.05
522	Kent Mercker	.05
523	Mike Jackson	.05
524	Troy Percival	.05
525	Tony Gwynn	1.25
526	Ron Coomer	.05
527	Darryl Hamilton	.05
528	Phil Plantier	.05
529	Norm Charlton	.05
530	Craig Paquette	.05
531	Dave Burba	.05
532	Mike Henneman	.05
533	Terrell Wade	.05
534	Eddie Williams	.05
535	Robin Ventura	.05
536	Chuck Knoblauch	.05
537	Les Norman	.05
538	Brady Anderson	.05
539	Roger Clemens	1.50
540	Mark Portugal	.05
541	Mike Matheny	.05
542	Jeff Parrett	.05
543	Roberto Kelly	.05
544	Damon Buford	.05
545	Chad Ogea	.05
546	Jose Offerman	.05
547	Brian Barber	.05
548	Danny Tartabull	.05
549	Duane Singleton	.05
550	Checklist (Tony Gwynn)	.75

1996 Donruss Press Proofs

The first 2,000 of each regular card issued in the 1996 Donruss set are distinguished by the addition of a gold-foil "PRESS PROOF" stamped along the right side. As opposed to regular-issue cards which have silver-and-black card numbers and personal data strip at bottom, the Press Proof cards have those elements printed in black-on-gold. Stated odds of finding a Press Proof are one per 12 packs in Series 1, one per 10 packs in Series 2, on average.

	NM/M
Complete Set (550):	150.00
Common Player:	.50

Diamond Kings

The most "common" of the '96 Donruss inserts are the popular Diamond Kings, featuring the portraits of Dick Perez on a black background within a mottled gold-foil frame. Once again, the DKs feature one player from each team, with 14 issued in each of Series 1 and 2. Like all '96 Donruss inserts, the DKs are numbered on back, within an edition of 10,000. Also on back are color action photos and career highlights. Diamond Kings are inserted at the rate of one per 60 foil packs (Series 1), and one per 30 packs (Series 2), on average.

	NM/M
Complete Set (31):	160.00
Common Player:	2.25
1 Frank Thomas	7.50
2 Mo Vaughn	2.50
3 Manny Ramirez	7.50
4 Mark McGwire	13.50
5 Juan Gonzalez	4.00
6 Roberto Alomar	3.00
7 Tim Salmon	2.50
8 Barry Bonds	15.00
9 Tony Gwynn	10.00
10 Reggie Sanders	2.50
11 Larry Walker	2.50
12 Pedro Martinez	7.50
13 Jeff King	2.50
14 Mark Grace	2.50
15 Greg Maddux	10.00
16 Don Mattingly	12.50
17 Gregg Jefferies	2.50
18 Chad Curtis	2.50
19 Jason Isringhausen	2.50
20 B.J. Surhoff	2.50
21 Jeff Conine	2.50
22 Kirby Puckett	10.00
23 Derek Bell	2.50
24 Wally Joyner	2.50
25 Brian Jordan	2.50
26 Edgar Martinez	2.50
27 Hideo Nomo	4.00
28 Mike Mussina	5.00
29 Eddie Murray	7.50
30 Cal Ripken Jr.	15.00
31 Checklist	.25

Elite

The Elite series continued as a Donruss insert in 1996, and they are the elite of the chase cards, being found on average only once per 140 packs (Series 1) or once per 75 packs (Series 2). The '96 Elite cards have a classic look bespeaking value. Player action photos at top center are framed in mottled silver foil and bordered in bright silver. Backs have another action photo, a few words about the player and a serial number from within an edition of 10,000 cards each. As usual, card numbering continues from the previous year.

	NM/M
Complete Set (12):	55.00
Complete Series 1 (61-66):	25.00
Complete Series 2 (67-72):	30.00
Common Player Series 1:	2.50
Common Player Series 2:	2.00
61 Cal Ripken Jr.	12.00
62 Hideo Nomo	3.00
63 Reggie Sanders	2.00
64 Mo Vaughn	2.00
65 Tim Salmon	2.50
66 Chipper Jones	8.00
67 Manny Ramirez	6.00
68 Greg Maddux	10.00
69 Frank Thomas	6.00
70 Ken Griffey Jr.	10.00
71 Dante Bichette	2.00
72 Tony Gwynn	8.00

Freeze Frame

One of two insert sets exclusive to Series 2 Donruss is the Freeze Frame issue. Printed on heavy, round-cornered cardboard stock, the inserts feature multiple photos of the player on both front and back. Fronts combine matte and glossy finish plus a gold-foil Donruss logo. Backs are conventionally printed, include 1995 season highlights and a serial number from within the edition of 5,000. Stated odds of pulling a Freeze Frame insert are one per 60 packs.

	NM/M
Complete Set (8):	16.00
Common Player:	1.00
1 Frank Thomas	2.00
2 Ken Griffey Jr.	3.00
3 Cal Ripken Jr.	4.00
4 Hideo Nomo	1.50
5 Greg Maddux	2.50
6 Albert Belle	1.00
7 Chipper Jones	2.50
8 Mike Piazza	3.00

Hit List

Printed on metallic foil with gold-foil graphic highlights, players who hit for high average with power or who collected milestone hits are featured in this insert set. Eight inserts were included in each of Series 1 and 2. Backs have a color action photo, a description of the player's batting prowess and a serial number from an edition of 10,000 cards each. Hit List inserts are found at an average rate of once per 106 foil packs in Series 1 and once per 60 packs in Series 2.

	NM/M
Complete Set (16):	30.00
Common Player:	.60
1 Tony Gwynn	3.00
2 Ken Griffey Jr.	5.00
3 Will Clark	.60
4 Mike Piazza	5.00
5 Carlos Baerga	.60
6 Mo Vaughn	.60
7 Mark Grace	.60
8 Kirby Puckett	3.00
9 Frank Thomas	2.00
10 Barry Bonds	6.00
11 Jeff Bagwell	2.00
12 Edgar Martinez	.60
13 Tim Salmon	.60
14 Wade Boggs	3.00
15 Don Mattingly	4.00
16 Eddie Murray	2.50

Long Ball Leaders

Once again the previous season's longest home runs are recalled in this retail-only insert set, found at an average rate of once per 96 packs in Series 1 only. Fronts are bordered and trimmed in bright silver foil and feature the player in his home run stroke against a black background. The date, location and distance of his tape-measure shot are in an arc across the card front. Backs feature another batting action photo, further details of the home run and a serial number within an edition of 5,000.

	NM/M
Complete Set (8):	45.00
Common Player:	1.50
1 Barry Bonds	15.00
2 Ryan Klesko	1.50
3 Mark McGwire	15.00

		NM/M
4	Raul Mondesi	1.50
5	Cecil Fielder	1.50
6	Ken Griffey Jr.	12.00
7	Larry Walker	1.50
8	Frank Thomas	6.00

Power Alley

Among the most visually dazzling of 1996's inserts is this hobby-only chase set featuring baseball's top sluggers. Action batting photos are found within several layers of prismatic foil in geometric patterns on front. Backs are horizontally formatted, feature portrait photos at left and power stats at right and bottom. In the lower-left corner is an individual serial number from within an edition of 5,000 cards each. The first 500 of each player's cards are specially die-cut at left- and right-center. Found only in Series 1 hobby foil packs, Power Alley inserts are a one per 92 pack pick.

		NM/M
Complete Set (10):		30.00
Common Player:		2.00
Die-cuts		2X
1	Frank Thomas	4.00
2	Barry Bonds	7.50
3	Reggie Sanders	2.00
4	Albert Belle	2.00
5	Tim Salmon	2.00
6	Dante Bichette	2.00
7	Mo Vaughn	2.00
8	Jim Edmonds	2.00
9	Manny Ramirez	4.00
10	Ken Griffey Jr.	6.00

Pure Power

These cards were random inserts found only in Series 2 retail packs. Fronts are printed on foil backgrounds and at bottom have a die-cut hole giving the impression a baseball has been batted through the card. On back the inserts are individually serial numbered within an edition of 5,000.

		NM/M
Complete Set (8):		25.00
Common Player:		2.25
1	Raul Mondesi	2.25
2	Barry Bonds	10.00
3	Albert Belle	2.25
4	Frank Thomas	4.50
5	Mike Piazza	7.50
6	Dante Bichette	2.25
7	Manny Ramirez	4.50
8	Mo Vaughn	2.25

Round Trippers

An embossed white home plate design bearing the player's 1995 dinger output is featured on this Series 2 insert set. The entire background has been rendered in gold-flecked sepia tones. Typography on front is in bronze foil. Backs repeat the sepia background photo and include a

month-by-month bar graph of the player's 1995 and career homers. Within the white home plate frame is the card's unique serial number from within an edition of 5,000. Odds of finding a Round Trippers card are stated at one per 55 packs, in hobby packs only.

		NM/M
Complete Set (10):		35.00
Common Player:		2.50
1	Albert Belle	2.50
2	Barry Bonds	7.50
3	Jeff Bagwell	4.00
4	Tim Salmon	2.50
5	Mo Vaughn	2.50
6	Ken Griffey Jr.	5.00
7	Mike Piazza	5.00
8	Cal Ripken Jr.	7.50
9	Frank Thomas	4.00
9p	Frank Thomas (Promo)	2.50
10	Dante Bichette	2.50

Showdown

Baseball's top hitters and pitchers are matched on a silver and black foil background in this insert set. Gold-foil graphic highlights complete the horizontal front design. Backs are printed on a black and gold background with color action photos and write-ups about each player. At top is a serial number from within an edition of 10,000 cards each. Showdown inserts are found at an average rate of one per Series 1 foil packs.

		NM/M
Complete Set (8):		22.50
Common Player:		.75
1	Frank Thomas, Hideo Nomo	3.00
2	Barry Bonds, Randy Johnson	6.00
3	Greg Maddux, Ken Griffey Jr.	5.00
4	Roger Clemens, Tony Gwynn	4.50
5	Mike Piazza, Mike Mussina	5.00
6	Cal Ripken Jr., Pedro Martinez	6.00
7	Tim Wakefield, Matt Williams	.75
8	Manny Ramirez, Carlos Perez	2.50

1997 Donruss

Donruss' 1997 Series 1 features 270 base cards with a full-bleed color action photo on the front. Horizontal backs have a photo, career statistics, a brief player profile and biographical tidbits. A Press Proofs parallel was made of the base cards in an edition of 2,000 each. Other Series 1 inserts include the annual Diamond Kings, Elites, Armed and Dangerous cards, Longball Leaders and Rocket Launchers. A 180-card Update set was released later as a follow-up to the regular '97 Donruss series. The Updates are numbered contiguously, #271-450, from the first series. Press Proofs and Gold Press Proof parallel inserts were available; other Update inserts include Dominators, Franchise Futures, Power Alley, Rookie Diamond Kings and a special Cal Ripken Jr. set.

		NM/M
Complete Set (450):		20.00
Series 1 (270):		10.00
Update Set (180):		10.00
Common Player:		.05
Common Press Proof:		.50
Press Proof Stars:		5X
Common Press Proof Gold:		2.00
Press Proof Gold Stars:		10X
Wax Pack (10):		1.50
Hobby Wax Box (18):		25.00
Retail Wax Box (36):		40.00
Magazine Pack (13):		1.50
Magazine Box (24):		20.00
Update Pack (10):		1.50
Update Wax Box (24):		30.00
1	Juan Gonzalez	.40
2	Jim Edmonds	.05
3	Tony Gwynn	1.00
4	Andres Galarraga	.05
5	Joe Carter	.05
6	Raul Mondesi	.05
7	Greg Maddux	1.00
8	Travis Fryman	.05
9	Brian Jordan	.05
10	Henry Rodriguez	.05
11	Manny Ramirez	.75
12	Mark McGwire	1.75
13	Marc Newfield	.05
14	Craig Biggio	.05
15	Sammy Sosa	1.00
16	Brady Anderson	.05
17	Wade Boggs	1.00
18	Charles Johnson	.05
19	Matt Williams	.05
20	Denny Neagle	.05
21	Ken Griffey Jr.	1.50
22	Robin Ventura	.05
23	Barry Larkin	.05
24	Todd Zeile	.05
25	Chuck Knoblauch	.05
26	Todd Hundley	.05
27	Roger Clemens	1.25
28	Michael Tucker	.05
29	Rondell White	.05
30	Osvaldo Fernandez	.05
31	Ivan Rodriguez	.65
32	Alex Fernandez	.05
33	Jason Isringhausen	.05
34	Chipper Jones	1.00
35	Paul O'Neill	.05
36	Hideo Nomo	.40
37	Roberto Alomar	.20
38	Derek Bell	.05
39	Paul Molitor	.75
40	Andy Benes	.05
41	Steve Trachsel	.05
42	J.T. Snow	.05
43	Jason Kendall	.05
44	Alex Rodriguez	1.75
45	Joey Hamilton	.05
46	Carlos Delgado	.05
47	Jason Giambi	.50
48	Larry Walker	.05
49	Derek Jeter	2.00
50	Kenny Lofton	.05
51	Devon White	.05
52	Matt Mieske	.05
53	Melvin Nieves	.05
54	Jose Canseco	.40
55	Tino Martinez	.05
56	Rafael Palmeiro	.65
57	Edgardo Alfonzo	.05
58	Jay Buhner	.05
59	Shane Reynolds	.05
60	Steve Finley	.05
61	Bobby Higginson	.05
62	Dean Palmer	.05
63	Terry Pendleton	.05
64	Marquis Grissom	.05
65	Mike Stanley	.05
66	Moises Alou	.05
67	Ray Lankford	.05
68	Marty Cordova	.05
69	John Olerud	.05
70	David Cone	.05
71	Benito Santiago	.05
72	Ryne Sandberg	1.00
73	Rickey Henderson	.75
74	Roger Cedeno	.05
75	Wilson Alvarez	.05
76	Tim Salmon	.05
77	Orlando Merced	.05
78	Vinny Castilla	.05
79	Ismael Valdes	.05
80	Dante Bichette	.05
81	Kevin Brown	.05
82	Andy Pettitte	.40
83	Scott Stahoviak	.05
84	Mickey Tettleton	.05
85	Jack McDowell	.05
86	Tom Glavine	.30
87	Gregg Jefferies	.05
88	Chili Davis	.05
89	Randy Johnson	.75
90	John Mabry	.05
91	Billy Wagner	.05
92	Jeff Cirillo	.05
93	Trevor Hoffman	.05
94	Juan Guzman	.05
95	Geronimo Berroa	.05
96	Bernard Gilkey	.05
97	Danny Tartabull	.05
98	Johnny Damon	.35
99	Charlie Hayes	.05
100	Reggie Sanders	.05
101	Robby Thompson	.05
102	Bobby Bonilla	.05
103	Reggie Jefferson	.05
104	John Smoltz	.05
105	Jim Thome	.05
106	Ruben Rivera	.05
107	Darren Oliver	.05
108	Mo Vaughn	.05
109	Roger Pavlik	.05
110	Terry Steinbach	.05
111	Jermaine Dye	.05
112	Mark Grudzielanek	.05
113	Rick Aguilera	.05
114	Jamey Wright	.05
115	Eddie Murray	.75
116	Brian Hunter	.05
117	Hal Morris	.05
118	Tom Pagnozzi	.05
119	Mike Mussina	.40
120	Mark Grace	.05
121	Cal Ripken Jr.	2.00
122	Tom Goodwin	.05
123	Paul Sorrento	.05
124	Jay Bell	.05
125	Todd Hollandsworth	.05
126	Edgar Martinez	.05
127	George Arias	.05
128	Greg Vaughn	.05
129	Roberto Hernandez	.05
130	Delino DeShields	.05
131	Bill Pulsipher	.05
132	Joey Cora	.05
133	Mariano Rivera	.15
134	Mike Piazza	1.50
135	Carlos Baerga	.05
136	Jose Mesa	.05
137	Will Clark	.05
138	Frank Thomas	.75
139	John Wetteland	.05
140	Shawn Estes	.05
141	Garret Anderson	.05
142	Andre Dawson	.25
143	Eddie Taubensee	.05
144	Ryan Klesko	.05
145	Rocky Coppinger	.05
146	Jeff Bagwell	.75
147	Donovan Osborne	.05
148	Greg Myers	.05
149	Brant Brown	.05
150	Kevin Elster	.05
151	Bob Wells	.05
152	Wally Joyner	.05
153	Rico Brogna	.05
154	Dwight Gooden	.05
155	Jermaine Allensworth	.05
156	Ray Durham	.05
157	Cecil Fielder	.05
158	Ryan Hancock	.05
159	Gary Sheffield	.30
160	Albert Belle	.05
161	Tomas Perez	.05
162	David Doster	.05
163	John Valentin	.05
164	Danny Graves	.05
165	Jose Paniagua	.05
166	Brian Giles **RC**	.50
167	Barry Bonds	2.00
168	Sterling Hitchcock	.05
169	Bernie Williams	.05
170	Fred McGriff	.05
171	George Williams	.05
172	Amaury Telemaco	.05
173	Ken Caminiti	.05
174	Ron Gant	.05
175	David Justice	.05
176	James Baldwin	.05
177	Pat Hentgen	.05
178	Ben McDonald	.05
179	Tim Naehring	.05
180	Jim Eisenreich	.05
181	Ken Hill	.05
182	Paul Wilson	.05
183	Marvin Benard	.05
184	Alan Benes	.05
185	Ellis Burks	.05
186	Scott Servais	.05
187	David Segui	.05
188	Scott Brosius	.05
189	Jose Offerman	.05
190	Eric Davis	.05
191	Brett Butler	.05
192	Curtis Pride	.05
193	Yamil Benitez	.05
194	Chan Ho Park	.05
195	Bret Boone	.05
196	Omar Vizquel	.05
197	Orlando Miller	.05
198	Ramon Martinez	.05
199	Harold Baines	.05
200	Eric Young	.05
201	Fernando Vina	.05
202	Alex Gonzalez	.05
203	Fernando Valenzuela	.05
204	Steve Avery	.05
205	Ernie Young	.05
206	Kevin Appier	.05
207	Randy Myers	.05
208	Jeff Suppan	.05
209	James Mouton	.05
210	Russ Davis	.05
211	Al Martin	.05
212	Troy Percival	.05
213	Al Leiter	.05
214	Dennis Eckersley	.65
215	Mark Johnson	.05
216	Eric Karros	.05
217	Royce Clayton	.05
218	Tony Phillips	.05
219	Tim Wakefield	.05
220	Alan Trammell	.05
221	Eduardo Perez	.05
222	Butch Huskey	.05
223	Tim Belcher	.05
224	Jamie Moyer	.05
225	F.P. Santangelo	.05
226	Rusty Greer	.05
227	Jeff Brantley	.05
228	Mark Langston	.05
229	Ray Montgomery	.05
230	Rich Becker	.05
231	Ozzie Smith	1.00
232	Rey Ordonez	.05
233	Ricky Otero	.05
234	Mike Cameron	.05
235	Mike Sweeney	.05
236	Mark Lewis	.05
237	Luis Gonzalez	.05
238	Marcus Jensen	.05
239	Ed Sprague	.05
240	Jose Valentin	.05
241	Jeff Frye	.05
242	Charles Nagy	.05
243	Carlos Garcia	.05
244	Mike Hampton	.05
245	B.J. Surhoff	.05
246	Wilton Guerrero	.05
247	Frank Rodriguez	.05
248	Gary Gaetti	.05
249	Lance Johnson	.05
250	Darren Bragg	.05
251	Darryl Hamilton	.05
252	John Jaha	.05
253	Craig Paquette	.05
254	Jaime Navarro	.05
255	Shawon Dunston	.05
256	Ron Wright	.05
257	Tim Belk	.05
258	Jeff Darwin	.05
259	Ruben Sierra	.05
260	Chuck Finley	.05
261	Darryl Strawberry	.05
262	Shannon Stewart	.05
263	Pedro Martinez	.05
264	Neifi Perez	.05
265	Jeff Conine	.05
266	Orel Hershiser	.05
267	Checklist 1-90 Eddie Murray (500 Career HR)	.05
268	Checklist 91-180 Paul Molitor (3,000 Career Hits)	.05
269	Checklist 181-270 Barry Bonds (300 Career HR)	.90
270	Checklist - inserts Mark McGwire (300 Career HR)	.75
271	Matt Williams	.05
272	Todd Zeile	.05
273	Roger Clemens	1.25
274	Michael Tucker	.05
275	J.T. Snow	.05
276	Kenny Lofton	.05
277	Jose Canseco	.40
278	Marquis Grissom	.05
279	Moises Alou	.05
280	Benito Santiago	.05
281	Willie McGee	.05
282	Chili Davis	.05
283	Ron Coomer	.05
284	Orlando Merced	.05
285	Delino DeShields	.05
286	John Wetteland	.05
287	Darren Daulton	.05
288	Lee Stevens	.05
289	Albert Belle	.05
290	Sterling Hitchcock	.05
291	David Justice	.05
292	Eric Davis	.05
293	Brian Hunter	.05
294	Darryl Hamilton	.05
295	Steve Avery	.05
296	Joe Vitiello	.05
297	Jaime Navarro	.05
298	Eddie Murray	.75
299	Randy Myers	.05
300	Francisco Cordova	.05
301	Javier Lopez	.05
302	Geronimo Berroa	.05
303	Jeffrey Hammonds	.05
304	Deion Sanders	.05
305	Jeff Fassero	.05
306	Curt Schilling	.25
307	Robb Nen	.05
308	Mark McLemore	.05
309	Jimmy Key	.05
310	Quilvio Veras	.05
311	Bip Roberts	.05
312	Esteban Loaiza	.05
313	Andy Ashby	.05
314	Sandy Alomar Jr.	.05
315	Shawn Green	.20
316	Luis Castillo	.05
317	Benji Gil	.05
318	Otis Nixon	.05
319	Aaron Sele	.05
320	Brad Ausmus	.05
321	Troy O'Leary	.05
322	Terrell Wade	.05
323	Jeff King	.05
324	Kevin Seitzer	.05
325	Mark Wohlers	.05
326	Edgar Renteria	.05
327	Dan Wilson	.05
328	Brian McRae	.05
329	Rod Beck	.05
330	Julio Franco	.05
331	Dave Nilsson	.05
332	Glenallen Hill	.05
333	Kevin Elster	.05
334	Joe Girardi	.05
335	David Wells	.05
336	Jeff Blauser	.05
337	Darryl Kile	.05
338	Jeff Kent	.05
339	Jim Leyritz	.05
340	Todd Stottlemyre	.05
341	Tony Clark	.05
342	Chris Hoiles	.05
343	Mike Lieberthal	.05
344	Matt Lawton	.05
345	Alex Ochoa	.05
346	Chris Snopek	.05
347	Rudy Pemberton	.05
348	Eric Owens	.05
349	Joe Randa	.05
350	John Olerud	.05
351	Steve Karsay	.05
352	Mark Whiten	.05
353	Bob Abreu	.10
354	Bartolo Colon	.05
355	Vladimir Guerrero	.75
356	Darin Erstad	.50
357	Scott Rolen	.60
358	Andruw Jones	.75
359	Scott Spiezio	.05
360	Karim Garcia	.05
361	Hideki Irabu **RC**	.25
362	Nomar Garciaparra	1.00
363	Dmitri Young	.05
364	Bubba Trammell **RC**	.25
365	Kevin Orie	.05
366	Jose Rosado	.05
367	Jose Guillen	.05
368	Brooks Kieschnick	.05
369	Pokey Reese	.05
370	Glendon Rusch	.05
371	Jason Dickson	.05
372	Todd Walker	.05
373	Justin Thompson	.05
374	Todd Greene	.05
375	Jeff Suppan	.05
376	Trey Beamon	.05
377	Damon Mashore	.05
378	Wendell Magee	.05
379	Shigetosi Hasegawa	.05
380	Bill Mueller	.05
381	Chris Widger	.05
382	Tony Grafannino	.05
383	Derrek Lee	.50
384	Brian Moehler	.05
385	Quinton McCracken	.05
386	Matt Morris	.05
387	Marvin Benard	.05
388	Deivi Cruz **RC**	.25
389	Javier Valentin **RC**	.05
390	Todd Dunwoody	.05
391	Derrick Gibson	.05
392	Raul Casanova	.05
393	George Arias	.05
394	Tony Womack **RC**	.25
395	Antone Williamson	.05
396	Jose Cruz Jr. **RC**	.50
397	Desi Relaford	.05
398	Frank Thomas/HL	.40
399	Ken Griffey Jr./HL	.65
400	Cal Ripken Jr./HL	1.00
401	Chipper Jones/HL	.50
402	Mike Piazza/HL	.65
403	Gary Sheffield/HL	.15
404	Alex Rodriguez/HL	.75
405	Wade Boggs/HL	.50
406	Juan Gonzalez/HL	.20
407	Tony Gwynn/HL	.50
408	Edgar Martinez/HL	.05
409	Jeff Bagwell/HL	.40
410	Larry Walker/HL	.05
411	Kenny Lofton/HL	.05
412	Manny Ramirez/HL	.40
413	Mark McGwire/HL	.75
414	Roberto Alomar/HL	.10
415	Derek Jeter/HL	1.00
416	Brady Anderson/HL	.05
417	Paul Molitor/HL	.35
418	Dante Bichette/HL	.05
419	Jim Edmonds/HL	.05
420	Mo Vaughn/HL	.05
421	Barry Bonds/HL	.90
422	Rusty Greer/HL	.05
423	Greg Maddux (King of the Hill)	.50
424	Andy Pettitte (King of the Hill)	.15

425	John Smoltz (King of the Hill)	.05
426	Randy Johnson (King of the Hill)	.40
427	Hideo Nomo (King of the Hill)	.20
428	Roger Clemens (King of the Hill)	.60
429	Tom Glavine (King of the Hill)	.15
430	Pat Hentgen (King of the Hill)	.05
431	Kevin Brown (King of the Hill)	.05
432	Mike Mussina (King of the Hill)	.20
433	Alex Fernandez (King of the Hill)	.05
434	Kevin Appier (King of the Hill)	.05
435	David Cone (King of the Hill)	.05
436	Jeff Fassero (King of the Hill)	.05
437	John Wetteland (King of the Hill)	.05
438	Barry Bonds, Ivan Rodriguez/IS	.90
439	Ken Griffey Jr., Andres Galarraga/IS	.65
440	Fred McGriff, Rafael Palmeiro/IS	.05
441	Barry Larkin, Jim Thome/IS	.05
442	Sammy Sosa, Albert Belle/IS	.50
443	Bernie Williams, Todd Hundley/IS	.05
444	Chuck Knoblauch, Brian Jordan/IS	.05
445	Mo Vaughn, Jeff Conine/IS	.05
446	Ken Caminiti, Jason Giambi/IS	.25
447	Raul Mondesi, Tim Salmon/IS	.05
448	Checklist (Cal Ripken Jr.)	.75
449	Checklist (Greg Maddux)	.60
450	Checklist (Ken Griffey Jr.)	.50

1997 Donruss Press Proofs

Each of the 450 cards in the Donruss base set was also produced in a Press Proof parallel edition of 2,000 cards. Virtually identical in design to the regular cards, the Press Proofs are printed on a metallic background with silver-foil highlights. Most Press Proof backs carry the notation "1 of 2000." Stated odds of finding a press proof are one per eight packs. A special "gold" press proof chase set features cards with gold-foil highlights, die-cut at top and bottom and the note "1 of 500" on back. Gold press proofs are found on average of once per 32 packs.

	NM/M
Common Player:	.50
Stars/Rookies:	5X
Common Gold Player:	2.00
Gold Stars/Rookies:	10X

Armed and Dangerous

These 15 cards are numbered up to 5,000. They were inserted in 1997 Donruss Series 1 retail packs only.

		NM/M
Complete Set (15):		35.00
Common Player:		1.00
1	Ken Griffey Jr.	4.00
2	Raul Mondesi	1.00
3	Chipper Jones	3.00
4	Ivan Rodriguez	1.50
5	Randy Johnson	2.00
6	Alex Rodriguez	5.00
7	Larry Walker	1.00
8	Cal Ripken Jr.	6.00
9	Kenny Lofton	1.00
10	Barry Bonds	6.00
11	Derek Jeter	6.00
12	Charles Johnson	1.00
13	Greg Maddux	3.00
14	Roberto Alomar	1.00
15	Barry Larkin	1.00

Diamond Kings

These 1997 Donruss Series 1 inserts have an action photo printed on a metallic foil background. Printed on the gold-foil border is a gauge with the player's 1996 home run total indicated. Horizontal backs have a player photo and record of career HRs by season. Each card is serially numbered within an edition of 5,000. The set was seeded in retail packs only.

		NM/M
Complete Set (15):		20.00
Common Player:		.50
1	Frank Thomas	2.00
2	Albert Belle	.50
3	Mo Vaughn	.50
4	Brady Anderson	.50
5	Greg Vaughn	.50
6	Ken Griffey Jr.	3.00
7	Jay Buhner	.50
8	Juan Gonzalez	.75
9	Mike Piazza	3.00
10	Jeff Bagwell	2.00
11	Sammy Sosa	2.50
12	Mark McGwire	4.00
13	Cecil Fielder	.50
14	Ryan Klesko	.50
15	Jose Canseco	.85

Rated Rookies

Although numbered more like an insert set, Rated Rookies are part of the regular-issue set. Cards are numbered 1-30, with no ratio given on packs. The cards are differentiated by a large silver-foil strip on the top right side with the words Rated Rookie.

		NM/M
Complete Set (30):		10.00
Common Player:		.50
1	Jason Thompson	.50
2	LaTroy Hawkins	.50
3	Scott Rolen	1.50
4	Trey Beamon	.50
5	Kimera Bartee	.50
6	Nerio Rodriguez	.50
7	Jeff D'Amico	.50
8	Quinton McCracken	.50
9	John Wasdin	.50
10	Robin Jennings	.50
11	Steve Gibralter	.50
12	Tyler Houston	.50
13	Tony Clark	.50
14	Ugueth Urbina	.50
15	Billy McMillon	.50
16	Raul Casanova	.50
17	Brooks Kieschnick	.50
18	Luis Castillo	.50
19	Edgar Renteria	.50
20	Andruw Jones	2.00
21	Chad Mottola	.50

3	Sammy Sosa	10.00
4	Barry Bonds	20.00
5	Chipper Jones	10.00
6	Alex Rodriguez	15.00
7	Ken Griffey Jr.	12.50
8	Jeff Bagwell	7.50
9	Cal Ripken Jr.	20.00
10	Mo Vaughn	3.00
11	Mike Piazza	12.50
12	Juan Gonzalez	4.50

Longball Leaders

22	Makoto Suzuki	.50
23	Justin Thompson	.50
24	Darin Erstad	1.00
25	Todd Walker	.50
26	Todd Greene	.50
27	Vladimir Guerrero	2.00
28	Darren Dreifort	.50
29	John Burke	.50
30	Damon Mashore	.50

1997 Donruss Jackie Robinson Rookie Reprint

In conjunction with its program of special issues and giveaways honoring the 50th anniversary of Robinson's major league debut, Donruss issued this "Commemorative Rookie Card." Printed in the same size as the 1949 Leaf Robinson, and on heavier, coarser stock than modern cards, the card carries a reprint notice and is serially numbered on back in gold foil from within an edition of 1,948.

		NM/M
79	Jackie Robinson	10.00

Jackie Robinson Sweepstakes Scratch-Off

This pack insert features inside a scratch-off contest in which genuine vintage 1948-49 Leaf Jackie Robinson cards were awarded. The 2-3/8" x 2-7/8" folder has a color photo of the Leaf Robinson rookie card on front. On back is information on ordering numbered lithographs of the Robinson card; an edition of 1,000 selling for $199 apiece, an edition of 500 autographed by his widow selling for $299 apiece.

		NM/M
	Jackie Robinson	.50

Rocket Launchers

These 1997 Donruss Series 1 inserts are limited to 5,000 each. They were only included in magazine packs.

		NM/M
Complete Set (15):		25.00
Common Player:		.75
1	Frank Thomas	2.50
2	Albert Belle	.75
3	Chipper Jones	3.00
4	Mike Piazza	4.00
5	Mo Vaughn	.75
6	Juan Gonzalez	1.00

7	Fred McGriff	.75
8	Jeff Bagwell	2.50
9	Matt Williams	.75
10	Gary Sheffield	1.00
11	Barry Bonds	5.00
12	Manny Ramirez	2.00
13	Henry Rodriguez	.75
14	Jason Giambi	1.50
15	Cal Ripken Jr.	5.00

Update Dominators

This 20-card insert highlights players known for being able to "take over a game." Each card features silver-foil highlights on front and stats on back.

		NM/M
Complete Set (20):		22.50
Common Player:		.50
1	Frank Thomas	1.25
2	Ken Griffey Jr.	2.25
3	Greg Maddux	1.50
4	Cal Ripken Jr.	3.00
5	Alex Rodriguez	2.50
6	Albert Belle	.50
7	Mark McGwire	2.50
8	Juan Gonzalez	.65
9	Chipper Jones	1.50
10	Hideo Nomo	.65
11	Roger Clemens	2.00
12	John Smoltz	.50
13	Mike Piazza	2.25
14	Sammy Sosa	1.50
15	Matt Williams	.50
16	Kenny Lofton	.50
17	Barry Larkin	.50
18	Rafael Palmeiro	1.00
19	Ken Caminiti	.50
20	Gary Sheffield	.75

Update Franchise Features

This hobby-exclusive insert consists of 15 cards designed with a movie poster theme. The double-front design highlights a top veteran player on one side with an up-and-coming rookie on the other. The side featuring the veteran has the designation "Now Playing," while the rookie side carries the banner "Coming Attraction." Each card is printed on an all-foil stock and numbered to 3,000.

		NM/M
Complete Set (15):		45.00
Common Player:		2.00
1	Ken Griffey Jr., Andruw Jones	4.00
2	Frank Thomas, Darin Erstad	2.50
3	Alex Rodriguez, Nomar Garciaparra	5.00
4	Chuck Knoblauch, Wilton Guerrero	2.00
5	Juan Gonzalez, Bubba Trammell	2.00
6	Chipper Jones, Todd Walker	3.00
7	Barry Bonds, Vladimir Guerrero	6.00
8	Mark McGwire, Dmitri Young	5.00
9	Mike Piazza, Mike Sweeney	4.00
10	Mo Vaughn, Tony Clark	2.00

11	Gary Sheffield, Jose Guillen	2.00
12	Kenny Lofton, Shannon Stewart	2.00
13	Cal Ripken Jr., Scott Rolen	6.00
14	Derek Jeter, Pokey Reese	6.00
15	Tony Gwynn, Bob Abreu	3.00

Update Power Alley

This 24-card insert is fractured into three different styles: Gold, Blue and Green. Each card is micro-etched and printed on holographic foil board. All cards are sequentially numbered, with the first 250 cards in each level being die-cut. Twelve players' cards feature a green finish and are numbered to 4,000. Eight players are printed on blue cards that are numbered to 2,000. Four players are found on gold cards numbered to 1,000.

		NM/M
Complete Set (24):		100.00
Common Gold:		7.50
Common Blue:		3.00
Common Green:		1.50
Die-Cuts:		3X
1	Frank Thomas (G)	7.50
2	Ken Griffey Jr. (G)	10.00
3	Cal Ripken Jr. (G)	15.00
4	Jeff Bagwell (B)	5.00
5	Mike Piazza (B)	7.50
6	Andruw Jones (GR)	3.50
7	Alex Rodriguez (G)	12.50
8	Albert Belle (GR)	1.50
9	Mo Vaughn (GR)	1.50
10	Chipper Jones (B)	6.00
11	Juan Gonzalez (B)	3.00
12	Ken Caminiti (B)	1.50
13	Manny Ramirez (GR)	3.50
14	Mark McGwire (GR)	6.00
15	Kenny Lofton (B)	3.00
16	Barry Bonds (B)	7.50
17	Gary Sheffield (GR)	1.50
18	Tony Gwynn (GR)	4.50
19	Vladimir Guerrero (B)	6.00
20	Ivan Rodriguez (B)	3.50
21	Paul Molitor (B)	5.00
22	Sammy Sosa (GR)	4.50
23	Matt Williams (GR)	1.50
24	Derek Jeter (GR)	7.50

1997 Donruss Update Press Proofs

This 180-card parallel set is printed on an all-foil stock with bright foil accents. Each card is numbered "1 of 2,000." Special die-cut gold versions are numbered as "1 of 500."

	NM/M
Common Player:	.50
Stars:	7X
Common Player, Gold:	5.00
Gold Stars:	15X

Update Cal Ripken

This 10-card set salutes Cal Ripken Jr. and is printed on an all-foil stock with foil highlights. Photos and text are taken from Ripken's autobiography, "The Only

---

These 2,500 sets of these insert cards made. The cards were randomly included in 1997 Donruss Series I packs. Fronts have a white marbled border and are graphically enhanced with silver foil, including a large script "E." On back is another photo, a career summary and a serial number from within the edition limit of 2,500. A promo card version of each card also exists.

		NM/M
Complete Set (12):		100.00
Common Player:		3.00
Promos: 50 Percent		
1	Frank Thomas	7.50
2	Paul Molitor	7.50

Elite Inserts

There were 2,500 sets of these insert cards made. The cards were randomly included in 1997 Donruss Series I packs.

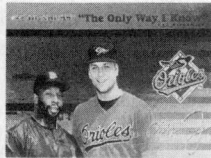

Way I Know." The first nine cards of the set were randomly inserted into packs. The 10th card was only available inside the book. Each card found within packs was numbered to 5,000.

	NM/M
Complete Set (10):	75.00
Common Card:	10.00
1-9 Cal Ripken Jr.	10.00
10 Cal Ripken Jr. (Book insert.)	10.00

Update Rookie Diamond Kings

This popular Donruss Update insert set features a new twist - all 10 cards feature promising rookies. Each card is sequentially numbered to 10,000, with the first 500 cards of each player printed on actual canvas.

	NM/M
Complete Set (10):	20.00
Common Player:	1.50
Canvas:	1.5X
1 Andruw Jones	4.00
2 Vladimir Guerrero	10.00
3 Scott Rolen	1.50
4 Todd Walker	1.50
5 Bartolo Colon	2.00
6 Jose Guillen	1.50
7 Nomar Garciaparra	6.00
8 Darin Erstad	2.00
9 Dmitri Young	1.50
10 Wilton Guerrero	1.50

1997 Donruss Team Sets

A total of 163 cards were part of the Donruss Team Set issue. Packs consisted solely of players from one of 11 different teams. In addition, a full 163-card parallel set called Pennant Edition was available, featuring red and gold foil and a special "Pennant Edition" logo. Cards were sold in five-card packs for $1.99 each. The Angels and Indians set were sold only at their teams' souvenir outlets. Cards #131 Bernie Williams and #144 Russ Davis were never issued. The Team Set cards utilize team-color foil highlights and the numbers on back differ from the regular-issue version.

	NM/M
Comp. Angels Set (1-15):	1.25
Comp. Braves Set (16-30):	3.00
Comp. Orioles Set (31-45):	2.50
Comp. Red Sox Set (46-60):	1.50
Comp. White Sox Set (61-75):	2.00
Comp. Indians Set (76-90):	1.50
Comp. Rockies Set (91-105):	1.50
Comp. Dodgers Set (106-120):	2.25
Comp. Yankees Set (121-135):	4.50
Comp. Mariners Set (136-150):	4.50
Comp. Cardinals Set (151-165):	2.00
Common Player:	.05
Pennant Edition Stars:	3X
1 Jim Edmonds	.05
2 Tim Salmon	.05
3 Tony Phillips	.05
4 Garret Anderson	.05
5 Troy Percival	.05
6 Mark Langston	.05
7 Chuck Finley	.05
8 Eddie Murray	.75
9 Jim Leyritz	.05
10 Darin Erstad	.30
11 Jason Dickson	.05
12 Allen Watson	.05
13 Shigetosi Hasegawa	.05
14 Dave Hollins	.05
15 Gary DiSarcina	.05
16 Greg Maddux	1.00
17 Denny Neagle	.05
18 Chipper Jones	1.00
19 Tom Glavine	.25
20 John Smoltz	.05
21 Ryan Klesko	.05
22 Fred McGriff	.05
23 Michael Tucker	.05
24 Kenny Lofton	.05
25 Javier Lopez	.05
26 Mark Wohlers	.05
27 Jeff Blauser	.05
28 Andruw Jones	.75
29 Tony Graffanino	.05
30 Terrell Wade	.05
31 Brady Anderson	.05
32 Roberto Alomar	.15
33 Rafael Palmeiro	.65
34 Mike Mussina	.35
35 Cal Ripken Jr.	2.00
36 Rocky Coppinger	.05
37 Randy Myers	.05
38 B.J. Surhoff	.05
39 Eric Davis	.05
40 Armando Benitez	.05
41 Jeffrey Hammonds	.05
42 Jimmy Key	.05
43 Chris Hoiles	.05
44 Mike Bordick	.05
45 Pete Incaviglia	.05
46 Mike Stanley	.05
47 Reggie Jefferson	.05
48 Mo Vaughn	.05
49 John Valentin	.05
50 Tim Naehring	.05
51 Jeff Suppan	.05
52 Tim Wakefield	.05
53 Jeff Frye	.05
54 Darren Bragg	.05
55 Steve Avery	.05
56 Shane Mack	.05
57 Aaron Sele	.05
58 Troy O'Leary	.05
59 Rudy Pemberton	.05
60 Nomar Garciaparra	1.00
61 Robin Ventura	.05
62 Wilson Alvarez	.05
63 Roberto Hernandez	.05
64 Frank Thomas	.75
65 Ray Durham	.05
66 James Baldwin	.05
67 Harold Baines	.05
68 Doug Drabek	.05
69 Mike Cameron	.05
70 Albert Belle	.05
71 Jaime Navarro	.05
72 Chris Snopek	.05
73 Lyle Mouton	.05
74 Dave Martinez	.05
75 Ozzie Guillen	.05
76 Manny Ramirez	.05
77 Jack McDowell	.05
78 Jim Thome	.50
79 Jose Mesa	.05
80 Brian Giles	.05
81 Omar Vizquel	.05
82 Charles Nagy	.05
83 Orel Hershiser	.05
84 Matt Williams	.05
85 Marquis Grissom	.05
86 David Justice	.05
87 Sandy Alomar	.05
88 Kevin Seitzer	.05
89 Julio Franco	.05
90 Bartolo Colon	.05
91 Andres Galarraga	.05
92 Larry Walker	.05
93 Vinny Castilla	.05
94 Dante Bichette	.05
95 Jamey Wright	.05
96 Ellis Burks	.05
97 Eric Young	.05
98 Neifi Perez	.05
99 Quinton McCracken	.05
100 Bruce Ruffin	.05
101 Walt Weiss	.05
102 Roger Bailey	.05
103 Jeff Reed	.05
104 Bill Swift	.05
105 Kirt Manwaring	.05
106 Raul Mondesi	.05
107 Hideo Nomo	.35
108 Roger Cedeno	.05
109 Ismael Valdes	.05
110 Todd Hollandsworth	.05
111 Mike Piazza	1.50
112 Brett Butler	.05
113 Chan Ho Park	.05
114 Ramon Martinez	.05
115 Eric Karros	.05
116 Wilton Guerrero	.05
117 Todd Zeile	.05
118 Karim Garcia	.05
119 Greg Gagne	.05
120 Darren Dreifort	.05
121 Wade Boggs	1.00
122 Paul O'Neill	.05
123 Derek Jeter	2.00
124 Tino Martinez	.05
125 David Cone	.05
126 Andy Pettitte	.25
127 Charlie Hayes	.05
128 Mariano Rivera	.15
129 Dwight Gooden	.05
130 Cecil Fielder	.05
132 Darryl Strawberry	.05
133 Joe Girardi	.05
134 David Wells	.05
135 Hideki Irabu	.05
136 Ken Griffey Jr.	1.25
137 Alex Rodriguez	1.50
138 Jay Buhner	.05
139 Randy Johnson	.75
140 Paul Sorrento	.05
141 Edgar Martinez	.05
142 Joey Cora	.05
143 Bob Wells	.05
145 Jamie Moyer	.05
146 Jeff Fassero	.05
147 Dan Wilson	.05
148 Jose Cruz, Jr.	.05
149 Scott Sanders	.05
150 Rich Amaral	.05
151 Brian Jordan	.05
152 Andy Benes	.05
153 Ray Lankford	.05
154 John Mabry	.05
155 Tom Pagnozzi	.05
156 Ron Gant	.05
157 Alan Benes	.05
158 Dennis Eckersley	.65
159 Royce Clayton	.05
160 Todd Stottlemyre	.05
161 Gary Gaetti	.05
162 Willie McGee	.05
163 Delino DeShields	.05
164 Dmitri Young	.05
165 Matt Morris	.05

1997 Donruss Team Sets MVP

The top players at each position were available in this 18-card insert set. Each card is sequentially numbered to 1,000. Fronts are printed with a textured foil background and holographic foil highlights. Backs have a portrait photo.

	NM/M
Complete Set (18):	45.00
Common Player:	.50
1 Ivan Rodriguez	1.50
2 Mike Piazza	5.50
3 Frank Thomas	2.50
4 Jeff Bagwell	2.50
5 Chuck Knoblauch	.50
6 Eric Young	.50
7 Alex Rodriguez	6.00
8 Barry Larkin	.50
9 Cal Ripken Jr.	7.50
10 Chipper Jones	4.00
11 Albert Belle	.50
12 Barry Bonds	7.50
13 Ken Griffey Jr.	5.50
14 Kenny Lofton	.50
15 Juan Gonzalez	1.00
16 Larry Walker	.50
17 Roger Clemens	5.00
18 Greg Maddux	4.00

1997 Donruss Elite

Donruss Elite Baseball is a 150-card, single-series set distributed as a hobby-only product. The regular-issue cards feature a silver border around the entire card, with a marblized frame around a color player photo at cen-

ter. Backs feature a color player photo and minimal statistics and personal data. Elite was accompanied by an Elite Stars parallel set and three inserts: Leather and Lumber, Passing the Torch and Turn of the Century.

	NM/M
Complete Set (150):	10.00
Common Player:	.10
Common Elite Star:	.50
Elite Stars Stars/RC's:	4X
Pack (6):	2.50
Wax Box (18):	35.00
1 Juan Gonzalez	.40
2 Alex Rodriguez	2.00
3 Frank Thomas	.75
4 Greg Maddux	1.00
5 Ken Griffey Jr.	1.50
6 Cal Ripken Jr.	2.50
7 Mike Piazza	1.50
8 Chipper Jones	1.00
9 Albert Belle	.75
10 Andruw Jones	.75
11 Vladimir Guerrero	.75
12 Mo Vaughn	.10
13 Ivan Rodriguez	.65
14 Andy Pettitte	.40
15 Tony Gwynn	1.00
16 Barry Bonds	2.50
17 Jeff Bagwell	.75
18 Manny Ramirez	.75
19 Kenny Lofton	.10
20 Roberto Alomar	.20
21 Mark McGwire	2.00
22 Ryan Klesko	.10
23 Tim Salmon	.10
24 Derek Jeter	2.50
25 Eddie Murray	.75
26 Jermaine Dye	.10
27 Ruben Rivera	.10
28 Jim Edmonds	.10
29 Mike Mussina	.40
30 Randy Johnson	.75
31 Sammy Sosa	1.00
32 Hideo Nomo	.40
33 Chuck Knoblauch	.10
34 Paul Molitor	.75
35 Rafael Palmeiro	.75
36 Brady Anderson	.10
37 Will Clark	.10
38 Craig Biggio	.10
39 Jason Giambi	.50
40 Roger Clemens	1.25
41 Jay Buhner	.10
42 Edgar Martinez	.10
43 Gary Sheffield	.35
44 Fred McGriff	.10
45 Bobby Bonilla	.10
46 Tom Glavine	.25
47 Wade Boggs	1.00
48 Jeff Conine	.10
49 John Smoltz	.10
50 Jim Thome	.60
51 Billy Wagner	.10
52 Jose Canseco	.40
53 Javy Lopez	.10
54 Cecil Fielder	.10
55 Garret Anderson	.10
56 Alex Ochoa	.10
57 Scott Rolen	.60
58 Darin Erstad	.30
59 Rey Ordonez	.10
60 Dante Bichette	.10
61 Joe Carter	.10
62 Moises Alou	.10
63 Jason Isringhausen	.10
64 Karim Garcia	.10
65 Brian Jordan	.10
66 Ruben Sierra	.10
67 Todd Hollandsworth	.10
68 Paul Wilson	.10
69 Ernie Young	.10
70 Ryne Sandberg	1.00
71 Raul Mondesi	.10
72 George Arias	.10
73 Ray Durham	.10
74 Dean Palmer	.10
75 Shawn Green	.30
76 Eric Young	.10
77 Jason Kendall	.10
78 Greg Vaughn	.10
79 Terrell Wade	.10
80 Bill Pulsipher	.10
81 Bobby Higginson	.10
82 Mark Grudzielanek	.10
83 Ken Caminiti	.10
84 Todd Greene	.10
85 Carlos Delgado	.50
86 Mark Grace	.10
87 Rondell White	.10
88 Barry Larkin	.10
89 J.T. Snow	.10
90 Alex Gonzalez	.10
91 Raul Casanova	.10
92 Marc Newfield	.10
93 Jermaine Allensworth	.10
94 John Mabry	.10
95 Kirby Puckett	1.00
96 Travis Fryman	.10
97 Kevin Brown	.15
98 Andres Galarraga	.10
99 Marty Cordova	.10
100 Henry Rodriguez	.10
101 Sterling Hitchcock	.10
102 Trey Beamon	.10
103 Brett Butler	.10
104 Rickey Henderson	.75
105 Tino Martinez	.10
106 Kevin Appier	.10
107 Brian Hunter	.10
108 Eric Karros	.10
109 Andre Dawson	.10
110 Darryl Strawberry	.10
111 James Baldwin	.10
112 Chad Mottola	.10
113 Dave Nilsson	.10
114 Carlos Baerga	.10
115 Chan Ho Park	.10
116 John Jaha	.10
117 Alan Benes	.10
118 Mariano Rivera	.20
119 Ellis Burks	.10
120 Tony Clark	.10
121 Todd Walker	.10
122 Dwight Gooden	.10
123 Ugueth Urbina	.10
124 David Cone	.10
125 Ozzie Smith	1.00
126 Kimera Bartee	.10
127 Rusty Greer	.10
128 Pat Hentgen	.10
129 Charles Johnson	.10
130 Quinton McCracken	.10
131 Troy Percival	.10
132 Shane Reynolds	.10
133 Charles Nagy	.10
134 Tom Goodwin	.10
135 Ron Gant	.10
136 Dan Wilson	.10
137 Matt Williams	.10
138 LaTroy Hawkins	.10
139 Kevin Seitzer	.10
140 Michael Tucker	.10
141 Todd Hundley	.10
142 Alex Fernandez	.10
143 Marquis Grissom	.10
144 Steve Finley	.10
145 Curtis Pride	.10
146 Derek Bell	.10
147 Butch Huskey	.10
148 Dwight Gooden	.10
149 Al Leiter	.10
150 Hideo Nomo	.40

1997 Donruss Elite Stars

Gold, rather than silver, foil differentiates the parallel set of Elite Stars from the regular-issue versions of each of the base cards in the Elite set. The parallels also have a small "Elite Stars" printed at top, flanking the position. Stated odds of finding a Stars insert are about one per five packs.

	NM/M
Common Player:	1.00

Leather & Lumber

Leather and Lumber is a 10-card insert set filled with veterans. Genuine leather is featured on one side of the card, while wood card stock is on the other. There were 500 sequentially numbered sets produced.

	NM/M
Complete Set (10):	140.00
Common Player:	4.00
1 Ken Griffey Jr.	20.00
2 Alex Rodriguez	25.00
3 Frank Thomas	9.00
4 Chipper Jones	12.50
5 Ivan Rodriguez	7.50
6 Cal Ripken Jr.	35.00
7 Barry Bonds	35.00
8 Chuck Knoblauch	4.00
9 Manny Ramirez	9.00
10 Mark McGwire	25.00

Passing the Torch

Passing the Torch is a 12-card insert limited to 1,500 individually numbered sets. It features eight different stars, each with their own cards and then featured on a double-sided card with another player from the set.

	NM/M
Complete Set (12):	110.00
Common Player:	4.50
1 Cal Ripken Jr.	20.00
2 Alex Rodriguez	15.00
3 Cal Ripken Jr., Alex Rodriguez	17.50
4 Kirby Puckett	10.00
5 Andruw Jones	7.50
6 Kirby Puckett, Andruw Jones	7.50
7 Cecil Fielder	4.50
8 Frank Thomas	7.50
9 Cecil Fielder, Frank Thomas	6.00
10 Ozzie Smith	10.00
11 Derek Jeter	20.00
12 Ozzie Smith, Derek Jeter	12.00

Passing the Torch Autographs

The first 150 individually numbered sets of the Passing the Torch insert were autographed. This means that cards 3, 6, 9 and 12 are dual-autographed on their double-sided format.

	NM/M
Common Card:	15.00
1 Cal Ripken Jr.	200.00
2 Alex Rodriguez	275.00
3 Cal Ripken Jr., Alex Rodriguez	750.00
4 Kirby Puckett	80.00
5 Andruw Jones	40.00
6 Kirby Puckett, Andruw Jones	140.00
7 Cecil Fielder	45.00
8 Frank Thomas	75.00

9	Cecil Fielder, Frank Thomas	125.00
10	Ozzie Smith	120.00
11	Derek Jeter	160.00
12	Ozzie Smith, Derek Jeter	325.00

Turn of the Century

Turn of the Century includes 20 potential year 2000 superstars on an insert set numbered to 3,500. The first 500 of these sets feature an external die-cut design. Cards feature the player over a framed background image on silver foil board, with black strips down each side. Backs have a color photo, a few words about the player and the serial number. Each card can also be found in an over-printed "SAMPLE" version.

		NM/M
Complete Set (20):		55.00
Common Player:		1.00
Die-Cuts:		3X
Samples:		1X
1	Alex Rodriguez	10.00
2	Andruw Jones	6.00
3	Chipper Jones	7.50
4	Todd Walker	1.00
5	Scott Rolen	4.00
6	Trey Beamon	1.00
7	Derek Jeter	12.50
8	Darin Erstad	3.00
9	Tony Clark	1.00
10	Todd Greene	1.00
11	Jason Giambi	3.00
12	Justin Thompson	1.00
13	Ernie Young	1.00
14	Jason Kendall	1.00
15	Alex Ochoa	1.00
16	Brooks Kieschnick	1.00
17	Bobby Higginson	1.00
18	Ruben Rivera	1.00
19	Chan Ho Park	1.00
20	Chad Mottola	1.00

1997 Donruss Limited

Each of the 200 base cards in this set features a double-front design showcasing an action photo on each side. The set is divided into four subsets. Counterparts (100 cards) highlights two different players from the same position; Double Team (40 cards) features some of the majors' top teammate duos; Star Factor (40 cards) consists of two photos of some of the hobby's favorite players; and Unlimited Potential/Talent (20 cards) combines a top veteran with a top prospect. The issue also includes a Limited Exposure parallel set and a multi-tiered insert called Fabric of the Game. Odds of finding any insert card were 1:5 packs. Less than 1,100 base sets were available. Cards were sold in five-card packs for $4.99.

	NM/M
Complete Set (200):	450.00
Common Counterpart:	.20
Common Double Team:	.75

Common Star Factor:	1.50
Common Unlimited Potential:	1.25
Pack (5):	2.00
Wax Box (24):	45.00

1	Ken Griffey Jr., Rondell White (Counterparts)	1.00
2	Greg Maddux, David Cone (Counterparts)	.75
3	Gary Sheffield, Moises Alou/DT	1.25
4	Frank Thomas/SF	10.00
5	Cal Ripken Jr., Kevin Orie (Counterparts)	2.00
6	Vladimir Guerrero, Barry Bonds (Unlimited Potential/Talent)	20.00
7	Eddie Murray, Reggie Jefferson (Counterparts)	.60
8	Manny Ramirez, Marquis Grissom/DT	2.50
9	Mike Piazza/SF	15.00
10	Barry Larkin, Rey Ordonez (Counterparts)	.20
11	Jeff Bagwell, Eric Karros (Counterparts)	.60
12	Chuck Knoblauch, Ray Durham (Counterparts)	.20
13	Alex Rodriguez, Edgar Renteria (Counterparts)	.20
14	Matt Williams, Vinny Castilla (Counterparts)	.20
15	Todd Hollandsworth, Bob Abreu (Counterparts)	.20
16	John Smoltz, Pedro Martinez (Counterparts)	.60
17	Jose Canseco, Chili Davis (Counterparts)	.40
18	Jose Cruz, Jr., Ken Griffey Jr./UPT	15.00
19	Ken Griffey Jr/SF	15.00
20	Paul Molitor, John Olerud (Counterparts)	.60
21	Roberto Alomar, Luis Castillo (Counterparts)	.35
22	Derek Jeter, Lou Collier (Counterparts)	2.00
23	Chipper Jones, Robin Ventura (Counterparts)	.75
24	Gary Sheffield, Ron Gant (Counterparts)	.25
25	Ramon Martinez, Bobby Jones (Counterparts)	.20
26	Mike Piazza, Raul Mondesi (Double Team)	7.50
27	Darin Erstad, Jeff Bagwell/UPT	7.50
28	Ivan Rodriguez/SF	7.50
29	J.T. Snow, Kevin Young (Counterparts)	.20
30	Ryne Sandberg, Julio Franco (Counterparts)	.75
31	Travis Fryman, Chris Snopek (Counterparts)	.20
32	Wade Boggs, Russ Davis (Counterparts)	.75
33	Brooks Kieschnick, Marty Cordova (Counterparts)	.20
34	Andy Pettitte, Denny Neagle (Counterparts)	.35
35	Paul Molitor, Matt Lawton (Double Team)	2.50
36	Scott Rolen, Cal Ripken Jr./UPT	20.00
37	Cal Ripken Jr./SF	20.00
38	Jim Thome, Dave Nilsson (Counterparts)	.50
39	Tony Womack RC, Carlos Baerga (Counterparts)	.20
40	Nomar Garciaparra, Mark Grudzielanek (Counterparts)	.75
41	Todd Greene, Chris Widger (Counterparts)	.20
42	Deion Sanders, Bernard Gilkey (Counterparts)	.20
43	Hideo Nomo, Charles Nagy (Counterparts)	.20
44	Ivan Rodriguez, Rusty Greer (Double Team)	2.00
45	Todd Walker, Chipper Jones/UPT	10.00
46	Greg Maddux/SF	12.00
47	Mo Vaughn, Cecil Fielder (Counterparts)	.20
48	Craig Biggio, Scott Spiezio (Counterparts)	.20
49	Pokey Reese, Jeff Blauser (Counterparts)	.20
50	Ken Caminiti, Joe Randa (Counterparts)	.20
51	Albert Belle, Shawn Green (Counterparts)	.20
52	Randy Johnson, Jason Dickson (Counterparts)	.60
53	Hideo Nomo, Chan Ho Park/DT	2.00
54	Scott Spiezio, Chuck Knoblauch/UPT	1.25
55	Chipper Jones/SF	12.00
56	Tino Martinez, Ryan McGuire (Counterparts)	.20
57	Eric Young, Wilton Guerrero (Counterparts)	.20
58	Ron Coomer, Dave Hollins (Counterparts)	.20
59	Sammy Sosa, Angel Echevarria (Counterparts)	.75
60	Dennis Reyes RC, Jimmy Key (Counterparts)	.20
61	Barry Larkin, Deion Sanders (Double Team)	.75
62	Wilton Guerrero, Roberto Alomar/UPT	2.00
63	Albert Belle/SF	1.50
64	Mark McGwire, Andres Galarraga (Counterparts)	1.50
65	Edgar Martinez, Todd Walker (Counterparts)	.20
66	Steve Finley, Rich Becker (Counterparts)	.20
67	Tom Glavine, Andy Ashby (Counterparts)	.30
68	Sammy Sosa, Ryne Sandberg/DT	5.00
69	Nomar Garciaparra, Alex Rodriguez/UPT	15.00
70	Jeff Bagwell/SF	10.00
71	Darin Erstad, Mark Grace (Counterparts)	.50
72	Scott Rolen, Edgardo Alfonzo (Counterparts)	.20
73	Kenny Lofton, Lance Johnson (Counterparts)	.20
74	Joey Hamilton, Brett Tomko (Counterparts)	.20
75	Eddie Murray, Tim Salmon (Double Team)	2.50
76	Dmitri Young, Mo Vaughn/UPT	1.25
77	Juan Gonzalez/SF	3.00
78	Frank Thomas, Tony Clark (Counterparts)	.60
79	Shannon Stewart, Bip Roberts (Counterparts)	.20
80	Shawn Estes, Alex Fernandez (Counterparts)	.20
81	John Smoltz, Javier Lopez (Double Team)	.75
82	Todd Greene, Mike Piazza/UPT	15.00
83	Derek Jeter/SF	20.00
84	Dmitri Young, Antone Williamson (Counterparts)	.20
85	Rickey Henderson, Darryl Hamilton (Counterparts)	.60
86	Billy Wagner, Dennis Eckersley (Counterparts)	.60
87	Larry Walker, Eric Young (Double Team)	.75
88	Mark Kotsay, Juan Gonzalez/UPT	3.00
89	Barry Bonds/SF	20.00
90	Will Clark, Jeff Conine (Counterparts)	.20
91	Tony Gwynn, Brett Butler (Counterparts)	.75
92	John Wetteland, Rod Beck (Counterparts)	.20
93	Bernie Williams, Tino Martinez/DT	1.25
94	Andruw Jones, Kenny Lofton/UPT	7.50
95	Mo Vaughn/SF	1.50
96	Joe Carter, Derrek Lee (Counterparts)	.20
97	John Mabry, F.P. Santangelo (Counterparts)	.20
98	Esteban Loaiza, Wilson Alvarez (Counterparts)	.20
99	Matt Williams, David Justice/SF	.75
100	Derrek Lee, Frank Thomas/UPT	7.50
101	Mark McGwire/SF	17.50
102	Fred McGriff, Paul Sorrento (Counterparts)	.20
103	Jermaine Allensworth, Bernie Williams (Counterparts)	.20
104	Ismael Valdes, Chris Holt (Counterparts)	.20
105	Fred McGriff, Ryan Klesko/DT	.75
106	Tony Clark, Mark McGwire/UPT	17.50
107	Tony Gwynn/SF	12.00
108	Jeffrey Hammonds, Ellis Burks (Counterparts)	.20
109	Shane Reynolds, Andy Benes (Counterparts)	.20
110	Roger Clemens, Carlos Delgado/DT	10.00
111	Karim Garcia, Albert Belle/UPT	1.25
112	Paul Molitor/SF	1.50
113	Trey Beamon, Eric Owens (Counterparts)	.20
114	Curt Schilling, Darryl Kile (Counterparts)	.30
115	Tom Glavine, Michael Tucker/DT	.75
116	Pokey Reese, Derek Jeter/UPT	20.00
117	Manny Ramirez/SF	10.00
118	Juan Gonzalez, Brant Brown (Counterparts)	.40
119	Juan Guzman, Francisco Cordova (Counterparts)	.20
120	Randy Johnson, Edgar Martinez/DT	2.50
121	Hideki Irabu, Greg Maddux/UPT	10.00
122	Alex Rodriguez/SF	17.50
123	Barry Bonds, Quinton McCracken (Counterparts)	2.00
124	Roger Clemens, Alan Benes (Counterparts)	.85
125	Wade Boggs, Paul O'Neill (Double Team)	1.75
126	Mike Cameron, Larry Walker/UPT	1.25
127	Gary Sheffield/SF	2.00
128	Andruw Jones, Raul Mondesi (Counterparts)	.75
129	Brian Anderson, Terrell Wade (Counterparts)	.20
130	Brady Anderson, Rafael Palmeiro (Counterparts)	2.00
131	Neifi Perez, Barry Larkin/UPT	1.25
132	Ken Caminiti/SF	1.50
133	Larry Walker, Rusty Greer (Counterparts)	.20
134	Mariano Rivera, Mark Wohlers (Counterparts)	.30
135	Hideki Irabu, Andy Pettitte/DT	1.50
136	Jose Guillen, Tony Gwynn/UPT	10.00
137	Hideo Nomo/SF	3.00
138	Vladimir Guerrero, Jim Edmonds (Counterparts)	.60
139	Justin Thompson, Dwight Gooden (Counterparts)	.20
140	Andres Galarraga, Dante Bichette/DT	.75
141	Kenny Lofton/SF	1.50
142	Tim Salmon, Manny Ramirez (Counterparts)	.60
143	Kevin Brown, Matt Morris (Counterparts)	.20
144	Craig Biggio, Bob Abreu/DT	.75
145	Roberto Alomar/SF	2.00
146	Jose Guillen, Brian Jordan (Counterparts)	.20
147	Bartolo Colon, Kevin Appier (Counterparts)	.20
148	Ray Lankford, Brian Jordan/DT	.75
149	Chuck Knoblauch/SF	1.50
150	Henry Rodriguez, Ray Lankford (Counterparts)	.20
151	Jaret Wright RC, Ben McDonald (Counterparts)	.20
152	Bobby Bonilla, Kevin Brown/DT	.75
153	Barry Larkin/SF	1.50
154	David Justice, Reggie Sanders (Counterparts)	.20
155	Mike Mussina, Ken Hill (Counterparts)	.40
156	Mark Grace, Brooks Kieschnick/DT	.50
157	Jim Thome/SF	2.50
158	Michael Tucker, Curtis Goodwin (Counterparts)	.20
159	Jeff Suppan, Jeff Fassero (Counterparts)	.20
160	Mike Mussina, Jeffrey Hammonds/DT	1.00
161	John Smoltz/SF	1.50
162	Moises Alou, Eric Davis (Counterparts)	.20
163	Sandy Alomar Jr., Dan Wilson (Counterparts)	.20
164	Rondell White, Henry Rodriguez/DT	.75
165	Roger Clemens/SF	12.50
166	Brady Anderson, Al Martin (Counterparts)	.20
167	Jason Kendall, Charles Johnson (Counterparts)	.20
168	Jason Giambi, Jose Canseco/DT	2.00
169	Larry Walker/SF	1.50
170	Jay Buhner, Geronimo Berroa (Counterparts)	.20
171	Ivan Rodriguez, Mike Sweeney (Counterparts)	.20
172	Kevin Appier, Jose Rosado/DT	.75
173	Bernie Williams/SF	1.50
174	Todd Dunwoody, Brian Giles RC (Counterparts)	.40
175	Javier Lopez, Scott Hatteberg (Counterparts)	.20
176	John Jaha, Jeff Cirillo/DT	.75
177	Andy Pettitte/SF	2.00
178	Dante Bichette, Butch Huskey (Counterparts)	.20
179	Raul Casanova, Todd Hundley (Counterparts)	.20
180	Jim Edmonds, Garret Anderson/DT	.75
181	Deion Sanders/SF	1.50
182	Ryan Klesko, Paul O'Neill (Counterparts)	.20
183	Joe Carter, Pat Hentgen/DT	.75
184	Brady Anderson/SF	1.50
185	Carlos Delgado, Wally Joyner (Counterparts)	.50
186	Jermaine Dye, Johnny Damon/DT	1.00
187	Randy Johnson/SF	7.50
188	Todd Hundley, Carlos Baerga/DT	.75
189	Tom Glavine/SF	2.50
190	Damon Mashore, Jason McDonald/DT	.75
191	Wade Boggs/SF	12.00
192	Al Martin, Jason Kendall/DT	.75
193	Matt Williams/SF	1.50
194	Will Clark, Dean Palmer/DT	.75
195	Sammy Sosa/SF	12.00
196	Jose Cruz, Jr., Jay Buhner/DT	.75
197	Eddie Murray/SF	10.00
198	Darin Erstad, Jason Dickson/DT	1.00
199	Fred McGriff/SF	1.50
200	Bubba Trammell, Bobby Higginson/DT	.75

Exposure

A complete 200-card parallel set printed with Holographic Poly-Chromium technology on both sides and featuring a special "Limited Exposure" stamp. Less than 40 sets of the Star Factor Limited Exposures are thought to exist.

	NM/M
Common Counterparts:	.75
Common Double Team:	3.00
Common Star Factor:	6.50
Common Unlimited:	4.50
Stars:	4X

Exposure Non-Glossy

In error, half (100 cards) of the Limited Exposure parallels were produced in regular technology (non-chrome) on regular (non-glossy) cardboard stock. These cards do carry the Limited Exposure identification in the card-number box on back, but do not carry the correct cards' higher values. No checklist of which 100 cards were involved in the error is available.

	NM/M
Common Non-Glossy:	.50
Stars: 25 Percent	

Fabric of the Game

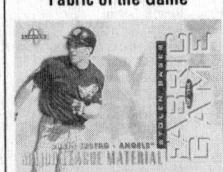

This fractured insert set consists of 69 different cards highlighting three different technologies representing three statistical categories: Canvas (stolen bases), Leather (doubles) and Wood (home runs). Each of the 23 cards in each category are found in vary-ing levels of scarcity: Legendary Material (one card per theme; numbered to 100), Hall of Fame Material (four cards numbered to 250), Superstar Material (five cards numbered to 500), Star Material (six cards numbered to 750), and Major League Material (seven cards numbered to 1,000).

		NM/M
Complete Set: (69):		275.00
Common Player:		1.50
Complete Canvas Set (23):		80.00
	Rickey Henderson/100	12.00
	Barry Bonds/250	15.00
	Kenny Lofton/250	2.50
	Roberto Alomar/250	4.50
	Ryne Sandberg/250	12.00
	Tony Gwynn/500	7.50
	Barry Larkin/500	2.00
	Brady Anderson/500	2.00
	Chuck Knoblauch/500	2.00
	Craig Biggio/750	2.00
	Sammy Sosa/750	7.50
	Gary Sheffield/750	2.00
	Eric Young/750	1.50
	Larry Walker/750	1.50
	Ken Griffey Jr./750	10.00
	Deion Sanders/750	1.50
	Raul Mondesi/1,000	1.50
	Rondell White/1,000	1.50
	Derek Jeter/1,000	10.00
	Nomar Garciaparra/1,000	6.00
	Wilton Guerrero/1,000	1.50
	Pokey Reese/1,000	1.50
	Darin Erstad/1,000	2.00
Complete Leather Set (23):		90.00
	Paul Molitor/100	15.00
	Wade Boggs/250	12.00
	Cal Ripken Jr./250	20.00
	Tony Gwynn/250	12.00
	Joe Carter/250	2.50
	Rafael Palmeiro/500	5.00
	Mark Grace/500	1.50
	Bobby Bonilla/500	1.50
	Andres Galarraga/500	1.50
	Edgar Martinez/500	1.50
	Ken Caminiti/750	1.50
	Ivan Rodriguez/750	4.50
	Frank Thomas/750	6.00
	Jeff Bagwell/750	6.00
	Albert Belle/750	1.50
	Bernie Williams/750	1.50
	Chipper Jones/1,000	7.50
	Rusty Greer/1,000	1.50
	Todd Walker/1,000	1.50
	Scott Rolen/1,000	3.00
	Bob Abreu/1,000	1.50
	Jose Guillen/1,000	1.50
	Jose Cruz, Jr./1,000	1.50
Complete Wood Set (23):		110.00
	Eddie Murray/100	12.00
	Cal Ripken Jr./250	20.00
	Barry Bonds/250	20.00
	Mark McGwire/250	17.50
	Fred McGriff/250	3.50
	Ken Griffey Jr./500	7.50
	Albert Belle/500	2.00
	Frank Thomas/500	6.50
	Juan Gonzalez/500	2.00
	Matt Williams/500	2.00
	Mike Piazza/750	6.00
	Jeff Bagwell/750	5.00
	Mo Vaughn/750	1.50
	Gary Sheffield/750	1.50
	Tim Salmon/750	1.50
	David Justice/750	1.50
	Manny Ramirez/1,000	5.00
	Jim Thome/1,000	2.50
	Tino Martinez/1,000	1.50
	Andruw Jones/1,000	3.50
	Vladimir Guerrero/1,000	5.00
	Tony Clark/1,000	1.50
	Dmitri Young/1,000	1.50

1997 Donruss Preferred

Each of the 200 base cards is printed on all-foil microetched stock. Conventional backs have a color player photo and a few stats. The set is fractured into four increasingly scarce levels: 100 Bronze cards, 70 Silver, 20 Gold and 10 Platinum. Instead of traditional packs, cards were sold in five-card collectible tins. Four different inserts were included with the product: Staremaster, X-Ponential Power, Cut To The Chase (a die-cut parallel) and Precious Metals. Odds of finding any insert were 1:4 packs.

	NM/M
Complete Set (200):	225.00
Common Bronze:	.10
Common Silver:	.60
Common Gold:	1.25
Common Platinum:	6.00
Cut to the Chase:	1.5X
Tin Pack (5):	2.50
Tin Box (24):	40.00
1 Frank Thomas/P	7.50
2 Ken Griffey Jr./P	12.50
3 Cecil Fielder/B	.10
4 Chuck Knoblauch/B	1.25
5 Garret Anderson/B	.10
6 Greg Maddux/P	10.00
7 Matt Williams/S	.60
8 Marquis Grissom/B	.60
9 Jason Isringhausen/B	.10
10 Larry Walker/S	.60
11 Charles Nagy/S	.10
12 Dan Wilson/B	.10
13 Albert Belle/G	1.25
14 Javier Lopez/B	.10
15 David Cone/B	.10
16 Bernard Gilkey/B	.10
17 Andres Galarraga/S	.60
18 Bill Pulsipher/B	.10
19 Alex Fernandez/B	.10
20 Andy Pettitte/B	1.25
21 Mark Grudzielanek/B	.10
22 Juan Gonzalez/P	6.00
23 Reggie Sanders/B	.10
24 Kenny Lofton/G	1.25
25 Andy Ashby/B	.10
26 John Wetteland/B	.10
27 Bobby Bonilla/B	.10
28 Hideo Nomo/G	2.50
29 Joe Carter/B	.10
30 Jose Canseco/B	.40
31 Ellis Burks/B	.10
32 Edgar Martinez/S	.60
33 Chan Ho Park/B	.10
34 David Justice/B	.10
35 Carlos Delgado/B	.50
36 Jeff Cirillo/B	.60
37 Charles Johnson/B	.10
38 Manny Ramirez/G	4.50
39 Greg Vaughn/B	.10
40 Henry Rodriguez/B	.10
41 Darryl Strawberry/B	.10
42 Jim Thome/G	2.50
43 Ryan Klesko/S	.60
44 Jermaine Allensworth/B	.10
45 Brian Jordan/B	1.25
46 Tony Gwynn/P	10.00
47 Rafael Palmeiro/S	3.50
48 Dante Bichette/S	.60
49 Ivan Rodriguez/S	3.50
50 Mark McGwire/G	8.00
51 Tim Salmon/B	.60
52 Roger Clemens/B	1.50
53 Matt Lawton/B	.10
54 Wade Boggs/S	3.50
55 Travis Fryman/B	.10
56 Bobby Higginson/S	.60
57 John Jaha/B	.60
58 Rondell White/B	.60
59 Tom Glavine/S	1.25
60 Eddie Murray/S	2.50
61 Vinny Castilla/B	.10
62 Todd Hundley/B	.10
63 Jay Buhner/S	.60
64 Paul O'Neill/B	.10
65 Steve Finley/B	.10
66 Kevin Appier/B	.10
67 Ray Durham/B	.10
68 Dave Nilsson/B	.10
69 Jeff Bagwell/G	4.50
70 Al Martin/B	.60
71 Paul Molitor/S	4.50
72 Kevin Brown/B	.60
73 Ron Gant/B	.10
74 Dwight Gooden/B	.10
75 Quinton McCracken/B	.10
76 Rusty Greer/B	.60
77 Juan Guzman/B	.60
78 Fred McGriff/S	.60
79 Tino Martinez/S	.60
80 Ray Lankford/B	.10
81 Ken Caminiti/B	1.25
82 James Baldwin/B	.10
83 Jermaine Dye/G	1.25
84 Mark Grace/S	.60
85 Pat Hentgen/B	.60
86 Jason Giambi/S	1.50
87 Brian Hunter/B	.10
88 Andy Benes/B	.10
89 Jose Rosado/B	.10
90 Shawn Green/B	.25
91 Jason Kendall/B	.10
92 Alex Rodriguez/P	15.00
93 Chipper Jones/P	10.00
94 Barry Bonds/B	10.00
95 Brady Anderson/G	1.25
96 Ryne Sandberg/S	3.50
97 Lance Johnson/B	.10
98 Cal Ripken Jr./P	17.50
99 Craig Biggio/S	.60
100 Dean Palmer/B	.10

101 Gary Sheffield/G	1.50
102 Johnny Damon/B	.35
103 Mo Vaughn/G	1.25
104 Randy Johnson/S	2.50
105 Raul Mondesi/G	.60
106 Roberto Alomar/G	2.00
107 Mike Piazza/P	12.50
108 Rey Ordonez/B	.10
109 Barry Larkin/S	1.25
110 Tony Clark/S	.60
111 Bernie Williams/S	.60
112 John Smoltz/G	1.25
113 Moises Alou/B	.10
114 Will Clark/B	.10
115 Sammy Sosa/G	6.00
116 Jim Edmonds/S	.60
117 Jeff Conine/S	.60
118 Joey Hamilton/B	.10
119 Todd Hollandsworth/B	.10
120 Troy Percival/B	.10
121 Paul Wilson/B	.10
122 Ken Hill/B	.10
123 Mariano Rivera/S	.75
124 Eric Karros/B	.10
125 Derek Jeter/G	10.00
126 Eric Young/B	.60
127 John Mabry/B	.10
128 Gregg Jefferies/B	.10
129 Ismael Valdes/S	.60
130 Marty Cordova/B	.10
131 Omar Vizquel/B	.10
132 Mike Mussina/S	1.25
133 Darin Erstad/B	.30
134 Edgar Renteria/B	.60
135 Billy Wagner/B	.10
136 Alex Ochoa/B	.10
137 Luis Castillo/B	.10
138 Rocky Coppinger/B	.10
139 Mike Sweeney/B	.10
140 Michael Tucker/B	.10
141 Chris Snopek/B	.10
142 Dmitri Young/S	.60
143 Andruw Jones/P	7.50
144 Mike Cameron/S	.60
145 Brant Brown/B	.10
146 Todd Walker/B	1.25
147 Nomar Garciaparra/S	6.00
148 Glendon Rusch/B	.10
149 Karim Garcia/B	.10
150 Bubba Trammell/S RC	.60
151 Todd Greene/B	.10
152 Wilton Guerrero/G	1.25
153 Scott Spiezio/B	.10
154 Brooks Kieschnick/B	.10
155 Vladimir Guerrero/G	4.50
156 Brian Giles/S RC	1.50
157 Pokey Reese/B	.10
158 Jason Dickson/S	1.25
159 Kevin Orie/B	.60
160 Scott Rolen/S	3.00
161 Bartolo Colon/B	.60
162 Shannon Stewart/G	1.25
163 Wendell Magee/B	.10
164 Jose Guillen/B	.60
165 Bob Abreu/S	.10
166 Deivi Cruz/B RC	.25
167 Alex Rodriguez	
(National Treasures)	3.00
168 Frank Thomas/B	
(National Treasures)	.75
169 Cal Ripken Jr./B	
(National Treasures)	4.00
170 Chipper Jones/B	
(National Treasures)	1.50
171 Mike Piazza/B	
(National Treasures)	2.50
172 Tony Gwynn/B	
(National Treasures)	3.50
173 Juan Gonzalez/B	
(National Treasures)	.40
174 Kenny Lofton/B	
(National Treasures)	.60
175 Ken Griffey Jr./B	
(National Treasures)	2.50
176 Mark McGwire/B	
(National Treasures)	3.00
177 Jeff Bagwell/B	
(National Treasures)	.75
178 Paul Molitor/S	
(National Treasures)	2.50
179 Andruw Jones/S	
(National Treasures)	.75
180 Manny Ramirez/S	
(National Treasures)	2.50
181 Ken Caminiti/S	
(National Treasures)	.60
182 Barry Bonds/S	
(National Treasures)	4.00
183 Mo Vaughn/G	
(National Treasures)	.10
184 Derek Jeter/S	
(National Treasures)	4.00
185 Barry Larkin/S	
(National Treasures)	.60
186 Ivan Rodriguez/B	
(National Treasures)	.65
187 Albert Belle/S	
(National Treasures)	.60
188 John Smoltz/B	
(National Treasures)	.60
189 Chuck Knoblauch/B	
(National Treasures)	.10
190 Brian Jordan/B	
(National Treasures)	.60
191 Gary Sheffield/S	
(National Treasures)	1.00
192 Jim Thome/S	
(National Treasures)	2.00

193 Brady Anderson/S	
(National Treasures)	.60
194 Hideo Nomo/S	
(National Treasures)	1.50
195 Sammy Sosa/S	
(National Treasures)	3.50
196 Greg Maddux/B	
(National Treasures)	1.25
197 Checklist	
(Vladimir Guerrero/B)	.40
198 Checklist (Scott Rolen/B)	.15
199 Checklist (Todd Walker/B)	.10
200 Checklist	
(Nomar Garciaparra/B)	.60

Cut To The Chase

Each of the cards in the Donruss Preferred series can also be found in this parallel set with die-cut borders, in the same bronze, silver, gold and platinum finishes. Multiplier values of the die-cuts are inverse to that usually found, with platinum cards the lowest, followed by gold, silver and bronze. Besides die-cutting, the chase cards feature a "CUT TO THE CHASE" designation at bottom.

Typical Value: 1.5X

Precious Metals

This 25-card partial parallel set features cards printed on actual silver, gold and platinum stock. Only 100 of each card were produced.

	NM/M
Common Player:	7.50
1 Frank Thomas/P	45.00
2 Ken Griffey Jr./P	75.00
3 Greg Maddux/P	60.00
4 Albert Belle/G	7.50
5 Juan Gonzalez/P	25.00
6 Kenny Lofton/S	7.50
7 Tony Gwynn/P	60.00
8 Ivan Rodriguez/G	30.00
9 Mark McGwire/G	90.00
10 Matt Williams/S	7.50
11 Wade Boggs/S	60.00
12 Eddie Murray/S	45.00
13 Jeff Bagwell/S	45.00
14 Ken Caminiti/G	7.50
15 Alex Rodriguez/P	90.00
16 Chipper Jones/P	60.00
17 Barry Bonds/S	125.00
18 Cal Ripken Jr./P	125.00
19 Mo Vaughn/G	7.50
20 Mike Piazza/P	75.00
21 Derek Jeter/P	125.00
22 Bernie Williams/S	7.50
23 Andruw Jones/P	45.00
24 Vladimir Guerrero/G	45.00
25 Jose Guillen/S	7.50

Staremasters

A 20-card insert printed on foil stock and accented with holographic foil, Staremasters is designed to show up-close "game-face" photography. Each card is sequentially numbered to 1,500. Each of the Staremasters inserts can also be found in a version overprinted with a large diagonal black "SAMPLE" on front and

back. These were distributed to dealers and the media. The sample cards have a "PROMO/1500" on back in place of a serial number.

	NM/M
Complete Set (20):	55.00
Common Player:	1.00
Samples: 50 Percent	
1 Alex Rodriguez	6.00
2 Frank Thomas	3.00
3 Chipper Jones	4.00
4 Cal Ripken Jr.	7.50
5 Mike Piazza	4.50
6 Juan Gonzalez	2.25
7 Derek Jeter	7.50
8 Jeff Bagwell	3.00
9 Ken Griffey Jr.	4.50
10 Tony Gwynn	4.00
11 Barry Bonds	7.50
12 Albert Belle	1.00
13 Greg Maddux	.50
14 Mark McGwire	6.00
15 Ken Caminiti	1.00
16 Hideo Nomo	2.25
17 Gary Sheffield	1.50
18 Andruw Jones	3.00
19 Mo Vaughn	1.00
20 Ivan Rodriguez	2.25

X-Ponential Power

This 20-card die-cut insert contains two top hitters from 10 different teams. Placing the cards of teammates together forms an "X" shape. Cards are printed on thick plastic stock and gold holographic foil stamping and are sequentially numbered to 3,000.

	NM/M
Complete Set (20):	50.00
Common Player:	1.00
1A Manny Ramirez	3.50
1B Jim Thome	3.00
2A Paul Molitor	3.50
2B Chuck Knoblauch	1.00
3A Ivan Rodriguez	2.50
3B Juan Gonzalez	2.25
4A Albert Belle	1.00
4B Frank Thomas	3.50
5A Roberto Alomar	1.25
5B Cal Ripken Jr.	9.00
6A Tim Salmon	1.00
6B Jim Edmonds	1.00
7A Ken Griffey Jr.	6.00
7B Alex Rodriguez	7.50
8A Chipper Jones	5.00
8B Andruw Jones	3.00
9A Mike Piazza	6.00
9B Raul Mondesi	1.00
10A Tony Gwynn	4.50
10B Ken Caminiti	1.00

1997 Donruss Preferred Tins

Twenty-five different players are featured on the lithographed steel tins which were the "packs" of Donruss Preferred baseball. The 3" x 4-1/2" x 5/8" tins are hinged along the left side and were produced in two versions. Predominantly blue tins are the standard package. A premium parallel version is gold-colored and serially numbered within an edition of 1,200. Gold tins were packed one

per 24-pack box of Preferred. Values shown are for opened tins. Shrink-wrapped unopened tins are valued about 1.5-3X the figures shown.

	NM/M
Complete Set, Blue (25):	10.00
Common Tin:	.25
Gold:	10X
1 Frank Thomas	.40
2 Ken Griffey Jr.	.60
3 Andruw Jones	.40
4 Cal Ripken Jr.	1.00
5 Mike Piazza	.60
6 Chipper Jones	.50
7 Alex Rodriguez	.75
8 Derek Jeter	1.00
9 Juan Gonzalez	.40
10 Albert Belle	.25
11 Tony Gwynn	.50
12 Greg Maddux	.50
13 Jeff Bagwell	.40
14 Roger Clemens	.55
15 Mark McGwire	.75
16 Gary Sheffield	.30
17 Manny Ramirez	.40
18 Hideo Nomo	.25
19 Kenny Lofton	.25
20 Mo Vaughn	.25
21 Ryne Sandberg	.50
22 Barry Bonds	1.00
23 Sammy Sosa	.50
24 John Smoltz	.25
25 Ivan Rodriguez	.35

1997 Donruss Preferred Tin Boxes

Twenty-five different players are featured on the lithographed steel boxes in which the "packs" of Donruss Preferred baseball were sold. Boxes measure about 5-1/4" x 9-1/4" x 5-3/8". Inside the removable lid is a serial number from within an edition of 1,200 (blue) or 299 (gold). The gold versions are a later, hobby-only release.

	NM/M
Complete Set, Blue (25):	70.00
Common Box:	2.00
Gold:	4X
1 Frank Thomas	3.00
2 Ken Griffey Jr.	5.00
3 Andruw Jones	3.00
4 Cal Ripken Jr.	7.50
5 Mike Piazza	5.00
6 Chipper Jones	4.00
7 Alex Rodriguez	6.00
8 Derek Jeter	7.50
9 Juan Gonzalez	2.50
10 Albert Belle	2.00
11 Tony Gwynn	4.00
12 Greg Maddux	4.00
13 Jeff Bagwell	3.00
14 Roger Clemens	4.00
15 Mark McGwire	6.00
16 Gary Sheffield	2.50
17 Manny Ramirez	3.00
18 Hideo Nomo	2.50
19 Kenny Lofton	2.00
20 Mo Vaughn	2.00
21 Ryne Sandberg	4.00
22 Barry Bonds	7.50
23 Sammy Sosa	4.00
24 John Smoltz	2.00
25 Ivan Rodriguez	2.50

1997 Donruss Signature

Donruss ventured in the autograph-per-pack market with this series featuring 100 base cards

(unsigned) and various types and versions of authentically autographed cards. The suggested retail price for each five-card pack was $14.99. Base cards have textured silver-foil borders and highlights on front. Backs have a second photo and lengthy stats. A parallel insert edition of each base card was also issued, labeled "Platinum Press Proof," the parallels have blue metallic foil on front and are designated "1 of 150" on the back.

	NM/M
Complete Set (100):	15.00
Common Player:	.10
Platinum Stars/RC's:	12X
Pack (5):	7.50
Wax Box (12):	80.00
1 Mark McGwire	1.25
2 Kenny Lofton	.10
3 Tony Gwynn	.75
4 Tony Clark	.10
5 Tim Salmon	.10
6 Ken Griffey Jr.	1.00
7 Mike Piazza	1.00
8 Greg Maddux	.75
9 Roberto Alomar	.20
10 Andres Galarraga	.10
11 Roger Clemens	.90
12 Bernie Williams	.10
13 Rondell White	.10
14 Kevin Appler	.10
15 Ray Lankford	.10
16 Frank Thomas	.65
17 Will Clark	.10
18 Chipper Jones	.75
19 Jeff Bagwell	.65
20 Manny Ramirez	.65
21 Ryne Sandberg	.75
22 Paul Molitor	.65
23 Gary Sheffield	.10
24 Jim Edmonds	.10
25 Barry Larkin	.10
26 Rafael Palmeiro	.60
27 Alan Benes	.10
28 David Justice	.10
29 Randy Johnson	.65
30 Barry Bonds	1.50
31 Mo Vaughn	.10
32 Michael Tucker	.10
33 Larry Walker	.10
34 Tino Martinez	.10
35 Jose Guillen	.10
36 Carlos Delgado	.40
37 Jason Dickson	.10
38 Tom Glavine	.25
39 Raul Mondesi	.10
40 Jose Cruz Jr. RC	.50
41 Johnny Damon	.20
42 Mark Grace	.25
43 Juan Gonzalez	.35
44 Vladimir Guerrero	.65
45 Kevin Brown	.10
46 Justin Thompson	.10
47 Eric Young	.10
48 Ron Coomer	.10
49 Mark Kotsay	.10
50 Scott Rolen	.60
51 Derek Jeter	1.50
52 Jim Thome	.50
53 Fred McGriff	.10
54 Albert Belle	.10
55 Garret Anderson	.10
56 Wilton Guerrero	.10
57 Jose Canseco	.40
58 Cal Ripken Jr.	1.50
59 Sammy Sosa	.75
60 Dmitri Young	.10
61 Alex Rodriguez	1.25
62 Javier Lopez	.10
63 Sandy Alomar Jr.	.10
64 Joe Carter	.10
65 Dante Bichette	.10
66 Al Martin	.10
67 Darin Erstad	.30
68 Pokey Reese	.10
69 Brady Anderson	.10
70 Andruw Jones	.65
71 Ivan Rodriguez	.50
72 Nomar Garciaparra	.75
73 Moises Alou	.10
74 Andy Pettitte	.35
75 Jay Buhner	.10
76 Craig Biggio	.10

77	Wade Boggs	.75
78	Shawn Estes	.10
79	Neifi Perez	.10
80	Rusty Greer	.10
81	Pedro Martinez	.60
82	Mike Mussina	.40
83	Jason Giambi	.40
84	Hideo Nomo	.35
85	Todd Hundley	.10
86	Deion Sanders	.10
87	Mike Cameron	.10
88	Bobby Bonilla	.10
89	Todd Greene	.10
90	Kevin Orie	.10
91	Ken Caminiti	.10
92	Chuck Knoblauch	.10
93	Matt Morris	.10
94	Matt Williams	.10
95	Pat Hentgen	.10
96	John Smoltz	.10
97	Edgar Martinez	.10
98	Jason Kendall	.10
99	Checklist (Ken Griffey Jr.)	.50
100	Checklist (Frank Thomas)	.30

1997 Donruss Signature Platinum Press Proofs

This parallel insert set features metallic blue borders and graphics on front and has a "1 of 150" notation on back.

	NM/M
Common Player:	2.00
Stars:	12X

1997 Donruss Signature Autographs Promo

The "autograph" on the front of this promo card is a facsimile signature, rather than hand-penned. The sample is identical in format to the common red base level autographs in the set, but Thomas does not appear in that format.

	NM/M
Frank Thomas	6.00

Autographs (Red)

The basic level of authentically autographed cards found one per ($15) pack in Donruss Signature is the unnumbered "red" version. Cards have the background of the front photo printed only in red. For

most players, 3,900 cards of the red version were autographed for insertion. Some players, however, signed fewer reds. Exchange cards had to be issued for Raul Mondesi and Edgar Renteria, whose signed cards were not ready when the set was first issued. It has been reported that Mondesi never signed any of the red version autograph cards. Cards are checklisted here in alphabetical order, in concordance with the larger Millenium checklist. The reported number of red cards signed appears in parentheses. This list differs significantly from the original list announced by Donruss in November 1997 due to last minute editions and deletions. Players signed in black and/or blue ink. Some players also added personal touches to some or all of their signatures, such as Bible verse citations, uniform numbers, etc.

		NM/M
Complete Set (116):		700.00
Common Player:		2.00
(1)	Jeff Abbott/3,900	2.00
(2)	Bob Abreu/3,900	8.00
(3)	Edgardo Alfonzo/3,900	3.00
(4)	Roberto Alomar/150	50.00
(5)	Sandy Alomar Jr./1,400	4.00
(6)	Moises Alou/900	10.00
(7)	Garret Anderson/3,900	7.00
(8)	Andy Ashby/3,900	3.00
(10)	Trey Beamon/3,900	2.00
(12)	Alan Benes/3,900	2.00
(13)	Geronimo Berroa/3,900	2.00
(14)	Wade Boggs/3,900	175.00
(18)	Kevin L. Brown/3,900	2.00
(20)	Brett Butler/1,400	3.50
(21)	Mike Cameron/3,900	7.00
(22)	Giovanni Carrara/2,900	2.00
(23)	Luis Castillo/3,900	4.00
(24)	Tony Clark/3,900	3.00
(25)	Will Clark/1,400	12.00
(27)	Lou Collier/3,900	2.00
(28)	Bartolo Colon/3,900	12.50
(29)	Ron Coomer/3,900	2.00
(30)	Marty Cordova/3,900	3.00
(31)	Jacob Cruz/3,900	2.00
(32)	Jose Cruz Jr./900	8.00
(33)	Russ Davis/3,900	3.00
(34)	Jason Dickson/3,900	2.00
(35)	Todd Dunwoody/3,900	2.00
(36)	Jermaine Dye/3,900	3.00
(37)	Jim Edmonds/3,900	12.00
(38)	Darin Erstad/3,900	8.00
(39)	Bobby Estalella/3,900	3.00
(40)	Shawn Estes/3,900	3.00
(41)	Jeff Fassero/3,900	2.00
(42)	Andres Galarraga/900	6.00
(43)	Karim Garcia/3,900	3.00
(45)	Derrick Gibson/3,900	3.00
(46)	Brian Giles/3,900	8.00
(47)	Tom Glavine/150	50.00
(49)	Rick Gorecki/900	4.50
(50)	Shawn Green/1,900	15.00
(51)	Todd Greene/3,900	3.00
(52)	Rusty Greer/3,900	3.00
(53)	Ben Grieve/3,900	3.00
(54)	Mark Grudzielanek/3,900	3.00
(55)	Vladimir Guerrero/1,900	20.00
(56)	Wilton Guerrero/2,150	3.00
(57)	Jose Guillen/2,900	2.00
(59)	Jeffrey Hammonds/2,150	3.50
(60)	Todd Helton/1,400	16.00
(61)	Todd Hollandsworth/ 2,900	3.00
(62)	Trenidad Hubbard/900	4.00
(63)	Todd Hundley/1,400	3.00
(66)	Bobby Jones/3,900	2.00
(68)	Brian Jordan/1,400	4.00
(69)	David Justice/900	10.00
(70)	Eric Karros/650	4.50
(71)	Jason Kendall/3,900	6.00
(72)	Jimmy Key/3,900	5.00
(73)	Brooks Kieschnick/3,900	2.00
(75)	Ryan Klesko/3,900	10.00
(76)	Paul Konerko/3,900	10.00
(77)	Mark Kotsay/2,400	3.00
(78)	Ray Lankford/3,900	4.00
(79)	Barry Larkin/150	35.00
(80)	Derrek Lee/3,900	10.00
(81)	Esteban Loaiza/3,900	3.00
(83)	Javier Lopez/1,400	10.00
(84)	Edgar Martinez/150	50.00
(85)	Pedro Martinez/900	35.00
(87)	Rafael Medina/3,900	2.00
(88)	Raul Mondesi (Exchange Card)	3.00
(89)	Matt Morris/3,900	3.00
(92)	Paul O'Neill/900	15.00
(93)	Kevin Orie/3,900	2.00
(94)	David Ortiz/3,900	50.00
(95)	Rafael Palmeiro/3,900	30.00
(96)	Jay Payton/3,900	2.50
(97)	Neifi Perez/3,900	2.00
(99)	Manny Ramirez/900	40.00
(100)	Joe Randa/3,900	2.00
(101)	Calvin Reese/3,900	2.00
(102)	Edgar Renteria (?)	20.00

(102)	Edgar Renteria (Exchange Card)	3.00
(103)	Dennis Reyes/3,900	2.00
(106)	Henry Rodriguez/3,900	2.00
(108)	Scott Rolen (1,900)	25.00
(109)	Kirk Rueter/2,900	3.00
(110)	Ryne Sandberg (400)	60.00
(112)	Dwight Smith/2,900	3.00
(113)	J.T. Snow/900	4.00
(114)	Scott Spiezio/3,900	2.00
(115)	Shannon Stewart/2,900	3.00
(116)	Jeff Suppan/1,900	3.00
(117)	Mike Sweeney/3,900	6.00
(118)	Miguel Tejada/3,900	25.00
(121)	Justin Thompson/2,400	3.00
(122)	Brett Tomko/3,900	3.00
(123)	Bubba Trammell/3,900	2.50
(124)	Michael Tucker/3,900	2.00
(125)	Javier Valentin/3,900	2.00
(126)	Mo Vaughn/150	12.00
(127)	Robin Ventura/1,400	8.00
(128)	Terrell Wade/3,900	2.00
(129)	Billy Wagner/3,900	12.00
(130)	Larry Walker/900	3.00
(131)	Todd Walker/2,400	3.00
(132)	Rondell White/3,900	6.00
(133)	Kevin Wickander/900	4.00
(134)	Chris Widger/3,900	2.00
(136)	Matt Williams/150	25.00
(137)	Antone Williamson/3,900	2.00
(138)	Dan Wilson/3,900	2.00
(139)	Tony Womack/3,900	5.00
(140)	Jaret Wright/3,900	12.00
(141)	Dmitri Young/3,900	8.00
(142)	Eric Young/3,900	2.50
(143)	Kevin Young/3,900	2.50

Century Marks (Blue)

Virtually identical to the more common red and green (Millenium) versions, the Century Marks are identifiable at first glance by the use of blue ink in the background of the front photo and the "Century Marks" designation at top. On back, the cards are numbered from 0001 through 0100 in metallic foil at center. Several players initially had to be represented in the set by exchange cards. The unnumbered cards are checklisted here alphabetically.

		NM/M
Common Player:		20.00
(1)	Jeff Abbott	20.00
(2)	Bob Abreu	30.00
(3)	Edgardo Alfonzo	20.00
(4)	Roberto Alomar	75.00
(5)	Sandy Alomar Jr.	25.00
(6)	Moises Alou	35.00
(7)	Garret Anderson	60.00
(8)	Andy Ashby	20.00
(9)	Jeff Bagwell	80.00
(10)	Trey Beamon	20.00
(11)	Albert Belle	30.00
(12)	Alan Benes	20.00
(13)	Geronimo Berroa	20.00
(14)	Wade Boggs	100.00
(15)	Barry Bonds	300.00
(16)	Bobby Bonilla	20.00
(17)	Kevin Brown	75.00
(18)	Kevin L. Brown	20.00
(19)	Jay Buhner	30.00
(20)	Brett Butler	30.00
(21)	Mike Cameron	25.00
(22)	Giovanni Carrara	20.00
(23)	Luis Castillo	20.00
(24)	Tony Clark	20.00
(25)	Will Clark	100.00
(26)	Roger Clemens	200.00
(27)	Lou Collier	20.00
(28)	Bartolo Colon	30.00
(29)	Ron Coomer	20.00
(30)	Marty Cordova	20.00
(31)	Jacob Cruz	20.00
(32)	Jose Cruz Jr.	30.00
(33)	Russ Davis	20.00
(34)	Jason Dickson	25.00
(35)	Todd Dunwoody	25.00
(36)	Jermaine Dye	60.00
(37)	Jim Edmonds	40.00
(38)	Darin Erstad	40.00
(39)	Bobby Estalella	20.00
(40)	Shawn Estes	20.00
(41)	Jeff Fassero	20.00
(42)	Andres Galarraga	30.00

(43)	Karim Garcia	20.00
(44)	Nomar Garciaparra/ SP/62	225.00
(45)	Derrick Gibson	20.00
(46)	Brian Giles	30.00
(47)	Tom Glavine	100.00
(48)	Juan Gonzalez	55.00
(49)	Rick Gorecki	20.00
(50)	Shawn Green	90.00
(51)	Todd Greene	20.00
(52)	Rusty Greer	20.00
(53)	Ben Grieve	20.00
(54)	Mark Grudzielanek	20.00
(55)	Vladimir Guerrero	100.00
(56)	Wilton Guerrero	20.00
(57)	Jose Guillen	30.00
(58)	Tony Gwynn	95.00
(59)	Jeffrey Hammonds	20.00
(60)	Todd Helton	60.00
(61)	Todd Hollandsworth	20.00
(62)	Trenidad Hubbard	20.00
(63)	Todd Hundley	25.00
(64)	Derek Jeter	200.00
(65)	Andruw Jones	50.00
(66)	Bobby Jones	20.00
(67)	Chipper Jones	100.00
(68)	Brian Jordan	35.00
(69)	David Justice	30.00
(70)	Eric Karros	25.00
(71)	Jason Kendall	30.00
(72)	Jimmy Key	50.00
(73)	Brooks Kieschnick	20.00
(74)	Ryan Klesko	25.00
(75)	Chuck Knoblauch	20.00
(76)	Paul Konerko	25.00
(77)	Mark Kotsay	20.00
(78)	Ray Lankford	20.00
(79)	Barry Larkin	60.00
(80)	Derrek Lee	40.00
(81)	Esteban Loaiza	20.00
(82)	Javy Lopez	45.00
(83)	Greg Maddux	175.00
(84)	Edgar Martinez	50.00
(85)	Pedro Martinez	100.00
(86)	Tino Martinez	50.00
(87)	Rafael Medina	20.00
(88)	Raul Mondesi	35.00
(88)	Raul Mondesi (Exchange card.)	5.00
(89)	Matt Morris	40.00
(90)	Eddie Murray	75.00
(91)	Mike Mussina	80.00
(92)	Paul O'Neill	40.00
(93)	Kevin Orie	20.00
(94)	David Ortiz	100.00
(95)	Rafael Palmeiro	80.00
(96)	Jay Payton	20.00
(97)	Neifi Perez	20.00
(98)	Andy Petitte	50.00
(99)	Manny Ramirez	100.00
(100)	Joe Randa	20.00
(101)	Calvin Reese	20.00
(102)	Edgar Renteria	50.00
(102)	Edgar Renteria (Exchange card.)	5.00
(103)	Dennis Reyes	20.00
(104)	Cal Ripken Jr.	225.00
(105)	Alex Rodriguez	180.00
(106)	Henry Rodriguez	20.00
(107)	Ivan Rodriguez	75.00
(108)	Scott Rolen	75.00
(109)	Kirk Rueter	20.00
(110)	Ryne Sandberg	125.00
(111)	Gary Sheffield	50.00
(112)	Dwight Smith	20.00
(113)	J.T. Snow	25.00
(114)	Scott Spiezio	20.00
(115)	Shannon Stewart	25.00
(116)	Jeff Suppan	20.00
(117)	Mike Sweeney	25.00
(118)	Miguel Tejada	120.00
(119)	Frank Thomas	80.00
(120)	Jim Thome	75.00
(120)	Jim Thome (Exchange card.)	5.00
(121)	Justin Thompson	20.00
(122)	Brett Tomko	20.00
(123)	Bubba Trammell	20.00
(124)	Michael Tucker	20.00
(125)	Javier Valentin	20.00
(126)	Mo Vaughn	25.00
(127)	Robin Ventura	30.00
(128)	Terrell Wade	20.00
(129)	Billy Wagner	40.00
(130)	Larry Walker	80.00
(131)	Todd Walker	25.00
(132)	Rondell White	25.00
(133)	Kevin Wickander	20.00
(134)	Chris Widger	20.00
(135)	Bernie Williams	75.00
(136)	Matt Williams	30.00
(137)	Antone Williamson	20.00
(138)	Dan Wilson	20.00
(139)	Tony Womack	25.00
(140)	Jaret Wright	35.00
(141)	Dmitri Young	30.00
(142)	Eric Young	30.00
(143)	Kevin Young	20.00

Millennium Marks (Green)

One thousand cards of most of the players who signed Signature Autographs are found in an edition marked on front as "Millenium Marks." These cards are also distinguished by the use of green ink in the background of the front photo.

On back, the cards have a silver-foil serial number between (generally) 0101-1,000. Some cards as noted in the alphabetical checklist here were produced in lower numbers. The MM autographs were a random insert among the one-per-pack autographed cards found in $15 packs of Donruss Signature. Packs carried exchange cards redeemable for autographed cards of Raul Mondesi, Edgar Renteria and Jim Thome. This checklist differs significantly from that released in November 1997 by Donruss due to the last-minute addition, deletion and substitution of players. It is possible that cards exist of players not shown here.

		NM/M
Complete Set (143):		1,450
Common Player:		2.00
(1)	Jeff Abbott	2.00
(2)	Bob Abreu	8.00
(3)	Edgardo Alfonzo	5.00
(4)	Roberto Alomar	20.00
(5)	Sandy Alomar Jr.	8.00
(6)	Moises Alou	15.00
(7)	Garret Anderson	10.00
(8)	Andy Ashby	5.00
(9)	Jeff Bagwell/400	75.00
(10)	Trey Beamon	2.00
(11)	Albert Belle/400	12.50
(12)	Alan Benes	2.00
(13)	Geronimo Berroa	2.00
(14)	Wade Boggs	30.00
(15)	Barry Bonds/400	200.00
(16)	Bobby Bonilla/900	7.50
(17)	Kevin Brown/900	20.00
(18)	Kevin L. Brown	10.00
(19)	Jay Buhner/900	10.00
(20)	Brett Butler	6.00
(21)	Mike Cameron	4.00
(22)	Giovanni Carrara	2.00
(23)	Luis Castillo	5.00
(24)	Tony Clark	5.00
(25)	Will Clark	12.00
(26)	Roger Clemens/400	120.00
(27)	Lou Collier	2.00
(28)	Bartolo Colon	5.00
(29)	Ron Coomer	2.00
(30)	Marty Cordova	2.00
(31)	Jacob Cruz	2.00
(32)	Jose Cruz Jr.	6.00
(33)	Russ Davis	2.00
(34)	Jason Dickson	5.00
(35)	Todd Dunwoody	5.00
(36)	Jermaine Dye	5.00
(37)	Jim Edmonds	30.00
(38)	Darin Erstad	10.00
(39)	Bobby Estalella	3.00
(40)	Shawn Estes	2.00
(41)	Jeff Fassero	4.00
(42)	Andres Galarraga	10.00
(43)	Karim Garcia	3.50
(44)	Nomar Garciaparra/650	75.00
(45)	Derrick Gibson	4.00
(46)	Brian Giles	8.00
(47)	Tom Glavine	25.00
(48)	Juan Gonzalez/900	25.00
(49)	Rick Gorecki	2.00
(50)	Shawn Green	22.00
(51)	Todd Greene	7.50
(52)	Rusty Greer	7.50
(53)	Ben Grieve	5.00
(54)	Mark Grudzielanek	2.00
(55)	Vladimir Guerrero	25.00
(56)	Wilton Guerrero	2.00
(57)	Jose Guillen	6.00
(58)	Tony Gwynn/900	30.00
(59)	Jeffrey Hammonds	2.00
(60)	Todd Helton	30.00
(61)	Todd Hollandsworth	2.00
(62)	Trenidad Hubbard	2.00
(63)	Todd Hundley	6.00
(64)	Derek Jeter/400	100.00
(65)	Andruw Jones/900	15.00
(66)	Bobby Jones	2.00
(67)	Chipper Jones	30.00
(68)	Brian Jordan	7.50
(69)	David Justice	10.00
(70)	Eric Karros	6.00
(71)	Jason Kendall	8.00
(72)	Jimmy Key	2.00
(73)	Brooks Kieschnick	4.00
(74)	Ryan Klesko	5.00
(75)	Chuck Knoblauch/900	5.00
(76)	Paul Konerko	5.00
(77)	Mark Kotsay	6.00
(78)	Ray Lankford	2.00
(79)	Barry Larkin	30.00
(80)	Derrek Lee	20.00
(81)	Esteban Loaiza	2.00
(82)	Javy Lopez	8.00
(83)	Greg Maddux/400	80.00
(84)	Edgar Martinez	25.00
(85)	Pedro Martinez	40.00
(86)	Tino Martinez/900	15.00
(87)	Rafael Medina	2.00
(88)	Raul Mondesi	10.00
(88)	Raul Mondesi (Exchange card.)	2.00
(89)	Matt Morris	15.00
(90)	Eddie Murray/900	27.50
(91)	Mike Mussina/900	20.00
(92)	Paul O'Neill	12.50
(93)	Kevin Orie	2.00
(94)	David Justice	40.00
(95)	Rafael Palmeiro	30.00
(96)	Jay Payton	5.00
(97)	Neifi Perez	2.00
(98)	Andy Petitte/900	25.00
(99)	Manny Ramirez	30.00
(100)	Joe Randa	2.00
(101)	Calvin Reese	2.00
(102)	Edgar Renteria	30.00
(102)	Edgar Renteria (Exchange card.)	2.00
(103)	Dennis Reyes	3.00
(104)	Cal Ripken Jr./400	135.00
(105)	Alex Rodriguez/400	100.00
(106)	Henry Rodriguez	3.00
(107)	Ivan Rodriguez/900	20.00
(108)	Scott Rolen	25.00
(109)	Kirk Rueter	2.00
(110)	Ryne Sandberg	40.00
(111)	Gary Sheffield/400	25.00
(112)	Dwight Smith	2.00
(113)	J.T. Snow	7.50
(114)	Scott Spiezio	5.00
(115)	Shannon Stewart	2.00
(116)	Jeff Suppan	2.00
(117)	Mike Sweeney	5.00
(118)	Miguel Tejada	40.00
(119)	Frank Thomas/400	50.00
(120)	Jim Thome/900	30.00
(120)	Jim Thome (Exchange card.)	2.00
(121)	Justin Thompson	2.00
(122)	Brett Tomko	2.00
(123)	Bubba Trammell	4.00
(124)	Michael Tucker	2.00
(125)	Javier Valentin	2.00
(126)	Mo Vaughn	8.00
(127)	Robin Ventura	8.00
(128)	Terrell Wade	2.00
(129)	Billy Wagner	10.00
(130)	Larry Walker	20.00
(131)	Todd Walker	6.00
(132)	Rondell White	6.00
(133)	Kevin Wickander	2.00
(134)	Chris Widger	2.00
(135)	Bernie Williams/400	60.00
(136)	Matt Williams	10.00
(137)	Antone Williamson	2.00
(138)	Dan Wilson	2.00
(139)	Tony Womack	2.00
(140)	Jaret Wright	15.00
(141)	Dmitri Young	5.00
(142)	Eric Young	5.00
(143)	Kevin Young	2.00

Notable Nicknames

Current and former players whose nicknames are instantly recognized are featured in this Signature Series insert. The autographs are generally enhanced by the appearance of those nicknames, though Roger Clemens omitted "The Rocket" from many of his cards. Backs have a serial number from within an edition of 200 of each card.

		NM/M
Common Player:		20.00
(1)	Ernie Banks (Mr. Cub)	150.00
(2)	Tony Clark (The Tiger)	30.00
(3)	Roger Clemens (The Rocket)	300.00

		NM/M
(4)	Reggie Jackson (Mr. October)	125.00
(5)	Randy Johnson (Big Unit)	300.00
(6)	Stan Musial (The Man)	180.00
(7)	Ivan Rodriguez (Pudge)	100.00
(8)	Frank Thomas (The Big Hurt)	125.00
(9)	Mo Vaughn (Hit Dog)	20.00
(10)	Billy Wagner (The Kid)	40.00

Significant Signatures

Retired superstars from the early 1960s through the mid 1990s are featured in this insert series. Cards are horizontal in format with color photos on front and back. Generally autographed on front, each card is serially numbered on back from within an edition of 2,000. The unnumbered cards are listed here in alphabetical order.

		NM/M
Common Player:		15.00
(1)	Ernie Banks	25.00
(2)	Johnny Bench	30.00
(3)	Yogi Berra	30.00
(4)	George Brett	40.00
(5)	Lou Brock	25.00
(6)	Rod Carew	25.00
(7)	Steve Carlton	20.00
(8)	Larry Doby	35.00
(9)	Carlton Fisk	30.00
(10)	Bob Gibson	25.00
(11)	Reggie Jackson	25.00
(12)	Al Kaline	25.00
(13)	Harmon Killebrew	30.00
(14)	Don Mattingly	40.00
(15)	Stan Musial	45.00
(16)	Jim Palmer	15.00
(17)	Brooks Robinson	30.00
(18)	Frank Robinson	15.00
(19)	Mike Schmidt	35.00
(20)	Tom Seaver	30.00
(21)	Duke Snider	20.00
(22)	Carl Yastrzemski	25.00

1997 Donruss Frank Thomas The Big Heart

In one of several specialty card charitable endeavors, Thomas and Donruss teamed up to issue this set as a fund raiser for "The Big Hurt's" charitable foundation. Each of the cards was available in an edition limited to 2,500 for a $20 donation. Cards are standard 2-1/2" x 3-1/2" with posed photos on front and "THE BIG HEART," a play on his nickname. Backs have information on the foundation, a second photo and a gold-foil serial number.

		NM/M
Complete Set (4):		20.00
Common Card:		5.00
1	Frank Thomas, Rod Carew	5.00
2	Frank Thomas	5.00
3	Frank Thomas	5.00
4	Frank Thomas	5.00

1997 Donruss VXP 1.0

This set was issued to accompany the hobby's first major effort to bring baseball cards into the computer age. The standard-format cards have motion-variable portrait and action photos on front

and another photo on back. Cards were sold in packs of 10 with one of six CD ROMs for about $10.

		NM/M
Complete Set (50):		17.50
Common Player:		.25
1	Darin Erstad	.40
2	Jim Thome	.50
3	Alex Rodriguez	1.50
4	Greg Maddux	1.00
5	Scott Rolen	.65
6	Roberto Alomar	.30
7	Tony Clark	.25
8	Randy Johnson	.75
9	Sammy Sosa	1.00
10	Jose Guillen	.25
11	Cal Ripken Jr.	2.00
12	Paul Molitor	.75
13	Jose Cruz Jr.	.20
14	Barry Larkin	.25
15	Ken Caminiti	.25
16	Rafael Palmeiro	.65
17	Chuck Knoblauch	.25
18	Juan Gonzalez	.40
19	Larry Walker	.25
20	Tony Gwynn	1.00
21	Brady Anderson	.25
22	Derek Jeter	2.00
23	Rusty Greer	.25
24	Gary Sheffield	.35
25	Barry Bonds	.25
26	Mo Vaughn	.20
27	Tino Martinez	.25
28	Ivan Rodriguez	.65
29	Jeff Bagwell	.75
30	Tim Salmon	.25
31	Nomar Garciaparra	1.00
32	Bernie Williams	.25
33	Kenny Lofton	.25
34	Mike Piazza	1.25
35	Jim Edmonds	.25
36	Frank Thomas	.75
37	Andy Pettitte	.35
38	Andruw Jones	.75
39	Raul Mondesi	.25
40	John Smoltz	.25
41	Albert Belle	.25
42	Mark McGwire	1.50
43	Chipper Jones	1.00
44	Hideo Nomo	.40
45	David Justice	.25
46	Manny Ramirez	.75
47	Ken Griffey Jr.	1.25
48	Roger Clemens	1.00
49	Vladimir Guerrero	.75
50	Ryne Sandberg	1.00

1997 Donruss VXP 1.0 CDs

One of the earliest attempts to bring baseball cards into the computer age was Donruss "VXP 1.0 CD ROM" trading cards. Retailed, with 10 special-series player cards for about $10, the 4" x 2-3/4" "card" is a CD with player portrait and action photos on front. The CD was sold in a cardboard folder with the player's picture on front and instructions for use inside. CDs feature player stats, action footage and other interactive elements.

		NM/M
Complete Set (6):		12.00
Common Player:		2.00
(1)	Ken Griffey Jr.	2.25
(2)	Greg Maddux	2.00
(3)	Mike Piazza	2.25
(4)	Cal Ripken Jr.	3.00
(5)	Alex Rodriguez	2.50
(6)	Frank Thomas	2.00

1998 Donruss

This 170-card set includes 155 regular player cards, the 10-card Fan Club subset and five checklists.

The cards have color photos and the player's name listed at the bottom. The backs have a horizontal layout with stats and a biography on the left and another photo on the right. The base set is paralleled twice. Silver Press Proofs is a silver foil and die-cut parallel numbered "1 of 1,500." Gold Press Proofs is die-cut, has gold foil and is numbered "1 of 500." The inserts are Crusade, Diamond Kings, Longball Leaders, Production Line and Rated Rookies.

		NM/M
Complete Set (420):		30.00
Complete Series 1 (170):		10.00
Complete Update 2 (250):		15.00
Common Player:		.05
Silver Press Proofs:		3X
Production 1,500 Sets		
Gold Press Proofs:		8X
Production 500 Sets		
Pack (10):		1.00
Wax Box (24):		16.00
1	Paul Molitor	.75
2	Juan Gonzalez	.40
3	Darryl Kile	.05
4	Randy Johnson	.75
5	Tom Glavine	.25
6	Pat Hentgen	.05
7	David Justice	.05
8	Kevin Brown	.05
9	Mike Mussina	.45
10	Ken Caminiti	.05
11	Todd Hundley	.05
12	Frank Thomas	.75
13	Ray Lankford	.05
14	Justin Thompson	.05
15	Jason Dickson	.05
16	Kenny Lofton	.05
17	Ivan Rodriguez	.65
18	Pedro Martinez	.75
19	Brady Anderson	.05
20	Barry Larkin	.05
21	Chipper Jones	1.50
22	Tony Gwynn	1.50
23	Roger Clemens	1.50
24	Sandy Alomar Jr.	.05
25	Tino Martinez	.25
26	Jeff Bagwell	.75
27	Shawn Estes	.05
28	Ken Griffey Jr.	1.75
29	Javier Lopez	.05
30	Denny Neagle	.05
31	Mike Piazza	1.75
32	Andres Galarraga	.05
33	Larry Walker	.05
34	Alex Rodriguez	2.00
35	Greg Maddux	1.50
36	Albert Belle	.25
37	Barry Bonds	2.50
38	Mo Vaughn	.05
39	Kevin Appier	.05
40	Wade Boggs	1.50
41	Garret Anderson	.05
42	Jeffrey Hammonds	.05
43	Marquis Grissom	.05
44	Jim Edmonds	.05
45	Brian Jordan	.05
46	Raul Mondesi	.05
47	John Valentin	.05
48	Brad Radke	.05
49	Ismael Valdes	.05
50	Matt Stairs	.05
51	Matt Williams	.05
52	Reggie Jefferson	.05
53	Alan Benes	.05
54	Charles Johnson	.05
55	Chuck Knoblauch	.05
56	Edgar Martinez	.05
57	Nomar Garciaparra	1.50
58	Craig Biggio	.25
59	Bernie Williams	.05
60	David Cone	.05
61	Cal Ripken Jr.	2.50
62	Mark McGwire	2.00
63	Roberto Alomar	.20
64	Fred McGriff	.05
65	Eric Karros	.05
66	Robin Ventura	.05
67	Darin Erstad	.30
68	Michael Tucker	.05
69	Jim Thome	.60
70	Mark Grace	.05
71	Lou Collier	.05

72	Karim Garcia	.05
73	Alex Fernandez	.05
74	J.T. Snow	.05
75	Reggie Sanders	.05
76	John Smoltz	.05
77	Tim Salmon	.05
78	Paul O'Neill	.05
79	Vinny Castilla	.05
80	Rafael Palmeiro	.65
81	Jaret Wright	.05
82	Jay Buhner	.05
83	Brett Butler	.05
84	Todd Greene	.05
85	Scott Rolen	.65
86	Sammy Sosa	1.50
87	Jason Giambi	.50
88	Carlos Delgado	.50
89	Deion Sanders	.05
90	Wilton Guerrero	.05
91	Andy Pettitte	.30
92	Brian Giles	.05
93	Dmitri Young	.05
94	Ron Coomer	.05
95	Mike Cameron	.05
96	Edgardo Alfonzo	.05
97	Jimmy Key	.05
98	Ryan Klesko	.05
99	Andy Benes	.05
100	Derek Jeter	2.50
101	Jeff Fassero	.05
102	Neifi Perez	.05
103	Hideo Nomo	.40
104	Andruw Jones	.75
105	Todd Helton	.50
106	Livan Hernandez	.05
107	Brett Tomko	.05
108	Shannon Stewart	.05
109	Bartolo Colon	.05
110	Matt Morris	.05
111	Miguel Tejada	.20
112	Pokey Reese	.05
113	Fernando Tatis	.05
114	Todd Dunwoody	.05
115	Jose Cruz Jr.	.05
116	Chan Ho Park	.05
117	Kevin Young	.05
118	Rickey Henderson	.75
119	Hideki Irabu	.05
120	Francisco Cordova	.05
121	Al Martin	.05
122	Tony Clark	.05
123	Curt Schilling	.25
124	Rusty Greer	.05
125	Jose Canseco	.40
126	Edgar Renteria	.05
127	Todd Walker	.05
128	Wally Joyner	.05
129	Bill Mueller	.05
130	Jose Guillen	.05
131	Manny Ramirez	.75
132	Bobby Higginson	.05
133	Kevin Orie	.05
134	Will Clark	.05
135	Dave Nilsson	.05
136	Jason Kendall	.05
137	Ivan Cruz	.05
138	Gary Sheffield	.25
139	Bubba Trammell	.05
140	Vladimir Guerrero	.75
141	Dennis Reyes	.05
142	Bobby Bonilla	.05
143	Ruben Rivera	.05
144	Ben Grieve	.25
145	Moises Alou	.05
146	Tony Womack	.05
147	Eric Young	.05
148	Paul Konerko	.10
149	Dante Bichette	.05
150	Joe Carter	.05
151	Rondell White	.05
152	Chris Holt	.05
153	Shawn Green	.05
154	Mark Grudzielanek	.05
155	Jermaine Dye	.05
156	Ken Griffey Jr. (Fan Club)	.90
157	Frank Thomas (Fan Club)	.50
158	Chipper Jones (Fan Club)	.75
159	Mike Piazza (Fan Club)	.90
160	Cal Ripken Jr. (Fan Club)	1.25
161	Greg Maddux (Fan Club)	.75
162	Juan Gonzalez (Fan Club)	.20
163	Alex Rodriguez (Fan Club)	1.00
164	Mark McGwire (Fan Club)	1.00
165	Derek Jeter (Fan Club)	1.25
166	Checklist (Larry Walker)	.05
167	Checklist (Tony Gwynn)	.60
168	Checklist (Tino Martinez)	.05
169	Checklist (Scott Rolen)	.15
170	Checklist (Nomar Garciaparra)	.60
171	Mike Sweeney	.05
172	Dustin Hermanson	.05
173	Darren Dreifort	.05
174	Ron Gant	.05
175	Todd Hollandsworth	.05
176	John Jaha	.05
177	Kerry Wood	.30
178	Chris Stynes	.05
179	Kevin Elster	.05
180	Derek Bell	.05
181	Darryl Strawberry	.05
182	Damion Easley	.05
183	Jeff Cirillo	.05
184	John Thomson	.05
185	Dan Wilson	.05
186	Jay Bell	.05

187	Bernard Gilkey	.05
188	Marc Valdes	.05
189	Ramon Martinez	.05
190	Charles Nagy	.05
191	Derek Lowe	.05
192	Andy Benes	.05
193	Delino DeShields	.05
194	Ryan Jackson RC	.05
195	Kenny Lofton	.05
196	Chuck Knoblauch	.05
197	Andres Galarraga	.05
198	Jose Canseco	.50
199	John Olerud	.05
200	Lance Johnson	.05
201	Darryl Kile	.05
202	Luis Castillo	.05
203	Joe Carter	.05
204	Dennis Eckersley	.65
205	Steve Finley	.05
206	Esteban Loaiza	.05
207	Ryan Christenson RC	.05
208	Deivi Cruz	.05
209	Mariano Rivera	.15
210	Mike Judd RC	.05
211	Billy Wagner	.05
212	Scott Spiezio	.05
213	Russ Davis	.05
214	Jeff Suppan	.05
215	Doug Glanville	.05
216	Dmitri Young	.05
217	Rey Ordonez	.05
218	Cecil Fielder	.05
219	Masato Yoshii RC	.10
220	Raul Casanova	.05
221	Rolando Arrojo RC	.20
222	Ellis Burks	.05
223	Butch Huskey	.05
224	Brian Hunter	.05
225	Marquis Grissom	.05
226	Kevin Brown	.05
227	Joe Randa	.05
228	Henry Rodriguez	.05
229	Omar Vizquel	.05
230	Fred McGriff	.05
231	Matt Williams	.05
232	Moises Alou	.05
233	Travis Fryman	.05
234	Wade Boggs	1.50
235	Pedro Martinez	.75
236	Rickey Henderson	.05
237	Bubba Trammell	.05
238	Mike Caruso	.05
239	Wilson Alvarez	.05
240	Geronimo Berroa	.05
241	Eric Milton	.05
242	Scott Erickson	.05
243	Todd Erdos RC	.05
244	Bobby Hughes	.05
245	Dave Hollins	.05
246	Dean Palmer	.05
247	Carlos Baerga	.05
248	Jose Silva	.05
249	Jose Cabrera RC	.05
250	Tom Evans	.05
251	Marty Cordova	.05
252	Hanley Frias RC	.05
253	Javier Valentin	.05
254	Mario Valdez	.05
255	Joey Cora	.05
256	Mike Lansing	.05
257	Jeff Kent	.05
258	David Dellucci RC	.10
259	Curtis King RC	.05
260	David Segui	.05
261	Royce Clayton	.05
262	Jeff Blauser	.05
263	Manny Aybar RC	.05
264	Mike Cather RC	.05
265	Todd Zeile	.05
266	Richard Hidalgo	.05
267	Dante Powell	.05
268	Mike DeJean RC	.05
269	Ken Cloude	.05
270	Danny Klassen	.05
271	Sean Casey	.15
272	A.J. Hinch	.05
273	Rich Butler RC	.05
274	Ben Ford RC	.05
275	Billy McMillon	.05
276	Wilson Delgado	.05
277	Orlando Cabrera	.05
278	Geoff Jenkins	.05
279	Enrique Wilson	.05
280	Derrek Lee	.60
281	Marc Pisciotta RC	.05
282	Abraham Nunez	.05
283	Aaron Boone	.05
284	Brad Fullmer	.05
285	Rob Stanifer RC	.05
286	Preston Wilson	.05
287	Greg Norton	.05
288	Bobby Smith	.05
289	Josh Booty	.05
290	Russell Branyan	.05
291	Jeremi Gonzalez	.05
292	Michael Coleman	.05
293	Cliff Politte	.05
294	Eric Ludwick	.05
295	Rafael Medina	.05
296	Jason Varitek	.05
297	Ron Wright	.05
298	Mark Kotsay	.05
299	David Ortiz	.50
300	Frank Catalanotto RC	.20
301	Robinson Checo	.05
302	Kevin Millwood RC	.75
303	Jacob Cruz	.05
304	Javier Vazquez	.05

305	Magglio Ordonez RC	1.50
306	Kevin Witt	.05
307	Derrick Gibson	.05
308	Shane Monahan	.05
309	Brian Rose	.05
310	Bobby Estalella	.05
311	Felix Heredia	.05
312	Desi Relaford	.05
313	Esteban Yan RC	.05
314	Ricky Ledee	.05
315	Steve Woodard RC	.05
316	Pat Watkins	.05
317	Damian Moss	.05
318	Bob Abreu	.05
319	Jeff Abbott	.05
320	Miguel Cairo	.05
321	Rigo Beltran RC	.05
322	Tony Saunders	.05
323	Randall Simon	.05
324	Hiram Bocachica	.05
325	Richie Sexson	.05
326	Karim Garcia	.05
327	Mike Lowell RC	1.00
328	Pat Cline	.05
329	Matt Clement	.05
330	Scott Elarton	.05
331	Manuel Barrios RC	.05
332	Bruce Chen	.05
333	Juan Encarnacion	.05
334	Travis Lee	.05
335	Wes Helms	.05
336	Chad Fox RC	.05
337	Donnie Sadler	.05
338	Carlos Mendoza RC	.05
339	Damian Jackson	.05
340	Julio Ramirez RC	.05
341	John Halama RC	.05
342	Edwin Diaz	.05
343	Felix Martinez	.05
344	Eli Marrero	.05
345	Carl Pavano	.05
346	Vladimir Guerrero/HL	.40
347	Barry Bonds/HL	1.25
348	Darin Erstad/HL	.10
349	Albert Belle/HL	.05
350	Kenny Lofton/HL	.05
351	Mo Vaughn/HL	.05
352	Jose Cruz Jr./HL	.05
353	Tony Clark/HL	.05
354	Roberto Alomar/HL	.10
355	Manny Ramirez/HL	.40
356	Paul Molitor/HL	.40
357	Jim Thome/HL	.05
358	Tino Martinez/HL	.05
359	Tim Salmon/HL	.05
360	David Justice/HL	.05
361	Raul Mondesi/HL	.05
362	Mark Grace/HL	.05
363	Craig Biggio/HL	.05
364	Larry Walker/HL	.05
365	Mark McGwire/HL	1.00
366	Juan Gonzalez/HL	.20
367	Derek Jeter/HL	1.25
368	Chipper Jones/HL	.75
369	Frank Thomas/HL	.50
370	Alex Rodriguez/HL	1.00
371	Mike Piazza/HL	.90
372	Tony Gwynn/HL	.75
373	Jeff Bagwell/HL	.40
374	Nomar Garciaparra/HL	.75
375	Ken Griffey Jr./HL	.90
376	Livan Hernandez (Untouchables)	.05
377	Chan Ho Park (Untouchables)	.05
378	Mike Mussina (Untouchables)	.20
379	Andy Pettitte (Untouchables)	.05
380	Greg Maddux (Untouchables)	.75
381	Hideo Nomo (Untouchables)	.20
382	Roger Clemens (Untouchables)	.80
383	Randy Johnson (Untouchables)	.40
384	Pedro Martinez (Untouchables)	.40
385	Jaret Wright (Untouchables)	.05
386	Ken Griffey Jr. (Spirit of the Game)	.90
387	Todd Helton (Spirit of the Game)	.05
388	Paul Konerko (Spirit of the Game)	.05
389	Cal Ripken Jr. (Spirit of the Game)	1.25
390	Larry Walker (Spirit of the Game)	.05
391	Ken Caminiti (Spirit of the Game)	.05
392	Jose Guillen (Spirit of the Game)	.05
393	Jim Edmonds (Spirit of the Game)	.05
394	Barry Larkin (Spirit of the Game)	.05
395	Bernie Williams (Spirit of the Game)	.05
396	Tony Clark (Spirit of the Game)	.05
397	Jose Cruz Jr. (Spirit of the Game)	.05
398	Ivan Rodriguez (Spirit of the Game)	.30

		NM/M
399	Darin Erstad (Spirit of the Game)	.10
400	Scott Rolen (Spirit of the Game)	.15
401	Mark McGwire (Spirit of the Game)	1.00
402	Andruw Jones (Spirit of the Game)	.40
403	Juan Gonzalez (Spirit of the Game)	.20
404	Derek Jeter (Spirit of the Game)	1.25
405	Chipper Jones (Spirit of the Game)	.75
406	Greg Maddux (Spirit of the Game)	.75
407	Frank Thomas (Spirit of the Game)	.50
408	Alex Rodriguez (Spirit of the Game)	1.00
409	Mike Piazza (Spirit of the Game)	.90
410	Tony Gwynn (Spirit of the Game)	.75
411	Jeff Bagwell (Spirit of the Game)	.40
412	Nomar Garciaparra (Spirit of the Game)	.75
413	Hideo Nomo (Spirit of the Game)	.20
414	Barry Bonds (Spirit of the Game)	1.25
415	Ben Grieve (Spirit of the Game)	.05
416	Checklist (Barry Bonds)	1.25
417	Checklist (Mark McGwire)	1.00
418	Checklist (Roger Clemens)	.65
419	Checklist (Livan Hernandez)	.05
420	Checklist (Ken Griffey Jr.)	.75

1998 Donruss Silver Press Proofs

Silver Press Proofs paralleled all 420 cards in the Donruss and Donruss Update Baseball. Cards featured silver foil stamping and a die-cut top right corner. Backs had a silver tint and were numbered "1 of 1500" in the bottom left corner.

	NM/M
Complete Set (420):	150.00
Common Player:	.50
Stars/RC's:	2X
Production 1,500 Sets	

1998 Donruss Gold Press Proofs

All 420 cards in Donruss and Donruss Update were also issued in Gold Press Proofs. These cards were die-cut on the top right corner and contained gold foil stamping. Backs featured a gold tint and "1 of 500" was printed in black in the bottom-left corner.

	NM/M
Common Player:	1.00
Stars/RC's:	6X
Production 500 Sets	

Crusade

This 100-card insert was included in 1998 Donruss (40 cards), Leaf (30) and Donruss Update (30).

The cards use refractive technology and the background features heraldic-style lions. The cards are sequentially numbered to 250. Crusade Purple (numbered to 100) and Red (25) parallels were also inserted in the three products.

		NM/M
Common Player:		4.00
Production 250 Sets		
Purples (100 Sets):		1X
Reds (25 Sets):		4X
5	Jason Dickson	4.00
6	Todd Greene	4.00
7	Roberto Alomar	5.00
8	Cal Ripken Jr.	40.00
12	Mo Vaughn	4.00
13	Nomar Garciaparra	15.00
16	Mike Cameron	4.00
20	Sandy Alomar Jr.	4.00
21	David Justice	4.00
25	Justin Thompson	4.00
27	Kevin Appier	4.00
33	Tino Martinez	4.00
36	Hideki Irabu	4.00
37	Jose Canseco	8.00
39	Ken Griffey Jr.	30.00
42	Edgar Martinez	4.00
45	Will Clark	6.00
47	Rusty Greer	4.00
50	Shawn Green	5.00
51	Jose Cruz Jr.	4.00
52	Kenny Lofton	4.00
53	Chipper Jones	15.00
62	Kevin Orie	4.00
65	Deion Sanders	6.00
67	Larry Walker	6.00
68	Dante Bichette	4.00
71	Todd Helton	10.00
74	Bobby Bonilla	4.00
75	Kevin Brown	4.00
78	Craig Biggio	6.00
82	Wilton Guerrero	4.00
85	Pedro Martinez	15.00
86	Edgardo Alfonzo	4.00
88	Scott Rolen	10.00
89	Francisco Cordova	4.00
90	Jose Guillen	4.00
92	Ray Lankford	4.00
93	Mark McGwire	20.00
94	Matt Morris	4.00
100	Shawn Estes	4.00

1998 Donruss Days

Similar in design, but featuring heavier stock, a metallic foil background and gold-foil graphic highlights on front, these cards were part of a ballpark promotion conducted by Donruss during the 1998 baseball season. Fans were given exchange cards at selected ballparks which could be traded at specially designated card shops in those locales for one of these premium star cards. Production was reportedly fewer than 10,000 of each card. Backs are numbered "X of 14," but are otherwise identical to the regular-issue version.

		NM/M
Complete Set (14):		16.00
Common Player:		.50
Production 5,000 Sets		
1	Frank Thomas	1.00
2	Ken Griffey Jr.	5.00
3	Mark McGwire	6.00
4	Tino Martinez	1.00
5	Barry Bonds	7.50
6	Frank Thomas	3.00
7	Albert Belle	1.00
8	Mike Piazza	5.00
9	Chipper Jones	4.00
10	Vladimir Guerrero	3.00
11	Matt Williams	1.00
11	Sammy Sosa	4.00

		NM/M
2	Tony Clark	.50
3	Ivan Rodriguez	.65
4	David Justice	.50
5	Nomar Garciaparra	1.50
6	Mark McGwire	2.50
7	Travis Lee	.50
8	Cal Ripken Jr.	3.00
9	Jeff Bagwell	1.00
10	Barry Bonds	3.00
11	Ken Griffey Jr.	2.00
12	Derek Jeter	3.00
13	Raul Mondesi	.50
14	Greg Maddux	1.50

Diamond Kings

Diamond Kings is a 20-card insert featuring a painted portrait by Dan Gardiner. Backs have a ghosted image of the portrait with a player biography and the card's number overprinted. A total of 10,000 sets were produced with the first 500 of each card printed on canvas. A Frank Thomas sample card was also created.

		NM/M
Complete Set (20):		65.00
Common Player:		2.00
Production 9,500 Sets		
Canvas (1st 500 Sets):		2X
1	Cal Ripken Jr.	9.00
2	Greg Maddux	4.50
3	Ivan Rodriguez	2.50
4	Tony Gwynn	4.50
5	Paul Molitor	3.00
6	Kenny Lofton	2.00
7	Andy Pettitte	2.00
8	Darin Erstad	2.00
9	Randy Johnson	3.00
10	Derek Jeter	9.00
11	Hideo Nomo	2.50
12	David Justice	2.00
13	Bernie Williams	2.00
14	Roger Clemens	5.00
15	Barry Larkin	2.00
16	Andruw Jones	4.00
17	Mike Piazza	6.50
18	Frank Thomas	3.00
18s	Frank Thomas (Sample)	3.00
19	Alex Rodriguez	7.50
20	Ken Griffey Jr.	6.50

Longball Leaders

Longball Leaders features 24 top home run hitters. The right border features a home run meter with zero at the bottom, 61 at the top and the player's 1997 home run total marked. Each card is sequentially numbered to 5,000.

		NM/M
Complete Set (24):		50.00
Common Player:		1.00
Production 5,000 Sets		
1	Frank Thomas/1,067	5.00
2	Mark McGwire/1,039	12.00
3	Barry Bonds/1,031	12.50
4	Jeff Bagwell/1,017	5.00
5	Ken Griffey Jr./1,028	10.00
6	Alex Rodriguez/846	12.00
7	Chipper Jones/850	7.00
8	Mike Piazza/1,070	10.00
9	Mo Vaughn/980	1.50
10	Brady Anderson/863	1.50
11	Manny Ramirez/953	5.00
12	Albert Belle/823	1.50
13	Jim Thome/1,001	2.50
14	Bernie Williams/952	1.50
15	Scott Rolen/846	2.00
16	Vladimir Guerrero/833	5.00

		NM/M
12	Tim Salmon	1.00
13	Raul Mondesi	1.00
14	Jeff Bagwell	3.00
15	Mo Vaughn	1.00
16	Manny Ramirez	3.00
17	Jim Thome	2.00
18	Jim Edmonds	1.00
19	Tony Clark	1.00
20	Nomar Garciaparra	4.00
21	Juan Gonzalez	1.50
22	Scott Rolen	2.00
23	Larry Walker	1.00
24	Andres Galarraga	1.00

Production Line-ob

This 20-card insert is printed on holographic foil board. Inserted in magazine packs, this insert features player's with a high on-base percentage in 1997. Each player's card is sequentially numbered to his on-base percentage from that season. The card back has a player photo and a list of the 20 players with their stat.

		NM/M
Complete Set (20):		85.00
Common Player:		1.50
1	Frank Thomas/456	6.00
2	Edgar Martinez/456	1.50
3	Roberto Alomar/390	2.00
4	Chuck Knoblauch/390	1.50
5	Mike Piazza/431	10.00
6	Barry Larkin/440	1.50
7	Kenny Lofton/409	1.50
8	Jeff Bagwell/425	6.00
9	Barry Bonds/446	15.00
10	Rusty Greer/405	1.50
11	Gary Sheffield/424	2.00
12	Mark McGwire/393	12.00
13	Chipper Jones/371	8.00
14	Tony Gwynn/409	8.00
15	Craig Biggio/415	1.50
16	Mo Vaughn/420	1.50
17	Bernie Williams/408	1.50
18	Ken Griffey Jr./382	10.00
19	Brady Anderson/393	1.50
20	Derek Jeter/370	15.00

Production Line-Pi

This 20-card insert was printed on holographic board. The set features players with a high power index from 1997. Each card is sequentially numbered to that player's power index from that season.

		NM/M
Complete Set (20):		85.00
Common Player:		1.50
1	Frank Thomas/1,067	5.00
2	Mark McGwire/1,039	12.00
3	Barry Bonds/1,031	12.50
4	Jeff Bagwell/1,017	5.00
5	Ken Griffey Jr./1,028	10.00
6	Alex Rodriguez/846	12.00
7	Chipper Jones/850	7.00
8	Mike Piazza/1,070	10.00
9	Mo Vaughn/980	1.50
10	Brady Anderson/863	1.50
11	Manny Ramirez/953	5.00
12	Albert Belle/823	1.50
13	Jim Thome/1,001	2.50
14	Bernie Williams/952	1.50
15	Scott Rolen/846	2.00
16	Vladimir Guerrero/833	5.00

		NM/M
17	Larry Walker/1,172	1.50
18	David Justice/1,013	1.50
19	Tino Martinez/948	1.50
20	Tony Gwynn/957	7.00

Production Line-Sg

This 20-card insert was printed on holographic board. It featured players with high slugging percentages in 1997. Each card is sequentially numbered to the player's slugging percentage from that season.

		NM/M
Complete Set (20):		135.00
Common Player:		3.00
1	Mark McGwire/646	20.00
2	Ken Griffey Jr./646	12.50
3	Andres Galarraga/585	3.00
4	Barry Bonds/585	22.50
5	Juan Gonzalez/589	4.50
6	Mike Piazza/638	12.50
7	Jeff Bagwell/592	7.50
8	Manny Ramirez/538	7.50
9	Jim Thome/579	4.50
10	Mo Vaughn/560	3.00
11	Larry Walker/720	3.00
12	Tino Martinez/577	3.00
13	Frank Thomas/611	7.50
14	Tim Salmon/517	3.00
15	Raul Mondesi/541	3.00
16	Alex Rodriguez/496	15.00
17	Nomar Garciaparra/534	10.00
18	Jose Cruz Jr./499	3.00
19	Tony Clark/500	3.00
20	Cal Ripken Jr./402	25.00

Rated Rookies

This 30-card insert features top young players. The fronts have a color player photo in front of a stars and stripes background, with "Rated Rookies" and the player's name printed on the right. The backs have another photo, basic player information and career highlights. A rare (250 each) Medalist version is micro-etched on gold holographic foil.

		NM/M
Complete Set (30):		32.50
Common Player:		1.00
Medalists (250 Sets):		6X
1	Mark Kotsay	1.00
2	Neifi Perez	1.00
3	Paul Konerko	1.50
4	Jose Cruz Jr.	1.00
5	Hideki Irabu	1.00
6	Mike Cameron	1.00
7	Jeff Suppan	1.00
8	Kevin Orie	1.00
9	Pokey Reese	1.00
10	Todd Dunwoody	1.00
11	Miguel Tejada	1.50
12	Jose Guillen	1.00
13	Bartolo Colon	1.50
14	Derrek Lee	2.50
15	Antone Williamson	1.00
16	Wilton Guerrero	1.00
17	Jaret Wright	1.00
18	Todd Helton	4.00
19	Shannon Stewart	1.00
20	Nomar Garciaparra	6.00
21	Brett Tomko	1.00
22	Fernando Tatis	1.00
23	Raul Ibanez	1.00

		NM/M
24	Dennis Reyes	1.00
25	Bobby Estalella	1.00
26	Lou Collier	1.00
27	Bubba Trammell	1.00
28	Ben Grieve	1.00
29	Ivan Cruz	1.00
30	Karim Garcia	1.00

Update Crusade

This 30-card insert is continued from 1998 Donruss and Leaf baseball sets. Each card features a color action photo in front of a Medieval background. The player's name and background are green and each card is serial numbered to 250. Purple (numbered to 100) and Red (25) parallel versions were also created. Crusade is a 130-card cross-brand insert with 40 cards included in 1998 Donruss and 30 each in 1998 Leaf and Leaf Rookies & Stars.

		NM/M
Complete Set, Green (30):		325.00
Common Player:		6.00
Production 250 Sets		
Purples (100 Sets):		3X
Reds (25 Sets):		10X
1	Tim Salmon	6.00
2	Garret Anderson	6.00
9	Rafael Palmeiro	15.00
10	Brady Anderson	6.00
14	Frank Thomas	15.00
17	Robin Ventura	6.00
22	Matt Williams	6.00
23	Tony Clark	6.00
29	Chuck Knoblauch	6.00
30	Bernie Williams	6.00
32	Derek Jeter	50.00
38	Jason Giambi	10.00
43	Jay Buhner	6.00
44	Juan Gonzalez	7.50
49	Carlos Delgado	9.00
55	Greg Maddux	20.00
59	Tom Glavine	9.00
60	Mark Grace	6.00
61	Sammy Sosa	20.00
63	Barry Larkin	6.00
69	Neifi Perez	6.00
72	Gary Sheffield	7.50
77	Jeff Bagwell	15.00
80	Raul Mondesi	6.00
81	Hideo Nomo	7.50
83	Rondell White	6.00
84	Vladimir Guerrero	15.00
87	Todd Hundley	6.00
96	Brian Jordan	6.00
99	Barry Bonds	50.00

Update Dominators

This 30-card insert features color player photos and holographic foil.

		NM/M
Complete Set (30):		25.00
Common Player:		.25
Approx. 1:12		
1	Roger Clemens	1.50
2	Tony Clark	.25
3	Darin Erstad	.50
4	Jeff Bagwell	1.00
5	Ken Griffey Jr.	1.75
6	Andruw Jones	1.00
7	Juan Gonzalez	.50
8	Ivan Rodriguez	1.00
9	Randy Johnson	1.00
10	Tino Martinez	.25
11	Mark McGwire	2.00
12	Chuck Knoblauch	.25
13	Jim Thome	.65
14	Alex Rodriguez	1.00
15	Hideo Nomo	.50
16	Jose Cruz Jr.	.25
17	Chipper Jones	1.50
18	Tony Gwynn	1.50
19	Barry Bonds	.25
20	Mo Vaughn	.25
21	Cal Ripken Jr.	2.50
22	Greg Maddux	1.50
23	Manny Ramirez	1.00
24	Andres Galarraga	.25
25	Vladimir Guerrero	.50
26	Albert Belle	.25

#	Player	Price
27	Nomar Garciaparra	1.50
28	Kenny Lofton	.25
29	Mike Piazza	1.75
30	Frank Thomas	1.00

Update Elite

This 20-card insert features color player photos in a diamond-shaped pattern at the top with the Elite Series logo and player's name at the bottom. The fronts have a cream-colored border.

		NM/M
Complete Set (20):		115.00
Common Player:		3.00
Production 2,500 Sets		
1	Jeff Bagwell	4.50
2	Andruw Jones	4.50
3	Ken Griffey Jr.	7.50
4	Derek Jeter	15.00
5	Juan Gonzalez	3.50
6	Mark McGwire	10.00
7	Ivan Rodriguez	3.50
8	Paul Molitor	4.50
9	Hideo Nomo	3.50
10	Mo Vaughn	3.00
11	Chipper Jones	6.00
12	Nomar Garciaparra	6.00
13	Mike Piazza	7.50
14	Frank Thomas	4.50
15	Greg Maddux	6.00
16	Cal Ripken Jr.	15.00
17	Alex Rodriguez	10.00
18	Scott Rolen	3.50
19	Barry Bonds	15.00
20	Tony Gwynn	6.00

Update FANtasy Team

This 20-card set features the top vote getters from the Donruss online Fan Club ballot box. The top 10 make up the 1st Team FANtasy Team and are sequentially numbered to 2,000. The other players are included in the 2nd Team FANtasy Team and are numbered to 4,000. The first 250 cards of each player are die-cut. The front of the cards feature a color photo inside a stars and stripes border.

		NM/M
Complete Set (20):		35.00
Common Player (1-10) (1,750 Sets):		1.50
Common Player (11-20) (3,750 Sets):		1.00
Die-Cuts (250 Each):		2X
1	Frank Thomas	4.00
2	Ken Griffey Jr.	3.50
3	Cal Ripken Jr.	5.00
4	Jose Cruz Jr.	1.00
5	Travis Lee	1.00
6	Greg Maddux	2.50
7	Alex Rodriguez	4.00
8	Mark McGwire	4.00
9	Chipper Jones	2.50
10	Andruw Jones	2.00
11	Mike Piazza	3.50
12	Tony Gwynn	2.50
13	Larry Walker	1.00
14	Nomar Garciaparra	3.00
15	Jaret Wright	1.00
16	Livan Hernandez	1.00
17	Roger Clemens	2.75
18	Derek Jeter	5.00
19	Scott Rolen	1.25
20	Jeff Bagwell	1.50

Update Rookie Diamond Kings

The Rookie Diamond Kings insert features color portraits by artist Dan Gardiner of young players inside a golden border. Player identification and Rookie Diamond Kings logo are at the bottom. Each card is sequentially numbered to 10,000 with the first 500 printed on canvas.

		NM/M
Complete Set (12):		20.00
Common Player:		2.00
Production 9,500 Sets		
Canvas (500 Sets):		2X
1	Travis Lee	4.00
2	Fernando Tatis	2.00
3	Livan Hernandez	2.00
4	Todd Helton	5.00
5	Derek Lee	3.50
6	Jaret Wright	2.00
7	Ben Grieve	2.00
8	Paul Konerko	2.50
9	Jose Cruz Jr.	2.00
10	Mark Kotsay	2.00
11	Todd Greene	2.00
12	Brad Fullmer	2.00

Update Sony MLB 99

This 20-card set promotes the MLB '99 game for Sony PlayStation systems. The card front has a color player photo with a red border on two sides. The Donruss, PlayStation and MLB '99 logos appear on the front as well. The backs have a MLB '99 Tip and instructions on entering the PlayStation MLB '99 Sweepstakes.

		NM/M
Complete Set (20):		3.00
Common Player:		.05
1	Cal Ripken Jr.	.75
2	Nomar Garciaparra	.40
3	Barry Bonds	.75
4	Mike Mussina	.20
5	Pedro Martinez	.25
6	Derek Jeter	.75
7	Andruw Jones	.25
8	Kenny Lofton	.05
9	Gary Sheffield	.15
10	Raul Mondesi	.05
11	Jeff Bagwell	.25
12	Tim Salmon	.05
13	Tom Glavine	.15
14	Ben Grieve	.05
15	Matt Williams	.05
16	Juan Gonzalez	.15
17	Mark McGwire	.05
18	Bernie Williams	.05
19	Andres Galarraga	.05

1998 Donruss Collections

Collections consists of a 750-card base set made up of cards from the Donruss (200 cards), Leaf (200), Donruss Elite (150) and Donruss Preferred (200) sets. The cards were reproduced with a chromium finish and have the scripted word "Collections" vertically at left-front. The Collections logo is repeated on back and each card has a second number within the 750-piece set. The Donruss and Leaf cards were inserted two per pack, Elite was inserted one per pack and Preferred cards had a production run of less than 1,400, averaging one card per two packs. The 200 Collections versions of Donruss cards can be found with a large black "SAMPLE" overprint value on back.

		NM/M
Complete Donruss Set (200):		100.00
Complete Leaf Set (200):		125.00
Complete Elite Set (150):		125.00
Complete Preferred Set (200):		300.00
Prized Collections Parallel:		2X
Pack (5):		4.00
Wax Box (20):		75.00
Samples:		6X
1	Paul Molitor	2.00
2	Juan Gonzalez	1.00
3	Darryl Kile	.25
4	Randy Johnson	2.00
5	Tom Glavine	.50
6	Pat Hentgen	.25
7	David Justice	.25
8	Kevin Brown	.25
9	Mike Mussina	.50
10	Ken Caminiti	.25
11	Todd Hundley	.25
12	Frank Thomas	2.00
13	Ray Lankford	.25
14	Justin Thompson	.25
15	Jason Dickson	.25
16	Kenny Lofton	.25
17	Ivan Rodriguez	1.50
18	Pedro Martinez	2.00
19	Brady Anderson	.25
20	Barry Larkin	.25
21	Chipper Jones	3.00
22	Tony Gwynn	3.00
23	Roger Clemens	3.25
24	Sandy Alomar Jr.	.25
25	Tino Martinez	.25
26	Jeff Bagwell	2.00
27	Shawn Estes	.25
28	Ken Griffey Jr.	3.50
29	Javier Lopez	.25
30	Denny Neagle	.25
31	Mike Piazza	3.50
32	Andres Galarraga	.25
33	Larry Walker	.25
34	Alex Rodriguez	4.50
35	Greg Maddux	3.00
36	Albert Belle	.25
37	Barry Bonds	6.00
38	Mo Vaughn	.25
39	Kevin Appier	.25
40	Wade Boggs	3.00
41	Garret Anderson	.25
42	Jeffrey Hammonds	.25
43	Marquis Grissom	.25
44	Jim Edmonds	.25
45	Brian Jordan	.25
46	Raul Mondesi	.25
47	John Valentin	.25
48	Brad Radke	.25
49	Ismael Valdes	.25
50	Matt Stairs	.25
51	Matt Williams	.25
52	Reggie Jefferson	.25
53	Alan Benes	.25
54	Charles Johnson	.25
55	Chuck Knoblauch	.25
56	Edgar Martinez	.25
57	Nomar Garciaparra	3.00
58	Craig Biggio	.25
59	Bernie Williams	.50
60	David Cone	.25
61	Cal Ripken Jr.	6.00
62	Mark McGwire	4.50
63	Roberto Alomar	.25
64	Fred McGriff	.25
65	Eric Karros	.25
66	Robin Ventura	.25
67	Darin Erstad	.50
68	Michael Tucker	.25
69	Jim Thome	1.00
70	Mark Grace	.25
71	Lou Collier	.25
72	Karim Garcia	.25
73	Alex Fernandez	.25
74	J.T. Snow	.25
75	Reggie Sanders	.25
76	John Smoltz	.25
77	Tim Salmon	.25
78	Paul O'Neill	.25
79	Vinny Castilla	.25
80	Rafael Palmeiro	1.50
81	Jaret Wright	.25
82	Jay Buhner	.25
83	Brett Butler	.25
84	Todd Greene	.25
85	Scott Rolen	1.50
86	Sammy Sosa	3.00
87	Jason Giambi	1.00
88	Carlos Delgado	.75
89	Deion Sanders	.25
90	Wilton Guerrero	.25
91	Andy Pettitte	.45
92	Brian Giles	.25
93	Dmitri Young	.25
94	Ron Coomer	.25
95	Mike Cameron	.25
96	Edgardo Alfonzo	.25
97	Jimmy Key	.25
98	Ryan Klesko	.25
99	Andy Benes	.25
100	Derek Jeter	6.00
101	Jeff Fassero	.25
102	Neifi Perez	.25
103	Hideo Nomo	1.00
104	Andruw Jones	2.00
105	Todd Helton	1.50
106	Livan Hernandez	.25
107	Brett Tomko	.25
108	Shannon Stewart	.25
109	Bartolo Colon	.25
110	Matt Morris	.25
111	Miguel Tejada	.40
112	Pokey Reese	.25
113	Fernando Tatis	.25
114	Todd Dunwoody	.25
115	Jose Cruz Jr.	.25
116	Chan Ho Park	.25
117	Kevin Young	.25
118	Rickey Henderson	2.00
119	Hideki Irabu	.25
120	Francisco Cordova	.25
121	Al Martin	.25
122	Tony Clark	.25
123	Curt Schilling	.40
124	Rusty Greer	.25
125	Jose Canseco	.60
126	Edgar Renteria	.25
127	Todd Walker	.25
128	Wally Joyner	.25
129	Bill Mueller	.25
130	Jose Guillen	.25
131	Manny Ramirez	2.00
132	Bobby Higginson	.25
133	Kevin Orie	.25
134	Will Clark	.25
135	Dave Nilsson	.25
136	Jason Kendall	.25
137	Ivan Cruz	.25
138	Gary Sheffield	.40
139	Bubba Trammell	.25
140	Vladimir Guerrero	2.00
141	Dennis Reyes	.25
142	Bobby Bonilla	.25
143	Ruben Rivera	.25
144	Ben Grieve	.25
145	Moises Alou	.25
146	Tony Womack	.25
147	Eric Young	.25
148	Paul Konerko	.35
149	Dante Bichette	.25
150	Joe Carter	.25
151	Rondell White	.25
152	Chris Holt	.25
153	Shawn Green	.40
154	Mark Grudzielanek	.25
155	Jermaine Dye	.25
156	Ken Griffey Jr. (Fan Club)	1.75
157	Frank Thomas (Fan Club)	1.00
158	Chipper Jones (Fan Club)	1.75
159	Mike Piazza (Fan Club)	1.75
160	Cal Ripken Jr. (Fan Club)	3.00
161	Greg Maddux (Fan Club)	1.50
162	Juan Gonzalez (Fan Club)	1.00
163	Alex Rodriguez (Fan Club)	2.25
164	Mark McGwire (Fan Club)	2.25
165	Derek Jeter (Fan Club)	3.00
166	Larry Walker (Checklist)	.25
167	Tony Gwynn (Checklist)	.75
168	Tino Martinez (Checklist)	.25
169	Scott Rolen (Checklist)	.40
170	Nomar Garciaparra (Checklist)	.75
1	Mark Kotsay	.50
2	Neifi Perez	.50
3	Paul Konerko	1.00
4	Jose Cruz Jr.	.50
5	Hideki Irabu	.50
6	Mike Cameron	.50
7	Jeff Suppan	.50
8	Kevin Orie	.50
9	Pokey Reese	.50
10	Todd Dunwoody	.50
11	Miguel Tejada	.50
12	Jose Guillen	.50
13	Bartolo Colon	.50
14	Derek Lee	.75
15	Antone Williamson	.50
16	Wilton Guerrero	.50
17	Jaret Wright	.50
18	Todd Helton	2.00
19	Shannon Stewart	.25
20	Nomar Garciaparra	3.00
21	Brett Tomko	.50
22	Fernando Tatis	.50
23	Raul Ibanez	.50
24	Dennis Reyes	.50
25	Bobby Estalella	.50
26	Lou Collier	.50
27	Bubba Trammell	.50
28	Ben Grieve	.50
29	Ivan Cruz	.50
30	Karim Garcia	.50
1	Rusty Greer	.25
2	Tino Martinez	.25
3	Bobby Bonilla	.25
4	Jason Giambi	.65
5	Matt Morris	.25
6	Craig Counsell	.25
7	Reggie Jefferson	.25
8	Brian Rose	.25
9	Ruben Rivera	.25
10	Shawn Estes	.25
11	Tony Gwynn	3.00
12	Jeff Abbott	.25
13	Jose Cruz Jr.	.25
14	Francisco Cordova	.25
15	Ryan Klesko	.25
16	Tim Salmon	.25
17	Brett Tomko	.25
18	Matt Williams	.25
19	Joe Carter	.25
20	Harold Baines	.25
21	Gary Sheffield	.40
22	Charles Johnson	.25
23	Aaron Boone	.35
24	Eddie Murray	2.00
25	Matt Stairs	.25
26	David Cone	.25
27	Jon Nunnally	.25
28	Chris Stynes	.25
29	Enrique Wilson	.25
30	Randy Johnson	2.00
31	Garret Anderson	.25
32	Manny Ramirez	2.00
33	Jeff Suppan	.25
34	Rickey Henderson	2.00
35	Scott Spiezio	.25
36	Rondell White	.25
37	Todd Greene	.25
38	Delino DeShields	.25
39	Kevin Brown	.25
40	Chili Davis	.25
41	Jimmy Key	.25
42	Mike Mussina	1.00
44	Joe Randa	.25
45	Chan Ho Park	.25
46	Brad Radke	.25
47	Geronimo Berroa	.25
48	Wade Boggs	3.00
49	Kevin Appier	.25
50	Moises Alou	.25
51	David Justice	.25
52	Ivan Rodriguez	1.50
53	J.T. Snow	.25
54	Brian Giles	.25
55	Will Clark	.25
56	Justin Thompson	.25
57	Javier Lopez	.25
58	Hideki Irabu	.25
59	Mark Grudzielanek	.25
60	Abraham Nunez	.25
61	Todd Hollandsworth	.25
62	Jay Bell	.25
63	Nomar Garciaparra	3.00
64	Vinny Castilla	.25
65	Lou Collier	.25
66	Kevin Orie	.25
67	John Valentin	.25
68	Robin Ventura	.25
69	Denny Neagle	.25
70	Tony Womack	.25
71	Dennis Reyes	.25
72	Wally Joyner	.25
73	Kevin Brown	.35
74	Ray Durham	.25
75	Mike Cameron	.25
76	Dante Bichette	.25
77	Jose Guillen	.25
78	Carlos Delgado	.60
79	Paul Molitor	2.00
80	Jason Kendall	.25
81	Mark Belhorn	.25
82	Damian Jackson	.25
83	Bill Mueller	.25
84	Kevin Young	.25
85	Curt Schilling	.50
86	Jeffrey Hammonds	.25
87	Sandy Alomar Jr.	.25
88	Bartolo Colon	.25
89	Wilton Guerrero	.25
90	Bernie Williams	.25
91	Deion Sanders	.25
92	Mike Piazza	3.50
93	Butch Huskey	.25
94	Edgardo Alfonzo	.25
95	Alan Benes	.25
96	Craig Biggio	.25
97	Mark Grace	.25
98	Shawn Green	.40
99	Derek Lee	1.00
100	Ken Griffey Jr.	3.50
101	Tim Raines	.25
102	Pokey Reese	.25
103	Lee Stevens	.25
104	Shannon Stewart	.25
105	John Smoltz	.25
106	Frank Thomas	2.00
107	Jeff Fassero	.25
108	Jay Buhner	.25
109	Jose Canseco	.45
110	Omar Vizquel	.25
111	Travis Fryman	.25
112	Dave Nilsson	.25
113	John Olerud	.25
114	Larry Walker	.25
115	Jim Edmonds	.25
116	Bobby Higginson	.25
117	Todd Hundley	.25
118	Paul O'Neill	.25
119	Bip Roberts	.25
120	Ismael Valdes	.25
121	Pedro Martinez	2.00
122	Jeff Cirillo	.25
123	Andy Benes	.25
124	Bobby Jones	.25
125	Brian Hunter	.25
126	Darryl Kile	.25
127	Pat Hentgen	.25
128	Marquis Grissom	.25
129	Eric Davis	.25
130	Chipper Jones	3.00
131	Edgar Martinez	.25
132	Andy Pettitte	.50
133	Cal Ripken Jr.	6.00
134	Scott Rolen	1.50
135	Ron Coomer	.25
136	Luis Castillo	.25
137	Fred McGriff	.25
138	Neifi Perez	.25
139	Eric Karros	.25
140	Alex Fernandez	.25
141	Jason Dickson	.25
142	Lance Johnson	.25
143	Ray Lankford	.25
144	Sammy Sosa	3.00
145	Eric Young	.25
146	Bubba Trammell	.25
147	Todd Walker	.25
148	Mo Vaughn/CC	.25
149	Jeff Bagwell/CC	2.00
150	Kenny Lofton/CC	.25
151	Raul Mondesi/CC	.25
152	Mike Piazza/CC	3.50
153	Chipper Jones/CC	3.00
154	Larry Walker/CC	.25
155	Greg Maddux/CC	3.00
156	Ken Griffey Jr./CC	3.50
157	Frank Thomas/CC	2.00
158	Darin Erstad/GLS	.25
159	Roberto Alomar/GLS	1.50
160	Albert Belle/GLS	1.00
161	Jim Thome/GLS	2.00
162	Tony Clark/GLS	1.00
163	Chuck Knoblauch/GLS	1.00
164	Derek Jeter/GLS	12.00
165	Alex Rodriguez/GLS	8.00
166	Tony Gwynn/GLS	6.00
167	Roger Clemens/GLS	7.00
168	Barry Larkin/GLS	1.00
169	Andres Galarraga/GLS	1.00
170	Vladimir Guerrero/GLS	4.50
171	Mark McGwire/GLS	8.00
172	Barry Bonds/GLS	12.00
173	Juan Gonzalez/GLS	2.50
174	Andruw Jones/GLS	4.50
175	Paul Molitor/GLS	4.50
176	Hideo Nomo/GLS	2.50
177	Cal Ripken Jr./GLS	12.50
178	Brad Fullmer/GLR	1.00
179	Jaret Wright/GLR	1.00
180	Bobby Estalella/GLR	1.00
181	Ben Grieve/GLR	2.00
182	Paul Konerko/GLR	1.50
183	David Ortiz/GLR	3.00
184	Todd Helton/GLR	3.00
185	Juan Encarnacion/GLR	1.00
186	Miguel Tejada/GLR	1.50
187	Jacob Cruz/GLR	1.00
188	Mark Kotsay/GLR	1.00
189	Fernando Tatis/GLR	1.00
190	Ricky Ledee/GLR	1.00
191	Richard Hidalgo/GLR	1.00
192	Richie Sexson/GLR	1.00
193	Luis Ordaz/GLR	1.00
194	Eli Marrero/GLR	1.00
195	Livan Hernandez/GLR	1.00
196	Homer Bush/GLR	1.00
197	Raul Ibanez/GLR	1.00
198	Checklist (Nomar Garciaparra)	1.00
199	Checklist (Scott Rolen)	.75
200	Checklist (Jose Cruz Jr.)	.25
201	Al Martin	.25
1	Ken Griffey Jr.	4.00
2	Frank Thomas	2.50
3	Alex Rodriguez	6.00
4	Mike Piazza	3.00
5	Greg Maddux	3.00
6	Cal Ripken Jr.	7.00
7	Chipper Jones	3.00
8	Derek Jeter	7.00
9	Tony Gwynn	3.00
10	Andruw Jones	2.50
11	Juan Gonzalez	2.50
12	Jeff Bagwell	2.50
13	Mark McGwire	6.00
14	Roger Clemens	2.50
15	Albert Belle	.50
16	Barry Bonds	7.00
17	Kenny Lofton	.25
18	Ivan Rodriguez	2.00
19	Manny Ramirez	2.50
20	Jim Thome	1.50

#	Player	Price
21	Chuck Knoblauch	.50
22	Paul Molitor	2.50
23	Barry Larkin	.50
24	Andy Pettitte	1.00
25	John Smoltz	.50
26	Randy Johnson	2.50
27	Bernie Williams	.50
28	Larry Walker	.50
29	Mo Vaughn	.50
30	Bobby Higginson	.50
31	Edgardo Alfonzo	.50
32	Justin Thompson	.50
33	Jeff Suppan	.50
34	Roberto Alomar	1.00
35	Hideo Nomo	1.25
36	Rusty Greer	.50
37	Tim Salmon	.50
38	Jim Edmonds	.50
39	Gary Sheffield	.75
40	Ken Caminiti	.50
41	Sammy Sosa	3.00
42	Tony Womack	.50
43	Matt Williams	.50
44	Andres Galarraga	.50
45	Garret Anderson	.50
46	Rafael Palmeiro	2.00
47	Mike Mussina	1.00
48	Craig Biggio	.50
49	Wade Boggs	3.00
50	Tom Glavine	.75
51	Jason Giambi	1.00
52	Will Clark	.50
53	David Justice	.50
54	Sandy Alomar Jr.	.50
55	Edgar Martinez	.50
56	Brady Anderson	.50
57	Eric Young	.50
58	Ray Lankford	.50
59	Kevin Brown	.60
60	Raul Mondesi	.50
61	Bobby Bonilla	.50
62	Javier Lopez	.50
63	Fred McGriff	.50
64	Rondell White	.50
65	Todd Hundley	.50
66	Mark Grace	.50
67	Alan Benes	.50
68	Jeff Abbott	.50
69	Bob Abreu	.50
70	Deion Sanders	.50
71	Tino Martinez	.50
72	Shannon Stewart	.50
73	Homer Bush	.50
74	Carlos Delgado	1.50
75	Raul Ibanez	.50
76	Hideki Irabu	.50
77	Jose Cruz Jr.	.50
78	Tony Clark	.50
79	Wilton Guerrero	.50
80	Vladimir Guerrero	2.50
81	Scott Rolen	2.25
82	Nomar Garciaparra	3.00
83	Darin Erstad	1.00
84	Chan Ho Park	.50
85	Mike Cameron	.50
86	Todd Walker	.50
87	Todd Dunwoody	.50
88	Neifi Perez	.50
89	Brett Tomko	.50
90	Jose Guillen	.50
91	Matt Morris	.50
92	Bartolo Colon	.50
93	Jaret Wright	.50
94	Shawn Estes	.50
95	Livan Hernandez	.50
96	Bobby Estalella	.50
97	Ben Grieve	.50
98	Paul Konerko	.75
99	David Ortiz	1.00
100	Todd Helton	2.00
101	Juan Encarnacion	.50
102	Bubba Trammell	.50
103	Miguel Tejada	1.00
104	Jacob Cruz	.50
105	Todd Greene	.50
106	Kevin Orie	.50
107	Mark Kotsay	.50
108	Fernando Tatis	.50
109	Jay Payton	.50
110	Pokey Reese	.50
111	Derrek Lee	1.50
112	Richard Hidalgo	.50
113	Ricky Ledee	.50
114	Lou Collier	.50
115	Ruben Rivera	.50
116	Shawn Green	1.00
117	Moises Alou	.50
118	Ken Griffey Jr. (Generations)	2.00
119	Frank Thomas (Generations)	1.25
120	Alex Rodriguez (Generations)	3.00
121	Mike Piazza (Generations)	2.00
122	Greg Maddux (Generations)	1.75
123	Cal Ripken Jr. (Generations)	3.50
124	Chipper Jones (Generations)	2.00
125	Derek Jeter (Generations)	3.50
126	Tony Gwynn (Generations)	1.75
127	Andruw Jones (Generations)	1.25
128	Juan Gonzalez (Generations)	.75
129	Jeff Bagwell (Generations)	1.25
130	Mark McGwire (Generations)	3.00
131	Roger Clemens (Generations)	1.75
132	Albert Belle (Generations)	.50
133	Barry Bonds (Generations)	3.50
134	Kenny Lofton (Generations)	.50
135	Ivan Rodriguez (Generations)	1.00
136	Manny Ramirez (Generations)	1.25
137	Jim Thome (Generations)	1.00
138	Chuck Knoblauch (Generations)	.50
139	Paul Molitor (Generations)	1.25
140	Barry Larkin (Generations)	.50
141	Mo Vaughn (Generations)	.50
142	Hideki Irabu (Generations)	.50
143	Jose Cruz Jr. (Generations)	.50
144	Tony Clark (Generations)	.50
145	Vladimir Guerrero (Generations)	1.25
146	Scott Rolen (Generations)	1.00
147	Nomar Garciaparra (Generations)	2.00
148	Checklist (Nomar Garciaparra)	1.00
149	Checklist (Larry Walker)	.50
150	Checklist (Tino Martinez)	.50
1	Ken Griffey Jr./EX	12.00
2	Frank Thomas/EX	7.50
3	Cal Ripken Jr./EX	17.50
4	Alex Rodriguez/EX	15.00
5	Greg Maddux/EX	10.00
6	Mike Piazza/EX	12.00
7	Chipper Jones/EX	10.00
8	Tony Gwynn/FB	10.00
9	Derek Jeter/FB	17.50
10	Jeff Bagwell/EX	7.50
11	Juan Gonzalez/EX	4.00
12	Nomar Garciaparra/EX	10.00
13	Andruw Jones/FB	7.50
14	Hideo Nomo/FB	4.00
15	Roger Clemens/FB	13.50
16	Mark McGwire/FB	15.00
17	Scott Rolen/FB	6.00
18	Vladimir Guerrero/FB	7.50
19	Barry Bonds/FB	17.50
20	Darin Erstad/FB	4.00
21	Albert Belle/FB	2.00
22	Kenny Lofton/FB	2.00
23	Mo Vaughn/FB	2.00
24	Tony Clark/FB	2.00
25	Ivan Rodriguez/FB	6.00
26	Larry Walker/CL	2.00
27	Eddie Murray/CL	7.50
28	Andy Pettitte/CL	4.00
29	Roberto Alomar/CL	2.00
30	Randy Johnson/CL	7.50
31	Manny Ramirez/CL	7.50
32	Paul Molitor/CL	7.50
33	Mike Mussina/CL	4.00
34	Jim Thome/FB	2.00
35	Tino Martinez/CL	2.00
36	Gary Sheffield/CL	3.00
37	Chuck Knoblauch/CL	2.00
38	Bernie Williams/CL	2.00
39	Tim Salmon/CL	2.00
40	Sammy Sosa/CL	10.00
41	Wade Boggs/CL	10.00
42	Will Clark/CL	2.00
43	Andres Galarraga/CL	2.00
44	Raul Mondesi/CL	2.00
45	Rickey Henderson/GS	6.50
46	Jose Canseco/GS	4.00
47	Pedro Martinez/GS	6.50
48	Jay Buhner/GS	2.00
49	Ryan Klesko/GS	2.00
50	Barry Larkin/CL	2.00
51	Charles Johnson/GS	2.00
52	Tom Glavine/GS	3.00
53	Edgar Martinez/CL	2.00
54	Fred McGriff/GS	2.00
55	Moises Alou/MZ	2.00
56	Dante Bichette/GS	2.00
57	Jim Edmonds/CL	2.00
58	Mark Grace/MZ	2.00
59	Chan Ho Park/MZ	2.00
60	Justin Thompson/MZ	2.00
61	John Smoltz/MZ	2.00
62	Craig Biggio/CL	2.00
63	Ken Caminiti/MZ	2.00
64	Deion Sanders/MZ	2.00
65	Carlos Delgado/CL	4.00
66	David Justice/CL	2.00
67	J.T. Snow/GS	2.00
68	Jason Giambi/CL	4.00
69	Garret Anderson/MZ	2.00
70	Rondell White/MZ	2.00
71	Matt Williams/MZ	2.00
72	Brady Anderson/MZ	2.00
73	Eric Karros/GS	2.00
74	Javier Lopez/GS	2.00
75	Pat Hentgen/GS	2.00
76	Todd Hundley/GS	2.00
77	Ray Lankford/GS	2.00
78	Denny Neagle/GS	2.00
79	Henry Rodriguez/GS	2.00
80	Sandy Alomar Jr./MZ	2.00
81	Rafael Palmeiro/MZ	5.00
82	Robin Ventura/GS	2.00
83	John Olerud/GS	2.00
84	Omar Vizquel/GS	2.00
85	Joe Randa/GS	2.00
86	Lance Johnson/GS	2.00
87	Kevin Brown/GS	2.00
88	Curt Schilling/GS	4.00
89	Ismael Valdes/GS	2.00
90	Francisco Cordova/GS	2.00
91	David Cone/GS	2.00
92	Paul O'Neill/GS	2.00
93	Jimmy Key/GS	2.00
94	Brad Radke/GS	2.00
95	Kevin Appier/GS	2.00
96	Al Martin/GS	2.00
97	Rusty Greer/MZ	2.00
98	Reggie Jefferson/GS	2.00
99	Ron Coomer/GS	2.00
100	Vinny Castilla/GS	2.00
101	Bobby Bonilla/MZ	2.00
102	Eric Young/GS	2.00
103	Tony Womack/GS	2.00
104	Jason Kendall/GS	2.00
105	Jeff Suppan/GS	2.00
106	Shawn Estes/MZ	2.00
107	Shawn Green/GS	2.00
108	Edgardo Alfonzo/GS	2.00
109	Alan Benes/MZ	2.00
110	Bobby Higginson/GS	2.00
111	Mark Grudzielanek/GS	2.00
112	Wilton Guerrero/GS	2.00
113	Todd Greene/MZ	2.00
114	Pokey Reese/GS	2.00
115	Jose Guillen/CL	2.00
116	Neifi Perez/MZ	2.00
117	Luis Castillo/GS	2.00
118	Edgar Renteria/GS	2.00
119	Karim Garcia/GS	2.00
120	Butch Huskey/GS	2.00
121	Michael Tucker/GS	2.00
122	Jason Dickson/GS	2.00
123	Todd Walker/MZ	2.00
124	Brian Jordan/GS	2.00
125	Joe Carter/GS	2.00
126	Matt Morris/MZ	2.00
127	Brett Tomko/MZ	2.00
128	Mike Cameron/CL	2.00
129	Russ Davis/GS	2.00
130	Shannon Stewart/MZ	2.00
131	Kevin Orie/GS	2.00
132	Scott Spiezio/GS	2.00
133	Brian Giles/GS	2.00
134	Raul Casanova/MZ	2.00
135	Jose Cruz Jr./CL	2.00
136	Hideki Irabu/MZ	2.00
137	Bubba Trammell/GS	2.00
138	Richard Hidalgo/MZ	2.00
139	Paul Konerko/CL	2.50
140	Todd Helton/MZ	5.00
141	Miguel Tejada/CL	3.00
142	Fernando Tatis/MZ	2.00
143	Ben Grieve/FB	2.00
144	Travis Lee/FB	2.00
145	Mark Kotsay/MZ	2.00
146	Eli Marrero/MZ	2.00
147	David Ortiz/CL	4.00
148	Juan Encarnacion/MZ	2.00
149	Jaret Wright/MZ	2.00
150	Livan Hernandez/MZ	2.00
151	Ruben Rivera/GS	2.00
152	Brad Fullmer/MZ	2.00
153	Dennis Reyes/MZ	2.00
154	Enrique Wilson/MZ	2.00
155	Todd Dunwoody/MZ	2.00
156	Derrick Gibson/MZ	2.00
157	Aaron Boone/MZ	2.00
158	Ron Wright/MZ	2.00
159	Preston Wilson/MZ	2.00
160	Abraham Nunez/MZ	2.00
161	Shane Monahan/GS	2.00
162	Carl Pavano/GS	2.00
163	Derek Lee/GS	4.00
164	Jeff Abbott/GS	2.00
165	Wes Helms/MZ	2.00
166	Brian Rose/GS	2.00
167	Bobby Estalella/GS	2.00
168	Ken Griffey Jr./GS	9.00
169	Frank Thomas/GS	6.00
170	Cal Ripken Jr./GS	15.00
171	Alex Rodriguez/GS	12.00
172	Greg Maddux/GS	7.50
173	Mike Piazza/GS	9.00
174	Chipper Jones/GS	8.00
175	Tony Gwynn/GS	7.50
176	Derek Jeter/GS	15.00
177	Jeff Bagwell/GS	6.00
178	Juan Gonzalez/GS	6.00
179	Nomar Garciaparra/GS	7.50
180	Andruw Jones/GS	6.00
181	Hideo Nomo/GS	3.00
182	Roger Clemens/GS	8.00
183	Mark McGwire/GS	12.00
184	Scott Rolen/GS	3.00
185	Barry Bonds/GS	15.00
186	Darin Erstad/GS	3.00
187	Mo Vaughn/GS	3.00
188	Ivan Rodriguez/GS	5.00
189	Larry Walker/MZ	2.00
190	Andy Pettitte/GS	3.00
191	Randy Johnson/MZ	6.00
192	Paul Molitor/GS	6.00
193	Jim Thome/GS	4.00
194	Tino Martinez/MZ	2.00
195	Gary Sheffield/GS	3.00
196	Albert Belle/GS	2.00
197	Jose Cruz Jr./GS	2.00
198	Todd Helton/GS	5.00
199	Ben Grieve/GS	2.00
200	Paul Konerko/GS	2.50

1998 Donruss Elite

Donruss Elite consists of a 150-card base set with two parallels and five inserts. The base cards feature a foil background with player photo on front. Another photo is on the back with stats and basic player information. The Aspirations parallel is numbered to 750 and the Status parallel is numbered to 100. The base set also includes the 30-card Generations subset and three checklists. The inserts are Back to the Future, Back to the Future Autographs, Craftsmen, Prime Numbers and Prime Numbers Die-Cuts.

	NM/M
Complete Set (150):	15.00
Common Player:	.10
Aspirations (750 Sets):	2.5X
Status (100 Sets):	15X
Pack (5):	2.50
Wax Box (18):	40.00

#	Player	Price
1	Ken Griffey Jr.	1.50
2	Frank Thomas	.75
3	Alex Rodriguez	2.00
4	Mike Piazza	1.50
5	Greg Maddux	1.00
6	Cal Ripken Jr.	2.50
7	Chipper Jones	1.00
8	Derek Jeter	2.50
9	Tony Gwynn	1.00
10	Andruw Jones	.75
11	Juan Gonzalez	.40
12	Jeff Bagwell	.75
13	Mark McGwire	2.00
14	Roger Clemens	1.25
15	Albert Belle	.10
16	Barry Bonds	2.50
17	Kenny Lofton	.10
18	Ivan Rodriguez	.65
19	Manny Ramirez	.75
20	Jim Thome	.50
21	Chuck Knoblauch	.10
22	Paul Molitor	.75
23	Barry Larkin	.10
24	Andy Pettitte	.40
25	John Smoltz	.10
26	Randy Johnson	.75
27	Bernie Williams	.10
28	Larry Walker	.10
29	Mo Vaughn	.10
30	Bobby Higginson	.10
31	Edgardo Alfonzo	.10
32	Justin Thompson	.10
33	Jeff Suppan	.10
34	Roberto Alomar	.30
35	Hideo Nomo	.40
36	Rusty Greer	.10
37	Tim Salmon	.10
38	Jim Edmonds	.10
39	Gary Sheffield	.25
40	Ken Caminiti	.10
41	Sammy Sosa	1.00
42	Tony Womack	.10
43	Matt Williams	.10
44	Andres Galarraga	.10
45	Garret Anderson	.10
46	Rafael Palmeiro	.65
47	Mike Mussina	.40
48	Craig Biggio	.10
49	Wade Boggs	1.00
50	Tom Glavine	.25
51	Jason Giambi	.50
52	Will Clark	.10
53	David Justice	.10
54	Sandy Alomar Jr.	.10
55	Edgar Martinez	.10
56	Brady Anderson	.10
57	Eric Young	.10
58	Ray Lankford	.10
59	Kevin Brown	.10
60	Raul Mondesi	.10
61	Bobby Bonilla	.10
62	Javier Lopez	.10
63	Fred McGriff	.10
64	Rondell White	.10
65	Todd Hundley	.10
66	Mark Grace	.10
67	Alan Benes	.10
68	Jeff Abbott	.10
69	Bob Abreu	.10
70	Deion Sanders	.10
71	Tino Martinez	.10
72	Shannon Stewart	.10
73	Homer Bush	.10
74	Carlos Delgado	.50
75	Raul Ibanez	.10
76	Hideki Irabu	.10
77	Jose Cruz Jr.	.10
78	Tony Clark	.10
79	Wilton Guerrero	.10
80	Vladimir Guerrero	.75
81	Scott Rolen	.60
82	Nomar Garciaparra	1.00
83	Darin Erstad	.30
84	Chan Ho Park	.10
85	Mike Cameron	.10
86	Todd Walker	.10
87	Todd Dunwoody	.10
88	Neifi Perez	.10
89	Brett Tomko	.10
90	Jose Guillen	.10
91	Matt Morris	.10
92	Bartolo Colon	.10
93	Jaret Wright	.10
94	Shawn Estes	.10
95	Livan Hernandez	.10
96	Bobby Estalella	.10
97	Ben Grieve	.10
98	Paul Konerko	.15
99	David Ortiz	.40
100	Todd Helton	.65
101	Juan Encarnacion	.10
102	Bubba Trammell	.10
103	Miguel Tejada	.25
104	Jacob Cruz	.10
105	Todd Greene	.10
106	Kevin Orie	.10
107	Mark Kotsay	.10
108	Fernando Tatis	.10
109	Jay Payton	.10
110	Pokey Reese	.10
111	Derek Lee	.10
112	Richard Hidalgo	.10
113	Ricky Ledee	.10
114	Lou Collier	.10
115	Ruben Rivera	.10
116	Shawn Green	.10
117	Moises Alou	.10
118	Ken Griffey Jr. (Generations)	.65
119	Frank Thomas (Generations)	.40
120	Alex Rodriguez (Generations)	.75
121	Mike Piazza (Generations)	.65
122	Greg Maddux (Generations)	.50
123	Cal Ripken Jr. (Generations)	1.00
124	Chipper Jones (Generations)	.50
125	Derek Jeter (Generations)	1.00
126	Tony Gwynn (Generations)	.50
127	Andruw Jones (Generations)	.40
128	Juan Gonzalez (Generations)	.20
129	Jeff Bagwell (Generations)	.40
130	Mark McGwire (Generations)	.75
131	Roger Clemens (Generations)	.65
132	Albert Belle (Generations)	.10
133	Barry Bonds (Generations)	1.00
134	Kenny Lofton (Generations)	.10
135	Ivan Rodriguez (Generations)	.25
136	Manny Ramirez (Generations)	.40
137	Jim Thome (Generations)	.25
138	Chuck Knoblauch (Generations)	.10
139	Paul Molitor (Generations)	.40
140	Barry Larkin (Generations)	.10
141	Mo Vaughn (Generations)	.10
142	Hideki Irabu (Generations)	.10
143	Jose Cruz Jr. (Generations)	.10
144	Tony Clark (Generations)	.10
145	Vladimir Guerrero (Generations)	.40
146	Scott Rolen (Generations)	.20
147	Nomar Garciaparra (Generations)	.50
148	Checklist (Nomar Garciaparra (Hit Streaks))	.40
149	Checklist Larry Walker (Long HR-Coors)	.10
150	Checklist Tino Martinez (3 HR in game)	.10

1998 Donruss Elite Aspirations

A parallel edition of 750 of each player are found in this die-cut set. Cards have a scalloped treatment cut into the top and sides and red, rather than silver metallic borders. The word "ASPI-

RATIONS" in printed on front at bottom-right. Backs have the notation "1 of 750."

	NM/M
Common Player:	.50
Stars/Rookies:	2.5X

1998 Donruss Elite Status

Just 100 serially numbered cards of each player are found in this die-cut parallel set. Cards have a scalloped treatment cut into the top and sides and red, rather than silver metallic borders.

	NM/M
Common Player:	1.50
Stars/Rookies:	15X

Back to the Future

These double-front cards feature a veteran or retired star on one side and a young player on the other. Each player's name, team and "Back to the Future" are printed in the border. The cards are numbered to 1,500, with the first 100 of each card signed by both players. Exceptions are cards #1 and #6. Ripken and Konerko did not sign the same cards and Frank Thomas did not sign his Back to the Future card. Thomas instead signed 100 copies of his Elite base set card which was specially marked.

		NM/M
Complete Set (8):		40.00
Common Player:		2.50
Production 1,400 Sets		
1	Cal Ripken Jr., Paul Konerko	9.00
2	Jeff Bagwell, Todd Helton	4.50
3	Eddie Mathews, Chipper Jones	5.00
4	Juan Gonzalez, Ben Grieve	2.50
5	Hank Aaron, Jose Cruz Jr.	10.00
6	Frank Thomas, David Ortiz	4.50
7	Nolan Ryan, Greg Maddux	9.00
8	Alex Rodriguez, Nomar Garciaparra	9.00

Back to the Future Autographs

The first 100 of each card in the Back to the Future insert was autographed by both players. Exceptions are cards #1 and #6. Ripken and Konerko did not sign the same cards and Frank Thomas did not sign his Back to the Future card. Thomas instead signed 100 specially marked copies of his Elite base-set card.

		NM/M
Production 100 Sets		
1a	Paul Konerko	30.00
1b	Cal Ripken Jr.	150.00

#	Player	NM/M
2	Jeff Bagwell, Todd Helton	120.00
3	Eddie Mathews, Chipper Jones	200.00
4	Juan Gonzalez, Ben Grieve	30.00
5	Hank Aaron, Jose Cruz Jr.	250.00
7	Nolan Ryan, Greg Maddux	850.00
8	Alex Rodriguez, Nomar Garciaparra	450.00
2	Frank Thomas (Specially autographed Elite)	45.00

Craftsmen

This 30-card insert has color player photos on the front and back. The set is sequentially numbered to 3,500. The Master Craftsmen parallel is numbered to 100.

		NM/M
Complete Set (30):		40.00
Common Player:		.50
Production 3,500 Sets		
Master Craftsman (100 Sets):		10X
1	Ken Griffey Jr.	3.00
2	Frank Thomas	1.50
3	Alex Rodriguez	4.00
4	Cal Ripken Jr.	5.00
5	Greg Maddux	2.00
6	Mike Piazza	3.00
7	Chipper Jones	2.00
8	Derek Jeter	5.00
9	Tony Gwynn	2.00
10	Nomar Garciaparra	2.00
11	Scott Rolen	1.25
12	Jose Cruz Jr.	.50
13	Tony Clark	.50
14	Vladimir Guerrero	1.50
15	Todd Helton	1.25
16	Ben Grieve	.50
17	Andruw Jones	1.50
18	Jeff Bagwell	1.50
19	Mark McGwire	4.00
20	Juan Gonzalez	.75
21	Roger Clemens	2.50
22	Albert Belle	.50
23	Barry Bonds	5.00
24	Kenny Lofton	.50
25	Ivan Rodriguez	1.25
26	Paul Molitor	1.50
27	Barry Larkin (Incorrect "CARDINALS" on front.)	.50
28	Mo Vaughn	.50
29	Larry Walker	.50
30	Tino Martinez	.50

Prime Numbers

This 36-card insert includes three cards for each of 12 players. Each card has a single number in the background. The three numbers for each player represent a key statistic for the player (ex. Mark McGwire's cards are 3-8-7; his career home run total at the time was 387). Each card in the set is sequentially numbered. The total is dependent upon the player's statistic. Promo versions with no serial number and a large "SAMPLE" on back exist for each card.

		NM/M
Common Card:		5.00
Samples: 50 Percent Player's Common		
1A	Ken Griffey Jr. 2/94	25.00
1B	Ken Griffey Jr. 9/204	20.00
1C	Ken Griffey Jr. 4/290	17.50
2A	Frank Thomas 4/56	25.00
2B	Frank Thomas 5/406	7.50
2C	Frank Thomas 6/450	7.50
3A	Mark McGwire 3/87	30.00
3B	Mark McGwire 8/307	20.00
3C	Mark McGwire 7/380	20.00
4A	Cal Ripken Jr. 5/17	135.00
4B	Cal Ripken Jr. 1/507	13.50
4C	Cal Ripken Jr. 7/510	13.50
5A	Mike Piazza 5/76	30.00
5B	Mike Piazza 7/506	12.00
5C	Mike Piazza 6/570	12.00
6A	Chipper Jones 4/89	25.00
6B	Chipper Jones 8/409	10.00
6C	Chipper Jones 9/480	10.00
7A	Tony Gwynn 3/72	25.00
7B	Tony Gwynn 7/302	9.00
7C	Tony Gwynn 2/370	9.00
8A	Barry Bonds 3/74	45.00
8B	Barry Bonds 7/304	12.00
8C	Barry Bonds 4/370	12.00
9A	Jeff Bagwell 4/25	25.00
9B	Jeff Bagwell 2/405	7.50
9C	Jeff Bagwell 5/420	7.50
10A	Juan Gonzalez 5/89	9.00
10B	Juan Gonzalez 8/509	6.00
10C	Juan Gonzalez 9/580	6.00
11A	Alex Rodriguez 5/34	55.00
11B	Alex Rodriguez 3/504	12.00
11C	Alex Rodriguez 4/530	12.00
12A	Kenny Lofton 3/54	15.00
12B	Kenny Lofton 5/304	5.00
12C	Kenny Lofton 4/350	5.00

Prime Numbers Die-Cuts

This set is a die-cut parallel of the Prime Numbers insert. Each card is sequentially numbered. The production run for each player is the number featured on his first card times 100, his second card times 10 and his third card is sequentially numbered to the number featured on the card.

		NM/M
Common Player:		4.00
1A	Ken Griffey Jr. 2/200	20.00
1B	Ken Griffey Jr. 9/90	35.00
1C	Ken Griffey Jr. 4/4	130.00
2A	Frank Thomas 4/400	6.00
2B	Frank Thomas 5/50	20.00
2C	Frank Thomas 6/6	60.00
3A	Mark McGwire 3/300	17.50
3B	Mark McGwire 8/80	50.00
3C	Mark McGwire 7/7	110.00
4A	Cal Ripken Jr. 5/500	12.50
4B	Cal Ripken Jr. 1/10	95.00
4C	Cal Ripken Jr. 7/7	120.00
5A	Mike Piazza 5/500	10.00
5B	Mike Piazza 7/70	30.00
5C	Mike Piazza 6/6	75.00
6A	Chipper Jones 4/400	7.50
6B	Chipper Jones 8/80	25.00
6C	Chipper Jones 9/9	55.00
7A	Tony Gwynn 3/300	9.00
7B	Tony Gwynn 7/70	25.00
7C	Tony Gwynn 2/2	160.00
8A	Barry Bonds 3/300	10.00
8B	Barry Bonds 7/70	35.00
8C	Barry Bonds 4/4	160.00
9A	Jeff Bagwell 4/400	4.00
9B	Jeff Bagwell 2/20	25.00
9C	Jeff Bagwell 5/5	55.00
10A	Juan Gonzalez 5/500	4.00
10B	Juan Gonzalez 8/80	15.00
10C	Juan Gonzalez 9/9	55.00
11A	Alex Rodriguez 5/500	8.00
11B	Alex Rodriguez 3/30	60.00
11C	Alex Rodriguez 4/4	160.00
12A	Kenny Lofton 3/300	4.00
12B	Kenny Lofton 5/50	7.50
12C	Kenny Lofton 4/4	30.00

1998 Donruss Preferred

The Donruss Preferred 200-card base set is broken down into five subsets: 100 Grand Stand cards (5:1), 40 Mezzanine (1:6), 30 Club Level (1:12), 20 Field Box (1:23) and 10 Executive Suite (1:65). The base set is paralleled in the Preferred Seating set. Each

subset has a different die-cut in the parallel. Inserts in this product include Great X-Pectations, Precious Metals and Title Waves.

		NM/M
Complete Set (200):		90.00
Common Grand Stand (5:1):		.10
Common Mezzanine (1:6):		.20
Common Club Level (1:12):		.30
Common Field Box (1:23):		.40
Common Executive Suite (1:65):		1.50
Tin Pack (5):		3.00
Tin Box (24):		40.00
1	Ken Griffey Jr./EX	4.00
2	Frank Thomas/EX	2.50
3	Cal Ripken Jr./EX	7.50
4	Alex Rodriguez/EX	5.00
5	Greg Maddux/EX	4.00
6	Mike Piazza/EX	4.00
7	Chipper Jones/EX	3.00
8	Tony Gwynn/FB	2.50
9	Derek Jeter/FB	6.00
10	Jeff Bagwell/EX	2.50
11	Juan Gonzalez/EX	4.00
12	Nomar Garciaparra/EX	3.00
13	Andruw Jones/FB	2.00
14	Hideo Nomo/FB	.65
15	Roger Clemens/FB	3.00
16	Mark McGwire/FB	5.00
17	Scott Rolen/FB	.75
18	Vladimir Guerrero/FB	2.00
19	Barry Bonds/FB	6.00
20	Darin Erstad/FB	.60
21	Albert Belle/FB	.40
22	Kenny Lofton/FB	.40
23	Mo Vaughn/FB	.40
24	Tony Clark/FB	.40
25	Ivan Rodriguez/FB	1.50
26	Larry Walker/CL	.30
27	Eddie Murray/CL	1.00
28	Andy Pettitte/CL	.45
29	Roberto Alomar/CL	.40
30	Randy Johnson/CL	1.00
31	Manny Ramirez/CL	.40
32	Paul Molitor/FB	2.00
33	Mike Mussina/CL	.50
34	Jim Thome/FB	.75
35	Tino Martinez/CL	.30
36	Gary Sheffield/CL	.45
37	Chuck Knoblauch/CL	.30
38	Bernie Williams/CL	.30
39	Tim Salmon/CL	.30
40	Sammy Sosa/CL	1.50
41	Wade Boggs/MZ	.75
42	Will Clark/CL	.10
43	Andres Galarraga/CL	.30
44	Raul Mondesi/CL	.30
45	Rickey Henderson/GS	.50
46	Jose Canseco/GS	.35
47	Pedro Martinez/CL	.50
48	Jay Buhner/GS	.10
49	Ryan Klesko/CL	.10
50	Barry Larkin/CL	.30
51	Charles Johnson/GS	.10
52	Tom Glavine/CL	.25
53	Edgar Martinez/CL	.30
54	Fred McGriff/GS	.30
55	Moises Alou/MZ	.20
56	Dante Bichette/GS	.10
57	Jim Edmonds/CL	.30
58	Mark Grace/MZ	.20
59	Chan Ho Park/MZ	.20
60	Justin Thompson/MZ	.20
61	John Smoltz/MZ	.20
62	Craig Biggio/CL	.30
63	Ken Caminiti/MZ	.20
64	Deion Sanders/MZ	.20
65	Carlos Delgado/GS	.30
66	David Justice/GS	.10
67	J.T. Snow/GS	.10
68	Jason Giambi/CL	.50
69	Garret Anderson/MZ	.20
70	Rondell White/MZ	.20
71	Matt Williams/GS	.20
72	Brady Anderson/MZ	.20
73	Eric Karros/GS	.20
74	Javier Lopez/GS	.10
75	Pat Hentgen/GS	.10
76	Todd Hundley/GS	.10
77	Ray Lankford/GS	.10
78	Denny Neagle/GS	.10
79	Henry Rodriguez/GS	.10
80	Sandy Alomar Jr./MZ	.20
81	Rafael Palmeiro/GS	.50
82	Robin Ventura/GS	.10
83	John Olerud/GS	.10
84	Omar Vizquel/GS	.10
85	Joe Randa/GS	.10
86	Lance Johnson/GS	.10
87	Kevin Brown/GS	.10
88	Curt Schilling/GS	.25
89	Ismael Valdes/GS	.10
90	Francisco Cordova/GS	.10
91	David Cone/GS	.10
92	Paul O'Neill/GS	.10
93	Jimmy Key/GS	.10
94	Brad Radke/GS	.10
95	Kevin Appier/GS	.10
96	Al Martin/GS	.10
97	Rusty Greer/MZ	.20
98	Reggie Jefferson/GS	.10
99	Ron Coomer/GS	.10
100	Vinny Castilla/GS	.20
101	Bobby Bonilla/MZ	.20
102	Eric Young/GS	.10
103	Tony Womack/GS	.10
104	Jason Kendall/GS	.10
105	Jeff Suppan/GS	.10
106	Shawn Estes/MZ	.20
107	Shawn Green/GS	.25
108	Edgardo Alfonzo/MZ	.20
109	Alan Benes/MZ	.20
110	Bobby Higginson/GS	.10
111	Mark Grudzielanek/GS	.10
112	Wilton Guerrero/GS	.10
113	Todd Greene/MZ	.20
114	Pokey Reese/GS	.10
115	Jose Guillen/CL	.30
116	Neifi Perez/MZ	.20
117	Luis Castillo/GS	.10
118	Edgar Renteria/GS	.10
119	Karim Garcia/GS	.10
120	Butch Huskey/GS	.10
121	Michael Tucker/GS	.10
122	Jason Dickson/GS	.10
123	Todd Walker/MZ	.20
124	Brian Jordan/GS	.10
125	Joe Carter/GS	.10
126	Matt Morris/MZ	.20
127	Brett Tomko/MZ	.20
128	Mike Cameron/CL	.30
129	Russ Davis/GS	.10
130	Shannon Stewart/MZ	.20
131	Kevin Orie/GS	.10
132	Scott Spiezio/GS	.10
133	Brian Giles/GS	.10
134	Raul Casanova/GS	.10
135	Jose Cruz Jr./CL	.30
136	Hideki Irabu/GS	.10
137	Bubba Trammell/GS	.10
138	Richard Hidalgo/GS	.30
139	Paul Konerko/CL	.35
140	Todd Helton/GS	1.00
141	Miguel Tejada/CL	.40
142	Fernando Tatis/MZ	.20
143	Ben Grieve/FB	.40
144	Travis Lee/FB	.65
145	Mark Kotsay/CL	.30
146	Eli Marrero/MZ	.20
147	David Ortiz/CL	.20
148	Juan Encarnacion/GS	.20
149	Jaret Wright/MZ	.20
150	Livan Hernandez/CL	.30
151	Ruben Rivera/GS	.10
152	Brad Fullmer/MZ	.20
153	Dennis Reyes/GS	.10
154	Enrique Wilson/MZ	.20
155	Todd Dunwoody/MZ	.20
156	Derrick Gibson/MZ	.20
157	Aaron Boone/MZ	.20
158	Ron Wright/MZ	.20
159	Preston Wilson/MZ	.20
160	Abraham Nunez/GS	.10
161	Shane Monahan/GS	.10
162	Carl Pavano/GS	.10
163	Derrek Lee/GS	.35
164	Jeff Abbott/GS	.20
165	Wes Helms/MZ	.20
166	Brian Rose/GS	.10
167	Bobby Estalella/GS	.10
168	Ken Griffey Jr./GS	.75
169	Frank Thomas/GS	.50
170	Cal Ripken Jr./GS	1.50
171	Alex Rodriguez/GS	1.00
172	Greg Maddux/GS	.60
173	Mike Piazza/GS	.75
174	Chipper Jones/GS	.60
175	Tony Gwynn/GS	.60
176	Derek Jeter/GS	1.50
177	Jeff Bagwell/GS	.50
178	Juan Gonzalez/GS	.30
179	Nomar Garciaparra/GS	.60
180	Andruw Jones/GS	.50
181	Hideo Nomo/GS	.30
182	Roger Clemens/GS	.65
183	Mark McGwire/GS	1.00
184	Scott Rolen/GS	.35
185	Barry Bonds/GS	1.50
186	Darin Erstad/GS	.25
187	Mo Vaughn/GS	.10
188	Ivan Rodriguez/GS	.40
189	Larry Walker/MZ	.20
190	Andy Pettitte/GS	.30
191	Randy Johnson/MZ	.60
192	Paul Molitor/GS	.50
193	Jim Thome/GS	.35
194	Tino Martinez/MZ	.20
195	Gary Sheffield/GS	.30
196	Albert Belle/GS	.10
197	Jose Cruz Jr./GS	.20
198	Todd Helton/GS	.40
199	Ben Grieve/GS	.10
200	Paul Konerko/GS	.20

Seating

Preferred Seating is a die-cut parallel of the base set. Each section of the base set has a different die-cut.

	NM/M
Common Grand Stand:	.50
Stars and Rookies:	4X
Common Mezzanine:	.50
Stars and Rookies:	2X
Common Club Level:	.50
Stars and Rookies:	2X
Common Field Box:	1.00
Stars and Rookies:	1.5X
Common Executive Suite:	2.50
Stars and Rookies:	1X

Great X-pectations

This 26-card insert features a veteran player on one side and a young player on the other. A large "GX" appears in the background on each side. The cards are sequentially numbered to 2,700, with the first 300 of each die-cut around the "GX".

		NM/M
Complete Set (26):		35.00
Common Player:		.75
Die-Cuts:		3X
Samples:		1X
1	Jeff Bagwell, Travis Lee	1.25
2	Jose Cruz Jr., Ken Griffey Jr.	2.00
3	Larry Walker, Ben Grieve	.75
4	Frank Thomas, Todd Helton	1.25
5	Jim Thome, Paul Konerko	1.00
6	Alex Rodriguez, Miguel Tejada	2.50
7	Greg Maddux, Livan Hernandez	1.75
8	Roger Clemens, Jaret Wright	1.75
9	Albert Belle, Juan Encarnacion	.75
10	Mo Vaughn, David Ortiz	1.00
11	Manny Ramirez, Mark Kotsay	1.25
12	Tim Salmon, Brad Fullmer	.75
13	Cal Ripken Jr., Fernando Tatis	3.50
14	Hideo Nomo, Hideki Irabu	1.50
15	Mike Piazza, Todd Greene	2.00
16	Gary Sheffield, Richard Hidalgo	.75
17	Paul Molitor, Darin Erstad	1.25
18	Ivan Rodriguez, Eli Marrero	1.00
19	Ken Caminiti, Todd Walker	.75
20	Tony Gwynn, Jose Guillen	1.75
21	Derek Jeter, Nomar Garciaparra	3.50
22	Chipper Jones, Scott Rolen	1.75
23	Juan Gonzalez, Andruw Jones	1.25
24	Barry Bonds, Vladimir Guerrero	3.50
25	Mark McGwire, Tony Clark	2.50
26	Bernie Williams, Mike Cameron	.75

Precious Metals

Precious Metals is a 30-card partial parallel of the Preferred base set. Each card was printed on stock using real silver, gold or platinum. Fifty complete sets were produced.

		NM/M
Complete Set (30):		850.00
Common Player:		7.50
1	Ken Griffey Jr.	50.00
2	Frank Thomas	35.00
3	Cal Ripken Jr.	75.00
4	Alex Rodriguez	60.00
5	Greg Maddux	45.00
6	Mike Piazza	50.00
7	Chipper Jones	45.00
8	Tony Gwynn	45.00
9	Derek Jeter	75.00
10	Jeff Bagwell	35.00
11	Juan Gonzalez	15.00
12	Nomar Garciaparra	45.00
13	Andruw Jones	35.00
14	Hideo Nomo	15.00
15	Roger Clemens	45.00
16	Mark McGwire	60.00
17	Scott Rolen	25.00
18	Barry Bonds	75.00
19	Darin Erstad	15.00
20	Kenny Lofton	7.50
21	Mo Vaughn	7.50
22	Ivan Rodriguez	25.00
23	Randy Johnson	35.00
24	Paul Molitor	35.00
25	Jose Cruz Jr.	7.50
26	Paul Konerko	7.50
27	Todd Helton	25.00
28	Ben Grieve	7.50
29	Travis Lee	7.50
30	Mark Kotsay	7.50

Title Waves

This 30-card set features players who won awards or titles between 1993-1997. Printed on plastic stock, each card is sequentially numbered to the year the player won the award. The card fronts feature the Title Waves logo, a color player photo in front of a background of fans and the name of the award the player won.

		NM/M
Complete Set (30):		100.00
Common Player:		1.00
1	Nomar Garciaparra	5.00
2	Scott Rolen	2.50
3	Roger Clemens	5.50
4	Gary Sheffield	1.50
5	Jeff Bagwell	3.50
6	Cal Ripken Jr.	10.00
7	Frank Thomas	3.50
8	Ken Griffey Jr.	6.00
9	Larry Walker	3.50
10	Derek Jeter	10.00
11	Juan Gonzalez	2.00
12	Bernie Williams	1.00
13	Andruw Jones	3.50
14	Andy Pettitte	1.50
15	Ivan Rodriguez	2.50
16	Alex Rodriguez	8.00

17	Mark McGwire	8.00
18	Andres Galarraga	1.00
19	Hideo Nomo	2.00
20	Mo Vaughn	1.00
21	Randy Johnson	3.50
22	Chipper Jones	5.00
23	Greg Maddux	5.00
24	Manny Ramirez	3.50
25	Tony Gwynn	5.00
26	Albert Belle	1.00
27	Kenny Lofton	1.00
28	Mike Piazza	6.00
29	Paul Molitor	3.50
30	Barry Bonds	10.00

Tins

Donruss Preferred was packaged in collectible tins. Each tin contained five cards and featured one of 24 players on the top. Silver (numbered to 999) and gold (199) parallel tins were also produced and included in hobby-only boxes. The values shown are for empty tins.

		NM/M
Complete Set (24):		17.50
Common Player:		.25
Gold Tins (199):		3X
Silver Tins (999):		1.5X
1	Todd Helton	.65
2	Ben Grieve	.25
3	Cal Ripken Jr.	2.50
4	Alex Rodriguez	2.00
5	Greg Maddux	1.00
6	Mike Piazza	1.50
7	Chipper Jones	1.00
8	Travis Lee	.25
9	Derek Jeter	2.50
10	Jeff Bagwell	.75
11	Juan Gonzalez	.50
12	Mark McGwire	2.00
13	Hideo Nomo	.50
14	Roger Clemens	1.25
15	Andruw Jones	.75
16	Paul Molitor	.75
17	Vladimir Guerrero	.75
18	Jose Cruz Jr.	.25
19	Nomar Garciaparra	1.00
20	Scott Rolen	.65
21	Ken Griffey Jr.	1.50
22	Larry Walker	.25
23	Frank Thomas	.75
24	Tony Gwynn	1.00

1998 Donruss Preferred Double-Wide Tins

Double-wide flip-top tins of Donruss Preferred cards were a reail exclusive with a price tag of about $6. The double-wide retail tins use the same player checklist and photo as the green hobby-version single tins, but have predominantly blue color. Values shown are for opened tins.

		NM/M
Complete Set (12):		12.00
Common Tin:		.65
1	Todd Helton, Ben Grieve	.65
2	Cal Ripken Jr., Alex Rodriguez	2.00
3	Greg Maddux, Mike Piazza	1.25
4	Chipper Jones, Travis Lee	1.00
5	Derek Jeter, Jeff Bagwell	2.00
6	Juan Gonzalez, Mark McGwire	1.50
7	Hideo Nomo, Roger Clemens	.75
8	Andruw Jones, Paul Molitor	.75
9	Vladimir Guerrero, Jose Cruz Jr.	.75
10	Nomar Garciaparra, Scott Rolen	1.00
11	Ken Griffey Jr., Larry Walker	1.25
12	Tony Gwynn, Frank Thomas	1.00

1998 Donruss Preferred Tin Boxes

The boxes for 1998 Donruss Preferred consisted of a lithographed steel lidded box which contained 24 tin packs. The basic tin box was green in color and individually serial numbered to 999. A parallel gold box issue was randomly inserted in Preferred cases and had boxes numbered to 199. Values shown are for empty boxes.

		NM/M
Complete Set (24):		85.00
Common Player:		1.00
Gold:		1.5X
1	Todd Helton	2.50
2	Ben Grieve	1.00
3	Cal Ripken Jr.	10.00
4	Alex Rodriguez	7.50
5	Greg Maddux	5.00
6	Mike Piazza	6.00
7	Chipper Jones	5.00
8	Travis Lee	1.00
9	Derek Jeter	10.00
10	Jeff Bagwell	3.00
11	Juan Gonzalez	1.50
12	Mark McGwire	7.50
13	Hideo Nomo	1.50
14	Roger Clemens	3.00
15	Andruw Jones	3.00
16	Paul Molitor	3.00
17	Vladimir Guerrero	3.00
18	Jose Cruz Jr.	1.00
19	Nomar Garciaparra	5.00
20	Scott Rolen	2.00
21	Ken Griffey Jr.	6.00
22	Larry Walker	1.00
23	Frank Thomas	5.00
24	Tony Gwynn	5.00

Signature Series Preview Autographs

This insert was a surprise addition to Donruss Update. The set features autographs from top rookies and stars. The number of cards produced varies for each player. The card fronts have a color player photo in front of a gold checkered border with the signature in a white area near the bottom. Cards of a number of players (Alou, Casey, Jenkins, Wilson, etc.) were never officially released, having been returned too late by the players; specimens, have, however made their way into the hobby market in unknown numbers.

		NM/M
Common Player:		10.00
(1)	Sandy Alomar Jr./96	30.00
(2)	Moises Alou	10.00
(3)	Andy Benes/135	15.00
(4)	Russell Branyan/188	15.00
(5)	Sean Casey	85.00
(6)	Tony Clark/188	15.00
(7)	Juan Encarnacion/193	15.00
(8)	Brad Fullmer/396	10.00
(9)	Juan Gonzalez/108	115.00
(10)	Ben Grieve/100	35.00
(11)	Todd Helton/101	50.00
(12)	Richard Hidalgo/380	10.00
(13)	A.J. Hinch/400	10.00
(14)	Damian Jackson/15	65.00
(15)	Geoff Jenkins	185.00
(16)	Derek Jeter	1,225
(17)	Chipper Jones/112	125.00
(18)	Chuck Knoblauch/98	50.00
(19)	Travis Lee/101	20.00
(20)	Mike Lowell/450	15.00
(21)	Greg Maddux/92	165.00
(22)	Kevin Millwood/395	30.00
(23)	Magglio Ordonez/420	50.00

(24)	David Ortiz/393	75.00
(25)	Rafael Palmeiro/107	50.00
(26)	Cal Ripken Jr./22	850.00
(27)	Alex Rodriguez/23	1,150
(28)	Curt Schilling/100	100.00
(29)	Randall Simon/380	10.00
(30)	Fernando Tatis/400	10.00
(31)	Miguel Tejada/375	40.00
(32)	Robin Ventura/95	30.00
(33)	Dan Wilson	85.00
(34)	Kerry Wood/373	40.00

1998 Donruss Signature Series

The 140-card base set has a white border encasing the player photo with the logo stamped with silver foil. Card backs have a small photo and complete year-by-year statistics. Signature Proofs are a parallel to the base set utilizing holo-foil treatment and "Signature Proof" written down the left edge of the card front. Each card is numbered "1 of 150" on the card back.

		NM/M
Complete Set (140):		30.00
Common Player:		.10
Signature Proofs:		12X
Pack (5):		12.50
Wax Box (12):		150.00
1	David Justice	.10
2	Derek Jeter	2.50
3	Nomar Garciaparra	1.00
4	Ryan Klesko	.10
5	Jeff Bagwell	.75
6	Dante Bichette	.10
7	Ivan Rodriguez	.65
8	Albert Belle	.10
9	Cal Ripken Jr.	2.50
10	Craig Biggio	.10
11	Barry Larkin	.10
12	Jose Guillen	.10
13	Will Clark	.10
14	J.T. Snow	.10
15	Chuck Knoblauch	.10
16	Todd Walker	.10
17	Scott Rolen	.60
18	Rickey Henderson	.75
19	Juan Gonzalez	.40
20	Justin Thompson	.10
21	Roger Clemens	1.25
22	Ray Lankford	.10
23	Jose Cruz Jr.	.10
24	Ken Griffey Jr.	1.50
25	Andruw Jones	.75
26	Darin Erstad	.30
27	Jim Thome	.50
28	Wade Boggs	1.00
29	Ken Caminiti	.10
30	Todd Hundley	.10
31	Mike Piazza	1.50
32	Sammy Sosa	1.00
33	Larry Walker	.10
34	Matt Williams	.10
35	Frank Thomas	.75
36	Gary Sheffield	.30
37	Alex Rodriguez	2.00
38	Hideo Nomo	.40
39	Kenny Lofton	.10
40	John Smoltz	.10
41	Mo Vaughn	.10
42	Edgar Martinez	.10
43	Paul Molitor	.75
44	Rafael Palmeiro	.65
45	Barry Bonds	2.50
46	Vladimir Guerrero	.75
47	Carlos Delgado	.50
48	Bobby Higginson	.10
49	Greg Maddux	1.00
50	Jim Edmonds	.10
51	Randy Johnson	.75
52	Mark McGwire	2.00
53	Rondell White	.10
54	Raul Mondesi	.10
55	Manny Ramirez	.75
56	Pedro Martinez	.75
57	Tim Salmon	.10
58	Moises Alou	.10
59	Fred McGriff	.10
60	Garret Anderson	.10
61	Sandy Alomar Jr.	.10
62	Chan Ho Park	.10
63	Mark Kotsay	.10
64	Mike Mussina	.50

65	Tom Glavine	.25
66	Tony Clark	.10
67	Mark Grace	.10
68	Tony Gwynn	.10
69	Tino Martinez	.10
70	Kevin Brown	.10
71	Todd Greene	.10
72	Andy Pettitte	.30
73	Livan Hernandez	.10
74	Curt Schilling	.25
75	Andres Galarraga	.10
76	Rusty Greer	.10
77	Jay Buhner	.10
78	Bobby Bonilla	.10
79	Chipper Jones	1.00
80	Eric Young	.10
81	Jason Giambi	.50
82	Javy Lopez	.10
83	Roberto Alomar	.25
84	Bernie Williams	.10
85	A.J. Hinch	.10
86	Kerry Wood	.40
87	Juan Encarnacion	.10
88	Brad Fullmer	.10
89	Ben Grieve	.10
90	Magglio Ordonez RC	2.00
91	Todd Helton	.65
92	Richard Hidalgo	.15
93	Paul Konerko	.15
94	Aramis Ramirez	.10
95	Ricky Ledee	.10
96	Derek Lee	.50
97	Travis Lee	.15
98	Matt Anderson RC	.25
99	Jaret Wright	.10
100	David Ortiz	.35
101	Carl Pavano	.10
102	Orlando Hernandez RC	.50
103	Fernando Tatis	.10
104	Miguel Tejada	.30
105	Rolando Arrojo RC	.50
106	Kevin Millwood RC	.50
107	Ken Griffey Jr. (Checklist)	.50
108	Frank Thomas (Checklist)	.30
109	Cal Ripken Jr. (Checklist)	.75
110	Greg Maddux (Checklist)	.40
111	John Olerud	.10
112	David Cone	.10
113	Vinny Castilla	.10
114	Jason Kendall	.10
115	Brian Jordan	.10
116	Hideki Irabu	.10
117	Bartolo Colon	.10
118	Greg Vaughn	.10
119	David Segui	.10
120	Bruce Chen	.10
121	Julio Ramirez RC	.10
122	Troy Glaus RC	4.00
123	Jeremy Giambi RC	.50
124	Ryan Minor RC	.15
125	Richie Sexson	.10
126	Dermal Brown	.10
127	Adrian Beltre	.15
128	Eric Chavez	.30
129	J.D. Drew RC	4.00
130	Gabe Kapler RC	.30
131	Masato Yoshii RC	.25
132	Mike Lowell RC	2.00
133	Jim Parque RC	.25
134	Roy Halladay	.10
135	Carlos Lee RC	1.00
136	Jin Ho Cho RC	.25
137	Michael Barrett	.10
138	Fernando Seguignol RC	.40
139	Odalis Perez RC	.10
140	Mark McGwire (Checklist)	.65

Proofs

This parallel set differs from the regular issue Signature Series base cards in the presence at leftfront of a vertical stack of gold refractive foil strips on which SIGNATURE PROOF is spelled out. Also, backs of the proofs have a gold, rather than white, background.

	NM/M
Complete Set (140):	450.00
Common Player:	1.00
Stars/Rookies:	12X

1998 Donruss Signature Series Autographs Samples

An unknown number of cards can be found with facsimile signatures on front and a "SAMPLE" overprint on back.

SAMPLE

Will remains one of the game's premier hitters as he enters his 13th big-league season. His .302 career batting average ranks sixth best among active major-leaguers with at least 1,500 hits while his on-base percentage of .381 ranks 10th best in baseball.

	NM/M
Adrian Beltre (Century)	12.50
Will Clark (Century)	12.50
Travis Lee (Red)	3.00

Autographs (Red)

Autographs were inserted one per pack and feature the player photo over a silver and red foil background. The featured player's autograph appears on the bottom portion on front with the Donruss logo stamped in gold foil. Autographs are un-numbered. The first 100 cards signed by each player are blue, sequentially numbered and designated as "Century Marks." The next 1,000 signed are green, sequentially numbered and designated as "Millennium Marks." Greg Maddux signed only 12 regular Donruss Signature Autographs.

		NM/M
Common Player:		2.50
(1)	Roberto Alomar/150	35.00
(2)	Sandy Alomar Jr./700	10.00
(3)	Moises Alou/900	15.00
(4)	Gabe Alvarez/2,900	4.00
(5)	Wilson Alvarez/1,600	4.00
(6)	Jay Bell/1,500	4.00
(7)	Adrian Beltre/1,900	25.00
(8)	Andy Benes/2,600	4.00
(9)	Aaron Boone/3,400	8.00
(10)	Russell Branyan/1,650	4.00
(11)	Orlando Cabrera/3,100	8.00
(12)	Mike Cameron/1,150	8.00
(13)	Joe Carter/400	10.00
(14)	Sean Casey/2,275	8.00
(15)	Bruce Chen/150	5.00
(16)	Tony Clark/2,275	5.00
(17)	Will Clark/1,400	15.00
(18)	Matt Clement/1,400	4.00
(19)	Pat Cline/400	5.00
(20)	Ken Cloude/3,400	2.50
(21)	Michael Coleman/2,800	2.50
(22)	David Cone/3,400	50.00
(23)	Jeff Conine/1,400	5.00
(24)	Jacob Cruz/3,200	2.50
(25)	Russ Davis/3,500	2.50
(26)	Jason Dickson/1,400	4.00
(27)	Todd Dunwoody/3,500	2.50
(28)	Juan Encarnacion/3,400	5.00
(29)	Darin Erstad/700	10.00
(30)	Bobby Estalella/3,400	4.00
(31)	Jeff Fassero/3,400	2.50
(32)	John Franco/1,800	2.50
(33)	Brad Fullmer/3,100	5.00
(34)	Jason Giambi/3,100	15.00
(35)	Derrick Gibson/1,200	5.00
(36)	Todd Greene/1,400	5.00
(37)	Ben Grieve/1,400	5.00
(38)	Mark Grudzielanek/3,200	4.00
(39)	Vladimir Guerrero/2,100	25.00
(40)	Wilton Guerrero/1,900	4.00
(41)	Jose Guillen/2,400	5.00
(42)	Todd Helton/1,300	20.00
(43)	Richard Hidalgo/3,100	4.00
(44)	A.J. Hinch/2,900	4.00
(45)	Butch Huskey/1,900	4.00
(46)	Raul Ibanez/3,300	2.50
(47)	Damian Jackson/1,400	4.00
(48)	Geoff Jenkins/3,100	6.00
(49)	Eric Karros/650	8.00
(50)	Ryan Klesko/400	8.00

(51)	Mark Kotsay/3,600	5.00
(52)	Ricky Ledee/2,200	5.00
(53)	Derrek Lee/3,400	15.00
(54)	Travis Lee/150	10.00
(54s)	Travis Lee (Facsimile autograph, "SAMPLE" on back.)	3.00
(55)	Javier Lopez/650	8.00
(56)	Mike Lowell/3,500	10.00
(57)	Greg Maddux/12	625.00
(58)	Eli Marrero/3,400	5.00
(59)	Al Martin/1,300	4.00
(60)	Rafael Medina/1,400	2.50
(61)	Scott Morgan/900	4.50
(62)	Abraham Nunez/3,500	2.50
(63)	Paul O'Neill/1,000	20.00
(64)	Luis Ordaz/2,700	2.50
(65)	Magglio Ordonez/3,200	15.00
(66)	Kevin Orie/1,350	5.00
(67)	David Ortiz/3,400	25.00
(68)	Rafael Palmeiro/1,000	25.00
(69)	Carl Pavano/2,600	5.00
(70)	Neifi Perez/3,300	2.50
(71)	Dante Powell/3,050	2.50
(72)	Aramis Ramirez/2,800	10.00
(73)	Mariano Rivera/900	35.00
(74)	Felix Rodriguez/1,400	3.00
(75)	Henry Rodriguez/3,400	3.00
(76)	Scott Rolen/1,900	30.00
(77)	Brian Rose/1,400	3.00
(78)	Curt Schilling/3,400	30.00
(79)	Richie Sexson/3,500	8.00
(80)	Randall Simon/3,500	3.00
(81)	J.T. Snow/400	10.00
(82)	Jeff Suppan/1,400	5.00
(83)	Fernando Tatis/3,900	3.00
(84)	Miguel Tejada/3,800	15.00
(85)	Brett Tomko/3,400	2.50
(86)	Bubba Trammell/3,900	2.50
(87)	Ismael Valdez/1,900	5.00
(88)	Robin Ventura/1,400	5.00
(89)	Billy Wagner/3,900	10.00
(90)	Todd Walker/1,900	5.00
(91)	Daryle Ward/400	4.00
(92)	Rondell White/3,400	5.00
(93)	Antone Williamson/3,350	2.50
(94)	Dan Wilson/2,400	4.00
(95)	Enrique Wilson/3,400	2.50
(96)	Preston Wilson/2,100	5.00
(97)	Tony Womack/3,500	2.50
(98)	Kerry Wood/3,500	10.00

Century Marks (Blue)

This 121-card set is a serially numbered, blue-foil parallel of the Autographs insert set and limited to 100 cards signed by each featured player (unless otherwise shown in the checklist). Jason Kendall's cards were never signed or returned to Donruss for packaging. A few have made their way into the hobby.

		NM/M
Common Player:		10.00
(1)	Roberto Alomar	60.00
(2)	Sandy Alomar Jr.	15.00
(3)	Moises Alou	40.00
(4)	Gabe Alvarez	10.00
(5)	Wilson Alvarez	10.00
(6)	Brady Anderson	15.00
(7)	Jay Bell	15.00
(8)	Albert Belle	20.00
(9)	Adrian Beltre	25.00
(10)	Andy Benes	10.00
(11)	Wade Boggs	60.00
(12)	Barry Bonds	250.00
(13)	Aaron Boone	25.00
(14)	Russell Branyan	10.00
(15)	Jay Buhner	10.00
(16)	Ellis Burks	10.00
(17)	Orlando Cabrera	25.00
(18)	Mike Cameron	25.00
(19)	Ken Caminiti	25.00
(20)	Joe Carter	20.00
(21)	Sean Casey	15.00
(22)	Bruce Chen	10.00
(23)	Tony Clark	10.00
(24)	Will Clark	40.00
(25)	Roger Clemens	200.00
(26)	Matt Clement	10.00
(27)	Pat Cline	10.00
(28)	Ken Cloude	10.00
(29)	Michael Coleman	10.00
(30)	David Cone	25.00
(31)	Jeff Conine	10.00

(32)	Jacob Cruz	10.00
(33)	Jose Cruz Jr.	15.00
(34)	Russ Davis	10.00
(35)	Jason Dickson	10.00
(36)	Todd Dunwoody	10.00
(37)	Scott Elarton	10.00
(38)	Darin Erstad	25.00
(39)	Bobby Estalella	10.00
(40)	Jeff Fassero	10.00
(41)	John Franco	10.00
(42)	Brad Fullmer	10.00
(43)	Andres Galarraga	15.00
(44)	Nomar Garciaparra	80.00
(45)	Jason Giambi	40.00
(46)	Derrick Gibson	10.00
(47)	Tom Glavine	75.00
(48)	Juan Gonzalez	50.00
(49)	Todd Greene	10.00
(50)	Ben Grieve	10.00
(51)	Mark Grudzielanek	10.00
(52)	Vladimir Guerrero	75.00
(53)	Wilton Guerrero	10.00
(54)	Jose Guillen	10.00
(55)	Tony Gwynn	80.00
(56)	Todd Helton	60.00
(57)	Richard Hidalgo	10.00
(58)	A.J. Hinch	10.00
(59)	Butch Huskey	10.00
(60)	Raul Ibanez	10.00
(61)	Damian Jackson	10.00
(62)	Geoff Jenkins	10.00
(63)	Derek Jeter	200.00
(64)	Randy Johnson	150.00
(65)	Chipper Jones	120.00
(66)	Eric Karros/50	15.00
(67)	Jason Kendall (Unsigned)	20.00
(68)	Ryan Klesko	10.00
(69)	Chuck Knoblauch	10.00
(70)	Mark Kotsay	10.00
(71)	Ricky Ledee	10.00
(72)	Derrek Lee	25.00
(73)	Travis Lee	15.00
(74)	Javier Lopez	25.00
(75)	Mike Lowell	30.00
(76)	Greg Maddux	150.00
(77)	Eli Marrero	10.00
(78)	Al Martin	10.00
(79)	Rafael Medina	10.00
(80)	Paul Molitor	50.00
(81)	Scott Morgan	10.00
(82)	Mike Mussina	75.00
(83)	Abraham Nunez	15.00
(84)	Paul O'Neill	40.00
(85)	Luis Ordaz	10.00
(86)	Magglio Ordonez	30.00
(87)	Kevin Orie	10.00
(88)	David Ortiz	75.00
(89)	Rafael Palmeiro	75.00
(90)	Carl Pavano	25.00
(91)	Neifi Perez	10.00
(92)	Andy Pettitte	50.00
(93)	Aramis Ramirez	25.00
(94)	Cal Ripken Jr.	200.00
(95)	Mariano Rivera	75.00
(96)	Alex Rodriguez	200.00
(97)	Felix Rodriguez	10.00
(98)	Henry Rodriguez	10.00
(99)	Scott Rolen	70.00
(100)	Brian Rose	10.00
(101)	Curt Schilling	50.00
(102)	Richie Sexson	20.00
(103)	Randall Simon	10.00
(104)	J.T. Snow	10.00
(105)	Darryl Strawberry	40.00
(106)	Jeff Suppan	10.00
(107)	Fernando Tatis	10.00
(108)	Brett Tomko	10.00
(109)	Bubba Trammell	10.00
(110)	Ismael Valdez	10.00
(111)	Robin Ventura	20.00
(112)	Billy Wagner	40.00
(113)	Todd Walker	15.00
(114)	Daryle Ward	10.00
(115)	Rondell White	20.00
(116)	Matt Williams/80	35.00
(117)	Antone Williamson	10.00
(118)	Dan Wilson	15.00
(119)	Enrique Wilson	10.00
(120)	Preston Wilson	15.00
(121)	Tony Womack	15.00
(122)	Kerry Wood	40.00

Millennium Marks (Green)

This is a green-foil parallel version of the Autographs insert set and features 1,000 cards

---

signed by the featured player (unless otherwise shown in the checklist). Cards are not numbered.

		NM/M
Common Player:		3.00
(1)	Roberto Alomar	25.00
(2)	Sandy Alomar Jr.	5.00
(3)	Moises Alou	10.00
(4)	Gabe Alvarez	3.00
(5)	Wilson Alvarez	3.00
(6)	Brady Anderson/800	8.00
(7)	Jay Bell	3.00
(8)	Albert Belle/400	10.00
(9)	Adrian Beltre	3.00
(10)	Andy Benes	3.00
(11)	Wade Boggs/900	20.00
(12)	Barry Bonds/400	150.00
(13)	Aaron Boone	4.00
(14)	Russell Branyan	3.00
(15)	Jay Buhner/400	10.00
(16)	Ellis Burks/900	5.00
(17)	Orlando Cabrera	6.00
(18)	Mike Cameron	5.00
(19)	Ken Caminiti/900	20.00
(20)	Joe Carter	8.00
(21)	Sean Casey	3.00
(22)	Bruce Chen	3.00
(23)	Tony Clark	5.00
(24)	Will Clark	25.00
(25)	Roger Clemens/400	75.00
(26)	Matt Clement/900	8.00
(27)	Pat Cline	3.00
(28)	Ken Cloude	3.00
(29)	Michael Coleman	3.00
(30)	David Cone	10.00
(31)	Jeff Conine	3.00
(32)	Jacob Cruz	3.00
(33)	Jose Cruz Jr./850	5.00
(34)	Russ Davis/950	3.00
(35)	Jason Dickson/950	3.00
(36)	Todd Dunwoody	3.00
(37)	Scott Elarton/900	3.00
(38)	Juan Encarnacion	5.00
(39)	Darin Erstad	25.00
(40)	Bobby Estalella	3.00
(41)	Jeff Fassero	3.00
(42)	John Franco/950	5.00
(43)	Brad Fullmer	3.00
(44)	Andres Galarraga/900	10.00
(45)	Nomar Garciaparra/400	60.00
(46)	Jason Giambi	20.00
(47)	Derrick Gibson	3.00
(48)	Tom Glavine/700	25.00
(49)	Juan Gonzalez	20.00
(50)	Todd Greene	3.00
(51)	Ben Grieve	4.00
(52)	Mark Grudzielanek	3.00
(53)	Vladimir Guerrero	30.00
(54)	Wilton Guerrero	3.00
(55)	Jose Guillen	3.00
(56)	Tony Gwynn/900	30.00
(57)	Todd Helton	20.00
(58)	Richard Hidalgo	3.00
(59)	A.J. Hinch	3.00
(60)	Butch Huskey	3.00
(61)	Raul Ibanez	3.00
(62)	Damian Jackson	3.00
(63)	Geoff Jenkins	3.00
(64)	Derek Jeter/400)	100.00
(65)	Randy Johnson/800	50.00
(66)	Chipper Jones/900	30.00
(67)	Eric Karros	5.00
(68)	Ryan Klesko	5.00
(69)	Chuck Knoblauch/900	10.00
(70)	Mark Kotsay	3.00
(71)	Ricky Ledee	3.00
(72)	Derrek Lee	20.00
(73)	Travis Lee	5.00
(74)	Javier Lopez/800	10.00
(75)	Mike Lowell	10.00
(76)	Greg Maddux/400	85.00
(77)	Eli Marrero	3.00
(78)	Al Martin/950	3.00
(79)	Rafael Medina/850	3.00
(80)	Paul Molitor/900	20.00
(81)	Scott Morgan	3.00
(82)	Mike Mussina/900	15.00
(83)	Abraham Nunez	3.00
(84)	Paul O'Neill/900	20.00
(85)	Luis Ordaz	3.00
(86)	Magglio Ordonez	15.00
(87)	Kevin Orie	3.00
(88)	David Ortiz	40.00
(89)	Rafael Palmeiro/900	30.00
(90)	Carl Pavano	10.00
(91)	Neifi Perez	3.00
(92)	Andy Pettitte/900	20.00
(93)	Dante Powell/950	3.00
(94)	Aramis Ramirez	10.00
(95)	Cal Ripken Jr./375	100.00
(96)	Mariano Rivera	30.00
(97)	Alex Rodriguez/350	75.00
(98)	Felix Rodriguez	5.00
(99)	Henry Rodriguez	3.00
(100)	Scott Rolen	20.00
(101)	Brian Rose	3.00
(102)	Curt Schilling	20.00
(103)	Richie Sexson	8.00
(104)	Randall Simon	3.00
(105)	J.T. Snow	4.00
(106)	Darryl Strawberry/900	40.00
(107)	Jeff Suppan	3.00
(108)	Fernando Tatis	5.00
(109)	Miguel Tejada	40.00
(110)	Brett Tomko	3.00
(111)	Bubba Trammell	3.00
(112)	Ismael Valdes	3.00
(113)	Robin Ventura	5.00
(114)	Billy Wagner/900	10.00
(115)	Todd Walker	4.00
(116)	Daryle Ward	3.00
(117)	Rondell White	5.00
(118)	Matt Williams/820	8.00
(119)	Antone Williamson	3.00
(120)	Dan Wilson	3.00
(121)	Enrique Wilson	3.00
(122)	Preston Wilson/400	10.00
(123)	Tony Womack	3.00
(124)	Kerry Wood	20.00

Significant Signatures

This 18-card autographed set features some of baseball's all-time great players. Each card is sequentially numbered to 2,000. The Sandy Koufax autographs weren't received in time prior to release and was redeemable by sending in the Billy Williams autograph, the collector would then receive both the Williams and Koufax back. Exchange cards were also initially released for Nolan Ryan and Ozzie Smith. Early in the 2000s, a large quantity of the Koufax cards found its way into the hobby market.

	NM/M
Complete Set (18):	425.00
Common Player:	10.00
Ernie Banks	25.00
Yogi Berra	25.00
George Brett	40.00
Catfish Hunter	35.00
Al Kaline	25.00
Harmon Killebrew	25.00
Ralph Kiner	10.00
Sandy Koufax	100.00
Eddie Mathews	25.00
Don Mattingly	50.00
Willie McCovey	25.00
Stan Musial	40.00
Phil Rizzuto (Edition of 1,000.)	20.00
Nolan Ryan	60.00
Nolan Ryan (Exchange card.)	5.00
Ozzie Smith	20.00
Ozzie Smith (Exchange card.)	5.00
Duke Snider	25.00
Don Sutton	12.00
Billy Williams	12.00

Redemption Baseballs

Redemption cards for authentically autographed baseballs were randomly inserted in Donruss Signature Series packs. Baseballs are laser burned with a Donruss seal to ensure authenticity. Every ball, except Ben Grieve's, is serial numbered within the edition limit shown. Signing Bonus redemption cards, no longer valid, are valued about 10 percent of the corresponding ball.

		NM/M
Common Autographed Ball:		15.00
Redemption Card: 10 Percent		
(1)	Roberto Alomar/60	35.00
(2)	Sandy Alomar Jr./60	20.00
(3)	Ernie Banks/12	85.00
(4)	Ken Caminiti/60	20.00
(5)	Tony Clark/60	20.00
(6)	Jacob Cruz/12	20.00
(7)	Russ Davis/60	15.00
(8)	Juan Encarnacion/60	20.00
(9)	Bobby Estalella/60	15.00
(10)	Jeff Fassero/60	15.00
(11)	Mark Grudzielanek/60	15.00
(12)	Ben Grieve/30	20.00
(13)	Jose Guillen/120	20.00
(14)	Tony Gwynn/60	100.00
(15)	Al Kaline/12	75.00
(16)	Paul Konerko/100	15.00
(17)	Travis Lee/100	20.00
(18)	Mike Lowell/60	15.00
(19)	Eli Marrero/60	15.00
(20)	Eddie Mathews/12	80.00
(21)	Paul Molitor/60	65.00

---

(22)	Stan Musial/12	125.00
(23)	Abraham Nunez/12	20.00
(24)	Luis Ordaz/12	20.00
(25)	Magglio Ordonez/12	50.00
(26)	Scott Rolen/60	45.00
(27)	Bubba Trammell/24	25.00
(28)	Robin Ventura/60	20.00
(29)	Billy Wagner/60	20.00
(30)	Rondell White/60	20.00
(31)	Antone Williamson/12	15.00
(32)	Tony Womack/60	15.00

2001 Donruss

	NM/M
Complete Set (220):	
Common Player:	.15
Common Rated Rookie (151-200):	4.00
Production 2001	
Hobby Pack (5):	6.00
Hobby Box (24):	120.00
The Rookies Coupon:	1.00
Inserted 1:72	
Baseball's Best Coupon:	1.00
Inserted 1:720	
Exchange Deadline 11/01/01	
1	Alex Rodriguez	2.00
2	Barry Bonds	2.50
3	Cal Ripken Jr.	2.50
4	Chipper Jones	2.50
5	Derek Jeter	2.50
6	Troy Glaus	.50
7	Frank Thomas	.75
8	Greg Maddux	1.00
9	Ivan Rodriguez	.50
10	Jeff Bagwell	.50
11	Jose Canseco	.40
12	Todd Helton	.50
13	Ken Griffey Jr.	1.50
14	Manny Ramirez	.75
15	Mark McGwire	2.00
16	Mike Piazza	1.50
17	Nomar Garciaparra	.75
18	Pedro Martinez	1.00
19	Randy Johnson	.75
20	Rick Ankiel	.40
21	Ricky Henderson	.75
22	Roger Clemens	1.50
23	Sammy Sosa	.75
24	Tony Gwynn	1.00
25	Vladimir Guerrero	.75
26	Eric Davis	.15
27	Roberto Alomar	.25
28	Mark Mulder	.25
29	Pat Burrell	.40
30	Harold Baines	.15
31	Carlos Delgado	.40
32	J.D. Drew	.40
33	Jim Edmonds	.40
34	Darin Erstad	.25
35	Jason Giambi	.50
36	Tom Glavine	.50
37	Juan Gonzalez	.40
38	Mark Grace	.25
39	Shawn Green	.25
40	Tim Hudson	.25
41	Andruw Jones	.50
42	David Justice	.25
43	Jeff Kent	.25
44	Barry Larkin	.25
45	Pokey Reese	.15
46	Mike Mussina	.40
47	Hideo Nomo	.40
48	Rafael Palmeiro	.50
49	Adam Piatt	.15
50	Scott Rolen	.75
51	Gary Sheffield	.40
52	Bernie Williams	.25
53	Bob Abreu	.40
54	Edgardo Alfonzo	.25
55	Jermaine Clark RC	.15
56	Albert Belle	.25
57	Craig Biggio	.25
58	Andres Galarraga	.15
59	Edgar Martinez	.15
60	Fred McGriff	.25
61	Magglio Ordonez	.40
62	Jim Thome	.50
63	Matt Williams	.25
64	Kerry Wood	.25
65	Moises Alou	.25
66	Brady Anderson	.15
67	Garret Anderson	.25
68	Tony Armas Jr.	.15
69	Tony Batista	.15
70	Jose Cruz Jr.	.15
71	Carlos Beltran	.50
72	Adrian Beltre	.25

73	Kris Benson	.15
74	Lance Berkman	.50
75	Kevin Brown	.15
76	Jay Buhner	.15
77	Jeromy Burnitz	.15
78	Ken Caminiti	.15
79	Sean Casey	.25
80	Luis Castillo	.15
81	Eric Chavez	.25
82	Jeff Cirillo	.15
83	Bartolo Colon	.15
84	David Cone	.15
85	Freddy Garcia	.15
86	Johnny Damon	.50
87	Ray Durham	.15
88	Jermaine Dye	.15
89	Juan Encarnacion	.15
90	Terrence Long	.15
91	Carl Everett	.15
92	Steve Finley	.15
93	Cliff Floyd	.15
94	Brad Fullmer	.15
95	Brian Giles	.15
96	Luis Gonzalez	.15
97	Rusty Greer	.15
98	Jeffrey Hammonds	.15
99	Mike Hampton	.15
100	Orlando Hernandez	.15
101	Richard Hidalgo	.15
102	Geoff Jenkins	.15
103	Jacque Jones	.15
104	Brian Jordan	.15
105	Gabe Kapler	.15
106	Eric Karros	.15
107	Jason Kendall	.15
108	Adam Kennedy	.15
109	Byung-Hyun Kim	.15
110	Ryan Klesko	.15
111	Chuck Knoblauch	.15
112	Paul Konerko	.40
113	Carlos Lee	.40
114	Kenny Lofton	.15
115	Javy Lopez	.15
116	Tino Martinez	.25
117	Ruben Mateo	.15
118	Kevin Millwood	.15
119	Ben Molina	.15
120	Raul Mondesi	.15
121	Trot Nixon	.15
122	John Olerud	.15
123	Paul O'Neill	.25
124	Chan Ho Park	.25
125	Andy Pettitte	.25
126	Jorge Posada	.25
127	Mark Quinn	.15
128	Aramis Ramirez	.15
129	Mariano Rivera	.40
130	Tim Salmon	.15
131	Curt Schilling	.75
132	Richie Sexson	.40
133	John Smoltz	.40
134	J.T. Snow	.15
135	Jay Payton	.15
136	Shannon Stewart	.15
137	B.J. Surhoff	.15
138	Mike Sweeney	.15
139	Fernando Tatis	.15
140	Miguel Tejada	.40
141	Jason Varitek	.40
142	Greg Vaughn	.15
143	Mo Vaughn	.15
144	Robin Ventura	.15
145	Jose Vidro	.15
146	Omar Vizquel	.15
147	Larry Walker	.15
148	David Wells	.15
149	Rondell White	.15
150	Preston Wilson	.15
151	Brent Abernathy	4.00
152	Cory Aldridge RC	4.00
153	Gene Altman RC	4.00
154	Josh Beckett	8.00
155	Wilson Betemit RC	8.00
156	Albert Pujols/500 RC	250.00
157	Joe Crede	8.00
158	Jack Cust	4.00
159	Ben Sheets/500	40.00
160	Alex Escobar	4.00
161	Adrian Hernandez RC	4.00
162	Pedro Feliz	4.00
163	Nate Frese RC	4.00
164	Carlos Garcia RC	4.00
165	Marcus Giles	4.00
166	Alexis Gomez RC	4.00
167	Jason Hart	4.00
168	Eric Hinske RC	8.00
169	Cesar Izturis	4.00
170	Nick Johnson	4.00
171	Mike Young	4.00
172	Brian Lawrence RC	4.00
173	Steve Lomasney	4.00
174	Nick Maness RC	4.00
175	Jose Mieses RC	4.00
176	Greg Miller RC	4.00
177	Eric Munson	4.00
178	Xavier Nady	4.00
179	Blaine Neal RC	4.00
180	Abraham Nunez	4.00
181	Jose Ortiz	4.00
182	Jeremy Owens RC	4.00
183	Neifi Perez	8.00
184	Corey Patterson	4.00
185	Carlos Pena	6.00
186	Wily Mo Pena	4.00
187	Timo Perez	4.00
188	Adam Pettyjohn RC	4.00
189	Luis Rivas	4.00
190	Jackson Melian RC	4.00

191	Wilken Ruan RC	4.00
192	Duaner Sanchez RC	4.00
193	Alfonso Soriano	8.00
194	Rafael Soriano RC	4.00
195	Ichiro Suzuki RC	60.00
196	Billy Sylvester RC	4.00
197	Juan Uribe RC	4.00
198	Eric Valent	4.00
199	Carlos Valderrama RC	4.00
200	Matt White RC	4.00
201	Alex Rodriguez	2.50
202	Barry Bonds	3.00
203	Cal Ripken Jr.	3.00
204	Chipper Jones	1.00
205	Derek Jeter	2.50
206	Troy Glaus	.50
207	Frank Thomas	.75
208	Greg Maddux	1.50
209	Ivan Rodriguez	.50
210	Jeff Bagwell	.50
211	Todd Helton	.50
212	Ken Griffey Jr.	1.50
213	Manny Ramirez	.75
214	Mark McGwire	1.50
215	Mike Piazza	1.50
216	Pedro Martinez	.75
217	Sammy Sosa	1.00
218	Tony Gwynn	1.00
219	Vladimir Guerrero	.75
220	Nomar Garciaparra	.75

2001 Donruss Baseball's Best

This up-scale version of 2001 Donruss was available to those who not only beat the 1:720 pack insertion odds, but also paid $105 to redeem the "winning" coupon. The boxed set contains 330 cards comprised of the 220-card '01 Donruss base set, the 105-card The Rookies set and the five Rookies Diamond King cards. The cards are printed on a thicker, glossy stock and have a "Baseball's Best" logo foil stamped on front in either bronze, silver or gold. Those redeeming coupons had an apparently random chance of receiving one of 999 bronze sets, 499 silver sets or 99 gold sets. Coupons expired in January 2002.

	NM/M
Complete Set, Bronze (330):	100.00
999 Produced	
Stars:	2-3X
Complete Set, Silver (330):	300.00
499 Produced	
Stars:	2-4X
Complete Set, Gold (330):	550.00
99 Produced	
Stars:	4-8X

All-Time Diamond Kings

	NM/M
Complete Set (10):	150.00
Common Player:	8.00
Production 2,500 Sets	
Studio Series:	2-3X
Production 250	
#9 Undetermined Redemp.	
1a	Frank Robinson	8.00
1b	Willie Mays (Should have been ATDK-9.)	25.00

2	Harmon Killebrew	8.00
3	Mike Schmidt	20.00
4	Reggie Jackson	8.00
5	Nolan Ryan	35.00
6	George Brett	20.00
7	Tom Seaver	10.00
8	Hank Aaron	25.00
10	Stan Musial	20.00

All-Time Diamond Kings Autograph

NM/M
Production 50 Sets

1	Frank Robinson	75.00
1	Willie Mays	200.00
2	Harmon Killebrew	80.00
3	Mike Schmidt	150.00
4	Reggie Jackson	80.00
5	Nolan Ryan	250.00
6	George Brett	200.00
7	Tom Seaver	85.00
8	Hank Aaron	275.00
10	Stan Musial	120.00

Bat Kings

NM/M
Common Card: 10.00
Production 250 Sets

1	Ivan Rodriguez	10.00
2	Tony Gwynn	25.00
3	Barry Bonds	50.00
4	Todd Helton	10.00
5	Troy Glaus	10.00
6	Mike Schmidt	40.00
7	Reggie Jackson	15.00
8	Harmon Killebrew	15.00
9	Frank Robinson	15.00
10	Hank Aaron	75.00

Bat Kings Autograph

NM/M
Production 50 Sets

1	Ivan Rodriguez	75.00
2	Tony Gwynn	120.00
3	Barry Bonds/No Auto.	50.00
3	Barry Bonds/Auto.	200.00
4	Todd Helton	65.00
5	Troy Glaus	65.00
6	Mike Schmidt	150.00
7	Reggie Jackson	100.00
8	Harmon Killebrew	100.00
9	Frank Robinson	100.00
10	Hank Aaron	300.00

2001 Donruss Diamond Kings Hawaii Promo

The first look at the resurrected Donruss brand under Playoff ownership was provided at the 2001 Hawaii trade show where a special promotional Diamond King card was distributed in two versions. The cards feature a Dan Gardiner artwork portrait with gold-foil graphic highlights on front, including a "HAWAII 2001" logo. Cards have a color photo on back. A special autographed version of the card was also created, signed on front and numbered in gold-foil on back from within an edition of 100.

NM/M
HDK-1 Alex Rodriguez 3.00

HDK-1 Alex Rodriguez/Auto. 150.00

2001 Diamond Kings

NM/M
Complete Set (20): 150.00
Common Player: 5.00
Production 2,500 Sets
Studio Canvas Parallel: 1-2X
Production 250

1	Alex Rodriguez	12.50
2	Cal Ripken Jr.	15.00
3	Mark McGwire	12.50
4	Ken Griffey Jr.	15.00
5	Derek Jeter	15.00
6	Nomar Garciaparra	10.00
7	Mike Piazza	10.00
8	Roger Clemens	9.00
9	Greg Maddux	8.00
10	Chipper Jones	8.00
11	Tony Gwynn	8.00
12	Barry Bonds	15.00
13	Sammy Sosa	10.00
14	Vladimir Guerrero	6.00
15	Frank Thomas	6.00
16	Troy Glaus	6.00
17	Todd Helton	6.00
18	Ivan Rodriguez	5.00
19	Pedro Martinez	5.00
20	Carlos Delgado	5.00

2001 Diamond Kings Studio Series Autograph

NM/M
Common Autograph: 50.00
Production 50 Sets

1	Alex Rodriguez	180.00
2	Cal Ripken Jr.	250.00
8	Roger Clemens	150.00
9	Greg Maddux	150.00
11	Chipper Jones	100.00
14	Vladimir Guerrero	100.00
15	Tony Gwynn	80.00
16	Troy Glaus	50.00
17	Todd Helton	60.00
18	Ivan Rodriguez	60.00

Diamond Kings Reprints

NM/M
Complete Set (20): 160.00
Common Player: 5.00
#'d to yr. produced

1	Rod Carew	5.00
2	Nolan Ryan	25.00
3	Tom Seaver	10.00
4	Carlton Fisk	5.00
5	Reggie Jackson	12.00
6	Steve Carlton	5.00
7	Johnny Bench	10.00
8	Joe Morgan	5.00
9	Mike Schmidt	20.00
10	Wade Boggs	15.00
11	Cal Ripken Jr.	25.00
12	Tony Gwynn	15.00
13	Andre Dawson	5.00
14	Ozzie Smith	15.00
15	George Brett	20.00
16	Dave Winfield	10.00
17	Paul Molitor	10.00
18	Will Clark	5.00
19	Robin Yount	10.00
20	Ken Griffey Jr.	17.50

Diamond Kings Reprints Autograph

NM/M
Common Player:

DKR1	Rod Carew/82	40.00
DKR2	Nolan Ryan/82	150.00
DKR3	Tom SeaveR/82	75.00
DKR4	Carlton Fisk/82	65.00
DKR5	Reggie Jackson/83	60.00
DKR6	Steve Carlton/83	40.00
DKR7	Johnny Bench/83	80.00
DKR8	Joe Morgan/83	30.00
DKR9	Mike Schmidt/84	120.00
DKR10	Wade Boggs/84	60.00
DKR11	Cal Ripken Jr./85	180.00
DKR12	Tony Gwynn/86	80.00
DKR13	Andre Dawson/86	35.00
DKR14	Ozzie Smith/87	60.00
DKR15	George Brett/87	120.00
DKR16	Dave Winfield/87	40.00
DKR17	Paul Molitor/88	60.00
DKR18	Will Clark/88	75.00
DKR19	Robin Yount/89	60.00
DKR20	Ken Griffey Jr./89/ No auto.	25.00

Elite Series

NM/M
Complete Set (20): 75.00
Common Player: 2.00
Production 2,500 Sets
Dominators: 5-8X
Production 25 Sets

1	Vladimir Guerrero	4.00
2	Cal Ripken Jr.	10.00
3	Greg Maddux	5.00
4	Alex Rodriguez	8.00
5	Barry Bonds	10.00
6	Chipper Jones	5.00
7	Derek Jeter	10.00
8	Ivan Rodriguez	2.50
9	Ken Griffey Jr.	7.00
10	Mark McGwire	8.00
11	Mike Piazza	7.00
12	Nomar Garciaparra	7.00
13	Pedro Martinez	4.00
14	Randy Johnson	4.00
15	Roger Clemens	6.00
16	Sammy Sosa	7.00
17	Tony Gwynn	5.00
18	Darin Erstad	3.00
19	Andruw Jones	4.00
20	Bernie Williams	2.00

Jersey Kings

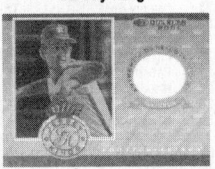

NM/M
Common Card: 25.00
Production 250 Sets

1	Vladimir Guerrero	15.00
2	Cal Ripken Jr.	50.00
3	Greg Maddux	25.00
4	Chipper Jones	15.00
5	Roger Clemens	25.00
6	George Brett	30.00
7	Tom Seaver	15.00
8	Nolan Ryan	50.00
9	Stan Musial	30.00

Jersey Kings Autographs

NM/M
Production 50 Sets

1	Vladimir Guerrero	90.00
2	Cal Ripken Jr.	225.00
3	Greg Maddux	150.00
4	Chipper Jones	100.00
5	Roger Clemens	150.00
6	George Brett	200.00
7	Tom Seaver	75.00
8	Nolan Ryan	200.00
9	Stan Musial	120.00
10	Ozzie Smith	100.00

Longball Leaders

NM/M
Complete Set (20): 50.00

Common Player: 1.00
Production 1,000 Sets
Die-Cut Parallel: 3-5X
#'d to '00 HR Total

1	Vladimir Guerrero	4.00
2	Alex Rodriguez	8.00
3	Barry Bonds	10.00
4	Troy Glaus	4.00
5	Frank Thomas	4.00
6	Jeff Bagwell	4.00
7	Todd Helton	4.00
8	Ken Griffey Jr.	6.00
9	Manny Ramirez	4.00
10	Mike Piazza	6.00
11	Sammy Sosa	6.00
12	Carlos Delgado	2.00
13	Jim Edmonds	1.00
14	Jason Giambi	3.00
15	David Justice	1.00
16	Rafael Palmeiro	3.00
17	Gary Sheffield	2.00
18	Jim Thome	1.00
19	Tony Batista	1.00
20	Richard Hidalgo	1.00

Production Line

NM/M
Complete Set (60): 150.00
Common Player: 1.00
Die-Cut OBP (1-20): 1-2X
Die-Cut SLG (21-40): 1-2.5X
Die-Cut PI (41-60): 1.5-3X
Production 100 Sets

1	Jason Giambi/476	3.00
2	Carlos Delgado/470	2.00
3	Todd Helton/463	3.00
4	Manny Ramirez/457	3.00
5	Barry Bonds/440	15.00
6	Gary Sheffield/438	2.00
7	Frank Thomas/436	3.00
8	Nomar Garciaparra/434	10.00
9	Brian Giles/432	1.00
10	Edgardo Alfonzo/425	.50
11	Jeff Kent/424	.75
12	Jeff Bagwell/424	3.00
13	Edgar Martinez/423	.75
14	Alex Rodriguez/420	10.00
15	Luis Castillo/418	.50
16	Will Clark/418	2.50
17	Jorge Posada/417	2.00
18	Derek Jeter/416	12.00
19	Bob Abreu/416	1.00
20	Moises Alou/416	.75
21	Todd Helton/698	3.00
22	Manny Ramirez/697	3.00
23	Barry Bonds/688	15.00
24	Carlos Delgado/664	2.00
25	Vladimir Guerrero/664	3.00
26	Jason Giambi/647	3.00
27	Gary Sheffield/643	2.00
28	Richard Hidalgo/636	.50
29	Sammy Sosa/634	8.00
30	Frank Thomas/625	3.00
31	Moises Alou/623	.75
32	Jeff Bagwell/615	3.00
33	Mike Piazza/614	8.00
34	Alex Rodriguez/606	10.00
35	Troy Glaus/604	3.00
36	Nomar Garciaparra/599	10.00
37	Jeff Kent/596	.75
38	Brian Giles/594	.75
39	Geoff Jenkins/588	.50
40	Carl Everett/587	.50
41	Todd Helton/1161	3.00
42	Manny Ramirez/1154	3.00
43	Carlos Delgado/1134	2.00
44	Barry Bonds/1128	12.00
45	Jason Giambi/1123	3.00
46	Gary Sheffield/1081	2.00
47	Vladimir Guerrero/1074	3.00
48	Frank Thomas/1061	3.00
49	Sammy Sosa/1040	8.00
50	Moises Alou/1039	1.00
51	Jeff Bagwell/1039	3.00
52	Nomar Garciaparra/1033	10.00
53	Richard Hidalgo/1027	.50
54	Alex Rodriguez/1026	10.00
55	Brian Giles/1026	1.00
56	Jeff Kent/1020	1.00
57	Mike Piazza/1012	8.00
58	Troy Glaus/1008	3.00
59	Edgar Martinez/1002	1.00
60	Jim Edmonds/994	1.00

Rookie Reprints

NM/M
Complete Set (40): 200.00
Common Player: 3.00
#'d to Original Yr. issued

1	Cal Ripken Jr.	20.00
2	Wade Boggs	10.00
3	Tony Gwynn	10.00
4	Ryne Sandberg	10.00
5	Don Mattingly	12.00
6	Joe Carter	3.00
7	Roger Clemens	15.00
8	Kirby Puckett	10.00
9	Orel Hershiser	3.00
10	Andres Galarraga	5.00
11	Jose Canseco	5.00
12	Fred McGriff	3.00
13	Paul O'Neill	3.00
14	Mark McGwire	15.00
15	Barry Bonds	20.00
16	Kevin Brown	3.00
17	David Cone	3.00
18	Rafael Palmeiro	8.00
19	Barry Larkin	3.00
20	Bo Jackson	5.00
21	Greg Maddux	10.00
22	Roberto Alomar	4.00
23	Mark Grace	3.00
24	David Wells	3.00
25	Tom Glavine	4.00
26	Matt Williams	3.00
27	Ken Griffey Jr.	12.00
28	Randy Johnson	8.00
29	Gary Sheffield	5.00
30	Craig Biggio	3.00
31	Curt Schilling	5.00
32	Larry Walker	3.00
33	Bernie Williams	4.00
34	Sammy Sosa	12.00
35	Juan Gonzalez	8.00
36	David Justice	3.00
37	Ivan Rodriguez	6.00
38	Jeff Bagwell	8.00
39	Jeff Kent	3.00
40	Manny Ramirez	8.00

Rookie Reprints Autographs

NM/M
Common Player:
#'d to last 2 digits of yr. issued.

1	Cal Ripken/82	150.00
2	Wade Boggs/83	40.00
3	Tony Gwynn/83	75.00
4	Ryne Sandberg/83	100.00
5	Don Mattingly/84	100.00
6	Joe Carter/84	20.00
7	Roger Clemens/85	200.00
8	Kirby Puckett/85	60.00
9	Orel Hershiser/85	25.00
10	Andres Galarraga/86	30.00
11	Barry Bonds/87	200.00
16	Kevin Brown/87	30.00
17	David Cone/87	30.00
18	Rafael Palmeiro/87	50.00
20	Bo Jackson/87	85.00
21	Greg Maddux/87	150.00
22	Roberto Alomar/88	40.00
24	David Wells/88	25.00
25	Tom Glavine/88	40.00
28	Randy Johnson/89	100.00
29	Gary Sheffield/89	50.00
31	Curt Schilling/89	40.00
34	Juan Gonzalez/90	40.00
36	David Justice/91	40.00
37	Ivan Rodriguez/91	100.00
39	Manny Ramirez/92	100.00

Stat Line Career

NM/M
Cards #1-150 print run 251-400: 3-6X
1-150 p/r 201-250: 4-8X

1-150 p/r 151-200: 4-8X
1-150 p/r 101-150: 5-10X
1-150 p/r 61-100: 10-20X
1-150 p/r 41-60: 20-30X
1-150 p/r 21-40: 25-40X
1-150 p/r 15-20: 30-60X
Common (151-200) p/r 251-400: 1.00
Common (151-200) p/r 151-250: 1.00
Common (151-200) p/r 101-150: 2.00
Common (151-200) p/r 76-100: 2.00
Common (151-200) p/r 31-75: 4.00
Common (151-200) p/r 20-30: 1-2X
cards 201-220 p/r 201-400: 1-2X
201-220 p/r 101-200: 2-4X
201-220 p/r 75-100: 3-5X
201-220 p/r 40-74: 4-8X

156	Albert Pujols/154	150.00
190	Jackson Melian/26	50.00
195	Ichiro Suzuki/106	200.00

Stat Line Season

NM/M
Cards #1-150 print run 151-200: 4-8X
1-150 p/r 101-150: 4-8X
1-150 p/r 76-100: 10-20X
1-150 p/r 51-75: 10-20X
1-150 p/r 36-50: 15-25X
1-150 p/r 21-35: 20-40X
Common (151-200) p/r 151-200: 1.00
Common (151-200) p/r 101-150: 1.00
Common (151-200) p/r 101-150: 1.00
Common (151-200) p/r 76-100: 2.00
Common (151-200) p/r 31-75: 3.00
Common (151-200) p/r 20-30: 1.00
cards 201-220 p/r 151-200: 1-30X
201-220 p/r 101-150: 2-4X
201-220 p/r 75-100: 3-5X
201-220 p/r 40-74: 4-8X

156	Albert Pujols/17	400.00
190	Jackson Melian/73	40.00
195	Ichiro Suzuki/153	150.00

1999 Retro

NM/M
Complete Set (100): 200.00
Common Player: .25
Inserted 1:Hobby Pack
Common (81-100): 3.00
Production 1,999

1	Ken Griffey Jr.	2.00
2	Nomar Garciaparra	2.00
3	Alex Rodriguez	3.00
4	Mark McGwire	3.00

#	Player	Price
5	Sammy Sosa	2.00
6	Chipper Jones	1.50
7	Mike Piazza	2.00
8	Barry Larkin	.50
9	Andruw Jones	1.00
10	Albert Belle	.25
11	Jeff Bagwell	1.00
12	Tony Gwynn	1.50
13	Manny Ramirez	1.00
14	Mo Vaughn	.25
15	Barry Bonds	4.00
16	Frank Thomas	1.00
17	Vladimir Guerrero	1.00
18	Derek Jeter	3.00
19	Randy Johnson	1.00
20	Greg Maddux	1.50
21	Pedro Martinez	1.00
22	Cal Ripken Jr.	3.00
23	Ivan Rodriguez	.75
24	Matt Williams	.25
25	Javy Lopez	.25
26	Tim Salmon	.25
27	Raul Mondesi	.25
28	Todd Helton	1.00
29	Magglio Ordonez	.75
30	Sean Casey	.25
31	Jeromy Burnitz	.25
32	Jeff Kent	.25
33	Jim Edmonds	.25
34	Jim Thome	.25
35	Dante Bichette	.25
36	Larry Walker	.25
37	Will Clark	.50
38	Omar Vizquel	.25
39	Mike Mussina	.50
40	Eric Karros	.25
41	Kenny Lofton	.25
42	David Justice	.25
43	Craig Biggio	.25
44	J.D. Drew	.25
45	Rickey Henderson	1.00
46	Bernie Williams	.50
47	Brian Giles	.25
48	Paul O'Neill	.25
49	Orlando Hernandez	.25
50	Jason Giambi	.50
51	Curt Schilling	1.00
52	Scott Rolen	1.00
53	Mark Grace	.50
54	Moises Alou	.50
55	Jason Kendall	.25
56	Ray Lankford	.25
57	Kerry Wood	.50
58	Gary Sheffield	.75
59	Ruben Mateo	.25
60	Darin Erstad	.25
61	Troy Glaus	1.00
62	Jose Canseco	.50
63	Wade Boggs	1.50
64	Tom Glavine	.50
65	Gabe Kapler	.25
66	Juan Gonzalez	1.00
67	Rafael Palmeiro	.75
68	Richie Sexson	.50
69	Carl Everett	.25
70	David Wells	.25
71	Carlos Delgado	.75
72	Eric Davis	.25
73	Shawn Green	.50
74	Andres Galarraga	.25
75	Edgar Martinez	.25
76	Roberto Alomar	.50
77	John Olerud	.25
78	Luis Gonzalez	.25
79	Kevin Brown	.25
80	Roger Clemens	2.00
81	Josh Beckett	5.00
82	Alfonso Soriano	8.00
83	Alex Escobar	.50
84	Pat Burrell	.50
85	Eric Chavez	.50
86	Erubiel Durazo	.50
87	Abraham Nunez	.50
88	Carlos Pena	2.00
89	Nick Johnson	.50
90	Eric Munson	.50
91	Corey Patterson	.50
92	Wily Mo Pena	.50
93	Rafael Furcal	1.00
94	Eric Valent	.50
95	Mark Mulder	.50
96	Chad Hutchinson	1.00
97	Freddy Garcia	.50
98	Tim Hudson	1.00
99	Rick Ankiel	1.00
100	Kip Wells	.50

1999 Diamond Kings

NM/M

Complete Set (5): 40.00
Common Player: 8.00
Production 2,500 Sets

#	Player	Price
1	Scott Rolen	8.00
2	Sammy Sosa	10.00
3	Juan Gonzalez	8.00
4	Ken Griffey Jr.	10.00
5	Derek Jeter	20.00

1999 Retro Stat Line Career

NM/M

Cards #1-80 print run 251-400: 2-3X
(1-80) p/r 151-250: 2-4X
(1-80) p/r 101-150: 3-6X
(1-80) p/r 76-100: 4-8X
(1-80) p/r 51-75: 5-10X
(1-80) p/r 30-50: 8-15X

#	Player	Print	Price
1	Ken Griffey Jr.	/350	20.00
2	Nomar Garciaparra	/309	20.00
3	Alex Rodriguez	/313	20.00
4	Mark McGwire	/219	25.00
5	Sammy Sosa	/312	12.00
6	Chipper Jones	/297	15.00
7	Mike Piazza	/333	20.00
8	Barry Larkin	/305	5.00
9	Andruw Jones	/273	6.00
10	Albert Belle	/321	2.50
11	Jeff Bagwell	/304	8.00
12	Tony Gwynn	/339	12.00
13	Manny Ramirez	/154	15.00
14	Mo Vaughn	/304	2.50
15	Barry Bonds	/290	12.00
16	Frank Thomas	/286	10.00
17	Vladimir Guerrero	/305	10.00
18	Derek Jeter	/308	25.00
19	Randy Johnson	/336	8.00
20	Greg Maddux	/202	20.00
21	Pedro Martinez	/298	10.00
22	Cal Ripken Jr.	/276	25.00
23	Ivan Rodriguez	/232	8.00
24	Matt Williams	/299	4.00
25	Javy Lopez	/333	2.50
26	Tim Salmon	/179	4.00
27	Raul Mondesi	/295	2.50
28	Todd Helton	/310	8.00
29	Magglio Ordonez	/173	4.00
30	Sean Casey	/269	2.50
31	Jeromy Burnitz	/294	2.50
32	Jeff Kent	/193	5.00
33	Jim Edmonds	/294	5.00
34	Jim Thome	/163	4.00
35	Dante Bichette	/300	2.50
36	Larry Walker	/225	8.00
37	Will Clark	/302	6.00
38	Omar Vizquel	/196	4.00
39	Mike Mussina	/118	10.00
40	Eric Karros	/177	4.00
41	Kenny Lofton	/311	2.50
42	David Justice	/214	5.00
43	Craig Biggio	/318	2.50
44	J.D. Drew	/35	25.00
45	Rickey Henderson	/283	6.00
46	Bernie Williams	/213	6.00
47	Brian Giles	/157	4.00
48	Paul O'Neill	/223	5.00
49	Orlando Hernandez	/313	2.50
50	Jason Giambi	/73	15.00
51	Curt Schilling	/336	2.50
52	Scott Rolen	/220	5.00
53	Mark Grace	/310	6.00
54	Moises Alou	/201	3.00
55	Jason Kendall	/225	2.50
56	Ray Lankford	/225	3.00
57	Kerry Wood	/233	3.00
58	Gary Sheffield	/202	5.00
59	Ruben Mateo	/384	2.50
60	Darin Erstad	/179	8.00
61	Troy Glaus	/218	10.00
62	Jose Canseco	/296	6.00
63	Wade Boggs	/329	8.00
64	Tom Glavine	/331	5.00
65	Juan Gonzalez	/301	8.00
66	Rafael Palmeiro	/314	6.00
67	Richie Sexson	/308	2.50
68	Carl Everett	/209	3.00
69	David Wells	/124	5.00
70	Carlos Delgado	/333	6.00
71	Eric Davis	/342	2.50
72	Shawn Green	/77	15.00
73	Andres Galarraga	/364	4.00
74	Edgar Martinez	/318	4.00
75	Roberto Alomar	/302	5.00
76	John Olerud	/301	2.50
77	Luis Gonzalez	/237	3.00
78	Kevin Brown	/330	2.50
79	Roger Clemens	/295	12.00
80	Alfonso Soriano	/113	15.00
83	Alex Escobar	/181	10.00
84	Pat Burrell	/303	12.00
85	Eric Chavez	/314	2.50
86	Erubiel Durazo	/147	5.00
87	Abraham Nunez	/106	15.00
88	Carlos Pena	/46	25.00
89	Nick Johnson	/259	6.00
90	Eric Munson	/392	6.00
91	Corey Patterson	/117	15.00
92	Wily Mo Pena	/247	6.00
93	Rafael Furcal	/137	20.00
94	Eric Valent	/53	10.00
95	Mark Mulder	/340	4.00
97	Freddy Garcia	/397	6.00
98	Tim Hudson	/17	50.00
99	Rick Ankiel	/222	10.00
100	Kip Wells	/371	2.50

1999 Retro Stat Line Season

NM/M

Cards #1-80 print run 251-400: 2-3X
(1-80) p/r 151-250: 2-4X
(1-80) p/r 101-150: 3-6X
(1-80) p/r 76-100: 4-8X
(1-80) p/r 51-75: 5-10X
(1-80) p/r 30-50: 8-15X

#	Player	Print	Price
1	Ken Griffey Jr.	/56	70.00
2	Nomar Garciaparra	/35	100.00
3	Alex Rodriguez	/42	100.00
4	Mark McGwire	/70	80.00
5	Sammy Sosa	/66	40.00
6	Chipper Jones	/123	30.00
7	Mike Piazza	/191	50.00
8	Barry Larkin	/166	8.00
9	Andruw Jones	/31	30.00
10	Albert Belle	/49	8.00
11	Jeff Bagwell	/164	12.00
12	Tony Gwynn	/148	25.00
13	Manny Ramirez	/145	20.00
14	Mo Vaughn	/40	10.00
15	Barry Bonds	/120	25.00
16	Frank Thomas	/155	15.00
17	Vladimir Guerrero	/38	40.00
18	Derek Jeter	/127	60.00
19	Randy Johnson	/19	75.00
20	Pedro Martinez	/19	80.00
21	Cal Ripken Jr.	/163	40.00
22	Ivan Rodriguez	/186	12.00
23	Matt Williams	/136	8.00
24	Javy Lopez	/106	8.00
25	Tim Salmon	/139	5.00
26	Raul Mondesi	/162	4.00
27	Todd Helton	/25	60.00
28	Magglio Ordonez	/151	4.00
29	Sean Casey	/82	8.00
30	Jeromy Burnitz	/125	5.00
31	Jeff Kent	/128	8.00
32	Jim Edmonds	/115	12.00
33	Jim Thome	/129	5.00
34	Dante Bichette	/122	5.00
35	Larry Walker	/113	15.00
36	Will Clark	/169	10.00
37	Omar Vizquel	/166	4.00
38	Mike Mussina	/175	10.00
39	Eric Karros	/150	5.00
40	Kenny Lofton	/54	10.00
41	David Justice	/151	6.00
42	Craig Biggio	/51	10.00
43	Rickey Henderson	/66	25.00
44	Bernie Williams	/26	30.00
45	Brian Giles	/94	6.00
46	Paul O'Neill	/116	10.00
47	Orlando Hernandez	/12	35.00
48	Jason Giambi	/166	10.00
49	Curt Schilling	/15	40.00
50	Scott Rolen	/31	30.00
51	Mark Grace	/92	15.00
52	Moises Alou	/124	5.00
53	Jason Kendall	/175	4.00
54	Ray Lankford	/154	4.00
55	Kerry Wood	/13	50.00
56	Gary Sheffield	/132	10.00
57	Ruben Mateo	/134	5.00
58	Darin Erstad	/159	10.00
59	Jose Canseco	/46	30.00
60	Wade Boggs	/122	15.00
61	Tom Glavine	/50	50.00
62	Gabe Kapler	/25	20.00
63	Juan Gonzalez	/50	20.00
64	Rafael Palmeiro	/121	10.00
65	Carl Everett	/138	5.00
66	David Wells	/163	5.00
67	Carlos Delgado	/155	10.00
68	Eric Davis	/148	5.00
69	Shawn Green	/100	12.00
70	Andres Galarraga	/44	20.00
71	Edgar Martinez	/102	10.00
72	Roberto Alomar	/166	15.00
77	John Olerud	/22	20.00
78	Luis Gonzalez	/146	5.00
79	Kevin Brown	/18	25.00
80	Roger Clemens	/20	120.00
81	Josh Beckett	/178	10.00
83	Alex Escobar	/27	40.00
85	Eric Chavez	/33	15.00
86	Erubiel Durazo	/19	25.00
87	Abraham Nunez	/95	10.00
88	Carlos Pena	/319	6.00
89	Nick Johnson	/17	50.00
90	Eric Munson	/16	40.00
91	Corey Patterson	/22	40.00
93	Rafael Furcal	/88	20.00
96	Chad Hutchinson	/51	6.00
98	Tim Hudson	/152	15.00
99	Rick Ankiel	/12	40.00
100	Kip Wells	/135	2.50

2000 Retro

NM/M

Complete Set (100): 90.00
Common Player: .25
Common (81-100): 3.00
Production 2,000

#	Player	Price
1	Vladimir Guerrero	1.00
2	Alex Rodriguez	4.00
3	Ken Griffey Jr.	4.00
4	Nomar Garciaparra	1.00
5	Mike Piazza	.25
6	Mark McGwire	2.00
7	Sammy Sosa	1.50
8	Chipper Jones	1.50
9	Jim Edmonds	.50
10	Tony Gwynn	1.00
11	Andruw Jones	.75
12	Albert Belle	.25
13	Jeff Bagwell	.75
14	Manny Ramirez	1.00
15	Mo Vaughn	.25
16	Barry Bonds	4.00
17	Frank Thomas	1.00
18	Ivan Rodriguez	.75
19	Derek Jeter	4.00
20	Randy Johnson	1.00
21	Greg Maddux	1.50
22	Pedro Martinez	1.00
23	Cal Ripken Jr.	4.00
24	Mark Grace	.50
25	Javy Lopez	.25
26	Ray Durham	.25
27	Todd Helton	1.00
28	Magglio Ordonez	.75
29	Sean Casey	.25
30	Darin Erstad	.50
31	Barry Larkin	.50
32	Will Clark	.50
33	Jim Thome	.75
34	Dante Bichette	.25
35	Larry Walker	.50
36	Ken Caminiti	.25
37	Omar Vizquel	.25
38	Miguel Tejada	.75
39	Eric Karros	.25
40	Gary Sheffield	.75
41	Jeff Cirillo	.25
42	Rondell White	.25
43	Rickey Henderson	.75
44	Bernie Williams	.50
45	Brian Giles	.25
46	Paul O'Neill	.50
47	Orlando Hernandez	.25
48	Ben Grieve	.25
49	Jason Giambi	.50
50	Curt Schilling	1.00
51	Scott Rolen	1.00
52	Bobby Abreu	.50
53	Jason Kendall	.25
54	Fernando Tatis	.25
55	Jeff Kent	.25
56	Mike Mussina	.50
57	Troy Glaus	.75
58	Jose Canseco	.50
59	Wade Boggs	1.00
60	Fred McGriff	.25
61	Juan Gonzalez	.75
62	Rafael Palmeiro	.75
63	Rusty Greer	.25
64	Carl Everett	.25
65	David Wells	.25
66	Carlos Delgado	.25
67	Shawn Green	.40
68	David Justice	.25
69	Edgar Martinez	.25
70	Roberto Alomar	.50
71	Jermaine Dye	.25
72	Jermaine Dye	.25
73	John Olerud	.25
74	Luis Gonzalez	.25
75	Craig Biggio	.50
76	Kevin Millwood	.25
77	Kevin Brown	.25
78	John Smoltz	.50
79	Roger Clemens	3.00
80	Mike Hampton	.25
81	Tomas De La Rosa	.25
82	C.C. Sabathia	1.00
83	Ryan Christenson	.25
84	Pedro Feliz	.25
85	Jose Ortiz	.25
86	Xavier Nady	.50
87	Julio Zuleta	.25
88	Jason Hart	.25
89	Keith Ginter	.25
90	Brent Abernathy	.25
91	Timo Perez	.25
92	Juan Pierre	.50
93	Tike Redman	.25
94	Mike Lamb	.50
95	Ben Sheets	1.00
96	Kazuhiro Sasaki	.50
97	Barry Zito	1.00
98	Adam Bernero	.25
99	Chad Durbin	.25
100	Matt Ginter	.25

2000 Diamond Kings

NM/M

Complete Set (5): 35.00
Common Player: 8.00
Production 2,500 Sets
Studio: 1-2X
Production 250 Sets

#	Player	Price
1	Frank Thomas	8.00
2	Greg Maddux	9.00
3	Alex Rodriguez	10.00
4	Jeff Bagwell	8.00
5	Manny Ramirez	8.00

2000 Retro Stat Line Career

NM/M

Cards #1-80 print run 251-400: 2-3X
1-80 p/r 151-250: 2-4X
1-80 p/r 101-150: 3-6X
1-80 p/r 76-100: 4-8X
1-80 p/r 51-75: 5-10X
1-80 p/r 31-50: 8-15X
1-80 p/r 21-30: 15-25X
Common (81-100) p/r 251-400: 1.00
Common (81-100) p/r 151-250: 1.00
Common (81-100) p/r 101-150: 2.00
Common (81-100) p/r 76-100: 2.00
Common (81-100) p/r 31-75: 2.00

2000 Retro Stat Line Season

NM/M

Cards #1-80 print run 251-400: 2-3X
1-80 p/r 151-250: 2-4X
1-80 p/r 101-150: 3-6X
1-80 p/r 76-100: 4-8X
1-80 p/r 51-75: 5-10X
1-80 p/r 31-50: 8-15X
1-80 p/r 21-30: 15-25X
Common (81-100) p/r 151-200: 1.00
Common (81-100) p/r 101-150: 2.00
Common (81-100) p/r 51-80: 2.00

2001 Donruss Classics

NM/M

Common Player: .50
Common SP (101-150): 5.00
Production 585
Common SP (151-200): 3.00
Production 1,755
Pack (6): 12.00
Box (18): 180.00

#	Player	Price
1	Alex Rodriguez	5.00
2	Barry Bonds	3.00
3	Cal Ripken Jr.	4.00
4	Chipper Jones	2.00
5	Derek Jeter	3.00
6	Troy Glaus	.75
7	Frank Thomas	2.00
8	Greg Maddux	2.00
9	Ivan Rodriguez	1.00
10	Jeff Bagwell	2.00
11	Cliff Floyd	.50
12	Todd Helton	1.00
13	Ken Griffey Jr.	2.00
14	Manny Ramirez	2.00
15	Mark McGwire	3.00
16	Mike Piazza	2.00
17	Nomar Garciaparra	2.00
18	Pedro Martinez	1.50
19	Randy Johnson	1.50
20	Rick Ankiel	.50
21	Rickey Henderson	.75
22	Roger Clemens	3.00
23	Sammy Sosa	2.50
24	Tony Gwynn	1.50
25	Vladimir Guerrero	1.50
26	Kazuhiro Sasaki	.50
27	Roberto Alomar	.75
28	Barry Zito	.75
29	Pat Burrell	.75
30	Harold Baines	.50
31	Carlos Delgado	.50
32	J.D. Drew	.50
33	Jim Edmonds	.75
34	Darin Erstad	.50
35	Jason Giambi	1.00
36	Tom Glavine	.75
37	Juan Gonzalez	1.00
38	Mark Grace	.75
39	Shawn Green	.75
40	Tim Hudson	.50
41	Andruw Jones	.75
42	Jeff Kent	.50
43	Barry Larkin	.50
44	Rafael Furcal	.50
45	Mike Mussina	.75
46	Hideo Nomo	.75
47	Rafael Palmeiro	1.00
48	Scott Rolen	1.00
49	Gary Sheffield	.75
50	Bernie Williams	.75
51	Bob Abreu	.50
52	Edgardo Alfonzo	.50
53	Edgar Martinez	.50
54	Magglio Ordonez	.75
55	Kerry Wood	.75
56	Adrian Beltre	.50
57	Lance Berkman	.75
58	Kevin Brown	.75
59	Sean Casey	.75
60	Eric Chavez	.75
61	Bartolo Colon	.50
62	Johnny Damon	.50
63	Jermaine Dye	.50
64	Juan Encarnacion	.50
65	Carl Everett	.50
66	Brian Giles	.75
67	Mike Hampton	.50
68	Richard Hidalgo	.50
69	Geoff Jenkins	.75
70	Jacque Jones	.50
71	Jason Kendall	.50
72	Ryan Klesko	.50
73	Chan Ho Park	.50
74	Richie Sexson	.75
75	Mike Sweeney	.50
76	Fernando Tatis	.50
77	Miguel Tejada	.50
78	Jose Vidro	.50
79	Larry Walker	.75
80	Preston Wilson	.50
81	Craig Biggio	.75
82	Fred McGriff	.50
83	Jim Thome	1.00
84	Garret Anderson	.75
85	Russell Branyan	.50
86	Tony Batista	.50
87	Terrence Long	.50
88	Brad Fullmer	.50
89	Rusty Greer	.50
90	Orlando Hernandez	.50
91	Gabe Kapler	.50
92	Paul Konerko	.50
93	Carlos Lee	.50
94	Kenny Lofton	.75
95	Raul Mondesi	.50
96	Jorge Posada	.75
97	Tim Salmon	.75
98	Greg Maddux	.75
99	Mo Vaughn	.50
100	Omar Vizquel	.50
101	Aubrey Huff	5.00
102	Jimmy Rollins	5.00
103	Cory Aldridge RC	5.00
104	Wilmy Caceres RC	5.00
105	Josh Beckett	6.00
106	Wilson Betemit RC	5.00
107	Timo Perez	5.00
108	Albert Pujols RC	240.00
109	Bud Smith RC	5.00
110	Jack Wilson RC	10.00
111	Alex Escobar	5.00
112	Johnny Estrada RC	10.00
113	Pedro Feliz	5.00
114	Nate Frese RC	5.00
115	Carlos Garcia	5.00
116	Brandon Larson RC	5.00
117	Alexis Gomez RC	5.00
118	Jason Hart	5.00
119	Adam Dunn	5.00
120	Marcus Giles	5.00
121	Christian Parker RC	5.00
122	Jackson Melian RC	5.00
123	Eric Chavez	5.00
124	Adrian Hernandez RC	5.00
125	Joe Kennedy RC	5.00
126	Jose Mieses RC	5.00
127	C.C. Sabathia	5.00
128	Eric Munson	5.00
129	Xavier Nady	5.00
130	Horacio Ramirez RC	10.00
131	Abraham Nunez	5.00
132	Jose Ortiz	5.00
133	Jeremy Owens RC	5.00
134	Claudio Vargas RC	5.00
135	Corey Patterson	5.00
136	Audres Torres RC	5.00
137	Ben Sheets	5.00

138	Joe Crede	5.00
139	Adam Pettyjohn RC	5.00
140	Elpidio Guzman RC	5.00
141	Jay Gibbons RC	10.00
142	Wilkin Ruan RC	5.00
143	Tsuyoshi Shinjo RC	10.00
144	Alfonso Soriano RC	5.00
145	Nick Johnson RC	5.00
146	Ichiro Suzuki RC	80.00
147	Juan Uribe RC	5.00
148	Jack Cust	5.00
149	Carlos Valderrama RC	5.00
150	Matt White RC	5.00
151	Hank Aaron	10.00
152	Ernie Banks	4.00
153	Johnny Bench	6.00
154	George Brett	10.00
155	Lou Brock	3.00
156	Rod Carew	3.00
157	Steve Carlton	3.00
158	Bob Feller	3.00
159	Bob Gibson	5.00
160	Reggie Jackson	5.00
161	Al Kaline	6.00
162	Sandy Koufax	600.00
163	Don Mattingly	10.00
164	Willie Mays	10.00
165	Willie McCovey	3.00
166	Joe Morgan	3.00
167	Stan Musial	8.00
168	Jim Palmer	3.00
169	Brooks Robinson	3.00
170	Frank Robinson	3.00
171	Nolan Ryan	15.00
172	Mike Schmidt	10.00
173	Tom Seaver	5.00
174	Warren Spahn	4.00
175	Robin Yount	5.00
176	Wade Boggs	4.00
177	Ty Cobb	10.00
178	Lou Gehrig	10.00
179	Luis Aparicio	3.00
180	Babe Ruth	15.00
181	Ryne Sandberg	10.00
182	Yogi Berra	5.00
183	Roberto Clemente	10.00
184	Eddie Murray	5.00
185	Robin Roberts	3.00
186	Duke Snider	5.00
187	Orlando Cepeda	3.00
188	Billy Williams	3.00
189	Juan Marichal	3.00
190	Harmon Killebrew	5.00
191	Kirby Puckett	8.00
192	Carlton Fisk	4.00
193	Dave Winfield	3.00
194	Whitey Ford	4.00
195	Paul Molitor	3.00
196	Tony Perez	3.00
197	Ozzie Smith	6.00
198	Ralph Kiner	3.00
199	Fergie Jenkins	3.00
200	Phil Rizzuto	4.00

Timeless Tributes

Stars (1-100):	4-8X
SP's (101-150):	1-1.5X
SP's (151-200):	1-2.5X
Production 100 Sets	

Benchmarks

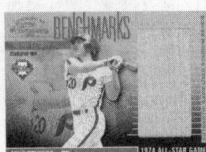

		NM/M
Common Player:		5.00
Inserted 1:18		
1	Todd Helton	5.00
2	Roberto Clemente	40.00
3	Mark McGwire	30.00
4	Barry Bonds	40.00
5	Bob Gibson	10.00
6	Ken Griffey Jr.	20.00
7	Frank Robinson	8.00
8	Greg Maddux	15.00
9	Reggie Jackson	10.00
10	Sammy Sosa	20.00
11	Willie Stargell	8.00
12	Vladimir Guerrero	8.00
13	Johnny Bench	15.00

14	Tony Gwynn	10.00
15	Mike Schmidt	17.50
16	Ivan Rodriguez	6.00
17	Jeff Bagwell	8.00
18	Cal Ripken Jr.	40.00
20	Kirby Puckett	15.00
21	Frank Thomas	8.00
22	Joe Morgan	5.00
23	Mike Piazza	20.00
25	Andruw Jones	5.00

Benchmarks Autographs

		NM/M
5	Bob Gibson	60.00
7	Frank Robinson	50.00
9	Reggie Jackson	100.00
15	Mike Schmidt	100.00
22	Joe Morgan	50.00
25	Andruw Jones	5.00

Classic Combos

		NM/M
Common Card:		20.00
1	Roberto Clemente	125.00
2	Willie Stargell	25.00
3	Babe Ruth	450.00
4	Lou Gehrig	300.00
5	Hank Aaron	100.00
6	Eddie Mathews	30.00
7	Johnny Bench	40.00
8	Joe Morgan	20.00
9	Robin Yount	45.00
10	Paul Molitor	35.00
11	Steve Carlton	25.00
12	Mike Schmidt	75.00
13	Stan Musial	75.00
14	Lou Brock	20.00
15	Yogi Berra	30.00
16	Phil Rizzuto	25.00
17	Ernie Banks	40.00
18	Billy Williams	20.00
19	Don Mattingly	70.00
21	Jackie Robinson	100.00
22	Duke Snider	30.00
23	Frank Robinson	25.00
24	Brooks Robinson	40.00
26	Willie McCovey	30.00
27	Ryne Sandberg	60.00
29	Harmon Killebrew	40.00
30	Rod Carew	40.00
31	Roberto Clemente, Willie Stargell	200.00
32	Babe Ruth, Lou Gehrig	1,000
33	Hank Aaron, Eddie Mathews	200.00
34	Johnny Bench, Joe Morgan	80.00
35	Robin Yount, Paul Molitor	100.00
36	Steve Carlton, Mike Schmidt	200.00
37	Stan Musial, Lou Brock	150.00
38	Phil Rizzuto, Yogi Berra	100.00
41	Jackie Robinson, Duke Snider	150.00
42	Brooks Robinson, Frank Robinson	75.00
43	Willie McCovey, Orlando Cepeda	60.00
45	Harmon Killebrew, Rod Carew	100.00

Classic Combos Autographs

No pricing due to scarcity.

Legendary Lumberjacks

		NM/M
Common Player:		5.00
Inserted 1:18		
1	Hack Wilson/244	75.00
2	Chipper Jones	10.00
3	Rogers Hornsby/SP/301	85.00
4	Nellie Fox	75.00
5	Ivan Rodriguez	10.00
6	Jimmie Foxx/300	120.00
7	Hank Aaron	50.00
8	Yogi Berra	15.00
9	Ernie Banks/SP/300	50.00
10	George Brett	25.00
11	Ty Cobb/SP/100	150.00
12	Roberto Clemente	125.00
13	Carlton Fisk	5.00
14	Reggie Jackson	10.00
15	Al Kaline	15.00
16	Harmon Killebrew	15.00

17	Ralph Kiner	5.00
18	Roger Maris/SP/275	120.00
19	Eddie Mathews	25.00
20	Ted Williams/SP/300	125.00
21	Willie McCovey	5.00
22	Eddie Murray	10.00
23	Joe Morgan/SP/268	8.00
24	Frank Robinson	10.00
25	Tony Perez	5.00
26	Mike Schmidt	20.00
27	Ryne Sandberg	25.00
28	Duke Snider/SP/300	7.00
29	Billy Williams	5.00
30	Dave Winfield	5.00
31	Robin Yount	10.00
32	Barry Bonds	30.00
34	Stan Musial/SP/300	35.00
35	Johnny Bench/SP/300	20.00
36	Orlando Cepeda	5.00
37	Jeff Bagwell	8.00
38	Frank Thomas	8.00
39	Juan Gonzalez	5.00
40	Cal Ripken Jr.	40.00
41	Rafael Palmeiro	5.00
42	Troy Glaus/SP/100	15.00
43	Manny Ramirez	5.00
44	Paul Molitor	15.00
45	Tony Gwynn	8.00
46	Rod Carew	8.00
47	Lou Brock	8.00
48	Wade Boggs	5.00
49	Babe Ruth/SP	225.00
50	Lou Gehrig/SP	150.00

Legendary Lumberjacks Autographs

		NM/M
No pricing due to scarcity.		
LL24	Frank Robinson	200.00

Significant Signatures

		NM/M
Common Autograph:		5.00
Inserted 1:18		
101	Aubrey Huff	6.00
103	Cory Aldridge	5.00
105	Josh Beckett/SP	30.00
106	Wilson Betemit	5.00
107	Timo Perez	5.00
108	Albert Pujols	600.00
110	Jack Wilson	10.00
111	Alex Escobar	5.00
112	Johnny Estrada	20.00
113	Pedro Feliz	5.00
114	Nate Frese	5.00
115	Carlos Garcia	5.00
116	Brandon Larson	8.00
118	Jason Hart	5.00
119	Adam Dunn/SP	25.00
120	Marcus Giles	8.00
121	Christian Parker	5.00
126	Jose Mieses	5.00
127	C.C. Sabathia	25.00
129	Xavier Nady	8.00
130	Horacio Ramirez	10.00
131	Abraham Nunez	5.00
132	Jose Ortiz	5.00
133	Jeremy Owens	5.00
134	Claudio Vargas	5.00
135	Corey Patterson/SP	20.00
136	Andres Torres	5.00
137	Ben Sheets/SP	25.00
138	Joe Crede	8.00
139	Adam Pettyjohn	5.00
140	Elpidio Guzman	5.00
141	Jay Gibbons	15.00
142	Wilkin Ruan	5.00
144	Alfonso Soriano/SP	40.00
145	Nick Johnson	10.00
147	Juan Uribe	10.00
149	Carlos Valderrama	5.00
151	Hank Aaron/SP	400.00
152	Ernie Banks	35.00
153	Johnny Bench/SP	100.00
154	George Brett/SP	150.00
155	Lou Brock	15.00
156	Rod Carew	25.00
157	Steve Carlton	25.00
158	Bob Feller	15.00
159	Bob Gibson	25.00
160	Reggie Jackson/SP	65.00
161	Al Kaline	40.00
162	Nolan Ryan/SP	150.00
163	Don Mattingly	80.00
164	Willie Mays/SP	160.00
165	Willie McCovey	20.00
166	Joe Morgan	10.00

167	Stan Musial/SP	85.00
168	Jim Palmer	15.00
169	Brooks Robinson	40.00
170	Frank Robinson	20.00
171	Nolan Ryan/SP	150.00
172	Mike Schmidt	75.00
173	Tom Seaver	30.00
174	Warren Spahn	40.00
175	Robin Yount/SP	100.00
176	Wade Boggs/SP	50.00
179	Luis Aparicio	10.00
181	Ryne Sandberg	75.00
182	Yogi Berra	30.00
184	Eddie Murray	50.00
185	Ron Santo	25.00
186	Duke Snider	25.00
187	Orlando Cepeda	10.00
188	Billy Williams	10.00
189	Juan Marichal	15.00
190	Harmon Killebrew	40.00
191	Kirby Puckett/SP	60.00
192	Carlton Fisk	20.00
193	Dave Winfield/SP	50.00
194	Whitey Ford	25.00
195	Paul Molitor/SP	50.00
196	Tony Perez	15.00
197	Ozzie Smith/SP	80.00
198	Ralph Kiner	25.00
199	Fergie Jenkins	10.00
200	Phil Rizzuto	40.00

Stadium Stars

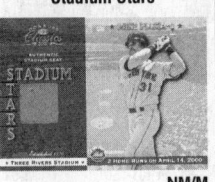

		NM/M
Common Player:		4.00
Inserted 1:18		
1	Babe Ruth	40.00
2	Cal Ripken Jr.	20.00
3	Brooks Robinson	8.00
4	Tony Gwynn	10.00
5	Ty Cobb	25.00
6	Vladimir Guerrero	8.00
7	Lou Gehrig	35.00
8	Nomar Garciaparra	12.00
9	Sammy Sosa	12.00
10	Reggie Jackson	8.00
11	Alex Rodriguez	12.00
12	Derek Jeter	20.00
13	Willie McCovey	4.00
14	Mark McGwire	15.00
15	Chipper Jones	10.00
16	Honus Wagner	10.00
17	Ken Griffey Jr.	12.00
18	Frank Robinson	8.00
19	Barry Bonds	20.00
20	Yogi Berra	8.00
21	Mike Piazza	12.00
22	Roger Clemens	10.00
23	Duke Snider	8.00
24	Frank Thomas	8.00
25	Andruw Jones	8.00

Timeless Treasures

		NM/M
Inserted 1:420		
1	Mark McGwire/Ball	200.00
2	Babe Ruth/Seat	60.00
3	Harmon Killebrew/Bat	30.00
4	Derek Jeter/Base	25.00
5	Barry Bonds/Ball	85.00

2001 Donruss Class of 2001 Samples

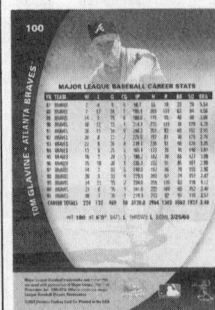

Each February 2002 issue of Beckett Baseball Card Monthly included a sample Donruss Class of 2001 card rubber-cemented inside.

The cards differ from the issued version only in the appearance on back of a (usually) silver-foil "SAMPLE" notation. Some cards were produced with the overprint in gold-foil, in much more limited quantities. The number of different players' cards involved in the promotion is unknown.

	NM/M
Common Player:	.10
Stars:	1.5-2X
Gold:	20X

2001 Donruss Class of 2001

Complete Set (300):	
Common Player:	.20
Common (101-200):	3.00
Production 1,875	
Common (201-300):	3.00
Production 625	
Pack (3):	6.00
Box (24 + Bobble Head):	125.00
1	Alex Rodriguez	2.00
2	Barry Bonds	2.50
3	Vladimir Guerrero	.75
4	Jim Edmonds	.20
5	Derek Jeter	2.50
6	Jose Canseco	.40
7	Rafael Furcal	.20
8	Cal Ripken Jr.	2.50
9	Brad Radke	.20
10	Miguel Tejada	.40
11	Pat Burrell	.50
12	Ken Griffey Jr.	1.50
13	Cliff Floyd	.20
14	Luis Gonzalez	.20
15	Frank Thomas	.75
16	Mike Sweeney	.20
17	Paul LoDuca	.20
18	Lance Berkman	.20
19	Tony Gwynn	1.00
20	Chipper Jones	1.00
21	Eric Chavez	.40
22	Kerry Wood	.35
23	Jorge Posada	.40
24	J.D. Drew	.50
25	Garret Anderson	.20
26	Mike Piazza	1.50
27	Kenny Lofton	.20
28	Mike Mussina	.40
29	Paul Konerko	.20
30	Bernie Williams	.20
31	Eric Milton	.20
32	Shawn Green	.40
33	Paul O'Neill	.20
34	Juan Gonzalez	.35
35	Andres Galarraga	.20
36	Gary Sheffield	.40
38	Ben Grieve	.20
39	Scott Rolen	.60
40	Mark Grace	.20
40	Hideo Nomo	.35
41	Barry Zito	.50
42	Edgar Martinez	.20
43	Jarrod Washburn	.20
44	Greg Maddux	1.00
45	Mark Buehrle	.20
46	Larry Walker	.20
47	Trot Nixon	.20
48	Nomar Garciaparra	1.50
49	Robert Fick	.20
50	Sean Casey	.40
51	Joe Mays	.20
52	Roger Clemens	1.50
53	Chan Ho Park	.20
54	Carlos Delgado	.50
55	Phil Nevin	.20
56	Jason Giambi	.50
57	Raul Mondesi	.20
58	Roberto Alomar	.35
59	Ryan Klesko	.20
60	Andruw Jones	.75
61	Gabe Kapler	.20
62	Darin Erstad	.35
63	Cristian Guzman	.20
64	Kazuhiro Sasaki	.20
65	Doug Mientkiewicz	.20
66	Sammy Sosa	1.50
67	Mike Hampton	.20
68	Rickey Henderson	.75
69	Mark Mulder	.30
70	Mark McGwire	2.00
71	Freddy Garcia	.20
72	Ivan Rodriguez	.60

73	Terrence Long	.20
74	Jeff Bagwell	.20
75	Moises Alou	.20
76	Todd Helton	.65
77	Preston Wilson	.20
78	Pedro Martinez	.75
79	Bobby Abreu	.20
80	Manny Ramirez	.75
81	Jose Vidro	.20
82	Randy Johnson	.75
83	Richie Sexson	.20
84	Troy Glaus	.65
85	Kevin Brown	.20
86	Carlos Lee	.20
87	Adrian Beltre	.30
88	Brian Giles	.20
89	Jermaine Dye	.20
90	Craig Biggio	.20
91	Richard Hidalgo	.20
92	Magglio Ordonez	.20
93	Aramis Ramirez	.20
94	Jeff Kent	.20
95	Curt Schilling	.50
96	Tim Hudson	.40
97	Fred McGriff	.20
98	Barry Larkin	.20
99	Jim Thome	.60
100	Tom Glavine	.40
101	Sean Douglass	3.00
102	Rob Mackowiak RC	3.00
103	Jeremy Fikac RC	3.00
104	Henry Mateo RC	3.00
105	Geronimo Gil RC	3.00
106	Ramon Vazquez RC	5.00
107	Pedro Santana RC	3.00
108	Ryan Jensen RC	3.00
109	Paul Phillips RC	3.00
110	Saul Rivera RC	3.00
111	Larry Bigbie	3.00
112	Josh Phelps	3.00
113	Justin Kaye RC	3.00
114	Kris Keller RC	3.00
115	Adam Bernero	3.00
116	Victor Zambrano RC	3.00
117	Felipe Lopez	3.00
118	Brian Roberts RC	10.00
119	Kurt Ainsworth	3.00
120	George Perez RC	3.00
121	Wilson Guzman RC	3.00
122	Derrick Lewis RC	3.00
123	Nate Teut RC	3.00
124	Martin Vargas RC	3.00
125	Brandon Inge	3.00
126	Travis Phelps RC	3.00
127	Les Walrond RC	3.00
128	Justin Atchley RC	3.00
129	Stubby Clapp RC	3.00
130	Bret Prinz RC	3.00
131	Bert Snow RC	3.00
132	Joe Crede	3.00
133	Nick Punto RC	3.00
134	Carlos Hernandez RC	3.00
135	Ken Vining RC	3.00
136	Luis Pineda RC	3.00
137	Winston Abreu RC	3.00
138	Matt Ginter	3.00
139	Jason Smith RC	3.00
140	Gene Altman RC	3.00
141	Brian Rogers RC	3.00
142	Michael Cuddyer	3.00
143	Mike Penney RC	3.00
144	Scott Podsednik RC	10.00
145	Esix Snead RC	3.00
146	Steve Watkins RC	3.00
147	Orlando Woodards RC	3.00
148	Mike Young	3.00
149	Chris George	3.00
150	Blaine Neal RC	3.00
151	Ben Sheets	3.00
152	Scott Stewart RC	3.00
153	Mike Koplove RC	3.00
154	Kyle Lohse RC	8.00
155	Dee Brown	3.00
156	Aubrey Huff	3.00
157	Pablo Ozuna	3.00
158	Bill Ortega	3.00
159	Toby Hall	3.00
160	Kevin Olsen RC	3.00
161	Will Ohman RC	3.00
162	Nate Cornejo	3.00
163	Jack Cust	3.00
164	Juan Rivera	3.00
165	Jerrod Riggan RC	3.00
166	Dustan Mohr RC	3.00
167	Doug Nickle RC	3.00
168	Craig Monroe RC	3.00
169	Jason Jennings	3.00
170	Bart Miadich RC	3.00
171	Luis Rivas	3.00
172	Tim Christman RC	3.00
173	Luke Hudson RC	3.00
174	Brett Jodie RC	3.00
175	Jorge Julio RC	4.00
176	David Espinosa	3.00
177	Mike Maroth RC	3.00
178	Keith Ginter	3.00
179	Juan Moreno RC	3.00
180	Brandon Knight RC	3.00
181	Steve Lomasney	3.00
182	John Grabow RC	3.00
183	Steve Green RC	3.00
184	Jason Karnuth RC	3.00
185	Bob File RC	3.00
186	Brent Abernathy	3.00
187	Morgan Ensberg RC	5.00
188	Wily Mo Pena	3.00
189	Ken Harvey	3.00
190	Josh Pearce RC	3.00

191	Cesar Izturis	3.00
192	Eric Hinske RC	5.00
193	Joe Beimel RC	3.00
194	Timo Perez RC	3.00
195	Troy Mattes RC	3.00
196	Eric Valent RC	3.00
197	Ed Rogers RC	3.00
198	Grant Balfour RC	3.00
199	Benito Baez RC	3.00
200	Vernon Wells RC	3.00
201	Joe Kennedy RC	3.00
202	Wilson Betemit RC	8.00
203	Christian Parker RC	3.00
204	Jay Gibbons RC	5.00
205	Carlos Garcia RC	4.00
206	Jack Wilson RC	3.00
207	Johnny Estrada RC	5.00
208	Wilkin Ruan RC	3.00
209	Brandon Duckworth RC	5.00
210	Willie Harris RC	5.00
211	Marlon Byrd RC	5.00
212	C.C. Sabathia RC	3.00
213	Dennis Tankersley RC	5.00
214	Brandon Larson RC	5.00
215	Alexis Gomez RC	3.00
216	Bill Hall RC	8.00
217	Antonio Perez RC	3.00
218	Jeremy Affeldt RC	5.00
219	Junior Spivey RC	5.00
220	Casey Fossum RC	5.00
221	Brandon Lyon RC	4.00
222	Angel Santos RC	4.00
223	Lance Davis RC	3.00
224	Zach Day RC	4.00
225	David Williams RC	3.00
226	Cesar Crespo RC	3.00
227	Jose Acevedo RC	3.00
228	Travis Hafner RC	20.00
229	Orlando Hudson RC	10.00
230	Jose Mieses RC	3.00
231	Ricardo Rodriguez RC	3.00
232	Alfonso Soriano	3.00
233	Jason Hart RC	3.00
234	Endy Chavez RC	3.00
235	Delvin James RC	3.00
236	Ryan Drese RC	3.00
237	Jeremy Owens RC	3.00
238	Brad Voyles RC	3.00
239	Nate Frese RC	3.00
240	Josh Beckett RC	3.00
241	Roy Oswalt RC	3.00
242	Juan Uribe RC	5.00
243	Cory Aldridge RC	3.00
244	Adam Dunn RC	3.00
245	Bud Smith RC	3.00
246	Adrian Hernandez RC	3.00
247	Matt Guerrier RC	3.00
248	Jimmy Rollins RC	3.00
249	Wilmy Caceres RC	3.00
250	Jason Michaels RC	3.00
251	Ichiro Suzuki RC	50.00
252	John Buck RC	3.00
253	Andres Torres RC	3.00
254	Alfredo Amezaga RC	3.00
255	Corky Miller RC	3.00
256	Rafael Soriano RC	10.00
257	Donaldo Mendez RC	3.00
258	Victor Martinez RC	40.00
259	Cory Patterson RC	3.00
260	Horacio Ramirez RC	3.00
261	Elpidio Guzman RC	3.00
262	Juan Diaz RC	3.00
263	Mike Rivera RC	3.00
264	Brian Lawrence RC	3.00
265	Josue Perez RC	3.00
266	Jose Nunez RC	3.00
267	Erik Bedard RC	20.00
268	Albert Pujols RC	150.00
269	Duaner Sanchez RC	3.00
270	Cody Ransom RC	3.00
271	Greg Miller RC	3.00
272	Adam Pettyjohn RC	3.00
273	Tsuyoshi Shinjo RC	3.00
274	Claudio Vargas RC	3.00
275	Justin Duchscherer RC	8.00
276	Tim Spooneybarger RC	3.00
277	Rick Bauer RC	3.00
278	Josh Fogg RC	5.00
279	Brian Reith RC	3.00
280	Scott MacRae RC	3.00
281	Ryan Ludwick RC	15.00
282	Erick Almonte RC	3.00
283	Josh Towers RC	5.00
284	Juan Pena RC	3.00
285	David Brous RC	3.00
286	Erik Hiljus RC	3.00
287	Nick Neugebauer RC	3.00
288	Jackson Melian RC	3.00
289	Billy Sylvester RC	3.00
290	Carlos Valderrama RC	3.00
291	Jose Cueto RC	3.00
292	Matt White RC	3.00
293	Nick Maness RC	3.00
294	Jason Lane RC	5.00
295	Brandon Berger RC	3.00
296	Angel Berroa RC	5.00
297	Juan Cruz RC	4.00
298	Dewon Brazelton RC	3.00
299	Mark Prior RC	10.00
300	Mark Teixeira RC	40.00

First Class
Stars (1-100): 5-10X
Production 100

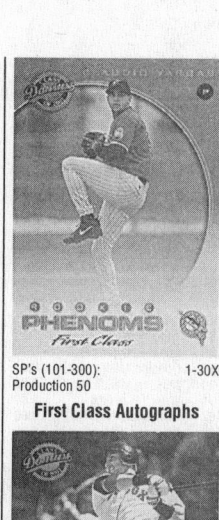

SP's (101-300): 1-30X
Production 50

First Class Autographs

NM/M
Common Player:

10	Miguel Tejada/75	30.00
17	Paul LoDuca/75	20.00
21	Eric Chavez/100	15.00
41	Mark Buehrle/100	20.00
49	Robert Fick/100	10.00
50	Sean Casey/100	10.00
51	Joe Mays/100	10.00
59	Ryan Klesko/50	10.00
69	Mark Mulder/100	10.00
73	Terrence Long/100	10.00
81	Jose Vidro/100	10.00
83	Richie Sexson/100	15.00
84	Troy Glaus/100	20.00
89	Jermaine Dye/100	15.00
91	Richard Hidalgo/100	8.00
93	Aramis Ramirez/100	25.00
96	Tim Hudson/100	25.00

Rookie Autographs

NM/M
Common Autograph: 8.00

109	Paul Phillips/250	8.00
114	Kris Keller/250	8.00
115	Adam Bernero/250	8.00
120	George Perez/250	8.00
123	Nate Teut/250	8.00
124	Martin Vargas/250	8.00
127	Les Walrond/250	8.00
132	Joe Crede/250	10.00
137	Winston Abreu/250	8.00
138	Matt Ginter/250	8.00
140	Gene Altman/250	8.00
142	Michael Cuddyer/250	8.00
143	Mike Penney/250	8.00
146	Esix Snead/250	8.00
147	Orlando Woodards/250	8.00
148	Jeff Deardorff/100	8.00
150	Blaine Neal/250	8.00
156	Aubrey Huff/250	10.00
157	Pablo Ozuna/250	8.00
158	Bill Ortega/250	8.00
160	Kevin Olsen/250	8.00
161	Will Ohman/250	8.00
163	Jack Cust/250	10.00
168	Craig Monroe/250	8.00
169	Jason Jennings/250	8.00
171	Luis Rivas/250	8.00
173	Luke Hudson/250	12.00
176	David Espinosa/250	8.00
177	Mike Maroth/250	8.00
178	Keith Ginter/250	8.00
181	Steve Lomasney/250	8.00
182	John Grabow/250	8.00
184	Jason Karnuth/250	8.00
186	Brent Abernathy/250	8.00
188	Wily Mo Pena/250	15.00
191	Cesar Izturis/250	8.00
192	Eric Hinske/250	10.00
194	Timo Perez/100	8.00
196	Eric Valent/250	8.00
201	Joe Kennedy/100	8.00
202	Wilson Betemit/100	15.00
203	Christian Parker/100	8.00
204	Jay Gibbons/100	20.00
205	Carlos Garcia/200	8.00
206	Jack Wilson/100	15.00
207	Johnny Estrada/200	20.00
208	Wilkin Ruan/200	8.00
209	Brandon Duckworth/100	8.00
211	Marlon Byrd/200	20.00
213	Dennis Tankersley/200	10.00
214	Brandon Larson/200	8.00
215	Alexis Gomez/200	10.00
216	Bill Hall/100	8.00
217	Antonio Perez/200	8.00
218	Jeremy Affeldt/200	10.00
220	Casey Fossum/200	10.00
224	Zach Day/200	8.00
225	David Williams/200	8.00
227	Jose Acevedo/200	8.00
229	Orlando Hudson/100	25.00
230	Jose Mieses/200	8.00
231	Ric Rodriguez/200	8.00
232	Alfonso Soriano/200	40.00
233	Jason Hart/200	8.00
234	Endy Chavez/200	8.00
235	Delvin James/100	8.00
237	Jeremy Owens/200	8.00
238	Brad Voyles/200	8.00
239	Nate Frese/200	8.00
240	Josh Beckett/25	80.00
241	Roy Oswalt/100	25.00
242	Juan Uribe/150	12.00
243	Cory Aldridge/200	8.00
244	Adam Dunn/100	30.00
245	Bud Smith/100	8.00
246	Adrian Hernandez/100	8.00
249	Wilmy Caceres/200	8.00
250	Jason Michaels/200	8.00
252	John Buck/100	15.00
253	Andres Torres/100	8.00
255	Corky Miller/250	8.00
256	Rafael Soriano/100	10.00
257	Donaldo Mendez/200	8.00
259	Corey Patterson/100	15.00
260	Horacio Ramirez/200	8.00
261	Elpidio Guzman/200	8.00
262	Juan Diaz/200	8.00
264	Brian Lawrence/200	10.00
265	Josue Perez/200	8.00
266	Jose Nunez/200	8.00
268	Albert Pujols/100	500.00
269	Duaner Sanchez/200	8.00
271	Greg Miller/200	8.00
272	Adam Pettyjohn/200	8.00
274	Claudio Vargas/200	8.00
279	Brian Reith/200	8.00
283	Josh Towers/100	8.00
285	David Brous/200	8.00
287	Nick Neugebauer/100	8.00
289	Billy Sylvester/200	8.00
290	Carlos Valderrama/200	8.00
292	Matt White/200	8.00
293	Nick Maness/200	8.00
296	Angel Berroa/100	15.00
297	Juan Cruz/100	8.00
298	Dewon Brazelton/100	8.00
299	Mark Prior/100	40.00
300	Mark Teixeira/100	250.00

Aces

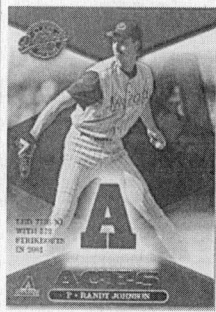

NM/M
Complete Set (20): 70.00
Common Player: 3.00
Inserted 1:30

1	Roger Clemens	12.00
2	Randy Johnson	7.50
3	Freddy Garcia	3.00
4	Greg Maddux	10.00
5	Tim Hudson	5.00
6	Curt Schilling	5.00
7	Mark Buehrle	3.00
8	Matt Morris	3.00
9	Joe Mays	3.00
10	Javier Vazquez	3.00
11	Mark Mulder	4.00
12	Wade Miller	3.00
13	Barry Zito	3.00
14	Pedro Martinez	7.50
15	Al Leiter	3.00
16	Chan Ho Park	3.00
17	John Burkett	3.00
18	C.C. Sabathia	3.00
19	Jamie Moyer	3.00
20	Mike Mussina	5.00

Diamond Aces

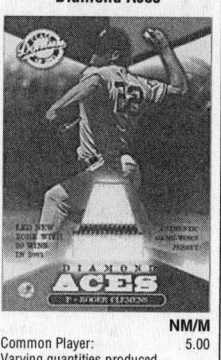

NM/M
Common Player: 5.00
Varying quantities produced.

1	Roger Clemens/200	30.00
2	Randy Johnson/750	10.00
3	Freddy Garcia/350	5.00
4	Greg Maddux/750	20.00
5	Tim Hudson/550	8.00
6	Curt Schilling/525	8.00
7	Mark Buehrle/750	5.00
9	Joe Mays/750	5.00
10	Javier Vazquez/500	5.00
11	Mark Mulder/300	6.00
12	Wade Miller/525	5.00
13	Barry Zito/550	5.00
14	Pedro Martinez/550	15.00
15	Al Leiter/525	5.00
16	Chan Ho Park/400	5.00
17	John Burkett/100	5.00
18	C.C. Sabathia/550	5.00
19	Jamie Moyer/700	5.00

Bobblehead

NM/M
Common Bobblehead: 10.00
One per box.

1	Ichiro Suzuki	40.00
2	Cal Ripken Jr.	40.00
3	Derek Jeter	35.00
4	Mark McGwire	35.00
5	Albert Pujols	40.00
6	Ken Griffey Jr.	20.00
7	Nomar Garciaparra	20.00
8	Mike Piazza	20.00
9	Alex Rodriguez	20.00
10	Manny Ramirez	10.00
11	Tsuyoshi Shinjo	10.00
12	Hideo Nomo	10.00
13	Chipper Jones	15.00
14	Sammy Sosa	20.00
15	Roger Clemens	17.50
16	Tony Gwynn	10.00
17	Barry Bonds	35.00
18	Kazuhiro Sasaki	10.00
19	Pedro Martinez	10.00
20	Jeff Bagwell	10.00
21	Ichiro Suzuki ROY	40.00
22	Albert Pujols ROY	40.00

Bobblehead Cards

NM/M
Common Player: 4.00
1-20 2,000 Produced
21-22 1,000 Produced

1	Ichiro Suzuki	15.00
2	Cal Ripken Jr.	12.00
3	Derek Jeter	12.00
4	Mark McGwire	10.00
5	Albert Pujols	10.00
6	Ken Griffey Jr.	8.00
7	Nomar Garciaparra	8.00
8	Mike Piazza	8.00
9	Alex Rodriguez	8.00
10	Manny Ramirez	8.00
11	Tsuyoshi Shinjo	4.00
12	Hideo Nomo	4.00
13	Chipper Jones	6.00
14	Sammy Sosa	6.00
15	Roger Clemens	7.00
16	Tony Gwynn	6.00
17	Barry Bonds	15.00
18	Kazuhiro Sasaki	4.00
19	Pedro Martinez	5.00
20	Jeff Bagwell	5.00
21	Ichiro Suzuki	15.00
22	Albert Pujols	15.00

Crusade

NM/M
Complete Set (25): 125.00
Common Player: 3.00

1	Roger Clemens/275	15.00
2	Luis Gonzalez/275	3.00
3	Troy Glaus/275	6.00
4	Freddy Garcia/300	3.00
5	Sean Casey/285	5.00
6	Bobby Abreu/300	5.00
7	Matt Morris/300	3.00
8	Cal Ripken Jr./275	25.00
9	Miguel Tejada/285	5.00
10	Vladimir Guerrero/275	8.00
11	Mark Buehrle/100	5.00
12	Mike Sweeney/300	5.00
13	Ivan Rodriguez/275	8.00
14	Jeff Bagwell/275	8.00
15	Joe Mays/250	3.00
16	Cliff Floyd/300	5.00
17	Lance Berkman/300	5.00
18	Aramis Ramirez/100	5.00
19	Tony Gwynn/300	10.00
20	Shannon Stewart/100	5.00
21	Todd Helton/275	8.00
22	Chipper Jones/275	12.00
23	Javier Vazquez/100	5.00
24	Shawn Green/275	5.00
25	Barry Bonds/200	25.00

Rookie Crusade

NM/M
Complete Set (25): 110.00
Common Player: 3.00

26	Albert Pujols/250	30.00
27	Wilson Betemit/100	3.00
28	C.C. Sabathia/290	5.00
29	Roy Oswalt/100	4.00
30	Johnny Estrada/100	3.00
31	Nick Johnson/100	4.00
32	Aubrey Huff/100	3.00
33	Corey Patterson/200	5.00
34	Jay Gibbons/100	4.00
35	Marcus Giles/100	4.00
36	Juan Cruz/100	3.00
37	Tsuyoshi Shinjo/300	3.00
38	Ben Sheets/285	3.00
39	Bud Smith/100	3.00
40	Alex Escobar/100	3.00
41	Joe Kennedy/100	3.00
42	Alexis Gomez/100	3.00
43	Jimmy Rollins/300	3.00
44	Josh Towers/100	3.00
45	Joe Crede/100	3.00
46	Brandon Duckworth/100	3.00
47	Ichiro Suzuki/250	40.00
48	Jose Ortiz/100	3.00
49	Casey Fossum/100	3.00
50	Adam Dunn/200	5.00

Crusade Autographs

NM/M
Common Player:

11	Mark Buehrle/200	10.00
15	Joe Mays/50	10.00
18	Aramis Ramirez/200	8.00
20	Shannon Stewart/200	8.00
23	Javier Vazquez/200	10.00
26	Albert Pujols/50	750.00
27	Wilson Betemit/100	10.00
29	Roy Oswalt/200	12.00
30	Johnny Estrada/200	8.00
31	Nick Johnson/200	12.00
32	Aubrey Huff/200	8.00
33	Corey Patterson/200	10.00
34	Jay Gibbons/200	20.00
35	Marcus Giles/200	8.00
38	Juan Cruz/200	8.00
39	Bud Smith/200	8.00
40	Alex Escobar/200	8.00
41	Joe Kennedy/200	8.00
42	Alexis Gomez/200	10.00
45	Josh Towers/200	8.00
46	Brandon Duckworth/200	12.00
48	Jose Ortiz/200	8.00
49	Casey Fossum/200	12.00
50	Adam Dunn/100	30.00

Dominators

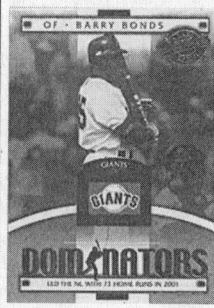

NM/M
Complete Set (30): 90.00
Common Player: 2.00
Inserted 1:20

1	Manny Ramirez	4.00
2	Lance Berkman	2.00
3	Juan Gonzalez	4.00
4	Albert Pujols	10.00
5	Jason Giambi	3.00
6	Mike Sweeney	2.00
7	Rafael Palmeiro	4.00
8	Luis Gonzalez	2.00
9	Ichiro Suzuki	10.00
10	Cliff Floyd	2.00
11	Roberto Alomar	4.00
12	Paul LoDuca	2.00
13	Shannon Stewart	2.00
14	Barry Bonds	10.00
15	Larry Walker	2.00
16	Shawn Green	3.00
17	Moises Alou	2.00
18	Cal Ripken Jr.	10.00
19	Brian Giles	3.00
20	Magglio Ordonez	3.00
21	Jose Vidro	2.00
22	Edgar Martinez	2.00
23	Aramis Ramirez	2.00
24	Tony Gwynn	5.00
25	Richie Sexson	2.00
26	Todd Helton	4.00
27	Garret Anderson	2.00
28	Chipper Jones	5.00
29	Troy Glaus	2.00
30	Jeff Bagwell	4.00

Diamond Dominators

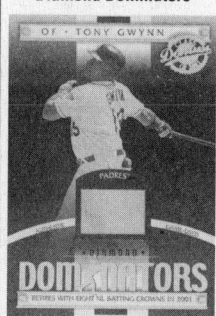

NM/M
Common Player: 4.00
Varying quantities produced.

1	Manny Ramirez/725	8.00
2	Lance Berkman/725	4.00
3	Juan Gonzalez/500	6.00

#	Player	Price
4	Albert Pujols/125	65.00
5	Jason Giambi/250	8.00
6	Mike Sweeney/325	4.00
7	Rafael Palmeiro/550	8.00
8	Luis Gonzalez/725	4.00
10	Cliff Floyd/725	4.00
11	Roberto Alomar/200	8.00
12	Paul LoDuca/600	4.00
13	Shannon Stewart/725	6.00
14	Barry Bonds/250	30.00
15	Larry Walker/725	6.00
16	Shawn Green/500	6.00
17	Moises Alou/550	4.00
18	Cal Ripken/250	50.00
19	Brian Giles/725	8.00
20	Magglio Ordonez/725	5.00
21	Jose Vidro/725	4.00
22	Edgar Martinez/200	6.00
23	Aramis Ramirez/200	5.00
24	Tony Gwynn/500	10.00
25	Richie Sexson/725	6.00
26	Todd Helton/725	8.00
27	Garret Anderson/725	6.00
28	Chipper Jones/725	12.00
29	Troy Glaus/200	8.00
30	Jeff Bagwell/325	8.00

Rewards

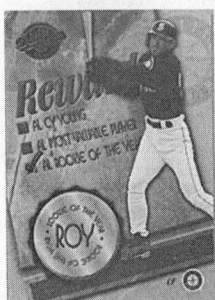

NM/M

Common Player: 5.00
Inserted 1:212

#	Player	Price
1	Jason Giambi	7.50
2	Ichiro Suzuki	40.00
3	Roger Clemens	20.00
4	Freddy Garcia	5.00
5	Ichiro Suzuki	40.00
6	Albert Pujols	30.00
7	Barry Bonds	30.00
8	Albert Pujols	30.00
9	Randy Johnson	10.00
10	Matt Morris	5.00

Final Rewards

NM/M

Common Player: 5.00
Varying quantities produced.

#	Player	Price
1	Jason Giambi/250	10.00
2	Ichiro Suzuki/50	120.00
3	Roger Clemens/200	30.00
4	Freddy Garcia/250	5.00
5	Ichiro Suzuki/50	120.00
6	Albert Pujols/125	60.00
7	Barry Bonds/200	40.00
8	Albert Pujols/125	60.00
9	Randy Johnson/250	15.00

Rookie Team

NM/M

Complete Set (15): 65.00

Common Player: 3.00
Inserted 1:83

#	Player	Price
1	Jay Gibbons	5.00
2	Alfonso Soriano	4.00
3	Jimmy Rollins	3.00
4	Wilson Betemit	3.00
5	Albert Pujols	20.00
6	Johnny Estrada	3.00
7	Ichiro Suzuki	15.00
8	Tsuyoshi Shinjo	4.00
9	Adam Dunn	3.00
10	C.C. Sabathia	3.00
11	Ben Sheets	3.00
12	Roy Oswalt	4.00
13	Bud Smith	3.00
14	Josh Towers	3.00
15	Juan Cruz	3.00

Rookie Team Materials

NM/M

Common Player: 5.00
Varying quantities produced.

#	Player	Price
1	Jay Gibbons/100	8.00
2	Alfonso Soriano/100	15.00
3	Jimmy Rollins/200	5.00
4	Albert Pujols/100	65.00
5	Johnny Estrada/100	5.00
6	Ichiro Suzuki/50	120.00
7	Tsuyoshi Shinjo/200	10.00
8	Adam Dunn/200	8.00
10	C.C. Sabathia/200	5.00
11	Ben Sheets/200	5.00
13	Bud Smith/250	5.00
14	Josh Towers/200	5.00
15	Juan Cruz/200	5.00

Yearbook

NM/M

Complete Set (25): 85.00
Common Player: 2.00
Inserted 1:24

#	Player	Price
1	Barry Bonds	12.00
2	Mark Mulder	3.00
3	Luis Gonzalez	2.00
4	Lance Berkman	2.00
5	Matt Morris	2.00
6	Roy Oswalt	2.50
7	Todd Helton	2.00
8	Tsuyoshi Shinjo	2.00
9	C.C. Sabathia	2.00
10	Curt Schilling	3.00
11	Rickey Henderson	3.00
12	Jamie Moyer	2.00
13	Shawn Green	3.00
14	Randy Johnson	4.00
15	Jim Thome	2.00
16	Larry Walker	2.00
17	Jimmy Rollins	2.00
18	Kazuhiro Sasaki	2.00
19	Hideo Nomo	3.00
20	Roger Clemens	7.50
21	Bud Smith	2.00
22	Ichiro Suzuki	10.00
23	Albert Pujols	15.00
24	Cal Ripken Jr.	15.00
25	Tony Gwynn	3.00

Yearbook Scrapbook

NM/M

Common Player: 4.00
Varying quantities produced.

#	Player	Price
1	Barry Bonds/525	30.00
2	Mark Mulder/500	6.00
3	Luis Gonzalez/500	4.00
4	Lance Berkman/525	4.00
5	Matt Morris/500	4.00
6	Roy Oswalt/150	6.00
7	Todd Helton/525	6.00
8	Tsuyoshi Shinjo/75	15.00
9	C.C. Sabathia/500	4.00
10	Curt Schilling/525	6.00
11	Rickey Henderson/200	15.00
12	Jamie Moyer/500	4.00
13	Shawn Green/525	5.00
14	Randy Johnson/500	8.00
15	Jim Thome/400	4.00
16	Larry Walker/500	4.00
18	Kazuhiro Sasaki/500	4.00
19	Hideo Nomo/150	50.00
20	Roger Clemens/475	20.00
21	Bud Smith/525	5.00
22	Ichiro Suzuki/75	80.00
23	Albert Pujols/150	50.00
24	Cal Ripken/525	30.00
25	Tony Gwynn/500	10.00

2001 Donruss Elite

NM/M

Complete Set (200):
Common Player: .25
Common (151-200): 5.00
Production 900
Common 201-250: 4.00
(#201-250 available by redemption.)
Pack (5): 12.00
Box (18): 200.00

#	Player	Price
1	Alex Rodriguez	2.00
2	Barry Bonds	2.50
3	Cal Ripken Jr.	2.50
4	Chipper Jones	1.50
5	Derek Jeter	2.50
6	Troy Glaus	.75
7	Frank Thomas	1.00
8	Greg Maddux	1.50
9	Ivan Rodriguez	.75
10	Jeff Bagwell	1.00
11	Jose Canseco	.50
12	Todd Helton	.75
13	Ken Griffey Jr.	1.75
14	Manny Ramirez	1.00
15	Mark McGwire	2.00
16	Mike Piazza	1.75
17	Nomar Garciaparra	1.50
18	Pedro Martinez	1.00
19	Randy Johnson	1.00
20	Rick Ankiel	.25
21	Ricky Henderson	1.00
22	Roger Clemens	1.75
23	Sammy Sosa	1.50
24	Tony Gwynn	1.50
25	Vladimir Guerrero	1.00
26	Eric Davis	.25
27	Roberto Alomar	.35
28	Mark Mulder	.35
29	Pat Burrell	.50
30	Harold Baines	.25
31	Carlos Delgado	.60
32	J.D. Drew	.40
33	Jim Edmonds	.25
34	Darin Erstad	.35
35	Jason Giambi	.50
36	Tom Glavine	.50
37	Juan Gonzalez	.50
38	Mark Grace	.25
39	Shawn Green	.40
40	Tim Hudson	.40
41	Andruw Jones	1.00
42	David Justice	.25
43	Jeff Kent	.25
44	Barry Larkin	.25
45	Pokey Reese	.25
46	Mike Mussina	.40
47	Hideo Nomo	.50
48	Rafael Palmeiro	.65
49	Adam Piatt	.25
50	Scott Rolen	.65
51	Gary Sheffield	.40
52	Bernie Williams	.25
53	Bob Abreu	.25
54	Edgardo Alfonzo	.25
55	Jermaine Clark RC	.25
56	Albert Belle	.25
57	Craig Biggio	.25
58	Andres Galarraga	.25
59	Edgar Martinez	.25
60	Fred McGriff	.25
61	Magglio Ordonez	.25
62	Jim Thome	.65
63	Matt Williams	.25
64	Kerry Wood	.50
65	Moises Alou	.25
66	Brady Anderson	.25
67	Garret Anderson	.25
68	Tony Armas Jr.	.25
69	Tony Batista	.25
70	Jose Cruz Jr.	.25
71	Carlos Beltran	.50
72	Adrian Beltre	.40
73	Kris Benson	.25
74	Lance Berkman	.25
75	Kevin Brown	.25
76	Jay Buhner	.25
77	Jeromy Burnitz	.25
78	Ken Caminiti	.25
79	Sean Casey	.40
80	Luis Castillo	.25
81	Eric Chavez	.40
82	Jeff Cirillo	.25
83	Bartolo Colon	.25
84	David Cone	.25
85	Freddy Garcia	.25
86	Johnny Damon	.50
87	Ray Durham	.25
88	Jermaine Dye	.25
89	Juan Encarnacion	.25
90	Terrence Long	.25
91	Carl Everett	.25
92	Steve Finley	.25
93	Cliff Floyd	.25
94	Brad Fulmer	.25
95	Brian Giles	.25
96	Luis Gonzalez	.25
97	Rusty Greer	.25
98	Jeffrey Hammonds	.25
99	Mike Hampton	.25
100	Orlando Hernandez	.35
101	Richard Hidalgo	.25
102	Geoff Jenkins	.25
103	Jacque Jones	.25
104	Brian Jordan	.25
105	Gabe Kapler	.25
106	Eric Karros	.25
107	Jason Kendall	.25
108	Adam Kennedy	.25
109	Byung-Hyun Kim	.25
110	Ryan Klesko	.25
111	Chuck Knoblauch	.25
112	Paul Konerko	.25
113	Carlos Lee	.25
114	Kenny Lofton	.25
115	Javy Lopez	.25
116	Tino Martinez	.25
117	Ruben Mateo	.25
118	Kevin Millwood	.25
119	Ben Molina	.25
120	Raul Mondesi	.25
121	Trot Nixon	.25
122	John Olerud	.25
123	Paul O'Neill	.25
124	Chan Ho Park	.25
125	Andy Pettitte	.40
126	Jorge Posada	.35
127	Mark Quinn	.25
128	Aramis Ramirez	.25
129	Mariano Rivera	.35
130	Tim Salmon	.25
131	Curt Schilling	.40
132	Richie Sexson	.25
133	John Smoltz	.25
134	J.T. Snow	.25
135	Jay Payton	.25
136	Shannon Stewart	.25
137	B.J. Surhoff	.25
138	Mike Sweeney	.25
139	Fernando Tatis	.25
140	Miguel Tejada	.40
141	Jason Varitek	.25
142	Greg Vaughn	.25
143	Mo Vaughn	.25
144	Robin Ventura	.25
145	Jose Vidro	.25
146	Omar Vizquel	.25
147	Larry Walker	.25
148	David Wells	.25
149	Rondell White	.25
150	Preston Wilson	.25
151	Brent Abernathy	5.00
152	Cory Aldridge RC	5.00
153	Gene Altman RC	5.00
154	Josh Beckett	6.00
155	Wilson Betemit RC	5.00
156	Albert Pujols RC	400.00
157	Joe Crede	5.00
158	Jack Cust	5.00
159	Ben Sheets	5.00
160	Alex Escobar	5.00
161	Adrian Hernandez RC	5.00
162	Pedro Feliz	5.00
163	Nate Frese RC	5.00
164	Carlos Garcia RC	5.00
165	Marcus Giles	5.00
166	Alexis Gomez RC	5.00
167	Jason Hart	5.00
168	Aubrey Huff	5.00
169	Cesar Izturis	5.00
170	Nick Johnson	5.00
171	Jack Wilson RC	10.00
172	Brian Lawrence RC	5.00
173	Christian Parker RC	5.00
174	Nick Maness RC	5.00
175	Jose Mieses RC	5.00
176	Greg Miller RC	5.00
177	Eric Munson	5.00
178	Xavier Nady RC	5.00
179	Blaine Neal RC	5.00
180	Abraham Nunez	5.00
181	Jose Ortiz	5.00
182	Jeremy Owens RC	5.00
183	Jay Gibbons RC	10.00
184	Corey Patterson	5.00
185	Carlos Pena	5.00
186	C.C. Sabathia	5.00
187	Timo Perez	5.00
188	Adam Pettyjohn RC	5.00
189	Donaldo Mendez RC	5.00
190	Jackson Melian RC	5.00
191	Wilken Ruan RC	5.00
192	Duaner Sanchez RC	5.00
193	Alfonso Soriano	5.00
194	Rafael Soriano RC	10.00
195	Ichiro Suzuki RC	150.00
196	Billy Sylvester RC	5.00
197	Juan Uribe RC	5.00
198	Tsuyoshi Shinjo RC	10.00
199	Carlos Valderrama RC	5.00
200	Matt White RC	5.00
201	Adam Dunn	6.00
202	Joe Kennedy	4.00
203	Mike Rivera	4.00
204	Erick Almonte	4.00
205	Brandon Duckworth	4.00
206	Victor Martinez RC	100.00
207	Rick Bauer	4.00
208	Jeff Deardorff	4.00
209	Antonio Perez	4.00
210	Bill Hall	30.00
211	Dennis Tankersley	6.00
212	Jeremy Affeldt	8.00
213	Junior Spivey	8.00
214	Casey Fossum	6.00
215	Brandon Lyon	4.00
216	Angel Santos	4.00
217	Cody Ransom	4.00
218	Jason Lane	35.00
219	David Williams	4.00
220	Alex Herrera	4.00
221	Ryan Drese	4.00
222	Travis Hafner	40.00
223	Bud Smith	4.00
224	Johnny Estrada	25.00
225	Ricardo Rodriguez	4.00
226	Brandon Berger	4.00
227	Claudio Vargas	4.00
228	Luis Garcia	4.00
229	Marlon Byrd	20.00
230	Hee Seop Choi	20.00
231	Corky Miller	4.00
232	Justin Duchscherer	6.00
233	Tim Spooneybarger	4.00
234	Roy Oswalt	4.00
235	Willie Harris	4.00
236	Josh Towers	4.00
237	Juan Pena	4.00
238	Alfredo Amezaga	4.00
239	Geronimo Gil	4.00
240	Juan Cruz	4.00
241	Ed Rogers	4.00
242	Joe Thurston	4.00
243	Orlando Hudson RC	10.00
244	John Buck RC	8.00
245	Martin Vargas	4.00
246	David Brous	4.00
247	Dewon Brazelton	4.00
248	Mark Prior	50.00
249	Angel Berroa	10.00
250	Mark Teixeira	100.00

Aspirations

Cards 1-150 print run 76-100: 5-10X
1-150 p/r 51-75: 8-15X
1-150 p/r 26-50: 10-25X
Cards 151-200 print run 76-100: 1X
151-200 p/r 51-75: 1.5X
151-200 p/r 26-50: 1.5-2X
Varying quantities produced.

Status

Cards 1-150 print run 76-100: 5-10X
1-150 p/r 51-75: 8-15X
1-150 p/r 26-50: 10-25X
Cards 151-200 print run 76-100: 1X
151-200 p/r 51-75: 1.5X
151-200 p/r 26-50: 1.5-2X
Varying quantities produced.

Back 2 Back Jacks

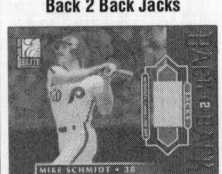

NM/M

Common Player: 15.00
Singles production 100.
Doubles production 50.
SP print runs listed.

#	Player	Price
1	Ernie Banks/75	20.00
2	Ryne Sandberg/75	40.00
3	Babe Ruth	200.00
4	Lou Gehrig	150.00
5	Eddie Matthews	25.00
6	Troy Glaus	15.00
7	Don Mattingly/50	50.00
8	Todd Helton	20.00
9	Wade Boggs	15.00
10	Tony Gwynn	25.00
11	Robin Yount	25.00
12	Paul Molitor/50	25.00
13	Mike Schmidt/50	40.00
14	Scott Rolen/75	25.00
15	Reggie Jackson	20.00
16	Dave Winfield	15.00
17	Johnny Bench/50	25.00
18	Joe Morgan	15.00
19	Brooks Robinson/50	15.00
20	Cal Ripken Jr.	50.00
21	Ty Cobb	100.00
22	Al Kaline/50	40.00
23	Frank Robinson/50	25.00
24	Frank Thomas	20.00
25	Roberto Clemente	25.00
26	Vladimir Guerrero/50	25.00
27	Harmon Killebrew/50	15.00
28	Kirby Puckett	20.00
29	Yogi Berra/75	35.00
30	Phil Rizzuto/75	30.00
31	Ernie Banks, Ryne Sandberg	80.00
32	Babe Ruth, Lou Gehrig	350.00
33	Troy Glaus, Eddie Matthews	40.00
34	Don Mattingly, Todd Helton	100.00
35	Tony Gwynn, Wade Boggs	75.00
36	Paul Molitor, Robin Yount	50.00
37	Mike Schmidt, Scott Rolen	80.00
38	Dave Winfield, Reggie Jackson	40.00
39	Joe Morgan, Johnny Bench	50.00
40	Brooks Robinson, Cal Ripken Jr.	100.00
41	Al Kaline, Ty Cobb	175.00
42	Frank Robinson, Frank Thomas	40.00
43	Roberto Clemente, Vladimir Guerrero	100.00
44	Harmon Killebrew, Kirby Puckett	50.00
45	Phil Rizzuto, Yogi Berra/25	100.00

Back 2 Back Jacks Autograph

NM/M

Common Autograph: 60.00
Print runs listed.

#	Player	Price
1	Ernie Banks/25	200.00
2	Ryne Sandberg/25	250.00
6	Troy Glaus/25	50.00
7	Don Mattingly/25	200.00
12	Paul Molitor/50	75.00
13	Mike Schmidt/50	150.00
14	Scott Rolen/25	60.00
17	Johnny Bench/50	100.00
19	Brooks Robinson/50	75.00
22	Al Kaline/50	100.00
23	Frank Robinson/50	100.00
26	Vladimir Guerrero/50	100.00
27	Harmon Killebrew/50	100.00
29	Yogi Berra/25	125.00
30	Phil Rizzuto/25	125.00
45	Phil Rizzuto, Yogi Berra/25	200.00

Passing the Torch

NM/M

Common Player: 4.00
Singles production 1,000.
Doubles production 500.

#	Player	Price
1	Stan Musial	8.00
2	Tony Gwynn	6.00
3	Willie Mays	10.00
4	Barry Bonds	15.00
5	Mike Schmidt	10.00
6	Scott Rolen	4.00
7	Cal Ripken Jr.	15.00
8	Alex Rodriguez	10.00
9	Hank Aaron	15.00
10	Andruw Jones	4.00
11	Nolan Ryan	15.00
12	Pedro Martinez	6.00
13	Wade Boggs	8.00
14	Nomar Garciaparra	8.00
15	Don Mattingly	10.00
16	Todd Helton	5.00
17	Stan Musial, Tony Gwynn	10.00
18	Barry Bonds, Willie Mays	20.00
19	Mike Schmidt, Scott Rolen	

20	Alex Rodriguez, Cal Ripken Jr.	25.00
21	Andruw Jones, Hank Aaron	15.00
22	Nolan Ryan, Pedro Martinez	25.00
23	Nomar Garciaparra, Wade Boggs	15.00
24	Don Mattingly, Todd Helton	15.00

Passing the Torch Autographs

		NM/M
Common Player:		30.00

Singles production 100.
Doubles production 50.

1	Stan Musial	100.00
2	Tony Gwynn	75.00
3	Willie Mays	200.00
4	Barry Bonds	275.00
5	Mike Schmidt	100.00
6	Scott Rolen	50.00
7	Cal Ripken Jr.	150.00
8	Alex Rodriguez	120.00
9	Hank Aaron	275.00
10	Andruw Jones	30.00
11	Nolan Ryan	125.00
12	Pedro Martinez	75.00
13	Wade Boggs	30.00
14	Nomar Garciaparra	50.00
15	Don Mattingly	100.00
16	Todd Helton	40.00
17	Stan Musial, Tony Gwynn	175.00
18	Barry Bonds, Willie Mays	900.00
19	Mike Schmidt, Scott Rolen	150.00
20	Alex Rodriguez, Cal Ripken Jr.	400.00
21	Andruw Jones, Hank Aaron	350.00
22	Nolan Ryan, Pedro Martinez	300.00
22	Nolan Ryan, Roger Clemens FB redemp.	375.00
23	Wade Boggs FB Redemp.	25.00
24	Don Mattingly, Todd Helton	200.00

Primary Colors

		NM/M
Complete Set (40):		100.00
Common Player:		1.00

Production 975 Sets

Red Die-Cut:	3-5X

Production 25

Blues:	1-1.5X

Production 200

Blue Die-Cut:	1.5-3X

Production 50

Yellows:	3-5X

Production 25

Yellow Die-Cut:	1.5-2X

Production 75

1	Alex Rodriguez	8.00
2	Barry Bonds	10.00
3	Cal Ripken Jr.	10.00
4	Chipper Jones	5.00
5	Derek Jeter	10.00
6	Troy Glaus	4.00
7	Frank Thomas	4.00
8	Greg Maddux	5.00
9	Ivan Rodriguez	2.50
10	Jeff Bagwell	4.00
11	Todd Helton	4.00

12	Ken Griffey Jr.	6.00
13	Manny Ramirez	4.00
14	Mark McGwire	8.00
15	Mike Piazza	6.00
16	Nomar Garciaparra	4.00
17	Pedro Martinez	4.00
18	Randy Johnson	4.00
19	Rick Ankiel	1.25
20	Roger Clemens	5.50
21	Sammy Sosa	6.00
22	Tony Gwynn	5.00
23	Vladimir Guerrero	4.00
24	Carlos Delgado	2.00
25	Jason Giambi	2.50
26	Andruw Jones	4.00
27	Bernie Williams	1.50
28	Roberto Alomar	1.50
29	Shawn Green	1.50
30	Barry Larkin	1.00
31	Scott Rolen	3.00
32	Gary Sheffield	2.00
33	Rafael Palmeiro	3.00
34	Albert Belle	1.00
35	Magglio Ordonez	1.50
36	Jim Thome	1.00
37	Jim Edmonds	1.00
38	Darin Erstad	2.00
39	Kris Benson	1.00
40	Sean Casey	1.50

Prime Numbers

		NM/M

Print runs listed.

1a	Alex Rodriguez/300	8.00
1b	Alex Rodriguez/308	8.00
1c	Alex Rodriguez/350	8.00
2a	Ken Griffey Jr./400	6.00
2b	Ken Griffey Jr./408	6.00
2c	Ken Griffey Jr./430	6.00
3a	Mark McGwire/500	8.00
3b	Mark McGwire/504	8.00
3c	Mark McGwire/550	8.00
4a	Cal Ripken Jr./400	10.00
4b	Cal Ripken Jr./407	10.00
4c	Cal Ripken Jr./410	10.00
5a	Derek Jeter/300	10.00
5b	Derek Jeter/302	10.00
5c	Derek Jeter/320	10.00
6a	Mike Piazza/300	6.00
6b	Mike Piazza/302	6.00
6c	Mike Piazza/360	6.00
7a	Nomar Garciaparra/300	6.00
7b	Nomar Garciaparra/302	6.00
7c	Nomar Garciaparra/370	6.00
8a	Sammy Sosa/300	6.00
8b	Sammy Sosa/306	6.00
8c	Sammy Sosa/380	6.00
9a	Vladimir Guerrero/300	4.00
9b	Vladimir Guerrero/305	4.00
9c	Vladimir Guerrero/340	4.00
10a	Tony Gwynn/300	4.00
10b	Tony Gwynn/304	4.00
10c	Tony Gwynn/390	4.00

Prime Numbers Die-Cut

		NM/M

Print runs listed.

1a	Alex Rodriguez/58	25.00
1b	Alex Rodriguez/50	25.00
2a	Ken Griffey Jr./38	20.00
2b	Ken Griffey Jr./30	20.00
3a	Mark McGwire/54	25.00
3b	Mark McGwire/25	25.00
5a	Derek Jeter/22	75.00
5b	Derek Jeter/20	75.00
6a	Mike Piazza/62	15.00
6b	Mike Piazza/60	15.00
7a	Nomar Garciaparra/72	15.00
7b	Nomar Garciaparra/70	15.00
8a	Sammy Sosa/86	15.00
8b	Sammy Sosa/80	15.00
9a	Vladimir Guerrero/45	10.00
9b	Vladimir Guerrero/40	10.00
10a	Tony Gwynn/94	10.00
10b	Tony Gwynn/90	10.00

Throwback Threads

Title Waves

		NM/M
Common Player:		1.00

Numbered to title year.

Holofoil:	2-3X

Production 100 Sets

1	Alex Rodriguez	3.00

		NM/M
Common Player:		15.00

Singles production 100.
Doubles production 50.
SP production listed.

1	Stan Musial/75	50.00
2	Tony Gwynn/75	25.00
3	Willie McCovey	15.00
4	Barry Bonds	50.00
5	Babe Ruth	250.00
6	Lou Gehrig	200.00
7	Mike Schmidt/75	40.00
8	Scott Rolen	20.00
9	Harmon Killebrew/75	30.00
10	Kirby Puckett	20.00
11	Al Kaline/75	40.00
12	Eddie Matthews	25.00
13	Hank Aaron/75	60.00
14	Andruw Jones/50	20.00
15	Lou Brock	15.00
16	Ozzie Smith	25.00
17	Ernie Banks/75	35.00
18	Ryne Sandberg	50.00
19	Roberto Clemente	100.00
20	Vladimir Guerrero/50	20.00
21	Frank Robinson/50	25.00
22	Frank Thomas	15.00
23	Brooks Robinson/50	25.00
24	Cal Ripken Jr.	50.00
25	Roger Clemens	30.00
26	Pedro Martinez	20.00
27	Reggie Jackson	15.00
28	Dave Winfield	15.00
29	Don Mattingly/50	60.00
30	Todd Helton	15.00
31	Stan Musial, Tony Gwynn/25	120.00
32	Barry Bonds, Willie McCovey	85.00
33	Babe Ruth, Lou Gehrig	500.00
34	Mike Schmidt, Scott Rolen/25	150.00
35	Harmon Killebrew, Kirby Puckett	50.00
36	Al Kaline, Eddie Matthews	50.00
37	Andruw Jones, Hank Aaron	85.00
38	Lou Brock, Ozzie Smith	50.00
39	Ernie Banks, Ryne Sandberg/25	125.00
40	Roberto Clemente, Vladimir Guerrero	90.00
41	Frank Robinson, Frank Thomas	40.00
42	Brooks Robinson, Cal Ripken Jr.	85.00
43	Pedro Martinez, Roger Clemens	60.00
44	Dave Winfield, Reggie Jackson	30.00
45	Don Mattingly, Todd Helton	75.00

Throwback Threads Autograph

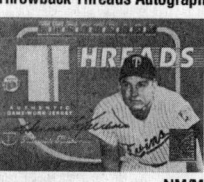

		NM/M

Production Listed
Football Exchange for 21 & 22 will be redeemed for #'s listed for 21 & 22.

1	Stan Musial/25	150.00
2	Tony Gwynn/25	100.00
7	Mike Schmidt/25	200.00
9	Harmon Killebrew/25	125.00
11	Al Kaline/25	120.00
13	Hank Aaron/25	250.00
14	Andruw Jones/50	50.00
17	Ernie Banks/25	150.00
20	Vladimir Guerrero/50	75.00
21	Frank Robinson/ 50 FB Redemp	40.00
22	Frank Thomas/ 50 FB redemp	50.00
23	Brooks Robinson/50	100.00
29	Don Mattingly/50	150.00
31	Stan Musial, Tony Gwynn/25	225.00
34	Mike Schmidt, Scott Rolen/25	225.00
39	Ernie Banks, Ryne Sandberg/25	250.00

1	Tony Gwynn/1994	5.00
2	Todd Helton/2000	4.00
3	Nomar Garciaparra/2000	6.00
4	Frank Thomas/1997	4.00
5	Alex Rodriguez/1996	8.00
6	Jeff Bagwell/1994	4.00
7	Mark McGwire/1998	8.00
8	Sammy Sosa/2000	6.00
9	Ken Griffey Jr./1997	6.00
10	Albert Belle/1995	1.00
11	Barry Bonds/1993	8.00
12	Jose Canseco/1991	2.00
13	Manny Ramirez/1999	4.00
14	Sammy Sosa/1998	6.00
15	Andres Galarraga/1996	1.00
16	Todd Helton/2000	4.00
17	Ken Griffey Jr./1997	6.00
18	Jeff Bagwell/1994	4.00
19	Mike Piazza/1995	6.00
20	Alex Rodriguez/1995	8.00
21	Jason Giambi/2000	2.00
22	Ivan Rodriguez/2000	2.50
23	Greg Maddux/1997	5.00
24	Pedro Martinez/1994	4.00
25	Derek Jeter/2000	10.00
26	Bernie Williams/1998	1.50
27	Roger Clemens/1999	8.00
28	Chipper Jones/1995	4.00
29	Mark McGwire/1990	8.00
30	Cal Ripken Jr./1983	10.00

Turn of the Century Autographs

		NM/M
Common Autograph:		8.00

Production 100 Sets
Redemp. deadline 5/01/03.

151	Brent Abernathy	8.00
152	Cory Aldridge	8.00
153	Gene Altman	8.00
154	Josh Beckett	80.00
155	Wilson Betemit	25.00
156	Albert Pujols	900.00
157	Joe Crede	30.00
158	Jack Cust	10.00
159	Ben Sheets	30.00
160	Alex Escobar	8.00
161	Adrian Hernandez	8.00
162	Pedro Feliz	8.00
163	Nate Frese	8.00
164	Carlos Garcia	8.00
165	Marcus Giles	20.00
166	Alexis Gomez	10.00
167	Jason Hart	8.00
168	Aubrey Huff	20.00
169	Cesar Izturis	10.00
170	Nick Johnson	20.00
171	Jack Wilson	15.00
172	Brian Lawrence	10.00
173	Christian Parker	8.00
174	Nick Maness	8.00
175	Jose Mieses	10.00
176	Greg Miller	8.00
177	Eric Munson	10.00
178	Xavier Nady	15.00
179	Blaine Neal	8.00
180	Abraham Nunez	10.00
181	Jose Ortiz	10.00
182	Jeremy Owens	8.00
183	Jay Gibbons	25.00
184	Corey Patterson	20.00
185	Carlos Pena	25.00
186	C.C. Sabathia	40.00
187	Timoniel Perez	8.00
188	Adam Pettyjohn	8.00
189	Donaldo Mendez	8.00
190	Jackson Melian	8.00
191	Wilken Ruan	8.00
192	Duaner Sanchez	8.00
193	Alfonso Soriano	60.00
194	Rafael Soriano	10.00
196	Billy Sylvester	8.00
197	Juan Uribe	20.00
199	Carlos Valderrama	8.00
200	Matt White	10.00

2001 Donruss Signature Series

		NM/M
Complete Set (311):		
Common Player:		.50
Common (111-165):		8.00
Auto. print run 330		
Common (166-311):		4.00

Production 800

Box:		100.00
1	Alex Rodriguez	3.00

2	Barry Bonds	4.00
3	Cal Ripken Jr.	4.00
4	Chipper Jones	2.00
5	Derek Jeter	4.00
6	Troy Glaus	1.50
7	Frank Thomas	1.50
8	Greg Maddux	2.00
9	Ivan Rodriguez	1.00
10	Jeff Bagwell	.50
11	John Olerud	.50
12	Todd Helton	1.50
13	Ken Griffey Jr.	2.50
14	Manny Ramirez	1.50
15	Mark McGwire	3.00
16	Mike Piazza	2.50
17	Nomar Garciaparra	2.50
18	Moises Alou	.50
19	Aramis Ramirez	.50
20	Curt Schilling	.75
21	Pat Burrell	.75
22	Doug Mientkiewicz	.50
23	Carlos Delgado	.75
24	J.D. Drew	.75
25	Cliff Floyd	.50
26	Freddy Garcia	.75
27	Roberto Alomar	.75
28	Barry Zito	.75
29	Juan Encarnacion	.50
30	Paul Konerko	.50
31	Mark Mulder	.75
32	Andy Pettitte	.75
33	Jim Edmonds	.50
34	Darin Erstad	1.00
35	Jason Giambi	1.00
36	Tom Glavine	.75
37	Juan Gonzalez	1.50
38	Fred McGriff	.75
39	Shawn Green	.75
40	Tim Hudson	.75
41	Andruw Jones	1.50
42	Jeff Kent	.50
43	Barry Larkin	.50
44	Brad Radke	.50
45	Mike Mussina	.75
46	Hideo Nomo	.75
47	Rafael Palmeiro	1.50
48	Scott Rolen	1.50
49	Gary Sheffield	.75
50	Bernie Williams	.75
51	Bobby Abreu	.50
52	Edgardo Alfonzo	.50
53	Edgar Martinez	.50
54	Magglio Ordonez	.75
55	Kerry Wood	.50
56	Adrian Beltre	.75
57	Lance Berkman	.50
58	Kevin Brown	.65
59	Sean Casey	.65
60	Eric Chavez	.50
61	Bartolo Colon	.50
62	Sammy Sosa	2.50
63	Jermaine Dye	.50
64	Tony Gwynn	2.00
65	Carl Everett	.50
66	Brian Giles	.50
67	Mike Hampton	.50
68	Richard Hidalgo	.50
69	Geoff Jenkins	.50
70	Tony Clark	.50
71	Roger Clemens	2.25
72	Ryan Klesko	.50
73	Chan Ho Park	.50
74	Richie Sexson	.50
75	Mike Sweeney	.50
76	Kazuhiro Sasaki	.50
77	Miguel Tejada	.75
78	Jose Vidro	.50
79	Larry Walker	.50
80	Preston Wilson	.50
81	Craig Biggio	.50
82	Andres Galarraga	.50
83	Jim Thome	.50
84	Vladimir Guerrero	1.50
85	Rafael Furcal	.50
86	Cristian Guzman	.50
87	Terrence Long	.50
88	Bret Boone	.50
89	Wade Miller	.50
90	Eric Milton	.50
91	Gabe Kapler	.50
92	Johnny Damon	.50
93	Carlos Lee	.50
94	Kenny Lofton	.50
95	Raul Mondesi	.50
96	Jorge Posada	.50
97	Mark Grace	.65
98	Robert Fick	.50
99	Joe Mays	.50

100	Aaron Sele	.50
101	Ben Grieve	.50
102	Luis Gonzalez	.65
103	Ray Durham	.50
104	Mark Quinn	.50
105	Jose Canseco	1.00
106	David Justice	.50
107	Pedro Martinez	1.50
108	Randy Johnson	1.50
109	Phil Nevin	.50
110	Ricky Henderson	1.50
111	Alex Escobar/Auto.	8.00
112	Johnny Estrada/ Auto. RC	15.00
113	Pedro Feliz/Auto.	8.00
114	Nate Frese/Auto.	8.00
115	Ricardo Rodriguez/ Auto. RC	8.00
116	Brandon Larson/ Auto. RC	8.00
117	Alexis Gomez/Auto. RC	8.00
118	Jason Hart/Auto.	8.00
119	C.C. Sabathia/Auto.	20.00
120	Endy Chavez/Auto. RC	8.00
121	Christian Parker/ Auto. RC	8.00
122	Jackson Melian RC	8.00
123	Joe Kennedy/Auto. RC	10.00
124	Adrian Hernandez/ Auto. RC	8.00
125	Cesar Izturis/Auto.	10.00
126	Jose Mieses/Auto. RC	8.00
127	Roy Oswalt/Auto.	30.00
128	Eric Munson/Auto.	8.00
129	Xavier Nady/Auto.	8.00
130	Horacio Ramirez/ Auto. RC	15.00
131	Abraham Nunez/Auto.	8.00
132	Jose Ortiz/Auto.	8.00
133	Jeremy Owens/Auto. RC	8.00
134	Claudio Vargas/Auto. RC	8.00
135	Corey Patterson/Auto.	15.00
136	Carlos Pena	15.00
137	Bud Smith/Auto. RC	8.00
138	Adam Dunn/Auto.	25.00
139	Adam Pettyjohn/Auto.	8.00
140	Elpidio Guzman/Auto. RC	8.00
141	Jay Gibbons/Auto. RC	15.00
142	Wilken Ruan/Auto. RC	8.00
143	Tsuyoshi Shinjo RC	8.00
144	Alfonso Soriano/Auto.	30.00
145	Marcus Giles/Auto.	10.00
146	Ichiro Suzuki RC	75.00
147	Juan Uribe/Auto.	10.00
148	David Williams/Auto. RC	8.00
149	Carlos Valderrama/ Auto. RC	8.00
150	Matt White/Auto. RC	8.00
151	Albert Pujols/Auto. RC	700.00
152	Donaldo Mendez/ Auto. RC	8.00
153	Cory Aldridge/Auto. RC	8.00
154	Brandon Duckworth/ Auto. RC	8.00
155	Josh Beckett/Auto.	30.00
156	Wilson Betemit/ Auto. RC	15.00
157	Ben Sheets/Auto.	25.00
158	Andres Torres/Auto. RC	8.00
159	Aubrey Huff/Auto.	15.00
160	Jack Wilson/Auto. RC	15.00
161	Rafael Soriano/Auto. RC	8.00
162	Nick Johnson/Auto.	12.00
163	Carlos Garcia/Auto. RC	8.00
164	Josh Towers/Auto. RC	10.00
165	Jason Michaels/Auto. RC	8.00
166	Ryan Drese RC	4.00
167	Dewon Brazelton RC	4.00
168	Kevin Olsen RC	4.00
169	Benito Baez RC	4.00
170	Mark Prior RC	20.00
171	Wilmy Caceres RC	4.00
172	Mark Teixeira RC	35.00
173	Willie Harris RC	4.00
174	Mike Koplove RC	4.00
175	Brandon Knight RC	4.00
176	John Grabow RC	4.00
177	Jeremy Affeldt RC	4.00
178	Brandon Inge RC	4.00
179	Casey Fossum RC	6.00
180	Scott Stewart RC	4.00
181	Luke Hudson RC	4.00
182	Ken Vining RC	4.00
183	Toby Hall RC	4.00
184	Eric Knott RC	4.00
185	Kris Foster RC	4.00
186	David Brous RC	4.00
187	Roy Smith RC	4.00
188	Grant Balfour RC	4.00
189	Jeremy Fikac RC	4.00
190	Morgan Ensberg RC	10.00
191	Ryan Freel RC	4.00
192	Ryan Jensen RC	4.00
193	Lance Davis RC	4.00
194	Delvin James RC	4.00
195	Timo Perez	4.00
196	Michael Cuddyer RC	4.00
197	Bob File RC	4.00
198	Martin Vargas RC	4.00
199	Kris Keller RC	4.00
200	Tim Spooneybarger RC	4.00
201	Adam Everett RC	4.00
202	Josh Fogg RC	6.00
203	Kip Wells RC	4.00
204	Rick Bauer RC	4.00
205	Brent Abernathy	4.00
206	Erick Almonte RC	4.00
207	Pedro Santana RC	4.00

208 Ken Harvey 4.00
209 Jerrod Riggan RC 4.00
210 Nick Punto RC 4.00
211 Steve Green RC 4.00
212 Nick Neugebauer RC 4.00
213 Chris George 4.00
214 Mike Penny 4.00
215 Bret Prinz RC 4.00
216 Tim Christman RC 4.00
217 Sean Douglass RC 4.00
218 Brett Jodie RC 4.00
219 Juan Diaz RC 4.00
220 Carlos Hernandez RC 4.00
221 Alex Cintron RC 4.00
222 Juan Cruz RC 4.00
223 Larry Bigbie 4.00
224 Junior Spivey RC 8.00
225 Luis Rivas 4.00
226 Brandon Lyon RC 4.00
227 Tony Cogan RC 4.00
228 Justin Duchscherer RC 6.00
229 Tike Redman 4.00
230 Jimmy Rollins 4.00
231 Scott Podsednik RC 15.00
232 Jose Acevedo RC 4.00
233 Luis Pineda RC 4.00
234 Josh Phelps 4.00
235 Paul Phillips RC 4.00
236 Brian Roberts RC 10.00
237 Orlando Woodwards RC 4.00
238 Bart Miadich RC 4.00
239 Les Walrond RC 4.00
240 Brad Voyles RC 4.00
241 Joe Crede 8.00
242 Juan Moreno RC 4.00
243 Matt Ginter 4.00
244 Brian Rogers RC 4.00
245 Pablo Ozuna RC 4.00
246 Geronimo Gil 4.00
247 Mike Maroth RC 4.00
248 Josue Perez RC 4.00
249 Dee Brown 4.00
250 Victor Zambrano RC 4.00
251 Nick Maness RC 4.00
252 Kyle Lohse RC 6.00
253 Greg Miller RC 4.00
254 Henry Mateo RC 4.00
255 Duaner Sanchez RC 6.00
256 Rob Mackowiak RC 6.00
257 Steve Lomasney 4.00
258 Angel Santos RC 4.00
259 Winston Abreu RC 4.00
260 Brandon Berger RC 4.00
261 Tomas De La Rosa RC 4.00
262 Ramon Vazquez RC 4.00
263 Mickey Callaway 4.00
264 Corky Miller RC 4.00
265 Keith Ginter 4.00
266 Cody Ransom RC 4.00
267 Doug Nickle RC 4.00
268 Derrick Lewis RC 4.00
269 Eric Hinske RC 6.00
270 Travis Phelps RC 4.00
271 Eric Valent 4.00
272 Michael Rivera RC 4.00
273 Esix Snead RC 4.00
274 Troy Mattes RC 4.00
275 Jermaine Clark RC 4.00
276 Nate Cornejo RC 4.00
277 George Perez RC 4.00
278 Juan Rivera RC 4.00
279 Justin Atchley RC 4.00
280 Adam Johnson 4.00
281 Gene Altman RC 4.00
282 Jason Jennings 4.00
283 Scott MacRae RC 4.00
284 Craig Monroe RC 6.00
285 Bert Snow RC 4.00
286 Stubby Clapp RC 4.00
287 Jack Cust 4.00
288 Will Ohman RC 4.00
289 Wily Mo Pena 4.00
290 Joe Beimel RC 4.00
291 Jason Karnuth RC 4.00
292 Bill Ortega 4.00
293 Nate Teut RC 4.00
294 Erik Hiljus RC 4.00
295 Jason Smith RC 4.00
296 Juan Pena 4.00
297 David Espinosa 4.00
298 Tim Redding 4.00
299 Brian Lawrence RC 4.00
300 Brian Reith RC 4.00
301 Chad Durbin 4.00
302 Kurt Ainsworth 4.00
303 Blaine Neal RC 4.00
304 Jorge Julio RC 4.00
305 Adam Bernero 4.00
306 Travis Hafner RC 20.00
307 Dustan Mohr RC 4.00
308 Cesar Crespo RC 4.00
309 Billy Sylvester RC 4.00
310 Zach Day RC 6.00
311 Angel Berroa RC 8.00

Signature Proofs
Stars (1-110): 2-3X

Production 175
Cards (111-311) Production 25

Award Winning Signatures

NM/M
Common Player: 20.00
Jeff Bagwell/94 65.00
Carlos Beltran/99 40.00
Johnny Bench/68 75.00
Yogi Berra/55 50.00
Craig Biggio/97 25.00
Barry Bonds/93 200.00
Rod Carew/77 50.00
Orlando Cepeda/67 20.00
Andre Dawson/77 20.00
Dennis Eckersley/92 25.00
Dennis Eckersley/92 25.00
Whitey Ford/61 50.00
Jason Giambi/100 20.00
Bob Gibson/68 40.00
Juan Gonzalez/96 35.00
Orel Hershiser/88 25.00
Al Kaline/67 75.00
Fred Lynn/75 15.00
Fred Lynn/75 15.00
Jim Palmer/76 25.00
Cal Ripken/83 150.00
Phil Rizzuto/50 40.00
Brooks Robinson/64 40.00
Scott Rolen/97 30.00
Ryne Sandberg/84 90.00
Warren Spahn/57 50.00
Frank Thomas/94 35.00
Billy Williams/61 20.00
Kerry Wood/98 40.00
Robin Yount/89 60.00

Century Marks

NM/M
Common Autograph: 5.00
Brent Abernathy/184 5.00
Roberto Alomar/102 40.00
Rick Ankiel/119 15.00
Lance Berkman/121 15.00
Mark Buehrle/224 10.00
Wilmy Caceres/194 5.00
Eric Chavez/170 10.00
Joe Crede/154 5.00
Jack Cust/178 10.00
Brandon Duckworth/183 5.00
David Espinosa/199 5.00
Johnny Estrada/198 5.00
Pedro Feliz/180 5.00
Robert Fick/232 5.00
Cliff Floyd/146 8.00
Casey Fossum/100 10.00
Jay Gibbons/175 5.00
Keith Ginter/163 4.00
Troy Glaus/144 20.00
Luis Gonzalez/101 10.00
Vladimir Guerrero/187 30.00
Richard Hidalgo/173 5.00
Tim Hudson/125 25.00
Adam Johnson/130 5.00
Gabe Kapler/150 8.00
Joe Kennedy/219 5.00
Ryan Klesko/176 10.00
Carlos Lee/179 8.00

Terrence Long/180 5.00
Edgar Martinez/110 20.00
Joe Mays/209 5.00
Greg Miller/194 5.00
Wade Miller/180 5.00
Mark Mulder/203 20.00
Xavier Nady/180 5.00
Magglio Ordonez/104 10.00
Jose Ortiz/187 5.00
Roy Oswalt/192 20.00
Wily Mo Pena/203 10.00
Brad Penny/198 5.00
Aramis Ramirez/241 20.00
Luis Rivas/163 5.00
Alex Rodriguez/110 120.00
Scott Rolen/106 30.00
Mike Sweeney/99 10.00
Eric Valent/163 5.00
Kip Wells/223 5.00
Kerry Wood/109 25.00

Milestone Marks

NM/M
Common Player: 10.00
Ernie Banks/285 35.00
Yogi Berra/120 50.00
Wade Boggs/88 60.00
Barry Bonds/55 200.00
George Brett/27 150.00
George Brett/23 150.00
Lou Brock/83 25.00
Rod Carew/110 30.00
Steve Carlton/75 35.00
Gary Carter/213 20.00
Bobby Doerr/192 15.00
Bob Feller/202 15.00
Whitey Ford/186 25.00
Steve Garvey/175 10.00
Tony Gwynn/99 50.00
Fergie Jenkins/149 15.00
Al Kaline/149 15.00
Harmon Killebrew/127 40.00
Ralph Kiner/105 20.00
Willie McCovey/80 75.00
Paul Molitor/96 40.00
Eddie Murray/46 70.00
Stan Musial/109 75.00
Phil Niekro/300 10.00
Tony Perez/146 15.00
Cal Ripken/25 200.00
Frank Robinson/136 20.00
Mike Schmidt/40 125.00
Mike Schmidt/23 150.00
Enos Slaughter/117 20.00
Warren Spahn/300 40.00
Alan Trammell/154 25.00
Hoyt Wilhelm/227 10.00
Dave Winfield/31 50.00
Dave Winfield/15 80.00

Notable Nicknames

NM/M
Common Player: 30.00
Production 100
Ernie Banks 75.00
Orlando Cepeda 40.00
Will Clark 80.00
Roger Clemens/50 250.00
Andre Dawson 30.00
Bob Feller 50.00
Carlton Fisk 70.00
Andres Galarraga 40.00
Luis Gonzalez 30.00
Reggie Jackson 75.00
Harmon Killebrew 80.00
Stan Musial 120.00
Brooks Robinson 80.00
Nolan Ryan 250.00

Ryne Sandberg 150.00
Enos Slaughter 60.00
Duke Snider 75.00
Frank Thomas 100.00

Signature Stats

Quantity produced listed.
Roberto Alomar/120 40.00
Moises Alou/124 6.00
Luis Aparicio/313 10.00
Lance Berkman/297 15.00
Wade Boggs/51 75.00
Lou Brock/118 15.00
Gary Carter/32 50.00
Joe Carter/121 5.00
Sean Casey/103 10.00
Darin Erstad/100 15.00
Bob Feller/26 50.00
Cliff Floyd/45 15.00
Whitey Ford/72 40.00
Andres Galarraga/150 8.00
Bob Gibson/112 25.00
Brian Giles/123 10.00
Troy Glaus/102 20.00
Luis Gonzalez/114 10.00
Vladimir Guerrero/131 30.00
Richard Hidalgo/314 6.00
Bo Jackson/32 85.00
Al Kaline/128 45.00
Gabe Kapler/302 6.00
Ralph Kiner/54 30.00
Carlos Lee/261 10.00
Kenny Lofton/210 6.00
Edgar Martinez/145 20.00
Joe Mays/115 6.00
Paul Molitor/41 50.00
Mark Mulder/88 25.00
Magglio Ordonez/126 10.00
Rafael Palmeiro/47 40.00
Kirby Puckett/31 100.00
Manny Ramirez/45 60.00
Alex Rodriguez/132 85.00
Ivan Rodriguez/113 30.00
Shannon Stewart/319 6.00
Mike Sweeney/144 6.00
Miguel Tejada/115 35.00
Joe Torre/230 25.00
Javier Vazquez/405 6.00
Jose Vidro/330 6.00
Hoyt Wilhelm/243 6.00

Team Trademarks

NM/M
Rick Ankiel/179 10.00
Ernie Banks/180 50.00
Johnny Bench/20 75.00
Yogi Berra/124 40.00
Wade Boggs/89 75.00
Barry Bonds/77 200.00
Lou Brock/29 35.00
Steve Carlton/174 25.00
Sean Casey/123 15.00
Orlando Cepeda/100 20.00
Roger Clemens/30 (Red Sox) 125.00
Roger Clemens/21 (Yankees) 150.00
Andre Dawson/176 15.00
Bobby Doerr/193 20.00
Whitey Ford/94 40.00
Steve Garvey/182 20.00
Bob Gibson/30 30.00
Juan Gonzalez/70 40.00
Shawn Green/109 15.00
Orel Hershiser/210 25.00
Reggie Jackson/73 50.00
Fergie Jenkins/213 15.00
Chipper Jones/74 50.00
Pedro Martinez/37 85.00
Willie Mays/197 125.00
Willie McCovey/70 70.00
Joe Morgan/33 80.00
Eddie Murray/45 75.00
Stan Musial/65 90.00
Mike Mussina/85 (Orioles) 40.00

Mike Mussina/95 (Yankees) 50.00
Phil Niekro/187 10.00
Rafael Palmeiro/99 30.00
Jim Palmer/142 15.00
Tony Perez/73 15.00
Manny Ramirez/57 50.00
Cal Ripken Jr./47 200.00
Phil Rizzuto/98 40.00
Brooks Robinson/146 25.00
Frank Robinson /118 (Orioles) 25.00
Frank Robinson/116 (Reds) 25.00
Alex Rodriguez/100 100.00
Ivan Rodriguez/62 50.00
Scott Rolen/39 40.00
Nolan Ryan/153 100.00
Ryne Sandberg/100 50.00
Curt Schilling/163 40.00
Mike Schmidt/107 75.00
Tom Seaver/25 125.00
Gary Sheffield/194 20.00
Enos Slaughter/215 20.00
Duke Snider/47 50.00
Warren Spahn/140 40.00
Joe Torre/90 40.00
Billy Williams/194 10.00
Kerry Wood/52 40.00

2001 Donruss Signature Series Hawaii

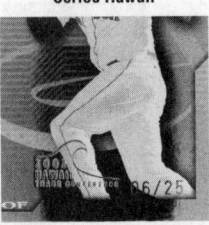

As part of its participation in the 2002 Hawaii Trade Conference, Donruss created special gold-foil enhanced versions of many of the base cards, inserts, parallels and autographs of its Signature Series issues. Cards all carry individual serial numbers from editions as low as 1-of-1 and as high as 25. Because of their scarcity and widely fluctuating demand, values cannot be quoted.

2001 Donruss Studio

Jason Giambi · 1B
OAKLAND ATHLETICS

NM/M
Complete Set (200):
Common Player: .25
Common SP (151-200): 4.00
Production 700
Pack (6): 8.00
Box (18) + 5x7 Auto. 140.00
1 Alex Rodriguez 2.00
2 Barry Bonds 2.50
3 Cal Ripken Jr. 2.50
4 Chipper Jones 1.00
5 Derek Jeter 2.50
6 Troy Glaus .65
7 Frank Thomas .75
8 Greg Maddux 1.00
9 Ivan Rodriguez .65
10 Jeff Bagwell .75
11 Mark Quinn .25
12 Todd Helton .65
13 Ken Griffey Jr. 1.50
14 Manny Ramirez .75
15 Mark McGwire 2.00
16 Mike Piazza 1.50
17 Nomar Garciaparra 1.00
18 Robin Ventura .25
19 Aramis Ramirez .25
20 J.T. Snow .25
21 Pat Burrell .60
22 Curt Schilling .25
23 Carlos Delgado .50
24 J.D. Drew .40
25 Cliff Floyd .25
26 Brian Jordan .25
27 Roberto Alomar .35
28 Barry Zito .40
29 Harold Baines .25

30 Brad Penny .25
31 Jose Cruz .25
32 Andy Pettitte .25
33 Jim Edmonds .35
34 Darin Erstad .35
35 Jason Giambi .60
36 Tom Glavine .50
37 Juan Gonzalez .50
38 Mark Grace .25
39 Shawn Green .50
40 Tim Hudson .50
41 Andruw Jones .75
42 Jeff Kent .25
43 Barry Larkin .25
44 Rafael Furcal .50
45 Mike Mussina .50
46 Hideo Nomo .50
47 Rafael Palmeiro .65
48 Scott Rolen .60
49 Gary Sheffield .25
50 Bernie Williams .25
51 Bobby Abreu .25
52 Edgardo Alfonzo .25
53 Edgar Martinez .25
54 Magglio Ordonez .25
55 Kerry Wood .50
56 Matt Morris .25
57 Lance Berkman .25
58 Kevin Brown .25
59 Sean Casey .40
60 Eric Chavez .25
61 Bartolo Colon .25
62 Johnny Damon .50
63 Jermaine Dye .25
64 Juan Encarnacion .25
65 Carl Everett .25
66 Brian Giles .25
67 Mike Hampton .25
68 Richard Hidalgo .25
69 Geoff Jenkins .25
70 Jacque Jones .25
71 Jason Kendall .25
72 Ryan Klesko .25
73 Chan Ho Park .25
74 Richie Sexson .25
75 Mike Sweeney .25
76 Fernando Tatis .25
77 Miguel Tejada .50
78 Jose Vidro .25
79 Larry Walker .25
80 Preston Wilson .25
81 Craig Biggio .25
82 Fred McGriff .25
83 Jim Thome .65
84 Garret Anderson .25
85 Mark Mulder .40
86 Tony Batista .25
87 Terrence Long .25
88 Brad Fullmer .25
89 Rusty Greer .25
90 Orlando Hernandez .25
91 Gabe Kapler .25
92 Paul Konerko .25
93 Carlos Lee .25
94 Kenny Lofton .25
95 Raul Mondesi .25
96 Jorge Posada .40
97 Tim Salmon .25
98 Greg Vaughn .25
99 Mo Vaughn .25
100 Omar Vizquel .25
101 Ben Grieve .25
102 Luis Gonzalez .25
103 Ray Durham .25
104 Ryan Dempster .25
105 Eric Karros .25
106 David Justice .25
107 Pedro Martinez .75
108 Randy Johnson .75
109 Rick Ankiel .25
110 Rickey Henderson .75
111 Roger Clemens .75
112 Sammy Sosa 1.00
113 Tony Gwynn 1.00
114 Vladimir Guerrero .75
115 Kazuhiro Sasaki .25
116 Phil Nevin .25
117 Ruben Mateo .25
118 Shannon Stewart .25
119 Matt Williams .25
120 Tino Martinez .25
121 Ken Caminiti .25
122 Edgar Renteria .25
123 Charles Johnson .25
124 Aaron Sele .25
125 Javy Lopez .25
126 Mariano Rivera .25
127 Shea Hillenbrand .25
128 Jeff D'Amico .25
129 Brady Anderson .25
130 Kevin Millwood .25
131 Trot Nixon .25
132 Mike Lieberthal .25
133 Juan Pierre .25
134 Russ Ortiz .25
135 Jose Macias .25
136 John Smoltz .25
137 Jason Varitek .25
138 Dean Palmer .25
139 Jeff Cirillo .25
140 Paul O'Neill .25
141 Andres Galarraga .25
142 David Wells .25
143 Brad Radke .25
144 Wade Miller .25
145 John Olerud .25
146 Moises Alou .25
147 Carlos Beltran .25

(Base set, continued)

148 Jeromy Burnitz .25
149 Steve Finley .25
150 Joe Mays .25
151 Alex Escobar 4.00
152 Johnny Estrada RC 8.00
153 Pedro Feliz 4.00
154 Nate Frese RC 4.00
155 Dee Brown 4.00
156 Brandon Larson RC 5.00
157 Alexis Gomez RC 4.00
158 Jason Hart 4.00
159 C.C. Sabathia 4.00
160 Josh Towers RC 5.00
161 Christian Parker RC 4.00
162 Jackson Melian RC 4.00
163 Joe Kennedy RC 4.00
164 Adrian Hernandez RC 4.00
165 Jimmy Rollins 4.00
166 Jose Mieses RC 4.00
167 Roy Oswalt 5.00
168 Eric Munson 4.00
169 Xavier Nady 4.00
170 Horacio Ramirez RC 8.00
171 Abraham Nunez 4.00
172 Jose Ortiz 4.00
173 Jeremy Owens RC 4.00
174 Claudio Vargas RC 4.00
175 Corey Patterson 4.00
176 Carlos Pena 4.00
177 Bud Smith RC 4.00
178 Adam Dunn 4.00
179 Adam Pettyjohn RC 4.00
180 Elpidio Guzman RC 4.00
181 Jay Gibbons RC 5.00
182 Wilkin Ruan RC 4.00
183 Tsuyoshi Shinjo RC 4.00
184 Alfonso Soriano 6.00
185 Marcus Giles 4.00
186 Ichiro Suzuki RC 85.00
187 Juan Uribe RC 5.00
188 David Williams RC 4.00
189 Carlos Valderrama RC 4.00
190 Matt White RC 4.00
191 Albert Pujols RC 240.00
192 Donaldo Mendez 4.00
193 Cory Aldridge RC 4.00
194 Endy Chavez RC 4.00
195 Josh Beckett 4.00
196 Wilson Betemit RC 4.00
197 Ben Sheets 4.00
198 Andres Torres RC 4.00
199 Aubrey Huff 4.00
200 Jack Wilson RC 8.00

Proofs

Chipper Jones • 3B
ATLANTA BRAVES

This parallel insert has a metallic holo-foil seal on front and is serially numbered to 25 each.
Values Undetermined
Production 25 Sets

Diamond Collection

NM/M
Common Player: 5.00
1 Vladimir Guerrero 10.00
2 Barry Bonds 30.00
3 Cal Ripken Jr. 30.00
4 Nomar Garciaparra 20.00
5 Greg Maddux 15.00
6 Frank Thomas 10.00
7 Roger Clemens 20.00
8 Luis Gonzalez/SP 6.00
9 Tony Gwynn 15.00
10 Carlos Lee/SP 6.00
11 Troy Glaus 8.00
12 Randy Johnson 15.00
13 Manny Ramirez/SP 10.00
14 Pedro Martinez 10.00
15 Todd Helton 10.00
16 Jeff Bagwell 10.00
17 Rickey Henderson 10.00
18 Kazuhiro Sasaki 5.00
19 Albert Pujols/SP 50.00
20 Ivan Rodriguez 10.00
21 Darin Erstad 6.00
22 Andruw Jones 8.00
23 Roberto Alomar 6.00
25 Juan Gonzalez 10.00
26 Shawn Green 7.50
27 Lance Berkman 5.00
28 Scott Rolen 9.00
29 Rafael Palmeiro 8.00
30 J.D. Drew 5.00
31 Kerry Wood 8.00
32 Jim Edmonds 5.00
33 Tom Glavine/SP 8.00
34 Hideo Nomo/SP 50.00
36 Tim Hudson 5.00
37 Miguel Tejada 5.00
38 Chipper Jones 15.00
39 Edgar Martinez/SP 8.00
40 Chan Ho Park 5.00
41 Magglio Ordonez 5.00
42 Sean Casey 5.00
43 Larry Walker 5.00
44 Cliff Floyd 5.00
45 Mike Sweeney 5.00
46 Kevin Brown 5.00
47 Richie Sexson 5.00
48 Jermaine Dye 5.00
49 Craig Biggio 5.00

Leather & Lumber

Bobby Abreu Jr. • Phillies

NM/M
Common Player: 5.00
Combos: No Pricing
Production 25 Sets
1 Barry Bonds 25.00
2 Cal Ripken Jr. 25.00
3 Miguel Tejada 5.00
4 Frank Thomas 8.00
5 Greg Maddux 10.00
6 Ivan Rodriguez 8.00
7 Jeff Bagwell/SP 10.00
8 Sean Casey/SP 6.00
9 Todd Helton 8.00
10 Cliff Floyd 5.00
11 Hideo Nomo 40.00
12 Chipper Jones 10.00
13 Rickey Henderson 8.00
14 Richard Hidalgo 5.00
15 Mike Piazza 15.00
16 Larry Walker 5.00
17 Tony Gwynn 10.00
18 Vladimir Guerrero 8.00
19 Rafael Furcal 5.00
20 Roberto Alomar/SP 8.00
21 Albert Pujols 60.00
22 Raul Mondesi 5.00
23 Jim Edmonds 5.00
24 Darin Erstad/SP 6.00
25 Craig Biggio 5.00
26 Kenny Lofton 5.00
27 Juan Gonzalez 8.00
28 John Olerud 5.00
29 Shawn Green 5.00
30 Andruw Jones/SP 8.00
31 Moises Alou 5.00
32 Jeff Kent 5.00
33 Ryan Klesko 5.00
34 Luis Gonzalez 5.00
35 Rafael Palmeiro 8.00
36 Scott Rolen 8.00
37 Carlos Lee 5.00
38 Bobby Abreu 5.00
39 Edgardo Alfonzo 5.00
40 Bernie Williams 5.00
41 Jermaine Dye 5.00
42 Lance Berkman 5.00
43 Edgar Martinez 5.00
44 Richie Sexson 5.00
45 Magglio Ordonez 5.00

Masterstokes

NM/M
Common Player: 8.00
Production 200 Sets
1 Tony Gwynn 25.00
2 Ivan Rodriguez 10.00
3 J.D. Drew 8.00
4 Cal Ripken Jr. 60.00
5 Hideo Nomo 50.00
6 Darin Erstad 8.00
7 Frank Thomas 12.00
8 Andruw Jones 12.00
9 Roberto Alomar 8.00
10 Larry Walker 8.00
11 Vladimir Guerrero 12.00
12 Barry Bonds 65.00
13 Luis Gonzalez 8.00
14 Juan Gonzalez 12.00
17 Todd Helton 12.00
18 Jeff Bagwell 12.00
19 Albert Pujols 75.00
21 Shawn Green 8.00
21 Magglio Ordonez 8.00
22 Scott Rolen 12.00
23 Rafael Palmeiro 10.00
24 Sean Casey 8.00
25 Jim Edmonds 8.00
26 Chipper Jones 20.00
27 Cliff Floyd 8.00
28 Carlos Lee 8.00
29 Edgar Martinez 8.00
30 Lance Berkman 8.00

Private Signings

Rick Ankiel • P
ST. LOUIS CARDINALS

NM/M
Common Player: 8.00
Inserted 1:Hobby Box
1 Alex Rodriguez 80.00
2 Miguel Tejada 25.00
3 Ben Sheets 15.00
4 Tony Gwynn/SP/190 60.00
5 Wilson Betemit 8.00
6 Rick Ankiel 8.00
7 Ivan Rodriguez/SP/150 30.00
8 Ryan Klesko 8.00
9 Jason Giambi/SP/250 15.00
10 Brad Penny 8.00
11 Gabe Kapler 8.00
12 Vladimir Guerrero 30.00
13 Alex Escobar 8.00
14 Edgar Martinez 15.00
15 Cal Ripken/SP/50 200.00
16 Brian Giles 8.00
17 Todd Helton/SP/125 25.00
18 Mike Sweeney 8.00
19 Cliff Floyd 8.00
20 Corey Patterson 12.00
21 Alfonso Soriano 40.00
22 Bobby Abreu 8.00
23 Shawn Green/SP/190 20.00
24 C.C. Sabathia 25.00
25 Luis Gonzalez 8.00
26 Barry Bonds/SP/95 200.00
27 Rafael Palmeiro/SP/190 40.00
28 Mike Mussina/SP/144 40.00
29 Roger Clemens/SP/190 100.00
30 Greg Maddux/SP/200 80.00
31 Troy Glaus 20.00
32 Kerry Wood 15.00
33 Roberto Alomar/SP/200 30.00
34 Tom Glavine 40.00
35 Frank Thomas 20.00
36 Carlos Lee 8.00
37 Scott Rolen 20.00
38 Andruw Jones/SP/250 20.00
39 Manny Ramirez/SP/115 40.00
40 Magglio Ordonez 12.00
41 Lance Berkman 8.00
42 Josh Beckett 30.00
43 Adam Dunn 15.00
44 Albert Pujols/SP/50 600.00
45 Darin Erstad 12.00
46 Curt Schilling 40.00
47 Barry Zito 12.00
48 Sean Casey 8.00

Round Trip Tickets

ROUND TRIP TICKETS
AUTHENTIC

No Pricing
Production 25 Sets

Warning Track

NM/M
Common Player: 4.00
1 Andruw Jones 8.00
2 Rafael Palmeiro 7.00
3 Gary Sheffield 5.00
4 Larry Walker 4.00
5 Shawn Green 4.00
6 Mike Piazza 12.00
7 Barry Bonds 20.00
8 J.D. Drew 4.00
9 Magglio Ordonez 4.00
10 Todd Helton 8.00
11 Juan Gonzalez 8.00
12 Pat Burrell 5.00
13 Mark McGwire 15.00
14 Frank Robinson 8.00
15 Manny Ramirez 8.00
16 Lance Berkman 8.00
17 Johnny Bench 10.00
18 Chipper Jones 10.00
19 Mike Schmidt 15.00
21 Vladimir Guerrero 8.00
22 Sammy Sosa 12.00
23 Cal Ripken Jr. 20.00
24 Roberto Alomar 8.00
25 Willie Stargell 4.00
27 Scott Rolen 7.00
28 Roberto Clemente/SP 50.00
29 Tony Gwynn 10.00
30 Ivan Rodriguez 8.00
31 Sean Casey 4.00
32 Frank Thomas 8.00
33 Jeff Bagwell 8.00
34 Jeff Kent 4.00
35 Reggie Jackson 8.00

2001 Donruss The Rookies

MARK TEIXEIRA
TEXAS RANGERS • 3B

NM/M
Complete Set (105): 80.00
Complete Factory Set (106): 100.00
Common Player: .25
1 Adam Dunn .50
2 Ryan Drese RC .40
3 Bud Smith RC .25
4 Tsuyoshi Shinjo RC .50
5 Roy Oswalt .50
6 Wilmy Caceres RC .25
7 Willie Harris RC .25
8 Andres Torres RC .25
9 Brandon Knight RC .25
10 Horacio Ramirez RC .75
11 Benito Baez RC .25
12 Jeremy Affeldt RC .25
13 Ryan Jensen RC .25
14 Casey Fossum RC .50
15 Ramon Vazquez RC .50
16 Dustan Mohr RC .25
17 Saul Rivera RC .25
18 Zach Day RC .25
19 Erik Hiljus RC .25
20 Cesar Crespo RC .25
21 Wilson Guzman RC .25
22 Travis Hafner RC 6.00
23 Grant Balfour RC .25
24 Johnny Estrada RC 1.50
25 Morgan Ensberg RC 1.00
26 Jack Wilson RC 1.50
27 Aubrey Huff .25
28 Endy Chavez RC .50
29 Delvin James RC .25
30 Michael Cuddyer .25
31 Jason Michaels RC .25
32 Martin Vargas RC .25
33 Donaldo Mendez RC .25
34 Jorge Julio RC .25
35 Tim Spooneybarger RC .25
36 Kurt Ainsworth RC .25
37 Josh Fogg RC .50
38 Brian Reith RC .25
39 Rick Baurer RC .25
40 Tim Redding .25
41 Erick Almonte RC .50
42 Juan Pena .25
43 Ken Harvey RC .25
44 David Brous RC .25
45 Kevin Olsen RC .25
46 Henry Mateo RC .25
47 Nick Neugebauer RC .25
48 Mike Penney RC .25
49 Jay Gibbons RC 1.00
50 Tim Christman RC .25
51 Brandon Duckworth RC .50
52 Brett Jodie RC .25
53 Christian Parker RC .25
54 Carlos Hernandez RC .25
55 Brandon Larson RC .50
56 Nick Punto RC .25
57 Elpidio Guzman RC .25
58 Joe Beimel RC .25
59 Junior Spivey RC .25
60 Will Ohman RC .25
61 Brandon Lyon RC .25
62 Stubby Clapp RC .25
63 Justin Duchscherer RC 1.50
64 Jimmy Rollins .40
65 David Williams RC .40
66 Craig Monroe RC .40
67 Jose Acevedo RC .25
68 Jason Jennings .25
69 Josh Phelps .25
70 Brian Roberts RC 2.00
71 Claudio Vargas RC .25
72 Adam Johnson .25
73 Bart Miadich RC .25
74 Juan Rivera .25
75 Brad Voyles RC .25
76 Nate Cornejo .25
77 Juan Moreno RC .25
78 Brian Rogers RC .25
79 Ricardo Rodriguez RC .25
80 Geronimo Gil RC .25
81 Joe Kennedy RC .25
82 Kevin Joseph RC .25
83 Josue Perez RC .25
84 Victor Zambrano RC .40
85 Josh Towers RC .40
86 Mike Rivera RC .25
87 Mark Prior RC 6.00
88 Juan Cruz RC .40
89 Dewon Brazelton RC .40
90 Angel Berroa RC 1.00
91 Mark Teixeira RC 15.00
92 Cody Ransom RC .25
93 Angel Santos RC .25
94 Corky Miller RC .40
95 Brandon Berger RC .40
96 Corey Patterson .25
97 Albert Pujols 60.00
98 Josh Beckett .50
99 C.C. Sabathia .25
100 Alfonso Soriano .75
101 Ben Sheets .25
102 Rafael Soriano RC .50
103 Wilson Betemit RC .50
104 Ichiro Suzuki RC 10.00
105 Jose Ortiz .25

Rookie Diamond Kings

NM/M
Complete Set (5): 40.00
Inserted 1:Rookies Set
106 C.C. Sabathia 5.00
107 Tsuyoshi Shinjo 8.00
108 Albert Pujols 25.00
109 Roy Oswalt 8.00
110 Ichiro Suzuki 12.00

2002 Donruss Samples

Each March 2002, issue of Beckett Baseball Card Monthly included a sample 2002 Donruss card rubber-cemented inside. The cards differ from the issued version only in the appearance on back of a (usually) silver-foil silver-foil "SAMPLE" notation. Some cards were produced with the overprint in gold-foil, in much more limited quantities. The number of different players, cards involved in the promotion is unknown.

NM/M
Common Player: .10
Stars: 1.5-2X
Gold: 10X

2002 Donruss

NM/M
Complete Set (220): 100.00
Common Player: .15

Common (151-200): 1.00
Inserted 1:4
Common (201-220): 1.00
Inserted 1:8
Pack (5): 2.00
Box (24): 40.00
1 Alex Rodriguez 1.50
2 Barry Bonds 2.00
3 Derek Jeter 2.00
4 Robert Fick .15
5 Juan Pierre .20
6 Torii Hunter .25
7 Todd Helton .75
8 Cal Ripken Jr. 2.00
9 Manny Ramirez .75
10 Johnny Damon .25
11 Mike Piazza 1.25
12 Nomar Garciaparra 1.25
13 Pedro Martinez .75
14 Brian Giles .15
15 Albert Pujols 1.50
16 Roger Clemens 1.00
17 Sammy Sosa 1.25
18 Vladimir Guerrero .75
19 Tony Gwynn 1.00
20 Pat Burrell .35
21 Carlos Delgado .50
22 Tino Martinez .15
23 Jim Edmonds .15
24 Jason Giambi .50
25 Tom Glavine .30
26 Mark Grace .20
27 Tony Armas Jr. .15
28 Andruw Jones .75
29 Ben Sheets .15
30 Jeff Kent .15
31 Barry Larkin .15
32 Joe Mays .15
33 Mike Mussina .40
34 Hideo Nomo .60
35 Rafael Palmeiro .65
36 Scott Brosius .15
37 Scott Rolen .65
38 Gary Sheffield .35
39 Bernie Williams .35
40 Bobby Abreu .15
41 Edgardo Alfonzo .15
42 C.C. Sabathia .15
43 Jeremy Giambi .15
44 Craig Biggio .15
45 Andres Galarraga .15
46 Edgar Martinez .15
47 Fred McGriff .25
48 Magglio Ordonez .25
49 Jim Thome .15
50 Matt Williams .15
51 Kerry Wood .50
52 Moises Alou .15
53 Brady Anderson .15
54 Garret Anderson .15
55 Juan Gonzalez .75
56 Bret Boone .15
57 Jose Cruz Jr. .15
58 Carlos Beltran .50
59 Adrian Beltre .25
60 Joe Kennedy .15
61 Lance Berkman .25
62 Kevin Brown .15
63 Tim Hudson .35
64 Jeromy Burnitz .15
65 Jarrod Washburn .15
66 Sean Casey .20
67 Eric Chavez .25
68 Bartolo Colon .15
69 Freddy Garcia .15
70 Jermaine Dye .15
71 Terrence Long .15
72 Cliff Floyd .15
73 Luis Gonzalez .15
74 Ichiro Suzuki 1.50
75 Mike Hampton .15
76 Richard Hidalgo .15
77 Geoff Jenkins .15
78 Gabe Kapler .15
79 Ken Griffey Jr. 1.25
80 Jason Kendall .15
81 Josh Towers .15
82 Ryan Klesko .15
83 Paul Konerko .15
84 Carlos Lee .15
85 Kenny Lofton .15
86 Josh Beckett .40
87 Raul Mondesi .15
88 Trot Nixon .15
89 John Olerud .15
90 Paul O'Neill .15
91 Chan Ho Park .15
92 Andy Pettitte .35

93	Jorge Posada	.30
94	Mark Quinn	.15
95	Aramis Ramirez	.15
96	Curt Schilling	.40
97	Richie Sexson	.15
98	John Smoltz	.15
99	Wilson Betemit	.15
100	Shannon Stewart	.15
101	Alfonso Soriano	.75
102	Mike Sweeney	.15
103	Miguel Tejada	.40
104	Greg Vaughn	.15
105	Robin Ventura	.15
106	Jose Vidro	.15
107	Larry Walker	.15
108	Preston Wilson	.15
109	Corey Patterson	.20
110	Mark Mulder	.25
111	Tony Clark	.15
112	Roy Oswalt	.25
113	Jimmy Rollins	.40
114	Kazuhiro Sasaki	.15
115	Barry Zito	.40
116	Javier Vazquez	.15
117	Mike Cameron	.15
118	Phil Nevin	.15
119	Bud Smith	.15
120	Cristian Guzman	.15
121	Al Leiter	.15
122	Brad Radke	.15
123	Bobby Higginson	.15
124	Robert Person	.15
125	Adam Dunn	.50
126	Ben Grieve	.15
127	Rafael Furcal	.15
128	Jay Gibbons	.15
129	Paul LoDuca	.15
130	Wade Miller	.15
131	Tsuyoshi Shinjo	.15
132	Eric Milton	.15
133	Rickey Henderson	.75
134	Roberto Alomar	.40
135	Darin Erstad	.50
136	J.D. Drew	.35
137	Shawn Green	.25
138	Randy Johnson	.75
139	Mark McGwire	1.50
140	Jose Canseco	.40
141	Jeff Bagwell	.75
142	Greg Maddux	1.00
143	Mark Buehrle	.15
144	Ivan Rodriguez	.65
145	Frank Thomas	.75
146	Rich Aurilia	.15
147	Troy Glaus	.75
148	Ryan Dempster	.15
149	Chipper Jones	1.00
150	Matt Morris	.15
151	Marlon Byrd	2.00
152	Ben Howard RC	4.00
153	Brandon Backe RC	2.00
154	Jorge De La Rosa RC	2.00
155	Corky Miller	1.00
156	Dennis Tankersley	1.00
157	Kyle Kane RC	3.00
158	Justin Duchscherer	1.00
159	Brian Mallette RC	3.00
160	Chris Baker RC	3.00
161	Jason Lane	1.00
162	Hee Seop Choi	1.50
163	Juan Cruz	1.00
164	Rodrigo Rosario RC	2.00
165	Matt Guerrier	1.00
166	Anderson Machado RC	3.00
167	Geronimo Gil	1.00
168	Dewon Brazelton	1.00
169	Mark Prior	5.00
170	Bill Hall	1.00
171	Jorge Padilla RC	4.00
172	Jose Cueto	1.00
173	Allan Simpson RC	3.00
174	Doug DeVore RC	3.00
175	Josh Pearce	1.00
176	Angel Berroa	1.00
177	Steve Bechler RC	3.00
178	Antonio Perez	1.00
179	Mark Teixeira	4.00
180	Erick Almonte	1.00
181	Orlando Hudson	1.00
182	Mike Rivera	1.00
183	Raul Chavez RC	2.00
184	Juan Pena	1.00
185	Travis Hughes RC	2.00
186	Ryan Ludwick	1.00
187	Ed Rogers	1.00
188	Andy Pratt RC	2.00
189	Nick Neugebauer	1.00
190	Tom Shearn RC	3.00
191	Eric Cyr RC	3.00
192	Victor Martinez	1.00
193	Brandon Berger	1.00
194	Erik Bedard	1.00
195	Fernando Rodney	1.00
196	Joe Thurston	1.00
197	John Buck	1.00
198	Jeff Deardorff RC	2.00
199	Ryan Jamison RC	2.00
200	Alfredo Amezaga	1.00
201	Luis Gonzalez	1.00
202	Roger Clemens	1.25
203	Barry Zito	1.25
204	Bud Smith	1.00
205	Magglio Ordonez	1.25
206	Kerry Wood	1.50
207	Freddy Garcia	1.00
208	Adam Dunn	1.50
209	Curt Schilling	2.00
210	Lance Berkman	1.50
211	Rafael Palmeiro	2.00
212	Ichiro Suzuki	4.00
213	Bobby Abreu	1.00
214	Mark Mulder	1.00
215	Roy Oswalt	1.50
216	Mike Sweeney	1.00
217	Paul LoDuca	1.00
218	Aramis Ramirez	1.00
219	Randy Johnson	2.00
220	Albert Pujols	5.00

Stat Line Career

Cards 1-150 print run 251-400:			2-4X
1-150 p/r 151-250:			3-6X
1-150 p/r 101-150:			4-8X
1-150 p/r 61-100:			5-10X
1-150 p/r 31-60:			8-20X
1-150 p/r 15-30:			15-30X
Common 151-200 p/r 251-400:			1.00
Common 151-200 p/r 151-250:			1.00
Common 151-200 p/r 76-150:			2.00
Common 151-200 p/r 30-75:			4.00

Stat Line Season

NM/M

cards 1-150 print run 151-200:		3-6X
1-150 p/r 101-150:		4-8X
1-150 p/r 76-100:		5-10X
1-150 p/r 51-75:		6-12X
1-150 p/r 31-50:		8-20X
1-150 p/r 15-30:		15-30X
Comm. 151-200 p/r 151-200:		1.00
Comm. 151-200 p/r 101-150:		1.50
Comm. 151-200 p/r 76-100:		2.00
Comm. 151-200 p/r 30-75:		4.00

Autographs

NM/M
Common Autograph: 15.00
Varying quantities produced.

203	Barry Zito/200	20.00
204	Bud Smith/200	10.00
205	Magglio Ordonez/200	20.00
206	Kerry Wood/200	30.00
207	Freddy Garcia/200	10.00
208	Adam Dunn/200	25.00
210	Lance Berkman/175	20.00
211	Rafael Palmeiro/25	20.00
213	Bobby Abreu/200	15.00
214	Mark Mulder/200	15.00
215	Roy Oswalt/200	15.00
216	Mike Sweeney/200	15.00
217	Paul LoDuca/200	15.00
218	Aramis Ramirez/200	20.00
220	Albert Pujols/200	150.00

All-Time Diamond Kings

NM/M
Complete Set (10): 80.00
Common Player: 5.00
Production 2,500 Sets
Studio Series: 2-3X
Production 250 Sets

1	Ted Williams	15.00
2	Cal Ripken Jr.	15.00
3	Lou Gehrig	10.00
4	Babe Ruth	15.00
5	Roberto Clemente	10.00
6	Don Mattingly	10.00
7	Kirby Puckett	8.00
8	Stan Musial	8.00
9	Yogi Berra	5.00
10	Ernie Banks	5.00

Bat Kings

NM/M
Quantities produced listed.
Studio Series: 1.5-3X
Production 25 or 50

1	Jason Giambi/250	15.00
2	Alex Rodriguez/250	25.00
3	Mike Piazza/250	20.00
4	Roberto Clemente/125	100.00
5	Babe Ruth/125	220.00

Diamond Kings

NM/M
Complete Set (20): 80.00
Common Player: 2.00
Production 2,500 Sets
Studio Series: 2-3X
Production 250 Sets

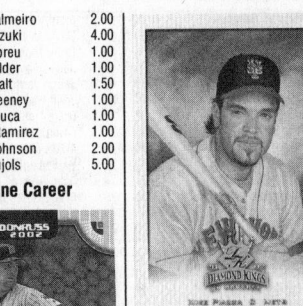

1	Nomar Garciaparra	6.00
2	Shawn Green	4.00
3	Randy Johnson	4.00
4	Derek Jeter	7.50
5	Carlos Delgado	3.00
6	Roger Clemens	5.00
7	Jeff Bagwell	4.00
8	Vladimir Guerrero	4.00
9	Luis Gonzalez	2.00
10	Mike Piazza	6.00
11	Ichiro Suzuki	6.00
12	Pedro Martinez	4.00
13	Todd Helton	4.00
14	Sammy Sosa	6.00
15	Ivan Rodriguez	3.50
16	Barry Bonds	7.50
17	Albert Pujols	6.00
18	Jim Thome	2.00
19	Alex Rodriguez	6.00
20	Jason Giambi	3.00

Elite Series

NM/M
Complete Set (15): 30.00
Common Player: 2.00
Production 2,500 Sets
Autographs: No Pricing
Production 25

1	Barry Bonds	8.00
2	Lance Berkman	2.00
3	Jason Giambi	2.50
4	Nomar Garciaparra	6.00
5	Curt Schilling	2.50
6	Vladimir Guerrero	3.00
7	Shawn Green	2.00
8	Troy Glaus	3.00
9	Jeff Bagwell	3.00
10	Manny Ramirez	3.00
11	Eric Chavez	2.00
12	Carlos Delgado	2.50
13	Mike Sweeney	2.00
14	Todd Helton	3.00
15	Luis Gonzalez	2.00

Elite Series Legends

NM/M
Complete Set (5): 15.00
Common Player: 3.00
Production 2,500

16	Enos Slaughter	3.00
17	Frank Robinson	4.00
18	Bob Gibson	4.00
19	Warren Spahn	4.00
20	Whitey Ford	4.00

Elite Series Legends Autographs

NM/M
Production 250 Sets

16	Enos Slaughter	30.00
17	Frank Robinson	30.00
18	Bob Gibson	35.00
19	Warren Spahn	40.00
20	Whitey Ford	40.00

Jersey Kings

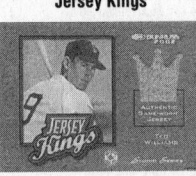

NM/M
Quantity produced listed.
Studio Series: 1.5-3X
Production 25 or 50

1	Alex Rodriguez/250	15.00
2	Jason Giambi/250	10.00
3	Carlos Delgado/250	8.00
4	Barry Bonds/250	25.00
5	Randy Johnson/250	10.00
6	Jim Thome/250	8.00
7	Shawn Green/250	8.00
8	Pedro Martinez/250	10.00
9	Jeff Bagwell/250	8.00
10	Vladimir Guerrero/250	10.00
11	Ivan Rodriguez/250	10.00
12	Nomar Garciaparra/250	15.00
13	Don Mattingly/125	80.00
14	Ted Williams/125	125.00
15	Lou Gehrig/125	200.00

Longball Leaders

NM/M
Complete Set (20): 40.00
Common Player: 1.00
Production 1,000 Sets
Seasonal Sum Parallel: 2-4X
Parallel #'d to 2001 HR Total.

1	Barry Bonds	8.00
2	Sammy Sosa	6.00
3	Luis Gonzalez	1.00
4	Alex Rodriguez	6.00
5	Shawn Green	1.50
6	Todd Helton	3.00
7	Jim Thome	1.00
8	Rafael Palmeiro	2.50
9	Richie Sexson	1.00
10	Troy Glaus	3.00
11	Manny Ramirez	3.00
12	Phil Nevin	1.00
13	Jeff Bagwell	3.00
14	Carlos Delgado	2.00
15	Jason Giambi	2.00
16	Chipper Jones	4.00
17	Larry Walker	1.00
18	Albert Pujols	6.00
19	Brian Giles	1.00
20	Bret Boone	1.00

Production Line

NM/M
Common Card: 2.00
Numbered to category stat.

1	Barry Bonds/515	8.00
2	Jason Giambi/477	4.00
3	Larry Walker/449	2.50
4	Sammy Sosa/437	6.00
5	Todd Helton/432	3.00
6	Lance Berkman/430	2.00
7	Luis Gonzalez/429	2.00
8	Chipper Jones/427	6.00
9	Edgar Martinez/423	2.00
10	Gary Sheffield/417	2.00
11	Jim Thome/416	3.00
12	Roberto Alomar/415	3.00
13	J.D. Drew/414	2.00
14	Jim Edmonds/410	2.00
15	Carlos Delgado/408	2.00
16	Manny Ramirez/405	4.00
17	Brian Giles/404	2.00
18	Albert Pujols/403	8.00
19	John Olerud/401	2.00
20	Alex Rodriguez/399	8.00
21	Barry Bonds/863	6.00
22	Sammy Sosa/737	1.50
23	Luis Gonzalez/688	1.50
24	Todd Helton/685	2.00
25	Larry Walker/662	1.50
26	Jason Giambi/660	2.00
27	Jim Thome/624	2.00
28	Alex Rodriguez/620	5.00
29	Lance Berkman/620	1.50
30	J.D. Drew/613	1.50
31	Albert Pujols/610	5.00
32	Manny Ramirez/609	2.00
33	Chipper Jones/605	3.00
34	Shawn Green/598	1.50
35	Brian Giles/590	1.50
36	Juan Gonzalez/590	2.00
37	Phil Nevin/588	1.50
38	Gary Sheffield/583	1.50
39	Bret Boone/578	1.50
40	Cliff Floyd/578	1.50
41	Barry Bonds/1,378	5.00
42	Sammy Sosa/1,174	4.00
43	Jason Giambi/1,137	1.50
44	Todd Helton/1,117	1.50
45	Luis Gonzalez/1,117	1.00
46	Larry Walker/1,111	1.00
47	Lance Berkman/1,050	1.50
48	Jim Thome/1,040	1.50
49	Chipper Jones/1,032	2.50
50	J.D. Drew/1,027	1.00
51	Alex Rodriguez/1,021	4.00
52	Manny Ramirez/1,014	1.50
53	Albert Pujols/1,013	4.00
54	Gary Sheffield/1,000	1.50
55	Brian Giles/994	1.00
56	Phil Nevin/976	1.00
57	Jim Edmonds/974	1.50
58	Shawn Green/970	1.00
59	Cliff Floyd/968	1.00
60	Edgar Martinez/966	1.00

Recollection Collection

NM/M
Complete Set (47):
Common Player:

6	Steve Carlton 83/30	40.00
7	Steve Carlton 87/30	40.00
8	Gary Carter 87/100	25.00
9	Gary Carter 89/100	25.00
10	Joe Carter 87/45	25.00
11	Andre Dawson 81/50	20.00
12	Andre Dawson 83/50	20.00
13	Andre Dawson 85/30	20.00
14	Andre Dawson 87/45	20.00
17	Dennis Eckersley 81/45	20.00
24	Steve Garvey 87/75	20.00
26	Fergie Jenkins 81/40	25.00
46	Tom Seaver 87/60	60.00
47	Don Sutton 87/200	15.00

Rookie Year Materials - Bats

NM/M
Production 250 Sets

1	Barry Bonds	40.00
2	Cal Ripken Jr.	40.00
3	Kirby Puckett	15.00
4	Johnny Bench	15.00

Rookie Year Materials - Bats Autograph

NM/M
Numbered to debut year.

1	Barry Bonds/86	125.00
2	Cal Ripken Jr/81	140.00
3	Kirby Puckett/84	120.00
4	Johnny Bench/68	75.00

Rookie Year Materials - Jerseys

NM/M
Quantity produced listed.
Parallel #'d to 25 or 50.

1	Nomar Garciaparra/250	20.00
2	Randy Johnson/250	10.00
3	Ivan Rodriguez/250	10.00
4	Vladimir Guerrero/250	15.00
5	Stan Musial/50	80.00
6	Yogi Berra/50	50.00

2002 Donruss Classics Samples

Each August 2002 issue of Beckett Baseball Card Monthly included a sample Donruss Classics card rubber-cemented inside. The cards differ from the issued version only in the appearance on back of a (usually) silver-foil "SAMPLE" notation. Some cards were produced with the overprint in gold-foil, in much more limited quantities. Cards #1-100 from the set can be found in this Sample version.

NM/M

Common Player:	.10
Stars:	1.5-2X
Gold:	10X

2002 Donruss Classics

NM/M
Complete Set (200):
Common Player: .50
Common (101-150): 3.00
Common (151-200): 2.00
Production 1,500
Pack (6): 5.00
Box (18): 70.00

1	Alex Rodriguez	3.00
2	Barry Bonds	5.00
3	C.C. Sabathia	.50
4	Chipper Jones	2.00
5	Derek Jeter	4.00
6	Troy Glaus	1.50
7	Frank Thomas	1.50
8	Greg Maddux	2.00
9	Ivan Rodriguez	1.50
10	Jeff Bagwell	1.50
11	Mark Buehrle	.50
12	Todd Helton	1.50
13	Ken Griffey Jr.	2.50
14	Manny Ramirez	1.50
15	Brad Penny	.50
16	Mike Piazza	2.50
17	Nomar Garciaparra	1.50
18	Pedro J. Martinez	1.50
19	Randy Johnson	1.50
20	Bud Smith	.50
21	Rickey Henderson	.50
22	Roger Clemens	2.25
23	Sammy Sosa	2.50
24	Brandon Duckworth	.50
25	Vladimir Guerrero	.50
26	Kazuhiro Sasaki	.50
27	Roberto Alomar	.65
28	Barry Zito	.75
29	Rich Aurilia	.50
30	Ben Sheets	.50
31	Carlos Delgado	1.00
32	J.D. Drew	.75
33	Jermaine Dye	.50
34	Darin Erstad	.50
35	Jason Giambi	1.00
36	Tom Glavine	.60
37	Juan Gonzalez	1.50
38	Luis Gonzalez	.35
39	Shawn Green	.50
40	Tim Hudson	.65
41	Andruw Jones	1.50
42	Shannon Stewart	.50
43	Barry Larkin	.50
44	Wade Miller	.50
45	Mike Mussina	.65
46	Hideo Nomo	1.00
47	Rafael Palmeiro	1.25
48	Scott Rolen	.75
49	Gary Sheffield	.75
50	Bernie Williams	.65
51	Bobby Abreu	.50
52	Javier Vazquez	.50
53	Edgar Martinez	.50
54	Magglio Ordonez	.75
55	Kerry Wood	.50
56	Adrian Beltre	.65
57	Lance Berkman	.50
58	Kevin Brown	.50
59	Sean Casey	.50
60	Eric Chavez	.75
61	Robert Person	.50
62	Jeremy Giambi	.50
63	Freddy Garcia	.50
64	Alfonso Soriano	1.50
65	Doug Davis	.50
66	Brian Giles	.50
67	Moises Alou	.50
68	Richard Hidalgo	.50
69	Paul LoDuca	.50
70	Aramis Ramirez	.50
71	Andres Galarraga	.50
72	Ryan Klesko	.50
73	Chan Ho Park	.50
74	Richie Sexson	.50
75	Mike Sweeney	.50
76	Aubrey Huff	.50
77	Miguel Tejada	.75
78	Jose Vidro	.50
79	Larry Walker	.50
80	Roy Oswalt	.75
81	Craig Biggio	.50
82	Juan Pierre	.50
83	Jim Thome	.50
84	Josh Towers	.50
85	Alex Escobar	.50
86	Cliff Floyd	.50
87	Terrence Long	.50
88	Curt Schilling	.75
89	Carlos Beltran	1.00
90	Albert Pujols	2.50
91	Gabe Kapler	.50
92	Mark Mulder	.50
93	Carlos Lee	.50
94	Robert Fick	.50
95	Raul Mondesi	.50
96	Ichiro Suzuki	2.50
97	Adam Dunn	.75
98	Corey Patterson	.75
99	Tsuyoshi Shinjo	.50
100	Joe Mays	.50
101	Juan Cruz	3.00
102	Marlon Byrd	3.00
103	Luis Garcia	3.00
104	Jorge Padilla RC	6.00
105	Dennis Tankersley	3.00
106	Josh Pearce	3.00
107	Ramon Vazquez	3.00
108	Chris Baker RC	5.00
109	Eric Cyr RC	3.00
110	Reed Johnson RC	5.00
111	Ryan Jamison RC	3.00
112	Antonio Perez	3.00
113	Satoru Komiyama RC	3.00
114	Austin Kearns	5.00
115	Juan Pena	3.00
116	Orlando Hudson	3.00
117	Kazuhiro Ishii RC	6.00
118	Eric Bedard	3.00
119	Luis Ugueto RC	3.00
120	Ben Howard RC	4.00
121	Morgan Ensberg	3.00
122	Doug DeVore RC	4.00
123	Josh Phelps	3.00
124	Angel Berroa	4.00
125	Ed Rogers	3.00
126	Takahito Nomura RC	3.00
127	John Ennis RC	3.00
128	Bill Hall	3.00
129	Dewon Brazelton	3.00
130	Hank Blalock	5.00
131	So Taguchi RC	5.00
132	Jorge De La Rosa RC	3.00
133	Matt Thornton	3.00
134	Brandon Backe RC	3.00
135	Jeff Deardorff RC	3.00
136	Steve Smyth	3.00
137	Anderson Machado RC	5.00
138	John Buck	3.00
139	Mark Prior	15.00
140	Sean Burroughs	3.00
141	Alex Herrera	3.00
142	Francis Beltran RC	3.00
143	Jason Romano	3.00
144	Michael Cuddyer	3.00
145	Steve Bechler RC	3.00
146	Alfredo Amezaga	3.00
147	Ryan Ludwick	3.00
148	Martin Vargas	3.00
149	Allan Simpson RC	3.00
150	Mark Teixeira	3.00

151	Hank Aaron	8.00
152	Ernie Banks	6.00
153	Johnny Bench	6.00
154	George Brett	10.00
155	Lou Brock	3.00
156	Rod Carew	4.00
157	Steve Carlton	4.00
158	Joe Torre	3.00
159	Dennis Eckersley	2.50
160	Reggie Jackson	5.00
161	Al Kaline	6.00
162	Dave Parker	2.00
163	Don Mattingly	10.00
164	Tony Gwynn	6.00
165	Willie McCovey	3.00
166	Joe Morgan	3.00
167	Stan Musial	8.00
168	Jim Palmer	3.00
169	Brooks Robinson	5.00
170	Bo Jackson	6.00
171	Nolan Ryan	15.00
172	Mike Schmidt	8.00
173	Tom Seaver	6.00
174	Cal Ripken Jr.	15.00
175	Robin Yount	6.00
176	Wade Boggs	5.00
177	Gary Carter	3.00
178	Ron Santo	2.00
179	Luis Aparicio	4.00
180	Bobby Doerr	3.00
181	Ryne Sandberg	6.00
182	Yogi Berra	5.00
183	Will Clark	5.00
184	Eddie Murray	4.00
185	Andre Dawson	3.00
186	Duke Snider	4.00
187	Orlando Cepeda	3.00
188	Billy Williams	2.00
189	Juan Marichal	4.00
190	Harmon Killebrew	5.00
191	Kirby Puckett	6.00
192	Carlton Fisk	4.00
193	Dave Winfield	3.00
194	Alan Trammell	3.00
195	Paul Molitor	6.00
196	Tony Perez	3.00
197	Ozzie Smith	6.00
198	Ralph Kiner	3.00
199	Fergie Jenkins	2.00
200	Phil Rizzuto	3.00

Timeless Tributes
Stars (1-100): 2-4X
SP's (101-150): 1-2X
SP's (151-200): 2-3X
Production 100 Sets

Classic Singles
NM/M
Common Player: 10.00
Some too scarce to price.

1	Cal Ripken Jr/Jsy/100	40.00
2	Eddie Murray/Jsy/100	15.00
3	George Brett/Jsy/100	35.00
4	Bo Jackson/Jsy/100	20.00
5	Ted Williams/Bat/50	200.00
6	Jimmie Foxx/Bat/50	60.00
7	Reggie Jackson/Jsy/100	15.00
8	Steve Carlton/Jsy/50	30.00
9	Mel Ott/Jsy/50	70.00
10	"Catfish" Hunter/Jsy/100	10.00
11	Nolan Ryan/Jsy/100	40.00
12	Rickey Henderson/Jsy/100	25.00
13	Robin Yount/Jsy/100	25.00
14	Orlando Cepeda/Jsy/100	15.00
15	Ty Cobb/Bat/50	150.00
16	Babe Ruth/Bat/50	275.00
17	Dave Parker/Jsy/100	10.00
18	Willie Stargell/Jsy/100	15.00
19	Ernie Banks/Bat/100	35.00
20	Mike Schmidt/Jsy/100	35.00
21	Duke Snider/Jsy/50	25.00
22	Jackie Robinson/Jsy/50	75.00
23	Rickey Henderson/Bat/100	25.00
25	Lou Gehrig/Bat/50	175.00
26	Jimmie Foxx/Bat/50	65.00
27	Tony Gwynn/Bat/100	20.00
29	Bobby Doerr/Jsy/100	15.00
30	Joe Torre/Jsy/100	10.00

Classic Combos

Too scarce to price.

Legendary Hats

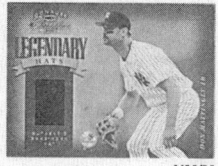

NM/M
50 sets produced.

1	Don Mattingly/50	150.00
2	George Brett	150.00
3	Wade Boggs	30.00
5	Ryne Sandberg	120.00

Legendary Leather

NM/M
50 sets produced.

1	Don Mattingly	125.00
2	Wade Boggs	30.00
3	Kirby Puckett	50.00
5	Mike Schmidt	80.00

Legendary Lumberjacks
NM/M
Varying quantities produced.

1	Don Mattingly/500	20.00
2	George Brett/400	20.00
3	Stan Musial/100	35.00
4	Lou Gehrig/50	175.00
5	Mike Piazza/500	10.00
6	Mel Ott/500	75.00
7	Ted Williams/50	150.00
8	Bo Jackson/500	8.00
9	Kirby Puckett/500	15.00
10	Rafael Palmeiro/500	10.00
11	Andre Dawson/500	5.00
12	Ozzie Smith/500	15.00
13	Paul Molitor/500	15.00
14	Babe Ruth/50	220.00
15	Carlton Fisk/500	8.00
16	Rickey Henderson/500	10.00
17	Gary Carter/500	5.00
18	Cal Ripken Jr/100	20.00
19	Eddie Matthews/100	20.00
20	Luis Aparicio/500	5.00
21	Al Kaline/100	25.00
22	Eddie Murray/100	8.00
23	Yogi Berra/100	25.00
24	Alex Rodriguez/500	10.00
25	Tony Gwynn/500	10.00
26	Roberto Clemente/100	80.00
27	Mike Schmidt/400	20.00
28	Reggie Jackson/500	10.00
29	Ryne Sandberg/500	20.00
30	Joe Morgan/400	5.00
31	Joe Torre/500	5.00
32	Gary Sheffield/500	5.00
33	Nomar Garciaparra/500	10.00
34	Jeff Bagwell/500	5.00
35	Manny Ramirez/500	8.00

Legendary Spikes

NM/M
50 Sets Produced

1	Don Mattingly	125.00
2	Eddie Murray	30.00
3	Paul Molitor	50.00
4	Harmon Killebrew	40.00
5	Mike Schmidt	100.00

New Millennium Classics

NM/M
Common Player: 4.00
Varying quantities produced
All jerseys unless noted.

1	Curt Schilling/500	6.00
2	Vladimir Guerrero/100	15.00
3	Jim Thome/500	8.00
4	Troy Glaus/400	6.00
5	Ivan Rodriguez/200	6.00
6	Todd Helton/400	8.00
7	Sean Casey/500	4.00
8	Scott Rolen/475	8.00
9	Ken Griffey Jr./150/Base	10.00
10	Hideo Nomo/100	25.00
11	Tom Glavine/350	5.00
12	Pedro Martinez/500	15.00
13	Cliff Floyd/500	4.00
14	Shawn Green/125	8.00
15	Rafael Palmeiro/250	8.00
16	Luis Gonzalez/100	5.00
17	Lance Berkman/100	6.00
18	Frank Thomas/500	8.00
19	Randy Johnson/400	8.00
20	Moises Alou/500	5.00
21	Chipper Jones/500	8.00
22	Larry Walker/300	4.00
23	Mike Sweeney/500	4.00
24	Juan Gonzalez/300	5.00
25	Roger Clemens/100	20.00
26	Albert Pujols/300/Base	15.00
27	Magglio Ordonez/500	5.00
28	Alex Rodriguez/400	10.00
29	Jeff Bagwell/100	10.00
30	Kazuhiro Sasaki/500	4.00
31	Barry Larkin/300	6.00
32	Andruw Jones/350	4.00
33	Kerry Wood/200	8.00
34	Rickey Henderson/100	5.00
35	Greg Maddux/100	15.00
36	Brian Giles/400	4.00
37	Craig Biggio/100	5.00
38	Roberto Alomar/400	6.00
39	Mike Piazza/400	10.00
40	Bernie Williams/100	10.00
41	Ichiro Suzuki/150/Ball	30.00
42	Kenny Lofton/450	4.00
43	Mark Mulder/500	4.00
44	Kazuhisa Ishii/100	15.00
45	Darin Erstad/500	4.00
46	Jose Vidro/500	4.00
47	Miguel Tejada/475	6.00
48	Roy Oswalt/500	5.00
49	Barry Zito/500	6.00
50	Manny Ramirez/400	8.00
51	Nomar Garciaparra/400	10.00
52	C.C. Sabathia/500	4.00
53	Carlos Delgado/500	6.00
54	Gary Sheffield/500	6.00
55	J.D. Drew/500	4.00
56	Barry Bonds/150/Ball	25.00
57	Derek Jeter/150/Bat	25.00
58	Edgar Martinez/400	4.00
59	Sammy Sosa/150/Ball	15.00

Significant Signatures

NM/M
Common Prospect Autograph: 5.00
Varying quantities produced,
many not priced due to scarcity.

101	Juan Cruz/400	6.00
102	Marlon Byrd/500	10.00
103	Luis Garcia/500	6.00
104	Jorge Padilla/500	5.00
105	Dennis Tankersley/250	10.00
106	Josh Pearce/500	5.00
107	Ramon Vazquez/500	5.00
108	Chris Baker/500 RC	8.00
109	Eric Cyr/500	6.00
110	Reed Johnson/500	10.00
111	Ryan Jamison/500	5.00
112	Antonio Perez/500	5.00
113	Satoru Komiyama/50	40.00
114	Austin Kearns/500	15.00
115	Juan Pena/500	5.00
116	Orlando Hudson/500	8.00
117	Kazuhisa Ishii/50	40.00
118	Eric Bedard/500	15.00
119	Luis Ugueto/250	10.00
120	Ben Howard/500	8.00
121	Morgan Ensberg/500	5.00
122	Doug DeVore/500	8.00
123	Josh Phelps/500	8.00
124	Angel Berroa/500	10.00
125	Ed Rogers/500	5.00
126	John Ennis/500	5.00
127	Bill Hall/400	10.00
128	Dewon Brazelton/400	8.00
129	Hank Blalock/100	20.00
130	So Taguchi/150	30.00
131	Jorge De La Rosa/500	5.00
132	Matt Thornton/500	5.00
133	Brandon Backe/500	5.00
134	Jeff Deardorff/500	5.00
135	Steve Smyth/400	5.00
136	Anderson Machado/500	10.00
137	John Buck/500	8.00
138	Mark Prior/250	25.00
139	Sean Burroughs/500	10.00
140	Alex Herrera/500	5.00
141	Francis Beltran/500	5.00
142	Jason Romano/500	5.00
143	Michael Cuddyer/400	8.00
144	Steve Bechler/500	8.00
145	Alfredo Amezaga/500	5.00
146	Ryan Ludwick/500	15.00
147	Martin Vargas/500	5.00
148	Allan Simpson/500	5.00
149	Mark Teixeira/200	30.00

152	Ernie Banks/25	100.00
153	Johnny Bench/25	125.00
154	George Brett/25	260.00
155	Lou Brock/100	30.00
157	Steve Carlton/125	35.00
159	Dennis Eckersley/500	15.00
161	Al Kaline/125	35.00
162	Dave Parker/500	10.00
163	Don Mattingly/50	75.00
168	Jim Palmer/125	25.00
169	Brooks Robinson/125	40.00
177	Gary Carter/150	25.00
178	Ron Santo/500	20.00
179	Luis Aparicio/400	10.00
180	Bobby Doerr/500	15.00
182	Yogi Berra/25	80.00
184	Eddie Murray/25	60.00
185	Andre Dawson/200	20.00
186	Duke Snider/25	70.00
187	Orlando Cepeda/125	25.00
188	Billy Williams/200	15.00
189	Juan Marichal/500	15.00
190	Harmon Killebrew/100	50.00
194	Alan Trammell/200	25.00
195	Paul Molitor/25	60.00
196	Tony Perez/150	25.00
198	Ralph Kiner/125	20.00
199	Fergie Jenkins/200	15.00
200	Phil Rizzuto/125	40.00

Timeless Treasures

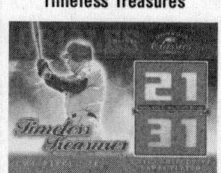

NM/M
Some not priced.

5	Ted Williams/Bat/42	140.00
6	Ted Williams/Bat/47	140.00
7	Ted Williams/Bat/46	140.00
8	Ted Williams/Bat/49	140.00
10	Cal Ripken Jr./Jsy/98	50.00
11	Cal Ripken Jr./Jsy/82	50.00
12	Cal Ripken Jr./Jsy/83	50.00
13	Cal Ripken Jr./Jsy/91	50.00

2002 Donruss Diamond Kings Samples

Each May and July 2002 issue of Beckett Baseball Card Monthly included a sample DK card rubber-cemented inside. The cards differ from the issued version only in the appearance on back of a (usually) silver-foil "SAMPLE" notation and, on some cards, the lack of silver-foil graphics on front. Some cards were produced with the back overprint in gold-foil in much more limited quantities. Cards #1-100 were issued in May, and 101-150 in July.

NM/M
Common Player: .25
Stars: 1.5-2X
Gold: 10X

2002 Donruss Diamond Kings

NM/M
Complete Set (150): 150.00
Common Player: .40
Common SP (101-150): 2.00
Inserted 1:3
Pack (4): 4.50
Box (24): 80.00

1	Vladimir Guerrero	1.00
2	Adam Dunn	.75
3	Tsuyoshi Shinjo	.40
4	Adrian Beltre	.60
5	Troy Glaus	1.00
6	Albert Pujols	2.00
7	Trot Nixon	.40
8	Alex Rodriguez	2.50
9	Tom Glavine	.50
10	Alfonso Soriano	1.00
11	Todd Helton	1.00
12	Joe Torre	.40
13	Tim Hudson	.50
14	Andruw Jones	.50
15	Shawn Green	.40
16	Aramis Ramirez	.40
17	Shannon Stewart	.40
18	Barry Bonds	3.00
19	Sean Casey	.40
20	Barry Larkin	.40
21	Scott Rolen	.75
22	Barry Zito	.50
23	Sammy Sosa	2.00
24	Bartolo Colon	.40
25	Ryan Klesko	.40
26	Ben Grieve	.40
27	Roy Oswalt	.50
28	Kazuhiro Sasaki	.40
29	Roger Clemens	1.75
30	Bernie Williams	.50
31	Roberto Alomar	.50
32	Bobby Abreu	.40
33	Robert Fick	.40
34	Bret Boone	.40
35	Rickey Henderson	1.00
36	Brian Giles	.40
37	Richie Sexson	.40
38	Bud Smith	.40
39	Richard Hidalgo	.40
40	C.C. Sabathia	.40
41	Rich Aurilia	.40
42	Carlos Beltran	.75
43	Raul Mondesi	.40
44	Carlos Delgado	.50
45	Randy Johnson	1.00
46	Chan Ho Park	.40
47	Rafael Palmeiro	.75
48	Chipper Jones	1.50
49	Phil Nevin	.40
50	Cliff Floyd	.40
51	Pedro Martinez	1.00
52	Craig Biggio	.40
53	Paul LoDuca	.40
54	Cristian Guzman	.40
55	Pat Burrell	.40
56	Curt Schilling	.50
57	Orlando Cabrera	.40
58	Darin Erstad	.65
59	Omar Vizquel	.40
60	Derek Jeter	3.00
61	Nomar Garciaparra	2.00
62	Edgar Martinez	.40
63	Moises Alou	.40
64	Eric Chavez	.50
65	Mike Sweeney	.40
66	Frank Thomas	1.00
67	Mike Piazza	2.00
68	Gary Sheffield	.50
69	Mike Mussina	.50
70	Greg Maddux	1.50
71	Juan Gonzalez	.50
72	Hideo Nomo	.65
73	Miguel Tejada	.50
74	Ichiro Suzuki	2.00
75	Matt Morris	.40
76	Ivan Rodriguez	.75
77	Mark Mulder	.40
78	J.D. Drew	.40
79	Mark Grace	.50
80	Jason Giambi	.50
81	Mark Buehrle	.40
82	Jose Vidro	.40
83	Manny Ramirez	1.00
84	Jeff Bagwell	1.00
85	Magglio Ordonez	.50
86	Ken Griffey Jr.	2.00
87	Luis Gonzalez	.40
88	Jim Edmonds	.40
89	Larry Walker	.40
90	Jim Thome	.40
91	Lance Berkman	.40
92	Jorge Posada	.40
93	Kevin Brown	.40
94	Joe Mays	.40
95	Kerry Wood	.75
96	Mark Ellis	.40
97	Austin Kearns	.75
98	Jorge De La Rosa RC	.50
99	Brandon Berger	.40
100	Ryan Ludwick	.40
101	Marlon Byrd	2.00
102	Brandon Backe RC	2.00
103	Juan Cruz	2.00
104	Anderson Machado RC	3.00
105	So Taguchi RC	2.00
106	Dewon Brazelton	2.00
107	Josh Beckett	3.00
108	John Buck	2.00
109	Jorge Padilla RC	3.00
110	Hee Seop Choi	2.00
111	Angel Berroa	2.00
112	Mark Teixeira	3.00
113	Victor Martinez	2.00
114	Kazuhisa Ishii RC	6.00
115	Dennis Tankersley	2.00
116	Wilson Valdez RC	2.00
117	Antonio Perez	2.00
118	Ed Rogers	2.00
119	Wilson Betemit	2.00
120	Mike Rivera	2.00
121	Mark Prior	6.00
122	Roberto Clemente	6.00
123	Roberto Clemente	6.00
124	Roberto Clemente	6.00
125	Roberto Clemente	6.00
126	Roberto Clemente	6.00
127	Babe Ruth	10.00
128	Ted Williams	8.00
129	Andre Dawson	2.00
130	Eddie Murray	3.00
131	Juan Marichal	3.00
132	Kirby Puckett	5.00
133	Alan Trammell	2.00
134	Bobby Doerr	2.00
135	Carlton Fisk	3.00
136	Eddie Mathews	4.00
137	Mike Schmidt	5.00
138	Jim "Catfish" Hunter	2.00
139	Nolan Ryan	10.00
140	George Brett	6.00
141	Gary Carter	2.00
142	Paul Molitor	4.00
143	Lou Gehrig	8.00
144	Ryne Sandberg	5.00
145	Tony Gwynn	5.00
146	Ron Santo	2.00
147	Cal Ripken Jr.	10.00
148	Al Kaline	4.00
149	Bo Jackson	3.00
150	Don Mattingly	8.00

Bronze Foil
Cards 1-100: 1-2X
Cards 101-150: .5X
Inserted 1:6
Gold Foil (1-100): 4-8X
Gold Foil (101-150): 2-3X
Production 100 Sets
Silver Foil (1-100): 3-4X
Silver Foil (101-150): 1-2X
Production 400 Sets

Diamond Cut

NM/M
Common Signature (1-30): 5.00

1	Vladimir Guerrero/400	30.00
2	Mark Prior/400	30.00
3	Victor Martinez/500	10.00
4	Marlon Byrd/500	15.00
5	Bud Smith/400	10.00
6	Joe Mays/500	10.00
7	Troy Glaus/500	20.00
8	Ron Santo/500	15.00
9	Roy Oswalt/500	20.00
10	Angel Berroa/500	10.00
11	Mark Buehrle/500	15.00
12	John Buck/500	10.00
13	Barry Larkin/250	40.00
14	Gary Carter/300	30.00
15	Mark Teixeira/500	20.00
16	Alan Trammell/500	20.00
17	Kazuhisa Ishii/500	10.00
18	Rafael Palmeiro/125	50.00
19	Austin Kearns/500	25.00
20	Joe Torre/125	20.00
21	J.D. Drew/400	20.00
22	So Taguchi/400	20.00
23	Juan Marichal/500	15.00
24	Bobby Doerr/500	20.00
25	Carlos Beltran/500	20.00
26	Robert Fick/500	10.00
27	Albert Pujols/200	180.00
28	Shannon Stewart/500	10.00
29	Antonio Perez/500	10.00
30	Wilson Betemit/500	10.00

Jerseys (31-80):

31	Alex Rodriguez/500	15.00
32	Curt Schilling/500	10.00
33	George Brett/300	30.00
34	Hideo Nomo/100	40.00
35	Ivan Rodriguez/500	10.00
36	Don Mattingly/200	40.00
37	Joe Mays/500	5.00
38	Lance Berkman/400	5.00
39	Tony Gwynn/500	10.00
40	Darin Erstad/400	5.00
41	Adrian Beltre/500	5.00
42	Frank Thomas/300	15.00
43	Cal Ripken Jr./300	30.00
44	Jose Vidro/500	5.00
45	Randy Johnson/300	10.00
46	Carlos Delgado/500	5.00
47	Roger Clemens/400	20.00
48	Luis Gonzalez/500	5.00
49	Marlon Byrd/500	5.00
50	Carlton Fisk/500	8.00
51	Manny Ramirez/500	8.00

52	Vladimir Guerrero/500	8.00
53	Barry Larkin/500	8.00
54	Aramis Ramirez/500	5.00
55	Todd Helton/300	5.00
56	Carlos Beltran/250	5.00
57	Jeff Bagwell/250	8.00
58	Larry Walker/500	5.00
59	Al Kaline/200	25.00
60	Chipper Jones/500	6.00
61	Bernie Williams/500	6.00
62	Bud Smith/500	5.00
63	Edgar Martinez/500	5.00
64	Pedro Martinez/500	6.00
65	Andre Dawson/200	6.00
66	Mike Piazza/100	40.00
67	Barry Zito/500	8.00
68	Bo Jackson/300	8.00
69	Nolan Ryan/400	50.00
70	Troy Glaus/500	6.00
71	Jorge Posada/500	8.00
72	Ted Williams/100	200.00
73	Nomar Garciaparra/500	15.00
74	"Catfish" Hunter/100	25.00
75	Gary Carter/500	8.00
76	Craig Biggio/500	5.00
77	Andruw Jones/500	8.00
78	Rickey Henderson/250	8.00
79	Greg Maddux/400	15.00
80	Kerry Wood/500	10.00

Bats (81-100):

81	Alex Rodriguez/500	20.00
82	Don Mattingly/425	30.00
83	Craig Biggio/500	5.00
84	Kazuhisa Ishii/375	8.00
85	Eddie Murray/500	8.00
86	Carlton Fisk/500	8.00
87	Tsuyoshi Shinjo/500	5.00
88	Bo Jackson/500	10.00
89	Eddie Mathews/100	30.00
90	Chipper Jones/500	8.00
91	Adam Dunn/375	8.00
92	Tony Gwynn/200	10.00
93	Kirby Puckett/500	15.00
94	Andre Dawson/500	5.00
95	Bernie Williams/500	5.00
96	Roberto Clemente/300	70.00
97	Babe Ruth/100	250.00
98	Roberto Alomar/500	8.00
99	Frank Thomas/500	8.00
100	So Taguchi/500	6.00

DK Originals

Complete Set (15):		50.00
Common Player:		2.00
Production 1,000 Sets		
1	Alex Rodriguez	7.00
2	Kazuhisa Ishii	2.00
3	Pedro Martinez	3.00
4	Nomar Garciaparra	6.00
5	Albert Pujols	6.00
6	Chipper Jones	5.00
7	So Taguchi	2.00
8	Jeff Bagwell	3.00
9	Vladimir Guerrero	3.00
10	Derek Jeter	8.00
11	Sammy Sosa	6.00
12	Ichiro Suzuki	6.00
13	Barry Bonds	8.00
14	Jason Giambi	3.00
15	Mike Piazza	6.00

Heritage Collection

		NM/M
Complete Set (25):		100.00
Common Player:		2.00
Inserted 1:23		
1	Lou Gehrig	8.00

2	Nolan Ryan	10.00
3	Ryne Sandberg	4.00
4	Ted Williams	8.00
5	Roberto Clemente	8.00
6	Mike Schmidt	6.00
7	Roger Clemens	5.00
8	Kirby Puckett	4.00
9	Andre Dawson	2.00
10	Carlton Fisk	2.00
11	Don Mattingly	8.00
12	Juan Marichal	2.00
13	George Brett	8.00
14	Bo Jackson	3.00
15	Eddie Mathews	3.00
16	Randy Johnson	3.00
17	Alan Trammell	2.00
18	Tony Gwynn	4.00
19	Paul Molitor	3.00
20	Barry Bonds	10.00
21	Eddie Murray	3.00
22	Jim "Catfish" Hunter	3.00
23	Rickey Henderson	3.00
24	Cal Ripken Jr.	10.00
25	Babe Ruth	10.00

Ramly T204

		NM/M
Complete Set (25):		120.00
Common Player:		3.00
Production 1,000 Sets		
1	Vladimir Guerrero	4.00
2	Jeff Bagwell	4.00
3	Barry Bonds	15.00
4	Rickey Henderson	4.00
5	Mike Piazza	8.00
6	Derek Jeter	15.00
7	Kazuhisa Ishii	3.00
8	Ichiro Suzuki	10.00
9	Chipper Jones	5.00
10	Sammy Sosa	8.00
11	Don Mattingly	10.00
12	Shawn Green	3.00
13	Nomar Garciaparra	10.00
14	Luis Gonzalez	3.00
15	Albert Pujols	8.00
16	Cal Ripken Jr.	15.00
17	Todd Helton	4.00
18	Hideo Nomo	3.00
19	Alex Rodriguez	10.00
20	So Taguchi	3.00
21	Lance Berkman	3.00
22	Tony Gwynn	5.00
23	Roger Clemens	6.00
24	Jason Giambi	4.00
25	Ken Griffey Jr.	8.00

Recollection Collection

		NM/M
Common Player:		
22	Fred Lynn 87 DK/28	15.00
30	Roy Oswalt 01 RDK Black/48	20.00
47	Alan Trammell 88 DK/110	30.00

Timeline

		NM/M
Complete Set (10):		60.00
Common Card:		3.00
Inserted 1:60		
1	Lou Gehrig, Don Mattingly	10.00
2	Hideo Nomo, Ichiro Suzuki	6.00
3	Cal Ripken Jr., Alex Rodriguez	10.00
4	Mike Schmidt, Scott Rolen	8.00
5	Ichiro Suzuki, Albert Pujols	8.00
6	Curt Schilling, Randy Johnson	5.00
7	Chipper Jones, Eddie Mathews	5.00
8	Lou Gehrig, Cal Ripken Jr.	10.00
9	Derek Jeter, Roger Clemens	10.00
10	Kazuhiko Ishimine, So Taguchi	3.00

2002 Donruss Diamond Kings - LCS Programs

A perforated sheet of Diamond King cards was inserted into some of the programs sold for the American and National League Championship Series. The 8-1/2" x 11" sheet features eight player cards and a header card advertising the brand. Each 2-1/2" x 3-1/2" card is perforated on all sides and differs from the regularly issued version only in the card number on back. Sheet cards have either an

---

"ALCS-" or "NLCS-" prefix to the number. Other programs could be found with similar sheets of Donruss Originals, Donruss Studio or Playoff Piece of the Game cards.

		NM/M
Complete Sheet Set (2):		20.00
Common Player:		.50
ALCS SHEET		10.00
1	Cal Ripken Jr.	3.00
2	Nomar Garciaparra	1.50
3	Roger Clemens	1.25
4	Alex Rodriguez	2.00
5	Troy Glaus	1.00
6	Miguel Tejada	.50
7	Alfonso Soriano	1.00
8	Ted Williams	2.50
--	Header Card	.10
NLCS SHEET		10.00
1	Randy Johnson	1.00
2	Josh Beckett	.75
3	Mike Piazza	1.50
4	Greg Maddux	1.25
5	Lance Berkman	.50
6	Mark Prior	2.00
7	Adam Dunn	1.00
8	Tony Gwynn	1.25
--	Header Card	.10

2002 Donruss Elite Samples

Each June 2002 issue of Beckett Baseball Card Monthly included a sample Elite Series card rubber-cemented inside. The cards differ from the issued version only in the appearance on back of a (usually) silver-foil "SAMPLE" notation. Some cards were produced with the overprint in gold-foil, in much more limited quantities. Cards #1-100 from the set can be found in this Sample version.

	NM/M
Common Player:	.25
Stars:	1.5-2X
Gold:	10X

2002 Donruss Elite

		NM/M
Complete Set (200):		
Common Player:		.25
Common (101-150):		2.00
Inserted 1:10		
Common (151-200):		4.00
Production 1,500		
Pack (5):		3.00
Box (20):		50.00

1	Vladimir Guerrero	.75
2	Bernie Williams	.35
3	Ichiro Suzuki	1.50
4	Roger Clemens	1.25
5	Greg Maddux	1.00
6	Fred McGriff	.25
7	Jermaine Dye	.25
8	Ken Griffey Jr.	1.50
9	Todd Helton	.75
10	Torii Hunter	.40
11	Pat Burrell	.40
12	Chipper Jones	1.00
13	Ivan Rodriguez	.50
14	Roy Oswalt	.40
15	Shannon Stewart	.25
16	Magglio Ordonez	.40
17	Lance Berkman	.25
18	Mark Mulder	.25
19	Al Leiter	.25
20	Sammy Sosa	1.50
21	Scott Rolen	.75
22	Aramis Ramirez	.25
23	Alfonso Soriano	.75
24	Phil Nevin	.25
25	Barry Bonds	2.50
26	Joe Mays	.25
27	Jeff Kent	.25
28	Mark Quinn	.25
29	Adrian Beltre	.35
30	Freddy Garcia	.25
31	Pedro J. Martinez	.75
32	Darryl Kile	.25
33	Mike Cameron	.25
34	Frank Catalanotto	.25
35	Jose Vidro	.25
36	Jim Thome	.75
37	Javy Lopez	.25
38	Paul Konerko	.25
39	Jeff Bagwell	.75
40	Curt Schilling	.40
41	Miguel Tejada	.40
42	Jim Edmonds	.25
43	Ellis Burks	.25
44	Mark Grace	.35
45	Robb Nen	.25
46	Jeff Conine	.25
47	Derek Jeter	2.50
48	Mike Lowell	.25
49	Javier Vazquez	.25
50	Manny Ramirez	.75
51	Bartolo Colon	.25
52	Carlos Beltran	.50
53	Tim Hudson	.40
54	Rafael Palmeiro	.65
55	Jimmy Rollins	.50
56	Andruw Jones	.75
57	Orlando Cabrera	.25
58	Dean Palmer	.25
59	Bret Boone	.25
60	Carlos Febles	.25
61	Ben Grieve	.25
62	Richie Sexson	.25
63	Alex Rodriguez	2.00
64	Juan Pierre	.25
65	Bobby Higginson	.25
66	Barry Zito	.40
67	Raul Mondesi	.25
68	Albert Pujols	2.00
69	Omar Vizquel	.25
70	Bobby Abreu	.25
71	Corey Koskie	.25
72	Tom Glavine	.40
73	Paul LoDuca	.25
74	Terrence Long	.25
75	Matt Morris	.25
76	Andy Pettitte	.40
77	Rich Aurilia	.25
78	Todd Walker	.25
79	John Olerud	.25
80	Mike Sweeney	.25
81	Ray Durham	.25
82	Fernando Vina	.25
83	Nomar Garciaparra	1.50
84	Mariano Rivera	.35
85	Mike Piazza	1.50
86	Mark Buehrle	.25
87	Adam Dunn	.50
88	Luis Gonzalez	.35
89	Richard Hidalgo	.25
90	Brad Radke	.25
91	Russ Ortiz	.25
92	Brian Giles	.25
93	Billy Wagner	.25
94	Cliff Floyd	.25
95	Eric Milton	.25
96	Bud Smith	.25
97	Wade Miller	.25
98	Jon Lieber	.25
99	Derrek Lee	.25
100	Jose Cruz Jr.	.25
101	Dmitri Young	2.00
102	Mo Vaughn	2.00
103	Tino Martinez	2.00
104	Larry Walker	2.50
105	Chuck Knoblauch	2.00
106	Troy Glaus	3.00
107	Jason Giambi	4.00
108	Travis Fryman	2.00
109	Josh Beckett	4.00
110	Edgar Martinez	2.00
111	Tim Salmon	2.00
112	C.C. Sabathia	4.00
113	Randy Johnson	5.00
114	Juan Gonzalez	3.00
115	Carlos Delgado	4.00
116	Hideo Nomo	4.00
117	Kerry Wood	4.00
118	Brian Jordan	2.00

119	Carlos Pena	2.00
120	Roger Cedeno	2.00
121	Chan Ho Park	2.00
122	Rafael Furcal	2.00
123	Frank Thomas	4.00
124	Mike Mussina	4.00
125	Rickey Henderson	5.00
126	Sean Casey	2.00
127	Barry Larkin	2.00
128	Kazuhiro Sasaki	2.00
129	Moises Alou	2.00
130	Jeff Cirillo	2.00
131	Jason Kendall	2.00
132	Gary Sheffield	3.00
133	Ryan Klesko	2.00
134	Kevin Brown	2.00
135	Darin Erstad	2.00
136	Roberto Alomar	3.00
137	Brad Fullmer	2.00
138	Eric Chavez	2.00
139	Ben Sheets	2.00
140	Trot Nixon	2.00
141	Garret Anderson	2.00
142	Shawn Green	2.50
143	Troy Percival	2.00
144	Craig Biggio	3.00
145	Jorge Posada	2.50
146	J.D. Drew	3.00
147	Johnny Damon	2.00
148	Jeromy Burnitz	2.00
149	Robin Ventura	2.00
150	Aaron Sele	2.00
151	Cam Esslinger RC	3.00
152	Ben Howard RC	4.00
153	Brandon Backe RC	3.00
154	Jorge De La Rosa RC	3.00
155	Austin Kearns	5.00
156	Carlos Zambrano	3.00
157	Kyle Kane RC	3.00
158	So Taguchi RC	5.00
159	Brian Mallette RC	3.00
160	Brett Jodie	3.00
161	Elio Serrano RC	3.00
162	Joe Thurston	3.00
163	Kevin Olsen	3.00
164	Rodrigo Rosario RC	4.00
165	Matt Guerrier	3.00
166	Anderson Machado RC	5.00
167	Bert Snow	3.00
168	Franklyn German RC	3.00
169	Brandon Claussen	3.00
170	Jason Romano	3.00
171	Jorge Padilla RC	5.00
172	Jose Cueto	3.00
173	Allan Simpson RC	3.00
174	Doug DeVore RC	3.00
175	Justin Duchscherer	3.00
176	Josh Pearce	3.00
177	Steve Bechler RC	3.00
178	Josh Phelps	3.00
179	Juan Diaz	3.00
180	Victor Alvarez RC	3.00
181	Ramon Vazquez	3.00
182	Mike Rivera	3.00
183	Kazuhisa Ishii RC	6.00
184	Henry Mateo	3.00
185	Travis Hughes RC	5.00
186	Zach Day	3.00
187	Brad Voyles	3.00
188	Sean Douglass	3.00
189	Nick Neugebauer	3.00
190	Tom Shearn RC	3.00
191	Eric Cyr RC	3.00
192	Adam Johnson	3.00
193	Michael Cuddyer	3.00
194	Erik Bedard	3.00
195	Mark Ellis	3.00
196	Carlos Hernandez	3.00
197	Deivi Santos	3.00
198	Morgan Ensberg	3.00
199	Ryan Jamison RC	3.00
200	Cody Ransom	3.00

Aspirations

1-100 print run 26-50:		15-30X
1-100 p/r 51-80:		8-15X
101-150 p/r 26-50:		1.5-3X
101-150 p/r 51-99:		1-2X

Status

1-100 print run 36-70:		10-20X
1-100 p/r 71-100:		5-10X
101-150 p/r 36-70:		1-2X
101-150 p/r 71-100:		1X

All-Star Salutes

	NM/M
Common Player:	1.00

Century:	1-2X
Production 100	

1	Ichiro Suzuki	5.00
2	Tony Gwynn	4.00
3	Magglio Ordonez	1.50
4	Cal Ripken Jr.	8.00
5	Tony Gwynn	4.00
6	Kazuhiro Sasaki	1.00
7	Freddy Garcia	1.00
8	Luis Gonzalez	1.00
9	Lance Berkman	1.00
10	Derek Jeter	8.00
11	Chipper Jones	4.00
12	Randy Johnson	3.00
13	Andruw Jones	3.00
14	Pedro J. Martinez	3.00
15	Jim Thome	1.00
16	Rafael Palmeiro	2.50
17	Barry Larkin	1.00
18	Ivan Rodriguez	2.50
19	Omar Vizquel	1.00
20	Edgar Martinez	1.00
21	Larry Walker	1.00
22	Javy Lopez	1.00
23	Mariano Rivera	1.25
24	Frank Thomas	3.00
25	Greg Maddux	4.00

Back to the Future

		NM/M
Complete Set (24):		75.00
Common Player:		2.00
Duals 500 produced, singles 1,000.		
1	Scott Rolen, Marlon Byrd	3.00
2	Joe Crede, Frank Thomas	6.00
3	Lance Berkman, Jeff Bagwell	6.00
4	Marcus Giles, Chipper Jones	10.00
5	Shawn Green, Paul LoDuca	4.00
7	Kerry Wood, Juan Cruz	4.00
8	Vladimir Guerrero, Orlando Cabrera	6.00
9	Scott Rolen	3.00
10	Marlon Byrd	2.00
11	Frank Thomas	3.00
12	Joe Crede	2.00
13	Jeff Bagwell	4.00
14	Lance Berkman	2.00
15	Chipper Jones	6.00
16	Marcus Giles	2.00
17	Shawn Green	2.50
18	Paul LoDuca	2.00
19	Jim Edmonds	3.00
20	Kerry Wood	3.00
22	Juan Cruz	2.00
23	Vladimir Guerrero	4.00
24	Orlando Cabrera	2.00

Back to the Future Threads

		NM/M
Common Card:		10.00
Duals 50 produced, singles 100.		
1	Scott Rolen, Marlon Byrd	30.00
2	Joe Crede, Frank Thomas	40.00
3	Lance Berkman, Jeff Bagwell	40.00
4	Marcus Giles, Chipper Jones	50.00
5	Shawn Green, Paul LoDuca	30.00
7	Kerry Wood, Juan Cruz	35.00
8	Vladimir Guerrero, Orlando Cabrera	40.00
9	Scott Rolen	15.00
10	Marlon Byrd	20.00
11	Frank Thomas	25.00
12	Joe Crede	10.00
13	Jeff Bagwell	25.00
14	Lance Berkman	15.00
15	Chipper Jones	25.00
16	Marcus Giles	10.00
17	Shawn Green	15.00
18	Paul LoDuca	10.00
19	Jim Edmonds	10.00
20	So Taguchi	50.00
21	Kerry Wood	15.00
22	Juan Cruz	10.00
23	Vladimir Guerrero	25.00
24	Orlando Cabrera	10.00

Back 2 Back Jacks

		NM/M
Common Card:		10.00
Dual Production 75		
Single Production 150		
1	Ivan Rodriguez, Alex Rodriguez	40.00
2	Kirby Puckett, Dave Winfield	50.00
3	Ted Williams, Nomar Garciaparra	150.00
4	Jeff Bagwell, Craig Biggio	25.00

5	Eddie Murray,	
	Cal Ripken Jr.	125.00
6	Andruw Jones,	
	Chipper Jones	25.00
7	Roberto Clemente,	
	Willie Stargell	120.00
8	Lou Gehrig,	
	Don Mattingly	180.00
9	Larry Walker,	
	Todd Helton	20.00
10	Manny Ramirez,	
	Trot Nixon	25.00
11	Alex Rodriguez	30.00
12	Ivan Rodriguez	15.00
13	Kirby Puckett	40.00
14	Dave Winfield	15.00
15	Ted Williams	100.00
16	Nomar Garciaparra	40.00
17	Jeff Bagwell	15.00
18	Craig Biggio	10.00
19	Eddie Murray	20.00
20	Cal Ripken Jr.	60.00
21	Andruw Jones	10.00
22	Chipper Jones	20.00
23	Roberto Clemente	80.00
25	Lou Gehrig	160.00
26	Don Mattingly	65.00
27	Larry Walker	10.00
28	Todd Helton	15.00
29	Manny Ramirez	20.00
30	Trot Nixon	10.00

Career Bests

	NM/M
Common Player:	2.00
1	Albert Pujols/1,013	8.00
2	Alex Rodriguez/52	20.00
3	Alex Rodriguez/135	15.00
4	Andruw Jones/104	6.00
5	Barry Bonds/73	25.00
6	Barry Bonds/1,379	10.00
7	Barry Bonds/177	20.00
8	C.C. Sabathia/171	4.00
9	Carlos Beltran/876	2.00
10	Chipper Jones/330	6.00
11	Derek Jeter/900	15.00
12	Eric Chavez/114	4.00
13	Frank Catalanotto/330	2.00
14	Ichiro Suzuki/838	10.00
15	Ichiro Suzuki/127	15.00
17	J.D. Drew/27	20.00
18	J.D. Drew/1,027	2.00
19	Jason Giambi/660	5.00
20	Jim Thome/49	25.00
21	Jim Thome/624	4.00
22	Jorge Posada/95	8.00
23	Jose Cruz Jr/856	2.00
24	Kazuhiro Sasaki/45	15.00
25	Kerry Wood/336	5.00
26	Lance Berkman/1,050	5.00
27	Magglio Ordonez/382	3.00
28	Mark Mulder/345	2.00
29	Pat Burrell/27	20.00
30	Pat Burrell/469	3.00
32	Randy Johnson/372	6.00
33	Richie Sexson/547	3.00
34	Roberto Alomar/956	4.00
35	Sammy Sosa/160	12.00
36	Sammy Sosa/1,174	6.00
37	Shawn Green/125	4.00
39	Trot Nixon/150	3.00
40	Troy Glaus/108	4.00

Passing the Torch

	NM/M
Common Card:	4.00
Dual 500, single 1,000 produced.	
1	Fergie Jenkins,	
	Mark Prior	10.00
2	Nolan Ryan, Roy Oswalt	25.00
3	Ozzie Smith, J.D. Drew	8.00
4	George Brett,	
	Carlos Beltran	15.00
5	Kirby Puckett,	
	Michael Cuddyer	10.00
	Johnny Bench,	
	Adam Dunn	8.00

7	Duke Snider,	
	Paul LoDuca	6.00
8	Tony Gwynn,	
	Xavier Nady	10.00
9	Fergie Jenkins	4.00
10	Mark Prior	8.00
11	Nolan Ryan	15.00
12	Roy Oswalt	5.00
13	Ozzie Smith	6.00
14	J.D. Drew	4.00
15	George Brett	10.00
16	Carlos Beltran	4.00
17	Kirby Puckett	6.00
18	Michael Cuddyer	4.00
19	Johnny Bench	6.00
20	Adam Dunn	6.00
21	Duke Snider	6.00
22	Paul LoDuca	4.00
23	Tony Gwynn	6.00
24	Xavier Nady	4.00

Passing the Torch Autographs

	NM/M
Common Autograph:	15.00
1	Ferguson Jenkins,	
	Mark Prior/50	100.00
2	Nolan Ryan,	
	Roy Oswalt/50	180.00
3	Ozzie Smith,	
	J.D. Drew/50	125.00
4	George Brett,	
	Carlos Beltran/25	300.00
5	Kirby Puckett,	
	Michael Cuddyer/50	100.00
6	Johnny Bench,	
	Adam Dunn/50	100.00
7	Duke Snider,	
	Paul LoDuca/50	80.00
8	Tony Gwynn,	
	Xavier Nady/50	120.00
9	Fergie Jenkins/50	40.00
10	Mark Prior/100	20.00
11	Nolan Ryan/100	125.00
12	Roy Oswalt/100	25.00
13	J.D. Drew/100	30.00
14	George Brett/25	300.00
15	Carlos Beltran/100	40.00
16	Kirby Puckett/25	150.00
17	Michael Cuddyer/100	15.00
18	Johnny Bench/100	50.00
19	Adam Dunn/100	40.00
20	Duke Snider/100	30.00
22	Paul LoDuca/100	15.00
23	Tony Gwynn/100	50.00
24	Xavier Nady/100	15.00

Recollection Collection

	NM/M
Common Player:	
2	Alfredo Amezaga 01/50	15.00
13	Orlando Hudson 01/50	20.00
20	Antonio Perez 01/50	15.00
20	Mike Rivera 01/50	15.00
22	Claudio Vargas 01/50	15.00
23	Martin Vargas 01/50	15.00

Throwback Threads

	NM/M
Common Card:	15.00
Dual 50, single 100 produced.	
1	Manny Ramirez,	
	Ted Williams	125.00
2	Mike Piazza,	
	Carlton Fisk	50.00
3	George Brett,	
	Bo Jackson	125.00
4	Randy Johnson,	
	Curt Schilling	40.00
5	Don Mattingly,	
	Lou Gehrig	250.00
6	Bernie Williams,	
	Dave Winfield	25.00
7	Rickey Henderson	75.00
8	Paul Molitor,	
	Robin Yount	75.00
9	J.D. Drew, Stan Musial	100.00
10	Andre Dawson,	
	Ryne Sandberg	100.00
11	Babe Ruth,	
	Reggie Jackson	325.00
12	Brooks Robinson,	
	Cal Ripken Jr.	120.00
13	Ted Williams,	
	Nomar Garciaparra	125.00
14	Shawn Green,	
	Jackie Robinson	80.00

15	Tony Gwynn,	
	Cal Ripken Jr.	120.00
16	Ted Williams	75.00
17	Manny Ramirez	20.00
18	Carlton Fisk	25.00
19	Mike Piazza	20.00
20	Bo Jackson	20.00
21	George Brett	50.00
22	Curt Schilling	20.00
23	Randy Johnson	20.00
24	Don Mattingly	50.00
25	Lou Gehrig	200.00
26	Bernie Williams	15.00
27	Dave Winfield	15.00
29	Rickey Henderson	40.00
30	Robin Yount	30.00
31	Paul Molitor	25.00
32	Stan Musial	65.00
33	J.D. Drew	15.00
34	Andre Dawson	15.00
35	Ryne Sandberg	50.00
36	Babe Ruth	250.00
37	Reggie Jackson	25.00
38	Brooks Robinson	25.00
39	Cal Ripken Jr.	75.00
40	Nomar Garciaparra	40.00
41	Jackie Robinson	80.00
42	Shawn Green	15.00
43	Pedro J. Martinez	20.00
44	Nolan Ryan	80.00
45	Kazuhiro Sasaki	15.00
46	Tony Gwynn	25.00
47	Carlton Fisk	20.00
48	Cal Ripken Jr.	75.00
49	Rod Carew	20.00
50	Nolan Ryan	80.00
51	Alex Rodriguez	25.00
52	Greg Maddux	25.00
53	Pedro J. Martinez	20.00
54	Rickey Henderson	30.00
55	Rod Carew	20.00
56	Roberto Clemente	100.00
57	Hideo Nomo	40.00
58	Rickey Henderson	40.00
59	Dave Parker	15.00
60	Eddie Mathews	25.00
61	Eddie Murray	20.00
62	Nolan Ryan	80.00
63	Tom Seaver	25.00
64	Roger Clemens	40.00
65	Rickey Henderson	40.00

Throwback Threads Autographs

Production 5-25

Turn of the Century

	NM/M
Common Player:	8.00
154	Jorge De La Rosa/50	8.00
156	Carlos Zambrano/50	8.00
157	Kyle Kane/50	8.00
158	So Taguchi/25	15.00
159	Brian Mallette/50	8.00
160	Brett Jodie/50	8.00
165	Matt Guerrier/50	8.00
168	Franklyn German/50	8.00
169	Brandon Claussen/50	15.00
171	Jorge Padilla/50	10.00
172	Jose Cueto/50	8.00
176	Josh Pearce/50	8.00
177	Steve Bechler/50	8.00
178	Josh Phelps/50	8.00
180	Victor Alvarez/50	8.00
182	Michael Rivera/50	8.00
183	Kazuhisa Ishii/125	20.00
184	Henry Mateo/50	8.00
186	Zach Day/50	8.00
189	Nick Neugebauer/100	8.00
192	Adam Johnson/125	8.00
193	Michael Cuddyer/50	8.00
194	Mark Ellis/25	10.00
196	Carlos Hernandez/150	8.00
198	Morgan Ensberg/50	8.00
200	Cody Ransom/150	8.00

Turn of the Century Autographs

	NM/M
Common Autograph:	10.00
151	Cam Esslinger/150	10.00
152	Ben Howard/150	10.00
153	Brandon Backe/150	15.00
154	Jorge De La Rosa/100	10.00
155	Austin Kearns/150	15.00
156	Carlos Zambrano/100	20.00
157	Kyle Kane/100	10.00
158	So Taguchi/125	20.00
159	Brian Mallette/100	10.00
160	Brett Jodie/100	10.00
161	Elio Serrano/150	10.00
162	Joe Thurston/150	10.00
163	Kevin Olsen/150	10.00
164	Rodrigo Rosario/150	10.00
165	Matt Guerrier/100	10.00
166	Anderson Machado/150	10.00
167	Bert Snow/150	10.00
168	Franklyn German/100	10.00
169	Brandon Claussen/150	15.00
170	Jason Romano/150	10.00
171	Jorge Padilla/100	15.00
172	Jose Cueto/100	10.00
173	Allan Simpson/150	10.00
174	Doug DeVore/150	15.00
175	Justin Duchscherer/150	10.00
176	Josh Pearce/100	10.00
177	Steve Bechler/100	10.00

178	Josh Phelps/100	15.00
179	Juan Diaz/150	10.00
180	Victor Alvarez/100	10.00
181	Ramon Vazquez/150	10.00
182	Michael Rivera/100	10.00
183	Kazuhisa Ishii/25	150.00
184	Henry Mateo/100	10.00
185	Travis Hughes/150	10.00
186	Zach Day/100	10.00
187	Brad Voyles/150	10.00
188	Sean Douglass/150	10.00
189	Nick Neugebauer/50	10.00
190	Tom Shearn/150	10.00
191	Eric Cyr/150	10.00
192	Adam Johnson/25	10.00
193	Michael Cuddyer/100	10.00
194	Erik Bedard/20	20.00
195	Mark Ellis/125	10.00
197	Deivis Santos/150	10.00
198	Morgan Ensberg/100	10.00
199	Ryan Jamison/150	10.00

2002 Donruss Fan Club

	NM/M
Complete Set (300):	
Common Player:	.25
Common (201-260):	3.00
Production 1,350	
Common (261-300):	2.00
Production 2,025	
Pack (5):	3.50
Box (20):	60.00
1	Alex Rodriguez	2.00
2	Pedro Martinez	.75
3	Vladimir Guerrero	.75
4	Jim Edmonds	.25
5	Derek Jeter	2.50
6	Johnny Damon	.40
7	Rafael Furcal	.25
8	Cal Ripken Jr.	2.50
9	Brad Radke	.25
10	Bret Boone	.25
11	Pat Burrell	.50
12	Roy Oswalt	.25
13	Cliff Floyd	.25
14	Robin Ventura	.25
15	Frank Thomas	.75
16	Mariano Rivera	.35
17	Paul LoDuca	.25
18	Geoff Jenkins	.25
19	Tony Gwynn	1.00
20	Chipper Jones	1.00
21	Eric Chavez	.25
22	Kerry Wood	.60
23	Jorge Posada	.35
24	J.D. Drew	.25
25	Garret Anderson	.25
26	Javier Vazquez	.25
27	Kenny Lofton	.25
28	Mike Mussina	.45
29	Paul Konerko	.25
30	Bernie Williams	.45
31	Eric Milton	.25
32	Craig Wilson	.25
33	Paul O'Neill	.25
34	Dmitri Young	.25
35	Andres Galarraga	.25
36	Gary Sheffield	.40
37	Ben Grieve	.25
38	Scott Rolen	.25
39	Mark Grace	.35
40	Albert Pujols	2.00
41	Barry Zito	.40
42	Edgar Martinez	.25
43	Jarrod Washburn	.25
44	Juan Pierre	.25
45	Mark Buehrle	.25
46	Larry Walker	.25
47	Trot Nixon	.25
48	Wade Miller	.25
49	Robert Fick	.25
50	Sean Casey	.40
51	Joe Mays	.25
52	Brad Fullmer	.25
53	Chan Ho Park	.25
54	Carlos Delgado	.50
55	Phil Nevin	.25
56	Mike Cameron	.25
57	Raul Mondesi	.25
58	Roberto Alomar	.40
59	Ryan Klesko	.25
60	Andruw Jones	.75
61	Gabe Kapler	.25
62	Darin Erstad	.65
63	Cristian Guzman	.25
64	Kazuhiro Sasaki	.25
65	Doug Mientkiewicz	.25
66	Sammy Sosa	1.50

67	Mike Hampton	.25
68	Rickey Henderson	.75
69	Mark Mulder	.35
70	Jeff Conine	.25
71	Freddy Garcia	.25
72	Ivan Rodriguez	.65
73	Terrence Long	.25
74	Adam Dunn	.50
75	Moises Alou	.25
76	Todd Helton	.75
77	Preston Wilson	.25
78	Roger Cedeno	.25
79	Tony Armas Jr.	.25
80	Manny Ramirez	.25
81	Jose Vidro	.25
82	Randy Johnson	.75
83	Richie Sexson	.25
84	Troy Glaus	.75
85	Kevin Brown	.35
86	Woody Williams	.25
87	Adrian Beltre	.40
88	Brian Giles	.25
89	Jermaine Dye	.25
90	Craig Biggio	.25
91	Richard Hidalgo	.25
92	Magglio Ordonez	.40
93	Al Leiter	.25
94	Jeff Kent	.25
95	Curt Schilling	.50
96	Tim Hudson	.25
97	Fred McGriff	.25
98	Barry Larkin	.25
99	Jim Thome	.25
100	Tom Glavine	.40
101	Alfonso Soriano	.75
102	Jamie Moyer	.25
103	Vinny Castilla	.25
104	Rich Aurilia	.25
105	Matt Morris	.25
106	Rafael Palmeiro	.65
107	Joe Crede	.25
108	Barry Bonds	2.50
109	Robert Person	.25
110	Nomar Garciaparra	1.50
111	Brandon Duckworth	.25
112	Russ Ortiz	.25
113	Jeff Weaver	.25
114	Carlos Beltran	.50
115	Ellis Burks	.25
116	Jeremy Giambi	.25
117	Carlos Lee	.25
118	Ken Griffey Jr.	1.50
119	Torii Hunter	.40
120	Andy Pettitte	.40
121	Jose Canseco	.40
122	Charles Johnson	.25
123	Nick Johnson	.25
124	Luis Gonzalez	.35
125	Rondell White	.25
126	Miguel Tejada	.50
127	Jose Cruz Jr.	.25
128	Brent Abernathy	.25
129	Scott Brosius	.25
130	Jon Lieber	.25
131	John Smoltz	.25
132	Mike Sweeney	.25
133	Shannon Stewart	.25
134	Derrek Lee	.25
135	Brian Jordan	.25
136	Rusty Greer	.25
137	Mike Piazza	1.50
138	Billy Wagner	.25
139	Shawn Green	.35
140	Orlando Cabrera	.25
141	Jeff Bagwell	.75
142	Aaron Sele	.25
143	Hideo Nomo	.75
144	Marlon Anderson	.25
145	Todd Walker	.25
146	Bobby Higginson	.25
147	Ichiro Suzuki	2.00
148	Juan Uribe	.25
149	Jason Kendall	.25
150	Mark Quinn	.25
151	Ben Sheets	.25
152	Paul Abbott	.25
153	Aubrey Huff	.25
154	Greg Maddux	1.00
155	Darryl Kile	.25
156	John Burkett	.25
157	Juan Gonzalez	.75
158	Javy Lopez	.25
159	Aramis Ramirez	.25
160	Lance Berkman	.25
161	David Cone	.25
162	Edgar Renteria	.25
163	Roger Clemens	1.25
164	Frank Catalanotto	.25
165	Bartolo Colon	.25
166	Mark McGwire	2.00
167	Jay Gibbons	.25
168	Tony Clark	.25
169	Tsuyoshi Shinjo	.25
170	Brad Penny	.25
171	Marcus Giles	.25
172	Matt Williams	.25
173	Bud Smith	.25
174	Tino Martinez	.25
175	Ryan Dempster	.25
176	Jimmy Rollins	.40
177	Edgardo Alfonzo	.25
178	Jason Giambi	.50
179	Aaron Boone	.25
180	Matt Dunigan	.25
181	Mike Lowell	.25
182	Jose Ortiz	.25
183	Johnny Estrada	.25
184	Shane Reynolds	.25

185	Joe Kennedy	.25
186	Corey Patterson	.25
187	Jeromy Burnitz	.25
188	C.C. Sabathia	.25
189	Doug Davis	.25
190	Omar Vizquel	.25
191	John Olerud	.25
192	Dee Brown	.25
193	Kip Wells	.25
194	A.J. Burnett	.25
195	Josh Towers	.25
196	Jason Varitek	.25
197	Jason Isringhausen	.25
198	Fernando Vina	.25
199	Ramon Ortiz	.25
200	Bobby Abreu	.25
201	Willie Harris	3.00
202	Angel Santos	3.00
203	Corky Miller	3.00
204	Mike Rivera	3.00
205	Justin Duchscherer	3.00
206	Rick Bauer	3.00
207	Angel Berroa	3.00
208	Juan Cruz	3.00
209	Dewon Brazelton	3.00
210	Mark Prior	10.00
211	Mark Teixeira	8.00
212	Geronimo Gil	3.00
213	Casey Fossum	3.00
214	Ken Harvey	3.00
215	Michael Cuddyer	3.00
216	Wilson Betemit	3.00
217	David Brous	3.00
218	Juan Pena	3.00
219	Travis Hafner	4.00
220	Erick Almonte	3.00
221	Morgan Ensberg	3.00
222	Martin Vargas	3.00
223	Brandon Berger	3.00
224	Zach Day	3.00
225	Brad Voyles	3.00
226	Jeremy Affeldt	3.00
227	Nick Neugebauer	3.00
228	Tim Redding	3.00
229	Adam Johnson	3.00
230	Doug DeVore RC	4.00
231	Cody Ransom	3.00
232	Marlon Byrd	3.00
233	Delvin James	3.00
234	Eric Munson	3.00
235	Dennis Tankersley	3.00
236	Josh Beckett	8.00
237	Bill Hall	3.00
238	Kevin Olsen	3.00
239	Francis Beltran RC	5.00
240	Antonio Perez	3.00
241	Orlando Hudson	3.00
242	Anderson Machado RC	6.00
243	Tom Shearn RC	5.00
244	Brian Mallette RC	4.00
245	Raul Chavez RC	4.00
246	Andy Pratt RC	4.00
247	Jorge De La Rosa RC	4.00
248	Jeff Deardorff RC	4.00
249	Ben Howard RC	4.00
250	Brandon Backe RC	4.00
251	Ed Rogers	3.00
252	Travis Hughes RC	5.00
253	Rodrigo Rosario RC	5.00
254	Alfredo Amezaga	3.00
255	Jorge Padilla RC	5.00
256	Victor Martinez	4.00
257	Steve Bechler RC	4.00
258	Chris Baker RC	4.00
259	Ryan Freel	3.00
260	Allan Simpson RC	4.00
261	Alex Rodriguez	6.00
262	Vladimir Guerrero	3.00
263	Bud Smith	2.00
264	Miguel Tejada	2.00
265	Craig Biggio	2.00
266	Luis Gonzalez	2.00
267	Ivan Rodriguez	2.00
268	C.C. Sabathia	2.00
269	Jeff Bagwell	3.00
270	Aramis Ramirez	2.00
271	Bobby Abreu	2.00
272	Rich Aurilia	2.00
273	Jason Giambi	3.00
274	Rickey Henderson	3.00
275	Wade Miller	2.00
276	Andruw Jones	3.00
277	Troy Glaus	3.00
278	Roy Oswalt	3.00
279	Tony Gwynn	3.00
280	Adam Dunn	2.00
281	Larry Walker	2.00
282	Jose Canseco	3.00
283	Todd Helton	3.00
284	Lance Berkman	2.00
285	Cal Ripken Jr.	10.00
286	Albert Pujols	8.00
287	Alfonso Soriano	2.00
288	Mark Mulder	2.00
289	Mike Hampton	2.00
290	Andres Galarraga	2.00
291	Barry Bonds	8.00
292	Ben Sheets	2.00
293	Ichiro Suzuki	8.00
294	J.D. Drew	2.00
295	Jose Ortiz	2.00
296	Kerry Wood	3.00
297	Mark McGwire	8.00
298	Mike Sweeney	2.00
299	Pat Burrell	3.00
300	Tim Hudson	3.00

Autographs

	NM/M
Common Player:	5.00
Varying quantities produced.	

201	Willie Harris/500	5.00
203	Corky Miller/500	5.00
205	Justin Duchscherer/500	10.00
207	Angel Berroa/100	8.00
208	Juan Cruz/175	8.00
209	Dewon Brazelton/52	15.00
210	Mark Prior/425	40.00
211	Mark Teixeira/425	25.00
213	Casey Fossum/100	10.00
215	Michael Cuddyer/52	15.00
216	Wilson Betemit/500	8.00
217	David Brous/500	5.00
218	Juan A. Pena/188	8.00
219	Travis Hafner/375	10.00
221	Morgan Ensberg/52	15.00
222	Martin Vargas/500	5.00
223	Brandon Berger/500	5.00
224	Zach Day/500	5.00
225	Brad Voyles/500	5.00
226	Jeremy Affeldt/250	5.00
227	Nick Neugebauer/225	8.00
228	Tim Redding/500	8.00
229	Adam Johnson/425	10.00
230	Doug DeVore/300	8.00
231	Cody Ransom/500	5.00
232	Marlon Byrd/475	15.00
233	Delvin James/375	5.00
234	Eric Munson/325	8.00
235	Dennis Tankersley/500	5.00
238	Kevin Olsen/325	5.00
240	Antonio Perez/525	5.00
241	Orlando Hudson/525	10.00
248	Jeff Deardorff/475	5.00
251	Ed Rogers/400	5.00
255	Jorge Padilla/450	15.00
260	Allan Simpson/475	5.00
278	Roy Oswalt/75	35.00

Artist
NM/M
Complete Set (14): 60.00
Common Player: 3.00
Production 300 Sets

1	Pedro Martinez	8.00
2	Curt Schilling	6.00
3	Kevin Brown	3.00
4	Tim Hudson	5.00
5	Kerry Wood	7.50
6	Barry Zito	4.00
7	Hideo Nomo	6.00
8	Randy Johnson	8.00
9	Greg Maddux	10.00
10	Roger Clemens	15.00
11	Kazuhiro Sasaki	3.00
12	Joe Mays	3.00
13	Mark Mulder	5.00
14	Javier Vazquez	3.00

Master Artists
NM/M
Common Player: 5.00
Production 150 Sets

1	Pedro Martinez	15.00
2	Curt Schilling	10.00
3	Kevin Brown	5.00
4	Tim Hudson	6.00
5	Kerry Wood	5.00
6	Barry Zito	8.00
7	Hideo Nomo	15.00
8	Randy Johnson	15.00
9	Greg Maddux	15.00
10	Roger Clemens	20.00
11	Kazuhiro Sasaki	5.00
12	Joe Mays	5.00
13	Mark Mulder	5.00
14	Javier Vazquez	3.00

Artist Autographs
NM/M
Production 15-100

6	Barry Zito/100	35.00

Craftsmen

NM/M
Complete Set (18): 80.00
Common Player: 3.00
Production 300 Sets

1	Ichiro Suzuki	10.00
2	Todd Helton	5.00
3	Manny Ramirez	5.00
4	Luis Gonzalez	3.00
5	Roberto Alomar	3.50
6	Moises Alou	3.00
7	Darin Erstad	3.00
8	Mike Piazza	10.00
9	Edgar Martinez	3.00
10	Vladimir Guerrero	6.00
11	Juan Gonzalez	5.00
12	Nomar Garciaparra	10.00
13	Tony Gwynn	6.00
14	Jeff Bagwell	5.00
15	Albert Pujols	15.00
16	Larry Walker	3.00
17	Paul LoDuca	3.00
18	Lance Berkman	3.00

Master Craftsmen

NM/M
Common Player: 5.00
Production 150 Sets/H

1	Ichiro Suzuki/Ball/51	75.00
2	Todd Helton	10.00
3	Manny Ramirez	10.00
4	Luis Gonzalez	8.00
5	Roberto Alomar	8.00
6	Moises Alou	8.00
7	Darin Erstad	8.00
8	Mike Piazza	15.00
9	Edgar Martinez	8.00
10	Vladimir Guerrero	15.00
11	Juan Gonzalez	8.00
12	Nomar Garciaparra	20.00
13	Tony Gwynn/175	20.00
14	Jeff Bagwell	8.00
15	Albert Pujols/175	25.00
16	Larry Walker/175	5.00
17	Paul LoDuca/175	5.00
18	Lance Berkman	8.00

Craftsmen Autographs
NM/M
Common Player:

17	Paul LoDuca/100	20.00

Double Features
NM/M
Complete Set (10): 80.00
Common Card: 8.00
Production 125 Sets

1	Larry Walker, Todd Helton	10.00
2	Jose Vidro, Vladimir Guerrero	10.00
3	Jason Giambi, Jeremy Giambi	8.00
4	Nomar Garciaparra, Manny Ramirez	15.00
5	Troy Glaus, Darin Erstad	8.00
6	Shawn Green, Paul LoDuca	8.00
7	Jeff Bagwell, Craig Biggio	10.00
8	Pedro Martinez, Hideo Nomo	12.00
9	Curt Schilling, Randy Johnson	10.00
10	Andruw Jones, Chipper Jones	12.00

Double Features Game-Used
NM/M
Common Card: 10.00
Production 50 Sets

1	Larry Walker, Todd Helton	15.00
2	Jose Vidro, Vladimir Guerrero	20.00
3	Jason Giambi, Jeremy Giambi	15.00
4	Nomar Garciaparra, Manny Ramirez	30.00
5	Troy Glaus, Darin Erstad	15.00
6	Shawn Green, Paul LoDuca	10.00
7	Jeff Bagwell, Craig Biggio	15.00
8	Pedro Martinez, Hideo Nomo	30.00
9	Curt Schilling, Randy Johnson	20.00
10	Andruw Jones, Chipper Jones	20.00

Franchise Features
NM/M
Complete Set (40): 180.00
Common Player: 3.00
Production 300 Sets

1	Cliff Floyd	3.00
2	Mike Piazza	12.00
3	Cal Ripken Jr.	25.00
4	Mike Sweeney	3.00
5	Curt Schilling	5.00
6	Aramis Ramirez	3.00
7	Vladimir Guerrero	8.00

8	Andruw Jones	8.00
9	Tim Hudson	3.00
10	Bernie Williams	3.00
11	Pedro Martinez	8.00
12	Roberto Alomar	3.00
13	Joe Mays	3.00
14	Jason Giambi	5.00
15	Kazuhiro Sasaki	3.00
16	Magglio Ordonez	5.00
17	Nomar Garciaparra	12.00
18	Juan Gonzalez	5.00
19	Carlos Beltran	3.00
20	Javier Vazquez	3.00
21	Miguel Tejada	5.00
22	Luis Gonzalez	3.00
23	Greg Maddux	10.00
24	Rafael Palmeiro	6.00
25	Freddy Garcia	3.00
26	Barry Zito	4.00
27	Paul LoDuca	3.00
28	Robert Fick	3.00
29	Roger Clemens	3.00
30	Eric Chavez	3.00
31	Ivan Rodriguez	8.00
32	Chipper Jones	10.00
33	Kerry Wood	6.00
34	Randy Johnson	8.00
35	Alex Rodriguez	12.00
36	Manny Ramirez	8.00
37	Mark Buehrle	3.00
38	Mark Mulder	3.00
39	Ichiro Suzuki	15.00
40	Troy Glaus	4.00

Franchise Features Autographs
NM/M
Production 15-100

6	Aramis Ramirez/100	20.00
9	Tim Hudson/50	25.00
13	Joe Mays/75	10.00
19	Carlos Beltran/100	20.00
25	Freddy Garcia/100	20.00
26	Barry Zito/100	30.00
27	Paul LoDuca/100	15.00
28	Robert Fick/100	15.00
30	Eric Chavez/50	20.00
37	Mark Buehrle/100	15.00

Franchise Features Game-Used
NM/M
Common Player: 4.00
Production 150 Sets
All Jerseys unless noted.

1	Cliff Floyd	4.00
2	Mike Piazza	15.00
3	Cal Ripken Jr.	30.00
4	Mike Sweeney	4.00
5	Curt Schilling	6.00
6	Aramis Ramirez	6.00
7	Vladimir Guerrero	8.00
8	Andruw Jones	8.00
9	Tim Hudson	6.00
10	Bernie Williams	6.00
11	Pedro Martinez	10.00
12	Roberto Alomar	6.00
13	Joe Mays	4.00
14	Jason Giambi	8.00
15	Kazuhiro Sasaki	5.00
16	Magglio Ordonez	6.00
17	Nomar Garciaparra	20.00
18	Juan Gonzalez	8.00
19	Carlos Beltran	4.00
20	Javier Vazquez	4.00
21	Miguel Tejada	5.00
22	Luis Gonzalez	4.00
23	Greg Maddux	15.00
24	Rafael Palmeiro	10.00
25	Freddy Garcia	4.00
26	Barry Zito	4.00
27	Paul LoDuca	4.00
28	Robert Fick	4.00
29	Roger Clemens	20.00
30	Eric Chavez/bat	4.00
31	Ivan Rodriguez	8.00
32	Chipper Jones	8.00
33	Kerry Wood	8.00
34	Randy Johnson	10.00
35	Alex Rodriguez	15.00
36	Manny Ramirez	8.00
37	Mark Buehrle	4.00
38	Mark Mulder	6.00
39	Ichiro Suzuki/Ball	80.00
40	Troy Glaus	6.00

League Leaders
NM/M
Common Player: 3.00
Production 300 Sets

1	Roger Clemens	12.00
2	Curt Schilling	5.00
3	Matt Morris	3.00
4	Randy Johnson	6.00
5	Mark Mulder	4.00
6	Curt Schilling	5.00
7	Mike Mussina	4.00
8	Joe Mays	3.00
9	Matt Morris	3.00
10	Tim Hudson	4.00
11	Mark Buehrle	3.00
12	Greg Maddux	10.00
13	Freddy Garcia	3.00
14	Randy Johnson	6.00
15	Curt Schilling	3.00
16	Chan Ho Park	3.00
17	Roger Clemens	12.00
18	Mike Mussina	4.00
19	Javier Vazquez	3.00
20	Kerry Wood	8.00
21	Randy Johnson	6.00
22	Barry Zito	4.00
23	Hideo Nomo	8.00
24	Ichiro Suzuki	10.00
25	Todd Helton	6.00
26	Albert Pujols	20.00
27	Alex Rodriguez	12.00
28	Shannon Stewart	3.00
29	Luis Gonzalez	3.00
30	Alex Rodriguez	12.00
31	Barry Bonds	20.00
32	Sammy Sosa	15.00
33	Luis Gonzalez	3.00
34	Todd Helton	6.00
35	Jim Thome	3.00
36	Shawn Green	4.00
37	Jeff Bagwell	7.50
38	Todd Helton	5.00
39	Luis Gonzalez	3.00
40	Lance Berkman	3.00
41	Juan Gonzalez	6.00
42	Larry Walker	3.00
43	Ichiro Suzuki	10.00
44	Lance Berkman	3.00
45	Todd Helton	5.00

League Leaders Autographs
NM/M
Production 15-100

5	Mark Mulder/100	20.00
11	Mark Buehrle/100	15.00
13	Freddy Garcia/100	15.00
19	Javier Vazquez/100	15.00
26	Albert Pujols/100	150.00
28	Shannon Stewart/100	15.00

League Leaders Game-Used
NM/M
Common Player: 4.00
Production 150 or 175

1	Roger Clemens	20.00
2	Curt Schilling	10.00
4	Randy Johnson	8.00
5	Mark Mulder	6.00
6	Curt Schilling	10.00
7	Mike Mussina/Shoe/50	25.00
8	Joe Mays	4.00
10	Tim Hudson	6.00
11	Mark Buehrle	4.00
12	Greg Maddux	15.00
13	Freddy Garcia	4.00
14	Randy Johnson	8.00
15	Curt Schilling	10.00
16	Chan Ho Park	4.00
17	Roger Clemens	20.00
18	Mike Mussina/Shoe/50	25.00
19	Javier Vazquez	4.00
20	Kerry Wood	10.00
21	Randy Johnson	8.00
22	Barry Zito	6.00
23	Hideo Nomo	15.00
24	Ichiro Suzuki/Ball/51	75.00
25	Todd Helton	8.00
26	Albert Pujols	20.00
27	Alex Rodriguez	15.00
28	Shannon Stewart	4.00
29	Luis Gonzalez	5.00
30	Alex Rodriguez	15.00
31	Barry Bonds	25.00
32	Sammy Sosa	15.00
33	Luis Gonzalez	4.00
34	Todd Helton	5.00
35	Jim Thome	10.00
36	Shawn Green	5.00
37	Jeff Bagwell	8.00
38	Todd Helton	5.00
39	Luis Gonzalez	4.00
40	Lance Berkman	6.00
41	Juan Gonzalez	6.00
42	Larry Walker	4.00
43	Ichiro Suzuki/Ball/51	75.00
44	Lance Berkman	4.00
45	Todd Helton	8.00

Pure Power
NM/M
Complete Set (18): 65.00
Common Player: 2.00
Production 300 Sets

1	Sammy Sosa	8.00
2	Lance Berkman	2.00
3	Chipper Jones	5.00
4	Troy Glaus	3.00
5	Barry Bonds	12.00
6	Todd Helton	4.00
7	Manny Ramirez	4.00
8	Jason Giambi	3.00
9	Juan Gonzalez	4.00
10	Albert Pujols	10.00
11	Jim Thome	2.00
12	Mike Piazza	8.00
13	Frank Thomas	4.00
14	Richie Sexson	2.00
15	Jeff Bagwell	4.00
16	Rafael Palmeiro	3.00
17	Luis Gonzalez	2.00
18	Shawn Green	2.50

Pure Power Masters

NM/M
Complete Set (18) 125.00
Common Player: 5.00
Production 150

1	Sammy Sosa	15.00
2	Lance Berkman	5.00
3	Chipper Jones	10.00
4	Troy Glaus	8.00
5	Barry Bonds	25.00
6	Todd Helton	8.00
7	Manny Ramirez	8.00
8	Jason Giambi	6.00
9	Juan Gonzalez	8.00
10	Albert Pujols	20.00
11	Jim Thome	5.00
12	Mike Piazza	15.00
13	Frank Thomas	8.00
14	Richie Sexson	5.00
15	Jeff Bagwell	8.00
16	Rafael Palmeiro	6.00
17	Luis Gonzalez	5.00
18	Shawn Green	6.00

Pure Power Autographs
NM/M
Varying quantities produced.

14	Richie Sexson/100	20.00

Records
NM/M
Complete Set (5): 50.00
Common Player: 8.00
Production 300

1-3	Barry Bonds	15.00
4-5	Rickey Henderson	8.00

Records Game-Used
NM/M
Production 150

1	Barry Bonds	40.00
2	Barry Bonds	40.00
3	Barry Bonds	40.00
4	Rickey Henderson	20.00
5	Rickey Henderson	20.00

2002 Donruss Originals Samples

Each November 2002 issue of Beckett Baseball Card Monthly included a sample '02 Donruss Originals card rubber-cemented inside. The cards differ from the issued version only in the appearance on back of a (usually) silver-foil silver-foil "SAMPLE" notation. Some cards were produced with the overprint in gold-foil, in much more limited quantities. The number of different players' cards involved in the promotion is unknown.

Common Player:
Stars: 1.5-2X
Gold: 10X

2002 Donruss Originals
NM/M
Complete Set (400): 75.00
Common Player: .10
Common Rated Rookie: .50
Pack (5): 2.00
Hobby Box (24): 40.00

1	So Taguchi/RR RC	.75
2	Allan Simpson/RR RC	.50
3	Brian Mallette/RR RC	.50

Mike Piazza c

4	Ben Howard/RR RC	.50
5	Kazuhisa Ishii/RR RC	2.00
6	Francis Beltran/RR RC	.50
7	Jorge Padilla/RR RC	.50
8	Brandon Puffer/RR RC	.50
9	Oliver Perez/RR RC	1.00
10	Kirk Saarloos/RR	.50
11	Travis Driskill/RR RC	.50
12	Jeremy Lambert/RR RC	.50
13	John Foster/RR RC	.50
14	Steve Kent/RR RC	.50
15	Shawn Sedlacek/RR RC	.50
16	Alex Rodriguez	1.25
17	Lance Berkman	.10
18	Kevin Brown	.10
19	Garret Anderson	.10
20	Bobby Abreu	.10
21	Richard Hidalgo	.10
22	Matt Morris	.10
23	Manny Ramirez	.60
24	Derek Jeter	1.50
25	Kerry Wood	.50
26	Mark Grace	.15
27	Edgar Martinez	.10
28	Nomar Garciaparra	1.00
29	Roberto Alomar	.25
30	Jason Giambi	.50
31	Juan Gonzalez	.50
32	Albert Pujols	1.00
33	Juan Cruz	.10
34	Troy Glaus	.60
35	Greg Maddux	.75
36	Adam Dunn	.40
37	J.D. Drew	.25
38	Tsuyoshi Shinjo	.10
39	Vladimir Guerrero	.60
40	Barry Bonds	1.50
41	Carlos Delgado	.40
42	Ken Griffey Jr.	1.00
43	Carlos Pena	.10
44	Jeff Kent	.10
45	Roger Clemens	.75
46	Frank Thomas	.60
47	Larry Walker	.10
48	Pedro J. Martinez	.60
49	Moises Alou	.10
50	Andruw Jones	.60
51	Luis Gonzalez	.25
52	Adrian Beltre	.10
53	Bobby Hill	.10
54	Roy Oswalt	.20
55	Tim Hudson	.10
56	Trot Nixon	.10
57	Jeff Bagwell	.60
58	Bernie Williams	.30
59	Magglio Ordonez	.40
60	Bartolo Colon	.10
61	Shawn Green	.20
62	Mark Buehrle	.10
63	Sean Casey	.10
64	Rickey Henderson	.60
65	Aramis Ramirez	.10
66	Ichiro Suzuki	1.00
67	Cliff Floyd	.10
68	Darin Erstad	.10
69	Paul LoDuca	.10
70	Ivan Rodriguez	.50
71	Mo Vaughn	.10
72	Todd Helton	.60
73	Raul Mondesi	.10
74	Sammy Sosa	1.00
75	Cristian Guzman	.10
76	Jimmy Rollins	.25
77	Hideo Nomo	.50
78	C.C. Sabathia	.10
79	Wade Miller	.10
80	Drew Henson	.10
81	Chipper Jones	.75
82	Miguel Tejada	.25
83	Freddy Garcia	.10
84	Richie Sexson	.10
85	Robin Ventura	.10
86	Jose Vidro	.10
87	Rich Aurilia	.10
88	Scott Rolen	.60
89	Carlos Beltran	.25
90	Austin Kearns	.25
91	Kazuhiro Sasaki	.10
92	Carlos Hernandez	.10
93	Randy Johnson	.60
94	Jim Thome	.40
95	Curt Schilling	.40
96	Alfonso Soriano	.50
97	Barry Larkin	.10
98	Rafael Palmeiro	.25
99	Tom Glavine	.25
100	Barry Zito	.20
101	Craig Biggio	.20

102	Mike Piazza	1.00
103	Ben Sheets	.20
104	Mark Mulder	.20
105	Mike Mussina	.25
106	Jim Edmonds	.10
107	Paul Konerko	.10
108	Pat Burrell	.25
109	Chan Ho Park	.10
110	Mike Sweeney	.10
111	Phil Nevin	.10
112	Brian Giles	.10
113	Eric Chavez	.20
114	Corey Patterson	.20
115	Gary Sheffield	.25
116	Kazuhisa Ishii/RR	2.00
117	Kyle Kane/RR RC	.50
118	Eric Junge/RR RC	.50
119	Luis Ugueto/RR RC	.50
120	Cam Esslinger/RR RC	.50
121	Earl Snyder/RR RC	.50
122	Oliver Perez/RR	1.00
123	Victor Alvarez/RR RC	.50
124	Tom Shearn/RR RC	.50
125	Corey Thurman/RR RC	.50
126	Satoru Komiyama/RR RC	.50
127	Hansel Izquierdo/RR RC	.50
128	Elio Serrano/RR RC	.50
129	Michael Crudale/RR RC	.50
130	Chris Snelling/RR	1.50
131	Nomar Garciaparra	1.00
132	Roger Clemens	.75
133	Hank Blalock	.25
134	Eric Chavez	.20
135	Corey Patterson	.20
136	Richie Sexson	.10
137	Freddy Garcia	.10
138	Miguel Tejada	.25
139	Alex Rodriguez/SP	1.50
140	Adrian Beltre	.10
141	Bobby Abreu	.10
142	Bret Boone	.10
143	Tim Hudson	.20
144	Roy Oswalt	.20
145	Derek Jeter	1.50
146	Rich Aurilia	.10
147	Mark Grace	.15
148	Kerry Wood/SP	1.00
149	Geronimo Gil	.10
150	Mark Buehrle	.10
151	Jim Edmonds	.10
152	Ichiro Suzuki	1.00
153	Juan Gonzalez	.60
154	Darin Erstad	.20
155	Barry Bonds/SP	2.50
156	Greg Maddux	.75
157	Adam Dunn	.40
158	Todd Helton	.60
159	Roberto Alomar	.25
160	Sammy Sosa	1.00
161	Sean Burroughs	.10
162	Albert Pujols	1.00
163	Carlos Delgado	.25
164	Frank Thomas	.60
165	Ken Griffey Jr.	1.00
166	Jason Giambi/SP	1.00
167	Chipper Jones	.75
168	Ivan Rodriguez	.50
169	Pedro Martinez/SP	1.00
170	Gary Sheffield	.25
171	Andruw Jones	.60
172	Luis Gonzalez	.25
173	Raul Mondesi	.10
174	Jose Vidro	.10
175	Garret Anderson/SP	.50
176	Scott Rolen	.60
177	Kazuhiro Sasaki	.10
178	Jeff Bagwell	.60
179	Manny Ramirez	.60
180	Jim Thome	.10
181	Ben Sheets	.20
182	Randy Johnson	.60
183	Lance Berkman	.10
184	Shawn Green	.20
185	Rickey Henderson	.60
186	Edgar Martinez	.10
187	Barry Larkin	.10
188	Bernie Williams	.30
189	Luis Aparicio	.10
190	Troy Glaus/SP	.50
191	Mike Mussina	.30
192	Pee Wee Reese	.20
193	Craig Biggio	.10
194	Vladimir Guerrero	.60
195	J.D. Drew	.20
196	Jeff Kent	.10
197	Dewon Brazelton	.10
198	Tsuyoshi Shinjo/SP	.40
199	Sean Casey	.10
200	Hideo Nomo	.50
201	C.C. Sabathia	.10
202	Larry Walker	.10
203	Mark Teixeira	.20
204	Mike Sweeney	.10
205	Moises Alou	.10
206	Mark Prior	.75
207	Javier Vazquez	.10
208	Phil Nevin	.10
209	Harmon Killebrew	.50
210	Brian Giles	.10
211	Carlos Beltran	.40
212	Don Drysdale	.40
213	Matt Morris	.10
214	Trot Nixon	.10
215	Magglio Ordonez	.25
216	Curt Schilling/SP	.75
217	Mark Mulder	.20
218	Alfonso Soriano	1.00
219	Rafael Palmeiro/SP	.75

220	Tom Glavine	.25
221	Barry Zito	.25
222	Mike Piazza	1.00
223	Bartolo Colon	.10
224	Cliff Floyd	.10
225	Paul LoDuca	.10
226	Cristian Guzman	.10
227	Mo Vaughn	.10
228	Aramis Ramirez	.10
229	Pat Burrell	.25
230	Chan Ho Park	.10
231	Satoru Komiyama/RR	.50
232	Brandon Backe/RR	.50
233	Anderson Machado/RR RC	.50
234	Doug DeVore/RR RC	.50
235	Steve Bechler/RR RC	.50
236	John Ennis/RR RC	.50
237	Rodrigo Rosario/RR RC	.50
238	Jorge Sosa/RR RC	.50
239	Ken Huckaby/RR RC	.50
240	Mike Moriarty/RR RC	.50
241	Kirk Saarloos/RR	1.00
242	Kevin Frederick/RR RC	.50
243	Aaron Guiel/RR	.50
244	Jose Rodriguez/RR	.50
245	So Taguchi/RR	1.00
246	Albert Pujols	1.00
247	Derek Jeter	.50
248	Brian Giles	.10
249	Mike Cameron	.10
250	Josh Beckett	.50
251	Ken Griffey Jr./SP	1.50
252	Aramis Ramirez	.15
253	Miguel Tejada	.25
254	Carlos Delgado	.25
255	Pedro J. Martinez	.60
256	Raul Mondesi	.10
257	Roger Clemens	.75
258	Gary Sheffield	.25
259	Jose Vidro	.10
260	Alex Rodriguez	1.25
261	Larry Walker	.10
262	Mark Mulder	.20
263	Scott Rolen	.60
264	Tim Hudson	.20
265	Manny Ramirez	.60
266	Rich Aurilia	.10
267	Roy Oswalt	.20
268	Mark Grace	.15
269	Lance Berkman	.10
270	Nomar Garciaparra	1.00
271	Barry Bonds	1.50
272	Ryan Klesko	.10
273	Ichiro Suzuki	1.00
274	Shawn Green	.20
275	Darin Erstad	.40
276	Bernie Williams	.30
277	Greg Maddux/SP	1.00
278	Eric Hinske	.10
279	Randy Johnson	.60
280	Todd Helton	.60
281	Sammy Sosa/SP	1.50
282	Nick Johnson	.10
283	Jose Cruz Jr.	.10
284	Frank Thomas	.60
285	Tsuyoshi Shinjo	.10
286	Troy Glaus	.60
287	Jason Giambi	.50
288	Chipper Jones/SP	1.00
289	Roberto Alomar	.30
290	Bobby Hill	.10
291	Garret Anderson	.10
292	Andruw Jones	.60
293	Luis Gonzalez	.15
294	Mike Mussina	.30
295	Ivan Rodriguez/SP	.75
296	Barry Larkin	.10
297	Kazuhiro Sasaki	.10
298	Alfonso Soriano	.50
299	Jeff Bagwell/SP	.75
300	Bobby Abreu	.10
301	Ben Sheets	.20
302	Curt Schilling	.40
303	Jim Thome	.10
304	Kerry Wood	.50
305	Mark Buehrle	.10
306	Rickey Henderson	.60
307	Rafael Palmeiro	.50
308	Jim Edmonds	.10
309	Mike Piazza	1.00
310	Edgar Martinez	.10
311	Tom Glavine	.25
312	Adrian Beltre	.10
313	Adam Dunn	.40
314	Craig Biggio	.10
315	Vladimir Guerrero/SP	1.00
316	Bret Boone	.10
317	Hideo Nomo/SP	.75
318	Jeff Kent	.10
319	Juan Gonzalez	.60
320	Sean Casey	.10
321	C.C. Sabathia	.10
322	J.D. Drew	.20
323	Torii Hunter/SP	.40
324	Chan Ho Park	.10
325	Mike Sweeney	.10
326	Javier Vazquez	.10
327	Jorge Posada	.25
328	Barry Zito	.25
329	Willie McCovey	.10
330	Kevin Brown	.20
331	Mo Vaughn	.10
332	Carlos Beltran	.40
333	Bobby Doerr	.10
334	Matt Morris	.10
335	Trot Nixon	.10
336	Magglio Ordonez	.25

337	Paul LoDuca	.10
338	Phil Nevin	.10
339	Eric Chavez	.20
340	Corey Patterson	.20
341	Richie Sexson	.10
342	Pat Burrell	.25
343	Freddy Garcia	.10
344	Bartolo Colon	.10
345	Cliff Floyd	.10
346	Deivis Santos/RR	.50
347	Felix Escalona/RR RC	.50
348	Miguel Asencio/RR RC	.50
349	Takahito Nomura/RR RC	.50
350	Jorge Padilla/RR	.50
351	Vladimir Guerrero	.60
352	Ichiro Suzuki	1.00
353	Jay Gibbons	.10
354	Alfonso Soriano	.50
355	Mark Buehrle	.10
356	Shawn Green	.20
357	Barry Larkin	.10
358	Josh Fogg	.10
359	Shannon Stewart	.10
360	Andruw Jones	.60
361	Juan Gonzalez	.60
362	Ken Griffey Jr.	1.00
363	Tim Hudson	.20
364	Roy Oswalt/SP	.60
365	Carlos Delgado	.40
366	Albert Pujols/SP	2.00
367	Willie Stargell	.25
368	Roger Clemens	.75
369	Luis Gonzalez	.25
370	Barry Zito	.25
371	Alex Rodriguez	1.25
372	Troy Glaus	.60
373	Vladimir Guerrero	.60
374	Jeff Bagwell	.60
375	Randy Johnson	.60
376	Manny Ramirez	.60
377	Derek Jeter/SP	2.00
378	C.C. Sabathia	.10
379	Rickey Henderson	.60
380	J.D. Drew	.20
381	Nomar Garciaparra	.60
382	Darin Erstad	.40
383	Ben Sheets	.20
884	Frank Thomas	.60
385	Barry Bonds	1.50
386	Pedro J. Martinez	.60
387	Mark Mulder	.20
388	Greg Maddux	.75
389	Todd Helton	.60
390	Lance Berkman	.10
391	Sammy Sosa	1.00
392	Mike Piazza	1.00
393	Chipper Jones	.75
394	Adam Dunn	.40
395	Jason Giambi	.50
396	Eric Chavez	.10
397	Bobby Abreu	.10
398	Aramis Ramirez	.10
399	Paul LoDuca	.10
400	Miguel Tejada	.25

Aqueous Glossy

Stars (1-400): 3-5X
Average of 1:Box

All-Stars

		NM/M
Complete Set (25):		90.00
Common Player:		2.00
Inserted 1:30		
1	George Brett	8.00
2	Rickey Henderson	4.00
3	Mike Schmidt	6.00
4	Vladimir Guerrero	3.00
5	Tony Gwynn	3.00
6	Curt Schilling	2.00
7	Don Mattingly	8.00
8	Roberto Alomar	2.00
9	Cal Ripken Jr.	8.00
10	Carlton Fisk	2.00
11	Roger Clemens	5.00
12	Jeff Bagwell	3.00
13	Kirby Puckett	8.00
14	Nolan Ryan	10.00
15	Ryne Sandberg	5.00
16	Ivan Rodriguez	2.00
17	Sammy Sosa	5.00
18	Greg Maddux	5.00
19	Alex Rodriguez	8.00
20	Todd Helton	2.00
21	Randy Johnson	3.00
22	Troy Glaus	2.00
23	Ichiro Suzuki	6.00
24	Barry Bonds	8.00
25	Derek Jeter	10.00

Champions

		NM/M
Complete Set (25):		75.00
Common Player:		2.00
Production 800 Sets		
1	Nolan Ryan	10.00
2	George Brett	6.00
3	Edgar Martinez	2.00
4	Mike Schmidt	4.00
5	Randy Johnson	3.00
6	Tony Gwynn	3.00
7	John Smoltz	2.00
8	Roger Clemens	3.00
9	Mel Ott	2.00
10	Todd Helton	3.00
11	Bernie Williams	2.00
12	Troy Glaus	3.00
13	Steve Carlton	2.00
14	Ryne Sandberg	4.00
15	Ted Williams	8.00
16	Alex Rodriguez	8.00
17	Lou Boudreau	2.00
18	Luis Gonzalez	2.00
19	Rickey Henderson	3.00
20	Jose Canseco	2.00
21	Stan Musial	5.00
22	Randy Johnson	3.00
23	Don Mattingly	6.00
24	Nomar Garciaparra	4.00
25	Wade Boggs	4.00

Champions Materials

		NM/M
Common Player:		8.00
Varying quantities produced.		
1	Nolan Ryan/78	65.00
2	George Brett/80	30.00
3	Edgar Martinez/92	10.00
4	Mike Schmidt/80	40.00
5	Randy Johnson/94	15.00
6	Tony Gwynn/84	20.00
7	John Smoltz/96	8.00
8	Roger Clemens/88	20.00
9	Todd Helton/100	10.00
10	Bernie Williams/98	10.00
11	Troy Glaus/100	10.00
12	Steve Carlton/80	15.00
13	Ryne Sandberg/90	40.00
14	Ted Williams/42	200.00
15	Alex Rodriguez/96	20.00
16	Lou Boudreau/44	15.00
17	Luis Gonzalez/99	8.00
18	Rickey Henderson/82	10.00
19	Stan Musial/50	60.00
20	Randy Johnson/88	15.00
21	Don Mattingly/84	60.00
22	Nomar Garciaparra/100	30.00
23	Wade Boggs/88	15.00

Gamers

		NM/M
Common Player:		3.00
Varying quantities produced.		
1	Alfonso Soriano/400	8.00
2	Shawn Green/500	5.00
3	Curt Schilling/250	8.00
4	Hideo Nomo/100	20.00
5	Toby Hall/500	4.00
6	Andruw Jones/500	8.00
7	Cliff Floyd/500	3.00
8	Mark Ellis/500	4.00
9	Gabe Kapler/500	3.00
10	Andres Galarraga/500	3.00
11	Freddy Garcia/500	3.00
12	Tsuyoshi Shinjo/200	4.00
13	Robin Ventura/500	3.00
14	Paul LoDuca/500	3.00
15	Manny Ramirez/500	8.00
16	Garret Anderson/250	6.00
17	Joe Kennedy/500	3.00
18	Roger Clemens/500	15.00
19	Gary Sheffield/500	6.00
20	Vernon Wells/500	4.00
21	Hideo Nomo/100	40.00
22	Tim Hudson/500	4.00
23	Larry Bigbie/500	3.00
24	Larry Walker/500	5.00
25	John Olerud/500	3.00
26	Chipper Jones/500	8.00
27	Tony Gwynn/500	10.00
28	Juan Gonzalez/500	8.00
29	Jacque Jones/500	3.00
30	Frank Thomas/500	8.00
31	Luis Gonzalez/500	4.00
32	Geoff Jenkins/500	3.00
33	J.D. Drew/500	5.00
34	Edgardo Alfonzo/500	3.00
37	Todd Helton/500	8.00
38	Brad Penny/500	4.00
39	Robert Fick/500	3.00
40	Will Clark/500	15.00
41	Tony Armas Jr./500	4.00
42	Nick Johnson/400	3.00
43	Ben Grieve/500	3.00
44	Vladimir Guerrero/500	8.00
45	Jason Jennings/500	3.00
46	Carlos Lee/500	3.00
47	Carlos Delgado/500	6.00
48	Chan Ho Park/500	3.00
49	Juan Diaz/500	3.00
50	Alex Rodriguez/400	15.00

Hit List

		NM/M
Complete Set (20):		40.00
Common Player:		1.00
Production 1,500 Sets		
1	Ichiro Suzuki	4.00
2	Shawn Green	1.00
3	Alex Rodriguez	5.00
4	Nomar Garciaparra	2.00
5	Derek Jeter	6.00
6	Barry Bonds	6.00
7	Mike Piazza	4.00
8	Albert Pujols	5.00
9	Chipper Jones	3.00
10	Sammy Sosa	4.00
11	Rickey Henderson	2.00
12	Frank Thomas	2.00
13	Jeff Bagwell	2.00
14	Vladimir Guerrero	2.00
15	Todd Helton	2.00
16	Adam Dunn	1.00
17	Rafael Palmeiro	1.00
18	Manny Ramirez	1.00
19	Lance Berkman	1.00
20	Jason Giambi	1.00

Hit List Total Bases

		NM/M
Common Player:		5.00
Numbered to career high total bases.		
1	Ichiro Suzuki/Base/316	15.00
2	Shawn Green/Bat/370	5.00
3	Alex Rodriguez/Bat/393	15.00
4	Nomar Garciaparra/Bat/365	10.00
5	Derek Jeter/346/Base	20.00
6	Barry Bonds/Base/411	20.00
7	Mike Piazza/Bat/355	8.00
8	Albert Pujols/Base/360	10.00
9	Chipper Jones/Bat/359	8.00
10	Sammy Sosa/Base/425	10.00
11	Rickey Henderson/Bat/285	10.00
12	Frank Thomas/Bat/364	8.00
13	Jeff Bagwell/Bat/363	8.00
14	Vladimir Guerrero/Bat/379	8.00
15	Todd Helton/Bat/405	8.00
16	Adam Dunn/Bat/141	8.00
17	Rafael Palmeiro/Bat/356	8.00
18	Manny Ramirez/Bat/346	8.00
19	Lance Berkman/Bat/358	5.00
20	Jason Giambi/Base/343	6.00

Making History

		NM/M
Complete Set (10):		30.00
Common Player:		2.00
Production 800 Sets		
1	Rafael Palmeiro	2.00
2	Roger Clemens	5.00
3	Greg Maddux	3.00
4	Randy Johnson	3.00
5	Barry Bonds	8.00
6	Mike Piazza	5.00
7	Roberto Alomar	2.00
8	Rickey Henderson	2.00
9	Sammy Sosa	6.00
10	Tom Glavine	2.00

Making History Materials

		NM/M
Production 100 Sets		
1	Rafael Palmeiro	15.00
2	Roger Clemens	20.00
3	Greg Maddux	15.00
4	Randy Johnson	10.00
5	Barry Bonds/Base	20.00
6	Mike Piazza	15.00
7	Roberto Alomar	8.00
8	Rickey Henderson	25.00
9	Sammy Sosa/Base	15.00
10	Tom Glavine	10.00

Mound Marvels

		NM/M
Complete Set (15):		30.00
Common Player:		1.00
Inserted 1:40		
1	Roger Clemens	6.00
2	Matt Morris	1.00
3	Pedro J. Martinez	5.00
4	Randy Johnson	5.00
5	Wade Miller	1.00
6	Tim Hudson	1.50
7	Mike Mussina	3.00
8	C.C. Sabathia	1.00
9	Kazuhisa Sasaki	1.00
10	Curt Schilling	4.00
11	Hideo Nomo	2.50
12	Roger Clemens	6.00
13	Mark Buehrle	1.50
14	Barry Zito	1.50
15	Roy Oswalt	1.50

Mound Marvels High Heat

		NM/M
Production 100 Sets		
1	Roger Clemens	25.00
2	Matt Morris	10.00
3	Pedro J. Martinez	20.00
4	Randy Johnson	15.00
5	Wade Miller	8.00
6	Tim Hudson	10.00
7	Mike Mussina	10.00
8	C.C. Sabathia	10.00
9	Kazuhiro Sasaki	10.00
10	Curt Schilling	15.00
11	Hideo Nomo	40.00
12	Roger Clemens	25.00
13	Mark Buehrle	8.00
14	Barry Zito	8.00
15	Roy Oswalt	8.00

Nifty Fifty Bats

		NM/M
Common Player:		5.00
Production 50 Sets		
1	Alex Rodriguez	20.00
2	Kerry Wood	15.00
3	Ivan Rodriguez	15.00
4	Geronimo Gil	5.00
5	Vladimir Guerrero	15.00
6	Corky Miller	5.00
7	Todd Helton	12.00
8	Rickey Henderson	15.00
9	Andruw Jones	10.00
10	Barry Bonds/Ball	30.00
11	Tom Glavine	10.00
12	Mark Teixeira	10.00
13	Mike Piazza	15.00
14	Austin Kearns	8.00
15	Rickey Henderson	15.00
16	Derek Jeter/Ball	20.00
17	Barry Larkin	8.00
18	Jeff Bagwell	10.00
19	Bernie Williams	10.00
20	Frank Thomas	10.00
21	Lance Berkman	8.00
22	Marlon Byrd	6.00
23	Randy Johnson	15.00
24	Ichiro Suzuki/Ball	40.00
25	Darin Erstad	8.00
26	Jason Lane	5.00
27	Roberto Alomar	8.00
28	Ken Griffey Jr./Ball	20.00
29	Tsuyoshi Shinjo	8.00
30	Pedro Martinez	15.00
31	Rickey Henderson	15.00
32	Albert Pujols/Ball	20.00
33	Nomar Garciaparra	15.00
34	Troy Glaus	10.00
35	Chipper Jones	15.00
36	Adam Dunn	15.00
37	Jason Giambi/Ball	15.00
38	Greg Maddux	20.00
39	Mike Piazza	15.00
40	So Taguchi	8.00
41	Manny Ramirez	10.00
42	Scott Rolen	15.00
43	Sammy Sosa/Ball	15.00
44	Shawn Green	8.00
45	Rickey Henderson	15.00
46	Alex Rodriguez	20.00
47	Hideo Nomo	30.00
48	Kazuhisa Ishii	8.00
49	Luis Gonzalez	8.00
50	Jim Thome	15.00

Nifty Fifty Jersey

		NM/M
Common Player:		5.00

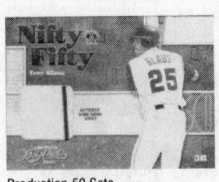

Nifty Fifty

Production 50 Sets

		NM/M
2	Kerry Wood	15.00
3	Ivan Rodriguez	15.00
4	Geronimo Gil	10.00
5	Vladimir Guerrero	15.00
6	Corky Miller	10.00
7	Todd Helton	12.00
8	Rickey Henderson	15.00
9	Andruw Jones	10.00
11	Tom Glavine	10.00
12	Mark Teixeira	15.00
13	Mike Piazza	15.00
14	Austin Kearns	8.00
15	Rickey Henderson	10.00
16	Derek Jeter/Base	20.00
17	Barry Larkin	8.00
18	Jeff Bagwell	10.00
19	Bernie Williams	10.00
20	Frank Thomas	10.00
21	Lance Berkman	8.00
22	Marlon Byrd	8.00
23	Randy Johnson	15.00
24	Ichiro Suzuki/Base	40.00
25	Darin Erstad	5.00
26	Jason Lane	5.00
27	Roberto Alomar	10.00
28	Ken Griffey Jr./Base	20.00
29	Tsuyoshi Shinjo	8.00
30	Pedro Martinez	15.00
31	Rickey Henderson	15.00
32	Albert Pujols/Base	20.00
33	Nomar Garciaparra	20.00
34	Troy Glaus	10.00
35	Chipper Jones	15.00
36	Adam Dunn	8.00
37	Jason Giambi/Base	10.00
38	Greg Maddux	20.00
39	Mike Piazza	15.00
40	So Taguchi	8.00
41	Manny Ramirez	10.00
42	Scott Rolen	15.00
43	Sammy Sosa/Base	15.00
44	Shawn Green	8.00
45	Rickey Henderson	15.00
46	Alex Rodriguez	20.00
47	Hideo Nomo	30.00
48	Kazuhisa Ishii	8.00
49	Luis Gonzalez	8.00
50	Jim Thome	15.00

Nifty Fifty Combos

Production 50 Sets
All bat & jerseys unless noted.

		NM/M
1	Alex Rodriguez	30.00
2	Kerry Wood	20.00
3	Ivan Rodriguez	20.00
4	Geronimo Gil	10.00
5	Vladimir Guerrero	20.00
6	Corky Miller	10.00
7	Todd Helton	20.00
8	Rickey Henderson	25.00
9	Andruw Jones	15.00
10	Barry Bonds/Base/Ball	40.00
11	Tom Glavine	20.00
12	Mark Teixeira	20.00
13	Mike Piazza	25.00
14	Austin Kearns	15.00
15	Rickey Henderson	25.00
16	Derek Jeter/Base/Ball	30.00
17	Barry Larkin	15.00
18	Jeff Bagwell	20.00
19	Bernie Williams	20.00
20	Frank Thomas	20.00
21	Lance Berkman	15.00
22	Marlon Byrd	15.00
23	Randy Johnson	20.00
24	Ichiro Suzuki/Base/Ball	60.00
25	Darin Erstad	15.00
26	Jason Lane	10.00
27	Roberto Alomar	15.00
28	Ken Griffey Jr./Base/Ball	25.00
29	Tsuyoshi Shinjo	10.00
30	Pedro Martinez	20.00
31	Rickey Henderson	25.00
32	Albert Pujols/Base/Ball	50.00
33	Nomar Garciaparra	30.00
34	Troy Glaus	15.00
35	Chipper Jones	20.00
36	Adam Dunn	15.00
37	Jason Giambi	20.00
38	Greg Maddux	25.00
39	Mike Piazza	25.00
40	So Taguchi	15.00
41	Manny Ramirez	20.00
42	Scott Rolen	20.00
43	Sammy Sosa/Base/Ball	25.00

On The Record

	NM/M
Complete Set (15):	60.00
Common Player:	3.00

Production 800 Sets

1	Ty Cobb	6.00
2	Jimmie Foxx	4.00
3	Lou Gehrig	10.00
4	Dale Murphy	5.00
5	Steve Carlton	3.00
6	Randy Johnson	4.00
7	Greg Maddux	6.00
8	Roger Clemens	8.00
9	Yogi Berra	5.00
10	Don Mattingly	8.00
11	Rickey Henderson	4.00
12	Stan Musial	6.00
13	Jackie Robinson	6.00
14	Roberto Clemente	10.00
15	Mike Schmidt	6.00

On the Record Materials

	NM/M
Varying quantities produced.

3	Lou Gehrig/34	220.00
4	Dale Murphy/83	10.00
5	Steve Carlton/72	10.00
6	Randy Johnson/100	10.00
7	Greg Maddux/93	15.00
8	Roger Clemens/87	20.00
9	Yogi Berra/51	12.00
10	Don Mattingly/85	25.00
11	Rickey Henderson/90	15.00
12	Jackie Robinson/49	50.00
14	Roberto Clemente/66	75.00
15	Mike Schmidt/80	25.00

Power Alley

	NM/M
Complete Set (15):	30.00
Common Player:	1.00

Production 1,500 Sets
Die-Cut Parallel: 1.5-2X
Production 100 Sets

1	Barry Bonds	6.00
2	Sammy Sosa	3.00
3	Lance Berkman	1.00
4	Luis Gonzalez	1.00
5	Alex Rodriguez	5.00
6	Troy Glaus	2.00
7	Vladimir Guerrero	2.00
8	Jason Giambi	1.50
9	Mike Piazza	3.00
10	Todd Helton	2.00
11	Mike Schmidt	4.00
12	Don Mattingly	4.00
13	Andre Dawson	1.50
14	Reggie Jackson	2.00
15	Dale Murphy	1.50

Recollection Collection

No Pricing

Signature Marks

	NM/M
Common Autograph:	5.00

Varying quantities produced.
Many not priced, lack of market info.

2	Eric Hinske/200	8.00
3	Cesar Izturis/200	5.00
4	Roy Oswalt/100	20.00
5	Jack Cust/200	8.00
6	Nick Johnson/200	8.00
7	Jason Hart/200	5.00
8	Mark Prior/100	30.00
9	Luis Garcia/200	5.00
10	Jay Gibbons/200	10.00
11	Corky Miller/200	8.00
12	Antonio Perez/100	8.00
13	Andres Torres/200	5.00
14	Brandon Claussen/200	8.00
15	Ed Rogers/200	5.00
16	Jorge Padilla/200	8.00
17	Francis Beltran/200	5.00
18	Kip Wells/200	8.00
19	Ryan Ludwick/200	10.00
20	Juan Cruz/100	8.00
21	Juan Diaz/200	8.00
22	Marcus Giles/200	10.00
23	Joe Kennedy/200	10.00
24	Wade Miller/100	10.00
25	Corey Patterson/100	10.00
26	Angel Berroa/200	10.00
27	Ricardo Rodriguez/200	5.00
28	Toby Hall/200	8.00
29	Carlos Pena/50	15.00
30	Jason Jennings/200	8.00
31	Rafael Soriano/200	10.00
32	Marlon Byrd/100	10.00
33	Rodrigo Rosario/200	5.00
35	Brent Abernathy/200	5.00
36	Bill Hall/200	15.00
37	Fernando Rodney/200	10.00
38	Josh Pearce/200	8.00
39	Brian Lawrence/200	8.00
40	Tim Redding/200	5.00
42	Jeremy Giambi/200	5.00
43	Victor Martinez/200	25.00
44	Hank Blalock/50	25.00
46	Geronimo Gil/200	5.00
47	So Taguchi/50	25.00
48	Austin Kearns/50	15.00
49	Alfonso Soriano/50	40.00

What If - Rookies

	NM/M
Complete Set (23):	75.00
Common Player:	1.50

Inserted 1:12

1	Wade Boggs	6.00
2	Ryne Sandberg	6.00
3	Cal Ripken Jr.	12.50
4	Tony Gwynn	6.00
5	Don Mattingly	10.00
6	Wade Boggs	6.00
7	Roger Clemens	7.50
8	Kirby Puckett	6.00
9	Eric Davis	1.50
10	Dwight Gooden	1.50
11	Eric Davis	1.50
12	Roger Clemens	7.50
13	Kirby Puckett	6.00
14	Dwight Gooden	1.50
15	Barry Bonds	12.50
16	Will Clark	1.50
17	Barry Larkin	1.50
18	Greg Maddux	6.00
19	Rafael Palmeiro	4.00
20	Craig Biggio	1.50
21	Gary Sheffield	1.50
22	Randy Johnson	5.00
23	Curt Schilling	3.00

What If - '78

	NM/M
Complete Set (27):	75.00
Common Player:	1.50

Inserted 1:12

1	Paul Molitor	4.00
2	Alan Trammell	1.50
3	Ozzie Smith	6.00
4	George Brett	10.00
5	Johnny Bench	6.00
6	Rod Carew	2.00
7	Carlton Fisk	1.50
8	Reggie Jackson	5.00
9	Dale Murphy	2.00
10	Joe Morgan	1.50
11	Eddie Murray	4.00
12	Jim Palmer	2.00
13	Tom Seaver	4.00
14	Willie Stargell	2.00
15	Dave Winfield	2.00
16	Dave Parker	1.50
17	Mike Schmidt	8.00
18	Eddie Mathews	4.00
19	Lou Brock	1.50
20	Willie McCovey	1.50
21	Andre Dawson	1.50
22	Dennis Eckersley	4.00
23	Robin Yount	4.00
24	Nolan Ryan	15.00
25	Steve Carlton	1.50
26	Paul Molitor	4.00
27	Ozzie Smith	6.00

What If - '80

	NM/M
Complete Set (25):	75.00
Common Player:	1.50

Inserted 1:12

1	Rickey Henderson	3.00
2	Johnny Bench	6.00
3	George Brett	10.00
4	Steve Carlton	2.50
5	Rod Carew	1.50
6	Gary Carter	1.50
7	Carlton Fisk	1.50
8	Reggie Jackson	5.00
9	Dave Parker	1.50
10	Dale Murphy	3.00
11	Paul Molitor	4.00
12	Mike Schmidt	8.00
13	Alan Trammell	1.50
14	Dave Winfield	1.50
15	Robin Yount	4.00
16	Joe Morgan	1.50
17	Jim Palmer	1.50
18	Nolan Ryan	15.00
19	Tom Seaver	4.00
20	Ozzie Smith	6.00
21	Willie McCovey	1.50
22	Andre Dawson	1.50
23	Eddie Murray	3.00
24	Al Kaline	5.00
25	Duke Snider	4.00

2002 Donruss Originals - LCS Programs

A perforated sheet of Donruss Originals cards was inserted into some of the programs sold for the American and National League Championship Series. The 8-1/2" x 11" sheet features eight player

cards and a header card advertising the brand. Each 2-1/2" x 3-1/2" card is perforated on all sides and differs from the regularly issued version only in the card number on back. Sheet cards have either an "ALCS-" or "NLCS-" prefix to the number. Other programs could be found with similar sheets of Donruss Diamond Kings, Donruss Studio or Playoff Piece of the Game cards.

	NM/M
Complete Sheet Set (2):	16.00
Common Player:	.50

ALCS SHEET 8.00

9	Manny Ramirez (1986 style)	1.00
10	Nolan Ryan/AS	2.50
11	Roger Clemens (Champions)	1.50
12	Alex Rodriguez/AS	2.00
13	Paul Konerko (1982 style)	.50
15	Don Mattingly/AS	1.50
16	Miguel Tejada (1984 style)	.50
	Rickey Henderson (Making History)	.50
---	Header Card	.10

NLCS SHEET 8.00

25	Mike Schmidt (Champions)	2.00
26	Andruw Jones (1986 style)	1.00
27	Lance Berkman (Power Alley)	.50
28	Vladimir Guerrero/AS	1.00
29	Roberto Clemente (On The Record)	3.00
30	Austin Kearns (1982 style)	.50
31	Curt Schilling/AS	.50
32	Kazuhisa Ishii (1984 style)	1.00
---	Header Card	.10

2002 Donruss Studio Samples

Each issue of the September 2002 Beckett Baseball Card Monthly included a sample 2002 Donruss Studio card rubber-cemented inside. The cards differ from the issued version only in the appearance on back of a (usually) silver-foil "SAMPLE" notation. Some cards were produced with the overprint in gold-foil, in much more limited quantities. The number of different players' cards involved in the promotion is unknown.

	NM/M
Common Player:	.10
Stars:	1.5-2X
Gold:	10X

2002 Donruss Studio

	NM/M
Complete Set (250):	150.00
Common Player:	.25
Common (201-250):	3.00

Production 1,500

Pack (5):		3.00
Box (18):		45.00
1	Vladimir Guerrero	.75
2	Chipper Jones	1.00
3	Bobby Abreu	.25
4	Barry Zito	.40

5	Larry Walker	.25
6	Miguel Tejada	.40
7	Mike Sweeney	.25
8	Shannon Stewart	.25
9	Sammy Sosa	1.50
10	Bud Smith	.25
11	Wilson Betemit	.25
12	Kevin Brown	.35
13	Ellis Burks	.25
15	Pat Burrell	.40
16	Marcus Giles	.25
17	Troy Glaus	.75
18	Barry Larkin	.25
19	Carlos Lee	.25
20	Brian Lawrence	.25
21	Paul LoDuca	.25
22	Ben Grieve	.25
23	Shawn Green	.40
24	Mike Cameron	.25
25	Roger Clemens	1.25
26	Joe Crede	.25
27	Jose Cruz	.25
28	Jeremy Affeldt	.25
29	Adrian Beltre	.25
30	Josh Beckett	.50
31	Roberto Alomar	.40
32	Toby Hall	.25
33	Mike Hampton	.25
34	Eric Milton	.25
35	Eric Munson	.25
36	Trot Nixon	.25
37	Roy Oswalt	.40
38	Chan Ho Park	.25
39	Charles Johnson	.25
41	Nick Johnson	.25
42	Tim Hudson	.40
43	Cristian Guzman	.25
44	Drew Henson	.25
45	Mark Grace	.35
46	Luis Gonzalez	.35
47	Pedro J. Martinez	.75
48	Joe Mays	.25
49	Jorge Posada	.40
50	Aramis Ramirez	.25
51	Kip Wells	.25
52	Moises Alou	.25
53	Omar Vizquel	.25
54	Ichiro Suzuki	1.50
55	Jimmy Rollins	.40
56	Freddy Garcia	.25
57	Steve Green	.25
58	Brian Jordan	.25
59	Paul Konerko	.35
60	Jack Cust	.25
61	Sean Casey	.25
62	Bret Boone	.25
63	Hideo Nomo	.60
64	Magglio Ordonez	.40
65	Frank Thomas	.75
66	Josh Towers	.25
67	Javier Vazquez	.25
68	Robin Ventura	.25
69	Aubrey Huff	.25
70	Richard Hidalgo	.25
71	Brandon Claussen	.25
72	Bartolo Colon	.25
73	John Buck	.25
74	Dee Brown	.25
75	Barry Bonds	2.00
76	Jason Giambi	.50
77	Erick Almonte	.25
78	Ryan Dempster	.25
79	Jim Edmonds	.40
80	Jay Gibbons	.25
81	Shigetoshi Hasegawa	.25
82	Todd Helton	.75
83	Erik Bedard	.25
84	Carlos Beltran	.50
85	Rafael Soriano	.25
86	Gary Sheffield	.25
87	Richie Sexson	.25
88	Mike Rivera	.25
89	Jose Ortiz	.25
90	Abraham Nunez	.25
91	Dave Williams	.25
92	Preston Wilson	.25
93	Jason Jennings	.25
94	Juan Diaz	.25
95	Steve Smyth	.25
96	Phil Nevin	.25
97	John Olerud	.25
98	Brad Penny	.25
99	Andy Pettitte	.40
100	Juan Pierre	.25
101	Manny Ramirez	.75
102	Edgardo Alfonzo	.25
103	Michael Cuddyer	.25

103	Johnny Damon	.40
104	Carlos Zambrano	.35
105	Jose Vidro	.25
106	Tsuyoshi Shinjo	.25
107	Ed Rogers	.25
108	Scott Rolen	.75
109	Mariano Rivera	.35
110	Tim Redding	.25
111	Josh Phelps	.25
112	Gabe Kapler	.25
113	Edgar Martinez	.25
114	Fred McGriff	.25
115	Raul Mondesi	.25
116	Wade Miller	.25
117	Mike Mussina	.40
118	Rafael Palmeiro	.65
119	Adam Johnson	.25
120	Rickey Henderson	.25
121	Bill Hall	.25
122	Ken Griffey Jr.	1.50
123	Geronimo Gil	.25
124	Robert Fick	.25
125	Darin Erstad	.50
126	Brandon Duckworth	.25
127	Garret Anderson	.25
128	Pedro Feliz	.25
129	Jeff Cirillo	.25
130	Brian Giles	.25
131	Craig Biggio	.25
132	Willie Harris	.25
133	Doug Davis	.25
134	Jeff Kent	.25
135	Terrence Long	.25
136	Carlos Delgado	.50
137	Tino Martinez	.25
138	Donaldo Mendez	.25
139	Sean Douglass	.25
140	Eric Chavez	.40
141	Rick Ankiel	.25
142	Jeremy Giambi	.25
143	Juan Pena	.25
144	Bernie Williams	.40
145	Craig Wilson	.25
146	Ricardo Rodriguez	.25
147	Albert Pujols	1.50
148	Antonio Perez	.25
149	Russ Ortiz	.25
150	Corky Miller	.25
151	Rich Aurilia	.25
152	Kerry Wood	.50
153	Joe Thurston	.25
154	Jeff Deardorff RC	.25
155	Jermaine Dye	.25
156	Andruw Jones	.75
157	Victor Martinez	.25
158	Nick Neugebauer	.25
159	Matt Morris	.25
160	Casey Fossum	.25
161	J.D. Drew	.40
162	Matt Childers RC	.50
163	Mark Buehrle	.50
164	Jeff Bagwell	.75
165	Kazuhiro Sasaki	.25
166	Ben Sheets	.25
167	Alex Rodriguez	1.50
168	Adam Pettyjohn	.25
169	Chris Snelling RC	.25
170	Robert Person	.25
171	Juan Uribe	.25
172	Mo Vaughn	.25
173	Alfredo Amezaga	.25
174	Ryan Drese	.25
175	Corey Thurman RC	.25
176	Jim Thome	.75
177	Orlando Cabrera	.25
178	Eric Cyr RC	.25
179	Greg Maddux	1.00
180	Earl Snyder RC	.25
181	C.C. Sabathia	.40
182	Mark Mulder	.40
183	Jose Mieses	.25
184	Joe Kennedy	.25
185	Randy Johnson	.75
186	Tom Glavine	.40
187	Eric Junge RC	.25
188	Mike Piazza	1.50
189	Corey Patterson	.25
190	Carlos Pena	.25
191	Curt Schilling	.25
192	Nomar Garciaparra	1.50
193	Lance Berkman	.25
194	Ryan Klesko	.25
195	Ivan Rodriguez	.75
196	Alfonso Soriano	.75
197	Derek Jeter	2.00
198	David Justice	.25
199	Juan Gonzalez	.75
200	Adam Dunn	.50
201	Victor Alvarez RC	3.00
202	Miguel Asencio RC	3.00
203	Brandon Backe RC	3.00
204	Chris Baker RC	4.00
205	Steve Bechler RC	4.00
206	Francis Beltran RC	4.00
207	Angel Berroa	4.00
208	Hank Blalock	4.00
209	Dewon Brazelton	3.00
210	Sean Burroughs	3.00
211	Marlon Byrd	3.00
212	Raul Chavez RC	4.00
213	Juan Cruz	3.00
214	Jorge De La Rosa RC	3.00
215	Doug DeVore RC	3.00
216	John Ennis RC	3.00
217	Felix Escalona RC	3.00
218	Morgan Ensberg RC	3.00
219	Cam Esslinger RC	3.00
220	Kevin Frederick RC	3.00

221	Franklyn German RC	3.00
222	Eric Hinske RC	4.00
223	Ben Howard RC	3.00
224	Orlando Hudson RC	3.00
225	Travis Hughes RC	5.00
226	Kazuhisa Ishii RC	6.00
227	Ryan Jamison RC	3.00
228	Reed Johnson RC	4.00
229	Kyle Kane RC	3.00
230	Austin Kearns	3.00
231	Satoru Komiyama RC	4.00
232	Jason Lane	3.00
233	Jeremy Lambert RC	3.00
234	Anderson Machado RC	4.00
235	Brian Mallette RC	3.00
236	Takahito Nomura RC	3.00
237	Jorge Padilla RC	4.00
238	Luis Ugueto RC	3.00
239	Mark Prior	10.00
240	Rene Reyes RC	3.00
241	Deivis Santos	3.00
242	Elio Serrano RC	3.00
243	Tom Shearn RC	3.00
244	Allan Simpson RC	3.00
245	So Taguchi RC	5.00
246	Dennis Tankersley	3.00
247	Mark Teixeira	6.00
248	Matt Thornton	3.00
249	Bobby Hill	3.00
250	Ramon Vazquez	3.00

Proof

Proofs (1-200):		4-8X
Proofs (201-250):		1-2X
Production 100 Sets		

Private Signings

		NM/M
Common Autograph:		5.00
Varying quantities produced.		
1	Vladimir Guerrero/25	75.00
2	Chipper Jones/15	150.00
3	Bobby Abreu/50	20.00
4	Barry Zito/25	25.00
6	Miguel Tejada/50	25.00
7	Mike Sweeney/50	15.00
9	Shannon Stewart/100	10.00
10	Bud Smith/100	5.00
11	Wilson Betemit/250	8.00
12	Kevin Brown/25	25.00
15	Cliff Floyd/50	15.00
16	Marcus Giles/250	10.00
17	Troy Glaus/50	25.00
18	Barry Larkin/50	50.00
19	Carlos Lee/25	20.00
20	Brian Lawrence/250	8.00
22	Paul LoDuca/50	15.00
25	Roger Clemens/15	175.00
26	Joe Crede/250	8.00
28	Jeremy Affeldt/250	8.00
29	Adrian Beltre/25	20.00
30	Josh Beckett/25	40.00
31	Roberto Alomar/25	50.00
32	Toby Hall/250	8.00
37	Roy Oswalt/50	20.00
40	Nick Johnson/250	8.00
42	Drew Henson/150	15.00
45	Luis Gonzalez/15	25.00
47	Joe Mays/100	8.00
49	Aramis Ramirez/50	20.00
50	Kip Wells/250	8.00
51	Moises Alou/15	25.00
55	Freddy Garcia/50	10.00
56	Steve Green/250	5.00
59	Jack Cust/250	10.00
60	Sean Casey/250	10.00
63	Magglio Ordonez/15	40.00
65	Josh Towers/250	8.00
66	Javier Vazquez/100	15.00
68	Aubrey Huff/250	10.00
69	Richard Hidalgo/25	15.00
70	Brandon Claussen/250	10.00
72	John Buck/250	5.00
73	Dee Brown/250	5.00
76	Erick Almonte/250	8.00
79	Jay Gibbons/250	15.00
81	Todd Helton/15	85.00
82	Erik Bedard/250	15.00
84	Rafael Soriano/250	10.00
85	Gary Sheffield/15	40.00
86	Richie Sexson/250	20.00
87	Mike Rivera/250	5.00
88	Jose Ortiz/250	8.00
89	Abraham Nunez/250	5.00
90	Dave Williams/250	8.00
92	Jason Jennings/250	8.00
93	Juan Diaz/250	5.00
96	Steve Smyth/250	5.00
97	Brad Penny/80	10.00
99	Juan Pierre/100	15.00
100	Manny Ramirez/50	75.00
102	Michael Cuddyer/250	10.00
104	Carlos Zambrano/250	15.00
105	Jose Vidro/100	10.00
107	Ed Rogers/250	5.00
110	Tim Redding/250	5.00
111	Josh Phelps/250	8.00
112	Gabe Kapler/100	10.00
113	Edgar Martinez/50	40.00
116	Wade Miller/250	10.00
118	Rafael Palmeiro/25	40.00
121	Bill Hall/250	10.00
123	Geronimo Gil/250	8.00
124	Robert Fick/150	8.00
126	Brandon Duckworth/250	8.00
128	Pedro Feliz/250	8.00
130	Brian Giles/15	25.00
131	Craig Biggio/15	40.00

132	Willie Harris/250	5.00
133	Doug Davis/250	8.00
135	Terrence Long/150	10.00
138	Donaldo Mendez/250	5.00
139	Sean Douglass/250	5.00
140	Eric Chavez/15	25.00
141	Rick Ankiel/250	20.00
142	Jeremy Giambi/100	6.00
143	Juan Pena/250	5.00
144	Bernie Williams/15	75.00
145	Craig Wilson/250	10.00
146	Ricardo Rodriguez/250	10.00
147	Albert Pujols/25	200.00
148	Antonio Perez/250	5.00
150	Corky Miller/250	5.00
151	Rich Aurilia/25	15.00
152	Kerry Wood/25	30.00
153	Joe Thurston/250	5.00
154	Jeff Deardorff/250	8.00
155	Jermaine Dye/15	25.00
157	Victor Martinez/250	15.00
158	Nick Neugebauer/150	5.00
160	Casey Fossum/250	8.00
161	J.D. Drew/25	25.00
162	Matt Childers/250	5.00
163	Mark Buehrle/100	10.00
166	Ben Sheets/250	15.00
167	Alex Rodriguez/15	165.00
168	Adam Pettyjohn/250	5.00
169	Chris Snelling/250	5.00
170	Robert Person/250	5.00
171	Juan Uribe/250	10.00
173	Alfredo Amezaga/250	5.00
175	Corey Thurman/250	5.00
178	Eric Cyr/250	5.00
179	Greg Maddux/25	200.00
180	Earl Snyder/250	5.00
181	C.C. Sabathia/50	20.00
182	Mark Mulder/50	15.00
183	Jose Mieses/250	5.00
184	Joe Kennedy/250	5.00
187	Eric Junge/250	5.00
189	Corey Patterson/205	20.00
190	Carlos Pena/250	8.00
191	Curt Schilling/15	80.00
195	Ivan Rodriguez/15	50.00
196	Alfonso Soriano/50	40.00
201	Victor Alvarez/250	5.00
203	Brandon Backe/250	5.00
204	Chris Baker/250	5.00
205	Steve Bechler/250	8.00
206	Francis Beltran/250	5.00
207	Angel Berroa/250	10.00
208	Hank Blalock/100	20.00
209	Dewon Brazelton/200	5.00
210	Sean Burroughs/250	20.00
211	Marlon Byrd/200	10.00
212	Raul Chavez/250	5.00
213	Juan Cruz/50	15.00
214	Jorge De La Rosa/250	5.00
215	Doug DeVore/250	5.00
216	John Ennis/250	5.00
217	Felix Escalona/250	5.00
218	Morgan Ensberg/250	10.00
219	Cam Esslinger/250	5.00
220	Kevin Frederick/250	5.00
221	Franklyn German/250	5.00
222	Eric Hinske/250	8.00
223	Ben Howard/250	5.00
224	Orlando Hudson/250	10.00
225	Travis Hughes/250	10.00
226	Kazuhisa Ishii/50	25.00
227	Ryan Jamison/250	5.00
228	Reed Johnson/250	5.00
229	Kyle Kane/250	5.00
230	Austin Kearns/250	20.00
231	Satoru Komiyama/250	10.00
232	Jason Lane/200	5.00
233	Jeremy Lambert/250	5.00
234	Anderson Machado/200	10.00
235	Brian Mallette/250	5.00
236	Takahito Nomura/100	20.00
237	Jorge Padilla/200	10.00
238	Luis Ugueto/250	5.00
239	Mark Prior/100	30.00
240	Rene Reyes/250	5.00
241	Deivis Santos/250	5.00
242	Elio Serrano/250	5.00
243	Tom Shearn/250	5.00
244	Allan Simpson/250	5.00
245	So Taguchi/100	15.00
246	Dennis Tankersley/100	10.00
247	Mark Teixeira/50	40.00
248	Matt Thornton/250	5.00
249	Bobby Hill/100	10.00
250	Ramon Vazquez/250	5.00

Classic Studio

WILLIE McCOVEY • 1B • SAN FRANCISCO GIANTS

		NM/M
Complete Set (25):		90.00
Common Player:		3.00
Production 1,000 Sets		
First Ballot:		3-4X
Print run based on HOF year.		
1	Kirby Puckett	5.00
2	George Brett	5.00
3	Nolan Ryan	10.00
4	Mike Schmidt	8.00
5	Steve Carlton	5.00
6	Reggie Jackson	5.00
7	Tom Seaver	3.00
8	Joe Morgan	3.00
9	Jim Palmer	3.00
10	Johnny Bench	5.00
11	Willie McCovey	3.00
12	Brooks Robinson	4.00
13	Al Kaline	5.00
14	Stan Musial	6.00
15	Ozzie Smith	5.00
16	Dave Winfield	3.00
17	Robin Yount	4.00
18	Rod Carew	3.00
19	Willie Stargell	3.00
20	Lou Brock	3.00
21	Ernie Banks	5.00
22	Ted Williams	10.00
23	Jackie Robinson	10.00
24	Roberto Clemente	10.00
25	Lou Gehrig	10.00

Classic Studio Autograph

Production 15-20

Diamond Collection

		NM/M
Complete Set (25):		65.00
Common Player:		1.50
Inserted 1:17		
1	Todd Helton	3.00
2	Chipper Jones	4.00
3	Lance Berkman	4.00
4	Derek Jeter	8.00
5	Hideo Nomo	4.00
6	Kazuhisa Ishii	1.50
7	Barry Bonds	8.00
8	Alex Rodriguez	6.00
9	Ichiro Suzuki	5.00
10	Mike Piazza	5.00
11	Jim Thome	1.50
12	Greg Maddux	5.00
13	Jeff Bagwell	3.00
14	Vladimir Guerrero	5.00
15	Ken Griffey Jr.	5.00
16	Jason Giambi	2.50
17	Nomar Garciaparra	5.00
18	Albert Pujols	6.00
19	Manny Ramirez	3.00
20	Pedro J. Martinez	3.00
21	Roger Clemens	4.50
22	Randy Johnson	3.00
23	Mark Prior	2.00
24	So Taguchi	1.50
25	Sammy Sosa	5.00

Diamond Collection Artist's Proof

		NM/M
Common Jersey Card:		4.00
Varying quantities produced.		
1	Todd Helton/250	8.00
2	Chipper Jones/150	10.00
3	Lance Berkman/200	6.00
4	Derek Jeter/200/Base	20.00
5	Hideo Nomo/150	25.00
6	Kazuhisa Ishii/150	8.00
7	Barry Bonds/200/Base	25.00
8	Alex Rodriguez/150	15.00
9	Ichiro Suzuki/200/Base	25.00
10	Mike Piazza/150	15.00
11	Jim Thome/150	8.00
12	Greg Maddux/150	15.00
13	Jeff Bagwell/150	8.00
14	Vladimir Guerrero/200	8.00
15	Ken Griffey Jr./200/Base	10.00
16	Jason Giambi/200/Base	10.00
17	Nomar Garciaparra/150	15.00
18	Albert Pujols/base/200	10.00
19	Manny Ramirez/150	8.00
20	Pedro Martinez/150	8.00
21	Roger Clemens/150	15.00
22	Randy Johnson/150	8.00
23	So Taguchi/150	8.00
25	Sammy Sosa/200/Base	15.00

Hats Off

		NM/M
Common Player:		8.00
Production 100		
MLB Logo:		No Pricing
Production One Set		
13	Carlos Lee	10.00
14	Mark Buehrle	10.00
16	Paul LoDuca	10.00
22	Brandon Duckworth	10.00

26	J.D. Drew	12.00
28	Wade Miller	10.00
30	Brian Giles	10.00
31	Lance Berkman	10.00
32	Shannon Stewart	10.00
34	Kazuhisa Ishii/50	20.00
35	Rafael Palmeiro	10.00
36	Roy Oswalt	15.00
37	Jason Lane	10.00
38	Andruw Jones	15.00
39	Brad Penny	15.00
40	Bud Smith	8.00
41	Carlos Beltran	15.00
42	Magglio Ordonez	20.00
43	Craig Biggio	15.00
45	Jeff Bagwell	25.00
47	Juan Cruz	8.00
48	Kerry Wood	25.00
49	Brandon Berger	8.00
50	Juan Pierre	8.00

Leather & Lumber

		NM/M
Common Player:		5.00
Production 200 unless noted.		
Artist's Proofs:		1.5-2X
Production 50		
1	Nomar Garciaparra	15.00
2	Jeff Bagwell/150	8.00
3	Alex Rodriguez	15.00
4	Vladimir Guerrero/100	10.00
5	Luis Gonzalez	8.00
6	Chipper Jones	10.00
7	Shawn Green	8.00
8	Kirby Puckett/100	15.00
9	Juan Gonzalez	8.00
10	Troy Glaus	8.00
11	Don Mattingly/100	30.00
12	Todd Helton	8.00
13	Jim Thome	10.00
14	Rickey Henderson	8.00
15	Mike Schmidt/100	35.00
16	Adam Dunn/100	10.00
17	Ivan Rodriguez	10.00
18	Manny Ramirez/150	10.00
19	Tsuyoshi Shinjo	8.00
20	Andruw Jones/150	10.00
21	Roberto Alomar	8.00
22	Lance Berkman	8.00
23	Derek Jeter/50/Ball	30.00
24	Ichiro Suzuki/50/Ball	60.00
25	Mike Piazza	15.00

Masterstrokes

		NM/M
Complete Set (25):		50.00
Common Player:		1.50
Inserted 1:17		
1	Vladimir Guerrero	3.00
2	Frank Thomas	3.00
3	Alex Rodriguez	6.00
4	Manny Ramirez	3.00
5	Jeff Bagwell	3.00
6	Jim Thome	1.50
7	Ichiro Suzuki	4.00
8	Andruw Jones	3.00
9	Troy Glaus	1.50
10	Chipper Jones	4.00
11	Juan Gonzalez	3.00
12	Lance Berkman	1.50
13	Mike Piazza	5.00
14	Darin Erstad	2.00
15	Albert Pujols	6.00
16	Kazuhisa Ishii	1.50
17	Shawn Green	1.50
18	Rafael Palmeiro	1.50
19	Todd Helton	3.00
20	Carlos Delgado	1.50
21	Ivan Rodriguez	2.00
22	Luis Gonzalez	1.50
23	Derek Jeter	8.00
24	Nomar Garciaparra	5.00
25	J.D. Drew	3.00

Masterstrokes Artist's Proof

		NM/M
All Jersey/bat unless noted.		
Varying quantities produced.		
1	Vladimir Guerrero/200	15.00
2	Frank Thomas/200	15.00
3	Alex Rodriguez/100	25.00
4	Manny Ramirez/200	10.00
5	Jeff Bagwell/150	10.00
6	Jim Thome/200	10.00
7	Ichiro Suzuki/100/ Ball/Base	50.00
8	Andruw Jones/200	10.00

9	Troy Glaus/200	10.00
10	Chipper Jones/200	15.00
11	Juan Gonzalez/200	10.00
12	Lance Berkman/200	8.00
13	Mike Piazza/200	25.00
14	Darin Erstad/200	10.00
15	Albert Pujols/100/ Ball/Base	30.00
16	Kazuhisa Ishii/150	15.00
17	Shawn Green/200	10.00
18	Rafael Palmeiro/200	15.00
19	Todd Helton/200	15.00
20	Carlos Delgado/200	10.00
21	Ivan Rodriguez/200	15.00
22	Luis Gonzalez/200	15.00
23	Derek Jeter/100/ Ball/Base	35.00
24	Nomar Garciaparra/150	25.00
25	J.D. Drew/150	8.00

Spirit of the Game

Spirit of the Game
Designated Hitter
EDGAR MARTINEZ • MARINERS

		NM/M
Complete Set (50):		60.00
Common Player:		1.00
Inserted 1:9		
1	Alex Rodriguez	5.00
2	Curt Schilling	1.50
3	Hideo Nomo	2.00
4	Derek Jeter	5.00
5	Mike Sweeney	1.00
6	Mike Piazza	4.00
7	Roger Clemens	3.00
8	Shawn Green	1.50
9	Vladimir Guerrero	2.00
10	Carlos Lee	1.00
11	Edgar Martinez	1.00
12	Albert Pujols	5.00
13	Mark Prior	1.00
14	Mark Buehrle	1.00
15	Chipper Jones	3.00
16	Paul LoDuca	1.00
17	Frank Thomas	2.00
18	Randy Johnson	1.00
19	Cliff Floyd	1.00
20	Todd Helton	1.00
21	Luis Gonzalez	1.00
22	Brandon Duckworth	1.00
23	Jason Giambi	1.00
24	Juan Uribe	1.00
25	Dewon Brazelton	1.00
26	J.D. Drew	1.00
27	Troy Glaus	1.00
28	Wade Miller	1.00
29	Darin Erstad	1.50
30	Brian Giles	1.00
31	Lance Berkman	1.00
32	Shannon Stewart	1.00
33	Kazuhisa Ishii	1.00
34	Corey Patterson	1.00
35	Rafael Palmeiro	1.50
36	Roy Oswalt	1.00
37	Jason Lane	1.00
38	Andruw Jones	2.00
39	Brad Penny	1.50
40	Bud Smith	1.00
41	Carlos Beltran	1.00
42	Magglio Ordonez	1.50
43	Craig Biggio	1.50
44	Hank Blalock	1.50
45	Jeff Bagwell	2.00
46	Josh Beckett	1.00
47	Juan Cruz	1.00
48	Kerry Wood	1.50
49	Brandon Berger	1.00
50	Juan Pierre	1.00

Studio Stars

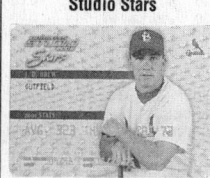

		NM/M
Complete Set (50):		60.00
Common Player:		1.00
Production 700 Sets		
Golds:		1.5-2X
Production 250 Sets		
Platinums:		3-5X
Production 50 Sets		
1	Mike Piazza	3.00
2	Ivan Rodriguez	1.50

3	Albert Pujols	4.00
4	Scott Rolen	2.00
5	Alex Rodriguez	4.00
6	Curt Schilling	1.50
7	Vladimir Guerrero	2.00
8	Jim Thome	1.00
9	Derek Jeter	5.00
10	C.C. Sabathia	1.00
11	Sammy Sosa	3.00
12	Adam Dunn	1.50
13	Bernie Williams	1.50
14	Ichiro Suzuki	4.00
15	Barry Bonds	5.00
16	Rickey Henderson	2.00
17	Ken Griffey Jr.	3.00
18	Kazuhisa Ishii	1.00
19	Kerry Wood	1.50
20	Todd Helton	1.50
21	Hideo Nomo	2.00
22	Frank Thomas	2.00
23	Manny Ramirez	2.00
24	Luis Gonzalez	1.00
25	Rafael Palmeiro	1.50
26	Mike Mussina	1.50
27	Roy Oswalt	1.00
28	Darin Erstad	1.00
29	Barry Larkin	1.00
30	Randy Johnson	2.00
31	Tom Glavine	1.00
32	Lance Berkman	1.00
33	Juan Gonzalez	2.00
34	Shawn Green	1.00
35	Nomar Garciaparra	3.00
36	Troy Glaus	2.00
37	Tim Hudson	1.00
38	Carlos Delgado	1.50
39	Jason Giambi	1.50
40	Andruw Jones	2.00
41	Roberto Alomar	1.00
42	Greg Maddux	2.50
43	Pedro J. Martinez	2.00
44	Tony Gwynn	3.00
45	Alfonso Soriano	1.50
46	Chipper Jones	2.50
47	J.D. Drew	1.00
48	Roger Clemens	2.75
49	Barry Zito	1.00
50	Jeff Bagwell	2.00

2002 Donruss Studio - LCS Programs

A perforated sheet of Donruss Studio cards was inserted into some of the programs sold for the American and National League Championship Series. The 8-1/2" x 11" sheet features eight player cards and a header card advertising the brand. Each 2-1/2" x 3-1/2" card is perforated on all sides and differs from the regularly issued version only in the card number on back. Sheet cards have either an "ALCS-" or "NLCS-" prefix to the number. Other programs could be found with similar sheets of Donruss Diamond Kings, Donruss Originals or Playoff Piece of the Game cards.

		NM/M
Complete Sheet Set (2):		16.00
Common Player:		.50
ALCS SHEET		8.00
25	Eric Hinske	.50
26	Edgar Martinez (Spirit/Game)	.50
27	Pedro Martinez	.75
28	Roger Clemens (Spirit/Game)	1.75
29	Alex Rodriguez (Spirit/Game)	2.50
30	George Brett (Classic)	2.00
31	Dewon Brazelton (Spirit/Game)	.50
32	Barry Zito	.60
---	Header Card	.10
NLCS SHEET		8.00
17	J.D. Drew (Spirit/Game)	.60
18	Randy Johnson	.75
19	Mike Piazza (Spirit/Game)	2.00
20	Ozzie Smith (Classic)	1.50
21	Jeff Kent	.50
22	Roy Oswalt (Spirit/Game)	.60
23	Pat Burrell	.50
24	Todd Helton (Spirit/Game)	.75
---	Header Card	.10

2002 Donruss The Rookies

		NM/M
Complete Set (110):		20.00
Common Player:		.15
Common Rookie:		.25
Pack (5):		2.00
Box (24):		40.00
1	Kazuhisa Ishii RC	1.00
2	P.J. Bevis RC	.25
3	Jason Simontacchi RC	.50
4	John Lackey RC	.15
5	Travis Driskill RC	.25
6	Carl Sadler RC	.25
7	Tim Kalita RC	.25
8	Nelson Castro RC	.25
9	Francis Beltran RC	.25
10	So Taguchi RC	.50
11	Ryan Bukvich RC	.25
12	Brian Fitzgerald RC	.15
13	Kevin Frederick RC	.25
14	Chone Figgins RC	.75
15	Marlon Byrd RC	.15
16	Ron Calloway RC	.25
17	Jason Lane RC	.15
18	Satoru Komiyama RC	.25
19	John Ennis RC	.25
20	Juan Brito RC	.25
21	Gustavo Chacin RC	.50
22	Josh Bard RC	.50
23	Brett Myers	.15
24	Mike Smith RC	.25
25	Eric Hinske	.15
26	Jake Peavy	.15
27	Todd Donovan RC	.25
28	Luis Ugueto RC	.25
29	Corey Thurman RC	.25
30	Takahito Nomura RC	.25
31	Andy Shibilo RC	.25
32	Mike Crudale RC	.25
33	Earl Snyder RC	.25
34	Brian Tallet RC	.50
35	Miguel Asencio RC	.25
36	Felix Escalona RC	.25
37	Drew Henson	.40
38	Steve Kent RC	.25
39	Rene Reyes RC	.25
40	Edwin Almonte RC	.25
41	Chris Snelling RC	.75
42	Franklyn German RC	.25
43	Jeriome Robertson RC	.25
44	Colin Young RC	.25
45	Jeremy Lambert RC	.25
46	Kirk Saarloos RC	.75
47	Matt Childers RC	.25
48	Justin Wayne	.15
49	Jose Valverde RC	.15
50	Wily Mo Pena	.15
51	Victor Alvarez RC	.25
52	Julius Matos RC	.25
53	Aaron Cook RC	.40
54	Jeff Austin RC	.25
55	Adrian Burnside RC	.25
56	Brandon Puffer RC	.25
57	Jeremy Hill RC	.25
58	Jaime Cerda RC	.25
59	Aaron Guiel RC	.25
60	Ron Chiavacci RC	.15
61	Kevin Cash RC	.25
62	Elio Serrano RC	.15
63	Julio Mateo RC	.25
64	Cam Esslinger RC	.25
65	Ken Huckaby RC	.25
66	Wiki Nieves RC	.25
67	Luis Martinez RC	.25
68	Scotty Layfield RC	.25
69	Jeremy Guthrie RC	.75
70	Hansel Izquierdo RC	.25
71	Shane Nance RC	.25
72	Jeff Baker RC	.50
73	Clifford Bartosh RC	.25
74	Mitch Wylie RC	.25
75	Oliver Perez RC	.75
76	Matt Thornton RC	.15
77	John Foster RC	.15
78	Joe Borchard	.15
79	Eric Junge RC	.25
80	Jorge Sosa RC	.25
81	Runelvys Hernandez RC	.25
82	Kevin Mench	.15
83	Ben Kozlowski RC	.50
84	Trey Hodges RC	.40
85	Reed Johnson RC	.25
86	Eric Eckenstahler RC	.25
87	Franklin Nunez RC	.25
88	Victor Martinez RC	.75
89	Kevin Gryboski RC	.25
90	Jason Jennings	.15
91	Jim Rushford RC	.25

92	Jeremy Ward RC	.25
93	Adam Walker RC	.25
94	Freddy Sanchez RC	.50
95	Wilson Valdez RC	.25
96	Lee Gardner RC	.15
97	Eric Good RC	.25
98	Hank Blalock	.50
99	Mark Corey	.15
100	Jason Davis RC	.40
101	Mike Gonzalez RC	.25
102	David Ross RC	.25
103	Tyler Yates RC	.25
104	Cliff Lee RC	1.00
105	Mike Moriarty RC	.25
106	Josh Hancock RC	.25
107	Jason Beverlin RC	.25
108	Clay Condrey RC	.25
109	Shawn Sedlacek RC	.25
110	Sean Burroughs	.15

Donruss Originals
401	Runelvys Hernandez RC	.50
402	Wilson Valdez RC	.25
403	Brian Tallet RC	1.00
404	Chone Figgins RC	.25
405	Jeriome Robertson RC	.50
406	Shane Nance RC	.25
407	Aaron Cook RC	.75
408	Trey Hodges RC	.75
409	Matt Childers RC	.40
410	Mitch Wylie RC	.25
411	Rene Reyes RC	.25
412	Mike Smith RC	.25
413	Jason Simontacchi RC	.75
414	Luis Martinez RC	.40
415	Kevin Cash RC	.40
416	Todd Donovan RC	.25
417	Scotty Layfield RC	.25
418	Joe Borchard RC	.25
419	Adrian Burnside RC	.25
420	Ben Kozlowski RC	.25
421	Clay Condrey RC	.25
422	Cliff Lee	1.00
423	Josh Bard	.25
424	Freddy Sanchez	1.00
425	Ron Calloway	.25

Donruss Studio
Common Studio RC:		3.00
Production 1,500		
251	Freddy Sanchez RC	5.00
252	Josh Bard RC	3.00
253	Trey Hodges RC	5.00
254	Jorge Sosa RC	3.00
255	Ben Kozlowski RC	3.00
256	Eric Good RC	3.00
257	Brian Tallet	5.00
258	P.J. Bevis RC	3.00
259	Rodrigo Rosario RC	3.00
260	Kirk Saarloos RC	5.00
261	Runelvys Hernandez RC	4.00
262	Josh Hancock RC	3.00
263	Tim Kalita RC	3.00
264	Jason Simontacchi RC	5.00
265	Clay Condrey RC	3.00
266	Cliff Lee RC	10.00
267	Aaron Guiel RC	4.00
268	Andy Pratt RC	4.00
269	Wilson Valdez RC	3.00
270	Oliver Perez RC	4.00
271	Joe Borchard	3.00
272	Jeriome Robertson RC	4.00
273	Aaron Cook RC	5.00
274	Kevin Cash RC	3.00
275	Chone Figgins RC	5.00

Best of Fan Club
Common Best of Fan Club RC:		3.00
Production 1,350		
Best of Fan Club Spotlights:		1.5-3X
Production 100 Sets		
201	Kirk Saarloos	4.00
202	Oliver Perez	4.00
203	So Taguchi	6.00
204	Runelvys Hernandez RC	5.00
205	Freddy Sanchez RC	5.00
206	Cliff Lee	10.00
207	Kazuhisa Ishii RC	8.00
208	Kevin Cash RC	5.00
209	Trey Hodges RC	6.00
210	Wilson Valdez RC	3.00
211	Satoru Komiyama RC	3.00
212	Luis Ugueto RC	3.00
213	Joe Borchard	3.00
214	Brian Tallet	4.00
215	Jeriome Robertson RC	5.00
216	Eric Junge RC	4.00
217	Aaron Cook RC	4.00
218	Jason Simontacchi RC	3.00
219	Miguel Asencio RC	3.00
220	Josh Bard RC	3.00
221	Earl Snyder RC	3.00
222	Felix Escalona RC	3.00
223	Rene Reyes RC	3.00
224	Chone Figgins RC	3.00
225	Chris Snelling RC	5.00

Fan Club
Inserted 1:4 Retail		
201	Kirk Saarloos	1.50
202	Oliver Perez	2.00
203	So Taguchi	2.00
204	Runelvys Hernandez RC	1.50
205	Freddy Sanchez RC	2.00
206	Cliff Lee	4.00
207	Kazuhisa Ishii RC	3.00
208	Kevin Cash	1.00
209	Trey Hodges	1.50
210	Wilson Valdez	.50
211	Satoru Komiyama RC	1.00
212	Luis Ugueto RC	1.50
213	Joe Borchard	2.00

214	Brian Tallet	3.00
215	Jeriome Robertson RC	1.50
216	Eric Junge	1.50
217	Aaron Cook	1.50
218	Jason Simontacchi	1.50
219	Miguel Asencio	1.50
220	Josh Bard	1.50
221	Earl Snyder	1.50
222	Felix Escalona	1.00
223	Rene Reyes	1.00
224	Chone Figgins	1.00
225	Chris Snelling RC	4.00

Elite
Common Elite RC:		4.00
Production 1,000		
Elite Turn of the Century:		1-2.5X
Production 100 Sets		
201	Chris Snelling RC	5.00
202	Satoru Komiyama RC	5.00
203	Jason Simontacchi RC	8.00
204	Tim Kalita RC	4.00
205	Runelvys Hernandez RC	5.00
206	Kirk Saarloos RC	4.00
207	Aaron Cook RC	6.00
208	Luis Ugueto RC	5.00
209	Gustavo Chacin RC	5.00
210	Francis Beltran RC	5.00
211	Takahito Nomura RC	5.00
212	Oliver Perez RC	6.00
213	Miguel Asencio RC	4.00
214	Rene Reyes RC	5.00
215	Jeff Baker RC	15.00
216	Jon Adkins RC	5.00
217	Carlos Rivera RC	5.00
218	Corey Thurman RC	5.00
219	Earl Snyder RC	5.00
220	Felix Escalona RC	5.00
221	Jeremy Guthrie RC	15.00
222	Josh Hancock RC	5.00
223	Ben Kozlowski RC	5.00
224	Eric Good RC	5.00
225	Eric Junge RC	5.00
226	Andy Pratt RC	5.00
227	Matt Thornton	5.00
228	Jorge Sosa RC	5.00
229	Mike Smith	5.00
230	Mitch Wylie RC	5.00
231	John Ennis RC	5.00
232	Reed Johnson RC	5.00
233	Joe Borchard	8.00
234	Ron Calloway RC	5.00
235	Brian Tallet	5.00
236	Chris Baker RC	5.00
237	Cliff Lee RC	20.00
238	Matt Childers RC	5.00
239	Freddy Sanchez RC	5.00
240	Chone Figgins RC	8.00
241	Kevin Cash RC	5.00
242	Josh Bard RC	5.00
243	Jeriome Robertson RC	5.00
244	Jeremy Hill RC	5.00
245	Shane Nance RC	5.00
246	Wes Obermueller RC	5.00
247	Trey Hodges RC	5.00
248	Eric Eckenstahler RC	5.00
249	Jim Rushford RC	5.00
250	Jose Castillo RC	10.00
251	Garrett Atkins RC	20.00
252	Alexis Rios RC	100.00
253	Ryan Church RC	8.00
254	Jimmy Gobble RC	8.00
255	Corwin Malone	6.00
256	Nic Jackson RC	8.00
257	Tommy Whiteman RC	8.00
258	Mario Ramos	5.00
260	Rob Bowen RC	5.00
261	Josh Wilson RC	5.00
262	Tim Hummel RC	5.00
264	Gerald Laird RC	15.00
265	Vinnie Chulk RC	5.00
266	Jesus Medrano RC	5.00
272	Adam LaRoche RC	20.00
273	Adam Morrissey RC	5.00
274	Henri Stanley RC	5.00
275	Walter Young RC	10.00

Donruss Classics
Common Classics RC:		3.00
Production 1,500		
Classics Timeless Tributes:		1.5-3X
Production 100 Sets		
201	Oliver Perez RC	4.00
202	Aaron Cook RC	5.00
203	Eric Junge RC	3.00
204	Freddy Sanchez RC	5.00
205	Cliff Lee	10.00
206	Runelvys Hernandez RC	5.00
207	Chone Figgins RC	5.00
208	Rodrigo Rosario RC	3.00
209	Kevin Cash RC	3.00
210	Josh Bard RC	3.00
211	Felix Escalona RC	3.00
212	Jeriome Robertson RC	5.00
213	Jason Simontacchi RC	5.00
214	Shane Nance RC	3.00
215	Ben Kozlowski RC	3.00
216	Brian Tallet	5.00
217	Earl Snyder RC	3.00
218	Andy Pratt RC	3.00
219	Trey Hodges RC	3.00
220	Kirk Saarloos	5.00
221	Rene Reyes RC	3.00
222	Joe Borchard	3.00
223	Wilson Valdez RC	3.00
224	Miguel Asencio RC	3.00
225	Chris Snelling RC	5.00

Diamond Kings
Common DK RC:		3.00
Inserted 1:10		

151	Chris Snelling RC	4.00
152	Satoru Komiyama RC	3.00
153	Oliver Perez RC	33.00
154	Kirk Saarloos RC	3.00
155	Rene Reyes RC	3.00
156	Runelvys Hernandez RC	3.00
157	Rodrigo Rosario RC	3.00
158	Jason Simontacchi RC	3.00
159	Miguel Asencio RC	3.00
160	Aaron Cook RC	3.00

Autographs

		NM/M
Production 15-100		5.00
Print runs listed.		
2	P.J. Bevis/50	20.00
9	Francis Beltran/100	5.00
13	Kevin Frederick/100	5.00
14	Chone Figgins/100	20.00
17	Marlon Byrd/100	10.00
19	Jason Lane/100	8.00
21	John Ennis/100	10.00
22	Josh Bard/100	10.00
25	Eric Hinske/100	10.00
28	Luis Ugueto/100	8.00
29	Corey Thurman/100	5.00
30	Takahito Nomura/100	20.00
33	Earl Snyder/100	10.00
34	Brian Tallet/100	15.00
37	Drew Henson/50	20.00
39	Rene Reyes/50	15.00
40	Edwin Almonte/50	15.00
41	Chris Snelling/50	20.00
42	Franklyn German/100	5.00
45	Jeremy Lambert/100	5.00
46	Kirk Saarloos/100	5.00
47	Matt Childers/100	5.00
50	Wily Mo Pena/100	15.00
51	Victor Alvarez/100	10.00
61	Kevin Cash/100	8.00
62	Elio Serrano/100	5.00
64	Cam Esslinger/100	5.00
69	Jeremy Guthrie/100	15.00
71	Shane Nance/100	8.00
72	Jeff Baker/100	20.00
76	Matt Thornton/100	10.00
78	Joe Borchard/100	8.00
82	Kevin Mench/100	10.00
83	Ben Kozlowski/100	8.00
84	Trey Hodges/100	10.00
85	Reed Johnson/100	15.00
88	Victor Martinez/100	25.00
90	Jason Jennings/100	8.00
95	Wilson Valdez/100	8.00
97	Eric Good/100	10.00
98	Hank Blalock/100	20.00
104	Cliff Lee/100	30.00
110	Sean Burroughs/50	10.00

Donruss Classics Signatures
		NM/M
Print runs listed.		
203	Eric Junge/50	10.00
205	Cliff Lee/100	40.00
207	Chone Figgins/100	10.00
208	Rodrigo Rosario/250	10.00
209	Kevin Cash/100	10.00
210	Josh Bard/100	10.00
214	Shane Nance/200	10.00
215	Ben Kozlowski/200	10.00
216	Brian Tallet/100	15.00
217	Earl Snyder/100	10.00
218	Andy Pratt/250	10.00
219	Trey Hodges/250	15.00
220	Kirk Saarloos/100	20.00
221	Rene Reyes/50	10.00
222	Joe Borchard/100	10.00
223	Wilson Valdez/100	10.00
225	Chris Snelling/100	25.00

Donruss Studio Private Signing
		NM/M
Print runs listed.		
252	Josh Bard/100	10.00
253	Trey Hodges/250	10.00
255	Ben Kozlowski/200	5.00
257	Brian Tallet/100	15.00
258	P.J. Bevis/100	15.00
259	Rodrigo Rosario/250	10.00
260	Kirk Saarloos/100	10.00
263	Tim Kalita/50	8.00
266	Cliff Lee/100	30.00
268	Andy Pratt/250	8.00
269	Wilson Valdez/200	10.00
271	Joe Borchard/100	15.00
274	Kevin Cash/100	8.00
275	Chone Figgins/100	8.00

Elite Turn of the Cent. Auto.
		NM/M
Common Autograph:		
Print runs listed.		
201	Chris Snelling/50	20.00
206	Kirk Saarloos/50	20.00
215	Jeff Baker/100	20.00
216	Jon Adkins/100	10.00
217	Carlos Rivera/100	15.00
221	Jeremy Guthrie/100	25.00
223	Ben Kozlowski/100	10.00
224	Eric Good/100	10.00
240	Chone Figgins/100	30.00
241	Kevin Cash/100	10.00
247	Trey Hodges/100	15.00
251	Garrett Atkins/100	50.00
253	Ryan Church/100	35.00
254	Jimmy Gobble/100	10.00
255	Corwin Malone/100	15.00
258	Tom Whiteman/100	10.00
259	Mario Ramos/100	10.00
260	Rob Bowen/100	10.00
261	Josh Wilson/100	10.00
262	Tim Hummel/100	10.00
264	Gerald Laird/100	25.00
266	Jesus Medrano/100	10.00
272	Adam LaRoche/100	30.00
273	Adam Morrissey/100	10.00
274	Henri Stanley/100	10.00

Fan Club Autograph
		NM/M
Common Autograph:		
Print runs listed.		
201	Kirk Saarloos/100	10.00
208	Kevin Cash/50	8.00
209	Trey Hodges/100	10.00
210	Wilson Valdez/50	10.00
212	Luis Ugueto/75	10.00
213	Joe Borchard/100	15.00
214	Brian Tallet/100	15.00
220	Josh Bard/100	8.00
221	Earl Snyder/100	8.00
223	Rene Reyes/50	8.00
224	Chone Figgins/100	8.00

Best of Fan Club Autograph

		NM/M
Production 10-100		
Print runs listed.		
201	Kirk Saarloos/100	10.00
208	Kevin Cash/50	10.00
209	Trey Hodges/100	10.00
210	Wilson Valdez/50	10.00
212	Luis Ugueto/75	10.00
213	Joe Borchard/50	15.00
214	Brian Tallet/50	15.00
220	Josh Bard/50	8.00
221	Earl Snyder/100	8.00
223	Rene Reyes/50	8.00
224	Chone Figgins/50	8.00
225	Chris Snelling/50	15.00

Phenoms

		NM/M
Common Player:		3.00
Production 1,000 Sets		
1	Kazuhisa Ishii	5.00
2	Eric Hinske	3.00
3	Jason Lane	3.00
4	Victor Martinez	5.00
5	Mark Prior	6.00
6	Antonio Perez	3.00
7	John Buck	3.00
8	Joe Borchard	3.00
9	Alexis Gomez	3.00
10	Sean Burroughs	3.00
11	Carlos Pena	3.00

12	Bill Hall	3.00
13	Alfredo Amezaga	3.00
14	Ed Rogers	3.00
15	Mark Teixeira	5.00
16	Chris Snelling	4.00
17	Nick Johnson	3.00
18	Angel Berroa	3.00
19	Orlando Hudson	3.00
20	Drew Henson	3.00
21	Austin Kearns	3.00
22	Dewon Brazelton	3.00
23	Dennis Tankersley	3.00
24	Josh Beckett	4.00
25	Marlon Byrd	4.00

Phenoms Autographs
		NM/M
Common Autograph:		5.00
Print runs listed.		
2	Eric Hinske/500	10.00
3	Jason Lane/500	5.00
4	Victor Martinez/225	5.00
5	Mark Prior/100	15.00
6	Antonio Perez/500	5.00
7	John Buck/100	8.00
8	Joe Borchard/100	10.00
9	Alexis Gomez/400	5.00
10	Sean Burroughs/150	10.00
11	Carlos Pena/150	8.00
12	Bill Hall/200	8.00
13	Alfredo Amezaga/500	5.00
14	Ed Rogers/500	5.00
15	Mark Teixeira/100	20.00
16	Chris Snelling/500	5.00
17	Nick Johnson/250	8.00
18	Angel Berroa/500	8.00
19	Orlando Hudson/400	15.00
20	Drew Henson/500	25.00
21	Austin Kearns/75	8.00
22	Dewon Brazelton/350	5.00
23	Dennis Tankersley/100	8.00
24	Josh Beckett/125	30.00
25	Marlon Byrd/500	10.00

Recollection Collection
No Pricing

Rookie Crusade

		NM/M
Common Player:		3.00
Production 1,500 Sets		
1	Corky Miller	3.00
2	Jack Cust	3.00
3	Erik Bedard	3.00
4	Andres Torres	3.00
5	Geronimo Gil	3.00
6	Rafael Soriano	3.00
7	Johnny Estrada	3.00
8	Steve Bechler	3.00
9	Adam Johnson	3.00
10	So Taguchi	3.00
11	Dee Brown	3.00
12	Kevin Frederick	3.00
13	Allan Simpson	3.00
14	Ricardo Rodriguez	3.00
15	Jason Hart	3.00
16	Matt Childers	3.00
17	Jason Jennings	3.00
18	Anderson Machado	3.00
19	Fernando Rodney	3.00
20	Brandon Larson	3.00
21	Satoru Komiyama	3.00
22	Francis Beltran	3.00
23	Joe Thurston	3.00
24	Josh Pearce	3.00
25	Carlos Hernandez	3.00
26	Ben Howard	3.00
27	Wilson Valdez	3.00
28	Victor Alvarez	3.00
29	Cesar Izturis	3.00
30	Endy Chavez	3.00
31	Michael Cuddyer	4.00
32	Bobby Hill	3.00
33	Willie Harris	3.00
34	Joe Crede	3.00
35	Jorge Padilla	3.00
36	Brandon Backe	3.00
37	Franklyn German	3.00
38	Xavier Nady	3.00
39	Raul Chavez	3.00
40	Shane Nance	3.00
41	Brandon Claussen	4.00
42	Tom Shearn	3.00
43	Freddy Sanchez	3.00
44	Chone Figgins	3.00
45	Cliff Lee	4.00
46	Brian Mallette	3.00
47	Mike Rivera	3.00

48	Elio Serrano	3.00
49	Rodrigo Rosario	3.00
50	Earl Snyder	3.00

Rookie Crusade Autograph

NM/M

Common Autograph: 5.00
Print runs listed.

1	Corky Miller/500	5.00
2	Jack Cust/500	6.00
3	Erik Bedard/100	10.00
4	Andres Torres/500	5.00
5	Geronimo Gil/500	5.00
6	Rafael Soriano/500	8.00
7	Johnny Estrada/400	5.00
8	Steve Bechler/500	6.00
9	Adam Johnson/500	5.00
11	Dee Brown/500	5.00
12	Kevin Frederick/150	5.00
13	Allan Simpson/150	5.00
14	Ricardo Rodriguez/500	5.00
15	Jason Hart/500	5.00
16	Matt Childers/150	5.00
17	Jason Jennings/500	5.00
18	Anderson Machado/500	8.00
19	Fernando Rodney/500	5.00
20	Brandon Larson/400	5.00
22	Francis Beltran/500	5.00
23	Joe Thurston/500	5.00
24	Josh Pearce/500	5.00
25	Carlos Hernandez/500	5.00
26	Ben Howard/500	6.00
27	Wilson Valdez/500	5.00
28	Victor Alvarez/500	5.00
29	Cesar Izturis/500	8.00
30	Endy Chavez/500	5.00
31	Michael Cuddyer/375	10.00
32	Bobby Hill/250	5.00
33	Willie Harris/300	5.00
34	Joe Crede/500	8.00
35	Jorge Padilla/475	10.00
36	Brandon Backe/350	5.00
37	Franklyn German/500	5.00
38	Xavier Nady/500	8.00
39	Raul Chavez/500	5.00
40	Shane Nance/500	5.00
41	Brandon Claussen/150	10.00
42	Tom Shearn/500	5.00
43	Chone Figgins/500	5.00
45	Cliff Lee/500	20.00
46	Brian Mallette/150	5.00
47	Mike Rivera/400	5.00
48	Elio Serrano/500	5.00
49	Rodrigo Rosario/100	10.00
50	Earl Snyder/100	5.00

2003 Donruss Samples

MIKE CAMERON 182

Each issue of the Jan., 2003, Beckett Baseball Card Monthly included a sample 2003 Donruss card rubber-cemented inside. The cards differ from the issued version only in the appearance on back of a (usually) silver-foil "SAMPLE" notation. Some cards were produced with the overprint in gold-foil, in much more limited quantities. The number of different players' cards involved in the promotion is unknown.

NM/M

Common Player: .10
Stars: 1.5-2X
Gold: 10X

2003 Donruss

GARRET ANDERSON OF

		NM/M
Complete Set (400):		40.00
Common Player:		.15
Pack (13):		1.50
Box (24):		30.00
1	Vladimir Guerrero	.75
2	Derek Jeter	2.00
3	Adam Dunn	.50
4	Greg Maddux	1.00
5	Lance Berkman	.40
6	Ichiro Suzuki	2.00
7	Mike Piazza	1.00
8	Alex Rodriguez	2.00
9	Tom Glavine	.25
10	Randy Johnson	.75
11	Nomar Garciaparra	1.00
12	Jason Giambi	.50
13	Sammy Sosa	1.00
14	Barry Zito	.25
15	Chipper Jones	1.00
16	Magglio Ordonez	.25
17	Larry Walker	.25
18	Alfonso Soriano	.75
19	Curt Schilling	.50
20	Barry Bonds	2.00
21	Joe Borchard	.15
22	Chris Snelling	.15
23	Brian Tallet	.15
24	Cliff Lee	.15
25	Freddy Sanchez	.15
26	Chone Figgins	.15
27	Kevin Cash	.15
28	Josh Bard	.15
29	Jeriome Robertson	.15
30	Jeremy Hill	.15
31	Shane Nance	.15
32	Jake Peavy Padres	.15
33	Trey Hodges	.15
34	Eric Eckenstahler	.15
35	Jim Rushford	.15
36	Oliver Perez	.15
37	Kirk Saarloos	.15
38	Hank Blalock	.15
39	Francisco Rodriguez	.25
40	Runelvys Hernandez	.15
41	Aaron Cook	.15
42	Josh Hancock	.15
43	P.J. Bevis	.15
44	Jon Adkins	.15
45	Tim Kalita	.15
46	Nelson Castro	.15
47	Colin Young	.15
48	Adrian Burnside	.15
49	Luis Martinez	.15
50	Peter Zamora	.15
51	Todd Donovan	.15
52	Jeremy Ward	.15
53	Wilson Valdez	.15
54	Eric Good	.15
55	Jeff Baker	.15
56	Mitch Wylie	.15
57	Ron Calloway	.15
58	Jose Valverde	.15
59	Jason Davis	.15
60	Scotty Layfield	.15
61	Matt Thornton	.15
62	Adam Walker	.15
63	Gustavo Chacin	.15
64	Ron Chiavacci	.15
65	Wiki Nieves	.15
66	Clifford Bartosh	.15
67	Mike Gonzalez	.15
68	Justin Wayne	.15
69	Eric Junge	.15
70	Ben Kozlowski	.15
71	Darin Erstad	.25
72	Garret Anderson	.40
73	Troy Glaus	.40
74	David Eckstein	.15
75	Adam Kennedy	.15
76	Kevin Appier	.15
77	Jarrod Washburn	.15
78	Scott Spiezio	.15
79	Tim Salmon	.25
80	Ramon Ortiz	.15
81	Bengie Molina	.15
82	Brad Fullmer	.15
83	Troy Percival	.15
84	David Segui	.15
85	Jay Gibbons	.15
86	Tony Batista	.15
87	Scott Erickson	.15
88	Jeff Conine	.15
89	Melvin Mora	.15
90	Buddy Groom	.15
91	Rodrigo Lopez	.15
92	Marty Cordova	.15
93	Geronimo Gil	.15
94	Kenny Lofton	.15
95	Shea Hillenbrand	.15
96	Manny Ramirez	.50
97	Pedro Martinez	.75
98	Nomar Garciaparra	1.00
99	Rickey Henderson	.40
100	Johnny Damon	.25
101	Trot Nixon	.15
102	Derek Lowe	.15
103	Hee Seop Choi	.15
104	Mark Teixeira	.40
105	Tim Wakefield	.15
106	Jason Varitek	.25
107	Frank Thomas	.50
108	Joe Crede	.15
109	Magglio Ordonez	.25
110	Ray Durham	.15
111	Mark Buehrle	.15
112	Paul Konerko	.25
113	Jose Valentin	.15
114	Carlos Lee	.15
115	Royce Clayton	.15
116	C.C. Sabathia	.15
117	Ellis Burks	.15
118	Omar Vizquel	.25
119	Jim Thome	.75
120	Matt Lawton	.15
121	Travis Fryman	.15
122	Earl Snyder	.15
123	Ricky Gutierrez	.15
124	Einar Diaz	.15
125	Danys Baez	.15
126	Robert Fick	.15
127	Bobby Higginson	.15
128	Steve Sparks	.15
129	Mike Rivera	.15
130	Wendell Magee	.15
131	Randall Simon	.15
132	Carlos Pena	.15
133	Mark Redman	.15
134	Juan Acevedo	.15
135	Mike Sweeney	.15
136	Aaron Guiel	.15
137	Carlos Beltran	.40
138	Joe Randa	.15
139	Paul Byrd	.15
140	Shawn Sedlacek	.15
141	Raul Ibanez	.15
142	Michael Tucker	.15
143	Torii Hunter	.40
144	Jacque Jones	.15
145	David Ortiz	.40
146	Corey Koskie	.15
147	Brad Radke	.15
148	Doug Mientkiewicz	.15
149	A.J. Pierzynski	.15
150	Dustan Mohr	.15
151	Michael Cuddyer	.15
152	Eddie Guardado	.15
153	Cristian Guzman	.15
154	Derek Jeter	2.00
155	Bernie Williams	.50
156	Roger Clemens	1.50
157	Mike Mussina	.50
158	Jorge Posada	.40
159	Alfonso Soriano	.75
160	Jason Giambi	.50
161	Robin Ventura	.15
162	Andy Pettitte	.25
163	David Wells	.15
164	Nick Johnson	.15
165	Jeff Weaver	.15
166	Raul Mondesi	.15
167	Rondell White	.15
168	Tim Hudson	.25
169	Barry Zito	.40
170	Mark Mulder	.25
171	Miguel Tejada	.25
172	Eric Chavez	.25
173	Billy Koch	.15
174	Jermaine Dye	.15
175	Scott Hatteberg	.15
176	Terrence Long	.15
177	David Justice	.25
178	Ramon Hernandez	.15
179	Ted Lilly	.15
180	Ichiro Suzuki	1.50
181	Edgar Martinez	.25
182	Mike Cameron	.15
183	John Olerud	.15
184	Bret Boone	.25
185	Dan Wilson	.15
186	Freddy Garcia	.15
187	Jamie Moyer	.15
188	Carlos Guillen	.15
189	Ruben Sierra	.15
190	Kazuhiro Sasaki	.15
191	Mark McLemore	.15
192	Chris Snelling	.15
193	Joel Pineiro	.15
194	Jeff Cirillo	.15
195	Rafael Soriano	.15
196	Ben Grieve	.15
197	Aubrey Huff	.15
198	Steve Cox	.15
199	Toby Hall	.15
200	Randy Winn	.15
201	Brent Abernathy	.15
202	Chris Gomez	.15
203	John Flaherty	.15
204	Paul Wilson	.15
205	Chan Ho Park	.15
206	Alex Rodriguez	2.00
207	Juan Gonzalez	.50
208	Rafael Palmeiro	.50
209	Ivan Rodriguez	.50
210	Rusty Greer	.15
211	Kenny Rogers	.15
212	Ismael Valdes	.15
213	Frank Catalanotto	.15
214	Hank Blalock	.50
215	Michael Young	.15
216	Kevin Mench	.15
217	Herbert Perry	.15
218	Gabe Kapler	.15
219	Carlos Delgado	.25
220	Shannon Stewart	.15
221	Eric Hinske	.15
222	Roy Halladay	.25
223	Felipe Lopez	.15
224	Vernon Wells	.15
225	Josh Phelps	.15
226	Jose Cruz	.15
227	Curt Schilling	.50
228	Randy Johnson	.75
229	Luis Gonzalez	.15
230	Mark Grace	.40
231	Junior Spivey	.15
232	Tony Womack	.15
233	Matt Williams	.25
234	Steve Finley	.15
235	Byung-Hyun Kim	.15
236	Craig Counsell	.15
237	Greg Maddux	1.00
238	Tom Glavine	.40
239	John Smoltz	.15
240	Chipper Jones	1.00
241	Gary Sheffield	.25
242	Andruw Jones	.40
243	Vinny Castilla	.15
244	Damian Moss	.15
245	Rafael Furcal	.15
246	Javy Lopez	.25
247	Kevin Millwood	.15
248	Kerry Wood	.75
249	Fred McGriff	.25
250	Sammy Sosa	1.00
251	Alex Gonzalez	.15
252	Corey Patterson	.25
253	Moises Alou	.15
254	Juan Cruz	.15
255	Jon Lieber	.15
256	Matt Clement	.15
257	Mark Prior	.75
258	Ken Griffey Jr.	1.00
259	Barry Larkin	.25
260	Adam Dunn	.50
261	Sean Casey	.15
262	Jose Rijo	.15
263	Elmer Dessens	.15
264	Austin Kearns	.25
265	Corky Miller	.15
266	Todd Walker	.15
267	Chris Reitsma	.15
268	Ryan Dempster	.15
269	Aaron Boone	.15
270	Danny Graves	.15
271	Brandon Larson	.15
272	Larry Walker	.25
273	Todd Helton	.50
274	Juan Uribe	.15
275	Juan Pierre	.15
276	Mike Hampton	.15
277	Todd Zeile	.15
278	Todd Hollandsworth	.15
279	Jason Jennings	.15
280	Josh Beckett	.25
281	Mike Lowell	.15
282	Derrek Lee	.25
283	A.J. Burnett	.15
284	Luis Castillo	.15
285	Tim Raines	.15
286	Preston Wilson	.15
287	Juan Encarnacion	.15
288	Charles Johnson	.15
289	Jeff Bagwell	.50
290	Craig Biggio	.25
291	Lance Berkman	.40
292	Daryle Ward	.15
293	Roy Oswalt	.40
294	Richard Hidalgo	.15
295	Octavio Dotel	.15
296	Wade Miller	.15
297	Julio Lugo	.15
298	Billy Wagner	.15
299	Shawn Green	.40
300	Adrian Beltre	.25
301	Paul LoDuca	.15
302	Eric Karros	.15
303	Kevin Brown	.15
304	Hideo Nomo	.40
305	Odalis Perez	.15
306	Eric Gagne	.40
307	Brian Jordan	.15
308	Cesar Izturis	.15
309	Mark Grudzielanek	.15
310	Kazuhisa Ishii	.15
311	Geoff Jenkins	.15
312	Richie Sexson	.40
313	Jose Hernandez	.15
314	Ben Sheets	.25
315	Ruben Quevedo	.15
316	Jeffrey Hammonds	.15
317	Alex Sanchez	.15
318	Eric Young	.15
319	Takahito Nomura	.15
320	Vladimir Guerrero	.75
321	Jose Vidro	.15
322	Orlando Cabrera	.15
323	Michael Barrett	.15
324	Javier Vazquez	.15
325	Tony Armas Jr.	.15
326	Andres Galarraga	.15
327	Tomokazu Ohka	.15
328	Bartolo Colon	.15
329	Fernando Tatis	.15
330	Brad Wilkerson	.15
331	Masato Yoshii	.15
332	Mike Piazza	1.00
333	Jeromy Burnitz	.15
334	Roberto Alomar	.50
335	Mo Vaughn	.15
336	Al Leiter	.15
337	Pedro Astacio	.15
338	Edgardo Alfonzo	.15
339	Armando Benitez	.15
340	Timoniel Perez	.15
341	Jay Payton	.15
342	Roger Cedeno	.15
343	Rey Ordonez	.15
344	Steve Trachsel	.15
345	Satoru Komiyama	.15
346	Scott Rolen	.75
347	Pat Burrell	.40
348	Bobby Abreu	.25
349	Mike Lieberthal	.15
350	Brandon Duckworth	.15
351	Jimmy Rollins	.25
352	Marlon Anderson	.15
353	Travis Lee	.15
354	Vicente Padilla	.15
355	Randy Wolf	.15
356	Jason Kendall	.15
357	Brian Giles	.25
358	Aramis Ramirez	.40
359	Pokey Reese	.15
360	Kip Wells	.15
361	Josh Fogg	.15
362	Mike Williams	.15
363	Jack Wilson	.15
364	Craig Wilson	.15
365	Kevin Young	.15
366	Ryan Klesko	.15
367	Phil Nevin	.15
368	Brian Lawrence	.15
369	Mark Kotsay	.15
370	Brett Tomko	.15
371	Trevor Hoffman	.15
372	Deivi Cruz	.15
373	Bubba Trammell	.15
374	Sean Burroughs	.15
375	Barry Bonds	2.00
376	Jeff Kent	.25
377	Rich Aurilia	.15
378	Tsuyoshi Shinjo	.15
379	Benito Santiago	.15
380	Kirk Rueter	.15
381	Livan Hernandez	.15
382	Russ Ortiz	.15
383	David Bell	.15
384	Jason Schmidt	.40
385	Reggie Sanders	.15
386	J.T. Snow	.15
387	Robb Nen	.15
388	Ryan Jensen	.15
389	Jim Edmonds	.40
390	J.D. Drew	.25
391	Albert Pujols	1.50
392	Fernando Vina	.15
393	Tino Martinez	.15
394	Edgar Renteria	.40
395	Matt Morris	.15
396	Woody Williams	.15
397	Jason Isringhausen	.15
398	Placido Polanco	.15
399	Eli Marrero	.15
400	Jason Simontacchi	.15

Stat Line Career

Cards serial numbered 251-400:	3-6X
Print run 151-250:	4-8X
Print run 101-150:	5-10X
Print run 61-100:	8-15X
Print run 31-60:	10-20X
Numbered to career stat.	

Stat Line Season

Cards serial numbered 151-200:	4-8X
Print run 101-150:	5-10X
Print run 61-100:	8-15X
Print run 31-60:	10-20X
Numbered to 2002 stat.	

All-Stars

		NM/M
Complete Set (10):		25.00
Common Player:		1.50
Retail only.		
1	Ichiro Suzuki	5.00
2	Alex Rodriguez	6.00
3	Nomar Garciaparra	3.00
4	Derek Jeter	6.00
5	Manny Ramirez	2.00
6	Barry Bonds	6.00
7	Adam Dunn	1.50
8	Mike Piazza	3.00
9	Sammy Sosa	4.00
10	Todd Helton	1.50

Anniversary 1983

ROBIN YOUNT

		NM/M
Complete Set (20):		50.00
Common Player:		1.50
Inserted 1:12		
1	Dale Murphy	2.00
2	Jim Palmer	2.00
3	Nolan Ryan	6.00
4	Ozzie Smith	4.00
5	Tom Seaver	4.00
6	Mike Schmidt	5.00
7	Steve Carlton	2.00
8	Robin Yount	3.00
9	Ryne Sandberg	4.00
10	Cal Ripken Jr.	8.00
11	Fernando Valenzuela	1.50
12	Andre Dawson	2.00
13	George Brett	6.00
14	Eddie Murray	3.00
15	Dave Winfield	2.00
16	Johnny Bench	4.00
17	Wade Boggs	4.00
18	Tony Gwynn	4.00
19	San Diego Chicken	1.50
20	Ty Cobb	5.00

Bat Kings

		NM/M
Common Player:		10.00
Studio Series:		1.5-3X
Production 25 or 50		
1	Scott Rolen/250	20.00
2	Frank Thomas/250	15.00
3	Chipper Jones/250	20.00
4	Ivan Rodriguez/250	15.00
5	Stan Musial/100	40.00
6	Nomar Garciaparra/250	25.00
7	Vladimir Guerrero/250	15.00
8	Adam Dunn/250	15.00
9	Lance Berkman/250	15.00
10	Magglio Ordonez/250	10.00
11	Ernie Banks/50	40.00
12	Manny Ramirez/100	25.00
13	Mike Piazza/100	40.00
14	Alex Rodriguez/100	25.00
15	Todd Helton/100	20.00
16	Andre Dawson/100	8.00
17	Cal Ripken Jr/100	60.00
18	Tony Gwynn/100	60.00
19	Don Mattingly/100	25.00
20	Ryne Sandberg/100	45.00

Diamond Kings

KINGS
ALEX RODRIGUEZ - TEXAS RANGER

		NM/M
Complete Set (20):		120.00
Common Player:		2.00
Production 2,500 Sets		
Studio Series:		1.5-3X
Production 250 Sets		
1	Vladimir Guerrero	5.00
2	Derek Jeter	15.00
3	Adam Dunn	5.00
4	Greg Maddux	8.00
5	Lance Berkman	8.00
6	Ichiro Suzuki	10.00
7	Mike Piazza	10.00
8	Alex Rodriguez	10.00
9	Tom Glavine	3.00
10	Randy Johnson	8.00
11	Nomar Garciaparra	10.00
12	Jason Giambi	5.00
13	Sammy Sosa	8.00

14	Barry Zito	3.00
15	Chipper Jones	8.00
16	Magglio Ordonez	2.00
17	Larry Walker	2.00
18	Alfonso Soriano	8.00
19	Curt Schilling	4.00
20	Barry Bonds	15.00

Elite Series

	NM/M
Complete Set (15):	50.00
Common Player:	2.00

Production 2,500 Sets
Dominators: No Pricing
Production 25 Sets

1	Alex Rodriguez	8.00
2	Barry Bonds	10.00
3	Ichiro Suzuki	8.00
4	Vladimir Guerrero	4.00
5	Randy Johnson	4.00
6	Pedro Martinez	4.00
7	Adam Dunn	3.00
8	Sammy Sosa	6.00
9	Jim Edmonds	2.00
10	Greg Maddux	6.00
11	Kazuhisa Ishii	2.00
12	Jason Giambi	3.00
13	Nomar Garciaparra	6.00
14	Tom Glavine	2.00
15	Todd Helton	3.00

Elite Dominators

No pricing, 25 sets produced.

Jersey Kings

	NM/M
Common Player:	10.00
Studio Series:	1.5-3X

Production 25 or 50

1	Juan Gonzalez/250	15.00
2	Greg Maddux/250	20.00
3	Nomar Garciaparra/250	20.00
4	Troy Glaus/250	10.00
5	Reggie Jackson/100	20.00
6	Alex Rodriguez/250	25.00
7	Alfonso Soriano/250	15.00
8	Curt Schilling/250	12.00
9	Vladimir Guerrero/250	15.00
10	Adam Dunn/250	15.00
11	Mark Grace/250	25.00
12	Roger Clemens/100	30.00
13	Jeff Bagwell/100	25.00
14	Tom Glavine/100	20.00
15	Mike Piazza/100	25.00
16	Rod Carew/100	20.00
17	Rickey Henderson/100	25.00
18	Mike Schmidt/100	40.00
19	Cal Ripken Jr/100	60.00
20	Dale Murphy/100	15.00

Longball Leaders

	NM/M
Complete Set (10):	30.00
Common Player:	1.50

Production 1,000 Sets
Seasonal Sum: 4-6X
Numbered to 2002 HR total.

1	Alex Rodriguez	6.00
2	Alfonso Soriano	4.00
3	Rafael Palmeiro	2.00
4	Jim Thome	3.00
5	Jason Giambi	3.00
6	Sammy Sosa	5.00
7	Barry Bonds	8.00
8	Lance Berkman	2.00
9	Shawn Green	1.50
10	Vladimir Guerrero	4.00

Production Line

	NM/M
Complete Set (30):	120.00
Common Player:	2.00

Numbered to selected stat.
Die-Cuts: 1-30X
Production 100 Sets

1	Alex Rodriguez/1,015	3.00
2	Jim Thome/1,122	3.00
3	Lance Berkman/982	2.00
4	Barry Bonds/1,381	8.00
5	Sammy Sosa/993	5.00
6	Vladimir Guerrero/1,010	3.00
7	Barry Bonds/582	10.00
8	Jason Giambi/435	6.00
9	Vladimir Guerrero/417	4.00
10	Adam Dunn/400	4.00
11	Chipper Jones/435	6.00
12	Todd Helton/429	3.00
13	Rafael Palmeiro/571	2.00
14	Sammy Sosa/594	6.00
15	Alex Rodriguez/623	8.00
16	Larry Walker/602	2.00
17	Lance Berkman/578	2.00
18	Alfonso Soriano/547	5.00
19	Ichiro Suzuki/321	6.00
20	Mike Sweeney/340	2.00
21	Manny Ramirez/349	4.00
22	Larry Walker/338	2.00
23	Barry Bonds/370	12.00
24	Jim Edmonds/311	2.00
25	Alfonso Soriano/300	6.00
26	Jason Giambi/335	6.00
27	Miguel Tejada/336	4.00
28	Brian Giles/309	3.00
29	Vladimir Guerrero/364	5.00
30	Pat Burrell/319	4.00

Timber and Threads

	NM/M
Common Player:	6.00

1	Al Kaline/Bat/125	25.00
2	Alex Rodriguez/Bat/350	20.00
3	Carlos Delgado/Bat/250	8.00
4	Cliff Floyd/Bat/250	8.00
5	Eddie Mathews/Bat/125	25.00
6	Edgar Martinez/Bat/125	10.00
7	Ernie Banks/Bat/50	40.00
8	Ivan Rodriguez/Bat/125	15.00
9	J.D. Drew/Bat/125	8.00
10	Jorge Posada/Bat/300	10.00
11	Lou Brock/Bat/125	20.00
12	Mike Piazza/Bat/125	15.00
13	Mike Schmidt/Bat/125	50.00
14	Reggie Jackson/Bat/125	20.00
15	Rickey Henderson/Bat/125	25.00
16	Robin Yount/Bat/125	35.00
17	Rod Carew/Bat/125	25.00
18	Scott Rolen/Bat/125	20.00
19	Shawn Green/Bat/200	8.00
20	Willie Stargell/Bat/125	15.00
21	Alex Rodriguez/Jsy/175	20.00
22	Andruw Jones/Jsy/275	8.00
23	Brooks Robinson/Jsy/150	25.00
24	Chipper Jones/Jsy/150	20.00
25	Greg Maddux/Jsy/175	20.00
26	Hideo Nomo/Jsy/300	40.00
27	Ivan Rodriguez/Jsy/225	10.00
28	Jack Morris/Jsy/150	8.00
29	J.D. Drew/Jsy/150	8.00
30	Jeff Bagwell/Jsy/500	15.00
31	Jim Thome/Jsy/200	8.00
32	John Smoltz/Jsy/175	8.00
33	John Olerud/Jsy/450	8.00
34	Kerry Wood/Jsy/200	15.00
35	Harmon Killebrew/Jsy/150	60.00
36	Larry Walker/Jsy/500	15.00
37	Magglio Ordonez/Jsy/150	10.00
38	Manny Ramirez/Jsy/500	15.00
39	Mike Piazza/Jsy/300	15.00
40	Mike Sweeney/Jsy/200	8.00
41	Nomar Garciaparra/Jsy/200	25.00
42	Paul Konerko/Jsy/500	10.00
43	Pedro Martinez/Jsy/175	15.00
44	Randy Johnson/Jsy/175	15.00
45	Roger Clemens/Jsy/350	20.00
46	Shawn Green/Jsy/250	8.00
47	Todd Helton/Jsy/175	8.00
48	Tom Glavine/Jsy/225	12.00
49	Tony Gwynn/Jsy/150	25.00
50	Vladimir Guerrero/Jsy/450	15.00

2003 Donruss Champions Samples

Each issue of the May 2003 Beckett Baseball Card Monthly included a sample 2003 Donruss Champions card rubber-cemented inside. The cards differ from the issued version only in the appearance on back of a (usually) silver-foil "SAMPLE" notation. Some cards were produced with the overprint in gold-foil, in much more limited quantities. The number of different players' cards involved in the promotion is unknown.

	NM/M
Common Player:	.10

Stars:	1.5-2X
Gold:	10X

2003 Donruss Champions

	NM/M
Complete Set (300):	40.00
Common Player:	.15
Pack (8):	2.00
Box (24):	40.00

1	Adam Kennedy	.15
2	Alfredo Amezaga	.15
3	Chone Figgins	.15
4	Darin Erstad	.25
5	David Eckstein	.15
6	Garret Anderson	.40
7	Jarrod Washburn	.15
8	Nolan Ryan	2.00
9	Tim Salmon	.25
10	Troy Glaus	.40
11	Troy Percival	.15
12	Curt Schilling	.50
13	Junior Spivey	.15
14	Luis Gonzalez	.25
15	Mark Grace	.50
16	Randy Johnson	1.00
17	Steve Finley	.15
18	Andruw Jones	.40
19	Chipper Jones	.75
20	Dale Murphy	.50
21	Gary Sheffield	.40
22	Greg Maddux	1.00
23	John Smoltz	.25
24	Andy Pratt	.15
25	Adam LaRoche	.15
26	Trey Hodges	.15
27	Warren Spahn	.75
28	Cal Ripken Jr.	3.00
29	Ed Rogers	.15
30	Brian Roberts	.15
31	Geronimo Gil	.15
32	Jay Gibbons	.15
33	Josh Towers	.15
34	Casey Fossum	.15
35	Cliff Floyd	.15
36	Derek Lowe	.15
37	Fred Lynn	.15
38	Freddy Sanchez	.15
39	Manny Ramirez	.50
40	Nomar Garciaparra	1.00
41	Pedro J. Martinez	.75
42	Rickey Henderson	.50
43	Shea Hillenbrand	.15
44	Trot Nixon	.15
45	Bobby Hill	.15
46	Corey Patterson	.25
47	Fred McGriff	.25
48	Hee Seop Choi	.15
49	Juan Cruz	.15
50	Kerry Wood	.75
51	Mark Prior	1.00
52	Moises Alou	.25
53	Nic Jackson	.15
54	Ryne Sandberg	1.00
55	Sammy Sosa	1.50
56	Carlos Lee	.15
57	Corwin Malone	.15
58	Frank Thomas	.50
59	Joe Borchard	.15
60	Joe Crede	.15
61	Magglio Ordonez	.25
62	Mark Buehrle	.25
63	Paul Konerko	.25
64	Tim Hummel	.15
65	Jon Adkins	.15
66	Adam Dunn	.50
67	Austin Kearns	.40
68	Barry Larkin	.40
69	Jose Acevedo	.15
70	Corky Miller	.15
71	Eric Davis	.15
72	Ken Griffey Jr.	.75
73	Sean Casey	.15
74	Wily Mo Pena	.15
75	Bob Feller	.50
76	Brian Tallet	.15
77	C.C. Sabathia	.15
78	Cliff Lee	.15
79	Earl Snyder	.15
80	Ellis Burks	.15
81	Jeremy Guthrie	.15
82	Travis Hafner	.25
83	Luis Garcia	.15
84	Omar Vizquel	.15
85	Ricardo Rodriguez	.15
86	Ryan Church	.15
87	Victor Martinez	.25
88	Brandon Phillips	.15
89	Jack Cust	.15
90	Jason Jennings	.15
91	Jeff Baker	.15
92	Garrett Atkins	.15
93	Juan Uribe	.15
94	Larry Walker	.25
95	Rene Reyes	.15
96	Todd Helton	.50
97	Alan Trammell	.25
98	Fernando Rodney	.15
99	Carlos Pena	.15
100	Jack Morris	.15
101	Bobby Higginson	.15
102	Mike Maroth	.15
103	Robert Fick	.15
104	Jesus Medrano	.15
105	Josh Beckett	.40
106	Luis Castillo	.15
107	Mike Lowell	.25
108	Juan Pierre	.15
109	Josh Wilson	.15
110	Tim Redding	.15
111	Carlos Hernandez	.15
112	Craig Biggio	.25
113	Henri Stanley	.15
114	Jason Lane	.15
115	Jeff Bagwell	.50
116	John Buck	.15
117	Kirk Saarloos	.15
118	Lance Berkman	.75
119	Nolan Ryan	2.00
120	Richard Hidalgo	.15
121	Rodrigo Rosario	.15
122	Roy Oswalt	.15
123	Tommy Whiteman RC	.15
124	Wade Miller	.15
125	Alexis Gomez	.15
126	Angel Berroa	.15
127	Brandon Berger	.15
128	Carlos Beltran	.40
129	George Brett	2.00
130	Jimmy Gobble	.15
131	Dee Brown	.15
132	Mike Sweeney	.15
133	Raul Ibanez	.15
134	Runelvys Hernandez	.15
135	Adrian Beltre	.40
136	Brian Jordan	.15
137	Cesar Izturis	.15
138	Victor Alvarez	.15
139	Hideo Nomo	.50
140	Joe Thurston	.15
141	Kazuhisa Ishii	.15
142	Kevin Brown	.25
143	Odalis Perez	.15
144	Paul LoDuca	.15
145	Shawn Green	.25
146	Ben Sheets	.15
147	Bill Hall	.15
148	Nick Neugebauer	.15
149	Richie Sexson	.40
150	Robin Yount	1.00
151	Shane Nance	.15
152	Takahito Nomura	.15
153	A.J. Pierzynski	.15
154	Joe Mays	.15
155	Kirby Puckett	1.00
156	Adam Johnson	.15
157	Rob Bowen	.15
158	Torii Hunter	.40
159	Andres Galarraga	.15
160	Endy Chavez	.15
161	Javier Vazquez	.15
162	Jose Vidro	.15
163	Vladimir Guerrero	.75
164	Dwight Gooden	.15
165	Mike Piazza	1.00
166	Roberto Alomar	.40
167	Tom Glavine	.40
168	Alfonso Soriano	.75
169	Bernie Williams	.40
170	Brandon Claussen	.15
171	Derek Jeter	2.00
172	Don Mattingly	1.50
173	Drew Henson	.15
174	Jason Giambi	.50
175	Joe Torre	.25
176	Jorge Posada	.40
177	Mike Mussina	.25
178	Nick Johnson	.15
179	Roger Clemens	1.50
180	Whitey Ford	.75
181	Adam Morrissey	.15
182	Barry Zito	.15
183	David Justice	.15
184	Eric Chavez	.40
185	Jermaine Dye	.15
186	Mark Mulder	.40
187	Miguel Tejada	.40
188	Reggie Jackson	.75
189	Terrence Long	.15
190	Tim Hudson	.25
191	Anderson Machado	.15
192	Bobby Abreu	.40
193	Brandon Duckworth	.15
194	Jim Thome	.75
195	Eric Junge	.15
196	Jeremy Giambi	.15
197	Johnny Estrada	.15
198	Jorge Padilla	.15
199	Marlon Byrd	.15
200	Mike Schmidt	1.50
201	Pat Burrell	.50
202	Steve Carlton	.25
203	Aramis Ramirez	.15
204	Brian Giles	.25
205	Carlos Rivera	.15
206	Craig Wilson	.15
207	Dave Williams	.15
208	Jack Wilson	.15
209	Jose Castillo	.15
210	Kip Wells	.15
211	Roberto Clemente	1.50
212	Walter Young	.15
213	Ben Howard	.15
214	Brian Lawrence	.15
215	Clifford Bartosh	.15
216	Dennis Tankersley	.15
217	Oliver Perez	.15
218	Phil Nevin	.15
219	Ryan Klesko	.25
220	Sean Burroughs	.15
221	Tony Gwynn	.75
222	Xavier Nady	.15
223	Mike Rivera	.15
224	Barry Bonds	2.00
225	Benito Santiago	.15
226	Jason Schmidt	.15
227	Jeff Kent	.25
228	Kenny Lofton	.15
229	Rich Aurilia	.15
230	Robb Nen	.15
231	Tsuyoshi Shinjo	.15
232	Bret Boone	.15
233	Chris Snelling	.15
234	Edgar Martinez	.25
235	Freddy Garcia	.15
236	Ichiro Suzuki	1.50
237	John Olerud	.25
238	Kazuhiro Sasaki	.15
239	Mike Cameron	.15
240	Rafael Soriano	.15
241	Albert Pujols	1.50
242	J.D. Drew	.40
243	Jim Edmonds	.40
244	Ozzie Smith	1.00
245	Scott Rolen	.75
246	So Taguchi	.15
247	Stan Musial	1.00
248	Antonio Perez	.15
249	Aubrey Huff	.15
250	Dewon Brazelton	.15
251	Delvin James	.15
252	Joe Kennedy	.15
253	Toby Hall	.15
254	Alex Rodriguez	2.00
255	Ben Kozlowski	.15
256	Gerald Laird	.15
257	Hank Blalock	.40
258	Ivan Rodriguez	.50
259	Juan Gonzalez	.50
260	Kevin Mench	.15
261	Mario Ramos	.15
262	Mark Teixeira	.25
263	Nolan Ryan	2.00
264	Rafael Palmeiro	.50
265	Alexis Rios	.15
266	Carlos Delgado	.40
267	Eric Hinske	.15
268	Josh Phelps	.15
269	Kevin Cash	.15
270	Orlando Hudson	.15
271	Roy Halladay	.15
272	Shannon Stewart	.15
273	Vernon Wells	.15
274	Vinnie Chulk	.15
275	Jason Anderson	.15
276	Craig Brazell RC	.50
277	Termrel Sledge RC	.50
278	Ryan Cameron RC	.50
279	Clint Barmes RC	.50
280	Jhonny Peralta	.50
281	Todd Wellemeyer RC	.50
282	Jon Leicester RC	.50
283	Brandon Webb RC	2.00
284	Tim Olson RC	.50
285	Matt Kata RC	.75
286	Rob Hammock RC	.50
287	Pete LaForest RC	.50
288	Nook Logan RC	.50
289	Prentice Redman RC	.40
290	Joe Valentine RC	.40
291	Jose Contreras RC	1.00
292	Josh Stewart RC	.40
293	Mike Nicolas RC	.40
294	Marshall McDougall	.15
295	Travis Chapman	.15
296	Jose Morban	.15
297	Michael Hessman RC	.40
298	Buddy Hernandez RC	.40
299	Shane Victorino RC	.40
300	Jason Dubois	.15
301	Hideki Matsui RC	3.00

Metalized

Stars:	4-8X
RC's:	1-30X

Production 100 Sets
Holofoils: No Pricing
Production 25 Sets

Autographs

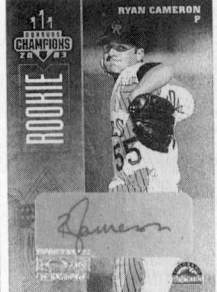

	NM/M
Common Autograph:	5.00

2	Alfredo Amezaga/325	5.00
3	Chone Figgins/375	10.00
12	Junior Spivey/45	8.00
14	Andy Pratt/475	8.00
25	Adam LaRoche/400	5.00
28	Trey Hodges/305	5.00
29	Ed Rogers/305	5.00
30	Brian Roberts/500	35.00
31	Geronimo Gil/150	8.00
32	Jay Gibbons/475	8.00
33	Josh Towers/500	10.00
34	Casey Fossum/160	5.00
35	Cliff Floyd/70	20.00
37	Fred Lynn/80	25.00
38	Freddy Sanchez/400	15.00
46	Corey Patterson/100	15.00
49	Juan Cruz/250	8.00
51	Mark Prior/50	30.00
53	Nic Jackson/100	10.00
57	Corwin Malone/400	8.00
59	Joe Borchard/215	8.00
64	Tim Hummel/400	5.00
65	Jon Adkins/400	5.00
66	Adam Dunn/300	30.00
67	Austin Kearns/50	20.00
69	Jose Acevedo/315	5.00
70	Corky Miller/295	5.00
74	Wily Mo Pena/450	15.00
76	Brian Tallet/250	8.00
78	Cliff Lee/330	15.00
79	Earl Snyder/225	8.00
81	Jeremy Guthrie/400	8.00
83	Luis Garcia/395	5.00
86	Ryan Church/395	10.00
87	Victor Martinez/250	25.00
88	Brandon Phillips/375	10.00
89	Jack Cust/498	10.00
90	Jason Jennings/375	8.00
91	Jeff Baker/400	8.00
92	Garrett Atkins/400	8.00
95	Rene Reyes/350	8.00
98	Fernando Rodney/500	8.00
100	Jack Morris/50	20.00
102	Mike Maroth/400	8.00
104	Jesus Medrano/500	8.00
110	Josh Wilson/400	8.00
110	Tim Redding/375	8.00
111	Carlos Hernandez/250	8.00
113	Henri Stanley/390	5.00
114	Jason Lane/250	10.00
117	Kirk Saarloos/500	8.00
120	Richard Hidalgo/120	8.00
121	Rodrigo Rosario/500	10.00
122	Roy Oswalt/200	20.00
124	Wade Miller/125	10.00
126	Angel Berroa/400	10.00
127	Brandon Berger/325	8.00
130	Jimmy Gobble/400	8.00
131	Dee Brown/500	8.00
132	Mike Sweeney/45	20.00
136	Runelvys Hernandez/225	5.00
138	Victor Alvarez/308	5.00
144	Paul LoDuca/200	20.00
146	Ben Sheets/50	20.00
147	Bill Hall/450	10.00
148	Nick Neugebauer/375	5.00
151	Shane Nance/150	8.00
152	Takahito Nomura/50	15.00
153	A.J. Pierzynski/250	10.00
156	Adam Johnson/500	8.00
157	Rob Bowen/375	8.00
158	Torii Hunter/45	20.00
160	Endy Chavez/280	8.00
161	Javier Vazquez/45	15.00
162	Jose Vidro/45	15.00
164	Dwight Gooden/45	30.00
170	Brandon Claussen/475	10.00
178	Nick Johnson/500	8.00
181	Adam Morrissey/395	8.00
185	Jermaine Dye/125	15.00
189	Terrence Long/250	8.00
191	Anderson Machado/500	8.00
193	Brandon Duckworth/100	10.00
195	Eric Junge/279	8.00
196	Jeremy Giambi/195	8.00
205	Carlos Rivera/400	5.00
206	Craig Wilson/245	8.00
207	Dave Williams/265	5.00
208	Jack Wilson/150	15.00

212	Walter Young/400	8.00
213	Ben Howard/500	8.00
214	Brian Lawrence/500	8.00
215	Clifford Bartosh/400	8.00
222	Xavier Nady/250	8.00
223	Mike Rivera/90	8.00
233	Chris Snelling/200	8.00
240	Rafael Soriano/500	8.00
248	Antonio Perez/500	8.00
249	Aubrey Huff/475	15.00
250	Dewon Brazelton/50	15.00
251	Delvin James/400	8.00
252	Joe Kennedy/250	8.00
253	Toby Hall/500	8.00
255	Ben Kozlowski/400	8.00
256	Gerald Laird/450	8.00
257	Hank Blalock/50	25.00
260	Kevin Mench/475	10.00
261	Mario Ramos/475	5.00
265	Mark Teixeira/40	40.00
265	Alexis Rios/400	20.00
266	Eric Hinske/390	10.00
269	Kevin Cash/375	8.00
274	Vinnie Chulk/100	10.00
275	Jason Anderson/493	15.00
276	Craig Brazell/500	15.00
277	Termel Sledge/500	10.00
278	Ryan Cameron/475	8.00
279	Clint Barmes/475	15.00
280	Jhonny Peralta/500	15.00
281	Todd Wellemeyer/477	10.00
282	Jon Leicester/480	8.00
283	Brandon Webb/500	50.00
284	Tim Olson/500	10.00
285	Matt Kata/487	10.00
286	Rob Hammock/486	10.00
287	Pete LaForest/500	10.00
288	Nook Logan/500	10.00
289	Prentice Redman/488	10.00
290	Joe Valentine/475	8.00
291	Jose Contreras/100	25.00
292	Josh Stewart/485	10.00
293	Mike Nicolas/500	10.00
295	Travis Chapman/100	15.00
296	Jose Morban/475	8.00
297	Michael Hessman/500	8.00
298	Buddy Hernandez/500	8.00
299	Shane Victorino/480	8.00
300	Jason Dubois/480	10.00
302	Ryan Wagner/500	15.00
303	Adam Loewen/100	10.00
304	Chien-Ming Wang/100	200.00
305	Hong-Chih Kuo/100	80.00
307	Dan Haren/100	25.00
309	Ramon Nivar/100	15.00

Call to the Hall

	NM/M
Complete Set (10):	30.00
Common Player:	2.00
Metalized:	2-4X
Production 100 Sets	
Holofoils:	No Pricing
Production 25 Sets	
1 Nolan Ryan/2,490	10.00
2 Tom Seaver/2,490	4.00
3 Phil Rizzuto/2,500	4.00
4 Orlando Cepeda/2,500	5.00
5 Al Kaline/2,500	5.00
6 Hoyt Wilhelm/2,500	2.00
7 Luis Aparicio/2,500	2.00
8 Billy Williams/2,500	2.00
9 Jim Palmer/2,500	2.00
10 Mike Schmidt/2,500	6.00

Call to the Hall Autographs
No Pricing
Quantity produced listed.

Grand Champions

	NM/M
Complete Set (25):	80.00
Common Player:	2.00
Inserted 1:18	
Metalized:	2-4X
Production 100 Sets	
Holo Foils:	No Pricing
Production 25 Sets	

1	Stan Musial	6.00
2	Bob Feller	2.00
3	Reggie Jackson	3.00
4	George Brett	8.00
5	Jim Palmer	2.00
6	Harmon Killebrew	4.00
7	Ernie Banks	4.00
8	Frank Robinson	2.00
9	Greg Maddux	4.00
10	Whitey Ford	4.00
11	Bob Gibson	4.00
12	Mike Schmidt	6.00
13	Nolan Ryan	10.00
14	Warren Spahn	4.00
15	Rod Carew	3.00
16	Hoyt Wilhelm	2.00
17	Duke Snider	4.00
18	Tom Seaver	4.00
19	Steve Carlton	3.00
20	Yogi Berra	4.00
21	Cal Ripken Jr.	10.00
22	Tony Gwynn	4.00
23	Wade Boggs	2.00
24	Rickey Henderson	3.00
25	Roger Clemens	3.00

Grand Champions Autographs
No Pricing

Numbers Game
Quantity produced listed.

1	Vladimir Guerrero/Jsy/200	10.00
2	Nomar Garciaparra/Jsy/200	20.00
3	Magglio Ordonez/Jsy/100	8.00
4	Garret Anderson/Jsy/50	15.00
5	Derek Jeter/Base/200	20.00
6	Jim Thome/Jsy/200	8.00
7	Torii Hunter/Jsy/200	10.00
8	Todd Helton/Jsy/200	10.00
9	Andruw Jones/Jsy/200	6.00
10	Luis Gonzalez/Jsy/200	5.00
11	Manny Ramirez/Jsy/200	12.00
12	Paul Konerko/Jsy/200	6.00
13	Alex Rodriguez/Jsy/200	20.00
14	Carlos Beltran/Jsy/200	4.00
15	Bernie Williams/Jsy/200	8.00
16	Barry Bonds/Base/200	20.00
17	Miguel Tejada/Jsy/50	15.00
18	Jason Giambi/Base/200	8.00
19	Ichiro Suzuki/Base/200	25.00
20	Ivan Rodriguez/Jsy/100	15.00
21	Rafael Palmeiro/Jsy/200	10.00
23	Carlos Delgado/Jsy/200	5.00
24	Vernon Wells/Jsy/200	4.00
25	Sammy Sosa/Jsy/200	20.00
26	Chipper Jones/Jsy/200	12.00
27	Adam Dunn/Jsy/44	25.00
28	Larry Walker/Jsy/100	8.00
29	Shawn Green/Jsy/100	10.00
30	Richie Sexson/Jsy/200	6.00
31	Jose Vidro/Jsy/200	4.00
32	Mike Piazza/Jsy/50	40.00
33	Roberto Alomar/Jsy/100	15.00
34	Bobby Abreu/Jsy/200	5.00
35	Pat Burrell/Jsy/200	8.00
36	Brian Giles/Jsy/200	6.00
37	Albert Pujols/Base/200	15.00
38	Lance Berkman/Jsy/200	15.00
39	Ryan Klesko/Jsy/200	6.00
40	Jeff Kent/Jsy/200	4.00

Statistical Champs

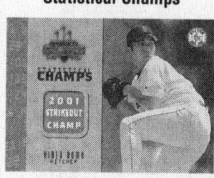

	NM/M
Complete Set (30):	40.00
Common Player:	1.00
Inserted 1:10	
1 Alex Rodriguez	5.00
2 Alfonso Soriano	1.50
3 Curt Schilling	1.50
4 Eddie Mathews	2.00
5 Fred Lynn	1.00
6 Harmon Killebrew	2.00
7 Hideo Nomo	1.00
8 Jim Thome	1.50
9 Kirby Puckett	4.00
10 Luis Gonzalez	1.00
11 Manny Ramirez	1.50
12 Jason Giambi	1.50
13 Mike Schmidt	4.00
14 Nomar Garciaparra	4.00
15 Lou Brock	1.50
16 Randy Johnson	4.00
17 Reggie Jackson	2.00
18 Rickey Henderson	1.50
19 Roberto Clemente	5.00
20 Barry Zito	1.50
21 Todd Helton	3.00
22 Tom Seaver	3.00
23 Tony Gwynn	2.00
24 Torii Hunter	1.00
25 Troy Glaus	1.00
26 Wade Boggs	1.50
27 Rod Carew	1.50
28 Juan Gonzalez	1.50
29 Sammy Sosa	3.00
30 Warren Spahn	2.00

Statistical Champs Materials

	NM/M
Quantity produced listed.	
1 Alex Rodriguez/Jsy/250	20.00
3 Curt Schilling/Jsy/225	8.00
5 Eddie Mathews/Jsy/200	20.00
6 Harmon Killebrew/Jsy/250	20.00
7 Hideo Nomo/Jsy/110	50.00
8 Jim Thome/Jsy/250	20.00
9 Kirby Puckett/Jsy/250	20.00
10 Luis Gonzalez/Jsy/250	5.00
11 Manny Ramirez/Jsy/155	10.00
12 Jason Giambi/Jsy/250	10.00
13 Mike Schmidt/Jsy/250	35.00
14 Nomar Garciaparra/Jsy/99	30.00
15 Lou Brock/Jsy/250	15.00
16 Randy Johnson/Jsy/100	15.00
17 Reggie Jackson/Jsy/200	15.00
18 Rickey Henderson/Jsy/184	15.00
19 Barry Zito/Jsy/100	15.00
20 Todd Helton/Jsy/250	10.00
21 Tom Seaver/Jsy/100	30.00
22 Tony Gwynn/Jsy/250	15.00
23 Torii Hunter/Jsy/250	15.00
24 Troy Glaus/Jsy/125	15.00
26 Wade Boggs/Jsy/250	15.00
27 Rod Carew/Hat/150	15.00
28 Juan Gonzalez/Jsy/250	8.00
29 Sammy Sosa/Jsy/250	20.00
30 Warren Spahn/Jsy/150	30.00

Team Colors

	NM/M
Complete Set (30):	60.00
Common Player:	1.00
Inserted 1:10	
1 Miguel Tejada	1.50
2 Mike Schmidt	5.00
3 George Brett	6.00
4 Magglio Ordonez	1.00
5 Ryne Sandberg	4.00
6 Adam Dunn	1.50
7 Mark Prior	2.00
8 Tony Gwynn	2.00
9 Troy Glaus	1.50
10 Stan Musial	4.00
11 Kirby Puckett	3.00
12 Don Mattingly	5.00
13 Bobby Abreu	1.00
14 Ichiro Suzuki	4.00
15 Cal Ripken Jr.	8.00
16 Chipper Jones	3.00
17 Carlos Beltran	1.50
18 Alfonso Soriano	2.00
19 Albert Pujols	5.00
20 Andruw Jones	1.50
21 Bernie Williams	1.50
22 Todd Helton	1.50
23 Roberto Clemente	6.00
24 Jim Thome	1.50
25 Carlos Delgado	1.00
26 Derek Jeter	6.00
27 Garret Anderson	1.00
28 Nomar Garciaparra	4.00
29 Torii Hunter	1.00
30 Vladimir Guerrero	1.50

Team Colors Materials

	NM/M
Quantity produced listed.	
1 Miguel Tejada/Jsy/50	15.00
2 Mike Schmidt/Jsy/200	35.00
3 George Brett/Jsy/200	35.00
4 Magglio Ordonez/Jsy/100	8.00
5 Ryne Sandberg/Jsy/44	20.00
7 Mark Prior/Jsy/200	15.00
8 Tony Gwynn/Jsy/200	15.00
9 Troy Glaus/Jsy/200	1.00
10 Stan Musial/Jsy/200	35.00
11 Kirby Puckett/Jsy/200	15.00
12 Don Mattingly/Jsy/200	40.00
13 Bobby Abreu/Jsy/200	8.00
14 Ichiro Suzuki/Base/200	25.00
15 Cal Ripken Jr./Jsy/200	40.00
16 Chipper Jones/Jsy/200	12.00
17 Carlos Beltran/Jsy/200	8.00
19 Albert Pujols/Base/200	15.00
20 Andruw Jones/Jsy/200	8.00
21 Bernie Williams/Jsy/200	8.00
22 Todd Helton/Jsy/200	10.00
23 Roberto Clemente/Jsy/200	80.00
24 Jim Thome/Jsy/200	8.00
25 Carlos Delgado/Jsy/200	8.00
26 Derek Jeter/Base/200	20.00
27 Garret Anderson/Jsy/50	12.00
28 Nomar Garciaparra/Jsy/200	10.00
29 Torii Hunter/Jsy/200	10.00
30 Vladimir Guerrero/Jsy/200	10.00

Total Game

	NM/M
Complete Set (40):	60.00
Common Player:	1.00
Inserted 1:9	
1 Vladimir Guerrero	2.00
2 Nomar Garciaparra	4.00
3 Magglio Ordonez	1.00
4 Garret Anderson	1.00
5 Derek Jeter	6.00
6 Jim Thome	1.50
7 Torii Hunter	1.50
8 Todd Helton	1.50
9 Andruw Jones	1.50
10 Alfonso Soriano	2.00
11 Luis Gonzalez	1.00
12 Manny Ramirez	1.50
13 Paul Konerko	1.00
14 Alex Rodriguez	5.00
15 Carlos Beltran	1.00
16 Bernie Williams	1.50
17 Barry Bonds	6.00
18 Miguel Tejada	1.00
19 Jason Giambi	1.00
20 Ichiro Suzuki	4.00
21 Ivan Rodriguez	1.50
22 Rafael Palmeiro	1.00
23 Carlos Delgado	1.00
24 Vernon Wells	1.00
25 Sammy Sosa	4.00
26 Chipper Jones	2.00
27 Adam Dunn	1.50
28 Larry Walker	1.00
29 Shawn Green	1.00
30 Richie Sexson	1.00
31 Jose Vidro	1.00
32 Mike Piazza	3.00
33 Roberto Alomar	1.50
34 Bobby Abreu	1.00
35 Pat Burrell	1.00
36 Brian Giles	1.00
37 Albert Pujols	5.00
38 Lance Berkman	1.00
39 Ryan Klesko	1.00
40 Jeff Kent	1.00

World Series Champions

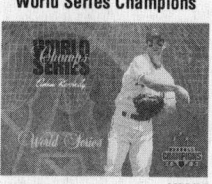

	NM/M
Complete Set (15):	20.00
Common Player:	1.50
Production 2,002 Sets	
Metalized:	2-3X
Production 100 Sets	
Holo Foil:	No Pricing
Production 25 Sets	
1 Troy Glaus	3.00
2 Jarrod Washburn	1.50
3 Darin Erstad	2.50
4 Troy Percival	1.50
5 David Eckstein	1.50
6 Francisco Rodriguez	2.00
7 Garret Anderson	2.50
8 John Lackey	1.50
9 Tim Salmon	2.00
10 Chone Figgins	1.50
11 Adam Kennedy	1.50
12 Scott Spiezio	1.50
13 Ben Molina	1.50
14 Brad Fullmer	1.50
15 Troy Glaus MVP	3.00

World Series Champions Autograph
No Pricing

2003 Donruss Classics Samples

Each issue of the June, 2003, Beckett Baseball Card Monthly included a sample 2003 Donruss Classics card rubber-cemented in-

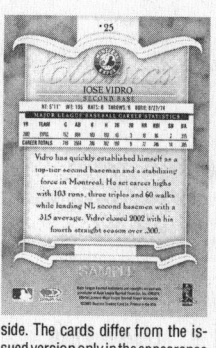

side. The cards differ from the issued version only in the appearance on back of a (usually) silver-foil "SAMPLE" notation. Some cards were produced with the overprint in gold-foil, in much more limited quantities. The number of different players' cards involved in the promotion is unknown.

	NM/M
Common Player:	.10
Stars:	1.5-2X
Gold:	10X

2003 Donruss Classics

	NM/M
Complete Set (200):	
Common Player:	.40
Common Legends (101-150):	3.00
Production 1,500	
Common Prospect (151-200):	3.00
Production 1,500	
Pack (7):	4.50
Box (18):	70.00
1 Troy Glaus	.50
2 Barry Bonds	3.00
3 Miguel Tejada	.50
4 Randy Johnson	1.00
5 Eric Hinske	.40
6 Barry Zito	.50
7 Jason Jennings	.40
8 Derek Jeter	3.00
9 Vladimir Guerrero	1.00
10 Corey Patterson	.50
11 Manny Ramirez	.75
12 Edgar Martinez	.50
13 Roy Oswalt	.50
14 Andruw Jones	.75
15 Alex Rodriguez	3.00
16 Mark Mulder	.50
17 Kazuhisa Ishii	.40
18 Gary Sheffield	.50
19 Jay Gibbons	.40
20 Roberto Alomar	.50
21 A.J. Pierzynski	.40
22 Eric Chavez	.50
23 Roger Clemens	2.00
24 C.C. Sabathia	.50
25 Jose Vidro	.40
26 Shannon Stewart	.40
27 Mark Teixeira	.50
28 Joe Thurston	.40
29 Josh Beckett	.75
30 Jeff Bagwell	.75
31 Geronimo Gil	.40
32 Curt Schilling	.75
33 Frank Thomas	.75
34 Lance Berkman	.50
35 Adam Dunn	.75
36 Christian Parker	.40
37 Jim Thome	1.00
38 Shawn Green	.50
39 Drew Henson	.40
40 Chipper Jones	1.00
41 Kevin Mench	.40
42 Hideo Nomo	.50
43 Andres Galarraga	.40
44 Doug Davis	.40
45 Mark Prior	1.00
46 Sean Casey	.40
47 Magglio Ordonez	.50
48 Tom Glavine	.50
49 Marlon Byrd	.40
50 Albert Pujols	2.00
51 Mark Buehrle	.40
52 Aramis Ramirez	.50
53 Pat Burrell	.50
54 Craig Biggio	.50
55 Alfonso Soriano	1.00
56 Kerry Wood	1.00
57 Wade Miller	.40
58 Hank Blalock	.75
59 Cliff Floyd	.40
60 Jason Giambi	.50
61 Carlos Beltran	.50
62 Brian Roberts	.40
63 Paul LoDuca	.40
64 Tim Redding	.40
65 Sammy Sosa	2.00
66 Joe Borchard	.40
67 Ryan Klesko	.40
68 Richie Sexson	.50
69 Carlos Lee	.40
70 Rickey Henderson	.75
71 Brian Tallet	.40
72 Luis Gonzalez	.50
73 Satoru Komiyama	.40
74 Tim Hudson	.50
75 Ken Griffey Jr.	1.50
76 Adam Johnson	.40
77 Bobby Abreu	.60
78 Adrian Beltre	.40
79 Rafael Palmeiro	.75
80 Ichiro Suzuki	2.00
81 Kenny Lofton	.40
82 Brian Giles	.50
83 Barry Larkin	.50
84 Robert Fick	.40
85 Ben Sheets	.50
86 Scott Rolen	1.00
87 Nomar Garciaparra	1.50
88 Brandon Phillips	.40
89 Ben Kozlowski	.40
90 Bernie Williams	.75
91 Pedro J. Martinez	1.00
92 Todd Helton	.75
93 Jermaine Dye	.40
94 Carlos Delgado	.50
95 Mike Piazza	1.50
96 Junior Spivey	.40
97 Torii Hunter	.50
98 Mike Sweeney	.40
99 Ivan Rodriguez	.75
100 Greg Maddux	1.50
101 Ernie Banks	5.00
102 Steve Garvey	3.00
103 George Brett	8.00
104 Lou Brock	3.00
105 Hoyt Wilhelm	3.00
106 Steve Carlton	4.00
107 Joe Torre	3.00
108 Dennis Eckersley	3.00
109 Reggie Jackson	5.00
110 Al Kaline	8.00
111 Harold Reynolds	3.00
112 Don Mattingly	8.00
113 Tony Gwynn	8.00
114 Willie McCovey	4.00
115 Joe Morgan	3.00
116 Stan Musial	8.00
117 Jim Palmer	3.00
118 Brooks Robinson	5.00
119 Don Sutton	3.00
120 Nolan Ryan	10.00
121 Mike Schmidt	6.00
122 Tom Seaver	5.00
123 Cal Ripken Jr.	8.00
124 Robin Yount	5.00
125 Bob Feller	3.00
126 Joe Carter	3.00
127 Jack Morris	3.00
128 Luis Aparicio	3.00
129 Bobby Doerr	3.00
130 Dave Parker	3.00
131 Yogi Berra	5.00
132 Will Clark	3.00
133 Fred Lynn	3.00
134 Andre Dawson	3.00
135 Duke Snider	4.00
136 Orlando Cepeda	3.00
137 Billy Williams	3.00
138 Dale Murphy	3.00
139 Harmon Killebrew	5.00
140 Kirby Puckett	6.00
141 Carlton Fisk	4.00
142 Eric Davis	3.00
143 Alan Trammell	3.00
144 Paul Molitor	5.00
145 Jose Canseco	3.00
146 Ozzie Smith	5.00
147 Ralph Kiner	3.00
148 Dwight Gooden	3.00
149 Phil Rizzuto	5.00
150 Lenny Dykstra	3.00
151 Adam LaRoche	4.00
152 Tim Hummel	3.00
153 Matt Kata RC	4.00
154 Jeff Baker	3.00
155 Josh Stewart RC	3.00
156 Marshall McDougall	4.00
157 Jhonny Peralta	4.00
158 Mike Nicolas RC	3.00
159 Jeremy Guthrie	3.00
160 Craig Brazell RC	4.00
161 Joe Valentine RC	4.00
162 Buddy Hernandez	3.00
163 Freddy Sanchez	4.00
164 Shane Victorino RC	4.00
165 Corwin Malone	4.00
166 Jason Dubois	3.00
167 Josh Wilson	4.00
168 Tim Olson RC	3.00
169 Clifford Bartosh RC	3.00
170 Michael Hessman RC	4.00

#	Player	Price
171	Ryan Church	5.00
172	Garrett Atkins	4.00
173	Jose Morban	3.00
174	Ryan Cameron RC	3.00
175	Todd Wellemeyer RC	4.00
176	Travis Chapman	3.00
177	Jason Anderson	4.00
178	Adam Morrissey	3.00
179	Jose Contreras RC	5.00
180	Nic Jackson	3.00
181	Rob Hammock RC	4.00
182	Carlos Rivera	3.00
183	Vinnie Chulk	3.00
184	Pete LaForest RC	3.00
185	Jon Leicester RC	4.00
186	Termmel Sledge RC	3.00
187	Jose Castillo	3.00
188	Gerald Laird	3.00
189	Nook Logan RC	4.00
190	Clint Barmes RC	5.00
191	Jesus Medrano	3.00
192	Henri Stanley	4.00
193	Hideki Matsui RC	10.00
194	Walter Young	3.00
195	Jon Adkins	3.00
196	Tommy Whiteman RC	4.00
197	Rob Bowen	3.00
198	Brandon Webb RC	8.00
199	Prentice Redman RC	4.00
200	Jimmy Gobble	3.00

Dress Code

DRESS CODE...

		NM/M
Common Player:		4.00

Quantity produced listed.

#	Player	Price
1	Roger Clemens/Jsy/500	15.00
2	M. Tejada/Jsy/Hat/250	20.00
3	V. Guerrero/Jsy/425	8.00
4	Kazuhisa Ishii/Jsy/150	10.00
5	Chipper Jones/Jsy/425	10.00
6	Troy Glaus/Jsy/425	8.00
7	Rafael Palmeiro/Jsy/425	8.00
8	Rickey Henderson/Jsy/250	
9	Pedro Martinez/Jsy/425	8.00
10	Andruw Jones/Jsy/425	6.00
11	Nomar Garciaparra/Jsy/500	12.00
12	Carlos Delgado/Jsy/500	5.00
13	R.Henderson/Jsy/Hat/250	
14	K. Wood/Jsy/Hat/250	20.00
15	L. Berkman/Jsy/Hat/250	10.00
16	Tony Gwynn/Jsy/Quad/100	65.00
17	Mark Mulder/Jsy/425	8.00
18	Jim Thome/Jsy/500	8.00
19	Mike Piazza/Jsy/500	15.00
20	Mike Mussina/Jsy/500	5.00
21	Luis Gonzalez/Jsy/500	5.00
22	Ryan Klesko/Jsy/500	5.00
23	Richie Sexson/Jsy/500	5.00
24	Curt Schilling/Jsy/200	10.00
25	A. Rodriguez/Jsy/500	12.00
26	B. Williams/Jsy/425	8.00
27	Cal Ripken Jr/Jsy/500	35.00
28	C.C. Sabathia/Jsy/500	5.00
29	M. Piazza/Bat/Jsy/200	30.00
30	Rickey Henderson/Hat/Jsy/250	15.00
31	Torii Hunter/Jsy/425	8.00
32	Mark Teixeira/Jsy/425	10.00
33	D. Murphy/Jsy/Bat/300	15.00
34	Todd Helton/Jsy/425	8.00
35	Eric Chavez/Jsy/425	8.00
36	Vernon Wells/Jsy/425	5.00
37	J. Bagwell/Jsy/Hat/100	25.00
38	Nick Johnson/Jsy/425	5.00
39	Tim Hudson/Jsy/Hat/250	10.00
40	Shawn Green/Jsy/425	5.00
41	Mark Buehrle/Jsy/500	5.00
42	Garret Anderson/Jsy/500	5.00
43	Alex Rodriguez/Jsy/500	12.00
44	Jason Giambi/Jsy/500	8.00
45	Carlos Beltran/Jsy/500	5.00
46	Adam Dunn/Jsy/Hat/100	30.00
47	Jorge Posada/Jsy/425	8.00
48	Roy Oswalt/Jsy/Hat/200	15.00
49	Rich Aurilia/Jsy/500	5.00
50	Jason Jennings/Quad/250	15.00
51	Mark Prior/Quad/250	40.00
52	Jim Edmonds/Jsy/500	8.00
53	Fred McGriff/Jsy/500	5.00
54	A. Soriano/Jsy/Shoe/100	15.00
55	Jeff Kent/Jsy/425	5.00
56	Hideo Nomo/Jsy/200	30.00
57	Manny Ramirez/Jsy/425	8.00
58	J. Canseco/Jsy/Bat/350	15.00
59	M. Ordonez/Jsy/500	5.00
60	A. Trammell/Jsy/Bat/200	10.00
61	Bobby Abreu/Jsy/500	6.00

#	Player	Price
62	R.Henderson/Dual Jsy/200	20.00
63	Josh Beckett/Jsy/500	6.00
64	Barry Larkin/Jsy/500	
65	Randy Johnson/Jsy/200	10.00
66	Juan Gonzalez/Jsy/500	8.00
67	Barry Zito/Jsy/Hat/125	15.00
68	Roger Clemens/Jsy/500	15.00
69	Rickey Henderson/Hat/Jsy/100	25.00
70	Hideo Nomo/Jsy/100	50.00
71	Paul Konerko/Jsy/400	6.00
72	Pat Burrell/Jsy/400	8.00
73	F.Thomas/Jsy/Pants/250	
74	Sammy Sosa/Jsy/500	15.00
75	G. Maddux/Glove/Jsy/50	60.00

Legendary Hats

		NM/M

Varying quantities produced.

#	Player	Price
1	Roberto Clemente/80	100.00
2	Kirby Puckett/50	50.00
3	Mike Schmidt/50	75.00
4	Tony Gwynn/50	50.00
5	Rickey Henderson/50	60.00

Legendary Leather

		NM/M

Varying quantities produced.

#	Player	Price
1	Nolan Ryan/50	110.00

Legendary Lumberjacks

LEGENDARY LUMBERJACKS

		NM/M
Common Player:		10.00

Varying quantities produced.

#	Player	Price
1	Babe Ruth/100	180.00
2	Lou Gehrig/80	125.00
3	George Brett/250	25.00
4	Duke Snider/250	20.00
5	Roberto Clemente/25	165.00
6	Ryne Sandberg/400	35.00
7	Robin Yount/300	25.00
8	Harmon Killebrew/250	25.00
9	Al Kaline/250	25.00
10	Eddie Mathews/225	20.00
11	Brooks Robinson/400	15.00
12	Kirby Puckett/375	20.00
13	Jose Canseco/400	15.00
14	Nellie Fox/325	20.00
15	Don Mattingly/400	35.00
16	Joe Torre/250	10.00
17	Cal Ripken Jr/250	40.00
18	Richie Ashburn/250	20.00
19	Mike Schmidt/250	30.00
20	Dale Murphy/325	15.00
21	Thurman Munson/400	15.00
22	Tony Gwynn/400	10.00
23	Orlando Cepeda/225	10.00
24	Ty Cobb/25	225.00
25	Paul Molitor/325	10.00
26	Ralph Kiner/200	10.00
27	Frank Robinson/225	20.00
28	Yogi Berra/250	50.00
29	Reggie Jackson/375	15.00
30	Rod Carew/325	15.00
31	Carlton Fisk/325	15.00
32	Rogers Hornsby/50	60.00
33	Mel Ott/125	30.00
34	Jimmie Foxx/50	60.00

Legendary Spikes

		NM/M

Production 50 Sets

#	Player	Price
1	Kirby Puckett	60.00
2	Tony Gwynn	50.00
3	Don Mattingly	125.00
4	Frank Robinson	35.00
5	Gary Carter	30.00

Legends of the Fall

		NM/M
Complete Set (10):		40.00
Common Player:		3.00

Production 2,500 Sets

#	Player	Price
1	Reggie Jackson	4.00
2	Duke Snider	4.00
3	Roberto Clemente	8.00
4	Mel Ott	5.00
5	Yogi Berra	5.00
6	Jackie Robinson	6.00
7	Enos Slaughter	4.00
8	Willie Stargell	4.00
9	Bobby Doerr	4.00
10	Thurman Munson	5.00

Legends of the Fall Fabrics

		NM/M

Quantity produced listed. 3.00

#	Player	Price
1	Reggie Jackson/100	20.00
3	Roberto Clemente/100	120.00
6	Jackie Robinson/50	80.00
8	Willie Stargell/100	20.00
9	Bobby Doerr/100	20.00

Membership

JIMMIE FOXX

MEMBERSHIP

		NM/M
Complete Set (15):		65.00
Common Player:		3.00

Production 2,500 Sets

#	Player	Price
1	Babe Ruth	10.00
2	Steve Carlton	3.00
3	Honus Wagner	6.00
4	Warren Spahn	5.00
5	Eddie Mathews	5.00
6	Nolan Ryan	10.00
7	Rogers Hornsby	5.00
8	Ernie Banks	5.00
9	Harmon Killebrew	5.00
10	Tom Seaver	5.00
11	Jimmie Foxx	6.00
12	Ty Cobb	10.00
13	Frank Robinson	4.00
14	Mel Ott	5.00
15	Lou Gehrig	8.00

Membership VIP Memorabilia

		NM/M

Varying quantities produced.

#	Player	Price
1	Babe Ruth/Bat/29	325.00
2	Steve Carlton/Jsy/81	25.00
4	Warren Spahn/Jsy/61	50.00
6	Eddie Mathews/Bat/67	60.00
7	Nolan Ryan/Jsy/80	75.00
8	R. Hornsby/Bat/31	75.00
9	Ernie Banks/Jsy/70	35.00
10	H. Killebrew/Jsy/71	60.00
11	Tom Seaver/Jsy/81	30.00
12	Jimmie Foxx/Bat/40	60.00
13	F. Robinson/Jsy/71	25.00
14	Mel Ott/Jsy/45	50.00

Significant Signatures

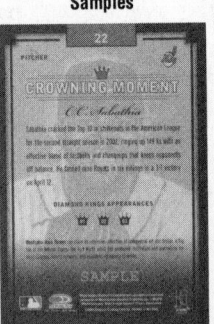

JEREMY GUTHRIE

		NM/M
Common Autograph:		8.00

#'s 201-211 exclusive to Donruss Rookies.

#	Player	Price
5	Eric Hinske/250	10.00
6	Barry Zito/25	40.00
7	Jason Jennings/250	10.00
10	Corey Patterson/100	15.00
13	Roy Oswalt/100	25.00
16	Mark Mulder/100	25.00
19	Jay Gibbons/250	10.00
21	A.J. Pierzynski/75	20.00
22	Eric Chavez/20	40.00
25	Jose Vidro/75	15.00
27	Mark Teixeira/40	40.00
31	Geronimo Gil/50	15.00
35	Adam Dunn/100	40.00
36	Christian Parker/250	10.00
39	Drew Henson/450	20.00
41	Kevin Mench/250	15.00
45	Mark Prior/50	30.00
56	Kerry Wood/15	60.00
57	Wade Miller/200	10.00
58	Hank Blalock/250	25.00
62	Brian Roberts/250	25.00
63	Paul LoDuca/100	15.00
64	Tim Redding/250	8.00
66	Joe Borchard/100	15.00
68	Richie Sexson/20	40.00
69	Carlos Lee/25	35.00
73	Satoru Komiyama/124	20.00

#	Player	Price
76	Adam Johnson/200	8.00
84	Robert Fick/50	10.00
88	Brandon Phillips/250	10.00
89	Ben Kozlowski/150	8.00
93	Jermaine Dye/100	20.00
96	Junior Spivey/100	15.00
102	Torii Hunter/50	25.00
108	Steve Garvey/50	30.00
111	Dennis Eckersley/50	30.00
118	Harold Reynolds/50	25.00
119	Don Sutton/100	20.00
122	Nolan Ryan/50	200.00
123	Cal Ripken Jr/50	220.00
126	Joe Carter/100	25.00
127	Jack Morris/100	20.00
128	Luis Aparicio/50	20.00
132	Will Clark/20	125.00
133	Fred Lynn/50	15.00
134	Andre Dawson/50	30.00
136	Orlando Cepeda/100	20.00
138	Billy Williams/100	15.00
142	Eric Davis/50	25.00
143	Alan Trammell/50	35.00
148	Dwight Gooden/50	40.00
149	Phil Rizzuto/20	75.00
150	Lenny Dykstra/50	25.00
151	Adam LaRoche/250	15.00
152	Tim Hummel/500	8.00
153	Matt Kata/500	15.00
154	Jeff Baker/500	15.00
155	Josh Stewart/177	10.00
156	Marshall McDougall/500	10.00
157	Jhonny Peralta/500	20.00
158	Mike Nicolas/500	10.00
159	Jeremy Guthrie/500	10.00
160	Craig Brazell/500	15.00
161	Joe Valentine/172	10.00
162	Buddy Hernandez/500	8.00
163	Freddy Sanchez/500	10.00
164	Shane Victorino/351	8.00
165	Corwin Malone/500	8.00
166	Jason Dubois/500	12.00
167	Jason Wilson/500	8.00
168	Tim Olson/500	10.00
169	Clifford Bartosh/500	8.00
170	Michael Hessman/427	8.00
171	Ryan Church/500	10.00
172	Garrett Atkins/500	8.00
173	Jose Morban/500	8.00
174	Ryan Cameron/500	10.00
175	Todd Wellemeyer/500	8.00
176	Travis Chapman/477	10.00
177	Jason Anderson/500	8.00
178	Adam Morrissey/500	8.00
179	Jose Contreras/100	20.00
180	Nic Jackson/500	10.00
181	Rob Hammock/500	10.00
182	Carlos Rivera/500	8.00
183	Vinnie Chulk/500	8.00
184	Pete LaForest/177	8.00
185	Jon Leicester/500	8.00
186	Termmel Sledge/500	8.00
187	Jose Castillo/500	10.00
188	Gerald Laird/500	8.00
189	Nook Logan/427	8.00
190	Clint Barmes/500	10.00
191	Jesus Medrano/500	8.00
192	Henri Stanley/500	8.00
194	Walter Young/500	10.00
195	Jon Adkins/500	8.00
196	Tommy Whiteman/500	8.00
197	Rob Bowen/500	8.00
198	Brandon Webb/500	40.00
199	Prentice Redman/127	10.00
200	Jimmy Gobble/500	10.00
201	Jeremy Bonderman/100	50.00
202	Adam Loewen/100	50.00
203	Chien-Ming Wang/50	220.00
205	Ryan Wagner/100	40.00
206	Dan Haren/100	40.00
209	Ramon Nivar/100	15.00

Singles

		NM/M
Common Player:		10.00

Varying quantities produced.

#	Player	Price
1	Babe Ruth/Jsy/100	275.00
2	Lou Gehrig/Jsy/80	200.00
3	Jackie Robinson/Jsy/80	75.00
5	Bobby Doerr/Jsy/100	15.00
7	Fred Lynn/Jsy/100	12.00
7	Honus Wagner/Seat/100	35.00
8	Roberto Clemente/Jsy/80	100.00
9	Kirby Puckett/Jsy/100	40.00
10	Torii Hunter/Jsy/100	10.00
11	Sammy Sosa/Jsy/100	25.00
12	Ryne Sandberg/Jsy/100	40.00
13	Hideo Nomo/Jsy/100	90.00
14	Kazuhisa Ishii/Jsy/100	35.00
15	Mike Schmidt/Jsy/100	45.00
16	Steve Carlton/Jsy/100	15.00
17	Robin Yount/Jsy/100	30.00
18	Paul Molitor/Jsy/100	25.00
19	Mike Piazza/Jsy/100	25.00
20	Duke Snider/Jsy/100	35.00
21	Al Kaline/Jsy/50	50.00
24	Don Mattingly/Jsy/100	60.00
25	Jason Giambi/Jsy/100	10.00
26	Ozzie Smith/Jsy/100	40.00
27	Roger Clemens/Jsy/100	20.00
28	Pedro Martinez/Jsy/100	20.00
29	Thurman Munson/Jsy/50	50.00
30	Yogi Berra/Jsy/25	70.00

Combos

		NM/M

Varying quantities produced.

#	Players	Price
CC1	Babe Ruth, Lou Gehrig/50	475.00
CC2	Jackie Robinson, Pee Wee Reese/50	80.00
CC3	Bobby Doerr, Fred Lynn/25	65.00
CC4	Honus Wagner, Roberto Clemente/50	150.00
CC5	Kirby Puckett, Torii Hunter/25	75.00
CC6	Sammy Sosa, Ryne Sandberg/25	100.00
CC7	Hideo Nomo, Kazuhisa Ishii/25	75.00
CC8	Mike Schmidt, Steve Carlton/25	150.00
CC9	Robin Yount, Paul Molitor/25	100.00
CC12	Don Mattingly, Jason Giambi/25	150.00
CC13	Stan Musial, Ozzie Smith/25	100.00

Timeless Treasures

		NM/M

Varying quantities produced.

#	Players	Price
1	Tony Gwynn, Stan Musial/50	100.00
3	Vladimir Guerrero, Roberto Clemente/50	125.00
5	Jason Giambi, Don Mattingly/50	100.00

Samples

CROWNING MOMENT
C.C. Sabathia
SAMPLE

Each April, 2003, issue of Beckett Baseball Card Monthly included a sample DK card rubber-cemented inside. The cards differ from the issued version only in the appearance on back of a (usually) silver-foil "SAMPLE" notation and, on some cards, the lack of silver-foil graphics on front. Some cards were produced with the back overprint in gold-foil in much more limited quantities.

		NM/M
Common Player:		.25
Stars:		1.5-2X
Gold:		10X

2003 Donruss Diamond Kings

JEFF BAGWELL-1B
Hometown Hitters

		NM/M
Complete Set (176):		90.00
Common Player:		.40
Common (151-176):		1.00
Pack (5):		4.00
Box (24):		75.00

#	Player	Price
1	Darin Erstad	.50
2	Garret Anderson	.50
3	Troy Glaus	.50
4	David Eckstein	.40
5	Jarrod Washburn	.40
6	Adam Kennedy	.40
7	Jay Gibbons	.40
8	Tony Batista	.40
9	Melvin Mora	.40
10	Rodrigo Lopez	.40
11	Manny Ramirez	.75
12	Pedro J. Martinez	1.00
13	Nomar Garciaparra	1.50
14	Rickey Henderson	.60
15	Johnny Damon	.50

#	Player	Price
16	Derek Lowe	.40
17	Cliff Floyd	.40
18	Frank Thomas	.75
19	Magglio Ordonez	.40
20	Paul Konerko	.40
21	Mark Buehrle	.40
22	C.C. Sabathia	.40
23	Omar Vizquel	.40
24	Jim Thome	.75
25	Ellis Burks	.40
26	Robert Fick	.40
27	Bobby Higginson	.40
28	Randall Simon	.40
29	Carlos Pena	.40
30	Carlos Beltran	.75
31	Paul Byrd	.40
32	Raul Ibanez	.40
33	Mike Sweeney	.40
34	Torii Hunter	.50
35	Corey Koskie	.40
36	A.J. Pierzynski	.40
37	Cristian Guzman	.40
38	Jacque Jones	.40
39	Derek Jeter	3.00
40	Bernie Williams	.60
41	Roger Clemens	2.00
42	Mike Mussina	.60
43	Jorge Posada	.50
44	Alfonso Soriano	1.00
45	Jason Giambi	.50
46	Robin Ventura	.40
47	David Wells	.40
48	Tim Hudson	.50
49	Barry Zito	.50
50	Mark Mulder	.50
51	Miguel Tejada	.50
52	Eric Chavez	.50
53	Jermaine Dye	.40
54	Ichiro Suzuki	2.00
55	Edgar Martinez	.50
56	John Olerud	.40
57	Dan Wilson	.40
58	Joel Pineiro	.40
59	Kazuhiro Sasaki	.40
60	Freddy Garcia	.40
61	Aubrey Huff	.40
62	Steve Cox	.40
63	Randy Winn	.40
64	Alex Rodriguez	2.50
65	Juan Gonzalez	.50
66	Rafael Palmeiro	.75
67	Ivan Rodriguez	.75
68	Kenny Rogers	.40
69	Carlos Delgado	.50
70	Eric Hinske	.40
71	Roy Halladay	.40
72	Vernon Wells	.40
73	Shannon Stewart	.40
74	Curt Schilling	.75
75	Randy Johnson	1.00
76	Luis Gonzalez	.40
77	Mark Grace	.50
78	Junior Spivey	.40
79	Greg Maddux	1.50
80	Tom Glavine	.50
81	John Smoltz	.50
82	Chipper Jones	1.00
83	Gary Sheffield	.40
84	Andruw Jones	1.00
85	Kerry Wood	.50
86	Fred McGriff	.50
87	Sammy Sosa	1.50
88	Mark Prior	1.00
89	Ken Griffey Jr	1.50
90	Barry Larkin	.50
91	Adam Dunn	.50
92	Sean Casey	.40
93	Austin Kearns	.40
94	Aaron Boone	.40
95	Larry Walker	.50
96	Todd Helton	.75
97	Jason Jennings	.40
98	Jay Payton	.40
99	Josh Beckett	.50
100	Mike Lowell	.40
101	A.J. Burnett	.40
102	Jeff Bagwell	.75
103	Craig da Luz	.40
104	Lance Berkman	.50
105	Roy Oswalt	.50
106	Wade Miller	.40
107	Shawn Green	.50
108	Adrian Beltre	.50
109	Hideo Nomo	.50
110	Kazuhisa Ishii	.40
111	Odalis Perez	.40
112	Paul LoDuca	.40
113	Ben Sheets	.40
114	Richie Sexson	.40
115	Jose Hernandez	.40
116	Vladimir Guerrero	.75
117	Jose Vidro	.40
118	Tomokazu Ohka	.40
119	Andres Galarraga	.40
120	Bartolo Colon	.40
121	Mike Piazza	1.00
122	Roberto Alomar	.50
123	Mo Vaughn	.50
124	Al Leiter	.40
125	Edgardo Alfonzo	.40
126	Pat Burrell	.50
127	Bobby Abreu	.50
128	Mike Lieberthal	.40
129	Vicente Padilla	.40
130	Marlon Byrd	.40
131	Jason Kendall	.40
132	Brian Giles	.40
133	Aramis Ramirez	.40

134	Kip Wells	.40
135	Ryan Klesko	.40
136	Phil Nevin	.40
137	Brian Lawrence	.40
138	Sean Burroughs	.40
139	Mark Kotsay	.40
140	Barry Bonds	3.00
141	Jeff Kent	.40
142	Benito Santiago	.40
143	Kirk Reuter	.40
144	Jason Schmidt	.50
145	Jim Edmonds	.50
146	J.D. Drew	.50
147	Albert Pujols	2.00
148	Tino Martinez	.40
149	Matt Morris	.40
150	Scott Rolen	1.00
151	Joe Borchard	2.00
152	Cliff Lee	1.00
153	Brian Tallet	1.00
154	Freddy Sanchez	1.00
155	Chone Figgins	1.00
156	Kevin Cash	1.00
157	Justin Wayne	1.00
158	Ben Kozlowski	1.00
159	Babe Ruth	6.00
160	Jackie Robinson	4.00
161	Ozzie Smith	4.00
162	Lou Gehrig	5.00
163	Stan Musial	4.00
164	Mike Schmidt	5.00
165	Carlton Fisk	2.00
166	George Brett	6.00
167	Dale Murphy	4.00
168	Cal Ripken Jr.	8.00
169	Tony Gwynn	3.00
170	Don Mattingly	6.00
171	Jack Morris	2.00
172	Ty Cobb	5.00
173	Nolan Ryan	6.00
174	Ryne Sandberg	5.00
175	Thurman Munson	4.00
176	Jose Contreras RC	8.00

Framed Portraits Bronze

Cards (1-150):	1-2.5X
Cards (151-176):	.75-1.5X
Silvers (1-150):	3-5X
Silvers (151-176):	2-3X
Production 400 Sets	
Golds (1-150):	5-10X
Golds (151-176):	3-6X
Production 100 Sets	

Diamond Cut

NM/M
Common Signature (1-25): 10.00
Quantity produced listed.

1	Barry Zito/75	50.00
2	Edgar Martinez/125	50.00
3	Jay Gibbons/150	25.00
4	Joe Borchard/150	20.00
5	Marlon Byrd/150	20.00
6	Adam Dunn/150	40.00
7	Torii Hunter/150	40.00
8	Vladimir Guerrero/25	150.00
9	Wade Miller/150	25.00
10	Alfonso Soriano/100	60.00
11	Brian Lawrence/150	25.00
12	Cliff Floyd/100	25.00
13	Dale Murphy/75	75.00
14	Jack Morris/150	25.00
15	Eric Hinske/150	25.00
16	Jason Jennings/150	20.00
17	Mark Buehrle/150	30.00
18	Mark Prior/150	40.00
19	Mark Mulder/150	35.00
20	Mike Sweeney/150	25.00
21	Nolan Ryan/50	200.00
22	Don Mattingly/75	100.00
23	Andruw Jones/150	40.00
24	Aubrey Huff/150	20.00

Common Jerseys (26-75): 5.00

26	Nolan Ryan/250	50.00
27	Ozzie Smith/400	15.00
28	Rickey Henderson/300	10.00
29	Jack Morris/500	5.00
30	George Brett/350	25.00
31	Cal Ripken Jr./300	40.00
32	Ryne Sandberg/450	20.00
33	Don Mattingly/400	25.00
34	Tony Gwynn/400	15.00
35	Dale Murphy/350	10.00
36	Carlton Fisk/400	10.00
38	Lou Gehrig/50	240.00
39	Garret Anderson/450	8.00
40	Pedro J. Martinez/400	8.00
41	Nomar Garciaparra/350	15.00
42	Magglio Ordonez/450	8.00
43	C.C. Sabathia/500	5.00
44	Omar Vizquel/250	8.00
45	Jim Thome/500	10.00
46	Torii Hunter/500	8.00
47	Roger Clemens/500	15.00
48	Alfonso Soriano/400	8.00
49	Tim Hudson/500	8.00
50	Barry Zito/350	6.00
51	Mark Mulder/500	6.00
52	Miguel Tejada/400	5.00
53	John Olerud/350	5.00
54	Alex Rodriguez/500	15.00
55	Rafael Palmeiro/500	8.00
56	Curt Schilling/500	8.00
57	Randy Johnson/400	10.00
58	Greg Maddux/350	12.00
59	John Smoltz/400	6.00
60	Chipper Jones/450	10.00
61	Andruw Jones/500	8.00
62	Kerry Wood/500	8.00
63	Mark Prior/500	10.00
64	Adam Dunn/350	10.00
65	Larry Walker/500	5.00
66	Todd Helton/500	8.00
67	Jeff Bagwell/500	10.00
68	Roy Oswalt/500	8.00
69	Hideo Nomo/150	15.00
70	Kazuhisa Ishii/250	5.00
71	Vladimir Guerrero/500	10.00
72	Mike Piazza/500	15.00
73	Joe Borchard/500	5.00
74	Ryan Klesko/500	5.00
75	Shawn Green/500	6.00

Common Bat (76-105): 5.00

76	George Brett/350	25.00
77	Ozzie Smith/450	15.00
78	Cal Ripken Jr/150	50.00
79	Don Mattingly/400	25.00
80	Babe Ruth/50	200.00
81	Dale Murphy/350	10.00
82	Rickey Henderson/500	10.00
83	Ivan Rodriguez/500	8.00
84	Marlon Byrd/500	8.00
85	Eric Chavez/500	8.00
86	Nomar Garciaparra/500	15.00
87	Alex Rodriguez/500	15.00
88	Vladimir Guerrero/500	10.00
89	Paul LoDuca/500	8.00
90	Richie Sexson/500	8.00
91	Mike Piazza/350	15.00
92	J.D. Drew/500	8.00
93	Juan Gonzalez/500	8.00
94	Pat Burrell/500	8.00
95	Adam Dunn/500	15.00
96	Mike Schmidt/500	20.00
97	Ryne Sandberg/500	20.00
98	Edgardo Alfonzo/500	8.00
99	Andruw Jones/500	8.00
100	Carlos Beltran/500	6.00
101	Jeff Bagwell/500	10.00
102	Lance Berkman/500	8.00
103	Luis Gonzalez/500	5.00
104	Carlos Delgado/500	6.00
105	Jim Edmonds/250	8.00

Combos (106-110):
Some Combos & Autos. not priced.

106	Alfonso Soriano/75	40.00
107	Greg Maddux/ Jsy/Auto./50	140.00
109	Adam Dunn/Bat/ Auto./50	60.00
110	Rickey Henderson/ Jsy/Bat/50	20.00

DK Evolution

NM/M
Complete Set (25): 85.00
Common Player: 2.00
Inserted 1:18

1	Cal Ripken Jr.	10.00
2	Ichiro Suzuki	6.00
3	Randy Johnson	4.00
4	Pedro J. Martinez	3.00
5	Nolan Ryan	10.00
6	Derek Jeter	10.00
7	Kerry Wood	4.00
8	Alex Rodriguez	8.00
9	Magglio Ordonez	2.00
10	Greg Maddux	5.00
11	Todd Helton	3.00
12	Sammy Sosa	3.00
13	Lou Gehrig	8.00
14	Lance Berkman	2.00
15	Barry Zito	2.00
16	Barry Bonds	10.00
17	Tom Glavine	2.00
18	Shawn Green	2.00
19	Roger Clemens	8.00
20	Nomar Garciaparra	6.00
21	Tony Gwynn	4.00
22	Vladimir Guerrero	3.00
23	Albert Pujols	8.00
24	Chipper Jones	4.00
25	Alfonso Soriano	4.00

Hall of Fame Heroes

NM/M
Complete Set (10): 40.00
Common Player: 3.00
Inserted 1:43

1	Bob Feller	3.00
2	Al Kaline	6.00
3	Lou Boudreau	4.00
4	Duke Snider	4.00
5	Jackie Robinson	6.00
6	Early Wynn	3.00
7	Yogi Berra	4.00
8	Stan Musial	6.00
9	Ty Cobb	6.00
10	Ted Williams	8.00

HOF Heroes Materials

NM/M
Common Player: 30.00
Production 50 Sets

1	Bob Feller/Jsy	70.00
2	Al Kaline/Bat	45.00
3	Lou Boudreau/Jsy	40.00
4	Duke Snider/Bat	30.00
6	Yogi Berra/Bat	40.00
7	Stan Musial/Bat	100.00
9	Ty Cobb/Bat	110.00
10	Ted Williams/Jsy	175.00

Heritage Collection

NM/M
Complete Set (25): 100.00
Common Player: 2.00
Inserted 1:23

1	Ozzie Smith	5.00
2	Lou Gehrig	8.00
3	Stan Musial	6.00
4	Mike Schmidt	6.00
5	Carlton Fisk	2.00
6	George Brett	10.00
7	Dale Murphy	4.00
8	Cal Ripken Jr.	10.00
9	Tony Gwynn	4.00
10	Don Mattingly	5.00
11	Jack Morris	2.00
12	Ty Cobb	8.00
13	Nolan Ryan	12.00
14	Ryne Sandberg	6.00
15	Thurman Munson	4.00
16	Ichiro Suzuki	6.00
17	Derek Jeter	10.00
18	Greg Maddux	5.00
19	Sammy Sosa	3.00
20	Pedro J. Martinez	3.00
21	Alex Rodriguez	8.00
22	Roger Clemens	5.00
23	Barry Bonds	10.00
24	Lance Berkman	2.00
25	Vladimir Guerrero	3.00

Recollection

Production 2-15

Recollection Autographs

NM/M
Common Player:

1	Adrian Beltre/40	15.00
8	Brandon Berger/99	10.00
9	Mark Buehrle/73	10.00
15	Andre Dawson/24	25.00
16	Andre Dawson/50	20.00
17	Andre Dawson/28	25.00
42	Jorge De La Rosa/148	10.00
24	Rob Fick/150	8.00
32	Tim Hudson/50	15.00
42	Ryan Ludwick/130	8.00
55	Roy Oswalt/65	15.00
56	Roy Oswalt/100	15.00
70	Bud Smith/114	5.00
72	Shannon Stewart/50	8.00

Team Timelines

NM/M
Complete Set (10): 85.00
Common Card: 4.00
Production 1,000 Sets

1	Nolan Ryan, Roy Oswalt	15.00
2	Dale Murphy, Chipper Jones	8.00
3	Stan Musial, Jim Edmonds	10.00
4	George Brett, Mike Sweeney	12.00
5	Tony Gwynn, Ryan Klesko	6.00
6	Carlton Fisk, Magglio Ordonez	4.00
7	Mike Schmidt, Pat Burrell	12.00
8	Don Mattingly, Bernie Williams	12.00
9	Ryne Sandberg, Kerry Wood	10.00
10	Lou Gehrig, Alfonso Soriano	10.00

Team Timelines Materials

NM/M
Common Card: 30.00
Production 100 unless noted.

1	Nolan Ryan, Roy Oswalt	120.00
2	Dale Murphy, Chipper Jones	40.00
3	Stan Musial, Jim Edmonds	45.00
4	George Brett, Mike Sweeney	65.00
5	Tony Gwynn, Ryan Klesko	40.00
6	Carlton Fisk, Magglio Ordonez	30.00
7	Mike Schmidt, Pat Burrell	90.00
8	Don Mattingly, Bernie Williams	70.00
9	Ryne Sandberg, Kerry Wood	60.00
10	Lou Gehrig, Alfonso Soriano/50	200.00

2003 Donruss Elite

NM/M
Complete Set (200):
Common Player: .25
Common Rookie (181-200): 3.00
Production 1,750
Pack (5): 3.50
Box (20): 60.00

1	Darin Erstad	.40
2	David Eckstein	.25
3	Garret Anderson	.40
4	Jarrod Washburn	.25
5	Tim Salmon	.40
6	Troy Glaus	.40
7	Marty Cordova	.25
8	Melvin Mora	.25
9	Rodrigo Lopez	.25
10	Tony Batista	.25
11	Derek Lowe	.25
12	Johnny Damon	.40
13	Manny Ramirez	.50
14	Nomar Garciaparra	1.50
15	Pedro J. Martinez	.75
16	Shea Hillenbrand	.25
17	Carlos Lee	.25
18	Joe Crede	.25
19	Frank Thomas	.50
20	Magglio Ordonez	.40
21	Mark Buehrle	.25
22	Paul Konerko	.25
23	C.C. Sabathia	.25
24	Ellis Burks	.25
25	Omar Vizquel	.40
26	Brian Tallet	.25
27	Bobby Higginson	.25
28	Carlos Pena	.25
29	Mark Redman	.25
30	Steve Sparks	.25
31	Carlos Beltran	.50
32	Joe Randa	.25
33	Mike Sweeney	.25
34	Raul Ibanez	.25
35	Runelvys Hernandez	.25
36	Brad Radke	.25
37	Corey Koskie	.25
38	Cristian Guzman	.25
39	David Ortiz	.50
40	Doug Mientkiewicz	.25
41	Jacque Jones	.25
42	Torii Hunter	.40
43	Alfonso Soriano	.40
44	Andy Pettitte	.40
45	Bernie Williams	.50
46	David Wells	.25
47	Derek Jeter	2.00
48	Jason Giambi	.40
49	Jeff Weaver	.25
50	Jorge Posada	.40
51	Mike Mussina	.50
52	Roger Clemens	1.50
53	Barry Zito	.40
54	Eric Chavez	.40
55	Jermaine Dye	.25
56	Mark Mulder	.40
57	Miguel Tejada	.40
58	Tim Hudson	.40
59	Bret Boone	.25
60	Chris Snelling	.25
61	Edgar Martinez	.40
62	Freddy Garcia	.25
63	Ichiro Suzuki	1.50
64	Jamie Moyer	.25
65	John Olerud	.25
66	Kazuhiro Sasaki	.25
67	Aubrey Huff	.25
68	Joe Kennedy	.25
69	Paul Wilson	.25
70	Alex Rodriguez	1.50
71	Chan Ho Park	.25
72	Hank Blalock	.50
73	Juan Gonzalez	.50
74	Kevin Mench	.25
75	Rafael Palmeiro	.50
76	Carlos Delgado	.40
77	Eric Hinske	.25
78	Josh Phelps	.25
79	Roy Halladay	.25
80	Shannon Stewart	.25
81	Vernon Wells	.25
82	Curt Schilling	.50
83	Junior Spivey	.25
84	Luis Gonzalez	.40
85	Mark Grace	.50
86	Randy Johnson	.75
87	Steve Finley	.25
88	Andruw Jones	.50
89	Chipper Jones	.75
90	Gary Sheffield	.50
91	Greg Maddux	1.00
92	John Smoltz	.40
93	Corey Patterson	.40
94	Kerry Wood	.75
95	Mark Prior	1.00
96	Moises Alou	.40
97	Sammy Sosa	1.50
98	Adam Dunn	.40
99	Austin Kearns	.40
100	Barry Larkin	.40
101	Ken Griffey Jr.	1.00
102	Sean Casey	.25
103	Jason Jennings	.25
104	Jay Payton	.25
105	Larry Walker	.40
106	Todd Helton	.50
107	A.J. Burnett	.25
108	Josh Beckett	.50
109	Juan Encarnacion	.25
110	Mike Lowell	.25
111	Craig Biggio	.40
112	Daryle Ward	.25
113	Jeff Bagwell	.50
114	Lance Berkman	.40
115	Roy Oswalt	.40
116	Jason Lane	.25
117	Adrian Beltre	.50
118	Hideo Nomo	.50
119	Kazuhisa Ishii	.25
120	Kevin Brown	.40
121	Odalis Perez	.25
122	Paul LoDuca	.25
123	Shawn Green	.40
124	Ben Sheets	.40
125	Jeffrey Hammonds	.25
126	Jose Hernandez	.25
127	Richie Sexson	.50
128	Bartolo Colon	.25
129	Brad Wilkerson	.25
130	Javier Vazquez	.25
131	Jose Vidro	.25
132	Michael Barrett	.25
133	Vladimir Guerrero	.75
134	Al Leiter	.25
135	Mike Piazza	1.00
136	Mo Vaughn	.25
137	Pedro Astacio	.25
138	Roberto Alomar	.40
139	Pat Burrell	.40
140	Vicente Padilla	.25
141	Jimmy Rollins	.40
142	Bobby Abreu	.40
143	Marlon Byrd	.40
144	Brian Giles	.40
145	Jason Kendall	.40
146	Aramis Ramirez	.25
147	Josh Fogg	.25
148	Ryan Klesko	.25
149	Phil Nevin	.25
150	Sean Burroughs	.25
151	Mark Kotsay	.25
152	Barry Bonds	2.00
153	Damian Moss	.25
154	Jason Schmidt	.50
155	Benito Santiago	.25
156	Rich Aurilia	.25
157	Scott Rolen	.75
158	J.D. Drew	.40
159	Jim Edmonds	.40
160	Matt Morris	.25
161	Tino Martinez	.25
162	Albert Pujols	1.50
163	Russ Ortiz	.25
164	Rey Ordonez	.25
165	Paul Byrd	.25
166	Kenny Lofton	.25
167	Kenny Rogers	.25
168	Rickey Henderson	.50
169	Fred McGriff	.50
170	Charles Johnson	.25
171	Mike Hampton	.25
172	Jim Thome	.75

2003 Donruss Diamond Kings Inserts Hawaii

At an invitation-only Donruss/Playoff reception during the SCD Hawaii Trade Conference, attendees were given a three-card pack with each card embossed with the show logo on front and gold-foil serial numbered on back. The packs had one each of the Diamond Kings inserts Heritage Collection (numbered to 20), Hall of Fame Heroes (50) and Team Timelines (50).

173	Travis Hafner	.25
174	Ivan Rodriguez	.50
175	Ray Durham	.25
176	Jeremy Giambi	.25
177	Jeff Kent	.40
178	Cliff Floyd	.25
179	Kevin Millwood	.25
180	Tom Glavine	.50
181	Hideki Matsui RC	10.00
182	Jose Contreras RC	5.00
183	Terrmel Sledge RC	3.00
184	Lew Ford RC	6.00
185	Jhonny Peralta	4.00
186	Alexis Rios	4.00
187	Jeff Baker	3.00
188	Jeremy Guthrie	3.00
189	Jose Castillo	3.00
190	Garrett Atkins	3.00
191	Jeremy Bonderman	3.00
192	Adam LaRoche	3.00
193	Vinnie Chulk	3.00
194	Walter Young	3.00
195	Jimmy Gobble	3.00
196	Prentice Redman RC	3.00
197	Jason Anderson	3.00
198	Nic Jackson	3.00
199	Travis Chapman	3.00
200	Shane Victorino RC	3.00

Aspirations

NM/M
Stars print run 25-50: 10-15X
Rookies (181-200) p/r 25-50: 1-30X
Stars p/r 51-99: 5-10X
Serial numbered to jersey number.
Gold One-of-One's exist.
181 Hideki Matsui/45 125.00

Status

NM/M
Stars print run 25-50: 10-15X
Rookies (181-200) p/r 25-50: 1-30X
Stars p/r 51-99: 5-10X
Gold Status: No Pricing
Production 24 Sets
181 Hideki Matsui/55 120.00

All-Time Career Best

NM/M
Complete Set (45): 120.00
Common Player: 2.00
Inserted 1:9
Gold print run 25-50: 4-8X
Gold print run 51-100: 3-5X
Gold p/r 101-239: 1.5-3X
Numbered to career stat.

1	Babe Ruth	6.00
2	Ty Cobb	4.00
3	Jackie Robinson	4.00
4	Lou Gehrig	5.00
5	Thurman Munson	2.00
6	Nolan Ryan	8.00
7	Mike Schmidt	4.00
8	Don Mattingly	5.00
9	Yogi Berra	3.00
10	Rod Carew	2.00
11	Reggie Jackson	3.00
12	Al Kaline	4.00
13	Harmon Killebrew	4.00
14	Eddie Mathews	3.00
15	Stan Musial	4.00
16	Jim Palmer	2.00
17	Phil Rizzuto	2.00
18	Brooks Robinson	3.00
19	Tom Seaver	3.00
20	Robin Yount	3.00
21	Carlton Fisk	3.00
22	Dale Murphy	4.00
23	Cal Ripken Jr.	8.00
24	Tony Gwynn	4.00
25	Andre Dawson	2.00
26	Derek Jeter	6.00
27	Ken Griffey Jr.	4.00
28	Albert Pujols	4.00
29	Sammy Sosa	4.00
30	Jason Giambi	3.00
31	Randy Johnson	3.00
32	Greg Maddux	4.00
33	Rickey Henderson	3.00
34	Pedro Martinez	3.00
35	Jeff Bagwell	3.00
36	Alex Rodriguez	5.00
37	Vladimir Guerrero	3.00
38	Chipper Jones	3.00
39	Shawn Green	2.00
40	Tom Glavine	2.00
41	Curt Schilling	2.00
42	Todd Helton	2.00
43	Roger Clemens	4.00
44	Lance Berkman	2.00
45	Nomar Garciaparra	5.00

All-Time Career Best Materials

NM/M
Common Player: 5.00
Varying quantities produced.

1	Babe Ruth/Bat/25	250.00
2	Ty Cobb/Bat/25	150.00
3	Jackie Robinson/Jsy/50	50.00
4	Lou Gehrig/Bat/100	100.00
5	Thurman Munson/ Bat/200	15.00
6	Nolan Ryan/Jsy/400	15.00
7	Mike Schmidt/Jsy/400	30.00
8	Don Mattingly/Jsy/400	40.00
9	Yogi Berra/Bat/100	25.00
10	Rod Carew/Bat/400	10.00
11	Reggie Jackson/Bat/400	10.00
12	Al Kaline/Bat/400	20.00
13	Harmon Killebrew/ Bat/400	15.00
14	Eddie Mathews/Bat/200	25.00
15	Stan Musial/Bat/100	10.00
16	Jim Palmer/Jsy/200	10.00
17	Phil Rizzuto/Bat/400	8.00
18	Brooks Robinson/ Bat/400	15.00
19	Tom Seaver/Jsy/400	15.00
20	Robin Yount/Bat/400	15.00
21	Carlton Fisk/Bat/400	15.00
22	Dale Murphy/Bat/400	8.00
23	Cal Ripken Jr/Bat/400	35.00
24	Tony Gwynn/Jsy/400	12.00
25	Andre Dawson/Bat/400	20.00
26	Derek Jeter/Base/400	15.00
27	Ken Griffey Jr./ Base/400	10.00
28	Albert Pujols/Bat/400	15.00
29	Sammy Sosa/Bat/400	12.00
30	Jason Giambi/Bat/400	8.00
31	Randy Johnson/Jsy/400	8.00
32	Greg Maddux/Jsy/400	15.00
33	Rickey Henderson/ Bat/400	10.00
34	Pedro Martinez/Jsy/400	10.00
35	Jeff Bagwell/Jsy/400	15.00
36	Alex Rodriguez/Bat/400	12.00
37	Vladimir Guerrero/ Bat/400	8.00
38	Chipper Jones/Bat/400	10.00
39	Shawn Green/Bat/400	5.00
40	Tom Glavine/Jsy/400	8.00
41	Curt Schilling/Jsy/400	8.00
42	Todd Helton/Bat/400	8.00
43	Roger Clemens/Jsy/400	20.00
44	Lance Berkman/Bat/400	5.00
45	Nomar Garciaparra/ Bat/400	15.00

All-Time Career Best Materials Gold

NM/M
Numbered to career stat.
Some not priced yet.

1	Babe Ruth/60	125.00
4	Lou Gehrig/49	125.00
5	Thurman Munson/105	25.00
7	Mike Schmidt/48	60.00
8	Don Mattingly/53	60.00
9	Yogi Berra/30	50.00
10	Rod Carew/239	10.00
11	Reggie Jackson/39	25.00
12	Al Kaline/29	50.00
13	Harmon Killebrew/140	25.00
14	Eddie Mathews/31	50.00
15	Stan Musial/39	60.00
18	Brooks Robinson/118	15.00
20	Robin Yount/49	40.00
21	Carlton Fisk/107	15.00
22	Dale Murphy/44	40.00
23	Cal Ripken Jr./211	45.00
24	Tony Gwynn/220	10.00
25	Andre Dawson/49	15.00
27	Ken Griffey Jr./56	25.00
28	Albert Pujols/37	30.00
29	Sammy Sosa/66	35.00
30	Jason Giambi/137	10.00
33	Rickey Henderson/130	20.00
35	Jeff Bagwell/47	15.00
36	Alex Rodriguez/393	10.00
37	Vladimir Guerrero/44	25.00
38	Chipper Jones/45	20.00
39	Shawn Green/49	15.00
41	Curt Schilling/35	20.00
42	Todd Helton/59	15.00
44	Lance Berkman/55	15.00
45	Nomar Garciaparra/35	50.00

Back to the Future

NM/M
Complete Set (15): 35.00
Common Card: 2.00
#'s 1-10 production 1,000:
#'s 11-15 production 500:

1	Kerry Wood	4.00
2	Mark Prior	4.00
3	Magglio Ordonez	2.50
4	Joe Borchard	2.00
5	Lance Berkman	3.00
6	Jason Lane	2.00
7	Rafael Palmeiro	3.00
8	Mark Teixeira	3.00
9	Carlos Delgado	3.00
10	Josh Phelps	2.00
11	Kerry Wood, Mark Prior	4.00
12	Joe Borchard, Magglio Ordonez	2.50
13	Jason Lane, Lance Berkman	3.00
14	Mark Teixeira, Rafael Palmeiro	
15	Carlos Delgado, Josh Phelps	3.00

Back to the Future Threads

NM/M
Common Card: 4.00
Singles production 250:
Doubles production 125:

1	Kerry Wood	10.00
2	Mark Prior	12.00
3	Magglio Ordonez	5.00
4	Joe Borchard	5.00
5	Lance Berkman	6.00
6	Jason Lane	4.00
7	Rafael Palmeiro	8.00
8	Mark Teixeira	10.00
9	Carlos Delgado	8.00
10	Josh Phelps	6.00
11	Kerry Wood, Mark Prior	20.00
12	Joe Borchard, Magglio Ordonez	8.00
13	Jason Lane, Lance Berkman	8.00
14	Mark Teixeira, Rafael Palmeiro	15.00
15	Carlos Delgado, Josh Phelps	8.00

Back 2 Back Jacks

NM/M
Common Player:

1	Adam Dunn/250	10.00
2	Alex Rodriguez/250	15.00
3	Alfonso Soriano/250	8.00
4	Andruw Jones/250	8.00
5	Chipper Jones/250	10.00
6	Jason Giambi/250	8.00
7	Jeff Bagwell/250	8.00
8	Jim Thome/250	8.00
9	Juan Gonzalez/250	8.00
10	Lance Berkman/250	6.00
11	Magglio Ordonez/250	4.00
12	Manny Ramirez/250	8.00
13	Miguel Tejada/250	6.00
14	Mike Piazza/250	15.00
15	Nomar Garciaparra/250	15.00
16	Rafael Palmeiro/250	8.00
17	Rickey Henderson/250	8.00
18	Sammy Sosa/250	15.00
19	Scott Rolen/250	8.00
20	Shawn Green/250	6.00
21	Todd Helton/250	8.00
22	Vladimir Guerrero/250	8.00
23	Ivan Rodriguez/250	8.00
24	Eric Chavez/250	6.00
25	Larry Walker/250	6.00
26	Troy Glaus/250, Garret Anderson	8.00
27	Adam Dunn, Austin Kearns/125	20.00
28	Alex Rodriguez, Rafael Palmeiro/125	20.00
29	Eric Chavez, Miguel Tejada/125	10.00
30	Frank Thomas, Magglio Ordonez/125	15.00
31	Jeff Bagwell, Lance Berkman/125	15.00
32	Manny Ramirez, Nomar Garciaparra/125	30.00
33	Jose Vidro, Vladimir Guerrero/125	15.00
34	Mike Piazza, Roberto Alomar/125	20.00
35	Larry Walker, Todd Helton/125	15.00
36	Babe Ruth/100	150.00
37	Cal Ripken Jr./100	65.00
38	Don Mattingly/100	50.00
39	Kirby Puckett/100	30.00
40	Roberto Clemente/100	75.00
41	Alfonso Soriano, Phil Rizzuto/75	25.00
42	Andre Dawson, Sammy Sosa/75	40.00
43	Ozzie Smith, Scott Rolen/75	60.00
44	Don Mattingly, Jason Giambi/75	75.00
45	Rickey Henderson, Ty Cobb/75	125.00
46	Joe Morgan, Johnny Bench/50	35.00
47	Brooks Robinson, Cal Ripken Jr./50	100.00
48	Bo Jackson, George Brett/50	100.00
49	Babe Ruth, Lou Gehrig/50	375.00
50	Thurman Munson, Yogi Berra/50	60.00

Career Best

NM/M
Common Player: 3.00
Numbered to statistic.

3	Garret Anderson/56	6.00
4	Andruw Jones/83	6.00
6	Magglio Ordonez/38	6.00
7	Magglio Ordonez/135	4.00
8	Adam Dunn/26	15.00
10	Lance Berkman/42	6.00
11	Lance Berkman/128	3.00
12	Shawn Green/385	3.00
13	Alfonso Soriano/39	12.00
14	Alfonso Soriano/300	5.00
15	Jason Giambi/120	5.00
16	Derek Jeter/32	8.00
17	Vladimir Guerrero/40	12.00
18	Vladimir Guerrero/417	5.00

19	Barry Zito/23	8.00
20	Miguel Tejada/34	8.00
21	Barry Bonds/198	15.00
22	Barry Bonds/370	15.00
23	Ichiro Suzuki/388	8.00
24	Alex Rodriguez/57	15.00
25	Alex Rodriguez/142	10.00

Career Best Materials

NM/M
Common Player: 4.00
Production 500 Sets

1	Randy Johnson/Jsy	8.00
2	Curt Schilling/Jsy	8.00
3	Garret Anderson/Bat	4.00
4	Andruw Jones/Bat	6.00
5	Kerry Wood/Shoe	10.00
6	Magglio Ordonez/Bat	4.00
7	Magglio Ordonez/Bat	4.00
8	Adam Dunn/Bat	6.00
9	Roy Oswalt/Jsy	5.00
10	Lance Berkman/Bat	5.00
11	Lance Berkman/Bat	5.00
12	Shawn Green/Bat	4.00
13	Alfonso Soriano/Bat	10.00
14	Alfonso Soriano/Bat	10.00
15	Jason Giambi/Bat	8.00
16	Derek Jeter/Base	15.00
17	Vladimir Guerrero/Bat	8.00
18	Vladimir Guerrero/Bat	8.00
19	Barry Zito/Jsy	6.00
20	Miguel Tejada/Bat	6.00
21	Barry Bonds/Base	15.00
22	Barry Bonds/Base	15.00
23	Ichiro Suzuki/Base	15.00
24	Alex Rodriguez/Jsy	10.00
25	Alex Rodriguez/Jsy	10.00

Career Best Materials Autograph

NM/M
Quantity produced listed.

3	Garret Anderson/Bat/75	35.00
8	Adam Dunn/Bat/100	50.00
9	Roy Oswalt/Jsy/250	30.00
17	Vladimir Guerrero/ Bat/50	75.00
18	Vladimir Guerrero/ Bat/50	75.00
19	Barry Zito/Jsy/75	40.00

Highlights

NM/M
Production 500 Sets

1	Sammy Sosa	10.00
2	Rafael Palmeiro	8.00
3	Hideki Matsui	10.00
4	Jose Contreras	4.00
5	Kevin Millwood	4.00

Highlights Autographs

NM/M
Production 50 Sets

1	Rafael Palmeiro	75.00
4	Jose Contreras	25.00

Passing the Torch

NM/M
Complete Set (15): 50.00
Common Player: 1.50

1	Stan Musial	6.00
2	Jim Edmonds	2.00
3	Dale Murphy	3.00
4	Andruw Jones	3.00
5	Roger Clemens	8.00
6	Mark Prior	3.00
7	Tom Seaver	3.00
8	Tom Glavine	1.50
9	Mike Schmidt	8.00
10	Pat Burrell	2.00
11	Jim Edmonds, Stan Musial	8.00
12	Andruw Jones, Dale Murphy	5.00
13	Mark Prior, Roger Clemens	8.00
14	Tom Glavine, Tom Seaver	5.00
15	Mike Schmidt, Pat Burrell	10.00

Passing the Torch Autograph

NM/M
Common Auto. (1-10): 30.00
#'s 1-10 Production 50
#'s 11-15 Production 25
No pricing for #'s 11-15.

1	Stan Musial	80.00
2	Jim Edmonds	40.00
3	Dale Murphy	50.00
4	Andruw Jones	30.00
5	Roger Clemens	125.00
6	Mark Prior	40.00
7	Tom Seaver	60.00
8	Tom Glavine	50.00
9	Mike Schmidt	100.00
10	Pat Burrell	30.00

Recollection Autographs

Some not priced due to scarcity.

1	Jeremy Affeldt/75	15.00
4	Erick Almonte/75	8.00
5	Adrian Beltre/36	30.00
7	Brandon Berger/83	8.00
8	Angel Berroa/28	25.00
13	Jeff Deardorff/53	8.00
14	Ryan Drese/100	25.00
21	Luis Garcia/28	15.00
28	Geronimo Gil/75	8.00
29	Travis Hafner Black/52	30.00
30	Bill Hall/27	15.00
36	Gerald Laird/46	30.00
42	Jason Lane/27	15.00
46	Victor Martinez/52	100.00
55	Roy Oswalt Black/61	20.00
56	Ricardo Rodriguez/75	8.00
57	Bud Smith/50	8.00
58	Bud Smith/28	10.00
59	Junior Spivey/45	20.00
60	Tim Spooneybarger/100	8.00
61	Shannon Stewart/35	20.00
64	Claudio Vargas/51	8.00

Throwback Threads

NM/M
Common Player: 4.00

1	Randy Johnson/Jsy	8.00
2	Randy Johnson/Hat	8.00
3	Roger Clemens/Jsy	20.00
4	Roger Clemens/Jsy	20.00
6	Manny Ramirez/Jsy	8.00
7	Greg Maddux/Jsy	15.00
8	Jason Giambi/Jsy	6.00
9	Alex Rodriguez/Jsy	10.00
10	Alex Rodriguez/Jsy	10.00
11	Miguel Tejada/Jsy	8.00
12	Alfonso Soriano/Jsy	8.00
13	Nomar Garciaparra/Jsy	15.00
14	Pedro J. Martinez/Jsy	8.00
15	Pedro J. Martinez/Jsy	8.00
16	Andruw Jones/Jsy	6.00
17	Chipper Jones/Jsy	8.00
18	Barry Zito/Jsy	8.00
19	Mark Mulder/Jsy	4.00
20	Lance Berkman/Jsy	6.00
21	Magglio Ordonez/Jsy	6.00
22	Mike Piazza/Jsy	15.00
23	Mike Piazza/Jsy	15.00
24	Rickey Henderson/Jsy	8.00
25	Rickey Henderson/Jsy	8.00
26	Rickey Henderson/Jsy	8.00
27	Sammy Sosa/Jsy	15.00
28	Shawn Green/Jsy	5.00
29	Troy Glaus/Jsy	6.00
30	Vladimir Guerrero/Jsy	8.00
31	Adam Dunn/Jsy	8.00
32	Jeff Bagwell/Jsy	8.00
33	Curt Schilling/Jsy	8.00
34	Hideo Nomo/Jsy	20.00
35	Hideo Nomo/Jsy	20.00
36	Hideo Nomo/Jsy	20.00
37	Kerry Wood/Jsy	10.00
38	Mark Prior/Jsy	8.00
39	Roberto Alomar/Jsy	6.00
40	Todd Helton/Jsy	8.00
41	Jim Thome/Jsy	8.00
42	Rafael Palmeiro/Jsy	8.00
43	Juan Gonzalez/Jsy	8.00
44	Vernon Wells/Jsy	4.00
45	Torii Hunter/Jsy	6.00
46	Randi Johnson/Jsy	15.00
47	Roger Clemens/Jsy	30.00
48	Jason Giambi/Jsy	10.00
49	Alex Rodriguez/Jsy	25.00
50	Pedro J. Martinez/Jsy	10.00
51	Mike Piazza/Jsy	25.00
52	Rickey Henderson	20.00
53	Rickey Henderson	20.00
54	Rickey Henderson/Hat, Rickey Henderson/20.00	
55	Hideo Nomo/Jsy	40.00
56	Randy Johnson/Jsy	15.00
57	Curt Schilling, Randy Johnson/Jsy	15.00
58	Alfonso Soriano, Ichiro Suzuki/Jsy	
59	Barry Zito, Mark Mulder	15.00
60	Andruw Jones, Chipper Jones/Jsy	20.00
61	Greg Maddux, Tom Glavine	40.00

62	Jeff Bagwell, Lance Berkman/Jsy	15.00
63	Mark Prior, Roger Clemens/Jsy	20.00
64	Alex Rodriguez, Rafael Palmeiro/Jsy	20.00
65	Jim Thome, Roberto Alomar/Jsy	20.00
66	Mike Piazza, Roberto Alomar/Jsy	25.00
67	Mark Grace, Sammy Sosa/Jsy	25.00
68	Larry Walker, Todd Helton/Jsy	20.00
69	Adam Dunn, Austin Kearns/Jsy	20.00
70	Alex Rodriguez, Ivan Rodriguez/Jsy	20.00
71	Bobby Abreu, Marlon Byrd/Jsy	15.00
72	Eric Chavez, Miguel Tejada/Jsy	15.00
73	Greg Maddux, John Smoltz/Jsy	30.00
74	Kerry Wood, Mark Prior/Jsy	10.00
75	Barry Zito, Tim Hudson/Jsy	10.00
76	Babe Ruth	250.00
77	Ty Cobb	100.00
78	Jackie Robinson	75.00
79	Lou Gehrig	125.00
80	Thurman Munson	30.00
81	Nolan Ryan	40.00
82	Don Mattingly	50.00
83	Mike Schmidt	40.00
84	Reggie Jackson	20.00
85	George Brett	40.00
86	Cal Ripken Jr.	50.00
87	Tony Gwynn	15.00
88	Yogi Berra	25.00
89	Stan Musial	40.00
90	Jim Palmer	10.00
91	Thurman Munson	50.00
92	Chipper Jones, Dale Murphy	50.00
93	Don Mattingly, Jason Giambi	80.00
94	Andre Dawson, Sammy Sosa	
95	Mark Prior, Nolan Ryan	50.00
96	Babe Ruth, Lou Gehrig	475.00
97	Joe Morgan, Tom Seaver	40.00
98	Harmon Killebrew, Rod Carew	40.00
99	Nolan Ryan	90.00
100	Reggie Jackson	35.00

Throwback Threads Autograph

NM/M
Production 5-75

		4.00
30	Vladimir Guerrero/50	75.00
31	Adam Dunn/50	75.00
34	Kerry Wood/50	75.00
38	Mark Prior/75	75.00
55	Roberto Alomar/50	75.00

Turn of the Century Autographs

NM/M
Common Autograph: 10.00
Production 50 Sets

182	Jose Contreras	40.00
183	Terrmel Sledge	15.00
184	Lew Ford	20.00
185	Jhonny Peralta	35.00
186	Alexis Rios	40.00
187	Jeff Baker	15.00
188	Jeremy Guthrie	15.00
189	Jose Castillo	15.00
190	Garrett Atkins	25.00
191	Jeremy Bonderman	40.00
192	Adam LaRoche	15.00
193	Vinnie Chulk	15.00
194	Walter Young	15.00
195	Jimmy Gobble	10.00
196	Prentice Redman	15.00
197	Jason Anderson	15.00
198	Nic Jackson	15.00
199	Travis Chapman	10.00
200	Shane Victorino	15.00

2003 Donruss Montreal Expos

Over the course of the season, in a series of stadium giveaways, fans attending selected games at

Olympic Stadium received a cello-wrapped pack of specially designed Donruss cards featuring many of the team's most popular players since entering the National League in 1969. Cards are the standard 2-1/2" x 3-1/2" format with either black-and-white or color photos on front, bordered in white with red and blue graphics. Backs have a dark blue background with personal data, a line of career stats and highlights.

	NM/M
Complete Set (59):	25.00
Common Player:	.25
Series 1, April 25	4.00
1 Claude Raymond	.75
2 Javier Vasquez	1.50
3 John Boccabella	.75
4 Bill Stoneman	.75
5 Carl Morton	.75
6 Ron Fairly	.75
Series 2, May 9	4.00
7 Bob Bailey	.25
8 Steve Renko	.25
9 Mike Marshall	.25
10 Ron Hunt	.25
11 Ken Singleton	.25
12 Pedro Martinez	3.00
Series 3, May 23	1.50
13 Tim Foli	.25
14 Mike Jorgensen	.25
15 Steve Rogers	.25
16 Willie Davis	.25
17 Larry Parrish	.25
18 Jerry White	.25
Series 4, June 20	8.00
19 Ellis Valentine	.25
20 Woody Fryman	.25
21 Andre Dawson	2.00
22 Warren Cromartie	.25
23 Vladimir Guerrero	4.00
24 Tony Perez	2.00
Series 5, July 11	1.50
25 Chris Speier	.25
26 Dan Schatzeder	.25
27 Ross Grimsley	.25
28 Scott Sanderson	.25
29 Tim Wallach	.25
30 Dave Cash	.25
Series 6, July 25	2.00
31 Bill Gullickson	.25
32 Tim Raines	1.00
33 Rodney Scott	.25
34 Ron LeFlore	.25
35 Charlie Lea	.25
36 Bill Lee	.25
Series 7, Aug. 1	3.00
37 Jeff Reardon	.25
38 Bryn Smith	.25
39 Al Oliver	.75
40 Hubie Brooks	.25
41 Terry Francona	.25
42 Gary Carter	2.00
Series 8, Aug. 15	4.00
43 Spike Owen	.25
44 Tim Burke	.25
45 Andres Galarraga	.50
46 Marquis Grissom	.50
47 Larry Walker	2.00
48 Moises Alou	.50
49 Dennis Martinez	.50
Series 9, Sept. 12	3.50
50 Denis Boucher	.25
51 Rondell White	.25
52 Mel Rojas	.25
53 Henry Rodriguez	.25
54 David Segui	.25
55 Ugueth Urbina	.25
56 Jose Vidro	1.00
57 Darrin Fletcher	.25
58 Orlando Cabrera	1.00
59 John Wetteland	.25

2003 Donruss Rookie & Traded

	NM/M
Complete Set (65):	8.00
Common Player:	.25
Pack (8):	8.00
Box (24):	150.00
1 Jeremy Bonderman	.50
2 Adam Loewen	.50
3 Dan Haren	.50

4 Jose Contreras **RC**	.50
5 Hideki Matsui **RC**	2.00
6 Arnie Munoz	.25
7 Miguel Cabrera	.25
8 Andrew Brown **RC**	.25
9 Josh Hall	.25
10 Josh Stewart **RC**	.25
11 Clint Barmes **RC**	.25
12 Luis Ayala **RC**	.25
13 Brandon Webb **RC**	1.50
14 Greg Aquino	.25
15 Chien-Ming Wang **RC**	2.00
16 Rickie Weeks **RC**	1.00
17 Edgar Gonzalez **RC**	.25
18 Dontrelle Willis	.25
19 Bo Hart **RC**	.25
20 Rosman Garcia **RC**	.25
21 Jeremy Griffiths	.25
22 Craig Brazell **RC**	.50
23 Daniel Cabrera **RC**	.50
24 Fernando Cabrera **RC**	.25
25 Terrmel Sledge **RC**	.25
26 Ramon Nivar	.25
27 Rob Hammock **RC**	.25
28 Francisco Rosario **RC**	.25
29 Cory Stewart	.25
30 Felix Sanchez	.25
31 Jorge Cordova	.25
32 Rocco Baldelli	.50
33 Beau Kemp **RC**	.25
34 Micheal Nakamura **RC**	.25
35 Rett Johnson **RC**	.25
36 Guillermo Quiroz **RC**	.25
37 Hong-Chih Kuo **RC**	1.00
38 Ian Ferguson **RC**	.25
39 Franklin Perez	.25
40 Tim Olson **RC**	.25
41 Jerome Williams	.25
42 Rich Fischer	.25
43 Phil Seibel **RC**	.25
44 Aaron Looper **RC**	.25
45 Jae Weong Seo	.25
46 Chad Gaudin **RC**	.25
47 Matt Kata **RC**	.25
48 Ryan Wagner **RC**	.25
49 Michel Hernandez **RC**	.25
50 Diegomar Markwell	.25
51 Doug Waechter	.25
52 Mike Nicolas	.25
53 Prentice Redman **RC**	.25
54 Shane Bazell	.25
55 Delmon Young **RC**	1.00
56 Brian Stokes	.25
57 Matt Bruback	.25
58 Nook Logan **RC**	.25
59 Oscar Villarreal **RC**	.25
60 Pete LaForest **RC**	.25
61 Shea Hillenbrand	.40
62 Aramis Ramirez	.40
63 Aaron Boone	.25
64 Roberto Alomar	.50
65 Rickey Henderson	.50

Team Heroes
Common Player (541-548):	.25
Team Heroes Glossy:	1-2X
541 Rickie Weeks **RC**	.75
542 Hideki Matsui **RC**	1.50
543 Ramon Nivar	.25
544 Adam Loewen **RC**	.25
545 Brandon Webb **RC**	1.50
546 Dan Haren	.50
547 Delmon Young **RC**	1.00
548 Ryan Wagner **RC**	.25

Champions
Common Player (302-309):	.25
Metalized:	4-8X
Production 100	
302 Ryan Wagner **RC**	.25
303 Adam Loewen **RC**	.25
304 Chien-Ming Wang **RC**	2.50
305 Hong-Chih Kuo **RC**	1.00
306 Delmon Young **RC**	1.50
307 Dan Haren	.50
308 Rickie Weeks **RC**	1.00
309 Ramon Nivar	.25

Leaf
Common Player (321-329):	.25
Leaf Red Press Proofs:	4-8X
Production 100	
Leaf Blue Press Proofs:	5-10X
Production 50	
321 Hideki Matsui **RC**	1.50
322 Ramon Nivar	.25
323 Adam Loewen **RC**	.25
324 Brandon Webb **RC**	2.00
325 Chien-Ming Wang **RC**	2.50
326 Delmon Young **RC**	1.50
327 Ryan Wagner **RC**	.25

328 Dan Haren	.50
329 Rickie Weeks **RC**	1.00

Playoff Prestige
Common Player (201-210):	.25
Prestige X-Tra Points:	5-10X
Production 50	
201 Jeremy Bonderman	.50
202 Brandon Webb **RC**	2.00
203 Adam Loewen **RC**	.25
204 Chien-Ming Wang **RC**	2.50
205 Hong-Chih Kuo **RC**	1.00
206 Delmon Young **RC**	1.50
207 Ryan Wagner **RC**	.25
208 Dan Haren	.50
209 Rickie Weeks **RC**	1.00
210 Ramon Nivar	.25

Classics
Common Player (201-211):	4.00
Production 1,000	
Classics Timeless Tributes:	.75-1.5X
Production 100	
201 Jeremy Bonderman	5.00
202 Adam Loewen **RC**	4.00
203 Chien-Ming Wang **RC**	20.00
204 Hong-Chih Kuo **RC**	4.00
205 Ryan Wagner **RC**	4.00
206 Dan Haren	6.00
207 Dontrelle Willis	4.00
208 Rickie Weeks **RC**	6.00
209 Ramon Nivar	4.00
210 Chad Gaudin **RC**	4.00
211 Delmon Young **RC**	8.00

Studio
Common Player (201-211):	3.00
Production 1,500	
Studio Proof:	1-1.5X
Production 100	
201 Adam Loewen **RC**	3.00
202 Jeremy Bonderman	5.00
203 Brandon Webb **RC**	10.00
204 Chien-Ming Wang **RC**	20.00
205 Chad Gaudin **RC**	3.00
206 Ryan Wagner **RC**	3.00
207 Hong-Chih Kuo **RC**	8.00
208 Dan Haren	6.00
209 Rickie Weeks **RC**	6.00
210 Ramon Nivar	3.00
211 Delmon Young **RC**	8.00

Diamond Kings
Common Player (177-201):	3.00
Inserted 1:30	
DK Portraits Bronze:	.5-1X
DK Portraits Silver:	1-1.5X
Production 1,000	
DK Portraits Gold:	1-2X
Production 500	
177 Hideki Matsui **RC**	10.00
178 Jeremy Bonderman	5.00
179 Brandon Webb **RC**	10.00
180 Adam Loewen **RC**	4.00
181 Chien-Ming Wang **RC**	15.00
182 Hong-Chih Kuo **RC**	6.00
183 Clint Barmes **RC**	3.00
184 Guillermo Quiroz **RC**	3.00
185 Edgar Gonzalez **RC**	3.00
186 Todd Wellemeyer **RC**	4.00
187 Dan Haren	4.00
188 Dustin McGowan	5.00
189 Preston Larrison	3.00
190 Kevin Youkilis	8.00
191 Kevin Youkilis	8.00
192 Bubba Nelson	3.00
193 Chris Burke	3.00
194 J.D. Durbin	3.00
195 Ryan Howard	20.00
196 Jason Kubel **RC**	5.00
197 Brendan Harris	5.00
198 Brian Bruney	3.00
199 Ramon Nivar	3.00
200 Rickie Weeks **RC**	5.00
201 Delmon Young **RC**	8.00

Leaf Certified Materials
Mirror Red Signature:	.75-1.5X
Production 100 or 50	
Mirror Blue Signature:	1-1.5X
Mirror Gold Signature:	No Pricing
Mirror Emerald Signature: No Pricing	
Mirror Reds:	.2-.4X
Production 100	
Mirror Blues:	.4-.6X
Production 50	
Mirror Golds:	No Pricing
Production 25	
251 Adam Loewen/ Auto./250 **RC**	15.00
252 Dan Haren/Auto./250	30.00
253 Dontrelle Willis/ Auto./250	20.00
254 Ramon Nivar/Auto./250	10.00
255 Chad Gaudin/Auto./250	10.00
256 Kevin Correia/ Auto./250 **RC**	10.00
257 Rickie Weeks/ Auto./100 **RC**	60.00
258 Ryan Wagner/ Auto./250 **RC**	10.00
259 Delmon Young/ Auto./100 **RC**	125.00

Playoff Absolute
Common Player (201-208):	4.00
Production 1,000	
Spectrum:	1-2X
Production 100	
201 Adam Loewen **RC**	4.00
202 Ramon Nivar	4.00
203 Dan Haren	6.00
204 Dontrelle Willis	4.00
205 Chad Gaudin	4.00
206 Rickie Weeks **RC**	

207 Ryan Wagner **RC**	4.00
208 Delmon Young **RC**	8.00

Elite Extra Edition
Common Player (1-58):	4.00
Production 900	
Elite Status:	1-30X
Numbered to Jersey Number	
Elite Aspirations:	1-2X
Varying quantities produced	
Turn of Century non-Auto.:	1-2X
Production 100	
Elite Gold Status:	No Pricing
Production 24	
1 Adam Loewen **RC**	5.00
2 Brandon Webb **RC**	15.00
3 Chien-Ming Wang **RC**	25.00
4 Hong-Chih Kuo **RC**	15.00
5 Clint Barmes **RC**	3.00
6 Guillermo Quiroz **RC**	3.00
7 Edgar Gonzalez **RC**	3.00
8 Todd Wellemeyer **RC**	6.00
9 Alfredo Gonzalez **RC**	3.00
10 Craig Brazell **RC**	3.00
11 Tim Olson **RC**	3.00
12 Rich Fischer	3.00
13 Daniel Cabrera **RC**	5.00
14 Francisco Rosario **RC**	4.00
15 Francisco Cruceta **RC**	4.00
16 Alejandro Machado **RC**	4.00
17 Andrew Brown **RC**	4.00
18 Rob Hammock **RC**	4.00
19 Arnie Munoz	4.00
20 Felix Sanchez	4.00
21 Nook Logan **RC**	4.00
22 Cory Stewart	4.00
23 Michel Hernandez **RC**	4.00
24 Rett Johnson **RC**	4.00
25 Josh Hall **RC**	4.00
26 Doug Waechter	4.00
27 Matt Kata **RC**	4.00
28 Dan Haren	8.00
29 Dontrelle Willis	4.00
30 Ramon Nivar	4.00
31 Chad Gaudin **RC**	5.00
32 Rickie Weeks **RC**	8.00
33 Ryan Wagner **RC**	4.00
34 Kevin Correia **RC**	4.00
35 Bo Hart **RC**	4.00
36 Oscar Villarreal **RC**	4.00
37 Josh Willingham **RC**	5.00
38 Jeff Duncan **RC**	5.00
39 David DeJesus **RC**	5.00
40 Dustin McGowan **RC**	8.00
41 Preston Larrison	4.00
42 Kevin Youkilis	8.00
43 Bubba Nelson	4.00
44 Chris Burke	6.00
45 J.D. Durbin	4.00
46 Ryan Howard	50.00
47 Jason Kubel **RC**	6.00
48 Brendan Harris	6.00
49 Brian Bruney	4.00
50 Byron Gettis	4.00
51 Edwin Jackson **RC**	6.00
52 Daniel Garcia	4.00
53 Chad Cordero **RC**	6.00
54 Delmon Young **RC**	15.00

Common Leaf Limited Phenom:
Silver Spotlights:	1X
Production 50	
Gold Spotlights:	No Pricing
Production 10 or 25	
201 Delmon Young/ Auto./99 **RC**	125.00
202 Rickie Weeks/ Auto./99 **RC**	60.00
203 Edwin Jackson/ Auto./99 **RC**	25.00
204 Dan Haren/Auto./99	40.00

Signature Series:
151 Delmon Young/ Auto./200 **RC**	80.00
152 Rickie Weeks/ Auto./200 **RC**	30.00
153 Edwin Jackson/ Auto./200	15.00

Autographs

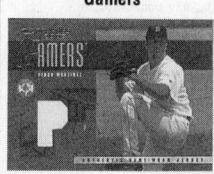

	NM/M
Common Autograph:	5.00
1 Jeremy Bonderman/50	40.00
2 Adam Loewen/500	10.00
3 Dan Haren/100	30.00
4 Jose Contreras/100	25.00
5 Arnie Munoz/584	5.00
6 Miguel Cabrera/50	50.00
7 Andrew Brown/584	5.00
8 Josh Hall/1000	10.00

10 Josh Stewart/300	5.00
11 Clint Barmes/129	15.00
12 Luis Ayala/1000	5.00
13 Brandon Webb/100	50.00
14 Greg Aquino/1000	5.00
15 Chien-Ming Wang/100	200.00
16 Edgar Gonzalez/400	5.00
17 Bo Hart/150	5.00
19 Rosman Garcia/250	5.00
21 Jeremy Griffiths/812	5.00
22 Craig Brazell/205	5.00
23 Daniel Cabrera/383	15.00
24 Fernando Cabrera/1000	5.00
25 Terrmel Sledge/250	5.00
26 Ramon Nivar/1000	5.00
27 Rob Hammock/201	10.00
28 Cory Stewart/1000	5.00
30 Felix Sanchez/1000	5.00
31 Jorge Cordova/1000	5.00
33 Beau Kemp/1000	5.00
34 Micheal Nakamura/1000	5.00
35 Rett Johnson/1000	5.00
36 Guillermo Quiroz/90	15.00
37 Hong-Chih Kuo/50	150.00
38 Ian Ferguson/1000	5.00
39 Franklin Perez/1000	5.00
40 Tim Olson/150	5.00
41 Jerome Williams/50	10.00
42 Rich Fischer/734	5.00
43 Phil Seibel/1000	5.00
44 Aaron Looper/513	5.00
45 Jae Weong Seo/50	30.00
47 Matt Kata/203	5.00
48 Ryan Wagner/100	10.00
50 Diegomar Markwell/1000	5.00
51 Doug Waechter/583	5.00
52 Mike Nicolas/1000	5.00
53 Prentice Redman/425	5.00
54 Shane Bazell/1000	5.00
55 Delmon Young/75	100.00
56 Brian Stokes/1000	5.00
57 Matt Bruback/513	5.00
58 Nook Logan/150	5.00
59 Oscar Villarreal/150	5.00
60 Pete LaForest/250	5.00

Gamers

	NM/M
Common Player:	4.00
Production 500	
Position:	1-2X
Production 100	
Number:	1-2X
Production 100	
Patch:	No Pricing
Production 25	
Rewards:	No Pricing
Production 10	
1 Nomar Garciaparra	8.00
2 Alex Rodriguez	8.00
3 Mike Piazza	8.00
4 Greg Maddux	8.00
5 Roger Clemens	10.00
6 Sammy Sosa	8.00
7 Randy Johnson	8.00
8 Albert Pujols	15.00
9 Alfonso Soriano	8.00
10 Chipper Jones	6.00
11 Mark Prior	8.00
12 Hideo Nomo	6.00
13 Adam Dunn	6.00
14 Juan Gonzalez	6.00
15 Vladimir Guerrero	8.00
16 Pedro J. Martinez	8.00
17 Jim Thome	6.00
18 Brandon Webb/200	6.00
19 Mike Mussina	6.00
20 Mark Teixeira	5.00
21 Barry Larkin	5.00
22 Ivan Rodriguez	6.00
23 Hank Blalock	6.00
24 Rafael Palmeiro	6.00
25 Curt Schilling	6.00
26 Troy Glaus	5.00
27 Bernie Williams	6.00
28 Scott Rolen	6.00
29 Torii Hunter	5.00
30 Nick Johnson	4.00
31 Kazuhisa Ishii	4.00
32 Shawn Green	5.00
33 Jeff Bagwell	6.00
34 Lance Berkman	5.00
35 Roy Oswalt	4.00
36 Kerry Wood	4.00
37 Todd Helton	6.00
38 Manny Ramirez	8.00
39 Andruw Jones	6.00
40 Frank Thomas	8.00
41 Gary Sheffield	5.00
42 Magglio Ordonez	6.00
43 Mike Sweeney	4.00
44 Carlos Beltran	6.00
45 Richie Sexson	4.00
46 Jeff Kent	5.00
47 Carlos Delgado	6.00
48 Vernon Wells	4.00
49 Dontrelle Willis	8.00
50 Jae Weong Seo	

Gamers Autograph

	NM/M
Production 5-50	4.00
Many not priced due to scarcity.	
20 Mark Teixeira/50	30.00
23 Hank Blalock/50	20.00
29 Torii Hunter/50	20.00
35 Roy Oswalt/50	20.00
43 Mike Sweeney/50	15.00
48 Vernon Wells/30	20.00
49 Dontrelle Willis/50	20.00

Playoff Prestige Autograph

	NM/M
Quantity produced listed.	
201 Jeremy Bonderman/100	40.00
202 Brandon Webb/100	50.00
203 Adam Loewen/100	25.00
204 Chien-Ming Wang/50	250.00
205 Hong-Chih Kuo/100	150.00
207 Ryan Wagner/100	25.00
208 Dan Haren/100	25.00
210 Ramon Nivar/100	5.00

Recollection Autographs

	NM/M
Common Player:	
7 Jack McDowell 88/75	20.00

Stat Line Season/Career

Cards serial #'d from 101-150: 1-2X
Cards serial #'d from 50-100: 2-3X
Cards serial #'d from 26-49: 3-4X
Cards numbered under 25 not priced.

Turn of the Century Autograph

	NM/M
Common Player:	10.00
Production 100	
Aspirations:	.75-1.5X
Varying quantities produced.	
1 Adam Loewen	15.00
2 Brandon Webb	125.00
3 Chien-Ming Wang	250.00
4 Hong-Chih Kuo	150.00
5 Clint Barmes	15.00
6 Guillermo Quiroz	10.00
7 Edgar Gonzalez	10.00
8 Todd Wellemeyer	10.00
9 Alfredo Gonzalez	10.00
10 Craig Brazell	10.00
11 Tim Olson	10.00
12 Rich Fischer	10.00
13 Daniel Cabrera	30.00
14 Francisco Rosario	10.00
15 Francisco Cruceta	10.00
16 Alejandro Machado	10.00
17 Andrew Brown	10.00
18 Rob Hammock	10.00
19 Arnie Munoz	10.00
20 Felix Sanchez	10.00
21 Nook Logan	10.00
22 Cory Stewart	10.00
23 Michel Hernandez	10.00
24 Rett Johnson	10.00
25 Josh Hall	15.00
26 Doug Waechter	10.00
27 Matt Kata	10.00
28 Dan Haren	75.00
29 Dontrelle Willis/25	40.00
30 Ramon Nivar	10.00
31 Chad Gaudin	20.00
32 Rickie Weeks/25	60.00
33 Ryan Wagner	10.00
35 Bo Hart	10.00
36 Oscar Villarreal	10.00
37 Josh Willingham	30.00
38 Jeff Duncan	15.00
40 Dustin McGowan	30.00
41 Preston Larrison	10.00
43 Kevin Youkilis	60.00
44 Bubba Nelson	15.00
45 Chris Burke	25.00
46 J.D. Durbin	15.00
47 Ryan Howard	500.00
48 Jason Kubel	30.00
49 Brendan Harris	20.00
51 Brian Bruney	10.00
52 Byron Gettis	10.00
53 Edwin Jackson	25.00
54 Daniel Garcia	10.00
55 Delmon Young	125.00

2003 Donruss Signature Series

	NM/M
Complete Set (150):	150.00

Common Player: .50
Common Rk (101-150): 1.00
Inserted 1:Tin
Tin: 35.00

#	Player	Price
1	Garret Anderson	.75
2	Tim Salmon	.75
3	Troy Glaus	.75
4	Curt Schilling	1.00
5	Luis Gonzalez	.75
6	Mark Grace	.75
7	Matt Williams	.50
8	Randy Johnson	1.50
9	Andruw Jones	1.00
10	Chipper Jones	1.50
11	Gary Sheffield	.75
12	Greg Maddux	2.00
13	Johnny Damon	.75
14	Manny Ramirez	1.00
15	Nomar Garciaparra	2.50
16	Pedro J. Martinez	1.50
17	Corey Patterson	.75
18	Kerry Wood	1.50
19	Mark Prior	2.00
20	Sammy Sosa	2.50
21	Bartolo Colon	.50
22	Frank Thomas	1.00
23	Magglio Ordonez	.50
24	Paul Konerko	.50
25	Adam Dunn	1.00
26	Austin Kearns	.75
27	Barry Larkin	.75
28	Ken Griffey Jr.	2.00
29	C.C. Sabathia	.50
30	Omar Vizquel	.50
31	Larry Walker	.50
32	Todd Helton	1.00
33	Ivan Rodriguez	1.00
34	Josh Beckett	.75
35	Craig Biggio	.75
36	Jeff Bagwell	1.00
37	Jeff Kent	.50
38	Lance Berkman	.75
39	Richard Hidalgo	.50
40	Roy Oswalt	.75
41	Carlos Beltran	1.00
42	Mike Sweeney	.50
43	Runelvys Hernandez	.50
44	Hideo Nomo	.75
45	Kazuhisa Ishii	.50
46	Paul LoDuca	.50
47	Shawn Green	.75
48	Ben Sheets	.75
49	Richie Sexson	.75
50	A.J. Pierzynski	.50
51	Torii Hunter	.75
52	Javier Vazquez	.50
53	Jose Vidro	.50
54	Vladimir Guerrero	1.50
55	Cliff Floyd	.50
56	David Cone	.50
57	Mike Piazza	2.00
58	Roberto Alomar	.75
59	Tom Glavine	.75
60	Alfonso Soriano	1.50
61	Derek Jeter	4.00
62	Drew Henson	.50
63	Jason Giambi	.75
64	Mike Mussina	1.00
65	Nick Johnson	.50
66	Roger Clemens	3.00
67	Barry Zito	.75
68	Eric Chavez	.75
69	Mark Mulder	.75
70	Miguel Tejada	.75
71	Tim Hudson	.75
72	Bobby Abreu	.75
73	Jim Thome	1.00
74	Kevin Millwood	.50
75	Pat Burrell	.50
76	Brian Giles	.50
77	Jason Kendall	.50
78	Kenny Lofton	.50
79	Phil Nevin	.50
80	Ryan Klesko	.50
81	Andres Galarraga	.50
82	Barry Bonds	4.00
83	Rich Aurilia	.50
84	Edgar Martinez	.50
85	Freddy Garcia	.50
86	Ichiro Suzuki	2.50
87	Albert Pujols	3.00
88	Jim Edmonds	.75
89	Scott Rolen	1.50
90	So Taguchi	.50
91	Rocco Baldelli	.50
92	Alex Rodriguez	3.00
93	Hank Blalock	1.00
94	Juan Gonzalez	1.00
95	Mark Teixeira	.75
96	Rafael Palmeiro	1.00
97	Carlos Delgado	1.00
98	Eric Hinske	.50
99	Roy Halladay	.75
100	Vernon Wells	.50
101	Hideki Matsui RC	10.00
102	Jose Contreras RC	3.00
103	Jeremy Bonderman RC	4.00
104	Bernie Castro RC	1.00
105	Alfredo Gonzalez RC	1.00
106	Arnie Munoz RC	1.00
107	Andrew Brown RC	1.50
108	Josh Hall RC	1.50
109	Josh Stewart RC	1.50
110	Clint Barmes RC	1.50
111	Brandon Webb RC	2.00
112	Chien-Ming Wang RC	15.00
113	Edgar Gonzalez RC	1.00
114	Alejandro Machado RC	1.00
115	Jeremy Griffiths	1.00
116	Craig Brazell RC	1.50
117	Shane Bazell RC	1.50
118	Fernando Cabrera RC	1.50
119	Termel Sledge RC	1.50
120	Rob Hammock RC	1.50
121	Francisco Rosario RC	1.50
122	Francisco Cruceta RC	1.50
123	Rett Johnson RC	1.50
124	Guillermo Quiroz RC	2.00
125	Hong-Chih Kuo RC	3.00
126	Ian Ferguson RC	1.50
127	Tim Olson RC	1.00
128	Todd Wellemeyer RC	2.50
129	Richard Fischer RC	1.00
130	Phil Seibel RC	1.00
131	Joe Valentine RC	1.00
132	Matt Kata RC	1.50
133	Michael Hessman RC	1.00
134	Michel Hernandez RC	1.00
135	Doug Waechter RC	1.50
136	Prentice Redman RC	1.50
137	Nook Logan RC	1.00
138	Oscar Villarreal RC	1.00
139	Pete LaForest RC	1.00
140	Matt Bruback RC	1.00
141	Dontrelle Willis RC	1.50
142	Greg Aquino RC	1.00
143	Lew Ford RC	2.00
144	Jeff Duncan RC	2.00
145	Dan Haren RC	2.00
146	Miguel Ojeda RC	1.00
147	Rosman Garcia RC	1.00
148	Felix Sanchez RC	1.00
149	Jon Leicester RC	1.00
150	Roger Deago RC	1.00

Century Proofs
Stars (1-100): 2-4X
Century (101-150): 1-2X
Production 100 Sets

Decade Proofs
Production 10 Sets
No pricing due to scarcity.

Authentic Cuts
Quantity produced listed.

Autographs
NM/M
Common Auto.: 8.00
Some not priced due to scarcity.

#	Player	Price
1	Garret Anderson	15.00
6	Mark Grace/141	40.00
8	Matt Williams	10.00
10	Randy Johnson/50	60.00
14	Chipper Jones/50	50.00
14	Manny Ramirez/50	40.00
17	Barry Larkin/159	25.00
33	Ivan Rodriguez/50	35.00
38	Lance Berkman/75	20.00
39	Richard Hidalgo	8.00
40	Roy Oswalt/150	15.00
42	Mike Sweeney	8.00
50	A.J. Pierzynski	8.00
51	Torii Hunter	15.00
53	Jose Vidro	6.00
54	Vladimir Guerrero	20.00
55	Cliff Floyd	8.00
56	David Cone/35	15.00
58	Roberto Alomar/50	30.00
65	Nick Johnson	10.00
67	Barry Zito/150	10.00
68	Eric Chavez	10.00
69	Mark Mulder/50	15.00
72	Bobby Abreu	15.00
78	Kenny Lofton/229	10.00
80	Ryan Klesko/100	10.00
81	Andres Galarraga	8.00
83	Rich Aurilia/122	8.00
84	Edgar Martinez	15.00
89	Scott Rolen/200	20.00
90	So Taguchi/220	10.00
95	Mark Teixeira/150	20.00
100	Vernon Wells	10.00
102	Jose Contreras	20.00
141	Dontrelle Willis/150	20.00

Century
NM/M
Common Auto: 15.00
Production 100 Sets
Decades: No Pricing
Production 10 Sets

#	Player	Price
1	Garret Anderson	15.00
7	Matt Williams	15.00
27	Barry Larkin	30.00
39	Richard Hidalgo	15.00
42	Mike Sweeney	15.00
50	A.J. Pierzynski	15.00
51	Torii Hunter	20.00
53	Jose Vidro	15.00
54	Vladimir Guerrero	30.00
55	Cliff Floyd	15.00
62	Drew Henson	15.00
65	Nick Johnson	15.00
69	Mark Mulder	25.00
72	Bobby Abreu	20.00
78	Kenny Lofton	15.00
81	Andres Galarraga	15.00
84	Edgar Martinez	25.00
89	Scott Rolen	30.00
90	So Taguchi	15.00
100	Vernon Wells	15.00
102	Jose Contreras	25.00

Century Notations
NM/M
Production 100 Sets
Decade Notations: No Pricing
Production 10 Sets

#	Player	Price
1	Garret Anderson	20.00
7	Matt Williams	15.00
50	A.J. Pierzynski	15.00
68	Eric Chavez	15.00
78	Kenny Lofton	15.00
84	Edgar Martinez	25.00

INKredible - Three
NM/M
Production 50 Sets
1 Barry Zito, Mark Mulder, Tim Hudson — 300.00
2 Andruw Jones, Chipper Jones, Greg Maddux — 325.00
3 Ernie Banks, Kerry Wood, Mark Prior — 300.00
4 Harmon Killebrew, Kirby Puckett, Torii Hunter — 175.00
5 Javier Vazquez, Jose Vidro, Vladimir Guerrero — 90.00

INKredible - Four
NM/M
Production 25 Sets
Limited pricing due to scarcity.
4 Brooks Robinson, Cal Ripken Jr., Frank Robinson, Jim Palmer — 500.00
6 Bo Jackson, Carlos Beltran, George Brett, Mike Sweeney — 225.00
7 Curt Schilling, Junior Spivey, Mark Grace, Randy Johnson — 475.00
10 Joe Carter, Roberto Alomar, Ryan Klesko, Tony Gwynn — 200.00

INKredible - Six
NM/M
Production 10 Sets
Limited pricing due to scarcity.
3 Andre Dawson, Ernie Banks, Kerry Wood, Mark Grace, Mark Prior, Ryne Sandberg — 1,500
5 Alex Rodriguez, Don Mattingly, George Brett, Hideo Nomo, Nolan Ryan, Roger Clemens — 3,100

Legends of Summer
NM/M
Complete Set (40): 125.00
Common Player: 3.00
Production 250 Sets
Century: 1X
Production 100 Sets
Decades: No Pricing
Production 10 Sets

#	Player	Price
1	Al Kaline	5.00
2	Alan Trammell	3.00
3	Andre Dawson	3.00
4	Babe Ruth	10.00
5	Billy Williams	3.00
6	Bo Jackson	4.00
7	Bob Feller	3.00
8	Bobby Doerr	3.00
9	Brooks Robinson	5.00
10	Dale Murphy	5.00
11	Dennis Eckersley	3.00
12	Don Mattingly	8.00
13	Duke Snider	3.00
14	Eric Davis	3.00
15	Frank Robinson	3.00
16	Fred Lynn	3.00
17	Gary Carter	3.00
18	Harmon Killebrew	5.00
19	Jack Morris	3.00
20	Jim Palmer	3.00
21	Jim Abbott	3.00
22	Joe Morgan	3.00
23	Joe Torre	3.00
24	Johnny Bench	5.00
25	Jose Canseco	3.00
26	Kirby Puckett	5.00
27	Lenny Dykstra	3.00
28	Lou Brock	3.00
29	Ralph Kiner	3.00
30	Mike Schmidt	6.00
31	Nolan Ryan	10.00
32	Nolan Ryan	10.00
33	Orel Hershiser	3.00
34	Phil Rizzuto	3.00
35	Orlando Cepeda	3.00
36	Ryne Sandberg	3.00
37	Stan Musial	6.00
38	Steve Garvey	3.00
39	Tony Perez	3.00
40	Ty Cobb	6.00

Legends of Summer Auto.
NM/M
Common Autograph: 8.00

#	Player	Price
1	Al Kaline	20.00
2	Alan Trammell	10.00
3	Andre Dawson	10.00
5	Billy Williams	8.00
6	Bo Jackson/100	50.00
7	Bob Feller	15.00
8	Bobby Doerr	15.00
9	Brooks Robinson	25.00
10	Dale Murphy/75	40.00
11	Dennis Eckersley	10.00
12	Don Mattingly/50	75.00
13	Duke Snider/225	20.00
14	Eric Davis	8.00
15	Frank Robinson	10.00
16	Fred Lynn	8.00
17	Gary Carter	10.00
18	Harmon Killebrew/171	20.00
19	Jack Morris	8.00
20	Jim Palmer	8.00
21	Jim Abbott	8.00
22	Joe Morgan/125	10.00
23	Joe Torre	10.00
24	Johnny Bench/75	30.00
25	Jose Canseco/75	30.00
26	Kirby Puckett/75	35.00
27	Lenny Dykstra	10.00
28	Lou Brock	15.00
29	Ralph Kiner	10.00
30	Mike Schmidt/75	60.00
31	Nolan Ryan/75	110.00
33	Orel Hershiser	20.00
34	Phil Rizzuto	15.00
35	Orlando Cepeda	15.00
36	Ryne Sandberg/75	60.00
37	Stan Musial/200	40.00
38	Steve Garvey	10.00
39	Tony Perez	10.00

Legends of Summer Century
NM/M
Production 100 Sets
Decades: No Pricing
Production 10 Sets

#	Player	Price
1	Al Kaline	25.00
2	Alan Trammell	20.00
3	Andre Dawson	15.00
5	Billy Williams	15.00
6	Bo Jackson	50.00
7	Bob Feller	25.00
8	Bobby Doerr	20.00
9	Brooks Robinson	30.00
11	Dennis Eckersley	15.00
12	Don Mattingly	65.00
14	Eric Davis	15.00
15	Frank Robinson	15.00
16	Fred Lynn	15.00
17	Gary Carter	20.00
19	Jack Morris	15.00
20	Jim Palmer	20.00
21	Jim Abbott	15.00
23	Joe Torre	15.00
27	Lenny Dykstra	15.00
28	Lou Brock	25.00
29	Ralph Kiner	15.00
33	Orel Hershiser	60.00
34	Phil Rizzuto	30.00
35	Orlando Cepeda	20.00
36	Ryne Sandberg	65.00
37	Stan Musial	60.00
38	Steve Garvey	15.00
39	Tony Perez	15.00

Legends of Summer Notations
NM/M
Common Autograph: 8.00

#	Player	Price
1	Al Kaline/200	20.00
2	Alan Trammell/250	10.00
3	Andre Dawson/165	10.00
3	Andre Dawson/250	10.00
5	Billy Williams/250	8.00
5	Billy Williams/150	8.00
7	Bob Feller/250	15.00
7	Bob Feller/200	15.00
8	Bobby Doerr/250	10.00
9	Brooks Robinson/150	20.00
9	Brooks Robinson/50	40.00
10	Dale Murphy/50	45.00
11	Dennis Eckersley/250	10.00
14	Eric Davis/250	8.00
14	Eric Davis/150	8.00
14	Eric Davis/50	8.00
16	Fred Lynn/240	10.00
16	Fred Lynn/250	10.00
18	Harmon Killebrew/75	10.00
18	Harmon Killebrew/50	40.00
18	Harmon Killebrew/125	30.00
19	Jack Morris/250	10.00
20	Jim Palmer/190	10.00
20	Jim Palmer/140	10.00
20	Jim Palmer/50	20.00
21	Jim Abbott/200	10.00
21	Jim Abbott/100	15.00
21	Jim Abbott/75	20.00
27	Lenny Dykstra/226	10.00
28	Lou Brock/50	35.00
29	Ralph Kiner/200	10.00
29	Ralph Kiner/100	10.00
29	Ralph Kiner/150	10.00
35	Orlando Cepeda/250	10.00
35	Orlando Cepeda/40	25.00
38	Steve Garvey/150	10.00
38	Steve Garvey/250	10.00
38	Steve Garvey/75	15.00
39	Tony Perez/250	10.00
39	Tony Perez/125	15.00
39	Tony Perez/75	20.00
39	Tony Perez/175	10.00

Notable Nicknames
NM/M
Complete Set (20): 75.00
Common Player: 3.00
Production 750 Sets
Century: 1-1.5X
Production 100 Sets
Decade: No Pricing
Production 10 Sets

#	Player	Price
1	Andre Dawson	3.00
2	Torii Hunter	3.00
3	Brooks Robinson	5.00
4	Carlton Fisk	3.00
5	Mike Mussina	4.00
6	Don Mattingly	8.00
7	Duke Snider	4.00
8	Eric Davis	3.00
9	Frank Thomas	4.00
10	Randy Johnson	5.00
11	Lenny Dykstra	3.00
12	Ivan Rodriguez	3.00
13	Nolan Ryan	10.00
14	Phil Rizzuto	3.00
15	Reggie Jackson	4.00
16	Roger Clemens	8.00
17	Ryne Sandberg	8.00
18	Stan Musial	6.00
19	Luis Gonzalez	3.00
20	Will Clark	4.00

Notable Nicknames Auto.
NM/M
Quantity produced listed.
Decades: No Pricing
Production 10 Sets

#	Player	Price
1	Andre "The Hawk" Dawson/100	30.00
2	Torii "Spiderman" Hunter/100	30.00
3	Brooks "Hoover" Robinson	60.00
4	Carlton "Pudge" Fisk/100	50.00
5	Mike "Moose" Mussina/100	80.00
6	Don "Donnie Baseball" Mattingly/100	100.00
7	Duke "Duke of Flatbush" Snider/100	60.00
8	Eric "The Red" Davis/40	50.00
9	Frank "The Big Hurt" Thomas/100	60.00
10	Randy "Big Unit" Johnson/100	100.00
11	Lenny "Nails" Dykstra/100	20.00
12	Ivan "Pudge" Rodriguez/75	50.00
14	Phil "Scooter" Rizzuto/100	50.00
15	Reggie "Mr. October" Jackson/100	60.00
16	Roger "The Rocket" Clemens/100	150.00
17	Ryne "Ryno" Sandberg/100	75.00
18	Stan "The Man" Musial/100	85.00
19	Luis "Gonzo" Gonzalez/100	25.00
20	Will "The Thrill" Clark/100	60.00

Notations
NM/M
Varying quantities produced.
Many not priced due to scarcity.

#	Player	Price
1	Garret Anderson/75	20.00
7	Matt Williams/250	10.00
7	Matt Williams/50	20.00
45	Kazuhisa Ishii/35	35.00
50	A.J. Pierzynski/200	10.00
53	Jose Vidro/40	15.00
62	Drew Henson/73	20.00
68	Eric Chavez/50	20.00
78	Kenny Lofton/150	10.00
80	Ryan Klesko/75	20.00
83	Rich Aurilia/61	15.00
84	Edgar Martinez/250	10.00
84	Edgar Martinez/60	20.00
100	Vernon Wells/75	15.00

Players Collection Auto.
NM/M
Quantity produced listed.

Player	Price
Roberto Alomar/75	30.00
Adrian Beltre/104	30.00
Lance Berkman/50	20.00
Craig Biggio/26	35.00
Joe Borchard/53	10.00
J.D. Drew/52	15.00
Jim Edmonds/52	25.00
Todd Helton/50	40.00
Jason Jennings/49	15.00
Chipper Jones/51	50.00
Paul LoDuca/227	20.00
Magglio Ordonez/102	20.00
Mark Prior/27	100.00
Ivan Rodriguez/52	35.00
Richie Sexson/50	20.00
Matt Williams/482	8.00

Signature Cuts
NM/M
Some not priced due to scarcity.

Decades
No Pricing
Production 10 Sets

#	Player	Price
8	Randy Johnson/40	60.00
33	Ivan Rodriguez/122	30.00
54	Vladimir Guerrero/34	35.00
58	Roberto Alomar/100	40.00
64	Mike Mussina/82	40.00
73	Jim Thome/127	30.00
80	Ryan Klesko/35	20.00
81	Andres Galarraga/51	20.00
89	Scott Rolen/36	40.00

Team Trademarks
NM/M
Complete Set (40): 150.00
Common Player: 3.00
Production 100 Sets
Century: 1X
Production 100 Sets
Decade: No Pricing
Production 10 Sets

#	Player	Price
1	Adam Dunn	3.00
2	Andre Dawson	3.00
3	Babe Ruth	10.00
4	Barry Bonds	10.00
5	Brooks Robinson	4.00
6	Cal Ripken Jr.	10.00
7	Derek Jeter	8.00
8	Don Mattingly	3.00
9	Frank Robinson	3.00
10	Fred Lynn	3.00
11	Gary Carter	3.00
12	George Brett	5.00
13	Greg Maddux	5.00
14	Ichiro Suzuki	6.00
15	Jim Palmer	3.00
16	Jose Contreras	3.00
17	Kerry Wood	4.00
18	Lou Gehrig	8.00
19	Magglio Ordonez	3.00
20	Mark Grace	3.00
21	Mike Schmidt	8.00
22	Nolan Ryan	10.00
23	Nolan Ryan	10.00
24	Reggie Jackson	4.00
25	Rickey Henderson	3.00
26	Roberto Clemente	6.00
27	Roger Clemens	6.00
28	Roger Clemens	6.00
29	Ryne Sandberg	6.00
30	Sammy Sosa	6.00
31	Stan Musial	6.00
32	Steve Carlton	3.00
33	Tim Hudson	3.00
34	Tom Glavine	3.00
35	Tom Seaver	4.00
36	Tony Gwynn	3.00
37	Torii Hunter	3.00
38	Ty Cobb	3.00
39	Vladimir Guerrero	4.00
40	Will Clark	3.00

Team Trademarks Century
NM/M
Production 100 Sets
Decade: No Pricing
Production 10 Sets

#	Player	Price
2	Andre Dawson	15.00
5	Brooks Robinson	30.00
9	Frank Robinson	15.00
10	Fred Lynn	15.00
11	Gary Carter	15.00
15	Jim Palmer	15.00
16	Jose Contreras	15.00
20	Mark Grace	60.00
29	Ryne Sandberg	65.00
31	Stan Musial	65.00
32	Steve Carlton	25.00
34	Tom Glavine	25.00
37	Steve Hunter	15.00
39	Vladimir Guerrero	25.00

Team Trademarks Autograph

NM/M
Quantity produced listed.

#	Player	Price
1	Adam Dunn/50	35.00
2	Andre Dawson/250	10.00
5	Brooks Robinson/250	20.00
6	Cal Ripken Jr./50	200.00
8	Don Mattingly/75	85.00
10	Fred Lynn/250	10.00
11	Gary Carter/250	10.00
12	George Brett/50	100.00
13	Greg Maddux/50	85.00
16	Jose Contreras/250	15.00
17	Kerry Wood/50	40.00
19	Magglio Ordonez/75	15.00
20	Mark Grace/25	90.00
22	Nolan Ryan/50	110.00
24	Reggie Jackson/75	25.00
26	Rickey Henderson/50	110.00
27	Roger Clemens/50	110.00
28	Roger Clemens/50	110.00
29	Ryne Sandberg/100	60.00
31	Stan Musial/200	50.00
32	Steve Carlton/150	20.00
33	Tim Hudson/100	35.00
34	Tom Glavine/50	35.00
35	Tom Seaver/50	35.00

36 Tony Gwynn/50 60.00
37 Torii Hunter/250 10.00
39 Vladimir Guerrero/250 20.00
40 Will Clark/125 30.00

Team Trademarks Notations
NM/M
Quantity produced listed.
2 Andre Dawson/250 10.00
2 Andre Dawson/150 10.00
5 Brooks Robinson/75 35.00
5 Brooks Robinson/125 20.00
10 Fred Lynn/50 20.00
15 Jim Palmer/32 25.00
15 Jim Palmer/128 15.00
15 Jim Palmer/150 15.00
29 Ryne Sandberg/40 80.00
29 Ryne Sandberg/50 75.00
32 Steve Carlton/50 35.00
33 Tim Hudson/50 45.00
40 Will Clark/52 60.00

2003 Donruss Studio Samples

Each August 2003 issue of Beckett Baseball Card Monthly included a sample Donruss Studio card rubber-cemented inside. The cards differ from the issued version only in the appearance on back of a (usually) silver-foil "SAMPLE" notation. Some cards were produced with the back overprint in gold-foil in much more limited quantities. The number of different players' cards involved in the promotion is unknown.

NM/M
Common Player: .10
Stars: 1.5X
Gold: 20X

2003 Donruss Studio

NM/M
Complete Set (200): 35.00
Common Player: .25
Pack (6): 4.00
Box (20): 60.00
1 Darin Erstad .40
2 David Eckstein .25
3 Garret Anderson .50
4 Jarrod Washburn .25
5 Tim Salmon .50
6 Troy Glaus .50
7 Jay Gibbons .25
8 Melvin Mora .25
9 Rodrigo Lopez .25
10 Tony Batista .25
11 Freddy Sanchez .25
12 Derek Lowe .25
13 Johnny Damon .40
14 Manny Ramirez .50
15 Nomar Garciaparra .75
16 Pedro J. Martinez 1.00
17 Rickey Henderson .50
18 Shea Hillenbrand .25
19 Carlos Lee .25
20 Frank Thomas .75
21 Magglio Ordonez .40
22 Bartolo Colon .25
23 Paul Konerko .25
24 Josh Stewart RC .50
25 C.C. Sabathia .25
26 Jeremy Guthrie .25
27 Ellis Burks .25
28 Omar Vizquel .40
29 Victor Martinez .25
30 Cliff Lee .25

31 Jhonny Peralta .50
32 Brian Tallet .25
33 Bobby Higginson .25
34 Carlos Pena .25
35 Nook Logan RC .25
36 Steve Sparks .25
37 Travis Chapman .25
38 Carlos Beltran .75
39 Joe Randa .25
40 Mike Sweeney .25
41 Jimmy Gobble .25
42 Michael Tucker .25
43 Runelvys Hernandez .25
44 Brad Radke .25
45 Corey Koskie .25
46 Cristian Guzman .25
47 J.C. Romero .25
48 Doug Mientkiewicz .25
49 Lew Ford RC 1.50
50 Jacque Jones .40
51 Torii Hunter .50
52 Alfonso Soriano .75
53 Nick Johnson .25
54 Bernie Williams .50
55 Jose Contreras RC 1.50
56 Derek Jeter 3.00
57 Jason Giambi .50
58 Brandon Claussen .25
59 Jorge Posada .50
60 Mike Mussina .50
61 Roger Clemens 2.00
62 Hideki Matsui RC 5.00
63 Barry Zito .50
64 Adam Morrissey .25
65 Eric Chavez .40
66 Jermaine Dye .25
67 Mark Mulder .40
68 Miguel Tejada .50
69 Joe Valentine RC .25
70 Tim Hudson .50
71 Bret Boone .40
72 Chris Snelling .25
73 Edgar Martinez .25
74 Freddy Garcia .25
75 Ichiro Suzuki 2.00
76 Jamie Moyer .25
77 John Olerud .40
78 Kazuhiro Sasaki .25
79 Aubrey Huff .25
80 Joe Kennedy .25
81 Dewon Brazelton .25
82 Pete LaForest RC .25
83 Alex Rodriguez 2.50
84 Chan Ho Park .25
85 Hank Blalock .75
86 Juan Gonzalez .75
87 Kevin Mench .25
88 Rafael Palmeiro .75
89 Carlos Delgado .50
90 Eric Hinske .25
91 Josh Phelps .25
92 Roy Halladay .40
93 Shannon Stewart .25
94 Vernon Wells .40
95 Vinnie Chulk .25
96 Curt Schilling .75
97 Junior Spivey .25
98 Luis Gonzalez .50
99 Mark Grace .50
100 Randy Johnson 1.00
101 Andruw Jones .75
102 Chipper Jones 1.00
103 Gary Sheffield .50
104 Greg Maddux 1.50
105 John Smoltz .50
106 Mike Hampton .25
107 Adam LaRoche .50
108 Michael Hessman RC .50
109 Corey Patterson .40
110 Kerry Wood 1.00
111 Mark Prior 1.00
112 Moises Alou .50
113 Sammy Sosa 1.50
114 Adam Dunn .75
115 Austin Kearns .40
116 Barry Larkin .50
117 Ken Griffey Jr. 1.50
118 Sean Casey .25
119 Jason Jennings .25
120 Jay Payton .25
121 Larry Walker .40
122 Todd Helton .75
123 Jeff Baker .25
124 Clint Barmes RC 1.00
125 Ivan Rodriguez .75
126 Josh Beckett .50
127 Juan Encarnacion .25
128 Mike Lowell .50
129 Craig Biggio .40
130 Jason Lane .25
131 Jeff Bagwell .75
132 Lance Berkman .50
133 Roy Oswalt .40
134 Jeff Kent .25
135 Hideo Nomo .50
136 Kazuhisa Ishii .25
137 Kevin Brown .25
138 Odalis Perez .25
139 Paul LoDuca .25
140 Shawn Green .50
141 Adrian Beltre .25
142 Ben Sheets .40
143 Bill Hall .25
144 Jeffrey Hammonds .25
145 Richie Sexson .50
146 Termmel Sledge RC .75
147 Brad Wilkerson .25
148 Javier Vazquez .25

149 Jose Vidro .25
150 Michael Barrett .25
151 Vladimir Guerrero .75
152 Al Leiter .25
153 Mike Piazza 2.00
154 Mo Vaughn .25
155 Cliff Floyd .25
156 Roberto Alomar .50
157 Roger Cedeno .25
158 Tom Glavine .50
159 Prentice Redman RC .50
160 Bobby Abreu .25
161 Jimmy Rollins .40
162 Mike Lieberthal .25
163 Pat Burrell .50
164 Vicente Padilla .25
165 Jim Thome .75
166 Kevin Millwood .40
167 Aramis Ramirez .25
168 Brian Giles .40
169 Jason Kendall .25
170 Josh Fogg .25
171 Kip Wells .25
172 Jose Castillo .25
173 Mark Kotsay .25
174 Oliver Perez .25
175 Phil Nevin .40
176 Ryan Klesko .40
177 Sean Burroughs .25
178 Brian Lawrence .25
179 Shane Victorino RC .25
180 Barry Bonds 3.00
181 Benito Santiago .25
182 Ray Durham .25
183 Rich Aurilia .25
184 Damian Moss .25
185 Albert Pujols 2.00
186 J.D. Drew .25
187 Jim Edmonds .50
188 Matt Morris .40
189 Tino Martinez .25
190 Scott Rolen .75
191 Troy Glaus, Tim Salmon .25
192 Sean Casey, Corky Miller .25
193 Carlos Lee, Frank Thomas .25
194 Lance Berkman, Jeff Kent .25
195 Jose Contreras, Mariano Rivera 1.00
196 Alex Rodriguez, Juan Gonzalez 1.00
197 Andy Pettitte, David Wells .25
198 Shawn Green, Dave Roberts .25
199 Mike Lieberthal, Jimmy Rollins .40
200 Mike Mussina, Hideki Matsui 2.00

Proofs
NM/M
Stars (1-200): 4-8X
Rookies (1-200): 2-3X
Production 100 Sets

Private Signings
NM/M
7 Jay Gibbons/100 10.00
11 Freddy Sanchez/150 25.00
24 Josh Stewart/100 8.00
26 Jeremy Guthrie/125 8.00
30 Victor Martinez/200 20.00
31 Cliff Lee/150 15.00
35 Jhonny Peralta/200 20.00
36 Nook Logan/100 8.00
37 Travis Chapman/150 8.00
41 Jimmy Gobble/200 8.00
47 J.C. Romero/200 8.00
49 Lew Ford/200 15.00
51 Torii Hunter/50 10.00
53 Nick Johnson/100 10.00
55 Jose Contreras/100 10.00
58 Brandon Claussen/200 10.00
69 Joe Valentine/200 8.00
79 Aubrey Huff/50 10.00
81 Dewon Brazelton/75 10.00
82 Pete LaForest/200 10.00
85 Hank Blalock/200 20.00
87 Kevin Mench/100 8.00
90 Eric Hinske/125 8.00
95 Vinnie Chulk/100 8.00
97 Junior Spivey/50 10.00
107 Adam LaRoche/100 15.00
108 Michael Hessman/200 8.00
111 Mark Prior/50 20.00
119 Jason Jennings/50 10.00
123 Jeff Baker/75 10.00
124 Clint Barmes/200 10.00
130 Jason Lane/100 15.00
139 Paul LoDuca/75 15.00
143 Bill Hall/50 10.00
146 Termmel Sledge/125 10.00
149 Jose Vidro/50 15.00
159 Prentice Redman/200 10.00
160 Bobby Abreu/50 20.00
171 Kip Wells/100 8.00
172 Jose Castillo/175 8.00
178 Brian Lawrence/100 10.00
179 Shane Victorino/100 10.00
201 Adam Loewen/100 20.00
202 Jeremy Bonderman/50 30.00
203 Brandon Webb/100 50.00
204 Chien-Ming Wang/50 250.00
206 Ryan Wagner/100 10.00
207 Hong-Chih Kuo/25 175.00
208 Dan Haren/100 25.00
210 Ramon Nivar/100 10.00

Big League Challenge
NM/M
Complete Set (50): 125.00
Common Player: 1.50

Production 400 Sets
Proofs 4-8X
Production 25 Sets
1 Jose Canseco 2.00
2 Magglio Ordonez 1.50
3 Alex Rodriguez 5.00
4 Lance Berkman 1.50
5 Rafael Palmeiro 3.00
6 Nomar Garciaparra 5.00
7 Nomar Garciaparra 5.00
8 Nomar Garciaparra 5.00
9 Troy Glaus 2.00
10 Mark McGwire 6.00
11 Mark McGwire 6.00
12 Mark McGwire 6.00
13 Jim Thome 3.00
14 Chipper Jones 3.00
15 Shawn Green 1.50
16 Alex Rodriguez 5.00
17 Alex Rodriguez 5.00
18 Alex Rodriguez 5.00
19 Alex Rodriguez 5.00
20 Jason Giambi 2.00
21 Pat Burrell 1.50
22 Mike Piazza 4.00
23 Mike Piazza 4.00
24 Mike Piazza 4.00
25 Frank Thomas 2.00
26 Rafael Palmeiro 2.00
27 Todd Helton 2.00
28 Jose Canseco 2.00
29 Albert Pujols 5.00
30 Troy Glaus 2.00
31 Barry Bonds 6.00
32 Barry Bonds 6.00
33 Barry Bonds 6.00
34 Todd Helton 3.00
35 Rafael Palmeiro 3.00
36 Jim Thome 3.00
37 Ozzie Smith 3.00
38 Troy Glaus 2.00
39 Shawn Green 1.50
40 Barry Bonds 6.00
41 Barry Bonds 6.00
42 Barry Bonds 6.00
43 Magglio Ordonez 1.50
44 Alex Rodriguez 5.00
45 Alex Rodriguez 5.00
46 Alex Rodriguez 5.00
47 Lance Berkman 1.50
48 Rafael Palmeiro 3.00
49 Pat Burrell 1.50
50 Albert Pujols 5.00

Big League Challenge Materials
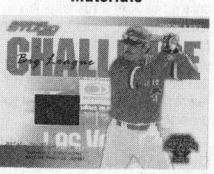
NM/M
Common Player: 4.00
Inserted 1:20
2 Magglio Ordonez/Jsy 4.00
3 Alex Rodriguez/Jsy 10.00
4 Lance Berkman/Jsy 4.00
5 Shawn Green/Jsy 4.00
29 Albert Pujols/Jsy 15.00
36 Jim Thome/Jsy 6.00
39 Shawn Green/Pants 4.00
40 Barry Bonds/Base 10.00
41 Barry Bonds/Base 10.00
42 Barry Bonds/Base 10.00
43 Magglio Ordonez/Jsy 4.00
45 Alex Rodriguez/Jsy 10.00
47 Lance Berkman/Pants 10.00
48 Rafael Palmeiro/Jsy 6.00
50 Albert Pujols/Pants 10.00

Big League Challenge Prime Material
NM/M
Common Player: 10.00
2 Magglio Ordonez/100 10.00
3 Alex Rodriguez/100 25.00
15 Shawn Green/50 15.00
29 Albert Pujols/100 25.00
36 Jim Thome/50 20.00
45 Alex Rodriguez/100 25.00
48 Rafael Palmeiro/100 15.00

Enshrinement

NM/M
Complete Set (50): 180.00
Common Player: 3.00
Production 750 Sets
Proofs 5-10X
Production 20 or 21
1 Gary Carter 4.00
2 Ozzie Smith 10.00

3 Kirby Puckett 6.00
4 Carlton Fisk 4.00
5 Tony Perez 3.00
6 Nolan Ryan 15.00
7 George Brett 12.00
8 Robin Yount 10.00
9 Orlando Cepeda 3.00
10 Phil Niekro 3.00
11 Mike Schmidt 10.00
12 Richie Ashburn 6.00
13 Steve Carlton 4.00
14 Phil Rizzuto 4.00
15 Reggie Jackson 6.00
16 Tom Seaver 5.00
17 Rollie Fingers 3.00
18 Rod Carew 5.00
19 Gaylord Perry 3.00
20 Fergie Jenkins 3.00
21 Jim Palmer 3.00
22 Joe Morgan 3.00
23 Johnny Bench 6.00
24 Willie Stargell 3.00
25 Billy Williams 3.00
26 Jim "Catfish" Hunter 3.00
27 Willie McCovey 3.00
28 Bobby Doerr 3.00
29 Lou Brock 3.00
30 Enos Slaughter 3.00
31 Hoyt Wilhelm 3.00
32 Harmon Killebrew 3.00
33 Pee Wee Reese 3.00
34 Luis Aparicio 3.00
35 Brooks Robinson 3.00
36 Juan Marichal 4.00
37 Frank Robinson 5.00
38 Bob Gibson 4.00
39 Al Kaline 6.00
40 Duke Snider 6.00
41 Eddie Mathews 5.00
42 Robin Roberts 3.00
43 Ralph Kiner 3.00
44 Whitey Ford 5.00
45 Roberto Clemente 10.00
46 Warren Spahn 5.00
47 Yogi Berra 5.00
48 Early Wynn 3.00
49 Stan Musial 6.00
50 Bob Feller 4.00

Enshrinement Autographs
NM/M
Varying quantities produced.
1 Gary Carter/50 30.00
5 Tony Perez/50 50.00
9 Orlando Cepeda/50 25.00
10 Phil Niekro/50 20.00
13 Steve Carlton/50 40.00
14 Phil Rizzuto/15 50.00
21 Fergie Jenkins/50 20.00
21 Jim Palmer/25 35.00
22 Joe Morgan/10 50.00
28 Bobby Doerr/100 50.00
31 Hoyt Wilhelm/50 25.00
34 Luis Aparicio/100 15.00
35 Brooks Robinson/65 65.00
43 Frank Robinson/25 50.00
43 Ralph Kiner/25 40.00
50 Bob Feller/100 25.00

Leather & Lumber
NM/M
Common Player: 5.00
1 Adam Dunn/400 10.00
2 Alex Rodriguez/250 12.00
4 Alfonso Soriano/250 10.00
4 Andruw Jones/400 8.00
4 Austin Kearns/400 8.00
7 Chipper Jones/400 10.00
9 Derek Jeter/100 35.00
9 Don Mattingly/100 40.00
10 Edgar Martinez 10.00
11 Frank Thomas/400 8.00
11 Fred McGriff/400 8.00
12 Greg Maddux/150 15.00
14 Hideki Matsui/Ball/100 40.00
14 Hideo Nomo/150 15.00
16 Ichiro Suzuki/Ball/100 40.00
17 Ivan Rodriguez/250 8.00
18 Jason Giambi/400 8.00
19 Jeff Bagwell/400 8.00
21 Jim Thome/400 10.00
23 Juan Gonzalez/400 8.00
23 Kerry Wood/250 10.00
25 Kirby Puckett/100 25.00
25 Lance Berkman/400 5.00
27 Magglio Ordonez/400 5.00
27 Manny Ramirez/250 8.00
27 Mark Prior/400 8.00
29 Miguel Tejada/200 5.00
30 Mike Piazza/400 10.00
31 Mike Schmidt/200 25.00
32 Nomar Garciaparra/400 15.00
34 Pat Burrell/400 8.00
34 Pedro Martinez/150 10.00
37 Randy Johnson/250 10.00
37 Rickey Henderson/175 8.00
39 Sammy Sosa/300 10.00
39 Shawn Green/400 5.00
40 Vladimir Guerrero/400 8.00

Leather & Lumber Dual
NM/M
Common Player:
Those without bat or ball are noted.
2 Adam Dunn/50 25.00
3 Alex Rodriguez/50 30.00
4 Andruw Jones/50 25.00
4 Austin Kearns/Shoe/25 25.00
7 Chipper Jones/25 45.00

8 Don Mattingly/25 80.00
10 Frank Thomas/50 30.00
13 Greg Maddux/Shoe/50 35.00
17 Ivan Rodriguez/25 25.00
19 Jeff Bagwell/25 35.00
23 Kerry Wood/50 25.00
24 Kirby Puckett/25 50.00
25 Lance Berkman/50 12.00
28 Mark Prior/Shoe/25 15.00
29 Miguel Tejada/25 15.00
33 Pat Burrell/25 20.00
36 Randy Johnson/25 40.00
38 Sammy Sosa/Shoe/50 60.00

Masterstrokes

NM/M
Complete Set (25): 50.00
Common Player: 1.00
Production 1,000 Sets
1 Adam Dunn 2.00
2 Albert Pujols 3.00
3 Alex Rodriguez 5.00
4 Alfonso Soriano 1.50
5 Andruw Jones 1.50
6 Chipper Jones 3.00
7 Derek Jeter 6.00
8 Greg Maddux 3.00
9 Hideki Matsui 8.00
10 Hideo Nomo 1.50
11 Ivan Rodriguez 1.50
12 Jason Giambi 1.50
13 Jeff Bagwell 2.00
14 Juan Gonzalez 1.50
15 Ken Griffey Jr. 3.00
16 Lance Berkman 1.00
17 Magglio Ordonez 1.00
18 Manny Ramirez 2.00
19 Mark Prior 2.00
20 Miguel Tejada 1.50
21 Mike Piazza 4.00
22 Nomar Garciaparra 2.00
23 Pat Burrell 1.50
24 Sammy Sosa 4.00
25 Vladimir Guerrero 2.00

Masterstrokes Artist's Proof
NM/M
Common Player: 15.00
Production 50 Sets
1 Adam Dunn 25.00
2 Albert Pujols 50.00
3 Alex Rodriguez 50.00
4 Alfonso Soriano 25.00
5 Andruw Jones 20.00
6 Chipper Jones 30.00
7 Derek Jeter 50.00
8 Greg Maddux 25.00
9 Hideki Matsui 75.00
10 Hideo Nomo 100.00
11 Ivan Rodriguez 20.00
12 Jason Giambi 15.00
13 Jeff Bagwell 25.00
14 Juan Gonzalez 25.00
15 Ken Griffey Jr. 30.00
16 Lance Berkman 15.00
17 Magglio Ordonez 15.00
18 Manny Ramirez 20.00
19 Mark Prior 20.00
20 Miguel Tejada 15.00
21 Mike Piazza 35.00
22 Nomar Garciaparra 40.00
23 Pat Burrell 15.00
24 Sammy Sosa 40.00
25 Vladimir Guerrero 25.00

Players Collection

NM/M
Common Player: 4.00

Production 300 Sets

#	Player	
1	Adam Dunn	8.00
2	Adrian Beltre	6.00
3	Alex Rodriguez	10.00
4	Alfonso Soriano	8.00
5	Andruw Jones	6.00
6	Andy Pettitte	4.00
7	Barry Larkin	6.00
8	Barry Zito	4.00
9	Ben Grieve	4.00
10	Bernie Williams	8.00
11	Cal Ripken Jr.	30.00
12	Carlos Delgado	5.00
13	C.C. Sabathia	4.00
14	Chipper Jones	10.00
15	Craig Biggio	6.00
16	Curt Schilling	6.00
17	Alex Rodriguez	10.00
18	Frank Thomas	8.00
19	Freddy Garcia	4.00
20	Jay Bell	4.00
21	Roger Clemens	12.00
22	Tony Gwynn	10.00
23	Ivan Rodriguez	6.00
24	Jason Giambi	6.00
25	Jason Jennings	4.00
26	Jay Payton	4.00
27	J.D. Drew	4.00
28	Jeff Bagwell	8.00
29	Jeromy Burnitz	4.00
30	Jim Edmonds	6.00
31	Jim Thome	8.00
32	Joe Borchard	4.00
33	Joe Mays	4.00
34	John Olerud	4.00
35	David Wells	4.00
36	Juan Gonzalez	6.00
37	Kazuhiro Sasaki	4.00
38	Chan Ho Park	4.00
39	Kerry Wood	8.00
40	Kevin Brown	5.00
41	Lance Berkman	4.00
42	Larry Walker	4.00
43	Bret Boone	4.00
44	Magglio Ordonez	4.00
45	Manny Ramirez	6.00
46	Mark Mulder	4.00
47	Mark Prior	8.00
48	Matt Williams	4.00
49	Miguel Tejada	6.00
50	Mike Piazza	10.00
51	Nomar Garciaparra	10.00
52	Doug Davis	4.00
53	Paul Konerko	4.00
54	Paul LoDuca	4.00
55	Pedro J. Martinez	8.00
56	Preston Wilson	4.00
57	Rafael Palmeiro	8.00
58	Marlon Byrd	4.00
59	Reggie Sanders	4.00
60	Richie Sexson	5.00
61	Rickey Henderson	10.00
62	Rickey Henderson	10.00
63	Robert Person	4.00
64	Jeff Bagwell	8.00
65	Roger Clemens	12.00
66	Roy Oswalt	4.00
67	Ryan Klesko	4.00
68	Sammy Sosa	12.00
69	Shawn Green	5.00
70	Steve Finley	4.00
71	Terrence Long	4.00
72	Tim Hudson	4.00
73	Toby Hall	4.00
74	Todd Helton	6.00
75	Travis Lee	4.00
76	Troy Glaus	6.00
77	Tsuyoshi Shinjo	4.00
78	Vernon Wells	4.00
79	Vladimir Guerrero	8.00
80	Wes Helms	4.00
81	Alex Rodriguez	10.00
82	Alfonso Soriano	8.00
83	Barry Larkin	6.00
84	Roberto Alomar	6.00
85	Ivan Rodriguez	6.00
86	Jason Giambi	6.00
87	Jeff Bagwell	8.00
88	Juan Gonzalez	6.00
89	Larry Walker	4.00
90	Luis Gonzalez	4.00
91	Magglio Ordonez	4.00
92	Manny Ramirez	8.00
93	Marlon Byrd	4.00
94	Mike Piazza	10.00
95	Pat Burrell	8.00
96	Todd Helton	6.00
97	Rickey Henderson	10.00
98	Andruw Jones	6.00
99	Craig Biggio	4.00
100	Mark Prior	8.00

Recollection Autographs 5x7

#	Player	NM/M
3	Sean Casey/125	15.00
5	Troy Glaus/82	20.00
8	Vladimir Guerrero/125	35.00
10	Todd Helton/55	35.00
12	Ryan Klesko/75	15.00
17	Ivan Rodriguez/50	40.00
19	C.C. Sabathia/50	20.00
20	Curt Schilling/75	30.00
23	Mike Sweeney/42	15.00
24	Miguel Tejada/44	30.00
26	Kerry Wood/200	25.00
27	Barry Zito/200	15.00

Spirit of the Game

	NM/M
Complete Set (35):	60.00

Common Player: 1.00
Production 1,250 Sets

#	Player	
1	Garret Anderson	1.00
2	Nomar Garciaparra	3.00
3	Pedro J. Martinez	2.00
4	Rickey Henderson	1.50
5	Magglio Ordonez	1.00
6	Torii Hunter	1.50
7	Alfonso Soriano	2.00
8	Jose Contreras	1.00
9	Derek Jeter	5.00
10	Jason Giambi	1.50
11	Roger Clemens	4.00
12	Hideki Matsui	6.00
13	Barry Zito	1.50
14	Ichiro Suzuki	3.00
15	Alex Rodriguez	4.00
16	Curt Schilling	2.00
17	Randy Johnson	2.00
18	Andruw Jones	1.50
19	Chipper Jones	3.00
20	Greg Maddux	3.00
21	Sammy Sosa	3.00
22	Adam Dunn	1.50
23	Ken Griffey Jr.	4.00
24	Todd Helton	2.00
25	Ivan Rodriguez	2.00
26	Lance Berkman	1.00
27	Hideo Nomo	1.50
28	Shawn Green	1.00
29	Vladimir Guerrero	2.00
30	Mike Piazza	3.00
31	Roberto Alomar	1.50
32	Jim Thome	2.00
33	Barry Bonds	5.00
34	Albert Pujols	3.00
35	Scott Rolen	2.00

Stars

	NM/M
Complete Set (50):	65.00
Common Player:	1.00
Inserted 1:5	
Golds:	3-5X

Production 100 Sets

#	Player	
1	Troy Glaus	1.50
2	Manny Ramirez	2.00
3	Nomar Garciaparra	3.00
4	Pedro J. Martinez	2.00
5	Rickey Henderson	1.50
6	Torii Hunter	1.50
7	Frank Thomas	1.50
8	Magglio Ordonez	1.00
9	Alfonso Soriano	2.00
10	Jose Contreras	1.00
11	Derek Jeter	5.00
12	Jason Giambi	1.50
13	Roger Clemens	4.00
14	Mike Mussina	1.50
15	Barry Zito	1.50
16	Miguel Tejada	1.50
17	Ichiro Suzuki	4.00
18	Alex Rodriguez	4.00
19	Juan Gonzalez	1.00
20	Rafael Palmeiro	2.00
21	Hank Blalock	2.00
22	Curt Schilling	2.00
23	Randy Johnson	2.00
24	Junior Spivey	1.00
25	Andruw Jones	1.50
26	Chipper Jones	2.00
27	Greg Maddux	3.00
28	Kerry Wood	2.00
29	Mark Prior	3.00
30	Sammy Sosa	3.00
31	Adam Dunn	2.00
32	Ken Griffey Jr.	3.00
33	Austin Kearns	1.50
34	Larry Walker	2.00
35	Todd Helton	2.00
36	Ivan Rodriguez	2.00
37	Jeff Bagwell	2.00
38	Lance Berkman	1.00
39	Craig Biggio	2.00
40	Hideo Nomo	1.50
41	Shawn Green	1.50
42	Vladimir Guerrero	2.00
43	Mike Piazza	3.00
44	Tom Glavine	1.50
45	Roberto Alomar	1.50
46	Pat Burrell	1.50
47	Jim Thome	2.00
48	Barry Bonds	5.00
49	Albert Pujols	4.00
50	Scott Rolen	2.00

2003 Donruss Team Heroes Samples

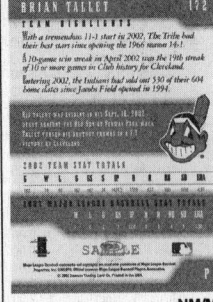

	NM/M
Common Player:	.10
Stars:	1.5-2X
Gold:	10X

2003 Donruss Team Heroes

Each issue of the February 2003 Beckett Baseball Card Monthly included a sample 2003 Donruss Team Heroes card rubber-cemented inside. The cards differ from the issued version only in the appearance on back of a (usually) silver-foil "SAMPLE" notation. Some cards were produced with the overprint in gold-foil, in much more limited quantities. The number of different players' cards involved in the promotion is unknown.

	NM/M
Complete Set (540):	55.00
Common Player:	.15
Pack (13):	1.50
Box (24):	25.00

#	Player	
1	Adam Kennedy	.15
2	Steve Green	.15
3	Rod Carew	.40
4	Alfredo Amezaga	.15
5	Reggie Jackson	.50
6	Jarrod Washburn	.15
7	Nolan Ryan	3.00
8	Tim Salmon	.25
9	Garret Anderson	.25
10	Darin Erstad	.25
11	Elpidio Guzman	.15
12	David Eckstein	.15
13	Troy Percival	.15
14	Troy Glaus	.75
15	Doug DeVore	.15
16	Tony Womack	.15
17	Matt Williams	.25
18	Junior Spivey	.15
19	Mark Grace	.50
20	Curt Schilling	.75
21	Erubiel Durazo	.15
22	Craig Counsell	.15
23	Byung-Hyun Kim	.15
24	Randy Johnson	1.00
25	Luis Gonzalez	.40
26	John Smoltz	.15
27	Tim Spooneybarger	.15
28	Dale Murphy	.50
29	Warren Spahn	.50
30	Jason Marquis	.15
31	Kevin Millwood	.15
32	Javy Lopez	.15
33	Vinny Castilla	.15
34	Julio Franco	.15
35	Trey Hodges	.15
36	Chipper Jones	1.50
37	Gary Sheffield	.25
38	Billy Sylvester	.15
39	Tom Glavine	.40
40	Rafael Furcal	.15
41	Cory Aldridge	.15
42	Greg Maddux	1.50
43	John Ennis	.15
44	Wes Helms	.15
45	Horacio Ramirez	.15
46	Derrick Lewis	.15
47	Marcus Giles	.15
48	Eddie Mathews	.75
49	Wilson Betemit	.15
50	Andruw Jones	.50
51	Josh Towers	.15
52	Ed Rogers	.15
53	Kris Foster	.15
54	Brooks Robinson	.75
55	Cal Ripken Jr.	3.00
56	Brian Roberts	.15
57	Luis Rivera	.15
58	Rodrigo Lopez	.15
59	Geronimo Gil	.15
60	Erik Bedard	.15
61	Jim Palmer	.40
62	Jay Gibbons	.15
63	Travis Driskill	.15
64	Larry Bigbie	.15
65	Eddie Murray	.40
66	Hoyt Wilhelm	.15
67	Bobby Doerr	.15
68	Pedro J. Martinez	1.00
69	Roger Clemens	1.50
70	Nomar Garciaparra	2.00
71	Trot Nixon	.15
72	Dennis Eckersley	.40
73	John Burkett	.15
74	Tim Wakefield	.15
75	Wade Boggs	.40
76	Cliff Floyd	.15
77	Casey Fossum	.15
78	Johnny Damon	.15
79	Fred Lynn	.15
80	Rickey Henderson	.40
81	Juan Diaz	.15
82	Manny Ramirez	.75
83	Carlton Fisk	.50
84	Jorge De La Rosa	.15
85	Shea Hillenbrand	.15
86	Derek Lowe	.15
87	Jason Varitek	.15
88	Carlos Baerga	.15
89	Freddy Sanchez	.15
90	Ugueth Urbina	.15
91	Rey Sanchez	.15
92	Josh Hancock	.15
93	Tony Clark	.15
94	Dustin Hermanson	.15
95	Ryne Sandberg	1.50
96	Fred McGriff	.25
97	Alex Gonzalez	.15
98	Mark Belhorn	.15
99	Fergie Jenkins	.25
100	Jon Lieber	.15
101	Francis Beltran	.15
102	Greg Maddux	1.50
103	Nate Frese	.15
104	Andre Dawson	.25
105	Carlos Zambrano	.15
106	Steve Smyth	.15
107	Ernie Banks	1.00
108	Will Ohman	.15
109	Kerry Wood	.50
110	Bobby Hill	.15
111	Moises Alou	.15
112	Hee Seop Choi	.15
113	Corey Patterson	.15
114	Sammy Sosa	1.50
115	Mark Prior	.50
116	Juan Cruz	.15
117	Ron Santo	.50
118	Billy Williams	.50
119	Antonio Alfonseca	.15
120	Matt Clement	.15
121	Carlton Fisk	.50
122	Joe Crede	.15
123	Magglio Ordonez	.40
124	Frank Thomas	.75
125	Joe Borchard	.15
126	Royce Clayton	.15
127	Luis Aparicio	.15
128	Willie Harris	.15
129	Kyle Kane	.15
130	Paul Konerko	.25
131	Matt Ginter	.15
132	Carlos Lee	.15
133	Mark Buehrle	.15
134	Adam Dunn	.75
135	Eric Davis	.15
136	Johnny Bench	1.00
137	Joe Morgan	.25
138	Austin Kearns	.40
139	Barry Larkin	.40
140	Ken Griffey Jr.	2.00
141	Luis Pineda	.15
142	Corky Miller	.15
143	Brandon Larson	.15
144	Wily Mo Pena	.15
145	Lance Davis	.15
146	Tom Seaver	1.00
147	Luke Hudson	.15
148	Sean Casey	.15
149	Tony Perez	.15
150	Todd Walker	.15
151	Aaron Boone	.15
152	Jose Rijo	.15
153	Ryan Dempster	.15
154	Danny Graves	.15
155	Matt Lawton	.15
156	Cliff Lee	.15
157	Ryan Drese	.15
158	Danys Baez	.15
159	Einar Diaz	.15
160	Milton Bradley	.15
161	Earl Snyder	.15
162	Ellis Burks	.15
163	Lou Boudreau	.15
164	Bob Feller	.75
165	Ricardo Rodriguez	.15
166	Victor Martinez	.15
167	Alex Herrera	.15
168	Omar Vizquel	.15
169	David Elder	.15
170	C.C. Sabathia	.15
171	Alex Escobar	.15
172	Brian Tallet	.15
173	Jim Thome	.75
174	Rene Reyes	.15
175	Juan Uribe	.15
176	Jason Romano	.15
177	Juan Pierre	.15
178	Jason Jennings	.15
179	Jose Ortiz	.15
180	Larry Walker	.25
181	Cam Esslinger	.15
182	Todd Helton	.50
183	Aaron Cook	.15
184	Jack Cust	.15
185	Jack Morris	.15
186	Mike Rivera	.15
187	Bobby Higginson	.15
188	Fernando Rodney	.15
189	Al Kaline	1.00
190	Carlos Pena	.15
191	Alan Trammell	.15
192	Mike Maroth	.15
193	Adam Pettyjohn	.15
194	David Espinosa	.15
195	Adam Bernero	.15
196	Franklyn German	.15
197	Robert Fick	.15
198	Andres Torres	.15
199	Luis Castillo	.15
200	Preston Wilson	.15
201	Pablo Ozuna	.15
202	Brad Penny	.15
203	Josh Beckett	.15
204	Charles Johnson	.15
205	Wilson Valdez	.15
206	A.J. Burnett	.15
207	Abraham Nunez	.15
208	Mike Lowell	.15
209	Jose Cueto	.15
210	Jeriome Robertson	.15
211	Jeff Bagwell	.75
212	Kirk Saarloos	.15
213	Craig Biggio	.25
214	Rodrigo Rosario	.15
215	Roy Oswalt	.15
216	John Buck	.15
217	Tim Redding	.15
218	Morgan Ensberg	.15
219	Richard Hidalgo	.15
220	Wade Miller	.15
221	Lance Berkman	.50
222	Raul Chavez	.15
223	Carlos Hernandez	.15
224	Greg Miller	.15
225	Tom Shearn	.15
226	Jason Lane	.15
227	Nolan Ryan	3.00
228	Billy Wagner	.15
229	Octavio Dotel	.15
230	Shane Reynolds	.15
231	Julio Lugo	.15
232	Daryle Ward	.15
233	Mike Sweeney	.15
234	Angel Berroa	.15
235	George Brett	1.50
236	Brad Voyles	.15
237	Brandon Berger	.15
238	Chad Durbin	.15
239	Alexis Gomez	.15
240	Jeremy Affeldt	.15
241	Bo Jackson	.75
242	Dee Brown	.15
243	Tony Cogan	.15
244	Carlos Beltran	.15
245	Joe Randa	.15
246	Pee Wee Reese	.25
247	Andy Ashby	.15
248	Cesar Izturis	.15
249	Duke Snider	.50
250	Mark Grudzielanek	.15
251	Chin-Feng Chen	.15
252	Brian Jordan	.15
253	Steve Garvey	.15
254	Odalis Perez	.15
255	Hideo Nomo	.50
256	Kevin Brown	.15
257	Eric Karros	.15
258	Joe Thurston	.15
259	Carlos Garcia	.15
260	Shawn Green	.40
261	Paul LoDuca	.15
262	Kazuhisa Ishii	.15
263	Victor Alvarez	.15
264	Eric Gagne	.15
265	Don Sutton	.15
266	Orel Hershiser	.15
267	Dave Roberts	.15
268	Adrian Beltre	.15
269	Don Drysdale	.50
270	Jackie Robinson	1.50
271	Tyler Houston	.15
272	Omar Daal	.15
273	Marquis Grissom	.15
274	Paul Quantrill	.15
275	Paul Molitor	.50
276	Jose Hernandez	.15
277	Takahito Nomura	.15
278	Nick Neugebauer	.15
279	Jose Mieses	.15
280	Richie Sexson	.40
281	Matt Childers	.15
282	Bill Hall	.15
283	Ben Sheets	.15
284	Brian Mallette	.15
285	Geoff Jenkins	.15
286	Robin Yount	.75
287	Jeff Deardorff	.15
288	Luis Rivas	.15
289	Harmon Killebrew	.15
290	Michael Cuddyer	.15
291	Torii Hunter	.15
292	Kevin Frederick	.15
293	Adam Johnson	.15
294	Jack Morris	.15
295	Rod Carew	.15
296	Kirby Puckett	1.50
297	Joe Mays	.15
298	Jacque Jones	.15
299	Cristian Guzman	.15
300	Kyle Lohse	.15
301	Eric Milton	.15
302	Brad Radke	.15
303	Doug Mientkiewicz	.15
304	Corey Koskie	.15
305	Jose Vidro	.15
306	Claudio Vargas	.15
307	Gary Carter	.25
308	Andre Dawson	.25
309	Henry Mateo	.15
310	Andres Galarraga	.15
311	Zach Day	.15
312	Bartolo Colon	.15
313	Endy Chavez	.15
314	Javier Vazquez	.15
315	Michael Barrett	.15
316	Vladimir Guerrero	1.00
317	Orlando Cabrera	.15
318	Al Leiter	.15
319	Timoniel Perez	.15
320	Rey Ordonez	.15
321	Gary Carter	.25
322	Armando Benitez	.15
323	Dwight Gooden	.15
324	Pedro Astacio	.15
325	Roberto Alomar	.50
326	Edgardo Alfonzo	.15
327	Nolan Ryan	3.00
328	Mo Vaughn	.25
329	Ryan Jamison	.15
330	Satoru Komiyama	.15
331	Mike Piazza	2.50
332	Tom Seaver	1.00
333	Jorge Posada	.25
334	Derek Jeter	2.50
335	Babe Ruth	3.00
336	Lou Gehrig	2.50
337	Andy Pettitte	.40
338	Mariano Rivera	.25
339	Robin Ventura	.15
340	Yogi Berra	1.00
341	Phil Rizzuto	.15
342	Bernie Williams	.50
343	Alfonso Soriano	1.50
344	Drew Henson	.15
345	Erick Almonte	.15
346	Rondell White	.15
347	Christian Parker	.15
348	Joe Torre	.25
349	Nick Johnson	.15
350	Raul Mondesi	.15
351	Brandon Claussen	.15
352	Reggie Jackson	.50
353	Roger Clemens	1.50
354	Don Mattingly	2.00
355	Jason Giambi	1.50
356	Adrian Hernandez	.15
357	Jeff Weaver	.15
358	Mike Mussina	.15
359	Brett Jodie	.15
360	David Wells	.15
361	Enos Slaughter	.15
362	Whitey Ford	.50
363	Eric Chavez	.25
364	Miguel Tejada	.40
365	Barry Zito	.15
366	Bert Snow	.15
367	Rickey Henderson	.50
368	Juan A. Pena	.15
369	Terrence Long	.15
370	Dennis Eckersley	.40
371	Mark Ellis	.15
372	Tim Hudson	.15
373	Jose Canseco	.50
374	Reggie Jackson	.50
375	Mark Mulder	.15
376	David Justice	.15
377	Jermaine Dye	.15
378	Brett Myers	.15
379	Lenny Dykstra	.15
380	Vicente Padilla	.15
381	Bobby Abreu	.15
382	Pat Burrell	.15
383	Jorge Padilla	.15
384	Jeremy Giambi	.15
385	Mike Liebenthal	.15
386	Anderson Machado	.15
387	Marlon Byrd	.15
388	Bud Smith	.15
389	Eric Valent	.15
390	Elio Serrano	.15
391	Jimmy Rollins	.15
392	Brandon Duckworth	.15
393	Robin Roberts	.15
394	Marlon Anderson	.15
395	Robert Person	.15
396	Johnny Estrada	.15
397	Mike Schmidt	.75
398	Eric Junge	.15
399	Jason Michaels	.15
400	Steve Carlton	.15
401	Placido Polanco	.15
402	John Grabow	.15
403	Tomas De La Rosa	.15

#	Player	Price
404	Tike Redman	.15
405	Willie Stargell	.40
406	Dave Williams	.15
407	John Candelaria	.15
408	Jack Wilson	.15
409	Matt Guerrier	.15
410	Jason Kendall	.15
411	Josh Fogg	.15
412	Aramis Ramirez	.15
413	Dave Parker	.15
414	Roberto Clemente	2.00
415	Kip Wells	.15
416	Brian Giles	.25
417	Honus Wagner	1.50
418	Ramon Vazquez	.15
419	Oliver Perez	.15
420	Ryan Klesko	.15
421	Brian Lawrence	.15
422	Ben Howard	.15
423	Ozzie Smith	1.00
424	Dennis Tankersley	.15
425	Tony Gwynn	1.00
426	Sean Burroughs	.15
427	Xavier Nady	.15
428	Phil Nevin	.15
429	Trevor Hoffman	.15
430	Jake Peavy	.15
431	Cody Ransom	.15
432	Kenny Lofton	.15
433	Mel Ott	.50
434	Tsuyoshi Shinjo	.15
435	Deivis Santos	.15
436	Rich Aurilia	.15
437	Will Clark	.15
438	Pedro Feliz	.15
439	J.T. Snow	.15
440	Robb Nen	.15
441	Carlos Valderrama	.15
442	Willie McCovey	.15
443	Jeff Kent	.25
444	Orlando Cepeda	.15
445	Barry Bonds	2.50
446	Alex Rodriguez	2.50
447	Allan Simpson	.15
448	Antonio Perez	.15
449	Edgar Martinez	.15
450	Freddy Garcia	.15
451	Chris Snelling	.15
452	Matt Thornton	.15
453	Kazuhiro Sasaki	.15
454	Harold Reynolds	.15
455	Randy Johnson	1.00
456	Bret Boone	.15
457	Rafael Soriano	.15
458	Luis Ugueto	.15
459	Ken Griffey Jr.	2.00
460	Ichiro Suzuki	2.00
461	Jamie Moyer	.15
462	Joel Pineiro	.15
463	Jeff Cirillo	.15
464	John Olerud	.15
465	Mike Cameron	.15
466	Ruben Sierra	.15
467	Mark McLemore	.15
468	Carlos Guillen	.15
469	Dan Wilson	.15
470	Shigetoshi Hasegawa	.15
471	Ben Davis	.15
472	Ozzie Smith	1.00
473	Matt Morris	.15
474	Edgar Renteria	.15
475	Les Walrond	.15
476	Albert Pujols	1.00
477	Stan Musial	1.50
478	J.D. Drew	.15
479	Josh Pearce	.15
480	Enos Slaughter	.15
481	Jason Simontacchi	.15
482	Jeremy Lambert	.15
483	Tino Martinez	.15
484	Rogers Hornsby	.50
485	Rick Ankiel	.25
486	Jim Edmonds	.25
487	Scott Rolen	.50
488	Kevin Joseph	.15
489	Fernando Vina	.15
490	Jason Isringhausen	.15
491	Lou Brock	.40
492	Joe Torre	.25
493	Bob Gibson	.50
494	Chuck Finley	.15
495	So Taguchi	.15
496	Ben Grieve	.15
497	Toby Hall	.15
498	Brent Abernathy	.15
499	Brandon Backe	.15
500	Felix Escalona	.15
501	Matt White	.15
502	Randy Winn	.15
503	Carl Crawford	.15
504	Dewon Brazelton	.15
505	Joe Kennedy	.15
506	Wade Boggs	.50
507	Aubrey Huff	.15
508	Alex Rodriguez	2.50
509	Ivan Rodriguez	.50
510	Will Clark	.75
511	Hank Blalock	.15
512	Travis Hughes	.15
513	Travis Hafner	.15
514	Ryan Ludwick	.15
515	Doug Davis	.15
516	Juan Gonzalez	.50
517	Jason Hart	.15
518	Mark Teixeira	.40
519	Nolan Ryan	3.00
520	Rafael Palmeiro	.50
521	Kevin Mench	.15

#	Player	Price
522	Chan Ho Park	.15
523	Kenny Rogers	.15
524	Rusty Greer	.15
525	Michael Young	.15
526	Carlos Delgado	.40
527	Vernon Wells	.15
528	Orlando Hudson	.15
529	Shannon Stewart	.15
530	Joe Carter	.15
531	Chris Baker	.15
532	Eric Hinske	.15
533	Corey Thurman	.15
534	Josh Phelps	.15
535	Reed Johnson	.15
536	Brian Bowles	.15
537	Roy Halladay	.15
538	Jose Cruz Jr.	.15
539	Kelvim Escobar	.15
540	Chris Carpenter	.15

Glossy
Stars: 1-2.5X
Inserted 1:1

Stat Line

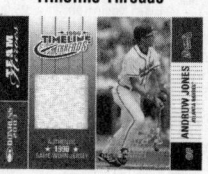

Cards serial numbered 151-250: 4-8X
Print run 101-150: 5-10X
Print run 51-100: 8-15X
Print run 26-50: 10-20X

Autographs
		NM/M
Common Player:		6.00

Some not priced due to scarcity.
#	Player	Price
4	Alfredo Amezaga/250	6.00
11	Elpidio Guzman/100	10.00
18	Doug DeVore/122	10.00
35	Trey Hodges/250	8.00
38	Billy Sylvester/250	6.00
41	Cory Aldridge/250	8.00
43	Horacio Ramirez/200	8.00
46	Derrick Lewis/250	6.00
47	Marcus Giles/200	8.00
49	Wilson Betemit/75	10.00
51	Josh Towers/110	6.00
52	Ed Rogers/250	6.00
53	Kris Foster/250	6.00
56	Brian Roberts/250	35.00
59	Geronimo Gil/60	8.00
60	Erik Bedard/250	8.00
62	Jay Gibbons/181	10.00
64	Larry Bigbie/100	10.00
67	Casey Fossum/250	6.00
79	Fred Lynn/250	20.00
81	Juan Diaz/250	6.00
84	Jorge De La Rosa/250	6.00
99	Fergie Jenkins/50	25.00
101	Francis Beltran/250	8.00
103	Nate Frese/250	6.00
105	Carlos Zambrano/150	20.00
108	Will Ohman/50	10.00
110	Bobby Hill/150	8.00
116	Mark Prior/150	40.00
122	Juan Cruz/50	10.00
125	Joe Crede/250	10.00
126	Joe Borchard/250	10.00
127	Luis Aparicio/50	20.00
128	Willie Harris/129	8.00
129	Kyle Kane/100	10.00
131	Matt Ginter/250	6.00
132	Carlos Lee/250	15.00
134	Mark Buehrle/50	20.00
135	Eric Davis/75	20.00
138	Austin Kearns/71	20.00
142	Corky Miller/250	6.00
143	Brandon Larson/143	10.00
144	Wily Mo Pena/250	15.00
147	Luke Hudson/50	12.00
149	Tony Perez/50	20.00
156	Cliff Lee/250	8.00
161	Earl Snyder/250	8.00
161	Ricardo Rodriguez/250	8.00
166	Victor Martinez/200	25.00
167	Alex Herrera/250	6.00
171	Alex Escobar/125	10.00
172	Brian Tallet/250	6.00
175	Rene Reyes/250	8.00
176	Jason Romano/50	15.00
177	Juan Pierre/66	15.00
178	Jason Jennings/250	15.00
179	Jose Ortiz/250	8.00
181	Cam Esslinger/250	6.00
184	Jack Cust/250	8.00
185	Jack Morris/250	20.00
186	Mike Rivera/250	6.00
188	Fernando Rodney/250	6.00
190	Carlos Pena/96	12.00
192	Mike Maroth/250	6.00

#	Player	Price
193	Adam Pettyjohn/250	6.00
194	David Espinosa/250	6.00
195	Adam Bernero/250	6.00
196	Franklyn German/250	6.00
197	Robert Fick/50	10.00
198	Andres Torres/250	6.00
201	Pablo Ozuna/250	6.00
205	Wilson Valdez/250	6.00
207	Abraham Nunez/250	6.00
212	Kirk Saarloos/250	8.00
214	Rodrigo Rosario/250	6.00
215	Roy Oswalt/50	20.00
217	Tim Redding/250	6.00
218	Morgan Ensberg/250	6.00
219	Richard Hidalgo/100	10.00
220	Wade Miller/250	6.00
222	Raul Chavez/125	15.00
223	Carlos Hernandez/250	6.00
224	Greg Miller/90	10.00
226	Jason Lane/250	6.00
234	Angel Berroa/200	10.00
236	Brad Voyles/250	10.00
237	Brandon Berger/250	6.00
238	Chad Durbin/250	8.00
239	Alexis Gomez/165	6.00
240	Jeremy Affeldt/250	6.00
242	Dee Brown/50	12.00
243	Tony Cogan/250	6.00
248	Cesar Izturis/200	10.00
253	Steve Garvey/75	30.00
258	Joe Thurston/108	6.00
259	Carlos Garcia/100	8.00
261	Paul LoDuca/50	20.00
263	Victor Alvarez/250	6.00
265	Don Sutton/50	20.00
277	Takahito Nomura/100	20.00
279	Jose Mieses/250	15.00
281	Matt Childers/50	12.00
283	Ben Sheets/100	20.00
284	Brian Mallette/250	6.00
287	Jeff Deardorff/100	6.00
288	Luis Rivas/200	8.00
290	Michael Cuddyer/250	10.00
291	Torii Hunter/250	25.00
294	Jack Morris/50	20.00
305	Jose Vidro/50	6.00
306	Claudio Vargas/150	6.00
309	Henry Mateo/250	6.00
311	Zach Day/250	6.00
313	Endy Chavez/250	6.00
314	Javier Vazquez/50	15.00
323	Dwight Gooden/75	25.00
344	Drew Henson/50	25.00
345	Erick Almonte/250	6.00
347	Christian Parker/200	6.00
351	Brandon Claussen/250	6.00
356	Adrian Hernandez/200	6.00
359	Brett Jodie/250	6.00
366	Bert Snow/250	6.00
368	Juan Pena/250	8.00
371	Mark Ellis/150	6.00
379	Lenny Dykstra/75	25.00
383	Jorge Padilla/250	6.00
384	Jeremy Giambi/100	10.00
386	Anderson Machado/250	6.00
387	Marlon Byrd/200	10.00
388	Bud Smith/125	10.00
389	Eric Valent/250	8.00
390	Elio Serrano/250	6.00
392	Brandon Duckworth/100	6.00
395	Robert Person/100	10.00
396	Johnny Estrada/209	15.00
398	Eric Junge/250	6.00
399	Jason Michaels/221	6.00
401	John Grabow/250	6.00
402	Dave Williams/250	6.00
406	John Candelaria/100	10.00
408	Jack Wilson/250	6.00
409	Matt Guerrier/200	6.00
412	Aramis Ramirez/50	30.00
413	Dave Parker/50	20.00
414	Kip Wells/50	8.00
419	Oliver Perez/150	10.00
421	Brian Lawrence/250	6.00
422	Ben Howard/250	6.00
427	Xavier Nady/50	15.00
435	Cody Ransom/100	8.00
435	Deivis Santos/100	6.00
438	Pedro Feliz/150	15.00
441	Carlos Valderrama/250	6.00
447	Allan Simpson/250	6.00
448	Antonio Perez/250	6.00
451	Chris Snelling/100	10.00
452	Matt Thornton/200	6.00
454	Harold Reynolds/250	15.00
457	Rafael Soriano/50	6.00
458	Luis Ugueto/50	6.00
475	Les Walrond/50	8.00
479	Josh Pearce/200	6.00
497	Toby Hall/250	6.00
498	Brent Abernathy/250	6.00
499	Brandon Backe/250	8.00
500	Felix Escalona/50	10.00
504	Dewon Brazelton/100	10.00
505	Joe Kennedy/200	6.00
507	Aubrey Huff/100	15.00
512	Travis Hughes/250	6.00
514	Ryan Ludwick/250	6.00
515	Doug Davis/25	8.00
517	Jason Hart/123	10.00
518	Mark Teixeira/250	40.00
521	Kevin Mench/250	10.00
528	Orlando Hudson/120	10.00
531	Chris Baker/200	6.00
532	Eric Hinske/250	10.00
533	Corey Thurman/250	8.00

#	Player	Price
534	Josh Phelps/150	10.00
535	Reed Johnson/250	6.00
536	Brian Bowles/250	6.00
543	Ramon Nivar/100	15.00
544	Adam Loewen/100	15.00
545	Brandon Webb/100	30.00
546	Dan Haren/100	25.00
548	Ryan Wagner/100	15.00

Timeline Threads

		NM/M
Common Player:		

Quantity produced listed.
#	Player	Price
	Bobby Doerr/39	20.00
2	Phil Rizzuto/47	30.00
3	Yogi Berra/47	35.00
5	Pee Wee Reese/58	15.00
6	Al Kaline/64	40.00
7	Orlando Cepeda/65	15.00
8	Eddie Mathews/66	40.00
9	Lou Brock/66	15.00
10	Juan Marichal/67	15.00
11	Ernie Banks/68	40.00
12	Willie Stargell/68	15.00
13	Jim Palmer/69	15.00
14	Luis Aparicio/69	15.00
15	Tom Seaver/69	30.00
16	Harmon Killebrew/71	50.00
17	Joe Morgan/74	15.00
18	Brooks Robinson/76	30.00
19	Mike Schmidt/81	65.00
20	Willie McCovey/77	15.00
21	Robin Yount/78	40.00
22	Reggie Jackson/79	20.00
23	Rod Carew/85	25.00
24	Nolan Ryan/91	80.00
25	Tony Gwynn/98	25.00
26	Alex Rodriguez/100	25.00
27	Carlos Delgado/101	10.00
28	Lance Berkman/102	12.00
29	Randy Johnson/100	20.00
30	Josh Beckett/101	15.00
31	Eric Davis/89	10.00
32	Todd Helton/100	15.00
33	Jose Canseco/89	25.00
34	Mike Piazza/101	25.00
35	Fred Lynn/75	15.00
36	Mike Sweeney/101	10.00
37	Miguel Tejada/101	15.00
38	Curt Schilling/101	15.00
39	Dale Murphy/87	40.00
40	Jim Thome/101	20.00
41	Adam Dunn/101	15.00
42	Nomar Garciaparra/100	25.00
43	Vladimir Guerrero/100	15.00
44	Alfonso Soriano/102	10.00
45	Wade Boggs/90	15.00
46	Randy Johnson/89	20.00
47	Hal Newhouser/55	15.00
48	Chipper Jones/93	20.00
49	Andruw Jones/96	15.00
50	Frank Thomas/94	15.00

2003 Donruss Team Heroes Hawaii

The base set and, it is believed, all inserts including autographs from the Team Heroes issue were produced in a special edition for attendees at the 2003 SCD Hawaii Trade Conference. Each card is gold-foil stamped with a show logo and "1/1" notation. Because of their unique nature, no catalog values are assigned.

2003 Donruss Timeless Treasures

	NM/M
Complete Set (100):	
Common Player:	2.00
Production 900 Sets	
Tin (4):	100.00
1	Adam Dunn	3.00
2	Al Kaline	5.00

#	Player	Price
3	Alan Trammell	2.00
4	Albert Pujols	8.00
5	Alex Rodriguez	8.00
6	Alfonso Soriano	4.00
7	Andre Dawson	2.00
8	Andruw Jones	3.00
9	Austin Kearns	2.00
10	Babe Ruth	10.00
11	Barry Bonds	10.00
12	Barry Larkin	2.00
13	Barry Zito	3.00
14	Bernie Williams	4.00
15	Bo Jackson	4.00
16	Brooks Robinson	4.00
17	Cal Ripken Jr.	10.00
18	Carlton Fisk	2.00
19	Chipper Jones	4.00
20	Curt Schilling	3.00
21	Dale Murphy	3.00
22	Derek Jeter	10.00
23	Don Mattingly	10.00
24	Duke Snider	4.00
25	Eddie Mathews	4.00
26	Frank Robinson	2.00
27	Frank Thomas	4.00
28	Garret Anderson	2.00
29	Gary Carter	2.00
30	George Brett	8.00
31	Greg Maddux	4.00
32	Harmon Killebrew	4.00
33	Hideki Matsui RC	10.00
34	Hideo Nomo	3.00
35	Ichiro Suzuki	6.00
36	Ivan Rodriguez	3.00
37	Jackie Robinson	6.00
38	Jason Giambi	3.00
39	Jeff Bagwell	4.00
40	Jim Edmonds	3.00
41	Jim Palmer	3.00
42	Jim Thome	4.00
43	Joe Morgan	2.00
44	Jorge Posada	4.00
45	Jose Contreras RC	5.00
46	Juan Gonzalez	3.00
47	Kazuhisa Ishii	2.00
48	Ken Griffey Jr.	5.00
49	Kerry Wood	2.00
50	Kirby Puckett	5.00
51	Lance Berkman	2.00
52	Larry Walker	2.00
53	Lou Brock	3.00
54	Lou Gehrig	10.00
55	Magglio Ordonez	2.00
56	Mark Prior	4.00
57	Miguel Tejada	3.00
58	Mike Mussina	3.00
59	Mike Piazza	6.00
60	Mike Schmidt	8.00
61	Nolan Ryan	10.00
62	Nomar Garciaparra	4.00
63	Ozzie Smith	5.00
64	Pat Burrell	2.00
65	Pedro J. Martinez	4.00
66	Pee Wee Reese	2.00
67	Phil Rizzuto	4.00
68	Rafael Palmeiro	3.00
69	Randy Johnson	5.00
70	Reggie Jackson	4.00
71	Richie Ashburn	2.00
72	Rickey Henderson	3.00
73	Roberto Alomar	2.00
74	Roberto Clemente	8.00
75	Robin Yount	4.00
76	Rod Carew	3.00
77	Roger Clemens	8.00
78	Rogers Hornsby	4.00
79	Roy Oswalt	2.00
80	Ryan Klesko	2.00
81	Ryne Sandberg	6.00
82	Sammy Sosa	8.00
83	Scott Rolen	4.00
84	Shawn Green	2.00
85	Stan Musial	8.00
86	Steve Carlton	3.00
87	Thurman Munson	4.00
88	Todd Helton	4.00
89	Tom Glavine	3.00
90	Tom Seaver	4.00
91	Tony Gwynn	5.00
92	Tony Perez	2.00
93	Torii Hunter	2.00
94	Troy Glaus	2.00
95	Ty Cobb	6.00
96	Vernon Wells	2.00
97	Vladimir Guerrero	4.00
98	Warren Spahn	4.00
99	Willie McCovey	3.00
100	Yogi Berra	5.00

Silver
Stars (1-100):		3-5X
Production 50 Sets		
Golds:		No Pricing
Production 10 Sets		
Platinum 1-of-1's exist.		

Award Materials
Quantity produced listed.
		NM/M
1	Ivan Rodriguez/100	10.00
2	Mike Schmidt/100	60.00
3	Roberto Clemente/50	80.00
4	Roger Clemens/50	25.00
5	Randy Johnson/100	15.00
6	Pedro J. Martinez/100	15.00
7	Ivan Rodriguez/100	10.00
8	Jeff Bagwell/100	15.00
9	Frank Thomas/100	15.00
10	Cal Ripken Jr./75	50.00
11	Tom Seaver/50	25.00

Award Prime Materials
Quantity produced listed.
		NM/M
6	Pedro J. Martinez/50	30.00
9	Frank Thomas/50	25.00

Award Materials Auto.
No Pricing

Award Winning MLB Logos
Complete Set (2):
Common Player:

Classic Combos
Quantity produced listed.
		NM/M
1	Jason Giambi/100	15.00
2	Adrian Beltre/100	10.00
3	Alex Rodriguez/100	15.00
4	Alfonso Soriano/100	30.00
6	Andruw Jones/100	15.00
7	Andre Dawson/100	15.00
8	Barry Larkin/100	15.00
9	Barry Zito/100	15.00
10	Cal Ripken Jr./100	60.00
11	Chipper Jones/100	50.00
12	Don Mattingly/10	50.00
13	Eric Chavez/100	15.00
14	Frank Thomas/100	15.00
15	Greg Maddux/100	25.00
16	Ivan Rodriguez/100	15.00
17	Jeff Bagwell/100	15.00
18	Jim Thome/100	15.00
19	Juan Gonzalez/100	15.00
20	Kazuhisa Ishii/100	15.00
21	Kerry Wood/100	15.00
22	Lance Berkman/100	10.00
23	Magglio Ordonez/100	10.00
24	Manny Ramirez/100	10.00
25	Miguel Tejada/100	10.00
26	Mike Piazza/100	20.00
27	Nomar Garciaparra/100	20.00
28	Pedro J. Martinez/100	20.00
29	Randy Johnson/100	15.00
30	Rickey Henderson/100	15.00
32	Ryne Sandberg/100	30.00
33	Shawn Green/100	15.00
34	Todd Helton/100	10.00
35	Tony Gwynn/100	20.00
36	Vladimir Guerrero/100	15.00

Classic Prime Combos
Quantity produced listed.
		NM/M
6	Andre Dawson/25	40.00
11	Don Mattingly/25	75.00
16	Jeff Bagwell/25	50.00

Classic Combos Auto.
Quantity produced listed.
		NM/M
8	Barry Zito/25	100.00
22	Magglio Ordonez/25	65.00
34	Tony Gwynn/25	100.00

Game Day Materials
Quantity produced listed.
		NM/M
1	Tony Gwynn/100	15.00
2	Magglio Ordonez/100	8.00
3	George Brett/100	40.00
4	Rickey Henderson/100	15.00
5	Billy Williams/100	15.00
6	Frank Thomas/100	15.00
7	Tony Gwynn/75	20.00
9	Ryne Sandberg/100	30.00
11	Miguel Tejada/100	15.00

Game Day Materials Auto.
Quantity produced listed.

HOF Cuts

		NM/M
	Production One Set	
	Ty Cobb (8/03 Auction)	6,500

HOF Combos

Quantity produced listed.

		NM/M
1	Al Kaline/50	50.00
4	Kirby Puckett/75	40.00
6	Mike Schmidt/100	50.00
7	Nolan Ryan/50	100.00
8	Phil Rizzuto/50	30.00
9	Reggie Jackson/25	40.00
11	Rod Carew/100	25.00
14	George Brett/50	85.00
15	Carlton Fisk/100	20.00

HOF Prime Combos

Quantity produced listed.

HOF Combos Autographs

Quantity produced listed.

HOF Induction Year Combos

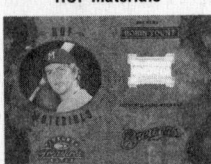

Production 25 Sets

		NM/M
6	Enos Slaughter, Lou Brock/25	60.00
8	Phil Rizzuto, Steve Carlton/25	45.00
10	George Brett, Robin Yount/25	185.00

HOF Letters

Quantity produced listed.

HOF Logos

Quantity produced listed.

		NM/M
29	Eddie Mathews/35	65.00
36	Nolan Ryan/35	100.00
37	Nolan Ryan/35	100.00
38	Nolan Ryan/35	100.00
43	Robin Yount/35	50.00

HOF Materials

Quantity produced listed.

		NM/M
1	Al Kaline	25.00
2	Babe Ruth/75	140.00
3	Carlton Fisk/100	15.00
4	Eddie Mathews/100	20.00
5	Gary Carter/100	15.00
6	George Brett/100	35.00
7	Harmon Killebrew/100	25.00
8	Joe Morgan/100	10.00
9	Kirby Puckett/100	20.00
10	Lou Gehrig/100	110.00
11	Luis Aparicio/100	10.00
12	Mike Schmidt/100	25.00
13	Ozzie Smith/100	25.00
14	Phil Rizzuto/100	10.00
15	Reggie Jackson/100	15.00
16	Richie Ashburn/100	15.00
17	Roberto Clemente/100	60.00
18	Robin Yount/100	20.00
19	Rod Carew/100	15.00
20	Rogers Hornsby/100	45.00
21	Stan Musial/100	35.00
22	Ty Cobb/100	120.00
23	Willie McCovey/100	10.00
24	Yogi Berra/100	30.00
25	Al Kaline/100	25.00
26	Babe Ruth/50	300.00
27	Bobby Doerr/100	15.00
28	Brooks Robinson/100	15.00
29	Eddie Mathews/100	15.00
30	Harmon Killebrew/100	25.00
31	Ty Cobb/50	150.00
32	Joe Morgan/100	10.00
33	Lou Brock/100	10.00

34	Lou Gehrig/50	225.00
35	Mike Schmidt/100	25.00
36	Nolan Ryan/100	40.00
37	Nolan Ryan/100	40.00
38	Nolan Ryan/100	40.00
39	Phil Rizzuto/100	10.00
40	Reggie Jackson/25	25.00
41	Reggie Jackson/100	15.00
42	Roberto Clemente/50	90.00
43	Robin Yount/100	20.00
44	Rod Carew/100	15.00
45	Stan Musial/100	35.00
46	Tom Seaver/100	20.00
47	Steve Carlton/100	15.00
48	Carlton Fisk/100	15.00
49	Pee Wee Reese/100	15.00
50	Jackie Robinson/50	85.00

HOF Materials Auto.

Quantity produced listed.

		NM/M
7	Harmon Killebrew/25	80.00
12	Mike Schmidt/15	180.00
24	Yogi Berra/15	150.00
28	Brooks Robinson/25	75.00
30	Harmon Killebrew/50	75.00
39	Phil Rizzuto/25	65.00
43	Robin Yount/25	175.00

HOF Numbers

Quantity produced listed.

		NM/M
35	Mike Schmidt/50	40.00
36	Nolan Ryan/35	100.00
43	Robin Yount/35	50.00
47	Steve Carlton/40	20.00
48	Carlton Fisk/35	45.00

Home Run Materials

Quantity produced listed.

		NM/M
1	Harmon Killebrew/100	20.00
2	Harmon Killebrew/100	20.00
3	Jose Canseco/100	15.00
4	Magglio Ordonez/100	8.00
5	Rafael Palmeiro/100	15.00
6	Rafael Palmeiro/100	15.00
7	Rafael Palmeiro/100	15.00
8	Alex Rodriguez/100	15.00
9	Alex Rodriguez/100	15.00
10	Alex Rodriguez/100	15.00
11	Alex Rodriguez/100	75.00
12	Adam Dunn/100	15.00

Home Run Materials Auto

Quantity produced listed.

		NM/M
1	Harmon Killebrew/25	80.00
3	Jose Canseco/25	100.00

Material Ink

Quantity produced listed.

		NM/M
1	Adam Dunn/50	45.00
2	Alan Trammell/100	30.00
3	Alex Rodriguez/100	150.00
4	Andre Dawson/100	30.00
6	Barry Zito/100	45.00
7	Bo Jackson/100	60.00
8	Bob Feller/25	70.00
9	Bobby Doerr/50	45.00
11	Cal Ripken Jr./50	200.00
12	Cal Ripken Jr./50	200.00
13	Cal Ripken Jr./50	225.00
14	Dale Murphy/50	45.00
15	Dave Parker/75	35.00
16	David Cone/100	30.00
17	Don Mattingly/100	85.00
18	Duke Snider/25	75.00
19	Edgar Martinez/50	50.00
20	Gary Carter/100	15.00
21	Harmon Killebrew/75	70.00
22	Jim Edmonds/25	55.00
23	Jim Thome/50	50.00
24	Joe Carter/100	30.00
25	Jose Canseco/50	50.00
26	Jose Vidro/100	20.00
27	Kazuhisa Ishii/50	40.00
28	Kerry Wood/50	60.00
29	Lance Berkman/50	40.00
31	Mark Mulder/25	65.00
32	Mike Schmidt/50	90.00
33	Nick Johnson/100	25.00
34	Nolan Ryan/25	225.00
35	Nolan Ryan/25	225.00
36	Nolan Ryan/25	225.00
37	Paul LoDuca/100	25.00
38	Paul Molitor/50	45.00
40	Reggie Jackson/40	85.00
41	Roberto Alomar/50	50.00
42	Roberto Alomar/100	40.00
43	Robin Yount/50	75.00
47	Ryan Klesko/75	25.00
48	Ryne Sandberg/25	140.00
50	Stan Musial/25	150.00
51	Steve Carlton/50	35.00
52	Steve Carlton/100	35.00
53	Todd Helton/50	60.00
54	Tom Seaver/50	50.00
55	Tony Gwynn/25	100.00
56	Torii Hunter/100	40.00
57	Vladimir Guerrero/100	40.00
58	Will Clark/50	85.00

Material MLB Logo Ink

No Pricing

Milestone Materials

Quantity produced listed.

		NM/M
3	Rickey Henderson/100	15.00

Past and Present

Production 100 Sets

		NM/M
1	Alex Rodriguez/100	20.00
2	Hideo Nomo/100	25.00
3	Jason Giambi/100	20.00
4	Juan Gonzalez/100	15.00
5	Mike Piazza/100	20.00
6	Pedro J. Martinez/100	15.00
7	Randy Johnson/100	15.00
8	Rickey Henderson/100	20.00
9	Roberto Alomar/100	15.00
10	Roger Clemens/100	20.00
11	Sammy Sosa/100	35.00

Past & Present Letters

Quantity produced listed.

		NM/M
1	Alex Rodriguez/75	30.00
2	Hideo Nomo/25	90.00
4	Juan Gonzalez/50	25.00
6	Pedro J. Martinez/75	35.00
7	Randy Johnson/75	40.00

Past and Present Logos

Quantity produced listed.

		NM/M
2	Hideo Nomo/25	90.00
3	Jason Giambi/75	40.00
5	Mike Piazza/50	40.00

Past & Present Numbers

Quantity produced listed.

		NM/M
2	Hideo Nomo/25	75.00
3	Jason Giambi/75	40.00
6	Pedro J. Martinez/50	40.00
7	Randy Johnson/50	40.00

Past & Present Patches

Quantity produced listed.

Post Season Materials

Quantity produced listed.

Post Season Prime Material

		NM/M

No Pricing

| 1 | Ozzie Smith/75 | 50.00 |

Post Season Materials Auto.

Quantity produced listed.

		NM/M
1	Ozzie Smith/15	125.00

Prime Materials

Quantity produced listed.

		NM/M
1	Tony Gwynn/100	15.00
2	Magglio Ordonez/100	8.00
4	Rickey Henderson/100	15.00
6	Frank Thomas/100	10.00
7	Tony Gwynn/75	20.00
10	Ryne Sandberg/100	30.00
11	Miguel Tejada/100	10.00

Prime Material Ink

Quantity produced listed.

		NM/M
2	Alan Trammell/50	50.00
5	Andre Dawson/25	40.00
7	Bo Jackson/25	100.00
20	Gary Carter/50	50.00
24	Joe Carter/50	50.00
26	Jose Vidro/25	40.00
27	Kazuhisa Ishii/50	50.00
33	Nick Johnson/50	45.00
53	Steve Carlton/50	50.00
56	Torii Hunter/50	50.00
59	Vladimir Guerrero/50	70.00
60	Will Clark/25	180.00

Rookie Year Combos

Quantity produced listed.

		NM/M
6	Mark Prior/50	40.00
7	Albert Pujols/50	80.00

Rookie Year Materials

		NM/M
	Common Player:	8.00
1	Cal Ripken Jr./100	50.00
2	Mike Schmidt/50	40.00
3	Rafael Palmeiro/100	15.00
4	Nomar Garciaparra/100	20.00
6	Stan Musial/42	70.00
8	Mike Piazza/100	30.00
9	Ivan Rodriguez/100	10.00
12	Vladimir Guerrero/100	10.00
13	Ivan Rodriguez/91	10.00
15	Andruw Jones/96	15.00
16	Andruw Jones/100	15.00
17	Fred Lynn/100	10.00

18	Jeff Kent/100	8.00
19	Gary Sheffield/100	10.00
20	Ron Santo/100	15.00
21	Juan Gonzalez/100	15.00
22	Alfonso Soriano/100	25.00
23	Ryan Klesko/92	10.00
24	Adam Dunn/100	12.00
25	Hideo Nomo/100	25.00
26	Mark Prior/100	15.00
27	Pat Burrell/99	10.00
28	Magglio Ordonez/100	8.00
29	Kirby Puckett/84	25.00
30	Albert Pujols/100	30.00
31	Albert Pujols/100	30.00

R.Y. Materials Auto.

Quantity produced listed.

		NM/M
7	Yogi Berra/15	150.00
26	Mark Prior/27	150.00
28	Magglio Ordonez/25	50.00

Rookie Year Materials Lett

Quantity produced listed.

		NM/M
4	Nomar Garciaparra/35	40.00
9	Ivan Rodriguez/35	25.00
12	Vladimir Guerrero/35	25.00
15	Andruw Jones/35	35.00
30	Albert Pujols/25	90.00

R.Y. Materials Logos

Quantity produced listed.

		NM/M
12	Vladimir Guerrero/50	25.00
15	Andruw Jones/50	25.00
17	Fred Lynn/25	25.00
19	Gary Sheffield/50	25.00
22	Alfonso Soriano/20	60.00
23	Ryan Klesko/50	15.00
30	Albert Pujols/50	75.00

R.Y. Materials Numbers

Quantity produced listed.

		NM/M
12	Vladimir Guerrero/50	25.00
15	Andruw Jones/15	25.00
17	Fred Lynn/30	25.00
18	Jeff Kent/20	20.00
19	Gary Sheffield/25	30.00
22	Alfonso Soriano/35	50.00
23	Ryan Klesko/35	20.00
26	Mark Prior/35	40.00
30	Albert Pujols/25	90.00

R.Y. Materials Patches

Quantity produced listed.

2003 Donruss/Playoff Babe Ruth Special Edition

Fifteen swatches from the jersey purchased in May 2003 for $265,000 were inserted into a special edition serially numbered card. Card No. 1 was given to Ruth's daughter. Some of the cards were reportedly given to Donruss/Playoff employees as year-end awards.

		NM/M
	Babe Ruth	2,100

2004 Donruss

Jeff Bagwell

		NM/M
	Complete Set (400):	75.00
	Common Player:	.10
	Pack (10):	3.50
	Box (24):	65.00
1	Derek Jeter	2.00
2	Greg Maddux	1.00
3	Albert Pujols	1.50
4	Ichiro Suzuki	1.00
5	Alex Rodriguez	1.50
6	Roger Clemens	1.50
7	Andruw Jones	.50

8	Barry Bonds	2.00
9	Jeff Bagwell	.50
10	Randy Johnson	.75
11	Scott Rolen	.50
12	Lance Berkman	.40
13	Barry Zito	.25
14	Manny Ramirez	.50
16	Carlos Delgado	.50
17	Alfonso Soriano	.75
18	Todd Helton	.50
19	Mike Mussina	.50
20	Nomar Garciaparra	1.50
21	Chipper Jones	1.00
22	Mark Prior	2.00
23	Jim Thome	.50
24	Vladimir Guerrero	.75
25	Pedro Martinez	.75
26	Sergio Mitre	.10
27	Adam Loewen	.10
28	Alfredo Gonzalez	.10
29	Miguel Ojeda	.10
30	Rosman Garcia	.10
31	Arnie Munoz	.10
32	Andrew Brown	.10
33	Josh Hall	.10
34	Josh Stewart	.10
35	Clint Barmes	.10
36	Brandon Webb	.10
37	Chien-Ming Wang	.40
38	Edgar Gonzalez	.10
39	Alejandro Machado	.10
40	Jeremy Griffiths	.10
42	Craig Brazell	.10
42	Daniel Cabrera	.10
43	Fernando Cabrera	.10
44	Terrmel Sledge	.10
45	Rob Hammock	.10
46	Francisco Rosario	.10
47	Francisco Cruceta	.10
48	Rett Johnson	.10
49	Guillermo Quiroz	.10
51	Hong-Chih Kuo	.10
51	Ian Ferguson	.10
52	Tim Olson	.10
53	Todd Wellemeyer	.10
54	Rich Fischer	.10
55	Phil Seibel	.10
56	Joe Valentine	.10
57	Matt Kata	.10
58	Michael Hessman	.10
59	Michel Hernandez	.10
60	Doug Waechter	.10
61	Prentice Redman	.10
62	Nook Logan	.10
63	Oscar Villarreal	.10
64	Pete LaForest	.10
65	Matt Bruback	.10
66	Dan Haren	.10
67	Greg Aquino	.10
68	Lew Ford	.10
69	Jeff Duncan	.10
70	Ryan Wagner	.10
71	Bengie Molina	.10
72	Brad Fullmer	.10
73	Darin Erstad	.10
74	David Eckstein	.10
75	Garret Anderson	.25
76	Jarrod Washburn	.10
77	Kevin Appier	.10
78	Scott Spiezio	.10
79	Tim Salmon	.25
80	Troy Glaus	.25
81	Troy Percival	.10
82	Jason Johnson	.10
83	Jay Gibbons	.10
84	Melvin Mora	.10
85	Sidney Ponson	.10
86	Tony Batista	.10
87	Bill Mueller	.10
88	Byung-Hyun Kim	.10
89	David Ortiz	.25
91	Derek Lowe	.10
91	Johnny Damon	.25
92	Casey Fossum	.10
93	Manny Ramirez	.50
94	Nomar Garciaparra	1.50
95	Pedro J. Martinez	.75
96	Todd Walker	.10
97	Trot Nixon	.10
98	Bartolo Colon	.25
99	Carlos Lee	.25
100	D'Angelo Jimenez	.10
101	Esteban Loaiza	.10
102	Frank Thomas	.50
103	Joe Crede	.10
104	Jose Valentin	.10
105	Magglio Ordonez	.25
106	Mark Buehrle	.10
107	Paul Konerko	.10
108	Brandon Phillips	.10
109	C.C. Sabathia	.10
110	Ellis Burks	.10
111	Jeremy Guthrie	.10
112	Josh Bard	.10
113	Matt Lawton	.10
114	Milton Bradley	.10
115	Omar Vizquel	.10
116	Travis Hafner	.10
117	Bobby Higginson	.10
118	Carlos Pena	.10
119	Dmitri Young	.20
120	Eric Munson	.10
121	Jeremy Bonderman	.10
122	Nate Cornejo	.10
123	Omar Infante	.10
124	Ramon Santiago	.10
125	Angel Berroa	.25
126	Carlos Beltran	.25

127	Desi Relaford	.10
128	Jeremy Affeldt	.10
129	Joe Randa	.10
130	Ken Harvey	.10
131	Mike MacDougal	.10
132	Michael Tucker	.10
133	Mike Sweeney	.20
134	Raul Ibanez	.20
135	Runelvys Hernandez	.10
136	A.J. Pierzynski	.10
137	Brad Radke	.10
138	Corey Koskie	.10
139	Cristian Guzman	.10
140	Doug Mientkiewicz	.10
141	Dustan Mohr	.10
142	Jacque Jones	.10
143	Kenny Rogers	.10
144	Bobby Kielty	.10
145	Kyle Lohse	.10
146	Luis Rivas	.10
147	Torii Hunter	.25
148	Alfonso Soriano	.75
149	Andy Pettitte	.40
150	Bernie Williams	.40
151	David Wells	.10
152	Derek Jeter	2.00
153	Hideki Matsui	2.00
154	Jason Giambi	.75
155	Jorge Posada	.50
156	Jose Contreras	.50
157	Mike Mussina	.50
158	Nick Johnson	.20
159	Robin Ventura	.20
160	Roger Clemens	1.50
161	Barry Zito	.25
162	Chris Singleton	.10
163	Eric Byrnes	.10
164	Eric Chavez	.25
165	Erubiel Durazo	.10
166	Keith Foulke	.10
167	Mark Ellis	.10
168	Miguel Tejada	.40
169	Mark Mulder	.25
170	Ramon Hernandez	.10
171	Ted Lilly	.10
172	Terrence Long	.10
173	Tim Hudson	.25
174	Bret Boone	.25
175	Carlos Guillen	.10
176	Dan Wilson	.10
177	Edgar Martinez	.25
178	Freddy Garcia	.10
179	Gil Meche	.10
180	Ichiro Suzuki	1.00
181	Jamie Moyer	.10
182	Joel Pineiro	.10
183	John Olerud	.20
184	Mike Cameron	.10
185	Randy Winn	.10
186	Ryan Franklin	.10
187	Kazuhiro Sasaki	.10
188	Aubrey Huff	.10
189	Carl Crawford	.25
190	Joe Kennedy	.10
191	Marlon Anderson	.10
192	Rey Ordonez	.10
193	Rocco Baldelli	.25
194	Toby Hall	.10
195	Travis Lee	.10
196	Alex Rodriguez	1.50
197	Carl Everett	.10
198	Chan Ho Park	.10
199	Einar Diaz	.10
200	Hank Blalock	.50
201	Ismael Valdes	.10
202	Juan Gonzalez	.50
203	Mark Teixeira	.50
204	Mike Young	.10
205	Rafael Palmeiro	.25
206	Carlos Delgado	.50
207	Kelvim Escobar	.10
208	Eric Hinske	.10
209	Frank Catalanotto	.10
210	Josh Phelps	.10
211	Orlando Hudson	.10
212	Roy Halladay	.25
213	Shannon Stewart	.10
214	Vernon Wells	.25
215	Carlos Baerga	.10
216	Curt Schilling	.40
217	Junior Spivey	.10
218	Luis Gonzalez	.25
219	Lyle Overbay	.10
220	Mark Grace	.25
221	Matt Williams	.20
222	Randy Johnson	.75
223	Shea Hillenbrand	.10
224	Steve Finley	.10
225	Andruw Jones	.25
226	Chipper Jones	1.00
227	Gary Sheffield	.40
228	Greg Maddux	1.00
229	Javy Lopez	.25
230	John Smoltz	.25
231	Marcus Giles	.10
232	Mike Hampton	.10
233	Rafael Furcal	.10
234	Robert Fick	.10
235	Russ Ortiz	.10
236	Alex Gonzalez	.10
237	Carlos Zambrano	.25
238	Corey Patterson	.10
239	Hee Seop Choi	.10
240	Kerry Wood	.25
241	Mark Belhorn	.10
242	Mark Prior	1.00
243	Moises Alou	.25
244	Sammy Sosa	1.00

#	Player	Price
245	Aaron Boone	.10
246	Adam Dunn	.40
247	Austin Kearns	.40
248	Barry Larkin	.25
249	Felipe Lopez	.10
250	Jose Guillen	.10
251	Ken Griffey Jr.	1.00
252	Jason LaRue	.10
253	Scott Williamson	.10
254	Sean Casey	.20
255	Shawn Chacon	.10
256	Chris Stynes	.10
257	Jason Jennings	.10
258	Jay Payton	.20
259	Jose Hernandez	.10
260	Larry Walker	.25
261	Preston Wilson	.20
262	Ronnie Belliard	.10
263	Todd Helton	.50
264	A.J. Burnett	.10
265	Alex Gonzalez	.10
266	Brad Penny	.10
267	Derrek Lee	.10
268	Ivan Rodriguez	.50
269	Josh Beckett	.50
270	Juan Encarnacion	.10
271	Juan Pierre	.10
272	Luis Castillo	.10
273	Mike Lowell	.10
274	Todd Hollandsworth	.10
275	Billy Wagner	.25
276	Brad Ausmus	.10
277	Craig Biggio	.25
278	Jeff Bagwell	.50
279	Jeff Kent	.25
280	Lance Berkman	.25
281	Richard Hidalgo	.10
282	Roy Oswalt	.25
283	Wade Miller	.10
284	Adrian Beltre	.10
285	Brian Jordan	.10
286	Cesar Izturis	.10
287	Dave Roberts	.10
288	Eric Gagne	.25
289	Fred McGriff	.25
290	Hideo Nomo	.40
291	Kazuhisa Ishii	.10
292	Kevin Brown	.25
293	Paul LoDuca	.10
294	Shawn Green	.40
295	Ben Sheets	.25
296	Geoff Jenkins	.25
297	Rey Sanchez	.10
298	Richie Sexson	.40
299	Wes Helms	.10
300	Brad Wilkerson	.10
301	Claudio Vargas	.10
302	Endy Chavez	.10
303	Fernando Tatis	.10
304	Javier Vazquez	.25
305	Jose Vidro	.10
306	Michael Barrett	.10
307	Orlando Cabrera	.20
308	Tony Armas Jr.	.10
309	Vladimir Guerrero	.75
310	Zach Day	.10
311	Al Leiter	.10
312	Cliff Floyd	.10
313	Jae Weong Seo	.10
314	Jeromy Burnitz	.10
315	Mike Piazza	1.00
316	Mo Vaughn	.10
317	Roberto Alomar	.40
318	Roger Cedeno	.10
319	Tom Glavine	.25
320	Jose Reyes	.40
321	Bobby Abreu	.20
322	Brett Myers	.10
323	David Bell	.10
324	Jim Thome	.50
325	Jimmy Rollins	.25
326	Kevin Millwood	.25
327	Marlon Byrd	.10
328	Mike Lieberthal	.10
329	Pat Burrell	.40
330	Randy Wolf	.10
331	Aramis Ramirez	.10
332	Brian Giles	.25
333	Jason Kendall	.20
334	Kenny Lofton	.20
335	Kip Wells	.10
336	Kris Benson	.10
337	Randall Simon	.10
338	Reggie Sanders	.10
339	Albert Pujols	2.00
340	Edgar Renteria	.10
341	Fernando Vina	.10
342	J.D. Drew	.10
343	Jim Edmonds	.25
344	Matt Morris	.10
345	Mike Matheny	.10
346	Scott Rolen	.50
347	Tino Martinez	.10
348	Woody Williams	.10
349	Brian Lawrence	.10
350	Mark Kotsay	.10
351	Mark Loretta	.10
352	Ramon Vazquez	.10
353	Rondell White	.10
354	Ryan Klesko	.25
355	Sean Burroughs	.10
356	Trevor Hoffman	.10
357	Xavier Nady	.10
358	Andres Galarraga	.10
359	Barry Bonds	2.00
360	Benito Santiago	.10
361	Deivi Cruz	.10
362	Edgardo Alfonzo	.10

#	Player	Price
363	J.T. Snow	.10
364	Jason Schmidt	.10
365	Kirk Rueter	.10
366	Kurt Ainsworth	.10
367	Marquis Grissom	.10
368	Ray Durham	.10
369	Rich Aurilia	.10
370	Tim Worrell	.10
371	Troy Glaus	.20
372	Melvin Mora	.10
373	Nomar Garciaparra	.75
374	Magglio Ordonez	.20
375	Omar Vizquel	.10
376	Dmitri Young	.10
377	Mike Sweeney	.10
378	Torii Hunter	.20
379	Derek Jeter	1.00
380	Barry Zito	.20
381	Ichiro Suzuki	.50
382	Rocco Baldelli	.20
383	Alex Rodriguez	.75
384	Carlos Delgado	.25
385	Randy Johnson	.40
386	Greg Maddux	.50
387	Sammy Sosa	.75
388	Ken Griffey Jr.	.50
389	Todd Helton	.25
390	Ivan Rodriguez	.25
391	Jeff Bagwell	.25
392	Hideo Nomo	.20
393	Richie Sexson	.20
394	Vladimir Guerrero	.40
395	Mike Piazza	.25
396	Jim Thome	.25
397	Jason Kendall	.10
398	Albert Pujols	1.00
399	Ryan Klesko	.10
400	Barry Bonds	1.00

Black Press Proofs

No pricing due to scarcity.
Production 10 Sets
Hot Pack exclusive.

Career Stat Line

Cards Serial #'d from 251-500: 3-5X
Print run 101-250: 4-6X
Print run 61-100: 4-8X
Print run 26-60: 8-15X
No pricing for P/R 25 or less.
Numbered to career statistic.

Season Stat Line

Print run 101-261: 4-6X
Print run 61-100: 4-8X
Print run 26-60: 8-15X
No pricing for P/R 25 or less.
Numbered to 2003 statistic.

All-Stars

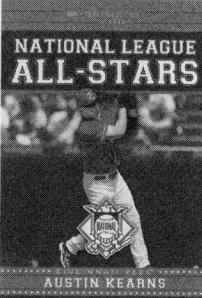

		NM/M
Complete Set (20):		40.00
Common Player:		1.50
Production 1,000 Sets		
Black:		1-2X
Production 250 Sets		
1	Alex Rodriguez	5.00
2	Roger Clemens	5.00
3	Ichiro Suzuki	3.00
4	Barry Zito	1.50
5	Garret Anderson	1.50
6	Derek Jeter	5.00
7	Manny Ramirez	2.00
8	Pedro J. Martinez	2.00
9	Alfonso Soriano	2.50
10	Carlos Delgado	1.50
11	Barry Bonds	5.00
12	Andruw Jones	2.00
13	Scott Rolen	1.50

Bat Kings

	NM/M
Common Player:	5.00
Studio Current Player:	1.5X
Production 50	
Studio Retired:	No Pricing
Production 25	
1 Alex Rodriguez/250	10.00
2 Albert Pujols/250	15.00
3 Chipper Jones/250	12.00
4 Lance Berkman/250	5.00
5 Cal Ripken Jr./100	50.00
6 George Brett/100	30.00
7 Don Mattingly/100	40.00
8 Roberto Clemente/100	75.00

Craftsmen

		NM/M
Complete Set (15):		40.00
Common Player:		2.00
Production 2,000 Sets		
Black:		1-2X
Production 275 Sets		
Master Craftsmen:		1-2X
Production 150 Sets		
1	Alex Rodriguez	5.00
2	Mark Prior	4.00
3	Ichiro Suzuki	3.00
4	Barry Bonds	5.00
5	Ken Griffey Jr.	3.00
6	Alfonso Soriano	3.00
7	Mike Piazza	3.00
8	Chipper Jones	5.00
9	Derek Jeter	5.00
10	Randy Johnson	2.50
11	Sammy Sosa	3.00
12	Roger Clemens	4.00
13	Nomar Garciaparra	4.00
14	Greg Maddux	3.00
15	Albert Pujols	5.00

Diamond Kings Insert

		NM/M
Complete Set (25):		80.00
Common Player:		2.00
Production 2,500 Sets		
Studio Series:		1-2X
Production 250 Sets		
Black:		1.5-2X
Production 100 Sets		
1	Derek Jeter	8.00
2	Greg Maddux	6.00
3	Albert Pujols	8.00
4	Ichiro Suzuki	6.00
5	Alex Rodriguez	6.00
6	Roger Clemens	6.00
7	Andruw Jones	3.00
8	Barry Bonds	8.00
9	Jeff Bagwell	3.00
10	Randy Johnson	3.00
11	Scott Rolen	3.00
12	Lance Berkman	2.00
13	Barry Zito	2.00
14	Manny Ramirez	3.00
15	Carlos Delgado	2.50
16	Alfonso Soriano	4.00
17	Todd Helton	3.00
18	Mike Mussina	2.00
19	Austin Kearns	2.00
20	Nomar Garciaparra	6.00

#	Player	Price
14	Austin Kearns	1.50
15	Mark Prior	4.00
16	Vladimir Guerrero	2.00
17	Jeff Bagwell	2.00
18	Mike Piazza	3.00
19	Albert Pujols	5.00
20	Randy Johnson	2.50

Elite Series

		NM/M
Complete Set (15):		60.00
Common Player:		2.00
Production 1,500 Sets		
Black:		1-2X
Production 150 Sets		
Dominators:		No Pricing
Production 25 Sets		
1	Albert Pujols	8.00
2	Barry Zito	3.00
3	Gary Sheffield	3.00
4	Mike Mussina	3.00
5	Lance Berkman	2.00
6	Alfonso Soriano	4.00
7	Randy Johnson	4.00
8	Nomar Garciaparra	8.00
9	Austin Kearns	3.00
10	Manny Ramirez	3.00
11	Mark Prior	6.00
12	Alex Rodriguez	6.00
13	Derek Jeter	8.00
14	Barry Bonds	8.00
15	Roger Clemens	6.00

Inside View

		NM/M
Complete Set (25):		50.00
Common Player:		1.00
Production 1,250 Sets		
1	Derek Jeter	4.00
2	Greg Maddux	3.00
3	Albert Pujols	5.00
4	Ichiro Suzuki	3.00
5	Alex Rodriguez	4.00
6	Roger Clemens	3.00
7	Andruw Jones	1.50
8	Barry Bonds	5.00
9	Jeff Bagwell	2.00
10	Randy Johnson	2.00
11	Scott Rolen	2.00
12	Lance Berkman	1.00
13	Barry Zito	1.50
14	Manny Ramirez	2.00
15	Carlos Delgado	1.50
16	Alfonso Soriano	2.00
17	Todd Helton	2.00
18	Mike Mussina	1.50
19	Austin Kearns	1.50
20	Nomar Garciaparra	4.00
21	Chipper Jones	3.00
22	Mark Prior	4.00
23	Jim Thome	2.00
24	Vladimir Guerrero	2.00
25	Pedro J. Martinez	2.50

Jersey Kings

		NM/M
Quantity produced listed.		
Studio Current Player:		1.5X
Production 50		
Studio Retired:		No Pricing
Production 25		
1	Alfonso Soriano/250	10.00
2	Sammy Sosa/250	15.00
3	Roger Clemens/250	15.00
4	Nomar Garciaparra/250	12.00
5	Mark Prior/250	10.00
6	Vladimir Guerrero/250	8.00
7	Don Mattingly/100	40.00
8	Roberto Clemente/100	80.00
9	George Brett/100	35.00

#	Player	Price
21	Chipper Jones	4.00
22	Mark Prior	4.00
23	Jim Thome	3.00
24	Vladimir Guerrero	3.00
25	Pedro J. Martinez	3.00

Longball Leaders

		NM/M
Complete Set (10):		20.00
Common Player:		1.50
Production 1,500 Sets		
Black:		1-2X
Production 250 Sets		
Die-Cuts:		1.5-3X
Production 50 Sets		
1	Barry Bonds	5.00
2	Alfonso Soriano	3.00
3	Adam Dunn	2.00
4	Alex Rodriguez	5.00
5	Jim Thome	2.00
6	Garret Anderson	1.50
7	Juan Gonzalez	1.50
8	Jeff Bagwell	2.00
9	Gary Sheffield	1.50
10	Sammy Sosa	4.00

Mound Marvels

		NM/M
Complete Set (15):		20.00
Common Player:		1.00
Production 750 Sets		
Black:		1-2X
Production 175 Sets		
1	Mark Prior	4.00
2	Curt Schilling	1.50
3	Mike Mussina	1.50
4	Kevin Brown	1.50
5	Pedro J. Martinez	2.50
6	Mark Mulder	1.00
7	Kerry Wood	1.50
8	Greg Maddux	3.00
9	Kevin Millwood	1.00
10	Barry Zito	1.50
11	Roger Clemens	5.00
12	Randy Johnson	2.50
13	Hideo Nomo	1.50
14	Tim Hudson	1.50
15	Tom Glavine	1.50

Power Alley Red

		NM/M
Complete Set (20):		50.00
Common Player:		2.00
Production 2,500 Sets		
Red Die-Cut:		1-2X
Production 250 Sets		
Blues:		1X
Production 1,000 Sets		
Blue Die-Cuts:		1.5-2X
Production 100 Sets		
Purples:		1-2X
Production 250 Sets		
Purple Die-Cuts:		No Pricing
Production 25 Sets		
Yellows:		1.5-2X
Production 100 Sets		
Yellow Die-Cuts:		No Pricing
Production 10 Sets		
Greens:		No Pricing
Production 25 Sets		
Green Die-Cuts:		No Pricing
Production 5 Sets		
1	Albert Pujols	8.00
2	Mike Piazza	5.00
3	Carlos Delgado	4.00
4	Barry Bonds	8.00
5	Jim Edmonds	4.00
6	Nomar Garciaparra	6.00
7	Alfonso Soriano	4.00
8	Alex Rodriguez	8.00

#	Player	Price
10	Nolan Ryan/100	40.00
11	Cal Ripken Jr./100	55.00
12	Mike Schmidt/100	40.00

#	Player	Price
9	Lance Berkman	2.00
10	Scott Rolen	3.00
11	Manny Ramirez	3.00
12	Rafael Palmeiro	3.00
13	Sammy Sosa	6.00
14	Adam Dunn	2.00
15	Andruw Jones	3.00
16	Jim Thome	3.00
17	Jason Giambi	3.00
18	Jeff Bagwell	3.00
19	Juan Gonzalez	3.00
20	Austin Kearns	2.00

Production Line Average

		NM/M
Complete Set (10):		35.00
Common Player:		
Die-Cuts:		1-2X
Production 100 Sets		
Black:		2-3X
Production 35 Sets		
1	Gary Sheffield/330	2.00
2	Ichiro Suzuki/312	5.00
3	Todd Helton/358	3.00
4	Manny Ramirez/325	3.00
5	Garret Anderson/315	2.00
6	Barry Bonds/341	8.00
7	Albert Pujols/359	8.00
8	Derek Jeter/324	8.00
9	Nomar Garciaparra/301	6.00
10	Hank Blalock/300	3.00

Production Line OBP

		NM/M
Complete Set (10):		25.00
Common Player:		2.00
Die-Cuts:		1-2X
Production 100 Sets		
Black:		2-3X
Production 40 Sets		
1	Todd Helton/458	3.00
2	Albert Pujols/439	6.00
3	Larry Walker/422	2.00
4	Barry Bonds/529	8.00
5	Chipper Jones/402	4.00
6	Manny Ramirez/427	3.00
7	Gary Sheffield/419	2.00
8	Lance Berkman/412	2.00
9	Alex Rodriguez/396	5.00
10	Jason Giambi/412	4.00

Production Line OPS

		NM/M
Complete Set (10):		25.00
Varying quanties produced.		
Black:		1-2X
Production 125 Sets		
Die-Cuts:		1-2X
Production 100 Sets		
1	Albert Pujols/1,106	5.00
2	Barry Bonds/1,278	5.00
3	Gary Sheffield/1,023	1.50
4	Todd Helton/1,088	2.00
5	Scott Rolen/910	3.00
6	Manny Ramirez/1,014	3.00
7	Alex Rodriguez/995	5.00
8	Jim Thome/958	2.00
9	Jason Giambi/939	3.00
10	Frank Thomas/952	3.00

Production Line Slugging

		NM/M
Complete Set (10):		25.00
Varying quantities produced.		
Black:		1-2X
Production 75 Sets		
Die-Cuts:		1-2X
Production 100 Sets		
1	Alex Rodriguez/604	6.00
2	Frank Thomas/562	3.00
3	Garret Anderson/541	2.00
4	Albert Pujols/667	6.00
5	Sammy Sosa/553	5.00
6	Gary Sheffield/604	3.00
7	Manny Ramirez/587	3.00
8	Jim Edmonds/617	4.00
9	Barry Bonds/688	6.00
10	Todd Helton/630	3.00

Timber & Threads

		NM/M
Common Player:		4.00
Inserted 1:40		
Studio Series:		1.5X
Production 50 Sets		
1	Adam Dunn	6.00
2	Alex Rodriguez/Blue	10.00
3	Alex Rodriguez/White	10.00
4	Andruw Jones	6.00
5	Austin Kearns	6.00
6	Carlos Beltran	4.00
7	Carlos Lee	4.00
8	Frank Thomas	8.00
9	Greg Maddux	10.00
10	Hideo Nomo	10.00
11	Jeff Bagwell	8.00
12	Lance Berkman	6.00

#	Player	NM/M
13	Magglio Ordonez	4.00
14	Mike Sweeney	4.00
15	Randy Johnson	8.00
16	Rocco Baldelli	10.00
17	Roger Clemens	12.00
18	Sammy Sosa	12.00
19	Shawn Green	4.00
20	Tom Glavine	6.00
21	Adam Dunn	4.00
22	Andruw Jones	6.00
23	Bobby Abreu	4.00
24	Hank Blalock	6.00
25	Ivan Rodriguez	6.00
26	Jim Edmonds	6.00
27	Josh Phelps	4.00
28	Juan Gonzalez	6.00
29	Lance Berkman	4.00
30	Larry Walker	4.00
31	Magglio Ordonez	4.00
32	Manny Ramirez	8.00
33	Mike Piazza	10.00
34	Nomar Garciaparra	10.00
35	Paul LoDuca	4.00
36	Roberto Alomar	4.00
37	Rocco Baldelli	10.00
38	Sammy Sosa	12.00
39	Vernon Wells	4.00
40	Vladimir Guerrero	8.00

2004 Donruss Classics

		NM/M
Complete Set (213):		90.00
Common Player:		.40
Common (151-210):		3.00
Production 1,999		
Pack (6):		6.00
Box (18):		90.00
1	Albert Pujols	2.50
2	Derek Jeter	3.00
3	Hank Blalock	.50
4	Shannon Stewart	.40
5	Jason Giambi	1.00
6	Carlos Lee	.40
7	Trot Nixon	.40
8	Bret Boone	.50
9	Mark Mulder	.40
10	Mariano Rivera	.50
11	Scott Podsednik	.75
12	Jim Edmonds	.50
13	Mike Lowell	.50
14	Robin Ventura	.40
15	Brian Giles	.50
16	Jose Vidro	.40
17	Manny Ramirez	.75
18	Alex Rodriguez	2.50
19	Carlos Beltran	.50
20	Hideki Matsui	2.50
21	Johan Santana	.40
22	Richie Sexson	.50
23	Chipper Jones	1.00
24	Steve Finley	.40
25	Mark Prior	1.50
26	Alexis Rios	.40
27	Rafael Palmeiro	.75
28	Jorge Posada	.50
29	Barry Zito	.50
30	Jamie Moyer	.40
31	Preston Wilson	.40
32	Miguel Cabrera	.75
33	Pedro Martinez	1.00
34	Curt Schilling	.75
35	Hee Seop Choi	.40
36	Dontrelle Willis	.50
37	Rafael Soriano	.40
38	Richard Fischer	.40
39	Brian Tallet	.40
40	Jose Castillo	.40
41	Wade Miller	.40
42	Jose Contreras	.40
43	Runelvys Hernandez	.40
44	Joe Borchard	.40
45	Kazuhisa Ishii	.40
46	Jose Reyes	.50
47	Adam Dunn	.50
48	Randy Johnson	1.00
49	Brandon Phillips	.40
50	Scott Rolen	1.00
51	Ken Griffey Jr.	1.50
52	Tom Glavine	.50
53	Cliff Lee	.50
54	Chien-Ming Wang	.50
55	Roy Oswalt	.50
56	Austin Kearns	.40
57	Jhonny Peralta	.40
58	Greg Maddux	1.50
59	Mark Grace	.50
60	Jae Weong Seo	.40
61	Nic Jackson	.40
62	Roger Clemens	2.50
63	Jimmy Gobble	.40
64	Travis Hafner	.40
65	Paul Konerko	.40
66	Jerome Williams	.40
67	Ryan Klesko	.50
68	Alexis Gomez	.40
69	Omar Vizquel	.40
70	Zach Day	.40
71	Rickey Henderson	.50
72	Morgan Ensberg	.40
73	Josh Beckett	.75
74	Garrett Atkins	.40
75	Sean Casey	.40
76	Julio Franco	.40
77	Lyle Overbay	.40
78	Josh Phelps	.40
79	Juan Gonzalez	.75
80	Rich Harden	.40
81	Bernie Williams	.50
82	Torii Hunter	.50
83	Angel Berroa	.40
84	Jody Gerut	.40
85	Roberto Alomar	.50
86	Byung-Hyun Kim	.40
87	Jay Gibbons	.40
88	Chone Figgins	.40
89	Fred McGriff	.50
90	Rich Aurilia	.40
91	Xavier Nady	.40
92	Marlon Byrd	.40
93	Mike Piazza	1.50
94	Vladimir Guerrero	1.00
95	Shawn Green	.50
96	Jeff Kent	.50
97	Ivan Rodriguez	.75
98	Jay Payton	.40
99	Barry Larkin	.50
100	Mike Sweeney	.40
101	Adrian Beltre	.40
102	Robby Hammock	.40
103	Orlando Hudson	.40
104	Mark Teixeira	.40
105	Hong-Chih Kuo	.40
106	Eric Chavez	.50
107	Nick Johnson	.40
108	Jacque Jones	.40
109	Ken Harvey	.40
110	Aramis Ramirez	.40
111	Victor Martinez	.40
112	Joe Crede	.40
113	Jason Varitek	.40
114	Troy Glaus	.50
115	Billy Wagner	.40
116	Kerry Wood	1.00
117	Hideo Nomo	.50
118	Brandon Webb	.40
119	Craig Biggio	.40
120	Orlando Cabrera	.40
121	Sammy Sosa	2.00
122	Bobby Abreu	.50
123	Andruw Jones	.75
124	Jeff Bagwell	.75
125	Jim Thome	1.00
126	Javy Lopez	.50
127	Luis Castillo	.40
128	Todd Helton	.75
129	Roy Halladay	.50
130	Mike Mussina	.50
131	Eric Byrnes	.40
132	Eric Hinske	.40
133	Nomar Garciaparra	2.00
134	Edgar Martinez	.50
135	Rocco Baldelli	.50
136	Miguel Tejada	.50
137	Alfonso Soriano	1.00
138	Carlos Delgado	.75
139	Rafael Furcal	.50
140	Ichiro Suzuki	2.00
141	Aubrey Huff	.40
142	Garret Anderson	.50
143	Vernon Wells	.40
144	Magglio Ordonez	.50
145	Brett Myers	.40
146	Luis Gonzalez	.40
147	Lance Berkman	.50
148	Frank Thomas	.75
149	Gary Sheffield	.50
150	Tim Hudson	.50
151	Duke Snider	3.00
152	Carl Yastrzemski	4.00
153	Whitey Ford	3.00
154	Cal Ripken Jr.	8.00
155	Dwight Gooden	2.00
156	Warren Spahn	4.00
157	Bob Gibson	3.00
158	Don Mattingly	6.00
159	Jack Morris	2.00
160	Jim Bunning	2.00
161	Fergie Jenkins	2.00
162	Brooks Robinson	3.00
163	George Kell	2.00
164	Darryl Strawberry	2.00
165	Robin Roberts	2.00
166	Monte Irvin	2.00
167	Ernie Banks	4.00
168	Wade Boggs	3.00
169	Gaylord Perry	2.00
170	Keith Hernandez	2.00
171	Lou Brock	3.00
172	Frank Robinson	3.00
173	Nolan Ryan	8.00
174	Stan Musial	3.00
175	Eddie Murray	3.00
176	Byron Gettis	.50
177	Merkin Valdez RC	5.00
178	Rickie Weeks	3.00
179	Akinori Otsuka RC	3.00
180	Brian Bruney	3.00
181	Freddy Guzman RC	3.00
182	Brendan Harris	3.00
183	John Gall RC	3.00
184	Jason Kubel	3.00
185	Delmon Young	4.00
186	Ryan Howard	3.00
187	Adam Loewen	3.00
188	J.D. Durbin	3.00
189	Dan Haren	3.00
190	Dustin McGowan	3.00
191	Chad Gaudin	3.00
192	Preston Larrison	3.00
193	Ramon Nivar	3.00
194	Ronald Belisario RC	3.00
195	Mike Gosling	3.00
196	Kevin Youkilis	3.00
197	Ryan Wagner	3.00
198	Bubba Nelson	3.00
199	Edwin Jackson	3.00
200	Chris Burke	3.00
201	Carlos Hines RC	3.00
202	Greg Dobbs RC	3.00
203	Jamie Brown RC	3.00
204	David Crouthers	3.00
205	Ian Snell RC	5.00
206	Gary Carter	3.00
207	Dale Murphy	3.00
208	Ryne Sandberg	5.00
209	Phil Niekro	2.00
210	Don Sutton	2.00
211	Alex Rodriguez/Yankees/SP	5.00
212	Alfonso Soriano/Rangers/SP	1.00
213	Greg Maddux/Cubs/SP	3.00

Timeless Tributes Green

Cards (1-150):	4-6X
Cards (151-210):	1-2X
Production 50 Sets	

Timeless Tributes Red

Red (1-150):	2-4X
Red (151-210):	1-1.5X
Production 100 Sets	

Timeless Tributes Platinum

No Pricing
Production One Set

Classic Singles Bat

NM/M
Quantity produced listed.

1	Babe Ruth/15	250.00
2	Stan Musial/25	30.00
3	Ted Williams/25	100.00
4	Lou Gehrig/25	125.00
5	Eddie Murray/50	15.00
7	Roy Campanella/50	20.00
8	Robin Yount/50	20.00
9	Roberto Clemente/25	70.00
10	Don Mattingly/50	25.00
12	Carl Yastrzemski/50	20.00
13	Mark Grace/50	15.00
15	Rickey Henderson/50	15.00
16	Reggie Jackson/50	15.00
18	Pee Wee Reese/50	15.00
20	Roger Maris/50	40.00
21	Cal Ripken Jr./50	60.00
23	Willie Stargell/50	15.00
24	Paul Molitor/50	20.00
26	Alan Trammell/50	12.00
27	Sammy Sosa/50	20.00
28	Bobby Doerr/50	8.00
29	Rod Carew/50	15.00
30	Yogi Berra/25	20.00
32	George Brett/50	30.00

Classic Singles Jersey

NM/M
Quantity produced listed.
Prime: No Pricing
Production One Set

2	Nolan Ryan/50	35.00
3	Stan Musial/15	50.00
6	Eddie Murray/100	10.00
7	Roy Campanella/Pants/50	
8	Robin Yount/100	15.00
9	Roberto Clemente/25	75.00
10	Don Mattingly/100	8.00
11	Bob Gibson/15	25.00
12	Carl Yastrzemski/50	20.00
13	Mark Grace/25	20.00
14	Jack Morris/100	6.00
15	Rickey Henderson/25	20.00
16	Reggie Jackson/50	15.00
17	Pee Wee Reese/25	25.00
18	Marty Marion/100	6.00
19	Tommy John/100	6.00
21	Roger Maris/50	50.00
21	Cal Ripken Jr./25	75.00
23	Red Schoendienst/25	10.00
23	Willie Stargell/100	15.00
24	Paul Molitor/100	10.00
25	Whitey Ford/50	25.00
26	Alan Trammell/100	10.00
27	Sammy Sosa/100	20.00
28	Bobby Doerr/50	8.00
29	Rod Carew/100	10.00
30	Yogi Berra/15	35.00
31	Phil Rizzuto/50	20.00
32	George Brett/25	40.00

Classic Singles Jersey-Bat

NM/M
Quantity produced listed.
Prime: No Pricing
Production One Set

2	Nolan Ryan/25	50.00
3	Stan Musial/15	45.00
6	Eddie Murray/25	25.00
7	Roy Campanella/Pants/25	35.00
8	Robin Yount/25	40.00
9	Roberto Clemente/25	125.00
10	Don Mattingly/25	40.00
12	Carl Yastrzemski/25	50.00
13	Mark Grace/25	20.00
15	Rickey Henderson/25	25.00
16	Reggie Jackson/25	25.00
17	Pee Wee Reese/25	25.00
20	Roger Maris/15	75.00
21	Cal Ripken Jr./25	75.00
23	Willie Stargell/25	20.00
24	Paul Molitor/25	25.00
26	Alan Trammell/25	20.00
27	Sammy Sosa/25	25.00
28	Bobby Doerr/25	25.00
29	Rod Carew/25	30.00
30	Yogi Berra/15	40.00
32	George Brett/25	50.00

Classic Combos Bat

NM/M
Quantity produced listed.

1	Babe Ruth, Lou Gehrig/25	375.00
2	Roy Campanella, Pee Wee Reese/50	25.00
3	Ted Williams, Carl Yastrzemski/25	125.00
4	Roberto Clemente, Willie Stargell/25	100.00
5	Eddie Murray, Cal Ripken Jr./50	50.00
6	Roger Maris, Yogi Berra/25	65.00
10	Nolan Ryan, Rod Carew/50	35.00
11	Don Mattingly, Rickey Henderson/50	40.00
15	Robin Yount, Paul Molitor/50	40.00
16	Mark Grace, Sammy Sosa/50	30.00
17	Ted Williams, Bobby Doerr/50	80.00
18	Reggie Jackson, Rod Carew/50	25.00

Classic Combos Jersey

NM/M
Quantity produced listed.
Prime: No Pricing
Production One Set

1	Babe Ruth Pants, Lou Gehrig/Pants/15	500.00
2	Roy Campanella/Pants, Pee Wee Reese/25	30.00
3	Ted Williams, Carl Yastrzemski/15	200.00
4	Roberto Clemente, Willie Stargell/25	85.00
5	Eddie Murray, Cal Ripken Jr./25	75.00
6	Roger Maris, Yogi Berra/25	65.00
8	Whitey Ford, Yogi Berra/25	30.00
9	Marty Marion, Stan Musial/25	40.00
10	Nolan Ryan, Rod Carew/25	40.00
11	Don Mattingly, Rickey Henderson/50	40.00
12	Jack Morris, Alan Trammell/50	15.00
13	Whitey Ford, Phil Rizzuto/25	30.00
14	Marty Marion, Red Schoendienst/25	15.00
15	Robin Yount, Paul Molitor/50	40.00
16	Mark Grace, Sammy Sosa/25	30.00
17	Ted Williams, Bobby Doerr/15	150.00
18	Reggie Jackson, Rod Carew/50	

Classic Combos Quad

NM/M
Quantity produced listed.
Prime: No Pricing
Production One Set

2	Roy Campanella/Pants, Pee Wee Reese/25	50.00
3	Ted Williams, Carl Yastrzemski/15	250.00
	Roberto Clemente, Willie Stargell/25	200.00
	Eddie Murray, Cal Ripken Jr./25	125.00
	Roger Maris, Yogi Berra/15	150.00
10	Nolan Ryan, Rod Carew/25	70.00
11	Don Mattingly, Rickey Henderson/25	80.00
15	Robin Yount, Paul Molitor/25	75.00
16	Mark Grace, Sammy Sosa/25	60.00
17	Ted Williams, Bobby Doerr/15	200.00
18	Reggie Jackson, Rod Carew/25	40.00

Dress Code Bat

		NM/M
Common Player:		5.00
Production 50 Sets		
Combo Material:		1-1.5X
Production 50 Sets		
1	Derek Jeter	25.00
2	Kerry Wood	15.00
3	Nomar Garciaparra	15.00
5	Jacque Jones	5.00
5	Mark Teixeira	6.00
6	Troy Glaus	8.00
7	Todd Helton	10.00
8	Miguel Tejada	6.00
9	Mike Piazza	12.00
11	Mike Sweeney	5.00
12	Albert Pujols	20.00
13	Rickey Henderson	10.00
14	Chipper Jones	10.00
15	Don Mattingly	25.00
16	Shawn Green	5.00
17	Mark Grace	10.00
18	Jason Giambi	8.00
19	Barry Zito	8.00
20	Sammy Sosa	15.00
22	Rafael Palmeiro	10.00
23	Frank Thomas	10.00
24	Manny Ramirez	8.00
25	Mike Mussina	10.00
27	Magglio Ordonez	6.00
28	Rocco Baldelli	12.00
28	Andruw Jones	8.00
29	Torii Hunter	6.00
31	Ivan Rodriguez	10.00
31	Jeff Bagwell	8.00
32	Mark Mulder	6.00
33	Trot Nixon	10.00
34	Cal Ripken Jr.	60.00
35	Dontrelle Willis	8.00
36	Hank Blalock	8.00
37	Brandon Webb	8.00
38	Miguel Cabrera	10.00
39	Hideo Nomo	8.00
40	Tim Hudson	8.00
42	Pedro Martinez	8.00
43	Hee Seop Choi	6.00
44	Randy Johnson	8.00
45	Tony Gwynn	15.00
46	Mark Prior	10.00
47	Eric Chavez	10.00
48	Alex Rodriguez	15.00
50	Alfonso Soriano	12.00

Dress Code Jersey

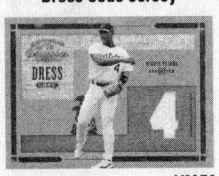

		NM/M
Common Player:		4.00
Production 100 Sets		
Number:		1X
Production 100 Sets		
Prime:		2X
Production 25 Sets		
1	Derek Jeter	25.00
2	Kerry Wood	10.00
3	Nomar Garciaparra	10.00
4	Jacque Jones	4.00
5	Mark Teixeira	5.00
6	Troy Glaus	6.00
7	Todd Helton	6.00
8	Miguel Tejada	6.00
9	Mike Piazza	10.00
11	Mike Sweeney	4.00
12	Albert Pujols	15.00
13	Rickey Henderson	8.00
14	Chipper Jones	
15	Don Mattingly	25.00
16	Shawn Green	5.00
17	Mark Grace	10.00
18	Jason Giambi	8.00
19	Barry Zito	8.00
20	Sammy Sosa	12.00
21	Jay Gibbons	4.00
22	Rafael Palmeiro	8.00
23	Frank Thomas	8.00
24	Manny Ramirez	8.00
25	Mike Mussina	8.00
26	Magglio Ordonez	6.00
27	Rocco Baldelli	6.00
28	Andruw Jones	6.00
29	Torii Hunter	6.00
30	Ivan Rodriguez	6.00
31	Jeff Bagwell	6.00
32	Mark Mulder	6.00
33	Trot Nixon	6.00
34	Cal Ripken Jr./25	80.00
35	Dontrelle Willis	6.00
36	Hank Blalock	5.00
37	Brandon Webb	4.00
38	Miguel Cabrera	12.00
39	Hideo Nomo	8.00
40	Shannon Stewart	4.00
41	Tim Hudson	6.00
42	Pedro Martinez	6.00
44	Hee Seop Choi	4.00
44	Randy Johnson	8.00
45	Tony Gwynn	10.00
46	Mark Prior	10.00
47	Eric Chavez	6.00
48	Alex Rodriguez	10.00
49	Johan Santana	4.00
50	Alfonso Soriano	8.00

Dress Code Combos Signature

NM/M
Quantity produced listed.
Prime: No Pricing
Production One Set

4	Jacque Jones/Jsy/25	15.00
21	Jay Gibbons/Jsy/25	15.00
32	Mark Mulder/Jsy/25	35.00
33	Trot Nixon/Jsy/25	50.00
35	Dontrelle Willis/Jsy/25	40.00
38	Miguel Cabrera/Jsy/25	70.00
40	Shannon Stewart/Jsy/25	20.00
49	Johan Santana/Jsy/25	40.00

Famous Foursomes

NM/M
Production 99 Sets

1	Roy Campanella, Pee Wee Reese, Jackie Robinson, Duke Snider	15.00
2	Stan Musial, Bob Gibson, Red Schoendienst, Clete Boyer	15.00

Famous Foursomes Jersey

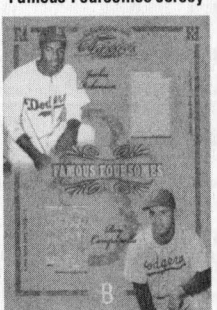

No Pricing
Production 10 Sets
Prime: No Pricing
Production One Set

Legendary Hats Material

NM/M
Quantity produced listed.

2	Mike Schmidt/25	50.00
6	George Brett/25	60.00
14	Cal Ripken Jr./25	100.00
16	Kirby Puckett/25	30.00
20	Reggie Jackson/Yanks/25	25.00
22	Ernie Banks/25	35.00
29	Dave Winfield/25	15.00
40	Wade Boggs/25	25.00
42	Rickey Henderson/A's/25	20.00
49	Reggie Jackson/Angels/25	25.00
51	Rafael Palmeiro/25	20.00
52	Sammy Sosa/25	20.00
55	Steve Carlton/25	15.00
56	Rod Carew Angels/25	20.00
60	R Henderson Angels/25	20.00

Legendary Jackets Material

NM/M
Production 100 Sets

2	Mike Schmidt	15.00
8	Reggie Jackson A's	15.00
17	Don Mattingly	

32	Gary Carter	5.00
54	Nolan Ryan	30.00
56	Rod Carew Angels	10.00

Legendary Jerseys Material

NM/M
Quantity produced listed.
Number: 1X
Production 3-50
No pricing for production 15 or less.
Prime: No Pricing
Production One Set

1	Tony Gwynn	20.00
2	Mike Schmidt/25	35.00
3	Johnny Bench/50	15.00
6	George Brett/25	50.00
7	Carlton Fisk/50	10.00
9	Reggie Jackson/25	30.00
9	Joe Morgan/25	15.00
10	Bo Jackson/25	50.00
12	Andre Dawson/50	10.00
13	R Henderson/25	20.00
14	Cal Ripken Jr./25	85.00
15	Dale Murphy/25	30.00
16	Kirby Puckett/50	15.00
17	Don Mattingly/50	25.00
18	Brooks Robinson/50	20.00
19	Orlando Cepeda/50	8.00
20	Reggie Jackson/25	25.00
21	Roberto Clemente/25	75.00
23	Frank Robinson/50	10.00
24	Harmon Killebrew/50	15.00
25	Willie Stargell/50	20.00
27	Carl Yastrzemski/50	25.00
29	Dave Winfield/50	10.00
30	Eddie Murray/50	20.00
31	Eddie Mathews/25	25.00
32	Gary Carter/50	20.00
33	Rod Carew/25	20.00
36	Paul Molitor/50	15.00
39	Robin Yount/50	25.00
40	Wade Boggs/50	15.00
42	Rickey Henderson/25	25.00
44	Yogi Berra/15	35.00
46	Luis Aparicio/25	8.00
47	Phil Rizzuto/25	20.00
48	Roger Maris/25	40.00
49	Reggie Jackson/25	15.00
51	Rafael Palmeiro/50	10.00
52	Sammy Sosa/50	20.00
53	Roger Clemens/50	25.00
54	Nolan Ryan/50	30.00
55	Steve Carlton/50	8.00
56	Rod Carew/50	15.00
57	Whitey Ford/25	35.00

Legendary Leather Material

NM/M
Quantity produced listed.

16	Kirby Puckett/Fld Glv/25	40.00
32	Gary Carter/Fld Glv/25	35.00
51	Rafael Palmeiro/Fld Glv/25	25.00
52	Sammy Sosa/Btg Glv/25	50.00
55	Steve Carlton/Fld Glv/25	15.00
58	Fergie Jenkins/Fld Glv/25	15.00

Legendary Lumberjacks

NM/M
Common Player: 2.00
Production 1,000 Sets
Spikes: 1-2X
Production 100 Sets
Bats: 2-3X
Production 50 Sets
Jackets: 2-3X

Production 50 Sets
Jerseys: 1X
Production 500 Sets
Leather: 1-2X
Production 100 Sets
Pants: 2-3X
Production 50 Sets

1	Tony Gwynn	3.00
2	Mike Schmidt	5.00
3	Johnny Bench	4.00
4	Roger Maris	5.00
5	Ted Williams	8.00
6	George Brett	6.00
7	Carlton Fisk	2.00
8	Reggie Jackson	3.00
9	Joe Morgan	2.00
10	Bo Jackson	3.00
11	Stan Musial	4.00
12	Andre Dawson	2.00
13	Rickey Henderson	2.00
14	Cal Ripken Jr.	8.00
15	Dale Murphy	2.00
16	Kirby Puckett	4.00
17	Don Mattingly	5.00
18	Brooks Robinson	3.00
19	Orlando Cepeda	2.00
20	Reggie Jackson	3.00
21	Roberto Clemente	6.00
22	Ernie Banks	4.00
23	Frank Robinson	3.00
24	Harmon Killebrew	3.00
25	Willie Stargell	3.00
26	Al Kaline	4.00
27	Carl Yastrzemski	4.00
28	Duke Snider	3.00
29	Dave Winfield	2.00
30	Eddie Murray	3.00
31	Eddie Matthews	3.00
32	Gary Carter	2.00
33	Rod Carew	3.00
34	Jimmie Foxx	4.00
35	Mel Ott	3.00
36	Paul Molitor	3.00
37	Thurman Munson	4.00
38	Rogers Hornsby	3.00
39	Robin Yount	4.00
40	Wade Boggs	3.00
41	Jackie Robinson	5.00
42	Rickey Henderson	2.00
43	Ty Cobb	5.00
44	Yogi Berra	3.00
45	Roy Campanella	4.00
46	Luis Aparicio	2.00
47	Phil Rizzuto	3.00
48	Roger Maris	5.00
49	Reggie Jackson	3.00
50	Lou Gehrig	6.00
51	Rafael Palmeiro	3.00
52	Sammy Sosa	5.00
53	Roger Clemens	6.00
54	Nolan Ryan	5.00
55	Steve Carlton	3.00
56	Rod Carew	3.00
57	Whitey Ford	3.00
58	Fergie Jenkins	2.00
59	Babe Ruth	8.00
	R Henderson	

Legendary Lumberjacks Material

NM/M
Quantity produced listed.

1	Tony Gwynn/100	15.00
2	Mike Schmidt/100	15.00
3	Johnny Bench/100	12.00
4	Roger Maris /25	40.00
5	Ted Williams/25	100.00
6	George Brett/100	25.00
7	Carlton Fisk/100	10.00
8	Reggie Jackson /100	12.00
9	Joe Morgan/100	10.00
10	Bo Jackson/100	15.00
11	Stan Musial/25	35.00
12	Andre Dawson/100	10.00
13	R Henderson/100	10.00
14	Cal Ripken Jr./100	40.00
15	Dale Murphy/100	10.00
16	Kirby Puckett/100	15.00
17	Don Mattingly/100	20.00
18	Brooks Robinson/100	15.00
19	Orlando Cepeda/100	10.00
20	Reggie Jackson/100	12.00
21	Roberto Clemente/25	65.00
22	Ernie Banks/100	15.00
23	Frank Robinson/100	15.00
24	Harmon Killebrew/100	20.00
25	Willie Stargell/100	15.00

26	Al Kaline/100	15.00
27	Carl Yastrzemski/100	15.00
28	Dave Winfield/100	5.00
30	Eddie Murray/100	15.00
31	Eddie Mathews/100	20.00
32	Gary Carter/100	8.00
33	Rod Carew/100	10.00
35	Mel Ott/25	35.00
36	Paul Molitor/100	10.00
37	Thurman Munson/50	20.00
38	Rogers Hornsby/25	50.00
39	Robin Yount/100	15.00
42	Wade Boggs/100	10.00
43	Rickey Henderson/50	10.00
44	Yogi Berra/25	20.00
45	Roy Campanella/25	30.00
46	Luis Aparicio/100	8.00
48	Roger Maris/25	40.00
49	Reggie Jackson/25	15.00
50	Lou Gehrig/25	125.00
51	Rafael Palmeiro/100	8.00
52	Sammy Sosa/100	15.00
56	Rod Carew/100	8.00
57	R Henderson/100	10.00

Legendary Pants Material

NM/M
Quantity produced listed.

1	Tony Gwynn/25	25.00
12	Andre Dawson/25	10.00
24	Harmon Killebrew/50	10.00
26	Al Kaline/50	30.00
45	Roy Campanella/25	25.00
46	Luis Aparicio/50	10.00
47	Phil Rizzuto/50	8.00
48	Roger Maris A's/25	30.00
51	Rafael Palmeiro/25	8.00
56	Rod Carew Angels/50	15.00
57	Whitey Ford/25	25.00
58	Fergie Jenkins/25	8.00

Legendary Spikes Material

NM/M
Quantity produced listed.

13	R Henderson Yanks/25	30.00
17	Don Mattingly/50	40.00
29	Dave Winfield/50	15.00
42	Rickey Henderson A's/25	30.00
51	Rafael Palmeiro/25	25.00
52	Sammy Sosa/50	30.00
60	R Henderson Angels/25	30.00

Membership

NM/M
Complete Set (25): 70.00
Common Player: 2.00
Production 2,499 Sets

1	Stan Musial	4.00
2	Ted Williams	5.00
3	Early Wynn	2.00
4	Roberto Clemente	5.00
5	Al Kaline	4.00
6	Bob Gibson	3.00
7	Lou Brock	2.00
8	Carl Yastrzemski	4.00
9	Gaylord Perry	2.00
10	Fergie Jenkins	2.00
11	Steve Carlton	2.00
12	Reggie Jackson	3.00
13	Rod Carew	3.00
14	Bert Blyleven	2.00
15	Mike Schmidt	4.00
16	Nolan Ryan	6.00
17	Robin Yount	4.00
18	George Brett	3.00
19	Eddie Murray	3.00
20	Tony Gwynn	3.00
21	Cal Ripken Jr.	8.00
22	Randy Johnson	4.00
23	Sammy Sosa	5.00
24	Rafael Palmeiro	3.00
25	Roger Clemens	5.00

Membership VIP Bat

NM/M
Quantity produced listed.

1	Stan Musial/25	40.00
2	Ted Williams/25	100.00
4	Roberto Clemente/25	65.00
5	Al Kaline/25	20.00
7	Lou Brock/25	20.00
8	Carl Yastrzemski/25	25.00
11	Steve Carlton/25	15.00
12	Reggie Jackson/25	25.00
13	Rod Carew/25	25.00
15	Mike Schmidt/25	30.00
17	Robin Yount/25	25.00
19	Eddie Murray/25	25.00
20	Tony Gwynn/25	25.00
22	Randy Johnson/25	30.00
23	Sammy Sosa/25	30.00
24	Rafael Palmeiro/25	20.00
25	Roger Clemens/25	25.00

Membership VIP Jersey

NM/M
Quantity produced listed.
Prime: No Pricing
Production One Set

1	Stan Musial/15	40.00
4	Roberto Clemente/25	75.00
5	Al Kaline/Pants/25	30.00
8	Carl Yastrzemski/25	30.00
9	Gaylord Perry/25	10.00
10	Fergie Jenkins/Pants/25	15.00
11	Steve Carlton/25	25.00
12	Reggie Jackson/25	25.00
13	Rod Carew/25	20.00
14	Bert Blyleven/25	10.00
15	Mike Schmidt/25	30.00
16	Nolan Ryan/25	35.00
17	George Brett/25	40.00
19	Eddie Murray/25	25.00
20	Tony Gwynn/25	25.00
21	Cal Ripken Jr./25	85.00
22	Randy Johnson/25	25.00
23	Sammy Sosa/25	30.00
24	Rafael Palmeiro/25	25.00
25	Roger Clemens/25	25.00

Membership VIP Signatures

NM/M
Quantity produced listed.

5	Al Kaline/20	50.00
9	Gaylord Perry/25	15.00
10	Fergie Jenkins/50	20.00
11	Steve Carlton/20	30.00
14	Bert Blyleven/25	10.00

Membership VIP Combos Material

NM/M
Quantity produced listed.
Prime: No Pricing
Production One Set

1	Stan Musial/Bat-Jsy/15	40.00
4	Roberto Clemente/Bat-Jsy/25	100.00
5	Al Kaline/Bat-Pants/25	30.00
8	Carl Yastrzemski/Bat-Jsy/25	50.00
10	Fergie Jenkins/Fld Glv-Pants/25	15.00
11	Steve Carlton/Bat-Jsy/25	-15.00
12	Reggie Jackson/Bat-Jsy/25	30.00
13	Rod Carew/Bat-Pants/25	25.00
15	Mike Schmidt/Bat-Jsy/25	40.00
16	Nolan Ryan/Bat-Jsy/25	40.00
17	Robin Yount/Bat-Jsy/25	40.00
18	George Brett/Bat-Jsy/25	50.00
19	Eddie Murray/Bat-Jsy/25	30.00
20	Tony Gwynn/Bat-Jsy/25	40.00
21	Cal Ripken Jr./Bat-Jsy/25	80.00
22	Randy Johnson/Bat-Jsy/25	25.00
23	Sammy Sosa/Bat-Jsy/25	35.00
24	Rafael Palmeiro/Bat-Jsy/25	25.00
25	Roger Clemens/Bat-Jsy/25	30.00

Membership VIP Combos Signature

NM/M
Quantity produced listed.
Prime: No Pricing
Production One Set

8	Al Kaline/Pants/25	50.00
9	Gaylord Perry/Jsy/50	15.00
10	Fergie Jenkins/Jsy/25	20.00
11	Steve Carlton/Jsy/50	40.00
14	Bert Blyleven/Jsy/25	15.00

2004 Donruss Classics National Trading Card Day

As part of its participation in NTCD on April 3, Donruss-Playoff issued a foil pack with four baseball player cards and two football, plus a header. Only the baseball players are listed here. Fronts have game-action photos on a ghosted background; backs have recent stats, biographical data and career highlights. The NTCD logo appears on front.

NM/M
Unopened Pack: 3.00
Common Player: .25

DP-1	Albert Pujols	.50
DP-2	Roger Clemens	.25
DP-3	Mike Piazza	.25
DP-4	Alfonso Soriano	.25

October Heroes

NM/M
Production 2,499 Sets

1	Reggie Jackson	3.00
2	Bob Gibson	3.00
3	Carlton Fisk	2.00
4	Whitey Ford	2.00
5	George Brett	5.00
6	Roberto Clemente	5.00
7	Roy Campanella	3.00
8	Babe Ruth	8.00

October Heroes Bat

NM/M
Quantity produced listed.

1	Reggie Jackson/25	25.00
3	Carlton Fisk/25	25.00
6	Roberto Clemente/25	65.00
7	Roy Campanella/25	25.00

October Heroes Fabric

NM/M
Quantity produced listed.

2	Bob Gibson/Jsy/15	30.00
3	Carlton Fisk/Jsy/25	25.00
4	Whitey Ford/Jsy/25	20.00
5	George Brett/Jsy/25	40.00
7	Roy Campanella/Pants/25	20.00

October Heroes Signature

NM/M
Quantity produced listed.

4	Whitey Ford/50	40.00

October Heroes Combos Material

NM/M
Quantity produced listed.

1	Reggie Jackson/Bat-Hat/25	40.00
3	Carlton Fisk/Bat-Jsy/25	30.00
5	George Brett/Bat-Jsy/25	50.00
7	Roy Campanella/Bat-Pants/25	35.00

October Heroes Combos Signature

NM/M
Quantity produced listed.

4	Whitey Ford Jsy/50	45.00

Significant Signatures Green

NM/M
Quantity produced listed.

3	Hank Blalock	40.00
5	Shannon Stewart/50	10.00
7	Trot Nixon/50	30.00
13	Mike Lowell/25	25.00
14	Robin Ventura/50	15.00
21	Carlos Beltran/50	50.00
21	Johan Santana/50	35.00
25	Steve Finley/25	25.00
26	Alexis Rios/100	15.00
32	Miguel Cabrera/50	50.00
36	Dontrelle Willis/25	25.00
37	Rafael Soriano/100	6.00
38	Richard Fischer/100	6.00
39	Brian Tallet/100	6.00
40	Jose Castillo/50	6.00
41	Wade Miller/25	20.00
44	Runelvys Hernandez/20	10.00
47	Joe Borchard/50	8.00
47	Adam Dunn/25	30.00
49	Brandon Phillips/50	6.00

53	Cliff Lee/50	20.00
54	Chien-Ming Wang/50	150.00
57	Jhonny Peralta/100	6.00
60	Jae Weong Seo/50	15.00
61	Nic Jackson/100	6.00
63	Jimmy Gobble/45	8.00
64	Travis Hafner/50	12.00
66	Jerome Williams/50	20.00
68	Alexis Gomez/50	6.00
70	Zach Day/50	8.00
72	Morgan Ensberg/50	8.00
74	Garrett Atkins/99	6.00
77	Lyle Overbay/100	6.00
78	Josh Phelps/25	10.00
79	Juan Gonzalez/25	45.00
80	Rich Harden/50	15.00
84	Jody Gerut/50	15.00
87	Jay Gibbons/50	15.00
88	Chone Figgins/50	10.00
99	Jay Payton/50	10.00
99	Barry Larkin/25	40.00
102	Robby Hammock/50	6.00
103	Orlando Hudson/50	8.00
105	Hong-Chih Kuo/50	30.00
106	Eric Chavez/35	35.00
108	Jacque Jones/50	10.00
109	Ken Harvey/100	8.00
110	Aramis Ramirez/50	20.00
111	Victor Martinez/50	20.00
112	Joe Crede/50	10.00
113	Jason Varitek/25	40.00
118	Brandon Webb/25	10.00
121	Sammy Sosa/21	150.00
127	Luis Castillo/25	10.00
134	Edgar Martinez/25	40.00
145	Brett Myers/50	8.00
149	Gary Sheffield/25	25.00
151	Duke Snider/25	35.00
153	Whitey Ford/25	40.00
155	Dwight Gooden/25	20.00
158	Don Mattingly/75	100.00
159	Jack Morris/25	10.00
160	Jim Bunning/25	25.00
161	Fergie Jenkins/25	15.00
163	George Kell/75	15.00
164	Darryl Strawberry/50	20.00
165	Robin Roberts/25	30.00
166	Monte Irvin/25	20.00
167	Ernie Banks/25	60.00
168	Wade Boggs/25	40.00
169	Gaylord Perry/50	10.00
170	Keith Hernandez/50	20.00
172	Frank Robinson/25	30.00
173	Nolan Ryan/25	120.00
174	Stan Musial/25	70.00
175	Eddie Murray/25	50.00
176	Byron Gettis/100	10.00
177	Merkin Valdez/100	20.00
178	Rickie Weeks/25	30.00
180	Brian Bruney/100	6.00
181	Freddy Guzman/100	6.00
182	Brendan Harris/100	6.00
183	John Gall/100	8.00
184	Jason Kubel/100	12.00
185	Delmon Young/50	30.00
186	Ryan Howard/100	80.00
187	Adam Loewen/100	15.00
188	J.D. Durbin/100	8.00
189	Dan Haren/100	10.00
190	Dustin McGowan/100	10.00
191	Chad Gaudin/100	6.00
192	Preston Larrison/100	6.00
193	Ramon Nivar/100	6.00
195	Mike Gosling/100	6.00
196	Kevin Youkilis/100	15.00
197	Ryan Wagner/100	10.00
198	Bubba Nelson/100	8.00
199	Edwin Jackson/100	10.00
200	Chris Burke/100	10.00
201	Carlos Hines/100	10.00
202	Greg Dobbs/50	6.00
203	Jamie Brown/100	8.00
204	David Crouthers/100	6.00
205	Ian Snell/100	30.00
206	Gary Carter/50	25.00
207	Dale Murphy/50	40.00
208	Ryne Sandberg/50	75.00
209	Phil Niekro/50	20.00
210	Don Sutton/50	15.00

Significant Signatures Red

NM/M
Quantity produced listed.

3	Hank Blalock/50	30.00
5	Shannon Stewart/25	8.00
6	Carlos Lee/25	20.00
7	Trot Nixon/50	20.00
9	Mark Mulder/25	30.00

#	Player	Price
12	Jim Edmonds/25	30.00
13	Mike Lowell/50	20.00
14	Robin Ventura/50	10.00
16	Jose Vidro/25	20.00
19	Carlos Beltran/25	50.00
21	Johan Santana/100	30.00
24	Steve Finley/100	20.00
26	Alexis Rios/250	6.00
27	Rafael Palmeiro/25	65.00
28	Jorge Posada/25	45.00
32	Miguel Cabrera/100	40.00
36	Dontrelle Willis/100	25.00
37	Rafael Soriano/25	6.00
38	Richard Fischer/250	6.00
39	Brian Tallet/250	6.00
40	Jose Castillo/250	6.00
41	Wade Miller/92	15.00
42	Jose Contreras/25	25.00
43	Runelvys Hernandez/50	8.00
44	Joe Borchard/250	6.00
47	Adam Dunn/25	30.00
49	Brandon Phillips/70	6.00
50	Scott Rolen/25	35.00
53	Cliff Lee/100	15.00
54	Chien-Ming Wang/250	100.00
55	Roy Oswalt/25	30.00
56	Austin Kearns/25	20.00
57	Jhonny Peralta/250	6.00
60	Jae Weong Seo/100	10.00
61	Nic Jackson/250	8.00
63	Jimmy Gobble/250	10.00
64	Travis Hafner/100	12.00
65	Paul Konerko/25	15.00
66	Jerome Williams/250	20.00
68	Alexis Gomez/100	6.00
70	Zach Day/100	8.00
72	Morgan Ensberg/100	8.00
74	Garrett Atkins/245	6.00
76	Julio Franco/25	20.00
77	Lyle Overbay/250	15.00
78	Josh Phelps/250	8.00
79	Juan Gonzalez/25	45.00
80	Rich Harden/150	10.00
82	Torii Hunter/250	30.00
84	Jody Gerut/100	15.00
87	Jay Gibbons/100	15.00
88	Chone Figgins/100	10.00
90	Rich Aurilia/25	15.00
92	Marlon Byrd/25	15.00
93	Jay Payton/100	8.00
99	Barry Larkin/25	40.00
102	Robby Hammock/150	6.00
103	Orlando Hudson/25	8.00
105	Hong-Chih Kuo/100	30.00
106	Eric Chavez/25	35.00
107	Nick Johnson/25	15.00
108	Jacque Jones/100	10.00
109	Ken Harvey/25	8.00
110	Aramis Ramirez/100	20.00
111	Victor Martinez/99	20.00
112	Joe Crede/250	10.00
113	Jason Varitek/50	35.00
114	Troy Glaus/25	30.00
118	Brandon Webb/50	15.00
119	Craig Biggio/25	30.00
120	Orlando Cabrera/25	10.00
121	Sammy Sosa/25	150.00
122	Bobby Abreu/25	15.00
123	Andruw Jones/25	30.00
124	Jeff Bagwell/25	65.00
127	Luis Castillo/25	10.00
131	Eric Byrnes/25	10.00
132	Eric Hinske/25	15.00
134	Edgar Martinez/50	30.00
135	Rocco Baldelli/25	40.00
143	Vernon Wells/25	40.00
144	Magglio Ordonez/25	30.00
145	Brett Myers/100	8.00
149	Gary Sheffield/50	20.00
150	Tim Hudson/25	40.00
151	Duke Snider/50	30.00
153	Whitey Ford/50	40.00
155	Dwight Gooden/100	20.00
156	Warren Spahn/25	45.00
158	Don Mattingly/25	100.00
159	Jack Morris/100	10.00
160	Jim Bunning/100	20.00
161	Fergie Jenkins/100	15.00
163	George Kell/100	15.00
164	Darryl Strawberry/100	20.00
165	Robin Roberts/100	15.00
166	Monte Irvin/100	15.00
167	Ernie Banks/50	50.00
168	Wade Boggs/50	30.00
169	Gaylord Perry/100	10.00
170	Keith Hernandez/100	20.00
171	Lou Brock/50	30.00
172	Frank Robinson/25	25.00
173	Nolan Ryan/50	85.00
174	Stan Musial/50	60.00
175	Eddie Murray/50	30.00
176	Byron Gettis/250	6.00
177	Merkin Valdez/250	15.00
178	Rickie Weeks/250	25.00
180	Brian Bruney/250	6.00
181	Freddy Guzman/250	6.00
182	Brendan Harris/250	6.00
183	John Gall/250	6.00
184	Jason Kubel/250	10.00
185	Delmon Young/100	30.00
186	Ryan Howard/250	70.00
187	Adam Loewen/250	15.00
188	J.D. Durbin/250	6.00
189	Dan Haren/250	10.00
190	Dustin McGowan/250	10.00
191	Chad Gaudin/250	6.00
192	Preston Larrison/250	6.00
193	Ramon Nivar/250	6.00
195	Mike Gosling/250	6.00
196	Kevin Youkilis/250	15.00
197	Ryan Wagner/250	10.00
198	Bubba Nelson/250	8.00
199	Edwin Jackson/250	10.00
200	Chris Burke/250	6.00
201	Carlos Hines/250	6.00
202	Greg Dobbs/250	6.00
203	Jamie Brown/250	8.00
204	David Crouthers/250	6.00
205	Ian Snell/250	25.00
206	Gary Carter/100	20.00
207	Dale Murphy/50	40.00
208	Ryne Sandberg/25	85.00
209	Phil Niekro/100	15.00
210	Don Sutton/100	15.00

Team Colors Bat
NM/M
Quantity produced listed.

#	Player	Price
2	Steve Garvey/50	10.00
3	Eric Davis/25	15.00
4	Al Oliver/50	8.00
6	Bobby Doerr/25	20.00
7	Paul Molitor/50	15.00
8	Dale Murphy/50	20.00
11	Jose Canseco/50	20.00
12	Jim Rice/50	12.00
13	Will Clark/50	25.00
14	Alan Trammell/50	12.00
18	Dwight Evans/50	15.00
21	Andre Dawson/Expos/50	10.00
22	Darryl Strawberry/Dgr/50	10.00
23	George Foster/50	8.00
26	Bo Jackson/50	30.00
27	Cal Ripken Jr./50	50.00
28	Deion Sanders/25	15.00
30	Don Mattingly/Jkt/25	25.00
31	Fred Lynn/50	8.00
33	Ernie Banks/25	30.00
34	Gary Carter/50	12.00
35	Roger Maris/50	40.00
36	Ron Santo/50	12.00
38	Tony Gwynn/50	15.00
40	Red Schoendienst/25	15.00
41	Steve Carlton/25	15.00
42	Wade Boggs/25	25.00
44	Luis Aparicio/50	15.00
46	Andre Dawson/Cubs/25	12.00
48	Darryl Strawberry/Mets/50	10.00
49	Dave Parker/Reds/50	8.00

Team Colors Jersey
NM/M
Quantity produced listed.
Prime: No Pricing
Production One Set

#	Player	Price
1	Lenny Dykstra/Mets Fld Glv/25	15.00
2	Steve Garvey/100	6.00
3	Eric Davis/25	15.00
5	Nolan Ryan/50	30.00
6	Bobby Doerr/25	15.00
7	Paul Molitor/100	10.00
8	Dale Murphy/50	20.00
9	Harold Baines/100	8.00
10	Dwight Gooden/50	10.00
11	Jose Canseco/100	15.00
12	Jim Rice/50	8.00
13	Will Clark/50	25.00
14	Alan Trammell/50	8.00
15	Lee Smith/100	5.00
16	Dwight Evans/50	15.00
17	Tony Oliva/100	8.00
18	Dave Parker/Pirates/25	10.00
19	Jack Morris/100	6.00
20	Luis Tiant/100	6.00
21	Andre Dawson/Expos/100	6.00
22	Darryl Strawberry/Dgr/100	8.00
23	George Foster/100	5.00
24	Marty Marion/100	6.00
25	Dennis Eckersley/100	6.00
26	Bo Jackson/50	30.00
27	Cal Ripken Jr./100	35.00
28	Deion Sanders/50	8.00
29	Don Mattingly/Jkt/100	20.00
30	Mark Grace/50	15.00
31	Fred Lynn/50	8.00
33	Ernie Banks/25	30.00
34	Gary Carter/Jkt/100	20.00
37	Keith Hernandez/25	15.00
38	Tony Gwynn/50	15.00
39	Jim Palmer/25	15.00
40	Red Schoendienst/25	15.00
41	Steve Carlton/25	15.00
43	Tommy John/50	15.00
44	Luis Aparicio/50	10.00
46	Andre Dawson/Cubs/25	15.00
47	Bert Blyleven/100	5.00
48	Darryl Strawberry/Mets/50	8.00
49	Dave Parker/Reds/100	5.00

Team Colors Signatures
NM/M
Quantity produced listed.

#	Player	Price
1	Lenny Dykstra/Mets/50	15.00
2	Steve Garvey/50	25.00
3	Eric Davis/50	20.00
4	Al Oliver/50	15.00
6	Bobby Doerr/50	20.00
9	Harold Baines/50	25.00
10	Dwight Gooden/50	20.00
12	Jim Rice/50	20.00
14	Alan Trammell/50	20.00
15	Lee Smith/50	15.00
16	Dwight Evans/50	20.00
17	Tony Oliva/50	20.00
18	Dave Parker/Pirates/50	15.00
19	Jack Morris/50	10.00
20	Luis Tiant/50	15.00
21	Andre Dawson/Expos/50	25.00
22	Darryl Strawberry/Dgr/50	20.00
23	George Foster/50	15.00
24	Marty Marion/50	15.00
25	Dennis Eckersley/25	25.00
31	Fred Lynn/50	15.00
35	Gary Carter/20	35.00
37	Keith Hernandez/25	35.00
39	Jim Palmer/20	35.00
40	Red Schoendienst/50	15.00
41	Steve Carlton/20	35.00
43	Tommy John/50	15.00
44	Luis Aparicio/50	20.00
45	Bob Feller/50	20.00
46	Andre Dawson/Cubs/25	25.00
47	Bert Blyleven/50	12.00
48	Darryl Strawberry/Mets/50	20.00
49	Dave Parker/Reds/50	15.00
50	Lenny Dykstra/Phils/50	15.00

Team Colors Combos Material
NM/M
Production 25 Sets
Prime: No Pricing
Production One Set

#	Player	Price
2	Steve Garvey/Bat-Jsy	15.00
3	Eric Davis/Bat-Jsy	15.00
5	Nolan Ryan/Bat-Jsy	50.00
6	Bobby Doerr/Bat-Jsy	25.00
7	Paul Molitor/Bat-Jsy	25.00
8	Dale Murphy/Bat-Jsy	25.00
11	Jose Canseco/Bat-Jsy	30.00
12	Jim Rice/Bat-Jsy	25.00
13	Will Clark/Bat-Jst	40.00
14	Alan Trammell/Bat-Jsy	25.00
16	Dwight Evans/Bat-Jsy	25.00
18	Dave Parker/Pirates Bat-Jsy	20.00
21	Andre Dawson/Expos Bat-Jsy	15.00
22	Darryl Strawberry/Dgr Bat-Jsy	20.00
23	George Foster/Bat-Jsy	15.00
26	Bo Jackson/Bat-Jsy	40.00
27	Cal Ripken Jr./Bat-Jsy	65.00
28	Deion Sanders/Bat-Jsy	25.00
29	Don Mattingly/Bat-Jsy	45.00
30	Mark Grace/Bat-Jsy	25.00
33	Ernie Banks/Bat-Jsy	45.00
34	Gary Carter/Bat-Jacket	25.00
38	Tony Gwynn/Bat-Jsy	40.00
40	Red Schoendienst/Bat-Jsy	15.00
41	Steve Carlton/Bat-Jsy	20.00
42	Wade Boggs/Bat-Jsy	20.00
45	Luis Aparicio/Bat-Jsy	15.00
46	Andre Dawson/Cubs Bat-Jsy	15.00
48	Darryl Strawberry/Mets Bat-Jsy	20.00
49	Dave Parker/Reds Bat-Jsy	20.00

Team Colors Combos Signature
NM/M
Quantity produced listed.
Prime: No Pricing
Production One Set

#	Player	Price
1	Lenny Dykstra/Mets Fld Glv/100	15.00
2	Steve Garvey/100	15.00
3	Eric Davis/Jsy/100	25.00
4	Al Oliver/Bat/100	20.00
6	Bobby Doerr/Jsy/100	20.00
9	Harold Baines/Jsy/100	20.00
10	Dwight Gooden/Jsy/100	25.00
12	Jim Rice/Jsy/100	20.00
14	Alan Trammell/Jsy/100	25.00
15	Lee Smith/Jsy/100	15.00
16	Dwight Evans/Jsy/100	25.00
17	Tony Oliva Jsy/100	20.00
18	Dave Parker/Pirates Jsy/100	15.00
19	Jack Morris/Jsy/100	20.00
20	Luis Tiant/Jsy/100	20.00
21	Andre Dawson/Expos Jsy/100	25.00
22	Darryl Strawberry/Dgr Jsy/100	25.00
23	George Foster/Jsy/100	20.00
24	Marty Marion/Jsy/100	20.00
25	Dennis Eckersley/Jsy/100	25.00
31	Fred Lynn/Jsy/100	15.00
33	Ernie Banks/Jsy/25	90.00
34	Gary Carter/Jkt/50	40.00
36	Ron Santo/Bat/25	50.00
37	Keith Hernandez/25	45.00
39	Jim Palmer/Jsy/25	35.00
40	Red Schoendienst/Jsy/100	15.00
41	Steve Carlton/Jsy/100	40.00
43	Tommy John/Jsy/100	20.00
44	Luis Aparicio/Jsy/100	15.00
46	Andre Dawson/Cubs Jsy/100	25.00
47	Darryl Strawberry/Mets Jsy/100	25.00
48	Dave Parker/Reds Jsy/100	15.00

Timeless Triples
NM/M
Complete Set (6): 40.00
Common Player:
Production 500 Sets

#	Players	Price
1	Ted Williams, Carl Yastrzemski, Carlton Fisk	10.00
2	Lou Gehrig, Roger Maris, Thurman Munson	8.00
3	Brooks Robinson, Frank Robinson, Cal Ripken Jr.	10.00
4	Roger Clemens, Andy Pettitte, Roy Oswalt	8.00
5	Greg Maddux, Mark Prior, Kerry Wood	8.00
6	Alex Rodriguez, Derek Jeter, Gary Sheffield	10.00

Timeless Triples Bat
NM/M
Production 25 Sets

#	Players	Price
1	Ted Williams, Carl Yastrzemski, Carlton Fisk	185.00
2	Lou Gehrig, Roger Maris, Thurman Munson	200.00
3	Brooks Robinson, Frank Robinson, Cal Ripken Jr.	140.00

Timeless Triples Jersey

NM/M
Quantity produced listed.
Prime: No Pricing
Production One Set

#	Players	Price
3	Brooks Robinson, Frank Robinson, Cal Ripken Jr./25	140.00

2004 Donruss Diamond Kings

NM/M
Complete Set (175): 75.00
Common Player: .25
Common (151-175): 1.50
Pack (5): 7.50
Box (12): 80.00

#	Player	Price
1	Alex Rodriguez	2.50
2	Andruw Jones	.75
3	Nomar Garciaparra	2.00
4	Kerry Wood	.75
5	Magglio Ordonez	.50
6	Victor Martinez	.25
7	Jeremy Bonderman	.25
8	Josh Beckett	.75
9	Jeff Kent	.40
10	Carlos Beltran	.50
11	Hideo Nomo	.50
12	Richie Sexson	.25
13	Jose Vidro	.25
14	Jae Weong Seo	.25
15	Alfonso Soriano	1.00
16	Barry Zito	.50
17	Brett Myers	.25
18	Brian Giles	.40
19	Edgar Martinez	.50
20	Jim Edmonds	.50
21	Rocco Baldelli	.75
22	Mark Teixeira	.50
23	Carlos Delgado	.50
24	Julius Matos	.25
25	Jose Reyes	.50
26	Marlon Byrd	.25
27	Albert Pujols	2.50
28	Vernon Wells	.40
29	Garret Anderson	.50
30	Jerome Williams	.25
31	Chipper Jones	1.00
32	Rich Harden	.50
33	Manny Ramirez	.75
34	Derek Jeter	3.00
35	Brandon Webb	.50
36	Mark Prior	1.50
37	Roy Halladay	.50
38	Frank Thomas	.75
39	Rafael Palmeiro	.75
40	Adam Dunn	.25
41	Aubrey Huff	.25
42	Todd Helton	.75
43	Matt Morris	.40
44	Dontrelle Willis	.40
45	Lance Berkman	.25
46	Mike Sweeney	.25
47	Kazuhisa Ishii	.25
48	Torii Hunter	.50
49	Vladimir Guerrero	.75
50	Mike Piazza	1.50
51	Alexis Rios	.25
52	Shannon Stewart	.25
53	Eric Hinske	.25
54	Jason Jennings	.25
55	Jason Giambi	1.00
56	Brandon Claussen	.25
57	Joe Thurston	.25
58	Ramon Nivar	.25
59	Jay Gibbons	.25
60	Eric Chavez	.50
61	Jimmy Gobble	.25
62	Walter Young	.25
63	Mark Grace	.50
64	Austin Kearns	.25
65	Bobby Abreu	.25
66	Hee Seop Choi	.25
67	Brandon Phillips	.25
68	Rickie Weeks	.50
69	Luis Gonzalez	.50
70	Mariano Rivera	.75
71	Jason Lane	.25
72	Xavier Nady	.25
73	Runelvys Hernandez	.25
74	Aramis Ramirez	.25
75	Ichiro Suzuki	2.00
76	Cliff Lee	.25
77	Chris Snelling	.25
78	Ryan Wagner	.25
79	Miguel Tejada	.50
80	Juan Gonzalez	.50
81	Joe Borchard	.25
82	Gary Sheffield	.50
83	Wade Miller	.25
84	Jeff Bagwell	.75
85	Ryan Church	.25
86	Adrian Beltre	.25
87	Jeff Baker	.25
88	Adam Loewen	.25
89	Bernie Williams	.50
90	Pedro J. Martinez	1.00
91	Carlos Rivera	.25
92	Junior Spivey	.25
93	Tim Hudson	.50
94	Troy Glaus	.50
95	Ken Griffey Jr.	1.50
96	Alexis Gomez	.25
97	Antonio Perez	.25
98	Dan Haren	.25
99	Ivan Rodriguez	.75
100	Randy Johnson	1.00
101	Lyle Overbay	.25
102	Oliver Perez	.25
103	Miguel Cabrera	.75
104	Scott Rolen	1.00
105	Roger Clemens	2.00
106	Brian Tallet	.25
107	Nic Jackson	.25
108	Angel Berroa	.25
109	Hank Blalock	.50
110	Ryan Klesko	.40
111	Jose Castillo	.25
112	Paul Konerko	.25
113	Greg Maddux	1.50
114	Mark Mulder	.50
115	Pat Burrell	.50
116	Garrett Atkins	.25
117	Jeremy Guthrie	.25
118	Orlando Cabrera	.25
119	Nick Johnson	.25
120	Tom Glavine	.50
121	Morgan Ensberg	.25
122	Sean Casey	.25
123	Orlando Hudson	.25
124	Hideki Matsui	2.50
125	Craig Biggio	.50
126	Adam LaRoche	.25
127	Hong-Chih Kuo	.25
128	Paul LoDuca	.25
129	Shawn Green	.50
130	Luis Castillo	.25
131	Joe Crede	.25
132	Ken Harvey	.25
133	Freddy Sanchez	.25
134	Roy Oswalt	.50
135	Curt Schilling	.75
136	Alfredo Amezaga	.25
137	Chien-Ming Wang	.50
138	Barry Larkin	.50
139	Trot Nixon	.25
140	Jim Thome	1.00
141	Bret Boone	.40
142	Jacque Jones	.25
143	Travis Hafner	.25
144	Sammy Sosa	2.00
145	Mike Mussina	.50
146	Vinnie Chulk	.25
147	Chad Gaudin	.25
148	Delmon Young	.50
149	Mike Lowell	.50
150	Rickey Henderson	.50
151	Roger Clemens	4.00
152	Mark Grace	2.00
153	Rickey Henderson	2.00
154	Alex Rodriguez	5.00
155	Rafael Palmeiro	2.00
156	Greg Maddux	3.00
157	Mike Piazza	3.00
158	Mike Mussina	1.50
159	Dale Murphy	1.50
160	Cal Ripken Jr.	2.00
161	Carl Yastrzemski	2.00
162	Marty Marion	1.50
163	Don Mattingly	4.00
164	Robin Yount	2.00
165	Andre Dawson	1.50
166	Jim Palmer	1.50
167	George Brett	2.00
168	Whitey Ford	2.00
169	Roy Campanella	2.00
170	Roger Maris	4.00
171	Duke Snider	2.00
172	Steve Carlton	2.00
173	Stan Musial	3.00
174	Nolan Ryan	6.00
175	Deion Sanders	1.50

Bronze
Bronze (1-150): 4-6X
Bronze (151-175): 2-3X
Production 100 Sets
Bronze Sepia: 2-3X
Production 100

Platinum
Platinum: No Pricing
Production One Set
Platinum Sepia: No Pricing
Production One Set

Silver
Silver (1-150): 5-10X
Silver (151-175): 2-4X
Production 50 Sets
Silver Sepia: 2-4X
Production 50

Framed Bronze
Framed Bronze (1-150): 2-3X
Framed Bronze (151-175): 1-2X
Framed Bronze Sepia: 1-2X
Inserted 1:6

Framed Platinum
Framed Platinum: No Pricing
Production One Set

Framed Silver
Framed Silver (1-150): 4-8X
Framed Silver (151-175): 2-3X
Production 100 Sets
Framed Silver Sepia: 2-3X
Production 100

Diamond Cut Bat
NM/M
Common Player: 6.00
Production 100 unless noted.

#	Player	Price
1	Alex Rodriguez	15.00
2	Nomar Garciaparra	12.00
3	Hideo Nomo	10.00
6	Alfonso Soriano	10.00
7	Edgar Martinez	10.00
8	Rocco Baldelli	10.00
9	Mark Teixeira	10.00
10	Albert Pujols	20.00
11	Vernon Wells	8.00
13	Garret Anderson	8.00
14	Brandon Webb	8.00
15	Mark Prior	15.00
16	Rafael Palmeiro	10.00
17	Adam Dunn	8.00
18	Dontrelle Willis	8.00
19	Kazuhisa Ishii	6.00
20	Torii Hunter	10.00
21	Vladimir Guerrero	10.00
22	Mike Piazza	10.00
23	Jason Giambi	10.00
26	Bobby Abreu	6.00
27	Hee Seop Choi	6.00
28	Rickie Weeks	12.00
30	Troy Glaus	8.00
31	Ivan Rodriguez	10.00
32	Hank Blalock	8.00
33	Greg Maddux	15.00
34	Nick Johnson	6.00
35	Shawn Green	8.00
36	Sammy Sosa	15.00
37	Dale Murphy/50	15.00
38	Cal Ripken Jr./50	50.00
39	Carl Yastrzemski/50	25.00
42	Don Mattingly	25.00
43	George Brett/50	15.00
46	Steve Carlton	15.00
47	Stan Musial/25	15.00
48	Nolan Ryan/50	35.00
50	Deion Sanders/50	15.00
50	Roberto Clemente/25	120.00

Diamond Cut Jersey
NM/M
Common Player: 15.00
Production 100 unless noted.

#	Player	Price
1	Alex Rodriguez	15.00
2	Nomar Garciaparra	15.00

#	Player	NM/M
3	Hideo Nomo/50	15.00
4	Alfonso Soriano	10.00
5	Brett Myers/50	10.00
6	Edgar Martinez	8.00
7	Rocco Baldelli	12.00
8	Mark Teixeira	10.00
9	Albert Pujols	20.00
10	Vernon Wells	8.00
11	Garret Anderson/50	8.00
12	Jerome Williams	8.00
13	Rich Harden	8.00
14	Brandon Webb	6.00
15	Mark Prior	15.00
16	Rafael Palmeiro	10.00
17	Adam Dunn	10.00
18	Dontrelle Willis	8.00
19	Kazuhisa Ishii	8.00
20	Torii Hunter	8.00
21	Vladimir Guerrero/50	15.00
22	Mike Piazza	15.00
23	Jason Giambi	10.00
25	Ramon Nivar	6.00
26	Bobby Abreu	6.00
27	Hee Seop Choi	6.00
29	Troy Glaus	8.00
31	Ivan Rodriguez	10.00
32	Hank Blalock	10.00
33	Greg Maddux	15.00
34	Nick Johnson	6.00
35	Shawn Green	8.00
36	Sammy Sosa	15.00
37	Dale Murphy/50	20.00
38	Cal Ripken Jr./50	50.00
39	Carl Yastrzemski	20.00
40	Marty Marion/50	15.00
41	Don Mattingly	25.00
42	Jim Palmer	20.00
43	George Brett/50	35.00
44	Whitey Ford/25	25.00
46	Steve Carlton	15.00
48	Nolan Ryan/50	40.00
49	Deion Sanders/50	15.00

Diamond Cut Signature

NM/M
Many not priced due to scarcity.

#	Player	
7	Rocco Baldelli/25	45.00
8	Mark Teixeira/25	30.00
13	Rich Harden/25	25.00
14	Brandon Webb/50	30.00
20	Torii Hunter/25	30.00
24	Ryan Wagner/50	20.00
25	Ramon Nivar/50	10.00
28	Rickie Weeks/50	30.00
29	Adam Loewen/50	20.00
32	Hank Blalock/25	30.00
40	Marty Marion/25	25.00
41	Don Mattingly/23	110.00
42	Jim Palmer/25	45.00
46	Steve Carlton/32	35.00
48	Nolan Ryan/34	125.00

Diamond Cut Combo

NM/M
Common Player: 10.00
Production 50 unless noted.

#	Player	
1	Alex Rodriguez	30.00
2	Nomar Garciaparra	25.00
3	Hideo Nomo/25	30.00
4	Alfonso Soriano	15.00
6	Edgar Martinez/25	15.00
7	Rocco Baldelli/25	25.00
9	Mark Teixeira/25	20.00
9	Albert Pujols	40.00
11	Vernon Wells/25	15.00
11	Garret Anderson/25	15.00
14	Brandon Webb/25	15.00
15	Mark Prior	20.00
16	Rafael Palmeiro/25	20.00
17	Adam Dunn/25	15.00
18	Dontrelle Willis/25	15.00
19	Kazuhisa Ishii/25	15.00
20	Torii Hunter/25	15.00
21	Vladimir Guerrero/25	25.00
22	Mike Piazza	20.00
23	Jason Giambi/25	25.00
26	Bobby Abreu	10.00
27	Hee Seop Choi	15.00
30	Troy Glaus/25	20.00
31	Ivan Rodriguez/25	20.00
32	Hank Blalock/25	20.00
33	Greg Maddux	25.00
34	Nick Johnson/25	12.00
36	Shawn Green/25	15.00
36	Sammy Sosa	25.00
41	Don Mattingly/23	50.00
42	Jim Palmer/22	45.00
46	Steve Carlton/32	20.00
48	Nolan Ryan/34	50.00
49	Deion Sanders/24	25.00
50	Roberto Clemente/21	150.00

Diamond Cut Signature Combo

NM/M
Varying quantities produced.

#	Player	
40	Marty Marion/25	30.00
46	Steve Carlton/32	45.00

DK Combos Bronze

NM/M
Varying quantities produced.

#	Player	
26	Marlon Byrd/Bat-Jsy/30	20.00
32	Rich Harden/Jsy/30	50.00
53	Eric Hinske/Bat-Jsy/30	20.00
57	Joe Thurston/Bat-Jsy/25	15.00
59	Jay Gibbons/Jsy-Jsy/30	35.00
65	Bob Abreu/Bat-Jsy/15	30.00
74	Aramis Ramirez/Bat-Jsy/25	25.00
92	Junior Spivey/Bat-Jsy/15	30.00
101	Lyle Overbay/Bat-Jsy/30	15.00
103	Miguel Cabrera/Bat-Jsy/30	35.00
108	Angel Berroa/Bat-Pants/30	15.00
109	Hank Blalock/Bat-Jsy/30	35.00
111	Jose Castillo/Bat-Bat/15	15.00
121	Morgan Ensberg/Bat-Jsy/30	15.00
123	Orlando Hudson/Bat-Jsy/30	15.00
126	Adam LaRoche/Bat-Bat/30	15.00
130	Luis Castillo/Bat-Jsy/30	15.00
143	Travis Hafner/Bat-Jsy/30	12.00
147	Chad Gaudin/Jsy-Jsy/25	12.00

DK Combos Gold

Gold Combos: No Pricing
Production 1-5
Gold Combos Sepia: No Pricing
Production One Set

DK Combos Platinum

Platinum Combos: No Pricing
Production One Set
Platinum Combos Sepia: No Pricing
Production One Set

DK Combos Silver

NM/M
Varying quantities produced.

#	Player	
26	Marlon Byrd/Bat/Bat/15	15.00
101	Lyle Overbay/Bat-Jsy/15	15.00
102	Miguel Cabrera/Bat-Jsy/15	50.00
108	Angel Berroa/Bat-Pants/15	20.00
109	Hank Blalock/Bat-Jsy/15	50.00
121	Morgan Ensberg/Bat-Jsy/15	20.00
123	Orlando Hudson/Bat-Jsy/15	15.00
126	Adam LaRoche/Bat-Bat/15	20.00

DK Combos Framed Bronze

NM/M
Varying quantities produced.

#	Player	
26	Marlon Byrd/Bat-Jsy/25	12.00
35	Brandon Webb/Bat-Jsy/25	25.00
53	Eric Hinske/Bat-Jsy/25	15.00
57	Joe Thurston/Bat-Jsy/25	12.00
59	Jay Gibbons/Jsy-Jsy/25	15.00
62	Walter Young/Bat-Bat/25	12.00
65	Bobby Abreu/Bat-Jsy/25	15.00
71	Jason Lane/Bat-Hat/25	15.00
74	Aramis Ramirez/Bat-Bat/25	20.00
77	Chris Snelling/Bat-Bat/25	12.00
81	Joe Borchard/Bat-Jsy/25	12.00
92	Junior Spivey/Bat-Jsy/25	12.00
97	Antonio Perez/Bat-Pants/25	12.00
98	Dan Haren/Bat-Jsy/25	15.00
101	Lyle Overbay/Bat-Jsy/25	10.00
103	Miguel Cabrera/Bat-Jsy/25	40.00
107	Nic Jackson/Bat-Bat/25	10.00
108	Angel Berroa/Bat-Pants/25	12.00
109	Hank Blalock/Bat-Jsy/25	30.00
110	Ryan Klesko/Bat-Jsy/15	20.00
111	Jose Castillo/Bat-Bat/25	10.00
121	Morgan Ensberg/Bat-Jsy/25	10.00
123	Orlando Hudson/Bat-Jsy/25	10.00
126	Adam LaRoche/Bat-Bat/25	15.00
127	Hong-Chih Kuo/Bat-Bat/25	10.00
130	Luis Castillo/Bat-Jsy/25	12.00
136	Alfredo Amezaga/Bat-Jsy/25	10.00
143	Travis Hafner/Bat-Jsy/25	10.00
147	Chad Gaudin/Jsy-Jsy/25	10.00

DK Combos Framed Gold

Framed Gold Combos: No Pricing
Production 1-5
Framed Gold Sepia: No Pricing
Production 1-5

DK Combos Framed Platinum

Framed Platinum: No Pricing
Production One Set

DK Combos Framed Silver

Framed Silver: No Pricing
Production 1-15
Framed Silver Sepia: No Pricing
Production 1-5

DK Materials Bronze

NM/M
Common Player:
No pricing for production 15 or less.

Framed Bronze:	1-1.5X
Production 5-100	
Framed Bronze Sepia:	1.5-2X
Production 5-50	
Silver:	1-2X
Production 5-50	
Silver Sepia:	1.5-2X
Production 1-30	
Framed Silver:	1-2X
Production 5-75	
Framed Silver Sepia:	1.5-2X
Production 1-30	
Gold:	1.5-2X
Production 1-50	
Gold Sepia:	No Pricing
Production 1-15	
Framed Gold:	1.5-2X
Production 5-50	
Framed Gold Sepia:	No Pricing
Production 1-15	
Platinums:	No Pricing

All Platinums limited to one set.

#	Player	
1	Alex Rodriguez/Bat-Jsy/150	20.00
2	Andruw Jones/Bat-Jsy/150	8.00
3	Nomar Garciaparra/Bat-Jsy/150	15.00
4	Kerry Wood/Bat-Jsy/150	15.00
5	Magglio Ordonez/Bat/150	8.00
6	Victor Martinez/Bat-Bat/100	6.00
7	Jeremy Bonderman/Jsy-Jsy/30	10.00
8	Josh Beckett/Bat-Jsy/150	10.00
9	Jeff Kent/Bat-Jsy/150	8.00
10	Carlos Beltran/Bat-Jsy/150	8.00
11	Hideo Nomo/Bat-Jsy/150	8.00
12	Richie Sexson/Bat-Jsy/150	10.00
13	Jose Vidro/Bat-Jsy/50	8.00
14	Jae Weong Seo/Jsy-Jsy/100	8.00
15	Alfonso Soriano/Bat-Jsy/150	10.00
16	Barry Zito/Bat-Jsy/150	10.00
17	Brett Myers/Bat-Jsy-Jsy/30	10.00
18	Brian Giles/Bat-Jsy/100	8.00
19	Edgar Martinez/Bat-Jsy/150	8.00
20	Jim Edmonds/Bat-Jsy/150	8.00
21	Rocco Baldelli/Bat-Jsy/150	12.00
22	Mark Teixeira/Bat-Jsy/150	10.00
23	Carlos Delgado/Bat-Jsy/150	8.00
25	Jose Reyes/Bat-Jsy/100	8.00
26	Marlon Byrd/Bat-Jsy/100	8.00
27	Albert Pujols/Bat-Jsy/150	25.00
28	Vernon Wells/Bat-Jsy/150	8.00
29	Garret Anderson/Bat-Jsy/15	20.00
30	Jerome Williams/Jsy-Jsy/150	8.00
31	Chipper Jones/Bat-Jsy/150	12.00
32	Rich Harden/Jsy-Jsy/100	8.00
33	Manny Ramirez/Bat-Jsy/150	10.00
34	Derek Jeter/Base-Base/150	20.00
35	Brandon Webb/Bat-Jsy/150	8.00
36	Mark Prior/Bat-Jsy/100	15.00
37	Roy Halladay/Jsy-Jsy/150	8.00
38	Frank Thomas/Bat-Jsy/150	12.00
39	Rafael Palmeiro/Bat-Jsy/150	8.00
40	Adam Dunn/Bat-Jsy/150	8.00
41	Aubrey Huff/Bat-Jsy/30	8.00
42	Todd Helton/Bat-Jsy/150	8.00
43	Matt Morris/Jsy-Jsy/100	8.00
44	Dontrelle Willis/Bat-Jsy/150	8.00
45	Lance Berkman/Bat-Jsy/150	6.00
46	Mike Sweeney/Bat-Jsy/100	8.00
47	Kazuhisa Ishii/Bat-Jsy/100	8.00
48	Torii Hunter/Bat-Jsy/150	8.00
49	Vladimir Guerrero/Bat-Jsy/150	15.00
50	Mike Piazza/Bat-Jsy/150	15.00
51	Alexis Rios/Bat-Bat/150	12.00
52	Shannon Stewart/Bat-Bat/100	6.00
53	Eric Hinske/Bat-Jsy/100	6.00
54	Jason Jennings/Bat-Jsy/150	6.00
55	Jason Giambi/Bat-Jsy/150	10.00
57	Joe Thurston/Bat-Jsy/150	6.00
58	Ramon Nivar/Bat-Jsy/150	6.00
59	Jay Gibbons/Jsy-Jsy/100	6.00
60	Eric Chavez/Bat-Jsy/150	8.00
62	Walter Young/Bat-Bat/100	6.00
63	Mark Grace/Bat-Jsy/150	10.00
64	Austin Kearns/Bat-Jsy/150	8.00
65	Bob Abreu/Bat-Jsy/150	8.00
66	Hee Seop Choi/Bat-Jsy/100	6.00
67	Brandon Phillips/Bat-Bat/100	6.00
68	Rickie Weeks/Bat-Bat/100	15.00
69	Luis Gonzalez/Bat-Jsy/150	6.00
70	Mariano Rivera/Jsy-Jsy/100	10.00
71	Jason Lane/Bat-Jsy/100	15.00
73	Runelvys Hernandez/Jsy-Jsy/100	8.00
75	Ichiro Suzuki/Ball-Base/15	50.00
77	Chris Snelling/Bat-Bat/30	8.00
79	Miguel Tejada/Bat-Jsy/150	8.00
80	Juan Gonzalez/Bat-Jsy/150	8.00
82	Gary Sheffield/Bat-Jsy/150	8.00
83	Wade Miller/Bat-Jsy/100	6.00
84	Jeff Bagwell/Bat-Jsy/150	8.00
86	Adrian Beltre/Bat-Jsy/150	6.00
87	Jeff Baker/Bat-Jsy/100	6.00
89	Bernie Williams/Bat-Jsy/100	8.00
90	Pedro J. Martinez/Bat-Jsy/100	10.00
92	Junior Spivey/Bat-Jsy/150	8.00
93	Tim Hudson/Bat-Jsy/150	8.00
94	Troy Glaus/Bat-Jsy/100	8.00
95	Ken Griffey Jr./Base-Base/100	15.00
96	Alexis Gomez/Bat-Bat/30	10.00
97	Antonio Perez/Bat-Pants/100	6.00
98	Dan Haren/Bat-Jsy/100	6.00
99	Ivan Rodriguez/Bat-Jsy/150	10.00
100	Randy Johnson/Bat-Jsy/100	12.00
101	Lyle Overbay/Bat-Jsy/100	6.00
103	Miguel Cabrera/Bat-Jsy/150	15.00
104	Scott Rolen/Bat-Jsy/150	8.00
105	Roger Clemens/Bat-Jsy/100	20.00
107	Nic Jackson/Bat-Bat/100	6.00
108	Angel Berroa/Bat-Pants/30	8.00
109	Hank Blalock/Bat-Jsy/150	8.00
110	Ryan Klesko/Bat-Jsy/100	8.00
111	Jose Castillo/Bat-Bat/100	6.00
112	Paul Konerko/Bat-Jsy/100	6.00
113	Greg Maddux/Bat-Jsy/150	15.00
114	Mark Mulder/Bat-Jsy/100	8.00
115	Pat Burrell/Bat-Jsy/100	8.00
116	Garrett Atkins/Jsy-Jsy/100	8.00
118	Orlando Cabrera/Bat-Jsy/100	6.00
119	Nick Johnson/Bat-Jsy/100	6.00
120	Tom Glavine/Bat-Jsy/100	10.00
122	Morgan Ensberg/Bat-Jsy/100	6.00
123	Orlando Hudson/Bat-Jsy/100	6.00
124	Hideki Matsui/Ball-Base/15	70.00
125	Craig Biggio/Bat-Jsy/100	8.00
126	Adam LaRoche/Bat-Bat/100	8.00
127	Hong-Chih Kuo/Bat-Bat/100	6.00
128	Paul LoDuca/Bat-Jsy/100	6.00
129	Shawn Green/Bat-Jsy/100	8.00
130	Luis Castillo/Bat-Jsy/100	6.00
132	Ken Harvey/Bat-Jsy/100	6.00
133	Freddy Sanchez/Bat-Bat/100	6.00
134	Roy Oswalt/Bat-Jsy/100	8.00
135	Curt Schilling/Bat-Jsy/15	15.00
136	Alfredo Amezaga/Bat-Jsy/15	6.00
139	Trot Nixon/Bat-Jsy/100	8.00
141	Jim Thome/Bat-Jsy/100	15.00
141	Bret Boone/Bat-Jsy/100	8.00
142	Jacque Jones/Bat-Jsy/150	6.00
143	Todd Hafner/Bat-Jsy/100	8.00
144	Sammy Sosa/Bat-Jsy/100	20.00
145	Mike Mussina/Bat-Jsy/100	12.00
147	Chad Gaudin/Jsy-Jsy/100	6.00
149	Mike Lowell/Bat-Jsy/100	8.00
150	Rickey Henderson/Bat-Jsy/15	15.00
151	Roger Clemens/FB Bat-Jsy/100	20.00
153	Rickey Henderson/FB Bat-Jsy/30	30.00
154	Alex Rodriguez/FB Bat-Jsy/100	20.00
155	Rafael Palmeiro/FB Bat-Jsy/100	10.00
156	Greg Maddux/FB Bat-Bat/100	15.00
157	Mike Piazza/FB Bat-Jsy/100	15.00
158	Mike Mussina/FB Bat-Jsy/100	12.00
159	Dale Murphy/LGD Bat-Jsy/100	20.00
160	Cal Ripken Jr./LGD Bat-Jsy/100	50.00
161	Carl Yastrzemski/LGD Bat-Jsy/100	25.00
162	Marty Marion/LGD Jsy-Jsy/30	10.00
163	Don Mattingly/LGD Bat-Jsy/100	25.00
164	Robin Yount/LGD Bat-Jsy/100	25.00
165	Andre Dawson/LGD Bat-Jsy/30	15.00
167	George Brett/LGD Bat-Jsy/50	50.00
168	Whitey Ford/LGD Bat-Jsy-Pants/30	20.00
172	Steve Carlton/LGD Jsy-Jsy/15	15.00
173	Stan Musial/LGD Bat-Jsy/30	25.00
174	Nolan Ryan/LGD Bat-Jsy/30	50.00
175	Deion Sanders/LGD Bat-Jsy/100	12.00

DK Signatures Bronze

NM/M
No pricing for prod. less than 15.
Framed Bronze: 1X
Production 1-50
Bronze Sepia: No Pricing
Production 1-15

#	Player	
6	Victor Martinez/200	10.00
13	Jose Vidro/200	10.00
14	Jae Weong Seo/200	15.00
17	Brett Myers/200	10.00
19	Edgar Martinez/200	40.00
26	Marlon Byrd/200	10.00
32	Rich Harden/200	8.00
35	Brandon Webb/25	30.00
41	Aubrey Huff/100	12.00
48	Torii Hunter/200	10.00
51	Alexis Rios/200	20.00
52	Shannon Stewart/200	6.00
53	Eric Hinske/25	20.00
56	Brandon Claussen/200	10.00
57	Joe Thurston/200	8.00
58	Ramon Nivar/100	6.00
59	Jay Gibbons/25	25.00
61	Jimmy Gobble/25	15.00
62	Walter Young/200	8.00
67	Brandon Phillips/100	6.00
68	Rickie Weeks/30	30.00
71	Jason Lane/200	8.00
73	Runelvys Hernandez/50	10.00
76	Aramis Ramirez/15	15.00
76	Cliff Lee/200	15.00
77	Chris Snelling/200	8.00
81	Joe Borchard/200	8.00
85	Ryan Church/200	8.00
87	Jeff Baker/100	8.00
88	Adam Loewen/100	20.00
91	Carlos Rivera/100	8.00
92	Junior Spivey/200	20.00
97	Antonio Perez/46	15.00
97	Alexis Gomez/200	8.00
98	Dan Haren/100	12.00
101	Lyle Overbay/200	8.00
102	Oliver Perez/100	8.00
103	Miguel Cabrera/100	35.00
106	Brian Tallet/200	8.00
107	Nic Jackson/200	8.00
108	Angel Berroa/200	15.00
109	Hank Blalock/25	35.00
111	Jose Castillo/200	8.00
114	Mark Mulder/25	30.00
117	Garrett Atkins/100	8.00
117	Jeremy Guthrie/200	8.00
118	Orlando Cabrera/75	12.00
121	Morgan Ensberg/200	10.00
123	Orlando Hudson/100	10.00
126	Adam LaRoche/100	10.00
127	Hong-Chih Kuo/25	75.00
130	Luis Castillo/100	20.00
131	Joe Crede/100	8.00
132	Ken Harvey/200	8.00
133	Freddy Sanchez/50	8.00
136	Alfredo Amezaga/90	8.00
137	Chien-Ming Wang/25	125.00
142	Jacque Jones/25	20.00
143	Travis Hafner/200	10.00
146	Vinnie Chulk/200	8.00
147	Chad Gaudin/100	8.00
149	Mike Lowell/25	20.00

DK Signatures Gold

NM/M
Many not priced due to scarcity.
Framed Gold: No Pricing
Production 1-5
Gold Sepia: No Pricing
Production 1-5

#	Player	
32	Rich Harden/50	20.00
51	Alexis Rios/50	25.00
56	Brandon Claussen/50	15.00
57	Joe Thurston/50	10.00
62	Walter Young/50	10.00
71	Jason Lane/40	10.00
77	Chris Snelling/50	15.00
81	Joe Borchard/50	15.00
85	Ryan Church/50	10.00
96	Alexis Gomez/50	10.00
101	Lyle Overbay/50	10.00
102	Oliver Perez/50	10.00
106	Brian Tallet/50	10.00
107	Nic Jackson/50	15.00
121	Morgan Ensberg/48	15.00
146	Vinnie Chulk/50	10.00

DK Signatures Platinum

No Pricing
Production One Set
Framed Platinum: No Pricing
Platinum Sepia: No Pricing
Production One Set

DK Signatures Silver

NM/M
No pricing for prod. less than 15.
Framed Silver: 1.5-2X
Production 1-25
Silver Sepia: No Pricing
Production 1-10

#	Player	
6	Victor Martinez/49	15.00
13	Jose Vidro/20	20.00
14	Jae Weong Seo/80	20.00
17	Brett Myers/90	15.00
26	Marlon Byrd/100	15.00
32	Rich Harden/100	15.00
35	Brandon Webb/15	35.00
41	Aubrey Huff/40	15.00
51	Alexis Rios/100	20.00
52	Shannon Stewart/30	15.00
56	Brandon Claussen/100	10.00
57	Joe Thurston/100	8.00
58	Ramon Nivar/30	15.00
61	Jimmy Gobble/30	20.00
62	Walter Young/30	15.00
67	Brandon Phillips/25	10.00
68	Rickie Weeks/100	40.00
71	Jason Lane/100	8.00
73	Runelvys Hernandez/25	10.00
74	Aramis Ramirez/30	25.00
76	Cliff Lee/100	15.00
77	Chris Snelling/50	15.00
78	Ryan Wagner/100	20.00
81	Joe Borchard/100	8.00
85	Ryan Church/100	8.00
87	Jeff Baker/25	15.00
88	Adam Loewen/30	25.00
96	Alexis Gomez/100	8.00
98	Dan Haren/30	15.00
101	Lyle Overbay/100	8.00
102	Oliver Perez/100	8.00
103	Miguel Cabrera/30	40.00
106	Brian Tallet/100	8.00
107	Nic Jackson/100	8.00
109	Hank Blalock/25	35.00
111	Jose Castillo/100	8.00
116	Garrett Atkins/100	10.00
117	Jeremy Guthrie/100	8.00
121	Morgan Ensberg/50	15.00
123	Orlando Hudson/100	15.00
126	Adam LaRoche/30	20.00
131	Joe Crede/35	10.00
132	Ken Harvey/15	15.00
136	Alfredo Amezaga/30	15.00
143	Travis Hafner/30	15.00
146	Vinnie Chulk/100	8.00

Gallery of Stars

NM/M
Complete Set (15): 50.00
Common Player: 2.00
Inserted 1:37

#	Player	
1	Nolan Ryan	8.00
2	Cal Ripken Jr.	8.00
3	George Brett	6.00
4	Don Mattingly	6.00
5	Deion Sanders	2.00
6	Mike Piazza	4.00
7	Hideo Nomo	2.00

8	Rickey Henderson	2.00
9	Roger Clemens	6.00
10	Greg Maddux	4.00
11	Albert Pujols	6.00
12	Alex Rodriguez	6.00
13	Dale Murphy	3.00
14	Mark Prior	4.00
15	Dontrelle Willis	2.00

Heritage Collection

		NM/M
Complete Set (25):		75.00
Common Player:		2.00
Inserted 1:22		
1	Dale Murphy	3.00
2	Cal Ripken Jr.	8.00
3	Carl Yastrzemski	4.00
4	Don Mattingly	6.00
5	Jim Palmer	4.00
6	Andre Dawson	2.00
7	Roy Campanella	3.00
8	George Brett	3.00
9	Duke Snider	3.00
10	Marty Marion	2.00
11	Deion Sanders	2.00
12	Whitey Ford	3.00
13	Stan Musial	5.00
14	Nolan Ryan	8.00
15	Steve Carlton	3.00
16	Robin Yount	3.00
17	Albert Pujols	6.00
18	Alex Rodriguez	6.00
19	Mike Piazza	4.00
20	Roger Clemens	4.00
21	Hideo Nomo	2.00
22	Mark Prior	4.00
23	Roger Maris	5.00
24	Greg Maddux	4.00
25	Mark Grace	2.00

Heritage Collection Auto.

No Pricing

Heritage Collection Bat

		NM/M
Production 50 unless noted.		
1	Dale Murphy	20.00
2	Cal Ripken Jr.	40.00
3	Carl Yastrzemski	20.00
4	Don Mattingly	30.00
6	Andre Dawson/25	20.00
7	Roy Campanella/25	30.00
8	George Brett/25	40.00
11	Deion Sanders	10.00
13	Stan Musial/25	35.00
14	Nolan Ryan/25	40.00
15	Steve Carlton/25	20.00
16	Robin Yount	20.00
17	Albert Pujols	25.00
18	Alex Rodriguez	25.00
19	Mike Piazza	15.00
20	Roger Clemens	25.00
21	Hideo Nomo	15.00
22	Mark Prior	15.00
23	Roger Maris/25	50.00
24	Greg Maddux	15.00
25	Mark Grace	10.00

Heritage Collection Jersey

		NM/M
Production 50 unless noted.		
1	Dale Murphy	15.00
2	Cal Ripken Jr.	40.00
3	Carl Yastrzemski	20.00
4	Don Mattingly	30.00
6	Andre Dawson/25	20.00
7	Roy Campanella/25	30.00
8	George Brett/25	40.00
10	Marty Marion	10.00
11	Deion Sanders	10.00
12	Whitey Ford/25	25.00
14	Nolan Ryan/25	40.00
15	Steve Carlton/25	20.00
16	Robin Yount	20.00
17	Albert Pujols	25.00
18	Alex Rodriguez	25.00
19	Mike Piazza	15.00
20	Roger Clemens	25.00
21	Hideo Nomo	15.00
22	Mark Prior	15.00
23	Roger Maris/25	50.00
24	Greg Maddux	15.00
25	Mark Grace	10.00

HOF Heroes

		NM/M
Common Player:		2.50
1	George Brett/1,000	6.00
2	George Brett/500	8.00
3	George Brett/250	12.00
4	Mike Schmidt/1,000	5.00
5	Mike Schmidt/250	8.00
6	Nolan Ryan/1,000	8.00
7	Nolan Ryan/500	10.00
8	Nolan Ryan/250	15.00
9	Roberto Clemente/1,000	6.00
10	Roberto Clemente/500	10.00

George Brett

11	Roberto Clemente/250	15.00
12	Roberto Clemente/100	20.00
13	Carl Yastrzemski/1,000	4.00
14	Robin Yount/1,000	4.00
15	Whitey Ford/1,000	4.00
16	Duke Snider/1,000	4.00
17	Duke Snider/1,000	8.00
18	Carlton Fisk/1,000	3.00
19	Ozzie Smith/1,000	5.00
20	Kirby Puckett/1,000	4.00
21	Bobby Doerr/1,000	2.50
22	Frank Robinson/1,000	3.00
23	Ralph Kiner/1,000	2.50
24	Al Kaline/1,000	4.00
25	Bob Feller/1,000	3.00
26	Yogi Berra/1,000	4.00
27	Stan Musial/1,000	5.00
28	Stan Musial/500	8.00
29	Stan Musial/250	10.00
30	Jim Palmer/1,000	2.50
31	Johnny Bench/1,000	4.00
32	Steve Carlton/1,000	3.00
33	Gary Carter/1,000	3.00
34	Roy Campanella/1,000	3.00
35	Roy Campanella/250	8.00

HOF Heroes Bat

		NM/M
Production 25 unless noted.		
1	George Brett	35.00
2	George Brett	35.00
3	George Brett	35.00
4	Mike Schmidt	35.00
5	Mike Schmidt	35.00
6	Nolan Ryan	40.00
7	Nolan Ryan	40.00
8	Nolan Ryan	40.00
13	Carl Yastrzemski	30.00
14	Robin Yount	35.00
15	Carlton Fisk	25.00
19	Ozzie Smith	30.00
20	Kirby Puckett	30.00
21	Bobby Doerr	20.00
22	Frank Robinson	15.00
23	Ralph Kiner	15.00
24	Al Kaline	25.00
31	Johnny Bench	25.00
32	Steve Carlton	20.00
33	Gary Carter	20.00
34	Roy Campanella	30.00
35	Roy Campanella	30.00

HOF Heroes Jersey

		NM/M
Production 25 unless noted.		
1	George Brett	35.00
2	George Brett	35.00
3	George Brett	35.00
4	Mike Schmidt	35.00
5	Mike Schmidt	35.00
6	Nolan Ryan	40.00
7	Nolan Ryan	40.00
8	Nolan Ryan	40.00
13	Carl Yastrzemski	30.00
14	Robin Yount	35.00
17	Whitey Ford	30.00
18	Carlton Fisk	25.00
19	Ozzie Smith	30.00
20	Kirby Puckett	30.00
21	Bobby Doerr	20.00
24	Al Kaline	25.00
32	Steve Carlton	20.00
33	Gary Carter	20.00
34	Roy Campanella	30.00
35	Roy Campanella	30.00

HOF Heroes Combo

Stan Musial

	NM/M
Production 25 unless noted.	

Column 3 (center)

1	George Brett	50.00
2	George Brett	50.00
3	George Brett	50.00
4	Mike Schmidt	40.00
5	Mike Schmidt	40.00
6	Nolan Ryan	50.00
7	Nolan Ryan	50.00
8	Nolan Ryan	50.00
13	Carl Yastrzemski	40.00
14	Robin Yount	40.00
15	Whitey Ford	30.00
18	Carlton Fisk	30.00
19	Ozzie Smith	40.00
20	Kirby Puckett	40.00
21	Bobby Doerr	25.00
23	Ralph Kiner	20.00
24	Al Kaline	35.00
32	Steve Carlton	30.00
33	Gary Carter	25.00
34	Roy Campanella	40.00
35	Roy Campanella	40.00

HOF Heroes Signature

		NM/M
Many not priced.		
14	Robin Yount/19	70.00
15	Whitey Ford/16	50.00
17	Frank Robinson/20	50.00
25	Bob Feller/19	40.00
31	Jim Palmer/22	40.00
32	Steve Carlton/32	35.00

Recollection Autographs

		NM/M
Varying quantities produced.		
6	Clint Barmes	
	03 DK Black/82	10.00
7	Clint Barmes	
	03 DK Blue/72	10.00
8	Carlos Beltran 02 DK/23	20.00
9	Carlos Beltran 03 DK/99	15.00
10	Adrian Beltre 02 DK/40	10.00
19	Chris Burke 03 DK/150	10.00
20	Marlon Byrd 02 DK/23	15.00
21	Marlon Byrd 03 DK/100	10.00
24	Kevin Cash 03 DK/103	10.00
25	Jose Cruz 85 DK/59	10.00
26	J.D. Durbin 03 DK/151	10.00
27	Jim Edmonds 03 DK/24	25.00
32	Julio Franco 87 DK/25	20.00
33	Freddy Garcia 03 DK/20	20.00
34	Jay Gibbons 03 DK/100	12.00
39	Brendan Harris	
	03 DK/150	8.00
42	Runelvys Hernandez	
	02 DK/100	8.00
43	Eric Hinske 03 DK/20	20.00
44	Tim Hudson 02 DK/25	30.00
45	Tim Hudson 03 DK/25	30.00
46	Aubrey Huff 03 DK/99	15.00
49	Jason Jennings	
	03 DK/50	10.00
50	Tommy John	
	88 DK Black/62	15.00
52	Howard Johnson	
	90 DK/52	10.00
54	Austin Kearns 02 DK/25	30.00
55	Austin Kearns 03 DK/25	30.00
59	Preston Larrison	
	03 DK Black/74	10.00
60	Preston Larrison	
	03 DK Blue/77	10.00
67	Dustin McGowan	
	03 DK/159	8.00
69	Melvin Mora 03 DK/101	8.00
71	Jack Morris 03 DK/60	10.00
72	Jack Morris	
	03 DK Her/19	20.00
74	Dale Murphy	
	03 DK Blue/47	30.00
82	Magglio Ordonez	
	03 DK/25	30.00
85	Dave Parker 82 DK/20	30.00
86	Dave Parker 90 DK/18	30.00
88	Jorge Posada 02 DK/25	50.00
89	Mark Prior 03 DK/25	100.00
92	Mike Rivera 02 DK/24	15.00
97	Ivan Rodriguez	
	03 DK/22	40.00
100	Rodrigo Rosario	
	02 DK/50	8.00
105	Ron Santo 02 DK/29	35.00
106	Richie Sexson	
	02 DK/25	25.00
107	Richie Sexson 03 DK/25	25.00
109	Chris Snelling 02 DK/46	12.00
119	Shannon Stewart	
	02 DK/50	15.00
120	Shannon Stewart	
	03 DK Black/92	12.00
126	Gorman Thomas	
	82 DK Black/22	20.00
127	Gorman Thomas	
	82 DK Blue/20	20.00
128	Alan Trammell	
	02 DK/29	30.00
129	Alan Trammell	
	02 DK Her/25	30.00
130	Robin Ventura	
	03 DK/25	20.00
131	Jose Vidro 03 DK/25	20.00
132	Rickie Weeks 03 DK/52	40.00
133	Kevin Youkilis	
	03 DK/153	15.00

Timeline

	NM/M
Common Player:	3.00

Inserted 1:92		
1	Roger Clemens	6.00
2	Mark Grace	3.00
3	Mike Mussina	3.00
4	Mike Piazza	4.00
5	Nolan Ryan	8.00
6	Rickey Henderson	3.00

Team Timeline

		NM/M
Complete Set (19):		65.00
Common Duo:		2.00
Inserted 1:29		
1	Deion Sanders,	
	Andruw Jones	2.00
2	Rickie Weeks,	
	Robin Yount	3.00
3	Don Mattingly,	
	Whitey Ford	8.00
4	Chipper Jones,	
	Dale Murphy	4.00
5	Nomar Garciaparra,	
	Bobby Doerr	5.00
6	Mark Prior, Sammy Sosa	5.00
7	Hideo Nomo,	
	Kazuhisa Ishii	2.00
8	Andre Dawson,	
	Mark Grace	3.00
9	Roger Clemens,	
	Carl Yastrzemski	6.00
10	Mike Mussina,	
	Cal Ripken Jr.	6.00
11	Stan Musial,	
	Albert Pujols	6.00
12	Jim Palmer,	
	Mike Mussina	2.00
13	Marty Marion,	
	Stan Musial	4.00
14	George Brett,	
	Mike Sweeney	6.00
15	Roger Clemens,	
	Roger Maris	6.00
16	Duke Snider,	
	Shawn Green	3.00
17	Jim Thome,	
	Mike Schmidt	6.00
18	Nolan Ryan,	
	Alex Rodriguez	8.00
19	Roy Campanella,	
	Mike Piazza	4.00

Team Timeline Bat

		NM/M
Production 25 unless noted.		
1	Deion Sanders,	
	Andruw Jones	15.00
2	Rickie Weeks,	
	Robin Yount	30.00
3	Don Mattingly,	
	Whitey Ford	60.00
4	Chipper Jones,	
	Dale Murphy	35.00
5	Nomar Garciaparra,	
	Bobby Doerr	30.00
6	Mark Prior,	
	Sammy Sosa	40.00
7	Hideo Nomo,	
	Kazuhisa Ishii	40.00
8	Andre Dawson,	
	Mark Grace	20.00
9	Roger Clemens,	
	Carl Yastrzemski	50.00
10	Mike Mussina,	
	Cal Ripken Jr.	75.00
11	Stan Musial,	
	Albert Pujols	65.00
12	Jim Palmer,	
	Mike Mussina	25.00
14	George Brett,	
	Mike Sweeney	30.00
15	Roger Clemens,	
	Roger Maris	60.00
17	Jim Thome,	
	Mike Schmidt	40.00
18	Nolan Ryan,	
	Alex Rodriguez	60.00
19	Roy Campanella,	
	Mike Piazza	40.00

Team Timeline Jersey

	NM/M
Production 25 Sets	
Prime:	No Pricing
Production One Set	
1	Deion Sanders,	
	Andruw Jones	15.00
2	Rickie Weeks,	
	Robin Yount	30.00

3	Don Mattingly,	
	Whitey Ford	60.00
4	Chipper Jones,	
	Dale Murphy	35.00
5	Nomar Garciaparra,	
	Bobby Doerr	30.00
6	Mark Prior,	
	Sammy Sosa	40.00
7	Hideo Nomo,	
	Kazuhisa Ishii	40.00
8	Andre Dawson,	
	Mark Grace	20.00
9	Roger Clemens,	
	Carl Yastrzemski	50.00
10	Mike Mussina,	
	Cal Ripken Jr.	75.00
14	George Brett,	
	Mike Sweeney	30.00
15	Roger Clemens,	
	Roger Maris	60.00
17	Jim Thome,	
	Mike Schmidt	40.00
18	Nolan Ryan,	
	Alex Rodriguez	60.00
19	Roy Campanella,	
	Mike Piazza	40.00

2004 Donruss Elite

	NM/M
Complete Set (205):	
Common Player:	.25
Common Auto. (151-180):	5.00
Production 250-1,000	
Common (181-200):	2.00
Production 1,000	
Pack (5):	5.00
Box (24):	100.00
1	Troy Glaus	.40
2	Darin Erstad	.25
3	Garret Anderson	.40
4	Tim Salmon	.40
5	Bartolo Colon	.40
6	Jose Guillen	.25
7	Miguel Tejada	.40
8	Adam Loewen	.25
9	Jay Gibbons	.25
10	Melvin Mora	.40
11	Javy Lopez	.40
12	Pedro J. Martinez	.75
13	Curt Schilling	.40
14	David Ortiz	.50
15	Keith Foulke	.25
16	Nomar Garciaparra	1.00
17	Magglio Ordonez	.40
18	Frank Thomas	.50
19	Carlos Lee	.40
20	Paul Konerko	.40
21	Mark Buehrle	.25
22	Jody Gerut	.25
23	Victor Martinez	.25
24	C.C. Sabathia	.25
25	Ellis Burks	.25
26	Bobby Higginson	.25
27	Jeremy Bonderman	.25
28	Fernando Vina	.25
29	Carlos Pena	.25
30	Dmitri Young	.25
31	Carlos Beltran	.50
32	Benito Santiago	.25
33	Mike Sweeney	.25
34	Angel Berroa	.25
35	Runelvys Hernandez	.25
36	Johan Santana	.25
37	Doug Mientkiewicz	.25
38	Shannon Stewart	.25
39	Torii Hunter	.40
40	Derek Jeter	2.00
41	Jason Giambi	.50
42	Bernie Williams	.40
43	Alfonso Soriano	.50
44	Gary Sheffield	.40
45	Mike Mussina	.50
46	Jorge Posada	.40
47	Hideki Matsui	1.00
48	Kevin Brown	.40
49	Javier Vazquez	.40
50	Mariano Rivera	.40
51	Eric Chavez	.40
52	Tim Hudson	.40
53	Mark Mulder	.40
54	Barry Zito	.40
55	Ichiro Suzuki	1.00
56	Edgar Martinez	.40
57	Bret Boone	.40
58	John Olerud	.40
59	Scott Spiezio	.25
60	Aubrey Huff	.40
61	Rocco Baldelli	.40

Column 6 (rightmost)

62	Jose Cruz Jr.	.25
63	Delmon Young	.40
64	Mark Teixeira	.40
65	Hank Blalock	.50
66	Michael Young	.40
67	Alex Rodriguez	2.00
68	Carlos Delgado	.25
69	Eric Hinske	.25
70	Roy Halladay	.40
71	Vernon Wells	.40
72	Randy Johnson	.75
73	Richie Sexson	.50
74	Brandon Webb	.25
75	Luis Gonzalez	.25
76	Steve Finley	.25
77	Chipper Jones	.50
78	Andruw Jones	.50
79	Marcus Giles	.25
80	Rafael Furcal	.25
81	J.D. Drew	.40
82	Sammy Sosa	1.50
83	Kerry Wood	.75
84	Mark Prior	1.00
85	Derek Lee	.40
86	Moises Alou	.40
87	Corey Patterson	.25
88	Ken Griffey Jr.	1.00
89	Austin Kearns	.40
90	Adam Dunn	.50
91	Barry Larkin	.40
92	Todd Helton	.50
93	Larry Walker	.40
94	Preston Wilson	.25
95	Charles Johnson	.25
96	Luis Castillo	.25
97	Josh Beckett	.40
98	Mike Lowell	.40
99	Miguel Cabrera	.75
100	Juan Pierre	.25
101	Dontrelle Willis	.25
102	Andy Pettitte	.40
103	Wade Miller	.25
104	Jeff Bagwell	.50
105	Craig Biggio	.40
106	Lance Berkman	.40
107	Jeff Kent	.40
108	Roy Oswalt	.40
109	Hideo Nomo	.40
110	Adrian Beltre	.25
111	Paul LoDuca	.25
112	Shawn Green	.40
113	Fred McGriff	.40
114	Eric Gagne	.40
115	Geoff Jenkins	.40
116	Rickie Weeks	.40
117	Scott Podsednik	.40
118	Nick Johnson	.25
119	Orlando Cabrera	.25
120	Jose Vidro	.25
121	Kazuo Matsui RC	5.00
122	Tom Glavine	.40
123	Al Leiter	.25
124	Mike Piazza	1.00
125	Jose Reyes	.50
126	Mike Cameron	.25
127	Pat Burrell	.40
128	Jim Thome	.75
129	Mike Lieberthal	.40
130	Bobby Abreu	.40
131	Kip Wells	.25
132	Jack Wilson	.40
133	Pokey Reese	.25
134	Brian Giles	.25
135	Sean Burroughs	.25
136	Ryan Klesko	.25
137	Trevor Hoffman	.25
138	Jason Schmidt	.25
139	J.T. Snow	.25
140	A.J. Pierzynski	.25
141	Ray Durham	.25
142	Jim Edmonds	.40
143	Albert Pujols	1.50
144	Edgar Renteria	.40
145	Scott Rolen	.75
146	Matt Morris	.25
147	Ivan Rodriguez	.75
148	Vladimir Guerrero	.50
149	Greg Maddux	1.00
150	Kevin Millwood	.40
151	Hector Gimenez	
	AU/750 RC	5.00
152	Willy Taveras	
	AU/750	15.00
153	Ruddy Yan AU/750	5.00
154	Graham Koonce AU/750	8.00
155	Jose Capellan	
	AU/750 RC	5.00
156	Onil Joseph AU/750 RC	5.00
157	John Gall AU/1000 RC	10.00
158	Carlos Hines AU/750 RC	5.00
159	Jerry Gil AU/750 RC	5.00
160	Mike Gosling AU/750 RC	5.00
161	Jason Frasor AU/750 RC	5.00
162	Justin Knoedler	
	AU/750 RC	5.00
163	Merkin Valdez	
	AU/750 RC	10.00
164	Angel Chavez	
	AU/1000 RC	5.00
165	Ivan Ochoa AU/750 RC	10.00
166	Greg Dobbs AU/750 RC	5.00
167	Ronald Belisario	
	AU/750 RC	5.00
168	Aaron Baldiris	
	AU/750 RC	10.00
170	David Crouthers AU/750	5.00
171	Freddy Guzman	
	AU/750 RC	5.00

172 Akinori Otsuka AU/250 **RC** 25.00
173 Ian Snell AU/750 **RC** 30.00
174 Nick Regilio AU/1000 **RC** 5.00
175 Jamie Brown AU/750 **RC** 5.00
176 Jerome Gamble AU/750 **RC** 5.00
177 Roberto Novoa AU/1000 **RC** 5.00
178 Sean Henn AU/1000 10.00
179 Ramon Ramirez AU/1000 **RC** 10.00
180 Jason Bartlett AU/1000 10.00
181 Bob Gibson/RET 2.00
182 Cal Ripken Jr./RET 8.00
183 Carl Yastrzemski/RET 4.00
184 Dale Murphy/RET 3.00
185 Don Mattingly/RET 6.00
186 Eddie Murray/RET 2.00
187 George Brett/RET 6.00
188 Jackie Robinson/RET 4.00
189 Jim Palmer/RET 2.00
190 Lou Gehrig/RET 5.00
191 Mike Schmidt/RET 5.00
192 Ozzie Smith/RET 5.00
193 Nolan Ryan/RET 8.00
194 Reggie Jackson/RET 3.00
195 Roberto Clemente/RET 6.00
196 Robin Yount/RET 4.00
197 Stan Musial/RET 5.00
198 Ted Williams/RET 8.00
199 Tony Gwynn/RET 3.00
200 Ty Cobb/RET 5.00
201 James Gandolfini/FG 3.00
202 Freddy Adu/FG 5.00
203 Summer Sanders/FG 1.50
204 Janet Evans/FG 1.50
205 Brandi Chastain/FG 1.50

Aspirations

Cards (1-150) print run 61-99: 4-8X
(1-150) p/r 41-60: 6-10X
(1-150) p/r 21-40: 8-15X
Autos. (151-180): .75-1.5X
(181-200): 2-3X
Production 19-99

Status

Cards (1-150) print run 61-81: 4-8X
(1-150) p/r 41-60: 6-10X
(1-150) p/r 21-40: 8-15X
Autos. (151-180): .75-1X
(181-200): 3-4X
Production 1-81

Status Gold
Gold (1-150): 10-20X
Gold (151-180): No Pricing
Gold (181-200): 3-6X
Production 24 Sets

Back to the Future
NM/M
#1-6
Production 500
#6-9
Production 250
Black: 1-2X
Production 25 or 50
Gold: .75-1.5X
Production 50 or 100
Red: 1X
Production 125 or 250
1 Tim Hudson 2.00
2 Rich Harden 1.50
3 Alex Rodriguez Rgr 3.00
4 Hank Blalock 3.00
5 Sammy Sosa 5.00
6 Hee Seop Choi 1.50
7 Tim Hudson, Rich Harden 3.00
8 Alex Rodriguez, Hank Blalock 6.00
9 Sammy Sosa, Hee Seop Choi 6.00

Back to the Future Bats
NM/M
#1-6
Production 200
#8-9
Production 100
1 Tim Hudson 4.00
2 Alex Rodriguez 10.00
3 Hank Blalock 6.00
4 Sammy Sosa 10.00
5 Hee Seop Choi 4.00
6 Alex Rodriguez, Hank Blalock 12.00
9 Sammy Sosa, Hee Seop Choi 12.00

Back to the Future Jerseys
NM/M
#1-6
Production 200
#7-9
Production 100
Prime: 1.5-2X
Production 25 or 50
1 Tim Hudson 4.00
2 Rich Harden 6.00
3 Alex Rodriguez/Rgr 10.00
4 Hank Blalock 6.00
5 Sammy Sosa 10.00
6 Hee Seop Choi 4.00
7 Tim Hudson, Rich Harden 8.00
8 Alex Rodriguez, Hank Blalock 12.00
9 Sammy Sosa, Hee Seop Choi 12.00

Back 2 Back Jacks
NM/M
Singles Production 25-125
Duals Production 25-50
1 Albert Pujols/125 15.00
2 Alex Rodriguez/125 10.00
3 Alfonso Soriano/125 8.00
4 Andruw Jones/125 5.00
5 Chipper Jones/125 8.00
6 Derek Jeter/125 20.00
7 Frank Thomas/125 8.00
8 Miguel Cabrera/125 8.00
9 Jason Giambi/125 8.00
10 Jim Thome/125 8.00
11 Mike Piazza/125 10.00
12 Nomar Garciaparra/25 35.00
13 Sammy Sosa/125 10.00
14 Shawn Green/125 4.00
15 Vladimir Guerrero/125 8.00
16 Andruw Jones, Chipper Jones/50 20.00
17 Alfonso Soriano, Derek Jeter/50 30.00
18 Jeff Bagwell, Lance Berkman/50 15.00
19 Alex Rodriguez, Rafael Palmeiro/50 20.00
20 Adam Dunn, Austin Kearns/25 20.00
21 Al Kaline/100 15.00
22 Babe Ruth/50 140.00
23 Cal Ripken Jr./100 40.00
24 Dale Murphy/100 10.00
25 Don Mattingly/100 15.00
26 George Brett/100 20.00
27 Lou Gehrig/100 85.00
28 Mike Schmidt/100 15.00
29 Roberto Clemente/100 50.00
30 Roy Campanella/100 15.00
31 Babe Ruth, Roger Maris/25 200.00
32 Harmon Killebrew, Kirby Puckett/50 35.00
33 Paul Molitor, Robin Yount/50 40.00
34 Reggie Jackson/50 15.00
35 Lou Gehrig, Ty Cobb/50 200.00
36 Don Mattingly, Jason Giambi/50 25.00
37 Ted Williams, Nomar Garciaparra/50 75.00
38 Andre Dawson, Sammy Sosa/50 25.00
39 Dale Murphy, Chipper Jones/50 15.00
40 Stan Musial, Jim Edmonds/50 25.00

Back 2 Back Jacks Combos
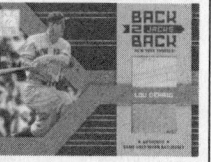
Singles Production 25-50
Duals Production 10-25
1 Albert Pujols/Bat-Jsy/50 30.00
2 Alex Rodriguez/Bat-Jsy/50 20.00
3 Alfonso Soriano/Bat-Jsy/50 15.00
4 Andruw Jones/Bat-Jsy/50 8.00
5 Chipper Jones/Bat-Jsy/50 12.00
6 Derek Jeter/Bat-Jsy/50 35.00
7 Frank Thomas/Bat-Jsy/50 15.00
8 Miguel Cabrera/Bat-Jsy/50 15.00
9 Jason Giambi/Bat-Jsy/50 15.00
10 Jim Thome/Bat-Jsy/50 15.00
11 Mike Piazza/Bat-Jsy/50 20.00
12 Nomar Garciaparra/Bat-Jsy/50 20.00
13 Sammy Sosa/Bat-Jsy/50 20.00
14 Shawn Green/Bat-Jsy/50 6.00
15 Vladimir Guerrero/Bat-Jsy/50 15.00
16 Andruw Jones, Chipper Jones/25 30.00
17 Alfonso Soriano, Lance Berkman/25 50.00
18 Jeff Bagwell, Lance Berkman/25 20.00
19 Alex Rodriguez, Rafael Palmeiro/25 30.00
20 Adam Dunn, Austin Kearns/25 20.00
21 Al Kaline/Bat-Jsy/50 25.00
22 Babe Ruth/Bat-Jsy/25 350.00
23 Cal Ripken Jr./Bat-Jsy/50 60.00
24 Dale Murphy/Bat-Jsy/50 15.00
25 Don Mattingly/Bat-Jsy/50 20.00
26 George Brett/Bat-Jsy/50 30.00
27 Lou Gehrig/Bat-Jsy/25 150.00
28 Mike Schmidt/Bat-Jsy/25 30.00
29 Roberto Clemente/Bat-Jsy/50 80.00
30 Roy Campanella/Bat-Jsy/50 25.00
31 Babe Ruth, Roger Maris/10 185.00
32 Harmon Killebrew, Kirby Puckett/25 50.00
33 Paul Molitor, Robin Yount/25 50.00
34 Reggie Jackson/25 25.00
35 Lou Gehrig, Ty Cobb/25 350.00
36 Don Mattingly, Jason Giambi/25 35.00
37 Ted Williams, Nomar Garciaparra 140.00
38 Andre Dawson, Sammy Sosa 40.00
39 Dale Murphy, Chipper Jones 20.00
40 Stan Musial, Jim Edmonds 35.00

Career Best

NM/M
Common Player: 1.00
Production 1,000 Sets
Black: 2X
Production 100 Sets
Gold Print Run 200-390: 1.5X
Gold P/R 101-200: 2X
Gold P/R 50-100: 3X
Gold P/R 26-50: 3-5X
Gold P/R 15-25: 5-8X
1 Albert Pujols 3.00
2 Alex Rodriguez 3.00
3 Alfonso Soriano 1.50
4 Andruw Jones 1.00
5 Barry Zito 1.00
6 Cal Ripken Jr. 5.00
7 Chipper Jones 1.50
8 Curt Schilling 1.00
9 Derek Jeter 4.00
10 Don Mattingly 4.00
11 Dontrelle Willis 1.00
12 Doc Gooden 1.00
13 Eddie Murray 1.50
14 Frank Thomas 1.50
15 Gary Sheffield 1.00
16 George Brett 4.00
17 Greg Maddux 2.00
18 Hideo Nomo 1.00
19 Ichiro Suzuki 2.00
20 Ivan Rodriguez 1.50
21 Jason Giambi 1.50
22 Jeff Bagwell 1.50
23 Jim Thome 1.50
24 Kerry Wood 1.50
25 Lance Berkman 1.00
26 Magglio Ordonez 1.00
27 Mark Prior 2.00
28 Mike Piazza 2.00
29 Mike Schmidt 3.00
30 Nomar Garciaparra 2.50
31 Pedro J. Martinez 2.00
32 Randy Johnson 2.00
33 Roger Clemens 3.00
34 Sammy Sosa 2.50
35 Tony Gwynn 1.50

Career Best Bats
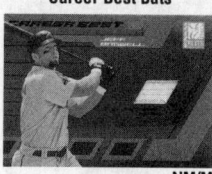
NM/M
Production 100 or 200
Combo Print Run 50: 1-2X
Combo P/R 25: 2X
Production 25 or 50
1 Albert Pujols/200 15.00
2 Alex Rodriguez/200 10.00
3 Alfonso Soriano/200 8.00
4 Andruw Jones/200 4.00
5 Barry Zito/200 4.00
6 Cal Ripken Jr./200 25.00
7 Chipper Jones/200 8.00
8 Curt Schilling/200 5.00
9 Derek Jeter/200 15.00
10 Don Mattingly/200 15.00
11 Dontrelle Willis/100 6.00
12 Doc Gooden/200 6.00
13 Eddie Murray/200 4.00
14 Frank Thomas/200 8.00
15 Gary Sheffield/200 5.00
16 George Brett/200 8.00
17 Greg Maddux/100 10.00
18 Hideo Nomo/100 6.00
19 Ivan Rodriguez/200 8.00
20 Jason Giambi/200 5.00
21 Jeff Bagwell/200 6.00
22 Jim Thome/200 8.00
23 Kerry Wood/100 6.00
24 Lance Berkman/200 4.00
25 Magglio Ordonez/200 4.00
26 Mark Prior/100 8.00
27 Mike Piazza/200 8.00
28 Mike Schmidt/100 10.00
29 Nomar Garciaparra/200 10.00
30 Pedro J. Martinez/200 8.00
31 Randy Johnson/200 8.00
32 Roger Clemens/200 15.00
33 Sammy Sosa/200 10.00
34 Tony Gwynn/200 8.00

Career Best Jerseys

NM/M
Quantity produced listed.
Prime: 1.5-2X
Production 25-50
1 Albert Pujols/200 15.00
2 Alex Rodriguez/200 10.00
3 Alfonso Soriano/200 8.00
4 Andruw Jones/200 5.00
5 Barry Zito/200 4.00
6 Cal Ripken Jr./50 40.00
7 Chipper Jones/200 8.00
8 Curt Schilling/200 5.00
9 Derek Jeter/200 15.00
10 Don Mattingly/50 20.00
11 Dontrelle Willis/200 6.00
12 Doc Gooden/200 6.00
13 Eddie Murray/200 6.00
14 Frank Thomas/200 8.00
15 Gary Sheffield/200 5.00
16 George Brett/50 25.00
17 Greg Maddux/200 10.00
18 Hideo Nomo/200 6.00
19 Ivan Rodriguez/200 8.00
20 Jason Giambi/200 6.00
21 Jeff Bagwell/200 6.00
22 Jim Thome/200 8.00
23 Kerry Wood/200 10.00
24 Lance Berkman/200 4.00
25 Magglio Ordonez/200 4.00
26 Mark Prior/200 8.00
27 Mike Piazza/200 8.00
28 Mike Schmidt/100 10.00
29 Nomar Garciaparra/200 10.00
30 Pedro J. Martinez/200 8.00
31 Randy Johnson/200 8.00
32 Roger Clemens/200 15.00
33 Sammy Sosa/200 8.00
34 Tony Gwynn/200 15.00

Passing the Torch

NM/M
#1-30
Production 1,000

Passing the Torch Autographs

NM/M
Quantity produced listed.
Many not priced due to scarcity.
4 Will Clark/15 100.00
8 Andre Dawson/50 15.00
9 Dale Murphy/50 30.00
11 Joe Morgan/15 25.00
14 Tim Hudson/15 45.00
15 Jim Rice/50 15.00
18 Mark Prior/15 80.00

24 Scott Rolen/15 50.00
30 Roy Oswalt/50 15.00

Passing the Torch Bats
NM/M
Quantity produced listed.
2 Andy Pettitte/200 4.00
3 Willie McCovey/100 6.00
4 Will Clark/100 25.00
5 Stan Musial/100 25.00
6 Albert Pujols/200 15.00
7 Andre Dawson/100 8.00
8 Vladimir Guerrero/100 8.00
10 Chipper Jones/200 8.00
11 Joe Morgan/200 4.00
12 Barry Larkin/200 5.00
14 Tim Hudson/200 5.00
15 Jim Rice/200 5.00
16 Manny Ramirez/200 8.00
17 Greg Maddux/200 10.00
18 Mark Prior/200 8.00
19 Don Mattingly/100 15.00
20 Jason Giambi/200 8.00
21 Roy Campanella/50 30.00
22 Mike Piazza/200 10.00
23 Ozzie Smith/100 15.00
24 Scott Rolen/200 8.00
25 Roger Clemens/200 15.00
26 Mike Mussina/200 8.00
27 Babe Ruth/25 150.00
28 Roger Maris/50 25.00
29 Nolan Ryan/100 25.00
30 Roy Oswalt/200 4.00
32 Willie McCovey, Will Clark/50 20.00
33 Stan Musial, Albert Pujols/50 50.00
34 Andre Dawson, Vladimir Guerrero/50 20.00
35 Dale Murphy, Chipper Jones/50 20.00
36 Joe Morgan, Barry Larkin/50 15.00
38 Jim Rice, Manny Ramirez/50 20.00
39 Greg Maddux, Mark Prior/50 25.00
40 Don Mattingly, Jason Giambi/50 35.00
41 Roy Campanella, Mike Piazza/25 35.00
42 Ozzie Smith, Scott Rolen/50 30.00
43 Roger Clemens, Mike Mussina/50 30.00
44 Babe Ruth, Roger Maris/25 200.00
45 Nolan Ryan, Roy Oswalt/50 35.00

Passing the Torch Jerseys
NM/M
Quantity produced listed.
1 Whitey Ford/100 15.00
2 Andy Pettitte/200 4.00
3 Willie McCovey/100 6.00
4 Will Clark/100 10.00
5 Stan Musial/200 25.00
6 Albert Pujols/200 15.00
7 Andre Dawson/200 8.00
8 Vladimir Guerrero/200 8.00
9 Dale Murphy/100 10.00
10 Chipper Jones/200 8.00
11 Joe Morgan/100 4.00
12 Barry Larkin/200 5.00
13 Jim "Catfish" Hunter/100 5.00
14 Tim Hudson/200 5.00
15 Jim Rice/200 5.00
16 Manny Ramirez/200 8.00
17 Mark Prior/200 8.00
19 Don Mattingly/100 15.00
20 Jason Giambi/200 8.00
21 Roy Campanella/50 30.00
22 Mike Piazza/200 10.00
23 Ozzie Smith/100 12.00
24 Scott Rolen/200 8.00
25 Roger Clemens/200 15.00
26 Mike Mussina/200 8.00
27 Babe Ruth/25 300.00
28 Roger Maris/50 50.00
29 Nolan Ryan/100 25.00
30 Roy Oswalt/200 4.00
31 Whitey Ford, Andy Pettitte/50 20.00
32 Willie McCovey, Will Clark/50 20.00
33 Stan Musial, Albert Pujols/50 50.00
34 Andre Dawson, Vladimir Guerrero/50 20.00
35 Dale Murphy, Chipper Jones/50 20.00
36 Joe Morgan, Barry Larkin/50 15.00
37 Jim "Catfish" Hunter, Tim Hudson/50 15.00
38 Jim Rice, Manny Ramirez/50 20.00
40 Don Mattingly, Jason Giambi/50 35.00
41 Roy Campanella, Mike Piazza 35.00
42 Ozzie Smith, Scott Rolen/50 30.00
43 Roger Clemens, Mike Mussina/50 30.00
45 Nolan Ryan, Roy Oswalt/50 35.00

Recollection Autographs

		NM/M
Common Autograph:		8.00
1	Jeremy Affeldt 01/25	15.00
2	Erick Almonte 01/26	10.00
4	Jeff Baker 02/25	30.00
5	Brandon Berger 01/25	8.00
6	Marlon Byrd 01/24	25.00
8	Ryan Drese 02/45	8.00
9	Brandon Duckworth 01/16	
10	Casey Fossum 01/23	15.00
11	Geronimo Gil 01/25	8.00
13	Jeremy Guthrie 02/25	20.00
14	Nic Jackson 02/95	8.00
21	Ricardo Rodriguez 01/25	8.00
23	Bud Smith 01/25	8.00
25	Junior Spivey 01/20	20.00
26	Tim Spooneybarger 01/25	10.00
28	Martin Vargas 01/37	8.00

Team

		NM/M
Production 1,500 Sets		
Black:		1X-2X
Production 150 Sets		
Gold:		1-1.5X
Production 250 Sets		
1	Cal Ripken Jr., Eddie Murray, Jim Palmer	4.00
2	Derek Jeter, Roger Clemens, Bernie Williams, Andy Pettitte	4.00
3	Johnny Bench, Tony Perez, George Foster, Dave Concepcion	
4	Josh Beckett, Dontrelle Willis, Ivan Rodriguez	2.00
5	Randy Johnson, Curt Schilling, Luis Gonzalez, Mark Grace	2.00
6	Derek Jeter, Wade Boggs, Darryl Strawberry	5.00
7	Chipper Jones, Tom Glavine, Greg Maddux, Ryan Klesko	4.00
8	Dwight Gooden, Gary Carter, Darryl Strawberry	2.00
9	Jackie Robinson, Roy Campanella, Duke Snider	3.00
10	Phil Rizzuto, Yogi Berra, Whitey Ford	2.00
11	Stan Musial, Curt Schilling, Marty Marion, Enos Slaughter	4.00

Team Bats

		NM/M
Production 100 Sets		
2	Derek Jeter, Roger Clemens, Bernie Williams, Andy Pettitte	30.00
3	Johnny Bench, Tony Perez, George Foster, Dave Concepcion	50.00
4	Josh Beckett, Dontrelle Willis, Ivan Rodriguez	15.00
5	Randy Johnson, Curt Schilling, Luis Gonzalez, Mark Grace	25.00
6	Derek Jeter, Wade Boggs, Darryl Strawberry	30.00
7	Chipper Jones, Tom Glavine, Greg Maddux, Ryan Klesko	25.00
8	Dwight Gooden, Gary Carter, Darryl Strawberry	20.00

Team Jerseys

		NM/M
Production 100 unless noted.		
1	Cal Ripken Jr., Eddie Murray, Jim Palmer	50.00
2	Derek Jeter, Roger Clemens, Bernie Williams, Andy Pettitte	40.00
4	Josh Beckett, Dontrelle Willis, Ivan Rodriguez	15.00
5	Randy Johnson, Curt Schilling, Luis Gonzalez, Mark Grace	25.00
6	Derek Jeter, Wade Boggs, Darryl Strawberry	
7	Chipper Jones, Tom Glavine, Greg Maddux, Ryan Klesko	25.00
9	Jackie Robinson, Roy Campanella, Duke Snider	75.00
10	Phil Rizzuto, Yogi Berra, Whitey Ford	35.00
11	Stan Musial, Curt Schilling, Marty Marion, Enos Slaughter	50.00

Throwback Threads

		NM/M
Quantity produced listed.		
Prime:		1.5-3X
Prime Singles Production 10-25		
Prime Duals Production 5-15		
1	Albert Pujols/150	60.00
2	Alex Rodriguez/ Rgr/150	125.00
3	Alfonso Soriano/150	175.00
4	Chipper Jones/150	120.00
5	Derek Jeter/150	15.00
6	Greg Maddux/150	10.00
7	Hideo Nomo/150	8.00
8	Miguel Cabrera/150	8.00
9	Ivan Rodriguez/150	8.00
10	Jason Giambi/150	8.00
11	Jeff Bagwell/150	8.00
12	Lance Berkman/150	4.00
13	Mark Prior/150	8.00
14	Mike Piazza/150	10.00
15	Nomar Garciaparra/150	10.00
16	Pedro J. Martinez/150	8.00
17	Randy Johnson/150	8.00
18	Sammy Sosa/150	10.00
19	Shawn Green/150	4.00
20	Vladimir Guerrero/150	8.00
21	Adam Dunn, Austin Kearns/75	20.00
22	Barry Zito, Mark Mulder/75	10.00
23	Curt Schilling/75	10.00
24	Derek Jeter, Jason Giambi/75	25.00
25	Dontrelle Willis, Josh Beckett/75	15.00
26	Frank Thomas, Magglio Ordonez/75	15.00
27	Jim Thome/75	15.00
28	Kerry Wood, Mark Prior/75	25.00
29	Hank Blalock, Mark Teixeira/75	15.00
30	Albert Pujols, Scott Rolen/75	40.00
31	Babe Ruth/50	280.00
32	Cal Ripken Jr./100	40.00
33	Carl Yastrzemski/100	20.00
34	Deion Sanders/100	10.00
35	Don Mattingly/100	20.00
36	George Brett/100	20.00
37	Jim Palmer/100	8.00
38	Kirby Puckett/100	15.00
39	Lou Gehrig/100	125.00
40	Mark Grace/100	10.00
41	Mike Schmidt/100	20.00
42	Nolan Ryan/100	25.00
43	Ozzie Smith/100	20.00
44	Reggie Jackson/100	10.00
45	Rickey Henderson/100	10.00
46	Roberto Clemente/100	75.00
47	Roger Clemens/100	15.00
48	Roger Maris/100	40.00
49	Roy Campanella/ Pants/100	20.00
50	Tony Gwynn/100	15.00
51	Babe Ruth, Lou Gehrig/25	400.00
52	Cal Ripken Jr., Eddie Murray/50	50.00
53	Ted Williams, Carl Yastrzemski/50	85.00
54	Andre Dawson, Gary Carter/50	20.00
55	Reggie Jackson, Rod Carew/50	20.00
56	Derek Jeter, Phil Rizzuto/50	40.00
57	Nolan Ryan, Roy Oswalt/50	40.00
58	Roger Clemens, Mike Mussina/50	25.00
59	Albert Pujols, Stan Musial/50	40.00
60	Nomar Garciaparra, Stan Musial/50	85.00

Throwback Threads Autographs

		NM/M
Production 25 Sets		

Throwback Threads Prime

Quantity produced listed.

Turn of the Century

Stars (1-150):		2-3X
Production 750		
Stars (181-200):		1X
Production 250		

2004 Donruss Elite Extra Edition

		NM/M
Complete Set (288):		
Common (1-150):		.25
Common (206-215):		2.00
Production 1,000		
Common No Auto.(216-355):		6.00
Common No Auto. (234-254):		3.00
No Auto. Production 1,000		
Pack (5):		14.00
Box (12):		150.00
Note: Cards 151-205 do not exist.		
1	Troy Glaus	.40
2	John Lackey	.25
3	Garret Anderson	.40
4	Francisco Rodriguez	.25
5	Casey Kotchman	.25
6	Jose Guillen	.25
7	Miguel Tejada	.50
8	Rafael Palmeiro	.50
9	Jay Gibbons	.25
10	Melvin Mora	.25
11	Javy Lopez	.25
12	Pedro Martinez	.75
13	Curt Schilling	.75
14	David Ortiz	.75
15	Manny Ramirez	.75
16	Nomar Garciaparra	1.00
17	Magglio Ordonez	.50
18	Frank Thomas	.75
19	Esteban Loaiza	.25
20	Paul Konerko	.50
21	Mark Buehrle	.25
22	Jody Gerut	.25
23	Victor Martinez	.40
24	C.C. Sabathia	.40
25	Travis Hafner	.50
26	Cliff Lee	.25
27	Jeremy Bonderman	.40
28	Dallas McPherson	.25
29	Jermaine Dye	.25
30	Carlos Guillen	.25
31	Carlos Beltran	.50
32	Ken Harvey	.25
33	Mike Sweeney	.25
34	Angel Berroa	.25
35	Johan Santana	.50
36	Joe Nathan	.25
37	Jacque Jones	.25
38	Shannon Stewart	.25
39	Torii Hunter	.40
40	Derek Jeter	2.00
41	Jason Giambi	.50
42	Danny Graves	.25
43	Alfonso Soriano	.75
44	Gary Sheffield	.50
45	Mike Mussina	.50
46	Jorge Posada	.50
47	Hideki Matsui	1.00
48	Francisco Cordero	.25
49	Javier Vazquez	.25
50	Mariano Rivera	.40
51	Eric Chavez	.40
52	Tim Hudson	.40
53	Mark Mulder	.40
54	Barry Zito	.40
55	Ichiro Suzuki	1.50
56	Edgar Martinez	.25
57	Bret Boone	.25
58	Lew Ford	.25
59	B.J. Upton	.40
60	Aubrey Huff	.25
61	Rocco Baldelli	.25
62	Carl Crawford	.40
63	Delmon Young	.40
64	Mark Teixeira	.50
65	Hank Blalock	.50
66	Michael Young	.25
67	Alex Rodriguez	1.50
68	Carlos Delgado	.40
69	Milton Bradley	.25
70	Roy Halladay	.40
71	Vernon Wells	.25
72	Randy Johnson	.75
73	Bobby Crosby	.25
74	Lyle Overbay	.25
75	Luis Gonzalez	.25
76	Steve Finley	.25
77	Chipper Jones	.75
78	Andruw Jones	.40
79	Marcus Giles	.25
80	Rafael Furcal	.25
81	J.D. Drew	.40
82	Sammy Sosa	1.00
83	Kerry Wood	.40
84	Mark Prior	.75
85	Derrek Lee	.50
86	Moises Alou	.40
87	Carlos Zambrano	.25
88	Ken Griffey Jr.	1.00
89	Austin Kearns	.40
90	Adam Dunn	.50
91	Barry Larkin	.40
92	Todd Helton	.50
93	Larry Walker	.40
94	Preston Wilson	.25
95	Sean Casey	.25
96	Luis Castillo	.25
97	Josh Beckett	.25
98	Mike Lowell	.25
99	Miguel Cabrera	.75
100	Brad Penny	.25
101	Dontrelle Willis	.40
102	Andy Pettitte	.40
103	Wade Miller	.25
104	Jeff Bagwell	.50
105	Craig Biggio	.40
106	Lance Berkman	.40
107	Jeff Kent	.25
108	Roy Oswalt	.40
109	Hideo Nomo	.40
110	Adrian Beltre	.40
111	Paul LoDuca	.25
112	Shawn Green	.40
113	Roger Clemens	2.00
114	Eric Gagne	.40
115	Danny Kolb	.25
116	Rickie Weeks	.25
117	Scott Podsednik	.25
118	Livan Hernandez	.25
119	Orlando Cabrera	.25
120	Jose Vidro	.25
121	Jose Reyes	.25
122	David Wright	1.50
123	Al Leiter	.25
124	Mike Piazza	1.00
125	Jose Reyes	.50
126	Richard Hidalgo	.25
127	Eric Milton	.25
128	Jim Thome	.75
129	Mike Lieberthal	.25
130	Bobby Abreu	.40
131	Kip Wells	.25
132	Jack Wilson	.25
133	Jason Bay	.40
134	Brian Giles	.25
135	Sean Burroughs	.25
136	Khalil Greene	.25
137	Jake Peavy	.25
138	Jason Schmidt	.40
139	J.T. Snow	.25
140	Craig Wilson	.25
141	Chase Utley	.50
142	Jim Edmonds	.40
143	Albert Pujols	2.00
144	Edgar Renteria	.40
145	Scott Rolen	.75
146	Matt Morris	.25
147	Ivan Rodriguez	.50
148	Vladimir Guerrero	.75
149	Greg Maddux	1.00
150	Ben Sheets	.25
206	Will Clark	2.00
207	Nolan Ryan	8.00
208	Bob Feller	2.00
209	Red Schoendienst	2.00
210	Brooks Robinson	3.00
211	Al Kaline	3.00
212	Ozzie Smith	4.00
213	Maury Wills	2.00
214	Steve Carlton	2.00
215	Duke Snider	3.00
216	Scott Lewis/ Auto./603 RC	10.00
217	Josh Johnson/ Auto./597 RC	10.00
218	Jeff Fiorentino/ Auto./597 RC	10.00
219	Grant Hansen/ Auto./599 RC	6.00
220	Yovani Gallardo/ Auto./803 RC	50.00
221	Eddie Prasch/ Auto./603 RC	10.00
222	Danny Hill/Auto./603 RC	6.00
223	Chuck Lofgren/ Auto./803 RC	15.00
224	Blake Johnson/ Auto./811 RC	6.00
225	Cory Dunlap/ Auto./599 RC	15.00
226	Carlos Vasquez/ Auto./869 RC	8.00
227	Jesse Crain/ Auto./1000 RC	10.00
228	Yhency Brazoban/ Auto./1000 RC	6.00
229	Abe Alvarez/ Auto./1000 RC	8.00
230	Scott Kazmir/Auto./350	60.00
231	J.A. Happ/Auto./1195 RC	8.00
232	Mark Jecmen/ Auto./1047 RC	6.00
234	Kameron Loe/1000 RC	3.00
235	Ervin Santana/1000 RC	5.00
239	Josh Karp/1000 RC	3.00
242	Alberto Callaspo/ 1000 RC	3.00
243	Jesse Hoover/ Auto./1191 RC	8.00
246	Justin Hoyman/ Auto./1124 RC	8.00
247	Juan Cedeno/1000 RC	8.00
250	Jake Dittler/1000	4.00
252	Benjamin Zobrist/ Auto./1178 RC	10.00
253	Jeff Salazar/1000 RC	3.00
254	Fausto Carmona/ 1000 RC	4.00
256	Jorge Vasquez/ Auto./1000 RC	6.00
257	Rafael Gonzalez/ Auto./603 RC	6.00
258	Andrew Dobies/ Auto./601 RC	10.00
259	Colby Miller/ Auto./997 RC	6.00
260	K.C. Herren/ Auto./735 RC	10.00
261	Ryan Meaux/ Auto./546 RC	6.00
262	Dustin Pedroia/ Auto./1114 RC	85.00
263	Fernando Nieve/ Auto./1000 RC	10.00
264	Mariano Gomez/ Auto./1000 RC	6.00
265	Eric Campbell/ Auto./260 RC	50.00
266	Billy Killian/Auto./703 RC	6.00
267	Mike Rouse/Auto./999	6.00
268	Kyle Bono/ Auto./1203 RC	8.00
269	Mitch Einertson/ Auto./1047 RC	10.00
270	Scott Proctor/ Auto./1000 RC	8.00
271	Tim Bittner/ Auto./1000 RC	6.00
272	Christian Garcia/ Auto./799 RC	10.00
273	Yadier Molina/ Auto./1000 RC	20.00
275	Charles Thomas/ Auto./907 RC	8.00
276	Travis Blackley/ Auto./621 RC	6.00
277	Frankie Francisco/ Auto./1000 RC	6.00
278	Dioner Navarro/ Auto./1000 RC	10.00
279	Joey Gathright/ Auto./1000 RC	8.00
280	Kazuhito Tadano/ Auto./1000 RC	15.00
281	Matt Bush/ Auto./1100 RC	20.00
282	David Haehnel/ Auto./865 RC	8.00
283	Tommy Hottovy/ Auto./825 RC	8.00
284	Chris Carter/ Auto./973 RC	25.00
285	Mark Rogers/ Auto./578 RC	15.00
286	Jeremy Sowers/ Auto./537 RC	25.00
287	Homer Bailey/ Auto./1571 RC	25.00
288	Mike Butia/Auto./825 RC	8.00
289	Chris Nelson/ Auto./465 RC	20.00
290	Thomas Diamond/ Auto./1055 RC	15.00
291	Neil Walker/ Auto./1343 RC	25.00
292	Sean Gamble/ Auto./1229 RC	8.00
293	Bill Bray/Auto./1073 RC	6.00
294	Reid Brignac/ Auto./522 RC	50.00
295	Ryan Klosterman/ Auto./865 RC	6.00
296	David Purcey/ Auto./1485 RC	8.00
297	Scott Elbert/ Auto./1617 RC	25.00
298	Josh Fields/ Auto./961 RC	25.00
299	Chris Lambert/ Auto./954 RC	8.00
300	Trevor Plouffe/ Auto./1329 RC	15.00
301	Greg Golson/ Auto./1334 RC	20.00
302	Josh Baker/ Auto./525 RC	8.00
303	Phillip Hughes/ Auto./1485 RC	50.00
304	Matt Macri/ Auto./979 RC	10.00
305	Kyle Waldrop/ Auto./823 RC	10.00
306	Richie Robnett/ Auto./1575 RC	15.00
307	Taylor Tankersley/ Auto./1073 RC	8.00
308	Blake DeWitt/ Auto./1562 RC	25.00
309	Daryl Jones/ Auto./575 RC	15.00
310	Eric Hurley/ Auto./1021 RC	30.00
311	J.P. Howell/ Auto./1453 RC	10.00
312	Zach Jackson/ Auto./1069 RC	8.00
313	Justin Orenduff/ Auto./473 RC	10.00
314	Tyler Lumsden/ Auto./473 RC	10.00
315	Matt Fox/Auto./473 RC	12.00
316	Danny Putnam/ Auto./473 RC	10.00
317	Jon Peterson/ Auto./464 RC	15.00
318	Gio Gonzalez/ Auto./473 RC	30.00
319	Jay Rainville/ Auto./823 RC	12.00
320	Huston Street/ Auto./709 RC	25.00
321	Jeff Marquez/ Auto./493 RC	15.00
322	Eric Beattie/ Auto./930 RC	8.00
323	B.J. Szymanski/ Auto./1327 RC	8.00
324	Seth Smith/ Auto./1065 RC	15.00
325	Robert Johnson/ Auto./790 RC	8.00
326	Wes Whisler/ Auto./473 RC	8.00
327	Billy Buckner/ Auto./673 RC	8.00
328	Jon Zeringue/ Auto./473 RC	15.00
329	Curtis Thigpen/ Auto./473 RC	10.00
330	Donny Lucy/ Auto./573 RC	6.00
331	Mike Ferris/ Auto./573 RC	10.00
332	Anthony Swarzak/ Auto./370 RC	25.00
333	Jason Jaramillo/ Auto./573 RC	8.00
334	Hunter Pence/ Auto./672 RC	80.00
335	Mike Rozier/ Auto./628 RC	8.00
336	Kurt Suzuki/ Auto./473 RC	15.00
337	Jason Vargas/ Auto./621 RC	15.00
338	Brian Bixler/ Auto./665 RC	10.00
340	Dexter Fowler/ Auto./623 RC	60.00
341	Mark Trumbo/ Auto./1321 RC	20.00
342	Jeff Frazier/ Auto./423 RC	15.00
343	Steven Register/ Auto./673 RC	8.00
344	Michael Schlact/ Auto./477 RC	8.00
345	Garrett Mock/ Auto./471 RC	12.00
346	Eric Haberer/ Auto./473 RC	8.00
347	Matt Tuiasosopo/ Auto./473 RC	20.00
348	Jason Windsor/ Auto./473 RC	15.00
349	Grant Johnson/ Auto./815 RC	10.00
350	J.C. Holt Auto./673 RC	10.00
351	Joseph Bauserman/ Auto./472 RC	8.00
352	Jamar Walton/ Auto./481 RC	15.00
353	Eric Patterson/ Auto.1571 RC	15.00

		NM/M
354	Tyler Johnson/	
	Auto/.775 **RC**	15.00
355	Nick Adenhart/	
	Auto/.653 **RC**	60.00

Aspirations

1-150 print run 61-99:	4-8X
1-150 p/r 41-60:	6-12X
1-150 p/r 26-40:	8-15X
1-150 p/r 25 or less:	No Pricing
206-355 p/r 51-99:	1-2X No Auto.
216-355 p/r 61-99:	.4-1X Auto.
216-355 p/r 41-60:	.5-1X Auto.
216-355 p/r 26-40:	.75-1X Auto.
No Pricing print run 25 or less.	

Aspirations Gold

Gold (1-150):	10-20X
Gold (206-215):	3-6X
Gold (216-355):	No Pricing
Production 25 Sets	

Status

1-150 print run 61-99:	4-8X
1-150 p/r 41-60:	6-12X
1-150 p/r 26-40:	8-15X
1-150 p/r 25 or less:	No Pricing
206-355 p/r 51-99:	1-2X No Auto.
216-355 p/r 61-99:	.4-1X Auto.
216-355 p/r 41-60:	.5-1X Auto.
216-355 p/r 26-40:	.75-1X Auto.
No pricing print run 25 or less.	

Status Gold

No Pricing
Production 10 Sets

Turn of the Century

(1-150):	3-5X
Production 250 Sets	
(206-215):	2-3X
(216-355 no auto.):	.5-1X
(216-355 auto.):	.2-.5X
206-355 production 100	

Back to Back Picks Sign.

		NM/M
Quantity produced listed.		
1	Delmon Young,	
	Rickie Weeks/25	40.00
3	Adam Dunn,	
	Austin Kearns/25	50.00
5	Michael Young,	
	Vernon Wells/25	35.00
6	Brian Roberts,	
	Larry Bigbie/25	30.00
7	Ron Cey,	
	Steve Garvey/50	35.00
8	Bill Madlock,	
	Dave Parker/50	40.00
9	Derrek Lee, Torii Hunter,	
	Trot Nixon/50	50.00
11	Chris Nelson, Matt Bush,	
	Reid Brignac/250	65.00
12	B.J. Szymanski, Greg Golson,	
	Jeff Frazier/250	40.00
13	Mark Trumbo, Nick Adenhart,	
	Tyler Johnson/250	40.00
14	Chris Carter, Danny Putnam,	
	Mark Jecmen/250	40.00
15	Billy Killian, Daryl Jones,	
	Matt Bush/100	40.00
16	Blake DeWitt, Justin Orenduff,	
	Scott Elbert/250	40.00
17	Jay Rainville, Kyle Waldrop,	
	Trevor Plouffe/250	40.00
18	Jeff Marquez, Jon Poterson,	
	Phillip Hughes/100	60.00
19	Wes Whisler, Tyler Lumsden,	
	Wes Whisler/100	40.00
20	Curtis Thigpen, David Purcey,	
	Zach Jackson/250	40.00

Career Best All-Stars

		NM/M
Common Player:		
Production 500 Sets		
1	Randy Johnson	3.00
2	David Ortiz	3.00
3	Edgar Renteria	2.00
4	Victor Martinez	2.00
5	Albert Pujols	6.00
6	Hideki Matsui	5.00
7	Mariano Rivera	2.00
8	Carlos Zambrano	2.00
9	Hank Blalock	2.00
10	Michael Young	2.00
11	Mike Piazza	4.00
12	Alfonso Soriano	3.00
13	Carl Crawford	2.00
14	Scott Rolen	2.00
15	Vladimir Guerrero	3.00
16	Lance Berkman	2.00
17	Todd Helton	2.00
18	Curt Schilling	2.00
19	Francisco Cordero	2.00
20	Mark Mulder	2.00
21	Sammy Sosa	4.00

22	Roger Clemens	6.00
23	Miguel Cabrera	3.00
24	Manny Ramirez	3.00
25	Jim Thome	3.00

Career Best A-S Jersey

		NM/M
Production 50 Sets		
Prime:		1X-2X
Production 5-25		
No pricing 15 or less.		
1	Randy Johnson	15.00
2	David Ortiz	15.00
3	Edgar Renteria	8.00
4	Victor Martinez	8.00
5	Albert Pujols	25.00
6	Hideki Matsui	40.00
7	Mariano Rivera	10.00
8	Carlos Zambrano	8.00
9	Hank Blalock	10.00
10	Michael Young	8.00
11	Mike Piazza	20.00
12	Alfonso Soriano	15.00
13	Carl Crawford	8.00
14	Scott Rolen	15.00
15	Vladimir Guerrero	15.00
16	Lance Berkman	8.00
17	Todd Helton	10.00
18	Curt Schilling	15.00
19	Francisco Cordero	8.00
20	Mark Mulder	8.00
21	Sammy Sosa	20.00
22	Roger Clemens	20.00
23	Miguel Cabrera	12.00
24	Manny Ramirez	15.00
25	Jim Thome	15.00

Career Best A-S Jersey Prime

		NM/M
2	David Ortiz/25	25.00
4	Victor Martinez/25	15.00
5	Albert Pujols/25	40.00
6	Hideki Matsui/25	75.00
8	Carlos Zambrano/25	15.00
9	Hank Blalock/25	20.00
10	Michael Young/25	15.00
11	Mike Piazza/25	30.00
12	Alfonso Soriano/25	25.00
13	Carl Crawford/25	15.00
14	Scott Rolen/25	25.00
15	Vladimir Guerrero/25	25.00
16	Lance Berkman/25	15.00
17	Todd Helton/25	20.00
18	Curt Schilling/25	25.00
20	Mark Mulder/25	15.00
21	Sammy Sosa/25	30.00
22	Roger Clemens/25	40.00
23	Miguel Cabrera/25	20.00
24	Manny Ramirez/25	25.00
25	Jim Thome/25	25.00

Career Best A-S Sig. Black

No Pricing
Production 1-5

Career Best A-S Sign. Gold

No Pricing
Production 1-10

Career Best A-S Sig. Jersey Go

		NM/M
Production 1-25		
2	David Ortiz/25	75.00
3	Edgar Renteria/25	40.00
4	Victor Martinez/25	40.00
8	Carlos Zambrano/25	40.00
10	Michael Young/25	35.00
13	Carl Crawford/25	30.00
19	Francisco Cordero/25	20.00

Career Best A-S Sig. Jersey Pr

No Pricing
Production 1-10

Draft Class

		NM/M
Common Duo:		2.00
Production 500 Sets		
1	Johnny Bench,	
	Nolan Ryan	10.00
2	Bert Blyleven,	
	Dwight Evans	2.00
3	Jim Rice,	
	Keith Hernandez	2.00
4	Dennis Eckersley,	
	Gary Carter	3.00
5	Fred Lynn, Robin Yount	5.00
	Andre Dawson,	
	Lee Smith	2.00
7	Alan Trammell,	
	Jack Morris	2.00
8	Harold Baines,	
	Paul Molitor	3.00
9	Cal Ripken Jr.,	
	Kirk Gibson	10.00
10	Don Mattingly,	
	Orel Hershiser	6.00
11	Darryl Strawberry,	
	Eric Davis	2.00
12	Dwight Gooden,	
	Jose Canseco	3.00
13	Rafael Palmeiro,	
	Randy Johnson	3.00

14	Curt Schilling,	
	Gary Sheffield	3.00
15	Mike Piazza,	
	Robin Ventura	4.00
16	Frank Thomas,	
	Jeff Bagwell	3.00
17	Chipper Jones,	
	Mike Mussina	3.00
18	Garret Anderson,	
	Jorge Posada	2.00
19	Scott Rolen, Torii Hunter	3.00
20	Kerry Wood, Todd Helton	3.00
21	Eric Chavez, Roy Oswalt	2.00
22	Johnny Estrada,	
	Vernon Wells	2.00
23	Lance Berkman,	
	Tim Hudson	2.00
24	Mark Buehrle,	
	Mark Mulder	2.00
25	C.C. Sabathia,	
	Sean Burroughs	2.00
26	Albert Pujols, Barry Zito	6.00
27	Rich Harden,	
	Rocco Baldelli	2.00
28	Bobby Crosby,	
	Mark Teixeira	2.00
29	Casey Kotchman,	
	Mark Prior	3.00
30	Dewon Brazelton,	
	Jeremy Bonderman	2.00
31	J.C. Holt, Jon Zeringue	3.00
32	Kyle Bono, Matt Fox	3.00
33	Dexter Fowler,	
	Mike Rozier	3.00
34	Huston Street,	
	J.P. Howell	4.00
35	Grant Johnson,	
	Matt Macri	3.00
36	Eric Beattie, Jeff Frazier	3.00
37	Jason Windsor,	
	Kurt Suzuki	5.00
38	Josh Fields,	
	Matt Tuiasosopo	3.00
39	Joseph Bauserman,	
	K.C. Herren	3.00
40	Chris Lambert, Eric Haberer,	
	Matt Tuiasosopo	3.00

Passing the Torch

		NM/M
Common Duo:		4.00
Production 500 Sets		
1	Dennis Eckersley,	
	Huston Street	4.00
2	Matt Bush, Tony Gwynn	6.00
3	Homer Bailey,	
	Tom Seaver	4.00
4	Bob Feller,	
	Jeremy Sowers	3.00
5	Josh Fields,	
	Robin Ventura	3.00
6	Nolan Ryan,	
	Thomas Diamond	8.00
7	Eric Patterson,	
	Ryne Sandberg	6.00
8	Richie Robnett,	
	Rickey Henderson	4.00
9	Mike Ferris, Stan Musial	5.00
10	Bobby Doerr,	
	Dustin Pedroia	3.00

Passing the Torch Auto. Black

No Pricing
Production 5-10 Sets

Passing the Torch Auto. Gold

		NM/M
Production 5-25		
2	Matt Bush,	
	Tony Gwynn/25	90.00
4	Bob Feller,	
	Jeremy Sowers/25	60.00
10	Bobby Doerr,	
	Dustin Pedroia/25	80.00

Round Numbers

		NM/M
Common Player:		2.00
Production 500 Sets		
1	Ozzie Smith	4.00
2	Derek Jeter	6.00
3	Alex Rodriguez	5.00
4	Paul Molitor	3.00
5	George Brett	6.00
6	Delmon Young	2.00
7	Dontrelle Willis	2.00
8	Gary Carter	2.00
9	Reggie Jackson	3.00
10	Andre Dawson	2.00
11	Neil Walker	2.00
12	Laynce Nix	2.00
13	Matt Bush	6.00
14	Lyle Overbay	2.00
15	Carlos Beltran	2.00
16	Todd Helton	2.00
17	Mark Grace	2.00
18	Fred Lynn	2.00
19	Robin Yount	4.00
20	Mike Schmidt	6.00
21	Roger Clemens	6.00
22	Will Clark	2.00
23	Don Mattingly	5.00
24	Blake DeWitt	2.00
25	Rafael Palmeiro	3.00
26	Wade Boggs	3.00

27	Mark Rogers	5.00
28	Billy Buckner	3.00
29	Jeff Baker	3.00
31	Nolan Ryan	8.00
32	Mike Piazza	4.00
33	Alexis Rios	2.00
34	Eddie Murray	3.00
35	Jose Canseco	3.00
36	Mike Mussina	3.00
37	Eric Beattie	3.00
38	Keith Hernandez	2.00
39	Michael Young	2.00
40	Dwight Evans	2.00
41	Adrian Gonzalez	2.00
42	Johnny Bench	3.00
43	Dennis Eckersley	2.00
44	Dale Murphy	2.00
45	Ryne Sandberg	4.00
46	David Wright	3.00
47	Hank Blalock	3.00
48	Orel Hershiser	2.00
49	Sean Casey	2.00
50	Albert Pujols	6.00

Round Numbers Signature

		NM/M
Production 5-250		
1	Ozzie Smith/25	65.00
2	Paul Molitor/25	35.00
6	Delmon Young/50	25.00
7	Dontrelle Willis/50	20.00
8	Gary Carter/50	20.00
10	Andre Dawson/50	20.00
11	Neil Walker/250	20.00
12	Laynce Nix/50	20.00
13	Matt Bush/100	40.00
14	Lyle Overbay/50	15.00
15	Carlos Beltran/50	50.00
17	Mark Grace/25	35.00
18	Fred Lynn/50	15.00
20	Mike Schmidt/25	85.00
22	Will Clark/20	60.00
23	Don Mattingly/25	80.00
24	Blake DeWitt/50	30.00
27	Mark Rogers/40	20.00
28	Billy Buckner/50	15.00
33	Alexis Rios/50	15.00
34	Jose Canseco/25	50.00
36	Eric Beattie/100	12.00
37	Keith Hernandez/50	20.00
38	Michael Young/50	25.00
39	Dwight Evans/50	25.00
40	Scott Elbert/250	15.00
41	Adrian Gonzalez/50	10.00
43	Dennis Eckersley/50	30.00
44	Dale Murphy/50	30.00
46	David Wright/25	75.00
47	Hank Blalock/25	20.00
49	Sean Casey/25	15.00

Signature

		NM/M
Production 1-50		
132	Jack Wilson/25	25.00
133	Jason Bay/25	25.00
231	J.A. Happ/10	10.00
233	Mark Jecmen/50	8.00
234	Kameron Loe/50	20.00
238	Ervin Santana/50	50.00
239	Josh Karp/50	15.00
243	Jesse Hoover/50	15.00
246	Justin Hoyman/50	15.00
247	Juan Cedeno/50	15.00
252	Benjamin Zobrist/50	10.00
253	Jeff Salazar/50	30.00
254	Fausto Carmona/50	20.00

Signature Aspirations

		NM/M
Production 1-100		
Golds:		No Pricing
Production 1-25		
216	Scott Lewis/50	15.00
217	Josh Johnson/50	15.00
218	Jeff Fiorentino/50	25.00
219	Grant Hansen/50	8.00
220	Yovani Gallardo/50	80.00
221	Eddie Prasch/50	10.00
222	Danny Hill/50	8.00
223	Chuck Lofgren/50	40.00
224	Blake Johnson/50	15.00
226	Cory Dunlap/50	20.00
226	Carlos Vasquez/50	10.00
227	Jesse Crain/50	15.00
228	Yhency Brazoban/50	10.00
229	Abe Alvarez/50	10.00
256	Jorge Vasquez/50	8.00
257	Rafael Gonzalez/50	8.00
258	Andrew Dobies/50	15.00
259	Colby Miller/49	10.00
260	K.C. Herren/50	10.00
261	Ryan Meaux/50	15.00
262	Dustin Pedroia/50	175.00
263	Fernando Nieve/50	8.00
265	Mariano Gomez/50	8.00
266	Billy Killian/50	8.00
267	Mike Rouse/50	8.00
268	Kyle Bono/50	8.00
269	Mitch Einertson/50	25.00
270	Scott Proctor/50	15.00
271	Tim Bittner/50	8.00
272	Christian Garcia/50	15.00
273	Yadier Molina/50	30.00
274	Justin Leone/50	15.00
275	Charles Thomas/50	10.00
276	Travis Blackley/50	10.00
277	Frankie Francisco/50	10.00

278	Dioner Navarro/50	15.00
279	Joey Gathright/50	10.00
280	Kazuhito Tadano/50	10.00
281	Matt Bush/50	30.00
282	David Haehnel/100	10.00
283	Tommy Hottovy/100	15.00
284	Chris Carter/50	30.00
286	Jeremy Sowers/50	40.00
287	Homer Bailey/50	30.00
288	Mike Butia/100	10.00
289	Chris Nelson/50	40.00
290	Thomas Diamond/100	30.00
291	Neil Walker/100	30.00
292	Sean Gamble/50	10.00
293	Bill Bray/100	8.00
294	Reid Brignac/50	75.00
295	Ryan Klosterman/.800	8.00
296	David Purcey/50	10.00
297	Scott Elbert/100	50.00
298	Josh Fields/50	50.00
299	Chris Lambert/50	10.00
300	Trevor Plouffe/100	25.00
301	Greg Golson/50	20.00
302	Josh Baker/100	10.00
303	Phillip Hughes/50	75.00
304	Matt Macri/50	12.00
305	Kyle Waldrop/50	10.00
306	Richie Robnett/50	25.00
307	Taylor Tankersley/100	10.00
308	Blake DeWitt/50	40.00
309	Daryl Jones/50	10.00
310	Eric Hurley/50	40.00
311	J.P. Howell/100	10.00
312	Zach Jackson/50	15.00
313	Justin Orenduff/100	20.00
314	Tyler Lumsden/100	15.00
315	Matt Fox/50	15.00
316	Danny Putnam/50	15.00
317	Jon Poterson/50	15.00
318	Gio Gonzalez/100	40.00
319	Jay Rainville/50	10.00
320	Huston Street/100	40.00
321	Jeff Marquez/100	15.00
322	Eric Beattie/100	10.00
323	B.J. Szymanski/100	10.00
324	Seth Smith/100	30.00
325	Robert Johnson/50	10.00
326	Wes Whisler/50	10.00
327	Billy Buckner/50	15.00
328	Jon Zeringue/50	30.00
329	Curtis Thigpen/50	12.00
330	Donny Lucy/50	10.00
331	Mike Ferris/50	10.00
333	Jason Jaramillo/50	15.00
334	Hunter Pence/50	125.00
335	Mike Rozier/50	10.00
336	Kurt Suzuki/50	25.00
337	Jason Vargas/50	50.00
338	Brian Bixler/50	15.00
340	Dexter Fowler/50	100.00
341	Mark Trumbo/50	40.00
342	Jeff Frazier/50	20.00
343	Steven Register/50	10.00
344	Michael Schlact/50	10.00
345	Garrett Mock/50	10.00
346	Eric Haberer/50	10.00
347	Matt Tuiasosopo/50	40.00
348	Jason Windsor/50	10.00
349	Grant Johnson/50	10.00
350	J.C. Holt/50	10.00
351	Joseph Bauserman/50	10.00
353	Jamar Walton/50	25.00
353	Eric Patterson/50	35.00
354	Tyler Johnson/50	15.00
355	Nick Adenhart/50	120.00

Sign. Turn of Century

		NM/M
216	Scott Lewis/100	12.00
217	Josh Johnson/100	12.00
218	Jeff Fiorentino/100	10.00
219	Grant Hansen/100	8.00
220	Yovani Gallardo/100	60.00
221	Eddie Prasch/100	8.00
222	Danny Hill/100	8.00
223	Chuck Lofgren/100	20.00
224	Blake Johnson/100	20.00
225	Cory Dunlap/100	10.00
226	Carlos Vasquez/100	10.00
227	Jesse Crain/100	15.00
228	Yhency Brazoban/100	10.00
229	Abe Alvarez/100	10.00
246	Justin Hoyman/250	10.00
252	Benjamin Zobrist/150	10.00
256	Jorge Vasquez/100	8.00
257	Rafael Gonzalez/100	8.00
258	Andrew Dobies/100	15.00
259	Colby Miller/100	10.00
260	K.C. Herren/100	15.00
261	Ryan Meaux/100	15.00
262	Dustin Pedroia/100	120.00
263	Fernando Nieve/100	10.00
264	Mariano Gomez/100	10.00
266	Billy Killian/100	8.00
267	Mike Rouse/100	10.00
268	Kyle Bono/100	8.00
269	Mitch Einertson/100	15.00
270	Scott Proctor/100	10.00
271	Tim Bittner/100	8.00
272	Christian Garcia/100	10.00
273	Yadier Molina/100	30.00
274	Justin Leone/100	15.00
275	Charles Thomas/100	10.00
276	Travis Blackley/100	10.00
277	Frankie Francisco/100	10.00
279	Joey Gathright/100	15.00
280	Kazuhito Tadano/100	15.00
281	Matt Bush/50	20.00
282	David Haehnel/250	8.00
283	Tommy Hottovy/250	8.00
284	Chris Carter/250	25.00
285	Mark Rogers/250	25.00
286	Jeremy Sowers/250	25.00
287	Homer Bailey/250	30.00
288	Mike Butia/250	8.00
289	Chris Nelson/100	25.00
291	Neil Walker/242	25.00
292	Sean Gamble/250	8.00
293	Bill Bray/250	8.00
294	Reid Brignac/100	60.00
295	Ryan Klosterman/250	8.00
296	David Purcey/250	8.00
298	Scott Elbert/250	40.00
299	Josh Fields/250	40.00
300	Chris Lambert/250	15.00
301	Trevor Plouffe/250	15.00
302	Greg Golson/250	20.00
303	Josh Baker/250	10.00
304	Phillip Hughes/250	60.00
305	Kyle Waldrop/250	15.00
307	Taylor Tankersley/250	15.00
308	Blake DeWitt/250	25.00
309	Daryl Jones/250	15.00
310	Eric Hurley/250	30.00
312	Zach Jackson/250	10.00
313	Justin Orenduff/100	15.00

Signature Status

		NM/M
Production 1-50		
Golds:		No Pricing
Production 1-10		
221	Eddie Prasch/25	15.00
224	Blake Johnson/25	20.00
229	Abe Alvarez/25	15.00
257	Rafael Gonzalez/25	10.00
268	Kyle Bono/25	15.00
272	Christian Garcia/25	15.00
276	Travis Blackley/25	10.00
281	Matt Bush/50	40.00
282	David Haehnel/250	8.00
283	Tommy Hottovy/250	8.00
284	Chris Carter/250	25.00
285	Mark Rogers/250	25.00
286	Jeremy Sowers/250	25.00
287	Homer Bailey/250	30.00
288	Mike Butia/250	8.00
289	Chris Nelson/100	25.00
290	Thomas Diamond/250	25.00
291	Neil Walker/242	25.00
292	Sean Gamble/250	8.00
293	Bill Bray/250	8.00
294	Reid Brignac/100	60.00
295	Ryan Klosterman/250	8.00
296	David Purcey/250	8.00
298	Scott Elbert/250	40.00
299	Josh Fields/250	40.00
300	Chris Lambert/250	15.00
301	Trevor Plouffe/250	15.00
302	Greg Golson/250	20.00
303	Josh Baker/250	10.00
304	Phillip Hughes/250	60.00
305	Kyle Waldrop/250	15.00
307	Taylor Tankersley/250	15.00
308	Blake DeWitt/250	25.00
309	Daryl Jones/250	15.00
310	Eric Hurley/250	30.00
312	Zach Jackson/250	10.00
313	Justin Orenduff/100	15.00

314 Tyler Lumsden/250 10.00
315 Matt Fox/250 12.00
316 Danny Putnam/250 12.00
317 Jon Poterson/238 12.00
318 Gio Gonzalez/250 30.00
319 Jay Rainville/250 20.00
320 Huston Street/250 25.00
321 Jeff Marquez/250 10.00
322 Eric Beattie/250 8.00
323 B.J. Szymanski/250 8.00
324 Seth Smith/250 20.00
325 Robert Johnson/100 10.00
326 Wes Whisler/100 8.00
327 Billy Buckner/100 10.00
328 Jon Zeringue/250 20.00
329 Curtis Thigpen/100 10.00
330 Donny Lucy/100 8.00
331 Mike Ferris/250 10.00
332 Anthony Swarzak/100 25.00
333 Jason Jaramillo/250 8.00
334 Hunter Pence/200 100.00
335 Mike Rozier/250 8.00
336 Kurt Suzuki/250 20.00
337 Jason Vargas/200 20.00
338 Brian Bixler/250 8.00
340 Dexter Fowler/250 60.00
341 Mark Trumbo/250 25.00
342 Jeff Frazier/50 20.00
343 Steven Register/250 8.00
344 Michael Schlact/200 15.00
345 Garrett Mock/250 15.00
346 Eric Haberer/100 8.00
347 Matt Tuiasosopo/250 25.00
348 Jason Windsor/100 15.00
349 Grant Johnson/250 8.00
350 J.C. Holt/100 8.00
351 Joseph Bauserman/100 8.00
352 Jamar Walton/200 12.00
353 Eric Patterson/250 25.00
354 Tyler Johnson/250 15.00
355 Nick Adenhart/100 75.00

Throwback Threads
NM/M
Production 50 Sets
1 Roger Maris 60.00
2 Ted Williams 80.00
3 Cal Ripken Jr. 75.00
4 Duke Snider 20.00
5 George Brett 40.00

Throwback Threads Auto.
No Pricing

2004 Donruss Leather & Lumber

NM/M
Complete Set (175):
Common Player (1-150): .25
Common Auto. (151-173): 6.00
Production 500
Pack (5): 5.00
Box (24): 100.00
1 Bartolo Colon .25
2 Garret Anderson .50
3 Tim Salmon .40
4 Troy Glaus .50
5 Vladimir Guerrero 1.00
6 Brandon Webb .25
7 Luis Gonzalez .40
8 Randy Johnson 1.00
9 Richie Sexson .50
10 Shea Hillenbrand .25
11 Adam LaRoche .25
12 Andruw Jones .50
13 Chipper Jones 1.00
14 Dale Murphy .75
15 J.D. Drew .50
16 Marcus Giles .25
17 Rafael Furcal .25
18 Cal Ripken Jr. 3.00
19 Javy Lopez .25
20 Jay Gibbons .25
21 Luis Matos .25
22 Miguel Tejada .50
23 Rafael Palmeiro .75
24 Curt Schilling .75
25 Jason Varitek .40
26 Manny Ramirez .75
27 Nomar Garciaparra 1.50
28 Pedro J. Martinez .75
29 Trot Nixon .25
30 Greg Maddux 1.50
31 Kerry Wood 1.00
32 Mark Prior 1.00
33 Ryne Sandberg 1.50
34 Sammy Sosa 2.00
35 Carlos Lee .25

36 Frank Thomas .75
37 Magglio Ordonez .40
38 Paul Konerko .25
39 Adam Dunn .75
40 Austin Kearns .25
41 Barry Larkin .50
42 Ken Griffey Jr. 1.50
43 Ryan Wagner .25
44 C.C. Sabathia .25
45 Jody Gerut .25
46 Omar Vizquel .25
47 Larry Walker .40
48 Preston Wilson .25
49 Todd Helton .75
50 Alan Trammell .50
51 Ivan Rodriguez .75
52 Jeremy Bonderman .25
53 Dontrelle Willis .25
54 Josh Beckett .50
55 Luis Castillo .25
56 Miguel Cabrera 1.00
57 Mike Lowell .25
58 Andy Pettitte .40
59 Craig Biggio .40
60 Jeff Bagwell .75
61 Jeff Kent .40
62 Lance Berkman .40
63 Roger Clemens 2.50
64 Roy Oswalt .40
65 Angel Berroa .25
66 Carlos Beltran .75
67 George Brett 2.00
68 Juan Gonzalez .50
69 Mike Sweeney .25
70 Eric Gagne .50
71 Hideo Nomo .25
72 Kazuhisa Ishii .25
73 Paul LoDuca .25
74 Shawn Green .50
75 Geoff Jenkins .25
76 Junior Spivey .25
77 Rickie Weeks .25
78 Robin Yount .75
79 Scott Podsednik .25
80 Jacque Jones .25
81 Johan Santana .50
82 Shannon Stewart .25
83 Torii Hunter .40
84 Andre Dawson .50
85 Chad Cordero .25
86 Jose Vidro .25
87 Nick Johnson .25
88 Orlando Cabrera .40
89 Gary Carter .50
90 Jae Weong Seo .25
91 Jose Reyes .50
92 Mike Piazza 1.50
93 Tom Glavine .50
94 Alex Rodriguez 2.50
95 Bernie Williams .50
96 Derek Jeter 2.50
97 Don Mattingly 2.00
98 Gary Sheffield .50
99 Hideki Matsui 1.50
100 Jason Giambi .50
101 Jorge Posada .50
102 Mike Mussina .50
103 Barry Zito .50
104 Bobby Crosby .25
105 Eric Chavez .40
106 Jermaine Dye .25
107 Mark Mulder .40
108 Rich Harden .25
109 Rickey Henderson .50
110 Tim Hudson .40
111 Bobby Abreu .25
112 Brett Myers .25
113 Jim Thome 1.00
114 Kevin Millwood .25
115 Marlon Byrd .25
116 Mike Schmidt 2.00
117 Pat Burrell .25
118 Dave Parker .25
119 Jason Bay .25
120 Jason Kendall .25
121 Brian Giles .25
122 Jay Payton .25
123 Ryan Klesko .25
124 Tony Gwynn 1.00
125 Edgardo Alfonzo .25
126 Jason Schmidt .50
127 Jerome Williams .25
128 Bret Boone .25
129 Edgar Martinez .50
130 Ichiro Suzuki 2.00
131 Jamie Moyer .25
132 John Olerud .25
133 Albert Pujols 2.00
134 Edgar Renteria .40
135 Jim Edmonds .25
136 Matt Morris .25
137 Scott Rolen 1.00
138 Aubrey Huff .25
139 Carl Crawford .25
140 Delmon Young .25
141 Rocco Baldelli .25
142 Alfonso Soriano 1.00
143 Hank Blalock .75
144 Mark Teixeira .25
145 Michael Young .25
146 Nolan Ryan 2.50
147 Carlos Delgado .50
148 Eric Hinske .25
149 Roy Halladay .25
150 Vernon Wells .25
151 Andres Blanco RC 8.00
152 Kevin Cave RC 6.00
153 Ryan Meaux RC 6.00

154 Tim Bausher RC 6.00
155 Jesse Harper RC 6.00
156 Mike Wuertz RC 8.00
157 Colby Miller RC 6.00
158 Donald Kelly RC 8.00
159 Edwin Moreno RC 6.00
160 Mike Johnston RC 6.00
161 Orlando Rodriguez RC 8.00
162 Phil Stockman RC 8.00
163 Yadier Molina RC 8.00
164 Jorge Vasquez RC 8.00
165 Scott Proctor RC 8.00
166 Jake Woods RC 6.00
167 Aarom Baldiris RC 8.00
168 Jason Bartlett RC 6.00
169 Casey Daigle RC 6.00
170 Dennis Sarfate RC 6.00
171 Edwardo Sierra RC 8.00
172 Merkin Valdez RC 8.00
173 Eddy Rodriguez RC 8.00
174 Kazuo Matsui RC 8.00
175 David Aardsma RC 4.00

Silver
Stars (1-150): 4-8X
SP's (151-175): .5X

Gold
Stars (1-150): 10-15X
SP's (151-175): No Pricing
Production 25 Sets

Platinum
No Pricing
Production One Set

B/W
NM/M
Common Player: 1.50
Production 1,000 Sets
Gold B/W: 4-6X
Production 25 Sets
Silver B/W: 2-3X
Production 100 Sets
Platinum B/W: No Pricing
Production One Set
13 Chipper Jones 2.00
14 Dale Murphy 1.50
18 Cal Ripken Jr. 8.00
27 Nomar Garciaparra 3.00
30 Greg Maddux 2.50
32 Mark Prior 1.50
33 Ryne Sandberg 3.00
34 Sammy Sosa 3.00
63 Roger Clemens 4.00
67 George Brett 4.00
78 Robin Yount 3.00
89 Gary Carter 1.50
92 Mike Piazza 3.00
94 Alex Rodriguez 5.00
96 Derek Jeter 5.00
97 Don Mattingly 4.00
99 Hideki Matsui 3.00
109 Rickey Henderson 1.50
116 Mike Schmidt 3.00
124 Tony Gwynn 2.00
130 Ichiro Suzuki 4.00
133 Albert Pujols 4.00
142 Alfonso Soriano 2.00
146 Nolan Ryan 5.00
174 Kazuo Matsui 6.00

Bat-Spikes
NM/M
Bat/Glove: .75-1.5X
Production 1-50
Bat/Ball: .75-1.5X
Production 5-25
No pricing 15 or less.
Barrel/Jersey: No Pricing
Production 1-5
1 Andruw Jones/25 15.00
3 Angel Berroa/25 10.00
5 Barry Zito/25 15.00
7 Ben Sheets/50 10.00
8 Brad Penny/50 8.00
9 Brian Giles/50 8.00
10 Carlos Lee/50 8.00
11 Corey Patterson/50 15.00
13 Don Mattingly/25 40.00
15 Gary Carter/50 12.00
17 Ivan Rodriguez/50 15.00
18 Jack Cust/50 8.00
20 Jason Jennings/50 8.00
21 Jim Edmonds/50 10.00
22 Joe Borchard/50 8.00
23 Joe Crede/50 8.00
24 Josh Beckett/25 15.00
25 Josh Phelps/50 8.00
26 Juan Pierre/50 8.00
27 Kenny Lofton/50 8.00
28 Lance Berkman/25 15.00
30 Magglio Ordonez/25 10.00
31 Marcus Giles/50 10.00
32 Mark Buehrle/50 8.00
33 Mark Prior/25 20.00
34 Mark Teixeira/25 15.00
35 Marlon Byrd/50 8.00
37 Mike Lowell/50 8.00
38 Nick Johnson/25 10.00
39 Orlando Hudson/50 8.00
40 Paul LoDuca/25 8.00
41 Rafael Palmeiro/25 20.00
42 Roy Oswalt/25 15.00
43 Roy Klesko/50 15.00
44 Ryan Klesko/50 15.00
45 Sean Casey/50 8.00
47 Travis Hafner/50 15.00
48 Travis Hafner/50 15.00
49 Victor Martinez/50 10.00
50 Wade Miller/50 10.00

Cuts

NM/M
Common Player:
1 Adam Dunn/192 20.00
2 Al Kaline/192 35.00
3 Alfonso Soriano/160 40.00
4 Andre Dawson/224 15.00
5 Angel Berroa/224
6 Harmon Killebrew/192 35.00
7 Bob Gibson/96 30.00
8 Brooks Robinson/192 30.00
9 Cal Ripken Jr./32 200.00
10 Dale Murphy/224 15.00
11 Darryl Strawberry/224 15.00
12 Delmon Young/192 20.00
13 Don Mattingly/96 65.00
14 Duke Snider/96 30.00
15 Dwight Gooden/224 15.00
16 Ozzie Smith/96 60.00
17 Garret Anderson/224 15.00
18 Gary Carter/160 20.00
19 George Kell/224 15.00
20 Hank Blalock/224 20.00
21 Jim Palmer/192 20.00
22 Kirk Gibson/160 15.00
23 Lou Brock/192 25.00
24 Ryne Sandberg/160 50.00
25 Mark Prior/160 40.00
26 Miguel Cabrera/224 15.00
27 Mike Lowell/160 15.00
28 Nolan Ryan/96 100.00
29 Luis Aparicio/224 15.00
30 Paul Molitor/160 30.00
31 Red Schoendienst/224 25.00
32 Rickie Weeks/224 10.00
33 Ron Santo/224 25.00
34 Roy Oswalt/224 20.00
35 Stan Musial/96 60.00
36 Steve Carlton/192 20.00
37 Tony Gwynn/192 35.00
38 Vernon Wells/160 20.00
39 Will Clark/192 35.00
40 Bob Feller/224 25.00
41 Bobby Doerr/224 20.00
42 Ralph Kiner/224 30.00
43 Torii Hunter/224 15.00
44 Rollie Fingers/224 15.00
45 Steve Garvey/224 15.00
46 Alan Trammell/224 15.00
47 Maury Wills/224 15.00
48 Gaylord Perry/224 15.00

Cuts Glove
NM/M
Quantity produced listed.
1 Adam Dunn/192 20.00
2 Al Kaline/192 35.00
3 Alfonso Soriano/160 40.00
4 Andre Dawson/224 15.00
5 Angel Berroa/224
6 Harmon Killebrew/192 35.00
7 Bob Gibson/96 30.00
8 Brooks Robinson/192 30.00
9 Cal Ripken Jr./32 200.00
10 Dale Murphy/224 15.00
11 Darryl Strawberry/224 15.00
12 Delmon Young/192 20.00
13 Don Mattingly/96 65.00
14 Duke Snider/96 30.00
15 Dwight Gooden/224 15.00
16 Ozzie Smith/96 60.00
17 Garret Anderson/224 15.00
18 Gary Carter/160 20.00
19 George Kell/224 15.00
20 Hank Blalock/224 20.00
21 Jim Palmer/192 20.00
22 Kirk Gibson/160 15.00
23 Lou Brock/192 25.00
24 Ryne Sandberg/160 50.00
25 Mark Prior/160 40.00
26 Miguel Cabrera/224 15.00
27 Mike Lowell/160 15.00
28 Nolan Ryan/96 100.00
29 Luis Aparicio/224 15.00
30 Paul Molitor/160 30.00
31 Red Schoendienst/224 25.00
32 Rickie Weeks/224 10.00
33 Ron Santo/224 25.00
34 Roy Oswalt/224 20.00
35 Stan Musial/96 60.00
36 Steve Carlton/192 20.00
37 Tony Gwynn/192 35.00
38 Vernon Wells/160 20.00
39 Will Clark/192 35.00
40 Bob Feller/224 25.00
41 Bobby Doerr/224 20.00
42 Ralph Kiner/224 30.00
43 Torii Hunter/224 15.00
44 Rollie Fingers/224 15.00
45 Steve Garvey/224 15.00
46 Alan Trammell/224 15.00
47 Maury Wills/224 15.00
48 Gaylord Perry/224 15.00

Hall of Fame
NM/M
Common Player: 2.00
Quantity produced listed.
Silver: 1-2X
Production 100 Sets
1 Carl Yastrzemski/1989 4.00
2 Carlton Fisk/2000 4.00
3 George Brett/1999 5.00
4 Johnny Bench/1989 4.00
5 Mike Schmidt/1995 6.00
6 Nolan Ryan/1999 6.00
7 Ozzie Smith/2002 4.00
8 Robin Yount/1999 4.00
9 Rod Carew/1991 3.00
10 Tom Seaver/1992 3.00

Hall of Fame Materials
NM/M
Quantity produced listed
1 Carl Yastrzemski/Jsy/250 15.00
2 Carlton Fisk/Jsy/250 10.00
3 George Brett/Jsy/250 15.00
4 Johnny Bench/Jsy/100 15.00
5 Mike Schmidt/Jkt/250 15.00
6 Nolan Ryan/Pants/100 25.00
7 Ozzie Smith/Jsy/100 15.00
8 Robin Yount/Jsy/250 12.00
9 Rod Carew/Jkt/250 15.00
10 Tom Seaver/Jsy/200 15.00

Leather Cuts Ball
No Pricing
Production 5-10

Leather in Leather

NM/M
Common Player:
Production 2,499 Sets
Silver: 1-2X
Production 100 Sets
1 Garret Anderson/BB 1.50
2 Albert Pujols/BB 5.00
3 John Smoltz/BB 1.50
4 Cal Ripken Jr./BB 5.00
5 Ichiro Suzuki/BB 5.00
6 Pedro J. Martinez/BB 2.00
7 Shawn Green/BB 1.50
8 Juan Gonzalez/BB 1.50
9 Mariano Rivera/BB 1.50
10 Jason Giambi/BB 1.50
11 Dave Parker/BG 1.50
12 Dwight Gooden/BG 1.50
13 Eric Munson/BG 1.50
14 Frank Thomas/BG 1.50
15 Joe Carter/BG 1.50
16 Jose Canseco/BG 1.50
17 Paul O'Neill/BG 1.50
18 Tony Gwynn/BG 3.00
19 Wade Boggs/BG 2.00
20 Xavier Nady/BG 1.50
21 Albert Pujols/FG 5.00
22 Alex Rodriguez/FG 6.00
23 Chipper Jones/FG 3.00
24 Derek Jeter/FG 6.00
25 Jack Wilson/FG 1.50
26 Lenny Dykstra/FG 1.50
27 Mark Grace/FG 2.00
28 Steve Carlton/FG 2.00
29 Tony Perez/FG 2.00
30 Vladimir Guerrero/FG 3.00
31 Bernie Williams/SH 2.00
32 Eddie Murray/SH 1.50
33 Frank Robinson/SH 2.00
34 Greg Maddux/SH 4.00
35 Harmon Killebrew/SH 3.00
36 Manny Ramirez/SH 2.00
37 Mike Piazza/SH 4.00
38 Paul Molitor/SH 3.00
39 Sammy Sosa/SH 4.00
40 Tim Hudson/SH 2.00

Leather Materials
NM/M
Quantity produced listed.
1 Garret Anderson/Ball/50 8.00
2 Albert Pujols/Ball/50 25.00

3 John Smoltz/Ball/50 20.00
4 Cal Ripken Jr./Ball/50 75.00
5 Ichiro Suzuki/Ball/50 60.00
6 Pedro J. Martinez/Ball/50 15.00
7 Shawn Green/Ball/50 10.00
8 Juan Gonzalez/Ball/50 10.00
9 Mariano Rivera/Ball/50 10.00
10 Jason Giambi/Ball/50 10.00
11 Dave Parker/Btg Glv/20 20.00
12 Dwight Gooden/Btg Glv/25
13 Eric Munson/Btg Glv/50 8.00
14 Frank Thomas/Btg Glv/50
15 Joe Carter/Btg Glv/50 10.00
16 Jose Canseco/Btg Glv/50 20.00
17 Paul O'Neill/Btg Glv/50
18 Tony Gwynn/Btg Glv/50 30.00
19 Wade Boggs/Btg Glv/25 20.00
20 Xavier Nady/Btg Glv/50 8.00
21 Alex Rodriguez/Fld Glv/25 35.00
23 Chipper Jones/Fld Glv/25
24 Derek Jeter/Fld Glv/25 50.00
25 Jack Wilson/Fld Glv/50 8.00
26 Lenny Dykstra/Fld Glv/25 10.00
27 Mark Grace/Fld Glv/50 15.00
28 Steve Carlton/Fld Glv/50 12.00
29 Tony Perez/Fld Glv/25 15.00
31 Bernie Williams/Spikes/50 10.00
32 Eddie Murray/Spikes/25 30.00
33 Frank Robinson/Spikes/25
34 Greg Maddux/Spikes/25 30.00
35 Harmon Killebrew/Spikes/25 35.00

Materials Bat B/W
NM/M
Production 100 unless noted.
13 Chipper Jones 8.00
14 Dale Murphy 15.00
18 Cal Ripken Jr. 30.00
27 Nomar Garciaparra 10.00
30 Greg Maddux 10.00
32 Mark Prior 8.00
33 Ryne Sandberg 30.00
34 Sammy Sosa 12.00
63 Roger Clemens/50 20.00
67 George Brett 15.00
78 Robin Yount 12.00
89 Gary Carter 10.00
92 Mike Piazza 10.00
94 Alex Rodriguez 15.00
96 Derek Jeter 20.00
97 Don Mattingly 20.00
109 Rickey Henderson 15.00
116 Mike Schmidt 15.00
124 Tony Gwynn 10.00
133 Albert Pujols 20.00
142 Alfonso Soriano 10.00
146 Nolan Ryan/25 65.00
174 Kazuo Matsui 20.00

Materials Jersey

NM/M
Common Jersey: 4.00
Quantity produced listed.
MLB Logo: No Pricing
Production One Set
Prime: 1-1.25X
Production 1-25
No pricing 15 or less.
Barrel: No Pricing
Production 1-5
2 Garret Anderson/50 8.00
3 Tim Salmon/250 4.00
4 Troy Glaus/250 4.00
5 Brandon Webb/100 4.00
7 Luis Gonzalez/250 4.00
8 Randy Johnson/100 10.00
12 Andruw Jones/250 4.00
13 Chipper Jones/250 8.00
14 Dale Murphy/250 10.00
16 Marcus Giles/250 4.00
17 Rafael Furcal/250 4.00
18 Cal Ripken Jr./100 30.00
19 Javy Lopez/250 4.00
20 Jay Gibbons/250 4.00
21 Luis Matos/250 4.00
22 Miguel Tejada/250 4.00
23 Rafael Palmeiro/250 4.00
25 Jason Varitek/250 4.00

26	Manny Ramirez/250	8.00
28	Pedro J. Martinez/250	8.00
29	Trot Nixon/250	10.00
30	Greg Maddux/100	10.00
31	Kerry Wood/250	10.00
32	Mark Prior/250	10.00
33	Ryne Sandberg/50	30.00
34	Sammy Sosa/250	10.00
35	Carlos Beltran/250	4.00
36	Frank Thomas/250	8.00
37	Magglio Ordonez/250	4.00
38	Paul Konerko/250	4.00
39	Adam Dunn/250	8.00
40	Austin Kearns/250	4.00
41	Barry Larkin/250	6.00
44	C.C. Sabathia/250	4.00
45	Jody Gerut/250	4.00
46	Omar Vizquel/250	4.00
47	Larry Walker/250	4.00
48	Preston Wilson/250	8.00
49	Todd Helton/250	8.00
50	Alan Trammell/50	10.00
51	Ivan Rodriguez/100	4.00
52	Jeremy Bonderman/150	4.00
53	Dontrelle Willis/100	4.00
54	Josh Beckett/250	4.00
55	Luis Castillo/250	4.00
56	Miguel Cabrera/50	15.00
57	Mike Lowell/25	10.00
58	Andy Pettitte/25	15.00
59	Craig Biggio/250	4.00
60	Jeff Bagwell/250	8.00
61	Jeff Kent/250	4.00
62	Lance Berkman/250	4.00
63	Roy Oswalt/250	4.00
65	Angel Berroa/50	6.00
66	Carlos Beltran/250	6.00
67	George Brett/250	15.00
69	Mike Sweeney/100	4.00
70	Hideo Nomo/250	6.00
71	Kazuhisa Ishii/250	4.00
72	Paul LoDuca/250	4.00
74	Shawn Green/250	4.00
75	Geoff Jenkins/250	4.00
77	Robin Yount/250	10.00
80	Jacque Jones/250	10.00
81	Johan Santana/250	8.00
82	Shannon Stewart/250	4.00
83	Torii Hunter/250	4.00
84	Andre Dawson/50	10.00
86	Jose Vidro/100	4.00
87	Orlando Cabrera/100	4.00
89	Gary Carter/250	8.00
90	Jae Weong Seo/100	4.00
91	Jose Reyes/250	6.00
92	Mike Piazza/250	10.00
93	Tom Glavine/250	6.00
94	Bernie Williams/250	6.00
95	Derek Jeter/150	20.00
96	Don Mattingly/250	15.00
97	Hideki Matsui/250	20.00
99	Jason Giambi/250	4.00
101	Jorge Posada/250	10.00
102	Mike Mussina/100	8.00
103	Barry Zito/250	4.00
105	Eric Chavez/250	4.00
107	Mark Mulder/250	4.00
108	Rich Harden/50	8.00
109	Rickey Henderson/100	10.00
111	Tim Hudson/250	4.00
112	Bobby Abreu/250	4.00
113	Brett Myers/250	4.00
114	Jim Thome/250	8.00
115	Kevin Millwood/250	4.00
116	Marlon Byrd/250	4.00
116	Mike Schmidt/50	25.00
117	Pat Burrell/250	4.00
118	Dave Parker/250	8.00
120	Jason Kendall/250	6.00
121	Ryan Klesko/250	4.00
124	Tony Gwynn/100	12.00
128	Jerome Williams/200	4.00
129	Edgar Martinez/250	6.00
131	Jamie Moyer/250	4.00
132	John Olerud/150	4.00
133	Albert Pujols/250	15.00
134	Edgar Renteria/100	6.00
135	Jim Edmonds/250	4.00
136	Matt Morris/250	4.00
137	Scott Rolen/250	8.00
138	Aubrey Huff/100	4.00
139	Carl Crawford/250	4.00
140	Rocco Baldelli/250	4.00
143	Hank Blalock/250	6.00
146	Nolan Ryan/250	30.00
147	Carlos Delgado/250	4.00
148	Eric Hinske/100	4.00
149	Roy Halladay/100	4.00
150	Vernon Wells/250	4.00

Materials Jersey B/W

NM/M
Common Player: 5.00
Jersey Prime B/W: No Pricing
Production 1-25

13	Chipper Jones/250	8.00
14	Dale Murphy/250	8.00
18	Cal Ripken Jr./100	35.00
30	Greg Maddux/100	10.00
32	Mark Prior/250	8.00
33	Ryne Sandberg/50	30.00
34	Sammy Sosa/250	12.00
67	George Brett/250	15.00
77	Robin Yount/150	10.00
89	Gary Carter/250	5.00
92	Mike Piazza/250	5.00
95	Derek Jeter/250	20.00
96	Don Mattingly/250	15.00
97	Hideki Matsui/250	20.00
109	Rickey Henderson/250	8.00
116	Mike Schmidt/250	25.00
124	Tony Gwynn/100	10.00
133	Albert Pujols/250	15.00
146	Nolan Ryan/100	25.00
174	Kazuo Matsui/50	25.00

Naturals

NM/M
Common Player: 1.50
Production 1,499 Sets
Silver: 1-2X
Production 100 Sets

1	Eric Chavez	1.50
2	Garret Anderson	1.50
3	Lance Berkman	1.50
4	Paul Molitor	3.00
5	Rafael Palmeiro	2.00
6	Ralph Kiner	3.00
7	Todd Helton	2.00
8	Tony Gwynn	4.00
9	Wade Boggs	2.00
10	Will Clark	2.00

Naturals Materials Bat

NM/M
Barrel: No Pricing
Production 1-5

1	Eric Chavez/20	12.00
2	Garret Anderson/250	5.00
3	Lance Berkman/250	5.00
4	Paul Molitor/250	8.00
5	Rafael Palmeiro/250	8.00
6	Ralph Kiner/250	10.00
7	Todd Helton/250	8.00
8	Tony Gwynn/250	12.00
9	Wade Boggs/250	8.00
10	Will Clark/250	10.00

Pennants/Pinstripes

NM/M
Common Player: 1.50
Production 1,499 Sets
Gold: 1-2X
Production 100 Sets

1	Reggie Jackson	2.50
2	Mike Schmidt	5.00
3	Steve Carlton	2.00
4	Dwight Gooden	1.50
5	Darryl Strawberry	1.50
6	Roger Clemens	5.00
7	Curt Schilling	2.00
8	Mark Grace	2.00
9	Ivan Rodriguez	2.00
10	Josh Beckett	1.50

Pennants/Pinstripes Materials

NM/M
Quantity produced listed.

1	Reggie Jackson/Pants/100	10.00
2	Mike Schmidt/Jsy/25	35.00
3	Steve Carlton/Jsy/100	4.00
4	Dwight Gooden/Jsy/250	8.00
5	Darryl Strawberry/Pants/250	5.00
6	Roger Clemens/Jsy/250	10.00
7	Curt Schilling/Jsy/250	8.00
8	Mark Grace/Jsy/250	8.00
9	Ivan Rodriguez/Jsy/250	8.00
10	Josh Beckett/Jsy/100	5.00

Rivals

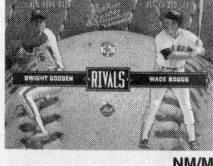

NM/M
Common Duo: No Pricing
Production 1,499 Sets

Silver: 1-2X
Production 100 Sets

1	Derek Jeter, Nomar Garciaparra	6.00
2	Mark Prior, Albert Pujols	4.00
3	Warren Spahn, Stan Musial	4.00
4	Don Sutton, Reggie Jackson	2.00
5	Roger Clemens, Mike Piazza	4.00
6	Dennis Eckersley, M. Williams	1.50
7	Kerry Wood, Frank Thomas	3.00
8	Jim Palmer, Willie Stargell	2.00
9	Tom Seaver, Mike Schmidt	5.00
10	Jack Morris, George Brett	5.00
11	Randy Johnson, Todd Helton	2.00
12	Tommy John, Rod Carew	2.00
13	Pedro J. Martinez, Jason Giambi	2.00
14	Dwight Gooden, Wade Boggs	1.50
15	Bob Gibson, Ernie Banks	3.00
16	Hideo Nomo, Barry Larkin	1.50
17	Roy Halladay, Vladimir Guerrero	2.00
18	Greg Maddux, Jeff Bagwell	3.00
19	Barry Zito, Alex Rodriguez	5.00
20	Steve Carlton, Andre Dawson	1.50
21	Mariano Rivera, Chipper Jones	2.00
22	Tom Glavine, Manny Ramirez	2.00
23	Whitey Ford, Harmon Killebrew	2.00
24	Carl Yastrzemski, Jim "Catfish" Hunter	2.00
25	Nolan Ryan, Robin Ventura	5.00
26	Carlton Fisk, Joe Morgan	1.50
27	Phil Rizzuto, Duke Snider	2.00
28	Fergie Jenkins, Lou Brock	1.50
29	Jose Canseco, Will Clark	1.50
30	Mike Mussina, Josh Beckett	1.50
31	Rickey Henderson, Ivan Rodriguez	2.00
32	Don Mattingly, Eddie Murray	5.00
33	Troy Glaus, Eric Chavez	1.50
34	Ryne Sandberg, Steve Garvey	2.00
35	Bob Gibson, Roger Maris	4.00
36	Roger Clemens, Cal Ripken Jr.	8.00
37	Orel Hershiser, Darryl Strawberry	1.50
38	Curt Schilling, Paul Molitor	2.00
39	Ichiro Suzuki, Hideki Matsui	5.00
40	Sammy Sosa, Jim Thome	4.00

Rivals Materials

NM/M
Quantity produced listed.

1	Derek Jeter/Jsy, Nomar Garciaparra/Bat/250	25.00
2	Mark Prior/Jsy, Albert Pujols/Jsy/250	20.00
3	Warren Spahn/Pants, Stan Musial/Jsy/100	30.00
5	Roger Clemens/Jsy/250, Mike Piazza/Jsy/250	20.00
6	Kerry Wood/Jsy, Frank Thomas/Jsy/250	10.00
7	Jim Palmer/Jsy, Willie Stargell/Jsy/250	
8	Tom Seaver/Jsy, Mike Schmidt/Jsy/250	20.00
9	Jack Morris/Jsy, George Brett/Jsy/250	15.00
10	Randy Johnson/Jsy, Todd Helton/Jsy/250	12.00
11	Tommy John/Pants, Rod Carew/Jkt/250	12.00
12	Pedro J. Martinez/Jsy, Jason Giambi/Jsy/250	12.00
13	Dwight Gooden/Jsy, Wade Boggs/Jsy/250	8.00
14	Bob Gibson/Jsy, Ernie Banks/Pants/100	20.00
15	Hideo Nomo/Jsy, Barry Larkin/Jsy/250	10.00
17	Roy Halladay/Jsy, Vladimir Guerrero/Jsy/250	10.00
18	Greg Maddux/Jsy, Jeff Bagwell/Jsy/250	15.00
19	Barry Zito/Jsy, Alex Rodriguez/Jsy/250	15.00
20	Steve Carlton/Jsy, Andre Dawson/Jsy/250	10.00
22	Tom Glavine/Jsy, Manny Ramirez/Jsy/250	10.00
23	Whitey Ford/Pants, Harmon Killebrew/Jsy/100	35.00
24	Carl Yastrzemski/Jsy, Jim "Catfish" Hunter/Jsy/250	20.00
25	Nolan Ryan/Pants, Robin Ventura/Jsy/250	25.00
26	Carlton Fisk/Jsy, Joe Morgan/Jsy/250	10.00
28	Fergie Jenkins/Pants, Lou Brock/Jsy/100	20.00
29	Jose Canseco/Bat, Will Clark/Bat/250	15.00
30	Mike Mussina/Jsy, Josh Beckett/Jsy/250	10.00
31	Rickey Henderson/Jsy, Ivan Rodriguez/Jsy	10.00
32	Don Mattingly/Jsy, Eddie Murray/Jsy/250	20.00
33	Troy Glaus/Jsy, Eric Chavez/Jsy/250	8.00
34	Ryne Sandberg/Jsy, Steve Garvey/Jsy/250	20.00
35	Bob Gibson/Jsy, Roger Maris/Jsy/100	40.00
36	Roger Clemens/Jsy, Cal Ripken Jr./Pants/250	30.00
38	Curt Schilling/Jsy, Paul Molitor/Bat/250	12.00
39	Ichiro Suzuki/Base, Hideki Matsui/Base/250	40.00
40	Sammy Sosa/Jsy, Jim Thome/Jsy/250	12.00

Signatures Bronze

NM/M 8.00
Quantity produced listed.

2	Garret Anderson/25	25.00
10	Shea Hillenbrand/100	10.00
11	Adam LaRoche/100	10.00
14	Dale Murphy/25	35.00
16	Marcus Giles/50	15.00
17	Rafael Furcal/50	20.00
21	Jay Gibbons/100	10.00
21	Luis Matos/100	10.00
35	Carlos Lee/100	10.00
39	Adam Dunn/50	30.00
44	C.C. Sabathia/100	10.00
48	Preston Wilson/50	15.00
50	Alan Trammell/50	10.00
52	Jeremy Bonderman/100	10.00
56	Miguel Cabrera/50	30.00
65	Angel Berroa/100	10.00
66	Carlos Beltran/100	25.00
79	Scott Podsednik/100	10.00
80	Jacque Jones/100	10.00
81	Johan Santana/100	40.00
82	Shannon Stewart/100	10.00
83	Torii Hunter/50	15.00
84	Andre Dawson/50	15.00
85	Chad Cordero/100	8.00
86	Jose Vidro/100	10.00
88	Orlando Cabrera/100	10.00
104	Bobby Crosby/100	10.00
106	Jermaine Dye/100	15.00
108	Rich Harden/50	10.00
115	Marlon Byrd/25	15.00
119	Jason Bay/50	15.00
122	Jay Payton/50	10.00
138	Aubrey Huff/50	15.00
139	Carl Crawford/50	20.00
145	Michael Young/100	15.00
151	Andres Blanco/100	10.00
152	Kevin Cave/100	10.00
153	Ryan Meaux/50	10.00
154	Tim Bausher/50	10.00
155	Jesse Harper/50	10.00
156	Mike Wuertz/50	10.00
158	Donald Kelly/50	8.00
159	Edwin Moreno/50	8.00
160	Mike Johnston/50	8.00
161	Orlando Rodriguez/50	8.00
164	Jorge Vasquez/50	10.00
166	Jake Woods/50	10.00
167	Aaron Baldiris/50	10.00
170	Dennis Sarfate/50	8.00
173	Eddy Rodriguez/50	10.00

Signatures Bronze B/W

No Pricing
Production 1-25

Signatures Silver

NM/M
Quantity produced listed.

2	Garret Anderson/25	20.00
10	Shea Hillenbrand/50	15.00
11	Adam LaRoche/50	15.00
14	Dale Murphy/50	25.00
16	Marcus Giles/50	10.00
17	Rafael Furcal/50	10.00
20	Jay Gibbons/50	10.00
21	Luis Matos/50	10.00
29	Trot Nixon/25	35.00
32	Mark Prior/25	40.00
35	Carlos Lee/50	10.00
39	Adam Dunn/25	30.00
40	Austin Kearns/25	30.00
43	Ryan Wagner/50	
44	C.C. Sabathia/25	15.00
45	Jody Gerut/50	15.00
48	Preston Wilson/50	15.00
50	Alan Trammell/50	20.00
52	Jeremy Bonderman/50	10.00
56	Miguel Cabrera/50	30.00
65	Angel Berroa/50	10.00
66	Carlos Beltran/50	30.00
73	Paul LoDuca/25	20.00
79	Scott Podsednik/50	10.00
80	Jacque Jones/50	10.00
81	Johan Santana/50	40.00
82	Shannon Stewart/50	15.00
83	Torii Hunter/50	15.00
84	Andre Dawson/50	15.00
85	Chad Cordero/50	8.00
86	Jose Vidro/50	10.00
88	Orlando Cabrera/50	12.00
104	Bobby Crosby/50	20.00
106	Jermaine Dye/50	15.00
107	Mark Mulder/25	20.00
108	Rich Harden/50	20.00
115	Marlon Byrd/50	10.00
119	Jason Bay/50	20.00
122	Jay Payton/50	10.00
138	Aubrey Huff/50	15.00
139	Carl Crawford/50	20.00
143	Hank Blalock/25	25.00
145	Michael Young/50	20.00
150	Vernon Wells/50	15.00
151	Andres Blanco/100	10.00
152	Kevin Cave/100	10.00
153	Ryan Meaux/100	8.00
154	Tim Bausher/100	8.00
155	Jesse Harper/100	8.00
156	Mike Wuertz/100	10.00
158	Donald Kelly/100	6.00
159	Edwin Moreno/100	6.00
160	Mike Johnston/100	6.00
161	Orlando Rodriguez/100	6.00
164	Jorge Vasquez/100	8.00
166	Jake Woods/100	8.00
167	Aaron Baldiris/100	8.00
170	Dennis Sarfate/100	8.00
173	Eddy Rodriguez/100	8.00

Signatures Silver B/W

No Pricing
Production 1-25

Signatures Gold

NM/M
Quantity produced listed.

2	Garret Anderson/25	25.00
10	Shea Hillenbrand/25	20.00
11	Adam LaRoche/25	15.00
14	Dale Murphy/25	35.00
16	Marcus Giles/25	20.00
17	Rafael Furcal/25	20.00
20	Jay Gibbons/25	15.00
21	Luis Matos/25	15.00
35	Carlos Lee/25	15.00
39	Adam Dunn/25	30.00
44	C.C. Sabathia/25	20.00
45	Jody Gerut/25	20.00
48	Preston Wilson/25	20.00
50	Alan Trammell/25	25.00
52	Jeremy Bonderman/25	10.00
56	Miguel Cabrera/25	35.00
65	Angel Berroa/25	10.00
66	Carlos Beltran/25	40.00
79	Scott Podsednik/25	10.00
80	Jacque Jones/25	10.00
81	Johan Santana/25	50.00
82	Shannon Stewart/25	20.00
83	Torii Hunter/25	20.00
84	Andre Dawson/25	20.00
85	Chad Cordero/25	10.00
86	Jose Vidro/25	15.00
88	Orlando Cabrera/25	15.00
104	Bobby Crosby/25	30.00
106	Jermaine Dye/25	20.00
115	Marlon Byrd/25	20.00
119	Jason Bay/25	25.00
122	Jay Payton/25	15.00
138	Aubrey Huff/25	20.00
139	Carl Crawford/25	25.00
145	Michael Young/25	30.00
151	Andres Blanco/100	10.00
152	Kevin Cave/100	10.00
153	Ryan Meaux/50	10.00
154	Tim Bausher/50	10.00
155	Jesse Harper/50	10.00
156	Mike Wuertz/50	10.00
158	Donald Kelly/50	8.00
159	Edwin Moreno/50	8.00
160	Mike Johnston/50	8.00
161	Orlando Rodriguez/50	8.00
164	Jorge Vasquez/50	10.00
166	Jake Woods/50	10.00
167	Aaron Baldiris/50	10.00
168	Jason Bartlett/50	12.00
170	Dennis Sarfate/50	8.00
173	Eddy Rodriguez/50	10.00

Signatures Gold B/W

No Pricing
Production 1-25

Signatures Platinum

No Pricing
Production One Set

Signatures Platinum B/W

No Pricing
Production One Set

2004 Donruss Studio

CHIPPER JONES

NM/M
Complete Set (220):
Common Player: .15
Common SP (201-221): 6.00
Production 400-800:
Pack (6): 4.00
Box (24): 75.00

1	Bartolo Colon	.15
2	Garret Anderson	.40
3	Tim Salmon	.25
4	Troy Glaus	.25
5	Vladimir Guerrero	.75
6	Brandon Webb	.15
7	Brian Bruney	.15
8	Casey Fossum	.15
9	Luis Gonzales	.15
10	Randy Johnson	1.00
11	Richie Sexson	.40
12	Robby Hammock	.15
13	Roberto Alomar	.40
14	Shea Hillenbrand	.15
15	Steve Finley	.15
16	Adam LaRoche	.15
17	Andruw Jones	.50
18	Bubba Nelson	.15
19	Chipper Jones	.75
20	Dale Murphy	.50
21	J.D. Drew	.25
22	Marcus Giles	.15
23	Michael Hessman	.15
24	Rafael Furcal	.25
25	Warren Spahn	.25
26	Adam Loewen	.15
27	Cal Ripken Jr.	3.00
28	Javy Lopez	.40
29	Jay Gibbons	.15
30	Luis Matos	.15
31	Miguel Tejada	.40
32	Rafael Palmeiro	.50
33	Curt Schilling	.25
34	Jason Varitek	.25
35	Kevin Youkilis	.15
36	Manny Ramirez	.50
37	Nomar Garciaparra	1.50
38	Pedro Martinez	.75
39	Trot Nixon	.25
40	Aramis Ramirez	.40
41	Brendan Harris	.15
42	Derrek Lee	.25
43	Ernie Banks	1.00
44	Greg Maddux	1.00
45	Kerry Wood	.75
46	Mark Prior	1.00
47	Ryne Sandberg	1.00
48	Sammy Sosa	1.50
49	Todd Wellemeyer	.15
50	Carlos Lee	.15
51	Edwin Almonte	.15
52	Frank Thomas	.50
53	Joe Borchard	.15
54	Joe Crede	.15
55	Magglio Ordonez	.25
56	Adam Dunn	.50
57	Austin Kearns	.25
58	Barry Larkin	.40
59	Brandon Larson	.15
60	Ken Griffey Jr.	1.00
61	Ryan Wagner	.15
62	Sean Casey	.25
63	Brian Tallet	.15
64	C.C. Sabathia	.15
65	Jeremy Guthrie	.15
66	Jody Gerut	.15
67	Travis Hafner	.25
68	Clint Barmes	.15
69	Jeff Baker	.15
70	Joe Kennedy	.15
71	Larry Walker	.25
72	Preston Wilson	.15
73	Todd Helton	.50
74	Dmitri Young	.15
75	Ivan Rodriguez	.50
76	Jeremy Bonderman	.15
77	Preston Larrison	.15
78	Dontrelle Willis	.25
79	Josh Beckett	.50
80	Juan Pierre	.15
81	Luis Castillo	.15
82	Miguel Cabrera	.50
83	Mike Lowell	.25
84	Andy Pettitte	.25
85	Chris Burke	.15
86	Craig Biggio	.25
87	Jeff Bagwell	.50
88	Jeff Kent	.25
89	Lance Berkman	.25
90	Morgan Ensberg	.15

#	Player	Price
91	Richard Hidalgo	.15
92	Roger Clemens	1.50
93	Roy Oswalt	.25
94	Wade Miller	.15
95	Angel Berroa	.15
96	Byron Gettis	.15
97	Carlos Beltran	.25
98	Juan Gonzalez	.50
99	Mike Sweeney	.15
100	Duke Snider	.50
101	Edwin Jackson	.15
102	Eric Gagne	.50
103	Hideo Nomo	.40
104	Hong-Chih Kuo	.15
105	Kazuhisa Ishii	.15
106	Paul Lo Duca	.15
107	Robin Ventura	.25
108	Shawn Green	.25
109	Junior Spivey	.15
110	Lyle Overbay	.25
111	Rickie Weeks	.25
112	Scott Podsednik	.25
113	J.D. Durbin	.15
114	Jacque Jones	.15
115	Jason Kubel	.15
116	Johan Santana	.15
117	Shannon Stewart	.15
118	Torii Hunter	.25
119	Brad Wilkerson	.15
120	Jose Vidro	.15
121	Nick Johnson	.15
122	Orlando Cabrera	.15
123	Zach Day	.15
124	Gary Carter	.40
125	Jae Weong Seo	.15
126	Kazuo Matsui RC	5.00
127	Mike Piazza	1.00
128	Tom Glavine	.40
129	Alex Rodriguez	2.00
130	Bernie Williams	.40
131	Chien-Ming Wang	.50
132	Derek Jeter	2.00
133	Don Mattingly	2.00
134	Gary Sheffield	.40
135	Hideki Matsui	1.00
136	Jason Giambi	.50
137	Javier Vazquez	.25
138	Jorge Posada	.40
139	Jose Contreras	.15
140	Kevin Brown	.25
141	Mariano Rivera	.40
142	Mike Mussina	.40
143	Whitey Ford	.50
144	Barry Zito	.25
145	Eric Chavez	.25
146	Mark Mulder	.25
147	Rich Harden	.15
148	Tim Hudson	.25
149	Bobby Abreu	.25
150	Jim Thome	.75
151	Kevin Millwood	.25
152	Marlon Byrd	.15
153	Mike Schmidt	1.00
154	Ryan Howard	.75
155	Jack Wilson	.15
156	Jason Kendall	.15
157	Akinori Otsuka RC	1.00
158	Brian Giles	.25
159	David Wells	.15
160	Jay Payton	.15
161	Phil Nevin	.15
162	Ryan Klesko	.15
163	Sean Burroughs	.15
164	A.J. Pierzynski	.15
165	J.T. Snow	.15
166	Jason Schmidt	.25
167	Jerome Williams	.15
168	Merkin Valdez RC	1.00
169	Will Clark	.50
170	Bret Boone	.25
171	Chris Snelling	.15
172	Edgar Martinez	.25
173	Ichiro Suzuki	1.00
174	Jamie Moyer	.15
175	Randy Winn	.15
176	Rich Aurilia	.15
177	Shigetoshi Hasegawa	.15
178	Albert Pujols	1.50
179	Dan Haren	.15
180	Edgar Renteria	.25
181	Jim Edmonds	.25
182	Matt Morris	.15
183	Scott Rolen	.75
184	Stan Musial	1.00
185	Aubrey Huff	.15
186	Chad Gaudin	.15
187	Delmon Young	.15
188	Fred McGriff	.25
189	Rocco Baldelli	.25
190	Alfonso Soriano	.75
191	Hank Blalock	.50
192	Mark Teixeira	.50
193	Nolan Ryan	2.50
194	Alexis Rios	.15
195	Carlos Delgado	.50
196	Dustin McGowan	.15
197	Guillermo Quiroz	.15
198	Josh Phelps	.15
199	Roy Halladay	.25
200	Vernon Wells	.25
201	Mike Gosling AU/400	8.00
202	Ronny Cedeno AU/76 RC	8.00
203	Ronald Belisario AU/400 RC	8.00
204	Justin Hampson AU/800 RC	6.00
205	Carlos Vasquez AU/800 RC	6.00

#	Player	Price
206	Lincoln Holdzkom AU/800 RC	6.00
207	Casey Daigle AU/550 RC	6.00
208	Jason Bartlett AU/700 RC	6.00
209	Mariano Gomez AU/800 RC	6.00
210	Mike House AU/800 RC	8.00
211	Chris Shelton AU/800 RC	25.00
212	Dennis Sarfate AU/800 RC	8.00
213	Shingo Takatsu AU/400 RC	35.00
214	Justin Leone AU/800 RC	15.00
215	Cory Sullivan AU/800 RC	8.00
216	Mike Wuertz AU/800 RC	8.00
217	Tim Bausher AU/800 RC	8.00
218	Jesse Harper AU/800 RC	8.00
219	Ryan Meaux AU/800 RC	8.00
221	Kevin Cave AU/800 RC	8.00

Proofs Silver
Silver (1-200): 3-6X
Silver (201-225): .25X
#220, 222-225 exist only in parallel set.
Production 100 Sets

Proofs Gold
Gold (1-200): 5-10X
Gold (201-225): .5X
#220, 222-225 exist only in parallel set.
Production 50 Sets

Proofs Platinum
No Pricing
Production 10 Sets

Big League Challenge

		NM/M
Production 999 Sets		6.00
Die-Cut:		1X
Production 500 Sets		
1	Albert Pujols/Left	6.00
2	Albert Pujols/Right	6.00
3	Alex Rodriguez/Rgr Left	5.00
4	Alex Rodriguez/Rgr Right	5.00
5	Magglio Ordonez	2.00
6	Rafael Palmeiro	3.00
7	Troy Glaus/Follow	2.00
8	Troy Glaus/Start	2.00
9	Albert Pujols/Bat Up	6.00
10	Alex Rodriguez/Rgr Bat Up	5.00

Big League Challenge Material

		NM/M
Production 100 Sets		15.00
Combo:		1-2X
Production 50 Sets		
1	Albert Pujols/Jsy	15.00
2	Albert Pujols/Pants	15.00
3	Alex Rodriguez/Rgr/Jsy	10.00
4	Alex Rodriguez/Rgr/Pants	10.00
5	Magglio Ordonez/Jsy	5.00
6	Rafael Palmeiro/Jsy	6.00
7	Troy Glaus/Jsy	6.00
8	Troy Glaus/Pants	6.00
9	Albert Pujols/Hat	15.00
10	Alex Rodriguez/Rgr/Hat	10.00

Diamond Cuts Combo Material

		NM/M
Quantity produced listed.		15.00
1	Derek Jeter/Bat/Jsy/50	40.00
2	Greg Maddux/Bat/Jsy/50	25.00
4	Miguel Cabrera/Bat/Jsy/50	20.00
5	Mark Mulder/Bat/Jsy/50	15.00
6	Rafael Furcal/Bat/Jsy/50	10.00
7	Mark Prior/Bat/Jsy/50	20.00
8	Roy Oswalt/Bat/Jsy/50	10.00
9	Dontrelle Willis/Bat/Jsy/25	15.00
10	Jay Gibbons/Bat/Jsy/50	10.00
11	Josh Beckett/Bat/Jsy/50	15.00
12	Angel Berroa/Bat/Jsy/50	10.00
13	Adam Dunn/Bat/Jsy/50	15.00
14	Hank Blalock/Bat/Jsy/50	15.00
15	Carlos Beltran/Bat/Jsy/50	10.00
16	Shannon Stewart/Bat/Jsy/50	10.00

#	Player	Price
17	Aubrey Huff/Bat/Jsy/50	10.00
18	Jeff Bagwell/Bat/Jsy/50	20.00
19	Trot Nixon/Bat/Jsy/50	15.00
20	Nolan Ryan/Jkt/Jsy/50	40.00
21	Tony Gwynn/Bat/Jsy/50	30.00
22	Andre Dawson/Bat/Jsy/50	15.00
23	Don Mattingly/Bat/Jkt/50	40.00
24	Dale Murphy/Bat/Jsy/50	20.00
25	Gary Carter/Bat/Jsy/50	15.00

Diamond Cuts Combo Material Signature

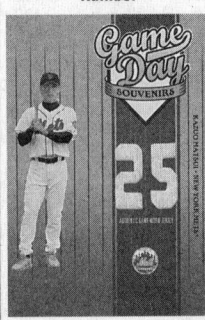

Production 1-5 Sets

Diamond Cuts Material Bat

		NM/M
Quantity produced listed		8.00
1	Derek Jeter/100	25.00
2	Greg Maddux/100	10.00
3	Nomar Garciaparra/200	10.00
4	Miguel Cabrera/200	8.00
5	Mark Mulder/200	6.00
6	Rafael Furcal/200	4.00
7	Mark Prior/200	8.00
8	Roy Oswalt/200	4.00
9	Dontrelle Willis/100	6.00
10	Jay Gibbons/200	4.00
11	Josh Beckett/200	6.00
12	Angel Berroa/200	4.00
13	Adam Dunn/200	8.00
14	Hank Blalock/200	8.00
15	Carlos Beltran/200	4.00
16	Shannon Stewart/200	4.00
17	Aubrey Huff/200	4.00
18	Jeff Bagwell/200	8.00
19	Trot Nixon/200	4.00
20	Tony Gwynn/200	10.00
22	Andre Dawson/200	6.00
23	Don Mattingly/200	15.00
24	Dale Murphy/200	10.00
25	Gary Carter/200	6.00

Diamond Cuts Material Jersey

		NM/M
Production 250 Sets		8.00
1	Derek Jeter	20.00
2	Greg Maddux	10.00
3	Nomar Garciaparra	10.00
4	Miguel Cabrera	8.00
5	Mark Mulder	4.00
6	Rafael Furcal	4.00
7	Mark Prior	8.00
8	Roy Oswalt	4.00
9	Dontrelle Willis	6.00
10	Jay Gibbons	4.00
11	Josh Beckett	6.00
12	Angel Berroa	4.00
13	Adam Dunn	8.00
14	Hank Blalock	8.00
15	Carlos Beltran	6.00
16	Shannon Stewart	4.00
17	Aubrey Huff	4.00
18	Jeff Bagwell	8.00
19	Trot Nixon	6.00
20	Nolan Ryan/Jacket	25.00
21	Tony Gwynn	10.00
22	Andre Dawson	6.00
23	Don Mattingly/Jacket	15.00
24	Dale Murphy	10.00
25	Gary Carter	6.00

Game Day Souvenirs Number

		NM/M
Quantity produced listed.		.5-1X
Position:		
Production 25-300		
1	Garret Anderson/Jsy/300	4.00
2	Troy Glaus/Jsy/300	6.00
3	Vladimir Guerrero/Jsy/300	8.00
4	Steve Finley/Jsy/250	4.00
5	Luis Gonzalez/Jsy/25	4.00
6	Richie Sexson/Jsy/250	6.00
7	Andruw Jones/Jsy/300	6.00
8	Chipper Jones/Jsy/300	8.00
9	Rafael Furcal/Jsy/250	4.00
13	Curt Schilling/Jsy/300	6.00
14	Pedro Martinez/Jsy/300	8.00
15	David Ortiz/Jsy/300	8.00
16	Sammy Sosa/Jsy/300	10.00
17	Corey Patterson/Jsy/250	6.00
18	Moises Alou/Jsy/300	4.00
19	Magglio Ordonez/Jsy/300	4.00
20	Paul Konerko/Jsy/300	4.00
21	Frank Thomas/Jsy/300	8.00
22	Austin Kearns/Jsy/50	8.00
23	Sean Casey/Jsy/200	6.00
24	Adam Dunn/Jsy/200	10.00
25	Omar Vizquel/Jsy/250	4.00
26	C.C. Sabathia/Jsy/300	4.00
27	Jody Gerut/Jsy/250	4.00
28	Todd Helton/Jsy/300	8.00
29	Vinny Castilla/Jsy/300	4.00
30	Jeromy Burnitz/Jsy/300	4.00
31	Fernando Vina/Jsy/150	4.00
32	Ivan Rodriguez/Jsy/300	8.00
33	Jeremy Bonderman/Jsy/300	4.00
34	Mike Lowell/Jsy/225	4.00
35	Luis Castillo/Jsy/250	4.00
36	Miguel Cabrera/Jsy/250	8.00
37	Roger Clemens/Jsy/300	10.00
38	Andy Pettitte/Jsy/300	6.00
39	Jeff Bagwell/Jsy/300	8.00
40	Mike Sweeney/Jsy/150	4.00
41	Carlos Beltran/Jsy/300	6.00
42	Angel Berroa/Jsy/300	4.00
43	Paul Lo Duca/Jsy/75	4.00
44	Shawn Green/Jsy/300	4.00
45	Adrian Beltre/Jsy/150	4.00
46	Ben Sheets/Jsy/300	4.00
47	Geoff Jenkins/Jsy/300	4.00
48	Junior Spivey/Jsy/300	4.00
49	Doug Mientkiewicz/Jsy/100	4.00
50	Shannon Stewart/Jsy/100	4.00
51	Torii Hunter/Jsy/300	6.00
52	Livan Hernandez/Jsy/300	4.00
53	Jose Vidro/Jsy/200	4.00
54	Orlando Cabrera/Jsy/300	4.00
55	Mike Piazza/Jsy/250	8.00
56	Mike Cameron/Jsy/250	4.00
57	Kazuo Matsui/Jsy/200	30.00
58	Derek Jeter/Jsy/50	30.00
59	Jason Giambi/Jsy/300	10.00
60	Barry Zito/Jsy/200	6.00
61	Eric Chavez/Jsy/150	4.00
62	Eric Byrnes/Jsy/150	4.00
63	Jim Thome/Jsy/300	8.00
64	Jimmy Rollins/Jsy/250	4.00
65	Jason Kendall/Jsy/250	4.00
66	Craig Wilson/Jsy/300	4.00
67	Jack Wilson/Jsy/250	4.00
68	Ryan Klesko/Jsy/300	4.00
69	Brian Giles/Jsy/300	4.00
70	Sean Burroughs/Jsy/300	4.00
71	A.J. Pierzynski/Jsy/300	4.00
72	J.T. Snow/Jsy/300	4.00
73	Michael Tucker/Jsy/300	4.00
74	Edgar Martinez/Jsy/50	10.00
75	Scott Rolen/Jsy/300	6.00
76	Albert Pujols/Jsy/300	15.00
77	Jim Edmonds/Jsy/300	4.00
78	Aubrey Huff/Jsy/100	4.00
79	Tino Martinez/Jsy/100	4.00
80	Rocco Baldelli/Jsy/100	6.00
81	Alfonso Soriano/Jsy/200	8.00
82	Michael Young/Jsy/250	4.00
83	Hank Blalock/Jsy/200	6.00
84	Eric Hinske/Jsy/200	4.00
85	Carlos Delgado/Jsy/300	4.00
86	Vernon Wells/Jsy/250	4.00

Game Day Souvenirs Signature Number
Production Five Sets

Heritage

		NM/M
Production 999 Sets		4.00
Die-Cut:		2-3X
Production 100 Sets		
1	George Brett	6.00
2	Nolan Ryan	8.00
3	Cal Ripken Jr.	8.00
4	Mike Schmidt	5.00
5	Roberto Clemente	6.00
6	Don Mattingly	5.00
7	Dale Murphy	4.00
8	Ryne Sandberg	4.00
9	Harmon Killebrew	4.00
10	Stan Musial	5.00

Heritage Material Bat

		NM/M
Production 50 Sets		15.00
1	George Brett	30.00
2	Cal Ripken Jr.	40.00
4	Mike Schmidt	20.00
5	Roberto Clemente	60.00
6	Don Mattingly	30.00
7	Dale Murphy	15.00
8	Ryne Sandberg	30.00
9	Harmon Killebrew	15.00
10	Stan Musial	35.00

Heritage Material Jersey

		NM/M
Quantity produced listed.		15.00
1	George Brett/200	15.00
2	Nolan Ryan/Jkt/200	20.00

#	Player	Price
3	Cal Ripken Jr./200	30.00
4	Mike Schmidt/Pants/200	15.00
5	Roberto Clemente/100	60.00
6	Don Mattingly/Jkt/200	15.00
7	Dale Murphy/200	8.00
8	Ryne Sandberg/200	20.00
9	Harmon Killebrew/Pants/200	15.00
10	Stan Musial/100	20.00

Heritage Signature Material Jersey

Production Five Sets

Heroes of the Hall

		NM/M
Production 999 Sets		4.00
Die-Cut:		1X
Production 500 Sets		
1	Fergie Jenkins	3.00
2	Gary Carter	3.00
3	Gaylord Perry	3.00
4	George Brett	6.00
5	Jim Palmer	3.00
6	Nolan Ryan	6.00
7	Paul Molitor	4.00
8	Rod Carew	4.00
9	Steve Carlton	3.00
10	Robin Yount	5.00

Heroes of the Hall Material Bat

		NM/M
Production 100 Sets		8.00
2	Gary Carter	8.00
4	George Brett	20.00
7	Paul Molitor	10.00
8	Rod Carew	8.00
9	Steve Carlton	8.00
10	Robin Yount	15.00

Heroes of the Hall Material Jersey

		NM/M
Production 200 unless noted.		
Prime:		No Pricing
Production 10 Sets		
1	Fergie Jenkins/Pants	8.00
2	Gary Carter	8.00
3	Gaylord Perry/100	8.00
4	George Brett	15.00
5	Jim Palmer	8.00
6	Nolan Ryan	25.00
7	Paul Molitor	10.00
8	Rod Carew	10.00
9	Steve Carlton	8.00
10	Robin Yount	15.00

Heroes of the Hall Material Signature

No Pricing
Production 1-10

Masterstrokes Material Bat

		NM/M
Production 200 Sets		6.00
1	Todd Helton	8.00
2	Jose Vidro	4.00
3	Edgar Renteria	6.00
4	Mike Lowell	4.00
5	Gary Sheffield	6.00
6	Albert Pujols	15.00
7	Javy Lopez	4.00
8	Carlos Delgado	6.00
9	Bret Boone	4.00
10	Alex Rodriguez	10.00
11	Vernon Wells	4.00
12	Manny Ramirez	6.00
13	Jorge Posada	4.00
14	Edgar Martinez	4.00
15	Bernie Williams	6.00
16	Magglio Ordonez	4.00
17	Garret Anderson	4.00
18	Eric Chavez	4.00
19	Alfonso Soriano	8.00
20	Jason Giambi	6.00
21	Jeff Kent	4.00
22	Scott Rolen	6.00
23	Vladimir Guerrero	8.00
24	Sammy Sosa	10.00
25	Mike Piazza	8.00

Masterstrokes Material Jersey

		NM/M
Prime:		No Pricing
Production Five Sets		
1	Todd Helton/250	8.00
2	Jose Vidro/250	4.00
3	Edgar Renteria/250	4.00
4	Mike Lowell/250	4.00
5	Gary Sheffield/250	6.00
6	Albert Pujols/250	15.00
7	Javy Lopez/250	6.00
8	Carlos Delgado/250	6.00
9	Bret Boone/250	4.00
10	Alex Rodriguez/250	10.00
11	Vernon Wells/250	4.00
12	Manny Ramirez/250	6.00
13	Jorge Posada/250	4.00
14	Edgar Martinez/250	4.00
15	Bernie Williams/250	4.00
16	Magglio Ordonez/250	4.00
17	Garret Anderson/250	4.00
18	Eric Chavez/250	4.00
19	Alfonso Soriano/150	4.00
20	Jason Giambi/250	6.00
21	Jeff Kent/250	4.00
22	Scott Rolen/250	6.00
23	Vladimir Guerrero/250	8.00
24	Sammy Sosa/250	8.00
25	Mike Piazza/250	8.00

Masterstrokes Combo Material

		NM/M
Production 50 Sets		10.00
1	Todd Helton/Bat-Jsy/50	15.00
2	Jose Vidro/Bat-Jsy/50	4.00
3	Edgar Renteria/Bat-Jsy/50	10.00
4	Mike Lowell/Bat-Jsy/50	10.00
5	Gary Sheffield/Bat-Jsy/50	10.00
6	Albert Pujols/Bat-Jsy/50	30.00
7	Javy Lopez/Bat-Jsy/50	8.00
8	Carlos Delgado/Bat-Jsy/50	10.00
9	Bret Boone/Bat-Jsy/50	8.00
10	Alex Rodriguez/Rgr Bat-Jsy/50	20.00
11	Vernon Wells/Bat-Jsy/50	8.00
12	Manny Ramirez/Bat-Jsy/50	10.00
13	Jorge Posada/Bat-Jsy/50	10.00
14	Edgar Martinez/Bat-Jsy/50	10.00
15	Bernie Williams/Bat-Jsy/50	10.00
16	Magglio Ordonez/Bat-Jsy/50	8.00
17	Garret Anderson/Bat-Jsy/50	8.00
18	Eric Chavez/Bat-Jsy/50	8.00
19	Alfonso Soriano/Bat-Jsy/50	15.00
20	Jason Giambi/Bat-Jsy/50	10.00
21	Jeff Kent/Bat-Jsy/50	8.00
22	Scott Rolen/Bat-Jsy/50	20.00
23	Vladimir Guerrero/Bat-Jsy/50	20.00
24	Sammy Sosa/Bat-Jsy/50	25.00
25	Mike Piazza/Bat-Jsy/50	20.00

Masterstrokes Combo Material Signature
No Pricing
Production 1-10

Players Collection Jersey

NM/M
Common Jersey:
Production 150 Sets
Platinum: 1-2X
Production 50 Sets

#	Player	NM/M
1	Adam Dunn/AS	6.00
2	Adam Dunn/Gray	6.00
3	Adam Dunn/White	6.00
4	Alex Rodriguez	10.00
5	Alex Rodriguez/AS	10.00
6	Alex Rodriguez/Blue	10.00
7	Alex Rodriguez/White	10.00
8	Andruw Jones/Home	6.00
9	Andruw Jones/Road	6.00
10	Austin Kearns	6.00
11	Brandon Webb	4.00
12	C.C. Sabathia	6.00
13	Cal Ripken Jr.	25.00
14	Carlos Beltran	6.00
15	Carlos Delgado	6.00
16	Carlos Lee	4.00
17	Chipper Jones/Home	8.00
18	Chipper Jones/Road	8.00
19	Craig Biggio	6.00
20	Curt Schilling	6.00
21	David Wells	4.00
22	Don Mattingly	20.00
23	Dontrelle Willis	6.00
24	Frank Thomas/Black	8.00
25	Frank Thomas/White	8.00
26	Fred McGriff	4.00
27	Garret Anderson/AS	6.00
28	Gary Sheffield	6.00
29	Gary Sheffield	6.00
30	Greg Maddux/Gray	8.00
31	Hank Blalock/Home	6.00
32	Hank Blalock/Road	6.00
33	Hee Seop Choi	6.00
34	Hideo Nomo/Gray	6.00
35	Hideo Nomo/Gray	6.00
36	Hideo Nomo/White	6.00
37	Ivan Rodriguez	6.00
38	Ivan Rodriguez	6.00
39	Jason Giambi/Home	6.00
40	Jim Edmonds	6.00
41	Jim Thorne	6.00
42	John Olerud	4.00
43	John Smoltz	6.00
44	Josh Beckett	6.00
45	Josh Phelps	4.00
46	Juan Gonzalez	6.00
47	Juan Gonzalez	6.00
48	Kazuhisa Ishii	6.00
49	Lance Berkman	6.00
50	Larry Walker/Home	4.00
51	Larry Walker/Road	4.00
52	Luis Gonzalez/AS	4.00
53	Magglio Ordonez/Home	4.00
54	Magglio Ordonez/Road	4.00
55	Manny Ramirez	8.00
56	Manny Ramirez/AS	8.00
57	Mark Prior/Home	8.00
58	Mark Prior/Road	8.00
59	Mark Teixeira	6.00
60	Mike Mussina	6.00
61	Mike Piazza/AS	8.00
62	Mike Piazza/Black	8.00
63	Mike Piazza/White	8.00
64	Nomar Garciaparra/Gray	8.00
65	Nomar Garciaparra/White	8.00
66	Pat Burrell	6.00
67	Paul Konerko	4.00
68	Paul Lo Duca	4.00
69	Pedro Martinez	8.00
70	Rafael Furcal	4.00
71	Rafael Palmeiro/Blue	6.00
72	Rafael Palmeiro/Gray	6.00
73	Ramon Hernandez	4.00
74	Rickey Henderson	6.00
75	Rickey Henderson/Black	6.00
76	Rickey Henderson/White	6.00
77	Roberto Alomar	6.00
78	Roberto Alomar	6.00
79	Robin Ventura/AS	4.00
80	Roger Clemens/Away	10.00
81	Roger Clemens/Home	10.00
82	Roy Halladay	6.00
83	Sammy Sosa/AS	12.00
84	Sammy Sosa/Gray	12.00
85	Sammy Sosa/White	12.00
86	Scott Rolen	8.00
87	Shannon Stewart	4.00
88	Shawn Green/Blue	4.00
89	Shawn Green/Gray	4.00
90	Shawn Green/White	4.00
91	Terrence Long	4.00
92	Tim Hudson	6.00
93	Todd Helton/Away	8.00
94	Todd Helton/Home	8.00
95	Tom Glavine	6.00
96	Tom Glavine	6.00
97	Torii Hunter	6.00
98	Vernon Wells	4.00
99	Vladimir Guerrero	8.00
100	Vladimir Guerrero/AS	8.00

Private Signings Silver

#	Player	NM/M
2	Garret Anderson/25	25.00
6	Brandon Webb/25	15.00
7	Brian Bruney/200	5.00
8	Casey Fossum/63	8.00
14	Shea Hillenbrand/25	20.00
18	Adam LaRoche/26	15.00
18	Bubba Nelson/250	8.00
22	Marcus Giles/25	30.00
24	Rafael Furcal/25	25.00
26	Adam Loewen/25	20.00
29	Jay Gibbons/50	15.00
30	Luis Matos/25	10.00
35	Kevin Youkilis/250	20.00
39	Trot Nixon/25	50.00
40	Aramis Ramirez/25	25.00
41	Brendan Harris/100	8.00
43	Ernie Banks/25	75.00
48	Sammy Sosa/21	150.00
50	Carlos Lee/25	20.00
51	Edwin Almonte/227	5.00
53	Joe Borchard/100	5.00
59	Brandon Larson/100	5.00
61	Ryan Wagner/50	10.00
63	Brian Tallet/50	5.00
65	Jeremy Guthrie/89	8.00
66	Jody Gerut/100	10.00
67	Travis Hafner/25	15.00
68	Clint Barmes/100	8.00
70	Joe Kennedy/100	5.00
72	Preston Wilson/25	25.00
77	Preston Larrison/100	8.00
81	Luis Castillo/25	15.00
82	Miguel Cabrera/25	60.00
85	Chris Burke/100	5.00
90	Morgan Ensberg/50	15.00
97	Byron Gettis/250	10.00
97	Carlos Beltran/50	35.00
101	Duke Snider/50	40.00
104	Edwin Jackson/100	15.00
104	Hong-Chih Kuo/250	30.00
		10.00
106	Paul Lo Duca/25	25.00
107	Robin Ventura/25	30.00
109	Junior Spivey/50	15.00
112	Scott Podsednik/100	20.00
113	J.D. Durbin/250	5.00
114	Jacque Jones/50	20.00
115	Jason Kubel/100	15.00
116	Johan Santana/25	25.00
117	Shannon Stewart/15	15.00
120	Jose Vidro/15	30.00
122	Orlando Cabrera/15	25.00
131	Gary Carter/25	25.00
131	Chien-Ming Wang/243	100.00
133	Don Mattingly/25	75.00
134	Gary Sheffield/25	25.00
147	Rich Harden/200	15.00
154	Ryan Howard/250	65.00
160	Jay Payton/50	10.00
167	Jerome Williams/57	25.00
168	Merkin Valdez/250	10.00
171	Will Clark/25	75.00
177	Chris Snelling/200	5.00
177	Shigetoshi Hasegawa/25	75.00
179	Dan Haren/250	8.00
184	Stan Musial/25	80.00
185	Aubrey Huff/250	10.00
187	Chad Gaudin/100	5.00
187	Delmon Young/25	40.00
192	Mark Teixeira/23	25.00
193	Nolan Ryan/34	100.00
194	Alexis Rios/250	10.00
196	Dustin McGowan/115	10.00
197	Guillermo Quiroz/120	8.00

Private Signings Platinum

No Pricing
Production 1-10

Private Signings Gold

#	Player	NM/M
2	Garret Anderson/16	35.00
6	Brandon Webb/55	10.00
7	Brian Bruney/100	5.00
14	Shea Hillenbrand/28	25.00
18	Adam LaRoche/25	15.00
18	Bubba Nelson/100	10.00
22	Marcus Giles/25	30.00
23	Michael Hessman/25	15.00

(continued — Private Signings)

#	Player	NM/M
29	Jay Gibbons/25	20.00
30	Luis Matos/100	10.00
35	Kevin Youkilis/100	25.00
41	Aramis Ramirez/16	35.00
41	Brendan Harris/75	10.00
47	Todd Wellemeyer/50	10.00
50	Carlos Lee/45	15.00
51	Edwin Almonte/56	10.00
53	Joe Borchard/25	10.00
54	Joe Crede/24	15.00
57	Austin Kearns/28	25.00
59	Brandon Larson/16	15.00
61	Ryan Wagner/38	15.00
63	Brian Tallet/50	10.00
65	Jeremy Guthrie/67	8.00
66	Jody Gerut/25	20.00
67	Travis Hafner/25	25.00
68	Clint Barmes/36	10.00
69	Jeff Baker/62	8.00
70	Joe Kennedy/37	15.00
73	Todd Helton/17	50.00
77	Preston Larrison/56	10.00
78	Dontrelle Willis/35	40.00
82	Miguel Cabrera/24	60.00
89	Chris Burke/46	8.00
89	Lance Berkman/17	50.00
90	Morgan Ensberg/25	15.00
97	Byron Gettis/100	8.00
97	Carlos Beltran/25	50.00
98	Juan Gonzalez/22	35.00
100	Duke Snider/25	50.00
101	Edwin Jackson/50	20.00
104	Hong-Chih Kuo/100	40.00
105	Kazuhisa Ishii/17	50.00
106	Paul Lo Duca/16	30.00
107	Robin Ventura/25	30.00
108	Shawn Green/15	30.00
109	Junior Spivey/37	15.00
112	Scott Podsednik/20	25.00
113	J.D. Durbin/31	15.00
114	Jacque Jones/25	25.00
116	Johan Santana/57	25.00
117	Shannon Stewart/23	15.00
121	Nick Johnson/21	15.00
122	Orlando Cabrera/18	25.00
124	Gary Carter/25	30.00
125	Jae Weong Seo/25	25.00
131	Chien-Ming Wang/100	125.00
167	Rich Harden/53	20.00
152	Marlon Byrd/29	15.00
154	Ryan Howard/100	75.00
160	Jay Payton/17	20.00
167	Jerome Williams/50	25.00
168	Merkin Valdez/100	15.00
171	Chris Snelling/32	10.00
177	Shigetoshi Hasegawa/17	75.00
179	Dan Haren/100	10.00
184	Stan Musial/25	80.00
186	Aubrey Huff/19	25.00
186	Chad Gaudin/100	5.00
187	Delmon Young/73	20.00
192	Mark Teixeira/25	25.00
194	Alexis Rios/25	20.00
194	Dustin McGowan/50	10.00
198	Josh Phelps/17	15.00

Rally Caps

NM/M
Production 999 Sets
Die-Cut: 1X
Production 500 Sets

#	Player	NM/M
1	Adam Dunn	2.00
2	Adrian Beltre	1.50
3	Albert Pujols	5.00
4	Alex Rodriguez	5.00
5	Andruw Jones	2.00
6	Angel Berroa	1.50
7	Aubrey Huff	1.50
8	Austin Kearns	1.50
9	Ben Sheets	2.00
10	Brad Penny	1.50
11	Carlos Beltran	2.00
12	Carlos Lee	1.50
13	Casey Fossum	1.50
14	Eric Hinske	1.50
15	Geoff Jenkins	1.50
16	Jack Wilson	1.50
17	Jason Jennings	1.50
18	Joe Kennedy	1.50
19	Lance Berkman	1.50
20	Magglio Ordonez	1.50
21	Kerry Wood	3.00
22	Mark Buehrle	1.50
23	Mark Prior	3.00
24	Mark Teixeira	2.00
25	Michael Cuddyer	1.50
26	Jeff Conine	1.50
27	Mike Mussina	2.50
28	Mike Piazza	4.00
29	Jose Reyes	2.00
30	Paul Lo Duca	1.50
31	Pedro Martinez	2.00
32	Roy Oswalt	2.00
33	Ryan Klesko	1.50
34	Sammy Sosa	4.00
35	Tim Hudson	1.50
36	Todd Helton	2.00
37	Torii Hunter	1.50
38	Vernon Wells	1.50
39	Craig Wilson	1.50
40	Edgar Renteria	1.50

Spirit of the Game

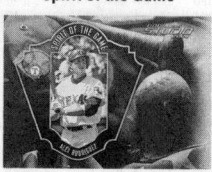

NM/M
Production 999 Sets
Die-Cut: 1X
Production 500 Sets

#	Player	NM/M
1	Sammy Sosa	4.00
2	Alex Rodriguez Rgr	4.00
3	Nomar Garciaparra	4.00
4	Derek Jeter	6.00
5	Albert Pujols	5.00
6	Roger Clemens	5.00
7	Mark Prior	3.00
8	Randy Johnson	2.00
9	Pedro Martinez	2.00
10	Vladimir Guerrero	2.00
11	Todd Helton	2.00
12	Jeff Bagwell	2.00
13	Mike Mussina	1.50
14	Josh Beckett	1.50
15	Hideo Nomo	1.50
16	Mike Piazza	4.00
17	Don Mattingly	5.00
18	George Brett	5.00
19	Nolan Ryan	8.00
20	Cal Ripken Jr.	8.00

Spirit of the Game Material Bat

#	Player	NM/M
1	Sammy Sosa/100	15.00
2	Alex Rodriguez/Rgr/100	10.00
3	Nomar Garciaparra/100	10.00
4	Derek Jeter/100	20.00
5	Albert Pujols/100	15.00
6	Roger Clemens/50	20.00
7	Mark Prior/100	8.00
8	Randy Johnson/100	10.00
9	Vladimir Guerrero/100	10.00
11	Todd Helton/100	10.00
12	Jeff Bagwell/100	8.00
13	Mike Mussina/50	10.00
14	Josh Beckett/100	8.00
15	Hideo Nomo/100	8.00
16	Mike Piazza/100	10.00
17	Don Mattingly/100	20.00
18	George Brett/100	20.00
20	Cal Ripken Jr./50	50.00

Spirit of the Game Material Jersey

NM/M
Prime: No Pricing
Production 1-5

#	Player	NM/M
1	Sammy Sosa/200	10.00
2	Alex Rodriguez/200	10.00
3	Nomar Garciaparra/100	10.00
4	Derek Jeter/200	20.00
5	Albert Pujols/100	20.00
7	Mark Prior/200	8.00
8	Randy Johnson/200	10.00
9	Pedro Martinez/200	10.00
11	Todd Helton/200	10.00
12	Jeff Bagwell/200	8.00
13	Mike Mussina/200	8.00
14	Josh Beckett/200	8.00
15	Hideo Nomo/200	8.00
16	Mike Piazza/200	12.00
17	Don Mattingly/Jkt/200	15.00
18	George Brett/200	15.00
19	Nolan Ryan/100	20.00
20	Cal Ripken Jr./100	40.00

Spirit of the Game Material Sig Jsy

No Pricing
Production 1-5

Stars

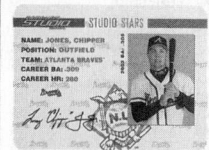

NM/M
Inserted 1:5
Gold: 1.5-3X
Production 100 Sets
Platinum: 3-5X
Production 25 Sets

#	Player	NM/M
1	Albert Pujols	3.00
2	Alex Rodriguez	4.00
3	Alfonso Soriano	1.50
4	Andy Pettitte	.50
5	Angel Berroa	.50
6	Aubrey Huff	.50
7	Austin Kearns	.75
8	Barry Zito	.75
9	Brian Giles	.75
10	Carlos Delgado	.75
11	Chipper Jones	1.50
12	Craig Biggio	.75
13	Curt Schilling	1.00
14	Derek Jeter	4.00
15	Edgar Martinez	.50
16	Eric Gagne	1.00
17	Frank Thomas	1.00
18	Hank Blalock	1.00
19	Hideki Matsui	3.00
20	Hideo Nomo	.75
21	Ichiro Suzuki	1.00
22	Ivan Rodriguez	1.00
23	Jason Kendall	.50
24	Jason Schmidt	.75
25	Jeff Bagwell	1.00
26	Jim Edmonds	1.00
27	Jim Thome	1.50
28	Josh Beckett	.75
29	Kazuo Matsui	4.00
30	Ken Griffey Jr.	2.50
31	Larry Walker	.50
32	Magglio Ordonez	.50
33	Manny Ramirez	1.00
34	Mark Mulder	.75
35	Mark Prior	1.00
36	Mark Teixeira	1.00
37	Miguel Tejada	1.00
38	Mike Mussina	1.00
39	Mike Piazza	2.50
40	Pedro Martinez	1.50
41	Randy Johnson	1.50
42	Roger Clemens	1.50
43	Roy Halladay	.50
44	Russ Ortiz	.50
45	Sammy Sosa	3.00
46	Scott Podsednik	.50
47	Tim Hudson	.75
48	Todd Helton	1.50
49	Vernon Wells	.50
50	Vladimir Guerrero	2.00

2004 Donruss Team Heroes

NM/M
Complete Set (465): 75.00
Common Player: .25
Common SP (441-465): .50
Pack (8): 2.00
Box (24): 40.00

#	Player	NM/M
1	Troy Glaus	.40
2	Garret Anderson	.40
3	John Lackey	.25
4	Jarrod Washburn	.25
5	Bengie Molina	.25
6	Adam Kennedy	.25
7	Francisco Rodriguez	.25
8	Darin Erstad	.25
9	Ramon Ortiz	.25
10	Chone Figgins	.25
11	Rich Fischer	.25
12	David Eckstein	.25
13	Troy Percival	.25
14	Tim Salmon	.40
15	Nolan Ryan Angels	2.00
16	Luis Gonzalez	.25
17	Matt Kata	.25
18	Randy Johnson	.75
19	Oscar Villarreal	.25
20	Tim Olson	.25
21	Rob Hammock	.25
22	Alex Cintron	.25
23	Brian Bruney	.25
24	Brandon Webb	.25
25	Greg Aquino	.25
26	Shea Hillenbrand	.25
27	Steve Finley	.25
28	Rod Barajas	.25
29	Mike Hampton	.25
30	Adam LaRoche	.25
31	Russ Ortiz	.25
32	Chipper Jones	.75
33	John Smoltz	.40
34	Andruw Jones	.50
35	Bubba Nelson	.25
36	Johnny Estrada	.25
37	Marcus Giles	.25
38	Rafael Furcal	.25
39	Horacio Ramirez	.25
40	Dale Murphy	.75
41	Gaylord Perry Braves	.25
42	Mark DeRosa	.25
43	Adam Loewen	.25
44	Jerry Hairston Jr.	.25
45	Jose Morban	.25
46	Daniel Cabrera	.25
47	Jay Gibbons	.25
48	Larry Bigbie	.25
49	Luis Matos	.25
50	Rodrigo Lopez	.25
51	Melvin Mora	.25
52	Cal Ripken Jr.	2.50
53	Geronimo Gil	.25
54	Tony Batista	.25
55	Jason Johnson	.25
56	Jason Varitek	.25
57	Bill Mueller	.25
58	Todd Walker	.25
59	Trot Nixon	.40
60	Tim Wakefield	.25
61	Kevin Youkilis	.50
62	David Ortiz	.50
63	Johnny Damon	.40
64	Derek Lowe	.25
65	Pedro J. Martinez	.75
66	Carl Yastrzemski	.75
67	Bobby Doerr	.25
68	Matt Clement	.25
69	Sammy Sosa	1.50
70	Randall Simon	.25
71	Nate Frese	.25
72	Carlos Zambrano	.40
73	Moises Alou	.40
74	Mark Prior	1.00
75	Jason Dubois	.25
76	Nic Jackson	.25
77	Corey Patterson	.40
78	John Webb	.25
79	Kerry Wood	.75
80	Aramis Ramirez	.40
81	Brendan Harris	.25
82	Kenny Lofton	.25
83	Alex Gonzalez	.25
84	Gary Matthews Sr.	.25
85	Mark Grace	.40
86	Mark Grudzielanek	.25
87	Joe Borowski	.25
88	Joe Crede	.25
89	Mark Buehrle	.25
90	Paul Konerko	.40
91	Magglio Ordonez	.40
92	Corwin Malone	.25
93	Frank Thomas	.50
94	Jose Valentin	.25
95	Miguel Olivo	.25
96	Esteban Loaiza	.25
97	Carlos Lee	.40
98	Harold Baines	.25
99	Jason LaRue	.25
100	Sean Casey	.40
101	Adam Dunn	.50
102	Josh Hall	.25
103	Danny Graves	.25
104	Barry Larkin	.40
105	Ken Griffey Jr.	1.00
106	Brandon Claussen	.25
107	Austin Kearns	.40
108	D'Angelo Jimenez	.25
109	Ryan Wagner	.25
110	Tim Hummel	.25
111	Johnny Bench	1.00
112	Eric Davis	.25
113	Jose Rijo	.25
114	Travis Hafner	.40
115	Jody Gerut	.25
116	Fernando Cabrera	.25
117	Jhonny Peralta	.25
118	Ryan Church	.25
119	Francisco Cruceta	.25
120	Omar Vizquel	.40
121	Jason Davis	.25
122	Jeremy Guthrie	.25
123	C.C. Sabathia	.25
124	Milton Bradley	.25

#	Player	Price
125	Cliff Lee	.25
126	Victor Martinez	.25
127	Bob Feller	.50
128	Casey Blake	.25
129	Josh Bard	.25
130	Billy Traber	.25
131	Coco Crisp	.25
132	Larry Walker	.40
133	Jason Jennings	.25
134	Garrett Atkins	.25
135	Rene Reyes	.25
136	Chin-Hui Tsao	.25
137	Preston Wilson	.25
138	Jeff Baker	.25
139	Charles Johnson	.25
140	Shawn Chacon	.25
141	Todd Helton	.50
142	Jay Payton	.25
143	Omar Infante	.25
144	Bobby Higginson	.25
145	Dmitri Young	.25
146	Jorge Cordova	.25
147	Jeremy Bonderman	.25
148	Brandon Inge	.25
149	Franklyn German	.25
150	Nook Logan	.25
151	Alex Sanchez	.25
152	Craig Monroe	.25
153	Preston Larrison	.25
154	Carlos Pena	.25
155	Alan Trammell	.50
156	Jack Morris	.25
157	Eric Munson	.25
158	Mike Maroth	.25
159	Josh Beckett	.40
160	Josh Willingham	.25
161	Mike Lowell	.40
162	Luis Castillo	.25
163	Wilson Valdez	.25
164	Miguel Cabrera	.75
165	Alex Gonzalez	.25
166	Carl Pavano	.25
167	Dontrelle Willis	.40
168	Juan Pierre	.25
169	Juan Encarnacion	.25
170	Brad Penny	.25
171	Ivan Rodriguez/Marlins	.50
172	Josh Wilson	.25
173	Jeff Conine	.25
174	Mark Redman	.25
175	A.J. Burnett	.25
176	Jeff Bagwell	.50
177	Octavio Dotel	.25
178	Craig Biggio	.40
179	John Buck	.25
180	Rodrigo Rosario	.25
181	Tommy Whiteman	.25
182	Kirk Saarloos	.25
183	Jason Lane	.25
184	Wade Miller	.25
185	Lance Berkman	.40
186	Roy Oswalt	.40
187	Tim Redding	.25
188	Jeff Kent	.40
189	Chris Burke	.25
190	Morgan Ensberg	.25
191	Nolan Ryan/Astros	2.00
192	Geoff Blum	.25
193	Jeremy Affeldt	.25
194	Mike Sweeney	.25
195	Angel Berroa	.25
196	Jimmy Gobble	.25
197	Ken Harvey	.25
198	Carlos Beltran	.50
199	Alexis Gomez	.25
200	Byron Gettis	.25
201	Mike MacDougal	.25
202	David DeJesus	.25
203	Runelvys Hernandez	.25
204	George Brett	1.50
205	Amos Otis	.25
206	Joe Randa	.25
207	Aaron Guiel	.25
208	Eric Gagne	.40
209	Shawn Green	.40
210	Kevin Brown	.40
211	Cesar Izturis	.25
212	Kazuhisa Ishii	.25
213	Joe Thurston	.25
214	Odalis Perez	.25
215	Rickey Henderson	.50
216	Hideo Nomo	.40
217	Hong-Chih Kuo	.25
218	Edwin Jackson	.25
219	Paul LoDuca	.25
220	Adrian Beltre	.25
221	Duke Snider	.75
222	Steve Garvey	.50
223	Rickie Weeks	.40
224	Bill Hall	.25
225	Doug Davis	.25
226	Geoff Jenkins	.40
227	Matt Childers	.25
228	Dan Kolb	.25
229	Scott Podsednik	.40
230	Pedro Liriano	.25
231	Ben Sheets	.40
232	Robin Yount	.75
233	Gorman Thomas	.25
234	Ben Oglivie	.25
235	Matt LeCroy	.25
236	Cristian Guzman	.25
237	Lew Ford	.25
238	J.C. Romero	.25
239	Rob Bowen	.25
240	Corey Koskie	.25
241	Jacque Jones	.25
242	Brad Radke	.25
243	Shannon Stewart	.25
244	J.D. Durbin	.25
245	Doug Mientkiewicz	.25
246	Jason Kubel	.25
247	Torii Hunter	.40
248	Johan Santana	.25
249	Kirby Puckett	.75
250	Luis Rivas	.25
251	Orlando Cabrera	.25
252	Tony Armas Jr.	.25
253	Brad Wilkerson	.25
254	Endy Chavez	.25
255	Jose Vidro	.25
256	Zach Day	.25
257	Livan Hernandez	.25
258	Termmel Sledge	.25
259	Michael Barrett	.25
260	Gary Carter	.50
261	Andre Dawson	.50
262	Craig Brazell	.25
263	Mike Piazza	1.00
264	Jeff Duncan	.25
265	Jason Anderson	.25
266	Tom Glavine	.40
267	Danny Garcia	.25
268	Ty Wigginton	.25
269	Al Leiter	.25
270	Jeremy Griffiths	.25
271	Jose Reyes	.40
272	Prentice Redman	.25
273	Cliff Floyd	.25
274	Jae Weong Seo	.25
275	Nolan Ryan/Mets	2.00
276	Keith Hernandez	.25
277	Jason Phillips	.25
278	Kazuo Matsui RC	3.00
279	Jose Contreras	.25
280	Aaron Boone	.25
281	Mike Mussina	.40
282	Jason Giambi	.50
283	Hideki Matsui	1.00
284	Derek Jeter	2.00
285	Mariano Rivera	.40
286	Chien-Ming Wang	.40
287	Bernie Williams	.25
288	Alfonso Soriano/Yanks	.50
289	Jorge Posada	.25
290	Michel Hernandez	.25
291	Erick Almonte	.25
292	Don Mattingly	1.50
293	Roger Clemens/Yanks	1.50
294	Gaylord Perry/Rgr	.25
295	Tommy John	.25
296	Tim Hudson	.40
297	Rich Harden	.25
298	Eric Chavez	.40
299	Adam Morrissey	.25
300	Mark Mulder	.40
301	Eric Byrnes	.25
302	Jermaine Dye	.25
303	Barry Zito	.25
304	Erubiel Durazo	.25
305	Mark Ellis	.25
306	Bobby Crosby	.25
307	Shane Bazzell	.25
308	Mario Ramos	.25
309	Jose Canseco	.50
310	Placido Polanco	.25
311	Jimmy Rollins	.25
312	Jim Thome	.75
313	Brett Myers	.25
314	Jason Michaels	.25
315	Vicente Padilla	.25
316	Bobby Abreu	.40
317	Ryan Howard	.25
318	Chase Utley	.50
319	Pat Burrell	.40
320	Randy Wolf	.25
321	Franklin Perez	.25
322	Marlon Byrd	.25
323	Kevin Millwood	.40
324	Mike Lieberthal	.25
325	Anderson Machado	.25
326	Travis Chapman	.25
327	Steve Carlton	.25
328	Greg Luzinski	.25
329	David Bell	.25
330	Craig Wilson	.40
331	Kris Benson	.25
332	Jose Castillo	.25
333	Josh Fogg	.25
334	Jason Kendall	.25
335	Walter Young	.25
336	Oliver Perez	.25
337	Jason Bay	.25
338	Duaner Sanchez	.25
339	Jack Wilson	.40
340	Carlos Rivera	.25
341	Kip Wells	.25
342	Freddy Sanchez	.25
343	Roberto Clemente	2.00
344	Al Oliver	.25
345	Phil Nevin	.25
346	Trevor Hoffman	.25
347	Ryan Klesko	.40
348	Khalil Greene	.25
349	Freddy Guzman RC	.25
350	Brian Giles	.25
351	Brian Lawrence	.25
352	Sean Burroughs	.25
353	Ben Howard	.25
354	Xavier Nady	.25
355	Mark Loretta	.25
356	Ramon Vazquez	.25
357	Tony Gwynn	.25
358	Adam Eaton	.25
359	Merkin Valdez RC	.75
360	Kevin Correia	.25
361	Edgardo Alfonzo	.25
362	Mike Cameron	.25
363	Ray Durham	.25
364	Jesse Foppert	.25
365	Robb Nen	.25
366	Marquis Grissom	.25
367	Jerome Williams	.25
368	Jason Schmidt	.40
369	Will Clark	.50
370	Bret Boone	.40
371	Freddy Garcia	.25
372	Dan Wilson	.25
373	Rett Johnson	.25
374	Kazuhiro Sasaki	.25
375	Ichiro Suzuki	1.00
376	Edgar Martinez	.25
377	Jamie Moyer	.25
378	Joel Pineiro	.25
379	Carlos Guillen	.25
380	Randy Winn	.25
381	J.J. Putz	.25
382	John Olerud	.40
383	Matt Thornton	.25
384	Rafael Soriano	.25
385	Gil Meche	.25
386	Albert Pujols	1.50
387	Woody Williams	.25
388	Dan Haren	.25
389	Matt Morris	.40
390	Jim Edmonds	.40
391	Edgar Renteria	.25
392	Scott Rolen	.75
393	J.D. Drew	.40
394	Bo Hart	.25
395	Stan Musial	1.00
396	Red Schoendienst	.25
397	Terry Pendleton	.25
398	Mike Matheny	.25
399	Dewon Brazelton	.25
400	Chad Gaudin	.25
401	Aubrey Huff	.25
402	Victor Zambrano	.25
403	Antonio Perez	.25
404	Carl Crawford	.25
405	Joe Kennedy	.25
406	Pete LaForest	.25
407	Delmon Young	.40
408	Rocco Baldelli	.40
409	Doug Waechter	.25
410	Brian Stokes	.25
411	Edwin Almonte	.25
412	Toby Hall	.25
413	Lance Carter	.25
414	Greg Maddux/Braves	1.00
415	Hank Blalock	.50
416	Colby Lewis	.25
417	Mark Teixeira	.40
418	Gerald Laird	.25
419	Ricardo Rodriguez	.25
420	Ben Kozlowski	.25
421	Kevin Mench	.25
422	Michael Young	.25
423	Ramon Nivar	.25
424	Laynce Nix	.25
425	Nolan Ryan/Rgr	2.00
426	Einar Diaz	.25
427	Carlos Delgado	.40
428	Eric Hinske	.25
429	Dustin McGowan	.25
430	Frank Catalanotto	.25
431	Kevin Cash	.25
432	Roy Halladay	.50
433	Orlando Hudson	.25
434	Francisco Rosario	.25
435	Guillermo Quiroz	.25
436	Vernon Wells	.25
437	Josh Phelps	.25
438	Alexis Rios	.25
439	Reed Johnson	.25
440	Chris Woodward	.25
441	Bartolo Colon/SP	.50
442	Richie Sexson/SP	.75
443	Greg Maddux/Cubs/SP	2.00
444	Javy Lopez/SP	.75
445	Gary Sheffield/SP	.75
446	Curt Schilling/SP	1.00
447	Nomar Garciaparra/SP	2.50
448	Manny Ramirez/SP	1.50
449	Derrek Lee/SP	.75
450	Roberto Alomar/SP	.75
451	Ivan Rodriguez Tigers/SP	1.50
452	Junior Spivey/SP	.50
453	Alfonso Soriano/Rgr/SP	1.50
454	Vladimir Guerrero/SP	1.50
455	Nick Johnson/SP	.50
456	Javier Vazquez/SP	.50
457	Andy Pettitte/SP	.75
458	Miguel Tejada/SP	.75
459	Rich Aurilia/SP	.50
460	A.J. Pierzynski/SP	.50
461	Raul Ibanez/SP	.50
462	Roger Clemens/Astros/SP	3.00
463	Juan Gonzalez/SP	1.00
464	Rafael Palmeiro/SP	1.00
465	Alex Rodriguez/Yanks/SP	4.00

Showdown Bronze
Bronze (1-440): 3-5X
Bronze (441-465): 2-3X
Production 150 Sets

Showdown Silver

Silver (1-440): 5-10X
Silver (441-465): 3-5X
Production 50 Sets

Showdown Gold
No Pricing
Production 10 Sets

Autographs

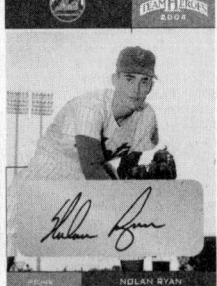

NM/M

Inserted 1:24

#	Player	Price
10	Chone Figgins	10.00
11	Rich Fischer	5.00
17	Matt Kata	5.00
18	Oscar Villarreal	5.00
20	Tim Olson	5.00
21	Rob Hammock/57	10.00
23	Brian Bruney	5.00
25	Greg Aquino	5.00
35	Bubba Nelson	5.00
46	Daniel Cabrera	5.00
61	Kevin Youkilis/50	15.00
71	Nate Frese	5.00
75	Jason Dubois	5.00
76	Nic Jackson	5.00
80	John Webb	5.00
81	Brendan Harris	10.00
84	Gary Matthews Sr.	10.00
90	Corwin Malone	5.00
102	Josh Hall/25	15.00
106	Brandon Claussen	10.00
116	Tim Hummel	5.00
117	Francisco Cabrera	5.00
118	Jhonny Peralta	8.00
118	Ryan Church	8.00
119	Francisco Cruceta/75	8.00
146	Jorge Cordova	5.00
149	Franklyn German	5.00
150	Nook Logan	5.00
153	Preston Larrison	5.00
160	Josh Willingham	8.00
163	Wilson Valdez	5.00
172	Josh Wilson	5.00
180	Rodrigo Rosario	8.00
181	Tommy Whiteman	5.00
189	Chris Burke	5.00
197	Ken Harvey	15.00
200	Byron Gettis	8.00
205	Amos Otis	10.00
211	Cesar Izturis	8.00
225	Doug Davis	5.00
227	Matt Childers	5.00
230	Pedro Liriano	5.00
233	Gorman Thomas	15.00
234	Ben Oglivie/86	15.00
237	Lew Ford	10.00
238	J.C. Romero	5.00
239	Rob Bowen	5.00
246	Jason Kubel/50	15.00
258	Termmel Sledge	5.00
262	Craig Brazell	5.00
264	Jeff Duncan	8.00
265	Jason Anderson	5.00
267	Danny Garcia	5.00
270	Jeremy Griffiths	5.00
272	Prentice Redman	8.00
291	Erick Almonte/66	8.00
307	Shane Bazzell	5.00
308	Mario Ramos	5.00
314	Jason Michaels/42	5.00
321	Franklin Perez	5.00
325	Anderson Machado/50	10.00
326	Travis Chapman	8.00
328	Greg Luzinski	15.00
331	Kris Benson	10.00
335	Walter Young/67	10.00
338	Duaner Sanchez	5.00
353	Ben Howard	5.00
359	Merkin Valdez/50	20.00
360	Kevin Correia	5.00
373	Rett Johnson/76	8.00
381	J.J. Putz	5.00
383	Matt Thornton/50	8.00
384	Rafael Soriano	8.00
406	Pete LaForest	5.00
410	Brian Stokes	5.00
411	Edwin Almonte	5.00
419	Ricardo Rodriguez	5.00
420	Ben Kozlowski	5.00
431	Kevin Cash	5.00
434	Francisco Rosario/48	8.00

2004 Donruss Throwback Threads

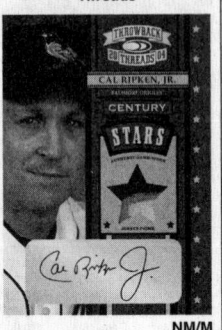

NM/M

Complete Set (250):
Common Player: .15
Common (201-225): 1.50
Common (226-250): 3.00
Production 1,000
Hobby Pack (5): 5.00
Hobby Box (24): 90.00

#	Player	Price
1	Bartolo Colon	.25
2	Darin Erstad	.25
3	David Eckstein	.15
4	Garret Anderson	.25
5	Tim Salmon	.25
6	Troy Glaus	.25
7	Vladimir Guerrero	.75
8	Brandon Webb	.25
9	Luis Gonzalez	.25
10	Randy Johnson	.75
11	Richie Sexson	.40
12	Roberto Alomar	.50
13	Shea Hillenbrand	.15
14	Steve Finley	.15
15	Adam LaRoche	.25
16	Andruw Jones	.50
17	Chipper Jones	.75
18	J.D. Drew	.25
19	John Smoltz	.25
20	Rafael Furcal	.15
21	Russ Ortiz	.15
22	Javy Lopez	.25
23	Jay Gibbons	.15
24	Larry Bigbie	.15
25	Luis Matos	.15
26	Melvin Mora	.15
27	Miguel Tejada	.40
28	Rafael Palmeiro	.50
29	Curt Schilling	.50
30	David Ortiz	.75
31	Derek Lowe	.25
32	Jason Varitek	.15
33	Johnny Damon	.25
34	Manny Ramirez	.50
35	Nomar Garciaparra	1.00
36	Pedro J. Martinez	.75
37	Trot Nixon	.15
38	Aramis Ramirez	.40
39	Corey Patterson	.15
40	Derrek Lee	.25
41	Greg Maddux	1.00
42	Kerry Wood	.75
43	Mark Prior	.75
44	Sammy Sosa	1.50
45	Carlos Lee	.25
46	Esteban Loaiza	.15
47	Frank Thomas	.50
48	Joe Borchard	.15
49	Magglio Ordonez	.25
50	Mark Buehrle	.15
51	Paul Konerko	.15
52	Adam Dunn	.50
53	Austin Kearns	.15
54	Barry Larkin	.40
55	Brandon Larson	.15
56	Ken Griffey Jr.	1.00
57	Ryan Wagner	.15
58	Sean Casey	.15
59	C.C. Sabathia	.25
60	Jody Gerut	.15
61	Omar Vizquel	.15
62	Travis Hafner	.15
63	Victor Martinez	.25
64	Charles Johnson	.15
65	Garrett Atkins	.15
66	Jason Jennings	.15
67	Joe Kennedy	.15
68	Larry Walker	.25
69	Preston Wilson	.15
70	Todd Helton	.50
71	Ivan Rodriguez	.50
72	Jeremy Bonderman	.15
73	A.J. Burnett	.15
74	Brad Penny	.15
75	Dontrelle Willis	.15
76	Josh Beckett	.50
77	Juan Pierre	.15
78	Luis Castillo	.15
79	Miguel Cabrera	.75
80	Mike Lowell	.25
81	Andy Pettitte	.25
82	Craig Biggio	.25
83	Jeff Bagwell	.50
84	Jeff Kent	.25
85	Lance Berkman	.25
86	Morgan Ensberg	.15
87	Richard Hidalgo	.15
88	Roger Clemens	1.50
89	Roy Oswalt	.25
90	Wade Miller	.15
91	Angel Berroa	.15
92	Carlos Beltran	.50
93	Juan Gonzalez	.40
94	Ken Harvey	.15
95	Mike Sweeney	.15
96	Runelvys Hernandez	.15
97	Adrian Beltre	.40
98	Edwin Jackson	.15
99	Eric Gagne	.40
100	Hideo Nomo	.25
101	Hong-Chih Kuo	.15
102	Kazuhisa Ishii	.15
103	Paul LoDuca	.15
104	Shawn Green	.25
105	Ben Sheets	.15
106	Geoff Jenkins	.15
107	Junior Spivey	.15
108	Rickie Weeks	.25
109	Scott Podsednik	.15
110	Corey Koskie	.15
111	Doug Mientkiewicz	.15
112	Jacque Jones	.15
113	Joe Mays	.15
114	Johan Santana	.15
115	Shannon Stewart	.15
116	Torii Hunter	.25
117	Brad Wilkerson	.15
118	Carl Everett	.15
119	Chad Cordero	.15
120	Jose Vidro	.15
121	Nick Johnson	.15
122	Orlando Cabrera	.25
123	Al Leiter	.15
124	Cliff Floyd	.15
125	Jae Weong Seo	.15
126	Jose Reyes	.25
127	Mike Cameron	.15
128	Mike Piazza	1.00
129	Tom Glavine	.25
130	Alex Rodriguez	2.00
131	Bernie Williams	.25
132	Chien-Ming Wang	.25
133	Derek Jeter	2.00
134	Gary Sheffield	.50
135	Hideki Matsui	1.00
136	Jason Giambi	.25
137	Javier Vazquez	.15
138	Jorge Posada	.25
139	Jose Contreras	.15
140	Kevin Brown	.15
141	Mariano Rivera	.25
142	Mike Mussina	.40
143	Barry Zito	.15
144	Bobby Crosby	.15
145	Eric Chavez	.25
146	Erubiel Durazo	.15
147	Jermaine Dye	.15
148	Mark Kotsay	.15
149	Mark Mulder	.25
150	Rich Harden	.15
151	Tim Hudson	.25
152	Billy Wagner	.15
153	Bobby Abreu	.25
154	Brett Myers	.15
155	Jim Thome	.75
156	Jimmy Rollins	.15
157	Kevin Millwood	.15
158	Marlon Byrd	.15
159	Pat Burrell	.15
160	Jason Bay	.15
161	Jason Kendall	.15
162	Brian Giles	.15
163	Jay Payton	.15
164	Ryan Klesko	.15
165	Edgardo Alfonzo	.15
166	Jason Schmidt	.40
167	Jerome Williams	.15
168	Todd Linden	.15
169	Bret Boone	.15
170	Edgar Martinez	.25
171	Freddy Garcia	.15
172	Ichiro Suzuki	1.50
173	Jamie Moyer	.15
174	John Olerud	.25
175	Shigetoshi Hasegawa	.15
176	Albert Pujols	1.50
177	Dan Haren	.15
178	Edgar Renteria	.15
179	Jim Edmonds	.25
180	Matt Morris	.15
181	Scott Rolen	.25
182	Aubrey Huff	.15
183	Carl Crawford	.25
184	Chad Gaudin	.15
185	Delmon Young	.25
186	Dewon Brazelton	.15
187	Fred McGriff	.25
188	Rocco Baldelli	.25
189	Alfonso Soriano	.25

#	Player	Price
190	Hank Blalock	.50
191	Laynce Nix	.15
192	Mark Teixeira	.25
193	Michael Young	.15
194	Carlos Delgado	.40
195	Eric Hinske	.15
196	Frank Catalanotto	.15
197	Josh Phelps	.15
198	Orlando Hudson	.15
199	Roy Halladay	.15
200	Vernon Wells	.15
201	Dale Murphy	2.00
202	Cal Ripken Jr.	10.00
203	Fred Lynn	1.50
204	Wade Boggs	2.00
205	Nolan Ryan	6.00
206	Rod Carew	2.00
207	Andre Dawson	1.50
208	Ernie Banks	3.00
209	Ryne Sandberg	5.00
210	Bo Jackson	3.00
211	Carlton Fisk	3.00
212	Dave Concepcion	1.50
213	Alan Trammell	1.50
214	George Brett	5.00
215	Robin Yount	4.00
216	Gary Carter	1.50
217	Darryl Strawberry	1.50
218	Dwight Gooden	1.50
219	Babe Ruth	6.00
220	Don Mattingly	5.00
221	Reggie Jackson	3.00
222	Mike Schmidt	5.00
223	Tony Gwynn	4.00
224	Keith Hernandez	1.50
225	Hector Gimenez RC	3.00
226	Graham Koonce	3.00
227	John Gall RC	5.00
228	Jerry Gil RC	3.00
229	Jason Frasor RC	3.00
230	Justin Knoedler RC	3.00
231	Ivan Ochoa RC	3.00
232	Greg Dobbs RC	3.00
233	Ronald Belisario RC	3.00
234	Jerome Gamble RC	3.00
235	Roberto Novoa RC	3.00
236	Sean Henn RC	3.00
237	Willy Taveras RC	3.00
238	Ramon Ramirez RC	3.00
239	Kazuo Matsui RC	8.00
240	Akinori Otsuka RC	4.00
241	Jason Bartlett RC	5.00
242	Fernando Nieve RC	3.00
243	Freddy Guzman RC	5.00
244	Aarom Baldiris RC	5.00
245	Merkin Valdez RC	3.00
246	Mike Gosling RC	3.00
247	Shingo Takatsu RC	8.00
248	William Bergolla RC	3.00
249	Shawn Hill RC	3.00
250	Justin Germano RC	3.00

Blast From the Past

Common Player: 1.50
Production 1,500 Sets
Spectrum: 2-3X
Production 100 Sets

#	Player	Price
1	Albert Pujols	5.00
2	Alex Rodriguez	4.00
3	Babe Ruth	6.00
4	Cal Ripken Jr.	8.00
5	Carlton Fisk	2.00
6	Eddie Mathews	3.00
7	Eddie Murray	2.00
8	Ernie Banks	3.00
9	Frank Robinson	2.00
10	George Foster	1.50
11	Harmon Killebrew	3.00
12	Jim Rice	1.50
13	Jim Thome	2.00
14	Johnny Bench	3.00
15	Jose Canseco	2.00
16	Juan Gonzalez	2.00
17	Ken Griffey Jr.	3.00
18	Mike Piazza	4.00
19	Mike Schmidt	5.00
20	Reggie Jackson	2.00
21	Roger Maris	5.00
22	Sammy Sosa	4.00
23	Stan Musial	4.00
24	Willie McCovey	2.00
25	Willie Stargell	2.00

Blast From the Past Bat
NM/M
Production 250 unless noted.

#	Player	Price
1	Albert Pujols	15.00

#	Player	Price
2	Alex Rodriguez	10.00
3	Babe Ruth	150.00
4	Cal Ripken Jr.	25.00
5	Carlton Fisk	8.00
6	Eddie Mathews	10.00
7	Eddie Murray	8.00
8	Ernie Banks	10.00
9	Frank Robinson	8.00
10	George Foster	6.00
11	Harmon Killebrew	10.00
12	Jim Rice	8.00
13	Jim Thome	8.00
14	Johnny Bench	10.00
15	Jose Canseco/100	8.00
16	Juan Gonzalez	8.00
18	Mike Piazza	10.00
19	Mike Schmidt	15.00
20	Reggie Jackson	8.00
21	Roger Maris	30.00
22	Sammy Sosa	10.00
23	Stan Musial	15.00
24	Willie McCovey	8.00
25	Willie Stargell	8.00

Century Coll. Material

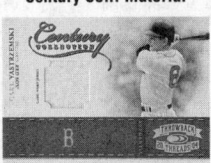

NM/M
All Jersey unless noted.
Prime: 1.5-3X
Production 10-25
Combo: .75-2X
Production 5-50
Combo Prime: 2-3X
Production 5-25
No pricing 15 or less.

#	Player	Price
1	Alan Trammell/250	8.00
2	Alex Rodriguez/250	10.00
3	Alfonso Soriano/250	8.00
4	Andre Dawson/250	6.00
5	Andy Pettitte/250	6.00
6	Bert Blyleven/250	6.00
7	Bo Jackson/250	12.00
8	Bobby Doerr/250	8.00
9	Brooks Robinson/25	30.00
10	Carl Yastrzemski/250	15.00
11	Carlos Delgado/250	4.00
12	Carlton Fisk Jkt/250	8.00
13	Curt Schilling/250	6.00
14	Darryl Strawberry/250	6.00
15	Dave Concepcion/250	6.00
16	Dave Parker/100	8.00
17	Dennis Eckersley/250	8.00
18	Don Sutton/250	10.00
19	Duke Snider/250	10.00
20	Dwight Gooden/250	6.00
21	Eddie Mathews/250	25.00
22	Enos Slaughter/100	8.00
23	Ernie Banks/Pants/25	15.00
24	Frankie Frisch/Jkt/250	12.00
25	Frank Robinson/50	8.00
26	Frank Thomas/250	10.00
27	Garret Anderson/250	6.00
28	Gary Carter/250	6.00
29	Gary Sheffield/250	6.00
30	Harmon Killebrew/50	25.00
31	Harold Baines/250	6.00
32	Hideo Nomo/250	6.00
33	Jack Morris/250	6.00
34	Jason Giambi/250	6.00
35	Jeff Kent/250	4.00
36	Jim "Catfish" Hunter/250	10.00
37	Jim Palmer/250	10.00
38	Jim Rice/250	10.00
39	Jim Thome/250	10.00
40	John Smoltz/250	8.00
41	Johnny Mize/Pants/250	8.00
42	Jose Canseco/250	8.00
43	Juan Gonzalez/250	8.00
44	Juan Marichal/250	8.00
45	Keith Hernandez/250	8.00
46	Kerry Wood/250	10.00
47	Kevin Brown/250	4.00
48	Lance Berkman/250	6.00
49	Larry Walker/250	6.00
50	Lee Smith/250	6.00
51	Lenny Dykstra/Bat/250	6.00
52	Luis Tiant/250	6.00
53	Magglio Ordonez/250	4.00
54	Manny Ramirez/250	8.00
55	Mariano Rivera/100	8.00
56	Mark Grace/250	8.00
57	Mark Mulder/250	6.00
58	Mark Teixeira/150	6.00
59	Marty Marion/25	15.00
60	Mike Mussina/Pants/250	8.00
61	Mike Piazza/250	8.00
62	Nellie Fox/Bat/250	15.00
63	Nolan Ryan/Jkt/250	20.00
65	Ozzie Smith/250	12.00
66	Pedro J. Martinez/250	8.00
67	Pee Wee Reese/Bat/250	8.00
68	Phil Niekro/250	8.00
69	Phil Rizzuto/Pants/250	8.00
70	Rafael Palmeiro/250	8.00
71	Ralph Kiner/Bat/250	8.00
72	Randy Johnson/250	10.00
73	Reggie Jackson/Jkt/250	8.00
74	Rickey Henderson/250	8.00
75	Roberto Alomar/250	8.00
76	Robin Ventura/250	8.00
77	Rod Carew/250	10.00
78	Roger Clemens/250	10.00
79	Ron Santo/Bat/250	10.00
80	Scott Rolen/250	6.00
81	Shawn Green/250	6.00
82	Steve Garvey/250	6.00
83	Tim Hudson/250	4.00
84	Tom Glavine/250	8.00
85	Tom Seaver/25	30.00
86	Adam Dunn/250	8.00
87	Tommy John/250	6.00
88	Tommy Lasorda/250	8.00
89	Tony Oliva/250	8.00
90	Tony Perez/Bat/250	8.00
91	Torii Hunter/250	4.00
92	Troy Glaus/250	4.00
93	Vernon Wells/250	4.00
94	Vladimir Guerrero/250	8.00
95	Wade Boggs/250	8.00
96	Warren Spahn/100	20.00
97	Will Clark/Bat/250	10.00
98	Willie McCovey/250	8.00
99	Willie Stargell/250	8.00
100	George Foster/250	8.00

Cent. Coll. Sign. Mat.
NM/M
All jersey unless noted.
Prime: No Pricing
Production 5-10
Combo: .75-1.5X
Production 5-25
No pricing 15 or less.
Combo Prime: No Pricing
Production 5-10

#	Player	Price
2	Alan Trammell/50	25.00
3	Alfonso Soriano/50	40.00
4	Andre Dawson/50	25.00
6	Bert Blyleven/50	25.00
7	Bobby Doerr/50	25.00
14	Darryl Strawberry/50	25.00
15	Dave Concepcion/50	25.00
16	Dave Parker/50	20.00
17	Dennis Eckersley/50	40.00
18	Don Sutton/50	25.00
19	Duke Snider/25	40.00
20	Dwight Gooden/50	25.00
27	Garret Anderson/50	25.00
28	Gary Carter/50	25.00
30	Gary Sheffield/25	30.00
31	Harold Baines/50	25.00
36	Jack Morris/50	15.00
37	Jim Palmer/25	25.00
38	Jim Rice/50	20.00
42	Jose Canseco/25	50.00
44	Juan Marichal/50	25.00
45	Keith Hernandez/50	25.00
50	Lee Smith/50	15.00
51	Lenny Dykstra Bat/50	25.00
52	Luis Tiant/50	15.00
53	Magglio Ordonez/50	25.00
56	Mark Grace/50	40.00
57	Mark Mulder/25	25.00
58	Mark Teixeira/25	40.00
59	Marty Marion/50	25.00
68	Phil Niekro/50	25.00
71	Ralph Kiner Bat/50	25.00
75	Roberto Alomar/25	50.00
76	Robin Ventura/50	20.00
82	Steve Garvey/50	15.00
84	Tommy John/50	15.00
90	Tony Perez Bat/50	30.00
91	Torii Hunter/25	30.00
93	Vernon Wells/50	25.00
94	Vladimir Guerrero/50	40.00
100	George Foster/50	20.00

Century Stars
NM/M
Common Player: 1.50
Production 1,500 Sets
Spectrum: 1.5-3X
Production 100 Sets

#	Player	Price
1	Al Kaline	2.00
2	Albert Pujols	5.00
3	Alex Rodriguez	4.00
4	Barry Larkin	2.00
5	Barry Zito	1.50
6	Billy Williams	2.00
7	Bob Feller	1.50
8	Bob Gibson	3.00
9	Cal Ripken Jr.	6.00
10	Chipper Jones	3.00
11	Curt Schilling	2.00
12	Dale Murphy	2.00
13	Dave Parker	1.50
14	Derek Jeter	6.00
15	Don Drysdale	1.50
16	Don Mattingly	5.00
17	Eddie Murray	2.00
18	Fergie Jenkins	2.00
19	Gary Carter	2.00
20	George Brett	5.00
21	Greg Maddux	3.00
22	Ivan Rodriguez	2.00
23	Jeff Bagwell	2.00
24	Joe Morgan	2.00
25	Johnny Bench	3.00
26	Kirby Puckett	3.00
27	Lou Boudreau	1.50
28	Lou Brock	1.50
29	Luis Aparicio	1.50
30	Manny Ramirez	2.00
31	Mark Prior	2.00
32	Miguel Tejada	2.00
33	Mike Mussina	2.00
34	Mike Piazza	3.00
35	Mike Schmidt	5.00
36	Nolan Ryan	5.00
37	Nomar Garciaparra	4.00
38	Ozzie Smith	3.00
39	Paul Molitor	3.00
40	Pedro J. Martinez	3.00
41	Rafael Palmeiro	3.00
42	Randy Johnson	3.00
43	Red Schoendienst	1.50
44	Reggie Jackson	3.00
45	Rickey Henderson	3.00
46	Roberto Alomar	2.00
47	Roberto Clemente	5.00
48	Robin Yount	3.00
49	Rod Carew	2.00
50	Roger Clemens	3.00
51	Ryne Sandberg	4.00
52	Sammy Sosa	4.00
53	Stan Musial	4.00
54	Steve Carlton	2.00
55	Todd Helton	2.00
56	Tom Glavine	2.00
57	Tom Seaver	3.00
58	Tony Gwynn	3.00
59	Wade Boggs	3.00
60	Whitey Ford	3.00

Century Stars Material
NM/M
All jersey unless noted.
Prime: No Pricing
Production Five Sets

#	Player	Price
1	Al Kaline Pants/25	30.00
2	Albert Pujols/50	25.00
4	Barry Larkin/50	6.00
5	Barry Zito/50	6.00
6	Billy Williams/50	8.00
8	Bob Gibson/25	20.00
9	Cal Ripken Jr./50	60.00
10	Chipper Jones/50	15.00
11	Curt Schilling/50	8.00
12	Dale Murphy/50	12.00
13	Dave Parker/50	8.00
14	Derek Jeter/50	35.00
15	Don Drysdale/50	12.00
16	Don Mattingly/Jkt/50	20.00
17	Eddie Murray/50	15.00
18	Fergie Jenkins/Pants/25	12.00
19	Gary Carter/Pants/50	8.00
20	George Brett/50	25.00
21	Greg Maddux/50	15.00
22	Ivan Rodriguez/50	12.00
23	Jeff Bagwell/50	10.00
24	Joe Morgan/25	20.00
25	Johnny Bench/50	25.00
26	Kirby Puckett/50	15.00
27	Lou Boudreau/50	8.00
28	Lou Brock/50	20.00
29	Luis Aparicio/Pants/50	8.00
30	Manny Ramirez/50	10.00
31	Mark Prior/50	8.00
32	Miguel Tejada/50	8.00
33	Mike Mussina/50	20.00
34	Mike Piazza/50	20.00
35	Mike Schmidt/50	25.00
36	Nolan Ryan/50	35.00
37	Nomar Garciaparra/50	15.00
38	Ozzie Smith/50	25.00
40	Pedro J. Martinez/50	10.00
41	Rafael Palmeiro/25	15.00
42	Randy Johnson/50	12.00
43	Red Schoendienst/50	8.00
44	Reggie Jackson/Pants/50	8.00
45	Rickey Henderson/50	15.00
46	Roberto Alomar/50	12.00
47	Robin Yount/50	15.00
48	Rod Carew/Jkt/50	10.00
50	Roger Clemens/50	15.00
51	Ryne Sandberg/50	20.00
52	Sammy Sosa/50	15.00
54	Steve Carlton/25	15.00
55	Todd Helton/50	12.00
56	Tom Glavine/50	10.00
57	Tom Seaver/50	15.00
58	Tony Gwynn/50	15.00
59	Wade Boggs/50	15.00

Century Stars Signature
NM/M
Signature Material: No Pricing
Production Five Sets
Sig. Material Prime: No Pricing
Production Five Sets

#	Player	Price
1	Al Kaline/25	50.00
6	Billy Williams/25	35.00
7	Bob Feller/25	30.00
8	Bob Gibson/25	35.00
12	Dale Murphy/25	40.00
13	Dave Parker/25	20.00
18	Fergie Jenkins/25	25.00
19	Gary Carter/25	25.00
24	Joe Morgan/25	30.00
28	Lou Brock/25	25.00
29	Luis Aparicio/25	20.00
35	Mike Schmidt/25	60.00
38	Ozzie Smith/25	75.00
53	Stan Musial/25	75.00

Dynasty

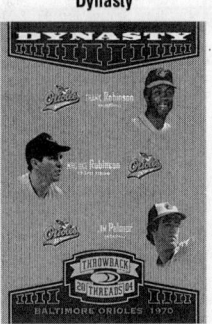

NM/M
Common Player: 3.00
Production 1,500 Sets
Spectrum: 2-3X
Production 100 Sets

#	Players	Price
1	Phil Rizzuto, Whitey Ford	3.00
2	Pee Wee Reese, Duke Snider, Tom Lasorda	3.00
3	Jim "Catfish" Hunter, Reggie Jackson	3.00
4	Roger Maris, Whitey Ford	5.00
5	Enos Slaughter, Shawn Marion, Stan Musial	5.00
6	Dwight Gooden, Gary Carter, Darryl Strawberry, Keith Hernandez	3.00
7	Johnny Bench, Tony Perez, Joe Morgan, George Foster	3.00
8	Derek Jeter, Jorge Posada, Bernie Williams, Andy Pettitte	6.00
9	Frank Robinson, Brooks Robinson, Jim Palmer	3.00
10	Willie Stargell, Dave Parker, Bill Madlock	3.00
11	Bob Gibson, Lou Brock, Ken Boyer	3.00
12	Rickey Henderson, Paul Molitor, Joe Carter, Roberto Alomar	3.00

Dynasty Material
NM/M
Quantity produced listed.
Prime: No Pricing
Production Five Sets

#	Players	Price
3	Jim "Catfish" Hunter, Reggie Jackson/50	25.00
6	Dwight Gooden, Gary Carter, Darryl Strawberry, Keith Hernandez/50	35.00
7	Johnny Bench, Tony Perez, Joe Morgan, George Foster/25	80.00
8	Derek Jeter, Jorge Posada, Bernie Williams, Andy Pettitte/50	
10	Willie Stargell, Dave Parker, Bill Madlock/25	30.00
11	Bob Gibson, Lou Brock, Ken Boyer/25	35.00
12	Rickey Henderson, Paul Molitor, Joe Carter, Roberto Alomar/25	60.00

Generations
NM/M
Common Duo: 1.50
Production 1,500 Sets
Spectrum: 2-3X
Production 100 Sets

#	Players	Price
1	George Brett, Albert Pujols	5.00
2	Wade Boggs, Aubrey Huff	
3	Jim "Catfish" Hunter, Tim Hudson	2.00
4	Steve Garvey, Shawn Green	1.50
5	Tony Gwynn, Garret Anderson	4.00
6	Fergie Jenkins, Mark Prior	2.00
7	Robin Yount, Rickie Weeks	4.00
8	Warren Spahn, Greg Maddux	4.00
9	Brooks Robinson, Cal Ripken Jr., Miguel Tejada	8.00
10	Bobby Doerr, Carl Yastrzemski, Manny Ramirez	5.00
11	Al Kaline, Alan Trammell, Ivan Rodriguez	2.50
12	Tom Seaver, Dwight Gooden, Tom Glavine	3.00
13	Stan Musial, Lou Brock, Jim Edmonds	4.00
14	George Foster, Dave Parker, Austin Kearns	1.50
15	Ed Mathews, Dale Murphy, Chipper Jones	3.00
16	Don Sutton, Nolan Ryan, Roger Clemens	8.00
17	Bernie Williams, Andre Dawson, Sammy Sosa	4.00
18	Whitey Ford, Tommy John, Andy Pettitte	2.00
19	Carlton Fisk, Roger Clemens, Nomar Garciaparra	4.00
20	Shawn Marion, Ozzie Smith, Edgar Renteria	4.00
21	Reggie Jackson, Rickey Henderson, Eric Chavez	2.00
22	Babe Ruth, Don Mattingly, Derek Jeter	8.00
23	Roberto Clemente Jr., Reggie Jackson, Sammy Sosa	6.00
24	Bob Feller, Tom Seaver, Roger Clemens	5.00
25	Ernie Banks, Cal Ripken Jr., Alex Rodriguez	8.00
26	Pee Wee Reese, Ozzie Smith, Derek Jeter	6.00
27	Harmon Killebrew, Mike Schmidt, Alex Rodriguez	5.00
28	Bob Gibson, Dwight Gooden, Josh Beckett	2.00

Generations Material
NM/M
Quantity produced listed.
Prime: No Pricing
Production Five Sets

#	Players	Price
1	George Brett, Albert Pujols/25	40.00
2	Wade Boggs, Aubrey Huff/50	10.00
3	Jim "Catfish" Hunter, Tim Hudson/25	20.00
5	Tony Gwynn, Garret Anderson/50	20.00
6	Fergie Jenkins, Mark Prior/25	15.00
7	Robin Yount, Rickie Weeks Bat/50	20.00
8	Warren Spahn, Greg Maddux/50	40.00
11	Al Kaline, Alan Trammell, Ivan Rodriguez Bat/25	40.00
14	George Foster, Dave Parker, Austin Kearns/25	20.00
16	Don Sutton, Nolan Ryan, Roger Clemens Bat/50	50.00
17	Billy Williams, Andre Dawson, Sammy Sosa/50	30.00
18	Whitey Ford, Tommy John, Andy Pettitte/25	40.00
19	Carlton Fisk, Roger Clemens, Nomar Garciaparra	
20	Marty Marion, Ozzie Smith, Edgar Renteria/25	40.00

21 Reggie Jackson, Rickey Henderson, Eric Chavez/50 30.00
24 Bob Feller, Tom Seaver, Roger Clemens/25 40.00
25 Ernie Banks, Cal Ripken Jr., Alex Rodriguez 65.00
26 Pee Wee Reese, Ozzie Smith, Derek Jeter/25 50.00
27 Harmon Killebrew, Mike Schmidt, Alex Rodriguez.Bat/25 50.00
28 Bob Gibson, Dwight Gooden, Josh Beckett/25 30.00

Material

NM/M
Common Player: 4.00
2 Darin Erstad/Jsy/100 .
4 Garret Anderson/Jsy/100 6.00
5 Tim Salmon/Jsy/100 6.00
6 Troy Glaus/Jsy/100 6.00
7 Vladimir Guerrero/Bat/100 10.00
8 Brandon Webb/Pants/100 4.00
9 Luis Gonzalez/Jsy/100 4.00
10 Randy Johnson/Jsy/100 10.00
11 Richie Sexson/Bat/50 8.00
12 Roberto Alomar/Bat/100 8.00
14 Steve Finley/Jsy/100 4.00
15 Adam LaRoche/Bat/100 4.00
16 Andruw Jones/Jsy/100 8.00
17 Chipper Jones/Jsy/100 8.00
19 J.D. Drew/Bat/100 4.00
19 John Smoltz/Jsy/100 8.00
20 Rafael Furcal/Jsy/100 4.00
22 Javy Lopez/Bat/100 6.00
23 Jay Gibbons/Jsy/100 4.00
24 Larry Bigbie/Jsy/100 4.00
25 Luis Matos/Jsy/100 4.00
26 Melvin Mora/Jsy/100 4.00
27 Miguel Tejada/Bat/100 6.00
28 Rafael Palmeiro/Jsy/100 8.00
29 Curt Schilling/Bat/100 4.00
30 David Ortiz/Bat/100 10.00
32 Jason Varitek/Bat/100 8.00
33 Johnny Damon/Bat/100 4.00
34 Manny Ramirez/Jsy/100 8.00
35 Nomar Garciaparra/Jsy/100 8.00
36 Pedro J. Martinez/Jsy/100 8.00
37 Trot Nixon/Bat/100 4.00
38 Aramis Ramirez/Jsy/100 6.00
39 Corey Patterson/Pants/100 6.00
41 Greg Maddux/Bat/100 10.00
42 Kerry Wood/Pants/100 4.00
43 Mark Prior/Jsy/100 6.00
44 Sammy Sosa/Jsy/100 12.00
45 Carlos Lee/Jsy/100 4.00
47 Frank Thomas/Pants/100 8.00
48 Joe Borchard/Jsy/100 4.00
49 Magglio Ordonez/Jsy/100 4.00
50 Mark Buehrle/Jsy/100 4.00
51 Paul Konerko/Jsy/100 4.00
52 Adam Dunn/Jsy/100 8.00
53 Austin Kearns/Jsy/100 6.00
54 Barry Larkin/Jsy/100 4.00
55 Brandon Larson/Fld Glv/100 4.00
58 Sean Casey/Jsy/100 4.00
59 C.C. Sabathia/Jsy/100 4.00
60 Jody Gerut/Jsy/100 4.00
61 Omar Vizquel/Jsy/100 4.00
62 Travis Hafner/Bat/100 6.00
63 Victor Martinez/Bat/100 6.00
64 Charles Johnson/Bat/100 4.00
65 Garrett Atkins/Jsy/100 4.00
66 Jason Jennings/Jsy/100 4.00
67 Joe Kennedy/Bat/100 4.00
69 Larry Walker/Jsy/100 6.00
69 Preston Wilson/Jsy/100 4.00
70 Todd Helton/Jsy/100 8.00
71 Ivan Rodriguez/Bat/100 8.00
72 Jeremy Bonderman/Jsy/100 4.00
73 A.J. Burnett/Jsy/100 4.00
74 Brad Penny/Jsy/100 4.00
75 Dontrelle Willis/Jsy/100 4.00
76 Josh Beckett/Jsy/100 6.00
77 Juan Pierre/Bat/100 4.00
78 Luis Castillo/Jsy/100 4.00
79 Miguel Cabrera/Jsy/100 8.00
80 Mike Lowell/Jsy/50 8.00
81 Andy Pettitte/Bat/100 6.00
82 Craig Biggio/Jsy/100 6.00
83 Jeff Bagwell/Jsy/100 8.00
84 Jeff Kent/Jsy/100 4.00
85 Lance Berkman/Jsy/100 4.00
86 Morgan Ensberg/Jsy/100 4.00
87 Richard Hidalgo/Pants/100 4.00
88 Roger Clemens/Bat/50 15.00
89 Roy Oswalt/Jsy/100 4.00
90 Wade Miller/Jsy/100 4.00
91 Angel Berroa/Pants/100 4.00
92 Carlos Beltran/Jsy/100 8.00
93 Juan Gonzalez/Bat/100 8.00
94 Ken Harvey/Bat/100 4.00
95 Mike Sweeney/Jsy/100 4.00
96 Runelvys Hernandez/Jsy/100 4.00
97 Adrian Beltre/Jsy/100 6.00
98 Edwin Jackson/Jsy/100 6.00
100 Hideo Nomo/Jsy/100 8.00
101 Hong-Chih Kuo/Bat/100 4.00
102 Kazuhisa Ishii/Jsy/100 4.00
103 Paul LoDuca/Jsy/100 4.00
104 Shawn Green/Jsy/100 6.00
105 Ben Sheets/Jsy/100 6.00
106 Geoff Jenkins/Jsy/100 4.00
107 Junior Spivey/Bat/100 4.00
108 Rickie Weeks/Bat/50 4.00
111 Doug Mientkiewicz/Bat/100 4.00
112 Jacque Jones/Jsy/100 4.00
113 Joe Mays/Jsy/100 4.00
114 Johan Santana/Jsy/100 8.00
115 Shannon Stewart/Jsy/100 4.00
116 Torii Hunter/Jsy/100 6.00
117 Brad Wilkerson/Bat/100 4.00
118 Carl Everett/Bat/100 4.00
120 Jose Vidro/Jsy/100 4.00
121 Nick Johnson/Bat/100 4.00
122 Orlando Cabrera/Jsy/100 4.00
123 Al Leiter/Jsy/100 4.00
124 Cliff Floyd/Bat/100 4.00
125 Jae Weong Seo/Jsy/100 4.00
126 Jose Reyes/Jsy/100 8.00
128 Mike Piazza/Jsy/100 10.00
129 Tom Glavine/Jsy/100 8.00
130 Alex Rodriguez/Bat/100 10.00
131 Bernie Williams/Jsy/100 6.00
133 Derek Jeter/Jsy/100 20.00
134 Gary Sheffield/Bat/100 6.00
135 Hideki Matsui/Jsy/100 20.00
136 Jason Giambi/Jsy/100 6.00
138 Jorge Posada/Jsy/100 6.00
141 Mariano Rivera/Jsy/50 15.00
142 Mike Mussina/Jsy/100 6.00
143 Barry Zito/Jsy/100 4.00
145 Eric Chavez/Jsy/100 4.00
146 Erubiel Durazo/Bat/100 4.00
147 Jermaine Dye/Bat/100 4.00
149 Mark Mulder/Jsy/100 6.00
150 Rich Harden/Jsy/100 4.00
151 Tim Hudson/Jsy/100 6.00
153 Bobby Abreu/Jsy/100 6.00
154 Brett Myers/Jsy/100 4.00
155 Jim Thome/Jsy/100 8.00
157 Kevin Millwood/Jsy/100 4.00
158 Marlon Byrd/Jsy/100 4.00
159 Pat Burrell/Jsy/100 6.00
161 Jason Kendall/Jsy/100 4.00
162 Brian Giles/Bat/100 4.00
164 Ryan Klesko/Bat/100 4.00
165 Edgardo Alfonzo/Bat/100 4.00
167 Jerome Williams/Jsy/100 4.00
169 Bret Boone/Jsy/29 4.00
170 Edgar Martinez/Jsy/100 8.00
171 Freddy Garcia/Jsy/100 4.00
173 Jamie Moyer/Jsy/100 4.00
174 John Olerud/Jsy/100 4.00
176 Albert Pujols/Jsy/100 20.00
177 Dan Haren/Jsy/100 4.00
178 Edgar Renteria/Jsy/100 6.00
179 Jim Edmonds/Jsy/100 6.00
180 Matt Morris/Jsy/100 4.00
181 Scott Rolen/Jsy/100 8.00
182 Aubrey Huff/Jsy/100 4.00
183 Carl Crawford/Jsy/100 4.00
184 Chad Gaudin/Jsy/100 4.00
185 Delmon Young/Bat/100 6.00
186 Dewon Brazelton/Jsy/100 4.00
187 Fred McGriff/Jsy/100 6.00
188 Rocco Baldelli/Jsy/100 4.00
189 Alfonso Soriano/Bat/100 8.00
190 Hank Blalock/Jsy/100 6.00
191 Laynce Nix/Bat/100 4.00
192 Mark Teixeira/Jsy/23 15.00
193 Michael Young/Bat/100 6.00
194 Carlos Delgado/Jsy/100 6.00
195 Eric Hinske/Jsy/100 4.00
196 Frank Catalanotto/Jsy/100 4.00
197 Josh Phelps/Jsy/100 4.00
198 Orlando Hudson/Jsy/100 4.00
199 Roy Halladay/Jsy/100 4.00
200 Vernon Wells/Jsy/100 4.00
201 Dale Murphy/Jsy/100 12.00
202 Cal Ripken Jr./Jsy/100 30.00
203 Fred Lynn/Bat/100 8.00
204 Wade Boggs/Jsy/100 8.00
205 Nolan Ryan/Jkt/100 25.00
206 Rod Carew/Bat/100 8.00
207 Andre Dawson/Pants/100 6.00
208 Ernie Banks/Pants/50 20.00
209 Ryne Sandberg/Jsy/50 12.00
210 Bo Jackson/Jsy/100 12.00
211 Carlton Fisk/Jsy/100 8.00
212 Dave Concepcion/Jsy/100 8.00
213 Alan Trammell/Bat/100 8.00
214 George Brett/Jsy/100 15.00
215 Robin Yount/Jsy/100 15.00
216 Gary Carter/Jsy/100 8.00
217 Darryl Strawberry/Pants/100 4.00
218 Dwight Gooden/Jsy/50 8.00
219 Babe Ruth/Jsy/25 400.00
220 Don Mattingly/Jkt/100 15.00
221 Reggie Jackson/Jkt/100 10.00
222 Mike Schmidt/Jkt/100 15.00
223 Tony Gwynn/Jsy/100 10.00
224 Keith Hernandez/Jsy/100 8.00

Player Threads

NM/M
Common Player: 4.00
Production 250 Sets
Prime: 2-3X
Production 10-25
No pricing 15 or less.
1 Aaron Boone 4.00
2 Alex Rodriguez/M's-Rgr 15.00
3 Andres Galarraga/Braves-Giants-Rgr 10.00
4 Aramis Ramirez 4.00
5 Bartolo Colon 4.00
6 Ben Grieve/A's-D'Rays 4.00
7 Brad Fullmer 4.00
8 Bret Boone/Braves-M's 4.00
9 Brian Giles 4.00
10 Brian Jordan 4.00
11 Byung-Hyun Kim 4.00
12 Casey Fossum 4.00
13 Cesar Izturis 4.00
14 Chan Ho Park 4.00
15 Charles Johnson 4.00
16 Cliff Floyd 4.00
17 Darryl Strawberry/Dgr-Met-Ynk 10.00
18 David Ortiz 10.00
19 David Wells/Jays-Yanks 4.00
20 Derrek Lee 6.00
21 Dmitri Young 4.00
22 Edgardo Alfonzo 4.00
23 Ellis Burks 4.00
24 Gary Sheffield/Braves-Brew-Dgr 8.00
25 Hee Seop Choi 4.00
26 Ivan Rodriguez/Marlins-Rgr 10.00
27 J.D. Drew 6.00
28 Javier Vazquez 4.00
29 Jay Payton 4.00
30 Jeff Kent/Astros-Giants-Jays 4.00
31 Jeromy Burnitz 4.00
32 Jim Thome/Indians-Phils 10.00
33 Joe Kennedy 4.00
34 Joe Torre 8.00
35 Jose Cruz Jr. 4.00
36 Juan Encarnacion 4.00
37 Juan Gonzalez/Indians-Rgr 4.00
38 Juan Pierre 4.00
39 Junior Spivey 4.00
40 Kenny Lofton/Brave-Tribe 8.00
41 Kevin Millwood 6.00
42 Manny Ramirez/Indians-Sox 12.00
43 Mark Grace/Cubs-D'backs 10.00
44 Mike Hampton 4.00
45 Mike Piazza/Dgr-Marlins-Mets 20.00
46 Milton Bradley 4.00
47 Moises Alou 4.00
48 Nick Johnson 4.00
49 Nolan Ryan/Ang/Jkt-Ast/Jkt-Rgr 50.00
50 Preston Wilson/Marlins-Rockies 6.00
51 Rafael Palmeiro/O's-Rgr 10.00
52 Ray Durham 4.00
53 Reggie Jackson/A's-Ang-Yank 15.00
54 Reggie Sanders 4.00
55 Rich Aurilia 4.00
56 Richie Sexson 4.00
57 Rickey Henderson/A's-M's-Yanks 50.00
58 Rickey Henderson/Dgr-Mets-Padres 20.00
59 Robert Fick 4.00
60 Roberto Alomar/Mets-Sox 8.00
61 Roberto Alomar/Indians-O's 8.00
62 Robin Ventura/Mets-Sox-Yanks 10.00
63 Rondell White/Cubs-Expos 6.00
64 Ryan Klesko/Braves-Padres 6.00
65 Sean Casey 6.00
66 Shannon Stewart/Jays-Twins 6.00
67 Shawn Green/Jays-Dgr 8.00
68 Shea Hillenbrand 4.00
69 Steve Carlton/Giants-Sox 8.00
70 Terrence Long 4.00
71 Tony Batista 4.00
72 Travis Hafner/Indians-Rgr 6.00
73 Travis Lee 4.00
74 Vladimir Guerrero 8.00
75 Wes Helms 4.00

Player Threads Signature

NM/M
Quantity produced listed.
4 Aramis Ramirez/25 30.00
17 Darryl Strawberry/Dgr-Met-Ynk/25 40.00
24 Gary Sheffield/Brave-Brw-Dgr/25 40.00
28 Javier Vazquez/25 20.00
29 Jay Payton/25 15.00
37 Juan Gonzalez/Indians-Rgr/25 20.00
39 Junior Spivey/25 15.00
50 Preston Wilson/25 25.00
55 Rich Aurilia/25 15.00
62 Robin Ventura/Mets-Sox-Yanks/25 40.00
68 Shea Hillenbrand/25 20.00
74 Vladimir Guerrero/25 60.00

Signature Marks

NM/M
Common Autograph: 8.00
4 Garret Anderson/25 25.00
8 Brandon Webb/50 15.00
13 Shea Hillenbrand/50 15.00
15 Adam LaRoche/50 15.00
20 Rafael Furcal/25 25.00
23 Jay Gibbons/50 15.00
24 Larry Bigbie/50 20.00
25 Luis Matos/50 10.00
26 Melvin Mora/50 15.00
30 David Ortiz/25 40.00
37 Trot Nixon/25 30.00
40 Derrek Lee/25 30.00
43 Mark Prior/25 30.00
45 Carlos Lee/50 10.00
46 Esteban Loaiza/50 12.00
48 Joe Borchard/50 10.00
50 Mark Buehrle/25 25.00
53 Austin Kearns/50 15.00
55 Brandon Larson/25 15.00
60 Jody Gerut/50 20.00
62 Travis Hafner/50 20.00
63 Victor Martinez/50 15.00
69 Preston Wilson/50 15.00
74 Brad Penny/50 10.00
79 Miguel Cabrera/25 40.00
80 Mike Lowell/25 20.00
86 Morgan Ensberg/25 6.00
89 Roy Oswalt/25 25.00
91 Angel Berroa/25 12.00
92 Carlos Beltran/25 35.00
98 Edwin Jackson/50 15.00
101 Hong-Chih Kuo/50 15.00
109 Scott Podsednik/50 15.00
112 Jacque Jones/50 15.00
114 Johan Santana/50 50.00
115 Shannon Stewart/50 15.00
116 Torii Hunter/25 15.00
119 Chad Cordero/50 8.00
120 Jose Vidro/50 15.00
122 Orlando Cabrera/50 15.00
132 Chien-Ming Wang/25 100.00
147 Jermaine Dye/50 15.00
160 Jason Bay/50 20.00
163 Jay Payton/50 15.00
168 Todd Linden/50 15.00
175 Shigetoshi Hasegawa/25 50.00
177 Dan Haren/50 15.00
181 Scott Rolen/25 50.00
182 Aubrey Huff/50 15.00
184 Chad Gaudin/50 10.00
186 Dewon Brazelton/50 10.00
187 Fred McGriff/25 40.00
189 Alfonso Soriano/50 50.00
193 Michael Young/50 20.00
203 Fred Lynn/50 15.00
207 Andre Dawson/50 20.00
216 Gary Carter/25 25.00
217 Darryl Strawberry/50 20.00
218 Dwight Gooden/50 15.00
225 Keith Hernandez/50 20.00
225 Hector Gimenez/100 8.00
226 Graham Koonce/100 8.00
228 Jerry Gil/100 8.00
229 Jason Frasor/100 8.00
230 Justin Knoedler/50 10.00
233 Ronald Belisario/200 8.00
234 Jerome Gamble/200 8.00
235 Roberto Novoa/200 8.00
236 Sean Henn/200 10.00
237 Willy Taveras/100 8.00
238 Ramon Ramirez/200 10.00
241 Jason Bartlett/25 20.00
242 Fernando Nieve/25 12.00
243 Freddy Guzman/25 20.00
248 William Bergolla/100 10.00
249 Shawn Hill/100 8.00
250 Justin Germano/100 8.00

2004 Donruss Timeless Treasures

NM/M
Complete Set (100): 200.00
Common Player: 1.50
Production 999 Sets
Tin (4): 125.00
1 Albert Pujols 6.00
2 Garret Anderson 2.00
3 Randy Johnson 3.00
4 Alex Rodriguez/Yanks 8.00
5 Manny Ramirez 3.00
7 Mark Prior 4.00
7 Roberto Alomar 2.00
8 Barry Larkin 2.00
9 Todd Helton 2.50
10 Ivan Rodriguez 3.00
11 Jacque Jones 1.50
12 Jeff Kent 2.00
13 Mike Sweeney 1.50
14 Shawn Green 2.00
15 Richie Sexson 2.00
16 Mike Piazza 5.00
17 Vladimir Guerrero 4.00
18 Mike Mussina 2.00
19 Barry Zito 2.00
20 Don Mattingly 6.00
21 Ichiro Suzuki 5.00
22 Rocco Baldelli 2.00
23 Rafael Palmeiro 3.00
24 Carlos Delgado 2.00
25 Roger Clemens 6.00
26 Luis Gonzalez 2.00
27 Gary Sheffield 2.00
28 Jay Gibbons 1.50
29 Nomar Garciaparra 5.00
30 Aramis Ramirez 2.00
31 Frank Thomas 3.00
32 Ryan Wagner 1.50
33 Preston Wilson 1.50
34 Hideki Matsui 4.00
35 Roy Oswalt 2.00
36 Angel Berroa 1.50
37 Kazuhisa Ishii 1.50
38 Scott Podsednik 2.00
39 Torii Hunter 2.00
40 Tom Glavine 2.00
41 Jason Giambi 3.00
42 Eric Chavez 2.00
43 Jim Thome 3.00
44 Tony Gwynn 3.00
45 Edgar Martinez 2.00
46 Jim Edmonds 2.00
47 Delmon Young 2.00
48 Hank Blalock 2.00
49 Vernon Wells 1.50
50 Curt Schilling 2.50
51 Chipper Jones 3.00
52 Cal Ripken Jr. 5.00
53 Jason Varitek 1.50
54 Kerry Wood 3.00
55 Magglio Ordonez 2.00
56 Adam Dunn 2.00
57 Jay Payton 1.50
58 Josh Beckett 2.00
59 Jeff Bagwell 3.00
60 Carlos Beltran 2.00
61 Hideo Nomo 2.00
62 Rickie Weeks 2.00
63 Alfonso Soriano 2.50
64 Miguel Tejada 2.00
65 Bret Boone 2.00
66 Scott Rolen 2.00
67 Aubrey Huff 1.50
68 Juan Gonzalez 2.50
69 Roy Halladay 2.50
70 Brandon Webb 1.50
71 Andruw Jones 2.50
72 Pedro J. Martinez 3.00
73 Carlos Lee 2.00
74 Lance Berkman 2.00
75 Paul LoDuca 1.50
76 Jorge Posada 2.00
77 Tim Hudson 2.00
78 Stan Musial 5.00
79 Mark Teixeira 2.00
80 Trot Nixon 1.50
81 Fred McGriff 1.50
82 Nick Johnson 1.50
83 Nolan Ryan 8.00
84 Ken Griffey Jr. 4.00
85 Mariano Rivera 2.00
86 Mark Mulder 2.00
87 Bob Gibson 2.50
88 Dale Murphy UER 2.50
89 Bernie Williams 2.00
90 Carl Yastrzemski 2.00
91 Sammy Sosa 5.00
92 Miguel Cabrera 4.00
93 Craig Biggio 2.00
94 George Brett 6.00
95 Rickey Henderson 3.00
96 Derek Jeter 8.00
97 Greg Maddux 4.00
98 Bob Abreu 2.00
99 Troy Glaus 2.00
100 Dontrelle Willis 2.00

Bronze
Bronze: 1-2X
Production 100 Sets

Silver
Silver: 2-4X
Production 25 Sets

Gold
Gold: No Pricing
Production 10 Sets

Platinum
Platinum: No Pricing
Production One Set

Award Materials

NM/M
Common Player: 10.00
Quantity produced listed.
Prime: 1-2X
Production 1-25
No pricing 10 or less.
Number: .75-1.5X
Production 3-51
No pricing 15 or less.
2 Stan Musial/Jsy/43 25.00
3 Lou Boudreau/Jsy/19 15.00
4 Roger Maris/Pants/61 40.00
5 Roger Maris/Jsy/61 40.00
6 Roberto Clemente/Bat/66 60.00
7 Bob Gibson 68 CY/Jsy/68
8 Bob Gibson 68 MVP/Jsy/68 20.00
9 Tom Seaver/Jsy/19 20.00
10 Fred Lynn/Jsy/75 8.00
11 Jim Rice/Jsy/78 10.00
12 Mike Schmidt 80 MVP/Jsy/80 15.00
13 Mike Schmidt 80 MVP/Pants/80 15.00
14 Mike Schmidt 80 MVP/Stir/80 15.00
15 Mike Schmidt 81 MVP/Jsy/81 15.00
16 Mike Schmidt 81 MVP/Bat/81 15.00
17 Dale Murphy/Jsy/82 15.00
18 Mike Schmidt 86 MVP/Hat/19 35.00
19 Mike Schmidt 86 MVP/Shoe/19
20 Mike Schmidt 86 MVP/Bat/86 15.00
21 Mike Schmidt 86 MVP/Stir/19 35.00
22 Jose Canseco/Jsy/88 10.00
23 Frank Thomas 93 MVP/Bat/93 10.00
24 Frank Thomas 93 MVP/Jsy/93
25 Jeff Bagwell/Pants/94 10.00
26 Frank Thomas 94 MVP/Jsy/94 10.00
27 Frank Thomas 94 MVP/Pants/94 10.00
28 Jeff Bagwell/Bat/94 10.00
29 Pedro J. Martinez 97/CY Jsy/97 10.00
30 Ivan Rodriguez/Bat/99 10.00
31 Randy Johnson 00 CY/Jsy/25 20.00
32 Pedro J. Martinez 00 CY/Jsy/25 20.00
33 Roger Clemens/Jsy/50 20.00
34 Randy Johnson 02 CY/Jsy/25 20.00
35 Miguel Tejada/Jsy/25 15.00

Award Materials Combos

NM/M
Prime: .75-1.5X
Production 19 Sets
4 Roger Maris/Bat-Pants/25 70.00
12 Mike Schmidt/80M/Jsy-Pants/25 40.00
13 Mike Schmidt 80M/Pant-Stir/25 30.00
14 Mike Schmidt 80M/Jsy-Stir/25 30.00
15 Mike Schmidt 81M/Bat-Jsy/25 40.00
16 Mike Schmidt 81M/Bat-Stir/50 30.00

18	Mike Schmidt 86M/ Hat-Shoe/50	30.00
19	Mike Schmidt 86M/ Hat-Bat/50	30.00
20	Mike Schmidt 86M/ Hat-Stir/50	30.00
21	Mike Schmidt 86M/ Bat-Shoe/50	30.00
23	Frank Thomas 93M/ Bat-Jsy/25	25.00
25	Jeff Bagwell/Bat-Jsy/25	25.00
32	Frank Thomas 94M/ Bat-Jsy/25	25.00
35	Miguel Tejada/ Bat-Jsy/25	15.00

Award Mat. Combo Prime
Production 19 Sets

Award Mater. Combo Sig.
No Pricing
Production Five Sets
Prime: No Pricing
Production One Set

Award Materials Number
Production 3-45

Award Mat. Sig. Number
No Pricing

Award Materials Prime
Production 1-25

Award Mat. Sig. Prime
No Pricing

Award Materials Sig.
NM/M
Common Autograph:
Quantity produced listed.
Number: 1-2X
Production 1-19
No pricing 10 or less.

7	Bob Gibson 68 CY/ Jsy/19	50.00
8	Bob Gibson 68 MVP/ Jsy/19	50.00
10	Fred Lynn Jsy/75	15.00
11	Jim Rice Jsy/78	30.00

Game Day Materials
NM/M
Quantity produced listed.

1	Nellie Fox/Bat/58	
2	Frank Robinson/Bat/61	10.00
3	George Brett/Bat/77	20.00
4	George Brett/Hat/82	30.00
5	Nolan Ryan/Hat/19	80.00
6	Cal Ripken Jr./Hat/85	50.00
7	Rod Carew/Hat/19	25.00
8	Ryne Sandberg/Bat/91	15.00
9	Kirby Puckett/Bat/92	15.00
10	Frank Thomas/Bat/93	10.00
12	Tony Gwynn/Pants/99	20.00
13	Vladimir Guerrero/ Bat/99	15.00
14	Tony Gwynn Hat/99	20.00
15	Magglio Ordonez/ Hat/15	15.00
16	Rickey Henderson/ Bat/50	10.00

Game Day Material Sig.
NM/M
Many not priced due to scarcity.

2	Frank Robinson/Bat	40.00
15	Magglio Ordonez/ Hat/25	30.00

HOF Materials Barrel
Production One Set

HOF Materials Bat
NM/M

1	Al Kaline/25	25.00
2	Babe Ruth/50	200.00
5	Bobby Doerr/25	10.00
6	Brooks Robinson/25	30.00
7	Carl Yastrzemski/25	30.00
8	Carlton Fisk/25	20.00
9	Dave Winfield/25	15.00
10	Eddie Murray/25	25.00
11	Ernie Banks/25	30.00
16	Frank Robinson/25	15.00
18	Joe Morgan/25	15.00
19	Johnny Bench/25	30.00
21	Kirby Puckett/25	30.00
22	Lou Brock/25	20.00
23	Lou Gehrig/50	125.00
24	Luis Aparicio/25	10.00
26	Mel Ott/25	40.00
27	Orlando Cepeda/25	15.00
28	Pee Wee Reese/25	15.00
29	Phil Rizzuto/25	15.00
30	Red Schoendienst/25	10.00
31	Roberto Clemente/25	65.00
32	Roy Campanella/25	25.00
33	Paul Molitor/25	20.00
34	Ty Cobb/25	100.00
35	Willie McCovey/25	15.00
36	Willie Stargell/25	15.00

HOF Materials Bat Sig.
NM/M

1	Al Kaline/50	40.00
2	Bobby Doerr/50	35.00
5	Brooks Robinson/50	40.00
11	Ernie Banks/25	75.00
17	Frank Robinson/50	35.00
18	Joe Morgan/25	40.00
19	Johnny Bench/50	60.00
22	Lou Brock/50	30.00
24	Luis Aparicio/50	30.00
26	Orlando Cepeda/50	25.00
28	Phil Rizzuto/50	35.00
29	Red Schoendienst/25	25.00
32	Paul Molitor/25	50.00

HOF Mat. Combo Bat-Jsy
NM/M
Quantity produced listed.
Prime: No Pricing
Production 1-5

1	Al Kaline/25	40.00
2	Babe Ruth/25	500.00
4	Bobby Doerr/25	15.00
5	Brooks Robinson/25	15.00
6	Carl Yastrzemski/50	40.00
7	Carlton Fisk/50	20.00
9	Dave Winfield/50	15.00
10	Eddie Murray/50	35.00
17	Frank Robinson/50	20.00
18	Joe Morgan/50	15.00
21	Kirby Puckett/50	30.00
22	Lou Brock/50	15.00
23	Lou Gehrig/25	220.00
24	Luis Aparicio/25	20.00
26	Mel Ott/25	60.00
27	Pee Wee Reese/50	20.00
28	Phil Rizzuto/50	40.00
29	Red Schoendienst/50	15.00
31	Roberto Clemente/50	80.00
32	Paul Molitor/50	30.00
34	Warren Spahn/25	65.00

HOF Mat. Combo Bat-Jsy Sig
NM/M
Quantity produced listed.
Prime: No Pricing
Production 1-5

4	Bobby Doerr/25	30.00
5	Brooks Robinson/25	80.00
11	Ernie Banks/25	80.00
13	Frank Robinson/25	65.00
18	Joe Morgan/25	40.00
22	Lou Brock/25	40.00
24	Luis Aparicio/25	30.00
29	Red Schoendienst/25	40.00
32	Paul Molitor/25	40.00

Mat. Bat-Jsy Sig. Prime
No Pricing

HOF Mat. Combo Bat-Pant
NM/M
Production 25 Sets

1	Al Kaline/25	35.00
2	Babe Ruth/25	350.00
12	Fergie Jenkins/ Fld Glv-Pants/25	15.00
23	Lou Gehrig/25	200.00
24	Luis Aparicio/25	15.00
25	Mel Ott/25	60.00
31	Roy Campanella/25	40.00
33	Ty Cobb/25	200.00

HOF Mat Combo Bat-Pant Sig
NM/M
Production 25 Sets

1	Al Kaline/25	75.00
12	Fergie Jenkins/ Fld Glv-Pants/25	35.00
24	Luis Aparicio/25	25.00

HOF Mat. Combo Jsy-Pant
NM/M

2	Babe Ruth/25	500.00
23	Lou Gehrig/25	220.00
24	Luis Aparicio/25	15.00

Mat. Combo Jsy-Pant Sig.
NM/M
Prime: No Pricing
Production 1-5

24	Luis Aparicio/25	25.00

Mat. Combo Jsy-Pant Prime
No Pricing

HOF Materials Jersey
NM/M
Quantity produced listed.
Prime: No Pricing
Production 1-10
Jersey Number: .75-1.5X
Production 1-44
No pricing 15 or less.

2	Babe Ruth/25	500.00
4	Bob Feller/10	10.00
5	Bobby Doerr/25	15.00
6	Brooks Robinson/50	15.00
7	Carl Yastrzemski/25	25.00
8	Carlton Fisk/50	15.00
9	Dave Winfield/50	25.00
10	Eddie Murray/25	15.00
13	Frank Robinson/25	15.00
14	Hal Newhouser/50	10.00
16	Hoyt Wilhelm/50	10.00
17	Jim Palmer/50	10.00
18	Joe Morgan/50	10.00
20	Juan Marichal/50	10.00
21	Kirby Puckett/50	20.00
22	Lou Brock/25	15.00
23	Lou Gehrig/25	140.00
25	Luis Aparicio/25	10.00
26	Mel Ott/25	20.00
27	Pee Wee Reese/50	15.00
28	Phil Rizzuto/50	15.00
30	Red Schoendienst/25	15.00
30	Roberto Clemente/50	60.00
32	Paul Molitor/50	15.00
34	Warren Spahn/50	20.00
35	Willie McCovey/50	15.00
36	Willie Stargell/50	15.00

HOF Materials Jsy Sig.
NM/M
Quantity produced listed.
Prime: No Pricing
Production 1-10
Number: 1X
Production 10-25

1	Al Kaline/25	50.00
4	Bobby Doerr/50	30.00
5	Brooks Robinson/50	30.00
13	Frank Robinson/50	35.00
15	Hoyt Wilhelm/50	25.00
17	Jim Palmer/50	30.00
18	Joe Morgan/50	25.00
20	Juan Marichal/50	35.00
22	Lou Brock/50	30.00
24	Luis Aparicio/50	20.00
26	Orlando Cepeda/25	25.00
28	Phil Rizzuto/50	40.00
32	Red Schoendienst/50	15.00
32	Paul Molitor/50	30.00
34	Warren Spahn/25	65.00

HOF Material Jsy Number
NM/M

16	Jackie Robinson/42	50.00

HOF Materials Jsy Prime
No Pricing

HOF Materials Pants
NM/M

1	Al Kaline/25	30.00
2	Babe Ruth/50	200.00
12	Fergie Jenkins/50	15.00
23	Lou Gehrig/50	125.00
24	Luis Aparicio/25	15.00
25	Mel Ott/25	40.00
31	Roy Campanella/25	30.00
33	Ty Cobb/25	125.00

HOF Mat. Pants Sig.
NM/M
Production 25 Sets

1	Al Kaline	50.00
12	Fergie Jenkins	30.00
24	Luis Aparicio	25.00
28	Phil Rizzuto	40.00

HOF Materials Sig.
NM/M
Quantity produced listed.
Prime: No Pricing
Production 1-10

1	Al Kaline/25	50.00
3	Bob Feller/25	50.00
5	Brooks Robinson/25	50.00
7	Carlton Fisk/27	50.00
9	Duke Snider/25	40.00
11	Ernie Banks/25	60.00
12	Fergie Jenkins/31	40.00
13	Frank Robinson/20	40.00
15	Hoyt Wilhelm/25	25.00
17	Jim Palmer/22	30.00
20	Juan Marichal/27	30.00
21	Kirby Puckett/25	60.00
22	Lou Brock/20	40.00
26	Orlando Cepeda/30	30.00
28	Phil Rizzuto/25	40.00
29	Red Schoendienst/25	40.00
32	Paul Molitor/25	50.00
34	Warren Spahn/21	50.00
35	Willie McCovey/25	40.00

HOF Mat. Jsy Sig Number
NM/M
No Pricing

HOF Mat. Jsy Sig. Prime
NM/M

23	Lou Gehrig/1 (7/04 Auction)	4,950

Home Away Gamers
NM/M
Quantity produced listed.
Prime: No Pricing
Production 3-5

1	Babe Ruth/Jsy-Jsy/25	600.00
3	Wade Boggs/ Jsy-Jsy/50	15.00
4	Tony Gwynn/Jsy-Jsy/50	30.00
5	Steve Carlton/ Jsy-Jsy/50	15.00
7	Ryne Sandberg/ Jsy-Jsy/50	35.00
9	Rod Carew/Jsy-Jsy/50	15.00
9	Rickey Henderson/ Jsy-Jsy/50	25.00
11	Ted Williams/ Jsy/Jsy/100	85.00
12	Ozzie Smith/Jsy-Jsy/25	25.00
13	Mike Schmidt/ Jsy-Jsy/50	30.00
14	Harmon Killebrew/ Jsy-Jsy/100	30.00
15	George Brett/ Jsy-Jsy/100	30.00
12	Don Mattingly/ Jsy/50	35.00
17	Dale Murphy/ Jsy-Jsy/50	15.00
17	Cal Ripken Jr./ Jsy-Jsy/100	50.00
19	Lou Gehrig/Jsy-Jsy/50	200.00
20	Nolan Ryan/ Jsy-Jsy/100	40.00

Home Away Gamers Sig.
NM/M

5	Steve Carlton/ Jsy-Jsy/25	40.00
13	Mike Schmidt/ Jsy-Jsy/100	100.00
14	Harmon Killebrew/ Jsy-Jsy/20	90.00
16	Don Mattingly/ Jsy-Jsy/25	120.00
17	Dale Murphy/ Jsy-Jsy/25	70.00
19	Lou Gehrig/Jsy-Jsy/1 (5/04 Auction)	7,100

Home Away Gamers Prime
No Pricing

Home Away Gamers Combos
NM/M
Quantity produced listed.
Prime: No Pricing
Production 3-10

1	Babe Ruth/25	800.00
4	Wade Boggs/50	25.00
5	Tony Gwynn/50	40.00
7	Steve Carlton/25	25.00
8	Stan Musial/25	85.00
9	Ryne Sandberg/50	40.00
9	Rod Carew/50	25.00
9	Rickey Henderson/50	25.00
11	Ted Williams/100	150.00
12	Ozzie Smith/50	40.00
13	Mike Schmidt/50	50.00
14	Harmon Killebrew/25	50.00
15	George Brett/100	50.00
16	Don Mattingly/50	60.00
17	Dale Murphy/50	25.00
18	Cal Ripken Jr./100	65.00
19	Lou Gehrig/25	400.00
20	Nolan Ryan/50	65.00

Home Away Gamer Combo Sig.
NM/M
No Pricing
Production 1-5
Prime: No Pricing
Production One Set

Home Away Gamer Combo Prime
No Pricing

Home Run Materials
NM/M

1	Roger Maris/Bat/61	40.00
3	Harmon Killebrew HR 570/Bat/75	20.00
4	Harmon Killebrew HR 565/Bat/75	20.00
5	Jose Canseco/Bat/96	10.00
6	Alex Rodriguez/Bat/100	15.00
7	Sammy Sosa/Jsy/100	15.00
8	Rafael Palmeiro/Jsy/25	20.00
9	Ivan Rodriguez/Jsy/25	20.00

Home Run Material Sig.
No Pricing

Material Ink Bat
NM/M

1	Adam Dunn/25	40.00
2	Alan Trammell/25	35.00
4	Andre Dawson/25	35.00
5	Bo Jackson/25	60.00
7	Dale Murphy/25	40.00
10	Don Mattingly/25	65.00
12	Mark Prior/25	80.00
25	Paul O'Neill/25	40.00
26	Ron Santo/50	35.00
30	Ryne Sandberg/25	85.00
32	Tony Gwynn/25	80.00
34	Will Clark/25	45.00

Material Ink Combos
NM/M
Quantity produced listed
Prime: No Pricing
Production 1-10

1	Adam Dunn/Bat-Jsy/25	40.00
2	Alan Trammell/ Bat-Jsy/25	35.00
4	Andre Dawson/ Bat-Jsy/25	35.00
5	Bo Jackson/Bat-Jsy/25	60.00
7	Dale Murphy/Bat-Jsy/25	40.00
12	Don Mattingly/ Bat-Jsy/25	100.00
17	Jose Canseco/ Bat-Jsy/25	50.00
30	Ryne Sandberg/ Bat-Jsy/25	85.00
32	Tony Gwynn/Bat-Jsy/25	80.00
34	Will Clark/Bat-Jsy/25	45.00

Mat. Ink Combo Prime
No Pricing

Material Ink Jersey
NM/M
Quantity produced listed.
Number: .75-1X
Production 1-100
No pricing 15 or less.
Prime: .75-1.5X
Production 1-25
No pricing 15 or less.

1	Adam Dunn/25	40.00
2	Alan Trammell/100	20.00
4	Andre Dawson/100	25.00
5	Bo Jackson/25	60.00
7	Dale Murphy/50	35.00
8	Darryl Strawberry/100	20.00
9	Dave Parker/25	20.00
11	Doc Gooden/100	20.00
12	Don Mattingly/65	65.00
13	Dontrelle Willis/25	40.00
15	Ivan Rodriguez/25	50.00
16	Joe Carter/25	35.00
17	Jose Canseco/25	50.00
19	Mark Prior/60	60.00
21	Mark Teixeira/25	50.00
22	Marty Marion/25	25.00
26	Rocco Baldelli/25	40.00
30	Ryne Sandberg/50	75.00
31	Ernie Banks/50	75.00
33	Vladimir Guerrero/25	60.00
34	Will Clark/50	25.00

Material Ink Jsy Number
NM/M
Quantity produced listed.

1	Adam Dunn/25	40.00
2	Alan Trammell/100	20.00
4	Andre Dawson/100	20.00
5	Bo Jackson/25	75.00
7	Dale Murphy/50	30.00
8	Darryl Strawberry/100	20.00
9	Dave Parker/25	30.00
11	Doc Gooden/100	15.00
12	Don Mattingly/50	75.00
13	Dontrelle Willis/25	40.00
16	Joe Carter/25	30.00
19	Mark Grace/25	40.00
21	Mark Teixeira/25	40.00
22	Marty Marion/25	20.00
26	Rocco Baldelli/25	25.00
31	Ernie Banks/50	65.00
33	Vladimir Guerrero/25	50.00
34	Will Clark/25	25.00

Milestone Materials
NM/M
Quantity produced listed
Number: .75-1.5X
Production 9-36
Prime: 1-2X
Production 25 Sets

Milestone Material Sig.
NM/M

4	Gaylord Perry/Jsy/82	20.00

Milestone Mat. Number
No Pricing

Mile. Mat. Sig. Number
NM/M

4	Gaylord Perry/Jsy/82	20.00

Milestone Mat. Prime
No Pricing

Mile. Mat. Sig. Prime
NM/M
Quantity produced listed.

4	Gaylord Perry/Jsy/19	30.00

No-Hitters Quad Sig.
No Pricing
Production One Set

Rookie Year Materials
NM/M
Quantity produced listed.
Prime: No Pricing
Production 5-10
Number: .75-1.5X
Production 3-51
No pricing 15 or less.

1	Stan Musial/Jsy/19	60.00
2	Yogi Berra/ Stripe Jsy/19	40.00
3	Yogi Berra/Gray Jsy/47	25.00
4	Whitey Ford/Jsy/72	20.00
5	Jim "Catfish" Hunter/ Jsy/65	10.00
6	Johnny Bench/Bat/68	15.00
8	Mike Schmidt/Bat/72	15.00
9	Gary Carter/Jsy/74	8.00
11	Robin Yount/Jsy/74	20.00
12	Cal Ripken Jr./Bat/81	40.00
12	Kirby Puckett/Bat/84	10.00
13	Roger Clemens/Jsy/84	20.00
15	Gary Sheffield/Jsy/89	8.00
16	Juan Gonzalez/Jsy/89	10.00
17	Randy Johnson/Jsy/89	10.00
18	Ivan Rodriguez/Jsy/91	10.00
20	Pedro J. Martinez/ Jsy/92	10.00
21	Mike Piazza/Jsy/93	10.00
22	Hideo Nomo/Jsy/95	10.00
23	Hideo Nomo/Pants/95	15.00
24	Alex Rodriguez/Jsy/95	15.00
26	Scott Rolen/Jsy/96	8.00
27	Andruw Jones/Jsy/96	8.00
28	Nomar Garciaparra/ Jsy/97	10.00
29	Vladimir Guerrero/ Jsy/97	10.00
31	Alfonso Soriano/ Jsy/100	10.00
32	Albert Pujols/ White Jsy/100	20.00
33	Albert Pujols/ Gray Jsy/100	20.00
34	Albert Pujols/Bat/100	20.00
36	Mark Prior/Blue Jsy/100	10.00
37	Mark Prior/ Jsy/100	10.00
38	Dontrelle Willis/Jsy/35	15.00

Rookie Year Mat. Sig.

NM/M
Quantity produced listed.
Prime: 1X
Number: 1X
No pricing 15 or less.

1	Stan Musial/Jsy/9	125.00
3	Yogi Berra/ Gray Jsy/19	100.00
4	Whitey Ford/Jsy/19	85.00
8	Gary Carter/Jsy/35	35.00
10	Fred Lynn/Jsy/75	15.00
14	Lenny Dykstra/ Fld Glv/85	20.00
16	Juan Gonzalez/Jsy/19	20.00
25	Garret Anderson/Jsy/95	20.00
30	Shannon Stewart/ Jsy/97	15.00
36	Mark Prior/Blue Jsy/22	80.00
37	Mark Prior/Gray Jsy/22	80.00
38	Dontrelle Willis/Jsy/35	40.00
39	Rocco Baldelli/Jsy/19	40.00

Rookie Year Mat. Combo
NM/M
Quantity produced listed.

2	Yogi Berra/Jsy/8	60.00
22	Hideo Nomo/ Jsy-Pants/16	30.00
36	Mark Prior/Jsy/22	30.00
38	Dontrelle Willis/ Jsy/35	10.00

R.Y. Materials Combos Sig.
NM/M
Quantity produced listed.

36	Mark Prior/Jsy/22	100.00
38	Dontrelle Willis/ Jsy/35	40.00

R.Y. Mat. Combos Prime
NM/M
Quantity produced listed.

36	Mark Prior/Jsy/22	30.00
38	Dontrelle Willis/ Jsy/35	10.00

R.Y. Mat. Combo Sig. Prime
NM/M
Quantity produced listed.

36	Mark Prior/Jsy/22	100.00
38	Dontrelle Willis/ Jsy/35	40.00

Rookie Year Mat. Dual
NM/M
Production 25 Sets
Prime: No Pricing
Production 10 Sets

40	Roger Clemens/Jsy, Nomar Garciaparra/Jsy	40.00
	Pedro J. Martinez/Jsy, Mike Piazza/Jsy	35.00
42	Mike Piazza/Jsy, Hideo Nomo/Jsy	35.00
43	Pedro J. Martinez/Jsy, Hideo Nomo/Jsy	20.00
44	Yogi Berra/Jsy, Whitey Ford/Jsy	50.00
45	Mike Schmidt/Bat, Scott Rolen/Jsy	40.00
	Stan Musial/Jsy, Albert Pujols/Jsy	75.00
47	Juan Gonzalez/Jsy, Ivan Rodriguez/Jsy	15.00

Rk. Year Mat. Dual Sig.
No Pricing
Production Five Sets

Rk. Year Mat. Dual Prime
No Pricing
Production 10 Sets

Rookie Year Mat. Number
Quantity produced listed.

Rk. Year Mat. Sig. Number
Quantity produced listed.

Rookie Year Mat. Prime
Quantity produced listed

Rk Year Mat. Sig. Prime
Quantity produced listed.

Signature Bronze

		NM/M
1	Albert Pujols/25	125.00
2	Garret Anderson/16	30.00
3	Alex Rodriguez/25	100.00
5	Manny Ramirez/24	40.00
6	Mark Prior/50	50.00
8	Barry Larkin/25	30.00
9	Todd Helton/17	50.00
14	Shawn Green/15	30.00
17	Vladimir Guerrero	50.00
20	Don Mattingly/50	60.00
23	Rafael Palmeiro/25	45.00
27	Gary Sheffield/50	25.00
37	Kazuhisa Ishii/17	40.00
40	Tom Glavine/25	30.00
42	Eric Chavez/25	25.00
44	Tony Gwynn/50	40.00
46	Jim Edmonds/15	35.00
47	Delmon Young/73	20.00
49	Vernon Wells/25	25.00
50	Curt Schilling/38	40.00
53	Jason Varitek/33	30.00
56	Adam Dunn/25	40.00
58	Josh Beckett/21	50.00
59	Jeff Bagwell/25	50.00
60	Carlos Beltran/15	40.00
68	Juan Gonzalez/25	40.00
71	Andruw Jones/25	40.00
76	Jorge Posada/25	40.00
78	Stan Musial/50	75.00
79	Mark Teixeira/23	35.00
83	Nolan Ryan/50	90.00
87	Bob Gibson/25	40.00
88	Dale Murphy/50	35.00
90	Carl Yastrzemski/25	60.00
91	Sammy Sosa/50	125.00
92	Miguel Cabrera/24	50.00
94	George Brett/25	100.00
95	Rickey Henderson/25	25.00
97	Greg Maddux/31	75.00
100	Dontrelle Willis/35	30.00

Signature Silver

		NM/M
	Quantity produced listed.	
2	Garret Anderson/10	10.00
6	Mark Prior/22	50.00
17	Vladimir Guerrero/27	50.00
20	Don Mattingly/23	90.00
27	Gary Sheffield/25	35.00
44	Tony Gwynn/19	75.00
47	Delmon Young/25	30.00
68	Juan Gonzalez/22	35.00
76	Jorge Posada/20	40.00
78	Stan Musial/25	75.00
83	Nolan Ryan/34	120.00
88	Dale Murphy/25	40.00
91	Sammy Sosa/21	125.00

Signature Gold
No Pricing
Production 1-11

Statistical Champions

		NM/M
	Number:	.75-1.5X
	Production 1-51	
	No pricing 15 or less.	
	Prime:	No Pricing
	Production 5-10	
2	Stan Musial 43 BA/Jsy/19	40.00
3	Ralph Kiner/Bat/49	10.00
4	Stan Musial 57 BA/Jsy/57	30.00
5	Ted Williams/Jsy/25	40.00
6	Warren Spahn/Jsy/25	30.00
7	Eddie Mathews/Jsy/19	40.00
8	Roger Maris 61 HR/Bat/61	40.00
9	Roger Maris 61 HR/Pants/61	40.00
10	Roger Maris 61 RBI/Bat/61	40.00
11	Roger Maris 61 RBI/Pants/61	40.00
12	Roberto Clemente/Jsy/19	100.00
13	Frank Robinson/Bat/66	10.00
14	Bob Gibson 68 ERA/Jsy/68	15.00
15	Bob Gibson 68 K/Jsy/68	15.00
16	Tom Seaver/Jsy/19	25.00
18	Harmon Killebrew/Pants/71	15.00
19	Mike Schmidt/Jsy/74	15.00
20	Reggie Jackson/Jsy/19	20.00
22	Rod Carew/Hat/78	15.00
23	Jim Rice 78 HR Jsy/78	10.00
24	Jim Rice 78 RBI Jsy/78	10.00
25	Reggie Jackson/Hat/80	15.00

26	Dale Murphy 82 RBI/Jsy/82	15.00
27	Steve Carlton/Jsy/83	10.00
28	Dale Murphy 85 HR/Jsy/85	15.00
29	Wade Boggs 86 BA/Jsy/86	15.00
30	Wade Boggs 87 BA/Jsy/87	15.00
31	Will Clark/Jsy/88	15.00
32	Nolan Ryan 89 K/Jsy/89	20.00
33	Nolan Ryan 90 K/Jsy/90	20.00
34	Nolan Ryan 90 K/Pants/90	20.00
35	Ryne Sandberg/Jsy/90	20.00
36	Roger Clemens 90 K/Jsy/90	20.00
37	George Brett/Jsy/90	20.00
38	Roger Clemens 92 ERA/Jsy/100	20.00
39	Roger Clemens 96 K/Jsy/100	20.00
40	Tony Gwynn/Jsy/25	35.00
41	Pedro Martinez/Expos/Jsy/25	20.00
42	Greg Maddux/Jsy/100	10.00
43	Juan Gonzalez/Pants/25	20.00
44	Manny Ramirez/Bat/25	15.00
45	Nomar Garciaparra 99 BA/Jsy/100	10.00
47	Nomar Garciaparra 00 BA/Jsy/100	10.00
48	Todd Helton 00 BA/Jsy/25	15.00
49	Todd Helton 00 RBI/Jsy/25	15.00
50	Troy Glaus/Jsy/25	15.00
51	Randy Johnson 00 K/Jsy/25	15.00
52	Tom Glavine/Jsy/25	10.00
53	Sammy Sosa 00 HR/Jsy/100	15.00
54	Alex Rodriguez 01 HR/Bat/100	15.00
55	Curt Schilling/Jsy/100	10.00
56	Pedro J. Martinez 99 K/Jsy/25	20.00
57	Alex Rodriguez 01 HR/Jsy/100	15.00
58	Mark Mulder/Jsy/25	10.00
59	Sammy Sosa 01 RBI/Jsy/100	15.00
60	Manny Ramirez/Jsy/25	10.00
61	Lance Berkman/Jsy/25	10.00
62	Randy Johnson 02 W/Jsy/25	15.00
63	Alex Rodriguez 02 HR/Jsy/100	15.00
64	Alex Rodriguez 02 RBI/Jsy/100	15.00
65	Alex Rodriguez 02 HR/Bat/100	15.00
66	Alex Rodriguez 02 RBI/Bat/100	15.00
67	Pedro J. Martinez 02 K/Jsy/25	20.00
68	Pedro J. Martinez 02 ERA/Jsy/25	20.00
69	Sammy Sosa 02 HR/Jsy/100	15.00
70	Jim Thome/Jsy/25	15.00
71	Alex Rodriguez 03 HR/Bat/100	15.00
72	Albert Pujols/Bat/100	20.00
73	Alex Rodriguez 03 HR/Jsy/100	15.00
74	Albert Pujols/Jsy/100	20.00

34	Nolan Ryan 90 K/Pants/25	120.00
35	Ryne Sandberg/Jsy/25	80.00
40	Tony Gwynn/Jsy/25	70.00
43	Juan Gonzalez/Pants/19	40.00
50	Troy Glaus/Jsy/25	35.00
52	Tom Glavine/Jsy/20	35.00
53	Sammy Sosa 00 HR/Jsy/25	150.00
55	Curt Schilling/Jsy/25	40.00
58	Mark Mulder/Jsy/25	30.00
59	Sammy Sosa 01 RBI/Jsy/25	150.00
61	Lance Berkman/Jsy/25	40.00
69	Sammy Sosa 02 HR/Jsy/25	150.00

Stat. Champ. Number
No Pricing

Stat. Champ. Sig. Number
No Pricing

Stat. Champ. Prime
No Pricing

Stat. Champ. Sig. Prime
No Pricing

World Series Materials

		NM/M
	Quantity produced listed.	
1	Frank Robinson/Bat/61	15.00
2	Ozzie Smith/Jsy/87	15.00
3	Rickey Henderson/Bat/93	15.00
4	Tom Glavine/Jsy/96	10.00
5	Roger Clemens/Jsy/100	15.00

World Series Mat. Sig.

		NM/M
	Quantity produced listed.	
	Prime:	No Pricing
	Production 9-10	
1	Frank Robinson/Bat/19	50.00
4	Tom Glavine/Jsy/19	40.00

World Series Mat. Prime

		NM/M
	Quantity produced listed.	
2	Ozzie Smith/Jsy/19	25.00
4	Tom Glavine/Jsy/19	20.00
5	Roger Clemens/Jsy/20	30.00

2004 Donruss Timelines

		NM/M
	Complete Set (50):	40.00
	Common Player:	.75
	Pack (5):	40.00
	Box (4):	120.00
1	Adam Dunn	.75
2	Albert Pujols	3.00
3	Alex Rodriguez	3.00
4	Alfonso Soriano	1.50
5	Andruw Jones	1.00
6	Austin Kearns	.75
7	Miguel Cabrera	1.00
8	Barry Zito	.75
9	Carlos Beltran	.75
10	Carlos Delgado	1.00
11	Chipper Jones	2.00
12	Curt Schilling	1.00
13	Derek Jeter	4.00
14	Frank Thomas	1.00
15	Garret Anderson	.75
16	Gary Sheffield	.75
17	Greg Maddux	2.00
18	Hank Blalock	.75
19	Hideki Matsui	3.00
20	Hideo Nomo	.75
21	Ichiro Suzuki	2.00
22	Ivan Rodriguez	1.00
23	Jason Giambi	1.50
24	Jeff Bagwell	1.00
25	Jim Thome	1.50
26	Juan Gonzalez	.75
27	Ken Griffey Jr.	2.00
28	Kevin Brown	.75
29	Kerry Wood	1.00
30	Lance Berkman	.75
31	Magglio Ordonez	.75
32	Manny Ramirez	1.00
33	Mark Prior	3.00
34	Mike Mussina	1.00
35	Mike Piazza	2.00
36	Nomar Garciaparra	3.00
37	Pedro J. Martinez	1.50
38	Rafael Palmeiro	1.00
39	Randy Johnson	1.50

Statistical Champ. Sig.

		NM/M
	No Pricing	
	Quantity produced listed.	
	Number:	.5-1.5X
	Production 1-47	
	Prime:	No Pricing
	Production 1-10	
3	Ralph Kiner/Bat/49	35.00
6	Warren Spahn/Jsy/25	40.00
13	Frank Robinson/Bat/66	40.00
14	Bob Gibson 68 ERA/Jsy/25	50.00
15	Bob Gibson 68 K/Jsy/25	50.00
17	Harmon Killebrew/Jsy/71	50.00
18	Harmon Killebrew/Pants/71	50.00
19	Mike Schmidt/Jsy/25	75.00
20	Reggie Jackson/Jsy/25	65.00
21	Phil Niekro/Jsy/25	30.00
22	Rod Carew/Hat/25	40.00
23	Jim Rice 78 HR Jsy/78	30.00
24	Jim Rice 78 RBI Jsy/78	30.00
25	Reggie Jackson/Hat/25	65.00
26	Dale Murphy 82 RBI/Jsy/25	50.00
27	Steve Carlton/Jsy/25	50.00
28	Dale Murphy 85 HR/Jsy/25	50.00
29	Wade Boggs 86 BA/Jsy/25	40.00
30	Wade Boggs 87 BA/Jsy/25	40.00
31	Will Clark/Jsy/88	30.00
32	Nolan Ryan 89 K/Jsy/25	120.00
33	Nolan Ryan 90 K/Jsy/25	120.00

40	Richie Sexson	.75
41	Roger Clemens	3.00
42	Roy Halladay	.75
43	Sammy Sosa	2.50
44	Scott Rolen	1.50
45	Shawn Green	.75
46	Tim Hudson	.75
47	Todd Helton	1.00
48	Torii Hunter	.75
49	Vernon Wells	.75
50	Vladimir Guerrero	1.50

Silver
Cards (1-50):	2X
Production 100 Sets	

Gold
Cards (1-50):	4-6X
Production 25 Sets	

Gold Autographs

		NM/M
	Production 25 Sets	30.00
1	Adam Dunn	40.00
7	Miguel Cabrera	80.00
9	Carlos Beltran	40.00
15	Garret Anderson	30.00
18	Hank Blalock	35.00
22	Ivan Rodriguez	60.00
26	Juan Gonzalez	50.00
31	Magglio Ordonez	40.00
33	Mark Prior	50.00
44	Scott Rolen	45.00
48	Torii Hunter	35.00
49	Vernon Wells	30.00
50	Vladimir Guerrero	70.00

Platinum
No Pricing
Production One Set

Platinum Autographs
No Pricing
Production One Set

Boys of Summer

		NM/M
	Complete Set (25):	75.00
	Common Player:	3.00
	Production 250 Sets	
	Silver:	1-1.5x
	Production 100 Sets	
	Gold:	3-4X
	Production 25 Sets	
	Platinum:	No Pricing
	Production One Set	
1	Alan Trammell	5.00
2	Marty Marion	3.00
3	Andre Dawson	3.00
4	Bo Jackson	5.00
5	Cal Ripken Jr.	10.00
6	Steve Garvey	3.00
7	Dale Murphy	3.00
8	Darren Daulton	3.00
9	Darryl Strawberry	3.00
10	Dave Parker	3.00
11	Doc Gooden	3.00
12	Don Mattingly	6.00
13	Eric Davis	3.00
14	Dwight Evans	3.00
15	Fred Lynn	3.00
16	Graig Nettles	3.00
17	Jay Buhner	3.00
18	Jim Rice	3.00
19	Jose Canseco	3.00
20	Keith Hernandez	3.00
21	Rickey Henderson	3.00
22	Jack Morris	3.00
23	Tony Gwynn	4.00
24	Vida Blue	3.00
25	Will Clark	3.00

Boys of Summer Autographs

		NM/M
	Common Autograph:	10.00
2	Marty Marion	10.00
3	Andre Dawson	15.00
6	Steve Garvey	12.00
8	Darren Daulton	10.00
9	Darryl Strawberry	15.00
10	Dave Parker	15.00
12	Doc Gooden	15.00
13	Eric Davis	12.00
15	Fred Lynn	12.00
16	Graig Nettles	15.00
17	Jay Buhner	15.00
20	Keith Hernandez	12.00
22	Jack Morris	12.00
24	Vida Blue	12.00

Boys of Summer Silver Auto

		NM/M
	Common Autograph:	12.00
	Production 100	
2	Marty Marion	12.00
3	Andre Dawson	15.00
6	Steve Garvey	20.00
8	Darren Daulton	12.00

Boys of Summer Gold Autographs

		NM/M
	Common Autograph:	20.00
	Production 25	
1	Alan Trammell	35.00
2	Marty Marion	20.00
3	Andre Dawson	20.00
6	Steve Garvey	20.00
8	Darren Daulton	20.00
9	Darryl Strawberry	20.00
10	Dave Parker	20.00
11	Doc Gooden	20.00
12	Don Mattingly	75.00
13	Eric Davis	20.00
14	Dwight Evans	25.00
15	Fred Lynn	25.00
16	Graig Nettles	20.00
17	Jay Buhner	25.00
18	Jim Rice	25.00
20	Keith Hernandez	20.00
22	Jack Morris	20.00
24	Vida Blue	20.00
25	Will Clark	100.00

Boys of Summer Platinum Auto.
No Pricing
Production One Set

Boys of Summer Materials

		NM/M
	Common Player:	5.00
	Combos:	1-2X
	Production 100 Sets	
	Prime:	1-2X
	Production 100 Sets	
3	Andre Dawson	5.00
4	Bo Jackson	10.00
5	Cal Ripken Jr.	20.00
7	Dale Murphy	6.00
9	Darryl Strawberry	5.00
11	Doc Gooden	5.00
12	Don Mattingly	15.00
19	Jose Canseco	6.00
21	Rickey Henderson	8.00
22	Jack Morris	5.00
23	Tony Gwynn	8.00
25	Will Clark	8.00

Boys of Summer Combo Materials

		NM/M
	Production 100 Sets	
3	Andre Dawson	10.00
4	Bo Jackson	15.00
5	Cal Ripken Jr.	30.00
7	Dale Murphy	10.00
12	Don Mattingly	25.00
19	Jose Canseco	10.00
21	Rickey Henderson	15.00
23	Tony Gwynn	10.00
25	Will Clark	10.00

Boys of Summer Material Auto.

		NM/M
	Varying quantities produced.	
3	Andre Dawson/50	25.00
9	Darryl Strawberry/150	25.00
11	Doc Gooden/100	25.00
12	Don Mattingly/150	80.00
22	Jack Morris/150	12.00

Boys of Summer Prime Materials

		NM/M
	Common Player:	8.00
	Production 100 Sets	
3	Andre Dawson	8.00
4	Bo Jackson	15.00
5	Cal Ripken Jr.	30.00
9	Darryl Strawberry	8.00
11	Doc Gooden	8.00
12	Don Mattingly	25.00
21	Rickey Henderson	15.00
23	Tony Gwynn	12.00
25	Will Clark	12.00

Boys/Summer Prime Materials Auto.
No Pricing
Production One Set

9	Darryl Strawberry	18.00
10	Dave Parker	12.00
11	Doc Gooden	20.00
12	Don Mattingly	65.00
13	Eric Davis	12.00
15	Fred Lynn	15.00
16	Graig Nettles	20.00
18	Jim Rice	20.00
20	Keith Hernandez	15.00
22	Jack Morris	15.00
24	Vida Blue	15.00

Call to the Hall

		NM/M
	Complete Set (25):	80.00
	Common Player:	3.00
	Production 250 Sets	
	Silver:	1X
	Production 100 Sets	
	Gold:	3-4X
	Production 25 Sets	
	Platinum:	No Pricing
	Production One Set	
1	Babe Ruth	10.00
2	Billy Williams	3.00
3	Bob Feller	3.00
4	Bobby Doerr	3.00
5	Carlton Fisk	3.00
6	Gary Carter	3.00
7	George Brett	8.00
8	Carl Yastrzemski	5.00
9	Harmon Killebrew	5.00
10	Jim Palmer	3.00
11	Joe Morgan	3.00
12	Johnny Bench	5.00
13	Kirby Puckett	5.00
14	Gaylord Perry	3.00
15	Mike Schmidt	6.00
16	Nolan Ryan	10.00
17	Ozzie Smith	5.00
18	Phil Rizzuto	3.00
19	Reggie Jackson	4.00
20	Roberto Clemente	6.00
21	Robin Yount	4.00
22	Rod Carew	3.00
23	Rollie Fingers	3.00
24	Steve Carlton	3.00
25	Tom Seaver	4.00

Call to the Hall Autographs

		NM/M
	Common Autograph:	15.00
	Silver Autos.:	1X
	Production 100	
3	Bob Feller	15.00
4	Bobby Doerr	15.00
14	Gaylord Perry	15.00
23	Rollie Fingers	15.00

Call to the Hall Gold Autographs

		NM/M
	Production 25 Sets	
2	Billy Williams	25.00
3	Bob Feller	40.00
6	Gary Carter	40.00
11	Jim Palmer	30.00
18	Phil Rizzuto	40.00
24	Steve Carlton	40.00

Call to the Hall Platinum Auto.
No Pricing
Production One Set

Call to the Hall Materials

		NM/M
	Common Player:	6.00
1	Babe Ruth/50	575.00
4	Bobby Doerr	8.00
6	Gary Carter	8.00
7	George Brett	12.00
8	Carl Yastrzemski	12.00
13	Kirby Puckett	10.00
15	Mike Schmidt	12.00
16	Nolan Ryan	20.00
17	Ozzie Smith	8.00
19	Reggie Jackson	20.00
20	Roberto Clemente/100	50.00

Call to the Hall Combo Materials

		NM/M
	Production 125 Sets	
6	Gary Carter	12.00
7	George Brett	25.00
13	Kirby Puckett	20.00

15	Mike Schmidt	25.00
16	Nolan Ryan	35.00
19	Reggie Jackson	20.00

Call to the Hall Material Auto.

NM/M
Varying quantities produced.

4	Bobby Doerr/100	25.00
6	Gary Carter/25	45.00
19	Reggie Jackson/25	50.00

Materials

NM/M
Common Player: 5.00
Combos: 1-2X
Production 125
Primes: 1-2X
Production 125

1	Adam Dunn	5.00
2	Albert Pujols	12.00
3	Alex Rodriguez	8.00
4	Alfonso Soriano	8.00
5	Andruw Jones	5.00
7	Miguel Cabrera/SP	10.00
10	Carlos Delgado	5.00
11	Chipper Jones	8.00
14	Frank Thomas	8.00
17	Greg Maddux	8.00
20	Hideo Nomo	6.00
22	Ivan Rodriguez	6.00
23	Jason Giambi	6.00
24	Jeff Bagwell	6.00
25	Jim Thome	6.00
26	Juan Gonzalez	6.00
30	Lance Berkman	5.00
33	Mark Prior	10.00
35	Mike Piazza	8.00
36	Nomar Garciaparra	10.00
37	Pedro J. Martinez	8.00
39	Randy Johnson	6.00
41	Roger Clemens	10.00
43	Sammy Sosa	10.00
45	Shawn Green	5.00
47	Todd Helton	10.00
49	Vernon Wells	5.00

Materials Autographs

NM/M
Varying quantities produced.

7	Miguel Cabrera/25	85.00
22	Ivan Rodriguez/25	65.00
33	Mark Prior/50	75.00
49	Vernon Wells/25	25.00

Materials Combo

NM/M
Common Player: 8.00
Production 125 Sets

2	Adam Dunn	8.00
2	Albert Pujols	20.00
3	Alex Rodriguez	15.00
4	Alfonso Soriano	10.00
5	Andruw Jones	8.00
7	Miguel Cabrera	20.00
11	Chipper Jones	15.00
14	Frank Thomas	12.00
17	Greg Maddux	15.00
20	Hideo Nomo	10.00
25	Jim Thome	12.00
30	Lance Berkman	8.00
33	Mark Prior	20.00
35	Mike Piazza	15.00
36	Nomar Garciaparra	15.00
37	Pedro J. Martinez	12.00
39	Randy Johnson	10.00
41	Roger Clemens	15.00
43	Sammy Sosa	15.00

45	Shawn Green	10.00
47	Todd Helton	10.00

Materials Prime

NM/M
Common Player: 8.00
Production 125 Sets

1	Adam Dunn	8.00
2	Albert Pujols	20.00
3	Alex Rodriguez	20.00
4	Alfonso Soriano	10.00
5	Andruw Jones	8.00
7	Miguel Cabrera	20.00
10	Carlos Delgado	8.00
11	Chipper Jones	15.00
14	Frank Thomas	12.00
17	Greg Maddux	15.00
20	Hideo Nomo	10.00
25	Jim Thome	12.00
30	Lance Berkman	8.00
33	Mark Prior	20.00
35	Mike Piazza	15.00
36	Nomar Garciaparra	15.00
37	Pedro J. Martinez	12.00
39	Randy Johnson	10.00
41	Roger Clemens	10.00
43	Sammy Sosa	15.00
45	Shawn Green	10.00
47	Todd Helton	10.00
49	Vernon Wells	5.00

Materials Prime Autograph

No Pricing
Production One Set

Recollection Autographs

Complete Set (1576):
Common Player:

2004 Donruss World Series

NM/M
Complete Set (200):
Common Player: .15
Common SP (176-200): 8.00
Pack (6): 6.00
Box (24): 120.00

1	Bartolo Colon	.15
2	Darin Erstad	.25
3	Garret Anderson	.25
4	Tim Salmon	.25
5	Troy Glaus	.25
6	Vladimir Guerrero	.75
7	Brandon Webb	.15
8	Luis Gonzalez	.15
9	Randy Johnson	.75
10	Roberto Alomar	.40
11	Shea Hillenbrand	.15
12	Steve Finley	.15
13	Andruw Jones	.40
14	Chipper Jones	.75
15	J.D. Drew	.25
16	Marcus Giles	.15
17	Rafael Furcal	.15
18	Javy Lopez	.25
19	Jay Gibbons	.15
20	Luis Matos	.15
21	Melvin Mora	.15
22	Miguel Tejada	.40
23	Rafael Palmeiro	.50
24	Curt Schilling	.75
25	Dwight Evans	.15
26	Fred Lynn	.15
27	Jason Varitek	.25
28	Jim Rice	.25
29	Johnny Damon	.40
30	Luis Tiant	.15
31	Manny Ramirez	.50
32	Nomar Garciaparra	1.00
33	Pedro Martinez	.75

34	Trot Nixon	.15
35	Aramis Ramirez	.15
36	Corey Patterson	.25
37	Derrek Lee	.25
38	Greg Maddux	1.00
39	Kerry Wood	.25
40	Mark Prior	.75
41	Moises Alou	.25
42	Sammy Sosa	1.50
43	Carlos Lee	.15
44	Frank Thomas	.50
45	Luis Aparicio	.15
46	Magglio Ordonez	.25
47	Mark Buehrle	.15
48	Paul Konerko	.25
49	Adam Dunn	.50
50	Austin Kearns	.15
51	Barry Larkin	.25
52	Dave Concepcion	.15
53	George Foster	.25
54	Joe Morgan	.15
55	Sean Casey	.25
56	Tony Perez	.25
57	C.C. Sabathia	.15
58	Jody Gerut	.15
59	Omar Vizquel	.15
60	Victor Martinez	.25
61	Charles Johnson	.15
62	Jeromy Burnitz	.15
63	Larry Walker	.25
64	Preston Wilson	.15
65	Todd Helton	.50
66	Alan Trammell	.15
67	Dmitri Young	.15
68	Ivan Rodriguez	.50
69	Jeremy Bonderman	.15
70	A.J. Burnett	.15
71	Brad Penny	.15
72	Dontrelle Willis	.15
73	Josh Beckett	.40
74	Juan Pierre	.15
75	Luis Castillo	.15
76	Miguel Cabrera	.75
77	Mike Lowell	.25
78	Andy Pettitte	.25
79	Craig Biggio	.25
80	Jeff Bagwell	.50
81	Jeff Kent	.25
82	Lance Berkman	.25
83	Roger Clemens	2.00
84	Roy Oswalt	.25
85	Wade Miller	.15
86	Angel Berroa	.15
87	Carlos Beltran	.50
88	Juan Gonzalez	.40
89	Ken Harvey	.15
90	Mike Sweeney	.15
91	Adrian Beltre	.40
92	Hideo Nomo	.40
93	Kazuhisa Ishii	.15
94	Milton Bradley	.15
95	Orel Hershiser	.15
96	Paul LoDuca	.15
97	Shawn Green	.25
98	Ben Sheets	.25
99	Geoff Jenkins	.15
100	Junior Spivey	.15
101	Rickie Weeks	.15
102	Scott Podsednik	.15
103	Jack Morris	.15
104	Jacque Jones	.15
105	Johan Santana	.50
106	Shannon Stewart	.15
107	Torii Hunter	.25
108	Jose Vidro	.15
109	Orlando Cabrera	.25
110	Al Leiter	.25
111	Darryl Strawberry	.25
112	Dwight Gooden	.25
113	Jose Reyes	.25
114	Kazuo Matsui RC	2.00
115	Keith Hernandez	.15
116	Lenny Dykstra	.15
117	Mike Piazza	1.00
118	Tom Glavine	.40
119	Alex Rodriguez	2.00
120	Bernie Williams	.40
121	Derek Jeter	2.00
122	Gary Sheffield	.50
123	Jason Giambi	.25
124	Javier Vazquez	.25
125	Jorge Posada	.25
126	Kenny Lofton	.15
127	Kevin Brown	.25
128	Mariano Rivera	.25
129	Mike Mussina	.40
130	Barry Zito	.25
131	Eric Chavez	.25
132	Jermaine Dye	.15
133	Mark Mulder	.25
134	Rich Harden	.25
135	Tim Hudson	.25
136	Brett Myers	.15
137	Jim Thome	.75
138	Kevin Millwood	.15
139	Marlon Byrd	.15
140	Mike Lieberthal	.15
141	Pat Burrell	.25
142	Steve Carlton	.25
143	Dave Parker	.15
144	Jason Kendall	.15
145	Brian Giles	.15
146	Jay Payton	.15
147	Ryan Klesko	.15
148	J.T. Snow	.15
149	Jason Schmidt	.25
150	Bret Boone	.15
151	Edgar Martinez	.25

152	Jamie Moyer	.15
153	Rich Aurilia	.15
154	Shigetoshi Hasegawa	.15
155	Albert Pujols	2.00
156	Dan Haren	.15
157	Edgar Renteria	.25
158	Fernando Vina	.15
159	Jim Edmonds	.40
160	Matt Morris	.15
161	Scott Rolen	.75
162	Aubrey Huff	.15
163	Carl Crawford	.25
164	Dewon Brazelton	.15
165	Fred McGriff	.25
166	Rocco Baldelli	.15
167	Alfonso Soriano	.75
168	Hank Blalock	.50
169	Kenny Rogers	.15
170	Mark Teixeira	.25
171	Michael Young	.15
172	Carlos Delgado	.40
173	Eric Hinske	.15
174	Roy Halladay	.15
175	Vernon Wells	.15
176	Ivan Ochoa/Auto./487 RC	8.00
177	Jason Bartlett/ Auto./1,000 RC	8.00
178	Josh Labandeira/ Auto./703 RC	8.00
179	Phil Stockman/ Auto./1,000 RC	8.00
180	Ronny Cedeno/ Auto./715 RC	8.00
181	Shawn Camp/ Auto./1,000 RC	8.00
182	Ruddy Yan Auto./1,000	8.00
183	Roberto Novoa/ Auto./568 RC	10.00
184	Justin Knoedler/ Auto./1,000 RC	8.00
185	Jesse Harper/ Auto./1,000 RC	8.00
186	Jason Szuminski/ Auto./1,000 RC	8.00
187	Jamie Brown/ Auto./800 RC	8.00
188	Eddy Rodriguez/ Auto./1,000 RC	8.00
189	Dennis Sarfate/ Auto./1,000 RC	8.00
190	Ryan Meaux/ Auto./1,000 RC	8.00
191	Charles Thomas/ Auto./1,000 RC	10.00
192	Frank Francisco/ Auto./1,000 RC	8.00
193	Orlando Rodriguez/ Auto./500 RC	8.00
194	Joey Gathright/ Auto./1,000 RC	8.00
195	Renyel Pinto/ Auto./1,000 RC	10.00
196	Justin Leone/ Auto./1,000 RC	10.00
197	Tim Bausher/ Auto./834 RC	8.00
198	Travis Blackley/ Auto./1,000 RC	10.00
199	Yadier Molina/ Auto./500 RC	15.00
200	Brad Halsey/ Auto./500 RC	10.00

HoloFoil 10

No Pricing
Production 10 Sets

HoloFoil 25

HoloFoil (1-175): 10-20X
HoloFoil (176-200): No Pricing
Production 25 Sets

HoloFoil 50

HoloFoil (1-175): 6-12X
HoloFoil (176-200): .75X
Production 50 Sets

HoloFoil 100

HoloFoil (1-175): 4-8X
HoloFoil (176-200): .5X
Production 100 Sets

2004 Donruss World Series Champions

NM/M
Complete Boxed Set (25): 25.00
Common Player: .50

201	Curt Schilling	3.00
202	Pedro Martinez	3.00
203	Derek Lowe	.50
204	Tim Wakefield	.50
205	Bronson Arroyo	.50
206	Mike Timlin	.50
207	Curt Leskanic	.50
208	Mike Myers	.50
209	Alan Embree	.50
210	Keith Foulke	.50
211	Jason Varitek	2.00
212	Doug Mirabelli	.50
213	Doug Mientkiewicz	.50
214	Mark Bellhorn	.50
215	Pokey Reese	.50
216	Orlando Cabrera	1.00
217	Bill Mueller	.50
218	Kevin Youkilis	.50
219	Manny Ramirez	3.00
220	Johnny Damon	3.00
221	Dave Roberts	.50

222	Trot Nixon	.50
223	Gabe Kapler	.50
224	David Ortiz	3.00

Box Topper

NM/M
Inserted 1:Set

WS1	World Series Champions	2.00

Blue

NM/M
Complete Set (100): 50.00
Common Player: .50
Inserted 1:1
HoloFoil 100: 2-4X
Production 100 Sets
HoloFoil 50: 4-6X
Production 50 Sets
HoloFoil 25: 6-10X
Production 25 Sets
HoloFoil 10: No Pricing
Production 10 Sets

1	Josh Beckett	.50
2	Miguel Cabrera	1.00
3	Derrek Lee	.50
4	Mike Lowell	.50
5	Brad Penny	.50
6	Ivan Rodriguez	1.00
7	Dontrelle Willis	.50
8	Luis Castillo	.50
9	Garret Anderson	.75
10	Troy Glaus	.75
11	John Lackey	.50
12	Chone Figgins	.50
13	Tim Salmon	.50
14	Darin Erstad	.50
15	Troy Percival	.50
16	Steve Finley	.50
17	Mark Grace	.75
18	Randy Johnson	1.00
19	Curt Schilling	.50
20	Luis Gonzalez	.50
21	Andy Pettitte	.75
22	Bernie Williams	.75
23	Jorge Posada	.75
24	Mariano Rivera	.75
25	Roger Clemens	3.00
26	Jose Canseco	1.00
27	David Justice	.50
28	Paul O'Neill	.75
29	Darryl Strawberry	.75
30	David Wells	.50
31	Wade Boggs	.75
32	Charles Johnson	.50
33	Cliff Floyd	.50
34	Moises Alou	.50
35	Edgar Renteria	.75
36	Chipper Jones	1.50
37	Tom Glavine	.75
38	John Smoltz	.75
39	Greg Maddux	1.50
40	Ryan Klesko	.50
41	Javy Lopez	.50
42	Fred McGriff	.50
43	Roberto Alomar	.50
44	Joe Carter	.50
45	Rickey Henderson	.50
46	Paul Molitor	1.00
47	Jack Morris	.50
48	Jack Morris	.50
49	Kirby Puckett	1.50
50	Eric Davis	.50
51	Barry Larkin	.75
52	Paul O'Neill	.75
53	Dennis Eckersley	.75
54	Jose Canseco	1.00
55	Rickey Henderson	.75
56	Dave Parker	.50
57	Orel Hershiser	.50
58	Kirk Gibson	.50
59	Bert Blyleven	.50
60	Dwight Gooden	.50
61	Gary Carter	.50
62	Lenny Dykstra	.50
63	Keith Hernandez	.50
64	Darryl Strawberry	.50
65	George Brett	3.00
66	Kirk Gibson	.50
67	Alan Trammell	.50
68	Jim Palmer	.75
69	Eddie Murray	.75
70	Cal Ripken Jr.	5.00
71	Keith Hernandez	.50
72	Ozzie Smith	1.50
73	Steve Garvey	.50
74	Steve Carlton	1.00
75	Mike Schmidt	4.00
76	John Candelaria	.50
77	Bert Blyleven	.50
78	Dave Parker	.50
79	Willie Stargell	.50
80	Reggie Jackson	1.00
81	Johnny Bench	2.00
82	Dave Concepcion	.50
83	George Foster	.50
84	Joe Morgan	.50
85	Tony Perez	.50

86	Rollie Fingers	.50
87	Jim "Catfish" Hunter	.50
88	Reggie Jackson	1.00
89	Al Oliver	.50
90	Roberto Clemente	3.00
91	Willie Stargell	.75
92	Brooks Robinson	1.00
93	Frank Robinson	.75
94	Nolan Ryan	4.00
95	Tom Seaver	1.50
96	Al Kaline	1.00
97	Bob Gibson	.75
98	Lou Brock	.75
99	Orlando Cepeda	.50
100	Duke Snider	1.00

Blue Material Bat

NM/M
Common Player: 5.00
Production 50 Sets

1	Josh Beckett	8.00
2	Miguel Cabrera	12.00
3	Derrek Lee	8.00
4	Mike Lowell	5.00
5	Brad Penny	5.00
6	Ivan Rodriguez	12.00
8	Luis Castillo	5.00
9	Garret Anderson	5.00
10	Troy Glaus	8.00
13	Tim Salmon	5.00
14	Darin Erstad	5.00
17	Mark Grace	12.00
19	Curt Schilling	12.00
20	Luis Gonzalez	5.00
21	Andy Pettitte	5.00
22	Bernie Williams	8.00
23	Jorge Posada	10.00
25	Roger Clemens	20.00
27	David Justice	5.00
28	Paul O'Neill	10.00
29	Darryl Strawberry	10.00
31	Wade Boggs	15.00
32	Charles Johnson	5.00
33	Cliff Floyd	5.00
34	Moises Alou	8.00
35	Edgar Renteria	8.00
36	Chipper Jones	15.00
37	Tom Glavine	10.00
39	Greg Maddux	20.00
40	Ryan Klesko	5.00
41	Javy Lopez	5.00
42	Fred McGriff	8.00
43	Roberto Alomar	5.00
44	Joe Carter	5.00
45	Rickey Henderson	15.00
46	Paul Molitor	15.00
49	Kirby Puckett	15.00
50	Eric Davis	5.00
51	Barry Larkin	8.00
52	Paul O'Neill	8.00
55	Rickey Henderson	15.00
56	Dave Parker	8.00
58	Kirk Gibson	10.00
60	Dwight Gooden	8.00
61	Gary Carter	8.00
62	Lenny Dykstra	5.00
63	Keith Hernandez	5.00
64	Darryl Strawberry	5.00
65	George Brett	25.00
66	Kirk Gibson	8.00
67	Alan Trammell	8.00
69	Eddie Murray	20.00
70	Cal Ripken Jr.	70.00
71	Keith Hernandez	8.00
72	Ozzie Smith	20.00
73	Steve Garvey	5.00
74	Steve Carlton	10.00
75	Mike Schmidt	25.00
78	Dave Parker	8.00
79	Willie Stargell	15.00
80	Reggie Jackson	15.00
81	Johnny Bench	20.00
82	Dave Concepcion	5.00
83	George Foster	5.00
84	Joe Morgan	8.00
85	Tony Perez	8.00
88	Reggie Jackson	15.00
89	Al Oliver	5.00
90	Roberto Clemente	60.00
91	Willie Stargell	15.00
92	Brooks Robinson	15.00
93	Frank Robinson	10.00
96	Al Kaline	15.00
98	Lou Brock	15.00
99	Orlando Cepeda	10.00

Blue Material Fabric

NM/M
Common Player: 4.00
Quantity produced listed.

1	Josh Beckett/Jsy/103	4.00
2	Miguel Cabrera/Jsy/103	8.00
3	Derrek Lee/Jsy/103	6.00
4	Mike Lowell/Jsy/103	4.00
5	Brad Penny/Jsy/103	4.00
6	Ivan Rodriguez/Jsy/103	8.00
7	Dontrelle Willis/Jsy/103	4.00
8	Garret Anderson/Jsy/102	4.00
10	Troy Glaus/Jsy/102	4.00
13	Tim Salmon/Jsy/102	4.00
14	Darin Erstad/Jsy/102	4.00
15	Tony Percival/Jsy/102	4.00
16	Steve Finley/Jsy/101	4.00
18	Randy Johnson/ Pants/101	8.00
19	Curt Schilling/Jsy/101	4.00
20	Luis Gonzalez/Jsy/101	4.00
21	Andy Pettitte/Jsy/100	6.00

Common Player: 8.00
Production 125 Sets

	Adam Dunn	8.00
	Albert Pujols	20.00
	Alex Rodriguez	15.00
	Alfonso Soriano	10.00
	Andruw Jones	8.00
	Miguel Cabrera	20.00
	Chipper Jones	15.00
	Frank Thomas	12.00
	Greg Maddux	15.00
	Hideo Nomo	10.00
	Jim Thome	12.00
	Lance Berkman	8.00
	Mark Prior	20.00
	Mike Piazza	15.00
	Nomar Garciaparra	15.00
	Pedro J. Martinez	12.00
	Randy Johnson	10.00
	Roger Clemens	15.00
	Sammy Sosa	15.00

22 Bernie Williams/Jsy/100 6.00
24 Mariano Rivera/Jsy/100 6.00
25 Roger Clemens/Jsy/100 12.00
29 Darryl Strawberry/Jsy/99 6.00
30 David Wells/Jsy/99 4.00
31 Wade Boggs/Jsy/96
32 Charles Johnson/Jsy/97 4.00
33 Cliff Floyd/Jsy/97
36 Chipper Jones/Jsy/95 8.00
37 Tom Glavine/Jsy/95 6.00
39 Greg Maddux/Jsy/95 10.00
40 Ryan Klesko/Jsy/95 4.00
41 Javy Lopez/Jsy/95
51 Barry Larkin/Jsy/90 8.00
54 Jose Canseco/Jsy/89 10.00
55 Rickey Henderson/Jsy/89 12.00
57 Orel Hershiser/Jsy/88 6.00
59 Bert Blyleven/Jsy/87
60 Dwight Gooden/Jsy/86 6.00
61 Gary Carter/Jkt/86
64 Darryl Strawberry/Jsy/86 6.00
65 George Brett/Jsy/85 20.00
68 Jim Palmer/Pants/83
69 Eddie Murray/Jsy/83 6.00
70 Cal Ripken Jr./Jsy/83 40.00
71 Keith Hernandez/Jsy/82 6.00
74 Steve Carlton/Jsy/80 6.00
75 Mike Schmidt/Jkt/80 15.00
78 Dave Parker/Jsy/79
79 Willie Stargell/Jsy/79 8.00
80 Reggie Jackson/Jsy/78 8.00
81 Johnny Bench/Jsy/75 12.00
82 Dave Concepcion/Jsy/75 4.00
83 George Foster/Jsy/75
86 Rollie Fingers/Jsy/74 4.00
87 Jim "Catfish" Hunter/Jsy/74 8.00
88 Reggie Jackson/Jkt/73 8.00
91 Willie Stargell/Jsy/71 8.00
98 Lou Brock/Jkt/67 8.00
100 Duke Snider/Pants/55 10.00

Blue Material Fabric AL/NL
NM/M
Common Player: 4.00
Quantity produced listed.
1 Josh Beckett/Jsy/100 4.00
2 Miguel Cabrera/Jsy/100 8.00
3 Derrek Lee/Jsy/100 4.00
4 Mike Lowell/Jsy/100 4.00
5 Brad Penny/Jsy/103 4.00
6 Ivan Rodriguez/Jsy/100 8.00
7 Dontrelle Willis/Jsy/100 4.00
9 Garret Anderson/Jsy/100 4.00
13 Troy Glaus/Jsy/100 4.00
14 Darin Erstad/Jsy/100 4.00
15 Tony Percival/Jsy/100 4.00
16 Steve Finley/Jsy/100 4.00
18 Randy Johnson/Pants/100 8.00
19 Curt Schilling/Jsy/100 4.00
20 Luis Gonzalez/Jsy/100 4.00
21 Andy Pettitte/Jsy/100 4.00
22 Bernie Williams/Jsy/100 6.00
24 Mariano Rivera/Jsy/100 6.00
25 Roger Clemens/Jsy/100 15.00
29 Darryl Strawberry/Jsy/100 4.00
30 David Wells/Jsy/10 4.00
31 Wade Boggs/Jsy/100 4.00
32 Charles Johnson/Jsy/100 4.00
33 Cliff Floyd/Jsy/100 4.00
36 Chipper Jones/Jsy/100 8.00
37 Tom Glavine/Jsy/100 6.00
39 Greg Maddux/Jsy/100 10.00
40 Ryan Klesko/Jsy/100 4.00
41 Javy Lopez/Jsy/10 4.00
51 Barry Larkin/Jsy/100 8.00
54 Jose Canseco/Jsy/100 10.00
55 Rickey Henderson/Jsy/100 10.00
57 Orel Hershiser/Jsy/100 8.00
59 Bert Blyleven/Jsy/50 8.00
60 Dwight Gooden/Jsy/50 8.00
61 Gary Carter/Jkt/100 6.00
64 Darryl Strawberry/Jsy/100 6.00
65 George Brett/Jsy/50 25.00
68 Jim Palmer/Pants/50 8.00
69 Eddie Murray/Jsy/50 15.00
70 Cal Ripken Jr./Jsy/50 65.00
71 Keith Hernandez/Jsy/50 8.00
74 Steve Carlton/Jsy/50 8.00
75 Mike Schmidt/Jkt/50 25.00
78 Dave Parker/Jsy/50 8.00
79 Willie Stargell/Jsy/50 15.00
80 Reggie Jackson/Jsy/50 15.00
82 Dave Concepcion/Jsy/50 8.00
83 George Foster/Jsy/50 8.00
86 Rollie Fingers/Jsy/50 8.00
87 Jim "Catfish" Hunter/Jsy/50 15.00
88 Reggie Jackson/Jkt/50 15.00
91 Willie Stargell/Jsy/50 15.00
98 Lou Brock/Jkt/50 15.00
100 Duke Snider/Pants/50 15.00

Blue Signature
NM/M
Quantity produced listed.
2 Miguel Cabrera/25 40.00
3 Derrek Lee/25 30.00
5 Brad Penny/25 15.00
9 Garret Anderson/25 20.00
11 John Lackey/50 10.00
12 Chone Figgins/25 15.00
16 Steve Finley/25 20.00
29 Darryl Strawberry/25 20.00
42 Fred McGriff/25 40.00
47 Jack Morris/25 20.00
48 Jack Morris/25 20.00
50 Eric Davis/25 25.00
53 Dennis Eckersley/25 40.00
56 Dave Parker/25 20.00
58 Bert Blyleven/25 25.00
60 Dwight Gooden/25 25.00
62 Lenny Dykstra/25 25.00
63 Keith Hernandez/25 25.00
64 Darryl Strawberry/25 25.00
67 Alan Trammell/25 25.00
68 Jim Palmer/25 25.00
71 Keith Hernandez/25 25.00
76 John Candelaria/25 25.00
77 Bert Blyleven/25 25.00
78 Dave Parker/25 20.00
82 Dave Concepcion/25 20.00
83 George Foster/25 20.00
85 Tony Perez/25 35.00
86 Rollie Fingers/25 25.00
89 Al Oliver/25 25.00

Face Off

NM/M
Complete Set (20): 75.00
Common Duo: 2.00
Production 500 Sets
HoloFoil: 2-4X
Production 25 Sets
1 Roger Clemens, Mike Piazza 6.00
2 Mike Mussina, Ivan Rodriguez 3.00
3 Mark Grace, Jorge Posada 4.00
4 Greg Maddux, Jim Thome 5.00
5 Rickey Henderson, Curt Schilling 4.00
6 Kirby Puckett, Tom Glavine 4.00
7 Dennis Eckersley, Will Clark 3.00
8 Bernie Williams, Randy Johnson 4.00
9 Cal Ripken Jr., Steve Carlton 12.00
10 Tom Seaver, Reggie Jackson 4.00
11 Mike Schmidt, George Brett 8.00
12 Wade Boggs, Keith Hernandez 3.00
13 Dwight Gooden, Dwight Evans 2.00
14 Johnny Bench, Jim "Catfish" Hunter 4.00
15 Jim Palmer, Dave Parker 4.00
16 Bob Gibson, Al Kaline 4.00
17 Carl Yastrzemski, Lou Brock 6.00
18 Duke Snider, Whitey Ford 4.00
19 Carlton Fisk, Tony Perez 4.00
20 Roberto Clemente, Frank Robinson 8.00

Face Off Material
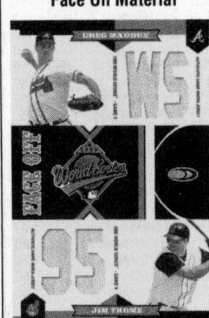
NM/M
Common Duo: 10.00
Quantity produced listed.
1 Roger Clemens/Jsy, Mike Piazza/Jsy 25.00
2 Mike Mussina/Jsy, Ivan Rodriguez/Jsy/100 20.00
4 Greg Maddux/Jsy, Jim Thome/Jsy 35.00
5 Rickey Henderson/Jsy, Curt Schilling/Jsy, 15.00
6 Kirby Puckett/Jsy, Tom Glavine/Jsy 25.00
8 Bernie Williams/Jsy, Randy Johnson/Pants/100 20.00
9 Cal Ripken Jr./Jsy, Steve Carlton/Jsy/50 75.00
11 Mike Schmidt/Jkt, George Brett/Jsy/50 40.00
13 Dwight Gooden/Jsy, Dwight Evans/Jsy/25 25.00
15 Jim Palmer/Jsy, Dave Parker/Jsy/50 10.00
17 Carl Yastrzemski/Jsy, Lou Brock/Jkt/50 40.00
18 Duke Snider/Pants, Whitey Ford/Jsy/50 25.00
19 Carlton Fisk/Jsy, Tony Perez/Fld Glv/50 20.00

Legends of the Fall

NM/M
Complete Set (20): 75.00
Common Player: 3.00
Production 500 Sets
HoloFoil: 2-4X
Production 25 Sets
1 Bob Gibson 4.00
2 Brooks Robinson 4.00
3 Cal Ripken Jr. 12.00
4 Carl Yastrzemski 6.00
5 Carlton Fisk 4.00
6 Derek Jeter 8.00
7 Duke Snider 4.00
8 Eddie Murray 4.00
9 Frank Robinson. 4.00
10 Gary Carter 3.00
11 George Brett 8.00
12 Jim Palmer 3.00
13 Johnny Bench 4.00
14 Marco Rivera 4.00
15 Mike Schmidt 8.00
16 Phil Rizzuto 3.00
17 Red Schoendienst 3.00
18 Reggie Jackson 4.00
19 Rickey Henderson 3.00
20 Whitey Ford 4.00

Legends of the Fall Material
NM/M
Common Player: 5.00
Quantity produced listed.
1 Bob Gibson/Jsy 12.00
2 Brooks Robinson/Bat/100 4.00
3 Cal Ripken Jr./Jkt/100 40.00
4 Carl Yastrzemski/Bat/50 10.00
5 Carlton Fisk/Bat/50 10.00
7 Duke Snider/Pants/50 15.00
8 Eddie Murray/Jsy/50 10.00
9 Frank Robinson/Bat/100 5.00
10 Gary Carter/Jsy/100 10.00
12 George Brett/Bat/50 25.00
12 Jim Palmer/Pants/25 12.00
13 Johnny Bench/Bat/100 12.00
14 Marco Rivera/Jsy/100 8.00
15 Mike Schmidt/Jkt/50 15.00
16 Phil Rizzuto/Pants/50 10.00
17 Red Schoendienst/Bat/100 5.00
18 Reggie Jackson/Bat/100 10.00
19 Rickey Henderson/Bat/100 10.00

Legends of the Fall Signature
NM/M
Common Player:
2 Brooks Robinson/25 30.00
3 Frank Robinson/25 35.00
10 Gary Carter/25 25.00
12 Jim Palmer/25 25.00
16 Phil Rizzuto/25 30.00
17 Red Schoendienst/25 30.00

Legends of the Fall Sign. Material
NM/M
Quantity produced listed.
1 Bob Gibson/Jsy/25 40.00
2 Brooks Robinson/Bat/50 35.00
7 Duke Snider/Pants/50 35.00
9 Frank Robinson/Bat/50 30.00
10 Gary Carter/Jkt/50 25.00
12 Jim Palmer/Pants/50 25.00
13 Johnny Bench/Bat/25 70.00
16 Phil Rizzuto/Pants/50 35.00
17 Red Schoendienst/Bat/100 20.00

Material Bat
NM/M
Common Player: 4.00
Production 100 Sets
2 Darin Erstad 4.00
3 Garret Anderson 4.00
4 Tim Salmon 4.00
5 Troy Glaus 4.00
6 Vladimir Guerrero 8.00
12 Luis Gonzalez 4.00
13 Andruw Jones 6.00
14 Chipper Jones 8.00
15 J.D. Drew 4.00
16 Marcus Giles 4.00
17 Rafael Furcal 4.00
18 Javy Lopez 4.00
19 Jay Gibbons 4.00
22 Miguel Tejada 6.00
23 Rafael Palmeiro 8.00
25 Dwight Evans 4.00
26 Fred Lynn 4.00
27 Jason Varitek 6.00
28 Jim Rice 6.00
29 Johnny Damon 10.00
31 Manny Ramirez 8.00
32 Nomar Garciaparra 10.00
33 Pedro Martinez 8.00
34 Trot Nixon 4.00
35 Aramis Ramirez 6.00
37 Derrek Lee 6.00
40 Mark Prior 6.00
41 Moises Alou 4.00
42 Sammy Sosa 12.00
43 Carlos Lee 4.00
44 Frank Thomas 8.00
45 Luis Aparicio 4.00
46 Magglio Ordonez 4.00
47 Mark Buehrle 4.00
48 Paul Konerko 4.00
49 Adam Dunn Jsy 4.00
50 Austin Kearns 4.00
51 Barry Larkin 8.00
52 Dave Concepcion 4.00
53 George Foster 4.00
54 Joe Morgan 8.00
55 Sean Casey 4.00
56 Tony Perez 4.00
59 Omar Vizquel 4.00
60 Victor Martinez 4.00
61 Charles Johnson 4.00
62 Larry Walker 8.00
63 Preston Wilson 4.00
64 Todd Helton 8.00
66 Alan Trammell 4.00
68 Ivan Rodriguez 8.00
71 Brad Penny 4.00
73 Josh Beckett 4.00
74 Juan Pierre 4.00
75 Luis Castillo 4.00
76 Miguel Cabrera 8.00
77 Mike Lowell 6.00
78 Andy Pettitte 4.00
80 Craig Biggio 6.00
80 Jeff Bagwell 8.00
81 Jeff Kent 4.00
82 Lance Berkman 4.00
83 Roger Clemens 15.00
84 Roy Oswalt 4.00
86 Angel Berroa 4.00
87 Carlos Beltran 8.00
88 Juan Gonzalez 8.00
89 Ken Harvey 4.00
90 Mike Sweeney 4.00
92 Adrian Beltre 6.00
93 Kazuhisa Ishii 4.00
96 Paul LoDuca 4.00
97 Shawn Green 4.00
98 Ben Sheets 4.00
99 Geoff Jenkins 4.00
104 Jacque Jones 4.00
106 Shannon Stewart 4.00
107 Torii Hunter 6.00
108 Jose Vidro 4.00
109 Orlando Cabrera 6.00
111 Darryl Strawberry 6.00
112 Dwight Gooden 6.00
113 Jose Reyes 6.00
114 Kazuo Matsui 10.00
115 Keith Hernandez 6.00
116 Lenny Dykstra 4.00
118 Tom Glavine 8.00
122 Gary Sheffield 6.00
123 Jason Giambi 4.00
125 Jorge Posada 8.00
126 Kenny Lofton 4.00
127 Kevin Brown 4.00
129 Mike Mussina 8.00
131 Eric Chavez 4.00
132 Jermaine Dye 4.00
133 Mark Mulder 4.00
135 Tim Hudson 6.00
137 Jim Thome 6.00
139 Marlon Byrd 4.00
141 Pat Burrell 4.00
142 Steve Carlton 6.00
143 Dave Parker 4.00
145 Brian Giles 4.00
147 Ryan Klesko 4.00
151 Edgar Martinez 4.00
153 Rich Aurilia 4.00
155 Albert Pujols 15.00
156 Dan Haren 4.00
157 Edgar Renteria 4.00
159 Jim Edmonds 6.00
161 Scott Rolen 6.00
162 Aubrey Huff 4.00
165 Fred McGriff 4.00
166 Rocco Baldelli 4.00
167 Alfonso Soriano 8.00
168 Hank Blalock 8.00
170 Mark Teixeira 8.00
171 Michael Young 4.00
172 Carlos Delgado 4.00
175 Vernon Wells 4.00

Material Fabric AL/NL

NM/M
Common Player: 4.00
Production 250 unless noted.
2 Darin Erstad/Jsy 4.00
3 Garret Anderson/Jsy 4.00
4 Tim Salmon/Jsy 4.00
5 Troy Glaus/Jsy 4.00
6 Vladimir Guerrero/Jsy 8.00
7 Brandon Webb/Pants 4.00
8 Luis Gonzalez/Jsy 4.00
9 Randy Johnson/Pants/100 10.00
12 Steve Finley/Jsy 4.00
13 Andruw Jones/Jsy 6.00
14 Chipper Jones/Jsy 8.00
16 Marcus Giles/Jsy 4.00
17 Rafael Furcal/Jsy 4.00
19 Jay Gibbons/Jsy 4.00
20 Luis Matos/Jsy 4.00
21 Melvin Mora/Jsy 4.00
22 Miguel Tejada/Jsy 6.00
23 Rafael Palmeiro/Jsy/100 8.00
25 Dwight Evans/Jsy 4.00
26 Fred Lynn/Jsy 4.00
28 Jim Rice/Jsy 6.00
31 Manny Ramirez/Jsy 8.00
33 Pedro Martinez/Jsy 8.00
35 Aramis Ramirez/Jsy 6.00
38 Greg Maddux/Jsy/100 12.00
40 Kerry Wood/Pants 6.00
42 Sammy Sosa/Jsy 10.00
43 Carlos Lee/Jsy 4.00
44 Frank Thomas/Jsy 8.00
47 Mark Buehrle/Jsy 4.00
48 Paul Konerko/Jsy 4.00
49 Adam Dunn/Jsy 8.00
50 Austin Kearns/Jsy 4.00
52 Dave Concepcion/Jsy 4.00
57 C.C. Sabathia/Jsy 4.00
58 Jody Gerut/Jsy 4.00
60 Omar Vizquel/Jsy 4.00
62 Victor Martinez/Jsy 4.00
63 Larry Walker/Jsy 8.00
64 Preston Wilson/Jsy 4.00
65 Todd Helton/Jsy 8.00
70 A.J. Burnett/Jsy 4.00
71 Brad Penny/Jsy 4.00
72 Dontrelle Willis/Jsy 4.00
73 Josh Beckett/Jsy 6.00
76 Miguel Cabrera/Jsy 8.00
77 Mike Lowell/Jsy 4.00
79 Craig Biggio/Jsy 8.00
80 Jeff Bagwell/Pants 8.00
81 Jeff Kent/Jsy 4.00
82 Lance Berkman/Jsy 4.00
86 Angel Berroa/Pants 4.00
90 Mike Sweeney/Jsy 4.00
91 Adrian Beltre/Jsy 6.00
92 Hideo Nomo/Jsy 4.00
93 Kazuhisa Ishii/Jsy 4.00
95 Orel Hershiser/Jsy/100 6.00
96 Paul LoDuca/Jsy 4.00
97 Shawn Green/Jsy 6.00
98 Ben Sheets/Pants 4.00
99 Geoff Jenkins/Jsy 4.00
104 Jacque Jones/Jsy 4.00
105 Johan Santana/Jsy 8.00
106 Shannon Stewart/Jsy 4.00
110 Al Leiter/Jsy 4.00
111 Darryl Strawberry/Jsy 4.00
117 Mike Piazza/Jsy 10.00
118 Tom Glavine/Jsy 8.00
120 Bernie Williams/Jsy 4.00
123 Jason Giambi/Jsy 4.00
128 Mariano Rivera/Jsy 8.00
129 Mike Mussina/Jsy 8.00
130 Barry Zito/Jsy 4.00
131 Eric Chavez/Jsy 4.00
133 Mark Mulder/Jsy 4.00
135 Tim Hudson/Jsy 6.00
136 Brett Myers/Jsy 4.00
137 Jim Thome/Jsy 8.00
138 Kevin Millwood/Jsy 4.00
139 Marlon Byrd/Jsy 4.00
141 Pat Burrell/Jsy 4.00
142 Steve Carlton/Jsy/100 6.00
143 Dave Parker/Jsy/100 4.00
147 Ryan Klesko/Jsy 4.00
152 Jamie Moyer/Jsy 4.00
155 Albert Pujols/Jsy/100 15.00
159 Jim Edmonds/Jsy 6.00
161 Scott Rolen/Jsy 8.00
162 Aubrey Huff/Jsy 4.00
163 Carl Crawford/Jsy 4.00
164 Dewon Brazelton/Jsy 4.00
165 Fred McGriff/Jsy 4.00
166 Rocco Baldelli/Jsy 4.00
168 Hank Blalock/Jsy 8.00
174 Roy Halladay/Jsy 4.00
175 Vernon Wells/Jsy 4.00

Material Fabric Number
NM/M
Common Player:
5 Troy Glaus/Jsy/25 10.00
6 Vladimir Guerrero/Jsy/27 20.00
7 Brandon Webb/Pants/55 6.00
8 Luis Gonzalez/Jsy/20 8.00
9 Randy Johnson/Pants/51 15.00
13 Andruw Jones/Jsy/25 10.00
16 Marcus Giles/Jsy/22 6.00
19 Jay Gibbons/Jsy/31 6.00
23 Rafael Palmeiro/Jsy/25 15.00
25 Dwight Evans/Jsy/24 15.00
26 Fred Lynn/Jsy/19 10.00
30 Luis Tiant/Jsy/23 6.00
31 Manny Ramirez/Jsy/24 20.00
33 Pedro Martinez/Jsy/45 15.00
38 Greg Maddux/Jsy/38 20.00
39 Kerry Wood/Pants/34 6.00
40 Mark Prior/Jsy/22 15.00
42 Sammy Sosa/Jsy/21 25.00
43 Carlos Lee/Jsy/45 6.00
44 Frank Thomas/Jsy/35 15.00
46 Magglio Ordonez/Jsy/30 8.00
47 Mark Buehrle/Jsy/56 6.00
49 Adam Dunn/Jsy/44 12.00
50 Austin Kearns/Jsy/28 6.00
57 C.C. Sabathia/Jsy/52 6.00
60 Victor Martinez/Jsy/41 8.00
63 Larry Walker/Jsy/33 10.00
64 Preston Wilson/Jsy/44 6.00
65 Todd Helton/Jsy/17 25.00
70 A.J. Burnett/Jsy/34 6.00
71 Brad Penny/Jsy/31 6.00
72 Dontrelle Willis/Jsy/35 6.00
73 Josh Beckett/Jsy/21 15.00
76 Miguel Cabrera/Jsy/29 20.00
90 Mike Sweeney/Jsy/29 6.00
91 Adrian Beltre/Jsy/29 15.00
95 Orel Hershiser/Jsy/29 15.00
105 Johan Santana/Jsy/57 15.00
106 Shannon Stewart/Jsy/23 8.00
107 Torii Hunter/Jsy/48 10.00
110 Al Leiter/Jsy/22 10.00
117 Mike Piazza/Jsy/31 15.00
118 Tom Glavine/Jsy/47 12.00
120 Bernie Williams/Jsy/35 12.00
123 Jason Giambi/Jsy/25 10.00
125 Jorge Posada/Jsy/20 15.00
128 Mariano Rivera/Jsy/42 10.00
129 Mike Mussina/Jsy/35 15.00
130 Barry Zito/Jsy/75 6.00
133 Mark Mulder/Jsy/20 15.00
136 Brett Myers/Jsy/39 6.00
137 Jim Thome/Jsy/29 20.00
138 Kevin Millwood/Jsy/34 8.00
139 Marlon Byrd/Jsy/29 6.00
142 Steve Carlton/Jsy/32 12.00
143 Dave Parker/Jsy/39 8.00
147 Ryan Klesko/Jsy/30 6.00
152 Jamie Moyer/Jsy/50 6.00
156 Dan Haren/Jsy/55 6.00
159 Jim Edmonds/Jsy/15 15.00
161 Scott Rolen/Jsy/27 15.00
164 Dewon Brazelton/Jsy/45 6.00
165 Fred McGriff/Jsy/29 15.00
174 Roy Halladay/Jsy/32 8.00

MVP
NM/M
Complete Set (15): 35.00
Common Player: 2.00
Production 1,000 Sets
HoloFoil: 2-4X
Production 50 Sets
1 Whitey Ford 3.00
2 Bob Gibson 3.00
3 Frank Robinson 2.00
4 Brooks Robinson 3.00
5 Roberto Clemente 3.00
6 Reggie Jackson 3.00
7 Rollie Fingers 2.00
8 Johnny Bench 3.00
9 Reggie Jackson 3.00
10 Mike Schmidt 3.00
11 Alan Trammell 2.00
12 Orel Hershiser 2.00
13 Jack Morris 2.00
14 Paul Molitor 2.00
15 Tom Glavine 3.00

MVP Material
NM/M
Quantity produced listed.
1 Whitey Ford/Jsy/50 10.00
2 Bob Gibson/Jsy/50 10.00

		NM/M
3	Frank Robinson/Jsy/25	12.00
6	Reggie Jackson/Jkt/100	8.00
9	Rollie Fingers/Jsy/100	5.00
9	Reggie Jackson/Jsy/25	20.00
10	Mike Schmidt/Jsy/50	25.00
12	Orel Hershiser/Jsy/100	5.00
15	Tom Glavine/Jsy/100	8.00

MVP Signature

		NM/M
	Quantity produced listed.	
11	Alan Trammell/25	20.00
13	Jack Morris/25	20.00

MVP Signature Material

		NM/M
	Quantity produced listed.	
2	Bob Gibson/Jsy/25	35.00
4	Frank Robinson/ Shoe/50	40.00
9	Rollie Fingers/Jsy/100	15.00
12	Orel Hershiser/Jsy/25	25.00

October Heroes

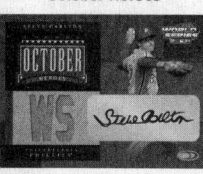

		NM/M
	Complete Set (20):	40.00
	Common Player:	2.00
	Production 500 Sets	
	HoloFoil:	2-4X
	Production 25 Sets	
1	Alan Trammell	2.00
2	Andy Pettitte	3.00
3	Jim "Catfish" Hunter	4.00
4	Chipper Jones	4.00
5	Dave Concepcion	2.00
6	David Wells	2.00
7	Jack Morris	2.00
8	Joe Morgan	5.00
9	Josh Beckett	2.00
10	Kirby Puckett	2.00
11	Kirk Gibson	2.00
12	Marty Marion	2.00
13	Miguel Cabrera	4.00
14	Paul Molitor	4.00
15	Paul O'Neill	2.00
16	Randy Johnson	4.00
17	Roger Clemens	6.00
18	Steve Carlton	3.00
19	Steve Garvey	2.00
20	Wade Boggs	3.00

October Heroes Material

		NM/M
	Common Player:	4.00
1	Alan Trammell/Jsy/25	10.00
2	Andy Pettitte/Jsy/25	4.00
3	Jim "Catfish" Hunter/ Jsy/25	15.00
4	Chipper Jones/Jsy/100	8.00
5	Dave Concepcion/ Jsy/100	4.00
6	David Wells/Jsy/25	8.00
9	Josh Beckett/Jsy/25	4.00
10	Kirby Puckett/Jsy/25	25.00
12	Marty Marion/Jsy/25	10.00
13	Miguel Cabrera/Jsy/100	8.00
16	Randy Johnson/ Pants/50	12.00
17	Roger Clemens/Jsy/100	12.00
18	Steve Carlton/Jsy/100	6.00
19	Steve Garvey/Jsy/100	4.00
20	Wade Boggs/Jsy/100	8.00

October Heroes Signatures

		NM/M
	Quantity produced listed.	
1	Alan Trammell/25	25.00
4	Dave Concepcion/25	20.00
7	Jack Morris/25	20.00
12	Marty Marion/25	20.00
13	Miguel Cabrera/25	40.00
18	Steve Carlton/25	35.00
19	Steve Garvey/25	20.00

October Heroes Sign. Material

		NM/M
1	Alan Trammell/Jsy/100	20.00
5	Dave Concepcion/ Jsy/100	15.00
12	Marty Marion/Jsy/100	15.00
13	Miguel Cabrera/Jsy/100	30.00
18	Steve Carlton/Jsy/50	35.00
19	Steve Garvey/Jsy/100	15.00

October Legends

		NM/M
	Complete Set (20):	60.00
	Common Player:	2.00
	Production 500 Sets	
	HoloFoil:	2-4X
	Production 25 Sets	
1	Bob Gibson	4.00
2	Cal Ripken Jr.	10.00
3	Carl Yastrzemski	6.00
4	Carlton Fisk	3.00
5	Duke Snider	4.00
6	Eddie Murray	4.00
7	Frank Robinson	3.00
8	George Brett	8.00
9	Joe Morgan	2.00
10	Johnny Bench	4.00
11	Lou Brock	3.00
12	Mike Schmidt	8.00
13	Paul Molitor	4.00
14	Phil Rizzuto	3.00
15	Reggie Jackson	4.00
16	Robin Yount	4.00
17	Stan Musial	6.00
18	Steve Carlton	2.00
19	Whitey Ford	3.00
20	Willie McCovey	4.00

October Legends Materials

		NM/M
	Common Player:	5.00
	Quantity produced listed.	
1	Bob Gibson/Jsy/50	10.00
2	Cal Ripken Jr./Jsy/50	50.00
3	Carl Yastrzemski/Jsy/25	20.00
4	Carlton Fisk/Jsy/100	8.00
5	Duke Snider/Jsy/25	20.00
6	Eddie Murray/Jsy/100	10.00
7	Frank Robinson/Jsy/25	8.00
8	George Brett/Jsy/50	25.00
10	Johnny Bench/Jsy/50	15.00
11	Lou Brock/Jkt/100	8.00
12	Mike Schmidt/Jkt/100	15.00
13	Phil Rizzuto/Pants/25	15.00
15	Reggie Jackson/Jkt/100	8.00
16	Robin Yount/Jsy/100	10.00
18	Steve Carlton/Jsy/100	5.00
19	Whitey Ford/Pants/25	14.00
20	Willie McCovey/Jsy/25	15.00

October Legends Signature

		NM/M
	Quantity produced listed.	
11	Lou Brock/25	35.00
14	Phil Rizzuto/25	35.00
18	Steve Carlton/25	30.00

October Legends Sig. Material

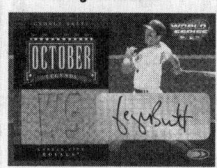

		NM/M
	Quantity produced listed	
1	Bob Gibson/Jsy/50	40.00
5	Duke Snider/Jsy/50	40.00
7	Frank Robinson/Jsy/50	30.00
11	Lou Brock/Jkt/100	25.00
13	Paul Molitor/Jsy/50	14.00
14	Phil Rizzuto/Pants/50	30.00
16	Robin Yount/Jsy/25	65.00
17	Stan Musial/Jsy/25	90.00
18	Steve Carlton/Jsy/100	25.00
19	Whitey Ford/Pants/25	14.00
20	Willie McCovey/Jsy/50	40.00

Playoff All-Stars

		NM/M
	Complete Set (20):	50.00
	Common Player:	2.00

		NM/M
	Production 500 Sets	
	HoloFoil:	2-4X
	Production 25 Sets	
1	Mark Prior	3.00
2	Sammy Sosa	6.00
3	Steve Finley	2.00
4	David Ortiz	4.00
5	Mike Piazza	5.00
6	Edgar Martinez	2.00
7	Roy Oswalt	2.00
8	Johan Santana	3.00
9	Jacque Jones	2.00
10	Will Clark	4.00
11	Albert Pujols	8.00
12	Andre Dawson	3.00
13	Nolan Ryan	10.00
14	Fred Lynn	2.00
15	Jim Rice	2.00
16	Dwight Evans	2.00
17	Harmon Killebrew	4.00
18	Maury Wills	2.00
19	Mark Mulder	2.00

Playoff All-Stars Material 1

		NM/M
	Quantity produced listed.	
1	Mark Prior/Jsy/100	6.00
2	Sammy Sosa/Jsy/50	10.00
3	Steve Finley/Jsy/100	4.00
4	David Ortiz/Jsy/100	10.00
5	Mike Piazza/Jsy/50	14.00
6	Edgar Martinez/Jsy/50	6.00
7	Roy Oswalt/Jsy/100	4.00
8	Johan Santana/Jsy/100	8.00
9	Jacque Jones/Jsy/100	4.00
10	Will Clark/Bat/100	10.00
11	Albert Pujols/Jsy/100	20.00
12	Andre Dawson/Jsy/100	6.00
13	Nolan Ryan/Jsy/25	25.00
14	Fred Lynn/Jsy/50	6.00
15	Jim Rice/Jsy/50	6.00
16	Dwight Evans/Jsy/50	6.00
17	Harmon Killebrew/ Jsy/50	20.00
19	Mark Mulder/Jsy/50	6.00
20	Frank Thomas/Jsy/50	8.00

Playoff All-Stars Material 2

		NM/M
	Common Dual:	6.00
1	Mark Prior/Jsy-Jsy/100	8.00
2	Sammy Sosa/ Jsy-Jsy/100	15.00
3	Steve Finley/ Jsy-Jsy/100	6.00
4	David Ortiz/Bat-Jsy/100	20.00
5	Mike Piazza/ Bat-Jsy/100	15.00
6	Edgar Martinez/ Bat-Jsy/100	10.00
7	Roy Oswalt/Bat-Jsy/100	6.00
8	Johan Santana/ Jsy-Jsy/100	10.00
9	Jacque Jones/ Bat-Jsy/100	6.00
11	Albert Pujols/ Jsy-Jsy/100	25.00
12	Andre Dawson/ Bat-Jsy/100	8.00
13	Nolan Ryan/Jkt-Jsy/50	40.00
14	Fred Lynn/Bat-Jsy/100	8.00
15	Jim Rice/Bat-Jsy/50	6.00
16	Dwight Evans/Bat-Jsy/50	6.00
17	Harmon Killebrew/ Bat-Jsy/50	25.00
19	Mark Mulder/ Bat-Jsy/100	6.00
20	Frank Thomas/ Bat-Jsy/100	12.00

Playoff All-Stars Material 3

		NM/M
	Common Triple:	10.00
1	Mark Prior/ Bat-Hat-Jsy/100	15.00
2	Sammy Sosa/ Bat-Jsy-Jsy/100	20.00
3	Steve Finley/ Jsy-Jsy-Jsy/100	10.00
4	David Ortiz/ Bat-Jsy-Jsy/100	25.00
5	Mike Piazza/ Bat-Jsy-Jsy/100	20.00
6	Edgar Martinez/ Bat-Jsy-Jsy/100	10.00
7	Roy Oswalt/ Bat-Fld Glv-Jsy/50	10.00
9	Jacque Jones/ Bat-Jsy-Jsy/100	10.00
11	Albert Pujols/ Bat-Jsy-Jsy/100	40.00
12	Andre Dawson/ Bat-Hat-Jsy/100	10.00
13	Nolan Ryan/ Bat-Jkt-Jsy/50	65.00
15	Jim Rice/ Bat-Jsy-Jsy/100	10.00
16	Dwight Evans/ Bat-Jsy-Jsy/100	10.00
17	Harmon Killebrew/ Bat-Jsy-Shoe/50	50.00
20	Frank Thomas/ Jsy-Jsy-Pants/100	20.00

Playoff All-Stars Signature

		NM/M
	Quantity produced listed.	
1	Mark Prior/25	40.00

3	Steve Finley/25	20.00
7	David Ortiz/25	60.00
8	Roy Oswalt/25	20.00
8	Johan Santana/25	40.00
9	Jacque Jones/25	15.00
10	Will Clark/25	50.00
13	Andre Dawson/25	20.00
13	Nolan Ryan/25	125.00
14	Fred Lynn/25	20.00
15	Jim Rice/25	25.00
16	Dwight Evans/25	30.00
18	Maury Wills/25	20.00

Playoff All-Stars Sig. Material 1

		NM/M
	Quantity produced listed.	
	Material 2:	.75-1.5X
	Production 5-100	
	Material 3:	.75-1.5X
	Production 5-100	
3	Steve Finley/Jsy/100	15.00
4	David Ortiz/Jsy/100	50.00
6	Edgar Martinez/Jsy/50	30.00
7	Roy Oswalt/Jsy/100	15.00
8	Johan Santana/Jsy/100	35.00
9	Jacque Jones/Jsy/100	15.00
10	Will Clark/Bat/25	65.00
12	Andre Dawson/Jsy/100	20.00
14	Fred Lynn/Jsy/25	20.00
15	Jim Rice/Jsy/25	25.00
19	Mark Mulder/Jsy/50	30.00
20	Frank Thomas/Jsy/25	50.00

Records

		NM/M
	Complete Set (5):	10.00
	Common Player:	3.00
	Production 1,000 Sets	
	HoloFoil:	2-4X
	Production 50 Sets	
1	Lou Brock	3.00
2	Yogi Berra	4.00
3	Reggie Jackson	3.00
4	Bob Gibson	3.00
5	Whitey Ford	3.00

Records Material

		NM/M
	Quantity produced listed.	
1	Lou Brock/Bat/100	10.00
2	Yogi Berra/Bat/50	20.00
3	Reggie Jackson/Bat/100	10.00
5	Whitey Ford/Pants/25	10.00

Records Signature

		NM/M
	Common Player:	
1	Lou Brock/25	30.00

Records Signature Material

		NM/M
	Quantity produced listed.	
1	Lou Brock/Bat/100	25.00
3	Reggie Jackson/Bat/20	40.00

Signature

		NM/M
	Common Autograph:	10.00
	201-222 Exclusive to Red Sox Champs Sets	
3	Garret Anderson/25	25.00
7	Brandon Webb/25	20.00
11	Shea Hillenbrand/25	20.00
12	Steve Finley/25	15.00
16	Marcus Giles/25	15.00
17	Rafael Furcal/25	20.00
19	Jay Gibbons/25	10.00
20	Luis Matos/25	10.00
21	Melvin Mora/25	20.00
25	Dwight Evans/25	30.00
26	Fred Lynn/25	25.00
28	Jim Rice/25	25.00
30	Luis Tiant/25	20.00
34	Trot Nixon/25	20.00
35	Aramis Ramirez/25	35.00
37	Derrek Lee/25	30.00
40	Mark Prior/25	40.00
43	Carlos Lee/25	10.00
45	Luis Aparicio/25	20.00
46	Magglio Ordonez/25	20.00
47	Mark Buehrle/25	10.00
49	Adam Dunn/25	40.00
50	Austin Kearns/25	20.00
52	Dave Concepcion/25	15.00
53	George Foster/25	15.00
56	Tony Perez/25	35.00
57	C.C. Sabathia/25	20.00
58	Jody Gerut/25	10.00
64	Victor Martinez/25	25.00
65	Preston Wilson/25	15.00
66	Alan Trammell/25	25.00
69	Jeremy Bonderman/25	10.00
71	Brad Penny/25	10.00
76	Miguel Cabrera/25	40.00
84	Roy Oswalt/25	20.00
85	Wade Miller/25	10.00
86	Angel Berroa/25	20.00
87	Carlos Beltran/25	50.00
89	Ken Harvey/25	10.00
94	Milton Bradley/25	20.00
96	Paul LoDuca/25	25.00
101	Rickie Weeks/25	20.00
102	Scott Podsednik/25	20.00
103	Jack Morris/25	20.00
104	Jacque Jones/25	15.00

105	Johan Santana/25	50.00
106	Shannon Stewart/25	15.00
107	Torii Hunter/25	25.00
108	Jose Vidro/25	15.00
109	Orlando Cabrera/25	40.00
111	Darryl Strawberry/25	25.00
112	Dwight Gooden/25	25.00
116	Keith Hernandez/25	25.00
116	Lenny Dykstra/25	20.00
132	Jermaine Dye/25	20.00
133	Mark Mulder/25	25.00
134	Rich Harden/25	25.00
139	Marlon Byrd/25	10.00
142	Steve Carlton/25	35.00
143	Dave Parker/25	25.00
146	Jay Payton/25	10.00
148	J.T. Snow/25	15.00
154	Shigetoshi Hasegawa/25	40.00
156	Dan Haren/25	15.00
162	Aubrey Huff/25	20.00
163	Carl Crawford/25	25.00
164	Dewon Brazelton/25	10.00
168	Hank Blalock/25	25.00
170	Mark Teixeira/25	35.00
171	Michael Young/25	20.00

Signature Trio

		NM/M
	Quantity produced listed.	
2	Derek Lee, Brad Penny, Mike Lowell/25	40.00
3	Garret Anderson, John Lackey, Chone Figgins/25	75.00
8	Roberto Alomar, Paul Molitor, Jack Morris/25	125.00
9	Eric Davis, Barry Larkin, Paul O'Neill/25	100.00
10	Dennis Eckersley, Jose Canseco, Dave Parker/25	125.00
11	Keith Hernandez, Dwight Gooden, Gary Carter/25	75.00
12	Lenny Dykstra, George Foster, Darryl Strawberry/25	65.00
13	Alan Trammell, Kirk Gibson, Jack Morris/25	100.00
15	Bert Blyleven, John Candelaria, Dave Parker/25	75.00

Souvenirs Playoff

		NM/M
	Common Player:	5.00
	Production 100 Sets	
1	Chipper Jones/Ball	10.00
2	Randy Johnson/Ball	10.00
3	Albert Pujols/Ball	20.00
4	Jason Schmidt/Ball	8.00
5	Gary Sheffield/Ball	8.00
6	Miguel Tejada/Ball	8.00
7	J.D. Drew/Ball	10.00
8	John Smoltz/Ball	10.00
9	Eric Milton/Ball	5.00
10	Mark Grace/Ball	10.00
11	Tim Hudson/Ball	5.00
12	Jeff Bagwell/Ball	10.00
13	Jim Edmonds/Ball	8.00
14	Sammy Sosa/Ball	15.00
15	Albert Pujols/Ball	20.00

Souvenirs World Series

		NM/M
	Common Player:	5.00
	Production 100 Sets	
1	Jason Schmidt/Ball	8.00
2	Troy Glaus/Base	5.00
3	Reggie Sanders/Base	5.00
4	Tim Salmon/Base	5.00
5	Garret Anderson/Base	5.00
6	Francisco Rodriguez/ Base	5.00
7	Rich Aurilia/Ball	5.00
8	Jeff Kent/Ball	5.00
9	Darin Erstad/Base	5.00
10	Troy Glaus/Base	5.00
11	Jeff Kent/Ball	5.00
12	Scott Spiezio/Base	5.00
13	Tony Percival/Base	5.00
14	Garret Anderson/Base	5.00
15	Darin Erstad/Base	5.00

Triple Threads

		NM/M
	Common Player:	10.00

1	Josh Beckett, Miguel Cabrera, Mike Lowell/100	15.00
2	Luis Castillo, Ivan Rodriguez, Dontrelle Willis/100	20.00
3	Garret Anderson, Troy Glaus, Tim Salmon/100	20.00
4	Curt Schilling, Mark Grace, Randy Johnson/50	25.00
5	Jorge Posada, Bernie Williams, Roger Clemens/25	25.00
6	Andy Pettitte, Wade Boggs, Mariano Rivera/50	20.00
7	Charles Johnson, Cliff Floyd, Moises Alou/100	10.00
8	Chipper Jones, Tom Glavine, Greg Maddux/25	30.00
9	Joe Carter, Rickey Henderson, David Wells/25	25.00
10	Eric Davis, Barry Larkin, Paul O'Neill/100	20.00
11	Dwight Gooden, Gary Carter, Darryl Strawberry/100	10.00
12	Frank White, Willie Wilson, George Brett/100	30.00
13	Jim Palmer, Eddie Murray, Cal Ripken Jr./50	125.00
14	Willie Stargell, Dave Parker, Bill Madlock/100	10.00
15	Johnny Bench, Joe Morgan, Tony Perez/100	35.00
16	Dave Concepcion, George Foster, Johnny Bench/50	40.00
17	Al Oliver, Roberto Clemente, Willie Stargell/50	20.00
18	Jim Palmer, Frank Robinson, Brooks Robinson/50	25.00
19	Bob Gibson, Lou Brock, Orlando Cepeda/50	25.00
20	Stan Musial, Red Schoendienst, Marty Marion/50	40.00

2005 Donruss

		NM/M
	Complete Set (400):	120.00
	Common-Player:	.15
	Common SP (1-70, 371-400):	1.00
	Inserted 1:6	
	Pack (10):	2.50
	Box (24):	50.00
1	Garret Anderson	1.00
2	Vladimir Guerrero	2.00
3	Manny Ramirez	2.00
4	Kerry Wood	1.00
5	Sammy Sosa	3.00
6	Magglio Ordonez	1.00
7	Adam Dunn	1.50
8	Todd Helton	1.50
9	Josh Beckett	1.00
10	Miguel Cabrera	2.00
11	Lance Berkman	1.00
12	Carlos Beltran	1.50
13	Shawn Green	1.00
14	Roger Clemens	4.00
15	Mike Piazza	2.50
16	Alex Rodriguez	3.00
17	Derek Jeter	4.00
18	Mark Mulder	1.00
19	Jim Thome	2.00
20	Albert Pujols	3.00
21	Scott Rolen	2.00
22	Aubrey Huff	1.00
23	Alfonso Soriano	2.00
24	Hank Blalock	1.50
25	Vernon Wells	1.00
26	Kazuo Matsui	1.50
27	B.J. Upton	1.50
28	Charles Thomas	1.00
29	Akinori Otsuka	1.00
30	David Aardsma	1.00
31	Travis Blackley	1.00
32	Brad Halsey	1.00
33	David Wright	5.00
34	Kazuhito Tadano	1.00
35	Casey Kotchman	1.50
36	Khalil Greene	2.00
37	Adrian Gonzalez	1.00
38	Zack Greinke	1.00
39	Chad Cordero	1.00
40	Scott Kazmir	4.00
41	Jeremy Guthrie	1.00
42	Noah Lowry	1.00
43	Chase Utley	1.00
44	Billy Traber	1.00
45	Aaron Baldiris	1.00

#	Player	Price
46	Abe Alvarez	1.00
47	Angel Chavez	1.00
48	Joe Mauer	1.00
49	Joey Gathright	1.00
50	John Gall	1.00
51	Ronald Belisario	1.00
52	Ryan Wing	1.00
53	Scott Proctor	1.00
54	Yadier Molina	1.00
55	Carlos Hines	1.00
56	Frankie Francisco	1.00
57	Graham Koonce	1.00
58	Jake Woods	1.00
59	Jason Bartlett	1.00
60	Mike Rouse	1.00
61	Phil Stockman	1.00
62	Renyel Pinto	1.00
63	Roberto Novoa	1.00
64	Ryan Meaux	1.00
65	David Crouthers	1.00
66	Justin Knoedler	1.00
67	Justin Leone	1.00
68	Nick Regilio	1.00
69	Mike Gosling	1.00
70	Onil Joseph	1.00
71	Bartolo Colon	.15
72	Brad Fullmer	.15
73	Chone Figgins	.15
74	Darin Erstad	.25
75	Francisco Rodriguez	.25
76	Garret Anderson	.25
77	Jarrod Washburn	.15
78	John Lackey	.15
79	Jose Guillen	.15
80	Robb Quinlan	.15
81	Tim Salmon	.25
82	Troy Glaus	.25
83	Troy Percival	.15
84	Vladimir Guerrero	.50
85	Brandon Webb	.15
86	Casey Fossum	.15
87	Luis Gonzalez	.15
88	Randy Johnson	.50
89	Richie Sexson	.25
90	Robby Hammock	.15
91	Roberto Alomar	.25
92	Adam LaRoche	.15
93	Andruw Jones	.25
94	Bubba Nelson	.15
95	Chipper Jones	.50
96	J.D. Drew	.25
97	John Smoltz	.25
98	Johnny Estrada	.15
99	Marcus Giles	.15
100	Mike Hampton	.15
101	Nick Green	.15
102	Rafael Furcal	.15
103	Russ Ortiz	.15
104	Adam Loewen	.15
105	Brian Roberts	.15
106	Javy Lopez	.25
107	Jay Gibbons	.15
108	Larry Bigbie	.15
109	Luis Matos	.15
110	Melvin Mora	.15
111	Miguel Tejada	.40
112	Rafael Palmeiro	.40
113	Rodrigo Lopez	.15
114	Sidney Ponson	.15
115	Bill Mueller	.15
116	Byung-Hyun Kim	.15
117	Curt Schilling	.40
118	David Ortiz	.40
119	Derek Lowe	.15
120	Doug Mientkiewicz	.15
121	Jason Varitek	.25
122	Johnny Damon	.25
123	Keith Foulke	.15
124	Kevin Youkilis	.25
125	Manny Ramirez	.50
126	Orlando Cabrera	.25
127	Pedro J. Martinez	.25
128	Trot Nixon	.15
129	Aramis Ramirez	.25
130	Carlos Zambrano	.25
131	Corey Patterson	.25
132	Derrek Lee	.25
133	Greg Maddux	.75
134	Kerry Wood	.25
135	Mark Prior	.50
136	Matt Clement	.15
137	Moises Alou	.25
138	Nomar Garciaparra	1.00
139	Sammy Sosa	1.00
140	Todd Walker	.15
141	Angel Guzman	.15
142	Billy Koch	.15
143	Carlos Lee	.15
144	Frank Thomas	.40
145	Magglio Ordonez	.25
146	Mark Buehrle	.25
147	Paul Konerko	.25
148	Wilson Valdez	.15
149	Adam Dunn	.40
150	Austin Kearns	.15
151	Barry Larkin	.25
152	Benito Santiago	.15
153	Jason LaRue	.15
154	Ken Griffey Jr.	.75
155	Ryan Wagner	.15
156	Sean Casey	.15
157	Brandon Phillips	.15
158	Brian Tallet	.15
159	C.C. Sabathia	.15
160	Cliff Lee	.15
161	Jeremy Guthrie	.25
162	Jody Gerut	.15
163	Matt Lawton	.15
164	Omar Vizquel	.15
165	Travis Hafner	.15
166	Victor Martinez	.25
167	Charles Johnson	.15
168	Garrett Atkins	.15
169	Jason Jennings	.15
170	Jay Payton	.15
171	Jeromy Burnitz	.15
172	Joe Kennedy	.15
173	Larry Walker	.25
174	Preston Wilson	.15
175	Todd Helton	.40
176	Vinny Castilla	.15
177	Bobby Higginson	.15
178	Brandon Inge	.15
179	Carlos Guillen	.15
180	Carlos Pena	.15
181	Craig Monroe	.15
182	Dmitri Young	.15
183	Eric Munson	.15
184	Fernando Vina	.15
185	Ivan Rodriguez	.40
186	Jeremy Bonderman	.15
187	Rondell White	.15
188	A.J. Burnett	.15
189	Dontrelle Willis	.25
190	Guillermo Mota	.15
191	Hee Seop Choi	.15
192	Jeff Conine	.15
193	Josh Beckett	.25
194	Juan Encarnacion	.15
195	Juan Pierre	.15
196	Luis Castillo	.15
197	Miguel Cabrera	.50
198	Mike Lowell	.15
199	Paul LoDuca	.15
200	Andy Pettitte	.25
201	Brad Ausmus	.15
202	Carlos Beltran	.40
203	Chris Burke	.15
204	Craig Biggio	.25
205	Jeff Bagwell	.25
206	Jeff Kent	.25
207	Lance Berkman	.25
208	Morgan Ensberg	.15
209	Octavio Dotel	.15
210	Roger Clemens	1.50
211	Roy Oswalt	.25
212	Tim Redding	.15
213	Angel Berroa	.15
214	Juan Gonzalez	.25
215	Ken Harvey	.15
216	Mike Sweeney	.15
217	Adrian Beltre	.25
218	Brad Penny	.15
219	Eric Gagne	.25
220	Hideo Nomo	.25
221	Hong-Chih Kuo	.15
222	Jeff Weaver	.15
223	Kazuhisa Ishii	.15
224	Milton Bradley	.15
225	Shawn Green	.25
226	Steve Finley	.15
227	Danny Kolb	.15
228	Geoff Jenkins	.15
229	Junior Spivey	.15
230	Lyle Overbay	.15
231	Rickie Weeks	.25
232	Scott Podsednik	.15
233	Brad Radke	.15
234	Corey Koskie	.15
235	Cristian Guzman	.15
236	Dustan Mohr	.15
237	Eddie Guardado	.15
238	J.D. Durbin	.15
239	Jacque Jones	.15
240	Joe Nathan	.15
241	Johan Santana	.40
242	Lew Ford	.15
243	Michael Cuddyer	.15
244	Shannon Stewart	.15
245	Torii Hunter	.25
246	Brad Wilkerson	.15
247	Carl Everett	.15
248	Jeff Fassero	.15
249	Jose Vidro	.15
250	Livan Hernandez	.15
251	Michael Barrett	.15
252	Tony Batista	.15
253	Zach Day	.15
254	Al Leiter	.15
255	Cliff Floyd	.15
256	Jae Weong Seo	.15
257	John Olerud	.15
258	Jose Reyes	.40
259	Mike Cameron	.15
260	Mike Piazza	1.00
261	Richard Hidalgo	.15
262	Tom Glavine	.25
263	Vance Wilson	.15
264	Alex Rodriguez	1.50
265	Armando Benitez	.15
266	Bernie Williams	.25
267	Bubba Crosby	.15
268	Chien-Ming Wang	.40
269	Derek Jeter	1.50
270	Esteban Loaiza	.15
271	Gary Sheffield	.25
272	Hideki Matsui	1.00
273	Jason Giambi	.25
274	Javier Vazquez	.15
275	Jorge Posada	.25
276	Jose Contreras	.15
277	Kenny Lofton	.15
278	Kevin Brown	.15
279	Mariano Rivera	.25
280	Mike Mussina	.25
281	Barry Zito	.25
282	Bobby Crosby	.15
283	Eric Byrnes	.15
284	Eric Chavez	.25
285	Erubiel Durazo	.15
286	Jermaine Dye	.15
287	Mark Kotsay	.15
288	Mark Mulder	.25
289	Rich Harden	.15
290	Tim Hudson	.15
291	Billy Wagner	.15
292	Bobby Abreu	.15
293	Brett Myers	.15
294	Eric Milton	.15
295	Jim Thome	.50
296	Jimmy Rollins	.25
297	Kevin Millwood	.15
298	Marlon Byrd	.15
299	Mike Lieberthal	.15
300	Pat Burrell	.15
301	Randy Wolf	.15
302	Craig Wilson	.15
303	Jack Wilson	.15
304	Jacob Cruz	.15
305	Jason Bay	.15
306	Jason Kendall	.15
307	Jose Castillo	.15
308	Kip Wells	.15
309	Brian Giles	.15
310	Brian Lawrence	.15
311	Chris Oxspring	.15
312	David Wells	.15
313	Freddy Guzman	.15
314	Jake Peavy	.15
315	Mark Loretta	.15
316	Ryan Klesko	.15
317	Sean Burroughs	.15
318	Trevor Hoffman	.15
319	Xavier Nady	.15
320	A.J. Pierzynski	.15
321	Edgardo Alfonzo	.15
322	J.T. Snow	.15
323	Jason Schmidt	.25
324	Jerome Williams	.15
325	Kirk Rueter	.15
326	Bret Boone	.15
327	Bucky Jacobsen	.15
328	Edgar Martinez	.15
329	Freddy Garcia	.15
330	Ichiro Suzuki	1.00
331	Jamie Moyer	.15
332	Joel Pineiro	.15
333	Scott Spiezio	.15
334	Shigetoshi Hasegawa	.15
335	Albert Pujols	1.50
336	Edgar Renteria	.25
337	Jason Isringhausen	.15
338	Jim Edmonds	.25
339	Matt Morris	.15
340	Mike Matheny	.15
341	Reggie Sanders	.15
342	Scott Rolen	.50
343	Woody Williams	.15
344	Jeff Suppan	.15
345	Aubrey Huff	.15
346	Carl Crawford	.25
347	Chad Gaudin	.15
348	Delmon Young	.15
349	Dewon Brazelton	.15
350	Jose Cruz Jr.	.15
351	Rocco Baldelli	.25
352	Tino Martinez	.15
353	Toby Hall	.15
354	Alfonso Soriano	.40
355	Brian Jordan	.15
356	Francisco Cordero	.15
357	Hank Blalock	.40
358	Kenny Rogers	.15
359	Kevin Mench	.15
360	Laynce Nix	.15
361	Mark Teixeira	.25
362	Michael Young	.15
363	Alex Gonzalez	.15
364	Alexis Rios	.15
365	Carlos Delgado	.15
366	Eric Hinske	.15
367	Frank Catalanotto	.15
368	Josh Phelps	.15
369	Roy Halladay	.15
370	Vernon Wells	.15
371	Vladimir Guerrero	2.00
372	Randy Johnson	2.00
373	Chipper Jones	2.00
374	Miguel Tejada	1.50
375	Pedro Martinez	3.00
376	Sammy Sosa	3.00
377	Frank Thomas	1.50
378	Ken Griffey Jr.	3.00
379	Victor Martinez	1.00
380	Todd Helton	1.50
381	Ivan Rodriguez	1.50
382	Miguel Cabrera	2.00
383	Roger Clemens	4.00
384	Ken Harvey	1.00
385	Eric Gagne	1.50
386	Lyle Overbay	1.00
387	Shannon Stewart	1.00
388	Brad Wilkerson	1.00
389	Mike Piazza	2.50
390	Alex Rodriguez	4.00
391	Mark Mulder	1.00
392	Jim Thome	2.00
393	Jack Wilson	1.00
394	Khalil Greene	1.50
395	Jason Schmidt	1.00
396	Ichiro Suzuki	6.00
397	Albert Pujols	4.00
398	Rocco Baldelli	1.00
399	Alfonso Soriano	3.00
400	Vernon Wells	1.00

Press Proofs Black
No Pricing
Production 10 Sets

Press Proofs Blue
Blue (71-370): 4-8X
Blue SP's: 2-3X
Production 100 Sets

Press Proofs Gold
Gold (71-370): 10-20X
Gold SP's: 3-6X
Production 25 Sets

Press Proofs Red
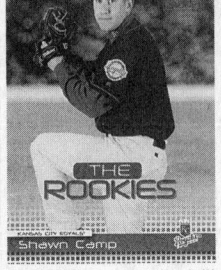

Red (71-370): 2-4X
Red SP's: .75-1.5X
Production 200 Sets

Stat Line Career

#71-370 print run 201-400:	2-4X
71-370 p/r 101-200:	3-6X
71-370 p/r 51-100:	4-8X
71-370 p/r 26-50:	6-12X
71-370 p/r 25 or less:	No Pricing
SP's print run 200 or more:	1-2X
SP's p/r 101-200:	1.5-2X
SP's p/r 51-100:	2-4X
SP's p/r 26-50:	3-5X
SP's p/r 25 or less:	No Pricing

Cards are numbered to career statistic.

Stat Line Season

#71-370 print run 101-200:	3-6X
71-370 p/r 51-100:	4-8X
71-370 p/r 26-50:	6-12X
71-370 p/r 25 or less:	No Pricing
SP's p/r 101 or more:	1.5-2X
SP's p/r 51-100:	2-4X
SP's p/r 26-50:	3-5X
SP's p/r 25 or less:	No Pricing

Cards are numbered to season statistic.

25th Anniversary
Stars: 10-20X
SP's (1-70, 371-400): 3-6X
Production 25 Sets

All-Stars AL
		NM/M
Common Player:		2.00
Production 1,000 Sets		
Gold:		1-2X
Production 100 Sets		
1	Alex Rodriguez	6.00
2	Alfonso Soriano	3.00
3	Curt Schilling	3.00
4	Derek Jeter	8.00
5	Hank Blalock	2.00
6	Hideki Matsui	6.00
7	Ichiro Suzuki	6.00
8	Ivan Rodriguez	3.00
9	Jason Giambi	3.00
10	Manny Ramirez	3.00
11	Mark Mulder	2.00
12	Michael Young	2.00
13	Tim Hudson	2.00
14	Victor Martinez	2.00
15	Vladimir Guerrero	3.00

All-Stars NL

		NM/M
Common Player:		2.00
Production 1,000 Sets		
Gold:		1-2X
Production 100 Sets		
1	Albert Pujols	8.00
2	Ben Sheets	2.00
3	Edgar Renteria	2.00
4	Eric Gagne	2.00
5	Jack Wilson	2.00
6	Jason Schmidt	2.00
7	Jeff Kent	2.00
8	Jim Thome	3.00
9	Ken Griffey Jr.	3.00
10	Mike Piazza	4.00
11	Roger Clemens	4.00
12	Sammy Sosa	5.00
13	Scott Rolen	3.00
14	Sean Casey	2.00
15	Todd Helton	2.00

Autographs
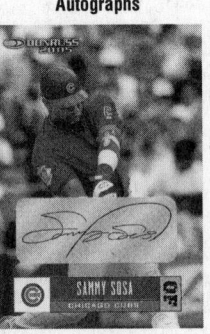

No Pricing

Bat Kings

		NM/M
Common Player:		5.00
Quantity produced listed.		
1	Garret Anderson/250	5.00
2	Vladimir Guerrero/250	8.00
3	Cal Ripken Jr./100	50.00
4	Manny Ramirez/250	8.00
5	Kerry Wood/250	8.00
6	Sammy Sosa/250	12.00
7	Magglio Ordonez/250	5.00
8	Adam Dunn/250	8.00
9	Todd Helton/250	8.00
10	Josh Beckett/250	5.00
11	Miguel Cabrera/250	8.00
12	Lance Berkman/250	8.00
13	Carlos Beltran/250	8.00
14	Shawn Green/250	5.00
15	Roger Clemens/100	15.00
16	Mike Piazza/250	12.00
17	Nolan Ryan/100	50.00
18	Mark Mulder/250	5.00
19	Jim Thome/250	8.00
20	Albert Pujols/250	20.00
21	Scott Rolen/250	10.00
22	Aubrey Huff/250	5.00
23	Alfonso Soriano/250	8.00

Bat Kings Signatures
No Pricing
Production 5 or 10

Craftsmen

	NM/M
Complete Set (30):	40.00
Common Player:	1.00
Production 1,000 Sets	
Black:	1.5-2X
Production 100 Sets	
Master:	1-2X
Production 250 Sets	

Master Black: No Pricing
Production 10 Sets

#	Player	Price
1	Albert Pujols	5.00
2	Alex Rodriguez	4.00
3	Alfonso Soriano	1.00
4	Andruw Jones	1.00
5	Carlos Beltran	1.50
6	Derek Jeter	5.00
7	Greg Maddux	2.50
8	Hank Blalock	1.50
9	Ichiro Suzuki	4.00
10	Jeff Bagwell	1.50
11	Jim Thome	2.00
12	Josh Beckett	1.50
13	Ken Griffey Jr.	2.50
14	Manny Ramirez	2.00
15	Mark Mulder	2.00
16	Mark Prior	2.00
17	Mark Teixeira	1.50
18	Miguel Tejada	1.50
19	Mike Mussina	1.50
20	Mike Piazza	2.50
21	Nomar Garciaparra	3.00
22	Pedro Martinez	1.50
23	Rafael Palmeiro	1.50
24	Randy Johnson	2.00
25	Roger Clemens	5.00
26	Sammy Sosa	2.00
27	Scott Rolen	2.00
28	Tim Hudson	1.00
29	Vernon Wells	1.00
30	Vladimir Guerrero	3.00

Diamond Kings Inserts
		NM/M
Complete Set (25):		40.00
Common Player:		1.50
Production 2,005 Sets		
Studio:		1.5-2X
Production 250 Sets		
Studio Black:		1.5-3X
Production 100 Sets		
1	Garret Anderson	1.50
2	Vladimir Guerrero	2.00
3	Manny Ramirez	1.50
4	Kerry Wood	1.50
5	Sammy Sosa	1.50
6	Magglio Ordonez	1.50
7	Adam Dunn	1.50
8	Todd Helton	1.50
9	Josh Beckett	1.50
10	Miguel Cabrera	1.50
11	Lance Berkman	1.50
12	Carlos Beltran	1.50
13	Shawn Green	1.50
14	Roger Clemens	3.00
15	Mike Piazza	3.00
16	Alex Rodriguez	6.00
17	Derek Jeter	6.00
18	Mark Mulder	1.50
19	Jim Thome	1.50
20	Albert Pujols	6.00
21	Scott Rolen	2.00
22	Aubrey Huff	1.50
23	Alfonso Soriano	2.00
24	Hank Blalock	1.50
25	Vernon Wells	1.50

Elite Series
		NM/M
Complete Set (25):		50.00
Common Player:		2.00
Production 1,500 Sets		
Black:		1-2X
Production 100 Sets		
Dominator:		1-1.5X
Production 250 Sets		
Dominator Black:		3-5X
Production 25 Sets		
1	Albert Pujols	6.00
2	Alex Rodriguez	5.00
3	Alfonso Soriano	2.00
4	Derek Jeter	5.00
5	Hank Blalock	1.50
6	Ichiro Suzuki	4.00
7	Ivan Rodriguez	2.00
8	Jim Thome	2.00
9	Ken Griffey Jr.	3.00
10	Manny Ramirez	2.00
11	Mark Mulder	1.50
12	Mark Prior	2.00
13	Michael Young	2.00
14	Miguel Cabrera	2.00
15	Miguel Tejada	2.00
16	Mike Piazza	2.00
17	Nomar Garciaparra	2.00
18	Rafael Palmeiro	1.50
19	Randy Johnson	2.00

20	Roger Clemens	6.00
21	Sammy Sosa	4.00
22	Scott Rolen	2.00
23	Tim Hudson	1.50
24	Todd Helton	1.50
25	Vladimir Guerrero	2.00

Fans of the Game

		NM/M
	Complete Set (5):	10.00
1	Jesse Ventura	3.00
2	John C. McGinley	2.00
3	Susie Essman	2.00
4	Dean Cain	2.00
5	Meat Loaf	3.00

Fans of the Game Signatures

		NM/M
1	Jesse Ventura	50.00
2	John C. McGinley/SP/300	50.00
3	Susie Essman	60.00
4	Dean Cain/SP/250	90.00
5	Meat Loaf	60.00

Jersey Kings

		NM/M
	Common Player:	5.00
1	Garret Anderson/250	5.00
2	Vladimir Guerrero/250	8.00
3	Cal Ripken Jr./100	50.00
4	Manny Ramirez/250	8.00
5	Kerry Wood/250	10.00
6	Sammy Sosa/250	12.00
7	Magglio Ordonez/250	5.00
8	Adam Dunn/250	8.00
9	Todd Helton/250	8.00
10	Josh Beckett/250	5.00
11	Miguel Cabrera/250	8.00
12	Lance Berkman/250	5.00
13	Carlos Beltran/250	8.00
14	Shawn Green/250	5.00
15	Roger Clemens/250	15.00
16	Mike Piazza/250	10.00
17	Nolan Ryan/100	50.00
18	Mark Mulder/250	5.00
19	Jim Thome/250	8.00
20	Albert Pujols/250	20.00
21	Scott Rolen/250	10.00
22	Aubrey Huff/250	5.00
23	Alfonso Soriano/250	8.00
24	Hank Blalock/250	8.00
25	Vernon Wells/250	5.00

Jersey Kings Signatures

No Pricing
Production 5 or 10

Longball Leaders

		NM/M
	Complete Set (15):	30.00
	Common Player:	2.00
	Black:	1-2X
	Production 250 Sets	
	Die-Cut:	2-3X
	Production 50 Sets	
	Black Die-Cut:	No Pricing
	Production 10 Sets	
1	Adam Dunn	3.00
2	Adrian Beltre	3.00
3	Albert Pujols	6.00
4	Alex Rodriguez	5.00
5	David Ortiz	3.00
6	Hank Blalock	3.00
7	J.D. Drew	2.00
8	Jeromy Burnitz	2.00
9	Jim Edmonds	2.50
10	Jim Thome	3.00
11	Manny Ramirez	3.00
12	Mark Teixeira	2.00
13	Moises Alou	2.00
14	Paul Konerko	2.00
15	Steve Finley	2.00

Mound Marvels

		NM/M
	Complete Set (15):	40.00
	Common Player:	2.00
	Production 1,000 Sets	
	Black:	No Pricing
	Production 10 Sets	
1	Curt Schilling	4.00
2	Dontrelle Willis	2.00
3	Eric Gagne	4.00
4	Greg Maddux	6.00
5	John Smoltz	3.00

6	Kenny Rogers	2.00
7	Kerry Wood	4.00
8	Mariano Rivera	3.00
9	Mark Mulder	2.00
10	Mark Prior	4.00
11	Mike Mussina	3.00
12	Pedro Martinez	4.00
13	Randy Johnson	4.00
14	Roger Clemens	8.00
15	Tim Hudson	2.00

Power Alley Red

	NM/M
Common Player:	1.50
Production 2,500 Sets	
Black:	No Pricing
Production 10 Sets	
Black Die-Cut:	No Pricing
Production Five Sets	
Blue:	1X
Production 1,000 Sets	
Blue Die-Cut:	2-3X
Production 100 Sets	
Green:	3-5X
Production 250 Sets	
Green Die-Cut:	No Pricing
Production 10 Sets	
Purple:	1-2X
Production 250 Sets	
Purple Die-Cut:	2-3X
Production 50 Sets	
Red Die-Cut:	1-2X
Production 250 Sets	
Yellow:	2-3X
Production 100 Sets	
Yellow Die-Cut:	3-5X
Production 25 Sets	

1	Adam Dunn	2.00
2	Adrian Beltre	2.00
3	Albert Pujols	6.00
4	Alex Rodriguez	5.00
5	Alfonso Soriano	3.00
6	Gary Sheffield	2.00
7	Hank Blalock	2.00
8	Hideki Matsui	4.00
9	J.D. Drew	1.50
10	Jeromy Burnitz	1.50
11	Jim Edmonds	2.00
12	Jim Thome	3.00
13	Ken Griffey Jr.	8.00
14	Manny Ramirez	2.00
15	Mark Teixeira	1.50
16	Miguel Cabrera	2.00
17	Miguel Tejada	2.00
18	Mike Lowell	1.50
19	Mike Piazza	3.00
20	Moises Alou	1.50
21	Paul Konerko	1.50
22	Sammy Sosa	4.00
23	Scott Rolen	3.00
24	Todd Helton	2.00
25	Vladimir Guerrero	3.00

Production Line BA

	NM/M
Common Player:	3.00
Black:	2-3X
Production 25 Sets	
Die-Cut:	1X
Production 100 Sets	
Black Die-Cut:	No Pricing
Production 10 Sets	

1	Ichiro Suzuki/372	8.00
2	Ivan Rodriguez/334	5.00
3	Juan Pierre/326	5.00
4	Adrian Beltre/334	5.00
5	Albert Pujols/331	10.00
6	Mark Loretta/335	3.00
7	Melvin Mora/340	3.00
8	Sean Casey/324	3.00
9	Todd Helton/347	5.00
10	Vladimir Guerrero/337	5.00

Production Line OBP

	NM/M
Common Player:	3.00
Black:	2-3X
Production 25 Sets	
Die-Cut:	1X
Production 100 Sets	
Black Die-Cut:	No Pricing
Production 10 Sets	

1	Albert Pujols/415	8.00
2	Bobby Abreu/428	3.00
3	Lance Berkman/450	3.00
4	J.D. Drew/436	3.00
5	Jorge Posada/400	3.00
6	Ichiro Suzuki/414	8.00

7	Manny Ramirez/397	4.00
8	Melvin Mora/419	3.00
9	Todd Helton/469	4.00
10	Travis Hafner/410	3.00

Production Line OPS

	NM/M
Common Player:	3.00
Black:	1.5-2X
Production 50 Sets	
Die-Cut:	1X
Production 100 Sets	
Black Die-Cut:	2-3X
Production 25 Sets	

1	Albert Pujols/1,072	8.00
2	Bobby Abreu/983	4.00
3	Lance Berkman/1,017	4.00
4	J.D. Drew/1,006	3.00
5	Jorge Posada/977	3.00
6	Ichiro Suzuki/1,016	3.00
7	Manny Ramirez/1,009	4.00
8	Melvin Mora/1,007	4.00
9	Todd Helton/1,088	4.00
10	Travis Hafner/993	3.00

Production Line Slugging

	NM/M
Common Player:	3.00
Black:	1.5-2X
Production 50 Sets	
Die-Cut:	1X
Production 100 Sets	
Black Die-Cut:	2-3X
Production 25 Sets	

1	Adrian Beltre/629	4.00
2	Albert Pujols/657	8.00
3	Todd Helton/620	4.00
4	J.D. Drew/569	3.00
5	Jim Edmonds/643	3.00
6	Jim Thome/581	4.00
7	Vladimir Guerrero/598	4.00
8	Manny Ramirez/613	4.00
9	Scott Rolen/598	4.00
10	Travis Hafner/583	3.00

Recollection Autographs

No Pricing
Production 1-5

Rookies

	NM/M
Common Player:	2.00
Inserted 1:23	
Black:	No Pricing
Production 10 Sets	
Blue:	1X
Production 100 Sets	
Gold:	2-3X
Production 25 Sets	
Red:	.75-1X
Production 200 Sets	

1	Fernando Nieve	2.00
2	Frankie Francisco	2.00
3	Jorge Vasquez	2.00
4	Travis Blackley	2.00
5	Joey Gathright	4.00
6	Kazuhito Tadano	2.00
7	Edwin Moreno	2.00
8	Lance Cormier	2.00
9	Justin Knoedler	2.00
10	Orlando Rodriguez	2.00
11	Renyel Pinto	2.00
12	Justin Leone	2.00
13	Dennis Sarfate	2.00
14	Sam Narron	2.00
15	Yadier Molina	4.00
16	Carlos Vasquez	2.00
17	Ryan Wing	2.00
18	Brad Halsey	2.00
19	Ryan Meaux	2.00
20	Mike Wuertz	2.00
21	Shawn Camp	2.00
22	Ruddy Yan	2.00
23	Donald Kelly	2.00
24	Jake Woods	2.00
25	Colby Miller	2.00
26	Abe Alvarez	2.00
27	Mike Rouse	2.00
28	Phil Stockman	2.00
29	Kevin Cave	2.00
30	Chris Shelton	4.00
31	Tim Bittner	2.00
32	Mariano Gomez	2.00
33	Angel Chavez	2.00
34	Carlos Hines	2.00
35	Aarom Baldiris	2.00
36	Kazuo Matsui	5.00
37	Nick Regilio	2.00
38	Ivan Ochoa	2.00

39	Graham Koonce	2.00
40	Merkin Valdez	3.00
41	Greg Dobbs	2.00
42	Chris Oxspring	2.00
43	David Crouthers	2.00
44	Freddy Guzman	2.00
45	Akinori Otsuka	3.00
46	Jesse Crain	2.00
47	Casey Daigle	2.00
48	Roberto Novoa	2.00
49	Eddy Rodriguez	2.00
50	Jason Bartlett	2.00

Rookies Stat Line Career

Print run 201-316:	1X
Print run 101-200:	1X
Print run 51-100:	1-1.5X
Print run 26-50:	1-2X
Print run 25 or less:	No Pricing
Cards are numbered to career statistic.	

Rookies Stat Line Season

Print run 101-200:	1X
Print run 51-100:	1-1.5X
Print run 26-50:	1-2X
Print run 25 or less:	No Pricing
Cards are numbered to season statistic.	

Rookies Autographs

		NM/M
	Common Autographs:	5.00
1	Fernando Nieve	5.00
2	Frankie Francisco	5.00
3	Jorge Vasquez	5.00
4	Travis Blackley	5.00
5	Joey Gathright	8.00
6	Edwin Moreno	5.00
7	Lance Cormier	5.00
8	Justin Knoedler	5.00
9	Orlando Rodriguez	5.00
10	Renyel Pinto	5.00
11	Dennis Sarfate	5.00
12	Yadier Molina	10.00
13	Carlos Vasquez	5.00
14	Ryan Wing/SP	10.00
15	Brad Halsey	8.00
16	Ryan Meaux	5.00
17	Mike Wuertz	5.00
18	Ruddy Yan	5.00
19	Donald Kelly	5.00
20	Jake Woods	5.00
21	Colby Miller	5.00
22	Abe Alvarez	8.00
23	Mike Rouse/SP	5.00
24	Phil Stockman	5.00
25	Kevin Cave	5.00
26	Chris Shelton/SP	10.00
27	Tim Bittner	5.00
28	Mariano Gomez	5.00
29	Angel Chavez	5.00
30	Carlos Hines	5.00
31	Aarom Baldiris	5.00
32	Nick Regilio	5.00
33	Ivan Ochoa	5.00
34	Graham Koonce	5.00
35	Chris Oxspring	5.00
36	David Crouthers	5.00
37	Roberto Novoa	5.00
38	Eddy Rodriguez	5.00
39	Jason Bartlett	5.00

Timber and Threads Bat

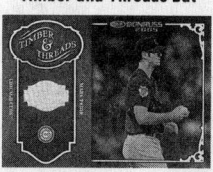

		NM/M
	Common Player:	5.00
1	Albert Pujols	15.00
2	Alfonso Soriano	8.00
3	Andre Dawson	8.00
4	Austin Kearns	5.00
5	Brad Penny	5.00
6	Carlos Beltran	8.00
7	Carlos Lee	5.00
8	Chipper Jones	8.00
9	Dale Murphy	8.00
10	Don Mattingly	20.00
11	Frank Thomas	8.00
12	Garret Anderson	5.00
13	Gary Carter	5.00
14	Hank Blalock	8.00
15	Jacque Jones	5.00
16	Jay Gibbons	5.00
17	Jeff Bagwell	8.00
18	Jermaine Dye	5.00
19	Jim Thome	8.00
20	Jose Vidro	5.00
21	Lance Berkman	5.00
22	Laynce Nix	5.00
23	Magglio Ordonez	5.00
24	Marcus Giles	5.00
25	Mark Prior	10.00
26	Mark Teixeira	5.00
27	Melvin Mora	5.00
28	Michael Young	5.00
29	Miguel Cabrera	8.00
30	Mike Lowell	5.00
31	Roy Oswalt	5.00
32	Sammy Sosa	8.00
33	Scott Rolen	10.00
34	Sean Burroughs	5.00
35	Sean Casey	5.00
36	Shannon Stewart	5.00

Timber and Threads Jersey Signature

		NM/M

39	Torii Hunter	5.00
40	Travis Hafner	5.00

Timber and Threads Bat Signature

No Pricing
Production 5 or 10

Timber and Threads Combo

		NM/M
1	Albert Pujols/Bat-Jsy	25.00
2	Alfonso Soriano/Bat-Jsy	10.00
3	Andre Dawson/Bat-Jsy	8.00
4	Austin Kearns/Bat-Jsy	8.00
5	Brad Penny/Bat-Jsy	6.00
6	Carlos Beltran/Bat-Jsy	12.00
7	Carlos Lee/Bat-Jsy	8.00
8	Chipper Jones/Bat-Jsy	12.00
9	Dale Murphy/Bat-Jsy	6.00
10	Don Mattingly/Bat-Jsy	25.00
11	Frank Thomas/Bat-Jsy	12.00
12	Garret Anderson/Bat-Jsy	8.00
13	Gary Carter/Bat-Jsy	10.00
14	Hank Blalock/Bat-Jsy	6.00
15	Jacque Jones/Bat-Jsy	6.00
16	Jay Gibbons/Bat-Jsy	6.00
17	Jeff Bagwell/Bat-Jsy	12.00
18	Jermaine Dye/Bat-Jsy	6.00
19	Jim Thome/Bat-Jsy	12.00
20	Jose Vidro/Bat-Jsy	6.00
21	Lance Berkman/Bat-Jsy	8.00
22	Laynce Nix/Bat-Jsy	6.00
23	Magglio Ordonez/Bat-Jsy	8.00
24	Marcus Giles/Bat-Jsy	6.00
25	Mark Prior/Bat-Jsy	15.00
26	Mark Teixeira/Bat-Jsy	8.00
27	Melvin Mora/Bat-Jsy	6.00
28	Michael Young/Bat-Jsy	8.00
29	Miguel Cabrera/Bat-Jsy	12.00
30	Mike Lowell/Bat-Jsy	8.00
31	Roy Oswalt/Bat-Jsy	6.00
32	Sammy Sosa/Bat-Jsy	15.00
33	Scott Rolen/Bat-Jsy	15.00
34	Sean Burroughs/Bat-Jsy	6.00
35	Sean Casey/Bat-Jsy	6.00
36	Torii Hunter/Bat-Jsy	8.00
37	Travis Hafner/Bat-Jsy	8.00

Timber and Threads Combo Signture

No Pricing
Production 5 or 10

Timber and Threads Jersey

		NM/M
	Common Player:	5.00
1	Albert Pujols	15.00
2	Alfonso Soriano	8.00
4	Austin Kearns	5.00
5	Brad Penny	5.00
6	Carlos Beltran	8.00
7	Carlos Lee	5.00
9	Dale Murphy	8.00
10	Don Mattingly	25.00
11	Frank Thomas	8.00
12	Garret Anderson	8.00
13	Gary Carter	8.00
14	Hank Blalock	8.00
16	Jacque Jones	5.00
17	Jay Gibbons	5.00
18	Jeff Bagwell	8.00
19	Jeremy Bonderman	5.00
20	Jermaine Dye	5.00
21	Jim Thome	8.00
22	Jose Vidro	5.00
23	Lance Berkman	5.00
24	Laynce Nix	5.00
25	Magglio Ordonez	5.00
26	Marcus Giles	5.00
27	Mark Prior	10.00
28	Mark Teixeira	5.00
29	Melvin Mora	5.00
30	Michael Young	5.00
31	Miguel Cabrera	8.00
32	Mike Lowell	5.00
33	Roy Oswalt	5.00
34	Sammy Sosa	8.00
35	Scott Rolen	10.00
36	Sean Burroughs	5.00
37	Sean Casey	5.00
38	Shannon Stewart	5.00
39	Torii Hunter	5.00
40	Travis Hafner	5.00

'85 Reprints

	NM/M
Complete Set (12):	40.00
Common Player:	2.00
Production 1,985 Sets	

1	Eddie Murray	3.00
2	George Brett	6.00
3	Nolan Ryan	8.00
4	Mike Schmidt	6.00
5	Tony Gwynn	3.00
7	Cal Ripken Jr.	10.00
8	Dwight Gooden	2.00
9	Roger Clemens	8.00
10	Don Mattingly	6.00
11	Kirby Puckett	4.00
12	Orel Hershiser	2.00

'85 Reprints Material

	NM/M
Production 85 Sets	

1	Eddie Murray/Jsy	20.00
2	George Brett/Jsy	35.00
3	Nolan Ryan/Jkt	40.00
4	Mike Schmidt/Jkt	35.00
5	Tony Gwynn/Jsy	20.00
7	Cal Ripken Jr./Jsy	50.00
9	Roger Clemens/Jsy	40.00
10	Don Mattingly/Jsy	35.00
11	Kirby Puckett/Jsy	20.00
12	Orel Hershiser/Jsy	10.00

2005 Donruss 1965 Minnesota Twins 40th Anniversary

To commemorate the 40th anniversary of the team's 1965 American League championship, this set was produced by Donruss as a stadium giveaway. Fifteen-card cello packs containing cards #1-15 were distributed on August 18. Cards #19-30 were given away the next day. Fronts have black-and-white photos bordered in blue.

	NM/M
Complete Set (30):	15.00
Common Player:	.25

1	Dave Boswell	.25
2	Jim Kaat	.50
3	Jim Merritt	.25
4	Mel Nelson	.25
5	Bill Pleis	.25
6	Dick Stigman	.25
7	Earl Battey	.25
8	Jerry Kindall	.25
9	Frank Quilici	.25
10	Zoilo Versalles	.50
11	Bob Allison	.50
12	Joe Nossek	.25
13	Tony Oliva	3.00
14	Sam Mele	.25
15	John Sain	.25
16	Jim "Mudcat" Grant	.35
17	Johnny Klippstein	.25
18	Camilo Pascual	.40
19	Jim Perry	.35
21	Al Worthington	.25
22	Jerry Zimmerman	.25
23	Harmon Killebrew	5.00
24	Don Mincher	.25
25	Rich Rollins	.25
26	Billy Martin	2.00
28	Jimmie Hall	.25
29	Sandy Valdespino	.25
30	Hal Naragon	.25
	Jim Lemon	.25

2005 Donruss Classics

	NM/M
Complete Set (250):	
Common Player (1-200):	.25
Common Auto. (201-225):	6.00
Common SP (226-250):	.25
Production 1,000	
Pack (5):	8.00
Box (18):	120.00

1	Scott Rolen	1.00
2	Derek Jeter	3.00
3	Jose Vidro	1.00
4	Johnny Damon	1.00
5	Nomar Garciaparra	2.00

#	Player	Price
6	Jose Guillen	.25
7	Trot Nixon	.25
8	Mark Loretta	.25
9	Jody Gerut	.25
10	Miguel Tejada	.75
11	Barry Larkin	.50
12	Jeff Kent	.40
13	Carl Crawford	.40
14	Paul Konerko	.40
15	Jim Edmonds	.50
16	Garret Anderson	.40
17	Jay Gibbons	.25
18	Moises Alou	.40
19	Mike Lowell	.25
20	Mark Mulder	.40
21	Josh Beckett	.50
22	Tim Salmon	.25
23	Shannon Stewart	.25
24	Miguel Cabrera	1.00
25	Jim Thome	1.00
26	Kevin Youkilis	.25
27	Justin Morneau	.75
28	Austin Kearns	.25
29	Cliff Lee	.25
30	Ken Griffey Jr.	1.50
31	Mike Piazza	1.50
32	Roy Halladay	.40
33	Larry Walker	.50
34	David Ortiz	1.00
35	Dontrelle Willis	.50
36	Craig Wilson	.25
37	Jeff Suppan	.25
38	Curt Schilling	1.00
39	Larry Bigbie	.25
40	Rich Harden	.40
41	Victor Martinez	.40
42	Jorge Posada	.50
43	Joey Gathright	.25
44	Adam Dunn	.75
45	Pedro Martinez	1.00
46	Dallas McPherson	.50
47	Tom Glavine	.40
48	Torii Hunter	.40
49	Angel Berroa	.25
50	Mark Prior	1.00
51	Ichiro Suzuki	2.00
52	C.C. Sabathia	.25
53	Bobby Abreu	.50
54	Shigetoshi Hasegawa	.25
55	Brandon Webb	.50
56	Mark Buehrle	.50
57	Johan Santana	.75
58	Francisco Rodriguez	.25
59	Roy Oswalt	.50
60	Mike Sweeney	.25
61	Jake Peavy	.50
62	Akinori Otsuka	.25
63	Dioner Navarro	.25
64	Kazuhito Tadano	.25
65	Ryan Wagner	.25
66	Abe Alvarez	.25
67	Mark Teixeira	.75
68	Jermaine Dye	.25
69	Todd Walker	.25
70	Octavio Dotel	.25
71	Frank Thomas	.75
72	Javy Lopez	.50
73	Scott Podsednik	.25
74	B.J. Upton	.75
75	Barry Zito	.40
76	Raul Ibanez	.25
77	Orlando Cabrera	.25
78	Sean Burroughs	.25
79	Esteban Loaiza	.25
80	Jason Schmidt	.50
81	Vinny Castilla	.25
82	Shingo Takatsu	.25
83	Juan Pierre	.25
84	David Dellucci	.25
85	Travis Blackley	.25
86	Brad Penny	.25
87	Nick Johnson	.25
88	Brian Roberts	.50
89	Kazuo Matsui	.25
90	Mike Lieberthal	.25
91	Craig Biggio	.40
92	Sean Casey	.25
93	Andy Pettitte	.50
94	Milton Bradley	.40
95	Rocco Baldelli	.25
96	Adrian Gonzalez	.25
97	Chad Tracy	.25
98	Chad Cordero	.25
99	Albert Pujols	3.00
100	Jason Kubel	.25
101	Rafael Furcal	.25
102	Jack Wilson	.25
103	Eric Chavez	.40
104	Casey Kotchman	.25
105	Jeff Bagwell	.75
106	Melvin Mora	.25
107	Bobby Crosby	.25
108	Preston Wilson	.25
109	Hank Blalock	.75
110	Vernon Wells	.40
111	Francisco Cordero	.25
112	Steve Finley	.25
113	Omar Vizquel	.25
114	Eric Byrnes	.25
115	Tim Hudson	.50
116	Aramis Ramirez	.50
117	Lance Berkman	.40
118	Shea Hillenbrand	.25
119	Aubrey Huff	.25
120	Lew Ford	.25
121	Sammy Sosa	2.00
122	Marcus Giles	.25
123	Rickie Weeks	.25
124	Manny Ramirez	1.00
125	Jason Giambi	.40
126	Adam LaRoche	.25
127	Vladimir Guerrero	1.00
128	Ken Harvey	.25
129	Adrian Beltre	.50
130	Magglio Ordonez	.25
131	Greg Maddux	1.50
132	Russ Ortiz	.25
133	Jason Varitek	.75
134	Kerry Wood	1.00
135	Mike Mussina	.75
136	Joe Nathan	.25
137	Troy Glaus	.50
138	Carlos Zambrano	.50
139	Ben Sheets	.50
140	Jae Weong Seo	.25
141	Derrek Lee	.50
142	Carlos Beltran	.50
143	John Lackey	.25
144	Aaron Rowand	.25
145	Dewon Brazelton	.25
146	Jason Bay	.25
147	Alfonso Soriano	1.00
148	Travis Hafner	.25
149	Ryan Church	.25
150	Bret Boone	.25
151	Bernie Williams	.50
152	Wade Miller	.25
153	Zack Greinke	.25
154	Scott Kazmir	.25
155	Hideki Matsui	2.00
156	Livan Hernandez	.25
157	Jose Capellan	.25
158	David Wright	1.00
159	Chone Figgins	.25
160	Jeremy Reed	.25
161	J.D. Drew	.40
162	Hideo Nomo	.50
163	Merkin Valdez	.25
164	Shawn Green	.40
165	Alexis Rios	.25
166	Johnny Estrada	.25
167	Danny Graves	.25
168	Carlos Lee	.25
169	John Van Benschoten	.25
170	Randy Johnson	1.00
171	Randy Wolf	.25
172	Luis Gonzalez	.40
173	Chipper Jones	1.00
174	Delmon Young	.50
175	Edwin Jackson	.25
176	Carlos Delgado	.50
177	Matt Clement	.25
178	Jacque Jones	.25
179	Gary Sheffield	.50
180	Laynce Nix	.25
181	Tom Gordon	.25
182	Jose Castillo	.25
183	Andruw Jones	.50
184	Brian Giles	.40
185	Paul LoDuca	.25
186	Roger Clemens	3.00
187	Todd Helton	.75
188	Keith Foulke	.25
189	Jeremy Bonderman	.25
190	Troy Percival	.25
191	Michael Young	.25
192	Carlos Guillen	.25
193	Rafael Palmeiro	.75
194	Brett Myers	.25
195	Carl Pavano	.40
196	Alex Rodriguez	2.50
197	Lyle Overbay	.25
198	Ivan Rodriguez	.75
199	Khalil Greene	.40
200	Edgar Renteria	.40
201	Justin Verlander AU/400 RC	40.00
202	Miguel Negron AU/1,300 RC	6.00
204	Paul Reynoso AU/1,200 RC	8.00
205	Colter Bean AU/1,200 RC	8.00
206	Raul Tablado AU/1,200 RC	8.00
207	Mark McLemore AU/1,500 RC	8.00
208	Russel Rohlicek AU/1,200 RC	8.00
210	Chris Seddon AU/785 RC	8.00
213	Mike Morse AU/1,200 RC	6.00
215	Randy Messenger AU/1,200 RC	8.00
217	Carlos Ruiz AU/1,200 RC	8.00
	Chris Roberson AU/1,200 RC	
219	Ryan Speier AU/1,200 RC	8.00
221	Ambiorix Burgos AU/1,200 RC	8.00
223	David Gassner AU/750 RC	6.00
224	Sean Tracey AU/1,200 RC	8.00
225	Casey Rogowski AU/1,500 RC	8.00
226	Billy Williams	3.00
227	Ralph Kiner	3.00
228	Ozzie Smith	5.00
229	Rod Carew	8.00
230	Nolan Ryan	8.00
231	Fergie Jenkins	3.00
232	Paul Molitor	4.00
233	Carlton Fisk	4.00
234	Rollie Fingers	3.00
235	Lou Brock	3.00
236	Gaylord Perry	3.00
237	Don Mattingly	6.00
238	Maury Wills	3.00
239	Luis Aparicio	3.00
240	George Brett	8.00
241	Mike Schmidt	6.00
242	Joe Morgan	3.00
243	Dennis Eckersley	3.00
244	Reggie Jackson	4.00
245	Bobby Doerr	3.00
246	Bob Feller	3.00
247	Cal Ripken Jr.	10.00
248	Harmon Killebrew	4.00
249	Frank Robinson	4.00
250	Stan Musial	5.00

Timeless Tributes Gold

Gold (1-200):	4-8X
Gold (201-225):	.4-.75X
Gold (226-250):	2-4X
Production 50 Sets	

Timeless Tributes Silver

Gold (1-200):	2-4X
Gold (201-225):	.25X
Gold (226-250):	1-2X
Production 100 Sets	

Timeless Tributes Platinum
No Pricing
Production One Set

Classic Combos

	NM/M
Common Combo:	4.00
Production 400 Sets	
Gold:	2-4X
Production 25 Sets	
Platinum:	No Pricing
Production One Set	
33	Babe Ruth, Ted Williams	10.00
34	Roberto Clemente, Vladimir Guerrero	8.00
35	Willie Mays, Willie McCovey	8.00
36	Yogi Berra, Mike Piazza	6.00
37	Sandy Koufax, Nolan Ryan	30.00
38	Harmon Killebrew, Mike Schmidt	8.00
39	Whitey Ford, Randy Johnson	4.00
40	Cal Ripken Jr., George Brett	15.00
41	Hank Aaron, Stan Musial	8.00
42	Carl Yastrzemski, Frank Robinson	6.00
43	Bob Feller, Roger Clemens	6.00
44	Bob Gibson, Tom Seaver	4.00
45	Roger Maris, Jim Thome	4.00
46	Albert Pujols, Don Mattingly	8.00
47	Duke Snider, Sammy Sosa	4.00
48	Rickey Henderson, Bo Jackson	4.00
49	Ernie Banks, Reggie Jackson	4.00
50	Burleigh Grimes, Greg Maddux	6.00

Classic Combos Bat
No Pricing
Production Five Sets

Classic Combos Jersey

	NM/M
Prime:	No Pricing
Production 1-5	
38	Harmon Killebrew, Mike Schmidt/50	30.00
39	Whitey Ford, Randy Johnson/25	25.00
40	Cal Ripken Jr., George Brett/50	50.00
45	Roger Maris, Jim Thome/50	50.00
46	Albert Pujols, Don Mattingly/50	40.00
47	Duke Snider, Sammy Sosa/25	30.00
48	Rickey Henderson, Bo Jackson/50	25.00

Classic Combos Materials

	NM/M
Prime:	No Pricing
Production Five Sets	
46	Albert Pujols, Don Mattingly/25	50.00
48	Rickey Henderson, Bo Jackson/25	30.00

Classic Combos Materials HR

	NM/M
Production 1-25	
46	Albert Pujols, Don Mattingly/25	50.00
48	Rickey Henderson, Bo Jackson/25	30.00

Classic Combos Signature
No Pricing
Production One Set

Classic Combos Signature Bat
No Pricing
Production One Set

Classic Combos Signature Jersey
No Pricing
Production 1-5

Classic Combos Signature Material
No Pricing
Production One Set

Classic Combos Sign. Materials HR
No Pricing
Production One Set

Classic Singles

	NM/M
Complete Set (32):	120.00
Common Player:	3.00
Production 400 Sets	
Gold:	2-4X
Production 25 Sets	
Platinum:	No Pricing
Production One Set	
1	Hank Aaron	8.00
2	Tom Seaver	4.00
3	Harmon Killebrew	4.00
4	Paul Molitor	4.00
5	Brooks Robinson	4.00
6	Stan Musial	4.00
7	Bobby Doerr	3.00
8	Cal Ripken Jr.	12.00
9	Phil Niekro	3.00
10	Eddie Murray	4.00
11	Randy Johnson	4.00
12	Steve Carlton	3.00
13	Rickey Henderson	3.00
14	Ernie Banks	4.00
15	Curt Schilling	4.00
16	Whitey Ford	4.00
17	Al Kaline	4.00
18	Gary Carter	3.00
19	Robin Yount	4.00
20	Johnny Bench	4.00
21	Bob Feller	3.00
22	Jim Palmer	3.00
23	Don Mattingly	6.00
24	Willie Mays	6.00
25	Dave Righetti	3.00
26	Roger Clemens	6.00
27	Juan Marichal	3.00
28	Tony Gwynn	4.00
29	Nolan Ryan	8.00
30	Carlton Fisk	3.00
31	Greg Maddux	5.00
32	Sandy Koufax	25.00

Classic Singles Bat

	NM/M
Production 25-50	
1	Hank Aaron/25	50.00
2	Tom Seaver/25	15.00
4	Paul Molitor/50	15.00
5	Brooks Robinson/50	15.00
6	Stan Musial/50	30.00
7	Bobby Doerr/25	10.00
8	Cal Ripken Jr./25	70.00
9	Phil Niekro/50	8.00
10	Eddie Murray/50	15.00
11	Randy Johnson/25	20.00
12	Steve Carlton/25	15.00
13	Rickey Henderson/50	15.00
14	Ernie Banks/50	20.00
17	Al Kaline/25	25.00
18	Gary Carter/50	8.00
19	Robin Yount/50	15.00
20	Johnny Bench/25	20.00
23	Don Mattingly/25	30.00
24	Willie Mays/50	50.00
28	Tony Gwynn/50	15.00
29	Nolan Ryan/25	40.00
30	Carlton Fisk/50	15.00

Classic Singles Jersey

	NM/M
Production 10-100	
Prime:	No Pricing
Production 1-5	
2	Tom Seaver/25	20.00
3	Harmon Killebrew/25	20.00
4	Paul Molitor/50	15.00
5	Brooks Robinson/50	15.00
6	Bobby Doerr/Pants/100	15.00
7	Cal Ripken Jr./25	70.00
9	Phil Niekro/50	8.00
10	Eddie Murray/50	15.00
11	Randy Johnson/50	12.00
12	Steve Carlton/25	12.00
13	Rickey Henderson/100	12.00
14	Ernie Banks/25	25.00
15	Curt Schilling/100	15.00
16	Whitey Ford/25	20.00
18	Gary Carter/100	8.00
19	Robin Yount/50	15.00
20	Johnny Bench/25	20.00
21	Bob Feller/Pants/25	20.00
22	Jim Palmer/100	8.00
23	Don Mattingly/100	25.00
24	Willie Mays/25	50.00
25	Dave Righetti/50	8.00
26	Roger Clemens/25	25.00
27	Juan Marichal/100	10.00
28	Tony Gwynn/100	15.00
29	Nolan Ryan/50	30.00
30	Carlton Fisk/25	15.00
31	Greg Maddux/100	15.00
32	Sandy Koufax/25	375.00

Classic Singles Materials

	NM/M
Production 10-25	
Prime:	No Pricing
Production 10-25	
2	Tom Seaver/Bat-Jsy/25	20.00
3	Harmon Killebrew/Bat-Jsy/25	25.00
4	Paul Molitor/Bat-Jsy/25	20.00
5	Brooks Robinson/Bat-Jsy/25	20.00
7	Bobby Doerr/Bat-Pants/25	10.00
11	Randy Johnson/Bat-Jsy/25	20.00
12	Steve Carlton/Bat-Jsy/25	15.00
13	Rickey Henderson/Bat-Jsy/25	30.00
18	Gary Carter/Bat-Jsy/25	15.00
19	Robin Yount/Bat-Jsy/25	25.00
20	Johnny Bench/Bat-Jsy/25	25.00
23	Don Mattingly/Bat-Jsy/25	35.00
28	Tony Gwynn/Bat-Jsy/25	25.00
29	Nolan Ryan/Bat-Jsy/25	25.00
30	Carlton Fisk/Bat-Jsy/25	15.00

Classic Singles Materials HR

	NM/M
Production 10-25	
2	Tom Seaver/Bat-Jsy/25	20.00
3	Harmon Killebrew/Bat-Jsy/25	25.00
4	Paul Molitor/Bat-Jsy/25	20.00

Classic Singles Signature
No Pricing
Production 1-5

Classic Singles Signature Bat
No Pricing
Production 1-10

Classic Singles Signature Jersey
No Pricing
Production 1-5

Classic Singles Sign. Materials
No Pricing
Production 1-10

Classic Singles Sign. Materials HR
No Pricing
Production 1-10

Dress Code Bat

	NM/M
Production 50-100	
1	Albert Pujols/100	25.00
2	Bernie Williams/50	10.00
4	Carlos Beltran/100	10.00
5	Chipper Jones/100	10.00
7	David Ortiz/100	12.00
8	Hank Blalock/100	6.00
9	Hideki Matsui/100	30.00
10	Jim Edmonds/100	8.00
11	Jim Thome/100	8.00
14	Mark Prior/50	8.00
15	Mark Teixeira/100	8.00
16	Miguel Cabrera/100	8.00
17	Miguel Tejada/100	6.00
18	Mike Piazza/100	12.00
22	Sammy Sosa/100	10.00
23	Scott Rolen/100	6.00
26	Torii Hunter/100	6.00
30	Vladimir Guerrero/100	10.00

Dress Code Jersey Number

	NM/M
Production 5-57	
2	Bernie Williams/51	10.00
4	Carlos Beltran/15	20.00
6	Curt Schilling/38	15.00
7	David Ortiz/34	20.00
9	Hideki Matsui/55	30.00
11	Jim Thome/25	15.00
12	Johan Santana/57	12.00
13	Mark Mulder/20	15.00
14	Mark Prior/22	15.00
15	Mark Teixeira/23	15.00
16	Miguel Cabrera/24	15.00
18	Mike Piazza/31	20.00
19	Pedro J. Martinez/45	10.00
20	Randy Johnson/Pants/51	12.00
21	Roger Clemens/23	25.00
22	Sammy Sosa/21	20.00
23	Scott Rolen/27	15.00
26	Torii Hunter/48	6.00
27	Travis Hafner/48	6.00
29	Victor Martinez/51	8.00
30	Vladimir Guerrero/27	20.00

Dress Code Jersey Prime

	NM/M
Production 25 Sets	
1	Albert Pujols	75.00
2	Bernie Williams	20.00
3	Carl Crawford	12.00
4	Carlos Beltran	25.00
5	Chipper Jones	30.00
6	Curt Schilling	30.00
7	David Ortiz	30.00
8	Hank Blalock	20.00
10	Jim Edmonds	20.00
11	Jim Thome	20.00
12	Johan Santana	30.00
13	Mark Mulder	20.00
14	Mark Prior	20.00
15	Mark Teixeira	25.00
16	Miguel Cabrera	25.00
17	Miguel Tejada	25.00
18	Mike Piazza	25.00
19	Pedro J. Martinez	25.00
20	Randy Johnson	30.00
21	Roger Clemens	50.00
22	Sammy Sosa	30.00
23	Scott Rolen	30.00
24	Tim Hudson	20.00
25	Todd Helton	20.00

#	Player	Price
26	Torii Hunter	15.00
27	Travis Hafner	10.00
28	Vernon Wells	10.00
29	Victor Martinez	15.00
30	Vladimir Guerrero	30.00

Dress Code Materials
NM/M
Production 5-100
Prime: No Pricing
Production Five Sets

#	Player	Price
1	Albert Pujols/Bat-Bat/Jsy/100	25.00
2	Bernie Williams/Bat-Jsy/100	10.00
4	Carlos Beltran/Bat-Bat/Jsy/100	10.00
5	Chipper Jones/Bat-Jsy/100	12.00
6	Curt Schilling/Bat-Jsy/100	15.00
7	David Ortiz/Bat-Hat/100	15.00
8	Hank Blalock/Bat-Jsy/100	8.00
9	Hideki Matsui/Bat-Jsy/100	30.00
10	Jim Edmonds/Jsy/Jsy/100	12.00
11	Jim Thome/Jsy/Jsy/100	12.00
15	Mark Teixeira/Bat-Jsy/100	8.00
16	Miguel Cabrera/Jsy/100	10.00
17	Miguel Tejada/Bat-Jsy/100	8.00
18	Mike Piazza/Bat-Jsy/100	12.00
19	Pedro J. Martinez/Bat-Jsy/100	12.00
22	Sammy Sosa/Bat-Jsy/100	12.00
23	Scott Rolen/Bat-Jsy/100	12.00
25	Todd Helton/Jsy-Jsy/100	8.00
26	Torii Hunter/Bat-Jsy/100	8.00
27	Travis Hafner/Jsy-Shoes/100	8.00
28	Vernon Wells/Jsy-Jsy/50	8.00
29	Victor Martinez/Jsy-Jsy/50	8.00
30	Vladimir Guerrero/Bat-Jsy/100	12.00

Dress Code Signature Bat
NM/M
Production 1-25

#	Player	Price
7	David Ortiz/25	50.00
8	Hank Blalock/25	30.00
16	Miguel Cabrera/25	50.00
26	Torii Hunter/25	30.00
27	Travis Hafner/25	25.00
28	Vernon Wells/25	25.00

Dress Code Signature Jersey
NM/M
Production 5-25

#	Player	Price
7	David Ortiz/25	50.00
8	Hank Blalock/25	30.00
13	Johan Santana/25	50.00
16	Miguel Cabrera/25	50.00
26	Torii Hunter/25	30.00
27	Travis Hafner/25	25.00
28	Vernon Wells/25	25.00
29	Victor Martinez/25	25.00

Dress Code Sign. Jersey Number
NM/M
Production 1-25
Prime: No Pricing
Production 1-5

#	Player	Price
7	David Ortiz/25	50.00
8	Hank Blalock/25	30.00
13	Johan Santana/25	50.00
26	Torii Hunter/25	30.00
27	Travis Hafner/25	25.00
29	Victor Martinez/25	25.00

Dress Code Signature Materials
No Pricing
Production 1-5

Home Run Heroes

NM/M

Complete Set (50):		90.00
Common Player:		1.50
Production 1,000 Sets		
Gold:		2-4X
Production 50 Sets		
Platinum:		No Pricing
Production One Set		
	Mike Schmidt	4.00
	Ken Griffey Jr.	6.00
	Babe Ruth	6.00
	Duke Snider	2.00
	Johnny Bench	3.00

#	Player	Price
6	Stan Musial	3.00
7	Willie McCovey	2.00
8	Willie Stargell	2.00
9	Ted Williams	5.00
10	Frank Thomas	2.00
12	Gary Sheffield	2.00
13	Jim Thome	2.00
14	Harmon Killebrew	2.00
14	Ernie Banks	3.00
15	George Foster	1.50
16	Albert Pujols	5.00
17	Tony Perez	1.50
18	Richie Sexson	1.50
19	Juan Gonzalez	1.50
20	Frank Robinson	2.00
21	Sammy Sosa	3.00
22	Jeff Bagwell	1.50
23	Mark Teixeira	1.50
24	Willie Mays	5.00
25	Rafael Palmeiro	2.00
26	Billy Williams	1.50
27	Vladimir Guerrero	2.00
28	Gary Carter	2.00
29	Fred McGriff	1.50
30	Orlando Cepeda	1.50
31	Dave Winfield	2.00
32	Shawn Green	1.50
33	Jose Canseco	1.50
34	Hideki Matsui	4.00
35	Roger Maris	4.00
36	Andre Dawson	2.00
37	Paul Konerko	1.50
38	Darryl Strawberry	1.50
39	Dave Parker	1.50
40	Adam Dunn	2.00
41	Ralph Kiner	2.00
42	Miguel Tejada	2.00
43	Dale Murphy	2.00
44	Hank Aaron	6.00
45	Mike Piazza	3.00
46	Reggie Jackson	2.00
47	Adrian Beltre	2.00
48	Cal Ripken Jr.	8.00
49	Manny Ramirez	2.00
50	Alex Rodriguez	5.00

Home Run Heroes Jersey HR
NM/M
Production 1-66
Prime: No Pricing
Production One Set

#	Player	Price
1	Mike Schmidt/48	25.00
3	Babe Ruth/25	165.00
5	Johnny Bench/45	15.00
7	Willie McCovey/23	15.00
8	Willie Stargell/48	15.00
9	Ted Williams/43	60.00
10	Frank Thomas/43	12.00
11	Gary Sheffield/36	8.00
12	Jim Thome/47	15.00
13	Harmon Killebrew/49	20.00
14	Ernie Banks Pants/47	20.00
15	Gene Foster/25	10.00
16	Albert Pujols/46	35.00
18	Richie Sexson/45	8.00
19	Juan Gonzalez/47	8.00
21	Sammy Sosa/66	15.00
22	Jeff Bagwell/47	10.00
23	Mark Teixeira/38	8.00
24	Willie Mays/51	50.00
25	Rafael Palmeiro/47	10.00
26	Billy Williams/26	8.00
27	Vladimir Guerrero/44	12.00
28	Gary Carter/31	10.00
29	Fred McGriff/32	12.00
30	Orlando Cepeda/Pants/46	8.00
31	Dave Winfield/34	10.00
32	Shawn Green/49	8.00
33	Jose Canseco/44	10.00
34	Hideki Matsui/Pants/31	40.00
35	Roger Maris/Pants/19	50.00
36	Andre Dawson/49	8.00
38	Darryl Strawberry/24	10.00
39	Dave Parker/34	8.00
40	Adam Dunn/46	8.00
42	Miguel Tejada/34	10.00
43	Dale Murphy/44	10.00
44	Hank Aaron/47	50.00
45	Mike Piazza/40	15.00
46	Reggie Jackson/39	8.00
47	Adrian Beltre/48	8.00
48	Cal Ripken Jr./34	50.00
49	Manny Ramirez/43	12.00

Home Run Heroes Materials
NM/M
Production 1-66
Prime: No Pricing
Production One Set

#	Player	Price
1	Mike Schmidt/Bat-Jsy/48	30.00
3	Babe Ruth/Bat-Jsy/25	300.00
5	Johnny Bench/Bat-Jsy/45	20.00
7	Willie McCovey/Bat-Jsy/23	20.00
8	Willie Stargell/Bat-Jsy/48	20.00
9	Ted Williams/Bat-Jsy/43	85.00
10	Frank Thomas/Jsy-Jsy/43	15.00
11	Gary Sheffield/Bat-Jsy/36	10.00
12	Jim Thome/Bat-Jsy/47	15.00

#	Player	Price
13	Harmon Killebrew/Bat-Jsy/49	25.00
14	Ernie Banks/Bat-Pants/47	25.00
15	George Foster/Bat-Jsy/52	10.00
16	Albert Pujols/Jsy/49	40.00
17	Tony Perez/Bat-Fld Glv/24	15.00
18	Richie Sexson/Bat-Jsy/45	10.00
19	Juan Gonzalez/Bat-Jsy/47	10.00
21	Sammy Sosa/Bat-Jsy/66	15.00
22	Jeff Bagwell/Bat-Jsy/47	12.00
23	Mark Teixeira/Bat-Jsy/38	10.00
24	Willie Mays/Bat-Jsy/51	50.00
25	Rafael Palmeiro/Bat-Jsy/47	12.00
26	Billy Williams/Bat-Jsy/26	10.00
27	Vladimir Guerrero/Bat-Jsy/44	15.00
28	Gary Carter/Bat-Jsy/31	12.00
29	Fred McGriff/Bat-Jsy/32	15.00
30	Orlando Cepeda/Bat-Pants/34	12.00
31	Dave Winfield/Bat-Jsy/34	15.00
32	Shawn Green/Bat-Jsy/49	10.00
33	Jose Canseco/Hat-Jsy/44	12.00
34	Hideki Matsui/Bat-Pants/31	60.00
35	Roger Maris/Bat-Pants/19	50.00
36	Andre Dawson/Bat-Jsy/49	10.00
38	Darryl Strawberry/Jsy-Pants/24	12.00
39	Dave Parker/Bat-Jsy/34	12.00
40	Adam Dunn/Bat-Jsy/46	15.00
42	Miguel Tejada/Bat-Jsy/34	15.00
43	Dale Murphy/Jsy/44	15.00
44	Hank Aaron/Bat-Jsy/47	50.00
45	Mike Piazza/Jsy-Jsy/40	15.00
46	Reggie Jackson/Bat-Jsy/39	15.00
47	Adrian Beltre/Bat-Jsy/48	12.00
48	Cal Ripken Jr./Bat-Jsy/25	60.00
49	Manny Ramirez/Bat-Jsy/43	15.00

Home Rune Heroes Signature
No Pricing
Production 1-10

Home Run Heroes Sign. Materials
No Pricing
Production 1-10

Legendary Lumberjacks
NM/M
Common Player: 2.00
Production 400 Sets
Gold: 2-4X
Production 50 Sets
Platinum: No Pricing
Production One Set

#	Player	Price
1	Al Kaline	4.00
2	Babe Ruth	8.00
3	Billy Williams	2.00
4	Bob Feller	3.00
5	Bob Gibson	3.00
6	Brooks Robinson	4.00
7	Cal Ripken Jr.	10.00
8	Carlton Fisk	3.00
9	Dennis Eckersley	2.00
10	Don Mattingly	6.00
11	Duke Snider	3.00
12	Eddie Murray	3.00
13	Ernie Banks	4.00
14	Fergie Jenkins	2.00
15	Frank Robinson	4.00
16	Gaylord Perry	2.00
17	George Brett	6.00
18	George Kell	2.00
19	Harmon Killebrew	4.00
20	Jim Palmer	4.00
21	Joe Morgan	2.00
22	Johnny Bench	5.00
23	Juan Marichal	2.00
24	Lou Brock	3.00
25	Maury Wills	2.00
26	Mike Schmidt	6.00
27	Nolan Ryan	8.00
28	Ozzie Smith	4.00
29	Paul Molitor	2.00
30	Pee Wee Reese	2.00
31	Phil Niekro	2.00
32	Phil Rizzuto	2.00
33	Ralph Kiner	2.00
34	Reggie Jackson	4.00
35	Rickey Henderson	3.00
36	Roberto Clemente	8.00
37	Robin Yount	4.00
38	Rod Carew	2.00

#	Player	Price
39	Roger Maris	5.00
40	Stan Musial	5.00
41	Steve Carlton	2.00
42	Ted Williams	8.00
43	Tom Seaver	3.00
44	Tony Gwynn	2.00
45	Tony Perez	2.00
46	Wade Boggs	3.00
47	Warren Spahn	4.00
48	Whitey Ford	4.00
49	Willie McCovey	3.00
50	Yogi Berra	4.00

Legendary Lumberjacks Bat
NM/M
Production 1-50

#	Player	Price
2	Babe Ruth/25	200.00
5	Brooks Robinson/50	15.00
7	Cal Ripken Jr./50	50.00
8	Carlton Fisk/50	10.00
10	Don Mattingly/50	25.00
12	Eddie Murray/50	15.00
13	Ernie Banks/50	15.00
15	Frank Robinson/50	15.00
17	George Brett/50	20.00
19	Harmon Killebrew/50	15.00
21	Joe Morgan/50	10.00
22	Johnny Bench/50	15.00
24	Lou Brock/50	10.00
26	Mike Schmidt/50	20.00
28	Ozzie Smith/50	15.00
29	Paul Molitor/50	12.00
30	Pee Wee Reese/50	15.00
34	Reggie Jackson/50	12.00
35	Rickey Henderson/50	12.00
36	Roberto Clemente/50	50.00
37	Robin Yount/50	15.00
38	Rod Carew/50	10.00
39	Roger Maris/25	40.00
41	Stan Musial/25	25.00
42	Ted Williams/25	60.00
44	Tony Gwynn/50	15.00
46	Wade Boggs/50	12.00
49	Willie McCovey/50	12.00
50	Yogi Berra/25	25.00

Legendary Lumberjacks Jersey
NM/M
Production 1-50

#	Player	Price
3	Billy Williams/25	15.00
5	Brooks Robinson/25	20.00
7	Cal Ripken Jr./50	50.00
8	Carlton Fisk/50	15.00
10	Don Mattingly/50	25.00
12	Eddie Murray/50	15.00
13	Ernie Banks/25	20.00
19	Harmon Killebrew/25	20.00
22	Johnny Bench/25	20.00
24	Lou Brock/25	12.00
25	Maury Wills/25	12.00
26	Mike Schmidt/25	25.00
28	Ozzie Smith/25	20.00
29	Paul Molitor/50	12.00
34	Reggie Jackson/25	15.00
35	Rickey Henderson/25	12.00
37	Robin Yount/50	15.00
38	Rod Carew/50	10.00

Legendary Lumberjacks Jersey HR
NM/M
Production 1-25

#	Player	Price
6	Brooks Robinson/25	20.00
7	Cal Ripken Jr./25	60.00
10	Don Mattingly/25	30.00
12	Eddie Murray/25	20.00
29	Paul Molitor/25	20.00
35	Rickey Henderson/25	20.00
37	Robin Yount/25	20.00
38	Rod Carew/25	15.00
44	Tony Gwynn/25	20.00
45	Tony Perez/25	15.00
46	Wade Boggs/25	15.00
49	Willie McCovey/25	15.00

Legendary Lumberjacks Materials
NM/M
Production 1-50

#	Player	Price
2	Babe Ruth/Bat-Jsy/25	300.00
6	Brooks Robinson/Bat-Jsy/50	20.00
7	Cal Ripken Jr./Bat-Jsy/50	60.00
8	Carlton Fisk/Bat-Jsy/25	15.00
10	Don Mattingly/Bat-Jsy/50	30.00
12	Eddie Murray/Bat-Jsy/50	20.00
13	Ernie Banks/Bat-Jsy/25	25.00
19	Harmon Killebrew/Bat-Jsy/25	20.00
22	Johnny Bench/Bat-Jsy/25	25.00
24	Lou Brock/Bat-Jsy/50	12.00
26	Mike Schmidt/Bat-Jsy/25	25.00
29	Paul Molitor/Bat-Jsy/50	15.00
34	Reggie Jackson/Bat-Jsy/20	15.00
36	Rickey Henderson/Bat-Jsy/15	
37	Robin Yount/Bat-Jsy/50	20.00
38	Rod Carew/Bat-Jsy/50	15.00
44	Tony Gwynn/Bat-Jsy/50	20.00
46	Wade Boggs/Bat-Jsy/50	15.00
47	Warren Spahn/Bat-Jsy/50	20.00
49	Willie McCovey/44	15.00

Legendary Players
NM/M
Common Player: 1.50
Production 800 Sets
Gold: 2-3X
Production 75 Sets
Platinum: No Pricing
Production One Set

#	Player	Price
1	Al Kaline	3.00
2	Babe Ruth	6.00
3	Billy Williams	1.50
4	Bob Feller	2.00
5	Bob Gibson	3.00
6	Brooks Robinson	3.00
7	Cal Ripken Jr.	8.00
8	Carlton Fisk	2.00
9	Dennis Eckersley	2.00
10	Don Mattingly	5.00
11	Duke Snider	2.00
12	Eddie Murray	2.00
13	Ernie Banks	2.00
14	Fergie Jenkins	1.50
15	Frank Robinson	3.00
16	Gaylord Perry	1.50
17	George Brett	5.00
18	George Kell	1.50
19	Harmon Killebrew	3.00
20	Jim Palmer	2.00
21	Joe Morgan	1.50
22	Johnny Bench	3.00
23	Juan Marichal	1.50
24	Lou Brock	2.00
25	Maury Wills	1.50
26	Mike Schmidt	5.00
27	Nolan Ryan	6.00
28	Ozzie Smith	3.00
29	Paul Molitor	2.00
30	Pee Wee Reese	1.50
31	Phil Niekro	1.50
32	Phil Rizzuto	1.50
33	Ralph Kiner	1.50
34	Reggie Jackson	2.00
35	Rickey Henderson	2.00
36	Roberto Clemente	6.00
37	Robin Yount	3.00
38	Rod Carew	2.00
39	Roger Maris	4.00
40	Stan Musial	4.00
41	Steve Carlton	1.50
42	Ted Williams	6.00
43	Tom Seaver	2.00
44	Tony Gwynn	2.00
45	Tony Perez	1.50
46	Wade Boggs	2.00
47	Warren Spahn	3.00
48	Whitey Ford	3.00
49	Willie McCovey	2.00
50	Yogi Berra	3.00

Legendary Players Hat
NM/M
Production 1-25

#	Player	Price
10	Don Mattingly/25	30.00
13	Ernie Banks/25	20.00
17	George Brett/25	30.00
20	Jim Palmer/25	10.00
26	Mike Schmidt/25	30.00
28	Ozzie Smith/25	25.00
37	Robin Yount/25	25.00
44	Tony Gwynn/25	20.00

Legendary Players Jacket
NM/M
Production 25 Sets

#	Player	Price
7	Cal Ripken Jr.	60.00
8	Carlton Fisk	12.00
10	Don Mattingly	40.00
24	Lou Brock	15.00
26	Mike Schmidt	35.00
27	Nolan Ryan	50.00
34	Reggie Jackson	15.00
35	Rickey Henderson	20.00
38	Rod Carew	20.00
42	Ted Williams	85.00

Legendary Players Jersey Number
NM/M
Production 1-44
Prime: No Pricing
Production One Set

#	Player	Price
3	Billy Williams/25	10.00
8	Carlton Fisk/72	10.00
9	Dennis Eckersley/43	10.00
10	Don Mattingly/23	30.00
12	Eddie Murray/33	15.00
16	Gaylord Perry/36	8.00
20	Jim Palmer/27	10.00
23	Juan Marichal/27	10.00
24	Lou Brock/20	15.00
25	Maury Wills/30	8.00
26	Mike Schmidt/20	30.00
27	Nolan Ryan/34	40.00
32	Phil Niekro/35	8.00
35	Rickey Henderson/24	15.00
37	Robin Yount/19	25.00
38	Rod Carew/29	15.00
41	Steve Carlton/32	10.00
43	Tom Seaver/41	15.00
44	Tony Gwynn/19	20.00
45	Tony Perez/27	10.00
46	Wade Boggs/26	15.00
47	Warren Spahn/20	12.00
49	Willie McCovey/44	12.00

Legendary Players Leather
NM/M
Production 10-25

#	Player	Price
10	Don Mattingly/Btg Glv/25	40.00
14	Fergie Jenkins/Fld Glv/25	15.00
26	Mike Schmidt/Fld Glv/25	40.00
35	Rickey Henderson/Btg Glv/25	25.00
41	Steve Carlton/Fld Glv/25	15.00
44	Tony Gwynn/Btg Glv/25	30.00
45	Tony Perez/Fld Glv/25	15.00

Legendary Players Pants
NM/M
Production 1-25

#	Player	Price
4	Bob Feller/19	20.00
7	Cal Ripken Jr./25	60.00
11	Duke Snider/25	20.00
12	Eddie Murray/25	20.00
14	Fergie Jenkins/25	15.00
20	Jim Palmer/25	10.00
23	Juan Marichal/25	10.00
28	Ozzie Smith/25	25.00
29	Paul Molitor/25	15.00
35	Rickey Henderson/25	15.00
38	Rod Carew/25	15.00
39	Roger Maris/25	50.00
43	Tom Seaver/25	15.00
44	Tony Gwynn/25	20.00
47	Warren Spahn/24	20.00
49	Willie McCovey/25	15.00

Legendary Players Signature
No Pricing
Production 1-10

Legendary Players Spikes
NM/M
Production 1-25

#	Player	Price
15	Frank Robinson/25	25.00
44	Tony Gwynn/25	30.00

Membership

NM/M
Common Player: 1.50
Production 1,000 Sets
Gold: 2-4X
Production 50 Sets
Platinum: No Pricing
Production One Set

#	Player	Price
1	Bobby Doerr	1.50
2	Tom Seaver	2.00
3	Cal Ripken Jr.	8.00
4	Paul Molitor	2.00
5	Brooks Robinson	2.00
6	Al Kaline	4.00
7	Steve Carlton	2.00
8	Carl Yastrzemski	4.00
9	Bob Feller	2.00
10	Fred Lynn	1.50
11	Luis Aparicio	1.50
12	Hank Aaron	6.00
13	Willie Mays	6.00
14	Bob Gibson	3.00
15	Joe Morgan	2.00
16	Whitey Ford	3.00
17	Don Sutton	1.50
18	Harmon Killebrew	3.00
19	Tony Gwynn	3.00
20	Lou Brock	1.50
21	Dennis Eckersley	1.50
22	Jim Palmer	1.50
23	Don Mattingly	5.00
24	Carlton Fisk	2.00
25	Gaylord Perry	1.50
26	Mike Schmidt	5.00
27	Nolan Ryan	6.00
28	Sandy Koufax	10.00
29	Rod Carew	2.00
30	Maury Wills	1.50

Membership VIP Bat
NM/M
Production 25 Sets

#	Player	Price
1	Bobby Doerr	10.00
2	Tom Seaver	20.00
3	Cal Ripken Jr.	60.00
4	Paul Molitor	15.00
5	Brooks Robinson	15.00
6	Al Kaline	20.00
7	Steve Carlton	10.00
8	Carl Yastrzemski	20.00
10	Fred Lynn	8.00
11	Luis Aparicio	8.00
12	Hank Aaron	40.00
13	Willie Mays	50.00
15	Joe Morgan	20.00
18	Harmon Killebrew	20.00
19	Tony Gwynn	20.00
20	Lou Brock	15.00
23	Don Mattingly	30.00
24	Carlton Fisk	15.00
29	Rod Carew	12.00

Membership VIP Jersey
NM/M
Production 5-50
Prime: No Pricing

Production One Set

#	Player	Price
7	Steve Carlton/25	10.00
10	Fred Lynn/25	10.00
11	Luis Aparicio/25	10.00
15	Joe Morgan/25	10.00
17	Don Sutton/50	8.00
19	Tony Gwynn/50	15.00
20	Lou Brock/25	15.00
21	Dennis Eckersley/50	8.00
22	Jim Palmer/25	10.00
23	Don Mattingly/25	30.00
24	Carlton Fisk/25	15.00
25	Gaylord Perry/50	8.00
26	Mike Schmidt/25	20.00
27	Nolan Ryan/25	40.00
29	Rod Carew/50	10.00

Membership VIP Materials
NM/M
Production 5-25
Prime: No Pricing
Production One Set

#	Player	Price
1	Bobby Doerr/Bat-Pants/25	10.00
2	Tom Seaver/Bat-Jsy/25	20.00
3	Cal Ripken Jr./Bat-Jsy/25	75.00
4	Paul Molitor/Bat-Jsy/25	20.00
5	Brooks Robinson/Bat-Jsy/25	25.00
7	Steve Carlton/Bat-Jsy/25	15.00
10	Fred Lynn/Bat-Jsy/25	10.00
11	Luis Aparicio/Bat-Jsy/25	
15	Joe Morgan/Bat-Jsy/25	12.00
18	Harmon Killebrew/Bat-Jsy/25	25.00
19	Tony Gwynn/Bat-Jsy/25	25.00
20	Lou Brock/Bat-Jsy/25	25.00
23	Don Mattingly/Bat-Jsy/25	35.00
27	Nolan Ryan/Bat-Jsy/25	50.00
29	Rod Carew/Bat-Jsy/25	20.00

Membership VIP Materials Awards
No Pricing
Production 5-10

Membership VIP Materials HOF
No Pricing
Production 10 Sets

Membership VIP Materials HR
NM/M
Production 6-49

#	Player	Price
1	Bobby Doerr/Jsy-Pants/27	15.00
3	Cal Ripken Jr./Jsy-Pants/34	60.00
4	Paul Molitor/Bat-Jsy/22	15.00
8	Carl Yastrzemski/Bat-Jsy/44	25.00
10	Fred Lynn/Bat-Jsy/39	50.00
12	Hank Aaron/Bat-Jsy/47	
15	Joe Morgan/Bat-Jsy/27	12.00
18	Harmon Killebrew/Bat-Jsy/49	20.00
20	Lou Brock/Bat-Jsy/21	15.00
23	Don Mattingly/Bat-Jsy/35	40.00
24	Carlton Fisk/Bat-Jsy/37	15.00
26	Mike Schmidt/Bat-Jsy/48	25.00

Membership VIP Materials Stats
No Pricing
Production 10 Sets

Membership VIP Signature
No Pricing
Production 1-5

Membership VIP Signature Bat
No Pricing
Production 1-10

Membership VIP Signature Jersey
No Pricing
Production 1-10

Membership VIP Signature Material
NM/M
Production 1-25
Prime: No Pricing
Production One Set

#	Player	Price
1	Bobby Doerr/Bat-Pants/25	35.00
10	Fred Lynn/Bat-Jsy/25	30.00
11	Luis Aparicio/Bat-Jsy/25	30.00
20	Lou Brock/Bat-Jsy/25	50.00

Membership VIP Sign. Mat. Awards
No Pricing
Production 1-10

Membership VIP Sig. Materials HOF
No Pricing
Production 1-10

Membership VIP Sign. Materials HR
No Pricing
Production 1-10

Membership VIP Sig. Mat. Stats
No Pricing
Production 5-10

Significant Signatures Silver
NM/M
Production 1-200
Gold: .75-1.5X
Production 1-100
No pricing 20 or less.
Platinum: No Pricing
Production One Set

#	Player	Price
17	Jay Gibbons/25	15.00
22	Tim Salmon/100	15.00
26	Kevin Youkilis/25	12.00
29	Cliff Lee/200	15.00
37	Jeff Suppan/200	10.00
39	Larry Bigbie/100	15.00
40	Rich Harden/100	15.00
41	Victor Martinez/25	20.00
43	Joey Gathright/100	8.00
61	Jake Peavy/25	40.00
63	Dioner Navarro/100	15.00
64	Kazuhito Tadano/100	15.00
65	Ryan Wagner/50	10.00
66	Abe Alvarez/100	15.00
67	Jermaine Dye/25	15.00
69	Todd Walker/25	15.00
70	Octavio Dotel/25	15.00
73	Scott Podsednik/25	20.00
76	Raul Ibanez/50	10.00
77	Orlando Cabrera/25	20.00
79	Esteban Loaiza/50	15.00
84	David Dellucci/50	20.00
85	Travis Blackley/200	8.00
86	Brad Penny/25	15.00
88	Brian Roberts/100	35.00
90	Mike Lieberthal/25	15.00
94	Milton Bradley/100	15.00
96	Adrian Gonzalez/200	12.00
97	Chad Tracy/100	10.00
98	Chad Cordero/100	8.00
100	Jason Kubel/200	12.00
102	Jack Wilson/100	15.00
104	Casey Kotchman/100	12.00
106	Melvin Mora/100	15.00
107	Bobby Crosby/100	15.00
111	Francisco Cordero/50	15.00
114	Eric Byrnes/50	15.00
118	Shea Hillenbrand/25	15.00
119	Aubrey Huff/25	20.00
120	Lew Ford/25	20.00
126	Adam LaRoche/25	15.00
128	Ken Harvey/50	10.00
132	Russ Ortiz/25	15.00
133	Jason Varitek/25	10.00
136	Joe Nathan/100	20.00
138	Carlos Zambrano/25	35.00
143	John Lackey/200	10.00
145	Dewon Brazelton/200	10.00
146	Jason Bay/25	25.00
148	Travis Hafner/100	12.00
152	Wade Miller/50	12.00
154	Scott Kazmir/25	35.00
156	Livan Hernandez/25	15.00
158	David Wright/25	85.00
159	Chone Figgins/50	12.00
163	Merkin Valdez/200	10.00
165	Alexis Rios/50	15.00
166	Johnny Estrada/200	10.00
167	Danny Graves/50	15.00
168	Carlos Lee/25	25.00
171	Randy Wolf/25	15.00
175	Edwin Jackson/25	12.00
178	Jacque Jones/25	10.00
180	Laynce Nix/200	10.00
181	Tom Gordon/25	12.00
182	Jose Castillo/100	12.00
188	Keith Foulke/25	60.00
189	Jeremy Bonderman/50	12.00
190	Troy Percival/25	15.00
194	Brett Myers/50	15.00
197	Lyle Overbay/25	20.00
202	Miguel Negron/100	8.00
204	Paulino Reynoso/100	8.00
205	Colter Bean/100	10.00
206	Raul Tablado/100	8.00
207	Mark McLemore/100	8.00
208	Russel Rohlicek/100	8.00
210	Chris Seddon/100	8.00
213	Mike Morse/100	20.00
217	Carlos Ruiz/100	15.00
218	Chris Roberson/100	8.00
219	Ryan Speier/100	8.00
221	Ambiorix Burgos/100	8.00
223	David Gassner/100	8.00
224	Sean Tracey/100	8.00
225	Casey Rogowski/100	8.00
236	Gaylord Perry/LGD/25	25.00
245	Bobby Doerr/LGD/25	25.00
246	Bob Feller/LGD/25	30.00

Stars of Summer
NM/M
Common Player: 1.50

Production 1,000 Sets
Gold: 2-4X
Production 50 Sets
Platinum: No Pricing
Production One Set

#	Player	Price
1	Andre Dawson	2.00
2	Bert Blyleven	2.00
3	Bill Madlock	1.50
4	Dale Murphy	3.00
5	Darryl Strawberry	2.00
6	Dave Parker	2.00
7	Dave Righetti	2.00
8	Dwight Evans	2.00
9	Dwight Gooden	2.00
10	Fred Lynn	1.50
11	George Foster	2.00
12	Harold Baines	2.00
13	Jack Morris	1.50
14	Jim Rice	3.00
15	Keith Hernandez	2.00
16	Kirk Gibson	2.00
17	Luis Aparicio	2.00
18	Mark Grace	2.00
19	Marty Marion	1.50
20	Orel Hershiser	2.00
21	Ron Guidry	3.00
22	Ron Santo	2.00
23	Steve Garvey	2.00
24	Tony Oliva	2.00
25	Will Clark	2.00

Stars of Summer Material
NM/M
Production 100-250

#	Player	Price
1	Andre Dawson/Jsy/250	8.00
2	Bert Blyleven/Jsy/150	8.00
3	Bill Madlock/Bat/250	5.00
4	Dale Murphy/Jsy/100	12.00
5	Darryl Strawberry/Jsy/250	8.00
6	Dave Parker/Jsy/100	10.00
7	Dave Righetti/Jsy/150	8.00
8	Dwight Evans/Bat/250	8.00
9	Dwight Gooden/Bat/150	8.00
10	Fred Lynn/Jsy/100	5.00
11	George Foster/Bat/250	5.00
12	Harold Baines/Jsy/250	5.00
13	Jack Morris/Jsy/100	5.00
14	Jim Rice/Pants/250	8.00
15	Keith Hernandez/Bat/100	5.00
16	Kirk Gibson/Jsy/250	8.00
17	Luis Aparicio/Bat/250	8.00
18	Mark Grace/Bat/250	8.00
22	Ron Santo/Bat/150	10.00
23	Steve Garvey/Jsy/250	8.00
24	Tony Oliva/Jsy/250	8.00
25	Will Clark/Bat/250	10.00

Stars of Summer Sign. Material

NM/M
Production 25-100

#	Player	Price
1	Andre Dawson/Jsy/100	20.00
2	Bert Blyleven/Jsy/50	20.00
3	Bill Madlock/Bat/100	20.00
4	Dale Murphy/Jsy/50	40.00
6	Dave Parker/Jsy/50	20.00
7	Dave Righetti/Jsy/50	20.00
8	Dwight Evans/Jsy/50	30.00
9	Dwight Gooden/Bat/25	25.00
10	Fred Lynn/Jsy/100	15.00
11	George Foster/Bat/50	20.00
12	Harold Baines/Jsy/100	20.00
13	Jack Morris/Jsy/100	15.00
14	Jim Rice/Pants/50	25.00
15	Keith Hernandez/Jsy/50	20.00
16	Kirk Gibson/Jsy/25	40.00
17	Luis Aparicio/Bat/100	20.00
18	Mark Grace/Bat/25	40.00
22	Ron Santo/Bat/50	35.00
23	Steve Garvey/Jsy/50	20.00
24	Tony Oliva/Jsy/50	20.00
25	Will Clark/Bat/25	40.00

Team Colors

NM/M
Common Player: 1.50
Production 800 Sets
Gold: 2-4X
Production 50 Sets
Platinum: No Pricing
Production One Set

#	Player	Price
1	Adam Dunn	2.00
2	Albert Pujols	6.00
3	Andruw Jones	2.00
4	Aramis Ramirez	2.00
5	Aubrey Huff	1.50
6	Bobby Abreu	2.00
7	Cal Ripken Jr.	8.00
8	Carlos Lee	1.50
9	Craig Biggio	2.00
10	Derek Lee	2.00
11	Garret Anderson	2.00
12	Gary Carter	2.00
13	Geoff Jenkins	1.50
14	Greg Maddux	4.00
15	Hank Blalock	2.00
16	Hideki Matsui	5.00
17	Jake Peavy	2.00
18	Jim Edmonds	2.00
19	Jim Palmer	2.00
20	Jose Guillen	1.50
21	Jose Vidro	1.50
22	Juan Pierre	1.50
23	Lew Ford	1.50
24	Lyle Overbay	1.50
25	Manny Ramirez	3.00
26	Mark Loretta	1.50
27	Mark Teixeira	3.00
28	Melvin Mora	1.50
29	Michael Young	2.00
30	Miguel Cabrera	4.00
31	Mike Lowell	2.00
32	Mike Mussina	2.00
33	Milton Bradley	2.00
34	Randy Johnson	4.00
35	Roger Clemens	6.00
36	Sean Casey	2.00
37	Shawn Green	2.00
38	Steve Carlton	2.00
39	Todd Helton	2.00
40	Travis Hafner	1.50

Team Colors Bat
NM/M
Production 100 Sets

#	Player	Price
1	Adam Dunn	8.00
2	Albert Pujols	20.00
3	Andruw Jones	5.00
4	Aramis Ramirez	5.00
7	Cal Ripken Jr.	30.00
9	Craig Biggio	8.00
10	Derek Lee	8.00
11	Garret Anderson	5.00
12	Gary Carter	5.00
15	Hank Blalock	5.00
16	Hideki Matsui	30.00
18	Jim Edmonds	10.00
21	Jose Vidro	5.00
22	Juan Pierre	5.00
23	Lew Ford	5.00
27	Mark Teixeira	5.00
28	Melvin Mora	5.00
29	Michael Young	10.00
30	Miguel Cabrera	10.00
31	Mike Lowell	5.00
36	Sean Casey	5.00
37	Shawn Green	5.00

Team Colors Materials
NM/M
Production 25-100
Prime: No Pricing
Production Five Sets

#	Player	Price
1	Adam Dunn/Bat-Jsy/100	10.00
2	Albert Pujols/Bat-Jsy/100	25.00
3	Andruw Jones/Bat-Jsy/100	8.00
4	Aramis Ramirez/Bat-Jsy/100	10.00
6	Bobby Abreu/Jsy-Jsy/100	10.00
7	Cal Ripken Jr./Bat-Jsy/100	40.00
8	Carlos Lee/Jsy-Jsy/100	8.00
9	Craig Biggio/Bat-Jsy/100	10.00
11	Garret Anderson/Bat-Jsy/100	8.00
12	Gary Carter/Bat-Jsy/25	8.00
13	Geoff Jenkins/...	
15	Hank Blalock/Bat-Jsy/100	10.00
16	Hideki Matsui/Bat/50	45.00
18	Jim Edmonds/Bat-Jkt/100	12.00
19	Jim Palmer/Jsy-Pants/25	12.00
21	Jose Vidro/Bat-Jsy/50	8.00
23	Lew Ford/Bat-Jsy/100	8.00
25	Manny Ramirez/Jsy-Jsy/100	15.00
27	Mark Teixeira/Bat-Jsy/100	10.00
28	Melvin Mora-Jsy/50	8.00
29	Michael Young/Bat-Jsy/100	8.00
30	Miguel Cabrera/Bat-Jsy/100	15.00
31	Mike Lowell/Bat-Jsy/100	8.00
36	Sean Casey/Bat-Jsy/100	8.00
37	Shawn Green	8.00
39	Todd Helton/Jsy-Jsy/50	10.00

Team Colors Signature
NM/M
Production 1-25

#	Player	Price
4	Aramis Ramirez/25	40.00
5	Aubrey Huff/25	20.00
8	Carlos Lee/25	25.00
17	Jake Peavy/25	40.00
20	Jose Guillen/25	25.00
21	Jose Vidro/25	20.00
23	Lew Ford/25	20.00
24	Lyle Overbay/25	25.00
26	Mark Loretta/25	25.00
28	Melvin Mora/25	25.00
33	Milton Bradley/25	25.00
40	Travis Hafner/25	20.00

Team Colors Signature Bat
NM/M
Production 5-25

#	Player	Price
1	Adam Dunn/25	40.00
4	Aramis Ramirez/25	40.00
5	Aubrey Huff/25	20.00
10	Derek Lee/25	35.00
11	Garret Anderson/25	30.00
15	Hank Blalock/25	30.00
21	Jose Vidro/25	20.00
23	Lew Ford/25	20.00
29	Michael Young/25	20.00

Team Colors Signature Jersey
NM/M
Production 1-25
Prime: No Pricing
Production One Set

#	Player	Price
1	Adam Dunn/25	40.00
4	Aramis Ramirez/50	40.00
5	Aubrey Huff/25	20.00
8	Carlos Lee/25	25.00
11	Garret Anderson/25	25.00
12	Gary Carter/25	25.00
15	Hank Blalock/25	30.00
21	Jose Vidro/25	20.00
23	Lew Ford/25	20.00
24	Lyle Overbay/25	25.00
28	Melvin Mora/25	25.00
29	Michael Young/25	20.00
40	Travis Hafner/25	20.00

Team Colors Signature Materials

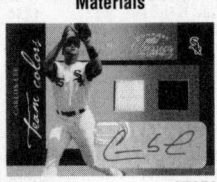

NM/M
Production 5-25
Prime: No Pricing
Production One Set

#	Player	Price
4	Aramis Ramirez/Bat-Jsy/25	50.00
5	Aubrey Huff/Jsy-Jsy/25	25.00
8	Carlos Lee/Jsy-Jsy/25	30.00
11	Garret Anderson/Bat-Jsy/25	30.00
15	Hank Blalock/Bat-Jsy/25	40.00
21	Jose Vidro/Bat-Jsy/25	25.00
23	Lew Ford/Bat-Jsy/25	25.00
28	Melvin Mora/Bat-Jsy/25	30.00
29	Michael Young/Jsy-Jsy/25	35.00
40	Travis Hafner/Jsy-Jsy/25	20.00

2005 Donruss Classics Texas Rangers Hall of Fame
This cello-wrapped set was a stadium giveaway.
NM/M
Complete Set (9): 7.00
Common Player: .25

#	Player	Price
(1)	Buddy Bell	.50
(2)	Mark Holtz (Broadcaster)	.25
(3)	Charlie Hough	.50

#	Player	Price
(4)	Ferguson Jenkins	.50
(5)	Johnny Oates	.50
(6)	Nolan Ryan	5.00
(7)	Jim Sundberg	.25
(8)	Tom Vandergriff (Broadcaster)	.25
(9)	John Wetteland	.50

2005 Donruss Diamond Kings

NM/M
Complete Set (300): 85.00
Complete Update Set (150): 40.00
Common Player: .25
Pack (5): 8.00
Box (12): 75.00
Update Pack (5): 5.00
Update Box (16): 75.00

#	Player	Price
1	Garret Anderson	.40
2	Vladimir Guerrero	.75
3	Jose Guillen	.40
4	Troy Glaus	.40
5	Tim Salmon	.25
6	Casey Kotchman	.25
7	Chone Figgins	.25
8	Robb Quinlan	.25
9	Francisco Rodriguez	.25
10	Troy Percival	.25
11	Randy Johnson	.75
12	Brandon Webb	.25
13	Richie Sexson	.40
14	Shea Hillenbrand	.25
15	Chad Tracy	.25
17	Alex Cintron	.25
18	Luis Gonzalez	.25
19	Rafael Furcal	.25
20	Andruw Jones	.50
21	Marcus Giles	.25
22	John Smoltz	.50
23	Adam LaRoche	.25
24	Russ Ortiz	.25
25	J.D. Drew	.25
26	Chipper Jones	.75
27	Nick Green	.25
28	Rafael Palmeiro	.50
29	Miguel Tejada	.50
30	Javy Lopez	.25
31	Luis Matos	.25
32	Larry Bigbie	.25
33	Rodrigo Lopez	.25
34	Brian Roberts	.25
35	Melvin Mora	.25
36	Adam Loewen	.25
37	Manny Ramirez	.75
38	Jason Varitek	.50
39	Trot Nixon	.25
40	Curt Schilling	.75
41	Keith Foulke	.25
42	Pedro Martinez	.75
43	Johnny Damon	.75
44	Kevin Youkilis	.25
45	Orlando Cabrera	.25
46	Abe Alvarez	.25
47	David Ortiz	.75
48	Kerry Wood	.25
49	Mark Prior	.75
50	Aramis Ramirez	.25
51	Greg Maddux	1.00
52	Carlos Zambrano	.25
53	Derrek Lee	.50
54	Corey Patterson	.25
55	Moises Alou	.25
56	Matt Clement	.25
57	Sammy Sosa	1.00
58	Nomar Garciaparra	.75
59	Todd Walker	.25
60	Angel Guzman	.25
61	Magglio Ordonez	.25
62	Carlos Lee	.25

No.	Player	Price
62	Joe Crede	.25
63	Paul Konerko	.25
64	Shingo Takatsu	.25
65	Frank Thomas	.50
66	Freddy Garcia	.25
67	Aaron Rowand	.25
68	Jose Contreras	.25
69	Adam Dunn	.50
70	Austin Kearns	.25
71	Barry Larkin	.40
72	Ken Griffey Jr.	1.00
73	Ryan Wagner	.25
74	Sean Casey	.25
75	Danny Graves	.25
76	C.C. Sabathia	.25
77	Jody Gerut	.25
78	Omar Vizquel	.40
79	Victor Martinez	.40
80	Matt Lawton	.25
81	Jake Westbrook	.25
82	Kazuhito Tadano	.25
83	Travis Hafner	.25
84	Todd Helton	.50
85	Preston Wilson	.25
86	Matt Holliday	.25
87	Jeromy Burnitz	.25
88	Vinny Castilla	.25
89	Jeremy Bonderman	.25
90	Ivan Rodriguez	.50
91	Carlos Guillen	.25
92	Brandon Inge	.25
93	Rondell White	.25
94	Dontrelle Willis	.25
95	Miguel Cabrera	.75
96	Josh Beckett	.40
97	Mike Lowell	.25
98	Luis Castillo	.25
99	Juan Pierre	.25
100	Paul LoDuca	.25
101	Guillermo Mota	.25
102	Craig Biggio	.25
103	Lance Berkman	.25
104	Roy Oswalt	.25
105	Roger Clemens	2.00
106	Jeff Kent	.25
107	Morgan Ensberg	.25
108	Jeff Bagwell	.50
109	Carlos Beltran	.50
110	Angel Berroa	.25
111	Mike Sweeney	.25
112	Jeremy Affeldt	.25
113	Zack Greinke	.25
114	Juan Gonzalez	.25
115	Andres Blanco	.25
116	Shawn Green	.25
117	Milton Bradley	.25
118	Adrian Beltre	.50
119	Hideo Nomo	.25
120	Steve Finley	.25
121	Eric Gagne	.25
122	Brad Penny	.25
123	Scott Podsednik	.25
124	Ben Sheets	.40
125	Lyle Overbay	.25
126	Junior Spivey	.25
127	Bill Hall	.25
128	Rickie Weeks	.25
129	Jacque Jones	.25
130	Torii Hunter	.40
131	Johan Santana	.25
132	Lew Ford	.25
133	Joe Mauer	.75
134	Justin Morneau	.50
135	Jason Kubel	.25
136	Jose Vidro	.25
137	Chad Cordero	.25
138	Brad Wilkerson	.25
139	Nick Johnson	.25
140	Livan Hernandez	.25
141	Tom Glavine	.40
142	Jae Weong Seo	.25
143	Jose Reyes	.50
144	Al Leiter	.25
145	Mike Piazza	1.00
146	Kazuo Matsui	.25
147	Richard Hidalgo	.25
148	David Wright	.75
149	Mariano Rivera	.50
150	Mike Mussina	.50
151	Alex Rodriguez	1.50
152	Derek Jeter	2.00
153	Jorge Posada	.50
154	Jason Giambi	.25
155	Gary Sheffield	.50
156	Bubba Crosby	.25
157	Javier Vazquez	.25
158	Kevin Brown	.25
159	Tom Gordon	.25
160	Esteban Loaiza	.25
161	Hideki Matsui	1.50
162	Eric Chavez	.40
163	Mark Mulder	.40
164	Barry Zito	.40
165	Tim Hudson	.40
166	Jermaine Dye	.25
167	Octavio Dotel	.25
168	Bobby Crosby	.25
169	Mark Kotsay	.25
170	Scott Hatteberg	.25
171	Jim Thome	.75
172	Bobby Abreu	.40
173	Kevin Millwood	.25
174	Mike Lieberthal	.25
175	Jimmy Rollins	.25
176	Chase Utley	.50
177	Randy Wolf	.25
178	Craig Wilson	.25
179	Jason Kendall	.25
180	Jack Wilson	.25
181	Jose Castillo	.25
182	Robert Mackowiak	.25
183	Oliver Perez	.25
184	Oliver Perez	.25
185	Sean Burroughs	.25
186	Jay Payton	.25
187	Brian Giles	.25
188	Akinori Otsuka	.25
189	Jake Peavy	.25
190	Phil Nevin	.25
191	Mark Loretta	.25
192	Khalil Greene	.40
193	Trevor Hoffman	.25
194	Freddy Guzman	.25
195	Jerome Williams	.25
196	Jason Schmidt	.40
197	Todd Linden	.25
198	Merkin Valdez	.25
199	J.T. Snow	.25
200	A.J. Pierzynski	.25
201	Edgar Martinez	.40
202	Ichiro Suzuki	1.50
203	Raul Ibanez	.25
204	Bret Boone	.25
205	Shigetoshi Hasegawa	.25
206	Miguel Olivo	.25
207	Bucky Jacobsen	.25
208	Jamie Moyer	.25
209	Jim Edmonds	.50
210	Scott Rolen	.75
211	Edgar Renteria	.50
212	Dan Haren	.25
213	Matt Morris	.25
214	Albert Pujols	2.00
215	Larry Walker	.40
216	Jason Isringhausen	.25
217	Chris Carpenter	.25
218	Jason Marquis	.25
219	Jeff Suppan	.25
220	Aubrey Huff	.25
221	Carl Crawford	.25
222	Rocco Baldelli	.25
223	Fred McGriff	.25
224	Dewon Brazelton	.25
225	B.J. Upton	.40
226	Joey Gathright	.25
227	Scott Kazmir	.40
228	Hank Blalock	.50
229	Mark Teixeira	.50
230	Michael Young	.25
231	Adrian Gonzalez	.25
232	Laynce Nix	.25
233	Alfonso Soriano	.75
234	Rafael Palmeiro	.50
235	Kevin Mench	.25
236	David Dellucci	.25
237	Francisco Cordero	.25
238	Kenny Rogers	.25
239	Roy Halladay	.25
240	Carlos Delgado	.40
241	Alexis Rios	.25
242	Vernon Wells	.25
243	Yadier Molina	.25
244	Rene Rivera	.25
245	Logan Kensing	.25
246	Gavin Floyd	.25
247	Russ Adams	.25
248	Dioner Navarro	.25
249	Ryan Howard	1.00
250	Ryan Church	.25
251	Jeff Francis	.25
252	John Van Benschoten	.25
253	Yhency Brazoban	.25
254	David Krynzel	.25
255	Victor Diaz	.25
256	Jairo Garcia	.25
257	Scott Proctor	.25
258	Shawn Hill	.25
259	Jeff Baker	.25
260	Matt Peterson	.25
261	Josh Kroeger	.25
262	Grady Sizemore	.40
263	Clint Nageotte	.25
264	Andy Green	.25
265	Justin Verlander RC	2.00
266	Jim Thome	.75
267	Larry Walker	.40
268	Ivan Rodriguez	.25
269	Brad Penny	.25
270	Carlos Beltran	.25
271	Paul LoDuca	.25
272	Orlando Cabrera	.25
273	Nomar Garciaparra	1.00
274	Esteban Loaiza	.25
275	Richard Hidalgo	.25
276	John Olerud	.25
277	Greg Maddux	1.00
278	Roger Clemens	2.00
279	Alfonso Soriano	.75
280	Dale Murphy	.50
281	Cal Ripken Jr.	4.00
282	Dwight Evans	.25
283	Ron Santo	.25
284	Andre Dawson	.25
285	Harold Baines	.25
286	Jack Morris	.25
287	Kirk Gibson	.25
288	Bo Jackson	.75
289	Orel Hershiser	.25
290	Maury Wills	.25
291	Tony Oliva	.25
292	Darryl Strawberry	.25
293	Roger Maris	1.00
294	Don Mattingly	2.00
295	Rickey Henderson	.50
296	Dave Stewart	.25
297	Dave Parker	.25
298	Steve Garvey	.25
299	Matt Williams	.25
300	Keith Hernandez	.25
301	John Lackey	.25
302	Vladimir Guerrero	.75
303	Garret Anderson	.25
304	Dallas McPherson	.25
305	Orlando Cabrera	.25
306	Steve Finley	.25
307	Luis Gonzalez	.25
308	Randy Johnson	.75
309	Scott Hairston	.25
310	Shawn Green	.25
311	Troy Glaus	.40
312	Javier Vazquez	.25
313	Russ Ortiz	.25
314	Chipper Jones	.75
315	Johnny Estrada	.25
316	Andruw Jones	.50
317	Tim Hudson	.50
318	Danny Kolb	.25
319	Jay Gibbons	.25
320	Melvin Mora	.25
321	Rafael Palmeiro	.50
322	Val Majewski	.25
323	David Ortiz	.75
324	Manny Ramirez	.75
325	Edgar Renteria	.25
326	Matt Clement	.25
327	Curt Schilling	.75
328	Sammy Sosa	1.00
329	Mark Prior	.75
330	Greg Maddux	1.00
331	Nomar Garciaparra	1.00
332	Frank Thomas	.50
333	Mark Buehrle	.25
334	Jermaine Dye	.25
335	Scott Podsednik	.25
336	Sean Casey	.25
337	Adam Dunn	.50
338	Ken Griffey Jr.	1.00
339	Travis Hafner	.25
340	Victor Martinez	.25
341	Cliff Lee	.25
342	Todd Helton	.50
343	Preston Wilson	.25
344	Ivan Rodriguez	.50
345	Dmitri Young	.25
346	Nate Robertson	.25
347	Miguel Cabrera	.75
348	Jeff Bagwell	.40
349	Andy Pettitte	.40
350	Roger Clemens	2.00
351	Ken Harvey	.25
352	Danny Bautista	.25
353	Hideo Nomo	.25
354	Kazuhisa Ishii	.25
355	Edwin Jackson	.25
356	J.D. Drew	.25
357	Jeff Kent	.25
358	Geoff Jenkins	.25
359	Carlos Lee	.25
360	Shannon Stewart	.25
361	Joe Nathan	.25
362	Johan Santana	.50
363	Mike Piazza	1.00
364	Hideki Matsui	.25
365	Carlos Beltran	.50
366	Pedro Martinez	.75
367	Ambiorix Concepcion RC	.40
368	Hideki Matsui	1.50
369	Bernie Williams	.40
370	Gary Sheffield	.50
371	Randy Johnson	.75
372	Jaret Wright	.25
373	Carl Pavano	.25
374	Derek Jeter	2.00
375	Alex Rodriguez	1.50
376	Eric Byrnes	.25
377	Rich Harden	.25
378	Mark Mulder	.40
379	Nick Swisher	.25
380	Eric Chavez	.25
381	Jason Kendall	.25
382	Marlon Byrd	.25
383	Pat Burrell	.25
384	Brett Myers	.25
385	Jim Thome	.50
386	Jason Bay	.25
387	Jake Peavy	.25
388	Moises Alou	.25
389	Omar Vizquel	.25
390	Travis Blackley	.25
391	Jose Lopez	.25
392	Jeremy Reed	.25
393	Adrian Beltre	.25
394	Richie Sexson	.25
395	Wladimir Balentien RC	1.50
396	Ichiro Suzuki	1.50
397	Albert Pujols	2.00
398	Scott Rolen	.75
399	Mark Mulder	.40
400	David Eckstein	.25
401	Delmon Young	.25
402	Aubrey Huff	.25
403	Alfonso Soriano	.25
404	Hank Blalock	.25
405	Richard Hidalgo	.25
406	Vernon Wells	.25
407	Orlando Hudson	.25
408	Alexis Rios	.25
409	Shea Hillenbrand	.25
410	Jose Guillen	.25
411	Vinny Castilla	.25
412	Jose Vidro	.25
413	Nick Johnson	.25
414	Livan Hernandez	.25
415	Miguel Tejada	.50
416	Gary Sheffield	.50
417	Curt Schilling	.75
418	Rafael Palmeiro	.50
419	Scott Rolen	.75
420	Aramis Ramirez	.40
421	Vladimir Guerrero	.75
422	Steve Finley	.50
423	Roger Clemens	2.00
424	Mike Piazza	1.00
425	Ivan Rodriguez	.50
426	David Justice	.25
427	Mark Grace	.40
428	Alan Trammell	.25
429	Bert Blyleven	.25
430	Dwight Gooden	.25
431	Deion Sanders	.25
432	Joe Torre	.25
433	Jose Canseco	.25
434	Tony Gwynn	.75
435	Will Clark	.40
436	Marty Marion	.25
437	Nolan Ryan	3.00
438	Billy Martin	.25
439	Carlos Delgado	.25
440	Magglio Ordonez	.25
441	Sammy Sosa	1.00
442	Keiichi Yabu RC	.50
443	Yuniesky Betancourt RC	1.00
444	Jeff Niemann RC	1.50
445	Brandon McCarthy RC	1.50
446	Philip Humber RC	1.50
447	Tadahito Iguchi RC	2.00
448	Cal Ripken Jr.	4.00
449	Ryne Sandberg	2.00
450	Willie Mays	2.00

Non-Canvas
No Pricing
Production 20 Sets

Bronze

Stars:	3-5X
Production 100 Sets	
Update Bronze (301-450):	3-5X
Production 50	

Silver
Silvers:	4-8X
Production 50 Sets	
Update (301-450):	No Pricing
Production 25 Sets	

Silver B/W
Silvers:	4-8X
Production 50 Sets	

Gold
Golds:	5-10X
Production 25 Sets	
Gold Update (301-450):	No Pricing
Production 10 Sets	

Platinum
No Pricing
Production One Set
Framed Platinums:	No Pricing
Production One Set	

Framed Black
Stars:	5-10X
Production 25 Sets	

Framed Blue

Stars:	5-10X
Production 25 Sets	

Framed Green
Stars:	4-8X
Production 50 Sets	

Framed Red
Stars:	1-30X
Inserted 1:3	

Diamond Cuts Bat

		NM/M
Common Player:		4.00
1	Adam Dunn/200	8.00
2	Adrian Beltre/200	6.00
3	Alfonso Soriano/50	8.00
4	Andruw Jones/200	6.00
5	Andy Pettitte/50	8.00
6	Aramis Ramirez/100	6.00
10	Carlos Beltran/200	8.00
12	Craig Wilson/200	4.00
13	Curt Schilling/50	10.00
14	Darin Erstad/200	6.00
16	Derek Lee/200	6.00
17	Fred McGriff/100	4.00
19	Ivan Rodriguez/200	8.00
21	Jason Bay/200	4.00
22	Jason Giambi/100	4.00
23	Jay Gibbons/200	4.00
24	John Olerud/200	4.00
26	Juan Gonzalez/200	4.00
27	Kazuhisa Ishii/200	6.00
29	Kevin Brown/100	4.00
31	Larry Walker/200	6.00
32	Mark Teixeira/200	6.00
33	Melvin Mora/50	8.00
34	Michael Young/200	4.00
35	Miguel Tejada/100	8.00
36	Mike Mussina/50	8.00
37	Paul LoDuca/200	4.00
38	Preston Wilson/200	4.00
39	Randy Johnson/50	10.00
41	Richie Sexson/200	4.00
42	Roger Clemens/50	15.00
43	Scott Rolen/100	8.00
44	Sean Burroughs/200	4.00
45	Sean Casey/200	4.00
46	Shannon Stewart/200	4.00
47	Shawn Green/200	4.00
48	Tim Salmon/200	4.00
49	Tom Glavine/200	6.00

Diamond Cuts Jersey

		NM/M
Common Player:		4.00
Prime:		No Pricing
Production One Set		
1	Adam Dunn/50	10.00
2	Adrian Beltre/200	6.00
3	Alfonso Soriano/50	8.00
4	Andruw Jones/200	4.00
5	Andy Pettitte/100	6.00
6	Aramis Ramirez/200	6.00
7	Brian Giles/200	4.00
8	C.C. Sabathia/200	4.00
9	Carl Crawford/200	4.00
10	Carlos Beltran/200	8.00
11	Carlos Lee/200	4.00
12	Craig Wilson/200	4.00
13	Curt Schilling/50	10.00
14	Darin Erstad/200	4.00
17	Fred McGriff/200	4.00
18	Greg Maddux/50	12.00
19	Ivan Rodriguez/200	8.00
20	Jason Bay/200	4.00
21	Jason Giambi/200	4.00
22	Jay Gibbons/100	4.00
23	Jeff Kent/200	4.00
24	John Olerud/200	4.00
25	Juan Gonzalez/Pants/200	4.00
26	Junior Spivey/200	4.00
27	Kazuhisa Ishii/200	6.00
29	Kevin Brown/200	4.00
28	Larry Walker/Rockies/200	6.00
30	Lyle Overbay/200	4.00
31	Mark Teixeira/100	6.00
32	Melvin Mora/200	4.00
33	Michael Young/200	4.00
34	Miguel Tejada/200	8.00
35	Mike Mussina/100	8.00
36	Paul LoDuca/50	6.00
37	Preston Wilson/200	4.00
38	Randy Johnson/100	8.00
39	Richie Sexson/200	4.00
40	Roger Clemens/50	15.00
41	Scott Rolen/50	10.00
42	Sean Burroughs/200	4.00
43	Sean Casey/200	4.00
44	Shannon Stewart/100	4.00
45	Shawn Green/200	4.00
48	Steve Finley/200	4.00
49	Tom Glavine/200	6.00
50	Travis Hafner/100	4.00

Diamond Cuts Combos

		NM/M
Common Player:		6.00
Prime:		No Pricing
Production One Set		
1	Adam Dunn/Bat-Jsy/100	10.00
2	Adrian Beltre/Bat-Jsy/100	8.00
3	Alfonso Soriano/Bat-Jsy/100	10.00
4	Andruw Jones/Bat-Jsy/100	8.00
5	Andy Pettitte/Jsy-Jsy/100	10.00
6	Aramis Ramirez/Bat-Jsy/100	8.00
7	Brian Giles/Bat-Jsy/100	6.00
10	Carlos Beltran/Bat-Jsy/50	15.00
11	Carlos Lee/Jsy-Jsy/100	6.00
12	Craig Wilson/Bat-Jsy/100	6.00
13	Curt Schilling/Bat-Jsy/100	12.00
14	Darin Erstad/Bat-Jsy/100	6.00
17	Fred McGriff/Bat-Jsy/100	6.00
19	Ivan Rodriguez/Bat-Jsy/100	10.00
21	Jason Giambi/Bat-Jsy/50	8.00
22	Jay Gibbons/Bat-Jsy/50	6.00
23	Jeff Kent/Bat-Jsy/100	6.00
24	John Olerud/Bat-Jsy/200	6.00
25	Juan Gonzalez/Bat-Pants/50	8.00
27	Kazuhisa Ishii/Bat-Jsy/100	8.00
28	Kevin Brown/Bat-Jsy/100	6.00
29	Larry Walker/Bat-Jsy/100	8.00
30	Mark Teixeira/Bat-Jsy/100	10.00
34	Miguel Tejada/Jsy-Jsy/100	10.00
35	Mike Mussina/Bat-Pants/50	12.00
36	Paul LoDuca/Bat-Jsy/50	8.00
37	Preston Wilson/Bat-Jsy/100	6.00
38	Randy Johnson/Bat-Jsy/50	15.00
40	Roger Clemens/Bat-Jsy/50	20.00
44	Shannon Stewart/Bat-Jsy/100	6.00
45	Shawn Green/Bat-Jsy/100	6.00
48	Tom Glavine/Bat-Jsy/100	8.00
49	Torii Hunter/Bat-Jsy/100	8.00

Diamond Cuts Signature

		NM/M
Production 1-100		
6	C.C. Sabathia/25	20.00
9	Carl Crawford/50	20.00
11	Carlos Lee/100	15.00
12	Craig Wilson/100	15.00
20	Jason Bay/100	15.00
22	Jay Gibbons/100	10.00
30	Lyle Overbay/100	15.00
32	Melvin Mora/50	15.00
44	Shannon Stewart/25	20.00
47	Tim Salmon/100	20.00
50	Travis Hafner/100	15.00

Diamond Cuts Signature Bat

		NM/M
Production 5-100		
1	Adam Dunn/25	40.00
6	Adrian Beltre/35	35.00
8	Aramis Ramirez/30	30.00
9	Carlos Beltran/50	40.00
12	Craig Wilson/100	15.00
16	Derek Lee/100	20.00
17	Fred McGriff/25	50.00
22	Jay Gibbons/100	10.00
31	Mark Teixeira/50	40.00
33	Michael Young/100	20.00
43	Paul LoDuca/25	25.00
44	Sean Casey/25	25.00
47	Torii Hunter/25	25.00

Diamond Cuts Sign. Jersey

		NM/M
Production 5-100		
Prime:		No Pricing
Production One Set		
2	Adrian Beltre/100	25.00
6	Aramis Ramirez/100	30.00
8	C.C. Sabathia/100	15.00
9	Carl Crawford/50	20.00
11	Carlos Lee/100	15.00
12	Craig Wilson/100	15.00
30	Lyle Overbay/100	15.00
31	Mark Teixeira/40	40.00
32	Melvin Mora/15	15.00
33	Michael Young/100	20.00
36	Paul LoDuca/25	25.00
42	Sean Burroughs/10	10.00
43	Sean Casey/25	25.00
44	Shannon Stewart/25	20.00
46	Steve Finley/25	25.00
50	Travis Hafner/50	25.00
57	Mark Kotsay/25	25.00
60	Victor Martinez/25	20.00

Diamond Cuts Sign. Combos

		NM/M
Prime:		No Pricing
Production One Set		
1	Adam Dunn/Bat-Jsy/25	40.00
2	Adrian Beltre/Bat-Bat/25	40.00

6	Aramis Ramirez/Bat-Jsy/100	30.00
8	C.C. Sabathia/Jsy-Jsy/100	25.00
11	Carlos Lee/Jsy-Jsy/100	20.00
12	Craig Wilson/Bat-Bat/100	15.00
17	Fred McGriff/Bat-Jsy/25	50.00
22	Jay Gibbons/Bat-Bat/50	10.00
25	Juan Gonzalez/Bat-Jsy/100	25.00
27	Kazuhisa Ishii/Bat-Jsy/25	50.00
31	Mark Teixeira/Bat-Bat/25	40.00
33	Michael Young/Bat-Jsy/50	25.00
36	Paul LoDuca/Bat-Bat/25	25.00
43	Sean Casey/Bat-Jsy/25	25.00
44	Shannon Stewart/Bat-Jsy/25	20.00
49	Torii Hunter/Bat-Jsy/25	25.00
50	Travis Hafner/Bat-Jsy/25	25.00
51	Aramis Ramirez/Jsy/24	25.00
60	Victor Martinez/25	20.00

Heritage Collection

NM/M

Common Player: 1.50
Inserted 1:21
#26-35 inserted 1:76
#26-35 are DK Update exclusive.

1	Andre Dawson	1.50
2	Bob Gibson	2.50
3	Cal Ripken Jr.	8.00
4	Dale Murphy	2.00
5	Darryl Strawberry	1.50
6	Dennis Eckersley	1.50
7	Don Mattingly	6.00
8	Duke Snider	3.00
9	Dwight Gooden	1.50
10	Eddie Murray	3.00
11	Frank Robinson	3.00
12	Gary Carter	2.00
13	George Brett	6.00
14	Harmon Killebrew	3.00
15	Jack Morris	1.50
16	Jim Palmer	1.50
17	Lou Brock	2.00
18	Mike Schmidt	6.00
19	Nolan Ryan	8.00
20	Ozzie Smith	4.00
21	Phil Niekro	1.50
22	Rod Carew	2.00
23	Rollie Fingers	1.50
24	Steve Carlton	1.50
25	Tony Gwynn	5.00
26	Curt Schilling	3.00
27	Bobby Doerr	1.50
28	Edgar Martinez	1.50
29	Jim Thorpe	4.00
30	Mark Grace	1.50
31	Matt Williams	1.50
32	Paul Molitor	2.50
33	Robin Yount	4.00
34	Ryne Sandberg	5.00
35	Will Clark	2.00

Heritage Collection Bat

NM/M

Production 50-100

1	Andre Dawson/50	8.00
3	Cal Ripken Jr./100	10.00
4	Dale Murphy/100	10.00
5	Darryl Strawberry/50	8.00
7	Don Mattingly/100	20.00
9	Dwight Gooden/100	5.00
10	Eddie Murray/100	15.00
11	Frank Robinson/100	8.00
12	Gary Carter/100	5.00
13	George Brett/100	15.00
14	Harmon Killebrew/100	10.00
17	Lou Brock/100	8.00
18	Mike Schmidt/100	20.00
19	Nolan Ryan/100	30.00
20	Ozzie Smith/100	15.00
21	Phil Niekro/50	8.00
22	Rod Carew/100	8.00
24	Steve Carlton/100	5.00
25	Tony Gwynn/100	10.00

Heritage Collection Jersey

NM/M

Production 25-100
Prime: No Pricing
Production One Set

1	Andre Dawson/100	8.00
2	Bob Gibson/50	10.00
3	Cal Ripken Jr./40	40.00
4	Dale Murphy/100	10.00
5	Darryl Strawberry/25	10.00
6	Dennis Eckersley/100	5.00
7	Don Mattingly/100	20.00
8	Duke Snider/50	15.00
9	Dwight Gooden/100	15.00
10	Eddie Murray/100	15.00

12	Gary Carter/100	5.00
13	George Brett/50	20.00
14	Harmon Killebrew/100	10.00
15	Jack Morris/100	5.00
16	Jim Palmer/100	5.00
17	Lou Brock/100	5.00
18	Mike Schmidt/Jkt/100	20.00
19	Nolan Ryan/100	25.00
20	Ozzie Smith/Pants/100	15.00
21	Phil Niekro/100	5.00
22	Rod Carew/100	8.00
23	Rollie Fingers/50	8.00
24	Steve Carlton/50	8.00
25	Tony Gwynn/100	10.00

Heritage Collection Combos

NM/M

Production 25-100
Prime: No Pricing
Production One Set

1	Andre Dawson/Bat-Jsy/50	8.00
3	Cal Ripken Jr./Bat-Jsy/50	60.00
4	Dale Murphy/Bat-Jsy/25	20.00
7	Don Mattingly/Bat-Jkt/100	25.00
8	Duke Snider/Jsy-Pants/25	20.00
9	Dwight Gooden/Bat-Jsy/100	10.00
10	Eddie Murray/Bat-Jsy/100	20.00
14	Harmon Killebrew/Bat-Jsy/100	15.00
16	Jim Palmer/Jsy-Jsy/100	10.00
17	Lou Brock/Bat-Jkt/50	10.00
18	Mike Schmidt/Bat-Jsy/100	25.00
19	Nolan Ryan/Jsy-Pants/50	40.00
20	Ozzie Smith/Bat-Jsy/100	20.00
21	Phil Niekro/Bat-Jsy/50	10.00
22	Rod Carew/Bat-Jsy/100	10.00
24	Steve Carlton/Bat-Jsy/100	10.00
25	Tony Gwynn/Bat-Jsy/50	15.00

Heritage Coll. Signature

NM/M

Production 1-50

1	Andre Dawson/50	25.00
5	Darryl Strawberry/50	25.00
9	Dwight Gooden/25	25.00
15	Jack Morris/50	20.00
23	Rollie Fingers/25	40.00

Heritage Coll. Sign. Bat

NM/M

Production 5-100
#26-35 are DK Update exclusive.

1	Andre Dawson/50	25.00
4	Dale Murphy/50	40.00
7	Don Mattingly/25	75.00
9	Dwight Gooden/100	15.00
11	Frank Robinson/25	40.00
14	Harmon Killebrew/50	40.00
17	Lou Brock/50	35.00
20	Ozzie Smith/25	65.00
21	Phil Niekro/20	30.00
22	Rod Carew/25	40.00
24	Steve Carlton/25	40.00
25	Tony Gwynn/25	50.00
28	Edgar Martinez/25	40.00
31	Matt Williams/25	35.00
35	Will Clark/25	40.00

Heritage Coll. Sign. Jersey

NM/M

Production 5-100
#26-35 are DK Update exclusive
Prime: No Pricing
Production One Set

1	Andre Dawson/100	25.00
2	Bob Gibson/25	40.00
4	Dale Murphy/50	40.00
5	Darryl Strawberry/Pants/100	25.00
6	Dennis Eckersley/50	25.00
7	Don Mattingly/25	85.00
8	Duke Snider/50	25.00
9	Dwight Gooden/100	20.00
11	Frank Robinson/25	40.00
12	Gary Carter/50	25.00
14	Harmon Killebrew/50	40.00
15	Jack Morris/50	15.00
16	Jim Palmer/25	35.00
17	Lou Brock/25	35.00
20	Ozzie Smith/25	60.00
21	Phil Niekro/25	30.00
22	Rod Carew/25	40.00
23	Rollie Fingers/25	40.00
24	Steve Carlton/25	40.00
27	Bobby Doerr/25	25.00
28	Edgar Martinez/25	35.00
31	Matt Williams/25	35.00
35	Will Clark/25	40.00

Heritage Coll. Sign. Combos

NM/M

Production 5-100
#26-35 are DK Update exclusive.
Prime: No Pricing
Production One Set

1	Andre Dawson/Bat-Jsy/50	25.00

4	Dale Murphy/Bat-Jsy/25	40.00
6	Dennis Eckersley/Jsy-Jsy/50	25.00
7	Don Mattingly/Bat-Jkt/25	80.00
9	Dwight Gooden/Bat-Jsy/100	25.00
12	Gary Carter/Jkt-Jsy/50	25.00
14	Harmon Killebrew/Bat-Bat/25	50.00
15	Jack Morris/Jsy-Jsy/25	30.00
16	Jim Palmer/Jsy-Jsy/25	25.00
17	Lou Brock/Bat-Jsy/50	40.00
21	Phil Niekro/Bat-Jsy/50	25.00
22	Rod Carew/Bat-Jkt/25	25.00
24	Steve Carlton/Bat-Jsy/25	40.00
25	Tony Gwynn/Bat-Jsy/25	50.00
27	Bobby Doerr/Jsy/Pants/25	25.00
28	Edgar Martinez/Bat-Jsy/25	40.00
31	Matt Williams/Bat-Jsy/25	35.00
35	Will Clark/Bat-Jsy/25	40.00

HOF Heroes

NM/M

#51-100 are DK Update exclusive.
Common Player: 1.50
Inserted 1:5
Non Canvas: No Pricing
Production 20 Sets
Bronze: 1-2X
Production 100 Sets
Gold: 3-5X
Production 25 Sets
Platinum: No Pricing
Production One Set
Silver: 2-4X
Production 50 Sets
Frame Black: 3-5X
Production 25 Sets
Frame Blue: 1-2X
Production 100 Sets
Frame Green: 2-4X
Production 50 Sets
Frame Red: 1X
Inserted 1:18

1	Phil Niekro	1.50
2	Brooks Robinson	2.00
3	Jim Palmer	2.00
4	Carl Yastrzemski	3.00
5	Ted Williams	5.00
6	Duke Snider	3.00
7	Burleigh Grimes	1.50
8	Don Sutton	1.50
9	Nolan Ryan	6.00
10	Fergie Jenkins	1.50
11	Carlton Fisk	2.00
12	Tom Seaver	3.00
13	Bob Feller	2.00
14	Nolan Ryan	6.00
15	George Brett	5.00
16	Warren Spahn	3.00
17	Paul Molitor	3.00
18	Rod Carew	3.00
19	Harmon Killebrew	3.00
20	Monte Irvin	2.00
21	Gary Carter	1.50
22	Phil Rizzuto	2.00
23	Babe Ruth	2.00
24	Reggie Jackson	2.00
25	Mike Schmidt	5.00
26	Roberto Clemente	1.50
27	Juan Marichal	1.50
28	Willie McCovey	2.00
29	Stan Musial	4.00
30	Ozzie Smith	3.00
31	Dennis Eckersley	1.50
32	Phil Niekro	1.50
33	Jim Palmer	2.00
34	Carl Yastrzemski	3.00
35	Duke Snider	3.00
36	Don Sutton	1.50
37	Nolan Ryan	6.00
38	Carlton Fisk	2.00
39	Tom Seaver	2.00
40	Bob Feller	2.00
41	Nolan Ryan	6.00
42	George Brett	5.00
43	Harmon Killebrew	3.00
44	Gary Carter	1.50
45	Mike Schmidt	5.00
46	Stan Musial	4.00
47	Ozzie Smith	3.00
48	Dennis Eckersley	1.50

49	Fergie Jenkins	1.50
50	Brooks Robinson	2.00
51	Eddie Murray	2.00
52	Frank Robinson	2.00
53	Carlton Fisk	1.50
54	Ted Williams	5.00
55	Rod Carew	3.00
56	Ernie Banks	3.00
57	Luis Aparicio	1.50
58	Johnny Bench	3.00
59	Al Kaline	2.00
60	George Kell	1.50
61	Robin Yount	3.00
62	Nolan Ryan	6.00
63	Whitey Ford	1.50
64	Reggie Jackson	2.00
65	Babe Ruth	6.00
66	Rollie Fingers	1.50
67	Steve Carlton	1.50
68	Robin Roberts	1.50
69	Ralph Kiner	1.50
70	Willie Stargell	2.00
71	Roberto Clemente	5.00
72	Gaylord Perry	1.50
73	Bob Gibson	2.00
74	Lou Brock	1.50
75	Frankie Frisch	1.50
76	Eddie Murray	2.00
77	Frank Robinson	2.00
78	Carlton Fisk	1.50
79	Ted Williams	5.00
80	Rod Carew	2.00
81	Ernie Banks	3.00
82	Luis Aparicio	1.50
83	Johnny Bench	3.00
84	Al Kaline	2.00
85	Willie Mays	5.00
86	Robin Yount	5.00
87	Nolan Ryan	5.00
88	Whitey Ford	2.00
89	Reggie Jackson	2.00
90	Babe Ruth	6.00
91	Rollie Fingers	1.50
92	Steve Carlton	1.50
93	Wade Boggs	2.00
94	Wade Boggs	2.00
95	Willie Stargell	2.00
96	Roberto Clemente	5.00
97	Gaylord Perry	1.50
98	Bob Gibson	2.00
99	Lou Brock	1.50
100	Frankie Frisch	1.50

HOF Heroes Materials Bronze

NM/M

Production 1-100
No pricing 20 or less.
Gold: .75-1.5X
Production 1-25
Silver: .75-1.5X
Production 10-50
Framed Black: No Pricing
Production 1-25
Framed Blue: .75-1.5X
Production 1-25
Framed Red: .75-1.5X
Production 10-50

1	Phil Niekro/Bat-Jsy/100	8.00
2	Brooks Robinson/Bat-Jsy/100	12.00
3	Jim Palmer/Jsy-Jsy/100	8.00
4	Carl Yastrzemski/Bat-Pants/50	20.00
6	Duke Snider/Jsy-Jsy/50	15.00
7	Burleigh Grimes/Pants-Pants/25	75.00
8	Don Sutton/Jsy-Jsy/100	8.00
9	Nolan Ryan/Bat-Jkt/50	40.00
10	Fergie Jenkins/Pants-Pants/100	8.00
11	Carlton Fisk/Bat-Jkt/100	12.00
12	Tom Seaver/Jsy-Pants/50	15.00
13	Bob Feller/Pants-Pants/25	20.00
14	Nolan Ryan/Bat-Jsy/50	40.00
15	George Brett/Bat-Bat/25	40.00
16	Warren Spahn/Jsy-Jsy/25	30.00
17	Paul Molitor/Bat-Jsy/100	15.00
18	Rod Carew/Jsy-Jsy/100	15.00
19	Harmon Killebrew/Bat-Jsy/50	20.00
21	Gary Carter/Bat-Jsy/100	8.00
23	Babe Ruth/Bat-Bat/25	300.00
24	Reggie Jackson/Bat-Jkt/100	15.00
25	Mike Schmidt/Bat-Jkt/50	30.00
26	Roberto Clemente/Bat-Bat/50	60.00
27	Juan Marichal/Pants-Pants/25	12.00
28	Willie McCovey/Jsy-Jsy/100	10.00
29	Stan Musial/Bat-Jsy/30	30.00
30	Ozzie Smith/Bat-Pants/100	20.00
31	Dennis Eckersley/Jsy-Jsy/100	8.00
32	Phil Niekro/Bat-Jsy/100	8.00
33	Jim Palmer/Jsy-Pants/25	12.00
34	Carl Yastrzemski/Bat-Pants/25	30.00
35	Duke Snider/Jsy-Pants 20.00	
36	Don Sutton/Jsy/100	8.00
37	Nolan Ryan/Bat-Jkt/50	50.00
38	Carlton Fisk/Bat-Jkt/100	12.00
39	Tom Seaver/Bat-Jsy/20	20.00
40	Bob Feller/Pants/25	20.00
41	Nolan Ryan/Bat-Jkt/25	50.00
42	George Brett/Bat-Bat/25	40.00
43	Harmon Killebrew/Bat-Jsy/25	25.00
44	Gary Carter/Bat-Jsy/100	8.00
45	Mike Schmidt/Jsy-Jsy/40	40.00
46	Stan Musial/Bat-Bat/30	30.00
47	Ozzie Smith/Jsy-Jsy/100	20.00
48	Dennis Eckersley/Jsy-Jsy/100	8.00
49	Fergie Jenkins/Pants-Pants/25	12.00
50	Brooks Robinson/Jsy/25	20.00
51	Eddie Murray/Bat/50	12.00
52	Frank Robinson/Bat/50	12.00
53	Carlton Fisk/Bat/Bat/50	10.00
54	Rod Carew/Bat/Jsy/50	12.00
55	Ernie Banks/Bat/Jsy/50	15.00
56		
57	Luis Aparicio/Bat/Bat/50	8.00
58	Johnny Bench/Bat/Jsy/50	15.00
59	Al Kaline/Bat/Jsy/50	20.00
61	Robin Yount/Bat/Jsy/50	15.00
62	Nolan Ryan/Bat/Jsy/25	50.00
63	Whitey Ford/Bat/Jsy/25	25.00
64	Reggie Jackson/Jsy/Jsy/50	15.00
66	Rollie Fingers/Bat/Bat/50	8.00
70	Willie Stargell/Bat/Jsy/50	15.00
72	Gaylord Perry/Jsy/Jsy/50	8.00
73	Bob Gibson/Jsy/Jsy/50	15.00
74	Lou Brock/Bat/Jsy/50	12.00
76	Eddie Murray/Bat/Bat/50	12.00
77	Frank Robinson/Bat/Bat/50	12.00
78	Carlton Fisk/Bat/Bat/50	10.00
80	Rod Carew/Bat/Jkt/50	12.00
81	Ernie Banks/Bat/Jsy/50	15.00
82	Luis Aparicio/Bat/Bat/50	8.00
83	Johnny Bench/Bat/Jsy/50	15.00
86	Robin Yount/Bat/Jsy/50	15.00
87	Nolan Ryan/Bat/Jsy/25	40.00
88	Whitey Ford/Bat/Jsy/25	25.00
89	Reggie Jackson/Jsy/Jsy/50	15.00
91	Rollie Fingers/Jsy/Jsy/50	8.00
92	Steve Carlton/Bat/Jsy/50	10.00
95	Willie Stargell/Jsy/Jsy/50	15.00
97	Gaylord Perry/Jsy/Jsy/50	8.00
99	Lou Brock/Jsy/Jsy/50	10.00

HOF Heroes Signatures Bronze

NM/M

Production 1-25
No pricing 20 or less.
Gold: No Pricing
Production 1-10
Platinum: No Pricing
Production One Set
Silver: 1X
Production 1-25
Framed Blue: No Pricing
Production One Set
Framed Black: No Pricing
Production 1-10
Framed Green: No Pricing
Production 1-25
Framed Red: No Pricing
Production 1-25
Cards #52-99 are seeded in DK Update.

13	Bob Feller/25	35.00
40	Bob Feller/25	35.00
52	Frank Robinson/25	35.00
57	Luis Aparicio/25	15.00
59	Al Kaline/25	40.00
60	George Kell/25	20.00
66	Rollie Fingers/25	15.00
67	Steve Carlton/25	20.00
68	Robin Roberts/25	20.00
69	Ralph Kiner/25	35.00
72	Gaylord Perry/15	15.00
74	Lou Brock/25	35.00
82	Luis Aparicio/25	15.00
84	Al Kaline/25	40.00
91	Rollie Fingers/25	15.00
92	Steve Carlton/25	20.00
93	Wade Boggs Yanks/25	30.00
94	Wade Boggs Sox/25	30.00
97	Gaylord Perry/25	15.00
99	Lou Brock/25	35.00

Signature Materials Bronze

NM/M

Production 5-50
No pricing 20 or less.

33	Jim Palmer/Jsy-Pants/25	12.00
34	Carl Yastrzemski/Bat-Pants/25	30.00
35	Duke Snider/Jsy-Pants	20.00
36	Don Sutton/Jsy/100	8.00
37	Nolan Ryan/Bat-Jkt/50	50.00
38	Carlton Fisk/Bat-Jkt/100	12.00
39	Tom Seaver/Bat-Jsy/20	20.00
40	Bob Feller/Pants/25	20.00
41	Nolan Ryan/Bat-Jkt/25	50.00
42	George Brett/Bat-Bat/25/40	40.00
43	Harmon Killebrew/Jsy-Jsy/25	25.00
44	Gary Carter/Bat-Jsy/100	8.00
45	Mike Schmidt/Jsy-Jsy/40	40.00
46	Stan Musial/Bat-Bat/30	30.00
47	Ozzie Smith/Jsy-Jsy/100	20.00
48	Dennis Eckersley/Jsy-Jsy/100	8.00
49	Fergie Jenkins/Pants-Pants/25	12.00
50	Brooks Robinson/Jsy/25	20.00
51	Eddie Murray/Bat/50	12.00
52	Frank Robinson/Bat/50	12.00

Gold:

Gold:		.75-1.5X
Production 5-25		
Platinum:		No Pricing
Production One Set		
Silver:		.75-1X
Production 5-50		
Framed Black:		No Pricing
Production 5-10		
Framed Blue:		.75-1.5X
Production 5-25		
Framed Green:		No Pricing
Production 1-10		
Framed Red:		.75-1.5X
Production 1-25		

#53-99 are found in DK Update.

2	Brooks Robinson/Bat-Jsy/25	50.00
3	Jim Palmer/Jsy-Pants/25	40.00
6	Duke Snider/Jsy-Jsy/25	40.00
8	Don Sutton/Jsy-Jsy/25	30.00
10	Fergie Jenkins/Pants-Pants/25	30.00
13	Bob Feller/Pants-Pants/50	35.00
18	Rod Carew/Bat-Jsy/50	40.00
19	Harmon Killebrew/Bat-Jsy/25	50.00
21	Gary Carter/Bat-Jsy/25	25.00
27	Juan Marichal/Pants-Pants/25	40.00
28	Willie McCovey/Jsy-Pants/25	50.00
29	Stan Musial/Bat-Bat/25	85.00
30	Ozzie Smith/Bat-Pants/25	75.00
31	Dennis Eckersley/Jsy-Jsy/25	35.00
32	Phil Niekro/Bat-Jsy/25	30.00
33	Jim Palmer/Jsy-Jsy/25	40.00
35	Duke Snider/Jsy-Pants/25	40.00
36	Don Sutton/Jsy-Jsy/25	30.00
40	Bob Feller/Pants-Pants/50	35.00
43	Harmon Killebrew/Bat-Jsy/25	40.00
44	Gary Carter/Bat-Jsy/25	25.00
47	Ozzie Smith/Bat-Bat/25	75.00
48	Dennis Eckersley/Jsy-Jsy/25	25.00
49	Fergie Jenkins/Pants-Pants/25	30.00
50	Brooks Robinson/Bat-Jsy/25	50.00
61	Robin Yount/Bat-Jsy/25	50.00
66	Rollie Fingers/Jsy-Jsy/50	15.00
72	Gaylord Perry/Jsy-Jsy/50	15.00
74	Lou Brock/Jsy-Jsy/50	30.00
80	Rod Carew/Bat-Jsy/50	25.00
99	Lou Brock/Bat-Jsy/50	40.00

Materials Bronze

NM/M

Production 10-200
No pricing 20 or less.
Gold: .75-1.5X
Production 25-50
Silver: .75-1.5X
Production 25-100
Platinum: No Pricing
Production One Set
Framed Black: No Pricing
Production 10 Sets
Framed Blue: .75-1.5X
Production 50 Sets
Framed Green: .75-1.5X
Production 25 Sets
Framed Red: .75-1.5X
Production 25-100
#302-450 are found in DK Update.

1	Garret Anderson/Bat-Jsy/200	5.0
2	Vladimir Guerrero/Bat-Jsy/200	10.0
4	Troy Glaus/Bat-Jsy/200	5.0
5	Tim Salmon/Bat-Jsy/200	5.0
7	Chone Figgins/Bat-Jsy/200	5.0
10	Tony Percival/Jsy-Jsy/200	5.0
12	Brandon Webb/Bat-Pants/200	5.0
13	Richie Sexson/Bat-Bat/200	5.0
17	Luis Gonzalez/Jsy-Jsy/200	5.0
18	Rafael Furcal/Bat-Jsy/200	5.0
19	Andruw Jones/Bat-Jsy/200	5.0
21	John Smoltz/Jsy-Jsy/200	8.0
23	J.D. Drew/Bat-Bat/200	5.0
25	Chipper Jones/Bat-Jsy/200	8.0
27	Rafael Palmeiro/Bat-Jsy/200	8.0
28	Miguel Tejada/Bat-Jsy/200	10.0
29	Javy Lopez/Bat-Jsy/25	5.0
30	Luis Matos/Jsy-Jsy/100	5.0
31	Larry Bigbie/Jsy-Jsy/200	5.0

32	Rodrigo Lopez/ Jsy-Jsy/200	5.00
34	Melvin Mora/Bat-Jsy/200	5.00
36	Manny Ramirez/ Bat-Jsy/200	10.00
38	Trot Nixon/Bat-Jsy/200	10.00
39	Curt Schilling/ Bat-Jsy/200	10.00
41	Pedro Martinez/ Bat-Jsy/200	10.00
42	Johnny Damon/ Bat-Bat/200	15.00
43	Kevin Youkilis/ Bat-Bat/200	5.00
46	David Ortiz/Bat-Jsy/200	10.00
47	Kerry Wood/ Jsy-Pants/200	10.00
48	Mark Prior/Bat-Jsy/200	8.00
49	Aramis Ramirez/ Bat-Jsy/200	8.00
50	Greg Maddux/ Bat-Jsy/100	15.00
51	Carlos Zambrano/ Jsy-Jsy/200	8.00
52	Derrek Lee/Bat-Bat/200	8.00
54	Moises Alou/Bat-Bat/200	8.00
56	Sammy Sosa/ Bat-Bat/200	10.00
57	Nomar Garciaparra/ Bat-Bat/200	10.00
60	Magglio Ordonez/ Bat-Bat/200	5.00
61	Carlos Lee/Bat-Jsy/200	5.00
62	Joe Crede/Bat-Bat/200	5.00
65	Frank Thomas/ Bat-Jsy/200	8.00
69	Adam Dunn/Bat-Bat/200	8.00
70	Austin Kearns/ Bat-Bat/200	5.00
74	Sean Casey/ Jsy-Pants/200	5.00
76	C.C. Sabathia/ Jsy-Jsy/200	5.00
77	Jody Gerut/Bat-Jsy/200	5.00
78	Omar Vizquel/ Bat-Jsy/200	5.00
79	Victor Martinez/ Bat-Bat/200	5.00
80	Matt Lawton/Bat-Bat/200	5.00
84	Todd Helton/Bat-Jsy/200	8.00
85	Preston Wilson/ Bat-Bat/200	5.00
90	Ivan Rodriguez/ Bat-Jsy/200	8.00
92	Brandon Inge/ Bat-Jsy/200	5.00
94	Dontrelle Willis/ Jsy-Jsy/200	5.00
95	Miguel Cabrera/ Bat-Jsy/200	10.00
96	Josh Beckett/Bat-Bat/100	5.00
97	Mike Lowell/Bat-Jsy/200	5.00
98	Luis Castillo/Bat-Bat/200	5.00
99	Juan Pierre/Bat-Bat/200	5.00
100	Paul LoDuca/Bat-Bat/200	5.00
102	Craig Biggio/ Bat-Pants/200	5.00
103	Lance Berkman/ Bat-Jsy/200	5.00
104	Roy Oswalt/Jsy-Jsy/200	5.00
105	Roger Clemens/ Bat-Jsy/200	15.00
106	Jeff Kent/Bat-Jsy/100	5.00
108	Jeff Bagwell/Bat-Jsy/100	8.00
109	Carlos Beltran/ Bat-Jsy/200	8.00
110	Angel Berroa/Bat-Bat/200	5.00
111	Mike Sweeney/ Bat-Jsy/200	5.00
112	Jeremy Affeldt/ Pants-Pants/200	5.00
114	Juan Gonzalez/ Bat-Jsy/200	8.00
116	Shawn Green/ Bat-Jsy/200	5.00
118	Adrian Beltre/ Bat-Jsy/200	8.00
119	Hideo Nomo/Bat-Jsy/200	8.00
123	Scott Podsednik/ Jsy-Jsy/200	5.00
124	Ben Sheets/ Bat-Pants/200	8.00
125	Lyle Overbay/ Jsy-Jsy/200	5.00
126	Junior Spivey/ Bat-Bat/200	5.00
127	Bill Hall/Bat-Jsy/200	5.00
129	Jacque Jones/ Bat-Jsy/200	5.00
130	Torii Hunter/Bat-Jsy/200	5.00
131	Johan Santana/ Jsy-Jsy/200	10.00
132	Lew Ford/Bat-Bat/200	5.00
136	Jose Vidro/Bat-Jsy/200	5.00
138	Brad Wilkerson/ Bat-Bat/100	5.00
139	Nick Johnson/ Bat-Bat/100	5.00
140	Livan Hernandez/ Jsy-Jsy/200	5.00
141	Tom Glavine/Bat-Bat/200	8.00
143	Jose Reyes/Bat-Jsy/200	6.00
144	Al Leiter/Jsy-Jsy/200	5.00
145	Mike Piazza/ Jsy-Jsy/100	15.00
146	Kazuo Matsui/ Bat-Jsy/200	8.00

147	Richard Hidalgo/ Bat-Bat/200	5.00
149	Mariano Rivera/ Jsy-Jsy/100	8.00
150	Mike Mussina/ Bat-Jsy/200	8.00
153	Jorge Posada/ Bat-Jsy/200	8.00
154	Jason Giambi/ Bat-Jsy/200	5.00
155	Gary Sheffield/ Bat-Jsy/200	8.00
158	Kevin Brown/Bat-Bat/100	5.00
160	Esteban Loaiza/ Bat-Bat/100	5.00
161	Hideki Matsui/ Jsy-Pants/200	20.00
162	Eric Chavez/Bat-Jsy/200	5.00
163	Mark Mulder/Bat-Bat/25	10.00
164	Barry Zito/Jsy-Jsy/200	8.00
166	Tim Hudson/Bat-Jsy/200	8.00
166	Jermaine Dye/ Bat-Jsy/200	5.00
168	Bobby Crosby/ Jsy-Jsy/200	8.00
171	Jim Thome/Bat-Jsy/200	8.00
172	Bobby Abreu/ Jsy-Jsy/200	8.00
173	Kevin Millwood/	
178	Craig Wilson/Bat-Jsy/200	5.00
181	Jack Wilson/Bat-Jsy/200	5.00
181	Jose Castillo/Bat-Jsy/200	5.00
185	Jason Bay/Bat-Jsy/200	5.00
185	Sean Burroughs/ Bat-Jsy/200	5.00
187	Brian Giles/Bat-Bat/100	5.00
193	Trevor Hoffman/ Jsy-Jsy/200	5.00
199	J.T. Snow/Jsy-Jsy/25	5.00
200	A.J. Pierzynski/ Jsy-Jsy/100	5.00
201	Edgar Martinez/ Bat-Bat/200	5.00
204	Bret Boone/Jsy-Jsy/200	5.00
208	Jamie Moyer/Jsy-Jsy/50	5.00
209	Jim Edmonds/ Bat-Jsy/200	8.00
210	Scott Rolen/ Bat-Jsy/200	10.00
211	Edgar Renteria/ Bat-Jsy/200	5.00
212	Dan Haren/Bat-Jsy/100	5.00
213	Matt Morris/Jsy-Jsy/100	5.00
214	Albert Pujols/ Jsy-Jsy/200	20.00
215	Larry Walker/Bat-Bat/200	8.00
220	Aubrey Huff/Bat-Bat/100	5.00
221	Carl Crawford/ Jsy-Jsy/200	5.00
222	Rocco Baldelli/ Bat-Jsy/200	5.00
223	Fred McGriff/Bat-Jsy/200	5.00
224	Dewon Brazelton/ Jsy-Jsy/200	5.00
225	B.J. Upton/Bat-Bat/200	8.00
226	Joey Gathright/ Bat-Jsy/200	5.00
228	Hank Blalock/ Bat-Jsy/100	8.00
229	Mark Teixeira/ Bat-Jsy/200	8.00
230	Michael Young/ Bat-Jsy/200	8.00
232	Laynce Nix/Bat-Jsy/200	5.00
233	Alfonso Soriano/ Bat-Jsy/200	8.00
234	Rafael Palmeiro/ Bat-Jsy/200	5.00
235	Kevin Mench/ Bat-Jsy/200	5.00
236	David Dellucci/ Jsy-Jsy/200	8.00
237	Francisco Cordero/ Jsy-Jsy/200	5.00
239	Roy Halladay/ Jsy-Jsy/200	8.00
240	Carlos Delgado/ Bat-Jsy/200	8.00
242	Vernon Wells/ Bat-Jsy/200	8.00
267	Larry Walker/ Bat-Jsy/200	8.00
268	Ivan Rodriguez/ Bat-Jsy/200	8.00
269	Brad Penny/Bat-Jsy/200	5.00
270	Carlos Beltran/ Bat-Jsy/200	8.00
271	Paul LoDuca/Bat-Jsy/200	5.00
273	Nomar Garciaparra/ Bat-Bat/100	10.00
274	Esteban Loaiza/ Bat-Bat/100	5.00
275	Richard Hidalgo/ Jkt-Pants/200	5.00
276	John Olerud/Bat-Jsy/200	5.00
277	Greg Maddux/ Jsy-Jsy/200	12.00
278	Roger Clemens/ Bat-Jsy/200	15.00
279	Alfonso Soriano/ Bat-Jsy/200	8.00
280	Dale Murphy/ Bat-Jsy/200	8.00
281	Cal Ripken Jr./ Bat-Jsy/200	30.00
282	Dwight Evans/ Bat-Jsy/200	5.00

283	Ron Santo/Bat-Bat/200	10.00
284	Andre Dawson/ Bat-Jsy/100	8.00
285	Harold Baines/ Bat-Jsy/200	8.00
286	Jack Morris/Jsy-Jsy/100	8.00
287	Kirk Gibson/Bat-Jsy/200	8.00
288	Bo Jackson/Bat-Jsy/200	10.00
289	Orel Hershiser/ Jsy-Jsy/50	8.00
291	Tony Oliva/Bat-Jsy/200	10.00
292	Darryl Strawberry/ Bat-Jsy/200	8.00
293	Roger Maris/ Jsy-Jsy/25	50.00
294	Don Mattingly/ Bat-Jsy/100	25.00
295	Rickey Henderson/ Jsy-Jsy/200	10.00
297	Dave Parker/Bat-Jsy/200	8.00
298	Steve Garvey/ Bat-Jsy/200	8.00
299	Matt Williams/ Bat-Jsy/200	8.00
300	Keith Hernandez/ Bat-Jsy/200	8.00
302	Vladimir Guerrero/ Bat-Jsy/200	10.00
303	Garret Anderson/ Bat-Bat/200	5.00
307	Luis Gonzalez/ Jsy-Jsy/200	5.00
310	Shawn Green/ Bat-Bat/200	5.00
311	Troy Glaus/Bat-Bat/200	5.00
314	Chipper Jones/ Jsy-Jsy/100	10.00
315	Johnny Estrada/ Bat-Jsy/200	5.00
316	Andruw Jones/ Bat-Jsy/200	8.00
319	Jay Gibbons/Bat-Jsy/200	5.00
320	Melvin Mora/Jsy-Jsy/200	5.00
321	Rafael Palmeiro/ Bat-Jsy/200	8.00
323	David Ortiz/Bat-Jsy/200	8.00
324	Manny Ramirez/ Jsy-Jsy/200	10.00
327	Curt Schilling/ Jsy-Jsy/200	10.00
328	Sammy Sosa/ Bat-Bat/200	10.00
329	Mark Prior/Bat-Jsy/200	8.00
330	Greg Maddux/ Jsy-Jsy/25	15.00
332	Frank Thomas/ Bat-Pants/200	10.00
333	Mark Buehrle/ Bat-Bat/200	5.00
336	Sean Casey/Bat-Jsy/200	5.00
337	Adam Dunn/Bat-Bat/200	8.00
339	Travis Hafner/ Jsy-Jsy/200	5.00
340	Victor Martinez/ Bat-Jsy/200	5.00
341	Cliff Lee/Jsy-Jsy/200	5.00
342	Todd Helton/Bat-Jsy/25	8.00
343	Preston Wilson/ Jsy-Jsy/200	5.00
344	Ivan Rodriguez/ Bat-Jsy/200	8.00
347	Miguel Cabrera/ Bat-Jsy/200	10.00
348	Jeff Bagwell/Bat-Jsy/200	8.00
349	Andy Pettitte/Bat-Jsy/200	8.00
350	Roger Clemens/ Bat-Jsy/200	15.00
351	Ken Harvey/Jsy-Jsy/200	5.00
353	Hideo Nomo/Bat-Jsy/200	8.00
354	Kazuhisa Ishii/ Jsy-Jsy/200	5.00
355	Edwin Jackson/ Jsy-Jsy/200	5.00
356	J.D. Drew/Bat-Bat/200	5.00
357	Jeff Kent/Bat-Bat/25	5.00
358	Geoff Jenkins/ Jsy-Pants/200	5.00
359	Carlos Lee/Bat-Bat/200	5.00
360	Shannon Stewart/ Jsy-Jsy/200	5.00
362	Johan Santana/ Jsy-Jsy/100	10.00
363	Mike Piazza/ Jsy-Jsy/200	12.00
364	Kazuo Matsui/ Jsy-Jsy/200	8.00
366	Pedro Martinez/ Bat-Jsy/100	10.00
368	Hideki Matsui/ Jsy-Jsy/100	20.00
369	Bernie Williams/ Bat-Jsy/200	8.00
370	Gary Sheffield/ Bat-Jsy/200	8.00
371	Randy Johnson/ Bat-Bat/25	10.00
378	Mark Mulder/Bat-Bat/200	8.00
381	Eric Chavez/Jsy-Jsy/100	5.00
382	Marlon Byrd/Bat-Jsy/200	5.00
383	Pat Burrell/Jsy-Jsy/200	5.00
388	Jim Thome/Bat-Jsy/200	8.00
388	Moises Alou/Bat-Jsy/200	5.00
394	Adrian Beltre/Bat-Jsy/200	5.00
394	Richie Sexson/ Bat-Bat/200	5.00
397	Albert Pujols/ Bat-Jsy/200	20.00

398	Scott Rolen/ Bat-Jsy/200	10.00
401	Delmon Young/ Bat-Bat/200	5.00
402	Aubrey Huff/Bat-Bat/50	5.00
403	Alfonso Soriano/ Bat-Jsy/200	8.00
404	Hank Blalock/ Bat-Jsy/200	5.00
405	Richard Hidalgo/ Bat-Jsy/200	5.00
406	Vernon Wells/ Jsy-Jsy/200	5.00
407	Orlando Hudson/ Bat-Jsy/200	5.00
412	Jose Vidro/Bat-Jsy/5	5.00
415	Miguel Tejada/ Bat-Jsy/200	8.00
416	Gary Sheffield/ Bat-Bat/200	8.00
417	Curt Schilling/ Jsy-Jsy/200	10.00
418	Rafael Palmeiro/ Bat-Pants/50	8.00
419	Scott Rolen/ Bat-Jsy/200	10.00
420	Aramis Ramirez/ Bat-Jsy/200	8.00
421	Vladimir Guerrero/ Bat-Bat/200	10.00
422	Steve Finley/Jsy-Jsy/200	5.00
423	Roger Clemens/ Bat-Jsy/25	15.00
424	Mike Piazza/ Jsy-Jsy/100	12.00
425	Ivan Rodriguez/ Bat-Bat/200	8.00
426	David Justice/ Bat-Jsy/200	5.00
427	Mark Grace/Bat-Jsy/25	8.00
428	Alan Trammell/ Bat-Jsy/200	5.00
430	Dwight Gooden/ Bat-Jsy/200	5.00
431	Deion Sanders/ Bat-Jsy/200	8.00
432	Joe Torre/Bat-Bat/100	5.00
433	Jose Canseco/ Bat-Jsy/200	8.00
434	Tony Gwynn/ Bat-Pants/200	10.00
435	Will Clark/Bat-Jsy/100	8.00
437	Nolan Ryan/Bat-Jsy/50	15.00
438	Billy Martin/ Bat-Jsy/200	10.00
439	Carlos Delgado/ Bat-Bat/100	5.00
440	Magglio Ordonez/ Bat-Bat/200	5.00
441	Sammy Sosa/ Bat-Bat/25	10.00
449	Ryne Sandberg/ Bat-Jsy/25	10.00

Recollection Autographs Gold

No Pricing	
Production One Set	
Silver:	No Pricing
Production One Set	
Platinum:	No Pricing
Production One Set	

Signature Bronze

	NM/M
Production 1-100	
No pricing 20 or less.	
Black:	No Pricing
Production One Set	
Gold:	.75-1.5X
Production 1-50	
Silver:	.75-1.5X
Production 1-100	
Platinum:	No Pricing
Production One Set	
Framed Blue:	.75-1.5X
Production 1-50	
Framed Green:	.75-1.5X
Production 1-25	
Framed Red:	.75-1.5X
Production 1-100	
#303-450 found in DK Update.	

3	Jose Guillen/100	15.00
5	Tim Salmon/100	20.00
6	Casey Kotchman/100	15.00
7	Chone Figgins/100	15.00
8	Robb Quinlan/100	8.00
9	Francisco Rodriguez/50	40.00
10	Troy Percival/100	15.00
14	Shea Hillenbrand/100	10.00
15	Chad Tracy/100	10.00
16	Alex Cintron/100	8.00
22	Adam LaRoche/100	10.00
23	Russ Ortiz/50	12.00
29	Nick Green/100	10.00
30	Luis Matos/100	10.00
31	Larry Bigbie/100	10.00
32	Rodrigo Lopez/100	15.00
33	Brian Roberts/100	25.00
37	Melvin Mora/100	15.00
40	Keith Foulke/50	40.00
43	Kevin Youkilis/100	15.00
44	Orlando Cabrera/50	20.00
45	Abe Alvarez/100	8.00
51	Carlos Zambrano/50	30.00
58	Todd Walker/50	15.00
59	Angel Guzman/100	15.00
61	Carlos Lee/100	15.00
73	Ryan Wagner/100	10.00

75	Danny Graves/100	12.00
76	C.C. Sabathia/50	20.00
77	Jody Gerut/100	8.00
79	Victor Martinez/100	20.00
82	Kazuhito Tadano/100	8.00
83	Travis Hafner/100	15.00
89	Jeremy Bonderman/100	15.00
92	Brandon Inge/100	10.00
101	Guillermo Mota/50	10.00
107	Morgan Ensberg/100	10.00
112	Jeremy Affeldt/100	10.00
117	Milton Bradley/100	10.00
122	Brad Penny/100	15.00
123	Scott Podsednik/50	15.00
125	Lyle Overbay/100	12.00
127	Bill Hall/100	8.00
132	Lew Ford/100	15.00
135	Jason Kubel/100	15.00
137	Chad Cordero/100	15.00
140	Livan Hernandez/25	15.00
156	Bubba Crosby/100	10.00
159	Tom Gordon/25	20.00
160	Esteban Loaiza/100	15.00
166	Jermaine Dye/100	15.00
167	Octavio Dotel/100	10.00
168	Bobby Crosby/100	20.00
174	Mike Lieberthal/100	12.00
177	Randy Wolf/100	10.00
178	Craig Wilson/100	8.00
180	Jack Wilson/100	12.00
181	Jose Castillo/100	10.00
184	Jason Bay/100	15.00
186	Jay Payton/50	10.00
189	Jake Peavy/30	30.00
194	Freddy Guzman/100	8.00
197	Todd Linden/100	10.00
198	Merkin Valdez/100	10.00
203	Raul Ibanez/100	10.00
206	Miguel Olivo/100	8.00
207	Bucky Jacobsen/100	12.00
208	Jamie Moyer/50	15.00
212	Dan Haren/100	12.00
219	Jeff Suppan/100	10.00
220	Aubrey Huff/50	15.00
221	Carl Crawford/25	20.00
224	Dewon Brazelton/100	8.00
226	Joey Gathright/100	10.00
227	Scott Kazmir/25	25.00
230	Michael Young/50	15.00
231	Adrian Gonzalez/100	10.00
232	Laynce Nix/100	15.00
236	David Dellucci/100	20.00
237	Francisco Cordero/100	15.00
241	Alexis Rios/100	15.00
248	Dioner Navarro/100	10.00
253	Yhency Brazoban/100	10.00
257	Scott Proctor/100	8.00
260	Matt Peterson/100	8.00
269	Brad Penny/50	10.00
272	Orlando Cabrera/50	15.00
274	Esteban Loaiza/100	15.00
284	Andre Dawson/50	20.00
285	Harold Baines/100	15.00
286	Jack Morris/100	15.00
290	Maury Wills/100	15.00
292	Darryl Strawberry/100	15.00
297	Dave Parker/100	15.00
299	Matt Williams/25	25.00
303	Garret Anderson/100	15.00
304	Dallas McPherson/100	15.00
305	Orlando Cabrera/25	15.00
306	Steve Finley/50	10.00
313	Russ Ortiz/50	10.00
315	Johnny Estrada/50	10.00
318	Danny Kolb/100	8.00
319	Jay Gibbons/50	10.00
320	Melvin Mora/50	10.00
325	Edgar Renteria/50	10.00
333	Mark Buehrle/50	20.00
336	Sean Casey/25	15.00
339	Travis Hafner/50	15.00
340	Victor Martinez/50	10.00
341	Cliff Lee/100	15.00
343	Preston Wilson/50	15.00
351	Ken Harvey/100	8.00
355	Edwin Jackson/50	10.00
359	Carlos Lee/100	10.00
360	Shannon Stewart/25	15.00
361	Joe Nathan/100	15.00
376	Eric Byrnes/100	15.00
377	Rich Harden/100	15.00
378	Mark Mulder/25	20.00
380	Eric Chavez/50	15.00
382	Marlon Byrd/100	8.00
384	Brett Myers/100	10.00
386	Jason Bay/100	15.00
387	Jake Peavy/25	25.00
402	Aubrey Huff/50	15.00
407	Orlando Hudson/25	15.00
410	Jose Guillen/25	15.00
429	Bert Blyleven/50	15.00
430	Dwight Gooden/50	15.00
436	Marty Marion/50	15.00

Signature Materials Bronze

	NM/M
Production 1-200	
No pricing 20 or less.	
Platinum:	No Pricing
Production One Set	
Framed Black:	No Pricing
Production 1-10	
Framed Blue:	No Pricing
Production 1-50	
Framed Green:	1-2X
Production 1-25	
Framed Red:	.75-1.5X
Production 1-100	

1	Garret Anderson/ Bat-Jsy/50	25.00
7	Chone Figgins/ Bat-Jsy/200	15.00
18	Rafael Furcal/ Bat-Jsy/50	20.00
19	Andruw Jones/ Bat-Jsy/25	35.00
31	Larry Bigbie/ Jsy-Jsy/200	15.00
32	Rodrigo Lopez/ Jsy-Jsy/200	15.00
38	Trot Nixon/Bat-Jsy/100	30.00
46	David Ortiz/Bat-Jsy/100	40.00
48	Mark Prior/Bat-Jsy/25	40.00
49	Aramis Ramirez/ Bat-Jsy/25	25.00
51	Carlos Zambrano/ Bat-Jsy/25	25.00
52	Derrek Lee/Bat-Bat/100	20.00
61	Carlos Lee/Bat-Bat/100	10.00
76	C.C. Sabathia/ Jsy-Jsy/200	20.00
78	Omar Vizquel/ Jsy-Jsy/25	40.00
95	Miguel Cabrera/ Bat-Jsy/25	50.00
109	Carlos Beltran/ Bat-Jsy/50	40.00
112	Jeremy Affeldt/ Pants-Pants/100	10.00
127	Bill Hall/Bat-Bat/100	10.00
129	Jacque Jones/ Bat-Jsy/50	20.00
131	Johan Santana/ Jsy-Jsy/50	40.00
132	Lew Ford/Bat-Jsy/200	15.00
139	Nick Johnson/ Bat-Bat/50	12.00
153	Jorge Posada/ Bat-Jsy/25	40.00
162	Eric Chavez/Bat-Jsy/25	25.00
178	Craig Wilson/ Bat-Jsy/15	15.00
185	Sean Burroughs/ Bat-Jsy/10	10.00
201	Edgar Martinez/ Bat-Bat/25	40.00
211	Edgar Renteria/ Bat-Jsy/30	30.00
221	Carl Crawford/ Jsy-Jsy/200	15.00
229	Mark Teixeira/ Bat-Jsy/40	40.00
230	Michael Young/ Bat-Jsy/20	20.00
232	Laynce Nix/Bat-Jsy/200	12.00
233	Alfonso Soriano/ Bat-Jsy/50	50.00
239	Roy Halladay/ Jsy-Jsy/25	25.00
269	Brad Penny/Bat-Jsy/100	10.00
280	Dale Murphy/ Bat-Jsy/50	35.00
282	Dwight Evans/ Bat-Jsy/25	25.00
283	Ron Santo/Bat-Bat/100	35.00
284	Andre Dawson/ Bat-Jsy/100	25.00
286	Jack Morris/ Jsy-Jsy/200	20.00
287	Kirk Gibson/Bat-Jsy/25	40.00
289	Orel Hershiser/ Jsy-Jsy/25	35.00
291	Tony Oliva/Bat-Jsy/200	25.00
294	Don Mattingly/ Jsy-Jsy/200	90.00
297	Dave Parker/ Bat-Jsy/25	25.00
298	Steve Garvey/ Bat-Jsy/50	25.00
300	Keith Hernandez/ Jsy-Jsy/200	20.00
303	Garret Anderson/ Bat-Jsy/200	20.00
315	Johnny Estrada/ Jsy-Jsy/200	12.00
319	Jay Gibbons/Bat-Jsy/50	12.00
320	Melvin Mora/Bat-Jsy/25	15.00
323	David Ortiz/Jsy-Jsy/25	50.00
333	Mark Buehrle/ Jsy-Jsy/25	25.00
339	Travis Hafner/ Jsy-Jsy/25	25.00
340	Victor Martinez/ Jsy-Jsy/25	20.00
341	Cliff Lee/Jsy-Jsy/25	20.00
343	Preston Wilson/ Jsy-Jsy/200	20.00
351	Ken Harvey/Jsy-Jsy/25	12.00
382	Marlon Byrd/Bat-Jsy/50	12.00
401	Delmon Young/ Bat-Jsy/25	25.00
407	Orlando Hudson/ Jsy-Jsy/25	25.00
419	Scott Rolen/Bat-Jsy/25	30.00
428	Alan Trammell/ Bat-Jsy/25	25.00
430	Dwight Gooden/ Bat-Jsy/25	25.00
434	Tony Gwynn/Bat-Jsy/25	40.00

Signature Materials Silver

	NM/M
Production 1-100	
7	Chone Figgins/ Bat-Jsy/100	15.00

#	Card	Price
18	Rafael Furcal/Bat-Jsy/25	30.00
31	Larry Bigbie/Jsy/100	15.00
32	Rodrigo Lopez/Jsy-Jsy/100	15.00
46	David Ortiz/Bat-Jsy/50	60.00
49	Aramis Ramirez/Bat-Jsy/50	35.00
51	Carlos Zambrano/Jsy/100	30.00
61	Carlos Lee/Bat-Jsy/100	10.00
76	C.C. Sabathia/Jsy/100	20.00
104	Roy Oswalt/Jsy-Jsy/50	30.00
112	Jeremy Affeldt/Pants-Pants/100	10.00
127	Bill Hall/Bat-Bat/100	10.00
129	Jacque Jones/Bat-Jsy/100	20.00
132	Lew Ford/Bat/Jsy/100	15.00
178	Craig Wilson/Bat-Jsy/100	15.00
221	Carl Crawford/Jsy-Jsy/100	15.00
230	Michael Young/Bat-Jsy/50	25.00
232	Laynce Nix/Bat-Jsy/100	15.00
269	Brad Penny/Bat-Jsy/100	15.00
280	Dale Murphy/Jsy-Jsy	50.00
282	Dwight Evans/Bat-Jsy	30.00
283	Ron Santo/Bat-Bat/50	45.00
284	Andre Dawson/Bat-Jsy/50	30.00
285	Harold Baines/Bat-Jsy	25.00
286	Jack Morris/Jsy-Jsy/50	25.00
291	Tony Oliva/Bat-Jsy/50	30.00
297	Dave Parker/Bat-Jsy/50	30.00
298	Steve Garvey/Bat-Jsy	30.00
299	Matt Williams/Jsy-Jsy	35.00
300	Keith Hernandez/Bat-Jsy	25.00

Signature Materials Gold
NM/M
Production 1-50

#	Card	Price
7	Chone Figgins/Bat-Jsy/25	20.00
18	Rafael Furcal/Bat-Jsy/25	30.00
31	Larry Bigbie/Jsy-Jsy/25	20.00
32	Rodrigo Lopez/Jsy-Jsy	
46	David Ortiz/Bat-Jsy/50	60.00
49	Aramis Ramirez/Bat-Jsy/50	35.00
51	Carlos Zambrano/Jsy	35.00
76	C.C. Sabathia/Jsy/50	25.00
104	Roy Oswalt/Jsy-Jsy/50	30.00
112	Jeremy Affeldt/Pants-Pants/50	15.00
127	Bill Hall/Bat-Bat/50	15.00
129	Jacque Jones/Bat-Jsy/50	20.00
132	Lew Ford/Bat-Jsy/50	20.00
178	Craig Wilson/Bat-Jsy/50	20.00
221	Carl Crawford/Jsy-Jsy/50	20.00
230	Michael Young/Bat-Jsy/50	25.00
269	Brad Penny/Bat-Jsy/50	15.00
280	Dale Murphy/Jsy-Jsy/25	50.00
282	Dwight Evans/Bat-Jsy	30.00
283	Ron Santo/Bat-Bat/50	45.00
284	Andre Dawson/Bat-Jsy/50	30.00
285	Harold Baines/Bat-Jsy	25.00
286	Jack Morris/Jsy-Jsy/50	25.00
291	Tony Oliva/Bat-Jsy/50	30.00
297	Dave Parker/Bat-Jsy/50	30.00
299	Matt Williams/Jsy/25	35.00

Team Timeline
NM/M
Complete Set (25): 65.00
Common Duo: 1.50
Inserted 1:21
#26-30 found in DK Update.

#	Card	Price
1	Albert Pujols, Scott Rolen	6.00
2	Roger Clemens, Andy Pettitte	6.00
3	Tim Hudson, Mark Mulder	1.50
4	Hank Blalock, Mark Teixeira	2.00
5	Miguel Cabrera, Mike Lowell	2.00
6	Greg Maddux, Sammy Sosa	4.00
7	Miguel Tejada, Cal Ripken Jr.	8.00
8	Vladimir Guerrero, Reggie Jackson	3.00
9	Mike Schmidt, Jim Thome	4.00
10	Chipper Jones, Greg Maddux	4.00
11	George Brett, Ken Harvey	5.00
12	Don Mattingly, Hideki Matsui	5.00
13	Torii Hunter, Johan Santana	2.00
14	Carlos Delgado, Vernon Wells	1.50
15	Todd Helton, Larry Walker	2.00
16	Duke Snider, Adrian Beltre	2.00
17	Al Kaline, Ivan Rodriguez	3.00
18	Rafael Palmeiro, Eddie Murray	2.00
19	Manny Ramirez, Carl Yastrzemski	3.00
20	Ralph Kiner, Jason Bay	1.50
21	Johnny Bench, Adam Dunn	3.00
22	Robin Yount, Lyle Overbay	4.00
23	Nolan Ryan, Randy Johnson	8.00
24	Gary Carter, Mike Piazza	4.00
25	Carlton Fisk, Frank Thomas	3.00
26	Nolan Ryan, Mike Piazza	8.00
27	Roger Clemens, Jeff Bagwell	8.00
28	Cal Ripken Jr., Sammy Sosa	8.00
29	Willie Mays, Jim Thorpe	8.00
30	Albert Pujols, Stan Musial	8.00

Team Timeline Materials Bat
NM/M
Production 25-100

#	Card	Price
2	Roger Clemens, Andy Pettitte/50	25.00
5	Miguel Cabrera, Mike Lowell/100	15.00
8	Vladimir Guerrero, Reggie Jackson/75	20.00
9	Mike Schmidt, Jim Thome/50	30.00
12	Don Mattingly, Hideki Matsui/50	50.00
15	Todd Helton, Larry Walker/100	10.00
17	Al Kaline, Ivan Rodriguez/25	30.00
18	Rafael Palmeiro, Eddie Murray/100	15.00
21	Johnny Bench, Adam Dunn/100	15.00
22	Robin Yount, Lyle Overbay/100	20.00
23	Nolan Ryan, Randy Johnson/25	40.00

Team Timeline Materials Jersey
NM/M
Common Duo: 8.00
Production 100 Sets
Prime: No Pricing
Production One Set
#26-30 found in DK Update.

#	Card	Price
1	Albert Pujols, Scott Rolen	40.00
2	Roger Clemens, Andy Pettitte	25.00
3	Tim Hudson, Mark Mulder	8.00
4	Hank Blalock, Mark Teixeira	10.00
7	Miguel Tejada, Cal Ripken Jr.	40.00
8	Vladimir Guerrero, Reggie Jackson	15.00
9	Mike Schmidt/Jkt, Jim Thome	30.00
10	Chipper Jones, Greg Maddux	20.00
12	Don Mattingly/Jkt, Hideki Matsui	50.00
14	Carlos Delgado, Vernon Wells	8.00
15	Todd Helton, Larry Walker	10.00
16	Duke Snider, Adrian Beltre	10.00
18	Rafael Palmeiro, Eddie Murray	15.00
19	Manny Ramirez, Carl Yastrzemski	25.00
21	Johnny Bench, Adam Dunn	15.00
22	Robin Yount, Lyle Overbay	15.00
24	Gary Carter, Mike Piazza	15.00
25	Carlton Fisk, Frank Thomas	15.00
26	Nolan Ryan, Mike Piazza	30.00
27	Roger Clemens, Jeff Bagwell	20.00
30	Albert Pujols, Stan Musial	40.00

Timeline
NM/M
Complete Set (25): 50.00
Common Player: 1.50
Inserted 1:21
#26-30 found in DK Update.

#	Card	Price
1	Roger Clemens	6.00
2	Nolan Ryan	8.00
3	Carlos Beltran	3.00
4	Ivan Rodriguez	3.00
5	Jim Thome	3.00
6	Mike Piazza	4.00
7	Miguel Tejada	3.00
8	Rafael Palmeiro	2.00
9	Greg Maddux	4.00
10	Tom Glavine	1.50
11	Vladimir Guerrero	3.00
12	Curt Schilling	3.00
13	Mike Mussina	2.00
14	Rickey Henderson	2.00
15	Scott Rolen	3.00
16	Alfonso Soriano	3.00
17	Gary Sheffield	2.00
18	Carlton Fisk	2.00
19	Aramis Ramirez	2.00
20	Mark Grace	1.50
21	Jason Giambi	1.50
22	Juan Gonzalez	1.50
23	Brad Penny	1.50
24	Nomar Garciaparra	4.00
25	Larry Walker	2.00
26	Curt Schilling	2.00
27	Reggie Jackson	2.00
28	Gary Carter	1.50
29	Roger Clemens	6.00
30	Nolan Ryan	8.00

Timeline Materials Bat
NM/M
Production 25-100

#	Card	Price
1	Roger Clemens	30.00
2	Nolan Ryan	50.00
3	Carlos Beltran	10.00
4	Ivan Rodriguez	10.00
5	Jim Thome	20.00
8	Rafael Palmeiro	10.00
9	Greg Maddux	30.00
10	Tom Glavine	10.00
11	Vladimir Guerrero	15.00
12	Curt Schilling	20.00
13	Mike Mussina	10.00
15	Rickey Henderson	10.00
16	Scott Rolen	20.00
17	Gary Sheffield	10.00
18	Carlton Fisk	10.00
19	Aramis Ramirez	10.00
21	Mark Grace	10.00
22	Juan Gonzalez	10.00
25	Larry Walker	10.00

Timeline Materials Jersey
NM/M
Production 50-200
Prime: No Pricing
Production One Set
#26-30 found in DK Update.

#	Card	Price
1	Roger Clemens	15.00
2	Nolan Ryan	25.00
4	Carlos Beltran	10.00
5	Ivan Rodriguez	8.00
6	Mike Piazza	15.00
7	Miguel Tejada	10.00
8	Rafael Palmeiro	10.00
9	Greg Maddux	15.00
11	Vladimir Guerrero	15.00
12	Curt Schilling	10.00
13	Mike Mussina	10.00
14	Rickey Henderson	10.00
15	Scott Rolen	15.00
16	Alfonso Soriano	10.00
18	Carlton Fisk	10.00
19	Aramis Ramirez	10.00
21	Jason Giambi	8.00
22	Juan Gonzalez	8.00
26	Curt Schilling	10.00
27	Reggie Jackson	10.00
29	Roger Clemens	15.00
30	Nolan Ryan	25.00

Update B/W
B/W: 1X
Inserted 1:2

Update Gallery of Stars
NM/M
Complete Set (25): 30.00
Common Player: 1.50
Inserted 1:8

#	Card	Price
1	Andre Dawson	1.50
2	Bob Feller	2.00
3	Bobby Doerr	1.50
4	C.C. Sabathia	1.50
5	Carl Crawford	1.50
6	Dale Murphy	2.00
7	Danny Kolb	1.50
8	Darryl Strawberry	1.50
9	Dave Parker	1.50
10	David Ortiz	3.00
11	Dwight Gooden	1.50
12	Garret Anderson	1.50
13	Jack Morris	1.50
14	Jacque Jones	1.50
15	Jim Palmer	2.00
16	Johan Santana	3.00
17	Ken Harvey	1.50
18	Lyle Overbay	1.50
19	Marty Marion	1.50
20	Melvin Mora	1.50
21	Michael Young	1.50
22	Miguel Cabrera	3.00
23	Preston Wilson	1.50
24	Sean Casey	1.50
25	Victor Martinez	1.50

Update Gallery of Stars Auto
NM/M
Production 5-100

#	Card	Price
1	Andre Dawson/100	15.00
2	Bob Feller/100	25.00
3	Bobby Doerr/100	15.00
4	C.C. Sabathia/25	20.00
5	Carl Crawford/100	12.00
6	Dale Murphy/100	20.00
7	Danny Kolb/100	15.00
8	Darryl Strawberry/100	15.00
9	Dave Parker/100	12.00
10	Dwight Gooden/100	15.00
13	Jack Morris/100	12.00
14	Jacque Jones/50	10.00
17	Ken Harvey/100	8.00
18	Lyle Overbay/100	10.00
19	Marty Marion/25	20.00
20	Melvin Mora/100	12.00
25	Victor Martinez/100	12.00

Update Gallery of Stars Bat
NM/M
Production 50-200

#	Card	Price
2	Andre Dawson/50	8.00
3	Bobby Doerr/100	4.00
6	Dale Murphy/100	8.00
8	Darryl Strawberry/100	4.00
9	Dave Parker/100	4.00
10	David Ortiz/200	10.00
11	Dwight Gooden/100	4.00
12	Garret Anderson/100	4.00
18	Lyle Overbay/50	4.00
21	Michael Young/200	4.00
22	Miguel Cabrera/100	8.00
23	Preston Wilson/200	4.00
24	Sean Casey/200	4.00

Update Gallery of Stars Bat Autograph
NM/M
Production 5-200

#	Card	Price
1	Andre Dawson/25	25.00
3	Bobby Doerr/200	15.00
9	Dave Parker/200	15.00
11	Dwight Gooden/100	20.00
12	Garret Anderson/100	15.00
14	Jacque Jones/100	15.00
17	Ken Harvey/100	12.00
21	Michael Young/100	15.00
22	Miguel Cabrera/100	35.00
24	Sean Casey/50	20.00

Update Gallery of Stars Jsy
NM/M
Production 25-100
Prime: No Pricing
Production One Set

#	Card	Price
1	Andre Dawson/100	6.00
2	Bob Feller/50	8.00
3	Bobby Doerr/100	6.00
4	C.C. Sabathia/100	4.00
6	Carl Crawford/100	4.00
6	Dale Murphy/100	8.00
8	Darryl Strawberry/25	6.00
9	Dave Parker/100	4.00
10	David Ortiz/100	8.00
11	Dwight Gooden/100	4.00
12	Garret Anderson/50	4.00
13	Jack Morris/100	4.00
14	Jacque Jones/100	4.00
15	Jim Palmer/50	6.00
17	Ken Harvey/100	4.00
18	Lyle Overbay/100	4.00
20	Melvin Mora/100	4.00
21	Michael Young/100	4.00
22	Miguel Cabrera/100	8.00
23	Preston Wilson/100	4.00
24	Sean Casey/100	4.00
25	Victor Martinez/25	6.00

Update Gallery of Stars Jersey Auto.
NM/M
Production 25-100
Prime: No Pricing
Production One Set

#	Card	Price
1	Andre Dawson/25	25.00
2	Bob Feller/50	30.00
3	Bobby Doerr/100	15.00
4	C.C. Sabathia/100	15.00
5	Carl Crawford/50	15.00
6	Dale Murphy/50	25.00
9	Dave Parker/100	15.00
10	David Ortiz/50	40.00
11	Dwight Gooden/50	20.00
12	Garret Anderson/50	20.00
13	Jack Morris/50	20.00
14	Jacque Jones/25	20.00
15	Jim Palmer/25	25.00
17	Ken Harvey/100	8.00
18	Lyle Overbay/100	10.00
19	Marty Marion/25	20.00
20	Melvin Mora/100	15.00
24	Sean Casey/25	20.00
25	Victor Martinez/100	20.00

Update Gallery of Star Combo
NM/M
Production 50-200 5.00
Prime: No Pricing
Production One Set

#	Card	Price
1	Andre Dawson/100	10.00
3	Bobby Doerr/100	8.00
4	C.C. Sabathia/100	5.00
6	Dale Murphy/100	10.00
9	Dave Parker/200	5.00
10	David Ortiz/200	12.00
11	Dwight Gooden/100	5.00
12	Garret Anderson/100	6.00
14	Jacque Jones/50	5.00
15	Jim Palmer/50	8.00
21	Michael Young/200	5.00
22	Miguel Cabrera/200	10.00
23	Preston Wilson/200	5.00
24	Sean Casey/200	5.00

Update Gallery of Stars Combo Auto.
NM/M
Production 25-200
Prime: No Pricing
Production One Set

#	Card	Price
1	Andre Dawson/50	25.00
3	Bobby Doerr/200	20.00
6	Dale Murphy/50	30.00
9	Dave Parker/100	15.00
10	David Ortiz/50	40.00
11	Dwight Gooden/100	20.00
12	Garret Anderson/100	20.00
14	Jacque Jones/50	20.00
15	Jim Palmer/25	25.00
17	Ken Harvey/50	15.00
21	Michael Young/50	20.00
22	Miguel Cabrera/50	35.00
24	Sean Casey/25	20.00
25	Victor Martinez/50	20.00

Update HOF Sluggers
NM/M
Common Player: 2.00

#	Card	Price
1	Duke Snider	2.00
2	Eddie Murray	2.00
3	Frank Robinson	2.00
4	George Brett	5.00
5	Harmon Killebrew	3.00
6	Mike Schmidt	5.00
7	Reggie Jackson	3.00
8	Roberto Clemente	5.00
9	Stan Musial	4.00
10	Willie Mays	5.00

Update HOF Sluggers Jersey
NM/M
Production 5-50

#	Card	Price
1	Duke Snider/Pants/25	10.00
2	Eddie Murray/50	10.00
5	Harmon Killebrew/25	15.00
6	Mike Schmidt/50	15.00
7	Reggie Jackson/Pants/50	8.00
9	Stan Musial/Pants/25	20.00
10	Willie Mays/Pants/25	25.00

Update Masters of the Game
NM/M
Common Player: 2.00

#	Card	Price
1	Albert Pujols	4.00
2	Cal Ripken Jr.	6.00
3	Don Mattingly	3.00
4	Greg Maddux	3.00
5	Jim Thorpe	2.00
6	Nolan Ryan	5.00
7	Randy Johnson	4.00
8	Roberto Clemente	6.00
9	Roger Clemens	4.00
10	Willie Mays	5.00

Update Masters of the Game Jersey
NM/M
Production 25-50

#	Card	Price
1	Albert Pujols/50	20.00
2	Cal Ripken Jr./50	30.00
3	Don Mattingly/25	30.00
4	Greg Maddux/50	10.00
5	Jim Thorpe/25	250.00
6	Nolan Ryan/50	20.00
7	Randy Johnson/25	10.00
9	Roger Clemens/50	10.00
10	Willie Mays/Pants/25	30.00

2005 Donruss Elite
NM/M
Complete Set (200):
Common Player (1-150): .25
Common SP (151-170): 3.00
Production 1,250
Common Auto. (171-200): 8.00
Production 500 to 1,500
Pack (5): 5.00
Box (20): 90.00

#	Card	Price
1	Bartolo Colon	.25
2	Casey Kotchman	.25
3	Chone Figgins	.25
4	Darin Erstad	.25
5	Garret Anderson	.40
6	Jose Guillen	.25
7	Vladimir Guerrero	.75
8	Luis Gonzalez	.25
9	Randy Johnson	.75
10	Troy Glaus	.40
11	Andruw Jones	.40
12	Chipper Jones	.75
13	J.D. Drew	.40
14	John Smoltz	.40
15	Johnny Estrada	.25
16	Marcus Giles	.25
17	Rafael Furcal	.40
18	Javy Lopez	.40
19	Jay Gibbons	.25
20	Melvin Mora	.25
21	Miguel Tejada	.50
22	Rafael Palmeiro	.50
23	Sidney Ponson	.25
24	Curt Schilling	.75
25	David Ortiz	.75
26	Derek Lowe	.40
27	Jason Varitek	.40
28	Johnny Damon	.75
29	Manny Ramirez	.75
30	Pedro Martinez	.75
31	Aramis Ramirez	.40
32	Carlos Zambrano	.25
33	Corey Patterson	.25
34	Derrek Lee	.50
35	Greg Maddux	1.00
36	Kerry Wood	.40
37	Mark Prior	.75
38	Moises Alou	.25
39	Nomar Garciaparra	1.00
40	Sammy Sosa	1.00
41	Carlos Lee	.25
42	Frank Thomas	.50
43	Jermaine Dye	.25
44	Magglio Ordonez	.25
45	Mark Buehrle	.25
46	Paul Konerko	.25
47	Adam Dunn	.50
48	Austin Kearns	.25
49	Barry Larkin	.40
50	Ken Griffey Jr.	1.00
51	Sean Casey	.25
52	C.C. Sabathia	.25
53	Cliff Lee	.25
54	Travis Hafner	.25
55	Victor Martinez	.25
56	Jeromy Burnitz	.25
57	Preston Wilson	.25
58	Todd Helton	.50
59	Brandon Inge	.25
60	Ivan Rodriguez	.50
61	Jeremy Bonderman	.25
62	Troy Percival	.25
63	Dontrelle Willis	.40
64	Josh Beckett	.40
65	Juan Pierre	.25
66	Miguel Cabrera	.75
67	Mike Lowell	.25
68	Paul LoDuca	.25
69	Andy Pettitte	.40
70	Brad Ausmus	.25
71	Carlos Beltran	.40
72	Craig Biggio	.40
73	Jeff Bagwell	.50
74	Lance Berkman	.40
75	Roger Clemens	2.00
76	Roy Oswalt	.40
77	Juan Gonzalez	.25
78	Mike Sweeney	.25
79	Zack Greinke	.40
80	Adrian Beltre	.25
81	Hideo Nomo	.25
82	Jeff Kent	.25
83	Milton Bradley	.25
84	Shawn Green	.25
85	Steve Finley	.25

86 Ben Sheets .25
87 Lyle Overbay .25
88 Scott Podsednik .25
89 Lew Ford .25
90 Shannon Stewart .25
91 Torii Hunter .25
92 David Wright .75
93 Jose Reyes .50
94 Kazuo Matsui .25
95 Mike Piazza 1.00
96 Tom Glavine .40
97 Alex Rodriguez 1.50
98 Bernie Williams .40
99 Derek Jeter 2.00
100 Gary Sheffield .50
101 Hideki Matsui 1.50
102 Jason Giambi .25
103 Kevin Brown .25
104 Mike Mussina .40
105 Barry Zito .25
106 Bobby Crosby .40
107 Eric Chavez .40
108 Jason Kendall .25
109 Mark Mulder .40
110 Bobby Abreu .25
111 Jim Thome .75
112 Kevin Millwood .25
113 Pat Burrell .25
114 Craig Wilson .25
115 Jack Wilson .25
116 Jason Bay .40
117 Brian Giles .25
118 Khalil Greene .40
119 Mark Loretta .25
120 Ryan Klesko .25
121 Sean Burroughs .25
122 Edgardo Alfonzo .25
123 J.T. Snow .25
124 Jason Schmidt .25
125 Omar Vizquel .25
126 Ichiro Suzuki 1.50
127 Jamie Moyer .25
128 Bret Boone .25
129 Richie Sexson .40
130 Albert Pujols 2.00
131 Edgar Renteria .40
132 Jeff Suppan .25
133 Jim Edmonds .40
134 Larry Walker .25
135 Scott Rolen .75
136 Aubrey Huff .25
137 B.J. Upton .25
138 Carl Crawford .25
139 Rocco Baldelli .25
140 Alfonso Soriano .75
141 Hank Blalock .40
142 Kenny Rogers .25
143 Laynce Nix .25
144 Mark Teixeira .50
145 Michael Young .25
146 Carlos Delgado .40
147 Eric Hinske .25
148 Roy Halladay .25
149 Vernon Wells .25
150 Jose Vidro .25
151 Bob Gibson 3.00
152 Brooks Robinson 5.00
153 Cal Ripken Jr. 10.00
154 Carl Yastrzemski 4.00
155 Don Mattingly 5.00
156 Eddie Murray 3.00
157 Ernie Banks 4.00
158 Frank Robinson 3.00
159 George Brett 5.00
160 Harmon Killebrew 4.00
161 Johnny Bench 4.00
162 Mike Schmidt 5.00
163 Nolan Ryan 6.00
164 Paul Molitor 4.00
165 Stan Musial 3.00
166 Steve Carlton 3.00
167 Tony Gwynn 4.00
168 Warren Spahn 4.00
169 Willie Mays 6.00
170 Willie McCovey 3.00
171 Miguel Negron AU/1,500 RC 8.00
172 Mike Morse AU/1,000 RC 15.00
173 Wladimir Balentien AU/1,500 RC 10.00
174 Alberto Concepcion AU/651 RC 10.00
175 Ubaldo Jimenez AU/500 RC 100.00
176 Justin Verlander AU/500 RC 50.00
177 Ryan Speier AU/1,000 RC 8.00
178 Geovany Soto AU/500 RC 40.00
179 Mark McLemore AU/1,200 RC 8.00
180 Ambiorix Burgos AU/599 RC 8.00
181 Chris Roberson AU/1,000 RC 8.00
182 Colter Bean AU/625 RC 10.00
183 Erick Threets AU/500 RC 8.00
184 Carlos Ruiz AU/1,000 RC 15.00
186 Jared Gothreaux AU/1,500 RC 10.00
187 Luis Hernandez AU/1,000 RC 8.00
188 Agustin Montero/1,000 RC 2.00

189 Paulino Reynoso/1,000 RC 2.00
190 Garrett Jones AU/500 RC 8.00
191 Sean Thompson AU/500 RC 8.00
192 Matt Lindstrom AU/1,500 RC 8.00
193 Nate McLouth AU/500 RC 15.00
194 Luke Scott AU/671 RC 25.00
195 Keith Hattig AU/500 10.00
196 Jason Hammel AU/1,500 RC 10.00
197 Danny Rueckel AU/671 RC 8.00
198 Justin Wechsler AU/500 RC 8.00
199 Chris Resop AU/500 RC 15.00
200 Jeff Miller AU/500 RC 10.00

Aspirations

Cards (1-150) print run 61-99: 4-8X
(1-150) p/r 41-60: 6-10X
(1-150) p/r 21-40: 8-15X
(151-170) p/r 36-80: 1.5-3X
Autos. (171-200) p/r 40-99: .5-1.5X
No pricing production 20 or less.
Production 15-99

Status

Cards (1-150) print run 61-81: 4-8X
(1-150) p/r 41-60: 6-10X
(1-150) p/r 21-40: 8-15X
(151-170) p/r 36-81: 1.5-3X
Autos. (171-200) p/r 40-81: .5-1.5X
No pricing production 20 or less.
Production 1-81

Status Gold

Gold (1-150): 10-20X
Gold (151-170): 3-5X
Gold (171-200): No Pricing
Production 24 Sets

Turn of the Century

Stars (1-150): 2-3X
Production 750
(151-170): 1X
Production 250
Rookies (171-200): .25-1X
Production 500

Back 2 Back Jacks

NM/M
1 Adam Dunn/200 8.00
3 Albert Pujols/100 15.00
4 Babe Ruth/50 160.00
5 Cal Ripken Jr./100 30.00
6 David Ortiz/200 10.00
7 Eddie Murray/150 8.00
8 Ernie Banks/50 15.00
9 Frank Robinson/50 8.00
10 Gary Sheffield/200 5.00
11 George Foster/125 5.00
12 Don Mattingly/10 15.00
13 Hideki Matsui/25 30.00
14 Jason Giambi/50 5.00
16 Jim Rice/125 8.00
17 Jim Thome/200 8.00
18 Johnny Bench/125 10.00
19 Lance Berkman/200 5.00
20 Manny Ramirez/200 10.00
21 Mike Piazza/200 10.00
22 Mike Schmidt/125 15.00
23 Rafael Palmeiro/200 8.00
24 Reggie Jackson/125 10.00
25 Sammy Sosa/100 8.00
26 Scott Rolen/200 8.00
27 Stan Musial/125 15.00
28 Willie Mays/50 40.00
29 Kirk Gibson/125 5.00
30 Will Clark/125 5.00
31 Willie Mays, Sammy Sosa/50 50.00
32 Eddie Murray, Mike Piazza/50 20.00
33 Mike Schmidt, Jim Thome/50 30.00
34 Rafael Palmeiro, Kirk Gibson/50 10.00
35 Jim Rice, Manny Ramirez/50 15.00
36 Adrian Beltre, Will Clark/50 15.00
37 Reggie Jackson, David Ortiz/50 15.00
38 Johnny Bench, Adam Dunn/50 20.00

Back 2 Back Jacks Combos

NM/M
1 Adam Dunn/Bat-Jsy/100 10.00
2 Adrian Beltre/Bat-Jsy/100 8.00
5 Cal Ripken Jr./Bat-Jsy/50 40.00
6 David Ortiz/Bat-Jsy/50 12.00
7 Eddie Murray/Bat-Jsy/50 10.00
9 Ernie Banks/Bat-Jsy/10 20.00
10 Gary Sheffield/Bat-Jsy/100 8.00
11 George Foster/Bat-Jsy/50 8.00
12 Don Mattingly/Bat-Jsy/20 20.00
13 Hideki Matsui/Bat-Jsy/25 40.00
14 Jason Giambi/Bat-Jsy/50 8.00
15 Jim Edmonds/Bat-Jsy/100 10.00
17 Jim Thome/Bat-Jsy/100 8.00
18 Johnny Bench/Bat-Jsy/100 15.00
19 Lance Berkman/Bat-Jsy/100 15.00
20 Manny Ramirez/Bat-Jsy/100 12.00
21 Mike Piazza/Bat-Jsy/25 15.00
22 Mike Schmidt/Bat-Jsy/50 20.00
23 Rafael Palmeiro/Bat-Jsy/50 10.00
24 Reggie Jackson/Bat-Jsy/50 15.00
25 Sammy Sosa/Bat-Jsy/50 15.00
26 Scott Rolen/Bat-Jsy/50 12.00
27 Stan Musial/Bat-Pants/50 25.00
28 Willie Mays/Bat-Jsy/50 60.00
29 Kirk Gibson/Bat-Jsy/50 12.00
30 Will Clark/Bat-Jsy/50 12.00
32 Eddie Murray, Mike Piazza/25 30.00
33 Mike Schmidt, Jim Thome/25 50.00
34 Rafael Palmeiro, Kirk Gibson/50 20.00
35 Jim Rice, Manny Ramirez/50 25.00
36 Adrian Beltre, Will Clark/50 15.00
37 Reggie Jackson, David Ortiz/50 30.00
38 Johnny Bench, Adam Dunn/50 30.00
40 Cal Ripken Jr., Albert Pujols/25 100.00

Career Best

NM/M
Common Player: 1.00
Production 1,500 Sets
Black: 1-2X
Production 150 Sets
Blue: 1-2X
Production 250 Sets
Gold: 1-1.5X
Production 500 Sets
1 Adam Dunn 1.50
2 Adrian Beltre 1.00
3 Albert Pujols 4.00
4 Andruw Jones 1.50
5 Ben Sheets 1.00
6 Bo Jackson 2.00
7 Brooks Robinson 2.00
8 Cal Ripken Jr. 6.00
9 Dale Murphy 1.50
10 Don Mattingly 3.00
11 Eddie Murray 1.50
12 George Brett 3.00
13 Hank Blalock 1.50
14 Ichiro Suzuki 3.00
15 Jim Thome 1.50
16 Kerry Wood 1.50
17 Lance Berkman 1.00
18 Mark Prior 2.00
19 Mark Teixeira 1.50
20 Mike Schmidt 3.00
21 Pedro Martinez 2.00
22 Randy Johnson 2.00
23 Rickey Henderson 1.50
24 Sammy Sosa 3.00
25 Tony Gwynn 2.00

Career Best Bats

NM/M
Production 50-250
1 Adam Dunn/250 8.00
2 Adrian Beltre/250 5.00
3 Albert Pujols/250 15.00
4 Andruw Jones/250 5.00
5 Ben Sheets/250 5.00
6 Bo Jackson/250 10.00
7 Brooks Robinson/250 8.00
8 Cal Ripken Jr./150 25.00
9 Dale Murphy/150 10.00
10 Don Mattingly/250 12.00
11 Eddie Murray/250 8.00
12 George Brett/250 15.00
13 Hank Blalock/250 8.00
14 Jim Thome/100 8.00
15 Kerry Wood/250 8.00
16 Lance Berkman/250 5.00
17 Mark Prior/150 6.00
18 Mark Teixeira/250 8.00
19 Mike Schmidt/250 12.00
20 Pedro Martinez/100 8.00
21 Randy Johnson/250 8.00
22 Rickey Henderson/250 8.00
23 Sammy Sosa/100 10.00
24 Tony Gwynn/100 10.00

Career Best Jerseys

NM/M
Production 100-250
1 Adam Dunn/250 8.00
2 Adrian Beltre/250 5.00
3 Albert Pujols/250 15.00
4 Andruw Jones/250 5.00
5 Ben Sheets/250 5.00
6 Bo Jackson/250 10.00
7 Brooks Robinson/50 10.00
8 Cal Ripken Jr./250 25.00
9 Dale Murphy/100 10.00
10 Don Mattingly/150 12.00
11 Eddie Murray/100 8.00
12 George Brett/100 15.00
13 Hank Blalock/250 8.00
14 Jim Thome/250 8.00
15 Kerry Wood/250 8.00
16 Lance Berkman/250 5.00
17 Mark Prior/250 6.00
18 Mark Teixeira/250 8.00
19 Mike Schmidt/100 12.00
20 Pedro Martinez/250 8.00
21 Randy Johnson/100 10.00
22 Rickey Henderson/50 10.00
23 Sammy Sosa/250 10.00
24 Tony Gwynn/250 10.00

Career Best Combos

NM/M
Production 25-150
1 Adam Dunn/Bat-Jsy/150 10.00
2 Adrian Beltre/Bat-Jsy/150 8.00
3 Albert Pujols/Bat-Jsy/150 20.00
4 Andruw Jones/Bat-Jsy/150 8.00
5 Ben Sheets/Bat-Jsy/150 8.00
6 Bo Jackson/Bat-Jsy/25 20.00
7 Brooks Robinson/Bat-Jsy/25 20.00
8 Cal Ripken Jr./Bat-Jsy/25 40.00
9 Dale Murphy/Bat-Jsy/25 10.00
10 Don Mattingly/Bat-Jsy/25 20.00
11 Eddie Murray/Bat-Jsy/25 12.00
12 George Brett/Bat-Jsy/25 25.00
13 Hank Blalock/Bat-Jsy/150 10.00
15 Jim Thome/Bat-Jsy/150 10.00
16 Kerry Wood/Bat-Pants/150 10.00
17 Lance Berkman/Bat-Jsy/150 8.00
18 Mark Prior/Bat-Jsy/150 8.00
19 Mark Teixeira/Bat-Jsy/150 12.00
21 Pedro Martinez/Bat-Jsy/125 10.00
23 Rickey Henderson/Bat-Jsy/25 15.00
24 Sammy Sosa/Bat-Jsy/150 12.00
25 Tony Gwynn/Bat-Jsy/25 15.00

Face 2 Face

NM/M
Complete Set (20): 35.00
Common Duo:
Production 1,500 Sets
Black: 1-1.5X
Production 500 Sets
Gold: 1-2X
Production 250 Sets
Red: 1X
Production 750 Sets
1 Roger Clemens, Scott Rolen 3.00
2 Greg Maddux, Jeff Bagwell 3.00
3 Mark Prior, Mike Piazza 3.00
4 Mike Mussina, Ivan Rodriguez 2.00
5 Josh Beckett, Sammy Sosa
6 Roy Oswalt, Miguel Cabrera
7 Roger Clemens, Albert Pujols 4.00
8 Pedro Martinez, Vladimir Guerrero 2.00
9 Randy Johnson, Jim Edmonds 2.00
10 Curt Schilling, Derek Jeter 4.00
11 Kerry Wood, Lance Berkman 1.50
12 Tim Hudson, Garret Anderson 1.00
13 Pedro Martinez, Gary Sheffield 2.00
14 Barry Zito, Magglio Ordonez 1.00
15 Kerry Wood, Shawn Green 1.50
16 Mike Mussina, Miguel Tejada 2.00
17 Randy Johnson, Albert Pujols 4.00
18 Nolan Ryan, George Brett 4.00
19 Tom Seaver, Mike Schmidt 3.00
20 Jim Palmer, Harmon Killebrew 2.00

Face 2 Face Bats

NM/M
Production 25-150
3 Mark Prior, Mike Piazza/10 8.00
4 Mike Mussina, Ivan Rodriguez/100 8.00
5 Josh Beckett, Sammy Sosa/50 10.00
6 Roy Oswalt, Miguel Cabrera/100 8.00
8 Pedro Martinez, Vladimir Guerrero/50 10.00
9 Randy Johnson, Jim Edmonds/250 10.00
11 Kerry Wood, Lance Berkman/150 8.00
12 Tim Hudson, Garret Anderson/150 8.00
13 Pedro Martinez, Gary Sheffield/150 8.00
14 Barry Zito, Magglio Ordonez/50 8.00
15 Kerry Wood, Shawn Green/150 8.00
18 Nolan Ryan, George Brett/100 25.00
19 Tom Seaver, Mike Schmidt/150 15.00

Face 2 Face Jerseys

NM/M
Production 25-200
1 Roger Clemens, Scott Rolen/200 15.00
2 Greg Maddux, Jeff Bagwell/75 10.00
3 Mark Prior, Mike Piazza/200 8.00
4 Mike Mussina, Ivan Rodriguez/200 8.00
5 Josh Beckett, Sammy Sosa/200 12.00
6 Roy Oswalt, Miguel Cabrera/200 8.00
7 Roger Clemens, Albert Pujols/200 8.00
8 Pedro Martinez, Vladimir Guerrero/75 10.00
11 Kerry Wood, Lance Berkman/200 8.00
12 Tim Hudson, Garret Anderson/75 8.00
13 Pedro Martinez, Gary Sheffield/75 10.00
14 Barry Zito, Magglio Ordonez/200 8.00
15 Kerry Wood, Shawn Green/200 8.00
16 Mike Mussina, Miguel Tejada/200 10.00
17 Randy Johnson, Albert Pujols/75 8.00
19 Tom Seaver, Mike Schmidt/50 20.00

Face 2 Face Combos

NM/M
Production 25-250
1 Roger Clemens/Jsy, Scott Rolen/Jsy/100 15.00
2 Greg Maddux/Jsy, Jeff Bagwell/Bat/100 10.00
3 Mark Prior/Jsy, Mike Piazza/Jsy 8.00
4 Mike Mussina/Jsy, Ivan Rodriguez/Bat/250 8.00
5 Josh Beckett/Jsy, Sammy Sosa/Bat/250 10.00
6 Roy Oswalt/Jsy, Miguel Cabrera/Bat/250 8.00
8 Pedro Martinez/Jsy, Vladimir Guerrero/Bat/75 10.00
11 Kerry Wood/Bat, Lance Berkman/Jsy/250 8.00
12 Tim Hudson/Jsy, Garret Anderson/Bat/100 8.00
13 Pedro Martinez/Jsy, Gary Sheffield/Jsy/75 12.00
14 Barry Zito/Jsy, Magglio Ordonez/Bat/250 8.00
15 Kerry Wood/Jsy, Shawn Green/Bat/250 8.00
16 Mike Mussina/Jsy, Miguel Tejada/Bat/250 10.00
19 Tom Seaver/Jsy, Mike Schmidt/Bat/50 20.00

Passing the Torch

NM/M
Common Player: 1.50
1-30 Production 1,000
31-45 Production 500
Black: 2-3X
1-30 Production 50
31-45 Production 25
Gold: 1-2X
1-30 Production 50
31-45 Production 50
Green: 1-1.5X
1-30 Production 250
31-45 Production 125
Red: 1X
1-30 Production 500
31-45 Production 250
1 Adrian Beltre 1.50
2 Albert Pujols 5.00
3 Alex Rodriguez 4.00
4 Andruw Jones 1.50
5 Babe Ruth 6.00
6 Ben Sheets 1.50
7 Brooks Robinson 2.00
8 Cal Ripken Jr. 4.00
9 Carl Yastrzemski 3.00
10 Dale Murphy 2.00
11 David Ortiz 2.00
12 Derek Jeter 5.00
13 Don Mattingly 4.00
14 George Brett 4.00
15 Greg Maddux 3.00
16 Hank Blalock 1.50
17 Jeff Bagwell 2.00
18 Johnny Bench 3.00
19 Magglio Ordonez 1.50
20 Mark Prior 2.00
21 Mark Teixeira 2.00
22 Miguel Cabrera 2.00
23 Mike Schmidt 3.00
24 Nolan Ryan 6.00
25 Pedro Martinez 2.00
26 Sammy Sosa 3.00
27 Scott Rolen 3.00
28 Tom Seaver 2.00
29 Vladimir Guerrero 2.00
30 Willie Mays 4.00
31 Carlton Fisk, Magglio Ordonez 3.00
32 Nolan Ryan, Ben Sheets 8.00
33 Babe Ruth, Alex Rodriguez 8.00
34 Cal Ripken Jr., B.J. Upton 10.00
35 Willie Mays, Andruw Jones 5.00
36 George Brett, Hank Blalock 5.00
37 Greg Maddux, Whitey Ford 4.00
38 Harmon Killebrew, Mark Prior
39 Tom Seaver, Mark Prior 3.00
40 Don Mattingly, Mark Teixeira 5.00
41 Stan Musial, Carlos Beltran 5.00
42 Dale Murphy, Lance Berkman
43 Willie McCovey, Jeff Bagwell 3.00
44 Andre Dawson, Miguel Cabrera 3.00
45 Brooks Robinson, Scott Rolen 4.00

Passing the Torch Autographs

NM/M
Production 5-100
1 Adrian Beltre/75 15.00
6 Ben Sheets/75 15.00
7 Brooks Robinson/100 25.00
10 Dale Murphy/50 20.00
13 Don Mattingly/50 50.00
18 Johnny Bench/25 50.00
19 Magglio Ordonez/75 10.00
20 Mark Prior/25 40.00
21 Mark Teixeira/75 25.00
22 Miguel Cabrera/75 25.00
23 Mike Schmidt/25 50.00
27 Scott Rolen/25 40.00
28 Tom Seaver/25 50.00
31 Carlton Fisk, Magglio Ordonez/25 50.00
44 Andre Dawson, Miguel Cabrera/25 50.00
45 Brooks Robinson, Scott Rolen/25 75.00

Passing the Torch Bats

NM/M
Production 25-250

#	Player	Price
1	Adrian Beltre/250	4.00
2	Albert Pujols/250	15.00
4	Andruw Jones/250	4.00
6	Ben Sheets/250	
7	Brooks Robinson/150	10.00
8	Cal Ripken Jr./150	25.00
9	Carl Yastrzemski/150	4.00
10	Dale Murphy/250	6.00
11	David Ortiz/250	8.00
13	Don Mattingly/150	10.00
16	George Brett/150	10.00
16	Hank Blalock/250	4.00
18	Jeff Bagwell/250	6.00
19	Magglio Ordonez/250	4.00
20	Mark Prior/50	10.00
21	Mark Teixeira/250	6.00
22	Miguel Cabrera/250	8.00
23	Mike Schmidt/150	10.00
24	Nolan Ryan/250	20.00
25	Pedro Martinez/150	8.00
26	Sammy Sosa/250	8.00
27	Scott Rolen/250	8.00
28	Tom Seaver/150	8.00
29	Vladimir Guerrero/250	8.00
30	Willie Mays/50	30.00
31	Carlton Fisk, Magglio Ordonez/250	6.00
32	Nolan Ryan, Ben Sheets/50	35.00
34	Cal Ripken Jr., B.J. Upton/50	50.00
35	Willie Mays, Andruw Jones/50	35.00
36	George Brett, Hank Blalock/150	15.00
39	Tom Seaver, Mark Prior/25	20.00
40	Don Mattingly, Mark Teixeira/150	15.00
42	Dale Murphy, Lance Berkman/50	12.00
43	Willie McCovey, Jeff Bagwell/25	20.00
44	Andre Dawson, Miguel Cabrera/250	10.00
45	Brooks Robinson, Scott Rolen/150	15.00

Passing the Torch Jerseys
NM/M
Production 25-250

#	Player	Price
1	Adrian Beltre/250	4.00
2	Albert Pujols/250	15.00
4	Andruw Jones/250	4.00
6	Ben Sheets/250	
8	Cal Ripken Jr./250	20.00
9	Carl Yastrzemski/Pants/50	10.00
10	Dale Murphy/250	6.00
13	David Ortiz/250	8.00
13	Don Mattingly/150	10.00
15	George Brett/150	12.00
16	Greg Maddux/250	10.00
16	Hank Blalock/250	4.00
17	Jeff Bagwell/250	6.00
18	Johnny Bench/Pants/150	10.00
19	Magglio Ordonez/250	4.00
20	Mark Prior/250	8.00
21	Mark Teixeira/250	6.00
22	Miguel Cabrera/250	8.00
23	Mike Schmidt/150	10.00
24	Nolan Ryan/50	20.00
25	Pedro Martinez/250	8.00
26	Sammy Sosa/250	8.00
27	Scott Rolen/250	8.00
28	Tom Seaver/50	8.00
29	Vladimir Guerrero/250	8.00
31	Carlton Fisk, Magglio Ordonez/50	8.00
32	Nolan Ryan, Ben Sheets/50	35.00
34	Cal Ripken Jr., B.J. Upton/50	50.00
35	Willie Mays, Andruw Jones/50	35.00
36	George Brett, Hank Blalock/50	15.00
39	Tom Seaver, Mark Prior/25	
40	Don Mattingly, Mark Teixeira/100	15.00
42	Dale Murphy, Lance Berkman/150	10.00
43	Willie McCovey, Jeff Bagwell/50	15.00
44	Andre Dawson, Miguel Cabrera/150	10.00

Recollection Autographs
Production 10-25

Teams
NM/M

Common Card:		
Production 1,500 Sets		
Black:		1X-2X
Production 250 Sets		
Blue:		1X
Production 1,000 Sets		
Gold:		2X-3X
Production 100 Sets		
Green:		1X-1.5X
Production 750 Sets		
Red:		1X-1.5X
Production 500 Sets		

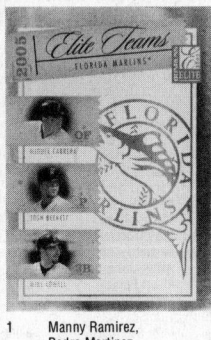

#	Player	Price
1	Manny Ramirez, Pedro Martinez, David Ortiz	4.00
2	Albert Pujols, Scott Rolen, Jim Edmonds	4.00
3	Roger Clemens, Jeff Bagwell, Lance Berkman, Craig Biggio	4.00
4	Miguel Cabrera, Josh Beckett, Mike Lowell	2.00
5	Kerry Wood, Mark Prior, Sammy Sosa, Greg Maddux	4.00
6	Adrian Beltre, Shawn Green, Hideo Nomo, Kazuhisa Ishii	2.00
7	Cal Ripken Jr., Eddie Murray, Jim Palmer	8.00
8	George Brett, Bo Jackson, Frank White	4.00
9	Roger Clemens, Mike Mussina, Alfonso Soriano, Bernie Williams	4.00
10	Tom Glavine, Greg Maddux, Ryan Klesko, David Justice	4.00

Teams Bats
NM/M
Production 50-100

#	Player	Price
1	Manny Ramirez, Pedro Martinez, David Ortiz/100	20.00
2	Albert Pujols, Scott Rolen, Jim Edmonds/100	40.00
3	Roger Clemens, Jeff Bagwell, Lance Berkman, Craig Biggio/50	35.00
4	Miguel Cabrera, Josh Beckett, Mike Lowell/100	10.00
6	Adrian Beltre, Shawn Green, Hideo Nomo, Kazuhisa Ishii/50	20.00
8	George Brett, Bo Jackson, Frank White/100	25.00

Teams Jerseys
NM/M
Production 50-150

#	Player	Price
1	Manny Ramirez, Pedro Martinez, David Ortiz/150	20.00
2	Albert Pujols, Scott Rolen, Jim Edmonds/150	30.00
3	Roger Clemens, Jeff Bagwell, Lance Berkman, Craig Biggio/150	25.00
4	Miguel Cabrera, Josh Beckett, Mike Lowell/150	15.00
5	Kerry Wood, Mark Prior, Sammy Sosa, Greg Maddux/150	25.00
6	Adrian Beltre, Shawn Green, Hideo Nomo, Kazuhisa Ishii/50	20.00
7	Cal Ripken Jr., Eddie Murray, Jim Palmer/100	35.00
9	Roger Clemens, Mike Mussina, Alfonso Soriano, Bernie Williams/100	25.00
10	Tom Glavine, Greg Maddux, Ryan Klesko, David Justice/100	30.00

Throwback Threads
NM/M
Production 10-200

#	Player	Price
1	Albert Pujols/200	15.00
3	Bert Blyleven/200	4.00
5	Bobby Doerr/Pants/200	8.00
6	Cal Ripken Jr./150	25.00
7	Carl Yastrzemski/Pants/150	12.00
8	Dale Murphy/150	8.00
9	Dennis Eckersley/50	8.00
10	Don Mattingly/200	10.00
11	Don Sutton/100	8.00
12	Early Wynn/50	6.00
14	Eddie Murray/100	8.00
16	Greg Maddux/150	8.00
17	Harmon Killebrew/100	8.00
18	Hoyt Wilhelm/150	6.00
19	Jim Edmonds/200	8.00
21	Lou Boudreau/100	8.00
22	Lou Brock/100	8.00
23	Miguel Cabrera/200	8.00
24	Mike Mussina/150	8.00
25	Mike Piazza/150	8.00
26	Mike Schmidt/150	15.00
27	Nolan Ryan/50	20.00
28	Phil Niekro/100	8.00
29	Randy Johnson/150	8.00
30	Rickey Henderson/150	8.00
31	Sammy Sosa/150	8.00
33	Scott Rolen/200	8.00
34	Steve Carlton/100	8.00
36	Tommy John/150	8.00
37	Vladimir Guerrero/200	8.00
38	Whitey Ford/25	15.00
39	Willie Mays/50	40.00
40	Willie McCovey/150	8.00
46	Lou Brock, Rickey Henderson/100	15.00
49	Bo Jackson, Deion Sanders/150	15.00
50	Nolan Ryan, Curt Schilling/100	25.00
51	Don Sutton, Greg Maddux/100	15.00
52	Harmon Killebrew, Rafael Palmeiro/100	15.00
53	Dale Murphy, Dwight Evans/150	12.00
55	Carl Yastrzemski, Vladimir Guerrero/50	8.00
56	Eddie Murray, Mike Piazza/100	12.00
57	Johnny Bench, Ivan Rodriguez/50	12.00
58	Jim Palmer, Tim Hudson/50	10.00
59	Cal Ripken Jr., Hank Blalock/50	35.00
60	Jim Rice, Manny Ramirez/100	12.00

Throwback Threads Autographs
NM/M
Production 5-100
Prime: No Pricing
Production 1-10

#	Player	Price
3	Bert Blyleven/100	15.00
4	Bobby Doerr/Pants/100	20.00
5	Brooks Robinson/30	30.00
9	Dale Murphy/100	25.00
9	Dennis Eckersley/75	20.00
17	Don Sutton/100	20.00
17	Harmon Killebrew/75	30.00
20	Jim Palmer/75	15.00
22	Lou Brock Jkt/75	30.00
23	Miguel Cabrera/75	30.00

Throwback Threads Prime
Production 1-25

2005 Donruss Greats
NM/M
Complete Set (150): 50.00
Common Player: .50
Pack (5): 9.00
Box (15): 120.00

#	Player	Price
1	Al Kaline	.75
2	Alan Trammell	.50
3	Andre Dawson	.50
4	Barry Larkin	.75
5	Bert Blyleven	.50
6	Billy Williams	.50
7	Bo Jackson	1.00
8	Bob Feller	.75
9	Bobby Doerr	.50
10	Brooks Robinson	1.00
11	Cal Ripken Jr.	4.00
12	Dale Murphy	.50
13	Darryl Strawberry	.50
14	Dave Parker	.50
15	Dave Stewart	.50
16	David Cone	.50
17	Dennis Eckersley	.50
18	Don Larsen	.50
19	Don Mattingly	2.00
20	Don Sutton	.50
21	Duke Snider	1.00
22	Dwight Evans	.50
23	Dwight Gooden	.50
24	Earl Weaver	.50
25	Fergie Jenkins	.50
26	Frank Robinson	1.00
27	Fred Lynn	.50
28	Gary Carter	.50
29	Gaylord Perry	.50
30	George Brett	2.50
31	George Foster	.50
32	George Kell	.50
33	Harmon Killebrew	1.50
34	Harold Baines	.50
35	Harold Reynolds	.50
36	Jack Morris	.50
37	Jim Abbott	.50
38	Jim Bunning	.50
39	Jim Palmer	.50
40	Jim Rice	.50
41	Jim Leyritz	.50
42	Joe Morgan	.50
43	John Kruk	.50
44	Johnny Bench	2.00
45	Johnny Podres	.50
46	Jose Canseco	1.00
47	Juan Marichal	.50
48	Keith Hernandez	.50
49	Kent Hrbek	.50
50	Kirby Puckett	2.00
51	Lee Smith	.50
52	Lenny Dykstra	.50
53	Luis Aparicio	.50
54	Luis Tiant	.50
55	Mark Grace	.50
56	Marty Marion	.50
57	Matt Williams	.50
58	Maury Wills	.50
59	Mike Schmidt	2.00
60	Minnie Minoso	.50
61	Nolan Ryan	3.00
62	Ozzie Smith	1.00
63	Paul Molitor	.75
64	Phil Rizzuto	.75
65	Ralph Kiner	.50
66	Randy Jones	.50
67	Red Schoendienst	.50
68	Rich "Goose" Gossage	.50
69	Rob Dibble	.50
70	Robin Roberts	.50
71	Rod Carew	.50
72	Rollie Fingers	.50
73	Ron Guidry	.50
74	Ron Santo	.50
75	Ryne Sandberg	2.00
76	Stan Musial	2.00
77	Steve Carlton	.50
78	Steve Garvey	.50
79	Steve Stone	.50
80	Terry Pendleton	.50
81	Terry Steinbach	.50
82	Tom Seaver	1.00
83	Tommy John	1.00
84	Tony Gwynn	1.00
85	Tony Oliva	.50
86	Whitey Ford	1.00
87	Will Clark	.75
88	Willie Mays	3.00
89	Willie McCovey	1.00
90	Roberto Clemente	2.50
91	Roger Maris	2.00
92	Bob Gibson	.75
93	Carl Yastrzemski	1.50
94	Jim "Catfish" Hunter	.50
95	Warren Spahn	1.00
96	Reggie Jackson	1.00
97	Lou Brock	.75
98	Joe Morgan	.50
99	Carlton Fisk	.50
100	Eddie Murray	.50
101	Roger Clemens	3.00
102	Greg Maddux	2.00
103	Derek Jeter	3.00
104	Albert Pujols	3.00
105	Ken Griffey Jr.	2.00
106	Alex Rodriguez	3.00
107	Mike Piazza	2.00
108	Manny Ramirez	1.00
109	Sammy Sosa	1.00
110	Rafael Palmeiro	.75
111	Randy Johnson	1.00
112	Vladimir Guerrero	1.00
113	Ichiro Suzuki	2.00
114	David Ortiz	1.00
115	Miguel Cabrera	1.00
116	Frank Thomas	2.00
117	Pedro Martinez	1.00
118	Chipper Jones	1.00
119	Todd Helton	.75
120	Alfonso Soriano	1.00
121	Ivan Rodriguez	.75
122	Carlos Delgado	.75
123	Carlos Beltran	.75
124	Jeff Kent	.75
125	Curt Schilling	.75
126	Derek Lee	.75
127	Jason Bay	.50
128	Mark Teixeira	.75
129	Craig Biggio	.50
130	Miguel Tejada	.75
131	Johan Santana	.75
132	Jim Thome	.75
133	Tim Hudson	.50
134	Barry Zito	.50
135	Mark Mulder	.50
136	Hideki Matsui	2.00
137	John Smoltz	.75
138	Mark Prior	.75
139	Andruw Jones	.75
140	Adam Dunn	.75
141	Prince Fielder	4.00
142	Tadahito Iguchi RC	2.00
143	Randy Johnson	1.00
144	Pedro Martinez	1.00
145	Alex Rodriguez	3.00
146	Roger Clemens	3.00
147	Vladimir Guerrero	1.00
148	Greg Maddux	2.00
149	Ken Griffey Jr.	2.00
150	Roger Clemens	3.00

Gold Holofoil
Gold Holofoil 3-4X
Production 100 Sets

Platinum Holofoil
Platinum Holofoil 3-5X
Production 50 Sets

Silver Holofoil
Silver Holofoil 1-2X
Inserted 1:3

Dodger Blues Brooklyn Material
NM/M
Common Player: 10.00
Prime: No Pricing
Production 10

#	Player	Price
1	Sandy Koufax/43	140.00
2	Duke Snider/27	40.00
3	Burleigh Grimes	40.00
4	Tommy Lasorda	10.00

Dodger Blues Brooklyn Sig. Material
NM/M

#	Player	Price
1	Sandy Koufax/37	300.00

Dodger Blues LA Material
NM/M
Common Player: No Pricing
Prime:
Production 1-10

#	Player	Price
1	Sandy Koufax/43	140.00
2	Duke Snider/55	35.00
4	Tommy Lasorda	10.00
5	Orel Hershiser	10.00
6	Don Sutton	10.00

Dodger Blues LA Signature Material
NM/M
Production 10-37
Prime: No Pricing
Production 1-5

#	Player	Price
1	Sandy Koufax/37	300.00

Hall of Fame Souvenirs
NM/M
Common Player: 2.00

#	Player	Price
1	Willie Mays/Giants	4.00
2	Hank Aaron/Mil	4.00
3	Hank Aaron/Atl	4.00
4	Willie Mays/Mets	4.00
5	Nolan Ryan	6.00
6	Roberto Clemente/Kneeling	4.00
7	Nellie Fox	2.00
8	Pee Wee Reese	3.00
9	Babe Ruth	6.00
10	Bobby Doerr	2.00
11	Brooks Robinson	3.00
12	Carlton Fisk	3.00
13	Eddie Murray	3.00
14	Ernie Banks	3.00
15	Frank Robinson	3.00
16	Gary Carter	2.00
17	Hack Wilson	2.00
18	Harmon Killebrew	2.00
19	Joe Morgan	2.00
20	Kirby Puckett	4.00
21	Lou Brock	2.00
22	Orlando Cepeda	2.00
23	Red Schoendienst	2.00
24	Richie Ashburn	2.00
25	Stan Musial	5.00
26	Roberto Clemente/Standing	6.00
27	Wade Boggs/Sox	3.00
28	Wade Boggs/Yanks	3.00

Hall of Fame Souvenirs Material Bat
NM/M
Common Player: 10.00

#	Player	Price
1	Willie Mays	25.00
2	Hank Aaron	25.00
3	Hank Aaron	25.00
4	Willie Mays	25.00
5	Nolan Ryan/30	40.00
6	Roberto Clemente	40.00
7	Nellie Fox	10.00
8	Pee Wee Reese	10.00
9	Babe Ruth	140.00
11	Brooks Robinson	10.00
12	Carlton Fisk	10.00
13	Eddie Murray	10.00
14	Ernie Banks	15.00
15	Frank Robinson	8.00
16	Gary Carter	8.00
17	Hack Wilson	30.00
18	Harmon Killebrew	8.00
19	Joe Morgan	8.00
20	Kirby Puckett	10.00
21	Lou Brock	8.00
22	Orlando Cepeda	8.00
23	Red Schoendienst	8.00
24	Richie Ashburn	8.00
25	Stan Musial	10.00
26	Roberto Clemente	40.00
27	Wade Boggs	10.00
28	Wade Boggs	10.00

HOF Souvenirs Material Combo
NM/M
Common Combo: 10.00

#	Player	Price
1	Willie Mays Giants	50.00
2	Hank Aaron Mil	50.00
3	Hank Aaron Atl	50.00
4	Willie Mays/25	50.00
5	Nolan Ryan/25	40.00
6	Pee Wee Reese/38	25.00
9	Babe Ruth/50	300.00
10	Bobby Doerr	10.00
11	Brooks Robinson/29	10.00
12	Carlton Fisk	10.00
13	Eddie Murray	10.00
14	Ernie Banks	20.00
15	Gary Carter	10.00
18	Harmon Killebrew	15.00
23	Red Schoendienst	10.00
26	Roberto Clemente	75.00
27	Wade Boggs	15.00
28	Wade Boggs	25.00

HOF Souvenirs Material Jersey
NM/M
Common Player: 10.00

#	Player	Price
1	Willie Mays/25	40.00
2	Hank Aaron/25	40.00
3	Hank Aaron/25	40.00
4	Willie Mays/25	40.00
5	Nolan Ryan/25	40.00
9	Babe Ruth/25	225.00
10	Bobby Doerr	10.00
12	Carlton Fisk	10.00
24	Richie Ashburn	10.00
25	Stan Musial	25.00
27	Wade Boggs	12.00

Hall of Fame Souvenirs Signature
No Pricing

HOF Souvenirs Sign. Material Bat
NM/M
No pricing production 22 or less.

#	Player	Price
10	Bobby Doerr	20.00
11	Brooks Robinson	30.00
12	Carlton Fisk	20.00
15	Frank Robinson	20.00
16	Gary Carter	20.00
18	Harmon Killebrew	30.00
19	Joe Morgan	20.00
20	Kirby Puckett/52	90.00
21	Lou Brock	25.00
22	Orlando Cepeda	25.00
23	Red Schoendienst	25.00
25	Stan Musial/50	60.00

HOF Souvenirs Sign. Material Combo
NM/M
Common Signature: 20.00

#	Player	Price
10	Bobby Doerr	20.00
11	Brooks Robinson	40.00
12	Carlton Fisk/50	20.00
15	Frank Robinson/39	30.00
16	Gary Carter	20.00
18	Harmon Killebrew	30.00
19	Joe Morgan/23	20.00
20	Kirby Puckett/45	125.00
22	Orlando Cepeda	25.00
25	Stan Musial	80.00
27	Wade Boggs/Sox	40.00
28	Wade Boggs/Yanks	40.00

HOF Souvenirs Sign. Material Jersey
NM/M
Common Signature: 20.00

#	Player	Price
10	Bobby Doerr	20.00
11	Brooks Robinson	20.00
12	Carlton Fisk	30.00
15	Frank Robinson	30.00
16	Gary Carter/63	20.00
18	Harmon Killebrew	30.00
22	Orlando Cepeda/68	20.00
23	Red Schoendienst	25.00
25	Stan Musial	65.00
27	Wade Boggs	40.00
28	Wade Boggs/3	40.00

Redbirds Material
NM/M
Common Player: 8.00
Prime: No Pricing
Production 1-25

#	Player	Price
1	Stan Musial w/Glove Jsy T2	35.00
2	Ozzie Smith/Jkt T2	
3	Enos Slaughter/Jsy T4	15.00
4	Frankie Frisch/Jkt T3	
5	Lou Brock/Jsy T2	15.00
6	Bob Gibson/Jsy T2	20.00
7	Ken Boyer/Jsy T3	25.00
8	Lee Smith/Jsy T4	8.00
9	Albert Pujols/Jsy T2	30.00
10	Stan Musial w/Bant Pants T2	35.00

Redbirds Signature Material
NM/M
Production 5-50
Prime: No Pricing
Production 1-5

#	Player	Price
8	Lee Smith/50	20.00

Signature Gold HoloFoil
NM/M
Tier 1 Production 1-50
Tier 2 Production 51-100
Tier 3 Production 101-250
Tier 4 Production 251-800
Tier 5 Production 801-1200
Tier 6 Production 1201-2000
Cards are not serial numbered.

#	Player	Price
1	Al Kaline T2	30.00
2	Alan Trammell T5	15.00
3	Andre Dawson T5	10.00
4	Barry Larkin T2/55	30.00
5	Bert Blyleven T4	10.00
6	Billy Williams T2/55	15.00
7	Bo Jackson T1/35	50.00
8	Bob Feller T6	10.00
9	Bobby Doerr T5	20.00
10	Brooks Robinson T2	30.00
11	Cal Ripken Jr. T3	120.00
12	Dale Murphy T3	

13	Darryl Strawberry T6	15.00
14	Dave Parker T3	10.00
15	Dave Stewart T4	15.00
16	David Cone T2	15.00
17	Dennis Eckersley T2	20.00
18	Don Larsen T4	20.00
19	Don Mattingly T1/45	75.00
20	Don Sutton T3	15.00
21	Duke Snider T2/55	15.00
22	Dwight Evans T3	15.00
23	Dwight Gooden T4	15.00
24	Earl Weaver T4	15.00
25	Fergie Jenkins T3	15.00
26	Frank Robinson T2	25.00
27	Fred Lynn T4	10.00
28	Gary Carter T2/55	15.00
29	Gaylord Perry T3	15.00
30	George Brett T1/35	75.00
31	George Foster T5	10.00
32	George Kell T6	15.00
33	Harmon Killebrew T2/55	30.00
34	Harold Baines T4	10.00
35	Harold Reynolds T4	10.00
36	Jack Morris T5	10.00
37	Jim Abbott T4	15.00
38	Jim Bunning T2	25.00
39	Jim Palmer T3	15.00
40	Jim Rice T2	20.00
41	Jim Leyritz T3	15.00
42	Joe Morgan T1/35	20.00
43	John Kruk T2	20.00
44	Johnny Bench T1/35	50.00
45	Johnny Podres T6	10.00
46	Jose Canseco T1/35	35.00
47	Juan Marichal T2	15.00
48	Keith Hernandez T5	15.00
49	Kent Hrbek T5	10.00
50	Kirby Puckett T1/35	85.00
51	Lee Smith T5	10.00
52	Lenny Dykstra T4	10.00
53	Luis Aparicio T3	15.00
54	Luis Tiant T3	15.00
55	Mark Grace T1/45	25.00
56	Marty Marion T4	15.00
57	Matt Williams T5	15.00
58	Maury Wills T4	15.00
59	Mike Schmidt T1/35	50.00
60	Minnie Minoso T5	15.00
61	Nolan Ryan T2/75	80.00
62	Ozzie Smith T2/55	40.00
63	Paul Molitor T2/55	30.00
64	Phil Rizzuto T2/55	30.00
65	Ralph Kiner T5	25.00
66	Randy Jones T4	10.00
67	Red Schoendienst T3	10.00
68	Rich "Goose" Gossage T5	10.00
69	Rob Dibble T4	30.00
70	Robin Roberts T2	30.00
71	Rod Carew T2/55	25.00
72	Rollie Fingers T3	15.00
73	Ron Guidry T3	25.00
74	Ron Santo T3	20.00
75	Ryne Sandberg T1/35	60.00
76	Stan Musial	20.00
77	Steve Carlton T2	15.00
78	Steve Garvey T3	15.00
79	Steve Stone T5	15.00
80	Terry Steinbach T3	10.00
81	Tom Seaver T1/35	40.00
82	Tommy John T6	10.00
83	Tony Gwynn T1/45	40.00
84	Tony Oliva T5	15.00
85	Whitey Ford T1/35	40.00
86	Will Clark T2/55	25.00
87	Willie Mays T2	150.00
88	Willie McCovey T1/45	35.00

Signature Platinum HoloFoil

NM/M

Production 1-50
Cards are not serial #'d.

	Andre Dawson	15.00
	Bert Blyleven	15.00
	Bob Feller	25.00
	Bobby Doerr	20.00
	Darryl Strawberry	15.00
	Dave Parker	15.00
	Don Larsen	30.00
	Dwight Gooden	20.00
	Fergie Jenkins	25.00
	Fred Lynn	15.00
	George Foster	15.00
	George Kell	25.00
	Harold Baines	20.00
	Harold Reynolds	15.00
	Jack Morris	15.00
	Jim Palmer	25.00
	Johnny Podres	20.00
	Keith Hernandez	15.00
	Kent Hrbek	20.00
	Lee Smith	15.00
	Lenny Dykstra	20.00
	Luis Tiant	20.00
	Marty Marion	25.00
	Matt Williams	20.00
	Maury Wills	20.00
	Minnie Minoso	25.00
	Ralph Kiner	40.00
	Randy Jones	15.00
	Red Schoendienst	25.00
	Rob Dibble	15.00
	Ron Santo	30.00
	Steve Stone	20.00
	Terry Steinbach	15.00
	Tommy John	15.00
	Tony Oliva	20.00

Souvenirs

NM/M

Common Player:		2.00
1	Jim Thorpe	4.00
2	Joe Carter	2.00
3	Will Clark	3.00
4	Cal Ripken Jr.	6.00
5	Dwight Evans	2.00
6	George Foster	2.00
7	Steve Garvey	2.00
8	Don Mattingly	4.00
9	Deion Sanders	3.00
10	Ron Santo	3.00
11	Alan Trammell	2.00
12	Robin Ventura	2.00
13	Matt Williams	3.00

Souvenirs Material Bat

NM/M

Common Player:		5.00
2	Joe Carter	5.00
3	Will Clark	8.00
5	Dwight Evans	5.00
6	George Foster	5.00
7	Steve Garvey	5.00
8	Don Mattingly	15.00
9	Deion Sanders	8.00
10	Ron Santo	8.00
11	Alan Trammell	8.00
12	Robin Ventura	5.00
13	Matt Williams	5.00

Souvenirs Material Combo

NM/M

Common Combo:		
2	Joe Carter/50	10.00
3	Will Clark	12.00
9	Deion Sanders	12.00
11	Alan Trammell	10.00

Souvenirs Material Jersey

NM/M

Common Player:		5.00
1	Jim Thorpe	120.00
3	Will Clark	10.00
4	Cal Ripken Jr.	25.00
9	Deion Sanders	10.00
11	Alan Trammell/48	10.00
12	Robin Ventura/48	5.00
13	Matt Williams	8.00

Souvenirs Signature

NM/M

Common Auto.:		15.00
3	Will Clark	25.00
5	Dwight Evans/25	20.00
7	Steve Garvey	15.00
10	Ron Santo	25.00
11	Alan Trammell	20.00

Souvenirs Signature Material Bat

NM/M

Common Player:		15.00
3	Will Clark	25.00
5	Dwight Evans	20.00
7	Steve Garvey	15.00
10	Ron Santo	25.00
11	Alan Trammell	20.00
12	Robin Ventura	15.00

Souvenirs Signature Material Combo

NM/M

Common Player:		20.00
3	Will Clark	30.00
7	Steve Garvey	20.00
11	Alan Trammell	20.00

Souvenirs Signature Material Jersey

NM/M

Common Player:		15.00
3	Will Clark	25.00
5	Dwight Evans	25.00
7	Steve Garvey	15.00
11	Alan Trammell	20.00

Sox Nation Material

NM/M

Common Player:		15.00
Prime:		No Pricing

Production 1-10

1	Ted Williams	75.00
2	Bobby Doerr	20.00
4	Roger Clemens/33	40.00
5	Carl Yastrzemski	25.00
6	Carl Yastrzemski	25.00
7	Jim Rice	15.00
9	Joe Cronin	15.00
10	Carlton Fisk	20.00
11	Fred Lynn	10.00
12	Wade Boggs	25.00
13	Wade Boggs/55	25.00

Sox Nation Signature Material

NM/M

Prime:		No Pricing

Production 1-5

2	Bobby Doerr/50	25.00
5	Jim Rice/50	25.00
7	Jim Rice/50	25.00
11	Fred Lynn/50	15.00

Yankee Clippings Material

NM/M

Common Player:		8.00
Prime:		No Pricing

Production 1-33

2	Babe Ruth	300.00
3	Billy Martin	40.00
4	Billy Martin	40.00
5	Bobby Murcer	15.00
6	Bucky Dent	10.00
7	Jim "Catfish" Hunter	15.00
8	Jim "Catfish" Hunter	15.00
9	Darryl Strawberry	8.00
10	Dave Righetti	8.00
11	Dave Winfield	15.00
12	Deion Sanders	15.00
13	Deion Sanders	15.00
14	Don Mattingly	35.00
15	Elston Howard	15.00
16	Graig Nettles	10.00
17	Roger Clemens/43	50.00
18	Luis Tiant	8.00
19	Mickey Rivers	15.00
20	Phil Rizzuto	15.00
21	Reggie Jackson	20.00
22	Rickey Henderson	15.00
23	Roger Maris	50.00
24	Roger Maris	50.00
25	Ron Guidry	15.00
26	Sparky Lyle	8.00
27	Phil Niekro	20.00
28	Tommy John	8.00
29	Whitey Ford	40.00
30	Yogi Berra	60.00

Yankee Clippings Signature Material

NM/M

Prime:		No Pricing

Production 1-5

9	Darryl Strawberry/25	30.00
18	Luis Tiant/50	30.00
20	Phil Rizzuto/25	60.00
25	Ron Guidry/25	50.00
28	Tommy John/25	30.00

2005 Donruss Leather & Lumber

NM/M

Complete Set (177):
Common Player (1-150): .25
Common Auto. (151-175): 8.00
Production 256
Card #176 doesn't exist.
Pack (5): 7.00
Box (18): 100.00

1	Adam Dunn	.50
2	Adrian Beltre	.40
3	Akinori Otsuka	.25
4	Al Leiter	.25
5	Albert Pujols	2.00
6	Alex Rodriguez	1.50
7	Alfonso Soriano	.75
8	Andy Pettitte	.40
9	Aramis Ramirez	.40
10	Aubrey Huff	.25
11	Austin Kearns	.25
12	Barry Larkin	.40
13	Barry Zito	.40
14	Bartolo Colon	.40
15	Bernie Williams	.40
16	Bobby Abreu	.40
17	Bobby Crosby	.40
18	Brad Penny	.25
19	Brian Giles	.25
20	C.C. Sabathia	.25
21	Carl Crawford	.40
22	Carl Pavano	.25
23	Carlos Beltran	.50
24	Carlos Delgado	.40
25	Carlos Lee	.40
26	Carlos Zambrano	.40
27	Casey Kotchman	.25
28	Chipper Jones	.75
29	Chone Figgins	.25
30	Craig Biggio	.40
31	Craig Monroe	.25
32	Cristian Guzman	.25
33	Curt Schilling	.75
34	Danny Haren	.25
35	Darin Erstad	.25
36	David Dellucci	.25
37	David Ortiz	.75
38	David Wells	.25
39	Derek Jeter	1.50
40	Dontrelle Willis	.40
41	Edgar Renteria	.40

42	Eric Gagne	.40
43	Frank Thomas	.50
44	Garret Anderson	.40
45	Gary Sheffield	.50
46	Geoff Jenkins	.25
47	Greg Maddux	1.50
48	Hideo Nomo	.40
49	Ichiro Suzuki	1.50
50	Ivan Rodriguez	.50
51	J.D. Drew	.25
52	Jake Peavy	.25
53	Jamie Moyer	.25
54	Jason Giambi	.25
55	Jason Kendall	.25
56	Jason Schmidt	.40
57	Jason Varitek	.40
58	Javy Lopez	.40
59	Jay Gibbons	.25
60	Jeff Bagwell	.50
61	Jeff Bagwell	.50
62	Jeremy Bonderman	.25
63	Jermaine Dye	.25
64	Jim Edmonds	.40
65	Jim Thome	.50
66	Joe Nathan	.25
67	Johan Santana	.50
68	John Olerud	.25
69	John Smoltz	.40
70	Johnny Damon	.75
71	Johnny Estrada	.25
72	Jose Reyes	.50
73	Jose Vidro	.25
74	Josh Beckett	.40
75	Juan Pierre	.25
76	Junior Spivey	.25
77	Justin Morneau	.40
78	Kazuhisa Ishii	.25
79	Kazuo Matsui	.25
80	Ken Griffey Jr.	1.50
81	Kerry Wood	.40
82	Kevin Brown	.25
83	Kevin Millwood	.25
84	Khalil Greene	.25
85	Lance Berkman	.25
86	Larry Walker	.40
87	Laynce Nix	.25
88	Lyle Overbay	.25
89	Magglio Ordonez	.25
90	Manny Ramirez	.50
91	Marcus Giles	.25
92	Mark Loretta	.25
93	Mark Mulder	.40
94	Mark Prior	.50
95	Mark Teixeira	.40
96	Melvin Mora	.25
97	Michael Young	.25
98	Miguel Tejada	.50
99	Mike Lieberthal	.25
100	Mike Lowell	.25
101	Mike Mussina	.40
102	Mike Piazza	1.00
103	Milton Bradley	.25
104	Moises Alou	.40
105	Morgan Ensberg	.25
106	Nomar Garciaparra	1.00
107	Omar Vizquel	.25
108	Paul Konerko	.40
109	Paul LoDuca	.25
110	Pedro Martinez	.75
111	Rafael Furcal	.25
112	Rafael Palmeiro	.40
113	Randy Johnson	.75
114	Richie Sexson	.40
115	Rocco Baldelli	.25
116	Roger Clemens	2.00
117	Roy Halladay	.40
118	Sammy Sosa	.75
119	Scott Podsednik	.40
120	Scott Rolen	.75
121	Sean Burroughs	.25
122	Sean Casey	.25
123	Shannon Stewart	.25
124	Shawn Green	.40
125	Steve Finley	.25
126	Tim Hudson	.40
127	Tim Salmon	.25
128	Todd Helton	.50
129	Tom Glavine	.40
130	Torii Hunter	.40
131	Travis Hafner	.25
132	Troy Glaus	.40
133	Troy Percival	.25
134	Vernon Wells	.40
135	Victor Martinez	.40
136	Vladimir Guerrero	.75
137	Andre Dawson	.40
138	Brooks Robinson	.75
139	Cal Ripken Jr.	3.00
140	Dale Murphy	.50
141	Darryl Strawberry	.40
142	George Brett	2.00
143	Harmon Killebrew	1.00
144	Jim Palmer	.50
145	Lou Brock	.75
146	Mike Schmidt	2.00
147	Nolan Ryan	2.00
148	Steve Carlton	.50
149	Tony Gwynn	1.00
150	Willie Mays	2.00
151	Agustin Montero RC	10.00
152	Carlos Ruiz RC	15.00
153	Casey Rogowski RC	8.00
154	Chris Resop RC	8.00
155	Chris Roberson RC	15.00
156	Colter Bean RC	15.00
157	Danny Rueckel RC	8.00
158	David Gassner RC	8.00
159	Geovany Soto RC	15.00

160	John Hattig Jr. RC	8.00
161	Justin Wechsler RC	10.00
162	Luke Scott RC	25.00
163	Mark McLemore RC	8.00
164	Miguel Negron RC	8.00
165	Mike Morse RC	20.00
166	Nate McLouth RC	8.00
167	Philip Humber RC	20.00
168	Randy Messenger RC	8.00
169	Raul Tablado RC	8.00
170	Russel Rohlicek RC	8.00
171	Ryan Speier RC	8.00
172	Scott Munter RC	10.00
173	Sean Thompson RC	10.00
174	Sean Tracey RC	10.00
175	Wladimir Balentien RC	15.00
176	Norihiro Nakamura/128 RC	75.00

Silver

Silver (1-150):	3-5X
Production 100 Sets	

Gold

Gold (1-150):	4-8X
Production 50 Sets	

Platinum

Platinum:	No Pricing
Production One Set	

Big Bang

NM/M

Common Player:	1.50
Production 2,000 Sets	
Gold:	1-2X
Production 100 Sets	
Silver:	1-2X
Production 200 Sets	
Platinum:	No Pricing
Production One Set	

1	Adam Dunn	2.00
2	Adrian Beltre	1.50
3	Albert Pujols	6.00
4	Alex Rodriguez	5.00
6	Chipper Jones	2.00
7	Dale Murphy	2.00
8	Darryl Strawberry	1.50
9	Dave Parker	1.50
10	David Ortiz	2.00
11	Duke Snider	2.00
12	Frank Robinson	1.50
13	Gary Sheffield	1.50
14	George Foster	1.50
15	Harmon Killebrew	3.00
16	Jim Edmonds	2.00
17	Jim Rice	1.50
18	Jim Thome	2.00
19	Ken Griffey Jr.	4.00
20	Manny Ramirez	2.00
21	Matt Williams	1.50
22	Mike Piazza	3.00
23	Mike Schmidt	5.00
24	Rafael Palmeiro	1.50
25	Sammy Sosa	3.00
25	Ted Williams	5.00

Big Bang Bat

NM/M

Production 50-250

3	Albert Pujols/250	15.00
8	Dave Parker/250	4.00
9	David Ortiz/250	8.00
13	Frank Robinson/100	8.00
13	George Foster/250	6.00
16	Jim Rice/50	6.00
18	Manny Ramirez/250	8.00
22	Mike Schmidt/100	15.00
23	Rafael Palmeiro/100	6.00
24	Sammy Sosa/250	8.00
25	Ted Williams/100	60.00

Big Bang Jersey

NM/M

Production 25-250	
Prime:	No Pricing

Production Five Sets

1	Adam Dunn/250	6.00
3	Albert Pujols/250	15.00
5	Chipper Jones/250	6.00
7	Dale Murphy/250	8.00
7	Darryl Strawberry/Pants/250	6.00
8	Dave Parker/250	4.00
9	David Ortiz/250	8.00
11	Duke Snider/250	12.00
12	Gary Sheffield/250	6.00
14	Harmon Killebrew/250	10.00
15	Jim Edmonds/250	6.00
16	Jim Rice/Pants/250	6.00
17	Jim Thome/250	8.00
19	Manny Ramirez/100	8.00
20	Matt Williams/250	6.00
21	Mike Piazza/250	10.00
23	Mike Schmidt/100	15.00
23	Rafael Palmeiro/Pants/250	6.00
24	Sammy Sosa/250	6.00
25	Ted Williams/Jkt/250	40.00

Big Bang Combos

NM/M

Production 25-100	
Prime:	No Pricing

Production Five Sets

1	Adam Dunn/Bat-Jsy/25	12.00
2	Adrian Beltre/Bat-Jsy/25	8.00

3	Albert Pujols/Bat-Jsy/100	25.00
7	Darryl Strawberry/Jsy-Pants/100	8.00
8	Dave Parker/Bat-Jsy/100	8.00
9	David Ortiz/Bat-Jsy/100	15.00
15	Jim Edmonds/Jsy-Jsy/100	10.00
16	Jim Rice/Jsy-Jsy/100	10.00
19	Manny Ramirez/Bat-Jsy/100	12.00
20	Matt Williams/Jsy-Jsy/100	
21	Mike Piazza/Bat-Jsy/50	15.00
22	Mike Schmidt/Bat-Jsy/100	20.00
23	Rafael Palmeiro/Bat-Jsy/100	10.00
24	Sammy Sosa/Bat-Jsy/100	12.00

Big Bang Signatures

No Pricing	
Production 1-10	

Game Ball Signatures

NM/M

Production 1-50

1	Ben Grieve/50	10.00
2	Eli Marrero/24	12.00
4	Jeff Fassero/24	25.00
5	Jose Guillen/47	25.00
7	Mark Grudzielanek/23	30.00
9	Paul Konerko/45	25.00

Great Gloves

NM/M

Common Player:	1.50
Production 2,000 Sets	
Gold:	2-3X
Production 50 Sets	
Silver:	1-2X
Production 100 Sets	
Platinum:	No Pricing
Production One Set	

1	Austin Kearns	1.50
2	Gary Carter	2.00
3	Ivan Rodriguez	2.00
4	Mark Grace	2.00
5	Mark Teixeira	2.00
6	Mike Schmidt	5.00
7	Omar Vizquel	1.50
8	Scott Rolen	3.00
9	Tony Gwynn	3.00
10	Willie Mays	5.00

Great Gloves Fielding Glv

NM/M

Production 25 Sets

1	Austin Kearns/25	10.00
2	Gary Carter/25	20.00
3	Ivan Rodriguez/25	15.00
4	Mark Grace/25	20.00
5	Mark Teixeira/25	15.00
6	Mike Schmidt/25	40.00
9	Tony Gwynn/25	20.00

Great Gloves Jersey

NM/M

Production 25-50	
Prime:	No Pricing

Production Five Sets

1	Austin Kearns/50	8.00
2	Gary Carter/50	8.00
3	Ivan Rodriguez/50	8.00
4	Mark Grace/50	10.00
5	Mark Teixeira/50	8.00
6	Mike Schmidt/50	20.00
7	Omar Vizquel/50	8.00
8	Scott Rolen/50	12.00
10	Willie Mays/25	40.00

Hitters Inc.

NM/M

Common Player:	1.50
Production 2,000 Sets	
Gold:	2-3X
Production 50 Sets	
Silver:	1-2X
Production 100 Sets	
Platinum:	No Pricing
Production One Set	

1	Albert Pujols	6.00
2	Alfonso Soriano	2.00
3	Cal Ripken Jr.	8.00
4	Don Mattingly	5.00
5	Dwight Evans	1.50
6	George Brett	5.00
7	Hank Blalock	1.50
8	Ichiro Suzuki	5.00
9	Ivan Rodriguez	2.00
10	Jack Wilson	1.50
11	Keith Hernandez	1.50
12	Larry Walker	1.50
13	Lou Brock	2.00
14	Lyle Overbay	1.50
15	Michael Young	2.00
16	Paul Molitor	2.00
17	Rod Carew	2.00
18	Sean Casey	1.50
19	Steve Garvey	2.00
20	Todd Helton	2.00
21	Tony Gwynn	3.00
22	Travis Hafner	1.50
23	Ted Williams	6.00
24	Wade Boggs	2.00
25	Willie Mays	5.00

Hitters Inc. Bat

NM/M

Production 25-100
1	Albert Pujols/100	15.00
2	Alfonso Soriano/50	15.00
3	Cal Ripken Jr./100	25.00
4	Don Mattingly/100	15.00
5	Dwight Evans/100	6.00
6	George Brett/100	15.00
7	Hank Blalock/50	6.00
9	Ivan Rodriguez/100	6.00
10	Jack Wilson/100	4.00
12	Larry Walker/100	6.00
13	Lou Brock/100	8.00
15	Michael Young/100	4.00
16	Paul Molitor/100	8.00
17	Rod Carew/100	8.00
18	Sean Casey/100	4.00
19	Steve Garvey/100	6.00
21	Tony Gwynn/100	10.00
23	Ted Williams/50	60.00
24	Wade Boggs/100	8.00
25	Willie Mays/25	40.00

Hitters Inc. Sign. Bat

NM/M

Production 5-25
5	Dwight Evans/25	20.00
7	Hank Blalock/25	25.00
10	Jack Wilson/25	15.00
13	Lou Brock/25	30.00
15	Michael Young/25	20.00
18	Sean Casey/25	15.00
19	Steve Garvey/25	30.00

Hitters Inc. Jersey

NM/M

Production 25-100
1	Albert Pujols/100	15.00
2	Alfonso Soriano/100	6.00
3	Cal Ripken Jr./100	25.00
4	Don Mattingly/100	15.00
5	Dwight Evans/100	6.00
7	Hank Blalock/100	4.00
9	Ivan Rodriguez/100	6.00
10	Jack Wilson/100	4.00
12	Larry Walker/100	6.00
13	Lou Brock/50	8.00
14	Lyle Overbay/100	4.00
16	Paul Molitor/100	8.00
17	Rod Carew/100	8.00
18	Sean Casey/100	4.00
19	Steve Garvey/100	6.00
20	Todd Helton/100	8.00
21	Tony Gwynn/100	10.00
22	Travis Hafner/100	6.00
23	Ted Williams/Jkt/100	40.00
24	Wade Boggs/100	8.00
25	Willie Mays/25	40.00

Hitters Inc. Sign. Jersey

NM/M

Production 5-25
5	Dwight Evans/25	20.00
7	Hank Blalock/25	25.00
10	Jack Wilson/25	15.00
13	Lou Brock/25	30.00
14	Lyle Overbay/25	15.00
18	Sean Casey/25	15.00
19	Steve Garvey/25	30.00
22	Travis Hafner/25	20.00

Hitters Inc. Signatures

No Pricing
Production 5-10

Leather Cuts

NM/M

Production 1-128
2	Andre Dawson/128	15.00
3	Bert Blyleven/128	15.00
4	Lee Smith/32	20.00
5	Billy Williams/64	15.00
6	Bob Feller/128	25.00
8	Joe Pepitone/128	20.00
9	Bobby Doerr/128	15.00
10	Juan Marichal/112	20.00
12	Dale Murphy/96	25.00
13	Darryl Strawberry/128	15.00
14	Johnny Podres/128	15.00
18	Duke Snider/128	25.00
20	Dwight Gooden/128	15.00
21	Fergie Jenkins/96	15.00
23	Fred Lynn/128	15.00
24	Justin Morneau/128	20.00
25	Gaylord Perry/128	15.00
27	George Foster/128	15.00
28	Harmon Killebrew/64	30.00
29	Jack Morris/128	15.00
30	Jim Palmer/128	15.00
31	Jim Rice/128	15.00
33	John Kruk/128	20.00
34	Randy Jones/128	15.00
35	Keith Hernandez/128	15.00
36	Lenny Dykstra/128	15.00
37	Lou Brock/64	35.00
38	Luis Aparicio/128	15.00
39	Lyle Overbay/128	10.00
40	Maury Wills/128	15.00
41	Earl Weaver/128	15.00
42	Miguel Cabrera/64	40.00
44	Monte Irvin/96	20.00
46	Red Schoendienst/128	15.00
48	Rich "Goose" Gossage/128	20.00
50	Minnie Minoso/128	20.00
51	Sean Casey/64	15.00

Leather Cuts Bat

NM/M

Production 6-128
1	Al Kaline/58	40.00
10	Cal Ripken Jr./60	125.00
13	Darryl Strawberry/96	15.00
19	Dwight Evans/128	25.00
20	Dwight Gooden/128	15.00
22	Frank Robinson/40	25.00
23	Fred Lynn/96	15.00
31	Jim Rice/32	25.00
36	Lenny Dykstra/128	15.00
37	Lou Brock/128	30.00
38	Luis Aparicio/128	15.00
39	Lyle Overbay/128	10.00
51	Sean Casey/32	15.00
55	Tommy John/128	15.00
57	Victor Martinez/128	15.00

Leather Cuts Jersey

NM/M

Production 1-128
2	Andre Dawson/128	20.00
3	Bert Blyleven/128	15.00
4	Lee Smith/96	15.00
9	Bobby Doerr/Pants/128	20.00
10	Juan Marichal/112	20.00
12	Dale Murphy/96	25.00
13	Darryl Strawberry/96	20.00
15	Dave Righetti/48	20.00
16	David Cone/120	15.00
19	Dwight Evans/44	30.00
20	Dwight Gooden/128	15.00
21	Fergie Jenkins/Pants/96	15.00
23	Fred Lynn/96	15.00
25	Gaylord Perry/128	15.00
28	Harmon Killebrew/32	40.00
29	Jack Morris/64	15.00
31	Jim Rice/Pants/128	20.00
33	John Kruk/128	20.00
35	Keith Hernandez/32	25.00
36	Lenny Dykstra/128	15.00
38	Luis Aparicio/128	15.00
39	Lyle Overbay/128	10.00
42	Miguel Cabrera/64	40.00
51	Sean Casey/32	15.00
55	Tommy John/128	15.00
57	Victor Martinez/128	15.00

Lumber Cuts

NM/M

Production 1-128
2	Andre Dawson/128	15.00
3	Bert Blyleven/128	15.00
4	Lee Smith/32	20.00
5	Billy Williams/64	15.00
6	Bob Feller/128	25.00
7	Joe Pepitone/128	20.00
8	Bobby Doerr/128	20.00
9	Juan Marichal/112	20.00
13	Dale Murphy/96	25.00
13	Darryl Strawberry/128	15.00
14	Johnny Podres/128	15.00
18	Duke Snider/128	25.00
20	Dwight Gooden/128	15.00
21	Fergie Jenkins/96	15.00
23	Fred Lynn/128	15.00
24	Justin Morneau/128	20.00
25	Gaylord Perry/128	15.00
27	George Foster/128	10.00
28	Harmon Killebrew/64	30.00
29	Jack Morris/128	15.00
30	Jim Palmer/128	15.00
31	Jim Rice/128	15.00
33	John Kruk/128	20.00
34	Randy Jones/128	15.00
35	Keith Hernandez/128	15.00
36	Lenny Dykstra/128	15.00
37	Lou Brock/64	35.00
38	Luis Aparicio/128	15.00
39	Lyle Overbay/128	10.00
40	Maury Wills/128	15.00
41	Earl Weaver/128	15.00
42	Miguel Cabrera/64	40.00
44	Monte Irvin/96	20.00
46	Red Schoendienst/128	15.00
48	Rich "Goose" Gossage/128	15.00
50	Minnie Minoso/128	20.00
51	Sean Casey/64	15.00

Lumber Cuts Bat

NM/M

Production 6-128
1	Al Kaline/58	40.00
10	Cal Ripken Jr./60	125.00
13	Darryl Strawberry/96	20.00
19	Dwight Evans/128	25.00
20	Dwight Gooden/128	15.00
22	Frank Robinson/40	25.00
23	Fred Lynn/96	15.00
31	Jim Rice/32	25.00
36	Lenny Dykstra/128	15.00
37	Lou Brock/128	30.00
38	Luis Aparicio/128	15.00

54	Steve Stone/128	15.00
55	Tommy John/128	15.00
57	Victor Martinez/128	15.00
61	Lee Smith/128	15.00

Leather Cuts Bat

NM/M

Production 6-128
1	Al Kaline/58	40.00
10	Cal Ripken Jr./60	125.00
13	Darryl Strawberry/96	15.00
19	Dwight Evans/128	25.00
20	Dwight Gooden/128	15.00
22	Frank Robinson/40	25.00
23	Fred Lynn/96	15.00
31	Jim Rice/32	25.00
36	Lenny Dykstra/128	15.00
37	Lou Brock/128	30.00
38	Luis Aparicio/128	15.00
39	Lyle Overbay/128	10.00
51	Sean Casey/32	15.00
55	Tommy John/128	15.00
57	Victor Martinez/128	15.00

Lumber Cuts Jersey

NM/M

Production 7-128
2	Andre Dawson/128	20.00
3	Bert Blyleven/128	15.00
4	Lee Smith/96	15.00
9	Bobby Doerr/Pants/128	20.00
10	Juan Marichal/112	20.00
12	Cal Ripken Jr./60	125.00
13	Dale Murphy/96	20.00
13	Darryl Strawberry/96	20.00
15	Dave Righetti/48	20.00
16	David Cone/120	15.00
19	Dwight Evans/44	30.00
20	Dwight Gooden/128	15.00
21	Fergie Jenkins/Pants/96	15.00
23	Fred Lynn/96	15.00
25	Gaylord Perry/128	15.00
28	Harmon Killebrew/32	40.00
29	Jack Morris/64	15.00
31	Jim Rice/Pants/128	20.00
33	John Kruk/128	20.00
35	Keith Hernandez/32	25.00
36	Lenny Dykstra/128	15.00
38	Luis Aparicio/128	15.00
39	Lyle Overbay/128	10.00
42	Miguel Cabrera/64	40.00
51	Sean Casey/32	15.00
55	Tommy John/128	15.00
57	Victor Martinez/128	15.00

Lumber/Leather

NM/M

Common Player: 1.50
Production 2,000 Sets
Gold: 2-3X
Production 50 Sets
Silver: 1-2X
Production 100 Sets
Platinum: No Pricing
Production One Set
1	Albert Pujols	6.00
2	Alex Rodriguez	5.00
3	Alfonso Soriano	2.00
4	Cal Ripken Jr.	8.00
5	Carlos Lee	2.00
6	Derek Jeter	8.00
7	Don Mattingly	5.00
8	Ichiro Suzuki	4.00
9	Ivan Rodriguez	2.00
10	Jack Wilson	1.50
11	Josh Beckett	1.50
12	Ken Griffey Jr.	4.00
13	Lance Berkman	1.50
14	Magglio Ordonez	1.50
15	Mark Grace	2.00
16	Mark Prior	2.00
17	Mark Teixeira	2.00
18	Mike Schmidt	4.00
19	Nolan Ryan	6.00
20	Nomar Garciaparra	3.00
21	Paul LoDuca	1.50
22	Rafael Palmeiro	2.00
23	Randy Johnson	2.00
24	Richie Sexson	1.50
25	Rickey Henderson	2.00
26	Roger Clemens	6.00
27	Ryan Klesko	1.50
28	Stan Musial	3.00
29	Steve Carlton	2.00
30	Tim Hudson	2.00
31	Tony Gwynn	1.50
32	Travis Hafner	1.50
33	Victor Martinez	1.50
34	Wade Boggs	2.00
35	Willie Mays	5.00

Lumber/Leather Barrel

No Pricing
Production One Set

L/L Barrel-Jersey

No Pricing
Production One Set

L/L Bat-Btg Glove

NM/M

Production 1-25
3	Alfonso Soriano/25	15.00
5	Carlos Lee/25	12.00
7	Don Mattingly/25	40.00
9	Ivan Rodriguez/25	15.00
13	Lance Berkman/25	15.00
18	Magglio Ordonez/25	15.00
19	Mike Schmidt/25	40.00
22	Paul LoDuca/25	15.00
24	Richie Sexson/25	15.00
25	Rickey Henderson/25	20.00
30	Ryan Klesko/25	15.00
31	Tony Gwynn/25	10.00

L/L Bat-Fld Glove

NM/M

Production 5-25

39	Lyle Overbay/128	10.00
51	Sean Casey/32	15.00
55	Tommy John/128	15.00
57	Victor Martinez/128	15.00

Lumber Cuts Jersey

NM/M

Production 1-128
2	Andre Dawson/128	20.00
3	Bert Blyleven/128	15.00
4	Lee Smith/96	15.00
9	Bobby Doerr/Pants/128	20.00
10	Cal Ripken Jr./60	125.00
12	Dale Murphy/96	20.00
13	Darryl Strawberry/96	20.00
15	Dave Righetti/48	20.00
16	David Cone/120	15.00
19	Dwight Evans/44	30.00
20	Dwight Gooden/128	15.00
21	Fergie Jenkins/Pants/96	15.00
23	Fred Lynn/96	15.00
42	Miguel Cabrera/64	40.00
51	Sean Casey/32	15.00
55	Tommy John/128	15.00
57	Victor Martinez/128	15.00

Lumber/Leather Bat-Spikes

NM/M

Production 1-25
1	Albert Pujols/25	40.00
5	Carlos Lee/25	12.00
9	Ivan Rodriguez/25	15.00
11	Josh Beckett/25	12.00
13	Lance Berkman/25	15.00
18	Magglio Ordonez/25	10.00
19	Mark Prior/25	15.00
22	Paul LoDuca/25	15.00
24	Rafael Palmeiro/25	15.00
25	Richie Sexson/25	15.00
27	Rickey Henderson/25	20.00
30	Ryan Klesko/25	15.00
31	Tim Hudson/25	15.00
31	Tony Gwynn/25	20.00

Materials Barrel

No Pricing
Production 1-4

Materials Bat

NM/M

Production 25-250
1	Adam Dunn/250	6.00
2	Adrian Beltre/100	4.00
5	Albert Pujols/150	15.00
7	Alfonso Soriano/100	4.00
8	Andy Pettitte/100	6.00
9	Aramis Ramirez/100	4.00
10	Aubrey Huff/250	4.00
11	Austin Kearns/100	4.00
12	Barry Larkin/200	5.00
13	Barry Zito/25	8.00
15	Bernie Williams/250	4.00
16	Brad Penny/75	4.00
19	Brian Giles/50	4.00
23	Carlos Beltran/100	8.00
24	Carlos Delgado/250	4.00
25	Carlos Lee/150	4.00
27	Casey Kotchman/250	4.00
29	Chone Figgins/250	4.00
30	Craig Biggio/250	6.00
31	Craig Monroe/250	4.00
33	Curt Schilling/100	8.00
35	Darin Erstad/250	4.00
36	David Ortiz/250	8.00
40	Dontrelle Willis/250	6.00
43	Frank Thomas/50	8.00
44	Garret Anderson/250	4.00
46	Geoff Jenkins/50	4.00
47	Greg Maddux/250	10.00
51	J.D. Drew/250	4.00
57	Jason Varitek/100	6.00
57	Javy Lopez/250	4.00
58	Jay Gibbons/250	4.00
59	Jeff Bagwell/250	6.00
61	Jeff Kent/250	4.00
68	John Olerud/250	4.00
72	Jose Reyes/250	6.00
73	Jose Vidro/250	4.00
75	Juan Pierre/250	4.00
81	Kerry Wood/100	6.00
82	Kevin Brown/100	4.00
85	Lance Berkman/250	4.00
87	Laynce Nix/250	4.00
89	Magglio Ordonez/250	4.00
90	Manny Ramirez/100	8.00
94	Mark Prior/100	8.00
97	Michael Young/250	6.00
106	Moises Alou/250	4.00
109	Nomar Garciaparra/100	8.00
109	Paul LoDuca/250	4.00
112	Rafael Furcal/250	4.00
114	Richie Sexson/250	6.00
115	Rocco Baldelli/250	4.00
118	Sammy Sosa/100	4.00
122	Sean Casey/100	4.00
123	Shannon Stewart/50	4.00
124	Shawn Green/250	4.00
126	Tim Hudson/250	6.00
128	Tim Salmon/250	4.00
129	Tom Glavine/250	4.00
130	Torii Hunter/250	4.00
132	Troy Glaus/250	4.00
138	Brooks Robinson/100	8.00
139	Cal Ripken Jr./50	30.00
145	Lou Brock/100	8.00
146	Mike Schmidt/50	15.00
147	Nolan Ryan/25	25.00
149	Tony Gwynn/100	10.00
150	Willie Mays/40	40.00

Materials Jersey

NM/M

Production 20-250
1	Adam Dunn/150	6.00
5	Albert Pujols/100	15.00
7	Alfonso Soriano/150	6.00
8	Andy Pettitte/150	4.00
9	Aramis Ramirez/250	4.00

5	Carlos Lee/25	12.00
9	Ivan Rodriguez/25	15.00
10	Jack Wilson/25	10.00
13	Lance Berkman/25	15.00
14	Mark Grace/25	20.00
16	Mark Prior/25	20.00
18	Mike Schmidt/25	40.00
21	Paul LoDuca/25	15.00
24	Richie Sexson/25	15.00
27	Ryan Klesko/25	10.00
30	Steve Carlton/25	15.00
31	Tony Gwynn/25	20.00

Materials Barrel

No Pricing
Production 1-4

Materials Bat

NM/M

Production 25-250
1	Adam Dunn/250	6.00
2	Adrian Beltre/100	4.00
5	Albert Pujols/100	15.00
7	Alfonso Soriano/100	4.00
8	Andy Pettitte/100	6.00
9	Aramis Ramirez/100	4.00
10	Aubrey Huff/250	4.00
12	Barry Larkin/25	6.00
13	Barry Zito/150	4.00
15	Bernie Williams/150	4.00
16	Bobby Abreu/250	4.00
17	Bobby Crosby/150	4.00
20	C.C. Sabathia/250	4.00
21	Carl Crawford/200	4.00
26	Carlos Zambrano/250	6.00
27	Casey Kotchman/140	4.00
28	Chipper Jones/250	8.00
29	Chone Figgins/200	4.00
30	Craig Biggio/200	6.00
33	Curt Schilling/250	4.00
35	Darin Erstad/150	4.00
36	David Dellucci/250	4.00
37	David Ortiz/250	8.00
40	Dontrelle Willis/250	4.00
43	Frank Thomas/Pants/150	8.00
44	Garret Anderson/250	4.00
45	Gary Sheffield/250	6.00
46	Geoff Jenkins/250	4.00
47	Greg Maddux/25	15.00
48	Hideo Nomo/250	6.00
50	Ivan Rodriguez/150	6.00
53	Jamie Moyer/50	6.00
54	Jason Giambi/250	4.00
57	Jason Varitek/100	10.00
57	Javy Lopez/150	4.00
58	Jay Gibbons/75	4.00
60	Jeff Bagwell/250	6.00
62	Jeremy Bonderman/150	4.00
64	Jim Edmonds/250	6.00
65	Jim Thome/150	6.00
67	Johan Santana/250	4.00
69	John Smoltz/250	6.00
70	Johnny Damon/250	6.00
71	Johnny Estrada/250	4.00
72	Jose Reyes/250	4.00
73	Jose Vidro/150	4.00
74	Josh Beckett/150	4.00
76	Junior Spivey/250	4.00
77	Justin Morneau/250	6.00
78	Kazuhisa Ishii/250	4.00
79	Kazuo Matsui/250	4.00
81	Kerry Wood/Pants/150	6.00
85	Lance Berkman/250	4.00
86	Larry Walker/250	4.00
87	Laynce Nix/250	4.00
88	Lyle Overbay/250	4.00
90	Manny Ramirez/250	8.00
93	Marcus Giles/150	4.00
94	Mark Prior/250	6.00
95	Mark Teixeira/250	6.00
96	Melvin Mora/100	4.00
97	Michael Young/25	8.00
98	Miguel Tejada/250	6.00
100	Mike Lowell/250	4.00
101	Mike Mussina/250	6.00
102	Mike Piazza/250	8.00
105	Morgan Ensberg/150	4.00
108	Paul Konerko/150	4.00
111	Rafael Furcal/150	4.00
112	Rafael Palmeiro/150	6.00
114	Rocco Baldelli/250	4.00
116	Roger Clemens/150	10.00
117	Roy Halladay/150	4.00
119	Scott Podsednik/250	4.00
120	Scott Rolen/250	6.00
121	Sean Burroughs/150	4.00
122	Sean Casey/250	4.00
123	Shannon Stewart/150	4.00
129	Todd Helton/250	6.00
130	Torii Hunter/250	4.00
131	Travis Hafner/250	6.00
134	Vernon Wells/250	4.00
135	Victor Martinez/150	4.00
136	Vladimir Guerrero/250	8.00
137	Andre Dawson/250	8.00
139	Cal Ripken Jr./250	20.00
140	Dale Murphy/250	6.00
141	Darryl Strawberry/Pants/150	4.00
143	Harmon Killebrew/100	8.00
145	Lou Brock/Jkt/250	8.00
146	Mike Schmidt/50	15.00
147	Nolan Ryan/150	15.00
148	Steve Carlton/25	10.00
149	Tony Gwynn/250	8.00
150	Willie Mays/Pants/25	40.00

Naturals

NM/M

Common Player: 1.50
Production 2,000 Sets
Gold: 2-3X
Production 50 Sets
Silver: 1-2X
Production 100 Sets
Platinum: No Pricing
Production One Set
1	Andruw Jones	2.00
2	Bernie Williams	1.50
3	Brooks Robinson	3.00
4	Cal Ripken Jr.	8.00
5	Casey Kotchman	1.50
6	Craig Biggio	2.00
7	Craig Wilson	1.50
8	David Ortiz	3.00
9	Eddie Murray	2.00
10	Javy Lopez	1.50
11	Jeff Bagwell	2.00
13	Lance Berkman	1.50
14	Magglio Ordonez	1.50
15	Michael Young	1.50
16	Rafael Palmeiro	2.00
17	Reggie Jackson	3.00
19	Rickey Henderson	2.00

Materials Jersey

NM/M

Production 20-250
1	Adam Dunn/150	6.00
5	Albert Pujols/100	15.00
7	Alfonso Soriano/150	6.00
13	Magglio Ordonez/100	4.00
15	Rafael Palmeiro	2.00
16	Reggie Jackson	2.00
17	Rickey Henderson	2.00

Naturals Barrel

No Pricing
Production 1-3

Naturals Bat

NM/M

Production 25-100
1	Andruw Jones/100	6.00
2	Bernie Williams/100	4.00
3	Brooks Robinson/100	8.00
4	Cal Ripken Jr./100	25.00
5	Casey Kotchman/100	4.00
6	Craig Biggio/100	6.00
7	Craig Wilson/100	4.00
8	David Ortiz/100	10.00
9	Eddie Murray/100	8.00
10	Javy Lopez/100	4.00
11	Jeff Bagwell/100	6.00
12	Lance Berkman/100	4.00
13	Magglio Ordonez/100	4.00
14	Michael Young/100	4.00
15	Rafael Palmeiro/100	6.00
16	Reggie Jackson/100	8.00
17	Rickey Henderson/100	8.00
18	Rocco Baldelli/100	4.00
19	Sammy Sosa/100	4.00
20	Shawn Green/100	4.00
21	Ted Williams/50	50.00
22	Tony Gwynn/100	10.00
23	Wade Boggs/100	8.00
24	Will Clark/100	8.00
25	Willie Mays/25	40.00

Naturals Jersey

NM/M

Production 25-100
Prime: No Pricing
Production Five Sets
1	Andruw Jones/100	6.00
2	Bernie Williams/100	6.00
4	Cal Ripken Jr./100	25.00
5	Casey Kotchman/100	4.00
6	Craig Biggio/100	6.00
7	Craig Wilson/100	4.00
8	David Ortiz/100	10.00
9	Eddie Murray/100	8.00
10	Javy Lopez/100	4.00
11	Jeff Bagwell/100	6.00
12	Lance Berkman/100	4.00
13	Magglio Ordonez/100	4.00
14	Michael Young/50	4.00
15	Rafael Palmeiro/100	6.00
16	Reggie Jackson/100	8.00
17	Rickey Henderson/Jkt/100	8.00
18	Rocco Baldelli/100	4.00
19	Sammy Sosa/100	4.00
20	Shawn Green/100	4.00
21	Ted Williams/Jkt/100	40.00
22	Tony Gwynn/100	10.00
23	Wade Boggs/100	4.00
24	Will Clark/50	8.00
25	Willie Mays/25	40.00

Naturals Combos

NM/M

Production 25-100
Prime: No Pricing
Production Five Sets
1	Andruw Jones/Bat-Jsy/100	8.00
2	Bernie Williams/Bat-Jsy/100	6.00
3	Brooks Robinson/Bat-Jsy/25	15.00
4	Cal Ripken Jr./Bat-Jsy/100	30.00
5	Casey Kotchman/Bat-Jsy/100	6.00
6	Craig Biggio/Bat-Jsy/100	6.00
7	Craig Wilson/Bat-Jsy/100	6.00
8	David Ortiz/Bat-Jsy/100	12.00
9	Eddie Murray/Bat-Jsy/100	10.00
10	Javy Lopez/Bat-Jsy/100	8.00
11	Jeff Bagwell/Bat-Jsy/100	8.00
12	Lance Berkman/Bat-Jsy/100	6.00
13	Magglio Ordonez/Bat-Jsy/25	8.00
14	Michael Young/Bat-Jsy/100	6.00
15	Rafael Palmeiro/Bat-Jsy/100	8.00
16	Reggie Jackson/Bat-Jsy/50	12.00
17	Rickey Henderson/Bat-Jkt/100	10.00
18	Rocco Baldelli/Bat-Jsy/100	6.00
19	Sammy Sosa/Bat-Jsy/100	6.00
20	Shawn Green/Bat-Jsy/100	6.00
21	Ted Williams/Bat-Jkt/50	60.00
22	Tony Gwynn/Bat-Jsy/100	
23	Wade Boggs/Bat-Jsy/100	

#	Player	Price
24	Will Clark/Bat-Jsy/50	10.00
25	Willie Mays/Bat-Jsy/25	50.00

Rivals

NM/M

Common Duo: 1.50
Production 2,000 Sets
Gold: 2-3X
Production 50 Sets
Silver: 1-2X
Production 100 Sets
Platinum: No Pricing
Production One Set

#	Player	Price
1	Ichiro Suzuki, Hideki Matsui	5.00
2	Mark Mulder, Vladimir Guerrero	2.00
3	Tim Hudson, Mark Teixeira	2.00
4	Roger Clemens, Albert Pujols	6.00
5	Greg Maddux, Jeff Bagwell	4.00
6	Randy Johnson, Adrian Beltre	3.00
7	Kerry Wood, Larry Walker	2.00
8	Mike Mussina, Manny Ramirez	2.00
9	C.C. Sabathia, Torii Hunter	1.50
10	Josh Beckett, Chipper Jones	2.00
11	Derek Jeter, Miguel Tejada	6.00
12	Alex Rodriguez, Hank Blalock	5.00
13	Carlos Beltran, Sammy Sosa	2.00
14	Mark Prior, Jim Thome	2.00
15	Miguel Cabrera, Andruw Jones	2.00
16	Johan Santana, Magglio Ordonez	2.00
17	Josh Beckett, Craig Biggio	2.00
18	Adam Dunn, Shawn Green	2.00
19	J. Morris, Rod Carew	2.00
20	Jim Palmer, Paul Molitor	2.00
21	Mike Schmidt, George Brett	5.00
22	Cal Ripken Jr., Don Mattingly	8.00
23	Bob Gibson, Ernie Banks	4.00
24	Eddie Murray, Bert Blyleven	3.00
25	Warren Spahn, Willie Mays	6.00

Rivals Bat

NM/M

Production 50-100

#	Player	Price
3	Tim Hudson, Mark Teixeira/50	10.00
4	Roger Clemens, Albert Pujols/25	25.00
5	Greg Maddux, Jeff Bagwell/100	15.00
7	Kerry Wood, Larry Walker/100	15.00
10	Josh Beckett, Chipper Jones/50	15.00
13	Carlos Beltran, Sammy Sosa/100	15.00
14	Mark Prior, Jim Thome/50	15.00
18	Adam Dunn, Shawn Green/100	10.00
21	Mike Schmidt, George Brett/100	20.00
22	Cal Ripken Jr., Don Mattingly/100	30.00

Rivals Jersey

NM/M

Production 50-250
Prime: No Pricing
Production Five Sets

#	Player	Price
2	Mark Mulder, Vladimir Guerrero/100	10.00
3	Tim Hudson, Mark Teixeira/250	10.00
4	Roger Clemens, Albert Pujols/100	20.00
5	Greg Maddux, Jeff Bagwell/250	10.00
7	Kerry Wood, Larry Walker/250	8.00
9	C.C. Sabathia, Torii Hunter/150	6.00
10	Josh Beckett Pants, Chipper Jones/150	6.00
13	Carlos Beltran, Sammy Sosa/250	10.00
14	Mark Prior, Jim Thome/250	6.00
15	Miguel Cabrera, Andruw Jones/250	6.00
16	Johan Santana, Magglio Ordonez/100	10.00
18	Adam Dunn, Shawn Green/100	10.00
19	J. Morris, Rod Carew/250	10.00
20	Mike Schmidt, George Brett/100	15.00
22	Cal Ripken Jr., Don Mattingly/100	40.00

#	Player	Price
23	Bob Gibson, Ernie Banks/50	15.00
24	Eddie Murray, Bert Blyleven	10.00
25	Warren Spahn/Pants, Willie Mays/Pants/50	60.00

Signatures Gold

NM/M

Production 5-100
Platinum: No Pricing
Production One Set

#	Player	Price
2	Adam Dunn/25	35.00
3	Adrian Beltre/25	25.00
9	Akinori Otsuka/30	30.00
10	Aubrey Huff/50	15.00
11	Austin Kearns/25	15.00
17	Bobby Crosby/100	15.00
18	Brad Penny/100	10.00
25	Carlos Lee/100	15.00
26	Carlos Zambrano/100	25.00
27	Casey Kotchman/100	15.00
29	Chone Figgins/100	15.00
31	Craig Monroe/100	15.00
34	Danny Haren/100	10.00
36	David Dellucci/100	15.00
52	Jake Peavy/100	25.00
53	Jamie Moyer/100	15.00
59	Jay Gibbons/100	15.00
62	Jeremy Bonderman/100	10.00
63	Jermaine Dye/100	12.00
66	Joe Nathan/100	15.00
71	Johnny Estrada/50	10.00
87	Laynce Nix/100	10.00
88	Lyle Overbay/100	10.00
92	Mark Loretta/100	15.00
99	Mike Lieberthal/100	10.00
103	Milton Bradley/100	12.00
105	Morgan Ensberg/100	12.00
108	Paul Konerko/25	20.00
111	Rafael Furcal/50	15.00
117	Roy Halladay/25	25.00
119	Scott Podsednik/50	15.00
121	Sean Burroughs/50	8.00
122	Sean Casey/25	15.00
123	Shannon Stewart/100	8.00
125	Steve Finley/50	15.00
126	Tim Hudson/25	30.00
127	Tim Salmon/100	15.00
130	Torii Hunter/25	20.00
131	Travis Hafner/100	12.00
133	Troy Percival/50	15.00
134	Vernon Wells/35	15.00
135	Victor Martinez/100	15.00
137	Andre Dawson/100	15.00
138	Brooks Robinson/25	30.00
140	Dale Murphy/50	25.00
141	Darryl Strawberry/100	15.00
143	Harmon Killebrew/50	30.00
144	Jim Palmer/25	20.00
145	Lou Brock/25	30.00
146	Mike Schmidt/25	60.00
148	Steve Carlton/25	25.00
149	Tony Gwynn/25	50.00

Signatures Lumber Cuts

NM/M

Production 256 Sets

#	Player	Price
151	Agustin Montero	8.00
152	Carlos Ruiz	8.00
153	Casey Rogowski	10.00
154	Chris Resop	15.00
155	Chris Roberson	10.00
156	Colter Bean	10.00
157	Danny Rueckel	8.00
158	David Gassner	8.00
159	Geovany Soto	15.00
160	John Hattig Jr.	8.00
161	Justin Wechsler	8.00
162	Luke Scott	15.00
163	Mark McLemore	8.00
164	Miguel Negron	8.00
165	Mike Morse	40.00
166	Nate McLouth/254	15.00
167	Philip Humber	20.00
168	Randy Messenger	8.00
169	Raul Tablado	8.00
170	Russel Rohlicek	8.00
171	Ryan Speier	8.00
172	Scott Munter	12.00
173	Sean Thompson	10.00
174	Sean Tracey	10.00
175	Wladimir Balentien	15.00
177	Norihiro Nakamura/128	75.00

2005 Donruss Cal Ripken 10th Anniversary

This card marking the 10th anniversary of Ripken's 2,131st consecutive game was issued in the September 4 issue of the Baltimore Sun newspaper.

NM/M

Cal Ripken Jr. 4.00

2005 Donruss Studio

NM/M

Complete Set (300):
Common Player: .25
Pack (6): 4.00
Box (24): 90.00

#	Player	Price
1	Casey Kotchman	.25
2	Chone Figgins	.25
3	Dallas McPherson	.25
4	Darin Erstad	.25
5	Ervin Santana	.25
6	Garret Anderson	.40
7	Norihiro Nakamura RC	2.00
8	John Lackey	.25
9	Orlando Cabrera	.25
10	Robb Quinlan	.25
11	Steve Finley	.25
12	Tim Salmon	.25
13	Vladimir Guerrero	.75
14	Brandon Webb	.25
15	Craig Counsell	.25
16	Javier Vazquez	.25
17	Luis Gonzalez	.25
18	Tony Pena RC	.40
19	Russ Ortiz	.25
20	Scott Hairston	.25
21	Shawn Green	.25
22	Jose Cruz Jr.	.25
23	Troy Glaus	.40
24	Adam LaRoche	.25
25	Andruw Jones	.50
26	Chipper Jones	.75
27	Danny Kolb	.25
28	John Smoltz	.40
29	Johnny Estrada	.25
30	Marcus Giles	.25
31	Nick Green	.25
32	Rafael Furcal	.25
33	Tim Hudson	.40
34	Brian Roberts	.25
35	Javy Lopez	.25
36	Jay Gibbons	.25
37	Melvin Mora	.25
38	Miguel Tejada	.40
39	Rafael Palmeiro	.50
40	Rodrigo Lopez	.25
41	Sidney Ponson	.25
42	Abe Alvarez	.25
43	Bill Mueller	.25
44	Curt Schilling	.75
45	David Ortiz	.75
46	David Wells	.25
47	Edgar Renteria	.25
48	Jason Varitek	.50
49	Jay Payton	.25
50	Johnny Damon	.75
51	Juan Cedeno	.25
52	Manny Ramirez	.75
53	Matt Clement	.25
54	Trot Nixon	.25
55	Wade Miller	.25
56	Aramis Ramirez	.40
57	Carlos Zambrano	.40
58	Corey Patterson	.25
59	Derek Lee	.50
60	Greg Maddux	1.50
61	Kerry Wood	.40
62	Mark Prior	.75
63	Nomar Garciaparra	.75
64	Sammy Sosa	1.00
65	Todd Walker	.25
66	A.J. Pierzynski	.25
67	Aaron Rowand	.25
68	Frank Thomas	.50
69	Freddy Garcia	.25
70	Jermaine Dye	.25
71	Mark Buehrle	.40
72	Paul Konerko	.40
73	Tadahito Iguchi RC	1.00
74	Pedro Lopez RC	.25
75	Scott Podsednik	.25
76	Shingo Takatsu	.25
77	Adam Dunn	.50
78	Austin Kearns	.25
79	Barry Larkin	.50
80	Bubba Nelson	.25
81	Danny Graves	.25
82	Eric Milton	.25
83	Ken Griffey Jr.	1.50
84	Ryan Wagner	.25
85	Sean Casey	.25
86	C.C. Sabathia	.40
87	Cliff Lee	.25
88	Fausto Carmona	.25
89	Grady Sizemore	.40
90	Jake Westbrook	.25
91	Jody Gerut	.25
92	Juan Gonzalez	.40
93	Kazuhito Tadano	.25
94	Travis Hafner	.40
95	Victor Martinez	.25
96	Charles Johnson	.25
97	Clint Barmes	.25
98	Cory Sullivan	.25
99	Jeff Baker	.25
100	Jeff Francis	.25
101	Jeff Salazar	.25
102	Jeromy Burnitz	.25

#	Player	Price
103	Joe Kennedy	.25
104	Matt Holliday	.50
105	Preston Wilson	.25
106	Todd Helton	.50
107	Ubaldo Jimenez RC	3.00
108	Brandon Inge	.25
109	Carlos Guillen	.25
110	Carlos Pena	.25
111	Craig Monroe	.25
112	Ivan Rodriguez	.50
113	Jeremy Bonderman	.25
114	Justin Verlander RC	2.00
115	Magglio Ordonez	.25
116	Troy Percival	.25
117	Vance Wilson	.25
118	A.J. Burnett	.25
119	Al Leiter	.25
120	Dontrelle Willis	.40
121	Josh Beckett	.40
122	Juan Pierre	.25
123	Miguel Cabrera	.75
124	Mike Lowell	.25
125	Paul LoDuca	.25
126	Randy Messenger RC	.40
127	Yorman Bazardo RC	.40
128	Andy Pettitte	.40
129	Brad Lidge	.25
130	Chris Burke	.25
131	Craig Biggio	.40
132	Fernando Nieve	.25
133	Jason Lane	.25
134	Jeff Bagwell	.50
135	Lance Berkman	.25
136	Morgan Ensberg	.25
137	Roger Clemens	2.00
138	Roy Oswalt	.25
139	Ambiorix Burgos RC	.25
140	David DeJesus	.25
141	Jeremy Affeldt	.25
142	Jose Lima	.25
143	Ken Harvey	.25
144	Mike MacDougal	.25
145	Mike Sweeney	.25
146	Terrence Long	.25
147	Zack Greinke	.25
148	Brad Penny	.25
149	Derek Lowe	.25
150	Dioner Navarro	.25
151	Edwin Jackson	.25
152	Eric Gagne	.25
153	Hee Seop Choi	.25
154	Hideo Nomo	.50
155	J.D. Drew	.40
156	Jeff Kent	.25
157	Jeff Weaver	.25
158	Milton Bradley	.25
159	Yhency Brazoban	.25
160	Ben Sheets	.25
161	Bill Hall	.25
162	Carlos Lee	.25
163	Gustavo Chacin	.25
164	Geoff Jenkins	.25
165	Jose Capellan	.25
166	Lyle Overbay	.25
167	Rickie Weeks	.40
168	Jacque Jones	.25
169	Joe Mauer	.50
170	Joe Nathan	.25
171	Johan Santana	.50
172	Justin Morneau	.40
173	Lew Ford	.25
174	Michael Cuddyer	.25
175	Shannon Stewart	.25
176	Torii Hunter	.25
177	Brad Radke	.25
178	Ambiorix Concepcion RC	.40
179	Carlos Beltran	.25
180	David Wright	.75
181	Jose Reyes	.50
182	Kazuo Matsui	.25
183	Kris Benson	.25
184	Mike Piazza	1.00
185	Pedro Martinez	.50
186	Philip Humber RC	1.00
187	Tom Glavine	.40
188	Alex Rodriguez	1.50
189	Carl Pavano	.25
190	Derek Jeter	2.00
191	Yuniesky Betancourt RC	1.00
192	Hideki Matsui	1.50
193	Jorge Posada	.40
194	Kevin Brown	.25
195	Mariano Rivera	.40
196	Mike Mussina	.40
197	Randy Johnson	.75
198	Scott Proctor	.25
199	Tom Gordon	.25
200	Barry Zito	.25
201	Bobby Crosby	.40
202	Danny Haren	.25
203	Eric Chavez	.40
204	Keiichi Yabu RC	.25
205	Jason Kendall	.25
206	Joe Blanton	.25
207	Mark Kotsay	.25
208	Nick Swisher	.40
209	Octavio Dotel	.25
210	Rich Harden	.40
211	Billy Wagner	.25
212	Bobby Abreu	.40
213	Chase Utley	.50
214	Gavin Floyd	.25
215	Jim Thome	.50
216	Jimmy Rollins	.50
217	Jon Lieber	.25
218	Kenny Lofton	.25
219	Mike Lieberthal	.25
220	Pat Burrell	.25

#	Player	Price
221	Randy Wolf	.25
222	Craig Wilson	.25
223	Jack Wilson	.25
224	Jason Bay	.25
225	John Van Benschoten	.25
226	Jose Castillo	.25
227	Kip Wells	.25
228	Matt Lawton	.25
229	Akinori Otsuka	.25
230	Brian Giles	.25
231	Freddy Guzman	.25
232	Jake Peavy	.40
233	Khalil Greene	.40
234	Mark Loretta	.25
235	Sean Burroughs	.25
236	Trevor Hoffman	.25
237	Woody Williams	.25
238	Armando Benitez	.25
239	Edgardo Alfonzo	.25
240	Erick Threets RC	.40
241	Jason Schmidt	.25
242	Marquis Grissom	.25
243	Merkin Valdez	.25
244	Michael Tucker	.25
245	Moises Alou	.25
246	Omar Vizquel	.25
247	Adrian Beltre	.25
248	Bret Boone	.25
249	Bucky Jacobsen	.25
250	Clint Nageotte	.25
251	Ichiro Suzuki	1.50
252	J.J. Putz	.25
253	Jeremy Reed	.25
254	Miguel Olivo	.25
255	Mike Morse RC	2.00
256	Richie Sexson	.40
257	Wladimir Balentien RC	1.00
258	Albert Pujols	2.00
259	Jason Isringhausen	.25
260	Jeff Suppan	.25
261	Jim Edmonds	.40
262	Larry Walker	.25
263	Mark Mulder	.40
264	Rick Ankiel	.25
265	Scott Rolen	.75
266	Yadier Molina	.25
267	Aubrey Huff	.25
268	B.J. Upton	.25
269	Carl Crawford	.25
270	Chris Seddon RC	.40
271	Delmon Young	.25
272	Dewon Brazelton	.25
273	Jeff Niemann RC	1.00
274	Rocco Baldelli	.25
275	Scott Kazmir	.25
276	Adrian Gonzalez	.25
277	Alfonso Soriano	.75
278	Francisco Cordero	.25
279	Hank Blalock	.40
280	Kameron Loe	.25
281	Kenny Rogers	.25
282	Laynce Nix	.25
283	Mark Teixeira	.40
284	Michael Young	.25
285	Corey Koskie	.25
286	David Bush	.25
287	Frank Catalanotto	.25
288	Gabe Gross	.25
289	Raul Tablado RC	.40
290	Roy Halladay	.40
291	Shea Hillenbrand	.25
292	Vernon Wells	.25
293	Chad Cordero	.25
294	Cristian Guzman	.25
295	Jose Guillen	.25
296	Jose Vidro	.25
297	Josh Karp	.25
298	Livan Hernandez	.25
299	Nick Johnson	.25
300	Vinny Castilla	.25

Proofs Silver

Stars: 3-5X
Production 100 Sets

Proofs Gold

Stars: 8-12X
Production 25 Sets

Proofs Platinum

No Pricing
Production 10 Sets

Autographs

No Pricing

Diamond Cuts

NM/M

Common Player: 1.00

Production 1,250 Sets

Die-Cut: 1-1.5X
Production 250 Sets
Die-Cut: 1.5-3X
Production 75 Sets

#	Player	Price
1	Roger Clemens	4.00
2	Manny Ramirez	1.50
3	Francisco Rodriguez	1.00
4	Brian Roberts	1.00
5	Javy Lopez	1.00
6	Vernon Wells	1.00
7	Johan Santana	1.50
8	Torii Hunter	1.00
9	Mike Mussina	1.50
10	Sammy Sosa	2.50
11	Ryan Wagner	1.00
12	Jack Wilson	1.00
13	Ichiro Suzuki	3.00
14	Greg Maddux	3.00
15	Albert Pujols	4.00
16	Jeremy Bonderman	1.00
17	Johnny Estrada	1.00
18	Mark Buehrle	1.00
19	Jorge Posada	1.00
20	Carl Crawford	1.00
21	Paul Konerko	1.00
22	Victor Martinez	1.00
23	Jose Vidro	1.00
24	Jim Thome	1.50
25	Andruw Jones	1.50

Diamond Cuts Bat

NM/M

Production 5-300

#	Player	Price
1	Roger Clemens/50	15.00
2	Manny Ramirez/200	8.00
5	Javy Lopez/300	4.00
8	Torii Hunter/300	4.00
10	Sammy Sosa/25	15.00
12	Jack Wilson/300	4.00
14	Greg Maddux/225	10.00
15	Albert Pujols/300	15.00
21	Paul Konerko/50	6.00
22	Victor Martinez/300	4.00
23	Jose Vidro/300	4.00
25	Andruw Jones/300	6.00

Diamond Cuts Jersey

NM/M

Production 15-250
Prime: No Pricing
Production 5-10

#	Player	Price
1	Roger Clemens/125	10.00
2	Manny Ramirez/250	4.00
3	Francisco Rodriguez/250	4.00
4	Brian Roberts/250	6.00
5	Javy Lopez/250	4.00
6	Vernon Wells/250	4.00
7	Johan Santana/175	8.00
8	Torii Hunter/250	4.00
9	Mike Mussina/250	6.00
10	Sammy Sosa/250	8.00
11	Ryan Wagner/250	4.00
14	Greg Maddux/250	8.00
15	Albert Pujols/250	20.00
16	Jeremy Bonderman/250	4.00
17	Johnny Estrada/250	4.00
18	Mark Buehrle/250	4.00
19	Jorge Posada/250	4.00
20	Carl Crawford/250	4.00
21	Paul Konerko/250	4.00
22	Victor Martinez/250	4.00
23	Jose Vidro/175	4.00
24	Jim Thome/250	6.00
25	Andruw Jones/250	6.00

Diamond Cuts Combo

NM/M

Production 5-50
Prime: No Pricing
Production 10 Sets

#	Player	Price
1	Roger Clemens/ Bat-Jsy/50	20.00
2	Manny Ramirez/ Bat-Jsy/50	12.00
3	Freddy Rodriguez/ Jsy-Jsy/50	10.00
5	Javy Lopez/Bat-Jsy/50	8.00
6	Vernon Wells/Jsy-Jsy/50	8.00
8	Torii Hunter/Jsy-Jsy/50	8.00
10	Sammy Sosa/ Jsy-Jsy/50	12.00
11	Ryan Wagner/Jsy-Jsy/50	8.00
12	Jack Wilson/Bat-Jsy/50	8.00
14	Greg Maddux/ Bat-Jsy/50	15.00
15	Albert Pujols/Bat-Jsy/50	30.00
17	Johnny Estrada/ Fld Glve-Jsy/50	8.00
21	Paul Konerko/ Jsy-Jsy/50	10.00
22	Victor Martinez/ Bat-Jsy/50	10.00
23	Jose Vidro/Bat-Jsy/50	8.00
24	Jim Thome/Jsy-Jsy/45	12.00
25	Andruw Jones/ Bat-Jsy/50	10.00

Diamond Cuts Signature Combo

NM/M

Production 25-50
Prime: No Pricing
Production 10 Sets

#	Player	Price
3	Freddy Rodriguez/ Jsy-Jsy/25	40.00

6 Vernon Wells/ Jsy-Jsy/25 25.00
8 Torii Hunter/Bat-Jsy/50 20.00
11 Ryan Wagner/ Jsy-Jsy/50 15.00
12 Jack Wilson/Bat-Jsy/50 20.00
16 Jeremy Bonderman/ Jsy-Jsy/50 20.00
17 Johnny Estrada/ Fld Glv-Jsy/50 15.00
21 Paul Konerko/ Jsy-Jsy/25 25.00

Heritage
NM/M
Common Player: 1.00
Production 1,000 Sets
Die-Cut: 1-1.5X
Production 200 Sets
Die-cut Gold: 2-3X
Production 50 Sets
1 Rickey Henderson 1.50
2 Jeff Bagwell 1.50
3 Steve Garvey 1.00
4 Albert Pujols 5.00
5 Don Mattingly 4.00
6 Frank Thomas 1.50
7 Tony Gwynn 2.00
8 Gary Sheffield 1.50
9 Dale Murphy 1.50
10 Kerry Wood 1.50
11 Cal Ripken Jr. 6.00
12 Miguel Cabrera 2.00
13 Dwight Gooden 1.00
14 Barry Zito 1.00
15 Darryl Strawberry 1.00

Heritage Bat
NM/M
Production 150 Sets
1 Rickey Henderson 8.00
2 Jeff Bagwell 6.00
3 Steve Garvey 4.00
4 Albert Pujols 15.00
5 Don Mattingly 10.00
6 Frank Thomas 6.00
7 Tony Gwynn 8.00
8 Gary Sheffield 6.00
9 Dale Murphy 6.00
11 Cal Ripken Jr. 20.00
12 Miguel Cabrera 6.00
13 Dwight Gooden 4.00
15 Darryl Strawberry 4.00

Heritage Jersey
NM/M
Production 50-250
Prime: No Pricing
Production 10 Sets
1 Rickey Henderson/250 8.00
2 Jeff Bagwell/250 6.00
3 Steve Garvey/250 4.00
4 Albert Pujols/250 15.00
5 Don Mattingly/250 12.00
6 Frank Thomas/250 6.00
7 Tony Gwynn/250 8.00
8 Dale Murphy/250 6.00
10 Kerry Wood/250 6.00
11 Cal Ripken Jr./250 20.00
12 Miguel Cabrera/250 8.00
13 Dwight Gooden/250 4.00
14 Barry Zito/250 4.00
15 Darryl Strawberry/250 4.00

Heritage Combo
NM/M
Production 10-50
Prime: No Pricing
Production 10 Sets
1 Rickey Henderson/ Bat-Jsy/50 15.00
2 Jeff Bagwell/Bat-Jsy/50 10.00
3 Steve Garvey/ Bat-Jsy/50 10.00
4 Albert Pujols/Bat-Jsy/50 25.00
5 Don Mattingly/ Bat-Jsy/50 20.00
6 Frank Thomas/ Bat-Jsy/50 10.00
7 Tony Gwynn/Bat-Jsy/50 15.00
8 Gary Sheffield/ Bat-Jsy/50 10.00
9 Dale Murphy/Bat-Jsy/50 12.00
10 Kerry Wood/ Jsy-Pants/25
11 Cal Ripken Jr./Bat-Jsy/50 4.00
12 Miguel Cabrera/ Bat-Jsy/50 12.00
13 Dwight Gooden/ Bat-Jsy/50 10.00
15 Darryl Strawberry/ Bat-Jsy/50 10.00

Heritage Signature Combo
NM/M
Production 10-50
Prime: No Pricing
Production 5-10
3 Steve Garvey/ Bat-Jsy/25 25.00
5 Don Mattingly/ Bat-Jsy/25 75.00
9 Dale Murphy/Bat-Jsy/25 40.00
11 Cal Ripken Jr./ Bat-Jsy/25 160.00
12 Miguel Cabrera/ Bat-Jsy/25 50.00
13 Dwight Gooden/ Bat-Jsy/25 25.00
15 Darryl Strawberry/ Bat-Jsy/25 25.00

Heroes of the Hall
NM/M
Common Player: 2.00
Production 350 Sets
Die-Cut: 1-1.5X
Production 75 Sets
Die-Cut Gold: 2-3X
Production 25 Sets
1 Luis Aparicio 2.00
2 Dennis Eckersley 2.00
3 Brooks Robinson 4.00
4 Carlton Fisk 4.00
5 Tom Seaver 4.00
6 Paul Molitor 4.00
7 Rod Carew 3.00
8 George Brett 6.00
9 Nolan Ryan 8.00
10 Mike Schmidt 6.00
11 Willie Mays 6.00
12 Gary Carter 2.00
13 Lou Brock 2.00
14 Steve Carlton 2.00
15 Harmon Killebrew 4.00

Heroes of the Hall Bat
NM/M
Production 100-150
1 Luis Aparicio/150 4.00
3 Brooks Robinson/150 8.00
4 Carlton Fisk/150 6.00
6 Paul Molitor/150 8.00
8 George Brett/150 12.00
10 Mike Schmidt/125 15.00
11 Willie Mays/100 35.00
12 Gary Carter/125 6.00
13 Lou Brock/150 6.00
15 Harmon Killebrew/150 8.00

Heroes of the Hall Jersey
NM/M
Production 50-150
Prime: No Pricing
Production 5-10
1 Luis Aparicio/150 4.00
2 Dennis Eckersley/150 6.00
3 Brooks Robinson/50 10.00
4 Carlton Fisk/50 6.00
5 Tom Seaver/150 8.00
6 Paul Molitor/150 8.00
7 Rod Carew/150 6.00
8 George Brett/150 12.00
9 Nolan Ryan/100 20.00
10 Mike Schmidt/100 15.00
11 Willie Mays/50 40.00
12 Gary Carter/150 6.00
14 Steve Carlton/150 4.00
15 Harmon Killebrew/150 8.00

Heroes of the Hall Combo
NM/M
Production 25-50
Prime: No Pricing
Production 5-10
1 Luis Aparicio/ Bat-Jsy/50 10.00
2 Dennis Eckersley/ Jsy-Pants/50 10.00
3 Brooks Robinson/ Bat-Jsy/50 15.00
4 Carlton Fisk/Bat-Jsy/50 12.00
5 Tom Seaver/ Jsy-Pants/50 15.00
6 Paul Molitor/Bat-Jsy/50 10.00
7 Rod Carew/Bat-Jsy/50 12.00
8 George Brett/Bat-Jsy/50 20.00
9 Nolan Ryan/Bat-Jsy/25 25.00
10 Mike Schmidt/ Bat-Jsy/50 20.00
11 Willie Mays/Bat-Jsy/25 60.00
12 Gary Carter/ Jsy-Pants/50 10.00
13 Lou Brock/Bat-Jkt/50 15.00
15 Harmon Killebrew/ Bat-Jsy/50 15.00

Heroes of the Hall Signature Combo
Production 5-50
Prime: No Pricing
Production 5-10
1 Luis Aparicio/ Bat-Jsy/50 20.00
2 Dennis Eckersley/ Jsy-Pants/25 30.00
4 Carlton Fisk/Bat-Jsy/25 40.00
6 Paul Molitor/Bat-Jsy/25 35.00
14 Steve Carlton/ Bat-Jsy/25 35.00
15 Harmon Killebrew/ Bat-Jsy/25 40.00

Masterstrokes
NM/M
Common Player: 1.50
Production 750 Sets
Die-Cut: 1-1.5X
Production 150 Sets
Die-Cut Gold: 1.5-2X
Production 50 Sets
1 Hideki Matsui 6.00
2 David Ortiz 3.00
3 Aramis Ramirez 2.00
4 Lance Berkman 1.50
5 Ichiro Suzuki 6.00
6 Mike Piazza 4.00
7 Ivan Rodriguez 2.00
8 Hideo Nomo 2.00
9 Jeff Bagwell 2.00
10 Travis Hafner 1.50
11 Casey Kotchman 1.50
12 Jim Edmonds 2.00
13 Michael Young 1.50
14 Lyle Overbay 1.50
15 Eric Chavez 2.00
16 Jason Bay 1.50
17 Hank Blalock 2.00
18 Frank Thomas 2.00
19 Craig Biggio 2.00
20 Miguel Cabrera 3.00
21 Vladimir Guerrero 2.00
22 Sammy Sosa 4.00
23 Chipper Jones 3.00
24 Rafael Palmeiro 2.00
25 Adam Dunn 2.00

Masterstrokes Bat
NM/M
Production 25-250
1 Hideki Matsui/25 30.00
2 David Ortiz/250 8.00
3 Aramis Ramirez/35 8.00
4 Lance Berkman/250 4.00
6 Mike Piazza/100 10.00
7 Ivan Rodriguez/250 6.00
9 Jeff Bagwell/250 6.00
10 Travis Hafner/250 4.00
11 Casey Kotchman/250 4.00
13 Michael Young/250 4.00
14 Lyle Overbay/250 4.00
16 Jason Bay/250 4.00
17 Hank Blalock/50 6.00
18 Frank Thomas/250 6.00
19 Craig Biggio/250 6.00
20 Miguel Cabrera/250 8.00
21 Vladimir Guerrero/250 8.00
22 Sammy Sosa/200 8.00
23 Chipper Jones/250 6.00
25 Adam Dunn/250 6.00

Masterstrokes Jersey
NM/M
Production 40-250
Prime: No Pricing
Production 10 Sets
1 Hideki Matsui/250 20.00
2 David Ortiz/250 8.00
3 Aramis Ramirez/250 6.00
4 Lance Berkman/250 4.00
6 Mike Piazza/250 8.00
7 Ivan Rodriguez/250 6.00
8 Hideo Nomo/250 6.00
9 Jeff Bagwell/250 6.00
10 Travis Hafner/200 6.00
11 Casey Kotchman/250 4.00
12 Jim Edmonds/250 6.00
13 Michael Young/150 6.00
14 Lyle Overbay/250 4.00
15 Eric Chavez/250 6.00
16 Jason Bay/150 4.00
17 Hank Blalock/250 4.00
18 Frank Thomas/250 6.00
19 Craig Biggio/250 6.00
20 Miguel Cabrera/250 8.00
21 Vladimir Guerrero/50 10.00
22 Sammy Sosa/250 8.00
23 Chipper Jones/225 6.00
24 Rafael Palmeiro/40 8.00
25 Adam Dunn/250 6.00

Masterstrokes Combo
NM/M
Production 15-50
Prime: No Pricing
Production 10 Sets
2 David Ortiz/Bat-Jsy/50 15.00
3 Aramis Ramirez/ Jsy-Jsy/50 10.00
4 Lance Berkman/ Bat-Jsy/50 8.00
6 Mike Piazza/Jsy-Jsy/50 15.00
7 Ivan Rodriguez/ Bat-Jsy/50 10.00
8 Hideo Nomo/Jsy-Jsy/50 12.00
9 Jeff Bagwell/Bat-Jsy/50 8.00
10 Travis Hafner/Bat-Jsy/50 8.00
11 Casey Kotchman/ Bat-Jsy/50 8.00
12 Jim Edmonds/ Jsy-Jsy/50 10.00
13 Michael Young/ Bat-Jsy/50 10.00
14 Lyle Overbay/Bat-Jsy/50 10.00
15 Eric Chavez/Bat-Jsy/50 10.00
16 Jason Bay/Bat-Jsy/50 8.00
17 Hank Blalock/ Jsy-Jsy/50 10.00
18 Frank Thomas/ Bat-Jsy/50 12.00
19 Craig Biggio/Bat-Jsy/50 10.00
20 Miguel Cabrera/ Bat-Jsy/50 15.00
21 Vladimir Guerrero/ Bat-Jsy/50 15.00
22 Sammy Sosa/ Bat-Jsy/50 15.00
23 Chipper Jones/ Bat-Jsy/50 12.00
24 Rafael Palmeiro/ Bat-Pants/50 12.00
25 Adam Dunn/Bat-Jsy/50 10.00

Masterstrokes Signature Combo
NM/M
Production 5-50
Prime: No Pricing
Production 5-10
10 Travis Hafner/ Bat-Jsy/50 25.00
11 Casey Kotchman/ Bat-Jsy/50 20.00
14 Lyle Overbay/ Bat-Jsy/50 12.00
15 Eric Chavez/Bat-Jsy/25 25.00
16 Jason Bay/Bat-Jsy/50 25.00
17 Hank Blalock/ Jsy-Jsy/25 30.00
20 Miguel Cabrera/ Bat-Jsy/25 50.00

Portraits Zenith White
NM/M
Common Player: 2.00
Production 70 Sets
Parallel #'d 40-60: .75-1X
Parallel #'d 20-35: .75-1.5X
No pricing 15 or less.
1 Ozzie Smith 6.00
2 Derek Jeter 8.00
3 Eric Chavez 2.00
4 Duke Snider 4.00
5 Albert Pujols 6.00
7 Ivan Rodriguez 3.00
8 Cal Ripken Jr. 15.00
9 Hank Blalock 2.00
11 Chipper Jones 3.00
12 Gary Sheffield 2.00
13 Alfonso Soriano 2.00
14 Carl Crawford 2.00
15 Lou Brock 2.00
16 Jim Edmonds 3.00
17 Bo Jackson 4.00
18 Todd Helton 3.00
19 Javy Lopez 2.00
20 Tony Gwynn 5.00
21 Mark Mulder 2.00
22 Sammy Sosa 4.00
23 Roger Clemens 6.00
24 Don Mattingly 8.00
25 Willie Mays 8.00
26 Andruw Jones 3.00
27 Steve Garvey 2.00
28 Scott Rolen 3.00
29 George Brett 8.00
30 Rod Carew 4.00
31 Ken Griffey Jr. 6.00
32 Mike Piazza 3.00
33 Steve Carlton 3.00
34 Larry Walker 2.00
35 Kerry Wood 2.00
36 Frank Thomas 3.00
37 Lance Berkman 2.00
38 Nomar Garciaparra 4.00
39 Curt Schilling 3.00
40 Carl Yastrzemski 6.00
41 Mark Grace 3.00
42 Tom Seaver 4.00
43 Mariano Rivera 3.00
44 Carlos Beltran 3.00
45 Reggie Jackson 4.00
46 Pedro Martinez 4.00
47 Richie Sexson 2.00
48 Tom Glavine 2.00
49 Torii Hunter 2.00
50 Ron Guidry 2.00
51 Michael Young 2.00
52 Ichiro Suzuki 6.00
53 C.C. Sabathia 2.00
54 Johnny Bench 4.00
55 Mark Teixeira 3.00
56 Hideki Matsui 6.00
57 Mike Mussina 3.00
58 Johan Santana 3.00
59 Fergie Jenkins 2.00
60 Hideo Nomo 2.00
61 Nolan Ryan 10.00
62 Whitey Ford 4.00
63 Jim Thome 3.00
64 Gary Carter 3.00
65 Randy Johnson 4.00
66 Vladimir Guerrero 3.00
67 Harmon Killebrew 3.00
68 Tim Hudson 3.00
69 Josh Beckett 2.00
70 Eddie Murray 4.00
70 Greg Maddux 5.00
71 J.D. Drew 2.00
72 Bob Feller 4.00
73 Adrian Beltre 2.00
74 Wade Boggs 4.00
75 Barry Zito 2.00
76 David Ortiz 3.00
77 Mike Schmidt 8.00
78 Miguel Cabrera 4.00
79 Carlos Delgado 2.00
80 Andre Dawson 2.00
81 Garret Anderson 2.00
82 Rickey Henderson 3.00
83 Shawn Green 2.00
84 Dale Murphy 3.00
85 Alex Rodriguez 6.00
86 Mark Prior 3.00
87 Paul Molitor 4.00
88 Jeff Bagwell 3.00
89 Eric Gagne 2.00
90 Troy Glaus 2.00
91 Robin Yount 4.00
92 Miguel Tejada 3.00
93 Kirk Gibson 2.00
94 Manny Ramirez 3.00
95 Rafael Palmeiro 3.00
96 Maury Wills 2.00
97 Craig Biggio 2.00
98 Jim Palmer 3.00
99 Adam Dunn 3.00
100 Carlton Fisk 8.00

Private Signings Silver
NM/M
Common Autograph: 8.00
Production 100 Sets
1 Casey Kotchman 15.00
2 Chone Figgins 8.00
5 Ervin Santana 8.00
9 Orlando Cabrera 12.00
18 Tim Salmon 12.00
19 Tony Pena 8.00
23 Russ Ortiz 8.00
27 Adam LaRoche 10.00
31 Danny Kolb 8.00
36 Nick Green 8.00
49 Jay Payton 8.00
51 Juan Cedeno 8.00
55 Wade Miller 8.00
57 Carlos Zambrano 20.00
70 Todd Walker 10.00
80 Jermaine Dye 12.00
81 Danny Graves 8.00
84 Ryan Wagner 8.00
87 Cliff Lee 15.00
88 Fausto Carmona 8.00
91 Jody Gerut 8.00
94 Travis Hafner 12.00
98 Cory Sullivan 8.00
101 Jeff Salazar 8.00
103 Joe Kennedy 8.00
108 Brandon Inge 8.00
111 Craig Monroe 8.00
113 Jeremy Bonderman 12.00
117 Vance Wilson 8.00
127 Yorman Bazardo 8.00
127 Yorman Bazardo 8.00
133 Jason Lane 8.00
136 Morgan Ensberg 12.00
141 Jeremy Affeldt 8.00
143 Ken Harvey 8.00
150 Dioner Navarro 8.00
151 Edwin Jackson 8.00
158 Milton Bradley 10.00
159 Yhency Brazoban 8.00
161 Bill Hall 8.00
162 Carlos Lee 12.00
166 Lyle Overbay 8.00
170 Joe Nathan 10.00
173 Lew Ford 8.00
191 Yuniesky Betancourt 25.00
198 Scott Proctor 8.00
201 Bobby Crosby 10.00
202 Danny Haren 8.00
209 Octavio Dotel 8.00
210 Rich Harden 12.00
219 Mike Lieberthal 12.00
221 Randy Wolf 8.00
222 Craig Wilson 8.00
223 Jack Wilson 8.00
224 Jason Bay 10.00
226 Jose Castillo 8.00
231 Freddy Guzman 8.00
232 Jake Peavy 25.00
234 Mark Loretta 10.00
250 Clint Nageotte 8.00
252 J.J. Putz 8.00
260 Jeff Suppan 10.00
276 Adrian Gonzalez 8.00
278 Francisco Cordero 8.00
280 Kameron Loe 8.00
282 Laynce Nix 8.00
291 Shea Hillenbrand 10.00
293 Chad Cordero 10.00
295 Jose Guillen 10.00
297 Josh Karp 8.00
298 Livan Hernandez 12.00

Private Signings Gold
NM/M
Common Autograph: 8.00
Production 50 Sets
1 Casey Kotchman 20.00
2 Chone Figgins 10.00
5 Ervin Santana 10.00
6 Garret Anderson 15.00
9 Orlando Cabrera 15.00
10 Robb Quinlan 8.00
11 Steve Finley 15.00
12 Tim Salmon 15.00
14 Brandon Webb 10.00
17 Tony Pena 10.00
19 Russ Ortiz 10.00
24 Adam LaRoche 12.00
27 Danny Kolb 8.00
29 Johnny Estrada 10.00
31 Nick Green 8.00
32 Rafael Furcal 15.00
34 Brian Roberts 20.00
36 Jay Gibbons 10.00
46 Rodrigo Lopez 10.00
47 Edgar Renteria 25.00
49 Jay Payton 10.00
51 Juan Cedeno 10.00
53 Matt Clement 30.00
54 Trot Nixon 20.00
55 Wade Miller 10.00
57 Carlos Zambrano 25.00
59 Derek Lee 40.00
65 Todd Walker 12.00
70 Jermaine Dye 15.00
71 Mark Buehrle 25.00
72 Paul Konerko 15.00
76 Shingo Takatsu 20.00
80 Austin Kearns 10.00
81 Danny Graves 8.00
84 Ryan Wagner 8.00
87 Cliff Lee 15.00
88 Fausto Carmona 8.00
91 Jody Gerut 8.00
93 Kazuhito Tadano 15.00
94 Travis Hafner 15.00
98 Cory Sullivan 8.00
101 Jeff Salazar 8.00
103 Joe Kennedy 8.00
108 Brandon Inge 10.00
111 Craig Monroe 8.00
113 Jeremy Bonderman 15.00
116 Troy Percival 8.00
117 Vance Wilson 8.00
123 Miguel Cabrera 35.00
127 Yorman Bazardo 8.00
133 Jason Lane 8.00
136 Morgan Ensberg 15.00
141 Jeremy Affeldt 8.00
143 Ken Harvey 8.00
148 Brad Penny 10.00
150 Dioner Navarro 15.00
151 Edwin Jackson 8.00
158 Milton Bradley 12.00
159 Yhency Brazoban 8.00
161 Bill Hall 10.00
162 Carlos Lee 15.00
166 Lyle Overbay 8.00
168 Jacque Jones 8.00
170 Joe Nathan 12.00
173 Lew Ford 10.00
175 Shannon Stewart 8.00
191 Yuniesky Betancourt 30.00
198 Scott Proctor 8.00
199 Tom Gordon 12.00
201 Bobby Crosby 20.00
202 Danny Haren 10.00
209 Octavio Dotel 10.00
210 Rich Harden 15.00
219 Mike Lieberthal 15.00
221 Randy Wolf 8.00
222 Craig Wilson 10.00
223 Jack Wilson 8.00
224 Jason Bay 15.00
226 Jose Castillo 10.00
229 Akinori Otsuka 20.00
231 Freddy Guzman 8.00
232 Jake Peavy 30.00
234 Mark Loretta 12.00
235 Sean Burroughs 8.00
243 Merkin Valdez 8.00
246 Omar Vizquel 8.00
249 Bucky Jacobsen 10.00
250 Clint Nageotte 15.00
252 J.J. Putz 15.00
254 Miguel Olivo 8.00
260 Jeff Suppan 12.00
266 Yadier Molina 12.00
267 Aubrey Huff 12.00
268 B.J. Upton 20.00
269 Carl Crawford 20.00
271 Delmon Young 25.00
272 Dewon Brazelton 10.00
276 Adrian Gonzalez 10.00
278 Francisco Cordero 10.00
280 Kameron Loe 10.00
282 Laynce Nix 10.00
284 Michael Young 15.00
291 Shea Hillenbrand 12.00
293 Chad Cordero 12.00
295 Jose Guillen 12.00
297 Josh Karp 8.00
298 Livan Hernandez 15.00
299 Nick Johnson 15.00

Spirit of the Game
NM/M
Common Player: 1.50
Production 600 Sets
Die-Cut: 1-1.5X
Production 125 Sets
Die-Cut Gold: 2-4X
Production 50 Sets
1 Mark Prior 3.00
2 Sean Casey 1.50
3 Ichiro Suzuki 5.00

#	Player	NM/M
4	Andruw Jones	2.00
5	Francisco Cordero	1.50
6	Ben Sheets	2.00
7	Rocco Baldelli	1.50
8	Rafael Furcal	1.50
9	Angel Berroa	1.50
10	Roy Oswalt	1.50
11	Jose Reyes	1.50
12	Shannon Stewart	1.50
13	Greg Maddux	5.00
14	Alfonso Soriano	3.00
15	Curt Schilling	3.00
16	Jody Gerut	1.50
17	Brandon Webb	1.50
18	Josh Beckett	2.00
19	Laynce Nix	1.50
20	Scott Rolen	1.50

Spirit of the Game Bat

NM/M

Production 75-300

#	Player	NM/M
1	Mark Prior/300	6.00
4	Andruw Jones/300	4.00
6	Ben Sheets/300	4.00
7	Rocco Baldelli/300	4.00
8	Rafael Furcal/300	4.00
9	Angel Berroa/300	4.00
11	Jose Reyes/300	4.00
12	Shannon Stewart/75	4.00
13	Greg Maddux/300	8.00
14	Alfonso Soriano/225	6.00
16	Jody Gerut/300	4.00
17	Brandon Webb/300	4.00
20	Laynce Nix/300	4.00

Spirit of the Game Jersey

NM/M

Production 125-250
Prime: No Pricing
Production 10 Sets

#	Player	NM/M
1	Mark Prior/250	6.00
2	Sean Casey/250	4.00
4	Andruw Jones/250	6.00
5	Francisco Cordero/250	4.00
6	Ben Sheets/250	4.00
7	Rocco Baldelli/250	4.00
8	Rafael Furcal/250	4.00
10	Roy Oswalt/250	4.00
11	Jose Reyes/250	4.00
12	Shannon Stewart/250	4.00
13	Greg Maddux/250	8.00
14	Alfonso Soriano/250	6.00
15	Curt Schilling/250	4.00
16	Jody Gerut/125	4.00
18	Josh Beckett/250	4.00
19	Laynce Nix/250	4.00
20	Scott Rolen/250	4.00

Spirit of the Game Combo

NM/M

Production 50 Sets
Prime: No Pricing
Production 10 Sets

#	Player	NM/M
1	Mark Prior/Bat-Jsy	12.00
2	Sean Casey/Jsy-Jsy	4.00
4	Andruw Jones/Bat-Jsy	8.00
6	Ben Sheets/Bat-Jsy	8.00
7	Rocco Baldelli/Bat-Jsy	8.00
8	Rafael Furcal/Bat-Jsy	6.00
10	Roy Oswalt/Bat-Jsy	8.00
11	Jose Reyes/Bat-Jsy	8.00
12	Shannon Stewart/Jsy-Jsy	8.00
13	Greg Maddux/Bat-Jsy	15.00
14	Alfonso Soriano/Jsy-Jsy	12.00
15	Curt Schilling/Bat-Jsy	12.00
16	Jody Gerut/Bat-Jsy	6.00
19	Laynce Nix/Bat-Jsy	6.00
20	Scott Rolen/Jsy-Jsy	12.00

Spirit of the Game Signature Combo

NM/M

Production 10-25
Prime: No Pricing
Production 5-10

#	Player	NM/M
	Sean Casey/Jsy-Jsy/25	20.00
	Rafael Furcal/Bat-Jsy/25	25.00
2	Shannon Stewart/Jsy/25	20.00
6	Jody Gerut/Bat-Jsy/25	15.00
9	Laynce Nix/Bat-Jsy/25	15.00

Stars

NM/M

Common Player: 1.00
Inserted 1:6
Gold: 1-2X
Production 500 Sets
Platinum: 2-4X
Production 50 Sets

Player	NM/M
Carlos Beltran	1.50
Sean Casey	1.00
Ichiro Suzuki	3.00
Vladimir Guerrero	1.50
Tim Hudson	1.50
Alex Rodriguez	4.00
Miguel Tejada	1.50
Curt Schilling	1.50
Roger Clemens	4.00
Ben Sheets	1.50
Todd Helton	1.50
Mark Mulder	1.00
Scott Podsednik	1.00
Victor Martinez	1.00
Mark Prior	1.00

#	Player	Price
16	Ivan Rodriguez	1.50
17	Dontrelle Willis	1.00
18	Andy Pettitte	1.00
19	Khalil Greene	1.50
20	Jeff Kent	1.00
21	Paul Konerko	1.00
22	Joe Mauer	1.50
23	Bobby Crosby	1.00
24	Pedro Martinez	2.00
25	John Smoltz	1.00
26	Derek Jeter	4.00
27	Moises Alou	1.00
28	Rich Harden	1.00
29	Jim Thome	1.50
30	Jason Bay	2.00
31	Aramis Ramirez	3.00
32	Carlos Lee	1.00
33	B.J. Upton	1.00
34	Nomar Garciaparra	1.00
35	Ken Griffey Jr.	1.00
36	Darin Erstad	1.00
37	Larry Walker	1.00
38	Jose Vidro	1.00
39	Zack Greinke	1.00
40	Michael Young	1.00
41	David Wright	2.00
42	Albert Pujols	4.00
43	Vernon Wells	1.00
44	Mark Teixeira	1.50
45	Jacque Jones	1.00
46	Brian Giles	1.00
47	Austin Kearns	1.00
48	Omar Vizquel	1.00
49	Randy Johnson	1.50
50	Jason Varitek	1.50

2005 Donruss Team Heroes

NM/M

Complete Set (440): 80.00
Common Player: .15
Pack (8): 1.75
Box (24): 35.00

#	Player	Price
1	Adam Kennedy	.15
2	Bartolo Colon	.15
3	Bengie Molina	.15
4	Casey Kotchman	.15
5	Chone Figgins	.15
6	Dallas McPherson	.25
7	Darin Erstad	.15
8	David Eckstein	.15
9	Francisco Rodriguez	.25
10	Garret Anderson	.25
11	Jarrod Washburn	.15
12	John Lackey	.15
13	Jose Guillen	.25
14	Robb Quinlan	.15
15	Tim Bittner	.15
16	Tim Salmon	.15
17	Vladimir Guerrero	.25
18	Alex Cintron	.15
19	Craig Counsell	.15
20	Brandon Webb	.15
21	Chad Tracy	.15
22	Doug DeVore	.15
23	Luis Gonzalez	.25
24	Mark Grace	.25
25	Randy Johnson	.75
26	Scott Hairston	.15
27	Shea Hillenbrand	.15
28	Tim Olson	.15
29	Adam LaRoche	.15
30	Andruw Jones	.40
31	Charles Thomas	.15
32	Chipper Jones	.75
33	Dale Murphy	.50
34	John Smoltz	.25
35	Johnny Estrada	.15
36	Jose Capellan	.15
37	Marcus Giles	.15
38	Nick Green	.15
39	Phil Niekro	.50
40	Rafael Furcal	.15
41	Brian Roberts	.50
42	Cal Ripken Jr.	4.00
43	Javy Lopez	.25
44	Jay Gibbons	.15
45	Larry Bigbie	.15
46	Luis Matos	.15
47	Melvin Mora	.15
48	Miguel Tejada	.50
49	Rafael Palmeiro	.50
50	Rodrigo Lopez	.15
51	Sidney Ponson	.15
52	Abe Alvarez	.15
53	Bill Mueller	.15
54	Curt Schilling	.75
55	David Ortiz	.75
56	Doug Mientkiewicz	.15
57	Dwight Evans	.15
58	Fred Lynn	.40
59	Jim Rice	.40
60	Johnny Damon	.75
61	Keith Foulke	.15
62	Kevin Youkilis	.15
63	Manny Ramirez	.75
64	Tim Wakefield	.15
65	Trot Nixon	.15
66	Angel Guzman	.15
67	Aramis Ramirez	.40
68	Carlos Zambrano	.15
69	Corey Patterson	.15
70	Derek Lee	.40
71	Greg Maddux	1.00
72	Kerry Wood	.75
73	Lee Smith	.15
74	Mark Prior	.75
75	Sammy Sosa	1.50
76	Aaron Rowand	.15
77	Carlos Lee	.25
78	Frank Thomas	.50
79	Freddy Garcia	.15
80	Harold Baines	.15
81	Jose Contreras	.15
82	Juan Uribe	.15
83	Mark Buehrle	.15
84	Paul Konerko	.15
85	Shingo Takatsu	.15
86	Adam Dunn	.50
87	Austin Kearns	.15
88	Danny Graves	.15
89	Eric Davis	.15
90	Jacob Cruz	.15
91	Jason LaRue	.15
92	Ken Griffey Jr.	1.50
93	Ryan Wagner	.15
94	Sean Casey	.25
95	Casey Blake	.15
96	C.C. Sabathia	.15
97	Cliff Lee	.15
98	Grady Sizemore	.25
99	Jake Westbrook	.15
100	Jody Gerut	.15
101	Kazuhito Tadano	.15
102	Matt Lawton	.15
103	Travis Hafner	.15
104	Victor Martinez	.15
105	Charles Johnson	.15
106	Clint Barmes	.25
107	Garrett Atkins	.15
108	Jason Jennings	.15
109	Jeff Francis	.15
110	Joe Kennedy	.15
111	Matt Holliday	.25
112	Preston Wilson	.15
113	Todd Helton	.50
114	Alan Trammell	.40
115	Bobby Higginson	.15
116	Brandon Inge	.15
117	Carlos Guillen	.15
118	Carlos Pena	.15
119	Craig Monroe	.15
120	Dmitri Young	.15
121	Eric Munson	.15
122	Ivan Rodriguez	.50
123	Jeremy Bonderman	.15
124	Roberto Novoa	.15
125	A.J. Burnett	.15
126	Alex Gonzalez	.15
127	Dontrelle Willis	.40
128	Guillermo Mota	.15
129	Josh Beckett	.40
130	Juan Pierre	.15
131	Luis Castillo	.15
132	Miguel Cabrera	.75
133	Paul LoDuca	.15
134	Adam Everett	.15
135	Andy Pettitte	.25
136	Brad Ausmus	.15
137	Chris Burke	.15
138	Craig Biggio	.25
139	Jeff Bagwell	.50
140	Lance Berkman	.15
141	Morgan Ensberg	.15
142	Nolan Ryan	3.00
143	Roger Clemens	2.00
144	Roy Oswalt	.25
145	Tim Redding	.15
146	Wade Miller	.15
147	Andres Blanco	.15
148	Angel Berroa	.15
149	Benito Santiago	.15
150	Byron Gettis	.15
151	George Brett	2.00
152	Jeremy Affeldt	.15
153	Ken Harvey	.15
154	Mike MacDougal	.15
155	Mike Sweeney	.15
156	Shawn Camp	.15
157	Zack Greinke	.15
158	Brad Penny	.15
159	Cesar Izturis	.15
160	Edwin Jackson	.15
161	Eric Gagne	.40
162	Jerry Hairston	.15
163	Jeff Weaver	.15
164	Kazuhisa Ishii	.15
165	Milton Bradley	.15
166	Orel Hershiser	.15
167	Shawn Green	.25
168	Steve Garvey	.15
169	Tommy John	.15
170	Yhency Brazoban	.15
171	Ben Sheets	.25
172	Bill Hall	.15
173	Danny Kolb	.15
174	Lyle Overbay	.15
175	Paul Molitor	.15
176	Robin Yount	1.00
177	Rollie Fingers	.15
178	Rickie Weeks	.15
179	Scott Podsednik	.15
180	Jack Morris	.15
181	Jacque Jones	.15
182	Jason Kubel	.15
183	Joe Mauer	.50
184	Johan Santana	.50
185	Justin Morneau	.25
186	Lew Ford	.15
187	Matthew LeCroy	.15
188	Rod Carew	.50
189	Shannon Stewart	.15
190	Torii Hunter	.25
191	Aarom Baldiris	.15
192	Cliff Floyd	.15
193	Darryl Strawberry	.15
195	Dwight Gooden	.15
196	David Wright	.75
197	Victor Zambrano	.15
198	Jose Reyes	.15
199	Kazuo Matsui	.15
200	Keith Hernandez	.15
201	Mike Piazza	1.00
202	Tom Glavine	.40
203	Vance Wilson	.15
204	Tom Seaver	.75
205	Alex Rodriguez	1.50
206	Bernie Williams	.40
207	Chien-Ming Wang	.40
208	Derek Jeter	2.00
209	Dioner Navarro	.15
210	Don Mattingly	1.50
211	Gary Sheffield	.50
212	Hideki Matsui	1.50
213	Jason Giambi	.25
214	Javier Vazquez	.15
215	Jim Leyritz	.15
216	Jorge Posada	.40
217	Kevin Brown	.15
218	Mariano Rivera	.40
219	Mike Mussina	.40
220	Scott Proctor	.15
221	Tom Gordon	.15
222	Barry Zito	.25
223	Bobby Crosby	.15
224	Dave Stewart	.15
225	Dennis Eckersley	.50
226	Eric Byrnes	.15
227	Eric Chavez	.25
228	Erubiel Durazo	.15
229	Mark Kotsay	.15
230	Mark Mulder	.40
231	Octavio Dotel	.15
232	Rich Harden	.15
233	Tim Hudson	.40
234	Billy Wagner	.15
235	Bobby Abreu	.15
236	Brett Myers	.15
237	Chase Utley	.25
238	Jim Thome	.75
239	Jimmy Rollins	.15
240	Lenny Dykstra	.15
241	Marlon Byrd	.15
242	Mike Lieberthal	.15
243	Mike Schmidt	1.50
244	Pat Burrell	.15
245	Randy Wolf	.15
246	Ryan Howard	.75
247	Steve Carlton	.15
248	Bert Blyleven	.15
249	Bill Madlock	.15
250	Dave Parker	.40
251	Craig Wilson	.15
252	Jack Wilson	.15
253	Jason Bay	.25
254	Jason Kendall	.15
255	Jose Castillo	.15
256	Kip Wells	.15
257	Akinori Otsuka	.15
258	Brian Giles	.25
259	Brian Lawrence	.15
260	Freddy Guzman	.15
261	Gaylord Perry	.15
262	Jake Peavy	.40
263	Jay Payton	.15
264	Khalil Greene	.25
265	Mark Loretta	.15
266	Phil Nevin	.15
267	Ryan Klesko	.15
268	Sean Burroughs	.15
269	Tony Gwynn	.75
270	Trevor Hoffman	.15
271	A.J. Pierzynski	.15
272	Dustan Mohr	.15
273	Edgardo Alfonzo	.15
274	Jason Schmidt	.40
275	Jerome Williams	.15
276	Matt Williams	.40
277	Merkin Valdez	.15
278	Todd Linden	.15
279	Will Clark	.50
280	Bret Boone	.15
281	Bucky Jacobsen	.15
282	Clint Nageotte	.15
283	Ichiro Suzuki	1.50
284	J.J. Putz	.15
285	Jamie Moyer	.15
286	Bobby Madritsch	.15
287	Mike Morse RC	.25
288	Shigetoshi Hasegawa	.15
289	Travis Blackley	.15
290	Albert Pujols	2.00
291	Dan Haren	.15
292	Jason Isringhausen	.15
293	Jason Marquis	.15
294	Jeff Suppan	.15
295	Jim Edmonds	.40
296	Larry Walker	.40
297	Reggie Sanders	.15
298	Scott Rolen	.75
299	Yadier Molina	.15
300	Aubrey Huff	.15
301	B.J. Upton	.15
302	Carl Crawford	.15
303	Chad Gaudin	.15
304	Delmon Young	.15
305	Dewon Brazelton	.15
306	Joey Gathright	.15
307	Jose Cruz Jr.	.15
308	Rocco Baldelli	.15
309	Wade Boggs	.50
310	Adrian Gonzalez	.15
311	Alfonso Soriano	.75
313	Francisco Cordero	.15
314	Frankie Francisco	.15
315	Hank Blalock	.50
316	Kenny Rogers	.15
317	Laynce Nix	.15
318	Mark Teixeira	.50
319	Michael Young	.15
320	Alexis Rios	.15
321	David Bush	.15
322	Eric Hinske	.15
323	Frank Catalanotto	.15
324	Gabe Gross	.15
325	Guillermo Quiroz	.15
326	Rickey Henderson	.50
327	Orlando Hudson	.15
328	Roy Halladay	.40
329	Ted Lilly	.15
330	Vernon Wells	.15
331	Alberto Callaspo	.15
332	Jeff Mathis	.15
333	Ervin Santana	.15
334	Troy Percival	.15
335	Troy Glaus	.40
336	Greg Aquino	.15
337	Tony Pena RC	.25
338	Luis Terrero	.15
339	J.D. Drew	.15
340	Jon Lieber	.15
341	Russ Ortiz	.15
342	Daniel Cabrera	.15
343	Kenny Lofton	.15
344	Val Majewski	.15
345	Orlando Cabrera	.15
346	Hanley Ramirez	.25
347	Jason Varitek	.50
348	Pedro Martinez	.75
349	Derek Lowe	.15
350	Juan Cedeno	.15
351	Todd Walker	.15
352	Matt Clement	.25
353	Moises Alou	.15
354	Nomar Garciaparra	1.00
355	Michael Barrett	.15
356	Todd Hollandsworth	.15
357	Jose Valentin	.15
358	Magglio Ordonez	.15
359	Pedro Lopez RC	.25
360	Barry Larkin	.15
361	Jaret Wright	.15
362	Elizardo Ramirez	.15
363	Omar Vizquel	.15
364	Fausto Carmona	.15
365	Jake Dittler	.15
366	Jeff Salazar	.15
367	Jeromy Burnitz	.15
368	Jayson Nix	.15
369	Ubaldo Jimenez RC	1.50
370	Vinny Castilla	.15
371	Justin Verlander RC	.75
372	Armando Benitez	.15
373	Carl Pavano	.25
374	Chris Aguila	.15
375	Logan Kensing	.15
376	Mike Lowell	.15
377	Yorman Bazardo RC	.25
378	Willy Taveras RC	.15
379	Jeff Kent	.25
380	Carlos Beltran	.50
381	Kevin Millwood	.15
382	Juan Gonzalez	.25
383	Steve Finley	.15
384	Hideo Nomo	.40
385	Adrian Beltre	.40
386	David Krynzel	.15
387	Richie Sexson	.40
388	Jesse Crain	.15
389	Brad Radke	.15
390	Jason Lane	.15
391	Corey Koskie	.15
392	Cristian Guzman	.15
393	Brad Wilkerson	.15
394	Brendan Harris	.15
395	Chad Cordero	.15
396	Endy Chavez	.15
397	Jose Vidro	.15
398	Josh Karp	.15
399	Livan Hernandez	.15
400	Nick Johnson	.15
401	Ryan Church	.15
402	Termel Sledge	.15
403	Philip Humber RC	.75
404	Ambiorix Concepcion RC	.25
405	Al Leiter	.15
406	Richard Hidalgo	.15
407	Kris Benson	.15
408	Mike Cameron	.15
409	Victor Diaz	.15
410	Tony Womack	.15
411	Ferdin Tejeda	.15
412	Nick Swisher	.15
413	Jairo Garcia	.15
414	Jermaine Dye	.15
415	Joe Blanton	.15
416	Eric Milton	.15
417	Gavin Floyd	.15
418	John Van Benschoten	.15
419	Matt Peterson	.15
420	David Wells	.15
421	J.T. Snow	.15
422	Willie Mays	2.00
423	Jeremy Reed	.15
424	Jose Lopez	.15
425	Raul Ibanez	.15
426	Wladimir Balentien RC	1.00
427	Matt Morris	.15
428	Mike Matheny	.15
429	Edgar Renteria	.25
430	Woody Williams	.15
431	Jeff Niemann RC	2.00
432	Scott Kazmir	.15
433	Tino Martinez	.15
434	Chris Young RC	.50
435	David Dellucci	.15
436	Kameron Loe	.15
437	Nolan Ryan	3.00
438	John-Ford Griffin	.15
439	Carlos Delgado	.40
440	Russ Adams	.15

Autographs

NM/M

#	Player	NM/M
4	Casey Kotchman/SP	20.00
14	Robb Quinlan	8.00
15	Tim Bittner	5.00
18	Alex Cintron/SP	8.00
22	Doug DeVore	5.00
28	Tim Olson	5.00
38	Nick Green	5.00
44	Jay Gibbons/SP	12.00
50	Rodrigo Lopez/SP	8.00
66	Angel Guzman	12.00
90	Jacob Cruz	5.00
97	Cliff Lee/SP	15.00
101	Kazuhito Tadano	20.00
104	Victor Martinez/SP	20.00
110	Joe Kennedy	5.00
116	Brandon Inge	10.00
119	Craig Monroe	5.00
124	Roberto Novoa	5.00
150	Byron Gettis/SP	8.00
152	Jeremy Affeldt	5.00
156	Shawn Camp	5.00
170	Yhency Brazoban	8.00
172	Bill Hall/SP	8.00
182	Jason Kubel/SP	12.00
192	Aarom Baldiris/SP	10.00
203	Vance Wilson	5.00
220	Scott Proctor	8.00
277	Merkin Valdez	5.00
278	Todd Linden	25.00
281	Bucky Jacobsen	5.00
282	Clint Nageotte	5.00
290	Travis Blackley	5.00
292	Dan Haren/SP	12.00
295	Jeff Suppan	10.00
300	Yadier Molina/SP	15.00
306	Dewon Brazelton	8.00
307	Joey Gathright/SP	10.00
311	Adrian Gonzalez	10.00
313	Francisco Cordero/SP	10.00
314	Frankie Francisco	5.00
317	Laynce Nix	8.00
333	Ervin Santana	10.00
337	Tony Pena	8.00
346	Hanley Ramirez	15.00
350	Juan Cedeno	8.00
359	Pedro Lopez	15.00
364	Fausto Carmona	15.00
365	Jake Dittler	5.00
366	Jeff Salazar	10.00
368	Jayson Nix	8.00
377	Yorman Bazardo	8.00
378	Willy Taveras/SP	15.00
398	Josh Karp	5.00
411	Ferdin Tejeda	5.00
419	Matt Peterson	5.00
435	David Dellucci/SP	20.00
436	Kameron Loe	5.00

Movie Gallery

NM/M

#	Player	NM/M
1	Cal Ripken Jr.	1.00

Showdown Blue

Blue: 3-5X

Showdown Bronze

Bronze: 4-6X
Production 100 Sets

Showdown Gold

Gold: No Pricing
Production 10 Sets

Showdown Red

Red: 1.5-3X

Showdown Silver

Silver: 6-8X
Production 50 Sets

2005 Donruss Team Heroes National Convention

These cello-wrapped team sets were available at the National Sports Collectors Convention to persons who redeemed a free coupon available at Wal-Mart. Cards share the basic design of Donruss Team Heroes but have a National Convention logo on front and are numbered "X of 6" on back.

		NM/M
Complete Set (12):		5.00
Common Player:		.25
Chicago Cubs Team Heroes (6)		3.00
1	Kerry Wood	.50
2	Aramis Ramirez	.25
3	Mark Prior	.50
4	Nomar Garciaparra	.50
5	Greg Maddux	.50
6	Derek Lee	1.00
Chicago White Sox Team Heroes (6)		2.00
1	Frank Thomas	1.00
2	Shingo Takatsu	.25
3	Aaron Rowand	.25
4	Paul Konerko	.25
5	Jermaine Dye	.25
6	Mark Buehrle	.25

2005 Donruss Throwback Threads

		NM/M
Complete Set (300):		
Common Player:		.20
Pack (5):		3.00
Box (24):		65.00
1	Luis Castillo	.20
2	Derek Jeter	1.50
3	Eric Chavez	.20
4	Angel Berroa	.20
5	Jeff Bagwell	.40
6	J.T. Snow	.20
7	Craig Biggio	.30
8	Michael Barrett	.20
9	Hank Blalock	.40
10	Chipper Jones	.50
11	Jacque Jones	.20
12	Mark Teixeira	.50
13	Omar Vizquel	.20
14	Paul LoDuca	.20
15	Jim Edmonds	.30
16	Aramis Ramirez	.30
17	Lance Berkman	.30
18	Javy Lopez	.30
19	Adam LaRoche	.20
20	Jorge Posada	.40
21	Sean Casey	.20
22	Mark Prior	.40
23	Phil Nevin	.20
24	Manny Ramirez	.50
25	Andruw Jones	.40
26	Matt Lawton	.20
27	Vladimir Guerrero	.50
28	Austin Kearns	.20
29	John Smoltz	.40
30	Ken Griffey Jr.	1.00
31	Mike Piazza	.75
32	Jason Jennings	.20
33	Jason Varitek	.40
34	David Ortiz	.40
35	Mike Mussina	.40
36	Joe Nathan	.20
37	Kenny Rogers	.20
38	Carlos Zambrano	.30
39	Eric Byrnes	.20
40	Clint Barmes	.20
41	Danny Kolb	.20
42	Mariano Rivera	.40
43	Joey Gathright	.40
44	Adam Dunn	.40
45	Carlos Lee	.20
46	Yhency Brazoban	.20
47	Roy Oswalt	.30
48	Torii Hunter	.20
49	Scott Podsednik	.20
50	Jason Hammel RC	.20
51	Ichiro Suzuki	1.00
52	C.C. Sabathia	.20
53	Bobby Abreu	.20
54	Jon Garland	.20
55	Brandon Webb	.20
56	Mark Buehrle	.30
57	Johan Santana	.50
58	Mike Sweeney	.20
59	Tadahito Iguchi RC	1.50
60	Edgar Renteria	.20
61	Aaron Rowand	.20
62	Craig Wilson	.20
63	J.D. Drew	.30
64	Bobby Crosby	.40
65	Justin Morneau	.50
66	Scott Rolen	.50
67	Jose Vidro	.20
68	Carlos Beltran	.40
69	Jeff Weaver	.20
70	Jason Schmidt	.20
71	Brad Wilkerson	.20
72	Yuniesky Betancourt RC	1.50
73	Octavio Dotel	.20
74	Mike Cameron	.20
75	Barry Zito	.40
76	Woody Williams	.20
77	Russel Rohlicek RC	.40
78	Mark Kotsay	.20
79	Jeff Suppan	.20
80	Eric Gagne	.40
81	Tim Salmon	.20
82	Troy Glaus	.40
83	Kevin Mench	.20
84	Ivan Rodriguez	.20
85	Sean Burroughs	.20
86	Dallas McPherson	.20
87	Jamie Moyer	.20
88	Orlando Cabrera	.20
89	Wladimir Balentien RC	1.00
90	Philip Humber RC	1.00
91	Francisco Cordero	.20
92	Danny Graves	.20
93	Bucky Jacobsen	.20
94	Cliff Lee	.40
95	Oliver Perez	.20
96	Jake Peavy	.30
97	Doug Mientkiewicz	.20
98	Brad Radke	.20
99	Jeremy Reed	.20
100	Garret Anderson	.30
101	Rafael Furcal	.20
102	Jack Wilson	.20
103	Bernie Williams	.20
104	Josh Beckett	.20
105	Albert Pujols	1.50
106	Ubaldo Jimenez RC	2.50
107	Richard Hidalgo	.20
108	Luke Scott RC	1.00
109	Hideo Nomo	.40
110	Vernon Wells	.40
111	Richie Sexson	.40
112	Chad Cordero	.20
113	Alex Rodriguez	1.50
114	Paul Konerko	.30
115	Carlos Guillen	.20
116	Francisco Rodriguez	.20
117	Johnny Damon	.50
118	David Wright	1.00
119	Lyle Overbay	.20
120	Brian Roberts	.20
121	Sammy Sosa	1.00
122	Roger Clemens	1.50
123	Rickie Weeks	.50
124	Larry Bigbie	.20
125	Rafael Palmeiro	.40
126	Jason Giambi	.30
127	Hideki Matsui	1.00
128	Brad Lidge	.20
129	Jeremy Affeldt	.20
130	Mike MacDougal	.20
131	Troy Percival	.20
132	Matt Morris	.20
133	David Gassner RC	.40
134	Kerry Wood	.40
135	Dontrelle Willis	.40
136	Michael Young	.40
137	Andy Pettitte	.40
138	Kris Benson	.20
139	Miguel Negron RC	.40
140	Rich Harden	.40
141	Bret Boone	.20
142	Danny Rueckel RC	.40
143	Jeff Niemann RC	1.00
144	Randy Messenger RC	.40
145	Pedro Martinez	.40
146	Kazuhisa Ishii	.20
147	Carlos Delgado	.30
148	Tom Glavine	.40
149	Russ Ortiz	.20
150	Gavin Floyd	.20
151	Randy Johnson	.50
152	Prince Fielder	10.00
153	Nomar Garciaparra	.75
154	Pat Burrell	.30
155	Melvin Mora	.20
156	Jose Reyes	.50
157	Trot Nixon	.20
158	B.J. Upton	.50
159	Jody Gerut	.20
160	Juan Pierre	.20
161	Miguel Tejada	.40
162	Barry Larkin	.40
163	Carl Crawford	.50
164	Ben Sheets	.40
165	Tim Hudson	.40
166	Darin Erstad	.20
167	Todd Helton	.40
168	Luis Gonzalez	.30
169	Mark Mulder	.40
170	David Dellucci	.20
171	Marcus Giles	.20
172	Shannon Stewart	.20
173	Zack Greinke	.40
174	Miguel Cabrera	.50
175	Nick Johnson	.20
176	Derrek Lee	.50
177	Jim Thome	.40
178	Ken Harvey	.20
179	Ambiorix Concepcion RC	.40
180	Roy Halladay	.30
181	Larry Walker	.20
182	Greg Maddux	1.00
183	Frank Thomas	.50
184	Travis Hafner	.30
185	Matt Holliday	.50
186	Victor Martinez	.20
187	Jason Isringhausen	.20
188	Bill Mueller	.20
189	Dewon Brazelton	.20
190	Adrian Beltre	.40
191	Tim Wakefield	.20
192	Alexis Rios	.20
193	Alfonso Soriano	.50
194	Fernando Vina	.20
195	Armando Benitez	.20
196	Bartolo Colon	.30
197	A.J. Burnett	.20
198	Milton Bradley	.20
199	Brad Penny	.20
200	Rocco Baldelli	.20
201	Curt Schilling	.50
202	Ryan Wagner	.20
203	Preston Wilson	.20
204	Akinori Otsuka	.20
205	Bill McCarthy RC	.40
206	Edgardo Alfonzo	.20
207	Mike Lieberthal	.20
208	Shea Hillenbrand	.20
209	Tom Gordon	.20
210	Kip Wells	.20
211	Frank Catalanotto	.20
212	Casey Kotchman	.20
213	Justin Verlander RC	1.50
214	Brandon Inge	.20
215	Terrmel Sledge	.20
216	Gary Sheffield	.40
217	Steve Finley	.20
218	Kenny Lofton	.20
219	Chris Carpenter	.30
220	Danny Haren	.20
221	Brett Myers	.20
222	Joe Mauer	.50
223	David Wells	.20
224	Brian Giles	.20
225	Moises Alou	.30
226	Casey Rogowski RC	.20
227	Chase Utley	.50
228	Corey Koskie	.20
229	Derek Lowe	.20
230	Erick Threets RC	.40
231	Grady Sizemore	.20
232	Jason Lane	.20
233	Jeremy Bonderman	.20
234	Livan Hernandez	.20
235	Ryan Klesko	.20
236	Sidney Ponson	.20
237	Jimmy Rollins	.40
238	Eric Milton	.20
239	Shingo Takatsu	.20
240	Scott Kazmir	.30
241	Shawn Green	.30
242	Nick Swisher	.40
243	Shawn Chacon	.20
244	Javier Vazquez	.20
245	Mark Loretta	.20
246	Dmitri Young	.20
247	Charles Johnson	.20
248	Magglio Ordonez	.30
249	Sean Thompson RC	.40
250	Jared Gothreaux RC	.40
251	Kevin Millwood	.20
252	Mike Lowell	.20
253	Cristian Guzman	.20
254	Nate McLouth RC	2.00
255	Delmon Young	.40
256	Jeromy Burnitz	.20
257	Garrett Atkins	.20
258	Junior Spivey	.20
259	Morgan Ensberg	.20
260	Chone Figgins	.20
261	Hayden Penn RC	.50
262	Jason Bay	.40
263	Jose Cruz Jr.	.20
264	Khalil Greene	.40
265	Ray Durham	.20
266	Juan Gonzalez	.40
267	Jeff Kent	.20
268	Dioner Navarro	.20
269	Rodrigo Lopez	.20
270	Geoff Jenkins	.20
271	Jermaine Dye	.20
272	Orlando Hudson	.20
273	Jose Lima	.20
274	Jeff Francis	.20
275	Luis Matos	.20
276	Jason Kendall	.20
277	Mike Hampton	.20
278	Al Kaline	.75
279	Bert Blyleven	.20
280	Bill Madlock	.40
281	Cal Ripken Jr.	3.00
282	Dale Murphy	.50
283	Gary Carter	.50
284	George Brett	2.00
285	Harmon Killebrew	1.00
286	Harold Baines	.40
287	John Kruk	.20
288	Keith Hernandez	.40
289	Willie Mays	3.00
290	Matt Williams	.20
291	Nolan Ryan	2.50
292	Paul Molitor	.50
293	Reggie Jackson	.75
294	Rickey Henderson	.40
295	Ron Cey	.20
296	Ryne Sandberg	1.00
297	Ted Williams	2.50
298	Tom Seaver	.50
299	Tony Gwynn	.75
300	Babe Ruth/SP	20.00

Century Proof Blue

Blue (1-299):	3-6X
Production 150 Sets	

Century Proof Green

Green (1-299):	3-6X

Century Proof Gold

Gold (1-299):	3-6X
Production 100 Sets	

Century Stars

		NM/M
Common Player:		1.00
Spectrum:		1.5-3X
Production 100 Sets		
1	Bobby Doerr	1.00
2	Derek Jeter	4.00
3	Harmon Killebrew	1.50
4	Paul Molitor	1.50
5	Brooks Robinson	1.50
6	Steve Garvey	1.00
7	Ivan Rodriguez	1.00
8	Carl Yastrzemski	2.50
9	Nomar Garciaparra	2.00
10	Miguel Tejada	1.00
11	Edgar Martinez	1.00
12	Kevin Brown	1.00
13	Alex Rodriguez	3.00
14	Carlton Fisk	1.50
15	Craig Biggio	1.00
16	Dwight Gooden	1.00
17	Jim Palmer	1.00
18	Ken Griffey Jr.	2.00
19	Bob Feller	1.50
20	Don Sutton	1.00
21	Al Kaline	1.50
22	Roger Clemens	4.00
23	Kirk Gibson	1.00
24	Willie Mays	3.00
25	Frank Robinson	1.00
26	Randy Johnson	1.00
27	Jim "Catfish" Hunter	1.00
28	Austin Kearns	1.00
29	John Smoltz	1.00
30	Nolan Ryan	4.00
31	Duke Snider	1.50
32	Bernie Williams	1.00
33	David Wells	1.00
34	Bo Jackson	1.50
35	Mike Mussina	1.00
36	Gaylord Perry	1.00
37	Andre Dawson	1.00
38	Curt Schilling	1.50
39	Darryl Strawberry	1.00
40	Willie McCovey	1.00
41	Tom Seaver	1.50
42	Mariano Rivera	1.00
43	Dennis Eckersley	1.00
44	David Cone	1.00
45	Bret Boone	1.00
46	Will Clark	1.00
47	Jack Morris	1.00
48	Ichiro Suzuki	3.00
49	Alan Trammell	1.00
50	Cal Ripken Jr.	4.00

Century Stars Material

		NM/M
Common Player:		4.00
Production 20-50		
Prime:		No Pricing
Production Five Sets		
1	Bobby Doerr/Pants/50	8.00
3	Harmon Killebrew/Jsy/50	15.00
4	Paul Molitor/Jsy/50	10.00
5	Brooks Robinson/Bat/50	10.00
6	Steve Garvey/Jsy/50	4.00
7	Ivan Rodriguez/Jsy/50	8.00
8	Carl Yastrzemski/Jsy/50	15.00
10	Miguel Tejada/Jsy/50	6.00
11	Edgar Martinez/Jsy/50	4.00
12	Kevin Brown/Jsy/50	4.00
14	Carlton Fisk/Jsy/50	8.00
15	Craig Biggio/Jsy/50	6.00
16	Dwight Gooden/Jsy/50	4.00
17	Jim Palmer/Jsy/50	6.00
20	Don Sutton/Jsy/50	4.00
21	Al Kaline/Bat/50	15.00
22	Roger Clemens/Jsy/50	15.00
23	Kirk Gibson/Jsy/50	4.00
25	Frank Robinson/Bat/50	6.00
26	Randy Johnson/Jsy/50	6.00
28	Austin Kearns/Jsy/50	4.00
29	John Smoltz/Jsy/50	4.00
30	Nolan Ryan/Jkt/50	25.00
32	Bernie Williams/Jsy/50	6.00
33	David Wells/Jsy/50	4.00
34	Bo Jackson/Jsy/50	10.00
35	Mike Mussina/Jsy/50	4.00
36	Gaylord Perry/Jsy/50	4.00
37	Andre Dawson/Jsy/50	4.00
38	Curt Schilling/Jsy/50	8.00
39	Darryl Strawberry/Jsy/50	4.00
40	Willie McCovey/Jsy/50	6.00
42	Mariano Rivera/Jsy/50	10.00
43	Dennis Eckersley/Jsy/50	6.00
44	David Cone/Jsy/50	4.00
45	Bret Boone/Jsy/50	4.00
47	Jack Morris/Jsy/50	4.00
49	Alan Trammell/Jsy/50	4.00
50	Cal Ripken Jr./Jsy/50	30.00

Century Stars Sign. Mat.

No Pricing
Production 10 Sets

Prime: No Pricing
Production Five Sets

Dynasty

		NM/M
Common Trio:		2.00
Spectrum:		1.25X
Production 100 Sets		
1	Reggie Jackson, Jim "Catfish" Hunter, Sparky Lyle	2.00
2	Cal Ripken Jr., Jim Palmer, Eddie Murray	8.00
3	Dwight Gooden, Gary Carter, Darryl Strawberry	2.00
5	Rickey Henderson, Dennis Eckersley, Jose Canseco	2.00
6	Chipper Jones, Greg Maddux, David Justice	3.00
7	Roger Clemens, Alfonso Soriano, Bernie Williams	6.00
7	Randy Johnson, Curt Schilling, Matt Williams	3.00
8	Troy Glaus, Garret Anderson, Francisco Rodriguez	2.00
9	Josh Beckett, Miguel Cabrera, Mike Lowell	2.00
10	Curt Schilling, Manny Ramirez, Jason Varitek	8.00

Dynasty Material

		NM/M
Production 20-50		
Prime:		No Pricing
Production Five Sets		
1	Reggie Jackson/Pants, Jim "Catfish" Hunter/Pants, Sparky Lyle/Pants/50	20.00
2	Cal Ripken Jr./Jsy, Jim Palmer/Jsy, Eddie Murray/Jsy/50	40.00
3	Dwight Gooden/Jsy, Gary Carter/Jsy, Darryl Strawberry/Pants/20	15.00
4	Rickey Henderson/Jsy, Dennis Eckersley/Pants, Jose Canseco/Jsy/50	35.00
5	Chipper Jones/Jsy, Greg Maddux/Jsy, David Justice/Jsy/50	25.00
6	Roger Clemens/Jsy, Alfonso Soriano/Jsy, Bernie Williams/Jsy/50	30.00
7	Randy Johnson/Jsy, Curt Schilling/Jsy, Matt Williams/Jsy/50	20.00
8	Troy Glaus/Jsy, Garret Anderson/Jsy, Francisco Rodriguez/Jsy/50	15.00
10	Curt Schilling/Jsy, Manny Ramirez/Jsy, Jason Varitek/Jsy/50	40.00

Generations

		NM/M
Common Player:		2.00
Spectrum:		1-2.5X
Production 100 Sets		
1	Duke Snider, Reggie Jackson, Sammy Sosa	2.00
2	Rod Carew, John Kruk, Eric Chavez	2.00
3	Bo Jackson, Deion Sanders, Brian Jordan	3.00
4	Brett George, Tony Gwynn, Todd Helton	4.00
5	Babe Ruth, Ted Williams, Willie Mays	5.00
6	Rickey Henderson, Lenny Dykstra, Ichiro Suzuki	3.00
7	Keith Hernandez, Don Mattingly, Casey Kotchman	2.00
8	Wade Boggs, Mark Grace, Hank Blalock	2.00
9	Gary Carter, Ivan Rodriguez, Victor Martinez	2.00
10	Gaylord Perry, Morris, Greg Maddux	2.00
11	Joe Morgan, Ryne Sandberg, Alfonso Soriano	2.00
12	Juan Marichal, Luis Tiant, Pedro Martinez	2.00
13	Stan Musial, Carl Yastrzemski, Lance Berkman	3.00
14	Johnny Bench, Carlton Fisk, Mike Piazza	3.00
15	Harmon Killebrew, Cal Ripken Jr., Albert Pujols	5.00
16	Frank Robinson, Andre Dawson, Gary Sheffield	
17	Bob Feller, Roger Clemens, Kerry Wood	4.00
18	Steve Carlton, Tom Glavine, Barry Zito	2.00
19	Murray, Rafael Palmeiro, Mark Teixeira	2.00
20	Brooks Robinson, Mike Schmidt, Scott Rolen	3.00
21	Luis Aparicio, Omar Vizquel, Rafael Furcal	3.00
22	Don Sutton, David Cone, Roy Oswalt	3.00
23	Fred Lynn, Dale Murphy, Jim Edmonds	3.00
24	Ozzie, Barry Larkin, B.J. Upton	3.00
25	Gibson, Nolan Ryan, Mark Prior	4.00

Generations Material

		NM/M
Production 20-50		
Prime:		No Pricing
Production 10 Sets		
2	Rod Carew/Jsy, John Kruk/Jsy, Eric Chavez/Jsy/50	15.00
3	Bo Jackson/Jsy, Deion Sanders/Jsy, Brian Jordan/Jsy/50	25.00
4	Brett George/Jsy, Tony Gwynn/Jsy, Todd Helton/Jsy/50	25.00
7	Keith Hernandez/Pants, Don Mattingly/Pants, Casey Kotchman/Jsy/20	30.00
8	Wade Boggs/Jsy, Mark Grace/Jsy, Hank Blalock/Jsy/50	15.00
9	Gary Carter/Jsy, Ivan Rodriguez/Jsy, Victor Martinez/Jsy/50	15.00
10	Gaylord Perry/Jsy, Morris/Jsy, Greg Maddux/Jsy/50	25.00
11	Joe Morgan/Jsy, Ryne Sandberg/Jsy, Alfonso Soriano/Jsy/50	35.00
12	Juan Marichal/Pants, Luis Tiant/Pants, Pedro Martinez/Jsy/20	20.00
14	Johnny Bench/Pants, Carlton Fisk/Jsy, Mike Piazza/Jsy/50	20.00
15	Harmon Killebrew/Jsy, Cal Ripken Jr./Jsy, Albert Pujols/Jsy/50	25.00
16	Frank Robinson/Bat, Andre Dawson/Jsy, Gary Sheffield/Jsy/20	15.00
17	Bob Feller/Pants, Roger Clemens/Jsy, Kerry Wood/Jsy/20	50.00
18	Steve Carlton/Jsy, Tom Glavine/Jsy, Barry Zito/Jsy/50	20.00
19	Murray/Jsy, Rafael Palmeiro/Jsy, Mark Teixeira/Jsy/50	20.00

Material Bat

		NM/M
Common Player:		4.00
Production 5-250		
1	Luis Castillo/250	4.00
4	Angel Berroa/250	4.00
5	Jeff Bagwell/250	6.00
7	Craig Biggio/250	6.00
14	Paul LoDuca/250	4.00
17	Lance Berkman/250	4.00
18	Javy Lopez/250	4.00
21	Sean Casey/250	4.00
25	Andruw Jones/250	6.00
26	Matt Lawton/250	4.00
28	Austin Kearns/250	4.00
32	Jason Jennings/250	4.00
33	Jason Varitek/50	12.00
34	David Ortiz/250	8.00
43	Joey Gathright/250	4.00
48	Torii Hunter/250	4.00
55	Brandon Webb/250	4.00
58	Mike Sweeney/250	4.00
62	Craig Wilson/250	4.00
63	J.D. Drew/250	4.00
67	Jose Vidro/250	6.00
68	Carlos Beltran/250	6.00
81	Tim Salmon/250	4.00
82	Troy Glaus/250	4.00
83	Kevin Mench/250	6.00
101	Rafael Furcal/150	4.00
102	Jack Wilson/250	4.00
103	Bernie Williams/250	6.00
107	Richard Hidalgo/250	6.00
111	Richie Sexson/100	6.00
121	Sammy Sosa/250	8.00
125	Rafael Palmeiro/250	6.00
135	Dontrelle Willis/50	6.00
136	Michael Young/250	6.00
141	Bret Boone/50	4.00
147	Carlos Delgado/250	6.00
148	Tom Glavine/250	4.00
153	Nomar Garciaparra/150	4.00
154	Pat Burrell/150	4.00
156	Jose Reyes/250	6.00
158	B.J. Upton/250	4.00
159	Jody Gerut/250	4.00
160	Juan Pierre/250	4.00
162	Barry Larkin/100	4.00
164	Ben Sheets/250	6.00
165	Tim Hudson/250	4.00
166	Darin Erstad/250	4.00
168	Luis Gonzalez/250	4.00

169	Mark Mulder/35	6.00
174	Miguel Cabrera/50	10.00
175	Nick Johnson/50	4.00
176	Derrek Lee/50	8.00
192	Alex Rios/50	4.00
197	A.J. Burnett/50	4.00
200	Rocco Baldelli/250	4.00
203	Preston Wilson/150	4.00
206	Edgardo Alfonzo/250	4.00
212	Casey Kotchman/250	4.00
215	Terrmel Sledge/250	4.00
218	Kenny Lofton/150	4.00
224	Brian Giles/35	6.00
225	Moises Alou/250	4.00
232	Jason Lane/250	4.00
235	Ryan Klesko/25	4.00
241	Shawn Green/250	4.00
247	Charles Johnson/250	4.00
248	Magglio Ordonez/250	4.00
252	Mike Lowell/50	4.00
255	Delmon Young/250	4.00
259	Morgan Ensberg/250	6.00
260	Chone Figgins/250	4.00
262	Jason Bay/175	6.00
265	Ray Durham/200	4.00
266	Juan Gonzalez/250	6.00
267	Jeff Kent/250	4.00
272	Orlando Hudson/250	4.00
280	Bill Madlock/100	4.00
281	Cal Ripken Jr./150	25.00
283	Gary Carter/25	8.00
284	George Brett/25	6.00
286	Harold Baines/25	6.00
288	Keith Hernandez/25	4.00
289	Willie Mays/35	35.00
291	Nolan Ryan/50	8.00
292	Paul Molitor/150	6.00
293	Reggie Jackson/25	10.00
294	Rickey Henderson/250	8.00
296	Ryne Sandberg/50	15.00
297	Ted Williams/25	50.00
299	Tony Gwynn/50	10.00
300	Babe Ruth/25	180.00

Material Jersey

SAMMY SOSA — OUTFIELD

		NM/M
Common Player:		4.00
Production 5-250		
Prime:		1-2X
Production 10-100		
No pricing 20 or less.		
	Luis Castillo/45	4.00
	Eric Chavez/250	4.00
	Jeff Bagwell/250	6.00
	J.T. Snow/250	4.00
	Craig Biggio/50	6.00
	Hank Blalock/25	6.00
	Chipper Jones/250	8.00
	Mark Teixeira/150	6.00
	Jacque Jones/250	4.00
	Jim Edmonds/250	6.00
	Aramis Ramirez/250	4.00
	Lance Berkman/250	4.00
	Javy Lopez/250	4.00
	Jorge Posada/250	6.00
	Sean Casey/250	4.00
	Mark Prior/50	8.00
	Phil Nevin/50	4.00
	Manny Ramirez/250	8.00
	Andruw Jones/250	6.00
	Vladimir Guerrero/250	8.00
	Austin Kearns/250	4.00
	John Smoltz/250	6.00
	Mike Piazza/250	8.00
	Jason Jennings/250	4.00
	David Ortiz/250	10.00
	Mike Mussina/250	6.00
	Carlos Zambrano/250	6.00
	Mariano Rivera/50	4.00
	Joey Gathright/100	4.00
	Adam Dunn/25	6.00
	Roy Oswalt/250	4.00
	Torii Hunter/100	4.00
	C.C. Sabathia/250	4.00
	Bobby Abreu/250	4.00
	Mark Buehrle/250	4.00
	Johan Santana/50	6.00
	Mike Sweeney/75	4.00
	Craig Wilson/250	4.00
	Bobby Crosby/100	6.00
	Scott Rolen/25	4.00
	Jose Vidro/75	4.00
	Mike Cameron/250	4.00
	Barry Zito/250	4.00
	Kevin Mench/250	4.00
	Ivan Rodriguez/250	6.00
	Jamie Moyer/50	4.00
	Francisco Cordero/250	4.00

94	Cliff Lee/250	4.00
98	Brad Radke/250	4.00
100	Garret Anderson/250	6.00
101	Rafael Furcal/100	4.00
103	Bernie Williams/250	6.00
104	Josh Beckett/25	4.00
105	Albert Pujols/250	15.00
109	Hideo Nomo/250	8.00
110	Vernon Wells/250	4.00
114	Paul Konerko/250	4.00
116	Francisco Rodriguez/250	4.00
117	Johnny Damon/250	8.00
118	David Wright/250	10.00
119	Lyle Overbay/250	4.00
120	Brian Roberts/250	4.00
122	Roger Clemens/100	12.00
124	Larry Bigbie/200	4.00
125	Rafael Palmeiro/250	4.00
126	Jason Giambi/250	6.00
127	Hideki Matsui/250	15.00
134	Kerry Wood/250	6.00
135	Dontrelle Willis/250	6.00
136	Michael Young/250	4.00
137	Andy Pettitte/250	6.00
141	Bret Boone/250	4.00
146	Kazuhisa Ishii/250	4.00
147	Carlos Delgado/250	4.00
148	Tom Glavine/250	4.00
154	Pat Burrell/250	4.00
155	Melvin Mora/250	4.00
156	Jose Reyes/200	4.00
157	Trot Nixon/250	4.00
158	B.J. Upton/250	4.00
159	Jody Gerut/100	4.00
161	Miguel Tejada/35	8.00
162	Barry Larkin/40	8.00
163	Carl Crawford/40	6.00
164	Ben Sheets/250	6.00
166	Darin Erstad/25	4.00
167	Todd Helton/150	6.00
168	Luis Gonzalez/250	4.00
170	David Dellucci/150	4.00
172	Shannon Stewart/250	4.00
174	Miguel Cabrera/100	8.00
176	Derrek Lee/250	8.00
177	Jim Thome/250	6.00
178	Ken Harvey/150	4.00
180	Roy Halladay/250	4.00
182	Greg Maddux/250	8.00
186	Victor Martinez/250	4.00
189	Dewon Brazelton/250	4.00
190	Adrian Beltre/250	4.00
193	Alfonso Soriano/250	4.00
197	A.J. Burnett/250	4.00
200	Rocco Baldelli/250	4.00
201	Curt Schilling/250	8.00
202	Ryan Wagner/250	4.00
203	Preston Wilson/250	4.00
211	Frank Catalanotto/250	4.00
212	Casey Kotchman/250	4.00
214	Brandon Inge/250	4.00
221	Brett Myers/250	4.00
232	Jason Lane/95	4.00
233	Jeremy Bonderman/250	4.00
234	Livan Hernandez/250	4.00
235	Ryan Klesko/250	4.00
237	Jimmy Rollins/35	6.00
252	Mike Lowell/250	4.00
257	Garrett Atkins/250	4.00
258	Junior Spivey/150	4.00
259	Morgan Ensberg/150	4.00
260	Chone Figgins/250	4.00
262	Jason Bay/250	6.00
269	Rodrigo Lopez/250	4.00
270	Geoff Jenkins/250	4.00
275	Luis Matos/250	4.00
279	Bert Blyleven/50	6.00
281	Cal Ripken Jr./250	30.00
282	Dale Murphy/250	10.00
283	Gary Carter/50	8.00
284	George Brett/50	15.00
285	Harmon Killebrew/25	15.00
286	Harold Baines/50	6.00
287	John Kruk/50	4.00
289	Willie Mays Pants/25	40.00
290	Matt Williams/25	8.00
291	Nolan Ryan/50	25.00
292	Paul Molitor/50	4.00
293	Reggie Jackson/25	8.00
294	Rickey Henderson/50	10.00
295	Ron Cey/50	4.00
296	Ryne Sandberg/50	5.00
297	Ted Williams/25	60.00
298	Tom Seaver/25	15.00
299	Tony Gwynn/50	12.00
300	Babe Ruth/25	200.00

Material Combo

		NM/M
Common Player:		6.00
Production 10-100		
Prime:		1-2X
Production 5-40		
No pricing 20 or less.		
1	Luis Castillo/Bat-Jsy/90	6.00
3	Eric Chavez/Bat-Jsy/5	8.00
5	Jeff Bagwell/Bat-Jsy/100	8.00
7	Craig Biggio/Bat-Jsy/25	10.00
12	Mark Teixeira/ Bat-Jsy/25	10.00
17	Lance Berkman/ Bat-Jsy/100	6.00
21	Sean Casey/Bat-Jsy/5	8.00
22	Mark Prior/Bat-Jsy/25	10.00
25	Andruw Jones/	
32	Jason Jennings/ Bat-Jsy/100	4.00

34	David Ortiz/Bat-Jsy/25	20.00
43	Joey Gathright/ Bat-Jsy/50	6.00
55	Brandon Webb/ Bat-Pants/100	6.00
58	Mike Sweeney/ Bat-Jsy/65	6.00
62	Craig Wilson/Bat-Jsy/100	6.00
67	Jose Vidro/Bat-Jsy/100	6.00
83	Kevin Mench/ Bat-Jsy/100	6.00
101	Rafael Furcal/Bat-Jsy/50	6.00
103	Bernie Williams/ Bat-Jsy/50	8.00
104	Josh Beckett/Bat-Jsy/25	8.00
110	Vernon Wells/ Hat-Jsy/50	4.00
124	Larry Bigbie/Jsy-Jsy/100	4.00
126	Jason Giambi/ Jsy-Jsy/100	6.00
136	Michael Young/ Bat-Jsy/50	6.00
146	Kazuhisa Ishii/ Hat-Jsy/25	10.00
154	Pat Burrell/Bat-Jsy/25	6.00
156	Jose Reyes/Bat-Jsy/25	8.00
157	Trot Nixon/Bat-Jsy/25	10.00
160	Juan Pierre/ Bat-Fld Glv/95	6.00
164	Ben Sheets/Bat-Jsy/100	8.00
168	Luis Gonzalez/ Jsy-Jsy/100	6.00
171	Marcus Giles/Hat-Jsy/50	6.00
172	Shannon Stewart/ Jsy-Jsy/30	6.00
174	Miguel Cabrera/ Bat-Jsy/25	12.00
180	Roy Halladay/Jsy-Jsy/85	8.00
183	Frank Thomas/ Hat-Jsy/25	15.00
186	Victor Martinez/ Fld Glv-Jsy/40	8.00
197	A.J. Burnett/Bat-Jsy/25	6.00
200	Rocco Baldelli/ Bat-Jsy/50	6.00
201	Curt Schilling/ Bat-Jsy/25	12.00
202	Ryan Wagner/ Jsy-Jsy/100	6.00
203	Preston Wilson/ Bat-Jsy/85	6.00
212	Casey Kotchman/ Bat-Jsy/50	6.00
218	Kenny Lofton/ Bat-Fld Glv/50	6.00
232	Jason Lane/Bat-Hat/50	6.00
235	Ryan Klesko/Hat-Jsy/100	6.00
252	Mike Lowell/Bat-Jsy/100	6.00
257	Garrett Atkins/ Jsy-Jsy/100	6.00
259	Morgan Ensberg/ Hat-Jsy/100	8.00
260	Chone Figgins/ Bat-Jsy/50	6.00
262	Jason Bay/Bat-Jsy/40	8.00
272	Orlando Hudson/ Bat-Jsy/40	6.00
275	Luis Matos/Jsy-Jsy/50	6.00
281	Cal Ripken Jr./ Bat-Jsy/50	40.00
283	Gary Carter/ Jsy-Pants/25	15.00
284	George Brett/Bat-Jsy/25	30.00
286	Harold Baines/ Bat-Jsy/25	10.00
288	Keith Hernandez/ Bat-Jsy/25	10.00
289	Willie Mays/ Bat-Pants/25	50.00
291	Nolan Ryan/Bat-Jsy/50	25.00
292	Paul Molitor/Bat-Jsy/50	15.00
293	Reggie Jackson/ Bat-Jsy/25	15.00
294	Rickey Henderson/ Bat-Jsy/50	6.00
296	Ryne Sandberg/ Bat-Jsy/25	25.00
297	Ted Williams/ Bat-Jsy/25	75.00
298	Tom Seaver/ Bat-Jsy/25	15.00
299	Tony Gwynn/ Jsy-Pants/25	15.00
300	Babe Ruth/Bat-Jsy/25	375.00

Player Timelines

		NM/M
Common Player:		1.00
Spectrum:		1-2.5X
Production 100 Sets		
1	Dale Murphy	2.00
2	Greg Maddux	3.00
3	Tom Glavine	2.00
4	David Ortiz	3.00
5	Bo Jackson	2.00
6	Lyle Overbay	1.00
7	Tommy John	1.00
8	Shawn Green	1.00
9	Aramis Ramirez	1.50
10	Javy Lopez	1.00
11	Vladimir Guerrero	3.00
12	Travis Hafner	1.00
13	Junior Spivey	1.00
14	Alfonso Soriano	1.00
15	Andre Dawson	1.00
16	Sammy Sosa	3.00
17	Andy Pettitte	1.50
18	Jim Edmonds	1.50

19	Willie McCovey	2.00
20	Scott Rolen	2.00
21	Jermaine Dye	1.00
23	Pedro Martinez	2.50
24	Don Sutton	1.00
25	Randy Johnson	2.00
26	Nolan Ryan	3.00
26	Dennis Eckersley	1.00
27	Reggie Jackson	2.00
28	Deion Sanders	1.00
29	Curt Schilling	2.00
30	Rickey Henderson	1.00
31	Mike Piazza	2.00
32	Gary Carter	1.00
33	Roberto Alomar	1.00
34	Hideo Nomo	1.00
35	Andres Galarraga	1.00
36	Juan Gonzalez	1.00
37	Roger Clemens	4.00
38	Jeff Kent	1.00
39	Steve Carlton	1.00
40	Wade Boggs	1.50

Player Timeline Material

		NM/M
Production 25-250		
1	Dale Murphy/50	10.00
2	Greg Maddux/100	10.00
3	Tom Glavine/50	8.00
4	David Ortiz/250	10.00
5	Bo Jackson/100	12.00
6	Lyle Overbay/250	4.00
7	Tommy John/Pants/250	4.00
8	Shawn Green/100	4.00
9	Aramis Ramirez/100	6.00
10	Javy Lopez/100	4.00
11	Vladimir Guerrero/25	15.00
12	Travis Hafner/25	8.00
13	Junior Spivey/25	4.00
14	Alfonso Soriano/100	6.00
16	Sammy Sosa/250	8.00
17	Andy Pettitte/100	8.00
18	Jim Edmonds/100	4.00
19	Willie McCovey/ Pants/50	12.00
20	Scott Rolen/50	10.00
21	Jermaine Dye/100	4.00
22	Pedro Martinez/100	12.00
23	Don Sutton/50	10.00
24	Randy Johnson/50	15.00
25	Nolan Ryan/Jkt/50	40.00
27	Reggie Jackson/ Pants/50	15.00
28	Deion Sanders/25	15.00
29	Curt Schilling/50	10.00
30	Rickey Henderson/ Pants/100	15.00
31	Mike Piazza/50	15.00
32	Gary Carter/Pants/50	10.00
33	Roberto Alomar/250	8.00
34	Hideo Nomo/50	15.00
35	Andres Galarraga/50	6.00
36	Juan Gonzalez/25	8.00
37	Roger Clemens/25	30.00
38	Jeff Kent/50	6.00

Player Timelines Sign. Mat.

		NM/M
Production 5-50		
Prime:		No Pricing
Production 5-10		
1	Dale Murphy/50	30.00
6	Lyle Overbay/50	12.00
7	Tommy John/Pants/50	15.00
12	Travis Hafner/25	20.00
13	Junior Spivey/25	12.00
15	Andre Dawson/25	25.00
21	Jermaine Dye/50	15.00
23	Don Sutton/25	20.00
32	Gary Carter/Pants/50	20.00
36	Juan Gonzalez/25	40.00

Polo Grounds 85 HIT Long Fly

	NM/M
Common Player:	1.50
Production 85 Sets	
Parallel #'d 40-75:	.75-1.5X
Parallel #'d 20-35:	1-2X
No pricing 15 or less.	
1 Ken Griffey Jr.	6.00
2 Roger Clemens	4.00
3 Barry Zito	2.00
4 Alex Rodriguez	5.00
5 Melvin Mora	1.50
6 Kevin Brown	1.50
7 Chipper Jones	3.00
8 Scott Kazmir	2.00

9	Kip Wells	1.50
10	Khalil Greene	2.00
11	Kevin Millwood	1.50
12	Kerry Wood	2.00
13	Mark Kotsay	1.50
14	Jeff Bagwell	2.00
15	Hank Blalock	2.00
16	Scott Rolen	2.00
17	Lance Berkman	2.00
18	Mike Mussina	2.00
19	Jim Edmonds	2.00
20	Jorge Posada	2.00
21	Curt Schilling	3.00
22	Vernon Wells	1.50
23	Pedro Martinez	2.00
24	Jeremy Reed	1.50
25	Hideki Matsui	4.00
26	Steve Finley	1.50
27	Gavin Floyd	1.50
28	Darin Erstad	1.50
29	Bernie Williams	2.00
30	Mark Mulder	2.00
31	Rafael Palmeiro	2.00
32	Andruw Jones	2.00
33	Roy Halladay	2.00
34	Dontrelle Willis	2.00
35	Bret Boone	1.50
36	Andy Pettitte	2.00
37	Vladimir Guerrero	3.00
38	Randy Johnson	3.00
39	Michael Young	2.00
40	Frank Thomas	2.00
41	Todd Helton	2.00
42	Johan Santana	3.00
43	Mark Teixeira	2.00
44	Justin Morneau	2.00
45	Brad Radke	1.50
46	Dallas McPherson	1.50
47	Tim Hudson	2.00
48	Carl Crawford	1.50
49	Eric Gagne	2.00
50	Mark Prior	3.00
51	Tom Glavine	2.00
52	Craig Biggio	2.00
53	John Smoltz	2.00
54	Manny Ramirez	3.00
55	Ivan Rodriguez	2.00
56	Gary Sheffield	2.00
57	Josh Beckett	2.00
58	Miguel Tejada	2.00
59	Bobby Abreu	2.00
60	Ichiro Suzuki	4.00
61	Sammy Sosa	2.50
62	Garret Anderson	2.00
63	Sean Casey	1.50
64	Troy Glaus	2.00
65	Larry Walker	2.00
66	Alfonso Soriano	2.00
67	Luis Gonzalez	2.00
68	Eric Chavez	2.00
69	Adrian Beltre	2.00
70	Miguel Cabrera	3.00
71	Carlos Beltran	2.00
72	Jim Thome	2.00
73	David Ortiz	3.00
74	Adam Dunn	2.00
75	Jacque Jones	1.50
76	Shawn Green	1.50
77	Victor Martinez	1.50
78	Torii Hunter	1.50
79	Carlos Lee	1.50
80	C.C. Sabathia	1.50
81	Joe Mauer	2.00
82	Kris Benson	1.50
83	Zack Greinke	1.50
84	Greg Maddux	4.00
85	David Wright	4.00
86	Mike Piazza	4.00
87	Johnny Damon	3.00
88	Derek Jeter	6.00
89	B.J. Upton	1.50
90	Albert Pujols	6.00
91	Cal Ripken Jr.	6.00
92	Nolan Ryan	5.00
93	George Brett	5.00
94	Don Mattingly	4.00
95	Ryne Sandberg	4.00
96	Rickey Henderson	3.00
97	Robin Yount	4.00
98	Mike Schmidt	4.00
99	Tony Gwynn	3.00
100	Willie Mays	5.00

Signature Marks

		NM/M
Production 5-1,000		
4	Angel Berroa/2	12.00
19	Adam LaRoche/50	4.00
36	Joe Nathan/25	20.00
38	Carlos Zambrano/25	30.00
39	Eric Byrnes/50	10.00
41	Danny Kolb/25	10.00
45	Carlos Lee/25	20.00
49	Scott Podsednik/20	20.00
52	C.C. Sabathia/25	15.00
54	Mark Buehrle/25	30.00
62	Craig Wilson/50	6.00
64	Bobby Crosby/100	15.00
67	Jose Vidro/25	12.00
73	Octavio Dotel/25	12.00
74	Russel Rohlicek/250	5.00
81	Tim Salmon/25	20.00
85	Sean Burroughs/25	10.00
87	Jamie Moyer/25	10.00
88	Orlando Cabrera/25	20.00
90	Philip Humber/25	20.00
91	Francisco Cordero/50	20.00
92	Danny Graves/25	10.00

93	Bucky Jacobsen/64	8.00
94	Cliff Lee/50	15.00
96	Jake Peavy/25	35.00
101	Rafael Furcal/25	20.00
102	Jack Wilson/100	10.00
108	Luke Scott/250	15.00
110	Vernon Wells/250	15.00
112	Chad Cordero/25	15.00
114	Paul Konerko/25	20.00
116	Francisco Rodriguez/25	20.00
118	David Wright/25	85.00
120	Lyle Overbay/25	10.00
123	Brian Roberts/25	15.00
124	Larry Bigbie/75	8.00
129	Jeremy Affeldt/50	8.00
131	Troy Percival/25	15.00
133	David Gassner/1,000	5.00
136	Michael Young/25	20.00
139	Miguel Negron/250	5.00
140	Rich Harden/50	25.00
142	Danny Rueckel/250	5.00
144	Randy Messenger/500	5.00
157	Russ Ortiz/25	15.00
157	Trot Nixon/25	25.00
158	B.J. Upton/25	20.00
159	Jody Gerut/25	10.00
170	David Dellucci/25	5.00
172	Shannon Stewart/25	15.00
175	Nick Johnson/25	15.00
178	Derrek Lee/25	40.00
178	Ken Harvey/25	8.00
179	Ambiorix Concepcion/ 500	8.00
184	Travis Hafner/25	15.00
191	Dewon Brazelton/66	15.00
192	Alexis Rios/25	15.00
198	Milton Bradley/100	12.00
199	Brad Penny/25	10.00
202	Ryan Wagner/25	10.00
204	Akinori Otsuka/25	20.00
207	Mike Lieberthal/25	10.00
208	Shea Hillenbrand/25	20.00
209	Tom Gordon/25	20.00
212	Casey Kotchman/100	10.00
213	Justin Verlander/50	40.00
220	Danny Haren/25	20.00
226	Casey Rogowski/250	5.00
230	Erick Threets/500	5.00
232	Jason Lane/25	10.00
233	Jeremy Bonderman/50	15.00
238	Livan Hernandez/25	15.00
239	Shingo Takatsu/25	20.00
245	Mark Loretta/25	5.00
250	Jared Gothreaux/1,000	5.00
254	Nate McLouth/1,000	15.00
258	Junior Spivey/25	10.00
259	Morgan Ensberg/25	15.00
262	Jason Bay/186	15.00
271	Jermaine Dye/25	15.00
272	Orlando Hudson/100	8.00
275	Luis Matos/25	10.00
279	Bert Blyleven/25	15.00
281	Bill Madlock/25	15.00
281	Cal Ripken Jr./25	150.00
282	Dale Murphy/25	30.00
286	Harold Baines/25	15.00
288	Keith Hernandez/25	15.00
290	Matt Williams/25	30.00

Throwback Collection

		NM/M
Common Player:		
Spectrum:		1-2.5X
Production 100 Sets		
1	Billy Martin	2.00
2	Tony Gwynn	2.00
3	Babe Ruth	4.00
4	Angel Berroa	1.00
5	Jeff Bagwell	1.50
6	Tony Oliva	1.00
7	Ivan Rodriguez	1.50
8	Gary Carter	1.50
9	Ted Williams	4.00
10	Chipper Jones	1.50
11	Al Oliver	1.00
12	Roberto Alomar	1.00
13	Omar Vizquel	1.00
14	Ernie Banks	2.00
15	Carlos Beltran	1.50
16	Garret Anderson	1.00
17	Mark Grace	1.00
18	Jason Giambi	1.00
19	Dave Righetti	1.00
20	Mike Schmidt	3.00
21	Roger Clemens	4.00
22	Juan Gonzalez	1.50
23	Carlos Delgado	1.50
24	Manny Ramirez	2.00
25	Jim Thome	1.50
26	Wade Boggs	2.00
27	Luis Tiant	1.00
28	Kerry Wood	1.50
29	Rod Carew	1.50
30	Dwight Evans	1.00
31	Mike Piazza	2.00
32	Billy Williams	1.00
33	Larry Walker	1.00
34	Nolan Ryan	4.00
35	Edgar Renteria	1.00
36	Greg Maddux	2.50
37	Gaylord Perry	1.00
38	Curt Schilling	1.00
39	Dave Parker	1.00
40	Andruw Jones	1.50
41	Orlando Cepeda	1.50
42	Fergie Jenkins	1.00

43	Kirby Puckett	2.00
44	Reggie Jackson	2.00
45	Bob Gibson	2.00
46	Rickey Henderson	2.00
47	Lee Smith	1.00
48	Lou Brock	1.50
49	Fred Lynn	1.00
50	Lance Berkman	1.00
51	Shawn Green	1.00
52	Hoyt Wilhelm	1.00
53	Sammy Sosa	2.50
54	Tim Hudson	1.50
55	Matt Williams	1.00
56	Marty Marion	1.00
57	Eric Chavez	1.00
58	Rafael Palmeiro	1.50
59	Randy Johnson	2.00
60	David Ortiz	2.00
61	Hank Blalock	1.00
62	Jim Rice	1.00
63	Mark Mulder	1.50
64	Kazuo Matsui	1.00
65	Pedro Martinez	2.00
66	Sean Casey	1.00
67	Carlos Lee	1.00
68	Stan Musial	3.00
69	Fred McGriff	1.00
70	Darryl Strawberry	1.00
71	Tommy John	1.00
72	Hideo Nomo	1.00
73	Johnny Bench	2.00
74	Cal Ripken Jr.	5.00
75	Harold Baines	1.00

Throwback Coll. Material

		NM/M
Production 5-500		
Prime:		1-2X
Production 5-25		
No pricing 20 or less.		
1	Billy Martin/Jsy/250	8.00
2	Tony Gwynn/Jsy/250	8.00
4	Angel Berroa/Pants/100	4.00
5	Jeff Bagwell/Jsy/250	6.00
6	Tony Oliva/Jsy/250	4.00
7	Ivan Rodriguez/Jsy/250	6.00
8	Gary Carter/Pants/250	6.00
10	Chipper Jones/Jsy/250	6.00
11	Al Oliver/Jsy/250	4.00
12	Roberto Alomar/Jsy/500	6.00
13	Omar Vizquel/Jsy/250	4.00
15	Carlos Beltran/Jsy/100	4.00
16	Garret Anderson/Jsy/400	4.00
17	Mark Grace/Jsy/250	4.00
18	Jason Giambi/Jsy/250	4.00
19	Dave Righetti/Jsy/250	4.00
21	Roger Clemens/Jsy/250	10.00
22	Juan Gonzalez/Jsy/250	4.00
23	Carlos Delgado/Jsy/150	4.00
24	Manny Ramirez/Jsy/250	10.00
25	Jim Thome/Jsy/500	4.00
26	Wade Boggs/Jsy/250	6.00
27	Luis Tiant/Pants/500	4.00
28	Kerry Wood/Jsy/50	4.00
29	Rod Carew/Jkt/250	6.00
30	Dwight Evans/Jsy/50	8.00
31	Mike Piazza/Jsy/100	8.00
32	Billy Williams/Jsy/100	4.00
33	Larry Walker/Jsy/100	4.00
34	Nolan Ryan/Pants/100	15.00
35	Edgar Renteria/Jsy/500	4.00
36	Greg Maddux/Jsy/375	8.00
37	Gaylord Perry/Jsyu/250	4.00
38	Curt Schilling/Jsy/500	4.00
39	Dave Parker/Jsy/500	4.00
40	Andruw Jones/Jsy/500	4.00
41	Orlando Cepeda/Pants/250	4.00
42	Fergie Jenkins/Jsy/250	4.00
43	Kirby Puckett/Jsy/400	6.00
44	Reggie Jackson/Jsy/250	6.00
45	Bob Gibson/Jsy/100	8.00
46	Rickey Henderson/Jsy/500	6.00
47	Lee Smith/Jsy/250	4.00
49	Fred Lynn/Jsy/250	4.00
50	Lance Berkman/Jsy/500	4.00
51	Shawn Green/Jsy/250	4.00
52	Hoyt Wilhelm/Jsy/250	4.00
53	Sammy Sosa/Jsy/250	8.00
54	Tim Hudson/Jsy/500	4.00
55	Matt Williams/Jsy/250	4.00
57	Eric Chavez/Jsy/500	4.00
58	Rafael Palmeiro/Jsy/500	6.00
59	Randy Johnson/Jsy/500	6.00
60	David Ortiz/Jsy/500	8.00
61	Hank Blalock/Jsy/500	4.00
62	Jim Rice/Pants/250	4.00
63	Mark Mulder/Jsy/100	4.00
64	Kazuo Matsui/Jsy/500	4.00
65	Pedro Martinez/Jsy/500	6.00
66	Sean Casey/Jsy/500	4.00
67	Carlos Lee/Jsy/500	4.00
68	Stan Musial/Jsy/500	20.00
69	Fred McGriff/Jsy/500	4.00
70	Darryl Strawberry/Jsy/	4.00
71	Tommy John/Jsy/250	4.00
72	Hideo Nomo/Jsy/500	4.00
73	Johnny Bench/Pants/100	8.00
74	Cal Ripken Jr./Jsy/250	20.00
75	Harold Baines/Jsy/250	4.00

Throwback Col. Mat. Combo

		NM/M
Production 5-100		
1	Billy Martin/Jsy-Pants/100	10.00

2	Tony Gwynn/Jsy-Pants/100	12.00
4	Angel Berroa/Bat-Pants/100	4.00
5	Jeff Bagwell/Jsy/100	8.00
6	Tony Oliva/Bat-Jsy/100	6.00
7	Ivan Rodriguez/Chest Prot-Jsy/100	8.00
8	Gary Carter/Jsy/100	4.00
10	Chipper Jones/Bat-Jsy/100	8.00
11	Al Oliver/Bat-Jsy/100	6.00
12	Roberto Alomar/Bat-Jsy/100	8.00
13	Omar Vizquel/Bat-Jsy/100	6.00
15	Carlos Beltran/Bat-Jsy/100	8.00
17	Mark Grace/Bat-Jsy/50	10.00
18	Jason Giambi/Jsy-Jsy/100	6.00
19	Dave Righetti/Jsy-Jsy/100	6.00
21	Roger Clemens/Jsy-Jsy/100	15.00
22	Juan Gonzalez/Jsy-Jsy/100	6.00
23	Carlos Delgado/Jsy-Jsy/100	4.00
26	Wade Boggs/Jsy-Jsy/100	10.00
33	Rod Carew/Jkt-Jsy/100	10.00
34	Nolan Ryan/Jsy-Jsy/100	6.00
36	Greg Maddux/Jsy-Jsy/100	12.00
38	Curt Schilling/Jsy-Jsy/100	6.00
40	Andruw Jones/Bat-Jsy/100	8.00
41	Orlando Cepeda/Bat-Pants/100	8.00
42	Kirby Puckett/Bat-Jsy/100	12.00
44	Reggie Jackson/Bat-Jsy/100	10.00
46	Rickey Henderson/Bat-Jsy/100	10.00
47	Lee Smith/Jsy-Jsy/100	6.00
49	Fred Lynn/Bat-Jsy/100	4.00
50	Lance Berkman/Bat-Jsy/100	4.00
51	Shawn Green/Bat-Jsy/100	4.00
52	Hoyt Wilhelm/Jsy-Jsy/100	4.00
53	Sammy Sosa/Jsy-Jsy/100	4.00
54	Tim Hudson/Jsy-Jsy/100	4.00
57	Eric Chavez/Jsy-Jsy/50	6.00
58	Rafael Palmeiro/Jsy/100	8.00
59	Randy Johnson/Jsy-Pants/100	10.00
60	David Ortiz/Jsy-Jsy/100	8.00
61	Hank Blalock/Jsy/50	6.00
62	Jim Rice/Jsy-Jsy/50	6.00
64	Kazuo Matsui/	
65	Pedro Martinez/Jsy-Jsy/100	8.00
66	Sean Casey/Jsy-Pants/100	
67	Carlos Lee/Hat-Jsy/100	4.00
69	Fred McGriff/Bat-Jsy/100	8.00
70	Darryl Strawberry/Jsy-Jsy/100	4.00
71	Tommy John/Bat-Jsy/100	4.00
72	Hideo Nomo/Jsy-Jsy/100	10.00
73	Johnny Bench/Bat-Pants/100	12.00
74	Cal Ripken Jr./Jsy-Jsy/100	30.00
75	Harold Baines/Bat-Jsy/100	4.00

Throwback Col. Sign. Mat.

		NM/M
Production 5-50		
2	Tony Gwynn/Jsy/50	40.00
4	Angel Berroa/Pants/50	10.00
6	Tony Oliva/Jsy/50	20.00
8	Gary Carter/Pants/50	20.00
12	Roberto Alomar/Jsy/30	30.00
13	Omar Vizquel/Jsy/50	30.00
15	Carlos Beltran/Jsy/50	30.00
17	Mark Grace/Jsy/50	20.00
19	Dave Righetti/Jsy/50	20.00
26	Wade Boggs/Jsy/50	35.00
27	Luis Tiant/Pants/50	20.00
29	Rod Carew/Jsy/50	30.00
30	Dwight Evans/Jsy/25	25.00
32	Billy Williams/Jsy/50	20.00
35	Edgar Renteria/Jsy/50	20.00
37	Gaylord Perry/Jsy/50	15.00
39	Dave Parker/Jsy/50	20.00
41	Orlando Cepeda/Pants/25	25.00
42	Fergie Jenkins/Jsy/50	20.00
44	Reggie Jackson/Jsy/50	50.00
45	Bob Gibson/Jsy/25	40.00
49	Fred Lynn/Jsy/50	20.00

54	Tim Hudson/Jsy/25	25.00
55	Matt Williams/Jsy/50	30.00
57	Eric Chavez/Jsy/50	20.00
62	Jim Rice/Jsy/50	25.00
63	Mark Mulder/Jsy/50	20.00
66	Sean Casey/Jsy/50	20.00
67	Carlos Lee/Jsy/50	20.00
68	Stan Musial/Pants/25	75.00
70	Darryl Strawberry/Jsy/50	20.00
71	Tommy John/Jsy/50	15.00
75	Harold Baines/Jsy/50	15.00

Throw. Col. Sign. Mat. Combo

		NM/M
Production 5-25		
2	Tony Gwynn/Jsy-Pants/25	50.00
4	Angel Berroa/Bat-Pants/25	15.00
6	Tony Oliva/Bat-Jsy/25	25.00
8	Gary Carter/Jsy/25	25.00
12	Roberto Alomar/Bat-Jsy/25	40.00
15	Carlos Beltran/Bat-Jsy/25	35.00
17	Mark Grace/Bat-Jsy/25	35.00
19	Dave Righetti/Jsy-Jsy/25	25.00
26	Wade Boggs/Bat-Jsy/25	40.00
29	Rod Carew/Jkt-Jsy/25	40.00
44	Reggie Jackson/Bat-Jsy/25	50.00
49	Fred Lynn/Bat-Jsy/25	30.00
62	Jim Rice/Jsy-Pants/25	30.00
67	Carlos Lee/Hat-Jsy/25	20.00
68	Stan Musial/Pants/25	75.00
70	Darryl Strawberry/Jsy/25	20.00
75	Harold Baines/Bat-Jsy/25	20.00

2005 Donruss Timeless Treasures

		NM/M
Complete Set (100):		100.00
Common Player:		1.50
Production 799 Sets		
Tin (4):		100.00
1	David Ortiz	3.00
2	Derek Jeter	8.00
3	Edgar Renteria	2.00
4	Paul Molitor	3.00
5	Jeff Bagwell	2.00
6	Melvin Mora	1.50
7	Bobby Crosby	1.50
8	Cal Ripken Jr.	10.00
9	Hank Blalock	2.00
10	Hideo Nomo	2.00
11	Gary Sheffield	3.00
12	Alfonso Soriano	3.00
13	Carl Crawford	1.50
14	Paul Konerko	1.50
15	Jim Edmonds	2.00
16	Garret Anderson	1.50
17	Lance Berkman	1.50
18	Javy Lopez	1.50
19	Tony Gwynn	3.00
20	Mark Mulder	1.50
21	Sammy Sosa	5.00
22	Roger Clemens	8.00
23	Mark Teixeira	2.00
24	Miguel Cabrera	3.00
25	Jim Thome	4.00
26	Mike Piazza	4.00
27	Vladimir Guerrero	3.00
28	Austin Kearns	1.50
29	Rod Carew	3.00
30	Ken Griffey Jr.	5.00
31	Mike Piazza	4.00
32	David Wright	4.00
33	Jason Varitek	2.00
34	Kerry Wood	2.00
35	Frank Thomas	3.00
36	Mark Prior	2.00
37	Mike Mussina	2.00
38	Curt Schilling	3.00
39	Greg Maddux	5.00
40	Miguel Tejada	3.00
41	Tom Seaver	3.00
42	Mariano Rivera	3.00
43	Jason Giambi	1.50
44	Roy Oswalt	1.50
45	Pedro Martinez	3.00

46	Jeff Niemann RC	5.00
47	Tom Glavine	1.50
48	Torii Hunter	1.50
49	Scott Rolen	3.00
50	Curt Schilling	3.00
51	Randy Johnson	3.00
52	C.C. Sabathia	1.50
53	Rafael Palmeiro	2.00
54	Jake Peavy	2.00
55	Hideki Matsui	6.00
56	Ichiro Suzuki	6.00
57	Johan Santana	3.00
58	Todd Helton	2.00
59	Justin Verlander RC	8.00
60	Kazuo Matsui	1.50
61	Rafael Palmeiro	1.50
62	Sean Casey	1.50
63	Nolan Ryan	8.00
64	Magglio Ordonez	1.50
65	Craig Biggio	2.00
66	Vernon Wells	1.50
67	Manny Ramirez	3.00
68	Aramis Ramirez	1.50
69	Omar Vizquel	1.50
70	Eric Gagne	1.50
71	Troy Glaus	2.00
72	Carlton Fisk	3.00
73	Victor Martinez	1.50
74	Adrian Beltre	2.00
75	Barry Zito	1.50
76	Josh Beckett	2.00
77	Michael Young	1.50
78	Eric Chavez	1.50
79	Hideo Nomo	2.00
80	Andruw Jones	2.00
81	Ivan Rodriguez	2.00
82	Don Mattingly	6.00
83	Larry Walker	2.00
84	Philip Humber RC	5.00
85	Juan Gonzalez	1.50
86	Tim Hudson	2.00
87	Alex Rodriguez	6.00
88	Greg Maddux	4.00
89	J.D. Drew	2.00
90	Shawn Green	1.50
91	Roger Clemens	8.00
92	Nomar Garciaparra	4.00
93	Andy Pettitte	2.00
94	Khalil Greene	1.50
95	Mike Schmidt	5.00
96	Carlos Beltran	2.00
97	Mike Mussina	2.00
98	Ben Sheets	1.50
99	Chipper Jones	3.00
100	Albert Pujols	8.00

Bronze
Bronze:	1-2X
Production 100 Sets	

Silver
Silver:	2-3X
Production 50 Sets	

Gold
Gold:	3-5X
Production 25 Sets	

Platinum
No Pricing	
Production One Set	

Award Materials Number
		NM/M
Production 1-29		
Prime:		No Pricing
Production 1-5		
9	Jim Palmer/Pants/22	12.00
10	Rod Carew/Jsy/29	15.00
12	Mike Schmidt/Jsy/25	20.00
13	Robin Yount/Jsy/19	25.00
15	Roger Clemens/Jsy/21	25.00

Award Mat. Sign. Number
No Pricing	
Production 1-5	

Award Materials Year
		NM/M
Production 1-99		
1	Lou Boudreau/Jsy/48	20.00
2	Roger Maris/Pants/61	40.00
6	Johnny Bench/Jsy/72	15.00
9	Jim Palmer/Pants/76	10.00
10	Rod Carew/Jsy/77	10.00
12	Mike Schmidt/Jsy/81	10.00
13	Robin Yount/Jsy/89	15.00
15	Dale Murphy/Jsy/83	10.00
16	Roger Clemens/Jsy/86	20.00
17	Tom Glavine/Jsy/91	8.00
18	Frank Thomas/Jsy/94	10.00
19	Jeff Bagwell/Jsy/94	8.00
20	Randy Johnson/Jsy/95	10.00
21	Pedro Martinez/Jsy/99	10.00
22	Ivan Rodriguez/Jsy/99	10.00

Award Mat. Sign. Year
		NM/M
Production 1-25		
Prime:		No Pricing
Production 1-5		
6	Johnny Bench/Jsy/25	60.00
9	Jim Palmer/Pants/25	35.00
10	Rod Carew/Jsy/25	50.00
12	Mike Schmidt/Jsy/25	75.00
14	Dale Murphy/Jsy/25	50.00

Game Day Materials
		NM/M
Production 5-100		

1	Rod Carew/Hat/25	20.00
2	Kirby Puckett/Bat/100	15.00
5	Nellie Fox/Bat/25	60.00
6	Vladimir Guerrero/Fld Glv/25	15.00
7	Tony Gwynn/Jsy/100	15.00
8	Rickey Henderson/Bat/100	10.00
9	David Ortiz/Hat/100	15.00
10	Carlos Beltran/Jsy/50	10.00

Game Day Mat. Sign.
		NM/M
Production 3-25		
7	Tony Gwynn/Jsy/25	50.00

Gamers NY
		NM/M
Production 25 Sets		
1	Jim Thorpe/Jsy-Jsy/25	450.00
2	Willie Mays/Jsy-Pants/25	75.00
3	Nolan Ryan/Bat-Jsy/25	65.00

Gamers NY Signatures
		NM/M
Production 5 Sets		
2	Willie Mays/Jsy-Pants/25	250.00
3	Nolan Ryan/Bat-Jsy/25	125.00

HOF Cuts
No Pricing	
Production 1-10	

HOF Cuts Materials
No Pricing	
Production 1-10	

HOF Materials Barrel
Production One Set	

HOF Materials Bat
		NM/M
Production 5-50		
1	Pee Wee Reese/25	20.00
3	Harmon Killebrew/25	20.00
4	Hack Wilson/25	65.00
5	Brooks Robinson/50	20.00
8	Stan Musial/50	30.00
9	Carl Yastrzemski/50	50.00
11	Ted Williams/50	50.00
12	Luis Aparicio/50	15.00
14	Bobby Doerr/25	15.00
15	Ernie Banks/50	20.00
20	Mike Schmidt/50	25.00
21	Roberto Clemente/50	75.00
24	Willie Mays/50	40.00
25	Willie Stargell/25	25.00
26	Frank Robinson/50	15.00
28	Reggie Jackson/50	15.00
30	Orlando Cepeda/50	10.00
34	Nolan Ryan/50	30.00
39	George Brett/50	25.00
43	Nellie Fox/50	40.00
44	Johnny Bench/50	20.00
47	Hank Aaron/50	40.00
50	Al Kaline/50	20.00

HOF Mat. Sign. Bat
		NM/M
Production 1-25		
3	Harmon Killebrew/25	50.00
5	Brooks Robinson/25	50.00
8	Stan Musial/25	85.00
11	Luis Aparicio/25	25.00
12	Bobby Doerr/25	25.00
15	Ralph Kiner/25	50.00
20	Mike Schmidt/25	75.00
24	Willie Mays/25	240.00
26	Frank Robinson/25	40.00
30	Orlando Cepeda/25	25.00
34	Nolan Ryan/25	120.00
43	Johnny Bench/25	60.00
50	Al Kaline/25	50.00

HOF Materials Hat
No Pricing	

HOF Materials Sign. Hat
Production 5-10	

HOF Materials Jersey
		NM/M
Production 1-100		
Prime:		No Pricing
Production 1-5		
3	Harmon Killebrew/100	15.00
5	Brooks Robinson/50	15.00
8	Stan Musial/100	25.00
9	Carl Yastrzemski/100	15.00
11	Ted Williams/100	60.00
14	Ernie Banks/100	15.00
17	Duke Snider/25	20.00
19	Willie McCovey/25	20.00
20	Mike Schmidt/50	25.00
22	Jim Palmer/25	15.00
23	Enos Slaughter/50	15.00
24	Willie Mays/100	40.00
25	Willie Stargell/50	25.00
28	Reggie Jackson/50	25.00
29	Warren Spahn/25	25.00
31	Hoyt Wilhelm/50	10.00
32	Sandy Koufax/25	250.00
33	Hal Newhouser/50	10.00
34	Nolan Ryan/50	30.00

35	George Brett/50	25.00
37	Jim "Catfish" Hunter/25	15.00
38	Frankie Frisch Jkt/50	15.00
40	Lou Boudreau/25	15.00
43	Johnny Bench/50	15.00
44	Hank Aaron/100	40.00
45	Joe Cronin/50	20.00
49	Early Wynn/50	15.00

HOF Mat. Sign. Jersey
		NM/M
Production 1-25		
Prime:		No Pricing
Production 1-5		
3	Harmon Killebrew/25	50.00
5	Brooks Robinson/25	50.00
8	Stan Musial/25	85.00
17	Duke Snider/25	40.00
18	Willie McCovey/25	50.00
20	Mike Schmidt/25	75.00
22	Jim Palmer/25	40.00
24	Willie Mays/25	240.00
34	Nolan Ryan/25	120.00
43	Johnny Bench/25	60.00

HOF Mat. Jersey Number
		NM/M
Production 1-44		
18	Willie McCovey/44	15.0
20	Mike Schmidt/44	30.0
22	Jim Palmer/22	12.0
24	Willie Mays/24	65.0
28	Reggie Jackson/44	15.0
29	Warren Spahn/21	25.0
31	Hoyt Wilhelm/31	10.0
32	Sandy Koufax/32	250.0
34	Nolan Ryan/34	30.0
37	Jim "Catfish" Hunter/29	15.0
44	Hank Aaron/44	50.0
49	Early Wynn/44	15.0

HOF Materials Sign. Jersey Number
		NM/M
Production 1-44		
18	Willie McCovey/44	50.0
20	Mike Schmidt/44	75.0
22	Jim Palmer/22	30.0
24	Willie Mays/24	240.0
34	Nolan Ryan/34	120.0

HOF Materials Combos
		NM/M
Production 1-25		
Prime:		No Pricin
Production 1-5		
3	Harmon Killebrew/Bat-Jsy/25	25.0
5	Brooks Robinson/Bat-Jsy/25	30.
8	Stan Musial/Bat-Jsy/25	40.
9	Carl Yastrzemski/Bat-Jsy/25	30.
9	Ted Williams/Bat-Jsy/25	85.
12	Bobby Doerr/Bat-Pants/25	15.
14	Ernie Banks/Bat-Jsy/25	25.
18	Willie McCovey/Jsy-Pants/25	
20	Mike Schmidt/Bat-Jsy/25	
24	Willie Mays/Bat-Jsy/25	75.
25	Willie Stargell/Bat-Jsy/25	
28	Reggie Jackson/Bat-Jsy/25	
29	Warren Spahn/Jsy-Pants/25	
34	Nolan Ryan/Jsy-Pants/25	50.
35	George Brett/Bat-Jsy/25	
43	Johnny Bench/Bat-Jsy/25	25.
44	Hank Aaron/Bat-Jsy/25	60.

HOF Mat. Sign. Combos
		NM/M
Production 1-25		
Prime:		No Pricin
Production 1-5		
3	Harmon Killebrew/Bat-Jsy/25	65.
5	Brooks Robinson/Bat-Jsy/25	65.
6	Stan Musial/Bat-Jsy/25	100.
12	Bobby Doerr/Bat-Pants/25	30.
18	Willie McCovey/Jsy-Pants/25	30.
20	Mike Schmidt/Bat-Jsy/25	85.
24	Willie Mays/Bat-Jsy/25	
30	Orlando Cepeda/Bat-Pants/25	
34	Nolan Ryan/Jsy-Jsy/25	
43	Johnny Bench/Bat-Jsy/25	

HOF Materials Pants
		NM/M
Production 1-50		
8	Stan Musial/50	30
9	Carl Yastrzemski/50	30
12	Bobby Doerr/50	

17 Duke Snider/25 20.00
18 Willie McCovey/50 15.00
19 Bob Feller/25 20.00
22 Jim Palmer/25 10.00
24 Willie Mays/50 40.00
29 Warren Spahn/25 25.00
30 Orlando Cepeda/50 10.00
34 Nolan Ryan/50 40.00
43 Burleigh Grimes/50 75.00
45 Johnny Bench/25 15.00
46 Fergie Jenkins/50 10.00

HOF Mat. Sign. Pants
NM/M
Production 1-50
6 Stan Musial/25 85.00
12 Bobby Doerr/50 25.00
17 Duke Snider/25 40.00
18 Willie McCovey/25 50.00
22 Jim Palmer/25 40.00
24 Willie Mays/25 240.00
30 Orlando Cepeda/25 25.00
34 Nolan Ryan/25 120.00
43 Johnny Bench/25 60.00
46 Fergie Jenkins/25 30.00

HOF Silver
NM/M
Common Player: 4.00
Production 500 Sets
Gold: 2-4X
Production 25 Sets
Platinum: No Pricing
Production One Set
1 Pee Wee Reese 4.00
2 Red Schoendienst 4.00
3 Harmon Killebrew 5.00
4 Hack Wilson 5.00
5 Brooks Robinson 4.00
6 Stan Musial 6.00
7 Al Simmons 4.00
8 Carl Yastrzemski 5.00
9 Ted Williams 8.00
10 Phil Rizzuto 4.00
11 Luis Aparicio 4.00
12 Bobby Doerr 4.00
13 Bob Lemon 4.00
14 Ernie Banks 5.00
15 Ralph Kiner 4.00
16 Whitey Ford 4.00
17 Duke Snider 4.00
18 Willie McCovey 4.00
19 Bob Feller 6.00
20 Mike Schmidt 6.00
21 Roberto Clemente 8.00
22 Jim Palmer 4.00
23 Enos Slaughter 4.00
24 Willie Mays 8.00
25 Willie Stargell 4.00
26 Frank Robinson 4.00
27 Carl Hubbell 4.00
28 Reggie Jackson 4.00
29 Warren Spahn 5.00
30 Orlando Cepeda 4.00
31 Hoyt Wilhelm 4.00
32 Sandy Koufax 15.00
33 Hal Newhouser 4.00
34 Nolan Ryan 8.00
35 George Brett 6.00
36 Bill Dickey 4.00
37 Jim "Catfish" Hunter 4.00
38 Frankie Frisch 4.00
39 Nellie Fox 4.00
40 Lou Boudreau 4.00
41 Hank Greenberg 5.00
42 Burleigh Grimes 4.00
43 Johnny Bench 5.00
44 Hank Aaron 8.00
45 Joe Cronin 4.00
46 Fergie Jenkins 4.00
47 Luke Appling 4.00
48 Yogi Berra 5.00
49 Early Wynn 4.00
50 Al Kaline 5.00

Home Road Gamers Duos
NM/M
Production 1-100
Prime: No Pricing
Production 1-10
3 Babe Ruth-Jsy-Jsy/25 450.00
4 Paul Molitor/Jsy-Pants/100 15.00
7 Ivan Rodriguez/Jsy-Jsy/100 10.00
9 Ted Williams/Jsy-Jsy/25 85.00
10 Andre Dawson/Jsy-Jsy/25 15.00
13 Darryl Strawberry/Jsy-Jsy/100 12.00
14 Ernie Banks/Jsy-Jsy/25 30.00
15 Jim Edmonds/Jsy-Jsy/25 15.00
16 Bo Jackson/Jsy-Jsy/20 20.00
17 Mark Grace/Jsy-Jsy/100 15.00
18 Albert Pujols/Jsy-Jsy/100 25.00
19 Tony Gwynn/Jsy-Jsy/100 15.00
20 Cal Ripken Jr./Jsy-Jsy/100 40.00
21 Chipper Jones/Jsy-Jsy/50 15.00
23 Don Mattingly/Jsy-Jsy/100 25.00

24 Willie Mays/Jsy-Jsy/25 80.00
25 Tony Oliva/Jsy-Jsy/25 10.00
28 Reggie Jackson/Jsy/100 15.00
29 Rod Carew/Jsy-Jsy/100 15.00
30 Harmon Killebrew/Jsy-Jsy/25 25.00
32 Nolan Ryan/Jsy/30 30.00
33 Eddie Murray/Jsy-Pants/100 15.00
35 Rickey Henderson/Jsy-Jsy/50 15.00
36 Jim Rice/Jsy-Jsy/50 12.00
37 Hoyt Wilhelm/Jsy/50 10.00
38 Curt Schilling/Jsy-Jsy/100 10.00
42 Greg Maddux/Jsy-Jsy/100 15.00
43 Dennis Eckersley/Jsy/25 10.00
44 Willie McCovey/Jsy-Pants/100 15.00
45 Willie Stargell/Jsy-Jsy/50 20.00
46 Mike Mussina/Jsy-Pants/50 15.00
47 Gary Carter/Jsy-Jsy/50 15.00
48 Dale Murphy/Jsy-Jsy/50 15.00
49 Mike Piazza/Jsy-Jsy/50 20.00
50 Jim Palmer/Jsy-Jsy/50 15.00

Home Road Gamers Sig. Duos
NM/M
Production 1-25
4 Paul Molitor/Jsy-Pants/25 60.00
11 Darryl Strawberry/Jsy-Jsy/25 30.00
17 Mark Grace/Jsy-Jsy/25 50.00
23 Tony Gwynn/Jsy-Jsy/25 50.00
25 Tony Oliva/Jsy-Jsy/25 30.00
29 Rod Carew/Jsy-Jsy/25 50.00
30 Harmon Killebrew/Jsy-Jsy/25 50.00
36 Jim Rice/Jsy-Jsy/25 35.00
43 Dennis Eckersley/Jsy-Jsy/25 30.00
44 Willie McCovey/Jsy-Pants/25 50.00
47 Gary Carter/Jsy-Jsy/25 30.00
48 Dale Murphy/Jsy-Jsy/25 50.00
50 Jim Palmer/Jsy-Pants/25 40.00

Home Road Gamer Sig. Trios
NM/M
Production 1-25
Prime: No Pricing
Production 1-5
4 Paul Molitor/Bat-Jsy-Pants/25 75.00
11 Darryl Strawberry/Fld Glv-Jsy/25 40.00
17 Mark Grace/Bat-Jsy/25 60.00
19 Tony Gwynn/Jsy-Jsy/25 70.00
23 Don Mattingly/Bat-Jsy/25 90.00
25 Tony Oliva/Bat-Jsy/25 35.00
29 Rod Carew/Bat-Jsy/25 60.00
30 Harmon Killebrew/Bat-Jsy/25 70.00
36 Jim Rice/Bat-Jsy/25 40.00

Home Road Gamers Trios
NM/M
Production 1-100
Prime: No Pricing
Production 1-10
4 Paul Molitor/Bat-Jsy-Pants/100 25.00
7 Ivan Rodriguez/Jsy-Jsy/100 15.00
9 Ted Williams/Bat-Jsy/25 120.00
11 Darryl Strawberry/Fld Glv-Jsy/20 20.00
14 Ernie Banks/Bat-Jsy-Jsy/25 40.00
15 Jim Edmonds/Bat-Jsy-Jsy/25 25.00
17 Mark Grace/Bat-Jsy-Jsy/25 40.00
18 Albert Pujols/Jsy-Jsy/100 40.00
19 Tony Gwynn/Jsy-Jsy/100 25.00
20 Cal Ripken Jr./Jsy-Jsy/100 60.00
21 Chipper Jones/Jsy-Jsy/100 20.00
23 Don Mattingly/Bat-Jsy/100 30.00

24 Willie Mays/Bat-Jsy-Jsy/25 75.00
25 Tony Oliva/Bat-Jsy-Jsy/25 20.00
28 Reggie Jackson/Bat-Jsy/100 15.00
29 Rod Carew/Bat-Jsy/100 25.00
30 Harmon Killebrew/Bat-Jsy/25 35.00
32 Nolan Ryan/Jkt-Jsy/100 35.00
33 Eddie Murray/Jsy-Pants/100 20.00
35 Rickey Henderson/Jsy-Jsy/50 20.00
36 Jim Rice/Bat-Jsy-Jsy/25 20.00
38 Curt Schilling/Bat-Jsy-Jsy/50 15.00
44 Willie McCovey/Bat-Jsy-Pants/25 20.00
45 Willie Stargell/Bat-Jsy/50 25.00
46 Mike Mussina/Bat-Jsy/25 35.00
47 Gary Carter/Bat-Jsy/25 25.00
48 Dale Murphy/Bat-Jsy-Jsy/50 30.00
49 Mike Piazza/Jsy-Jsy/25 35.00

Home Run Materials
NM/M
Production 1-100
1 Ernie Banks/Bat/60 15.00
2 Roger Maris/Bat/61 50.00
4 Johnny Bench/Pants/71 10.00
5 Harmon Killebrew/Bat/75 15.00
6 Jose Canseco/Bat/25 15.00
8 Sammy Sosa/Jsy/100 10.00
9 Jim Thome/Jsy/50 10.00
10 Rafael Palmeiro/Jsy/50 8.00

Home Run Materials Sig.
NM/M
Production 3-25
1 Ernie Banks/Bat/25 60.00
4 Johnny Bench/Pants/25 60.00
5 Harmon Killebrew/Bat/25 50.00

Material Ink Bat
No Pricing
Production 1-10

Material Ink Jersey
NM/M
Production 1-50
2 Fred Lynn/50 15.00
3 Dale Murphy/50 30.00
4 Paul Molitor/50 30.00
8 Alan Trammell/50 15.00
12 Gary Carter/50 20.00
14 Andre Dawson/50 20.00
15 Luis Aparicio/50 15.00
18 Darryl Strawberry/50 15.00
19 Kirk Gibson/50 20.00
20 Don Sutton/50 20.00
23 Don Mattingly/Jkt/75 75.00
24 Tony Perez/50 25.00
27 Carlton Fisk/25 40.00
29 Fred McGriff/25 40.00
30 John Kruk/25 20.00
32 Dwight Evans/25 25.00
33 Gary Sheffield/25 50.00
35 Bo Jackson/25 65.00
36 Gaylord Perry/25 20.00
39 Dave Parker/25 20.00
42 Harmon Killebrew/50 50.00
43 Dennis Eckersley/25 25.00
46 Willie McCovey/25 50.00
47 Luis Tiant/50 20.00
48 Mark Teixeira/25 40.00

Mat. Ink Jersey Number
NM/M
Production 1-44
2 Fred Lynn/19 30.00
4 Darryl Strawberry/44 20.00
20 Don Sutton/20 25.00
22 Mark Prior/22 50.00
23 Don Mattingly/Jkt/23 80.00
24 Tony Perez/34 40.00
27 Carlton Fisk/27 40.00
29 Fred McGriff/29 50.00
30 John Kruk/29 50.00
32 Dwight Evans/34 50.00
36 Gaylord Perry/36 20.00
40 Mark Teixeira/23 40.00
44 Dennis Eckersley/43 20.00
44 Willie McCovey/44 40.00
46 Luis Tiant/27 25.00

Material Ink Combos
NM/M
Production 1-25
Prime: No Pricing
Production 1-5
2 Fred Lynn/Bat-Jsy/25 35.00
3 Gary Carter/Bat-Jsy/25 30.00
10 Andre Dawson/Bat-Jsy/25 30.00
11 Luis Aparicio/Bat-Jsy/100 30.00

14 Darryl Strawberry/Bat-Jsy/25 30.00
27 Carlton Fisk/Bat-Jsy/25 40.00
37 Miguel Cabrera/Jsy/25 50.00
39 Dave Parker/Bat-Jsy/25 25.00
48 Mark Grace/Bat-Jsy/25 40.00

Milestone Mat. Number
NM/M
Production 1-31
2 Nolan Ryan/Jsy/30 35.00
10 Greg Maddux/Jsy/31 20.00

Milestone Materials Signature Number
No Pricing
Production 1-10

Milestone Material Year
NM/M
Production 10-25
Prime: No Pricing
Production 1-10
1 Roger Maris/Pants/25 40.00
2 Nolan Ryan/Jsy/25 30.00
5 Steve Garvey/Jsy/25 10.00
6 Wade Boggs/Jsy/25 10.00
7 Tony Gwynn/Jsy/25 20.00
8 Sammy Sosa/Jsy/25 10.00
9 Randy Johnson/Jsy/25 15.00
10 Greg Maddux/Jsy/25 20.00

Milestone Materials Signature Year
NM/M
Production 1-25
Prime: No Pricing
Production 1-5
2 Nolan Ryan/Jsy/25 120.00
5 Steve Garvey/Jsy/25 25.00
7 Tony Gwynn/Jsy/25 40.00

No-Hitters
NM/M
Production 3-25
7 Dennis Eckersley, Bert Blyleven/25 35.00
8 Juan Marichal, Gaylord Perry/25 35.00
9 Jim Palmer, Bob Gibson/25 40.00

Rookie Year Materials Number
NM/M
Production 1-44
1 Rod Carew/Jsy/29 20.00
6 Juan Marichal/Jsy/27 12.00
8 Jim Palmer/Hat/22 15.00
16 Kirk Gibson/Hat/23 15.00
18 Roger Clemens/Jsy/21 25.00
20 David Cone/Jsy/44 8.00
23 Deion Sanders/Jsy/21 20.00
28 Mike Piazza/Jsy/31 8.00
33 Andruw Jones/Jsy/10 10.00
34 Vladimir Guerrero/Jsy/27 15.00
37 Kerry Wood/Jsy/34 15.00
38 Magglio Ordonez/Jsy/30 8.00
40 Mark Mulder/Jsy/20 7.00
41 Lance Berkman/Jsy/17 10.00
42 Alfonso Soriano/Jsy/33 10.00
46 Mark Prior/Jsy/22 10.00
47 Mark Teixeira/Jsy/23 10.00
48 Miguel Cabrera/Jsy/20 15.00
50 Victor Martinez/Jsy/41 8.00

Rookie Year Material Signature Number
NM/M
Production 1-30
1 Rod Carew/Jsy/29 35.00
3 Duke Snider/Jsy/25 40.00
6 Juan Marichal/Jsy/25 25.00
11 Gary Carter/Jsy/25 30.00
12 Robin Yount/Jsy/19 65.00
13 Keith Hernandez/Jsy/18 35.00
15 Ozzie Smith/Jsy/25 20.00
20 David Cone/Jsy/25 25.00
21 Gary Sheffield/Jsy/25 40.00
24 Dwight Gooden/Jsy/16 25.00
38 Magglio Ordonez/Jsy/30 20.00
46 Mark Prior/Jsy/22 40.00
47 Mark Teixeira/Jsy/23 50.00
48 Miguel Cabrera/Jsy/20 50.00
50 Victor Martinez/Jsy/19 20.00

Rookie Year Materials Year
NM/M
Production 1-100
Prime: No Pricing
Production Five Sets
1 Rod Carew/Jsy/100 15.00
3 Duke Snider/Jsy/100 12.00
6 Juan Marichal/Jsy/100 10.00
11 Gary Carter/Jsy/100 8.00
12 Robin Yount/Jsy/100 15.00
13 Keith Hernandez/Jsy/100 10.00
15 Ozzie Smith/Jsy/100 10.00
17 Dave Righetti/Jsy/100 10.00
18 Roger Clemens/Jsy/100 15.00
19 Greg Maddux/Jsy/100 25.00
20 David Cone/Jsy/100 8.00
21 Gary Sheffield/Jsy/100 10.00
22 Randy Johnson/Jsy/100 10.00
23 Deion Sanders/Jsy/100 8.00
25 Dwight Gooden/Jsy/100 12.00
25 Ivan Rodriguez/Jsy/100 8.00
26 Jeff Bagwell/Pants/100 8.00
27 Pedro Martinez/Jsy/100 10.00
28 Mike Piazza/Jsy/100 12.00
29 Chipper Jones/Jsy/100 10.00
30 Hideo Nomo/Jsy/100 12.00
32 Scott Rolen/Jsy/100 10.00
33 Andruw Jones/Jsy/100 8.00
34 Vladimir Guerrero/Jsy/100 10.00
35 Sean Casey/Jsy/100 10.00
36 Paul LoDuca/Jsy/100 8.00
37 Kerry Wood/Jsy/100 12.00
38 Magglio Ordonez/Jsy/25 8.00
39 Vernon Wells/Jsy/100 8.00
40 Mark Mulder/Jsy/100 8.00
41 Lance Berkman/Jsy/100 8.00
42 Alfonso Soriano/Jsy/100 8.00
43 Albert Pujols/Jsy/100 20.00
44 Ben Sheets/Jsy/25 10.00
45 Roy Oswalt/Jsy/100 10.00
46 Mark Teixeira/Jsy/100 10.00
48 Miguel Cabrera/Jsy/100 10.00
49 Travis Hafner/Jsy/25 10.00
50 Victor Martinez/Jsy/25 10.00

Rookie Year Materials Signature Year
NM/M
Production 1-25
Prime: No Pricing
Production 1-5
1 Rod Carew/Jsy/25 35.00
3 Duke Snider/Jsy/25 40.00
6 Juan Marichal/Jsy/25 30.00
11 Gary Carter/Jsy/25 30.00
12 Robin Yount/Jsy/25 65.00
13 Keith Hernandez/Jsy/25 30.00
15 Ozzie Smith/Jsy/25 50.00
17 Dave Righetti/Jsy/25 20.00
21 David Cone/Jsy/25 25.00
24 Dwight Gooden/Jsy/25 40.00
32 Scott Rolen/Jsy/25 50.00
35 Sean Casey/Jsy/25 20.00
36 Paul LoDuca/Jsy/25 20.00
38 Magglio Ordonez/Jsy/25 20.00
39 Vernon Wells/Jsy/25 20.00
40 Mark Mulder/Jsy/25 25.00
42 Alfonso Soriano/Jsy/25 35.00
44 Ben Sheets/Jsy/25 25.00
46 Mark Prior/Jsy/25 40.00
47 Mark Teixeira/Jsy/25 40.00
48 Miguel Cabrera/Jsy/25 50.00
49 Travis Hafner/Jsy/25 20.00
50 Victor Martinez/Jsy/25 20.00

Salutations Signature
NM/M
Production 1-24
1 Al Kaline/24 70.00
5 Dale Murphy/24 50.00
7 Duke Snider/24 50.00
11 Johnny Bench/24 60.00
19 Steve Carlton/24 40.00

Signature Bronze
NM/M
Platinum: No Pricing
Production 10-100
Production One Set
3 Edgar Renteria/50 30.00
4 Paul Molitor/100 25.00
7 Bobby Crosby/25 25.00
8 Cal Ripken Jr./25 200.00
11 Hank Blalock/50 25.00
12 Gary Sheffield/50 35.00
14 Alfonso Soriano/50 25.00
15 Paul Konerko/50 30.00
16 Garret Anderson/50 30.00
19 Tony Gwynn/100 40.00
22 Mark Mulder/50 25.00
23 Mark Teixeira/50 30.00
28 Miguel Cabrera/50 30.00
28 Austin Kearns/50 15.00
32 Rod Carew/100 40.00
33 David Wright/25 75.00
35 Kerry Wood/50 35.00
36 Mark Prior/100 40.00
41 Tom Seaver/100 40.00
45 Roy Oswalt/50 25.00
46 Jeff Niemann/100 35.00
49 Torii Hunter/50 30.00
50 Scott Rolen/50 25.00
52 C.C. Sabathia/25 25.00
53 Rafael Palmeiro/50 30.00
57 Johan Santana/50 40.00
59 Justin Verlander/100 50.00
61 Rafael Palmeiro/50 30.00
62 Sean Casey/25 20.00
63 Nolan Ryan/50 85.00
66 Magglio Ordonez/50 15.00
67 Craig Biggio/50 20.00
68 Vernon Wells/25 20.00
69 Manny Ramirez/25 30.00
72 Omar Vizquel/50 40.00
73 Carlton Fisk/100 25.00
74 Victor Martinez/50 15.00
75 Adrian Beltre/50 25.00
76 Barry Zito/50 20.00

76 Josh Beckett/25 35.00
77 Michael Young/50 20.00
78 Eric Chavez/50 15.00
84 Don Mattingly/25 60.00
85 Philip Humber/100 25.00
86 Juan Gonzalez/25 25.00
86 Tim Hudson/25 30.00
90 Shawn Green/25 30.00
95 Mike Schmidt/100 50.00
98 Ben Sheets/25 25.00
99 Chipper Jones/25 60.00

Signature Silver
NM/M
Production 5-50
3 Edgar Renteria/25 40.00
4 Paul Molitor/50 30.00
8 Hank Blalock/25 25.00
11 Gary Sheffield/25 40.00
12 Alfonso Soriano/25 35.00
14 Paul Konerko/25 25.00
15 Jim Edmonds/25 35.00
16 Garret Anderson/25 25.00
19 Tony Gwynn/50 60.00
22 Mark Mulder/50 25.00
23 Mark Teixeira/25 40.00
24 Miguel Cabrera/25 40.00
28 Austin Kearns/25 20.00
29 Rod Carew/50 30.00
34 Kerry Wood/50 20.00
36 Mark Prior/50 40.00
41 Tom Seaver/50 50.00
46 Jeff Niemann/50 25.00
47 Torii Hunter/25 25.00
49 Scott Rolen/50 25.00
57 Johan Santana/25 50.00
59 Justin Verlander/25 35.00
63 Nolan Ryan/25 100.00
64 Magglio Ordonez/25 20.00
65 Craig Biggio/25 35.00
72 Omar Vizquel/25 40.00
72 Carlton Fisk/50 40.00
74 Victor Martinez/25 20.00
74 Adrian Beltre/25 25.00
75 Barry Zito/25 20.00
77 Michael Young/25 20.00
78 Eric Chavez/25 20.00
82 Don Mattingly/50 60.00
84 Philip Humber/50 40.00
86 Juan Gonzalez/25 30.00
86 Tim Hudson/25 30.00
95 Mike Schmidt/50 65.00

Signature Gold
NM/M
Production 3-25
4 Paul Molitor/25 35.00
19 Tony Gwynn/25 50.00
20 Mark Mulder/25 30.00
29 Rod Carew/25 50.00
36 Mark Prior/25 50.00
41 Tom Seaver/25 60.00
63 Nolan Ryan/25 120.00
72 Carlton Fisk/25 35.00
82 Don Mattingly/25 85.00
95 Mike Schmidt/25 85.00

Statistical Champions Material Number
NM/M
Production 1-47
1 Nolan Ryan/Jsy/34 30.00
2 Lee Smith/Jsy/47 8.00
6 Kerry Wood/Jsy/34 12.00
20 Curt Schilling/Jsy/38 10.00
20 Mark Mulder/Jsy/20 10.00
21 Roger Clemens/Jsy/21 25.00
22 Will Clark/Jsy/22 10.00
23 Don Mattingly/Jsy/23 25.00
24 Manny Ramirez/Jsy/24 12.00
25 Billy Williams/Jsy/50 10.00
26 Wade Boggs/Jsy/26 15.00
27 Kevin Brown/Jsy/27 8.00
32 Sandy Koufax/Jsy/32 250.00
33 Jose Canseco/Jsy/33 12.00
34 Kirby Puckett/Jsy/34 15.00
35 Rickey Henderson/Jsy/35 15.00
38 Curt Schilling/Jsy/38 10.00
41 Nolan Ryan/Jsy/34 30.00
44 Roy Oswalt/Jsy/44 8.00

Stat. Champion Materials Sign. Number
NM/M
Production 1-34
1 Nolan Ryan/Jsy/34 120.00
19 Tony Gwynn/Jsy/19 75.00
20 Mark Mulder/Jsy/20 25.00
22 Will Clark/Jsy/22 40.00
23 Don Mattingly/Jsy/23 75.00
26 Wade Boggs/Jsy/26 50.00
29 Adrian Beltre/Jsy/29 35.00
39 Don Sutton/Jsy/20 30.00
41 Nolan Ryan/Jsy/34 120.00

Statistical Champions Materials Year
NM/M
Production 1-100
Prime: No Pricing
Production 1-5
1 Nolan Ryan/Jsy/100 25.00
2 Lee Smith/Jsy/100 10.00
3 Harmon Killebrew/Jsy/100 12.00

4	Kerry Wood/Jsy/100	12.00
5	Albert Pujols/Jsy/100	20.00
6	Curt Schilling/Jsy/100	8.00
7	Joe Cronin/Pants/100	12.00
8	Cal Ripken Jr./Jsy/100	30.00
9	Barry Zito/Jsy/100	8.00
10	Miguel Tejada/Jsy/100	10.00
11	Edgar Martinez/Jsy/25	8.00
14	Andre Dawson/Jsy/100	10.00
17	Todd Helton/Jsy/100	8.00
19	Tony Gwynn/Jsy/100	12.00
20	Mark Mulder/Jsy/100	5.00
21	Roger Clemens/Jsy/100	15.00
22	Will Clark/Jsy/25	20.00
23	Don Mattingly/Jsy/100	20.00
24	Manny Ramirez/Jsy/25	10.00
25	Billy Williams/Jsy/100	8.00
26	Wade Boggs/Jsy/100	10.00
27	Kevin Brown/Jsy/100	5.00
28	George Brett/Jsy/100	20.00
29	Adrian Beltre/Jsy/100	10.00
30	Lance Berkman/Jsy/100	5.00
31	Sammy Sosa/Jsy/100	10.00
32	Sandy Koufax/Jsy/25	250.00
33	Jose Canseco/Jsy/25	15.00
34	Kirby Puckett/Jsy/100	10.00
35	Rickey Henderson/ Jsy/100	12.00
36	Juan Gonzalez/Jsy/100	8.00
38	Curt Schilling/Jsy/100	8.00
39	Don Sutton/Jsy/100	8.00
40	Johan Santana/Jsy/100	10.00
41	Nolan Ryan/Jsy/25	25.00
43	Lou Brock/Jsy/100	8.00
44	Roy Oswalt/Jsy/25	8.00
45	Dale Murphy/Jsy/100	10.00

Stat. Champions Materials Sign. Year

NM/M

Production 1-50
Prime: No Pricing
Production 1-5

1	Nolan Ryan/Jsy/50	100.00
3	Harmon Killebrew/ Jsy/50	40.00
4	Kerry Wood/Jsy/25	40.00
8	Cal Ripken Jr./Jsy/25	175.00
9	Barry Zito/Jsy/25	25.00
11	Edgar Martinez/Jsy/50	40.00
19	Tony Gwynn/Jsy/50	60.00
20	Mark Mulder/Jsy/25	25.00
22	Will Clark/Jsy/25	40.00
23	Don Mattingly/Jsy/50	60.00
26	Wade Boggs/Jsy/50	40.00
29	Adrian Beltre/Jsy/25	35.00
39	Don Sutton/Jsy/25	30.00
40	Johan Santana/Jsy/25	60.00
41	Nolan Ryan/Jsy/50	100.00
43	Lou Brock/Jsy/50	40.00
45	Dale Murphy/Jsy/50	30.00

World Series Materials

NM/M

Production 1-100

1	Frank Robinson/Bat/100	10.00
3	Carl Yastrzemski/ Bat/100	25.00
4	Jack Morris/Jsy/50	8.00
5	Wade Boggs/Bat/100	12.00
8	Andruw Jones/Jsy/100	8.00
10	Darryl Strawberry/ Jsy/25	10.00

World Series Materials Signatures

NM/M

Production 1-25
Prime: No Pricing
Production 1-10

4	Jack Morris/Jsy/25	25.00
5	Wade Boggs/Bat/25	40.00
10	Darryl Strawberry/ Jsy/25	25.00

2005 Donruss Zenith Promos

This 7-1/2" x 10" Dufex foil-technology card was distributed as a wrapper redemption at the National Sports Collectors Convention in Chicago. The back has a promo overprint.

NM/M

32	Sandy Koufax	12.00

2005 Donruss Zenith

NM/M

Complete Set (250):		50.00
Common Player:		.25
Hobby Pack (5):		5.00
Hobby Box (18):		80.00
1	Curt Schilling	.50
2	Jim Edmonds	.40
3	Ichiro Suzuki	1.50
4	Jody Gerut	.25
5	Carlos Beltran	.50
6	Miguel Tejada	.50
7	Ted Lilly	.25
8	Bobby Abreu	.40
9	Mark Teixeira	.50
10	Manny Ramirez	.75
11	Eric Gagne	.40
12	Adrian Beltre	.40
13	Dmitri Young	.25
14	Alfonso Soriano	.50
15	Vladimir Guerrero	.75
16	Carl Crawford	.25
17	David Ortiz	.75
18	Jose Guillen	.25
19	Miguel Cabrera	.75
20	Alex Rodriguez	2.00
21	Brad Lidge	.25
22	Francisco Rodriguez	.25
23	Carlos Lee	.25
24	Ben Sheets	.40
25	Jason Schmidt	.25
26	Cesar Izturis	.25
27	Corey Patterson	.25
28	Marcus Giles	.25
29	Melvin Mora	.25
30	Yadier Molina	.25
31	Juan Pierre	.25
32	Aubrey Huff	.25
33	Rafael Furcal	.25
34	David Dellucci	.25
35	Jake Peavy	.40
36	Aramis Ramirez	.40
37	Javy Lopez	.25
38	Aaron Rowand	.25
39	Raul Ibanez	.25
40	Jason Bay	.40
41	Michael Young	.25
42	Ivan Rodriguez	.50
43	Derrek Lee	.50
44	Adam Dunn	.50
45	Eric Chavez	.40
46	Pedro Martinez	.75
47	Roy Oswalt	.40
48	Kevin Millwood	.25
49	Carlos Delgado	.40
50	Derek Jeter	2.00
51	Johnny Damon	.50
52	Richie Sexson	.40
53	Nomar Garciaparra	.75
54	Edgar Renteria	.25
55	Carl Pavano	.25
56	Tim Wakefield	.25
57	Michael Barrett	.25
58	Johnny Estrada	.25
59	Jeff Kent	.25
60	Mark Loretta	.25
61	Greg Maddux	1.00
62	Hank Blalock	.40
63	Moises Alou	.40
64	Brad Radke	.25
65	Brad Wilkerson	.25
66	Sean Casey	.25
67	Oliver Perez	.40
68	Scott Hatteberg	.25
69	Mike Lowell	.25
70	Kazuo Matsui	.25
71	Mark Prior	.50
72	Hideki Matsui	1.50
73	Geoff Jenkins	.25
74	Gary Sheffield	.50
75	A.J. Burnett	.25
76	Vernon Wells	.25
77	Kenny Rogers	.25
78	Jose Reyes	.50
79	Victor Martinez	.25
80	Jorge Posada	.40
81	Rich Harden	.25
82	Travis Hafner	.25
83	Bret Boone	.25
84	Chipper Jones	.50
85	Bartolo Colon	.25
86	Scott Podsednik	.25
87	Coco Crisp	.25
88	Luis Castillo	.25
89	John Smoltz	.50
90	Andruw Jones	.50
91	Milton Bradley	.25

92	Torii Hunter	.25
93	Shawn Green	.40
94	Paul Konerko	.40
95	David Wells	.25
96	Scott Rolen	.50
97	Rodrigo Lopez	.25
98	Garret Anderson	.40
99	Tim Hudson	.40
100	Sammy Sosa	.75
101	Jason Varitek	.50
102	Lance Berkman	.40
103	Troy Glaus	.40
104	Carlos Guillen	.25
105	Jeff Bagwell	.50
106	Phil Nevin	.25
107	Freddy Garcia	.25
108	Jake Westbrook	.25
109	Marquis Grissom	.25
110	Johan Santana	.75
111	Kerry Wood	.40
112	Jose Vidro	.25
113	Mike Mussina	.40
114	Josh Beckett	.40
115	Matt Lawton	.25
116	Craig Biggio	.40
117	Reggie Sanders	.25
118	Jason Kendall	.25
119	Larry Walker	.40
120	Roger Clemens	2.00
121	C.C. Sabathia	.25
122	Javier Vazquez	.25
123	Barry Zito	.40
124	Jon Lieber	.25
125	Kris Benson	.25
126	Jacque Jones	.25
127	Ray Durham	.25
128	Mark Kotsay	.25
129	Jack Wilson	.25
130	Bobby Crosby	.25
131	Todd Helton	.50
132	Lyle Overbay	.25
133	Jon Garland	.25
134	Roy Halladay	.40
135	Orlando Cabrera	.25
136	Danny Kolb	.25
137	Austin Kearns	.25
138	Paul LoDuca	.25
139	Magglio Ordonez	.40
140	Rafael Palmeiro	.50
141	Omar Vizquel	.25
142	Mike Piazza	1.00
143	Mark Mulder	.40
144	Dontrelle Willis	.40
145	Tom Glavine	.40
146	Khalil Greene	.25
147	Ken Griffey Jr.	1.50
148	Mike Sweeney	.25
149	Trot Nixon	.25
150	Randy Johnson	.75
151	Doug Mientkiewicz	.25
152	Jeromy Burnitz	.25
153	Brandon Webb	.25
154	Kevin Brown	.25
155	Carlos Zambrano	.25
156	Shingo Takatsu	.25
157	Erubiel Durazo	.25
158	Jason Isringhausen	.25
159	Corey Koskie	.25
160	Aaron Boone	.25
161	Joe Nathan	.25
162	Nick Johnson	.25
163	Michael Tucker	.25
164	Chris Carpenter	.25
165	Preston Wilson	.25
166	J.T. Snow	.25
167	Hideo Nomo	.40
168	Miguel Olivo	.25
169	Jarrod Washburn	.25
170	Derek Lowe	.25
171	Eric Milton	.25
172	Andy Pettitte	.40
173	Jason Giambi	.40
174	Richard Hidalgo	.25
175	Jayson Werth	.25
176	Juan Gonzalez	.25
177	Rocco Baldelli	.25
178	Steve Finley	.25
179	Frank Thomas	.40
180	Kenny Lofton	.25
181	Randy Winn	.25
182	Brandon McCarthy RC	1.50
183	Lew Ford	.25
184	Mike Cameron	.25
185	Carlos Pena	.25
186	Brian Roberts	.25
187	Jeremy Bonderman	.25
188	Luis Gonzalez	.25
189	J.D. Drew	.25
190	Frank Catalanotto	.25
191	John Buck	.25
192	Pat Burrell	.25
193	Ryan Klesko	.25
194	Jermaine Dye	.25
195	Mariano Rivera	.40
196	Angel Berroa	.25
197	Carlos Zambrano	.25
198	Joel Pineiro	.25
199	Jay Gibbons	.25
200	Albert Pujols	2.00
201	Billy Wagner	.25
202	Darin Erstad	.25
203	Jim Thome	.50
204	Adam LaRoche	.25
205	Cliff Floyd	.25
206	Grady Sizemore	.50
207	Garrett Atkins	.25
208	Philip Humber RC	1.00
209	Zack Greinke	.25

210	Wladimir Balentien RC	1.00
211	Ubaldo Jimenez RC	5.00
212	Dallas McPherson	.25
213	Justin Verlander RC	3.00
214	Justin Morneau	.50
215	Chase Utley	.50
216	Casey Kotchman	.25
217	Tadahito Iguchi RC	3.00
218	Hanley Ramirez	.50
219	Scott Kazmir	.25
220	J.J. Hardy	.25
221	Ambiorix Concepcion RC	.50
222	Jeff Niemann RC	1.00
223	David Wright	1.00
224	Joe Mauer	.50
225	Rickie Weeks	.25
226	Yuniesky Betancourt RC	1.00
227	Brady Clark	.25
228	Keiichi Yabu RC	.50
229	Delmon Young	.50
230	Nick Swisher	.25
231	George Brett	1.00
232	Ryne Sandberg	1.00
233	Mike Schmidt	1.00
234	Tony Gwynn	.75
235	Rickey Henderson	.50
236	Ozzie Smith	1.00
237	Reggie Jackson	.75
238	Steve Carlton	.40
239	Robin Yount	1.00
240	Tom Seaver	.50
241	Ted Williams	1.50
242	Don Mattingly	1.00
243	Mark Grace	.40
244	Rod Carew	.40
245	Willie Mays	1.50
246	Gary Carter	.40
247	Wade Boggs	.50
248	Dale Murphy	.40
249	Nolan Ryan	2.00
250	Cal Ripken Jr.	3.00

Artist's Proofs Silver

Silver AP (1-250):	3-5X
Inserted 1:16	

Artist's Proofs Gold

Gold AP (1-250):	5-10X
Production 50 Sets	

Museum Collection

Museum (1-250):	2-3X
Inserted 1:3	

Epix Orange Play

NM/M

Common Player:	1.50
Production 750 Sets	
Black Game:	1-2X
Production 75 Sets	
Black Moment:	2-3X
Production 25 Sets	
Black Play:	1X
Production 100 Sets	
Black Season:	1-2X
Production 50 Sets	
Blue Game:	1X
Production 350	
Blue Moment:	1X
Production 150 Sets	
Blue Play:	1X
Production 500 Sets	
Blue Season:	1X
Production 250 Sets	
Emerald Game:	1X
Production 100 Sets	
Emerald Moment:	1-2X
Production 50 Sets	
Emerald Play:	1X
Production 150 Sets	
Emerald Season:	1X
Production 75 Sets	
Orange Game:	1X
Production 500 Sets	
Orange Moment:	1X
Production 250 Sets	
Orange Season:	1X
Production 350 Sets	
Purple Game:	1X
Production 250 Sets	
Purple Moment:	1X
Production 100 Sets	
Purple Play:	1X
Production 350 Sets	
Purple Season:	1X
Production 150 Sets	
Red Game:	1X
Production 150 Sets	
Red Moment:	1-2X
Production 50 Sets	
Red Play:	1X
Production 250 Sets	
Red Season:	1X
Production 100 Sets	
1 Vladimir Guerrero	3.00
2 Alex Rodriguez	6.00
3 Johan Santana	3.00
4 Todd Helton	3.00
5 Mark Teixeira	2.00
6 Manny Ramirez	3.00
7 Scott Rolen	2.00
8 Gary Sheffield	2.00
9 Miguel Cabrera	2.00
10 Jim Thome	2.00
11 Eric Chavez	2.00
12 Roger Clemens	6.00
13 Pedro Martinez	3.00
14 Roy Oswalt	1.50

15	Carlos Delgado	1.50
16	Nomar Garciaparra	2.00
17	Hideki Matsui	5.00
18	Shawn Green	1.50
19	Greg Maddux	4.00
20	Ted Williams	6.00
21	Don Mattingly	5.00
22	Cal Ripken Jr.	10.00
23	George Brett	6.00
24	Nolan Ryan	8.00
25	Willie Mays	6.00

Mozaics

NM/M

Common Trio:	1.00
Inserted 1:8	

1	Pedro Martinez, Carlos Beltran, Tom Glavine	2.00
2	Albert Pujols, Jim Edmonds, Mark Mulder	5.00
3	Sammy Sosa, Miguel Tejada, Rafael Palmeiro	2.00
4	Mark Teixeira, Hank Blalock, Michael Young	2.00
5	Andruw Jones, Rafael Furcal, Johnny Estrada	1.00
6	Bobby Crosby, Eric Chavez, Barry Zito	1.00
7	Shawn Green, Troy Glaus, Luis Gonzalez	1.00
8	Austin Kearns, Adam Dunn, Sean Casey	1.00
9	Jim Thome, Bobby Abreu, Pat Burrell	1.50
10	Lance Berkman, Jeff Bagwell, Craig Biggio	1.50
11	Orlando Cabrera, Steve Finley, Darin Erstad	1.00
12	J.D. Drew, Jeff Kent, Milton Bradley	1.00
13	Dontrelle Willis, Mike Lowell, A.J. Burnett	1.00
14	Adrian Beltre, Jeremy Reed, Richie Sexson	1.00
15	Joe Mauer, Justin Morneau, Jacque Jones	1.00
16	Gary Sheffield, Hideki Matsui, Mike Mussina	4.00

Mozaics Materials Single

NM/M

Common Player:		4.00
1	Pedro Martinez/Jsy	6.00
2	Albert Pujols/Bat	15.00
3	Miguel Tejada/Jsy	4.00
4	Mark Teixeira/Bat	6.00
7	Andruw Jones/Bat	6.00
8	Luis Gonzalez/Bat	4.00
9	Adam Dunn/Bat	4.00
10	Bobby Abreu/Jsy	4.00
11	Craig Biggio/Bat	4.00
12	Darin Erstad/Bat	4.00
13	J.D. Drew/Bat	4.00
14	A.J. Burnett/Bat	4.00
15	Richie Sexson/Bat	4.00
16	Jacque Jones/Bat	4.00
	Gary Sheffield/Fld Glv	6.00

Mozaics Materials Triple Jerseys

NM/M

Production 5-100
Prime: No Pricing
Production 5-10

4	Mark Teixeira, Hank Blalock, Michael Young/100	10.00
6	Bobby Crosby, Eric Chavez, Barry Zito/25	10.00
8	Austin Kearns, Adam Dunn, Sean Casey/100	10.00
9	Jim Thome, Bobby Abreu, Pat Burrell/100	10.00
10	Lance Berkman, Jeff Bagwell, Craig Biggio/100	10.00
16	Gary Sheffield, Hideki Matsui, Mike Mussina/50	25.00

Positions

NM/M

Common Card:	
Inserted 1:21	
Gold:	1-2X
Production 100 Sets	

1	Randy Johnson, Mark Prior, Roger Clemens	4.00
2	Ivan Rodriguez, Mike Piazza, Victor Martinez	2.00

3	Albert Pujols, Todd Helton, David Ortiz	5.00
4	Marcus Giles, Mark Loretta, Bret Boone	1.00
5	Scott Rolen, Aramis Ramirez, Chipper Jones	2.00
6	Kazuo Matsui, Miguel Tejada, Michael Young	1.00
7	Brian Giles, Manny Ramirez, Shannon Stewart	2.00
8	Rocco Baldelli, Andruw Jones, Vernon Wells	1.50
9	Miguel Cabrera, Lance Berkman, Vladimir Guerrero	2.00

Positions Materials Single

NM/M

Common Player:		4.00
1	Mark Prior/Bat	6.00
2	Ivan Rodriguez/Bat	6.00
3	Albert Pujols/Bat	15.00
4	Bret Boone/Jsy	4.00
5	Chipper Jones/Bat	6.00
6	Kazuo Matsui/Jsy	4.00
7	Manny Ramirez/Bat	4.00
8	Andruw Jones/Bat	6.00
9	Lance Berkman/Bat	4.00

Positions Materials Triple Jersey

NM/M

Production 5-100

2	Ivan Rodriguez, Mike Piazza, Victor Martinez/15	15.00
3	Albert Pujols, Todd Helton, David Ortiz/50	25.00
5	Scott Rolen, Aramis Ramirez, Chipper Jones/100	15.00
6	Kazuo Matsui, Miguel Tejada, Michael Young/75	10.00
8	Rocco Baldelli, Andruw Jones, Vernon Wells/100	10.00
9	Miguel Cabrera, Lance Berkman, Vladimir Guerrero/100	15.00

Positions Mat. Triple Jersey Prime

NM/M

Production 5-25

2	Ivan Rodriguez, Mike Piazza, Victor Martinez/25	35.00
5	Scott Rolen, Aramis Ramirez, Chipper Jones/25	35.00
6	Kazuo Matsui, Miguel Tejada, Michael Young/25	25.00
7	Brian Giles, Manny Ramirez, Shannon Stewart/25	20.00
8	Rocco Baldelli, Andruw Jones, Vernon Wells/25	25.00
9	Miguel Cabrera, Lance Berkman, Vladimir Guerrero/25	35.00

Red Hot

NM/M

Common Player:		
Inserted 1:16		
1	Scott Rolen	1.50
2	Johan Santana	1.50
3	Josh Beckett	1.00
4	Aubrey Huff	1.00
5	Alfonso Soriano	1.50
6	Jeff Bagwell	1.50
7	Ted Williams	5.00
8	Mark Prior	1.50
9	Todd Helton	1.50
10	Vladimir Guerrero	2.00

Red Hot Bats

NM/M

Production 50-150

1	Scott Rolen/150	6.00
4	Aubrey Huff/150	4.00
5	Alfonso Soriano/150	6.00
6	Jeff Bagwell/150	6.00
7	Ted Williams/25	40.00
8	Mark Prior/150	6.00
9	Todd Helton/150	6.00
10	Vladimir Guerrero/150	6.00

Red Hot Jerseys

NM/M

Production 25-300

1	Scott Rolen/150	6.00
2	Johan Santana/150	6.00
3	Josh Beckett/300	6.00
4	Aubrey Huff/25	6.00
5	Alfonso Soriano/150	6.00
6	Jeff Bagwell/300	6.00
7	Ted Williams/25	60.00
8	Mark Prior/250	6.00
9	Todd Helton/165	6.00
10	Vladimir Guerrero/150	6.00

Red Hot Jerseys Prime

Production 1-25

#	Player	NM/M
1	Scott Rolen/25	20.00
2	Johan Santana/25	20.00
3	Josh Beckett/25	15.00
4	Aubrey Huff/25	10.00
5	Alfonso Soriano/25	15.00
8	Jeff Bagwell/25	20.00
9	Mark Prior/25	20.00
10	Todd Helton/25	20.00
10	Vladimir Guerrero/25	25.00

White Hot

Common Player: Inserted 1:65

#	Player	NM/M
1	Scott Rolen	2.00
2	Johan Santana	2.00
3	Josh Beckett	1.50
4	Aubrey Huff	1.50
5	Alfonso Soriano	2.00
6	Jeff Bagwell	2.00
7	Ted Williams	6.00
8	Mark Prior	2.00
9	Todd Helton	2.00
10	Vladimir Guerrero	2.00

White Hot Bats

Production 50 Sets

#	Player	NM/M
1	Scott Rolen/50	8.00
4	Aubrey Huff/50	4.00
5	Alfonso Soriano/50	6.00
6	Jeff Bagwell/50	6.00
7	Ted Williams/50	40.00
9	Mark Prior/50	8.00
9	Todd Helton/50	6.00
10	Vladimir Guerrero/50	8.00

White Hot Jerseys

Production 1-200
Prime: No Pricing
Production 1-10

#	Player	NM/M
1	Scott Rolen/50	8.00
2	Johan Santana/50	8.00
3	Josh Beckett/185	4.00
5	Alfonso Soriano/50	6.00
6	Jeff Bagwell/200	6.00
9	Mark Prior/50	6.00
9	Todd Helton/151	6.00
10	Vladimir Guerrero/50	8.00

Roll Call Autographs

Inserted 1:24

#	Player	NM/M
1	Hanley Ramirez	20.00
2	Sean Tracey	8.00
3	Justin Wechsler	8.00
4	Matt Lindstrom	6.00
5	Garrett James	8.00
6	Ambiorix Concepcion	8.00
7	Casey Rogowski	8.00
8	Kelly Shoppach	6.00
9	Sean Thompson	8.00
10	Jeff Miller	6.00
11	Chris Resop	10.00
12	Justin Verlander	25.00
13	Geovany Soto	20.00
14	Paulino Reynoso	8.00
15	Chris Roberson	8.00
16	Justin Leone	6.00
17	Jeff Niemann	15.00
18	Mark Woodyard	6.00
19	Raul Tablado	8.00
20	Norihiro Nakamura	20.00
21	Tony Pena	8.00
22	Wladimir Balentien	15.00
23	Miguel Negron	6.00
24	Eude Brito	8.00
25	Ubaldo Jimenez	40.00
26	Mike Morse	10.00
27	Devon Lowery	6.00
28	Philip Humber	12.00
29	Nate McLouth	10.00
30	Jason Hammel	8.00

Spellbound

Common Maddux (1-4): 3.00
Common Clemens (5-9): 4.00
Common A-Rod (10-13): 4.00
Common Pujols (14-19): 4.00
Inserted 1:11

#	Player	NM/M
1	Greg Maddux/G	3.00
2	Greg Maddux/R	3.00
3	Greg Maddux/E	3.00
4	Greg Maddux/G	3.00
5	Roger Clemens/O	4.00
6	Roger Clemens/R	4.00
7	Roger Clemens/E	4.00
8	Roger Clemens/E	4.00
9	Roger Clemens/R	4.00
10	Alex Rodriguez/A	4.00
11	Alex Rodriguez/L	4.00
12	Alex Rodriguez/E	4.00
13	Alex Rodriguez/X	4.00
14	Albert Pujols/A	4.00
15	Albert Pujols/B	4.00
16	Albert Pujols/E	4.00
17	Albert Pujols/E	4.00
18	Albert Pujols/E	4.00
19	Albert Pujols/R	4.00

Spellbound Jerseys

Production 150-250

#	Player	NM/M
1	Greg Maddux G/150	12.00
2	Greg Maddux R/150	12.00
3	Greg Maddux E/150	12.00
4	Greg Maddux G/150	12.00
5	Roger Clemens R/150	15.00
6	Roger Clemens O/150	15.00
7	Roger Clemens E/150	15.00
8	Roger Clemens E/150	15.00
9	Roger Clemens R/150	15.00
14	Albert Pujols A/250	15.00
15	Albert Pujols L/250	15.00
16	Albert Pujols B/250	15.00
17	Albert Pujols E/250	15.00
18	Albert Pujols R/250	15.00
19	Albert Pujols T/250	15.00

Spellbound Jerseys Prime

Production 10-25

#	Player	NM/M
5	Roger Clemens R/25	40.00
6	Roger Clemens O/25	40.00
7	Roger Clemens E/25	40.00
8	Roger Clemens E/25	40.00
9	Roger Clemens R/25	40.00

Team Zenith

Common Player: Inserted 1:31
Gold: 1-2X
Production 100 Sets

#	Player	NM/M
1	Ichiro Suzuki	5.00
2	Jim Edmonds	2.00
3	Hideki Matsui	5.00
4	Alex Rodriguez	5.00
5	Derek Jeter	6.00
6	Alfonso Soriano	2.00
7	Jim Thome	2.00
8	Jorge Posada	1.50
9	Barry Zito	1.50
10	Curt Schilling	2.00
11	Willie Mays	4.00

Team Zenith Bats

Production 15-25

#	Player	NM/M
3	Hideki Matsui/50	25.00
7	Jim Thome/150	6.00
8	Jorge Posada/25	8.00
11	Willie Mays/25	70.00

Team Zenith Jerseys

Production 15-300

#	Player	NM/M
3	Hideki Matsui/165	20.00
7	Jim Thome/175	6.00
8	Jorge Posada/300	6.00
9	Barry Zito/150	4.00
10	Curt Schilling/150	6.00
11	Willie Mays/175	30.00

Team Zenith Jerseys Prime

Production 25 Sets

#	Player	NM/M
2	Jim Edmonds/25	15.00
4	Alfonso Soriano/25	15.00
7	Jim Thome/25	20.00
8	Jorge Posada/25	15.00
9	Barry Zito/25	15.00
10	Curt Schilling/25	20.00

Z-Graphs

WASHINGTON NATIONALS — NICK JOHNSON

Production 1-250

#	Player	NM/M
1	Danny Haren/250	10.00
2	Dallas McPherson/250	12.00
5	Jeremy Bonderman/200	12.00
7	Craig Wilson/250	8.00
8	Adam LaRoche/250	12.00
11	Nick Johnson/250	10.00
14	Dontrelle Willis/25	25.00
17	Morgan Ensberg/250	10.00
19	Trot Nixon/100	20.00
20	B.J. Upton/50	20.00
21	Brian Roberts/250	15.00
24	Omar Vizquel/100	20.00
27	Shannon Stewart/100	10.00
29	Angel Berroa/100	8.00
30	Brandon Webb/100	10.00
32	Magglio Ordonez/100	12.00
34	Cal Ripken Jr./100	90.00
35	Johnny Estrada/100	10.00
37	Austin Kearns/100	10.00
39	Nolan Ryan/34	80.00
40	Orlando Cabrera/100	10.00
42	Roy Oswalt/100	15.00
44	Roy Halladay/50	20.00
48	Bobby Crosby/50	20.00
49	Jack Wilson/25	15.00
40	Jacque Jones/100	12.00
41	Eric Byrnes/250	8.00
44	Tony Gwynn/25	40.00
52	Paul Molitor/25	30.00
55	Ryne Sandberg/25	12.00
57	Casey Kotchman/100	5.00
60	Paul Konerko/100	20.00
62	David Wright/100	40.00
66	Milton Bradley/100	12.00
67	Rich Harden/250	15.00
68	Travis Hafner/250	10.00
69	Victor Martinez/25	15.00
70	Vernon Wells/25	15.00
72	Francisco Rodriguez/100	20.00
75	Mark Prior/25	40.00
79	Sean Casey/50	15.00
80	Carlos Zambrano/50	15.00
81	Livan Hernandez/100	12.00
84	Mark Buehrle/100	15.00
85	Keith Foulke/100	20.00
86	Edgar Renteria/100	15.00
88	Derek Lee/100	25.00
89	Joe Nathan/100	10.00
91	Michael Young/50	15.00
93	Dale Murphy/100	15.00
93	Francisco Cordero/100	8.00
94	Jake Peavy/100	20.00
95	Aubrey Huff/100	10.00
96	Carlos Lee/25	15.00
98	Miguel Cabrera/25	40.00
99	Mark Teixeira/25	40.00

Z-Bats

Common Player: 4.00

#	Player	NM/M
3	Rickey Henderson	8.00
6	Andy Pettitte	4.00
7	Craig Wilson	4.00
9	Nick Johnson	4.00
10	Bernie Williams	6.00
11	Dontrelle Willis	6.00
12	Kenny Lofton	4.00
13	Tom Glavine	4.00
14	Kazuo Matsui/SP	6.00
15	Morgan Ensberg/SP	6.00
16	Mike Piazza	6.00
17	Trot Nixon/SP	8.00
18	Ryan Klesko/SP	4.00
19	B.J. Upton	4.00
21	Omar Vizquel	4.00
22	Shannon Stewart	4.00
23	Preston Wilson	4.00
24	Angel Berroa	4.00
26	Brandon Webb	4.00
27	Rafael Palmeiro	4.00
28	Mike Sweeney	4.00
29	Magglio Ordonez	4.00
30	Cal Ripken Jr.	25.00
31	Johnny Estrada	4.00
32	Austin Kearns	4.00
33	Nolan Ryan	20.00
34	Orlando Cabrera	4.00
35	Roy Oswalt	4.00
37	Lyle Overbay	4.00
39	Jack Wilson	4.00
40	Jacque Jones	4.00
44	Tony Gwynn	8.00
45	Mike Cameron	4.00
46	Geoff Jenkins	4.00
47	Bo Jackson	8.00
48	Luis Gonzalez	4.00
49	Craig Biggio	6.00
51	Josh Beckett	4.00
52	Paul Molitor	8.00
53	Kerry Wood	4.00
54	Lew Ford	4.00
55	Ryne Sandberg	10.00
56	Jeff Bagwell	6.00
57	Casey Kotchman	4.00
58	Chipper Jones	8.00
59	Chone Figgins	4.00
60	Paul Konerko	6.00
61	Kevin Mench	4.00
62	David Wright	10.00
64	Andruw Jones	4.00
65	Garret Anderson	4.00
66	Jorge Posada	6.00
68	Travis Hafner	4.00
69	Victor Martinez	4.00
70	Vernon Wells	4.00
71	A.J. Burnett	4.00
72	Francisco Rodriguez	4.00
73	Mark Prior	6.00
74	Mike Lowell	4.00
77	Sean Casey	4.00
77	Carlos Zambrano	4.00
79	Brad Radke	4.00
80	Moises Alou	4.00
81	Livan Hernandez	4.00
82	Hank Blalock	4.00
84	Reggie Jackson	8.00
84	Mark Buehrle	6.00
87	Edgar Renteria	4.00
88	Adam Dunn	6.00
89	Derek Lee	4.00
90	Michael Young	4.00
91	Dale Murphy	4.00
92	Aramis Ramirez	4.00
93	Francisco Cordero	4.00
95	Aubrey Huff	4.00
96	Ben Sheets	4.00
97	Carlos Lee	4.00
98	Miguel Cabrera	6.00
99	Mark Teixeira	6.00
100	Albert Pujols	15.00

Z-Batgraphs

Production 1-100

#	Player	NM/M
7	Craig Wilson/100	12.00
9	Nick Johnson/100	15.00
14	Dontrelle Willis/25	40.00
24	Angel Berroa/100	8.00
29	Magglio Ordonez/100	10.00
39	Jack Wilson/25	15.00
44	Tony Gwynn/25	50.00
52	Paul Molitor/25	40.00
55	Ryne Sandberg/25	65.00
57	Casey Kotchman/50	20.00
59	Chone Figgins/50	20.00
69	Victor Martinez/25	15.00
73	Mark Prior/25	50.00
90	Michael Young/100	15.00
91	Dale Murphy/100	15.00
97	Carlos Lee/50	20.00
99	Mark Teixeira/25	40.00

Z-Jerseys

Common Player: 4.00

#	Player	NM/M
1	Danny Haren	6.00
3	Rickey Henderson	8.00
4	Andy Pettitte	4.00
5	Jeremy Bonderman	4.00
6	Pat Burrell	4.00
7	Craig Wilson	4.00
10	Bernie Williams	6.00
11	Dontrelle Willis	6.00
13	Tom Glavine	4.00
14	Kazuo Matsui	8.00
16	Mike Piazza	8.00
17	Trot Nixon	4.00
19	Ryan Klesko	4.00
20	Brian Roberts	4.00
21	Omar Vizquel	4.00
22	Shannon Stewart	4.00
23	Preston Wilson	4.00
27	Garrett Atkins	4.00
28	Mike Sweeney	4.00
29	Magglio Ordonez	4.00
30	Cal Ripken Jr.	25.00
32	Austin Kearns	4.00
33	Nolan Ryan	20.00
34	Orlando Cabrera	4.00
36	Roy Oswalt	6.00
37	Lyle Overbay	4.00
39	Jack Wilson	4.00
41	Eric Byrnes	4.00
42	Barry Zito	4.00
43	C.C. Sabathia	4.00
44	Tony Gwynn	8.00
45	Mike Cameron	4.00
46	Geoff Jenkins	4.00
47	Bo Jackson	8.00
48	Luis Gonzalez	4.00
49	Johnny Damon	6.00
50	Craig Biggio	6.00
51	Josh Beckett	4.00
52	Paul Molitor	6.00
53	Kerry Wood	4.00
54	Lew Ford	4.00
55	Ryne Sandberg	10.00
56	Jeff Bagwell	6.00
57	Casey Kotchman	4.00
58	Chipper Jones	8.00
59	Chone Figgins	4.00
60	Paul Konerko	6.00
61	Kevin Mench	4.00
62	David Wright	10.00
64	Andruw Jones	4.00
65	Garret Anderson	4.00
66	Jorge Posada	6.00
68	Travis Hafner	4.00
69	Victor Martinez	4.00
70	Vernon Wells	4.00
71	A.J. Burnett	4.00
72	Francisco Rodriguez	4.00
73	Mark Prior	6.00
74	Mike Lowell	4.00
75	Sean Casey	4.00
77	Carlos Zambrano	4.00
78	Brad Radke	4.00
79	Moises Alou	4.00
80	Livan Hernandez	4.00
81	Hank Blalock	4.00
82	J.D. Drew	4.00
84	Reggie Jackson	8.00
84	Mark Buehrle	6.00
87	Edgar Renteria	4.00
88	Adam Dunn	6.00
89	Derek Lee	4.00
90	Michael Young	4.00
91	Dale Murphy	4.00
92	Aramis Ramirez	4.00
93	Francisco Cordero	4.00
95	Aubrey Huff	4.00
96	Ben Sheets	4.00
97	Carlos Lee	4.00
98	Miguel Cabrera	6.00
99	Mark Teixeira	8.00
100	Albert Pujols	15.00

Z-Jerseygraphs

Production 1-100

#	Player	NM/M
5	Jeremy Bonderman/100	20.00
9	Craig Wilson/100	10.00
11	Dontrelle Willis/25	35.00
15	Morgan Ensberg/50	15.00
17	Trot Nixon/50	25.00
19	B.J. Upton/50	25.00
20	Brian Roberts/100	15.00
22	Shannon Stewart/100	15.00
31	Johnny Estrada/100	15.00
35	Roy Oswalt/20	25.00
36	Roy Halladay/25	25.00
37	Lyle Overbay/25	15.00
38	Bobby Crosby/25	25.00
40	Jacque Jones/100	15.00
44	Tony Gwynn/25	50.00
52	Paul Molitor/25	35.00
55	Ryne Sandberg/25	65.00
57	Casey Kotchman/50	20.00
59	Chone Figgins/50	20.00
60	Paul Konerko/25	35.00
68	Travis Hafner/25	25.00
69	Victor Martinez/25	25.00
72	Francisco Rodriguez/100	25.00
73	Mark Prior/25	50.00
75	Sean Casey/25	20.00
80	Livan Hernandez/100	15.00
88	Mark Buehrle/25	25.00
90	Michael Young/100	25.00
91	Dale Murphy/100	25.00
93	Francisco Cordero/100	12.00
96	Ben Sheets/25	35.00
99	Mark Teixeira/25	50.00

Z-Jerseys Prime

Production 1-150

#	Player	NM/M
3	Rickey Henderson/150	15.00
4	Andy Pettitte/100	10.00
5	Jeremy Bonderman/150	10.00
6	Pat Burrell/100	8.00
7	Craig Wilson/150	8.00
10	Bernie Williams/100	10.00
11	Dontrelle Willis/100	8.00
14	Kazuo Matsui/150	8.00
17	Trot Nixon/100	12.00
18	Ryan Klesko/150	8.00
20	Brian Roberts/50	10.00
22	Shannon Stewart/150	8.00
23	Preston Wilson/150	8.00
25	Garrett Atkins/150	8.00
27	Rafael Palmeiro/150	10.00
28	Mike Sweeney/150	8.00
30	Cal Ripken Jr./50	50.00
31	Johnny Estrada/100	8.00
32	Austin Kearns/150	8.00
33	Nolan Ryan/100	30.00
35	Roy Oswalt/100	10.00
36	Roy Halladay/150	10.00
37	Lyle Overbay/100	8.00
40	Jacque Jones/150	8.00
41	Eric Byrnes/50	10.00
42	Barry Zito/150	10.00
43	C.C. Sabathia/150	8.00
44	Tony Gwynn/150	15.00
45	Mike Cameron/150	8.00
46	Geoff Jenkins/150	10.00
47	Bo Jackson/100	20.00
48	Luis Gonzalez/150	8.00
49	Johnny Damon/100	10.00
51	Josh Beckett/150	10.00
52	Paul Molitor/70	15.00
54	Lew Ford/150	8.00
55	Ryne Sandberg/50	25.00
56	Jeff Bagwell/150	12.00
57	Casey Kotchman/50	10.00
58	Chipper Jones/150	15.00
60	Paul Konerko/150	10.00
61	Kevin Mench/150	8.00
64	Andruw Jones/150	10.00
65	Garret Anderson/25	12.00
66	Jorge Posada/50	10.00
68	Travis Hafner/100	10.00
69	Victor Martinez/25	12.00
70	Vernon Wells/25	10.00
71	A.J. Burnett/150	10.00
72	Francisco Rodriguez/100	10.00
73	Mark Prior/50	15.00
74	Mike Lowell/150	10.00
75	Sean Casey/150	8.00
77	Carlos Zambrano/100	8.00
78	Brad Radke/100	8.00
81	Livan Hernandez/100	10.00
83	Hank Blalock/100	10.00
84	Reggie Jackson/150	15.00
84	Mark Buehrle/50	8.00
87	Adam Dunn/50	15.00
89	Derek Lee/50	15.00
91	Michael Young/100	10.00
92	Dale Murphy/50	20.00
93	Francisco Cordero/50	10.00
95	Aubrey Huff/50	8.00
96	Ben Sheets/150	10.00
98	Miguel Cabrera/150	15.00
99	Mark Teixeira/150	15.00

Z-Jerseygraphs Prime

Production 1-25

#	Player	NM/M
5	Jeremy Bonderman/25	35.00
7	Craig Wilson/25	25.00
11	Dontrelle Willis/25	50.00
17	Trot Nixon/25	40.00
19	B.J. Upton/25	35.00
20	Brian Roberts/25	40.00
22	Shannon Stewart/25	25.00
29	Angel Berroa/25	20.00
31	Johnny Estrada/25	20.00
32	Austin Kearns/25	20.00
35	Roy Oswalt/25	35.00
40	Jacque Jones/25	25.00
41	Eric Byrnes/25	20.00
55	Tony Gwynn/25	65.00
57	Casey Kotchman/25	30.00
60	Paul Konerko/25	50.00
68	Travis Hafner/25	35.00
69	Victor Martinez/25	35.00
70	Vernon Wells/25	35.00
73	Francisco Rodriguez/25	40.00
75	Mark Prior/25	60.00
77	Carlos Zambrano/25	30.00
80	Livan Hernandez/25	25.00
84	Mark Buehrle/25	30.00
88	Derek Lee/25	50.00
90	Michael Young/25	40.00
91	Dale Murphy/25	40.00
93	Francisco Cordero/25	20.00
95	Aubrey Huff/25	25.00
96	Ben Sheets/25	35.00
98	Miguel Cabrera/25	50.00
99	Mark Teixeira/25	60.00

Z-Combos

Production 1-150
Cards are bat/jsy unless noted.

#	Player	NM/M
6	Rickey Henderson/100	12.00
9	Craig Wilson/150	6.00
10	Bernie Williams/150	6.00
11	Dontrelle Willis/25	10.00
14	Kazuo Matsui/50	10.00
19	B.J. Upton/50	10.00
24	Angel Berroa/	
26	Brandon Webb/Bat-Pants/100	6.00
30	Cal Ripken Jr./100	30.00
33	Nolan Ryan/25	40.00
44	Tony Gwynn/100	12.00
47	Bo Jackson/100	12.00
50	Craig Biggio/25	6.00
52	Paul Molitor/50	12.00
53	Kerry Wood/25	10.00
54	Lew Ford/25	6.00
55	Ryne Sandberg/100	20.00
56	Jeff Bagwell/100	15.00
57	Casey Kotchman/100	8.00
58	Chipper Jones/100	6.00
59	Chone Figgins/100	6.00
61	Kevin Mench/100	6.00
64	Andruw Jones/100	10.00
69	Victor Martinez/100	8.00
71	A.J. Burnett/100	10.00
73	Mark Prior/100	10.00
81	Hank Blalock/100	10.00
87	Adam Dunn/25	10.00
88	Derek Lee/25	12.00
90	Michael Young/100	6.00
91	Dale Murphy/100	10.00
99	Mark Teixeira/Bat-Hat/100	12.00

Z-Combos Prime

Production 1-25
All are bat/patch.

#	Player	NM/M
3	Rickey Henderson/25	25.00
7	Craig Wilson/25	10.00
10	Bernie Williams/25	15.00
11	Dontrelle Willis/25	15.00
14	Kazuo Matsui/25	15.00
19	B.J. Upton/25	15.00
27	Rafael Palmeiro/25	15.00
30	Cal Ripken Jr./25	65.00
33	Nolan Ryan/25	50.00
44	Tony Gwynn/25	25.00
47	Bo Jackson/25	25.00
55	Ryne Sandberg/25	35.00
56	Jeff Bagwell/25	25.00
57	Casey Kotchman/25	15.00
58	Chipper Jones/25	15.00
61	Kevin Mench/25	10.00
64	Andruw Jones/25	15.00
65	Garret Anderson/25	15.00
69	Victor Martinez/25	15.00
71	A.J. Burnett/25	10.00
73	Mark Prior/25	15.00
74	Mike Lowell/25	15.00
81	Hank Blalock/25	15.00
87	Adam Dunn/25	15.00
88	Derek Lee/25	20.00
90	Michael Young/25	20.00
91	Dale Murphy/25	20.00
96	Ben Sheets/25	15.00
99	Mark Teixeira/25	25.00

Z-Team

TIM HUDSON

Common Player: Inserted 1:11
Gold: 1-2X
Production 100 Sets

#	Player	NM/M
1	Albert Pujols	5.00
2	Carlos Beltran	2.00
3	Randy Johnson	2.00
4	Miguel Tejada	1.50
5	Ichiro Suzuki	1.50
6	Eric Gagne	1.00
7	Adrian Beltre	1.50
8	Alfonso Soriano	1.50
9	Jim Edmonds	1.50

#	Player	Price
10	David Ortiz	2.00
11	Curt Schilling	2.00
12	Mariano Rivera	1.50
13	Derek Jeter	5.00
14	Ivan Rodriguez	1.50
15	Johnny Damon	2.00
16	Mark Prior	1.50
17	Vernon Wells	1.00
18	Chipper Jones	1.00
19	Torii Hunter	1.00
20	Tim Hudson	1.50
21	Lance Berkman	1.00
22	Troy Glaus	1.00
23	Mike Piazza	2.50
24	Mark Mulder	1.00
25	Ken Griffey Jr.	3.00

2007 Donruss Elite Extra Edition

NM/M

Common (1-92):		.25
Common Auto. (93-142):		8.00
Pack (5):		8.00
Box (20):		140.00

#	Player	Price
1	Andrew Brackman	1.00
2	Austin Gallagher	1.00
3	Brett Cecil	1.00
4	Darwin Barney	1.00
5	David Price	3.00
6	J.P. Arencibia	1.00
7	Josh Donaldson	.50
8	Brandon Hicks	.25
9	Brian Rike	.25
10	Bryan Morris	.50
11	Cale Iorg	.50
12	Casey Weathers	.25
13	Corey Kluber	.25
14	Daniel Moskos	1.00
15	Danny Payne	.25
16	David Kopp	.50
17	Dellin Betances	.50
18	Derrick Robinson	.25
19	Drew Stubbs	.50
20	Eric Eiland	.50
21	Francisco Pena	.25
22	Greg Reynolds	.25
23	Jeff Samardzija	1.00
24	Jess Todd	.50
25	John Tolisano	.50
26	Jordan Zimmerman	.50
27	Julian Sampson	.25
28	Luke Hochevar	1.00
29	Mat Latos	.50
30	Matt Mangini	.25
31	Matt Spencer	.50
32	Matthew Sweeney	.25
33	Max Scherzer	3.00
34	Mitch Canham	.50
35	Nick Schmidt	.25
36	Paul Kelly	.25
37	Ryan Pope	.75
38	Sam Runion	.50
39	Steven Souza	.50
40	Travis Mattair	.75
41	Trystan Magnuson	1.00
42	Willie Middlebrooks	1.00
43	Zack Cozart	.50
44	James Adkins	.50
45	Cory Luebke	.25
46	Aaron Poreda	.50
47	Clayton Mortensen	.50
48	Bradley Suttle	1.00
49	Tony Butler	.50
50	Zach Britton	.50
51	Scott Cousins	.25
52	Wendell Fairley	1.00
53	Eric Sogard	.50
54	Jonathan Lucroy	1.00
55	Lars Davis	.25
56	Demetris Nichols	.25
57	Aaron Gray	.25
58	Daequan Cook	.25
59	Derrick Byars	.25
60	Reyshawn Terry	.25
61	Taurean Green	.25
62	Don Haskins	.25
63	Jerry Tarkanian	.25
64	Rick Majerus	.25
65	Rollie Massimino	.25
66	Ara Parseghian	.25
67	Dale Brown	.25
68	Dean Smith	.25
69	Eddie Sutton	.25
70	Frank Broyles	.25
71	Gene Keady	.25
72	Jim Boeheim	.25
73	Norm Stewart	.25
74	Steve Spurrier	.25
75	Tom Osborne	.25
76	Vince Dooley	.25
77	Jennie Finch	.50
78	Amanda Beard	.75
79	Mike Powell	.25
80	Rebecca Lobo	.25
81	Brandi Chastain	.25
82	Clint Dolezel	.25
83	Elvin Hayes	.50
84	Cobi Jones	.25
85	Bill Walton	.50
86	Sidney Moncrief	.25
87	Dominique Wilkins	.50
88	Summer Sanders	.25
89	Michelle Akers	.25
90	Muggsy Bogues	.25
91	Charlie Culberson	.50
92	Jacob Smolinski	1.00
93	Blake Beaven/Auto./719	15.00
94	Brad Chalk/Auto./613	8.00
95	Brett Anderson/Auto./549	30.00
96	Chris Withrow//700	20.00
97	Clay Fuller/Auto./674	8.00
98	Damon Sublett/Auto./674	15.00
99	Devin Mesoraco/Auto./674	15.00
100	Drew Cumberland/Auto./744	15.00
101	Jack McGeary/Auto./744	20.00
102	Jake Arrieta/Auto./949	25.00
103	James Simmons/Auto./624	15.00
104	Jarrod Parker/Auto./499	30.00
105	Jason Dominguez/Auto./744	8.00
106	Jason Heyward/Auto./750	200.00
107	Joe Savery/Auto./750	15.00
108	Jon Gilmore/Auto./819	15.00
109	Jordan Walden/Auto./794	30.00
110	Josh Smoker/Auto./719	20.00
111	Josh Vitters/Auto./769	30.00
112	Julio Borbon/Auto./594	15.00
113	Justin Jackson/Auto./850	10.00
114	Kellen Kulbacki/Auto./549	15.00
115	Kevin Ahrens/Auto./794	25.00
116	Kyle Lotzkar/Auto./611	15.00
117	Madison Bumgarner/Auto./794	35.00
118	Matt Dominguez/Auto./769	25.00
119	Matt LaPorta/Auto./594	25.00
120	Matt Wieters/Auto./799	120.00
121	Michael Burgess/Auto./672	25.00
122	Michael Main/Auto./794	15.00
123	Michael Moustakas/Auto./999	50.00
124	Nathan Vineyard/Auto./700	10.00
125	Neil Ramirez/Auto./774	15.00
126	Nick Hagadone/Auto./544	25.00
127	Peter Kozma/Auto./719	15.00
128	Phillippe Aumont/Auto./674	25.00
129	Preston Mattingly/Auto./519	20.00
131	Ross Detwiler/Auto./650	15.00
132	Tim Alderson/Auto./719	25.00
133	Todd Frazier/Auto./774	20.00
134	Wes Roemer/Auto./694	15.00
135	Ben Revere/Auto./700	20.00
136	D.J. Strawberry/Auto./374	10.00
137	Alando Tucker/Auto./494	10.00
138	Jared Jordan/Auto./474	8.00
139	Marc Gasol/Auto./474	8.00
140	Stephane Lasme/Auto./674	8.00
141	Austin Jackson/Auto./794	50.00
142	Beau Mills/Auto./624	25.00

Aspirations

Aspirations (1-92):		4-8X
Non Auto. Aspir. (93-142):		.2-.25X
Production 100 Sets		

Black Status Autos.

Production One Set

Status

Status (1-92):	6-10X
Non Auto. Status (93-142):	.2-.3X
Production 50 Sets	
Gold Status (1-92):	8-15X
No Auto. Gold Status:	No Pricing
Production 25 Sets	

College Ties

NM/M

Common Duo:		2.00
Production 1,500 Sets		
Gold:		1X
Production 500 Sets		
Red:		1.5-3X
Production 100 Sets		

#	Players	Price
1	Daniel Moskos, David Kopp	2.00
2	Jess Todd, Nick Schmidt	2.00
3	J.P. Arencibia, Julio Borbon	2.00
4	Casey Weathers, David Price	3.00
5	Matt LaPorta, Taurean Green	3.00
6	Amanda Beard, Jennie Finch	3.00
7	Demetris Nichols, Jim Boeheim	3.00
8	Danny Payne, Matt Wieters	3.00
9	Darwin Barney, Mitch Canham	2.00
10	James Adkins, Luke Hochevar	2.00
11	Cory Luebke, Daequan Cook	2.00
12	Brett Cecil, D.J. Strawberry	2.00

College Ties Autograph

NM/M

Production 50 or 100

#	Players	Price
1	Daniel Moskos, David Kopp/100	15.00
2	Jess Todd, Nick Schmidt/100	15.00
3	J.P. Arencibia, Julio Borbon/100	15.00
4	Casey Weathers, David Price/100	40.00
5	Matt LaPorta, Taurean Green/100	30.00
6	Amanda Beard, Jennie Finch/50	50.00
7	Demetris Nichols, Jim Boeheim/50	15.00
8	Danny Payne, Matt Wieters/100	50.00
9	Darwin Barney, Mitch Canham/100	25.00
10	James Adkins, Luke Hochevar/50	25.00
11	Cory Luebke, Daequan Cook/100	20.00
12	Brett Cecil, D.J. Strawberry/50	15.00

College Ties Jerseys

NM/M

Production 50-500		
Prime:		No Pricing
Production 5-50		

#	Players	Price
1	Daniel Moskos, David Kopp/75	8.00
6	Amanda Beard, Jennie Finch/50	20.00
9	Darwin Barney, Mitch Canham/500	10.00

Collegiate Patches Auto.

NM/M

Production 25-250

#	Player	Price
1	Amanda Beard/100	40.00
2	Ara Parseghian/250	30.00
3	Burt Reynolds/25	100.00
5	Dale Brown/250	200.00
6	Dean Smith/250	60.00
7	Eddie Sutton/250	30.00
8	Frank Broyles/250	20.00
9	Gene Keady/250	20.00
11	Jennie Finch/249	50.00
12	Jim Boeheim/250	25.00
13	Sheryl Swoopes/250	20.00
14	Rebecca Lobo/250	20.00
15	Ron Howard/25	75.00
16	Steve Spurrier S.Carolina/100	40.00
17	Tom Osborne/249	40.00
18	Vince Dooley/250	25.00
19	Josh Donaldson/250	20.00
20	Cobi Jones/97	25.00
21	Bill Walton/250	40.00
22	Sidney Moncrief/250	20.00
23	Dominique Wilkins/100	40.00
24	Steve Spurrier Florida/100	40.00
25	Drew Stubbs/250	20.00
26	Andrew Brackman/250	30.00
27	Casey Weathers/250	20.00
28	Daniel Moskos/250	20.00
29	David Price/250	75.00
30	Greg Reynolds/250	15.00
31	J.P. Arencibia/249	15.00
32	Jeff Samardzija/150	50.00
33	Julio Borbon/250	15.00
34	Luke Hochevar/250	25.00
35	Matt LaPorta/250	50.00
36	Matt Mangini/250	15.00
37	Matt Wieters/250	120.00
38	Max Scherzer/182	75.00
39	Mitch Canham/250	25.00
40	Nick Schmidt/250	20.00
41	James Adkins/250	15.00
42	Demetris Nichols/250	10.00
43	Aaron Gray/250	15.00
44	Daequan Cook/250	20.00
45	Derrick Byars/250	10.00
46	Reyshawn Terry/250	15.00
47	Taurean Green/250	15.00
48	Summer Sanders/250	25.00
49	Bobby Hurley/250	20.00
50	Muggsy Bogues/250	15.00
51	Jerry Tarkanian/250	20.00
52	Cale Iorg/250	20.00
53	Lynette Woodard/249	15.00
54	Nick Hagadone/250	10.00
63	Trystan Magnuson/248	15.00
64	Matt Spencer/249	15.00
65	Darwin Barney/250	15.00
67	Connie Mack III/100	15.00
68	Mike Powell/99	25.00

School Colors

NM/M

Common Card:		2.00
Production 1,500 Sets		

#	Player	Price
1	David Price	3.00
2	Daniel Moskos	2.00
3	Greg Reynolds	2.00
4	Matt LaPorta	3.00
5	Matt Wieters	4.00
6	Luke Hochevar	2.00
7	Max Scherzer	4.00
8	Alando Tucker	2.00
9	Daequan Cook	2.00
10	Eddie Sutton	2.00
11	Dean Smith	3.00
12	Steve Spurrier	2.00
13	Tom Osborne	2.00
14	Don Haskins	2.00
15	Jerry Tarkanian	2.00
16	Rick Majerus	2.00
17	Rollie Massimino	2.00
18	Ara Parseghian	2.00
19	Dale Brown	2.00
20	Frank Broyles	2.00
21	Gene Keady	2.00
22	Jim Boeheim	2.00
23	Norm Stewart	2.00
24	Vince Dooley	2.00
25	Bill Walton	3.00
26	Nick Schmidt	2.00
27	Burt Reynolds	3.00
28	Ron Howard	2.00
29	Beau Mills	3.00
30	James Simmons	2.00
31	Joe Savery	2.00
32	Ross Detwiler	2.00
33	J.P. Arencibia	2.00
34	Drew Stubbs	2.00

School Colors Autos.

NM/M

Production 10-50

#	Player	Price
1	David Price/50	60.00
2	Daniel Moskos/50	15.00
3	Greg Reynolds/50	20.00
4	Matt LaPorta/50	40.00
5	Matt Wieters/50	100.00
6	Luke Hochevar/50	20.00
7	Max Scherzer/50	60.00
8	Alando Tucker/50	15.00
9	Daequan Cook/50	20.00
10	Eddie Sutton/50	30.00
12	Steve Spurrier/25	40.00
13	Tom Osborne/25	40.00
14	Don Haskins/25	20.00
15	Jerry Tarkanian/25	25.00
16	Rick Majerus/25	20.00
18	Ara Parseghian/25	30.00
19	Dale Brown/25	20.00
21	Frank Broyles/25	20.00
22	Gene Keady/25	20.00
23	Jim Boeheim/25	30.00
24	Norm Stewart/25	20.00
25	Vince Dooley/25	25.00
26	Bill Walton/25	30.00
29	Nick Schmidt/50	15.00
30	Beau Mills/50	15.00
31	James Simmons/50	15.00
32	Joe Savery/50	30.00
33	Ross Detwiler/50	15.00
34	J.P. Arencibia/50	20.00
	Drew Stubbs/25	25.00

Signature Aspirations

NM/M

Production 5-100

#	Player	Price
1	Andrew Brackman/100	20.00
2	Austin Gallagher/100	20.00
3	Brett Cecil/100	30.00
4	Darwin Barney/100	15.00
5	David Price/100	85.00
6	J.P. Arencibia/100	30.00
7	Josh Donaldson/250	25.00
8	Brandon Hicks/100	25.00
9	Brian Rike/100	20.00
10	Bryan Morris/100	20.00
11	Cale Iorg/100	20.00
12	Casey Weathers/100	20.00
13	Corey Kluber/100	20.00
14	Daniel Moskos/100	15.00
15	Danny Payne/50	15.00
16	David Kopp/36	15.00
17	Dellin Betances/100	30.00
18	Derrick Robinson/100	15.00
19	Drew Stubbs/100	20.00
20	Eric Eiland/100	15.00
21	Francisco Pena/100	20.00
22	Greg Reynolds/100	20.00
23	Jess Todd/50	30.00
24	John Tolisano/100	25.00
26	Jordan Zimmerman/75	30.00
27	Julian Sampson/100	15.00
29	Mat Latos/34	50.00
31	Matt Mangini/80	15.00
33	Matt Spencer/30	20.00
34	Matthew Sweeney/100	20.00
35	Mitch Canham/25	40.00
36	Nick Schmidt/25	20.00
37	Paul Kelly/15	15.00
38	Ryan Pope/100	25.00
39	Sam Runion/100	20.00
40	Steven Souza/100	20.00
41	Travis Mattair/50	20.00
42	Willie Middlebrooks/25	50.00
43	Zack Cozart/25	20.00
44	James Adkins/100	20.00
45	Cory Luebke/100	15.00
46	Aaron Poreda/100	20.00
47	Clayton Mortensen/100	10.00
48	Bradley Suttle/100	25.00
49	Tony Butler/100	20.00
50	Zach Britton/100	20.00
52	Scott Cousins/50	15.00
53	Wendell Fairley/100	35.00
54	Eric Sogard/100	10.00
55	Jonathan Lucroy/100	25.00
56	Lars Davis/100	15.00
57	Demetris Nichols/100	20.00
58	Aaron Gray/100	10.00
59	Daequan Cook/50	20.00
60	Derrick Byars/100	10.00
61	Reyshawn Terry/100	20.00
62	Taurean Green/75	15.00
63	Don Haskins/50	15.00
64	Jerry Tarkanian/50	20.00
66	Rick Majerus/50	15.00
67	Ara Parseghian/100	20.00
69	Eddie Sutton/50	20.00
70	Frank Broyles/50	15.00
72	Gene Keady/50	15.00
74	Jim Boeheim/50	20.00
75	Steve Spurrier/25	40.00
76	Tom Osborne/100	30.00
77	Vince Dooley/50	20.00
78	Jennie Finch/50	50.00
79	Mike Powell/100	20.00
80	Rebecca Lobo/100	30.00
81	Brandi Chastain/50	15.00
82	Clint Dolezel/100	10.00
83	Elvin Hayes/100	20.00
84	Cobi Jones/100	20.00
85	Bill Walton/25	25.00
86	Sidney Moncrief/50	15.00
87	Dominique Wilkins/50	20.00
88	Summer Sanders/50	20.00
89	Michelle Akers/100	15.00
90	Muggsy Bogues/100	15.00
91	Charlie Culberson/50	30.00
92	Jacob Smolinski/100	25.00
93	Blake Beaven/100	15.00
94	Brad Chalk/100	15.00
95	Brett Anderson/100	40.00
96	Chris Withrow/100	20.00
97	Clay Fuller/100	15.00
98	Damon Sublett/50	35.00
100	Devin Mesoraco/100	20.00
100	Drew Cumberland/100	20.00
101	Jack McGeary/100	25.00
102	Jake Arrieta/100	35.00
103	James Simmons/50	15.00
104	Jarrod Parker/50	30.00
105	Jason Dominguez/100	20.00
106	Jason Heyward/100	250.00
107	Joe Savery/100	30.00
108	Jon Gilmore/100	25.00
109	Jordan Walden/50	40.00
110	Josh Smoker/100	30.00
111	Josh Vitters/100	50.00
112	Julio Borbon/100	25.00
113	Justin Jackson/100	25.00
114	Kellen Kulbacki/100	40.00
115	Kevin Ahrens/100	40.00
116	Kyle Lotzkar/100	15.00
117	Madison Bumgarner/50	60.00
118	Matt Dominguez/100	40.00
119	Matt LaPorta/100	40.00
120	Matt Wieters/50	150.00
121	Michael Burgess/100	40.00
122	Michael Main/100	20.00
123	Michael Moustakas/100	80.00
124	Nathan Vineyard/100	15.00
125	Neil Ramirez/100	15.00
126	Nick Hagadone/100	20.00
127	Peter Kozma/100	20.00
128	Phillippe Aumont/100	40.00
129	Preston Mattingly/100	40.00
131	Ross Detwiler/100	25.00
132	Tim Alderson/100	20.00
133	Todd Frazier/100	20.00
134	Wes Roemer/100	15.00
135	Ben Revere/100	30.00
137	D.J. Strawberry/100	15.00
	Alando Tucker/50	15.00

Signature Status

NM/M

Production 1-50		
Gold Status:		No Pricing
Production 1-10		

#	Player	Price
1	Andrew Brackman/50	30.00
2	Austin Gallagher/50	30.00
3	Brett Cecil/50	35.00
4	Darwin Barney/50	20.00
5	David Price/50	100.00
6	J.P. Arencibia/50	40.00
7	Josh Donaldson/50	40.00
8	Brandon Hicks/50	25.00
9	Brian Rike/50	25.00
10	Bryan Morris/50	20.00
11	Cale Iorg/50	20.00
12	Casey Weathers/50	25.00
13	Corey Kluber/50	10.00
14	Daniel Moskos/50	20.00
15	Danny Payne/25	25.00
16	David Kopp/25	15.00
17	Dellin Betances/25	50.00
18	Derrick Robinson/50	20.00
19	Drew Stubbs/50	25.00
20	Eric Eiland/50	20.00
21	Francisco Pena/25	25.00
22	Greg Reynolds/25	25.00
24	Jess Todd/25	40.00
25	John Tolisano/50	30.00
26	Jordan Zimmerman/25	40.00
27	Julian Sampson/25	20.00
29	Mat Latos/25	50.00
31	Matt Mangini/50	20.00
34	Matthew Sweeney/25	25.00
36	Paul Kelly/25	25.00
37	Ryan Pope/25	25.00
38	Sam Runion/25	25.00
39	Steven Souza/25	25.00
40	Travis Mattair/25	25.00
41	Trystan Magnuson/25	25.00
44	James Adkins/25	25.00
45	Cory Luebke/50	20.00
46	Aaron Poreda/25	25.00
47	Clayton Mortensen/50	15.00
48	Bradley Suttle/25	25.00
49	Tony Butler/50	25.00
50	Zach Britton/25	25.00
52	Wendell Fairley/50	40.00
53	Eric Sogard/25	15.00
54	Jonathan Lucroy/50	30.00
55	Lars Davis/50	20.00
56	Demetris Nichols/50	15.00
57	Aaron Gray/25	20.00
58	Daequan Cook/25	20.00
59	Derrick Byars/50	20.00
60	Reyshawn Terry/50	10.00
61	Taurean Green/29	20.00
62	Don Haskins/50	20.00
63	Jerry Tarkanian/25	20.00
64	Rick Majerus/25	20.00
68	Ara Parseghian/25	20.00
69	Eddie Sutton/25	25.00
70	Frank Broyles/25	20.00
71	Gene Keady/25	20.00
72	Jim Boeheim/25	20.00
73	Tom Osborne/25	40.00
76	Vince Dooley/25	75.00
78	Jennie Finch/25	60.00
79	Mike Powell/25	25.00
80	Rebecca Lobo/50	40.00
81	Brandi Chastain/25	50.00
82	Clint Dolezel/50	10.00
83	Elvin Hayes/25	25.00
84	Cobi Jones/25	20.00
85	Bill Walton/50	30.00
86	Sidney Moncrief/25	20.00
87	Dominique Wilkins/25	25.00
88	Summer Sanders/25	25.00
89	Michelle Akers/50	15.00
90	Muggsy Bogues/50	15.00
91	Charlie Culberson/50	35.00
92	Jacob Smolinski/50	30.00
93	Blake Beaven/50	20.00
94	Brad Chalk/50	20.00
95	Brett Anderson/50	65.00
96	Chris Withrow/50	25.00
97	Clay Fuller/50	20.00
98	Damon Sublett/25	30.00
99	Devin Mesoraco/50	25.00
100	Drew Cumberland/50	25.00
101	Jack McGeary/50	30.00
102	Jake Arrieta/50	40.00
103	James Simmons/25	25.00
104	Jarrod Parker/50	50.00
105	Jason Dominguez/25	50.00
106	Jason Heyward/25	300.00
107	Joe Savery/25	30.00
108	Jon Gilmore/50	30.00
109	Jordan Walden/25	65.00
110	Josh Smoker/50	30.00
111	Josh Vitters/50	85.00
112	Julio Borbon/50	30.00
113	Justin Jackson/25	30.00
114	Kellen Kulbacki/50	20.00
115	Kevin Ahrens/50	20.00
116	Kyle Lotzkar/50	20.00
117	Madison Bumgarner/25	85.00
118	Matt Dominguez/25	40.00
119	Matt LaPorta/25	40.00
120	Matt Wieters/25	200.00
121	Michael Burgess/25	40.00

122	Michael Main/25	40.00
123	Michael Moustakas/50	90.00
124	Nathan Vineyard/50	20.00
125	Neil Ramirez/50	20.00
126	Nick Hagadone/25	50.00
127	Peter Kozma/50	25.00
128	Phillippe Aumont/50	50.00
129	Preston Mattingly/25	40.00
131	Ross Detwiler/50	30.00
132	Tim Alderson/50	50.00
133	Todd Frazier/50	30.00
134	Wes Roemer/50	20.00
135	Ben Revere/50	30.00
136	D.J. Strawberry/25	20.00
137	Alando Tucker/25	20.00
138	Jared Jordan/50	15.00
139	Marc Gasol/25	15.00
340	Stephane Lasme/50	10.00
141	Austin Jackson/25	150.00
142	Beau Mills/25	25.00

Sig. Turn of the Century

NM/M

Production 10-500

1	Andrew Brackman/500	25.00
2	Austin Gallagher/500	15.00
3	Brett Cecil/500	25.00
4	Darwin Barney/500	15.00
5	David Price/500	50.00
6	J.P. Arencibia/500	15.00
7	Josh Donaldson/500	15.00
8	Brandon Hicks/419	15.00
9	Brian Rike/500	15.00
10	Bryan Morris/500	15.00
11	Cale Iorg/397	15.00
12	Casey Weathers/500	20.00
13	Corey Kluber/419	8.00
14	Daniel Moskos/500	15.00
15	Danny Payne/394	15.00
16	David Kopp/449	10.00
17	Dellin Betances/494	20.00
18	Derrick Robinson/500	15.00
19	Drew Stubbs/494	25.00
20	Eric Eiland/419	15.00
21	Francisco Pena/396	20.00
22	Greg Reynolds/500	15.00
23	Jeff Samardzija/219	20.00
24	Jess Todd/394	20.00
25	John Tolisano/419	20.00
26	Jordan Zimmermann/469	20.00
27	Julian Sampson/494	15.00
28	Luke Hochevar/158	20.00
29	Mat Latos/499	25.00
30	Matt Mangini/500	15.00
31	Matt Spencer/500	10.00
32	Matthew Sweeney/500	20.00
33	Max Scherzer/250	50.00
34	Mitch Canham/250	10.00
35	Nick Schmidt/209	10.00
36	Paul Kelly/500	15.00
37	Ryan Pope/500	10.00
38	Sam Runion/494	15.00
39	Steven Souza/500	15.00
40	Travis Mattair/494	10.00
41	Trystan Magnuson/246	15.00
42	Willie Middlebrooks/409	
43	Zack Cozart/409	10.00
44	James Adkins/500	15.00
45	Cory Luebke/469	15.00
46	Aaron Poreda/500	15.00
47	Clayton Mortensen/500	8.00
48	Bradley Suttle/500	20.00
49	Tony Butler/419	15.00
50	Zach Britton/437	15.00
51	Scott Cousins/500	8.00
52	Wendell Fairley/500	15.00
53	Eric Sogard/500	8.00
54	Jonathan Lucroy/500	20.00
55	Lars Davis/500	10.00
56	Demetris Nichols/500	8.00
57	Aaron Gray/500	10.00
58	Daequan Cook/494	10.00
59	Derrick Byars/300	8.00
60	Reyshawn Terry/300	8.00
61	Taurean Green/500	10.00
62	Don Haskins/194	15.00
63	Jerry Tarkanian/144	15.00
64	Rick Majerus/194	15.00
65	Ara Parseghian/69	15.00
67	Dale Brown/89	15.00
68	Eddie Sutton/144	15.00
69	Frank Broyles/69	15.00
70	Gene Keady/144	15.00
71	Steve Spurrier/59	25.00
75	Tom Osborne/320	25.00
76	Vince Dooley/91	15.00
77	Jennie Finch/119	50.00
79	Mike Powell/119	20.00
80	Rebecca Lobo/234	25.00

81	Brandi Chastain/94	40.00
82	Clint Dolezel/243	8.00
83	Elvin Hayes/344	15.00
84	Cobi Jones/247	15.00
85	Sidney Moncrief/169	15.00
86	Summer Sanders/169	15.00
89	Michelle Akers/344	10.00
90	Muggsy Bogues/94	15.00
91	Charlie Culberson/500	25.00
92	Jacob Smolinski/500	20.00
93	Blake Beaven/100	25.00
94	Brad Chalk/100	15.00
95	Brett Anderson/145	40.00
96	Chris Withrow/168	25.00
97	Clay Fuller/145	15.00
98	Damon Sublett/220	30.00
99	Devin Mesoraco/145	20.00
100	Drew Cumberland/125	20.00
101	Jack McGeary/145	25.00
102	Jake Arrieta/145	30.00
103	James Simmons/100	15.00
104	Jarrod Parker/55	30.00
105	Jason Dominguez/100	10.00
106	Jason Heyward/169	250.00
107	Joe Savery/119	20.00
108	Jon Gilmore/100	25.00
109	Jordan Walden/100	35.00
110	Josh Smoker/200	20.00
111	Josh Vitters/150	50.00
112	Julio Borbon/100	20.00
113	Justin Jackson/100	20.00
114	Kellen Kulbacki/145	20.00
115	Kevin Ahrens/100	30.00
116	Kyle Lotzkar/100	15.00
117	Madison Bumgarner/100	40.00
118	Matt Dominguez/100	30.00
119	Matt LaPorta/100	30.00
120	Matt Wieters/100	150.00
121	Michael Burgess/100	30.00
122	Michael Main/100	25.00
123	Michael Moustakas/345	50.00
124	Nathan Vineyard/100	15.00
125	Neil Ramirez/145	15.00
126	Nick Hagadone/100	30.00
127	Peter Kozma/100	20.00
128	Phillippe Aumont/120	30.00
129	Preston Mattingly/100	25.00
131	Ross Detwiler/119	25.00
132	Tim Alderson/100	40.00
133	Todd Frazier/145	20.00
134	Wes Roemer/100	15.00
135	Ben Revere/119	30.00
136	D.J. Strawberry/100	10.00
137	Alando Tucker/100	10.00
138	Jared Jordan/100	10.00
139	Marc Gasol/100	10.00
140	Stephane Lasme/145	10.00
141	Austin Jackson/100	80.00
142	Beau Mills/100	30.00

Throwback Threads

NM/M

Common Player: 5.00
Production 500 unless noted.
Prime: No Pricing
Production 3-50

1	Brandi Chastain	20.00
2	Amanda Beard/44	15.00
3	Drew Stubbs	5.00
4	Drew Cumberland	5.00
5	Clint Dolezel	5.00
6	Mat Latos	5.00
7	Brett Cecil	5.00
8	Vince Dooley	8.00
9	Brett Anderson	5.00
10	Casey Weathers/75	5.00
11	Daniel Moskos	5.00
12	Darwin Barney	5.00
13	Kellen Kulbacki	5.00
14	Matt Dominguez	8.00
15	Matt Mangini	5.00
16	Mitch Canham	5.00
17	Willie Middlebrooks	8.00
18	Mike Powell	5.00
20	Steve Spurrier	5.00
21	Dale Brown	5.00
22	Don Haskins	5.00
23	Nick Schmidt	5.00
24	Zack Cozart	5.00

Throwback Threads Autos.

NM/M

Production 50 or 100
Prime Auto.: No Pricing
Production 1-25

1	Brandi Chastain/100	50.00
2	Amanda Beard/50	40.00
3	Drew Stubbs/100	15.00
4	Drew Cumberland/100	15.00
5	Clint Dolezel/100	15.00
6	Mat Latos/100	25.00
7	Brett Anderson/100	30.00
9	Casey Weathers/100	15.00
11	Daniel Moskos/100	15.00
12	Darwin Barney/100	25.00
13	Kellen Kulbacki/100	15.00
14	Matt Dominguez/100	30.00
15	Matt Mangini/100	20.00
16	Mitch Canham/100	20.00
17	Willie Middlebrooks/100	25.00
19	Mike Powell/100	15.00
20	Steve Spurrier/50	40.00
21	Dale Brown/50	15.00
22	Don Haskins/50	15.00
23	Nick Schmidt/50	10.00
24	Zack Cozart/100	15.00

2007 Donruss Americana

NM/M

Complete Set (100): 40.00
Common Player: .25

1	John Travolta	1.00
2	Stacy Keibler	2.00
3	Burt Reynolds	1.00
4	Steve Guttenberg	.25
5	William Shatner	1.00
6	Lee Majors	.50
7	Gretchen Wilson	.50
8	Ultimate Warrior	.50
9	Barbara Eden	.50
10	Carrie Fisher	.50
11	Lori Petty	.25
12	Morgan Fairchild	.50
13	Vince Neil	.50
14	Gail Kim	.25
15	Cedric the Entertainer	.50
16	Corin Nemec	.25
17	Billy Dee Williams	.50
18	Jim Furyk	.50
19	Dick Van Patten	.25
20	Debbie Reynolds	.25
21	William Fichtner	.25
22	Bob Eubanks	.25
23	Mike Huckabee	1.00
24	Jack Hanna	.25
25	Elliott Gould	.25
26	Lou Gossett Jr.	.25
27	Catherine Bach	.50
28	Tippi Hedren	.25
29	Walter Koenig	.25
30	Ernest Borgnine	.25
31	Cindy Williams	.25
32	Cindy Morgan	.25
33	Giovanni Ribisi	.25
34	Story Musgrave	.25
35	Esther Williams	.25
36	Connie Mack III	.25
37	Gilbert Gottfried	.25
38	Burt Ward	.50
39	Josh Duhamel	.25
40	Larry Hagman	.50
41	Catherine Hicks	.25
42	Karen Lynn Gorney	.25
43	Larry King	.50
44	Autumn Reeser	.25
45	Mickey Rooney	.50
46	Aidan Quinn	.25
47	Martin Klebba	.25
48	Michael Pare'	.25
49	Hugh O'Brian	.25
50	Molly Shannon	.25
51	Dee Snider	.75
52	Melissa Jo Hunter	.25
53	Jennie Finch	1.00
54	Henry Winkler	.50
55	Neil Patrick Harris	.25
56	Val Kilmer	.25
57	Peter Marshall	.25
58	Clint Howard	.25
59	Buzz Aldrin	.50
60	Heather Cox	.25
61	Angela Simmons	.25
62	Richard Kiel	.25
63	Leonard Nimoy	.25
64	Jan Rooney	.25
65	Shirley Jones	.25
66	Bruce Jenner	.25
67	Tom Green	.25
68	Dom DeLuise	.50
69	Bobby Allison	.50
70	Tony Curtis	.50
71	Shawnee Smith	.25
72	Wink Martindale	.25
73	Tara Conner	.25
74	Sheryl Swoopes	.25
75	Wayne Newton	.50
76	Justine Simmons	.25
77	Keiko Agena	.25
78	Tom Savini	.25
79	David Faustino	.25
80	Adam West	.25
81	Gina Phillips	.25
82	Dawn Wells	.25
83	George Allen	.25
84	Chris Sarandon	.25
85	Amanda Beard	.50
86	Katey Sagal	.50
87	Ed O'Neill	.50
88	Dina Meyer	.50
89	Ron Howard	.25
90	Randy Owen	.25
91	Yunjin Kim	.25
92	Chuck Woolery	.25
93	Ed McMahon	.50
94	Stephanie Powers	.25
95	Warwick Davis	.25
96	Scott Baio	.25
97	Russell Johnson	.25
98	Michael Berryman	.25
99	Bernie Mac	.50
100	Ashley Judd	1.00

Cinema Stars

NM/M

Common Card: 4.00
Production 500 Sets

1	John Travolta	5.00
2	Burt Reynolds	5.00
3	William Shatner	5.00
4	Carrie Fisher	5.00
5	Ron Howard	5.00
6	Elliott Gould	4.00
7	Lou Gossett Jr.	4.00
8	Ernest Borgnine	4.00

9	Giovanni Ribisi	4.00
10	Quentin Tarantino	4.00
11	Shirley Jones	4.00
12	Dom DeLuise	4.00
13	Adam West	4.00
14	Bernie Mac	4.00
15	Ashley Judd	5.00
16	Josh Duhamel	4.00
17	Catherine Bach	4.00
18	Cindy Morgan	4.00
19	Karen Lynn Gorney	4.00
20	Larry Hagman	4.00
21	Lee Majors	4.00
22	Morgan Fairchild	4.00
23	Richard Kiel	4.00
24	Tippi Hedren	4.00
25	Walter Koenig	4.00
26	Burt Ward	4.00
27	Barbara Eden	4.00
28	Cedric the Entertainer	5.00
29	Billy Dee Williams	5.00
30	Leonard Nimoy	5.00

Cinema Stars Directors Cut Sign.

NM/M

Production 10-100

2	Burt Reynolds/25	250.00
3	William Shatner/25	150.00
5	Ron Howard/25	125.00
11	Shirley Jones/25	80.00
12	Dom DeLuise/25	60.00
16	Josh Duhamel/25	80.00
17	Catherine Bach/50	100.00
18	Cindy Morgan/100	40.00
19	Karen Lynn Gorney/50	40.00
20	Larry Hagman/25	100.00
22	Morgan Fairchild/50	60.00
23	Richard Kiel/25	75.00
24	Tippi Hedren/25	100.00
25	Walter Koenig/25	100.00
27	Barbara Eden/25	125.00
29	Billy Dee Williams/25	150.00
30	Leonard Nimoy/25	200.00

Cinema Stars Materials

NM/M

Common Card: 8.00
Production 100-500
Golden Era: 1-1.5X
Production 5-50
Silver Screen: 1-1.5X
Production 25-100
Super Stars: 2-3X
Production 5-25
No pricing production 20 or less.

1	John Travolta/Jkt/500	20.00
2	Burt Reynolds/Shirt/500	15.00
3	William Shatner/ Shirt/500	15.00
4	Carrie Fisher/Shirt/250	25.00
6	Elliott Gould/Sweater/500	8.00
7	Lou Gossett Jr./ Shirt/500	8.00
8	Ernest Borgnine/ Shirt/500	10.00
9	Giovanni Ribisi/Shirt/380	8.00
11	Shirley Jones/Skirt/500	10.00
13	Adam West/Shirt/500	15.00
15	Ashley Judd/Shirt/400	20.00
16	Josh Duhamel/Shirt/350	8.00
17	Catherine Bach/ Shirt/500	15.00
18	Cindy Morgan/Shirt/500	8.00
19	Larry Hagman/Shirt/350	10.00
21	Lee Majors/ Pajamas/500	10.00
22	Morgan Fairchild/ Shirt/100	20.00
24	Tippi Hedren/Dress/500	10.00
26	Burt Ward/Shirt/400	10.00
27	Barbara Eden/Shirt/195	10.00
30	Leonard Nimoy/ Shirt/500	15.00

Cinema Stars Signatures

NM/M

Production 10-100
Signature Materials: 1-1.5X
Production 4-25

2	Burt Reynolds/25	80.00
3	William Shatner/25	140.00
4	Carrie Fisher/50	150.00
5	Ron Howard/75	75.00
6	Elliott Gould/100	25.00
7	Lou Gossett/50	30.00
8	Ernest Borgnine/50	60.00
9	Giovanni Ribisi/50	25.00
11	Shirley Jones/50	50.00
12	Dom DeLuise/50	40.00
13	Adam West/50	60.00
14	Bernie Mac/50	50.00
15	Ashley Judd/50	160.00
16	Josh Duhamel/50	50.00
17	Catherine Bach/25	75.00
18	Cindy Morgan/25	25.00
19	Karen Lynn Gorney/25	25.00
20	Larry Hagman/25	75.00
21	Lee Majors/25	60.00
22	Morgan Fairchild/25	60.00
23	Richard Kiel/50	50.00
24	Tippi Hedren/25	75.00
25	Walter Koenig/75	50.00
26	Burt Ward/50	50.00
27	Barbara Eden/25	75.00
28	Cedric the Entertainer/50	30.00

29	Billy Dee Williams/50	50.00
30	Leonard Nimoy/25	120.00

Co-Stars Materials

NM/M

Production 50 unless noted.
Golden Era: No Pricing
Production 10 Sets
Silver Screen: 1-1.5X
Production 25 Sets

1	Marilyn Monroe/Skirt, Bette Davis/Dress	150.00
2	Humphrey Bogart/Shirt, Ingrid Bergman/Dress	100.00
3	James Dean/Robe, Natalie Wood/Dress	100.00
4	Burt Reynolds/Shirt, Jackie Gleason/ Coat/100	50.00
5	William Shatner/Shirt, Leonard Nimoy/ Shirt/100	50.00
6	Adam West/Shirt, Burt Ward/Shirt/100	40.00
7	Rock Hudson/Jkt, James Dean/Robe	100.00
8	Ed O'Neill/Shirt, Katey Sagal/Blouse/100	30.00
9	Dawn Wells/Shirt, Russell Johnson/ Shirt/100	40.00
10	Ernest Borgnine/Shirt, Debbie Reynolds/ H'chief	40.00

Co-Stars Signatures

NM/M

Production 50 unless noted

1	S. Smith, D. Meyer	100.00
2	Barbara Eden, Larry Hagman	200.00
3	William Shatner, Leonard Nimoy/25	300.00
4	Adam West, Burt Ward	150.00
5	Ed O'Neill, Katey Sagal	150.00
6	Burt Reynolds, Dom DeLuise/25	150.00
7	Ron Howard, Henry Winkler/25	200.00
8	Billy Dee Williams, Carrie Fisher/25	200.00
9	Mickey Rooney, Jan Rooney/25	150.00
10	Dawn Wells, Russell Johnson	150.00

Hollywood Legends

NM/M

Common Card:
Production 500 Sets

1	James Dean	8.00
2	Ingrid Bergman	4.00
3	Gloria Swanson	4.00
4	Rock Hudson	4.00
5	Bette Davis	6.00
6	Jayne Mansfield	8.00
7	Greta Garbo	4.00
8	Ava Gardner	4.00
9	Mae West	4.00
10	Steve McQueen	4.00
11	Audrey Hepburn	6.00
12	Jean Harlow	4.00
13	Lillian Gish	4.00
14	Carole Lombard	4.00
15	James Cagney	4.00
16	Marilyn Monroe	10.00
17	Mary Pickford	4.00
18	Debbie Reynolds	4.00
19	Ginger Rogers	4.00
20	Glenn Ford	4.00
21	Eleanor Powell	4.00
22	Gene Tierney	4.00
23	Lana Turner	4.00
24	Esther Williams	4.00
25	Natalie Wood	4.00
26	Loretta Young	4.00
27	Humphrey Bogart	4.00
28	Marlon Brando	6.00
29	Dorothy Lamour	4.00
30	Tony Curtis	4.00
31	Bob Denver	4.00
32	Errol Flynn	4.00
33	Peter Sellers	4.00
34	Patricia Neal	4.00
35	Mickey Rooney	4.00
36	Marlene Dietrich	4.00
37	Jimmy Stewart	6.00
38	Yvonne De Carlo	4.00
39	Rudolph Valentino	4.00
40	Bing Crosby	4.00

Directors Cut Signatures

NM/M

Production 1-25

24	Esther Williams/25	200.00
34	Patricia Neal/25	150.00

Hollywood Legends Materials

NM/M

Common Card:
Production 25-350
Golden Era: 1-1.5X
Production 5-50
Silver Screen: 1-1.5X
Production 10-100
Super Stars: 2-3X

Production 1-25

1	James Dean/Robe/155	100.00
2	Ingrid Bergman/ Dress/250	35.00
3	Gloria Swanson/ Dress/350	25.00
4	Rock Hudson/Jkt/250	25.00
5	Bette Davis/Dress/250	35.00
6	Jayne Mansfield/ Shirt/325	40.00
7	Greta Garbo/Dress/350	35.00
8	Ava Gardner/Dress/325	35.00
9	Mae West/Coat/350	30.00
10	Steve McQueen/Jkt/350	30.00
11	Audrey Hepburn/ Dress/325	50.00
12	Jean Harlow/Coat/325	35.00
13	Lillian Gish/Coat/325	30.00
14	Carole Lombard/ Dress/350	30.00
15	James Cagney/Coat/350	35.00
16	Marilyn Monroe/ Skirt/250	125.00
17	Mary Pickford/ Dress/350	25.00
18	Debbie Reynolds/ Handkerchief/25	40.00
19	Ginger Rogers/Coat/325	30.00
20	Glenn Ford/Shirt/350	20.00
21	Eleanor Powell/ Tights/325	25.00
22	Gene Tierney/Dress/325	25.00
23	Lana Turner/Dress/325	30.00
24	Esther Williams/ Bathing Suit/100	25.00
25	Natalie Wood/ Dress/350	40.00
26	Loretta Young/Coat/350	25.00
27	Humphrey Bogart/ Shirt/350	50.00
28	Marlon Brando/ Pants/325	30.00
29	Dorothy Lamour/ Dress/325	30.00
30	Tony Curtis/Shirt/325	20.00
31	Bob Denver/Shirt/350	20.00
32	Errol Flynn/Jkt/325	40.00
33	Peter Sellers/Jkt/325	25.00
34	Patricia Neal/Shawl/350	25.00
35	Mickey Rooney/ Shirt/325	25.00
36	Marlene Dietrich/ Coat/350	30.00
37	Jimmy Stewart/ Coat/325	50.00
38	Yvonne De Carlo/ Coat/350	25.00
40	Bing Crosby/Shoes/25	200.00

Hollywood Legends Signatures

NM/M

Production 25 Sets
Signature Materials: 1-1.5X
Production 25 Sets

18	Debbie Reynolds	100.00
24	Esther Williams	100.00
30	Tony Curtis	100.00
35	Mickey Rooney	100.00

Private Signings

NM/M

Production 5-1,250

1	John Travolta/25	40.00
1	John Travolta/25	180.00
4	Stacy Keibler/250	50.00
4	Steve Guttenberg/300	20.00
5	William Shatner/25	120.00
7	Gretchen Wilson/200	60.00
8	Ultimate Warrior/250	50.00
9	Barbara Eden/25	75.00
10	Carrie Fisher/25	150.00
11	Lori Petty/200	15.00
12	Morgan Fairchild/150	50.00
13	Vince Neil/250	30.00
14	Gail Kim/250	30.00
15	Cedric the Entertainer/135	30.00
16	Corin Nemec/200	15.00
17	Billy Dee Williams/85	50.00
18	Jim Furyk/100	50.00
19	Dick Van Patten	50.00
21	William Fichtner/100	15.00
22	Bob Eubanks/50	50.00
23	Mike Huckabee/275	50.00
24	Jack Hanna/400	20.00
25	Elliott Gould/250	25.00
26	Lou Gossett Jr./50	30.00
28	Tippi Hedren	50.00
29	Walter Koenig/60	50.00
30	Ernest Borgnine/50	50.00
31	Cindy Williams/50	40.00
32	Cindy Morgan/330	15.00
33	Giovanni Ribisi/250	25.00
34	Story Musgrave/250	25.00
35	Esther Williams/50	50.00
36	Connie Mack III/150	15.00
37	Gilbert Gottfried/450	15.00
38	Burt Ward/75	50.00
39	Josh Duhamel/50	50.00
40	Larry Hagman/50	50.00
41	Catherine Hicks/350	20.00
42	Karen Lynn Gorney/418	15.00
43	Larry King/200	30.00
44	Autumn Reeser/364	25.00
45	Mickey Rooney/50	80.00
46	Aidan Quinn/168	15.00
47	Martin Klebba/1,250	10.00

48 Michael Pare'/1,250 10.00
49 Hugh O'Brian/70 25.00
50 Molly Shannon/250 25.00
51 Dee Snider 25.00
52 Melissa Jo Hunter/ 1,250 10.00
53 Jennie Finch/500 40.00
54 Henry Winkler/50 80.00
55 Neil Patrick Harris/100 30.00
56 Val Kilmer/100 40.00
57 Peter Marshall/200 15.00
58 Clint Howard/100 25.00
59 Buzz Aldrin/50 150.00
60 Heather Cox/500 25.00
61 Angela Simmons/159 15.00
62 Richard Kiel/100 50.00
63 Leonard Nimoy/25 125.00
64 Jan Rooney/175 20.00
66 Bruce Jenner/250 25.00
67 Tom Green/200 20.00
68 Dom DeLuise/105 40.00
69 Bobby Allison/100 25.00
70 Tony Curtis/25 80.00
71 Shawnee Smith 15.00
72 Wink Martindale/95 45.00
73 Tara Conner/150 40.00
74 Sheryl Swoopes/375 20.00
75 Wayne Newton/110 50.00
76 Justine Simmons/250 10.00
77 Keiko Agena/130 15.00
78 Tom Savini/364 15.00
79 David Faustino/150 20.00
80 Adam West/50 60.00
81 Gina Phillips/350 20.00
82 Dawn Wells/100 50.00
83 George Allen/224 15.00
84 Chris Sarandon/312 10.00
86 Katey Sagal/100 40.00
87 Ed O'Neill/100 40.00
88 Dina Meyer/100 40.00
89 Ron Howard/60 80.00
90 Randy Owen/200 25.00
91 Yunjin Kim/400 30.00
92 Chuck Woolery/100 15.00
93 Ed McMahon/470 25.00
94 Stephanie Powers/100 50.00
95 Warwick Davis/250 10.00
96 Scott Baio/250 25.00
97 Russell Johnson/100 40.00
98 Michael Berryman/314 15.00
99 Bernie Mac/85 40.00
100 Ashley Judd/50 180.00

Promos
No Pricing

Sports Legends
NM/M
Common Card: 4.00
Production 500 Sets
1 Willie Mays 8.00
2 Jackie Robinson 8.00
3 Walt Frazier 4.00
4 Lou Gehrig 10.00
5 Jim Courier 4.00
6 Tony Esposito 4.00
7 Martina Navratilova 4.00
8 Stan Musial 8.00
9 Patrick Roy 8.00
10 Larry Bird 8.00

Sports Legends Materials
NM/M
Production 25-500
1 Willie Mays/Jsy/100 40.00
2 Jackie Robinson/ Jkt/100 50.00
4 Walt Frazier/Jsy/100 10.00
5 Lou Gehrig/Jsy/100 150.00
6 Jim Courier/Shirt/500 10.00
7 Tony Esposito/Jsy/500 10.00
8 Stan Musial/Jsy/25 40.00

Sports Legends Signatures
NM/M
Production 25-50
Signature Materials: 1X
Production 25-50
1 Willie Mays/25 200.00
3 Walt Frazier/25 50.00
5 Jim Courier/50 40.00
7 Tony Esposito/25 50.00
7 Martina Navratilova/50 75.00
8 Stan Musial/25 75.00
9 Patrick Roy/25 125.00
10 Larry Bird/25 125.00

Stars Materials
NM/M
Common Card: 5.00
Production 10-250
1 John Travolta/Jkt/250 15.00
2 Stacy Keibler/Shirt/195 20.00
3 Burt Reynolds/Shirt/250 15.00
4 Steve Guttenberg/ Shirt/250 5.00
5 William Shatner/ Shirt/250 15.00
6 Lee Majors/ Pajamas/250 20.00
8 Ultimate Warrior/ Trunks/95 20.00
9 Barbara Eden/Shirt/50 25.00
10 Carrie Fisher/Shirt/50 25.00
11 Lori Petty/Shirt/250 8.00
12 Morgan Fairchild/ Shirt/50 25.00
13 Vince Neil/Shirt/250 60.00
16 Corin Nemec/Shirt/250 8.00
18 Jim Furyk/Shirt/250 15.00
19 Dick Van Patten/ Shirt/250 8.00
20 Debbie Reynolds/ Handkerchief/250 40.00
21 William Fichtner/ Shirt/250 8.00
22 Bob Eubanks/Shirt/250 8.00
23 Mike Huckabee/ Shirt/250 10.00
25 Elliott Gould/Sweater/250 8.00
26 Lou Gossett Jr./Shirt/250 8.00
27 Catherine Bach/ Shirt/250 5.00
28 Tippi Hedren/Dress/250 15.00
30 Ernest Borgnine/ Shirt/100 10.00
31 Cindy Williams/Shirt/100 5.00
32 Cindy Morgan/Shirt/190 8.00
33 Giovanni Ribisi/Shirt/100 8.00
35 Esther Williams/ Bathing Suit/100 25.00
36 Connie Mack III/ Shirt/250 5.00
37 Gilbert Gottfried/ Shirt/100 10.00
38 Burt Ward/Shirt/100 15.00
39 Josh Duhamel/ Shirt/100 10.00
40 Larry Hagman/Shirt/100 15.00
46 Mickey Rooney/Shirt/80 25.00
47 Aidan Quinn/Pants/250 5.00
48 Martin Klebba/Shirt/250 8.00
49 Hugh O'Brian/Shirt/250 8.00
52 Melissa Jo Hunter/ Shirt/25 25.00
55 Neil Patrick Harris/ Shirt/250 8.00
63 Leonard Nimoy/ Shirt/100 15.00
65 Shirley Jones/Shirt/100 5.00
66 Bruce Jenner/Shirt/250 8.00
67 Tom Green/Pants/250 5.00
69 Bobby Allison/Shirt/250 8.00
70 Tony Curtis/Shirt/85 20.00
72 Wink Martindale/ Shirt/250 5.00
73 Tara Conner/Shirt/100 20.00
76 Keiko Agena/Shirt/250 5.00
79 David Faustino/Shirt/250 8.00
80 Adam West/Shirt/100 15.00
83 George Allen/Pants/250 5.00
85 Amanda Beard/ Bathing Suit/25 30.00
86 Katey Sagal/Blouse/250 10.00
87 Ed O'Neill/Shirt/250 10.00
88 Dina Meyer/Shirt/55 15.00
92 Chuck Woolery/ Pants/250 5.00
96 Scott Baio/Shirt/250 5.00
97 Russell Johnson/ Shirt/100 15.00
100 Ashley Judd/Shirt/100 25.00

Stars Signature Materials
NM/M
Production 10-250
1 John Travolta/Jkt/25 180.00
2 Stacy Keibler/Shirt/25 80.00
3 Burt Reynolds/Shirt/25 80.00
5 William Shatner/ Shirt/25 120.00
6 Lee Majors/Pajamas/25 60.00
8 Ultimate Warrior/ Trunks/50 75.00
9 Barbara Eden/Shirt/100 60.00
10 Carrie Fisher/Shirt/25 160.00
11 Lori Petty/Shirt/200 15.00
12 Morgan Fairchild/ Shirt/150 50.00
13 Vince Neil/Shirt/250 30.00
14 Gail Kim/Trunks/150 30.00
16 Corin Nemec/Shirt/200 15.00
18 Jim Furyk/Shirt/100 50.00
19 Dick Van Patten/ Shirt/250 20.00
20 Debbie Reynolds/ Handkerchief/25 100.00
21 William Fichtner/ Shirt/250 15.00
22 Bob Eubanks/Shirt/150 20.00
23 Mike Huckabee/ Shirt/225 50.00
26 Lou Gossett Jr./Shirt/30 30.00
27 Catherine Bach/ Shirt/22 100.00
28 Tippi Hedren/Dress/25 80.00
30 Ernest Borgnine/ Shirt/100 50.00
31 Cindy Williams/ Shirt/200 25.00
33 Giovanni Ribisi/ Shirt/200 20.00
35 Esther Williams/ Bathing Suit/50 80.00
36 Connie Mack III/ Shirt/250 10.00
38 Burt Ward/Shirt/100 50.00
45 Mickey Rooney/Shirt/80 100.00
47 Aidan Quinn/Pants/200 15.00
48 Martin Klebba/Shirt/250 10.00
49 Hugh O'Brian/Shirt/200 30.00
52 Melissa Jo Hunter/ Shirt/250 15.00
55 Neil Patrick Harris/ Shirt/100 25.00
56 Val Kilmer/Coat/100 35.00
63 Leonard Nimoy/ Shirt/25 125.00
65 Shirley Jones/Skirt/250 50.00
66 Bruce Jenner/Shirt/250 25.00
67 Tom Green/Pants/200 20.00
69 Bobby Allison/Shirt/100 25.00
70 Tony Curtis/Shirt/50 75.00
72 Wink Martindale/ Shirt/150 20.00
73 Tara Conner/Shirt/100 50.00
77 Keiko Agena/Shirt/250 15.00
79 David Faustino/ Shirt/200 20.00
80 Adam West/Shirt/100 60.00
83 Dawn Wells/Shirt/100 50.00
86 George Allen/Blouse/100 40.00
87 Ed O'Neill/Shirt/100 50.00
88 Dina Meyer/Shirt/100 50.00
92 Chuck Woolery/ Pants/100 5.00
94 Stephanie Powers/ Handkerchief/25 60.00
96 Scott Baio/Shirt/100 20.00
97 Russell Johnson/ Shirt/100 40.00
100 Ashley Judd/Shirt/50 160.00

2008 Donruss Americana Legends
NM/M
Complete Set (144): 50.00
Common Legend: .50
Pack (5): 10.00
Box (10): 90.00
1 Ted Williams 1.50
2 Jim Brown 1.50
3 Larry Bird 1.50
4 Peggy Fleming .50
5 Willie Mays 1.50
6 Oscar Robertson 1.00
7 Bobby Allison .50
9 Joe Montana 2.00
10 Hank Aaron 2.00
11 Patrick Roy 1.50
12 John Wooden .50
13 Jake LaMotta .75
14 Clyde Lovellette .50
15 Nolan Ryan 1.50
16 John Elway 2.00
17 Ray Bourque .75
18 Johnny Weissmuller .50
19 Dan Issel .50
20 Stan Musial 1.00
21 Troy Aikman 1.50
22 Elvin Hayes .50
23 Bruce Jenner .50
24 Norm Ullman .50
25 Kevin McHale 1.00
26 Sidney Moncrief .50
27 Mike Powell .50
28 John Riggins 1.00
29 Satchel Paige 1.00
30 Summer Sanders .50
32 Walt Frazier .50
33 Michelle Akers .50
34 Bill Gadsby .50
35 Don Mattingly 1.00
36 Frank Gifford .50
37 John Bohman .50
38 Jim Courier .50
39 Bobby Wanzer .50
40 Bob Gibson 1.00
41 Roger Staubach 1.00
42 Marques Haynes .50
43 Ultimate Warrior .50
44 Dolph Schayes .50
45 Roberto Clemente 1.50
46 Urijah Faber .50
47 Dominique Wilkins .75
48 Cobi Jones .50
49 Alex English .50
50 Joe Jackson 1.50
52 Robert Parish .50
53 Steve Young 1.00
55 Gerry Cheevers .50
56 Bailey Howell .50
57 Amanda Beard .50
58 Don Haskins .50
59 Pierre Pilote .50
60 Earl Campbell .50
61 Yogi Berra 1.00
62 Dean Smith .50
63 Rollie Massimino .50
64 Pete Rose 2.00
65 Jim Kelly .50
66 Bob Feller .75
67 Brad Park .50
68 Dick Vitale .50
69 Lance Alworth .50
70 Brooks Robinson 1.00
72 Rick Majerus .50
73 Dan Marino 2.00
74 Al Cervi .50
75 Cal Ripken Jr. 2.00
76 Lisa Leslie .50
77 Jerry West 1.00
78 Tony Dorsett 1.00
79 Jeanette Lee .50
80 Carl Yastrzemski 1.00
81 Dominique Moceanu .50
82 Vince Dooley .50
83 Bob Griese .75
84 Alex Delvecchio .50
85 Carlton Fisk .75
86 Wes Unseld .50
87 Bill Walton .75
88 Jim Taylor 1.00
89 Arnie Risen .50
90 Duke Snider 1.00
91 Phil Esposito .50
92 Dennis Rodman .50
93 Bela Karolyi .50
94 Serena Williams 1.00
95 Eddie Murray .75
96 Eric Dickerson .75
97 Jim Boeheim .50
98 Tatu Pecorari .50
99 Pete Weber .50
100 Frank Robinson 1.00
101 Lefty Kreh .50
102 Jerry Tarkanian .50
103 Mike Bossy .50
104 Dan Fouts .50
105 Jim Palmer .75
106 Steve Cauthen .50
107 Lynette Woodard .50
108 Michael Irvin .75
109 Cale Yarborough .50
110 Johnny Bench 1.00
111 Paul Coffey .50
112 Muggsy Bogues .50
113 Dick Butkus 1.50
114 Hope Solo .50
115 Juan Marichal .75
116 Al Unser .50
117 Sheryl Swoopes .50
118 Gale Sayers 1.50
119 Mike Schmidt 1.00
120 Nate Thurmond .50
121 Whitey Ford .50
122 Jennie Finch .50
123 Cliff Hagan .50
124 Paul Molitor 1.00
125 Tony Esposito .50
126 Ron Turcotte .50
127 Cat Osterman .50
128 Tony Gwynn 1.00
129 Cat Osterman .50
130 Reggie Jackson 1.00
131 Lawrence Taylor 1.00
132 Pat LaFontaine .50
133 Martina Navratilova 1.00
134 George Gervin .50
135 Ryne Sandberg 1.00
136 Marion Jones .50
137 Richard Petty 1.00
138 Raymond Berry .50
139 Al Unser Jr. .50
140 Nolan Ryan 1.50
141 Jean Cruguet .50
142 Lenny Moore .50
143 Willie McCovey 1.00
144 Matt Serra .50
145 Al Kaline 1.00
146 Bobby Hurley .50
147 Eddie Sutton .50
148 Knute Rockne 1.00
149 David Thompson .50
150 Pete Rose 2.00

Mirror Black
Production One Set

Mirror Blue
Mirror Blue: 4-6X
Production 100 Sets

Mirror Blue Signatures
NM/M
Production 2-250
Emerald Autos.: No Pricing
Production 3-5
Mirror Gold: No Pricing
Production 4-25
Mirror Black: No Pricing
Production One Set
4 Peggy Fleming/50 30.00
5 Willie Mays/25 150.00
9 Bobby Allison/26 25.00
10 Joe Montana/25 100.00
11 Hank Aaron/25 200.00
12 John Wooden/25 80.00
13 Jake LaMotta/25 40.00
14 Clyde Lovellette/150 15.00
15 Nolan Ryan/25 75.00
17 Ray Bourque/25 30.00
19 Dan Issel/100 15.00
20 Stan Musial/25 60.00
23 Bruce Jenner/100 20.00
24 Norm Ullman/250 10.00
26 Kevin McHale/250 50.00
28 Mike Powell/250 10.00
32 Walt Frazier/50 25.00
34 Bill Gadsby/250 10.00
36 Frank Gifford/25 40.00
37 Parker Bohn/250 5.00
39 Bobby Wanzer/250 5.00
40 Bob Gibson/25 30.00
42 Marques Haynes/50 20.00
43 Ultimate Warrior/128 35.00
45 Dolph Schayes/143 15.00
46 Urijah Faber/35 10.00
52 Robert Parish/250 10.00
54 Gerry Cheevers/250 5.00
55 Bailey Howell/250 10.00
58 Pierre Pilote/250 10.00
60 Yogi Berra/25 75.00
62 Rollie Massimino/50 15.00
63 Pete Rose/50 100.00
65 Bob Feller/50 20.00
67 Brad Park/250 10.00
74 Al Cervi/250 10.00
75 Cal Ripken Jr./25 80.00
76 Lisa Leslie/100 20.00
77 Jerry West/25 60.00
79 Jeanette Lee/250 30.00
80 Carl Yastrzemski/25 50.00
81 Dominique Moceanu/ 100 25.00
83 Bob Griese/25 25.00
84 Alex Delvecchio/250 15.00
86 Wes Unseld/50 20.00
87 Bill Walton/25 50.00
89 Arnie Risen/25 15.00
90 Duke Snider/25 30.00
91 Phil Esposito/25 25.00
93 Dennis Rodman/25 35.00
94 Bela Karolyi/25 20.00
94 Serena Williams/25 75.00
95 Eddie Murray/25 35.00
98 Tatu Pecorari/25 15.00
99 Pete Weber/250 15.00
100 Frank Robinson/25 30.00
101 Lefty Kreh/250 5.00
103 Mike Bossy/50 15.00
104 Dan Fouts/25 30.00
105 Jim Palmer/25 25.00
106 Steve Cauthen/100 15.00
107 Lynette Woodard/50 15.00
108 Michael Irvin/25 30.00
109 Cale Yarborough/25 15.00
110 Johnny Bench/25 50.00
111 Paul Coffey/25 20.00
114 Hope Solo/30 30.00
115 Juan Marichal/25 30.00
116 Al Unser/25 15.00
121 Nate Thurmond/100 15.00
122 Whitey Ford/25 40.00
123 Jennie Finch/100 30.00
124 Cliff Hagan/150 15.00
125 Paul Molitor/25 30.00
126 Tony Esposito/25 15.00
127 Ron Turcotte/250 5.00
129 Cat Osterman/100 30.00
130 Reggie Jackson/25 35.00
132 Pat LaFontaine/250 5.00
134 George Gervin/50 20.00
135 Ryne Sandberg/25 40.00
136 Marion Jones/50 15.00
137 Richard Petty/65 35.00
139 Al Unser Jr./100 20.00
140 Nolan Ryan/25 75.00
141 Jean Cruguet/250 8.00
143 Lenny Moore/250 8.00
144 Matt Serra/50 20.00
145 Al Kaline/50 30.00
147 Eddie Sutton/27 25.00
149 David Thompson/250 15.00
150 Pete Rose/50 100.00

Mirror Emerald
No Pricing
Production 5 Sets

Mirror Gold
Mirror Gold: 10-15X
Production 25 Sets

Mirror Red
Mirror Red: 2-4x
Production 250 Sets

Mirror Red Materials
ELVIN HAYES
NM/M
Production 10-500
Mirror Black: No Pricing
Production One Set
Mirror Blue: 1-1.25X
Production 5-250
Emerald: No Pricing
Production 1-5
Gold: No Pricing
Production 1-25
1 Ted Williams/100 30.00
7 Oscar Robertson/500 8.00
8 Bobby Allison/500 8.00
9 Joe Montana/100 20.00
11 Hank Aaron/100 30.00
11 Patrick Roy/500 8.00
15 Nolan Ryan/500 15.00
16 John Elway/100 20.00
18 Johnny Weissmuller/500 5.00
19 Dan Issel/500 5.00
22 Elvin Hayes/500 5.00
23 Bruce Jenner/500 8.00
24 Norm Ullman/250 8.00
26 Sidney Moncrief/475 5.00
27 Mike Powell/250 5.00
29 John Riggins/25 20.00
30 Satchel Paige/25 40.00
31 Summer Sanders/100 20.00
32 Walt Frazier/500 8.00
33 Michelle Akers/500 5.00
34 Bill Gadsby/500 5.00
35 Don Mattingly/25 15.00
37 Parker Bohn/500 5.00
41 Roger Staubach/100 20.00
42 Marques Haynes/500 5.00
45 Roberto Clemente/250 10.00
46 Urijah Faber/450 10.00
47 Dominique Wilkins/300 8.00
48 Cobi Jones/500 5.00
50 Joe Jackson/50 200.00
52 Robert Parish/350 5.00
53 Steve Young/100 10.00
55 Bailey Howell/500 5.00
57 Don Haskins/475 5.00
58 Pierre Pilote/500 5.00
59 Earl Campbell/50 10.00
62 Rollie Massimino/500 5.00
63 Pete Rose/250 20.00
64 Jim Kelly/500 10.00
72 Rick Majerus/400 5.00
73 Dan Marino/100 25.00
75 Cal Ripken Jr./100 25.00
77 Jerry West/500 15.00
78 Tony Dorsett/100 5.00
79 Jeanette Lee/250 20.00
82 Vince Dooley/500 8.00
83 Bob Griese/50 8.00
85 Carlton Fisk/500 8.00
86 Wes Unseld/500 5.00
93 Bela Karolyi/500 5.00
96 Eric Dickerson/100 8.00
98 Tatu Pecorari/500 5.00
99 Pete Weber/450 5.00
100 Frank Robinson/100 8.00
104 Dan Fouts/100 8.00
106 Steve Cauthen/500 5.00
108 Michael Irvin/25 10.00
112 Muggsy Bogues/500 5.00
114 Hope Solo/500 10.00
120 Mike Schmidt/250 10.00
122 Whitey Ford/25 15.00
125 Paul Molitor/50 8.00
126 Tony Esposito/250 5.00
127 Ron Turcotte/500 5.00
128 Tony Gwynn/25 15.00
129 Cat Osterman/500 15.00
130 Reggie Jackson/250 8.00
137 Richard Petty/400 10.00
138 Raymond Berry/100 8.00
140 Nolan Ryan/25 15.00
142 Lenny Moore/100 8.00
143 Willie McCovey/25 10.00
148 Knute Rockne/500 25.00
150 Pete Rose/250 20.00

Mirror Red Signatures
PETE WEBER
BOWLING
NM/M
Production 25-1,370
4 Peggy Fleming/108 25.00
7 Oscar Robertson/25 50.00
12 John Wooden/25 35.00
13 Jake LaMotta/214 35.00
14 Clyde Lovellette/659 75.00
17 Ray Bourque/25 15.00
19 Dan Issel/501 15.00
22 Elvin Hayes/79 30.00
23 Bruce Jenner/369 10.00
24 Norm Ullman/714 15.00
25 Kevin McHale/369 15.00
28 Mike Powell/502 15.00
32 Walt Frazier/158 15.00
34 Bill Gadsby/564 15.00
35 Frank Gifford/25 80.00
37 Parker Bohn/1,369 20.00
38 Jim Courier/42 30.00
39 Bobby Wanzer/658 15.00
40 Bob Gibson/55 15.00
42 Marques Haynes/337 15.00
44 Dolph Schayes/655 12.00
46 Urijah Faber/519 20.00
52 Robert Parish/211 15.00
54 Gerry Cheevers/568 15.00
55 Bailey Howell/664 10.00
58 Pierre Pilote/539 10.00
62 Rollie Massimino/333 15.00
65 Bob Feller/100 25.00
66 Brad Park/269 15.00
67 Dick Vitale/133 40.00
74 Al Cervi/619 10.00
76 Lisa Leslie/396 15.00
77 Jerry West/25 60.00
79 Jeanette Lee/1,013 25.00
81 Dominique Moceanu/ 219 15.00
83 Bob Griese/55 20.00
84 Alex Delvecchio/563 15.00
86 Wes Unseld/283 15.00
87 Bill Walton/259 20.00
88 Jim Taylor/25 30.00

89	Arnie Risen/558	15.00
91	Phil Esposito/109	20.00
92	Dennis Rodman/179	35.00
93	Bela Karolyi/259	15.00
94	Serena Williams/25	15.00
98	Tatu Pecorari/539	15.00
99	Pete Weber/458	15.00
100	Frank Robinson/25	15.00
101	Lefty Kreh/1,250	15.00
103	Mike Bossy/269	15.00
106	Steve Cauthen/1,236	15.00
107	Lynette Woodard/112	15.00
108	Michael Irvin/25	15.00
109	Cale Yarborough/297	15.00
111	Paul Coffey/25	15.00
113	Dick Butkus/25	15.00
114	Hope Solo/182	15.00
116	Al Unser/219	15.00
121	Nate Thurmond/270	15.00
122	Whitey Ford/50	15.00
123	Jennie Finch/369	30.00
124	Cliff Hagan/556	15.00
125	Paul Molitor/50	30.00
126	Tony Esposito/93	15.00
127	Ron Turcotte/1,370	15.00
129	Cat Osterman/493	30.00
131	Lawrence Taylor/50	15.00
132	Pat LaFontaine/290	15.00
134	George Gervin/287	15.00
136	Marion Jones/182	25.00
139	Al Unser Jr./219	8.00
141	Jean Cruguet/1,103	15.00
142	Lenny Moore/50	25.00
144	Matt Serra/167	20.00
145	Al Kaline/100	30.00
149	David Thompson/767	15.00

Certified Cuts
NM/M
Production 1-100
1	Jerry West/50	60.00
4	Nate Thurmond/49	20.00
5	Alex Delvecchio/100	30.00
6	Larry Bird/50	75.00
7	Dennis Rodman/40	40.00
9	Oscar Robertson/125	125.00
10	Robert Parish/100	25.00
12	John Wooden/20	125.00
13	Jake LaMotta/45	140.00
18	Tatu Pecorari/40	25.00
21	Steve Cauthen/50	65.00
22	Jean Cruguet/100	35.00
25	Jeanette Lee/100	50.00

Certified Cuts 2
NM/M
Production 10-55
8	Dick Vitale/10	75.00
13	Jake LaMotta/55	140.00
21	Steve Cauthen/50	65.00

Champions

NM/M
Common Player:	2.00
Production 1,000 Sets
Gold:	1-1.5X
Production 100 Sets
1	Jerry West	3.00
2	Joe Montana	6.00
3	Whitey Ford	3.00
4	Jennie Finch	3.00
5	John Riggins	3.00
6	Bob Gibson	3.00
7	Larry Bird	5.00
8	Roger Staubach	3.00
9	Pete Rose	4.00
10	Dolph Schayes	2.00
11	Reggie Jackson	3.00
12	John Elway	5.00
13	Cliff Hagan	2.00
14	Don Larsen	3.00
15	Bill Walton	3.00
16	Dan Issel	2.00
17	Serena Williams	3.00
18	Jean Cruguet	2.00
19	Pete Weber	2.00
20	Steve Cauthen	2.00

Champions Materials
NM/M
Production 10-250
1	Jerry West/250	10.00
2	Joe Montana/250	20.00
3	John Riggins/250	10.00
8	Roger Staubach/250	15.00
9	Pete Rose/25	40.00
11	Reggie Jackson/150	20.00
12	John Elway/250	20.00

16	Dan Issel/100	10.00
19	Pete Weber/100	5.00
20	Steve Cauthen/100	5.00

Champions Signatures
NM/M
Production 1-100
1	Jerry West/50	50.00
3	Whitey Ford/25	40.00
4	Jennie Finch/50	30.00
6	Bob Gibson/25	30.00
9	Pete Rose/25	100.00
10	Dolph Schayes/100	15.00
13	Cliff Hagan/100	15.00
15	Bill Walton/25	40.00
16	Dan Issel/100	20.00
17	Serena Williams/50	60.00
18	Jean Cruguet/100	15.00
19	Pete Weber/100	20.00
20	Steve Cauthen/100	15.00

College Heroes

NM/M
Common Player:	2.00
Production 1,000 Sets
Gold:	1-1.5X
Production 100 Sets
1	Cat Osterman	2.00
2	Mike Powell	2.00
3	Adrian Peterson	5.00
4	Bo Jackson	4.00
5	Gordon Beckham	3.00
6	Oscar Robertson	3.00
7	Elvin Hayes	3.00
8	Buster Posey	5.00
9	Dan Issel	2.00

College Heroes Signatures
NM/M
Production 25-100
1	Cat Osterman/100	35.00
2	Mike Powell/100	10.00
3	Adrian Peterson\	100.00
4	Bo Jackson/25	60.00
5	Gordon Beckham/100	35.00
7	Elvin Hayes/100	15.00
8	Buster Posey/50	50.00
9	Dan Issel/100	15.00

College Heroes Materials
NM/M
Production 50-250
1	Cat Osterman/100	15.00
2	Mike Powell/150	5.00
3	Adrian Peterson/250	20.00
4	Bo Jackson/250	10.00
5	Gordon Beckham/250	10.00
6	Oscar Robertson/250	10.00
7	Elvin Hayes/250	8.00
8	Buster Posey/50	15.00
9	Dan Issel/250	5.00

Collegiate Legends Patches Auto.
NM/M
Production 25-250
1	Tom Seaver/50	50.00
2	Reggie Jackson/51	50.00
3	Lisa Leslie/250	25.00
4	Oscar Robertson/50	120.00
7	Jerry West/52	60.00
8	Hope Solo/244	30.00
9	Rick Majerus/150	15.00
10	Arnie Risen/98	20.00
11	John Wooden/100	100.00
12	Steve Spurrier/65	40.00
13	John Wooden/20	100.00
15	Dan Issel/100	40.00
16	Elvin Hayes/100	35.00
17	Clyde Lovellette/100	30.00
19	Alex English/100	20.00
20	David Thompson/100	40.00
21	Marion Jones/246	40.00
22	Bobby Hurley/100	25.00
23	Wes Unseld/100	25.00
24	Bo Jackson/25	100.00
25	Deion Sanders/50	60.00

Legends of the Game Combos
NM/M
Production 25-100
Prime:	No Pricing
Production 1-10
1	Knute Rockne, Pat O'Brien/25	80.00

2	Joe Jackson, Pete Rose/100	180.00
3	Joe Montana, Knute Rockne/100	60.00
6	Ron Turcotte, Steve Cauthen/100	20.00
7	Dan Fouts, Tony Gwynn/100	25.00
7	Nolan Ryan, Troy Aikman/100	40.00
8	Earl Campbell, Elvin Hayes/100	10.00
9	Dominique Wilkins, Hank Aaron/100	25.00
11	Earl Campbell, Nolan Ryan/100	30.00
12	Willie Mays, Cal Ripken Jr./50	50.00
15	Cal Ripken Jr., Raymond Berry/100	40.00

Museum Collection

NM/M
Common Player:	2.00
Production 1,000 Sets
Gold:	1-1.5X
Production 100 Sets
1	Hank Aaron	6.00
2	Joe Montana	6.00
3	Ray Bourque	2.00
4	Sam Snead	3.00
5	Joe Jackson	4.00
6	John Elway	5.00
7	Don Drysdale	3.00
8	Raymond Berry	2.00
9	Parker Bohn	3.00
10	Roger Staubach	4.00
11	Ted Williams	4.00
12	Cal Ripken Jr.	6.00
13	Satchel Paige	4.00
14	Steve Young	4.00
15	Tony Dorsett	4.00
16	Knute Rockne	5.00
17	Willie Mays	5.00
18	Dan Marino	4.00
19	Robert Parish	2.00
20	Lenny Moore	2.00
21	Casey Stengel	3.00
22	Eddie Mathews	3.00
23	Dominique Wilkins	2.00
24	Dan Fouts	3.00
25	Pete Rose	4.00
26	Eric Dickerson	2.00
27	Al Unser	2.00
28	Jeanette Lee	2.00
29	Pete Weber	2.00
30	Bill Walton	3.00
31	Bela Karolyi	2.00
32	Steve Cauthen	2.00
33	Lefty Kreh	2.00
34	Cale Yarborough	2.00
35	Mike Bossy	2.00

Museum Collection Materials
NM/M
Production 25-250
Prime:	No Pricing
Production 1-25
Curator Parallel:	1-1.2X
Production 10-100
Curator Prime:	No Pricing
Production 1-25
1	Hank Aaron/100	30.00
2	Joe Montana/100	25.00
4	Sam Snead/250	20.00
5	Joe Jackson/100	150.00
6	John Elway/100	20.00
7	Don Drysdale/50	15.00
9	Raymond Berry/250	15.00
10	Roger Staubach/100	40.00
11	Ted Williams/250	30.00
12	Cal Ripken Jr./100	30.00
13	Satchel Paige/50	40.00
14	Steve Young/250	10.00
15	Tony Dorsett/25	25.00
16	Knute Rockne/250	30.00
18	Dan Marino/100	30.00
20	Lenny Moore/250	10.00
22	Eddie Mathews/25	20.00
23	Dominique Wilkins/100	10.00
24	Dan Fouts/250	10.00
25	Pete Rose/250	25.00
26	Eric Dickerson/250	10.00
28	Jeanette Lee/100	10.00
29	Pete Weber/250	10.00
31	Bela Karolyi/250	5.00
32	Steve Cauthen/250	5.00

Museum Collection Signatures
NM/M
Production 1-250
Material Auto.:	No Pricing
Production 1-25
3	Ray Bourque/50	30.00
9	Parker Bohn/250	15.00
17	Willie Mays/25	150.00
19	Robert Parish/100	20.00
25	Pete Rose/25	100.00
27	Al Unser/50	25.00
28	Jeanette Lee/100	35.00
29	Pete Weber/50	25.00
30	Bill Walton/25	60.00
31	Bela Karolyi/50	20.00
32	Steve Cauthen/100	15.00
33	Lefty Kreh/250	10.00
34	Cale Yarborough/100	20.00
35	Mike Bossy/100	15.00

Signature Connection Combos
NM/M
Production 25 unless noted.
1	Kevin McHale, Larry Bird	160.00
2	Dan Fouts, Tony Gwynn	80.00
4	Nolan Ryan, Troy Aikman	150.00
5	Earl Campbell, Elvin Hayes	40.00
11	Bo Jackson, Deion Sanders	175.00
12	Bill Walton, Troy Aikman	75.00
13	Bill Gadsby, Pierre Pilote/100	30.00
14	Al Unser, Al Unser Jr./100	40.00
15	Gerry Cheevers, Phil Esposito/100	30.00
16	Al Unser, Richard Petty/100	65.00
17	Bela Karolyi, Dominique Moceanu/50	75.00

Sign. Connection Triples
NM/M
Production 25-250
1	Kevin McHale, Larry Bird, Robert Parish/25	275.00
2	Jean Cruguet, Ron Turcotte, Steve Cauthen/250	50.00
3	Bob Gibson, Lynette Woodard, Marques Haynes/50	50.00

2008 Donruss Celebrity Cuts
NM/M
Complete Set (100):	
Common Celebrity:	3.00
Production 499 Sets
Hobby Box (One Pack):	120.00
1	Adam West	3.00
2	Ashley Judd	3.00
3	Angie Dickinson	3.00
4	Barbara Eden	3.00
5	Bernie Mac	3.00
7	Billy Dee Williams	3.00
8	Bobby Allison	3.00
9	Burt Reynolds	5.00
10	Burt Ward	3.00
11	Buzz Aldrin	3.00
12	Carrie Fisher	3.00
13	Cedric the Entertainer	3.00
14	Cindy Williams	3.00
15	Dawn Wells	3.00
16	Debbie Reynolds	3.00
17	Dick Van Patten	3.00
18	Dolores Hart	3.00
19	Dom DeLuise	3.00
20	Christina Applegate	3.00
21	Doug Jones	3.00
22	Ed O'Neill	3.00
23	Elliott Gould	3.00
24	Ernest Borgnine	3.00
25	Erik Estrada	3.00
26	Esther Williams	3.00
27	Ed Asner	3.00
28	Joyce DeWitt	3.00
29	Helen Slater	3.00
30	Giovanni Ribisi	3.00
31	Gloria Stuart	3.00
32	Barbara Bush	3.00
33	Henry Winkler	3.00
34	Hugh O'Brian	3.00
35	Jonathan Winters	3.00
37	Julie Newmar	3.00
38	Jackie Robinson	8.00
39	James Dean	3.00
40	Jane Russell	5.00
41	Jerry Lewis	3.00
42	Jim Courier	3.00
43	Kathryn Grayson	3.00
44	John Travolta	5.00
45	Josh Duhamel	3.00
46	Katey Sagal	3.00
47	Knute Rockne	3.00
48	John Wooden	6.00
49	Larry Bird	6.00
50	Larry Hagman	3.00
51	Lee Majors	3.00
52	Leonard Nimoy	5.00
53	Kathie Lee Gifford	3.00
54	Lou Gossett Jr.	3.00

55	Margaret O'Brien	3.00
56	Marilyn Monroe	8.00
57	Lee Meriwether	3.00
58	Marlon Brando	3.00
59	Martina Navratilova	3.00
60	Maud Adams	3.00
61	Mickey Rooney	3.00
62	Molly Shannon	3.00
63	Lindsay Wagner	3.00
64	Mark Hamill	3.00
65	Neil Patrick Harris	3.00
66	George Bush	5.00
67	Patrick Roy	8.00
68	Kurt Russell	3.00
69	Peggy Fleming	3.00
70	Randy Couture	3.00
71	Quentin Tarantino	3.00
72	Richard Kiel	3.00
73	Richard Petty	3.00
74	Robert Wagner	3.00
75	Ricardo Montalban	3.00
76	Ron Howard	3.00
77	Russell Johnson	3.00
78	Scott Baio	3.00
79	Shawnee Smith	3.00
80	Shirley Jones	3.00
81	Stan Musial	6.00
82	Stella Stevens	3.00
83	Stephanie Powers	3.00
84	Steve Guttenberg	3.00
85	Rob Schneider	3.00
86	Ted Williams	8.00
87	Tippi Hedren	3.00
88	Tony Curtis	3.00
89	Tony Esposito	4.00
90	Ultimate Warrior	3.00
91	Val Kilmer	3.00
92	Walt Frazier	3.00
93	Walter Koenig	3.00
94	Wayne Newton	3.00
95	William Shatner	3.00
96	Willie Mays	6.00
97	Willie Nelson	3.00
98	Margot Kidder	3.00
99	Yunjin Kim	3.00
100	Priscilla Barnes	3.00

Century Silver
NM/M
Silver (1-100):	2X
Production 50 Sets

Century Gold
Gold (1-100):	3-4X
Production 25 Sets

Century Platinum
Production One Set

Century Gold Signatures
NM/M
Production 1-200
Platium Autos:	No Pricing
Production One Set
3	Angie Dickinson/200	40.00
6	Betty Garrett/200	25.00
8	Bobby Allison/200	25.00
11	Buzz Aldrin/50	150.00
13	Cedric the Entertainer/200	20.00
15	Dawn Wells/50	40.00
18	Dolores Hart/200	25.00
19	Dom DeLuise/50	30.00
20	Christina Applegate/25	100.00
21	Doug Jones/50	15.00
25	Erik Estrada/25	25.00
27	Ed Asner/200	25.00
28	Joyce DeWitt/100	30.00
29	Helen Slater/200	25.00
30	Giovanni Ribisi/50	25.00
31	Gloria Stuart/100	40.00
33	Henry Winkler/34	60.00
35	Jonathan Winters/100	30.00
36	Julie Newmar/200	50.00
39	Jane Russell/200	50.00
41	Jim Courier/200	20.00
44	Josh Duhamel/50	25.00
48	Larry Bird/200	75.00
52	Kathie Lee Gifford/200	30.00
55	Margaret O'Brien/200	30.00
57	Lee Meriwether/200	30.00
59	Martina Navratilova/100	30.00
62	Molly Shannon/50	25.00
63	Lindsay Wagner/50	40.00
65	Neil Patrick Harris/30	40.00
67	Patrick Roy/75	60.00
69	Peggy Fleming/200	40.00
70	Randy Couture/100	75.00
71	Quentin Tarantino/50	25.00
72	Richard Kiel/200	25.00
73	Richard Petty/200	25.00
74	Robert Wagner/200	25.00
78	Scott Baio/50	20.00
79	Shawnee Smith/100	10.00
81	Stan Musial/100	60.00
83	Stephanie Powers/60	60.00
84	Steve Guttenberg/99	25.00
85	Rob Schneider/36	40.00
87	Tippi Hedren/100	35.00
89	Tony Esposito/35	50.00
91	Val Kilmer/100	25.00
92	Walt Frazier/100	35.00
96	Willie Mays/50	125.00
97	Willie Nelson/50	25.00
98	Margot Kidder/200	15.00
100	Priscilla Barnes/200	30.00

Award Winners Autos.
NM/M
Production 25-55
1	Ernest Borgnine/55	60.00
2	Lou Gossett Jr./25	60.00
3	Quentin Tarantino/50	85.00

Celebrity Cuts
NM/M
Production 1-25
26	Ernest Borgnine/25	60.00
29	Patricia Neal/25	50.00

Century Materials
NM/M
Production 5-100
Combo Materials:	1-1.5X
Production 5-50
Prime Materials:	1.5-2X
Production 1-50
Combo Prime Materials:	No Pricing
Production 1-10
No pricing production 20 or less.
1	Adam West/75	15.00
2	Ashley Judd/50	20.00
4	Barbara Eden/100	20.00
5	Bernie Mac/50	15.00
8	Bobby Allison/100	10.00
9	Burt Reynolds/100	20.00
14	Cindy Williams/100	8.00
15	Dawn Wells/50	15.00
17	Dick Van Patten/100	8.00
20	Christina Applegate/100	20.00
21	Doug Jones/100	10.00
22	Ed O'Neill/100	15.00
23	Elliott Gould/75	8.00
24	Ernest Borgnine/50	10.00
25	Erik Estrada/50	8.00
27	Ed Asner/100	10.00
31	Gloria Stuart/100	25.00
32	Barbara Bush/50	15.00
33	Henry Winkler/50	15.00
34	Hugh O'Brian/50	8.00
35	Jonathan Winters/100	15.00
36	Julie Newmar/100	20.00
37	Jackie Robinson/100	30.00
38	James Dean/100	40.00
39	Jane Russell/100	15.00
40	Jerry Lewis/100	25.00
41	Jim Courier/100	8.00
42	Kathryn Grayson/100	20.00
43	John Travolta/100	15.00
45	Katey Sagal/100	10.00
46	Knute Rockne/100	75.00
48	Larry Bird/100	35.00
49	Larry Hagman/50	8.00
50	Lee Majors/100	15.00
52	Kathie Lee Gifford/100	15.00
53	Lou Gehrig/50	60.00
54	Lou Gossett Jr./50	15.00
55	Margaret O'Brien/100	15.00
56	Marilyn Monroe/100	100.00
57	Lee Meriwether/100	15.00
58	Marlon Brando/100	15.00
59	Martina Navratilova/50	15.00
62	Molly Shannon/100	10.00
65	Neil Patrick Harris/100	15.00
67	Patrick Roy/100	20.00
68	Kurt Russell/100	15.00
70	Randy Couture/100	30.00
73	Richard Petty/100	25.00
77	Russell Johnson/100	15.00
78	Scott Baio/100	8.00
81	Stan Musial/100	25.00
82	Stella Stevens/100	10.00
83	Stephanie Powers/36	15.00
84	Steve Guttenberg/100	10.00
85	Rob Schneider/100	10.00
87	Tippi Hedren/100	20.00
89	Tony Esposito/100	15.00
91	Val Kilmer/100	10.00
92	Walt Frazier/100	15.00
96	Willie Mays/100	25.00
99	Yunjin Kim/100	15.00
100	Priscilla Barnes/100	15.00

Century Signature Materials
NM/M
Production 1-50
Prime Autos.:	1-1.5X
Production 1-50
Combo Autos.:	No Pricing
Production 1-10
Combo Prime Autos.:	No Pricing
Production 1-25
No pricing production 20 or less.
1	Adam West/25	60.00
8	Bobby Allison/50	30.00
17	Dick Van Patten/50	25.00
21	Doug Jones/50	25.00
27	Ed Asner/50	25.00
33	Henry Winkler/50	60.00
41	Jim Courier/50	25.00
48	Larry Bird/50	90.00
49	Larry Hagman/50	35.00
55	Margaret O'Brien/50	40.00
62	Molly Shannon/50	30.00
85	Rob Schneider/25	50.00
96	Willie Mays/50	125.00

Combo Cuts
Production One Set

Hollywood Letter Autos.
NM/M
Production 45-99
1	Burt Reynolds/45	75.00

2 Debbie Reynolds/99 75.00
3 Ernest Borgnine/99 60.00
4 Lou Gossett Jr./45 50.00
5 Mickey Rooney/45 85.00
6 Ron Howard/72 85.00
7 Tony Curtis/45 75.00
8 Elliott Gould/45 50.00
10 Leonard Nimoy/44 100.00
11 Christina Applegate/45 100.00
12 Ricardo Montalban/45 80.00

Hollywood Icons

NM/M

Common Icon: 4.00
Production 200 Sets
Gold: 2-3X
Production 25 Sets

1 Audrey Hepburn 4.00
2 Ava Gardner 4.00
3 Bette Davis 4.00
4 Bing Crosby 4.00
5 Carole Lombard 4.00
6 Dorothy Lamour 4.00
7 Errol Flynn 4.00
8 Gene Tierney 4.00
9 Ginger Rogers 4.00
10 Gloria Swanson 4.00
11 Greta Garbo 4.00
12 Humphrey Bogart 4.00
13 Ingrid Bergman 4.00
14 Jackie Gleason 4.00
15 James Cagney 4.00
16 James Dean 6.00
17 Jimmy Stewart 6.00
18 Jayne Mansfield 4.00
19 Jean Harlow 4.00
20 Lana Turner 4.00
21 Lillian Gish 4.00
22 Loretta Young 4.00
23 Mae West 4.00
24 Marilyn Monroe 8.00
25 Marlene Dietrich 4.00
26 Marlon Brando 4.00
27 Mary Pickford 4.00
28 Natalie Wood 4.00
29 Rock Hudson 4.00
30 Steve McQueen 4.00
31 Yvonne De Carlo 4.00
32 Patricia Neal 4.00
33 Glenn Ford 4.00
34 Eleanor Powell 4.00
35 Bob Denver 4.00
36 Peter Sellers 4.00
37 Rudolph Valentino 4.00
38 Johnny Weissmuller 4.00
39 Montgomery Clift 4.00
40 Olivia de Havilland 4.00
41 Henry Fonda 6.00
42 John Wayne 6.00
43 Gene Kelly 4.00
44 Ed O'Neill 4.00
45 Katey Sagal 4.00
46 Ron Howard 4.00
47 Wayne Newton 4.00
48 Esther Williams 4.00
49 Ernest Borgnine 4.00
50 Shirley Jones 4.00
51 Lou Gossett Jr. 4.00
52 Debbie Reynolds 4.00
53 Tony Curtis 4.00
54 Mickey Rooney 4.00
55 John Travolta 4.00
56 Burt Reynolds 6.00
57 William Shatner 6.00
58 Lee Majors 4.00
59 Barbara Eden 4.00
60 Carrie Fisher 4.00
61 Elliott Gould 4.00
62 Val Kilmer 4.00
63 Larry Hagman 4.00
64 Quentin Tarantino 4.00
65 Leonard Nimoy 6.00
66 Adam West 4.00
67 Ashley Judd 4.00
68 Frank Sinatra 4.00
69 Fred Astaire 4.00
70 George Burns 4.00
71 Leslie Howard 4.00
72 John Gilbert 4.00
73 Orson Welles 4.00
74 William Holden 4.00
75 Rita Hayworth 4.00

Hollywood Icons Materials

NM/M

Production 100 unless noted.
Combo Materials: 1-1.5X
Production 5-50
Prime Materials: 1.5X
Production 1-50
Combo Prime Materials: No Pricing
Production 1-10
Prime Studio Die-Cuts: No Pricing
Production 1-10

1 Audrey Hepburn 50.00
2 Ava Gardner 20.00
3 Bette Davis 35.00
4 Bing Crosby/50 30.00
5 Carole Lombard 20.00
6 Dorothy Lamour 20.00
7 Errol Flynn 25.00
8 Gene Tierney 20.00
9 Ginger Rogers 25.00
10 Gloria Swanson 20.00
11 Greta Garbo 20.00
12 Humphrey Bogart 35.00
13 Ingrid Bergman 25.00
14 Jackie Gleason 35.00
15 James Cagney 35.00
16 James Dean 50.00
17 Jimmy Stewart 35.00
18 Jayne Mansfield 25.00
19 Jean Harlow 25.00
20 Lana Turner 20.00
21 Lillian Gish 20.00
22 Loretta Young 25.00
23 Mae West 25.00
24 Marilyn Monroe 80.00
25 Marlene Dietrich 20.00
26 Marlon Brando 25.00
27 Mary Pickford 20.00
28 Natalie Wood 35.00
29 Rock Hudson 20.00
30 Steve McQueen 25.00
31 Yvonne De Carlo 25.00
33 Glenn Ford 15.00
34 Eleanor Powell/50 20.00
35 Bob Denver 25.00
36 Peter Sellers 20.00
38 Johnny Weissmuller 15.00
39 Montgomery Clift 25.00
42 John Wayne 60.00
43 Gene Kelly 25.00
44 Ed O'Neill 15.00
45 Katey Sagal 15.00
49 Ernest Borgnine/50 15.00
51 Lou Gossett Jr. 15.00
52 Debbie Reynolds/50 25.00
55 John Travolta 20.00
56 Burt Reynolds 20.00
58 Lee Majors 15.00
59 Barbara Eden/25 35.00
61 Elliott Gould 15.00
62 Val Kilmer 15.00
63 Larry Hagman 15.00
66 Adam West/50 15.00
67 Ashley Judd/25 25.00
71 Leslie Howard 15.00
74 William Holden 20.00

Hollywood Icons Cut Sigs

NM/M

Production 1-100

31 Yvonne De Carlo/100 80.00
32 Patricia Neal/100 50.00
59 Barbara Eden/40 80.00
64 Quentin Tarantino/100 80.00
66 Adam West/25 125.00
67 Ashley Judd/25 150.00

Hollywood Icons Gold Autos

NM/M

No Pricing 4.00
Production 1-14
Platinum Autos: No Pricing
Production One Set

Hollywd Icons Sig Materials

NM/M

Production 1-25
Prime Autos.: No Pricing
Production 1-5
Combo Material Auto.: No Pricing
Production 1-25
Combo Prime Auto.: No Pricing
Production 1-10

56 Burt Reynolds/25 75.00
63 Larry Hagman/25 35.00

Hollywd. Icons Quad Die-Cut

NM/M

Production 25 unless noted.
Prime Quads: No Pricing
Production 1-25

1 Audrey Hepburn 180.00
2 Ava Gardner 50.00
3 Bette Davis 60.00
5 Carole Lombard 50.00
6 Dorothy Lamour 50.00
7 Errol Flynn 50.00
8 Gene Tierney 50.00
9 Ginger Rogers 60.00
10 Gloria Swanson 30.00
13 Ingrid Bergman 60.00
14 Jackie Gleason 60.00
15 James Cagney 75.00
16 James Dean 180.00
17 Jimmy Stewart 120.00
18 Jayne Mansfield 50.00
20 Lana Turner 50.00
21 Lillian Gish 40.00
22 Loretta Young 50.00
23 Mae West 40.00
24 Marilyn Monroe 200.00
25 Marlene Dietrich 60.00
27 Mary Pickford 40.00
30 Steve McQueen 60.00
31 Yvonne De Carlo 40.00
32 Patricia Neal 40.00
33 Glenn Ford 35.00
35 Bob Denver 50.00
36 Peter Sellers 40.00
38 Johnny Weissmuller 50.00
39 Montgomery Clift 50.00
42 John Wayne 120.00
45 Katey Sagal 30.00
55 John Travolta 50.00
56 Burt Reynolds 80.00
58 Lee Majors 30.00
59 Barbara Eden 50.00
62 Val Kilmer 40.00
74 William Holden 60.00

Movie Stars

NM/M

Common Movie Star: 4.00

Production 200 Sets
Gold: 2-3X
Production 25 Sets
Platinum: No Pricing
Production One Set

1 Adam West 4.00
2 Barbara Eden 4.00
3 Billy Dee Williams 4.00
4 Burt Reynolds 6.00
5 Burt Ward 4.00
6 Carrie Fisher 4.00
7 Debbie Reynolds 4.00
8 Ernest Borgnine 4.00
9 Esther Williams 4.00
10 Hugh O'Brian 4.00
11 Josh Duhamel 4.00
12 Larry Hagman 4.00
13 Lee Majors 4.00
14 Leonard Nimoy 6.00
15 Lou Gossett Jr. 4.00
16 Richard Kiel 4.00
17 Ashley Judd 6.00
18 Shirley Jones 4.00
19 Tippi Hedren 4.00
20 Tony Curtis 4.00
21 Walter Koenig 4.00
22 William Shatner 6.00
23 Mickey Rooney 4.00
24 John Travolta 4.00
25 Elliott Gould 4.00
26 Val Kilmer 4.00
27 Patricia Neal 4.00
28 Ricardo Montalban 4.00
29 Rob Schneider 4.00
30 Jerry Lewis 4.00

Movie Stars Gold Signatures

NM/M

Production 2-50
Platinum Autos.: No Pricing
Production 1-10

15 Larry Hagman/50 40.00
16 Richard Kiel/50 30.00
20 Tony Curtis/38 60.00
29 Rob Schneider/25 40.00
30 Jerry Lewis/25 75.00

Movie Stars Materials

NM/M

Production 1-100
Prime Materials: No Pricing
Production 1-20
Combo Materials: 1-1.5X
Production 5-100
Combo Prime Materials: No Pricing
Production 1-25

1 Adam West/50 20.00
2 Barbara Eden/100 25.00
4 Burt Reynolds/100 20.00
7 Debbie Reynolds/50 25.00
10 Hugh O'Brian/100 8.00
11 Josh Duhamel/100 8.00
12 Larry Hagman/100 10.00
13 Lee Majors/100 15.00
15 Lou Gossett Jr./50 15.00
17 Ashley Judd/25 25.00
19 Tippi Hedren/100 15.00
24 John Travolta/100 15.00
25 Elliott Gould/100 15.00
26 Val Kilmer/100 15.00
27 Patricia Neal/100 15.00
28 Ricardo Montalban/50 15.00
29 Rob Schneider/50 15.00
30 Jerry Lewis/50 10.00

Movie Stars Material Auto.

NM/M

Production 1-50 4.00
Prime Auto.: No Pricing
Production 1-5
Combo Material Auto.: 1-1.5X
Production 1-50
Combo Material Prime Auto.: No Pricing
Production 1-10

11 Josh Duhamel/50 40.00
12 Larry Hagman/50 40.00
19 Tippi Hedren/18 50.00
29 Rob Schneider/25 40.00
30 Jerry Lewis/25 75.00

Movie Stars Cut Auto. Var. 1

NM/M

Production 2-40

3 Billy Dee Williams/35 75.00
16 Richard Kiel/50 40.00
23 Mickey Rooney/25 100.00
27 Patricia Neal/25 50.00

Movie Stars Cut Auto. Var. 2

NM/M

Production 2-40

11 Josh Duhamel/22 50.00
19 Tippi Hedren/27 60.00
26 Val Kilmer/20 60.00

Movie Stars Cut Auto. Var. 3

NM/M

Production 2-23

11 Josh Duhamel/23 50.00
26 Val Kilmer/20 60.00

Movie Stars Cut Auto. Var. 4

NM/M

Production 4-20

26 Val Kilmer/20 60.00

Movie Stars Cut Auto. Var. 5

NM/M

Production 4-15

Movie Stars Cut Auto. Var. 6

NM/M

Production 3-20

26 Val Kilmer/20 60.00

Recollection Collection

NM/M

represents total autos. produced.

1 Catherine Bach/78 60.00
3 Lee Majors/52 70.00

Stardom Combo Autos.

No Pricing
Production 10 Sets

Stardom Triple Autos.

No Pricing
Production Five Sets

Donruss Celebrity Cuts Stardom Quad Autos.

No Pricing
Production Five Sets

2008 Donruss Elite Extra Edition

NM/M

Common Player (1-100): .50
Common Auto. (101-200): 8.00
Production 99-1,495
Pack (5): 4.00
Box (20): 60.00

1 Aaron Cunningham .50
2 Aaron Pribanic .50
3 Aaron Shafer .50
4 Adam Mills .50
5 Adam Moore .50
6 Beamer Weems .50
7 Beau Mills .75
8 Blake Tekotte .50
9 Bobby Lanigan .50
10 Brad Hand .50
11 Brandon Crawford .50
12 Brandon Waring 1.00
13 Brent Morel .50
14 Brett Jacobson .50
15 Caleb Gindl .50
16 Carlos Peguero .50
17 Charlie Blackmon .50
18 Charlie Furbush .50
19 Chris Davis .50
20 Chris Valaika .50
21 Clark Murphy .75
22 Clayton Cook .50
23 Cody Adams .50
24 Cody Satterwhite .50
25 Cole St. Clair .50
26 Corey Young .50
27 Curtis Petersen .50
28 Danny Rams .50
29 Dennis Raben .75
30 Derek Norris .50
31 Tyson Brummett .50
32 Dusty Coleman .50
33 Edgar Olmos .75
34 Engel Beltre 1.50
35 Eric Beaulac .50
36 Geison Aguasviva .50
37 Gerardo Parra .75
38 Graham Hicks .50
39 Greg Halman 1.50
40 Hector Gomez 1.00
41 J.D. Alfaro .50
42 Jack Egbert .50
43 James Darnell .75
44 Jay Austin .50
45 Jeremy Beckham .50
46 Jeremy Farrell .50
47 Jeremy Hamilton .50
48 Jericho Jones .75
49 Jesse Darcy .50
50 Jeudy Valdez .50
51 Jharmidy DeJesus 1.00
52 Joba Chamberlain .50
53 Johnny Giavotella .50
54 Jon Mark Owings .50
55 Jordan Meaker .50
56 Jose Duran .50
57 Josh Harrison .50
58 Josh Lindblom .50
59 Josh Reddick .50
60 Juan Carlos Sulbaran .50
61 Justin Bristow .50
62 Kenny Gilbert .50
63 Kirk Nieuwenhuis .50
64 Kyle Hudson .75
65 Kyle Russell .75
66 Kyle Weiland 1.00
67 L.J. Hoes .50
68 Mark Cohoon .50
69 Mark Sobolewski .75
70 Mat Gamel 1.50
71 Matt Harrison .75
72 Max Ramirez .75
73 Tony Delmonico .50
74 Mike Stanton 5.00
75 Mitch Abeita .50
76 Neftali Feliz 2.00
77 Neftali Soto 1.50
78 Niko Vasquez 1.00
79 Omar Aguilar .50
80 Petey Paramore .50
81 Ray Kruml .50
82 Rolando Gomez .50
83 Ryan Chaffee .50
84 Ryan Pressly .50
85 Sam Freeman .75
86 Sawyer Carroll 1.00
87 Scott Green .50
88 Sean Ratliff .50
89 Shane Peterson .50
90 T.J. Steele .50
91 Tim Federowicz .50
92 Tyler Chatwood .50
93 Tyler Cline .50
94 Tyler Ladendorf .50
95 Tyler Yockey .50
96 Wilmer Flores 1.50
97 Wilson Ramos 1.00
98 Zach McAllister .75
99 Zach Stewart .50
100 Zeke Spruill .75
101 Adrian Nieto/Auto./521 8.00
102 Alan Horne/Auto./349 12.00
103 Andrew Cashner/Auto./685 15.00
104 Anthony Hewitt/Auto./920 10.00
105 Brad Holt/Auto./432 25.00
106 Bryan Petersen/Auto./319 8.00
107 Bryan Price/Auto./572 15.00
108 Bud Norris/Auto./1,095 8.00
109 Carlos Gutierrez/Auto./202 15.00
110 Chase D'Arnaud/Auto./1,218 10.00
111 Chris Johnson/Auto./99 25.00
112 Christian Friedrich/Auto./402 12.00
113 Christian Marrero/Auto./662 15.00
114 Clayton Conner/Auto./819 8.00
115 Cole Rohrbough/Auto./719 10.00
116 Collin DeLome/Auto./819 15.00
117 Daniel Cortes/Auto./680 15.00
118 Dan Schlereth/Auto./570 8.00
119 Denny Almonte/Auto./821 10.00
120 Allan Dykstra/Auto./1,069 10.00
121 Dominic Brown/Auto./996 50.00
122 Evan Fredrickson/Auto./922 8.00
123 Gordon Beckham/Auto./710 35.00
124 Greg Veloz/Auto./819 30.00
125 Ike Davis/Auto./995 30.00
126 Isaac Galloway/Auto./1,099 10.00
127 Jacob Jefferies/Auto./819 15.00
128 Michael Kohn/Auto./199 12.00
129 Jared Goedert/Auto./819 8.00
130 Jason Knapp/Auto./999 15.00
131 Jhoulys Chacin/Auto./821 25.00
132 Jordy Mercer/Auto./483 15.00
133 Jorge Bucardo/Auto./819 10.00
134 Jose Ceda/Auto./1,470 8.00
135 Jose Martinez/Auto./868 8.00
136 Josh Roenicke/Auto./829 8.00
137 Juan Francisco/Auto./1,495 15.00
138 Justin Parker/Auto./719 8.00
139 Kyle Ginley/Auto./819 10.00
140 Lance Lynn/Auto./570 15.00
141 Logan Forsythe/Auto./162 20.00
142 Logan Morrison/Auto./360 25.00
143 Logan Schafer/Auto./793 8.00
144 Lorenzo Cain/Auto./817 10.00
145 Lucas Duda/Auto./124 10.00
146 Matt Mitchell/Auto./719 8.00
147 Danny Espinosa/Auto./443 15.00
148 Michael Taylor/Auto./720 25.00
149 Michel Inoa/Auto./1,199 20.00
150 Mike Montgomery/Auto./922 10.00
151 Cord Phelps/Auto./693 10.00
152 Pablo Sandoval/Auto./99 50.00
153 Quincy Latimore/Auto./819 10.00
154 R.J. Seidel/Auto./819 8.00
155 Raynor Contreras/Auto./1,349 10.00
156 Rick Porcello/Auto./1,299 25.00
157 Robert Hernandez/Auto./859 8.00
158 Ryan Kalish/Auto./1,129 10.00
159 Ryan Perry/Auto./745 15.00
160 Shelby Ford/Auto./819 15.00
161 Shooter Hunt/Auto./397 15.00
162 Tyler Kolodny/Auto./819 10.00
163 Tyler Sample/Auto./619 20.00
164 Tyson Ross/Auto./999 8.00
167 Waldis Joaquin/Auto./819 8.00
167 Welington Castillo/Auto./1,319 8.00
168 Wilin Rosario/Auto./1,099 10.00
169 Xavier Avery/Auto./199 20.00
170 Zach Collier/Auto./217 20.00
171 Zach Putnam/Auto./444 15.00
172 Anthony Gose/Auto./519 10.00
173 Roger Kieschnick/Auto./569 15.00
174 Andrew Liebel/Auto./219 10.00
175 Tim Murphy/Auto./244 8.00
176 Vance Worley/Auto./219 8.00
177 Buster Posey/Auto./934 50.00
178 Kenn Kasparek/Auto./694 8.00
179 J.P. Ramirez/Auto./719 15.00
180 Evan Bigley/Auto./819 15.00
181 Trey Haley/Auto./719 8.00
182 Robbie Grossman/Auto./719 15.00
183 Jordan Danks/Auto./254 25.00
185 Brett Hunter/Auto./269 10.00
185 Rafael Rodriguez/Auto./999 30.00
186 Yeicok Calderon/Auto./819 25.00
187 Gustavo Pierre/Auto./719 10.00
188 Will Smith/Auto./719 15.00
189 Daniel Thomas/Auto./719 10.00
190 Carson Blair/Auto./719 15.00
191 Chris Hicks/Auto./719 10.00
192 Rashun Dixon/Auto./199 25.00
193 Marcus Lemon/Auto./199 20.00
194 Kyle Nicholson/Auto./719 10.00
195 Mike Cisco/Auto./719 10.00
196 Jarek Cunningham/Auto./719 10.00
197 Cat Osterman/Auto./719 20.00
198 Derrick Rose/Auto./99 125.00
199 Michael Beasley/Auto./99 60.00
200 O.J. Mayo Auto/99 60.00

Aspirations

NM/M

Aspirations (1-100): 3-6X
Aspir. (101-200): .15-.25X
Common Aspiration (101-200): 2.00
Production 150 Sets

Aspirations Autos.

NM/M

Production 5-100

1 Aaron Cunningham/50 15.00
2 Aaron Pribanic/50 10.00
3 Aaron Shafer/100 15.00
4 Adam Mills/100 15.00
5 Adam Moore/100 15.00
6 Beamer Weems/50 10.00
7 Beau Mills/50 15.00
8 Blake Tekotte/25 15.00
9 Bobby Lanigan/100 10.00
10 Brad Hand/50 15.00
11 Brandon Crawford/50 20.00
12 Brandon Waring/100 20.00
13 Brent Morel/100 15.00
14 Brett Jacobson/100 15.00
15 Caleb Gindl/100 12.00
16 Carlos Peguero/100 15.00
17 Charlie Blackmon/50 15.00
18 Charlie Furbush/100 10.00
19 Chris Davis/100 20.00
20 Chris Valaika/100 15.00
21 Clark Murphy/50 15.00

22 Clayton Cook/100 15.00
23 Cody Adams/50 10.00
24 Cody Satterwhite/50 20.00
25 Cole St. Clair/100 15.00
26 Corey Young/100 15.00
27 Curtis Petersen/100 10.00
28 Danny Rams/100 10.00
29 Dennis Raben/50 20.00
30 Derek Norris/50 10.00
31 Tyson Brummett/100 15.00
32 Dusty Coleman/100 10.00
33 Edgar Olmos/100 20.00
34 Eric Beaulac/100 15.00
36 Geison Aguasviva/100 15.00
37 Gerardo Parra/100 20.00
38 Graham Hicks/100 15.00
39 Greg Halman/100 30.00
40 Hector Gomez/100 20.00
41 J.D. Alfaro/100 8.00
42 Jack Egbert/100 10.00
43 James Darnell/50 20.00
44 Jay Austin/50 15.00
45 Jeremy Beckham/100 12.00
46 Jeremy Farrell/100 15.00
47 Jeremy Hamilton/100 15.00
48 Jericho Jones/100 20.00
49 Jesse Darcy/100 15.00
50 Jeudy Valdez/100 10.00
51 Jharmidy DeJesus/50 20.00
52 Johnny Giavotella/100 15.00
54 Jon Mark Owings/100 8.00
55 Jordan Meaker/100 10.00
56 Jose Duran/100 10.00
57 Josh Harrison/100 15.00
58 Josh Lindblom/50 15.00
59 Josh Reddick/50 30.00
60 Juan Carlos Sulbaran/100 10.00
61 Justin Bristow/100 10.00
62 Kenny Gilbert/100 15.00
63 Kirk Nieuwenhuis/100 15.00
64 Kyle Hudson/50 15.00
65 Kyle Russell/50 20.00
66 Kyle Weiland/50 20.00
67 L.J. Hoes/50 15.00
68 Mark Cohoon/100 15.00
69 Mark Sobolewski/100 15.00
70 Mat Gamel/50 40.00
71 Matt Harrison/100 15.00
72 Max Ramirez/100 15.00
73 Tony Delmonico/50 20.00
74 Mike Stanton/25 300.00
75 Mitch Abeita/100 15.00
76 Neftali Feliz/50 60.00
77 Neftali Soto/50 40.00
78 Niko Vasquez/50 25.00
79 Omar Aguilar/100 10.00
80 Petey Paramore/100 15.00
81 Ray Kruml/100 15.00
82 Rolando Gomez/100 10.00
83 Ryan Chaffee/100 15.00
84 Ryan Pressly/100 10.00
85 Sam Freeman/100 15.00
86 Sawyer Carroll/100 15.00
87 Scott Green/100 10.00
88 Sean Ratliff/100 15.00
89 Shane Peterson/100 15.00
90 T.J. Steele/50 15.00
91 Tim Federowicz/100 15.00
92 Tyler Chatwood/100 10.00
93 Tyler Cline/100 15.00
94 Tyler Ladendorf/100 15.00
95 Tyler Yockey/100 15.00
96 Wilmer Flores/50 60.00
97 Wilson Ramos/100 15.00
98 Zach McAllister/100 20.00
99 Zach Stewart/100 15.00
100 Zeke Spruill/50 10.00
102 Alan Horne/100 15.00
106 Bryan Petersen/50 15.00
108 Bud Norris/50 15.00
113 Christian Marrero/50 15.00
114 Clayton Conner/50 10.00
116 Collin DeLome/50 20.00
119 Denny Almonte/50 15.00
123 Dominic Brown/50 100.00
124 Greg Veloz/50 15.00
127 Jacob Jefferies/50 20.00
129 Jared Goedert/50 15.00
130 Jason Knapp/50 30.00
131 Jhoulys Chacin/50 30.00
132 Jordy Mercer/75 20.00
133 Jorge Bucardo/50 15.00
134 Jose Ceda/100 10.00
135 Jose Martinez/75 15.00
136 Josh Roenicke/50 12.00
137 Juan Francisco/50 20.00
139 Kyle Ginley/50 15.00
143 Logan Schafer/50 12.00
148 Lorenzo Cain/50 15.00
149 Michael Taylor/50 40.00
153 Pablo Sandoval/50 100.00
155 Quincy Latimore/50 15.00
156 R.J. Seidel/50 15.00
157 Raynor Contreras/100 15.00
159 Robert Hernandez/50 15.00
160 Ryan Kalish/50 15.00
163 Shelby Ford/50 20.00
166 Tyler Kolodny/50 15.00
169 Waldis Joaquin/50 15.00
170 Welington Castillo/50 15.00
173 Roger Kieschnick/50 25.00
186 Evan Bigley/50 15.00
188 Yeicok Calderon/50 50.00

Status
Status (1-100): 5-10X
Status (101-200): .25-.4X

Production 50 Sets
Status Gold: No Pricing
Production 25 Sets

Turn of Century Autos.
NM/M
Production 8-999
1 Aaron Cunningham/150 15.00
2 Aaron Pribanic/269 8.00
3 Aaron Shafer/117 15.00
4 Adam Mills/841 10.00
5 Adam Moore/844 10.00
6 Beamer Weems/844 15.00
7 Beau Mills/64 15.00
8 Blake Tekotte/194 15.00
9 Bobby Lanigan/594 8.00
10 Brad Rand/447 8.00
11 Brandon Crawford/718 10.00
12 Brandon Waring/369 12.00
13 Brent Morel/269 15.00
14 Brett Jacobson/488 8.00
15 Caleb Gindl/245 10.00
16 Carlos Peguero/344 12.00
17 Charlie Blackmon/122 12.00
18 Charlie Furbush/469 8.00
19 Chris Davis/399 15.00
20 Chris Valaika/309 10.00
21 Clark Murphy/644 15.00
22 Clayton Cook/844 10.00
23 Cody Adams/447 8.00
24 Cody Satterwhite/322 15.00
25 Cole St. Clair/342 12.00
26 Corey Young/594 8.00
27 Curtis Petersen/199 8.00
28 Danny Rams/594 8.00
29 Dennis Raben/172 15.00
30 Derek Norris/744 8.00
31 Tyson Brummett/919 10.00
32 Dusty Coleman/719 8.00
33 Edgar Olmos/594 15.00
34 Eric Beaulac/594 10.00
36 Geison Aguasviva/368 12.00
37 Gerardo Parra/421 15.00
38 Graham Hicks/594 15.00
39 Greg Halman/429 12.00
40 Hector Gomez/320 15.00
41 J.D. Alfaro/790 8.00
42 Jack Egbert/844 8.00
43 James Darnell/89 20.00
44 Jay Austin/207 8.00
46 Jeremy Beckham/199 10.00
46 Jeremy Farrell/844 10.00
48 Jeremy Hamilton/844 10.00
48 Jericho Jones/844 15.00
49 Jesse Darcy/594 12.00
50 Jeudy Valdez/374 8.00
51 Jharmidy DeJesus/269 15.00
52 Joba Chamberlain/39 40.00
53 Johnny Giavotella/844 8.00
54 Jon Mark Owings/844 8.00
55 Jordan Meaker/844 8.00
56 Jose Duran/262 8.00
57 Josh Harrison/844 12.00
58 Josh Lindblom/131 12.00
59 Josh Reddick/320 30.00
60 Juan Carlos Sulbaran/844 8.00
61 Justin Bristow/594 8.00
62 Kenny Gilbert/842 12.00
63 Kirk Nieuwenhuis/844 12.00
64 Kyle Hudson/419 15.00
65 Kyle Russell/594 8.00
66 Kyle Weiland/394 20.00
67 L.J. Hoes/494 10.00
68 Mark Cohoon/844 8.00
69 Mark Sobolewski/269 15.00
70 Mat Gamel/145 40.00
71 Matt Harrison/244 15.00
72 Max Ramirez/604 12.00
73 Tony Delmonico/744 15.00
74 Mike Stanton/100 180.00
75 Mitch Abeita/769 12.00
76 Neftali Feliz/999 40.00
77 Neftali Soto/645 30.00
78 Niko Vasquez/494 20.00
79 Omar Aguilar/594 8.00
80 Petey Paramore/519 15.00
81 Ray Kruml/844 12.00
82 Rolando Gomez/544 8.00
83 Ryan Chaffee/594 8.00
84 Ryan Pressly/844 8.00
85 Sam Freeman/819 15.00
86 Sawyer Carroll/544 15.00
87 Scott Green/294 10.00
88 Sean Ratliff/544 10.00
89 Shane Peterson/132 15.00
90 T.J. Steele/122 15.00
91 Tim Federowicz/844 12.00
92 Tyler Chatwood/257 12.00
93 Tyler Cline/594 12.00
94 Tyler Ladendorf/227 8.00
95 Tyler Yockey/844 12.00
96 Wilmer Flores/99 60.00
97 Wilson Ramos/745 15.00
98 Zach McAllister/844 15.00
99 Zach Stewart/294 8.00
100 Zeke Spruill/99 10.00
101 Adrian Nieto/50 8.00
102 Alan Horne/125 15.00
104 Andrew Cashner/50 15.00
105 Anthony Hewitt/50 15.00
106 Brad Holt/50 25.00
107 Bryan Petersen/100 10.00
108 Bryan Price/50 10.00
109 Bud Norris/50 10.00
109 Carlos Gutierrez/50 20.00
110 Chase D'Arnaud/50 15.00
111 Chris Johnson/50 30.00

112 Christian Friedrich/50 15.00
113 Christian Marrero/100 15.00
114 Clayton Conner/50 15.00
115 Cole Rohrbough/50 15.00
116 Collin DeLome/100 15.00
117 Daniel Cortes/50 20.00
118 Dan Schlereth/50 10.00
119 Denny Almonte/100 10.00
120 Allan Dykstra/50 15.00
121 Dominic Brown/100 65.00
122 Evan Fredrickson/50 10.00
123 Gordon Beckham/50 40.00
124 Greg Veloz/100 10.00
125 Ike Davis/50 75.00
126 Isaac Galloway/50 15.00
127 Jacob Jefferies/100 20.00
128 Michael Kohn/40 15.00
129 Jared Goedert/100 10.00
130 Jason Knapp/125 20.00
131 Jhoulys Chacin/50 30.00
132 Jordy Mercer/50 20.00
133 Jorge Bucardo/100 15.00
134 Jose Ceda/250 10.00
135 Jose Martinez/100 10.00
136 Josh Roenicke/50 15.00
137 Juan Francisco/250 15.00
138 Justin Parker/50 12.00
139 Kyle Ginley/100 15.00
140 Lance Lynn/50 15.00
141 Logan Morrison/50 65.00
142 Logan Schafer/125 10.00
143 Lorenzo Cain/100 10.00
146 Matt Mitchell/50 10.00
147 Danny Espinosa/50 20.00
148 Michael Taylor/100 25.00
149 Michel Inoa/50 25.00
150 Mike Montgomery/50 15.00
151 Cord Phelps/50 15.00
152 Pablo Sandoval/100 80.00
153 Quincy Latimore/100 10.00
154 R.J. Seidel/100 10.00
155 Raynor Contreras/250 10.00
156 Rick Porcello/50 40.00
157 Robert Hernandez/100 10.00
158 Ryan Kalish/100 10.00
159 Ryan Perry/50 20.00
160 Shelby Ford/50 15.00
161 Shooter Hunt/50 10.00
162 Tyler Kolodny/100 15.00
163 Tyler Sample/50 15.00
164 Tyson Ross/50 15.00
166 Waldis Joaquin/100 10.00
167 Welington Castillo/100 10.00
168 Wilin Rosario/50 15.00
169 Xavier Avery/50 15.00
170 Zach Collier/50 20.00
171 Zach Putnam/50 20.00
172 Anthony Gose/50 12.00
173 Roger Kieschnick/50 20.00
174 Andrew Liebel/50 12.00
175 Tim Murphy/50 10.00
176 Vance Worley/50 10.00
177 Buster Posey/50 100.00
178 Kenn Kasparek/50 12.00
179 J.P. Ramirez/50 20.00
180 Evan Bigley/100 15.00
181 Trey Haley/50 10.00
182 Robbie Grossman/50 20.00
183 Jordan Danks/40 30.00
184 Brett Hunter/50 15.00
185 Rafael Rodriguez/50 35.00
186 Yeicok Calderon/100 15.00
187 Gustavo Pierre/50 15.00
188 Will Smith/50 20.00
189 Daniel Thomas/50 15.00
190 Carson Blair/50 15.00
191 Chris Hicks/50 10.00
193 Marcus Lemon/40 15.00
194 Kyle Nicholson/50 15.00
195 Mike Cisco/50 15.00
196 Jarek Cunningham/50 15.00
197 Cat Osterman/50 25.00

Red Status Autos.
NM/M
Production 5-50
Gold Status: No Pricing
Production 5 Sets
Black Status: No Pricing
Production One Set
1 Aaron Pribanic/50 10.00
3 Aaron Shafer/50 15.00
3 Adam Mills/50 10.00
4 Adam Moore/50 10.00
6 Beamer Weems/50 10.00
8 Bobby Lanigan/50 8.00
10 Brandon Waring/50 10.00
13 Brent Morel/50 15.00
14 Brett Jacobson/50 8.00
16 Caleb Gindl/50 12.00
16 Carlos Peguero/50 15.00
18 Charlie Furbush/50 8.00
19 Chris Davis/50 25.00
21 Chris Valaika/50 8.00
22 Clayton Cook/50 15.00
23 Cole St. Clair/50 8.00
26 Corey Young/50 8.00
28 Curtis Petersen/50 15.00
28 Danny Rams/50 8.00
31 Tyson Brummett/50 8.00
35 Edgar Olmos/50 20.00
36 Eric Beaulac/50 15.00
37 Geison Aguasviva/50 10.00
37 Gerardo Parra/50 20.00
38 Graham Hicks/50 10.00
39 Greg Halman/50 50.00
40 Hector Gomez/50 20.00
41 J.D. Alfaro/50 8.00

42 Jack Egbert/50 10.00
45 Jeremy Beckham/50 12.00
46 Jeremy Farrell/50 15.00
47 Jeremy Hamilton/50 15.00
48 Jericho Jones/50 20.00
49 Jesse Darcy/50 15.00
50 Jeudy Valdez/50 10.00
53 Johnny Giavotella/50 10.00
54 Jon Mark Owings/50 10.00
55 Jordan Meaker/50 10.00
56 Jose Duran/50 10.00
57 Josh Harrison/50 15.00
59 Josh Reddick/50 40.00
60 Juan Carlos Sulbaran/50 10.00
61 Justin Bristow/50 10.00
62 Kenny Gilbert/50 15.00
63 Kirk Nieuwenhuis/50 15.00
68 Mark Cohoon/50 15.00
69 Mark Sobolewski/50 15.00
71 Matt Harrison/50 15.00
72 Max Ramirez/50 15.00
75 Mitch Abeita/50 15.00
79 Omar Aguilar/50 10.00
80 Petey Paramore/50 15.00
81 Ray Kruml/50 15.00
83 Ryan Chaffee/50 15.00
84 Ryan Pressly/50 15.00
85 Sam Freeman/50 10.00
86 Sawyer Carroll/50 20.00
87 Scott Green/50 15.00
88 Sean Ratliff/50 15.00
91 Tim Federowicz/50 15.00
93 Tyler Cline/50 15.00
95 Tyler Yockey/50 15.00
97 Wilson Ramos/50 20.00
98 Zach McAllister/50 20.00
132 Jordy Mercer/40 20.00
134 Jose Ceda/250 10.00
135 Jose Martinez/50 15.00

College Ties Green
NM/M
Common Duo: 1.50
Production 1,500 Sets
Gold: 1-2X
Production 100 Sets
Red: 2-3X
Production 50 Sets
1 Cord Phelps, Sean Ratliff 1.50
2 Ryan Perry, T.J. Steele 2.00
3 Aaron Pribanic, Mitch Abeita 2.00
4 Dan Schlereth, Ryan Perry 1.50
5 Dan Schlereth, T.J. Steele 1.50
6 Jordy Mercer, Matt Mangini 2.00
7 Blake Tekotte, Mark Sobolewski 1.50
8 Logan Forsythe, Nick Schmidt 1.50
9 Matt Wieters, Charlie Blackmon 6.00
10 Joba Chamberlain, Mitch Abeita 4.00
11 Andrew Cashner, Andrew Walker 1.50
12 Sawyer Carroll, Scott Green 1.50
13 Kyle Russell, Taylor Teagarden 1.50
14 Carlos Gutierrez, Dennis Raben 2.00
15 Cody Satterwhite, Lance Lynn 1.50
16 Cat Osterman, Jordan Danks 1.50
17 Aaron Shafer, Dusty Coleman 2.00
19 Aaron Pribanic, Joba Chamberlain 4.00
19 Bryan Price, Cole St. Clair 1.50
20 Cat Osterman, Kenn Kasparek 1.50
21 Brandon Hicks, Jose Duran 2.00
22 Roger Kieschnick, Zach Stewart 1.50
23 Danny Espinosa, Shane Peterson 2.50
24 Brett Jacobson, David Price 3.00
25 Bryan Price, Joe Savery 1.50

26 Ike Davis, Petey Paramore 1.50
27 Brent Morel, Logan Schafer 2.00
28 Dennis Raben, Mark Sobolewski 1.50
29 Andrew Liebel, Shane Peterson 1.50
30 Buster Posey, Tony Thomas 4.00
31 Cole St. Clair, Joe Savery 1.50
32 Bradley Suttle, Cat Osterman 1.50
33 Blake Tekotte, Dennis Raben 2.00
34 Carlos Gutierrez, Mark Sobolewski 2.50
35 Blake Tekotte, Carlos Gutierrez 3.00

College Ties Jersey
NM/M
Common Duo: 5.00
Production 100-500
Prime: No Pricing
Production 25 Sets
6 Jordy Mercer, Matt Mangini/500 5.00
8 Logan Forsythe, Nick Schmidt/500 5.00
11 Andrew Cashner, Andrew Walker/500 8.00
15 Cody Satterwhite, Lance Lynn/500 5.00
16 Cat Osterman, Jordan Danks/50 10.00
20 Cat Osterman, Kenn Kasparek/100 15.00
21 Brandon Hicks, Jose Duran/50 8.00
30 Buster Posey, Tony Thomas/50 15.00
32 Bradley Suttle, Cat Osterman/100 10.00

College Ties Auto.
NM/M
Production 20-44
24 Brett Jacobson, David Price/44 50.00

Collegiate Patches
NM/M
Common Patch Auto.: 10.00
Production 25-250
1 Ryan Patterson/250 15.00
2 Mark Melancon/250 20.00
3 Buster Posey/250 50.00
4 O.J. Mayo/50 75.00
5 Gordon Beckham/250 50.00
6 Josh Roenicke/250 15.00
7 Michael Beasley/100 50.00
8 Jack Egbert/249 15.00
11 Tyson Brummett/250 15.00
12 Ike Davis/250 15.00
13 Andrew Cashner/250 15.00
14 Charlie Furbush/250 15.00
15 Ryan Perry/248 15.00
16 Sean Doolittle/250 25.00
17 Alan Horne/250 15.00
18 Dan Schlereth/250 15.00
19 Carlos Gutierrez/249 15.00
20 Shooter Hunt/250 20.00
21 Cat Osterman/250 40.00
22 Lance Lynn/249 20.00
23 Byron Wiley/248 15.00
24 Brad Mills/249 15.00
25 Bryan Price/249 15.00
26 Logan Forsythe/249 15.00
27 Brian Duensing/250 20.00
28 Tyson Ross/255 10.00
29 Shane Peterson/250 15.00
30 Josh Lindblom/249 10.00
31 Aaron Shafer/250 15.00
32 Dennis Raben/250 15.00
33 Cody Satterwhite/250 15.00
34 James Darnell/250 15.00
35 Charlie Blackmon/240 15.00
36 Blake Wood/250 15.00
37 Jordan Danks/250 20.00
38 Jordy Mercer/247 15.00
39 Roger Kieschnick/250 15.00
40 Zach Stewart/250 15.00
41 Daniel McCutchen/250 15.00
42 Brent Morel/250 15.00
43 Kyle Hudson/249 15.00
44 Tim Murphy/250 15.00
45 Petey Paramore/250 15.00
46 Kyle Russell/250 20.00
47 Andrew Liebel/248 15.00
49 Aaron Pribanic/250 15.00
50 Scott Green/250 10.00
51 Blake Tekotte/248 15.00
52 Vance Worley/250 10.00
53 Taylor Teagarden/250 15.00
54 Cord Phelps/250 10.00

55 Kyle Weiland/250 20.00
56 Allan Dykstra/250 15.00
57 Danny Espinosa/250 15.00
59 Zach Putnam/244 15.00
60 Mark Sobolewski/250 15.00
61 Regis Philbin/50 60.00
62 Randy Couture/50 60.00
63 Jose Duran/250 10.00
64 Lucas Duda/249 15.00
65 Ashley Judd/29 125.00

School Colors
NM/M
Common Player: 1.50
Production 1,500 Sets
1 T.J. Steele 2.00
2 Brett Jacobson 2.00
3 Buster Posey 5.00
4 O.J. Mayo 3.00
5 Gordon Beckham 4.00
6 Sean Ratliff 1.50
7 Michael Beasley 3.00
8 Jose Duran 1.50
9 Derrick Rose 1.50
10 Joba Chamberlain 5.00
11 Sam Freeman 1.50
12 Ike Davis 1.50
13 Andrew Cashner 1.50
14 Chase D'Arnaud 1.50
15 Ryan Perry 2.00
16 Blake Tekotte 1.50
17 Cole St. Clair 1.50
18 Dan Schlereth 1.50
19 Carlos Gutierrez 2.50
20 Shooter Hunt 2.00
21 Zach Putnam 1.50
22 Lance Lynn 1.50
23 Mitch Abeita 1.50
24 Jordan Danks 2.50
25 Bryan Price 1.50
26 Logan Forsythe 1.50
27 Brandon Crawford 1.50
28 Tyson Ross 1.50
29 Shane Peterson 2.00
30 Josh Lindblom 1.50
31 Aaron Shafer 2.00
32 Dennis Raben 2.00
33 Cody Satterwhite 2.00
34 James Darnell 2.00
35 Charlie Blackmon 1.50
36 Sawyer Carroll 1.50
37 Cat Osterman 2.00
38 Jordy Mercer 2.00
39 Roger Kieschnick 1.50
40 Zach Stewart 1.50
41 Kyle Weiland 3.00
42 Brent Morel 1.50
43 Lucas Duda 1.50
44 Tim Murphy 1.50
45 Petey Paramore 1.50
46 Kyle Russell 2.50
47 Logan Schafer 2.00
48 Andrew Liebel 1.50
49 Aaron Pribanic 1.50
50 Scott Green 1.50

School Colors Auto.
NM/M
Production 25 or 50
3 Buster Posey/50 65.00
5 Gordon Beckham/50 40.00
8 Jose Duran/50 15.00
12 Ike Davis/50 30.00
13 Andrew Cashner/50 15.00
14 Chase D'Arnaud/50 15.00
15 Ryan Perry/50 15.00
16 Blake Tekotte/50 15.00
18 Dan Schlereth/50 10.00
22 Lance Lynn/50 20.00
25 Bryan Price/50 15.00
31 Aaron Shafer/50 15.00
32 Dennis Raben/50 15.00
33 Cody Satterwhite/50 25.00
35 Charlie Blackmon/50 10.00
42 Brent Morel/50 15.00
45 Petey Paramore/50 15.00
46 Kyle Russell/50 20.00
47 Logan Schafer/50 15.00

School Colors Material
NM/M
Production 100 Sets
Prime: No Pricing
Production 25 Sets
3 Buster Posey 15.00
4 O.J. Mayo 15.00
5 Gordon Beckham 15.00
7 Michael Beasley 15.00

8 Jose Duran 8.00
9 Derrick Rose 15.00
13 Andrew Cashner 8.00
33 Cody Satterwhite 8.00
37 Cat Osterman 15.00

Throwback Threads
NM/M
Common Player:
Prime: 1.5-2X
Production 1-50
No pricing prod. less than 25.
1 Rick Porcello/500 10.00
2 Gordon Beckham/500
3 Andrew Cashner/500 5.00
6 Cody Satterwhite/500 8.00
9 Jose Duran/500 5.00
10 Derrick Rose/500 20.00
11 Michael Beasley/500 15.00
12 O.J. Mayo/400 15.00
13 Buster Posey/250 15.00
20 Cat Osterman/100 15.00
24 Tim Alderson/500 8.00
25 Michael Burgess/500 15.00

Throwback Threads Auto
NM/M
Common Player:
Prime: No Pricing
Production 1-25
1 Rick Porcello/100 75.00
2 Gordon Beckham/100 40.00
3 Andrew Cashner/100 15.00
5 Xavier Avery/35 30.00
6 Cody Satterwhite/100 15.00
9 Jose Duran/100 15.00
13 Buster Posey/100 60.00
20 Cat Osterman/50 40.00
24 Tim Alderson/40 25.00

2008 Donruss Threads

NM/M
Common Player (1-100): .25
Common Auto. (101-150): 8.00
Production 99-1,999
Common Letter Auto.
(151-187): 15.00
Production (240-280):
Pack (5): 4.00
Box (24): 85.00
1 Hank Aaron 2.00
2 Dale Murphy .50
3 Brooks Robinson .75
4 Cal Ripken Jr. 2.00
5 Eddie Murray .50
6 Carl Yastrzemski 1.00
7 Carlton Fisk .50
8 Wade Boggs .50
9 Joe Jackson 1.50
10 Johnny Pesky .25
11 Jim Rice .50
12 Fred Lynn .25
13 Duke Snider .75
14 Carl Erskine .25
15 Ernie Banks 1.00
16 Ryne Sandberg 1.00
17 Don Sutton .50
18 Luis Aparicio .50
19 Tom Seaver .75
20 Tony Perez .50
21 Pete Rose 2.00
22 Bob Feller .50
23 Al Kaline .75
24 Mark Fidrych .25
25 Kirk Gibson .25
26 Alan Trammell .25
27 George Brett 1.50
28 Steve Garvey .50
29 Robin Yount .75
30 Harmon Killebrew .75
31 Paul Molitor .50
32 Gary Carter .50
33 George Bush .50
34 Don Larsen .50
35 Don Mattingly 1.00
36 Reggie Jackson .75
37 Tim Raines .25
38 Mike Schmidt 1.00
39 Steve Carlton .50
40 Tony Gwynn .50
41 Juan Marichal .50
42 Willie Mays 1.50
43 Willie McCovey .50
44 Will Clark .25
45 Bob Gibson .50
46 Dennis Eckersley .25
47 Red Schoendienst .25
48 Stan Musial 1.00
49 Nolan Ryan 1.50
50 Frank Howard .25
51 Austin Romine .50
52 Chris Carter .50
53 Jordan Schafer .50
54 Michael Burgess .50
55 John Raynor .25
56 Lars Anderson 2.00
57 Josh Reddick .25
58 Luis Exposito .50
59 Aneury Rodriguez .50
60 Nick Weglarz 1.00
61 Hector Gomez .50
62 Jon Still .25
63 Brandon Hamilton .25
64 Bud Norris .50
65 Danny Duffy .25
66 Jovan Rosa .50
67 Sean O'Sullivan .25
68 Edilio Colina .25
69 Ryan Patterson .25
70 Brent Brewer .25
71 David Bromberg .25
72 Bryan Petersen .25
73 Lucas Duda .25
74 Ruben Tejada .25
75 Andrew Lambo 1.00
76 Jeff Corsaletti .50
77 Alexis Oliveras 1.00
78 Fernando Garcia .25
79 Jairo Heredia .50
80 Jesus Montero 2.00
81 Jose Tabata .50
82 Carlos Gonzalez .50
83 Patrick Ryan .25
84 Sean Doolittle .25
85 Carlos Carrasco .50
86 Luis Cruz .50
87 Yefri Carvajal .25
88 Stolmy Pimentel .50
89 Wilber Bucardo .50
90 Angel Villalona .50
91 Madison Bumgarner 2.00
92 Danny Carroll .25
93 Juan Ramirez .25
94 Louis Marson .75
95 Josh Vitters 1.00
96 Desmond Jennings 1.50
97 Abraham Almonte .25
98 Mat Gamel 1.00
99 Andrew LeFave .25
100 Elvis Andrus .50
101 Emilio Bonifacio/1,874 8.00
102 Wilin Rosario/999 8.00
103 Carlos Peguero/465 20.00
104 Tyler Flowers/999 40.00
105 Tyler Henson/999 10.00
106 Nevin Griffith/999 8.00
107 Caleb Gindl/465 10.00
108 Jose Ceda/999 8.00
109 Brandon Waring/465 20.00
110 Neftali Soto/999 30.00
111 Ryan Miller/999 8.00
112 Jack Egers/999 8.00
113 Juan Silverio/999 8.00
114 Jhoulys Chacin/1,999 25.00
115 Charlie Furbush/465 8.00
116 Hector Correa/999 8.00
117 Brad James/1,999 8.00
118 Keaton Hayenga/999 10.00
119 Brent Fisher/1,058 8.00
120 Juan Francisco/999 15.00
121 Andrew Romine/875 8.00
122 Mason Tobin/999 8.00
123 Anel De Los Santos/999 8.00
124 Andrew Walker/2,599 15.00
125 Alfredo Silverio/25,999 8.00
126 Mario Martinez/1,375 15.00
127 Taylor Green/999 10.00
128 D.J. Jones/399 8.00
129 Wilson Ramos/999 15.00
130 Trevor Reckling/875 15.00
131 Engel Beltre/465 20.00
132 Scott Moviel/1,000 8.00
133 Josh Tomlin/875 10.00
134 Dominic Brown/999 50.00
135 Neftali Feliz/465 40.00
136 Brian Friday/1,249 8.00
137 Drew Miller/1,999 8.00
138 Steve Garrison/1,999 8.00
139 Mike McBryde/950 8.00
140 Brian Duensing/575 8.00
141 Greg Halman/465 30.00
142 Jharmidy DeJesus/465 25.00
143 Mike Stanton/465 100.00
144 Wilmer Flores/99 80.00
145 Heath Rollins/999 8.00
146 Alex Cobb/999 8.00
147 Omar Poveda/999 8.00
148 Yohermyn Chavez/999 15.00
149 Gerardo Parra/999 10.00
150 Clayton Conner/250 15.00
151 Tyler Kolodny/280 20.00
152 Ryan Kalish/240 30.00
153 Rick Porcello/240 50.00
154 Shane Peterson/240 20.00
155 Tyler Ladendorf/240 15.00
156 Josh Lindblom/240 20.00
157 Tyler Chatwood/240 20.00
158 Logan Morrison/240 40.00
159 Collin DeLome/240 25.00
160 Daniel Cortes/240 20.00
161 Chris Johnson/280 40.00
162 Matt Mitchell/240 15.00
163 Denny Almonte/280 15.00
164 Greg Veloz/240 20.00
165 R.J. Seidel/240 15.00
167 Xavier Avery/250 25.00
168 Quincy Latimore/240 15.00
169 Aaron Shafer/280 15.00
170 Raynor Contreras/270 15.00
171 Waldis Joaquin/280 15.00
172 Jorge Bucardo/280 15.00
173 James Darnell/280 20.00
174 Logan Forsythe/280 15.00
175 Kyle Ginley/240 15.00
176 Ike Davis/250 40.00
177 Max Ramirez/244 20.00
178 Chris Davis/250 25.00
179 Jay Austin/240 15.00
180 Brad Holt/240 25.00
181 Carlos Gutierrez/270 15.00
182 Christian Friedrich/270 15.00
184 Zach Collier/280 20.00
186 Robert Hernandez/269 15.00
187 Christian Marrero/280 20.00

Gold Century Proof
Gold (1-100): 3-6X
Gold (1-150): .2-.25X
Production 50 Sets

Green Century Proof
Green (1-100): 2-4X
Green (101-150): .15-.2X
Production 250 Sets

Platinum Century Proof
Platinum (1-100): 10-15X
Platinum (101-150): .4-.5X
Production 25 Sets

Silver Century Proof
Silver (1-100): 3-5X
Silver (101-150): .2-.25X
Production 100 Sets

Baseball Americana
NM/M
Common Card: 2.00
1 Bud Abbott 2.00
2 Lou Costello 2.00
3 Don Mattingly 4.00
4 Eddie Murray 3.00
5 Ryne Sandberg 4.00
6 Pete Rose 5.00
7 Cal Ripken Jr. 5.00
8 Ernie Banks 3.00
9 George Brett 4.00
10 Mike Schmidt 3.00
11 Johnny Bench 3.00
12 Carlton Fisk 2.00
13 Tony Gwynn 3.00
14 Hank Aaron 5.00
15 Willie Mays 4.00
16 Joe Jackson 4.00
17 Ted Williams 4.00
18 Stan Musial 4.00
19 Nolan Ryan 5.00
20 Bob Feller 2.00
21 Kurt Russell 2.00
22 Burt Lancaster 2.00
23 Tab Hunter 2.00
24 Gary Cooper 2.00
25 Tony Curtis 2.00
26 John Cusack 2.00
27 Bernie Mac 2.00
28 Regis Philbin 2.00
29 Marcia Gay Harden 2.00
30 Albert Brooks 2.00
31 Billy Dee Williams 2.00
32 Esther Williams 2.00
33 Betty Garrett 2.00
34 Karen Allen 2.00
35 Ed Asner 2.00
36 Robert Wagner 2.00
37 Gary Coleman 2.00
38 Ed McMahon 2.00
39 Rob Schneider 2.00
40 Lori Petty 2.00
41 Bob Gibson 3.00
42 Dennis Eckersley 4.00
43 Carl Yastrzemski 4.00
44 Don Drysdale 3.00
45 Satchel Paige 4.00
46 Casey Stengel 3.00
47 Eddie Mathews 4.00
48 Early Wynn 2.00
49 Marilyn Monroe 5.00
50 George Bush 2.00

Baseball Americana Materials
NM/M
Production 1-500
Position: 1-2X
Production 1-250
No pricing prod. under 25.
1 Bud Abbott/500 15.00
2 Lou Costello/250 25.00
3 Don Mattingly/100 20.00
4 Eddie Murray/150 10.00
5 Pete Rose/250 35.00
6 Cal Ripken Jr./100 25.00
7 George Brett/75 15.00
8 Mike Schmidt/100 15.00
9 Tony Gwynn/250 8.00
10 Mike Schmidt/100 15.00
11 Nolan Ryan/100 15.00
12 Dale Murphy/100 8.00
13 Tony Gwynn/250 8.00
14 Dave Winfield/100 8.00
15 Paul Molitor/100 8.00
16 Barry Larkin/500 6.00
17 Kirk Gibson/500 8.00
18 Nolan Ryan/100 20.00
19 Pete Rose/500 40.00
20 Steve Garvey/100 8.00
21 Wade Boggs/100 6.00
22 Ted Williams/50 30.00
23 Steve Carlton/100 8.00
33 Betty Garrett/250 8.00
35 Ed Asner/500 5.00
36 Robert Wagner/500 5.00
38 Ed McMahon/500 5.00
39 Rob Schneider/350 5.00
40 Lori Petty/500 5.00
41 Bob Gibson/100 8.00
43 Carl Yastrzemski/500 15.00
44 Don Drysdale/100 15.00
45 Satchel Paige/100 30.00
46 Casey Stengel/500 15.00
47 Eddie Mathews/100 8.00
48 Early Wynn/500 8.00
49 TBD/500 40.00
50 TBD/500 20.00

Baseball Americana Signatures
NM/M
Production 3-100
3 Don Mattingly/25 50.00
6 Pete Rose/50 125.00
10 Mike Schmidt/25 40.00
11 Johnny Bench/50 40.00
12 Carlton Fisk/50 25.00
13 Tony Gwynn/25 40.00
20 Bob Feller/100 20.00
23 Tab Hunter/100 20.00
27 Bernie Mac/38 70.00
28 Regis Philbin/100 25.00
29 Marcia Gay Harden/100 15.00
30 Albert Brooks/100 15.00
41 Bob Gibson/100 20.00
42 Dennis Eckersley/100 15.00
43 Carl Yastrzemski/25 50.00

Baseball Americana Sign. Materials

NM/M
Production 3-100
3 Don Mattingly/25 50.00
6 Pete Rose/50 150.00
7 Cal Ripken Jr./25 100.00
10 Mike Schmidt/25 40.00
11 Johnny Bench/50 40.00
12 Carlton Fisk/50 25.00
13 Tony Gwynn/50 40.00
27 Bernie Mac/100 75.00
41 Bob Gibson/25 25.00

Bats
NM/M
Production 1-500
1 Hank Aaron/500 25.00
2 Joe Jackson/500 300.00
35 Don Mattingly/250 15.00
36 Reggie Jackson/500 8.00
38 Mike Schmidt/500 10.00
42 Willie Mays/50 30.00
52 Chris Carter/500 8.00
53 Jordan Schafer/500 8.00
54 Michael Burgess/500 8.00
70 Brent Brewer/500 5.00
81 Jose Tabata/500 8.00
84 Sean Doolittle/500 8.00
92 Danny Carroll/500 5.00
96 Desmond Jennings/50 5.00
127 Taylor Green/500 5.00
142 Greg Halman/500 5.00
143 Jharmidy DeJesus/500 5.00

Century Collection Materials
NM/M
Production 10-100
Prime: No Pricing
Production 3-10
1 Cal Ripken Jr./100 25.00
2 Ryne Sandberg/75 15.00
3 Pete Rose/50 40.00
4 Fred Lynn/100 8.00
5 Tom Seaver/100 10.00
6 George Brett/50 25.00
7 Don Mattingly/75 20.00
8 Mike Schmidt/100 15.00
9 Tony Gwynn/100 8.00
10 Dale Murphy/100 8.00
11 Nolan Ryan/100 15.00
12 Pete Rose/100 40.00
13 Dave Winfield/100 8.00
14 Paul Molitor/100 8.00
15 Kirk Gibson/100 8.00
24 Robin Yount/100 10.00
25 Luis Aparicio/100 6.00
26 Jim Rice/100 5.00
27 Jim Palmer/100 5.00
28 Harmon Killebrew/100 10.00
29 Gaylord Perry/100 5.00
30 Gary Carter/100 8.00
31 Eddie Murray/50 10.00
32 Don Drysdale/100 10.00
33 Satchel Paige/100 40.00
34 Casey Stengel/100 15.00
35 Eddie Mathews/100 8.00
36 Dennis Eckersley/100 8.00
37 Carlton Fisk/100 8.00
38 Carl Yastrzemski/100 15.00
39 Early Wynn/100 8.00
40 Lefty Grove/50 100.00

Century Legends

NM/M
Common Player: 1.50
Century Proof: 2-3X
Production 100 Sets
1 Stan Musial 2.00
2 Willie Mays 2.00
3 Hank Aaron 3.00
4 Ted Williams 2.00
5 Whitey Ford 1.50
6 Bob Gibson 1.50
7 Joe Jackson 2.00
8 Duke Snider 1.50
9 Ernie Banks 2.00
10 Bob Feller 1.50
11 Nolan Ryan 3.00
12 Mike Schmidt 2.00
13 Carl Yastrzemski 2.00
14 Pete Rose 2.00
15 Harmon Killebrew 2.00

Century Legends Materials
NM/M
Production 1-100
Prime: No Pricing
Production 1-25
1 Stan Musial/25 30.00
4 Ted Williams/50 30.00
6 Bob Gibson/50 10.00
11 Nolan Ryan/100 15.00
12 Mike Schmidt/100 15.00
13 Carl Yastrzemski/100 15.00
14 Pete Rose/100 40.00
15 Harmon Killebrew/100 10.00

Century Stars

NM/M
Common Player: 1.00
Century Proof: 2-3X
Production 100 Sets
1 Carlton Fisk 1.00
2 Harmon Killebrew 2.00
3 Ryne Sandberg 2.00
4 Cal Ripken Jr. 3.00
5 Mike Schmidt 2.00
6 Tony Gwynn 1.50
7 Pete Rose 2.00
8 Tim Raines 1.00
9 Dale Murphy 1.00
10 Steve Carlton 1.00
11 Bob Gibson 1.50
12 Nolan Ryan 3.00
13 Robin Yount 1.00
14 Paul Molitor 1.00
15 Kirk Gibson 1.00

Century Stars Materials
NM/M
Production 50 or 100
Prime: No Pricing
Production 1-10
1 Carlton Fisk/100 8.00
2 Harmon Killebrew/100 10.00
3 Ryne Sandberg/50 15.00
4 Cal Ripken Jr./100 25.00
5 Mike Schmidt/100 15.00
6 Tony Gwynn/100 8.00
7 Pete Rose/100 40.00
8 Dale Murphy/100 8.00
10 Steve Carlton/100 5.00
11 Bob Gibson/100 10.00
12 Nolan Ryan/100 15.00
13 Robin Yount/100 10.00
14 Paul Molitor/100 6.00
15 Kirk Gibson/50 5.00

College Greats

NM/M
Common Player: 1.00
1 Tom Seaver 2.00
2 Reggie Jackson 2.00
3 Frank Howard 1.00
4 Dave Winfield 2.00
5 Paul Molitor 1.50
6 Barry Larkin 1.00
7 Kirk Gibson 1.00
8 Robin Roberts 1.00
9 Will Clark 1.00
10 Bob Gibson 1.50
11 Steve Garvey 1.00
12 Fred Lynn 1.00

College Greats Signatures
NM/M
Production 5-50
1 Tom Seaver/25 40.00
2 Reggie Jackson/50 50.00
3 Frank Howard/50 25.00
4 Dave Winfield/25 50.00
5 Paul Molitor/25 40.00
6 Barry Larkin/50 50.00
8 Robin Roberts/40 30.00
10 Bob Gibson/50 30.00
12 Fred Lynn/50 30.00

College Greats Signature Combos
No Pricing
Production 5 Sets

Diamond Kings

NM/M
Common Player:
Framed Red: 1.5-2X
Production 100 Sets
Gold: 1.5-2X
Production 100 Sets
Silver: 1-2X
Production 250 Sets
Framed Blue: 2-3X
Production 50 Sets
Framed Green: 3-5X
Production 25 Sets
Framed Black: No Pricing
Production 10 Sets
Platinum: 3-5X
Production 25 Sets
1 Jordan Schafer 2.00
2 Nolan Reimold 2.00
3 Matt McBride 2.00
4 Lars Anderson 3.00
5 Blake Wood 2.00
6 Josh Vitters 2.00
7 Chris Valaika 2.00
8 Drew Stubbs 2.00
9 Rick Porcello 3.00
11 Anthony Rizzo 2.00

12	Jon Jay	1.00
13	Clay Fuller	1.00
14	Damon Sublett	3.00
16	Brett Anderson	1.00
16	Matt Spencer	1.00
17	Drew Cumberland	1.00
18	Tim Alderson	2.00
19	Madison Bumgarner	3.00
20	Jess Todd	1.00
21	Michael Hollimon	1.00
22	Taylor Teagarden	1.00
24	Daniel McCutchen	1.00
24	Trystan Magnuson	1.00
25	Michael Burgess	1.00
26	Hank Aaron	4.00
27	Cal Ripken Jr.	4.00
28	Jim Palmer	1.50
29	Bobby Doerr	1.50
30	Duke Snider	2.00
31	Rod Carew	1.50
32	Ernie Banks	2.00
33	Ryne Sandberg	3.00
34	Billy Williams	1.50
35	Fergie Jenkins	1.50
36	Pete Rose	3.00
37	George Kell	1.50
38	George Brett	3.00
39	Reggie Jackson	2.00
40	Don Mattingly	3.00
41	Phil Niekro	1.00
42	Whitey Ford	2.00
43	Yogi Berra	2.00
44	Mike Schmidt	2.00
45	Tony Gwynn	2.00
46	Willie Mays	3.00
47	Gaylord Perry	1.00
48	Stan Musial	2.00
49	Lou Brock	1.50
50	Nolan Ryan	3.00
51	Joe Jackson	3.00
52	Gordon Beckham	5.00
53	Derrick Rose	3.00
54	Michael Beasley	3.00
55	O.J. Mayo	3.00
56	Pete Rose	3.00
57	Rick Porcello	3.00
58	Nolan Ryan	3.00

Diamond Kings Materials

NM/M
Production 1-250
Prime: No Pricing
Production 1-25

1	Jordan Schafer/250	5.00
6	Josh Vitters/250	8.00
8	Mark Melancon/125	5.00
9	Drew Stubbs/250	5.00
10	Rick Porcello/250	10.00
13	Clay Fuller/250	5.00
14	Damon Sublett/250	10.00
15	Brett Anderson/250	5.00
16	Matt Spencer/250	8.00
17	Drew Cumberland/250	5.00
18	Tim Alderson/250	8.00
19	Madison Bumgarner/125	15.00
23	Jess Todd/250	8.00
24	Trystan Magnuson/250	10.00
25	Michael Burgess/250	10.00
27	Cal Ripken Jr./200	20.00
28	Jim Palmer/50	10.00
33	Ryne Sanberg/50	25.00
36	Pete Rose/250	50.00
38	George Brett/75	20.00
40	Don Mattingly/150	20.00
43	Yogi Berra/25	25.00
44	Mike Schmidt/75	20.00
45	Tony Gwynn/250	8.00
49	Lou Brock/100	20.00
50	Nolan Ryan/50	25.00
56	Pete Rose/100	40.00
57	Rick Porcello	15.00
58	Nolan Ryan	25.00

Diamond Kings Signatures

NM/M
Production 5-500

1	Jordan Schafer/199	20.00
2	Nolan Reimold/500	5.00
3	Matt McBride/500	10.00
4	Lars Anderson/474	35.00
5	Blake Wood/500	10.00
6	Chris Valaika/500	10.00
8	Mark Melancon/238	15.00
9	Drew Stubbs/465	15.00
10	Rick Porcello/300	40.00
11	Brett Anderson/315	15.00
12	Tim Alderson/215	15.00
19	Madison Bumgarner/223	30.00
21	Michael Hollimon/500	10.00
22	Taylor Teagarden/475	15.00
23	Daniel McCutchen/500	10.00
24	Trystan Magnuson/215	15.00
25	Michael Burgess/182	15.00
28	Jim Palmer/100	25.00
29	Bobby Doerr/250	20.00
30	Duke Snider/50	40.00
33	Fergie Jenkins/100	20.00
36	Pete Rose/50	125.00
39	Reggie Jackson/25	40.00
40	Don Mattingly/25	50.00
42	Whitey Ford/100	40.00
44	Mike Schmidt/25	40.00
47	Gaylord Perry/150	20.00
50	Lou Brock/25	25.00
50	Nolan Ryan/25	70.00
56	Pete Rose/25	125.00
57	Rick Porcello/25	80.00
58	Nolan Ryan/25	75.00

Diamond Kings Signatures Materials

NM/M
Production 5-100
Prime: No Pricing
Production 1-10

1	Jordan Schafer/25	30.00
10	Rick Porcello/25	100.00
18	Damon Sublett/25	50.00
18	Tim Alderson/25	25.00
19	Madison Bumgarner/25	40.00
27	Cal Ripken Jr./25	150.00
28	Jim Palmer/25	30.00
36	Pete Rose/25	160.00
40	Don Mattingly/25	60.00
49	Lou Brock/25	35.00
50	Nolan Ryan/25	85.00
56	Pete Rose/25	160.00
57	Rick Porcello/25	100.00

Dynasty

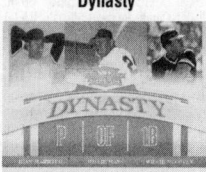

NM/M
Common Trio: 3.00
Century Proof: 2-3X
Production 100 Sets

1	Cal Ripken Jr., Eddie Murray, Jim Palmer	3.00
2	Joe Morgan, Johnny Bench, Pete Rose	3.00
3	Juan Marichal, Willie Mays, Willie McCovey	3.00

Dynasty Materials

NM/M
Production 50 or 100
Prime: No Pricing
Production 10 Sets

| 1 | Cal Ripken Jr., Eddie Murray, Jim Palmer/50 | 30.00 |
| 2 | Joe Morgan, Johnny Bench, Pete Rose/100 | 65.00 |

Generations

NM/M
Common Duo: 2.00
Century Proof: 2-3X
Production 100 Sets

1	Dale Murphy, Hank Aaron	3.00
2	Cal Ripken Jr., Eddie Murray	3.00
3	Ernie Banks, Ryne Sandberg	2.00
4	Willie Mays, Willie McCovey	3.00
5	Paul Molitor, Rod Carew	2.00

Generations Materials

NM/M
Production 10-100
Prime: No Pricing
Production 5-10

| 2 | Cal Ripken Jr., Eddie Murray/100 | 30.00 |

Jerseys

NM/M
Production 5-500
Prime: No Pricing
Production 1-25

2	Dale Murphy/350	8.00
3	Brooks Robinson/250	8.00
4	Cal Ripken Jr./350	20.00
5	Eddie Murray/350	8.00
6	Carl Yastrzemski/400	10.00
7	Carlton Fisk/150	5.00
8	Wade Boggs/500	8.00
11	Jim Rice/350	5.00
14	Fred Lynn/350	5.00
16	Ryne Sandberg/150	10.00
18	Luis Aparicio/200	5.00
19	Tom Seaver/350	8.00
21	Pete Rose/100	40.00
25	Kirk Gibson/250	5.00
26	Alan Trammell/250	5.00
27	George Brett/250	10.00
28	Steve Garvey/150	5.00
29	Robin Yount/500	10.00
30	Harmon Killebrew/150	10.00
31	Paul Molitor/300	5.00
32	Gary Carter/450	5.00
33	George Bush/500	20.00
35	Don Mattingly/150	20.00
36	Reggie Jackson/350	8.00
38	Mike Schmidt/350	10.00
39	Steve Carlton/250	8.00
42	Tony Gwynn/500	8.00
43	Willie McCovey/500	8.00
44	Will Clark/500	5.00
45	Bob Gibson/100	5.00
46	Dennis Eckersley/250	5.00
47	Red Schoendienst/300	5.00
49	Nolan Ryan/250	15.00
54	Michael Burgess/500	5.00
57	Madison Bumgarner/100	20.00
95	Josh Vitters/500	5.00
146	Heath Rollins/90	5.00
147	Alex Cobb/95	8.00

Signatures Gold

NM/M
Production 10-999
Platinum: No Pricing
Production 5-25

3	Brooks Robinson/50	25.00
4	Cal Ripken Jr./50	80.00
5	Eddie Murray/25	40.00
6	Carl Yastrzemski/50	40.00
8	Carlton Fisk/25	25.00
10	Johnny Pesky/100	15.00
11	Jim Rice/100	20.00
12	Fred Lynn/50	20.00
13	Duke Snider/50	40.00
14	Carl Erskine/75	15.00
16	Ryne Sandberg/50	40.00
18	Don Sutton/100	20.00
18	Luis Aparicio/50	20.00
19	Tom Seaver/50	40.00
20	Tony Perez/25	20.00
21	Pete Rose/75	120.00
22	Bob Feller/100	25.00
23	Al Kaline/50	35.00
24	Mark Fidrych/100	15.00
26	Alan Trammell/75	15.00
28	Steve Garvey/45	20.00
29	Robin Yount/50	25.00
31	Paul Molitor/50	20.00
32	Gary Carter/50	20.00
34	Don Larsen/50	25.00
35	Don Mattingly/50	60.00
36	Reggie Jackson/50	35.00
37	Tim Raines/25	30.00
38	Mike Schmidt/50	50.00
39	Steve Carlton/50	20.00
42	Tony Gwynn/50	35.00
43	Willie Mays/50	80.00
43	Willie McCovey/50	35.00
45	Bob Gibson/25	25.00
46	Dennis Eckersley/50	25.00
47	Red Schoendienst/100	20.00
48	Stan Musial/50	50.00
49	Nolan Ryan/50	75.00
50	Frank Howard/75	15.00
51	Austin Romine/725	20.00
52	Chris Carter/499	15.00
53	Jordan Schafer/275	15.00
55	John Raynor/575	15.00
56	Lars Anderson/499	35.00
57	Josh Reddick/499	30.00
58	Luis Exposito/971	10.00
59	Aneury Rodriguez/975	8.00
60	Nick Weglarz/999	15.00
61	Hector Gomez/499	15.00
62	Jon Still/725	8.00
63	Brandon Hamilton/972	8.00
64	Bud Norris/499	8.00
65	Danny Duffy/499	20.00
66	Jovan Rosa/973	15.00
67	Sean O'Sullivan/499	10.00
68	Edilio Colina/975	8.00
69	Ryan Patterson/775	8.00
70	Brent Brewer/470	8.00
71	David Bromberg/999	8.00
72	Bryan Petersen/475	8.00
73	Lucas Duda/250	10.00
74	Ruben Tejada/999	10.00
75	Jeff Corsaletti/975	10.00
76	Alexis Oliveras/975	10.00
77	Fernando Garcia/975	8.00
79	Jairo Heredia/999	10.00
80	Jesus Montero/975	35.00
81	Jose Tabata/975	20.00
82	Carlos Gonzalez/975	20.00
83	Patrick Ryan/499	8.00
84	Sean Doolittle/249	15.00
85	Carlos Carrasco/999	15.00
86	Luis Cruz/975	10.00
87	Yefri Carvajal/999	8.00
88	Stolmy Pimentel/975	15.00
89	Wilber Bucardo/420	8.00
91	Madison Bumgarner/250	30.00
92	Danny Carroll/999	8.00
93	Juan Ramirez/999	8.00
94	Louis Marson/725	20.00
96	Desmond Jennings/749	25.00
97	Abraham Almonte/975	8.00
99	Andrew LeFave/975	8.00
100	Elvis Andrus/749	20.00
102	Wilin Rosario/100	25.00
104	Tyler Flowers/100	50.00
105	Tyler Henson/100	10.00
106	Nevin Griffith/100	8.00
108	Jose Ceda/100	10.00
111	Ryan Miller/100	10.00
112	Jack Egbert/100	10.00
113	Juan Silverio/100	15.00
114	Jhoulys Chacin/30	30.00
116	Hector Correa/100	10.00
117	Brad James/100	10.00
119	Keaton Hayenga/100	20.00
120	Brent Fisher/100	10.00
121	Juan Francisco/100	25.00
122	Andrew Romine/100	15.00
123	Mason Tobin/100	15.00
124	Anel De Los Santos/100	10.00
126	Alfredo Silverio/100	15.00
127	Mario Martinez/100	10.00
128	Taylor Green/100	20.00
129	D.J. Jones/100	15.00
130	Wilson Ramos/100	15.00
131	Trevor Reckling/100	15.00
133	Scott Moviel/100	10.00
134	Josh Tomlin/100	10.00
135	Dominic Brown/100	75.00
137	Brian Friday/100	10.00
138	Drew Miller/100	10.00
139	Mike McBryde/100	10.00
141	Brian Duensing/100	10.00
146	Heath Rollins/100	15.00
148	Omar Poveda/100	15.00
149	Yohermyn Chavez/100	15.00
150	Gerardo Parra/100	15.00

2009 Donruss Americana

NM/M
Complete Set (100): 40.00
Common Card: .50
Pack (5): 20.00
Box (4): 75.00

1	Jackie Chan	2.00
2	Patrick Stewart	1.00
3	Marcia Gay Harden	.50
4	Michael Madsen	.50
5	Joseph Lawrence	.50
6	Randal Kleiser	.50
7	Sofia Milos	.50
8	Charlene Tilton	.50
9	Elena Verdugo	.50
10	Annette Charles	.50
11	Barry Pearl	.50
12	Edd Byrnes	.50
13	Jeffrey Tambor	.50
14	Eddie Deezen	.50
15	Lawrence Hilton-Jacobs	.50
16	Robert Hegyes	.50
17	Ron Palillo	.50
18	Tab Hunter	.50
19	Patty Duke	.50
20	John Cusack	.50
21	Ralph Macchio	.50
22	Connie Britton	.50
23	Barry Watson	.50
24	John Kerr	.50
25	Gary Sinise	1.00
26	Diane Farr	.50
27	Lauren Bacall	.50
28	Steve Kanaly	.50
29	Ty Hardin	.50
30	Lorna Luft	.50
31	Dylan McDermott	.50
32	Fred Willard	.50
33	Gerald Okamura	.50
34	Alessandro Nivola	.50
35	Marc McClure	.50
36	David Ladd	.50
37	John Buccigross	.50
38	Vicki Lawrence	.50
39	Jordan Ladd	.50
40	Bridgette Wilson-Sampras	.50
41	Natalie Zea	.50
42	Malcolm McDowell	.50
43	John C. McGinley	.50
44	Stephen Baldwin	.50
45	Nadine Velazquez	.50
46	Charlie Daniels	.50
47	Tracy Lawrence	.50
48	Michael Beck	.50
49	Denzel Whitaker	.50
50	Francesco Quinn	.50
51	Jon Provost	.50
52	George A. Romero	.50
53	Daniel Baldwin	.50
54	Debi Mazar	.50
55	Robert Vaughn	.50
56	Brigitte Nielsen	.50
57	Geoff Stults	.50
58	James Duval	.50
59	Michael Boatman	.50
60	Barry Williams	.50
61	Peter Graves	.50
62	Chazz Palminteri	.50
63	Elijah Wood	1.00
64	Emily Procter	.50
65	Yancy Butler	.50
66	Olesya Rulin	.50
67	Meredith Salenger	.50
68	Micky Dolenz	.50
69	Barry Bostwick	.50
70	Albert Brooks	.50
71	Tony Todd	.50
72	Anson Williams	.50
73	Deborah Shelton	.50
74	Corbin Bleu	.50
75	Marisol Nichols	.50
76	Erin Moran	.50
77	Taryn Manning	.50
78	Ami Dolenz	.50
79	Niecy Nash	.50
80	Paul Le Mat	.50
81	Swoosie Kurtz	.50
82	Alan Ruck	.50
83	Daniel Logan	.50
84	Aaron Tippin	.50
85	David Carradine	1.00
86	Dean McDermott	.50
87	Eric Roberts	.50
88	Erin Gray	.50
89	Irvin Kershner	.50
90	James Caan	1.00
91	Jamie Donnelly	.50
92	Jill-Michele Melean	.50
93	Luke Goss	.50
94	Marton Csokas	.50
95	Peter Brown	.50
96	Piper Laurie	.50
97	Teddy Gentry	.50
98	Tori Spelling	.50
99	William Forsythe	.50
100	Julia Louis-Dreyfus	1.00

Gold Proofs

Gold Proof (1-100): 4-6X
Production 50 Sets

Gold Proofs Retail

Gold Retail (1-100): 3-5X
Production 100 Sets

Platinum Proofs

No Pricing
Production 10 Sets

Platinum Proofs Retail

Platinum (1-100): 6-8X
Production 25 Sets

Silver Proofs

Silver Proof (1-100): 3-5X
Production 100 Sets

Silver Proofs Retail

Silver Proof (1-100): 2-3X
Production 250 Sets

Award Winners Letter Patch Auto.

NM/M
Production 25 or 30

| 2 | Richard Dreyfuss/30 | 40.00 |
| 3 | Goldie Hawn/30 | 60.00 |

Casting Call Autograph

NM/M
Production 20 or 30

| 1 | Christina Applegate, David Faustino, Ed O'Neill, Katey Sagal/30 | 180.00 |
| 3 | Corey Feldman, Susie Feldman/30 | 60.00 |

Celebrity Cut Autographs

NM/M
Production 1-100

1	Charlie Daniels/28	50.00
2	Goldie Hawn, 20 Foul Play	60.00
2	Goldie Hawn, 20 Shampoo	60.00
3	Ron Howard, 17 American Graffiti	75.00
3	Ron Howard, 17 Cocoon	75.00
3	Ron Howard, 17 Splash	75.00
3	Ron Howard, 17 Music Man	75.00
4	Willie Nelson/100	8.00
5	Richard Dreyfuss/20	75.00
5	Richard Dreyfuss/19	75.00

Cinema Stars

NM/M
Common Card: 2.00
Production 1,000 Sets

1	James Caan	3.00
2	Jordan Ladd	2.00
3	Malcolm McDowell	2.00
4	Michael Madsen	2.00
5	Goldie Hawn	3.00
6	Lauren Bacall	2.00
7	Tab Hunter	2.00
8	Marcia Gay Harden	2.00
9	Geoff Stults	2.00
10	Gary Sinise	3.00
11	Chazz Palminteri	2.00
12	Corbin Bleu	2.00
13	Ralph Macchio	2.00
14	Elijah Wood	3.00
15	Burt Reynolds	3.00
16	Albert Brooks	2.00
17	Richard Dreyfuss	2.00
18	Patrick Stewart	2.00
19	William Forsythe	2.00
20	Eric Roberts	2.00
21	David Carradine	2.00
22	Yancy Butler	2.00
23	Elena Verdugo	2.00
24	Patty Duke	2.00

Cinema Stars Material

NM/M
Production 5-500

3	Malcolm McDowell/100	15.00
5	Goldie Hawn/250	10.00
6	Lauren Bacall/250	15.00
7	Tab Hunter/150	8.00
8	Marcia Gay Harden/50	6.00
9	Geoff Stults/500	4.00
14	Elijah Wood/150	10.00
15	Burt Reynolds/250	5.00
16	Albert Brooks/250	4.00
18	Patrick Stewart/250	15.00
19	William Forsythe/250	5.00
20	Eric Roberts/250	4.00
21	David Carradine/250	15.00
22	Yancy Butler/500	6.00
23	Elena Verdugo/500	4.00

Cinema Stars Material Golden Era

NM/M
Production 5-50

3	Malcolm McDowell/100	10.00
5	Goldie Hawn/50	10.00
6	Lauren Bacall/50	15.00
7	Tab Hunter/50	10.00
8	Marcia Gay Harden/50	6.00
9	Geoff Stults/50	4.00
14	Elijah Wood/40	10.00
15	Burt Reynolds/50	10.00
16	Albert Brooks/50	4.00
18	Patrick Stewart/50	15.00
21	David Carradine/50	15.00
22	Yancy Butler/25	8.00
23	Elena Verdugo/50	4.00

Cinema Star Material Silver Screen

NM/M
Production 5-100

3	Malcolm McDowell/100	10.00
5	Goldie Hawn/100	10.00
6	Lauren Bacall/100	15.00
7	Tab Hunter/100	10.00
8	Marcia Gay Harden/50	4.00
9	Geoff Stults/100	4.00
14	Elijah Wood/75	10.00
15	Burt Reynolds/100	8.00
16	Albert Brooks/100	4.00
18	Patrick Stewart/100	15.00
19	William Forsythe/100	6.00
21	David Carradine/100	8.00
22	Yancy Butler/50	4.00
23	Elena Verdugo/100	4.00

Cinema Stars Signatures

NM/M
Production 25-75

2	James Caan/50	60.00
2	Jordan Ladd/50	20.00
3	Malcolm McDowell/25	30.00
5	Michael Madsen/25	25.00
5	Goldie Hawn/25	50.00
6	Lauren Bacall/25	60.00
7	Tab Hunter/25	20.00
8	Marcia Gay Harden/25	50.00
9	Geoff Stults/25	10.00
10	Gary Sinise/75	40.00
11	Chazz Palminteri/25	40.00
12	Corbin Bleu/25	40.00
13	Ralph Macchio/50	35.00
14	Elijah Wood/25	35.00
15	Burt Reynolds/25	35.00
16	Albert Brooks/25	20.00
17	Richard Dreyfuss/71	40.00
18	Patrick Stewart/50	50.00
19	William Forsythe/25	25.00
20	Eric Roberts/25	20.00
21	David Carradine/100	100.00
22	Yancy Butler/25	20.00
23	Elena Verdugo/25	15.00
24	Patty Duke/25	35.00

Cinema Stars Signature Materials

NM/M
Production 25-100

2	Jordan Ladd/25	25.00
3	Malcolm McDowell/25	30.00
4	Michael Madsen/100	20.00
5	Goldie Hawn/50	65.00
6	Lauren Bacall/25	40.00
7	Tab Hunter/100	15.00
8	Marcia Gay Harden/	20.00
9	Geoff Stults/25	10.00
10	Gary Sinise/25	50.00
11	Chazz Palminteri/75	35.00
12	Corbin Bleu/25	40.00
14	Elijah Wood/25	40.00
15	Burt Reynolds/25	35.00
16	Albert Brooks/100	25.00
18	Patrick Stewart/100	25.00
19	William Forsythe/100	25.00
20	Eric Roberts/25	20.00
21	David Carradine/100	100.00
22	Yancy Butler/75	25.00
23	Elena Verdugo/50	20.00

Cinema Stars Material Super Star

NM/M
Production 1-25

3	Malcolm McDowell/25	12.00
5	Goldie Hawn/25	40.00
6	Lauren Bacall/25	40.00
7	Tab Hunter/25	15.00
8	Marcia Gay Harden/25	10.00
15	Burt Reynolds/25	20.00
18	Patrick Stewart/25	30.00

| 19 | William Forsythe/25 | 10.00 |
| 21 | David Carradine/25 | 35.00 |

Co-Stars Materials
NM/M
Production 20-250

1	Judy Garland, Mickey Rooney/250	20.00
2	Leslie Howard, Vivian Leigh/250	15.00
3	Burt Lancaster, Gary Cooper/250	15.00
5	Douglas Fairbanks Jr., Edward G. Robinson/50	20.00
6	Ernest Borgnine, Telly Savalas/250	10.00
7	Judy Garland, Margaret O'Brien/25	30.00
8	Burt Lancaster, Telly Savalas/250	12.00
9	Douglas Fairbanks Jr., Leslie Howard/250	15.00
10	Carole Lombard, George Raft/25	30.00
11	George Raft, William Holden/25	25.00
13	George Raft, Marilyn Monroe/25	60.00
14	George Raft, Tony Curtis/25	25.00
15	Anthony Quinn, Ernest Borgnine/250	10.00
16	Anthony Quinn, Mickey Rooney/250	15.00

Co-Stars Materials Golden Era
NM/M
Production 10-50

1	Judy Garland, Mickey Rooney/50	20.00
2	Leslie Howard, Vivian Leigh/50	15.00
3	Burt Lancaster, Gary Cooper/50	20.00
6	Ernest Borgnine, Telly Savalas/50	10.00
7	Judy Garland, Margaret O'Brien/25	30.00
8	Burt Lancaster, Telly Savalas/50	15.00
9	Douglas Fairbanks Jr., Leslie Howard/50	15.00
11	George Raft, William Holden/20	25.00
13	George Raft, Marilyn Monroe/20	60.00
14	George Raft, Tony Curtis/20	25.00
15	Anthony Quinn, Ernest Borgnine/50	15.00
16	Anthony Quinn, Mickey Rooney/50	15.00

Co-Stars Materials Silver Screen
NM/M
Production 10-100

1	Judy Garland, Mickey Rooney/100	20.00
2	Leslie Howard, Vivian Leigh/100	15.00
3	Burt Lancaster, Gary Cooper/100	15.00
5	Douglas Fairbanks Jr., Edward G. Robinson/25	25.00
6	Ernest Borgnine, Telly Savalas/100	10.00
7	Judy Garland, Margaret O'Brien/25	30.00
8	Burt Lancaster, Telly Savalas/100	12.00
9	Douglas Fairbanks Jr., Leslie Howard/100	10.00
15	Anthony Quinn, Ernest Borgnine/100	10.00
16	Anthony Quinn, Mickey Rooney/100	15.00

Co-Stars Signatures
NM/M
Production 5-25

1	Charlene Tilton, Steve Kanaly/25	40.00
5	Francesco Quinn, Michael Madsen/25	35.00
7	Electra Avellan, James Duval/25	25.00
10	Elise Avellan, James Duval/25	25.00
11	David Prowse, Malcolm McDowell/25	70.00
12	Paul Le Mat, Richard Dreyfuss/25	75.00
13	Tony Todd, William Forsythe/25	25.00
14	Malcolm McDowell, William Forsythe/25	25.00
15	William Forsythe, Yancy Butler/25	35.00
16	Burt Reynolds, William Forsythe/25	40.00
19	Barry Bostwick, Michael Beck/25	20.00
20	Malcolm McDowell, Marton Csokas/25	40.00
21	Jordan Ladd, Kurt Russell/25	40.00
22	David Ladd, Jordan Ladd/25	20.00
23	David Carradine, Michael Madsen/25	100.00
29	Michael Madsen, Taryn Manning/25	35.00

Combo Cuts
NM/M
Production 1-26

| 3 | Erin Moran, Ron Howard/26 | 100.00 |
| 4 | Martin Kove, Ralph Macchio/20 | 75.00 |

Hollywood Legends
NM/M
Common Card: 2.00
Production 1,000 Sets

1	Burt Lancaster	3.00
2	Marilyn Monroe	5.00
3	Douglas Fairbanks Sr.	2.00
4	Edward G. Robinson	2.00
5	Gary Cooper	3.00
6	Judy Garland	2.00
7	Lou Costello	3.00
8	Vivian Leigh	2.00
9	Alan Ladd	2.00
10	Anthony Quinn	2.00
11	Donna Reed	2.00
12	Douglas Fairbanks Jr.	2.00
13	Edward G. Robinson Jr.	2.00
14	George Raft	2.00
15	Hedy Lamarr	2.00
16	Johnny Weissmuller	2.00
17	Pat Paulsen	2.00
18	Pat O'Brien	2.00
19	Redd Foxx	2.00
20	Telly Savalas	2.00
21	Tyrone Power	2.00
22	William Holden	2.00
23	Leslie Howard	2.00
24	Carole Lombard	2.00
25	Donald O'Connor	2.00
26	Duke Ellington	2.00

Hollywood Legends Directors Cut
NM/M
Production 1-80

| 19 | Redd Foxx/80 | 120.00 |

Hollywood Legends Material
NM/M
Production 25-500

2	Marilyn Monroe/500	30.00
5	Gary Cooper/500	10.00
6	Judy Garland/500	15.00
7	Lou Costello/500	15.00
8	Vivian Leigh/500	10.00
9	Alan Ladd/400	6.00
10	Anthony Quinn/500	6.00
11	Donna Reed/500	10.00
12	Douglas Fairbanks Jr./500	6.00
13	Edward G. Robinson Jr./150	8.00
14	George Raft/60	15.00
16	Hedy Lamarr/50	8.00
16	Johnny Weissmuller/25	30.00
17	Pat Paulsen/250	6.00
18	Pat O'Brien/50	10.00
19	Redd Foxx/50	15.00
20	Telly Savalas/500	8.00
21	Tyrone Power/500	8.00
22	William Holden/250	8.00
23	Leslie Howard/500	8.00
24	Carole Lombard/500	5.00
25	Donald O'Connor/500	8.00

Holly. Legends Mater. Golden Era
NM/M
Production 5-50

1	Burt Lancaster/50	20.00
2	Marilyn Monroe/50	60.00
5	Gary Cooper/50	20.00
6	Judy Garland/50	25.00
7	Lou Costello/50	25.00
8	Vivian Leigh/50	20.00
9	Alan Ladd/50	15.00
10	Anthony Quinn/50	10.00
11	Donna Reed/50	20.00
12	Douglas Fairbanks Jr./50	15.00
13	Edward G. Robinson Jr./50	15.00
15	Hedy Lamarr/50	15.00
17	Pat Paulsen/50	15.00
19	Redd Foxx/50	25.00
20	Telly Savalas/50	15.00
21	Tyrone Power/50	15.00
22	William Holden/50	15.00
23	Leslie Howard/50	15.00
24	Carole Lombard/50	15.00
25	Donald O'Connor/50	15.00

Holly Legends Mat. Silver Screen
NM/M
Production 10-100

1	Burt Lancaster/100	15.00
2	Marilyn Monroe/100	40.00
4	Edward G. Robinson/35	50.00
5	Gary Cooper/100	15.00
6	Judy Garland/100	20.00
7	Lou Costello/100	15.00
8	Vivian Leigh/100	15.00
9	Alan Ladd/100	12.00
10	Anthony Quinn/100	10.00
11	Donna Reed/100	15.00
12	Douglas Fairbanks Jr./100	10.00
13	Edward G. Robinson Jr./100	10.00
15	Hedy Lamarr/100	15.00
17	Pat Paulsen/100	12.00
18	Pat O'Brien/25	25.00
19	Redd Foxx/100	20.00
20	Telly Savalas/100	10.00
21	Tyrone Power/100	10.00
22	William Holden/75	10.00
23	Leslie Howard/100	10.00
24	Carole Lombard/100	10.00
25	Donald O'Connor/100	15.00

Holly. Legends Mater. Super Star
NM/M
Production 1-25

1	Burt Lancaster/25	30.00
2	Marilyn Monroe/25	150.00
6	Lou Costello/25	30.00
8	Vivian Leigh/25	40.00
9	Alan Ladd/25	25.00
11	Donna Reed/25	50.00
12	Douglas Fairbanks Jr./25	20.00
13	Edward G. Robinson Jr./25	30.00
20	Telly Savalas/25	30.00
21	Tyrone Power/25	30.00
22	William Holden/25	30.00
24	Carole Lombard/25	30.00
25	Donald O'Connor/25	30.00

Hollywood Letter Patch Autos.
NM/M
Production 9-46

1	Richard Dreyfuss/45	60.00
2	Elijah Wood/46	40.00
3	John Cusack/45	40.00
4	Jackie Chan/45	150.00
5	Lauren Bacall/45	80.00
6	Kurt Russell/45	65.00
7	Goldie Hawn/45	60.00
8	Vicki Lawrence/44	65.00
9	Jane Russell/42	65.00
10	James Caan/45	60.00

Movie Posters Materials
NM/M
Production 40-500

1	Orson Welles/500	15.00
2	Marlon Brando/500	30.00
3	William Holden/40	40.00
4	Bette Davis/500	20.00
5	Humphrey Bogart/250	20.00
6	Henry Fonda/500	15.00
7	Humphrey Bogart/250	20.00
8	Jimmy Stewart/250	15.00
9	Humphrey Bogart/500	20.00
10	Gary Cooper/500	15.00
11	Clark Gable/125	30.00
12	Cary Grant/500	20.00
13	Lillian Gish/500	15.00
14	Vivian Leigh/500	20.00
15	Cary Grant/500	20.00
17	Burt Lancaster/50	25.00
18	James Dean/75	35.00
19	Frank Sinatra/500	20.00
20	Charlie Chaplin/500	15.00
21	William Holden/40	40.00
22	Charlie Chaplin/500	15.00
23	Edward G. Robinson/50	40.00
24	Montgomery Clift/250	20.00
25	Jack Lemmon/500	20.00
26	John Wayne/500	15.00
27	Katherine Hepburn/500	15.00
28	Spencer Tracy/500	15.00
29	James Cagney/500	20.00
32	Henry Fonda/500	15.00
33	Fred Astaire/500	15.00
34	Katherine Hepburn/500	15.00
35	Spencer Tracy/500	15.00
36	Cary Grant/500	20.00
37	Cary Grant/500	20.00
38	Cary Grant/500	20.00
39	Cary Grant/500	20.00
41	Bette Davis/500	20.00
43	Greta Garbo/500	20.00
44	Jane Russell/500	20.00
45	Spencer Tracy/500	15.00
46	Marlene Dietrich/500	15.00
47	Fred Astaire/500	15.00
48	Gary Cooper/500	15.00
50	Greer Garson/500	20.00
52	John Wayne/500	25.00
54	Ginger Rogers/500	25.00
55	Mae West/500	20.00
56	Shirley Temple/500	40.00
57	Burt Lancaster/500	25.00
58	Humphrey Bogart/500	20.00
63	Katherine Hepburn/500	15.00
64	Gary Cooper/500	15.00
65	Marilyn Monroe/500	20.00

Movie Posters Combo Materials
NM/M
Production 10-500

1	Orson Welles, Agnes Moorehead/500	15.00
3	William Holden, Gloria Swanson/40	30.00
5	Katherine Hepburn, Humphrey Bogart/250	30.00
7	Humphrey Bogart, Mary Astor/250	35.00
11	Gary Cooper, Grace Kelly/500	15.00
12	Claudette Colbert, Clark Gable/125	40.00
13	Cary Grant, James Mason/500	25.00
15	Marlon Brando, Vivian Leigh/500	20.00
16	Cary Grant, Katherine Hepburn/500	20.00
17	Burt Lancaster, Montgomery Clift/50	35.00
18	James Dean, Natalie Wood/60	60.00
19	Janet Leigh, Frank Sinatra/500	20.00
21	Ernest Borgnine, William Holden/40	50.00
22	Charlie Chaplin, Claudette Colbert/500	20.00
24	Elizabeth Taylor, Montgomery Clift/250	20.00
26	John Wayne, Natalie Wood/500	30.00
27	Katherine Hepburn, Cary Grant/500	20.00
28	Katherine Hepburn, Spencer Tracy/500	20.00
31	Elizabeth Taylor, Richard Burton/500	20.00
33	Ginger Rogers, Fred Astaire/500	20.00
34	Ginger Rogers, Katherine Hepburn/500	15.00
35	Spencer Tracy, Katherine Hepburn/500	20.00
36	Cary Grant, Ingrid Bergman/500	20.00
37	Cary Grant, Rosalind Russell/500	25.00
38	Grace Kelly, Cary Grant/500	20.00
39	Cary Grant, Loretta Young/500	20.00
40	Bette Davis, Leslie Howard/250	20.00
41	Henry Fonda, Bette Davis/500	20.00
42	Katherine Hepburn, Gregory Peck/500	25.00
43	Greta Garbo, Joan Crawford/500	35.00
44	Marilyn Monroe, Jane Russell/500	35.00
45	Spencer Tracy, Mickey Rooney/500	20.00
49	Mickey Rooney, Elizabeth Taylor/500	20.00
51	Gary Cooper, Barbara Stanwyck/500	20.00
52	Barbara Stanwyck, Henry Fonda/500	40.00
61	Shelly Winters, Robert Mitchum/500	15.00
64	Gary Cooper, Teresa Wright/500	20.00

Movie Posters Quad Material
NM/M
Production 100

| 17 | Burt Lancaster, Montgomery Clift, Deborah Kerr, Donna Reed/50 | 50.00 |

Movie Posters Triple Material
NM/M
Production 15-100

16	Cary Grant, Katherine Hepburn, Jimmy Stewart/250	35.00
17	Burt Lancaster, Montgomery Clift, Deborah Kerr/50	30.00
18	James Dean, Natalie Wood, Sal Mineo/50	60.00
24	Montgomery Clift, Elizabeth Taylor, Shelly Winters/100	35.00
34	Katherine Hepburn, Ginger Rogers, Lucille Ball/500	25.00
40	Leslie Howard, Bette Davis, Humphrey Bogart/50	65.00
61	Robert Mitchum, Shelly Winters, Lillian Gish/500	20.00

Private Signings
NM/M
Production 10-466

1	Jackie Chan/50	125.00
2	Patrick Stewart/40	50.00
3	Marcia Gay Harden/50	20.00
5	Joseph Lawrence/25	25.00
6	Randal Kleiser/50	10.00
7	Sofia Milos/50	20.00
8	Charlene Tilton/55	20.00
9	Elena Verdugo/50	12.00
10	Annette Charles/50	15.00
11	Barry Pearl/50	10.00
12	Edd Byrnes/50	15.00
13	Jeffrey Tambor/50	20.00
14	Eddie Deezen/250	10.00
15	Lawrence Hilton-Jacobs/250	8.00
16	Robert Hegyes/250	8.00
17	Ron Palillo/250	12.00
18	Tab Hunter/56	20.00
19	Patty Duke/50	35.00
20	John Cusack/20	50.00
21	Ralph Macchio/50	35.00
22	Connie Britton/250	15.00
23	Barry Watson/50	8.00
24	John Kerr/50	10.00
25	Gary Sinise/54	40.00
26	Diane Farr/50	25.00
27	Lauren Bacall/43	50.00
28	Steve Kanaly/281	12.00
29	Ty Hardin/50	10.00
30	Lorna Luft/50	20.00
31	Dylan McDermott/80	15.00
32	Fred Willard/466	12.00
33	Gerald Okamura/415	6.00
34	Alessandro Nivola/372	8.00
35	Marc McClure/50	10.00
36	David Ladd/50	8.00
38	Vicki Lawrence/62	10.00
39	Jordan Ladd/50	20.00
40	Bridgette Wilson-Sampras/50	20.00
41	Natalie Zea/325	10.00
42	Malcolm McDowell/87	25.00
43	John C. McGinley/50	20.00
44	Stephen Baldwin/50	15.00
46	Nadine Velazquez/50	35.00
47	Charlie Daniels/50	40.00
48	Tracy Lawrence/50	20.00
49	Michael Beck/256	8.00
49	Denzel Whitaker/50	10.00
51	Francesco Quinn/50	10.00
52	Jon Provost/50	15.00
53	George A. Romero/50	30.00
53	Daniel Baldwin/50	15.00
55	Debi Mazar/50	20.00
55	Robert Vaughn/50	35.00
56	Brigitte Nielsen/250	15.00
57	Geoff Stults/428	8.00
58	James Duval/50	10.00
59	Michael Boatman/406	10.00
60	Barry Williams/50	15.00
61	Peter Graves/44	30.00
62	Chazz Palminteri/50	25.00
63	Elijah Wood/50	30.00
64	Emily Procter/50	40.00
65	Yancy Butler/106	20.00
66	Olesya Rulin/50	20.00
67	Meredith Salenger/50	30.00
68	Micky Dolenz/56	30.00
69	Barry Bostwick/50	15.00
70	Albert Brooks/50	20.00
71	Tony Todd/50	10.00
72	Anson Williams/50	10.00
73	Deborah Shelton/250	10.00
74	Corbin Bleu/250	20.00
75	Marisol Nichols/50	20.00
76	Erin Moran/50	30.00
77	Taryn Manning/50	15.00
78	Ami Dolenz/50	25.00
79	Niecy Nash/50	15.00
80	Paul Le Mat/50	10.00
81	Swoosie Kurtz/50	15.00
82	Alan Ruck/50	20.00
83	Daniel Logan/250	8.00
84	Aaron Tippin/50	10.00
86	Dean McDermott/145	10.00
87	Eric Roberts/50	15.00
88	Erin Gray/50	40.00
89	Irvin Kershner/104	30.00
90	James Caan/50	50.00
91	Jamie Donnelly/50	15.00
92	Jill-Michele Melean/50	10.00
93	Luke Goss/50	20.00
94	Marton Csokas/50	10.00
95	Peter Brown/50	10.00
96	Piper Laurie/50	15.00
97	Teddy Gentry/50	25.00
98	Tori Spelling/73	30.00
99	William Forsythe/53	20.00
100	Julia Louis-Dreyfus/50	50.00

Stars Material Gold Proof
NM/M
Production 1-25

Stars Material Silver Proof
NM/M
Production 5-100

1	Jackie Chan/100	20.00
2	Patrick Stewart/100	15.00
3	Marcia Gay Harden/50	5.00
5	Joseph Lawrence/50	8.00
7	Charlene Tilton/100	6.00
9	Elena Verdugo/50	4.00
11	Barry Pearl/50	4.00
14	Eddie Deezen/50	4.00
15	Lawrence Hilton-Jacobs/100	8.00
16	Robert Hegyes/100	4.00
17	Ron Palillo/100	4.00
18	Tab Hunter/100	15.00
20	John Cusack/100	10.00
22	Connie Britton/100	6.00
23	Barry Watson/50	4.00
24	John Kerr/100	6.00
26	Diane Farr/100	6.00
27	Lauren Bacall/100	15.00
28	Steve Kanaly/100	6.00
29	Ty Hardin/50	6.00
33	Gerald Okamura/100	4.00
34	Alessandro Nivola/100	4.00
36	David Ladd/100	4.00
37	John Buccigross/100	4.00
38	Vicki Lawrence/100	6.00
40	Bridgette Wilson-Sampras/100	6.00
41	Natalie Zea/100	6.00
42	Malcolm McDowell/100	8.00
44	Stephen Baldwin/100	8.00
46	Charlie Daniels/100	8.00
47	Tracy Lawrence/100	4.00
48	Michael Beck/100	4.00
49	Denzel Whitaker/100	4.00
50	Francesco Quinn/100	4.00
51	Jon Provost/100	4.00
52	George A. Romero/100	10.00
53	Daniel Baldwin/100	6.00
54	Debi Mazar/100	6.00
55	Robert Vaughn/50	6.00
56	Brigitte Nielsen/100	8.00
57	Geoff Stults/100	4.00
58	James Duval/100	4.00
60	Barry Williams/100	4.00
61	Peter Graves/100	6.00
63	Elijah Wood/100	10.00
64	Emily Procter/100	4.00
66	Olesya Rulin/100	6.00
67	Meredith Salenger/100	8.00
68	Micky Dolenz/100	8.00
70	Albert Brooks/100	4.00
71	Tony Todd/100	4.00
72	Anson Williams/100	8.00
75	Marisol Nichols/50	6.00
77	Taryn Manning/100	6.00
78	Ami Dolenz/100	6.00
80	Paul Le Mat/100	4.00
81	Swoosie Kurtz/100	4.00
83	Daniel Logan/100	4.00
84	Aaron Tippin/100	6.00
85	David Carradine/100	15.00
86	Dean McDermott/100	4.00
94	Marton Csokas/50	4.00
95	Piper Laurie/100	4.00
96	Piper Laurie/100	4.00
99	William Forsythe/100	6.00
100	Julia Louis-Dreyfus/100	10.00

Stars Signature Materials
NM/M
Production 25-100

1	Jackie Chan/100	140.00
2	Patrick Stewart/100	50.00
3	Marcia Gay Harden/100	15.00
4	Michael Madsen/25	25.00
5	Joseph Lawrence/25	25.00
7	Sofia Milos/50	20.00
8	Charlene Tilton/100	20.00
9	Elena Verdugo/50	15.00
14	Eddie Deezen/25	15.00
15	Lawrence Hilton-Jacobs/100	10.00
16	Robert Hegyes/100	10.00
17	Ron Palillo/100	15.00
18	Tab Hunter/100	15.00
20	John Cusack/50	50.00
22	Connie Britton/100	20.00
23	Barry Watson/50	8.00
24	John Kerr/100	15.00
25	Gary Sinise/25	50.00
26	Diane Farr/50	25.00
27	Lauren Bacall/50	60.00
28	Steve Kanaly/50	15.00
29	Ty Hardin/50	10.00
33	Gerald Okamura/100	10.00
34	Alessandro Nivola/100	10.00
36	David Ladd/50	8.00
37	John Buccigross/250	8.00
38	Vicki Lawrence/100	15.00
39	Jordan Ladd/25	25.00
40	Bridgette Wilson-Sampras/100	20.00
41	Natalie Zea/100	20.00
42	Malcolm McDowell/100	30.00
44	Stephen Baldwin/100	30.00
45	Nadine Velazquez/50	30.00
46	Charlie Daniels/100	35.00
47	Tracy Lawrence/100	15.00
48	Michael Beck/50	10.00
49	Denzel Whitaker/100	15.00
50	Francesco Quinn/100	15.00
51	Jon Provost/100	15.00
52	George A. Romero/100	35.00
53	Daniel Baldwin/100	15.00
54	Debi Mazar/100	30.00
55	Robert Vaughn/100	30.00
56	Brigitte Nielsen/100	15.00
57	Geoff Stults/100	8.00
58	James Duval/100	15.00
60	Barry Williams/100	15.00
61	Peter Graves/100	25.00
62	Chazz Palminteri/20	30.00
63	Elijah Wood/50	45.00
64	Emily Procter/100	25.00
65	Yancy Butler/50	25.00
66	Olesya Rulin/100	40.00
67	Meredith Salenger/100	40.00
68	Micky Dolenz/50	30.00
70	Albert Brooks/50	20.00
71	Tony Todd/50	10.00
72	Anson Williams/100	20.00
73	Deborah Shelton/100	15.00
74	Corbin Bleu/50	20.00

75	Marisol Nichols/100	20.00
77	Taryn Manning/100	15.00
78	Ami Dolenz/100	25.00
80	Paul Le Mat/100	15.00
81	Swoosie Kurtz/100	15.00
83	Daniel Logan/100	10.00
84	Aaron Tippin/250	10.00
85	David Carradine/100	75.00
86	Dean McDermott/50	
87	Eric Roberts/50	20.00
92	Jill-Michele Melean/ 100	15.00
94	Marton Csokas/50	15.00
95	Peter Brown/100	8.00
96	Piper Laurie/100	15.00
98	Tori Spelling/100	35.00
99	William Forsythe/100	20.00
100	Julia Louis-Dreyfus/ 100	60.00

TV Stars

		NM/M
Common Card:		2.00
Production 1,000 Sets		
1	Joey Lawrence	2.00
2	Sofia Milos	2.00
3	Charlene Tilton	2.00
4	Elena Verdugo	2.00
5	Patrick Stewart	3.00
6	Yancy Butler	2.00
7	Peter Graves	2.00
8	Nadine Velazquez	2.00
9	Jon Provost	2.00
10	Barry Watson	2.00
11	Patty Duke	2.00
12	John C. McGinley	2.00
13	Robert Vaughn	2.00
14	Barbara Eden	3.00
15	Ty Hardin	2.00
16	Ricardo Montalban	3.00
17	Micky Dolenz	2.00
18	Vicki Lawrence	2.00
19	Dylan McDermott	2.00
21	Tori Spelling	2.00
22	James Caan	3.00
23	Jill-Michele Melean	2.00
	Dean McDermott	2.00

TV Stars Signature

		NM/M
Production 25-50		
1	Joey Lawrence/25	25.00
2	Sofia Milos/25	20.00
3	Charlene Tilton/25	15.00
4	Elena Verdugo/25	15.00
5	Patrick Stewart/25	50.00
6	Yancy Butler/25	20.00
7	Peter Graves/25	30.00
8	Nadine Velazquez/25	15.00
9	Jon Provost/25	10.00
10	Barry Watson/25	10.00
11	Patty Duke/50	35.00
12	John C. McGinley/50	10.00
13	Robert Vaughn/25	30.00
14	Barbara Eden/50	40.00
15	Ty Hardin/25	10.00
16	Ricardo Montalban/30	75.00
17	Micky Dolenz/25	35.00
18	Vicki Lawrence/25	10.00
19	Dylan McDermott/50	15.00
20	Tori Spelling/25	30.00
21	James Caan/50	50.00
22	Jill-Michele Melean/25	15.00
23	Dean McDermott/25	15.00

TV Stars Signature Directors Cut

		NM/M
Production 10-60		
1	Joey Lawrence/40	15.00
2	Joey Lawrence/20	20.00
3	Charlene Tilton/60	20.00
4	Elena Verdugo/39	15.00
5	Patrick Stewart/25	60.00
6	Yancy Butler/40	25.00
7	Patty Duke/40	35.00
8	Micky Dolenz/20	50.00
22	Jill-Michele Melean/40	10.00

TV Stars Signature Material

		NM/M
Production 3-100		
1	Joey Lawrence/25	25.00
2	Sofia Milos/100	20.00
3	Charlene Tilton/100	15.00
4	Elena Verdugo/50	12.00
5	Patrick Stewart/100	10.00
6	Yancy Butler/75	20.00
7	Peter Graves/50	30.00
8	Nadine Velazquez/50	30.00
9	Jon Provost/100	8.00
10	Barry Watson/100	30.00
13	Robert Vaughn/100	30.00
15	Ty Hardin/100	10.00
17	Micky Dolenz/100	35.00
19	Vicki Lawrence/100	10.00
21	Tori Spelling/100	30.00
22	Jill-Michele Melean/ 100	15.00
23	Dean McDermott/50	15.00

TV Stars Material Big Screen

		NM/M
Production 1-50		
2	Joey Lawrence/25	8.00
3	Charlene Tilton/25	8.00
4	Elena Verdugo/50	5.00
5	Patrick Stewart/50	15.00

10	Barry Watson/50	6.00
17	Micky Dolenz/50	15.00
18	Vicki Lawrence/50	10.00
20	Tori Spelling/25	10.00
22	Jill-Michele Melean/25	6.00
23	Dean McDermott/45	6.00

TV Stars Material Small Screen

		NM/M
Production 25-500		
1	Joey Lawrence/100	6.00
3	Charlene Tilton/150	5.00
4	Elena Verdugo/150	4.00
5	Patrick Stewart/100	10.00
7	Peter Graves/500	5.00
9	Jon Provost/25	15.00
10	Barry Watson/250	4.00
13	Robert Vaughn/25	6.00
15	Ty Hardin/25	4.00
17	Micky Dolenz/250	8.00
18	Vicki Lawrence/500	6.00
20	Tori Spelling/50	5.00
22	Jill-Michele Melean/100	4.00
23	Dean McDermott/250	4.00

2009 Donruss Elite Extra Edition

Common Player (1-50):		.25
Common Auto. (51-150):		8.00
Pack (5):		5.00
Box (20):		90.00
1	Bobby Borchering	.50
2	Blake Smith	.25
3	Drew Storen	.50
4	J.R. Murphy	.25
5	Zack Wheeler	.50
6	Nolan Arenado	.25
7	Matt Bashore	.25
8	Josh Phegley	.25
9	Jacob Turner	.25
10	Mike Leake	.25
11	Kelly Dugan	.25
12	Bill Bullock	.25
13	Shelby Miller	.25
14	Alex Wilson	.25
16	Max Stassi	.75
17	Aaron Miller	.25
18	A.J. Pollock	.25
19	Brooks Pounders	.50
20	Shaver Hansen	.25
21	Tyler Skaggs	.50
22	Jiovanni Mier	.50
23	Everett Williams	.25
24	Rich Poythress	.25
25	Chad Jenkins	.25
26	Rey Fuentes	.25
27	Ryan Jackson	.25
28	Eric Arnett	.50
29	Chris Owings	.25
30	Garrett Gould	.25
31	Tyler Matzek	.50
32	Donnie Joseph	.25
33	Brandon Belt	.25
34	Jon Gaston	.25
35	Tracye Thompson	.25
36	Marc Krauss	.25
37	Kyrell Hudson	.75
38	Ben Tootle	.25
39	Jake Marisnick	.25
40	Aaron Baker	.25
41	Kent Matthes	.25
42	Andrew Oliver	.25
43	Cameron Garfield	.25
44	Adam Warren	.25
45	Dustin Dickerson	.75
46	James Jones	.25
47	Brooks Raley	.25
48	Jenrry Mejia	.50
49	Brock Holt	.25
50	Wes Hatton	.25
51	Dustin Ackley/ Auto./899	50.00
52	Donavan Tate/ Auto./999	30.00
53	Tony Sanchez/ Auto./435	20.00
54	Matt Hobgood/ Auto./681	15.00
55	Alex White/Auto./599	15.00
56	Jared Mitchell/ Auto./370	30.00
57	Mike Trout/Auto./495	30.00
58	Brett Jackson/ Auto./534	25.00
59	Mike Minor/Auto./570	15.00
60	Slade Heathcott/ Auto./754	25.00
61	Tom Mendonca/ Auto./569	15.00
62	Wil Myers/Auto./799	15.00
63	Jason Kipnis/Auto./319	15.00
64	Robert Stock/ Auto./569	15.00
65	Tim Wheeler/Auto./794	15.00
66	Mychal Givens/ Auto./794	15.00
67	Grant Green/Auto./444	20.00
68	D.J. LeMahieu/ Auto./645	15.00
69	Rex Brothers/Auto./699	8.00
70	Thomas Joseph/ Auto./99	15.00
71	Wade Gaynor/Auto./730	10.00
72	Ryan Wheeler/ Auto./690	15.00
73	Kyle Heckathorn/ Auto./599	15.00
74	Chad James/Auto./99	20.00

75	Victor Black/Auto./694	12.00
76	Todd Glaesmann/ Auto./494	12.00
77	Tyler Kehrer/Auto./99	25.00
78	Steve Baron/Auto./700	8.00
79	Matt Davidson/ Auto./599	10.00
80	Jeff Kobernus/ Auto./570	10.00
81	Kentrail Davis/ Auto./655	15.00
82	Kyle Gibson/Auto./645	20.00
83	Garrett Richards/ Auto./470	10.00
84	Brad Boxberger/ Auto./550	10.00
85	Evan Chambers/ Auto./695	8.00
86	Telvin Nash/Auto./725	10.00
87	Austin Kirk/Auto./599	10.00
88	Marquise Cooper/ Auto./99	30.00
89	Jason Christian/ Auto./730	8.00
90	Randal Grichuk/ Auto./770	15.00
91	Nick Franklin/ Auto./724	10.00
92	Eric Smith/Auto./99	25.00
93	Jeremy Hazelbaker/ Auto./640	15.00
94	Zach Dotson/Auto./699	8.00
95	Josh Fellhauer/ Auto./494	10.00
96	Jeff Malm/Auto./650	10.00
97	Caleb Cotham/ Auto./549	12.00
98	Trevor Holder/ Auto./649	8.00
99	Joe Kelly/Auto./690	10.00
100	Robbie Shields/ Auto./749	8.00
101	Kyle Bellamy/Auto./695	8.00
102	Braxton Lane/Auto./710	8.00
103	Justin Marks/Auto./99	15.00
104	Ryan Goins/Auto./599	8.00
105	Chase Anderson/ Auto./619	8.00
106	Kyle Seager/Auto./744	8.00
107	Colton Cain/Auto./99	40.00
108	David Renfroe/ Auto./695	20.00
109	Travis Banwart/ Auto./645	8.00
110	Joe Testa/Auto./699	8.00
111	Brandon Jacobs/ Auto./725	8.00
112	Brett Brach/Auto./699	8.00
113	Brad Brach/Auto./695	8.00
114	Keon Broxton/Auto./675	8.00
115	Nathan Karns/Auto./734	8.00
116	Kendal Volz/Auto./695	8.00
117	Charles Ruiz/Auto./594	8.00
118	Mike Spina/Auto./580	8.00
119	Jamie Johnson/ Auto./619	8.00
120	Bryan Mitchell/ Auto./699	10.00
121	Chad Bell/Auto./744	8.00
122	Dan Taylor/Auto./650	8.00
123	Khris Davis/Auto./150	15.00
124	Ashur Tolliver/ Auto./730	8.00
125	Cody Rogers/Auto./690	8.00
126	Trent Stevenson/ Auto./744	8.00
127	Dean Weaver/Auto./599	8.00
128	Matt Helm/Auto./790	15.00
129	Andrew Doyle/Auto./640	8.00
130	Matt Graham/Auto./690	8.00
131	Kevan Hess/Auto./719	8.00
132	Luke Bailey/Auto./475	8.00
133	Steve Matz/Auto./790	10.00
134	Tanner Bushue/ Auto./652	10.00
135	Neil Medchill/ Auto./710	15.00
136	Edward Paredes/ Auto./725	8.00
137	A.J. Jimenez/Auto./695	8.00
138	Grant Desme/Auto./744	10.00
139	Zack Von Rosenberg/ Auto./710	10.00
140	Daniel Fields Auto/749	15.00
141	Graham Stoneburner/ Auto./719	8.00
142	David Holmberg/ Auto./719	8.00
143	Chris Dominguez/ Auto./719	15.00
144	Luke Murton/Auto./750	10.00
145	Danny Rosenbaum/ Auto./695	8.00
146	Tyler Townsend/ Auto./99	25.00
147	Louis Coleman/ Auto./99	8.00
148	Patrick Schuster/ Auto./695	8.00
149	Jeff Hunt/Auto./99	25.00
150	Aroldis Chapman/ Auto./695	60.00

Aspirations

Aspirations (1-50):		4-8X
Aspirations (51-150):		.15-.25
Common Aspir.:		2.00
Production 150 Sets		
StatusStatus (1-50):		6-10X
Status (51-150):		.20-.30
Production 100 Sets		
Status Gold		
Gold (1-50):		6-12X
Gold (51-150):		.25-.35X
Production 50 Sets		
Back to Back Materials		
Production 35-250		
1	Ike Davis Reggie Jackson/250	15.00
	Jason Kipnis/250	10.00
2	Reggie Jackson/250 Robbie Grossman	10.00
3	Quincy Latimore/250	8.00
4	Buster Posey Will Clark/35	35.00

Back to the Future Autographs

Production 1-99		
1	Allan Dykstra/99	8.00
2	Alan Horne/99	8.00
3	Jim Palmer/49	20.00
4	Andrew Cashner/99	10.00
5	Andrew Lambo/99	15.00
6	Anthony Hewitt/99	8.00
8	Brandon Crawford/99	8.00
9	Brett Hunter/99	8.00
10	Bryan Price/99	8.00
11	Buster Posey/99	35.00
12	Chase D'Arnaud/99	8.00
14	Christian Friedrich/99	10.00
16	Dwight Gooden/99	15.00
18	Evan Frederickson/99	8.00
19	Mark Fidrych/49	30.00
20	George Brett/99	60.00
22	Ike Davis/99	15.00
23	Jason Knapp/99	8.00
26	Logan Schafer/99	8.00
27	Michael Ynoa/99	8.00
28	Mike Cisco/50	8.00
32	Pete Rose/99	75.00
33	Rafael Rodriguez/99	8.00
35	Robin Yount/49	40.00
37	Steve Garvey/50	25.00
39	Zach McAllister/99	8.00
40	Zeke Spruill/99	8.00

College Ties Autographs

Production 4-50		
1	Dustin Ackley Alex White/50 Mike Leake	50.00
2	Jason Kipnis/50 Mike Minor	20.00
3	Caleb Cotham/50 Jason Kipnis Ike Davis/50	20.00
4	Brad Boxberger Robert Stock/50	15.00
7	Chase Anderson Aaron Baker/50 Shaver Hansen	15.00
	Dustin Dickerson/50 Kendal Volz	
	Aaron Miller/50 Robert Stock	15.00
11	Grant Green/50 Chad Jenkins Kyle Heckathorn/50	30.00
13	Eric Arnett Josh Phegley/50	25.00
14	Matt Bashore Josh Phegley/25	15.00
16	Victor Black Ryan Goins/50	8.00
17	Brett Jackson Jeff Kobernus/25	25.00
18	Brett Jackson Blake Smith/50	10.00
19	Trevor Holder Rich Poythress/50	10.00

College Ties Green

Common Duo:		1.50
Gold:		1-2X
Production 100 Sets		
Red:		2-3X
Production 25 Sets		
1	Dustin Ackley Alex White Mike Leake	4.00
2	Jason Kipnis Mike Minor Caleb Cotham	3.00
3	Jason Kipnis Ike Davis	2.00
5	Brad Boxberger Robert Stock Garrett Richards	
6	Jamie Johnson Chase Anderson Aaron Baker	1.50
7	Shaver Hansen Dustin Dickerson Kendal Volz	1.50
8	Aaron Miller Brooks Raley Jose Duran	2.00
11	Robert Stock Grant Green	3.00
12	Chad Jenkins Kyle Heckathorn	1.50

13	Eric Arnett	
	Josh Phegley	2.50
14	Matt Bashore Josh Phegley	1.50
15	Jared Mitchell D.J. LeMahieu	
16	Victor Black Ryan Goins	2.00
17	Brett Jackson Jeff Kobernus Brett Jackson	3.00
18	Blake Smith	2.50
19	Trevor Holder Rich Poythress	1.50
20	Jordan Danks Brandon Belt	2.00

College Ties Jerseys

Production 250 Sets		
Prime:		No Pricing
Production 12-25		
7	Chase Anderson Aaron Baker	8.00
10	Brooks Raley Jose Duran	8.00

Collegiate Patch Autographs

Production 104-125		
1	Dustin Ackley/118	125.00
2	Tony Sanchez/125	30.00
3	Mike Minor/125	40.00
4	Mike Leake/125	30.00
5	Drew Storen/125	25.00
6	Grant Green/125	25.00
7	Alex White/124	35.00
8	A.J. Pollock/123	20.00
9	Jared Mitchell/125	10.00
10	Eric Arnett/125	20.00
11	Brett Jackson/125	20.00
12	Aaron Miller/117	10.00
13	Josh Phegley/125	15.00
14	Kentrail Davis/125	15.00
15	Garrett Richards/104	10.00
16	Brad Boxberger/125	15.00
17	Matt Bashore/124	10.00
18	Jeff Kobernus/125	10.00
19	Rich Poythress/124	20.00
21	Blake Smith/125	15.00
22	Andrew Oliver/125	15.00
23	Jason Kipnis/125	15.00
24	Marc Krauss/125	15.00
25	Robert Stock/125	15.00
26	Bill Bullock/125	15.00
27	Alex Wilson/125	15.00
28	D.J. LeMahieu/125	25.00
29	Trevor Holder/125	10.00
30	Donnie Joseph/125	15.00
31	Ben Paulsen/125	15.00
32	Kent Matthes/125	15.00
33	Adam Warren/125	20.00
34	Brandon Belt/125	10.00
35	Ryan Jackson/125	15.00
36	Caleb Cotham/125	20.00
37	Shaver Hansen/124	15.00
38	Josh Fellhauer/125	10.00
39	Jamie Johnson/125	10.00
40	Khris Davis/125	10.00
41	Dustin Dickerson/125	10.00
42	Brock Holt/125	10.00
43	Charles Ruiz/125	10.00
44	Aaron Baker/125	15.00
45	Mike Spina/125	10.00
46	Jim Abbott/125	40.00
47	Fred Lynn/125	15.00
48	John Olerud/125	35.00
49	Robin Ventura/125	10.00

Elite Series

Common Player:		1.00
1	Dustin Ackley	1.00
2	Donavan Tate	3.00
3	Mike Leake	1.00
4	Tony Sanchez	2.00
5	Al Kaline	3.00
6	Mike Minor	1.00
7	A.J. Pollock	1.00
8	Nolan Ryan	6.00
9	Will Clark	1.50
10	Albert Pujols	6.00

Elite Series Autographs

Production 20-199		
1	Dustin Ackley/100	50.00
2	Donavan Tate/199	40.00
3	Mike Leake/100	15.00
4	Tony Sanchez/100	25.00
5	Al Kaline/100	35.00
6	Mike Minor/40	25.00
7	A.J. Pollock/100	15.00
8	Nolan Ryan/50	40.00
9	Will Clark/52	40.00
10	Albert Pujols/30	375.00

Passing the Torch Autographs

Production 5-100		
1	Buster Posey Tony Sanchez/100	30.00

Private Signings

Production 5-250		
2	Al Kaline/20	50.00
3	Bobby Borchering/50	35.00
4	Donavan Tate/245	50.00
6	Drew Storen/100	50.00
7	Dustin Ackley/250	50.00
8	Frank Howard/25	50.00
9	Grant Green/50	25.00
10	Jacob Turner/100	40.00

13	Kyle Gibson/50	40.00
15	Matt Hobgood/100	30.00
16	Mike Leake/50	30.00
18	Mike Minor/50	20.00
20	Slade Heathcott/50	50.00
22	Steve Garvey/20	40.00
23	Tony Sanchez/50	30.00
24	Tyler Matzek/50	50.00
25	Zack Wheeler/100	40.00

School Colors

Common Player:		1.50
1	Dustin Ackley	4.00
2	Grant Green	1.50
3	Mike Leake	2.00
4	Drew Storen	2.00
5	Jared Mitchell	2.00
6	Ryan Jackson	1.50
7	Tom Mendonca	3.00
8	Josh Phegley	2.00
9	A.J. Pollock	1.50
10	Tony Sanchez	3.00
11	Marc Krauss	1.50
12	Garrett Richards	1.50
13	Shaver Hansen	1.50
14	Josh Fellhauer	1.50
15	Brandon Belt	1.50
16	Bill Bullock	1.50
17	Mike Minor	2.50
18	Kent Matthes	1.50
19	Ben Paulsen	1.50
24	Aaron Baker	1.50

School Colors Autographs

Production 20-100		
1	Dustin Ackley/100	50.00
2	Grant Green/100	20.00
3	Mike Leake/100	15.00
4	Drew Storen/100	10.00
5	Jared Mitchell/100	35.00
6	Ryan Jackson/100	10.00
7	Tom Mendonca/100	20.00
9	A.J. Pollock/100	15.00
10	Tony Sanchez/100	10.00
11	Marc Krauss/100	10.00
12	Garrett Richards/100	10.00
13	Shaver Hansen/100	10.00
14	Josh Fellhauer/100	8.00
15	Brandon Belt/100	8.00
16	Bill Bullock/100	10.00
18	Kent Matthes/100	10.00
19	Ben Paulsen/100	10.00
24	Aaron Baker/100	10.00

School Colors Materials

Production 250 Sets		
Prime:		No Pricing
Production 16-25		
5	Jared Mitchell	5.00
13	Shaver Hansen	5.00
16	Bill Bullock	5.00
17	Mike Minor	8.00
20	Aaron Baker	5.00

Signature Aspirations

Production 100 Sets		
1	Bobby Borchering	25.00
2	Blake Smith	15.00
3	Drew Storen	15.00
4	J.R. Murphy	20.00
5	Zack Wheeler	35.00
6	Nolan Arenado	20.00
7	Matt Bashore	15.00
8	Josh Phegley	15.00
9	Jacob Turner	40.00
10	Mike Leake	25.00
11	Kelly Dugan	20.00
12	Bill Bullock	12.00
13	Shelby Miller	30.00
14	Alex Wilson	10.00
15	Ben Paulsen	10.00
16	Max Stassi	15.00
17	A.J. Pollock	20.00
18	Aaron Miller	20.00
19	Brooks Pounders	15.00
20	Shaver Hansen	10.00
21	Tyler Skaggs	15.00
22	Jiovanni Mier	15.00
23	Everett Williams	15.00
25	Chad Jenkins	15.00
26	Ryan Jackson	20.00
28	Eric Arnett	20.00
29	Chris Owings	15.00
30	Garrett Gould	15.00
32	Donnie Joseph	15.00
33	Brandon Belt	15.00
34	Jon Gaston	15.00
35	Tracye Thompson	15.00
36	Marc Krauss	15.00
38	Ben Tootle	8.00
39	Jake Marisnick	15.00
40	Aaron Baker	15.00
41	Kent Matthes	12.00
42	Andrew Oliver	15.00
43	Cameron Garfield	15.00
44	Adam Warren	20.00
45	Dustin Dickerson	8.00
46	Brooks Raley	15.00
48	Jenrry Mejia	40.00
49	Brock Holt	8.00
50	Wes Hatton	15.00
51	Dustin Ackley	100.00
52	Donavan Tate	65.00
53	Tony Sanchez	25.00
54	Matt Hobgood	15.00
55	Alex White	15.00
56	Jared Mitchell	35.00
57	Mike Trout	30.00
58	Brett Jackson	35.00

#	Player	Price
59	Mike Minor	25.00
60	Slade Heathcott	40.00
61	Tom Mendonca	20.00
62	Wil Myers	40.00
63	Jason Kipnis	15.00
64	Robert Stock	25.00
65	Tim Wheeler	15.00
66	Mychal Givens	15.00
67	Grant Green	25.00
68	D.J. LeMahieu	20.00
69	Rex Brothers	10.00
71	Wade Gaynor	15.00
72	Ryan Wheeler	20.00
73	Kyle Heckathorn	15.00
75	Victor Black	12.00
76	Todd Glaesmann	15.00
78	Steve Baron	10.00
79	Matt Davidson	25.00
81	Jeff Kobernus	15.00
82	Kentrail Davis	20.00
82	Kyle Gibson	25.00
83	Garrett Richards	15.00
84	Brad Boxberger	15.00
85	Evan Chambers	8.00
86	Telvin Nash	12.00
87	Austin Kirk	10.00
89	Jason Christian	10.00
90	Randal Grichuk	20.00
91	Nick Franklin	25.00
93	Jeremy Hazelbaker	15.00
94	Zach Dotson	12.00
95	Josh Fellhauer	10.00
96	Jeff Malm	15.00
97	Caleb Cotham	20.00
98	Trevor Holder	8.00
99	Joe Kelly	15.00
100	Robbie Shields	8.00
101	Kyle Bellamy	8.00
102	Braxton Lane	15.00
104	Ryan Goins	8.00
105	Chase Anderson	8.00
106	Kyle Seager	10.00
107	David Renfroe	40.00
109	Travis Banwart	8.00
110	Joe Testa	10.00
111	Brandon Jacobs	15.00
112	Brett Brach	10.00
113	Brad Brach	8.00
114	Keon Broxton	20.00
115	Nathan Karns	8.00
116	Kendal Volz	10.00
117	Charles Ruiz	8.00
118	Mike Spina	15.00
119	Jamie Johnson	8.00
120	Bryan Mitchell	15.00
121	Chad Bell	8.00
122	Dan Taylor	10.00
125	Cody Rogers	15.00
126	Trent Stevenson	10.00
127	Dean Weaver	8.00
128	Matt Helm	20.00
129	Andrew Doyle	10.00
130	Matt Graham	10.00
131	Kevan Hess	10.00
132	Luke Bailey	20.00
133	Steve Matz	25.00
134	Tanner Bushue	15.00
135	Neil Medchill	20.00
136	Edward Paredes	8.00
137	A.J. Jimenez	8.00
138	Grant Desme	10.00
139	Zack Von Rosenberg	15.00
140	Daniel Fields	25.00
141	Graham Stoneburner	20.00
142	David Holmberg	10.00
143	Chris Dominguez	25.00
144	Luke Murton	20.00
145	Danny Rosenbaum	8.00
147	Louis Coleman	8.00
148	Patrick Schuster	10.00
150	Aroldis Chapman	100.00

Signature Status

Production 50 Sets
Black 1 of 1's exist
Gold:
Production 5 Sets   No Pricing

#	Player	Price
1	Bobby Borchering	30.00
2	Blake Smith	15.00
3	Drew Storen	25.00
4	J.R. Murphy	25.00
5	Zack Wheeler	40.00
6	Nolan Arenado	35.00
7	Matt Bashore	15.00
8	Josh Phegley	15.00
9	Jacob Turner	90.00
10	Mike Leake	20.00
11	Kelly Dugan	20.00
12	Bill Bullock	25.00
13	Shelby Miller	40.00
14	Alex Wilson	20.00
15	Ben Paulsen	12.00
16	Max Stassi	20.00
17	A.J. Pollock	25.00
18	Aaron Miller	25.00
19	Brooks Pounders	20.00
20	Shaver Hansen	12.00
21	Tyler Skaggs	20.00
22	Jiovanni Mier	20.00
23	Everett Williams	25.00
24	Chad Jenkins	20.00
25	Ryan Jackson	25.00
27	Eric Arnett	25.00
29	Chris Owings	25.00
30	Garrett Gould	20.00
32	Donnie Joseph	10.00
33	Brandon Belt	12.00
34	Jon Gaston	20.00
35	Tracye Thompson	15.00
36	Marc Krauss	20.00
38	Ben Tootle	10.00
39	Jake Marisnick	30.00
40	Aaron Baker	15.00
41	Kent Matthes	15.00
42	Andrew Oliver	20.00
43	Cameron Garfield	20.00
44	Adam Warren	25.00
45	Dustin Dickerson	12.00
47	Brooks Raley	20.00
48	Jenrry Mejia	60.00
49	Brock Holt	10.00
50	Wes Hatton	15.00
51	Dustin Ackley	150.00
52	Donavan Tate	80.00
53	Tony Sanchez	30.00
54	Matt Hobgood	30.00
55	Alex White	20.00
56	Jared Mitchell	50.00
57	Mike Trout	40.00
58	Brett Jackson	40.00
59	Mike Minor	25.00
60	Slade Heathcott	50.00
61	Tom Mendonca	20.00
62	Wil Myers	50.00
63	Jason Kipnis	20.00
64	Robert Stock	30.00
65	Tim Wheeler	20.00
66	Mychal Givens	20.00
67	Grant Green	40.00
68	D.J. LeMahieu	25.00
71	Rex Brothers	20.00
72	Wade Gaynor	20.00
73	Ryan Wheeler	30.00
74	Kyle Heckathorn	20.00
75	Victor Black	20.00
76	Todd Glaesmann	20.00
78	Steve Baron	20.00
79	Matt Davidson	30.00
80	Jeff Kobernus	20.00
81	Kentrail Davis	35.00
82	Kyle Gibson	40.00
83	Garrett Richards	20.00
84	Brad Boxberger	25.00
85	Evan Chambers	20.00
86	Telvin Nash	15.00
87	Austin Kirk	10.00
89	Jason Christian	10.00
90	Randal Grichuk	25.00
91	Nick Franklin	30.00
93	Jeremy Hazelbaker	15.00
94	Zach Dotson	15.00
95	Josh Fellhauer	20.00
96	Jeff Malm	25.00
97	Caleb Cotham	30.00
99	Trevor Holder	10.00
99	Joe Kelly	15.00
100	Robbie Shields	15.00
101	Kyle Bellamy	15.00
102	Braxton Lane	25.00
104	Ryan Goins	10.00
105	Chase Anderson	10.00
106	Kyle Seager	15.00
108	David Renfroe	60.00
109	Travis Banwart	10.00
110	Joe Testa	10.00
111	Brandon Jacobs	20.00
112	Brett Brach	15.00
113	Brad Brach	10.00
114	Keon Broxton	25.00
115	Nathan Karns	10.00
116	Kendal Volz	20.00
117	Charles Ruiz	10.00
118	Mike Spina	20.00
119	Jamie Johnson	10.00
120	Bryan Mitchell	10.00
121	Chad Bell	10.00
122	Dan Taylor	15.00
125	Cody Rogers	20.00
126	Trent Stevenson	15.00
127	Dean Weaver	10.00
128	Matt Helm	25.00
129	Andrew Doyle	10.00
130	Matt Graham	12.00
131	Kevan Hess	20.00
132	Luke Bailey	30.00
133	Steve Matz	30.00
134	Tanner Bushue	25.00
135	Neil Medchill	30.00
136	Edward Paredes	10.00
137	A.J. Jimenez	10.00
138	Grant Desme	20.00
139	Zack Von Rosenberg	20.00
140	Daniel Fields	35.00
141	Graham Stoneburner	15.00
142	David Holmberg	12.00
143	Chris Dominguez	40.00
144	Luke Murton	15.00
145	Danny Rosenbaum	12.00
147	Louis Coleman	12.00
148	Patrick Schuster	25.00
150	Aroldis Chapman	150.00

Turn of the Century Autos.

Production 10-844

#	Player/Serial	Price
1	Bobby Borchering/799	15.00
2	Blake Smith/794	8.00
3	Drew Storen/519	15.00
4	J.R. Murphy/840	15.00
5	Zack Wheeler/744	15.00
6	Nolan Arenado/844	12.00
7	Matt Bashore/655	8.00
8	Josh Phegley/613	15.00
9	Jacob Turner/799	25.00
10	Mike Leake/356	15.00
11	Kelly Dugan/799	8.00
12	Bill Bullock/370	10.00
13	Shelby Miller/690	20.00
14	Alex Wilson/710	8.00
15	Ben Paulsen/599	8.00
16	Max Stassi/810	15.00
17	A.J. Pollock/499	10.00
18	Aaron Miller/650	10.00
19	Brooks Pounders/844	10.00
20	Shaver Hansen/425	8.00
21	Tyler Skaggs/820	12.00
22	Jiovanni Mier/825	10.00
23	Everett Williams/799	12.00
24	Rich Poythress/150	15.00
25	Chad Jenkins/785	10.00
26	Rey Fuentes/99	30.00
27	Ryan Jackson/558	8.00
28	Eric Arnett/669	10.00
29	Chris Owings/799	10.00
30	Garrett Gould/799	10.00
31	Tyler Matzek/125	35.00
32	Donnie Joseph/699	8.00
33	Brandon Belt/610	10.00
34	Jon Gaston/725	10.00
35	Tracye Thompson/699	10.00
36	Marc Krauss/619	10.00
37	Kyrell Hudson/99	20.00
38	Ben Tootle/825	8.00
39	Jake Marisnick/799	10.00
40	Aaron Baker/359	8.00
41	Kent Matthes/619	10.00
42	Andrew Oliver/710	8.00
43	Cameron Garfield/844	8.00
44	Adam Warren/675	10.00
45	Dustin Dickerson/650	8.00
46	James Jones/99	35.00
47	Brooks Raley/494	8.00
48	Jenrry Mejia/844	20.00
49	Brock Holt/619	8.00
50	Wes Hatton/790	8.00
51	Dustin Ackley/75	75.00
52	Donavan Tate/225	40.00
53	Tony Sanchez/50	30.00
54	Matt Hobgood/75	20.00
55	Alex White/70	15.00
56	Jared Mitchell/40	50.00
57	Mike Trout/149	25.00
58	Brett Jackson/49	10.00
60	Slade Heathcott/40	50.00
61	Tom Mendonca/50	30.00
62	Wil Myers/50	50.00
63	Jason Kipnis/25	30.00
64	Robert Stock/30	30.00
66	Mychal Givens/299	15.00
69	Rex Brothers/100	10.00
71	Wade Gaynor/110	15.00
72	Ryan Wheeler/150	15.00
73	Kyle Heckathorn/99	15.00
75	Victor Black/100	12.00
76	Todd Glaesmann/50	20.00
78	Steve Baron/125	10.00
79	Matt Davidson/125	25.00
82	Jeff Kobernus/99	15.00
81	Kentrail Davis/50	35.00
82	Kyle Gibson/99	15.00
83	Garrett Richards/99	15.00
84	Brad Boxberger/110	15.00
85	Evan Chambers/149	8.00
86	Telvin Nash/99	12.00
87	Austin Kirk/199	10.00
89	Jason Christian/111	10.00
90	Randal Grichuk/204	10.00
91	Nick Franklin/120	25.00
93	Jeremy Hazelbaker/204	10.00
94	Zach Dotson/100	12.00
95	Josh Fellhauer/125	10.00
96	Jeff Malm/149	15.00
97	Caleb Cotham/50	30.00
98	Trevor Holder/100	8.00
99	Joe Kelly/99	15.00
100	Robbie Shields/99	10.00
101	Kyle Bellamy/149	8.00
102	Braxton Lane/125	8.00
104	Ryan Goins/150	8.00
105	Chase Anderson/25	15.00
106	Kyle Seager/100	10.00
108	David Renfroe/149	30.00
109	Travis Banwart/199	10.00
110	Joe Testa/125	10.00
111	Brandon Jacobs/100	12.00
112	Brett Brach/75	12.00
113	Brad Brach/100	8.00
114	Keon Broxton/114	8.00
115	Nathan Karns/110	8.00
116	Kendal Volz/99	10.00
117	Charles Ruiz/125	8.00
118	Mike Spina/115	15.00
119	Jamie Johnson/100	8.00
120	Bryan Mitchell/125	15.00
121	Chad Bell/100	8.00
122	Dan Taylor/175	8.00
125	Cody Rogers/150	12.00
126	Trent Stevenson/100	10.00
127	Dean Weaver/199	8.00
128	Matt Helm/50	25.00
129	Andrew Doyle/155	8.00
130	Matt Graham/150	10.00
131	Kevan Hess/125	8.00
132	Luke Bailey/100	10.00
133	Steve Matz/50	30.00
134	Tanner Bushue/190	10.00
135	Neil Medchill/125	10.00
136	Edward Paredes/110	8.00
137	A.J. Jimenez/149	8.00
138	Grant Desme/100	10.00
139	Zack Von Rosenberg/50	20.00
140	Daniel Fields/90	25.00
141	Graham Stoneburner/125	20.00
142	David Holmberg/110	10.00
143	Chris Dominguez/125	25.00
144	Luke Murton/90	20.00
145	Danny Rosenbaum/149	8.00
147	Louis Coleman/199	8.00
148	Patrick Schuster/149	10.00
150	Aroldis Chapman/149	75.00

Throwback Threads

Production 50-250
Prime: No Pricing
Production 1-10

#	Player/Serial	Price
1	Mike Trout/250	10.00
2	Shelby Miller/250	10.00
3	Mike Minor/250	8.00
4	Jason Kipnis/250	5.00
5	Bill Bullock/250	5.00
8	Jared Mitchell/250	8.00
9	Kyle Russell/250	5.00
10	Jose Duran/250	5.00
11	Buster Posey/149	5.00
14	Pete Rose/250	25.00
16	Robbie Grossman/250	5.00
17	Shaver Hansen/250	5.00
18	Tim Wheeler/250	5.00
19	Josh Vitters/50	5.00
20	Todd Glaesmann/250	5.00
21	Mike Cisco/250	5.00
22	Aaron Baker/250	5.00
23	Chase Anderson/250	5.00
24	Brooks Raley/250	5.00

Throwback Threads Autographs

Production 5-250

#	Player/Serial	Price
1	Mike Trout/100	30.00
2	Shelby Miller/250	25.00
3	Mike Minor/53	20.00
4	Jason Kipnis/100	15.00
5	Bill Bullock/199	5.00
8	Jared Mitchell/149	30.00
11	Buster Posey/25	40.00
14	Pete Rose/149	85.00
20	Todd Glaesmann/250	10.00
21	Mike Cisco/50	10.00
22	Aaron Baker/100	15.00
23	Chase Anderson/100	10.00
24	Brooks Raley/250	10.00

Throwback Threads Prime Autos.

Production 1-50

#	Player/Serial	Price
1	Mike Trout/50	35.00
2	Shelby Miller/50	30.00
3	Mike Minor/25	35.00
5	Bill Bullock/50	8.00
8	Jared Mitchell/50	50.00
20	Todd Glaesmann/50	15.00
23	Chase Anderson/50	15.00
24	Brooks Raley/50	15.00

1986 Dorman's Cheese

Found in specially-marked packages of Dorman's American Cheese Singles, this set consists of 10 two-card panels of baseball superstars. Labeled "Super Star Limited Edition," the panels measure 2" x 1-1/2" and have a perforation line in the center. Fronts have a color photo along with the Dorman's logo and the player's name, team and position. Due to a lack of MLB licensing, all team insignias have been airbrushed from the players' caps. Backs contain brief player statistics. The unnumbered panels and cards are listed here alphabetically by the player on the left.

		NM/M
Complete Panel Set (10):		5.00
Complete Singles Set (20):		4.00
Common Panel:		.50
Common Player:		.20
Panel 1		1.00
(1)	George Brett	.75
(2)	Jack Morris	.20
Panel 2		1.50
(3)	Gary Carter	.40
(4)	Cal Ripken Jr.	1.00
Panel 3		.65
(5)	Dwight Gooden	.20
(6)	Kent Hrbek	.20
Panel 4		1.00
(7)	Rickey Henderson	.40
(8)	Mike Schmidt	.75
Panel 5		.75
(9)	Keith Hernandez	.25
(10)	Dale Murphy	.25
Panel 6		1.00
(11)	Reggie Jackson	.60
(12)	Eddie Murray	.40
Panel 7		1.25
(13)	Don Mattingly	.75
(14)	Ryne Sandberg	.60
Panel 8		1.00
(15)	Willie McGee	.20
(16)	Robin Yount	.40
Panel 9		1.00
(17)	Rick Sutcliffe (Sutcliffe)	.20
(18)	Wade Boggs	.60
Panel 10		1.00
(19)	Dave Winfield	.40
(20)	Jim Rice	.25

1981 Drake's

Producing its first baseball card set since 1950, Drake Bakeries, in conjunction with Topps, issued a 33-card set entitled "Big Hitters." The cards, in standard 2-1/2" x 3-1/2" size, feature 19 American League and 14 National League sluggers. Full-color action photos, containing a facsimile autograph, are positioned in red frames for A.L. players and blue frames for N.L. hitters. The player's name, team, position, and Drake's logo are also on front. Backs, which are similar to the regular 1981 Topps issue, contain the card number, statistical and biographical information, and the Drake's logo.

		NM/M
Complete Set (33):		6.00
Common Player:		.25
1	Carl Yastrzemski	1.50
2	Rod Carew	1.00
3	Pete Rose	3.00
4	Dave Parker	.25
5	George Brett	2.00
6	Eddie Murray	1.00
7	Mike Schmidt	2.00
8	Jim Rice	.50
9	Fred Lynn	.25
10	Reggie Jackson	1.50
11	Steve Garvey	.50
12	Ken Singleton	.25
13	Bill Buckner	.25
14	Dave Winfield	1.00
15	Jack Clark	.25
16	Cecil Cooper	.25
17	Bob Horner	.25
18	George Foster	.25
19	Dave Kingman	.25
20	Cesar Cedeno	.25
21	Joe Charboneau	.75
22	George Hendrick	.25
23	Gary Carter	1.00
24	Al Oliver	.25
25	Bruce Bochte	.25
26	Jerry Mumphrey	.25
27	Steve Kemp	.25
28	Bob Watson	.25
29	John Castino	.25
30	Tony Armas	.25
31	John Mayberry	.25
32	Carlton Fisk	1.00
33	Lee Mazzilli	.25

1982 Drake's

Drake Bakeries produced, in conjunction with Topps, a "2nd Annual Collectors' Edition" in 1982. Thirty-three standard-size cards (2-1/2" x 3-1/2") make up the set. Like the previous year, the set is entitled "Big Hitters" and is comprised of 19 American League players and 14 from the National League. Fronts have a mounted photo appearance and contain a facsimile autograph. The player's name, team, position, and the Drake's logo also are on front. Backs, other than being numbered 1-33 and containing a Drake's copyright line, are identical to the regular 1982 Topps.

		NM/M
Complete Set (33):		5.00
Common Player:		.25
1	Tony Armas	.25
2	Buddy Bell	.25
3	Johnny Bench	.50
4	George Brett	1.00
5	Bill Buckner	.25
6	Rod Carew	.50
7	Gary Carter	.50
8	Jack Clark	.25
9	Cecil Cooper	.25
10	Jose Cruz	.25
11	Dwight Evans	.25
12	Carlton Fisk	.50
13	George Foster	.25
14	Steve Garvey	.40
15	Kirk Gibson	.25
16	Mike Hargrove	.25
17	George Hendrick	.25
18	Bob Horner	.25
19	Reggie Jackson	.75
20	Terry Kennedy	.25
21	Dave Kingman	.25
22	Greg Luzinski	.25
23	Bill Madlock	.25
24	John Mayberry	.25
25	Eddie Murray	.50
26	Graig Nettles	.25
27	Jim Rice	.40
28	Pete Rose	2.00
29	Mike Schmidt	1.00
30	Ken Singleton	.25
31	Dave Winfield	.50
32	Butch Wynegar	.25
33	Richie Zisk	.25

1983 Drake's

Seventeen American League and 16 National League "Big Hitters" make up the 33-card "3rd Annual Collectors' Edition" set issued by Drake Bakeries in 1983. The Topps-produced cards measure 2-1/2" x 3-1/2". Fronts are somewhat similar in design to the previous year's set. Backs are identical to the 1983 Topps regular issue except for being numbered 1-33 and containing a Drake's logo and copyright line.

		NM/M
Complete Set (33):		5.00
Common Player:		.25
1	Don Baylor	.25
2	Bill Buckner	.25
3	Rod Carew	.60
4	Gary Carter	.60
5	Jack Clark	.25
6	Cecil Cooper	.25
7	Dwight Evans	.25
8	George Foster	.25
9	Pedro Guerrero	.25
10	George Hendrick	.25
11	Bob Horner	.25
12	Reggie Jackson	.75
13	Steve Kemp	.25
14	Dave Kingman	.25
15	Bill Madlock	.25
16	Gary Matthews	.25
17	Hal McRae	.25
18	Dale Murphy	.40
19	Eddie Murray	.60
20	Ben Oglivie	.25
21	Al Oliver	.25
22	Jim Rice	.25
23	Cal Ripken, Jr.	3.00
24	Pete Rose	2.00
25	Mike Schmidt	.75
26	Ken Singleton	.25
27	Gorman Thomas	.25
28	Jason Thompson	.25

29	Mookie Wilson	.25
30	Willie Wilson	.25
31	Dave Winfield	.60
32	Carl Yastrzemski	.75
33	Robin Yount	.60

1984 Drake's

For the fourth year in a row, Drake Bakeries issued a 33-card "Big Hitters" set. The 1984 edition, produced again by Topps, includes 17 National League players and 16 from the American League. As in all previous years, card fronts feature the player in a batting pose. Backs are identical to the 1984 Topps regular issue except for being numbered 1-33 and carrying the Drake's logo and copyright line. The cards are the standard 2-1/2" x 3-1/2".

		NM/M
Complete Set (33):		4.00
Common Player:		.25
1	Don Baylor	.25
2	Wade Boggs	.75
3	George Brett	1.00
4	Bill Buckner	.25
5	Rod Carew	.50
6	Gary Carter	.25
7	Ron Cey	.25
8	Cecil Cooper	.25
9	Andre Dawson	.35
10	Steve Garvey	.35
11	Pedro Guerrero	.25
12	George Hendrick	.25
13	Keith Hernandez	.25
14	Bob Horner	.25
15	Reggie Jackson	.75
16	Steve Kemp	.25
17	Ron Kittle	.25
18	Greg Luzinski	.25
19	Fred Lynn	.25
20	Bill Madlock	.25
21	Gary Matthews	.25
22	Dale Murphy	.35
23	Eddie Murray	.50
24	Al Oliver	.25
25	Jim Rice	.25
26	Cal Ripken, Jr.	2.00
27	Pete Rose	1.25
28	Mike Schmidt	1.00
29	Darryl Strawberry	.25
30	Alan Trammell	.25
31	Mookie Wilson	.25
32	Dave Winfield	.50
33	Robin Yount	.50

1985 Drake's

The "5th Annual Collectors' Edition" set produced by Topps for Drake Bakeries consists of 33 "Big Hitters" and 11 "Super Pitchers." The new "Super Pitchers" feature increased the set's size from the usual 33 cards to 44. The 2-1/2" x 3-1/2" cards show the player in a game-action photo. Backs differ from the regular 1985 Topps issue only in that they are numbered 1-44 and carry the Drake's logo.

		NM/M
Complete Set (44):		3.00
Common Player:		.15
1	Tony Armas	.15
2	Harold Baines	.15
3	Don Baylor	.15
4	George Brett	.75
5	Gary Carter	.40
6	Ron Cey	.15
7	Jose Cruz	.15
8	Alvin Davis	.15
9	Chili Davis	.15
10	Dwight Evans	.15
11	Steve Garvey	.25
12	Kirk Gibson	.15
13	Pedro Guerrero	.15
14	Tony Gwynn	.50
15	Keith Hernandez	.15
16	Kent Hrbek	.15
17	Reggie Jackson	.50
18	Gary Matthews	.15
19	Don Mattingly	.75
20	Dale Murphy	.25
21	Eddie Murray	.40
22	Dave Parker	.15
23	Lance Parrish	.15
24	Tim Raines	.15
25	Jim Rice	.25
26	Cal Ripken, Jr.	1.50
27	Juan Samuel	.15
28	Ryne Sandberg	.50
29	Mike Schmidt	.75
30	Darryl Strawberry	.15
31	Alan Trammell	.15
32	Dave Winfield	.40
33	Robin Yount	.40
34	Mike Boddicker	.15
35	Steve Carlton	.40
36	Dwight Gooden	.15
37	Willie Hernandez	.15
38	Mark Langston	.15
39	Dan Quisenberry	.15
40	Dave Righetti	.15
41	Tom Seaver	.40
42	Bob Stanley	.15
43	Rick Sutcliffe	.15
44	Bruce Sutter	.30

1986 Drake's

For the sixth consecutive year, Drake Bakeries issued a baseball card set. The 1986 set was the first in that sequence not produced by Topps. Cards were available only by buying the snack products on whose boxes the cards were printed. Cards, measuring 2-1/2" x 3-1/2", were issued in either two-, three-, or four-card panels. Fourteen panels, consisting of 37 different players, comprise the set. The players who make up the set are tabbed as either "Big Hitters" or "Super Pitchers." Logos of various Drake's products can be found on the panel backs. The value of the set is higher when collected in either panel or complete box form.

		NM/M
Complete Panel Set (14):		20.00
Complete Singles Set (37):		12.00
Common Panel:		1.00
Common Player:		.25
Panel (1)		.75
1	Gary Carter	.40
2	Dwight Evans	.25
Panel (2)		1.00
3	Reggie Jackson	.50
4	Dave Parker	.25
Panel (3)		1.50
5	Rickey Henderson	.40
6	Pedro Guerrero	.25
Panel (4)		.75
7	Don Mattingly	.75
8	Mike Marshall	.25
9	Keith Moreland	.25
Panel (5)		4.00
10	Keith Hernandez	.25
11	Cal Ripken Jr.	2.50
Panel (6)		.50
12	Dale Murphy	.35
13	Jim Rice	.35
Panel (7)		3.00
14	George Brett	.75
15	Tim Raines	.25
Panel (8)		1.50
16	Darryl Strawberry	.25
17	Bill Buckner	.25
Panel (9)		3.00
18	Dave Winfield	.40
19	Ryne Sandberg	.50
20	Steve Balboni	.25
21	Tommy Herr	.25
Panel (10)		3.00
22	Pete Rose	1.50
23	Willie McGee	.25
24	Harold Baines	.25
25	Eddie Murray	.40
Panel (11)		3.00
26	Mike Schmidt	.75
27	Wade Boggs	.50
28	Kirk Gibson	.25
Panel (12)		1.50
29	Bret Saberhagen	.25
30	John Tudor	.25
31	Orel Hershiser	.25
Panel (13)		4.00
32	Ron Guidry	.25
33	Nolan Ryan	2.50
34	Dave Steib	.25
Panel (14)		1.50
35	Dwight Gooden	.25
36	Fernando Valenzuela	.25
37	Tom Browning	.25

1987 Drake's

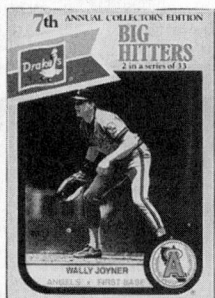

For the seventh consecutive season, Drake Bakeries produced a baseball card set. The 2-1/2" x 3-1/2" cards were printed in either two-, three-, or four-card panels on boxes of various snack products distributed in the eastern U.S. The set is comprised of 33 cards, with 25 players branded as "Big Hitters" and eight as "Super Pitchers." Fronts carry a game-action photo and the Drake's logo surrounded by a brown and yellow border. Backs have the player's complete major league record.

		NM/M
Complete Panel Set (12):		20.00
Complete Singles Set (33):		12.00
Common Panel:		1.50
Common Single Player:		.25
Panel (1)		1.00
1	Darryl Strawberry	.25
2	Wally Joyner	.25
Panel (2)		1.00
3	Von Hayes	.25
4	Jose Canseco	.40
Panel (3)		5.00
5	Dave Winfield	.60
6	Cal Ripken Jr.	2.50
7	Keith Moreland	.25
Panel (4)		2.50
8	Don Mattingly	1.00
9	Willie McGee	.25
Panel (5)		2.00
10	Keith Hernandez	.25
11	Tony Gwynn	.75
Panel (6)		.50
12	Rickey Henderson	.60
13	Dale Murphy	.35
14	George Brett	1.00
15	Jim Rice	.25
Panel (7)		5.00
16	Wade Boggs	.75
17	Kevin Bass	.25
18	Dave Parker	.25
19	Kirby Puckett	.25
Panel (8)		2.00
20	Gary Carter	.60
21	Ryne Sandberg	.75
22	Harold Baines	.25
Panel (9)		1.00
23	Mike Schmidt	1.00
24	Eddie Murray	.60
25	Steve Sax	.25
Panel (10)		1.00
26	Dwight Gooden	.25
27	Jack Morris	.25
Panel (11)		.75
28	Ron Darling	.25
29	Fernando Valenzuela	.25
30	John Tudor	.25
Panel (12)		7.50
31	Roger Clemens	1.00
32	Nolan Ryan	2.50
33	Mike Scott	.25

1988 Drake's

The 8th annual edition of this set includes 33 glossy full-color cards printed on cut-out panels of two, three

DRAKE'S 8TH ANNUAL "BIG HITTERS" & "SUPER PITCHERS" COLLECTORS EDITION BASEBALL CARD SERIES

of four cards on Drake's dessert snack boxes. Card fronts have white borders with a large red and blue "Super Pitchers" (6 cards) or "Big Hitters" (27 cards) caption upper-left, beside the "8th Annual Collector's Edition" label. Backs are printed in black and include the card number, personal data, batting/pitching record and sponsor logos.

		NM/M
Complete Panel Set (12):		20.00
Complete Singles Set (33):		10.00
Common Panel:		1.50
Common Player:		.25
Panel (1)		2.00
1	Don Mattingly	1.00
2	Tim Raines	.25
Panel (2)		1.00
3	Darryl Strawberry	.25
4	Wade Boggs	.75
Panel (3)		6.00
5	Keith Hernandez	.25
6	Mark McGwire	1.50
Panel (4)		3.00
7	Rickey Henderson	.60
8	Mike Schmidt	1.00
9	Dwight Evans	.25
Panel (5)		2.00
10	Gary Carter	.60
11	Paul Molitor	.60
Panel (6)		3.50
12	Dave Winfield	.60
13	Alan Trammell	.25
14	Tony Gwynn	.75
Panel (7)		2.50
15	Dale Murphy	.35
16	Andre Dawson	.35
17	Von Hayes	.25
18	Willie Randolph	.25
Panel (8)		3.50
19	Kirby Puckett	.75
20	Juan Samuel	.25
21	Eddie Murray	.60
Panel (9)		1.00
22	George Bell	.25
23	Larry Sheets	.25
24	Eric Davis	.25
Panel (10)		5.00
25	Cal Ripken Jr.	2.00
26	Pedro Guerrero	.25
27	Will Clark	.25
Panel (11)		1.00
28	Dwight Gooden	.25
29	Frank Viola	.25
Panel (12)		3.00
30	Roger Clemens	1.00
31	Rick Sutcliffe	.25
32	Jack Morris	.25
33	John Tudor	.25

1989 Dubuque Braves

Given away at Sunday home games to correspond with player appearances at a stadium autograph booth, these 2-3/8" x 3-1/2" cards were sponsored by the Braves hot dog concessionaire, Dubuque Meats. Cards have player photos centered within a dark blue border. A Braves cap is at upper-left, the hot dog company's logo at lower-left. The player's name, team and position are in white. Backs, printed in black on white, have the Braves logo, a few personal facts and figures and previous year/career stats. Because only 15,000 of each card were distributed over the course of the season, compilation of complete sets is extremely challenging. The checklist here is arranged in alphabetical order.

		NM/M
Complete Set (33):		40.00
Common Player:		.50
(1)	Paul Assenmacher	.50
(2)	Jim Acker	.50
(3)	Jose Alvarez	.50
(4)	Bruce Benedict	.50
(5)	Geronimo Berroa/SP	8.00
(6)	Jeff Blauser	.50
(7)	Joe Boever	.50
(8)	Marty Clary	.50
(9)	Bruce dal Canton	.50
(10)	Jody Davis	.50
(11)	Mark Eichhorn	.50
(12)	Ron Gant	1.50
(13)	Tom Glavine	5.00
(14)	Tommy Gregg	.50
(15)	Dion James/SP	4.00
(16)	Clarence Jones	.50
(17)	Derek Lilliquist	.50
(18)	Roy Majtyka	.50
(19)	Oddibe McDowell	.50
(20)	Dale Murphy	6.00
(21)	Russ Nixon	.50
(22)	Gerald Perry	.50
(23)	John Russell	.50
(24)	Lonnie Smith	.50
(25)	Pete Smith	.50
(26)	Zane Smith	.50
(27)	John Smoltz	4.00
(28)	Brian Snitker	.50
(29)	Andres Thomas	.50
(30)	Jeff Treadway	.50
(31)	Jeff Wetherby	.50
(32)	Ed Whited	.50
(33)	Bobby Wine	.50

1990 Dubuque Braves

For a second season, the Braves' hot dog vendor, Dubuque Meats, sponsored this season-long promotion. Up to four different player cards were given out at Sunday home games, corresponding with player appearances at an autograph booth. Some player cards were distributed more than once, while others, such as Dale Murphy, who was traded, were only given out one day. Players were added to the set right up through the final Sunday home game of the season. Complete sets are extremely difficult to assemble. The player photo on these 2-3/8" x 3-1/2" cards have a white border. A red banner beneath the photo has the player's name, uniform number and position printed in black. Backs are printed in dark blue and feature full minor and major league stats. The checklist here is arranged alphabetically.

		NM/M
Complete Set (35):		25.00
Common Player:		.50
(1)	Steve Avery	.50
(2)	Jeff Blauser	.50
(3)	Joe Boever	.50
(4)	Francisco Cabrera	.50
(5)	Pat Corrales	.50
(6)	Bobby Cox	.50
(7)	Nick Esasky	.50
(8)	Ron Gant	1.50
(9)	Tom Glavine	4.00
(10)	Mark Grant	.50
(11)	Tommy Gregg	.50
(12)	Dwayne Henry	.50
(13)	Alexis Infante	.50
(14)	Clarence Jones	.50
(15)	Dave Justice	4.50
(16)	Jimmy Kremers	.50
(17)	Charlie Leibrandt	.50
(18)	Mark Lemke	.50
(19)	Roy Majtyka	.50
(20)	Leo Mazzone	.50
(21)	Oddibe McDowell	.50
(22)	Dale Murphy	5.00
(23)	Phil Niekro	3.00
(24)	Greg Olson	.50
(25)	Jim Presley	.50
(26)	Lonnie Smith	.50
(27)	Pete Smith	.50
(28)	John Smoltz	1.50
(29)	Brian Snitker	.50
(30)	Andres Thomas	.50
(31)	Jeff Treadway	.50
(32)	Ernie Whitt	.50
(33)	Jimmy Williams	.50
(34)	Homer the Brave (Mascot)	.50
(35)	Rally (Mascot)	.50

1990 Dubuque Braves Team Photo Set

This three-panel team set was given away at an early-season game, commemorating the Braves 25th season in Atlanta. The sheet measures 11" x 28-1/2". The top panel is a team photo. The two lower panels contain 30 individual cards, 2-1/2" x 3-1/4", perforated to allow them to be separated. Backs are printed in red and blue. The perforated team set is much more common than the Dubuque cards given out a few at a time during Sunday home games. The checklist below is arranged according to uniform numbers which appear on the front of each card.

		NM/M
Complete Panel:		9.00
Common Player:		.25
1	Oddibe McDowell	.25
2	Russ Nixon	.25
3	Dale Murphy	3.00
4	Jeff Blauser	.25
5	Ron Gant	.50
10	Greg Olson	.25
11	Ernie Whitt	.25
14	Andres Thomas	.25
15	Jeff Treadway	.25
16	Tommy Gregg	.25
17	Nick Esasky	.25
18	Jim Presley	.25
19	Francisco Cabrera	.25
21	Mark Lemke	.25
23	Dave Justice	2.00
24	Derek Lilliquist	.25
25	Pete Smith	.25
27	Lonnie Smith	.25
30	John Smoltz	1.00
31	Mike Stanton	.25
32	Tony Castillo	.25
37	Joe Boever	.25
40	Charlie Kerfeld	.25
45	Charlie Leibrandt	.25
46	Dwayne Henry	.25
47	Tom Glavine	1.50
48	Marty Clary	.25
49	Rick Luecken	.25
58a	Joe Hesketh	.25
58b	Alexis Infante	.25

1991 Dubuque Braves

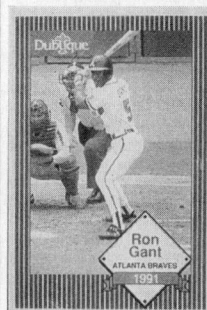

At each Sunday home game the Braves distributed some 15,000 of each of three to six player cards to kids under 14. The cards corresponded to appearances by those players at an autograph session. That method of distribution makes accumulation of complete sets very difficult. Sponsor of the set for the third straight year was the stadium's hot dog concessionaire, Dubuque Meats. Their logo appears in the upper-left corner of the player photo. At lower-right on the 2-1/4" x 3-1/2" cards is a baseball diamond figure with the team and player name and the year of issue. There is a white outer border on the card, with the photo framed in white-pinstriped dark blue. Backs are printed in dark blue, with logos, complete stats, biographical information and the player's uniform number. Cards are checklisted here in alphabetical order.

		NM/M
Complete Set (41):		25.00
Common Player:		.50
(1)	Steve Avery	.50
(2)	Jim Beauchamp	.50
(3)	Mike Bell	.50
(4)	Rafael Belliard	.50
(5)	Juan Berenguer	.50
(6)	Jeff Blauser	.50
(7)	Sid Bream	.50
(8)	Francisco Cabrera	.50
(9)	Jim Clancy	.50
(10)	Pat Corrales	.50
(11)	Bobby Cox	.50
(12)	Nick Esasky	.50
(13)	Marvin Freeman	.50
(14)	Ron Gant	1.00
(15)	Tom Glavine	3.00
(16)	Mark Grant	.50
(17)	Tommy Gregg	.50
(18)	Mike Heath	.50
(19)	Brian Hunter	.50
(20)	Clarence Jones	.50
(21)	David Justice	2.00
(22)	Charlie Leibrandt	.50
(23)	Mark Lemke	.50
(24)	Leo Mazzone	.50
(25)	Kent Mercker	.50
(26)	Keith Mitchell	.50
(27)	Otis Nixon	.50
(28)	Greg Olson	.50
(29)	Jeff Parrett	.50
(30)	Terry Pendleton	.50
(31)	Armando Reynoso	.50
(32)	Deion Sanders	3.00
(33)	Lonnie Smith	.50
(34)	Pete Smith	.50
(35)	John Smoltz	1.50
(36)	Mike Stanton	.50
(37)	Jeff Treadway	.50
(38)	Jimy Williams	.50
(39)	Ned Yost	.50
(40)	Homer the Brave (Mascot)	.50
(41)	Rally (Mascot)	.50

1991 Dubuque Braves Team Photo Set

This team photo/player card triptych was an early season giveaway. Each of the three fold-out panels measures about 9-1/2" x 10-1/2". The 30 individual player cards have perforated edges for easy removal from the sheet. The 2-1/8" x 3-1/8" cards have a player portrait photo at center, with blue diamond designs at the corners. A red box below the photo has the player's name and uniform number. Blue Braves and Dubuque logos appear at the lower corners of the white border. Backs are printed in red and blue and include full stats and a facsimile autograph, plus a few biographical details. The team sheet cards are considered much more common than the other Braves baseball card pro-

		NM/M
Complete Panel:		7.50
Common Player:		.25
2	Luis Rivera	.25
3	Jody Reed	.25
6	Tony Pena	.25
7	Rick Burleson	.25
11	Tim Naehring	.25
12	Ellis Burks	.25
16	Frank Viola	.25
17	Butch Hobson	.25
18	Carlos Quintana	.25
20	John Marzano	.25
21	Roger Clemens	6.00
23	Tom Brunansky	.25
25	Jack Clark	.25
26	Wade Boggs	3.00
27	Greg Harris	.25
29	Phil Plantier	.25
30	Matt Young	.25
32	Gary Allenson	.25
34	Don Zimmer	.25
37	Rich Gale	.25
38	Al Bumbry	.25
39	Mike Greenwell	.25
41	Jeff Reardon	.25
42	Mo Vaughn	.35
43	Kevin Morton	.25
44	Danny Darwin	.25
47	Mike Gardiner	.25
48	Tony Fossas	.25
50	Tom Bolton	.25
55	Joe Hesketh	.25

motional giveaways, especially in complete sets. Cards are checklisted here alphabetically.

		NM/M
Complete Panel:		15.00
Common Player:		.50
(1)	Steve Avery	.50
(2)	Rafael Belliard	.50
(3)	Juan Berenguer	.50
(4)	Jeff Blauser	.50
(5)	Sid Bream	.50
(6)	Francisco Cabrera	.50
(7)	Bobby Cox	.50
(8)	Nick Esasky	.50
(9)	Marvin Freeman	.50
(10)	Ron Gant	.75
(11)	Tom Glavine	3.00
(12)	Mark Grant	.50
(13)	Tommy Gregg	.50
(14)	Mike Heath	.50
(15)	Danny Heep	.50
(16)	David Justice	2.00
(17)	Charlie Leibrandt	.50
(18)	Mark Lemke	.50
(19)	Kent Mercker	.50
(20)	Otis Nixon	.50
(21)	Greg Olson	.50
(22)	Jeff Parrett	.50
(23)	Terry Pendleton	.50
(24)	Deion Sanders	2.00
(25)	Doug Sisk	.50
(26)	Lonnie Smith	.50
(27)	Pete Smith	.50
(28)	John Smoltz	1.50
(29)	Mike Stanton	.50
(30)	Jeff Treadway	.50

1992 Dunkin' Donuts Red Sox

The 1992 Boston Red Sox were the subject of a set of 30 cards, including the manager and coaches. Co-sponsored by Dunkin Donuts and WVIT-TV and released in May in Connecticut, the set was sold as an uncut, perforated sheet of 30 cards, measuring about 9-1/2" x 10-3/4". Individual perforated cards could be removed from the sheet; they measure 2-1/8" x 3-1/8". Fronts have a player photo framed in black on a white background. In the border beneath the photo are the player's name, position, uniform number and sponsors' logos. Backs have complete major and minor league stats. The cards are checklisted here by uniform number, which appears on the card front.

1993 Duracell Power Players

The Duracell battery company issued a 48-card set in 1993 that was presented in two 24-card series. The cards were available through the mail with proofs of purchase from selected Duracell products. Cards feature a Duracell logo at top, with a black and orange border surrounding a color photo of the player. The player's name is printed in yellow with team and position in white on top of a green background. Because the set was not licensed to use major league uniform logos, they were airbrushed off the photos. Backs have a player portrait photo, a facsimile autograph, recent stats and a few biographical and career details printed over a ballpark scene. Series I cards are number "X of 24;" Series II cards are so indicated beneath the card number.

		NM/M
Complete Set (48):		4.00
Common Player:		.10
Series 1		2.00
1	Roger Clemens	.60
2	Frank Thomas	.40
3	Andre Dawson	.25
4	Orel Hershiser	.10
5	Kirby Puckett	.50
6	Edgar Martinez	.10
7	Craig Biggio	.10
8	Terry Pendleton	.10
9	Mark McGwire	.75
10	Dave Stewart	.10
11	Ozzie Smith	.50
12	Doug Drabek	.10
13	Dwight Gooden	.10
14	Tony Gwynn	.50
15	Carlos Baerga	.10
16	Robin Yount	.40
17	Barry Bonds	1.00
18	Bip Roberts	.10
19	Don Mattingly	.60
20	Nolan Ryan	1.00
21	Tom Glavine	.25
22	Will Clark	.10
23	Cecil Fielder	.10
24	Dave Winfield	.40
Series 2		2.00
1	Cal Ripken, Jr.	1.00
2	Melido Perez	.10
3	John Kruk	.10
4	Charlie Hayes	.10
5	George Brett	.60
6	Ruben Sierra	.10
7	Deion Sanders	.15
8	Andy Van Slyke	.10
9	Fred McGriff	.10
10	Benito Santiago	.10
11	Charles Nagy	.10
12	Greg Maddux	.50
13	Ryne Sandberg	.50
14	Dennis Martinez	.10
15	Ken Griffey Jr.	.75
16	Jim Abbott	.10
17	Barry Larkin	.10
18	Gary Sheffield	.30
19	Jose Canseco	.25
20	Jack McDowell	.10
21	Darryl Strawberry	.10
22	Delino DeShields	.10
23	Dennis Eckersley	.40
24	Paul Molitor	.40

E

2003 Easton Gloves

A set of standard-format cards featuring members of the Easton Advisory Staff was issued as a premium for the purchase of youth model baseball gloves. The cards were distributed in four-card cello packs. Fronts have black bor-

ders, game-action photos, a facsimile autograph, player identification and Easton logos. Backs have a smaller photo, personal data and recent stats.

		NM/M
Complete Set (12):		20.00
Common Player:		2.00
1	Bobby Abreu	2.00
2	Luis Castillo	2.00
3	Eric Chavez	2.00
4	Eric Gagne	2.00
5	Luis Gonzalez	2.00
6	Eddie Guardado	2.00
7	Jeff Kent	2.00
8	Javy Lopez	2.00
9	John Olerud	2.00
10	Vicente Padilla	2.00
11	Sammy Sosa	7.50
12	Mike Williams	2.00

2005 Easton Gloves

A set of standard-format cards featuring members of the Easton Advisory Staff was issued as a premium for the purchase of youth model baseball gloves. Card fronts have game-action photos, a facsimile autograph and player identification. Backs have a smaller photo, personal data and recent stats.

		NM/M
Complete Set (12):		8.00
Common Player:		1.00
1	Sammy Sosa	2.50
2	Orlando Cabrera	1.00
3	Eric Chavez	1.00
4	Luis Gonzalez	1.00
5	Jeff Kent	1.00
6	Javy Lopez	1.00
7	Aramis Ramirez	1.00
8	Edgar Renteria	1.00
9	Luis Castillo	1.00
10	Eric Gagne	1.00
11	Michael Barrett	1.00
12	Bobby Abreu	1.00

1990 Eclipse Stars of the Negro Leagues

Better known in the field of comic books than baseball cards, Eclipse of California produced this set of cards honoring stars of the defunct Negro Leagues. The 2-1/2" x 3-1/2" cards have water color paintings (by Mark Chiarello) of the players on front. Well-written (by Jack Morelli) career summaries on back give a real flavor for this brand of pro ball and its era. Copyright lines for all parties are at bottom back. The issue was sold as a boxed set.

		NM/M
Complete Set (36):		16.00
Common Player:		.50
1	Header Card	.25
2a	Josh Gibson (Wrong picture, "H" on cap.)	4.00
2b	Josh Gibson (Correct picture, "G" on cap.)	4.00
3	Cannonball Redding	.50

4	Biz Mackey	2.00
5	Pop Lloyd	1.00
6	Bingo DeMoss	1.00
7	Willard Brown	2.00
8	John Donaldson	.50
9	Monte Irvin	1.50
10	Ben Taylor	2.00
11	Willie Wells	1.25
12	Dave Brown	.50
13	Leon Day	1.00
14	Ray Dandridge	1.00
15	Turkey Stearnes	1.00
16	Rube Foster	1.00
17	Oliver Marcelle	.50
18	Judy Johnson	1.00
19	Christobel Torrienti	2.00
20	Satchel Paige	4.00
21	Mule Suttles	2.00
22	John Beckwith	.50
23	Martin Dihigo	1.00
24	Willie Foster	.50
25	Dick Lundy	.50
26	Buck Leonard	1.00
27	Smokey Joe Williams	1.00
28	Cool Papa Bell	1.00
29	Bullet Rogan	1.00
30	Newt Allen	.75
31	Bruce Petway	.50
32	Jose Mendez	2.00
33	Louis Santop	2.00
34	Jud Wilson	2.00
35	Sammy Hughes	.50
36a	Oscar Charleston (Wrong picture, "G" on cap.)	1.00
36b	Oscar Charleston (Correct picture, "H" on cap.)	1.00

1992 Eclipse Negro League BPA - Paul Lee

Four Negro League baseball cards were handed out to the first 50,000 fans attending Negro League Baseball Players Association night at Shea Stadium on June 2. Cards feature the artwork of Paul Lee on front. Backs have a career summary and biographical details, along with the Mets and Eclipse logos.

		NM/M
Complete Set (4):		4.00
Common Player:		1.50
1	Monte Irvin	1.50
2	"Buck" Leonard	1.00
3	Josh Gibson	3.00
4	Ray Dandridge	1.00

1992 Eclipse Negro League BPA - John Clapp

Sponsored by Kraft, and produced by Eclipse, 15,000 sets of these cards were made for distribution at The Negro League Baseball Players Association night, August 9 at Lackawanna County Stadium, home of the Scranton Wilkes-Barre Red Barons. The 2-1/2" x 3-1/2" cards have watercolor player pictures on front, by artist John Clapp. Backs have career summaries, sponsor and issuer logos and copyright information.

		NM/M
Complete Set (18):		6.00

Common Player:		.50
1	Leon Day	1.50
2	Clinton (Casey) Jones	.50
3	Lester Lockett	.50
4	Monte Irvin	2.00
5	Armando Vazquez	.50
6	Jimmie Crutchfield	.50
7	Ted Radcliffe	.50
8	Albert Haywood	.50
9	Artie Wilson	1.50
10	Sam Jethroe	1.25
11	Edsall Walker	.50
12	Bill Wright	.50
13	Jim Cohen	.50
14	Andy Porter	.50
15	Tommy Sampson	.50
16	Buck Leonard	1.50
17	Josh Gibson	2.00
18	Martinez Jackson	1.50

2003 El Nueva Dia Montreal Expos

To commemorate the series played by the Expos in Puerto Rico, a local newspaper sponsored this set given away to fans at Hiram Bithorn Stadium on September 11 at the final San Juan "home" game. The cello-wrapped set has nine colorful 4-3/4" x 5-5/8" blank-back cards arranged like a newspaper page. At top is the sponsor's logo and the logo created for the historic series of games throughout the 2003 season. At bottom are one or two color photos with captions. In between are a headline and story summary about one of the series. All text is in Spanish. Each player named or prominently pictured on the card is listed.

		NM/M
Complete Set (9):		12.50
Common Card:		.60
1	Montreal pisa el 'home' (Jose Vidro, Wilfredo Cordero, Mark Grudzielanek)	1.25
2	Ovacion a Robero Alomar (Roberto Alomar)	2.50
3	Abuso casero de los Expos (Javier Vazquez, Javier Lopez, Marcus Giles)	1.25
4	Javy Lopez carga a los Bravos (Henry Mateo, Rocky Biddle, Javy Lopez, Andruw Jones)	.60
5	Reaccion por todo lo alto (Javier Vazquez, Brian Schneider)	1.25
6	Recibe el Bithorn a los campeones (Bengie Molina, Jose Molina)	.60
7	Puerto Rico (Juan Gonzalez)	2.50
8	Card' (Dontrelle Willis, Ivan Rodriguez, Braden Looper)	1.25
9	En la Isla Sosa con los Cachorros (Sammy Sosa)	5.00

1990 Elite Senior League

This 126-card set features the players of the first Senior League season. Cards are printed on high quality stock with full-color photos. The card backs feature statistics. Earl Weaver and Mike Easler cards were distributed as promo cards. Original retail price was about $12 per boxed set, the only manner of distribution.

		NM/M
Complete Set (126):		4.00
Common Player:		.05
1	Curt Flood	.15
2	Bob Tolan	.05
3	Dick Bosman	.05
4	Ivan DeJesus	.05
5	Dock Ellis	.05
6	Roy Howell	.05
7	Lamar Johnson	.05
8	Steve Kemp	.05
9	Ken Landreaux	.05
10	Randy Lerch	.05
11	Jon Matlack	.05
12	Gary Rajsich	.05
13	Lenny Randle	.05
14	Elias Sosa	.05
15	Ozzie Virgil	.05
16	Milt Wilcox	.05
17	Steve Henderson	.05
18	Ray Burris	.05
19	Mike Easler	.05
20	Juan Eichelberger	.05
21	Rollie Fingers	.50
22	Toby Harrah	.05
23	Randy Johnson	.05
24	Dave Kingman	.15
25	Lee Lacy	.05
26	Tito Landrum	.05
27	Paul Mirabella	.05
28	Mickey Rivers	.10
29	Rodney Scott	.05
30	Tim Stoddard	.05
31	Ron Washington	.05
32	Jerry White	.05
33	Dick Williams	.05
34	Clete Boyer	.10
35	Steve Dillard	.05
36	Garth Iorg	.05
37	Bruce Kison	.05
38	Wayne Krenchicki	.05
39	Ron LeFlore	.10
40	Tippy Martinez	.05
41	Omar Moreno	.05
42	Jim Morrison	.05
43	Graig Nettles	.15
44	Jim Nettles	.05
45	Wayne Nordhagen	.05
46	Al Oliver	.15
47	Jerry Royster	.05
48	Sammy Stewart	.05
49	Randy Bass	.05
50	Vida Blue	.10
51	Bruce Bochy	.05
52	Doug Corbett	.05
53	Jose Cruz	.05
54	Jamie Easterly	.05
55	Pete Falcone	.05
56	Bob Galasso	.05
57	Johnny Grubb	.05
58	Bake McBride	.05
59	Dyar Miller	.05
60	Tom Paciorek	.05
61	Ken Reitz	.05
62	U.L. Washington	.05
63	Alan Ashby	.05
64	Pat Dobson	.05
65	Doug Bird	.05
66	Marty Castillo	.05
67	Dan Driessen	.05
68	Wayne Garland	.05
69	Tim Ireland	.05
70	Ron Jackson	.05
71	Bobby Jones	.05
72	Dennis Leonard	.05
73	Rick Manning	.05
74	Amos Otis	.05
75	Pat Putnam	.05
76	Eric Rasmussen	.05
77	Paul Blair	.05
78	Bert Campaneris	.05
79	Cesar Cedeno	.10
80	Ed Figueroa	.05
81	Ross Grimsley	.05
82	George Hendrick	.05
83	Cliff Johnson	.05
84	Mike Kekich	.05
85	Rafael Landestoy	.05
86	Larry Milbourne	.05
87	Bobby Molinaro	.05
88	Sid Monge	.05
89	Rennie Stennett	.05
90	Derrell Thomas	.05
91	Earl Weaver	.30
92	Gary Allenson	.05
93	Pedro Borbon	.05
94	Al Bumbry	.05
95	Bill Campbell	.05
96	Bernie Carbo	.05
97	Ferguson Jenkins	.50
98	Pete LaCock	.05
99	Bill Lee	.05
100	Tommy McMillan	.05
101	Joe Pittman	.05
102	Gene Richards	.05
103	Leon Roberts	.05
104	Tony Scott	.05
105	Doug Simunic	.05
106	Rick Wise	.05

107	Willie Aikens	.05
108	Juan Beniquez	.05
109	Bobby Bonds	.10
110	Sergio Ferrer	.05
111	Chuck Ficks	.05
112	George Foster	.10
113	Dave Hilton	.05
114	Al Holland	.05
115	Clint Hurdle	.05
116	Bill Madlock	.10
117	Steve Ontiveros	.05
118	Roy Thomas	.05
119	Luis Tiant	.10
120	Walt Williams	.05
121	Vida Blue	.10
122	Bobby Bonds	.10
123	Rollie Fingers	.50
124	George Foster	.10
125	Fergie Jenkins	.50
126	Dave Kingman	.10

1983 English's Chicken Baltimore Orioles Lids

The World Champion O's were featured on this set of fried chicken bucket lids. Printed on thick cardboard discs with the blank backs heavily waxed, the lids come in two sizes, 8-3/8" diameter and 7-1/4". The design is the same on each, with a black, white and orange player portrait at center, flanked by some personal data and '83 stats. His name is in orange below, with his position and team in black beneath that. In the wide orange border is "English's Salutes / 1983 Champions." The player's union logo is at right of the portrait, but cap logos are missing because the issue was not licensed through MLB. The lids are not numbered.

		NM/M
Complete Set (13):		45.00
Common Player:		2.00
(1)	Mike Boddicker	2.00
(2)	Rich Dauer	2.00
(3)	Storm Davis	2.00
(4)	Mike Flanagan	2.00
(5)	John Lowenstein	2.00
(6)	Tippy Martinez	2.00
(7)	Gary Roenicke	2.00
(8)	Ken Singleton	2.00
(9)	Rick Dempsey	2.00
(10)	Scott McGregor	2.00
(11)	Eddie Murray	6.00
(12)	Jim Palmer	6.00
(13)	Cal Ripken, Jr.	30.00

1991 Enor Kevin Maas Story

This 20-card set was produced by one of the hobby's leading manufacturers of plastic supplies. Not surprisingly, the set was housed in a 6" x 8-1/4" plastic album with eight four-card plastic sheets inside. Besides the cards and album, the set came with a biographical brochure on the 1990 A.L. Rookie of the Year runner-up. Each of the 2-1/2" x 3-1/2" cards features one or more color photos of the player on front. A series of red stripes at the top of the card features the player's name in the uppermost stripe. Backs have the same stripe motif at top and include

career information or stats at center. The logos of MLB, the Yankees and Enor appear at the bottom.

	NM/M
Complete Set w/Album (20):	4.00
Single Card:	.10

F

1981 Family Fun Centers Padres

Six Padres players or staff are featured on these 13" x 10" coupon sheets. At the right end of each glossy paper sheet is a group of coupons and advertising for the recreation centers, printed in black, yellow and green. At left are six photos. Each of the 3" x 4" photos has a color player pose. At either top or bottom, depending on placement on the sheet, is the player name in black, "FAMILY FUN CENTER" in green and a red building logo. Backs are blank and the sheets are not perforated.

	NM/M
Complete Set (5):	110.00
Common Sheet:	10.00
(1)	Randy Bass, Frank Howard, Gary Lucas, Gene Richards, Ozzie Smith, Jerry Turner	60.00
(2)	Kurt Bevacqua, Dave Cash, Paul Dade, Rollie Fingers, Don Williams, Dave Winfield	25.00
(3)	Dan Boone, Chuck Estrada, Joe Lefebvre, Tim Lollar, Ed Stevens, Steve Swisher	10.00
(4)	John Curtis, Barry Evans, Tim Flannery, Terry Kennedy, Steve Mura, Bob Tolan	10.00
(5)	Von Joshua, Fred Kendall, Dennis Kinney, Jerry Mumphrey, Steve Mura, Dick Phillips	10.00

1994 FanFest Roberto Clemente Commemorative

In an unprecedented show of co-operation, the five Major League Baseball trading card licensees created this set of Roberto Clemente commemorative cards for distribution at the All-Star Fan Fest. Cards were available at participating manufacturers' booths, making complete sets somewhat difficult to assemble. Topps and Fleer based their commemorative cards on their companies' respective 1955 and 1963 Clemente cards. Donruss had artist Dick Perez create a Diamond King of Clemente, while Upper Deck and Score Select created new designs. It is believed fewer than 10,000 of each card exist.

		NM/M
Complete Set (5):		30.00
Common Card:		6.00
1	Roberto Clemente (Donruss Diamond King)	6.00
2	Roberto Clemente (Fleer 1963 reprint)	6.00
3	Roberto Clemente (Score Select)	6.00
4	Roberto Clemente (Topps 1955 reprint)	10.00
5	Roberto Clemente (Upper Deck)	6.00

1995 FanFest Nolan Ryan Commemorative

At the July 7-11,1995, FanFest, held in Dallas, Texas, site of the All-Star Game, five of Major League Baseball's principal licensees combined on a wrapper redemption program which offered Nolan Ryan Tribute cards. With 3,000 of the cards pegged as each day's maximum giveaway, only 15,000 total sets were available. Most of the companies opted for gold-leaf and/or foil-print extravaganzas, while Topps chose to re-create a single-player 1968-style Nolan Ryan rookie card with full career stats on back.

		NM/M
Complete Set (5):		16.00
Common Card:		4.00
1	Nolan Ryan (Upper Deck)	4.00
2	Nolan Ryan (Topps)	4.50
3	Nolan Ryan (Pinnacle)	4.00
4	Nolan Ryan (Fleer Ultra)	4.00
5	Nolan Ryan (Donruss)	4.00

1996 FanFest Steve Carlton Commemorative

Philadelphia's most famous Lefty (before Rocky Balboa) was chosen as the subject of the '96 All-Star FanFest multi-company card tribute. Each of the five largest baseball card licensees produced a Carlton card for use in a wrapper redemption promotion at the annual show. Each of the cards featured the Liberty Bell All-Star Game logo along with such bells and whistles as embossing, metallic-foil highlights, etc.

		NM/M
Complete Set (5):		12.50
Common Card:		3.00
1	Steve Carlton (Donruss)	3.00
2	Steve Carlton (Fleer Ultra)	3.00
3	Steve Carlton (Pinnacle)	3.00
4	Steve Carlton (Topps)	4.00
5	Steve Carlton (Upper Deck)	3.00

1997 FanFest Jackie Robinson Commemorative

1998 FanFest Lou Brock Commemorative

In the years before the Rockies joined the National League, Denver's "home team" was the St. Louis Cardinals. One of that team's greatest players of the 1960s and 1970s, Hall of Famer Lou Brock, was selected to be honored in the annual All-Star Fan-Fest commemorative series used by the card companies as a wrapper redemption premium (five wrappers for each card). Card fronts include the All-Star Game logo, backs have the Cooperstown Collection logo. Topps' card is a chromium version reproduction of Brock's 1962 rookie card, which depicts him as a Cub.

		NM/M
Complete Set (5):		3.00
Common Card:		.50
1	Lou Brock (Topps)	2.00
2	Lou Brock (Pinnacle)	1.00
3	Lou Brock (Fleer)	.50
4	Lou Brock (Donruss DK)	1.00
5	Lou Brock (Upper Deck)	.50

1999 FanFest Carl Yastrzemski Commemorative

One of the modern Red Sox most popular players of the of the 1960s-1980s, Hall of Famer Carl Yastrzemski, was selected to be honored in the 1999 Boston All-Star FanFest commemorative series used by the card companies as a wrapper redemption premium (five wrappers for each card). Card fronts include the All-Star Game logo.

		NM/M
Complete Set (4):		7.50
Common Card:		2.00
1	Carl Yastrzemski (Topps)	2.75
2	Carl Yastrzemski (Ultra)	2.00

3	Carl Yastrzemski (Upper Deck)	2.00
	Carl Yastrzemski (Pacific)	2.00

2000 FanFest Hank Aaron Commemorative

As in past years, each of Major League Baseball's major card licensees produced a special card in conjunction with FanFest in Atlanta prior to the All-Star Game. Visitors to the Collector's Showcase area of FanFest could obtain one card from each company's booth via a wrapper redemption.

		NM/M
Complete Set (4):		7.50
Common Card:		2.50
1	Hank Aaron (Topps)	2.50
2	Hank Aaron (Fleer)	2.50
3	Hank Aaron (Upper Deck)	2.50
4	Hank Aaron (Pacific)	2.50

2000 FanFest Hank Aaron Rookie Reprint

It has been reported that Topps originally intended to use this rookie reprint as its redemption card at FanFest, but later switched to a version of the Aaron card which appeared in 2000 Topps. It is said the rookie version was only distributed to a few of the vendors. Like the other cards in the redemption program, the '54 Topps reprint has the event logo on front. It is numbered "1 of 4" on back.

		NM/M
1	Hank Aaron (1954 Topps reprint)	4.00

2001 FanFest Seattle Mariners

A multi-manufacturer wrapper-redemption promotion at the July 6-10 All-Star FanFest in Seattle allowed collectors to acquire a special set of nine cards featuring current and former M's stars. Cards were generally available by visiting

In conjunction with FanFest in Cleveland, July 4-8, preceding the All-Star Game, five of the major card companies combined to create a card set honoring Jackie Robinson. Each company made its card available at the show in a wrapper redemption exchange. In most cases the tribute cards showcased the respective companies' technical expertise. Production of each card was limited to 15,000.

		NM/M
Complete Set (5):		12.00
Common Card:		2.50
1	Jackie Robinson (Pinnacle Dufex)	2.50
2	Jackie Robinson (Topps Finest '52 reprint)	3.00
3	Jackie Robinson (Upper Deck)	2.50
4	Jackie Robinson (Donruss - 1948 Leaf reprint)	2.50
5	Jackie Robinson (Fleer)	2.50

the booth of each manufacturer and opening five packs of that company's 2001 baseball cards. Original artwork, and metallic-foil highlights were featured on some cards. Production was 10,000 of each card.

		NM/M
Complete Set (9):		20.00
Common Player:		2.00
1	Ken Griffey Jr. (Upper Deck)	4.00
2	Alex Rodriguez (Donruss Diamond Kings)	5.00
3	Ichiro Suzuki (Fleer)	7.50
4	Edgar Martinez (Topps Gallery)	2.00
5	John Olerud (Topps Gallery)	2.00
6	Jay Buhner (Fleer)	2.00
7	Randy Johnson (Donruss Diamond Kings)	3.50
8	Lou Piniella (Upper Deck)	2.00
9	Alvin Davis, Harold Reynolds (Tuff Stuff)	2.00

2002 FanFest

All of the major baseball card licensees participated in a wrapper redemption program at the 2002 FanFest in Milwaukee. Each company produced one card of a Brewers star and one from another team. Five wrappers from selected products could be traded in for one of the cards. Wrappers from super-premium brands could be exchanged for cards featuring game-used base swatches. All cards carry special All-Star Game logos.

		NM/M
Complete Set (8):		10.00
Common Player:		2.00
1	Derek Jeter (Fleer)	3.00
2	Ichiro (Upper Deck)	4.00
3a	Sammy Sosa (Topps Finest)	2.50
3b	Sammy Sosa (Topps Finest Refractor)	12.00
4	Barry Bonds (Donruss Studio)	3.00
5	Robin Yount (Donruss Studio)	2.00
6	Geoff Jenkins (Topps Finest)	2.00
7	Ben Sheets (Upper Deck)	2.00
8	Richie Sexson (Fleer)	2.00

2002 FanFest Game-Used Base Cards

All of the major baseball card licensees participated in a wrapper redemption program at the 2002 FanFest in Milwaukee. Each company produced one card of a Brewers star and one from another team. Five wrappers from selected products could be traded in for one of the cards. Wrappers from super-premium brands could be exchanged for cards featuring game-used base swatches. All cards carry special All-Star Game logos.

		NM/M
Complete Set GU Base Cards (4):		35.00
Common Player:		5.00
GU1a	Derek Jeter (Fleer, First Base)	6.00
GU1b	Derek Jeter (Fleer, Second Base)	6.00

GU2	Ichiro (Upper Deck)	20.00
GU3	Sammy Sosa (Topps)	5.00
GU4	Barry Bonds (Donruss Studio)	7.50

2003 FanFest

By opening packs of specified brands at various card companies' FanFest booths, collectors could receive one of eight redemption cards. Low-priced card wrappers could be redeemed for base brand-type cards while opening high-priced packs would net a game-used base card. Cards feature the All-Star Game logo and are numbered within the edition of eight.

		NM/M
Complete Set (8):		35.00
Common Player:		2.00
1	Hideki Matsui (Upper Deck, g-u base)	7.50
2	Barry Bonds (Topps, g-u base)	10.00
3	Derek Jeter (Fleer, g-u base)	10.00
4	Sammy Sosa (Donruss, g-u base)	7.50
5	Frank Thomas (Upper Deck)	3.00
6	Bartolo Colon (Topps)	2.00
7	Paul Konerko (Fleer)	2.00
8	Magglio Ordonez (Donruss)	2.00

2004 FanFest

By opening packs of specified brands at various card companies' FanFest booths at the All-Star related event in Houston, collectors could receive one of 12 redemption cards featuring current and former (Ryan) Astros players. Low-priced card wrappers could be redeemed for base brand-type cards while opening high-priced packs would net a game-used base card. Ten thousand of each of the regular redemption and Ryan-Clemens cards were produced; the game-used cards were in an edition of 1,000 each. Cards feature the All-Star Game and FanFest logos and are numbered within the edition of 12.

		NM/M
Complete Set (12):		45.00
Common Player:		2.00
1	Roger Clemens (Fleer GU)	10.00
2	Andy Pettitte (Upper Deck GU)	5.00
3	Jeff Bagwell (Donruss GU)	7.50
4	Lance Berkman (Topps GU)	5.00
5	Roy Oswalt (Topps)	2.00
6	Craig Biggio (Donruss)	2.00
7	Jeff Kent (Upper Deck)	2.00
8	Adam Everett (Fleer)	2.00
9	Roger Clemens, Nolan Ryan (Fleer)	5.00
10	Roger Clemens, Nolan Ryan (Upper Deck)	5.00
11	Roger Clemens, Nolan Ryan (Donruss)	5.00
12	Roger Clemens, Nolan Ryan (Topps)	5.00

2005 FanFest

By opening packs of specified brands at various card companies' FanFest booths at the All-Star relat-

ed event in Detroit, collectors could receive one of nine redemption cards. Low-priced card wrappers could be redeemed for base brand-type cards while opening high-priced packs would net a game-used jersey card. Ten thousand of each of the regular redemption and dual-player cards were produced; the game-used cards were in an edition of 1,000 each. Cards feature the All-Star Game and FanFest logos.

		NM/M
Complete Set (9):		25.00
Common Player:		1.00
1	Ivan Rodriguez (Topps jersey)	12.50
2	Jeremy Bonderman (UD jersey)	6.00
3	Dmitri Young (Donruss jersey)	6.00
4	Derek Jeter (UD)	3.00
5	Alex Rodriguez (Topps)	3.00
6	Albert Pujols (Donruss)	3.00
7	Al Kaline, Ivan Rodriguez (UD)	1.00
8	Al Kaline, Ivan Rodriguez (Donruss)	1.00
9	Al Kaline, Ivan Rodriguez (Topps)	1.00

1988 Fantastic Sam's

This set of color player discs (2-1/2" diameter) was distributed during a Superstar Sweepstakes sponsored by Fantastic Sam's Family Haircutters' 1,800 stores nationwide. Each card consists of two connected discs (bright orange fronts, white backs) perforated for easy separation. One disc features the baseball player photo, the other carries the sweepstakes logo and a list of prizes. Player discs carry a Fantastic Sam's Baseball Superstars header curved above the photo, with player name, team and position printed in black. Backs are black-and-white and include personal info, card number and 1987 stats. Sweepstakes discs list contest prizes (Grand Prize was 4 tickets to a 1988 Championship game) on the front and an entry form on the flipside. Below the prize list is a silver scratch-off rectangle which may reveal an instant prize.

		NM/M
Complete Set (20):		4.00
Uncut Sheet:		10.00
Common Player:		.10
1	Kirby Puckett	.50
2	George Brett	.75
3	Mark McGwire	1.00
4	Wally Joyner	.10
5	Paul Molitor	.45
6	Alan Trammell	.10
7	George Bell	.10
8	Wade Boggs	.50
9	Don Mattingly	.75
10	Julio Franco	.10
11	Ozzie Smith	.50
12	Will Clark	.10
13	Dale Murphy	.15
14	Eric Davis	.25
15	Andre Dawson	.25
16	Tim Raines	.10
17	Darryl Strawberry	.10
18	Tony Gwynn	.50
19	Mike Schmidt	.75
20	Pedro Guerrero	.10

1984 Farmer Jack Detroit Tigers

Though there is no indication on the picutres themselves, this issue was a promotion by the Farmer Jack grocery store chain. Printed on semi-gloss paper, the color photos are bordered in white and measure 6" x 9". A facsimile autograph

is printed on front. The unnumbered pictures are blank-backed and are checklisted here in alphabetical order.

		NM/M
Complete Set (16):		15.00
Common Player:		.50
(1)	Dave Bergman	.50
(2)	Darrell Evans	1.25
(3)	Barbaro Garbey	.50
(4)	Kirk Gibson	1.00
(5)	John Grubb	.50
(6)	Willie Hernandez	.50
(7)	Larry Herndon	.50
(8)	Howard Johnson	.90
(9)	Chet Lemon	.75
(10)	Jack Morris	.90
(11)	Lance Parrish	1.00
(12)	Dan Petry	.50
(13)	Dave Rozema	.50
(14)	Alan Trammell	4.00
(15)	Lou Whitaker	2.50
(16)	Milt Wilcox	.50

1987 Farmland Dairies Mets

The New York Mets and Farmland Dairies produced a nine-card panel of baseball cards for members of the Junior Mets Club. Members of the club, kids 14 years of age and younger, received the perforated panel as part of a package featuring gifts and special privileges. The cards are the standard 2-1/2" x 3-1/2" with fronts containing a full-color photo encompassed by a blue border. The backs are designed on a vertical format and have player statistics and career highlights. The Farmland Dairies and Junior Mets Club logos are carried on the card backs.

		NM/M
Complete Panel Set:		4.50
Complete Singles Set (9):		3.00
Common Single Player:		.25
1	Mookie Wilson	.35
4	Lenny Dykstra	.35
8	Gary Carter	1.50
12	Ron Darling	.25
18	Darryl Strawberry	.35
19	Bob Ojeda	.25
22	Kevin McReynolds	.25
42	Roger McDowell	.25
---	Team Card	.25

1988 Farmland Dairies Mets

Part of the Junior Mets Fan Club membership package, this set of nine standard size cards was printed on a single panel. Card fronts feature full-color action shots framed in orange and blue. A white player name runs across the top border, with a large team logo, uniform number and position printed below the photo. Card backs are blue on brown and include personal data, stats and 1987 season highlights. The set was offered to fans 14 years and younger for a $6 fan club membership fee, with a $1 dis-

count for those who sent in two proofs of purchase from Farmland Dairies milk cartons.

		NM/M
Complete Panel Set:		4.50
Complete Singles Set (9):		2.50
Common Single Player:		.25
8	Gary Carter	1.50
16	Dwight Gooden	.25
17	Keith Hernandez	.40
18	Darryl Strawberry	.25
20	Howard Johnson	.25
21	Kevin Elster	.25
42	Roger McDowell	.25
48	Randy Myers	.25
50	Sid Fernandez	.25

1989 Farmland Dairies Mets

For the third consecutive year in 1989, Farmland Dairies sponsored the Junior Mets fan club. One of the club's membership benefits was a nine-card set issued on a 7-1/2 x 10-1/2" perforated sheet. Individual cards measure the standard 2-1/2" x 3-1/2" with team-color borders of blue and gold. Backs have the Junior Mets and Farmland Dairies logos along with 1988 highlights and stats, career stats and some biographical data. The checklist is by uniform number as shown on the cards' front.

		NM/M
Complete Set, Sheet		3.50
Complete Set, Singles (9):		3.00
Common Player:		.50
8	Gary Carter	1.50
9	Gregg Jefferies	.50
16	Dwight Gooden	.25
18	Darryl Strawberry	.25
22	Kevin McReynolds	.25
25	Keith Miller	.25
42	Roger McDowell	.25
44	David Cone	.50
---	1988 Eastern Division Champs (Team Photo)	.25

1993 Fax Pax

Roger Clemens

Titled "Fax Pax World of Sports," this 40-card set was issued in Great Britain and features top athletes from many sports around the world. The 2-1/2" x 3-1/2" cards have borderless color action photos on

front. A white strip near the bottom carries the player's name and the flag of his nation. Black, white and red backs have biographical data, stats and a career summary. Only the baseball players are listed here.

		NM/M
Common Player:		1.00
1	Roger Clemens	1.50
2	Ken Griffey Jr.	2.00
3	John Olerud	1.00
4	Nolan Ryan	3.00

1982 FBI Foods Discs

This set was issued in the form of a pair of 2-7/8" diameter discs printed on the bottoms of six-pack cartons of Canadian soft drinks. The discs have black-and-white player portrait photos at center, with cap logos airbrushed off. At top is a green and orange FBI logo. Player identification flanks the photo. The copyright and logo of the Players Association appear at right. The initials of the set's producer, Mike Schechter Associates, appear at lower-left. The unnumbered discs are checklisted here in alphabetical order. Because of their appearance on the bottom of a cardboard box, many cards suffer scuffing on the front, or show indentations from the soda cans. A premium of 25-50 percent attaches to intact boxes or panels.

		NM/M
Complete Set, Singles (30):		650.00
Common Player:		10.00
(1)	Vida Blue	10.00
(2)	George Brett	100.00
(3)	Rod Carew	25.00
(4)	Steve Carlton	30.00
(5)	Gary Carter	30.00
(6)	Warren Cromartie	10.00
(7)	Andre Dawson	15.00
(8)	Rollie Fingers	20.00
(9)	Carlton Fisk	30.00
(10)	Steve Garvey	15.00
(11)	Goose Gossage	10.00
(12)	Bill Gullickson	10.00
(13)	Steve Henderson	10.00
(14)	Keith Hernandez	10.00
(15)	John Mayberry	10.00
(16)	Al Oliver	10.00
(17)	Dave Parker	10.00
(18)	Tim Raines	10.00
(19)	Jim Rice	15.00
(20)	Steve Rogers	10.00
(21)	Pete Rose	150.00
(22)	Nolan Ryan	150.00
(23)	Mike Schmidt	100.00
(24)	Tom Seaver	30.00
(25)	Ken Singleton	10.00
(26)	Dave Steib	10.00
(27)	Bruce Sutter	20.00
(28)	Ellis Valentine	10.00
(29)	Fernando Valenzuela	10.00
(30)	Dave Winfield	30.00

1993 Finest Promos

Debuting at the 1993 National Convention in Chicago, this three-card set introduced the hobby to the Topps Finest baseball issue. While the promos are identical in high-tech format to the regular Finest cards issued later, including the same card numbers, there are differences in the promos; some subtle, some glaring. For instance, the

Ryan and Alomar cards were issued in promo form in the "gray" style of the basic set. In the regularly issued set, those cards were in the green All-Star format. Each of the promos is overprinted in red on the back, "Promotional Sample 1 of 5000." Of considerably greater rarity are refractor versions of these promo cards, with production numbers unknown.

		NM/M
Complete Set (3):		25.00
Complete Set, Refractors (3):		1,500
88	Roberto Alomar	3.50
88r	Roberto Alomar (Refractor)	300.00
98	Don Mattingly	10.00
98r	Don Mattingly (Refractor)	500.00
107	Nolan Ryan	15.00
107r	Nolan Ryan (Refractor)	750.00

1993 Finest

MIKE PIAZZA

This 199-card set uses a process of multi-color metallization; this chromium technology adds depth and dimension to the card. The set has a 33-card subset of All-Stars; a parallel version of these cards (Refractors) were also created with refracting foil using the metallization enhancement process. There is one refracting foil card in every nine packs. Packs have five cards. Each 18-count box contains a 5" x 7" version of one of the 33 All-Star players in the set.

		NM/M
Complete Set (199):		75.00
Common Player:		.50
Refractors:		40-50X
Pack (6):		15.00
Wax Box (18):		300.00
1	Dave Justice	.50
2	Lou Whitaker	.50
3	Bryan Harvey	.50
4	Carlos Garcia	.50
5	Sid Fernandez	.50
6	Brett Butler	.50
7	Scott Cooper	.50
8	B.J. Surhoff	.50
9	Steve Finley	.50
10	Curt Schilling	2.00
11	Jeff Bagwell	4.00
12	Alex Cole	.50
13	John Olerud	.50
14	John Smiley	.50
15	Bip Roberts	.50
16	Albert Belle	.50
17	Duane Ward	.50
18	Alan Trammell	.50
19	Andy Benes	.50
20	Reggie Sanders	.50
21	Todd Zeile	.50
22	Rick Aguilera	.50
23	Dave Hollins	.50
24	Jose Rijo	.50
25	Matt Williams	.50
26	Sandy Alomar	.50
27	Alex Fernandez	.50
28	Ozzie Smith	6.00
29	Ramon Martinez	.50
30	Bernie Williams	.50
31	Gary Sheffield	1.00
32	Eric Karros	.50
33	Frank Viola	.50
34	Kevin Young	.50
35	Ken Hill	.50
36	Tony Fernandez	.50
37	Tim Wakefield	.50
38	John Kruk	.50
39	Chris Sabo	.50
40	Marquis Grissom	.50
41	Glenn Davis	.50
42	Jeff Montgomery	.50
43	Kenny Lofton	.50
44	John Burkett	.50
45	Darryl Hamilton	.50
46	Jim Abbott	.50
47	Ivan Rodriguez	3.00
48	Eric Young	.50
49	Mitch Williams	.50
50	Harold Reynolds	.50
51	Brian Harper	.50
52	Rafael Palmeiro	3.00
53	Bret Saberhagen	.50
54	Jeff Conine	.50
55	Ivan Calderon	.50
56	Juan Guzman	.50
57	Carlos Baerga	.50
58	Charles Nagy	.50
59	Wally Joyner	.50
60	Charlie Hayes	.50
61	Shane Mack	.50
62	Pete Harnisch	.50
63	George Brett	8.00
64	Lance Johnson	.50
65	Ben McDonald	.50
66	Bobby Bonilla	.50
67	Terry Steinbach	.50
68	Ron Gant	.50
69	Doug Jones	.50
70	Paul Molitor	4.00
71	Brady Anderson	.50
72	Chuck Finley	.50
73	Mark Grace	.75
74	Mike Devereaux	.50
75	Tony Phillips	.50
76	Chuck Knoblauch	.50
77	Tony Gwynn	6.00
78	Kevin Appier	.50
79	Sammy Sosa	6.00
80	Mickey Tettleton	.50
81	Felix Jose	.50
82	Mark Langston	.50
83	Gregg Jefferies	.50
84	Andre Dawson/AS	1.00
85	Greg Maddux/AS	6.00
86	Rickey Henderson/AS	4.00
87	Tom Glavine/AS	2.50
88	Roberto Alomar/AS	1.00
89	Darryl Strawberry/AS	.50
90	Wade Boggs/AS	6.00
91	Bo Jackson/AS	1.00
92	Mark McGwire/AS	6.00
93	Robin Ventura/AS	.50
94	Joe Carter/AS	.50
95	Lee Smith/AS	.50
96	Cal Ripken, Jr./AS	10.00
97	Larry Walker/AS	.50
98	Don Mattingly/AS	8.00
99	Jose Canseco/AS	2.50
100	Dennis Eckersley/AS	3.00
101	Terry Pendleton/AS	.50
102	Frank Thomas/AS	4.00
103	Barry Bonds/AS	.50
104	Roger Clemens/AS	8.00
105	Ryne Sandberg/AS	6.00
106	Fred McGriff/AS	.50
107	Nolan Ryan/AS	10.00
108	Will Clark/AS	.50
109	Pat Listach/AS	.50
110	Ken Griffey Jr/AS	6.00
111	Cecil Fielder/AS	.50
112	Kirby Puckett/AS	6.00
113	Dwight Gooden/AS	.50
114	Barry Larkin/AS	.50
115	David Cone/AS	.50
116	Juan Gonzalez/AS	2.50
117	Kent Hrbek	.50
118	Tim Wallach	.50
119	Craig Biggio	.50
120	Bobby Kelly	.50
121	Greg Olson	.50
122	Eddie Murray	4.00
123	Wil Cordero	.50
124	Jay Buhner	.50
125	Carlton Fisk	4.00
126	Eric Davis	.50
127	Doug Drabek	.50
128	Ozzie Guillen	.50
129	John Wetteland	.50
130	Andres Galarraga	.50
131	Ken Caminiti	.50
132	Tom Candiotti	.50
133	Pat Borders	.50
134	Kevin Brown	.50
135	Travis Fryman	.50
136	Kevin Mitchell	.50
137	Greg Swindell	.50
138	Benny Santiago	.50
139	Reggie Jefferson	.50
140	Chris Bosio	.50
141	Deion Sanders	.60
142	Scott Erickson	.50
143	Howard Johnson	.50
144	Orestes Destrade	.50
145	Jose Guzman	.50
146	Chad Curtis	.50
147	Cal Eldred	.50
148	Willie Greene	.50
149	Tommy Greene	.50
150	Erik Hanson	.50
151	Bob Welch	.50
152	John Jaha	.50
153	Harold Baines	.50
154	Randy Johnson	4.00
155	Al Martin	.50
156	J.T. Snow RC	1.50
157	Mike Mussina	2.50
158	Ruben Sierra	.50
159	Dean Palmer	.50
160	Steve Avery	.50
161	Julio Franco	.50
162	Dave Winfield	4.00
163	Tim Salmon	.50
164	Tom Henke	.50
165	Mo Vaughn	.50
166	John Smoltz	.50
167	Danny Tartabull	.50
168	Delino DeShields	.50
169	Charlie Hough	.50
170	Paul O'Neill	.50
171	Darren Daulton	.50
172	Jack McDowell	.50
173	Junior Felix	.50
174	Jimmy Key	.50
175	George Bell	.50
176	Mike Stanton	.50
177	Len Dykstra	.50
178	Norm Charlton	.50
179	Eric Anthony	.50
180	Bob Dibble	.50
181	Otis Nixon	.50
182	Randy Myers	.50
183	Tim Raines	.50
184	Orel Hershiser	.50
185	Andy Van Slyke	.50
186	Mike Lansing RC	1.00
187	Ray Lankford	.50
188	Mike Morgan	.50
189	Moises Alou	.50
190	Edgar Martinez	.50
191	John Franco	.50
192	Robin Yount	5.00
193	Bob Tewksbury	.50
194	Jay Bell	.50
195	Luis Gonzalez	.50
196	Dave Fleming	.50
197	Mike Greenwell	.50
198	David Nied	.50
199	Mike Piazza	10.00

Refractors

This parallel insert set comprises each of the 199 cards from the regular Topps Finest set recreated with refracting foil using the metallization enhancement process. One refractor card was inserted in every nine packs, on average. Estimated production was about 250 of each card, though shortprints are known. In the mid 2000s large quantities of the refractors began appearing in the market, fueling speculation that some form of unissued remainder inventory had been released from the printer.

		NM/M
Common Player:		15.00
1	Dave Justice	15.00
2	Lou Whitaker	15.00
3	Bryan Harvey/SP	45.00
4	Carlos Garcia	15.00
5	Sid Fernandez	15.00
6	Brett Butler	15.00
7	Scott Cooper	15.00
8	B.J. Surhoff	15.00
9	Steve Finley	15.00
10	Curt Schilling	50.00
11	Jeff Bagwell	100.00
12	Alex Cole	15.00
13	John Olerud	15.00
14	John Smiley	15.00
15	Bip Roberts	15.00
16	Albert Belle	15.00
17	Duane Ward	15.00
18	Alan Trammell	15.00
19	Andy Benes	15.00
20	Reggie Sanders	15.00
21	Todd Zeile	15.00
22	Rick Aguilera	15.00
23	Dave Hollins	15.00
24	Jose Rijo	15.00
25	Matt Williams	15.00
26	Sandy Alomar	15.00
27	Alex Fernandez	15.00
28	Ozzie Smith	100.00
29	Ramon Martinez	15.00
30	Bernie Williams	15.00
31	Gary Sheffield	40.00
32	Eric Karros	15.00
33	Frank Viola	15.00
34	Kevin Young	15.00
35	Ken Hill	15.00
36	Tony Fernandez	15.00
37	Tim Wakefield	15.00
38	John Kruk	15.00
39	Chris Sabo/SP	75.00
40	Marquis Grissom	15.00
41	Glenn Davis/SP	50.00
42	Jeff Montgomery	15.00
43	Kenny Lofton	15.00
44	John Burkett	15.00
45	Darryl Hamilton	15.00
46	Jim Abbott	15.00
47	Ivan Rodriguez	150.00
48	Eric Young	15.00
49	Mitch Williams	15.00
50	Harold Reynolds	15.00
51	Brian Harper	15.00
52	Rafael Palmeiro	75.00
53	Bret Saberhagen	15.00
54	Jeff Conine	15.00
55	Ivan Calderon	15.00
56	Juan Guzman	15.00
57	Carlos Baerga	15.00
58	Charles Nagy	15.00
59	Wally Joyner	15.00
60	Charlie Hayes	15.00
61	Shane Mack	15.00
62	Pete Harnisch	15.00
63	George Brett	125.00
64	Lance Johnson	15.00
65	Ben McDonald	15.00
66	Bobby Bonilla	15.00
67	Terry Steinbach	15.00
68	Ron Gant	15.00
69	Doug Jones	15.00
70	Paul Molitor	100.00
71	Brady Anderson	15.00
72	Chuck Finley	15.00
73	Mark Grace	15.00
74	Mike Devereaux	15.00
75	Tony Phillips	15.00
76	Chuck Knoblauch	15.00
77	Tony Gwynn	100.00
78	Kevin Appier	15.00
79	Sammy Sosa	150.00
80	Mickey Tettleton	15.00
81	Felix Jose	15.00
82	Mark Langston	15.00
83	Gregg Jefferies	15.00
84	Andre Dawson/AS	35.00
85	Greg Maddux/AS	150.00
86	Rickey Henderson/AS	125.00
87	Tom Glavine/AS	50.00
88	Roberto Alomar/AS	45.00
89	Darryl Strawberry/AS	15.00
90	Wade Boggs/AS	100.00
91	Bo Jackson/AS	60.00
92	Mark McGwire/AS	200.00
93	Robin Ventura/AS	15.00
94	Joe Carter/AS/SP	50.00
95	Lee Smith/AS	15.00
96	Cal Ripken, Jr./AS	500.00
97	Larry Walker/AS/SP	15.00
98	Don Mattingly/AS	100.00
99	Jose Canseco/AS	50.00
100	Dennis Eckersley/AS	75.00
101	Terry Pendleton/AS	15.00
102	Frank Thomas/AS/SP	200.00
103	Barry Bonds/AS	300.00
104	Roger Clemens/AS	200.00
105	Ryne Sandberg/AS	125.00
106	Fred McGriff/AS	15.00
107	Nolan Ryan/AS	500.00
108	Will Clark/AS/SP	75.00
109	Pat Listach/AS	15.00
110	Ken Griffey Jr./AS	450.00
111	Cecil Fielder/AS	15.00
112	Kirby Puckett/AS	100.00
113	Dwight Gooden/AS	15.00
114	Barry Larkin/AS	15.00
115	David Cone/AS	15.00
116	Juan Gonzalez/AS/SP	150.00
117	Kent Hrbek	15.00
118	Tim Wallach	15.00
119	Craig Biggio	15.00
120	Bobby Kelly	15.00
121	Greg Olson	15.00
122	Eddie Murray	100.00
123	Wil Cordero	15.00
124	Jay Buhner	15.00
125	Carlton Fisk	75.00
126	Eric Davis	15.00
127	Doug Drabek	15.00
128	Ozzie Guillen	15.00
129	John Wetteland	15.00
130	Andres Galarraga	15.00
131	Ken Caminiti	15.00
132	Tom Candiotti	15.00
133	Pat Borders	15.00
134	Kevin Brown	15.00
135	Travis Fryman	15.00
136	Kevin Mitchell	15.00
137	Greg Swindell	15.00
138	Benny Santiago	15.00
139	Reggie Jefferson	15.00
140	Chris Bosio	15.00
141	Deion Sanders	15.00
142	Scott Erickson	15.00
143	Howard Johnson	15.00
144	Orestes Destrade	15.00
145	Jose Guzman	15.00
146	Chad Curtis	15.00
147	Cal Eldred	15.00
148	Willie Greene/SP	75.00
149	Tommy Greene	15.00
150	Erik Hanson	15.00
151	Bob Welch	15.00
152	John Jaha	15.00
153	Harold Baines	15.00
154	Randy Johnson	100.00
155	Al Martin	15.00
156	J.T. Snow	15.00
157	Mike Mussina	45.00
158	Ruben Sierra	15.00
159	Dean Palmer	15.00
160	Steve Avery	15.00
161	Julio Franco	15.00
162	Dave Winfield	100.00
163	Tim Salmon/SP	50.00
164	Tom Henke	15.00
165	Mo Vaughn	15.00
166	John Smoltz	15.00
167	Danny Tartabull	15.00
168	Delino DeShields	15.00
169	Charlie Hough	15.00
170	Paul O'Neill	15.00
171	Darren Daulton	15.00
172	Jack McDowell	15.00
173	Junior Felix	15.00
174	Jimmy Key	15.00
175	George Bell	15.00
176	Mike Stanton	15.00
177	Len Dykstra	15.00
178	Norm Charlton	15.00
179	Eric Anthony	15.00
180	Bob Dibble	15.00
181	Otis Nixon	15.00
182	Randy Myers	15.00
183	Tim Raines	15.00
184	Orel Hershiser	15.00
185	Andy Van Slyke	15.00
186	Mike Lansing	15.00
187	Ray Lankford	15.00
188	Mike Morgan	15.00
189	Moises Alou	15.00
190	Edgar Martinez	15.00
191	John Franco	15.00
192	Robin Yount	90.00
193	Bob Tewksbury	15.00
194	Jay Bell	15.00
195	Luis Gonzalez	15.00
196	Dave Fleming	15.00
197	Mike Greenwell	15.00
198	David Nied	15.00
199	Mike Piazza	250.00

Jumbo All-Stars

These 4-1/2" x 6" cards were produced using the chromium metallization process. Each 18-pack Finest box contains one of the All-Star jumbo cards. Based on '93 Finest production, it is estimated fewer than 1,500 of each were issued.

		NM/M
Complete Set (33):		185.00
Common Player:		2.00
84	Andre Dawson	2.50
85	Greg Maddux	10.00
86	Rickey Henderson	7.50
87	Tom Glavine	3.00
88	Roberto Alomar	3.00
89	Darryl Strawberry	2.00
90	Wade Boggs	10.00
91	Bo Jackson	2.00
92	Mark McGwire	20.00
93	Robin Ventura	2.00
94	Joe Carter	2.00
95	Lee Smith	2.00
96	Cal Ripken, Jr.	30.00
97	Larry Walker	2.00
98	Don Mattingly	12.00
99	Jose Canseco	3.50
100	Dennis Eckersley	6.00
101	Terry Pendleton	2.00
102	Frank Thomas	7.50
103	Barry Bonds	30.00
104	Roger Clemens	12.00
105	Ryne Sandberg	10.00
106	Fred McGriff	2.00
107	Nolan Ryan	30.00
108	Will Clark	2.50
109	Pat Listach	2.00
110	Ken Griffey Jr.	15.00
111	Cecil Fielder	2.00
112	Kirby Puckett	10.00
113	Dwight Gooden	2.00
114	Barry Larkin	2.00
115	David Cone	2.00
116	Juan Gonzalez	7.50

1994 Finest Pre-Production

Forty cards premiering the upcoming 1994 Topps Finest set were issued as a random insert in packs of Topps Series 2 regular-issue cards. The promos are in the same format as the regular-issue Finest cards and share the same card numbers. On back there is a red "Pre-Production" notice printed diagonally over the statistics.

Mark McGwire 1B

		NM/M
Complete Set (40):		35.00
Common Player:		1.00
22	Deion Sanders	1.00
23	Jose Offerman	1.00
26	Alex Fernandez	1.00
31	Steve Finley	1.00
35	Andres Galarraga	1.00
43	Reggie Sanders	1.00
47	Dave Hollins	1.00
52	David Cone	1.00
59	Dante Bichette	1.00
61	Orlando Merced	1.00
62	Brian McRae	1.00
66	Mike Mussina	2.50
76	Mike Stanley	1.00
78	Mark McGwire	6.00
79	Pat Listach	1.00
84	Phil Plantier	1.00
90	Jeff Russell	1.00
92	Gregg Jefferies	1.00
93	Jose Guzman	1.00
100	John Smoltz	1.00
102	Jim Thome	3.00
121	Moises Alou	1.00
125	Devon White	1.00
126	Ivan Rodriguez	3.00
130	Dave Magadan	1.00
136	Ozzie Smith	4.00
141	Chris Hoiles	1.00
149	Jim Abbott	1.00
151	Bill Swift	1.00
154	Edgar Martinez	1.00
157	J.T. Snow	1.00
159	Alan Trammell	1.00
163	Roberto Kelly	1.00
166	Scott Erickson	1.00
168	Scott Cooper	1.00
169	Rod Beck	1.00
177	Dean Palmer	1.00
182	Todd Van Poppel	1.00
185	Paul Sorrento	1.00

1994 Finest

Milt Thompson

The 1994 Finest set comprises two series of 220 cards each; subsets of 20 superstars and 20 top rookies are featured in each series. Each card has a metallic look to it, using Topps Finest technology. Backs picture the player on the top half and statistics on the bottom. Baseball's Finest was limited to 4,000 cases and available to dealers through an allocation process, based on their sales the previous year. Along with the regular-issue set, there was a parallel set, called Refractors, of 440 cards and a 4 x 6-inch version of the 80 subset cards.

		NM/M
Complete Set (440):		40.00
Common Player:		.15
Refractors:		3X
Series 1 or 2 Pack (7):		1.50
Series 1 or 2 Box (24):		25.00
1	Mike Piazza	3.00
2	Kevin Stocker	.15
3	Greg McMichael	.15
4	Jeff Conine	.15
5	Rene Arocha	.15
6	Aaron Sele	.15
7	Brent Gates	.15
8	Chuck Carr	.15
9	Kirk Rueter	.15

No.	Player	Value
10	Mike Lansing	.15
11	Al Martin	.15
12	Jason Bere	.15
13	Troy Neel	.15
14	Armando Reynoso	.15
15	Jeromy Burnitz	.15
16	Rich Amaral	.15
17	David McCarty	.15
18	Tim Salmon	.15
19	Steve Cooke	.15
20	Wil Cordero	.15
21	Kevin Tapani	.15
22	Deion Sanders	.15
23	Jose Offerman	.15
24	Mark Langston	.15
25	Ken Hill	.15
26	Alex Fernandez	.15
27	Jeff Blauser	.15
28	Royce Clayton	.15
29	Brad Ausmus	.15
30	Ryan Bowen	.15
31	Steve Finley	.15
32	Charlie Hayes	.15
33	Jeff Kent	.15
34	Mike Henneman	.15
35	Andres Galarraga	.15
36	Wayne Kirby	.15
37	Joe Oliver	.15
38	Terry Steinbach	.15
39	Ryan Thompson	.15
40	Luis Alicea	.15
41	Randy Velarde	.15
42	Bob Tewksbury	.15
43	Reggie Sanders	.15
44	Brian Williams	.15
45	Joe Orsulak	.15
46	Jose Lind	.15
47	Dave Hollins	.15
48	Graeme Lloyd	.15
49	Jim Gott	.15
50	Andre Dawson	.40
51	Steve Buechele	.15
52	David Cone	.15
53	Ricky Gutierrez	.15
54	Lance Johnson	.15
55	Tino Martinez	.15
56	Phil Hiatt	.15
57	Carlos Garcia	.15
58	Danny Darwin	.15
59	Dante Bichette	.15
60	Scott Kamieniecki	.15
61	Orlando Merced	.15
62	Brian McRae	.15
63	Pat Kelly	.15
64	Tom Henke	.15
65	Jeff King	.15
66	Mike Mussina	.75
67	Tim Pugh	.15
68	Robby Thompson	.15
69	Paul O'Neill	.15
70	Hal Morris	.15
71	Ron Karkovice	.15
72	Joe Girardi	.15
73	Eduardo Perez	.15
74	Raul Mondesi	.15
75	Mike Gallego	.15
76	Mike Stanley	.15
77	Kevin Roberson	.15
78	Mark McGwire	4.00
79	Pat Listach	.15
80	Eric Davis	.15
81	Mike Bordick	.15
82	Dwight Gooden	.15
83	Mike Moore	.15
84	Phil Plantier	.15
85	Darren Lewis	.15
86	Rick Wilkins	.15
87	Darryl Strawberry	.15
88	Rob Dibble	.15
89	Greg Vaughn	.15
90	Jeff Russell	.15
91	Mark Lewis	.15
92	Gregg Jefferies	.15
93	Jose Guzman	.15
94	Kenny Rogers	.15
95	Mark Lemke	.15
96	Mike Morgan	.15
97	Andujar Cedeno	.15
98	Orel Hershiser	.15
99	Greg Swindell	.15
100	John Smoltz	.15
101	Pedro Martinez	.15
102	Jim Thome	1.00
103	David Segui	.15
104	Charles Nagy	.15
105	Shane Mack	.15
106	John Jaha	.15
107	Tom Candiotti	.15
108	David Wells	.15
109	Bobby Jones	.15
110	Bob Hamelin	.15
111	Bernard Gilkey	.15
112	Chili Davis	.15
113	Todd Stottlemyre	.15
114	Derek Bell	.15
115	Mark McLemore	.15
116	Mark Whiten	.15
117	Mike Devereaux	.15
118	Terry Pendleton	.15
119	Pat Meares	.15
120	Pete Harnisch	.15
121	Moises Alou	.15
122	Jay Buhner	.15
123	Wes Chamberlain	.15
124	Mike Perez	.15
125	Devon White	.15
126	Ivan Rodriguez	1.25
127	Don Slaught	.15

No.	Player	Value
128	John Valentin	.15
129	Jaime Navarro	.15
130	Dave Magadan	.15
131	Brady Anderson	.15
132	Juan Guzman	.15
133	John Wetteland	.15
134	Dave Stewart	.15
135	Scott Servais	.15
136	Ozzie Smith	2.50
137	Darrin Fletcher	.15
138	Jose Mesa	.15
139	Wilson Alvarez	.15
140	Pete Incaviglia	.15
141	Chris Hoiles	.15
142	Darryl Hamilton	.15
143	Chuck Finley	.15
144	Archi Cianfrocco	.15
145	Bill Wegman	.15
146	Joey Cora	.15
147	Darrell Whitmore	.15
148	David Hulse	.15
149	Jim Abbott	.15
150	Curt Schilling	.40
151	Bill Swift	.15
152	Tommy Greene	.15
153	Roberto Mejia	.15
154	Edgar Martinez	.15
155	Roger Pavlik	.15
156	Randy Tomlin	.15
157	J.T. Snow	.15
158	Bob Welch	.15
159	Alan Trammell	.15
160	Ed Sprague	.15
161	Ben McDonald	.15
162	Derrick May	.15
163	Roberto Kelly	.15
164	Bryan Harvey	.15
165	Ron Gant	.15
166	Scott Erickson	.15
167	Anthony Young	.15
168	Scott Cooper	.15
169	Rod Beck	.15
170	John Franco	.15
171	Gary DiSarcina	.15
172	Dave Fleming	.15
173	Wade Boggs	2.50
174	Kevin Appier	.15
175	Jose Bautista	.15
176	Wally Joyner	.15
177	Dean Palmer	.15
178	Tony Phillips	.15
179	John Smiley	.15
180	Charlie Hough	.15
181	Scott Fletcher	.15
182	Todd Van Poppel	.15
183	Mike Blowers	.15
184	Willie McGee	.15
185	Paul Sorrento	.15
186	Eric Young	.15
187	Bret Barberie	.15
188	Manuel Lee	.15
189	Jeff Branson	.15
190	Jim Deshaies	.15
191	Ken Caminiti	.15
192	Tim Raines	.15
193	Joe Grahe	.15
194	Hipolito Pichardo	.15
195	Denny Neagle	.15
196	Dave Staton	.15
197	Mike Benjamin	.15
198	Milt Thompson	.15
199	Bruce Ruffin	.15
200	Chris Hammond	.15
201	Tony Gwynn	2.50
202	Robin Ventura	.15
203	Frank Thomas	1.50
204	Kirby Puckett	2.50
205	Roberto Alomar	.30
206	Dennis Eckersley	1.25
207	Joe Carter	.15
208	Albert Belle	.15
209	Greg Maddux	2.50
210	Ryne Sandberg	2.50
211	Juan Gonzalez	.75
212	Jeff Bagwell	1.50
213	Randy Johnson	1.50
214	Matt Williams	.15
215	Dave Winfield	1.50
216	Larry Walker	.15
217	Roger Clemens	2.75
218	Kenny Lofton	.15
219	Cecil Fielder	.15
220	Darren Daulton	.15
221	John Olerud	.15
222	Jose Canseco	.75
223	Rickey Henderson	1.50
224	Fred McGriff	.15
225	Gary Sheffield	.50
226	Jack McDowell	.15
227	Rafael Palmeiro	1.25
228	Travis Fryman	.15
229	Marquis Grissom	.15
230	Barry Bonds	5.00
231	Carlos Baerga	.15
232	Ken Griffey Jr.	3.00
233	Dave Justice	.15
234	Bobby Bonilla	.15
235	Cal Ripken	5.00
236	Sammy Sosa	2.50
237	Len Dykstra	.15
238	Will Clark	.15
239	Paul Molitor	1.50
240	Barry Larkin	.15
241	Matt Williams	.15
242	Mitch Williams	.15
243	Ron Darling	.15
244	Darryl Kile	.15
245	Geronimo Berroa	.15

No.	Player	Value
246	Gregg Olson	.15
247	Brian Harper	.15
248	Rheal Cormier	.15
249	Rey Sanchez	.15
250	Jeff Fassero	.15
251	Sandy Alomar	.15
252	Chris Bosio	.15
253	Andy Stankiewicz	.15
254	Harold Baines	.15
255	Andy Ashby	.15
256	Tyler Green	.15
257	Kevin Brown	.15
258	Mo Vaughn	.15
259	Mike Harkey	.15
260	Dave Henderson	.15
261	Kent Hrbek	.15
262	Darrin Jackson	.15
263	Bob Wickman	.15
264	Spike Owen	.15
265	Todd Jones	.15
266	Pat Borders	.15
267	Tom Glavine	.45
268	Dave Nilsson	.15
269	Rich Batchelor	.15
270	Delino DeShields	.15
271	Felix Fermin	.15
272	Orestes Destrade	.15
273	Mickey Morandini	.15
274	Otis Nixon	.15
275	Ellis Burks	.15
276	Greg Gagne	.15
277	John Doherty	.15
278	Julio Franco	.15
279	Bernie Williams	.15
280	Rick Aguilera	.15
281	Mickey Tettleton	.15
282	David Nied	.15
283	Johnny Ruffin	.15
284	Dan Wilson	.15
285	Omar Vizquel	.15
286	Willie Banks	.15
287	Erik Pappas	.15
288	Cal Eldred	.15
289	Bobby Witt	.15
290	Luis Gonzalez	.15
291	Greg Pirkl	.15
292	Alex Cole	.15
293	Ricky Bones	.15
294	Denis Boucher	.15
295	John Burkett	.15
296	Steve Trachsel	.15
297	Ricky Jordan	.15
298	Mark Dewey	.15
299	Jimmy Key	.15
300	Mike MacFarlane	.15
301	Tim Belcher	.15
302	Carlos Reyes	.15
303	Greg Harris	.15
304	Brian Anderson **RC**	.15
305	Terry Mulholland	.15
306	Felix Jose	.15
307	Darren Holmes	.15
308	Jose Rijo	.15
309	Paul Wagner	.15
310	Bob Scanlan	.15
311	Mike Jackson	.15
312	Jose Vizcaino	.15
313	Rob Butler	.15
314	Kevin Seitzer	.15
315	Geronimo Pena	.15
316	Hector Carrasco	.15
317	Eddie Murray	1.50
318	Roger Salkeld	.15
319	Todd Hundley	.15
320	Danny Jackson	.15
321	Kevin Young	.15
322	Mike Greenwell	.15
323	Kevin Mitchell	.15
324	Chuck Knoblauch	.15
325	Danny Tartabull	.15
326	Vince Coleman	.15
327	Marvin Freeman	.15
328	Andy Benes	.15
329	Mike Kelly	.15
330	Karl Rhodes	.15
331	Allen Watson	.15
332	Damion Easley	.15
333	Reggie Jefferson	.15
334	Kevin McReynolds	.15
335	Arthur Rhodes	.15
336	Brian Hunter	.15
337	Tom Browning	.15
338	Pedro Munoz	.15
339	Billy Ripken	.15
340	Gene Harris	.15
341	Fernando Vina	.15
342	Sean Berry	.15
343	Pedro Astacio	.15
344	B.J. Surhoff	.15
345	Doug Drabek	.15
346	Jody Reed	.15
347	Ray Lankford	.15
348	Steve Farr	.15
349	Eric Anthony	.15
350	Pete Smith	.15
351	Lee Smith	.15
352	Mariano Duncan	.15
353	Doug Strange	.15
354	Tim Bogar	.15
355	Dave Weathers	.15
356	Eric Karros	.15
357	Randy Myers	.15
358	Chad Curtis	.15
359	Steve Avery	.15
360	Brian Jordan	.15
361	Tim Wallach	.15
362	Pedro Martinez	1.50
363	Bip Roberts	.15

No.	Player	Value
364	Lou Whitaker	.15
365	Luis Polonia	.15
366	Benny Santiago	.15
367	Brett Butler	.15
368	Shawon Dunston	.15
369	Kelly Stinnett	.15
370	Chris Turner	.15
371	Ruben Sierra	.15
372	Greg Harris	.15
373	Xavier Hernandez	.15
374	Howard Johnson	.15
375	Duane Ward	.15
376	Roberto Hernandez	.15
377	Scott Leius	.15
378	Dave Valle	.15
379	Sid Fernandez	.15
380	Doug Jones	.15
381	Zane Smith	.15
382	Craig Biggio	.15
383	Rick White	.15
384	Tom Pagnozzi	.15
385	Chris James	.15
386	Bret Boone	.15
387	Jeff Montgomery	.15
388	Chad Kreuter	.15
389	Greg Hibbard	.15
390	Mark Grace	.15
391	Phil Leftwich	.15
392	Don Mattingly	2.75
393	Ozzie Guillen	.15
394	Gary Gaetti	.15
395	Erik Hanson	.15
396	Scott Brosius	.15
397	Tom Gordon	.15
398	Bill Gullickson	.15
399	Matt Mieske	.15
400	Pat Hentgen	.15
401	Walt Weiss	.15
402	Greg Blosser	.15
403	Stan Javier	.15
404	Doug Henry	.15
405	Ramon Martinez	.15
406	Frank Viola	.15
407	Mike Hampton	.15
408	Andy Van Slyke	.15
409	Bobby Ayala	.15
410	Todd Zeile	.15
411	Jay Bell	.15
412	Denny Martinez	.15
413	Mark Portugal	.15
414	Bobby Munoz	.15
415	Kirt Manwaring	.15
416	John Kruk	.15
417	Trevor Hoffman	.15
418	Chris Sabo	.15
419	Bret Saberhagen	.15
420	Chris Nabholz	.15
421	James Mouton	.15
422	Tony Tarasco	.15
423	Carlos Delgado	.75
424	Rondell White	.15
425	Javier Lopez	.15
426	Chan Ho Park **RC**	1.00
427	Cliff Floyd	.15
428	Dave Staton	.15
429	J.R. Phillips	.15
430	Manny Ramirez	1.50
431	Kurt Abbott	.15
432	Melvin Nieves	.15
433	Alex Gonzalez	.15
434	Rick Helling	.15
435	Danny Bautista	.15
436	Matt Walbeck	.15
437	Ryan Klesko	.15
438	Steve Karsay	.15
439	Salomon Torres	.15
440	Scott Ruffcorn	.15

Refractors

It takes an experienced eye and good light to detect a Refractor parallel card from a regular-issue Topps Finest. The Refractor utilizes a variation of the Finest metallic printing process to produce rainbow-effect highlights on the card front. The Refractors share the checklist with the regular-issue Finest and were inserted at a rate of about one per 10 packs.

	NM/M
Complete Set (440):	300.00
Common Player:	1.00
Stars/Rookies:	3X

Superstar Jumbos

Identical in format to the Superstars subset in the Finest issue, these cards measure about 4" x 5-1/2" and were distributed one per box in Finest foil packs. Backs carry a card number under the banner with the player's name and position. There were 20 rookies and 20 superstars from both Series 1 and Series 2.

No.	Player	NM/M
	Complete Set (80):	140.00
	Common Player:	1.00
1	Mike Piazza	12.50
2	Kevin Stocker	1.00
3	Greg McMichael	1.00
4	Jeff Conine	1.00
5	Rene Arocha	1.00
6	Aaron Sele	1.00
7	Brent Gates	1.00
8	Chuck Carr	1.00
9	Kirk Rueter	1.00
10	Mike Lansing	1.00
11	Al Martin	1.00
12	Jason Bere	1.00
13	Troy Neel	1.00
14	Armando Reynoso	1.00
15	Jeromy Burnitz	1.00
16	Rich Amaral	1.00
17	David McCarty	1.00
18	Tim Salmon	1.00
19	Steve Cooke	1.00
20	Wil Cordero	1.00
201	Tony Gwynn	7.50
202	Robin Ventura	1.00
203	Frank Thomas	6.00
204	Kirby Puckett	7.50
205	Roberto Alomar	2.00
206	Dennis Eckersley	5.00
207	Joe Carter	1.00
208	Albert Belle	1.00
209	Greg Maddux	7.50
210	Ryne Sandberg	7.50
211	Juan Gonzalez	3.00
212	Jeff Bagwell	6.00
213	Randy Johnson	6.00
214	Matt Williams	1.00
215	Dave Winfield	6.00
216	Larry Walker	1.00
217	Roger Clemens	10.00
218	Kenny Lofton	1.00
219	Cecil Fielder	1.00
220	Darren Daulton	1.00
221	John Olerud	1.00
222	Jose Canseco	4.00
223	Rickey Henderson	6.00
224	Fred McGriff	1.00
225	Gary Sheffield	2.00
226	Jack McDowell	1.00
227	Rafael Palmeiro	5.00
228	Travis Fryman	1.00
229	Marquis Grissom	1.00
230	Barry Bonds	20.00
231	Carlos Baerga	1.00
232	Ken Griffey Jr.	12.50
233	Dave Justice	1.00
234	Bobby Bonilla	1.00
235	Cal Ripken	20.00
236	Sammy Sosa	7.50
237	Len Dykstra	1.00
238	Will Clark	1.00
239	Paul Molitor	6.00
240	Barry Larkin	1.00
421	James Mouton	1.00
422	Tony Tarasco	1.00
423	Carlos Delgado	3.00
424	Rondell White	1.00
425	Javier Lopez	1.00
426	Chan Ho Park	1.00
427	Cliff Floyd	1.00
428	Dave Staton	1.00
429	J.R. Phillips	1.00
430	Manny Ramirez	6.00
431	Kurt Abbott	1.00
432	Melvin Nieves	1.00
433	Alex Gonzalez	1.00
434	Rick Helling	1.00
435	Danny Bautista	1.00
436	Matt Walbeck	1.00
437	Ryan Klesko	1.00
438	Steve Karsay	1.00
439	Salomon Torres	1.00
440	Scott Ruffcorn	1.00

Superstar Sampler

This special version of 45 of the biggest-name stars from the 1994 Topps Finest set was issued in a three-card cello pack with the same player's '94 Bowman and Stadium Club cards. The packs were available only in 1994 Topps retail factory sets. Cards are identical to the regular-issue Finest cards except for a round, red "Topps Superstar Sampler" logo printed at bottom center on back.

No.	Player	NM/M
	Complete Set (45):	400.00
	Common Player:	4.00
1	Mike Piazza	35.00
18	Tim Salmon	4.00
35	Andres Galarraga	4.00
74	Raul Mondesi	4.00
92	Gregg Jefferies	4.00
201	Tony Gwynn	20.00
203	Frank Thomas	15.00
204	Kirby Puckett	20.00
205	Roberto Alomar	6.00
207	Joe Carter	4.00
208	Albert Belle	4.00
209	Greg Maddux	20.00
210	Ryne Sandberg	20.00
211	Juan Gonzalez	7.50
212	Jeff Bagwell	15.00
213	Randy Johnson	15.00
214	Matt Williams	4.00
216	Larry Walker	4.00
217	Roger Clemens	30.00
219	Cecil Fielder	4.00
220	Darren Daulton	4.00
221	John Olerud	4.00
222	Jose Canseco	7.50
224	Fred McGriff	4.00
225	Gary Sheffield	6.00
226	Jack McDowell	4.00
227	Rafael Palmeiro	12.00
229	Marquis Grissom	4.00
230	Barry Bonds	65.00
231	Carlos Baerga	4.00
232	Ken Griffey Jr.	35.00
233	Dave Justice	4.00
234	Bobby Bonilla	4.00
235	Cal Ripken Jr.	65.00
237	Len Dykstra	4.00
238	Will Clark	4.00
239	Paul Molitor	15.00
240	Barry Larkin	4.00
258	Mo Vaughn	4.00
267	Tom Glavine	7.50
390	Mark Grace	4.00
392	Don Mattingly	30.00
408	Andy Van Slyke	4.00
427	Cliff Floyd	4.00
430	Manny Ramirez	15.00

Bronze

This three-card set was included as part of the purchase of a 1994 Topps Stadium Club Members Only set, but was also made available on a limited basis via newspaper ads. The cards feature a version of Topps' Finest technology with the multi-colored front design laminated to a bronze base by a heavy lucite overlay. Backs are engraved in black on bronze and contain complete major and minor league stats and a few personal data. The Finest bronze cards are slightly larger than current standard size, measuring 2-3/4" x 3-3/4".

	NM/M
Complete Set (3):	40.00

		NM/M
	Common Player:	10.00
1	Barry Bonds	20.00
2	Ken Griffey Jr.	15.00
3	Frank Thomas	10.00

1995 Finest

In its third year Finest baseball was reduced to a 220-card base set. All cards feature the chrome-printing technology associated with the Finest logo and include a peel-off plastic protector on the card front. Backgrounds are green with gold pinstripes. Behind the action photo at center is a large diamond with each corner intersected by a silver semi-circle. On the Finest Rookies subset which makes up the first 30 cards of the issue, the diamond has a graduated pink to orange center, with flecks of red throughout. Veterans cards have a graduated blue to purple center of the diamond. On the rookies cards there is a teal brand name at top, while the vets show a gold "FINEST." Backs repeat the front background motif in shades of green. There is a player photo at right, with biographical data, 1994 and career stats, and a "Finest Moment" career highlight at left. Finest was sold in seven-card packs with a suggested retail price of $4.99.

		NM/M
	Complete Set (220):	75.00
	Common Player:	.25
	Refractors:	5X
	Series 1 or 2 Pack (7):	2.00
	Series 1 or 2 Wax Box (24):	30.00
1	Raul Mondesi (Rookie Theme)	.25
2	Kurt Abbott (Rookie Theme)	.25
3	Chris Gomez (Rookie Theme)	.25
4	Manny Ramirez (Rookie Theme)	1.50
5	Rondell White (Rookie Theme)	.25
6	William Van Landingham (Rookie Theme)	.25
7	Jon Lieber (Rookie Theme)	.25
8	Ryan Klesko (Rookie Theme)	.25
9	John Hudek (Rookie Theme)	.25
10	Joey Hamilton (Rookie Theme)	.25
11	Bob Hamelin (Rookie Theme)	.25
12	Brian Anderson (Rookie Theme)	.25
13	Mike Lieberthal (Rookie Theme)	.25
14	Rico Brogna (Rookie Theme)	.25
15	Rusty Greer (Rookie Theme)	.25
16	Carlos Delgado (Rookie Theme)	1.00
17	Jim Edmonds (Rookie Theme)	.65
18	Steve Trachsel (Rookie Theme)	.25
19	Matt Walbeck (Rookie Theme)	.25
20	Armando Benitez (Rookie Theme)	.25
21	Steve Karsay (Rookie Theme)	.25
22	Jose Oliva (Rookie Theme)	.25
23	Cliff Floyd (Rookie Theme)	.25
24	Kevin Foster (Rookie Theme)	.25
25	Javier Lopez (Rookie Theme)	.25
26	Jose Valentin (Rookie Theme)	.25
27	James Mouton (Rookie Theme)	.25

28	Hector Carrasco (Rookie Theme)	.25
29	Orlando Miller (Rookie Theme)	.25
30	Garret Anderson (Rookie Theme)	.25
31	Marvin Freeman	.25
32	Brett Butler	.25
33	Roberto Kelly	.25
34	Rod Beck	.25
35	Jose Rijo	.25
36	Edgar Martinez	.25
37	Jim Thome	.65
38	Rick Wilkins	.25
39	Wally Joyner	.25
40	Wil Cordero	.25
41	Tommy Greene	.25
42	Travis Fryman	.25
43	Don Slaught	.25
44	Brady Anderson	.25
45	Matt Williams	.25
46	Rene Arocha	.25
47	Rickey Henderson	1.50
48	Mike Mussina	.75
49	Greg McMichael	.25
50	Jody Reed	.25
51	Tino Martinez	.25
52	Dave Clark	.25
53	John Valentin	.25
54	Bret Boone	.25
55	Walt Weiss	.25
56	Kenny Lofton	.25
57	Scott Leius	.25
58	Eric Karros	.25
59	John Olerud	.25
60	Chris Hoiles	.25
61	Sandy Alomar	.25
62	Tim Wallach	.25
63	Cal Eldred	.25
64	Tom Glavine	.50
65	Mark Grace	.25
66	Rey Sanchez	.25
67	Bobby Ayala	.25
68	Dante Bichette	.25
69	Andres Galarraga	.25
70	Chuck Carr	.25
71	Bobby Witt	.25
72	Steve Avery	.25
73	Bobby Jones	.25
74	Delino DeShields	.25
75	Kevin Tapani	.25
76	Randy Johnson	1.50
77	David Nied	.25
78	Pat Hentgen	.25
79	Tim Salmon	.25
80	Todd Zeile	.25
81	John Wetteland	.25
82	Albert Belle	.25
83	Ben McDonald	.25
84	Bobby Munoz	.25
85	Bip Roberts	.25
86	Mo Vaughn	.25
87	Chuck Finley	.25
88	Chuck Knoblauch	.25
89	Frank Thomas	1.50
90	Danny Tartabull	.25
91	Dean Palmer	.25
92	Len Dykstra	.25
93	J.R. Phillips	.25
94	Tom Candiotti	.25
95	Marquis Grissom	.25
96	Barry Larkin	.25
97	Bryan Harvey	.25
98	Dave Justice	.25
99	David Cone	.25
100	Wade Boggs	2.50
101	Jason Bere	.25
102	Hal Morris	.25
103	Fred McGriff	.25
104	Bobby Bonilla	.25
105	Jay Buhner	.25
106	Allen Watson	.25
107	Mickey Tettleton	.25
108	Kevin Appier	.25
109	Ivan Rodriguez	1.00
110	Carlos Garcia	.25
111	Andy Benes	.25
112	Eddie Murray	1.50
113	Mike Piazza	3.50
114	Greg Vaughn	.25
115	Paul Molitor	1.50
116	Terry Steinbach	.25
117	Jeff Bagwell	1.50
118	Ken Griffey Jr.	3.50
119	Gary Sheffield	.75
120	Cal Ripken Jr.	5.00
121	Jeff Kent	.25
122	Jay Bell	.25
123	Will Clark	.25
124	Cecil Fielder	.25
125	Alex Fernandez	.25
126	Don Mattingly	3.00
127	Reggie Sanders	.25
128	Moises Alou	.25
129	Craig Biggio	.25
130	Eddie Williams	.25
131	John Franco	.25
132	John Kruk	.25
133	Jeff King	.25
134	Royce Clayton	.25
135	Doug Drabek	.25
136	Ray Lankford	.25
137	Roberto Alomar	.50
138	Todd Hundley	.25
139	Alex Cole	.25
140	Shawon Dunston	.25
141	John Roper	.25
142	Mark Langston	.25

143	Tom Pagnozzi	.25
144	Wilson Alvarez	.25
145	Scott Cooper	.25
146	Kevin Mitchell	.25
147	Mark Whiten	.25
148	Jeff Conine	.25
149	Chili Davis	.25
150	Luis Gonzalez	.25
151	Juan Guzman	.25
152	Mike Greenwell	.25
153	Mike Henneman	.25
154	Rick Aguilera	.25
155	Dennis Eckersley	1.00
156	Darrin Fletcher	.25
157	Darren Lewis	.25
158	Juan Gonzalez	.75
159	Dave Hollins	.25
160	Jimmy Key	.25
161	Roberto Hernandez	.25
162	Randy Myers	.25
163	Joe Carter	.25
164	Darren Daulton	.25
165	Mike MacFarlane	.25
166	Bret Saberhagen	.25
167	Kirby Puckett	2.50
168	Lance Johnson	.25
169	Mark McGwire	4.00
170	Jose Canseco	.75
171	Mike Stanley	.25
172	Lee Smith	.25
173	Robin Ventura	.25
174	Greg Gagne	.25
175	Brian McRae	.25
176	Mike Bordick	.25
177	Rafael Palmeiro	1.00
178	Kenny Rogers	.25
179	Chad Curtis	.25
180	Devon White	.25
181	Paul O'Neill	.25
182	Ken Caminiti	.25
183	Dave Nilsson	.25
184	Tim Naehring	.25
185	Roger Clemens	3.00
186	Otis Nixon	.25
187	Tim Raines	.25
188	Dennis Martinez	.25
189	Pedro Martinez	1.50
190	Jim Abbott	.25
191	Ryan Thompson	.25
192	Barry Bonds	5.00
193	Joe Girardi	.25
194	Steve Finley	.25
195	John Jaha	.25
196	Tony Gwynn	2.50
197	Sammy Sosa	2.50
198	John Burkett	.25
199	Carlos Baerga	.25
200	Ramon Martinez	.25
201	Aaron Sele	.25
202	Eduardo Perez	.25
203	Alan Trammell	.25
204	Orlando Merced	.25
205	Deion Sanders	.35
206	Robb Nen	.25
207	Jack McDowell	.25
208	Ruben Sierra	.25
209	Bernie Williams	.25
210	Kevin Seitzer	.25
211	Charles Nagy	.25
212	Tony Phillips	.25
213	Greg Maddux	2.50
214	Jeff Montgomery	.25
215	Larry Walker	.25
216	Andy Van Slyke	.25
217	Ozzie Smith	2.50
218	Geronimo Pena	.25
219	Gregg Jefferies	.25
220	Lou Whitaker	.25

Refractors

A parallel set with a counterpart to each of the 220 cards in the regular Finest emission, the Refractors are printed in a version of the Finest chrome technology that produces a rainbow effect when viewed at the proper angle. The relatively open spaces of the 1995 Finest design make the Refractors easier to spot than the previous years' versions, but just to assist the identification process, Topps placed a small black "REFRACTOR" in the dark green background on the cards' backs, as well. Advertised rate of insertion for the Refractors was about one per 12 packs.

		NM/M
	Complete Set (220):	400.00
	Common Player:	1.00
	Stars:	5X

Flame Throwers

The scarcest of the Finest inserts is the nine-card set of baseball's hardest throwing pitchers. Flame Throwers cards are found at an average rate of one per 48 packs. Fronts have a central photo of a pitcher bringing his best heat. Behind the photo is the Flame Throwers typographic logo in tones of red, yellow and orange. Backs have another photo and a bar graph rating the pitcher's skill levels.

		NM/M
	Complete Set (9):	20.00
	Common Player:	1.50
1	Jason Bere	1.50
2	Roger Clemens	8.00
3	Juan Guzman	1.50
4	John Hudek	1.50
5	Randy Johnson	5.00
6	Pedro Martinez	4.00
7	Jose Rijo	1.50
8	Bret Saberhagen	1.50
9	John Wetteland	1.50

Power Kings

The emphasis is on youth in this chase set of baseball's top distance threats. Found at a rate of one per 24 packs, on average, the Power Kings inserts have a central photo of the player in batting action. The background, in shades of blue, features lightning strokes. Backs feature another pair of player photos and a bar graph charting the hitter's power skills.

		NM/M
	Complete Set (18):	35.00
	Common Player:	.75
1	Bob Hamelin	.75
2	Raul Mondesi	.75
3	Ryan Klesko	.75
4	Carlos Delgado	1.50
5	Manny Ramirez	3.00
6	Mike Piazza	5.00
7	Jeff Bagwell	3.00
8	Mo Vaughn	.75
9	Frank Thomas	3.00
10	Ken Griffey Jr.	5.00
11	Albert Belle	.75
12	Sammy Sosa	4.00
13	Dante Bichette	.75
14	Gary Sheffield	.75
15	Matt Williams	.75
16	Fred McGriff	.75
17	Barry Bonds	7.50
18	Cecil Fielder	.75

Update

Players who changed teams through trades or free agent signings and more of the season's rookie play-

er crop are included in the Finest Update series of 110 cards. The cards are numbered contiguously with the base Finest set and share the same design. Once again, Refractor cards were found on an average of once per 12 packs. Finest Update was sold in seven-card packs with a suggested retail price of $4.99.

		NM/M
	Complete Set (110):	20.00
	Common Player:	.25
	Refractors:	5X
	Wax Pack (7):	1.25
	Wax Box (24):	20.00
221	Chipper Jones	2.50
222	Benji Gil	.25
223	Tony Phillips	.25
224	Trevor Wilson	.25
225	Tony Tarasco	.25
226	Roberto Petagine	.25
227	Mike MacFarlane	.25
228	Hideo Nomo RC	3.00
229	Mark McLemore	.25
230	Ron Gant	.25
231	Andujar Cedeno	.25
232	Mike Mimbs RC	.25
233	Jim Abbott	.25
234	Ricky Bones	.25
235	Marty Cordova	.25
236	Mark Johnson	.25
237	Marquis Grissom	.25
238	Tom Henke	.25
239	Terry Pendleton	.25
240	John Wetteland	.25
241	Lee Smith	.25
242	Jaime Navarro	.25
243	Luis Alicea	.25
244	Scott Cooper	.25
245	Gary Gaetti	.25
246	Edgardo Alfonzo	.25
247	Brad Clontz	.25
248	Dave Mlicki	.25
249	Dave Winfield	.75
250	Mark Grudzielanek RC	.50
251	Alex Gonzalez	.25
252	Kevin Brown	.25
253	Esteban Loaiza	.25
254	Vaughn Eshelman	.25
255	Bill Swift	.25
256	Brian McRae	.25
257	Bobby Higginson RC	.50
258	Jack McDowell	.25
259	Scott Stahoviak	.25
260	Jon Nunnally	.25
261	Charlie Hayes	.25
262	Jacob Brumfield	.25
263	Chad Curtis	.25
264	Heathcliff Slocumb	.25
265	Mark Whiten	.25
266	Mickey Tettleton	.25
267	Jose Mesa	.25
268	Doug Jones	.25
269	Trevor Hoffman	.25
270	Paul Sorrento	.25
271	Shane Andrews	.25
272	Brett Butler	.25
273	Curtis Goodwin	.25
274	Larry Walker	.25
275	Phil Plantier	.25
276	Ken Hill	.25
277	Vinny Castilla	.25
278	Billy Ashley	.25
279	Derek Jeter	6.00
280	Bob Tewksbury	.25
281	Jose Offerman	.25
282	Glenallen Hill	.25
283	Tony Fernandez	.25
284	Mike Devereaux	.25
285	John Burkett	.25
286	Geronimo Berroa	.25
287	Quilvio Veras	.25
288	Jason Bates	.25
289	Lee Tinsley	.25
290	Derek Bell	.25
291	Jeff Fassero	.25
292	Ray Durham	.25
293	Chad Ogea	.25
294	Bill Pulsipher	.25
295	Phil Nevin	.25
296	Carlos Perez RC	.25
297	Roberto Kelly	.25
298	Tim Wakefield	.25
299	Jeff Manto	.25
300	Brian Hunter	.25
301	C.J. Nitkowski	.25

302	Dustin Hermanson	.25
303	John Mabry	.25
304	Orel Hershiser	.25
305	Ron Villone	.25
306	Sean Bergman	.25
307	Tom Goodwin	.25
308	Al Reyes	.25
309	Todd Stottlemyre	.25
310	Rich Becker	.25
311	Joey Cora	.25
312	Ed Sprague	.25
313	John Smoltz	.25
314	Frank Castillo	.25
315	Chris Hammond	.25
316	Ismael Valdes	.25
317	Pete Harnisch	.25
318	Bernard Gilkey	.25
319	John Kruk	.25
320	Marc Newfield	.25
321	Brian Johnson	.25
322	Mark Portugal	.25
323	David Hulse	.25
324	Luis Ortiz	.25
325	Mike Benjamin	.25
326	Brian Jordan	.25
327	Shawn Green	.75
328	Joe Oliver	.25
329	Felipe Lira	.25
330	Andre Dawson	.75

Update Refractors

The special version of Topps' chromium printing process which creates a rainbow effect was applied to a limited number of each card in the Finest Update set to create a parallel Refractor edition. To assist in identification, a small black "REFRACTOR" is printed on the cards' backs, as well. Refractors are found on average once every 12 packs of Finest Update.

		NM/M
	Complete Set (110):	100.00
	Common Player:	1.00
	Stars:	5X

Bronze League Leaders

Available only by mail directly from Topps, this set features N.L. and A.L. leaders in various batting categories for the 1994 season. Fronts employ Topps' Finest technology with a stained-glass effect in the background, overlaid with a heavy layer of resin. Backs are bronze and feature 1994 stats and highlights embossed in blue. The cards are oversized, measuring 2-3/4" x 3-3/4".

		NM/M
	Complete Set (6):	20.00
	Common Player:	2.50
1	Matt Williams	2.50
2	Tony Gwynn	6.50
3	Jeff Bagwell	5.00
4	Ken Griffey Jr.	9.00
5	Paul O'Neill	2.50
6	Frank Thomas	5.00

1996 Finest

Utilizing three levels of basecard scarcity, the 359-card Finest set comprises 220 Commons (Bronze), 91 Uncommons (Silver)

and 49 Rares (Gold). Cards were somewhat randomly assigned a status. Uncommon cards are found one in four packs; Rare cards are seeded one per 24 packs. The set has eight themes. Series 1 themes are Phenoms, Intimidators, Gamers and Sterling, the latter of which consists of star players already included within the first three themes. Series 2 themes are Franchise, Additions, Prodigies and Sterling. Regular-issue cards are not only numbered from 1-359 in the set as a whole, but also numbered within each subset. Finest Refractor parallel cards were also made. Rare Refractor cards are found one every 288 packs (fewer than 150 of each produced), while Uncommon Refractors are found one per 48 packs. Common Refractors are seeded 1:12.

	NM/M
Complete Set (359):	300.00
Bronze Set (220):	60.00
Common Bronze:	.15
Silver Set (91):	90.00
Typical Silver:	.50
Gold Set (47):	200.00
Typical Gold:	2.00
Series 1 Pack (6):	1.50
Series 1 Wax Box (24):	30.00
Series 2 Pack (6):	1.50
Series 2 Wax Box (24):	30.00
1 Greg Maddux/S (Intimidators)	3.00
2 Bernie Williams/S (Gamers)	.50
3 Ivan Rodriguez/S (Intimidators)	1.50
4 Marty Cordova/G (Phenoms)	2.00
5 Roberto Hernandez (Intimidators)	.15
6 Tony Gwynn/G (Gamers)	7.50
7 Barry Larkin/S (Sterling)	.50
8 Terry Pendleton (Gamers)	.15
9 Albert Belle/G (Sterling)	2.00
10 Ray Lankford/S (Gamers)	.50
11 Mike Piazza/S (Sterling)	4.00
12 Ken Caminiti (Gamers)	.15
13 Larry Walker/S (Intimidators)	.50
14 Matt Williams/S (Intimidators)	.50
15 Dan Miceli (Phenoms)	.15
16 Chipper Jones (Sterling)	2.00
17 John Wetteland (Intimidators)	.15
18 Kirby Puckett/S (Sterling)	7.50
19 Tim Naehring (Gamers)	.15
20 Karim Garcia/G (Phenoms)	2.00
21 Eddie Murray (Gamers)	1.25
22 Tim Salmon/S (Intimidators)	.50
23 Kevin Appier (Intimidators)	.15
24 Ken Griffey Jr. (Sterling)	3.00
25 Cal Ripken Jr./G (Gamers)	15.00
26 Brian McRae (Gamers)	.15
27 Pedro Martinez (Intimidators)	1.25
28 Brian Jordan (Gamers)	.15
29 Mike Fetters (Intimidators)	.15
30 Carlos Delgado (Phenoms)	.65
31 Shane Reynolds (Intimidators)	.15
32 Terry Steinbach (Gamers)	.15
33 Hideo Nomo/G (Sterling)	2.50
34 Mark Leiter (Gamers)	.15
35 Edgar Martinez/S (Intimidators)	.50
36 David Segui (Gamers)	.15
37 Gregg Jefferies (Gamers)	.50
38 Bill Pulsipher/S (Phenoms)	.50
39 Ryne Sandberg/G (Gamers)	7.50
40 Fred McGriff (Intimidators)	1.25
41 Shawn Green/S (Phenoms)	.75
42 Jeff Bagwell/G (Sterling)	5.00
43 Jim Abbott/S (Gamers)	.50
44 Glenallen Hill (Intimidators)	.15
45 Brady Anderson (Gamers)	.15
46 Roger Clemens/S (Intimidators)	3.50
47 Jim Thome (Gamers)	.60
48 Frank Thomas (Sterling)	1.25
49 Chuck Knoblauch (Gamers)	.15
50 Lenny Dykstra (Gamers)	.15
51 Jason Isringhausen/G (Phenoms)	2.00
52 Rondell White/S (Phenoms)	.50
53 Tom Pagnozzi (Gamers)	.15
54 Dennis Eckersley/S (Intimidators)	1.50
55 Ricky Bones (Gamers)	.15
56 David Justice (Intimidators)	.15
57 Steve Avery (Gamers)	.15
58 Robby Thompson (Gamers)	.15
59 Hideo Nomo/S (Phenoms)	1.00
60 Gary Sheffield/S (Intimidators)	.75
61 Tony Gwynn (Sterling)	2.00
62 Will Clark/S (Gamers)	.50
63 Denny Neagle (Gamers)	.15
64 Mo Vaughn/G (Intimidators)	2.00
65 Bret Boone/S (Gamers)	.50
66 Dante Bichette/G (Sterling)	2.00
67 Robin Ventura (Gamers)	.15
68 Rafael Palmeiro/S (Intimidators)	1.50
69 Carlos Baerga/S (Gamers)	.50
70 Kevin Seitzer (Gamers)	.15
71 Ramon Martinez (Intimidators)	.15
72 Tom Glavine/S (Gamers)	1.00
73 Garret Anderson/S (Phenoms)	.50
74 Mark McGwire/G (Intimidators)	12.00
75 Brian Hunter (Phenoms)	.15
76 Alan Benes (Phenoms)	.15
77 Randy Johnson/S (Intimidators)	2.00
78 Jeff King/S (Gamers)	.50
79 Kirby Puckett/S (Intimidators)	3.00
80 Ozzie Guillen (Gamers)	.15
81 Kenny Lofton/S (Intimidators)	2.00
82 Benji Gil (Phenoms)	.15
83 Jim Edmonds/S (Gamers)	2.00
84 Cecil Fielder/S (Gamers)	.50
85 Todd Hundley (Gamers)	.15
86 Reggie Sanders/S (Intimidators)	.50
87 Pat Hentgen (Gamers)	.15
88 Ryan Klesko/S (Intimidators)	.50
89 Chuck Finley (Gamers)	.15
90 Mike Mussina/S (Intimidators)	2.50
91 John Valentin/S (Intimidators)	.50
92 Derek Jeter (Phenoms)	4.00
93 Paul O'Neill (Intimidators)	.15
94 Darrin Fletcher (Gamers)	.15
95 Manny Ramirez/S (Phenoms)	2.00
96 Delino DeShields (Gamers)	.15
97 Tim Salmon (Sterling)	.15
98 John Olerud (Gamers)	.15
99 Vinny Castilla/S (Intimidators)	.50
100 Jeff Conine/G (Gamers)	2.00
101 Tim Wakefield (Gamers)	.15
102 Johnny Damon/S (Phenoms)	3.50
103 Dave Stevens (Gamers)	.15
104 Orlando Merced (Gamers)	.15
105 Barry Bonds/S (Sterling)	15.00
106 Jay Bell (Gamers)	.15
107 John Burkett (Gamers)	.15
108 Chris Hoiles (Gamers)	.15
109 Carlos Perez/S (Phenoms)	.50
110 Dave Nilsson (Gamers)	.15
111 Rod Beck (Intimidators)	.15
112 Craig Biggio/S (Gamers)	.50
113 Mike Piazza (Intimidators)	3.00
114 Mark Langston (Gamers)	.15
115 Juan Gonzalez/S (Intimidators)	1.00
116 Rico Brogna (Gamers)	.15
117 Jose Canseco/S (Intimidators)	3.00
118 Tom Goodwin (Gamers)	.15
119 Bryan Rekar (Phenoms)	.15
120 David Cone (Intimidators)	.15
121 Ray Durham/S (Phenoms)	.50
122 Andy Pettitte (Phenoms)	.40
123 Chili Davis (Intimidators)	.15
124 John Smoltz (Gamers)	.15
125 Heathcliff Slocumb (Intimidators)	.15
126 Dante Bichette (Intimidators)	.15
127 C.J. Nitkowski/S (Phenoms)	.15
128 Alex Gonzalez (Phenoms)	.15
129 Jeff Montgomery (Intimidators)	.15
130 Raul Mondesi/S (Intimidators)	.15
131 Denny Martinez (Gamers)	.15
132 Mel Rojas (Intimidators)	.15
133 Derek Bell (Gamers)	.15
134 Trevor Hoffman (Intimidators)	.15
135 Ken Griffey Jr./G (Intimidators)	9.00
136 Darren Daulton (Gamers)	.15
137 Pete Schourek (Gamers)	.15
138 Phil Nevin (Phenoms)	.15
139 Andres Galarraga (Intimidators)	.15
140 Chad Fonville (Phenoms)	.15
141 Chipper Jones/S (Phenoms)	8.00
142 Lee Smith/S (Intimidators)	.50
143 Joe Carter/S (Gamers)	.50
144 J.T. Snow (Gamers)	.15
145 Greg Maddux/S (Sterling)	7.50
146 Barry Bonds (Intimidators)	4.00
147 Orel Hershiser (Gamers)	.15
148 Quilvio Veras (Phenoms)	.15
149 Will Clark (Sterling)	.15
150 Jose Rijo (Gamers)	.15
151 Mo Vaughn/S (Sterling)	.50
152 Travis Fryman (Gamers)	.15
153 Frank Rodriguez/S (Phenoms)	.50
154 Alex Fernandez (Gamers)	.15
155 Wade Boggs (Gamers)	2.00
156 Troy Percival (Phenoms)	.15
157 Moises Alou (Gamers)	.15
158 Javy Lopez (Gamers)	.15
159 Jason Giambi (Phenoms)	.50
160 Steve Finley/S (Gamers)	.15
161 Jeff Bagwell/S (Intimidators)	2.00
162 Mark McGwire (Sterling)	3.50
163 Eric Karros (Gamers)	.15
164 Jay Buhner/G (Intimidators)	2.00
165 Cal Ripken Jr./S (Sterling)	6.00
166 Mickey Tettleton (Intimidators)	.15
167 Barry Larkin (Intimidators)	.15
168 Lyle Mouton/S (Phenoms)	.50
169 Ruben Sierra (Intimidators)	.15
170 Bill Swift (Gamers)	.15
171 Sammy Sosa/S (Intimidators)	3.00
172 Chad Curtis (Gamers)	.15
173 Dean Palmer (Gamers)	.15
174 John Franco/S (Gamers)	.50
175 Bobby Bonilla (Intimidators)	.15
176 Greg Colbrunn (Gamers)	.15
177 Jose Mesa (Intimidators)	.15
178 Mike Greenwell (Gamers)	.15
179 Greg Vaughn/S (Intimidators)	.50
180 Mark Wohlers (Intimidators)	.15
181 Doug Drabek (Gamers)	.15
182 Paul O'Neill/S (Sterling)	.50
183 Wilson Alvarez (Gamers)	.15
184 Marty Cordova (Sterling)	.15
185 Hal Morris (Gamers)	.15
186 Frank Thomas/S (Intimidators)	6.00
187 Carlos Garcia (Gamers)	.15
188 Albert Belle/S (Intimidators)	.50
189 Mark Grace/S (Gamers)	.50
190 Marquis Grissom (Gamers)	.15
191 Checklist	.15
192 Chipper Jones/G (Phenoms)	8.00
193 Will Clark (Gamers)	.15
194 Paul Molitor (Gamers)	1.25
195 Kenny Rogers (Gamers)	.15
196 Reggie Sanders (Gamers)	.15
197 Roberto Alomar/G (Gamers)	2.50
198 Dennis Eckersley (Gamers)	4.00
199 Raul Mondesi (Gamers)	.15
200 Lance Johnson (Gamers)	.15
201 Alvin Mormon (Gamers)	.15
202 George Arias/G (Phenoms)	2.00
203 Jack McDowell (Gamers)	.15
204 Randy Myers (Gamers)	.15
205 Harold Baines (Gamers)	.15
206 Marty Cordova (Gamers)	.15
207 Rich Hunter RC (Gamers)	.15
208 Al Leiter (Gamers)	.15
209 Greg Gagne (Gamers)	.15
210 Ben McDonald (Gamers)	.15
211 Ernie Young/S (Gamers)	.50
212 Terry Adams (Gamers)	.15
213 Paul Sorrento (Gamers)	.15
214 Albert Belle (Gamers)	.15
215 Mike Blowers (Gamers)	.15
216 Jim Edmonds (Gamers)	.15
217 Felipe Crespo (Gamers)	.15
218 Fred McGriff/S (Gamers)	.50
219 Shawon Dunston (Gamers)	.15
220 Jimmy Haynes (Gamers)	.15
221 Jose Canseco (Gamers)	.50
222 Eric Davis (Gamers)	.15
223 Kimera Bartee/S (Gamers)	.50
224 Tim Raines (Gamers)	.15
225 Tony Phillips (Gamers)	.15
226 Charlie Hayes (Gamers)	.15
227 Eric Owens (Gamers)	.15
228 Roberto Alomar (Gamers)	.30
229 Rickey Henderson/S (Gamers)	2.00
230 Sterling Hitchcock/S (Gamers)	.50
231 Bernard Gilkey/S (Gamers)	.50
232 Hideo Nomo/S (Gamers)	2.50
233 Kenny Lofton (Gamers)	.15
234 Ryne Sandberg/S (Gamers)	3.00
235 Greg Maddux/S (Gamers)	3.00
236 Mark McGwire (Gamers)	3.50
237 Jay Buhner (Gamers)	.15
238 Craig Biggio (Gamers)	.15
239 Todd Stottlemyre/S (Gamers)	.50
240 Barry Bonds (Gamers)	4.00
241 Jason Kendall/S (Gamers)	.50
242 Paul O'Neill/S (Gamers)	.50
243 Chris Snopek/G (Gamers)	.15
244 Ron Gant (Gamers)	.15
245 Paul Wilson (Gamers)	.15
246 Todd Hollandsworth (Gamers)	.15
247 Todd Zeile (Gamers)	.15
248 David Justice (Gamers)	.15
249 Tim Salmon/G (Gamers)	2.00
250 Moises Alou (Gamers)	.15
251 Bob Wolcott (Gamers)	.15
252 David Wells (Gamers)	.15
253 Juan Gonzalez (Gamers)	.65
254 Andres Galarraga (Gamers)	.15
255 Dave Hollins (Gamers)	.15
256 Devon White/S (Gamers)	.50
257 Sammy Sosa (Gamers)	2.00
258 Ivan Rodriguez (Gamers)	.75
259 Bip Roberts (Gamers)	.15
260 Tino Martinez (Gamers)	.15
261 Chuck Knoblauch/S (Gamers)	.50
262 Mike Stanley (Gamers)	.15
263 Wally Joyner/S (Gamers)	.50
264 Butch Huskey (Gamers)	.15
265 Jeff Conine (Gamers)	.15
266 Matt Williams/G (Gamers)	2.00
267 Mark Grace (Gamers)	.15
268 Jason Schmidt (Gamers)	.15
269 Otis Nixon (Gamers)	.15
270 Randy Johnson/G (Gamers)	5.00
271 Kirby Puckett (Gamers)	2.00
272 Andy Fox/S RC (Gamers)	.50
273 Andy Benes (Gamers)	.15
274 Sean Berry/S (Gamers)	.50
275 Mike Piazza (Gamers)	3.00
276 Rey Ordonez (Gamers)	.15
277 Benito Santiago/S (Gamers)	.50
278 Gary Gaetti (Gamers)	.15
279 Paul Molitor/S (Gamers)	5.00
280 Robin Ventura (Gamers)	.15
281 Cal Ripken Jr. (Gamers)	4.00
282 Carlos Baerga (Gamers)	.15
283 Roger Cedeno (Gamers)	.15
284 Chad Mottola/S (Gamers)	.50
285 Terrell Wade (Gamers)	.15
286 Kevin Brown (Gamers)	.15
287 Rafael Palmeiro (Gamers)	1.00
288 Mo Vaughn (Gamers)	.15
289 Dante Bichette/S (Gamers)	.50
290 Cecil Fielder/S (Gamers)	.50
291 Doc Gooden (Gamers)	.50
292 Bob Tewksbury (Gamers)	.15
293 Kevin Mitchell/S (Gamers)	.50
294 Livan Hernandez/G RC (Gamers)	2.00
295 Russ Davis/S (Gamers)	.50
296 Chan Ho Park/S (Gamers)	.50
297 T.J. mathews (Gamers)	.15
298 Manny Ramirez (Gamers)	1.25
299 Jeff Bagwell (Gamers)	1.25
300 Marty Janzen/G RC (Gamers)	2.00
301 Wade Boggs (Gamers)	2.00
302 Larry Walker/S (Gamers)	.50
303 Steve Gibralter (Gamers)	.15
304 B.J. Surhoff (Gamers)	.15
305 Ken Griffey Jr./S (Gamers)	4.00
306 Royce Clayton (Gamers)	.15
307 Sal Fasano (Gamers)	.15
308 Ron Gant/G (Gamers)	2.00
309 Gary Sheffield (Gamers)	.40
310 Ken Hill (Gamers)	.15
311 Joe Girardi (Gamers)	.15
312 Matt Lawton RC (Gamers)	.15
313 Billy Wagner/S (Gamers)	.50
314 Julio Franco (Gamers)	.15
315 Joe Carter (Gamers)	.15
316 Brooks Kieschnick (Gamers)	.15
317 Mike Grace/S RC (Gamers)	.50
318 Heathcliff Slocumb (Gamers)	.15
319 Barry Larkin (Gamers)	.15
320 Tony Gwynn (Gamers)	2.00
321 Ryan Klesko/S (Gamers)	2.00
322 Frank Thomas (Gamers)	1.25
323 Edgar Martinez (Gamers)	.15
324 Jermaine Dye/S (Gamers)	.50
325 Henry Rodriguez (Gamers)	.15
326 Marvin Benard RC (Gamers)	.50
327 Kenny Lofton/S (Gamers)	.50
328 Derek Bell/S (Gamers)	.50
329 Ugueth Urbina (Gamers)	.15
330 Jason Giambi (Gamers)	3.00
331 Roger Salkeld (Gamers)	.15
332 Edgar Renteria (Gamers)	.15
333 Ryan Klesko (Gamers)	.15
334 Ray Lankford (Gamers)	.15
335 Edgar Martinez/G (Gamers)	2.00
336 Justin Thompson (Gamers)	.15
337 Gary Sheffield/S (Gamers)	.75
338 Rey Ordonez/S (Gamers)	2.00
339 Mark Clark (Gamers)	.15
340 Ruben Rivera (Gamers)	.15
341 Mark Grace/S (Gamers)	.50
342 Matt Williams (Gamers)	.15
343 Francisco Cordova RC (Gamers)	.25
344 Cecil Fielder (Gamers)	.15
345 Andres Galarraga/S (Gamers)	.50
346 Brady Anderson/S (Gamers)	.50
347 Sammy Sosa/G (Gamers)	7.50
348 Mark Grudzielanek (Gamers)	.15
349 Ron Coomer (Gamers)	.15
350 Derek Jeter/S (Gamers)	6.00
351 Rich Aurilia (Gamers)	.15
352 Jose Herrera (Gamers)	.15
353 Jay Buhner/S	.50
354 Juan Gonzalez/G	2.50
355 Craig Biggio/G	2.00
356 Tony Clark	.15
357 Tino Martinez/S	.15
358 Dan Naulty RC	.15
359 Checklist	.15

Refractors

Finest Refractor cards were created as a parallel set to Topps' 1996 Finest set. Rare Refractor cards are found about one per 288 packs (less than 150 of these sets were produced), while Uncommon Refractors are found one every 48 packs. Common Refractors are seeded one every 12 packs.

	NM/M
Complete Set (359):	900.00
Bronze Set (220):	300.00
Common Bronze:	1.00
Bronze Stars:	4X
Silver Set (91):	250.00
Typical Silver:	2.00
Silver Stars:	2.5X
Gold Set (48):	600.00
Typical Gold:	6.00
Gold Stars:	2X

1997 Finest Samples

Many of the subsets included in the 1997 Finest issue were previewed with a cello-wrapped pack of five cards distributed to hobby dealers. Cards are virtually identical to the issued versions and are designated a Refractor on back. Overprinted on back is a red notice, "PROMOTIONAL SAMPLE / NOT FOR RESALE."

	NM/M
Complete Set (5):	15.00
Common Player:	2.50
1 Barry Bonds	3.50
15 Derek Jeter	3.50
30 Mark McGwire	3.00
143 Hideo Nomo	2.50
159 Jeff Bagwell	2.50

1997 Finest

Finest returned for 1997 in its three-tiered format from 1996, but added several new twists. Issued in two series of 175 cards each, cards numbered 1-100 and 176-275 are bronze; 101-150 and 276-325 are silver and 151-175 and 326-350 are gold. All cards are designated among one of five different subsets per series. In Series 1 they are: Warriors, Blue Chips, Power, Hurlers and Masters. Series 2 subsets are: Power, Masters, Blue Chips, Competitors and Acquisitions. The bronze cards are the "common" card, while silvers are found every four packs and golds every 24 packs. Each card has a parallel Refractor version: bronze (1:12), silver (1:48) and gold (1:288). In addition, silver and gold cards have an additional parallel set. Silvers are found in an embossed version (1:16) and embossed Refractor version (1:192), while golds are found in a die-cut embossed version (1:96) and a die-cut embossed Refractor (1:1152).

	NM/M
Complete Set (350):	200.00
Bronze Set (200):	15.00
Common Bronze:	.15
Silver Set (100):	75.00
Typical Silver:	.50
Embossed Silvers:	2X
Gold Set (50):	150.00
Typical Gold:	2.00
Embossed Die-Cut Golds:	1.5X
Series 1 or 2 Pack (6):	1.50
Series 1 or 2 Wax Box (24):	25.00
1 Barry Bonds/B	2.00
2 Ryne Sandberg/B	.75
3 Brian Jordan/B	.15
4 Rocky Coppinger/B	.15
5 Dante Bichette/B	.15
6 Al Martin/B	.15
7 Charles Nagy/B	.15
8 Otis Nixon/B	.15
9 Mark Johnson/B	.15
10 Jeff Bagwell/B	.60
11 Ken Hill/B	.15
12 Willie Adams/B	.15
13 Raul Mondesi/B	.15
14 Reggie Sanders/B	.15
15 Derek Jeter/B	2.00
16 Jermaine Dye/B	.15
17 Edgar Renteria/B	.15
18 Travis Fryman/B	.15
19 Roberto Hernandez/B	.15
20 Sammy Sosa/B	.75
21 Garret Anderson/B	.15
22 Rey Ordonez/B	.15
23 Glenallen Hill/B	.15
24 Dave Nilsson/B	.15
25 Kevin Brown/B	.15
26 Brian McRae/B	.15
27 Joey Hamilton/B	.15
28 Jamey Wright/B	.15
29 Frank Thomas/B	.60
30 Mark McGwire/B	1.50
31 Ramon Martinez/B	.15
32 Jaime Bluma/B	.15
33 Frank Rodriguez/B	.15
34 Andy Benes/B	.15
35 Jay Buhner/B	.15
36 Justin Thompson/B	.15
37 Darin Erstad/B	.30
38 Gregg Jefferies/B	.15
39 Jeff D'Amico/B	.15
40 Pedro Martinez/B	.60
41 Nomar Garciaparra/B	.75
42 Jose Valentin/B	.15
43 Pat Hentgen/B	.15
44 Will Clark/B	.15
45 Bernie Williams/B	.15
46 Luis Castillo/B	.15
47 B.J. Surhoff/B	.15
48 Greg Gagne/B	.15
49 Pete Schourek/B	.15
50 Mike Piazza/B	1.00
51 Dwight Gooden/B	.15
52 Javy Lopez/B	.15
53 Chuck Finley/B	.15
54 James Baldwin/B	.15
55 Jack McDowell/B	.15
56 Royce Clayton/B	.15
57 Carlos Delgado/B	.35
58 Neifi Perez/B	.15
59 Eddie Taubensee/B	.15
60 Rafael Palmeiro/B	.50
61 Marty Cordova/B	.15
62 Wade Boggs/B	.75
63 Rickey Henderson/B	.60
64 Mike Hampton/B	.15
65 Troy Percival/B	.15
66 Barry Larkin/B	.15
67 Jermaine Allensworth/B	.15
68 Mark Clark/B	.15
69 Mike Lansing/B	.15
70 Mark Grudzielanek/B	.15
71 Todd Stottlemyre/B	.15
72 Juan Guzman/B	.15
73 John Burkett/B	.15
74 Wilson Alvarez/B	.15
75 Ellis Burks/B	.15
76 Bobby Higginson/B	.15
77 Ricky Bottalico/B	.15

#	Player	Price		#	Player	Price		#	Player	Price
78	Omar Vizquel/B	.15		195	Chris Hoiles/B	.15		313	Barry Bonds/S	5.00
79	Paul Sorrento/B	.15		196	Orlando Merced/B	.15		314	Steve Finley/S	.50
80	Denny Neagle/B	.15		197	Brett Butler/B	.15		315	Vladimir Guerrero/S	1.50
81	Roger Pavlik/B	.15		198	Derek Bell/B	.15		316	Matt Morris/S	.50
82	Mike Liebenthal/B	.15		199	Bobby Bonilla/B	.15		317	Tom Glavine/S	1.00
83	Devon White/B	.15		200	Alex Ochoa/B	.15		318	Jeff Bagwell/S	1.50
84	John Olerud/B	.15		201	Wally Joyner/B	.15		319	Albert Belle/S	.50
85	Kevin Appier/B	.15		202	Mo Vaughn/B	.15		320	Hideki Irabu/S RC	1.00
86	Joe Girardi/ B	.15		203	Doug Drabek/B	.15		321	Andres Galarraga/S	.50
87	Paul O'Neill/B	.15		204	Tino Martinez/B	.15		322	Cecil Fielder/S	.50
88	Mike Sweeney/B	.15		205	Roberto Alomar/B	.30		323	Barry Larkin/S	.50
89	John Smiley/B	.15		206	Brian Giles/B RC	.75		324	Todd Hundley/S	.50
90	Ivan Rodriguez/B	.50		207	Todd Worrell/B	.15		325	Fred McGriff/S	.50
91	Randy Myers/B	.15		208	Alan Benes/B	.15		326	Gary Sheffield/G	3.00
92	Bip Roberts/B	.15		209	Jim Leyritz/B	.15		327	Craig Biggio/G	2.00
93	Jose Mesa/B	.15		210	Darryl Hamilton/B	.15		328	Raul Mondesi/G	2.00
94	Paul Wilson/B	.15		211	Jimmy Key/B	.15		329	Edgar Martinez/G	2.00
95	Mike Mussina/B	.30		212	Juan Gonzalez/B	.35		330	Chipper Jones/G	8.00
96	Ben McDonald/B	.15		213	Vinny Castilla/B	.15		331	Bernie Williams/G	3.00
97	John Mabry/B	.15		214	Chuck Knoblauch/B	.15		332	Juan Gonzalez/G	3.00
98	Tom Goodwin/B	.15		215	Tony Phillips/B	.15		333	Ron Gant/G	2.00
99	Edgar Martinez/B	.15		216	Jeff Cirillo/B	.15		334	Cal Ripken Jr./G	12.00
100	Andruw Jones/B	.60		217	Carlos Garcia/B	.15		335	Larry Walker/G	2.00
101	Jose Canseco/S	.75		218	Brooks Kieschnick/B	.15		336	Matt Williams/G	2.00
102	Billy Wagner/S	.50		219	Marquis Grissom/B	.15		337	Jose Cruz Jr./G	2.00
103	Dante Bichette/S	.50		220	Dan Wilson/B	.15		338	Joe Carter/G	2.00
104	Curt Schilling/S	1.00		221	Greg Vaughn/B	.15		339	Wilton Guerrero/G	2.00
105	Dean Palmer/S	.50		222	John Wetteland/B	.15		340	Cecil Fielder/G	2.00
106	Larry Walker/S	.50		223	Andres Galarraga/B	.15		341	Todd Walker/G	2.00
107	Bernie Williams/S	.50		224	Ozzie Guillen/B	.15		342	Ken Griffey Jr./G	10.00
108	Chipper Jones/S	2.00		225	Kevin Elster/B	.15		343	Ryan Klesko/G	2.00
109	Gary Sheffield/S	1.00		226	Bernard Gilkey/B	.15		344	Roger Clemens/G	10.00
110	Randy Johnson/S	1.50		227	Mike MacFarlane/B	.15		345	Hideo Nomo/G	3.00
111	Roberto Alomar/S	.75		228	Heathcliff Slocumb/B	.15		346	Dante Bichette/G	2.00
112	Todd Walker/S	.50		229	Wendell Magee Jr./B	.15		347	Albert Belle/G	2.00
113	Sandy Alomar/S	.50		230	Carlos Baerga/B	.15		348	Randy Johnson/G	6.00
114	John Jaha/S	.50		231	Kevin Seitzer/B	.15		349	Manny Ramirez/G	6.00
115	Ken Caminiti/S	.50		232	Henry Rodriguez/B	.15		350	John Smoltz/G	2.00
116	Ryan Klesko/S	.50		233	Roger Clemens/B	1.00				
117	Mariano Rivera/S	.75		234	Mark Wohlers/B	.15				
118	Jason Giambi/S	1.00		235	Eddie Murray/B	.60				
119	Lance Johnson/S	.50		236	Todd Zeile/B	.15				
120	Robin Ventura/S	.50		237	J.T. Snow/B	.15				
121	Todd Hollandsworth/S	.50		238	Ken Griffey Jr./B	1.00				
122	Johnny Damon/S	.75		239	Sterling Hitchcock/B	.15				
123	William Van Landingham/S	.50		240	Albert Belle/B	.15				
124	Jason Kendall/S	.50		241	Terry Steinbach/B	.15				
125	Vinny Castilla/S	.50		242	Robb Nen/B	.15				
126	Harold Baines/S	.50		243	Mark McLemore/B	.15				
127	Joe Carter/S	.50		244	Jeff King/B	.15				
128	Craig Biggio/S	.50		245	Tony Clark/B	.15				
129	Tony Clark/S	.50		246	Tim Salmon/B	.15				
130	Ron Gant/S	.50		247	Benito Santiago/B	.15				
131	David Segui/S	.50		248	Robin Ventura/B	.15				
132	Steve Trachsel/S	.50		249	Bubba Trammell/B RC	.15				
133	Scott Rolen/S	1.00		250	Chili Davis/B	.15				
134	Mike Stanley/S	.50		251	John Valentin/B	.15				
135	Cal Ripken Jr./S	5.00		252	Cal Ripken Jr./B	2.00				
136	John Smoltz/S	.50		253	Matt Williams/B	.15				
137	Bobby Jones/S	.50		254	Jeff Kent/B	.15				
138	Manny Ramirez/S	1.50		255	Eric Karros/B	.15				
139	Ken Griffey Jr./S	3.00		256	Ray Lankford/B	.15				
140	Chuck Knoblauch/S	.50		257	Ed Sprague/B	.15				
141	Mark Grace/S	.50		258	Shane Reynolds/B	.15				
142	Chris Snopek/S	.50		259	Jaime Navarro/B	.15				
143	Hideo Nomo/S	.75		260	Eric Davis/B	.15				
144	Tim Salmon/S	.50		261	Orel Hershiser/B	.15				
145	David Cone/S	.50		262	Mark Grace/B	.15				
146	Eric Young/S	.50		263	Rod Beck/B	.15				
147	Jeff Brantley/S	.50		264	Ismael Valdes/B	.15				
148	Jim Thome/S	1.00		265	Manny Ramirez/B	.60				
149	Trevor Hoffman/S	.50		266	Ken Caminiti/B	.15				
150	Juan Gonzalez/S	.75		267	Tim Naehring/B	.15				
151	Mike Piazza/S	8.00		268	Jose Rosado/B	.15				
152	Ivan Rodriguez/G	4.00		269	Greg Colbrunn/B	.15				
153	Mo Vaughn/G	2.00		270	Dean Palmer/B	.15				
154	Brady Anderson/G	2.00		271	David Justice/B	.15				
155	Mark McGwire/G	8.00		272	Scott Spiezio/B	.15				
156	Rafael Palmeiro/G	4.00		273	Chipper Jones/B	.75				
157	Barry Larkin/G	2.00		274	Mel Rojas/B	.15				
158	Greg Maddux/G	7.50		275	Bartolo Colon/B	.15				
159	Jeff Bagwell/G	5.00		276	Darin Erstad/S	1.00				
160	Frank Thomas/G	6.00		277	Sammy Sosa/S	2.00				
161	Ken Caminiti/G	2.00		278	Rafael Palmeiro/S	1.00				
162	Andruw Jones/G	5.00		279	Frank Thomas/S	1.50				
163	Dennis Eckersley/G	4.00		280	Ruben Rivera/S	.50				
164	Jeff Conine/G	2.00		281	Hal Morris/S	.50				
165	Jim Edmonds/G	2.00		282	Jay Buhner/S	.50				
166	Derek Jeter/G	12.00		283	Kenny Lofton/S	.50				
167	Vladimir Guerrero/G	6.00		284	Jose Canseco/S	.75				
168	Sammy Sosa/G	5.00		285	Alex Fernandez/S	.50				
169	Tony Gwynn/G	6.00		286	Todd Helton/S	1.25				
170	Andres Galarraga/G	2.00		287	Andy Pettitte/S	1.00				
171	Todd Hundley/G	2.00		288	John Franco/S	.50				
172	Jay Buhner/G	2.00		289	Ivan Rodriguez/S	1.25				
173	Paul Molitor/G	6.00		290	Ellis Burks/S	.50				
174	Kenny Lofton/G	2.00		291	Julio Franco/S	.50				
175	Barry Bonds/G	12.00		292	Mike Piazza/S	3.00				
176	Gary Sheffield/G	.35		293	Brian Jordan/S	.50				
177	Dmitri Young/B	.15		294	Greg Maddux/S	2.00				
178	Jay Bell/B	.15		295	Bob Abreu/S	.50				
179	David Wells/B	.15		296	Rondell White/S	.50				
180	Walt Weiss/B	.15		297	Moises Alou/S	.50				
181	Paul Molitor/B	.60		298	Tony Gwynn/S	2.00				
182	Jose Guillen/B	.15		299	Deion Sanders/S	.50				
183	Al Leiter/B	.15		300	Jeff Montgomery/S	.50				
184	Mike Fetters/B	.15		301	Ray Durham/S	.50				
185	Mark Langston/B	.15		302	John Wasdin/S	.50				
186	Fred McGriff/B	.15		303	Ryne Sandberg/S	.50				
187	Darrin Fletcher/B	.15		304	Delino DeShields/S	.50				
188	Brant Brown/B	.15		305	Mark McGwire/S	4.00				
189	Geronimo Berroa/B	.15		306	Andruw Jones/S	1.50				
190	Jim Thome/B	.50		307	Kevin Orie/S	.50				
191	Jose Vizcaino/B	.15		308	Matt Williams/S	.50				
192	Andy Ashby/B	.15		309	Karim Garcia/S	.50				
193	Rusty Greer/B	.15		310	Derek Jeter/S	5.00				
194	Brian Hunter/B	.15		311	Mo Vaughn/S	.50				
				312	Brady Anderson/S	.50				

Embossed

Each Uncommon (silver) and Rare (gold) card in both Series 1 and 2 Finest was also issued in a parallel Embossed version. The Embossed Silver were a 1:16 find, while the die-cut Embossed Gold were found on average of just one per 96 packs.

	NM/M
Common Embossed Silver:	1.00
Embossed Silver Stars:	2X
Common Embossed Gold:	3.00
Embossed/Die-Cut Gold Stars:	1.5X

Refractors

Every card in '97 Finest - both regular and embossed parallel - has a Refractor version. The Uncommon parallel set of Refractors features a mosaic pattern in the background while the Rare embossed die-cut parallel set of Refractors is produced with a hyper-plaid foil design. The number of cards and the insertion ratios for each level of Refractors is as follows: Common (200 cards, 1:12 packs), Uncommon (100, 1:48), Rare (50, 1:288), Embossed Uncommon (100, 1:192), Embossed Die-Cut Rare (50, 1:1152).

	NM/M
Common Bronze:	2.00
Bronze Stars:	6X
Typical Silver:	3.00
Silver Stars:	3X
Typical Gold:	8.00
Gold Stars:	2X
Typical Embossed Silver:	7.50
Embossed Silver Stars:	7X
Typical Embossed Gold:	20.00
Embossed Gold Stars:	5X

1998 Finest Pre-Production

Five-card cello packs of '98 Finest were distributed in the hobby market to preview the always-popular issue. The cards are virtually identical to the issued versions except for the card number, which bears a "PP" prefix.

		NM/M
Complete Set (5):		8.00
Common Player:		2.00
1	Nomar Garciaparra	2.25
2	Mark McGwire	3.00
3	Ivan Rodriguez	2.00
4	Ken Griffey Jr.	2.50
5	Roger Clemens	2.25

1998 Finest

Finest dropped its three-tiered format in 1998 and produced a 275-card set on a thicker 26-point stock, with 150 cards in Series 1 and 125 in Series 2. The catch in 1998 was that each card arrived in Protector, No-Protector, Protector Refractor and No-Protector Refractor versions. Six-card packs sold for a suggested retail price of $5. Finest also included insert sets for the first time since 1995. Included in Series 1 packs were Centurions, Mystery Finest and Power Zone inserts. Series 2 had Mystery Finest, Stadium Stars and The Man. Throughout both series, Finest Protector cards are considered base cards, while No-Protector are inserted one per two packs (HTA odds 1:1), No-Protector Refractors are seeded 1:24 packs (HTA odds 1:10) and Finest Refractors are seeded 1:12 packs (HTA odds 1:5).

		NM/M
Complete Set (275):		30.00
Common Player:		.15
No-Protector:		2.5X
Refractors:		4X
No-Protector Refractor:		8X
Pack (6):		1.50
Wax Box (24):		25.00
Jumbo Pack (13):		2.50
Jumbo Box (12):		25.00

#	Player	Price		#	Player	Price		#	Player	Price
1	Larry Walker	.15		33	Kevin Orie	.15		151	Frank Thomas	.75
2	Andruw Jones	.75		34	Royce Clayton	.15		152	John Wetteland	.15
3	Ramon Martinez	.15		35	Edgar Martinez	.15		153	Mike Lansing	.15
4	Geronimo Berroa	.15		36	Neifi Perez	.15		154	Pedro Martinez	.75
5	David Justice	.15		37	Kevin Appier	.15		155	Rico Brogna	.15
6	Rusty Greer	.15		38	Darryl Hamilton	.15		156	Kevin Brown	.15
7	Chad Ogea	.15		39	Michael Tucker	.15		157	Alex Rodriguez	2.00
8	Tom Goodwin	.15		40	Roger Clemens	1.25		158	Wade Boggs	1.00
9	Tino Martinez	.15		41	Carl Everett	.15		159	Richard Hidalgo	.15
10	Jose Guillen	.15		42	Mike Sweeney	.15		160	Mark Grace	.15
11	Jeffrey Hammonds	.15		43	Pat Meares	.15		161	Jose Mesa	.15
12	Brian McRae	.15		44	Brian Giles	.15		162	John Olerud	.15
13	Jeremi Gonzalez	.15		45	Matt Morris	.15		163	Tim Belcher	.15
14	Craig Counsell	.15		46	Jason Dickson	.15		164	Chuck Finley	.15
15	Mike Piazza	1.50		47	Rich Loiselle	.15		165	Brian Hunter	.15
16	Greg Maddux	1.00		48	Joe Girardi	.15		166	Joe Carter	.15
17	Todd Greene	.15		49	Steve Trachsel	.15		167	Stan Javier	.15
18	Rondell White	.15		50	Ben Grieve	.15		168	Jay Bell	.15
19	Kirk Rueter	.15		51	Jose Vizcaino	.15		169	Ray Lankford	.15
20	Tony Clark	.15		52	Hideki Irabu	.15		170	John Smoltz	.15
21	Brad Radke	.15		53	J.T. Snow	.15		171	Ed Sprague	.15
22	Jaret Wright	.15		54	Mike Hampton	.15		172	Jason Giambi	.50
23	Carlos Delgado	.50		55	Dave Nilsson	.15		173	Todd Walker	.15
24	Dustin Hermanson	.15		56	Alex Fernandez	.15		174	Paul Konerko	.15
25	Gary Sheffield	.40		57	Brett Tomko	.15		175	Rey Ordonez	.15
26	Jose Canseco	.35		58	Wally Joyner	.15		176	Dante Bichette	.15
27	Kevin Young	.15		59	Kelvim Escobar	.15		177	Bernie Williams	.15
28	David Wells	.15		60	Roberto Alomar	.30		178	Jon Nunnally	.15
29	Mariano Rivera	.25		61	Todd Jones	.15		179	Rafael Palmeiro	.60
30	Reggie Sanders	.15		62	Paul O'Neill	.15		180	Jay Buhner	.15
31	Mike Cameron	.15		63	Jamie Moyer	.15		181	Devon White	.15
32	Bobby Witt	.15		64	Mark Wohlers	.15		182	Jeff D'Amico	.15
				65	Jose Cruz Jr.	.15		183	Walt Weiss	.15
				66	Troy Percival	.15		184	Scott Spiezio	.15
				67	Rick Reed	.15		185	Moises Alou	.15
				68	Will Clark	.15		186	Carlos Baerga	.15
				69	Jamey Wright	.15		187	Todd Zeile	.15
				70	Mike Mussina	.35		188	Gregg Jefferies	.15
				71	David Cone	.15		189	Mo Vaughn	.15
				72	Ryan Klesko	.15		190	Terry Steinbach	.15
				73	Scott Hatteberg	.15		191	Ray Durham	.15
				74	James Baldwin	.15		192	Robin Ventura	.15
				75	Tony Womack	.15		193	Jeff Reed	.15
				76	Carlos Perez	.15		194	Ken Caminiti	.15
				77	Charles Nagy	.15		195	Eric Karros	.15
				78	Jeromy Burnitz	.15		196	Wilson Alvarez	.15
				79	Shane Reynolds	.15		197	Gary Gaetti	.15
				80	Cliff Floyd	.15		198	Andres Galarraga	.15
				81	Jason Kendall	.15		199	Alex Gonzalez	.15
				82	Chad Curtis	.15		200	Garret Anderson	.15
				83	Matt Karchner	.15		201	Andy Benes	.15
				84	Ricky Bottalico	.15		202	Harold Baines	.15
				85	Sammy Sosa	1.00		203	Ron Coomer	.15
				86	Javy Lopez	.15		204	Dean Palmer	.15
				87	Jeff Kent	.15		205	Reggie Jefferson	.15
				88	Shawn Green	.25		206	John Burkett	.15
				89	Devon White	.15		207	Jermaine Allensworth	.15
				90	Tony Gwynn	1.00		208	Bernard Gilkey	.15
				91	Bob Tewksbury	.15		209	Jeff Bagwell	.75
				92	Derek Jeter	2.50		210	Kenny Lofton	.15
				93	Eric Davis	.15		211	Bobby Jones	.15
				94	Jeff Fassero	.15		212	Bartolo Colon	.15
				95	Denny Neagle	.15		213	Jim Edmonds	.15
				96	Ismael Valdes	.15		214	Pat Hentgen	.15
				97	Tim Salmon	.15		215	Matt Williams	.15
				98	Mark Grudzielanek	.15		216	Bob Abreu	.15
				99	Curt Schilling	.35		217	Jorge Posada	.15
				100	Ken Griffey Jr.	1.50		218	Marty Cordova	.15
				101	Edgardo Alfonzo	.15		219	Ken Hill	.15
				102	Vinny Castilla	.15		220	Steve Finley	.15
				103	Jose Rosado	.15		221	Jeff King	.15
				104	Scott Erickson	.15		222	Quinton McCracken	.15
				105	Alan Benes	.15		223	Matt Stairs	.15
				106	Shannon Stewart	.15		224	Darin Erstad	.35
				107	Delino DeShields	.15		225	Fred McGriff	.15
				108	Mark Loretta	.15		226	Marquis Grissom	.15
				109	Todd Hundley	.15		227	Doug Glanville	.15
				110	Chuck Knoblauch	.15		228	Tom Glavine	.35
				111	Quinton McCracken	.15		229	John Franco	.15
				112	F.P. Santangelo	.15		230	Darren Bragg	.15
				113	Gerald Williams	.15		231	Barry Larkin	.15
				114	Omar Vizquel	.15		232	Trevor Hoffman	.15
				115	John Valentin	.15		233	Brady Anderson	.15
				116	Damion Easley	.15		234	Al Martin	.15
				117	Matt Lawton	.15		235	B.J. Surhoff	.15
				118	Jim Thome	.60		236	Ellis Burks	.15
				119	Sandy Alomar	.15		237	Randy Johnson	.75
				120	Albert Belle	.15		238	Mark Clark	.15
				121	Chris Stynes	.15		239	Tony Saunders	.15
				122	Butch Huskey	.15		240	Hideo Nomo	.40
				123	Shawn Estes	.15		241	Brad Fullmer	.15
				124	Terry Adams	.15		242	Chipper Jones	1.00
				125	Ivan Rodriguez	.60		243	Jose Valentin	.15
				126	Ron Gant	.15		244	Manny Ramirez	.75
				127	John Mabry	.15		245	Derrek Lee	.50
				128	Jeff Shaw	.15		246	Jimmy Key	.15
				129	Jeff Montgomery	.15		247	Tim Naehring	.15
				130	Justin Thompson	.15		248	Bobby Higginson	.15
				131	Livan Hernandez	.15		249	Charles Johnson	.15
				132	Ugueth Urbina	.15		250	Chili Davis	.15
				133	Doug Glanville	.15		251	Tom Gordon	.15
				134	Troy O'Leary	.15		252	Mike Lieberthal	.15
				135	Cal Ripken Jr.	2.50		253	Billy Wagner	.15
				136	Quivio Veras	.15		254	Juan Guzman	.15
				137	Pedro Astacio	.15		255	Todd Stottlemyre	.15
				138	Willie Greene	.15		256	Brian Jordan	.15
				139	Lance Johnson	.15		257	Barry Bonds	2.50
				140	Nomar Garciaparra	1.00		258	Dan Wilson	.15
				141	Jose Offerman	.15		259	Paul Molitor	.75
				142	Scott Rolen	.60		260	Juan Gonzalez	.40
				143	Derek Bell	.15		261	Francisco Cordova	.15
				144	Johnny Damon	.35		262	Cecil Fielder	.15
				145	Mark McGwire	2.00		263	Travis Lee	.15
				146	Chan Ho Park	.15		264	Kevin Tapani	.15
				147	Edgar Renteria	.15		265	Raul Mondesi	.15
				148	Eric Young	.15		266	Travis Fryman	.15
				149	Craig Biggio	.15		267	Armando Benitez	.15
				150	Checklist 1-150	.15		268	Pokey Reese	.15

269	Rick Aguilera	.15
270	Andy Pettitte	.35
271	Jose Vizcaino	.15
272	Kerry Wood	.40
273	Vladimir Guerrero	.75
274	John Smiley	.15
275	Checklist 151-275	.15

Refractors

All 275 cards from Finest Series 1 and 2 are available in a Refractor version. seeded one per 12 packs. Besides the refractive quality of the printing of front, Refractors are designated with an "R" suffix to the card number on back.

		NM/M
Complete Set (275):		200.00
Common Player:		1.00
Stars/Rookies:		4X

No-Protector

This parallel to the 275-card base set foregoes the peel-off front protector and adds Finest technology to the back of the card. Stated insertion rates were one per two packs or one per pack in Home Team Advantage (HTA) boxes.

		NM/M
Complete Set (275):		150.00
Common Player:		.50
Stars/Rookies:		2.5X

No-Protector Refractor

A Refractor parallel to the 275 No-Protector parallel cards was a 1:24 pack insert. In Series 1, only the refractive quality of the front and back printing reveals this insert. Series 2 No-Protector Refractors have an "R" suffix to the card number on back.

		NM/M
Complete Set (275):		400.00
Common Player:		2.00
Stars/Rookies:		8X

Centurions

Centurions is a 20-card insert found only Series 1 hobby (1:153) and Home Team Advantage packs (1:71). The theme of the insert to

top players who will lead the game into the next century. Each card is sequentially numbered on the back to 500, while Refractor versions are numbered to 75.

		NM/M
Complete Set (20):		75.00
Common Player:		1.50
Production 500 Sets		
Refractors (75 Sets):		4X
C1	Andruw Jones	4.50
C2	Vladimir Guerrero	4.50
C3	Nomar Garciaparra	6.00
C4	Scott Rolen	3.50
C5	Ken Griffey Jr.	8.00
C6	Jose Cruz Jr.	1.50
C7	Barry Bonds	12.00
C8	Mark McGwire	10.00
C9	Juan Gonzalez	2.50
C10	Jeff Bagwell	4.50
C11	Frank Thomas	4.50
C12	Paul Konerko	2.00
C13	Alex Rodriguez	10.00
C14	Mike Piazza	8.00
C15	Travis Lee	1.50
C16	Chipper Jones	6.00
C17	Larry Walker	1.50
C18	Mo Vaughn	1.50
C19	Livan Hernandez	1.50
C20	Jaret Wright	1.50

Mystery Finest

This 50-card insert was seeded one per 36 Series 1 packs and one per 15 HTA packs. The set includes 20 top players, each matched on a double-sided card with three other players and once with himself. Each side of the card is printed on a chromium finish and arrives with a black opaque protector. Mystery Finest inserts are numbered with an "M" prefix. Refractor versions were seeded one per 64 packs (HTA odds 1:15).

		NM/M
Complete Set (50):		125.00
Common Player:		1.50
Refractors:		4X
M1	Frank Thomas, Ken Griffey Jr.	3.00
M2	Frank Thomas, Mike Piazza	3.00
M3	Frank Thomas, Mark McGwire	4.00
M4	Frank Thomas, Frank Thomas	2.00
M5	Ken Griffey Jr., Mike Piazza	3.00
M6	Ken Griffey Jr., Mark McGwire	4.00
M7	Ken Griffey Jr., Frank Thomas	4.00
M8	Mike Piazza, Mark McGwire	4.00
M9	Mike Piazza, Mike Piazza	4.00
M10	Mike Piazza, Mark McGwire	6.00
M11	Nomar Garciaparra, Jose Cruz Jr.	2.50
M12	Nomar Garciaparra, Derek Jeter	3.50
M13	Nomar Garciaparra, Andruw Jones	2.50
M14	Nomar Garciaparra, Nomar Garciaparra	3.00
M15	Jose Cruz Jr., Derek Jeter	5.00
M16	Jose Cruz Jr., Andruw Jones	1.50
M17	Jose Cruz Jr., Jose Cruz Jr.	1.50
M18	Derek Jeter, Andruw Jones	5.00
M19	Derek Jeter, Derek Jeter	7.50
M20	Andruw Jones, Andruw Jones	2.00
M21	Cal Ripken Jr., Tony Gwynn	5.00
M22	Cal Ripken Jr., Barry Bonds	5.00
M23	Cal Ripken Jr., Greg Maddux	5.00
M24	Cal Ripken Jr., Cal Ripken Jr.	7.50
M25	Tony Gwynn, Barry Bonds	5.00
M26	Tony Gwynn, Greg Maddux	2.50
M27	Tony Gwynn, Tony Gwynn	3.00
M28	Barry Bonds, Greg Maddux	5.00
M29	Barry Bonds, Barry Bonds	7.50
M30	Greg Maddux, Greg Maddux	4.50
M31	Juan Gonzalez, Larry Walker	1.50
M32	Juan Gonzalez, Andres Galarraga	1.50
M33	Juan Gonzalez, Chipper Jones	2.50
M34	Juan Gonzalez, Juan Gonzalez	1.50
M35	Larry Walker, Andres Galarraga	1.50
M36	Larry Walker, Chipper Jones	2.50
M37	Larry Walker, Larry Walker	1.50
M38	Andres Galarraga, Chipper Jones	2.50
M39	Andres Galarraga, Andres Galarraga	1.50
M40	Chipper Jones, Chipper Jones	3.00
M41	Gary Sheffield, Sammy Sosa	3.00
M42	Gary Sheffield, Jeff Bagwell	1.50
M43	Gary Sheffield, Tino Martinez	1.50
M44	Gary Sheffield, Gary Sheffield	2.00
M45	Sammy Sosa, Jeff Bagwell	3.00
M46	Sammy Sosa, Tino Martinez	3.00
M47	Sammy Sosa, Sammy Sosa	3.00
M48	Jeff Bagwell, Tino Martinez	1.50
M49	Jeff Bagwell, Jeff Bagwell	2.00
M50	Tino Martinez, Tino Martinez	1.50

Mystery Finest 2

Forty more Mystery Finest inserts were seeded in Series 2 packs at a rate of one per 36 packs (HTA odds 1:15), with Refrators every 1:144 packs (HTA odds 1:64). As with Series 1, 20 players are in the checklist; some players are found with another player on the back or by himself on each side. Each side is printed in Finest technology with an opaque black protector.

		NM/M
Complete Set (40):		100.00
Common Player:		1.50
Refractors:		4X
M1	Nomar Garciaparra, Frank Thomas	3.50
M2	Nomar Garciaparra, Albert Belle	3.50
M3	Nomar Garciaparra, Scott Rolen	3.50
M4	Frank Thomas, Albert Belle	2.50
M5	Frank Thomas, Scott Rolen	2.50
M6	Albert Belle, Scott Rolen	1.50
M7	Ken Griffey Jr., Jose Cruz	4.00
M8	Ken Griffey Jr., Alex Rodriguez	6.00
M9	Ken Griffey Jr., Roger Clemens	4.50
M10	Jose Cruz, Alex Rodriguez	6.00
M11	Jose Cruz, Roger Clemens	3.00
M12	Alex Rodriguez, Roger Clemens	6.00
M13	Mike Piazza, Barry Bonds	6.00
M14	Mike Piazza, Derek Jeter	6.00
M15	Mike Piazza, Bernie Williams	4.50
M16	Barry Bonds, Derek Jeter	6.50
M17	Barry Bonds, Bernie Williams	4.00
M18	Derek Jeter, Bernie Williams	6.00
M19	Mark McGwire, Jeff Bagwell	4.50
M20	Mark McGwire, Mo Vaughn	5.00
M21	Mark McGwire, Jim Thome	5.00
M22	Jeff Bagwell, Mo Vaughn	1.50
M23	Jeff Bagwell, Jim Thome	1.50
M24	Mo Vaughn, Jim Thome	1.50
M25	Juan Gonzalez, Travis Lee	1.50
M26	Juan Gonzalez, Ben Grieve	1.50
M27	Juan Gonzalez, Fred McGriff	1.50
M28	Travis Lee, Ben Grieve	1.50
M29	Travis Lee, Fred McGriff	1.50
M30	Ben Grieve, Fred McGriff	1.50
M31	Albert Belle, Albert Belle	1.50
M32	Scott Rolen, Scott Rolen	2.00
M33	Mike Piazza, Alex Rodriguez	6.00
M34	Roger Clemens, Roger Clemens	4.00
M35	Bernie Williams, Bernie Williams	1.50
M36	Mo Vaughn, Mo Vaughn	1.50
M37	Jim Thome, Jim Thome	2.00
M38	Travis Lee, Travis Lee	1.50
M39	Fred McGriff, Fred McGriff	1.50
M40	Ben Grieve, Ben Grieve	1.50

Mystery Finest Jumbo

Series 2 Home Team Advantage (HTA) boxes were the exclusive venue for these large-format (3" x 5") versions of Mystery Finest. Regular cards were found one per six boxes of HTA, while Refractor versions were a 1:12 seed.

		NM/M
Complete Set (3):		12.50
Common Card:		4.00
Refractor:		1.5X
1	Ken Griffey Jr., Alex Rodriguez	4.00
2	Derek Jeter, Bernie Williams	5.00
3	Mark McGwire, Jeff Bagwell	4.00

Power Zone

This Series 1 insert features Topps' new "Flop Inks" technology which changes the color of the card depending at what angle it is viewed. They are inserted one per 72 hobby packs (HTA odds 1:32). Cards are numbered with a "P" prefix.

		NM/M
Complete Set (20):		25.00
Common Player:		.50
1	Ken Griffey Jr.	3.00
2	Jeff Bagwell	2.00
3	Jose Cruz Jr.	.50
4	Barry Bonds	5.00
5	Mark McGwire	4.00
6	Jim Thome	1.50
7	Mo Vaughn	.50

8	Gary Sheffield	1.00
9	Andres Galarraga	.50
10	Nomar Garciaparra	2.50
11	Rafael Palmeiro	1.50
12	Sammy Sosa	2.50
13	Jay Buhner	.50
14	Tony Clark	.50
15	Mike Piazza	3.00
16	Larry Walker	.50
17	Albert Belle	.50
18	Tino Martinez	.50
19	Juan Gonzalez	1.25
20	Frank Thomas	2.00

Stadium Stars

Stadium Stars is a 24-card insert that features Topps' new lenticular holographic chromium technology. These are exclusive to Series 2 packs and carried an insertion rate of one per 72 packs (HTA odds 1:32).

		NM/M
Complete Set (24):		95.00
Common Player:		1.00
SS1	Ken Griffey Jr.	8.00
SS2	Alex Rodriguez	10.00
SS3	Mo Vaughn	1.00
SS4	Nomar Garciaparra	6.00
SS5	Frank Thomas	4.50
SS6	Albert Belle	1.00
SS7	Derek Jeter	12.00
SS8	Chipper Jones	6.00
SS9	Cal Ripken Jr.	12.00
SS10	Jim Thome	3.00
SS11	Mike Piazza	8.00
SS12	Juan Gonzalez	2.50
SS13	Jeff Bagwell	4.50
SS14	Sammy Sosa	6.00
SS15	Jose Cruz Jr.	1.50
SS16	Gary Sheffield	2.00
SS17	Larry Walker	1.00
SS18	Tony Gwynn	6.00
SS19	Mark McGwire	10.00
SS20	Barry Bonds	12.00
SS21	Tino Martinez	1.00
SS22	Manny Ramirez	4.50
SS23	Ken Caminiti	1.00
SS24	Andres Galarraga	1.00

The Man

This 20-card insert features the top players in baseball and was exlusively found in Series 2 packs. Regular versions are sequentially numbered to 500 and inserted one per 119 packs, while Refractor versions are numbered to 75 and inserted one per 793 packs.

		NM/M
Complete Set (20):		125.00
Common Player:		1.50
Refractors:		3X
TM1	Ken Griffey Jr.	10.00
TM2	Barry Bonds	15.00
TM3	Frank Thomas	6.00
TM4	Chipper Jones	7.50
TM5	Cal Ripken Jr.	15.00
TM6	Nomar Garciaparra	7.50
TM7	Mark McGwire	12.50
TM8	Mike Piazza	10.00
TM9	Derek Jeter	15.00
TM10	Alex Rodriguez	12.50
TM11	Jose Cruz Jr.	1.50
TM12	Larry Walker	1.50
TM13	Jeff Bagwell	6.00

TM14	Tony Gwynn	7.50
TM15	Travis Lee	2.00
TM16	Juan Gonzalez	6.00
TM17	Scott Rolen	6.00
TM18	Randy Johnson	6.00
TM19	Roger Clemens	9.00
TM20	Greg Maddux	15.00

Jumbo

Eight oversized cards were inserted into both Series 1 and Series 2 boxes as box toppers. The cards measure 3" x 5" and are inserted one per three boxes, with Refractor versions every six boxes. The oversized cards are similar to the regular-issue cards except for the numbering which designates each "X of 8."

		NM/M
Complete Set (16):		30.00
Common Player:		1.00
Refractors:		1.5X
1	Mark McGwire	4.00
2	Cal Ripken Jr.	5.00
3	Nomar Garciaparra	2.00
4	Mike Piazza	3.00
5	Greg Maddux	2.00
6	Jose Cruz Jr.	1.00
7	Roger Clemens	2.00
8	Ken Griffey Jr.	3.00
1	Frank Thomas	1.50
2	Bernie Williams	1.00
3	Randy Johnson	1.50
4	Chipper Jones	2.00
5	Manny Ramirez	1.50
6	Barry Bonds	5.00
7	Juan Gonzalez	1.25
8	Jeff Bagwell	1.50

1999 Finest

Released in two series, with each consisting of 100 regular and 50 subset cards divided into three categories: Gems, Sensations and Rookies in Series 1, and Sterling, Gamers and Rookies in the second series. The subset cards are short-printed, seeded one per pack. Cards are printed on 27-point stock utilizing chromium technology. There are two parallels: Refractors and die-cut Gold Refractors. Refractors are seeded 1:12 packs, while Gold Refractors are numbered to 100 sets. Six-cards packs carried an SRP of $4.99.

		NM/M
Complete Set (300):		80.00
Complete Series 1 (150):		30.00
Complete Series 2 (150):		50.00
Common Player:		.15
Common SP (101-150, 251-300):		.50
Star Refractors:		6X
SP Refractors:		3X
Star Gold Refractors:		15X
SP Gold Refractors:		10X
Pack (6):		1.50
Wax Box (24):		30.00
1	Darin Erstad	.15
2	Javy Lopez	.15
3	Vinny Castilla	.15
4	Jim Thome	.15
5	Tino Martinez	.15

No.	Player	NM/M
6	Mark Grace	.15
7	Shawn Green	.40
8	Dustin Hermanson	.15
9	Kevin Young	.15
10	Tony Clark	.15
11	Scott Brosius	.15
12	Craig Biggio	.15
13	Brian McRae	.15
14	Chan Ho Park	.15
15	Manny Ramirez	1.00
16	Chipper Jones	1.50
17	Rico Brogna	.15
18	Quinton McCracken	.15
19	J.T. Snow Jr.	.15
20	Tony Gwynn	1.50
21	Juan Guzman	.15
22	John Valentin	.15
23	Rick Helling	.15
24	Sandy Alomar	.15
25	Frank Thomas	1.00
26	Jorge Posada	.15
27	Dmitri Young	.15
28	Rick Reed	.15
29	Kevin Tapani	.15
30	Troy Glaus	.75
31	Kenny Rogers	.15
32	Jeromy Burnitz	.15
33	Mark Grudzielanek	.15
34	Mike Mussina	.50
35	Scott Rolen	.75
36	Neifi Perez	.15
37	Brad Radke	.15
38	Darryl Strawberry	.15
39	Robb Nen	.15
40	Moises Alou	.15
41	Eric Young	.15
42	Livan Hernandez	.15
43	John Wetteland	.15
44	Matt Lawton	.15
45	Ben Grieve	.15
46	Fernando Tatis	.15
47	Travis Fryman	.15
48	David Segui	.15
49	Bob Abreu	.15
50	Nomar Garciaparra	1.50
51	Paul O'Neill	.15
52	Jeff King	.15
53	Francisco Cordova	.15
54	John Olerud	.15
55	Vladimir Guerrero	1.00
56	Fernando Vina	.15
57	Shane Reynolds	.15
58	Chuck Finley	.15
59	Rondell White	.15
60	Greg Maddux	.15
61	Ryan Minor	.15
62	Tom Gordon	.15
63	Damion Easley	.15
64	Ray Durham	.15
65	Orlando Hernandez	.15
66	Bartolo Colon	.15
67	Jaret Wright	.15
68	Royce Clayton	.15
69	Tim Salmon	.15
70	Mark McGwire	2.50
71	Alex Gonzalez	.15
72	Tom Glavine	.40
73	David Justice	.15
74	Omar Vizquel	.15
75	Juan Gonzalez	.50
76	Bobby Higginson	.15
77	Todd Walker	.15
78	Dante Bichette	.15
79	Kevin Millwood	.15
80	Roger Clemens	1.75
81	Kerry Wood	.50
82	Cal Ripken Jr.	3.00
83	Jay Bell	.15
84	Barry Bonds	3.00
85	Alex Rodriguez	2.50
86	Doug Glanville	.15
87	Jason Kendall	.15
88	Sean Casey	.25
89	Aaron Sele	.15
90	Derek Jeter	3.00
91	Andy Ashby	.15
92	Rusty Greer	.15
93	Rod Beck	.15
94	Matt Williams	.15
95	Mike Piazza	2.00
96	Wally Joyner	.15
97	Barry Larkin	.15
98	Eric Milton	.15
99	Gary Sheffield	.50
100	Greg Maddux	1.50
101	Ken Griffey Jr. (Gem)	4.00
102	Frank Thomas (Gem)	2.00
103	Nomar Garciaparra (Gem)	3.00
104	Mark McGwire (Gem)	5.00
105	Alex Rodriguez (Gem)	5.00
106	Tony Gwynn (Gem)	3.00
107	Juan Gonzalez (Gem)	.75
108	Jeff Bagwell (Gem)	2.00
109	Sammy Sosa (Gem)	2.00
110	Vladimir Guerrero (Gem)	2.00
111	Roger Clemens (Gem)	3.50
112	Barry Bonds (Gem)	6.00
113	Darin Erstad (Gem)	3.00
114	Mike Piazza (Gem)	4.00
115	Derek Jeter (Gem)	6.00
116	Chipper Jones (Gem)	6.00
117	Larry Walker (Gem)	.50
118	Scott Rolen (Gem)	1.50
119	Cal Ripken Jr. (Gem)	6.00
120	Greg Maddux (Gem)	3.00
121	Troy Glaus (Sensations)	3.00
122	Ben Grieve (Sensations)	.50
123	Ryan Minor (Sensations)	.50
124	Kerry Wood (Sensations)	.50
125	Travis Lee (Sensations)	.50
126	Adrian Beltre (Sensations)	.50
127	Brad Fullmer (Sensations)	.50
128	Aramis Ramirez (Sensations)	.50
129	Eric Chavez (Sensations)	.50
130	Todd Helton (Sensations)	1.50
131	Pat Burrell RC (Finest Rookies)	4.00
132	Ryan Mills RC (Finest Rookies)	.50
133	Austin Kearns RC (Finest Rookies)	3.00
134	Josh McKinley RC (Finest Rookies)	.50
135	Adam Everett RC (Finest Rookies)	.75
136	Marlon Anderson	.50
137	Bruce Chen	.50
138	Matt Clement	.50
139	Alex Gonzalez	.50
140	Roy Halladay	.50
141	Calvin Pickering	.50
142	Randy Wolf	.50
143	Ryan Anderson	.50
144	Ruben Mateo	.50
145	Alex Escobar RC	.50
146	Jeremy Giambi	.50
147	Lance Berkman	.50
148	Michael Barrett	.50
149	Preston Wilson	.50
150	Gabe Kapler	.50
151	Roger Clemens	1.75
152	Jay Buhner	.15
153	Brad Fullmer	.15
154	Ray Lankford	.15
155	Jim Edmonds	.15
156	Jason Giambi	.60
157	Bret Boone	.15
158	Jeff Cirillo	.15
159	Rickey Henderson	1.00
160	Edgar Martinez	.15
161	Ron Gant	.15
162	Mark Kotsay	.15
163	Trevor Hoffman	.15
164	Jason Schmidt	.15
165	Brett Tomko	.15
166	David Ortiz	.50
167	Dean Palmer	.15
168	Hideki Irabu	.15
169	Mike Cameron	.15
170	Pedro Martinez	1.00
171	Tom Goodwin	.15
172	Brian Hunter	.15
173	Al Leiter	.15
174	Charles Johnson	.15
175	Curt Schilling	.50
176	Robin Ventura	.15
177	Travis Lee	.15
178	Jeff Shaw	.15
179	Ugueth Urbina	.15
180	Roberto Alomar	.30
181	Cliff Floyd	.15
182	Adrian Beltre	.25
183	Tony Womack	.15
184	Brian Jordan	.15
185	Randy Johnson	1.00
186	Mickey Morandini	.15
187	Todd Hundley	.15
188	Jose Valentin	.15
189	Eric Davis	.15
190	Ken Caminiti	.15
191	David Wells	.15
192	Ryan Klesko	.15
193	Garret Anderson	.15
194	Eric Karros	.15
195	Ivan Rodriguez	.75
196	Aramis Ramirez	.15
197	Mike Lieberthal	.15
198	Will Clark	.15
199	Rey Ordonez	.15
200	Ken Griffey Jr.	2.00
201	Jose Guillen	.15
202	Scott Erickson	.15
203	Paul Konerko	.15
204	Johnny Damon	.40
205	Larry Walker	.15
206	Denny Neagle	.15
207	Jose Offerman	.15
208	Andy Pettitte	.30
209	Bobby Jones	.15
210	Kevin Brown	.15
211	John Smoltz	.15
212	Henry Rodriguez	.15
213	Tim Belcher	.15
214	Carlos Delgado	.50
215	Andruw Jones	1.00
216	Andy Benes	.15
217	Fred McGriff	.15
218	Edgar Renteria	.25
219	Miguel Tejada	.25
220	Bernie Williams	.15
221	Justin Thompson	.15
222	Marty Cordova	.15
223	Delino DeShields	.15
224	Ellis Burks	.15
225	Kenny Lofton	.15
226	Steve Finley	.15
227	Eric Chavez	.25
228	Jose Cruz Jr.	.15
229	Marquis Grissom	.15
230	Jeff Bagwell	1.00
231	Jose Canseco	.50
232	Edgardo Alfonzo	.15
233	Richie Sexson	.15
234	Jeff Kent	.15
235	Rafael Palmeiro	.75
236	David Cone	.15
237	Gregg Jefferies	.15
238	Mike Lansing	.15
239	Mariano Rivera	.25
240	Albert Belle	.15
241	Chuck Knoblauch	.15
242	Derek Bell	.15
243	Pat Hentgen	.15
244	Andres Galarraga	.15
245	Mo Vaughn	.15
246	Wade Boggs	1.50
247	Devon White	.15
248	Todd Helton	.75
249	Raul Mondesi	.15
250	Sammy Sosa	1.50
251	Nomar Garciaparra (Sterling)	
252	Mark McGwire (Sterling)	5.00
253	Alex Rodriguez (Sterling)	5.00
254	Juan Gonzalez (Sterling)	.75
255	Vladimir Guerrero (Sterling)	
256	Ken Griffey Jr. (Sterling)	4.00
257	Mike Piazza (Sterling)	4.00
258	Derek Jeter (Sterling)	6.00
259	Albert Belle (Sterling)	.50
260	Greg Vaughn (Sterling)	.50
261	Sammy Sosa (Sterling)	3.00
262	Greg Maddux (Sterling)	3.00
263	Frank Thomas (Sterling)	2.00
264	Mark Grace (Sterling)	.50
265	Ivan Rodriguez (Sterling)	1.25
266	Roger Clemens (Gamers)	3.50
267	Mo Vaughn (Gamers)	.50
268	Jim Thome (Gamers)	.75
269	Darin Erstad (Gamers)	.65
270	Chipper Jones (Gamers)	2.50
271	Larry Walker (Gamers)	.50
272	Cal Ripken Jr. (Gamers)	6.00
273	Scott Rolen (Gamers)	1.25
274	Randy Johnson (Gamers)	2.00
275	Tony Gwynn (Gamers)	2.50
276	Barry Bonds (Gamers)	6.00
277	Sean Burroughs RC	1.50
278	J.M. Gold RC	.50
279	Carlos Lee	.50
280	George Lombard	.50
281	Carlos Beltran	1.50
282	Fernando Seguignol	.50
283	Eric Chavez	.65
284	Carlos Pena RC	3.00
285	Corey Patterson RC	2.00
286	Alfonso Soriano RC	12.00
287	Nick Johnson RC	2.00
288	Jorge Toca RC	.50
289	A.J. Burnett RC	1.00
290	Andy Brown RC	.50
291	Doug Mientkiewicz RC	1.00
292	Bobby Seay RC	.50
293	Chip Ambres RC	.50
294	C.C. Sabathia RC	3.00
295	Choo Freeman RC	1.00
296	Eric Valent RC	.50
297	Matt Belisle RC	.50
298	Jason Tyner RC	.50
299	Masao Kida RC	.50
300	Hank Aaron, Mark McGwire (Homerun Kings)	3.00

Refractors

Inserted at the rate of one card per 12 packs, Refractors use special technology to impart a more colorful sheen to the card fronts. To eliminate doubt, the backs have the word "REFRACTOR" printed to the right of the card number at top.

	NM/M
Complete Set (300):	750.00
Common Player:	1.00
Stars:	6X
SP's:	3X

Gold Refractors

At the top of Finest's chase-card line-up for 1999 are the Gold Refractors. Fronts have an overall gold tone in the background. Backs are individually serial numbered in gold foil with an edition of 100 each, and have the words "GOLD RE-FRACTOR" printed at top, to the right of the card number. The Gold

Refractors are die-cut along the edges to create a deckled effect. Stated pack insertion rates were between 1:26 and 1:82 depending on series and type.

	NM/M
Common Player:	3.00
Stars:	15X
SP's:	10X

Complements

This Series 2 insert set pairs two players on a "split-screen" card front. There are three different versions for each card, Non-Refractor/Refractor (1:56), Refractor/Non-Refractor (1:56) and Refractor/Refractor (1:168). Each card is numbered with a "C" prefix. Values shown are for cards with either the left- or right-side player as Refractor; dual-refractor cards valued at 2X.

		NM/M
Complete Set (7):		25.00
Common Player:		2.50
Inserted 1:56		
Dual-Refractors:		2X
Inserted 1:168		
1	Mike Piazza, Ivan Rodriguez	4.00
2	Tony Gwynn, Wade Boggs	3.00
3	Kerry Wood, Roger Clemens	3.50
4	Juan Gonzalez, Sammy Sosa	3.00
5	Derek Jeter, Nomar Garciaparra	6.00
6	Mark McGwire, Frank Thomas	5.00
7	Vladimir Guerrero, Andruw Jones	2.50

Double Feature

Similar to Finest Complements, this Series 2 set utilizes split-screen fronts to accomodate two players on a horizontal format. Each card has three versions: Non-Refractor/Refractor (1:56), Refractor/Non-Refractor (1:56) and Refractor/Refractor (1:168). Card numbers have a "DF" prefix. Values shown are for cards with either left- or right-side Refractor; Dual-Refractor cards are valued at 2X.

		NM/M
Complete Set (7):		30.00
Common Player:		2.00
Dual-Refractors:		2X
1	Ken Griffey Jr., Alex Rodriguez	10.00
2	Chipper Jones, Andruw Jones	6.00
3	Darin Erstad, Mo Vaughn	5.00
4	Craig Biggio, Jeff Bagwell	4.00
5	Ben Grieve, Eric Chavez	2.00
6	Albert Belle, Cal Ripken Jr.	10.00
7	Scott Rolen, Pat Burrell	3.00

Franchise Records

This Series 2 insert set focuses on players who led their teams

in various statistical categories. They are randomly seeded in 1:129 packs, while a parallel Refractor version is inserted 1:378. Card numbers have a "FR" prefix.

		NM/M
Complete Set (10):		35.00
Common Player:		2.00
Refractors:		3X
1	Frank Thomas	2.50
2	Ken Griffey Jr.	5.00
3	Mark McGwire	6.00
4	Juan Gonzalez	2.00
5	Nomar Garciaparra	3.00
6	Mike Piazza	5.00
7	Cal Ripken Jr.	7.50
8	Sammy Sosa	3.00
9	Barry Bonds	7.50
10	Tony Gwynn	3.00

Future's Finest

This Series 2 insert focuses on up-and-coming players who are primed to emerge as superstars. These are seeded 1:171 packs and limited to 500 numbered sets. Card numbers have a "FF" prefix.

		NM/M
Complete Set (10):		35.00
Common Player:		2.00
1	Pat Burrell	10.00
2	Troy Glaus	12.50
3	Eric Chavez	3.00
4	Ryan Anderson	2.00
5	Ruben Mateo	2.00
6	Gabe Kapler	2.00
7	Alex Gonzalez	2.00
8	Michael Barrett	2.00
9	Lance Berkman	2.00
10	Fernando Seguignol	2.00

Hank Aaron Award Contenders

This insert set focuses on nine players who had the best chance to win baseball's newest award. Production varies from card to card, with nine times as many of card #9 as of card #1, and so on. Insertion odds thus vary greatly, from 1:12 to 1:216. Refractor versions are found at odds which vary from 1:96 to 1:1728. Card numbers have an "HA" prefix.

		NM/M
Complete Set (9):		20.00
Common Player:		2.00
Refractors:		3X
1	Juan Gonzalez	2.00
2	Vladimir Guerrero	2.50
3	Nomar Garciaparra	3.00
4	Albert Belle	2.00
5	Frank Thomas	2.50
6	Sammy Sosa	3.00
7	Alex Rodriguez	5.00
8	Ken Griffey Jr.	4.00
9	Mark McGwire	5.00

Leading Indicators

Utilizing a heat-sensitive, thermal ink technology, these cards highlight the 1998 home run totals of 10 players. Touching the left, right or center field portion of the card behind each player's image reveals his 1998 season home run total in that specific direction. These are seeded in Series 1 packs.

		NM/M
Complete Set (10):		20.00
Common Player:		.50
Inserted 1:24		
L1	Mark McGwire	5.00
L2	Sammy Sosa	3.00
L3	Ken Griffey Jr.	4.00
L4	Greg Vaughn	.50
L5	Albert Belle	.50
L6	Juan Gonzalez	.75
L7	Andres Galarraga	.50
L8	Alex Rodriguez	5.00
L9	Barry Bonds	6.00
L10	Jeff Bagwell	1.50

Milestones

This Series 2 insert set is fractured into four subsets, each focusing on a statistical category: Hits, Home Runs, RBIs and Doubles. The Hits category is limited to 3,000 numbered sets. Home Runs are limited to 500 numbered sets. RBIs are limited to 1,400 numbered sets and Doubles is limited to 500 numbered sets. Each card number carries an "M" prefix.

		NM/M
Complete Set (40):		125.00
Common Hits (1-10):		.50
Common Homeruns (11-20):		2.00
Common RBI (21-30):		1.00
Common Doubles (31-40):		2.00
1	Tony Gwynn (Hits)	1.50
2	Cal Ripken Jr. (Hits)	3.00
3	Wade Boggs (Hits)	1.50
4	Ken Griffey Jr. (Hits)	2.00
5	Frank Thomas (Hits)	1.00
6	Barry Bonds (Hits)	3.00
7	Travis Lee (Hits)	.50
8	Alex Rodriguez (Hits)	2.50
9	Derek Jeter (Hits)	3.00
10	Vladimir Guerrero (Hits)	1.00
11	Mark McGwire (Home Runs)	8.00
12	Ken Griffey Jr. (Home Runs)	7.00
13	Vladimir Guerrero (Home Runs)	4.00

14	Alex Rodriguez (Home Runs)	8.00
15	Barry Bonds (Home Runs)	10.00
16	Sammy Sosa (Home Runs)	5.00
17	Albert Belle (Home Runs)	2.00
18	Frank Thomas (Home Runs)	4.00
19	Jose Canseco (Home Runs)	3.00
20	Mike Piazza (Home Runs)	7.00
21	Jeff Bagwell (RBI)	2.00
22	Barry Bonds (RBI)	6.00
23	Ken Griffey Jr. (RBI)	4.00
24	Albert Belle (RBI)	1.00
25	Juan Gonzalez (RBI)	1.50
26	Vinny Castilla (RBI)	1.00
27	Mark McGwire (RBI)	5.00
28	Alex Rodriguez (RBI)	5.00
29	Nomar Garciaparra (RBI)	3.00
30	Frank Thomas (RBI)	2.50
31	Barry Bonds (Doubles)	10.00
32	Albert Belle (Doubles)	2.00
33	Ben Grieve (Doubles)	2.00
34	Craig Biggio (Doubles)	2.00
35	Vladimir Guerrero (Doubles)	4.00
36	Nomar Garciaparra (Doubles)	5.00
37	Alex Rodriguez (Doubles)	7.00
38	Derek Jeter (Doubles)	10.00
39	Ken Griffey Jr. (Doubles)	7.00
40	Brad Fullmer (Doubles)	2.00

Peel & Reveal

This Series 1 insert offers 20 players produced in varying levels of scarcity designated by background design: Sparkle is common, Hyperplaid is uncommon and Stadium Stars is rare. Each card has a peel-off opaque protective coating on both front and back. Stated insertion odds are: Sparkle 1:30; Hyperplaid 1:60, and Stadium Stars 1:120. Home Team Advantage (HTA) boxes have odds which are twice as good.

		NM/M
Complete Set (20):		40.00
Common Player:		1.00
Hyperplaid:		1.5X
Stadium Stars:		2.5X
1	Kerry Wood	1.50
2	Mark McGwire	5.00
3	Sammy Sosa	3.00
4	Ken Griffey Jr.	4.00
5	Nomar Garciaparra	3.00
6	Greg Maddux	3.00
7	Derek Jeter	6.00
8	Andres Galarraga	1.00
9	Alex Rodriguez	5.00
10	Frank Thomas	2.00
11	Roger Clemens	3.50
12	Juan Gonzalez	1.50
13	Ben Grieve	1.00
14	Jeff Bagwell	2.00
15	Todd Helton	2.00
16	Chipper Jones	3.00
17	Barry Bonds	6.00
18	Travis Lee	1.00
19	Vladimir Guerrero	2.00
20	Pat Burrell	1.50

Prominent Figures

Fifty cards on Refractor technology highlight superstars chasing the all-time records in five different statistical categories: Home Runs, Slugging Percentage, Batting Average, RBIs and Total Bases. Ten players are featured in each category, each sequentially numbered to the all-time single season record statistic for that category. Home Run category is numbered to 70, Slugging Percentage to 847, Batting Average to 424, RBIs to 190 and Total Bases to 457.

PROMINENT FIGURES

		NM/M
Complete Set (50):		250.00
Common Home Runs (1-10); #'d to 70:		3.00
Common Slugging % (11-20); #'d to 847:		1.00
Common Batting Ave. (21-30); #'d to 424:		1.75
Common RBIs (31-40); #'d to 190:		
Common Total Bases (41-50); #'d to 457:		1.75
1	Mark McGwire (HR)	25.00
2	Sammy Sosa (HR)	10.00
3	Ken Griffey Jr. (HR)	15.00
4	Mike Piazza (HR)	15.00
5	Juan Gonzalez (HR)	5.00
6	Greg Vaughn (HR)	3.00
7	Alex Rodriguez (HR)	25.00
8	Manny Ramirez (HR)	7.50
9	Jeff Bagwell (HR)	7.50
10	Andres Galarraga (HR)	5.00
11	Mark McGwire (S%)	6.00
12	Sammy Sosa (S%)	5.00
13	Juan Gonzalez (S%)	2.50
14	Ken Griffey Jr. (S%)	5.00
15	Barry Bonds (S%)	7.50
16	Greg Vaughn (S%)	1.00
17	Larry Walker (S%)	1.00
18	Andres Galarraga (S%)	1.00
19	Jeff Bagwell (S%)	2.50
20	Albert Belle (S%)	1.00
21	Tony Gwynn (BA)	5.00
22	Mike Piazza (BA)	6.00
23	Larry Walker (BA)	1.75
24	Alex Rodriguez (BA)	7.50
25	John Olerud (BA)	1.75
26	Frank Thomas (BA)	3.50
27	Bernie Williams (BA)	1.75
28	Chipper Jones (BA)	5.00
29	Jim Thome (BA)	2.50
30	Barry Bonds (BA)	9.00
31	Juan Gonzalez (RBI)	3.00
32	Sammy Sosa (RBI)	9.00
33	Mark McGwire (RBI)	20.00
34	Albert Belle (RBI)	2.00
35	Ken Griffey Jr. (RBI)	15.00
36	Jeff Bagwell (RBI)	6.00
37	Chipper Jones (RBI)	10.00
38	Vinny Castilla (RBI)	2.00
39	Alex Rodriguez (RBI)	20.00
40	Andres Galarraga (RBI)	2.00
41	Sammy Sosa (TB)	6.00
42	Mark McGwire (TB)	7.50
43	Albert Belle (TB)	1.75
44	Ken Griffey Jr. (TB)	6.00
45	Jeff Bagwell (TB)	3.50
46	Juan Gonzalez (TB)	3.50
47	Barry Bonds (TB)	9.00
48	Vladimir Guerrero (TB)	3.50
49	Larry Walker (TB)	1.75
50	Alex Rodriguez (TB)	7.50

Split Screen

Players who share a common bond are highlighted in this Series 1 insert set which includes 14 paired players. Each card is available in three variations: Non-Refractor (1:28), Refractor/Non-Refractor (1:28) and Refractor/Refractor (1:84). Values shown are for a card with either left- or right-side Refractor; dual-Refractor cards are worth 2X.

		NM/M
Complete Set (14):		30.00
Common Card:		1.00
Dual-Refractor:		2X
1	Mark McGwire, Sammy Sosa	4.00
2	Ken Griffey Jr., Alex Rodriguez	4.00
3	Nomar Garciaparra, Derek Jeter	5.00
4	Barry Bonds, Albert Belle	4.00
5	Cal Ripken Jr., Tony Gwynn	4.00
6	Manny Ramirez, Juan Gonzalez	1.50
7	Frank Thomas, Andres Galarraga	1.50
8	Scott Rolen, Chipper Jones	2.00
9	Ivan Rodriguez, Mike Piazza	3.00
10	Kerry Wood, Roger Clemens	2.50
11	Greg Maddux, Tom Glavine	2.00
12	Troy Glaus, Eric Chavez	1.00
13	Ben Grieve, Todd Helton	1.00
14	Travis Lee, Pat Burrell	2.50

Team Finest

The first 10 cards are showcased in Series 1 while the last 10 cards showcased in Series 2. Team Finest are available in three colors: Blue, Red and Gold (Red and Gold are only available in Home Team Advantage packs). All Team Finest are serially numbered as follows: Blue, numbered to 1,500; Blue Refractors to 150; Red to 500; Red Refractors to 50; Gold to 250 and Gold Refractors to 25. Cards have a TF prefix to the card number.

		NM/M
Complete Set (20):		25.00
Common Blue:		1.00
Production 1,500 Sets		
Blue Refractors:		3X
Production 150 Sets		
Reds:		1.5X
Production 500 Sets		
Red Refractors:		7X
Production 50 Sets		
Golds:		2X
Production 250 Sets		
Gold Refractors:		10X
Production 25 Sets		
1	Greg Maddux	2.50
2	Mark McGwire	4.50
3	Sammy Sosa	2.50
4	Juan Gonzalez	1.25
5	Alex Rodriguez	4.50
6	Travis Lee	1.00
7	Roger Clemens	2.75
8	Darin Erstad	1.25
9	Todd Helton	1.75
10	Mike Piazza	3.50
11	Kerry Wood	1.25
12	Ken Griffey Jr.	3.50
13	Frank Thomas	2.00
14	Jeff Bagwell	2.00
15	Nomar Garciaparra	2.50
16	Derek Jeter	6.00
17	Chipper Jones	2.50
18	Barry Bonds	6.00
19	Tony Gwynn	2.50
20	Ben Grieve	1.00

2000 Finest

The 286-card base set has the traditional chromium finish with the Topps Finest logo in the upper left portion on the front. Also in the upper left portion is a partial image of a baseball with seams in the background of the player photo. Card backs have a small photo with '99 stats and career totals. The rookies from Series 1 are serial numbered to 2,000 and in Series 2 to 3,000.

		NM/M
Complete Set (286):		250.00
Complete Series 1 (147):		175.00
Complete Series 2 (140):		125.00
Common Player:		.25
Common Rookie (101-120):		4.00
Production 2,000		
Common Rookie (247-266):		4.00
Production 3,000		
Common Counterpart (267-276):		.75
Inserted 1:8		
Common Gem (136-145):		1.50
Inserted 1:24		
Pack (6):		2.00
Series 1 & 2 Box (24):		40.00
1	Nomar Garciaparra	2.00
2	Chipper Jones	1.50
3	Erubiel Durazo	.25
4	Robin Ventura	.25
5	Garret Anderson	.25
6	Dean Palmer	.25
7	Mariano Rivera	.35
8	Rusty Greer	.25
9	Jim Thome	.25
10	Jeff Bagwell	1.00
11	Jason Giambi	.75
12	Jeromy Burnitz	.25
13	Mark Grace	.35
14	Russ Ortiz	.25
15	Kevin Brown	.25
16	Kevin Millwood	.25
17	Scott Williamson	.25
18	Orlando Hernandez	.25
19	Todd Walker	.25
20	Carlos Beltran	.50
21	Ruben Rivera	.25
22	Curt Schilling	.40
23	Brian Giles	.25
24	Eric Karros	.25
25	Preston Wilson	.25
26	Al Leiter	.25
27	Juan Encarnacion	.25
28	Tim Salmon	.40
29	B.J. Surhoff	.25
30	Bernie Williams	.45
31	Lee Stevens	.25
32	Pokey Reese	.25
33	Mike Sweeney	.25
34	Corey Koskie	.25
35	Roberto Alomar	.40
36	Tim Hudson	.40
37	Tom Glavine	.40
38	Jeff Kent	.25
39	Mike Lieberthal	.25
40	Barry Larkin	.25
41	Paul O'Neill	.25
42	Rico Brogna	.25
43	Brian Daubach	.25
44	Rich Aurilia	.25
45	Vladimir Guerrero	1.00
46	Luis Castillo	.25
47	Bartolo Colon	.25
48	Kevin Appier	.25
49	Mo Vaughn	.25
50	Alex Rodriguez	2.50
51	Randy Johnson	1.00
52	Kris Benson	.25
53	Tony Clark	.25
54	Chad Allen	.25
55	Larry Walker	.25
56	Freddy Garcia	.25
57	Paul Konerko	.35
58	Edgardo Alfonzo	.25
59	Brady Anderson	.25
60	Derek Jeter	3.00
61	Mike Hampton	.25
62	Jeff Cirillo	.25
63	Shannon Stewart	.25
64	Greg Maddux	1.50
65	Mark McGwire	2.00
66	Gary Sheffield	.50
67	Kevin Young	.25
68	Tony Gwynn	1.50
69	Rey Ordonez	.25
70	Cal Ripken Jr.	3.00
71	Todd Helton	1.00
72	Brian Jordan	.25
73	Jose Canseco	.50
74	Luis Gonzalez	.40
75	Barry Bonds	3.00
76	Jermaine Dye	.25
77	Jose Offerman	.25
78	Magglio Ordonez	.40
79	Fred McGriff	.25
80	Ivan Rodriguez	.60
81	Josh Hamilton (Prospects)	.50
82	Vernon Wells (Prospects)	.25
83	Mark Mulder (Prospects)	.35
84	John Patterson (Prospects)	.25
85	Nick Johnson (Prospects)	.50
86	Pablo Ozuna (Prospects)	.25
87	A.J. Burnett (Prospects)	.25
88	Jack Cust (Prospects)	.25
89	Adam Piatt (Prospects)	.25
90	Rob Ryan (Prospects)	.25
91	Sean Burroughs (Prospects)	.35
92	D'Angelo Jimenez (Prospects)	.25
93	Chad Hermansen (Prospects)	.25
94	Rob Fick (Prospects)	.25
95	Ruben Mateo (Prospects)	.25
96	Alex Escobar (Prospects)	.25
97	Willi Mo Pena (Prospects)	.25
98	Corey Patterson (Prospects)	.50
99	Eric Munson (Prospects)	.25
100	Pat Burrell (Prospects)	.75
101	Michael Tejera RC	.25
102	Bobby Bradley RC	4.00
103	Larry Bigbie RC	6.00
104	B.J. Garbe RC	4.00
105	Josh Kalinowski RC	4.00
106	Brett Myers RC	15.00
107	Chris Mears RC	4.00
108	Aaron Rowand RC	10.00
109	Corey Myers RC	4.00
110	John Sneed RC	4.00
111	Ryan Christensen RC	4.00
112	Kyle Snyder RC	4.00
113	Mike Paradis RC	4.00
114	Chance Caple RC	4.00
115	Ben Christiansen RC	4.00
116	Brad Baker RC	4.00
117	Rob Purvis RC	4.00
118	Rick Asadoorian RC	4.00
119	Ruben Salazar RC	4.00
120	Julio Zuleta RC	4.00
121	Ken Griffey Jr., Alex Rodriguez (Features)	4.00
122	Nomar Garciaparra, Derek Jeter (Features)	5.00
123	Mark McGwire, Sammy Sosa (Features)	4.00
124	Randy Johnson, Pedro Martinez (Features)	2.00
125	Mike Piazza, Ivan Rodriguez (Features)	3.00
126	Manny Ramirez, Roberto Alomar (Features)	2.00
127	Chipper Jones, Andruw Jones (Features)	3.00
128	Cal Ripken Jr., Tony Gwynn (Features)	5.00
129	Jeff Bagwell, Craig Biggio (Features)	1.50
130	Vladimir Guerrero, Barry Bonds (Features)	5.00
131	Alfonso Soriano, Nick Johnson (Features)	2.00
132	Josh Hamilton, Pat Burrell (Features)	1.50
133	Corey Patterson, Ruben Mateo (Features)	.75
134	Larry Walker, Todd Helton (Features)	1.50
135	Edgardo Alfonzo, Rey Ordonez (Features)	.75
136	Derek Jeter (Gems)	10.00
137	Alex Rodriguez (Gems)	8.00
138	Chipper Jones (Gems)	5.00
139	Mike Piazza (Gems)	6.00
140	Mark McGwire (Gems)	8.00
141	Juan Gonzalez (Gems)	4.00
142	Cal Ripken Jr. (Gems)	10.00
143	Vladimir Guerrero (Gems)	3.00
144	Randy Johnson (Gems)	3.00
145	Jeff Bagwell (Gems)	3.00
146	Ken Griffey Jr. field	1.50
146a	Ken Griffey Jr. press	1.50
147	Andruw Jones	.25
148	Kerry Wood	.50
149	Jim Edmonds	.25
150	Pedro Martinez	1.00
151	Warren Morris	.25
152	Trevor Hoffman	.25
153	Eric Young	.25
154	Andy Pettitte	.40
155	Frank Thomas	1.00
156	Damion Easley	.25
157	Cliff Floyd	.25
158	Ben Davis	.25
159	John Valentin	.25
160	Rafael Palmeiro	.65
161	Andy Ashby	.25
162	J.D. Drew	.40
163	Jay Bell	.25
164	Adam Kennedy	.25
165	Manny Ramirez	1.00
166	John Halama	.25
167	Octavio Dotel	.25
168	Darin Erstad	.40
169	Jose Lima	.25
170	Andres Galarraga	.25
171	Scott Rolen	.75
172	Delino DeShields	.25
173	J.T. Snow Jr.	.25
174	Tony Womack	.25
175	John Olerud	.25
176	Jason Kendall	.25
177	Carlos Lee	.25
178	Eric Milton	.25
179	Jeff Cirillo	.25
180	Gabe Kapler	.25
181	Greg Vaughn	.25
182	Denny Neagle	.25
183	Tino Martinez	.25
184	Doug Mientkiewicz	.25
185	Juan Gonzalez	1.00
186	Ellis Burks	.25
187	Mike Hampton	.25
188	Royce Clayton	.25
189	Mike Mussina	.50
190	Carlos Delgado	.50
191	Ben Grieve	.25
192	Fernando Tatis	.25
193	Matt Williams	.25
194	Rondell White	.25
195	Shawn Green	.50
196	Justin Thompson	.25
197	Troy Glaus	1.00
198	Roger Cedeno	.25
199	Ray Lankford	.25
200	Sammy Sosa	2.00
201	Kenny Lofton	.25
202	Edgar Martinez	.25
203	Mark Kotsay	.25
204	David Wells	.25
205	Craig Biggio	.25
206	Ray Durham	.25
207	Troy O'Leary	.25
208	Rickey Henderson	.75
209	Bob Abreu	.25
210	Neifi Perez	.25
211	Carlos Febles	.25
212	Chuck Knoblauch	.25
213	Moises Alou	.25
214	Omar Vizquel	.25
215	Vinny Castilla	.25
216	Javy Lopez	.25
217	Johnny Damon	.25
218	Roger Clemens	1.75
219	Miguel Tejada	.40
220	Deion Sanders	.35
221	Matt Lawton	.25
222	Albert Belle	.25
223	Adrian Beltre	.50
224	Dante Bichette	.25
225	Raul Mondesi	.25
226	Mike Piazza	2.00
227	Brad Penny (Prospects)	.25
228	Kip Wells (Prospects)	.25
229	Adam Everett (Prospects)	.25
230	Eddie Yarnall (Prospects)	.25
231	Matt LeCroy (Prospects)	.25
232	Ryan Anderson (Prospects)	.25
233	Rick Ankiel (Prospects)	.25
234	Daryle Ward (Prospects)	.25
235	Rafael Furcal (Prospects)	.25
236	Dee Brown (Prospects)	.25
237	Travis Dawkins (Prospects)	.25
238	Eric Valent (Prospects)	.25
239	Peter Bergeron (Prospects)	.25
240	Alfonso Soriano (Prospects)	1.50
241	John Patterson (Prospects)	.25
242	Jorge Toca (Prospects)	.25
243	Ryan Anderson (Prospects)	.25
244	Jason Dallaero (Prospects)	.25
245	Jason Grilli (Prospects)	.25
246	Chad Hermansen (Prospects)	.25
247	Scott Downs RC	4.00
248	Keith Reed RC	4.00
249	Edgar Cruz RC	4.00
250	Wes Anderson RC	10.00
251	Lyle Overbay RC	4.00
252	Mike Lamb RC	4.00
253	Vince Faison RC	4.00
254	Chad Alexander RC	4.00
255	Chris Wakeland RC	4.00
256	Aaron McNeal RC	4.00
257	Tomokazu Ohka RC	4.00
258	Ty Howington RC	6.00
259	Javier Colina RC	4.00
260	Jason Jennings RC	4.00
261	Ramon Santiago RC	4.00
262	Johan Santana RC	150.00
263	Quincey Foster RC	4.00
264	Junior Brignac RC	4.00
265	Rico Washington RC	4.00
266	Scott Sobkowiak RC	4.00
267	Pedro Martinez, Rick Ankiel (Counterparts)	2.00
268	Manny Ramirez, Vladimir Guerrero (Counterparts)	2.00
269	A.J. Burnett, Mark Mulder (Counterparts)	.75
270	Mike Piazza, Eric Munson (Counterparts)	1.00
271	Josh Hamilton, Corey Patterson (Counterparts)	1.00
272	Ken Griffey Jr., Sammy Sosa (Counterparts)	3.00
273	Derek Jeter, Alfonso Soriano (Counterparts)	3.00
274	Mark McGwire, Pat Burrell (Counterparts)	5.00
275	Chipper Jones, Cal Ripken Jr. (Counterparts)	5.00
276	Nomar Garciaparra, Alex Rodriguez (Counterparts)	4.00
277	Pedro Martinez (Gems)	3.00
278	Tony Gwynn (Gems)	5.00
279	Barry Bonds (Gems)	10.00
280	Juan Gonzalez (Gems)	3.00
281	Larry Walker (Gems)	3.00
282	Nomar Garciaparra (Gems)	6.00
283	Ken Griffey Jr. (Gems)	6.00
284	Manny Ramirez (Gems)	.25

285	Shawn Green (Gems)	2.00
286	Sammy Sosa (Gems)	6.00

Refractor

These are a parallel to the base set and have a mirror like sheen. Card backs have "refractor" written underneath the card number.

Stars (1-100):	5-10X
Inserted 1:24	
Rookies (101-120,247-266):	.5-1X
Production 500 Sets	
Features (121-135):	2-3X
Inserted 1:96	
Counterparts (267-276):	2-3X
Inserted 1:96	
Gems (136-145,277-286):	2-3X
Inserted 1:288	

Gold Refractor

A parallel to the base set, these have the usual mirror like appearance with a deckle edged border. Regular cards are seeded 1:240 packs, Rookies are limited to 100 serial numbered sets, Features and Counterparts subsets (1:960) and Gems (1:2,880).

Stars (1-100):	20-40X
Inserted 1:240	
Rookies (101-120, 247-266):	1-2X
Production 100 Sets	
Features:	4-8X
Inserted 1:960	
Counterparts:	4-8X
Inserted 1:960	
Gems:	5-10X
Inserted 1:2,880	

Ballpark Bounties

Seeded across both Series 1 and 2 these inserts use Serigraph Fresnal technology and have a metallic looking image of a baseball in the background of the player photo. Card backs are numbered with a "BB" prefix.

	NM/M
Complete Set (30):	85.00
Complete Series 1 (15):	45.00
Complete Series 2 (15):	45.00
Common Player:	1.50
Inserted 1:24	
	Chipper Jones	5.00
	Mike Piazza	6.00
	Vladimir Guerrero	3.00
	Sammy Sosa	6.00
	Nomar Garciaparra	6.00
	Manny Ramirez	3.00
	Jeff Bagwell	3.00
	Scott Rolen	2.00
	Carlos Beltran	2.50
	Pedro Martinez	3.00
	Greg Maddux	5.00
	Josh Hamilton	2.00
	Adam Piatt	1.50
	Pat Burrell	2.00
	Alfonso Soriano	5.00
	Alex Rodriguez	8.00
	Derek Jeter	10.00
	Cal Ripken Jr.	10.00
	Larry Walker	1.50
	Barry Bonds	6.00
	Ken Griffey Jr.	6.00
	Mark McGwire	8.00

23	Ivan Rodriguez	2.00
24	Andruw Jones	2.50
25	Todd Helton	2.50
26	Randy Johnson	3.00
27	Ruben Mateo	1.50
28	Corey Patterson	1.50
29	Sean Burroughs	1.50
30	Eric Munson	1.50

Dream Cast

These inserts are found exclusively in Series 2 packs and utilize Duflex technology. The card fronts try to portray a "dream sequence" with sky and clouds in the background. They are numbered with a "DC" prefix on the card back.

	NM/M
Complete Set (10):	40.00
Common Player:	2.00
Inserted 1:36	
1	Mark McGwire	8.00
2	Roberto Alomar	2.00
3	Chipper Jones	5.00
4	Derek Jeter	10.00
5	Barry Bonds	10.00
6	Ken Griffey Jr.	6.00
7	Sammy Sosa	6.00
8	Mike Piazza	6.00
9	Pedro Martinez	3.00
10	Randy Johnson	3.00

Finest Moments

This four-card set pays tribute to milestone achievements accomplished during the 1999 season. They are numbered with a "FM" prefix. A Refractor parallel version is seeded 1:20 packs.

	NM/M
Complete Set (4):	6.00
Common Player:	1.00
Inserted 1:9	
Refractor:	1-2X
Inserted 1:20	
1	Chipper Jones	3.00
2	Ivan Rodriguez	1.50
3	Tony Gwynn	3.00
4	Wade Boggs	3.00

Moments Autographs

An autographed version of the four-card set, these were seeded 1:425 packs.

For The Record

Printed on Finest Clear Card technology, each of the 10 players featured has three cards. Each card sequentially numbered to the distance of the outfield wall in their home ballpark (left, center and right). Combining all three cards forms a panoramic view of the stadium.

		NM/M
Complete Set (30):		300.00
Common Player:		8.00
Inserted 1:24		
1A	Derek Jeter/318	20.00
1B	Derek Jeter/408	20.00
1C	Derek Jeter/314	20.00
2A	Mark McGwire/330	15.00
2B	Mark McGwire/402	15.00
2C	Mark McGwire/330	15.00
3A	Ken Griffey Jr./331	10.00
3B	Ken Griffey Jr./405	10.00
3C	Ken Griffey Jr./327	10.00
4A	Alex Rodriguez/331	15.00
4B	Alex Rodriguez/405	15.00
4C	Alex Rodriguez/327	15.00
5A	Nomar Garciaparra/310	10.00
5B	Nomar Garciaparra/390	10.00
5C	Nomar Garciaparra/302	10.00
6A	Cal Ripken Jr./333	20.00
6B	Cal Ripken Jr./410	20.00
6C	Cal Ripken Jr./318	20.00
7A	Sammy Sosa/355	10.00
7B	Sammy Sosa/400	10.00
7C	Sammy Sosa/353	10.00
8A	Manny Ramirez/325	8.00
8B	Manny Ramirez/410	8.00
8C	Manny Ramirez/325	8.00
9A	Mike Piazza/338	10.00
9B	Mike Piazza/410	10.00
9C	Mike Piazza/338	10.00
10A	Chipper Jones/335	9.00
10B	Chipper Jones/401	10.00
10C	Chipper Jones/330	10.00

Gems Oversized

Each of the 10 Gems subset cards in series 1 and 2 were also done on an oversized format. The oversized cards were added as a box topper to each box. Home Team Advantage stores received Refractor versions of the Gems Oversized cards as a box topper.

		NM/M
Complete Set (20):		50.00
Common Player:		1.00
Inserted 1:Box		
1	Derek Jeter	6.00
2	Alex Rodriguez	5.00
3	Chipper Jones	3.00
4	Mike Piazza	4.00
5	Mark McGwire	5.00
6	Ivan Rodriguez	1.25
7	Cal Ripken Jr.	6.00
8	Vladimir Guerrero	2.00
9	Randy Johnson	1.00
10	Jeff Bagwell	2.00

	NM/M
Common Autograph:	25.00
Inserted 1:425	
1	Chipper Jones	50.00
2	Ivan Rodriguez	25.00
3	Tony Gwynn	50.00
4	Wade Boggs	25.00

Going the Distance

This 12-card set highlights the top hitters in baseball, utilizing Photopolymer hologram technology. Card backs are numbered with a "GTD" prefix.

	NM/M
Complete Set (12):	45.00
Common Player:	3.00
Inserted 1:24	
1	Tony Gwynn	3.50
2	Alex Rodriguez	6.00
3	Derek Jeter	8.00
4	Chipper Jones	4.00
5	Nomar Garciaparra	4.00
6	Sammy Sosa	4.00
7	Ken Griffey Jr.	4.00
8	Vladimir Guerrero	3.00
9	Mark McGwire	6.00
10	Mike Piazza	4.00
11	Manny Ramirez	3.00
12	Cal Ripken Jr.	8.00

2001 Finest

		NM/M
Complete Set (140):		250.00
Common Player:		.25
Common Standout Veteran (10):	5.00
Production 1999		
Common Rookie (111-140):		4.00
Production 999		
Pack (6):		8.00
Box (20):		140.00
1	Mike Piazza/SV	10.00
2	Andruw Jones	.50
3	Jason Giambi	.75
4	Fred McGriff	.25
5	Vladimir Guerrero/SV	6.00
6	Adrian Gonzalez	.40
7	Pedro Martinez	1.00
8	Mike Lieberthal	.25
9	Warren Morris	.25
10	Juan Gonzalez	.50
11	Jose Canseco	.50
12	Jose Valentin	.25
13	Jeff Cirillo	.25
14	Pokey Reese	.25
15	Scott Rolen	.75
16	Greg Maddux	1.50
17	Carlos Delgado	.50
18	Rick Ankiel	.50
19	Steve Finley	.25
20	Shawn Green	.40
21	Orlando Cabrerra	.25
22	Roberto Alomar	.40
23	John Olerud	.25
24	Albert Belle	.25
25	Edgardo Alfonzo	.25
26	Rafael Palmeiro	.75
27	Mike Sweeney	.25
28	Bernie Williams	.40
29	Larry Walker	.25
30	Barry Bonds/SV	15.00
31	Orlando Hernandez	.25
32	Randy Johnson	1.00
33	Shannon Stewart	.25

34	Mark Grace	.40
35	Alex Rodriguez/SV	12.00
36	Tino Martinez	.40
37	Carlos Febles	.25
38	Al Leiter	.25
39	Omar Vizquel	.25
40	Chuck Knoblauch	.25
41	Tim Salmon	.40
42	Brian Jordan	.25
43	Edgar Renteria	.25
44	Preston Wilson	.25
45	Mariano Rivera	.50
46	Gabe Kapler	.25
47	Jason Kendall	.25
48	Rickey Henderson	.75
49	Luis Gonzalez	.40
50	Tom Glavine	.50
51	Jeromy Burnitz	.25
52	Garret Anderson	.25
53	Craig Biggio	.25
54	Vinny Castilla	.25
55	Jeff Kent	.25
56	Gary Sheffield	.50
57	Jorge Posada	.50
58	Sean Casey	.25
59	Johnny Damon	.50
60	Dean Palmer	.25
61	Todd Helton	.75
62	Barry Larkin	.50
63	Robin Ventura	.25
64	Kenny Lofton	.25
65	Sammy Sosa/SV	8.00
66	Rafael Furcal	.50
67	Jay Bell	.25
68	J.T. Snow Jr.	.25
69	Jose Vidro	.25
70	Ivan Rodriguez	.75
71	Jermaine Dye	.25
72	Chipper Jones/SV	10.00
73	Fernando Vina	.25
74	Ben Grieve	.25
75	Mark McGwire/SV	10.00
76	Matt Williams	.25
77	Mark Grudzielanek	.25
78	Mike Hampton	.25
79	Brian Giles	.25
80	Tony Gwynn	1.50
81	Carlos Beltran	.50
82	Ray Durham	.25
83	Brad Radke	.25
84	David Justice	.25
85	Frank Thomas	1.00
86	Todd Zeile	.25
87	Pat Burrell	.75
88	Jim Thome	.25
89	Greg Vaughn	.25
90	Ken Griffey Jr./SV	10.00
91	Mike Mussina	.50
92	Magglio Ordonez	.50
93	Bobby Abreu	.25
94	Alex Gonzalez	.25
95	Kevin Brown	.25
96	Jay Buhner	.25
97	Roger Clemens	2.00
98	Nomar Garciaparra/SV	5.00
99	Derrek Lee	.50
100	Derek Jeter/SV	15.00
101	Adrian Beltre	.40
102	Geoff Jenkins	.25
103	Javy Lopez	.25
104	Raul Mondesi	.25
105	Troy Glaus	.50
106	Jeff Bagwell	.75
107	Eric Karros	.25
108	Mo Vaughn	.25
109	Cal Ripken Jr.	3.00
110	Manny Ramirez	1.00
111	Scott Heard RC	4.00
112	Luis Montanez RC	5.00
113	Ben Diggins RC	4.00
114	Shaun Boyd RC	4.00
115	Sean Burnett RC	4.00
116	Carmen Cali RC	4.00
117	Derek Thompson RC	4.00
118	David Parrish RC	4.00
119	Dominic Rich RC	4.00
120	Chad Petty RC	4.00
121	Steve Smyth RC	4.00
122	John Lackey	6.00
123	Matt Galante RC	4.00
124	Danny Borrell RC	4.00
125	Bob Keppel RC	4.00
126	Justin Wayne RC	4.00
127	J.R. House	4.00
128	Brian Sellier RC	4.00
129	Dan Moylan RC	4.00
130	Scott Pratt RC	4.00
131	Victor Hall RC	4.00
132	Joel Pineiro	4.00
133	Josh Axelson RC	4.00
134	Jose Reyes RC	120.00
135	Greg Runser RC	4.00
136	Bryan Hebson RC	4.00
137	Sammy Serrano RC	4.00
138	Kevin Joseph RC	4.00
139	Juan Richardson RC	4.00
140	Mark Fischer RC	4.00

Finest Refractors

		NM/M
Stars (1-110):		4-8X
Production 499		
SP's:		.5-1.5X
Production 399		
Cards (111-140):		1-2X
Production 241		

All-Stars

	NM/M
Complete Set (10):	30.00

Mike Piazza

	NM/M
Common Player:	2.00
Inserted 1:10	
Refractors:	1.5-2X
Inserted 1:40	
1	Mark McGwire	4.00
2	Derek Jeter	6.00
3	Alex Rodriguez	5.00
4	Chipper Jones	4.00
5	Nomar Garciaparra	2.00
6	Sammy Sosa	4.00
7	Mike Piazza	4.00
8	Barry Bonds	6.00
9	Vladimir Guerrero	2.00
10	Ken Griffey Jr.	4.00

Autographed

	NM/M
Common Player:	5.00
Inserted 1:22	
MB	Milton Bradley	15.00
SB	Sean Burnett	5.00
BKC	Brian Cole	5.00
JC	Joe Crede	10.00
BC	Brad Creese	5.00
BD	Ben Diggins	5.00
CD	Chad Durham	5.00
TF	Troy Farnsworth	5.00
RF	Rafael Furcal	15.00
KG	Keith Ginter	5.00
AG	Adrian Gonzalez	20.00
JHH	Josh Hamilton	40.00
JH	Jason Hart	5.00
JRH	J.R. House	5.00
AH	Adam Hyzdu	5.00
DKC	David Kelton	5.00
AK	Adam Kennedy	5.00
DK	David Krynzel	5.00
ML	Mike Lamb	5.00
TL	Terrence Long	5.00
KM	Kevin Mench	5.00
BM	Ben Molina	8.00
JM	Justin Morneau	75.00
CM	Chad Mottola	5.00
JO	Jose Ortiz	5.00
DP	David Parrish	5.00
DCP	Corey Patterson	8.00
JP	Jay Payton	5.00
CP	Carlos Pena	10.00
AP	Albert Pujols	300.00
MQ	Mark Quinn	5.00
MR	Mark Redman	5.00
BS	Ben Sheets	15.00
JS	Juan Silvestre	5.00
JNS	Jamal Strong	5.00
BZ	Barry Zito	15.00

Moments

	NM/M
Complete Set (25):	45.00
Common Player:	1.00
Inserted 1:12	
Refractors:	1.5-2X
Inserted 1:40	
1	Pat Burrell	2.00
2	Adam Kennedy	1.00
3	Mike Lamb	1.00
4	Rafael Furcal	1.50
5	Terrence Long	1.00

6	Jay Payton	1.00
7	Mark Quinn	1.00
8	Ben Molina	1.00
9	Kazuhiro Sasaki	1.00
10	Mark Redman	1.00
11	Barry Bonds	8.00
12	Alex Rodriguez	6.00
13	Roger Clemens	5.00
14	Jim Edmonds	1.00
15	Jason Giambi	2.00
16	Todd Helton	2.50
17	Troy Glaus	2.00
18	Carlos Delgado	2.00
19	Darin Erstad	2.00
20	Cal Ripken Jr.	8.00
21	Paul Molitor	3.00
22	Robin Yount	2.50
23	George Brett	5.00
24	Dave Winfield	2.50
25	Wade Boggs	3.00

Moments Autographs

NM/M
Inserted 1:250

BB	Barry Bonds	150.00
GB	George Brett	75.00
JG	Jason Giambi	25.00
TG	Troy Glaus	20.00
TH	Todd Helton	30.00
PM	Paul Molitor	30.00
EM	Eddie Murray	20.00
CR	Cal Ripken Jr.	125.00
DW	Dave Winfield	20.00
RY	Robin Yount	50.00

Origins

NM/M
Complete Set (15): 18.00
Common Player: 1.00
Inserted 1:7
Refractors: 1.5-2X
Inserted 1:40

1	Derek Jeter	5.00
2	Jason Kendall	1.00
3	Jose Vidro	1.00
4	Preston Wilson	1.00
5	Jim Edmonds	1.00
6	Vladimir Guerrero	2.00
7	Andruw Jones	1.50
8	Scott Rolen	1.50
9	Edgardo Alfonzo	1.00
10	Mike Sweeney	1.00
11	Alex Rodriguez	4.00
12	Jermaine Dye	1.00
13	Charles Johnson	1.00
14	Darren Dreifort	1.00
15	Neifi Perez	1.00

2002 Finest

NM/M
Complete Set (110): 125.00
Common Player: .25
Common SP Auto. (101-110): 8.00
Pack (5): 4.00
Box (18): 60.00

1	Mike Mussina	.50
2	Steve Sparks	.25
3	Randy Johnson	1.00
4	Orlando Cabrera	.25
5	Jeff Kent	.25
6	Carlos Delgado	.75
7	Ivan Rodriguez	.75
8	Jose Cruz	.25
9	Jason Giambi	.75
10	Brad Penny	.25
11	Moises Alou	.25
12	Mike Piazza	2.00
13	Ben Grieve	.25

14	Derek Jeter	3.00
15	Roy Oswalt	.40
16	Pat Burrell	.65
17	Preston Wilson	.25
18	Kevin Brown	.25
19	Barry Bonds	3.00
20	Phil Nevin	.25
21	Juan Gonzalez	1.00
22	Carlos Beltran	.60
23	Chipper Jones	1.50
24	Curt Schilling	.50
25	Jorge Posada	.40
26	Alfonso Soriano	1.00
27	Cliff Floyd	.25
28	Rafael Palmeiro	.75
29	Terrence Long	.25
30	Ken Griffey Jr.	2.00
31	Jason Kendall	.25
32	Jose Vidro	.25
33	Jermaine Dye	.25
34	Bobby Higginson	.25
35	Albert Pujols	2.50
36	Miguel Tejada	.40
37	Jim Edmonds	.25
38	Barry Zito	.40
39	Jimmy Rollins	.50
40	Rafael Furcal	.25
41	Omar Vizquel	.25
42	Kazuhiro Sasaki	.25
43	Brian Giles	.25
44	Darin Erstad	.50
45	Mariano Rivera	.40
46	Troy Percival	.25
47	Mike Sweeney	.25
48	Vladimir Guerrero	1.00
49	Troy Glaus	1.00
50	Hideo Nomo	.65
51	Edgardo Alfonzo	.25
52	Roger Clemens	1.75
53	Eric Chavez	.40
54	Alex Rodriguez	2.50
55	Cristian Guzman	.25
56	Jeff Bagwell	1.00
57	Bernie Williams	.40
58	Kerry Wood	.60
59	Ryan Klesko	.25
60	Ichiro Suzuki	2.00
61	Larry Walker	.25
62	Nomar Garciaparra	2.00
63	Craig Biggio	.25
64	J.D. Drew	.40
65	Juan Pierre	.25
66	Roberto Alomar	.50
67	Luis Gonzalez	.40
68	Bud Smith	.25
69	Magglio Ordonez	.25
70	Scott Rolen	1.00
71	Tsuyoshi Shinjo	.25
72	Reggie Sanders	.25
73	Garret Anderson	.40
74	Tim Hudson	.40
75	Adam Dunn	.75
76	Gary Sheffield	.50
77	Johnny Damon	.40
78	Todd Helton	1.00
79	Geoff Jenkins	.25
80	Shawn Green	.40
81	C.C. Sabathia	.50
82	Kazuhisa Ishii RC	2.00
83	Rich Aurilia	.25
84	Mike Hampton	.25
85	Ben Sheets	.25
86	Andruw Jones	1.00
87	Richie Sexson	.25
88	Jim Thome	.75
89	Sammy Sosa	2.00
90	Greg Maddux	1.50
91	Pedro Martinez	1.00
92	Jeromy Burnitz	.25
93	Raul Mondesi	.25
94	Bret Boone	.25
95	Jerry Hairston Jr.	.25
96	Carlos Pena	.25
97	Juan Cruz	.25
98	Morgan Ensberg	.25
99	Nathan Haynes	.25
100	Xavier Nady	.25
101	Nic Jackson/Auto. RC	10.00
102	Mauricio Lara/Auto. RC	8.00
103	Freddy Sanchez/ Auto. RC	20.00
104	Clint Nageotte/Auto. RC	15.00
105	Beltran Perez/Auto. RC	8.00
106	Garrett Gentry/Auto. RC	8.00
107	Chad Qualls/Auto. RC	8.00
108	Jason Bay/Auto. RC	35.00
109	Michael Hill/Auto. RC	8.00
110	Brian Tallet/Auto.	10.00

Refractors

Star Refractors: 2-5X
Numbered to 499
X-Fractors: 3-6X
Numbered to 299
X-Fractor Protector: 5-10X
X-Fract. Protector (101-110): 1-2X
Numbered to 99

Moments Autographs

Common Autograph: 10.00
Inserted 1:18

LA	Luis Aparicio	15.00
YB	Yogi Berra	30.00
JB	Jim Bunning	10.00
BG	Bob Gibson	25.00
GG	Rich "Goose" Gossage	15.00
FJ	Fergie Jenkins	15.00
DL	Don Larsen	15.00
DM	Don Mattingly	75.00
GP	Gaylord Perry	10.00
BR	Bobby Richardson	10.00
BRO	Brooks Robinson	35.00
JS	Johnny Sain	10.00
MS	Mike Schmidt	50.00
RS	Red Schoendienst	10.00
BT	Bobby Thomson	15.00

Bat Relics

Common Player: 5.00
Inserted 1:72

BB	Barry Bonds	25.00
BBO	Bret Boone	5.00
NG	Nomar Garciaparra	15.00
LG	Luis Gonzalez	5.00
TG	Tony Gwynn	10.00
TH	Todd Helton	8.00
AJ	Andruw Jones	5.00
CJ	Chipper Jones	10.00
MP	Mike Piazza	10.00
AP	Albert Pujols	20.00
AR	Alex Rodriguez	10.00
IR	Ivan Rodriguez	8.00
TS	Tsuyoshi Shinjo	5.00
AS	Alfonso Soriano	5.00
BW	Bernie Williams	8.00

Team Topps Legends

Common Autograph

Uniform Relics

Common Player: 5.00
Inserted 1:24

RA	Roberto Alomar	8.00
JB	Jeff Bagwell	8.00
BB	Barry Bonds	20.00
BBO	Bret Boone	5.00
CD	Carlos Delgado	8.00
LG	Luis Gonzalez	8.00
MG	Mark Grace	8.00
SG	Shawn Green	8.00
TG	Tony Gwynn	10.00
TH	Todd Helton	8.00
RH	Rickey Henderson	15.00
AJ	Andruw Jones	8.00
CJ	Chipper Jones	10.00
GM	Greg Maddux	10.00
PM	Pedro Martinez	10.00
HN	Hideo Nomo	20.00
RP	Rafael Palmeiro	10.00
MP	Mike Piazza	10.00
AR	Alex Rodriguez	10.00
IR	Ivan Rodriguez	8.00
CS	Curt Schilling	10.00
TS	Tsuyoshi Shinjo	5.00
FT	Frank Thomas	8.00
LW	Larry Walker	5.00

2003 Finest

NM/M
Complete Set (110):
Common Player: .25
Common Auto. (101-110):
Pack (5): 4.00
Box (18): 50.00

1	Sammy Sosa	1.00
2	Paul Konerko	.25
3	Todd Helton	.75
4	Mike Lowell	.25
5	Lance Berkman	.25
6	Kazuhisa Ishii	.25
7	A.J. Pierzynski	.25
8	Jose Vidro	.25
9	Roberto Alomar	.40
10	Derek Jeter	3.00
11	Barry Zito	.40
12	Jimmy Rollins	.75
13	Brian Giles	.25
14	Ryan Klesko	.25
15	Rich Aurilia	.25
16	Jim Edmonds	.25
17	Aubrey Huff	.25
18	Ivan Rodriguez	.50
19	Eric Hinske	.25
20	Barry Bonds	3.00
21	Darin Erstad	.40
22	Curt Schilling	.50
23	Andruw Jones	.25
24	Jay Gibbons	.25
25	Nomar Garciaparra	.50
26	Kerry Wood	.50
27	Magglio Ordonez	.50
28	Austin Kearns	.25
29	Jason Jennings	.25
30	Jason Giambi	.50
31	Tim Hudson	.40
32	Edgar Martinez	.25
33	Carl Crawford	.25
34	Hee Seop Choi	.50
35	Vladimir Guerrero	.75
36	Jeff Kent	.25
37	John Smoltz	.25
38	Frank Thomas	.75
39	Cliff Floyd	.25
40	Mike Piazza	1.50
41	Mark Prior	.50
42	Tim Salmon	.40
43	Shawn Green	.50
44	Bernie Williams	.40
45	Jim Thome	.25
46	John Olerud	.25
47	Orlando Hudson	.25
48	Mark Teixeira	.75
49	Gary Sheffield	.50
50	Ichiro Suzuki	2.00
51	Tom Glavine	.40
52	Torii Hunter	.25
53	Craig Biggio	.25
54	Carlos Beltran	.75
55	Bartolo Colon	.25
56	Jorge Posada	.35
57	Pat Burrell	.50
58	Edgar Renteria	.25
59	Rafael Palmeiro	.50
60	Alfonso Soriano	.75
61	Brandon Phillips	.25
62	Luis Gonzalez	.40
63	Manny Ramirez	.75
64	Garret Anderson	.25
65	Ken Griffey Jr.	1.50
66	A.J. Burnett	.25
67	Mike Sweeney	.25
68	Doug Mientkiewicz	.25
69	Eric Chavez	.50
70	Adam Dunn	.75
71	Shea Hillenbrand	.25
72	Troy Glaus	.50
73	Rodrigo Lopez	.25
74	Moises Alou	.25
75	Chipper Jones	1.50
76	Bobby Abreu	.25
77	Mark Mulder	.40
78	Kevin Brown	.25

79	Josh Beckett	.75
80	Larry Walker	.25
81	Randy Johnson	.75
82	Greg Maddux	1.50
83	Johnny Damon	.40
84	Omar Vizquel	.25
85	Jeff Bagwell	.50
86	Carlos Pena	.25
87	Roy Oswalt	.40
88	Richie Sexson	.25
89	Roger Clemens	1.25
90	Miguel Tejada	.40
91	Vicente Padilla	.25
92	Phil Nevin	.25
93	Edgardo Alfonzo	.25
94	Bret Boone	.25
95	Albert Pujols	2.00
96	Carlos Delgado	.50
97	Marlon Byrd	.25
98	Scott Rolen	.50
99	Pedro J. Martinez	.75
100	Alex Rodriguez	2.00
101	Adam LaRoche	15.00
102	Andy Marte RC	10.00
103	Daryl Clark RC	10.00
104	J.D. Durbin RC	10.00
105	Craig Brazell RC	10.00
106	Brian Burgamy RC	10.00
107	Tyler Johnson RC	10.00
108	Joey Gomes	10.00
109	Bryan Bullington RC	10.00
110	Byron Gettis RC	10.00

Refractors

Stars (1-100): 2-4X
Rookie Autos.(101-110): .75-1.5X
Inserted 1:6

X-Fractors

Stars (1-100): 5-10X
Rookie Autos.(101-110): 1-2.5X
Production 99 Sets
X-Fractor Golds (1-100): 3-6X
Golds Rk Autos.(101-110): 1-2X
Production 199 Sets

Bat Relics

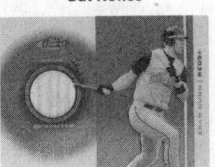

NM/M
Common Player: 8.00
Inserted 1:6

JB	Jeff Bagwell	8.00
LB	Lance Berkman	8.00
WB	Wade Boggs	8.00
BB	Barry Bonds	20.00
RC	Rod Carew	10.00
RCL	Roger Clemens	15.00
AD	Adam Dunn	8.00
NG	Nomar Garciaparra	20.00
TH	Todd Helton	8.00
RH	Rickey Henderson	8.00
CJ	Chipper Jones	10.00
AK	Austin Kearns	8.00
GM	Greg Maddux	15.00
PM	Paul Molitor	8.00
DM	Dale Murphy	15.00
RP	Rafael Palmeiro	8.00
MP	Mike Piazza	15.00
KP	Kirby Puckett	15.00
AP	Albert Pujols	15.00
MR	Manny Ramirez	8.00
CR	Cal Ripken Jr.	35.00
AR	Alex Rodriguez	12.00
IR	Ivan Rodriguez	8.00
MS	Mike Schmidt	20.00
AS	Alfonso Soriano	10.00
MT	Miguel Tejada	8.00
JT	Jim Thome	10.00

Moments Autographs

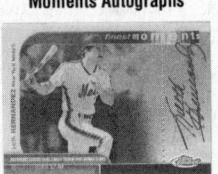

NM/M
Common Player: 10.00

EB	Ernie Banks	60.00
PB	Paul Blair	10.00
LB	Lou Brock	25.00
GC	Gary Carter	15.00
OC	Orlando Cepeda	15.00
GF	George Foster	15.00
GG	Rich "Goose" Gossage	15.00
KH	Keith Hernandez	15.00
DL	Don Larsen	15.00
WMA	Willie Mays	150.00
JP	Jim Palmer	15.00
GP	Gaylord Perry	15.00
JS	Johnny Sain	10.00

Team Topps Legends
Autograph

NM/M
Common Autograph: 10.00

Luis Aparicio	15.00
Paul Blair	10.00
Lou Brock	25.00
Rich "Goose" Gossage	15.00
Al Kaline	35.00
Don Larsen	20.00
Vern Law	12.00
Stan Musial	75.00

Uniform Relics

NM/M
Common Player: 5.00

BB	Barry Bonds	20.00
EC	Eric Chavez	5.00
AD	Adam Dunn	10.00
LG	Luis Gonzalez	5.00
TH	Todd Helton	8.00
RJ	Randy Johnson	8.00
AJ	Andruw Jones	8.00
CJ	Chipper Jones	8.00
GM	Greg Maddux	12.00
WM	Willie Mays	30.00
MM	Mark Mulder	6.00
RO	Roy Oswalt	5.00
RP	Rafael Palmeiro	8.00
MP	Mike Piazza	12.00
AP	Albert Pujols	15.00
MR	Manny Ramirez	8.00
AR	Alex Rodriguez	15.00
CS	Curt Schilling	5.00
AS	Alfonso Soriano	10.00
SS	Sammy Sosa	15.00
MSW	Mike Sweeney	5.00
LW	Larry Walker	5.00

2004 Finest

NM/M
Complete Set (122):
Common Player: .40
Common Star Relic (101-110): 8.00
Inserted 1:42
Common FYP Autograph (111-122): 10.00
Inserted 1:18
Pack (5): 6.00
Box (18): 85.00
Mini-Box (6): 30.00

1	Juan Pierre	.40
2	Derek Jeter	3.00
3	Garret Anderson	.50
4	Javy Lopez	.50
5	Corey Patterson	.50
6	Todd Helton	.75
7	Roy Oswalt	.50
8	Shawn Green	.50
9	Vladimir Guerrero	1.00
10	Jorge Posada	.50
11	Jason Kendall	.40
12	Scott Rolen	1.00
13	Randy Johnson	1.00
14	Bill Mueller	.40
15	Magglio Ordonez	.50
16	Larry Walker	.50
17	Lance Berkman	.50
18	Richie Sexson	.75
19	Orlando Cabrera	.40
20	Alfonso Soriano	.50
21	Kevin Millwood	.50
22	Edgar Martinez	.50
23	Aubrey Huff	.50
24	Carlos Delgado	.50
25	Vernon Wells	.50
26	Mark Teixeira	.50
27	Troy Glaus	.50
28	Jeff Kent	.50
29	Hideo Nomo	.50
30	Torii Hunter	.50
31	Hank Blalock	.50
32	Brandon Webb	.50
33	Tony Batista	.50
34	Bret Boone	.50
35	Ryan Klesko	

#	Player	Price
36	Barry Zito	.50
37	Aaron Boone	.40
38	Geoff Jenkins	.50
39	Jeff Bagwell	.75
40	Dontrelle Willis	.50
41	Adam Dunn	.75
42	Mark Buehrle	.40
43	Esteban Loaiza	.40
44	Angel Berroa	.40
45	Ivan Rodriguez	.75
46	Jose Vidro	.40
47	Mark Mulder	.50
48	Marlon Byrd	.40
49	Jim Edmonds	.50
50	Eric Gagne	.50
51	Marcus Giles	.40
52	Curt Schilling	.75
53	Ken Griffey Jr.	1.50
54	Jason Schmidt	.40
55	Miguel Tejada	.50
56	Dmitri Young	.40
57	Mike Lowell	.50
58	Mike Sweeney	.40
59	Scott Podsednik	.75
60	Miguel Cabrera	1.00
61	Johan Santana	.40
62	Bernie Williams	.50
63	Eric Chavez	.50
64	Bobby Abreu	.50
65	Brian Giles	.40
66	Michael Young	.40
67	Paul LoDuca	.40
68	Austin Kearns	.40
69	Jody Gerut	.40
70	Kerry Wood	1.00
71	Luis Matos	.40
72	Greg Maddux	1.50
73	Alex Rodriguez	4.00
74	Mike Lieberthal	.40
75	Jim Thome	1.00
76	Javier Vazquez	.40
77	Bartolo Colon	.50
78	Manny Ramirez	.75
79	Jacque Jones	.40
80	Johnny Damon	.40
81	Carlos Beltran	.75
82	C.C. Sabathia	.40
83	Preston Wilson	.40
84	Luis Castillo	.50
85	Kevin Brown	.50
86	Shannon Stewart	.40
87	Cliff Floyd	.40
88	Mike Mussina	.50
89	Rafael Furcal	.40
90	Roy Halladay	.50
91	Frank Thomas	.75
92	Melvin Mora	.40
93	Andruw Jones	.75
94	Luis Gonzalez	.50
95	David Ortiz	.75
96	Gary Sheffield	.50
97	Tim Hudson	.50
98	Phil Nevin	.40
99	Ichiro Suzuki	2.00
100	Albert Pujols	2.50
101	Nomar Garciaparra	15.00
102	Sammy Sosa	15.00
103	Josh Beckett	8.00
104	Jason Giambi	8.00
105	Rocco Baldelli	8.00
106	Jose Reyes	8.00
107	Chipper Jones	10.00
108	Pedro J. Martinez	10.00
109	Mike Piazza	8.00
110	Mark Prior	8.00
111	Craig Ansman RC	10.00
112	Jeff Allison	15.00
113	David Murphy	20.00
114	Jason Hirsh	20.00
115	Matt Moses	20.00
116	Estee Harris RC	10.00
117	Logan Kensing RC	10.00
118	Lastings Milledge	40.00
119	Merkin Valdez RC	15.00
120	Travis Blackley RC	15.00
121	Vito Chiaravalloti RC	15.00
122	Dioner Navarro RC	25.00

Refractor

...fractor (1-100):		2-4X
...serted 1:6		
...fractor (101-110):		1-2X
...serted 1:156		
...fractor (111-122):		1-2X
...serted 1:132		

Gold Refractor

...ld Refractor (1-100):		6-12X
...ld Refr. (101-110):		1.5-2X
...ld Refr. (111-122):		2-4X
...duction 50 Sets		

Uncirculated X-Fractor

...ars (1-100):		4-8X
...tors (101-110):		1-2X
...tographs (111-122):		1-2X

Inserted as a box topper.
Production 139 Sets

Moments Autographs

		NM/M
Common Autograph:		10.00
JA	Jim Abbott	15.00
VB	Vida Blue	12.00
OC	Orlando Cepeda	12.00
LD	Lenny Dykstra	10.00
GS	George Foster	10.00
EK	Ed Kranepool	10.00
WM	Willie Mays	100.00
JP	Johnny Podres	10.00
DS	Duke Snider	40.00
RY	Robin Yount	75.00

Relics

		NM/M
Common Player:		4.00
JB	Jeff Bagwell	8.00
RB1	Rocco Baldelli/Jsy	6.00
RB3	Rocco Baldelli/Jsy	6.00
JPB1	Josh Beckett	8.00
LB1	Lance Berkman/Bat	5.00
LB2	Lance Berkman/Jsy	5.00
AB	Angel Berroa	4.00
HB1	Hank Blalock/Bat	8.00
HB2	Hank Blalock/Jsy	8.00
PB	Pat Burrell	10.00
SB	Sean Burroughs	5.00
MB	Marlon Byrd	4.00
MC	Miguel Cabrera	10.00
EC	Eric Chavez	5.00
AD	Adam Dunn	8.00
DE	Darin Erstad	4.00
NG	Nomar Garciaparra	12.00
TG	Troy Glaus	6.00
AG	Adrian Gonzalez	4.00
LG	Luis Gonzalez	4.00
SG	Shawn Green	6.00
VG	Vladimir Guerrero	8.00
CG	Cristian Guzman	4.00
RH	Rich Harden	5.00
TH1	Todd Helton/Bat	8.00
TH2	Todd Helton/Jsy	8.00
TH	Tim Hudson	5.00
TKH1	Torii Hunter/Bat	6.00
TKH2	Torii Hunter/Jsy	6.00
KI	Kazuhisa Ishii	4.00
RJ	Randy Johnson	6.00
AJ	Andruw Jones	6.00
JL	Javy Lopez	4.00
DL	Derek Lowe	6.00
ML1	Mike Lowell/Jsy	5.00
ML2	Mike Lowell/Jsy	5.00
GM	Greg Maddux	10.00
KM	Kevin Millwood	6.00

MM	Mark Mulder	4.00
BM1	Brett Myers/Jsy	4.00
BM2	Brett Myers/Jsy	4.00
MO1	Magglio Ordonez/Jsy	6.00
MO2	Magglio Ordonez/Bat	6.00
RP1	Rafael Palmeiro/Bat	8.00
RP2	Rafael Palmeiro/Jsy	8.00
RP3	Rafael Palmeiro/Jsy	8.00
AP	Andy Pettitte	6.00
JP	Juan Pierre	4.00
MP	Mark Prior	10.00
AP1	Albert Pujols/Jsy	15.00
AP2	Albert Pujols/Bat	15.00
JR1	Jose Reyes/Jsy	8.00
JR2	Jose Reyes/Bat	8.00
JR3	Jose Reyes/Jsy	8.00
MR	Mariano Rivera	10.00
AR1	Alex Rodriguez/Rangers	10.00
AR2	Alex Rodriguez/Yankees	20.00
IR1	Ivan Rodriguez/Jsy	4.00
IR2	Ivan Rodriguez/Jsy	8.00
IR3	Ivan Rodriguez/Bat	8.00
SR	Scott Rolen	8.00
CCS	C.C. Sabathia	6.00
KS	Kazuhiro Sasaki	4.00
CS	Curt Schilling	6.00
GS	Gary Sheffield	6.00
JS	John Smoltz	8.00
AS	Alfonso Soriano	8.00
SS	Sammy Sosa	12.00
MT1	Miguel Tejada/Bat	6.00
MT2	Miguel Tejada/Jsy	6.00
FT	Frank Thomas	8.00
JT	Jim Thome	10.00
LW	Larry Walker	4.00
VW	Vernon Wells	5.00
BW	Bernie Williams	6.00
DW	Dontrelle Willis	5.00
PW	Preston Wilson	4.00
KW1	Kerry Wood/Jsy	10.00
KW2	Kerry Wood/Bat	10.00
DY	Delmon Young	8.00
BZ	Barry Zito	8.00

2005 Finest

		NM/M
Complete Set (166):		
Common Player:		.40
Common Auto. (141-156).		10.00
Production 970, unless noted.		
Pack (5):		10.00
Box (18):		150.00
1	Alexis Rios	.40
2	Hank Blalock	.50
3	Bobby Abreu	.50
4	Curt Schilling	1.00
5	Albert Pujols	2.00
6	Aaron Rowand	.40
7	B.J. Upton	.50
8	Andruw Jones	.50
9	Jeff Francis	.40
10	Sammy Sosa	1.00
11	Aramis Ramirez	.75
12	Carl Pavano	.40
13	Bartolo Colon	.40
14	Greg Maddux	2.00
15	Scott Kazmir	.40
16	Melvin Mora	.40
17	Brandon Backe	.40
18	Bobby Crosby	.40
19	Carlos Lee	.50
20	Carl Crawford	.50
21	Brian Giles	.40
22	Jeff Bagwell	.75
23	J.D. Drew	.50
24	C.C. Sabathia	.40
25	Alfonso Soriano	1.00
26	Chipper Jones	1.00
27	Austin Kearns	.40
28	Carlos Delgado	.50
29	Jack Wilson	.40
30	Dmitri Young	.40
31	Carlos Guillen	.50
32	Jim Thome	1.00
33	Eric Chavez	.50
34	Jason Schmidt	.50
35	Brad Radke	.40
36	Frank Thomas	.75
37	Darin Erstad	.40
38	Javier Vazquez	.40
39	Garret Anderson	.50
40	David Ortiz	1.00
41	Javy Lopez	.40
42	Geoff Jenkins	.40
43	Jose Vidro	.40
44	Aubrey Huff	.40
45	Bernie Williams	.50
46	Dontrelle Willis	.50

47	Jim Edmonds	.50
48	Ivan Rodriguez	.50
49	Gary Sheffield	.50
50	Alex Rodriguez	2.50
51	John Buck	.40
52	Andy Pettitte	.50
53	Ichiro Suzuki	2.50
54	Johnny Estrada	.40
55	Jake Peavy	.50
56	Carlos Zambrano	.50
57	Jose Reyes	1.00
58	Bret Boone	.40
59	Jason Bay	.50
60	David Wright	1.50
61	Jeromy Burnitz	.40
62	Corey Patterson	.40
63	Juan Pierre	.50
64	Zack Greinke	.40
65	Mike Lowell	.40
66	Ken Griffey Jr.	2.00
67	Marcus Giles	.50
68	Edgar Renteria	.50
69	Ken Harvey	.40
70	Pedro Martinez	1.00
71	Johnny Damon	.50
72	Lyle Overbay	.40
73	Mike Maroth	.40
74	Jorge Posada	.50
75	Carlos Beltran	.75
76	Mark Buehrle	.40
77	Khalil Greene	.40
78	Josh Beckett	.50
79	Mark Loretta	.40
80	Rafael Palmeiro	.75
81	Justin Morneau	.75
82	Rocco Baldelli	.50
83	Ben Sheets	.50
84	Kerry Wood	.50
85	Miguel Tejada	.75
86	Magglio Ordonez	.50
87	Livan Hernandez	.40
88	Kazuo Matsui	.40
89	Manny Ramirez	1.00
90	Hideki Matsui	2.00
91	Jeff Kent	.50
92	Matt Lawton	.40
93	Richie Sexson	.50
94	Mike Mussina	.75
95	Adam Dunn	.75
96	Johan Santana	.75
97	Nomar Garciaparra	.50
98	Michael Young	.40
99	Victor Martinez	.50
100	Barry Bonds	3.00
101	Oliver Perez	.40
102	Randy Johnson	1.00
103	Mark Mulder	.50
104	Pat Burrell	.40
105	Mike Sweeney	.40
106	Mark Teixeira	.75
107	Paul LoDuca	.40
108	Jon Lieber	.40
109	Mike Piazza	1.50
110	Roger Clemens	2.00
111	Rafael Furcal	.50
112	Troy Glaus	.50
113	Miguel Cabrera	1.00
114	Randy Wolf	.40
115	Lance Berkman	.75
116	Mark Prior	.50
117	Rich Harden	.50
118	Preston Wilson	.40
119	Roy Oswalt	.50
120	Luis Gonzalez	.50
121	Ronnie Belliard	.40
122	Sean Casey	.50
123	Barry Zito	.50
124	Larry Walker	.50
125	Derek Jeter	3.00
126	Tim Hudson	.50
127	Tom Glavine	.50
128	Scott Rolen	1.00
129	Torii Hunter	.50
130	Paul Konerko	.75
131	Shawn Green	.40
132	Travis Hafner	.50
133	Vernon Wells	.50
134	Sidney Ponson	.40
135	Vladimir Guerrero	1.00
136	Mark Kotsay	.40
137	Todd Helton	.75
138	Adrian Beltre	.50
139	Wily Mo Pena	.40
140	Joe Mauer	.75
141	Brian Stavisky RC	10.00
142	Nate McLouth RC	24.00
143	Glen Perkins/375 RC	20.00
144	Chip Cannon RC	15.00
145	Shane Costa RC	15.00
146	Wes Swackhamer RC	10.00
147	Kevin Melillo RC	15.00
148	Billy Butler RC	40.00
149	Landon Powell RC	10.00
150	Scott Mathieson RC	10.00
151	Chris Roberson RC	10.00
152	Chad Orvella/375 RC	15.00
153	Eric Nielsen RC	10.00
154	Matt Campbell RC	10.00
155	Mike Rogers RC	15.00
156	Melky Cabrera RC	25.00
157	Nolan Ryan	3.00
158	Bo Jackson	1.00
159	Wade Boggs	1.00
160	Andre Dawson	.75
161	Dave Winfield	1.00
162	Reggie Jackson	1.00
163	David Justice	.40
164	Dale Murphy	1.00

165	Paul O'Neill	.75
166	Tom Seaver	1.50

Refractors

Refrac. (1-140, 157-166):		2-4X
Autograph (141-156):		.5-1X
Production 399 Sets		

Refractors Black

Refrac. (1-140, 157-166):		4-8X
Autograph (141-156):		1-2X
Production 99 Sets		

Refractors Blue

Refrac. (1-140, 157-166):		2-4X
Autograph (141-156):		.5-1X
Production 299 Sets		

Refractors Gold

Refrac. (1-140, 157-166):		5-10X
Autograph (141-156):		2-4X
Production 49 Sets		

Refractors Green

Refrac. (1-140, 157-166):		2-4X
Autograph (141-156):		.5-1.5X
Production 199 Sets		

Refractors White Framed

No Pricing	
Production One Set	

Super Fractor

No Pricing	
Production One Set	

X-Fractor

Refrac. (1-140, 157-166):		2-4X
Autograph (141-156):		.5-1X
Production 250 Sets		

X-Fractor Black

Refrac. (1-140, 157-166):		8-15X
Autograph (141-156):		No Pricing
Production 25 Sets		

X-Fractor Blue

Refrac. (1-140, 157-166):		3-5X
Autograph (141-156):		.5-1.5X
Production 150 Sets		

X-Fractor Gold

No Pricing	
Production 10 Sets	

X-Fractor Green

Refrac. (1-140, 157-166):		5-10X
Autograph (141-156):		1.5-3X
Production 50 Sets		

X-Fractor White Framed

No Pricing	
Production One Set	

Autographs

		NM/M
X-Fractor:		1.5-2X
Production 25 Sets		
JB	Jason Bay	25.00
CB	Carlos Beltran	30.00
BB	Barry Bonds	150.00
MB	Milton Bradley	15.00
EC	Eric Chavez	20.00
JE	Johnny Estrada	15.00
EG	Eric Gagne	30.00
KM	Kevin Millar	15.00
DO	David Ortiz	50.00
MR	Mariano Rivera	60.00
JS	Johan Santana	40.00
GS	Gary Sheffield	30.00

AS	Alfonso Soriano	30.00
JST	Jacob Stevens	10.00
DW	David Wright	80.00

Moment Autographs

		NM/M
Production 50		
PM	Pedro Martinez	75.00
CS	Curt Schilling	120.00

Printing Plates

No Pricing
Production one set for each color.

Alex Rodriguez Finest Moments

		NM/M
A-Rod 1-49:		10.00
Production 190 Sets		
FAM1-49	Alex Rodriguez	10.00

Alex Rodriguez Finest Moments Autograph

		NM/M
Production 13 Sets		
A-Rod Auto. 1-49:		150.00

2 of a Kind Autographs

No Pricing
Production 13

2006 Finest

		NM/M
Complete Set (155):		
Common Player:		.40
Common Auto. (141-155):		10.00
Pack (5):		9.00
Box (18):		150.00
1	Vladimir Guerrero	1.00
2	Troy Glaus	.50
3	Andruw Jones	.75
4	Miguel Tejada	.75
5	Manny Ramirez	1.00
6	Curt Schilling	1.00
7	Mark Prior	.50
8	Kerry Wood	.50
9	Tadahito Iguchi	.40
10	Freddy Garcia	.40
11	Ryan Howard	1.50
12	Mark Buehrle	.40
13	Wily Mo Pena	.40
14	C.C. Sabathia	.75
15	Garret Anderson	.40
16	Shawn Green	.40
17	Rafael Furcal	.75
18	Jeff Francoeur	.75
19	Ken Griffey Jr.	2.00
20	Derek Lee	.75

#	Player	Price
21	Paul Konerko	.75
22	Rickie Weeks	.50
23	Magglio Ordonez	.75
24	Juan Pierre	.40
25	Felix Hernandez	1.00
26	Roger Clemens	3.00
27	Zack Greinke	.40
28	Johan Santana	1.00
29	Jose Reyes	1.00
30	Bobby Crosby	.40
31	Jason Schmidt	.40
32	Khalil Greene	.40
33	Richie Sexson	.50
34	Mark Mulder	.50
35	Mark Teixeira	.75
36	Nick Johnson	.40
37	Vernon Wells	.50
38	Scott Kazmir	.75
39	Jim Edmonds	.50
40	Adrian Beltre	.50
41	Dan Johnson	.40
42	Carlos Lee	.75
43	Lance Berkman	.75
44	Josh Beckett	.75
45	Morgan Ensberg	.40
46	Garrett Atkins	.75
47	Chase Utley	1.00
48	Joe Mauer	.75
49	Travis Hafner	.75
50	Alex Rodriguez	3.00
51	Austin Kearns	.40
52	Scott Podsednik	.40
53	Jose Contreras	.40
54	Greg Maddux	2.00
55	Hideki Matsui	2.00
56	Matt Clement	.40
57	Javy Lopez	.50
58	Tim Hudson	.75
59	Luis Gonzalez	.40
60	Bartolo Colon	.50
61	Marcus Giles	.40
62	Justin Morneau	.75
63	Nomar Garciaparra	1.00
64	Robinson Cano	1.00
65	Ervin Santana	.50
66	Brady Clark	.40
67	Edgar Renteria	.40
68	Jon Garland	.40
69	Felipe Lopez	.50
70	Ivan Rodriguez	.75
71	Dontrelle Willis	.75
72	Carlos Guillen	.50
73	J.D. Drew	.40
74	Rich Harden	.50
75	Albert Pujols	3.00
76	Livan Hernandez	.40
77	Roy Halladay	.50
78	Hank Blalock	.50
79	David Wright	1.50
80	Jimmy Rollins	1.00
81	John Smoltz	.75
82	Miguel Cabrera	1.00
83	David DeJesus	.40
84	Torii Hunter	.50
85	Adam Dunn	.75
86	Randy Johnson	1.00
87	Roy Oswalt	.75
88	Bobby Abreu	.75
89	Rocco Baldelli	.40
90	Ichiro Suzuki	2.00
91	Jorge Cantu	.40
92	Jack Wilson	.40
93	Jose Vidro	.40
94	Kevin Millwood	.50
95	David Ortiz	1.00
96	Victor Martinez	.75
97	Jeremy Bonderman	.40
98	Todd Helton	.75
99	Carlos Beltran	.75
100	Gustavo Chacin	.40
101	Jeff Kent	.50
102	Mike Sweeney	.40
103	Ben Sheets	.40
104	Melvin Mora	.40
105	Gary Sheffield	.75
106	Craig Wilson	.40
107	Chris Carpenter	.75
108	Michael Young	.50
109	Gustavo Chacin	.40
110	Chipper Jones	1.00
111	Mark Loretta	.40
112	Andy Pettitte	.75
113	Carlos Delgado	.75
114	Pat Burrell	.50
115	Jason Bay	.50
116	Brian Roberts	.50
117	Joe Crede	.40
118	Jake Peavy	.75
119	Aubrey Huff	.40
120	Pedro Martinez	1.00
121	Jorge Posada	.50
122	Barry Zito	.50
123	Scott Rolen	.75
124	Brett Myers	.40
125	Derek Jeter	3.00
126	Eric Chavez	.50
127	Carl Crawford	.50
128	Jim Thome	.75
129	Johnny Damon	1.00
130	Alfonso Soriano	.75
131	Clint Barmes	.40
132	Dustin Nippert RC	1.00
133	Hanley Ramirez RC	5.00
134	Matt Capps RC	1.00
135	Miguel Perez RC	1.00
136	Tom Gorzelanny RC	1.00
137	Charlton Jimerson RC	1.00
138	Bryan Bullington RC	1.00
139	Kenji Johjima RC	1.00
140	Craig Hansen RC	1.00
141	Craig Breslow RC	10.00
142	Adam Wainwright RC	30.00
143	Joey Devine RC	10.00
144	Hong-Chih Kuo RC	20.00
145	Jason Botts RC	10.00
146	Josh Johnson RC	15.00
147	Jason Bergmann RC	10.00
148	Scott Olsen RC	15.00
149	Darrell Rasner RC	10.00
150	Daniel Ortmeier RC	10.00
151	Chuck James RC	10.00
152	Ryan Garko RC	10.00
153	Nelson Cruz RC	30.00
154	Anthony Lerew RC	10.00
155	Francisco Liriano RC	20.00

SuperFractor
No Pricing
Production One Set

Gold Refractor
Stars (1-140): 6-12X
Autos. (141-155): 2-3X
Production 49 Sets

Black Refractor
Stars (1-140): 4-8X
Autos. (141-155): 1-2X
Production 99 Sets

Green Refractor
Stars (1-140): 2-5X
Autos. (141-155): .75-1.5X
Production 199 Sets

Blue Refractor
Stars (1-140): 2-5X
Autos. (141-155): .75-1X
Production 299 Sets

Refractor
Stars (1-140): 2-4X
Autos. (141-155): .5-1X
Production 399 Sets

White Framed Refractor
No Pricing
Production One Set

Gold X-Fractor
No Pricing
Production 10 Sets

Black X-Fractor
Stars (1-140): 8-15X
Autos. (141-155): No Pricing
Production 25 Sets

Green X-Fractor
Stars (1-140): 6-12X
Autos. (141-155): 2-3X
Production 50 Sets

Blue X-Fractor
Stars (1-140): 3-5X
Autos. (141-155): 1-1.5X
Production 150 Sets

X-Fractor
Stars (1-140): 2-5X
Autos. (141-155): .75-1X
Production 250 Sets

Mickey Mantle Finest Moments

Common Mantle: 10.00
Production 850 Sets
Refractor: 1X
Production 399 Sets
Blue Refractor: 1-1.5X
Production 299 Sets
Green Refractor: 1-2X
Production 199 Sets
Black Refractor: 1.5-3X
Production 99 Sets
Gold Refractor: 3-4X
Production 49 Sets
X-Fractor: 1-1.5X
Production 250 Sets
Blue X-Fractor: 1-2X
Production 150 Sets
Green X-Fractor: 3-4X
Production 50 Sets
Black X-Fractor: 4-6X
Production 25 Sets
Gold X-Fractor: No Pricing
Production 10 Sets
1-20 Mickey Mantle 10.00

Autographs
NM/M
Common Auto.: 8.00
X-Fractor: 1-2X
Production 25 Sets
SuperFractor: No Pricing
Production One Set
Printing plates one set per color.

Code	Player	Price
JB	Jason Bay	15.00
MC	Miguel Cabrera	30.00
RC	Robinson Cano	30.00
EC	Eric Chavez	8.00
MG	Marcus Giles	8.00
VG	Vladimir Guerrero	30.00
JG	Jose Guillen	8.00
RH	Rich Harden	10.00
KJ	Kenji Johjima	20.00
AJ	Andruw Jones	15.00
CJ	Chipper Jones	60.00
DL	Derrek Lee	30.00
RO	Roy Oswalt	25.00
AR	Alex Rodriguez	140.00
GS	Gary Sheffield	20.00
DWI	Dontrelle Willis	10.00
CW	Craig Wilson	8.00
DW	David Wright	60.00

Barry Bonds Finest Moments Autographs
No Pricing

Barry Bonds Finest Moments

NM/M
Common Bonds: 10.00
Production 425 Sets
Gold Refractor: 1-2X
Production 199 Sets
1-25 Barry Bonds 10.00

Mickey Mantle Finest Moments Cut Signature
No Pricing
Production One Set

2007 Finest

GREG MADDUX
SAN DIEGO PADRES
PITCHER

NM/M
Complete Set (165):
Common Player (1-135): .25
Common RC (136-150): 1.00
Common RC Auto. (151-165): 10.00
Pack (5): 8.00
Box (18): 125.00

#	Player	Price
1	David Wright	2.00
2	Jered Weaver	.50
3	Chipper Jones	1.00
4	Magglio Ordonez	.50
5	Ben Sheets	.50
6	Nick Johnson	.25
7	Melvin Mora	.25
8	Chien-Ming Wang	.50
9	Andre Ethier	.50
10	Carlos Beltran	1.00
11	Ryan Zimmerman	1.00
12	Troy Glaus	.50
13	Hanley Ramirez	1.00
14	Mark Buehrle	.50
15	Dan Uggla	.50
16	Richie Sexson	.25
17	Scott Kazmir	.50
18	Garrett Atkins	.50
19	Matt Cain	.50
20	Jorge Posada	.50
21	Brett Myers	.50
22	Jeff Francoeur	.50
23	Scott Rolen	1.00
24	Derrek Lee	.75
25	Manny Ramirez	1.00
26	Johnny Damon	1.00
27	Mark Teixeira	1.00
28	Mark Prior	.50
29	Victor Martinez	.50
30	Greg Maddux	2.00
31	Prince Fielder	1.50
32	Jeremy Bonderman	.50
33	Paul LoDuca	.50
34	Brandon Webb	.50
35	Robinson Cano	1.00
36	Josh Beckett	.75
37	David DeJesus	.25
38	Kenny Rogers	.25
39	Jim Thome	1.00
40	Brian McCann	.50
41	Lance Berkman	.50
42	Adam Dunn	.75
43	Rocco Baldelli	.50
44	Brian Roberts	.50
45	Vladimir Guerrero	1.00
46	Dontrelle Willis	.50
47	Eric Chavez	.25
48	Carlos Zambrano	.50
49	Ivan Rodriguez	1.00
50	Alex Rodriguez	3.00
51	Curt Schilling	1.00
52	Carlos Delgado	.50
53	Matt Holliday	1.00
54	Mark Teahen	.25
55	Frank Thomas	1.00
56	Grady Sizemore	.75
57	Aramis Ramirez	.50
58	Rafael Furcal	.50
59	David Ortiz	1.00
60	Paul Konerko	.50
61	Barry Zito	.25
62	Travis Hafner	.50
63	Nick Swisher	.50
64	Johan Santana	1.00
65	Miguel Tejada	.75
66	Carl Crawford	.50
67	Kenji Johjima	.50
68	Derek Jeter	3.00
69	Francisco Liriano	.50
70	Ken Griffey Jr.	2.00
71	Pat Burrell	.50
72	Adrian Gonzalez	.50
73	Miguel Cabrera	1.00
74	Albert Pujols	3.00
75	Justin Verlander	.75
76	Carlos Lee	.50
77	John Smoltz	.50
78	Orlando Hudson	.25
79	Joe Mauer	.50
80	Freddy Sanchez	.25
81	Bobby Abreu	.50
82	Pedro Martinez	1.00
83	Vernon Wells	.50
84	Justin Morneau	.75
85	Bill Hall	.50
86	Jason Schmidt	.50
87	Michael Young	.50
88	Tadahito Iguchi	.25
89	Kevin Millwood	.50
90	Randy Johnson	1.00
91	Roy Halladay	.50
92	Mike Lowell	.50
93	Jake Peavy	.50
94	Jason Varitek	.75
95	Todd Helton	.50
96	Mark Loretta	.25
97	Gary Matthews	.25
98	Ryan Howard	2.00
99	Jose Reyes	1.00
100	Chris Carpenter	.50
101	Hideki Matsui	2.00
102	Brian Giles	.25
103	Torii Hunter	.50
104	Rich Harden	.25
105	Ichiro Suzuki	2.00
106	Chase Utley	1.00
107	Nicholas Markakis	.50
108	Marcus Giles	.25
109	Gary Sheffield	.75
110	Jim Edmonds	.50
111	Brandon Phillips	.50
112	Roy Oswalt	.50
113	Jeff Kent	.50
114	Jason Bay	.50
115	Raul Ibanez	.25
116	Stephen Drew	.50
117	Hank Blalock	.50
118	Tom Glavine	.50
119	Andruw Jones	.75
120	Alfonso Soriano	1.00
121	Mariano Rivera	.50
122	Garret Anderson	.25
123	Erik Bedard	.50
124	Huston Street	.25
125	Austin Kearns	.50
126	Jermaine Dye	.25
127	C.C. Sabathia	.50
128	Joe Nathan	.25
129	Craig Monroe	.25
130	Aubrey Huff	.25
131	Billy Wagner	.25
132	Jorge Cantu	.25
133	Trevor Hoffman	.25
134	Ronnie Belliard	.25
135	B.J. Ryan	.25
136	Adam Lind (RC)	2.00
137	Hector Gimenez (RC)	1.00
138	Shawn Riggans (RC)	1.00
139	Joaquin Arias (RC)	1.00
140	Drew Anderson (RC)	1.00
141	Mike Rabelo RC	1.00
142	Chris Narveson (RC)	1.00
143	Ryan Feierabend (RC)	1.00
144	Vinny Rottino (RC)	1.00
145	Jon Knott (RC)	1.00
146	Oswaldo Navarro RC	1.00
147	Brian Stokes (RC)	1.00
148	Glen Perkins (RC)	1.00
149	Mitch Maier (RC)	1.00
150	Delmon Young (RC)	1.50
151	Andrew Miller/Auto. RC	15.00
152	Troy Tulowitzki/Auto. (RC)	25.00
153	Philip Humber/Auto. (RC)	15.00
154	Kevin Kouzmanoff/Auto. (RC)	15.00
155	Michael Bourn/Auto. (RC)	15.00
156	Miguel Montero/Auto. (RC)	15.00
157	David Murphy/Auto. (RC)	15.00
158	Ryan Sweeney/Auto. (RC)	15.00
159	Jeff Baker/Auto. (RC)	10.00
160	Jeff Salazar/Auto. (RC)	10.00
161	Jose Garcia/Auto. (RC)	10.00
162	Josh Fields/Auto. (RC)	10.00
163	Delwyn Young/Auto. (RC)	10.00
164	Fred Lewis/Auto. (RC)	10.00
165	Scott Moore/Auto. (RC)	10.00

Printing Plates
Production one set per color.

SuperFractor
Production One Set

X-Fractor
X-Fractor (1-135): 10-20X
RC Autos: No Pricing
Production 25 Sets

Gold Refractor
Gold Refractor (1-150): 5-10X
Production 50
RC Autos.: 2X
Production 49

Black Refractor
Black Refractor (1-150): 4-8X
RC Autos.: 1.5X
Production 99 Sets

Green Refractor
Green Refractor (1-150): 2-5X
RC Autos.: 1-1.5X
Production 199 Sets

Blue Refractor
Blue Refractor (1-150): 2-5X
Production 399 Sets
RC Autos.: .75-1X
Production 299

Refractor
Refractor (1-150): 2-4X
RC Autographs: .5-1X
Production 399 only autos serial #'d.

Rookies Finest Moments Autograph

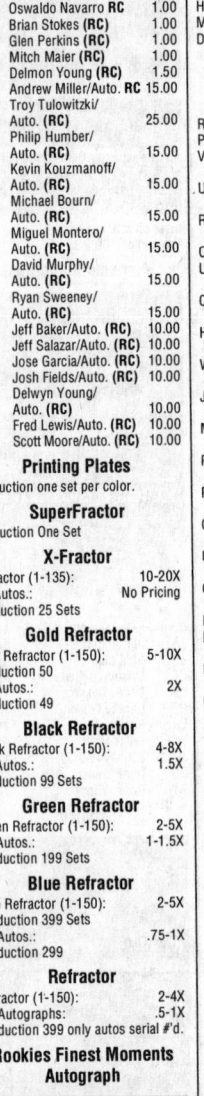

Brandon Phillips
Phillips Tags Twins

NM/M
Common Autograph: 10.00
Refractors: No Pricing
Production 25 Sets

Code	Player	Price
DO	David Ortiz	50.00
DW	David Wright	75.00
JN	Joe Nathan	10.00
AR	Alex Rodriguez	125.00
TH	Travis Hafner	20.00
RH	Ryan Howard	100.00
AS	Anibal Sanchez	15.00
BP	Brandon Phillips	10.00
CH	Cole Hamels	40.00
DWW	Dontrelle Willis	15.00
LM	Lastings Milledge	25.00
RC	Robinson Cano	50.00
MN	Michael Napoli	20.00
DU	Dan Uggla	15.00
BW	Brad Wilkerson	10.00
MC	Melky Cabrera	25.00
AW	Adam Wainwright	30.00
CQ	Carlos Quentin	15.00
RJH	Rich Hill	15.00
YP	Yusmeiro Petit	15.00
FC	Fausto Carmona	15.00
CJ	Chuck James	10.00
JM	Justin Morneau	25.00
RZ	Ryan Zimmerman	25.00
RM	Russell Martin	20.00
JP	Jonathan Papelbon	20.00
HR	Hanley Ramirez	40.00
MTC	Matt Cain	25.00
DY	Delmon Young	15.00

Dual Rookies Finest Moments Autograph
NM/M
Refractors: No Pricing
Production 25 Sets

Code	Players	Price
VR	Justin Verlander, Hanley Ramirez	60.00
US	Dan Uggla, Anibal Sanchez	25.00
RP	Mariano Rivera, Jorge Posada	80.00
OP	Roy Oswalt, Mark Prior	40.00
UW	Chase Utley, David Wright	100.00
CY	Robinson Cano, Michael Young	50.00
HR	Travis Hafner, Manny Ramirez	40.00
WW	Chien-Ming Wang, Brandon Webb	120.00
JH	Chuck James, Cole Hamels	40.00
MNA	Russell Martin, Michael Napoli	20.00
PO	Yusmeiro Petit, Scott Olsen	20.00
PP	Jonathan Papelbon, Dustin Pedroia	50.00
CC	Eric Chavez, Miguel Cabrera	40.00
UG	Dan Uggla, Marcus Giles	15.00
CK	Nelson Cruz, Matthew Kemp	25.00
HJ	Rich Hill, Josh Johnson	30.00
HM	Cole Hamels, Brett Myers	40.00
MC	Lastings Milledge, Melky Cabrera	35.00
CR	Matt Cain, Anthony Reyes	25.00
ZC	Joel Zumaya, Fausto Carmona	20.00
BM	Jason Bay, Justin Morneau	35.00
MG	Russell Martin, Ryan Garko	25.00
MN	Kendry Morales, Michael Napoli	25.00
MK	Lastings Milledge, Matthew Kemp	30.00
RU	Hanley Ramirez, Dan Uggla	40.00

A-Rod Road to 500
NM/M
Common A-Rod (26-50): 2.00
Inserted 2:Box

Ryan Howard HR History

Home Run 50 9.3.06 RYAN HOWARD

NM/M
Common Howard (1-58): 4.00
Inserted 2:Box
Production 459 Sets
Refractor: 1.5-2...
Production 149 Sets
X-Fractor: 2-4...
Production 50 Sets
Gold Refractor: No Pricin...
Production One Set

Mantle Cut Signature
Production One

Rookies Finest Moments
NM/M
Common Player:
Refractor: 2-3...
Blue Refractor: 2-4...
Production 299 Sets
Green Refractor: 2-4...
Production 199 Sets
Black Refractor: 4-8...
Production 99 Sets
Gold Refractor:
Production 50 Sets
X-Fractor: 10-15...
Production 25 Sets

AD	Adam Dunn	1.00
AJ	Andruw Jones	1.50
AP	Albert Pujols	4.00
AR	Alex Rodriguez	4.00
CB	Carlos Beltran	1.50
CC	Carl Crawford	.50
CJ	Chipper Jones	1.50
DJ	Derek Jeter	4.00
DL	Derrek Lee	1.50
DO	David Ortiz	1.50
DW	David Wright	2.50
DWW	Dontrelle Willis	.50
HM	Hideki Matsui	2.50
IS	Ichiro Suzuki	2.50
JB	Jason Bay	1.00
JM	Joe Mauer	1.00
JR	Jose Reyes	2.00
KG	Ken Griffey Jr.	3.00
MC	Miguel Cabrera	1.50
MP	Mike Piazza	2.00
MR	Manny Ramirez	1.50
MT	Miguel Tejada	1.00
NG	Nomar Garciaparra	1.50
RH	Ryan Howard	3.00
VG	Vladimir Guerrero	1.50
AS	Anibal Sanchez	.50
JP	Jonathan Papelbon	1.50
DU	Dan Uggla	.50
HR	Hanley Ramirez	1.00
JV	Justin Verlander	1.00
FL	Francisco Liriano	1.00
SD	Stephen Drew	1.00
JW	Jered Weaver	1.00
JS	Jeremy Sowers	.50
KJ	Kenji Johjima	1.00
MCA	Melky Cabrera	1.00
NM	Nicholas Markakis	1.00
PF	Prince Fielder	2.00
RM	Russell Martin	.50
AE	Andre Ethier	1.00
MK	Matthew Kemp	1.00
JH	Jason Hirsh	.50
CH	Cole Hamels	2.00
JBA	Josh Barfield	.50
IK	Ian Kinsler	.50
AW	Adam Wainwright	1.00
JST	Brian Stokes	.50
MN	Michael Napoli	.50
CQ	Carlos Quentin	1.00
NC	Nelson Cruz	.50

Rookie Redemption

RYAN BRAUN
MILWAUKEE BREWERS

NM/M

Complete Set (10):
Common Card: 10.00
Inserted 1:3 Mini Box

1	Hideki Okajima RC	10.00
2	Elijah Dukes RC	10.00
3	Akinori Iwamura RC	10.00
4	Tim Lincecum RC	30.00
5	Daisuke Matsuzaka RC	15.00
6	Ryan Braun (RC)	20.00
7	Daisuke Matsuzaka, Hideki Okajima	
8	Justin Upton RC	25.00
9	Phil Hughes (RC)	20.00
10	Joba Chamberlain/ Auto. RC	40.00

2008 Finest

NM/M

Common Player (1-125): .25
Common RC (126-150): 1.00
Common RC Auto. (151-166): 1.00
Pack (5): 10.00
Box (15): 140.00

1	Daisuke Matsuzaka	1.00
2	Justin Upton	1.00
3	Andruw Jones	.50
4	John Lackey	.50
5	Brandon Phillips	.50
6	Ryan Zimmerman	.50
7	Tim Lincecum	.75
8	Johnny Damon	.75
9	Garrett Atkins	.50
10	Magglio Ordonez	.50
11	Tom Gorzelanny	.25
12	Eric Chavez	.25
13	Troy Tulowitzki	1.00
14	Mike Lowell	.50
15	Brandon Webb	.50
16	Chipper Jones	1.00
17	Alex Gordon	.75
18	Ken Griffey Jr.	2.00
19	Roy Oswalt	.50
20	Miguel Cabrera	1.00
21	Chase Utley	1.00
22	Scott Kazmir	.50
23	Kenji Johjima	.25
24	Frank Thomas	1.00
25	Ryan Braun	1.50
26	Carlos Pena	.50
27	Robinson Cano	.75
28	Ben Sheets	.50
29	Russell Martin	.50
30	Joe Mauer	1.00
31	Gary Sheffield	.50
32	Carlos Zambrano	.50
33	Jermaine Dye	.25
34	Dan Uggla	.50
35	Erik Bedard	.50
36	Tim Hudson	.50
37	David Ortiz	1.00
38	Tom Glavine	.50
39	Adrian Gonzalez	.50
40	Jorge Posada	.50
41	Noah Lowry	.25
42	Vernon Wells	.50
43	Johan Santana	1.00
44	Dmitri Young	.25
45	Manny Ramirez	1.00
46	Jim Edmonds	.25
47	Roy Halladay	.50
48	Delmon Young	.50
49	Nick Swisher	.25
50	David Wright	1.50
51	Paul Konerko	.50
52	Curt Schilling	.75
53	Torii Hunter	.50
54	Gary Matthews Jr.	.25
55	Derrek Lee	.75
56	John Smoltz	.50
57	Adam Dunn	.75
58	C.C. Sabathia	.50
59	Chris Young	.50
60	Jake Peavy	.50
61	Joba Chamberlain	1.50
62	Jason Bay	.50
63	Chris Carpenter	.50
64	Jimmy Rollins	.75
65	Grady Sizemore	.75
66	Joe Blanton	.25
67	Justin Morneau	.50
68	Lance Berkman	.50
69	Jeff Francis	.25
70	Nicholas Markakis	.50
71	Orlando Cabrera	.50
72	Barry Zito	.25
73	Eric Byrnes	.50
74	Brian McCann	.50
75	Albert Pujols	3.00
76	Josh Beckett	.75
77	Jim Thome	.75
78	Fausto Carmona	.50
79	Brad Hawpe	.25
80	Prince Fielder	1.00
81	Justin Verlander	.75
82	Billy Butler	.25
83	J.J. Hardy	.25
84	Hideki Matsui	1.50
85	Matt Holliday	.75
86	Bobby Crosby	.25
87	Orlando Hudson	.25
88	Ichiro Suzuki	2.00
89	Troy Glaus	.50
90	Hanley Ramirez	1.00
91	Carlos Beltran	.75
92	Mark Buehrle	.25
93	Andy Pettitte	.50
94	Mark Teixeira	.75
95	Curtis Granderson	.75
96	Cole Hamels	.50
97	Jarrod Saltalamacchia	.25
98	Carl Crawford	.50
99	Dontrelle Willis	.25
100	Alex Rodriguez	3.00
101	Brad Penny	.25
102	Michael Young	.25
103	Greg Maddux	1.50
104	Brian Roberts	.50
105	Hunter Pence	.75
106	Aaron Harang	.25
107	Ivan Rodriguez	.50
108	Danny Haren	.50
109	Freddy Sanchez	.25
110	Alfonso Soriano	1.00
111	Hank Blalock	.25
112	Chien-Ming Wang	1.00
113	Carlos Delgado	.50
114	Aramis Ramirez	.50
115	Jose Reyes	1.00
116	Victor Martinez	.50
117	Carlos Lee	.50
118	Jeff Kent	.25
119	Miguel Tejada	.50
120	Vladimir Guerrero	1.00
121	Travis Hafner	.50
122	Todd Helton	.50
123	Chris Young	.50
124	Derek Jeter	3.00
125	Ryan Howard	1.00
126	Alberto Gonzalez (RC)	1.00
127	Felipe Paulino RC	1.00
128	Donny Lucy (RC)	1.00
129	Nick Blackburn RC	2.00
130	Luke Hochevar RC	1.50
131	Bronson Sardinha (RC)	1.00
132	Heath Phillips RC	1.00
133	Bryan Bullington (RC)	1.00
134	Jeff Clement (RC)	1.00
135	Josh Banks RC	1.50
136	Emilio Bonifacio RC	1.00
137	Ryan Hanigan RC	1.00
138	Erick Threets (RC)	1.00
139	Seth Smith (RC)	1.50
140	Billy Buckner (RC)	1.00
141	Bill Murphy (RC)	1.00
142	Radhames Liz RC	1.00
143	Joey Votto (RC)	2.50
144	Mel Stocker RC	1.50
145	Dan Meyer (RC)	1.00
146	Rob Johnson (RC)	1.00
147	Josh Newman RC	1.00
148	Daniel Giese (RC)	1.00
149	Luis Mendoza (RC)	1.00
150	Wladimir Balentien (RC)	2.00
151	Brandon Jones/ Auto. RC	20.00
152	Rich Thompson/ Auto. (RC)	10.00
153	Chin-Lung Hu/ Auto. (RC)	50.00
154	Chris Seddon/ Auto. (RC)	10.00
155	Steve Pearce/Auto. RC	15.00
156	Lance Broadway/ Auto. RC	10.00
157	Nyjer Morgan/ Auto. RC	15.00
158	Jonathan Meloan/ Auto. RC	10.00
159	Josh Anderson/ Auto. (RC)	10.00
160	Clay Buchholz/ Auto. (RC)	40.00
161	Joe Koshansky/ Auto. (RC)	10.00
162	Clint Sammons/ Auto. (RC)	15.00
163	Daric Barton/Auto. (RC)	15.00
164	Ross Detwiler/Auto. RC	20.00
165	Sam Fuld/Auto. RC	15.00
166	Justin Ruggiano/ Auto. RC	15.00

Refractor

NM/M

Refractor (1-150): 2-4X
RC Autographs: 1X
Production 499 only autos serial #'d.

Blue Refractor

CHRIS YOUNG

Blue Refractor (1-150): 2-5X
Production 299 Sets
RC Autos.: .75-1X
Production 399

Green Refractor

NOAH LOWRY

Green Refractor (1-150): 2-5X
RC Autos.: 1-1.5X
Production 199 Sets

Black Refractor

Black Refractor (1-150): 4-8X
RC Autos.: 1.5X
Production 99 Sets

Gold Refractor

Gold Refractor (1-150): 5-10X
RC Autos.: 2X
Production 50 Sets

Red Refractor

ROY HALLADAY

Red Refractor (1-150): 8-15X
RC Autos.: 3-4X
Production 25 Sets

White X-Fractor

Production One Set

Printing Plates

Production one set per color.

Moments

JOHAN SANTANA
2-Time CY Young Award Winner

NM/M

Common Player: .50
Refractor: 2-3X
Blue Refractor: 2-4X
Production 299 Sets
Green Refractor: 2-4X
Production 199 Sets
Black Refractor: 4-6X
Production 99 Sets
Gold Refractor: 4-8X
Production 50 Sets
Red Refractor: 8-15X
Production 25 Sets

AR	Alex Rodriguez	3.00
JT	Jim Thome	1.00
SS	Sammy Sosa	1.00
TG	Tom Glavine	1.00
TH	Trevor Hoffman	.50
RA	Rick Ankiel	1.00
MB	Mark Buehrle	.50
JV	Justin Verlander	1.00
CB	Clay Buchholz	1.00
FT	Frank Thomas	1.00
CG	Curtis Granderson	1.00
DW	David Wright	2.00
RH	Ryan Howard	2.00
PM	Pedro Martinez	1.00
ROH	Roy Halladay	1.00
TT	Troy Tulowitzki	2.00
JS	John Smoltz	1.00
PF	Prince Fielder	2.00
IS	Ichiro Suzuki	2.00
CP	Carlos Pena	1.00
DJ	Derek Jeter	3.00
JR	Jose Reyes	2.00
AP	Andy Pettitte	.50
TOH	Todd Helton	1.00
ISS	Ichiro Suzuki	2.00
DO	David Ortiz	2.00
BP	Brandon Phillips	1.00
JSA	Jarrod Saltalamacchia	.50
BW	Brandon Webb	1.00
APU	Albert Pujols	3.00
CF	Chone Figgins	.50
MH	Matt Holliday	1.50
DH	Danny Haren	1.00
FH	Felix Hernandez	1.00
EB	Eric Byrnes	.50
AG	Adrian Gonzalez	.75
VG	Vladimir Guerrero	1.00
RB	Ryan Braun	1.50
HP	Hunter Pence	1.00
FC	Fausto Carmona	.50
HR	Hanley Ramirez	1.50
AS	Andrew Sonnantine	.50
CH	Cole Hamels	1.00
JAS	Johan Santana	1.50
MR	Mark Reynolds	1.00
JMC	Miguel Cabrera	1.50
BPB	Brian Bannister	1.00
DL	Derrek Lee	1.00
ME	Mark Ellis	1.00
CS	C.C. Sabathia	1.00

Moments Autographs

BRAUN — FINEST 2007 SEASON MOMENTS

NM/M

Common Auto.:
Red Refractor: No Pricing
Production 25 Sets

RH	Ryan Howard	60.00
BP	Brandon Phillips	15.00
JC	Jack Cust	10.00
JR	Jose Reyes	50.00
HR	Hanley Ramirez	30.00
RB	Ryan Braun	40.00
ME	Mark Ellis	10.00
JD	Justin Duchscherer	10.00
MR	Mark Reynolds	15.00
AS	Andrew Sonnantine	10.00
DW	David Wright	60.00
NM	Nicholas Markakis	20.00
MC	Miguel Cabrera	30.00
BPB	Brian Bannister	15.00
CH	Cole Hamels	30.00
JA	Jeremy Accardo	10.00
PH	Phil Hughes	25.00
JS	Jarrod Saltalamacchia	15.00
CMW	Chien-Ming Wang	75.00
CG	Curtis Granderson	30.00
RZ	Ryan Zimmerman	20.00
JH	Josh Hamilton	15.00
FC	Fausto Carmona	10.00
VG	Vladimir Guerrero	35.00

Topps Team Favorites

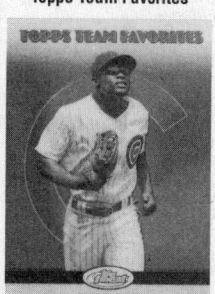

FELIX PIE
CHICAGO CUBS

NM/M

Complete Set (8): 10.00
Common Player: 1.00
Refractors: 2-4X

JR	Jose Reyes	3.00
DW	David Wright	4.00
MC	Melky Cabrera	1.50
RC	Robinson Cano	2.00
AS	Alfonso Soriano	2.00
FP	Felix Pie	1.50
EC	Eric Chavez	2.00
BC	Bobby Crosby	1.00

Topps Team Favorites Autographs

NM/M

Production 100 Sets
Red Refractor: No Pricing
Production 25 Sets

JR	Jose Reyes	50.00
DW	David Wright	60.00
MC	Melky Cabrera	20.00
RC	Robinson Cano	40.00
AS	Alfonso Soriano	30.00
FP	Felix Pie	10.00
EC	Eric Chavez	10.00
BC	Bobby Crosby	10.00

Topps Team Favorites Dual

NM/M

Common Duo: 2.00
Red Refractor: No Pricing
Production 25 Sets

RW	Jose Reyes, David Wright	4.00
CC	Melky Cabrera, Robinson Cano	3.00
SP	Alfonso Soriano, Felix Pie	2.00
EB	Eric Chavez, Bobby Crosby	2.00

Topps Team Favorites Dual Autographs

NM/M

Production 74 Sets
Red Refractor: No Pricing
Production 25 Sets

RW	Jose Reyes, David Wright	180.00
CC	Melky Cabrera, Robinson Cano	50.00
SP	Alfonso Soriano, Felix Pie	40.00
EB	Eric Chavez, Bobby Crosby	15.00

Topps Team Favorites Cut Signatures

Production One Set

Rookie Redemption

NM/M

Inserted 1:15

1	Johnny Cueto	12.00
2	Jay Bruce/Auto.	30.00
3	Kosuke Fukudome	10.00
4	Jeff Samardzija	5.00
5	Chris Davis	5.00
6	Justin Masterson	5.00
7	Clayton Kershaw	15.00
8	Daniel Murphy	5.00
9	Denard Span	8.00
10	Jed Lowrie Auto	20.00

2009 Finest

RYAN BRAUN

NM/M

Common Player (1-150): .25
Common RC Letter Auto.
(151-164): 15.00
Pack (5): 6.00
Box (18): 100.00

1	Kosuke Fukudome	.50
2	Derek Jeter	3.00
3	Evan Longoria	2.00
4	Alex Gordon	.50
5	David Wright	1.50
6	Ryan Howard	1.50
7	Jose Reyes	1.50
8	Ryan Braun	1.50
9	Hunter Pence	.50
10	Chipper Jones	1.00
11	Jimmy Rollins	1.00
12	Alfonso Soriano	.75
13	Alex Rodriguez	2.50
14	Paul Konerko	.50
15	Dustin Pedroia	1.00
16	Brian McCann	.50
17	Ken Griffey Jr.	2.00
18	Daisuke Matsuzaka	.75
19	Josh Beckett	.75
20	Jorge Posada	.50
21	Nick Markakis	.25
22	Xavier Nady	.25
23	Carlos Pena	.50
24	Grady Sizemore	1.00
25	Mark Teixeira	.75
26	Chase Utley	1.00
27	Vladimir Guerrero	1.00
28	Prince Fielder	1.00
29	Brian Roberts	.50

#	Player	Price
30	Magglio Ordonez	.50
31	Cliff Lee	.25
32	Josh Hamilton	1.50
33	Justin Morneau	.75
34	David Ortiz	1.00
35	Cole Hamels	.50
36	Edinson Volquez	.25
37	Hanley Ramirez	1.00
38	Carlos Zambrano	.50
39	Brett Myers	.25
40	Chien-Ming Wang	.50
41	John Lackey	.50
42	B.J. Upton	.50
43	Gary Sheffield	.50
44	Jake Peavy	.50
45	Carlos Lee	.50
46	Jacoby Ellsbury	1.00
47	Francisco Liriano	.50
48	Torii Hunter	.50
49	Eric Chavez	.25
50	Jamie Moyer	.25
51	Ichiro Suzuki	1.50
52	C.C. Sabathia	1.00
53	Matt Holliday	.50
54	Ervin Santana	.25
55	Hideki Matsui	.75
56	Mark Buehrle	.25
57	Johan Santana	1.00
58	Francisco Rodriguez	.50
59	Jorge Cantu	.25
60	Joe Mauer	.50
61	Ian Kinsler	.75
62	Joba Chamberlain	.75
63	Stephen Drew	.50
64	J.D. Drew	.25
65	Justin Upton	.50
66	Troy Glaus	.25
67	Chone Figgins	.25
68	David DeJesus	.25
69	Joey Votto	.75
70	Alex Rios	.50
71	Adam Jones	.50
72	Miguel Tejada	.50
73	Michael Young	.25
74	Vernon Wells	.50
75	Tim Lincecum	1.00
76	Ryan Zimmerman	.50
77	Nate McLouth	.50
78	Carl Crawford	.50
79	Dan Haren	.50
80	Brandon Webb	.50
81	Tim Hudson	.25
82	Rafael Furcal	.50
83	Ryan Dempster	.25
84	Carlos Beltran	.75
85	Lance Berkman	.75
86	Jhonny Peralta	.25
87	Aramis Ramirez	.25
88	Aubrey Huff	.25
89	Johnny Damon	.75
90	Carlos Quentin	.75
91	Yunel Escobar	.25
92	Scott Kazmir	.50
93	Delmon Young	.50
94	Jermaine Dye	.50
95	Miguel Cabrera	1.00
96	Zack Greinke	.50
97	Chris Young	.50
98	Derrek Lee	.75
99	Orlando Hudson	.25
100	Jay Bruce	1.00
101	Garrett Atkins	.50
102	Curtis Granderson	.75
103	Adrian Gonzalez	.50
104	Raul Ibanez	.50
105	Roy Halladay	.50
106	Jon Lester	.75
107	Adam Dunn	.75
108	A.J. Burnett	.25
109	Gavin Floyd	.25
110	Russell Martin	.50
111	Dan Uggla	.50
112	Andre Ethier	.50
113	Casey Kotchman	.25
114	Matt Garza	.25
115	Kevin Youkilis	.75
116	Felix Hernandez	.25
117	Rich Harden	.25
118	Roy Oswalt	.50
119	Jason Bay	.50
120	Geovany Soto	.50
121	Ryan Ludwick	.50
122	Joe Saunders	.25
123	Gil Meche	.25
124	Jim Thome	.50
125	Albert Pujols	2.00
126	Andrew Carpenter RC	1.00
127	Aaron Cunningham RC	1.00
128	Phil Coke RC	1.50
129	Alcides Escobar RC	1.50
130	Dexter Fowler (RC)	1.50
131	Michael Hinckley (RC)	1.00
132	Brad Nelson (RC)	1.00
133	Scott Lewis (RC)	1.00
134	Juan Miranda RC	1.00
135	Jason Motte (RC)	1.50
136	Travis Snider (RC)	3.00
137	Wade LeBlanc RC	1.00
138	Matt Tuiasosopo (RC)	1.00
139	Humberto Sanchez (RC)	1.00
140	Freddy Sandoval (RC)	1.00
141	Chris Lambert (RC)	1.00
142	John Jaso RC	1.00
143	James McDonald (RC)	1.00
144	Luis Valbuena (RC)	1.00
145	Richard Rundles (RC)	1.00
146	Josh Whitesell (RC)	1.00
147	Jeff Baisley RC	1.00

#	Player		Price
148	Ramon Ramirez (RC)		1.00
149	Jason Bourgeois (RC)		1.00
150	Jesus Delgado RC		1.00
151	Mat Gamel Letter/		
		Auto./285 RC	30.00
152	Travis Snider Letter/		
		Auto./170 RC	25.00
153	Angel Salome Letter/		
		Auto./218 (RC)	15.00
154	Will Venable Letter/		
		Auto./170 RC	15.00
155	Michael Bowden Letter/		
		Auto./218 (RC)	25.00
156	Conor Gillaspie Letter/		
		Auto./107 RC	20.00
157	Matt Antonelli Letter/		
		Auto./107 RC	15.00
158	Greg Golson Letter/		
		Auto./218 (RC)	15.00
159	Kila Ka'aihue Letter/		
		Auto./170 RC	15.00
160	Bobby Parnell Letter/		
		Auto./170 RC	15.00
161	Gaby Sanchez Letter/		
		Auto./170 RC	20.00
162	Jon Niese Letter/		
		Auto./285 RC	15.00
163	Dexter Fowler Letter/		
		Auto./285 (RC)	20.00
164	David Price Letter/		
		Auto./285 RC	50.00

Refractor
Refractor (1-150):		2-3X
Letter Auto. (151-164):		1-1.2X
Letter Autos. production 75		

Blue Refractor
Blue Refractor (1-150):		3-5X
Production 399		
Letter Auto. (151-164):		1-1.5X
Auto. production 25.		

Green Refractor
Green Refractor (1-150):		4-8X
Production 99 Sets		

Gold Refractor
Gold Refractor (1-150):		5-10X
Production 50		
Letter Auto. (151-164):		No Pricing
Auto. production 10.		

X-Fractor
Production One Set

Red Refractor
Red Refractor (1-150):		10-20X
Production 25		
Letter Auto. (151-164):		No Pricing
Production 5		

Rookie Redemption

		NM/M
Refractor Redemp:		1-1.5X
Production 199		
Gold Refractor Redemp.:		3-5X
Production 50		
1	Matt LaPorta	15.00
2	Tommy Hanson	25.00
3	Andrew Bailey	10.00
4	Julio Borbon	12.00
5	Colby Rasmus	15.00
6	Kyle Blanks	10.00
7	Neftali Feliz	12.00
8	Nolan Reimold	12.00
9	Rick Porcello	20.00
10	Tommy Hanson/Auto.	60.00

Moments Autographs

		NM/M
Common Auto.:		15.00
Red Refractor:		No Pricing
Production 25 Sets		
JR	Jose Reyes	35.00
AC	Asdrubal Cabrera	15.00
JL	Jon Lester	30.00
JB	Jay Bruce	35.00
JC	Joba Chamberlain	40.00

		Price
DW	David Wright	50.00
EV	Evan Longoria	50.00
AI	Akinori Iwamura	15.00
HP	Hunter Pence	25.00
RC	Robinson Cano	25.00
JBA	Jason Bay	15.00
DO	David Ortiz	50.00
JV	Joey Votto	40.00
RH	Ryan Howard	65.00

2010 Finest
Common Player:		.25
Common RC Auto. (151-164):		10.00
RC Auto # represents total print run		
Pack (5):		10.00
Box (12):		100.00
1	Tim Lincecum	1.00
2	Evan Longoria	1.50
3	Alex Rodriguez	1.50
4	Ryan Braun	1.00
5	Grady Sizemore	.50
6	David Wright	1.00
7	Albert Pujols	2.00
8	Derrek Lee	.50
9	Ichiro Suzuki	1.50
10	Justin Morneau	.50
11	Johan Santana	.75
12	Matt Kemp	.50
13	Daisuke Matsuzaka	.50
14	Derek Jeter	2.00
15	Mark Buehrle	.25
16	Chipper Jones	1.00
17	Prince Fielder	1.00
18	Ryan Howard	1.00
19	Vladimir Guerrero	.50
20	Alexei Ramirez	.25
21	Joba Chamberlain	.50
22	Russell Martin	.25
23	CC Sabathia	.75
24	Adam Dunn	.40
25	Jose Reyes	.50
26	Michael Young	.25
27	Joe Mauer	.75
28	Mark Teixeira	.75
29	Jason Bartlett	.25
30	Johnny Damon	.50
31	Miguel Cabrera	.75
32	Adam Wainwright	.50
33	Brandon Webb	.50
34	Carlos Pena	.50
35	Jorge Posada	.50
36	Pablo Sandoval	.50
37	Manny Ramirez	.50
38	Robinson Cano	.50
39	Nick Markakis	.50
40	Justin Upton	.75
41	Adrian Gonzalez	.50
42	Ian Kinsler	.50
43	Ryan Zimmerman	.50
44	Mark Reynolds	.40
45	Raul Ibanez	.40
46	Jason Bay	.50
47	Kendry Morales	.40
48	Todd Helton	.40
49	Dan Uggla	.40
50	Adam Lind	.50
51	Victor Martinez	.50
52	Mariano Rivera	.75
53	Chase Utley	1.00
54	Kevin Youkilis	.50
55	Carlos Lee	.40
56	Josh Hamilton	.50
57	Brad Hawpe	.25
58	Brandon Inge	.25
59	Bobby Abreu	.40
60	Nelson Cruz	.50
61	James Loney	.40
62	Jason Kubel	.40
63	Russell Branyan	.25
64	Curtis Granderson	.50
65	Ken Griffey Jr.	1.00
66	Troy Tulowitzki	.50
67	Jermaine Dye	.25
68	Paul Konerko	.40
69	Josh Johnson	.40
70	David Ortiz	.50
71	Hideki Matsui	.75
72	Dustin Pedroia	.75
73	Jon Lester	.50
74	Joey Votto	.75
75	Josh Beckett	.50
76	Billy Butler	.40
77	David DeJesus	.40
78	Nick Swisher	.40
79	Brian Roberts	.50
80	Felix Hernandez	.50
81	J.A. Happ	.40
82	Marco Scutaro	.25
83	Hanley Ramirez	1.00
84	Lance Berkman	.40
85	Dan Haren	.40
86	Yunel Escobar	.25
87	Justin Verlander	.50
88	Carlos Beltran	.40
89	Shane Victorino	.50
90	Carl Crawford	.50
91	Adam Jones	.40
92	Jason Marquis	.25
93	Everth Cabrera	.25
94	B.J. Upton	.50
95	Ted Lilly	.25
96	Ubaldo Jimenez	.50
97	Aaron Hill	.25
98	Kosuke Fukudome	.50
99	Jorge Cantu	.25
100	Jose Lopez	.25
101	Rick Porcello	.50
102	Matt Cain	.50

#	Player	Price
103	Chone Figgins	.25
104	Tommy Hanson	.75
105	Jacoby Ellsbury	.75
105	Clayton Kershaw	.50
107	Miguel Tejada	.40
108	Yovani Gallardo	.40
109	Andrew McCutchen	.75
110	Felipe Lopez	.25
111	Asdrubal Cabrera	.25
112	Roy Halladay	.75
113	Hunter Pence	.40
114	Gordon Beckham	.75
115	Cole Hamels	.75
116	Brian McCann	.50
117	Michael Cuddyer	.40
118	Cliff Lee	.50
119	Roy Oswalt	.50
120	A.J. Pierzynski	.25
121	Jayson Werth	.50
122	Mike Lowell	.40
123	John Lannan	.25
124	Luis Castillo	.25
125	Andy Pettitte	.40
126	Neil Walker (RC)	1.50
127	Brad Kilby RC	1.50
128	Chris Johnson RC	1.50
129	Tommy Manzella (RC)	1.50
130	Sergio Escalona (RC)	1.00
131	Chris Pettit RC	1.00
132	Kevin Richardson RC	1.00
133	Armando Gabino RC	1.00
134	Reid Gorecki RC	2.00
135	Justin Turner RC	1.00
136	Adam Moore RC	1.00
137	Kyle Phillips RC	1.00
138	John Hester RC	2.00
139	Dusty Hughes RC	1.00
140	Waldis Joaquin RC	1.50
141	Jeff Manship RC	1.50
142	Dan Runzler RC	2.00
143	Pedro Viola RC	1.00
144	Craig Gentry RC	1.00
145	Brent Dlugach (RC)	2.00
146	Esmil Rogers RC	1.00
147	Josh Butler RC	1.00
148	Dustin Richardson RC	1.00
149	Matt Carson (RC)	1.00
150	Henry Rodriguez RC	2.00
151	Brandon Allen	
	AU/1420 (RC)	15.00
152	Tyler Colvin	
	AU/1302 RC	25.00
153	Daniel Hudson	
	AU/1302 RC	15.00
154	Juan Francisco	
	AU/954 RC	15.00
155	Drew Stubbs	
	AU/1302 RC	15.00
156	Michael Brantley	
	AU/1072 RC	15.00
157	Tobi Stoner	
	AU/1302 RC	15.00
158	Josh Thole	
	AU/1420 RC	15.00
159	Daniel McCutchen	
	AU/954 RC	10.00
160	Eric Hacker	
	AU/1302 RC	10.00
161	Madison Bumgarner	
	AU/954 RC	20.00
162	Buster Posey	
	AU/1420 RC	30.00
163	Dan Runzler AU/1190	10.00
164	Ian Desmond	
	AU/1190 (RC)	15.00
165	Dustin Richardson	
	AU/2170	10.00

Printing Plates
Production one set per color.

Refractors
Refractor (1-125):		2-4X
Refractor RC (126-150):		1-2X
Production 599		
Auto. (151-165):		1.25X
Each Letter #'d to 75		

Refractor Blue
Blue (1-125):		4-6X
Blue RC (126-150):		2-3X
Production 299		
Blue Auto. (151-165):		1.5X
Each Letter #'d to 25		

Refractors Gold
Gold (1-125):		10-15X
Gold RC (126-150):		4-8X
Production 50 Sets		
Gold Auto. (151-165):		1-2X
Each Letter #'d to 10		

Refractors Green
Green (1-125):		6-10X
Green RC (126-150):		2-4X
Production 99 Sets		

Refractors Purple
Production One Set

Refractors Red
Red (1-125):		20-30X
Red RC (126-150):		6-10X
Production 25 Sets		
Red Auto. (151-165):		2-4X
Each Letter #'d to 5		

Finest Moments Autographs
Red Refractor:		1-1.5X
Production 25 Sets		
Purple 1 of 1's exist		
AE	Andre Ethier	20.00

		Price
AH	Aaron Hill	10.00
CF	Chone Figgins	12.00
CJ	Chipper Jones	75.00
CK	Clayton Kershaw	20.00
DP	Dustin Pedroia	25.00
DW	David Wright	35.00
JF	Jeff Francoeur	15.00
JM	Justin Morneau	25.00
JS	Joe Saunders	8.00
MS	Max Scherzer	8.00
PF	Prince Fielder	30.00
RC	Robinson Cano	25.00
RH	Ryan Howard	60.00
RP	Rick Porcello	30.00
UJ	Ubaldo Jimenez	20.00
YG	Yovani Gallardo	20.00
ZG	Zack Greinke	30.00

Rookie Logo Patch
Production 50 Sets		
Purple 1 of 1's exist		
126	Neil Walker	20.00
127	Brad Kilby	15.00
128	Chris Johnson	15.00
129	Tommy Manzella	10.00
130	Sergio Escalona	10.00
131	Chris Pettit	15.00
132	Kevin Richardson	12.00
133	Armando Gabino	15.00
134	Reid Gorecki	15.00
135	Justin Turner	15.00
136	Adam Moore	15.00
137	Kyle Phillips	10.00
138	John Hester	15.00
139	Dusty Hughes	12.00
140	Waldis Joaquin	10.00
141	Jeff Manship	10.00
142	Dan Runzler	15.00
143	Pedro Viola	10.00
144	Craig Gentry	15.00
145	Brent Dlugach	10.00
146	Esmil Rogers	15.00
147	Josh Butler	15.00
148	Dustin Richardson	15.00
149	Matt Carson	20.00
150	Henry Rodriguez	15.00

Rookie Redemption
Common Redemption:		20.00
Blue Refractor:		1.5X
Gold Refractor:		2-3X
1. Jason Heyward		100.00
2. Ike Davis		20.00

1993 Flair Promos

Among the scarcest modern baseball promo cards are those produced to introduce Fleer's new premium product for 1993, Flair. Basically similar to the issued versions, the promo cards have "000" in place of the card number on back. The promos are checklisted here in alphabetical order.

		NM/M
Complete Set (8):		200.00
Common Player:		10.00
(1)	Will Clark	10.00
(2)	Darren Daulton	10.00
(3)	Andres Galarraga	10.00
(4)	Bryan Harvey	10.00
(5)	David Justice	10.00
(6)	Jody Reed	10.00
(7)	Nolan Ryan	100.00
(8)	Sammy Sosa	60.00

1993 Flair

Designed as Fleer's super-premium card brand, this 300-card set contains extra-thick cards which feature gold-foil highlights and UV coating front and back. Portrait and action photos are combined in a high-tech front picture and there is a muted photo on the back, as well.

		NM/M
Complete Set (300):		15.00
Common Player:		.10
Pack (10):		1.50
Wax Box (24):		20.00
1	Steve Avery	.10
2	Jeff Blauser	.10
3	Ron Gant	.10
4	Tom Glavine	.25
5	Dave Justice	.10
6	Mark Lemke	.10
7	Greg Maddux	1.00
8	Fred McGriff	.10
9	Terry Pendleton	.10
10	Deion Sanders	.15
11	John Smoltz	.10
12	Mike Stanton	.10
13	Steve Buechele	.10
14	Mark Grace	.10
15	Greg Hibbard	.10
16	Derrick May	.10
17	Chuck McElroy	.10
18	Mike Morgan	.10
19	Randy Myers	.10
20	Ryne Sandberg	1.00
21	Dwight Smith	.10
22	Sammy Sosa	1.00
23	Jose Vizcaino	.10
24	Tim Belcher	.10
25	Rob Dibble	.10
26	Roberto Kelly	.10
27	Barry Larkin	.25
28	Kevin Mitchell	.10
29	Hal Morris	.10
30	Joe Oliver	.10
31	Jose Rijo	.10
32	Bip Roberts	.10
33	Chris Sabo	.10
34	Reggie Sanders	.10
35	Dante Bichette	.10
36	Willie Blair	.10
37	Jerald Clark	.10
38	Alex Cole	.10
39	Andres Galarraga	.10
40	Joe Girardi	.10
41	Charlie Hayes	.10
42	Chris Jones	.10
43	David Nied	.10
44	Eric Young	.10
45	Alex Arias	.10
46	Jack Armstrong	.10
47	Bret Barberie	.10
48	Chuck Carr	.10
49	Jeff Conine	.10
50	Orestes Destrade	.10
51	Chris Hammond	.10
52	Bryan Harvey	.10
53	Benito Santiago	.10
54	Gary Sheffield	.35
55	Walt Weiss	.10
56	Eric Anthony	.10
57	Jeff Bagwell	.75
58	Craig Biggio	.50
59	Ken Caminiti	.10
60	Andujar Cedeno	.10
61	Doug Drabek	.10
62	Steve Finley	.10
63	Luis Gonzalez	.10
64	Pete Harnisch	.10
65	Doug Jones	.10
66	Darryl Kile	.10
67	Greg Swindell	.10
68	Brett Butler	.10
69	Jim Gott	.10
70	Orel Hershiser	.10
71	Eric Karros	.10
72	Pedro Martinez	.75
73	Ramon Martinez	.10
74	Roger McDowell	.10
75	Mike Piazza	1.50
76	Jody Reed	.10
77	Tim Wallach	.10
78	Moises Alou	.10
79	Greg Colbrunn	.10
80	Wil Cordero	.10
81	Delino DeShields	.10
82	Jeff Fassero	.10
83	Marquis Grissom	.10
84	Ken Hill	.10
85	Mike Lansing RC	.10
86	Dennis Martinez	.10
87	Larry Walker	.25
88	John Wetteland	.10
89	Bobby Bonilla	.10
90	Vince Coleman	.10
91	Dwight Gooden	.10
92	Todd Hundley	.10
93	Howard Johnson	.10
94	Eddie Murray	.75
95	Joe Orsulak	.10
96	Bret Saberhagen	.10
97	Darren Daulton	.10
98	Mariano Duncan	.10
99	Len Dykstra	.10
100	Jim Eisenreich	.10
101	Tommy Greene	.10
102	Dave Hollins	.10

103 Pete Incaviglia .10
104 Danny Jackson .10
105 John Kruk .10
106 Terry Mulholland .10
107 Curt Schilling .25
108 Mitch Williams .10
109 Stan Belinda .10
110 Jay Bell .10
111 Steve Cooke .10
112 Carlos Garcia .10
113 Jeff King .10
114 Al Martin .10
115 Orlando Merced .10
116 Don Slaught .10
117 Andy Van Slyke .10
118 Tim Wakefield .10
119 Rene Arocha RC .10
120 Bernard Gilkey .10
121 Gregg Jefferies .10
122 Ray Lankford .10
123 Donovan Osborne .10
124 Tom Pagnozzi .10
125 Erik Pappas .10
126 Geronimo Pena .10
127 Lee Smith .10
128 Ozzie Smith 1.00
129 Bob Tewksbury .10
130 Mark Whiten .10
131 Derek Bell .10
132 Andy Benes .10
133 Tony Gwynn 1.00
134 Gene Harris .10
135 Trevor Hoffman .10
136 Phil Plantier .10
137 Rod Beck .10
138 Barry Bonds 2.50
139 John Burkett .10
140 Will Clark .10
141 Royce Clayton .10
142 Mike Jackson .10
143 Darren Lewis .10
144 Kirt Manwaring .10
145 Willie McGee .10
146 Bill Swift .10
147 Robby Thompson .10
148 Matt Williams .10
149 Brady Anderson .10
150 Mike Devereaux .10
151 Chris Hoiles .10
152 Ben McDonald .10
153 Mark McLemore .10
154 Mike Mussina .40
155 Gregg Olson .10
156 Harold Reynolds .10
157 Cal Ripken, Jr. 2.50
158 Rick Sutcliffe .10
159 Fernando Valenzuela .10
160 Roger Clemens 1.25
161 Scott Cooper .10
162 Andre Dawson .30
163 Scott Fletcher .10
164 Mike Greenwell .10
165 Greg Harris .10
166 Billy Hatcher .10
167 Jeff Russell .10
168 Mo Vaughn .10
169 Frank Viola .10
170 Chad Curtis .10
171 Chili Davis .10
172 Gary DiSarcina .10
173 Damion Easley .10
174 Chuck Finley .10
175 Mark Langston .10
176 Luis Polonia .10
177 Tim Salmon .10
178 Scott Sanderson .10
179 J.T. Snow RC .50
180 Wilson Alvarez .10
181 Ellis Burks .10
182 Joey Cora .10
183 Alex Fernandez .10
184 Ozzie Guillen .10
185 Roberto Hernandez .10
186 Bo Jackson .20
187 Lance Johnson .10
188 Jack McDowell .10
189 Frank Thomas .75
190 Robin Ventura .10
191 Carlos Baerga .10
192 Albert Belle .10
193 Wayne Kirby .10
194 Derek Lilliquist .10
195 Kenny Lofton .10
196 Carlos Martinez .10
197 Jose Mesa .10
198 Eric Plunk .10
199 Paul Sorrento .10
200 Jon Doherty .10
201 Cecil Fielder .10
202 Travis Fryman .10
203 Kirk Gibson .10
204 Mike Henneman .10
205 Chad Kreuter .10
206 Scott Livingstone .10
207 Tony Phillips .10
208 Mickey Tettleton .10
209 Alan Trammell .10
210 David Wells .10
211 Lou Whitaker .10
212 Kevin Appier .10
213 George Brett 1.25
214 David Cone .10
215 Tom Gordon .10
216 Phil Hiatt .10
217 Felix Jose .10
218 Wally Joyner .10
219 Jose Lind .10
220 Mike Macfarlane .10

221 Brian McRae .10
222 Jeff Montgomery .10
223 Cal Eldred .10
224 Darryl Hamilton .10
225 John Jaha .10
226 Pat Listach .10
227 Graeme Lloyd RC .10
228 Kevin Reimer .10
229 Bill Spiers .10
230 B.J. Surhoff .10
231 Greg Vaughn .10
232 Robin Yount .75
233 Rick Aguilera .10
234 Jim Deshaies .10
235 Brian Harper .10
236 Kent Hrbek .10
237 Chuck Knoblauch .10
238 Shane Mack .10
239 David McCarty .10
240 Pedro Munoz .10
241 Mike Pagliarulo .10
242 Kirby Puckett 1.00
243 Dave Winfield .75
244 Jim Abbott .10
245 Wade Boggs 1.00
246 Pat Kelly .10
247 Jimmy Key .10
248 Jim Leyritz .10
249 Don Mattingly 1.25
250 Matt Nokes .10
251 Paul O'Neill .10
252 Mike Stanley .10
253 Danny Tartabull .10
254 Bob Wickman .10
255 Bernie Williams .10
256 Mike Bordick .10
257 Dennis Eckersley .60
258 Brent Gates .10
259 Goose Gossage .10
260 Rickey Henderson .75
261 Mark McGwire 2.00
262 Ruben Sierra .10
263 Terry Steinbach .10
264 Bob Welch .10
265 Bobby Witt .10
266 Rich Amaral .10
267 Chris Bosio .10
268 Jay Buhner .10
269 Norm Charlton .10
270 Ken Griffey Jr. 1.50
271 Erik Hanson .10
272 Randy Johnson .75
273 Edgar Martinez .10
274 Tino Martinez .10
275 Dave Valle .10
276 Omar Vizquel .10
277 Kevin Brown .10
278 Jose Canseco .45
279 Julio Franco .10
280 Juan Gonzalez .40
281 Tom Henke .10
282 David Hulse .10
283 Rafael Palmeiro .65
284 Dean Palmer .10
285 Ivan Rodriguez .65
286 Nolan Ryan 2.50
287 Roberto Alomar .25
288 Pat Borders .10
289 Joe Carter .10
290 Juan Guzman .10
291 Pat Hentgen .10
292 Paul Molitor .75
293 John Olerud .10
294 Ed Sprague .10
295 Dave Stewart .10
296 Duane Ward .10
297 Devon White .10
298 Checklist .05
299 Checklist .05
300 Checklist .05

Wave of the Future

The game's top prospects are featured in this insert issue randomly packaged in Flair packs. Cards #19-20, Darrell Whitmore and Nigel Wilson, were printed with each other's back; no corrected version was made.

NM/M
Complete Set (20): 6.00
Common Player: .15
1 Jason Bere .15
2 Jeremy Burnitz .15
3 Russ Davis .15
4 Jim Edmonds .25
5 Cliff Floyd .15
6 Jeffrey Hammonds .15
7 Trevor Hoffman .15
8 Domingo Jean .15
9 David McCarty .15
10 Bobby Munoz .15
11 Brad Pennington .15
12 Mike Piazza 3.00
13 Manny Ramirez 2.00
14 John Roper .15
15 Tim Salmon .25
16 Aaron Sele .15
17 Allen Watson .15
18 Rondell White .15
19 Darell Whitmore .15
20 Nigel Wilson .15

1994 Flair

One of the success stories of 1993 returned with the release of Fleer Flair for 1994. At $4 per pack this was pricey stuff, but collectors apparently liked the look that includes an extremely thick card stock, full-bleed photos and gold-foil graphics on both sides with a protective polyester laminate described as "far beyond mere UV coating." In addition to the 250 regular-issue cards, there are three 10-card insert sets; Wave of the Future, Outfield Power and Hot Numbers in Series 1, the last with players' images printed on 100 percent etched foil. Series 2 has 200 base cards and Hot Glove, Infield Power and 10 more Wave of the Future insert cards.

NM/M
Complete Set (450): 60.00
Common Player: .10
Series 1 Pack (10): 1.50
Series 1 Box (24): 20.00
Series 2 Pack (10): 3.00
Series 2 Box (24): 50.00
1 Harold Baines .10
2 Jeffrey Hammonds .10
3 Chris Hoiles .10
4 Ben McDonald .10
5 Mark McLemore .10
6 Jamie Moyer .10
7 Jim Poole .10
8 Cal Ripken, Jr. 3.00
9 Chris Sabo .10
10 Scott Bankhead .10
11 Scott Cooper .10
12 Danny Darwin .10
13 Andre Dawson .30
14 Billy Hatcher .10
15 Aaron Sele .10
15a Aaron Sele/OPS 2.00
16 John Valentin .10
17 Dave Valle .10
18 Mo Vaughn .10
19 Brian Anderson RC .50
20 Gary DiSarcina .10
21 Jim Edmonds .10
22 Chuck Finley .10
23 Bo Jackson .20
24 Mark Leiter .10
25 Greg Myers .10
26 Eduardo Perez .10
27 Tim Salmon .10
28 Wilson Alvarez .10
29 Jason Bere .10
30 Alex Fernandez .10
31 Ozzie Guillen .10
32 Joe Hall .10
33 Darrin Jackson .10
34 Kirk McCaskill .10
35 Tim Raines .10
36 Frank Thomas 1.00
37 Carlos Baerga .10
38 Albert Belle .10
39 Mark Clark .10
40 Wayne Kirby .10
41 Dennis Martinez .10
42 Charles Nagy .10
43 Manny Ramirez 1.00
44 Paul Sorrento .10
45 Jim Thome .65
46 Eric Davis .10
47 John Doherty .10
48 Junior Felix .10
49 Cecil Fielder .10

50 Kirk Gibson .10
51 Mike Moore .10
52 Tony Phillips .10
53 Alan Trammell .10
54 Kevin Appier .10
55 Stan Belinda .10
56 Vince Coleman .10
57 Greg Gagne .10
58 Bob Hamelin .10
59 Dave Henderson .10
60 Wally Joyner .10
61 Mike Macfarlane .10
62 Jeff Montgomery .10
63 Ricky Bones .10
64 Jeff Bronkey .10
65 Alex Diaz .10
66 Cal Eldred .10
67 Darryl Hamilton .10
68 John Jaha .10
69 Mark Kiefer .10
70 Kevin Seitzer .10
71 Turner Ward .10
72 Rich Becker .10
73 Scott Erickson .10
74 Keith Garagozzo .10
75 Kent Hrbek .10
76 Scott Leius .10
77 Kirby Puckett 1.50
78 Matt Walkbeck .10
79 Dave Winfield 1.00
80 Mike Gallego .10
81 Xavier Hernandez .10
82 Jimmy Key .10
83 Jim Leyritz .10
84 Don Mattingly 1.75
85 Matt Nokes .10
86 Paul O'Neill .10
87 Melido Perez .10
88 Danny Tartabull .10
89 Mike Bordick .10
90 Ron Darling .10
91 Dennis Eckersley .75
92 Stan Javier .10
93 Steve Karsay .10
94 Mark McGwire 2.50
95 Troy Neel .10
96 Terry Steinbach .10
97 Bill Taylor .10
98 Eric Anthony .10
99 Chris Bosio .10
100 Tim Davis .10
101 Felix Fermin .10
102 Dave Fleming .10
103 Ken Griffey Jr. 2.00
104 Greg Hibbard .10
105 Reggie Jefferson .10
106 Tino Martinez .10
107 Jack Armstrong .10
108 Will Clark .10
109 Juan Gonzalez .50
110 Rick Helling .10
111 Tom Henke .10
112 David Hulse .10
113 Manuel Lee .10
114 Doug Strange .10
115 Roberto Alomar .25
116 Joe Carter .10
117 Carlos Delgado .50
118 Pat Hentgen .10
119 Paul Molitor 1.00
120 John Olerud .10
121 Dave Stewart .10
122 Todd Stottlemyre .10
123 Mike Timlin .10
124 Jeff Blauser .10
125 Tom Glavine .30
126 Dave Justice .10
127 Mike Kelly .10
128 Ryan Klesko .10
129 Javier Lopez .10
130 Greg Maddux 1.50
131 Fred McGriff .10
132 Kent Mercker .10
133 Mark Wohlers .10
134 Willie Banks .10
135 Steve Buechele .10
136 Shawon Dunston .10
137 Jose Guzman .10
138 Glenallen Hill .10
139 Randy Myers .10
140 Karl Rhodes .10
141 Ryne Sandberg 1.50
142 Steve Trachsel .10
143 Bret Boone .10
144 Tom Browning .10
145 Hector Carrasco .10
146 Barry Larkin .10
147 Hal Morris .10
148 Jose Rijo .10
149 Reggie Sanders .10
150 John Smiley .10
151 Dante Bichette .10
152 Ellis Burks .10
153 Joe Girardi .10
154 Mike Harkey .10
155 Roberto Mejia .10
156 Marcus Moore .10
157 Armando Reynoso .10
158 Bruce Ruffin .10
159 Eric Young .10
160 Kurt Abbott RC .10
161 Jeff Conine .10
162 Orestes Destrade .10
163 Chris Hammond .10
164 Bryan Harvey .10
165 Dave Magadan .10
166 Gary Sheffield .40
167 David Weathers .10

168 Andujar Cedeno .10
169 Tom Edens .10
170 Luis Gonzalez .10
171 Pete Harnisch .10
172 Todd Jones .10
173 Darryl Kile .10
174 James Mouton .10
175 Scott Servais .10
176 Mitch Williams .10
177 Pedro Astacio .10
178 Orel Hershiser .10
179 Raul Mondesi .10
180 Jose Offerman .10
181 Chan Ho Park RC 1.00
182 Mike Piazza 2.00
183 Cory Snyder .10
184 Tim Wallach .10
185 Todd Worrell .10
186 Sean Berry .10
187 Wil Cordero .10
188 Darrin Fletcher .10
189 Cliff Floyd .10
190 Marquis Grissom .10
191 Rod Henderson .10
192 Ken Hill .10
193 Pedro Martinez 1.00
194 Kirk Rueter .10
195 Jeromy Burnitz .10
196 John Franco .10
197 Dwight Gooden .10
198 Todd Hundley .10
199 Bobby Jones .10
200 Jeff Kent .10
201 Mike Maddux .10
202 Ryan Thompson .10
203 Jose Vizcaino .10
204 Darren Daulton .10
205 Len Dykstra .10
206 Jim Eisenreich .10
207 Dave Hollins .10
208 Danny Jackson .10
209 Doug Jones .10
210 Jeff Juden .10
211 Ben Rivera .10
212 Kevin Stocker .10
213 Milt Thompson .10
214 Jay Bell .10
215 Steve Cooke .10
216 Mark Dewey .10
217 Al Martin .10
218 Orlando Merced .10
219 Don Slaught .10
220 Zane Smith .10
221 Rick White .10
222 Kevin Young .10
223 Rene Arocha .10
224 Rheal Cormier .10
225 Brian Jordan .10
226 Ray Lankford .10
227 Mike Perez .10
228 Ozzie Smith 1.50
229 Mark Whiten .10
230 Todd Zeile .10
231 Derek Bell .10
232 Archi Cianfrocco .10
233 Ricky Gutierrez .10
234 Trevor Hoffman .10
235 Phil Plantier .10
236 Dave Staton .10
237 Wally Whitehurst .10
238 Todd Benzinger .10
239 Barry Bonds 3.00
240 John Burkett .10
241 Royce Clayton .10
242 Bryan Hickerson .10
243 Mike Jackson .10
244 Darren Lewis .10
245 Kirt Manwaring .10
246 Mark Portugal .10
247 Salomon Torres .10
248 Checklist .10
249 Checklist .10
250 Checklist .10
251 Brady Anderson .10
252 Mike Devereaux .10
253 Sid Fernandez .10
254 Leo Gomez .10
255 Mike Mussina .40
256 Mike Oquist .10
257 Rafael Palmeiro .75
258 Lee Smith .10
259 Damon Berryhill .10
260 Wes Chamberlain .10
261 Roger Clemens 1.75
262 Gar Finnvold .10
263 Mike Greenwell .10
264 Tim Naehring .10
265 Otis Nixon .10
266 Ken Ryan .10
267 Chad Curtis .10
268 Chili Davis .10
269 Damion Easley .10
270 Jorge Fabregas .10
271 Mark Langston .10
272 Phil Leftwich .10
273 Harold Reynolds .10
274 J.T. Snow .10
275 Joey Cora .10
276 Julio Franco .10
277 Roberto Hernandez .10
278 Lance Johnson .10
279 Ron Karkovice .10
280 Jack McDowell .10
281 Robin Ventura .10
282 Sandy Alomar Jr. .10
283 Kenny Lofton .10
284 Jose Mesa .10
285 Jack Morris .10

286 Eddie Murray 1.00
287 Chad Ogea .10
288 Eric Plunk .10
289 Paul Shuey .10
290 Omar Vizquel .10
291 Danny Bautista .10
292 Travis Fryman .10
293 Greg Gohr .10
294 Chris Gomez .10
295 Mickey Tettleton .10
296 Lou Whitaker .10
297 David Cone .10
298 Gary Gaetti .10
299 Tom Gordon .10
300 Felix Jose .10
301 Jose Lind .10
302 Brian McRae .10
303 Mike Fetters .10
304 Brian Harper .10
305 Pat Listach .10
306 Matt Mieske .10
307 Dave Nilsson .10
308 Jody Reed .10
309 Greg Vaughn .10
310 Bill Wegman .10
311 Rick Aguilera .10
312 Alex Cole .10
313 Denny Hocking .10
314 Chuck Knoblauch .10
315 Shane Mack .10
316 Pat Meares .10
317 Kevin Tapani .10
318 Jim Abbott .10
319 Wade Boggs 1.00
320 Sterling Hitchcock .10
321 Pat Kelly .10
322 Terry Mulholland .10
323 Luis Polonia .10
324 Mike Stanley .10
325 Bob Wickman .10
326 Bernie Williams .10
327 Mark Acre .10
328 Geronimo Berroa .10
329 Scott Brosius .10
330 Brent Gates .10
331 Rickey Henderson 1.00
332 Carlos Reyes .10
333 Ruben Sierra .10
334 Bobby Witt .10
335 Bobby Ayala .10
336 Jay Buhner .10
337 Randy Johnson 1.00
338 Edgar Martinez .10
339 Bill Risley .10
340 Alex Rodriguez RC 40.00
341 Roger Salkeld .10
342 Dan Wilson .10
343 Kevin Brown .10
344 Jose Canseco .45
345 Dean Palmer .10
346 Ivan Rodriguez .75
347 Kenny Rogers .10
348 Pat Borders .10
349 Juan Guzman .10
350 Ed Sprague .10
351 Devon White .10
352 Steve Avery .10
353 Roberto Kelly .10
354 Mark Lemke .10
355 Greg McMichael .10
356 Terry Pendleton .10
357 John Smoltz .10
358 Mike Stanton .10
359 Tony Tarasco .10
360 Mark Grace .10
361 Derrick May .10
362 Rey Sanchez .10
363 Sammy Sosa 1.50
364 Rick Wilkins .10
365 Jeff Brantley .10
366 Tony Fernandez .10
367 Chuck McElroy .10
368 Kevin Mitchell .10
369 John Roper .10
370 Johnny Ruffin .10
371 Deion Sanders .15
372 Marvin Freeman .10
373 Andres Galarraga .10
374 Charlie Hayes .10
375 Nelson Liriano .10
376 David Nied .10
377 Walt Weiss .10
378 Bret Barberie .10
379 Jerry Browne .10
380 Chuck Carr .10
381 Greg Colbrunn .10
382 Charlie Hough .10
383 Kurt Miller .10
384 Benito Santiago .10
385 Jeff Bagwell 1.00
386 Craig Biggio .10
387 Ken Caminiti .10
388 Doug Drabek .10
389 Steve Finley .10
390 John Hudek .10
391 Orlando Miller .10
392 Shane Reynolds .10
393 Brett Butler .10
394 Tom Candiotti .10
395 Delino DeShields .10
396 Kevin Gross .10
397 Eric Karros .10
398 Ramon Martinez .10
399 Henry Rodriguez .10
400 Moises Alou .10
401 Jeff Fassero .10
402 Mike Lansing .10
403 Mel Rojas .10

404	Larry Walker	.10
405	John Wetteland	.10
406	Gabe White	.10
407	Bobby Bonilla	.10
408	Josias Manzanillo	.10
409	Bret Saberhagen	.10
410	David Segui	.10
411	Mariano Duncan	.10
412	Tommy Greene	.10
413	Billy Hatcher	.10
414	Ricky Jordan	.10
415	John Kruk	.10
416	Bobby Munoz	.10
417	Curt Schilling	.30
418	Fernando Valenzuela	.10
419	David West	.10
420	Carlos Garcia	.10
421	Brian Hunter	.10
422	Jeff King	.10
423	Jon Lieber	.10
424	Ravelo Manzanillo	.10
425	Denny Neagle	.10
426	Andy Van Slyke	.10
427	Bryan Eversgerd	.10
428	Bernard Gilkey	.10
429	Gregg Jefferies	.10
430	Tom Pagnozzi	.10
431	Bob Tewksbury	.10
432	Allen Watson	.10
433	Andy Ashby	.10
434	Andy Benes	.10
435	Donnie Elliott	.10
436	Tony Gwynn	1.50
437	Joey Hamilton	.10
438	Tim Hyers	.10
439	Luis Lopez	.10
440	Bip Roberts	.10
441	Scott Sanders	.10
442	Rod Beck	.10
443	Dave Burba	.10
444	Darryl Strawberry	.10
445	Bill Swift	.10
446	Robby Thompson	.10
447	William Van Landingham RC	.10
448	Matt Williams	.10
449	Checklist	.10
450	Checklist	.10

Hot Gloves

Hot Glove is a 10-card Series 2 insert set. It focuses on players with outstanding defensive ability. Cards feature a die-cut design, with the player photo in front of a baseball glove. Player identification and a "Hot Glove" logo are in gold foil in the lower-left corner.

		NM/M
Complete Set (10):		40.00
Common Player:		2.00
1	Barry Bonds	10.00
2	Will Clark	2.00
3	Ken Griffey Jr.	7.50
4	Kenny Lofton	2.00
5	Greg Maddux	5.00
6	Don Mattingly	6.50
7	Kirby Puckett	5.00
8	Cal Ripken, Jr.	10.00
9	Tim Salmon	2.00
10	Matt Williams	2.00

Hot Numbers

Hot Numbers is an insert set found in Series 1 packs at an average rate of 1:24. Each card is printed on 100 percent etched foil and displays the player in the forefront with a background made up of floating numbers. The player's name is in gold foil across the bottom-right side and a large foil "Hot Numbers" and that player's uniform number are in a square at bottom-left.

		NM/M
Complete Set (10):		15.00
Common Player:		.50
1	Roberto Alomar	1.00
2	Carlos Baerga	.50
3	Will Clark	.50
4	Fred McGriff	.50
5	Paul Molitor	3.00
6	John Olerud	.50
7	Mike Piazza	4.50
8	Cal Ripken, Jr.	6.00
9	Ryne Sandberg	4.00
10	Frank Thomas	3.00

Infield Power

Infield Power is a horizontally formatted insert set. Cards show the player batting on one half and in the field on the other half of the card, divided by a black, diagonal strip that reads "Infield Power" and the player's name. The set spotlights infielders that often hit the longball. Infield Power was inserted into Series 2 packs at an average rate of 1:5.

		NM/M
Complete Set (10):		5.00
Common Player:		.25
1	Jeff Bagwell	.75
2	Will Clark	.25
3	Darren Daulton	.25
4	Don Mattingly	1.25
5	Fred McGriff	.25
6	Rafael Palmeiro	.65
7	Mike Piazza	1.50
8	Cal Ripken, Jr.	2.50
9	Frank Thomas	.75
10	Matt Williams	.25

Outfield Power

Flair's Outfield Power was randomly inserted in Series 1 packs at a 1:5 rate. This vertically formatted card shows the player in the field on top, while the bottom half shows the player at the plate. The photos divided by a black strip with "Outfield Power" and the player's name on it.

		NM/M
Complete Set (10):		5.00
Common Player:		.30
1	Albert Belle	.30
2	Barry Bonds	2.00
3	Joe Carter	.30
4	Len Dykstra	.30
5	Juan Gonzalez	.45
6	Ken Griffey Jr.	1.50
7	Dave Justice	.30
8	Kirby Puckett	1.00
9	Tim Salmon	.30
10	Dave Winfield	.75

Wave of the Future 1

Series 1 Wave of the Future is horizontally formatted and depicts 10 outstanding 1994 rookies who have the potential to become superstars. Each player is featured on a colorful wavelike background. A Wave of the Future gold-foil stamp is placed in the bottom-right corner with the player name in gold foil starting in the opposite bottom corner and running across the bottom. Advertised insertion rate was 1:5.

		NM/M
Complete Set (10):		6.00
Common Player:		.25
1	Kurt Abbott	.25
2	Carlos Delgado	5.00
3	Steve Karsay	.25
4	Ryan Klesko	.25
5	Javier Lopez	.25
6	Raul Mondesi	.25
7	James Mouton	.25
8	Chan Ho Park	.25
9	Dave Staton	.25
10	Rick White	.25

Wave of the Future 2

Series 2 Flair also has a Wave of the Future insert set. Unlike the earlier series, this 10-card set is vertically formated. The Wave of the Future logo appears in the bottom-left with the player's name stretching across the rest of the bottom. The background has a swirling water effect, on which the player is superimposed. Insertion rate is one per five packs.

		NM/M
Complete Set (10):		22.50
Common Player:		.50
1	Mark Acre	.50
2	Chris Gomez	.50
3	Joey Hamilton	.50
4	John Hudek	.50
5	Jon Lieber	.50
6	Matt Mieske	.50
7	Orlando Miller	.50
8	Alex Rodriguez	20.00
9	Tony Tarasco	.50
10	Bill VanLandingham	.50

1995 Flair

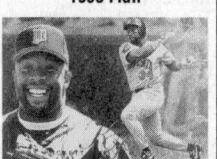

There's no mistaking that 1995 Flair is Fleer's super-premium brand. Cards are printed on double-thick cardboard with a background of etched metallic foil: Gold for National Leaguers, silver for American. A portrait and an action photo are featured on the horizontal front design. Backs are vertically formatted with a borderless action photo, several years worth of stats and foil trim. The basic set was issued in two series of 216 basic cards each, along with several insert sets exclusive to each series. Cards were sold in a hard pack of nine with a suggested retail price of $5.

		NM/M
Complete Set (432):		30.00
Common Player:		.10
Series 1 or 2 Pack (9):		1.00
Series 1 or 2 Wax Box (24):		15.00
1	Brady Anderson	.10
2	Harold Baines	.10
3	Leo Gomez	.10
4	Alan Mills	.10
5	Jamie Moyer	.10
6	Mike Mussina	.40
7	Mike Oquist	.10
8	Arthur Rhodes	.10
9	Cal Ripken Jr.	3.00
10	Roger Clemens	1.75
11	Scott Cooper	.10
12	Mike Greenwell	.10
13	Aaron Sele	.10
14	John Valentin	.10
15	Mo Vaughn	.10
16	Chad Curtis	.10
17	Gary DiSarcina	.10
18	Chuck Finley	.10
19	Andrew Lorraine	.10
20	Spike Owen	.10
21	Tim Salmon	.10
22	J.T. Snow	.10
23	Wilson Alvarez	.10
24	Jason Bere	.10
25	Ozzie Guillen	.10
26	Mike LaValliere	.10
27	Frank Thomas	1.00
28	Robin Ventura	.10
29	Carlos Baerga	.10
30	Albert Belle	.10
31	Jason Grimsley	.10
32	Dennis Martinez	.10
33	Eddie Murray	1.00
34	Charles Nagy	.10
35	Manny Ramirez	1.00
36	Paul Sorrento	.10
37	John Doherty	.10
38	Cecil Fielder	.10
39	Travis Fryman	.10
40	Chris Gomez	.10
41	Tony Phillips	.10
42	Lou Whitaker	.10
43	David Cone	.10
44	Gary Gaetti	.10
45	Mark Gubicza	.10
46	Bob Hamelin	.10
47	Wally Joyner	.10
48	Rusty Meacham	.10
49	Jeff Montgomery	.10
50	Ricky Bones	.10
51	Cal Eldred	.10
52	Pat Listach	.10
53	Matt Mieske	.10
54	Dave Nilsson	.10
55	Greg Vaughn	.10
56	Bill Wegman	.10
57	Chuck Knoblauch	.10
58	Scott Leius	.10
59	Pat Mahomes	.10
60	Pat Meares	.10
61	Pedro Munoz	.10
62	Kirby Puckett	1.50
63	Wade Boggs	1.00
64	Jimmy Key	.10
65	Jim Leyritz	.10
66	Don Mattingly	1.75
67	Paul O'Neill	.10
68	Melido Perez	.10
69	Danny Tartabull	.10
70	John Briscoe	.10
71	Scott Brosius	.10
72	Ron Darling	.10
73	Brent Gates	.10
74	Rickey Henderson	1.00
75	Stan Javier	.10
76	Mark McGwire	2.50
77	Todd Van Poppel	.10
78	Bobby Ayala	.10
79	Mike Blowers	.10
80	Jay Buhner	.10
81	Ken Griffey Jr.	2.00
82	Randy Johnson	1.00
83	Tino Martinez	.10
84	Jeff Nelson	.10
85	Alex Rodriguez	2.50
86	Will Clark	.10
87	Jeff Frye	.10
88	Juan Gonzalez	.50
89	Rusty Greer	.10
90	Darren Oliver	.10
91	Dean Palmer	.10
92	Ivan Rodriguez	.75
93	Matt Whiteside	.10
94	Roberto Alomar	.25
95	Joe Carter	.10
96	Tony Castillo	.10
97	Juan Guzman	.10
98	Pat Hentgen	.10
99	Mike Huff	.10
100	John Olerud	.10
101	Woody Williams	.10
102	Roberto Kelly	.10
103	Ryan Klesko	.10
104	Javier Lopez	.10
105	Greg Maddux	1.50
106	Fred McGriff	.10
107	Jose Oliva	.10
108	John Smoltz	.10
109	Tony Tarasco	.10
110	Mark Wohlers	.10
111	Jim Bullinger	.10
112	Shawon Dunston	.10
113	Derrick May	.10
114	Randy Myers	.10
115	Karl Rhodes	.10
116	Rey Sanchez	.10
117	Steve Trachsel	.10
118	Eddie Zambrano	.10
119	Bret Boone	.10
120	Brian Dorsett	.10
121	Hal Morris	.10
122	Jose Rijo	.10
123	John Roper	.10
124	Reggie Sanders	.10
125	Pete Schourek	.10
126	John Smiley	.10
127	Ellis Burks	.10
128	Vinny Castilla	.10
129	Marvin Freeman	.10
130	Andres Galarraga	.10
131	Mike Munoz	.10
132	David Nied	.10
133	Bruce Ruffin	.10
134	Walt Weiss	.10
135	Eric Young	.10
136	Greg Colbrunn	.10
137	Jeff Conine	.10
138	Jeremy Hernandez	.10
139	Charles Johnson	.10
140	Robb Nen	.10
141	Gary Sheffield	.40
142	Dave Weathers	.10
143	Jeff Bagwell	1.00
144	Craig Biggio	.10
145	Tony Eusebio	.10
146	Luis Gonzalez	.10
147	John Hudek	.10
148	Darryl Kile	.10
149	Dave Veres	.10
150	Billy Ashley	.10
151	Pedro Astacio	.10
152	Rafael Bournigal	.10
153	Delino DeShields	.10
154	Raul Mondesi	.10
155	Mike Piazza	2.00
156	Rudy Seanez	.10
157	Ismael Valdes	.10
158	Tim Wallach	.10
159	Todd Worrell	.10
160	Moises Alou	.10
161	Cliff Floyd	.10
162	Gil Heredia	.10
163	Mike Lansing	.10
164	Pedro Martinez	1.00
165	Kirk Rueter	.10
166	Tim Scott	.10
167	Jeff Shaw	.10
168	Rondell White	.10
169	Bobby Bonilla	.10
170	Rico Brogna	.10
171	Todd Hundley	.10
172	Jeff Kent	.10
173	Jim Lindeman	.10
174	Joe Orsulak	.10
175	Bret Saberhagen	.10
176	Toby Borland	.10
177	Darren Daulton	.10
178	Lenny Dykstra	.10
179	Jim Eisenreich	.10
180	Tommy Greene	.10
181	Tony Longmire	.10
182	Bobby Munoz	.10
183	Kevin Stocker	.10
184	Jay Bell	.10
185	Steve Cooke	.10
186	Ravelo Manzanillo	.10
187	Al Martin	.10
188	Denny Neagle	.10
189	Don Slaught	.10
190	Paul Wagner	.10
191	Rene Arocha	.10
192	Bernard Gilkey	.10
193	Jose Oquendo	.10
194	Tom Pagnozzi	.10
195	Ozzie Smith	1.50
196	Allen Watson	.10
197	Mark Whiten	.10
198	Andy Ashby	.10
199	Donnie Elliott	.10
200	Bryce Florie	.10
201	Tony Gwynn	1.50
202	Trevor Hoffman	.10
203	Brian Johnson	.10
204	Tim Mauser	.10
205	Bip Roberts	.10
206	Rod Beck	.10
207	Barry Bonds	3.00
208	Royce Clayton	.10
209	Darren Lewis	.10
210	Mark Portugal	.10
211	Kevin Rogers	.10
212	William Van Landingham	.10
213	Matt Williams	.10
214	Checklist	.10
215	Checklist	.10
216	Checklist	.10
217	Bret Barberie	.10
218	Armando Benitez	.10
219	Kevin Brown	.10
220	Sid Fernandez	.10
221	Chris Hoiles	.10
222	Doug Jones	.10
223	Ben McDonald	.10
224	Rafael Palmeiro	.75
225	Andy Van Slyke	.10
226	Jose Canseco	.40
227	Vaughn Eshelman	.10
228	Mike Macfarlane	.10
229	Tim Naehring	.10
230	Frank Rodriguez	.10
231	Lee Tinsley	.10
232	Mark Whiten	.10
233	Garret Anderson	.10
234	Chili Davis	.10
235	Jim Edmonds	.10
236	Mark Langston	.10
237	Troy Percival	.10
238	Tony Phillips	.10
239	Lee Smith	.10
240	Jim Abbott	.10
241	James Baldwin	.10
242	Mike Devereaux	.10
243	Ray Durham	.10
244	Alex Fernandez	.10
245	Roberto Hernandez	.10
246	Lance Johnson	.10
247	Ron Karkovice	.10
248	Tim Raines	.10
249	Sandy Alomar Jr.	.10
250	Orel Hershiser	.10
251	Julian Tavarez	.10
252	Jim Thome	.65
253	Omar Vizquel	.10
254	Dave Winfield	1.00
255	Chad Curtis	.10
256	Kirk Gibson	.10
257	Mike Henneman	.10
258	Bob Higginson RC	.25
259	Felipe Lira	.10
260	Rudy Pemberton	.10
261	Alan Trammell	.10
262	Kevin Appier	.10
263	Pat Borders	.10
264	Tom Gordon	.10
265	Jose Lind	.10
266	Jon Nunnally	.10
267	Dilson Torres	.10
268	Michael Tucker	.10
269	Jeff Cirillo	.10
270	Darryl Hamilton	.10
271	David Hulse	.10
272	Mark Kiefer	.10
273	Graeme Lloyd	.10
274	Joe Oliver	.10
275	Al Reyes	.10
276	Kevin Seitzer	.10
277	Rick Aguilera	.10
278	Marty Cordova	.10
279	Scott Erickson	.10
280	LaTroy Hawkins	.10
281	Brad Radke	.10
282	Kevin Tapani	.10
283	Tony Fernandez	.10
284	Sterling Hitchcock	.10
285	Pat Kelly	.10
286	Jack McDowell	.10
287	Andy Pettitte	.30
288	Mike Stanley	.10
289	John Wetteland	.10
290	Bernie Williams	.10
291	Mark Acre	.10
292	Geronimo Berroa	.10
293	Dennis Eckersley	.75
294	Steve Ontiveros	.10
295	Ruben Sierra	.10
296	Terry Steinbach	.10
297	Dave Stewart	.10
298	Todd Stottlemyre	.10
299	Darren Bragg	.10
300	Joey Cora	.10
301	Edgar Martinez	.10
302	Bill Risley	.10
303	Ron Villone	.10
304	Dan Wilson	.10
305	Benji Gil	.10
306	Wilson Heredia	.10
307	Mark McLemore	.10
308	Otis Nixon	.10
309	Kenny Rogers	.10
310	Jeff Russell	.10
311	Mickey Tettleton	.10
312	Bob Tewksbury	.10
313	David Cone	.10
314	Carlos Delgado	.50
315	Alex Gonzalez	.10
316	Shawn Green	.10
317	Paul Molitor	1.00
318	Ed Sprague	.10
319	Devon White	.10
320	Steve Avery	.10
321	Jeff Blauser	.10
322	Brad Clontz	.10
323	Tom Glavine	.30
324	Marquis Grissom	.10
325	Chipper Jones	1.50
326	Dave Justice	.10
327	Mark Lemke	.10
328	Kent Mercker	.10
329	Jason Schmidt	.10
330	Steve Buechele	.10
331	Kevin Foster	.10
332	Mark Grace	.10
333	Brian McRae	.10
334	Sammy Sosa	1.50
335	Ozzie Timmons	.10
336	Rick Wilkins	.10
337	Hector Carrasco	.10
338	Ron Gant	.10
339	Barry Larkin	.10
340	Deion Sanders	.15
341	Benito Santiago	.10
342	Roger Bailey	.10
343	Jason Bates	.10
344	Dante Bichette	.10
345	Joe Girardi	.10
346	Bill Swift	.10
347	Mark Thompson	.10
348	Larry Walker	.10
349	Kurt Abbott	.10
350	John Burkett	.10
351	Chuck Carr	.10
352	Andre Dawson	.30
353	Chris Hammond	.10
354	Charles Johnson	.10
355	Terry Pendleton	.10
356	Quilvio Veras	.10
357	Derek Bell	.10
358	Jim Dougherty	.10
359	Doug Drabek	.10

360	Todd Jones	.10
361	Orlando Miller	.10
362	James Mouton	.10
363	Phil Plantier	.10
364	Shane Reynolds	.10
365	Todd Hollandsworth	.10
366	Eric Karros	.10
367	Ramon Martinez	.10
368	Hideo Nomo RC	3.00
369	Jose Offerman	.10
370	Antonio Osuna	.10
371	Todd Williams	.10
372	Shane Andrews	.10
373	Wil Cordero	.10
374	Jeff Fassero	.10
375	Darrin Fletcher	.10
376	Mark Grudzielanek RC	.50
377	Carlos Perez RC	.25
378	Mel Rojas	.10
379	Tony Tarasco	.10
380	Edgardo Alfonzo	.10
381	Brett Butler	.10
382	Carl Everett	.10
383	John Franco	.10
384	Pete Harnisch	.10
385	Bobby Jones	.10
386	Dave Mlicki	.10
387	Jose Vizcaino	.10
388	Ricky Bottalico	.10
389	Tyler Green	.10
390	Charlie Hayes	.10
391	Dave Hollins	.10
392	Gregg Jefferies	.10
393	Michael Mimbs RC	.10
394	Mickey Morandini	.10
395	Curt Schilling	.30
396	Heathcliff Slocumb	.10
397	Jason Christiansen	.10
398	Midre Cummings	.10
399	Carlos Garcia	.10
400	Mark Johnson	.10
401	Jeff King	.10
402	Jon Lieber	.10
403	Esteban Loaiza	.10
404	Orlando Merced	.10
405	Gary Wilson RC	.10
406	Scott Cooper	.10
407	Tom Henke	.10
408	Ken Hill	.10
409	Danny Jackson	.10
410	Brian Jordan	.10
411	Ray Lankford	.10
412	John Mabry	.10
413	Todd Zeile	.10
414	Andy Benes	.10
415	Andres Berumen	.10
416	Ken Caminiti	.10
417	Andujar Cedeno	.10
418	Steve Finley	.10
419	Joey Hamilton	.10
420	Dustin Hermanson	.10
421	Melvin Nieves	.10
422	Roberto Petagine	.10
423	Eddie Williams	.10
424	Glenallen Hill	.10
425	Kirt Manwaring	.10
426	Terry Mulholland	.10
427	J.R. Phillips	.10
428	Joe Rosselli	.10
429	Robby Thompson	.10
430	Checklist	.10
431	Checklist	.10
432	Checklist	.10

Cal Ripken, Jr. Enduring Flair

The career of Cal Ripken, Jr., is traced in this insert set found in Series 2 Flair at the average rate of once per dozen packs. Each card has a vintage photo on front, with large silver-foil "ENDURING" logo toward bottom. Backs have another color photo, a quote and other information about the milestone. The series was extended by a special mail-in offer for five additional cards which chronicled Ripken's record-breaking 1995 season.

	NM/M
Complete Set (15):	40.00
Common Card:	4.00
Rookie Of The Year	4.00
1st MVP Season	4.00
World Series Highlight	4.00
Family Tradition	4.00

5	8,243 Consecutive Innings	4.00
6	95 Consecutive Errorless Games	4.00
7	All-Star MVP	4.00
8	1,000th RBI	4.00
9	287th Home Run	4.00
10	2,000th Consecutive Game	4.00
11	Record-tying Game	6.00
12	Record-breaking Game	6.00
13	Defensive Prowess	4.00
14	Literacy Work	6.00
15	2,153 and Counting	6.00

Hot Gloves

The cream of the crop among Series 2 Flair inserts is this set featuring fine fielders. Cards have a background of an embossed gold-foil glove, with a color player photo centered in front. Silver foil comprises the card title and player name at bottom and the Flair logo at top. Backs have a white background, a photo of a glove with a career summary overprinted and a player portrait photo in a lower corner. These inserts are found at the average rate of once per 25 packs.

		NM/M
Complete Set (12):		35.00
Common Player:		1.25
1	Roberto Alomar	2.00
2	Barry Bonds	10.00
3	Ken Griffey Jr.	7.50
4	Marquis Grissom	1.25
5	Barry Larkin	1.25
6	Darren Lewis	1.25
7	Kenny Lofton	1.25
8	Don Mattingly	6.00
9	Cal Ripken Jr.	10.00
10	Ivan Rodriguez	2.50
11	Devon White	1.25
12	Matt Williams	1.25

Hot Numbers

These Series 1 inserts are a 1:9 find. Gold metallic-foil background with 1994 seasonal stat numbers are the background for a color action photo on front. Horizontal backs have a ghosted portrait photo at right and career highlights at left.

		NM/M
Complete Set (10):		10.00
Common Player:		.50
1	Jeff Bagwell	1.00
2	Albert Belle	.50
3	Barry Bonds	2.25
4	Ken Griffey Jr.	2.00
5	Kenny Lofton	.50
6	Greg Maddux	1.25
7	Mike Piazza	2.00
8	Cal Ripken Jr.	2.25
9	Frank Thomas	1.00
10	Matt Williams	.50

Infield Power

Power rays and waves emitting from the player's bat in an action photo are the front design of this Series 2 chase set. The card ti-

tle, name and team at bottom, and the Flair logo at top are in silver foil. Backs repeat the wave theme with a player photo on one end and a career summary at the other. These inserts are seeded at the average rate of one per five packs.

		NM/M
Complete Set (10):		4.00
Common Player:		.25
1	Jeff Bagwell	.75
2	Darren Daulton	.25
3	Cecil Fielder	.25
4	Andres Galarraga	.25
5	Fred McGriff	.25
6	Rafael Palmeiro	.65
7	Mike Piazza	1.50
8	Frank Thomas	1.00
9	Mo Vaughn	.25
10	Matt Williams	.25

Outfield Power

Laser-like colored rays are the background to the action photo on front and portrait on back of this series. The card title, player identification and Flair logo on front are in silver foil. Backs are horizontal, silver-foil enhanced and include a career summary. This chase set is seeded at the average rate of one card per six packs of Series 1 Flair.

		NM/M
Complete Set (10):		4.00
Common Player:		.25
1	Albert Belle	.25
2	Dante Bichette	.25
3	Barry Bonds	2.00
4	Jose Canseco	.50
5	Joe Carter	.25
6	Juan Gonzalez	.50
7	Ken Griffey Jr.	1.00
8	Kirby Puckett	.75
9	Gary Sheffield	.50
10	Ruben Sierra	.25

Today's Spotlight

The premier insert set in Flair Series I, found once every 30 packs or so, this die-cut issue has the player action photo spotlighted in a 2-3/8" bright white oval, with the rest of the photo muted in gray and dark gray. The card title, Flair logo, play- er name and team are in silver foil. The horizontal backs have a player portrait photo in the spotlight and career summary on the side.

		NM/M
Complete Set (12):		15.00
Common Player:		1.00
1	Jeff Bagwell	3.00
2	Jason Bere	1.00
3	Cliff Floyd	1.00
4	Chuck Knoblauch	1.00
5	Kenny Lofton	1.00
6	Javier Lopez	1.00
7	Raul Mondesi	1.00
8	Mike Mussina	1.50
9	Mike Piazza	5.00
10	Manny Ramirez	3.00
11	Tim Salmon	1.00
12	Frank Thomas	3.00

Wave Of The Future

The cream of baseball's rookie crop is featured in this Series 2 insert set, found once per eight packs on average. Fronts have a graduated color background with a baseball/wave morph, which is repeated at the bottom in silver foil, along with the player name. A color action photo is at center. The player's name, team and "Wave of the Future" are repeated in horizontal rows behind the photo. Horizontal backs repeat the wave logo, have another player photo and a career summary.

		NM/M
Complete Set (10):		7.50
Common Player:		.35
1	Jason Bates	.25
2	Armando Benitez	.25
3	Marty Cordova	.25
4	Ray Durham	.25
5	Vaughn Eshelman	.25
6	Carl Everett	.25
7	Shawn Green	1.50
8	Dustin Hermanson	.25
9	Chipper Jones	4.00
10	Hideo Nomo	1.50

1996 Flair Promotional Sheet

Three samples of Flair's 1996 issue and an information card are included on this 5" x 7" promotional sheet. Sheets are found with either a gold or silver finish.

	NM/M
Complete Sheet:	5.00

1996 Flair

Fleer's 1996 Flair baseball set has 400 cards, a parallel set and four insert types. Regular card fronts have two photos of the featured player; backs have a photo and career statistics. All cards have a silver-foil version and a gold-foil version, with each version appearing in equal numbers. Seven-card packs carried an issue price of $4.99.

		NM/M
Complete Set (400):		50.00

		NM/M
Common Player:		.15
Pack (9):		3.00
Wax Box (18):		40.00
1	Roberto Alomar	.30
2	Brady Anderson	.15
3	Bobby Bonilla	.15
4	Scott Erickson	.15
5	Jeffrey Hammonds	.15
6	Jimmy Haynes	.15
7	Chris Hoiles	.15
8	Kent Mercker	.15
9	Mike Mussina	.50
10	Randy Myers	.15
11	Rafael Palmeiro	.75
12	Cal Ripken Jr.	3.00
(12p)	Cal Ripken Jr./OPS (No card #.)	3.00
13	B.J. Surhoff	.15
14	David Wells	.15
15	Jose Canseco	.50
16	Roger Clemens	1.75
17	Wil Cordero	.15
18	Tom Gordon	.15
19	Mike Greenwell	.15
20	Dwayne Hosey	.15
21	Jose Malave	.15
22	Tim Naehring	.15
23	Troy O'Leary	.15
24	Aaron Sele	.15
25	Heathcliff Slocumb	.15
26	Mike Stanley	.15
27	Jeff Suppan	.15
28	John Valentin	.15
29	Mo Vaughn	.15
30	Tim Wakefield	.15
31	Jim Abbott	.15
32	Garret Anderson	.15
33	George Arias	.15
34	Chili Davis	.15
35	Gary DiSarcina	.15
36	Jim Edmonds	.15
37	Chuck Finley	.15
38	Todd Greene	.15
39	Mark Langston	.15
40	Troy Percival	.15
41	Tim Salmon	.15
42	Lee Smith	.15
43	J.T. Snow	.15
44	Randy Velarde	.15
45	Tim Wallach	.15
46	Wilson Alvarez	.15
47	Harold Baines	.15
48	Jason Bere	.15
49	Ray Durham	.15
50	Alex Fernandez	.15
51	Ozzie Guillen	.15
52	Roberto Hernandez	.15
53	Ron Karkovice	.15
54	Darren Lewis	.15
55	Lyle Mouton	.15
56	Tony Phillips	.15
57	Chris Snopek	.15
58	Kevin Tapani	.15
59	Danny Tartabull	.15
60	Frank Thomas	1.00
61	Robin Ventura	.15
62	Sandy Alomar	.15
63	Carlos Baerga	.15
64	Albert Belle	.15
65	Julio Franco	.15
66	Orel Hershiser	.15
67	Kenny Lofton	.15
68	Dennis Martinez	.15
69	Jack McDowell	.15
70	Jose Mesa	.15
71	Eddie Murray	1.00
72	Charles Nagy	.15
73	Tony Pena	.15
74	Manny Ramirez	1.00
75	Julian Tavarez	.15
76	Jim Thome	.65
77	Omar Vizquel	.15
78	Chad Curtis	.15
79	Cecil Fielder	.15
80	Travis Fryman	.15
81	Chris Gomez	.15
82	Bob Higginson	.15
83	Mark Lewis	.15
84	Felipe Lira	.15
85	Alan Trammell	.15
86	Kevin Appier	.15
87	Johnny Damon	.50
88	Tom Goodwin	.15
89	Mark Gubicza	.15
90	Bob Hamelin	.15
91	Keith Lockhart	.15
92	Jeff Montgomery	.15
93	Jon Nunnally	.15
94	Bip Roberts	.15
95	Michael Tucker	.15
96	Joe Vitiello	.15
97	Ricky Bones	.15
98	Chuck Carr	.15
99	Jeff Cirillo	.15
100	Mike Fetters	.15
101	John Jaha	.15
102	Mike Matheny	.15
103	Ben McDonald	.15
104	Matt Mieske	.15
105	Dave Nilsson	.15
106	Kevin Seitzer	.15
107	Steve Sparks	.15
108	Jose Valentin	.15
109	Greg Vaughn	.15
110	Rick Aguilera	.15
111	Rich Becker	.15
112	Marty Cordova	.15
113	LaTroy Hawkins	.15
114	Dave Hollins	.15
115	Roberto Kelly	.15
116	Chuck Knoblauch	.15
117	Matt Lawton RC	.50
118	Pat Meares	.15
119	Paul Molitor	1.00
120	Kirby Puckett	1.50
121	Brad Radke	.15
122	Frank Rodriguez	.15
123	Scott Stahoviak	.15
124	Matt Walbeck	.15
125	Wade Boggs	1.00
126	David Cone	.15
127	Joe Girardi	.15
128	Dwight Gooden	.15
129	Derek Jeter	3.00
130	Jimmy Key	.15
131	Jim Leyritz	.15
132	Tino Martinez	.15
133	Paul O'Neill	.40
134	Andy Pettitte	.15
135	Tim Raines	.15
136	Ruben Rivera	.15
137	Kenny Rogers	.15
138	Ruben Sierra	.15
139	John Wetteland	.15
140	Bernie Williams	.15
141	Tony Batista RC	.50
142	Allen Battle	.15
143	Geronimo Berroa	.15
144	Mike Bordick	.15
145	Scott Brosius	.15
146	Steve Cox	.15
147	Brent Gates	.15
148	Jason Giambi	.65
149	Doug Johns	.15
150	Mark McGwire	2.50
151	Pedro Munoz	.15
152	Ariel Prieto	.15
153	Terry Steinbach	.15
154	Todd Van Poppel	.15
155	Bobby Ayala	.15
156	Chris Bosio	.15
157	Jay Buhner	.15
158	Joey Cora	.15
159	Russ Davis	.15
160	Ken Griffey Jr.	2.00
161	Sterling Hitchcock	.15
162	Randy Johnson	1.00
163	Edgar Martinez	.15
164	Alex Rodriguez	2.50
165	Paul Sorrento	.15
166	Dan Wilson	.15
167	Will Clark	.15
168	Benji Gil	.15
169	Juan Gonzalez	.50
170	Rusty Greer	.15
171	Kevin Gross	.15
172	Darryl Hamilton	.15
173	Mike Henneman	.15
174	Ken Hill	.15
175	Mark McLemore	.15
176	Dean Palmer	.15
177	Roger Pavlik	.15
178	Ivan Rodriguez	.75
179	Mickey Tettleton	.15
180	Bobby Witt	.15
181	Joe Carter	.15
182	Felipe Crespo	.15
183	Alex Gonzalez	.15
184	Shawn Green	.40
185	Juan Guzman	.15
186	Erik Hanson	.15
187	Pat Hentgen	.15
188	Sandy Martinez RC	.15
189	Otis Nixon	.15
190	John Olerud	.15
191	Paul Quantrill	.15
192	Bill Risley	.15
193	Ed Sprague	.15
194	Steve Avery	.15
195	Jeff Blauser	.15
196	Brad Clontz	.15
197	Jermaine Dye	.15
198	Tom Glavine	.40
199	Marquis Grissom	.15
200	Chipper Jones	1.50
201	David Justice	.15
202	Ryan Klesko	.15
203	Mark Lemke	.15
204	Javier Lopez	.15
205	Greg Maddux	1.50
206	Fred McGriff	.15
207	Greg McMichael	.15
208	Wonderful Monds	.15
209	Jason Schmidt	.15
210	John Smoltz	.15
211	Mark Wohlers	.15

#	Player	Price
212	Jim Bullinger	.15
213	Frank Castillo	.15
214	Kevin Foster	.15
215	Luis Gonzalez	.15
216	Mark Grace	.15
217	Robin Jennings RC	.15
218	Doug Jones	.15
219	Dave Magadan	.15
220	Brian McRae	.15
221	Jaime Navarro	.15
222	Rey Sanchez	.15
223	Ryne Sandberg	1.50
224	Scott Servais	.15
225	Sammy Sosa	1.50
226	Ozzie Timmons	.15
227	Bret Boone	.15
228	Jeff Branson	.15
229	Jeff Brantley	.15
230	Dave Burba	.15
231	Vince Coleman	.15
232	Steve Gibralter	.15
233	Mike Kelly	.15
234	Barry Larkin	.15
235	Hal Morris	.15
236	Mark Portugal	.15
237	Jose Rijo	.15
238	Reggie Sanders	.15
239	Pete Schourek	.15
240	John Smiley	.15
241	Eddie Taubensee	.15
242	Jason Bates	.15
243	Dante Bichette	.15
244	Ellis Burks	.15
245	Vinny Castilla	.15
246	Andres Galarraga	.15
247	Darren Holmes	.15
248	Curt Leskanic	.15
249	Steve Reed	.15
250	Kevin Ritz	.15
251	Bret Saberhagen	.15
252	Bill Swift	.15
253	Larry Walker	.15
254	Walt Weiss	.15
255	Eric Young	.15
256	Kurt Abbott	.15
257	Kevin Brown	.15
258	John Burkett	.15
259	Greg Colbrunn	.15
260	Jeff Conine	.15
261	Andre Dawson	.40
262	Chris Hammond	.15
263	Charles Johnson	.15
264	Al Leiter	.15
265	Robb Nen	.15
266	Terry Pendleton	.15
267	Pat Rapp	.15
268	Gary Sheffield	.50
269	Quilvio Veras	.15
270	Devon White	.15
271	Bob Abreu	.15
272	Jeff Bagwell	1.00
273	Derek Bell	.15
274	Sean Berry	.15
275	Craig Biggio	.15
276	Doug Drabek	.15
277	Tony Eusebio	.15
278	Richard Hidalgo	.15
279	Brian Hunter	.15
280	Todd Jones	.15
281	Derrick May	.15
282	Orlando Miller	.15
283	James Mouton	.15
284	Shane Reynolds	.15
285	Greg Swindell	.15
286	Mike Blowers	.15
287	Brett Butler	.15
288	Tom Candiotti	.15
289	Roger Cedeno	.15
290	Delino DeShields	.15
291	Greg Gagne	.15
292	Karim Garcia	.15
293	Todd Hollandsworth	.15
294	Eric Karros	.15
295	Ramon Martinez	.15
296	Raul Mondesi	.15
297	Hideo Nomo	.50
298	Mike Piazza	2.00
299	Ismael Valdes	.15
300	Todd Worrell	.15
301	Moises Alou	.15
302	Shane Andrews	.15
303	Yamil Benitez	.15
304	Jeff Fassero	.15
305	Darrin Fletcher	.15
306	Cliff Floyd	.15
307	Mark Grudzielanek	.15
308	Mike Lansing	.15
309	Pedro Martinez	1.00
310	Ryan McGuire	.15
311	Carlos Perez	.15
312	Mel Rojas	.15
313	David Segui	.15
314	Rondell White	.15
315	Edgardo Alfonzo	.15
316	Rico Brogna	.15
317	Carl Everett	.15
318	John Franco	.15
319	Bernard Gilkey	.15
320	Todd Hundley	.15
321	Jason Isringhausen	.15
322	Lance Johnson	.15
323	Bobby Jones	.15
324	Jeff Kent	.15
325	Rey Ordonez	.15
326	Bill Pulsipher	.15
327	Jose Vizcaino	.15
328	Paul Wilson	.15
329	Ricky Bottalico	.15

#	Player	Price
330	Darren Daulton	.15
331	David Doster RC	.15
332	Lenny Dykstra	.15
333	Jim Eisenreich	.15
334	Sid Fernandez	.15
335	Gregg Jefferies	.15
336	Mickey Morandini	.15
337	Benito Santiago	.15
338	Curt Schilling	.40
339	Kevin Stocker	.15
340	David West	.15
341	Mark Whiten	.15
342	Todd Zeile	.15
343	Jay Bell	.15
344	John Ericks	.15
345	Carlos Garcia	.15
346	Charlie Hayes	.15
347	Jason Kendall	.15
348	Jeff King	.15
349	Mike Kingery	.15
350	Al Martin	.15
351	Orlando Merced	.15
352	Dan Miceli	.15
353	Denny Neagle	.15
354	Alan Benes	.15
355	Andy Benes	.15
356	Royce Clayton	.15
357	Dennis Eckersley	.75
358	Gary Gaetti	.15
359	Ron Gant	.15
360	Brian Jordan	.15
361	Ray Lankford	.15
362	John Mabry	.15
363	T.J. Mathews	.15
364	Mike Morgan	.15
365	Donovan Osborne	.15
366	Tom Pagnozzi	.15
367	Ozzie Smith	1.50
368	Todd Stottlemyre	.15
369	Andy Ashby	.15
370	Brad Ausmus	.15
371	Ken Caminiti	.15
372	Andujar Cedeno	.15
373	Steve Finley	.15
374	Tony Gwynn	1.50
375	Joey Hamilton	.15
376	Rickey Henderson	1.00
377	Trevor Hoffman	.15
378	Wally Joyner	.15
379	Marc Newfield	.15
380	Jody Reed	.15
381	Bob Tewksbury	.15
382	Fernando Valenzuela	.15
383	Rod Beck	.15
384	Barry Bonds	3.00
385	Mark Carreon	.15
386	Shawon Dunston	.15
387	Osvaldo Fernandez RC	.40
388	Glenallen Hill	.15
389	Stan Javier	.15
390	Mark Leiter	.15
391	Kirt Manwaring	.15
392	Robby Thompson	.15
393	William Van Landingham	.15
394	Allen Watson	.15
395	Matt Williams	.15
396	Checklist	.15
397	Checklist	.15
398	Checklist	.15
399	Checklist	.15
400	Checklist	.15

cards, a design first made popular in 1994. Hot Gloves can only be found in hobby packs, at a rate of one per every 90 packs.

		NM/M
Complete Set (10):		60.00
Common Player:		3.00
1	Roberto Alomar	4.00
2	Barry Bonds	15.00
3	Will Clark	3.00
4	Ken Griffey Jr.	10.00
5	Kenny Lofton	3.00
6	Greg Maddux	7.50
7	Mike Piazza	10.00
8	Cal Ripken Jr.	15.00
9	Ivan Rodriguez	4.00
10	Matt Williams	3.00

Powerline

Ten of baseball's top sluggers are featured on these Flair inserts. They are the easiest of the Flair inserts to obtain; seeded one per six packs. Fronts combine yellow-green artwork with the player photo. Backs have a vertical color photo and career information.

		NM/M
Complete Set (10):		6.00
Common Player:		.25
1	Albert Belle	.25
2	Barry Bonds	2.00
3	Juan Gonzalez	.35
4	Ken Griffey Jr.	.75
5	Mark McGwire	1.00
6	Mike Piazza	.75
7	Manny Ramirez	.50
8	Sammy Sosa	.65
9	Frank Thomas	.50
10	Matt Williams	.25

Wave of the Future

These inserts feature up-and-coming young talent in baseball. Twenty 1996 rookies and prospects are printed on lenticular cards. They are seeded one per every 72 packs.

		NM/M
Complete Set (20):		30.00
Common Player:		2.00
1	Bob Abreu	3.00
2	George Arias	2.00
3	Tony Batista	2.00

4	Alan Benes	2.00
5	Yamil Benitez	2.00
6	Steve Cox	2.00
7	David Doster	2.00
8	Jermaine Dye	2.00
9	Osvaldo Fernandez	2.00
10	Karim Garcia	3.00
11	Steve Gibralter	2.00
12	Todd Greene	2.00
13	Richard Hidalgo	2.00
14	Robin Jennings	2.00
15	Jason Kendall	2.00
16	Jose Malave	2.00
17	Wonderful Monds	2.00
18	Rey Ordonez	2.00
19	Ruben Rivera	2.00
20	Paul Wilson	2.00

1997 Flair Showcase Promo Strip

The concept of Flair Showcase's Style-Grace-Showcase set composition is debuted on this 7-1/2" x 3-1/2" strip featuring three cards of Alex Rodriguez. The cards are overprinted in gold on front and black on back with "PROMOTIONAL SAMPLE."

	NM/M
Complete Strip (3):	5.00

Row 2 (Style)

The 1997 Flair issue is actually three different versions of a 180-player set printed on a super-glossy thick stock. The most common version, Style, is designated Row 2 on back. Fronts have a color action photo with a black-and-white portrait image in the background, all printed on silver foil. Cards #1-60 are designated "Showtime" on back; #61-120 are "Showpiece" and #121-180 are labeled "Showstopper" and were inserted in varying ratios: Showtime - 1.5:1; Showpiece 1:1.5 and Showstopper 1:1. Cards were sold exclusively at hobby shops in five-card packs for $4.99.

	NM/M
Complete Set (180):	15.00
Common Showtime (1-60):	.15
Common Showpiece (61-120):	.25
Common Showstopper (121-180):	.20
A-Rod Glove Exchange:	125.00
Pack (5):	2.00
Wax Box (24):	35.00
1	Andruw Jones	1.25
2	Derek Jeter	3.00
3	Alex Rodriguez	2.25
4	Paul Molitor	1.25
5	Jeff Bagwell	1.25
6	Scott Rolen	1.00
7	Kenny Lofton	.15
8	Cal Ripken Jr.	3.00
9	Brady Anderson	.15
10	Chipper Jones	1.50
11	Todd Greene	.15
12	Todd Walker	.15
13	Billy Wagner	.15
14	Craig Biggio	.15
15	Kevin Orie	.15
16	Hideo Nomo	.65
17	Kevin Appier	.15
18	Bubba Trammell RC	.65
19	Juan Gonzalez	.65
20	Randy Johnson	1.25
21	Roger Clemens	1.75
22	Johnny Damon	.35
23	Ryne Sandberg	1.50
24	Ken Griffey Jr.	2.00
25	Barry Bonds	.75
26	Nomar Garciaparra	1.50
27	Vladimir Guerrero	1.25
28	Ron Gant	.15

29	Joe Carter	.15
30	Tim Salmon	.15
31	Mike Piazza	2.00
32	Barry Larkin	.15
33	Manny Ramirez	1.25
34	Sammy Sosa	1.50
35	Frank Thomas	1.50
36	Melvin Nieves	.15
37	Tony Gwynn	1.50
38	Gary Sheffield	.35
39	Darin Erstad	.50
40	Ken Caminiti	.15
41	Jermaine Dye	.15
42	Mo Vaughn	.35
43	Raul Mondesi	.15
44	Greg Maddux	1.50
45	Chuck Knoblauch	.15
46	Andy Pettitte	.50
47	Deion Sanders	.15
48	Albert Belle	.15
49	Jamey Wright	.15
50	Rey Ordonez	.15
51	Bernie Williams	.15
52	Mark McGwire	2.25
53	Mike Mussina	.50
54	Bob Abreu	.20
55	Reggie Sanders	.15
56	Brian Jordan	.15
57	Ivan Rodriguez	1.00
58	Roberto Alomar	.30
59	Tim Naehring	.15
60	Edgar Renteria	.15
61	Dean Palmer	.25
62	Benito Santiago	.25
63	David Cone	.25
64	Carlos Delgado	.75
65	Brian Giles RC	.75
66	Alex Ochoa	.25
67	Rondell White	.25
68	Robin Ventura	.25
69	Eric Karros	.25
70	Jose Valentin	.25
71	Rafael Palmeiro	1.00
72	Chris Snopek	.25
73	David Justice	.25
74	Tom Glavine	.45
75	Rudy Pemberton	.25
76	Larry Walker	.75
77	Jim Thome	.75
78	Charles Johnson	.25
79	Dante Powell	.25
80	Derrek Lee	.75
81	Jason Kendall	.25
82	Todd Hollandsworth	.25
83	Bernard Gilkey	.25
84	Mel Rojas	.25
85	Dmitri Young	.25
86	Bret Boone	.25
87	Pat Hentgen	.25
88	Bobby Bonilla	.25
89	John Wetteland	.25
90	Todd Hundley	.25
91	Wilton Guerrero	.25
92	Geronimo Berroa	.25
93	Al Martin	.25
94	Danny Tartabull	.25
95	Brian McRae	.25
96	Steve Finley	.25
97	Todd Stottlemyre	.25
98	John Smoltz	.25
99	Matt Williams	.25
100	Eddie Murray	1.25
101	Henry Rodriguez	.25
102	Marty Cordova	.25
103	Juan Guzman	.25
104	Chili Davis	.25
105	Eric Young	.25
106	Jeff Abbott	.25
107	Shannon Stewart	.25
108	Rocky Coppinger	.25
109	Jose Canseco	.65
110	Dante Bichette	.25
111	Dwight Gooden	.25
112	Scott Brosius	.25
113	Steve Avery	.25
114	Andres Galarraga	.25
115	Sandy Alomar Jr.	.25
116	Ray Lankford	.25
117	Jorge Posada	.25
118	Ryan Klesko	.25
119	Jay Buhner	.25
120	Jose Guillen	.25
121	Paul O'Neill	.20
122	Jimmy Key	.20
123	Hal Morris	.20
124	Travis Fryman	.20
125	Jim Edmonds	.20
126	Jeff Cirillo	.20
127	Fred McGriff	.20
128	Alan Benes	.20
129	Derek Bell	.20
130	Tony Graffanino	.20
131	Shawn Green	.40
132	Denny Neagle	.20
133	Alex Fernandez	.20
134	Mickey Morandini	.20
135	Royce Clayton	.20
136	Jose Mesa	.20
137	Edgar Martinez	.20
138	Curt Schilling	.40
139	Lance Johnson	.20
140	Andy Benes	.20
141	Charles Nagy	.20
142	Mariano Rivera	.40
143	Mark Wohlers	.20
144	Ken Hill	.20
145	Jay Bell	.20
146	Bob Higginson	.20

147	Mark Grudzielanek	.20
148	Ray Durham	.20
149	John Olerud	.20
150	Joey Hamilton	.20
151	Trevor Hoffman	.20
152	Dan Wilson	.20
153	J.T. Snow	.20
155	Marquis Grissom	.20
156	Yamil Benitez	.20
156	Rusty Greer	.20
157	Darryl Kile	.20
158	Ismael Valdes	.20
159	Jeff Conine	.20
160	Darren Daulton	.20
161	Chan Ho Park	.20
162	Troy Percival	.20
163	Wade Boggs	1.50
164	Dave Nilsson	.20
165	Vinny Castilla	.20
166	Kevin Brown	.20
167	Dennis Eckersley	1.00
168	Wendell Magee Jr.	.20
169	John Jaha	.20
170	Garret Anderson	.20
171	Jason Giambi	.75
172	Mark Grace	.15
173	Tony Clark	.20
174	Moises Alou	.20
175	Brett Butler	.20
176	Cecil Fielder	.20
177	Chris Widger	.20
178	Doug Drabek	.20
179	Ellis Burks	.20
180	Shigetosi Hasegawa	.20

Row 1 (Grace)

The second level of '97 Flair scarcity is represented by the Row 1/Grace cards (so designated on back). These are visually differentiated on front by the use of a full background to the action photo and the addition of a color portrait. Row 1/Grace cards are further broken down by their designation on back as: "Showstopper" (#1-60 seeded 1:2.5 packs), "Showtime" (#61-120; 1:2) and "Showpiece" (#121-180; 1:3) with varying insertion rates as shown.

	NM/M
Complete Set (180):	50.00
Common Showstopper (1-60):	.35
Stars:	1.5X
Common Showtime (#61-120):	.1X
Stars:	.1X
Common Showpiece (#121-180):	.6X
Stars:	1.5X

Row 0 (Showcase)

The scarcest level of '97 Flair is the Row 0/Showcase cards (so designated on front and back). These are identifiable on front by the use of a color portrait in the foreground, with a large action photo behind, printed on a gold-flecked metallic background. Row 0/Showcase cards are further broken down by their designation on back as: "Showpiece" (#1-60 seeded 1:24 packs), "Showstopper" (#61-120; 1:12) and "Showtime" (#121-180; 1:5) with varying insertion rates as shown.

	NM/M
Complete Set (180):	200.
Common Showpiece (1-60):	1.
Stars:	
Common Showstopper (61-120):	
Stars:	
Common Showtime (121-180):	
Stars:	

Legacy Collection

This 540-card parallel set printed on matte-finish stock rather than the high-gloss of the regular cards. Front graphic highlights are in blue foil, as is the serial number on back from within each card...

Diamond Cuts

Ten of the game's top stars are showcased on these 1996 Flair inserts. They are seeded one per 20 packs. Fronts have a textured background rainbow metallic foil and silver glitter.

		NM/M
Complete Set (12):		25.00
Common Player:		1.00
1	Jeff Bagwell	2.50
2	Albert Belle	1.00
3	Barry Bonds	6.00
4	Juan Gonzalez	1.25
5	Ken Griffey Jr.	4.00
6	Greg Maddux	3.00
7	Eddie Murray	2.50
8	Mike Piazza	4.00
9	Cal Ripken Jr.	6.00
10	Frank Thomas	2.50
11	Mo Vaughn	1.00
12	Matt Williams	1.00

Hot Gloves

Ten top defensive players are highlighted on these die-cut insert edition of just 100. Stated odds of insertion are one per 30 packs. Because all Legacies are printed in identical numbers, there is no premium for cards of different rows.

	NM/M
Common Player:	10.00
Stars:	25X

Legacy Masterpiece

The insert card chase reached its inevitable zenith with the creation of this series of one-of-a-kind inserts. Each of the 180 players' three cards (Row 2/Style, Row 1/Grace, Row 0/Showcase) in the '97 Flair Legacy Collection was also produced in an edition of one card and inserted at a rate of about one per 3,000 packs. Instead of the blue metallic foil highlights on front and back of the regular Legacy cards, the one-of-a-kind Masterpieces are highlighted in purple and carry a notation on back, "The Only 1 of 1 Masterpiece." Because of the unique nature of each card, value depends solely on demand, thus presentation of meaningful "catalog" values is not possible.

	NM/M
Common Player:	100.00

Diamond Cuts

This 20-card insert, found 1:20 packs, features a die-cut design with an action photo of the player appearing above a baseball diamond in the lower background.

		NM/M
Complete Set (20):		55.00
Common Player:		1.50
1	Jeff Bagwell	3.00
2	Albert Belle	1.50
3	Ken Caminiti	1.50
4	Juan Gonzalez	2.00
5	Ken Griffey Jr.	4.50
6	Tony Gwynn	4.00
7	Todd Hundley	1.50
8	Andruw Jones	3.00
9	Chipper Jones	4.00
10	Greg Maddux	4.00
11	Mark McGwire	5.00
12	Mike Piazza	4.50

13	Derek Jeter	6.00
14	Manny Ramirez	3.00
15	Cal Ripken Jr.	6.00
16	Alex Rodriguez	5.00
17	Frank Thomas	3.00
18	Mo Vaughn	1.50
19	Bernie Williams	1.50
20	Matt Williams	1.50

Hot Gloves

Inserted 1:90 packs, Hot Gloves features 15 cards with a die-cut "flaming glove" design printed in thermally active inks and saluting some of baseball's best defensive players.

		NM/M
Complete Set (15):		125.00
Common Player:		2.50
1	Roberto Alomar	3.00
2	Barry Bonds	20.00
3	Juan Gonzalez	6.00
4	Ken Griffey Jr.	15.00
5	Marquis Grissom	2.50
6	Derek Jeter	20.00
7	Chipper Jones	12.00
8	Barry Larkin	2.50
9	Kenny Lofton	2.50
10	Greg Maddux	12.00
11	Mike Piazza	15.00
12	Cal Ripken Jr.	20.00
13	Alex Rodriguez	17.50
14	Ivan Rodriguez	7.50
15	Frank Thomas	10.00

Wave of the Future

This insert focuses on some of the up-and-coming young stars in the game. Cards were seeded 1:4 packs. A large ocean wave makes up the background of each card front.

		NM/M
Complete Set (27):		10.00
Common Player:		.25
1	Todd Greene	.25
2	Andruw Jones	1.50
3	Randall Simon	.25
4	Wady Almonte	.25
5	Pat Cline	.25
6	Jeff Abbott	.25
7	Justin Towle	.25
8	Richie Sexson	.25
9	Bubba Trammell	.25
10	Bob Abreu	.35
11	David Arias (Last name actually Ortiz.)	9.00
12	Todd Walker	.25
13	Orlando Cabrera	.25
14	Vladimir Guerrero	1.50
15	Ricky Ledee	.25
16	Jorge Posada	.25
17	Ruben Rivera	.25
18	Scott Spiezio	.25
19	Scott Rolen	1.00
20	Emil Brown	.25
21	Jose Guillen	.25
22	T.J. Staton	.25
23	Elieser Marrero	.25
24	Fernando Tatis	.25
25	Ryan Jones	.25
WF1	Hideki Irabu	.25
WF2	Jose Cruz Jr.	.25

1998 Flair Showcase Promo Strip

Each of the Row 0, 1, 2 and 3 variations of Cal Ripken's cards are

featured on this 10" x 3-1/2" promo strip. The front of each card has "PROMOTIONAL SAMPLE" printed diagonally in gold; on the back the notice is printed in black-and-white.

	NM/M
Complete Promo Strip:	5.00

1998 Flair Showcase Row 3

Row 3, or Flair, cards are considered the base cards of '98 Showcase. They feature a close-up black-and-white portrait photo in the background and an action shot in front, overprinted on a silver-foil background. Flair/Showtime (#1-30) cards are inserted 1:.9 packs, Flair/Showstopper (#31-60) are found 1:1.1 packs, Flair/Showdown (#61-90) cards are inserted 1:1.5 packs and Flair/Showdown (#91-120) cards are inserted 1:2 packs.

		NM/M
Complete Set (120):		20.00
Common Player (1-30):		.25
Common Player (31-60):		.25
Common Player (61-90):		.35
Common Player (91-120):		.45
Pack (5):		2.50
Wax Box (24):		45.00
1	Ken Griffey Jr.	2.00
2	Travis Lee	.25
3	Frank Thomas	1.25
4	Ben Grieve	.25
5	Nomar Garciaparra	1.50
6	Jose Cruz Jr.	.25
7	Alex Rodriguez	2.50
8	Cal Ripken Jr.	3.00
9	Mark McGwire	2.50
10	Chipper Jones	1.50
11	Paul Konerko	.40
12	Todd Helton	1.00
13	Greg Maddux	1.50
14	Derek Jeter	3.00
15	Jaret Wright	.25
16	Livan Hernandez	.25
17	Mike Piazza	2.00
18	Juan Encarnacion	.25
19	Tony Gwynn	1.50
20	Scott Rolen	1.00
21	Roger Clemens	1.75
22	Tony Clark	.25
23	Albert Belle	.25
24	Mo Vaughn	.25
25	Andruw Jones	1.25
26	Jason Dickson	.25
27	Fernando Tatis	.25
28	Ivan Rodriguez	.75
29	Ricky Ledee	.25
30	Darin Erstad	.50
31	Brian Rose	.25
32	Magglio Ordonez RC	3.00
33	Larry Walker	.25
34	Bobby Higginson	.25
35	Chili Davis	.25
36	Barry Bonds	3.00
37	Vladimir Guerrero	1.25
38	Jeff Bagwell	1.25
39	Kenny Lofton	.25
40	Ryan Klesko	.25
41	Mike Cameron	.25
42	Charles Johnson	.25
43	Andy Pettitte	.40
44	Juan Gonzalez	1.25
45	Tim Salmon	.25
46	Hideki Irabu	.25
47	Paul Molitor	1.25
48	Edgar Renteria	.25
49	Manny Ramirez	1.25
50	Jim Edmonds	.25
51	Bernie Williams	.25
52	Roberto Alomar	.40
53	David Justice	.25
54	Rey Ordonez	.25
55	Ken Caminiti	.25
56	Jose Guillen	.25
57	Randy Johnson	1.25
58	Brady Anderson	.25
59	Hideo Nomo	.50

60	Tino Martinez	.25
61	John Smoltz	.35
62	Joe Carter	.35
63	Matt Williams	.35
64	Robin Ventura	.35
65	Barry Larkin	.35
66	Dante Bichette	.35
67	Travis Fryman	.35
68	Gary Sheffield	.60
69	Eric Karros	.35
70	Matt Stairs	.35
71	Al Martin	.35
72	Jay Buhner	.35
73	Ray Lankford	.35
74	Carlos Delgado	.65
75	Edgardo Alfonzo	.35
76	Rondell White	.35
77	Chuck Knoblauch	.35
78	Raul Mondesi	.35
79	Johnny Damon	.60
80	Matt Morris	.35
81	Tom Glavine	.60
82	Kevin Brown	.35
83	Garret Anderson	.35
84	Mike Mussina	.40
85	Pedro Martinez	1.25
86	Craig Biggio	.35
87	Darryl Kile	.35
88	Rafael Palmeiro	.75
89	Jim Thome	.60
90	Andres Galarraga	.35
91	Sammy Sosa	1.50
92	Willie Greene	.45
93	Vinny Castilla	.45
94	Justin Thompson	.45
95	Jeff King	.45
96	Jeff Cirillo	.45
97	Mark Grudzielanek	.45
98	Brad Radke	.45
99	John Olerud	.45
100	Curt Schilling	.65
101	Steve Finley	.45
102	J.T. Snow	.45
103	Edgar Martinez	.45
104	Wilson Alvarez	.45
105	Rusty Greer	.45
106	Pat Hentgen	.45
107	David Cone	.45
108	Fred McGriff	.45
109	Jason Giambi	.75
110	Tony Womack	.45
111	Bernard Gilkey	.45
112	Alan Benes	.45
113	Mark Grace	.45
114	Reggie Sanders	.45
115	Moises Alou	.45
116	John Jaha	.45
117	Henry Rodriguez	.45
118	Dean Palmer	.45
119	Mike Lieberthal	.45
120	Shawn Estes	.45

Row 2

Row 2, or Style (as they are designated on front) cards in Flair Showcase are the second easiest type of card to pull from packs. Fronts are similar to Row 3 base cards, but include the entire background of the action photo and have a color portrait photo. Cards #1-30 are inserted one per three packs, #31-60 are found 1:2.5 packs, #61-90 cards are inserted 1:4 and #91-120 are inserted one per three packs.

	NM/M
Complete Set (120):	40.00
Common Player:	.50
Stars:	1.5-2X

Row 1

Row 1, also referred to as Grace, was the second most difficult type of card to pull from Flair Showcase. The front design has an action photo overprinted on a large portrait which is printed on a rainbow metallic-foil background. Cards #1-30 are seeded one per 16 packs, #31-60 are 1:24, #61-90 are 1:6 and #91-120 are 1:10.

	NM/M
Complete Set (1-120):	100.00
Commons (1-30):	1.00
Stars:	2X
Commons (31-60):	1.25
Stars:	3X
Commons (61-90):	.35
Stars:	1X
Commons (91-120):	.75
Stars:	1.5X

Row 0

Row 0 is the most difficult of the four tiers to obtain from packs. Two action photos are combined on a horizontal format with one in a prismatic foil background. The first 30 cards are serially numbered to 250, cards #30-60 are numbered to 500, #61-90 are numbered to 1,000, and #91-120 are numbered within an edition of 2,000.

	NM/M
Complete Set (120):	350.00
Common Player (1-30):	5.00
Stars:	10X
Common Player (31-60):	3.00
Stars:	8X
Common Player (61-90):	2.00
Stars:	6X
Common Player (91-120):	1.00
Stars:	4X

Legacy Collection

Legacy Collection parallels all 480 cards in the Flair Showcase set. Each Legacy Collection card displays the player's name in black plate laminated on the back, with the card's sequential numbering to 100 in gold foil.

	NM/M
Common Player:	7.50
Stars:	25X

Legacy Masterpiece

Each of the 120 players' four cards (Rows 3, 2, 1 and 0) in the '98 Flair Legacy Collection was also produced in an edition of one card and inserted at a rate of about one per 3,000 packs. The one-of-a-kind cards carry a notation on back: "The Only 1 of 1 Masterpiece." With supply a fixed quantity, value depends on demand at any particular time, thus it is not possible to present meaningful "catalog" values.

	NM/M
Common Player:	50.00

Perfect 10

Perfect 10 features the game's most popular players on a silk-screen technology design. The cards were serial numbered to 10 on the back and were inserted into packs of Flair Showcase.

		NM/M
Complete Set (10):		1,600
Common Player:		100.00
1	Ken Griffey Jr.	200.00
2	Cal Ripken Jr.	300.00
3	Frank Thomas	125.00
4	Mike Piazza	200.00
5	Greg Maddux	150.00
6	Nomar Garciaparra	150.00
7	Mark McGwire	250.00
8	Scott Rolen	100.00
9	Alex Rodriguez	250.00
10	Roger Clemens	175.00

Wave of the Future

Twelve up-and-coming players with hot minor league stats and Major League potential are displayed in Wave of the Future. The cards contain a clear acetate card inside a plastic covering that is filled with vegetable oil and glitter. These were inserted one per 20 packs and are numbered with a "WF" prefix.

		NM/M
Complete Set (12):		10.00
Common Player:		.50
WF1	Travis Lee	.50
WF2	Todd Helton	5.00
WF3	Ben Grieve	.50
WF4	Juan Encarnacion	.50
WF5	Brad Fullmer	.50
WF6	Ruben Rivera	.50
WF7	Paul Konerko	.75
WF8	Derrek Lee	1.50
WF9	Mike Lowell	.50
WF10	Magglio Ordonez	2.00
WF11	Rich Butler	.50
WF12	Eli Marrero	.50

1999 Flair Showcase Row 3 (Power)

Power is one of three tiers in 1999 Showcase. The front on this base-level version is rainbow holo-

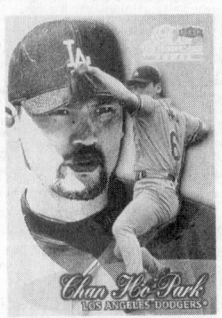

foil including the large portrait photo in the background. In the foreground is a color action photo. Matte textured silver spot embossing is printed over the player's name and team at lower-right. All three Rows of Showcase can be found with three different back designs. Showtime presents traditional annual and career stats. Horizontally formatted Showcase cards have a black-and-white player photo as a "Classic Matchup" of the player's stats to those of a past star. Showdown backs have a color action photo on a brightly-colored wave-pattern background. A stat box at center offers career numbers in four unique categories like day-night, grass-turf, etc. Each of these three back-design levels of scarcity has a different advertised insertion rate. Within Row 3/Power, these vary only between one card in .9 packs, and one card in 1.2 packs, thus there is no practical value differential. Five-card packs of Flair Showcase had a $4.99 SRP.

	NM/M
Complete Set (144):	25.00
Common Player:	.25
Pack (5):	3.00
Wax Box (24):	45.00
1 Mark McGwire	2.50
2 Sammy Sosa	1.50
3 Ken Griffey Jr.	2.00
4 Chipper Jones	1.50
5 Ben Grieve	.25
6 J.D. Drew	.75
7 Jeff Bagwell	1.00
8 Cal Ripken Jr.	3.00
9 Tony Gwynn	1.50
10 Nomar Garciaparra	1.50
11 Travis Lee	.35
12 Troy Glaus	.75
13 Mike Piazza	2.00
14 Alex Rodriguez	2.50
15 Kevin Brown	.25
16 Darin Erstad	.50
17 Scott Rolen	.50
18 Micah Bowie RC	.25
19 Juan Gonzalez	.50
20 Kerry Wood	.50
21 Roger Clemens	1.75
22 Derek Jeter	3.00
23 Pat Burrell RC	3.00
24 Tim Salmon	.25
25 Barry Bonds	3.00
26 Roosevelt Brown RC	.25
27 Vladimir Guerrero	1.00
28 Randy Johnson	.25
29 Mo Vaughn	.25
30 Fernando Seguignol	.25
31 Greg Maddux	1.50
32 Tony Clark	.25
33 Eric Chavez	.40
34 Kris Benson	.25
35 Frank Thomas	1.00
36 Mario Encarnacion	.25
37 Gabe Kapler	.25
38 Jeremy Giambi	.25
39 Peter Tucci RC	.25
40 Manny Ramirez	1.00
41 Albert Belle	.25
42 Warren Morris	.25
43 Michael Barrett	.25
44 Andruw Jones	1.00
45 Carlos Delgado	.60
46 Jaret Wright	.25
47 Juan Encarnacion	.25
48 Scott Hunter	.25
49 Tino Martinez	.25
50 Craig Biggio	.25
51 Jim Thome	.60
52 Vinny Castilla	.25
53 Tom Glavine	.40
54 Bob Higginson	.25
55 Moises Alou	.25
56 Robin Ventura	.25
57 Bernie Williams	.25
58 Pedro J. Martinez	1.00
59 Greg Vaughn	.25
60 Ray Lankford	.25

61 Jose Canseco	.40
62 Ivan Rodriguez	.75
63 Shawn Green	.40
64 Rafael Palmeiro	.75
65 Ellis Burks	.25
66 Jason Kendall	.25
67 David Wells	.25
68 Rondell White	.25
69 Gary Sheffield	.40
70 Ken Caminiti	.25
71 Cliff Floyd	.25
72 Larry Walker	.25
73 Bartolo Colon	.25
74 Barry Larkin	.25
75 Calvin Pickering	.25
76 Jim Edmonds	.25
77 Henry Rodriguez	.25
78 Roberto Alomar	.40
79 Andres Galarraga	.25
80 Richie Sexson	.75
81 Todd Helton	.75
82 Damion Easley	.25
83 Livan Hernandez	.25
84 Carlos Beltran	.60
85 Todd Hundley	.25
86 Todd Walker	.25
87 Scott Brosius	.25
88 Bob Abreu	.25
89 Corey Koskie	.25
90 Ruben Rivera	.25
91 Edgar Renteria	.25
92 Quinton McCracken	.25
93 Bernard Gilkey	.25
94 Shannon Stewart	.25
95 Dustin Hermanson	.25
96 Mike Caruso	.25
97 Alex Gonzalez	.25
98 Raul Mondesi	.25
99 David Cone	.25
100 Curt Schilling	.40
101 Brian Giles	.25
102 Edgar Martinez	.25
103 Rolando Arrojo	.25
104 Derek Bell	.25
105 Denny Neagle	.25
106 Marquis Grissom	.25
107 Bret Boone	.25
108 Mike Mussina	.50
109 John Smoltz	.25
110 Brett Tomko	.25
111 David Justice	.25
112 Andy Pettitte	.40
113 Eric Karros	.25
114 Dante Bichette	.25
115 Jeromy Burnitz	.25
116 Paul Konerko	.40
117 Steve Finley	.25
118 Ricky Ledee	.25
119 Edgardo Alfonzo	.25
120 Dean Palmer	.25
121 Rusty Greer	.25
122 Luis Gonzalez	.25
123 Randy Winn	.25
124 Jeff Kent	.25
125 Doug Glanville	.25
126 Justin Thompson	.25
127 Bret Saberhagen	.25
128 Wade Boggs	1.50
129 Al Leiter	.25
130 Paul O'Neill	.25
131 Chan Ho Park	.25
132 Johnny Damon	.60
133 Darryl Kile	.25
134 Reggie Sanders	.25
135 Kevin Millwood	.25
136 Charles Johnson	.25
137 Ray Durham	.25
138 Rico Brogna	.25
139 Matt Williams	.25
140 Sandy Alomar	.25
141 Jeff Cirillo	.25
142 Devon White	.25
143 Andy Benes	.25
144 Mike Stanley	.25
Checklist Card	.05

FRow 2 (Passion)

The metallic-foil background in the second level of Flair Showcase - Row 2/Passion - has an action photo printed in front of large textured numerals representing the player's number. In the foreground is another action shot. Backs have the same three designs

as Row 3, but only vary in insertion rate from one card per 1.3 packs to one card per three packs.

	NM/M
Complete Set (144):	65.00
Common Player:	.25
Showdown (1-48):	2X
Showpiece (49-96):	1X
Showtime (97-144):	1X

Row 1 (Showcase)

Showcase level - Row 1 - presents two portraits and an action photo and the player's uniform number on a plastic laminate in a horizontal format. A gold-foil serial number is stamped into the upper-left corner in one of three levels of scarcity: Showpiece (#1-48) is limited to 1,500 numbered sets, Showtime (#49-96) is limited to 3,000 sets and Showdown (#97-144) is numbered to 6,000 sets.

	NM/M
Complete Set (144):	300.00
Common Showpiece (1-48):	2.00
Showpiece Stars:	5X
Common Showtime (49-96):	1.00
Showtime Stars:	3X
Common Showdown (97-144):	.50
Showdown Stars:	2X

Legacy / Masterpiece

Each of the 432 total cards in Flair Showcase was also produced in a pair of extremely limited parallels. The blue-foil enhanced Legacy Collection cards are serially numbered within an edition of just 99. The presence of purple foil on front signifies a Legacy Masterpiece card, which is identified on front by the notation, "The Only 1 of 1 Masterpiece." Because of their unique nature, determination of a "book value" for Masterpiece cards is not possible.

	NM/M
Common Legacy:	6.00
Legacy Stars:	20X
Common Masterpiece:	50.00

Measure of Greatness

This 15-card set captures baseball's top superstars who were closing in on milestones during the 1999 season. Each card is sequentially numbered to 500.

	NM/M
Complete Set (15):	100.00
Common Player:	3.00
Production 500 Sets	
1 Roger Clemens	7.50
2 Nomar Garciaparra	6.50
3 Juan Gonzalez	3.00
4 Ken Griffey Jr.	8.00
5 Vladimir Guerrero	5.00
6 Tony Gwynn	6.50
7 Derek Jeter	15.00
8 Chipper Jones	8.00

9 Mark McGwire	12.50
10 Mike Piazza	9.00
11 Manny Ramirez	5.00
12 Cal Ripken Jr.	15.00
13 Alex Rodriguez	12.50
14 Sammy Sosa	6.50
15 Frank Thomas	5.00

Wave of the Future

This insert set spotlights young stars on the rise and is limited to 1,000 serial numbered sets.

	NM/M
Complete Set (15):	40.00
Common Player:	1.50
Production 1,000 Sets	
1 Kerry Wood	4.00
2 Ben Grieve	1.50
3 J.D. Drew	4.00
4 Juan Encarnacion	1.50
5 Travis Lee	2.00
6 Todd Helton	7.50
7 Troy Glaus	7.50
8 Ricky Ledee	1.50
9 Eric Chavez	2.00
10 Ben Davis	1.50
11 George Lombard	1.50
12 Jeremy Giambi	1.50
13 Roosevelt Brown	1.50
14 Pat Burrell	6.00
15 Preston Wilson	1.50

2003 Flair

	NM/M
Complete Set (125):	
Common Player:	.25
Common SP (91-125):	4.00
Production 500	
Pack (5):	3.50
Box (20):	50.00
1 Hideo Nomo	.60
2 Derek Jeter	3.00
3 Junior Spivey	.25
4 Rich Aurilia	.25
5 Luis Gonzalez	.35
6 Sean Burroughs	.25
7 Pedro J. Martinez	1.00
8 Randy Winn	.25
9 Carlos Delgado	.50
10 Pat Burrell	.50
11 Barry Larkin	.40
12 Roberto Alomar	.40
13 Tony Batista	.25
14 Barry Bonds	3.00
15 Craig Biggio	.25
16 Ivan Rodriguez	.65
17 Javier Vazquez	.25
18 Joe Borchard	.25
19 Josh Phelps	.25
20 Omar Vizquel	.25
21 Tom Glavine	.40
22 Darin Erstad	.50
23 Hee Seop Choi	.25
24 Roger Clemens	1.75
25 Michael Cuddyer	.25
26 Mike Sweeney	.25
27 Phil Nevin	.25
28 Torii Hunter	.25
29 Vladimir Guerrero	1.00
30 Ellis Burks	.25
31 Jimmy Rollins	.50
32 Ken Griffey Jr.	2.00
33 Magglio Ordonez	.40
34 Mark Prior	1.00
35 Mike Lieberthal	.25
36 Jorge Posada	.30
37 Rodrigo Lopez	.25
38 Todd Helton	1.00

39 Adam Kennedy	.25
40 Curt Schilling	.40
41 Jim Thome	.25
42 Josh Beckett	.25
43 Carlos Pena	.25
44 Jason Kendall	.25
45 Sammy Sosa	2.00
46 Scott Rolen	.75
47 Alex Rodriguez	2.50
48 Aubrey Huff	.25
49 Bobby Abreu	.25
50 Jeff Kent	.25
51 Joe Randa	.25
52 Lance Berkman	.25
53 Orlando Cabrera	.25
54 Richie Sexson	.25
55 Albert Pujols	2.00
56 Alfonso Soriano	.50
57 Greg Maddux	1.50
58 Jason Giambi	.75
59 Jeff Bagwell	1.00
60 Kerry Wood	.50
61 Manny Ramirez	1.00
62 Eric Chavez	.40
63 Preston Wilson	.25
64 Shawn Green	.50
65 Shea Hillenbrand	.25
66 Austin Kearns	.75
67 Cliff Floyd	.25
68 Edgardo Alfonzo	.25
69 J.D. Drew	.40
70 Larry Walker	.25
71 Mike Piazza	2.00
72 Andruw Jones	.75
73 Ben Grieve	.25
74 Eric Hinske	.25
75 Geoff Jenkins	.25
76 Kazuhiro Sasaki	.25
77 Matt Morris	.25
78 Miguel Tejada	.40
79 Aramis Ramirez	.25
80 Troy Glaus	1.00
81 Ichiro Suzuki	2.00
82 Mark Teixeira	.50
83 Nomar Garciaparra	2.00
84 Chipper Jones	1.50
85 Frank Thomas	1.00
86 Paul LoDuca	.25
87 Bernie Williams	.35
88 Adam Dunn	.75
89 Randy Johnson	1.00
90 Barry Zito	.40
91 Lew Ford RC	8.00
92 Joe Valentine RC	3.00
93 Jhonny Peralta	4.00
94 Hideki Matsui RC	20.00
95 Francisco Rosario RC	3.00
96 Adam LaRoche	4.00
97 Josh Hall RC	6.00
98 Chien-Ming Wang RC	25.00
99 Josh Willingham RC	6.00
100 Guillermo Quiroz RC	6.00
101 Terrmel Sledge RC	3.00
102 Prentice Redman RC	3.00
103 Matt Bruback RC	6.00
104 Alejandro Machado RC	3.00
105 Shane Victorino RC	6.00
106 Chris Waters RC	3.00
107 Jose Contreras RC	8.00
108 Pete LaForest RC	3.00
109 Nook Logan RC	3.00
110 Hector Luna RC	8.00
111 Daniel Cabrera RC	6.00
112 Matt Kata RC	6.00
113 Rontrez Johnson RC	8.00
114 Josh Stewart RC	8.00
115 Michael Hessman RC	3.00
116 Felix Sanchez RC	6.00
117 Michel Hernandez RC	3.00
118 Arnaldo Munoz RC	3.00
119 Ian Ferguson RC	3.00
120 Clint Barmes RC	6.00
121 Brian Stokes RC	3.00
122 Craig Brazell RC	6.00
123 John Webb	3.00
124 Tim Olson RC	6.00
125 Jeremy Bonderman	10.00

Row 1

	NM/M
Stars (1-90):	5-10X
Rookies (91-125):	.75-1.5X
Production 150 Sets	
Row 2:	No Pricing
Production 25 Sets	

Diamond Cuts

	NM/M
Common Player:	4.00
Inserted 1:10	
Golds:	1-2X
Production 100 Sets	
1DC Alex Rodriguez	12.00
2DC Roberto Alomar	4.00
3DC Scott Rolen	5.00
4DC Alfonso Soriano	6.00
5DC Chipper Jones	7.50
6DC Pat Burrell	5.00
7DC Derek Jeter	15.00

8DC Mike Piazza	10.00
9DC J.D. Drew	4.00
10DC Vladimir Guerrero	6.00
11DC Greg Maddux	7.50
12DC Barry Zito	4.00
13DC Troy Glaus	5.00
14DC Roy Oswalt	4.00
15DC Roger Clemens	9.00

Hot Numbers

	NM/M
Common Player:	15.00
Production 100 Sets	
1HN Alex Rodriguez	35.00
2HN Roberto Alomar	15.00
3HN Scott Rolen	30.00
4HN Alfonso Soriano	15.00
5HN Chipper Jones	25.00
6HN Pat Burrell	25.00
7HN Derek Jeter	40.00
8HN Mike Piazza	30.00
9HN J.D. Drew	15.00
10HN Vladimir Guerrero	20.00
11HN Greg Maddux	30.00
12HN Barry Zito	15.00
13HN Troy Glaus	15.00
14HN Roy Oswalt	15.00

Hot Numbers Dual

Production 25 Sets	No Pricing

Power Tools

	NM/M
Common Player:	5.00
Production 500 Sets	
Golds:	1-1.5X
Production 100 Sets	
1PT Nomar Garciaparra	15.00
2PT Derek Jeter	25.00
3PT Sammy Sosa	12.00
4PT Miguel Tejada	5.00
5PT Austin Kearns	10.00
6PT Jason Giambi	8.00
7PT Adam Dunn	8.00
8PT Jim Thome	8.00
9PT Lance Berkman	8.00
10PT Alfonso Soriano	15.00
12PT Alex Rodriguez	15.00
13PT Mike Piazza	10.00
14PT Bernie Williams	10.00
15PT Jeff Bagwell	8.00
16PT Andruw Jones	5.00
17PT Scott Rolen	12.00
19PT Juan Gonzalez	6.00

Power Tools - Dual

	NM/M
Common Duo:	
Production 200 Sets	
1PTD Nomar Garciaparra, Derek Jeter	40.00
3PTD Adam Dunn, Austin Kearns	25.00
4PTD Jim Thome, Sammy Sosa	15.00
5PTD Alex Rodriguez, Nomar Garciaparra	20.00
6PTD Jason Giambi, Bernie Williams	15.00
7PTD Derek Jeter, Alfonso Soriano	25.00
8PTD Lance Berkman, Jeff Bagwell	10.00
9PTD Miguel Tejada, Alex Rodriguez	20.00
10PTD Jason Giambi, Mike Piazza	20.00

Sweet Swatch

	NM/M
Common Player:	5.00
Production 250 Sets	
Derek Jeter	20.00
Sammy Sosa	15.00
Hideo Nomo	20.00
Vladimir Guerrero	6.00
Jason Giambi	8.00
Nomar Garciaparra	15.00
Randy Johnson	12.00
Miguel Tejada	5.00
Pedro J. Martinez	10.00
Adam Dunn	8.00
Roger Clemens	15.00
Mark Prior	10.00
Chipper Jones	10.00
Alex Rodriguez	10.00
Bernie Williams	8.00
Lance Berkman	8.00

Kazuhiro Sasaki 6.00
Alfonso Soriano 12.00

Sweet Swatch Oversized

NM/M
Common Player: 6.00
1:Hobby Box
Masterpiece One-of-One's exist.

Derek Jeter/150	20.00
Sammy Sosa/279	15.00
Hideo Nomo/970	12.00
Jason Giambi/350	15.00
Nomar Garciaparra/727	15.00
Randy Johnson/274	15.00
Miguel Tejada/518	6.00
Pedro Martinez/1,480	10.00
Adam Dunn/1,090	8.00
Roger Clemens/97	25.00
Mark Prior/1,195	10.00
Chipper Jones/80	15.00
Alex Rodriguez/150	15.00
Bernie Williams/1,420	8.00
Lance Berkman/1,465	6.00
Kazuhiro Sasaki/505	10.00

Sweet Swatch Autograph Oversized

NM/M
Common Player:
Golds: 1.5-2X
Production 25, Jeter 50
Masterpiece One-of-Ones exist.

Derek Jeter/312	90.00
Randy Johnson/218	60.00
Adam Dunn/218	30.00
Jeff Bagwell/218	40.00

Sweet Swatch Patch

NM/M
Common Player: 15.00
Production 50 Sets

Sammy Sosa	50.00
Hideo Nomo	50.00
Jason Giambi	20.00
Nomar Garciaparra	45.00
Randy Johnson	40.00
Miguel Tejada	15.00
Pedro J. Martinez	40.00
Adam Dunn	35.00
Roger Clemens	50.00
Mark Prior	25.00
Alex Rodriguez	45.00
Bernie Williams	20.00
Kazuhiro Sasaki	30.00
Alfonso Soriano	35.00

Sweet Swatch Patch Oversized

NM/M
Common Player: 15.00

Derek Jeter/35	75.00
Sammy Sosa/190	40.00
Hideo Nomo/114	50.00
Vladimir Guerrero/290	35.00
Nomar Garciaparra/124	40.00
Miguel Tejada/183	15.00
Pedro Martinez/185	40.00
Adam Dunn/130	30.00
Mark Prior/290	25.00
Chipper Jones/284	25.00
Alex Rodriguez/298	40.00
Bernie Williams/123	25.00
Lance Berkman/287	25.00
Kazuhiro Sasaki/90	40.00

Sweet Swatch Dual Oversized

Production 25 Sets: No Pricing

Wave of the Future

NM/M
Common Player: 3.00
Production 500 Sets
Golds: 1-2X
Production 100 Sets

WOF Francisco Rodriguez	3.00
WOF Carl Crawford	4.00
WOF Austin Kearns	10.00
WOF Hank Blalock	3.00
WOF Marlon Byrd	3.00
WOF Michael Restovich	3.00
WOF Joe Borchard	3.00
WOF Sean Burroughs	4.00
WOF Aubrey Huff	3.00
WOF Josh Phelps	5.00

2003 Flair Greats of the Game

NM/M
Complete Set (95): 35.00

Common Player: .40
Pack (5): 6.00
Box (20): 100.00

1	Ozzie Smith	1.00
2	Red Schoendienst	.40
3	Harmon Killebrew	1.50
4	Ralph Kiner	.40
5	Johnny Bench	2.00
6	Al Kaline	1.00
7	Bobby Doerr	.40
8	Cal Ripken Jr.	4.00
9	Enos Slaughter	.40
10	Phil Rizzuto	1.00
11	Luis Aparicio	.40
12	Pee Wee Reese	.40
13	Richie Ashburn	.40
14	Ernie Banks	2.00
15	Earl Weaver	.40
16	Whitey Ford	1.50
17	Brooks Robinson	1.00
18	Lou Boudreau	.40
19	Robin Yount	1.00
20	Mike Schmidt	2.50
21	Bob Lemon	.40
22	Stan Musial	2.50
23	Joe Morgan	.60
24	Early Wynn	.40
25	Willie Stargell	.75
26	Yogi Berra	2.00
27	Juan Marichal	.40
28	Rick Ferrell	.40
29	Rod Carew	.75
30	Jim Bunning	.40
31	Ferguson Jenkins	.40
32	Steve Carlton	.75
33	Larry Doby	.40
34	Nolan Ryan	4.00
35	Phil Niekro	.40
36	Billy Williams	.40
37	Hal Newhouser	.40
38	Bob Feller	.75
39	Lou Brock	.75
40	Monte Irvin	.75
41	Eddie Mathews	1.00
42	Rollie Fingers	.40
43	Gaylord Perry	.40
44	Reggie Jackson	1.50
45	Bob Gibson	1.00
46	Robin Roberts	.40
47	Tom Seaver	1.00
48	Willie McCovey	.40
49	Hoyt Wilhelm	.40
50	George Kell	.40
51	Warren Spahn	1.00
52	Jim "Catfish" Hunter	.40
53	Dom DiMaggio	.40
54	Joe Medwick	.40
55	Johnny Pesky	.40
56	Steve Garvey	.40
57	Harry Heilmann	.40
58	Dave Winfield	.75
59	Andre Dawson	.40
60	Jimmie Foxx	1.00
61	Buddy Bell	.40
62	Gabby Hartnett	.40
63	Babe Ruth	4.00
64	Dizzy Dean	1.50
65	Hank Greenberg	.40
66	Don Drysdale	.75
67	Gary Carter	.40
68	Wade Boggs	.75
69	Tony Perez	.40
70	Mickey Cochrane	.75
71	Bill Dickey	.40
72	George Brett	3.00
73	Honus Wagner	3.00
74	George Sisler	1.00
75	Walter Johnson	1.00
76	Ron Santo	.40
77	Roy Campanella	1.00
78	Roger Maris	2.50
79	Kirby Puckett	2.50
80	Alan Trammell	.40
81	Don Mattingly	3.00
82	Ty Cobb	3.00
83	Lou Gehrig	3.00
84	Jackie Robinson	3.00
85	Billy Martin	.75
86	Paul Molitor	.75
87	Duke Snider	1.00
88	Thurman Munson	1.50
89	Luke Appling	.40
90	Ernie Lombardi	.40
91	Rube Waddell	.40
92	Travis Jackson	.40
93	Joe Sewell	.40
94	King Kelly	.40
95	Heinie Manush	.40

Common Home Team (96-133): 2.00

96HT	Bobby Doerr	2.00
97HT	Johnny Pesky	2.00
98HT	Wade Boggs	3.00
99HT	Tony Conigliaro	2.00
100HT	Carlton Fisk	3.00
101HT	Rico Petrocelli	2.00
102HT	Jim Rice	2.00
103HT	Al Lopez	2.00
104HT	Pee Wee Reese	2.00
105HT	Tommy Lasorda	2.00
106HT	Gil Hodges	3.00
107HT	Jackie Robinson	6.00
108HT	Duke Snider	4.00
109HT	Don Drysdale	4.00
110HT	Steve Garvey	2.00
111HT	Hoyt Wilhelm	2.00
112HT	Bob Gibson	4.00
113HT	Monte Irvin	3.00
114HT	Willie McCovey	3.00
115HT	Travis Jackson	2.00
116HT	Bobby Bonds	2.00
117HT	Orlando Cepeda	2.00
118HT	Whitey Ford	4.00
119HT	Phil Rizzuto	4.00
120HT	Reggie Jackson	4.00
121HT	Yogi Berra	5.00
122HT	Roger Maris	6.00
123HT	Don Mattingly	10.00
124HT	Babe Ruth	10.00
125HT	Dave Winfield	3.00
126HT	Bob Gibson	4.00
127HT	Enos Slaughter	2.00
128HT	Joe Medwick	2.00
129HT	Lou Brock	3.00
130HT	Ozzie Smith	5.00
131HT	Stan Musial	6.00
132HT	Steve Carlton	3.00
133HT	Dizzy Dean	4.00

Ballpark Heroes

NM/M
Complete Set (9): 25.00
Common Player: 2.00
Inserted 1:10

1BH	Nolan Ryan	5.00
2BH	Babe Ruth	5.00
3BH	Honus Wagner	3.00
4BH	Ty Cobb	4.00
5BH	Ernie Banks	3.00
6BH	Mike Schmidt	3.00
7BH	Duke Snider	2.00
8BH	Cal Ripken Jr.	5.00
9BH	Stan Musial	3.00

Bat Rack Triple

Common Card: 15.00
Production 300

Eddie Murray, Cal Ripken Jr., Brooks Robinson	75.00
Ryne Sandberg, Ron Santo, Billy Williams	45.00
Johnny Bench, Joe Morgan, Tony Perez	35.00
Eddie Mathews, Paul Molitor, Robin Yount	40.00
Tommie Agee, Jerry Grote, Bud Harrelson	15.00
Reggie Jackson, Don Mattingly, Dave Winfield	45.00
Dave Parker, Willie Stargell	20.00

Bat Rack Quad

NM/M
Common Card: 50.00
Numbered to 150.

Don Mattingly, Joe Morgan, Cal Ripken Jr., Brooks Robinson	90.00
Ryne Sandberg, Ron Santo, Billy Williams, Andre Dawson	60.00
Dave Winfield, Cal Ripken Jr., Paul Molitor, Robin Yount	80.00

Eddie Murray, Eddie Mathews, Reggie Jackson, Willie McCovey 50.00

Classic Numbers

NM/M
Complete Set (13): 50.00
Common Player: 3.00
Inserted 1:20

1CN	Jackie Robinson	6.00
2CN	Willie McCovey	3.00
3CN	Brooks Robinson	5.00
4CN	Reggie Jackson	6.00
5CN	Ozzie Smith	6.00
6CN	Johnny Bench	6.00
7CN	Yogi Berra	6.00
8CN	Cal Ripken Jr.	10.00
9CN	George Brett	8.00
10CN	Thurman Munson	6.00
11CN	Joe Morgan	3.00
12CN	Nolan Ryan	10.00
13CN	Steve Carlton	3.00

Classic Numbers Game-Used

NM/M
Common Player: 10.00
Inserted 1:24

Willie McCovey	12.00
George Brett	20.00
Joe Morgan	10.00
Yogi Berra	20.00
Cal Ripken Jr.	25.00
Nolan Ryan	35.00
Ozzie Smith	15.00
Johnny Bench	15.00
Ryne Sandberg	25.00
Thurman Munson	20.00
Steve Carlton	10.00

Classic Numbers Dual-side

NM/M
Common Card: 25.00
Production 250 Sets

Yogi Berra, Thurman Munson	45.00
Nolan Ryan, Steve Carlton	65.00
Johnny Bench, Thurman Munson	35.00
Cal Ripken Jr., Ozzie Smith	60.00
Joe Morgan, Ryne Sandberg	35.00
Willie McCovey, Johnny Bench	25.00
Yogi Berra, Cal Ripken Jr.	50.00
George Brett, Nolan Ryan	75.00

Cut of History

NM/M
Common Player: 5.00
Inserted 1:10

Paul O'Neill	5.00
Dennis Eckersley	8.00
Jim Palmer	6.00
Graig Nettles	8.00
Frank Baker	30.00
Wade Boggs	8.00
Roger Maris	60.00
Jim "Catfish" Hunter	8.00
Alan Trammell	12.00
Eddie Murray	20.00
Steve Carlton	8.00
Tom Seaver	8.00
Gary Carter	8.00
Phil Niekro	6.00
Luis Aparicio	8.00
Reggie Jackson	12.00
Fergie Jenkins	8.00
Kirby Puckett	15.00
Billy Martin	15.00
Joe Medwick	25.00
Buddy Bell	5.00
Early Wynn	10.00
Cal Ripken Jr.	25.00
Hoyt Wilhelm	8.00
Willie McCovey	10.00

Cut of History Auto.

NM/M
Common Player:

Alan Trammell/211	25.00
Steve Carlton/506	30.00
Cal Ripken Jr./155	150.00
Johnny Bench/161	50.00

Greats of the Grain

NM/M
Production 50 Sets

1GOG	Ty Cobb	100.00
2GOG	Mike Schmidt	50.00
3GOG	Babe Ruth	140.00
4GOG	Lou Gehrig	80.00
5GOG	George Brett	160.00
6GOG	Stan Musial	75.00
7GOG	Don Mattingly	110.00
8GOG	Cal Ripken Jr.	100.00
9GOG	Eddie Mathews	75.00

HOF Postmark

NM/M
Production 2,002

Ozzie Smith	20.00
Ozzie Smith/Auto./202	100.00

Home Team Cut

NM/M
Common Player: 8.00
Patch: 2-5X
Production 25 Sets

Wade Boggs	15.00
Carlton Fisk	20.00
Jim Rice	15.00
Pee Wee Reese	15.00
Duke Snider	20.00
Steve Garvey	10.00
Tommy Lasorda	15.00
Juan Marichal	10.00
Bobby Bonds	8.00
Willie McCovey	10.00
Billy Martin	15.00
Roger Maris	65.00
Reggie Jackson	15.00
Dave Winfield	12.00
Red Schoendienst	8.00
Ozzie Smith	35.00
Joe Medwick	25.00

Sweet Swatch bat

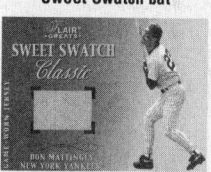

NM/M
Common Player: 15.00

Cal Ripken Jr/305	40.00
George Brett/320	30.00
Johnny Bench/175	20.00
Reggie Jackson/155	20.00
Don Mattingly/340	40.00
Willie McCovey/155	15.00
Jose Canseco/175	25.00
Kirby Puckett/251	30.00
Orlando Cepeda/165	15.00
Eddie Mathews/185	40.00
Pee Wee Reese/165	30.00
Andre Dawson/310	15.00

Sweet Swatch jersey

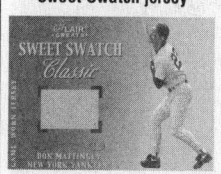

NM/M
Common Player: 15.00

Jerry Coleman/528	20.00
Ryne Sandberg/374	25.00
Johnny Bench/410	20.00
Paul Molitor/592	15.00
Cal Ripken Jr/557	45.00
Gil Hodges/545	20.00
Carlton Fisk/1,200	15.00
Nolan Ryan/590	40.00
Tom Seaver/385	20.00
Don Mattingly/880	35.00
Jose Canseco/1,329	15.00
George Brett/384	30.00
Jim Palmer/335	15.00
Kirby Puckett/445	20.00
Juan Marichal/385	15.00
Robin Yount/340	15.00
Andre Dawson/335	15.00

Sweet Swatch Jersey Auto.

NM/M
Common Autograph:

Cal Ripken Jr/40	240.00
Johnny Bench/40	130.00
Alan Trammell/40	75.00

2003 Flair/Poland Springs Yankees Greats

The "Official Bottled Water of the N.Y. Yankees" sponsored this stadium giveaway card set. The first 18,000 youngsters through the gates at the May 14 game received five-card cello packs which

---

included four player cards and a sponsor's card. The player cards are virtually identical to the regular-issue versions except for the addition on a Poland Springs logo on front and, in the case of Berra, a card number change on back.

NM/M
Complete Set (5): 6.00
Common Player: 1.50

8	Yogi Berra	2.00
10	Phil Rizzuto	1.50
16	Whitey Ford	2.00
44	Reggie Jackson	2.00
---	Sponsor's Card	.10

2006 Flair Showcase

NM/M
Complete Set (200):
Common Player (1-100): .50
Common Player (101-150): 1.50
Inserted 1:4 Hobby
Common Player (151-200): 2.00
Inserted 1:8 Hobby
Pack (5): 3.00
Box (18): 50.00

1	Jeremy Hermida RC	.50
2	Albert Pujols	3.00
3	Ryan Shealy RC	.50
4	Mark Prior	.50
5	Chuck James RC	1.00
6	Shawn Green	.50
7	Rickie Weeks	.75
8	Roy Halladay	.75
9	Luis Gonzalez	.50
10	David Ortiz	1.50
11	Josh Beckett	1.00
12	Gary Sheffield	.75
13	Jose Reyes	1.00
14	Brandon Watson RC	.50
15	Tadahito Iguchi	.50
16	Rich Harden	.50
17	Skip Schumaker RC	.50
18	Vladimir Guerrero	1.00
19	Chris Carpenter	.75
20	Brian Roberts	.50
21	Roy Oswalt	.75
22	Ben Johnson RC	.50
23	Todd Helton	.75
24	Wilbert Nieves RC	.50
25	Michael Young	.50
26	A.J. Burnett	.50
27	J.D. Drew	.50
28	Adrian Beltre	.75
29	Tim Hudson	.50
30	Jake Peavy	.75
31	Magglio Ordonez	.75
32	Brad Wilkerson	.50
33	Ryan Freel	.50
34	Javier Vazquez	.50
35	Tom Glavine	.75
36	Jason Bergmann RC	1.00
37	Marcus Giles	.50
38	Jim Thome	.75
39	Ichiro Suzuki	2.00
40	Jeff Harris RC	.75
41	Miguel Cabrera	1.00
42	Nomar Garciaparra	.75
43	Brian Giles	.50
44	Jeremy Accardo RC	.50
45	Taylor Buchholz RC	.50
46	Mike Jacobs	.50
47	Chris Denorfia RC	.50
48	Ivan Rodriguez	.75
49	Mike Piazza	1.00
50	Curt Schilling	1.00
51	Kelly Stoppach RC	.50

52	Jason Kubel **RC**	.50
53	Craig Biggio	.75
54	Livan Hernandez	.50
55	Joe Mauer	.75
56	Scott Feldman **RC**	1.00
57	Garret Anderson	.50
58	Steve Stemle **RC**	1.00
59	Boof Bonser **RC**	.50
60	Jose Guillen	.50
61	Rafael Furcal	.75
62	John Van Benschoten **RC**	.50
63	Dontrelle Willis	.50
64	Jose Vidro	.50
65	David Wright	2.00
66	Alfonso Soriano	1.00
67	Scott Podsednik	.50
68	Felix Hernandez	.75
69	Richie Sexson	.75
70	Jeff Francoeur	.75
71	Conor Jackson	.50
72	Javy Lopez	.50
73	Jonathan Papelbon **RC**	5.00
74	Frank Thomas	.75
75	Greg Maddux	2.00
76	Josh Rupe **RC**	.50
77	Eric Chavez	.50
78	Ben Sheets	.75
79	Chase Utley	1.00
80	Derrek Lee	.75
81	Manny Ramirez	1.00
82	Pedro Martinez	1.00
83	Hideki Matsui	2.00
84	Jeremy Bonderman	.50
85	Ronny Cedeno	.50
86	Trevor Hoffman	.50
87	Mark Buehrle	.50
88	Jason Bay	.75
89	Reggie Sanders	.50
90	Brian Anderson **RC**	.75
91	Travis Hafner	.75
92	Carlos Beltran	.75
93	Cody Ross **RC**	.50
94	Melvin Mora	.50
95	Chris Duffy	.50
96	Vernon Wells	.50
97	Bartolo Colon	.50
98	Aubrey Huff	.50
99	Paul Konerko	.75
100	Cesar Izturis	.50
101	Josh Willingham **RC**	1.50
102	Matt Cain **RC**	2.00
103	Macay McBride **RC**	1.50
104	Jeff Mathis	1.50
105	Alex Rodriguez	8.00
106	Justin Morneau	2.00
107	Felipe Lopez	1.50
108	Justin Verlander **RC**	8.00
109	Ryan Howard	5.00
110	Mike Sweeney	1.50
111	Scott Rolen	2.00
112	Hank Blalock	1.50
113	Kerry Wood	1.50
114	B.J. Ryan	1.50
115	Garrett Atkins	2.00
116	Carlos Delgado	2.00
117	Zack Greinke	2.00
118	Chad Cordero	1.50
119	Julio Lugo	1.50
120	Bobby Crosby	1.50
121	Barry Zito	1.50
122	Jhonny Peralta	1.50
123	Miguel Tejada	2.50
124	Grady Sizemore	3.00
125	Derek Jeter	8.00
126	Cliff Lee	1.50
127	Khalil Greene	2.00
128	Lance Berkman	2.00
129	Huston Street	1.50
130	Jermaine Dye	2.00
131	Chone Figgins	2.00
132	Torii Hunter	2.00
133	Jorge Cantu	1.50
134	Jason Giambi	2.00
135	Johan Santana	3.00
136	Chad Tracy	1.50
137	Troy Glaus	2.00
138	Moises Alou	2.00
139	Jason Schmidt	1.50
140	Ken Griffey Jr.	6.00
141	Jason Varitek	3.00
142	John Smoltz	2.50
143	Andy Pettitte	2.00
144	Jeff Kent	2.00
145	Coco Crisp	1.50
146	Jonny Gomes	1.50
147	Aaron Rowand	1.50
148	Mike Mussina	2.50
149	Johnny Damon	4.00
150	Edgar Renteria	1.50
151	Scott Kazmir	2.00
152	Lyle Overbay	1.50
153	Placido Polanco	2.00
154	Mariano Rivera	4.00
155	Hanley Ramirez **RC**	3.00
156	Morgan Ensberg	1.50
157	Kenny Rogers	2.00
158	Brad Lidge	2.00
159	A.J. Pierzynski	1.50
160	Aramis Ramirez	3.00
161	Mark Teixeira	3.00
162	Carl Crawford	3.00
163	Ryan Zimmerman **RC**	6.00
164	Adam Dunn	3.00
165	Joe Nathan	2.00
166	Juan Pierre	2.00
167	Pat Burrell	3.00
168	Carlos Lee	2.00
169	Billy Wagner	2.00

170	Prince Fielder **RC**	10.00
171	Randy Johnson	4.00
172	Andruw Jones	3.00
173	Francisco Rodriguez	2.00
174	Robinson Cano	3.00
175	Matt Holliday	3.00
176	Jim Edmonds	2.00
177	Josh Barfield **RC**	2.00
178	Chipper Jones	4.00
179	Bobby Jenks	2.00
180	Carlos Zambrano	3.00
181	Bobby Abreu	3.00
182	Brandon Webb	2.00
183	Kevin Millwood	2.00
184	Zachary Duke	2.00
185	Randy Winn	2.00
186	Eric Gagne	2.00
187	Kenji Johjima **RC**	5.00
188	John Patterson	2.00
189	Mark Loretta	2.00
190	Anderson Hernandez **RC**	2.00
191	Chris Resop **RC**	2.00
192	Ian Kinsler **RC**	2.00
193	Francisco Liriano **RC**	5.00
194	Noah Lowry	2.00
195	Brett Myers	2.00
196	Rocco Baldelli	2.00
197	Cliff Floyd	2.00
198	Sean Casey	2.00
199	Geoff Jenkins	2.00
200	Clint Barmes	2.00

Printing Plates

No Pricing
Production one set per color.

Legacy Blue

Blue (1-100):	2-4X
Blue (101-150):	1-1.5X
Blue (151-200):	1X

Production 150 Sets

Legacy Emerald

Emerald (1-100):	2-4X
Emerald (101-150):	1-1.5X
Emerald (151-200):	1X

Production 150 Sets

Autographics

		NM/M
Common Autograph:		8.00
BA	Bronson Arroyo	20.00
JB	Jason Bay	15.00
HB	Hank Blalock	15.00
BO	Jeremy Bonderman	15.00
SC	Sean Casey/SP	15.00
GC	Gustavo Chacin	15.00
BC	Brandon Claussen	10.00
CH	Chad Cordero	15.00
CO	Craig Counsell	10.00
CA	Carl Crawford	15.00
CC	Coco Crisp	15.00
KG	Ken Griffey Jr./SP	75.00
JG	Jose Guillen	15.00
TH	Travis Hafner/SP	15.00
AH	Aaron Harang	15.00
LH	Livan Hernandez	8.00
CI	Cesar Izturis	8.00
MK	Mark Kotsay	8.00
CL	Cliff Lee	15.00
JM	Justin Morneau	15.00
XN	Xavier Nady	10.00
RO	Roy Oswalt/SP	15.00
WP	Wily Mo Pena	10.00
JH	Jhonny Peralta	10.00
JP	Joel Pineiro	10.00
RA	Aramis Ramirez	10.00
AR	Aaron Rowand	15.00
CU	Chase Utley/SP/100	40.00

JV	Javier Vazquez/SP	8.00
OV	Omar Vizquel	20.00
RZ	Ryan Zimmerman	30.00

Fresh Ink

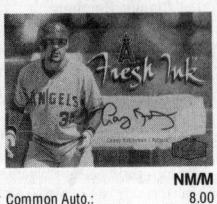

		NM/M
Common Auto.:		8.00
GA	Garrett Atkins	10.00
CB	Clint Barmes/SP	10.00
JB	Joe Blanton	8.00
MC	Miguel Cabrera/SP	25.00
MA	Matt Cain/SP	25.00
BC	Bobby Crosby	8.00
DD	David DeJesus	10.00
GF	Gavin Floyd	15.00
JG	Jonny Gomes	8.00
KG	Khalil Greene/SP	25.00
ZG	Zack Greinke	20.00
HA	Rich Harden	15.00
DH	Danny Haren	10.00
RH	Rich Hill	15.00
TI	Tadahito Iguchi	40.00
SK	Scott Kazmir	15.00
CK	Casey Kotchman	10.00
NL	Noah Lowry	8.00
VM	Victor Martinez	15.00
BM	Brandon McCarthy	8.00
OP	Odalis Perez	8.00
RE	Jeremy Reed	8.00
BR	Brian Roberts	15.00
ES	Ervin Santana	15.00
JS	Johan Santana/SP	50.00
CS	Chris Shelton	8.00
HS	Huston Street	15.00
MT	Mark Teahen	8.00
DW	Dontrelle Willis	15.00
WR	David Wright/SP/100	60.00
KY	Kevin Youkilis	15.00
MY	Michael Young/SP/100	20.00

Hot Gloves

		NM/M
Common Player:		10.00
Inserted 1:108 Hobby		
1	Derrek Lee	15.00
2	Andruw Jones	10.00
3	Bobby Abreu	10.00
4	Luis Castillo	10.00
5	Mike Matheny	10.00
6	Cesar Izturis	10.00
7	Craig Biggio	10.00
8	Darin Erstad	10.00
9	Derek Jeter	40.00
10	Eric Chavez	10.00
11	Greg Maddux	40.00
12	Ichiro Suzuki	35.00
13	Ivan Rodriguez	10.00
14	J.T. Snow	10.00
15	Jim Edmonds	10.00
16	Steve Finley	10.00
17	Kenny Rogers	10.00
18	Jason Varitek	20.00
19	Ken Griffey Jr.	40.00
20	Mark Teixeira	15.00
21	Orlando Hudson	10.00
22	Mike Hampton	10.00
23	Mike Mussina	10.00
24	Vernon Wells	15.00
25	Omar Vizquel	10.00
26	Alex Rodriguez	40.00
27	Mike Cameron	10.00
28	Scott Rolen	15.00
29	Todd Helton	15.00
30	Torii Hunter	15.00

Hot Numbers

		NM/M
Common Player:		1.50
Inserted 1:6 Hobby		
1	Albert Pujols	8.00
2	Alex Rodriguez	8.00
3	Andruw Jones	2.00
4	Bobby Abreu	1.50
5	Chipper Jones	3.00
6	Curt Schilling	2.00
7	David Ortiz	3.00
8	David Wright	5.00
9	Derek Jeter	8.00

10	Derrek Lee	3.00
11	Eric Gagne	1.50
12	Greg Maddux	5.00
13	Hideki Matsui	5.00
14	Ichiro Suzuki	5.00
15	Ivan Rodriguez	2.00
16	Johan Santana	3.00
17	Johnny Damon	3.00
18	Ken Griffey Jr.	5.00
19	Manny Ramirez	3.00
20	Mark Prior	1.50
21	Mark Teixeira	2.00
22	Miguel Cabrera	3.00
23	Miguel Tejada	2.00
24	Pedro Martinez	3.00
25	Randy Johnson	3.00
26	Rickie Weeks	1.50
27	Roger Clemens	5.00
28	Todd Helton	2.00
29	Torii Hunter	1.50
30	Vladimir Guerrero	3.00

Lettermen

No Pricing
Production 3-9

Showcase Signatures

		NM/M
Production 35 Sets		
JE	Jeremy Bonderman	30.00
SC	Sean Casey	20.00
CD	Chad Cordero	10.00
JG	Jose Guillen	10.00
AH	Aaron Harang	20.00
HA	Rich Harden	30.00
CI	Cesar Izturis	10.00
XN	Xavier Nady	20.00
RO	Roy Oswalt	20.00
WM	Wily Mo Pena	20.00
PE	Jhonny Peralta	15.00
BR	Brian Roberts	30.00
CS	Chris Shelton	20.00
KY	Kevin Youkilis	20.00
RZ	Ryan Zimmerman	50.00

Stitches

		NM/M
Common Player:		4.00
Inserted 1:9		
BA	Bobby Abreu	6.00
MA	Moises Alou	4.00
RB	Rocco Baldelli	6.00
JO	Josh Beckett	8.00
CB	Carlos Beltran	8.00
AB	Adrian Beltre	4.00
LB	Lance Berkman	6.00
HB	Hank Blalock	6.00
BO	Jeremy Bonderman	4.00
MB	Mark Buehrle	4.00
MC	Miguel Cabrera	10.00
RC	Robinson Cano	12.00
JC	Jorge Cantu	6.00
EC	Eric Chavez	4.00
CO	Michael Collins	4.00
CA	Carl Crawford	6.00
BC	Bobby Crosby	4.00
JD	Johnny Damon	10.00
CD	Carlos Delgado	6.00
DR	J.D. Drew	6.00
AD	Adam Dunn	6.00
JE	Jim Edmonds	6.00
RF	Rafael Furcal	4.00
EG	Eric Gagne	4.00
FG	Freddy Garcia	4.00
JG	Jason Giambi	4.00
BG	Brian Giles	4.00
TG	Tom Glavine	8.00
LG	Luis Gonzalez	4.00
GR	Khalil Greene	4.00
KG	Ken Griffey Jr.	10.00
VG	Vladimir Guerrero	8.00
TR	Travis Hafner	6.00
RH	Roy Halladay	6.00
RI	Rich Harden	6.00
HA	J.J. Hardy	4.00
TH	Todd Helton	8.00
HO	Trevor Hoffman	6.00
MH	Matt Holliday	8.00
HU	Tim Hudson	6.00
TO	Torii Hunter	6.00
DJ	Derek Jeter	20.00
RJ	Randy Johnson	8.00
AJ	Andruw Jones	6.00
CJ	Chipper Jones	8.00
JJ	Jacque Jones	4.00
SK	Scott Kazmir	6.00
JK	Jeff Kent	6.00
CL	Carlos Lee	4.00
DL	Derek Lee	8.00
PL	Paul LoDuca	6.00
JL	Javy Lopez	4.00
GM	Greg Maddux	10.00
PM	Pedro Martinez	8.00
KM	Kazuo Matsui	6.00
DM	Daisuke Matsuzaka	50.00
JM	Joe Mauer	8.00
KE	Kevin Millwood	4.00

MM	Mike Mussina	8.00
TN	Trot Nixon	8.00
DO	David Ortiz	15.00
JP	Jake Peavy	6.00
AN	Andy Pettitte	6.00
MI	Mike Piazza	10.00
MP	Mark Prior	6.00
AP	Albert Pujols	20.00
AR	Aramis Ramirez	6.00
MR	Manny Ramirez	8.00
RE	Jeremy Reed	4.00
JR	Jose Reyes	10.00
BR	Brian Roberts	4.00
FR	Francisco Rodriguez	6.00
IR	Ivan Rodriguez	8.00
SR	Scott Rolen	8.00
CC	C.C. Sabathia	4.00
JS	Johan Santana	8.00
CS	Curt Schilling	8.00
JA	Jason Schmidt	6.00
RS	Richie Sexson	4.00
BS	Ben Sheets	4.00
GS	Gary Sheffield	6.00
SM	John Smoltz	8.00
AS	Alfonso Soriano	4.00
SW	Mike Sweeney	4.00
MT	Mark Teixeira	8.00
TE	Miguel Tejada	8.00
FT	Frank Thomas	10.00
JT	Jim Thome	8.00
JU	Juan Uribe	4.00
JV	Jason Varitek	10.00
OV	Omar Vizquel	6.00
RW	Rickie Weeks	5.00
VW	Vernon Wells	6.00
DW	Dontrelle Willis	6.00
PW	Preston Wilson	4.00
KW	Kerry Wood	6.00
WR	David Wright	15.00
MY	Michael Young	6.00
BZ	Barry Zito	4.00

Wave of the Future

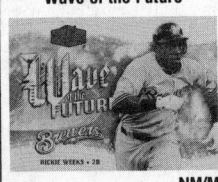

		NM/M
Common Player:		1.00
Inserted 1:2		
WF-1	Jeremy Hermida	1.00
WF-2	Kelly Stoppach	1.00
WF-3	Adam Wainwright	1.00
WF-4	Ryan Zimmerman	4.00
WF-5	Josh Willingham	1.00
WF-6	Brandon McCarthy	1.00
WF-7	Conor Jackson	1.00
WF-8	Grady Sizemore	2.00
WF-9	Curtis Granderson	1.50
WF-10	Jose Capellan	1.00
WF-11	Mike Jacobs	1.00
WF-12	Gavin Floyd	1.00
WF-13	Hanley Ramirez	2.00
WF-14	Jason Kubel	1.00
WF-15	Nate McLouth	1.00
WF-16	Felix Hernandez	1.50
WF-17	Jeff Francoeur	1.50
WF-18	Wilbert Nieves	1.00
WF-19	Cody Ross	1.00
WF-20	Justin Verlander	5.00
WF-21	Ben Johnson	1.00
WF-22	Guillermo Quiroz	1.00
WF-23	Jonathan Papelbon	4.00
WF-24	Prince Fielder	3.00
WF-25	Rickie Weeks	1.50
WF-26	Robinson Cano	2.00
WF-27	Kenji Johjima	3.00
WF-28	Anderson Hernandez	1.00
WF-29	Yuniesky Betancourt	1.00
WF-30	Zachary Duke	1.00

WBC Classic Moments

		NM/M
Common Player:		1.50
Inserted 1:8		
CM-1	Adam Stern	1.50
CM-2	Jason Bay	2.00
CM-3	Wei Wang	1.50
CM-4	Yung-Chi Chen	3.00
CM-5	Pedro Luis Lazo	1.50
CM-6	Yoandy Garlobo	1.50
CM-7	Ormari Romero	1.50

CM-8	Frederich Cepeda	1.50
CM-9	Yulieski Gourriel	1.50
CM-10	Yadel Marti	1.50
CM-11	David Ortiz	5.00
CM-12	Albert Pujols	5.00
CM-13	Adrian Beltre	1.50
CM-14	Alberto Castillo	1.50
CM-15	Odalis Perez	1.50
CM-16	Jason Grilli	1.50
CM-17	Daisuke Matsuzaka	5.00
CM-18	Sadaharu Oh	10.00
CM-19	Nobuhiko Matsunaka	3.00
CM-20	Ichiro Suzuki	5.00
CM-21	Akinori Otsuka	3.00
CM-22	Koji Uehara	3.00
CM-23	Kosuke Fukudome	5.00
CM-24	Daisuke Matsuzaka	5.00
CM-25	Ichiro Suzuki	5.00
CM-26	Seung-Yeop Lee	2.00
CM-27	Seung-Yeop Lee	2.00
CM-28	Jong Beom Lee	1.50
CM-29	Jae Weong Seo	1.50
CM-30	Chan Ho Park	1.50
CM-31	Hee Seop Choi	1.50
CM-32	Jorge Cantu	1.50
CM-33	Oliver Perez	1.50
CM-34	Vinny Castilla	1.50
CM-35	Esteban Loaiza	1.50
CM-36	Shairon Martis	1.50
CM-37	Bernie Williams	2.00
CM-38	Javier Vazquez	1.50
CM-39	Carlos Beltran	2.00
CM-40	Bernie Williams	2.00
CM-41	Roger Clemens	5.00
CM-42	Ken Griffey Jr.	5.00
CM-43	Alex Rodriguez	5.00
CM-44	Derek Jeter	5.00
CM-45	Derek Jeter	5.00
CM-46	Chipper Jones	2.00
CM-47	Miguel Cabrera	2.00
CM-48	Francisco Rodriguez	1.50
CM-49	Victor Martinez	1.50
CM-50	Freddy Garcia	1.50

1981 Fleer

For the first time in 18 years Fleer issued a baseball card set featuring current players. The 660 card effort included numerous errors in the first print run which were subsequently corrected. The 2-1/2" x 3-1/2" cards are numbered by team in order of the previous season's finish. Card fronts feature full-color photo inside a border which is color-coded by team. Backs are printed in black, gray and yellow on white stock and carry full player statistical information. The player's batting average or earned run average is located in a circle in the upper-right corner of the back. The complete set price in the checklist that follows does not include the higher priced variations.

		NM/M
Complete Set (660):		30.00
Common Player:		.05
Wax Pack (17):		1.75
Wax Box (38):		50.00
Vending Box (500):		20.00
1	Pete Rose	3.00
2	Larry Bowa	.05
3	Manny Trillo	.05
4	Bob Boone	.05
5a	Mike Schmidt/Portrait	2.50
5b	Mike Schmidt/Btg	2.00
6a	Steve Carlton ("Lefty" on front.)	
6b	Steve Carlton (Pitcher of the Year on front. date 1066 on back.)	2.00
6c	Steve Carlton (Pitcher of the Year on front. date 1966 on back.)	.50
7a	Tug McGraw (Game Saver on front.)	
7b	Tug McGraw (Pitcher on front.)	
8	Larry Christenson	.05
9	Bake McBride	.05
10	Greg Luzinski	.10
11	Ron Reed	.05
12	Dickie Noles	.05

No.	Player	Value
13	Keith Moreland RC	.15
14	Bob Walk RC	.05
15	Lonnie Smith	.05
16	Dick Ruthven	.05
17	Sparky Lyle	.05
18	Greg Gross	.05
19	Garry Maddox	.05
20	Nino Espinosa	.05
21	George Vukovich	.05
22	John Vukovich	.05
23	Ramon Aviles	.05
24a	Kevin Saucier (Ken Saucier on back.)	.10
24b	Kevin Saucier (Kevin Saucier on back.)	.50
25	Randy Lerch	.05
26	Del Unser	.05
27	Tim McCarver	.15
28a	George Brett/Btg	2.00
28b	George Brett/Portait	2.00
29a	Willie Wilson/Portait	.50
29b	Willie Wilson/Btg	.15
30	Paul Splittorff	.05
31	Dan Quisenberry	.05
32a	Amos Otis/Btg	.50
32b	Amos Otis (Portrait)	.10
33	Steve Busby	.05
34	U.L. Washington	.05
35	Dave Chalk	.05
36	Darrell Porter	.05
37	Marty Pattin	.05
38	Larry Gura	.05
39	Renie Martin	.05
40	Rich Gale	.05
41a	Hal McRae (Dark blue "Royals" on front.)	.40
41b	Hal McRae (Light blue "Royals" on front.)	.10
42	Dennis Leonard	.05
43	Willie Aikens	.05
44	Frank White	.05
45	Clint Hurdle	.05
46	John Wathan	.05
47	Pete LaCock	.05
48	Rance Mulliniks	.05
49	Jeff Twitty	.05
50	Jamie Quirk	.05
51	Art Howe	.05
52	Ken Forsch	.05
53	Vern Ruhle	.05
54	Joe Niekro	.05
55	Frank LaCorte	.05
56	J.R. Richard	.05
57	Nolan Ryan	4.00
58	Enos Cabell	.05
59	Cesar Cedeno	.05
60	Jose Cruz	.05
61	Bill Virdon	.05
62	Terry Puhl	.05
63	Joaquin Andujar	.05
64	Alan Ashby	.05
65	Joe Sambito	.05
66	Denny Walling	.05
67	Jeff Leonard	.05
68	Luis Pujols	.05
69	Bruce Bochy	.05
70	Rafael Landestoy	.05
71	Dave Smith RC	.05
72	Danny Heep RC	.05
73	Julio Gonzalez	.05
74	Craig Reynolds	.05
75	Gary Woods	.05
76	Dave Bergman	.05
77	Randy Niemann	.05
78	Joe Morgan	1.00
79a	Reggie Jackson/Portrait	2.50
79b	Reggie Jackson/Btg	2.00
80	Bucky Dent	.10
81	Tommy John	.10
82	Luis Tiant	.05
83	Rick Cerone	.05
84	Dick Howser	.05
85	Lou Piniella	.10
86	Ron Davis	.05
87a	Graig Nettles (Craig on back.)	4.50
87b	Graig Nettles (Graig on back.)	.15
88	Ron Guidry	.10
89	Rich Gossage	.10
90	Rudy May	.05
91	Gaylord Perry	.75
92	Eric Soderholm	.05
93	Bob Watson	.05
94	Bobby Murcer	.10
95	Bobby Brown	.05
96	Jim Spencer	.05
97	Tom Underwood	.05
98	Oscar Gamble	.05
99	Johnny Oates	.05
100	Fred Stanley	.05
101	Ruppert Jones	.05
102	Dennis Werth	.05
103	Joe Lefebvre	.05
104	Brian Doyle	.05
105	Aurelio Rodriguez	.05
106	Doug Bird	.05
107	Mike Griffin	.05
108	Tim Lollar	.05
109	Willie Randolph	.05
110	Steve Garvey	.30
111	Reggie Smith	.05
112	Don Sutton	.75
113	Burt Hooton	.05
114a	Davy Lopes (Davey) (No finger on back.)	.05
114b	Davy Lopes (Davey) (Small finger on back.)	.50
115	Dusty Baker	.05
116	Tom Lasorda	.10
117	Bill Russell	.05
118	Jerry Reuss	.05
119	Terry Forster	.05
120a	Bob Welch (Bob on back.)	.10
120b	Bob Welch (Robert)	.50
121	Don Stanhouse	.05
122	Rick Monday	.05
123	Derrel Thomas	.05
124	Joe Ferguson	.05
125	Rick Sutcliffe	.10
126a	Ron Cey (No finger on back.)	.05
126b	Ron Cey (Small finger on back.)	.50
127	Dave Goltz	.05
128	Jay Johnstone	.05
129	Steve Yeager	.05
130	Gary Weiss	.05
131	Mike Scioscia RC	.50
132	Vic Davalillo	.05
133	Doug Rau	.05
134	Pepe Frias	.05
135	Mickey Hatcher	.05
136	Steve Howe RC	.10
137	Robert Castillo	.05
138	Gary Thomasson	.05
139	Rudy Law	.05
140	Fernando Valenzuela RC	1.50
141	Manny Mota	.05
142	Gary Carter	1.00
143	Steve Rogers	.05
144	Warren Cromartie	.05
145	Andre Dawson	.40
146	Larry Parrish	.05
147	Rowland Office	.05
148	Ellis Valentine	.05
149	Dick Williams	.05
150	Bill Gullickson RC	.15
151	Elias Sosa	.05
152	John Tamargo	.05
153	Chris Speier	.05
154	Ron LeFlore	.05
155	Rodney Scott	.05
156	Stan Bahnsen	.05
157	Bill Lee	.05
158	Fred Norman	.05
159	Woodie Fryman	.05
160	Dave Palmer	.05
161	Jerry White	.05
162	Roberto Ramos	.05
163	John D'Acquisto	.05
164	Tommy Hutton	.05
165	Charlie Lea RC	.15
166	Scott Sanderson	.05
167	Ken Macha	.05
168	Tony Bernazard	.05
169	Jim Palmer	1.00
170	Steve Stone	.10
171	Mike Flanagan	.05
172	Al Bumbry	.05
173	Doug DeCinces	.05
174	Scott McGregor	.05
175	Mark Belanger	.05
176	Tim Stoddard	.05
177a	Rick Dempsey (No finger on front.)	.05
177b	Rick Dempsey (Small finger on front.)	.50
178	Earl Weaver	.25
179	Tippy Martinez	.05
180	Dennis Martinez	.05
181	Sammy Stewart	.05
182	Rich Dauer	.05
183	Lee May	.05
184	Eddie Murray	1.00
185	Benny Ayala	.05
186	John Lowenstein	.05
187	Gary Roenicke	.05
188	Ken Singleton	.05
189	Dan Graham	.05
190	Terry Crowley	.05
191	Kiko Garcia	.05
192	Dave Ford	.05
193	Mark Corey	.05
194	Lenn Sakata	.05
195	Doug DeCinces	.05
196	Johnny Bench	1.00
197	Dave Concepcion	.05
198	Ray Knight	.05
199	Ken Griffey	.05
200	Tom Seaver	1.00
201	Dave Collins	.05
202	George Foster	.05
203	Junior Kennedy	.05
204	Frank Pastore	.05
205	Dan Driessen	.05
206	Hector Cruz	.05
207	Paul Moskau	.05
208	Charlie Leibrandt RC	.25
209	Harry Spilman	.05
210	Joe Price RC	.05
211	Tom Hume	.05
212	Joe Nolan	.05
213	Doug Bair	.05
214	Mario Soto	.05
215a	Bill Bonham (No finger on back.)	.05
215b	Bill Bonham (Small finger on back.)	.50
216a	George Foster (Slugger on front.)	.25
216b	George Foster (Outfield on front.)	.15
217	Paul Householder	.05
218	Ron Oester	.05
219	Sam Mejias	.05
220	Sheldon Burnside	.05
221	Carl Yastrzemski	1.00
222	Jim Rice	.40
223	Fred Lynn	.05
224	Carlton Fisk	1.00
225	Rick Burleson	.05
226	Dennis Eckersley	.75
227	Butch Hobson	.05
228	Tom Burgmeier	.05
229	Garry Hancock	.05
230	Don Zimmer	.05
231	Steve Renko	.05
232	Dwight Evans	.05
233	Mike Torrez	.05
234	Bob Stanley	.05
235	Jim Dwyer	.05
236	Dave Stapleton	.05
237	Glenn Hoffman	.05
238	Jerry Remy	.05
239	Dick Drago	.05
240	Bill Campbell	.05
241	Tony Perez	.75
242	Phil Niekro	.75
243	Dale Murphy	.30
244	Bob Horner	.05
245	Jeff Burroughs	.05
246	Rick Camp	.05
247	Bob Cox	.25
248	Bruce Benedict	.05
249	Gene Garber	.05
250	Jerry Royster	.05
251a	Gary Matthews (No finger on back.)	.05
251b	Gary Matthews (Small finger on back.)	.50
252	Chris Chambliss	.05
253	Luis Gomez	.05
254	Bill Nahorodny	.05
255	Doyle Alexander	.05
256	Brian Asselstine	.05
257	Biff Pocoroba	.05
258	Mike Lum	.05
259	Charlie Spikes	.05
260	Glenn Hubbard	.05
261	Tommy Boggs	.05
262	Al Hrabosky	.05
263	Rick Matula	.05
264	Preston Hanna	.05
265	Larry Bradford	.05
266	Rafael Ramirez RC	.05
267	Larry McWilliams	.05
268	Rod Carew	1.00
269	Bobby Grich	.05
270	Carney Lansford	.05
271	Don Baylor	.05
272	Joe Rudi	.05
273	Dan Ford	.05
274	Jim Fregosi	.05
275	Dave Frost	.05
276	Frank Tanana	.05
277	Dickie Thon	.05
278	Jason Thompson	.05
279	Rick Miller	.05
280	Bert Campaneris	.05
281	Tom Donohue	.05
282	Brian Downing	.05
283	Fred Patek	.05
284	Bruce Kison	.05
285	Dave LaRoche	.05
286	Don Aase	.05
287	Jim Barr	.05
288	Alfredo Martinez	.05
289	Larry Harlow	.05
290	Andy Hassler	.05
291	Dave Kingman	.05
292	Bill Buckner	.05
293	Rick Reuschel	.05
294	Bruce Sutter	.75
295	Jerry Martin	.05
296	Scot Thompson	.05
297	Ivan DeJesus	.05
298	Steve Dillard	.05
299	Dick Tidrow	.05
300	Randy Martz	.05
301	Lenny Randle	.05
302	Lynn McGlothen	.05
303	Cliff Johnson	.05
304	Tim Blackwell	.05
305	Dennis Lamp	.05
306	Bill Caudill	.05
307	Carlos Lezcano	.05
308	Jim Tracy	.05
309	Doug Capilla	.05
310	Willie Hernandez	.05
311	Mike Vail	.05
312	Mike Krukow	.05
313	Barry Foote	.05
314	Larry Biittner	.05
315	Mike Tyson	.05
316	Lee Mazzilli	.05
317	John Stearns	.05
318	Alex Trevino	.05
319	Craig Swan	.05
320	Frank Taveras	.05
321	Steve Henderson	.05
322	Neil Allen	.05
323	Mark Bomback	.05
324	Mike Jorgensen	.05
325	Joe Torre	.25
326	Elliott Maddox	.05
327	Pete Falcone	.05
328	Ray Burris	.05
329	Claudell Washington	.05
330	Doug Flynn	.05
331	Joel Youngblood	.05
332	Bill Almon	.05
333	Tom Hausman	.05
334	Pat Zachry	.05
335	Jeff Reardon RC	2.00
336	Wally Backman RC	.15
337	Dan Norman	.05
338	Jerry Morales	.05
339	Ed Farmer	.05
340	Bob Molinaro	.05
341	Todd Cruz	.05
342a	Britt Burns RC (No finger on front.)	.10
342b	Britt Burns RC (Small finger on front.)	.50
343	Kevin Bell	.05
344	Tony LaRussa	.25
345	Steve Trout	.05
346	Harold Baines RC	3.00
347	Richard Wortham	.05
348	Wayne Nordhagen	.05
349	Mike Squires	.05
350	Lamar Johnson	.05
351	Rickey Henderson	2.50
352	Francisco Barrios	.05
353	Thad Bosley	.05
354	Chet Lemon	.05
355	Bruce Kimm	.05
356	Richard Dotson RC	.05
357	Jim Morrison	.05
358	Mike Proly	.05
359	Greg Pryor	.05
360	Dave Parker	.05
361	Omar Moreno	.05
362a	Kent Tekulve (1071 Waterbury on back)	.15
362b	Kent Tekulve (1971 Waterbury on back)	.05
363	Willie Stargell	1.00
364	Phil Garner	.05
365	Ed Ott	.05
366	Don Robinson	.05
367	Chuck Tanner	.05
368	Jim Rooker	.05
369	Dale Berra	.05
370	Jim Bibby	.05
371	Steve Nicosia	.05
372	Mike Easler	.05
373	Bill Robinson	.05
374	Lee Lacy	.05
375	John Candelaria	.05
376	Manny Sanguillen	.05
377	Rick Rhoden	.05
378	Grant Jackson	.05
379	Tim Foli	.05
380	Rod Scurry RC	.05
381	Bill Madlock	.05
382a	Kurt Bevacqua (Photo reversed, backwards "P" on cap.)	.15
382b	Kurt Bevacqua (Correct photo.)	.50
383	Bert Blyleven	.10
384	Eddie Solomon	.05
385	Enrique Romo	.05
386	John Milner	.05
387	Mike Hargrove	.05
388	Jorge Orta	.05
389	Toby Harrah	.05
390	Tom Veryzer	.05
391	Miguel Dilone	.05
392	Dan Spillner	.05
393	Jack Brohamer	.05
394	Wayne Garland	.05
395	Sid Monge	.05
396	Rick Waits	.05
397	Joe Charboneau RC	.50
398	Gary Alexander	.05
399	Jerry Dybzinski	.05
400	Mike Stanton	.05
401	Mike Paxton	.05
402	Gary Gray	.05
403	Rick Manning	.05
404	Bo Diaz	.05
405	Ron Hassey	.05
406	Ross Grimsley	.05
407	Victor Cruz	.05
408	Len Barker	.05
409	Bob Bailor	.05
410	Otto Velez	.05
411	Ernie Whitt	.05
412	Jim Clancy	.05
413	Barry Bonnell	.05
414	Dave Stieb	.05
415	Damaso Garcia RC	.05
416	John Mayberry	.05
417	Roy Howell	.05
418	Dan Ainge RC	3.00
419a	Jesse Jefferson (Pirates on back.)	.10
419b	Jesse Jefferson (Blue Jays on back.)	.50
420	Joey McLaughlin	.05
421	Lloyd Moseby RC	.10
422	Al Woods	.05
423	Garth Iorg	.05
424	Doug Ault	.05
425	Ken Schrom RC	.05
426	Mike Willis	.05
427	Steve Braun	.05
428	Bob Davis	.05
429	Jerry Garvin	.05
430	Alfredo Griffin	.05
431	Bob Mattick	.05
432	Vida Blue	.05
433	Jack Clark	.05
434	Willie McCovey	1.00
435	Mike Ivie	.05
436a	Darrel Evans (Darrel on front.)	.15
436b	Darrell Evans (Darrell on front.)	.50
437	Terry Whitfield	.05
438	Rennie Stennett	.05
439	John Montefusco	.05
440	Jim Wohlford	.05
441	Bill North	.05
442	Milt May	.05
443	Max Venable	.05
444	Ed Whitson	.05
445	Al Holland RC	.05
446	Randy Moffitt	.05
447	Bob Knepper	.05
448	Gary Lavelle	.05
449	Greg Minton	.05
450	Johnnie LeMaster	.05
451	Larry Herndon	.05
452	Rich Murray	.05
453	Joe Pettini	.05
454	Allen Ripley	.05
455	Dennis Littlejohn	.05
456	Tom Griffin	.05
457	Alan Hargesheimer	.05
458	Joe Strain	.05
459	Steve Kemp	.05
460	Sparky Anderson	.25
461	Alan Trammell	.05
462	Mark Fidrych	.25
463	Lou Whitaker	.05
464	Dave Rozema	.05
465	Milt Wilcox	.05
466	Champ Summers	.05
467	Lance Parrish	.05
468	Dan Petry	.05
469	Pat Underwood	.05
470	Rick Peters	.05
471	Al Cowens	.05
472	John Wockenfuss	.05
473	Tom Brookens	.05
474	Richie Hebner	.05
475	Jack Morris	.05
476	Jim Lentine	.05
477	Bruce Robbins	.05
478	Mark Wagner	.05
479	Tim Corcoran	.05
480a	Stan Papi (Pitcher on front.)	.15
480b	Stan Papi (Shortstop on front.)	.50
481	Kirk Gibson RC	5.00
482	Dan Schatzeder	.05
483	Amos Otis	.05
484	Dave Winfield	1.00
485	Rollie Fingers	.75
486	Gene Richards	.05
487	Randy Jones	.05
488	Ozzie Smith	2.00
489	Gene Tenace	.05
490	Bill Fahey	.05
491	John Curtis	.05
492	Dave Cash	.05
493a	Tim Flannery (Photo reversed, batting righty.)	.15
493b	Tim Flannery (Photo correct, batting lefty.)	.50
494	Jerry Mumphrey	.05
495	Bob Shirley	.05
496	Steve Mura	.05
497	Eric Rasmussen	.05
498	Broderick Perkins	.05
499	Barry Evans	.05
500	Chuck Baker	.05
501	Luis Salazar RC	.05
502	Gary Lucas	.05
503	Mike Armstrong	.05
504	Jerry Turner	.05
505	Dennis Kinney	.05
506	Willy Montanez (Willie)	.05
507	Gorman Thomas	.05
508	Ben Oglivie	.05
509	Larry Hisle	.05
510	Sal Bando	.05
511	Robin Yount	1.00
512	Mike Caldwell	.05
513	Sixto Lezcano	.05
514a	Jerry Augustine (Billy Travers photo.)	.15
514b	Billy Travers (Correct name with photo.)	.50
515	Paul Molitor	1.00
516	Moose Haas	.05
517	Bill Castro	.05
518	Jim Slaton	.05
519	Lary Sorensen	.05
520	Bob McClure	.05
521	Charlie Moore	.05
522	Jim Gantner	.05
523	Reggie Cleveland	.05
524	Don Money	.05
525	Billy Travers	.05
526	Buck Martinez	.05
527	Dick Davis	.05
528	Ted Simmons	.05
529	Garry Templeton	.05
530	Ken Reitz	.05
531	Tony Scott	.05
532	Ken Oberkfell	.05
533	Bob Sykes	.05
534	Keith Smith	.05
535	John Littlefield	.05
536	Jim Kaat	.05
537	Bob Forsch	.05
538	Mike Phillips	.05
539	Terry Landrum RC	.05
540	Leon Durham RC	.05
541	Terry Kennedy	.05
542	George Hendrick	.05
543	Dane Iorg	.05
544	Mark Littell (Photo actually Jeff Little.)	.05
545	Keith Hernandez	.05
546	Silvio Martinez	.05
547a	Pete Vuckovich (Photo actually Don Hood.)	.15
547b	Don Hood (Correct name with photo.)	.50
548	Bobby Bonds	.10
549	Mike Ramsey	.05
550	Tom Herr	.05
551	Roy Smalley	.05
552	Jerry Koosman	.05
553	Ken Landreaux	.05
554	John Castino	.05
555	Doug Corbett	.05
556	Bombo Rivera	.05
557	Ron Jackson	.05
558	Butch Wynegar	.05
559	Hosken Powell	.05
560	Pete Redfern	.05
561	Roger Erickson	.05
562	Glenn Adams	.05
563	Rick Sofield	.05
564	Geoff Zahn	.05
565	Pete Mackanin	.05
566	Mike Cubbage	.05
567	Darrell Jackson	.05
568	Dave Edwards	.05
569	Rob Wilfong	.05
570	Sal Butera	.05
571	Jose Morales	.05
572	Rick Langford	.05
573	Mike Norris	.05
574	Rickey Henderson	2.50
575	Tony Armas	.05
576	Dave Revering	.05
577	Jeff Newman	.05
578	Bob Lacey	.05
579	Brian Kingman (Photo actually Alan Wirth.)	.05
580	Mitchell Page	.05
581	Billy Martin	.25
582	Rob Picciolo	.05
583	Mike Heath	.05
584	Mickey Klutts	.05
585	Orlando Gonzalez	.05
586	Mike Davis RC	.05
587	Wayne Gross	.05
588	Matt Keough	.05
589	Steve McCatty	.05
590	Dwayne Murphy	.05
591	Mario Guerrero	.05
592	Dave McKay	.05
593	Jim Essian	.05
594	Dave Heaverlo	.05
595	Maury Wills	.10
596	Juan Beniquez	.05
597	Rodney Craig	.05
598	Jim Anderson	.05
599	Floyd Bannister	.05
600	Bruce Bochte	.05
601	Julio Cruz	.05
602	Ted Cox	.05
603	Dan Meyer	.05
604	Larry Cox	.05
605	Bill Stein	.05
606	Steve Garvey	.30
607	Dave Roberts	.05
608	Leon Roberts	.05
609	Reggie Walton	.05
610	Dave Edler	.05
611	Larry Milbourne	.05
612	Kim Allen	.05
613	Mario Mendoza	.05
614	Tom Paciorek	.05
615	Glenn Abbott	.05
616	Joe Simpson	.05
617	Mickey Rivers	.05
618	Jim Kern	.05
619	Jim Sundberg	.05
620	Richie Zisk	.05
621	Jon Matlack	.05
622	Fergie Jenkins	.75
623	Pat Corrales	.05
624	Ed Figueroa	.05
625	Buddy Bell	.05
626	Al Oliver	.05
627	Doc Medich	.05
628	Bump Wills	.05
629	Rusty Staub	.05
630	Pat Putnam	.05
631	John Grubb	.05
632	Danny Darwin	.05
633	Ken Clay	.05
634	Jim Norris	.05
635	John Butcher	.05
636	Dave Roberts	.05
637	Billy Sample	.05
638	Carl Yastrzemski	1.00
639	Cecil Cooper	.05
640	Mike Schmidt	2.00
641a	Checklist 1-50 (41 Hal McRae)	.10
641b	Checklist 1-50 (41 Hal McRae Double Threat)	.10
642	Checklist 51-109	.05
643	Checklist 110-168	.05
644a	Checklist 169-220 (202 George Foster)	.10
644b	Checklist 169-220 (202 George Foster "Slugger")	.10
(645a)	Triple Threat (Larry Bowa, Pete Rose, Mike Schmidt (No number on back.))	2.00
645b	Triple Threat (Pete Rose, Larry Bowa, Mike Schmidt (Number on back.))	2.00
646	Checklist 221-267	.05
647	Checklist 268-315	.05

648	Checklist 316-359	.05
649	Checklist 360-408	.05
650	Reggie Jackson	2.00
651	Checklist 409-458	.05
652a	Checklist 459-509 (483 Aurelio Lopez)	.10
652b	Checklist 459-506 (No 483.)	.10
653	Willie Wilson	.05
654a	Checklist 507-550 (514 Jerry Augustine)	.10
654b	Checklist 507-550 (514 Billy Travers)	.05
655	George Brett	3.00
656	Checklist 551-593	.05
657	Tug McGraw	.05
658	Checklist 594-637	.05
659a	Checklist 640-660 (Last number on front is 551.)	.10
659b	Checklist 640-660 (Last number on front is 483.)	.15
660a	Steve Carlton (Date 1066 on back.)	1.00
660b	Steve Carlton (Date 1966 on back.)	2.00

All-Star Game/Team Logo Stickers

Highlights of previous All-Star Games are presented in Robert Laughlin cartoons on the cardboard backings of these stickers which feature team logos, caps or patches. Though none of the players are named on the cards, many are identifiable by the pictures, uniform numbers and/or game-action descriptions on the cards. Where a specific player is clearly depicted, his name is listed.

		NM/M
	Complete Set (47):	15.00
	Common Card:	.50
1933	AL wins newsman's first "Dream Game" (Babe Ruth)	1.00
1934	out (Carl Hubbell, Babe Ruth, Lou Gehrig, Jimmie Foxx, Al Simmons, Joe Cronin)	.50
1935	in row (Mel Harder, Lefty Gomez)	.60
1936	first time (Dizzy Dean)	.75
1937	lineup (Lou Gehrig)	.75
1938	gets strong pitching (Johnny VanderMeer)	.60
1939	in World's Fair city (Joe DiMaggio)	.75
1940	shutout (Paul Derringer)	.50
1941	Two-out homer in 9th wins for AL (Ted Williams)	.65
1942	victory (Lou Boudreau, Rudy York)	.50
1943	anyway	.50
1944	easiest win	.50
1946	most lopsided win	.50
1947	AL pinch hits break up pitchers' battle	.50
1948	AL wins despite stars on injury list	.50
1949	gains 12-4 series lead (George Kell, Johnny Mize)	.50
1950	park	.50
1951	NL bombs rivals with four homers (Ralph Kiner)	.60
1952	Two NL homers win rain-shortened game (Jackie Robinson, Hank Sauer)	.65
1953	first eight innings (Red Schoendienst, Minnie Minoso)	.50
1954	slugfest (Al Rosen)	.50
1955	in 12th (Stan Musial)	.65
1956	NL scores in five straight innings (Ted Williams)	.75
1957	in ninth (Mickey Mantle)	1.00
1958	of no extra-base hits (Nellie Fox)	.65
1959	two games(Frank Robinson, Al Kaline)	.60
1960	NL wins both games in AL parks	.50
1961	for only tie (Stu Miller)	.50
1962	year of two games is split	.50
1963	NL is outhit 11-6 but wins anyway	.50
1964	All-Star series	.50
1965	All-Star series (Willie Mays)	.75
1966	NL takes pitchers' battle in 10th (Juan Marichal, Denny McLain)	.60
1967	30 batters fan in 15-inning marathon	.50
1968	AL scoreless streak reaches 18 innings	.50
1969	runaway (Willie McCovey)	.60
1970	12th (Bud Harrelson)	.50
1971	triumph from 1963 to 1980 (Reggie Jackson, Harmon Killebrew, Frank Robinson)	.65
1972	games (Hank Aaron)	.75
1973	they win again	.50
1974	Dodgers are heroes in easy NL victory	.50
1975	9th	.50
1976	NL breezes	.50
1977	win again	.50
1978	with four in 8th	.50
1979	row to win seesaw 50th game	.50
1980	series lead of 32-18 (1 tie)	.50

Star Stickers

JOHNNY BENCH — REDS — CATCHER

The 128-card 1981 Fleer Star Sticker set was designed to allow the card fronts to be peeled away from the cardboard backs. Fronts feature color photos with blue and yellow trim. Backs are identical in design to the regular 1981 Fleer set except for color and numbering. The set contains three unnumbered checklist cards whose fronts depict Reggie Jackson, George Brett and Mike Schmidt. The sticker-cards, which are the standard 2-1/2" x 3-1/2", were issued in gum wax packs.

		NM/M
	Complete Set (128):	15.00
	Common Player:	.15
	Wax Pack (5):	1.25
	Wax Box (36):	15.00
1	Steve Garvey	.40
2	Ron LeFlore	.15
3	Ron Cey	.15
4	Dave Revering	.15
5	Tony Armas	.15
6	Mike Norris	.15
7	Steve Kemp	.15
8	Bruce Bochte	.15
9	Mike Schmidt	2.00
10	Scott McGregor	.15
11	Buddy Bell	.15
12	Carney Lansford	.15
13	Carl Yastrzemski	1.00
14	Ben Oglivie	.15
15	Willie Stargell	1.00
16	Cecil Cooper	.15
17	Gene Richards	.15
18	Jim Kern	.15
19	Jerry Koosman	.15
20	Larry Bowa	.15
21	Kent Tekulve	.15
22	Dan Driessen	.15
23	Phil Niekro	.75
24	Dan Quisenberry	.15
25	Dave Winfield	1.00
26	Dave Parker	.15
27	Rick Langford	.15
28	Amos Otis	.15
29	Bill Buckner	.15
30	Al Bumbry	.15
31	Bake McBride	.15
32	Mickey Rivers	.15
33	Rick Burleson	.15
34	Dennis Eckersley	.75
35	Cesar Cedeno	.15
36	Enos Cabell	.15
37	Johnny Bench	1.00
38	Robin Yount	1.00
39	Mark Belanger	.15
40	Rod Carew	1.00
41	George Foster	.15
42	Lee Mazzilli	.15
43	Triple Threat (Larry Bowa, Pete Rose, Mike Schmidt)	2.00
44	J.R. Richard	.15
45	Lou Piniella	.15
46	Ken Landreaux	.15
47	Rollie Fingers	.75
48	Joaquin Andujar	.15
49	Tom Seaver	1.00
50	Bobby Grich	.15
51	Jon Matlack	.15
52	Jack Clark	.15
53	Jim Rice	.15
54	Rickey Henderson	3.00
55	Roy Smalley	.15
56	Mike Flanagan	.15
57	Steve Rogers	.15
58	Carlton Fisk	1.00
59	Don Sutton	.75
60	Ken Griffey	.15
61	Burt Hooton	.15
62	Dusty Baker	.15
63	Vida Blue	.15
64	Al Oliver	.15
65	Jim Bibby	.15
66	Tony Perez	.75
67	Davy Lopes (Davey)	.15
68	Bill Russell	.15
69	Larry Parrish	.15
70	Garry Maddox	.15
71	Phil Garner	.15
72	Graig Nettles	.20
73	Gary Carter	1.00
74	Pete Rose	3.00
75	Greg Luzinski	.15
76	Ron Guidry	.15
77	Gorman Thomas	.15
78	Jose Cruz	.15
79	Bob Boone	.15
80	Bruce Sutter	.75
81	Chris Chambliss	.15
82	Paul Molitor	1.00
83	Tug McGraw	.15
84	Ferguson Jenkins	.75
85	Steve Carlton	1.00
86	Miguel Dilone	.15
87	Reggie Smith	.15
88	Rick Cerone	.15
89	Alan Trammell	.15
90	Doug DeCinces	.15
91	Sparky Lyle	.15
92	Warren Cromartie	.15
93	Rick Reuschel	.15
94	Larry Hisle	.15
95	Paul Splittorff	.15
96	Manny Trillo	.15
97	Frank White	.15
98	Fred Lynn	.15
99	Bob Horner	.15
100	Omar Moreno	.15
101	Dave Concepcion	.15
102	Larry Gura	.15
103	Ken Singleton	.15
104	Steve Stone	.15
105	Richie Zisk	.15
106	Willie Wilson	.15
107	Willie Randolph	.15
108	Nolan Ryan	3.00
109	Joe Morgan	1.00
110	Bucky Dent	.20
111	Dave Kingman	.15
112	John Castino	.15
113	Joe Rudi	.15
114	Ed Farmer	.15
115	Reggie Jackson	2.50
116	George Brett	2.00
117	Eddie Murray	1.00
118	Rich Gossage	.20
119	Dale Murphy	.40
120	Ted Simmons	.15
121	Tommy John	.20
122	Don Baylor	.15
123	Andre Dawson	.60
124	Jim Palmer	1.00
125	Garry Templeton	.15
----	Checklist 1-42 (Reggie Jackson)	.50
----	Checklist 43-83 (George Brett)	.50
----	Checklist 84-125 (Mike Schmidt)	.50

Superstar Stickers

FLEER MICKEY MANTLE super star

While these small (about 1-1/2" x 2") stickers carry the Fleer name and were, indeed, produced by Fleer, they are more akin to collectors' issues than a legitimate product. Wrappers of 1981 Fleer Star Stickers offered the opportunity to put one's own photo, or the photo of someone else, on 24 stickers for a couple of dollars and proofs of purchase. Some enterprising hobbyists sent in several different pictures of Mickey Mantle and pictures of then-current stars and had them made into stickers. Because they are un-authorized by Mantle, or the other players seen (Boggs, Mattingly, Yaz, etc.), there is no collector value.

1982 Fleer

Cardinals 28 — Tom Herr — SECOND BASE

Fleer's 1982 set did not match the quality of the previous year's effort. Many of the card photos are blurred and have muddied backgrounds. The 2-1/2" x 3-1/2" cards feature color photos bordered by a frame which is color-coded by team. Backs are blue, white, and yellow and contain the player's team logo plus the logos of Major League Baseball and the Major League Baseball Players Association. Due to a lawsuit by Topps, Fleer was forced to issue the set with team logo stickers rather than gum. The complete set price does not include the higher priced variations.

		NM/M
	Complete Set (660):	45.00
	Common Player:	.05
	Wax Pack (15):	3.00
	Wax Box (36):	85.00
	Cello Pack (28):	4.00
	Cello Box (24):	85.00
	Vending Box (500):	40.00
1	Dusty Baker	.05
2	Robert Castillo	.05
3	Ron Cey	.05
4	Terry Forster	.05
5	Steve Garvey	.30
6	Dave Goltz	.05
7	Pedro Guerrero	.05
8	Burt Hooton	.05
9	Steve Howe	.05
10	Jay Johnstone	.05
11	Ken Landreaux	.05
12	Davey Lopes	.05
13	Mike Marshall RC	.15
14	Bobby Mitchell	.05
15	Rick Monday	.05
16	Tom Niedenfuer RC	.05
17	Ted Power RC	.05
18	Jerry Reuss	.05
19	Ron Roenicke	.05
20	Bill Russell	.05
21	Steve Sax RC	.45
22	Mike Scioscia	.05
23	Reggie Smith	.05
24	Dave Stewart RC	1.50
25	Rick Sutcliffe	.05
26	Derrel Thomas	.05
27	Fernando Valenzuela	.10
28	Bob Welch	.05
29	Steve Yeager	.05
30	Bobby Brown	.05
31	Rick Cerone	.05
32	Ron Davis	.05
33	Bucky Dent	.10
34	Barry Foote	.05
35	George Frazier	.05
36	Oscar Gamble	.05
37	Rich Gossage	.10
38	Ron Guidry	.10
39	Reggie Jackson	1.50
40	Tommy John	.10
41	Rudy May	.05
42	Larry Milbourne	.05
43	Jerry Mumphrey	.05
44	Bobby Murcer	.05
45	Gene Nelson RC	.05
46	Graig Nettles	.05
47	Johnny Oates	.05
48	Lou Piniella	.10
49	Willie Randolph	.05
50	Rick Reuschel	.05
51	Dave Revering	.05
52	Dave Righetti RC	.45
53	Aurelio Rodriguez	.05
54	Bob Watson	.05
55	Dennis Werth	.05
56	Dave Winfield	1.00
57	Johnny Bench	1.00
58	Bruce Berenyi	.05
59	Larry Biittner	.05
60	Scott Brown	.05
61	Dave Collins	.05
62	Geoff Combe	.05
63	Dave Concepcion	.05
64	Dan Driessen	.05
65	Joe Edelen	.05
66	George Foster	.05
67	Ken Griffey	.05
68	Paul Householder	.05
69	Tom Hume	.05
70	Junior Kennedy	.05
71	Ray Knight	.05
72	Mike LaCoss	.05
73	Rafael Landestoy	.05
74	Charlie Leibrandt	.05
75	Sam Mejias	.05
76	Paul Moskau	.05
77	Joe Nolan	.05
78	Mike O'Berry	.05
79	Ron Oester	.05
80	Frank Pastore	.05
81	Joe Price	.05
82	Tom Seaver	1.00
83	Mario Soto	.05
84	Mike Vail	.05
85	Tony Armas	.05
86	Shooty Babitt	.05
87	Dave Beard	.05
88	Rick Bosetti	.05
89	Keith Drumright	.05
90	Wayne Gross	.05
91	Mike Heath	.05
92	Rickey Henderson	1.00
93	Cliff Johnson	.05
94	Jeff Jones	.05
95	Matt Keough	.05
96	Brian Kingman	.05
97	Mickey Klutts	.05
98	Rick Langford	.05
99	Steve McCatty	.05
100	Dave McKay	.05
101	Dwayne Murphy	.05
102	Jeff Newman	.05
103	Mike Norris	.05
104	Bob Owchinko	.05
105	Mitchell Page	.05
106	Rob Picciolo	.05
107	Jim Spencer	.05
108	Fred Stanley	.05
109	Tom Underwood	.05
110	Joaquin Andujar	.05
111	Steve Braun	.05
112	Bob Forsch	.05
113	George Hendrick	.05
114	Keith Hernandez	.05
115	Tom Herr	.05
116	Dane Iorg	.05
117	Jim Kaat	.10
118	Tito Landrum	.05
119	Sixto Lezcano	.05
120	Mark Littell	.05
121	John Martin	.05
122	Silvio Martinez	.05
123	Ken Oberkfell	.05
124	Darrell Porter	.05
125	Mike Ramsey	.05
126	Orlando Sanchez	.05
127	Bob Shirley	.05
128	Lary Sorensen	.05
129	Bruce Sutter	.75
130	Bob Sykes	.05
131	Garry Templeton	.05
132	Gene Tenace	.05
133	Jerry Augustine	.05
134	Sal Bando	.05
135	Mark Brouhard	.05
136	Mike Caldwell	.05
137	Reggie Cleveland	.05
138	Cecil Cooper	.05
139	Jamie Easterly	.05
140	Marshall Edwards	.05
141	Rollie Fingers	.75
142	Jim Gantner	.05
143	Moose Haas	.05
144	Larry Hisle	.05
145	Roy Howell	.05
146	Rickey Keeton	.05
147	Randy Lerch	.05
148	Paul Molitor	1.00
149	Don Money	.05
150	Charlie Moore	.05
151	Ben Oglivie	.05
152	Ted Simmons	.05
153	Jim Slaton	.05
154	Gorman Thomas	.05
155	Robin Yount	1.00
156	Pete Vukovich	.05
157	Benny Ayala	.05
158	Mark Belanger	.05
159	Al Bumbry	.05
160	Terry Crowley	.05
161	Rich Dauer	.05
162	Doug DeCinces	.05
163	Rick Dempsey	.05
164	Jim Dwyer	.05
165	Mike Flanagan	.05
166	Dave Ford	.05
167	Dan Graham	.05
168	Wayne Krenchicki	.05
169	John Lowenstein	.05
170	Dennis Martinez	.05
171	Tippy Martinez	.05
172	Scott McGregor	.05
173	Jose Morales	.05
174	Eddie Murray	1.00
175	Jim Palmer	1.00
176	Cal Ripken, Jr. RC	40.00
177	Gary Roenicke	.05
178	Lenn Sakata	.05
179	Ken Singleton	.05
180	Sammy Stewart	.05
181	Tim Stoddard	.05
182	Steve Stone	.05
183	Stan Bahnsen	.05
184	Ray Burris	.05
185	Gary Carter	1.00
186	Warren Cromartie	.05
187	Andre Dawson	.50
188	Terry Francona RC	.05
189	Woodie Fryman	.05
190	Bill Gullickson	.05
191	Grant Jackson	.05
192	Wallace Johnson	.05
193	Charlie Lea	.05
194	Bill Lee	.05
195	Jerry Manuel	.05
196	Brad Mills	.05
197	John Milner	.05
198	Rowland Office	.05
199	David Palmer	.05
200	Larry Parrish	.05
201	Mike Phillips	.05
202	Tim Raines	.25
203	Bobby Ramos	.05
204	Jeff Reardon	.05
205	Steve Rogers	.05
206	Scott Sanderson	.05
207	Rodney Scott (Photo actually Tim Raines.)	.10
208	Elias Sosa	.05
209	Chris Speier	.05
210	Tim Wallach RC	1.00
211	Jerry White	.05
212	Alan Ashby	.05
213	Cesar Cedeno	.05
214	Jose Cruz	.05
215	Kiko Garcia	.05
216	Phil Garner	.05
217	Danny Heep	.05
218	Art Howe	.05
219	Bob Knepper	.05
220	Frank LaCorte	.05
221	Joe Niekro	.05
222	Joe Pittman	.05
223	Terry Puhl	.05
224	Luis Pujols	.05
225	Craig Reynolds	.05
226	J.R. Richard	.05
227	Dave Roberts	.05
228	Vern Ruhle	.05
229	Nolan Ryan	3.0..
230	Joe Sambito	.0..
231	Tony Scott	.0..
232	Dave Smith	.0..
233	Harry Spilman	.0..
234	Don Sutton	.7..
235	Dickie Thon	.0..
236	Denny Walling	.0..
237	Gary Woods	.0..
238	Luis Aguayo RC	.0..
239	Ramon Aviles	.0..
240	Bob Boone	.0..
241	Larry Bowa	.0..
242	Warren Brusstar	.0..
243	Steve Carlton	.7..
244	Larry Christenson	.0..
245	Dick Davis	.0..
246	Greg Gross	.0..
247	Sparky Lyle	.0..
248	Garry Maddox	.0..
249	Gary Matthews	.0..
250	Bake McBride	.0..
251	Tug McGraw	.0..
252	Keith Moreland	.0..
253	Dickie Noles	.0..
254	Mike Proly	.0..
255	Ron Reed	.0..
256	Pete Rose	2.5..
257	Dick Ruthven	.0..
258	Mike Schmidt	
259	Lonnie Smith	.0..
260	Manny Trillo	.0..
261	Del Unser	.0..
262	George Vukovich	.0..
263	Tom Brookens	.0..
264	George Cappuzzello	.0..
265	Marty Castillo	.0..
266	Al Cowens	.0..
267	Kirk Gibson	.0..
268	Richie Hebner	.0..
269	Ron Jackson	.0..
270	Lynn Jones	.0..
271	Steve Kemp	.0..
272	Rick Leach RC	.0..
273	Aurelio Lopez	.0..
274	Jack Morris	.0..
275	Kevin Saucier	.0..
276	Lance Parrish	.0..
277	Rick Peters	.0..
278	Dan Petry	.0..
279	David Rozema	.0..
280	Stan Papi	.0..
281	Dan Schatzeder	.0..
282	Champ Summers	.0..
283	Alan Trammell	.0..
284	Lou Whitaker	.0..
285	Milt Wilcox	.0..
286	John Wockenfuss	.0..
287	Gary Allenson	.0..
288	Tom Burgmeier	.0..
289	Bill Campbell	.0..
290	Mark Clear	.0..
291	Steve Crawford	.0..
292	Dennis Eckersley	.0..
293	Dwight Evans	.0..
294	Rich Gedman RC	.0..
295	Garry Hancock	.0..
296	Glenn Hoffman	.0..
297	Bruce Hurst	.0..
298	Carney Lansford	.0..
299	Rick Miller	.0..
300	Reid Nichols	.0..

301	Bob Ojeda RC	.25
302	Tony Perez	.75
303	Chuck Rainey	.05
304	Jerry Remy	.05
305	Jim Rice	.50
306	Joe Rudi	.05
307	Bob Stanley	.05
308	Dave Stapleton	.05
309	Frank Tanana	.05
310	Mike Torrez	.05
311	John Tudor	.05
312	Carl Yastrzemski	1.00
313	Buddy Bell	.05
314	Steve Comer	.05
315	Danny Darwin	.05
316	John Ellis	.05
317	John Grubb	.05
318	Rick Honeycutt	.05
319	Charlie Hough	.05
320	Fergie Jenkins	.75
321	John Henry Johnson	.05
322	Jim Kern	.05
323	Jon Matlack	.05
324	Doc Medich	.05
325	Mario Mendoza	.05
326	Al Oliver	.05
327	Pat Putnam	.05
328	Mickey Rivers	.05
329	Leon Roberts	.05
330	Billy Sample	.05
331	Bill Stein	.05
332	Jim Sundberg	.05
333	Mark Wagner	.05
334	Bump Wills	.05
335	Bill Almon	.05
336	Harold Baines	.05
337	Ross Baumgarten	.05
338	Tony Bernazard	.05
339	Britt Burns	.05
340	Richard Dotson	.05
341	Jim Essian	.05
342	Ed Farmer	.05
343	Carlton Fisk	1.00
344	Kevin Hickey	.05
345	Lamarr Hoyt (LaMarr)	.05
346	Lamar Johnson	.05
347	Jerry Koosman	.05
348	Rusty Kuntz	.05
349	Dennis Lamp	.05
350	Ron LeFlore	.05
351	Chet Lemon	.05
352	Greg Luzinski	.05
353	Bob Molinaro	.05
354	Jim Morrison	.05
355	Wayne Nordhagen	.05
356	Greg Pryor	.05
357	Mike Squires	.05
358	Steve Trout	.05
359	Alan Bannister	.05
360	Len Barker	.05
361	Bert Blyleven	.10
362	Joe Charboneau	.10
363	John Denny	.05
364	Bo Diaz	.05
365	Miguel Dilone	.05
366	Jerry Dybzinski	.05
367	Wayne Garland	.05
368	Mike Hargrove	.05
369	Toby Harrah	.05
370	Ron Hassey	.05
371	Von Hayes RC	.25
372	Pat Kelly	.05
373	Duane Kuiper	.05
374	Rick Manning	.05
375	Sid Monge	.05
376	Jorge Orta	.05
377	Dave Rosello	.05
378	Dan Spillner	.05
379	Mike Stanton	.05
380	Andre Thornton	.05
381	Tom Veryzer	.05
382	Rick Waits	.05
383	Doyle Alexander	.05
384	Vida Blue	.05
385	Fred Breining	.05
386	Enos Cabell	.05
387	Jack Clark	.05
388	Darrell Evans	.05
389	Tom Griffin	.05
390	Larry Herndon	.05
391	Al Holland	.05
392	Gary Lavelle	.05
393	Johnnie LeMaster	.05
394	Jerry Martin	.05
395	Milt May	.05
396	Greg Minton	.05
397	Joe Morgan	1.00
398	Joe Pettini	.05
399	Alan Ripley	.05
400	Billy Smith	.05
401	Rennie Stennett	.05
402	Ed Whitson	.05
403	Jim Wohlford	.05
404	Willie Aikens	.05
405	George Brett	2.00
406	Ken Brett	.05
407	Dave Chalk	.05
408	Rich Gale	.05
409	Cesar Geronimo	.05
410	Larry Gura	.05
411	Clint Hurdle	.05
412	Mike Jones	.05
413	Dennis Leonard	.05
414	Renie Martin	.05
415	Lee May	.05
416	Hal McRae	.05
417	Darryl Motley	.05
418	Rance Mulliniks	.05

419	Amos Otis	.05
420	Ken Phelps RC	.05
421	Jamie Quirk	.05
422	Dan Quisenberry	.05
423	Paul Splittorff	.05
424	U.L. Washington	.05
425	John Wathan	.05
426	Frank White	.05
427	Willie Wilson	.05
428	Brian Asselstine	.05
429	Bruce Benedict	.05
430	Tom Boggs	.05
431	Larry Bradford	.05
432	Rick Camp	.05
433	Chris Chambliss	.05
434	Gene Garber	.05
435	Preston Hanna	.05
436	Bob Horner	.05
437	Glenn Hubbard	.05
438a	Al Hrabosky (All Hrabosky, 5'1" on back.)	4.50
438b	Al Hrabosky (Al Hrabosky, 5'1" on back.)	1.00
438c	Al Hrabosky (Al Hrabosky, 5'10" on back.)	.25
439	Rufino Linares	.05
440	Rick Mahler RC	.05
441	Ed Miller	.05
442	John Montefusco	.05
443	Dale Murphy	.50
444	Phil Niekro	.75
445	Gaylord Perry	.75
446	Biff Pocoroba	.05
447	Rafael Ramirez	.05
448	Jerry Royster	.05
449	Claudell Washington	.05
450	Don Aase	.05
451	Don Baylor	.05
452	Juan Beniquez	.05
453	Rick Burleson	.05
454	Bert Campaneris	.05
455	Rod Carew	1.00
456	Bob Clark	.05
457	Brian Downing	.05
458	Dan Ford	.05
459	Ken Forsch	.05
460	Dave Frost	.05
461	Bobby Grich	.05
462	Larry Harlow	.05
463	John Harris	.05
464	Andy Hassler	.05
465	Butch Hobson	.05
466	Jesse Jefferson	.05
467	Bruce Kison	.05
468	Fred Lynn	.05
469	Angel Moreno	.05
470	Ed Ott	.05
471	Fred Patek	.05
472	Steve Renko	.05
473	Mike Witt RC	.10
474	Geoff Zahn	.05
475	Gary Alexander	.05
476	Dale Berra	.05
477	Kurt Bevacqua	.05
478	Jim Bibby	.05
479	John Candelaria	.05
480	Victor Cruz	.05
481	Mike Easler	.05
482	Tim Foli	.05
483	Lee Lacy	.05
484	Vance Law	.05
485	Bill Madlock	.05
486	Willie Montanez	.05
487	Omar Moreno	.05
488	Steve Nicosia	.05
489	Dave Parker	.05
490	Tony Pena	.05
491	Pascual Perez	.05
492	Johnny Ray RC	.05
493	Rick Rhoden	.05
494	Bill Robinson	.05
495	Don Robinson	.05
496	Enrique Romo	.05
497	Rod Scurry	.05
498	Eddie Solomon	.05
499	Willie Stargell	1.00
500	Kent Tekulve	.05
501	Jason Thompson	.05
502	Glenn Abbott	.05
503	Jim Anderson	.05
504	Floyd Bannister	.05
505	Bruce Bochte	.05
506	Jeff Burroughs	.05
507	Bryan Clark	.05
508	Ken Clay	.05
509	Julio Cruz	.05
510	Dick Drago	.05
511	Gary Gray	.05
512	Dan Meyer	.05
513	Jerry Narron	.05
514	Tom Paciorek	.05
515	Casey Parsons	.05
516	Lenny Randle	.05
517	Shane Rawley	.05
518	Joe Simpson	.05
519	Richie Zisk	.05
520	Neil Allen	.05
521	Bob Bailor	.05
522	Hubie Brooks	.05
523	Mike Cubbage	.05
524	Pete Falcone	.05
525	Doug Flynn	.05
526	Tom Hausman	.05
527	Ron Hodges	.05
528	Randy Jones	.05
529	Mike Jorgensen	.05
530	Dave Kingman	.05
531	Ed Lynch	.05

532	Mike Marshall	.05
533	Lee Mazzilli	.05
534	Dyar Miller	.05
535	Mike Scott	.05
536	Rusty Staub	.05
537	John Stearns	.05
538	Craig Swan	.05
539	Frank Taveras	.05
540	Alex Trevino	.05
541	Ellis Valentine	.05
542	Mookie Wilson	.05
543	Joel Youngblood	.05
544	Pat Zachry	.05
545	Glenn Adams	.05
546	Fernando Arroyo	.05
547	John Verhoeven	.05
548	Sal Butera	.05
549	John Castino	.05
550	Don Cooper	.05
551	Doug Corbett	.05
552	Dave Engle	.05
553	Roger Erickson	.05
554	Danny Goodwin	.05
555a	Darrell Jackson (Black cap.)	.65
555b	Darrell Jackson (Red cap w/speck of white.)	3.00
555c	Darrell Jackson (Red cap w/white T.)	.10
556	Pete Mackanin	.05
557	Jack O'Connor	.05
558	Hosken Powell	.05
559	Pete Redfern	.05
560	Roy Smalley	.05
561	Chuck Baker	.05
562	Gary Ward	.05
563	Rob Wilfong	.05
564	Al Williams	.05
565	Butch Wynegar	.05
566	Randy Bass	.05
567	Juan Bonilla	.05
568	Danny Boone	.05
569	John Curtis	.05
570	Juan Eichelberger	.05
571	Barry Evans	.05
572	Tim Flannery	.05
573	Ruppert Jones	.05
574	Terry Kennedy	.05
575	Joe Lefebvre	.05
576a	John Littlefield (Pitching lefty.)	80.00
576b	John Littlefield (Pitching righty.)	.05
577	Gary Lucas	.05
578	Steve Mura	.05
579	Broderick Perkins	.05
580	Gene Richards	.05
581	Luis Salazar	.05
582	Ozzie Smith	1.50
583	John Urrea	.05
584	Chris Welsh	.05
585	Rick Wise	.05
586	Doug Bird	.05
587	Tim Blackwell	.05
588	Bobby Bonds	.10
589	Bill Buckner	.05
590	Bill Caudill	.05
591	Hector Cruz	.05
592	Jody Davis RC	.10
593	Ivan DeJesus	.05
594	Steve Dillard	.05
595	Leon Durham	.05
596	Rawly Eastwick	.05
597	Steve Henderson	.05
598	Mike Krukow	.05
599	Mike Lum	.05
600	Randy Martz	.05
601	Jerry Morales	.05
602	Ken Reitz	.05
603a	Lee Smith RC (Cubs logo reversed on back.)	2.50
603b	Lee Smith RC (corrected)	2.50
604	Dick Tidrow	.05
605	Jim Tracy	.05
606	Mike Tyson	.05
607	Ty Waller	.05
608	Danny Ainge	.50
609	Jorge Bell RC	1.00
610	Mark Bomback	.05
611	Barry Bonnell	.05
612	Jim Clancy	.05
613	Damaso Garcia	.05
614	Jerry Garvin	.05
615	Alfredo Griffin	.05
616	Garth Iorg	.05
617	Luis Leal	.05
618	Ken Macha	.05
619	John Mayberry	.05
620	Joey McLaughlin	.05
621	Lloyd Moseby	.05
622	Dave Stieb	.05
623	Jackson Todd	.05
624	Willie Upshaw RC	.05
625	Otto Velez	.05
626	Ernie Whitt	.05
627	Al Woods	.05
628	1981 All-Star Game	.05
629	All-Star Infielders (Bucky Dent, Frank White)	.05
630	Big Red Machine (Dave Concepcion, Dan Driessen, George Foster)	.30
631	Top N.L. Relief Pitcher (Bruce Sutter)	.30
632	Steve & Carlton (Steve Carlton, Carlton Fisk)	.25

633	3000th Game, May 25, 1981 (Carl Yastrzemski)	.35
634	Dynamic Duo (Johnny Bench, Tom Seaver)	.30
635	West Meets East (Gary Carter, Fernando Valenzuela)	.20
636a	N.L. Strikeout King (Fernando Valenzuela ("...led the National League..."))	.50
636b	N.L. Strikeout King (Fernando Valenzuela ("...led the National League..."))	.25
637	Home Run King (Mike Schmidt)	.50
638	N.L. All-Stars (Gary Carter, Dave Parker)	.25
639	Perfect Game! (Len Barker, Bo Diaz)	.25
640	Pete Rose, Pete Rose, Jr. (Re-Pete)	2.00
641	Phillies' Finest (Steve Carlton, Mike Schmidt, Lonnie Smith)	.50
642	Red Sox Reunion (Dwight Evans, Fred Lynn)	.10
643	Most Hits and Runs (Rickey Henderson)	1.00
644	Most Saves 1981 A.L. (Rollie Fingers)	.15
645	Most 1981 Wins (Tom Seaver)	.25
646a	Yankee Powerhouse (Reggie Jackson, Dave Winfield (Comma after "outfielder" on back.))	1.50
646b	Yankee Powerhouse (Reggie Jackson, Dave Winfield (No comma.))	2.00
647	Checklist 1-56	.05
648	Checklist 57-109	.05
649	Checklist 110-156	.05
650	Checklist 157-211	.05
651	Checklist 212-262	.05
652	Checklist 263-312	.05
653	Checklist 313-358	.05
654	Checklist 359-403	.05
655	Checklist 404-449	.05
656	Checklist 450-501	.05
657	Checklist 502-544	.05
658	Checklist 545-585	.05
659	Checklist 586-627	.05
660	Checklist 628-646	.05

Proofs

More than two dozen proof cards which differ significantly from the issued versions in 1982 Fleer are known, though the quantities in which they have made their way into the hobby market are not known. Blank-backed and hand-cut from press sheets, the proofs include a number of Hall of Famers and high-demand stars. The manner in which the proof card differs from the issued version is listed parenthetically.

		NM/M
---	Dave Patterson (No issued version.)	75.00
4	Terry Forster (Green photo border.)	50.00
31	Rick Cerone/Catching (Game-action.)	75.00
37	Rich Gossage (Pose to knees.)	75.00
48	Lou Piniella/Trotting (Game-action.)	75.00
49	Willie Randolph/Btg (Game-action.)	75.00
61	Dave Collins/Btg (Game-action.)	50.00
67	Ken Griffey (Home uniform.)	60.00
82	Tom Seaver/Pitching (Game-action.)	60.00
312	Carl Yastrzemski (Misspelled "Yastremski.")	350.00
395	Milt May (Ed Whitson photo.)	60.00
402	Ed Whitson (Milt May photo.)	60.00
416	Hal McRae (Position: OF.)	25.00
427	Willie Wilson (Pose, no microphone.)	50.00
449	Claudell Washington (Game-action, batting.)	50.00
503	Jim Anderson (Incorrect name: Mike.)	25.00
555	Darrell Jackson (Pictures unidentified pitcher.)	45.00
629	All-Star Infielders (Captioned: "Dent & White.")	25.00
632	Steve & Carlton (Captioned: "Carlton & Steve / FISK & CARLTON.")	40.00
635	West Meets East (Captioned: "East Meets West.")	25.00
644	N.L. All-Stars (Captioned: "Parker & Carter.")	25.00
646	Most Saves 1981 (Captioned: "A.L. Most Saves in 1981.")	25.00
652	Yankee Powerhouse (Captioned: "Winfield & Jackson.")	45.00
652	Checklist (Lists #275 as Stan Papi.)	15.00
660	Checklist (McRae's position: OF.)	15.00
660	Checklist (White border, incorrect captions as above.)	15.00

Test Cards

To test a proposed cardboard stock from International Paper Co., a run of 100 sheets of test cards was printed and delivered to Fleer officials. The cards on the sheet include various combinations of correct picture/name combinations, incorrect picture/name combinations and cards with no player identification. All cards have the words "TEST CARD" overprinted in black in the player identification area at bottom center, along with the letters "o," "n" or both vertically at the left end of the oblong. Backs are blank. At least half of the 132-card test sheets have made their way into the hobby where they are offered both as complete sheets and as hand-cut single cards or panels. A number of the photos seen on the test cards did not appear in Fleer's 1982 card set. The checklist here is arranged by row and card number on the sheets. Player names are as printed, if the photo is not that player it is identified in parentheses. Each of the 66 cards is double-printed on the sheet.

		NM/M
Complete Sheet (132):		1,500
Complete Sheet (66):		900.00
Common Card:		10.00
1-1	Jon Matlack (Steve Christmas)	10.00
1-2	Wayne Gross (Jose Brito)	10.00
1-3	Mario Mendoza (John Lickert)	10.00
1-4	Mike Heath (Daryl Sconiers)	10.00
1-5	Bump Wills (Lee Mazzilli)	10.00
1-6	Steve McCatty (Jose Rodriguez)	10.00
1-7	Steve Stone	25.00
1-8	No identification (Brian Harper)	10.00
1-9	Dennis Martinez (Cubs player)	15.00
1-10	No identification (Julio Valdez)	10.00
1-11	Jim Palmer (Del Unser)	25.00
2-1	Billy Sample (Bill Doran)	10.00
2-2	Tony Armas (Tony Armas)	10.00
2-3	Rick Honeycutt (Rick Honeycutt)	10.00
2-4	Cliff Jackson (Tim Ireland)	10.00
2-5	John Ellis (Floyd Rayford)	10.00
2-6	Dave McKay (Jim Wright)	10.00
2-7	Ken Singleton (Larry Milbourne)	10.00
2-8	No identification (Steve Balboni)	10.00
2-9	John Lowenstein (Mickey Mahler)	10.00
2-10	No identification (Ty Waller)	10.00
2-11	Doug DeCinces (Mike Patterson)	10.00
3-1	Mickey Rivers (Pat Putnam)	10.00
3-2	Rickey Henderson (Mike Norris)	25.00
3-3	Jim Sundberg (Jim Kern)	10.00
3-4	Bob Owchinko (Fred Stanley)	10.00
3-5	Buddy Bell (Danny Darwin)	10.00
3-6	Shooty Babbitt (Rick Langford)	10.00
3-7	Sammy Stewart (Tippy Martinez)	10.00
3-8	No identification (Juan Eichelberger)	10.00
3-9	Lenn Sakata (Eddie Murray)	25.00
3-10	No identification (Juan Bonilla)	10.00
3-11	Benny Ayala (Terry Crowley)	10.00
4-1	Al Oliver (Bill Stein)	10.00
4-2	Dwayne Murphy (Matt Keough)	10.00
4-3	Leon Roberts (John Grubb)	10.00
4-4	Rob Picciolo (Brian Kingman)	10.00
4-5	Mark Wagner (Steve Comer)	10.00
4-6	Jeff Jones (Jeff Neumann)	10.00
4-7	Tim Stoddard (Mike Flanagan)	10.00
4-8	No identification (John Urrea)	10.00
4-9	Rick Dempsey (Mark Belanger)	10.00
4-10	No identification (Luis Salazar)	10.00
4-11	Dave Ford (Cal Ripken Jr.)	250.00
5-1	Pat Putnam	15.00
5-2	Mike Norris	15.00
5-3	Jim Kern	15.00
5-4	Fred Stanley	15.00
5-5	Danny Darwin	15.00
5-6	Rick Langford	15.00
5-7	Tippy Martinez	15.00
5-8	No identification (Juan Eichelberger)	10.00
5-9	Eddie Murray	30.00
5-10	No identification (Juan Bonilla)	10.00
5-11	Terry Crowley	15.00
6-1	Bill Stein	15.00
6-2	Matt Keough	15.00
6-3	John Grubb	15.00
6-4	Brian Kingman	15.00
6-5	Steve Comer	15.00
6-6	Jeff Neumann	15.00
6-7	Mike Flanagan	15.00
6-8	No identification (John Urrea)	10.00
6-9	Mark Belanger	15.00
6-10	No identification (Luis Salazar)	10.00
6-11	Cal Ripken, Jr.	400.00

1982 Fleer Stamps

Issued by Fleer in 1982, this set consists of 242 player stamps, each measuring 1-13/16" x 2-1/2". Originally issued in perforated strips of 10, the full-color stamps are numbered in the lower-left corner and were designed to be placed in an album. Six stamps feature two players each.

	NM/M
Complete Set (242):	10.00
Common Player:	.05
Stamp Album:	1.50
Wax Pack (10):	.35
Wax Box (12):	12.50

1	Fernando Valenzuela	.05
2	Rick Monday	.05
3	Ron Cey	.05
4	Dusty Baker	.05
5	Burt Hooton	.05
6	Pedro Guerrero	.05
7	Jerry Reuss	.05

1982 Fleer Stamps (continued)

#	Player	Price	#	Player	Price
8	Bill Russell	.05	122	Dwayne Murphy	.05
9	Steve Garvey	.15	123	Rickey Henderson	.25
10	Davey Lopes	.05	124	Wayne Gross	.05
11	Tom Seaver	.25	125	Mike Norris	.05
12	George Foster	.05	126	Rick Langford	.05
13	Frank Pastore	.05	127	Jim Spencer	.05
14	Dave Collins	.05	128	Tony Armas	.05
15	Dave Concepcion	.05	129	Matt Keough	.05
16	Ken Griffey	.05	130	Jeff Jones	.05
17	Johnny Bench	.25	131	Steve McCatty	.05
18	Ray Knight	.05	132	Rollie Fingers	.20
19	Mario Soto	.05	133	Jim Gantner	.05
20	Ron Oester	.05	134	Gorman Thomas	.05
21	Ken Oberkfell	.05	135	Robin Yount	.25
22	Bob Forsch	.05	136	Paul Molitor	.25
23	Keith Hernandez	.05	137	Ted Simmons	.05
24	Dane Iorg	.05	138	Ben Oglivie	.05
25	George Hendrick	.05	139	Moose Haas	.05
26	Gene Tenace	.05	140	Cecil Cooper	.05
27	Garry Templeton	.05	141	Pete Vuckovich	.05
28	Bruce Sutter	.20	142	Doug DeCinces	.05
29	Darrell Porter	.05	143	Jim Palmer	.25
30	Tom Herr	.05	144	Steve Stone	.05
31	Tim Raines	.05	145	Mike Flanagan	.05
32	Chris Speier	.05	146	Rick Dempsey	.05
33	Warren Cromartie	.05	147	Al Bumbry	.05
34	Larry Parrish	.05	148	Mark Belanger	.05
35	Andre Dawson	.25	149	Scott McGregor	.05
36	Steve Rogers	.05	150	Ken Singleton	.05
37	Jeff Reardon	.05	151	Eddie Murray	.25
38	Rodney Scott	.05	152	Lance Parrish	.05
39	Gary Carter	.25	153	David Rozema	.05
40	Scott Sanderson	.05	154	Champ Summers	.05
41	Cesar Cedeno	.05	155	Alan Trammell	.25
42	Nolan Ryan	1.00	156	Lou Whitaker	.05
43	Don Sutton	.20	157	Milt Wilcox	.05
44	Terry Puhl	.05	158	Kevin Saucier	.05
45	Joe Niekro	.05	159	Jack Morris	.05
46	Tony Scott	.05	160	Steve Kemp	.05
47	Joe Sambito	.05	161	Kirk Gibson	.05
48	Art Howe	.05	162	Carl Yastrzemski	.25
49	Bob Knepper	.05	163	Jim Rice	.20
50	Jose Cruz	.05	164	Carney Lansford	.05
51	Pete Rose	.50	165	Dennis Eckersley	.20
52	Dick Ruthven	.05	166	Mike Torrez	.05
53	Mike Schmidt	.35	167	Dwight Evans	.05
54	Steve Carlton	.25	168	Glenn Hoffman	.05
55	Tug McGraw	.05	169	Bob Stanley	.05
56	Larry Bowa	.05	170	Tony Perez	.20
57	Garry Maddox	.05	171	Jerry Remy	.05
58	Gary Matthews	.05	172	Buddy Bell	.05
59	Manny Trillo	.05	173	Ferguson Jenkins	.20
60	Lonnie Smith	.05	174	Mickey Rivers	.05
61	Vida Blue	.05	175	Bump Wills	.05
62	Milt May	.05	176	Jon Matlack	.05
63	Joe Morgan	.25	177	Steve Comer	.05
64	Enos Cabell	.05	178	Al Oliver	.05
65	Jack Clark	.05	179	Bill Stein	.05
66	Claudell Washington	.05	180	Pat Putnam	.05
67	Gaylord Perry	.20	181	Jim Sundberg	.05
68	Phil Niekro	.20	182	Ron LeFlore	.05
69	Bob Horner	.05	183	Carlton Fisk	.25
70	Chris Chambliss	.05	184	Harold Baines	.05
71	Dave Parker	.05	185	Bill Almon	.05
72	Tony Pena	.05	186	Richard Dotson	.05
73	Kent Tekulve	.05	187	Greg Luzinski	.05
74	Mike Easler	.05	188	Mike Squires	.05
75	Tim Foli	.05	189	Britt Burns	.05
76	Willie Stargell	.25	190	Lamarr Hoyt	.05
77	Bill Madlock	.05	191	Chet Lemon	.05
78	Jim Bibby	.05	192	Joe Charboneau	.10
79	Omar Moreno	.05	193	Toby Harrah	.05
80	Lee Lacy	.05	194	John Denny	.05
81	Hubie Brooks	.05	195	Rick Manning	.05
82	Rusty Staub	.05	196	Miguel Dilone	.05
83	Ellis Valentine	.05	197	Bo Diaz	.05
84	Neil Allen	.05	198	Mike Hargrove	.05
85	Dave Kingman	.05	199	Bert Blyleven	.05
86	Mookie Wilson	.05	200	Len Barker	.05
87	Doug Flynn	.05	201	Andre Thornton	.05
88	Pat Zachry	.05	202	George Brett	.35
89	John Stearns	.05	203	U.L. Washington	.05
90	Lee Mazzilli	.05	204	Dan Quisenberry	.05
91	Ken Reitz	.05	205	Larry Gura	.05
92	Mike Krukow	.05	206	Willie Aikens	.05
93	Jerry Morales	.05	207	Willie Wilson	.05
94	Leon Durham	.05	208	Dennis Leonard	.05
95	Ivan DeJesus	.05	209	Frank White	.05
96	Bill Buckner	.05	210	Hal McRae	.05
97	Jim Tracy	.05	211	Amos Otis	.05
98	Steve Henderson	.05	212	Don Aase	.05
99	Dick Tidrow	.05	213	Butch Hobson	.05
100	Mike Tyson	.05	214	Fred Lynn	.05
101	Ozzie Smith	.35	215	Brian Downing	.05
102	Ruppert Jones	.05	216	Dan Ford	.05
103	Broderick Perkins	.05	217	Rod Carew	.25
104	Gene Richrds	.05	218	Bobby Grich	.05
105	Terry Kennedy	.05	219	Rick Burleson	.05
106	Jim Bibby, Willie Stargell	.10	220	Don Baylor	.05
107	Larry Bowa, Pete Rose	.25	221	Ken Forsch	.05
108	Warren Spahn, Fernando Valenzuela	.10	222	Bruce Bochte	.05
109	Dave Concepcion, Pete Rose	.25	223	Richie Zisk	.05
110	Reggie Jackson, Dave Winfield	.20	224	Tom Paciorek	.05
111	Tom Lasorda, Fernando Valenzuela	.20	225	Julio Cruz	.05
112	Reggie Jackson	.35	226	Jeff Burroughs	.05
113	Dave Winfield	.20	227	Doug Corbett	.05
114	Lou Piniella	.10	228	Roy Smalley	.05
115	Tommy John	.10	229	Gary Ward	.05
116	Rich Gossage	.10	230	John Castino	.05
117	Ron Davis	.05	231	Rob Wilfong	.05
118	Rick Cerone	.05	232	Dave Stieb	.05
119	Graig Nettles	.05	233	Otto Velez	.05
120	Ron Guidry	.05	234	Damaso Garcia	.05
121	Willie Randolph	.05	235	John Mayberry	.05
			236	Alfredo Griffin	.05
			237	Ted Williams, Carl Yastrzemski	.50
			238	Rick Cerone, Graig Nettles	.05
239	Buddy Bell, George Brett	.15			
240	Steve Carlton, Jim Kaat	.10			
241	Steve Carlton, Dave Parker	.10			
242	Ron Davis, Nolan Ryan	.40			

1983 Fleer Promo Sheet

The consumer, rather than dealer, was the target audience for this sheet premiering '83 Fleer. Six player cards, identical to the issued versions, appear on the 9-5/8" x 7-1/2" sheet, along with advertising messages on front and back. Versions of the sheet can be found with the name of hobby publications which inserted the sample into their issues.

	NM/M
Uncut Sheet:	5.00

1983 Fleer

The 1983 Fleer set features color photos set inside a light brown border. The cards are standard 2-1/2" x 3-1/2". A team logo is located at the card bottom and the word "Fleer" is found at the top. The card backs are designed on a vertical format and include a small black and white photo of the player along with biographical and statistical information. The reverses are done in two shades of brown on white stock. The set was issued with team logo stickers.

	NM/M
Complete Set (660):	40.00
Common Player:	.05
Wax Pack (15):	3.00
Wax Box (38):	100.00
Cello Pack (28):	4.00
Cello Box (24):	80.00
Vending Box (500):	35.00

#	Player	Price	#	Player	Price	#	Player	Price
1	Joaquin Andujar	.05	34	Jim Gantner	.05	152	Larry Whisenton	.05
2	Doug Bair	.05	35	Moose Haas	.05	153	Porfirio Altamirano	.05
3	Steve Braun	.05	36	Roy Howell	.05	154	Marty Bystrom	.05
4	Glenn Brummer	.05	37	Peter Ladd	.05	155	Steve Carlton	.75
5	Bob Forsch	.05	38	Bob McClure	.05	156	Larry Christenson	.05
6	David Green	.05	39	Doc Medich	.05	157	Ivan DeJesus	.05
7	George Hendrick	.05	40	Paul Molitor	.75	158	John Denny	.05
8	Keith Hernandez	.05	41	Don Money	.05	159	Bob Dernier	.05
9	Tom Herr	.05	42	Charlie Moore	.05	160	Bo Diaz	.05
10	Dane Iorg	.05	43	Ben Oglivie	.05	161	Ed Farmer	.05
11	Jim Kaat	.10	44	Ed Romero	.05	162	Greg Gross	.05
12	Jeff Lahti	.05	45	Ted Simmons	.05	163	Mike Krukow	.05
13	Tito Landrum	.05	46	Jim Slaton	.05	164	Garry Maddox	.05
14	Dave LaPoint RC	.05	47	Don Sutton	.65	165	Gary Matthews	.05
15	Willie McGee RC	1.50	48	Gorman Thomas	.05	166	Tug McGraw	.05
16	Steve Mura	.05	49	Pete Vuckovich	.05	167	Bob Molinaro	.05
17	Ken Oberkfell	.05	50	Ned Yost	.05	168	Sid Monge	.05
18	Darrell Porter	.05	51	Robin Yount	.75	169	Ron Reed	.05
19	Mike Ramsey	.05	52	Benny Ayala	.05	170	Bill Robinson	.05
20	Gene Roof	.05	53	Bob Bonner	.05	171	Pete Rose	3.00
21	Lonnie Smith	.05	54	Al Bumbry	.05	172	Dick Ruthven	.05
22	Ozzie Smith	1.50	55	Terry Crowley	.05	173	Mike Schmidt	2.00
23	John Stuper	.05	56	Storm Davis RC	.10	174	Manny Trillo	.05
24	Bruce Sutter	.65	57	Rich Dauer	.05	175	Ozzie Virgil	.05
25	Gene Tenace	.05	58	Rick Dempsey	.05	176	George Vukovich	.05
26	Jerry Augustine	.05	59	Jim Dwyer	.05	177	Gary Allenson	.05
27	Dwight Bernard	.05	60	Mike Flanagan	.05	178	Luis Aponte	.05
28	Mark Brouhard	.05	61	Dan Ford	.05	179	Wade Boggs RC	10.00
29	Mike Caldwell	.05	62	Glenn Gulliver	.05	180	Tom Burgmeier	.05
30	Cecil Cooper	.05	63	John Lowenstein	.05	181	Mark Clear	.05
31	Jamie Easterly	.05	64	Dennis Martinez	.05	182	Dennis Eckersley	.65
32	Marshall Edwards	.05	65	Tippy Martinez	.05	183	Dwight Evans	.05
33	Rollie Fingers	.65	66	Scott McGregor	.05	184	Rich Gedman	.05
			67	Eddie Murray	.75	185	Glenn Hoffman	.05
			68	Joe Nolan	.05	186	Bruce Hurst	.05
			69	Jim Palmer	.75	187	Carney Lansford	.05
			70	Cal Ripken, Jr.	6.00	188	Rick Miller	.05
			71	Gary Roenicke	.05	189	Reid Nichols	.05
			72	Lenn Sakata	.05	190	Bob Ojeda	.05
			73	Ken Singleton	.05	191	Tony Perez	.65
			74	Sammy Stewart	.05	192	Chuck Rainey	.05
			75	Tim Stoddard	.05	193	Jerry Remy	.05
			76	Don Aase	.05	194	Jim Rice	.35
			77	Don Baylor	.05	195	Bob Stanley	.05
			78	Juan Beniquez	.05	196	Dave Stapleton	.05
			79	Bob Boone	.05	197	Mike Torrez	.05
			80	Rick Burleson	.05	198	John Tudor	.05
			81	Rod Carew	.75	199	Julio Valdez	.05
			82	Bobby Clark	.05	200	Carl Yastrzemski	.75
			83	Doug Corbett	.05	201	Dusty Baker	.05
			84	John Curtis	.05	202	Joe Beckwith	.05
			85	Doug DeCinces	.05	203	Greg Brock RC	.05
			86	Brian Downing	.05	204	Ron Cey	.05
			87	Joe Ferguson	.05	205	Terry Forster	.05
			88	Tim Foli	.05	206	Steve Garvey	.30
			89	Ken Forsch	.05	207	Pedro Guerrero	.05
			90	Dave Goltz	.05	208	Burt Hooton	.05
			91	Bobby Grich	.05	209	Steve Howe	.05
			92	Andy Hassler	.05	210	Ken Landreaux	.05
			93	Reggie Jackson	1.50	211	Mike Marshall	.05
			94	Ron Jackson	.05	212	Candy Maldonado RC	.05
			95	Tommy John	.10	213	Rick Monday	.05
			96	Bruce Kison	.05	214	Tom Niedenfuer	.05
			97	Fred Lynn	.05	215	Jorge Orta	.05
			98	Ed Ott	.05	216	Jerry Reuss	.05
			99	Steve Renko	.05	217	Ron Roenicke	.05
			100	Luis Sanchez	.05	218	Vicente Romo	.05
			101	Rob Wilfong	.05	219	Bill Russell	.05
			102	Mike Witt	.05	220	Steve Sax	.05
			103	Geoff Zahn	.05	221	Mike Scioscia	.05
			104	Willie Aikens	.05	222	Dave Stewart	.05
			105	Mike Armstrong	.05	223	Derrel Thomas	.05
			106	Vida Blue	.05	224	Fernando Valenzuela	.05
			107	Bud Black RC	.50	225	Bob Welch	.05
			108	George Brett	2.00	226	Ricky Wright	.05
			109	Bill Castro	.05	227	Steve Yeager	.05
			110	Onix Concepcion	.05	228	Bill Almon	.05
			111	Dave Frost	.05	229	Harold Baines	.05
			112	Cesar Geronimo	.05	230	Salome Barojas	.05
			113	Larry Gura	.05	231	Tony Bernazard	.05
			114	Steve Hammond	.05	232	Britt Burns	.05
			115	Don Hood	.05	233	Richard Dotson	.05
			116	Dennis Leonard	.05	234	Ernesto Escarrega	.05
			117	Jerry Martin	.05	235	Carlton Fisk	.75
			118	Lee May	.05	236	Jerry Hairston Sr.	.05
			119	Hal McRae	.05	237	Kevin Hickey	.05
			120	Amos Otis	.05	238	LaMarr Hoyt	.05
			121	Greg Pryor	.05	239	Steve Kemp	.05
			122	Dan Quisenberry	.05	240	Jim Kern	.05
			123	Don Slaught RC	.20	241	Ron Kittle RC	.25
			124	Paul Splittorff	.05	242	Jerry Koosman	.05
			125	U.L. Washington	.05	243	Dennis Lamp	.05
			126	John Wathan	.05	244	Rudy Law	.05
			127	Frank White	.05	245	Vance Law	.05
			128	Willie Wilson	.05	246	Ron LeFlore	.05
			129	Steve Bedrosian	.05	247	Greg Luzinski	.05
			130	Bruce Benedict	.05	248	Tom Paciorek	.05
			131	Tommy Boggs	.05	249	Aurelio Rodriguez	.05
			132	Brett Butler	.05	250	Mike Squires	.05
			133	Rick Camp	.05	251	Steve Trout	.05
			134	Chris Chambliss	.05	252	Jim Barr	.05
			135	Ken Dayley	.05	253	Dave Bergman	.05
			136	Gene Garber	.05	254	Fred Breining	.05
			137	Terry Harper	.05	255	Bob Brenly	.05
			138	Bob Horner	.05	256	Jack Clark	.05
			139	Glenn Hubbard	.05	257	Chili Davis	.05
			140	Rufino Linares	.05	258	Darrell Evans	.05
			141	Rick Mahler	.05	259	Alan Fowlkes	.05
			142	Dale Murphy	.50	260	Rich Gale	.05
			143	Phil Niekro	.65	261	Atlee Hammaker	.05
			144	Pascual Perez	.05	262	Al Holland	.05
			145	Biff Pocoroba	.05	263	Duane Kuiper	.05
			146	Rafael Ramirez	.05	264	Bill Laskey	.05
			147	Jerry Royster	.05	265	Gary Lavelle	.05
			148	Ken Smith	.05	266	Johnnie LeMaster	.05
			149	Bob Walk	.05	267	Renie Martin	.05
			150	Claudell Washington	.05	268	Milt May	.05
			151	Bob Watson	.05	269	Greg Minton	.05
270	Joe Morgan	.75						
271	Tom O'Malley	.05						
272	Reggie Smith	.05						
273	Guy Sularz	.05						
274	Champ Summers	.05						
275	Max Venable	.05						
276	Jim Wohlford	.05						
277	Ray Burris	.05						
278	Gary Carter	.75						
279	Warren Cromartie	.05						
280	Andre Dawson	.40						
281	Terry Francona	.05						
282	Doug Flynn	.05						
283	Woody Fryman	.05						
284	Bill Gullickson	.05						
285	Wallace Johnson	.05						
286	Charlie Lea	.05						
287	Randy Lerch	.05						
288	Brad Mills	.05						
289	Dan Norman	.05						
290	Al Oliver	.05						
291	David Palmer	.05						
292	Tim Raines	.05						
293	Jeff Reardon	.05						
294	Steve Rogers	.05						
295	Scott Sanderson	.05						
296	Dan Schatzeder	.05						
297	Bryn Smith	.05						
298	Chris Speier	.05						
299	Tim Wallach	.05						
300	Jerry White	.05						
301	Joel Youngblood	.05						
302	Ross Baumgarten	.05						
303	Dale Berra	.05						
304	John Candelaria	.05						
305	Dick Davis	.05						
306	Mike Easler	.05						
307	Richie Hebner	.05						
308	Lee Lacy	.05						
309	Bill Madlock	.05						
310	Larry McWilliams	.05						
311	John Milner	.05						
312	Omar Moreno	.05						
313	Jim Morrison	.05						
314	Steve Nicosia	.05						
315	Dave Parker	.05						
316	Tony Pena	.05						
317	Johnny Ray	.05						
318	Rick Rhoden	.05						
319	Don Robinson	.05						
320	Enrique Romo	.05						
321	Manny Sarmiento	.05						
322	Rod Scurry	.05						
323	Jim Smith	.05						
324	Willie Stargell	.75						
325	Jason Thompson	.05						
326	Kent Tekulve	.05						
327a	Tom Brookens (Narrow (1/4") brown box at bottom on back.)	.45						
327b	Tom Brookens (Wide (1-1/4") brown box at bottom on back.)	.05						
328	Enos Cabell	.05						
329	Kirk Gibson	.05						
330	Larry Herndon	.05						
331	Mike Ivie	.05						
332	Howard Johnson RC	1.00						
333	Lynn Jones	.05						
334	Rick Leach	.05						
335	Chet Lemon	.05						
336	Jack Morris	.05						
337	Lance Parrish	.05						
338	Larry Pashnick	.05						
339	Dan Petry	.05						
340	Dave Rozema	.05						
341	Dave Rucker	.05						
342	Elias Sosa	.05						
343	Dave Tobik	.05						
344	Alan Trammell	.05						
345	Jerry Turner	.05						
346	Jerry Ujdur	.05						
347	Pat Underwood	.05						
348	Lou Whitaker	.05						
349	Milt Wilcox	.05						
350	Glenn Wilson RC	.05						
351	John Wockenfuss	.05						
352	Kurt Bevacqua	.05						
353	Juan Bonilla	.05						
354	Floyd Chiffer	.05						
355	Luis DeLeon	.05						
356	Dave Dravecky RC	.30						
357	Dave Edwards	.05						
358	Juan Eichelberger	.05						
359	Tim Flannery	.05						
360	Tony Gwynn RC	15.00						
361	Ruppert Jones	.05						
362	Terry Kennedy	.05						
363	Joe Lefebvre	.05						
364	Sixto Lezcano	.05						
365	Tim Lollar	.05						
366	Gary Lucas	.05						
367	John Montefusco	.05						
368	Broderick Perkins	.05						
369	Joe Pittman	.05						
370	Gene Richards	.05						
371	Luis Salazar	.05						
372	Eric Show RC	.05						
373	Garry Templeton	.05						
374	Chris Welsh	.05						
375	Alan Wiggins	.05						
376	Rick Cerone	.05						
377	Dave Collins	.05						
378	Roger Erickson	.05						
379	George Frazier	.05						
380	Oscar Gamble	.05						
381	Goose Gossage	.10						
382	Ken Griffey	.05						

#	Player	Price
383	Ron Guidry	.10
384	Dave LaRoche	.05
385	Rudy May	.05
386	John Mayberry	.05
387	Lee Mazzilli	.05
388	Mike Morgan	.05
389	Jerry Mumphrey	.05
390	Bobby Murcer	.10
391	Graig Nettles	.10
392	Lou Piniella	.10
393	Willie Randolph	.05
394	Shane Rawley	.05
395	Dave Righetti	.05
396	Andre Robertson	.05
397	Roy Smalley	.05
398	Dave Winfield	.75
399	Butch Wynegar	.05
400	Chris Bando	.05
401	Alan Bannister	.05
402	Len Barker	.05
403	Tom Brennan	.05
404	Carmelo Castillo RC	.05
405	Miguel Dilone	.05
406	Jerry Dybzinski	.05
407	Mike Fischlin	.05
408	Ed Glynn (Photo actually Bud Anderson.)	.05
409	Mike Hargrove	.05
410	Toby Harrah	.05
411	Ron Hassey	.05
412	Von Hayes	.05
413	Rick Manning	.05
414	Bake McBride	.05
415	Larry Milbourne	.05
416	Bill Nahorodny	.05
417	Jack Perconte	.05
418	Larry Sorensen	.05
419	Dan Spillner	.05
420	Rick Sutcliffe	.05
421	Andre Thornton	.05
422	Rick Waits	.05
423	Eddie Whitson	.05
424	Jesse Barfield	.05
425	Barry Bonnell	.05
426	Jim Clancy	.05
427	Damaso Garcia	.05
428	Jerry Garvin	.05
429	Alfredo Griffin	.05
430	Garth Iorg	.05
431	Roy Lee Jackson	.05
432	Luis Leal	.05
433	Buck Martinez	.05
434	Joey McLaughlin	.05
435	Lloyd Moseby	.05
436	Rance Mulliniks	.05
437	Dale Murray	.05
438	Wayne Nordhagen	.05
439	Gene Petralli RC	.05
440	Hosken Powell	.05
441	Dave Stieb	.05
442	Willie Upshaw	.05
443	Ernie Whitt	.05
444	Al Woods	.05
445	Alan Ashby	.05
446	Jose Cruz	.05
447	Kiko Garcia	.05
448	Phil Garner	.05
449	Danny Heep	.05
450	Art Howe	.05
451	Bob Knepper	.05
452	Alan Knicely	.05
453	Ray Knight	.05
454	Frank LaCorte	.05
455	Mike LaCoss	.05
456	Randy Moffitt	.05
457	Joe Niekro	.05
458	Terry Puhl	.05
459	Luis Pujols	.05
460	Craig Reynolds	.05
461	Bert Roberge	.05
462	Vern Ruhle	.05
463	Nolan Ryan	4.00
464	Joe Sambito	.05
465	Tony Scott	.05
466	Dave Smith	.05
467	Harry Spilman	.05
468	Dickie Thon	.05
469	Denny Walling	.05
470	Larry Andersen	.05
471	Floyd Bannister	.05
472	Jim Beattie	.05
473	Bruce Bochte	.05
474	Manny Castillo	.05
475	Bill Caudill	.05
476	Bryan Clark	.05
477	Al Cowens	.05
478	Julio Cruz	.05
479	Todd Cruz	.05
480	Gary Gray	.05
481	Dave Henderson	.05
482	Mike Moore RC	.05
483	Gaylord Perry	.65
484	Dave Revering	.05
485	Joe Simpson	.05
486	Mike Stanton	.05
487	Rick Sweet	.05
488	Ed Vande Berg RC	.05
489	Richie Zisk	.05
490	Doug Bird	.05
491	Larry Bowa	.05
492	Bill Buckner	.05
493	Bill Campbell	.05
494	Jody Davis	.05
495	Leon Durham	.05
496	Steve Henderson	.05
497	Willie Hernandez	.05
498	Fergie Jenkins	.65
499	Jay Johnstone	.05

#	Player	Price
500	Junior Kennedy	.05
501	Randy Martz	.05
502	Jerry Morales	.05
503	Keith Moreland	.05
504	Dickie Noles	.05
505	Mike Proly	.05
506	Allen Ripley	.05
507	Ryne Sandberg RC	10.00
508	Lee Smith	1.00
509	Pat Tabler	.05
510	Dick Tidrow	.05
511	Bump Wills	.05
512	Gary Woods	.05
513	Tony Armas	.05
514	Dave Beard	.05
515	Jeff Burroughs	.05
516	John D'Acquisto	.05
517	Wayne Gross	.05
518	Mike Heath	.05
519	Rickey Henderson	.75
520	Cliff Johnson	.05
521	Matt Keough	.05
522	Brian Kingman	.05
523	Rick Langford	.05
524	Davey Lopes	.05
525	Steve McCatty	.05
526	Dave McKay	.05
527	Dan Meyer	.05
528	Dwayne Murphy	.05
529	Jeff Newman	.05
530	Mike Norris	.05
531	Bob Owchinko	.05
532	Joe Rudi	.05
533	Jimmy Sexton	.05
534	Fred Stanley	.05
535	Tom Underwood	.05
536	Neil Allen	.05
537	Wally Backman	.05
538	Bob Bailor	.05
539	Hubie Brooks	.05
540	Carlos Diaz	.05
541	Pete Falcone	.05
542	George Foster	.05
543	Ron Gardenhire	.05
544	Brian Giles	.05
545	Ron Hodges	.05
546	Randy Jones	.05
547	Mike Jorgensen	.05
548	Dave Kingman	.05
549	Ed Lynch	.05
550	Jesse Orosco	.05
551	Rick Ownbey	.05
552	Charlie Puleo RC	.05
553	Gary Rajsich	.05
554	Mike Scott	.05
555	Rusty Staub	.05
556	John Stearns	.05
557	Craig Swan	.05
558	Ellis Valentine	.05
559	Tom Veryzer	.05
560	Mookie Wilson	.05
561	Pat Zachry	.05
562	Buddy Bell	.05
563	John Butcher	.05
564	Steve Comer	.05
565	Danny Darwin	.05
566	Bucky Dent	.05
567	John Grubb	.05
568	Rick Honeycutt	.05
569	Dave Hostetler	.05
570	Charlie Hough	.05
571	Lamar Johnson	.05
572	Jon Matlack	.05
573	Paul Mirabella	.05
574	Larry Parrish	.05
575	Mike Richardt	.05
576	Mickey Rivers	.05
577	Billy Sample	.05
578	Dave Schmidt RC	.05
579	Bill Stein	.05
580	Jim Sundberg	.05
581	Frank Tanana	.05
582	Mark Wagner	.05
583	George Wright	.05
584	Johnny Bench	.75
585	Bruce Berenyi	.05
586	Larry Biittner	.05
587	Cesar Cedeno	.05
588	Dave Concepcion	.05
589	Dan Driessen	.05
590	Greg Harris	.05
591	Ben Hayes	.05
592	Paul Householder	.05
593	Tom Hume	.05
594	Wayne Krenchicki	.05
595	Rafael Landestoy	.05
596	Charlie Leibrandt	.05
597	Eddie Milner RC	.05
598	Ron Oester	.05
599	Frank Pastore	.05
600	Joe Price	.05
601	Tom Seaver	.75
602	Bob Shirley	.05
603	Mario Soto	.05
604	Alex Trevino	.05
605	Mike Vail	.05
606	Duane Walker	.05
607	Tom Brunansky	.05
608	Bobby Castillo	.05
609	John Castino	.05
610	Ron Davis	.05
611	Lenny Faedo	.05
612	Terry Felton	.05
613	Gary Gaetti RC	.35
614	Mickey Hatcher	.05
615	Brad Havens	.05
616	Kent Hrbek	.05
617	Randy S. Johnson	.05

#	Player	Price
618	Tim Laudner	.05
619	Jeff Little	.05
620	Bob Mitchell	.05
621	Jack O'Connor	.05
622	John Pacella	.05
623	Pete Redfern	.05
624	Jesus Vega	.05
625	Frank Viola RC	1.00
626	Ron Washington	.05
627	Gary Ward	.05
628	Al Williams	.05
629	Red Sox All-Stars (Mark Clear, Dennis Eckersley, Carl Yastrzemski)	.25
630	300 Career Wins (Terry Bulling, Gaylord Perry)	.10
631	Pride of Venezuela (Dave Concepcion, Manny Trillo)	.10
632	All-Star Infielders (Buddy Bell, Robin Yount)	.20
633	Mr. Vet & Mr. Rookie (Kent Hrbek, Dave Winfield)	.25
634	Fountain of Youth (Pete Rose, Willie Stargell)	.40
635	Big Chiefs (Toby Harrah, Andre Thornton)	.05
636	"Smith Bros." (Lonnie Smith, Ozzie Smith)	.15
637	Base Stealers' Threat (Gary Carter, Bo Diaz)	.10
638	All-Star Catchers (Gary Carter, Carlton Fisk)	.15
639	Rickey Henderson/IA	.50
640	Home Run Threats (Reggie Jackson, Ben Oglivie)	.25
641	Two Teams - Same Day (Joel Youngblood)	.05
642	Last Perfect Game (Len Barker, Ron Hassey)	.05
643	Blue (Vida Blue)	.05
644	Black & (Bud Black)	.05
645	Power (Reggie Jackson)	.30
646	Speed & (Rickey Henderson)	.30
647	Checklist 1-51	.05
648	Checklist 52-103	.05
649	Checklist 104-152	.05
650	Checklist 153-200	.05
651	Checklist 201-251	.05
652	Checklist 252-301	.05
653	Checklist 302-351	.05
654	Checklist 352-399	.05
655	Checklist 400-444	.05
656	Checklist 445-489	.05
657	Checklist 490-535	.05
658	Checklist 536-583	.05
659	Checklist 584-628	.05
660	Checklist 629-646	.05

Star Stamps

The 1983 Fleer Stamp set consists of 288 stamps, including 224 player stamps and 64 team logo stamps. They were originally issued on four different sheets of 72 stamps each (checklisted below) and in "Vend-A-Stamp" dispensers of 18 stamps each. Sixteen different dispenser strips were needed to complete the set (strips 1-4 comprise Sheet 1; strips 5-8 comprise Sheet 2; strips 9-12 comprise Sheet 3; strips 13-16 comprise Sheet 4.) Stamps measure 1-1/4" x 1-13/16".

		NM/M
Complete Sheet Set (4):		5.00
Complete Vend-A-Stamp Set (288):		5.00
Common Sheet:		2.50
Common Stamp Dispenser:		.35
Common Single Stamp:		.01
1	Sheet 1 (A's Logo, Angels Logo, Astros Logo, Cardinals Logo, Cubs Logo, Dodgers Logo, Expos Logo, Giants Logo, Indians Logo, Mets Logo, Orioles Logo, Phillies Logo, Pirates Logo, Red Sox Logo, Twins Logo, White Sox Logo, Neil Allen, Harold Baines,	

	Buddy Bell, Dale Berra, Wade Boggs, George Brett, Bill Buckner, Jack Clark, Dave Concepcion, Warren Cromartie, Doug DeCinces, Luis DeLeon, Brian Downing, Dan Driessen, Mike Flanagan, Bob Forsch, Ken Forsch, Toby)	2.50
2	Sheet 2 (Angels Logo, Astros Logo, Braves Logo, Cardinals logo, Dodgers Logo, Expos Logo, Indians Logo, Mariners Logo, Mets Logo, Phillies Logo, Pirates Logo, Rangers Logo, Reds Logo, Royals Logo, Tigers Logo, Yankees Logo, Willie Aikens, Bob Bailor, Dusty Baker, Floyd Bannister, Len Barker, Hubie Brooks, Tom Brunansky, Chris Chambliss, Mark Clear, Andre Dawson, Bo Diaz, Dennis Eckersley, Rollie Fingers, George Foster, Goose Gossage, Ken Griffey, Ron Guid)	2.50
3	Sheet 3 (A's Logo, Angels Logo, Blue Jays Logo, Braves Logo, Brewers Logo, Dodgers Logo, Giants Logo, Indians Logo, Mariners Logo, Orioles Logo, Padres Logo, Reds Logo, Royals Logo, Tigers Logo, Twins Logo, White Sox Logo, Alan Ashby, Dave Beard, Jim Beattie, Johnny Bench, Larry Biittner, Bob Boone, Rod Carew, Gary Carter, Bobby Castillo, Bill Caudill, Cecil Cooper, Mike Easler, Dwight Evans, Carlton Fisk, Gene Garber, Damaso Garcia, Larry Herndon, Al Hol)	2.50
4	Sheet 4 (Blue Jays Logo, Braves logo, Brewers Logo, Cubs Logo, Expos Logo, Giants Logo, Padres Logo, Phillies Logo, Pirates Logo, Rangers Logo, Red Sox Logo, Reds Logo, Royals Logo, Twins Logo, White Sox Logo, Yankees Logo, Joaquin Andujar, Don Baylor, Vida Blue, Bruce Bochte, Larry Bowa, Al Bumbry, Jeff Burroughs, Enos Cabell, Steve Carlton, Cesar Cedeno, Rick Cerone, Ron Cey, Larry Christenson, Jim Clancy, Jose Cruz, Danny Darwin, Rich Dauer, Ron Davis,)	2.50

Star Stamps Poster

Available via a wrapper redemption offer, this huge (31-3/4" x 21-3/4") poster is printed in red and blue on glossy white paper stock. Besides blue-tone photos of each stamp, the poster has trivia questions and the logos of each team, league, MLB and the players' association. Sheets were folded to 9-1/2" x 12-1/2" for mailing.

	NM/M
Star Stamp Poster	10.00

1983 Fleer Stickers

This 270-sticker set consists of both player stickers and team logo stickers, all measuring 1-13/16" x 2-1/2". The player stickers are numbered on the back. The front features a full-color photo surrounded by a blue border with two stars at the top. The stickers were issued in strips of 10 player stickers plus two team logo stickers. The 26 logo stickers have been assigned numbers 271 through 296.

ROD CAREW

		NM/M
Complete Set (296):		10.00
Common Player:		.05
Wax Pack (12):		.30
Wax Box (48):		10.00
1	Bruce Sutter	.20
2	Willie McGee	.05
3	Darrell Porter	.05
4	Lonnie Smith	.05
5	Dane Iorg	.05
6	Keith Hernandez	.05
7	Joaquin Andujar	.05
8	Ken Oberkfell	.05
9	John Stuper	.05
10	Ozzie Smith	.40
11	Bob Forsch	.05
12	Jim Gantner	.05
13	Rollie Fingers	.20
14	Pete Vuckovich	.05
15	Ben Oglivie	.05
16	Don Sutton	.20
17	Bob McClure	.05
18	Robin Yount	.25
19	Paul Molitor	.25
20	Gorman Thomas	.05
21	Mike Caldwell	.05
22	Ted Simmons	.05
23	Cecil Cooper	.05
24	Steve Renko	.05
25	Tommy John	.10
26	Rod Carew	.25
27	Bruce Kison	.05
28	Ken Forsch	.05
29	Geoff Zahn	.05
30	Doug DiCinces	.05
31	Fred Lynn	.05
32	Reggie Jackson	.40
33	Don Baylor	.05
34	Bob Boone	.05
35	Brian Downing	.05
36	Goose Gossage	.05
37	Roy Smalley	.05
38	Graig Nettles	.05
39	Dave Winfield	.25
40	Lee Mazzilli	.05
41	Jerry Mumphrey	.05
42	Dave Collins	.05
43	Rick Cerone	.05
44	Willie Randolph	.05
45	Lou Piniella	.10
46	Ken Griffey	.05
47	Ron Guidry	.05
48	Jack Clark	.05
49	Reggie Smith	.05
50	Atlee Hammaker	.05
51	Fred Breining	.05
52	Gary Lavelle	.05
53	Chili Davis	.05
54	Greg Minton	.05
55	Joe Morgan	.25
56	Al Holland	.05
57	Bill Laskey	.05
58	Duane Kuiper	.05
59	Tom Burgmeier	.05
60	Carl Yastrzemski	.25
61	Mark Clear	.05
62	Mike Torrez	.05
63	Dennis Eckersley	.20
64	Wade Boggs	.50
65	Bob Stanley	.05
66	Jim Rice	.15
67	Carney Lansford	.05
68	Jerry Remy	.05
69	Dwight Evans	.05
70	John Candelaria	.05
71	Bill Madlock	.05
72	Dave Parker	.05
73	Kent Tekulve	.05
74	Tony Pena	.05
75	Manny Sarmiento	.05
76	Johnny Ray	.05
77	Dale Berra	.05
78	Lee Lacy	.05
79	Jason Thompson	.05
80	Mike Easler	.05
81	Willie Stargell	.25
82	Rick Camp	.05
83	Bob Watson	.05
84	Bob Horner	.05
85	Rafael Ramirez	.05
86	Chris Chambliss	.05
87	Gene Garber	.05
88	Claudell Washington	.05
89	Steve Bedrosian	.05
90	Dale Murphy	.15
91	Phil Niekro	.20
92	Jerry Royster	.05
93	Bob Walk	.05
94	Frank White	.05

#	Player	Price
95	Dennis Leonard	.05
96	Vida Blue	.05
97	U.L. Washington	.05
98	George Brett	.45
99	Amos Otis	.05
100	Dan Quisenberry	.05
101	Willie Aikens	.05
102	Hal McRae	.05
103	Larry Gura	.05
104	Willie Wilson	.05
105	Damaso Garcia	.05
106	Hosken Powell	.05
107	Joey McLaughlin	.05
108	Jim Clancy	.05
109	Barry Bonnell	.05
110	Garth Iorg	.05
111	Dave Stieb	.05
112	Fernando Valenzuela	.05
113	Steve Garvey	.10
114	Rick Monday	.05
115	Burt Hooton	.05
116	Bill Russell	.05
117	Pedro Guerrero	.05
118	Steve Sax	.05
119	Steve Howe	.05
120	Ken Landreaux	.05
121	Dusty Baker	.05
122	Ron Cey	.05
123	Jerry Reuss	.05
124	Bump Wills	.05
125	Keith Moreland	.05
126	Dick Tidrow	.05
127	Bill Campbell	.05
128	Larry Bowa	.05
129	Randy Martz	.05
130	Ferguson Jenkins	.20
131	Leon Durham	.05
132	Bill Buckner	.05
133	Ron Davis	.05
134	Jack O'Connor	.05
135	Kent Hrbek	.05
136	Gary Ward	.05
137	Al Williams	.05
138	Tom Brunansky	.05
139	Bobby Castillo	.05
140	Dusty Baker, Dale Murphy	.10
141	Nolan Ryan	.65
142	Lee Lacey (Lacy),	
	Omar Moreno	.05
143	Al Oliver, Pete Rose	.25
144	Rickey Henderson	.25
145	Ray Knight, Pete Rose, Mike Schmidt	.30
146	Hal McRae, Ben Oglivie	.05
147	Tom Hume, Ray Knight	.05
148	Buddy Bell, Carlton Fisk	.05
149	Steve Kemp	.05
150	Rudy Law	.05
151	Ron LeFlore	.05
152	Jerry Koosman	.05
153	Carlton Fisk	.25
154	Salome Barojas	.05
155	Harold Baines	.05
156	Britt Burns	.05
157	Tom Paciorek	.05
158	Greg Luzinski	.05
159	LaMarr Hoyt	.05
160	George Wright	.05
161	Danny Darwin	.05
162	Lamar Johnson	.05
163	Charlie Hough	.05
164	Buddy Bell	.05
165	John Matlack (Jon)	.05
166	Billy Sample	.05
167	John Grubb	.05
168	Larry Parrish	.05
169	Ivan DeJesus	.05
170	Mike Schmidt	.45
171	Tug McGraw	.05
172	Ron Reed	.05
173	Garry Maddox	.05
174	Pete Rose	.50
175	Manny Trillo	.05
176	Steve Carlton	.25
177	Bo Diaz	.05
178	Gary Matthews	.05
179	Bill Caudill	.05
180	Ed Vande Berg	.05
181	Gaylord Perry	.20
182	Floyd Bannister	.05
183	Richie Zisk	.05
184	Al Cowens	.05
185	Bruce Bochte	.05
186	Jeff Burroughs	.05
187	Dave Beard	.05
188	Davey Lopes	.05
189	Dwayne Murphy	.05
190	Rick Langford	.05
191	Tom Underwood	.05
192	Rickey Henderson	.25
193	Mike Flanagan	.05
194	Scott McGregor	.05
195	Ken Singleton	.05
196	Rich Dauer	.05
197	John Lowenstein	.05
198	Cal Ripken, Jr.	1.00
199	Dennis Martinez	.05
200	Jim Palmer	.25
201	Tippy Martinez	.05
202	Eddie Murray	.25
203	Al Bumbry	.05
204	Dickie Thon	.05
205	Phil Garner	.05
206	Jose Cruz	.05
207	Nolan Ryan	.65
208	Ray Knight	.05
209	Terry Puhl	.05
210	Joe Niekro	.05

#	Player	NM/M
211	Art Howe	
212	Alan Ashby	.05
213	Tom Hume	.05
214	Johnny Bench	.25
215	Larry Biittner	.05
216	Mario Soto	.05
217	Dan Driessen	.05
218	Tom Seaver	.25
219	Dave Concepcion	.05
220	Wayne Krenchicki	.05
221	Cesar Cedeno	.05
222	Ruppert Jones	.05
223	Terry Kennedy	.05
224	Luis DeLeon	.05
225	Eric Show	.05
226	Tim Flannery	.05
227	Garry Templeton	.05
228	Tim Lollar	.05
229	Sixto Lezcano	.05
230	Bob Bailor	.05
231	Craig Swan	.05
232	Dave Kingman	.05
233	Mookie Wilson	.05
234	John Stearns	.05
235	Ellis Valentine	.05
236	Neil Allen	.05
237	Pat Zachry	.05
238	Rusty Staub	.05
239	George Foster	.05
240	Rick Sutcliffe	.05
241	Andre Thornton	.05
242	Mike Hargrove	.05
243	Dan Spillner	.05
244	Lary Sorensen	.05
245	Len Barker	.05
246	Rick Manning	.05
247	Toby Harrah	.05
248	Milt Wilcox	.05
249	Lou Whitaker	.05
250	Tom Brookens	.05
251	Chet Lemon	.05
252	Jack Morris	.05
253	Alan Trammell	.05
254	John Wockenfuss	.05
255	Lance Parrish	.05
256	Larry Herndon	.05
257	Chris Speier	.05
258	Woody Fryman	.05
259	Scott Sanderson	.05
260	Steve Rogers	.05
261	Warren Cromartie	.05
262	Gary Carter	.25
263	Bill Gullickson	.05
264	Andre Dawson	.15
265	Tim Raines	.05
266	Charlie Lea	.05
267	Jeff Reardon	.05
268	Al Oliver	.05
269	George Hendrick	.05
270	John Montefusco	.05
(271)	A's Logo	.05
(272)	Angels Logo	.05
(273)	Astros Logo	.05
(274)	Blue Jays Logo	.05
(275)	Braves Logo	.05
(276)	Brewers Logo	.05
(277)	Cardinals Logo	.05
(278)	Cubs Logo	.05
(279)	Dodgers Logo	.05
(280)	Expos Logo	.05
(281)	Giants Logo	.05
(282)	Indians Logo	.05
(283)	Mariners Logo	.05
(284)	Mets Logo	.05
(285)	Orioles Logo	.05
(286)	Padres Logo	.05
(287)	Phillies Logo	.05
(288)	Pirates Logo	.05
(289)	Rangers Logo	.05
(290)	Red Sox Logo	.05
(291)	Reds Logo	.05
(292)	Royals Logo	.05
(293)	Tigers Logo	.05
(294)	Twins Logo	.05
(295)	Yankees Logo	.05
(296)	White Sox Logo	.05

1984 Fleer Sample Sheet

Reportedly available only as an insert in a trade magazine for the grocery industry, this full-color 7-7/8" x 10-7/8" sheet is printed on glossy paper rather than cardboard. The full-color front reproduces nine cards from the forthcoming '84 Fleer issue. The black and red back has details of the cards and ordering informartion.

NM/M

Sample Sheet:
George Foster,
Keith Hernandez, Ron Oester,
Charlie Puleo, Steve Rogers,
Dan Schatzeder, Bill Scherrer,
Bryn Smith,
Darryl Strawberry ... 10.00

1984 Fleer

Kent Hrbek — FIRST BASE

The 1984 Fleer set contained 660 cards for the fourth consecutive year. The 2-1/2" x 3-1/2" cards feature a color photo surrounded by white borders and horizontal dark blue stripes. The top stripe contains the word "Fleer" with the lower carrying the player's name. Backs have a small black-and-white player photo and are done in blue ink on white stock. The set was issued with team logo stickers.

	NM/M
Complete Set (660):	40.00
Common Player:	.05
Wax Pack (15):	2.50
Wax Box (36):	75.00
Cello Pack (28):	4.50
Cello Box (24):	85.00
Vending Box (500):	40.00

#	Player	NM/M
1	Mike Boddicker RC	.05
2	Al Bumbry	.05
3	Todd Cruz	.05
4	Rich Dauer	.05
5	Storm Davis	.05
6	Rick Dempsey	.05
7	Jim Dwyer	.05
8	Mike Flanagan	.05
9	Dan Ford	.05
10	John Lowenstein	.05
11	Dennis Martinez	.05
12	Tippy Martinez	.05
13	Scott McGregor	.05
14	Eddie Murray	1.00
15	Joe Nolan	.05
16	Jim Palmer	1.00
17	Cal Ripken, Jr.	4.00
18	Gary Roenicke	.05
19	Lenn Sakata	.05
20	John Shelby RC	.05
21	Ken Singleton	.05
22	Sammy Stewart	.05
23	Tim Stoddard	.05
24	Marty Bystrom	.05
25	Steve Carlton	1.00
26	Ivan DeJesus	.05
27	John Denny	.05
28	Bob Dernier	.05
29	Bo Diaz	.05
30	Kiko Garcia	.05
31	Greg Gross	.05
32	Kevin Gross RC	.05
33	Von Hayes	.05
34	Willie Hernandez	.05
35	Al Holland	.05
36	Charles Hudson RC	.05
37	Joe Lefebvre	.05
38	Sixto Lezcano	.05
39	Garry Maddox	.05
40	Gary Matthews	.05
41	Len Matuszek	.05
42	Tug McGraw	.05
43	Joe Morgan	1.00
44	Tony Perez	.75
45	Ron Reed	.05
46	Pete Rose	3.00
47	Juan Samuel RC	.25
48	Mike Schmidt	2.50
49	Ozzie Virgil	.05
50	Juan Agosto RC	.05
51	Harold Baines	.05
52	Floyd Bannister	.05
53	Salome Barojas	.05
54	Britt Burns	.05
55	Julio Cruz	.05
56	Richard Dotson	.05
57	Jerry Dybzinski	.05
58	Carlton Fisk	1.00
59	Scott Fletcher RC	.05
60	Jerry Hairston Sr.	.05
61	Kevin Hickey	.05
62	Marc Hill	.05
63	LaMarr Hoyt	.05
64	Ron Kittle	.05
65	Jerry Koosman	.05
66	Dennis Lamp	.05
67	Rudy Law	.05
68	Vance Law	.05
69	Greg Luzinski	.05
70	Tom Paciorek	.05
71	Mike Squires	.05
72	Dick Tidrow	.05
73	Greg Walker RC	.05
74	Glenn Abbott	.05
75	Howard Bailey	.05
76	Doug Bair	.05
77	Juan Berenguer	.05
78	Tom Brookens	.05
79	Enos Cabell	.05
80	Kirk Gibson	.05
81	John Grubb	.05
82	Larry Herndon	.05
83	Wayne Krenchicki	.05
84	Rick Leach	.05
85	Chet Lemon	.05
86	Aurelio Lopez	.05
87	Jack Morris	.05
88	Lance Parrish	.05
89	Dan Petry	.05
90	Dave Rozema	.05
91	Alan Trammell	.05
92	Lou Whitaker	.05
93	Milt Wilcox	.05
94	Glenn Wilson	.05
95	John Wockenfuss	.05
96	Dusty Baker	.05
97	Joe Beckwith	.05
98	Greg Brock	.05
99	Jack Fimple	.05
100	Pedro Guerrero	.05
101	Rick Honeycutt	.05
102	Burt Hooton	.05
103	Steve Howe	.05
104	Ken Landreaux	.05
105	Mike Marshall	.05
106	Rick Monday	.05
107	Jose Morales	.05
108	Tom Niedenfuer	.05
109	Alejandro Pena RC	.05
110	Jerry Reuss	.05
111	Bill Russell	.05
112	Steve Sax	.05
113	Mike Scioscia	.05
114	Derrel Thomas	.05
115	Fernando Valenzuela	.05
116	Bob Welch	.05
117	Steve Yeager	.05
118	Pat Zachry	.05
119	Don Baylor	.05
120	Bert Campaneris	.05
121	Rick Cerone	.05
122	Ray Fontenot RC	.05
123	George Frazier	.05
124	Oscar Gamble	.05
125	Goose Gossage	.10
126	Ken Griffey	.05
127	Ron Guidry	.10
128	Jay Howell RC	.05
129	Steve Kemp	.05
130	Matt Keough	.05
131	Don Mattingly RC	20.00
132	John Montefusco	.05
133	Omar Moreno	.05
134	Dale Murray	.05
135	Graig Nettles	.05
136	Lou Piniella	.10
137	Willie Randolph	.05
138	Shane Rawley	.05
139	Dave Righetti	.05
140	Andre Robertson	.05
141	Bob Shirley	.05
142	Roy Smalley	.05
143	Dave Winfield	1.00
144	Butch Wynegar	.05
145	Jim Acker RC	.05
146	Doyle Alexander	.05
147	Jesse Barfield	.05
148	George Bell	.05
149	Barry Bonnell	.05
150	Jim Clancy	.05
151	Dave Collins	.05
152	Tony Fernandez RC	.50
153	Damaso Garcia	.05
154	Dave Geisel	.05
155	Jim Gott RC	.05
156	Alfredo Griffin	.05
157	Garth Iorg	.05
158	Roy Lee Jackson	.05
159	Cliff Johnson	.05
160	Luis Leal	.05
161	Buck Martinez	.05
162	Joey McLaughlin	.05
163	Randy Moffitt	.05
164	Lloyd Moseby	.05
165	Rance Mullinks	.05
166	Jorge Orta	.05
167	Dave Stieb	.05
168	Willie Upshaw	.05
169	Ernie Whitt	.05
170	Len Barker	.05
171	Steve Bedrosian	.05
172	Bruce Benedict	.05
173	Brett Butler	.05
174	Rick Camp	.05
175	Chris Chambliss	.05
176	Ken Dayley	.05
177	Pete Falcone	.05
178	Terry Forster	.05
179	Gene Garber	.05
180	Terry Harper	.05
181	Bob Horner	.05
182	Glenn Hubbard	.05
183	Randy Johnson	.05
184	Craig McMurtry RC	.05
185	Donnie Moore RC	.05
186	Dale Murphy	.60
187	Phil Niekro	.75
188	Pascual Perez	.05
189	Biff Pocoroba	.05
190	Rafael Ramirez	.05
191	Jerry Royster	.05
192	Claudell Washington	.05
193	Bob Watson	.05
194	Jerry Augustine	.05
195	Mark Brouhard	.05
196	Mike Caldwell	.05
197	Tom Candiotti RC	.25
198	Cecil Cooper	.05
199	Rollie Fingers	.75
200	Jim Gantner	.05
201	Bob L. Gibson	.05
202	Moose Haas	.05
203	Roy Howell	.05
204	Pete Ladd	.05
205	Rick Manning	.05
206	Bob McClure	.05
207	Paul Molitor	1.00
208	Don Money	.05
209	Charlie Moore	.05
210	Ben Oglivie	.05
211	Chuck Porter	.05
212	Ed Romero	.05
213	Ted Simmons	.05
214	Jim Slaton	.05
215	Don Sutton	.75
216	Tom Tellmann	.05
217	Pete Vuckovich	.05
218	Ned Yost	.05
219	Robin Yount	1.00
220	Alan Ashby	.05
221	Kevin Bass RC	.05
222	Jose Cruz	.05
223	Bill Dawley RC	.05
224	Frank DiPino	.05
225	Bill Doran RC	.05
226	Phil Garner	.05
227	Art Howe	.05
228	Bob Knepper	.05
229	Ray Knight	.05
230	Frank LaCorte	.05
231	Mike LaCoss	.05
232	Mike Madden	.05
233	Jerry Mumphrey	.05
234	Joe Niekro	.05
235	Terry Puhl	.05
236	Luis Pujols	.05
237	Craig Reynolds	.05
238	Vern Ruhle	.05
239	Nolan Ryan	4.00
240	Mike Scott	.05
241	Tony Scott	.05
242	Dave Smith	.05
243	Dickie Thon	.05
244	Denny Walling	.05
245	Dale Berra	.05
246	Jim Bibby	.05
247	John Candelaria	.05
248	Jose DeLeon RC	.05
249	Mike Easler	.05
250	Cecilio Guante RC	.05
251	Richie Hebner	.05
252	Lee Lacy	.05
253	Bill Madlock	.05
254	Milt May	.05
255	Lee Mazzilli	.05
256	Larry McWilliams	.05
257	Jim Morrison	.05
258	Dave Parker	.05
259	Tony Pena	.05
260	Johnny Ray	.05
261	Rick Rhoden	.05
262	Don Robinson	.05
263	Manny Sarmiento	.05
264	Rod Scurry	.05
265	Kent Tekulve	.05
266	Gene Tenace	.05
267	Jason Thompson	.05
268	Lee Tunnell RC	.05
269	Marvell Wynne RC	.05
270	Ray Burris	.05
271	Gary Carter	1.00
272	Warren Cromartie	.05
273	Andre Dawson	.30
274	Doug Flynn	.05
275	Terry Francona	.05
276	Bill Gullickson	.05
277	Bob James	.05
278	Charlie Lea	.05
279	Bryan Little	.05
280	Al Oliver	.05
281	Tim Raines	.05
282	Bobby Ramos	.05
283	Jeff Reardon	.05
284	Steve Rogers	.05
285	Scott Sanderson	.05
286	Dan Schatzeder	.05
287	Bryn Smith	.05
288	Chris Speier	.05
289	Manny Trillo	.05
290	Mike Vail	.05
291	Tim Wallach	.05
292	Chris Welsh	.05
293	Jim Wohlford	.05
294	Kurt Bevacqua	.05
295	Juan Bonilla	.05
296	Bobby Brown	.05
297	Luis DeLeon	.05
298	Dave Dravecky	.05
299	Tim Flannery	.05
300	Steve Garvey	.25
301	Tony Gwynn	2.00
302	Andy Hawkins RC	.10
303	Ruppert Jones	.05
304	Terry Kennedy	.05
305	Tim Lollar	.05
306	Gary Lucas	.05
307	Kevin McReynolds RC	.25
308	Sid Monge	.05
309	Mario Ramirez	.05
310	Gene Richards	.05
311	Luis Salazar	.05
312	Eric Show	.05
313	Elias Sosa	.05
314	Garry Templeton	.05
315	Mark Thurmond RC	.05
316	Ed Whitson	.05
317	Alan Wiggins	.05
318	Neil Allen	.05
319	Joaquin Andujar	.05
320	Steve Braun	.05
321	Glenn Brummer	.05
322	Bob Forsch	.05
323	David Green	.05
324	George Hendrick	.05
325	Tom Herr	.05
326	Dane Iorg	.05
327	Jeff Lahti	.05
328	Dave LaPoint	.05
329	Willie McGee	.05
330	Ken Oberkfell	.05
331	Darrell Porter	.05
332	Jamie Quirk	.05
333	Mike Ramsey	.05
334	Floyd Rayford	.05
335	Lonnie Smith	.05
336	Ozzie Smith	2.00
337	John Stuper	.05
338	Bruce Sutter	.75
339	Andy Van Slyke RC	1.00
340	Dave Von Ohlen	.05
341	Willie Aikens	.05
342	Mike Armstrong	.05
343	Bud Black	.05
344	George Brett	2.50
345	Onix Concepcion	.05
346	Keith Creel	.05
347	Larry Gura	.05
348	Don Hood	.05
349	Dennis Leonard	.05
350	Hal McRae	.05
351	Amos Otis	.05
352	Gaylord Perry	.75
353	Greg Pryor	.05
354	Dan Quisenberry	.05
355	Steve Renko	.05
356	Leon Roberts	.05
357	Pat Sheridan RC	.05
358	Joe Simpson	.05
359	Don Slaught	.05
360	Paul Splittorff	.05
361	U.L. Washington	.05
362	John Wathan	.05
363	Frank White	.05
364	Willie Wilson	.05
365	Jim Barr	.05
366	Dave Bergman	.05
367	Fred Breining	.05
368	Bob Brenly	.05
369	Jack Clark	.05
370	Chili Davis	.05
371	Mark Davis RC	.05
372	Darrell Evans	.05
373	Atlee Hammaker	.05
374	Mike Krukow	.05
375	Duane Kuiper	.05
376	Bill Laskey	.05
377	Gary Lavelle	.05
378	Johnnie LeMaster	.05
379	Jeff Leonard	.05
380	Randy Lerch	.05
381	Renie Martin	.05
382	Andy McGaffigan	.05
383	Greg Minton	.05
384	Tom O'Malley	.05
385	Max Venable	.05
386	Brad Wellman	.05
387	Joel Youngblood	.05
388	Gary Allenson	.05
389	Luis Aponte	.05
390	Tony Armas	.05
391	Doug Bird	.05
392	Wade Boggs	2.00
393	Dennis Boyd RC	.05
394	Mike Brown	.05
395	Mark Clear	.05
396	Dennis Eckersley	.75
397	Dwight Evans	.05
398	Rich Gedman	.05
399	Glenn Hoffman	.05
400	Bruce Hurst	.05
401	John Henry Johnson	.05
402	Ed Jurak	.05
403	Rick Miller	.05
404	Jeff Newman	.05
405	Reid Nichols	.05
406	Bob Ojeda	.05
407	Jerry Remy	.05
408	Jim Rice	.05
409	Bob Stanley	.05
410	Dave Stapleton	.05
411	John Tudor	.05
412	Carl Yastrzemski	1.50
413	Buddy Bell	.05
414	Larry Biittner	.05
415	John Butcher	.05
416	Danny Darwin	.05
417	Bucky Dent	.05
418	Dave Hostetler	.05
419	Charlie Hough	.05
420	Bobby Johnson	.05
421	Odell Jones	.05
422	Jon Matlack	.05
423	Pete O'Brien RC	.05
424	Larry Parrish	.05
425	Mickey Rivers	.05
426	Billy Sample	.05
427	Dave Schmidt	.05
428	Mike Smithson RC	.05
429	Bill Stein	.05
430	Dave Stewart	.05
431	Jim Sundberg	.05
432	Frank Tanana	.05
433	Dave Tobik	.05
434	Wayne Tolleson RC	.05
435	George Wright	.05
436	Bill Almon	.05
437	Keith Atherton RC	.05
438	Dave Beard	.05
439	Tom Burgmeier	.05
440	Jeff Burroughs	.05
441	Chris Codiroli RC	.05
442	Tim Conroy RC	.05
443	Mike Davis	.05
444	Wayne Gross	.05
445	Garry Hancock	.05
446	Mike Heath	.05
447	Rickey Henderson	1.00
448	Don Hill RC	.05
449	Bob Kearney	.05
450	Bill Krueger	.05
451	Rick Langford	.05
452	Carney Lansford	.05
453	Davey Lopes	.05
454	Steve McCatty	.05
455	Dan Meyer	.05
456	Dwayne Murphy	.05
457	Mike Norris	.05
458	Ricky Peters	.05
459	Tony Phillips	.05
460	Tom Underwood	.05
461	Mike Warren	.05
462	Johnny Bench	1.50
463	Bruce Berenyi	.05
464	Dann Bilardello	.05
465	Cesar Cedeno	.05
466	Dave Concepcion	.05
467	Dan Driessen	.05
468	Nick Esasky RC	.05
469	Rich Gale	.05
470	Ben Hayes	.05
471	Paul Householder	.05
472	Tom Hume	.05
473	Alan Knicely	.05
474	Eddie Milner	.05
475	Ron Oester	.05
476	Kelly Paris	.05
477	Frank Pastore	.05
478	Ted Power	.05
479	Joe Price	.05
480	Charlie Puleo	.05
481	Gary Redus RC	.05
482	Bill Scherrer	.05
483	Mario Soto	.05
484	Alex Trevino	.05
485	Duane Walker	.05
486	Larry Bowa	.05
487	Warren Brusstar	.05
488	Bill Buckner	.05
489	Bill Campbell	.05
490	Ron Cey	.05
491	Jody Davis	.05
492	Leon Durham	.05
493	Mel Hall RC	.05
494	Fergie Jenkins	.75
495	Jay Johnstone	.05
496	Craig Lefferts RC	.10
497	Carmelo Martinez RC	.05
498	Jerry Morales	.05
499	Keith Moreland	.05
500	Dickie Noles	.05
501	Mike Proly	.05
502	Chuck Rainey	.05
503	Dick Ruthven	.05
504	Ryne Sandberg	2.00
505	Lee Smith	.05
506	Steve Trout	.05
507	Gary Woods	.05
508	Juan Beniquez	.05
509	Bob Boone	.05
510	Rick Burleson	.05
511	Rod Carew	1.00
512	Bobby Clark	.05
513	John Curtis	.05
514	Doug DeCinces	.05
515	Brian Downing	.05
516	Tim Foli	.05
517	Ken Forsch	.05
518	Bobby Grich	.05
519	Andy Hassler	.05
520	Reggie Jackson	1.50
521	Ron Jackson	.05
522	Tommy John	.10
523	Bruce Kison	.05
524	Steve Lubratich	.05
525	Fred Lynn	.05
526	Gary Pettis RC	.05
527	Luis Sanchez	.05
528	Daryl Sconiers	.05
529	Ellis Valentine	.05
530	Rob Wilfong	.05
531	Mike Witt	.05
532	Geoff Zahn	.05
533	Bud Anderson	.05
534	Chris Bando	.05
535	Alan Bannister	.05
536	Bert Blyleven	.05
537	Tom Brennan	.05
538	Jamie Easterly	.05

539	Juan Eichelberger	.05
540	Jim Essian	.05
541	Mike Fischlin	.05
542	Julio Franco	.05
543	Mike Hargrove	.05
544	Toby Harrah	.05
545	Ron Hassey	.05
546	Neal Heaton RC	.05
547	Bake McBride	.05
548	Broderick Perkins	.05
549	Lary Sorensen	.05
550	Dan Spillner	.05
551	Rick Sutcliffe	.05
552	Pat Tabler	.05
553	Gorman Thomas	.05
554	Andre Thornton	.05
555	George Vukovich	.05
556	Darrell Brown	.05
557	Tom Brunansky	.05
558	Randy Bush RC	.05
559	Bobby Castillo	.05
560	John Castino	.05
561	Ron Davis	.05
562	Dave Engle	.05
563	Lenny Faedo	.05
564	Pete Filson	.05
565	Gary Gaetti	.05
566	Mickey Hatcher	.05
567	Kent Hrbek	.05
568	Rusty Kuntz	.05
569	Tim Laudner	.05
570	Rick Lysander	.05
571	Bobby Mitchell	.05
572	Ken Schrom	.05
573	Ray Smith	.05
574	Tim Teufel RC	.05
575	Frank Viola	.05
576	Gary Ward	.05
577	Ron Washington	.05
578	Len Whitehouse	.05
579	Al Williams	.05
580	Bob Bailor	.05
581	Mark Bradley	.05
582	Hubie Brooks	.05
583	Carlos Diaz	.05
584	George Foster	.05
585	Brian Giles	.05
586	Danny Heep	.05
587	Keith Hernandez	.05
588	Ron Hodges	.05
589	Scott Holman	.05
590	Dave Kingman	.05
591	Ed Lynch	.05
592	Jose Oquendo RC	.05
593	Jesse Orosco	.05
594	Junior Ortiz RC	.05
595	Tom Seaver	1.00
596	Doug Sisk RC	.05
597	Rusty Staub	.05
598	John Stearns	.05
599	Darryl Strawberry	.25
600	Craig Swan	.05
601	Walt Terrell RC	.05
602	Mike Torrez	.05
603	Mookie Wilson	.05
604	Jamie Allen	.05
605	Jim Beattie	.05
606	Tony Bernazard	.05
607	Manny Castillo	.05
608	Bill Caudill	.05
609	Bryan Clark	.05
610	Al Cowens	.05
611	Dave Henderson	.05
612	Steve Henderson	.05
613	Orlando Mercado	.05
614	Mike Moore	.05
615	Ricky Nelson	.05
616	Spike Owen RC	.10
617	Pat Putnam	.05
618	Ron Roenicke	.05
619	Mike Stanton	.05
620	Bob Stoddard	.05
621	Rick Sweet	.05
622	Roy Thomas	.05
623	Ed Vande Berg	.05
624	Matt Young RC	.05
625	Richie Zisk	.05
626	'83 All-Star Game Record Breaker (Fred Lynn)	.05
627	'83 All-Star Game Record Breaker (Manny Trillo)	.05
628	N.L. Iron Man (Steve Garvey)	.10
629	A.L. Batting Runner-Up (Rod Carew)	.15
630	A.L. Batting Champion (Wade Boggs)	.50
631	Letting Go Of The Raines (Tim Raines)	.10
632	Double Trouble (Al Oliver)	.05
633	All-Star Second Base (Steve Sax)	.05
634	All-Star Shortstop (Dickie Thon)	.05
635	Ace Firemen (Tippy Martinez, Dan Quisenberry)	.05
636	Reds Reunited (Joe Morgan, Tony Perez, Pete Rose)	.75
637	Backstop Stars (Bob Boone, Lance Parrish)	.05
638	The Pine Tar Incident, 7/24/83 (George Brett, Gaylord Perry)	.05
639	1983 No-Hitters (Bob Forsch, Dave Righetti, Mike Warren)	.05

640	Retiring Superstars (Johnny Bench, Carl Yastrzemski)	.50
641	Going Out In Style (Gaylord Perry)	.05
642	300 Club & Strikeout Record (Steve Carlton)	.10
643	The Managers (Joe Altobelli, Paul Owens)	.05
644	The MVP (Rick Dempsey)	.05
645	The Rookie Winner (Mike Boddicker)	.05
646	The Clincher (Scott McGregor)	.05
647	Checklist: Orioles/Royals (Joe Altobelli)	.05
648	Checklist: Phillies/Giants (Paul Owens)	.05
649	Checklist: White Sox/Red Sox (Tony LaRussa)	.05
650	Checklist: Tigers/Rangers (Sparky Anderson)	.10
651	Checklist: Dodgers/A's (Tommy Lasorda)	.10
652	Checklist: Yankees/Reds (Billy Martin)	.10
653	Checklist: Blue Jays/Cubs (Bobby Cox)	.10
654	Checklist: Braves/Angels (Joe Torre)	.10
655	Checklist: Brewers/Indians (Rene Lacheman)	.05
656	Checklist: Astros/Twins (Bob Lillis)	.05
657	Checklist: Pirates/Mets (Chuck Tanner)	.05
658	Checklist: Expos/Mariners (Bill Virdon)	.05
659	Checklist: Padres/Specials (Dick Williams)	.05
660	Checklist: Cardinals/Specials (Whitey Herzog)	.05

Fleer Update

Brett Butler
OUTFIELD

Following the lead of Topps, Fleer issued near the end of the baseball season a 132-card set to update player trades and include rookies not depicted in the regular issue. The cards are identical in design to the regular issue but are numbered U-1 through U-132. Available only as a boxed set through hobby dealers, the set was printed in limited quantities. Sets were not factory sealed.

		NM/M
Complete Set (132):		220.00
Common Player:		.25
1	Willie Aikens	.25
2	Luis Aponte	.25
3	Mark Bailey	.25
4	Bob Bailor	.25
5	Dusty Baker	.25
6	Steve Balboni	.25
7	Alan Bannister	.25
8	Marty Barrett	.25
9	Dave Beard	.25
10	Joe Beckwith	.25
11	Dave Bergman	.25
12	Tony Bernazard	.25
13	Bruce Bochte	.25
14	Barry Bonnell	.25
15	Phil Bradley	.25
16	Fred Breining	.25
17	Mike Brown	.25
18	Bill Buckner	.25
19	Ray Burris	.25
20	John Butcher	.25
21	Brett Butler	.25
22	Enos Cabell	.25
23	Bill Campbell	.25
24	Bill Caudill	.25
25	Bobby Clark	.25
26	Bryan Clark	.25
27	Roger Clemens RC	140.00
28	Jaime Cocanower	.25
29	Ron Darling RC	1.00
30	Alvin Davis RC	.25
31	Bob Dernier	.25
32	Carlos Diaz	.25
33	Mike Easler	.25
34	Dennis Eckersley	4.00
35	Jim Essian	.25
36	Darrell Evans	.25

37	Mike Fitzgerald	.25
38	Tim Foli	.25
39	John Franco RC	3.00
40	George Frazier	.25
41	Rich Gale	.25
42	Barbaro Garbey	.25
43	Dwight Gooden RC	7.50
44	Goose Gossage	.40
45	Wayne Gross	.25
46	Mark Gubicza	1.00
47	Jackie Gutierrez	.25
48	Toby Harrah	.25
49	Ron Hassey	.25
50	Richie Hebner	.25
51	Willie Hernandez	.25
52	Ed Hodge	.25
53	Ricky Horton	.25
54	Art Howe	.25
55	Dane Iorg	.25
56	Brook Jacoby	.25
57	Dion James RC	.25
58	Mike Jeffcoat RC	.25
59	Ruppert Jones	.25
60	Bob Kearney	.25
61	Jimmy Key RC	1.00
62	Dave Kingman	.25
63	Brad Komminsk RC	.25
64	Jerry Koosman	.25
65	Wayne Krenchicki	.25
66	Rusty Kuntz	.25
67	Frank LaCorte	.25
68	Dennis Lamp	.25
69	Tito Landrum	.25
70	Mark Langston RC	4.00
71	Rick Leach	.25
72	Craig Lefferts	.25
73	Gary Lucas	.25
74	Jerry Martin	.25
75	Carmelo Martinez	.25
76	Mike Mason RC	.25
77	Gary Matthews	.25
78	Andy McGaffigan	.25
79	Joey McLaughlin	.25
80	Joe Morgan	5.00
81	Darryl Motley	.25
82	Graig Nettles	.40
83	Phil Niekro	3.00
84	Ken Oberkfell	.25
85	Al Oliver	.25
86	Jorge Orta	.25
87	Amos Otis	.25
88	Bob Owchinko	.25
89	Dave Parker	.25
90	Jack Perconte	.25
91	Tony Perez	3.00
92	Gerald Perry	.25
93	Kirby Puckett RC	75.00
94	Shane Rawley	.25
95	Floyd Rayford	.25
96	Ron Reed	.25
97	R.J. Reynolds	.25
98	Gene Richards	.25
99	Jose Rijo RC	1.00
100	Jeff Robinson	.25
101	Ron Romanick	.25
102	Pete Rose	10.00
103	Bret Saberhagen RC	5.00
104	Scott Sanderson	.25
105	Dick Schofield RC	.25
106	Tom Seaver	7.50
107	Jim Slaton	.25
108	Mike Smithson	.25
109	Lary Sorensen	.25
110	Tim Stoddard	.25
111	Jeff Stone	.25
112	Champ Summers	.25
113	Jim Sundberg	.25
114	Rick Sutcliffe	.35
115	Craig Swan	.25
116	Derrel Thomas	.25
117	Gorman Thomas	.25
118	Alex Trevino	.25
119	Manny Trillo	.25
120	John Tudor	.25
121	Tom Underwood	.25
122	Mike Vail	.25
123	Tom Waddell	.25
124	Gary Ward	.25
125	Terry Whitfield	.25
126	Curtis Wilkerson	.25
127	Frank Williams	.25
128	Glenn Wilson	.25
129	John Wockenfuss	.25
130	Ned Yost	.25
131	Mike Young RC	.25
132	Checklist 1-132	.10

1984 Fleer Stickers

This set was designed to be housed in a special collector's album that was organized according to various league leader categories, resulting in some players being pictured on more than one sticker. Each full-color sticker measures 1-15/16" x 2-1/2" and is framed with a beige border. The stickers, which were sold in packs of six, are numbered on the back.

		NM/M
Complete Set (126):		9.00
Common Player:		.05
Sticker Album:		1.00
Wax Box (100):		12.00
1	Dickie Thon	.05
2	Ken Landreaux	.05
3	Darrell Evans	.05
4	Harold Baines	.05
5	Dave Winfield	.25
6	Bill Madlock	.05
7	Lonnie Smith	.05
8	Jose Cruz	.05
9	George Hendrick	.05
10	Ray Knight	.05
11	Wade Boggs	.30
12	Rod Carew	.05
13	Lou Whitaker	.05
14	Alan Trammell	.05
15	Cal Ripken, Jr.	.50
16	Mike Schmidt	.40
17	Dale Murphy	.20
18	Andre Dawson	.15
19	Pedro Guerrero	.05
20	Jim Rice	.15
21	Tony Armas	.05
22	Ron Kittle	.05
23	Eddie Murray	.05
24	Jose Cruz	.05
25	Andre Dawson	.15
26	Rafael Ramirez	.05
27	Al Oliver	.05
28	Wade Boggs	.30
29	Cal Ripken, Jr.	.50
30	Lou Whitaker	.05
31	Cecil Cooper	.05
32	Dale Murphy	.20
33	Andre Dawson	.15
34	Pedro Guerrero	.05
35	Mike Schmidt	.40
36	George Brett	.40
37	Jim Rice	.15
38	Eddie Murray	.25
39	Carlton Fisk	.25
40	Rusty Staub	.05
41	Duane Walker	.05
42	Steve Braun	.05
43	Kurt Bevacqua	.05
44	Hal McRae	.05
45	Don Baylor	.05
46	Ken Singleton	.05
47	Greg Luzinski	.05
48	Mike Schmidt	.40
49	Keith Hernandez	.05
50	Dale Murphy	.20
51	Tim Raines	.05
52	Wade Boggs	.30
53	Rickey Henderson	.25
54	Rod Carew	.25
55	Ken Singleton	.05
56	John Denny	.05
57	John Candelaria	.05
58	Larry McWilliams	.05
59	Pascual Perez	.05
60	Jesse Orosco	.05
61	Moose Haas	.05
62	Richard Dotson	.05
63	Mike Flanagan	.05
64	Scott McGregor	.05
65	Atlee Hammaker	.05
66	Rick Honeycutt	.05
67	Lee Smith	.05
68	Al Holland	.05
69	Greg Minton	.05
70	Bruce Sutter	.20
71	Jeff Reardon	.05
72	Frank DiPino	.05
73	Dan Quisenberry	.05
74	Bob Stanley	.05
75	Ron Davis	.05
76	Bill Caudill	.05
77	Peter Ladd	.05
78	Steve Carlton	.25
79	Mario Soto	.05
80	Larry McWilliams	.05
81	Fernando Valenzuela	.05
82	Nolan Ryan	.75
83	Jack Morris	.05
84	Floyd Bannister	.05
85	Dave Stieb	.05
86	Dave Righetti	.05
87	Rick Sutcliffe	.05
88	Tim Raines	.05
89	Alan Wiggins	.05
90	Steve Sax	.05
91	Mookie Wilson	.05
92	Rickey Henderson	.25
93	Rudy Law	.05
94	Willie Wilson	.05
95	Julio Cruz	.05
96	Johnny Bench	.30
97	Carl Yastrzemski	.25
98	Gaylord Perry	.15
99	Pete Rose	.45

100	Joe Morgan	.25
101	Steve Carlton	.25
102	Jim Palmer	.25
103	Rod Carew	.25
104	Darryl Strawberry	.20
105	Craig McMurtry	.05
106	Mel Hall	.05
107	Lee Tunnell	.05
108	Bill Dawley	.05
109	Ron Kittle	.05
110	Mike Boddicker	.05
111	Julio Franco	.05
112	Daryl Sconiers	.05
113	Neal Heaton	.05
114	John Shelby	.05
115	Rick Dempsey	.05
116	John Lowenstein	.05
117	Jim Dwyer	.05
118	Bo Diaz	.05
119	Pete Rose	.45
120	Joe Morgan	.25
121	Gary Matthews	.05
122	Garry Maddox	.05
123	Paul Owens	.05
124	Tom Lasorda	.05
125	Joe Altobelli	.05
126	Tony LaRussa	.05

1985 Fleer

The 1985 Fleer set consists of 660 cards, each measuring 2-1/2" x 3-1/2". Card fronts feature a color photo plus the player's team logo and the word "Fleer." The photos have a color-coded frame which corresponds to the player's team. A gray border surrounds the frame. Backs are similar in design to previous years, but have two shades of red and black ink on white stock. For the fourth consecutive year, Fleer included special cards and team checklists in the set. Also incorporated in a set for the first time were 10 "Major League Prospect" cards, each featuring two rookie hopefuls. The set was issued with team logo stickers.

		NM/M
Unopened Factory Set (660):		50.00
Complete Set (660):		40.00
Common Player:		.05
Wax Pack (15):		4.50
Wax Box (36):		150.00
Cello Pack (28):		6.00
Cello Box (24):		150.00
Rack Pack (45):		8.00
Vending Box (500):		35.00
1	Doug Bair	.05
2	Juan Berenguer	.05
3	Dave Bergman	.05
4	Tom Brookens	.05
5	Marty Castillo	.05
6	Darrell Evans	.05
7	Barbaro Garbey	.05
8	Kirk Gibson	.05
9	John Grubb	.05
10	Willie Hernandez	.05
11	Larry Herndon	.05
12	Howard Johnson	.05
13	Ruppert Jones	.05
14	Rusty Kuntz	.05
15	Chet Lemon	.05
16	Aurelio Lopez	.05
17	Sid Monge	.05
18	Jack Morris	.05
19	Lance Parrish	.05
20	Dan Petry	.05
21	Dave Rozema	.05
22	Bill Scherrer	.05
23	Alan Trammell	.05
24	Lou Whitaker	.05
25	Milt Wilcox	.05
26	Kurt Bevacqua	.05
27	Greg Booker RC	.05
28	Bobby Brown	.05
29	Luis DeLeon	.05
30	Dave Dravecky	.05
31	Tim Flannery	.05
32	Steve Garvey	.40
33	Goose Gossage	.10
34	Tony Gwynn	2.00
35	Greg Harris	.05
36	Andy Hawkins	.05
37	Terry Kennedy	.05

38	Craig Lefferts	.05
39	Tim Lollar	.05
40	Carmelo Martinez	.05
41	Kevin McReynolds	.05
42	Graig Nettles	.05
43	Luis Salazar	.05
44	Eric Show	.05
45	Garry Templeton	.05
46	Mark Thurmond	.05
47	Ed Whitson	.05
48	Alan Wiggins	.05
49	Rich Bordi	.05
50	Larry Bowa	.05
51	Warren Brusstar	.05
52	Ron Cey	.05
53	Henry Cotto RC	.05
54	Jody Davis	.05
55	Bob Dernier	.05
56	Leon Durham	.05
57	Dennis Eckersley	.75
58	George Frazier	.05
59	Richie Hebner	.05
60	Dave Lopes	.05
61	Gary Matthews	.05
62	Keith Moreland	.05
63	Rick Reuschel	.05
64	Dick Ruthven	.05
65	Ryne Sandberg	2.00
66	Scott Sanderson	.05
67	Lee Smith	.05
68	Tim Stoddard	.05
69	Rick Sutcliffe	.05
70	Steve Trout	.05
71	Gary Woods	.05
72	Wally Backman	.05
73	Bruce Berenyi	.05
74	Hubie Brooks	.05
75	Kelvin Chapman	.05
76	Ron Darling	.05
77	Sid Fernandez RC	.05
78	Mike Fitzgerald	.05
79	George Foster	.05
80	Brent Gaff	.05
81	Ron Gardenhire	.05
82	Dwight Gooden	.25
83	Tom Gorman	.05
84	Danny Heep	.05
85	Keith Hernandez	.05
86	Ray Knight	.05
87	Ed Lynch	.05
88	Jose Oquendo	.05
89	Jesse Orosco	.05
90	Rafael Santana RC	.05
91	Doug Sisk	.05
92	Rusty Staub	.05
93	Darryl Strawberry	.10
94	Walt Terrell	.05
95	Mookie Wilson	.05
96	Jim Acker	.05
97	Willie Aikens	.05
98	Doyle Alexander	.05
99	Jesse Barfield	.05
100	George Bell	.05
101	Jim Clancy	.05
102	Dave Collins	.05
103	Tony Fernandez	.05
104	Damaso Garcia	.05
105	Jim Gott	.05
106	Alfredo Griffin	.05
107	Garth Iorg	.05
108	Roy Lee Jackson	.05
109	Cliff Johnson	.05
110	Jimmy Key	.05
111	Dennis Lamp	.05
112	Rick Leach	.05
113	Luis Leal	.05
114	Buck Martinez	.05
115	Lloyd Moseby	.05
116	Rance Mulliniks	.05
117	Dave Stieb	.05
118	Willie Upshaw	.05
119	Ernie Whitt	.05
120	Mike Armstrong	.05
121	Don Baylor	.05
122	Marty Bystrom	.05
123	Rick Cerone	.05
124	Joe Cowley RC	.05
125	Brian Dayett RC	.05
126	Tim Foli	.05
127	Ray Fontenot	.05
128	Ken Griffey	.05
129	Ron Guidry	.10
130	Toby Harrah	.05
131	Jay Howell	.05
132	Steve Kemp	.05
133	Don Mattingly	2.50
134	Bobby Meacham	.05
135	John Montefusco	.05
136	Omar Moreno	.05
137	Dale Murray	.05
138	Phil Niekro	.75
139	Mike Pagliarulo RC	.20
140	Willie Randolph	.05
141	Dennis Rasmussen RC	.05
142	Dave Righetti	.05
143	Jose Rijo	.05
144	Andre Robertson	.05
145	Bob Shirley	.05
146	Dave Winfield	1.00
147	Butch Wynegar	.05
148	Gary Allenson	.05
149	Tony Armas	.05
150	Marty Barrett	.05
151	Wade Boggs	2.00
152	Dennis Boyd	.05
153	Bill Buckner	.05
154	Mark Clear	.05
155	Roger Clemens	25.00

No.	Player	Price
156	Steve Crawford	.05
157	Mike Easler	.05
158	Dwight Evans	.05
159	Rich Gedman	.05
160	Jackie Gutierrez	.05
161	Bruce Hurst	.05
162	John Henry Johnson	.05
163	Rick Miller	.05
164	Reid Nichols	.05
165	Al Nipper RC	.05
166	Bob Ojeda	.05
167	Jerry Remy	.05
168	Jim Rice	.25
169	Bob Stanley	.05
170	Mike Boddicker	.05
171	Al Bumbry	.05
172	Todd Cruz	.05
173	Rich Dauer	.05
174	Storm Davis	.05
175	Rick Dempsey	.05
176	Jim Dwyer	.05
177	Mike Flanagan	.05
178	Dan Ford	.05
179	Wayne Gross	.05
180	John Lowenstein	.05
181	Dennis Martinez	.05
182	Tippy Martinez	.05
183	Scott McGregor	.05
184	Eddie Murray	1.00
185	Joe Nolan	.05
186	Floyd Rayford	.05
187	Cal Ripken, Jr.	4.00
188	Gary Roenicke	.05
189	Lenn Sakata	.05
190	John Shelby	.05
191	Ken Singleton	.05
192	Sammy Stewart	.05
193	Bill Swaggerty	.05
194	Tom Underwood	.05
195	Mike Young	.05
196	Steve Balboni	.05
197	Joe Beckwith	.05
198	Bud Black	.05
199	George Brett	2.50
200	Onix Concepcion	.05
201	Mark Gubicza RC	.50
202	Larry Gura	.05
203	Mark Huismann RC	.05
204	Dane Iorg	.05
205	Danny Jackson RC	.05
206	Charlie Leibrandt	.05
207	Hal McRae	.05
208	Darryl Motley	.05
209	Jorge Orta	.05
210	Greg Pryor	.05
211	Dan Quisenberry	.05
212	Bret Saberhagen	.25
213	Pat Sheridan	.05
214	Don Slaught	.05
215	U.L. Washington	.05
216	John Wathan	.05
217	Frank White	.05
218	Willie Wilson	.05
219	Neil Allen	.05
220	Joaquin Andujar	.05
221	Steve Braun	.05
222	Danny Cox RC	.05
223	Bob Forsch	.05
224	David Green	.05
225	George Hendrick	.05
226	Tom Herr	.05
227	Ricky Horton RC	.05
228	Art Howe	.05
229	Mike Jorgensen	.05
230	Kurt Kepshire	.05
231	Jeff Lahti	.05
232	Tito Landrum	.05
233	Dave LaPoint	.05
234	Willie McGee	.05
235	Tom Nieto RC	.05
236	Terry Pendleton RC	1.00
237	Darrell Porter	.05
238	Dave Rucker	.05
239	Lonnie Smith	.05
240	Ozzie Smith	2.00
241	Bruce Sutter	.75
242	Andy Van Slyke	.05
243	Dave Von Ohlen	.05
244	Larry Andersen	.05
245	Bill Campbell	.05
246	Steve Carlton	1.00
247	Tim Corcoran	.05
248	Ivan DeJesus	.05
249	John Denny	.05
250	Bo Diaz	.05
251	Greg Gross	.05
252	Kevin Gross	.05
253	Von Hayes	.05
254	Al Holland	.05
255	Charles Hudson	.05
256	Jerry Koosman	.05
257	Joe Lefebvre	.05
258	Sixto Lezcano	.05
259	Garry Maddox	.05
260	Len Matuszek	.05
261	Tug McGraw	.05
262	Al Oliver	.05
263	Shane Rawley	.05
264	Juan Samuel	.05
265	Mike Schmidt	2.50
266	Jeff Stone RC	.05
267	Ozzie Virgil	.05
268	Glenn Wilson	.05
269	John Wockenfuss	.05
270	Darrell Brown	.05
271	Tom Brunansky	.05
272	Randy Bush	.05
273	John Butcher	.05
274	Bobby Castillo	.05
275	Ron Davis	.05
276	Dave Engle	.05
277	Pete Filson	.05
278	Gary Gaetti	.05
279	Mickey Hatcher	.05
280	Ed Hodge	.05
281	Kent Hrbek	.05
282	Houston Jimenez	.05
283	Tim Laudner	.05
284	Rick Lysander	.05
285	Dave Meier	.05
286	Kirby Puckett	8.00
287	Pat Putnam	.05
288	Ken Schrom	.05
289	Mike Smithson	.05
290	Tim Teufel	.05
291	Frank Viola	.05
292	Ron Washington	.05
293	Don Aase	.05
294	Juan Beniquez	.05
295	Bob Boone	.05
296	Mike Brown	.05
297	Rod Carew	1.00
298	Doug Corbett	.05
299	Doug DeCinces	.05
300	Brian Downing	.05
301	Ken Forsch	.05
302	Bobby Grich	.05
303	Reggie Jackson	2.00
304	Tommy John	.10
305	Curt Kaufman	.05
306	Bruce Kison	.05
307	Fred Lynn	.05
308	Gary Pettis	.05
309	Ron Romanick RC	.05
310	Luis Sanchez	.05
311	Dick Schofield	.05
312	Daryl Sconiers	.05
313	Jim Slaton	.05
314	Derrel Thomas	.05
315	Rob Wilfong	.05
316	Mike Witt	.05
317	Geoff Zahn	.05
318	Len Barker	.05
319	Steve Bedrosian	.05
320	Bruce Benedict	.05
321	Rick Camp	.05
322	Chris Chambliss	.05
323	Jeff Dedmon RC	.05
324	Terry Forster	.05
325	Gene Garber	.05
326	Albert Hall RC	.05
327	Terry Harper	.05
328	Bob Horner	.05
329	Glenn Hubbard	.05
330	Randy Johnson	.05
331	Brad Komminsk	.05
332	Rick Mahler	.05
333	Craig McMurtry	.05
334	Donnie Moore	.05
335	Dale Murphy	.40
336	Ken Oberkfell	.05
337	Pascual Perez	.05
338	Gerald Perry	.05
339	Rafael Ramirez	.05
340	Jerry Royster	.05
341	Alex Trevino	.05
342	Claudell Washington	.05
343	Alan Ashby	.05
344	Mark Bailey RC	.05
345	Kevin Bass	.05
346	Enos Cabell	.05
347	Jose Cruz	.05
348	Bill Dawley	.05
349	Frank DiPino	.05
350	Bill Doran	.05
351	Phil Garner	.05
352	Bob Knepper	.05
353	Mike LaCoss	.05
354	Jerry Mumphrey	.05
355	Joe Niekro	.05
356	Terry Puhl	.05
357	Craig Reynolds	.05
358	Vern Ruhle	.05
359	Nolan Ryan	4.00
360	Joe Sambito	.05
361	Mike Scott	.05
362	Dave Smith	.05
363	Julio Solano RC	.05
364	Dickie Thon	.05
365	Denny Walling	.05
366	Dave Anderson	.05
367	Bob Bailor	.05
368	Greg Brock	.05
369	Carlos Diaz	.05
370	Pedro Guerrero	.05
371	Rick Honeycutt	.05
372	Burt Hooton	.05
373	Ken Howell RC	.05
374	Ken Landreaux	.05
375	Candy Maldonado	.05
376	Mike Marshall	.05
377	Tom Niedenfuer	.05
378	Alejandro Pena	.05
379	Jerry Reuss	.05
380	R.J. Reynolds RC	.05
381	German Rivera	.05
382	Bill Russell	.05
383	Steve Sax	.05
384	Mike Scioscia	.05
385	Franklin Stubbs RC	.05
386	Fernando Valenzuela	.05
387	Bob Welch	.05
388	Terry Whitfield	.05
389	Steve Yeager	.05
390	Pat Zachry	.05
392	Fred Breining	.05
393	Gary Carter	1.00
394	Andre Dawson	.25
395	Miguel Dilone	.05
396	Dan Driessen	.05
397	Doug Flynn	.05
398	Terry Francona	.05
399	Bill Gullickson	.05
400	Bob James	.05
401	Charlie Lea	.05
402	Bryan Little	.05
403	Gary Lucas	.05
404	David Palmer	.05
405	Tim Raines	.05
406	Mike Ramsey	.05
407	Jeff Reardon	.05
408	Steve Rogers	.05
409	Dan Schatzeder	.05
410	Bryn Smith	.05
411	Mike Stenhouse	.05
412	Tim Wallach	.05
413	Jim Wohlford	.05
414	Bill Almon	.05
415	Keith Atherton	.05
416	Bruce Bochte	.05
417	Tom Burgmeier	.05
418	Ray Burris	.05
419	Bill Caudill	.05
420	Chris Codiroli	.05
421	Tim Conroy	.05
422	Mike Davis	.05
423	Jim Essian	.05
424	Mike Heath	.05
425	Rickey Henderson	1.00
426	Donnie Hill	.05
427	Dave Kingman	.05
428	Bill Krueger	.05
429	Carney Lansford	.05
430	Steve McCatty	.05
431	Joe Morgan	1.00
432	Dwayne Murphy	.05
433	Tony Phillips	.05
434	Lary Sorensen	.05
435	Mike Warren	.05
436	Curt Young RC	.05
437	Luis Aponte	.05
438	Chris Bando	.05
439	Tony Bernazard	.05
440	Bert Blyleven	.10
441	Brett Butler	.05
442	Ernie Camacho	.05
443	Joe Carter	.25
444	Carmelo Castillo	.05
445	Jamie Easterly	.05
446	Steve Farr RC	.05
447	Mike Fischlin	.05
448	Julio Franco	.05
449	Mel Hall	.05
450	Mike Hargrove	.05
451	Neal Heaton	.05
452	Brook Jacoby	.05
453	Mike Jeffcoat RC	.05
454	Don Schulze RC	.05
455	Roy Smith	.05
456	Pat Tabler	.05
457	Andre Thornton	.05
458	George Vukovich	.05
459	Tom Waddell	.05
460	Jerry Willard	.05
461	Dale Berra	.05
462	John Candelaria	.05
463	Jose DeLeon	.05
464	Doug Frobel	.05
465	Cecilio Guante	.05
466	Brian Harper	.05
467	Lee Lacy	.05
468	Bill Madlock	.05
469	Lee Mazzilli	.05
470	Larry McWilliams	.05
471	Jim Morrison	.05
472	Tony Pena	.05
473	Johnny Ray	.05
474	Rick Rhoden	.05
475	Don Robinson	.05
476	Rod Scurry	.05
477	Kent Tekulve	.05
478	Jason Thompson	.05
479	John Tudor	.05
480	Lee Tunnell	.05
481	Marvell Wynne	.05
482	Salome Barojas	.05
483	Dave Beard	.05
484	Jim Beattie	.05
485	Barry Bonnell	.05
486	Phil Bradley RC	.05
487	Al Cowens	.05
488	Alvin Davis	.05
489	Dave Henderson	.05
490	Steve Henderson	.05
491	Bob Kearney	.05
492	Mark Langston	.15
493	Larry Milbourne	.05
494	Paul Mirabella	.05
495	Mike Moore	.05
496	Edwin Nunez RC	.05
497	Spike Owen	.05
498	Jack Perconte	.05
499	Ken Phelps	.05
500	Jim Presley RC	.05
501	Mike Stanton	.05
502	Bob Stoddard	.05
503	Gorman Thomas	.05
504	Ed Vande Berg	.05
505	Matt Young	.05
506	Juan Agosto	.05
507	Harold Baines	.05
508	Floyd Bannister	.05
509	Britt Burns	.05
510	Julio Cruz	.05
511	Richard Dotson	.05
512	Jerry Dybzinski	.05
513	Carlton Fisk	1.00
514	Scott Fletcher	.05
515	Jerry Hairston Sr.	.05
516	Marc Hill	.05
517	LaMarr Hoyt	.05
518	Ron Kittle	.05
519	Rudy Law	.05
520	Vance Law	.05
521	Greg Luzinski	.05
522	Gene Nelson	.05
523	Tom Paciorek	.05
524	Ron Reed	.05
525	Bert Roberge	.05
526	Tom Seaver	1.00
527	Roy Smalley	.05
528	Dan Spillner	.05
529	Mike Squires	.05
530	Greg Walker	.05
531	Cesar Cedeno	.05
532	Dave Concepcion	.05
533	Eric Davis RC	2.00
534	Nick Esasky	.05
535	Tom Foley	.05
536	John Franco	.05
537	Brad Gulden	.05
538	Tom Hume	.05
539	Wayne Krenchicki	.05
540	Andy McGaffigan	.05
541	Eddie Milner	.05
542	Ron Oester	.05
543	Bob Owchinko	.05
544	Dave Parker	.05
545	Frank Pastore	.05
546	Tony Perez	.75
547	Ted Power	.05
548	Joe Price	.05
549	Gary Redus	.05
550	Pete Rose	3.00
551	Jeff Russell RC	.05
552	Mario Soto	.05
553	Jay Tibbs RC	.05
554	Duane Walker	.05
555	Alan Bannister	.05
556	Buddy Bell	.05
557	Danny Darwin	.05
558	Charlie Hough	.05
559	Bobby Jones	.05
560	Odell Jones	.05
561	Jeff Kunkel RC	.05
562	Mike Mason RC	.05
563	Pete O'Brien	.05
564	Larry Parrish	.05
565	Mickey Rivers	.05
566	Billy Sample	.05
567	Dave Schmidt	.05
568	Donnie Scott	.05
569	Dave Stewart	.05
570	Frank Tanana	.05
571	Wayne Tolleson	.05
572	Gary Ward	.05
573	Curtis Wilkerson	.05
574	George Wright	.05
575	Ned Yost	.05
576	Mark Brouhard	.05
577	Mike Caldwell	.05
578	Bobby Clark	.05
579	Jaime Cocanower	.05
580	Cecil Cooper	.05
581	Rollie Fingers	.75
582	Jim Gantner	.05
583	Moose Haas	.05
584	Dion James	.05
585	Pete Ladd	.05
586	Rick Manning	.05
587	Bob McClure	.05
588	Paul Molitor	1.00
589	Charlie Moore	.05
590	Ben Oglivie	.05
591	Chuck Porter	.05
592	Randy Ready RC	.05
593	Ed Romero	.05
594	Bill Schroeder RC	.05
595	Ray Searage	.05
596	Ted Simmons	.05
597	Jim Sundberg	.05
598	Don Sutton	.75
599	Tom Tellmann	.05
600	Rick Waits	.05
601	Robin Yount	1.00
602	Dusty Baker	.05
603	Bob Brenly	.05
604	Jack Clark	.05
605	Chili Davis	.05
606	Mark Davis	.05
607	Dan Gladden RC	.25
608	Atlee Hammaker	.05
609	Mike Krukow	.05
610	Duane Kuiper	.05
611	Bob Lacey	.05
612	Bill Laskey	.05
613	Gary Lavelle	.05
614	Johnnie LeMaster	.05
615	Jeff Leonard	.05
616	Randy Lerch	.05
617	Greg Minton	.05
618	Steve Nicosia	.05
619	Gene Richards	.05
620	Jeff Robinson RC	.05
621	Scot Thompson	.05
622	Manny Trillo	.05
623	Brad Wellman	.05
624	Frank Williams RC	.05
625	Joel Youngblood	.05
626	Cal Ripken, Jr./IA	1.00
627	Mike Schmidt/IA	.50
628	Giving the Signs (Sparky Anderson)	.10
629	A.L. Pitcher's Nightmare (Rickey Henderson, Dave Winfield)	.50
630	N.L. Pitcher's Nightmare (Ryne Sandberg, Mike Schmidt)	1.00
631	N.L. All-Stars (Gary Carter, Steve Garvey, Ozzie Smith, Darryl Strawberry)	.25
632	All-Star Game Winning Battery (Gary Carter, Charlie Lea)	.10
633	N.L. Pennant Clinchers (Steve Garvey, Goose Gossage)	.10
634	N.L. Rookie Phenoms (Dwight Gooden, Juan Samuel)	.05
635	Toronto's Big Guns (Willie Upshaw)	.05
636	Toronto's Big Guns (Lloyd Moseby)	.05
637	Holland (Al Holland)	.05
638	Tunnell (Lee Tunnell)	.05
639	Reggie Jackson/IA	.50
640	Pete Rose/IA	.75
641	Father & Son (Cal Ripken, Jr., Cal Ripken, Sr.)	1.00
642	Cubs team	.05
643	1984's Two Perfect Games & One No-Hitter (Jack Morris, David Palmer, Mike Witt)	.05
644	Major League Prospect (Willie Lozado, Vic Mata)	.05
645	Major League Prospect (Kelly Gruber RC, Randy O'Neal RC)	.15
646	Major League Prospect (Jose Roman RC, Joel Skinner RC)	.05
647	Major League Prospect (Steve Kiefer RC, Danny Tartabull RC)	.50
648	Major League Prospect (Rob Deer RC, Alejandro Sanchez RC)	.25
649	Major League Prospect (Shawon Dunston RC, Bill Hatcher RC)	1.00
650	Major League Prospect (Mike Bielecki RC, Ron Robinson RC)	.10
651	Major League Prospect (Zane Smith RC, Paul Zuvella RC)	.10
652	Major League Prospect (Glenn Davis RC, Joe Hesketh RC)	.20
653	Major League Prospect (Steve Jeltz RC, John Russell RC)	.10
654	Checklist 1-95	.05
655	Checklist 96-195	.05
656	Checklist 196-292	.05
657	Checklist 293-391	.05
658	Checklist 392-481	.05
659	Checklist 482-575	.05
660	Checklist 576-660	.05

Fleer Update

For the second straight year, Fleer issued a 132-card update set. Cards portray traded players on their new teams and also include rookies not depicted in the regular issue. The cards are identical in design to the 1985 Fleer set but are numbered U-1 through U-132. The set was issued with team logo stickers in a specially designed box and was available only through hobby dealers.

No.	Player	NM/M
	Complete Set (132):	5.00
	Common Player:	.10
1	Don Aase	.10
2	Bill Almon	.10
3	Dusty Baker	.10
4	Dale Berra	.10
5	Karl Best RC	.10
6	Tim Birtsas RC	.10
7	Vida Blue	.10
8	Rich Bordi	.10
9	Daryl Boston RC	.10
10	Hubie Brooks	.10
11	Chris Brown RC	.10
12	Tom Browning RC	.10
13	Al Bumbry	.10
14	Tim Burke RC	.10
15	Ray Burris	.10
16	Jeff Burroughs	.10
17	Ivan Calderon RC	.10
18	Jeff Calhoun	.10
19	Bill Campbell	.10
20	Don Carman RC	.10
21	Gary Carter	.50
22	Bobby Castillo	.10
23	Bill Caudill	.10
24	Rick Cerone	.10
25	Jack Clark	.10
26	Pat Clements RC	.10
27	Stewart Cliburn RC	.10
28	Vince Coleman RC	.10
29	Dave Collins	.10
30	Fritz Connally	.10
31	Henry Cotto RC	.10
32	Danny Darwin	.10
33	Darren Daulton RC	1.00
34	Jerry Davis	.10
35	Brian Dayett	.10
36	Ken Dixon RC	.10
37	Tommy Dunbar	.10
38	Mariano Duncan RC	.10
39	Bob Fallon	.10
40	Brian Fisher RC	.10
41	Mike Fitzgerald	.10
42	Ray Fontenot	.10
43	Greg Gagne RC	.10
44	Oscar Gamble	.10
45	Jim Gott	.10
46	David Green	.10
47	Alfredo Griffin	.10
48	Ozzie Guillen RC	2.00
49	Toby Harrah	.10
50	Ron Hassey	.10
51	Rickey Henderson	3.00
52	Steve Henderson	.10
53	George Hendrick	.10
54	Teddy Higuera RC	.10
55	Al Holland	.10
56	Burt Hooton	.10
57	Jay Howell	.10
58	LaMarr Hoyt	.10
59	Tim Hulett RC	.10
60	Bob James	.10
61	Cliff Johnson	.10
62	Howard Johnson	.10
63	Ruppert Jones	.10
64	Steve Kemp	.10
65	Bruce Kison	.10
66	Mike LaCoss	.10
67	Lee Lacy	.10
68	Dave LaPoint	.10
69	Gary Lavelle	.10
70	Vance Law	.10
71	Manny Lee RC	.10
72	Sixto Lezcano	.10
73	Tim Lollar	.10
74	Urbano Lugo RC	.10
75	Fred Lynn	.10
76	Steve Lyons RC	.10
77	Mickey Mahler	.10
78	Ron Mathis RC	.10
79	Len Matuszek	.10
80	Oddibe McDowell RC	.10
81	Roger McDowell RC	.10
82	Donnie Moore	.10
83	Ron Musselman	.10
84	Al Oliver	.10
85	Joe Orsulak RC	.10
86	Dan Pasqua RC	.10
87	Chris Pittaro RC	.10
88	Rick Reuschel	.10
89	Earnie Riles RC	.10
90	Jerry Royster	.10
91	Dave Rozema	.10
92	Dave Rucker	.10
93	Vern Ruhle	.10
94	Mark Salas RC	.10
95	Luis Salazar	.10
96	Joe Sambito	.10
97	Billy Sample	.10
98	Alex Sanchez	.10
99	Calvin Schiraldi RC	.10
100	Rick Schu RC	.10
101	Larry Sheets RC	.10
102	Ron Shepherd	.10
103	Nelson Simmons RC	.10
104	Don Slaught	.10
105	Roy Smalley	.10
106	Lonnie Smith	.10
107	Nate Snell RC	.10
108	Lary Sorensen	.10
109	Chris Speier	.10
110	Mike Stenhouse	.10
111	Tim Stoddard	.10
112	John Stuper	.10
113	Jim Sundberg	.10
114	Bruce Sutter	.10
115	Don Sutton	.10
116	Bruce Tanner RC	.10
117	Kent Tekulve	.10
118	Walt Terrell	.10
119	Mickey Tettleton RC	.10
120	Rich Thompson	.10
121	Louis Thornton RC	.10
122	Alex Trevino	.10
123	John Tudor	.10
124	Jose Uribe RC	.10
125	Dave Valle RC	.10
126	Dave Von Ohlen	.10
127	Curt Wardle	.10

#	Player	Price
128	U.L. Washington	.10
129	Ed Whitson	.10
130	Herm Winningham RC	.10
131	Rich Yett RC	.10
132	Checklist	.10

1985 Fleer Limited Edition

The 1985 Fleer Limited Edition boxed set was distributed through several chains of retail stores. The cards, which are the standard 2-1/2" x 3-1/2", have full-color photos inside a red and yellow frame. The backs are set in black type against two different shades of yellow and contain the player's personal and statistical information. The set was issued in a specially designed box which carried the complete checklist for the set on the back. Six team logo stickers were also included with the set.

NM/M
#	Player	Price
	Complete Set (44):	4.00
	Common Player:	.10
1	Buddy Bell	.10
2	Bert Blyleven	.10
3	Wade Boggs	.60
4	George Brett	.75
5	Rod Carew	.50
6	Steve Carlton	.50
7	Alvin Davis	.10
8	Andre Dawson	.25
9	Steve Garvey	.15
10	Goose Gossage	.15
11	Tony Gwynn	.60
12	Keith Hernandez	.10
13	Kent Hrbek	.10
14	Reggie Jackson	.60
15	Dave Kingman	.10
16	Ron Kittle	.10
17	Mark Langston	.10
18	Jeff Leonard	.10
19	Bill Madlock	.10
20	Don Mattingly	.75
21	Jack Morris	.10
22	Dale Murphy	.15
23	Eddie Murray	.50
24	Tony Pena	.10
25	Dan Quisenberry	.10
26	Tim Raines	.10
27	Jim Rice	.25
28	Cal Ripken, Jr.	1.00
29	Pete Rose	.85
30	Nolan Ryan	1.00
31	Ryne Sandberg	.60
32	Steve Sax	.10
33	Mike Schmidt	.75
34	Tom Seaver	.50
35	Ozzie Smith	.60
36	Mario Soto	.10
37	Dave Stieb	.10
38	Darryl Strawberry	.10
39	Rick Sutcliffe	.10
40	Alan Trammell	.10
41	Willie Upshaw	.10
42	Fernando Valenzuela	.10
43	Dave Winfield	.50
44	Robin Yount	.50

1985 Fleer Star Stickers

The 1985 Fleer sticker set consists of 126 player stickers, each measuring 1-15/16" x 2-1/2". Numbered on the back, the stickers were designed to be put in a special album. Distributed in packs of six, the 1985 stickers are the scarcest of all Fleer baseball sticker issues.

NM/M
#	Player	Price
	Complete Set (126):	12.50
	Common Player:	.05
	Sticker Album:	1.25
	Wax Pack (6):	.25
	Wax Box (100):	16.00
1	Pete Rose	1.00
2	Pete Rose	1.00
3	Pete Rose	1.00
4	Don Mattingly	1.50
5	Dave Winfield	.40
6	Wade Boggs	.50
7	Buddy Bell	.05
8	Tony Gwynn	.40
9	Lee Lacy	.05
10	Chili Davis	.05
11	Ryne Sandberg	.50
12	Tony Armas	.05
13	Jim Rice	.15
14	Dave Kingman	.05
15	Alvin Davis	.05
16	Gary Carter	.25
17	Mike Schmidt	1.00
18	Dale Murphy	.20
19	Ron Cey	.05
20	Eddie Murray	.40
21	Harold Baines	.05
22	Kirk Gibson	.05
23	Jim Rice	.15
24	Gary Matthews	.05
25	Keith Hernandez	.05
26	Gary Carter	.25
27	George Hendrick	.05
28	Tony Armas	.05
29	Dave Kingman	.05
30	Dwayne Murphy	.05
31	Lance Parrish	.05
32	Andre Thornton	.05
33	Dale Murphy	.20
34	Mike Schmidt	1.00
35	Gary Carter	.25
36	Darryl Strawberry	.05
37	Don Mattingly	1.50
38	Larry Parrish	.05
39	George Bell	.05
40	Dwight Evans	.05
41	Cal Ripken, Jr.	2.00
42	Tim Raines	.05
43	Johnny Ray	.05
44	Juan Samuel	.05
45	Ryne Sandberg	.50
46	Mike Easler	.05
47	Andre Thornton	.05
48	Dave Kingman	.05
49	Don Baylor	.05
50	Rusty Staub	.05
51	Steve Braun	.05
52	Kevin Bass	.05
53	Greg Gross	.05
54	Rickey Henderson	.40
55	Dave Collins	.05
56	Brett Butler	.05
57	Gary Pettis	.05
58	Tim Raines	.05
59	Juan Samuel	.05
60	Alan Wiggins	.05
61	Lonnie Smith	.05
62	Eddie Murray	.05
63	Eddie Murray	.05
64	Eddie Murray	.05
65	Eddie Murray	.05
66	Eddie Murray	.05
67	Eddie Murray	.05
68	Tom Seaver	.05
69	Tom Seaver	.05
70	Tom Seaver	.05
71	Tom Seaver	.05
72	Tom Seaver	.05
73	Tom Seaver	.05
74	Mike Schmidt	.25
75	Mike Schmidt	.25
76	Mike Schmidt	.25
77	Mike Schmidt	.25
78	Mike Schmidt	.25
79	Mike Schmidt	.25
80	Mike Boddicker	.05
81	Bert Blyleven	.05
82	Jack Morris	.05
83	Dan Petry	.05
84	Frank Viola	.05
85	Joaquin Andujar	.05
86	Mario Soto	.05
87	Dwight Gooden	.05
88	Joe Niekro	.05
89	Rick Sutcliffe	.05
90	Mike Boddicker	.05
91	Dave Stieb	.05
92	Bert Blyleven	.05
93	Phil Niekro	.25
94	Alejandro Pena	.05
95	Dwight Gooden	.05
96	Orel Hershiser	.15
97	Rick Rhoden	.05
98	John Candelaria	.05
99	Dan Quisenberry	.05
100	Bill Caudill	.05
101	Willie Hernandez	.05
102	Dave Righetti	.05
103	Ron Davis	.05
104	Bruce Sutter	.20
105	Lee Smith	.05
106	Jesse Orosco	.05
107	Al Holland	.05
108	Goose Gossage	.05
109	Mark Langston	.05
110	Dave Stieb	.05
111	Mike Witt	.05
112	Bert Blyleven	.05
113	Dwight Gooden	.05
114	Fernando Valenzuela	.05
115	Nolan Ryan	2.00
116	Mario Soto	.05
117	Ron Darling	.05
118	Dan Gladden	.05
119	Jeff Stone	.05
120	John Franco	.05
121	Barbaro Garbey	.05
122	Kirby Puckett	1.50
123	Roger Clemens	7.50
124	Bret Saberhagen	.05
125	Sparky Anderson	.05
126	Dick Williams	.05

1986 Fleer

The 1986 Fleer set contains 660 color cards measuring 2-1/2" x 3-1/2". The card fronts feature a player photo enclosed by a dark blue border. The card backs are minus the black-and-white photo that was included in past Fleer efforts. Player biographical and statistical information appear in black and yellow on white stock. As in 1985, Fleer devoted 10 cards, entitled "Major League Prospects," to 20 promising rookie players. The 1986 set, as in the previous four years was issued with team logo stickers.

NM/M
#	Player	Price
	Unopened Fact. Set (660):	30.00
	Complete Set (660):	25.00
	Common Player:	.05
	Wax Pack (15):	1.50
	Wax Box (36):	45.00
	Cello Pack (28):	2.00
	Cello Box (24):	40.00
	Rack Pack (45):	4.00
	Rack Box (24):	65.00
1	Steve Balboni	.05
2	Joe Beckwith	.05
3	Buddy Biancalana	.05
4	Bud Black	.05
5	George Brett	2.00
6	Onix Concepcion	.05
7	Steve Farr	.05
8	Mark Gubicza	.05
9	Dane Iorg	.05
10	Danny Jackson	.05
11	Lynn Jones	.05
12	Mike Jones	.05
13	Charlie Leibrandt	.05
14	Hal McRae	.05
15	Omar Moreno	.05
16	Darryl Motley	.05
17	Jorge Orta	.05
18	Dan Quisenberry	.05
19	Bret Saberhagen	.05
20	Pat Sheridan	.05
21	Lonnie Smith	.05
22	Jim Sundberg	.05
23	John Wathan	.05
24	Frank White	.05
25	Willie Wilson	.05
26	Joaquin Andujar	.05
27	Steve Braun	.05
28	Bill Campbell	.05
29	Cesar Cedeno	.05
30	Jack Clark	.05
31	Vince Coleman	.05
32	Danny Cox	.05
33	Ken Dayley	.05
34	Ivan DeJesus	.05
35	Bob Forsch	.05
36	Brian Harper	.05
37	Tom Herr	.05
38	Ricky Horton	.05
39	Kurt Kepshire	.05
40	Jeff Lahti	.05
41	Tito Landrum	.05
42	Willie McGee	.05
43	Tom Nieto	.05
44	Terry Pendleton	.05
45	Darrell Porter	.05
46	Ozzie Smith	1.50
47	John Tudor	.05
48	Andy Van Slyke	.05
49	Todd Worrell RC	.25
50	Jim Acker	.05
51	Doyle Alexander	.05
52	Jesse Barfield	.05
53	George Bell	.05
54	Jeff Burroughs	.05
55	Bill Caudill	.05
56	Jim Clancy	.05
57	Tony Fernandez	.05
58	Tom Filer	.05
59	Damaso Garcia	.05
60	Tom Henke RC	.05
61	Garth Iorg	.05
62	Cliff Johnson	.05
63	Jimmy Key	.05
64	Dennis Lamp	.05
65	Gary Lavelle	.05
66	Buck Martinez	.05
67	Lloyd Moseby	.05
68	Rance Mulliniks	.05
69	Al Oliver	.05
70	Dave Stieb	.05
71	Louis Thornton	.05
72	Willie Upshaw	.05
73	Ernie Whitt	.05
74	Rick Aguilera RC	.75
75	Wally Backman	.05
76	Gary Carter	1.00
77	Ron Darling	.05
78	Len Dykstra RC	2.00
79	Sid Fernandez	.05
80	George Foster	.05
81	Dwight Gooden	.05
82	Tom Gorman	.05
83	Danny Heep	.05
84	Keith Hernandez	.05
85	Howard Johnson	.05
86	Ray Knight	.05
87	Terry Leach	.05
88	Ed Lynch	.05
89	Roger McDowell	.05
90	Jesse Orosco	.05
91	Tom Paciorek	.05
92	Ronn Reynolds	.05
93	Rafael Santana	.05
94	Doug Sisk	.05
95	Rusty Staub	.05
96	Darryl Strawberry	.05
97	Mookie Wilson	.05
98	Neil Allen	.05
99	Don Baylor	.05
100	Dale Berra	.05
101	Rich Bordi	.05
102	Marty Bystrom	.05
103	Joe Cowley	.05
104	Brian Fisher RC	.05
105	Ken Griffey	.05
106	Ron Guidry	.10
107	Ron Hassey	.05
108	Rickey Henderson	1.00
109	Don Mattingly	2.00
110	Bobby Meacham	.05
111	John Montefusco	.05
112	Phil Niekro	.75
113	Mike Pagliarulo	.05
114	Dan Pasqua	.05
115	Willie Randolph	.05
116	Dave Righetti	.05
117	Andre Robertson	.05
118	Billy Sample	.05
119	Bob Shirley	.05
120	Ed Whitson	.05
121	Dave Winfield	1.00
122	Butch Wynegar	.05
123	Dave Anderson	.05
124	Bob Bailor	.05
125	Greg Brock	.05
126	Enos Cabell	.05
127	Bobby Castillo	.05
128	Carlos Diaz	.05
129	Mariano Duncan	.05
130	Pedro Guerrero	.05
131	Orel Hershiser	.05
132	Rick Honeycutt	.05
133	Ken Howell	.05
134	Ken Landreaux	.05
135	Bill Madlock	.05
136	Candy Maldonado	.05
137	Mike Marshall	.05
138	Len Matuszek	.05
139	Tom Niedenfuer	.05
140	Alejandro Pena	.05
141	Jerry Reuss	.05
142	Bill Russell	.05
143	Steve Sax	.05
144	Mike Scioscia	.05
145	Fernando Valenzuela	.05
146	Bob Welch	.05
147	Terry Whitfield	.05
148	Juan Beniquez	.05
149	Bob Boone	.05
150	John Candelaria	.05
151	Rod Carew	1.00
152	Stewart Cliburn RC	.05
153	Doug DeCinces	.05
154	Brian Downing	.05
155	Ken Forsch	.05
156	Craig Gerber	.05
157	Bobby Grich	.05
158	George Hendrick	.05
159	Al Holland	.05
160	Reggie Jackson	1.50
161	Ruppert Jones	.05
162	Urbano Lugo RC	.05
163	Kirk McCaskill RC	.25
164	Donnie Moore	.05
165	Gary Pettis	.05
166	Ron Romanick	.05
167	Dick Schofield	.05
168	Daryl Sconiers	.05
169	Jim Slaton	.05
170	Don Sutton	.75
171	Mike Witt	.05
172	Buddy Bell	.05
173	Tom Browning	.05
174	Dave Concepcion	.05
175	Eric Davis	.05
176	Bo Diaz	.05
177	Nick Esasky	.05
178	John Franco	.05
179	Tom Hume	.05
180	Wayne Krenchicki	.05
181	Andy McGaffigan	.05
182	Eddie Milner	.05
183	Ron Oester	.05
184	Dave Parker	.05
185	Frank Pastore	.05
186	Tony Perez	.75
187	Ted Power	.05
188	Joe Price	.05
189	Gary Redus	.05
190	Ron Robinson	.05
191	Pete Rose	2.50
192	Mario Soto	.05
193	John Stuper	.05
194	Jay Tibbs	.05
195	Dave Van Gorder	.05
196	Max Venable	.05
197	Juan Agosto	.05
198	Harold Baines	.05
199	Floyd Bannister	.05
200	Britt Burns	.05
201	Julio Cruz	.05
202	Joel Davis RC	.05
203	Richard Dotson	.05
204	Carlton Fisk	1.00
205	Scott Fletcher	.05
206	Ozzie Guillen	.05
207	Jerry Hairston Sr.	.05
208	Tim Hulett	.05
209	Bob James	.05
210	Ron Kittle	.05
211	Rudy Law	.05
212	Bryan Little	.05
213	Gene Nelson	.05
214	Reid Nichols	.05
215	Luis Salazar	.05
216	Tom Seaver	1.00
217	Dan Spillner	.05
218	Bruce Tanner	.05
219	Greg Walker	.05
220	Dave Wehrmeister	.05
221	Juan Berenguer	.05
222	Dave Bergman	.05
223	Tom Brookens	.05
224	Darrell Evans	.05
225	Barbaro Garbey	.05
226	Kirk Gibson	.05
227	John Grubb	.05
228	Willie Hernandez	.05
229	Larry Herndon	.05
230	Chet Lemon	.05
231	Aurelio Lopez	.05
232	Jack Morris	.05
233	Randy O'Neal	.05
234	Lance Parrish	.05
235	Dan Petry	.05
236	Alex Sanchez	.05
237	Bill Scherrer	.05
238	Nelson Simmons	.05
239	Frank Tanana	.05
240	Walt Terrell	.05
241	Alan Trammell	.05
242	Lou Whitaker	.05
243	Milt Wilcox	.05
244	Hubie Brooks	.05
245	Tim Burke RC	.05
246	Andre Dawson	.35
247	Mike Fitzgerald	.05
248	Terry Francona	.05
249	Bill Gullickson	.05
250	Joe Hesketh	.05
251	Bill Laskey	.05
252	Vance Law	.05
253	Charlie Lea	.05
254	Gary Lucas	.05
255	David Palmer	.05
256	Tim Raines	.05
257	Jeff Reardon	.05
258	Bert Roberge	.05
259	Dan Schatzeder	.05
260	Bryn Smith	.05
261	Randy St. Claire RC	.05
262	Scot Thompson	.05
263	Tim Wallach	.05
264	U.L. Washington	.05
265	Mitch Webster RC	.05
266	Herm Winningham RC	.05
267	Floyd Youmans RC	.05
268	Don Aase	.05
269	Mike Boddicker	.05
270	Rich Dauer	.05
271	Storm Davis	.05
272	Rick Dempsey	.05
273	Ken Dixon	.05
274	Jim Dwyer	.05
275	Mike Flanagan	.05
276	Wayne Gross	.05
277	Lee Lacy	.05
278	Fred Lynn	.05
279	Tippy Martinez	.05
280	Dennis Martinez	.05
281	Scott McGregor	.05
282	Eddie Murray	1.00
283	Floyd Rayford	.05
284	Cal Ripken, Jr.	3.00
285	Gary Roenicke	.05
286	Larry Sheets	.05
287	John Shelby	.05
288	Nate Snell	.05
289	Sammy Stewart	.05
290	Alan Wiggins	.05
291	Mike Young	.05
292	Alan Ashby	.05
293	Mark Bailey	.05
294	Kevin Bass	.05
295	Jeff Calhoun	.05
296	Jose Cruz	.05
297	Glenn Davis	.05
298	Bill Dawley	.05
299	Frank DiPino	.05
300	Bill Doran	.05
301	Phil Garner	.05
302	Jeff Heathcock RC	.05
303	Charlie Kerfeld RC	.05
304	Bob Knepper	.05
305	Ron Mathis	.05
306	Jerry Mumphrey	.05
307	Jim Pankovits	.05
308	Terry Puhl	.05
309	Craig Reynolds	.05
310	Nolan Ryan	3.00
311	Mike Scott	.05
312	Dave Smith	.05
313	Dickie Thon	.05
314	Denny Walling	.05
315	Kurt Bevacqua	.05
316	Al Bumbry	.05
317	Jerry Davis	.05
318	Luis DeLeon	.05
319	Dave Dravecky	.05
320	Tim Flannery	.05
321	Steve Garvey	.30
322	Goose Gossage	.05
323	Tony Gwynn	1.50
324	Andy Hawkins	.05
325	LaMarr Hoyt	.05
326	Roy Lee Jackson	.05
327	Terry Kennedy	.05
328	Craig Lefferts	.05
329	Carmelo Martinez	.05
330	Lance McCullers RC	.05
331	Kevin McReynolds	.05
332	Graig Nettles	.05
333	Jerry Royster	.05
334	Eric Show	.05
335	Tim Stoddard	.05
336	Garry Templeton	.05
337	Mark Thurmond	.05
338	Ed Wojna	.05
339	Tony Armas	.05
340	Marty Barrett	.05
341	Wade Boggs	1.50
342	Dennis Boyd	.05
343	Bill Buckner	.05
344	Mark Clear	.05
345	Roger Clemens	2.00
346	Steve Crawford	.05
347	Mike Easler	.05
348	Dwight Evans	.05
349	Rich Gedman	.05
350	Jackie Gutierrez	.05
351	Glenn Hoffman	.05
352	Bruce Hurst	.05
353	Bruce Kison	.05
354	Tim Lollar	.05
355	Steve Lyons	.05
356	Al Nipper	.05
357	Bob Ojeda	.05
358	Jim Rice	.30
359	Bob Stanley	.05
360	Mike Trujillo	.05
361	Thad Bosley	.05
362	Warren Brusstar	.05
363	Ron Cey	.05
364	Jody Davis	.05
365	Bob Dernier	.05
366	Shawon Dunston	.05
367	Leon Durham	.05
368	Dennis Eckersley	.75
369	Ray Fontenot	.05
370	George Frazier	.05
371	Bill Hatcher	.05
372	Dave Lopes	.05
373	Gary Matthews	.05
374	Ron Meredith	.05
375	Keith Moreland	.05
376	Reggie Patterson	.05
377	Dick Ruthven	.05
378	Ryne Sandberg	1.50
379	Scott Sanderson	.05
380	Lee Smith	.05
381	Lary Sorensen	.05
382	Chris Speier	.05
383	Rick Sutcliffe	.05
384	Steve Trout	.05
385	Gary Woods	.05
386	Bert Blyleven	.10
387	Tom Brunansky	.05
388	Randy Bush	.05
389	John Butcher	.05
390	Ron Davis	.05
391	Dave Engle	.05
392	Frank Eufemia	.05
393	Pete Filson	.05
394	Gary Gaetti	.05
395	Greg Gagne	.05
396	Mickey Hatcher	.05
397	Kent Hrbek	.05
398	Tim Laudner	.05
399	Rick Lysander	.05
400	Dave Meier	.05
401	Kirby Puckett	1.50
402	Mark Salas	.05
403	Ken Schrom	.05
404	Roy Smalley	.05
405	Mike Smithson	.05

No.	Player	Price
406	Mike Stenhouse	.05
407	Tim Teufel	.05
408	Frank Viola	.05
409	Ron Washington	.05
410	Keith Atherton	.05
411	Dusty Baker	.05
412	Tim Birtsas RC	.05
413	Bruce Bochte	.05
414	Chris Codiroli	.05
415	Dave Collins	.05
416	Mike Davis	.05
417	Alfredo Griffin	.05
418	Mike Heath	.05
419	Steve Henderson	.05
420	Donnie Hill	.05
421	Jay Howell	.05
422	Tommy John	.10
423	Dave Kingman	.05
424	Bill Krueger	.05
425	Rick Langford	.05
426	Carney Lansford	.05
427	Steve McCatty	.05
428	Dwayne Murphy	.05
429	Steve Ontiveros RC	.05
430	Tony Phillips	.05
431	Jose Rijo	.05
432	Mickey Tettleton	.05
433	Luis Aguayo	.05
434	Larry Andersen	.05
435	Steve Carlton	1.00
436	Don Carman RC	.05
437	Tim Corcoran	.05
438	Darren Daulton	.05
439	John Denny	.05
440	Tom Foley	.05
441	Greg Gross	.05
442	Kevin Gross	.05
443	Von Hayes	.05
444	Charles Hudson	.05
445	Garry Maddox	.05
446	Shane Rawley	.05
447	Dave Rucker	.05
448	John Russell	.05
449	Juan Samuel	.05
450	Mike Schmidt	2.00
451	Rick Schu	.05
452	Dave Shipanoff	.05
453	Dave Stewart	.05
454	Jeff Stone	.05
455	Kent Tekulve	.05
456	Ozzie Virgil	.05
457	Glenn Wilson	.05
458	Jim Beattie	.05
459	Karl Best	.05
460	Barry Bonnell	.05
461	Phil Bradley	.05
462	Ivan Calderon RC	.05
463	Al Cowens	.05
464	Alvin Davis	.05
465	Dave Henderson	.05
466	Bob Kearney	.05
467	Mark Langston	.05
468	Bob Long	.05
469	Mike Moore	.05
470	Edwin Nunez	.05
471	Spike Owen	.05
472	Jack Perconte	.05
473	Jim Presley	.05
474	Donnie Scott	.05
475	Bill Swift RC	.05
476	Danny Tartabull	.05
477	Gorman Thomas	.05
478	Roy Thomas	.05
479	Ed Vande Berg	.05
480	Frank Wills	.05
481	Matt Young	.05
482	Ray Burris	.05
483	Jaime Cocanower	.05
484	Cecil Cooper	.05
485	Danny Darwin	.05
486	Rollie Fingers	.75
487	Jim Gantner	.05
488	Bob Gibson	.05
489	Moose Haas	.05
490	Teddy Higuera RC	.05
491	Paul Householder	.05
492	Pete Ladd	.05
493	Rick Manning	.05
494	Bob McClure	.05
495	Paul Molitor	1.00
496	Charlie Moore	.05
497	Ben Oglivie	.05
498	Randy Ready	.05
499	Earnie Riles RC	.05
500	Ed Romero	.05
501	Bill Schroeder	.05
502	Ray Searage	.05
503	Ted Simmons	.05
504	Pete Vuckovich	.05
505	Rick Waits	.05
506	Robin Yount	1.00
507	Len Barker	.05
508	Steve Bedrosian	.05
509	Bruce Benedict	.05
510	Rick Camp	.05
511	Rick Cerone	.05
512	Chris Chambliss	.05
513	Jeff Dedmon	.05
514	Terry Forster	.05
515	Gene Garber	.05
516	Terry Harper	.05
517	Bob Horner	.05
518	Glenn Hubbard	.05
519	Joe Johnson RC	.05
520	Brad Komminsk	.05
521	Rick Mahler	.05
522	Dale Murphy	.30
523	Ken Oberkfell	.05
524	Pascual Perez	.05
525	Gerald Perry	.05
526	Rafael Ramirez	.05
527	Steve Shields RC	.05
528	Zane Smith	.05
529	Bruce Sutter	.75
530	Milt Thompson RC	.05
531	Claudell Washington	.05
532	Paul Zuvella	.05
533	Vida Blue	.05
534	Bob Brenly	.05
535	Chris Brown RC	.05
536	Chili Davis	.05
537	Mark Davis	.05
538	Rob Deer	.05
539	Dan Driessen	.05
540	Scott Garrelts	.05
541	Dan Gladden	.05
542	Jim Gott	.05
543	David Green	.05
544	Atlee Hammaker	.05
545	Mike Jeffcoat	.05
546	Mike Krukow	.05
547	Dave LaPoint	.05
548	Jeff Leonard	.05
549	Greg Minton	.05
550	Alex Trevino	.05
551	Manny Trillo	.05
552	Jose Uribe RC	.05
553	Brad Wellman	.05
554	Frank Williams	.05
555	Joel Youngblood	.05
556	Alan Bannister	.05
557	Glenn Brummer	.05
558	Steve Buechele RC	.05
559	Jose Guzman RC	.05
560	Toby Harrah	.05
561	Greg Harris	.05
562	Dwayne Henry RC	.05
563	Burt Hooton	.05
564	Charlie Hough	.05
565	Mike Mason	.05
566	Oddibe McDowell RC	.05
567	Dickie Noles	.05
568	Pete O'Brien	.05
569	Larry Parrish	.05
570	Dave Rozema	.05
571	Dave Schmidt	.05
572	Don Slaught	.05
573	Wayne Tolleson	.05
574	Duane Walker	.05
575	Gary Ward	.05
576	Chris Welsh	.05
577	Curtis Wilkerson	.05
578	George Wright	.05
579	Chris Bando	.05
580	Tony Bernazard	.05
581	Brett Butler	.05
582	Ernie Camacho	.05
583	Joe Carter	.05
584	Carmello Castillo (Carmelo)	.05
585	Jamie Easterly	.05
586	Julio Franco	.05
587	Mel Hall	.05
588	Mike Hargrove	.05
589	Neal Heaton	.05
590	Brook Jacoby	.05
591	Otis Nixon RC	.25
592	Jerry Reed	.05
593	Vern Ruhle	.05
594	Pat Tabler	.05
595	Rich Thompson	.05
596	Andre Thornton	.05
597	Dave Von Ohlen	.05
598	George Vukovich	.05
599	Tom Waddell	.05
600	Curt Wardle	.05
601	Jerry Willard	.05
602	Bill Almon	.05
603	Mike Bielecki	.05
604	Sid Bream	.05
605	Mike Brown	.05
606	Pat Clements RC	.05
607	Jose DeLeon	.05
608	Denny Gonzalez	.05
609	Cecilio Guante	.05
610	Steve Kemp	.05
611	Sam Khalifa	.05
612	Lee Mazzilli	.05
613	Larry McWilliams	.05
614	Jim Morrison	.05
615	Joe Orsulak RC	.25
616	Tony Pena	.05
617	Johnny Ray	.05
618	Rick Reuschel	.05
619	R.J. Reynolds	.05
620	Rick Rhoden	.05
621	Don Robinson	.05
622	Jason Thompson	.05
623	Lee Tunnell	.05
624	Jim Winn	.05
625	Marvell Wynne	.05
626	Dwight Gooden/IA	.05
627	Don Mattingly/IA	.50
628	Pete Rose (4,192 Hits)	.50
629	Rod Carew (3,000 Hits)	.25
630	Phil Niekro, Tom Seaver (300 Wins)	.25
631	Ouch! (Don Baylor)	.05
632	Instant Offense (Tim Raines, Darryl Strawberry)	.05
633	Shortstops Supreme (Cal Ripken, Jr., Alan Trammell)	1.00
634	Boggs & "Hero" (Wade Boggs, George Brett)	1.00
635	Braves Dynamic Duo (Bob Horner, Dale Murphy)	.25
636	Cardinal Ignitors (Vince Coleman, Willie McGee)	.25
637	Terror on the Basepaths (Vince Coleman)	.05
638	Charlie Hustle & Dr. K (Dwight Gooden, Pete Rose)	.50
639	1984 and 1985 A.L. Batting Champs (Wade Boggs, Don Mattingly)	1.00
640	N.L. West Sluggers (Steve Garvey, Dale Murphy, Dave Parker)	.25
641	Staff Aces (Dwight Gooden, Fernando Valenzuela)	.10
642	Blue Jay Stoppers (Jimmy Key, Dave Stieb)	.05
643	A.L. All-Star Backstops (Carlton Fisk, Rich Gedman)	.10
644	Major League Prospect (Benito Santiago RC, Gene Walter RC)	1.00
645	Major League Prospect (Colin Ward RC, Mike Woodard RC)	.10
646	Major League Prospect (Kal Daniels RC, Paul O'Neill RC)	2.00
647	Major League Prospect (Andres Galarraga RC, Fred Toliver RC)	3.00
648	Major League Prospect (Curt Ford RC, Bob Kipper RC)	.10
649	Major League Prospect (Jose Canseco, Eric Plunk RC)	5.00
650	Major League Prospect (Mark McLemore RC, Gus Polidor RC)	.75
651	Major League Prospect (Mickey Brantley RC, Rob Woodward RC)	.10
652	Major League Prospect (Mark Funderburk RC, Billy Joe Robidoux RC)	.10
653	Major League Prospect (Cecil Fielder RC, Cory Snyder RC)	1.50
654	Checklist 1-97	.05
655	Checklist 98-196	.05
656	Checklist 197-291	.05
657	Checklist 292-385	.05
658	Checklist 386-482	.05
659	Checklist 483-578	.05
660	Checklist 579-660	.05

are the standard 2-1/2" x 3-1/2" and were randomly inserted in three-pack rack packs. Card fronts feature a player photo set against a blue background with horizontal light blue stripes. Backs are printed in black on blue and feature career highlights in narrative form.

		NM/M
Complete Set (6):		5.00
Common Player:		.75
1	Pete Rose	2.00
2	Steve Carlton	.75
3	Tom Seaver	.75
4	Rod Carew	.75
5	Nolan Ryan	3.00
6	Reggie Jackson	1.00

Box Panels

Picking up on a Donruss idea, Fleer issued eight cards in panels of four on the bottoms of the wax and cello pack boxes. The cards are numbered C-1 through C-8 and are 2-1/2" x 3-1/2", with a complete panel measuring 5" x 7-1/8". Included in the eight cards are six players and two team logo/checklist cards.

		NM/M
Complete Panel Set (2):		4.00
Complete Singles Set (8):		4.00
Common Single Player:		.20
Panel		2.50
1	Royals Logo/Checklist	.05
2	George Brett	2.00
3	Ozzie Guillen	.20
4	Dale Murphy	.40
Panel		1.50
5	Cardinals Logo/Checklist	.20
6	Tom Browning	.20
7	Gary Carter	1.00
8	Carlton Fisk	1.00

Fleer Update

Issued near the end of the baseball season, the 1986 Fleer Update set consists of cards numbered U-1 through U-132. The 2-1/2" x 3-1/2" cards are identical in design to the regular 1986 Fleer set. The purpose of the set is to update player trades and include rookies not depicted in the regular issue. The set was issued with team logo stickers in a specially designed box and was available only through hobby dealers.

		NM/M
Unopened Fact. Set (132):		40.00
Complete Set (132):		30.00
Common Player:		.05
1	Mike Aldrete RC	.05
2	Andy Allanson RC	.05
3	Neil Allen	.05
4	Joaquin Andujar	.05
5	Paul Assenmacher RC	.05
6	Scott Bailes RC	.05
7	Jay Baller RC	.05
8	Scott Bankhead RC	.05
9	Bill Bathe RC	.05
10	Don Baylor	.05
11	Billy Beane RC	.05
12	Steve Bedrosian	.05
13	Juan Beniquez	.05
14	Barry Bonds RC	25.00
15	Bobby Bonilla RC	1.00
16	Rich Bordi	.05
17	Bill Campbell	.05
18	Tom Candiotti	.05
19	John Cangelosi RC	.05
20	Jose Canseco	4.00
21	Chuck Cary RC	.05
22	Juan Castillo RC	.05
23	Rick Cerone	.05
24	John Cerutti RC	.05
25	Will Clark RC	1.00
26	Mark Clear	.05
27	Darnell Coles RC	.05
28	Dave Collins	.05
29	Tim Conroy	.05
30	Ed Correa RC	.05
31	Joe Cowley	.05
32	Bill Dawley	.05
33	Rob Deer	.05
34	John Denny	.05
35	Jim DeShaies	.05
36	Doug Drabek RC	1.00
37	Mike Easler	.05
38	Mark Eichhorn RC	.05
39	Dave Engle	.05
40	Mike Fischlin	.05
41	Scott Fletcher	.05
42	Terry Forster	.05
43	Terry Francona	.05
44	Andres Galarraga	.50
45	Lee Guetterman RC	.05
46	Bill Gullickson	.05
47	Jackie Gutierrez	.05
48	Moose Haas	.05
49	Billy Hatcher	.05
50	Mike Heath	.05
51	Guy Hoffman RC	.05
52	Tom Hume	.05
53	Pete Incaviglia RC	.50
54	Dane Iorg	.05
55	Chris James RC	.05
56	Stan Javier RC	.05
57	Tommy John	.15
58	Tracy Jones RC	.05
59	Wally Joyner RC	1.00
60	Wayne Krenchicki	.05
61	John Kruk RC	1.00
62	Mike LaCoss	.05
63	Pete Ladd	.05
64	Dave LaPoint	.05
65	Mike LaValliere RC	.05
66	Rudy Law	.05
67	Dennis Leonard	.05
68	Steve Lombardozzi RC	.05
69	Aurelio Lopez	.05
70	Mickey Mahler	.05
71	Candy Maldonado	.05
72	Roger Mason RC	.05
73	Greg Mathews RC	.05
74	Andy McGaffigan	.05
75	Joel McKeon RC	.05
76	Kevin Mitchell RC	.50
77	Bill Mooneyham RC	.05
78	Omar Moreno	.05
79	Jerry Mumphrey	.05
80	Al Newman RC	.05
81	Phil Niekro	.50
82	Randy Niemann	.05
83	Juan Nieves RC	.05
84	Bob Ojeda	.05
85	Rick Ownbey	.05
86	Tom Paciorek	.05
87	David Palmer	.05
88	Jeff Parrett RC	.05
89	Pat Perry RC	.05
90	Dan Plesac RC	.05
91	Darrell Porter	.05
92	Luis Quinones RC	.05
93	Rey Quinonez RC	.05
94	Gary Redus	.05
95	Jeff Reed RC	.05
96	Bip Roberts RC	.05
97	Billy Joe Robidoux	.05
98	Gary Roenicke	.05
99	Ron Roenicke	.05
100	Angel Salazar	.05
101	Joe Sambito	.05
102	Billy Sample	.05
103	Dave Schmidt	.05
104	Ken Schrom	.05
105	Ruben Sierra RC	.75
106	Ted Simmons	.05
107	Sammy Stewart	.05
108	Kurt Stillwell RC	.05
109	Dale Sveum RC	.05
110	Tim Teufel	.05
111	Bob Tewksbury RC	.05
112	Andres Thomas RC	.05
113	Jason Thompson	.05
114	Milt Thompson	.05
115	Rob Thompson RC	.05
116	Jay Tibbs	.05
117	Fred Toliver	.05
118	Wayne Tolleson	.05
119	Alex Trevino	.05
120	Manny Trillo	.05
121	Ed Vande Berg	.05
122	Ozzie Virgil	.05
123	Tony Walker RC	.05
124	Gene Walter	.05
125	Duane Ward RC	.05
126	Jerry Willard	.05
127	Mitch Williams RC	.05
128	Reggie Williams RC	.05
129	Bobby Witt RC	.05
130	Marvell Wynne	.05
131	Steve Yeager	.05
132	Checklist	.05

Baseball's Best

The 1986 Fleer Baseball's Best set was produced for the McCrory's retail chain and its affiliated stores. Subtitled "Sluggers vs. Pitchers," the set contains 22 each of the game's best hitters and pitchers. The 2-1/2" x 3-1/2" cards have color action photos on front. Backs are done in blue and red and carry players' personal and statistical data. The sets were issued in a specially designed box with six team logo stickers.

		NM/M
Complete Set (44):		4.00
Common Player:		.10
1	Bert Blyleven	.25
2	Wade Boggs	.75
3	George Brett	1.00
4	Tom Browning	.10
5	Jose Canseco	.60
6	Will Clark	.15
7	Roger Clemens	1.00
8	Alvin Davis	.10
9	Julio Franco	.10
10	Kirk Gibson	.10
11	Dwight Gooden	.10
12	Goose Gossage	.10
13	Pedro Guerrero	.10
14	Ron Guidry	.10
15	Tony Gwynn	.75
16	Orel Hershiser	.10
17	Kent Hrbek	.10
18	Reggie Jackson	.75
19	Wally Joyner	.15
20	Charlie Leibrandt	.10
21	Don Mattingly	1.00
22	Willie McGee	.10
23	Jack Morris	.10
24	Dale Murphy	.25
25	Eddie Murray	.50
26	Jeff Reardon	.10
27	Rick Reuschel	.10
28	Cal Ripken, Jr.	1.00
29	Pete Rose	1.50
30	Nolan Ryan	2.00
31	Bret Saberhagen	.10
32	Ryne Sandberg	.75
33	Mike Schmidt	1.00
34	Tom Seaver	.50
35	Bryn Smith	.10
36	Mario Soto	.10
37	Dave Stieb	.10
38	Darryl Strawberry	.10
39	Rick Sutcliffe	.10
40	John Tudor	.10
41	Fernando Valenzuela	.10
42	Bobby Witt	.10
43	Mike Witt	.10
44	Robin Yount	.50

League Leaders

Fleer's 1986 "League Leaders" set features 44 of the game's top players and was issued through the Walgreen's drug store chain. Fronts contain a color photo and feature player name, team and position in a blue band near the bottom of the card. The words "League Leaders" appear in a red

All-Stars

Fleer's choices for a major league All-Star team make up this 12-card set. The cards were randomly inserted in 35¢ wax packs and 59¢ cello packs. The card fronts have a color photo set against a bright red background for A.L. players or a bright blue background for N.L. players. Backs feature the player's career highlights on a red and blue background.

		NM/M
Complete Set (12):		7.50
Common Player:		.10
1	Don Mattingly	2.00
2	Tom Herr	.10
3	George Brett	2.00
4	Gary Carter	.75
5	Cal Ripken, Jr.	4.00
6	Dave Parker	.10
7	Rickey Henderson	.75
8	Pedro Guerrero	.10
9	Dan Quisenberry	.10
10	Dwight Gooden	.10
11	Gorman Thomas	.10
12	John Tudor	.10

Future Hall Of Famers

The 1986 Future Hall of Famers set is comprised of six players Fleer felt would gain eventual entrance into the Baseball Hall of Fame. The cards band at the top of the card. The background for the card fronts is alternating blue and white stripes. The card backs are printed in blue, red and white and carry statistical information and team logo. Cards are the standard 2-1/2" x 3-1/2". The set was issued in a special cardboard box, along with six team logo stickers.

		NM/M
Complete Set (44):		4.00
Common Player:		.10
1	Wade Boggs	.60
2	George Brett	.75
3	Jose Canseco	.60
4	Rod Carew	.40
5	Gary Carter	.40
6	Jack Clark	.10
7	Vince Coleman	.10
8	Jose Cruz	.10
9	Alvin Davis	.10
10	Mariano Duncan	.10
11	Leon Durham	.10
12	Carlton Fisk	.40
13	Julio Franco	.10
14	Scott Garrelts	.10
15	Steve Garvey	.25
16	Dwight Gooden	.10
17	Ozzie Guillen	.10
18	Willie Hernandez	.10
19	Bob Horner	.10
20	Kent Hrbek	.10
21	Charlie Leibrandt	.10
22	Don Mattingly	.75
23	Oddibe McDowell	.10
24	Willie McGee	.10
25	Keith Moreland	.10
26	Lloyd Moseby	.10
27	Dale Murphy	.25
28	Phil Niekro	.35
29	Joe Orsulak	.10
30	Dave Parker	.10
31	Lance Parrish	.10
32	Kirby Puckett	.60
33	Tim Raines	.10
34	Earnie Riles	.10
35	Cal Ripken, Jr.	1.50
36	Pete Rose	1.00
37	Bret Saberhagen	.10
38	Juan Samuel	.10
39	Ryne Sandberg	.60
40	Tom Seaver	.40
41	Lee Smith	.10
42	Ozzie Smith	.60
43	Dave Stieb	.10
44	Robin Yount	.40

Limited Edition

Produced for the McCrory's store chain and its affiliates for the second year in a row, the Limited Edition set contains 44 cards. In standard 2-1/2" x 3-1/2" size, cards have color photos enclosed by green, red and yellow trim. Backs carry black print on two shades of red. The set was issued in a special cardboard box, along with six team logo stickers.

		NM/M
Complete Set (44):		4.00
Common Player:		.10
1	Doyle Alexander	.10
2	Joaquin Andujar	.10
3	Harold Baines	.10
4	Wade Boggs	.60
5	Phil Bradley	.10
6	George Brett	.75
7	Hubie Brooks	.10
8	Chris Brown	.10
9	Tom Brunansky	.10
10	Gary Carter	.50
11	Vince Coleman	.10
12	Cecil Cooper	.10
13	Jose Cruz	.10
14	Mike Davis	.10
15	Carlton Fisk	.50
16	Julio Franco	.10
17	Damaso Garcia	.10
18	Rich Gedman	.10
19	Kirk Gibson	.10
20	Dwight Gooden	.10
21	Pedro Guerrero	.60
22	Tony Gwynn	.60
23	Rickey Henderson	.10
24	Orel Hershiser	.10
25	LaMarr Hoyt	.10
26	Reggie Jackson	.60
27	Don Mattingly	.75
28	Oddibe McDowell	.10
29	Willie McGee	.10
30	Paul Molitor	.10
31	Dale Murphy	.20
32	Eddie Murray	.50
33	Dave Parker	.10
34	Tony Pena	.10
35	Jeff Reardon	.10
36	Cal Ripken, Jr.	1.50
37	Pete Rose	1.00
38	Bret Saberhagen	.10
39	Juan Samuel	.10
40	Ryne Sandberg	.60
41	Mike Schmidt	.75
42	Lee Smith	.10
43	Don Sutton	.40
44	Lou Whitaker	.10

Mini

Fleer's 1986 "Classic Miniatures" set contains 120 cards that measure 1-13/16" x 2-9/16". The design of the high-gloss cards is identical to the regular 1986 Fleer set but the player photos are entirely different. The set, which was issued in a specially designed box along with 18 team logo stickers, was available only through hobby dealers.

		NM/M
Complete Set (120):		3.50
Common Player:		.05
1	George Brett	.65
2	Dan Quisenberry	.05
3	Bret Saberhagen	.05
4	Lonnie Smith	.05
5	Willie Wilson	.05
6	Jack Clark	.05
7	Vince Coleman	.05
8	Tom Herr	.05
9	Willie McGee	.05
10	Ozzie Smith	.50
11	John Tudor	.05
12	Jesse Barfield	.05
13	George Bell	.05
14	Tony Fernandez	.05
15	Damaso Garcia	.05
16	Dave Stieb	.05
17	Gary Carter	.40
18	Ron Darling	.05
19	Dwight Gooden	.05
20	Keith Hernandez	.05
21	Darryl Strawberry	.05
22	Ron Guidry	.05
23	Rickey Henderson	.05
24	Don Mattingly	.65
25	Dave Righetti	.05
26	Dave Winfield	.40
27	Mariano Duncan	.05
28	Pedro Guerrero	.05
29	Bill Madlock	.05
30	Mike Marshall	.05
31	Fernando Valenzuela	.05
32	Reggie Jackson	.50
33	Gary Pettis	.05
34	Ron Romanick	.05
35	Don Sutton	.30
36	Mike Witt	.05
37	Buddy Bell	.05
38	Tom Browning	.05
39	Dave Parker	.05
40	Pete Rose	.75
41	Mario Soto	.05
42	Harold Baines	.05
43	Carlton Fisk	.40
44	Ozzie Guillen	.05
45	Ron Kittle	.05
46	Tom Seaver	.40
47	Kirk Gibson	.05
48	Jack Morris	.05
49	Lance Parrish	.05
50	Alan Trammell	.05
51	Lou Whitaker	.05
52	Hubie Brooks	.05
53	Andre Dawson	.25
54	Tim Raines	.05
55	Bryn Smith	.05
56	Tim Wallach	.05
57	Mike Boddicker	.05
58	Eddie Murray	.40
59	Cal Ripken, Jr.	1.25
60	John Shelby	.05
61	Mike Young	.05
62	Jose Cruz	.05
63	Glenn Davis	.05
64	Phil Garner	.05
65	Nolan Ryan	1.25
66	Mike Scott	.05
67	Steve Garvey	.15
68	Goose Gossage	.05
69	Tony Gwynn	.50
70	Andy Hawkins	.05
71	Garry Templeton	.05
72	Wade Boggs	.50
73	Roger Clemens	.65
74	Dwight Evans	.05
75	Rich Gedman	.05
76	Jim Rice	.25
77	Shawon Dunston	.05
78	Leon Durham	.05
79	Keith Moreland	.05
80	Ryne Sandberg	.50
81	Rick Sutcliffe	.05
82	Bert Blyleven	.05
83	Tom Brunansky	.05
84	Kent Hrbek	.05
85	Kirby Puckett	.50
86	Bruce Bochte	.05
87	Jose Canseco	.40
88	Mike Davis	.05
89	Jay Howell	.05
90	Dwayne Murphy	.05
91	Steve Carlton	.40
92	Von Hayes	.05
93	Juan Samuel	.05
94	Mike Schmidt	.65
95	Glenn Wilson	.05
96	Phil Bradley	.05
97	Alvin Davis	.05
98	Jim Presley	.05
99	Danny Tartabull	.05
100	Cecil Cooper	.05
101	Paul Molitor	.40
102	Earnie Riles	.05
103	Robin Yount	.05
104	Bob Horner	.05
105	Dale Murphy	.20
106	Bruce Sutter	.30
107	Claudell Washington	.05
108	Chris Brown	.05
109	Chili Davis	.05
110	Scott Garrelts	.05
111	Oddibe McDowell	.05
112	Pete O'Brien	.05
113	Gary Ward	.05
114	Brett Butler	.05
115	Julio Franco	.05
116	Brook Jacoby	.05
117	Mike Brown	.05
118	Joe Orsulak	.05
119	Tony Pena	.05
120	R.J. Reynolds	.05

Star Stickers

Fleer's 1986 sticker-card set again measures 2-1/2" x 3-1/2" and features color photos inside dark maroon borders. Backs are identical to the 1986 baseball card issue except for the 1-132 numbering system and blue ink instead of yellow. Card #132 is a multi-player card featuring Dwight Gooden and Dale Murphy on the front and a complete checklist for the set on the reverse. The cards were sold in wax packs with team logo stickers.

		NM/M
Complete Set (132):		7.00
Common Player:		.05
Wax Pack (5):		1.00
Wax Box (36):		12.00
1	Harold Baines	.05
2	Jesse Barfield	.05
3	Don Baylor	.05
4	Juan Beniquez	.05
5	Tim Birtsas	.05
6	Bert Blyleven	.10
7	Bruce Bochte	.05
8	Wade Boggs	.50
9	Dennis Boyd	.05
10	Phil Bradley	.05
11	George Brett	.65
12	Hubie Brooks	.05
13	Chris Brown	.05
14	Tom Browning	.05
15	Tom Brunansky	.05
16	Bill Buckner	.05
17	Britt Burns	.05
18	Brett Butler	.05
19	Jose Canseco	.40
20	Rod Carew	.40
21	Steve Carlton	.40
22	Don Carman	.05
23	Gary Carter	.40
24	Jack Clark	.05
25	Vince Coleman	.05
26	Cecil Cooper	.05
27	Jose Cruz	.05
28	Ron Darling	.05
29	Alvin Davis	.05
30	Jody Davis	.05
31	Mike Davis	.05
32	Andre Dawson	.25
33	Mariano Duncan	.05
34	Shawon Dunston	.05
35	Leon Durham	.05
36	Darrell Evans	.05
37	Tony Fernandez	.05
38	Carlton Fisk	.40
39	John Franco	.05
40	Julio Franco	.05
41	Damaso Garcia	.05
42	Scott Garrelts	.05
43	Steve Garvey	.15
44	Rich Gedman	.05
45	Kirk Gibson	.05
46	Dwight Gooden	.05
47	Pedro Guerrero	.05
48	Ron Guidry	.05
49	Ozzie Guillen	.05
50	Tony Gwynn	.50
51	Andy Hawkins	.05
52	Von Hayes	.05
53	Rickey Henderson	.40
54	Tom Henke	.05
55	Keith Hernandez	.05
56	Willie Hernandez	.05
57	Tom Herr	.05
58	Orel Hershiser	.05
59	Teddy Higuera	.05
60	Bob Horner	.05
61	Charlie Hough	.05
62	Jay Howell	.05
63	LaMarr Hoyt	.05
64	Kent Hrbek	.05
65	Reggie Jackson	.50
66	Bob James	.05
67	Dave Kingman	.05
68	Ron Kittle	.05
69	Charlie Leibrandt	.05
70	Fred Lynn	.05
71	Mike Marshall	.05
72	Don Mattingly	.65
73	Oddibe McDowell	.05
74	Willie McGee	.05
75	Scott McGregor	.05
76	Paul Molitor	.40
77	Donnie Moore	.05
78	Keith Moreland	.05
79	Jack Morris	.05
80	Dale Murphy	.15
81	Eddie Murray	.40
82	Phil Niekro	.35
83	Joe Orsulak	.05
84	Dave Parker	.05
85	Lance Parrish	.05
86	Larry Parrish	.05
87	Tony Pena	.05
88	Gary Pettis	.05
89	Jim Presley	.05
90	Kirby Puckett	.50
91	Dan Quisenberry	.05
92	Tim Raines	.05
93	Johnny Ray	.05
94	Jeff Reardon	.05
95	Rick Reuschel	.05
96	Jim Rice	.25
97	Dave Righetti	.05
98	Earnie Riles	.05
99	Cal Ripken, Jr.	1.25
100	Ron Romanick	.05
101	Pete Rose	.85
102	Nolan Ryan	1.25
103	Bret Saberhagen	.05
104	Mark Salas	.05
105	Juan Samuel	.05
106	Ryne Sandberg	.50
107	Mike Schmidt	.65
108	Mike Scott	.05
109	Tom Seaver	.40
110	Bryn Smith	.05
111	Dave Smith	.05
112	Lee Smith	.05
113	Ozzie Smith	.50
114	Mario Soto	.05
115	Dave Stieb	.05
116	Darryl Strawberry	.05
117	Bruce Sutter	.35
118	Garry Templeton	.05
119	Gorman Thomas	.05
120	Andre Thornton	.05
121	Alan Trammell	.05
122	John Tudor	.05
123	Fernando Valenzuela	.05
124	Frank Viola	.05
125	Gary Ward	.05
126	Lou Whitaker	.05
127	Frank White	.05
128	Glenn Wilson	.05
129	Willie Wilson	.05
130	Dave Winfield	.40
131	Robin Yount	.40
132	Dwight Gooden, Dale Murphy	.10

Star Stickers Box Panels

Four cards, numbered S-1 through S-4, were placed on the bottoms of 1986 Fleer Star Stickers wax pack boxes. The cards are nearly identical in format to the regular issue sticker cards. Individual cards measure 2-1/2" x 3-1/2" in size, while a complete panel of four measures 5" x 7-1/8".

		NM/M
Complete Panel Set:		2.00
Complete Singles Set (4):		2.00
Common Single Player:		.30
1	Dodgers Logo	.05
2	Wade Boggs	1.25
3	Steve Garvey	.30
4	Dave Winfield	1.00

1987 Fleer

The 1987 Fleer set consists of 660 cards. Fronts feature a graduated blue-to-white border design. The player's name and position appear in the upper-left corner of the card; his team logo is located in the lower-right. Backs are done in blue, red and white and contain an innovative "Pro Scouts Report" feature which rates the player's batting or pitching skills. For the third year in a row, Fleer included its "Major League Prospects" subset. Fleer produced a glossy-finish Collectors Edition set which came housed in a specially-designed tin box. After experiencing a dramatic hike in price during 1987, the glossy set now sells for only a few dollars more than the regular issue.

		NM/M
Unopened Fact. Set (672):		65.00
Complete Set (660):		50.00
Common Player:		.05
Wax Pack (15/17):		3.00
Wax Box (36):		100.00
Cello Pack (28):		5.00
Cello Box (24):		100.00
Rack Pack (51):		8.00
Rack Box (24):		160.00
1	Rick Aguilera	.05
2	Richard Anderson	.05
3	Wally Backman	.05
4	Gary Carter	.75
5	Ron Darling	.05
6	Len Dykstra	.05
7	Kevin Elster RC	.15
8	Sid Fernandez	.05
9	Dwight Gooden	.05
10	Ed Hearn RC	.05
11	Danny Heep	.05
12	Keith Hernandez	.05
13	Howard Johnson	.05
14	Ray Knight	.05
15	Lee Mazzilli	.05
16	Roger McDowell	.05
17	Kevin Mitchell	.05
18	Randy Niemann	.05
19	Bob Ojeda	.05
20	Jesse Orosco	.05
21	Rafael Santana	.05
22	Doug Sisk	.05
23	Darryl Strawberry	.05
24	Tim Teufel	.05
25	Mookie Wilson	.05
26	Tony Armas	.05
27	Marty Barrett	.05
28	Don Baylor	.05
29	Wade Boggs	1.00
30	Oil Can Boyd	.05
31	Bill Buckner	.05
32	Roger Clemens	2.00
33	Steve Crawford	.05
34	Dwight Evans	.05
35	Rich Gedman	.05
36	Dave Henderson	.05
37	Bruce Hurst	.05
38	Tim Lollar	.05
39	Al Nipper	.05
40	Spike Owen	.05
41	Jim Rice	.30
42	Ed Romero	.05
43	Joe Sambito	.05
44	Calvin Schiraldi	.05
45	Tom Seaver	.75
46	Jeff Sellers RC	.05
47	Bob Stanley	.05
48	Sammy Stewart	.05
49	Larry Andersen	.05
50	Alan Ashby	.05
51	Kevin Bass	.05
52	Jeff Calhoun	.05
53	Jose Cruz	.05
54	Danny Darwin	.05
55	Glenn Davis	.05
56	Jim Deshaies RC	.10
57	Bill Doran	.05
58	Phil Garner	.05
59	Billy Hatcher	.05
60	Charlie Kerfeld	.05
61	Bob Knepper	.05
62	Dave Lopes	.05
63	Aurelio Lopez	.05
64	Jim Pankovits	.05
65	Terry Puhl	.05
66	Craig Reynolds	.05
67	Nolan Ryan	3.00
68	Mike Scott	.05
69	Dave Smith	.05
70	Dickie Thon	.05
71	Tony Walker	.05
72	Denny Walling	.05
73	Bob Boone	.05
74	Rick Burleson	.05
75	John Candelaria	.05
76	Doug Corbett	.05
77	Doug DeCinces	.05
78	Brian Downing	.05
79	Chuck Finley RC	1.00
80	Terry Forster	.05
81	Bobby Grich	.05
82	George Hendrick	.05
83	Jack Howell RC	.05
84	Reggie Jackson	1.00
85	Ruppert Jones	.05
86	Wally Joyner	.05
87	Gary Lucas	.05
88	Kirk McCaskill	.05
89	Donnie Moore	.05
90	Gary Pettis	.05
91	Vern Ruhle	.05
92	Dick Schofield	.05
93	Don Sutton	.65
94	Rob Wilfong	.05
95	Mike Witt	.05
96	Doug Drabek	.05
97	Mike Easler	.05
98	Mike Fischlin	.05
99	Brian Fisher	.05
100	Ron Guidry	.10
101	Rickey Henderson	.75
102	Tommy John	.10
103	Ron Kittle	.05
104	Don Mattingly	2.00
105	Bobby Meacham	.05
106	Joe Niekro	.05
107	Mike Pagliarulo	.05
108	Dan Pasqua	.05
109	Willie Randolph	.05
110	Dennis Rasmussen	.05
111	Dave Righetti	.05
112	Gary Roenicke	.05
113	Rod Scurry	.05
114	Bob Shirley	.05
115	Joel Skinner	.05

#	Player	Price
116	Tim Stoddard	.05
117	Bob Tewksbury RC	.35
118	Wayne Tolleson	.05
119	Claudell Washington	.05
120	Dave Winfield	.75
121	Steve Buechele	.05
122	Ed Correa RC	.05
123	Scott Fletcher	.05
124	Jose Guzman	.05
125	Toby Harrah	.05
126	Greg Harris	.05
127	Charlie Hough	.05
128	Pete Incaviglia	.05
129	Mike Mason	.05
130	Oddibe McDowell	.05
131	Dale Mohorcic RC	.05
132	Pete O'Brien	.05
133	Tom Paciorek	.05
134	Larry Parrish	.05
135	Geno Petralli	.05
136	Darrell Porter	.05
137	Jeff Russell	.05
138	Ruben Sierra	.05
139	Don Slaught	.05
140	Gary Ward	.05
141	Curtis Wilkerson	.05
142	Mitch Williams RC	.10
143	Bobby Witt RC	.10
144	Dave Bergman	.05
145	Tom Brookens	.05
146	Bill Campbell	.05
147	Chuck Cary RC	.05
148	Darnell Coles	.05
149	Dave Collins	.05
150	Darrell Evans	.05
151	Kirk Gibson	.05
152	John Grubb	.05
153	Willie Hernandez	.05
154	Larry Herndon	.05
155	Eric King RC	.05
156	Chet Lemon	.05
157	Dwight Lowry	.05
158	Jack Morris	.05
159	Randy O'Neal	.05
160	Lance Parrish	.05
161	Dan Petry	.05
162	Pat Sheridan	.05
163	Jim Slaton	.05
164	Frank Tanana	.05
165	Walt Terrell	.05
166	Mark Thurmond	.05
167	Alan Trammell	.05
168	Lou Whitaker	.05
169	Luis Aguayo	.05
170	Steve Bedrosian	.05
171	Don Carman	.05
172	Darren Daulton	.05
173	Greg Gross	.05
174	Kevin Gross	.05
175	Von Hayes	.05
176	Charles Hudson	.05
177	Tom Hume	.05
178	Steve Jeltz	.05
179	Mike Maddux RC	.05
180	Shane Rawley	.05
181	Gary Redus	.05
182	Ron Roenicke	.05
183	Bruce Ruffin RC	.10
184	John Russell	.05
185	Juan Samuel	.05
186	Dan Schatzeder	.05
187	Mike Schmidt	2.00
188	Rick Schu	.05
189	Jeff Stone	.05
190	Kent Tekulve	.05
191	Milt Thompson	.05
192	Glenn Wilson	.05
193	Buddy Bell	.05
194	Tom Browning	.05
195	Sal Butera	.05
196	Dave Concepcion	.05
197	Kal Daniels	.05
198	Eric Davis	.35
199	John Denny	.05
200	Bo Diaz	.05
201	Nick Esasky	.05
202	John Franco	.05
203	Bill Gullickson	.05
204	Barry Larkin RC	2.00
205	Eddie Milner	.05
206	Rob Murphy RC	.05
207	Ron Oester	.05
208	Dave Parker	.65
209	Tony Perez	.05
210	Ted Power	.05
211	Joe Price	.05
212	Ron Robinson	.05
213	Pete Rose	2.50
214	Mario Soto	.05
215	Kurt Stillwell RC	.05
216	Max Venable	.05
217	Chris Welsh	.05
218	Carl Willis RC	.05
219	Jesse Barfield	.05
220	George Bell	.05
221	Bill Caudill	.05
222	John Cerutti RC	.05
223	Jim Clancy	.05
224	Mark Eichhorn RC	.10
225	Tony Fernandez	.05
226	Damaso Garcia	.05
227	Kelly Gruber	.05
228	Tom Henke	.05
229	Garth Iorg	.05
230	Cliff Johnson	.05
231	Joe Johnson	.05
232	Jimmy Key	.05
233	Dennis Lamp	.05
234	Rick Leach	.05
235	Buck Martinez	.05
236	Lloyd Moseby	.05
237	Rance Mulliniks	.05
238	Dave Stieb	.05
239	Willie Upshaw	.05
240	Ernie Whitt	.05
241	Andy Allanson RC	.05
242	Scott Bailes RC	.05
243	Chris Bando	.05
244	Tony Bernazard	.05
245	John Butcher	.05
246	Brett Butler	.05
247	Ernie Camacho	.05
248	Tom Candiotti	.05
249	Joe Carter	.05
250	Carmen Castillo	.05
251	Julio Franco	.05
252	Mel Hall	.05
253	Brook Jacoby	.05
254	Phil Niekro	.65
255	Otis Nixon	.05
256	Dickie Noles	.05
257	Bryan Oelkers	.05
258	Ken Schrom	.05
259	Don Schulze	.05
260	Cory Snyder	.10
261	Pat Tabler	.05
262	Andre Thornton	.05
263	Rich Yett RC	.05
264	Mike Aldrete RC	.05
265	Juan Berenguer	.05
266	Vida Blue	.05
267	Bob Brenly	.05
268	Chris Brown	.05
269	Will Clark	.05
270	Chili Davis	.05
271	Mark Davis	.05
272	Kelly Downs RC	.05
273	Scott Garrelts	.05
274	Dan Gladden	.05
275	Mike Krukow	.05
276	Randy Kutcher RC	.05
277	Mike LaCoss	.05
278	Jeff Leonard	.05
279	Candy Maldonado	.05
280	Roger Mason	.05
281	Bob Melvin RC	.05
282	Greg Minton	.05
283	Jeff Robinson	.05
284	Harry Spilman	.05
285	Rob Thompson RC	.05
286	Jose Uribe	.05
287	Frank Williams	.05
288	Joel Youngblood	.05
289	Jack Clark	.05
290	Vince Coleman	.05
291	Tim Conroy	.05
292	Danny Cox	.05
293	Ken Dayley	.05
294	Curt Ford	.05
295	Bob Forsch	.05
296	Tom Herr	.05
297	Ricky Horton	.05
298	Clint Hurdle	.05
299	Jeff Lahti	.05
300	Steve Lake	.05
301	Tito Landrum	.05
302	Mike LaValliere RC	.05
303	Greg Mathews RC	.05
304	Willie McGee	.05
305	Jose Oquendo	.05
306	Terry Pendleton	.05
307	Pat Perry	.05
308	Ozzie Smith	1.50
309	Ray Soff	.05
310	John Tudor	.05
311	Andy Van Slyke	.05
312	Todd Worrell	.05
313	Dann Bilardello	.05
314	Hubie Brooks	.05
315	Tim Burke	.05
316	Andre Dawson	.35
317	Mike Fitzgerald	.05
318	Tom Foley	.05
319	Andres Galarraga	.05
320	Joe Hesketh	.05
321	Wallace Johnson	.05
322	Wayne Krenchicki	.05
323	Vance Law	.05
324	Dennis Martinez	.05
325	Bob McClure	.05
326	Andy McGaffigan	.05
327	Al Newman RC	.05
328	Tim Raines	.05
329	Jeff Reardon	.05
330	Luis Rivera RC	.05
331	Bob Sebra RC	.05
332	Bryn Smith	.05
333	Jay Tibbs	.05
334	Tim Wallach	.05
335	Mitch Webster	.05
336	Jim Wohlford	.05
337	Floyd Youmans	.05
338	Chris Bosio RC	.25
339	Glenn Braggs RC	.05
340	Rick Cerone	.05
341	Mark Clear	.05
342	Bryan Clutterbuck RC	.05
343	Cecil Cooper	.05
344	Rob Deer	.05
345	Jim Gantner	.05
346	Ted Higuera	.05
347	John Henry Johnson	.05
348	Tim Leary RC	.05
349	Rick Manning	.05
350	Paul Molitor	.75
351	Charlie Moore	.05
352	Juan Nieves	.05
353	Ben Oglivie	.05
354	Dan Plesac RC	.10
355	Ernest Riles	.05
356	Billy Joe Robidoux	.05
357	Bill Schroeder	.05
358	Dale Sveum RC	.05
359	Gorman Thomas	.05
360	Bill Wegman RC	.05
361	Robin Yount	.75
362	Steve Balboni	.05
363	Scott Bankhead RC	.05
364	Buddy Biancalana	.05
365	Bud Black	.05
366	George Brett	2.00
367	Steve Farr	.05
368	Mark Gubicza	.05
369	Bo Jackson	.75
370	Danny Jackson	.05
371	Mike Kingery RC	.05
372	Rudy Law	.05
373	Charlie Leibrandt	.05
374	Dennis Leonard	.05
375	Hal McRae	.05
376	Jorge Orta	.05
377	Jamie Quirk	.05
378	Dan Quisenberry	.05
379	Bret Saberhagen	.05
380	Angel Salazar	.05
381	Lonnie Smith	.05
382	Jim Sundberg	.05
383	Frank White	.05
384	Willie Wilson	.05
385	Joaquin Andujar	.05
386	Doug Bair	.05
387	Dusty Baker	.05
388	Bruce Bochte	.05
389	Jose Canseco	.65
390	Chris Codiroli	.05
391	Mike Davis	.05
392	Alfredo Griffin	.05
393	Moose Haas	.05
394	Donnie Hill	.05
395	Jay Howell	.05
396	Dave Kingman	.05
397	Carney Lansford	.05
398	David Leiper RC	.05
399	Bill Mooneyham RC	.05
400	Dwayne Murphy	.05
401	Steve Ontiveros	.05
402	Tony Phillips	.05
403	Eric Plunk	.05
404	Jose Rijo	.05
405	Terry Steinbach RC	.50
406	Dave Stewart	.05
407	Mickey Tettleton	.05
408	Dave Von Ohlen	.05
409	Jerry Willard	.05
410	Curt Young	.05
411	Bruce Bochy	.05
412	Dave Dravecky	.05
413	Tim Flannery	.05
414	Steve Garvey	.25
415	Goose Gossage	.10
416	Tony Gwynn	1.50
417	Andy Hawkins	.05
418	LaMarr Hoyt	.05
419	Terry Kennedy	.05
420	John Kruk	.05
421	Dave LaPoint	.05
422	Craig Lefferts	.05
423	Carmelo Martinez	.05
424	Lance McCullers	.05
425	Kevin McReynolds	.05
426	Graig Nettles	.05
427	Bip Roberts	.05
428	Jerry Royster	.05
429	Benito Santiago	.05
430	Eric Show	.05
431	Bob Stoddard	.05
432	Garry Templeton	.05
433	Gene Walter	.05
434	Ed Whitson	.05
435	Marvell Wynne	.05
436	Dave Anderson	.05
437	Greg Brock	.05
438	Enos Cabell	.05
439	Mariano Duncan	.05
440	Pedro Guerrero	.05
441	Orel Hershiser	.05
442	Rick Honeycutt	.05
443	Ken Howell	.05
444	Ken Landreaux	.05
445	Bill Madlock	.05
446	Mike Marshall	.05
447	Len Matuszek	.05
448	Tom Niedenfuer	.05
449	Alejandro Pena	.05
450	Dennis Powell RC	.05
451	Jerry Reuss	.05
452	Bill Russell	.05
453	Steve Sax	.05
454	Mike Scioscia	.05
455	Franklin Stubbs	.05
456	Alex Trevino	.05
457	Fernando Valenzuela	.05
458	Ed Vande Berg	.05
459	Bob Welch	.05
460	Reggie Williams RC	.05
461	Don Aase	.05
462	Juan Beniquez	.05
463	Mike Boddicker	.05
464	Juan Bonilla	.05
465	Rich Bordi	.05
466	Storm Davis	.05
467	Rick Dempsey	.05
468	Ken Dixon	.05
469	Jim Dwyer	.05
470	Mike Flanagan	.05
471	Jackie Gutierrez	.05
472	Brad Havens	.05
473	Lee Lacy	.05
474	Fred Lynn	.05
475	Scott McGregor	.05
476	Eddie Murray	.75
477	Tom O'Malley	.05
478	Cal Ripken, Jr.	3.00
479	Larry Sheets	.05
480	John Shelby	.05
481	Nate Snell	.05
482	Jim Traber RC	.05
483	Mike Young	.05
484	Neil Allen	.05
485	Harold Baines	.05
486	Floyd Bannister	.05
487	Daryl Boston	.05
488	Ivan Calderon	.05
489	John Cangelosi RC	.05
490	Steve Carlton	.75
491	Joe Cowley	.05
492	Julio Cruz	.05
493	Bill Dawley	.05
494	Jose DeLeon	.05
495	Richard Dotson	.05
496	Carlton Fisk	.75
497	Ozzie Guillen	.05
498	Jerry Hairston Sr.	.05
499	Ron Hassey	.05
500	Tim Hulett	.05
501	Bob James	.05
502	Steve Lyons	.05
503	Joel McKeon RC	.05
504	Gene Nelson	.05
505	Dave Schmidt	.05
506	Ray Searage	.05
507	Bobby Thigpen RC	.15
508	Greg Walker	.05
509	Jim Acker	.05
510	Doyle Alexander	.05
511	Paul Assenmacher RC	.05
512	Bruce Benedict	.05
513	Chris Chambliss	.05
514	Jeff Dedmon	.05
515	Gene Garber	.05
516	Ken Griffey	.05
517	Terry Harper	.05
518	Bob Horner	.05
519	Glenn Hubbard	.05
520	Rick Mahler	.05
521	Omar Moreno	.05
522	Dale Murphy	.35
523	Ken Oberkfell	.05
524	Ed Olwine	.05
525	David Palmer	.05
526	Rafael Ramirez	.05
527	Billy Sample	.05
528	Ted Simmons	.05
529	Zane Smith	.05
530	Bruce Sutter	.65
531	Andres Thomas RC	.05
532	Ozzie Virgil	.05
533	Allan Anderson RC	.05
534	Keith Atherton	.05
535	Billy Beane	.05
536	Bert Blyleven	.10
537	Tom Brunansky	.05
538	Randy Bush	.05
539	George Frazier	.05
540	Gary Gaetti	.05
541	Greg Gagne	.05
542	Mickey Hatcher	.05
543	Neal Heaton	.05
544	Kent Hrbek	.05
545	Roy Lee Jackson	.05
546	Tim Laudner	.05
547	Steve Lombardozzi	.05
548	Mark Portugal RC	.10
549	Kirby Puckett	1.50
550	Jeff Reed	.05
551	Mark Salas	.05
552	Roy Smalley	.05
553	Mike Smithson	.05
554	Frank Viola	.05
555	Thad Bosley	.05
556	Ron Cey	.05
557	Jody Davis	.05
558	Ron Davis	.05
559	Bob Dernier	.05
560	Frank DiPino	.05
561	Shawon Dunston	.05
562	Leon Durham	.05
563	Dennis Eckersley	.65
564	Terry Francona	.05
565	Dave Gumpert	.05
566	Guy Hoffman	.05
567	Ed Lynch	.05
568	Gary Matthews	.05
569	Keith Moreland	.05
570	Jamie Moyer RC	.20
571	Jerry Mumphrey	.05
572	Ryne Sandberg	1.00
573	Scott Sanderson	.05
574	Lee Smith	.05
575	Chris Speier	.05
576	Rick Sutcliffe	.05
577	Manny Trillo	.05
578	Steve Trout	.05
579	Karl Best	.05
580	Scott Bradley RC	.05
581	Phil Bradley	.05
582	Mickey Brantley	.05
583	Mike Brown	.05
584	Alvin Davis	.05
585	Lee Guetterman RC	.10
586	Mark Huismann	.05
587	Bob Kearney	.05
588	Pete Ladd	.05
589	Mark Langston	.05
590	Mike Moore	.05
591	Mike Morgan	.05
592	John Moses	.05
593	Ken Phelps	.05
594	Jim Presley	.05
595	Rey Quinonez (Quinones) RC	.05
596	Harold Reynolds	.05
597	Billy Swift	.05
598	Danny Tartabull	.05
599	Steve Yeager	.05
600	Matt Young	.05
601	Bill Almon	.05
602	Rafael Belliard RC	.05
603	Mike Bielecki	.05
604	Barry Bonds	40.00
605	Bobby Bonilla	.05
606	Sid Bream	.05
607	Mike Brown	.05
608	Pat Clements	.05
609	Mike Diaz RC	.05
610	Cecilio Guante	.05
611	Barry Jones RC	.05
612	Bob Kipper	.05
613	Larry McWilliams	.05
614	Jim Morrison	.05
615	Joe Orsulak	.05
616	Junior Ortiz	.05
617	Tony Pena	.05
618	Johnny Ray	.05
619	Rick Reuschel	.05
620	R.J. Reynolds	.05
621	Rick Rhoden	.05
622	Don Robinson	.05
623	Bob Walk	.05
624	Jim Winn	.05
625	Youthful Power (Jose Canseco, Pete Incaviglia)	.15
626	300 Game Winners (Phil Niekro, Don Sutton)	.25
627	A.L. Firemen (Don Aase, Dave Righetti)	.25
628	Rookie All-Stars (Jose Canseco, Wally Joyner)	.15
629	Magic Mets (Gary Carter, Dwight Gooden, Keith Hernandez, Darryl Strawberry)	.15
630	N.L. Best Righties (Mike Krukow, Mike Scott)	.05
631	Sensational Southpaws (John Franco, Fernando Valenzuela)	.05
632	Count 'Em (Bob Horner)	.05
633	A.L. Pitcher's Nightmare (Jose Canseco, Kirby Puckett, Jim Rice)	.25
634	All-Star Battery (Gary Carter, Roger Clemens)	.50
635	4,000 Strikeouts (Steve Carlton)	.15
636	Big Bats At First Sack (Glenn Davis, Eddie Murray)	.15
637	On Base (Wade Boggs, Keith Hernandez)	.25
638	Sluggers From Left Side (Don Mattingly, Darryl Strawberry)	.50
639	Former MVP's (Dave Parker, Ryne Sandberg)	.25
640	Dr. K. & Super K (Roger Clemens, Dwight Gooden)	.50
641	A.L. West Stoppers (Charlie Hough, Mike Witt)	.05
642	Doubles & Triples (Tim Raines, Juan Samuel)	.05
643	Outfielders With Punch (Harold Baines, Jesse Barfield)	.05
644	Major League Prospects (Dave Clark RC, Greg Swindell RC)	.35
645	Major League Prospects (Ron Karkovice RC, Russ Morman RC)	.05
646	Major League Prospects (Willie Fraser RC, Devon White RC)	1.00
647	Major League Prospects (Jerry Browne RC, Mike Stanley RC)	.25
648	Major League Prospects (Phil Lombardi RC, Dave Magadan RC)	.20
649	Major League Prospects (Ralph Bryant RC, Jose Gonzalez RC)	.10
650	Major League Prospects (Randy Asadoor RC, Jimmy Jones RC)	.10
651	Major League Prospects (Marvin Freeman RC, Tracy Jones RC)	.10
652	Major League Prospects (Kevin Seitzer RC, John Stefero RC)	.25
653	Major League Prospects (Steve Fireovid RC, Rob Nelson RC)	.10
654	Checklist 1-95	.05
655	Checklist 96-192	.05
656	Checklist 193-288	.05
657	Checklist 289-384	.05
658	Checklist 385-483	.05
659	Checklist 484-578	.05
660	Checklist 579-660	.05

All-Stars

As in 1986, Fleer All-Star Team cards were randomly inserted in wax and cello packs. Twelve cards, measuring the standard 2-1/2" x 3-1/2", comprise the set. Fronts feature a full-color player photo set against a gray background for American League players and a black background for National Leaguers. Backs are printed in black, red and white and feature a lengthy player biography. Fleer's choices for a major league All-Star team is once again the theme for the set.

		NM/M
Complete Set (12):		8.00
Common Player:		.25
1	Don Mattingly	2.00
2	Gary Carter	1.00
3	Tony Fernandez	.25
4	Steve Sax	.25
5	Kirby Puckett	1.50
6	Mike Schmidt	.25
7	Mike Easler	.25
8	Todd Worrell	.25
9	George Bell	.25
10	Fernando Valenzuela	.25
11	Roger Clemens	2.00
12	Tim Raines	.25

Headliners

A continuation of the 1986 Future Hall of Famers idea, Fleer encountered legal problems with using the Hall of Fame name and abated them by entitling the set "Headliners." The cards were randomly inserted in three-pack rack packs. Fronts feature a player photo set against a beige background with bright red stripes. Backs are printed in black, red and gray and offer a brief biography with an emphasis on the player's performance during the 1986 season.

		NM/M
Complete Set (6):		4.00
Common Player:		
1	Wade Boggs	1.50
2	Jose Canseco	1.00
3	Dwight Gooden	.50
4	Rickey Henderson	1.00
5	Keith Hernandez	.50
6	Jim Rice	.75

'86 World Series

Fleer issued a set of 12 cards highlighting the 1986 World Series between the Boston Red Sox and New York Mets. The sets were available only with Fleer factory sets, both regular and glossy. The cards, 2-1/2" x 3-1/2", have either horizontal or vertical formats. The fronts are bordered in red, white and blue stars and stripes with a thin gold frame around the photo. Backs are printed in red and blue on white stock and include information regarding the photo on the card fronts.

		NM/M
Complete Set, Regular (12):		6.00
Complete Set, Glossy (12):		6.00
Common Card:		.25
1	Left-Hand Finesse Beats Mets (Bruce Hurst)	.25
2	Wade Boggs, Keith Hernandez	1.25
3	Roger Clemens	4.00
4	Gary Carter	1.00
5	Ron Darling	.25
6	.433 Series Batting Average (Marty Barrett)	.25
7	Dwight Gooden	.50
8	Strategy At Work	.25
9	Dewey! (Dwight Evans)	.25
10	One Strike From Boston Victory (Dave Henderson, Spike Owen)	.25
11	Ray Knight, Darryl Strawberry	.25
12	Series M.V.P. (Ray Knight)	.25

Box Panels

For the second straight year, Fleer produced a special set of cards designed to stimulate sales of their wax and cello pack boxes. In 1987, Fleer issued 16 cards in panels of four on the bottoms of retail boxes. The cards are numbered C-1 through C-16 and are 2-1/2" x 3-1/2" in size. The cards have the same design as the regular issue set with the player photos and card numbers being different.

		NM/M
Complete Panel Set (4):		6.00
Complete Singles Set (16):		6.00
Common Panel:		1.50
Common Single Player:		.15
Panel		1.50
1	Mets Logo	.05
6	Keith Hernandez	.25
9	Dale Murphy	.45
14	Ryne Sandberg	1.00
Panel		2.50
3	Jesse Barfield	.15
3	George Brett	1.50
	Red Sox Logo	.05
11	Kirby Puckett	1.00
Panel		1.50
8	Dwight Gooden	.15
9	Astros Logo	.05
10	Dave Parker	.15
15	Mike Schmidt	1.50
Panel		1.00
7	Wally Joyner	.25
12	Dave Righetti	.15
	Angels Logo	.05
16	Robin Yount	.75

Glossy Tin

The three-year run of limited edition, glossy collectors' issues by Fleer from 1987-89 has become known to the hobby as "tins" for the colorful lithographed metal boxes in which complete sets were sold. In

their debut year a reported 100,000 sets were made, each serial numbered on a sticker attached to the shrink-wrapped tin box. While the glossy version of the 1987 Fleer set once enjoyed a significant premium over regular cards, today that premium has evaporated and, indeed, it can be harder to find a buyer for the glossy version.

	NM/M
Unopened Set (672):	75.00
Complete Set (672):	50.00
Common Player:	.10

Fleer Update

The 1987 update edition brings the regular Fleer set up to date by including traded players and hot rookies. The cards measure 2-1/2" x 3-1/2" and are housed in a specially designed box with 25 team logo stickers. A glossy-coated Fleer Collectors Edition set was also produced.

		NM/M
Complete Set (132):		9.00
Common Player:		.05
1	Scott Bankhead	.05
2	Eric Bell RC	.05
3	Juan Beniquez	.05
4	Juan Berenguer	.05
5	Mike Birkbeck RC	.05
6	Randy Bockus RC	.05
7	Rod Booker RC	.05
8	Thad Bosley	.05
9	Greg Brock	.05
10	Bob Brower RC	.05
11	Chris Brown	.05
12	Jerry Browne RC	.05
13	Ralph Bryant	.05
14	DeWayne Buice RC	.05
15	Ellis Burks RC	.05
16	Casey Candaele RC	.05
17	Steve Carlton	.50
18	Juan Castillo	.05
19	Chuck Crim RC	.05
20	Mark Davidson RC	.05
21	Mark Davis	.05
22	Storm Davis	.05
23	Bill Dawley	.05
24	Andre Dawson	.30
25	Brian Dayett	.05
26	Rick Dempsey	.05
27	Ken Dowell RC	.05
28	Dave Dravecky	.05
29	Mike Dunne RC	.05
30	Dennis Eckersley	.40
31	Cecil Fielder	.05
32	Brian Fisher	.05
33	Willie Fraser	.05
34	Ken Gerhart RC	.05
35	Jim Gott	.05
36	Dan Gladden	.05
37	Mike Greenwell RC	.05
38	Cecilio Guante	.05
39	Albert Hall	.05
40	Atlee Hammaker	.05
41	Mickey Hatcher	.05
42	Mike Heath	.05
43	Neal Heaton	.05
44	Mike Henneman RC	.05
45	Guy Hoffman	.05
46	Charles Hudson	.05
47	Chuck Jackson RC	.05
48	Mike Jackson RC	.05
49	Reggie Jackson	.75
50	Chris James	.05
51	Dion James	.05
52	Stan Javier	.05
53	Stan Jefferson RC	.05
54	Jimmy Jones	.05
55	Tracy Jones	.05
56	Terry Kennedy	.05
57	Mike Kingery	.05
58	Ray Knight	.05
59	Gene Larkin RC	.05
60	Mike LaValliere RC	.05
61	Jack Lazorko RC	.05
62	Terry Leach	.05
63	Rick Leach	.05
64	Craig Lefferts	.05
65	Jim Lindeman RC	.05
66	Bill Long RC	.05
67	Mike Loynd RC	.05
68	Greg Maddux RC	8.00
69	Bill Madlock	.05
70	Dave Magadan	.05
71	Joe Magrane RC	.05
72	Fred Manrique RC	.05
73	Mike Mason	.05
74	Lloyd McClendon RC	.05
75	Fred McGriff RC	.05
76	Mark McGwire	3.00
77	Mark McLemore	.05
78	Kevin McReynolds	.05
79	Dave Meads RC	.05
80	Greg Minton	.05
81	John Mitchell RC	.05
82	Kevin Mitchell	.05
83	John Morris	.05
84	Jeff Musselman RC	.05
85	Randy Myers RC	.05
86	Gene Nelson	.05
87	Joe Niekro	.05
88	Tom Nieto	.05
89	Reid Nichols	.05
90	Matt Nokes RC	.05
91	Dickie Noles	.05
92	Edwin Nunez	.05
93	Jose Nunez RC	.05
94	Paul O'Neill	.05
95	Jim Paciorek RC	.05
96	Lance Parrish	.05
97	Bill Pecota RC	.05
98	Tony Pena	.05
99	Luis Polonia RC	.05
100	Randy Ready	.05
101	Jeff Reardon	.05
102	Gary Redus	.05
103	Rick Rhoden	.05
104	Wally Ritchie RC	.05
105	Jeff Robinson RC	.05
106	Mark Salas	.05
107	Dave Schmidt	.05
108	Kevin Seitzer	.05
109	John Shelby	.05
110	John Smiley RC	.05
111	Lary Sorensen	.05
112	Chris Speier	.05
113	Randy St. Claire	.05
114	Jim Sundberg	.05
115	B.J. Surhoff RC	.05
116	Greg Swindell	.05
117	Danny Tartabull	.05
118	Dorn Taylor RC	.05
119	Lee Tunnell	.05
120	Ed Vande Berg	.05
121	Andy Van Slyke	.05
122	Gary Ward	.05
123	Devon White	.05
124	Alan Wiggins	.05
125	Bill Wilkinson RC	.05
126	Jim Winn	.05
127	Frank Williams	.05
128	Ken Williams RC	.05
129	Matt Williams RC	1.00
130	Herm Winningham	.05
131	Matt Young	.05
132	Checklist 1-132	.05

Update Glossy Tin

The 1987 Fleer glossy update set is identical to the regular-issue updates, except for the high-gloss coating on the cards' fronts and the lithographed metal box in which the sets were sold. Production was estimated at 100,000. Because of perceived overproduction, the glossy tin update set and singles currently carry little, if any, premium over the regular-issue updates.

	NM/M
Unopened Set (132):	12.00
Complete Set (132):	7.50
Common Player:	.10

Award Winners

Cardinal Comeback Player of the Year

The 1987 Fleer Award Winners boxed set was prepared for distribution by 7-Eleven stores. The 2-1/2" x 3-1/2" cards feature players who have won various major league awards during their careers. Fronts contain full-color photos surrounded by a yellow border. The name of the award the player won is printed at the bottom of the card in an oval-shaped band designed to resemble a metal nameplate on a trophy. Backs are printed in black, yellow and white, and include lifetime major and minor league statistics along with typical personal information. Each boxed set contained six team logo stickers.

		NM/M
Complete Set (44):		5.00
Common Player:		.10
1	Marty Barrett	.10
2	George Bell	.10
3	Bert Blyleven	.20
4	Bob Boone	.10
5	John Candelaria	.10
6	Jose Canseco	.45
7	Gary Carter	.50
8	Joe Carter	.10
9	Roger Clemens	1.00
10	Cecil Cooper	.10
11	Eric Davis	.10
12	Tony Fernandez	.10
13	Scott Fletcher	.10
14	Bob Forsch	.10
15	Dwight Gooden	.10
16	Ron Guidry	.10
17	Ozzie Guillen	.10
18	Bill Gullickson	.10
19	Tony Gwynn	.75
20	Bob Knepper	.10
21	Ray Knight	.10
22	Mark Langston	.10
23	Candy Maldonado	.10
24	Don Mattingly	1.00
25	Roger McDowell	.10
26	Dale Murphy	.20
27	Dave Parker	.10
28	Lance Parrish	.10
29	Gary Pettis	.10
30	Kirby Puckett	.75
31	Johnny Ray	.10
32	Dave Righetti	.10
33	Cal Ripken, Jr.	1.50
34	Bret Saberhagen	.10
35	Ryne Sandberg	.75
36	Mike Schmidt	1.00
37	Mike Scott	.10
38	Ozzie Smith	.75
39	Robbie Thompson	.10
40	Fernando Valenzuela	.10
41	Mitch Webster	.10
42	Frank White	.10
43	Mike Witt	.10
44	Todd Worrell	.10

Baseball All-Stars

Produced by Fleer for exclusive distribution through Ben Franklin stores, the "Baseball All-Stars" set is comprised of 44 cards in the standard 2-1/2" x 3-1/2" format. Cards have full-color photos surrounded by a bright red border with white pinstripes at the top and bottom. Backs are printed in blue, white and dark red and include complete major and minor league statistics. The set was issued in a special cardboard box with a handful of team logo stickers.

		NM/M
Complete Set (44):		5.00
Common Player:		.10
1	Harold Baines	.10
2	Jesse Barfield	.10
3	Wade Boggs	.65
4	Dennis "Oil Can" Boyd	.10
5	Scott Bradley	.10
6	Jose Canseco	.40
7	Gary Carter	.50
8	Joe Carter	.10
9	Mark Clear	.10
10	Roger Clemens	.85
11	Jose Cruz	.10
12	Chili Davis	.10
13	Jody Davis	.10
14	Rob Deer	.10
15	Brian Downing	.10
16	Sid Fernandez	.10
17	John Franco	.10
18	Andres Galarraga	.10
19	Dwight Gooden	.10
20	Tony Gwynn	.65
21	Charlie Hough	.10
22	Bruce Hurst	.10
23	Wally Joyner	.10
24	Carney Lansford	.10
25	Fred Lynn	.10
26	Don Mattingly	.85
27	Willie McGee	.10
28	Jack Morris	.10
29	Dale Murphy	.20
30	Bob Ojeda	.10
31	Tony Pena	.10
32	Kirby Puckett	.65
33	Dan Quisenberry	.10
34	Tim Raines	.10
35	Willie Randolph	.10
36	Cal Ripken, Jr.	1.50
37	Pete Rose	1.00
38	Nolan Ryan	1.50
39	Juan Samuel	.10
40	Mike Schmidt	.85
41	Ozzie Smith	.65
42	Andres Thomas	.10
43	Fernando Valenzuela	.10
44	Mike Witt	.10

Baseball's Best

For a second straight baseball card season, Fleer produced for McCrory's stores and their affiliates a 44-card "Baseball's Best" set. Subtitled "Sluggers vs. Pitchers," 28 everyday players and 16 pitchers are featured. The card design is nearly identical to the previous year's effort. The cards were sold in a specially designed box along with six team logo stickers.

		NM/M
Complete Set (44):		4.00
Common Player:		.10
1	Kevin Bass	.10
2	Jesse Barfield	.10
3	George Bell	.10
4	Wade Boggs	.65
5	Sid Bream	.10
6	George Brett	.85
7	Ivan Calderon	.10
8	Jose Canseco	.50
9	Jack Clark	.10
10	Roger Clemens	.85
11	Eric Davis	.10
12	Andre Dawson	.25
13	Sid Fernandez	.10
14	John Franco	.10
15	Dwight Gooden	.10
16	Pedro Guerrero	.10
17	Tony Gwynn	.65
18	Rickey Henderson	.60
19	Tom Henke	.10
20	Ted Higuera	.10
21	Pete Incaviglia	.10
22	Wally Joyner	.10
23	Jeff Leonard	.10
24	Joe Magrane	.10
25	Don Mattingly	.85
26	Mark McGwire	1.00
27	Jack Morris	.10
28	Dale Murphy	.20
29	Dave Parker	.10
30	Ken Phelps	.10
31	Kirby Puckett	.65
32	Tim Raines	.10
33	Jeff Reardon	.10
34	Dave Righetti	.10
35	Cal Ripken, Jr.	1.50
36	Bret Saberhagen	.10
37	Mike Schmidt	.85
38	Mike Scott	.10
39	Kevin Seitzer	.10
40	Darryl Strawberry	.10
41	Rick Sutcliffe	.10
42	Pat Tabler	.10
43	Fernando Valenzuela	.10
44	Mike Witt	.10

Baseball's Best Box Bottom

These special cards were printed on the bottom of retail boxes of Fleer's "Baseball's Best" boxed sets. The box-bottom cards are in the same format as the boxed cards, with red, white and blue borders and a yellow title strip at top. Backs are also similar in design to the regular-issue cards, carrying player data and stats. Cards are numbered with a "M" prefix.

		NM/M
Complete Panel (6):		3.00
Complete Set (6):		3.00
Common Player:		.50
1	Steve Bedrosian	.50
2	Will Clark	1.00
3	Vince Coleman	.50
4	Bo Jackson	2.00
5	Cory Snyder	.50
---	K.C. Royals Logo	.10

Exciting Stars

Another entry into the Fleer line-up of individual boxed sets, the "Baseball's Exciting Stars" set was produced for Cumberland Farms stores. The card fronts feature a red, white and blue border with the words "Exciting Stars" printed in yellow at the top. The backs are printed in red and blue and carry complete major and minor league statistics. Included with the boxed set of 44 cards were six team logo stickers.

		NM/M
Complete Set (44):		4.00
Common Player:		.10
1	Don Aase	.10
2	Rick Aguilera	.10
3	Jesse Barfield	.10
4	Wade Boggs	.65
5	Dennis "Oil Can" Boyd	.10
6	Sid Bream	.10
7	Jose Canseco	.45
8	Steve Carlton	.50
9	Gary Carter	.50
10	Will Clark	.10
11	Roger Clemens	.85
12	Danny Cox	.10
13	Alvin Davis	.10
14	Eric Davis	.10
15	Rob Deer	.10
16	Brian Downing	.10
17	Gene Garber	.10
18	Steve Garvey	.20
19	Dwight Gooden	.10
20	Mark Gubicza	.10
21	Mel Hall	.10
22	Terry Harper	.10
23	Von Hayes	.10
24	Rickey Henderson	.50
25	Tom Henke	.10
26	Willie Hernandez	.10
27	Ted Higuera	.10
28	Rick Honeycutt	.10
29	Kent Hrbek	.08
30	Wally Joyner	.10
31	Charlie Kerfeld	.10
32	Fred Lynn	.10
33	Don Mattingly	.85
34	Tim Raines	.10
35	Dennis Rasmussen	.10
36	Johnny Ray	.10
37	Jim Rice	.25
38	Pete Rose	1.00
39	Lee Smith	.10
40	Cory Snyder	.10

41	Darryl Strawberry	.10
42	Kent Tekulve	.10
43	Willie Wilson	.10
44	Bobby Witt	.10

Game Winners

The 1987 Fleer "Baseball's Game Winners" boxed set was produced for distribution through Bi-Mart Discount Drug, Pay'n-Save, Mott's 5 & 10, M.E. Moses, and Winn's stores. Cards have a light blue border with the player's name and game winning RBI or games-won statistics in a yellow oval band at the top. Backs are similar to the regular-issue 1987 Fleer, with full professional stats. Included with the boxed set were six team logo stickers.

		NM/M
Complete Set (44):		4.00
Common Player:		.10
1	Harold Baines	.10
2	Don Baylor	.10
3	George Bell	.10
4	Tony Bernazard	.10
5	Wade Boggs	.75
6	George Brett	.85
7	Hubie Brooks	.10
8	Jose Canseco	.50
9	Gary Carter	.60
10	Roger Clemens	.85
11	Eric Davis	.10
12	Glenn Davis	.10
13	Shawon Dunston	.10
14	Mark Eichhorn	.10
15	Gary Gaetti	.10
16	Steve Garvey	.15
17	Kirk Gibson	.10
18	Dwight Gooden	.10
19	Von Hayes	.10
20	Willie Hernandez	.10
21	Ted Higuera	.10
22	Wally Joyner	.10
23	Bob Knepper	.10
24	Mike Krukow	.10
25	Jeff Leonard	.10
26	Don Mattingly	.85
27	Kirk McCaskill	.10
28	Kevin McReynolds	.10
29	Jim Morrison	.10
30	Dale Murphy	.10
31	Pete O'Brien	.10
32	Bob Ojeda	.10
33	Larry Parrish	.10
34	Ken Phelps	.10
35	Dennis Rasmussen	.10
36	Ernest Riles	.10
37	Cal Ripken, Jr.	1.00
38	Ron Robinson	.10
39	Steve Sax	.10
40	Mike Schmidt	.85
41	John Tudor	.10
42	Fernando Valenzuela	.10
43	Mike Witt	.10
44	Curt Young	.10

Hottest Stars

The "Baseball's Hottest Stars" set was produced by Fleer for the Revco Drug Store chain. Measuring the standard 2-1/2" x 3-1/2", the cards feature full-color photos surrounded by a red, white and blue border. Card backs are printed in red, white and black and contain the player's lifetime professional statistics. The set was sold in a special cardboard box with six team logo stickers.

		NM/M
Unopened Set (44):		45.00
Complete Set (44):		25.00
Common Player:		.10
1	Joaquin Andujar	.10
2	Harold Baines	.10
3	Kevin Bass	.10
4	Don Baylor	.10
5	Barry Bonds	20.00
6	George Brett	1.00
7	Tom Brunansky	.10
8	Brett Butler	.10
9	Jose Canseco	.60
10	Roger Clemens	1.00
11	Ron Darling	.10
12	Eric Davis	.10
13	Andre Dawson	.25
14	Doug DeCinces	.10
15	Leon Durham	.10
16	Mark Eichhorn	.10
17	Scott Garrelts	.10
18	Dwight Gooden	.10
19	Dave Henderson	.10
20	Rickey Henderson	.60
21	Keith Hernandez	.10
22	Ted Higuera	.10
23	Bob Horner	.10
24	Pete Incaviglia	.10
25	Wally Joyner	.10
26	Mark Langston	.10
27	Don Mattingly	1.00
28	Dale Murphy	.20
29	Kirk McCaskill	.10
30	Willie McGee	.10
31	Dave Righetti	.10
32	Pete Rose	1.50
33	Bruce Ruffin	.10
34	Steve Sax	.10
35	Mike Schmidt	1.00
36	Larry Sheets	.10
37	Eric Show	.10
38	Dave Smith	.10
39	Cory Snyder	.10
40	Frank Tanana	.10
41	Alan Trammell	.10
42	Reggie Williams	.10
43	Mookie Wilson	.10
44	Todd Worrell	.10

League Leaders

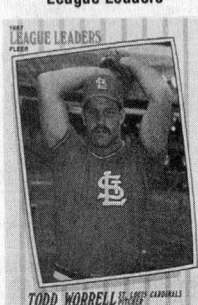

For a second year, Fleer produced a 44-card "League Leaders" set for Walgreens. The card fronts feature a border style which is identical to that used in 1986. However, a trapezoidal shaped full-color player photo is placed diagonally on the front. "1987 Fleer League Leaders" appears in the upper left corner of the front although nowhere on the card does it state in which pitching, hitting or fielding department was the player a league leader. Backs are printed in red and blue on white stock. The cards in the boxed set are the standard 2-1/2" x 3-1/2" size.

		NM/M
Complete Set (44):		4.00
Common Player:		.10
1	Jesse Barfield	.10
2	Mike Boddicker	.10
3	Wade Boggs	.65
4	Phil Bradley	.10
5	George Brett	.85
6	Hubie Brooks	.10
7	Chris Brown	.10
8	Jose Canseco	.50
9	Joe Carter	.10
10	Roger Clemens	.85
11	Vince Coleman	.10
12	Joe Cowley	.10
13	Kal Daniels	.10
14	Glenn Davis	.10
15	Jody Davis	.10
16	Darrell Evans	.10
17	Dwight Evans	.10
18	John Franco	.10
19	Julio Franco	.10
20	Dwight Gooden	.10
21	Goose Gossage	.10
22	Tom Herr	.10
23	Ted Higuera	.10
24	Bob Horner	.10
25	Pete Incaviglia	.10
26	Wally Joyner	.10
27	Dave Kingman	.10
28	Don Mattingly	.85
29	Willie McGee	.10
30	Donnie Moore	.10
31	Keith Moreland	.10
32	Eddie Murray	.60
33	Mike Pagliarulo	.10
34	Larry Parrish	.10
35	Tony Pena	.10
36	Kirby Puckett	.65
37	Pete Rose	1.00
38	Juan Samuel	.10
39	Ryne Sandberg	.65
40	Mike Schmidt	.85
41	Darryl Strawberry	.10
42	Greg Walker	.10
43	Bob Welch	.10
44	Todd Worrell	.10

Limited Edition

For the third straight year, Fleer produced a Limited Edition set for the McCrory's store chain and its affiliates. The cards are the standard 2-1/2" x 3-1/2" and feature light blue borders at the top and bottom and a diagonal red and white border running along both sides. The set was issued in a specially prepared cardboard box, along with six team logo stickers.

		NM/M
Complete Set (44):		4.00
Common Player:		.10
1	Floyd Bannister	.10
2	Marty Barrett	.10
3	Steve Bedrosian	.10
4	George Bell	.10
5	George Brett	.85
6	Jose Canseco	.40
7	Joe Carter	.10
8	Will Clark	.10
9	Roger Clemens	.85
10	Vince Coleman	.10
11	Glenn Davis	.10
12	Mike Davis	.10
13	Len Dykstra	.10
14	John Franco	.10
15	Julio Franco	.10
16	Steve Garvey	.25
17	Kirk Gibson	.10
18	Dwight Gooden	.10
19	Tony Gwynn	.65
20	Keith Hernandez	.10
21	Teddy Higuera	.10
22	Kent Hrbek	.10
23	Wally Joyner	.10
24	Mike Krukow	.10
25	Mike Marshall	.10
26	Don Mattingly	.85
27	Oddibe McDowell	.10
28	Jack Morris	.10
29	Lloyd Moseby	.10
30	Dale Murphy	.20
31	Eddie Murray	.50
32	Tony Pena	.10
33	Jim Presley	.10
34	Jeff Reardon	.10
35	Jim Rice	.25
36	Pete Rose	1.00
37	Mike Schmidt	.85
38	Mike Scott	.10
39	Lee Smith	.10
40	Lonnie Smith	.10
41	Gary Ward	.10
42	Dave Winfield	.50
43	Todd Worrell	.10
44	Robin Yount	.50

Limited Edition Box Bottom

These special cards were printed on the bottom of retail boxes of Fleer's "Limited Edition" boxed sets. The box-bottom cards are in the same format as the boxed cards, with red, white and blue borders. Backs are also similar in design to the regular-issue cards, carrying player data and stats.

		NM/M
Complete Panel:		2.00
Complete Set (6):		2.00
Common Player:		.50
C1	Ron Darling	.50
C2	Bill Buckner	.50
C3	John Candelaria	.50
C4	Jack Clark	.50
C5	Bret Saberhagen	.50
C6	Houston Astros Logo	.25

Mini

Continuing with an idea originated the previous year, the Fleer "Classic Miniatures" set consists of 120 cards that measure 1-13/16" x 2-9/16". The cards are identical in design to the regular-issue set, but use completely different photos. The set was issued in a specially prepared collectors box along with 18 team logo stickers. The mini set was available only through hobby dealers.

		NM/M
Complete Set (120):		4.00
Common Player:		.05
1	Don Aase	.05
2	Joaquin Andujar	.05
3	Harold Baines	.05
4	Jesse Barfield	.05
5	Kevin Bass	.05
6	Don Baylor	.05
7	George Bell	.05
8	Tony Bernazard	.05
9	Bert Blyleven	.05
10	Wade Boggs	.65
11	Phil Bradley	.05
12	Sid Bream	.05
13	George Brett	.85
14	Hubie Brooks	.05
15	Chris Brown	.05
16	Tom Candiotti	.05
17	Jose Canseco	.40
18	Gary Carter	.50
19	Joe Carter	.05
20	Roger Clemens	.85
21	Vince Coleman	.05
22	Cecil Cooper	.05
23	Ron Darling	.05
24	Alvin Davis	.05
25	Chili Davis	.05
26	Eric Davis	.05
27	Glenn Davis	.05
28	Mike Davis	.05
29	Doug DeCinces	.05
30	Rob Deer	.05
31	Jim Deshaies	.05
32	Bo Diaz	.05
33	Richard Dotson	.05
34	Brian Downing	.05
35	Shawon Dunston	.05
36	Mark Eichhorn	.05
37	Dwight Evans	.05
38	Tony Fernandez	.05
39	Julio Franco	.05
40	Gary Gaetti	.05
41	Andres Galarraga	.05
42	Scott Garrelts	.05
43	Steve Garvey	.15
44	Kirk Gibson	.05
45	Dwight Gooden	.05
46	Ken Griffey	.05
47	Mark Gubicza	.05
48	Ozzie Guillen	.05
49	Bill Gullickson	.05
50	Tony Gwynn	.65
51	Von Hayes	.05
52	Rickey Henderson	.50
53	Keith Hernandez	.05
54	Willie Hernandez	.05
55	Ted Higuera	.05
56	Charlie Hough	.05
57	Kent Hrbek	.05
58	Pete Incaviglia	.05
59	Wally Joyner	.05
60	Bob Knepper	.05
61	Mike Krukow	.05
62	Mark Langston	.05
63	Carney Lansford	.05
64	Jim Lindeman	.05
65	Bill Madlock	.05
66	Don Mattingly	.85
67	Kirk McCaskill	.05
68	Lance McCullers	.05
69	Keith Moreland	.05
70	Jack Morris	.05
71	Jim Morrison	.05
72	Lloyd Moseby	.05
73	Jerry Mumphrey	.05
74	Dale Murphy	.15
75	Eddie Murray	.50
76	Pete O'Brien	.05
77	Bob Ojeda	.05
78	Jesse Orosco	.05
79	Dan Pasqua	.05
80	Dave Parker	.05
81	Larry Parrish	.05
82	Jim Presley	.05
83	Kirby Puckett	.65
84	Dan Quisenberry	.05
85	Tim Raines	.05
86	Dennis Rasmussen	.05
87	Johnny Ray	.05
88	Jeff Reardon	.05
89	Jim Rice	.25
90	Dave Righetti	.05
91	Earnest Riles	.05
92	Cal Ripken, Jr.	1.50
93	Ron Robinson	.05
94	Juan Samuel	.05
95	Ryne Sandberg	.65
96	Steve Sax	.05
97	Mike Schmidt	.85
98	Ken Schrom	.05
99	Mike Scott	.05
100	Ruben Sierra	.05
101	Lee Smith	.05
102	Ozzie Smith	.65
103	Cory Snyder	.05
104	Kent Tekulve	.05
105	Andres Thomas	.05
106	Rob Thompson	.05
107	Alan Trammell	.05
108	John Tudor	.05
109	Fernando Valenzuela	.05
110	Greg Walker	.05
111	Mitch Webster	.05
112	Lou Whitaker	.05
113	Frank White	.05
114	Reggie Williams	.05
115	Glenn Wilson	.05
116	Willie Wilson	.05
117	Dave Winfield	.50
118	Mike Witt	.05
119	Todd Worrell	.05
120	Floyd Youmans	.05

Record Setters

Produced by Fleer for the Eckerd Drug chain, the Record Setters set contains 44 cards in standard 2-1/2" x 3-1/2" size. Although the set is titled "Record Setters," the actual records the players have set is not specified anywhere on the cards. Given that several players included in the set were young prospects, a better title for those cards might have been "Possible Record Setters." The set came housed in a special cardboard box with six team logo stickers.

		NM/M
Complete Set (44):		4.00
Common Player:		.10
1	George Brett	.85
2	Chris Brown	.10
3	Jose Canseco	.40
4	Roger Clemens	.85
5	Alvin Davis	.10
6	Shawon Dunston	.10
7	Tony Fernandez	.10
8	Carlton Fisk	.45
9	Gary Gaetti	.10
10	Gene Garber	.10
11	Rich Gedman	.10
12	Dwight Gooden	.10
13	Ozzie Guillen	.10
14	Bill Gullickson	.10
15	Billy Hatcher	.10
16	Orel Hershiser	.10
17	Wally Joyner	.10
18	Ray Knight	.10
19	Craig Lefferts	.10
20	Don Mattingly	.85
21	Kevin Mitchell	.10
22	Lloyd Moseby	.10
23	Dale Murphy	.15
24	Eddie Murray	.45
25	Phil Niekro	.30
26	Ben Oglivie	.10
27	Jesse Orosco	.10
28	Joe Orsulak	.10
29	Larry Parrish	.10
30	Tim Raines	.10
31	Shane Rawley	.10
32	Dave Righetti	.10
33	Pete Rose	1.00
34	Steve Sax	.10
35	Mike Schmidt	.85
36	Mike Scott	.10
37	Don Sutton	.30
38	Alan Trammell	.10
39	John Tudor	.10
40	Gary Ward	.10
41	Lou Whitaker	.10
42	Willie Wilson	.10
43	Todd Worrell	.10
44	Floyd Youmans	.10

Star Stickers

The 1987 Fleer Star Stickers set contains 132 cards which become stickers if the back is bent and peeled off. As in the previous year, the card backs are identical, save the numbering system, to the regular-issue cards. The cards measure 2-1/2" x 3-1/2" and were sold in wax packs with team logo stickers. The fronts have a green border with a red and white banner wrapped across the upper left corner and the sides. The backs are printed in green and yellow.

		NM/M
Complete Set (132):		6.00
Common Player:		.05
Wax Pack (5):		.50
Wax Box (36):		12.00
1	Don Aase	.05
2	Harold Baines	.05
3	Floyd Bannister	.05
4	Jesse Barfield	.05
5	Marty Barrett	.05
6	Kevin Bass	.05
7	Don Baylor	.05
8	Steve Bedrosian	.05
9	George Bell	.05
10	Bert Blyleven	.05
11	Mike Boddicker	.05
12	Wade Boggs	.85
13	Phil Bradley	.05
14	Sid Bream	.05
15	George Brett	.85
16	Hubie Brooks	.05
17	Tom Brunansky	.05
18	Tom Candiotti	.05
19	Jose Canseco	.40
20	Gary Carter	.50
21	Joe Carter	.05
22	Will Clark	.85
23	Mark Clear	.05
24	Roger Clemens	.85
25	Vince Coleman	.05
26	Jose Cruz	.05
27	Ron Darling	.05
28	Alvin Davis	.05
29	Chili Davis	.05
30	Eric Davis	.05
31	Glenn Davis	.05
32	Mike Davis	.05
33	Andre Dawson	.25
34	Doug DeCinces	.05
35	Brian Downing	.05
36	Shawon Dunston	.05
37	Mark Eichhorn	.05
38	Dwight Evans	.05
39	Tony Fernandez	.05
40	Bob Forsch	.05
41	John Franco	.05
42	Julio Franco	.05
43	Gary Gaetti	.05
44	Gene Garber	.05
45	Scott Garrelts	.05
46	Steve Garvey	.05
47	Kirk Gibson	.05
48	Dwight Gooden	.05
49	Ken Griffey	.05
50	Ozzie Guillen	.05
51	Bill Gullickson	.05
52	Tony Gwynn	.65
53	Mel Hall	.05
54	Greg Harris	.05

#	Player	Price
55	Von Hayes	.05
56	Rickey Henderson	.50
57	Tom Henke	.05
58	Keith Hernandez	.05
59	Willie Hernandez	.05
60	Ted Higuera	.05
61	Bob Horner	.05
62	Charlie Hough	.05
63	Jay Howell	.05
64	Kent Hrbek	.05
65	Bruce Hurst	.05
66	Pete Incaviglia	.05
67	Bob James	.05
68	Wally Joyner	.05
69	Mike Krukow	.05
70	Mark Langston	.05
71	Carney Lansford	.05
72	Fred Lynn	.05
73	Bill Madlock	.05
74	Don Mattingly	.85
75	Kirk McCaskill	.05
76	Lance McCullers	.05
77	Oddibe McDowell	.05
78	Paul Molitor	.50
79	Keith Moreland	.05
80	Jack Morris	.05
81	Jim Morrison	.05
82	Jerry Mumphrey	.05
83	Dale Murphy	.20
84	Eddie Murray	.50
85	Ben Oglivie	.05
86	Bob Ojeda	.05
87	Jesse Orosco	.05
88	Dave Parker	.05
89	Larry Parrish	.05
90	Tony Pena	.05
91	Jim Presley	.05
92	Kirby Puckett	.65
93	Dan Quisenberry	.05
94	Tim Raines	.05
95	Dennis Rasmussen	.05
96	Shane Rawley	.05
97	Johnny Ray	.05
98	Jeff Reardon	.05
99	Jim Rice	.25
100	Dave Righetti	.05
101	Cal Ripken, Jr.	2.00
102	Pete Rose	1.00
103	Nolan Ryan	2.00
104	Juan Samuel	.05
105	Ryne Sandberg	.65
106	Steve Sax	.05
107	Mike Schmidt	.85
108	Mike Scott	.05
109	Dave Smith	.05
110	Lee Smith	.05
111	Lonnie Smith	.05
112	Ozzie Smith	.65
113	Cory Snyder	.05
114	Darryl Strawberry	.05
115	Don Sutton	.45
116	Kent Tekulve	.05
117	Gorman Thomas	.05
118	Alan Trammell	.05
119	John Tudor	.05
120	Fernando Valenzuela	.05
121	Bob Welch	.05
122	Lou Whitaker	.05
123	Frank White	.05
124	Reggie Williams	.05
125	Willie Wilson	.05
126	Dave Winfield	.50
127	Mike Witt	.05
128	Todd Worrell	.05
129	Curt Young	.05
130	Robin Yount	.50
131	Checklist (Jose Canseco, Don Mattingly)	.25
132	Checklist (Bo Jackson, Eric Davis)	.05

Star Stickers Box Panels

Fleer issued on the bottoms of its Fleer Star Stickers wax pack boxes six player cards plus two team logo/checklist cards. The cards, which measure 2-1/2" x 3-1/2", are numbered S-1 through S-8, and are identical in design to the Star Stickers.

		NM/M
Complete Panel Set (2):		2.50
Complete Singles Set (8):		2.50
Common Single Player:		.10
Panel		2.00
2	Wade Boggs	.75
3	Bert Blyleven	.10
5	Phillies Logo	.05
6	Don Mattingly	1.50

Panel		1.00
1	Tigers Logo	.05
3	Jose Cruz	.05
5	Glenn Davis	.10
7	Bob Horner	.10

1988 Fleer

Alan Trammell
SHORTSTOP

A clean, uncluttered look was featured in the 1988 Fleer set. Cards in the standard 2-1/2" x 3-1/2" format feature blue and red diagonal lines on a white background. Player identification and team logo appears at top. Backs include personal information and career statistics, plus a new feature called "At Their Best." This feature graphically shows a player's pitching or hitting statistics for home and road games and how he fared during day games as opposed to night contests. The set includes 19 special cards (#622-640) and 12 "Major League Prospects" cards.

		NM/M
Retail Factory Set (672):		12.00
Hobby Factory Set (672):		10.00
Complete Set (660):		8.00
Common Player:		.05
Wax Pack (15):		.75
Wax Box (36):		12.00
Cello Pack (28):		1.25
Cello Box (24):		16.00
1	Keith Atherton	.05
2	Don Baylor	.05
3	Juan Berenguer	.05
4	Bert Blyleven	.10
5	Tom Brunansky	.05
6	Randy Bush	.05
7	Steve Carlton	.50
8	Mark Davidson RC	.05
9	George Frazier	.05
10	Gary Gaetti	.05
11	Greg Gagne	.05
12	Dan Gladden	.05
13	Kent Hrbek	.05
14	Gene Larkin RC	.05
15	Tim Laudner	.05
16	Steve Lombardozzi	.05
17	Al Newman	.05
18	Joe Niekro	.05
19	Kirby Puckett	.65
20	Jeff Reardon	.05
21a	Dan Schatzader (Incorrect spelling.)	.10
21b	Dan Schatzader (Correct spelling.)	.05
22	Roy Smalley	.05
23	Mike Smithson	.05
24	Les Straker RC	.05
25	Frank Viola	.05
26	Jack Clark	.05
27	Vince Coleman	.05
28	Danny Cox	.05
29	Bill Dawley	.05
30	Ken Dayley	.05
31	Doug DeCinces	.05
32	Curt Ford	.05
33	Bob Forsch	.05
34	David Green	.05
35	Tom Herr	.05
36	Ricky Horton	.05
37	Lance Johnson RC	.25
38	Steve Lake	.05
39	Jim Lindeman	.05
40	Joe Magrane RC	.10
41	Greg Mathews	.05
42	Willie McGee	.05
43	John Morris	.05
44	Jose Oquendo	.05
45	Tony Pena	.05
46	Terry Pendleton	.05
47	Ozzie Smith	.65
48	John Tudor	.05
49	Lee Tunnell	.05
50	Todd Worrell	.05
51	Doyle Alexander	.05
52	Dave Bergman	.05
53	Tom Brookens	.05
54	Darrell Evans	.05
55	Kirk Gibson	.05
56	Mike Heath	.05
57	Mike Henneman RC	.05
58	Willie Hernandez	.05
59	Larry Herndon	.05

60	Eric King	.05
61	Chet Lemon	.05
62	Scott Lusader RC	.05
63	Bill Madlock	.05
64	Jack Morris	.05
65	Jim Morrison	.05
66	Matt Nokes	.05
67	Dan Petry	.05
68a	Jeff Robinson RC (Born 12-13-60 on back.)	.25
68b	Jeff Robinson RC (Born 12/14/61 on back.)	.10
69	Pat Sheridan	.05
70	Nate Snell	.05
71	Frank Tanana	.05
72	Walt Terrell	.05
73	Mark Thurmond	.05
74	Alan Trammell	.05
75	Lou Whitaker	.05
76	Mike Aldrete	.05
77	Bob Brenly	.05
78	Will Clark	.05
79	Chili Davis	.05
80	Kelly Downs	.05
81	Dave Dravecky	.05
82	Scott Garrelts	.05
83	Atlee Hammaker	.05
84	Dave Henderson	.05
85	Mike Krukow	.05
86	Mike LaCoss	.05
87	Craig Lefferts	.05
88	Jeff Leonard	.05
89	Candy Maldonado	.05
90	Ed Milner	.05
91	Bob Melvin	.05
92	Kevin Mitchell	.05
93	Jon Perlman RC	.05
94	Rick Reuschel	.05
95	Don Robinson	.05
96	Chris Speier	.05
97	Harry Spilman	.05
98	Robbie Thompson	.05
99	Jose Uribe	.05
100	Mark Wasinger RC	.05
101	Matt Williams	.05
102	Jesse Barfield	.05
103	George Bell	.05
104	Juan Beniquez	.05
105	John Cerutti	.05
106	Jim Clancy	.05
107	Rob Ducey RC	.05
108	Mark Eichhorn	.05
109	Tony Fernandez	.05
110	Cecil Fielder	.05
111	Kelly Gruber	.05
112	Tom Henke	.05
113	Garth Iorg (lorg)	.05
114	Jimmy Key	.05
115	Rick Leach	.05
116	Manny Lee	.05
117	Nelson Liriano RC	.05
118	Fred McGriff	.05
119	Lloyd Moseby	.05
120	Rance Mulliniks	.05
121	Jeff Musselman	.05
122	Jose Nunez RC	.05
123	Dave Stieb	.05
124	Willie Upshaw	.05
125	Duane Ward RC	.05
126	Ernie Whitt	.05
127	Rick Aguilera	.05
128	Wally Backman	.05
129	Mark Carreon	.10
130	Gary Carter	.50
131	David Cone RC	.05
132	Ron Darling	.05
133	Len Dykstra	.05
134	Sid Fernandez	.05
135	Dwight Gooden	.05
136	Keith Hernandez	.05
137	Gregg Jefferies RC	.50
138	Howard Johnson	.05
139	Terry Leach	.05
140	Barry Lyons RC	.05
141	Dave Magadan	.05
142	Roger McDowell	.05
143	Kevin McReynolds	.05
144	Keith Miller RC	.05
145	John Mitchell RC	.05
146	Randy Myers	.05
147	Bob Ojeda	.05
148	Jesse Orosco	.05
149	Rafael Santana	.05
150	Doug Sisk	.05
151	Darryl Strawberry	.05
152	Tim Teufel	.05
153	Gene Walter	.05
154	Mookie Wilson	.05
155	Jay Aldrich RC	.05
156	Chris Bosio	.05
157	Glenn Braggs	.05
158	Greg Brock	.05
159	Juan Castillo	.05
160	Mark Clear	.05
161	Cecil Cooper	.05
162	Chuck Crim RC	.05
163	Rob Deer	.05
164	Mike Felder	.05
165	Jim Gantner	.05
166	Ted Higuera	.05
167	Steve Kiefer	.05
168	Rick Manning	.05
169	Paul Molitor	.50
170	Juan Nieves	.05
171	Dan Plesac	.05
172	Earnest Riles	.05
173	Bill Schroeder	.05
174	Steve Stanicek RC	.05

175	B.J. Surhoff	.05
176	Dale Sveum	.05
177	Bill Wegman	.05
178	Robin Yount	.50
179	Hubie Brooks	.05
180	Tim Burke	.05
181	Casey Candaele	.05
182	Mike Fitzgerald	.05
183	Tom Foley	.05
184	Andres Galarraga	.05
185	Neal Heaton	.05
186	Wallace Johnson	.05
187	Vance Law	.05
188	Dennis Martinez	.05
189	Bob McClure	.05
190	Andy McGaffigan	.05
191	Reid Nichols	.05
192	Pascual Perez	.05
193	Tim Raines	.05
194	Jeff Reed	.05
195	Bob Sebra	.05
196	Bryn Smith	.05
197	Randy St. Claire	.05
198	Tim Wallach	.05
199	Mitch Webster	.05
200	Herm Winningham	.05
201	Floyd Youmans	.05
202	Brad Arnsberg RC	.05
203	Rick Cerone	.05
204	Pat Clements	.05
205	Henry Cotto	.05
206	Mike Easler	.05
207	Ron Guidry	.10
208	Bill Gullickson	.05
209	Rickey Henderson	.50
210	Charles Hudson	.05
211	Tommy John	.10
212	Roberto Kelly RC	.25
213	Ron Kittle	.05
214	Don Mattingly	.75
215	Bobby Meacham	.05
216	Mike Pagliarulo	.05
217	Dan Pasqua	.05
218	Willie Randolph	.05
219	Rick Rhoden	.05
220	Dave Righetti	.05
221	Jerry Royster	.05
222	Tim Stoddard	.05
223	Wayne Tolleson	.05
224	Gary Ward	.05
225	Claudell Washington	.05
226	Dave Winfield	.50
227	Buddy Bell	.05
228	Tom Browning	.05
229	Dave Concepcion	.05
230	Kal Daniels	.05
231	Eric Davis	.05
232	Bo Diaz	.05
233	Nick Esasky	.05
234	John Franco	.05
235	Guy Hoffman	.05
236	Tom Hume	.05
237	Tracy Jones	.05
238	Bill Landrum RC	.05
239	Barry Larkin	.05
240	Terry McGriff RC	.05
241	Rob Murphy	.05
242	Ron Oester	.05
243	Dave Parker	.05
244	Pat Perry	.05
245	Ted Power	.05
246	Dennis Rasmussen	.05
247	Ron Robinson	.05
248	Kurt Stillwell	.05
249	Jeff Treadway RC	.05
250	Frank Williams	.05
251	Steve Balboni	.05
252	Bud Black	.05
253	Thad Bosley	.05
254	George Brett	.75
255	John Davis RC	.05
256	Steve Farr	.05
257	Gene Garber	.05
258	Jerry Gleaton	.05
259	Mark Gubicza	.05
260	Bo Jackson	.10
261	Danny Jackson	.05
262	Ross Jones RC	.05
263	Charlie Leibrandt	.05
264	Bill Pecota RC	.05
265	Melido Perez RC	.05
266	Jamie Quirk	.05
267	Dan Quisenberry	.05
268	Bret Saberhagen	.05
269	Angel Salazar	.05
270	Kevin Seitzer	.05
271	Danny Tartabull	.05
272	Gary Thurman RC	.05
273	Frank White	.05
274	Willie Wilson	.05
275	Tony Bernazard	.05
276	Jose Canseco	.30
277	Mike Davis	.05
278	Storm Davis	.05
279	Dennis Eckersley	.40
280	Alfredo Griffin	.05
281	Rick Honeycutt	.05
282	Jay Howell	.05
283	Reggie Jackson	.65
284	Dennis Lamp	.05
285	Carney Lansford	.05
286	Mark McGwire	.75
287	Dwayne Murphy	.05
288	Gene Nelson	.05
289	Steve Ontiveros	.05
290	Tony Phillips	.05
291	Eric Plunk	.05
292	Luis Polonia RC	.15

293	Rick Rodriguez RC	.05
294	Terry Steinbach	.05
295	Dave Stewart	.05
296	Curt Young	.05
297	Luis Aguayo	.05
298	Steve Bedrosian	.05
299	Jeff Calhoun	.05
300	Don Carman	.05
301	Todd Frohwirth RC	.05
302	Greg Gross	.05
303	Kevin Gross	.05
304	Von Hayes	.05
305	Keith Hughes RC	.05
306	Mike Jackson RC	.05
307	Chris James	.05
308	Steve Jeltz	.05
309	Mike Maddux	.05
310	Lance Parrish	.05
311	Shane Rawley	.05
312	Wally Ritchie RC	.05
313	Bruce Ruffin	.05
314	Juan Samuel	.05
315	Mike Schmidt	.75
316	Rick Schu	.05
317	Jeff Stone	.05
318	Kent Tekulve	.05
319	Milt Thompson	.05
320	Glenn Wilson	.05
321	Rafael Belliard	.05
322	Barry Bonds	1.00
323	Bobby Bonilla	.05
324	Sid Bream	.05
325	John Cangelosi	.05
326	Mike Diaz	.05
327	Doug Drabek	.05
328	Mike Dunne RC	.05
329	Brian Fisher	.05
330	Brett Gideon RC	.05
331	Terry Harper	.05
332	Bob Kipper	.05
333	Mike LaValliere	.05
334	Jose Lind RC	.15
335	Junior Ortiz	.05
336	Vicente Palacios RC	.05
337	Bob Patterson RC	.05
338	Al Pedrique RC	.05
339	R.J. Reynolds	.05
340	John Smiley	.05
341	Andy Van Slyke	.05
342	Bob Walk	.05
343	Marty Barrett	.05
344	Todd Benzinger RC	.05
345	Wade Boggs	.65
346	Tom Bolton RC	.05
347	Oil Can Boyd	.05
348	Ellis Burks	.05
349	Roger Clemens	.75
350	Steve Crawford	.05
351	Dwight Evans	.05
352	Wes Gardner RC	.05
353	Rich Gedman	.05
354	Mike Greenwell	.05
355	Sam Horn RC	.05
356	Bruce Hurst	.05
357	John Marzano RC	.05
358	Al Nipper	.05
359	Spike Owen	.05
360	Jody Reed RC	.15
361	Jim Rice	.20
362	Ed Romero	.05
363	Kevin Romine RC	.05
364	Joe Sambito	.05
365	Calvin Schiraldi	.05
366	Jeff Sellers	.05
367	Bob Stanley	.05
368	Scott Bankhead	.05
369	Phil Bradley	.05
370	Scott Bradley	.05
371	Mickey Brantley	.05
372	Mike Campbell RC	.05
373	Alvin Davis	.05
374	Lee Guetterman	.05
375	Dave Hengel RC	.05
376	Mike Kingery	.05
377	Mark Langston	.05
378	Edgar Martinez RC	1.00
379	Mike Moore	.05
380	Mike Morgan	.05
381	John Moses	.05
382	Donnell Nixon RC	.05
383	Edwin Nunez	.05
384	Ken Phelps	.05
385	Jim Presley	.05
386	Rey Quinones	.05
387	Jerry Reed	.05
388	Harold Reynolds	.05
389	Dave Valle	.05
390	Bill Wilkinson RC	.05
391	Harold Baines	.05
392	Floyd Bannister	.05
393	Daryl Boston	.05
394	Ivan Calderon	.05
395	Jose DeLeon	.05
396	Richard Dotson	.05
397	Carlton Fisk	.50
398	Ozzie Guillen	.05
399	Ron Hassey	.05
400	Donnie Hill	.05
401	Bob James	.05
402	Dave LaPoint	.05
403	Bill Lindsey RC	.05
404	Bill Long RC	.05
405	Steve Lyons	.05
406	Fred Manrique RC	.05
407	Jack McDowell RC	.25
408	Gary Redus	.05
409	Ray Searage	.05
410	Bobby Thigpen	.05

411	Greg Walker	.05
412	Kenny Williams RC	.05
413	Jim Winn	.05
414	Jody Davis	.05
415	Andre Dawson	.25
416	Brian Dayett	.05
417	Bob Dernier	.05
418	Frank DiPino	.05
419	Shawon Dunston	.05
420	Leon Durham	.05
421	Les Lancaster RC	.10
422	Ed Lynch	.05
423	Greg Maddux	.75
424	Dave Martinez	.05
425a	Keith Moreland (Bunting, photo actually Jody Davis.)	2.00
425b	Keith Moreland (Standing upright, correct photo.)	.05
426	Jamie Moyer	.05
427	Jerry Mumphrey	.05
428	Paul Noce RC	.05
429	Rafael Palmeiro	.40
430	Wade Rowdon RC	.05
431	Ryne Sandberg	.65
432	Scott Sanderson	.05
433	Lee Smith	.05
434	Jim Sundberg	.05
435	Rick Sutcliffe	.05
436	Manny Trillo	.05
437	Juan Agosto	.05
438	Larry Andersen	.05
439	Alan Ashby	.05
440	Kevin Bass	.05
441	Ken Caminiti RC	.25
442	Rocky Childress RC	.05
443	Jose Cruz	.05
444	Danny Darwin	.05
445	Glenn Davis	.05
446	Jim Deshaies	.05
447	Bill Doran	.05
448	Ty Gainey	.05
449	Billy Hatcher	.05
450	Jeff Heathcock	.05
451	Bob Knepper	.05
452	Rob Mallicoat RC	.05
453	Dave Meads RC	.05
454	Craig Reynolds	.05
455	Nolan Ryan	1.00
456	Mike Scott	.05
457	Dave Smith	.05
458	Denny Walling	.05
459	Robbie Wine RC	.05
460	Gerald Young RC	.05
461	Bob Brower	.05
462a	Jerry Browne (White player, photo actually Bob Brower.)	2.00
462b	Jerry Browne (Black player, correct photo.)	.05
463	Steve Buechele	.05
464	Edwin Correa	.05
465	Cecil Espy RC	.05
466	Scott Fletcher	.05
467	Jose Guzman	.05
468	Greg Harris	.05
469	Charlie Hough	.05
470	Pete Incaviglia	.05
471	Paul Kilgus RC	.05
472	Mike Loynd	.05
473	Oddibe McDowell	.05
474	Dale Mohorcic	.05
475	Pete O'Brien	.05
476	Larry Parrish	.05
477	Geno Petralli	.05
478	Jeff Russell	.05
479	Ruben Sierra	.05
480	Mike Stanley	.05
481	Curtis Wilkerson	.05
482	Mitch Williams	.05
483	Bobby Witt	.05
484	Tony Armas	.05
485	Bob Boone	.05
486	Bill Buckner	.05
487	DeWayne Buice RC	.05
488	Brian Downing	.05
489	Chuck Finley	.05
490	Willie Fraser	.05
491	Jack Howell	.05
492	Ruppert Jones	.05
493	Wally Joyner	.05
494	Jack Lazorko	.05
495	Gary Lucas	.05
496	Kirk McCaskill	.05
497	Mark McLemore	.05
498	Darrell Miller	.05
499	Greg Minton	.05
500	Donnie Moore	.05
501	Gus Polidor	.05
502	Johnny Ray	.05
503	Mark Ryal RC	.05
504	Dick Schofield	.05
505	Don Sutton	.40
506	Devon White	.05
507	Mike Witt	.05
508	Dave Anderson	.05
509	Tim Belcher RC	.05
510	Ralph Bryant	.05
511	Tim Crews RC	.15
512	Mike Devereaux RC	.10
513	Mariano Duncan	.05
514	Pedro Guerrero	.05
515	Jeff Hamilton RC	.05
516	Mickey Hatcher	.05
517	Brad Havens	.05
518	Orel Hershiser	.05
519	Shawn Hillegas RC	.05
520	Ken Howell	.05

521	Tim Leary	.05
522	Mike Marshall	.05
523	Steve Sax	.05
524	Mike Scioscia	.05
525	Mike Sharperson RC	.05
526	John Shelby	.05
527	Franklin Stubbs	.05
528	Fernando Valenzuela	.05
529	Bob Welch	.05
530	Matt Young	.05
531	Jim Acker	.05
532	Paul Assenmacher	.05
533	Jeff Blauser RC	.10
534	Joe Boever RC	.05
535	Martin Clary RC	.05
536	Kevin Coffman RC	.05
537	Jeff Dedmon	.05
538	Ron Gant RC	.50
539	Tom Glavine RC	2.00
540	Ken Griffey	.05
541	Al Hall	.05
542	Glenn Hubbard	.05
543	Dion James	.05
544	Dale Murphy	.20
545	Ken Oberkfell	.05
546	David Palmer	.05
547	Gerald Perry	.05
548	Charlie Puleo	.05
549	Ted Simmons	.05
550	Zane Smith	.05
551	Andres Thomas	.05
552	Ozzie Virgil	.05
553	Don Aase	.05
554	Jeff Ballard RC	.05
555	Eric Bell	.05
556	Mike Boddicker	.05
557	Ken Dixon	.05
558	Jim Dwyer	.05
559	Ken Gerhart	.05
560	Rene Gonzales RC	.05
561	Mike Griffin	.05
562	John Hayban (Habyan)	.05
563	Terry Kennedy	.05
564	Ray Knight	.05
565	Lee Lacy	.05
566	Fred Lynn	.05
567	Eddie Murray	.50
568	Tom Niedenfuer	.05
569	Bill Ripken RC	.05
570	Cal Ripken, Jr.	1.00
571	Dave Schmidt	.05
572	Larry Sheets	.05
573	Pete Stanicek RC	.05
574	Mark Williamson RC	.05
575	Mike Young	.05
576	Shawn Abner RC	.05
577	Greg Booker	.05
578	Chris Brown	.05
579	Keith Comstock RC	.05
580	Joey Cora RC	.05
581	Mark Davis	.05
582	Tim Flannery	.05
583	Goose Gossage	.05
584	Mark Grant	.05
585	Tony Gwynn	.65
586	Andy Hawkins	.05
587	Stan Jefferson	.05
588	Jimmy Jones	.05
589	John Kruk	.05
590	Shane Mack	.10
591	Carmelo Martinez	.05
592	Lance McCullers	.05
593	Eric Nolte RC	.05
594	Randy Ready	.05
595	Luis Salazar	.05
596	Benito Santiago	.05
597	Eric Show	.05
598	Garry Templeton	.05
599	Ed Whitson	.05
600	Scott Bailes	.05
601	Chris Bando	.05
602	Jay Bell RC	.50
603	Brett Butler	.05
604	Tom Candiotti	.05
605	Joe Carter	.05
606	Carmen Castillo	.05
607	Brian Dorsett RC	.05
608	John Farrell RC	.05
609	Julio Franco	.05
610	Mel Hall	.05
611	Tommy Hinzo RC	.05
612	Brook Jacoby	.05
613	Doug Jones RC	.10
614	Ken Schrom	.05
615	Cory Snyder	.05
616	Sammy Stewart	.05
617	Greg Swindell	.05
618	Pat Tabler	.05
619	Ed Vande Berg	.05
620	Eddie Williams RC	.05
621	Rich Yett	.05

622	Slugging Sophomores (Wally Joyner, Cory Snyder)	.10
623	Dominican Dynamite (George Bell, Pedro Guerrero)	.05
624	Oakland's Power Team (Jose Canseco, Mark McGwire)	.50
625	Classic Relief (Dan Plesac, Dave Righetti)	.05
626	All-Star Righties (Jack Morris, Bret Saberhagen, Mike Witt)	.05
627	Game Closers (Steve Bedrosian, John Franco)	.05
628	Masters of the Double Play (Ryne Sandberg, Ozzie Smith)	.50
629	Rookie Record Setter (Mark McGwire)	.50
630	Changing the Guard in Boston (Todd Benzinger, Ellis Burks, Mike Greenwell)	.10
631	N.L. Batting Champs (Tony Gwynn, Tim Raines)	.20
632	Pitching Magic (Orel Hershiser, Mike Scott)	.05
633	Big Bats At First (Mark McGwire, Pat Tabler)	.50
634	Hitting King and the Thief (Tony Gwynn, Vince Coleman)	.15
635	A.L. Slugging Shortstops (Tony Fernandez, Cal Ripken, Jr., Alan Trammell)	.40
636	Tried and True Sluggers (Gary Carter, Mike Schmidt)	.40
637	Crunch Time (Eric Davis)	.05
638	A.L. All-Stars (Matt Nokes, Kirby Puckett)	.25
639	N.L. All-Stars (Keith Hernandez, Dale Murphy)	.10
640	The "O's" Brothers (Bill Ripken, Cal Ripken, Jr.)	.50
641	Major League Prospects (Mark Grace RC, Darrin Jackson RC)	1.00
642	Major League Prospects (Damon Berryhill RC, Jeff Montgomery)	.20
643	Major League Prospects (Felix Fermin RC, Jessie Reid RC)	.05
644	Major League Prospects (Greg Myers RC, Greg Tabor RC)	.05
645	Major League Prospects (Jim Eppard RC, Joey Meyer RC)	.05
646	Major League Prospects (Adam Peterson RC, Randy Velarde RC)	.10
647	Major League Prospects (Chris Gwynn RC, Peter Smith RC)	.15
648	Major League Prospects (Greg Jelks RC, Tom Newell RC)	.05
649	Major League Prospects (Mario Diaz RC, Clay Parker RC)	.05
650	Major League Prospects (Jack Savage RC, Todd Simmons RC)	.05
651	Major League Prospects (John Burkett RC, Kirt Manwaring RC)	.30
652	Major League Prospects (Dave Otto RC, Walt Weiss RC)	.25
653	Major League Prospects (Randell Byers (Randall) RC, Jeff King RC)	.25
654a	Checklist 1-101 (21 is Schatzader)	.10
654b	Checklist 1-101 (21 is Schatzeder)	.05
655	Checklist 102-201	.05
656	Checklist 202-296	.05
657	Checklist 297-390	.05
658	Checklist 391-483	.05
659	Checklist 484-575	.05
660	Checklist 576-660	.05

Headliners

This six-card set was inserted in Fleer three-packs, sold by retail outlets and hobby dealers nationwide. The card fronts feature crisp full-color player cut-outs printed on a gray and white facsimile sports page. "Fleer Headliners 1988" is printed in black and red on a white banner across the top of the card, both front and back. A similar white banner across the card bottom bears the black and white National or American League logo and a red player/team name. Card backs are black on gray with red accents and include the card number and a narrative career summary.

		NM/M
Complete Set (6):		3.00
Common Player:		.25
1	Don Mattingly	1.50
2	Mark McGwire	2.00
3	Jack Morris	.15
4	Darryl Strawberry	.15
5	Dwight Gooden	.15
6	Tim Raines	.15

'87 World Series

Highlights of the 1987 Series are captured in this full-color insert set found only in Fleer's regular 660-card factory sets. This second World Series edition by Fleer features cards framed in red, with a blue and white starred bunting draped over the upper edges of the photo and a brief photo caption printed on a yellow band across the lower border. Numbered card backs are red, white and blue and include a description of the action pictured on the front, with stats for the Series.

		NM/M
Complete Set (12):		2.50
Common Player:		.25
1	"Grand" Hero In Game 1 (Dan Gladden)	.25
2	The Cardinals' "Bush" Whacked (Randy Bush, Tony Pena)	.25
3	Masterful Performance Turns Momentum (John Tudor)	.25
4	Throw Smoke! (Tony Pena, Todd Worrell)	.25
5	Cardinal Attack - Disruptive Speed (Vince Coleman)	.25

All-Stars

For the third consecutive year, Fleer randomly inserted All-Star Team cards in its wax and cello packs. Twelve cards make up the set, with players chosen for the set being Fleer's idea of a major league All-Star team.

	NM/M
Complete Set (12):	3.00
Common Player:	.10

1	Matt Nokes	.10
2	Tom Henke	.10
3	Ted Higuera	.10
4	Roger Clemens	1.50
5	George Bell	.10
6	Andre Dawson	.25
7	Eric Davis	.10
8	Wade Boggs	.85
9	Alan Trammell	.10
10	Juan Samuel	.10
11	Jack Clark	.10
12	Paul Molitor	.75

Box Panels

Fleer's third annual box-bottom issue once again included 16 full-color trading cards printed on the bottoms of four different wax and cello pack retail display boxes. Each box contains three player cards and one team logo card. Player cards follow the same design as the basic 1988 Fleer issue. Standard size, the cards are numbered C-1 through C-16.

		NM/M
Complete Panel Set (4):		4.00
Complete Singles Set (16):		4.00
Common Panel:		1.00
Common Single Player:		.10
Panel		1.50
1	Cardinals Logo	.05
11	Mike Schmidt	1.00
14	Dave Stewart	.10
15	Tim Wallach	.10
Panel		1.00
2	Dwight Evans	.10
8	Shane Rawley	.10
9	Ryne Sandberg	.75
13	Tigers Logo	.05
Panel		1.25
3	Andres Galarraga	.10
9	Dale Murphy	.45
6	Giants Logo	.05
12	Kevin Seitzer	.10
Panel		1.00
4	Wally Joyner	.10
5	Twins Logo	.05
7	Kirby Puckett	1.00
16	Todd Worrell	.10

Glossy Tin

In its second year of production, Fleer radically reduced production numbers on its glossy version of the 1988 baseball card set. With production estimates in the 60,000 set range, values of the '88 tin glossies are about double those of the regular issue cards. Once again the issue was sold only as complete sets in colorful lithographed metal boxes.

	NM/M
Complete Set (672):	20.00
Common Player:	.15

Update

This update set (numbered U-1 through U-132 are 2-1/2" x 3-1/2") features traded veterans and rookies in a mixture of full-color action shots and close-ups, framed by white borders with red and blue stripes. The backs are red, white and blue-gray and include personal info, along with yearly and "At Their Best" (day, night, home, road) stats charts. The set was packaged in white cardboard boxes with red and blue stripes. A glossy-coated edition of the update set was issued in its own box and is valued at two times the regular issue.

		NM/M
Complete Set (132):		5.00
Common Player:		.05
1	Jose Bautista RC	.05
2	Joe Orsulak	.05
3	Doug Sisk	.05
4	Craig Worthington RC	.05
5	Mike Boddicker	.05
6	Rick Cerone	.05
7	Larry Parrish	.05
8	Lee Smith	.10
9	Mike Smithson	.05
10	John Trautwein RC	.05
11	Sherman Corbett RC	.05
12	Chili Davis	.05
13	Jim Eppard	.05
14	Bryan Harvey RC	.05
15	John Davis	.05
16	Dave Gallagher RC	.05
17	Ricky Horton	.05
18	Dan Pasqua	.05
19	Melido Perez	.05
20	Jose Segura RC	.05
21	Andy Allanson	.05
22	Jon Perlman	.05
23	Domingo Ramos	.05
24	Rick Rodriguez	.05
25	Willie Upshaw	.05
26	Paul Gibson RC	.05
27	Don Heinkel RC	.05
28	Ray Knight	.05
29	Gary Pettis	.05
30	Luis Salazar	.05
31	Mike MacFarlane	.05
32	Jeff Montgomery	.05
33	Ted Power	.05
34	Israel Sanchez RC	.05
35	Kurt Stillwell	.05
36	Pat Tabler	.05
37	Don August RC	.05
38	Darryl Hamilton RC	.05
39	Jeff Leonard	.05
40	Joey Meyer	.05
41	Allan Anderson	.05
42	Brian Harper	.05
43	Tom Herr	.05
44	Charlie Lea	.05
45	John Moses	.05
46	John Candelaria	.05
47	Jack Clark	.05
48	Richard Dotson	.05
49	Al Leiter RC	.05
50	Rafael Santana	.05
51	Don Slaught	.05
52	Todd Burns RC	.05
53	Dave Henderson	.05
54	Doug Jennings RC	.05
55	Dave Parker	.05
56	Walt Weiss	.05
57	Bob Welch	.05
58	Henry Cotto	.05
59	Marion Diaz (Mario)	.05
60	Mike Jackson	.05
61	Bill Swift	.05
62	Jose Cecena RC	.05
63	Ray Hayward RC	.05
64	Jim Steels RC	.05
65	Pat Borders RC	.05
66	Sil Campusano RC	.05
67	Mike Flanagan	.05
68	Todd Stottlemyre RC	.05
69	David Wells RC	.05
70	Jose Alvarez RC	.05
71	Paul Runge	.05
72	Cesar Jimenez RC (German)	.05
73	Pete Smith	.05
74	John Smoltz RC	1.50
75	Damon Berryhill	.05
76	Goose Gossage	.05
77	Mark Grace	.10
78	Darrin Jackson	.05
79	Vance Law	.05
80	Jeff Pico RC	.05
81	Gary Varsho RC	.05
82	Tim Birtsas	.05
83	Rob Dibble RC	.05
84	Danny Jackson	.05
85	Paul O'Neill	.05
86	Jose Rijo	.05
87	Chris Sabo RC	.25
88	John Fishel RC	.05
89	Craig Biggio RC	4.00
90	Terry Puhl	.05
91	Rafael Ramirez	.05
92	Louie Meadows RC	.05
93	Kirk Gibson	.05
94	Alfredo Griffin	.05
95	Jay Howell	.05
96	Jesse Orosco	.05
97	Alejandro Pena	.05
98	Tracy Woodson RC	.05
99	John Dopson RC	.05
100	Brian Holman RC	.05
101	Rex Hudler RC	.05

102	Jeff Parrett RC	.05
103	Nelson Santovenia RC	.05
104	Kevin Elster	.05
105	Jeff Innis RC	.05
106	Mackey Sasser RC	.05
107	Phil Bradley	.05
108	Danny Clay RC	.05
109	Greg Harris	.05
110	Ricky Jordan RC	.05
111	David Palmer	.05
112	Jim Gott	.05
113	Tommy Gregg RC (Photo actually Randy Milligan.)	.05
114	Barry Jones	.05
115	Randy Milligan RC	.05
116	Luis Alicea RC	.05
117	Tom Brunansky	.05
118	John Costello RC	.05
119	Jose DeLeon	.05
120	Bob Horner	.05
121	Scott Terry RC	.05
122	Roberto Alomar RC	1.50
123	Dave Leiper	.05
124	Keith Moreland	.05
125	Mark Parent RC	.05
126	Dennis Rasmussen	.05
127	Randy Bockus	.05
128	Brett Butler	.05
129	Donell Nixon	.05
130	Earnest Riles	.05
131	Roger Samuels RC	.05
132	Checklist	.05

Update Glossy Tin

The glossy version of the 1988 Fleer Update set differs from the regular-issue Update set only in the high-gloss finish applied to the cards' fronts and the lithographed metal box in which sets were sold.

	NM/M
Complete Set (132):	9.00
Common Player:	.15

Award Winners

This limited edition boxed set of 1987 award-winning player cards also includes six team logo sticker cards. Red, white, blue and yellow bands border the sharp, full-color player photos printed below a "Fleer Award Winners 1988" banner. The player's name and award are printed beneath the photo. Flip sides are red, white and blue and list personal information, career data, team logo and card number. This set was sold exclusively at 7-11 stores nationwide.

		NM/M
Complete Set (44):		3.50
Common Player:		.05
1	Steve Bedrosian	.05
2	George Bell	.05
3	Wade Boggs	.65
4	Jose Canseco	.30
5	Will Clark	.05
6	Roger Clemens	.75
7	Kal Daniels	.05
8	Eric Davis	.05
9	Andre Dawson	.25
10	Mike Dunne	.05
11	Dwight Evans	.05
12	Carlton Fisk	.50
13	Julio Franco	.05
14	Dwight Gooden	.05
15	Pedro Guerrero	.05
16	Tony Gwynn	.65
17	Orel Hershiser	.05
18	Tom Henke	.05
19	Ted Higuera	.05
20	Charlie Hough	.05
21	Wally Joyner	.05
22	Jimmy Key	.05
23	Don Mattingly	.75
24	Mark McGwire	1.50
25	Paul Molitor	.50
26	Jack Morris	.05
27	Dale Murphy	.20
28	Terry Pendleton	.05
29	Kirby Puckett	.65
30	Tim Raines	.05
31	Jeff Reardon	.05
32	Harold Reynolds	.05
33	Dave Righetti	.05

34	Benito Santiago	.05
35	Mike Schmidt	.75
36	Mike Scott	.05
37	Kevin Seitzer	.05
38	Larry Sheets	.05
39	Ozzie Smith	.65
40	Darryl Strawberry	.05
41	Rick Sutcliffe	.05
42	Danny Tartabull	.05
43	Alan Trammell	.05
44	Tim Wallach	.05

Baseball All-Stars

This limited edition boxed set features major league All-Stars. The standard-size cards feature a sporty bright blue and yellow striped background. Card backs feature a blue and white striped design with a yellow highlighted section at the top that contains the player name, card number, team, position and personal data, followed by lifetime career stats. Fleer All-Stars are cellowrapped in blue and yellow striped boxes with checklist backs. The set includes six team logo sticker cards that feature black-and-white aerial shots of major league ballparks. The set was marketed exclusively by Ben Franklin stores.

		NM/M
Complete Set (44):		4.00
Common Player:		.05
1	George Bell	.05
2	Wade Boggs	.65
3	Bobby Bonilla	.05
4	George Brett	.85
5	Jose Canseco	.35
6	Jack Clark	.05
7	Will Clark	.05
8	Roger Clemens	.85
9	Eric Davis	.05
10	Andre Dawson	.25
11	Julio Franco	.05
12	Dwight Gooden	.05
13	Tony Gwynn	.65
14	Orel Hershiser	.05
15	Teddy Higuera	.05
16	Charlie Hough	.05
17	Kent Hrbek	.05
18	Bruce Hurst	.05
19	Wally Joyner	.05
20	Mark Langston	.05
21	Dave LaPoint	.05
22	Candy Maldonado	.05
23	Don Mattingly	.85
24	Roger McDowell	.05
25	Mark McGwire	1.00
26	Jack Morris	.05
27	Dale Murphy	.20
28	Eddie Murray	.50
29	Matt Nokes	.05
30	Kirby Puckett	.65
31	Tim Raines	.05
32	Willie Randolph	.05
33	Jeff Reardon	.05
34	Nolan Ryan	1.00
35	Juan Samuel	.05
36	Mike Schmidt	.85
37	Mike Scott	.05
38	Kevin Seitzer	.05
39	Ozzie Smith	.65
40	Darryl Strawberry	.05
41	Rick Sutcliffe	.05
42	Alan Trammell	.05
43	Tim Wallach	.05
44	Dave Winfield	.50

Baseball's Best

This boxed set of 44 standard-size cards (2-1/2" x 3-1/2") and six team logo stickers is the third annual issue from Fleer highlighting the best major league sluggers and pitchers. Five additional player cards were printed on retail display box bottoms, along with a checklist logo card (numbered C-1 through C-6). Full-color player photos are framed by a green border that fades to yellow. A red (slugger) or blue (pitcher) player name is printed be-

neath the photo. Backs are printed in green on a white background with yellow highlights. Card number, player name and personal info appear in a green vertical box on the left-hand side of the card back with a yellow cartoon-style team logo overprinted across a stats chart on the right. This set was produced by Fleer for exclusive distribution by McCrory's stores (McCrory, McClellan, J.J. Newberry, H.L. Green, TG&Y).

		NM/M
Complete Set (44):		4.00
Common Player:		.05
1	George Bell	.05
2	Wade Boggs	.65
3	Bobby Bonilla	.05
4	Tom Brunansky	.05
5	Ellis Burks	.05
6	Jose Canseco	.40
7	Joe Carter	.05
8	Will Clark	.05
9	Roger Clemens	.85
10	Eric Davis	.05
11	Glenn Davis	.05
12	Andre Dawson	.25
13	Dennis Eckersley	.45
14	Andres Galarraga	.05
15	Dwight Gooden	.05
16	Pedro Guerrero	.05
17	Tony Gwynn	.65
18	Orel Hershiser	.05
19	Ted Higuera	.05
20	Pete Incaviglia	.05
21	Danny Jackson	.05
22	Doug Jennings	.05
23	Mark Langston	.05
24	Dave LaPoint	.05
25	Mike LaValliere	.05
26	Don Mattingly	.85
27	Mark McGwire	1.00
28	Dale Murphy	.20
29	Ken Phelps	.05
30	Kirby Puckett	.65
31	Johnny Ray	.05
32	Jeff Reardon	.05
33	Dave Righetti	.05
34	Cal Ripkin, Jr. (Ripken)	1.50
35	Chris Sabo	.05
36	Mike Schmidt	.85
37	Mike Scott	.05
38	Kevin Seitzer	.05
39	Dave Stewart	.05
40	Darryl Strawberry	.05
41	Greg Swindell	.05
42	Frank Tanana	.05
43	Dave Winfield	.50
44	Todd Worrell	.05

Baseball's Best Box Panel

Six cards were placed on the bottoms of retail boxes of the Fleer Baseball's Best boxed sets in 1988. The cards, 2-1/2" x 3-1/2", are identical in design to cards found in the 44-card set. The cards are numbered C-1 through C-6 and were produced for distribution by McCrory stores and its affiliates.

		NM/M
Complete Panel Set:		1.50
Complete Singles Set (6):		1.50
Common Single Player:		.10
1	Ron Darling	.10
2	Rickey Henderson	.75
3	Carney Lansford	.10
4	Rafael Palmeiro	.60
5	Frank Viola	.10
6	Minnesota Twins Logo	.05

Exciting Stars

This boxed set showcases star major leaguers. Player photos are slanted upwards to the right, framed by a blue border with a red and white stripe across the middle. Card backs are numbered and printed in red, white and blue. The set was packaged in a checklist box, with six team logo sticker cards featuring black-and-white stadium photos on the flip sides. Exciting Stars was distributed via Cumberland Farm stores throughout the northeastern U.S. and Florida.

		NM/M
Complete Set (44):		3.00
Common Player:		.05
1	Harold Baines	.05
2	Kevin Bass	.05
3	George Bell	.05
4	Wade Boggs	.65
5	Mickey Brantley	.05
6	Sid Bream	.05
7	Jose Canseco	.30
8	Jack Clark	.05
9	Will Clark	.05
10	Roger Clemens	.85
11	Vince Coleman	.05
12	Eric Davis	.05
13	Andre Dawson	.25
14	Julio Franco	.05
15	Dwight Gooden	.05
16	Mike Greenwell	.05
17	Tony Gwynn	.65
18	Von Hayes	.02
19	Tom Henke	.05
20	Orel Hershiser	.05
21	Teddy Higuera	.05
22	Brook Jacoby	.05
23	Wally Joyner	.05
24	Jimmy Key	.05
25	Don Mattingly	.85
26	Mark McGwire	1.00
27	Jack Morris	.05
28	Dale Murphy	.20
29	Matt Nokes	.05
30	Kirby Puckett	.65
31	Tim Raines	.05
32	Ryne Sandberg	.65
33	Benito Santiago	.05
34	Mike Schmidt	.85
35	Mike Scott	.05
36	Kevin Seitzer	.05
37	Larry Sheets	.05
38	Ruben Sierra	.05
39	Darryl Strawberry	.05
40	Rick Sutcliffe	.05
41	Danny Tartabull	.05
42	Alan Trammell	.05
43	Fernando Valenzuela	.05
44	Devon White	.05

Hottest Stars

This boxed set of standard-size player cards and six team logo stickers was produced by Fleer for exclusive distribution at Revco drug stores nationwide. Card fronts feature full-color photos of players representing every major league team. Photos are framed in red, orange and yellow, with a blue-and-

white player name printed at bottom. A flaming baseball logo bearing the words "Hottest Stars" appears in the lower-left corner of the photo. Card backs are red, white and blue. The player's name, position, card number and team logo are printed at top, followed by a stats box and personal data. The set also includes six team logo sticker cards with flipside stadium photos in black-and-white.

		NM/M
Complete Set (44):		3.50
Common Player:		.05
1	George Bell	.05
2	Wade Boggs	.65
3	Bobby Bonilla	.05
4	George Brett	.85
5	Jose Canseco	.30
6	Will Clark	.05
7	Roger Clemens	.85
8	Eric Davis	.05
9	Andre Dawson	.25
10	Tony Fernandez	.05
11	Julio Franco	.05
12	Gary Gaetti	.05
13	Dwight Gooden	.05
14	Mike Greenwell	.05
15	Tony Gwynn	.65
16	Rickey Henderson	.50
17	Keith Hernandez	.05
18	Tom Herr	.05
19	Orel Hershiser	.05
20	Ted Higuera	.05
21	Wally Joyner	.05
22	Jimmy Key	.05
23	Mark Langston	.05
24	Don Mattingly	.85
25	Jack McDowell	.05
26	Mark McGwire	1.00
27	Kevin Mitchell	.05
28	Jack Morris	.05
29	Dale Murphy	.20
30	Kirby Puckett	.65
31	Tim Raines	.05
32	Shane Rawley	.05
33	Benito Santiago	.05
34	Mike Schmidt	.85
35	Mike Scott	.05
36	Kevin Seitzer	.05
37	Larry Sheets	.05
38	Ruben Sierra	.05
39	Dave Smith	.05
40	Ozzie Smith	.05
41	Darryl Strawberry	.05
42	Rick Sutcliffe	.05
43	Pat Tabler	.05
44	Alan Trammell	.05

League Leaders

This boxed set is the third annual limited edition set from Fleer highlighting leading players. The 1988 edition contains the same type of information, front and back, as the previous sets, with a new color scheme and design. Card fronts have bright blue borders, solid on the lower portion, striped on the upper, with a gold bar separating the two sections. The full-color player photo is centered above a yellow name banner. The numbered card backs are blue, pink and white, and contain player stats and personal notes. Six team logo sticker cards, with flipside black-and-white photos of ballparks, accompany this set which was marketed exclusively by Walgreen drug stores.

		NM/M
Complete Set (44):		3.50
Common Player:		.05
1	George Bell	.05
2	Wade Boggs	.65
3	Ivan Calderon	.05
4	Jose Canseco	.30
5	Will Clark	.05
6	Roger Clemens	.85
7	Vince Coleman	.05
8	Eric Davis	.05
9	Andre Dawson	.25
10	Bill Doran	.05
11	Dwight Evans	.05
12	Julio Franco	.05
13	Gary Gaetti	.05
14	Andres Galarraga	.05
15	Dwight Gooden	.05
16	Tony Gwynn	.65
17	Tom Henke	.05
18	Keith Hernandez	.05
19	Orel Hershiser	.05
20	Ted Higuera	.05
21	Kent Hrbek	.05
22	Wally Joyner	.05
23	Jimmy Key	.05
24	Mark Langston	.05
25	Don Mattingly	.85
26	Mark McGwire	1.00
27	Paul Molitor	.50
28	Jack Morris	.05
29	Dale Murphy	.20
30	Kirby Puckett	.65
31	Tim Raines	.05
32	Rick Rueschel	.05
33	Bret Saberhagen	.05
34	Benito Santiago	.05
35	Mike Schmidt	.85
36	Mike Scott	.05
37	Kevin Seitzer	.05
38	Larry Sheets	.05
39	Ruben Sierra	.05
40	Darryl Strawberry	.05
41	Rick Sutcliffe	.05
42	Alan Trammell	.05
43	Andy Van Slyke	.05
44	Todd Worrell	.05

Mini

This third annual issue of miniatures (1-7/8" x 2-5/8") includes 120 high-gloss cards featuring new photos, not copies from the regular issue, although the card designs are identical. Card backs are red, white and blue and include personal data, yearly career stats and a stats breakdown of batting average, slugging percentage and on-base average, listed for day, night, home and road games. Card backs are numbered in alphabetical order by teams which are also listed alphabetically. The set includes 18 team logo stickers with black-and-white aerial stadium photos on the flip sides.

		NM/M
Complete Set (120):		3.50
Common Player:		.05
1	Eddie Murray	.50
2	Dave Schmidt	.05
3	Larry Sheets	.05
4	Wade Boggs	.65
5	Roger Clemens	.85
6	Dwight Evans	.05
7	Mike Greenwell	.05
8	Sam Horn	.05
9	Lee Smith	.05
10	Brian Downing	.05
11	Wally Joyner	.05
12	Devon White	.05
13	Mike Witt	.05
14	Ivan Calderon	.05
15	Ozzie Guillen	.05
16	Jack McDowell	.05
17	Kenny Williams	.05
18	Joe Carter	.05
19	Julio Franco	.05
20	Pat Tabler	.05
21	Doyle Alexander	.05
22	Jack Morris	.05
23	Matt Nokes	.05
24	Walt Terrell	.05
25	Alan Trammell	.05
26	Bret Saberhagen	.05
27	Kevin Seitzer	.05
28	Danny Tartabull	.05
29	Gary Thurman	.05
30	Ted Higuera	.05
31	Paul Molitor	.50
32	Dan Plesac	.05
33	Robin Yount	.50
34	Gary Gaetti	.05
35	Kent Hrbek	.05
36	Kirby Puckett	.65

9	Andre Dawson	.25
10	Bill Doran	.05
11	Dwight Evans	.05
12	Julio Franco	.05
13	Gary Gaetti	.05
14	Andres Galarraga	.05
15	Dwight Gooden	.05
16	Tony Gwynn	.65
17	Tom Henke	.05
18	Keith Hernandez	.05
19	Orel Hershiser	.05
20	Ted Higuera	.05
21	Kent Hrbek	.05
22	Wally Joyner	.05
23	Jimmy Key	.05
24	Mark Langston	.05
25	Don Mattingly	.85
26	Mark McGwire	1.00
27	Paul Molitor	.50
28	Jack Morris	.05
29	Dale Murphy	.20
30	Kirby Puckett	.65
31	Tim Raines	.05
32	Rick Rueschel	.05
33	Bret Saberhagen	.05
34	Benito Santiago	.05
35	Mike Schmidt	.85
36	Mike Scott	.05
37	Kevin Seitzer	.05
38	Larry Sheets	.05
39	Ruben Sierra	.05
40	Darryl Strawberry	.05
41	Rick Sutcliffe	.05
42	Alan Trammell	.05
43	Andy Van Slyke	.05
44	Todd Worrell	.05

37	Jeff Reardon	.05
38	Frank Viola	.05
39	Jack Clark	.05
40	Rickey Henderson	.50
41	Don Mattingly	.85
42	Willie Randolph	.05
43	Dave Righetti	.05
44	Dave Winfield	.50
45	Jose Canseco	.30
46	Mark McGwire	1.00
47	Dave Parker	.05
48	Dave Stewart	.05
49	Walt Weiss	.05
50	Bob Welch	.05
51	Mickey Brantley	.05
52	Mark Langston	.05
53	Harold Reynolds	.05
54	Scott Fletcher	.05
55	Charlie Hough	.05
56	Pete Incaviglia	.05
57	Larry Parrish	.05
58	Ruben Sierra	.05
59	George Bell	.05
60	Mark Eichhorn	.05
61	Tony Fernandez	.05
62	Tom Henke	.05
63	Jimmy Key	.05
64	Dion James	.05
65	Dale Murphy	.20
66	Zane Smith	.05
67	Andre Dawson	.25
68	Mark Grace	.25
69	Jerry Mumphrey	.05
70	Ryne Sandberg	.65
71	Rick Sutcliffe	.05
72	Kal Daniels	.05
73	Eric Davis	.05
74	John Franco	.05
75	Ron Robinson	.05
76	Jeff Treadway	.05
77	Kevin Bass	.05
78	Glenn Davis	.05
79	Nolan Ryan	1.00
80	Mike Scott	.05
81	Dave Smith	.05
82	Kirk Gibson	.05
83	Pedro Guerrero	.05
84	Orel Hershiser	.05
85	Steve Sax	.05
86	Fernando Valenzuela	.05
87	Tim Burke	.05
88	Andres Galarraga	.05
89	Neal Heaton	.05
90	Tim Raines	.05
91	Tim Wallach	.05
92	Dwight Gooden	.05
93	Keith Hernandez	.05
94	Gregg Jefferies	.10
95	Howard Johnson	.05
96	Roger McDowell	.05
97	Darryl Strawberry	.05
98	Steve Bedrosian	.05
99	Von Hayes	.05
100	Shane Rawley	.05
101	Juan Samuel	.05
102	Mike Schmidt	.85
103	Bobby Bonilla	.05
104	Mike Dunne	.05
105	Andy Van Slyke	.05
106	Vince Coleman	.05
107	Bob Horner	.05
108	Willie McGee	.05
109	Ozzie Smith	.65
110	John Tudor	.05
111	Todd Worrell	.05
112	Tony Gwynn	.65
113	John Kruk	.05
114	Lance McCullers	.05
115	Benito Santiago	.05
116	Will Clark	.05
117	Jeff Leonard	.05
118	Candy Maldonado	.05
119	Kirt Manwaring	.05
120	Don Robinson	.05

MVP

This boxed set of 44 standard-size cards and six team logo stickers was produced by Fleer for exclusive distribution at Toys "R" Us stores. This premiere edition features full-color player photos framed by a yellow and blue border. Card backs are yellow and blue on a white background. The player's team, position and personal data are followed by stats, logo and a blue banner bearing the player's name, team logo and card number. The six sticker cards feature black-and-white stadium photos on the backs.

		NM/M
Complete Set (44):		3.50
Common Player:		.05
1	George Bell	.05
2	Wade Boggs	.65
3	Jose Canseco	.30
4	Ivan Calderon	.05
5	Will Clark	.85
6	Roger Clemens	.85
7	Vince Coleman	.05
8	Eric Davis	.05
9	Andre Dawson	.25
10	Dave Dravecky	.05
11	Mike Dunne	.05
12	Dwight Evans	.05
13	Sid Fernandez	.05
14	Tony Fernandez	.05
15	Julio Franco	.05
16	Dwight Gooden	.05
17	Tony Gwynn	.65
18	Ted Higuera	.05
19	Charlie Hough	.05
20	Wally Joyner	.05
21	Mark Langston	.05
22	Don Mattingly	.85
23	Mark McGwire	1.00
24	Jack Morris	.05
25	Dale Murphy	.20
26	Kirby Puckett	.65
27	Tim Raines	.05
28	Willie Randolph	.05
29	Ryne Sandberg	.65
30	Benito Santiago	.05
31	Mike Schmidt	.85
32	Mike Scott	.05
33	Kevin Seitzer	.05
34	Larry Sheets	.05
35	Ozzie Smith	.65
36	Dave Stewart	.05
37	Darryl Strawberry	.05
38	Rick Sutcliffe	.05
39	Alan Trammell	.05
40	Fernando Valenzuela	.05
41	Frank Viola	.05
42	Tim Wallach	.05
43	Dave Winfield	.50
44	Robin Yount	.50

Record Setters

1988 FLEER RECORD SETTERS — DALE MURPHY

For the second consecutive year, Fleer issued this set for exclusive distribution by Eckerd Drug stores. Cards are standard size with red and blue borders framing the full-color player photos. Card backs list personal information and career stats in red and blue on a white background. Each 44-card set comes cello-wrapped with a checklist box that contains six additional cards with peel-off team logo stickers. The sticker cards feature black-and-white aerial photos of major league ballparks, along with stadium statistics such as field size, seating capacity and date of the first game played.

		NM/M
Complete Set (44):		3.50
Common Player:		.05
1	Jesse Barfield	.05
2	George Bell	.05
3	Wade Boggs	.65
4	Jose Canseco	.35
5	Jack Clark	.05
6	Will Clark	.85
7	Roger Clemens	.85
8	Alvin Davis	.05
9	Eric Davis	.05
10	Andre Dawson	.25
11	Mike Dunne	.05
12	John Franco	.05
13	Julio Franco	.05
14	Dwight Gooden	.05
15	Mark Gubicza	.05
16	Ozzie Guillen	.05
17	Tony Gwynn	.65
18	Orel Hershiser	.05
19	Teddy Higuera	.05
20	Howard Johnson	.05
21	Wally Joyner	.05
22	Jimmy Key	.05
23	Jeff Leonard	.05
24	Don Mattingly	.85
25	Mark McGwire	1.00
26	Jack Morris	.05
27	Dale Murphy	.20
28	Larry Parrish	.05
29	Kirby Puckett	.65
30	Tim Raines	.05
31	Harold Reynolds	.05
32	Dave Righetti	.05
33	Cal Ripken, Jr.	1.00
34	Benito Santiago	.05
35	Mike Schmidt	.85
36	Mike Scott	.05
37	Kevin Seitzer	.05
38	Ozzie Smith	.65
39	Darryl Strawberry	.05
40	Rick Sutcliffe	.05
41	Alan Trammell	.05
42	Frank Viola	.05
43	Mitch Williams	.05
44	Todd Worrell	.05

Star Stickers

ALAN TRAMMELL — TIGERS SHORTSTOP

This set of 132 standard-size sticker cards (including a checklist card) features exclusive player photos, different from those in the Fleer regular issue. Card fronts have light gray borders sprinkled with multi-colored stars. Card backs are printed in red, gray and black on white and include personal data and a breakdown of pitching and batting stats into day, night, home and road categories. Cards were marketed in two different display boxes that feature six players and two team logos on the bottoms.

		NM/M
Complete Set (132):		7.50
Common Player:		.05
Wax Pack (5):		.50
Wax Box (36):		10.00
1	Mike Boddicker	.05
2	Eddie Murray	.50
3	Cal Ripken, Jr.	1.50
4	Larry Sheets	.05
5	Wade Boggs	.65
6	Ellis Burks	.05
7	Roger Clemens	.85
8	Dwight Evans	.05
9	Mike Greenwell	.05
10	Bruce Hurst	.05
11	Brian Downing	.05
12	Wally Joyner	.05
13	Mike Witt	.05
14	Ivan Calderon	.05
15	Jose DeLeon	.05
16	Ozzie Guillen	.05
17	Bobby Thigpen	.05
18	Joe Carter	.05
19	Julio Franco	.05
20	Brook Jacoby	.05
21	Cory Snyder	.05
22	Pat Tabler	.05
23	Doyle Alexander	.05
24	Kirk Gibson	.05
25	Mike Henneman	.05
26	Jack Morris	.05
27	Matt Nokes	.05
28	Walt Terrell	.05
29	Alan Trammell	.85
30	George Brett	.85
31	Charlie Leibrandt	.05
32	Bret Saberhagen	.05
33	Kevin Seitzer	.05
34	Danny Tartabull	.05
35	Frank White	.05
36	Rob Deer	.05
37	Ted Higuera	.05
38	Paul Molitor	.50
39	Dan Plesac	.05
40	Robin Yount	.65
41	Bert Blyleven	.05
42	Tom Brunansky	.05
43	Gary Gaetti	.05
44	Kent Hrbek	.05
45	Kirby Puckett	.65
46	Jeff Reardon	.05
47	Frank Viola	.05
48	Don Mattingly	.85
49	Mike Pagliarulo	.05
50	Willie Randolph	.05
51	Rick Rhoden	.05
52	Dave Righetti	.05
53	Dave Winfield	.50
54	Jose Canseco	.30
55	Carney Lansford	.05
56	Mark McGwire	1.00
57	Dave Stewart	.05
58	Curt Young	.05
59	Alvin Davis	.05
60	Mark Langston	.05
61	Ken Phelps	.05
62	Harold Reynolds	.05
63	Scott Fletcher	.05
64	Charlie Hough	.05
65	Pete Incaviglia	.05
66	Oddibe McDowell	.05
67	Pete O'Brien	.05
68	Larry Parrish	.05
69	Ruben Sierra	.05
70	Jesse Barfield	.05
71	George Bell	.05
72	Tony Fernandez	.05
73	Tom Henke	.05
74	Jimmy Key	.05
75	Lloyd Moseby	.05
76	Dion James	.05
77	Dale Murphy	.20
78	Zane Smith	.05
79	Andre Dawson	.25
80	Ryne Sandberg	.65
81	Rick Sutcliffe	.05
82	Kal Daniels	.05
83	Eric Davis	.05
84	John Franco	.05
85	Kevin Bass	.05
86	Glenn Davis	.05
87	Bill Doran	.05
88	Nolan Ryan	1.50
89	Mike Scott	.05
90	Dave Smith	.05
91	Pedro Guerrero	.05
92	Orel Hershiser	.05
93	Steve Sax	.05
94	Fernando Valenzuela	.05
95	Tim Burke	.05
96	Andres Galarraga	.05
97	Tim Raines	.05
98	Tim Wallach	.05
99	Mitch Webster	.05
100	Ron Darling	.05
101	Sid Fernandez	.05
102	Dwight Gooden	.05
103	Keith Hernandez	.05
104	Howard Johnson	.05
105	Roger McDowell	.05
106	Darryl Strawberry	.05
107	Steve Bedrosian	.05
108	Von Hayes	.05
109	Shane Rawley	.05
110	Juan Samuel	.05
111	Mike Schmidt	.85
112	Milt Thompson	.05
113	Sid Bream	.05
114	Bobby Bonilla	.05
115	Mike Dunne	.05
116	Andy Van Slyke	.05
117	Vince Coleman	.05
118	Willie McGee	.05
119	Terry Pendleton	.05
120	Ozzie Smith	.65
121	John Tudor	.05
122	Todd Worrell	.05
123	Tony Gwynn	.65
124	John Kruk	.05
125	Benito Santiago	.05
126	Will Clark	.05
127	Dave Dravecky	.05
128	Jeff Leonard	.05
129	Candy Maldonado	.05
130	Rick Rueschel	.05
131	Don Robinson	.05
132	Checklist	.05

Star Stickers Box Panels

RON GUIDRY — YANKEES PITCHER

This set of eight box-bottom cards was printed on two different retail display boxes. Six players and two team logo sticker cards are included in the set, three player photos and one team photo per box. The full-color player photos are exclusive to the Fleer Star Sticker set. The cards, which measure 2-1/2" x 3-1/2", have a light gray border sprinkled with multi-color stars. The backs are printed in navy blue and red.

		NM/M
Complete Panel Set (2):		1.50
Complete Singles Set (8):		1.50
Common Singles Player:		.15
Panel		1.00
1	Eric Davis	.10
3	Kevin Mitchell	.10
5	Rickey Henderson	.75
7	Tigers Logo	.05
Panel		1.00
2	Gary Carter	.75
4	Ron Guidry	.10
6	Don Baylor	.10
8	Giants Logo	.05

Superstars

OREL HERSHISER — Dodgers • Pitcher

This is the fourth edition of Fleer boxed sets produced for distribution by McCrory's (1985-87 issues were titled "Fleer Limited Edition"). The Superstars standard-size card set features full-color player photos framed by red, white and blue striped top and bottom borders. Card fronts have a semi-glossy slightly textured finish. Card backs are red and blue on white and include card numbers, personal data and statistics. Six team logo sticker cards are also included in this set which was marketed in red, white and blue boxes with checklist backs. Boxed sets were sold exclusively at McCrory's stores and its affiliates.

		NM/M
Complete Set (44):		5.00
Common Player:		.10
1	Steve Bedrosian	.10
2	George Bell	.10
3	Wade Boggs	.65
4	Barry Bonds	1.50
5	Jose Canseco	.45
6	Joe Carter	.10
7	Jack Clark	.10
8	Will Clark	.85
9	Roger Clemens	.85
10	Alvin Davis	.10
11	Eric Davis	.10
12	Glenn Davis	.10
13	Andre Dawson	.25
14	Dwight Gooden	.10
15	Orel Hershiser	.10
16	Teddy Higuera	.10
17	Kent Hrbek	.10
18	Wally Joyner	.10
19	Jimmy Key	.10
20	John Kruk	.10
21	Jeff Leonard	.10
22	Don Mattingly	.85
23	Mark McGwire	1.00
24	Kevin McReynolds	.10
25	Dale Murphy	.15
26	Matt Nokes	.10
27	Terry Pendleton	.10
28	Kirby Puckett	.65
29	Tim Raines	.10
30	Rick Rhoden	.10
31	Cal Ripken, Jr.	1.50
32	Benito Santiago	.10
33	Mike Schmidt	.85
34	Mike Scott	.10
35	Kevin Seitzer	.10
36	Ruben Sierra	.10
37	Cory Snyder	.10
38	Darryl Strawberry	.10
39	Rick Sutcliffe	.10
40	Danny Tartabull	.10
41	Alan Trammell	.10
42	Ken Williams	.10
43	Mike Witt	.10
44	Robin Yount	.50

Superstars Box Panel

Six cards were placed on the bottoms of retail boxes of the Fleer Superstars boxed sets. in 1988. The cards, 2-1/2" x 3-1/2", are identical in design to cards found in the 44-card set. The cards are num-

FLEER 1988 — SHANE RAWLEY — Phillies • Pitcher

bered C-1 through C-6 and were produced for distribution by McCrory stores and its affiliates.

		NM/M
Complete Panel:		2.50
Complete Set (6):		2.50
Common Player:		.25
C1	Pete Incaviglia	.15
C2	Rickey Henderson	1.00
C3	Tony Fernandez	.15
C4	Shane Rawley	.15
C5	Ryne Sandberg	1.50
C6	St. Louis Cardinals Logo/Checklist	.10

1989 Fleer

KEVIN ROMINE — OUTFIELD — FLEER

This set includes 660 standard-size cards and was issued with 45 team logo stickers. Individual card fronts feature a gray and white striped background with full-color player photos framed by a bright line of color that slants upward to the right. The set also includes two subsets: 15 Major League Prospects and 12 SuperStar Specials. A special bonus set of 12 All-Star Team cards was randomly inserted in individual wax packs of 15 cards. The last seven cards in the set are checklists, with players listed alphabetically by teams.

		NM/M
Retail Factory Set (660):		17.50
Hobby Factory Set (672):		20.00
Complete Set (660):		15.00
Common Player:		.05
Wax Pack (15):		1.00
Wax Box (36):		25.00
Cello Pack (36):		1.50
Cello Box (24):		20.00
Rack Pack (42+1):		1.50
Rack Box (24):		25.00
1	Don Baylor	.05
2	Lance Blankenship RC	.05
3	Todd Burns RC	.05
4	Greg Cadaret RC	.05
5	Jose Canseco	.35
6	Storm Davis	.05
7	Dennis Eckersley	.35
8	Mike Gallego RC	.05
9	Ron Hassey	.05
10	Dave Henderson	.05
11	Rick Honeycutt	.05
12	Glenn Hubbard	.05
13	Stan Javier	.05
14	Doug Jennings RC	.05
15	Felix Jose RC	.05
16	Carney Lansford	.05
17	Mark McGwire	.65
18	Gene Nelson	.05
19	Dave Parker	.05
20	Eric Plunk	.05
21	Luis Polonia	.05
22	Terry Steinbach	.05
23	Dave Stewart	.05
24	Walt Weiss	.05
25	Bob Welch	.05
26	Curt Young	.05
27	Rick Aguilera	.05
28	Wally Backman	.05
29	Mark Carreon	.40
30	Gary Carter	.05
31	David Cone	.05
32	Ron Darling	.05
33	Len Dykstra	.05
34	Kevin Elster	.05
35	Sid Fernandez	.05
36	Dwight Gooden	.05
37	Keith Hernandez	.05
38	Gregg Jefferies	.05
39	Howard Johnson	.05
40	Terry Leach	.05
41	Dave Magadan	.05
42	Bob McClure	.05
43	Roger McDowell	.05
44	Kevin McReynolds	.05
45	Keith Miller	.05
46	Randy Myers	.05
47	Bob Ojeda	.05
48	Mackey Sasser	.05
49	Darryl Strawberry	.05
50	Tim Teufel	.05
51	Dave West RC	.05
52	Mookie Wilson	.05
53	Dave Anderson	.05
54	Tim Belcher	.05
55	Mike Davis	.05
56	Mike Devereaux	.05
57	Kirk Gibson	.05
58	Alfredo Griffin	.05
59	Chris Gwynn	.05
60	Jeff Hamilton	.05
61a	Danny Heep (Home: San Antonio, TX)	.25
61b	Danny Heep (Home: Lake Hills, TX)	.05
62	Orel Hershiser	.05
63	Brian Holton RC	.05
64	Jay Howell	.05
65	Tim Leary	.05
66	Mike Marshall	.05
67	Ramon Martinez RC	.25
68	Jesse Orosco	.05
69	Alejandro Pena	.05
70	Steve Sax	.05
71	Mike Scioscia	.05
72	Mike Sharperson	.05
73	John Shelby	.05
74	Franklin Stubbs	.05
75	John Tudor	.05
76	Fernando Valenzuela	.05
77	Tracy Woodson	.05
78	Marty Barrett	.05
79	Todd Benzinger	.05
80	Mike Boddicker	.05
81	Wade Boggs	.50
82	"Oil Can" Boyd	.05
83	Ellis Burks	.05
84	Rick Cerone	.05
85	Roger Clemens	.75
86	Steve Curry RC	.05
87	Dwight Evans	.05
88	Wes Gardner	.05
89	Rich Gedman	.05
90	Mike Greenwell	.05
91	Bruce Hurst	.05
92	Dennis Lamp	.05
93	Spike Owen	.05
94	Larry Parrish	.05
95	Carlos Quintana RC	.05
96	Jody Reed	.05
97	Jim Rice	.25
98a	Kevin Romine (Batting follow-thru, photo actually Randy Kutcher.)	.25
98b	Kevin Romine (Arms crossed on chest, correct photo.)	.05
99	Lee Smith	.05
100	Mike Smithson	.05
101	Bob Stanley	.05
102	Allan Anderson	.05
103	Keith Atherton	.05
104	Juan Berenguer	.05
105	Bert Blyleven	.10
106	Eric Bullock RC	.05
107	Randy Bush	.05
108	John Christensen RC	.05
109	Mark Davidson	.05
110	Gary Gaetti	.05
111	Greg Gagne	.05
112	Dan Gladden	.05
113	German Gonzalez RC	.05
114	Brian Harper	.05
115	Tom Herr	.05
116	Kent Hrbek	.05
117	Gene Larkin	.05
118	Tim Laudner	.05
119	Charlie Lea	.05
120	Steve Lombardozzi	.05
121a	John Moses (Home: Phoenix, AZ)	.25
121b	John Moses (Home: Tempe, AZ)	.05
122	Al Newman	.05
123	Mark Portugal	.05
124	Kirby Puckett	.50
125	Jeff Reardon	.05
126	Fred Toliver	.05
127	Frank Viola	.05
128	Doyle Alexander	.05
129	Dave Bergman	.05
130a	Tom Brookens (Mike Heath stats on back.)	.25
130b	Tom Brookens (Correct stats on back.)	.05
131	Paul Gibson RC	.05
132a	Mike Heath (Tom Brookens stats on back.)	.25
132b	Mike Heath (Correct stats on back.)	.05
133	Don Heinkel RC	.05
134	Mike Henneman	.05
135	Guillermo Hernandez	.05

No.	Name	Price
136	Eric King	.05
137	Chet Lemon	.05
138	Fred Lynn	.05
139	Jack Morris	.05
140	Matt Nokes	.05
141	Gary Pettis	.05
142	Ted Power	.05
143	Jeff Robinson	.05
144	Luis Salazar	.05
145	Steve Searcy RC	.05
146	Pat Sheridan	.05
147	Frank Tanana	.05
148	Alan Trammell	.05
149	Walt Terrell	.05
150	Jim Walewander RC	.05
151	Lou Whitaker	.05
152	Tim Birtsas	.05
153	Tom Browning	.05
154	Keith Brown RC	.05
155	Norm Charlton RC	.15
156	Dave Concepcion	.05
157	Kal Daniels	.05
158	Eric Davis	.05
159	Bo Diaz	.05
160	Rob Dibble	.05
161	Nick Esasky	.05
162	John Franco	.05
163	Danny Jackson	.05
164	Barry Larkin	.05
165	Rob Murphy	.05
166	Paul O'Neill	.05
167	Jeff Reed	.05
168	Jose Rijo	.05
169	Ron Robinson	.05
170	Chris Sabo	.05
171	Candy Sierra RC	.05
172	Van Snider RC	.05
173a	Jeff Treadway (Blue "target" above head.)	75.00
173b	Jeff Treadway (No "target.")	.05
174	Frank Williams	.05
175	Herm Winningham	.05
176	Jim Adduci RC	.05
177	Don August	.05
178	Mike Birkbeck	.05
179	Chris Bosio	.05
180	Glenn Braggs	.05
181	Greg Brock	.05
182	Mark Clear	.05
183	Chuck Crim	.05
184	Rob Deer	.05
185	Tom Filer	.05
186	Jim Gantner	.05
187	Darryl Hamilton	.05
188	Ted Higuera	.05
189	Odell Jones	.05
190	Jeffrey Leonard	.05
191	Joey Meyer	.05
192	Paul Mirabella	.05
193	Paul Molitor	.40
194	Charlie O'Brien RC	.05
195	Dan Plesac	.05
196	Gary Sheffield RC	1.00
197	B.J. Surhoff	.05
198	Dale Sveum	.05
199	Bill Wegman	.05
200	Robin Yount	.40
201	Rafael Belliard	.05
202	Barry Bonds	.75
203	Bobby Bonilla	.05
204	Sid Bream	.05
205	Benny Distefano RC	.05
206	Doug Drabek	.05
207	Mike Dunne	.05
208	Felix Fermin	.05
209	Brian Fisher	.05
210	Jim Gott	.05
211	Bob Kipper	.05
212	Dave LaPoint	.05
213	Mike LaValliere	.05
214	Jose Lind	.05
215	Junior Ortiz	.05
216	Vicente Palacios RC	.05
217	Tom Prince RC	.05
218	Gary Redus	.05
219	R.J. Reynolds	.05
220	Jeff Robinson	.05
221	John Smiley	.05
222	Andy Van Slyke	.05
223	Bob Walk	.05
224	Glenn Wilson	.05
225	Jesse Barfield	.05
226	George Bell	.05
227	Pat Borders	.05
228	John Cerutti	.05
229	Jim Clancy	.05
230	Mark Eichhorn	.05
231	Tony Fernandez	.05
232	Cecil Fielder	.05
233	Mike Flanagan	.05
234	Kelly Gruber	.05
235	Tom Henke	.05
236	Jimmy Key	.05
237	Rick Leach	.05
238	Manny Lee	.05
239	Nelson Liriano	.05
240	Fred McGriff	.05
241	Lloyd Moseby	.05
242	Rance Mulliniks	.05
243	Jeff Musselman	.05
244	Dave Stieb	.05
245	Todd Stottlemyre RC	.05
246	Duane Ward	.05
247	David Wells	.05
248	Ernie Whitt	.05
249	Luis Aguayo	.05
250a	Neil Allen (Home: Sarasota, FL)	.25
250b	Neil Allen (Home: Syosset, NY)	.25
251	John Candelaria	.05
252	Jack Clark	.05
253	Richard Dotson	.05
254	Rickey Henderson	.40
255	Tommy John	.10
256	Roberto Kelly	.05
257	Al Leiter	.05
258	Don Mattingly	.60
259	Dale Mohorcic	.05
260	Hal Morris RC	.25
261	Scott Nielsen RC	.05
262	Mike Pagliarulo	.05
263	Hipolito Pena RC	.05
264	Ken Phelps	.05
265	Willie Randolph	.05
266	Rick Rhoden	.05
267	Dave Righetti	.05
268	Rafael Santana	.05
269	Steve Shields RC	.05
270	Joel Skinner	.05
271	Don Slaught	.05
272	Claudell Washington	.05
273	Gary Ward	.05
274	Dave Winfield	.40
275	Luis Aquino RC	.05
276	Floyd Bannister	.05
277	George Brett	.60
278	Bill Buckner	.05
279	Nick Capra RC	.05
280	Jose DeJesus RC	.05
281	Steve Farr	.05
282	Jerry Gleaton	.05
283	Mark Gubicza	.05
284	Tom Gordon RC	.25
285	Bo Jackson	.35
286	Charlie Leibrandt	.05
287	Mike Macfarlane RC	.10
288	Jeff Montgomery	.05
289	Bill Pecota	.05
290	Jamie Quirk	.05
291	Bret Saberhagen	.05
292	Kevin Seitzer	.05
293	Kurt Stillwell	.05
294	Pat Tabler	.05
295	Danny Tartabull	.05
296	Gary Thurman	.05
297	Frank White	.05
298	Willie Wilson	.05
299	Roberto Alomar	.20
300	Sandy Alomar, Jr. RC	.25
301	Chris Brown	.05
302	Mike Brumley RC	.05
303	Mark Davis	.05
304	Mark Grant	.05
305	Tony Gwynn	.50
306	Greg Harris RC	.05
307	Andy Hawkins	.05
308	Jimmy Jones	.05
309	John Kruk	.05
310	Dave Leiper	.05
311	Carmelo Martinez	.05
312	Lance McCullers	.05
313	Keith Moreland	.05
314	Dennis Rasmussen	.05
315	Randy Ready	.05
316	Benito Santiago	.05
317	Eric Show	.05
318	Todd Simmons	.05
319	Garry Templeton	.05
320	Dickie Thon	.05
321	Ed Whitson	.05
322	Marvell Wynne	.05
323	Mike Aldrete	.05
324	Brett Butler	.05
325	Will Clark	.05
326	Kelly Downs	.05
327	Dave Dravecky	.05
328	Scott Garrelts	.05
329	Atlee Hammaker	.05
330	Charlie Hayes RC	.10
331	Mike Krukow	.05
332	Craig Lefferts	.05
333	Candy Maldonado	.05
334	Kirt Manwaring	.05
335	Bob Melvin	.05
336	Kevin Mitchell	.05
337	Donell Nixon	.05
338	Tony Perezchica RC	.05
339	Joe Price	.05
340	Rick Reuschel	.05
341	Earnest Riles	.05
342	Don Robinson	.05
343	Chris Speier	.05
344	Robby Thompson	.05
345	Jose Uribe	.05
346	Matt Williams	.05
347	Trevor Wilson RC	.15
348	Juan Agosto	.05
349	Larry Andersen	.05
350a	Alan Ashby ("Throws Right")	.25
350b	Alan Ashby ("Throws Right")	.25
351	Kevin Bass	.05
352	Buddy Bell	.05
353	Craig Biggio	.05
354	Danny Darwin	.05
355	Glenn Davis	.05
356	Jim Deshaies	.05
357	Bill Doran	.05
358	John Fishel RC	.05
359	Billy Hatcher	.05
360	Bob Knepper	.05
361	Louie Meadows RC	.05
362	Dave Meads	.05
363	Jim Pankovits	.05
364	Terry Puhl	.05
365	Rafael Ramirez	.05
366	Craig Reynolds	.05
367	Mike Scott	.05
368	Nolan Ryan	.75
369	Dave Smith	.05
370	Gerald Young	.05
371	Hubie Brooks	.05
372	Tim Burke	.05
373	John Dopson RC	.05
374	Mike Fitzgerald	.05
375	Tom Foley	.05
376	Andres Galarraga	.05
377	Neal Heaton	.05
378	Joe Hesketh	.05
379	Brian Holman RC	.05
380	Rex Hudler	.05
381a	Randy Johnson RC (Marlboro ad on scoreboard.)	40.00
381b	Randy Johnson (Ad partially obscured.)	10.00
381c	Randy Johnson RC (Ad completely blacked out.)	3.00
382	Wallace Johnson	.05
383	Tracy Jones	.05
384	Dave Martinez	.05
385	Dennis Martinez	.05
386	Andy McGaffigan	.05
387	Otis Nixon	.05
388	Johnny Paredes RC	.05
389	Jeff Parrett	.05
390	Pascual Perez	.05
391	Tim Raines	.05
392	Luis Rivera	.05
393	Nelson Santovenia RC	.05
394	Bryn Smith	.05
395	Tim Wallach	.05
396	Andy Allanson	.05
397	Rod Allen RC	.05
398	Scott Bailes	.05
399	Tom Candiotti	.05
400	Joe Carter	.05
401	Carmen Castillo	.05
402	Dave Clark	.05
403	John Farrell	.05
404	Julio Franco	.05
405	Don Gordon	.05
406	Mel Hall	.05
407	Brad Havens	.05
408	Brook Jacoby	.05
409	Doug Jones	.05
410	Jeff Kaiser RC	.05
411	Luis Medina RC	.05
412	Cory Snyder	.05
413	Greg Swindell	.05
414	Ron Tingley RC	.05
415	Willie Upshaw	.05
416	Ron Washington	.05
417	Rich Yett	.05
418	Damon Berryhill	.05
419	Mike Bielecki	.05
420	Doug Dascenzo RC	.05
421	Jody Davis	.05
422	Andre Dawson	.25
423	Frank DiPino	.05
424	Shawon Dunston	.05
425	"Goose" Gossage	.10
426	Mark Grace	.05
427	Mike Harkey RC	.05
428	Darrin Jackson	.05
429	Les Lancaster	.05
430	Vance Law	.05
431	Greg Maddux	.50
432	Jamie Moyer	.05
433	Al Nipper	.05
434	Rafael Palmeiro	.35
435	Pat Perry	.05
436	Jeff Pico RC	.05
437	Ryne Sandberg	.50
438	Calvin Schiraldi	.05
439	Rick Sutcliffe	.05
440a	Manny Trillo ("Throws Rig")	.35
440b	Manny Trillo ("Throws Right")	.05
441	Gary Varsho RC	.05
442	Mitch Webster	.05
443	Luis Alicea	.05
444	Tom Brunansky	.05
445	Vince Coleman	.05
446	John Costello RC	.05
447	Danny Cox	.05
448	Ken Dayley	.05
449	Jose DeLeon	.05
450	Curt Ford	.05
451	Pedro Guerrero	.05
452	Bob Horner	.05
453	Tim Jones RC	.05
454	Steve Lake	.05
455	Joe Magrane	.05
456	Greg Mathews	.05
457	Willie McGee	.05
458	Larry McWilliams	.05
459	Jose Oquendo	.05
460	Tony Pena	.05
461	Terry Pendleton	.05
462	Steve Peters RC	.05
463	Ozzie Smith	.50
464	Scott Terry	.05
465	Denny Walling	.05
466	Todd Worrell	.05
467	Tony Armas	.05
468	Dante Bichette RC	.25
469	Bob Boone	.05
470	Terry Clark RC	.05
471	Stew Cliburn	.05
472	Mike Cook RC	.05
473	Sherman Corbett RC	.05
474	Chili Davis	.05
475	Brian Downing	.05
476	Jim Eppard	.05
477	Chuck Finley	.05
478	Willie Fraser	.05
479	Bryan Harvey	.05
480	Jack Howell	.05
481	Wally Joyner	.05
482	Jack Lazorko	.05
483	Kirk McCaskill	.05
484	Mark McLemore	.05
485	Greg Minton	.05
486	Dan Petry	.05
487	Johnny Ray	.05
488	Dick Schofield	.05
489	Devon White	.05
490	Mike Witt	.05
491	Harold Baines	.05
492	Daryl Boston	.05
493	Ivan Calderon	.05
494	Mike Diaz	.05
495	Carlton Fisk	.40
496	Dave Gallagher RC	.05
497	Ozzie Guillen	.05
498	Shawn Hillegas	.05
499	Lance Johnson	.05
500	Barry Jones	.05
501	Bill Long	.05
502	Steve Lyons	.05
503	Fred Manrique	.05
504	Jack McDowell	.05
505	Donn Pall RC	.05
506	Kelly Paris	.05
507	Dan Pasqua	.05
508	Ken Patterson RC	.05
509	Melido Perez	.05
510	Jerry Reuss	.05
511	Mark Salas	.05
512	Bobby Thigpen	.05
513	Mike Woodard	.05
514	Bob Brower	.05
515	Steve Buechele	.05
516	Jose Cecena RC	.05
517	Cecil Espy	.05
518	Scott Fletcher	.05
519	Cecilio Guante	.05
520	Jose Guzman	.05
521	Ray Hayward	.05
522	Charlie Hough	.05
523	Pete Incaviglia	.05
524	Mike Jeffcoat	.05
525	Paul Kilgus	.05
526	Chad Kreuter RC	.15
527	Jeff Kunkel	.05
528	Oddibe McDowell	.05
529	Pete O'Brien	.05
530	Geno Petralli	.05
531	Jeff Russell	.05
532	Ruben Sierra	.05
533	Mike Stanley	.05
534	Ed Vande Berg	.05
535	Curtis Wilkerson	.05
536	Mitch Williams	.05
537	Bobby Witt	.05
538	Steve Balboni	.05
539	Scott Bankhead	.05
540	Scott Bradley	.05
541	Mickey Brantley	.05
542	Jay Buhner	.05
543	Mike Campbell	.05
544	Darnell Coles	.05
545	Henry Cotto	.05
546	Alvin Davis	.05
547	Mario Diaz	.05
548	Ken Griffey Jr. RC	6.00
549	Erik Hanson RC	.05
550	Mike Jackson	.05
551	Mark Langston	.05
552	Edgar Martinez	.05
553	Bill McGuire RC	.05
554	Mike Moore	.05
555	Jim Presley	.05
556	Rey Quinones	.05
557	Jerry Reed	.05
558	Harold Reynolds	.05
559	Mike Schooler RC	.05
560	Bill Swift	.05
561	Dave Valle	.05
562	Steve Bedrosian	.05
563	Phil Bradley	.05
564	Don Carman	.05
565	Bob Dernier	.05
566	Marvin Freeman	.05
567	Todd Frohwirth	.05
568	Greg Gross	.05
569	Kevin Gross	.05
570	Greg Harris	.05
571	Von Hayes	.05
572	Chris James	.05
573	Steve Jeltz	.05
574	Ron Jones RC	.05
575	Ricky Jordan RC	.05
576	Mike Maddux	.05
577	David Palmer	.05
578	Lance Parrish	.05
579	Shane Rawley	.05
580	Bruce Ruffin	.05
581	Juan Samuel	.05
582	Mike Schmidt	.60
583	Kent Tekulve	.05
584	Milt Thompson	.05
585	Jose Alvarez RC	.05
586	Paul Assenmacher	.05
587	Bruce Benedict	.05
588	Jeff Blauser	.05
589	Terry Blocker RC	.05
590	Ron Gant	.05
591	Tom Glavine	.30
592	Tommy Gregg	.05
593	Albert Hall	.05
594	Dion James	.05
595	Rick Mahler	.05
596	Dale Murphy	.25
597	Gerald Perry	.05
598	Charlie Puleo	.05
599	Ted Simmons	.05
600	Pete Smith	.05
601	Zane Smith	.05
602	John Smoltz	.50
603	Bruce Sutter	.35
604	Andres Thomas	.05
605	Ozzie Virgil	.05
606	Brady Anderson	.05
607	Jeff Ballard	.05
608	Jose Bautista RC	.05
609	Ken Gerhart	.05
610	Terry Kennedy	.05
611	Eddie Murray	.40
612	Carl Nichols	.05
613	Tom Niedenfuer	.05
614	Joe Orsulak	.05
615	Oswaldo Peraza RC (Oswald)	.05
616a	Bill Ripken (Vulgarity on bat knob.)	8.00
616b	Bill Ripken (Scribble over vulgarity.)	6.00
616c	Bill Ripken (Black box over vulgarity.)	.10
616d	Bill Ripken (Vulgarity whited out.(Many fake "white out" cards exist, created by erasures.)	250.00
616e	Billy Ripken (Strip cut out of bottom of card.)	.10
617	Cal Ripken, Jr.	.60
618	Dave Schmidt	.05
619	Rick Schu	.05
620	Larry Sheets	.05
621	Doug Sisk	.05
622	Pete Stanicek	.05
623	Mickey Tettleton	.05
624	Jay Tibbs	.05
625	Jim Traber	.05
626	Mark Williamson	.05
627	Craig Worthington RC	.05
628	Speed and Power (Jose Canseco)	.20
629	Pitcher Perfect (Tom Browning)	.05
630	Like Father Like Sons (Roberto Alomar, Sandy Alomar, Jr.)	.20
631	N.L. All-Stars (Will Clark, Rafael Palmeiro)	.10
632	Homeruns Coast to Coast (Will Clark, Darryl Strawberry)	.05
633	Hot Corner's Hot Hitters (Wade Boggs, Carney Lansford)	.05
634	Triple A's (Jose Canseco, Mark McGwire, Terry Steinbach)	.40
635	Dual Heat (Mark Davis, Dwight Gooden)	.05
636	N.L. Pitching Power (David Cone, Danny Jackson)	.05
637	Cannon Arms (Bobby Bonilla, Chris Sabo)	.05
638	Double Trouble (Andres Galarraga, Gerald Perry)	.05
639	Power Center (Eric Davis)	.05
640	Major League Prospects (Cameron Drew RC, Steve Wilson RC)	.05
641	Major League Prospects (Kevin Brown, Kevin Reimer RC)	.30
642	Major League Prospects (Jerald Clark RC, Brad Pounders RC)	.05
643	Major League Prospects (Mike Capel RC, Drew Hall RC)	.05
644	Major League Prospects (Joe Girardi RC, Rolando Roomes RC)	.20
645	Major League Prospects (Marty Brown RC, Lenny Harris RC)	.15
646	Major League Prospects (Luis de los Santos RC, Jim Campbell RC)	.05
647	Major League Prospects (Miguel Garcia RC, Randy Kramer RC)	.05
648	Major League Prospects (Torey Lovullo RC, Robert Palacios RC)	.05
649	Major League Prospects (Jim Corsi RC, Bob Milacki RC)	.05
650	Major League Prospects (Grady Hall RC, Mike Rochford RC)	.05
651	Major League Prospects (Vance Lovelace RC, Terry Taylor RC)	.05
652	Major League Prospects (Dennis Cook RC, Ken Hill RC)	.20
653	Major League Prospects (Scott Service RC, Shane Turner RC)	.05
654	Checklist 1-101	.05
655	Checklist 102-200	.05
656	Checklist 201-298	.05
657	Checklist 299-395	.05
658	Checklist 396-490	.05
659	Checklist 491-584	.05
660	Checklist 585-660	.05

All-Star Team

'89 FLEER ALL-STAR TEAM

FRANK VIOLA — LEFT HAND PITCHER-TWINS

This special 12-card set represents Fleer's choices for its 1989 Major League All-Star Team. For the fourth consecutive year, Fleer inserted the special cards randomly in wax and cello packs. The cards feature two player photos set against a green background with the "'89 Fleer All-Star Team" logo bannered across the top, and the player's name, position and team in the lower left corner. The backs contain a narrative player profile.

		NM/M
	Complete Set (12):	2.50
	Common Player:	.25
1	Bobby Bonilla	.25
2	Jose Canseco	.75
3	Will Clark	.40
4	Dennis Eckersley	.50
5	Julio Franco	.25
6	Mike Greenwell	.25
7	Orel Hershiser	.25
8	Paul Molitor	1.00
9	Mike Scioscia	.25
10	Darryl Strawberry	.25
11	Alan Trammell	.25
12	Frank Viola	.25

For The Record

FOR THE RECORD — FLEER

Greg Maddux CUBS PITCHER

Fleer's "For the Record" set features six players and their achievements from 1988. Fronts of the standard 2-1/2" x 3-1/2" cards feature a photo of the player set against a red scoreboard background. Card backs are grey and describe individual accomplishments. The cards were distributed randomly in rack packs.

		NM/M
	Complete Set (6):	2.50
	Common Player:	.25
1	Wade Boggs	.75
2	Roger Clemens	1.00
3	Andres Galarraga	.25
4	Kirk Gibson	.75
5	Greg Maddux	.75
6	Don Mattingly	1.00

World Series

This 12-card set, which depicts highlights of the 1988 World Series, was included as a special sub-set with the regular and glossy factory-collated Fleer set. It was not available as individual cards in wax packs, cello packs or any other form.

NM/M
Complete Set, Regular (12): 2.00
Common Card: .10
1 Dodgers Secret Weapon (Mickey Hatcher) .10
2 Rookie Starts Series (Tim Belcher) .10
3 Jose Canseco .25
4 Dramatic Comeback (Mike Scioscia) .10
5 Kirk Gibson .25
6 Orel Hershiser .15
7 One Swings, Three RBIs (Mike Marshall) .10
8 Mark McGwire 1.00
9 Sax's Speed Wins Game 4 (Steve Sax) .10
10 Series Caps Award Winning Year (Walt Weiss) .10
11 Orel Hershiser .15
12 Dodger Blue, World Champs .25

Box Panels

For the fourth consecutive year, Fleer issued a series of cards on the bottom panels of its regular 1989 Fleer wax pack boxes. The 28-card set includes 20 players and eight team logo cards, all designed in the identical style of the regular 1989 Fleer set. The box-bottom cards were randomly printed, four cards (three player cards and one team logo) on each bottom panel. Cards are numbered C-1 to C-28.

NM/M
Complete Panel Set (7): 6.00
Complete Singles Set (28): 3.00
Common Single Player: .15
1 Mets Logo .05
2 Wade Boggs .75
3 George Brett 1.25
4 Jose Canseco .50
5 A's Logo .05
6 Will Clark .10
7 David Cone .10
8 Andres Galarraga .10
9 Dodgers Logo .05
10 Kirk Gibson .10
11 Mike Greenwell .10
12 Tony Gwynn .75
13 Tigers Logo .05
14 Orel Hershiser .10
15 Danny Jackson .10
16 Wally Joyner .10
17 Red Sox Logo .05
18 Yankees Logo .05
19 Fred McGriff .10
20 Kirby Puckett .75
21 Chris Sabo .10
22 Kevin Seitzer .10
23 Pirates Logo .05
24 Astros Logo .05
25 Darryl Strawberry .10
26 Alan Trammell .10
27 Andy Van Slyke .10
28 Frank Viola .10

Glossy Tin

The last of the limited-edition, collector-version glossy tin sets is estimated to have been produced in an edition of 30,000-60,000, creating a significant premium over their counterparts in the regular

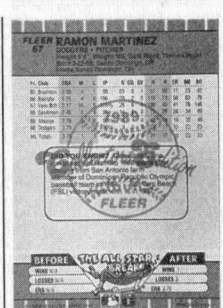

Fleer set. The issue was sold only in complete-set form in a lithographed metal box. The 1989 glossies differ from the regular cards on back in the use of blue, rather than yellow ink, and the appearance at center of a large baseball logo with 1989 / Collector's Edition / Fleer at center. No glossy version of the '89 Update set was made. Fleer glossy sets were originally wholesaled at $40 each.

NM/M
Unopened Set (672): 75.00
Complete Set (672): 50.00
Common Player: .25

Update

Fleer produced its sixth consecutive "Update" set in 1989 to supplement the company's regular set. As in the past, the set consisted of 132 cards (numbered U-1 through U-132) that were sold by hobby dealers in special collector's boxes.

NM/M
Complete Set (132): 6.00
Common Player: .05
1 Phil Bradley .05
2 Mike Devereaux .05
3 Steve Finley RC .05
4 Kevin Hickey .05
5 Brian Holton .05
6 Bob Milacki .05
7 Randy Milligan .05
8 John Dopson .05
9 Nick Esasky .05
10 Rob Murphy .05
11 Jim Abbott RC .05
12 Bert Blyleven .10
13 Jeff Manto RC .05
14 Bob McClure .05
15 Lance Parrish .05
16 Lee Stevens RC .05
17 Claudell Washington .05
18 Mark Davis .05
19 Eric King .05
20 Ron Kittle .05
21 Matt Merullo RC .05
22 Steve Rosenberg RC .05
23 Robin Ventura RC .25
24 Keith Atherton .05
25 Joey (Albert) Belle RC 1.00
26 Jerry Browne .05
27 Felix Fermin .05
28 Brad Komminsk .05
29 Pete O'Brien .05
30 Mike Brumley .05
31 Tracy Jones .05
32 Mike Schwabe RC .05
33 Gary Ward .05
34 Frank Williams .05
35 Kevin Appier RC .25
36 Bob Boone .05
37 Luis de los Santos RC .05
38 Jim Eisenreich RC .05
39 Jaime Navarro RC .05
40 Bill Spiers RC .05
41 Greg Vaughn RC .25
42 Randy Veres RC .05
43 Wally Backman .05
44 Shane Rawley .05
45 Steve Balboni .05
46 Jesse Barfield .05

47 Alvaro Espinoza RC .05
48 Bob Geren RC .05
49 Mel Hall .05
50 Andy Hawkins .05
51 Hensley Meulens RC .05
52 Steve Sax .05
53 Deion Sanders RC .75
54 Rickey Henderson .40
55 Mike Moore .05
56 Tony Phillips .05
57 Greg Briley .05
58 Gene Harris .05
59 Randy Johnson 2.00
60 Jeffrey Leonard .05
61 Dennis Powell .05
62 Omar Vizquel .05
63 Kevin Brown .05
64 Julio Franco .05
65 Jamie Moyer .05
66 Rafael Palmeiro .35
67 Nolan Ryan 1.00
68 Francisco Cabrera RC .05
69 Junior Felix RC .05
70 Al Leiter .05
71 Alex Sanchez RC .05
72 Geronimo Berroa RC .05
73 Derek Lilliquist RC .05
74 Lonnie Smith .05
75 Jeff Treadway .05
76 Paul Kilgus .05
77 Lloyd McClendon .05
78 Scott Sanderson .05
79 Dwight Smith RC .05
80 Jerome Walton RC .05
81 Mitch Williams .05
82 Steve Wilson .05
83 Todd Benzinger .05
84 Ken Griffey .05
85 Rick Mahler .05
86 Rolando Roomes .05
87 Scott Scudder RC .05
88 Jim Clancy .05
89 Rick Rhoden .05
90 Dan Schatzeder .05
91 Mike Morgan .05
92 Eddie Murray .40
93 Willie Randolph .05
94 Ray Searage .05
95 Mike Aldrete .05
96 Kevin Gross .05
97 Mark Langston .05
98 Spike Owen .05
99 Zane Smith .05
100 Don Aase .05
101 Barry Lyons .05
102 Juan Samuel .05
103 Wally Whitehurst RC .05
104 Dennis Cook .05
105 Len Dykstra .05
106 Charlie Hayes RC .05
107 Tommy Herr .05
108 Ken Howell .05
109 John Kruk .05
110 Roger McDowell .05
111 Terry Mulholland RC .05
112 Jeff Parrett .05
113 Neal Heaton .05
114 Jeff King .05
115 Randy Kramer .05
116 Bill Landrum .05
117 Cris Carpenter RC .05
118 Frank DiPino .05
119 Ken Hill .05
120 Dan Quisenberry .05
121 Milt Thompson .05
122 Todd Zeile RC .25
123 Jack Clark .05
124 Bruce Hurst .05
125 Mark Parent .05
126 Bip Roberts .05
127 Jeff Brantley RC .05
128 Terry Kennedy .05
129 Mike LaCoss .05
130 Greg Litton RC .05
131 Mike Schmidt .65
132 Checklist .05

Bill Ripken FF 'Test'

At the height of the furor over the vulgarity shown on the initial print run of Bill Ripken's card, when genuine examples were selling for as high as $125, this fantasy card surfaced to prey on collectors. In standard size, the card is printed in black-and-white on front and back,

reproducing a genuine card. On the back, typography was also added to make the piece look like a test card. This fraudulent product has no collectible value.

Baseball All-Stars

This specially-boxed set was produced by Fleer for the Ben Franklin store chain. The full-color player photos are surrounded by a border of pink and yellow vertical bands. "Fleer Baseball All-Stars" appears along the top in red, white and blue. The set was sold in a box with a checklist on the back.

NM/M
Complete Set (44): 4.00
Common Player: .10
1 Doyle Alexander .10
2 George Bell .10
3 Wade Boggs .65
4 Bobby Bonilla .10
5 Jose Canseco .40
6 Will Clark .10
7 Roger Clemens .75
8 Vince Coleman .10
9 David Cone .10
10 Mark Davis .10
11 Andre Dawson .25
12 Dennis Eckersley .45
13 Andres Galarraga .10
14 Kirk Gibson .10
15 Dwight Gooden .10
16 Mike Greenwell .10
17 Mark Gubicza .10
18 Ozzie Guillen .10
19 Tony Gwynn .10
20 Rickey Henderson .50
21 Orel Hershiser .10
22 Danny Jackson .10
23 Doug Jones .10
24 Ricky Jordan .10
25 Bob Knepper .10
26 Barry Larkin .10
27 Vance Law .10
28 Don Mattingly .75
29 Mark McGwire 1.00
30 Paul Molitor .50
31 Gerald Perry .10
32 Kirby Puckett .65
33 Johnny Ray .10
34 Harold Reynolds .10
35 Cal Ripken, Jr. 1.50
36 Don Robinson .10
37 Ruben Sierra .10
38 Dave Smith .10
39 Darryl Strawberry .10
40 Dave Steib .10
41 Alan Trammell .10
42 Andy Van Slyke .10
43 Frank Viola .10
44 Dave Winfield .50

Exciting Stars

Sold exclusively in Cumberland Farm stores, this boxed set pictures the game's top stars. The card fronts feature a color player photo surrounded by a blue border with "Baseball's Exciting Stars" along the top. The cards were num-

bered alphabetically and packed in a special box with a complete checklist on the back.

NM/M
Complete Set (44): 4.00
Common Player: .10
1 Harold Baines .10
2 Wade Boggs .65
3 Jose Canseco .50
4 Joe Carter .10
5 Will Clark .10
6 Roger Clemens .75
7 Vince Coleman .10
8 David Cone .10
9 Eric Davis .10
10 Glenn Davis .10
11 Andre Dawson .25
12 Dwight Evans .10
13 Andres Galarraga .10
14 Kirk Gibson .10
15 Dwight Gooden .10
16 Jim Gott .10
17 Mark Grace .10
18 Mike Greenwell .10
19 Mark Gubicza .10
20 Tony Gwynn .65
21 Rickey Henderson .60
22 Tom Henke .10
23 Mike Henneman .10
24 Orel Hershiser .10
25 Danny Jackson .10
26 Gregg Jefferies .10
27 Ricky Jordan .10
28 Wally Joyner .10
29 Mark Langston .10
30 Tim Leary .10
31 Don Mattingly .75
32 Mark McGwire 1.50
33 Dale Murphy .15
34 Kirby Puckett .65
35 Chris Sabo .10
36 Kevin Seitzer .10
37 Ruben Sierra .10
38 Ozzie Smith .65
39 Dave Stewart .10
40 Darryl Strawberry .10
41 Alan Trammell .10
42 Frank Viola .10
43 Dave Winfield .60
44 Robin Yount .60

Heroes of Baseball

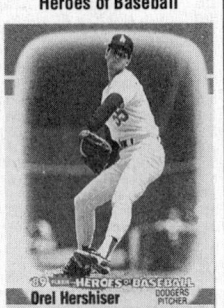

This boxed set was produced by Fleer for the Woolworth store chain. The fronts of the cards are designed in a red and blue color scheme and feature full-color photos that fade into a soft focus on all edges. The set is numbered alphabetically and was packaged in a special box with a checklist on the back.

NM/M
Complete Set (44): 4.00
Common Player: .10
1 George Bell .75
2 Wade Boggs .75
3 Barry Bonds 1.50
4 Tom Brunansky .10
5 Jose Canseco .40
6 Joe Carter .10
7 Will Clark .10
8 Roger Clemens .85
9 David Cone .10
10 Eric Davis .10
11 Glenn Davis .10
12 Andre Dawson .25
13 Dennis Eckersley .50
14 John Franco .10
15 Gary Gaetti .10
16 Andres Galarraga .10
17 Kirk Gibson .10
18 Dwight Gooden .10
19 Mike Greenwell .10
20 Tony Gwynn .75
21 Bryan Harvey .10
22 Orel Hershiser .10
23 Ted Higuera .10
24 Danny Jackson .10
25 Ricky Jordan .10
26 Don Mattingly .85
27 Fred McGriff .10
28 Mark McGwire 1.00
29 Kevin McReynolds .10
30 Gerald Perry .10
31 Kirby Puckett .75

32 Johnny Ray .10
33 Harold Reynolds .10
34 Cal Ripken, Jr. 1.50
35 Ryne Sandberg .10
36 Kevin Seitzer .10
37 Ruben Sierra .10
38 Darryl Strawberry .10
39 Bobby Thigpen .10
40 Alan Trammell .10
41 Andy Van Slyke .10
42 Frank Viola .10
43 Dave Winfield .65
44 Robin Yount .65

League Leaders

Another of the various small, boxed sets issued by Fleer, "League Leaders" was produced for Walgreen stores. The standard-size cards feature color photos on the front surrounded by a red border with "Fleer League Leaders" across the top. The backs include player stats and data and the team logo. The cards are numbered alphabetically and packaged in a special box that includes the full checklist on the back.

NM/M
Complete Set (44): 3.00
Common Player: .10
1 Allan Anderson .10
2 Wade Boggs .75
3 Jose Canseco .50
4 Will Clark .10
5 Roger Clemens .85
6 Vince Coleman .10
7 David Cone .10
8 Kal Daniels .10
9 Chili Davis .10
10 Eric Davis .10
11 Glenn Davis .10
12 Andre Dawson .25
13 John Franco .10
14 Andres Galarraga .10
15 Kirk Gibson .10
16 Dwight Gooden .10
17 Mark Grace .10
18 Mike Greenwell .10
19 Tony Gwynn .75
20 Orel Hershiser .10
21 Pete Incaviglia .10
22 Danny Jackson .10
23 Gregg Jefferies .10
24 Joe Magrane .10
25 Don Mattingly .85
26 Fred McGriff .10
27 Mark McGwire 1.00
28 Dale Murphy .10
29 Dan Plesac .10
30 Kirby Puckett .75
31 Harold Reynolds .10
32 Cal Ripken, Jr. 1.50
33 Jeff Robinson .10
34 Mike Scott .10
35 Ozzie Smith .75
36 Dave Stewart .10
37 Darryl Strawberry .10
38 Greg Swindell .10
39 Bobby Thigpen .10
40 Alan Trammell .10
41 Andy Van Slyke .10
42 Frank Viola .10
43 Dave Winfield .65
44 Robin Yount .65

MVP

Filled with superstars, this boxed set was produced by Fleer in 1989 for the Toys "R" Us chain. The fronts of the cards are designed in a yellow and green color scheme and include a "Fleer Baseball MVP" logo above the color player photo. The backs are printed in shades of green and yellow and include biographical notes and stats. The set was issued in a special box with a checklist on the back.

		NM/M
Complete Set (44):		5.00
Common Player:		.10
1	Steve Bedrosian	.10
2	George Bell	.10
3	Wade Boggs	.75
4	George Brett	.85
5	Hubie Brooks	.10
6	Jose Canseco	.50
7	Will Clark	.10
8	Roger Clemens	.85
9	Eric Davis	.10
10	Glenn Davis	.10
11	Andre Dawson	.25
12	Andres Galarraga	.10
13	Kirk Gibson	.10
14	Dwight Gooden	.10
15	Mark Grace	.10
16	Mike Greenwell	.10
17	Tony Gwynn	.75
18	Bryan Harvey	.10
19	Orel Hershiser	.10
20	Ted Higuera	.10
21	Danny Jackson	.10
22	Mike Jackson	.10
23	Doug Jones	.10
24	Greg Maddux	.75
25	Mike Marshall	.10
26	Don Mattingly	.85
27	Fred McGriff	.10
28	Mark McGwire	1.50
29	Kevin McReynolds	.10
30	Jack Morris	.10
31	Gerald Perry	.10
32	Kirby Puckett	.75
33	Chris Sabo	.10
34	Mike Scott	.10
35	Ruben Sierra	.10
36	Darryl Strawberry	.10
37	Danny Tartabull	.10
38	Bobby Thigpen	.10
39	Alan Trammell	.10
40	Andy Van Slyke	.10
41	Frank Viola	.10
42	Walt Weiss	.10
43	Dave Winfield	.65
44	Todd Worrell	.10

Superstars

This boxed set was produced by Fleer for the McCrory store chain. The cards are standard 2-1/2" x 3-1/2" and the full-color player photos are outlined in red with a tan-and-white striped border. The backs carry yellow and white stripes and include the Fleer "SuperStars" logo, player stats and biographical information. The cards are numbered alphabetically and packaged in a special box that includes a checklist on the back.

		NM/M
Complete Set (44):		4.00
Common Player:		.10
1	Roberto Alomar	.35
2	Harold Baines	.10
3	Tim Belcher	.10
4	Wade Boggs	.65
5	George Brett	.85
6	Jose Canseco	.50
7	Gary Carter	.60
8	Will Clark	.10
9	Roger Clemens	.85
10	Kal Daniels	.10
11	Eric Davis	.10
12	Andre Dawson	.25
13	Tony Fernandez	.10
14	Scott Fletcher	.10
15	Andres Galarraga	.10
16	Kirk Gibson	.10
17	Dwight Gooden	.10
18	Jim Gott	.10
19	Mark Grace	.10
20	Mike Greenwell	.10
21	Tony Gwynn	.75
22	Rickey Henderson	.60
23	Orel Hershiser	.10
24	Ted Higuera	.10
25	Gregg Jefferies	.10
26	Wally Joyner	.10
27	Mark Langston	.10
28	Greg Maddux	.75
29	Don Mattingly	.85
30	Fred McGriff	.10
31	Mark McGwire	1.50
32	Dan Plesac	.10
33	Kirby Puckett	.75
34	Jeff Reardon	.10
35	Chris Sabo	.10
36	Mike Schmidt	.85
37	Mike Scott	.10
38	Cory Snyder	.10
39	Darryl Strawberry	.10
40	Alan Trammell	.10
41	Frank Viola	.10
42	Walt Weiss	.10
43	Dave Winfield	.60
44	Todd Worrell	.10

1990 Fleer

George Brett / FIRST BASE

Fleer's 1990 set, its 10th annual baseball card offering, again consisted of 660 cards numbered by team. The front of the cards feature mostly action photos surrounded by one of several different color bands and a white border. The set includes various special cards, including a series of "Major League Prospects," Players of the Decade, team checklist cards and a series of multi-player cards. The backs include complete career stats, player data, and a special "Vital Signs" section showing on-base percentage, slugging percentage, etc. for batters; and strikeout and walk ratios, opposing batting averages, etc. for pitchers.

		NM/M
Factory Hobby Set (672):		12.50
Retail Hobby Set (660):		12.00
Complete Set (660):		10.00
Common Player:		.05
Wax Pack (15):		.50
Wax Box (36):		10.00
Cello Pack (33):		1.00
Cello Box (24):		12.00
1	Lance Blankenship	.05
2	Todd Burns	.05
3	Jose Canseco	.30
4	Jim Corsi	.05
5	Storm Davis	.05
6	Dennis Eckersley	.35
7	Mike Gallego	.05
8	Ron Hassey	.05
9	Dave Henderson	.05
10	Rickey Henderson	.40
11	Rick Honeycutt	.05
12	Stan Javier	.05
13	Felix Jose	.05
14	Carney Lansford	.05
15	Mark McGwire	.65
16	Mike Moore	.05
17	Gene Nelson	.05
18	Dave Parker	.05
19	Tony Phillips	.05
20	Terry Steinbach	.05
21	Dave Stewart	.05
22	Walt Weiss	.05
23	Bob Welch	.05
24	Curt Young	.05
25	Paul Assenmacher	.05
26	Damon Berryhill	.05
27	Mike Bielecki	.05
28	Kevin Blankenship	.05
29	Andre Dawson	.25
30	Shawon Dunston	.05
31	Joe Girardi	.05
32	Mark Grace	.05
33	Mike Harkey	.05
34	Paul Kilgus	.05
35	Les Lancaster	.05
36	Vance Law	.05
37	Greg Maddux	.50
38	Lloyd McClendon	.05
39	Jeff Pico	.05
40	Ryne Sandberg	.50
41	Scott Sanderson	.05
42	Dwight Smith	.05
43	Rick Sutcliffe	.05
44	Jerome Walton RC	.05
45	Mitch Webster	.05
46	Curt Wilkerson	.05
47	Dean Wilkins RC	.05
48	Mitch Williams	.05
49	Steve Wilson	.05
50	Steve Bedrosian	.05
51	Mike Benjamin RC	.05
52	Jeff Brantley RC	.10
53	Brett Butler	.05
54	Will Clark	.05
55	Kelly Downs	.05
56	Scott Garrelts	.05
57	Atlee Hammaker	.05
58	Terry Kennedy	.05
59	Mike LaCoss	.05
60	Craig Lefferts	.05
61	Greg Litton RC	.05
62	Candy Maldonado	.05
63	Kirt Manwaring	.05
64	Randy McCament RC	.05
65	Kevin Mitchell	.05
66	Donell Nixon	.05
67	Ken Oberkfell	.05
68	Rick Reuschel	.05
69	Ernest Riles	.05
70	Don Robinson	.05
71	Pat Sheridan	.05
72	Chris Speier	.05
73	Robby Thompson	.05
74	Jose Uribe	.05
75	Matt Williams	.05
76	George Bell	.05
77	Pat Borders	.05
78	John Cerutti	.05
79	Junior Felix RC	.05
80	Tony Fernandez	.05
81	Mike Flanagan	.05
82	Mauro Gozzo RC	.05
83	Kelly Gruber	.05
84	Tom Henke	.05
85	Jimmy Key	.05
86	Manny Lee	.05
87	Nelson Liriano	.05
88	Lee Mazzilli	.05
89	Fred McGriff	.05
90	Lloyd Moseby	.05
91	Rance Mulliniks	.05
92	Alex Sanchez	.05
93	Dave Steib	.05
94	Todd Stottlemyre	.05
95	Duane Ward	.05
96	David Wells	.05
97	Ernie Whitt	.05
98	Frank Wills	.05
99	Mookie Wilson	.05
100	Kevin Appier	.05
101	Luis Aquino	.05
102	Bob Boone	.05
103	George Brett	.60
104	Jose DeJesus	.05
105	Luis de los Santos	.05
106	Jim Eisenreich	.05
107	Steve Farr	.05
108	Tom Gordon	.05
109	Mark Gubicza	.05
110	Bo Jackson	.10
111	Terry Leach	.05
112	Charlie Leibrandt	.05
113	Rick Luecken RC	.05
114	Mike Macfarlane	.05
115	Jeff Montgomery	.05
116	Bret Saberhagen	.05
117	Kevin Seitzer	.05
118	Kurt Stillwell	.05
119	Pat Tabler	.05
120	Danny Tartabull	.05
121	Gary Thurman	.05
122	Frank White	.05
123	Willie Wilson	.05
124	Matt Winters	.05
125	Jim Abbott	.05
126	Tony Armas	.05
127	Dante Bichette	.05
128	Bert Blyleven	.10
129	Chili Davis	.05
130	Brian Downing	.05
131	Mike Fetters RC	.05
132	Chuck Finley	.05
133	Willie Fraser	.05
134	Bryan Harvey	.05
135	Jack Howell	.05
136	Wally Joyner	.05
137	Jeff Manto RC	.05
138	Kirk McCaskill	.05
139	Bob McClure	.05
140	Greg Minton	.05
141	Lance Parrish	.05
142	Dan Petry	.05
143	Johnny Ray	.05
144	Dick Schofield	.05
145	Lee Stevens RC	.05
146	Claudell Washington	.05
147	Devon White	.05
148	Mike Witt	.05
149	Roberto Alomar	.20
150	Sandy Alomar, Jr.	.05
151	Andy Benes	.05
152	Jack Clark	.05
153	Pat Clements	.05
154	Joey Cora	.05
155	Mark Davis	.05
156	Mark Grant	.05
157	Tony Gwynn	.50
158	Greg Harris	.05
159	Bruce Hurst	.05
160	Darrin Jackson	.05
161	Chris James	.05
162	Carmelo Martinez	.05
163	Mike Pagliarulo	.05
164	Mark Parent	.05
165	Dennis Rasmussen	.05
166	Bip Roberts	.05
167	Benito Santiago	.05
168	Calvin Schiraldi	.05
169	Eric Show	.05
170	Garry Templeton	.05
171	Ed Whitson	.05
172	Brady Anderson	.05
173	Jeff Ballard	.05
174	Phil Bradley	.05
175	Mike Devereaux	.05
176	Steve Finley	.05
177	Pete Harnisch RC	.05
178	Kevin Hickey	.05
179	Brian Holton	.05
180	Ben McDonald RC	.15
181	Bob Melvin	.05
182	Bob Milacki	.05
183	Randy Milligan	.05
184	Gregg Olson RC	.05
185	Joe Orsulak	.05
186	Bill Ripken	.05
187	Cal Ripken, Jr.	.75
188	Dave Schmidt	.05
189	Larry Sheets	.05
190	Mickey Tettleton	.05
191	Mark Thurmond	.05
192	Jay Tibbs	.05
193	Jim Traber	.05
194	Mark Williamson	.05
195	Craig Worthington	.05
196	Don Aase	.05
197	Blaine Beatty RC	.05
198	Mark Carreon	.05
199	Gary Carter	.40
200	David Cone	.05
201	Ron Darling	.05
202	Kevin Elster	.05
203	Sid Fernandez	.05
204	Dwight Gooden	.05
205	Keith Hernandez	.05
206	Jeff Innis RC	.05
207	Gregg Jefferies	.05
208	Howard Johnson	.05
209	Barry Lyons	.05
210	Dave Magadan	.05
211	Kevin McReynolds	.05
212	Jeff Musselman	.05
213	Randy Myers	.05
214	Bob Ojeda	.05
215	Juan Samuel	.05
216	Mackey Sasser	.05
217	Darryl Strawberry	.05
218	Tim Teufel	.05
219	Frank Viola	.05
220	Juan Agosto	.05
221	Larry Anderson	.05
222	Eric Anthony RC	.10
223	Kevin Bass	.05
224	Craig Biggio	.05
225	Ken Caminiti	.05
226	Jim Clancy	.05
227	Danny Darwin	.05
228	Glenn Davis	.05
229	Jim Deshaies	.05
230	Bill Doran	.05
231	Bob Forsch	.05
232	Brian Meyer	.05
233	Terry Puhl	.05
234	Rafael Ramirez	.05
235	Rick Rhoden	.05
236	Dan Schatzeder	.05
237	Mike Scott	.05
238	Dave Smith	.05
239	Alex Trevino	.05
240	Glenn Wilson	.05
241	Gerald Young	.05
242	Tom Brunansky	.05
243	Cris Carpenter	.05
244	Alex Cole RC	.05
245	Vince Coleman	.05
246	John Costello	.05
247	Ken Dayley	.05
248	Jose DeLeon	.05
249	Frank DiPino	.05
250	Pedro Guerrero	.05
251	Ken Hill	.05
252	Joe Magrane	.05
253	Willie McGee	.05
254	John Morris	.05
255	Jose Oquendo	.05
256	Tony Pena	.05
257	Terry Pendleton	.05
258	Ted Power	.05
259	Dan Quisenberry	.05
260	Ozzie Smith	.50
261	Scott Terry	.05
262	Milt Thompson	.05
263	Denny Walling	.05
264	Todd Worrell	.05
265	Todd Zeile	.05
266	Marty Barrett	.05
267	Mike Boddicker	.05
268	Wade Boggs	.50
269	Ellis Burks	.05
270	Rick Cerone	.05
271	Roger Clemens	.60
272	John Dopson	.05
273	Nick Esasky	.05
274	Dwight Evans	.05
275	Wes Gardner	.05
276	Rich Gedman	.05
277	Mike Greenwell	.05
278	Danny Heep	.05
279	Eric Hetzel	.05
280	Dennis Lamp	.05
281	Rob Murphy	.05
282	Joe Price	.05
283	Carlos Quintana	.05
284	Jody Reed	.05
285	Luis Rivera	.05
286	Kevin Romine	.05
287	Lee Smith	.05
288	Mike Smithson	.05
289	Bob Stanley	.05
290	Harold Baines	.06
291	Kevin Brown	.05
292	Steve Buechele	.05
293	Scott Coolbaugh RC	.05
294	Jack Daugherty RC	.05
295	Cecil Espy	.05
296	Julio Franco	.05
297	Juan Gonzalez RC	2.00
298	Cecilio Guante	.05
299	Drew Hall	.05
300	Charlie Hough	.05
301	Pete Incaviglia	.05
302	Mike Jeffcoat	.05
303	Chad Kreuter	.05
304	Jeff Kunkel	.05
305	Rick Leach	.05
306	Fred Manrique	.05
307	Jamie Moyer	.05
308	Rafael Palmeiro	.35
309	Geno Petralli	.05
310	Kevin Reimer	.05
311	Kenny Rogers RC	.10
312	Jeff Russell	.05
313	Nolan Ryan	.75
314	Ruben Sierra	.05
315	Bobby Witt	.05
316	Chris Bosio	.05
317	Glenn Braggs	.05
318	Greg Brock	.05
319	Chuck Crim	.05
320	Rob Deer	.05
321	Mike Felder	.05
322	Tom Filer	.05
323	Tony Fossas RC	.05
324	Jim Gantner	.05
325	Darryl Hamilton	.05
326	Ted Higuera	.05
327	Mark Knudson RC	.05
328	Bill Krueger	.05
329	Tim McIntosh RC	.05
330	Paul Molitor	.40
331	Jaime Navarro	.05
332	Charlie O'Brien	.05
333	Jeff Peterek RC	.05
334	Dan Plesac	.05
335	Jerry Reuss	.05
336	Gary Sheffield	.35
337	Bill Spiers RC	.05
338	B.J. Surhoff	.05
339	Greg Vaughn	.05
340	Robin Yount	.40
341	Hubie Brooks	.05
342	Tim Burke	.05
343	Mike Fitzgerald	.05
344	Tom Foley	.05
345	Andres Galarraga	.05
346	Damaso Garcia	.05
347	Marquis Grissom RC	.50
348	Kevin Gross	.05
349	Joe Hesketh	.05
350	Jeff Huson RC	.05
351	Wallace Johnson	.05
352	Mark Langston	.05
353a	Dave Martinez	.05
	(Yellow 90.)	6.00
353b	Dave Martinez (Red 90.)	.05
354	Dennis Martinez	.05
355	Andy McGaffigan	.05
356	Otis Nixon	.05
357	Spike Owen	.05
358	Pascual Perez	.05
359	Tim Raines	.05
360	Nelson Santovenia	.05
361	Bryn Smith	.05
362	Zane Smith	.05
363	Larry Walker RC	.75
364	Tim Wallach	.05
365	Rick Aguilera	.05
366	Allan Anderson	.05
367	Wally Backman	.05
368	Doug Baker RC	.05
369	Juan Berenguer	.05
370	Randy Bush	.05
371	Carmen Castillo	.05
372	Mike Dyer RC	.05
373	Gary Gaetti	.05
374	Greg Gagne	.05
375	Dan Gladden	.05
376	German Gonzalez	.05
377	Brian Harper	.05
378	Kent Hrbek	.05
379	Gene Larkin	.05
380	Tim Laudner	.05
381	John Moses	.05
382	Al Newman	.05
383	Kirby Puckett	.50
384	Shane Rawley	.05
385	Jeff Reardon	.05
386	Roy Smith	.05
387	Gary Wayne RC	.05
388	Dave West	.05
389	Tim Belcher	.05
390	Tim Crews	.05
391	Mike Davis	.05
392	Rick Dempsey	.05
393	Kirk Gibson	.05
394	Jose Gonzalez	.05
395	Alfredo Griffin	.05
396	Jeff Hamilton	.05
397	Lenny Harris	.05
398	Mickey Hatcher	.05
399	Orel Hershiser	.05
400	Jay Howell	.05
401	Mike Marshall	.05
402	Ramon Martinez	.05
403	Mike Morgan	.05
404	Eddie Murray	.40
405	Alejandro Pena	.05
406	Willie Randolph	.05
407	Mike Scioscia	.05
408	Ray Searage	.05
409	Fernando Valenzuela	.05
410	Jose Vizcaino RC	.10
411	John Wetteland RC	.20
412	Jack Armstrong	.05
413	Todd Benzinger	.05
414	Tim Birtsas	.05
415	Tom Browning	.05
416	Norm Charlton	.05
417	Eric Davis	.05
418	Rob Dibble	.05
419	John Franco	.05
420	Ken Griffey Sr.	.05
421	Chris Hammond RC	.15
422	Danny Jackson	.05
423	Barry Larkin	.05
424	Tim Leary	.05
425	Rick Mahler	.05
426	Joe Oliver RC	.05
427	Paul O'Neill	.05
428	Luis Quinones	.05
429	Jeff Reed	.05
430	Jose Rijo	.05
431	Ron Robinson	.05
432	Rolando Roomes	.05
433	Chris Sabo	.05
434	Scott Scudder RC	.05
435	Herm Winningham	.05
436	Steve Balboni	.05
437	Jesse Barfield	.05
438	Mike Blowers RC	.05
439	Tom Brookens	.05
440	Greg Cadaret	.05
441	Alvaro Espinoza	.05
442	Bob Geren RC	.05
443	Lee Guetterman	.05
444	Mel Hall	.05
445	Andy Hawkins	.05
446	Roberto Kelly	.05
447	Don Mattingly	.60
448	Lance McCullers	.05
449	Hensley Meulens	.05
450	Dale Mohorcic	.05
451	Clay Parker	.05
452	Eric Plunk	.05
453	Dave Righetti	.05
454	Deion Sanders	.10
455	Steve Sax	.05
456	Don Slaught	.05
457	Walt Terrell	.05
458	Dave Winfield	.40
459	Jay Bell	.05
460	Rafael Belliard	.05
461	Barry Bonds	.75
462	Bobby Bonilla	.05
463	Sid Bream	.05
464	Benny Distefano	.05
465	Doug Drabek	.05
466	Jim Gott	.05
467	Billy Hatcher	.05
468	Neal Heaton	.05
469	Jeff King	.05
470	Bob Kipper	.05
471	Randy Kramer	.05
472	Bill Landrum	.05
473	Mike LaValliere	.05
474	Jose Lind	.05
475	Junior Ortiz	.05
476	Gary Redus	.05
477	Rick Reed RC	.05
478	R.J. Reynolds	.05
479	Jeff Robinson	.05
480	John Smiley	.05
481	Andy Van Slyke	.05
482	Bob Walk	.05
483	Andy Allanson	.05
484	Scott Bailes	.05
485	Albert Belle	.05
486	Bud Black	.05
487	Jerry Browne	.05
488	Tom Candiotti	.05
489	Joe Carter	.05
490	David Clark	.05
491	John Farrell	.05
492	Felix Fermin	.05
493	Brook Jacoby	.05
494	Dion James	.05
495	Doug Jones	.05
496	Brad Komminsk	.05
497	Rod Nichols	.05
498	Pete O'Brien	.05
499	Steve Olin RC	.05
500	Jesse Orosco	.05
501	Joel Skinner	.05
502	Cory Snyder	.05
503	Greg Swindell	.05
504	Rich Yett	.05
505	Scott Bankhead	.05
506	Scott Bradley	.05
507	Greg Briley	.05

508	Jay Buhner	.05
509	Darnell Coles	.05
510	Keith Comstock	.05
511	Henry Cotto	.05
512	Alvin Davis	.05
513	Ken Griffey Jr.	.65
514	Erik Hanson	.05
515	Gene Harris	.05
516	Brian Holman	.05
517	Mike Jackson	.05
518	Randy Johnson	.40
519	Jeffrey Leonard	.05
520	Edgar Martinez	.05
521	Dennis Powell	.05
522	Jim Presley	.05
523	Jerry Reed	.05
524	Harold Reynolds	.05
525	Mike Schooler	.05
526	Bill Swift	.05
527	David Valle	.05
528	Omar Vizquel	.05
529	Ivan Calderon	.05
530	Carlton Fisk	.40
531	Scott Fletcher	.05
532	Dave Gallagher	.05
533	Ozzie Guillen	.05
534	Greg Hibbard RC	.05
535	Shawn Hillegas	.05
536	Lance Johnson	.05
537	Eric King	.05
538	Ron Kittle	.05
539	Steve Lyons	.05
540	Carlos Martinez	.05
541	Tom McCarthy RC	.05
542	Matt Merullo RC	.05
543	Donn Pall	.05
544	Dan Pasqua	.05
545	Ken Patterson	.05
546	Melido Perez	.05
547	Steve Rosenberg	.05
548	Sammy Sosa RC	5.00
549	Bobby Thigpen	.05
550	Robin Ventura	.05
551	Greg Walker	.05
552	Don Carman	.05
553	Pat Combs RC	.05
554	Dennis Cook	.05
555	Darren Daulton	.05
556	Len Dykstra	.05
557	Curt Ford	.05
558	Charlie Hayes	.05
559	Von Hayes	.05
560	Tom Herr	.05
561	Ken Howell	.05
562	Steve Jeltz	.05
563	Ron Jones	.05
564	Ricky Jordan	.05
565	John Kruk	.05
566	Steve Lake	.05
567	Roger McDowell	.05
568	Terry Mulholland	.05
569	Dwayne Murphy	.05
570	Jeff Parrett	.05
571	Randy Ready	.05
572	Bruce Ruffin	.05
573	Dickie Thon	.05
574	Jose Alvarez	.05
575	Geronimo Berroa	.05
576	Jeff Blauser	.05
577	Joe Boever	.05
578	Marty Clary	.05
579	Jody Davis	.05
580	Mark Eichhorn	.05
581	Darrell Evans	.05
582	Ron Gant	.05
583	Tom Glavine	.25
584	Tommy Greene RC	.05
585	Tommy Gregg	.05
586	Dave Justice RC	.40
587	Mark Lemke RC	.05
588	Derek Lilliquist	.05
589	Oddibe McDowell	.05
590	Kent Mercker RC	.05
591	Dale Murphy	.20
592	Gerald Perry	.05
593	Lonnie Smith	.05
594	Pete Smith	.05
595	John Smoltz	.05
596	Mike Stanton RC	.05
597	Andres Thomas	.05
598	Jeff Treadway	.05
599	Doyle Alexander	.05
600	Dave Bergman	.05
601	Brian Dubois RC	.05
602	Paul Gibson	.05
603	Mike Heath	.05
604	Mike Henneman	.05
605	Guillermo Hernandez	.05
606	Shawn Holman RC	.05
607	Tracy Jones	.05
608	Chet Lemon	.05
609	Fred Lynn	.05
610	Jack Morris	.05
611	Matt Nokes	.05
612	Gary Pettis	.05
613	Kevin Ritz RC	.05
614	Jeff Robinson	.05
615	Steve Searcy	.05
616	Frank Tanana	.05
617	Alan Trammell	.05
618	Gary Ward	.05
619	Lou Whitaker	.05
620	Frank Williams	.05

		NM/M
621a	Players of the Decade/1980 (George Brett (... 10 .390 hitting ...))	1.00
621b	Players of the Decade/1980 (George Brett)	.25

622	Players of the Decade/1981 (Fernando Valenzuela)	.05
623	Players of the Decade/1982 (Dale Murphy)	.05
624a	Players of the Decade/1983 (Cal Ripkin, Jr. (Ripken))	1.50
624b	Players of the Decade/1983 (Cal Ripken, Jr.)	.30
625	Players of the Decade/1984 (Ryne Sandberg)	.25
626	Players of the Decade/1985 (Don Mattingly)	.30
627	Players of the Decade/1986 (Roger Clemens)	.30
628	Players of the Decade/1987 (George Bell)	.05
629	Players of the Decade/1988 (Jose Canseco)	.10
630a	Players of the Decade/1989 (Will Clark (Total bases 32.))	.35
630b	Players of the Decade/1989 (Will Clark (Total bases 321.))	.05
631	Game Savers (Mark Davis, Mitch Williams)	.05
632	Boston Igniters (Wade Boggs, Mike Greenwell)	.15
633	Starter & Stopper (Mark Gubicza, Jeff Russell)	.05
634	League's Best Shortstops (Tony Fernandez, Cal Ripken Jr.)	.30
635	Human Dynamos (Kirby Puckett, Bo Jackson)	.20
636	300 Strikeout Club (Mike Scott, Nolan Ryan)	.30
637	The Dynamic Duo (Will Clark, Kevin Mitchell)	.05
638	A.L. All-Stars (Don Mattingly, Mark McGwire)	.65
639	N.L. East Rivals (Howard Johnson, Ryne Sandberg)	.20
640	Major League Prospects (Rudy Seanez RC, Colin Charland RC)	.05
641	Major League Prospects (George Canale RC, Kevin Maas RC)	.10
642	Major League Prospects (Kelly Mann RC, Dave Hansen RC)	.05
643	Major League Prospects (Greg Smith RC, Stu Tate RC)	.05
644	Major League Prospects (Tom Drees RC, Dan Howitt RC)	.05
645	Major League Prospects (Mike Roesler RC, Derrick May RC)	.05
646	Major League Prospects (Scott Hemond RC, Mark Gardner RC)	.10
647	Major League Prospects (John Orton RC, Scott Leius RC)	.10
648	Major League Prospects (Rich Monteleone RC, Dana Williams RC)	.05
649	Major League Prospects (Mike Huff RC, Steve Frey RC)	.05
650	Major League Prospects (Chuck McElroy RC, Moises Alou RC)	.50
651	Major League Prospects (Bobby Rose RC, Mike Hartley RC)	.10
652	Major League Prospects (Matt Kinzer RC, Wayne Edwards RC)	.05
653	Major League Prospects (Delino DeShields RC, Jason Grimsley RC)	.15
654	Athletics, Cubs, Giants & Blue Jays (Checklist)	.05
655	Royals, Angels, Padres & Orioles (Checklist)	.05
656	Mets, Astros, Cardinals & Red Sox (Checklist)	.05
657	Rangers, Brewers, Expos & Twins (Checklist)	.05
658	Dodgers, Reds, Yankees & Pirates (Checklist)	.05
659	Indians, Mariners, White Sox & Phillies (Checklist)	.05
660	Braves, Tigers & Special Cards (Checklist)	.05

All-Stars

The top players at each position, as selected by Fleer, are featured in this 12-card set inserted in cello packs and some wax packs. The cards measure 2-1/2" x 3-1/2" and feature a unique two-photo format on the card fronts.

		NM/M
Complete Set (12):		4.00
Common Player:		.20
1	Harold Baines	.20
2	Will Clark	.25

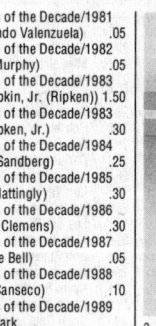

3	Mark Davis	.20
4	Howard Johnson	.20
5	Joe Magrane	.20
6	Kevin Mitchell	.20
7	Kirby Puckett	1.00
8	Cal Ripken	2.00
9	Ryne Sandberg	1.00
10	Mike Scott	.20
11	Ruben Sierra	.20
12	Mickey Tettleton	.25

League Standouts

Fleer's "League Standouts" are six of baseball's top players distributed randomly in Fleer rack packs. Fronts feature full color photos with a six-dimensional effect. A black and gold frame borders the photo. Backs are yellow and describe the player's accomplishments. The cards measure 2-1/2" x 3-1/2".

		NM/M
Complete Set (6):		3.00
Common Player:		.50
1	Barry Larkin	.50
2	Don Mattingly	1.50
3	Darryl Strawberry	.50
4	Jose Canseco	.75
5	Wade Boggs	1.00
6	Mark Grace	.50

Soaring Stars

Cards from this 12-card set could be found in 1990 Fleer jumbo cello packs. The cards are styled with a cartoon flavor, featuring astronomical graphics surrounding the player. Backs feature information about the promising young player.

		NM/M
Complete Set (12):		5.00
Common Player:		.10
1	Todd Zeile	.25
2	Mike Stanton	.25
3	Larry Walker	.50
4	Robin Ventura	.50
5	Scott Coolbaugh	.25
6	Ken Griffey Jr.	4.00
7	Tom Gordon	.25
8	Jerome Walton	.25
9	Junior Felix	.25
10	Jim Abbott	.25
11	Ricky Jordan	.25
12	Dwight Smith	.25

World Series

This 12-card set depicts highlights of the 1989 World Series and was included in the factory-collated Fleer set. Single World Series cards were discovered in cello and rack packs, but this was not intended to happen. Fronts of the 2-1/2" x 3-1/2" cards feature action photos set against a white background with a red and blue "'89 World Series" banner. Backs are pink and white and describe the events of the 1989 Fall Classic.

		NM/M
Complete Set (12):		1.50
Common Player:		.10
1	The Final Piece To The Puzzle (Mike Moore)	.10
2	Kevin Mitchell	.15
3	Game Two's Crushing Blow	.10
4	Will Clark	.15
5	Jose Canseco	.75
6	Great Leather in the Field	.10
7	Game One And A's Break Out On Top	.10
8	Dave Stewart	.10
9	Parker's Bat Produces Power (Dave Parker)	.25
10	World Series Record Book Game 3	.10
11	Rickey Henderson	.75
12	Oakland A's - Baseball's Best In '89	.25

Box Panels

For the fifth consecutive year, Fleer issued a series of cards on the bottom panels of its wax pack boxes. This 28-card set features both players and team logo cards. The cards were numbered C-1 to C-28.

		NM/M
Complete Set, Panels (7):		7.00
Complete Set, Singles (28):		7.00
Common Player:		.05
1	Giants Logo	.05
2	Tim Belcher	.05
3	Roger Clemens	1.00
4	Eric Davis	.05
5	Glenn Davis	.05
6	Cubs Logo	.05
7	John Franco	.05
8	Mike Greenwell	.05
9	Athletics logo	.05
10	Ken Griffey Jr.	2.00
11	Pedro Guerrero	.05
12	Tony Gwynn	.75
13	Blue Jays Logo	.05
14	Orel Hershiser	.05
15	Bo Jackson	.10
16	Howard Johnson	.05
17	Mets Logo	.05
18	Cardinals Logo	.05
19	Don Mattingly	1.00
20	Mark McGwire	2.00
21	Kevin Mitchell	.05
22	Kirby Puckett	.75
23	Royals Logo	.05
24	Orioles Logo	.05
25	Ruben Sierra	.05
26	Dave Stewart	.05
27	Jerome Walton	.05
28	Robin Yount	.60

Printed in Canada

Whether these cards were printed for distribution in Canada or simply the work of a Canadian printer engaged by Fleer to meet U.S. demand is unknown. Each of the 660 cards in the 1990 Fleer issue can be found with a "1990 FLEER LTD./LTEE PTD. IN CANADA" copyright notice on back in the bottom border. Except for various superstar cards, little demand attaches to this variation.

	NM/M
Complete Set (660):	25.00
Common Player:	.25
Wax Pack (10):	1.50
Wax Box (48):	50.00

Update

Fleer produced its seventh consecutive "Update" set in 1990. As in the past, the set consists of 132 cards (numbered U-1 through U-132) that were sold to hobby dealers in special collectors boxes. The cards are designed in the same style as the regular issue. A special Nolan Ryan commemorative card is included in the set.

		NM/M
Complete Set (132):		5.00
Common Player:		.05
1	Steve Avery RC	.05
2	Francisco Cabrera	.05
3	Nick Esasky	.05
4	Jim Kremers RC	.05
5	Greg Olson RC	.05
6	Jim Presley	.05
7	Shawn Boskie RC	.05
8	Joe Kraemer RC	.05
9	Luis Salazar	.05
10	Hector Villanueva RC	.05
11	Glenn Braggs	.05
12	Mariano Duncan	.05
13	Billy Hatcher	.05
14	Tim Layana RC	.05
15	Hal Morris	.05
16	Javier Ortiz RC	.05
17	Dave Rohde RC	.05
18	Eric Yelding RC	.05
19	Hubie Brooks	.05
20	Kal Daniels	.05
21	Dave Hansen	.05
22	Mike Hartley	.05
23	Stan Javier	.05
24	Jose Offerman RC	.05
25	Juan Samuel	.05
26	Dennis Boyd	.05
27	Delino DeShields	.05
28	Steve Frey	.05
29	Mark Gardner	.05
30	Chris Nabholz RC	.05
31	Bill Sampen RC	.05
32	Dave Schmidt	.05
33	Daryl Boston	.05
34	Chuck Carr RC	.05
35	John Franco	.05
36	Todd Hundley RC	.25
37	Julio Machado RC	.05
38	Alejandro Pena	.05
39	Darren Reed RC	.05
40	Kelvin Torve RC	.05
41	Darrel Akerfelds RC	.05
42	Jose DeJesus	.05
43	Dave Hollins RC	.05
44	Carmelo Martinez	.05
45	Brad Moore RC	.05
46	Dale Murphy	.15
47	Wally Backman	.05
48	Stan Belinda RC	.05
49	Bob Patterson	.05
50	Ted Power	.05
51	Don Slaught	.05

52	Geronimo Pena RC	.05
53	Lee Smith	.05
54	John Tudor	.05
55	Joe Carter	.05
56	Tom Howard RC	.05
57	Craig Lefferts	.05
58	Rafael Valdez RC	.05
59	Dave Anderson	.05
60	Kevin Bass	.05
61	John Burkett	.05
62	Gary Carter	.40
63	Rick Parker RC	.05
64	Trevor Wilson	.05
65	Chris Hoiles RC	.05
66	Tim Hulett	.05
67	Dave Johnson RC	.05
68	Curt Schilling RC	.35
69	David Segui RC	.05
70	Tom Brunansky	.05
71	Greg Harris	.05
72	Dana Kiecker RC	.05
73	Tim Naehring RC	.05
74	Tony Pena	.05
75	Jeff Reardon	.05
76	Jerry Reed	.05
77	Mark Eichhorn	.05
78	Mark Langston	.05
79	John Orton	.05
80	Luis Polonia	.05
81	Dave Winfield	.40
82	Cliff Young RC	.05
83	Wayne Edwards	.05
84	Alex Fernandez RC	.05
85	Craig Grebeck RC	.05
86	Scott Radinsky RC	.05
87	Frank Thomas RC	3.00
88	Beau Allred RC	.05
89	Sandy Alomar, Jr.	.05
90	Carlos Baerga RC	.10
91	Kevin Bearse RC	.05
92	Chris James	.05
93	Candy Maldonado	.05
94	Jeff Manto	.05
95	Cecil Fielder	.05
96	Travis Fryman RC	.25
97	Lloyd Moseby	.05
98	Edwin Nunez	.05
99	Tony Phillips	.05
100	Larry Sheets	.05
101	Mark Davis	.05
102	Storm Davis	.05
103	Gerald Perry	.05
104	Terry Shumpert	.05
105	Edgar Diaz RC	.05
106	Dave Parker	.05
107	Tim Drummond RC	.05
108	Junior Ortiz	.05
109	Park Pittman RC	.05
110	Kevin Tapani RC	.05
111	Oscar Azocar RC	.05
112	Jim Leyritz RC	.05
113	Kevin Maas	.05
114	Alan Mills RC	.05
115	Matt Nokes	.05
116	Pascual Perez	.05
117	Ozzie Canseco RC	.05
118	Scott Sanderson	.05
119	Tino Martinez RC	.05
120	Jeff Schaefer RC	.05
121	Matt Young	.05
122	Brian Bohanon RC	.05
123	Jeff Huson	.05
124	Ramon Manon RC	.05
125	Gary Mielke RC	.05
126	Willie Blair RC	.05
127	Glenallen Hill RC	.05
128	John Olerud RC	.35
129	Luis Sojo RC	.05
130	Mark Whiten RC	.05
131	Three Decades of No Hitters (Nolan Ryan)	1.00
132	Checklist	.05

Award Winners

Hill's department stores and 7-Eleven outlets exclusively sold the 1990 Fleer "Award Winners." This 44-card boxed set includes baseball's statistical leaders of 1989. Card fronts feature a full-color player photo framed by a winner's cup design and blue border. Backs showcase player statistics in blue on a yellow and white background. The cards measure 2-1/2" x 3-1/2". The checklist provided on the back of each box is not correct. It incorrectly lists Bob Boone's team as the Angels and card #10 as Ron Darling. Darryl Strawberry (#38) is not checklisted and all cards #10-38 are off by a number. This is one of the scarcer Fleer box sets of the era.

		NM/M
Complete Set (44):		6.00
Common Player:		.05
1	Jeff Ballard	.05
2	Tim Belcher	.05
3	Bert Blyleven	.05
4	Wade Boggs	.75
5	Bob Boone	.05
6	Jose Canseco	.50
7	Will Clark	.05
8	Jack Clark	.05
9	Vince Coleman	.05
10	Eric Davis	.05
11	Jose DeLeon	.05
12	Tony Fernandez	.05
13	Carlton Fisk	.60
14	Scott Garrelts	.05
15	Tom Gordon	.05
16	Ken Griffey Jr.	1.50
17	Von Hayes	.05
18	Rickey Henderson	.60
19	Bo Jackson	.10
20	Howard Johnson	.05
21	Don Mattingly	1.00
22	Fred McGriff	.05
23	Kevin Mitchell	.05
24	Gregg Olson	.05
25	Gary Pettis	.05
26	Kirby Puckett	.75
27	Harold Reynolds	.05
28	Jeff Russell	.05
29	Nolan Ryan	2.00
30	Bret Saberhagen	.05
31	Ryne Sandberg	.75
32	Benito Santiago	.05
33	Mike Scott	.05
34	Ruben Sierra	.05
35	Lonnie Smith	.05
36	Ozzie Smith	.75
37	Dave Stewart	.05
38	Darryl Strawberry	.05
39	Greg Swindell	.05
40	Andy Van Slyke	.05
41	Tim Wallach	.05
42	Jerome Walton	.05
43	Mitch Williams	.05
44	Robin Yount	.60

Baseball All-Stars

ERIC DAVIS REDS OUTFIELD

Sold exclusively in Ben Franklin stores, this boxed set showcases the game's top players. Fronts feature a player photo surrounded by a pin-striped tan border. Backs have statistics and data printed in shades of red and dark blue. The cards measure 2-1/2" x 3-1/2" and are packed in a special box with a complete checklist on the back. Like other Fleer boxed sets, the cards are numbered alphabetically. All cards carry a "Printed in Canada" note on back.

		NM/M
Complete Set (44):		6.00
Common Player:		.05
1	Wade Boggs	.75
2	Bobby Bonilla	.05
3	Tim Burke	.05
4	Jose Canseco	.50
5	Will Clark	.05
6	Eric Davis	.05
7	Glenn Davis	.05
8	Julio Franco	.05
9	Tony Fernandez	.05
10	Gary Gaetti	.05
11	Scott Garrelts	.05
12	Mark Grace	.05
13	Mike Greenwell	.05
14	Ken Griffey Jr.	1.00
15	Mark Gubicza	.05
16	Pedro Guerrero	.05
17	Von Hayes	.05
18	Orel Hershiser	.05
19	Bruce Hurst	.05
20	Bo Jackson	.10
21	Howard Johnson	.05
22	Doug Jones	.05
23	Barry Larkin	.05
24	Don Mattingly	.85
25	Mark McGwire	1.00
26	Kevin McReynolds	.05
27	Kevin Mitchell	.05
28	Dan Plesac	.05
29	Kirby Puckett	.75
30	Cal Ripken, Jr.	1.50
31	Bret Saberhagen	.05
32	Ryne Sandberg	.75
33	Steve Sax	.05
34	Ruben Sierra	.75
35	Ozzie Smith	.75
36	John Smoltz	.05
37	Darryl Strawberry	.05
38	Terry Steinbach	.05
39	Dave Stewart	.05
40	Bobby Thigpen	.05
41	Alan Trammell	.05
42	Devon White	.05
43	Mitch Williams	.05
44	Robin Yount	.60

League Leaders

TIM BELCHER DODGERS PITCHER

For the fifth consecutive year Fleer released a "League Leaders" boxed set of 44 top Major League players. Card number 42 (Jerome Walton) pictures a player other than Walton. The 2-1/2" x 3-1/2" cards display a full-color photo bordered by a blue frame. Backs feature complete statistics. The cards are numbered alphabetically and a complete checklist is displayed on the back of the box. The set was available at Walgreen drug stores. Cards carry a "Printed in Canada" notice on back.

		NM/M
Complete Set (44):		6.00
Common Player:		.10
1	Roberto Alomar	.25
2	Tim Belcher	.10
3	George Bell	.10
4	Wade Boggs	.75
5	Jose Canseco	.50
6	Will Clark	.10
7	David Cone	.10
8	Eric Davis	.10
9	Glenn Davis	.10
10	Nick Esasky	.10
11	Dennis Eckersley	.55
12	Mark Grace	.10
13	Mike Greenwell	.10
14	Ken Griffey Jr.	1.25
15	Mark Gubicza	.10
16	Pedro Guerrero	.10
17	Tony Gwynn	.75
18	Rickey Henderson	.60
19	Bo Jackson	.15
20	Doug Jones	.10
21	Ricky Jordan	.10
22	Barry Larkin	.10
23	Don Mattingly	.85
24	Fred McGriff	.10
25	Mark McGwire	1.25
26	Kevin Mitchell	.10
27	Jack Morris	.10
28	Gregg Olson	.10
29	Dan Plesac	.10
30	Kirby Puckett	.75
31	Nolan Ryan	1.50
32	Bret Saberhagen	.75
33	Ryne Sandberg	.75
34	Steve Sax	.10
35	Mike Scott	.10
36	Ruben Sierra	.10
37	Lonnie Smith	.10
38	Darryl Strawberry	.10
39	Bobby Thigpen	.10
40	Andy Van Slyke	.10
41	Tim Wallach	.10
42	Jerome Walton	.10
43	Devon White	.10
44	Robin Yount	.60

MVP

This 44-card boxed set was produced by Fleer for the Toys R Us chain. Fronts are designed with graduating black-to-white borders, surrounding a color player photo.

GEORGE BELL BLUE JAYS OUTFIELD

Backs contain individual data and career statistics. The back of each box carries a checklist of all the players in the set. Six peel-off team logo stickers featuring a baseball trivia quiz on the back are also included with each set. The cards are 2-1/2" x 3-1/2" and numbered alphabetically. All cards carry a "Printed in Canada" notation on the back at bottom.

		NM/M
Complete Set (44):		6.00
Common Player:		.10
1	George Bell	.10
2	Bert Blyleven	.10
3	Wade Boggs	.65
4	Bobby Bonilla	.10
5	George Brett	.85
6	Jose Canseco	.45
7	Will Clark	.10
8	Roger Clemens	.85
9	Eric Davis	.10
10	Glenn Davis	.10
11	Tony Fernandez	.10
12	Dwight Gooden	.10
13	Mike Greenwell	.10
14	Ken Griffey Jr.	1.25
15	Pedro Guerrero	.10
16	Tony Gwynn	.65
17	Rickey Henderson	.50
18	Tom Herr	.10
19	Orel Hershiser	.10
20	Kent Hrbek	.10
21	Bo Jackson	.15
22	Howard Johnson	.10
23	Don Mattingly	.85
24	Fred McGriff	.10
25	Mark McGwire	1.25
26	Kevin Mitchell	.10
27	Paul Molitor	.50
28	Dale Murphy	.25
29	Kirby Puckett	.65
30	Tim Raines	.10
31	Cal Ripken, Jr.	1.50
32	Bret Saberhagen	.10
33	Ryne Sandberg	.65
34	Ruben Sierra	.10
35	Dwight Smith	.10
36	Ozzie Smith	.65
37	Darryl Strawberry	.10
38	Dave Stewart	.10
39	Greg Swindell	.10
40	Bobby Thigpen	.10
41	Alan Trammell	.10
42	Jerome Walton	.10
43	Mitch Williams	.10
44	Robin Yount	.50

1991 Fleer Promo Strip

This three-card strip was issued to introduce Fleer's 1991 baseball card set. The cards on the 7-1/2" x 3-1/2" strip are identical to the players' regular issue cards.

	NM/M
Three-Card Strip:	4.00

1991 Fleer

Fleer expanded its 1991 set to include 720 cards. The cards feature yellow borders surrounding full-color action photos. Backs feature a circular portrait photo, biographical information, complete statistics, and career highlights. Once again these cards are numbered alphabetically within team. Because Fleer used more than one printer, many minor variations in photo cropping and typography can be found. The most notable are included in the checklist here.

DAVID CONE METS P

		NM/M
Unopened Factory Set (732):		12.00
Complete Set (720):		10.00
Common Player:		.05
Wax Pack (15):		.50
Wax Box (36):		12.50
Jumbo Wax Pack (53):		1.25
Jumbo Wax Box (24):		20.00
Cello Pack (30):		1.00
Cello Box (24):		16.00
1	Troy Afenir RC	.05
2	Harold Baines	.05
3	Lance Blankenship	.05
4	Todd Burns	.05
5	Jose Canseco	.30
6	Dennis Eckersley	.35
7	Mike Gallego	.05
8	Ron Hassey	.05
9	Dave Henderson	.05
10	Rickey Henderson	.40
11	Rick Honeycutt	.05
12	Doug Jennings	.05
13	Joe Klink RC	.05
14	Carney Lansford	.05
15	Darren Lewis RC	.05
16	Willie McGee	.05
17a	Mark McGwire (Six-line career summary.)	.65
17b	Mark McGwire (Seven-line career summary.)	.65
18	Mike Moore	.05
19	Gene Nelson	.05
20	Dave Otto	.05
21	Jamie Quirk	.05
22	Willie Randolph	.05
23	Scott Sanderson	.05
24	Terry Steinbach	.05
25	Dave Stewart	.05
26	Walt Weiss	.05
27	Bob Welch	.05
28	Curt Young	.05
29	Wally Backman	.05
30	Stan Belinda RC	.05
31	Jay Bell	.05
32	Rafael Belliard	.05
33	Barry Bonds	.75
34	Bobby Bonilla	.05
35	Sid Bream	.05
36	Doug Drabek	.05
37	Carlos Garcia RC	.10
38	Neal Heaton	.05
39	Jeff King	.05
40	Bob Kipper	.05
41	Bill Landrum	.05
42	Mike LaValliere	.05
43	Jose Lind	.05
44	Carmelo Martinez	.05
45	Bob Patterson	.05
46	Ted Power	.05
47	Gary Redus	.05
48	R.J. Reynolds	.05
49	Don Slaught	.05
50	John Smiley	.05
51	Zane Smith	.05
52	Randy Tomlin RC	.10
53	Andy Van Slyke	.05
54	Bob Walk	.05
55	Jack Armstrong	.05
56	Todd Benzinger	.05
57	Glenn Braggs	.05
58	Keith Brown	.05
59	Tom Browning	.05
60	Norm Charlton	.05
61	Eric Davis	.05
62	Rob Dibble	.05
63	Bill Doran	.05
64	Mariano Duncan	.05
65	Chris Hammond	.05
66	Billy Hatcher	.05
67	Danny Jackson	.05
68	Barry Larkin	.05
69	Tim Layana RC	.05
70	Terry Lee RC	.05
71	Rick Mahler	.05
72	Hal Morris	.05
73	Randy Myers	.05
74	Ron Oester	.05
75	Joe Oliver	.05
76	Paul O'Neill	.05
77	Luis Quinones	.05
78	Jeff Reed	.05
79	Jose Rijo	.05
80	Chris Sabo	.05
81	Scott Scudder	.05
82	Herm Winningham	.05
83	Larry Andersen	.05
84	Marty Barrett	.05
85	Mike Boddicker	.05
86	Wade Boggs	.50
87	Tom Bolton	.05
88	Tom Brunansky	.05
89	Ellis Burks	.05
90	Roger Clemens	.55
91	Scott Cooper RC	.05
92	John Dopson	.05
93	Dwight Evans	.05
94	Wes Gardner	.05
95	Jeff Gray RC	.05
96	Mike Greenwell	.05
97	Greg Harris	.05
98	Daryl Irvine RC	.05
99	Dana Kiecker RC	.05
100	Randy Kutcher	.05
101	Dennis Lamp	.05
102	Mike Marshall	.05
103	John Marzano	.05
104	Rob Murphy	.05
105a	Tim Naehring RC (Seven-line career summary.)	.05
105b	Tim Naehring RC (Nine-line career summary.)	.05
106	Tony Pena	.05
107	Phil Plantier RC	.05
108	Carlos Quintana	.05
109	Jeff Reardon	.05
110	Jerry Reed	.05
111	Jody Reed	.05
112	Luis Rivera	.05
113a	Kevin Romine (One-line career summary.)	.05
113b	Kevin Romine (Two-line career summary.)	.05
114	Phil Bradley	.05
115	Ivan Calderon	.05
116	Wayne Edwards	.05
117	Alex Fernandez	.05
118	Carlton Fisk	.40
119	Scott Fletcher	.05
120	Craig Grebeck RC	.05
121	Ozzie Guillen	.05
122	Greg Hibbard	.05
123	Lance Johnson	.05
124	Barry Jones	.05
125a	Ron Karkovice (Two-line career summary.)	.05
125b	Ron Karkovice (One-line career summary.)	.05
126	Eric King	.05
127	Steve Lyons	.05
128	Carlos Martinez	.05
129	Jack McDowell	.05
130	Donn Pall	.05
131	Dan Pasqua	.05
132	Ken Patterson	.05
133	Melido Perez	.05
134	Adam Peterson	.05
135	Scott Radinsky RC	.05
136	Sammy Sosa	.50
137	Bobby Thigpen	.05
138	Frank Thomas	.40
139	Robin Ventura	.05
140	Daryl Boston	.05
141	Chuck Carr RC	.05
142	Mark Carreon	.05
143	David Cone	.05
144	Ron Darling	.05
145	Kevin Elster	.05
146	Sid Fernandez	.05
147	John Franco	.05
148	Dwight Gooden	.05
149	Tom Herr	.05
150	Todd Hundley	.05
151	Gregg Jefferies	.05
152	Howard Johnson	.05
153	Dave Magadan	.05
154	Kevin McReynolds	.05
155	Keith Miller	.05
156	Bob Ojeda	.05
157	Tom O'Malley	.05
158	Alejandro Pena	.05
159	Darren Reed RC	.05
160	Mackey Sasser	.05
161	Darryl Strawberry	.05
162	Tim Teufel	.05
163	Kelvin Torve	.05
164	Julio Valera	.05
165	Frank Viola	.05
166	Wally Whitehurst	.05
167	Jim Acker	.05
168	Derek Bell RC	.05
169	George Bell	.05
170	Willie Blair RC	.05
171	Pat Borders	.05
172	John Cerutti	.05
173	Junior Felix	.05
174	Tony Fernandez	.05
175	Kelly Gruber	.05
176	Tom Henke	.05
177	Glenallen Hill	.05
178	Jimmy Key	.05
179	Manny Lee	.05
180	Fred McGriff	.05
181	Rance Mulliniks	.05
182	Greg Myers	.05
183	John Olerud	.05
184	Luis Sojo	.05
185	Dave Steib	.05
186	Todd Stottlemyre	.05
187	Duane Ward	.05
188	David Wells	.05
189	Mark Whiten RC	.05
190	Ken Williams	.05
191	Frank Wills	.05
192	Mookie Wilson	.05
193	Don Aase	.05
194	Tim Belcher	.05
195	Hubie Brooks	.05
196	Dennis Cook	.05
197	Tim Crews	.05
198	Kal Daniels	.05
199	Kirk Gibson	.05
200	Jim Gott	.05
201	Alfredo Griffin	.05
202	Chris Gwynn	.05
203	Dave Hansen	.05
204	Lenny Harris	.05
205	Mike Hartley	.05
206	Mickey Hatcher	.05
207	Carlos Hernandez RC	.05
208	Orel Hershiser	.05
209	Jay Howell	.05
210	Mike Huff	.05
211	Stan Javier	.05
212	Ramon Martinez	.05
213	Mike Morgan	.05
214	Eddie Murray	.40
215	Jim Neidlinger RC	.05
216	Jose Offerman	.05
217	Jim Poole RC	.05
218	Juan Samuel	.05
219	Mike Scioscia	.05
220	Ray Searage	.05
221	Mike Sharperson	.05
222	Fernando Valenzuela	.05
223	Jose Vizcaino	.05
224	Mike Aldrete	.05
225	Scott Anderson RC	.05
226	Dennis Boyd	.05
227	Tim Burke	.05
228	Delino DeShields	.05
229	Mike Fitzgerald	.05
230	Tom Foley	.05
231	Steve Frey	.05
232	Andres Galarraga	.05
233	Mark Gardner	.05
234	Marquis Grissom	.05
235	Kevin Gross	.05
236	Drew Hall	.05
237	Dave Martinez	.05
238	Dennis Martinez	.05
239	Dale Mohorcic	.05
240	Chris Nabholz RC	.05
241	Otis Nixon	.05
242	Junior Noboa RC	.05
243	Spike Owen	.05
244	Tim Raines	.05
245	Mel Rojas RC	.10
246	Scott Ruskin RC	.05
247	Bill Sampen RC	.05
248	Nelson Santovenia	.05
249	Dave Schmidt	.05
250	Larry Walker	.05
251	Tim Wallach	.05
252	Dave Anderson	.05
253	Kevin Bass	.05
254	Steve Bedrosian	.05
255	Jeff Brantley	.05
256	John Burkett	.05
257	Brett Butler	.05
258	Gary Carter	.40
259	Will Clark	.05
260	Steve Decker RC	.05
261	Kelly Downs	.05
262	Scott Garrelts	.05
263	Terry Kennedy	.05
264	Mike LaCoss (Photo on back actually Ken Oberkfell.)	.05
265	Mark Leonard RC	.05
266	Greg Litton	.05
267	Kevin Mitchell	.05
268	Randy O'Neal RC	.05
269	Rick Parker RC	.05
270	Rick Reuschel	.05
271	Ernest Riles	.05
272	Don Robinson	.05
273	Robby Thompson	.05
274	Mark Thurmond	.05
275	Jose Uribe	.05
276	Matt Williams	.05
277	Trevor Wilson	.05
278	Gerald Alexander RC	.05
279	Brad Arnsberg	.05
280	Kevin Belcher RC	.05
281	Joe Bitker RC	.05
282	Kevin Brown	.05
283	Steve Buechele	.05
284	Jack Daugherty	.05
285	Julio Franco	.05
286	Juan Gonzalez	.20
287	Bill Haselman RC	.05
288	Charlie Hough	.05
289	Jeff Huson	.05
290	Pete Incaviglia	.05
291	Mike Jeffcoat	.05
292	Jeff Kunkel	.05
293	Gary Mielke	.05
294	Jamie Moyer	.05
295	Rafael Palmeiro	.35
296	Geno Petralli	.05
297	Gary Pettis	.05
298	Kevin Reimer	.05
299	Kenny Rogers	.05
300	Jeff Russell	.05
301	John Russell	.05
302a	Nolan Ryan (First horizontal line between 1979/1980.)	.75
302b	Nolan Ryan (First horizontal line between 1980/1981.)	.75
303	Ruben Sierra	.05
304	Bobby Witt	.05
305	Jim Abbott	.05
306	Kent Anderson RC	.05
307	Dante Bichette	.05
308	Bert Blyleven	.05

309 Chili Davis .05
310 Brian Downing .05
311 Mark Eichhorn .05
312 Mike Fetters .05
313 Chuck Finley .05
314 Willie Fraser .05
315 Bryan Harvey .05
316 Donnie Hill .05
317 Wally Joyner .05
318 Mark Langston .05
319 Kirk McCaskill .05
320 John Orton .05
321 Lance Parrish .05
322 Luis Polonia .05
323 Johnny Ray .05
324 Bobby Rose .05
325 Dick Schofield .05
326 Rick Schu .05
327a Lee Stevens (Six-line career summary.)
327b Lee Stevens (Seven-line career summary.) .05
328 Devon White .05
329 Dave Winfield .40
330 Cliff Young RC .05
331 Dave Bergman .05
332 Phil Clark RC .05
333 Darnell Coles .05
334 Milt Cuyler RC .05
335 Cecil Fielder .05
336 Travis Fryman .05
337 Paul Gibson .05
338 Jerry Don Gleaton .05
339 Mike Heath .05
340 Mike Henneman .05
341 Chet Lemon .05
342 Lance McCullers .05
343 Jack Morris .05
344 Lloyd Moseby .05
345 Edwin Nunez .05
346 Clay Parker .05
347 Dan Petry .05
348 Tony Phillips .05
349 Jeff Robinson .05
350 Mike Salas .05
351 Mike Schwabe RC .05
352 Larry Sheets .05
353 John Shelby .05
354 Frank Tanana .05
355 Alan Trammell .05
356 Gary Ward .05
357 Lou Whitaker .05
358 Beau Allred .05
359 Sandy Alomar,Jr. .05
360 Carlos Baerga .05
361 Kevin Bearse RC .05
362 Tom Brookens .05
363 Jerry Browne .05
364 Tom Candiotti .05
365 Alex Cole .05
366 John Farrell .05
367 Felix Fermin .05
368 Keith Hernandez .05
369 Brook Jacoby .05
370 Chris James .05
371 Dion James .05
372 Doug Jones .05
373 Candy Maldonado .05
374 Steve Olin .05
375 Jesse Orosco .05
376 Rudy Seanez .05
377 Joel Skinner .05
378 Cory Snyder .05
379 Greg Swindell .05
380 Sergio Valdez RC .05
381 Mike Walker RC .05
382 Colby Ward RC .05
383 Turner Ward RC .05
384 Mitch Webster .05
385 Kevin Wickander RC .05
386 Darrel Akerfelds .05
387 Joe Boever .05
388a Rod Booker (No 1981 stats.)
388b Rod Booker (1981 stats included) .05
389 Sil Campusano .05
390 Don Carman .05
391 Wes Chamberlain RC .05
392 Pat Combs .05
393 Darren Daulton .05
394 Jose DeJesus .05
395 Len Dykstra .05
396 Jason Grimsley .05
397 Charlie Hayes .05
398 Von Hayes .05
399 Dave Hollins RC .05
400 Ken Howell .05
401 Ricky Jordan .05
402 John Kruk .05
403 Steve Lake .05
404 Chuck Malone RC .05
405 Roger McDowell .05
406 Chuck McElroy .05
407 Mickey Morandini RC .05
408 Terry Mulholland .05
409 Dale Murphy .15
410 Randy Ready .05
411 Bruce Ruffin .05
412 Dickie Thon .05
413 Paul Assenmacher .05
414 Damon Berryhill .05
415 Mike Bielecki .05
416 Shawn Boskie RC .05
417 Dave Clark .05
418 Doug Dascenzo .05
419a Andre Dawson (No 1976 stats.) .25

419b Andre Dawson (1976 stats included) .25
420 Shawon Dunston .05
421 Joe Girardi .05
422 Mark Grace .05
423 Mike Harkey .05
424 Les Lancaster .05
425 Bill Long .05
426 Greg Maddux .50
427 Derrick May .05
428 Jeff Pico .05
429 Domingo Ramos .05
430 Luis Salazar .05
431 Ryne Sandberg .50
432 Dwight Smith .05
433 Greg Smith .05
434 Rick Sutcliffe .05
435 Gary Varsho .05
436 Hector Villanueva RC .05
437 Jerome Walton .05
438 Curtis Wilkerson .05
439 Mitch Williams .05
440 Steve Wilson .05
441 Marvell Wynne .05
442 Scott Bankhead .05
443 Scott Bradley .05
444 Greg Briley .05
445 Mike Brumley .05
446 Jay Buhner .05
447 Dave Burba RC .05
448 Henry Cotto .05
449 Alvin Davis .05
450 Ken Griffey Jr. .60
451 Erik Hanson .05
452 Gene Harris .05
453 Brian Holman .05
454 Mike Jackson .05
455 Randy Johnson .40
456 Jeffrey Leonard .05
457 Edgar Martinez .05
458 Tino Martinez .05
459 Pete O'Brien .05
460 Harold Reynolds .05
461 Mike Schooler .05
462 Bill Swift .05
463 David Valle .05
464 Omar Vizquel .05
465 Matt Young .05
466 Brady Anderson .05
467 Jeff Ballard .05
468 Juan Bell RC .05
469a Mike Devereaux ("Six" last word in career summary top line.)
469b Mike Devereaux ("Runs" last word in career summary top line.) .05
470 Steve Finley .05
471 Dave Gallagher .05
472 Leo Gomez RC .05
473 Rene Gonzales .05
474 Pete Harnisch .05
475 Kevin Hickey .05
476 Chris Hoiles RC .10
477 Sam Horn .05
478 Tim Hulett .05
479 Dave Johnson .05
480 Ron Kittle .05
481 Ben McDonald .05
482 Bob Melvin .05
483 Bob Milacki .05
484 Randy Milligan .05
485 John Mitchell RC .05
486 Gregg Olson .05
487 Joe Orsulak .05
488 Joe Price .05
489 Bill Ripken .05
490 Cal Ripken, Jr. .75
491 Curt Schilling .25
492 David Segui RC .10
493 Anthony Telford RC .05
494 Mickey Tettleton .05
495 Mark Williamson .05
496 Craig Worthington .05
497 Juan Agosto .05
498 Eric Anthony .05
499 Craig Biggio .05
500 Ken Caminiti .05
501 Casey Candaele .05
502 Andujar Cedeno RC .05
503 Danny Darwin .05
504 Mark Davidson .05
505 Glenn Davis .05
506 Jim Deshaies .05
507 Luis Gonzalez RC 1.00
508 Bill Gullickson .05
509 Xavier Hernandez RC .05
510 Brian Meyer .05
511 Ken Oberkfell .05
512 Mark Portugal .05
513 Rafael Ramirez .05
514 Karl Rhodes RC .10
515 Mike Scott .05
516 Mike Simms RC .05
517 Dave Smith .05
518 Franklin Stubbs .05
519 Glenn Wilson .05
520 Eric Yelding .05
521 Gerald Young .05
522 Shawn Abner .05
523 Roberto Alomar .20
524 Andy Benes .05
525 Joe Carter .05
526 Jack Clark .05
527 Joey Cora .05
528 Paul Faries RC .05
529 Tony Gwynn .50
530 Atlee Hammaker .05

531 Greg Harris .05
532 Thomas Howard RC .05
533 Bruce Hurst .05
534 Craig Lefferts .05
535 Derek Lilliquist .05
536 Fred Lynn .05
537 Mike Pagliarulo .05
538 Mark Parent .05
539 Dennis Rasmussen .05
540 Bip Roberts .05
541 Richard Rodriguez RC .05
542 Benito Santiago .05
543 Calvin Schiraldi .05
544 Eric Show .05
545 Phil Stephenson .05
546 Garry Templeton .05
547 Ed Whitson .05
548 Eddie Williams .05
549 Kevin Appier .05
550 Luis Aquino .05
551 Bob Boone .05
552 George Brett .55
553 Jeff Conine RC .30
554 Steve Crawford .05
555 Mark Davis .05
556 Storm Davis .05
557 Jim Eisenreich .05
558 Steve Farr .05
559 Tom Gordon .05
560 Mark Gubicza .05
561 Bo Jackson .10
562 Mike Macfarlane .05
563 Brian McRae RC .10
564 Jeff Montgomery .05
565 Bill Pecota .05
566 Gerald Perry .05
567 Bret Saberhagen .05
568 Jeff Schulz RC .10
569 Kevin Seitzer .05
570 Terry Shumpert RC .05
571 Kurt Stillwell .05
572 Danny Tartabull .05
573 Gary Thurman .05
574 Frank White .05
575 Willie Wilson .05
576 Chris Bosio .05
577 Greg Brock .05
578 George Canale .05
579 Chuck Crim .05
580 Rob Deer .05
581 Edgar Diaz RC .05
582 Tom Edens RC .05
583 Mike Felder .05
584 Jim Gantner .05
585 Darryl Hamilton .05
586 Ted Higuera .05
587 Mark Knudson .05
588 Bill Krueger .05
589 Tim McIntosh .05
590 Paul Mirabella .05
591 Paul Molitor .40
592 Jaime Navarro .05
593 Dave Parker .05
594 Dan Plesac .05
595 Ron Robinson .05
596 Gary Sheffield .30
597 Bill Spiers .05
598 B.J. Surhoff .05
599 Greg Vaughn .05
600 Randy Veres .05
601 Robin Yount .40
602a Rick Aguilera (Five-line career summary.) .05
602b Rick Aguilera (Four-line career summary.) .05
603 Allan Anderson .05
604 Juan Berenguer .05
605 Randy Bush .05
606 Carmen Castillo .05
607 Tim Drummond .05
608 Scott Erickson RC .10
609 Gary Gaetti .05
610a Greg Gagne (Horizontal lines under 82 Ft. Lauderdale, 84 Toledo and 87 Twins.) .05
610b Greg Gagne (Horizontal lines under 82 Orlando, 84 Twins and 88 Twins.) .05
611 Dan Gladden .05
612 Mark Guthrie RC .05
613 Brian Harper .05
614 Kent Hrbek .05
615 Gene Larkin .05
616 Terry Leach .05
617 Nelson Liriano .05
618 Shane Mack .05
619 John Moses .05
620 Pedro Munoz RC .05
621 Al Newman .05
622 Junior Ortiz .05
623 Kirby Puckett .50
624 Roy Smith .05
625 Kevin Tapani .05
626 Gary Wayne .05
627 David West .05
628 Cris Carpenter .05
629 Vince Coleman .05
630 Ken Dayley .05
631 Jose DeLeon .05
632 Frank DiPino .05
633 Bernard Gilkey RC .05
634 Pedro Guerrero .05
635 Ken Hill .05
636 Felix Jose .05
637 Ray Lankford RC .25
638 Joe Magrane .05
639 Tom Niedenfuer .05
640 Jose Oquendo .05

641 Tom Pagnozzi .05
642 Terry Pendleton .05
643 Mike Perez RC .05
644 Bryn Smith .05
645 Lee Smith .05
646 Ozzie Smith .50
647 Scott Terry .05
648 Bob Tewksbury .05
649 Milt Thompson .05
650 John Tudor .05
651 Denny Walling .05
652 Craig Wilson RC .05
653 Todd Worrell .05
654 Todd Zeile .05
655 Oscar Azocar RC .05
656 Steve Balboni .05
657 Jesse Barfield .05
658 Greg Cadaret .05
659 Chuck Cary .05
660 Rick Cerone .05
661 Dave Eiland .05
662a Alvaro Espinoza (No 1979-80 stats.) .05
662b Alvaro Espinoza (1979-80 stats included) .05
663 Bob Geren .05
664 Lee Guetterman .05
665 Mel Hall .05
666a Andy Hawkins (No 1978 stats.) .05
666b Andy Hawkins (1978 stats included) .05
667 Jimmy Jones .05
668 Roberto Kelly .05
669 Dave LaPoint .05
670 Tim Leary .05
671 Jim Leyritz RC .10
672 Kevin Maas .05
673 Don Mattingly .60
674 Matt Nokes .05
675 Pascual Perez .05
676 Eric Plunk .05
677 Dave Righetti .05
678 Jeff Robinson .05
679 Steve Sax .05
680 Mike Witt .05
681 Steve Avery .05
682 Mike Bell .05
683 Jeff Blauser .05
684 Francisco Cabrera .05
685 Tony Castillo RC .05
686 Marty Clary .05
687 Nick Esasky .05
688 Ron Gant .05
689 Tom Glavine .25
690 Mark Grant .05
691 Tommy Gregg .05
692 Dwayne Henry .05
693 Dave Justice .05
694 Jimmy Kremers RC .05
695 Charlie Leibrandt .05
696 Mark Lemke .05
697 Oddibe McDowell .05
698 Greg Olson .05
699 Jeff Parrett .05
700 Jim Presley .05
701 Victor Rosario RC .05
702 Lonnie Smith .05
703 Pete Smith .05
704 John Smoltz .05
705 Mike Stanton .05
706 Andres Thomas .05
707 Jeff Treadway .05
708 Jim Vatcher RC .05
709 Home Run Kings (Ryne Sandberg, Cecil Fielder) .10
710 Second Generation Superstars (Barry Bonds, Ken Griffey Jr.) .65
711 NLCS Team Leaders (Bobby Bonilla, Barry Larkin) .05
712 Top Game Savers (Bobby Thigpen, John Franco) .05
713 Chicago's 100 Club (Andre Dawson, Ryne Sandberg) .10
714 Checklists (Athletics, Pirates, Reds, Red Sox) .05
715 Dodgers .05
716 Checklists (Expos, Giants, Rangers, Angels) .05
717 Checklists (Tigers, Indians, Phillies, Cubs) .05
718 Checklists (Mariners, Orioles, Astros, Padres) .05
719 Checklists (Royals, Brewers, Twins, Cardinals) .05
720 Checklists (Yankees, Braves, Super Stars) .05

All-Stars

Three player photos are featured on each card in this special insert set. An action shot and portrait close-up are featured on the front, while a full-figure pose is showcased on the back. The cards were inserted into 1991 Fleer cello packs.

		NM/M
Complete Set (10):		5.00
Common Player:		.25
1	Ryne Sandberg	.75
2	Barry Larkin	.25
3	Matt Williams	.25
4	Cecil Fielder	.25
5	Barry Bonds	2.00
6	Rickey Henderson	.50
7	Ken Griffey Jr.	1.50
8	Jose Canseco	.25
9	Benito Santiago	.25
10	Roger Clemens	1.00

World Series

Once again Fleer released a set in honor of the World Series from the previous season. The 1991 issue features only eight cards compared to 12 in 1990. The cards feature white borders surrounding full-color action shots from the 1990 Fall Classic. The card backs feature an overview of the World Series action.

		NM/M
Complete Set (8):		1.50
Common Player:		.25
1	Eric Davis	.25
2	Billy Hatcher	.25
3	Jose Canseco	.35
4	Rickey Henderson	.45
5	Chris Sabo, Carney Lansford	.25
6	Dave Stewart	.25
7	Jose Rijo	.25
8	Reds Celebrate	.25

Box Panels

Unlike past box panel sets, the 1991 Fleer box panels feature a theme; 1990 no-hitters are celebrated on the three different boxes. The cards feature blank backs and are numbered in order of no-hitter on the front. A team logo was included on each box. The card fronts are styled after the 1991 Fleer cards. A special no-hitter logo appears in the lower left corner.

		NM/M
Complete Set, Singles (10):		3.00
Complete Set, Panels (3):		3.00
Common Player:		.10
1	Mark Langston, Mike Witt	.10
2	Randy Johnson	1.00
3	Nolan Ryan	2.00
4	Dave Stewart	.10
5	Fernando Valenzuela	.10
6	Andy Hawkins	.10
7	Melido Perez	.10
8	Terry Mulholland	.10
9	Dave Steib	.10
----	Team Logos	.05

TIM RAINES

WHITE SOX • OF

Update

Fleer produced its eighth consecutive "Update" set in 1991 to supplement the company's regular set. As in the past, the set consists of 132 cards that were sold by hobby dealers in special collectors boxes. The cards are designed in the same style as the regular Fleer issue.

		NM/M
Complete Set (132):		3.00
Common Player:		.05
1	Glenn Davis	.05
2	Dwight Evans	.05
3	Jose Mesa RC	.05
4	Jack Clark	.05
5	Danny Darwin	.05
6	Steve Lyons	.05
7	Mo Vaughn RC	.05
8	Floyd Bannister	.05
9	Gary Gaetti	.05
10	Dave Parker	.05
11	Joey Cora	.05
12	Charlie Hough	.05
13	Matt Merullo	.05
14	Warren Newson RC	.05
15	Tim Raines	.05
16	Albert Belle	.05
17	Glenallen Hill	.05
18	Shawn Hillegas	.05
19	Mark Lewis	.05
20	Charles Nagy RC	.05
21	Mark Whiten	.05
22	John Cerutti	.05
23	Rob Deer	.05
24	Mickey Tettleton	.05
25	Warren Cromartie	.05
26	Kirk Gibson	.05
27	David Howard RC	.05
28	Brent Mayne RC	.05
29	Dante Bichette	.05
30	Mark Lee RC	.05
31	Julio Machado	.05
32	Edwin Nunez	.05
33	Willie Randolph	.05
34	Franklin Stubbs	.05
35	Bill Wegman	.05
36	Chili Davis	.05
37	Chuck Knoblauch RC	.05
38	Scott Leius	.05
39	Jack Morris	.05
40	Mike Pagliarulo	.05
41	Lenny Webster RC	.05
42	John Habyan RC	.05
43	Steve Howe	.05
44	Jeff Johnson RC	.05
45	Scott Kamienicki RC	.05
46	Pat Kelly RC	.05
47	Hensley Meulens	.05
48	Wade Taylor RC	.05
49	Bernie Williams RC	.20
50	Kirk Dressendorfer RC	.05
51	Ernest Riles	.05
52	Rich DeLucia RC	.05
53	Tracy Jones	.05
54	Bill Krueger	.05
55	Alonzo Powell RC	.05
56	Jeff Schaefer	.05
57	Russ Swan RC	.05
58	John Barfield RC	.05
59	Rich Gossage	.10
60	Jose Guzman	.05
61	Dean Palmer RC	.05
62	Ivan Rodriguez RC	1.50
63	Roberto Alomar	.20
64	Tom Candiotti	.05
65	Joe Carter	.05
66	Ed Sprague RC	.05
67	Pat Tabler	.05
68	Mike Timlin RC	.05
69	Devon White	.05
70	Rafael Belliard	.05
71	Juan Berenguer	.05
72	Sid Bream	.05
73	Marvin Freeman	.05
74	Kent Mercker	.05
75	Otis Nixon	.05
76	Terry Pendleton	.05
77	George Bell	.05
78	Danny Jackson	.05
79	Chuck McElroy	.05
80	Gary Scott RC	.05
81	Heathcliff Slocumb RC	.05
82	Dave Smith	.05
83	Rick Wilkins RC	.05
84	Freddie Benavides RC	.05

#	Player	Price
85	Ted Power	.05
86	Mo Sanford RC	.05
87	Jeff Bagwell RC	2.00
88	Steve Finley	.05
89	Pete Harnisch	.05
90	Darryl Kile RC	.05
91	Brett Butler	.05
92	John Candelaria	.05
93	Gary Carter	.40
94	Kevin Gross	.05
95	Bob Ojeda	.05
96	Darryl Strawberry	.05
97	Ivan Calderon	.05
98	Ron Hassey	.05
99	Gilberto Reyes	.05
100	Hubie Brooks	.05
101	Rick Cerone	.05
102	Vince Coleman	.05
103	Jeff Innis	.05
104	Pete Schourek RC	.05
105	Andy Ashby RC	.05
106	Wally Backman	.05
107	Darrin Fletcher RC	.05
108	Tommy Greene	.05
109	John Morris	.05
110	Mitch Williams	.05
111	Lloyd McClendon	.05
112	Orlando Merced RC	.05
113	Vicente Palacios	.05
114	Gary Varsho	.05
115	John Wehner RC	.05
116	Rex Hudler	.05
117	Tim Jones	.05
118	Geronimo Pena RC	.05
119	Gerald Perry	.05
120	Larry Andersen	.05
121	Jerald Clark	.05
122	Scott Coolbaugh	.05
123	Tony Fernandez	.05
124	Darrin Jackson	.05
125	Fred McGriff	.05
126	Jose Mota RC	.05
127	Tim Teufel	.05
128	Bud Black	.05
129	Mike Felder	.05
130	Willie McGee	.05
131	Dave Righetti	.05
132	Checklist	.05

ProVisions

RICKEY HENDERSON

The illustrations of artist Terry Smith are showcased in this special set. Twelve fantasy portraits were produced for cards inserted in rack packs. Four other ProVision cards were inserted into factory sets. The rack pack cards feature black borders, while the factory set cards have white borders. Information on the card backs explains the manner in which Smith painted each player. Factory insert ProVisions are indicated by an "F" suffix in the checklist here.

		NM/M
Complete Set (12):		5.00
Common Player:		.15
Complete Factory Set (4):		5.00
Common Player:		.25
1	Kirby Puckett	.75
2	Will Clark	.15
3	Ruben Sierra	.15
4	Mark McGwire	1.50
5	Bo Jackson	.25
6	Jose Canseco	.50
7	Dwight Gooden	.15
8	Mike Greenwell	.15
9	Roger Clemens	1.00
10	Eric Davis	.15
11	Don Mattingly	1.00
12	Darryl Strawberry	.15
1F	Barry Bonds	3.50
2F	Rickey Henderson	.50
3F	Ryne Sandberg	1.00
4F	Dave Stewart	.25

1992 Fleer Promo

It has been reported that only 100 of this sample card were made for distribution at the 1991 FanFest event. The card differs from the issued Kirby Puckett card in the '92 Fleer set in the card number, the absence of 1991 stats and the overprinting of a sample card notice, all on the back.

		NM/M
123	Kirby Puckett	400.00

1992 Fleer

For the second consecutive year, Fleer produced a 720-card set. The standard card fronts feature full-color action photos bordered in green with the player's name, position and team logo on the right border. The backs feature another full-color action photo, biographical information and statistics. A special 12-card Roger Clemens subset is also included in the 1992 Fleer set. Three more Clemens cards were available through a mail-in offer, and 2,000 Roger Clemens autographed cards were inserted in 1992 packs. Once again the cards are numbered according to team. Subsets in the issue included Major League Propects (#652-680), Record Setters (#681-687), League Leaders (#688-697), Superstar Specials (#698-707) and ProVisions (#708-713), which for the first time were part of the regular numbered set rather than limited edition insert cards.

		NM/M
Unopened Factory Set (732):		17.50
Complete Set (720):		8.00
Common Player:		.05
Wax Pack (15):		.45
Wax Box (36):		10.00
Cello Pack (35):		1.00
Cello Box (24):		16.00
1	Brady Anderson	.05
2	Jose Bautista	.05
3	Juan Bell	.05
4	Glenn Davis	.05
5	Mike Devereaux	.05
6	Dwight Evans	.05
7	Mike Flanagan	.05
8	Leo Gomez	.05
9	Chris Hoiles	.05
10	Sam Horn	.05
11	Tim Hulett	.05
12	Dave Johnson	.05
13	Chito Martinez RC	.05
14	Ben McDonald	.05
15	Bob Melvin	.05
16	Luis Mercedes RC	.10
17	Jose Mesa	.05
18	Bob Milacki	.05
19	Randy Milligan	.05
20	Mike Mussina	.30
21	Gregg Olson	.05
22	Joe Orsulak	.05
23	Jim Poole	.05
24	Arthur Rhodes RC	.10
25	Billy Ripken	.05
26	Cal Ripken, Jr.	1.00
27	David Segui	.05
28	Roy Smith	.05
29	Anthony Telford	.05
30	Mark Williamson	.05
31	Craig Worthington	.05
32	Wade Boggs	.55
33	Tom Bolton	.05
34	Tom Brunansky	.05
35	Ellis Burks	.05
36	Jack Clark	.05
37	Roger Clemens	.60
38	Danny Darwin	.05
39	Mike Greenwell	.05
40	Joe Hesketh	.05
41	Daryl Irvine	.05
42	Dennis Lamp	.05
43	Tony Pena	.05
44	Phil Plantier	.05
45	Carlos Quintana	.05
46	Jeff Reardon	.05
47	Jody Reed	.05
48	Luis Rivera	.05
49	Mo Vaughn	.05
50	Jim Abbott	.05
51	Kyle Abbott	.05
52	Ruben Amaro Jr. RC	.05
53	Scott Bailes	.05
54	Chris Beasley RC	.05
55	Mark Eichhorn	.05
56	Mike Fetters	.05
57	Chuck Finley	.05
58	Gary Gaetti	.05
59	Dave Gallagher	.05
60	Donnie Hill	.05
61	Bryan Harvey	.05
62	Wally Joyner	.05
63	Mark Langston	.05
64	Kirk McCaskill	.05
65	John Orton	.05
66	Lance Parrish	.05
67	Luis Polonia	.05
68	Bobby Rose	.05
69	Dick Schofield	.05
70	Luis Sojo	.05
71	Lee Stevens	.05
72	Dave Winfield	.50
73	Cliff Young	.05
74	Wilson Alvarez	.05
75	Esteban Beltre RC	.05
76	Joey Cora	.05
77	Brian Drahman RC	.05
78	Alex Fernandez	.05
79	Carlton Fisk	.50
80	Scott Fletcher	.05
81	Craig Grebeck	.05
82	Ozzie Guillen	.05
83	Greg Hibbard	.05
84	Charlie Hough	.05
85	Mike Huff	.05
86	Bo Jackson	.10
87	Lance Johnson	.05
88	Ron Karkovice	.05
89	Jack McDowell	.05
90	Matt Merullo	.05
91	Warren Newson RC	.05
92	Donn Pall	.05
93	Dan Pasqua	.05
94	Ken Patterson	.05
95	Melido Perez	.05
96	Scott Radinsky	.05
97	Tim Raines	.05
98	Sammy Sosa	.55
99	Bobby Thigpen	.05
100	Frank Thomas	.50
101	Robin Ventura	.05
102	Mike Aldrete	.05
103	Sandy Alomar, Jr.	.05
104	Carlos Baerga	.05
105	Albert Belle	.05
106	Willie Blair	.05
107	Jerry Browne	.05
108	Alex Cole	.05
109	Felix Fermin	.05
110	Glenallen Hill	.05
111	Shawn Hillegas	.05
112	Chris James	.05
113	Reggie Jefferson RC	.05
114	Doug Jones	.05
115	Eric King	.05
116	Mark Lewis	.05
117	Carlos Martinez	.05
118	Charles Nagy	.05
119	Rod Nichols	.05
120	Steve Olin	.05
121	Jesse Orosco	.05
122	Rudy Seanez	.05
123	Joel Skinner	.05
124	Greg Swindell	.05
125	Jim Thome RC	.50
126	Mark Whiten	.05
127	Scott Aldred	.05
128	Andy Allanson	.05
129	John Cerutti	.05
130	Milt Cuyler	.05
131	Mike Dalton RC	.05
132	Rob Deer	.05
133	Cecil Fielder	.05
134	Travis Fryman	.05
135	Dan Gakeler RC	.05
136	Paul Gibson	.05
137	Bill Gullickson	.05
138	Mike Henneman	.05
139	Pete Incaviglia	.05
140	Mark Leiter RC	.05
141	Scott Livingstone RC	.10
142	Lloyd Moseby	.05
143	Tony Phillips	.05
144	Mark Salas	.05
145	Frank Tanana	.05
146	Walt Terrell	.05
147	Mickey Tettleton	.05
148	Alan Trammell	.05
149	Lou Whitaker	.05
150	Kevin Appier	.05
151	Luis Aquino	.05
152	Todd Benzinger	.05
153	Mike Boddicker	.05
154	George Brett	.60
155	Storm Davis	.05
156	Jim Eisenreich	.05
157	Kirk Gibson	.05
158	Tom Gordon	.05
159	Mark Gubicza	.05
160	David Howard RC	.05
161	Mike Macfarlane	.05
162	Brent Mayne	.05
163	Brian McRae	.05
164	Jeff Montgomery	.05
165	Bill Pecota	.05
166	Harvey Pulliam RC	.05
167	Bret Saberhagen	.05
168	Kevin Seitzer	.05
169	Terry Shumpert	.05
170	Kurt Stillwell	.05
171	Danny Tartabull	.05
172	Gary Thurman	.05
173	Dante Bichette	.05
174	Kevin Brown	.05
175	Chuck Crim	.05
176	Jim Gantner	.05
177	Darryl Hamilton	.05
178	Ted Higuera	.05
179	Darren Holmes	.05
180	Mark Lee	.05
181	Julio Machado	.05
182	Paul Molitor	.50
183	Jaime Navarro	.05
184	Edwin Nunez	.05
185	Dan Plesac	.05
186	Willie Randolph	.05
187	Ron Robinson	.05
188	Gary Sheffield	.30
189	Bill Spiers	.05
190	B.J. Surhoff	.05
191	Dale Sveum	.05
192	Greg Vaughn	.05
193	Bill Wegman	.05
194	Robin Yount	.50
195	Rick Aguilera	.05
196	Allan Anderson	.05
197	Steve Bedrosian	.05
198	Randy Bush	.05
199	Larry Casian RC	.05
200	Chili Davis	.05
201	Scott Erickson	.05
202	Greg Gagne	.05
203	Dan Gladden	.05
204	Brian Harper	.05
205	Kent Hrbek	.05
206	Chuck Knoblauch	.05
207	Gene Larkin	.05
208	Terry Leach	.05
209	Scott Leius	.05
210	Shane Mack	.05
211	Jack Morris	.05
212	Pedro Munoz RC	.05
213	Denny Neagle RC	.10
214	Al Newman	.05
215	Junior Ortiz	.05
216	Mike Pagliarulo	.05
217	Kirby Puckett	.55
218	Paul Sorrento	.05
219	Kevin Tapani	.05
220	Lenny Webster	.05
221	Jesse Barfield	.05
222	Greg Cadaret	.05
223	Dave Eiland	.05
224	Alvaro Espinoza	.05
225	Steve Farr	.05
226	Bob Geren	.05
227	Lee Guetterman	.05
228	John Habyan	.05
229	Mel Hall	.05
230	Steve Howe	.05
231	Mike Humphreys RC	.05
232	Scott Kamieniecki	.10
233	Pat Kelly	.05
234	Roberto Kelly	.05
235	Tim Leary	.05
236	Kevin Maas	.05
237	Don Mattingly	.60
238	Hensley Meulens	.05
239	Matt Nokes	.05
240	Pascual Perez	.05
241	Eric Plunk	.05
242	John Ramos RC	.05
243	Scott Sanderson	.05
244	Steve Sax	.05
245	Wade Taylor RC	.05
246	Randy Velarde	.05
247	Bernie Williams	.05
248	Troy Afenir	.05
249	Harold Baines	.05
250	Lance Blankenship	.05
251	Mike Bordick RC	.10
252	Jose Canseco	.30
253	Steve Chitren	.05
254	Ron Darling	.05
255	Dennis Eckersley	.45
256	Mike Gallego	.05
257	Dave Henderson	.05
258	Rickey Henderson	.50
259	Rick Honeycutt	.05
260	Brook Jacoby	.05
261	Carney Lansford	.05
262	Mark McGwire	.75
263	Mike Moore	.05
264	Gene Nelson	.05
265	Jamie Quirk	.05
266	Joe Slusarski RC	.10
267	Terry Steinbach	.05
268	Dave Stewart	.05
269	Todd Van Poppel RC	.05
270	Walt Weiss	.05
271	Bob Welch	.05
272	Curt Young	.05
273	Scott Bradley	.05
274	Greg Briley	.05
275	Jay Buhner	.05
276	Henry Cotto	.05
277	Alvin Davis	.05
278	Rich DeLucia	.05
279	Ken Griffey Jr.	.65
280	Erik Hanson	.05
281	Brian Holman	.05
282	Mike Jackson	.05
283	Randy Johnson	.50
284	Tracy Jones	.05
285	Bill Krueger	.05
286	Edgar Martinez	.05
287	Tino Martinez	.05
288	Rob Murphy	.05
289	Pete O'Brien	.05
290	Alonzo Powell	.05
291	Harold Reynolds	.05
292	Mike Schooler	.05
293	Russ Swan	.05
294	Bill Swift	.05
295	Dave Valle	.05
296	Omar Vizquel	.05
297	Gerald Alexander	.05
298	Brad Arnsberg	.05
299	Kevin Brown	.05
300	Jack Daugherty	.05
301	Mario Diaz	.05
302	Brian Downing	.05
303	Julio Franco	.05
304	Juan Gonzalez	.25
305	Rich Gossage	.10
306	Jose Guzman	.05
307	Jose Hernandez RC	.05
308	Jeff Huson	.05
309	Mike Jeffcoat	.05
310	Terry Mathews RC	.05
311	Rafael Palmeiro	.45
312	Dean Palmer	.05
313	Geno Petralli	.05
314	Gary Pettis	.05
315	Kevin Reimer	.05
316	Ivan Rodriguez	.45
317	Kenny Rogers	.05
318	Wayne Rosenthal RC	.05
319	Jeff Russell	.05
320	Nolan Ryan	1.00
321	Ruben Sierra	.05
322	Jim Acker	.05
323	Roberto Alomar	.20
324	Derek Bell	.05
325	Pat Borders	.05
326	Tom Candiotti	.05
327	Joe Carter	.05
328	Rob Ducey	.05
329	Kelly Gruber	.05
330	Juan Guzman RC	.25
331	Tom Henke	.05
332	Jimmy Key	.05
333	Manny Lee	.05
334	Al Leiter	.05
335	Bob MacDonald RC	.05
336	Candy Maldonado	.05
337	Rance Mulliniks	.05
338	Greg Myers	.05
339	John Olerud	.05
340	Ed Sprague RC	.10
341	Dave Stieb	.05
342	Todd Stottlemyre	.05
343	Mike Timlin RC	.10
344	Duane Ward	.05
345	David Wells	.05
346	Devon White	.05
347	Mookie Wilson	.05
348	Eddie Zosky	.05
349	Steve Avery	.05
350	Mike Bell RC	.05
351	Rafael Belliard	.05
352	Juan Berenguer	.05
353	Jeff Blauser	.05
354	Sid Bream	.05
355	Francisco Cabrera	.05
356	Marvin Freeman	.05
357	Ron Gant	.05
358	Tom Glavine	.30
359	Brian Hunter RC	.05
360	Dave Justice	.05
361	Charlie Leibrandt	.05
362	Mark Lemke	.05
363	Kent Mercker	.05
364	Keith Mitchell RC	.05
365	Greg Olson	.05
366	Terry Pendleton	.05
367	Armando Reynoso RC	.05
368	Deion Sanders	.10
369	Lonnie Smith	.05
370	Pete Smith	.05
371	John Smoltz	.05
372	Mike Stanton	.05
373	Jeff Treadway	.05
374	Mark Wohlers RC	.05
375	Paul Assenmacher	.05
376	George Bell	.05
377	Shawn Boskie	.05
378	Frank Castillo RC	.05
379	Andre Dawson	.25
380	Shawon Dunston	.05
381	Mark Grace	.05
382	Mike Harkey	.05
383	Danny Jackson	.05
384	Les Lancaster	.05
385	Cedric Landrum RC	.05
386	Greg Maddux	.55
387	Derrick May	.05
388	Chuck McElroy	.05
389	Ryne Sandberg	.55
390	Heathcliff Slocumb RC	.10
391	Dave Smith	.05
392	Dwight Smith	.05
393	Rick Sutcliffe	.05
394	Hector Villanueva	.05
395	Chico Walker RC	.05
396	Jerome Walton	.05
397	Rick Wilkins RC	.15
398	Jack Armstrong	.05
399	Freddie Benavides RC	.05
400	Glenn Braggs	.05
401	Tom Browning	.05
402	Norm Charlton	.05
403	Eric Davis	.05
404	Rob Dibble	.05
405	Bill Doran	.05
406	Mariano Duncan	.05
407	Kip Gross RC	.05
408	Chris Hammond	.05
409	Billy Hatcher	.05
410	Chris Jones RC	.05
411	Barry Larkin	.05
412	Hal Morris	.05
413	Randy Myers	.05
414	Joe Oliver	.05
415	Paul O'Neill	.05
416	Ted Power	.05
417	Luis Quinones	.05
418	Jeff Reed	.05
419	Jose Rijo	.05
420	Chris Sabo	.05
421	Reggie Sanders RC	.05
422	Scott Scudder	.05
423	Glenn Sutko	.05
424	Eric Anthony	.05
425	Jeff Bagwell	.50
426	Craig Biggio	.05
427	Ken Caminiti	.05
428	Casey Candaele	.05
429	Mike Capel	.05
430	Andujar Cedeno	.05
431	Jim Corsi	.05
432	Mark Davidson	.05
433	Steve Finley	.05
434	Luis Gonzalez	.05
435	Pete Harnisch	.05
436	Dwayne Henry	.05
437	Xavier Hernandez	.05
438	Jimmy Jones	.05
439	Darryl Kile	.05
440	Rob Mallicoat RC	.05
441	Andy Mota RC	.05
442	Al Osuna	.05
443	Mark Portugal	.05
444	Scott Servais RC	.10
445	Mike Simms	.05
446	Gerald Young	.05
447	Tim Belcher	.05
448	Brett Butler	.05
449	John Candelaria	.05
450	Gary Carter	.50
451	Dennis Cook	.05
452	Tim Crews	.05
453	Kal Daniels	.05
454	Jim Gott	.05
455	Alfredo Griffin	.05
456	Kevin Gross	.05
457	Chris Gwynn	.05
458	Lenny Harris	.05
459	Orel Hershiser	.05
460	Jay Howell	.05
461	Stan Javier	.05
462	Eric Karros	.05
463	Ramon Martinez	.05
464	Roger McDowell	.05
465	Mike Morgan	.05
466	Eddie Murray	.50
467	Jose Offerman	.05
468	Bob Ojeda	.05
469	Juan Samuel	.05
470	Mike Scioscia	.05
471	Darryl Strawberry	.05
472	Bret Barberie RC	.10
473	Brian Barnes	.05
474	Eric Bullock	.05
475	Ivan Calderon	.05
476	Delino DeShields	.05
477	Jeff Fassero RC	.10
478	Mike Fitzgerald	.05
479	Steve Frey	.05
480	Andres Galarraga	.05
481	Mark Gardner	.05
482	Marquis Grissom	.05
483	Chris Haney RC	.05
484	Barry Jones	.05
485	Dave Martinez	.05
486	Dennis Martinez	.05
487	Chris Nabholz	.05
488	Spike Owen	.05
489	Gilberto Reyes	.05
490	Mel Rojas	.05
491	Scott Ruskin	.05
492	Bill Sampen	.05
493	Larry Walker	.05
494	Tim Wallach	.05
495	Daryl Boston	.05
496	Hubie Brooks	.05
497	Tim Burke	.05
498	Mark Carreon	.05
499	Tony Castillo	.05
500	Vince Coleman	.05
501	David Cone	.05
502	Kevin Elster	.05
503	Sid Fernandez	.05
504	John Franco	.05
505	Dwight Gooden	.05
506	Todd Hundley	.05
507	Jeff Innis	.05
508	Gregg Jefferies	.05
509	Howard Johnson	.05
510	Dave Magadan	.05
511	Terry McDaniel RC	.05
512	Kevin McReynolds	.05
513	Keith Miller	.05
514	Charlie O'Brien	.05
515	Mackey Sasser	.05
516	Pete Schourek RC	.05
517	Julio Valera	.05
518	Frank Viola	.05
519	Wally Whitehurst	.05
520	Anthony Young RC	.05
521	Andy Ashby RC	.10
522	Kim Batiste RC	.05
523	Joe Boever	.05
524	Wes Chamberlain	.05

525	Pat Combs	.05
526	Danny Cox	.05
527	Darren Daulton	.05
528	Jose DeJesus	.05
529	Len Dykstra	.05
530	Darrin Fletcher	.05
531	Tommy Greene	.05
532	Jason Grimsley	.05
533	Charlie Hayes	.05
534	Von Hayes	.05
535	Dave Hollins	.05
536	Ricky Jordan	.05
537	John Kruk	.05
538	Jim Lindeman	.05
539	Mickey Morandini	.05
540	Terry Mulholland	.05
541	Dale Murphy	.20
542	Randy Ready	.05
543	Wally Ritchie	.05
544	Bruce Ruffin	.05
545	Steve Searcy	.05
546	Dickie Thon	.05
547	Mitch Williams	.05
548	Stan Belinda	.05
549	Jay Bell	.05
550	Barry Bonds	1.00
551	Bobby Bonilla	.05
552	Steve Buechele	.05
553	Doug Drabek	.05
554	Neal Heaton	.05
555	Jeff King	.05
556	Bob Kipper	.05
557	Bill Landrum	.05
558	Mike LaValliere	.05
559	Jose Lind	.05
560	Lloyd McClendon	.05
561	Orlando Merced	.05
562	Bob Patterson	.05
563	Joe Redfield RC	.05
564	Gary Redus	.05
565	Rosario Rodriguez	.05
566	Don Slaught	.05
567	John Smiley	.05
568	Zane Smith	.05
569	Randy Tomlin	.05
570	Andy Van Slyke	.05
571	Gary Varsho	.05
572	Bob Walk	.05
573	John Wehner RC	.05
574	Juan Agosto	.05
575	Cris Carpenter	.05
576	Jose DeLeon	.05
577	Rich Gedman	.05
578	Bernard Gilkey	.05
579	Pedro Guerrero	.05
580	Ken Hill	.05
581	Rex Hudler	.05
582	Felix Jose	.05
583	Ray Lankford	.05
584	Omar Olivares	.05
585	Jose Oquendo	.05
586	Tom Pagnozzi	.05
587	Geronimo Pena	.05
588	Mike Perez	.05
589	Gerald Perry	.05
590	Bryn Smith	.05
591	Lee Smith	.05
592	Ozzie Smith	.55
593	Scott Terry	.05
594	Bob Tewksbury	.05
595	Milt Thompson	.05
596	Todd Zeile	.05
597	Larry Andersen	.05
598	Oscar Azocar	.05
599	Andy Benes	.05
600	Ricky Bones RC	.05
601	Jerald Clark	.05
602	Pat Clements	.05
603	Paul Faries	.05
604	Tony Fernandez	.05
605	Tony Gwynn	.55
606	Greg Harris	.05
607	Thomas Howard	.05
608	Bruce Hurst	.05
609	Darrin Jackson	.05
610	Tom Lampkin	.05
611	Craig Lefferts	.05
612	Jim Lewis RC	.05
613	Mike Maddux	.05
614	Fred McGriff	.05
615	Jose Melendez RC	.05
616	Jose Mota RC	.05
617	Dennis Rasmussen	.05
618	Bip Roberts	.05
619	Rich Rodriguez	.05
620	Benito Santiago	.05
621	Craig Shipley RC	.05
622	Tim Teufel	.05
623	Kevin Ward RC	.05
624	Ed Whitson	.05
625	Dave Anderson	.05
626	Kevin Bass	.05
627	Rod Beck RC	.10
628	Bud Black	.05
629	Jeff Brantley	.05
630	John Burkett	.05
631	Will Clark	.05
632	Royce Clayton RC	.05
633	Steve Decker	.05
634	Kelly Downs	.05
635	Mike Felder	.05
636	Scott Garrelts	.05
637	Eric Gunderson	.05
638	Bryan Hickerson RC	.05
639	Darren Lewis	.05
640	Greg Litton	.05
641	Kirt Manwaring	.05
642	Paul McClellan RC	.05

643	Willie McGee	.05
644	Kevin Mitchell	.05
645	Francisco Olivares	.05
646	Mike Remlinger RC	.10
647	Dave Righetti	.05
648	Robby Thompson	.05
649	Jose Uribe	.05
650	Matt Williams	.05
651	Trevor Wilson	.05
652	Tom Goodwin RC (Prospects)	.05
653	Terry Bross RC (Prospects)	.05
654	Mike Christopher RC (Prospects)	.05
655	Kenny Lofton (Prospects)	.05
656	Chris Cron RC (Prospects)	.05
657	Willie Banks RC (Prospects)	.05
658	Pat Rice RC (Prospects)	.05
659a	Rob Mauer RC (Prospects) (Last name misspelled.)	.75
659b	Rob Maurer RC (Prospects)(Corrected)	.05
660	Don Harris RC (Prospects)	.05
661	Henry Rodriguez (Prospects)	.05
662	Cliff Brantley RC (Prospects)	.05
663	Mike Linskey RC (Prospects)	.05
664	Gary Disarcina RC (Prospects)	.05
665	Gil Heredia RC (Prospects)	.10
666	Vinny Castilla RC (Prospects)	.05
667	Paul Abbott RC (Prospects)	.05
668	Monty Fariss RC (Prospects)	.05
669	Jarvis Brown RC (Prospects)	.05
670	Wayne Kirby RC (Prospects)	.05
671	Scott Brosius RC (Prospects)	.05
672	Bob Hamelin (Prospects)	.05
673	Joel Johnston RC (Prospects)	.05
674	Tim Spehr RC (Prospects)	.05
675	Jeff Gardner RC (Prospects)	.05
676	Rico Rossy RC (Prospects)	.05
677	Roberto Hernandez RC (Prospects)	.20
678	Ted Wood RC (Prospects)	.05
679	Cal Eldred (Prospects)	.05
680	Sean Berry RC (Prospects)	.05
681	Rickey Henderson (Stolen Base Record)	.05
682	Nolan Ryan (Record 7th No-hitter)	.25
683	Dennis Martinez (Perfect Game)	.05
684	Wilson Alvarez (Rookie No-hitter)	.05
685	Joe Carter (3 100 RBI Seasons)	.05
686	Dave Winfield (400 Home Runs)	.20
687	David Cone (Ties NL Record Strikeouts)	.05
688	Jose Canseco (League Leaders)	.15
689	Howard Johnson (League Leaders)	.05
690	Julio Franco (League Leaders)	.05
691	Terry Pendleton (League Leaders)	.05
692	Cecil Fielder (League Leaders)	.05
693	Scott Erickson (League Leaders)	.05
694	Tom Glavine (League Leaders)	.05
695	Dennis Martinez (League Leaders)	.05
696	Bryan Harvey (League Leaders)	.05
697	Lee Smith (League Leaders)	.05
698	Super Siblings (Roberto & Sandy Alomar, Roberto & Sandy Alomar)	.10
699	The Indispensables (Bobby Bonilla, Will Clark)	.05
700	Teamwork (Mark Wohlers, Kent Mercker, Alejandro Pena)	.05
701	Tiger Tandems (Chris Jones, Bo Jackson, Gregg Olson, Frank Thomas)	.05
702	The Ignitors (Brett Butler, Paul Molitor)	.10
703	The Indispensables II (Cal Ripken Jr., Joe Carter)	.20
704	Power Packs (Barry Larkin, Kirby Puckett)	.15
705	Today and Tomorrow (Mo Vaughn, Cecil Fielder)	.05
706	Teenage Sensations (Ramon Martinez, Ozzie Guillen)	.05

707	Designated Hitters (Harold Baines, Wade Boggs)	.20
708	Robin Yount (ProVision)	.35
709	Ken Griffey Jr. (ProVision)	.60
710	Nolan Ryan (ProVision)	.75
711	Cal Ripken, Jr. (ProVision)	.75
712	Frank Thomas (ProVision)	.50
713	Dave Justice (ProVision)	.05
714	Checklist 1-101	.05
715	Checklist 102-194	.05
716	Checklist 195-296	.05
717	Checklist 297-397	.05
718	Checklist 398-494	.05
719	Checklist 495-596	.05
720a	Checklist 597-720 (659 Rob Mauer)	.05
720b	Checklist 597-720 (659 Rob Maurer)	.05

All-Stars

Black borders with gold highlights are featured on these special wax pack insert cards. The fronts feature glossy action photos with a portrait photo inset. Backs feature career highlights.

		NM/M
Complete Set (24):		8.00
Common Player:		.10
1	Felix Jose	.10
2	Tony Gwynn	1.25
3	Barry Bonds	3.00
4	Bobby Bonilla	.10
5	Mike LaValliere	.10
6	Tom Glavine	.40
7	Ramon Martinez	.10
8	Lee Smith	.10
9	Mickey Tettleton	.10
10	Scott Erickson	.10
11	Frank Thomas	.75
12	Danny Tartabull	.10
13	Will Clark	.10
14	Ryne Sandberg	1.25
15	Terry Pendleton	.10
16	Barry Larkin	.10
17	Rafael Palmeiro	.65
18	Julio Franco	.10
19	Robin Ventura	.10
20	Cal Ripken, Jr.	3.00
21	Joe Carter	.10
22	Kirby Puckett	1.25
23	Ken Griffey Jr.	2.25
24	Jose Canseco	.50

Roger Clemens

This set chronicles the career highlights of Roger Clemens. The initial 12 cards from the set were inserted in 1992 Fleer wax packs. A limited number of autographed cards were inserted as well. The additional three cards from the set were available through a mail-in offer. The card fronts feature black borders with metallic gold type. The flip side is yellow with black borders.

		NM/M
Complete Set (15):		6.00
Common Card:		.50
Autographed Card:		40.00
1	Quiet Storm	.50
2	Courted by the Mets and Twins	.50
3	The Show	.50
4	A Rocket Launched	.50
5	Time of Trial	.50
6	Break Through	.50
7	Play it Again Roger	.50
8	Business as Usual	.50
9	Heee's Back	.50
10	Blood, Sweat and Tears	.50
11	Prime of Life	.50
12	Man for Every Season	.50
13	Cooperstown Bound	1.50
14	The Heat of the Moment	1.50
15	Final Words	1.50

Lumber Co.

Baseball's top power hitters at each position are featured in this nine-card set. Fronts feature full-color action photos bordered in black. Backs feature posed player photos and career highlights. The set was included only in factory sets released to the hobby trade.

		NM/M
Complete Set (9):		5.00
Common Player:		.25
1	Cecil Fielder	.25
2	Mickey Tettleton	.25
3	Darryl Strawberry	.25
4	Ryne Sandberg	1.00
5	Jose Canseco	.40
6	Matt Williams	.25
7	Cal Ripken, Jr.	2.00
8	Barry Bonds	2.00
9	Ron Gant	.25

Rookie Sensations

This 20-card set features the top rookies of 1991 and rookie prospects from 1992. The card fronts feature blue borders with "Rookie Sensations" in gold along the top border. The flip sides feature background information on the player. The cards were randomly inserted in 1992 Fleer cello packs. This issue saw very high prices when initially released then suffered long-term declines as the hobby became inundated with more and more insert sets.

		NM/M
Complete Set (20):		13.50
Common Player:		.35
1	Frank Thomas	6.00
2	Todd Van Poppel	.35
3	Orlando Merced	.35
4	Jeff Bagwell	6.00
5	Jeff Fassero	.35
6	Darren Lewis	.35
7	Milt Cuyler	.35
8	Mike Timlin	.35
9	Brian McRae	.35
10	Chuck Knoblauch	.35
11	Rich DeLucia	.35
12	Ivan Rodriguez	4.50
13	Juan Guzman	.35
14	Steve Chitren	.35
15	Mark Wohlers	.35
16	Wes Chamberlain	.35
17	Ray Lankford	.35
18	Chito Martinez	.35
19	Phil Plantier	.35
20	Scott Leius	.35

Smoke 'N Heat

STEVE AVERY

This 12-card set of top pitchers was included in factory sets designated for sale within the general retail trade. Card numbers have an "S" prefix.

		NM/M
Complete Set (12):		7.50
Common Player:		.25
1	Lee Smith	.25
2	Jack McDowell	.25
3	David Cone	.25
4	Roger Clemens	2.00
5	Nolan Ryan	3.00
6	Scott Erickson	.25
7	Tom Glavine	.50
8	Dwight Gooden	.25
9	Andy Benes	.25
10	Steve Avery	.25
11	Randy Johnson	1.00
12	Jim Abbott	.25

Team Leaders

RAFAEL PALMEIRO

White and green borders highlight this insert set from Fleer. The card fronts also feature a special gold-foil "team leaders" logo beneath the full-color player photo. The card backs feature player information. The cards were randomly inserted in 1992 Fleer rack packs.

		NM/M
Complete Set (20):		10.00
Common Player:		.50
1	Don Mattingly	2.00
2	Howard Johnson	.50
3	Chris Sabo	.50
4	Carlton Fisk	1.25
5	Kirby Puckett	1.50
6	Cecil Fielder	1.50
7	Tony Gwynn	1.50
8	Will Clark	1.50
9	Bobby Bonilla	.50
10	Len Dykstra	.50
11	Tom Glavine	.75
12	Rafael Palmeiro	1.00
13	Wade Boggs	1.50
14	Joe Carter	.50
15	Ken Griffey Jr.	2.50
16	Darryl Strawberry	.50
17	Cal Ripken, Jr.	3.00
18	Danny Tartabull	.50
19	Jose Canseco	.75
20	Andre Dawson	.50

Update

RYAN THOMPSON
OUTFIELD

This 132-card set was released in boxed set form and features traded players, free agents and top rookies from 1992. The cards are styled after the regular 1992 Fleer and are numbered alphabetically according to team. This set marks the ninth year that Fleer has released an update set. The set includes four black-bordered "Headliner" cards.

		NM/M
Complete Set (136):		60.00
Common Player:		.05
H1	1992 All-Star Game MVP (Ken Griffey Jr.)	1.50
H2	3000 Career Hits (Robin Yount)	.75
H3	Major League Career Saves Record (Jeff Reardon)	.10
H4	Record RBI Performance (Cecil Fielder)	.05
1	Todd Frohwirth	.05
2	Alan Mills	.05
3	Rick Sutcliffe	.05
4	John Valentin RC	.25
5	Frank Viola	.05
6	Bob Zupcic RC	.05
7	Mike Butcher RC	.05
8	Chad Curtis RC	.50
9	Damion Easley RC	.50
10	Tim Salmon RC	.50
11	Julio Valera	.05
12	George Bell	.05
13	Roberto Hernandez RC	.05
14	Shawn Jeter RC	.05
15	Thomas Howard	.05
16	Jesse Levis RC	.05
17	Kenny Lofton	.05
18	Paul Sorrento	.05
19	Rico Brogna RC	.05
20	John Doherty RC	.05
21	Dan Gladden	.05
22	Buddy Groom RC	.05
23	Shawn Hare RC	.05
24	John Kiely RC	.05
25	Kurt Knudsen RC	.05
26	Gregg Jefferies	.05
27	Wally Joyner	.05
28	Kevin Koslofski RC	.05
29	Kevin McReynolds	.05
30	Rusty Meacham	.05
31	Keith Miller	.05
32	Hipolito Pichardo RC	.05
33	James Austin RC	.05
34	Scott Fletcher	.05
35	John Jaha RC	.05
36	Pat Listach RC	.05
37	Dave Nilsson RC	.05
38	Kevin Seitzer	.05
39	Tom Edens	.05
40	Pat Mahomes RC	.05
41	John Smiley	.05
42	Charlie Hayes	.05
43	Sam Militello RC	.05
44	Andy Stankiewicz RC	.05
45	Danny Tartabull	.05
46	Bob Wickman RC	.05
47	Jerry Browne	.05
48	Kevin Campbell RC	.05
49	Vince Horsman RC	.05
50	Troy Neel RC	.05
51	Ruben Sierra	.05
52	Bruce Walton RC	.05
53	Willie Wilson	.05
54	Bret Boone RC	.50
55	Dave Fleming RC	.05
56	Kevin Mitchell	.05
57	Jeff Nelson RC	.05
58	Shane Turner RC	.05
59	Jose Canseco	.65
60	Jeff Frye RC	.05
61	Damilo Leon RC	.05
62	Roger Pavlik RC	.05
63	David Cone	.05
64	Pat Hentgen RC	.05
65	Randy Knorr RC	.05
66	Jack Morris	.05
67	Dave Winfield	1.00
68	David Nied RC	.05
69	Otis Nixon	.05
70	Alejandro Pena	.05
71	Jeff Reardon	.05
72	Alex Arias RC	.05
73	Jim Bullinger RC	.05
74	Mike Morgan	.05
75	Rey Sanchez RC	.05
76	Bob Scanlan	.05
77	Sammy Sosa	3.00
78	Scott Bankhead	.05
79	Tim Belcher	.05
80	Steve Foster RC	.05
81	Willie Greene RC	.05
82	Bip Roberts	.05
83	Scott Ruskin	.05
84	Greg Swindell	.05
85	Juan Guerrero RC	.05
86	Butch Henry RC	.05
87	Doug Jones	.05
88	Brian Williams RC	.05
89	Tom Candiotti	.05
90	Eric Davis	.05
91	Carlos Hernandez RC	.05
92	Mike Piazza RC	45.00
93	Mike Sharperson	.05

94	Eric Young RC	.05
95	Moises Alou	.05
96	Greg Colbrunn	.05
97	Wil Cordero RC	.05
98	Ken Hill	.05
99	John Vander Wal RC	.05
100	John Wetteland	.05
101	Bobby Bonilla	.05
102	Eric Hilman RC	.05
103	Pat Howell RC	.05
104	Jeff Kent RC	15.00
105	Dick Schofield	.05
106	Ryan Thompson RC	.05
107	Chico Walker	.05
108	Juan Bell	.05
109	Mariano Duncan	.05
110	Jeff Grotewold RC	.05
111	Ben Rivera RC	.05
112	Curt Schilling	.65
113	Victor Cole RC	.05
114	Al Martin RC	.05
115	Roger Mason	.05
116	Blas Minor RC	.05
117	Tim Wakefield RC	4.00
118	Mark Clark	.05
119	Rheal Cormier RC	.05
120	Donovan Osborne RC	.05
121	Todd Worrell	.05
122	Jeremy Hernandez RC	.05
123	Randy Myers	.05
124	Frank Seminara RC	.05
125	Gary Sheffield	.75
126	Dan Walters RC	.05
127	Steve Hosey RC	.05
128	Mike Jackson	.05
129	Jim Pena RC	.05
130	Cory Snyder	.05
131	Bill Swift	.05
132	Checklist	.05

7-Eleven

The 1992 Performer Collection was a combined effort from Fleer and 7-11. Customers at 7-11 stores received a packet of five cards with gasoline purchases to build the 24-card set of major stars. The cards are standard size, with virtually the identical design to the regular issue Fleer set of 1992, with only the addition of "The Performer" logo on the front of the card and a pair of sponsors' logos on back.

		NM/M
	Complete Set (24):	9.00
	Common Player:	.20
1	Nolan Ryan	1.50
2	Frank Thomas	.65
3	Ryne Sandberg	.75
4	Ken Griffey Jr.	1.00
5	Cal Ripken, Jr.	1.50
6	Roger Clemens	.85
7	Cecil Fielder	.20
8	Dave Justice	.40
9	Wade Boggs	.75
10	Tony Gwynn	.75
11	Kirby Puckett	.75
12	Darryl Strawberry	.20
13	Jose Canseco	.50
14	Barry Larkin	.20
15	Terry Pendleton	.20
16	Don Mattingly	.85
17	Rickey Henderson	.65
18	Ruben Sierra	.65
19	Jeff Bagwell	.65
20	Tom Glavine	.45
21	Ramon Martinez	.20
22	Will Clark	.45
23	Barry Bonds	1.50
24	Roberto Alomar	.40

1993 Fleer

The card fronts feature silver borders with the player's name, team and position in a banner along the left side of the card. The backs feature an action photo of the player with his name in bold behind him. A box featuring biographical information, statistics and player information is located to the right of the action photo. The cards are numbered alphabetically by team. The basic Fleer issue for 1993 was is-

sued in two series of 360 cards each. The 720-card set included a number of subsets and could be found in many different types of packaging with an unprecedented number of inserts sets to spice up each offering.

		NM/M
	Complete Set (720):	10.00
	Common Player:	.05
	Series 1 or 2 Pack (15):	.05
	Series 1 or 2 Box (36):	12.50
1	Steve Avery	.05
2	Sid Bream	.05
3	Ron Gant	.05
4	Tom Glavine	.25
5	Brian Hunter	.05
6	Ryan Klesko	.05
7	Charlie Leibrandt	.05
8	Kent Mercker	.05
9	David Nied	.05
10	Otis Nixon	.05
11	Greg Olson	.05
12	Terry Pendleton	.05
13	Deion Sanders	.10
14	John Smoltz	.05
15	Mike Stanton	.05
16	Mark Wohlers	.05
17	Paul Assenmacher	.05
18	Steve Buechele	.05
19	Shawon Dunston	.05
20	Mark Grace	.05
21	Derrick May	.05
22	Chuck McElroy	.05
23	Mike Morgan	.05
24	Rey Sanchez	.05
25	Ryne Sandberg	.60
26	Bob Scanlan	.05
27	Sammy Sosa	.60
28	Rick Wilkins	.05
29	Bobby Ayala RC	.05
30	Tim Belcher	.05
31	Jeff Branson RC	.05
32	Norm Charlton	.05
33	Steve Foster RC	.05
34	Willie Greene RC	.05
35	Chris Hammond	.05
36	Milt Hill RC	.05
37	Hal Morris	.05
38	Joe Oliver	.05
39	Paul O'Neill	.05
40	Tim Pugh RC	.05
41	Jose Rijo	.05
42	Bip Roberts	.05
43	Chris Sabo	.05
44	Reggie Sanders	.05
45	Eric Anthony	.05
46	Jeff Bagwell	.50
47	Craig Biggio	.05
48	Joe Boever	.05
49	Casey Candaele	.05
50	Steve Finley	.05
51	Luis Gonzalez	.05
52	Pete Harnisch	.05
53	Xavier Hernandez	.05
54	Doug Jones	.05
55	Eddie Taubensee	.05
56	Brian Williams	.05
57	Pedro Astacio RC	.10
58	Todd Benzinger	.05
59	Brett Butler	.05
60	Tom Candiotti	.05
61	Lenny Harris	.05
62	Carlos Hernandez	.05
63	Orel Hershiser	.05
64	Eric Karros	.05
65	Ramon Martinez	.05
66	Jose Offerman	.05
67	Mike Scioscia	.05
68	Mike Sharperson	.05
69	Eric Young RC	.10
70	Moises Alou	.05
71	Ivan Calderon	.05
72	Archi Cianfrocco RC	.05
73	Wil Cordero	.05
74	Delino DeShields	.05
75	Mark Gardner	.05
76	Ken Hill	.05
77	Tim Laker RC	.05
78	Chris Nabholz	.05
79	Mel Rojas	.05
80	John Vander Wal RC	.10
81	Larry Walker	.05
82	Tim Wallach	.05
83	John Wetteland	.05
84	Bobby Bonilla	.05

85	Daryl Boston	.05
86	Sid Fernandez	.05
87	Eric Hillman RC	.05
88	Todd Hundley	.05
89	Howard Johnson	.05
90	Jeff Kent	.05
91	Eddie Murray	.50
92	Bill Pecota	.05
93	Bret Saberhagen	.05
94	Dick Schofield	.05
95	Pete Schourek	.05
96	Anthony Young	.05
97	Ruben Amaro Jr.	.05
98	Juan Bell	.05
99	Wes Chamberlain	.05
100	Darren Daulton	.05
101	Mariano Duncan	.05
102	Mike Hartley	.05
103	Ricky Jordan	.05
104	John Kruk	.05
105	Mickey Morandini	.05
106	Terry Mulholland	.05
107	Ben Rivera RC	.05
108	Curt Schilling	.25
109	Keith Shepherd RC	.05
110	Stan Belinda	.05
111	Jay Bell	.05
112	Barry Bonds	1.00
113	Jeff King	.05
114	Mike LaValliere	.05
115	Jose Lind	.05
116	Roger Mason	.05
117	Orlando Merced	.05
118	Bob Patterson	.05
119	Don Slaught	.05
120	Zane Smith	.05
121	Randy Tomlin	.05
122	Andy Van Slyke	.05
123	Tim Wakefield RC	.10
124	Rheal Cormier	.05
125	Bernard Gilkey	.05
126	Felix Jose	.05
127	Ray Lankford	.05
128	Bob McClure	.05
129	Donovan Osborne	.05
130	Tom Pagnozzi	.05
131	Geronimo Pena	.05
132	Mike Perez	.05
133	Lee Smith	.05
134	Bob Tewksbury	.05
135	Todd Worrell	.05
136	Todd Zeile	.05
137	Jerald Clark	.05
138	Tony Gwynn	.60
139	Greg Harris	.05
140	Jeremy Hernandez	.05
141	Darrin Jackson	.05
142	Mike Maddux	.05
143	Fred McGriff	.05
144	Jose Melendez	.05
145	Rich Rodriguez	.05
146	Frank Seminara	.05
147	Gary Sheffield	.35
148	Kurt Stillwell	.05
149	Dan Walters RC	.05
150	Rod Beck	.05
151	Bud Black	.05
152	Jeff Brantley	.05
153	John Burkett	.05
154	Will Clark	.05
155	Royce Clayton	.05
156	Mike Jackson	.05
157	Darren Lewis	.05
158	Kirt Manwaring	.05
159	Willie McGee	.05
160	Cory Snyder	.05
161	Bill Swift	.05
162	Trevor Wilson	.05
163	Brady Anderson	.05
164	Glenn Davis	.05
165	Mike Devereaux	.05
166	Todd Frohwirth	.05
167	Leo Gomez	.05
168	Chris Hoiles	.05
169	Ben McDonald	.05
170	Randy Milligan	.05
171	Alan Mills	.05
172	Mike Mussina	.30
173	Gregg Olson	.05
174	Arthur Rhodes	.05
175	David Segui	.05
176	Ellis Burks	.05
177	Roger Clemens	.60
178	Scott Cooper	.05
179	Danny Darwin	.05
180	Tony Fossas	.05
181	Paul Quantrill RC	.10
182	Jody Reed	.05
183	John Valentin RC	.10
184	Mo Vaughn	.05
185	Frank Viola	.05
186	Bob Zupcic	.05
187	Jim Abbott	.05
188	Gary DiSarcina	.05
189	Damion Easley RC	.05
190	Junior Felix	.05
191	Chuck Finley	.05
192	Joe Grahe	.05
193	Bryan Harvey	.05
194	Mark Langston	.05
195	John Orton	.05
196	Luis Polonia	.05
197	Tim Salmon	.05
198	Luis Sojo	.05
199	Wilson Alvarez	.05
200	Gary Bell	.05
201	Alex Fernandez	.05
202	Craig Grebeck	.05

203	Ozzie Guillen	.05
204	Lance Johnson	.05
205	Ron Karkovice	.05
206	Kirk McCaskill	.05
207	Jack McDowell	.05
208	Scott Radinsky	.05
209	Tim Raines	.05
210	Frank Thomas	.50
211	Robin Ventura	.05
212	Sandy Alomar Jr.	.05
213	Carlos Baerga	.05
214	Dennis Cook	.05
215	Thomas Howard	.05
216	Mark Lewis	.05
217	Derek Lilliquist	.05
218	Kenny Lofton	.05
219	Charles Nagy	.05
220	Steve Olin	.05
221	Paul Sorrento	.05
222	Jim Thome	.40
223	Mark Whiten	.05
224	Milt Cuyler	.05
225	Rob Deer	.05
226	John Doherty RC	.05
227	Cecil Fielder	.05
228	Travis Fryman	.05
229	Mike Henneman	.05
230	John Kiely RC	.05
231	Kurt Knudsen RC	.05
232	Scott Livingstone	.05
233	Tony Phillips	.05
234	Mickey Tettleton	.05
235	Kevin Appier	.05
236	George Brett	.65
237	Tom Gordon	.05
238	Gregg Jefferies	.05
239	Wally Joyner	.05
240	Kevin Koslofski RC	.05
241	Mike Macfarlane	.05
242	Brian McRae	.05
243	Rusty Meacham	.05
244	Keith Miller	.05
245	Jeff Montgomery	.05
246	Hipolito Pichardo RC	.05
247	Ricky Bones	.05
248	Cal Eldred	.05
249	Mike Fetters	.05
250	Darryl Hamilton	.05
251	Doug Henry	.05
252	John Jaha RC	.05
253	Pat Listach	.05
254	Paul Molitor	.50
255	Jaime Navarro	.05
256	Kevin Seitzer	.05
257	B.J. Surhoff	.05
258	Greg Vaughn	.05
259	Bill Wegman	.05
260	Robin Yount	.50
261	Rick Aguilera	.05
262	Chili Davis	.05
263	Scott Erickson	.05
264	Greg Gagne	.05
265	Mark Guthrie	.05
266	Brian Harper	.05
267	Kent Hrbek	.05
268	Terry Jorgensen	.05
269	Gene Larkin	.05
270	Scott Leius	.05
271	Pat Mahomes	.05
272	Pedro Munoz	.05
273	Kirby Puckett	.60
274	Kevin Tapani	.05
275	Carl Willis	.05
276	Steve Farr	.05
277	John Habyan	.05
278	Mel Hall	.05
279	Charlie Hayes	.05
280	Pat Kelly	.05
281	Don Mattingly	.65
282	Sam Militello	.05
283	Matt Nokes	.05
284	Melido Perez	.05
285	Andy Stankiewicz	.05
286	Danny Tartabull	.05
287	Randy Velarde	.05
288	Bob Wickman	.05
289	Bernie Williams	.05
290	Lance Blankenship	.05
291	Mike Bordick	.05
292	Jerry Browne	.05
293	Dennis Eckersley	.40
294	Rickey Henderson	.50
295	Vince Horsman RC	.05
296	Mark McGwire	.85
297	Jeff Parrett	.05
298	Ruben Sierra	.05
299	Terry Steinbach	.05
300	Walt Weiss	.05
301	Bob Welch	.05
302	Willie Wilson	.05
303	Bobby Witt	.05
304	Bret Boone	.05
305	Jay Buhner	.05
306	Dave Fleming	.05
307	Ken Griffey Jr.	.75
308	Erik Hanson	.05
309	Edgar Martinez	.05
310	Tino Martinez	.05
311	Jeff Nelson	.05
312	Dennis Powell	.05
313	Mike Schooler	.05
314	Russ Swan	.05
315	Dave Valle	.05
316	Omar Vizquel	.05
317	Kevin Brown	.05
318	Todd Burns	.05
319	Jose Canseco	.35
320	Julio Franco	.05

321	Jeff Frye	.05
322	Juan Gonzalez	.30
323	Jose Guzman	.05
324	Jeff Huson	.05
325	Dean Palmer	.05
326	Kevin Reimer	.05
327	Ivan Rodriguez	.40
328	Kenny Rogers	.05
329	Dan Smith RC	.05
330	Roberto Alomar	.20
331	Derek Bell	.05
332	Pat Borders	.05
333	Joe Carter	.05
334	Kelly Gruber	.05
335	Tom Henke	.05
336	Jimmy Key	.05
337	Manuel Lee	.05
338	Candy Maldonado	.05
339	John Olerud	.05
340	Todd Stottlemyre	.05
341	Duane Ward	.05
342	Devon White	.05
343	Dave Winfield	.50
344	Edgar Martinez (League Leaders)	.05
345	Cecil Fielder (League Leaders)	.05
346	Kenny Lofton (League Leaders)	.05
347	Jack Morris (League Leaders)	.05
348	Roger Clemens (League Leaders)	.35
349	Fred McGriff (Round Trippers)	.05
350	Barry Bonds (Round Trippers)	.60
351	Gary Sheffield (Round Trippers)	.05
352	Darren Daulton (Round Trippers)	.05
353	Dave Hollins (Round Trippers)	.05
354	Brothers In Blue (Pedro Martinez, Ramon Martinez)	.25
355	Power Packs (Ivan Rodriguez, Kirby Puckett)	.25
356	Triple Threats (Ryne Sandberg, Gary Sheffield)	.20
357	Infield Trifecta (Roberto Alomar, Chuck Knoblauch, Carlos Baerga)	.05
358	Checklist	.05
359	Checklist	.05
360	Checklist	.05
361	Rafael Belliard	.05
362	Damon Berryhill	.05
363	Mike Bielecki	.05
364	Jeff Blauser	.05
365	Francisco Cabrera	.05
366	Marvin Freeman	.05
367	Dave Justice	.05
368	Mark Lemke	.05
369	Alejandro Pena	.05
370	Jeff Reardon	.05
371	Lonnie Smith	.05
372	Pete Smith	.05
373	Shawn Boskie	.05
374	Jim Bullinger	.05
375	Frank Castillo	.05
376	Doug Dascenzo	.05
377	Andre Dawson	.25
378	Mike Harkey	.05
379	Greg Hibbard	.05
380	Greg Maddux	.60
381	Ken Patterson	.05
382	Jeff Robinson	.05
383	Luis Salazar	.05
384	Dwight Smith	.05
385	Jose Vizcaino	.05
386	Scott Bankhead	.05
387	Tom Browning	.05
388	Darnell Coles	.05
389	Rob Dibble	.05
390	Bill Doran	.05
391	Dwayne Henry	.05
392	Cesar Hernandez	.05
393	Roberto Kelly	.05
394	Barry Larkin	.05
395	Dave Martinez	.05
396	Kevin Mitchell	.05
397	Jeff Reed	.05
398	Scott Ruskin	.05
399	Greg Swindell	.05
400	Dan Wilson	.05
401	Andy Ashby	.05
402	Freddie Benavides	.05
403	Dante Bichette	.05
404	Willie Blair	.05
405	Denis Boucher	.05
406	Vinny Castilla	.05
407	Braulio Castillo	.05
408	Alex Cole	.05
409	Andres Galarraga	.05
410	Joe Girardi	.05
411	Butch Henry	.05
412	Darren Holmes	.05
413	Calvin Jones	.05
414	Steve Reed RC	.05
415	Kevin Ritz	.05
416	Jim Tatum RC	.05
417	Jack Armstrong	.05
418	Bret Barberie	.05
419	Ryan Bowen	.05
420	Cris Carpenter	.05

421	Chuck Carr	.05
422	Scott Chiamparino	.05
423	Jeff Conine	.05
424	Jim Corsi	.05
425	Steve Decker	.05
426	Chris Donnels	.05
427	Monty Fariss	.05
428	Bob Natal	.05
429	Pat Rapp RC	.05
430	Dave Weathers	.05
431	Nigel Wilson RC	.05
432	Ken Caminiti	.05
433	Andujar Cedeno	.05
434	Tom Edens	.05
435	Juan Guerrero	.05
436	Pete Incaviglia	.05
437	Jimmy Jones	.05
438	Darryl Kile	.05
439	Rob Murphy	.05
440	Al Osuna	.05
441	Mark Portugal	.05
442	Scott Servais	.05
443	John Candelaria	.05
444	Tim Crews	.05
445	Eric Davis	.05
446	Tom Goodwin	.05
447	Jim Gott	.05
448	Kevin Gross	.05
449	Dave Hansen	.05
450	Jay Howell	.05
451	Roger McDowell	.05
452	Bob Ojeda	.05
453	Henry Rodriguez	.05
454	Darryl Strawberry	.05
455	Mitch Webster	.05
456	Steve Wilson	.05
457	Brian Barnes	.05
458	Sean Berry	.05
459	Jeff Fassero	.05
460	Darrin Fletcher	.05
461	Marquis Grissom	.05
462	Dennis Martinez	.05
463	Spike Owen	.05
464	Matt Stairs	.05
465	Sergio Valdez	.05
466	Kevin Bass	.05
467	Vince Coleman	.05
468	Mark Dewey	.05
469	Kevin Elster	.05
470	Tony Fernandez	.05
471	John Franco	.05
472	Dave Gallagher	.05
473	Paul Gibson	.05
474	Dwight Gooden	.05
475	Lee Guetterman	.05
476	Jeff Innis	.05
477	Dave Magadan	.05
478	Charlie O'Brien	.05
479	Willie Randolph	.05
480	Mackey Sasser	.05
481	Ryan Thompson	.05
482	Chico Walker	.05
483	Kyle Abbott	.05
484	Bob Ayrault	.05
485	Kim Batiste	.05
486	Cliff Brantley	.05
487	Jose DeLeon	.05
488	Len Dykstra	.05
489	Tommy Greene	.05
490	Jeff Grotewold	.05
491	Dave Hollins	.05
492	Danny Jackson	.05
493	Stan Javier	.05
494	Tom Marsh	.05
495	Greg Matthews	.05
496	Dale Murphy	.15
497	Todd Pratt RC	.05
498	Mitch Williams	.05
499	Danny Cox	.05
500	Doug Drabek	.05
501	Carlos Garcia	.05
502	Lloyd McClendon	.05
503	Denny Neagle	.05
504	Gary Redus	.05
505	Bob Walk	.05
506	John Wehner	.05
507	Luis Alicea	.05
508	Mark Clark	.05
509	Pedro Guerrero	.05
510	Rex Hudler	.05
511	Brian Jordan	.05
512	Omar Olivares	.05
513	Jose Oquendo	.05
514	Gerald Perry	.05
515	Bryn Smith	.05
516	Craig Wilson	.05
517	Tracy Woodson	.05
518	Larry Anderson	.05
519	Andy Benes	.05
520	Jim Deshaies	.05
521	Bruce Hurst	.05
522	Randy Myers	.05
523	Benito Santiago	.05
524	Tim Scott	.05
525	Tim Teufel	.05
526	Mike Benjamin	.05
527	Dave Burba	.05
528	Craig Colbert	.05
529	Mike Felder	.05
530	Bryan Hickerson	.05
531	Chris James	.05
532	Mark Leonard	.05
533	Greg Litton	.05
534	Francisco Oliveras	.05
535	John Patterson	.05
536	Jim Pena	.05
537	Dave Righetti	.05
538	Robby Thompson	.05

#	Player	Price		#	Player	Price
539	Jose Uribe	.05		657	Gerald Williams	.05
540	Matt Williams	.05		658	Curt Young	.05
541	Storm Davis	.05		659	Harold Baines	.05
542	Sam Horn	.05		660	Kevin Campbell	.05
543	Tim Hulett	.05		661	Ron Darling	.05
544	Craig Lefferts	.05		662	Kelly Downs	.05
545	Chito Martinez	.05		663	Eric Fox	.05
546	Mark McLemore	.05		664	Dave Henderson	.05
547	Luis Mercedes	.05		665	Rick Honeycutt	.05
548	Bob Milacki	.05		666	Mike Moore	.05
549	Joe Orsulak	.05		667	Jamie Quirk	.05
550	Billy Ripken	.05		668	Jeff Russell	.05
551	Cal Ripken, Jr.	1.00		669	Dave Stewart	.05
552	Rick Sutcliffe	.05		670	Greg Briley	.05
553	Jeff Tackett	.05		671	Dave Cochrane	.05
554	Wade Boggs	.60		672	Henry Cotto	.05
555	Tom Brunansky	.05		673	Rich DeLucia	.05
556	Jack Clark	.05		674	Brian Fisher	.05
557	John Dopson	.05		675	Mark Grant	.05
558	Mike Gardiner	.05		676	Randy Johnson	.50
559	Mike Greenwell	.05		677	Tim Leary	.05
560	Greg Harris	.05		678	Pete O'Brien	.05
561	Billy Hatcher	.05		679	Lance Parrish	.05
562	Joe Hesketh	.05		680	Harold Reynolds	.05
563	Tony Pena	.05		681	Shane Turner	.05
564	Phil Plantier	.05		682	Jack Daugherty	.05
565	Luis Rivera	.05		683	David Hulse RC	.05
566	Herm Winningham	.05		684	Terry Mathews	.05
567	Matt Young	.05		685	Al Newman	.05
568	Bert Blyleven	.05		686	Edwin Nunez	.05
569	Mike Butcher	.05		687	Rafael Palmeiro	.40
570	Chuck Crim	.05		688	Roger Pavlik	.05
571	Chad Curtis RC	.15		689	Geno Petralli	.05
572	Tim Fortugno	.05		690	Nolan Ryan	1.00
573	Steve Frey	.05		691	David Cone	.05
574	Gary Gaetti	.05		692	Alfredo Griffin	.05
575	Scott Lewis	.05		693	Juan Guzman	.05
576	Lee Stevens	.05		694	Pat Hentgen	.05
577	Ron Tingley	.05		695	Randy Knorr	.05
578	Julio Valera	.05		696	Bob MacDonald	.05
579	Shawn Abner	.05		697	Jack Morris	.05
580	Joey Cora	.05		698	Ed Sprague	.05
581	Chris Cron	.05		699	Dave Stieb	.05
582	Carlton Fisk	.50		700	Pat Tabler	.05
583	Roberto Hernandez	.05		701	Mike Timlin	.05
584	Charlie Hough	.05		702	David Wells	.05
585	Terry Leach	.05		703	Eddie Zosky	.05
586	Donn Pall	.05		704	Gary Sheffield	
587	Dan Pasqua	.05			(League Leaders)	.05
588	Steve Sax	.05		705	Darren Daulton	
589	Bobby Thigpen	.05			(League Leaders)	.05
590	Albert Belle	.05		706	Marquis Grissom	
591	Felix Fermin	.05			(League Leaders)	.05
592	Glenallen Hill	.05		707	Greg Maddux	
593	Brook Jacoby	.05			(League Leaders)	.10
594	Reggie Jefferson	.05		708	Bill Swift	
595	Carlos Martinez	.05			(League Leaders)	.05
596	Jose Mesa	.05		709	Juan Gonzalez	
597	Rod Nichols	.05			(Round Trippers)	.15
598	Junior Ortiz	.05		710	Mark McGwire	
599	Eric Plunk	.05			(Round Trippers)	.50
600	Ted Power	.05		711	Cecil Fielder	
601	Scott Scudder	.05			(Round Trippers)	.05
602	Kevin Wickander	.05		712	Albert Belle	
603	Skeeter Barnes	.05			(Round Trippers)	.05
604	Mark Carreon	.05		713	Joe Carter	
605	Dan Gladden	.05			(Round Trippers)	.05
606	Bill Gullickson	.05		714	Power Brokers	
607	Chad Kreuter	.05			(Frank Thomas,	
608	Mark Leiter	.05			Cecil Fielder)	.10
609	Mike Munoz	.05		715	Unsung Heroes	
610	Rich Rowland	.05			(Larry Walker,	
611	Frank Tanana	.05			Darren Daulton)	.05
612	Walt Terrell	.05		716	Hot Corner Hammers	
613	Alan Trammell	.05			(Edgar Martinez,	
614	Lou Whitaker	.05			Robin Ventura)	.05
615	Luis Aquino	.05		717	Start to Finish	
616	Mike Boddicker	.05			(Roger Clemens,	
617	Jim Eisenreich	.05			Dennis Eckersley)	.25
618	Mark Gubicza	.05		718	Checklist	.05
619	David Howard	.05		719	Checklist	.05
620	Mike Magnante	.05		720	Checklist	.05
621	Brent Mayne	.05				
622	Kevin McReynolds	.05			**All-Stars**	
623	Eddie Pierce RC	.05				
624	Bill Sampen	.05				
625	Steve Shifflett	.05				
626	Gary Thurman	.05				
627	Curtis Wikerson	.05				
628	Chris Bosio	.05				
629	Scott Fletcher	.05				
630	Jim Gantner	.05				
631	Dave Nilsson	.05				
632	Jesse Orosco	.05				
633	Dan Plesac	.05				
634	Ron Robinson	.05			Horizontal-format All-Star	
635	Bill Spiers	.05				
636	Franklin Stubbs	.05				
637	Willie Banks	.05				
638	Randy Bush	.05				
639	Chuck Knoblauch	.05				
640	Shane Mack	.05				
641	Mike Pagliarulo	.05				
642	Jeff Reboulet	.05				
643	John Smiley	.05				
644	Mike Trombley RC	.05				
645	Gary Wayne	.05				
646	Lenny Webster	.05				
647	Tim Burke	.05				
648	Mike Gallego	.05				
649	Dion James	.05				
650	Jeff Johnson	.05				
651	Scott Kamieniecki	.05				
652	Kevin Maas	.05				
653	Rich Monteleone	.05				
654	Jerry Nielsen	.05				
655	Scott Sanderson	.05				
656	Mike Stanley	.05				

8	Joe Carter	.15
9	Kirby Puckett	1.00
10	Brian Harper	.15
11	Dave Fleming	.15
12	Jack McDowell	.15

NATIONAL LEAGUE

1	Fred McGriff	.15
2	Delino DeShields	.15
3	Gary Sheffield	.40
4	Barry Larkin	.15
5	Felix Jose	.15
6	Larry Walker	.15
7	Barry Bonds	2.50
8	Andy Van Slyke	.15
9	Darren Daulton	.15
10	Greg Maddux	.75
11	Tom Glavine	.25
12	Lee Smith	.15

Tom Glavine Career Highlights

This 15-card insert set spotlighted career highlights of Fleer's 1993 spokesman, Tom Glavine. Twelve cards were available in Series 1 and Series 2 packs; cards #13-15 could be obtained only via a special mail offer. A limited number of certified autograph cards were also inserted into packs. Cards #1-4 and 7-10 can each be found with two variations on the back. The versions found in Series 2 packaging are the "correct" backs. Neither version carries a premium value.

	NM/M
Complete Set (15):	5.00
Common Card:	.50
Autographed Card:	30.00
1-15 Tom Glavine	.50

Golden Moments

Three cards of this insert set were available in both series of wax packs. Fronts feature black borders with gold-foil baseballs in the corners. The player's name appears in a "Golden Moments" banner at the bottom of the photo. Backs have a portrait photo of the player at top-center and a information on the highlight. The cards are unnumbered and are checklisted here alphabetically within series.

	NM/M
Complete Set (6):	4.00
Common Player:	.25
SERIES 1	2.00
(1) George Brett	1.50
(2) Mickey Morandini	.25
(3) Dave Winfield	.50
SERIES 2	2.00
(1) Dennis Eckersley	.40
(2) Bip Roberts	.25
(3) Frank Thomas, Juan Gonzalez	1.50

Major League Prospects

Yet another way to package currently hot rookies and future prospects to increase sales of the

base product, there were 18 insert cards found in each series' wax packs. Fronts are bordered in black and have gold-foil highlights. Most of the depicted players were a few seasons away from everyday play in the major leagues.

	NM/M
Complete Set (36):	7.50
Common Player:	.15
SERIES 1	5.00
1 Melvin Nieves	.15
2 Sterling Hitchcock	.15
3 Tim Costo	.15
4 Manny Alexander	.15
5 Alan Embree	.15
6 Kevin Young	.15
7 J.T. Snow	.15
8 Russ Springer	.15
9 Billy Ashley	.15
10 Kevin Rogers	.15
11 Steve Hosey	.15
12 Eric Wedge	.15
13 Mike Piazza	3.50
14 Jesse Levis	.15
15 Rico Brogna	.15
16 Alex Arias	.15
17 Rod Brewer	.15
18 Troy Neel	.15
SERIES 2	2.50
1 Scooter Tucker	.15
2 Kerry Woodson	.15
3 Greg Colbrunn	.15
4 Pedro Martinez	1.50
5 Dave Silvestri	.15
6 Kent Bottenfield	.15
7 Rafael Bournigal	.15
8 J.T. Bruett	.15
9 Dave Mlicki	.15
10 Paul Wagner	.15
11 Mike Williams	.15
12 Henry Mercedes	.15
13 Scott Taylor	.15
14 Dennis Moeller	.15
15 Javier Lopez	.15
16 Steve Cooke	.15
17 Pete Young	.15
18 Ken Ryan	.15

ProVisions

This three-card insert set in Series I wax packs features the baseball art of Wayne Still. Black-bordered fronts feature a player-fantasy painting at center, with the player's name gold-foil stamped beneath. Backs are also bordered in black and have a white box with a career summary.

	NM/M
Complete Set (6):	3.00
Common Player:	.40
SERIES 1	2.00
1 Roberto Alomar	.65
2 Dennis Eckersley	1.00
3 Gary Sheffield	.75
SERIES 2	1.00
1 Andy Van Slyke	.40
2 Tom Glavine	.75
3 Cecil Fielder	.40

Rookie Sensations

Ten rookie sensations - some of whom had not been true rookies for several seasons - were featured

in this insert issue packaged exclusively in Series 1 and Series 2 cello packs. Card fronts have a player photo set against a silver background and surrounded by a blue border. The player's name and other front printing are in gold foil. Backs are also printed in silver with a blue border. There is a player portrait photo and career summary.

	NM/M
Complete Set (20):	6.25
Common Player:	.25
SERIES 1	3.00
1 Kenny Lofton	.50
2 Cal Eldred	.25
3 Pat Listach	.25
4 Roberto Hernandez	.25
5 Dave Fleming	.25
6 Eric Karros	.25
7 Reggie Sanders	.25
8 Derrick May	.25
9 Mike Perez	.25
10 Donovan Osborne	.25
SERIES 2	2.00
1 Moises Alou	.50
2 Pedro Astacio	.25
3 Jim Austin	.25
4 Chad Curtis	.25
5 Gary DiSarcina	.25
6 Scott Livingstone	.25
7 Sam Militello	.25
8 Arthur Rhodes	.25
9 Tim Wakefield	.35
10 Bob Zupcic	.25

Team Leaders

This 20-card insert issue was exclusive to Series 1 and 2 rack packs. Fronts feature a portrait photo, with a small action photo superimposed. At the side is a colored bar with the player's name and "Team Leaders" printed vertically. On back is a career summary. Card borders are a light metallic green and both sides of the card are UV coated.

	NM/M
Complete Set (20):	12.50
Common Player:	.40
SERIES 1	10.00
1 Kirby Puckett	1.25
2 Mark McGwire	3.00
3 Pat Listach	.40
4 Roger Clemens	1.50
5 Frank Thomas	1.00
6 Carlos Baerga	.40
7 Brady Anderson	.40
8 Juan Gonzalez	.50
9 Roberto Alomar	.60
10 Ken Griffey Jr.	2.00
SERIES 2	4.00
1 Will Clark	.40
2 Terry Pendleton	.40
3 Ray Lankford	.40
4 Eric Karros	.40
5 Gary Sheffield	.75
6 Ryne Sandberg	1.25
7 Marquis Grissom	.40
8 John Kruk	.40
9 Jeff Bagwell	1.00
10 Andy Van Slyke	.40

Final Edition

This 310-card set was sold as a complete set in its own box. Card numbers have the prefix "F." The set also includes 10 Diamond Tribute cards, which are numbered DT1-DT10.

	NM/M
Complete Set (310):	7.50
Common Player:	.05
1 Steve Bedrosian	.05
2 Jay Howell	.05
3 Greg Maddux	.65
4 Greg McMichael RC	.05
5 Tony Tarasco RC	.05
6 Jose Bautista	.05
7 Jose Guzman	.05
8 Greg Hibbard	.05
9 Candy Maldonado	.05
10 Randy Myers	.05
11 Matt Walbeck RC	.05
12 Turk Wendell	.05
13 Willie Nelson	.05
14 Greg Cadaret	.05
15 Roberto Kelly	.05
16 Randy Milligan	.05
17 Kevin Mitchell	.05
18 Jeff Reardon	.05
19 John Roper	.05
20 John Smiley	.05
21 Andy Ashby	.05
22 Dante Bichette	.05
23 Willie Blair	.05
24 Pedro Castellano	.05
25 Vinny Castilla	.05
26 Jerald Clark	.05
27 Alex Cole	.05
28 Scott Fredrickson RC	.05
29 Jay Gainer RC	.05
30 Andres Galarraga	.05
31 Joe Girardi	.05
32 Ryan Hawblitzel	.05
33 Charlie Hayes	.05
34 Darren Holmes	.05
35 Chris Jones	.05
36 David Nied	.05
37 J. Owens RC	.05
38 Lance Painter RC	.05
39 Jeff Parrett	.05
40 Steve Reed RC	.05
41 Armando Reynoso	.05
42 Bruce Ruffin	.05
43 Danny Sheaffer RC	.05
44 Keith Shepherd	.05
45 Jim Tatum	.05
46 Gary Wayne	.05
47 Eric Young	.05
48 Luis Aquino	.05
49 Alex Arias	.05
50 Jack Armstrong	.05
51 Bret Barberie	.05
52 Geronimo Berroa	.05
53 Ryan Bowen	.05
54 Greg Briley	.05
55 Chris Carpenter	.05
56 Chuck Carr	.05
57 Jeff Conine	.05
58 Jim Corsi	.05
59 Orestes Destrade	.05
60 Junior Felix	.05
61 Chris Hammond	.05
62 Bryan Harvey	.05
63 Charlie Hough	.05
64 Joe Klink	.05
65 Richie Lewis RC	.05
66 Mitch Lyden RC	.05
67 Bob Natal	.05
68 Scott Pose RC	.05
69 Rich Renteria	.05
70 Benito Santiago	.05
71 Gary Sheffield	.15
72 Matt Turner RC	.05
73 Walt Weiss	.05
74 Darrell Whitmore RC	.05
75 Nigel Wilson	.05
76 Kevin Bass	.05
77 Doug Drabek	.05
78 Tom Edens	.05
79 Chris James	.05
80 Greg Swindell	.05
81 Omar Daal RC	.05
82 Raul Mondesi	.05
83 Jody Reed	.05
84 Cory Snyder	.05
85 Rick Trlicek	.05
86 Tim Wallach	.05
87 Todd Worrell	.05

All-Stars (description)

Horizontal-format All-Star cards comprised one of the many 1993 Fleer insert issues. Twelve cards of National League All-Stars were included in Series I wax packs, while a dozen American League All-Stars were found in Series II packs. They are among the more popular and valuable of the '93 Fleer inserts.

	NM/M
Complete Set A.L. (12):	6.00
Complete Set N.L. (12):	3.75
Common Player:	.15

AMERICAN LEAGUE

1	Frank Thomas	.85
2	Roberto Alomar	.40
3	Edgar Martinez	.15
4	Pat Listach	.15
5	Cecil Fielder	.15
6	Juan Gonzalez	.40
7	Ken Griffey Jr.	2.00

#	Player	Price
88	Tavo Alvarez	.05
89	Frank Bolick	.05
90	Kent Bottenfield	.05
91	Greg Colbrunn	.05
92	Cliff Floyd	.05
93	Lou Frazier RC	.05
94	Mike Gardiner	.05
95	Mike Lansing RC	.25
96	Bill Risley	.05
97	Jeff Shaw	.05
98	Kevin Baez	.05
99	Tim Bogar RC	.05
100	Jeromy Burnitz	.05
101	Mike Draper	.05
102	Darrin Jackson	.05
103	Mike Maddux	.05
104	Joe Orsulak	.05
105	Doug Saunders	.05
106	Frank Tanana	.05
107	Dave Telgheder	.05
108	Larry Anderson	.05
109	Jim Eisenreich	.05
110	Pete Incaviglia	.05
111	Danny Jackson	.05
112	David West	.05
113	Al Martin	.05
114	Blas Minor	.05
115	Dennis Moeller	.05
116	Will Pennyfeather	.05
117	Rich Robertson	.05
118	Ben Shelton	.05
119	Lonnie Smith	.05
120	Freddie Toliver	.05
121	Paul Wagner	.05
122	Kevin Young	.05
123	Rene Arocha RC	.05
124	Gregg Jefferies	.05
125	Paul Kilgus	.05
126	Les Lancaster	.05
127	Joe Magrane	.05
128	Rob Murphy	.05
129	Erik Pappas	.05
130	Stan Royer	.05
131	Ozzie Smith	.65
132	Tom Urbani	.05
133	Mark Whiten	.05
134	Derek Bell	.05
135	Doug Brocail	.05
136	Phil Clark	.05
137	Mark Ettles RC	.05
138	Jeff Gardner	.05
139	Pat Gomez RC	.05
140	Ricky Gutierrez	.05
141	Gene Harris	.05
142	Kevin Higgins RC	.05
143	Trevor Hoffman	.05
144	Phil Plantier	.05
145	Kerry Taylor RC	.05
146	Guillermo Velasquez	.05
147	Wally Whitehurst	.05
148	Tim Worrell RC	.05
149	Todd Benzinger	.05
150	Barry Bonds	2.00
151	Greg Brummett	.05
152	Mark Carreon	.05
153	Dave Martinez	.05
154	Jeff Reed	.05
155	Kevin Rogers	.05
156	Harold Baines	.05
157	Damon Buford	.05
158	Paul Carey RC	.05
159	Jeffrey Hammonds	.05
160	Jamie Moyer	.05
161	Sherman Obando RC	.05
162	John O'Donoghue RC	.05
163	Brad Pennington	.05
164	Jim Poole	.05
165	Harold Reynolds	.05
166	Fernando Valenzuela	.05
167	Jack Voight RC	.05
168	Mark Williamson	.05
169	Scott Bankhead	.05
170	Greg Blosser	.05
171	Jim Byrd RC	.05
172	Ivan Calderon	.05
173	Andre Dawson	.25
174	Scott Fletcher	.05
175	Jose Melendez	.05
176	Carlos Quintana	.05
177	Jeff Russell	.05
178	Aaron Sele	.05
179	Rod Correia RC	.05
180	Chili Davis	.05
181	Jim Edmonds RC	3.00
182	Rene Gonzales	.05
183	Hilly Hathaway RC	.05
184	Torey Lovullo	.05
185	Greg Myers	.05
186	Gene Nelson	.05
187	Troy Percival	.05
188	Scott Sanderson	.05
189	Darryl Scott RC	.05
190	J.T. Snow RC	.50
191	Russ Springer	.05
192	Jason Bere	.05
193	Rodney Bolton	.05
194	Ellis Burks	.05
195	Bo Jackson	.15
196	Mike LaValliere	.05
197	Scott Ruffcorn	.05
198	Jeff Schwartz RC	.05
199	Jerry DiPoto	.05
200	Alvaro Espinoza	.05
201	Wayne Kirby	.05
202	Tom Kramer RC	.05
203	Jesse Levis	.05
204	Manny Ramirez	.50
205	Jeff Treadway	.05
206	Bill Wertz RC	.05
207	Cliff Young	.05
208	Matt Young	.05
209	Kirk Gibson	.05
210	Greg Gohr	.05
211	Bill Krueger	.05
212	Bob MacDonald	.05
213	Mike Moore	.05
214	David Wells	.05
215	Billy Brewer RC	.05
216	David Cone	.05
217	Greg Gagne	.05
218	Mark Gardner	.05
219	Chis Haney	.05
220	Phil Hiatt	.05
221	Jose Lind	.05
222	Juan Bell	.05
223	Tom Brunansky	.05
224	Mike Ignasiak	.05
225	Joe Kmak	.05
226	Tom Lampkin	.05
227	Graeme Lloyd RC	.05
228	Carlos Maldonado	.05
229	Matt Mieske	.05
230	Angel Miranda	.05
231	Troy O'Leary RC	.10
232	Kevin Reimer	.05
233	Larry Casian	.05
234	Jim Deshaies	.05
235	Eddie Guardado RC	.10
236	Chip Hale	.05
237	Mike Maksudian RC	.05
238	David McCarty	.05
239	Pat Meares RC	.05
240	George Tsamis RC	.05
241	Dave Winfield	.50
242	Jim Abbott	.05
243	Wade Boggs	.65
244	Andy Cook RC	.05
245	Russ Davis RC	.10
246	Mike Humphreys	.05
247	Jimmy Key	.05
248	Jim Leyritz	.05
249	Bobby Munoz	.05
250	Paul O'Neill	.05
251	Spike Owen	.05
252	Dave Silvestri	.05
253	Marcos Armas RC	.05
254	Brent Gates	.05
255	Goose Gossage	.05
256	Scott Lydy RC	.05
257	Henry Mercedes	.05
258	Mike Mohler RC	.05
259	Troy Neel	.05
260	Edwin Nunez	.05
261	Craig Paquette	.05
262	Kevin Seitzer	.05
263	Rich Amaral	.05
264	Mike Blowers	.05
265	Chris Bosio	.05
266	Norm Charlton	.05
267	Jim Converse RC	.05
268	John Cummings RC	.05
269	Mike Felder	.05
270	Mike Hampton	.05
271	Bill Haselman	.05
272	Dwayne Henry	.05
273	Greg Litton	.05
274	Mackey Sasser	.05
275	Lee Tinsley	.05
276	David Wainhouse	.05
277	Jeff Bronkey RC	.05
278	Benji Gil	.05
279	Tom Henke	.05
280	Charlie Leibrandt	.05
281	Robb Nen	.05
282	Bill Ripken	.05
283	Jon Shave RC	.05
284	Doug Strange	.05
285	Matt Whiteside RC	.05
286	Scott Brow RC	.05
287	Willie Canate RC	.05
288	Tony Castillo	.05
289	Domingo Cedeno RC	.05
290	Darnell Coles	.05
291	Danny Cox	.05
292	Mark Eichhorn	.05
293	Tony Fernandez	.05
294	Al Leiter	.05
295	Paul Molitor	.50
296	Dave Stewart	.05
297	Woody Williams RC	.05
298	Checklist	.05
299	Checklist	.05
300	Checklist	.05
1DT	Wade Boggs	.65
2DT	George Brett	.75
3DT	Andre Dawson	.50
4DT	Carlton Fisk	.50
5DT	Paul Molitor	.50
6DT	Nolan Ryan	2.00
7DT	Lee Smith	.05
8DT	Ozzie Smith	.65
9DT	Dave Winfield	.50
10DT	Robin Yount	.50

Atlantic

The Atlantic Collectors Edition set of 1993 features 24 of the top players in the game (plus one checklist) portrayed in a style matching the regular-issue Fleer set, with the addition of the Atlantic logo and a gold border. The cards were given away five at a time with

gasoline purchases at gas stations in New York and Pennsylvania during the summer.

		NM/M
	Complete Set (25):	3.50
	Common Player:	.12
1	Roberto Alomar	.20
2	Barry Bonds	1.00
3	Bobby Bonilla	.10
4	Will Clark	.10
5	Roger Clemens	.60
6	Darren Daulton	.10
7	Dennis Eckersley	.30
8	Cecil Fielder	.10
9	Tom Glavine	.25
10	Juan Gonzalez	.25
11	Ken Griffey Jr.	.75
12	John Kruk	.10
13	Greg Maddux	.50
14	Don Mattingly	.60
15	Fred McGriff	.10
16	Mark McGwire	.85
17	Terry Pendleton	.10
18	Kirby Puckett	.50
19	Cal Ripken Jr.	1.00
20	Nolan Ryan	1.00
21	Ryne Sandberg	.50
22	Gary Sheffield	.25
23	Frank Thomas	.40
24	Andy Van Slyke	.10
25	Checklist	.05

Fruit of the Loom

Fruit of the Loom and Fleer combined to create a 66-card baseball set in 1993 that featured many of the top players in the game. The cards, with the same design as the regular-issue Fleer cards, also display the Fruit of the Loom logo in the upper-left corner. Three cards were inserted in specially marked packages of the company's products.

		NM/M
	Complete Set (66):	30.00
	Common Player:	.25
1	Roberto Alomar	.45
2	Brady Anderson	.25
3	Jeff Bagwell	1.00
4	Albert Belle	.25
5	Craig Biggio	.25
6	Barry Bonds	3.00
7	George Brett	1.75
8	Brett Butler	.25
9	Jose Canseco	.65
10	Joe Carter	.25
11	Will Clark	.25
12	Roger Clemens	1.75
13	Darren Daulton	.25
14	Andre Dawson	.40
15	Delino DeShields	.25
16	Rob Dibble	.25
17	Doug Drabek	.25
18	Dennis Eckersley	.85
19	Cecil Fielder	.25
20	Travis Fryman	.25
21	Tom Glavine	.45
22	Juan Gonzalez	.50
23	Dwight Gooden	.25
24	Mark Grace	.25
25	Ken Griffey Jr.	2.00
26	Marquis Grissom	.25
27	Juan Guzman	.25
28	Tony Gwynn	1.50
29	Rickey Henderson	1.00
30	David Justice	.25
31	Eric Karros	.25
32	Chuck Knoblauch	.25
33	John Kruk	.25
34	Ray Lankford	.25
35	Barry Larkin	.25
36	Pat Listach	.25
37	Kenny Lofton	.25
38	Shane Mack	.25
39	Greg Maddux	1.50
40	Dennis Martinez	.25
41	Edgar Martinez	.25
42	Ramon Martinez	.25
43	Don Mattingly	1.75
44	Jack McDowell	.25
45	Fred McGriff	.25
46	Mark McGwire	2.50
47	Jeff Montgomery	.25
48	Eddie Murray	1.00
49	Charles Nagy	.25
50	Tom Pagnozzi	.25
51	Terry Pendleton	.25
52	Kirby Puckett	1.50
53	Jose Rijo	.25
54	Cal Ripken, Jr.	3.00
55	Nolan Ryan	3.00
56	Ryne Sandberg	1.50
57	Gary Sheffield	.65
58	Bill Swift	.25
59	Danny Tartabull	.25
60	Mickey Tettleton	.25
61	Frank Thomas	1.00
62	Andy Van Slyke	.25
63	Robin Ventura	.25
64	Larry Walker	.25
65	Robin Yount	1.00
66	Checklist	.05

1994 Fleer "Highlights" Promo Sheet

To introduce its special insert card series honoring 1993 A.L. Rookie of the Year Tim Salmon and Phillies stars John Kruk and Darren Daulton, Fleer issued this 5" x 7" promo sheet. The three player cards on the sheet are similar to the issued versions except they have black overprinting on front and back which reads, "PROMOTIONAL SAMPLE." The non-player segment of the sheet has details about the inserts and special mail-in offers for additional cards.

	NM/M
Sheet:	6.00

1994 Fleer

Fleer's 720-card 1994 set, released in one series, includes another 204 insert cards to be pursued by collectors. Every pack includes one of the cards, randomly inserted from among the 12 insert sets. Regular cards have action photos on front, with a team logo in one of the lower corners. The player's name and position is stamped in gold foil around the logo. On back, another color player photo is overprinted with color boxes, data and stats, leaving a clear image of the player's face, 1-1/2" x 1-3/4" in size. Cards are UV coated on both sides.

#	Player	NM/M
	Complete Set (720):	12.50
	Common Player:	.05
	Pack (15):	.50
	Wax Box (36):	12.50
1	Brady Anderson	.05
2	Harold Baines	.05
3	Mike Devereaux	.05
4	Todd Frohwirth	.05
5	Jeffrey Hammonds	.05
6	Chris Hoiles	.05
7	Tim Hulett	.05
8	Ben McDonald	.05
9	Mark McLemore	.05
10	Alan Mills	.05
11	Jamie Moyer	.05
12	Mike Mussina	.40
13	Gregg Olson	.05
14	Mike Pagliarulo	.05
15	Brad Pennington	.05
16	Jim Poole	.05
17	Harold Reynolds	.05
18	Arthur Rhodes	.05
19	Cal Ripken, Jr.	2.00
20	David Segui	.05
21	Rick Sutcliffe	.05
22	Fernando Valenzuela	.05
23	Jack Voigt	.05
24	Mark Williamson	.05
25	Scott Bankhead	.05
26	Roger Clemens	1.00
27	Scott Cooper	.05
28	Danny Darwin	.05
29	Andre Dawson	.25
30	Rob Deer	.05
31	John Dopson	.05
32	Scott Fletcher	.05
33	Mike Greenwell	.05
34	Greg Harris	.05
35	Billy Hatcher	.05
36	Bob Melvin	.05
37	Tony Pena	.05
38	Paul Quantrill	.05
39	Carlos Quintana	.05
40	Ernest Riles	.05
41	Jeff Russell	.05
42	Ken Ryan	.05
43	Aaron Sele	.05
44	John Valentin	.05
45	Mo Vaughn	.05
46	Frank Viola	.05
47	Bob Zupcic	.05
48	Mike Butcher	.05
49	Rod Correia	.05
50	Chad Curtis	.05
51	Chili Davis	.05
52	Gary DiSarcina	.05
53	Damion Easley	.05
54	Jim Edmonds	.05
55	Chuck Finley	.05
56	Steve Frey	.05
57	Rene Gonzales	.05
58	Joe Grahe	.05
59	Hilly Hathaway	.05
60	Stan Javier	.05
61	Mark Langston	.05
62	Phil Leftwich	.05
63	Torey Lovullo	.05
64	Joe Magrane	.05
65	Greg Myers	.05
66	Ken Patterson	.05
67	Eduardo Perez	.05
68	Luis Polonia	.05
69	Tim Salmon	.20
69a	Tim Salmon/OPS	2.00
70	J.T. Snow	.05
71	Ron Tingley	.05
72	Julio Valera	.05
73	Wilson Alvarez	.05
74	Tim Belcher	.05
75	George Bell	.05
76	Jason Bere	.05
77	Rod Bolton	.05
78	Ellis Burks	.05
79	Joey Cora	.05
80	Alex Fernandez	.05
81	Craig Grebeck	.05
82	Ozzie Guillen	.05
83	Roberto Hernandez	.05
84	Bo Jackson	.10
85	Lance Johnson	.05
86	Ron Karkovice	.05
87	Mike LaValliere	.05
88	Kirk McCaskill	.05
89	Jack McDowell	.05
90	Warren Newson	.05
91	Dan Pasqua	.05
92	Scott Radinsky	.05
93	Tim Raines	.05
94	Steve Sax	.05
95	Jeff Schwartz	.05
96	Frank Thomas	.75
97	Robin Ventura	.05
98	Sandy Alomar, Jr.	.05
99	Carlos Baerga	.05
100	Albert Belle	.05
101	Mark Clark	.05
102	Jerry DiPoto	.05
103	Alvaro Espinoza	.05
104	Felix Fermin	.05
105	Jeremy Hernandez	.05
106	Reggie Jefferson	.05
107	Wayne Kirby	.05
108	Tom Kramer	.05
109	Mark Lewis	.05
110	Derek Lilliquist	.05
111	Kenny Lofton	.05
112	Candy Maldonado	.05
113	Jose Mesa	.05
114	Jeff Mutis	.05
115	Charles Nagy	.05
116	Bob Ojeda	.05
117	Junior Ortiz	.05
118	Eric Plunk	.05
119	Manny Ramirez	.75
120	Paul Sorrento	.05
121	Jim Thome	.60
122	Jeff Treadway	.05
123	Bill Wertz	.05
124	Skeeter Barnes	.05
125	Milt Cuyler	.05
126	Eric Davis	.05
127	John Doherty	.05
128	Cecil Fielder	.05
129	Travis Fryman	.05
130	Kirk Gibson	.05
131	Dan Gladden	.05
132	Greg Gohr	.05
133	Chris Gomez	.05
134	Bill Gullickson	.05
135	Mike Henneman	.05
136	Kurt Knudsen	.05
137	Chad Kreuter	.05
138	Bill Krueger	.05
139	Scott Livingstone	.05
140	Bob MacDonald	.05
141	Mike Moore	.05
142	Tony Phillips	.05
143	Mickey Tettleton	.05
144	Alan Trammell	.05
145	David Wells	.05
146	Lou Whitaker	.05
147	Kevin Appier	.05
148	Stan Belinda	.05
149	George Brett	1.00
150	Billy Brewer	.05
151	Hubie Brooks	.05
152	David Cone	.05
153	Gary Gaetti	.05
154	Greg Gagne	.05
155	Tom Gordon	.05
156	Mark Gubicza	.05
157	Chris Gwynn	.05
158	John Habyan	.05
159	Chris Haney	.05
160	Phil Hiatt	.05
161	Felix Jose	.05
162	Wally Joyner	.05
163	Jose Lind	.05
164	Mike Macfarlane	.05
165	Mike Magnante	.05
166	Brent Mayne	.05
167	Brian McRae	.05
168	Kevin McReynolds	.05
169	Keith Miller	.05
170	Jeff Montgomery	.05
171	Hipolito Pichardo	.05
172	Rico Rossy	.05
173	Juan Bell	.05
174	Ricky Bones	.05
175	Cal Eldred	.05
176	Mike Fetters	.05
177	Darryl Hamilton	.05
178	Doug Henry	.05
179	Mike Ignasiak	.05
180	John Jaha	.05
181	Pat Listach	.05
182	Graeme Lloyd	.05
183	Matt Mieske	.05
184	Angel Miranda	.05
185	Jaime Navarro	.05
186	Dave Nilsson	.05
187	Troy O'Leary	.05
188	Jesse Orosco	.05
189	Kevin Reimer	.05
190	Kevin Seitzer	.05
191	Bill Spiers	.05
192	B.J. Surhoff	.05
193	Dickie Thon	.05
194	Jose Valentin	.05
195	Greg Vaughn	.05
196	Bill Wegman	.05
197	Robin Yount	.75
198	Rick Aguilera	.05
199	Willie Banks	.05
200	Bernardo Brito	.05
201	Larry Casian	.05
202	Scott Erickson	.05
203	Eddie Guardado	.05
204	Mark Guthrie	.05
205	Chip Hale	.05
206	Brian Harper	.05
207	Mike Hartley	.05
208	Kent Hrbek	.05
209	Terry Jorgensen	.05
210	Chuck Knoblauch	.05
211	Gene Larkin	.05
212	Shane Mack	.05
213	David McCarty	.05
214	Pat Meares	.05
215	Pedro Munoz	.05
216	Derek Parks	.05
217	Kirby Puckett	.85
218	Jeff Reboulet	.05
219	Kevin Tapani	.05
220	Mike Trombley	.05
221	George Tsamis	.05
222	Carl Willis	.05
223	Dave Winfield	.75
224	Jim Abbott	.05
225	Paul Assenmacher	.05
226	Wade Boggs	.85

#	Player	Price
227	Russ Davis	.05
228	Steve Farr	.05
229	Mike Gallego	.05
230	Paul Gibson	.05
231	Steve Howe	.05
232	Dion James	.05
233	Domingo Jean	.05
234	Scott Kamieniecki	.05
235	Pat Kelly	.05
236	Jimmy Key	.05
237	Jim Leyritz	.05
238	Kevin Maas	.05
239	Don Mattingly	1.00
240	Rich Monteleone	.05
241	Bobby Munoz	.05
242	Matt Nokes	.05
243	Paul O'Neill	.05
244	Spike Owen	.05
245	Melido Perez	.05
246	Lee Smith	.05
247	Mike Stanley	.05
248	Danny Tartabull	.05
249	Randy Velarde	.05
250	Bob Wickman	.05
251	Bernie Williams	.20
252	Mike Aldrete	.05
253	Marcos Armas	.05
254	Lance Blankenship	.05
255	Mike Bordick	.05
256	Scott Brosius	.05
257	Jerry Browne	.05
258	Ron Darling	.05
259	Kelly Downs	.05
260	Dennis Eckersley	.60
261	Brent Gates	.05
262	Goose Gossage	.05
263	Scott Hemond	.05
264	Dave Henderson	.05
265	Rick Honeycutt	.05
266	Vince Horsman	.05
267	Scott Lydy	.05
268	Mark McGwire	1.50
269	Mike Mohler	.05
270	Troy Neel	.05
271	Edwin Nunez	.05
272	Craig Paquette	.05
273	Ruben Sierra	.05
274	Terry Steinbach	.05
275	Todd Van Poppel	.05
276	Bob Welch	.05
277	Bobby Witt	.05
278	Rich Amaral	.05
279	Mike Blowers	.05
280	Bret Boone	.05
281	Chris Bosio	.05
282	Jay Buhner	.05
283	Norm Charlton	.05
284	Mike Felder	.05
285	Dave Fleming	.05
286	Ken Griffey Jr.	1.25
287	Erik Hanson	.05
288	Bill Haselman	.05
289	Brad Holman RC	.05
290	Randy Johnson	.75
291	Tim Leary	.05
292	Greg Litton	.05
293	Dave Magadan	.05
294	Edgar Martinez	.05
295	Tino Martinez	.05
296	Jeff Nelson	.05
297	Erik Plantenberg RC	.05
298	Mackey Sasser	.05
299	Brian Turang RC	.05
300	Dave Valle	.05
301	Omar Vizquel	.05
302	Brian Bohanon	.05
303	Kevin Brown	.05
304	Jose Canseco	.40
305	Mario Diaz	.05
306	Julio Franco	.05
307	Juan Gonzalez	.75
308	Tom Henke	.05
309	David Hulse	.05
310	Manuel Lee	.05
311	Craig Lefferts	.05
312	Charlie Leibrandt	.05
313	Rafael Palmeiro	.75
314	Dean Palmer	.05
315	Roger Pavlik	.05
316	Dan Peltier	.05
317	Geno Petralli	.05
318	Gary Redus	.05
319	Ivan Rodriguez	.65
320	Kenny Rogers	.05
321	Nolan Ryan	2.00
322	Doug Strange	.05
323	Matt Whiteside	.05
324	Roberto Alomar	.30
325	Pat Borders	.05
326	Joe Carter	.05
327	Tony Castillo	.05
328	Darnell Coles	.05
329	Danny Cox	.05
330	Mark Eichhorn	.05
331	Tony Fernandez	.05
332	Alfredo Griffin	.05
333	Juan Guzman	.05
334	Rickey Henderson	.75
335	Pat Hentgen	.05
336	Randy Knorr	.05
337	Al Leiter	.05
338	Paul Molitor	.75
339	Jack Morris	.05
340	John Olerud	.05
341	Dick Schofield	.05
342	Ed Sprague	.05
343	Dave Stewart	.05
344	Todd Stottlemyre	.05
345	Mike Timlin	.05
346	Duane Ward	.05
347	Turner Ward	.05
348	Devon White	.05
349	Woody Williams	.05
350	Steve Avery	.05
351	Steve Bedrosian	.05
352	Rafael Belliard	.05
353	Damon Berryhill	.05
354	Jeff Blauser	.05
355	Sid Bream	.05
356	Francisco Cabrera	.05
357	Marvin Freeman	.05
358	Ron Gant	.05
359	Tom Glavine	.25
360	Jay Howell	.05
361	Dave Justice	.05
362	Ryan Klesko	.05
363	Mark Lemke	.05
364	Javier Lopez	.05
365	Greg Maddux	.85
366	Fred McGriff	.05
367	Greg McMichael	.05
368	Kent Mercker	.05
369	Otis Nixon	.05
370	Greg Olson	.05
371	Bill Pecota	.05
372	Terry Pendleton	.05
373	Deion Sanders	.05
374	Pete Smith	.05
375	John Smoltz	.05
376	Mike Stanton	.05
377	Tony Tarasco	.05
378	Mark Wohlers	.05
379	Jose Bautista	.05
380	Shawn Boskie	.05
381	Steve Buechele	.05
382	Frank Castillo	.05
383	Mark Grace	.10
384	Jose Guzman	.05
385	Mike Harkey	.05
386	Greg Hibbard	.05
387	Glenallen Hill	.05
388	Steve Lake	.05
389	Derrick May	.05
390	Chuck McElroy	.05
391	Mike Morgan	.05
392	Randy Myers	.05
393	Dan Plesac	.05
394	Kevin Roberson	.05
395	Rey Sanchez	.05
396	Ryne Sandberg	.85
397	Bob Scanlan	.05
398	Dwight Smith	.05
399	Sammy Sosa	1.25
400	Jose Vizcaino	.05
401	Rick Wilkins	.05
402	Willie Wilson	.05
403	Eric Yelding	.05
404	Bobby Ayala	.05
405	Jeff Branson	.05
406	Tom Browning	.05
407	Jacob Brumfield	.05
408	Tim Costo	.05
409	Rob Dibble	.05
410	Willie Greene	.05
411	Thomas Howard	.05
412	Roberto Kelly	.05
413	Bill Landrum	.05
414	Barry Larkin	.05
415	Larry Luebbers RC	.05
416	Kevin Mitchell	.05
417	Hal Morris	.05
418	Joe Oliver	.05
419	Tim Pugh	.05
420	Jeff Reardon	.05
421	Jose Rijo	.05
422	Bip Roberts	.05
423	John Roper	.05
424	Johnny Ruffin	.05
425	Chris Sabo	.05
426	Juan Samuel	.05
427	Reggie Sanders	.05
428	Scott Service	.05
429	John Smiley	.05
430	Jerry Spradlin RC	.05
431	Kevin Wickander	.05
432	Freddie Benavides	.05
433	Dante Bichette	.05
434	Willie Blair	.05
435	Daryl Boston	.05
436	Kent Bottenfield	.05
437	Vinny Castilla	.05
438	Jerald Clark	.05
439	Alex Cole	.05
440	Andres Galarraga	.05
441	Joe Girardi	.05
442	Greg Harris	.05
443	Charlie Hayes	.05
444	Darren Holmes	.05
445	Chris Jones	.05
446	Roberto Mejia	.05
447	David Nied	.05
448	J. Owens	.05
449	Jeff Parrett	.05
450	Steve Reed	.05
451	Armando Reynoso	.05
452	Bruce Ruffin	.05
453	Mo Sanford	.05
454	Danny Sheaffer	.05
455	Jim Tatum	.05
456	Gary Wayne	.05
457	Eric Young	.05
458	Luis Aquino	.05
459	Alex Arias	.05
460	Jack Armstrong	.05
461	Bret Barberie	.05
462	Ryan Bowen	.05
463	Chuck Carr	.05
464	Jeff Conine	.05
465	Henry Cotto	.05
466	Orestes Destrade	.05
467	Chris Hammond	.05
468	Bryan Harvey	.05
469	Charlie Hough	.05
470	Joe Klink	.05
471	Richie Lewis	.05
472	Bob Natal RC	.05
473	Pat Rapp RC	.05
474	Rich Renteria RC	.10
475	Rich Rodriguez	.05
476	Benito Santiago	.05
477	Gary Sheffield	.35
478	Matt Turner	.05
479	David Weathers	.05
480	Walt Weiss	.05
481	Darrell Whitmore	.05
482	Eric Anthony	.05
483	Jeff Bagwell	.75
484	Kevin Bass	.05
485	Craig Biggio	.05
486	Ken Caminiti	.05
487	Andujar Cedeno	.05
488	Chris Donnels	.05
489	Doug Drabek	.05
490	Steve Finley	.05
491	Luis Gonzalez	.25
492	Pete Harnisch	.05
493	Xavier Hernandez	.05
494	Doug Jones	.05
495	Todd Jones	.05
496	Darryl Kile	.05
497	Al Osuna	.05
498	Mark Portugal	.05
499	Scott Servais	.05
500	Greg Swindell	.05
501	Eddie Taubensee	.05
502	Jose Uribe	.05
503	Brian Williams	.05
504	Billy Ashley	.05
505	Pedro Astacio	.05
506	Brett Butler	.05
507	Tom Candiotti	.05
508	Omar Daal	.05
509	Jim Gott	.05
510	Kevin Gross	.05
511	Dave Hansen	.05
512	Carlos Hernandez	.05
513	Orel Hershiser	.05
514	Eric Karros	.05
515	Pedro Martinez	.75
516	Ramon Martinez	.05
517	Roger McDowell	.05
518	Raul Mondesi	.05
519	Jose Offerman	.05
520	Mike Piazza	1.25
521	Jody Reed	.05
522	Henry Rodriguez	.05
523	Mike Sharperson	.05
524	Cory Snyder	.05
525	Darryl Strawberry	.05
526	Rick Trlicek	.05
527	Tim Wallach	.05
528	Mitch Webster	.05
529	Steve Wilson	.05
530	Todd Worrell	.05
531	Moises Alou	.05
532	Brian Barnes	.05
533	Sean Berry	.05
534	Greg Colbrunn	.05
535	Delino DeShields	.05
536	Jeff Fassero	.05
537	Darrin Fletcher	.05
538	Cliff Floyd	.05
539	Lou Frazier	.05
540	Marquis Grissom	.05
541	Butch Henry	.05
542	Ken Hill	.05
543	Mike Lansing	.05
544	Brian Looney RC	.05
545	Dennis Martinez	.05
546	Chris Nabholz	.05
547	Randy Ready	.05
548	Mel Rojas	.05
549	Kirk Rueter	.05
550	Tim Scott	.05
551	Jeff Shaw	.05
552	Tim Spehr	.05
553	John VanderWal	.05
554	Larry Walker	.05
555	John Wetteland	.05
556	Rondell White	.05
557	Tim Bogar	.05
558	Bobby Bonilla	.05
559	Jeromy Burnitz	.05
560	Sid Fernandez	.05
561	John Franco	.05
562	Dave Gallagher	.05
563	Dwight Gooden	.05
564	Eric Hillman	.05
565	Todd Hundley	.05
566	Jeff Innis	.05
567	Darrin Jackson	.05
568	Howard Johnson	.05
569	Bobby Jones	.05
570	Jeff Kent	.05
571	Mike Maddux	.05
572	Jeff McKnight	.05
573	Eddie Murray	.75
574	Charlie O'Brien	.05
575	Joe Orsulak	.05
576	Bret Saberhagen	.05
577	Pete Schourek	.05
578	Dave Telgheder	.05
579	Ryan Thompson	.05
580	Anthony Young	.05
581	Ruben Amaro	.05
582	Larry Andersen	.05
583	Kim Batiste	.05
584	Wes Chamberlain	.05
585	Darren Daulton	.05
586	Mariano Duncan	.05
587	Len Dykstra	.05
588	Jim Eisenreich	.05
589	Tommy Greene	.05
590	Dave Hollins	.10
591	Pete Incaviglia	.05
592	Danny Jackson	.05
593	Ricky Jordan	.05
594	John Kruk	.05
595	Roger Mason	.05
596	Mickey Morandini	.05
597	Terry Mulholland	.05
598	Todd Pratt	.05
599	Ben Rivera	.05
600	Curt Schilling	.25
601	Kevin Stocker	.05
602	Milt Thompson	.05
603	David West	.05
604	Mitch Williams	.05
605	Jay Bell	.05
606	Dave Clark	.05
607	Steve Cooke	.05
608	Tom Foley	.05
609	Carlos Garcia	.05
610	Joel Johnston	.05
611	Jeff King	.05
612	Al Martin	.05
613	Lloyd McClendon	.05
614	Orlando Merced	.05
615	Blas Minor	.05
616	Denny Neagle	.05
617	Mark Petkovsek RC	.05
618	Tom Prince	.05
619	Don Slaught	.05
620	Zane Smith	.05
621	Randy Tomlin	.05
622	Andy Van Slyke	.05
623	Paul Wagner	.05
624	Tim Wakefield	.05
625	Bob Walk	.05
626	Kevin Young	.05
627	Luis Alicea	.05
628	Rene Arocha	.05
629	Rod Brewer	.05
630	Rheal Cormier	.05
631	Bernard Gilkey	.05
632	Lee Guetterman	.05
633	Gregg Jefferies	.05
634	Brian Jordan	.05
635	Les Lancaster	.05
636	Ray Lankford	.05
637	Rob Murphy	.05
638	Omar Olivares	.05
639	Jose Oquendo	.05
640	Donovan Osborne	.05
641	Tom Pagnozzi	.05
642	Erik Pappas	.05
643	Geronimo Pena	.05
644	Mike Perez	.05
645	Gerald Perry	.05
646	Ozzie Smith	.85
647	Bob Tewksbury	.05
648	Allen Watson	.05
649	Mark Whiten	.05
650	Tracy Woodson	.05
651	Todd Zeile	.05
652	Andy Ashby	.05
653	Brad Ausmus	.05
654	Billy Bean	.05
655	Derek Bell	.05
656	Andy Benes	.05
657	Doug Brocail	.05
658	Jarvis Brown	.05
659	Archi Cianfrocco	.05
660	Phil Clark	.05
661	Mark Davis	.05
662	Jeff Gardner	.05
663	Pat Gomez	.05
664	Ricky Gutierrez	.05
665	Tony Gwynn	.85
666	Gene Harris	.05
667	Kevin Higgins	.05
668	Trevor Hoffman	.05
669	Pedro A. Martinez RC	.05
670	Tim Mauser	.05
671	Melvin Nieves	.05
672	Phil Plantier	.05
673	Frank Seminara	.05
674	Craig Shipley	.05
675	Kerry Taylor	.05
676	Tim Teufel	.05
677	Guillermo Velasquez	.05
678	Wally Whitehurst	.05
679	Tim Worrell	.05
680	Rod Beck	.05
681	Mike Benjamin	.05
682	Todd Benzinger	.05
683	Bud Black	.05
684	Barry Bonds	2.00
685	Jeff Brantley	.05
686	Dave Burba	.05
687	John Burkett	.05
688	Mark Carreon	.05
689	Will Clark	.10
690	Royce Clayton	.05
691	Bryan Hickerson	.05
692	Mike Jackson	.05
693	Darren Lewis	.05
694	Kirt Manwaring	.05
695	Dave Martinez	.05
696	Willie McGee	.05
697	John Patterson	.05
698	Jeff Reed	.05
699	Kevin Rogers	.05
700	Scott Sanderson	.05
701	Steve Scarsone	.05
702	Billy Swift	.05
703	Robby Thompson	.05
704	Matt Williams	.05
705	Trevor Wilson	.05
706	"Brave New World" (Fred McGriff, Ron Gant, Dave Justice)	.10
707	"1-2 Punch" (Paul Molitor, John Olerud)	.10
708	"American Heat" (Mike Mussina, Jack McDowell)	.10
709	"Together Again" (Lou Whitaker, Alan Trammell)	.10
710	"Lone Star Lumber" (Rafael Palmeiro, Juan Gonzalez)	.20
711	"Batmen" (Brett Butler, Tony Gwynn)	.10
712	"Twin Peaks" (Kirby Puckett, Chuck Knoblauch)	.20
713	"Back to Back" (Mike Piazza, Eric Karros)	.25
714	Checklist	.05
715	Checklist	.05
716	Checklist	.05
717	Checklist	.05
718	Checklist	.05
719	Checklist	.05
720	Checklist	.05

Award Winners

The 1993 MVP, Cy Young and Rookie of the Year award winners from each league are featured in this insert set. Cards are UV coated on both sides. Three different croppings of the same player action photo are featured on the front, with the player's name and other printing in gold foil. Backs have a player portrait and short summary of his previous season's performance. According to the company, odds of finding one of these horizontal-format inserts were one in 37 packs.

		NM/M
Complete Set (6):		4.50
Common Player:		.25
1	Frank Thomas	.75
2	Barry Bonds	2.00
3	Jack McDowell	.25
4	Greg Maddux	1.00
5	Tim Salmon	.50
6	Mike Piazza	1.50

All-Stars

Each league's 25 representatives for the 1993 All-Star Game are featured in this insert set. Fronts have a player action photo with a rippling American flag in the top half of the background. The '93 All-Star logo is featured at the bottom, along with a gold-foil impression of the player's name. The flag motif is repeated at top of the card back, along with a player portrait photo set against a red (American League) or blue (National League) background. Odds of finding one of the 50 All-Star inserts are one in every two 15-card foil packs.

		NM/M
Complete Set (50):		10.00
Common Player:		.10
1	Roberto Alomar	.20
2	Carlos Baerga	.10
3	Albert Belle	.10
4	Wade Boggs	.75
5	Joe Carter	.10
6	Scott Cooper	.10
7	Cecil Fielder	.10
8	Travis Fryman	.10
9	Juan Gonzalez	.60
10	Ken Griffey Jr.	1.50
11	Pat Hentgen	.10
12	Randy Johnson	.60
13	Jimmy Key	.10
14	Mark Langston	.10
15	Jack McDowell	.10
16	Paul Molitor	.60
17	Jeff Montgomery	.10
18	Mike Mussina	.40
19	John Olerud	.10
20	Kirby Puckett	.75
21	Cal Ripken, Jr.	2.00
22	Ivan Rodriguez	.50
23	Frank Thomas	.65
24	Greg Vaughn	.10
25	Duane Ward	.10
26	Steve Avery	.10
27	Rod Beck	.10
28	Jay Bell	.10
29	Andy Benes	.10
30	Jeff Blauser	.10
31	Barry Bonds	2.00
32	Bobby Bonilla	.10
33	John Burkett	.10
34	Darren Daulton	.10
35	Andres Galarraga	.10
36	Tom Glavine	.30
37	Mark Grace	.25
38	Marquis Grissom	.10
39	Tony Gwynn	.75
40	Bryan Harvey	.10
41	Dave Hollins	.10
42	Dave Justice	.10
43	Darryl Kile	.10
44	John Kruk	.10
45	Barry Larkin	.05
46	Terry Mulholland	.05
47	Mike Piazza	1.50
48	Ryne Sandberg	.75
49	Gary Sheffield	.30
50	John Smoltz	.10

Golden Moments

FRANK THOMAS ENTERS 5th DIMENSION

Ten highlights from the 1993 Major League baseball season are commemorated in this insert set. Each of the cards has a title which summarizes the historical moment. These inserts are available exclusively in Fleer cards packaged for large retail outlets.

		NM/M
Complete Set (10):		5.00
Common Player:		.10
1	"Four in One" (Mark Whiten)	.10
2	"Left and Right" (Carlos Baerga)	.10
3	"3,000 Hit Club" (Dave Winfield)	.50
4	"Eight Straight" (Ken Griffey Jr.)	1.50
5	"Triumphant Return" (Bo Jackson)	.25
6	"Farewell to Baseball" (George Brett)	1.00
7	"Farewell to Baseball" (Nolan Ryan)	2.00
8	"Thirty Times Six" (Fred McGriff)	.10
9	"Enters 5th Dimension" (Frank Thomas)	.75
10	"The No-Hit Parade" (Chris Bosio, Jim Abbott, Darryl Kile)	.10

Golden Moments Super

Super-size (3-1/2" x 5") versions of the Golden Moments insert set were included in hobby cases at the rate of one set, in a specially-printed folder, per 20-box case. Each card carries a serial number designating its position in an edition of 10,000.

	NM/M
Complete Set (10):	7.50
Common Player:	

		NM/M
1	"Four in One" (Mark Whiten)	.50
2	"Left and Right" (Carlos Baerga)	.50
3	"3,000 Hit Club" (Dave Winfield)	.75
4	"Eight Straight" (Ken Griffey Jr.)	2.00
5	"Triumphant Return" (Bo Jackson)	.75
6	"Farewell to Baseball" (George Brett)	1.50
7	"Farewell to Baseball" (Nolan Ryan)	2.50
8	"Thirty Times Six" (Fred McGriff)	.50
9	"Enters 5th Dimension" (Frank Thomas)	1.00
10	"The No-Hit Parade" (Chris Bosio, Jim Abbott, Darryl Kile)	.50

League Leaders

Twelve players who led the major leagues in various statistical categories in 1993 are featured in this insert set. Cards are UV coated and have gold-foil stamping on both sides. Within a light metallic green border, card fronts feature a color action photo superimposed over a similar photo in black-and-white. The category in which the player led his league is printed down the right border. Other printing is gold-foil. On back is a color photo and details of the league-leading performance. Stated odds of finding a League Leaders card were one per 17 packs.

		NM/M
Complete Set (12):		3.00
Common Player:		.10
1	John Olerud	.10
2	Albert Belle	.10
3	Rafael Palmeiro	.75
4	Kenny Lofton	.10
5	Jack McDowell	.10
6	Kevin Appier	.10
7	Andres Galarraga	.10
8	Barry Bonds	2.00
9	Len Dykstra	.10
10	Chuck Carr	.10
11	Tom Glavine	.30
12	Greg Maddux	1.00

Lumber Co.

This insert set features the major leagues' top home run hitters. Inserted only in 21-card jumbo packs, odds of finding one were given as one per five packs. Card fronts feature player action photos against a background resembling the label area of a baseball bat. On back is a background photo of a row of bats on the dirt. A player write-up and close-up photo complete the design.

	NM/M
Complete Set (10):	7.50
Common Player:	.40

		NM/M
1	Albert Belle	.40
2	Barry Bonds	2.50
3	Ron Gant	.40
4	Juan Gonzalez	1.00
5	Ken Griffey Jr.	2.00
6	Dave Justice	.40
7	Fred McGriff	.40
8	Rafael Palmeiro	.75
9	Frank Thomas	1.25
10	Matt Williams	.40

Major League Prospects

Thirty-five of the game's promising young stars are featured in this insert set. A light green metallic border frames a player photo, with his team logo lightly printed over the background. Most of the printing is gold-foil stamped. Backs have a player photo against a pinstriped background. A light blue box contains career details. Given odds of finding a "Major League Prospects" card are one in six packs.

		NM/M
Complete Set (35):		4.00
Common Player:		.10
1	Kurt Abbott	.10
2	Brian Anderson	.10
3	Rich Aude	.10
4	Cory Bailey	.10
5	Danny Bautista	.10
6	Marty Cordova	.10
7	Tripp Cromer	.10
8	Midre Cummings	.10
9	Carlos Delgado	1.50
10	Steve Dreyer	.10
11	Steve Dunn	.10
12	Jeff Granger	.10
13	Tyrone Hill	.10
14	Denny Hocking	.10
15	John Hope	.10
16	Butch Huskey	.10
17	Miguel Jimenez	.10
18	Chipper Jones	2.50
19	Steve Karsay	.10
20	Mike Kelly	.10
21	Mike Lieberthal	.20
22	Albie Lopez	.10
23	Jeff McNeely	.10
24	Dan Miceli	.10
25	Nate Minchey	.10
26	Marc Newfield	.10
27	Darren Oliver	.10
28	Luis Ortiz	.10
29	Curtis Pride	.10
30	Roger Salkeld	.10
31	Scott Sanders	.10
32	Dave Staton	.10
33	Salomon Torres	.10
34	Steve Trachsel	.10
35	Chris Turner	.10

ProVisions

Nine players are featured in this insert set. Cards feature the fantasy artwork of Wayne Still in a format that produces one large image when all nine cards are properly arranged. Besides the art, card fronts feature the player's name in gold-foil. Backs have a background in several shades of red, with the player's name and team at the top in white. A short ca-

reer summary is printed in black. Odds of finding this particular insert in a pack are one in 12.

		NM/M
Complete Set (9):		4.00
Common Player:		.25
1	Darren Daulton	.25
2	John Olerud	.25
3	Matt Williams	.25
4	Carlos Baerga	.25
5	Ozzie Smith	1.00
6	Juan Gonzalez	.75
7	Jack McDowell	.25
8	Mike Piazza	2.00
9	Tony Gwynn	1.00

Rookie Sensations

This insert set features the top rookies from 1993. These inserts were available only in 21-card jumbo packs, with stated odds of one in four packs. Full-bleed fronts have a pair of player photos - one highlighted by a neon outline - superimposed on a graduated background approximating the team colors. Team uniform logo details appear vertically at the right or left side. The player's name is gold-foil stamped in a banner at bottom. The Rookie Sensations and Fleer logos are also gold-imprinted. On back, the team uniform logo is repeated on a white background, along with another player photo and a short write-up.

		NM/M
Complete Set (20):		6.00
Common Player:		.25
1	Rene Arocha	.25
2	Jason Bere	.25
3	Jeromy Burnitz	.25
4	Chuck Carr	.25
5	Jeff Conine	.25
6	Steve Cooke	.25
7	Cliff Floyd	.25
8	Jeffrey Hammonds	.25
9	Wayne Kirby	.25
10	Mike Lansing	.25
11	Al Martin	.25
12	Greg McMichael	.25
13	Troy Neel	.25
14	Mike Piazza	4.00
15	Armando Reynoso	.25
16	Kirk Rueter	.25
17	Tim Salmon	1.00
18	Aaron Sele	.25
19	J.T. Snow	.25
20	Kevin Stocker	.25

Tim Salmon A.L. Rookie of the Year

The popular Angels Rookie of the Year is featured in a 15-card set produced in what Fleer terms "metallized" format. The first 12 cards in the set were inserted into foil packs at the rate of about one card per box. Three additional cards could be obtained by sending $1.50 and 10 '94 Fleer wrappers to a mail-in offer. On

both front and back, the cards have a color player photo set against a metallic-image background.

		NM/M
Complete Set (15):		12.50
Common Card:		1.00
Autograph/2,000:		15.00
1-12	Tim Salmon	1.00
13-15	Tim Salmon	1.50

Smoke N' Heat

Among the scarcest of the '94 Fleer inserts, available at a stated rate of one per 30 packs, these feature 10 of the top strikeout pitchers in the major leagues. "Metallized" card fronts have a player photo set against an infernal background with large letters, "Smoke 'N Heat." The player's name is in gold foil at bottom. Backs have a similar chaotic hot-red background, a player photo and career summary.

		NM/M
Complete Set (12):		10.00
Common Player:		.20
1	Roger Clemens	4.00
2	David Cone	.25
3	Juan Guzman	.25
4	Pete Harnisch	.25
5	Randy Johnson	2.00
6	Mark Langston	.25
7	Greg Maddux	3.00
8	Mike Mussina	1.00
9	Jose Rijo	.25
10	Nolan Ryan	5.00
11	Curt Schilling	1.00
12	John Smoltz	.75

Team Leaders

A player from each major league team has been chosen for this 28-card insert set. Fronts feature a team logo against a background of graduated team colors. Player portrait and action photos are superimposed. At bottom is the player name, team and position, all in gold foil. Backs have a team logo and player photo set against a white background, with a short write-up justifying the player's selection as

a "Team Leader." Odds of finding one of these inserts were given as one in eight packs.

		NM/M
Complete Set (28):		7.50
Common Player:		.10
1	Cal Ripken, Jr.	2.00
2	Mo Vaughn	.10
3	Tim Salmon	.15
4	Frank Thomas	.50
5	Carlos Baerga	.10
6	Cecil Fielder	.10
7	Brian McRae	.10
8	Greg Vaughn	.10
9	Kirby Puckett	.65
10	Don Mattingly	.75
11	Mark McGwire	1.50
12	Ken Griffey Jr.	1.00
13	Juan Gonzalez	.50
14	Paul Molitor	.50
15	Dave Justice	.10
16	Ryne Sandberg	.65
17	Barry Larkin	.10
18	Andres Galarraga	.10
19	Gary Sheffield	.25
20	Jeff Bagwell	.50
21	Mike Piazza	1.00
22	Marquis Grissom	.10
23	Bobby Bonilla	.10
24	Len Dykstra	.10
25	Jay Bell	.10
26	Gregg Jefferies	.10
27	Tony Gwynn	.65
28	Will Clark	.15

All-Rookie Team

Sharing the format of the basic 1994 Fleer issue, this nine-card set of rookies was available only by redemption of a trade card randomly inserted into foil packs. The exchange card expired Sept. 30, 1994. The cards are numbered with an "M" prefix.

		NM/M
Complete Set (9):		3.00
Common Player:		.25
Exchange Card:		.25
1	Kurt Abbott	.25
2	Rich Becker	.25
3	Carlos Delgado	2.00
4	Jorge Fabregas	.25
5	Bob Hamelin	.25
6	John Hudek	.25
7	Tim Hyers	.25
8	Luis Lopez	.25
9	James Mouton	.25

Update

Rookies, traded players and free agents who changed teams were included in the annual update issue. In the same format as the regular-issue '94 Fleer set, cards are numbered alphabetically within team. Ten special Diamond Tribute cards included in the Update set feature baseball's proven superstars.

		NM/M
Complete Set (210):		50.00
Common Player:		.05
1	Mark Eichhorn	.05
2	Sid Fernandez	.05
3	Leo Gomez	.05
4	Mike Oquist	.05
5	Rafael Palmeiro	.60
6	Chris Sabo	.05
7	Dwight Smith	.05
8	Lee Smith	.05
9	Damon Berryhill	.05
10	Wes Chamberlain	.05
11	Gar Finnvold	.05
12	Chris Howard	.05
13	Tim Naehring	.05
14	Otis Nixon	.05
15	Brian Anderson	.05
16	Jorge Fabregas	.05
17	Rex Hudler	.05
18	Bo Jackson	.15
19	Mark Leiter	.05
20	Spike Owen	.05
21	Harold Reynolds	.05
22	Chris Turner	.05
23	Dennis Cook	.05
24	Jose DeLeon	.05
25	Julio Franco	.05
26	Joe Hall	.05
27	Darrin Jackson	.05
28	Dane Johnson	.05
29	Norberto Martin	.05
30	Scott Sanderson	.05
31	Jason Grimsley	.05
32	Dennis Martinez	.05
33	Jack Morris	.05
34	Eddie Murray	.75
35	Chad Ogea	.05
36	Tony Pena	.05
37	Paul Shuey	.05
38	Omar Vizquel	.05
39	Danny Bautista	.05
40	Tim Belcher	.05
41	Joe Boever	.05
42	Storm Davis	.05
43	Junior Felix	.05
44	Mike Gardiner	.05
45	Buddy Groom	.05
46	Juan Samuel	.05
47	Vince Coleman	.05
48	Bob Hamelin	.05
49	Dave Henderson	.05
50	Rusty Meacham	.05
51	Terry Shumpert	.05
52	Jeff Bronkey	.05
53	Alex Diaz	.05
54	Brian Harper	.05
55	Jose Mercedes	.05
56	Jody Reed	.05
57	Bob Scanlan	.05
58	Turner Ward	.05
59	Rich Becker	.05
60	Alex Cole	.05
61	Denny Hocking	.05
62	Scott Leius	.05
63	Pat Mahomes	.05
64	Carlos Pulido	.05
65	Dave Stevens	.05
66	Matt Walbeck	.05
67	Xavier Hernandez	.05
68	Sterling Hitchcock	.05
69	Terry Mulholland	.05
70	Luis Polonia	.05
71	Gerald Williams	.05
72	Mark Acre	.05
73	Geronimo Berroa	.05
74	Rickey Henderson	.75
75	Stan Javier	.05
76	Steve Karsay	.05
77	Carlos Reyes	.05
78	Bill Taylor	.05
79	Eric Anthony	.05
80	Bobby Ayala	.05
81	Tim Davis	.05
82	Felix Fermin	.05
83	Reggie Jefferson	.05
84	Keith Mitchell	.05
85	Bill Risley	.05
86	Alex Rodriguez RC	40.00
87	Roger Salkeld	.05
88	Dan Wilson	.05
89	Cris Carpenter	.05
90	Will Clark	.10
91	Jeff Frye	.05
92	Rick Helling	.05
93	Chris James	.05
94	Oddibe McDowell	.05
95	Billy Ripken	.05
96	Carlos Delgado	.60
97	Alex Gonzalez	.05
98	Shawn Green	.50
99	Darren Hall	.05
100	Mike Huff	.05
101	Mike Kelly	.05
102	Roberto Kelly	.05
103	Charlie O'Brien	.05
104	Jose Oliva	.05
105	Gregg Olson	.05
106	Willie Banks	.05
107	Jim Bullinger	.05
108	Chuck Crim	.05
109	Shawon Dunston	.05
110	Karl Rhodes	.05
111	Steve Trachsel	.05
112	Anthony Young	.05
113	Eddie Zambrano	.05
114	Bret Boone	.05
115	Jeff Brantley	.05
116	Hector Carrasco	.05
117	Tony Fernandez	.05
118	Tim Fortugno	.05
119	Erik Hanson	.05
120	Chuck McElroy	.05
121	Deion Sanders	.05

#	Player	Price
122	Ellis Burks	.05
123	Marvin Freeman	.05
124	Mike Harkey	.05
125	Howard Johnson	.05
126	Mike Kingery	.05
127	Nelson Liriano	.05
128	Marcus Moore	.05
129	Mike Munoz	.05
130	Kevin Ritz	.05
131	Walt Weiss	.05
132	Kurt Abbott	.05
133	Jerry Browne	.05
134	Greg Colbrunn	.05
135	Jeremy Hernandez	.05
136	Dave Magadan	.05
137	Kurt Miller	.05
138	Robb Nen	.05
139	Jesus Tavarez	.05
140	Sid Bream	.05
141	Tom Edens	.05
142	Tony Eusebio	.05
143	John Hudek	.05
144	Brian Hunter	.05
145	Orlando Miller	.05
146	James Mouton	.05
147	Shane Reynolds	.05
148	Rafael Bournigal	.05
149	Delino DeShields	.05
150	Garey Ingram	.05
151	Chan Ho Park	.05
152	Wil Cordero	.05
153	Pedro Martinez	.75
154	Randy Milligan	.05
155	Lenny Webster	.05
156	Rico Brogna	.05
157	Josias Manzanillo	.05
158	Kevin McReynolds	.05
159	Mike Remlinger	.05
160	David Segui	.05
161	Pete Smith	.05
162	Kelly Stinnett	.05
163	Jose Vizcaino	.05
164	Billy Hatcher	.05
165	Doug Jones	.05
166	Mike Lieberthal	.05
167	Tony Longmire	.05
168	Bobby Munoz	.05
169	Paul Quantrill	.05
170	Heathcliff Slocumb	.05
171	Fernando Valenzuela	.05
172	Mark Dewey	.05
173	Brian Hunter	.05
174	Jon Lieber	.05
175	Ravelo Manzanillo	.05
176	Dan Miceli	.05
177	Rick White	.05
178	Bryan Eversgerd	.05
179	John Habyan	.05
180	Terry McGriff	.05
181	Vicente Palacios	.05
182	Rich Rodriguez	.05
183	Rick Sutcliffe	.05
184	Donnie Elliott	.05
185	Joey Hamilton	.05
186	Tim Hyers	.05
187	Luis Lopez	.05
188	Ray McDavid	.05
189	Bip Roberts	.05
190	Scott Sanders	.05
191	Eddie Williams	.05
192	Steve Frey	.05
193	Pat Gomez	.05
194	Rich Monteleone	.05
195	Mark Portugal	.05
196	Darryl Strawberry	.05
197	Salomon Torres	.05
198	W. Van Landingham	.05
199	Checklist	.05
200	Checklist	.05

DIAMOND TRIBUTE

#	Player	Price
DT1	Barry Bonds	2.00
DT2	Joe Carter	.05
DT3	Will Clark	.10
DT4	Roger Clemens	1.50
DT5	Tony Gwynn	1.00
DT6	Don Mattingly	1.50
DT7	Fred McGriff	.05
DT8	Eddie Murray	.75
DT9	Kirby Puckett	1.00
DT10	Cal Ripken Jr.	2.00

Atlantic

Five-card packs of this special Fleer set were given away with an eight-gallon premium gasoline purchase at Atlantic/Sunoco stations in the Eastern U.S. between June 1 and July 31. Many of the cards suffered damaged borders from the packaging process. Cards are in the basic 1994 Fleer format, though the name and position around the team logo at top are in white on these cards, rather than gold-foil. Different front and back photos are used in this set. Backs include the gas station logos at bottom.

		NM/M
Complete Set (25):		3.00
Common Player:		.10
1	Roberto Alomar	.20
2	Carlos Baerga	.10
3	Jeff Bagwell	.40
4	Jay Bell	.05
5	Barry Bonds	1.00
6	Joe Carter	.10
7	Roger Clemens	.60
8	Darren Daulton	.10
9	Lenny Dykstra	.10
10	Cecil Fielder	.10
11	Tom Glavine	.35
12	Juan Gonzalez	.40
13	Ken Griffey Jr.	.75
14	Dave Justice	.10
15	John Kruk	.10
16	Greg Maddux	.50
17	Don Mattingly	.60
18	Jack McDowell	.10
19	John Olerud	.10
20	Mike Piazza	.75
21	Kirby Puckett	.50
22	Tim Salmon	.25
23	Frank Thomas	.40
24	Andy Van Slyke	.10
25	Checklist	.05

Extra Bases

Extra Bases was a 400-card, oversized set, plus 80 insert cards in four different subsets. The cards, 4-11/16" by 2-1/2", have a full-bleed photo on the front and back, as well as UV coating and color coding by team. As was the case in other Fleer products, Extra Bases contained an insert card in every pack. All 80 insert cards feature gold or silver foil stamping.

		NM/M
Complete Set (400):		15.00
Common Player:		.10
Wax Pack:		.45
Wax Box (36):		10.00
1	Brady Anderson	.10
2	Harold Baines	.10
3	Mike Devereaux	.10
4	Sid Fernandez	.10
5	Jeffrey Hammonds	.10
6	Chris Hoiles	.10
7	Ben McDonald	.10
8	Mark McLemore	.10
9	Mike Mussina	.40
10	Mike Oquist	.10
11	Rafael Palmeiro	.75
12	Cal Ripken, Jr.	2.50
13	Chris Sabo	.10
14	Lee Smith	.10
15	Wes Chamberlain	.10
16	Roger Clemens	1.25
17	Scott Cooper	.10
18	Danny Darwin	.10
19	Andre Dawson	.25
20	Mike Greenwell	.10
21	Tim Naehring	.10
22	Otis Nixon	.10
23	Jeff Russell	.10
24	Ken Ryan	.10
25	Aaron Sele	.10
26	John Valentin	.10
27	Mo Vaughn	.10
28	Frank Viola	.10
29	Brian Anderson RC	.15
30	Chad Curtis	.10
31	Chili Davis	.10
32	Gary DiSarcina	.10
33	Damion Easley	.10
34	Jim Edmonds	.10
35	Chuck Finley	.10
36	Bo Jackson	.15
37	Mark Langston	.10
38	Harold Reynolds	.10
39	Tim Salmon	.20
40	Wilson Alvarez	.10
41	James Baldwin	.10
42	Jason Bere	.10
43	Joey Cora	.10
44	Ray Durham RC	.50
45	Alex Fernandez	.10
46	Julio Franco	.10
47	Ozzie Guillen	.10
48	Darrin Jackson	.10
49	Lance Johnson	.10
50	Ron Karkovice	.10
51	Jack McDowell	.10
52	Tim Raines	.10
53	Frank Thomas	.75
54	Robin Ventura	.10
55	Sandy Alomar Jr.	.10
56	Carlos Baerga	.10
57	Albert Belle	.10
58	Mark Clark	.10
59	Wayne Kirby	.10
60	Kenny Lofton	.10
61	Dennis Martinez	.10
62	Jose Mesa	.10
63	Jack Morris	.10
64	Eddie Murray	.75
65	Charles Nagy	.10
66	Manny Ramirez	.75
67	Paul Shuey	.10
68	Paul Sorrento	.10
69	Jim Thome	.50
70	Omar Vizquel	.10
71	Eric Davis	.10
72	John Doherty	.10
73	Cecil Fielder	.10
74	Travis Fryman	.10
75	Kirk Gibson	.10
76	Gene Harris	.10
77	Mike Henneman	.10
78	Mike Moore	.10
79	Tony Phillips	.10
80	Mickey Tettleton	.10
81	Alan Trammell	.10
82	Lou Whitaker	.10
83	Kevin Appier	.10
84	Vince Coleman	.10
85	David Cone	.10
86	Gary Gaetti	.10
87	Greg Gagne	.10
88	Tom Gordon	.10
89	Jeff Granger	.10
90	Bob Hamelin	.10
91	Dave Henderson	.10
92	Felix Jose	.10
93	Wally Joyner	.10
94	Jose Lind	.10
95	Mike Macfarlane	.10
96	Brian McRae	.10
97	Jeff Montgomery	.10
98	Ricky Bones	.10
99	Jeff Bronkey	.10
100	Alex Diaz	.10
101	Cal Eldred	.10
102	Darryl Hamilton	.10
103	Brian Harper	.10
104	John Jaha	.10
105	Pat Listach	.10
106	Dave Nilsson	.10
107	Jody Reed	.10
108	Kevin Seitzer	.10
109	Greg Vaughn	.10
110	Turner Ward	.10
111	Wes Weger	.10
112	Bill Wegman	.10
113	Rick Aguilera	.10
114	Rich Becker	.10
115	Alex Cole	.10
116	Scott Erickson	.10
117	Kent Hrbek	.10
118	Chuck Knoblauch	.10
119	Scott Leius	.10
120	Shane Mack	.10
121	Pat Mahomes	.10
122	Pat Meares	.10
123	Kirby Puckett	1.00
124	Kevin Tapani	.10
125	Matt Walbeck	.10
126	Dave Winfield	.75
127	Jim Abbott	.10
128	Wade Boggs	1.00
129	Mike Gallego	.10
130	Xavier Hernandez	.10
131	Pat Kelly	.10
132	Jimmy Key	.10
133	Don Mattingly	1.25
134	Terry Mulholland	.10
135	Matt Nokes	.10
136	Paul O'Neill	.10
137	Melido Perez	.10
138	Luis Polonia	.10
139	Mike Stanley	.10
140	Danny Tartabull	.10
141	Randy Velarde	.10
142	Bernie Williams	.20
143	Mark Acre	.10
144	Geronimo Berroa	.10
145	Mike Bordick	.10
146	Scott Brosius	.10
147	Ron Darling	.10
148	Dennis Eckersley	.65
149	Brent Gates	.10
150	Rickey Henderson	.75
151	Stan Javier	.10
152	Steve Karsay	.10
153	Mark McGwire	2.00
154	Troy Neel	.10
155	Ruben Sierra	.10
156	Terry Steinbach	.10
157	Bill Taylor	.10
158	Rich Amaral	.10
159	Eric Anthony	.10
160	Bobby Ayala	.10
161	Chris Bosio	.10
162	Jay Buhner	.10
163	Tim Davis	.10
164	Felix Fermin	.10
165	Dave Fleming	.10
166	Ken Griffey Jr.	1.50
167	Reggie Jefferson	.10
168	Randy Johnson	.75
169	Edgar Martinez	.10
170	Tino Martinez	.10
171	Bill Risley	.10
172	Roger Salkeld	.10
173	Mac Suzuki RC	.20
174	Dan Wilson	.10
175	Kevin Brown	.10
176	Jose Canseco	.40
177	Will Clark	.15
178	Juan Gonzalez	.75
179	Rick Helling	.10
180	Tom Henke	.10
181	Chris James	.10
182	Manuel Lee	.10
183	Dean Palmer	.10
184	Ivan Rodriguez	.65
185	Kenny Rogers	.10
186	Roberto Alomar	.20
187	Pat Borders	.10
188	Joe Carter	.10
189	Carlos Delgado	.50
190	Juan Guzman	.10
191	Pat Hentgen	.10
192	Paul Molitor	.75
192a	Paul Molitor (Promotional sample.)	2.00
193	John Olerud	.10
194	Ed Sprague	.10
195	Dave Stewart	.10
196	Todd Stottlemyre	.10
197	Duane Ward	.10
198	Devon White	.10
199	Steve Avery	.10
200	Jeff Blauser	.10
201	Tom Glavine	.30
202	Dave Justice	.10
203	Mike Kelly	.10
204	Roberto Kelly	.10
205	Ryan Klesko	.10
206	Mark Lemke	.10
207	Javier Lopez	.10
208	Greg Maddux	1.00
209	Fred McGriff	.10
210	Greg McMichael	.10
211	Kent Mercker	.10
212	Terry Pendleton	.10
213	John Smoltz	.10
214	Tony Tarasco	.10
215	Willie Banks	.10
216	Steve Buechele	.10
217	Shawon Dunston	.10
218	Mark Grace	.15
219	Brooks Kieschnick RC	.10
220	Derrick May	.10
221	Randy Myers	.10
222	Karl Rhodes	.10
223	Rey Sanchez	.10
224	Sammy Sosa	1.50
225	Steve Traschel	.10
226	Rick Wilkins	.10
227	Bret Boone	.15
228	Jeff Brantley	.10
229	Tom Browning	.10
230	Hector Carrasco	.10
231	Rob Dibble	.10
232	Erik Hanson	.10
233	Barry Larkin	.10
234	Kevin Mitchell	.10
235	Hal Morris	.10
236	Joe Oliver	.10
237	Jose Rijo	.10
238	Johnny Ruffin	.10
239	Deion Sanders	.15
240	Reggie Sanders	.10
241	John Smiley	.10
242	Dante Bichette	.10
243	Ellis Burks	.10
244	Andres Galarraga	.10
245	Joe Girardi	.10
246	Greg Harris	.10
247	Charlie Hayes	.10
248	Howard Johnson	.10
249	Roberto Mejia	.10
250	Marcus Moore	.10
251	David Nied	.10
252	Armando Reynoso	.10
253	Bruce Ruffin	.10
254	Mark Thompson	.10
255	Walt Weiss	.10
256	Kurt Abbott RC	.20
257	Bret Barberie	.10
258	Chuck Carr	.10
259	Jeff Conine	.10
260	Chris Hammond	.10
261	Bryan Harvey	.10
262	Jeremy Hernandez	.10
263	Charlie Hough	.10
264	Dave Magadan	.10
265	Benito Santiago	.10
266	Gary Sheffield	.25
267	David Weathers	.10
268	Jeff Bagwell	.75
269	Craig Biggio	.10
270	Ken Caminiti	.10
271	Andujar Cedeno	.10
272	Doug Drabek	.10
273	Steve Finley	.10
274	Luis Gonzalez	.20
275	Pete Harnisch	.10
276	John Hudek	.10
277	Darryl Kile	.10
278	Orlando Miller	.10
279	James Mouton	.10
280	Shane Reynolds	.10
281	Scott Servais	.10
282	Greg Swindell	.10
283	Pedro Astacio	.10
284	Brett Butler	.10
285	Tom Candiotti	.10
286	Delino DeShields	.10
287	Kevin Gross	.10
288	Orel Hershiser	.10
289	Eric Karros	.10
290	Ramon Martinez	.10
291	Raul Mondesi	.10
292	Jose Offerman	.10
293	Chan Ho Park RC	.75
294	Mike Piazza	1.50
295	Henry Rodriguez	.10
296	Cory Snyder	.10
297	Tim Wallach	.10
298	Todd Worrell	.10
299	Moises Alou	.10
300	Sean Berry	.10
301	Wil Cordero	.10
302	Joey Eischen	.10
303	Jeff Fassero	.10
304	Darrin Fletcher	.10
305	Cliff Floyd	.10
306	Marquis Grissom	.10
307	Ken Hill	.10
308	Mike Lansing	.10
309	Pedro Martinez	.75
310	Mel Rojas	.10
311	Kirk Rueter	.10
312	Larry Walker	.10
313	John Wetteland	.10
314	Rondell White	.10
315	Bobby Bonilla	.10
316	John Franco	.10
317	Dwight Gooden	.10
318	Todd Hundley	.10
319	Bobby Jones	.10
320	Jeff Kent	.10
321	Kevin McReynolds	.10
322	Bill Pulsipher	.10
323	Bret Saberhagen	.10
324	David Segui	.10
325	Pete Smith	.10
326	Kelly Stinnett	.10
327	Ryan Thompson	.10
328	Jose Vizcaino	.10
329	Ricky Bottalico	.10
330	Darren Daulton	.10
331	Mariano Duncan	.10
332	Len Dykstra	.10
333	Tommy Greene	.10
334	Billy Hatcher	.10
335	Dave Hollins	.10
336	Pete Incaviglia	.10
337	Danny Jackson	.10
338	Doug Jones	.10
339	Ricky Jordan	.10
340	John Kruk	.10
341	Curt Schilling	.30
342	Kevin Stocker	.10
343	Jay Bell	.10
344	Steve Cooke	.10
345	Carlos Garcia	.10
346	Brian Hunter	.10
347	Jeff King	.10
348	Al Martin	.10
349	Orlando Merced	.10
350	Denny Neagle	.10
351	Don Slaught	.10
352	Andy Van Slyke	.10
353	Paul Wagner	.10
354	Rick White	.10
355	Luis Alicea	.10
356	Rene Arocha	.10
357	Rheal Cormier	.10
358	Bernard Gilkey	.10
359	Gregg Jefferies	.10
360	Ray Lankford	.10
361	Tom Pagnozzi	.10
362	Mike Perez	.10
363	Ozzie Smith	1.00
364	Bob Tewksbury	.10
365	Mark Whiten	.10
366	Todd Zeile	.10
367	Andy Ashby	.10
368	Brad Ausmus	.10
369	Derek Bell	.10
370	Andy Benes	.10
371	Archi Cianfrocco	.10
372	Tony Gwynn	1.00
373	Trevor Hoffman	.10
374	Tim Hyers	.10
375	Pedro Martinez	.10
376	Phil Plantier	.10
377	Bip Roberts	.10
378	Scott Sanders	.10
379	Dave Staton	.10
380	Wally Whitehurst	.10
381	Rod Beck	.10
382	Todd Benzinger	.10
383	Barry Bonds	2.50
384	John Burkett	.10
385	Royce Clayton	.10
386	Bryan Hickerson	.10
387	Mike Jackson	.10
388	Darren Lewis	.10
389	Kirt Manwaring	.10
390	Willie McGee	.10
391	Mark Portugal	.10
392	Bill Swift	.10
393	Robby Thompson	.10
394	Salomon Torres	.10
395	Matt Williams	.10
396	Checklist	.10
397	Checklist	.10
398	Checklist	.10
399	Checklist	.10
400	Checklist	.10

Game Breakers

Game Breakers featured 30 big-name stars from both leagues who have exhibited offensive fire-power. This insert set was done in a horizontal format picturing the player in two different shots, one close-up and one slightly further away. The words "Game Breakers" is written across the bottom, with the player name and team in much smaller letters, printed under it.

		NM/M
Complete Set (30):		15.00
Common Player:		.25
1	Jeff Bagwell	.75
2	Rod Beck	.25
3	Albert Belle	.25
4	Barry Bonds	3.00
5	Jose Canseco	.65
6	Joe Carter	.25
7	Roger Clemens	1.50
8	Darren Daulton	.25
9	Len Dykstra	.25
10	Cecil Fielder	.25
11	Tom Glavine	.50
12	Juan Gonzalez	.75
13	Mark Grace	.35
14	Ken Griffey Jr.	2.00
15	Dave Justice	.25
16	Greg Maddux	1.25
17	Don Mattingly	1.50
18	Ben McDonald	.25
19	Fred McGriff	.25
20	Paul Molitor	.75
21	John Olerud	.25
22	Mike Piazza	2.00
23	Kirby Puckett	1.25
24	Cal Ripken, Jr.	3.00
25	Tim Salmon	.35
26	Gary Sheffield	.50
27	Frank Thomas	1.00
28	Mo Vaughn	.25
29	Matt Williams	.25
30	Dave Winfield	.75

Major League Hopefuls

Minor league standouts with impressive credentials were showcased in Major League Hopefuls. Each card in this insert set shows the player over a computer enhanced background, with three smaller photos running down the top half, on the left side of the card. The insert set title runs across the bottom and the player's name is just under it on a black strip.

		NM/M
Complete Set (10):		2.00
Common Player:		.25

1	James Baldwin	.25
2	Ricky Bottalico	.25
3	Ray Durham	.25
4	Joey Eischen	.25
5	Brooks Kieschnick	.25
6	Orlando Miller	.25
7	Bill Pulsipher	.25
8	Mac Suzuki	.25
9	Mark Thompson	.25
10	Wes Weger	.25

Rookie Standouts

Rookie Standouts highlights 20 of the best and brightest first-year players of the 1994 season. Cards picture the player on a baseball background, with a black, jagged-edged "aura" around the player. Names and teams were placed in the bottom-left corner, running up the side. The Rookie Standouts logo, which is a gold glove with a baseball in it and "Rookie Standouts" printed under it, was placed in the bottom-right corner and the Extra Bases logo appears in the upper-left.

		NM/M
Complete Set (20):		7.50
Common Player:		.25
1	Kurt Abbott	.25
2	Brian Anderson	.25
3	Hector Carrasco	.25
4	Tim Davis	.25
5	Carlos Delgado	2.50
6	Cliff Floyd	.25
7	Bob Hamelin	.25
8	Jeffrey Hammonds	.25
9	Rick Helling	.25
10	Steve Karsay	.25
11	Ryan Klesko	.25
12	Javier Lopez	.25
13	Raul Mondesi	.25
14	James Mouton	.25
15	Chan Ho Park	.25
16	Manny Ramirez	3.00
17	Tony Tarasco	.25
18	Steve Trachsel	.25
19	Rick White	.25
20	Rondell White	.25

Second Year Stars

Second-Year Stars contains 1993 rookies who were expected to have an even bigger impact in the 1994 season. Each card features five photos of the player. Four are in a filmstrip down the left side; the remaining two-thirds of the card contain a larger photo. "Second-Year Stars" is printed across the

bottom, along with the player name and team. Backs repeat the film-strip motif.

		NM/M
Complete Set (20):		5.00
Common Player:		.25
1	Bobby Ayala	.25
2	Jason Bere	.25
3	Chuck Carr	.25
4	Jeff Conine	.25
5	Steve Cooke	.25
6	Wil Cordero	.25
7	Carlos Garcia	.25
8	Brent Gates	.25
9	Trevor Hoffman	.25
10	Wayne Kirby	.25
11	Al Martin	.25
12	Pedro Martinez	1.50
13	Greg McMichael	.25
14	Troy Neel	.25
15	David Nied	.25
16	Mike Piazza	3.00
17	Kirk Rueter	.25
18	Tim Salmon	.50
19	Aaron Sele	.25
20	Kevin Stocker	.25

Pitcher's Duel

Pitcher's Duel was available to collectors who mailed in 10 Extra Bases wrappers. The set features 20 of the top pitchers in baseball. Contained in the set were five American League and five National League cards, with two pitchers from the same league on each card. The front background pictures a wide-angle photo of a major league stadium, viewed from above the diamond, behind home plate. Backs have two more action photos set against a sepia-toned background photo of an Old West street to enhance the shootout theme of the set. Cards are numbered with an "M" prefix.

		NM/M
Complete Set (10):		7.50
Common Player:		.50
1	Roger Clemens, Jack McDowell	2.50
2	Ben McDowell, Randy Johnson	1.50
3	Jimmy Key, David Cone	.50
4	Mike Mussina, Aaron Sele	1.00
5	Chuck Finley, Wilson Alvarez	.50
6	Steve Avery, Curt Schilling	.75
7	Greg Maddux, Jose Rijo	2.00
8	Bret Saberhagen, Bob Tewksbury	.50
9	Tom Glavine, Bill Swift	.75
10	Doug Drabek, Orel Hershiser	.50

1995 Fleer Promos

This eight-player (plus a header card), cello-wrapped promo set was included in a special "Fleer" national newsstand magazine in early 1995. At first glance the cards seem identical to the regularly issued cards of the same players, but there are subtle differences on the back of each card.

		NM/M
Complete Set (9):		4.00
Common Player:		.50
26	Roger Clemens (1988 291 SO and 1992 2.41 ERA boxed)	2.00
78	Paul O'Neill (1991 boxed)	.50
155	David Cone (1990 233 SO boxed, white shadow on team names)	.50
235	Tim Salmon (No box on 1992 101 R.)	.50
285	Marquis Grissom (Black stats, 1993 boxed.)	1.00
351	Marquis Grissom (No box on 1988 291 AB.)	.50
509	Ozzie Smith (Black stats, no box on 1986 Cardinals.)	1.50
514	Dante Bichette (Black stats.)	.50
--	Header Card "Different by Design"	.05

1995 Fleer

Fleer baseball in 1995 offered six different designs, one for each division. The basic set contains 600 cards and was sold in 12- and 18-card packs. National League West cards feature many smaller pictures in the background that are identical to the picture in the forefront, while AL West cards contain an action photo over top of a close-up on the right side and a water colored look on the left side. AL Central cards exhibit numbers pertinent to each player throughout the front design, with the player in the middle. NL East players appear in action on the left half of the card with a colorful, encripted look on the rest. National League Central and American League East feature more standard designs with the player in the forefront, with vital numbers and a color background.

		NM/M
Complete Set (600):		15.00
Common Player:		.05
Pack (12):		.75
Wax Box (36):		17.50
1	Brady Anderson	.05
2	Harold Baines	.05
3	Damon Buford	.05
4	Mike Devereaux	.05
5	Mark Eichhorn	.05
6	Sid Fernandez	.05
7	Leo Gomez	.05
8	Jeffrey Hammonds	.05
9	Chris Hoiles	.05
10	Rick Krivda	.05
11	Ben McDonald	.05
12	Mark McLemore	.05
13	Alan Mills	.05
14	Jamie Moyer	.05
15	Mike Mussina	.40
16	Mike Oquist	.05
17	Rafael Palmeiro	.65
18	Arthur Rhodes	.05
19	Cal Ripken, Jr.	2.50
20	Chris Sabo	.05
21	Lee Smith	.05
22	Jack Voight	.05
23	Damon Berryhill	.05
24	Tom Brunansky	.05
25	Wes Chamberlain	.05
26	Roger Clemens	1.25
27	Scott Cooper	.05
28	Andre Dawson	.25
29	Gar Finnvold	.05
30	Tony Fossas	.05
31	Mike Greenwell	.05
32	Joe Hesketh	.05
33	Chris Howard	.05
34	Chris Nabholz	.05
35	Tim Naehring	.05
36	Otis Nixon	.05
37	Carlos Rodriguez	.05
38	Rich Rowland	.05
39	Ken Ryan	.05
40	Aaron Sele	.05
41	John Valentin	.05
42	Mo Vaughn	.05
43	Frank Viola	.05
44	Danny Bautista	.05
45	Joe Boever	.05
46	Milt Cuyler	.05
47	Storm Davis	.05
48	John Doherty	.05
49	Junior Felix	.05
50	Cecil Fielder	.05
51	Travis Fryman	.05
52	Mike Gardiner	.05
53	Kirk Gibson	.05
54	Chris Gomez	.05
55	Buddy Groom	.05
56	Mike Henneman	.05
57	Chad Kreuter	.05
58	Mike Moore	.05
59	Tony Phillips	.05
60	Juan Samuel	.05
61	Mickey Tettleton	.05
62	Alan Trammell	.05
63	David Wells	.05
64	Lou Whitaker	.05
65	Jim Abbott	.05
66	Joe Ausanio	.05
67	Wade Boggs	1.00
68	Mike Gallego	.05
69	Xavier Hernandez	.05
70	Sterling Hitchcock	.05
71	Steve Howe	.05
72	Scott Kamieniecki	.05
73	Pat Kelly	.05
74	Jimmy Key	.05
75	Jim Leyritz	.05
76	Don Mattingly	1.25
77	Terry Mulholland	.05
78	Paul O'Neill	.05
79	Melido Perez	.05
80	Luis Polonia	.05
81	Mike Stanley	.05
82	Danny Tartabull	.05
83	Randy Velarde	.05
84	Bob Wickman	.05
85	Bernie Williams	.10
86	Gerald Williams	.05
87	Roberto Alomar	.10
88	Pat Borders	.05
89	Joe Carter	.05
90	Tony Castillo	.05
91	Brad Cornett	.05
92	Carlos Delgado	.50
93	Alex Gonzalez	.05
94	Shawn Green	.40
95	Juan Guzman	.05
96	Darren Hall	.05
97	Pat Hentgen	.05
98	Mike Huff	.05
99	Randy Knorr	.05
100	Al Leiter	.05
101	Paul Molitor	.75
102	John Olerud	.05
103	Dick Schofield	.05
104	Ed Sprague	.05
105	Dave Stewart	.05
106	Todd Stottlemyre	.05
107	Devon White	.05
108	Woody Williams	.05
109	Wilson Alvarez	.05
110	Paul Assenmacher	.05
111	Jason Bere	.05
112	Dennis Cook	.05
113	Joey Cora	.05
114	Jose DeLeon	.05
115	Alex Fernandez	.05
116	Julio Franco	.05
117	Craig Graboeck	.05
118	Ozzie Guillen	.05
119	Roberto Hernandez	.05
120	Darrin Jackson	.05
121	Lance Johnson	.05
122	Ron Karkovice	.05
123	Mike LaValliere	.05
124	Norberto Martin	.05
125	Kirk McCaskill	.05
126	Jack McDowell	.05
127	Tim Raines	.05
128	Frank Thomas	.75
129	Robin Ventura	.05
130	Sandy Alomar Jr.	.05
131	Carlos Baerga	.05
132	Albert Belle	.75
133	Mark Clark	.05
134	Alvaro Espinoza	.05
135	Jason Grimsley	.05
136	Wayne Kirby	.05
137	Kenny Lofton	.05
138	Albie Lopez	.05
139	Dennis Martinez	.05
140	Jose Mesa	.05
141	Eddie Murray	.75
142	Charles Nagy	.05
143	Tony Pena	.05
144	Eric Plunk	.05
145	Manny Ramirez	.75
146	Jeff Russell	.05
147	Paul Shuey	.05
148	Paul Sorrento	.05
149	Jim Thome	.65
150	Omar Vizquel	.05
151	Dave Winfield	.75
152	Kevin Appier	.05
153	Billy Brewer	.05
154	Vince Coleman	.05
155	David Cone	.05
156	Gary Gaetti	.05
157	Greg Gagne	.05
158	Tom Gordon	.05
159	Mark Gubicza	.05
160	Bob Hamelin	.05
161	Dave Henderson	.05
162	Felix Jose	.05
163	Wally Joyner	.05
164	Jose Lind	.05
165	Mike Macfarlane	.05
166	Mike Magnante	.05
167	Brent Mayne	.05
168	Brian McRae	.05
169	Rusty Meacham	.05
170	Jeff Montgomery	.05
171	Hipolito Pichardo	.05
172	Terry Shumpert	.05
173	Michael Tucker	.05
174	Ricky Bones	.05
175	Jeff Cirillo RC	.30
176	Alex Diaz	.05
177	Cal Eldred	.05
178	Mike Fetters	.05
179	Darryl Hamilton	.05
180	Brian Harper	.05
181	John Jaha	.05
182	Pat Listach	.05
183	Graeme Lloyd	.05
184	Jose Mercedes	.05
185	Matt Mieske	.05
186	Dave Nilsson	.05
187	Jody Reed	.05
188	Bob Scanlan	.05
189	Kevin Seitzer	.05
190	Bill Spiers	.05
191	B.J. Surhoff	.05
192	Jose Valentin	.05
193	Greg Vaughn	.05
194	Turner Ward	.05
195	Bill Wegman	.05
196	Rick Aguilera	.05
197	Rich Becker	.05
198	Alex Cole	.05
199	Marty Cordova	.05
200	Steve Dunn	.05
201	Scott Erickson	.05
202	Mark Guthrie	.05
203	Chip Hale	.05
204	LaTroy Hawkins	.05
205	Denny Hocking	.05
206	Chuck Knoblauch	.05
207	Scott Leius	.05
208	Shane Mack	.05
209	Pat Mahomes	.05
210	Pat Meares	.05
211	Pedro Munoz	.05
212	Kirby Puckett	1.00
213	Jeff Reboulet	.05
214	Dave Stevens	.05
215	Kevin Tapani	.05
216	Matt Walbeck	.05
217	Carl Willis	.05
218	Brian Anderson	.05
219	Chad Curtis	.05
220	Chili Davis	.05
221	Gary DiSarcina	.05
222	Damion Easley	.05
223	Jim Edmonds	.05
224	Chuck Finley	.05
225	Joe Grahe	.05
226	Rex Hudler	.05
227	Bo Jackson	.10
228	Mark Langston	.05
229	Phil Leftwich	.05
230	Mark Leiter	.05
231	Spike Owen	.05
232	Bob Patterson	.05
233	Troy Percival	.05
234	Eduardo Perez	.05
235	Tim Salmon	.10
236	J.T. Snow	.05
237	Chris Turner	.05
238	Mark Acre	.05
239	Geronimo Berroa	.05
240	Mike Bordick	.05
241	John Briscoe	.05
242	Scott Brosius	.05
243	Ron Darling	.05
244	Dennis Eckersley	.65
245	Brent Gates	.05
246	Rickey Henderson	.75
247	Stan Javier	.05
248	Steve Karsay	.05
249	Mark McGwire	2.00
250	Troy Neel	.05
251	Steve Ontiveros	.05
252	Carlos Reyes	.05
253	Ruben Sierra	.05
254	Terry Steinbach	.05
255	Bill Taylor	.05
256	Todd Van Poppel	.05
257	Bobby Witt	.05
258	Rich Amaral	.05
259	Eric Anthony	.05
260	Bobby Ayala	.05
261	Mike Blowers	.05
262	Chris Bosio	.05
263	Jay Buhner	.05
264	John Cummings	.05
265	Tim Davis	.05
266	Felix Fermin	.05
267	Dave Fleming	.05
268	Goose Gossage	.05
269	Ken Griffey Jr.	1.50
270	Reggie Jefferson	.05
271	Randy Johnson	.75
272	Edgar Martinez	.05
273	Tino Martinez	.05
274	Greg Pirkl	.05
275	Bill Risley	.05
276	Roger Salkeld	.05
277	Luis Sojo	.05
278	Mac Suzuki	.05
279	Dan Wilson	.05
280	Kevin Brown	.05
281	Jose Canseco	.40
282	Cris Carpenter	.05
283	Will Clark	.10
284	Jeff Frye	.05
285	Juan Gonzalez	.65
286	Rick Helling	.05
287	Tom Henke	.05
288	David Hulse	.05
289	Chris James	.05
290	Manuel Lee	.05
291	Oddibe McDowell	.05
292	Dean Palmer	.05
293	Roger Pavlik	.05
294	Bill Ripken	.05
295	Ivan Rodriguez	.65
296	Kenny Rogers	.05
297	Doug Strange	.05
298	Matt Whiteside	.05
299	Steve Avery	.05
300	Steve Bedrosian	.05
301	Rafael Belliard	.05
302	Jeff Blauser	.05
303	Dave Gallagher	.05
304	Tom Glavine	.30
305	Dave Justice	.05
306	Mike Kelly	.05
307	Roberto Kelly	.05
308	Ryan Klesko	.05
309	Mark Lemke	.05
310	Javier Lopez	.05
311	Greg Maddux	1.00
312	Fred McGriff	.05
313	Greg McMichael	.05
314	Kent Mercker	.05
315	Charlie O'Brien	.05
316	Jose Oliva	.05
317	Terry Pendleton	.05
318	John Smoltz	.05
319	Mike Stanton	.05
320	Tony Tarasco	.05
321	Terrell Wade	.05
322	Mark Wohlers	.05
323	Kurt Abbott	.05
324	Luis Aquino	.05
325	Bret Barberie	.05
326	Ryan Bowen	.05
327	Jerry Browne	.05
328	Chuck Carr	.05
329	Matias Carrillo	.05
330	Greg Colbrunn	.05
331	Jeff Conine	.05
332	Mark Gardner	.05
333	Chris Hammond	.05
334	Bryan Harvey	.05
335	Richie Lewis	.05
336	Dave Magadan	.05
337	Terry Mathews	.05
338	Robb Nen	.05
339	Yorkis Perez	.05
340	Pat Rapp	.05
341	Benito Santiago	.05
342	Gary Sheffield	.40
343	Dave Weathers	.05
344	Moises Alou	.05
345	Sean Berry	.05
346	Wil Cordero	.05
347	Joe Eischen	.05
348	Jeff Fassero	.05
349	Darrin Fletcher	.05
350	Cliff Floyd	.05
351	Marquis Grissom	.05
352	Butch Henry	.05
353	Gil Heredia	.05
354	Ken Hill	.05
355	Mike Lansing	.05
356	Pedro Martinez	.75
357	Mel Rojas	.05
358	Kirk Rueter	.05
359	Tim Scott	.05
360	Jeff Shaw	.05
361	Larry Walker	.05
362	Lenny Webster	.05
363	John Wetteland	.05
364	Rondell White	.05
365	Bobby Bonilla	.05
366	Rico Brogna	.05
367	Jeromy Burnitz	.05
368	John Franco	.05
369	Dwight Gooden	.05
370	Todd Hundley	.05
371	Jason Jacome	.05
372	Bobby Jones	.05
373	Jeff Kent	.05
374	Jim Lindeman	.05
375	Josias Manzanillo	.05
376	Roger Mason	.05
377	Kevin McReynolds	.05
378	Joe Orsulak	.05
379	Bill Pulsipher	.05
380	Bret Saberhagen	.05
381	David Segui	.05
382	Pete Smith	.05
383	Kelly Stinnett	.05
384	Ryan Thompson	.05
385	Jose Vizcaino	.05
386	Toby Borland	.05
387	Ricky Bottalico	.05
388	Darren Daulton	.05
389	Mariano Duncan	.05
390	Len Dykstra	.05
391	Jim Eisenreich	.05
392	Tommy Greene	.05
393	Dave Hollins	.05
394	Pete Incaviglia	.05
395	Danny Jackson	.05
396	Doug Jones	.05
397	Ricky Jordan	.05
398	John Kruk	.05
399	Mike Lieberthal	.05
400	Tony Longmire	.05
401	Mickey Morandini	.05
402	Bobby Munoz	.05
403	Curt Schilling	.25

No.	Player	Price		No.	Player	Price
404	Heathcliff Slocumb	.05		522	Mike Kingery	.05
405	Kevin Stocker	.05		523	Nelson Liriano	.05
406	Fernando Valenzuela	.05		524	Mike Munoz	.05
407	David West	.05		525	David Nied	.05
408	Willie Banks	.05		526	Steve Reed	.05
409	Jose Bautista	.05		527	Kevin Ritz	.05
410	Steve Buechele	.05		528	Bruce Ruffin	.05
411	Jim Bullinger	.05		529	John Vander Wal	.05
412	Chuck Crim	.05		530	Walt Weiss	.05
413	Shawon Dunston	.05		531	Eric Young	.05
414	Kevin Foster	.05		532	Billy Ashley	.05
415	Mark Grace	.10		533	Pedro Astacio	.05
416	Jose Hernandez	.05		534	Rafael Bournigal	.05
417	Glenallen Hill	.05		535	Brett Butler	.05
418	Brooks Kieschnick	.05		536	Tom Candiotti	.05
419	Derrick May	.05		537	Omar Daal	.05
420	Randy Myers	.05		538	Delino DeShields	.05
421	Dan Plesac	.05		539	Darren Dreifort	.05
422	Karl Rhodes	.05		540	Kevin Gross	.05
423	Rey Sanchez	.05		541	Orel Hershiser	.05
424	Sammy Sosa	1.50		542	Garey Ingram	.05
425	Steve Trachsel	.05		543	Eric Karros	.05
426	Rick Wilkins	.05		544	Ramon Martinez	.05
427	Anthony Young	.05		545	Raul Mondesi	.05
428	Eddie Zambrano	.05		546	Chan Ho Park	.05
429	Bret Boone	.05		547	Mike Piazza	1.50
430	Jeff Branson	.05		548	Henry Rodriguez	.05
431	Jeff Brantley	.05		549	Rudy Seanez	.05
432	Hector Carrasco	.05		550	Ismael Valdes	.05
433	Brian Dorsett	.05		551	Tim Wallach	.05
434	Tony Fernandez	.05		552	Todd Worrell	.05
435	Tim Fortugno	.05		553	Andy Ashby	.05
436	Erik Hanson	.05		554	Brad Ausmus	.05
437	Thomas Howard	.05		555	Derek Bell	.05
438	Kevin Jarvis	.05		556	Andy Benes	.05
439	Barry Larkin	.05		557	Phil Clark	.05
440	Chuck McElroy	.05		558	Donnie Elliott	.05
441	Kevin Mitchell	.05		559	Ricky Gutierrez	.05
442	Hal Morris	.05		560	Tony Gwynn	1.00
443	Jose Rijo	.05		561	Joey Hamilton	.05
444	John Roper	.05		562	Trevor Hoffman	.05
445	Johnny Ruffin	.05		563	Luis Lopez	.05
446	Deion Sanders	.05		564	Pedro Martinez	.05
447	Reggie Sanders	.05		565	Tim Mauser	.05
448	Pete Schourek	.05		566	Phil Plantier	.05
449	John Smiley	.05		567	Bip Roberts	.05
450	Eddie Taubensee	.05		568	Scott Sanders	.05
451	Jeff Bagwell	.75		569	Craig Shipley	.05
452	Kevin Bass	.05		570	Jeff Tabaka	.05
453	Craig Biggio	.05		571	Eddie Williams	.05
454	Ken Caminiti	.05		572	Rod Beck	.05
455	Andujar Cedeno	.05		573	Mike Benjamin	.05
456	Doug Drabek	.05		574	Barry Bonds	2.50
457	Tony Eusebio	.05		575	Dave Burba	.05
458	Mike Felder	.05		576	John Burkett	.05
459	Steve Finley	.05		577	Mark Carreon	.05
460	Luis Gonzalez	.10		578	Royce Clayton	.05
461	Mike Hampton	.05		579	Steve Frey	.05
462	Pete Harnisch	.05		580	Bryan Hickerson	.05
463	John Hudek	.05		581	Mike Jackson	.05
464	Todd Jones	.05		582	Darren Lewis	.05
465	Darryl Kile	.05		583	Kirt Manwaring	.05
466	James Mouton	.05		584	Rich Monteleone	.05
467	Shane Reynolds	.05		585	John Patterson	.05
468	Scott Servais	.05		586	J.R. Phillips	.05
469	Greg Swindell	.05		587	Mark Portugal	.05
470	Dave Veres	.05		588	Joe Rosselli	.05
471	Brian Williams	.05		589	Darryl Strawberry	.05
472	Jay Bell	.05		590	Bill Swift	.05
473	Jacob Brumfield	.05		591	Robby Thompson	.05
474	Dave Clark	.05		592	William Van Landingham	.05
475	Steve Cooke	.05		593	Matt Williams	.05
476	Midre Cummings	.05		594	Checklist	.05
477	Mark Dewey	.05		595	Checklist	.05
478	Tom Foley	.05		596	Checklist	.05
479	Carlos Garcia	.05		597	Checklist	.05
480	Jeff King	.05		598	Checklist	.05
481	Jon Lieber	.05		599	Checklist	.05
482	Ravelo Manzanillo	.05		600	Checklist	.05
483	Al Martin	.05				
484	Orlando Merced	.05				
485	Danny Miceli	.05				
486	Denny Neagle	.05				
487	Lance Parrish	.05				
488	Don Slaught	.05				
489	Zane Smith	.05				
490	Andy Van Slyke	.05				
491	Paul Wagner	.05				
492	Rick White	.05				
493	Luis Alicea	.05				
494	Rene Arocha	.05				
495	Rheal Cormier	.05				
496	Bryan Eversgerd	.05				
497	Bernard Gilkey	.05				
498	John Habyan	.05				
499	Gregg Jefferies	.05				
500	Brian Jordan	.05				
501	Ray Lankford	.05				
502	John Mabry	.05				
503	Terry McGriff	.05				
504	Tom Pagnozzi	.05				
505	Vicente Palacios	.05				
506	Geronimo Pena	.05				
507	Gerald Perry	.05				
508	Rich Rodriguez	.05				
509	Ozzie Smith	1.00				
510	Bob Tewksbury	.05				
511	Allen Watson	.05				
512	Mark Whiten	.05				
513	Todd Zeile	.05				
514	Dante Bichette	.05				
515	Willie Blair	.05				
516	Ellis Burks	.05				
517	Marvin Freeman	.05				
518	Andres Galarraga	.05				
519	Joe Girardi	.05				
520	Greg Harris	.05				
521	Charlie Hayes	.05				

		NM/M
Common Player:		.40
1	Jeff Bagwell	1.50
2	Albert Belle	.40
3	Barry Bonds	3.50
4	Jose Canseco	.75
5	Joe Carter	.40
6	Ken Griffey Jr.	2.50
7	Fred McGriff	.40
8	Kevin Mitchell	.40
9	Frank Thomas	1.75
10	Matt Williams	.40

Award Winners

Fleer Award Winners contain Fleer's choices of baseball's most outstanding players. This six-card set was only inserted at a rate of one per 24 packs. Each card has an embossed gold foil design, with the gold strip running up the left side and containing the words "Fleer Award Winner" and the player name.

		NM/M
Complete Set (6):		4.00
Common Player:		.25
1	Frank Thomas	1.50
2	Jeff Bagwell	1.50
3	David Cone	.25
4	Greg Maddux	2.00
5	Bob Hamelin	.25
6	Raul Mondesi	.25

League Leaders

League Leaders feature players on a horizontal format from 10 statistical categories from both leagues. "League Leader" is placed in a blue strip down the left-side of the card, with their respective league and their name in it. These were inserted at a rate of one per 12 packs.

		NM/M
Complete Set (10):		4.00
Common Player:		.25
1	Paul O'Neill	.25
2	Ken Griffey Jr.	1.50
3	Kirby Puckett	.75
4	Jimmy Key	.25
5	Randy Johnson	.65
6	Tony Gwynn	.75
7	Matt Williams	.75
8	Jeff Bagwell	.50
9	Greg Maddux, Ken Hill	.75
10	Andy Benes	.25

Lumber Company

Ten of the top longball hitters were featured in Lumber Co., which were inserted into every 24 12-card retailer packs. They show the power hitter in action, with a wood-grain Lumber Co. logo across the bottom, contain the player's name and team.

		NM/M
Complete Set (10):		12.00
Common Player:		.25
1	Mike Mussina	.40
2	Raul Mondesi	.25
3	Jeff Bagwell	.25
4	Greg Maddux	1.00
5	Tim Salmon	.25
6	Manny Ramirez	.75

All-Stars

All-Stars are a horizontal, two-sided insert set consisting of 25 cards. A National League All-Star is on one side, while an American League All-Star is on the other, by position. All-Stars are the most common insert in Fleer 1995 baseball, with an insertion ratio of one per three packs.

		NM/M
Complete Set (25):		8.00
Common Card:		.20
1	Ivan Rodriguez, Mike Piazza	.75
2	Frank Thomas, Gregg Jefferies	.50
3	Roberto Alomar, Mariano Duncan	.40
4	Wade Boggs, Matt Williams	.65
5	Cal Ripken, Jr., Ozzie Smith	1.50
6	Joe Carter, Barry Bonds	1.50
7	Ken Griffey Jr., Tony Gwynn	.75
8	Kirby Puckett, Dave Justice	.65
9	Jimmy Key, Greg Maddux	.65
10	Chuck Knoblauch, Wil Cordero	.20
11	Scott Cooper, Ken Caminiti	.20
12	Will Clark, Carlos Garcia	.50
13	Paul Molitor, Jeff Bagwell	.50
14	Travis Fryman, Craig Biggio	.20
15	Mickey Tettleton, Fred McGriff	.20
16	Kenny Lofton, Moises Alou	.20
17	Albert Belle, Marquis Grissom	.20
18	Paul O'Neill, Dante Bichette	.20
19	David Cone, Ken Hill	.20
20	Mike Mussina, Doug Drabek	.50
21	Randy Johnson, John Hudek	.50
22	Pat Hentgen, Danny Jackson	.20
23	Wilson Alvarez, Rod Beck	.20
24	Lee Smith, Randy Myers	.20
25	Jason Bere, Doug Jones	.20

Major League Prospects

Major League Prospects showcases 10 of 1995's most promising young players. The set title is repeatedly printed across the background, with the player's name and team in a gray strip across the bottom. These cards were inserted into one every six packs.

		NM/M
Complete Set (10):		6.00
Common Player:		.25
1	Garret Anderson	.50
2	James Baldwin	.25
3	Alan Benes	.25
4	Armando Benitez	.25
5	Ray Durham	.25
6	Brian Hunter	.25
7a	Derek Jeter (No licensor logos on back.)	4.00
7b	Derek Jeter (Licensor logos on back.)	4.00
8	Charles Johnson	.25
9	Orlando Miller	.25
10	Alex Rodriguez	3.00

Pro-Visions

Pro-Visions contain six interlocking cards that form one giant picture. These original art cards exhibit the player in a fantasy art background and are inserted into every nine packs.

		NM/M
Complete Set (6):		2.00
Common Player:		.25
1	Mike Mussina	.40
2	Raul Mondesi	.25
3	Jeff Bagwell	.25
4	Greg Maddux	1.00
5	Tim Salmon	.25
6	Manny Ramirez	.75

Rookie Sensations

A perennial favorite within Fleer products, Rookie Sensations cards were inserted in 18-card packs only, at a rate of one per 16 packs. This 20-card set featured the top rookies from the 1994 season. The player's name and team run up the right side of the card, while the words "Rookie Sensations" appear in the bottom-left corner, separated by a colorful, zig-zagged image of a player.

		NM/M
Complete Set (20):		5.00
Common Player:		.25
1	Kurt Abbott	.25
2	Rico Brogna	.25
3	Hector Carrasco	.25
4	Kevin Foster	.25
5	Chris Gomez	.25
6	Darren Hall	.25
7	Bob Hamelin	.25
8	Joey Hamilton	.25
9	John Hudek	.25
10	Ryan Klesko	.25
11	Javier Lopez	.25
12	Matt Mieske	.25
13	Raul Mondesi	.25
14	Manny Ramirez	4.00
15	Shane Reynolds	.25
16	Bill Risley	.25
17	Johnny Ruffin	.25
18	Steve Trachsel	.25
19	William Van Landingham	.25
20	Rondell White	.25

Team Leaders

Team Leaders are two-player cards featuring the leading hitter and pitcher from each major league team, one on each side. Inserted at a rate of one per 24 packs, these are only found in 12-card hobby packs. Team Leaders consisted of 28 cards and included a Team Leader logo in the bottom-left corner.

		NM/M
Complete Set (28):		50.00
Common Card:		.50
1	Cal Ripken, Jr., Mike Mussina	7.50
2	Mo Vaughn, Roger Clemens	4.50
3	Tim Salmon, Chuck Finley	.75
4	Frank Thomas, Jack McDowell	2.50
5	Albert Belle, Dennis Martinez	.50
6	Cecil Fielder, Mike Moore	.50
7	Bob Hamelin, David Cone	.50
8	Greg Vaughn, Ricky Bones	.50
9	Kirby Puckett, Rick Aguilera	3.00
10	Don Mattingly, Jimmy Key	4.50
11	Ruben Sierra, Dennis Eckersley	1.50
12	Ken Griffey Jr., Randy Johnson	6.00
13	Jose Canseco, Kenny Rogers	1.00
14	Joe Carter, Pat Hentgen	.50
15	Dave Justice, Greg Maddux	3.00
16	Sammy Sosa, Steve Trachsel	5.00
17	Kevin Mitchell, Jose Rijo	.50
18	Dante Bichette, Bruce Ruffin	.50
19	Jeff Conine, Robb Nen	.50
20	Jeff Bagwell, Doug Drabek	2.50
21	Mike Piazza, Ramon Martinez	5.00
22	Moises Alou, Ken Hill	.50
23	Bobby Bonilla, Bret Saberhagen	.50
24	Darren Daulton, Danny Jackson	.50
25	Jay Bell, Zane Smith	.50
26	Gregg Jefferies, Bob Tewksbury	.50
27	Tony Gwynn, Andy Benes	3.00
28	Matt Williams, Rod Beck	.50

All-Fleer 9

Available only by mailing in 10 Fleer wrappers and $3, this set presents an all-star lineup in a unique design. Colored scribbles down one side of the card front offer a background for gold-foil printing of the card title, player name, position and team. Backs repeat the colored scribbles across virtually the entire surface, making it extremely difficult to read the career summary printed in white over it.

		NM/M
Complete Set (9):		4.00
Common Player:		.25
1	Mike Piazza	1.00
2	Frank Thomas	.50
3	Roberto Alomar	.40
4	Cal Ripken Jr.	2.50
5	Matt Williams	.25
6	Barry Bonds	2.50
7	Ken Griffey Jr.	1.00
8	Tony Gwynn	.65
9	Greg Maddux	.65

All-Rookies

This mail-in set was available by redeeming a randomly inserted trade card found in packs. The cards feature action player photos on a muted background, with the player ID in gold-foil beneath a huge rookie banner. Horizontal backs have a player photo at left and professional highlights at right. Cards have an "M" prefix to the card number.

		NM/M
Complete Set (9):		1.50
Common Player:		.25
Trade card:		2X
1	Edgardo Alfonzo	.25
2	Jason Bates	.25
3	Brian Boehringer	.25
4	Darren Bragg	.25
5	Brad Clontz	.25
6	Jim Dougherty	.25
7	Todd Hollandsworth	.25
8	Rudy Pemberton	.25
9	Frank Rodriguez	.25

Update

Fleer carried its "different by design" concept of six formats (one for each division in each league) from the regular set into its 1995 Update issue. The issue consists of 200 cards of 1995's traded, rookie and free agent players, plus five different insert sets. One insert card was found in each regular (12-card, $1.49) and jumbo (18-card, $2.29) pack. Cards are numbered with a "U" prefix.

		NM/M
Complete Set (200):		7.00
Common Player:		.05
Pack (12):		.50
Wax Box (36):		7.50
1	Manny Alexander	.05
2	Bret Barberie	.05
3	Armando Benitez	.05
4	Kevin Brown	.05
5	Doug Jones	.05
6	Sherman Obando	.05
7	Andy Van Slyke	.05
8	Stan Belinda	.05
9	Jose Canseco	.30
10	Vaughn Eshelman	.05
11	Mike Macfarlane	.05
12	Troy O'Leary	.05
13	Steve Rodriguez	.05
14	Lee Tinsley	.05
15	Tim Vanegmond	.05
16	Mark Whiten	.05
17	Sean Bergman	.05
18	Chad Curtis	.05
19	John Flaherty	.05
20	Bob Higginson RC	.15
21	Felipe Lira	.05
22	Shannon Penn	.05
23	Todd Steverson	.05
24	Sean Whiteside	.05
25	Tony Fernandez	.05
26	Jack McDowell	.05
27	Andy Pettitte	.15
28	John Wetteland	.05
29	David Cone	.05
30	Mike Timlin	.05
31	Duane Ward	.05
32	Jim Abbott	.05
33	James Baldwin	.05
34	Mike Devereaux	.05
35	Ray Durham	.05
36	Tim Fortugno	.05
37	Scott Ruffcorn	.05
38	Chris Sabo	.05
39	Paul Assenmacher	.05
40	Bud Black	.05
41	Orel Hershiser	.05
42	Julian Tavarez	.05
43	Dave Winfield	.60
44	Pat Borders	.05
45	Melvin Bunch RC	.05
46	Tom Goodwin	.05
47	Jon Nunnally	.05
48	Joe Randa	.05
49	Dilson Torres RC	.05
50	Joe Vitiello	.05
51	David Hulse	.05
52	Scott Karl	.05
53	Mark Kiefer	.05
54	Derrick May	.05
55	Joe Oliver	.05
56	Al Reyes	.05
57	Steve Sparks RC	.05
58	Jerald Clark	.05
59	Eddie Guardado	.05
60	Kevin Maas	.05
61	David McCarty	.05
62	Brad Radke RC	.50
63	Scott Stahoviak	.05
64	Garret Anderson	.05
65	Shawn Boskie	.05
66	Mike James	.05
67	Tony Phillips	.05
68	Lee Smith	.05
69	Mitch Williams	.05
70	Jim Corsi	.05
71	Mark Harkey	.05
72	Dave Stewart	.05
73	Todd Stottlemyre	.05
74	Joey Cora	.05
75	Chad Kreuter	.05
76	Jeff Nelson	.05
77	Alex Rodriguez	2.00
78	Ron Villone	.05
79	Bob Wells RC	.05
80	Jose Alberro RC	.05
81	Terry Burrows	.05
82	Kevin Gross	.05
83	Wilson Heredia	.05
84	Mark McLemore	.05
85	Otis Nixon	.05
86	Jeff Russell	.05
87	Mickey Tettleton	.05
88	Bob Tewksbury	.05
89	Pedro Borbon	.05
90	Marquis Grissom	.05
91	Chipper Jones	.75
92	Mike Mordecai	.05
93	Jason Schmidt	.15
94	John Burkett	.05
95	Andre Dawson	.25
96	Matt Dunbar RC	.05
97	Charles Johnson	.05
98	Terry Pendleton	.05
99	Rich Scheid	.05
100	Quilvio Veras	.05
101	Bobby Witt	.05
102	Eddie Zosky	.05
103	Shane Andrews	.05
104	Reid Cornelius	.05
105	Chad Fonville RC	.05
106	Mark Grudzielanek RC	.25
107	Roberto Kelly	.05
108	Carlos Perez RC	.05
109	Tony Tarasco	.05
110	Brett Butler	.05
111	Carl Everett	.05
112	Pete Harnisch	.05
113	Doug Henry	.05
114	Kevin Lomon	.05
115	Blas Minor	.05
116	Dave Mlicki	.05
117	Ricky Otero RC	.05
118	Norm Charlton	.05
119	Tyler Green	.05
120	Gene Harris	.05
121	Charlie Hayes	.05
122	Gregg Jefferies	.05
123	Michael Mimbs RC	.05
124	Paul Quantrill	.05
125	Frank Castillo	.05
126	Brian McRae	.05
127	Jaime Navarro	.05
128	Mike Perez	.05
129	Tanyon Sturtze	.05
130	Ozzie Timmons	.05
131	John Courtright	.05
132	Ron Gant	.05
133	Xavier Hernandez	.05
134	Brian Hunter	.05
135	Benito Santiago	.05
136	Pete Smith	.05
137	Scott Sullivan	.05
138	Derek Bell	.05
139	Doug Brocail	.05
140	Ricky Gutierrez	.05
141	Pedro Martinez	.05
142	Orlando Miller	.05
143	Phil Plantier	.05
144	Craig Shipley	.05
145	Rich Aude	.05
146	Jason Christiansen RC	.05
147	Freddy Garcia RC	.25
148	Jim Gott	.05
149	Mark Johnson RC	.05
150	Esteban Loaiza	.05
151	Dan Plesac	.05
152	Gary Wilson RC	.05
153	Allen Battle	.05
154	Terry Bradshaw	.05
155	Scott Cooper	.05
156	Tripp Cromer	.05
157	John Frascatore	.05
158	John Habyan	.05
159	Tom Henke	.05
160	Ken Hill	.05
161	Danny Jackson	.05
162	Donovan Osborne	.05
163	Tom Urbani	.05
164	Roger Bailey	.05
165	Jorge Brito RC	.05
166	Vinny Castilla	.05
167	Darren Holmes	.05
168	Roberto Mejia	.05
169	Bill Swift	.05
170	Mark Thompson	.05
171	Larry Walker	.05
172	Greg Hansell	.05
173	Dave Hansen	.05
174	Carlos Hernandez	.05
175	Hideo Nomo RC	2.00
176	Jose Offerman	.05
177	Antonio Osuna	.05
178	Reggie Williams	.05
179	Todd Williams	.05
180	Andres Berumen	.05
181	Ken Caminiti	.05
182	Andujar Cedeno	.05
183	Steve Finley	.05
184	Bryce Florie	.05
185	Dustin Hermanson	.05
186	Ray Holbert	.05
187	Melvin Nieves	.05
188	Roberto Petagine	.05
189	Jody Reed	.05
190	Fernando Valenzuela	.05
191	Brian Williams	.05
192	Mark Dewey	.05
193	Glenallen Hill	.05
194	Chris Hook RC	.05
195	Terry Mulholland	.05
196	Steve Scarsone	.05
197	Trevor Wilson	.05
198	Checklist	.05
199	Checklist	.05
200	Checklist	.05

Update Diamond Tribute

Borderless action photos and gold-foil graphics are front features of this chase set honoring perhaps the 10 top names among baseball's veteran players. The backs have another photo and a few sentences describing what makes the player worthy of inclusion in such a set. The Diamond Tribute cards are found on the average of one per five packs.

		NM/M
Complete Set (10):		6.00
Common Player:		.25
1	Jeff Bagwell	.75
2	Albert Belle	.25
3	Barry Bonds	3.00
4	David Cone	.25
5	Dennis Eckersley	.50
6	Ken Griffey Jr.	1.50
7	Rickey Henderson	.60
8	Greg Maddux	1.00
9	Frank Thomas	.75
10	Matt Williams	.25

Update Headliners

The most common of the Fleer Update inserts are the Headliners cards found on average of one per three packs. Fronts have an action photo set against a collage of newspaper clippings. The graphics are gold-foil. Backs have another color photo and a "Fleer Times" newspaper background with career summary and/or quotes about the featured player.

		NM/M
Complete Set (20):		8.00
Common Player:		.10
1	Jeff Bagwell	.50
2	Albert Belle	.15
3	Barry Bonds	3.00
4	Jose Canseco	.40
5	Joe Carter	.15
6	Will Clark	.25
7	Roger Clemens	2.00
8	Lenny Dykstra	.15
9	Cecil Fielder	.15
10	Juan Gonzalez	.40
11	Ken Griffey Jr.	2.00
12	Kenny Lofton	.15
13	Greg Maddux	.75
14	Fred McGriff	.15
15	Mike Piazza	1.50
16	Kirby Puckett	.75
17	Tim Salmon	.15
18	Frank Thomas	.50
19	Mo Vaughn	.15
20	Matt Williams	.15

Update Rookie Update

Ten of 1995's top rookies are featured in this horizontally-formatted insert set. Fronts have an action photo with a large gold-foil "ROOKIE UPDATE" headline at top. Backs

have another photo and career summary. Rookie Update chase cards are found on the average of one per four packs.

		NM/M
Complete Set (10):		4.00
Common Player:		.10
1	Shane Andrews	.10
2	Ray Durham	.10
3	Shawn Green	.40
4	Charles Johnson	.10
5	Chipper Jones	1.50
6	Esteban Loaiza	.10
7	Hideo Nomo	1.00
8	Jon Nunnally	.10
9	Alex Rodriguez	2.00
10	Julian Tavarez	.10

Update Smooth Leather

These inserts featuring top fielders were found only in pre-priced (magazine) foil packs, at an average rate of one card per 12 packs. Fronts are highlighted with gold-foil graphics. Backs have a glove in the background and explain the player's defensive abilities.

		NM/M
Complete Set (10):		7.50
Common Player:		.25
1	Roberto Alomar	.50
2	Barry Bonds	2.50
3	Ken Griffey Jr.	1.50
4	Marquis Grissom	.25
5	Darren Lewis	.25
6	Kenny Lofton	.25
7	Don Mattingly	1.00
8	Cal Ripken Jr.	2.50
9	Ivan Rodriguez	.75
10	Matt Williams	.25

Update Soaring Stars

A metallic foil-etched background behind the color player action photo identifies this chase set as the toughest among those in the 1995 Fleer Update issue. The Soaring Star cards are found at the average rate of one per box. Backs are conventionally printed and featured a colorful posterized version of the front background, along with another color photo and a career summary.

		NM/M
Complete Set (9):		3.50
Common Player:		.15
1	Moises Alou	.35
2	Jason Bere	.25
3	Jeff Conine	.25
4	Cliff Floyd	.25
5	Pat Hentgen	.25
6	Kenny Lofton	.25
7	Raul Mondesi	.25
8	Mike Piazza	3.00
9	Tim Salmon	.35

Panini Stickers

Following Fleer's purchase of the well-known Italian sticker company, Panini, it was no surprise to see the companies produce a 1995 baseball issue. Titled "Major League Baseball All-Stars," the set consists of 156 player and team logo stickers. A 36-page color album to house the stickers was sold for $1.19. Sold in six-sticker packs for about .50, the individual stickers measure 1-15/16" x 3". Borders are team color-coded and have the player name and team logo at bottom, with the position abbreviation in a diamond at top-right. Backs are printed in black-and-white and include a sticker number, copyright notice and large logos of the licensors and Fleer/Panini. Each sticker can be found with backs that do, or do not, include a promotional message beginning, "Collect all 156 ..."

		NM/M
Complete Set (156):		3.00
Common Player:		.05
Album:		1.00
Wax Pack (6):		.25
Wax Box (100):		15.00
1	Tom Glavine	.15
2	Doug Drabek	.05
3	Rod Beck	.05
4	Pedro J. Martinez	.25
5	Danny Jackson	.05
6	Greg Maddux	.30
7	Bret Saberhagen	.05
8	Ken Hill	.05
9	Marvin Freeman	.05
10	Andy Benes	.05
11	Wilson Alvarez	.05
12	Jimmy Key	.05
13	Mike Mussina	.15
14	Roger Clemens	.35
15	Pat Hentgen	.05
16	Randy Johnson	.25
17	Lee Smith	.05
18	David Cone	.05
19	Jason Bere	.05
20	Dennis Martinez	.05
21	Darren Daulton	.05
22	Darrin Fletcher	.05
23	Tom Pagnozzi	.05
24	Mike Piazza	.40
25	Benito Santiago	.05
26	Sandy Alomar Jr.	.05
27	Chris Hoiles	.05
28	Ivan Rodriguez	.20
29	Mike Stanley	.05
30	Dave Nilsson	.05
31	Jeff Bagwell	.25
32	Mark Grace	.10
33	Gregg Jefferies	.05
34	Andres Galarraga	.05
35	Fred McGriff	.10
36	Will Clark	.10
37	Mo Vaughn	.35
38	Don Mattingly	.35
39	Frank Thomas	.25
40	Cecil Fielder	.05
41	Robby Thompson	.05
42	Delino DeShields	.05
43	Carlos Garcia	.05
44	Bret Boone	.05
45	Craig Biggio	.05
46	Roberto Alomar	.10
47	Chuck Knoblauch	.05
48	Jose Lind	.05
49	Carlos Baerga	.05
50	Lou Whitaker	.05
51	Bobby Bonilla	.05
52	Tim Wallach	.05
53	Todd Zeile	.05
54	Matt Williams	.05
55	Ken Caminiti	.05
56	Robin Ventura	.05
57	Wade Boggs	.30
58	Scott Cooper	.05
59	Travis Fryman	.05
60	Dean Palmer	.05
61	Jay Bell	.05
62	Barry Larkin	.05
63	Ozzie Smith	.30
64	Wil Cordero	.05
65	Royce Clayton	.05
66	Chris Gomez	.05
67	Ozzie Guillen	.05
68	Cal Ripken Jr.	.50
69	Omar Vizquel	.05
70	Gary DiSarcina	.05
71	Dante Bichette	.05
72	Lenny Dykstra	.05
73	Barry Bonds	.50
74	Gary Sheffield	.20
75	Larry Walker	.05
76	Raul Mondesi	.05
77	Dave Justice	.05
78	Moises Alou	.05
79	Tony Gwynn	.30
80	Deion Sanders	.05
81	Kenny Lofton	.05
82	Kirby Puckett	.30
83	Juan Gonzalez	.20
84	Jay Buhner	.05
85	Joe Carter	.05
86	Ken Griffey Jr.	.40
87	Ruben Sierra	.05
88	Tim Salmon	.05
89	Paul O'Neill	.05
90	Albert Belle	.05
91	Danny Tartabull	.05
92	Jose Canseco	.05
93	Harold Baines	.05
94	Kirk Gibson	.05
95	Chili Davis	.05
96	Eddie Murray	.25
97	Bob Hamelin	.05
98	Paul Molitor	.25
99	Raul Mondesi	.05
100	Ryan Klesko	.05
101	Cliff Floyd	.05
102	William Van Landingham	.05
103	Joey Hamilton	.05
104	John Hudek	.05
105	Manny Ramirez	.25
106	Bob Hamelin	.05
107	Rusty Greer	.05
108	Chris Gomez	.05
109	Greg Maddux	.20
110	Jeff Bagwell	.15
111	Raul Mondesi	.05
112	David Cone	.05
113	Frank Thomas	.25
114	Bob Hamelin	.05
115	Tony Gwynn	.20
116	Matt Williams	.05
117	Jeff Bagwell	.15
118	Craig Biggio	.05
119	Andy Benes	.05
120	Greg Maddux	.20
121	John Franco	.05
122	Paul O'Neill	.05
123	Ken Griffey Jr.	.35
124	Kirby Puckett	.05
125	Kenny Lofton	.05
126	Randy Johnson	.05
127	Jimmy Key	.05
128	Lee Smith	.05
129	San Francisco Giants Logo	.05
130	Montreal Expos Logo	.05
131	Cincinnati Reds Logo	.05
132	Los Angeles Dodgers Logo	.05
133	New York Mets Logo	.05
134	San Diego Padres Logo	.05
135	Colorado Rockies Logo	.05
136	Pittsburgh Pirates Logo	.05
137	Florida Marlins Logo	.05
138	Philadelphia Phillies Logo	.05
139	Atlanta Braves Logo	.05
140	Houston Astros Logo	.05
141	St. Louis Cardinals Logo	.05
142	Chicago Cubs Logo	.05
143	Cleveland Indians Logo	.05
144	New York Yankees Logo	.05
145	Kansas City Royals Logo	.05
146	Chicago White Sox Logo	.05
147	Baltimore Orioles Logo	.05
148	Seattle Mariners Logo	.05
149	Boston Red Sox Logo	.05
150	California Angels Logo	.05
151	Toronto Blue Jays Logo	.05
152	Detroit Tigers Logo	.05
153	Texas Rangers Logo	.05
154	Oakland A's Logo	.05
155	Milwaukee Brewers Logo	.05
156	Minnesota Twins Logo	.05

Revco Cleveland Indians

In the midst of their pennant winning season in 1995, the Cleveland Indians were the subject of a special "Update" set produced by Fleer and sold exclusively by Revco stores and the team itself. Seventeen of the 20 cards in the set are virtually identical to the regular-issue 1995 Fleer cards, except for a change in card number on the back, designating each card as "X of 20," and the use of silver foil on front, as opposed to the gold foil found on regular cards. The Dave Winfield card in the Update issue pictures him in an Indians uniform, instead of the Twins uniform in which he appears in the regular set. Logo and checklist cards were added to the team set. Cards were sold in 10-card foil packs.

		NM/M
Complete Set (20):		6.00
Common Player:		.10
1	Sandy Alomar Jr.	.10
2	Carlos Baerga	.10
3	Albert Belle	.10
4	Mark Clark	.10
5	Alvaro Espinoza	.10
6	Wayne Kirby	.10
7	Kenny Lofton	.10
8	Dennis Martinez	.10
9	Jose Mesa	.10
10	Eddie Murray	2.00
11	Charles Nagy	.10
12	Tony Pena	.10
13	Eric Plunk	.10
14	Manny Ramirez	2.00
15	Paul Sorrento	.10
16	Jim Thome	1.00
17	Omar Vizquel	.10
18	Dave Winfield	2.00
19	Indians/Fleer Logo Card	.05
20	Checklist/Indians Logo	.05

1996 Fleer

In a radical departure from the UV-coated standard for even base-brand baseball cards, Fleer's 1996 issue is printed on a matte surface. Fronts feature borderless game-action photos with minimal (player ID, Fleer logo) graphic enhancement in gold foil. Backs have a white background, a portrait photo, full pro stats and a few career highlights. The single-series set was sold in basic 11-card packs with one of nearly a dozen insert-set cards in each 1.49 pack. The set is arranged alphabetically by player within team and league. A glossy-surface Tiffany Collection parallel was included in each pack.

		NM/M
Complete Set (600):		20.00
Common Player:		.05
Complete Tiffany Set (600):		100.00
Tiffanies:		2X
Pack (11):		.75
Wax Box (36):		16.00
1	Manny Alexander	.05
2	Brady Anderson	.05
3	Harold Baines	.05
4	Armando Benitez	.05
5	Bobby Bonilla	.05
6	Kevin Brown	.05
7	Scott Erickson	.05
8	Curtis Goodwin	.05
9	Jeffrey Hammonds	.05
10	Jimmy Haynes	.05
11	Chris Hoiles	.05
12	Doug Jones	.05
13	Rick Krivda	.05
14	Jeff Manto	.05
15	Ben McDonald	.05
16	Jamie Moyer	.05
17	Mike Mussina	.50
18	Jesse Orosco	.05
19	Rafael Palmeiro	.65

No	Player	Price
20	Cal Ripken Jr.	2.50
20(p)	Cal Ripken Jr./OPS	2.50
21	Rick Aguilera	.05
22	Luis Alicea	.05
23	Stan Belinda	.05
24	Jose Canseco	.50
25	Roger Clemens	1.25
26	Vaughn Eshelman	.05
27	Mike Greenwell	.05
28	Erik Hanson	.05
29	Dwayne Hosey	.05
30	Mike Macfarlane	.05
31	Tim Naehring	.05
32	Troy O'Leary	.05
33	Aaron Sele	.05
34	Zane Smith	.05
35	Jeff Suppan	.05
36	Lee Tinsley	.05
37	John Valentin	.05
38	Mo Vaughn	.05
39	Tim Wakefield	.05
40	Jim Abbott	.05
41	Brian Anderson	.05
42	Garret Anderson	.05
43	Chili Davis	.05
44	Gary DiSarcina	.05
45	Damion Easley	.05
46	Jim Edmonds	.05
47	Chuck Finley	.05
48	Todd Greene	.05
49	Mike Harkey	.05
50	Mike James	.05
51	Mark Langston	.05
52	Greg Myers	.05
53	Orlando Palmeiro	.05
54	Bob Patterson	.05
55	Troy Percival	.05
56	Tony Phillips	.05
57	Tim Salmon	.10
58	Lee Smith	.05
59	J.T. Snow	.05
60	Randy Velarde	.05
61	Wilson Alvarez	.05
62	Luis Andujar RC	.05
63	Jason Bere	.05
64	Ray Durham	.05
65	Alex Fernandez	.05
66	Ozzie Guillen	.05
67	Roberto Hernandez	.05
68	Lance Johnson	.05
69	Matt Karchner	.05
70	Ron Karkovice	.05
71	Norberto Martin	.05
72	Dave Martinez	.05
73	Kirk McCaskill	.05
74	Lyle Mouton	.05
75	Tim Raines	.05
76	Mike Sirotka RC	.05
77	Frank Thomas	.75
78	Larry Thomas	.05
79	Robin Ventura	.05
80	Sandy Alomar Jr.	.05
81	Paul Assenmacher	.05
82	Carlos Baerga	.05
83	Albert Belle	.05
84	Mark Clark	.05
85	Alan Embree	.05
86	Alvaro Espinoza	.05
87	Orel Hershiser	.05
88	Ken Hill	.05
89	Kenny Lofton	.05
90	Dennis Martinez	.05
91	Jose Mesa	.05
92	Eddie Murray	.75
93	Charles Nagy	.05
94	Chad Ogea	.05
95	Tony Pena	.05
96	Herb Perry	.05
97	Eric Plunk	.05
98	Jim Poole	.05
99	Manny Ramirez	.75
100	Paul Sorrento	.05
101	Julian Tavarez	.05
102	Jim Thome	.60
103	Omar Vizquel	.05
104	Dave Winfield	.75
105	Danny Bautista	.05
106	Joe Boever	.05
107	Chad Curtis	.05
108	John Doherty	.05
109	Cecil Fielder	.05
110	John Flaherty	.05
111	Travis Fryman	.05
112	Chris Gomez	.05
113	Bob Higginson	.05
114	Mark Lewis	.05
115	Jose Lima	.05
116	Felipe Lira	.05
117	Brian Maxcy	.05
118	C.J. Nitkowski	.05
119	Phil Plantier	.05
120	Clint Sodowsky	.05
121	Alan Trammell	.05
122	Lou Whitaker	.05
123	Kevin Appier	.05
124	Johnny Damon	.35
125	Gary Gaetti	.05
126	Tom Goodwin	.05
127	Tom Gordon	.05
128	Mark Gubicza	.05
129	Bob Hamelin	.05
130	David Howard	.05
131	Jason Jacome	.05
132	Wally Joyner	.05
133	Keith Lockhart	.05
134	Brent Mayne	.05
135	Jeff Montgomery	.05
136	Jon Nunnally	.05
137	Juan Samuel	.05
138	Mike Sweeney RC	.50
139	Michael Tucker	.05
140	Joe Vitiello	.05
141	Ricky Bones	.05
142	Chuck Carr	.05
143	Jeff Cirillo	.05
144	Mike Fetters	.05
145	Darryl Hamilton	.05
146	David Hulse	.05
147	John Jaha	.05
148	Scott Karl	.05
149	Mark Kiefer	.05
150	Pat Listach	.05
151	Mark Loretta	.05
152	Mike Matheny	.05
153	Matt Mieske	.05
154	Dave Nilsson	.05
155	Joe Oliver	.05
156	Al Reyes	.05
157	Kevin Seitzer	.05
158	Steve Sparks	.05
159	B.J. Surhoff	.05
160	Jose Valentin	.05
161	Greg Vaughn	.05
162	Fernando Vina	.05
163	Rich Becker	.05
164	Ron Coomer	.05
165	Marty Cordova	.05
166	Chuck Knoblauch	.05
167	Matt Lawton RC	.30
168	Pat Meares	.05
169	Paul Molitor	.75
170	Pedro Munoz	.05
171	Jose Parra	.05
172	Kirby Puckett	1.00
173	Brad Radke	.05
174	Jeff Reboulet	.05
175	Rich Robertson	.05
176	Frank Rodriguez	.05
177	Scott Stahoviak	.05
178	Dave Stevens	.05
179	Matt Walbeck	.05
180	Wade Boggs	1.00
181	David Cone	.05
182	Tony Fernandez	.05
183	Joe Girardi	.05
184	Derek Jeter	2.50
185	Scott Kamieniecki	.05
186	Pat Kelly	.05
187	Jim Leyritz	.05
188	Tino Martinez	.05
189	Don Mattingly	1.25
190	Jack McDowell	.05
191	Jeff Nelson	.05
192	Paul O'Neill	.05
193	Melido Perez	.05
194	Andy Pettitte	.30
195	Mariano Rivera	.15
196	Ruben Sierra	.05
197	Mike Stanley	.05
198	Darryl Strawberry	.05
199	John Wetteland	.05
200	Bob Wickman	.05
201	Bernie Williams	.10
202	Mark Acre	.05
203	Geronimo Berroa	.05
204	Mike Bordick	.05
205	Scott Brosius	.05
206	Dennis Eckersley	.65
207	Brent Gates	.05
208	Jason Giambi	.60
209	Rickey Henderson	.75
210	Jose Herrera	.05
211	Stan Javier	.05
212	Doug Johns	.05
213	Mark McGwire	2.00
214	Steve Ontiveros	.05
215	Craig Paquette	.05
216	Ariel Prieto	.05
217	Carlos Reyes	.05
218	Terry Steinbach	.05
219	Todd Stottlemyre	.05
220	Danny Tartabull	.05
221	Todd Van Poppel	.05
222	John Wasdin	.05
223	George Williams	.05
224	Steve Wojciechowski	.05
225	Rich Amaral	.05
226	Bobby Ayala	.05
227	Tim Belcher	.05
228	Andy Benes	.05
229	Chris Bosio	.05
230	Darren Bragg	.05
231	Jay Buhner	.05
232	Norm Charlton	.05
233	Vince Coleman	.05
234	Joey Cora	.05
235	Russ Davis	.05
236	Alex Diaz	.05
237	Felix Fermin	.05
238	Ken Griffey Jr.	1.75
239	Sterling Hitchcock	.05
240	Randy Johnson	.75
241	Edgar Martinez	.05
242	Bill Risley	.05
243	Alex Rodriquez	2.00
244	Luis Sojo	.05
245	Dan Wilson	.05
246	Bob Wolcott	.05
247	Will Clark	.10
248	Jeff Frye	.05
249	Benji Gil	.05
250	Juan Gonzalez	.65
251	Rusty Greer	.05
252	Kevin Gross	.05
253	Roger McDowell	.05
254	Mark McLemore	.05
255	Otis Nixon	.05
256	Luis Ortiz	.05
257	Mike Pagliarulo	.05
258	Dean Palmer	.05
259	Roger Pavlik	.05
260	Ivan Rodriguez	.65
261	Kenny Rogers	.05
262	Jeff Russell	.05
263	Mickey Tettleton	.05
264	Bob Tewksbury	.05
265	Dave Valle	.05
266	Matt Whiteside	.05
267	Roberto Alomar	.10
268	Joe Carter	.05
269	Tony Castillo	.05
270	Domingo Cedeno	.05
271	Timothy Crabtree	.05
272	Carlos Delgado	.60
273	Alex Gonzalez	.05
274	Shawn Green	.20
275	Juan Guzman	.05
276	Pat Hentgen	.05
277	Al Leiter	.05
278	Sandy Martinez RC	.05
279	Paul Menhart	.05
280	John Olerud	.05
281	Paul Quantrill	.05
282	Ken Robinson	.05
283	Ed Sprague	.05
284	Mike Timlin	.05
285	Steve Avery	.05
286	Rafael Belliard	.05
287	Jeff Blauser	.05
288	Pedro Borbon	.05
289	Brad Clontz	.05
290	Mike Devereaux	.05
291	Tom Glavine	.25
292	Marquis Grissom	.05
293	Chipper Jones	1.00
294	David Justice	.05
295	Mike Kelly	.05
296	Ryan Klesko	.05
297	Mark Lemke	.05
298	Javier Lopez	.05
299	Greg Maddux	1.00
300	Fred McGriff	.05
301	Greg McMichael	.05
302	Ken Mercker	.05
303	Mike Mordecai	.05
304	Charlie O'Brien	.05
305	Eduardo Perez	.05
306	Luis Polonia	.05
307	Jason Schmidt	.05
308	John Smoltz	.05
309	Terrell Wade	.05
310	Mark Wohlers	.05
311	Scott Bullett	.05
312	Jim Bullinger	.05
313	Larry Casian	.05
314	Frank Castillo	.05
315	Shawon Dunston	.05
316	Kevin Foster	.05
317	Matt Franco	.05
318	Luis Gonzalez	.10
319	Mark Grace	.10
320	Jose Hernandez	.05
321	Mike Hubbard	.05
322	Brian McRae	.05
323	Randy Myers	.05
324	Jaime Navarro	.05
325	Mark Parent	.05
326	Mike Perez	.05
327	Rey Sanchez	.05
328	Ryne Sandberg	1.00
329	Scott Servais	.05
330	Sammy Sosa	1.50
331	Ozzie Timmons	.05
332	Steve Trachsel	.05
333	Todd Zeile	.05
334	Bret Boone	.10
335	Jeff Branson	.05
336	Jeff Brantley	.05
337	Dave Burba	.05
338	Hector Carrasco	.05
339	Mariano Duncan	.05
340	Ron Gant	.05
341	Lenny Harris	.05
342	Xavier Hernandez	.05
343	Thomas Howard	.05
344	Mike Jackson	.05
345	Barry Larkin	.05
346	Darren Lewis	.05
347	Hal Morris	.05
348	Eric Owens	.05
349	Mark Portugal	.05
350	Jose Rijo	.05
351	Reggie Sanders	.05
352	Benito Santiago	.05
353	Pete Schourek	.05
354	John Smiley	.05
355	Eddie Taubensee	.05
356	Jerome Walton	.05
357	David Wells	.05
358	Roger Bailey	.05
359	Jason Bates	.05
360	Dante Bichette	.05
361	Ellis Burks	.05
362	Vinny Castilla	.05
363	Andres Galarraga	.05
364	Darren Holmes	.05
365	Mike Kingery	.05
366	Curt Leskanic	.05
367	Quinton McCracken	.05
368	Mike Munoz	.05
369	David Nied	.05
370	Steve Reed	.05
371	Bryan Rekar	.05
372	Kevin Ritz	.05
373	Bruce Ruffin	.05
374	Bret Saberhagen	.05
375	Bill Swift	.05
376	John Vander Wal	.05
377	Larry Walker	.05
378	Walt Weiss	.05
379	Eric Young	.05
380	Kurt Abbott	.05
381	Alex Arias	.05
382	Jerry Browne	.05
383	John Burkett	.05
384	Greg Colbrunn	.05
385	Jeff Conine	.05
386	Andre Dawson	.35
387	Chris Hammond	.05
388	Charles Johnson	.05
389	Terry Mathews	.05
390	Robb Nen	.05
391	Joe Orsulak	.05
392	Terry Pendleton	.05
393	Pat Rapp	.05
394	Gary Sheffield	.45
395	Jesus Tavarez	.05
396	Marc Valdes	.05
397	Quilvio Veras	.05
398	Randy Veres	.05
399	Devon White	.05
400	Jeff Bagwell	.75
401	Derek Bell	.05
402	Craig Biggio	.05
403	John Cangelosi	.05
404	Jim Dougherty	.05
405	Doug Drabek	.05
406	Tony Eusebio	.05
407	Ricky Gutierrez	.05
408	Mike Hampton	.05
409	Dean Hartgraves	.05
410	John Hudek	.05
411	Brian Hunter	.05
412	Todd Jones	.05
413	Darryl Kile	.05
414	Dave Magadan	.05
415	Derrick May	.05
416	Orlando Miller	.05
417	James Mouton	.05
418	Shane Reynolds	.05
419	Greg Swindell	.05
420	Jeff Tabaka	.05
421	Dave Veres	.05
422	Billy Wagner	.05
423	Donne Wall RC	.05
424	Rick Wilkins	.05
425	Billy Ashley	.05
426	Mike Blowers	.05
427	Brett Butler	.05
428	Tom Candiotti	.05
429	Juan Castro	.05
430	John Cummings	.05
431	Delino DeShields	.05
432	Joey Eischen	.05
433	Chad Fonville	.05
434	Greg Gagne	.05
435	Dave Hansen	.05
436	Carlos Hernandez	.05
437	Todd Hollandsworth	.05
438	Eric Karros	.05
439	Roberto Kelly	.05
440	Ramon Martinez	.05
441	Raul Mondesi	.05
442	Hideo Nomo	.65
443	Antonio Osuna	.05
444	Chan Ho Park	.05
445	Mike Piazza	1.75
446	Felix Rodriguez	.05
447	Kevin Tapani	.05
448	Ismael Valdes	.05
449	Todd Worrell	.05
450	Moises Alou	.05
451	Shane Andrews	.05
452	Yamil Benitez	.05
453	Sean Berry	.05
454	Wil Cordero	.05
455	Jeff Fassero	.05
456	Darrin Fletcher	.05
457	Cliff Floyd	.05
458	Mark Grudzielanek	.05
459	Gil Heredia	.05
460	Tim Laker	.05
461	Mike Lansing	.05
462	Pedro Martinez	.75
463	Carlos Perez	.05
464	Curtis Pride	.05
465	Mel Rojas	.05
466	Kirk Rueter	.05
467	F.P. Santangelo RC	.05
468	Tim Scott	.05
469	David Segui	.05
470	Tony Tarasco	.05
471	Rondell White	.05
472	Edgardo Alfonzo	.05
473	Tim Bogar	.05
474	Rico Brogna	.05
475	Damon Buford	.05
476	Paul Byrd	.05
477	Carl Everett	.10
478	John Franco	.05
479	Todd Hundley	.05
480	Butch Huskey	.05
481	Jason Isringhausen	.05
482	Bobby Jones	.05
483	Chris Jones	.05
484	Jeff Kent	.10
485	Dave Mlicki	.05
486	Robert Person	.05
487	Bill Pulsipher	.05
488	Kelly Stinnett	.05
489	Ryan Thompson	.05
490	Jose Vizcaino	.05
491	Howard Battle	.05
492	Toby Borland	.05
493	Ricky Bottalico	.05
494	Darren Daulton	.05
495	Lenny Dykstra	.05
496	Jim Eisenreich	.05
497	Sid Fernandez	.05
498	Tyler Green	.05
499	Charlie Hayes	.05
500	Gregg Jefferies	.05
501	Kevin Jordan	.05
502	Tony Longmire	.05
503	Tom Marsh	.05
504	Michael Mimbs	.05
505	Mickey Morandini	.05
506	Gene Schall	.05
507	Curt Schilling	.25
508	Heathcliff Slocumb	.05
509	Kevin Stocker	.05
510	Andy Van Slyke	.05
511	Lenny Webster	.05
512	Mark Whiten	.05
513	Mike Williams	.05
514	Jay Bell	.05
515	Jacob Brumfield	.05
516	Jason Christiansen	.05
517	Dave Clark	.05
518	Midre Cummings	.05
519	Angelo Encarnacion	.05
520	John Ericks	.05
521	Carlos Garcia	.05
522	Mark Johnson	.05
523	Jeff King	.05
524	Nelson Liriano	.05
525	Esteban Loaiza	.05
526	Al Martin	.05
527	Orlando Merced	.05
528	Dan Miceli	.05
529	Ramon Morel	.05
530	Denny Neagle	.05
531	Steve Parris	.05
532	Dan Plesac	.05
533	Don Slaught	.05
534	Paul Wagner	.05
535	John Wehner	.05
536	Kevin Young	.05
537	Allen Battle	.05
538	David Bell	.05
539	Alan Benes	.05
540	Scott Cooper	.05
541	Tripp Cromer	.05
542	Tony Fossas	.05
543	Bernard Gilkey	.05
544	Tom Henke	.05
545	Brian Jordan	.05
546	Ray Lankford	.05
547	John Mabry	.05
548	T.J. Mathews	.05
549	Mike Morgan	.05
550	Jose Oliva	.05
551	Jose Oquendo	.05
552	Donovan Osborne	.05
553	Tom Pagnozzi	.05
554	Mark Petkovsek	.05
555	Danny Sheaffer	.05
556	Ozzie Smith	1.00
557	Mark Sweeney	.05
558	Allen Watson	.05
559	Andy Ashby	.05
560	Brad Ausmus	.05
561	Willie Blair	.05
562	Ken Caminiti	.05
563	Andujar Cedeno	.05
564	Glenn Dishman	.05
565	Steve Finley	.05
566	Bryce Florie	.05
567	Tony Gwynn	1.00
568	Joey Hamilton	.05
569	Dustin Hermanson	.05
570	Trevor Hoffman	.05
571	Brian Johnson	.05
572	Marc Kroon	.05
573	Scott Livingstone	.05
574	Marc Newfield	.05
575	Melvin Nieves	.05
576	Jody Reed	.05
577	Bip Roberts	.05
578	Scott Sanders	.05
579	Fernando Valenzuela	.05
580	Eddie Williams	.05
581	Rod Beck	.05
582	Marvin Benard RC	.10
583	Barry Bonds	2.50
584	Jamie Brewington	.05
585	Mark Carreon	.05
586	Royce Clayton	.05
587	Shawn Estes	.05
588	Glenallen Hill	.05
589	Mark Leiter	.05
590	Kirt Manwaring	.05
591	David McCarty	.05
592	Terry Mulholland	.05
593	John Patterson	.05
594	J.R. Phillips	.05
595	Deion Sanders	.05
596	Steve Scarsone	.05
597	Robby Thompson	.05
598	Sergio Valdez	.05
599	William Van Landingham	.05
600	Matt Williams	.05

Tiffany

While Fleer's basic card set for 1996 feature matte-surface cards, a glossy version of each regular card was also issued as a parallel insert set. Other than the UV coat...

ing on front and back and the use of silver- rather than gold-foil typography on front, the cards are identical to the regular '96 Fleer player cards. One glossy version card is found in each pack.

	NM/M
Complete Set (600):	100.00
Common Player:	.15
Stars:	2X

Checklists

Checklist cards are treated as an insert set in 1996 Fleer, appearing on average once every six packs. Like all other Fleer hobby inserts in the baseball set, the checklists are UV-coated front and back, in contrast to the matte-finish regular issue cards. Checklists have borderless game-action photos on front, with gold-foil typography. Backs have a large Fleer logo and checklist data on a white background.

		NM/M
Complete Set (10):		5.00
Common Player:		.25
1	Barry Bonds	2.00
2	Ken Griffey Jr.	1.00
3	Chipper Jones	.75
4	Greg Maddux	.75
5	Mike Piazza	1.00
6	Manny Ramirez	.60
7	Cal Ripken Jr.	2.00
8	Frank Thomas	.60
9	Mo Vaughn	.25
10	Matt Williams	.25

Golden Memories

Some of the 1995 season's greatest moments are captured in this insert set, a one per 10 pack pick. Fronts have two photos of the player, one in full color in the foreground and one in monochrome as a backdrop. Typography is in prismatic foil vertically down one side. Backs have another player photo, along with details of the milestone. Two of the cards feature multiple players.

	NM/M
Complete Set (10):	6.00

		NM/M
Common Player:		.10
1	Albert Belle	.10
2	Barry Bonds,	
	Sammy Sosa	1.50
3	Greg Maddux	1.00
4	Edgar Martinez	.10
5	Ramon Martinez	.10
6	Mark McGwire	1.50
7	Eddie Murray	.75
8	Cal Ripken Jr.	2.00
9	Frank Thomas	.75
10	Alan Trammell,	
	Lou Whitaker	.15

Lumber Company

Once again for 1996, a Fleer "Lumber Company" chase set honors the game's top sluggers. The '96 version has a horizontal format with a rather small player action photo on a background resembling the trademark area of a bat. The "trademark" is actually the player and team name along with the "Lumber Company" ID, printed in textured glossy black ink. Backs repeat the trademark motif and also include a close-up player photo and a few words about his power-hitting numbers. Lumber Company cards are a one per nine pack pick, on average, found only in retail packs.

		NM/M
Complete Set (12):		12.50
Common Player:		.50
1	Albert Belle	.50
2	Dante Bichette	.50
3	Barry Bonds	3.00
4	Ken Griffey Jr.	1.50
5	Mark McGwire	2.00
6	Mike Piazza	1.50
7	Manny Ramirez	1.00
8	Tim Salmon	.60
9	Sammy Sosa	1.25
10	Frank Thomas	1.00
11	Mo Vaughn	.50
12	Matt Williams	.50

Post-Season Glory

Highlights of the 1995 postseason are featured in this small chase card set. Against a stadium background are multiple photos of the featured player, arranged horizontally. The vertical backs have another player photo down one side, and a description of his playoff performance on the other. Stated odds of picking one of these cards are one per five packs.

		NM/M
Complete Set (5):		1.50
Common Player:		.15
1	Tom Glavine	.25
2	Ken Griffey Jr.	1.00
3	Orel Hershiser	.15
4	Randy Johnson	.50
5	Jim Thome	.50

Prospects

Some of the 1995 season's greatest moments are captured in

	NM/M
Complete Set (10):	6.00

Minor leaguers who are expected to make it big in the big time are featured in this insert issue. Fronts feature large portrait photos against pastel backgrounds with player and set ID in prismatic foil. Backs have an action photo and repeat the front background color in a box which details the player's potential and career to date. Average odds of finding a Prospects card are one per six packs.

		NM/M
Complete Set (10):		1.00
Common Player:		.15
1	Yamil Benitez	.15
2	Roger Cedeno	.15
3	Tony Clark	.15
4	Micah Franklin	.15
5	Karim Garcia	.30
6	Todd Greene	.15
7	Alex Ochoa	.15
8	Ruben Rivera	.15
9	Chris Snopek	.15
10	Shannon Stewart	.15

Road Warriors

A black-and-white country highway photo is the background for the color player action photo on this insert set. Front typography is in silver foil. The players featured are those whose performance on the road is considered outstanding. Backs have a white background, portrait photo and stats bearing out the away-game superiority. These inserts are found at an average pace of one per 13 packs.

		NM/M
Complete Set (10):		9.00
Common Player:		.40
1	Derek Bell	.40
2	Tony Gwynn	1.25
3	Greg Maddux	1.25
4	Mark McGwire	2.50
5	Mike Piazza	2.00
6	Manny Ramirez	1.00
7	Tim Salmon	.50
8	Frank Thomas	1.00
9	Mo Vaughn	.50
10	Matt Williams	.40

Rookie Sensations

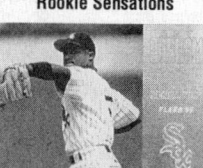

Top rookies of the 1995 season are featured on this chase card set. Horizontally formatted, the cards have an action photo on one side and a large prismatic-foil end strip which displays the player name, team logo and card company identifiers. Backs have a portrait photo on a white background with a few sentences about the player's rookie season. Stated odds of finding one of these inserts is one per 11 packs, on average.

		NM/M
Complete Set (15):		5.00
Common Player:		.25
1	Garret Anderson	.40
2	Marty Cordova	.25
3	Johnny Damon	1.00
4	Ray Durham	.25
5	Carl Everett	.25
6	Shawn Green	.50
7	Brian Hunter	.25
8	Jason Isringhausen	.25
9	Charles Johnson	.25

10	Chipper Jones	2.00
11	John Mabry	.25
12	Hideo Nomo	.50
13	Troy Percival	.25
14	Andy Pettitte	.50
15	Quilvio Veras	.25

Smoke 'N Heat

Once more using the "Smoke 'N Heat" identifier for a chase set of the game's hardest throwers, Fleer presents these select pitchers in action photos against a black-and-flame background. Front typography is in gold foil. Backs have a large portrait photo, repeat the flame motif as background and have a description of the pitcher's prowess in a black box. The cards are found, on average, once per nine packs.

		NM/M
Complete Set (10):		4.00
Common Player:		.15
1	Kevin Appier	.15
2	Roger Clemens	1.50
3	David Cone	.15
4	Chuck Finley	.15
5	Randy Johnson	.75
6	Greg Maddux	1.00
7	Pedro Martinez	.75
8	Hideo Nomo	.50
9	John Smoltz	.30
10	Todd Stottlemyre	.15

Team Leaders

One player from each club has been selected for inclusion in the "Team Leaders" chase set. Fronts have action player photos on a background of metallic foil littered with multiple representations of the team logo. Gold-foil lettering identifies the player, team and chase set. Backs have a white background, portrait photo and description of the player's leadership role. Stated rate of insertion for this set is one card per nine packs, on average, found only in hobby packs.

		NM/M
Complete Set (28):		30.00
Common Player:		.50
1	Cal Ripken Jr.	6.00
2	Mo Vaughn	.50
3	Jim Edmonds	1.00
4	Frank Thomas	2.00
5	Kenny Lofton	.50
6	Travis Fryman	.50
7	Gary Gaetti	.50
8	B.J. Surhoff	.50
9	Kirby Puckett	2.50
10	Don Mattingly	3.00
11	Mark McGwire	4.00
12	Ken Griffey Jr.	3.00
13	Juan Gonzalez	1.00
14	Joe Carter	.50
15	Greg Maddux	2.50
16	Sammy Sosa	3.00
17	Barry Larkin	.50
18	Dante Bichette	.50
19	Jeff Conine	.50
20	Jeff Bagwell	2.00
21	Mike Piazza	3.00

22	Rondell White	.50
23	Rico Brogna	.50
24	Darren Daulton	.50
25	Jeff King	.50
26	Ray Lankford	.50
27	Tony Gwynn	2.50
28	Barry Bonds	6.00

Tomorrow's Legends

In this insert set the projected stars of tomorrow are featured in action poses on a busy multi-colored, quartered background of baseball symbols and the globe. Typography is in silver foil. Backs have a portrait photo and large team logo along with an early-career summary. Odds of finding a "Tomorrow's Legends" card are posted at one per 13 packs, on average.

		NM/M
Complete Set (10):		3.50
Common Player:		.25
1	Garret Anderson	.25
2	Jim Edmonds	.50
3	Brian Hunter	.25
4	Jason Isringhausen	.25
5	Charles Johnson	.25
6	Chipper Jones	2.00
7	Ryan Klesko	.25
8	Hideo Nomo	1.00
9	Manny Ramirez	1.50
10	Rondell White	.25

Zone

The toughest pull (one in 90 packs, average) among the '96 Fleer chase cards is this set evoking the "zone" that the game's great players seek in which their performance is at its peak. The cards have action photos with a background of prismatic foil. Backs are conventionally printed but simulate the foil background and include a player portrait photo plus quotes about the player.

		NM/M
Complete Set (12):		20.00
Common Player:		.75
1	Albert Belle	.75
2	Barry Bonds	6.00
3	Ken Griffey Jr.	4.00
4	Tony Gwynn	3.00
5	Randy Johnson	2.00
6	Kenny Lofton	.75
7	Greg Maddux	3.00
8	Edgar Martinez	.75
9	Mike Piazza	4.00
10	Frank Thomas	2.00
11	Mo Vaughn	.75
12	Matt Williams	.75

Update

Fleer Update Baseball has 250 cards, including more than 55 rookies, plus traded players and free agents in their new uniforms, 35 Encore subset cards and five checklists. Each card in the regular-issue set also has a parallel "Tiffany Collection" version, which has UV coating and holographic foil stamp-

---

ing in contrast to the matte finish and gold foil of the regular cards. Insert cards include Diamond Tribute, New Horizons, Smooth Leather and Soaring Stars. Each pack also contains a Fleer "Thanks a Million" scratch-off game card, redeemable for prizes. Cards are numbered with a "U" prefix.

		NM/M
Complete Set (250):		12.00
Common Player:		.05
Complete Tiffany Set (250):		40.00
Tiffany Stars:		2X
Pack (11):		1.00
Wax Box (24):		15.00
1	Roberto Alomar	.10
2	Mike Devereaux	.05
3	Scott McClain RC	.05
4	Roger McDowell	.05
5	Kent Mercker	.05
6	Jimmy Myers	.05
7	Randy Myers	.05
8	B.J. Surhoff	.05
9	Tony Tarasco	.05
10	David Wells	.05
11	Wil Cordero	.05
12	Tom Gordon	.05
13	Reggie Jefferson	.05
14	Jose Malave	.05
15	Kevin Mitchell	.05
16	Jamie Moyer	.05
17	Heathcliff Slocumb	.05
18	Mike Stanley	.05
19	George Arias	.05
20	Jorge Fabregas	.05
21	Don Slaught	.05
22	Randy Velarde	.05
23	Harold Baines	.05
24	Mike Cameron RC	.75
25	Darren Lewis	.05
26	Tony Phillips	.05
27	Bill Simas	.05
28	Chris Snopek	.05
29	Kevin Tapani	.05
30	Danny Tartabull	.05
31	Julio Franco	.05
32	Jack McDowell	.05
33	Kimera Bartee	.05
34	Mark Lewis	.05
35	Melvin Nieves	.05
36	Mark Parent	.05
37	Eddie Williams	.05
38	Tim Belcher	.05
39	Sal Fasano	.05
40	Chris Haney	.05
41	Mike Macfarlane	.05
42	Jose Offerman	.05
43	Joe Randa	.05
44	Bip Roberts	.05
45	Chuck Carr	.05
46	Bobby Hughes	.05
47	Graeme Lloyd	.05
48	Ben McDonald	.05
49	Kevin Wickander	.05
50	Rick Aguilera	.05
51	Mike Durant	.05
52	Chip Hale	.05
53	LaTroy Hawkins	.05
54	Dave Hollins	.05
55	Roberto Kelly	.05
56	Paul Molitor	.75
57	Dan Naulty RC	.05
58	Mariano Duncan	.05
59	Andy Fox RC	.05
60	Joe Girardi	.05
61	Dwight Gooden	.05
62	Jimmy Key	.05
63	Matt Luke RC	.05
64	Tino Martinez	.05
65	Jeff Nelson	.05
66	Tim Raines	.05
67	Ruben Rivera	.05
68	Kenny Rogers	.05
69	Gerald Williams	.05
70	Tony Batista RC	.50
71	Allen Battle	.05
72	Jim Corsi	.05
73	Steve Cox	.05
74	Pedro Munoz	.05
75	Phil Plantier	.05
76	Scott Spiezio	.05
77	Ernie Young	.05
78	Russ Davis	.05
79	Sterling Hitchcock	.05
80	Edwin Hurtado	.05

81	Raul Ibanez RC	.05
82	Mike Jackson	.05
83	Ricky Jordan	.05
84	Paul Sorrento	.05
85	Doug Strange	.05
86	Mark Brandenburg	.05
87	Damon Buford	.05
88	Kevin Elster	.05
89	Darryl Hamilton	.05
90	Ken Hill	.05
91	Ed Vosberg	.05
92	Craig Worthington	.05
93	Tilson Brito	.05
94	Giovanni Carrara	.05
95	Felipe Crespo	.05
96	Erik Hanson	.05
97	Marty Janzen RC	.05
98	Otis Nixon	.05
99	Charlie O'Brien	.05
100	Robert Perez	.05
101	Paul Quantrill	.05
102	Bill Risley	.05
103	Juan Samuel	.05
104	Jermaine Dye	.05
105	Wonderful Monds	.05
106	Dwight Smith	.05
107	Jerome Walton	.05
108	Terry Adams	.05
109	Leo Gomez	.05
110	Robin Jennings RC	.05
111	Doug Jones	.05
112	Brooks Kieschnick	.05
113	Dave Magadan	.05
114	Jason Maxwell RC	.05
115	Rodney Myers	.05
116	Eric Anthony	.05
117	Vince Coleman	.05
118	Eric Davis	.05
119	Steve Gibralter	.05
120	Curtis Goodwin	.05
121	Willie Greene	.05
122	Mike Kelly	.05
123	Marcus Moore	.05
124	Chad Mottola	.05
125	Chris Sabo	.05
126	Roger Salkeld	.05
127	Pedro Castellano	.05
128	Trenidad Hubbard	.05
129	Jayhawk Owens	.05
130	Jeff Reed	.05
131	Kevin Brown	.05
132	Al Leiter	.05
133	Matt Mantei RC	.05
134	Dave Weathers	.05
135	Devon White	.05
136	Bob Abreu	.05
137	Sean Berry	.05
138	Doug Brocail	.05
139	Richard Hidalgo	.05
140	Alvin Morman	.05
141	Mike Blowers	.05
142	Roger Cedeno	.05
143	Greg Gagne	.05
144	Karim Garcia	.10
145	Wilton Guerrero RC	.05
146	Israel Alcantara RC	.05
147	Omar Daal	.05
148	Ryan McGuire	.05
149	Sherman Obando	.05
150	Jose Paniagua	.05
151	Henry Rodriguez	.05
152	Andy Stankiewicz	.05
153	Dave Veres	.05
154	Juan Acevedo	.05
155	Mark Clark	.05
156	Bernard Gilkey	.05
157	Pete Harnisch	.05
158	Lance Johnson	.05
159	Brent Mayne	.05
160	Rey Ordonez	.05
161	Kevin Roberson	.05
162	Paul Wilson	.05
163	David Doster RC	.05
164	Mike Grace RC	.05
165	Rich Hunter RC	.05
166	Pete Incaviglia	.05
167	Mike Lieberthal	.05
168	Terry Mulholland	.05
169	Ken Ryan	.05
170	Benito Santiago	.05
171	Kevin Sefcik RC	.05
172	Lee Tinsley	.05
173	Todd Zeile	.05
174	Francisco Cordova RC	.05
175	Danny Darwin	.05
176	Charlie Hayes	.05
177	Jason Kendall	.05
178	Mike Kingery	.05
179	Jon Lieber	.05
180	Zane Smith	.05
181	Luis Alicea	.05
182	Cory Bailey	.05
183	Andy Benes	.05
184	Pat Borders	.05
185	Mike Busby RC	.05
186	Royce Clayton	.05
187	Dennis Eckersley	.65
188	Gary Gaetti	.05
189	Ron Gant	.05
190	Aaron Holbert	.05
191	Willie McGee	.05
192	Miguel Mejia RC	.05
193	Jeff Parrett	.05
194	Todd Stottlemyre	.05
195	Sean Bergman	.05
196	Archi Cianfrocco	.05
197	Rickey Henderson	.75
198	Wally Joyner	.05
199	Craig Shipley	.05
200	Bob Tewksbury	.05
201	Tim Worrell	.05
202	Rich Aurilia RC	.05
203	Doug Creek	.05
204	Shawon Dunston	.05
205	Osvaldo Fernandez RC	.05
206	Mark Gardner	.05
207	Stan Javier	.05
208	Marcus Jensen	.05
209	Chris Singleton RC	.05
210	Allen Watson	.05
211	Jeff Bagwell (Encore)	.75
212	Derek Bell (Encore)	.05
213	Albert Belle (Encore)	.05
214	Wade Boggs (Encore)	1.00
215	Barry Bonds (Encore)	2.00
216	Jose Canseco (Encore)	.50
217	Marty Cordova (Encore)	.05
218	Jim Edmonds (Encore)	.05
219	Cecil Fielder (Encore)	.05
220	Andres Galarraga (Encore)	.05
221	Juan Gonzalez (Encore)	.65
222	Mark Grace (Encore)	.10
223	Ken Griffey Jr. (Encore)	1.50
224	Tony Gwynn (Encore)	1.00
225	Jason Isringhausen (Encore)	.05
226	Derek Jeter (Encore)	2.00
227	Randy Johnson (Encore)	.75
228	Chipper Jones (Encore)	1.00
229	Ryan Klesko (Encore)	.05
230	Barry Larkin (Encore)	.05
231	Kenny Lofton (Encore)	.05
232	Greg Maddux (Encore)	1.00
233	Raul Mondesi (Encore)	.05
234	Hideo Nomo (Encore)	.65
235	Mike Piazza (Encore)	1.50
236	Manny Ramirez (Encore)	.05
237	Cal Ripken Jr. (Encore)	2.00
238	Tim Salmon (Encore)	.10
239	Ryne Sandberg (Encore)	1.00
240	Reggie Sanders (Encore)	.05
241	Gary Sheffield (Encore)	.30
242	Sammy Sosa (Encore)	1.25
243	Frank Thomas (Encore)	.75
244	Mo Vaughn (Encore)	.05
245	Matt Williams (Encore)	.05
246	Checklist	.05
247	Checklist	.05
248	Checklist	.05
249	Checklist	.05
250	Checklist	.05

Update Tiffany

	NM/M
Complete Set (250):	45.00
Common Player:	.15
Glossy Stars:	2X

Update Diamond Tribute

These insert cards are the most difficult to pull from 1996 Fleer Update packs; they are seeded one per every 100 packs. The 10-card set features cards of future Hall of Famers on stock utilizing two different holographic foils and a diamond design, similar to the "Zone" insert cards in Fleer Baseball.

		NM/M
Complete Set (10):		50.00
Common Player:		4.00
1	Wade Boggs	6.00
2	Barry Bonds	10.00
3	Ken Griffey Jr.	7.50
4	Tony Gwynn	6.00
5	Rickey Henderson	4.00
6	Greg Maddux	6.00
7	Eddie Murray	4.00
8	Cal Ripken Jr.	10.00
9	Ozzie Smith	6.00
10	Frank Thomas	5.00

Update Headliners

These 20 cards feature newsmakers from 1996. The cards were random inserts in 1996 Fleer Update packs, one per every five retail packs.

		NM/M
Complete Set (20):		20.00
Common Player:		.25
1	Roberto Alomar	.50
2	Jeff Bagwell	1.00
3	Albert Belle	.25
4	Barry Bonds	3.50
5	Cecil Fielder	.25
6	Juan Gonzalez	.75
7	Ken Griffey Jr.	2.25
8	Tony Gwynn	1.50
9	Randy Johnson	1.00
10	Chipper Jones	1.50
11	Ryan Klesko	.25
12	Kenny Lofton	.25
13	Greg Maddux	1.50
14	Hideo Nomo	.75
15	Mike Piazza	2.25
16	Manny Ramirez	1.00
17	Cal Ripken Jr.	3.50
18	Tim Salmon	.40
19	Frank Thomas	1.00
20	Matt Williams	.25

Update New Horizons

These 1996 Fleer Update inserts feature 20 promising youngsters with bright futures in the majors. The cards were seeded one per every five hobby packs.

		NM/M
Complete Set (20):		2.00
Common Player:		.25
1	Bob Abreu	.45
2	George Arias	.25
3	Tony Batista	.25
4	Steve Cox	.25
5	David Doster	.25
6	Jermaine Dye	.25
7	Andy Fox	.25
8	Mike Grace	.25
9	Todd Greene	.25
10	Wilton Guerrero	.25
11	Richard Hidalgo	.25
12	Raul Ibanez	.25
13	Robin Jennings	.25
14	Marcus Jensen	.25
15	Jason Kendall	.35
16	Brooks Kieschnick	.25
17	Ryan McGuire	.25
18	Miguel Mejia	.25
19	Rey Ordonez	.25
20	Paul Wilson	.25

Update Smooth Leather

Ten of the game's top fielders are showcased on these 1996 Fleer Update insert cards. The cards were seeded one per every five packs.

		NM/M
Complete Set (10):		7.00
Common Player:		.40
1	Roberto Alomar	.50
1p	Roberto Alomar (Promo)	2.00
2	Barry Bonds	2.50
3	Will Clark	.45
4	Ken Griffey Jr.	1.75
5	Kenny Lofton	.40
6	Greg Maddux	1.00
7	Raul Mondesi	.40
8	Rey Ordonez	.40
9	Cal Ripken Jr.	2.50
9p	Cal Ripken Jr. (Promo)	6.00
10	Matt Williams	.40

Update Soaring Stars

Ten of the game's top players are spotlighted on these 1996 Fleer Update inserts. The cards were seeded one per every 11 packs.

		NM/M
Complete Set (10):		6.00
Common Player:		.25
1	Jeff Bagwell	.75
2	Barry Bonds	2.00
3	Juan Gonzalez	.75
4	Ken Griffey Jr.	1.50
5	Chipper Jones	1.00
6	Greg Maddux	1.00
7	Mike Piazza	1.50
8	Manny Ramirez	.75
9	Frank Thomas	.75
10	Matt Williams	.25

Baseball '96

For a second consecutive year Fleer issued a special version of its Cleveland Indians cards for sale at Revco stores and Jacobs Field. Sold in 10-card packs with a suggested retail price of $1.49, the Revco version Indians team set differs from the regular Fleer cards in the application of UV coating on front and back, the use of silver-rather than gold-foil highlights and the numbering "X of 20." Following up on the Indians team-set issue, Fleer also issued 20-card sets for several other teams, distributed regionally. They were also sold in 10-card packs ($1.99 SRP) and feature UV coating, silver-foil graphics and special numbering. Some cards were updated and feature new photos reflecting trades, free agent signings, etc.

		NM/M
Complete Set (180):		27.00
Common Player:		.09
Atlanta Braves Team Set:		4.00
1	Steve Avery	.10
2	Jeff Blauser	.10
3	Brad Clontz	.10
4	Tom Glavine	.35
5	Marquis Grissom	.10
6	Chipper Jones	1.25
7	David Justice	.10
8	Ryan Klesko	.10
9	Mark Lemke	.10
10	Javier Lopez	.10
11	Greg Maddux	1.25
12	Fred McGriff	.10
13	Greg McMichael	.10
14	Eddie Perez	.10
15	Jason Schmidt	.10
16	John Smoltz	.10
17	Terrell Wade	.10
18	Mark Wohlers	.10
19	Logo Card	.10
20	Checklist	.10
Baltimore Orioles Team Set:		5.00
1	Roberto Alomar	.20
2	Brady Anderson	.10
3	Armando Benitez	.10
4	Bobby Bonilla	.10
5	Scott Erickson	.10
6	Jeffrey Hammonds	.10
7	Jimmy Haynes	.10
8	Chris Hoiles	.10
9	Rick Krivda	.10
10	Kent Mercker	.10
11	Mike Mussina	.45
12	Randy Myers	.10
13	Jesse Orosco	.10
14	Rafael Palmeiro	.75
15	Cal Ripken Jr.	2.50
16	B.J. Surhoff	.10
17	Tony Tarasco	.10
18	David Wells	.10
19	Logo Card	.10
20	Checklist	.10
Boston Red Sox Team Set:		3.00
1	Stan Belinda	.10
2	Jose Canseco	.50
3	Roger Clemens	2.00
4	Wil Cordero	.10
5	Vaughn Eshelman	.10
6	Tom Gordon	.10
7	Mike Greenwell	.10
8	Dwayne Hosey	.10
9	Kevin Mitchell	.10
10	Tim Naehring	.10
11	Troy O'Leary	.10
12	Aaron Sele	.10
13	Heathcliff Slocumb	.10
14	Mike Stanley	.10
15	Jeff Suppan	.10
16	John Valentin	.10
17	Mo Vaughn	.10
18	Tim Wakefield	.10
19	Logo Card	.10
20	Checklist	.10
Chicago Cubs Team Set:		4.00
1	Terry Adams	.10
2	Jim Bullinger	.10
3	Frank Castillo	.10
4	Kevin Foster	.10
5	Leo Gomez	.10
6	Luis Gonzalez	.20
7	Mark Grace	.15
8	Jose Hernandez	.10
9	Robin Jennings RC	.10
10	Doug Jones	.10
11	Brooks Kieschnick	.10
12	Brian McRae	.10
13	Jaime Navarro	.10
14	Rey Sanchez	.10
15	Ryne Sandberg	1.25
16	Scott Servais	.10
17	Sammy Sosa	1.50
18	Steve Trachsel	.10
19	Logo Card	.10
20	Checklist	.10
Chicago White Sox Team Set:		4.00
1	Wilson Alvarez	.10
2	Harold Baines	.10
3	Jason Bere	.10
4	Ray Durham	.10
5	Alex Fernandez	.10
6	Ozzie Guillen	.10
7	Roberto Hernandez	.10
8	Matt Karchner	.10
9	Ron Karkovice	.10
10	Darren Lewis	.10
11	Dave Martinez	.10
12	Lyle Mouton	.10
13	Tony Phillips	.10
14	Chris Snopek	.10
15	Kevin Tapani	.10
16	Danny Tartabull	.10
17	Frank Thomas	1.00
18	Robin Ventura	.10
19	Logo Card	.10
20	Checklist	.10
Cleveland Indians Team Set:		4.00
1	Sandy Alomar Jr.	.10
2	Paul Assenmacher	.10
3	Carlos Baerga	.10
4	Albert Belle	.09
5	Orel Hershiser	.10
6	Kenny Lofton	.10
7	Dennis Martinez	.10
8	Jose Mesa	.10
9	Eddie Murray	1.00
10	Charles Nagy	.10
11	Tony Pena	.10
12	Herb Perry	.10
13	Eric Plunk	.10
14	Jim Poole	.10
15	Manny Ramirez	1.00
16	Julian Tavarez	.10
17	Jim Thome	.75
18	Omar Vizquel	.10
19	Logo Card	.10
20	Checklist	.10
Colorado Rockies Team Set:		2.75
1	Jason Bates	.10
2	Dante Bichette	.10
3	Ellis Burks	.10
4	Vinny Castilla	.10
5	Andres Galarraga	.10
6	Darren Holmes	.10
7	Curt Leskanic	.10
8	Quinton McCracken	.10
9	Mike Munoz	.10
10	Jayhawk Owens	.10
11	Steve Reed	.10
12	Kevin Ritz	.10
13	Bret Saberhagen	.10
14	Bill Swift	.10
15	John Vander Wal	.10
16	Larry Walker	.10
17	Walt Weiss	.10
18	Eric Young	.10
19	Logo Card	.10
20	Checklist	.10
L.A. Dodgers Team Set:		4.00
1	Mike Blowers	.10
2	Brett Butler	.10
3	Tom Candiotti	.10
4	Roger Cedeno	.10
5	Delino DeShields	.10
6	Chad Fonville	.10
7	Greg Gagne	.10
8	Karim Garcia	.15
9	Todd Hollandsworth	.10
10	Eric Karros	.10
11	Ramon Martinez	.10
12	Raul Mondesi	.10
13	Hideo Nomo	.75
14	Antonio Osuna	.10
15	Chan Ho Park	.10
16	Mike Piazza	2.00
17	Ismael Valdes	.10
18	Todd Worrell	.10
19	Logo Card	.10
20	Checklist	.10
Texas Rangers Team Set:		2.75
1	Mark Brandenburg	.10
2	Damon Buford	.10
3	Will Clark	.10
4	Kevin Elster	.10
5	Benji Gil	.10
6	Juan Gonzalez	.75
7	Rusty Greer	.10
8	Kevin Gross	.10
9	Darryl Hamilton	.10
10	Ken Hill	.10
11	Mark McLemore	.10
12	Dean Palmer	.10
13	Roger Pavlik	.10
14	Ivan Rodriguez	.75
15	Mickey Tettleton	.10
16	Dave Valle	.10
17	Ed Vosberg	.10
18	Matt Whiteside	.10
19	Logo Card	.10
20	Checklist	.10

Panini Stickers

For the second year of distribution by Fleer/SkyBox, the annual baseball sticker set once again used Panini as the dominant brand identification. Printed in Italy, the stickers were sold in packs of six for 49 cents in the U.S., 69 cents in Canada. At 2-1/8" x 3", the basic player stickers have a green border around the color action photo; a second, ghosted, version of the photo appear in the background. Team logo and player ID are in a bar at bottom. Backs are printed in blue with the sticker number, Panini and licensor logos, along with copyright information. Team logo and special rookie stickers were printed on silver foil. A 60-page album was issued to house the set.

		NM/M
Complete Set (246):		4.00
Common Player:		.05
Album:		.75
1	David Justice	.05
2	Tom Glavine	.20
3	Javier Lopez	.05
4	Greg Maddux	.45
5	Marquis Grissom	.05
6	Braves Logo	.05
7	Ryan Klesko	.05
8	Chipper Jones	.45
9	Quilvio Veras	.05
10	Chris Hammond	.05
11	Charles Johnson	.05
12	John Burkett	.05
13	Marlins Logo	.05
14	Jeff Conine	.05
15	Gary Sheffield	.25
16	Greg Colbrunn	.05
17	Moises Alou	.05
18	Pedro J. Martinez	.35
19	Rondell White	.05
20	Tony Tarasco	.05
21	Expos Logo	.05
22	Carlos Perez	.05
23	David Segui	.05
24	Wil Cordero	.05
25	Jason Isringhausen	.05
26	Rico Brogna	.05
27	Edgardo Alfonzo	.05
28	Todd Hundley	.05
29	Mets Logo	.05
30	Bill Pulsipher	.05
31	Carl Everett	.05

#	Player	Price
32	Jose Vizcaino	.05
33	Lenny Dykstra	.05
34	Charlie Hayes	.05
35	Heathcliff Slocumb	.05
36	Darren Daulton	.05
37	Phillies Logo	.05
38	Mickey Morandini	.05
39	Gregg Jefferies	.05
40	Jim Eisenreich	.05
41	Brian McRae	.05
42	Luis Gonzalez	.10
43	Randy Myers	.05
44	Shawon Dunston	.05
45	Cubs Logo	.05
46	Jaime Navarro	.05
47	Mark Grace	.10
48	Sammy Sosa	.50
49	Barry Larkin	.05
50	Pete Schourek	.05
51	John Smiley	.05
52	Reggie Sanders	.05
53	Reds Logo	.05
54	Hal Morris	.05
55	Ron Gant	.05
56	Bret Boone	.05
57	Craig Biggio	.05
58	Brian L. Hunter	.05
59	Jeff Bagwell	.35
60	Shane Reynolds	.05
61	Astros Logo	.05
62	Derek Bell	.05
63	Doug Drabek	.05
64	Orlando Miller	.05
65	Jay Bell	.05
66	Dan Miceli	.05
67	Orlando Merced	.05
68	Jeff King	.05
69	Carlos Garcia	.05
70	Pirates Logo	.05
71	Al Martin	.05
72	Denny Neagle	.05
73	Ray Lankford	.05
74	Ozzie Smith	.45
75	Bernard Gilkey	.05
76	John Mabry	.05
77	Cardinals Logo	.05
78	Brian Jordan	.05
79	Scott Cooper	.05
80	Allen Watson	.05
81	Dante Bichette	.05
82	Bret Saberhagen	.05
83	Walt Weiss	.05
84	Andres Galarraga	.05
85	Rockies Logo	.05
86	Larry Walker	.05
87	Bill Swift	.05
88	Vinny Castilla	.05
89	Raul Mondesi	.05
90	Roger Cedeno	.05
91	Chad Fonville	.05
92	Hideo Nomo	.30
93	Dodgers Logo	.05
94	Ramon Martinez	.05
95	Mike Piazza	.60
96	Eric Karros	.05
97	Tony Gwynn	.45
98	Brad Ausmus	.05
99	Trevor Hoffman	.05
100	Ken Caminiti	.05
101	Padres Logo	.05
102	Andy Ashby	.05
103	Steve Finley	.05
104	Joey Hamilton	.05
105	Matt Williams	.05
106	Rod Beck	.05
107	Barry Bonds	.75
108	William Van Landingham	.05
109	Giants Logo	.05
110	Deion Sanders	.05
111	Royce Clayton	.05
112	Glenallen Hill	.05
113	Tony Gwynn (League Leader - BA)	.20
114	Dante Bichette (League Leader - HR)	.05
115	Dante Bichette (League Leader - RBI)	.05
116	Quilvio Veras (League Leader - SB)	.05
117	Hideo Nomo (League Leader - K)	.15
118	Greg Maddux (League Leader - W)	.20
119	Randy Myers (League Leader - Saves)	.05
120	Edgar Martinez (League Leader - BA)	.05
121	Albert Belle (League Leader - HR)	.05
122	Mo Vaughn (League Leader - RBI)	.05
123	Kenny Lofton (League Leader - SB)	.05
124	Randy Johnson (League Leader - K)	.15
125	Mike Mussina (League Leader - W)	.10
126	Jose Mesa (League Leader - Saves)	.05
127	Mike Mussina	.20
128	Cal Ripken Jr.	.75
129	Rafael Palmeiro	.30
130	Ben McDonald	.05
131	Orioles Logo	.05
132	Chris Hoiles	.05
133	Bobby Bonilla	.05
134	Brady Anderson	.05
135	Jose Canseco	.20
136	Roger Clemens	.50
137	Mo Vaughn	.05
138	Mike Greenwell	.05
139	Red Sox Logo	.05
140	Tim Wakefield	.05
141	John Valentin	.05
142	Tim Naehring	.05
143	Travis Fryman	.05
144	Chad Curtis	.05
145	Felipe Lira	.05
146	Cecil Fielder	.05
147	Tigers Logo	.05
148	John Flaherty	.05
149	Chris Gomez	.05
150	Sean Bergman	.05
151	Don Mattingly	.50
152	Andy Pettitte	.15
153	Wade Boggs	.45
154	Paul O'Neill	.05
155	Yankees Logo	.05
156	Bernie Williams	.10
157	Jack McDowell	.05
158	David Cone	.05
159	Roberto Alomar	.35
160	Paul Molitor	.35
161	Shawn Green	.15
162	Joe Carter	.05
163	Blue Jays Logo	.05
164	Alex Gonzalez	.05
165	Al Leiter	.05
166	John Olerud	.05
167	Alex Fernandez	.05
168	Ray Durham	.05
169	Lance Johnson	.05
170	Ozzie Guillen	.05
171	White Sox Logo	.05
172	Robin Ventura	.05
173	Frank Thomas	.35
174	Tim Raines	.05
175	Albert Belle	.05
176	Manny Ramirez	.35
177	Eddie Murray	.35
178	Orel Hershiser	.05
179	Indians Logo	.05
180	Kenny Lofton	.05
181	Carlos Baerga	.05
182	Jose Mesa	.05
183	Gary Gaetti	.05
184	Tom Goodwin	.05
185	Kevin Appier	.05
186	Jon Nunnally	.05
187	Royals Logo	.05
188	Wally Joyner	.05
189	Jeff Montgomery	.05
190	Johnny Damon	.25
191	B.J. Surhoff	.05
192	Ricky Bones	.05
193	John Jaha	.05
194	Dave Nilsson	.05
195	Brewers Logo	.05
196	Greg Vaughn	.05
197	Kevin Seitzer	.05
198	Joe Oliver	.05
199	Chuck Knoblauch	.05
200	Kirby Puckett	.45
201	Marty Cordova	.05
202	Pat Meares	.05
203	Twins Logo	.05
204	Scott Stahoviak	.05
205	Matt Walbeck	.05
206	Pedro Munoz	.05
207	Garret Anderson	.05
208	Chili Davis	.05
209	Tim Salmon	.10
210	J.T. Snow	.05
211	Angels Logo	.05
212	Jim Edmonds	.05
213	Chuck Finley	.05
214	Mark Langston	.05
215	Dennis Eckersley	.30
216	Todd Stottlemyre	.05
217	Geronimo Berroa	.05
218	Mark McGwire	.65
219	A's Logo	.05
220	Brent Gates	.05
221	Terry Steinbach	.05
222	Rickey Henderson	.35
223	Ken Griffey Jr.	.60
224	Alex Rodriguez	.65
225	Tino Martinez	.05
226	Randy Johnson	.35
227	Mariners Logo	.05
228	Jay Buhner	.05
229	Vince Coleman	.05
230	Edgar Martinez	.05
231	Will Clark	.10
232	Juan Gonzalez	.35
233	Kenny Rogers	.05
234	Ivan Rodriguez	.30
235	Rangers Logo	.05
236	Mickey Tettleton	.05
237	Dean Palmer	.05
238	Otis Nixon	.05
239	Hideo Nomo (Rookie)	.20
240	Quilvio Veras (Rookie)	.05
241	Jason Isringhausen (Rookie)	.05
242	Andy Pettitte (Rookie)	.05
243	Chipper Jones (Rookie)	.25
244	Garret Anderson (Rookie)	.05
245	Charles Johnson (Rookie)	.05
246	Marty Cordova (Rookie)	.05

issue Series 1 has 500 cards equipped with icons designating All-Stars, League Leaders and World Series cards. There were also 10 checklist cards in the regular-issue set, featuring stars on the front. Fleer arrived in 10-card packs and had a Tiffany Collection parallel set and six different insert sets, including Rookie Sensations, Golden Memories, Team Leaders, Night and Day, Zone and Lumber Company. Series 2 comprises 261 cards plus inserts Decade of Excellence, Bleacher Bashers, Diamond Tributes, Goudey Greats, Headliners, New Horizons and Soaring Stars.

	NM/M
Complete Set (761):	100.00
Complete Series 1 Set (500):	30.00
Complete Series 2 Set (261):	70.00
Common Player:	.05
Complete Tiffany Set (1-761):	500.00
Tiffany Stars/RC's:	8X
A. Jones Circa AU/200:	35.00
Series 2 Pack (10):	3.00
Series 2 Wax Box (36):	90.00

1997 Fleer

Fleer maintained its matte-finish coating for 1997 after it debuted in the 1996 product. The regular-

#	Player	Price
1	Roberto Alomar	.10
2	Brady Anderson	.05
3	Bobby Bonilla	.05
4	Rocky Coppinger	.05
5	Cesar Devarez	.05
6	Scott Erickson	.05
7	Jeffrey Hammonds	.05
8	Chris Hoiles	.05
9	Eddie Murray	.05
10	Mike Mussina	.40
11	Randy Myers	.05
12	Rafael Palmeiro	.75
13	Cal Ripken Jr.	2.50
14	B.J. Surhoff	.05
15	David Wells	.05
16	Todd Zeile	.05
17	Darren Bragg	.05
18	Jose Canseco	.40
19	Roger Clemens	1.75
20	Wil Cordero	.05
21	Jeff Frye	.05
22	Nomar Garciaparra	1.75
23	Tom Gordon	.05
24	Mike Greenwell	.05
25	Reggie Jefferson	.05
26	Jose Malave	.05
27	Tim Naehring	.05
28	Troy O'Leary	.05
29	Heathcliff Slocumb	.05
30	Mike Stanley	.05
31	John Valentin	.05
32	Mo Vaughn	.05
33	Tim Wakefield	.05
34	Garret Anderson	.05
35	George Arias	.05
36	Shawn Boskie	.05
37	Chili Davis	.05
38	Jason Dickson	.05
39	Gary DiSarcina	.05
40	Darin Erstad	.10
41	Jorge Fabregas	.05
42	Chuck Finley	.05
43	Todd Greene	.05
44	Mike Holtz RC	.05
45	Rex Hudler	.05
46	Mike James	.05
47	Mark Langston	.05
48	Mark Langston	.05
49	Troy Percival	.05
50	Tim Salmon	.15
51	Jeff Schmidt	.05
52	J.T. Snow	.05
53	Randy Velarde	.05
54	Wilson Alvarez	.05
55	Harold Baines	.05
56	James Baldwin	.05
57	Jason Bere	.05
58	Mike Cameron	.05
59	Ray Durham	.05
60	Alex Fernandez	.05
61	Ozzie Guillen	.05
62	Roberto Hernandez	.05
63	Ron Karkovice	.05
64	Darren Lewis	.05
65	Dave Martinez	.05
66	Lyle Mouton	.05
67	Greg Norton	.05
68	Tony Phillips	.05
69	Chris Snopek	.05
70	Kevin Tapani	.05
71	Danny Tartabull	.05
72	Frank Thomas	1.00
73	Robin Ventura	.05
74	Sandy Alomar Jr.	.05
75	Albert Belle	.05
76	Mark Carreon	.05
77	Julio Franco	.05
78	Brian Giles RC	1.00
79	Orel Hershiser	.05
80	Kenny Lofton	.05
81	Dennis Martinez	.05
82	Jack McDowell	.05
83	Jose Mesa	.05
84	Charles Nagy	.05
85	Chad Ogea	.05
86	Eric Plunk	.05
87	Manny Ramirez	1.00
88	Kevin Seitzer	.05
89	Julian Tavarez	.05
90	Jim Thome	.65
91	Jose Vizcaino	.05
92	Omar Vizquel	.05
93	Brad Ausmus	.05
94	Kimera Bartee	.05
95	Raul Casanova	.05
96	Tony Clark	.05
97	John Cummings	.05
98	Travis Fryman	.05
99	Bob Higginson	.05
100	Mark Lewis	.05
101	Felipe Lira	.05
102	Phil Nevin	.05
103	Melvin Nieves	.05
104	Curtis Pride	.05
105	A.J. Sager	.05
106	Ruben Sierra	.05
107	Justin Thompson	.05
108	Alan Trammell	.05
109	Kevin Appier	.05
110	Tim Belcher	.05
111	Jaime Bluma	.05
112	Johnny Damon	.35
113	Tom Goodwin	.05
114	Chris Haney	.05
115	Keith Lockhart	.05
116	Mike Macfarlane	.05
117	Jeff Montgomery	.05
118	Jose Offerman	.05
119	Craig Paquette	.05
120	Joe Randa	.05
121	Bip Roberts	.05
122	Jose Rosado	.05
123	Mike Sweeney	.05
124	Michael Tucker	.05
125	Jeremy Burnitz	.05
126	Jeff Cirillo	.05
127	Jeff D'Amico	.05
128	Mike Fetters	.05
129	John Jaha	.05
130	Scott Karl	.05
131	Jesse Levis	.05
132	Mark Loretta	.05
133	Mike Matheny	.05
134	Ben McDonald	.05
135	Matt Mieske	.05
136	Marc Newfield	.05
137	Dave Nilsson	.05
138	Jose Valentin	.05
139	Fernando Vina	.05
140	Bob Wickman	.05
141	Gerald Williams	.05
142	Rick Aguilera	.05
143	Rich Becker	.05
144	Ron Coomer	.05
145	Marty Cordova	.05
146	Roberto Kelly	.05
147	Chuck Knoblauch	.05
148	Matt Lawton	.05
149	Pat Meares	.05
150	Travis Miller	.05
151	Paul Molitor	1.00
152	Greg Myers	.05
153	Dan Naulty	.05
154	Kirby Puckett	1.50
155	Brad Radke	.05
156	Frank Rodriguez	.05
157	Scott Stahoviak	.05
158	Dave Stevens	.05
159	Matt Walbeck	.05
160	Todd Walker	.05
161	Wade Boggs	1.50
162	David Cone	.05
163	Mariano Duncan	.05
164	Cecil Fielder	.05
165	Joe Girardi	.05
166	Dwight Gooden	.05
167	Charlie Hayes	.05
168	Derek Jeter	2.50
169	Jimmy Key	.05
170	Jim Leyritz	.05
171	Tino Martinez	.05
172	Ramiro Mendoza RC	.10
173	Jeff Nelson	.05
174	Paul O'Neill	.05
175	Andy Pettitte	.35
176	Mariano Rivera	.15
177	Ruben Rivera	.05
178	Kenny Rogers	.05
179	Darryl Strawberry	.05
180	John Wetteland	.05
181	Bernie Williams	.10
182	Willie Adams	.05
183	Tony Batista	.05
184	Geronimo Berroa	.05
185	Mike Bordick	.05
186	Scott Brosius	.05
187	Bobby Chouinard	.05
188	Jim Corsi	.05
189	Brent Gates	.05
190	Jason Giambi	.50
191	Jose Herrera	.05
192	Damon Mashore RC	.05
193	Mark McGwire	2.25
194	Mike Mohler	.05
195	Scott Spiezio	.05
196	Terry Steinbach	.05
197	Bill Taylor	.05
198	John Wasdin	.05
199	Steve Wojciechowski	.05
200	Ernie Young	.05
201	Rich Amaral	.05
202	Jay Buhner	.05
203	Norm Charlton	.05
204	Joey Cora	.05
205	Russ Davis	.05
206	Ken Griffey Jr.	2.00
207	Sterling Hitchcock	.05
208	Brian Hunter	.05
209	Raul Ibanez	.05
210	Randy Johnson	1.00
211	Edgar Martinez	.05
212	Jamie Moyer	.05
213	Alex Rodriguez	2.25
214	Paul Sorrento	.05
215	Matt Wagner	.05
216	Bob Wells	.05
217	Dan Wilson	.05
218	Damon Buford	.05
219	Will Clark	.10
220	Kevin Elster	.05
221	Juan Gonzalez	.75
222	Rusty Greer	.05
223	Kevin Gross	.05
224	Darryl Hamilton	.05
225	Mike Henneman	.05
226	Ken Hill	.05
227	Mark McLemore	.05
228	Darren Oliver	.05
229	Dean Palmer	.05
230	Roger Pavlik	.05
231	Ivan Rodriguez	.75
232	Mickey Tettleton	.05
233	Bobby Witt	.05
234	Jacob Brumfield	.05
235	Joe Carter	.05
236	Tim Crabtree	.05
237	Carlos Delgado	.50
238	Huck Flener	.05
239	Alex Gonzalez	.05
240	Shawn Green	.20
241	Juan Guzman	.05
242	Pat Hentgen	.05
243	Marty Janzen	.05
244	Sandy Martinez	.05
245	Otis Nixon	.05
246	Charlie O'Brien	.05
247	John Olerud	.05
248	Robert Perez	.05
249	Ed Sprague	.05
250	Mike Timlin	.05
251	Steve Avery	.05
252	Jeff Blauser	.05
253	Brad Clontz	.05
254	Jermaine Dye	.05
255	Tom Glavine	.30
256	Marquis Grissom	.05
257	Andruw Jones	1.00
258	Chipper Jones	1.50
259	David Justice	.05
260	Ryan Klesko	.05
261	Mark Lemke	.05
262	Javier Lopez	.05
263	Greg Maddux	1.50
264	Fred McGriff	.05
265	Greg McMichael	.05
266	Denny Neagle	.05
267	Terry Pendleton	.05
268	Eddie Perez	.05
269	John Smoltz	.05
270	Terrell Wade	.05
271	Mark Wohlers	.05
272	Terry Adams	.05
273	Brant Brown	.05
274	Leo Gomez	.05
275	Luis Gonzalez	.10
276	Mark Grace	.10
277	Tyler Houston	.05
278	Robin Jennings	.05
279	Brooks Kieschnick	.05
280	Brian McRae	.05
281	Jaime Navarro	.05
282	Ryne Sandberg	1.50
283	Scott Servais	.05
284	Sammy Sosa	1.75
285	Dave Swartzbaugh RC	.05
286	Amaury Telemaco	.05
287	Steve Trachsel	.05
288	Pedro Valdes RC	.05
289	Turk Wendell	.05
290	Bret Boone	.05
291	Jeff Branson	.05
292	Jeff Brantley	.05
293	Eric Davis	.05
294	Willie Greene	.05
295	Thomas Howard	.05
296	Barry Larkin	.05
297	Kevin Mitchell	.05
298	Hal Morris	.05
299	Chad Mottola	.05
300	Joe Oliver	.05
301	Mark Portugal	.05
302	Roger Salkeld	.05
303	Reggie Sanders	.05
304	Pete Schourek	.05
305	John Smiley	.05
306	Eddie Taubensee	.05
307	Dante Bichette	.05
308	Ellis Burks	.05
309	Vinny Castilla	.05
310	Andres Galarraga	.05
311	Curt Leskanic	.05
312	Quinton McCracken	.05
313	Neifi Perez	.05
314	Jeff Reed	.05
315	Steve Reed	.05
316	Armando Reynoso	.05
317	Kevin Ritz	.05
318	Bruce Ruffin	.05
319	Larry Walker	.05
320	Walt Weiss	.05
321	Jamey Wright	.05
322	Eric Young	.05
323	Kurt Abbott	.05
324	Alex Arias	.05
325	Kevin Brown	.05
326	Luis Castillo	.05
327	Greg Colbrunn	.05
328	Jeff Conine	.05
329	Andre Dawson	.25
330	Charles Johnson	.05
331	Al Leiter	.05
332	Ralph Milliard	.05
333	Robb Nen	.05
334	Pat Rapp	.05
335	Edgar Renteria	.05
336	Gary Sheffield	.35
337	Devon White	.05
338	Bob Abreu	.05
339	Jeff Bagwell	1.00
340	Derek Bell	.05
341	Sean Berry	.05
342	Craig Biggio	.05
343	Doug Drabek	.05
344	Tony Eusebio	.05
345	Ricky Gutierrez	.05
346	Mike Hampton	.05
347	Brian Hunter	.05
348	Todd Jones	.05
349	Darryl Kile	.05
350	Derrick May	.05
351	Orlando Miller	.05
352	James Mouton	.05
353	Shane Reynolds	.05
354	Billy Wagner	.05
355	Donne Wall	.05
356	Mike Blowers	.05
357	Brett Butler	.05
358	Roger Cedeno	.05
359	Chad Curtis	.05
360	Delino DeShields	.05
361	Greg Gagne	.05
362	Karim Garcia	.10
363	Wilton Guerrero	.05
364	Todd Hollandsworth	.05
365	Eric Karros	.05
366	Ramon Martinez	.05
367	Raul Mondesi	.05
368	Hideo Nomo	.75
369	Antonio Osuna	.05
370	Chan Ho Park	.05
371	Mike Piazza	2.00
372	Ismael Valdes	.05
373	Todd Worrell	.05
374	Moises Alou	.05
375	Shane Andrews	.05
376	Yamil Benitez	.05
377	Jeff Fassero	.05
378	Darrin Fletcher	.05
379	Cliff Floyd	.05
380	Mark Grudzielanek	.05
381	Mike Lansing	.05
382	Barry Manuel	.05
383	Pedro Martinez	1.00
384	Henry Rodriguez	.05
385	Mel Rojas	.05
386	F.P. Santangelo	.05
387	David Segui	.05
388	Ugueth Urbina	.05
389	Rondell White	.05
390	Edgardo Alfonzo	.05
391	Carlos Baerga	.05
392	Mark Clark	.05
393	Alvaro Espinoza	.05
394	John Franco	.05
395	Bernard Gilkey	.05
396	Pete Harnisch	.05
397	Todd Hundley	.05
398	Butch Huskey	.05
399	Jason Isringhausen	.05
400	Lance Johnson	.05
401	Bobby Jones	.05
402	Alex Ochoa	.05
403	Rey Ordonez	.05
404	Robert Person	.05
405	Paul Wilson	.05
406	Matt Beech	.05
407	Ron Blazier	.05
408	Ricky Bottalico	.05
409	Lenny Dykstra	.05
410	Jim Eisenreich	.05
411	Bobby Estalella	.05
412	Mike Grace	.05
413	Gregg Jefferies	.05
414	Mike Lieberthal	.05
415	Wendell Magee Jr.	.05
416	Mickey Morandini	.05
417	Ricky Otero	.05
418	Scott Rolen	.75
419	Ken Ryan	.05
420	Benito Santiago	.05
421	Curt Schilling	.25
422	Kevin Sefcik	.05

423	Jermaine Allensworth	.05
424	Trey Beamon	.05
425	Jay Bell	.05
426	Francisco Cordova	.05
427	Carlos Garcia	.05
428	Mark Johnson	.05
429	Jason Kendall	.05
430	Jeff King	.05
431	Jon Lieber	.05
432	Al Martin	.05
433	Orlando Merced	.05
434	Ramon Morel	.05
435	Matt Ruebel	.05
436	Jason Schmidt	.05
437	Marc Wilkins RC	.05
438	Alan Benes	.05
439	Andy Benes	.05
440	Royce Clayton	.05
441	Dennis Eckersley	.65
442	Gary Gaetti	.05
443	Ron Gant	.05
444	Aaron Holbert	.05
445	Brian Jordan	.05
446	Ray Lankford	.05
447	John Mabry	.05
448	T.J. Mathews	.05
449	Willie McGee	.05
450	Donovan Osborne	.05
451	Tom Pagnozzi	.05
452	Ozzie Smith	1.50
453	Todd Stottlemyre	.05
454	Mark Sweeney	.05
455	Dmitri Young	.05
456	Andy Ashby	.05
457	Ken Caminiti	.05
458	Archi Cianfrocco	.05
459	Steve Finley	.05
460	John Flaherty	.05
461	Chris Gomez	.05
462	Tony Gwynn	1.50
463	Joey Hamilton	.05
464	Rickey Henderson	1.00
465	Trevor Hoffman	.05
466	Brian Johnson	.05
467	Wally Joyner	.05
468	Jody Reed	.05
469	Scott Sanders	.05
470	Bob Tewksbury	.05
471	Fernando Valenzuela	.05
472	Greg Vaughn	.05
473	Tim Worrell	.05
474	Rich Aurilia	.05
475	Rod Beck	.05
476	Marvin Benard	.05
477	Barry Bonds	2.50
478	Jay Canizaro	.05
479	Shawon Dunston	.05
480	Shawn Estes	.05
481	Mark Gardner	.05
482	Glenallen Hill	.05
483	Stan Javier	.05
484	Marcus Jensen	.05
485	Bill Mueller RC	1.50
486	William Van Landingham	.05
487	Allen Watson	.05
488	Rick Wilkins	.05
489	Matt Williams	.05
489p	Matt Williams ("PROMOTIONAL SAMPLE")	1.50
490	Desi Wilson	.05
491	Checklist (Albert Belle)	.05
492	Checklist (Ken Griffey Jr.)	.85
493	Checklist (Andruw Jones)	.40
494	Checklist (Chipper Jones)	.60
495	Checklist (Mark McGwire)	1.00
496	Checklist (Paul Molitor)	.45
497	Checklist (Mike Piazza)	.85
498	Checklist (Cal Ripken Jr.)	1.25
499	Checklist (Alex Rodriguez)	.85
500	Checklist (Frank Thomas)	.45
501	Kenny Lofton	.05
502	Carlos Perez	.05
503	Tim Raines	.05
504	Danny Patterson RC	.05
505	Derrick May	.05
506	Dave Hollins	.05
507	Felipe Crespo	.05
508	Brian Banks	.05
509	Jeff Kent	.05
510	Bubba Trammell RC	.25
511	Robert Person	.05
512	David Arias RC (Ortiz)	40.00
513	Ryan Jones	.05
514	David Justice	.05
515	Will Cunnane	.05
516	Russ Johnson	.05
517	John Burkett	.05
518	Robinson Checo RC	.05
519	Ricardo Rincon RC	.05
520	Woody Williams	.05
521	Rick Helling	.05
522	Jorge Posada	.05
523	Kevin Orie	.05
524	Fernando Tatis RC	.15
525	Jermaine Dye	.05
526	Brian Hunter	.05
527	Greg McMichael	.05
528	Matt Wagner	.05
529	Richie Sexson	.05
530	Scott Ruffcorn	.05
531	Luis Gonzalez	.10
532	Mike Johnson	.05
533	Mark Petkovsek	.05
534	Doug Drabek	.05
535	Jose Canseco	.40
536	Bobby Bonilla	.05
537	J.T. Snow	.05
538	Shawon Dunston	.05
539	John Ericks	.05
540	Terry Steinbach	.05
541	Jay Bell	.05
542	Joe Borowski	.05
543	David Wells	.05
544	Justin Towle RC	.10
545	Mike Blowers	.05
546	Shannon Stewart	.05
547	Rudy Pemberton	.05
548	Bill Swift	.05
549	Osvaldo Fernandez	.05
550	Eddie Murray	1.00
551	Don Wengert	.05
552	Brad Ausmus	.05
553	Carlos Garcia	.05
554	Jose Guillen	.05
555	Rheal Cormier	.05
556	Doug Brocail	.05
557	Rex Hudler	.05
558	Armando Benitez	.05
559	Elieser Marrero	.05
560	Ricky Ledee RC	.25
561	Bartolo Colon	.05
562	Quilvio Veras	.05
563	Alex Fernandez	.05
564	Darren Dreifort	.05
565	Benji Gil	.05
566	Kent Mercker	.05
567	Glendon Rusch	.05
568	Ramon Tatis RC	.05
569	Roger Clemens	1.75
570	Mark Lewis	.05
571	Emil Brown RC	.05
572	Jaime Navarro	.05
573	Sherman Obando	.05
574	John Wasdin	.05
575	Calvin Maduro	.05
576	Todd Jones	.05
577	Orlando Merced	.05
578	Cal Eldred	.05
579	Mark Gubicza	.05
580	Michael Tucker	.05
581	Tony Saunders RC	.05
582	Garvin Alston	.05
583	Joe Roa	.05
584	Brady Raggio RC	.05
585	Jimmy Key	.05
586	Marc Sagmoen RC	.05
587	Jim Bullinger	.05
588	Yorkis Perez	.05
589	Jose Cruz Jr. RC	.75
590	Mike Stanton	.05
591	Deivi Cruz RC	.25
592	Steve Karsay	.05
593	Mike Trombley	.05
594	Doug Glanville	.05
595	Scott Sanders	.05
596	Thomas Howard	.05
597	T.J. Staton	.05
598	Garrett Stephenson	.05
599	Rico Brogna	.05
600	Albert Belle	.05
601	Jose Vizcaino	.05
602	Chili Davis	.05
603	Shane Mack	.05
604	Jim Eisenreich	.05
605	Todd Zeile	.05
606	Brian Boehringer	.05
607	Paul Shuey	.05
608	Kevin Tapani	.05
609	John Wetteland	.05
610	Jim Leyritz	.05
611	Ray Montgomery	.05
612	Doug Bochtler	.05
613	Wady Almonte	.05
614	Danny Tartabull	.05
615	Orlando Miller	.05
616	Bobby Ayala	.05
617	Tony Graffanino	.05
618	Marc Valdes	.05
619	Ron Villone	.05
620	Derrek Lee	.05
621	Greg Colbrunn	.05
622	Felix Heredia RC	.10
623	Carl Everett	.05
624	Mark Thompson	.05
625	Jeff Granger	.05
626	Damian Jackson	.05
627	Mark Leiter	.05
628	Chris Holt	.05
629	Dario Veras RC	.05
630	Dave Burba	.05
631	Darryl Hamilton	.05
632	Mark Acre	.05
633	Fernando Hernandez	.05
634	Terry Mulholland	.05
635	Dustin Hermanson	.05
636	Delino DeShields	.05
637	Steve Avery	.05
638	Tony Womack RC	.10
639	Mark Whiten	.05
640	Marquis Grissom	.05
641	Xavier Hernandez	.05
642	Eric Davis	.05
643	Bob Tewksbury	.05
644	Dante Powell	.05
645	Carlos Castillo	.05
646	Chris Widger	.05
647	Moises Alou	.05
648	Pat Listach	.05
649	Edgar Ramos	.05
650	Deion Sanders	.05
651	John Olerud	.05
652	Todd Dunwoody	.05
653	Randall Simon RC	.10
654	Dan Carlson	.05
655	Matt Williams	.05
656	Jeff King	.05
657	Luis Alicea	.05
658	Brian Moehler	.05
659	Ariel Prieto	.05
660	Kevin Elster	.05
661	Mark Hutton	.05
662	Aaron Sele	.05
663	Graeme Lloyd	.05
664	John Burke	.05
665	Mel Rojas	.05
666	Sid Fernandez	.05
667	Pedro Astacio	.05
668	Jeff Abbott	.05
669	Darren Daulton	.05
670	Mike Bordick	.05
671	Sterling Hitchcock	.05
672	Damion Easley	.05
673	Armando Reynoso	.05
674	Pat Cline	.05
675	Orlando Cabrera RC	.50
676	Alan Embree	.05
677	Brian Bevil	.05
678	David Weathers	.05
679	Cliff Floyd	.05
680	Joe Randa	.05
681	Bill Haselman	.05
682	Jeff Fassero	.05
683	Matt Morris	.05
684	Mark Portugal	.05
685	Lee Smith	.05
686	Pokey Reese	.05
687	Benito Santiago	.05
688	Brian Johnson	.05
689	Brent Brede RC	.05
690	Shigetosi Hasegawa	.05
691	Julio Santana	.05
692	Steve Kline	.05
693	Julian Tavarez	.05
694	John Hudek	.05
695	Manny Alexander	.05
696	Roberto Alomar (Encore)	.10
697	Jeff Bagwell (Encore)	.45
698	Barry Bonds (Encore)	1.25
699	Ken Caminiti (Encore)	.05
700	Juan Gonzalez (Encore)	.35
701	Ken Griffey Jr. (Encore)	.85
702	Tony Gwynn (Encore)	.60
703	Derek Jeter (Encore)	1.25
704	Andruw Jones (Encore)	.45
705	Chipper Jones (Encore)	.60
706	Barry Larkin (Encore)	.05
707	Greg Maddux (Encore)	.45
708	Mark McGwire (Encore)	1.00
709	Paul Molitor (Encore)	.45
710	Hideo Nomo (Encore)	.35
711	Andy Pettitte (Encore)	.30
712	Mike Piazza (Encore)	.85
713	Manny Ramirez (Encore)	.45
714	Cal Ripken Jr. (Encore)	1.25
715	Alex Rodriguez (Encore)	.60
716	Ryne Sandberg (Encore)	.60
717	John Smoltz (Encore)	.05
718	Frank Thomas (Encore)	.50
719	Mo Vaughn (Encore)	.05
720	Bernie Williams (Encore)	.10
721	Checklist (Tim Salmon)	.60
722	Checklist (Greg Maddux)	.60
723	Checklist (Cal Ripken Jr.)	1.25
724	Checklist (Mo Vaughn)	.05
725	Checklist (Ryne Sandberg)	.45
726	Checklist (Frank Thomas)	.50
727	Checklist (Barry Larkin)	.05
728	Checklist (Manny Ramirez)	.45
729	Checklist (Andres Galarraga)	.05
730	Checklist (Tony Clark)	.05
731	Checklist (Gary Sheffield)	.20
732	Checklist (Jeff Bagwell)	.40
733	Checklist (Kevin Appier)	.05
734	Checklist (Mike Piazza)	.85
735	Checklist (Jeff Cirillo)	.05
736	Checklist (Paul Molitor)	.40
737	Checklist (Henry Rodriguez)	.05
738	Checklist (Todd Hundley)	.05
739	Checklist (Derek Jeter)	1.25
740	Checklist (Mark McGwire)	1.00
741	Checklist (Curt Schilling)	.15
742	Checklist (Jason Kendall)	.05
743	Checklist (Tony Gwynn)	.60
744	Checklist (Barry Bonds)	1.25
745	Checklist (Ken Griffey Jr.)	.85
746	Checklist (Brian Jordan)	.05
747	Checklist (Juan Gonzalez)	.40
748	Checklist (Joe Carter)	.05
749	Arizona Diamondbacks	.05
750	Tampa Bay Devil Rays	.05
751	Hideki Irabu	.15
752	Jeremi Gonzalez RC	.15
753	Mario Valdez RC	.05
754	Aaron Boone	.05
755	Brett Tomko	.05
756	Jaret Wright RC	1.00
757	Ryan McGuire	.05
758	Jason McDonald	.05
759	Adrian Brown RC	.05
760	Keith Foulke RC	.25
761	Checklist	.05

Tiffany

Insertion odds were considerably lengthened for the UV-coated Tiffany Collection parallels in 1997 Fleer - to one card per 20 packs.

	NM/M
Complete Set (761):	500.00
Common Player:	1.00
Stars/Rcs:	8X
512 David Arias (Ortiz)	140.00

Bleacher Blasters

This 10-card insert features some of the game's top power hitters and was found in retail packs only. Cards featured a die-cut "burst" pattern on an etched foil background. Backs have a portrait photo and career highlights. Cards were inserted 1:36 packs.

		NM/M
	Complete Set (10):	40.00
	Common Player:	1.50
1	Albert Belle	1.50
2	Barry Bonds	10.00
3	Juan Gonzalez	2.00
4	Ken Griffey Jr.	6.00
5	Mark McGwire	8.00
6	Mike Piazza	6.00
7	Alex Rodriguez	8.00
8	Frank Thomas	4.00
9	Mo Vaughn	1.50
10	Matt Williams	1.50

Decade of Excellence

A 12-card insert found 1:36 in hobby shop packs, cards are in a format similar to the 1987 Fleer set and feature vintage photos of players who started their careers no later than the '87 season. Ten percent of the press run (1:360 packs) received a special foil treatment and designation as "Rare Traditions."

		NM/M
	Complete Set (12):	35.00
	Common Player:	1.50
	Rare Tradition:	12X
1	Wade Boggs	4.50
2	Barry Bonds	9.00
3	Roger Clemens	6.00
4	Tony Gwynn	4.50
5	Rickey Henderson	3.00
6	Greg Maddux	4.50
7	Mark McGwire	6.00
8	Paul Molitor	3.00
9	Eddie Murray	3.00
10	Cal Ripken Jr.	9.00
11	Ryne Sandberg	4.50
12	Matt Williams	1.50

Diamond Tribute

Twelve of the game's top stars are highlighted in this set. Fronts feature an embossed rainbow prismatic foil background and gold lettering. Backs have an action photo and a few sentences about the player. They were inserted 1:288 packs.

		NM/M
	Complete Set (12):	120.00
	Common Player:	3.00
1	Albert Belle	3.00
2	Barry Bonds	20.00
3	Juan Gonzalez	5.00
4	Ken Griffey Jr.	12.50
5	Tony Gwynn	10.00
6	Greg Maddux	5.00

7	Mark McGwire	15.00
8	Eddie Murray	8.00
9	Mike Piazza	12.50
10	Cal Ripken Jr.	20.00
11	Alex Rodriguez	15.00
12	Frank Thomas	8.00

Golden Memories

Golden Memories captures 10 different highlights from the 1996 season, and is inserted one per 16 packs. Moments like Dwight Gooden's no hit, Paul Molitor's 3000th hit and Eddie Murray's 500th home run are highlighted on a horizontal format.

		NM/M
	Complete Set (10):	6.00
	Common Player:	.25
1	Barry Bonds	2.00
2	Dwight Gooden	.25
3	Todd Hundley	.25
4	Mark McGwire	1.50
5	Paul Molitor	.75
6	Eddie Murray	.75
7	Hideo Nomo	.50
8	Mike Piazza	1.25
9	Cal Ripken Jr.	2.00
10	Ozzie Smith	1.00

Goudey Greats

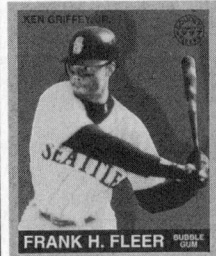

Using a 2-3/8" x 2-7/8" format reminiscent of 1933 Goudey cards, this 15-card insert offers today's top players in classic old-time design. Cards were inserted 1:8 packs. A limited number (1 percent of press run) of cards received a special gold-foil treatment and were found only in hobby packs.

		NM/M
	Complete Set (15):	20.00
	Common Player:	.50
	Foils:	15X
1	Barry Bonds	4.00
2	Ken Griffey Jr.	3.00
3	Tony Gwynn	2.00
4	Derek Jeter	4.00
5	Chipper Jones	2.00
6	Kenny Lofton	.50
7	Greg Maddux	2.00
8	Mark McGwire	3.50
9	Eddie Murray	1.50
10	Mike Piazza	3.00
11	Cal Ripken Jr.	4.00
12	Alex Rodriguez	3.50
13	Ryne Sandberg	2.00
14	Frank Thomas	1.50
15	Mo Vaughn	2.00

Headliners

This 20-card insert highlights the personal achievements of each of the players depicted. Cards are inserted 1:2 packs and feature multi-color foil stamping on the fronts and a newspaper-style account of the player's achievement on the back.

		NM/M
	Complete Set (20):	5.00
	Common Player:	.10
1	Jeff Bagwell	.25
2	Albert Belle	.10
3	Barry Bonds	1.00
4	Ken Caminiti	.10
5	Juan Gonzalez	.20
6	Ken Griffey Jr.	.60
7	Tony Gwynn	.40
8	Derek Jeter	1.00
9	Andruw Jones	.40
10	Chipper Jones	.40
11	Greg Maddux	.40
12	Mark McGwire	.25
13	Paul Molitor	.25
14	Eddie Murray	.25
15	Mike Piazza	.25
16	Cal Ripken Jr.	1.00
17	Alex Rodriguez	.75
18	Ryne Sandberg	.40
19	John Smoltz	.05
20	Frank Thomas	.25

Lumber Company

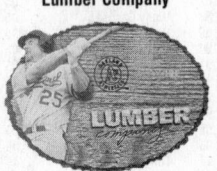

Lumber Company inserts were found every 48 retail packs. The cards were printed on a die-cut, spherical wood-like pattern, with the player imposed on the left side. Eighteen of the top power hitters in baseball are highlighted.

		NM/M
	Complete Set (18):	45.00
	Common Player:	1.00
1	Brady Anderson	1.00
2	Jeff Bagwell	3.00
3	Albert Belle	1.00
4	Barry Bonds	8.00
5	Jay Buhner	1.00
6	Ellis Burks	1.00
7	Andres Galarraga	1.00
8	Juan Gonzalez	2.00
9	Ken Griffey Jr.	5.00
10	Todd Hundley	1.00
11	Ryan Klesko	1.00
12	Mark McGwire	6.00
13	Mike Piazza	6.00
14	Alex Rodriguez	6.00
15	Gary Sheffield	1.00
16	Sammy Sosa	4.00
17	Frank Thomas	3.00
18	Mo Vaughn	1.00

Million Dollar Moments

By assembling a complete set of 50 baseball "Million Dollar Moments" cards prior to July 31, 1998, a collector could win $50,000 a year through 2018. The catch, of course, is that cards #46-50 were printed in very limited quantities, with only one card #50. (Stated odds of winning the million were one in nearly 46,000,000.) The Moments cards have player action photos on front vignetted into a black border. The Fleer Million Dollar Moments logo is at top, with the player name and the date and details of his highlight at bottom in orange and white. Backs have the contest rules in fine print. Instant Win versions of some cards were also issued.

		NM/M
Complete Set (45):		2.00
Common Player:		.05
1	Checklist	.05
2	Derek Jeter	.45
3	Babe Ruth	.25
4	Barry Bonds	.45
5	Brooks Robinson	.05
6	Todd Hundley	.05
7	Johnny Vander Meer	.05
8	Cal Ripken Jr.	.45
9	Bill Mazeroski	.05
10	Chipper Jones	.25
11	Frank Robinson	.05
12	Roger Clemens	.35
13	Bob Feller	.05
14	Mike Piazza	.30
15	Joe Nuxhall	.05
16	Hideo Nomo	.15
17	Jackie Robinson	.25
18	Orel Hershiser	.05
19	Bobby Thomson	.05
20	Joe Carter	.05
21	Al Kaline	.05
22	Bernie Williams	.05
23	Don Larsen	.05
24	Rickey Henderson	.15
25	Maury Wills	.05
26	Andruw Jones	.15
27	Bobby Richardson	.05
28	Alex Rodriguez	.35
29	Jim Bunning	.05
30	Ken Caminiti	.05
31	Bob Gibson	.05
32	Frank Thomas	.20
33	Mickey Lolich	.05
34	John Smoltz	.05
35	Ron Swoboda	.05
36	Albert Belle	.05
37	Chris Chambliss	.05
38	Juan Gonzalez	.10
39	Ron Blomberg	.05
40	John Wetteland	.05
41	Carlton Fisk	.05
42	Mo Vaughn	.05
43	Bucky Dent	.05
44	Greg Maddux	.25
45	Willie Stargell	.05

New Horizons

Rookies and prospects expected to make an impact during the 1996 season were featured in this 15-card insert set. Card fronts feature a rainbow foil background with the words "New Horizon" featured prominently on the bottom under the player's name. Cards were inserted 1:4 packs.

		NM/M
Complete Set (15):		2.00
Common Player:		.05
1	Bob Abreu	.10
2	Jose Cruz Jr.	.05
3	Darin Erstad	.10
4	Nomar Garciaparra	.75
5	Vladimir Guerrero	.60
6	Wilton Guerrero	.05
7	Jose Guillen	.05
8	Hideki Irabu	.05
9	Andruw Jones	.05
10	Kevin Orie	.05
11	Scott Rolen	.50
12	Scott Spiezio	.05
13	Bubba Trammell	.05

14	Todd Walker	.05
15	Dmitri Young	.05

Night & Day

Night and Day spotlighted 10 stars with unusual prowess during night or day games. These lenticular cards carried the toughest insert ratios in Fleer Baseball at one per 288 packs.

		NM/M
Complete Set (10):		45.00
Common Player:		1.00
1	Barry Bonds	12.00
2	Ellis Burks	1.00
3	Juan Gonzalez	2.00
4	Ken Griffey Jr.	6.00
5	Mark McGwire	7.50
6	Mike Piazza	6.00
7	Manny Ramirez	4.00
8	Alex Rodriguez	8.00
9	John Smoltz	2.00
10	Frank Thomas	4.00

Rookie Sensations

Rookies Sensations showcased 20 of the top up-and-coming stars in baseball. Appearing every six packs, these inserts have the feaured player in the foreground, with the background look of painted brush strokes.

		NM/M
Complete Set (20):		6.00
Common Player:		.25
1	Jermaine Allensworth	.25
2	James Baldwin	.25
3	Alan Benes	.25
4	Jermaine Dye	.25
5	Darin Erstad	.50
6	Todd Hollandsworth	.25
7	Derek Jeter	2.50
8	Jason Kendall	.25
9	Alex Ochoa	.25
10	Rey Ordonez	.25
11	Edgar Renteria	.25
12	Bob Abreu	.50
13	Nomar Garciaparra	1.50
14	Wilton Guerrero	.25
15	Andruw Jones	1.00
16	Wendell Magee	.25
17	Neifi Perez	.25
18	Scott Rolen	.75
19	Scott Spiezio	.25
20	Todd Walker	.25

Soaring Stars

A 12-card insert found 1:12 packs designed to profile players with outstanding statistical performances early in their careers. Fronts have player action photos set against a background of rainbow holographic stars which appear, disappear and twinkle as the viewing angle is changed. Conventionally printed backs have another player photo and a few sentences about his career. A parallel version on which the background stars glow was issued at a greatly reduced rate.

		NM/M
Complete Set (12):		10.00
Common Player:		.25
Glowing:		6X
1	Albert Belle	.25
2	Barry Bonds	2.00
3	Juan Gonzalez	.50
4	Ken Griffey Jr.	1.25
5	Derek Jeter	2.00
6	Andruw Jones	.60
7	Chipper Jones	1.00
8	Greg Maddux	1.00
9	Mark McGwire	1.50
10	Mike Piazza	1.25
11	Alex Rodriguez	1.50
12	Frank Thomas	.75

Team Leaders

Team Leaders captured the statistical and/or inspirational leaders from all 28 teams. Inserted every 20 packs, these inserts were printed on a horizontal format, with the player's face die-cut in the perimeter of the card.

		NM/M
Complete Set (28):		25.00
Common Player:		.25
1	Cal Ripken Jr.	5.00
2	Mo Vaughn	.25
3	Jim Edmonds	.40
4	Frank Thomas	1.50
5	Albert Belle	.25
6	Bob Higginson	.25
7	Kevin Appier	.25
8	John Jaha	.25
9	Paul Molitor	1.50
10	Andy Pettitte	.65
11	Mark McGwire	4.00
12	Ken Griffey Jr.	3.00
13	Juan Gonzalez	.75
14	Pat Hentgen	.25
15	Chipper Jones	2.00
16	Mark Grace	.35
17	Barry Larkin	.25
18	Ellis Burks	.25
19	Gary Sheffield	.60
20	Jeff Bagwell	1.50
21	Mike Piazza	3.00
22	Henry Rodriguez	.25
23	Todd Hundley	.25
24	Curt Schilling	.60
25	Jeff King	.25
26	Brian Jordan	.25
27	Tony Gwynn	1.50
28	Barry Bonds	5.00

Zone

Twenty of the top hitters in baseball are featured on these holographic cards with the words Zone printed across the front. Zone inserts were found only in hobby packs at a rate of one per 80.

FLEER '97		

		NM/M
Complete Set (20):		80.00
Common Player:		1.50
1	Jeff Bagwell	5.00
2	Albert Belle	1.50
3	Barry Bonds	15.00
4	Ken Caminiti	1.50
5	Andres Galarraga	1.50
6	Juan Gonzalez	2.50
7	Ken Griffey Jr.	8.00
8	Tony Gwynn	6.00
9	Chipper Jones	6.00
10	Greg Maddux	6.00
11	Mark McGwire	10.00
12	Dean Palmer	1.50
13	Andy Petitte	3.00
14	Mike Piazza	8.00
15	Alex Rodriguez	12.00
16	Gary Sheffield	2.50
17	John Smoltz	2.50
18	Frank Thomas	5.00
19	Jim Thome	4.00
20	Matt Williams	1.50

1998 Fleer

Fleer was issued in two series in 1998, with 350 cards in Series 1 and 250 in Series 2. Each card features a borderless color action shot, with backs containing player information. Subsets in Series 1 included Smoke 'N Heat (301-310), Golden Memories (311-320) and Tale of the Tape (321-340). Golden Memories (1:6 packs) and Tale of the Tape (1:4) were shortprinted. Series 2 subsets included 25 short-printed (1:4) Unforgettable Moments (571-595). Inserts in Series 1 were Vintage '63, Vintage '63 Classic, Decade of Excellence, Decade of Excellence Rare Traditions, Diamond Ink, Diamond Standouts, Lumber Company, Power Game, Rookie Sensations and Zone. Series 2 inserts include: Vintage '63, Vintage '63 Classic, Promising Forecast, In the Clutch, Mickey Mantle: Monumental Moments, Mickey Mantle: Monumental Moments Gold Edition, Diamond Tribute and Diamond Ink.

		NM/M
Complete Set (600):		65.00
Complete Series 1 (350):		40.00
Complete Series 2 (250):		25.00
Common Player:		.05
Series 1 or 2 Pack (10):		1.00
Series 1 or 2 Wax Box (36):		20.00
1	Ken Griffey Jr.	1.50
2	Derek Jeter	2.50
3	Gerald Williams	.05
4	Carlos Delgado	.50
5	Nomar Garciaparra	1.50
6	Gary Sheffield	.30
7	Jeff King	.05
8	Cal Ripken Jr.	2.50
9	Matt Williams	.05
10	Chipper Jones	1.00
11	Chuck Knoblauch	.05
12	Mark Grudzielanek	.05
13	Edgardo Alfonzo	.05
14	Andres Galarraga	.15
15	Tim Salmon	.15
16	Reggie Sanders	.05
17	Tony Clark	.05
18	Jason Kendall	.05
19	Juan Gonzalez	.65
20	Ben Grieve	.10
21	Roger Clemens	1.25
22	Raul Mondesi	.05
23	Robin Ventura	.05
24	Derek Lee	.05
25	Mark McGwire	2.00
26	Luis Gonzalez	.10
27	Kevin Brown	.05
28	Kirk Rueter	.05
29	Bobby Estalella	.05
30	Shawn Green	.35
31	Greg Maddux	1.00
32	Jorge Velandia	.05
33	Larry Walker	.05
34	Joey Cora	.05
35	Frank Thomas	.85

36	Curtis King RC	.05
37	Aaron Boone	.05
38	Curt Schilling	.25
39	Bruce Aven	.05
40	Ben McDonald	.05
41	Andy Ashby	.05
42	Jason McDonald	.05
43	Eric Davis	.05
44	Mark Grace	.10
45	Pedro Martinez	.75
46	Lou Collier	.05
47	Chan Ho Park	.05
48	Shane Halter	.05
49	Brian Hunter	.05
50	Jeff Bagwell	.75
51	Bernie Williams	.10
52	J.T. Snow	.05
53	Todd Greene	.05
54	Shannon Stewart	.05
55	Darren Bragg	.05
56	Fernando Tatis	.05
57	Darryl Kile	.05
58	Chris Stynes	.05
59	Javier Valentin	.05
60	Brian McRae	.05
61	Tom Evans	.05
62	Randall Simon	.05
63	Darrin Fletcher	.05
64	Jaret Wright	.05
65	Luis Ordaz	.05
66	Jose Canseco	.40
67	Edgar Renteria	.05
68	Jay Buhner	.05
69	Paul Konerko	.10
70	Adrian Brown	.05
71	Chris Carpenter	.05
72	Mike Lieberthal	.05
73	Dean Palmer	.05
74	Jorge Fabregas	.05
75	Stan Javier	.05
76	Damion Easley	.05
77	David Cone	.05
78	Aaron Sele	.05
79	Antonio Alfonseca	.05
80	Bobby Jones	.05
81	David Justice	.05
82	Jeffrey Hammonds	.05
83	Doug Glanville	.05
84	Jason Dickson	.05
85	Brad Radke	.05
86	David Segui	.05
87	Greg Vaughn	.05
88	Mike Cather RC	.05
89	Alex Fernandez	.05
90	Billy Taylor	.05
91	Jason Schmidt	.05
92	Mike DeJean RC	.05
93	Domingo Cedeno	.05
94	Jeff Cirillo	.05
95	Manny Aybar RC	.10
96	Jaime Navarro	.05
97	Dennis Reyes	.05
98	Barry Larkin	.25
99	Troy O'Leary	.05
100	Alex Rodriguez	2.00
100p	Alex Rodriguez/OPS	2.00
101	Pat Hentgen	.05
102	Bubba Trammell	.05
103	Glendon Rusch	.05
104	Kenny Lofton	.05
105	Craig Biggio	.05
106	Kelvim Escobar	.05
107	Mark Kotsay	.05
108	Rondell White	.05
109	Darren Oliver	.05
110	Jim Thome	.65
111	Rich Becker	.05
112	Chad Curtis	.05
113	Dave Hollins	.05
114	Bill Mueller	.05
115	Antone Williamson	.05
116	Tony Womack	.05
117	Randy Myers	.05
118	Rico Brogna	.05
119	Pat Watkins	.05
120	Eli Marrero	.05
121	Jay Bell	.05
122	Kevin Tapani	.05
123	Todd Erdos RC	.10
124	Neifi Perez	.05
125	Todd Hundley	.05
126	Jeff Abbott	.05
127	Todd Zeile	.05
128	Travis Fryman	.05
129	Sandy Alomar	.05
130	Fred McGriff	.05
131	Richard Hidalgo	.05
132	Scott Spiezio	.05
133	John Valentin	.05
134	Quivilio Veras	.05
135	Mike Lansing	.05
136	Paul Molitor	.75
137	Randy Johnson	.75
138	Harold Baines	.05
139	Doug Jones	.05
140	Abraham Nunez	.05
141	Alan Benes	.05
142	Matt Perisho	.05
143	Chris Clemons	.05
144	Andy Pettitte	.30
145	Jason Giambi	.40
146	Moises Alou	.05
147	Chad Fox RC	.05
148	Felix Martinez	.05
149	Carlos Mendoza RC	.05
150	Scott Rolen	.65
151	Jose Cabrera RC	.05
152	Justin Thompson	.05

153	Ellis Burks	.05
154	Pokey Reese	.05
155	Bartolo Colon	.05
156	Ray Durham	.05
157	Ugueth Urbina	.05
158	Tom Goodwin	.05
159	David Dellucci RC	.25
160	Rod Beck	.05
161	Ramon Martinez	.05
162	Joe Carter	.05
163	Kevin Orie	.05
164	Trevor Hoffman	.05
165	Emil Brown	.05
166	Robb Nen	.05
167	Paul O'Neill	.05
168	Ryan Long	.05
169	Ray Lankford	.05
170	Ivan Rodriguez	.65
171	Rick Aguilera	.05
172	Deivi Cruz	.05
173	Ricky Bottalico	.05
174	Garret Anderson	.05
175	Jose Vizcaino	.05
176	Omar Vizquel	.05
177	Jeff Blauser	.05
178	Orlando Cabrera	.05
179	Russ Johnson	.05
180	Matt Stairs	.05
181	Will Cunnane	.05
182	Adam Riggs	.05
183	Matt Morris	.05
184	Mario Valdez	.05
185	Larry Sutton	.05
186	Marc Pisciotta RC	.05
187	Dan Wilson	.05
188	John Franco	.05
189	Darren Daulton	.05
190	Todd Helton	.75
191	Brady Anderson	.05
192	Ricardo Rincon	.05
193	Kevin Stocker	.05
194	Jose Valentin	.05
195	Ed Sprague	.05
196	Ryan McGuire	.05
197	Scott Eyre RC	.05
198	Steve Finley	.05
199	T.J. Mathews	.05
200	Mike Piazza	1.50
201	Mark Wohlers	.05
202	Brian Giles	.05
203	Eduardo Perez	.05
204	Shigetosi Hasegawa	.05
205	Mariano Rivera	.15
206	Jose Rosado	.05
207	Michael Coleman	.05
208	James Baldwin	.05
209	Russ Davis	.05
210	Billy Wagner	.05
211	Sammy Sosa	1.50
212	Frank Catalanotto RC	.15
213	Delino DeShields	.05
214	John Olerud	.05
215	Heath Murray	.05
216	Jose Vidro	.05
217	Jim Edmonds	.05
218	Shawon Dunston	.05
219	Homer Bush	.05
220	Midre Cummings	.05
221	Tony Saunders	.05
222	Jeromy Burnitz	.05
223	Enrique Wilson	.05
224	Chili Davis	.05
225	Jerry DiPoto	.05
226	Dante Powell	.05
227	Javier Lopez	.05
228	Kevin Polcovich RC	.10
229	Deion Sanders	.05
230	Jimmy Key	.05
231	Rusty Greer	.05
232	Reggie Jefferson	.05
233	Ron Coomer	.05
234	Bobby Higginson	.05
235	Magglio Ordonez RC	2.00
236	Miguel Tejada	.25
237	Rick Gorecki	.05
238	Charles Johnson	.05
239	Lance Johnson	.05
240	Derek Bell	.05
241	Will Clark	.10
242	Brady Raggio	.05
243	Orel Hershiser	.05
244	Vladimir Guerrero	.75
245	John LeRoy	.05
246	Shawn Estes	.05
247	Brett Tomko	.05
248	Dave Nilsson	.05
249	Edgar Martinez	.05
250	Tony Gwynn	1.00
251	Mark Bellhorn	.05
252	Jed Hansen	.05
253	Butch Huskey	.05
254	Eric Young	.05
255	Vinny Castilla	.05
256	Hideki Irabu	.05
257	Mike Cameron	.05
258	Juan Encarnacion	.05
259	Brian Rose	.05
260	Brad Ausmus	.05
261	Dan Serafini	.05
262	Willie Greene	.05
263	Troy Percival	.05
264	Jeff Wallace RC	.05
265	Richie Sexson	.05
266	Rafael Palmeiro	.65
267	Brad Fullmer	.05
268	Jeremi Gonzalez	.05
269	Rob Stanifer RC	.05
270	Mickey Morandini	.05

#	Player	Price
271	Andruw Jones	.75
272	Royce Clayton	.05
273	Takashi Kashiwada	.05
274	Steve Woodard RC	.10
275	Jose Cruz Jr.	.05
276	Keith Foulke	.05
277	Brad Rigby	.05
278	Tino Martinez	.05
279	Todd Jones	.05
280	John Wetteland	.05
281	Alex Gonzalez	.05
282	Ken Cloude	.05
283	Jose Guillen	.05
284	Danny Clyburn	.05
285	David Ortiz	.05
286	John Thomson	.05
287	Kevin Appier	.05
288	Ismael Valdes	.05
289	Gary DiSarcina	.05
290	Todd Dunwoody	.05
291	Wally Joyner	.05
292	Charles Nagy	.05
293	Jeff Shaw	.05
294	Kevin Millwood RC	1.00
295	Rigo Beltran RC	.05
296	Jeff Frye	.05
297	Oscar Henriquez	.05
298	Mike Thurman	.05
299	Garrett Stephenson	.05
300	Barry Bonds	2.50
301	Roger Clemens (Smoke 'N Heat)	.75
302	David Cone (Smoke 'N Heat)	.05
303	Hideki Irabu (Smoke 'N Heat)	.05
304	Randy Johnson (Smoke 'N Heat)	.40
305	Greg Maddux (Smoke 'N Heat)	.50
306	Pedro Martinez (Smoke 'N Heat)	.35
307	Mike Mussina (Smoke 'N Heat)	.25
308	Andy Pettitte (Smoke 'N Heat)	.15
309	Curt Schilling (Smoke 'N Heat)	.10
310	John Smoltz (Smoke 'N Heat)	.05
311	Roger Clemens (Golden Memories)	1.00
312	Jose Cruz Jr. (Golden Memories)	.25
313	Nomar Garciaparra (Golden Memories)	1.00
314	Ken Griffey Jr. (Golden Memories)	1.00
315	Tony Gwynn (Golden Memories)	.75
316	Hideki Irabu (Golden Memories)	.25
317	Randy Johnson (Golden Memories)	.60
318	Mark McGwire (Golden Memories)	1.50
319	Curt Schilling (Golden Memories)	.35
320	Larry Walker (Golden Memories)	.15
321	Jeff Bagwell (Tale of the Tape)	.60
322	Albert Belle (Tale of the Tape)	.15
323	Barry Bonds (Tale of the Tape)	1.50
324	Jay Buhner (Tale of the Tape)	.15
325	Tony Clark (Tale of the Tape)	.15
326	Jose Cruz Jr. (Tale of the Tape)	.15
327	Andres Galarraga (Tale of the Tape)	.15
328	Juan Gonzalez (Tale of the Tape)	.30
329	Ken Griffey Jr. (Tale of the Tape)	.85
330	Andruw Jones (Tale of the Tape)	.60
331	Tino Martinez (Tale of the Tape)	.15
332	Mark McGwire (Tale of the Tape)	1.00
333	Rafael Palmeiro (Tale of the Tape)	.50
334	Mike Piazza (Tale of the Tape)	.85
335	Manny Ramirez (Tale of the Tape)	.65
336	Alex Rodriguez (Tale of the Tape)	1.00
337	Frank Thomas (Tale of the Tape)	.65
338	Jim Thome (Tale of the Tape)	.65
339	Mo Vaughn (Tale of the Tape)	.15
340	Larry Walker (Tale of the Tape)	.15
341	Checklist (Jose Cruz Jr.)	.15
342	Checklist (Ken Griffey Jr.)	.65
343	Checklist (Derek Jeter)	1.00
344	Checklist (Andruw Jones)	.40
345	Checklist (Chipper Jones)	.50
346	Checklist (Greg Maddux)	.50
347	Checklist (Mike Piazza)	.65
348	Checklist (Cal Ripken Jr.)	1.00
349	Checklist (Alex Rodriguez)	.75
350	Checklist (Frank Thomas)	.45
351	Mo Vaughn	.05
352	Andres Galarraga	.05
353	Roberto Alomar	.10
354	Darin Erstad	.10
355	Albert Belle	.05
356	Matt Williams	.05
357	Darryl Kile	.05
358	Kenny Lofton	.05
359	Orel Hershiser	.05
360	Bob Abreu	.05
361	Chris Widger	.05
362	Glenallen Hill	.05
363	Chili Davis	.05
364	Kevin Brown	.05
365	Marquis Grissom	.05
366	Livan Hernandez	.05
367	Moises Alou	.05
368	Matt Lawton	.05
369	Rey Ordonez	.05
370	Kenny Rogers	.05
371	Lee Stevens	.05
372	Wade Boggs	1.00
373	Luis Gonzalez	.05
374	Jeff Conine	.05
375	Esteban Loaiza	.05
376	Jose Canseco	.40
377	Henry Rodriguez	.05
378	Dave Burba	.05
379	Todd Hollandsworth	.05
380	Ron Gant	.05
381	Pedro Martinez	.75
382	Ryan Klesko	.05
383	Derrek Lee	.05
384	Doug Glanville	.05
385	David Wells	.05
386	Ken Caminiti	.05
387	Damon Hollins	.05
388	Manny Ramirez	.75
389	Mike Mussina	.45
390	Jay Bell	.05
391	Mike Piazza	1.50
392	Mike Lansing	.05
393	Mike Hampton	.05
394	Geoff Jenkins	.05
395	Jimmy Haynes	.05
396	Scott Servais	.05
397	Kent Mercker	.05
398	Jeff Kent	.05
399	Kevin Elster	.05
400	Masato Yoshii RC	.50
401	Jose Vizcaino	.05
402	Javier Martinez	.05
403	David Segui	.05
404	Tony Saunders	.05
405	Karim Garcia	.05
406	Armando Benitez	.05
407	Joe Randa	.05
408	Vic Darensbourg	.05
409	Sean Casey	.20
410	Eric Milton	.05
411	Trey Moore	.05
412	Mike Stanley	.05
413	Tom Gordon	.05
414	Hal Morris	.05
415	Braden Looper	.05
416	Mike Kelly	.05
417	John Smoltz	.05
418	Roger Cedeno	.05
419	Al Leiter	.05
420	Chuck Knoblauch	.05
421	Felix Rodriguez	.05
422	Bip Roberts	.05
423	Ken Hill	.05
424	Jermaine Allensworth	.05
425	Esteban Yan	.05
426	Scott Karl	.05
427	Sean Berry	.05
428	Rafael Medina	.05
429	Javier Vazquez	.05
430	Rickey Henderson	.75
431	Adam Butler RC	.05
432	Todd Stottlemyre	.05
433	Yamil Benitez	.05
434	Sterling Hitchcock	.05
435	Paul Sorrento	.05
436	Bobby Ayala	.05
437	Tim Raines	.05
438	Chris Hoiles	.05
439	Rod Beck	.05
440	Donnie Sadler	.05
441	Charles Johnson	.05
442	Russ Ortiz	.05
443	Pedro Astacio	.05
444	Wilson Alvarez	.05
445	Mike Blowers	.05
446	Todd Zeile	.05
447	Mel Rojas	.05
448	F.P. Santangelo	.05
449	Dmitri Young	.05
450	Brian Anderson	.05
451	Cecil Fielder	.05
452	Roberto Hernandez	.05
453	Todd Walker	.05
454	Tyler Green	.05
455	Jorge Posada	.05
456	Geronimo Berroa	.05
457	Jose Silva	.05
458	Bobby Bonilla	.05
459	Walt Weiss	.05
460	Darren Dreifort	.05
461	B.J. Surhoff	.05
462	Quinton McCracken	.05
463	Derek Lowe	.05
464	Jorge Fabregas	.05
465	Joey Hamilton	.05
466	Brian Jordan	.05
467	Allen Watson	.05
468	John Jaha	.05
469	Heathcliff Slocumb	.05
470	Gregg Jefferies	.05
471	Scott Brosius	.05
472	Chad Ogea	.05
473	A.J. Hinch	.05
474	Bobby Smith	.05
475	Brian Moehler	.05
476	DaRond Stovall	.05
477	Kevin Young	.05
478	Jeff Suppan	.05
479	Marty Cordova	.05
480	John Halama RC	.25
481	Bubba Trammell	.05
482	Mike Caruso	.05
483	Eric Karros	.05
484	Jamey Wright	.05
485	Mike Sweeney	.05
486	Aaron Sele	.05
487	Cliff Floyd	.05
488	Jeff Brantley	.05
489	Jim Leyritz	.05
490	Denny Neagle	.05
491	Travis Fryman	.05
492	Carlos Baerga	.05
493	Eddie Taubensee	.05
494	Darryl Strawberry	.05
495	Brian Johnson	.05
496	Randy Myers	.05
497	Jeff Blauser	.05
498	Jason Wood	.05
499	Rolando Arrojo RC	.25
500	Johnny Damon	.05
501	Jose Mercedes	.05
502	Tony Batista	.05
503	Mike Piazza	1.50
504	Hideo Nomo	.65
505	Chris Gomez	.05
506	Jesus Sanchez RC	.05
507	Al Martin	.05
508	Brian Edmondson	.05
509	Joe Girardi	.05
510	Shayne Bennett	.05
511	Joe Carter	.05
512	Dave Mlicki	.05
513	Rich Butler RC	.10
514	Dennis Eckersley	.65
515	Travis Lee	.10
516	John Mabry	.05
517	Jose Mesa	.05
518	Phil Nevin	.05
519	Raul Casanova	.05
520	Mike Fetters	.05
521	Gary Sheffield	.30
522	Terry Steinbach	.05
523	Steve Trachsel	.05
524	Josh Booty	.05
525	Darryl Hamilton	.05
526	Mark McLemore	.05
527	Kevin Stocker	.05
528	Bret Boone	.05
529	Shane Andrews	.05
530	Robb Nen	.05
531	Carl Everett	.05
532	LaTroy Hawkins	.05
533	Fernando Vina	.05
534	Michael Tucker	.05
535	Mark Langston	.05
536	Mickey Mantle	2.00
537	Bernard Gilkey	.05
538	Francisco Cordova	.05
539	Mike Bordick	.05
540	Fred McGriff	.05
541	Cliff Politte	.05
542	Jason Varitek	.05
543	Shawon Dunston	.05
544	Brian Meadows	.05
545	Pat Meares	.05
546	Carlos Perez	.05
547	Desi Relaford	.05
548	Antonio Osuna	.05
549	Devon White	.05
550	Sean Runyan	.05
551	Mickey Morandini	.05
552	Dave Martinez	.05
553	Jeff Fassero	.05
554	Ryan Jackson RC	.05
555	Stan Javier	.05
556	Jaime Navarro	.05
557	Jose Offerman	.05
558	Mike Lowell RC	1.00
559	Darrin Fletcher	.05
560	Mark Lewis	.05
561	Dante Bichette	.05
562	Chuck Finley	.05
563	Kerry Wood	.35
564	Andy Benes	.05
565	Freddy Garcia	.05
566	Tom Glavine	.25
567	Jon Nunnally	.05
568	Miguel Cairo	.05
569	Shane Reynolds	.05
570	Roberto Kelly	.05
571	Checklist (Jose Cruz Jr.)	.25
572	Checklist (Ken Griffey Jr.)	.65
573	Checklist (Mark McGwire)	.75
574	Checklist (Cal Ripken Jr.)	1.00
575	Checklist (Frank Thomas)	.45
576	Jeff Bagwell (Unforgettable Moments)	1.00
577	Barry Bonds (Unforgettable Moments)	3.00
578	Tony Clark (Unforgettable Moments)	.25
579	Roger Clemens (Unforgettable Moments)	2.00
580	Jose Cruz Jr. (Unforgettable Moments)	.25
581	Nomar Garciaparra (Unforgettable Moments)	1.50
582	Juan Gonzalez (Unforgettable Moments)	1.00
583	Ben Grieve (Unforgettable Moments)	.25
584	Ken Griffey Jr. (Unforgettable Moments)	2.00
585	Tony Gwynn (Unforgettable Moments)	1.50
586	Derek Jeter (Unforgettable Moments)	3.00
587	Randy Johnson (Unforgettable Moments)	1.00
588	Chipper Jones (Unforgettable Moments)	1.50
589	Greg Maddux (Unforgettable Moments)	1.50
590	Mark McGwire (Unforgettable Moments)	2.50
591	Andy Pettitte (Unforgettable Moments)	.45
592	Paul Molitor (Unforgettable Moments)	1.00
593	Cal Ripken Jr. (Unforgettable Moments)	3.00
594	Alex Rodriguez (Unforgettable Moments)	2.50
595	Scott Rolen (Unforgettable Moments)	.50
596	Curt Schilling (Unforgettable Moments)	.50
597	Frank Thomas (Unforgettable Moments)	1.25
598	Jim Thome (Unforgettable Moments)	.75
599	Larry Walker (Unforgettable Moments)	.25
600	Bernie Williams (Unforgettable Moments)	.30

Decade of Excellence

Decade of Excellence inserts were found in one per 72 Series 1 hobby packs of Fleer Tradition. The 12-card set features 1988 season photos in Fleer's 1988 card design. The set includes only those current players who have been in baseball for 10 years or more. The use of blue and red metallic foil stripes in the background differentiates a scarcer (1:720 hobby packs) "Rare Traditions" parallel to the insert.

		NM/M
Complete Set (12):		35.00
Common Player:		1.00
Inserted 1:72		
Rare Traditions:		3X
Inserted 1:720		
1	Roberto Alomar	1.50
2	Barry Bonds	8.00
3	Roger Clemens	5.00
4	David Cone	1.00
5	Andres Galarraga	1.00
6	Mark Grace	1.00
7	Tony Gwynn	4.00
8	Randy Johnson	3.00
9	Greg Maddux	4.00
10	Mark McGwire	6.00
11	Paul O'Neill	1.00
12	Cal Ripken Jr.	8.00

Diamond Ink

These one-per-pack inserts offer collectors a chance to acquire genuine autographed baseballs. Issued in denominations of 1, 5 and 10 points, the cards had to be accumulated to a total of 500 points of the same player to be redeemed for an autographed ball of that player. Cards are the standard 3-1/2" x 2-1/2" and are printed in black and purple on front and black and yellow on back. The point value of each card is embossed at center to prevent counterfeiting. The rules of the exchange program are printed on back. The deadline for redemption was Dec. 31, 1998. Values shown are for 1-pt. cards. The unnumbered players in the series are listed alphabetically.

		NM/M
Complete Set, 1 pt. (11):		1.00
Common Player, 1 pt.:		.05
5-pt. Cards:		5X
10-pt. Cards:		10X
(1)	Jay Buhner	.05
(2)	Roger Clemens	.20
(3)	Jose Cruz Jr.	.05
(4)	Nomar Garciaparra	.20
(5)	Tony Gwynn	.15
(6)	Roberto Hernandez	.05
(7)	Greg Maddux	.15
(8)	Cal Ripken Jr.	.30
(9)	Alex Rodriguez	.25
(10)	Scott Rolen	.10
(11)	Tony Womack	.05

Diamond Standouts

Diamond Standouts were inserted into Series I packs at a rate of one per 12. The 20-card insert set features players over a diamond design silver foil background.

		NM/M
Complete Set (20):		25.00
Common Player:		.50
1	Jeff Bagwell	1.00
2	Barry Bonds	4.00
3	Roger Clemens	2.00
4	Jose Cruz Jr.	.50
5	Andres Galarraga	.50
6	Nomar Garciaparra	2.00
7	Juan Gonzalez	.75
8	Ken Griffey Jr.	2.00
9	Derek Jeter	4.00
10	Randy Johnson	1.00
11	Chipper Jones	1.50
12	Kenny Lofton	.50
13	Greg Maddux	1.50
14	Pedro Martinez	1.00
15	Mark McGwire	3.00
16	Mike Piazza	2.00
17	Alex Rodriguez	3.00
18	Curt Schilling	.75
19	Frank Thomas	1.00
20	Larry Walker	.50

Diamond Tribute

This 10-card insert was exclusive to Series 2 packs and seeded one per 300 packs. Cards were printed on a leather-like laminated stock and had silver holofoil stamping.

		NM/M
Complete Set (10):		90.00
Common Player:		5.00
DT1	Jeff Bagwell	7.50
DT2	Roger Clemens	10.00
DT3	Nomar Garciaparra	10.00
DT4	Juan Gonzalez	5.00
DT5	Ken Griffey Jr.	12.00
DT6	Mark McGwire	15.00
DT7	Mike Piazza	12.00
DT8	Cal Ripken Jr.	20.00
DT9	Alex Rodriguez	15.00
DT10	Frank Thomas	7.50

Heroes For Kids Commemorative Card

More than two dozen nominees for Players Choice Awards are featured in action photos on both sides of this 11" x 8-1/2" card.

	NM/M
Commemorative Card:	3.00

In the Clutch

This Series 2 insert features stars who can stand up to pressure of big league ball. Fronts have embossed action photos on a prismatic metallic foil background. Backs have a portrait photo and a few words about the player. Stated insertion rate for the inserts was one per 20 packs on average.

		NM/M
Complete Set (15):		25.00
Common Player:		.40
IC1	Jeff Bagwell	1.00
IC2	Barry Bonds	2.00
IC3	Roger Clemens	2.00
IC4	Jose Cruz Jr.	.40
IC5	Nomar Garciaparra	2.00
IC6	Juan Gonzalez	.75
IC7	Ken Griffey Jr.	2.50
IC8	Tony Gwynn	1.50
IC9	Derek Jeter	5.00
IC10	Chipper Jones	1.50
IC11	Greg Maddux	1.50
IC12	Mark McGwire	4.00
IC13	Mike Piazza	2.50
IC14	Frank Thomas	1.00
IC15	Larry Walker	.50

Lumber Company

This 15-card set was exclusive to Series I retail packs and inserted one per 36 packs. It included power hitters and featured the insert name in large letters across the top.

		NM/M
Complete Set (15):		50.00
Common Player:		.75
Inserted 1:36 R		
1	Jeff Bagwell	2.50
2	Barry Bonds	8.00
3	Jose Cruz Jr.	.75
4	Nomar Garciaparra	4.00
5	Juan Gonzalez	1.50
6	Ken Griffey Jr.	5.00
7	Tony Gwynn	3.00
8	Chipper Jones	3.00
9	Tino Martinez	.75
10	Mark McGwire	6.00
11	Mike Piazza	6.00
12	Cal Ripken Jr.	8.00
13	Alex Rodriguez	6.00
14	Frank Thomas	6.00
15	Larry Walker	.75

Mickey Mantle Monumental Moments

This 10-card insert honors Hall of Famer Mickey Mantle's legendary career and was seeded one per 68 packs of Series 2. Fleer/SkyBox worked closely with Mantle's family with each photo in the set personally selected by them. A gold-enhanced version was issued with each card serially numbered to 51.

	NM/M
Complete Set (10):	40.00
Common Card:	5.00
Inserted 1:68	
Gold (51 Sets):	3X
1 Armed and Dangerous	5.00
2 Getting Ready in Spring Training	5.00
3 Mantle and Rizzuto Celebrate	5.00
4 Posed for Action	5.00
5 Signed, Sealed and Ready to Deliver	5.00
6 Triple Crown 1956 Season	5.00
7 Number 7 . . .	5.00
8 Mantle's Powerful Swing . . .	5.00
9 Old-Timers Day Introduction	5.00
10 Portrait of Determination	5.00

Promising Forecast

Potential future stars are showcased in this Series 2 insert. Both front and back have a background of a colorful weather map. Fronts have a glossy player action photo on a matte-finish background. Backs are all-glossy and have a second photo and a few words about the player's potential. Average odds of pulling a Promising Forecast card were stated as one per 12 packs.

	NM/M
Complete Set (20):	7.00
Common Player:	.25
Inserted 1:12	
PF1 Rolando Arrojo	.25
PF2 Sean Casey	.40
PF3 Brad Fullmer	.25
PF4 Karim Garcia	.35
PF5 Ben Grieve	.25
PF6 Todd Helton	3.00
PF7 Richard Hidalgo	.25
PF8 A.J. Hinch	.25
PF9 Paul Konerko	.35
PF10 Mark Kotsay	.25
PF11 Derrek Lee	1.00
PF12 Travis Lee	.35
PF13 Eric Milton	.25
PF14 Magglio Ordonez	.50
PF15 David Ortiz	.50
PF16 Brian Rose	.25
PF17 Miguel Tejada	.35
PF18 Jason Varitek	.35
PF19 Enrique Wilson	.25
PF20 Kerry Wood	1.00

Rookie Sensations

Rookie Sensations included 20 gray-bordered cards of the 1997

most promising players who were eligible for the Rookie of the Year award. Each card contained a multi-colored background and was inserted one per 18 packs.

	NM/M
Complete Set (20):	12.00
Common Player:	.50
Inserted 1:18	
1 Mike Cameron	.50
2 Jose Cruz Jr.	.50
3 Jason Dickson	.50
4 Kelvim Escobar	.50
5 Nomar Garciaparra	3.00
6 Ben Grieve	.50
7 Vladimir Guerrero	3.00
8 Wilton Guerrero	.50
9 Jose Guillen	.50
10 Todd Helton	2.00
11 Livan Hernandez	.50
12 Hideki Irabu	.50
13 Andruw Jones	3.00
14 Matt Morris	.50
15 Magglio Ordonez	1.00
16 Neifi Perez	.50
17 Scott Rolen	2.00
18 Fernando Tatis	.50
19 Brett Tomko	.50
20 Jaret Wright	.50

The Power Game

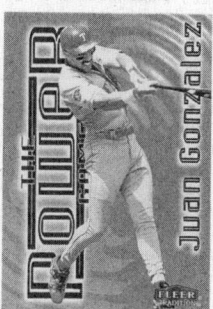

Pitchers and hitters are pictured over a purple metallic background with UV coating in this 20-card insert. Power Game inserts were exclusive to Series I and seeded one per 36 packs.

	NM/M
Complete Set (20):	30.00
Common Player:	.50
Inserted 1:36	
1 Jeff Bagwell	2.00
2 Albert Belle	.50
3 Barry Bonds	6.00
4 Tony Clark	.50
5 Roger Clemens	3.50
6 Jose Cruz Jr.	.50
7 Andres Galarraga	.50
8 Nomar Garciaparra	3.50
9 Juan Gonzalez	1.00
10 Ken Griffey Jr.	4.00
11 Randy Johnson	2.00
12 Greg Maddux	3.00
13 Pedro Martinez	2.00
14 Tino Martinez	.50
15 Mark McGwire	5.00
16 Mike Piazza	4.00
17 Curt Schilling	.75
18 Frank Thomas	2.00
19 Jim Thome	2.00
20 Larry Walker	.50

Vintage '63

Vintage featured 126 different players, with 63 in Series I and 63 in Series II, on the design of 1963 Fleer cards. The insert commemorated the 35th anniversary of Fleer and was seeded one per hobby pack. In addition, Series II featured Mickey Mantle on card No. 67, which completed the original 1963 Fleer set that ended at card No. 66 and wasn't able to include Mantle

MARK McGWIRE
St. Louis Cardinals.—1B

for licensing reasons. The Mantle card was printed in vintage looking stock and was purposely made to look and feel like the originals. Fleer also printed a Classic parallel version to this insert that contained gold foil on the front and was sequentially numbered to 63 with a "C" prefix on the back.

	NM/M
Complete Set (126):	20.00
Complete Series 1 (63):	10.00
Complete Series 2 (63):	10.00
Common Player:	.10
Classics (63 sets):	20X
1 Jason Dickson	.10
2 Tim Salmon	.25
3 Andruw Jones	.75
4 Chipper Jones	1.00
5 Kenny Lofton	.10
6 Greg Maddux	1.00
7 Rafael Palmeiro	.65
8 Cal Ripken Jr.	2.50
9 Nomar Garciaparra	1.25
10 Mark Grace	.10
11 Sammy Sosa	1.25
12 Frank Thomas	.75
13 Deion Sanders	.10
14 Sandy Alomar	.10
15 David Justice	.10
16 Jim Thome	.75
17 Matt Williams	.10
18 Jaret Wright	.10
19 Vinny Castilla	.10
20 Andres Galarraga	.10
21 Todd Helton	.75
22 Larry Walker	.10
23 Tony Clark	.10
24 Moises Alou	.10
25 Kevin Brown	.10
26 Charles Johnson	.10
27 Edgar Renteria	.10
28 Gary Sheffield	.10
29 Jeff Bagwell	.75
30 Craig Biggio	.10
31 Raul Mondesi	.10
32 Mike Piazza	1.50
33 Chuck Knoblauch	.10
34 Paul Molitor	.75
35 Vladimir Guerrero	.75
36 Pedro Martinez	.75
37 Todd Hundley	.10
38 Derek Jeter	2.50
39 Tino Martinez	.10
40 Paul O'Neill	.10
41 Andy Pettitte	.35
42 Mariano Rivera	.20
43 Bernie Williams	.20
44 Ben Grieve	.10
45 Scott Rolen	.65
46 Curt Schilling	.45
47 Jason Kendall	.10
48 Tony Womack	.10
49 Ray Lankford	.10
50 Mark McGwire	2.00
51 Matt Morris	.10
52 Tony Gwynn	1.00
53 Barry Bonds	2.50
54 Jay Buhner	.10
55 Ken Griffey Jr.	1.50
56 Randy Johnson	.75
57 Edgar Martinez	.10
58 Alex Rodriguez	2.00
59 Juan Gonzalez	.65
60 Rusty Greer	.10
61 Ivan Rodriguez	.65
62 Roger Clemens	1.25
63 Jose Cruz Jr.	.10
Checklist #1-63	.10
64 Darin Erstad	.20
65 Jay Bell	.10
66 Andy Benes	.10
67 Mickey Mantle	2.00
68 Karim Garcia	.10
69 Travis Lee	.10
70 Matt Williams	.10
71 Andres Galarraga	.10
72 Tom Glavine	.35
73 Ryan Klesko	.10
74 Denny Neagle	.10
75 John Smoltz	.10
76 Roberto Alomar	.20
77 Joe Carter	.10
78 Mike Mussina	.50
79 B.J. Surhoff	.10
80 Dennis Eckersley	.65
81 Pedro Martinez	.75
82 Mo Vaughn	.10
83 Jeff Blauser	.10
84 Henry Rodriguez	.10
85 Albert Belle	.10
86 Sean Casey	.25
87 Travis Fryman	.10
88 Kenny Lofton	.10
89 Darryl Kile	.10
90 Mike Lansing	.10
91 Bobby Bonilla	.10
92 Cliff Floyd	.10
93 Livan Hernandez	.10
94 Derrek Lee	.10
95 Moises Alou	.10
96 Shane Reynolds	.10
97 Jeff Conine	.10
98 Johnny Damon	.35
99 Eric Karros	.10
100 Hideo Nomo	.65
101 Marquis Grissom	.10
102 Matt Lawton	.10
103 Todd Walker	.10
104 Gary Sheffield	.50
105 Bernard Gilkey	.10
106 Rey Ordonez	.10
107 Chili Davis	.10
108 Chuck Knoblauch	.10
109 Charles Johnson	.10
110 Rickey Henderson	.75
111 Bob Abreu	.10
112 Doug Glanville	.10
113 Gregg Jefferies	.10
114 Al Martin	.10
115 Kevin Young	.10
116 Ron Gant	.10
117 Kevin Brown	.10
118 Ken Caminiti	.10
119 Joey Hamilton	.10
120 Jeff Kent	.10
121 Wade Boggs	1.00
122 Quinton McCracken	.10
123 Fred McGriff	.10
124 Paul Sorrento	.10
125 Jose Canseco	.50
126 Randy Myers	.10
Checklist #64-126	.10

Vintage '63 Classic

Vintage '63 Classic paralleled all 126 Vintage '63 inserts throughout Series 1 and 2, plus the checklists. These cards feature gold-foil stamping on front, specifically around the diamond in the lower-left corner, and are sequentially numbered to 63 sets. Cards have a "C" suffix to the card number.

	NM/M
Complete Set (128):	650.00
Common Player:	4.00
Stars/RC's:	20X

Zone

Inserted in one per 288 packs of Series I Fleer Tradition, Zone featured 15 top players printed on rainbow foil and etching.

	NM/M
Complete Set (15):	130.00
Common Player:	4.00
Inserted 1:288	
1 Jeff Bagwell	7.50
2 Barry Bonds	25.00
3 Roger Clemens	10.00
4 Jose Cruz Jr.	4.00

5 Nomar Garciaparra	10.00
6 Juan Gonzalez	6.00
7 Ken Griffey Jr.	12.00
8 Tony Gwynn	9.00
9 Chipper Jones	9.00
10 Greg Maddux	9.00
11 Mark McGwire	15.00
12 Mike Piazza	12.00
13 Alex Rodriguez	20.00
14 Frank Thomas	7.50
15 Larry Walker	4.00

Update

Fleer's first Update set since 1994 is this 100-card boxed set. It arrived soon after the conclusion of the 1998 World Series and focused on rookies who made their major league debut in September and had not yet had a rookie card. The set had 70 rookies, including 15 making their major league debut, 20 traded players and free agents. There was one subset called Season's Highlights that focused on feats like Mark McGwire's 70th home run, Sammy Sosa's single-month home run record and Kerry Wood's 20 strikeout performance.

	NM/M
Complete Set (100):	12.50
Common Player:	.05
U1 Mark McGwire (Season Highlights)	.75
U2 Sammy Sosa (Season Highlights)	.45
U3 Roger Clemens (Season Highlights)	.45
U4 Barry Bonds (Season Highlights)	1.00
U5 Kerry Wood (Season Highlights)	.20
U6 Paul Molitor (Season Highlights)	.25
U7 Ken Griffey Jr. (Season Highlights)	.50
U8 Cal Ripken Jr. (Season Highlights)	1.00
U9 David Wells (Season Highlights)	.05
U10 Alex Rodriguez (Season Highlights)	.75
U11 Angel Pena RC	.25
U12 Bruce Chen	.05
U13 Craig Wilson	.05
U14 Orlando Hernandez RC	1.50
U15 Aramis Ramirez	.05
U16 Aaron Boone	.05
U17 Bob Henley	.05
U18 Juan Guzman	.05
U19 Darryl Hamilton	.05
U20 Jay Payton	.05
U21 Jeremy Powell RC	.05
U22 Ben Davis	.05
U23 Preston Wilson	.10
U24 Jim Parque RC	.15
U25 Odalis Perez RC	.25
U26 Ron Belliard	.05
U27 Royce Clayton	.05
U28 George Lombard	.05
U29 Tony Phillips	.05
U30 Fernando Seguignol RC	.15
U31 Armando Rios RC	.10
U32 Jerry Hairston Jr. RC	.05
U33 Justin Baughman RC	.05
U34 Seth Greisinger	.05
U35 Alex Gonzalez	.05
U36 Michael Barrett	.05
U37 Carlos Beltran	.35
U38 Ellis Burks	.05
U39 Jose Jimenez	.05
U40 Carlos Guillen	.05
U41 Marlon Anderson	.05
U42 Scott Elarton	.05
U43 Glenallen Hill	.05
U44 Shane Monahan	.05
U45 Dennis Martinez	.05
U46 Carlos Febles RC	.20
U47 Carlos Perez	.05
U48 Wilton Guerrero	.05
U49 Randy Johnson	.45
U50 Brian Simmons RC	.05
U51 Carlton Loewer	.05
U52 Mark DeRosa RC	.50
U53 Tim Young RC	.05
U54 Gary Gaetti	.05
U55 Eric Chavez	.25
U56 Carl Pavano	.15
U57 Mike Stanley	.05
U58 Todd Stottlemyre	.05
U59 Gabe Kapler RC	.50
U60 Mike Jerzembeck RC	.05
U61 Mitch Meluskey RC	.15
U62 Bill Pulsipher	.05
U63 Derrick Gibson	.05
U64 John Rocker RC	.75
U65 Calvin Pickering	.05
U66 Blake Stein	.05
U67 Fernando Tatis	.05
U68 Gabe Alvarez	.05
U69 Jeffrey Hammonds	.05
U70 Adrian Beltre	.25
U71 Ryan Bradley RC	.10
U72 Edgar Clemente RC	.05
U73 Rick Croushore RC	.05
U74 Matt Clement	.15
U75 Dermal Brown	.05
U76 Paul Bako	.05
U77 Placido Polanco RC	1.00
U78 Jay Tessmer	.05
U79 Jarrod Washburn	.05
U80 Kevin Witt	.05
U81 Mike Metcalfe	.05
U82 Daryle Ward	.05
U83 Benj Sampson RC	.05
U84 Mike Kinkade RC	.20
U85 Randy Winn	.05
U86 Jeff Shaw	.05
U87 Troy Glaus RC	4.00
U88 Hideo Nomo	.35
U89 Mark Grudzielanek	.05
U90 Mike Frank RC	.05
U91 Bobby Howry RC	.10
U92 Ryan Minor RC	.15
U93 Corey Koskie RC	1.00
U94 Matt Anderson RC	.20
U95 Joe Carter	.05
U96 Paul Konerko	.15
U97 Sidney Ponson	.05
U98 Jeremy Giambi RC	.25
U99 Jeff Kubenka RC	.05
U100 J.D. Drew RC	5.00

Diamond Skills Commemorative Sheet

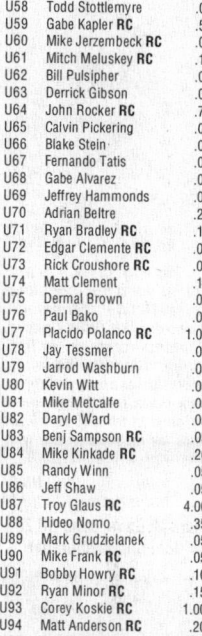

In conjunction with its sponsorship of the Diamond Skills program, Fleer and its 2,500 direct dealers distributed this eight-player sheet to 7-14 year olds participating in the event. Participants could get a sheet by redeeming Fleer wrappers at a local card store. The 10" x 9" sheet features full size Fleer Tradition card reproductions. At top is a list of 1997 Diamond Skills winners.

	NM/M
Complete Sheet:	2.00

Mantle & Sons

As part of its participation in SportsFest in May, 1998, Fleer issued a promotional card featuring a vintage color photo of Mickey Mantle and his sons, David and Danny. The back of the card announced Fleer's first-ever inclusion of Mickey Mantle cards in some of its forthcoming releases.

	NM/M
Mickey Mantle, Danny Mantle, David Mantle	3.00

Mickey Mantle Promo Postcard

This 4-1/4" x 5-1/2" color postcard was sent to Fleer dealers to announce a Mickey Mantle commemorative series in its Series 2 product. The address side has the Fleer Tradition logo in black, blue and red. The picture side has a color photo of one of the Mantle cards to be issued in the format of the 1963 Fleer issue. Cards are individually serial numbered within an edition of 3,500.

	NM/M
Mickey Mantle	4.00

Mark McGwire 62nd HR 23K Gold Commemorative

Marketed as a retail-exclusive "Official 62nd HR 23 Kt. Gold Commemorative Card," this 2-1/2" x 3-1/2" card was sold in a colorful blister pack. Embossed in 23-karat gold foil is an image of McGwire in action. Also on front are a 62-HR logo and a facsimile autograph, along with the legend "Smashing the Record." On back is a small picture of McGwire with the large 9-8-98 date and the details of the record blast. There are appropriate licensing logos and a serial number from within an edition of 200,000.

	NM/M
Mark McGwire	5.00

National Convention Commemorative Set

In conjunction with its participation at the 19th National Sports Collectors Convention in Chicago in August 1998, Fleer distributed this commemorative set to persons purchasing VIP admission packages. The set includes a specially numbered (NC1) Fleer Tradition Mickey Mantle card, a card picturing Mick with his sons, one of seven large-format (3-1/2" x 5") cards reproducing Mantle Monumental Moments inserts, and an unnumbered header card. The Monumental Moments reproductions are printed on a pin-striped-sky background.

		NM/M
Complete Set (8):		15.00
Common Card:		2.25
NC1	Mickey Mantle (Fleer Tradition)	2.25
NC2	Mickey Mantle (With sons.)	2.25
NC3	Mickey Mantle (Monumental Moments - accepting trophy.)	2.25
NC4	Mickey Mantle (Monumental Moments - making a throw.)	2.25
NC5	Mickey Mantle (Monumental Moments - sliding pit.)	2.25
NC6	Mickey Mantle (Monumental Moments - batting.)	2.25
NC7	Mickey Mantle (Monumental Moments - number retired.)	2.25
	Header Card	.25

1999 Fleer

Released as a single series in 10-card packs with a suggested retail price of $1.59, the base set consists of 600 cards, including 10 checklists and a 15-card Franchise Futures subset. Cards are UV coated, with borderless photos and gold-foil graphics. Backs have personal bio-information along with year-by-year career stats and a small photo. There are two parallels, Starting Nine, which are hobby-exclusive, numbered to nine sets with blue foil stamping and Warning Track. Found exclusively in retail packs, Warning Tracks can be identified by red foil stamping and a Warning Track logo.

	NM/M
Complete Set (600):	25.00
Common Player:	.05
Warning Track:	2X
Inserted 1:1 R	
Pack (10):	1.00
Wax Box (36):	25.00

#	Player	Price
1	Mark McGwire	2.00
2	Sammy Sosa	1.25
3	Ken Griffey Jr.	1.50
4	Kerry Wood	.30
5	Derek Jeter	2.50
6	Stan Musial	2.00
7	J.D. Drew	.65
7p	J.D. Drew/OPS	1.50
8	Cal Ripken Jr.	2.50
9	Alex Rodriguez	2.00
10	Travis Lee	.15
11	Andres Galarraga	.05
12	Nomar Garciaparra	1.25
13	Albert Belle	.05
14	Barry Larkin	.05
15	Dante Bichette	.05
16	Tony Clark	.05
17	Moises Alou	.05
18	Rafael Palmeiro	.65
19	Raul Mondesi	.05
20	Vladimir Guerrero	.75
21	John Olerud	.05
22	Bernie Williams	.10
23	Ben Grieve	.65
24	Scott Rolen	.65
25	Jeromy Burnitz	.05
26	Ken Caminiti	.05
27	Barry Bonds	2.50
28	Todd Helton	.75
29	Juan Gonzalez	.65
30	Roger Clemens	1.25
31	Andruw Jones	.75
32	Mo Vaughn	.05
33	Larry Walker	.05
34	Frank Thomas	.75
35	Manny Ramirez	.75
36	Randy Johnson	.75
37	Vinny Castilla	.05
38	Juan Encarnacion	.05
39	Jeff Bagwell	.75
40	Gary Sheffield	.50
41	Mike Piazza	1.50
42	Richie Sexson	.05
43	Tony Gwynn	1.00
44	Chipper Jones	1.00
45	Jim Thome	.65
46	Craig Biggio	.05
47	Carlos Delgado	.40
48	Greg Vaughn	.05
49	Greg Maddux	1.00
50	Troy Glaus	.65
51	Roberto Alomar	.10
52	Dennis Eckersley	.60
53	Mike Caruso	.05
54	Bruce Chen	.05
55	Aaron Boone	.05
56	Bartolo Colon	.05
57	Derrick Gibson	.05
58	Brian Anderson	.05
59	Gabe Alvarez	.05
60	Todd Dunwoody	.05
61	Rod Beck	.05
62	Derek Bell	.05
63	Francisco Cordova	.05
64	Johnny Damon	.25
65	Adrian Beltre	.15
66	Garret Anderson	.05
67	Armando Benitez	.05
68	Edgardo Alfonzo	.05
69	Ryan Bradley	.05
70	Eric Chavez	.30
71	Bobby Abreu	.05
72	Andy Ashby	.05
73	Ellis Burks	.05
74	Jeff Cirillo	.05
75	Jay Buhner	.05
76	Ron Gant	.05
77	Rolando Arrojo	.05
78	Will Clark	.10
79	Chris Carpenter	.05
80	Jim Edmonds	.05
81	Tony Batista	.05
82	Shane Andrews	.05
83	Mark DeRosa	.05
84	Brady Anderson	.05
85	Tony Gordon	.05
86	Brant Brown	.05
87	Ray Durham	.05
88	Ron Coomer	.05
89	Bret Boone	.05
90	Travis Fryman	.05
91	Darryl Kile	.05
92	Paul Bako	.05
93	Cliff Floyd	.05
94	Scott Elarton	.05
95	Jeremy Giambi	.05
96	Darren Dreifort	.05
97	Marquis Grissom	.05
98	Marty Cordova	.05
99	Fernando Seguignol	.05
100	Orlando Hernandez	.05
101	Jose Cruz Jr.	.05
102	Jason Giambi	.60
103	Damion Easley	.05
104	Freddy Garcia	.05
105	Marlon Anderson	.05
106	Kevin Brown	.05
107	Joe Carter	.05
108	Russ Davis	.05
109	Brian Jordan	.05
110	Wade Boggs	1.00
111	Tom Goodwin	.05
112	Scott Brosius	.05
113	Darin Erstad	.10
114	Jay Bell	.05
115	Tom Glavine	.25
116	Pedro Martinez	.75
117	Mark Grace	.10
118	Russ Ortiz	.05
119	Magglio Ordonez	.10
120	Sean Casey	.15
121	Rafael Roque RC	.05
122	Brian Giles	.05
123	Mike Lansing	.05
124	David Cone	.05
125	Alex Gonzalez	.05
126	Carl Everett	.05
127	Jeff King	.05
128	Charles Johnson	.05
129	Geoff Jenkins	.05
130	Corey Koskie	.05
131	Brad Fullmer	.05
132	Al Leiter	.05
133	Rickey Henderson	.75
134	Rico Brogna	.05
135	Jose Guillen	.05
136	Matt Clement	.05
137	Carlos Guillen	.05
138	Orel Hershiser	.05
139	Ray Lankford	.05
140	Miguel Cairo	.05
141	Chuck Finley	.05
142	Rusty Greer	.05
143	Kelvim Escobar	.05
144	Ryan Klesko	.05
145	Andy Benes	.05
146	Eric Davis	.05
147	David Wells	.05
148	Trot Nixon	.05
149	Jose Hernandez	.05
150	Mark Johnson	.05
151	Mike Frank	.05
152	Joey Hamilton	.05
153	David Justice	.05
154	Mike Mussina	.40
155	Neifi Perez	.05
156	Luis Gonzalez	.10
157	Livan Hernandez	.05
158	Dermal Brown	.05
159	Jose Lima	.05
160	Eric Karros	.05
161	Ronnie Belliard	.05
162	Matt Lawton	.05
163	Dustin Hermanson	.05
164	Brian McRae	.05
165	Mike Kinkade	.05
166	A.J. Hinch	.05
167	Doug Glanville	.05
168	Hideo Nomo	.65
169	Jason Kendall	.05
170	Steve Finley	.05
171	Jeff Kent	.05
172	Ben Davis	.05
173	Edgar Martinez	.05
174	Eli Marrero	.05
175	Quinton McCracken	.05
176	Rick Helling	.05
177	Tom Evans	.05
178	Carl Pavano	.10
179	Todd Greene	.05
180	Omar Daal	.05
181	George Lombard	.05
182	Ryan Minor	.05
183	Troy O'Leary	.05
184	Robb Nen	.05
185	Mickey Morandini	.05
186	Robin Ventura	.05
187	Pete Harnisch	.05
188	Kenny Lofton	.05
189	Eric Milton	.05
190	Bobby Higginson	.05
191	Jamie Moyer	.05
192	Mark Kotsay	.05
193	Shane Reynolds	.05
194	Carlos Febles	.05
195	Jeff Kubenka	.05
196	Chuck Knoblauch	.05
197	Kenny Rogers	.05
198	Bill Mueller	.05
199	Shane Monahan	.05
200	Matt Morris	.05
201	Fred McGriff	.05
202	Ivan Rodriguez	.65
203	Kevin Witt	.05
204	Troy Percival	.05
205	David Dellucci	.05
206	Kevin Millwood	.05
207	Jerry Hairston Jr.	.05
208	Mike Stanley	.05
209	Henry Rodriguez	.05
210	Trevor Hoffman	.05
211	Craig Wilson	.05
212	Reggie Sanders	.05
213	Carlton Loewer	.05
214	Omar Vizquel	.05
215	Gabe Kapler	.05
216	Derrek Lee	.05
217	Billy Wagner	.05
218	Dean Palmer	.05
219	Chan Ho Park	.05
220	Fernando Vina	.05
221	Roy Halladay	.75
222	Paul Molitor	.75
223	Ugueth Urbina	.05
224	Rey Ordonez	.05
225	Ricky Ledee	.05
226	Scott Spiezio	.05
227	Wendell Magee Jr.	.05
228	Aramis Ramirez	.05
229	Brian Simmons	.05
230	Fernando Tatis	.05
231	Bobby Smith	.05
232	Aaron Sele	.05
233	Shawn Green	.20
234	Mariano Rivera	.15
235	Tim Salmon	.10
236	Andy Fox	.05
237	Denny Neagle	.05
238	John Valentin	.05
239	Kevin Tapani	.05
240	Paul Konerko	.10
241	Robert Fick	.05
242	Edgar Renteria	.05
243	Brett Tomko	.05
244	Daryle Ward	.05
245	Carlos Beltran	.30
246	Angel Pena	.05
247	Steve Woodard	.05
248	David Ortiz	.05
249	Justin Thompson	.05
250	Rondell White	.05
251	Jaret Wright	.05
252	Ed Sprague	.05
253	Jay Payton	.05
254	Mike Lowell	.05
255	Orlando Cabrera	.05
256	Jason Schmidt	.05
257	David Segui	.05
258	Paul Sorrento	.05
259	John Wetteland	.05
260	Devon White	.05
261	Odalis Perez	.05
262	Calvin Pickering	.05
263	Alex Ramirez	.05
264	Preston Wilson	.05
265	Brad Radke	.05
266	Walt Weiss	.05
267	Tim Young	.05
268	Tino Martinez	.05
269	Matt Stairs	.05
270	Curt Schilling	.25
271	Tony Womack	.05
272	Ismael Valdes	.05
273	Wally Joyner	.05
274	Armando Rios	.05
275	Andy Pettitte	.25
276	Bubba Trammell	.05
277	Todd Zeile	.05
278	Shannon Stewart	.05
279	Matt Williams	.05
280	John Rocker	.05
281	B.J. Surhoff	.05
282	Eric Young	.05
283	Dmitri Young	.05
284	John Smoltz	.05
285	Todd Walker	.05
286	Paul O'Neill	.05
287	Blake Stein	.05
288	Kevin Young	.05
289	Quivilo Veras	.05
290	Kirk Rueter	.05
291	Randy Winn	.05
292	Miguel Tejada	.05
293	J.T. Snow	.05
294	Michael Tucker	.05
295	Jay Tessmer	.05
296	Scott Erickson	.05
297	Tim Wakefield	.05
298	Jeff Abbott	.05
299	Eddie Taubensee	.05
300	Darryl Hamilton	.05
301	Kevin Orie	.05
302	Jose Offerman	.05
303	Scott Karl	.05
304	Chris Widger	.05
305	Todd Hundley	.05
306	Desi Relaford	.05
307	Sterling Hitchcock	.05
308	Delino DeShields	.05
309	Alex Gonzalez	.05
310	Justin Baughman	.05
311	Jamey Wright	.05
312	Wes Helms	.05
313	Dante Powell	.05
314	Jim Abbott	.05
315	Manny Alexander	.05
316	Harold Baines	.05
317	Danny Graves	.05
318	Sandy Alomar	.05
319	Pedro Astacio	.05
320	Jermaine Allensworth	.05
321	Matt Anderson	.05
322	Chad Curtis	.05
323	Antonio Osuna	.05
324	Brad Ausmus	.05
325	Steve Trachsel	.05
326	Mike Blowers	.05
327	Brian Bohanon	.05
328	Chris Gomez	.05
329	Valerio de los Santos	.05
330	Rich Aurilia	.05
331	Michael Barrett	.05
332	Rick Aguilera	.05
333	Adrian Brown	.05
334	Bill Spiers	.05
335	Matt Beech	.05
336	David Bell	.05
337	Juan Acevedo	.05
338	Jose Canseco	.50
339	Wilson Alvarez	.05
340	Luis Alicea	.05
341	Jason Dickson	.05
342	Mike Bordick	.05
343	Ben Ford	.05
344	Keith Lockhart	.05
345	Jason Christiansen	.05
346	Darren Bragg	.05
347	Doug Brocail	.05
348	Jeff Blauser	.05
349	James Baldwin	.05
350	Jeffrey Hammonds	.05
351	Ricky Bottalico	.05
352	Russ Branyon	.05
353	Mark Brownson	.05
354	Dave Berg	.05
355	Sean Bergman	.05
356	Jeff Conine	.05
357	Shayne Bennett	.05
358	Bobby Bonilla	.05
359	Bob Wickman	.05
360	Carlos Baerga	.05
361	Chris Fussell	.05
362	Chili Davis	.05
363	Jerry Spradlin	.05
364	Carlos Hernandez	.05
365	Roberto Hernandez	.05
366	Marvin Benard	.05
367	Ken Cloude	.05
368	Tony Fernandez	.05
369	John Burkett	.05
370	Gary DiSarcina	.05
371	Alan Benes	.05
372	Karim Garcia	.05
373	Carlos Perez	.05
374	Damon Buford	.05
375	Mark Clark	.05
376	Edgard Clemente RC	.05
377	Chad Bradford	.05
378	Frank Catalanotto	.05
379	Vic Darensbourg	.05
380	Sean Berry	.05
381	Dave Burba	.05
382	Sal Fasano	.05
383	Steve Parris	.05
384	Roger Cedeno	.05
385	Chad Fox	.05
386	Wilton Guerrero	.05
387	Dennis Cook	.05
388	Joe Girardi	.05
389	LaTroy Hawkins	.05
390	Ryan Christenson	.05
391	Paul Byrd	.05
392	Lou Collier	.05
393	Jeff Fassero	.05
394	Jim Leyritz	.05
395	Shawn Estes	.05
396	Mike Kelly	.05
397	Rich Croushore	.05
398	Royce Clayton	.05
399	Rudy Seanez	.05
400	Darrin Fletcher	.05
401	Shigetosi Hasegawa	.05
402	Bernard Gilkey	.05
403	Juan Guzman	.05
404	Jeff Frye	.05
405	Marino Santana	.05
406	Alex Fernandez	.05
407	Gary Gaetti	.05
408	Dan Miceli	.05
409	Mike Cameron	.05
410	Mike Remlinger	.05
411	Joey Cora	.05
412	Mark Gardner	.05
413	Aaron Ledesma	.05
414	Jerry Dipoto	.05
415	Ricky Gutierrez	.05
416	John Franco	.05
417	Mendy Lopez	.05
418	Hideki Irabu	.05
419	Mark Grudzielanek	.05
420	Bobby Hughes	.05
421	Pat Meares	.05
422	Jimmy Haynes	.05
423	Bob Henley	.05
424	Bobby Estalella	.05
425	Jon Lieber	.05
426	Giomar Guevara RC	.05
427	Jose Jimenez	.05
428	Deivi Cruz	.05
429	Jonathan Johnson	.05
430	Ken Hill	.05
431	Craig Grebeck	.05
432	Jose Rosado	.05
433	Danny Klassen	.05
434	Bobby Howry	.05
435	Gerald Williams	.05
436	Omar Olivares	.05
437	Chris Hoiles	.05
438	Seth Greisinger	.05
439	Scott Hatteberg	.05
440	Jeremi Gonzalez	.05
441	Wil Cordero	.05
442	Jeff Montgomery	.05
443	Chris Stynes	.05
444	Tony Saunders	.05
445	Einar Diaz	.05
446	Laril Gonzalez	.05
447	Ryan Jackson	.05
448	Mike Hampton	.05
449	Todd Hollandsworth	.05
450	Gabe White	.05
451	John Jaha	.05
452	Bret Saberhagen	.05
453	Otis Nixon	.05
454	Steve Kline	.05
455	Butch Huskey	.05
456	Mike Jerzembeck	.05
457	Wayne Gomes	.05
458	Mike Macfarlane	.05
459	Jesus Sanchez	.05
460	Al Martin	.05
461	Dwight Gooden	.05
462	Ruben Rivera	.05
463	Pat Hentgen	.05
464	Jose Valentin	.05
465	Vladimir Nunez	.05
466	Charlie Hayes	.05
467	Jay Powell	.05
468	Raul Ibanez	.05
469	Kent Mercker	.05
470	John Mabry	.05
471	Woody Williams	.05
472	Roberto Kelly	.05
473	Jim Mecir	.05
474	Dave Hollins	.05
475	Rafael Medina	.05
476	Darren Lewis	.05
477	Felix Heredia	.05
478	Brian Hunter	.05
479	Matt Mantei	.05
480	Richard Hidalgo	.05
481	Bobby Jones	.05
482	Hal Morris	.05
483	Ramiro Mendoza	.05
484	Matt Luke	.05
485	Esteban Loaiza	.05
486	Mark Loretta	.05
487	A.J. Pierzynski	.05
488	Charles Nagy	.05
489	Kevin Sefcik	.05
490	Jason McDonald	.05
491	Jeremy Powell	.05
492	Scott Servais	.05
493	Abraham Nunez	.05
494	Stan Spencer	.05
495	Stan Javier	.05
496	Jose Paniagua	.05
497	Gregg Jefferies	.05
498	Gregg Olson	.05
499	Derek Lowe	.05
500	Willis Otanez	.05
501	Brian Moehler	.05
502	Glenallen Hill	.05
503	Bobby Jones	.05
504	Greg Norton	.05
505	Mike Jackson	.05
506	Kirt Manwaring	.05

507	Eric Weaver	.05
508	Mitch Meluskey	.05
509	Todd Jones	.05
510	Mike Matheny	.05
511	Benj Sampson	.05
512	Tony Phillips	.05
513	Mike Thurman	.05
514	Jorge Posada	.05
515	Bill Taylor	.05
516	Mike Sweeney	.05
517	Jose Silva	.05
518	Mark Lewis	.05
519	Chris Peters	.05
520	Brian Johnson	.05
521	Mike Timlin	.05
522	Mark McLemore	.05
523	Dan Plesac	.05
524	Kelly Stinnett	.05
525	Sidney Ponson	.05
526	Jim Parque	.05
527	Tyler Houston	.05
528	John Thomson	.05
529	Mike Metcalfe	.05
530	Robert Person	.05
531	Marc Newfield	.05
532	Javier Vazquez	.05
533	Terry Steinbach	.05
534	Turk Wendell	.05
535	Tim Raines	.05
536	Brian Meadows	.05
537	Mike Lieberthal	.05
538	Ricardo Rincon	.05
539	Dan Wilson	.05
540	John Johnstone	.05
541	Todd Stottlemyre	.05
542	Kevin Stocker	.05
543	Ramon Martinez	.05
544	Mike Simms	.05
545	Paul Quantrill	.05
546	Matt Walbeck	.05
547	Turner Ward	.05
548	Bill Pulsipher	.05
549	Donnie Sadler	.05
550	Lance Johnson	.05
551	Bill Simas	.05
552	Jeff Reed	.05
553	Jeff Shaw	.05
554	Joe Randa	.05
555	Paul Shuey	.05
556	Mike Redmond	.05
557	Sean Runyan	.05
558	Enrique Wilson	.05
559	Scott Radinsky	.05
560	Larry Sutton	.05
561	Masato Yoshii	.05
562	David Nilsson	.05
563	Mike Trombley	.05
564	Darryl Strawberry	.05
565	Dave Mlicki	.05
566	Placido Polanco	.05
567	Yorkis Perez	.05
568	Esteban Yan	.05
569	Lee Stevens	.05
570	Steve Sinclair	.05
571	Jarrod Washburn	.05
572	Lenny Webster	.05
573	Mike Sirotka	.05
574	Jason Varitek	.05
575	Terry Mulholland	.05
576	Adrian Beltre (Franchise Futures)	.10
577	Eric Chavez (Franchise Futures)	.20
578	J.D. Drew (Franchise Futures)	.35
579	Juan Encarnacion (Franchise Futures)	.05
580	Nomar Garciaparra (Franchise Futures)	.65
581	Troy Glaus (Franchise Futures)	.35
582	Ben Grieve (Franchise Futures)	.05
583	Vladimir Guerrero (Franchise Futures)	.40
584	Todd Helton (Franchise Futures)	.35
585	Derek Jeter (Franchise Futures)	1.25
586	Travis Lee (Franchise Futures)	.10
587	Alex Rodriguez (Franchise Futures)	1.00
588	Scott Rolen (Franchise Futures)	.30
589	Richie Sexson (Franchise Futures)	.05
590	Kerry Wood (Franchise Futures)	.20
591	Ken Griffey Jr. (Checklist)	.75
592	Chipper Jones (Checklist)	.50
593	Alex Rodriguez (Checklist)	1.00
594	Sammy Sosa (Checklist)	.65
595	Mark McGwire (Checklist)	1.00
596	Cal Ripken Jr. (Checklist)	1.25
597	Nomar Garciaparra (Checklist)	.65
598	Derek Jeter (Checklist)	1.25
599	Kerry Wood (Checklist)	.20
600	J.D. Drew (Checklist)	.40

Starting Nine

This ultra-scarce, hobby-only parallel insert, found at the rate of about two cards per case, includes

just nine cards of each player. Sharing the basic design of the Fleer Traditional set, the cards have blue metallic foil printing on front, including a "STARTING 9 NINE" logo at lower-right. At bottom right, the card's individual serial number from within the edition of nine is printed. Backs have an "S" suffix to the card number.

	NM/M
Common Player:	20.00

Warning Track Collection

Each of the cards in '99 Fleer Tradition was paralleled in this retail-only issue found one per pack. Warning Track cards are distinguished by the use of red metallic foil on front for the player's name, team, position that are in gold-foil on the regular version. There is also a special "Warning Track Collection" logo in red foil at bottom-right. On back, WTC cards have a "W" suffix to the card number.

	NM/M
Complete Set (600):	160.00
Common Player:	.50
Stars:	2X

Fleer Date With Destiny

This 10-card set takes a look at what Hall of Fame plaques might look like for some of today's great players. These are serially numbered to 100 sets.

		NM/M
Complete Set (10):		300.00
Common Player:		20.00
Production 100 Sets		
1	Barry Bonds	60.00
2	Roger Clemens	35.00
3	Ken Griffey Jr.	40.00
4	Tony Gwynn	30.00
5	Greg Maddux	30.00
6	Mark McGwire	50.00
7	Mike Piazza	40.00
8	Cal Ripken Jr.	60.00
9	Alex Rodriguez	50.00
10	Frank Thomas	20.00

Diamond Magic

A multi-layer card, where collectors turn a "wheel" for a kaleidoscope effect behind the player image. These are seeded 1:96 packs.

		NM/M
Complete Set (15):		50.00
Common Player:		1.00
Inserted 1:96		
1	Barry Bonds	9.00
2	Roger Clemens	4.50
3	Nomar Garciaparra	4.50
4	Ken Griffey Jr.	5.00
5	Tony Gwynn	3.75
6	Orlando Hernandez	1.00
7	Derek Jeter	9.00
8	Randy Johnson	3.00
9	Chipper Jones	3.75
10	Greg Maddux	3.75
11	Mark McGwire	6.00
12	Alex Rodriguez	7.50
13	Sammy Sosa	4.50
14	Bernie Williams	1.50
15	Kerry Wood	2.00

Going Yard

This 15-card set features the top home run hitters from the '98 season. These 1:18 pack inserts unfold to be twice as wide as regular cards and takes an unorthodox look at how far the longest home runs went.

		NM/M
Complete Set (15):		4.00
Common Player:		.10
Inserted 1:18		
1	Moises Alou	.10
2	Albert Belle	.10
3	Jose Canseco	.30
4	Vinny Castilla	.10
5	Andres Galarraga	.10
6	Juan Gonzalez	.20
7	Ken Griffey Jr.	.75
8	Chipper Jones	.50
9	Mark McGwire	1.00
10	Rafael Palmeiro	.35
11	Mike Piazza	.75
12	Alex Rodriguez	1.00
13	Sammy Sosa	.65
14	Greg Vaughn	.10
15	Mo Vaughn	.10

Golden Memories

This 15-card set pays tribute to the great moments from the 1998 season including David Wells perfect

game and McGwire's record breaking season. These are seeded 1:54 packs on an embossed frame design.

		NM/M
Complete Set (15):		45.00
Common Player:		.75
Inserted 1:54		
1	Albert Belle	.75
2	Barry Bonds	7.50
3	Roger Clemens	4.50
4	Nomar Garciaparra	4.50
5	Juan Gonzalez	1.50
6	Ken Griffey Jr.	3.75
7	Randy Johnson	2.75
8	Greg Maddux	3.25
9	Mark McGwire	5.00
10	Mike Piazza	3.75
11	Cal Ripken Jr.	7.50
12	Alex Rodriguez	6.00
13	Sammy Sosa	4.50
14	David Wells	.75
15	Kerry Wood	2.00

Home Run Heroes

These cards were part of an unannounced multi-manufacturer (Fleer, Upper Deck, Topps, Pacific) insert program which was exclusive to Wal-Mart. Each company produced cards of Mark McGwire and Sammy Sosa, along with two other premier sluggers. Each company's cards share a "Power Elite" logo at top and "Home Run Heroes" logo vertically at right.

		NM/M
Complete Set (4):		7.50
Common Player:		1.50
1	Mark McGwire (Tradition)	3.00
2	Sammy Sosa (Sports Illustrated)	2.00
3	Mike Piazza (SkyBox Thunder)	2.00
4	Nomar Garciaparra (SkyBox Thunder)	2.00

Stan Musial Monumental Moments

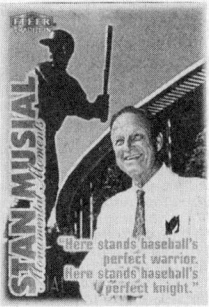

Great moments and insight from and about the St. Louis Cardinals great. This 10-card tribute set chronicles Musial's legendary career. These are seeded 1:36 packs with 500 autographed cards randomly seeded.

		NM/M
Complete Set (10):		15.00
Common Musial:		2.00
Autographed Card:		60.00
1	Life in Donora	2.00
2	Values	2.00
3	In the Beginning	2.00
4	In the Navy	2.00
5	The 1948 Season (W/Red Schoendienst.)	2.00
6	Success Stories (W/Pres. Kennedy.)	2.00
7	Mr. Cardinal	2.00
8	Most Valuable Player	2.00
9	... baseball's perfect knight	2.00
10	Hall of Fame	2.00

Rookie Flashback

This 15-card set features the impact rookies from the 1998 season. These are seeded 1:6 packs and feature sculpture embossing.

		NM/M
Complete Set (15):		5.00
Common Player:		.25
Inserted 1:6		
1	Matt Anderson	.25
2	Rolando Arrojo	.25
3	Adrian Beltre	.50
4	Mike Caruso	.25
5	Eric Chavez	.40
6	J.D. Drew	.75
7	Juan Encarnacion	.25
8	Brad Fullmer	.25
9	Troy Glaus	1.50
10	Ben Grieve	.25
11	Todd Helton	1.50
12	Orlando Hernandez	.25
13	Travis Lee	.40
14	Richie Sexson	.25
15	Kerry Wood	.65

Vintage '61

This 50-card set takes the first 50 cards from the base set and showcases them in the 1961 Fleer "Baseball Greats" card design. These are seeded one per hobby pack.

		NM/M
Complete Set (50):		7.50
Common Player:		.05
Inserted 1:1		
1	Mark McGwire	.75
2	Sammy Sosa	.50
3	Ken Griffey Jr.	.60
4	Kerry Wood	.25
5	Derek Jeter	1.00
6	Stan Musial	.75
7	J.D. Drew	.30
8	Cal Ripken Jr.	1.00
9	Alex Rodriguez	.75
10	Travis Lee	.10
11	Andres Galarraga	.05
12	Nomar Garciaparra	.50
13	Albert Belle	.05
14	Barry Larkin	.05
15	Dante Bichette	.05
16	Tony Clark	.05
17	Moises Alou	.05
18	Rafael Palmeiro	.30
19	Raul Mondesi	.05
20	Vladimir Guerrero	.35
21	John Olerud	.05
22	Bernie Williams	.10
23	Ben Grieve	.05
24	Scott Rolen	.30
25	Jeromy Burnitz	.05
26	Ken Caminiti	.05
27	Barry Bonds	1.00
28	Todd Helton	.35
29	Juan Gonzalez	.25
30	Roger Clemens	.50
31	Andruw Jones	.35
32	Mo Vaughn	.05
33	Larry Walker	.05
34	Frank Thomas	.35
35	Manny Ramirez	.35
36	Randy Johnson	.35
37	Vinny Castilla	.05
38	Juan Encarnacion	.05
39	Jeff Bagwell	.35
40	Gary Sheffield	.25
41	Mike Piazza	.60

42	Richie Sexson	.05
43	Tony Gwynn	.45
44	Chipper Jones	.45
45	Jim Thome	.30
46	Craig Biggio	.05
47	Carlos Delgado	.25
48	Greg Vaughn	.05
49	Greg Maddux	.45
50	Troy Glaus	.35

Update

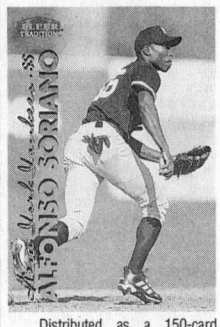

Distributed as a 150-card boxed set, the main focus for this release is the inclusion of rookie cards of players called up late in the '99 season, including Rick Ankiel. Besides rookies, the set also features 10 traded players/ free agents and a 10-card Season Highlights subset.

		NM/M
Complete Set (150):		25.00
Common Player:		.10
1	Rick Ankiel RC	5.00
2	Peter Bergeron RC	.25
3	Pat Burrell RC	1.50
4	Eric Munson RC	.35
5	Alfonso Soriano RC	3.00
6	Tim Hudson RC	2.00
7	Erubiel Durazo RC	.25
8	Chad Hermansen	.10
9	Jeff Zimmerman	.10
10	Jesus Pena RC	.10
11	Ramon Hernandez	.25
12	Trent Durrington RC	.10
13	Tony Armas Jr.	.10
14	Mike Fyhrie RC	.10
15	Danny Kolb RC	.10
16	Mike Porzio RC	.10
17	Will Brunson RC	.10
18	Mike Duvall RC	.10
19	Doug Mientkiewicz RC	.75
20	Gabe Molina RC	.15
21	Luis Vizcaino RC	.20
22	Robinson Cancel RC	.10
23	Brett Laxton RC	.10
24	Joe McEwing RC	.25
25	Justin Speier RC	.20
26	Kip Wells RC	.25
27	Armando Almanza RC	.10
28	Joe Davenport RC	.10
29	Yamid Haad RC	.10
30	John Halama	.10
31	Adam Kennedy	.10
32	Vicente Padilla RC	.25
33	Travis Dawkins RC	.25
34	Ryan Rupe RC	.25
35	B.J. Ryan RC	.10
36	Chance Sanford RC	.10
37	Anthony Shumaker RC	.10
38	Ryan Glynn RC	.10
39	Matt Herges RC	.20
40	Ben Molina	.10
41	Scott Williamson	.10
42	Eric Gagne RC	1.50
43	John McDonald RC	.10
44	Scott Sauerbeck RC	.10
45	Mike Venafro RC	.10
46	Edwards Guzman RC	.10
47	Richard Barker RC	.10
48	Braden Looper	.10
49	Chad Meyers RC	.10
50	Scott Strickland RC	.10
51	Billy Koch	.10
52	Dave Newhan RC	.10
53	David Riske RC	.10
54	Jose Santiago	.10
55	Miguel Del Toro RC	.10
56	Orber Moreno RC	.10
57	Dave Roberts	.10
58	Tim Byrdak RC	.10
59	David Lee RC	.10
60	Guillermo Mota RC	.15
61	Wilton Veras RC	.15
62	Joe Mays RC	.35
63	Jose Fernandez RC	.10
64	Ray King RC	.10
65	Chris Petersen RC	.15
66	Vernon Wells	.15
67	Ruben Mateo	.10
68	Ben Petrick	.10
69	Chris Tremie RC	.10
70	Lance Berkman	.10
71	Dan Smith	.10
72	Carlos Hernandez RC	.10
73	Chad Harville RC	.25
74	Damaso Marte	.10

75	Aaron Myette RC	.15
76	Willis Roberts RC	.10
77	Erik Sabel RC	.10
78	Hector Almonte RC	.10
79	Kris Benson RC	.10
80	Pat Daneker RC	.10
81	Freddy Garcia RC	.50
82	Byung-Hyun Kim RC	.25
83	Wily Pena RC	1.00
84	Dan Wheeler RC	.15
85	Tim Harikkala RC	.10
86	Derrin Ebert RC	.10
87	Horacio Estrada RC	.10
88	Liu Rodriguez RC	.10
89	Jordan Zimmerman RC	.10
90	A.J. Burnett RC	.40
91	Doug Davis RC	.10
92	Robert Ramsey RC	.10
93	Ryan Franklin RC	.10
94	Charlie Greene RC	.10
95	Bo Porter RC	.10
96	Jorge Toca RC	.10
97	Casey Blake RC	.20
98	Amaury Garcia RC	.10
99	Jose Molina RC	.10
100	Melvin Mora RC	1.00
101	Joe Nathan RC	.10
102	Juan Pena RC	.25
103	Dave Borkowski RC	.10
104	Eddie Gaillard RC	.10
105	Rob Radlosky RC	.10
106	Brett Hinchliffe RC	.10
107	Carlos Lee RC	.10
108	Rob Ryan RC	.10
109	Jeff Weaver RC	.50
110	Ed Yarnall RC	.10
111	Nelson Cruz RC	.10
112	Cleatus Davidson RC	.10
113	Tim Kubinski RC	.10
114	Sean Spencer RC	.10
115	Joe Winkelsas RC	.10
116	Chris Clapinski RC	.10
117	Tom Davey RC	.10
118	Warren Morris RC	.10
119	Dan Murray RC	.10
120	Jose Nieves RC	.10
121	Mark Quinn RC	.10
122	Josh Beckett RC	10.00
123	Chad Allen RC	.10
124	Mike Figga	.10
125	Beiker Graterol RC	.10
126	Aaron Scheffer RC	.10
127	Wiki Gonzalez RC	.10
128	Ramon E. Martinez	.10
129	Matt Riley RC	.25
130	Chris Woodward RC	.10
131	Albert Belle	.10
132	Roger Cedeno	.10
133	Roger Clemens	.75
134	Brian Giles	.10
135	Rickey Henderson	.60
136	Randy Johnson	.60
137	Brian Jordan	.10
138	Paul Konerko	.15
139	Hideo Nomo	.50
140	Kenny Rogers	.10
141	Wade Boggs	.65
142	Jose Canseco	.45
143	Roger Clemens	.75
144	David Cone	.10
145	Tony Gwynn	.65
146	Mark McGwire	1.00
147	Cal Ripken Jr.	1.50
148	Alex Rodriguez	1.00
149	Fernando Tatis	.10
150	Robin Ventura	.10

Millennium

This special edition of '99 Fleer Tradition was issued only in factory sets, for sale on Shop at Home. Besides the 600 cards in the regular Tradition issue, these sets include 20 renumbered rookie and highlight cards from the Fleer Update set. Each set is sealed with gold-foil on which is a serial number from with an edition of 5,000 sets. Each card in the edition has a special gold-foil "2000" logo on front.

NM/M
Complete Factory Set (620): 30.00
Common Player: .50
Stars: 5X
601 Rick Ankiel .75

602	Peter Bergeron	.50
603	Pat Burrell	2.00
604	Eric Munson	.50
605	Alfonso Soriano	2.00
606	Tim Hudson	1.25
607	Erubiel Durazo	.50
608	Chad Hermansen	.50
609	Jeff Zimmerman	.50
610	Jesus Pena	.50
611	Wade Boggs (Highlights)	.75
612	Jose Canseco (Highlights)	.50
613	Roger Clemens (Highlights)	1.00
614	David Cone (Highlights)	.50
615	Tony Gwynn (Highlights)	.75
616	Mark McGwire (Highlights)	1.50
617	Cal Ripken Jr. (Highlights)	2.00
618	Alex Rodriguez (Highlights)	1.50
619	Fernando Tatis (Highlights)	.50
620	Robin Ventura (Highlights)	.50

Brilliants Sample

To preview the introduction of its Brilliants brand of premium quality cards into baseball, Fleer issued a promo card of J.D. Drew. Like the issued cards, the sample is printed on plastic with a mirrored silver background on front. Both front and back are overprinted, "PROMOTIONAL SAMPLE."

NM/M
J.D. Drew 3.00

1999 Fleer Brilliants

This 175-card set features an action photo on a complete silver-foiled background swirl pattern. The featured player's name, team and postion are stamped in gold foil. Card backs have a small photo, vital information, 1998 statistics and a brief overview of the player's '98 season. Cards numbered 126-175 are part of a short-printed Rookies subset and are seeded 1:2 packs.

NM/M
Complete Set (175): 60.00
Common Player: .25
Common SP (126-175): .50
Blues (1:3): 1.5X
SP Blues (1:6): 1X
Golds: 8X
SP Golds: 3X
Production 99 Sets
24 Karat Golds: 40X
SP's: 15X
Production 24 Sets
Pack (5): 2.00
Wax Box (24): 32.50

1	Mark McGwire	2.50
2	Derek Jeter	3.00
3	Nomar Garciaparra	1.75
4	Travis Lee	.25
5	Jeff Bagwell	.75
6	Andres Galarraga	.25
7	Pedro Martinez	.75
8	Cal Ripken Jr.	3.00
9	Vladimir Guerrero	.75
10	Chipper Jones	1.50
11	Rusty Greer	.25
12	Omar Vizquel	.25
13	Quinton McCracken	.25
14	Jaret Wright	.25
15	Mike Mussina	.50
16	Jason Giambi	.60
17	Tony Clark	.25
18	Troy O'Leary	.25
19	Troy Percival	.25
20	Kerry Wood	.50
21	Vinny Castilla	.25
22	Chris Carpenter	.25
23	Richie Sexson	.25
24	Ken Griffey Jr.	2.00
25	Barry Bonds	3.00
26	Carlos Delgado	.60
27	Frank Thomas	.75
28	Manny Ramirez	.75
29	Shawn Green	.50
30	Mike Piazza	2.00
31	Tino Martinez	.25
32	Dante Bichette	.25
33	Scott Rolen	.65
34	Gabe Alvarez	.25
35	Raul Mondesi	.25
36	Damion Easley	.25
37	Jeff Kent	.25
38	Al Leiter	.25
39	Alex Rodriguez	2.50
40	Jeff King	.25
41	Mark Grace	.25
42	Larry Walker	.25
43	Moises Alou	.25
44	Juan Gonzalez	.65
45	Rolando Arrojo	.25
46	Tom Glavine	.45
47	Johnny Damon	.25
48	Livan Hernandez	.25
49	Craig Biggio	.25
50	Dmitri Young	.25
51	Chan Ho Park	.25
52	Todd Walker	.25
53	Derek Lee	.25
54	Todd Helton	.75
55	Ray Lankford	.25
56	Jim Thome	.65
57	Matt Lawton	.25
58	Matt Anderson	.25
59	Jose Offerman	.25
60	Eric Karros	.25
61	Orlando Hernandez	.25
62	Ben Grieve	.25
63	Bobby Abreu	.25
64	Kevin Young	.25
65	John Olerud	.25
66	Sammy Sosa	1.75
67	Andy Ashby	.25
68	Juan Encarnacion	.25
69	Shane Reynolds	.25
70	Bernie Williams	.35
71	Mike Cameron	.25
72	Troy Glaus	.75
73	Gary Sheffield	.60
74	Jeromy Burnitz	.25
75	Mike Caruso	.25
76	Chuck Knoblauch	.25
77	Kenny Rogers	.25
78	David Cone	.25
79	Tony Gwynn	1.50
80	Aramis Ramirez	.25
81	Paul O'Neill	.25
82	Charles Nagy	.25
83	Javy Lopez	.25
84	Scott Erickson	.25
85	Trevor Hoffman	.25
86	Andruw Jones	.75
87	Ray Durham	.25
88	Jorge Posada	.25
89	Edgar Martinez	.25
90	Tim Salmon	.35
91	Bobby Higginson	.25
92	Adrian Beltre	.45
93	Jason Kendall	.25
94	Henry Rodriguez	.25
95	Greg Maddux	1.50
96	David Justice	.25
97	Ivan Rodriguez	.65
98	Curt Schilling	.45
99	Matt Williams	.25
100	Darin Erstad	.50
101	Rafael Palmeiro	.65
102	David Wells	.25
103	Barry Larkin	.25
104	Robin Ventura	.25
105	Edgar Renteria	.25
106	Andy Pettitte	.50
107	Albert Belle	.45
108	Steve Finley	.25
109	Fernando Vina	.25
110	Rondell White	.25
111	Kevin Brown	.25
112	Jose Canseco	.50
113	Roger Clemens	1.75
114	Todd Hundley	.25
115	Will Clark	.35
116	Jim Edmonds	.25
117	Randy Johnson	.75
118	Denny Neagle	.25
119	Brian Jordan	.25
120	Dean Palmer	.25
121	Roberto Alomar	.45
122	Ken Caminiti	.25
123	Brian Giles	.25
124	Todd Stottlemyre	.25
125	Mo Vaughn	.25
126	J.D. Drew	1.00
127	Ryan Minor	.25
128	Gabe Kapler	.50
129	Jeremy Giambi	.50
130	Eric Chavez	1.00
131	Ben Davis	.50
132	Rob Fick	.50
133	George Lombard	.50
134	Calvin Pickering	.50
135	Preston Wilson	.50
136	Corey Koskie	.75
137	Russell Branyan	.50
138	Bruce Chen	.50
139	Matt Clement	.50
140	Pat Burrell RC	2.50
141	Freddy Garcia RC	1.00
142	Brian Simmons	.50
143	Carlos Febles	.50
144	Carlos Guillen	.50
145	Fernando Seguignol	.50
146	Carlos Beltran	1.00
147	Edgard Clemente	.50
148	Mitch Meluskey	.50
149	Ryan Bradley	.50
150	Marlon Anderson	.50
151	A.J. Burnett RC	1.00
152	Scott Hunter RC	.50
153	Mark Johnson	.50
154	Angel Pena	.50
155	Roy Halladay	.75
156	Chad Allen RC	.50
157	Trot Nixon	.75
158	Ricky Ledee	.50
159	Gary Bennett RC	.50
160	Micah Bowie RC	.60
161	Doug Mientkiewicz	.60
162	Danny Klassen	.50
163	Willis Otanez	.50
164	Jin Ho Cho	.50
165	Mike Lowell	.60
166	Armando Rios	.50
167	Tom Evans	.50
168	Michael Barrett	.50
169	Alex Gonzalez	.50
170	Masao Kida RC	.60
171	Peter Tucci RC	.50
172	Luis Saturria	.50
173	Kris Benson	.50
174	Mario Encarnacion RC	.50
175	Roosevelt Brown RC	.50

Blue/Golds

The 175 Fleer Brilliants base cards are paralleled in three insert sets of differing degrees of scarcity. Brilliant Blue parallels have a mirrored blue foil background on front and a "B" suffix to the card number on back. They are seeded one per three packs (125 veterans) and one per six packs (50 rookies). Gold parallels are printed with gold foil background and a "G" suffix. Each card is serially numbered on back within an edition of 99. The 24-karat Gold parallels have gold rainbow holographic foil backgrounds, a 24-karat gold logo and are serially numbered to just 24 of each card; numbers have a TG sugffix.

NM/M
Brilliants Blue Common: .50
Brilliants Blue Stars: 1.5X
Brilliants Blue Rookies: 1X
Brilliants Gold Common: 3.00
Brilliants Gold Stars: 8X
Brilliants Gold Rookies: 3X
Brilliants 24K Gold Common: 10.00
Brilliants 24K Gold Stars: 40X
Brilliants 24K Gold Rookies: 15X

Illuminators

This 15-card set highlights baseball's top young prospects on a team color-coded fully foiled front. Card backs are numbered with an "I" suffix and are inserted 1:10 packs.

NM/M
Complete Set (15): 10.00
Common Player: .75
Inserted 1:10

1	Kerry Wood	2.00
2	Ben Grieve	.75
3	J.D. Drew	1.50
4	Juan Encarnacion	.75
5	Travis Lee	.75
6	Todd Helton	3.00
7	Troy Glaus	2.00
8	Ricky Ledee	.75
9	Eric Chavez	1.50
10	Ben Davis	.75
11	George Lombard	.75
12	Jeremy Giambi	.75
13	Richie Sexson	.75
14	Corey Koskie	.75
15	Russell Branyan	.75

Shining Stars

Shining Stars is a 15-card set printed on styrene with two-sided mirrored foil. Card backs are numbered with a "S" suffix and are seeded 1:20 packs. Pulsars are a parallel set that are printed on two-sided rainbow holographic foil and styrene with an embossed star pattern in the background. Pulsars are seeded 1:400 packs.

NM/M
Complete Set (15): 30.00
Common Player: 1.50
Inserted 1:20
Pulsars: 4X
Inserted 1:400

1	Ken Griffey Jr.	2.50
2	Mark McGwire	3.00
3	Sammy Sosa	2.25
4	Derek Jeter	4.00
5	Nomar Garciaparra	2.25
6	Alex Rodriguez	3.00
7	Mike Piazza	2.50
8	Juan Gonzalez	1.50
9	Chipper Jones	2.00
10	Cal Ripken Jr.	4.00
11	Frank Thomas	1.50
12	Greg Maddux	2.00
13	Roger Clemens	2.25
14	Vladimir Guerrero	1.50
15	Manny Ramirez	1.50

1999 Fleer Mystique

The "Mystique" of this issue lay partly in the fact that each four-card $4.99 pack included a card which was covered with a peel-off coating, either a short-printed star card from the #1-100 base set, one of the short-printed Rookie (#101-150) or Stars (#151-160) cards or one of the inserts. The Rookie cards are serial numbered to 2,999 apiece, while the red-foil highlighted Stars cards are in an edition of 2,500 each. Fronts have metallic foil backgrounds, backs have a player portrait photo, biographical and career notes and stats.

NM/M
Complete Set (160): 125.00
Common Player: .20
Common SP (1-100): .75
Common (101-150): 1.00
Production 2,999 Sets
Common (151-160): 2.00
Production 2,500 Sets
Pack (4): 3.00
Wax Box (24): 60.00

1	Ken Griffey Jr./SP	2.50
2	Livan Hernandez	.20
3	Jeff Kent	.20
4	Brian Jordan	.20
5	Kevin Young	.20
6	Vinny Castilla	.20
7	Orlando Hernandez/SP	.75
8	Bobby Abreu	.20
9	Vladimir Guerrero	1.50
10	Chuck Knoblauch	.20
11	Nomar Garciaparra/SP	2.25
12	Jeff Bagwell	1.00
13	Todd Walker	.20
14	Johnny Damon	.45
15	Mike Caruso	.20
16	Cliff Floyd	.20
17	Andy Pettitte	.35
18	Cal Ripken Jr./SP	4.00
19	Brian Giles	.20
20	Robin Ventura	.20
21	Alex Gonzalez	.20
22	Randy Johnson	.75
23	Raul Mondesi	.20
24	Ken Caminiti	.20
25	Tom Glavine	.20
26	Derek Jeter/SP	4.00
27	Carlos Delgado	.50
28	Adrian Beltre	.35
29	Tino Martinez	.20
30	Todd Helton	1.00
31	Juan Gonzalez/SP	1.25
32	Henry Rodriguez	.20
33	Jim Thome	.65
34	Paul O'Neill	.20
35	Scott Rolen/SP	1.25
36	Rafael Palmeiro	.65
37	Will Clark	.25
38	Todd Hundley	.20
39	Andruw Jones/SP	1.50
40	Luis Rolando Arrojo	.20
41	Barry Larkin	.20
42	Tim Salmon	.25
43	Rondell White	.20
44	Curt Schilling	.40
45	Chipper Jones/SP	2.00
46	Jeromy Burnitz	.20
47	Mo Vaughn	.20
48	Tony Clark	.20
49	Fernando Tatis	.20
50	Dmitri Young	.20
51	Wade Boggs	1.50
52	Rickey Henderson	.75
53	Manny Ramirez/SP	1.50
54	Edgar Martinez	.20
55	Jason Giambi	.65
56	Jason Kendall	.20
57	Eric Karros	.20
58	Jose Canseco/SP	1.00
59	Shawn Green	.40
60	Ellis Burks	.20
61	Derek Bell	.20
62	Shannon Stewart	.20
63	Roger Clemens/SP	2.25
64	Sean Casey/SP	.75
65	Jose Offerman	.20
66	Sammy Sosa/SP	2.25
67	Frank Thomas/SP	1.50
68	Tony Gwynn/SP	2.00
69	Roberto Alomar	.35
70	Mark McGwire/SP	3.00
71	Troy Glaus	1.00
72	Ray Durham	.20
73	Jeff Cirillo	.20
74	Alex Rodriguez/SP	3.00
75	Jose Cruz Jr.	.20
76	Juan Encarnacion	.20
77	Mark Grace	.20
78	Barry Bonds/SP	4.00
79	Ivan Rodriguez/SP	1.25
80	Greg Vaughn	.20
81	Greg Maddux/SP	2.00
82	Albert Belle	.20
83	John Olerud	.20
84	Kenny Lofton	.20
85	Bernie Williams	.30
86	Matt Williams	.20
87	Ray Lankford	.20
88	Darin Erstad	.20
89	Ben Grieve	.20
90	Craig Biggio	.20
91	Dean Palmer	.20
92	Reggie Sanders	.20
93	Dante Bichette	.20
94	Pedro Martinez/SP	1.50
95	Larry Walker	.20
96	David Wells	.20
97	Travis Leev	.20
98	Mike Piazza/SP	2.50
99	Mike Mussina	.45
100	Kevin Brown	.20

101	Ruben Mateo (Rookie)	1.00
102	Roberto Ramirez (Rookie)	1.00
103	Glen Barker RC (Rookie)	1.00
104	Clay Bellinger RC (Rookie)	1.00
105	Carlos Guillen (Rookie)	1.00
106	Scott Schoeneweis (Rookie)	1.00
107	Creighton Gubanich (Rookie)	1.00
108	Scott Williamson (Rookie)	1.00
109	Edwards Guzman RC (Rookie)	1.00
110	A.J. Burnett RC (Rookie)	4.00
111	Jeremy Giambi (Rookie)	1.00
112	Trot Nixon (Rookie)	1.50
113	J.D. Drew (Rookie)	3.00
114	Roy Halladay (Rookie)	1.50
115	Jose Macias RC (Rookie)	2.00
116	Corey Koskie (Rookie)	1.50
117	Ryan Rupe RC (Rookie)	1.50
118	Scott Hunter (Rookie)	1.00
119	Rob Fick (Rookie)	1.00
120	McKay Christensen (Rookie)	1.50
121	Carlos Febles (Rookie)	2.00
122	Gabe Kapler (Rookie)	1.50
123	Jeff Liefer (Rookie)	1.00
124	Warren Morris (Rookie)	1.00
125	Chris Pritchett (Rookie)	1.00
126	Torii Hunter (Rookie)	3.00
127	Armando Rios (Rookie)	1.00
128	Ricky Ledee (Rookie)	1.00
129	Kelly Dransfeldt RC (Rookie)	1.00
130	Jeff Zimmerman (Rookie)	1.50
131	Eric Chavez (Rookie)	2.00
132	Freddy Garcia (Rookie)	3.00
133	Jose Jimenez (Rookie)	1.00
134	Pat Burrell RC (Rookie)	20.00
135	Joe McEwing RC (Rookie)	1.50
136	Kris Benson (Rookie)	1.00
137	Joe Mays RC (Rookie)	2.00
138	Rafael Roque (Rookie)	1.00
139	Cristian Guzman (Rookie)	1.50
140	Michael Barrett (Rookie)	1.50
141	Doug Mientkiewicz (Rookie)	1.50
142	Jeff Weaver RC (Rookie)	4.00
143	Mike Lowell (Rookie)	1.50
144	Jason Phillips RC (Rookie)	2.00
145	Marlon Anderson (Rookie)	1.50
146	Brett Hinchliffe RC (Rookie)	1.00
147	Matt Clement (Rookie)	1.50
148	Terrence Long (Rookie)	1.00
149	Carlos Beltran (Rookie)	2.50
150	Preston Wilson (Rookie)	1.50
151	Ken Griffey Jr. (Stars)	2.00
152	Mark McGwire (Stars)	3.00
153	Sammy Sosa (Stars)	1.50
154	Mike Piazza (Stars)	2.00
155	Alex Rodriguez (Stars)	3.00
156	Nomar Garciaparra (Stars)	1.50
157	Cal Ripken Jr. (Stars)	4.00
158	Greg Maddux (Stars)	1.50
159	Derek Jeter (Stars)	4.00
160	Juan Gonzalez (Stars)	1.00
	Checklist Card	.10

Mystique Gold

The first 100 cards of the base set are paralleled in this insert which features gold-foil highlights on front. Gold versions are found in one of eight packs, on average.

	NM/M
Common Player:	1.00
Stars (1-100):	1.5X
Inserted 1:8	

Masterpiece

Each of the cards in Fleer Mystique was also produced in a unique Masterpiece version. The super-rarities are labeled on front "The Only 1 of 1 / Masterpiece."

	NM/M
Common Player:	50.00

Mystique Destiny

A silver holofoil background on front and a serial number within an edition of 999 each marks this insert set. Backs have another photo along with career highlights.

	NM/M
Complete Set (10):	35.00
Common Player:	2.00
Production 999 Sets	
1 Tony Gwynn	5.00
2 Juan Gonzalez	3.00
3 Scott Rolen	4.00
4 Nomar Garciaparra	6.00
5 Orlando Hernandez	2.00
6 Andruw Jones	4.00
7 Vladimir Guerrero	4.00
8 Darin Erstad	2.00
9 Manny Ramirez	4.00
10 Roger Clemens	6.00

Established

A plastic stock, red holofoil background and silver foil highlights complement the action photo of a top star in this insert set. Backs have another photo, some career highlights and a serial number from within an edition of 100 each.

	NM/M
Complete Set (10):	300.00
Common Player:	15.00
Production 100 Sets	
1 Ken Griffey Jr.	30.00
2 Derek Jeter	60.00
3 Chipper Jones	20.00
4 Greg Maddux	20.00
5 Mark McGwire	45.00
6 Mike Piazza	60.00
7 Cal Ripken Jr.	60.00
8 Alex Rodriguez	45.00
9 Sammy Sosa	25.00
10 Frank Thomas	15.00

Feel the Game

Swatches of various game-used equipment are featured in this insert series. Each card is hand-numbered from editions which range between 345 and 450.

	NM/M
Common Player:	10.00
Adrian Beltre/Shoe/430	15.00
J.D. Drew/Jsy/450	15.00
Juan Gonzalez/ Bat Glv/415	10.00
Tony Gwynn/Jsy/435	15.00
Kevin Millwood/Jsy/435	10.00
Alex Rodriguez/ Bat Glv/345	30.00
Frank Thomas/Jsy/450	15.00

Fresh Ink

These inserts, found about one per 48 packs, have a white oval at bottom front containing an autograph of the player pictured. At bottom is a white panel with a hand-printed serial number from within each card's edition, which ranged from 140 to 1,000. Backs have a Fleer seal and statement of authenticity pertinent to the autograph. The unnumbered cards are listed here in alphabetical order.

	NM/M
Complete Set (26):	300.00
Common Player:	4.00
Inserted 1:48	
Roberto Alomar/500	10.00
Michael Barrett/1,000	4.00
Kris Benson/500	8.00
Micah Bowie/1,000	4.00
A.J. Burnett/500	10.00
Pat Burrell/500	15.00
Ken Caminiti/250	10.00
Jose Canseco/250	25.00
Sean Casey/1,000	8.00
Edgard Clemente/1,000	4.00
Bartolo Colon/500	8.00
J.D. Drew/400	15.00
Juan Encarnacion/1,000	4.00
Troy Glaus/400	15.00
Juan Gonzalez/250	15.00
Shawn Green/250	15.00
Tony Gwynn/250	30.00
Chipper Jones/250	35.00
Gabe Kapler/750	6.00
Barry Larkin/250	25.00
Doug Mientkiewicz/500	6.00
Alex Rodriguez/200	80.00
Scott Rolen/140	30.00
Fernando Tatis/750	4.00
Robin Ventura/500	6.00
Todd Walker/1,000	6.00

Prophetic

Blue holofoil with silver highlights is the graphic treatment found on this insert set of young stars. Each card is numbered from within an edition of 1,999. Backs have a portrait photo and a few words about the player.

	NM/M
Complete Set (10):	15.00
Common Player:	1.00
Production 1,999 Sets	
1 Eric Chavez	1.50
2 J.D. Drew	2.00
3 A.J. Burnett	1.00
4 Ben Grieve	1.00
5 Gabe Kapler	1.00
6 Todd Helton	2.50
7 Troy Glaus	4.00
8 Travis Lee	1.00
9 Pat Burrell	5.00
10 Kerry Wood	1.50

Diamond Skills Commemorative Sheet

In conjunction with its sponsorship of the Diamond Skills program, Fleer distributed this eight-player sheet to 7-14 year olds par-ticipating in the event. Participants could get a sheet by redeeming Fleer wrappers at a local card store. The 10" x 9" sheet features full size Fleer Tradition cards. At top is a list of 1997 Diamond Skills winners.

	NM/M
Complete Sheet:	3.00

National Convention Commemorative Set

In conjunction with its participation at the 20th National Sports Collectors Convention in Atlanta in July 1999 Fleer distributed this cello-wrapped commemorative set to persons purchasing VIP admission packages. The set includes a specially numbered (NC1) version of the Stan Musial card from '99 Fleer Tradition, three large-format (3-1/2" x5") cards reproducing Musial Monumental Moments inserts, and an unnumbered header card. The Monumental Moments reproductions are printed on a red background with the famed St. Louis arch.

		NM/M
Complete Set (5):		10.00
Common Card:		2.00
NC1	Stan Musial (Fleer Tradition)	2.00
NC2	Stan Musial (Life in Donora - Monumental Moment)	2.00
NC3	Stan Musial (The 1948 Season - Monumental Moment)	2.00
NC4	Stan Musial (Hall of Fame - Monumental Season)	2.00
	Header Card	.25

2000 Fleer Focus

The 250-card base set has two versions for the Prospects subset card numbers 226-250. The portrait versions are serial numbered from 1-999, while the remaining serial numbered from 1,000 to 3,999 capture an action shot. The base set design has a white border with gold foil stamping. Card backs have complete year-by-year statistics along with a career note and small photo.

		NM/M
Complete Set (250):		100.00
Common Player:		.15
Common Prospect (226-250):		4.00

Production 2,999 Sets		
Common Portrait (226-250):		8.00
Portraits:		2X
Production 999 Sets		
Pack:		2.00
Wax Box (24):		35.00
1	Nomar Garciaparra	1.25
2	Adrian Beltre	.35
3	Miguel Tejada	.35
4	Joe Randa	.15
5	Larry Walker	.15
6	Jeff Weaver	.15
7	Jay Bell	.15
8	Ivan Rodriguez	.50
9	Edgar Martinez	.15
10	Desi Relaford	.15
11	Derek Jeter	2.50
12	Delino DeShields	.15
13	Craig Biggio	.15
14	Chuck Knoblauch	.15
15	Chuck Finley	.15
16	Brett Tomko	.15
17	Bobby Higginson	.15
18	Pedro Martinez	.75
19	Troy O'Leary	.15
20	Rickey Henderson	.75
21	Robb Nen	.15
22	Rolando Arrojo	.15
23	Rondell White	.15
24	Royce Clayton	.15
25	Rusty Greer	.15
26	Stan Spencer	.15
27	Steve Finley	.15
28	Tom Goodwin	.15
29	Troy Percival	.15
30	Wilton Guerrero	.15
31	Roberto Alomar	.30
32	Mike Hampton	.15
33	Michael Barrett	.15
34	Curt Schilling	.40
35	Bill Mueller	.15
36	Bernie Williams	.30
37	John Smoltz	.15
38	B.J. Surhoff	.15
39	Pete Harnisch	.15
40	Juan Encarnacion	.15
41	Derrek Lee	.15
42	Jeff Shaw	.15
43	David Cone	.15
44	Jason Christiansen	.15
45	Jeff Kent	.15
46	Randy Johnson	.75
47	Todd Walker	.15
48	Jose Lima	.15
49	Jason Giambi	.50
50	Ken Griffey Jr.	1.50
51	Bartolo Colon	.15
52	Mike Lieberthal	.15
53	Shane Reynolds	.15
54	Travis Lee	.15
55	Travis Fryman	.15
56	John Valentin	.15
57	Joey Hamilton	.15
58	Jay Buhner	.15
59	Brad Radke	.15
60	A.J. Burnett	.15
61	Roy Halladay	.25
62	Raul Mondesi	.15
63	Matt Mantei	.15
64	Mark Grace	.15
65	David Justice	.15
66	Billy Wagner	.15
67	Eric Milton	.15
68	Eric Chavez	.25
69	Doug Glanville	.15
70	Ray Durham	.15
71	Mike Sirotka	.15
72	Greg Vaughn	.15
73	Brian Jordan	.15
74	Alex Gonzalez	.15
75	Alex Rodriguez	2.00
76	David Nilsson	.15
77	Robin Ventura	.15
78	Kevin Young	.15
79	Wilson Alvarez	.15
80	Matt Williams	.15
81	Ismael Valdes	.15
82	Kenny Lofton	.15
83	Carlos Beltran	.45
84	Doug Mientkiewicz	.15
85	Wally Joyner	.15
86	J.D. Drew	.35
87	Carlos Delgado	.50
88	Tony Womack	.15
89	Eric Young	.15
90	Manny Ramirez	.75
91	Johnny Damon	.15
92	Torii Hunter	.25
93	Kenny Rogers	.15
94	Trevor Hoffman	.15
95	John Wetteland	.15
96	Ray Lankford	.15
97	Tom Glavine	.30
98	Carlos Lee	.15
99	Richie Sexson	.15
100	Carlos Febles	.15
101	Chad Allen	.15
102	Sterling Hitchcock	.15
103	Joe McEwing	.15
104	Justin Thompson	.15
105	Jim Edmonds	.15
106	Kerry Wood	.40
107	Jim Thome	.65
108	Jeremy Giambi	.15
109	Mike Piazza	1.50
110	Darryl Kile	.15
111	Darin Erstad	.30
112	Kyle Farnsworth	.15
113	Omar Vizquel	.15
114	Orber Moreno	.15
115	Al Leiter	.15
116	John Olerud	.15
117	Aaron Sele	.15
118	Chipper Jones	1.00
119	Paul Konerko	.25
120	Chris Singleton	.15
121	Fernando Vina	.15
122	Andy Ashby	.15
123	Eli Marrero	.15
124	Edgar Renteria	.15
125	Roberto Hernandez	.15
126	Andruw Jones	.75
127	Magglio Ordonez	.25
128	Bob Wickman	.15
129	Tony Gwynn	1.00
130	Mark McGwire	2.00
131	Albert Belle	.15
132	Pokey Reese	.15
133	Tony Clark	.15
134	Jeff Bagwell	.75
135	Mark Grudzielanek	.15
136	Dustin Hermanson	.15
137	Reggie Sanders	.15
138	Ryan Rupe	.15
139	Kevin Millwood	.15
140	Bret Saberhagen	.15
141	Juan Guzman	.15
142	Alex Gonzalez	.15
143	Gary Sheffield	.30
144	Roger Clemens	1.25
145	Ben Grieve	.15
146	Bobby Abreu	.15
147	Brian Giles	.15
148	Quinton McCracken	.15
149	Freddy Garcia	.15
150	Erubiel Durazo	.15
151	Sidney Ponson	.15
152	Scott Williamson	.15
153	Ken Caminiti	.15
154	Vladimir Guerrero	.75
155	Andy Pettitte	.25
156	Edwards Guzman	.15
157	Shannon Stewart	.15
158	Greg Maddux	1.00
159	Mike Stanley	.15
160	Sean Casey	.25
161	Cliff Floyd	.15
162	Devon White	.15
163	Scott Brosius	.15
164	Marlon Anderson	.15
165	Jason Kendall	.15
166	Ryan Klesko	.15
167	Sammy Sosa	1.25
168	Frank Thomas	.75
169	Geoff Jenkins	.15
170	Jason Schmidt	.15
171	Dan Wilson	.15
172	Jose Canseco	.40
173	Troy Glaus	.75
174	Mariano Rivera	.20
175	Scott Rolen	.65
176	J.T. Snow	.15
177	Rafael Palmeiro	.65
178	A.J. Hinch	.15
179	Jose Offerman	.15
180	Jeff Cirillo	.15
181	Dean Palmer	.15
182	Jose Rosado	.15
183	Armando Benitez	.15
184	Brady Anderson	.15
185	Cal Ripken Jr.	2.50
186	Barry Larkin	.15
187	Damion Easley	.15
188	Moises Alou	.15
189	Todd Hundley	.15
190	Tim Hudson	.25
191	Livan Hernandez	.15
192	Fred McGriff	.15
193	Orlando Hernandez	.25
194	Tim Salmon	.20
195	Mike Mussina	.40
196	Todd Helton	.75
197	Juan Gonzalez	.50
198	Kevin Brown	.15
199	Ugueth Urbina	.15
200	Matt Stairs	.15
201	Shawn Estes	.15
202	Gabe Kapler	.15
203	Javy Lopez	.15
204	Henry Rodriguez	.15
205	Dante Bichette	.15
206	Jeromy Burnitz	.15
207	Todd Zeile	.15
208	Rico Brogna	.15
209	Warren Morris	.15
210	David Segui	.15
211	Vinny Castilla	.15
212	Mo Vaughn	.15
213	Charles Johnson	.15
214	Neifi Perez	.15
215	Shawn Green	.40
216	Carl Pavano	.15
217	Tino Martinez	.15
218	Barry Bonds	2.50
219	David Wells	.15
220	Paul O'Neill	.15
221	Masato Yoshii	.15
222	Kris Benson	.15
223	Fernando Tatis	.15
224	Lee Stevens	.15
225	Jose Cruz Jr.	.15
226	Rick Ankiel (Prospect)	4.00
227	Matt Riley (Prospect)	4.00
228	Norm Hutchins (Prospect)	4.00
229	Ruben Mateo (Prospect)	4.00

230	Ben Petrick (Prospect)	4.00
231	Mario Encarnacion (Prospect)	4.00
232	Nick Johnson (Prospect)	6.00
233	Adam Piatt (Prospect)	6.00
234	Mike Darr (Prospect)	4.00
235	Chad Hermansen (Prospect)	4.00
236	Wily Pena (Prospect)	6.00
237	Octavio Dotel (Prospect)	4.00
238	Vernon Wells (Prospect)	6.00
239	Daryle Ward (Prospect)	4.00
240	Adam Kennedy (Prospect)	4.00
241	Angel Pena (Prospect)	4.00
242	Lance Berkman (Prospect)	6.00
243	Gabe Molina (Prospect)	4.00
244	Steve Lomasney (Prospect)	4.00
245	Jacob Cruz (Prospect)	4.00
246	Mark Quinn (Prospect)	4.00
247	Eric Munson (Prospect)	4.00
248	Alfonso Soriano (Prospect)	6.00
249	Kip Wells (Prospect)	6.00
250	Josh Beckett (Prospect)	6.00
	Checklist #171	.05
	Checklist #172-25, Inserts	.05
	Checklist Inserts	.05

Green

Green, rather than gold, ink is used on front for the player name, team and position to distinguish this parallel insert set. On back, each card is numbered from within an edition of 300 each.

	NM/M
Common Player:	3.00
Stars:	5-10X
Yng Stars & RC's (226-250):	1-2X
Production 300 Sets	

Masterpiece

Each of the cards in Fleer Focus was issued in a parallel edition of just one piece each. Fronts of Masterpiece 1/1s have purple metallic ink, instead of gold, for the player identification. On back, there is a notation "The Only 1 of 1 Masterpiece" along with an "M" suffix to the card number. An error version has all the attributes of the true Masterpiece, but lacks the "Only 1 . . ." notation on back (see 2000 Fleer Focus Masterpiece Errors).

	NM/M
Common Player:	100.00

Masterpiece Errors

Thousands of collectors' hopes were crushed when it was determined that an unknown number of uncompleted Masterpiece 1-of-1 cards were erroneously inserted in Focus foil packs. Like the true Masterpiece cards, the fronts of the error cards have the player name, team and position at bottom front in purple, rather than gold foil. On back, the cards even have the "M"

suffix to the card number at lower-right. Unfortunately, these do not have the foil-stamped "The Only 1 of 1 Masterpiece" notation on back; greatly reducing the value.

	NM/M
Complete Set (25):	250.00
Common Player:	4.00
50M	Ken Griffey Jr.	100.00
202M	Gabe Kapler	8.00
203M	Javy Lopez	6.00
204M	Henry Rodriguez	4.00
205M	Dante Bichette	5.00
206M	Jeromy Burnitz	5.00
207M	Todd Zeile	4.00
208M	Rico Brogna	4.00
209M	Warren Morris	4.00
210M	David Segui	4.00
211M	Vinny Castilla	5.00
212M	Mo Vaughn	6.00
213M	Charles Johnson	5.00
214M	Neifi Perez	5.00
215M	Shawn Green	20.00
216M	Carl Pavano	4.00
217M	Tino Martinez	5.00
218M	Barry Bonds	30.00
219M	David Wells	8.00
220M	Paul O'Neill	6.00
221M	Masato Yoshii	5.00
222M	Kris Benson	8.00
223M	Fernando Tatis	6.00
224M	Lee Stevens	4.00
225M	Jose Cruz Jr.	6.00

Club 3000

These inserts are die-cut around the numbers 3,000 and features three players who either have 3,000 hits or strikeouts, this set spotlights Stan Musial, Steve Carlton and Paul Molitor. These are seeded 1:36 packs.

	NM/M
Complete Set (3):	4.00
Common Player:	1.50
(1)	Steve Carlton	1.50
(2)	Paul Molitor	1.50
(3)	Stan Musial	1.50

Club 3000 Memorabilia

Five tiers featuring memorabilia from game-used bats, caps etc... make up this hand numbered set. Besides a bat and cap insert others include jersey, bat and jersey combo and a bat, jersey and cap combo.

	NM/M
Steve Carlton/Bat/325	25.00
Steve Carlton/Hat/65	75.00
Steve Carlton/Jsy/750	20.00
Steve Carlton/Bat/Hat/Jsy/25	200.00
Paul Molitor/Bat/355	30.00
Paul Molitor/Hat/65	85.00
Paul Molitor/Jsy/975	20.00
Paul Molitor/Bat/Jsy/100	60.00
Stan Musial/Bat/325	50.00
Stan Musial/Hat/65	125.00
Stan Musial/Jsy/975	35.00
Stan Musial/Bat/Jsy/100	80.00

Feel the Game

This 10-card set offers pieces of player-worn jersey from some of baseball's biggest stars embedded into the card front. These were seeded 1:288 packs.

	NM/M
Common Player:	5.00
Inserted 1:288	
Adrian Beltre	7.50
Tom Glavine	10.00
Vladimir Guerrero	15.00
Randy Johnson	15.00
Javy Lopez	5.00
Alex Rodriguez	30.00
Scott Rolen	10.00

Cal Ripken Jr.	40.00
Tim Salmon	6.00
Miguel Tejada	10.00

Focal Points

This 15-card set has silver foil etching around the border and silver foil stamping. These were seeded 1:6 packs and are numbered with an "F" suffix on the card back.

	NM/M
Complete Set (15):	15.00
Common Player:	.75
Inserted 1:6	
1	Mark McGwire	2.50
2	Tony Gwynn	1.00
3	Nomar Garciaparra	2.00
4	Juan Gonzalez	.75
5	Jeff Bagwell	.75
6	Chipper Jones	1.00
7	Cal Ripken Jr.	3.00
8	Alex Rodriguez	2.50
9	Scott Rolen	.75
10	Vladimir Guerrero	.75
11	Mike Piazza	1.50
12	Frank Thomas	.75
13	Ken Griffey Jr.	1.50
14	Sammy Sosa	1.50
15	Derek Jeter	3.00

Focus Pocus

This 10-card set has a silver prismatic, holofoil background with silver foil stamping. These were seeded 1:14 packs and are numbered with an "FP" suffix.

	NM/M
Complete Set (10):	12.00
Common Player:	1.00
Inserted 1:14	
1	Cal Ripken Jr.	3.00
2	Tony Gwynn	1.50
3	Nomar Garciaparra	2.00
4	Juan Gonzalez	1.00
5	Mike Piazza	2.00
6	Mark McGwire	2.00
7	Chipper Jones	1.50
8	Ken Griffey Jr.	2.00
9	Derek Jeter	3.00
10	Alex Rodriguez	2.50

Fresh Ink

These autographed inserts are seeded 1:96 packs.

	NM/M
Common Player:	5.00
Inserted 1:96	
Chad Allen	5.00
Michael Barrett	5.00
Josh Beckett	30.00
Rob Bell	5.00
Adrian Beltre	15.00
Milton Bradley	8.00
Rico Brogna	5.00
Mike Cameron	8.00
Eric Chavez	15.00
Bruce Chen	5.00
Johnny Damon	20.00
Ben Davis	5.00
J.D. Drew	15.00
Erubiel Durazo	10.00
Jeremy Giambi	6.00
Jason Giambi	25.00
Doug Glanville	6.00
Troy Glaus	25.00
Shawn Green	20.00
Mike Hampton	10.00
Tim Hudson	15.00
John Jaha	5.00
Derek Jeter	150.00
D'Angelo Jimenez	5.00
Nick Johnson	8.00
Andruw Jones	20.00
Jason Kendall	10.00
Adam Kennedy	6.00
Mike Lieberthal	8.00
Edgar Martinez	15.00
Aaron McNeal	5.00
Kevin Millwood	10.00
Mike Mussina	30.00
Magglio Ordonez	15.00
Eric Owens	5.00
Rafael Palmeiro	20.00
Wily Pena	15.00
Adam Piatt	8.00
Cal Ripken Jr.	100.00
Alex Rodriguez	65.00
Scott Rolen	20.00
Tim Salmon	15.00
Chris Singleton	5.00
Mike Sweeney	10.00
Jose Vidro	5.00
Rondell White	8.00
Jaret Wright	5.00

Future Vision

This 15-card set highlights the top prospects over a holo-foiled background with red foil etching and stamping. These were seeded 1:9 packs and are numbered with an "FV" suffix.

	NM/M
Complete Set (15):	8.00
Common Player:	.40
Inserted 1:9	
1	Rick Ankiel	.50
2	Matt Riley	.40
3	Ruben Mateo	.40
4	Ben Petrick	.40
5	Mario Encarnacion	.40
6	Octavio Dotel	.40
7	Vernon Wells	.65
8	Adam Kennedy	.40
9	Lance Berkman	.40
10	Chad Hermansen	.40
11	Mark Quinn	.40
12	Eric Munson	.40
13	Alfonso Soriano	2.00
14	Kip Wells	.40
15	Josh Beckett	.75

2000 Fleer Gamers

The 120-card base set has silver foil etching down the left portion of the card with vertical stripes running down the right portion of the card front. The card back has career statistical totals as well as a small photo. Two short-printed subsets also make up the 120-card set. Next Gamers (91-110) are seeded 1:3 packs and Fame Game (111-120) are seeded 1:8 packs.

	NM/M
Complete Set (120):	50.00
Common Player (1-90):	.15
Common (91-110):	1.00
Inserted 1:3	
Common (111-120):	1.50
Inserted 1:8	
Pack:	2.00
Wax Box:	35.00
1	Cal Ripken Jr.	3.00
2	Derek Jeter	2.00
3	Alex Rodriguez	1.50
4	Alex Gonzalez	.15
5	Nomar Garciaparra	1.25
6	Brian Giles	.15
7	Chris Singleton	.15
8	Kevin Brown	.15
9	J.D. Drew	.25
10	Raul Mondesi	.15
11	Sammy Sosa	1.25
12	Carlos Beltran	.50
13	Eric Chavez	.25
14	Gabe Kapler	.15
15	Tim Salmon	.25
16	Manny Ramirez	.75
17	Orlando Hernandez	.15
18	Jeff Kent	.15
19	Juan Gonzalez	.75
20	Moises Alou	.15
21	Jason Giambi	.50
22	Ivan Rodriguez	.60
23	Geoff Jenkins	.15
24	Ken Griffey Jr.	1.25
25	Mark McGwire	1.50
26	Jose Canseco	.40
27	Roberto Alomar	.40
28	Craig Biggio	.15
29	Scott Rolen	.65
30	Vinny Castilla	.15
31	Greg Maddux	1.00
32	Pedro J. Martinez	.75
33	Mike Piazza	1.25
34	Albert Belle	.25
35	Frank Thomas	.75
36	Bobby Abreu	.15
37	Edgar Martinez	.15
38	Pokey Reese	.15
39	Preston Wilson	.15
40	Mike Lieberthal	.15
41	Andruw Jones	.75
42	Damion Easley	.15
43	Mike Cameron	.15
44	Todd Walker	.15
45	Jason Kendall	.15
46	Sean Casey	.25
47	Corey Koskie	.15
48	Warren Morris	.15
49	Andres Galarraga	.15
50	Dean Palmer	.15
51	Jose Vidro	.15
52	Brian Jordan	.15
53	Tony Clark	.15
54	Vladimir Guerrero	.75
55	Mo Vaughn	.15
56	Richie Sexson	.15
57	Tino Martinez	.15
58	Eric Owens	.15
59	Matt Williams	.15
60	Omar Vizquel	.15
61	Rickey Henderson	.75
62	J.T. Snow	.15
63	Mark Grace	.25
64	Carlos Febles	.15
65	Paul O'Neill	.15
66	Randy Johnson	.75
67	Kenny Lofton	.15
68	Roger Cedeno	.15
69	Shawn Green	.35
70	Chipper Jones	1.00
71	Jeff Cirillo	.15
72	Robin Ventura	.15
73	Paul Konerko	.15
74	Jeromy Burnitz	.15
75	Ben Grieve	.15
76	Troy Glaus	.75
77	Jim Thome	.15
78	Bernie Williams	.25
79	Barry Bonds	2.00
80	Ray Durham	.15
81	Adrian Beltre	.15
82	Ray Lankford	.15
83	Carlos Delgado	.50
84	Erubiel Durazo	.15
85	Larry Walker	.15
86	Edgardo Alfonzo	.15
87	Rafael Palmeiro	.65
88	Magglio Ordonez	.25
89	Jeff Bagwell	.75
90	Tony Gwynn	1.00
91	Norm Hutchins (Next Gamers)	1.00
92	Derrick Turnbow **RC** (Next Gamers)	1.50
93	Matt Riley (Next Gamers)	1.00
94	David Eckstein (Next Gamers)	1.00
95	Dernell Stenson (Next Gamers)	1.00
96	Joe Crede (Next Gamers)	1.00
97	Ben Petrick (Next Gamers)	1.00
98	Eric Munson (Next Gamers)	1.00
99	Pablo Ozuna (Next Gamers)	1.00
100	Josh Beckett (Next Gamers)	3.00
101	Aaron McNeal **RC** (Next Gamers)	1.50
102	Milton Bradley (Next Gamers)	1.50
103	Alex Escobar (Next Gamers)	1.50
104	Alfonso Soriano (Next Gamers)	4.00
105	Wily Pena (Next Gamers)	1.50
106	Nick Johnson (Next Gamers)	1.50
107	Adam Piatt (Next Gamers)	1.50
108	Pat Burrell (Next Gamers)	2.00
109	Rick Ankiel (Next Gamers)	1.00
110	Vernon Wells (Next Gamers)	2.00
111	Alex Rodriguez (Fame Game)	3.00
112	Cal Ripken Jr. (Fame Game)	4.00
113	Mark McGwire (Fame Game)	3.00
114	Ken Griffey Jr. (Fame Game)	3.00
115	Mike Piazza (Fame Game)	2.00
116	Nomar Garciaparra (Fame Game)	3.00
117	Derek Jeter (Fame Game)	4.00
118	Chipper Jones (Fame Game)	1.50
119	Sammy Sosa (Fame Game)	2.00
120	Tony Gwynn (Fame Game)	1.50

Extra

A parallel to the 120-card base set, the gold foiled card front and "Extra" written down the right portion of the card can be used to differentiate these from regular cards. "Extra" is also written underneath the card number on the back as well. Extras 1-90 are seeded 1:24 packs and numbers 91-120 are seeded 1:36 packs.

Stars (1-90):	5-10X
Inserted 1:24	
Next Gamers (91-110):	1-2X
Inserted 1:36	
Fame Game (110-120):	1-2X
Inserted 1:36	

Cal to Greatness

This 15-card tribute insert set to baseball's "Iron Man" is broken into three tiers. Cards 1-5 are seeded 1:9 packs, cards 6-10 are found

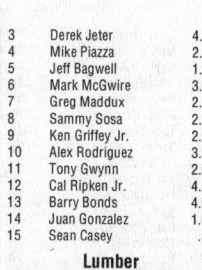

1:25 packs and cards 11-15 are inserted 1:144 packs. Card backs are numbered with a "C" suffix.

	NM/M
Complete Set (15)	100.00
Common Ripken (1-5)	3.00
Inserted 1:9	
Common Ripken (6-10)	6.00
Inserted 1:25	
Common Ripken (11-15)	20.00
Inserted 1:144	
1-5 Cal Ripken Jr.	3.00
6-10 Cal Ripken Jr.	6.00
11-15 Cal Ripken Jr.	20.00

Change the Game

This 15-card set has a holo-foiled front with Change the Game printed behind the player image. Seeded 1:24 packs, card backs are numbered with a "CG" suffix.

	NM/M
Complete Set (15)	50.00
Common Player	1.50
Inserted 1:24	
1 Alex Rodriguez	6.00
2 Cal Ripken Jr.	7.50
3 Chipper Jones	3.00
4 Derek Jeter	7.50
5 Ken Griffey Jr.	4.00
6 Mark McGwire	6.00
7 Mike Piazza	4.00
8 Nomar Garciaparra	4.00
9 Sammy Sosa	4.00
10 Tony Gwynn	3.00
11 Ivan Rodriguez	1.50
12 Pedro Martinez	2.00
13 Juan Gonzalez	2.00
14 Vladimir Guerrero	2.00
15 Manny Ramirez	2.00

Determined

This 15-card set has a holo-foiled front with two player images on the card front. The second player photo is smaller than the primary image and is a close-up shot. Card backs are numbered with a "D" suffix and are seeded 1:12 packs.

	NM/M
Complete Set (15)	25.00
Common Player	.50
Inserted 1:12	
1 Nomar Garciaparra	2.50
2 Chipper Jones	2.00

3 Derek Jeter	4.00
4 Mike Piazza	2.50
5 Jeff Bagwell	1.00
6 Mark McGwire	3.00
7 Greg Maddux	2.00
8 Sammy Sosa	2.50
9 Ken Griffey Jr.	2.50
10 Alex Rodriguez	3.00
11 Tony Gwynn	2.00
12 Cal Ripken Jr.	4.00
13 Barry Bonds	4.00
14 Juan Gonzalez	1.00
15 Sean Casey	.50

Lumber

Seeded 1:36 packs, these inserts have a piece of game-used bat embedded into the card front and are numbered with an "GL" suffix

	NM/M
Common Player	5.00
Inserted 1:36	
1 Alex Rodriguez	30.00
2 Carlos Delgado	10.00
3 Jose Vidro	5.00
4 Carlos Febles	5.00
5 J.D. Drew	7.50
6 Mike Cameron	5.00
7 Derek Jeter	40.00
8 Eric Chavez	6.00
9 Cal Ripken Jr.	40.00
10 Gabe Kapler	5.00
11 Damion Easley	5.00
12 Frank Thomas	15.00
13 Chris Singleton	5.00
14 Norm Hutchins	5.00
15 Pokey Reese	5.00
16 Rafael Palmeiro	12.00
17 Ray Durham	5.00
18 Ray Lankford	5.00
19 Roger Cedeno	5.00
20 Shawn Green	6.00
21 Wade Boggs	20.00
22 Roberto Alomar	7.50
23 Moises Alou	5.00
24 Adrian Beltre	6.00
25 Barry Bonds	40.00
26 Jason Giambi	10.00
27 Jason Kendall	5.00
28 Paul Konerko	5.00
29 Mike Lieberthal	5.00
30 Edgar Martinez	5.00
31 Raul Mondesi	5.00
32 Scott Rolen	12.00
33 Alfonso Soriano	10.00
34 Ivan Rodriguez	10.00
35 Magglio Ordonez	7.50
36 Chipper Jones	20.00
37 Sean Casey	6.00
38 Edgardo Alfonzo	5.00
39 Robin Ventura	5.00
40 Bernie Williams	6.00
41 Vladimir Guerrero	15.00
42 Tony Clark	5.00
43 Carlos Beltran	10.00
44 Warren Morris	5.00
45 Jim Thome	5.00
46 Jeromy Burnitz	5.00
47 Matt Williams	5.00
48 Erubiel Durazo	5.00

Lumber Autograph

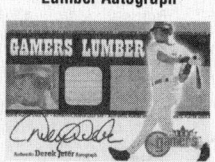

Twelve players also signed a limited number of their Lumber inserts. The number signed by each player is listed after the player name. These were seeded 1:287 packs.

	NM/M
Common Player	15.00
Inserted 1:287	
1 Derek Jeter	150.00
2 Eric Chavez	20.00
3 Rafael Palmeiro	40.00
4 Shawn Green	35.00
5 Roberto Alomar	45.00
6 Paul Konerko	15.00
7 Sean Casey	15.00
8 Alex Rodriguez	80.00
9 Robin Ventura	20.00
10 Erubiel Durazo	15.00
11 Tony Clark	15.00
12 Alfonso Soriano	60.00

2000 Fleer Greats of the Game

Satchel Paige of the St. Louis Browns

The base set consists of 107-cards of retired stars. Card fronts have a brown border with "Fleer Greats of the Game" stamped in silver foil. Backs have a small photo along with complete career statistics and a brief career highlight.

	NM/M
Complete Set (108)	50.00
Common Player	.50
Pack (6)	10.00
Wax Box (24)	200.00
1 Mickey Mantle	8.00
2 Gil Hodges	1.00
3 Monte Irvin	1.00
4 Satchel Paige	2.50
5 Roy Campanella	2.00
6 Richie Ashburn	1.00
7 Roger Maris	3.00
8 Ozzie Smith	2.00
9 Reggie Jackson	2.50
10 Eddie Mathews	2.50
11 Dave Righetti	.50
12 Dave Winfield	1.00
13 Lou Whitaker	.50
14 Phil Garner	.50
15 Ron Cey	.50
16 Brooks Robinson	2.50
17 Bruce Sutter	.50
18 Dave Parker	.50
19 Johnny Bench	2.50
20 Fernando Valenzuela	.50
21 George Brett	4.00
22 Paul Molitor	2.00
23 Hoyt Wilhelm	.50
24 Luis Aparicio	.50
25 Frank White	.50
26 Herb Score	.50
27 Kirk Gibson	.50
28 Mike Schmidt	3.00
29 Don Baylor	.50
30 Joe Pepitone	.50
31 Hal McRae	.50
32 Lee Smith	.50
33 Nolan Ryan	7.00
34 Nolan Ryan/OPS	5.00
35 Bill Mazeroski	.75
36 Bobby Doerr	.50
37 Duke Snider	1.00
38 Dick Groat	.50
39 Larry Doby	.50
40 Kirby Puckett	2.00
41 Steve Carlton	1.00
42 Dennis Eckersley	.50
43 Jim Bunning	.50
44 Ron Guidry	.50
45 Alan Trammell	1.00
46 Bob Feller	1.50
47 Dave Concepcion	.50
48 Dwight Evans	.50
49 Enos Slaughter	.50
50 Tom Seaver	2.50
51 Tony Oliva	1.00
52 Mel Stottlemyre	.50
53 Tommy John	.50
54 Willie McCovey	1.00
55 Red Schoendienst	.50
56 Gorman Thomas	.50
57 Ralph Kiner	1.00
58 Robin Yount	2.00
59 Andre Dawson	1.00
60 Al Kaline	2.50
61 Dom DiMaggio	.50
62 Juan Marichal	1.00
63 Jack Morris	.50
64 Warren Spahn	1.50
65 Preacher Roe	.50
66 Darrell Evans	.50
67 Jim Bouton	.50
68 Rocky Colavito	.75
69 Bob Gibson	1.50
70 Whitey Ford	1.50
71 Moose Skowron	.50
72 Boog Powell	1.00
73 Al Lopez	.50
74 Lou Brock	1.00
75 Mickey Lolich	.50
76 Rod Carew	2.00
77 Bob Lemon	.50
78 Frank Howard	.50
79 Phil Rizzuto	1.50
80 Carl Yastrzemski	2.00
81 Rico Carty	.50
82 Jim Kaat	.50

82 Bert Blyleven	.50
83 George Kell	.50
84 Jim Palmer	1.00
85 Maury Wills	1.00
86 Jim Rice	.50
87 Joe Carter	.50
88 Clete Boyer	.50
89 Yogi Berra	2.00
90 Cecil Cooper	.50
91 Davey Johnson	.50
92 Lou Boudreau	.50
93 Orlando Cepeda	1.00
94 Tommy Henrich	.50
95 Hank Bauer	.50
96 Don Larsen	1.50
97 Vida Blue	1.00
98 Ben Oglivie	.50
99 Don Mattingly	5.00
100 Dale Murphy	1.00
101 Ferguson Jenkins	1.00
102 Bobby Bonds	.75
103 Dick Allen	.50
104 Stan Musial	3.00
105 Gaylord Perry	.50
106 Willie Randolph	.50
107 Willie Stargell	1.50
108 Checklist	.50

Autographs

George Brett [signature]

Seeded in every six packs, Autographs feature the signature on the bottom half of the card front in black Sharpie. The autographed set features 89 retired players. Some cards were issued in considerably lower quantities than others, as noted in the checklist.

	NM/M
Common Player	10.00
Inserted 1:6	
Luis Aparicio	25.00
Hank Bauer	10.00
Don Baylor	20.00
Johnny Bench	200.00
Yogi Berra	180.00
Vida Blue	20.00
Bert Blyleven	10.00
Bobby Bonds	40.00
Lou Boudreau	120.00
Jim Bouton	20.00
Clete Boyer	15.00
George Brett	
(275 or less)	300.00
Lou Brock	40.00
Jim Bunning	40.00
Rod Carew	50.00
Steve Carlton	20.00
Joe Carter/SP	75.00
Orlando Cepeda	25.00
Ron Cey	15.00
Rocky Colavito	30.00
Dave Concepcion	
(Black autograph.)	15.00
Dave Concepcion	
(Red autograph.)	15.00
Cecil Cooper	10.00
Andre Dawson	25.00
Dom DiMaggio	75.00
Bobby Doerr	15.00
Darrell Evans	15.00
Bob Feller	30.00
Whitey Ford	
(300 or less)	150.00
Phil Garner	10.00
Bob Gibson	40.00
Kirk Gibson	20.00
Dick Groat	25.00
Ron Guidry	20.00
Tommy Henrich	
(300 or less)	180.00
Frank Howard	20.00
Reggie Jackson	
(250 or less)	180.00
Ferguson Jenkins	20.00
Tommy John	20.00
Davey Johnson	10.00
Jim Kaat	20.00
Al Kaline	50.00
George Kell	20.00
Ralph Kiner	30.00
Don Larsen	25.00
Mickey Lolich	10.00
Juan Marichal	40.00
Eddie Mathews	150.00
Don Mattingly	
(300 or less)	350.00

Bill Mazeroski	50.00
Willie McCovey	150.00
Hal McRae	10.00
Paul Molitor	50.00
Jack Morris	10.00
Dale Murphy	40.00
Stan Musial	150.00
Ben Oglivie	10.00
Tony Oliva	15.00
Jim Palmer/SP	150.00
Dave Parker	20.00
Joe Pepitone	10.00
Gaylord Perry	15.00
Boog Powell	15.00
Kirby Puckett	
(200 or less)	350.00
Willie Randolph	20.00
Jim Rice	30.00
Dave Righetti	15.00
Phil Rizzuto	
(200 or less)	200.00
Brooks Robinson	40.00
Preacher Roe	15.00
Nolan Ryan	180.00
Mike Schmidt	
(175 or less)	500.00
Red Schoendienst	20.00
Herb Score	25.00
Tom Seaver	100.00
Moose Skowron	20.00
Enos Slaughter	30.00
Lee Smith	10.00
Ozzie Smith/SP	200.00
Duke Snider/SP	200.00
Warren Spahn/SP	275.00
Bruce Sutter	15.00
Gorman Thomas	10.00
Alan Trammell	20.00
Frank White	10.00
Hoyt Wilhelm	15.00
Maury Wills	15.00
Dave Winfield	300.00
Carl Yastrzemski	75.00
Robin Yount/SP	250.00

Memorable Moments Auto.

	NM/M
Common Player	60.00
1 Ron Guidry/78	75.00
2 Nolan Ryan/99	300.00
3 Herb Score/55	40.00
4 Tom Seaver/69	180.00

Retrospection

The 15-card Retrospection insert set highlights some of the all-time greats with a design borrowed from 1960 Fleer. Former greats including Stan Musial and Al Kaline are featured. They were seeded 1:6 packs.

	NM/M
Complete Set (15)	75.00
Common Player	4.00
Inserted 1:6	
1 Rod Carew	4.00
2 Stan Musial	8.00
3 Nolan Ryan	15.00
4 Tom Seaver	6.00
5 Brooks Robinson	5.00
6 Al Kaline	6.00
7 Mike Schmidt	10.00
8 Thurman Munson	8.00
9 Steve Carlton	4.00
10 Roger Maris	8.00
11 Duke Snider	6.00
12 Yogi Berra	6.00
13 Carl Yastrzemski	5.00
14 Reggie Jackson	6.00
15 Johnny Bench	8.00

Yankees Clippings

This 15-card memorabilia insert features an actual piece of New York Yankee uniform worn by former stars. The jersey swatch is formed in the shape of the interlocking "NY" logo and are seeded 1:48 packs.

	NM/M
Common Player	20.00
Inserted 1:48	
1 Mickey Mantle	200.00
2 Ron Guidry	40.00
3 Don Larsen	40.00
4 Elston Howard	40.00
5 Mel Stottlemyre	25.00
6 Don Mattingly	100.00
7 Reggie Jackson	50.00
8 Tommy John	20.00
9 Dave Winfield	25.00
10 Willie Randolph	20.00
11 Tommy Henrich	20.00
12 Billy Martin	50.00
13 Dave Righetti	20.00
14 Joe Pepitone	20.00
15 Thurman Munson	80.00

2000 Fleer Impact

Roger Clemens p.

The base set consists of 200 cards with 25 of those being Prospect subset cards. The featured player's team logo appears beside the player name on the bottom portion with the Impact logo on the top left portion. Card backs have a maximum of 10 years of statistics along with a small photo and vital information. Impact was sold in 10-card packs with an SRP of $.99 per pack.

	NM/M
Complete Set (200)	15.00
Common Player	.10
Pack (10)	1.00
Box (36)	20.00
1 Cal Ripken Jr.	1.50
2 Jose Canseco	.25
3 Manny Ramirez	.60
4 Bernie Williams	.30
5 Troy Glaus	.60
6 Jeff Bagwell	.60
7 Corey Koskie	.10
8 Barry Larkin	.10
9 Mark Quinn	.10
10 Russ Ortiz	.10
11 Tim Salmon	.15
12 Preston Wilson	.10
13 Mo Vaughn	.10
14 Ray Lankford	.10
15 Sterling Hitchcock	.10
16 Al Leiter	.10
17 Jim Morris	.10
18 Freddy Garcia	.10
19 Adrian Beltre	.20
20 Eric Chavez	.20
21 Robinson Cancel	.10
22 Edgar Renteria	.10
23 John Jaha	.10
24 Chuck Finley	.10
25 Andres Galarraga	.10
26 Paul Byrd	.10
27 John Halama	.10
28 Eric Karros	.10
29 Mike Piazza	1.00
30 Ryan Rupe	.10
31 Frank Thomas	.60
32 Randy Velarde	.10
33 Bobby Abreu	.10
34 Randy Johnson	.60
35 Matt Williams	.10
36 Tony Gwynn	.75
37 Dean Palmer	.10
38 Aaron Sele	.10
39 Rondell White	.10
40 Erubiel Durazo	.10
41 Curt Schilling	.25
42 Kip Wells	.10
43 Craig Biggio	.10
44 Tom Glavine	.25
45 Trevor Hoffman	.10
46 Greg Vaughn	.10
47 Edgar Martinez	.10
48 Magglio Ordonez	.20
49 Mark Mulder	.10
50 John Rocker	.10
51 Kenny Rogers	.10
52 Gary Sheffield	.25
53 Brian Simmons	.10
54 Tony Womack	.10
55 Ken Caminiti	.10
56 Jeff Cirillo	.10

57	Ray Durham	.10
58	Mike Lieberthal	.10
59	Ruben Mateo	.10
60	Mike Cameron	.10
61	Rusty Greer	.10
62	Alex Rodriguez	1.25
63	Robin Ventura	.10
64	Pokey Reese	.10
65	Jose Lima	.10
66	Neifi Perez	.10
67	Rafael Palmeiro	.50
68	Scott Rolen	.50
69	Mike Hampton	.10
70	Sammy Sosa	1.00
71	Mike Stanley	.10
72	Dan Wilson	.10
73	Kerry Wood	.50
74	Mike Mussina	.30
75	Masato Yoshii	.10
76	Peter Bergeron	.10
77	Carlos Delgado	.50
78	Juan Encarnacion	.10
79	Nomar Garciaparra	1.00
80	Jason Kendall	.10
81	Pedro Martinez	.60
82	Darin Erstad	.40
83	Larry Walker	.10
84	Rick Ankiel	.10
85	Scott Erickson	.10
86	Roger Clemens	.85
87	Matt Lawton	.10
88	Jon Lieber	.10
89	Shane Reynolds	.10
90	Ivan Rodriguez	.50
91	Pat Burrell	.50
92	Kent Bottenfield	.10
93	David Cone	.10
94	Mark Grace	.15
95	Paul Konerko	.10
96	Eric Milton	.10
97	Lee Stevens	.10
98	B.J. Surhoff	.10
99	Billy Wagner	.10
100	Ken Griffey Jr.	1.00
101	Randy Wolf	.10
102	Henry Rodriguez	.10
103	Carlos Beltran	.40
104	Rich Aurilia	.10
105	Chipper Jones	.75
106	Homer Bush	.10
107	Johnny Damon	.10
108	J.D. Drew	.40
109	Orlando Hernandez	.10
110	Brad Radke	.10
111	Wilton Veras	.10
112	Dmitri Young	.10
113	Jermaine Dye	.10
114	Kris Benson	.10
115	Derek Jeter	1.50
116	Cole Liniak	.10
117	Jim Thome	.10
118	Pedro Astacio	.10
119	Carlos Febles	.10
120	Darryl Kile	.10
121	Alfonso Soriano	.50
122	Michael Barrett	.10
123	Ellis Burks	.10
124	Chad Hermansen	.10
125	Trot Nixon	.10
126	Bobby Higginson	.10
127	Rick Helling	.10
128	Chris Carpenter	.10
129	Vinny Castilla	.10
130	Brian Giles	.10
131	Todd Helton	.60
132	Jason Varitek	.10
133	Rob Ducey	.10
134	Octavio Dotel	.10
135	Adam Kennedy	.10
136	Jeff Kent	.10
137	Aaron Boone	.10
138	Todd Walker	.10
139	Jeromy Burnitz	.10
140	Roberto Hernandez	.10
141	Matt LeCroy	.10
142	Ugueth Urbina	.10
143	David Wells	.10
144	Luis Gonzalez	.25
145	Andruw Jones	.50
146	Juan Gonzalez	.60
147	Moises Alou	.10
148	Michael Tejera	.10
149	Brian Jordan	.10
150	Mark McGwire	1.25
151	Shawn Green	.25
152	Jay Bell	.10
153	Fred McGriff	.10
154	Rey Ordonez	.10
155	Matt Stairs	.10
156	A.J. Burnett	.10
157	Omar Vizquel	.10
158	Damion Easley	.10
159	Dante Bichette	.10
160	Javy Lopez	.10
161	Fernando Seguignol	.10
162	Richie Sexson	.10
163	Vladimir Guerrero	.60
164	Kevin Young	.10
165	Josh Beckett	.15
166	Albert Belle	.10
167	Cliff Floyd	.10
168	Gabe Kapler	.10
169	Nick Johnson	.15
170	Raul Mondesi	.10
171	Warren Morris	.10
172	Kenny Lofton	.10
173	Reggie Sanders	.10
174	Mike Sweeney	.10
175	Robert Fick	.10
176	Barry Bonds	1.50
177	Luis Castillo	.10
178	Roger Cedeno	.10
179	Jim Edmonds	.10
180	Geoff Jenkins	.10
181	Adam Piatt	.10
182	Phil Nevin	.10
183	Roberto Alomar	.30
184	Kevin Brown	.10
185	D.T. Cromer	.10
186	Jason Giambi	.50
187	Fernando Tatis	.10
188	Brady Anderson	.10
189	Tony Clark	.10
190	Alex Fernandez	.10
191	Matt Blank	.10
192	Greg Maddux	.75
193	Kevin Millwood	.10
194	Jason Schmidt	.10
195	Shannon Stewart	.10
196	Rolando Arrojo	.10
197	Darren Dreifort	.10
198	Ben Grieve	.10
199	Bartolo Colon	.10
200	Sean Casey	.10

Autographics

This autographed set has the player signature on the bottom portion of the card. These were seeded 1:216 packs.

		NM/M
Common Player:		5.00
Inserted 1:216		
Silvers:		1-2X
Production 250 Sets		
Golds:		1-2X
Production 50 Sets		
1	Bobby Abreu	15.00
2	Marlon Anderson	5.00
3	Rick Ankiel	15.00
4	Rob Bell	5.00
5	Carlos Beltran	25.00
6	Wade Boggs	30.00
7	Barry Bonds	200.00
8	Milton Bradley	8.00
9	Pat Burrell	25.00
10	Orlando Cabrera	10.00
11	Chris Carpenter	5.00
12	Sean Casey	8.00
13	Carlos Delgado	20.00
14	J.D. Drew	15.00
15	Ray Durham	8.00
16	Kelvim Escobar	6.00
17	Vladimir Guerrero	30.00
18	Tony Gwynn	35.00
19	Jerry Hairston Jr.	5.00
20	Todd Helton	25.00
21	Nick Johnson	8.00
22	Jason Kendall	8.00
23	Mark Kotsay	8.00
24	Cole Liniak	5.00
25	Jose Macias	5.00
26	Greg Maddux	60.00
27	Ruben Mateo	8.00
28	Ober Moreno	5.00
29	Eric Munson	8.00
30	Joe Nathan	5.00
31	Angel Pena	5.00
32	Adam Piatt	5.00
33	Matt Riley	5.00
34	Cal Ripken Jr.	100.00
35	Alex Rodriguez	75.00
36	Scott Rolen	25.00
37	Jimmy Rollins	15.00
38	B.J. Ryan	5.00
39	Alfonso Soriano	40.00
40	Frank Thomas	25.00
41	Wilton Veras	5.00
42	Billy Wagner	5.00
43	Jeff Weaver	8.00
44	Scott Williamson	6.00

Genuine Coverage

This memorabilia insert set has pieces of game-used batting gloves embedded into the card front. They were seeded 1:720 packs.

		NM/M
Common Player:		5.00
Inserted 1:720		
1	Alex Rodriguez	65.00
2	Cole Liniak	5.00
3	Barry Bonds	75.00
4	Ben Davis	5.00
5	Bobby Abreu	7.50
6	Mike Sweeney	7.50
7	Rafael Palmeiro	35.00
8	Carlos Lee	5.00
9	Glen Barker	5.00
10	Jason Giambi	30.00
11	Jacque Jones	7.50
12	Joe Nathan	5.00
13	Jason LaRue	5.00
14	Magglio Ordonez	7.50
15	Shannon Stewart	5.00
16	Matt Lawton	5.00
17	Trevor Hoffman	5.00

Mighty Fine in '99

This 40-card set honors the 1999 World Series Champion New York Yankees as well as other various award winners from the '99 season. These were seeded one per pack.

		NM/M
Complete Set (40):		8.00
Common Player:		.15
Inserted 1:1		
1	Clay Bellinger	.15
2	Scott Brosius	.15
3	Roger Clemens	.75
4	David Cone	.15
5	Chad Curtis	.15
6	Chili Davis	.15
7	Joe Girardi	.15
8	Jason Grimsley	.15
9	Orlando Hernandez	.15
10	Hideki Irabu	.15
11	Derek Jeter	2.00
12	Chuck Knoblauch	.15
13	Ricky Ledee	.15
14	Jim Leyritz	.15
15	Tino Martinez	.15
16	Ramiro Mendoza	.15
17	Jeff Nelson	.15
18	Paul O'Neill	.15
19	Andy Pettitte	.25
20	Jorge Posada	.25
21	Mariano Rivera	.25
22	Luis Sojo	.15
23	Mike Stanton	.15
24	Allen Watson	.15
25	Bernie Williams	.30
26	Chipper Jones	.60
27	Ivan Rodriguez	.45
28	Randy Johnson	.50
29	Pedro Martinez	.50
30	Scott Williamson	.15
31	Carlos Beltran	.40
32	Mark McGwire	1.50
33	Ken Griffey Jr.	1.00
34	Robin Ventura	.15
35	Tony Gwynn	.60
36	Wade Boggs	.60
37	Cal Ripken Jr.	2.00
38	Jose Canseco	.50
39	Alex Rodriguez	1.50
40	Fernando Tatis	.15

Point of Impact

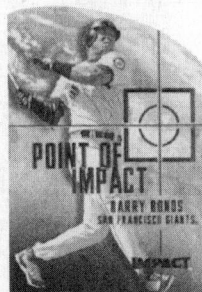

Point of Impact honors some of the game's top sluggers on a die-cut design. Card fronts have silver foil stamping and cross hairs where the featured player finds his sweet spot. These were seeded 1:30 packs and are numbered with an "PI" suffix on the card back.

		NM/M
Complete Set (10):		20.00
Common Player:		1.00
Inserted 1:30		
1	Ken Griffey Jr.	2.00
2	Mark McGwire	3.00
3	Sammy Sosa	2.00
4	Jeff Bagwell	1.00
5	Derek Jeter	4.00
6	Chipper Jones	1.50
7	Nomar Garciaparra	2.00
8	Cal Ripken Jr.	4.00
9	Barry Bonds	4.00
10	Alex Rodriguez	3.00

2000 Fleer Mystique

The base set consists of 175-cards including a 50-card Prospects subset that each card is serially numbered to 2,000 and covered. The card fronts have a full bleed design with gold foil stamping. Card backs have complete year-by-year statistics and a small photo.

		NM/M
Complete Set (175):		350.00
Common Player:		.20
Common 126-175:		6.00
Production 2,000 sets		
Pack (5):		3.00
Box (20):		50.00
1	Derek Jeter	3.00
2	David Justice	.20
3	Kevin Brown	.20
4	Jason Giambi	.75
5	Jose Canseco	.50
6	Mark Grace	.20
7	Hideo Nomo	.65
8	Edgardo Alfonzo	.20
9	Barry Bonds	3.00
10	Pedro Martinez	1.00
11	Juan Gonzalez	1.00
12	Vladimir Guerrero	1.00
13	Chuck Finley	.20
14	Brian Jordan	.20
15	Richie Sexson	.20
16	Chan Ho Park	.20
17	Tim Hudson	.40
18	Fred McGriff	.20
19	Darin Erstad	.60
20	Chris Singleton	.20
21	Jeff Bagwell	1.00
22	David Cone	.20
23	Edgar Martinez	.20
24	Greg Maddux	1.50
25	Jim Thome	.20
26	Eric Karros	.20
27	Bobby Abreu	.20
28	Greg Vaughn	.20
29	Kevin Millwood	.20
30	Omar Vizquel	.20
31	Marquis Grissom	.20
32	Mike Lieberthal	.20
33	Gabe Kapler	.20
34	Brady Anderson	.20
35	Jeff Cirillo	.20
36	Geoff Jenkins	.20
37	Scott Rolen	.75
38	Rafael Palmeiro	.65
39	Randy Johnson	1.00
40	Barry Larkin	.20
41	Johnny Damon	.40
42	Andy Pettitte	.40
43	Mark McGwire	2.50
44	Albert Belle	.20
45	Derrick Gibson	.20
46	Corey Koskie	.20
47	Curt Schilling	.50
48	Ivan Rodriguez	.65
49	Mike Mussina	.50
50	Todd Helton	1.00
51	Matt Lawton	.20
52	Jason Kendall	.20
53	Kenny Rogers	.20
54	Cal Ripken Jr.	3.00
55	Larry Walker	.20
56	Eric Milton	.20
57	Warren Morris	.20
58	Carlos Delgado	.50
59	Kerry Wood	.65
60	Cliff Floyd	.20
61	Mike Piazza	2.00
62	Jeff Kent	.20
63	Sammy Sosa	2.00
64	Alex Fernandez	.20
65	Mike Hampton	.20
66	Livan Hernandez	.20
67	Matt Williams	.20
68	Roberto Alomar	.45
69	Jermaine Dye	.20
70	Ken Griffey Jr.	2.00
71	Bernie Williams	.35
72	Edgar Renteria	.20
73	Tom Glavine	.40
74	Bartolo Colon	.20
75	Jason Varitek	.20
76	Eric Chavez	.40
77	Fernando Tatis	.20
78	Adrian Beltre	.40
79	Paul Konerko	.20
80	Mike Lowell	.20
81	Robin Ventura	.20
82	Russ Ortiz	.20
83	Troy Glaus	1.00
84	Frank Thomas	1.00
85	Craig Biggio	.20
86	Orlando Hernandez	.20
87	John Olerud	.20
88	Chipper Jones	1.50
89	Manny Ramirez	1.00
90	Shawn Green	.40
91	Ben Grieve	.20
92	Vinny Castilla	.20
93	Tim Salmon	.35
94	Dante Bichette	.20
95	Ken Caminiti	.20
96	Andruw Jones	.75
97	Alex Rodriguez	2.50
98	Erubiel Durazo	.20
99	Sean Casey	.30
100	Carlos Beltran	.50
101	Paul O'Neill	.20
102	Ray Lankford	.20
103	Troy O'Leary	.20
104	Bobby Higginson	.20
105	Rondell White	.20
106	Tony Gwynn	1.50
107	Magglio Ordonez	.40
108	Jim Edmonds	.20
109	Preston Wilson	.20
110	Roger Clemens	1.75
111	Ken Griffey Jr.	2.00
112	Nomar Garciaparra	2.00
113	Juan Encarnacion	.20
114	Michael Barrett	.20
115	Matt Clement	.20
116	David Wells	.20
117	Mo Vaughn	.20
118	Mike Cameron	.20
119	Jose Lima	.20
120	Tino Martinez	.20
121	J.D. Drew	.40
122	Carl Everett	.20
123	Tony Clark	.20
124	Brad Radke	.20
125	Kevin Young	.20
126	Raul Mondesi	.20
127	Cole Liniak (Prospects)	6.00
128	Alfonso Soriano (Prospects)	8.00
129	Lance Berkman (Prospects)	8.00
130	Danny Young (Prospects)	6.00
131	Francisco Cordero (Prospects)	6.00
132	Rob Fick (Prospects)	6.00
133	Matt LeCroy (Prospects)	6.00
134	Adam Piatt (Prospects)	6.00
135	Derrick Turnbow RC (Prospects)	6.00
136	Mark Quinn (Prospects)	6.00
137	Kip Wells (Prospects)	6.00
138	Rob Bell (Prospects)	6.00
139	Brad Penny (Prospects)	6.00
140	Pat Burrell (Prospects)	10.00
141	Danys Baez RC (Prospects)	6.00
142	Chad Hermansen (Prospects)	6.00
143	Steve Lomasney (Prospects)	6.00
144	Peter Bergeron (Prospects)	6.00
145	Jimmy Anderson (Prospects)	6.00
146	Mike Darr (Prospects)	6.00
147	Jacob Cruz (Prospects)	6.00
148	Kazuhiro Sasaki RC (Prospects)	10.00
149	Ben Petrick (Prospects)	6.00
150	Rick Ankiel (Prospects)	8.00
151	Aaron McNeal RC (Prospects)	6.00
152	Octavio Dotel (Prospects)	6.00
153	Juan Pena (Prospects)	6.00
154	Nick Johnson (Prospects)	8.00
155	Wilton Veras (Prospects)	6.00
156	Wily Pena (Prospects)	6.00
157	Mark Mulder (Prospects)	6.00
158	Daryle Ward (Prospects)	6.00
159	Chad Durbin RC (Prospects)	6.00
160	Angel Pena (Prospects)	6.00
161	Dewayne Wise (Prospects)	6.00
162	Tarrik Brock (Prospects)	6.00
163	Marcus Jensen (Prospects)	6.00
164	Kevin Barker (Prospects)	6.00
165	B.J. Ryan (Prospects)	6.00
166	Cesar King (Prospects)	6.00
167	Geoff Blum (Prospects)	6.00
167	Ruben Mateo (Prospects)	6.00
168	Ramon Ortiz (Prospects)	6.00
169	Eric Munson (Prospects)	6.00
170	Josh Beckett (Prospects)	8.00
171	Rafael Furcal (Prospects)	6.00
172	Matt Riley (Prospects)	6.00
173	Johan Santana RC (Prospects)	60.00
174	Mark Johnson (Prospects)	6.00
175	Adam Kennedy (Prospects)	6.00

Gold

These parallel inserts to the 175-card base set are identical to the base cards besides gold highlights throughout the background of the player photo. The word "Gold" also appears underneath the card number on the back. These were seeded 1:20 packs.

Stars (1-125):	4-8X
SP's (126-175):	1X
Inserted 1:20	

Club 3000

This three-card set is die-cut around the 3,000 numerals with a date on the left side when the featured player reached the 3,000 milestone. The player name is stamped in silver holo-foil. Card backs are not numbered and have a brief career note. These were seeded 1:20 packs.

		NM/M
Complete Set (3):		6.00
Common Player:		1.50
Inserted 1:20		
1	Cal Ripken Jr.	5.00
2	Bob Gibson	1.50
3	Dave Winfield	1.50

Club 3000 Memorabilia

Five different memorabilia versions of each player exist, using pieces of game-used bat, jersey and cap which are embedded into each card. The amount of each card produced is listed after the player name.

	NM/M
Cal Ripken Jr./Jsy/825	40.00
Cal Ripken Jr./Bat/265	75.00
Cal Ripken Jr./Hat/55	120.00
Cal Ripken Jr./Bat/Jsy/100	100.00
Bob Gibson/Jsy/825	20.00
Bob Gibson/Bat/265	30.00
Bob Gibson/Bat/Jsy/100	50.00
Bob Gibson/Hat/Jsy/100	50.00
Bob Gibson/Hat/55	75.00
Dave Winfield/Jsy/825	15.00
Dave Winfield/Bat/270	25.00
Dave Winfield/Bat/Jsy/100	50.00
Dave Winfield/Hat/55	60.00

Diamond Dominators

This 10-card set spotlights baseball's most dominating performers. Card fronts have a holofoil appearance. These were seeded 1:5 packs and are numbered with an "DD" suffix.

	NM/M
Complete Set (10):	15.00
Common Player:	.75
Inserted 1:5	
1 Manny Ramirez	1.00
2 Pedro Martinez	1.00
3 Sean Casey	.75
4 Vladimir Guerrero	1.00
5 Sammy Sosa	1.50
6 Nomar Garciaparra	1.50
7 Mark McGwire	2.50
8 Ken Griffey Jr.	1.50
9 Derek Jeter	3.00
10 Alex Rodriguez	2.50

Feel the Game

This game-used memorabilia set features either game-used jerseys or bats from today's top stars. These were seeded 1:120 packs.

	NM/M
Common Player:	5.00
Inserted 1:120	
1 Tony Gwynn/Jsy	20.00
2 Alex Rodriguez/Jsy	25.00
3 Chipper Jones/Jsy	20.00
4 Cal Ripken Jr./Jsy	40.00
5 Derek Jeter/Pants	40.00
6 Alex Rodriguez/Bat	30.00
7 Frank Thomas/Bat	15.00
8 Barry Bonds/Bat	40.00
9 Carlos Beltran/Bat	5.00
10 Shawn Green/Bat	8.00
11 Michael Barrett/Bat	10.00
12 Rafael Palmeiro/Bat	10.00
13 Vladimir Guerrero/Bat	15.00
14 Pat Burrell/Bat	12.00

Fresh Ink

This autographed set features signatures from many of the game's top players and are seeded 1:40 packs.

	NM/M
Common Player:	5.00
Inserted 1:40	
1 Chad Allen	5.00
2 Glen Barker	5.00
3 Michael Barrett	5.00
4 Josh Beckett	30.00
5 Rob Bell	5.00
6 Lance Berkman	25.00
7 Kent Bottenfield	5.00
8 Milton Bradley	8.00
9 Orlando Cabrera	10.00
10 Sean Casey	6.00
11 Roger Cedeno	5.00
12 Will Clark	25.00
13 Russ Davis	5.00
14 Carlos Delgado	15.00
15 Einar Diaz	5.00
16 J.D. Drew	10.00
17 Erubiel Durazo	10.00
18 Damion Easley	5.00
19 Carlos Febles	5.00
20 Doug Glanville	6.00
21 Alex Gonzalez	5.00
22 Tony Gwynn	40.00
23 Mike Hampton	8.00
24 Bobby Howry	5.00
25 John Jaha	5.00
26 Nick Johnson	20.00
27 Andruw Jones	20.00
28 Adam Kennedy	8.00
29 Mike Lieberthal	8.00
30 Jose Macias	5.00
31 Ruben Mateo	8.00
32 Raul Mondesi	8.00

33 Heath Murray	5.00
34 Mike Mussina	30.00
35 Hideo Nomo	250.00
36 Magglio Ordonez	15.00
37 Eric Owens	5.00
38 Adam Piatt	5.00
39 Cal Ripken Jr.	100.00
40 Tim Salmon	15.00
41 Chris Singleton	5.00
42 J.T. Snow	8.00
43 Mike Sweeney	10.00
44 Wilton Veras	5.00
45 Jose Vidro	8.00
46 Rondell White	10.00
47 Jaret Wright	5.00

High Praise

This 10-card set has a holofoiled card front with a "sky" background. These were inserted 1:20 packs and are numbered on the card back with an "HP" suffix.

	NM/M
Complete Set (10):	18.00
Common Player:	.75
Inserted 1:20	
1 Mark McGwire	3.00
2 Ken Griffey Jr.	2.00
3 Alex Rodriguez	3.00
4 Derek Jeter	4.00
5 Sammy Sosa	2.00
6 Mike Piazza	2.00
7 Nomar Garciaparra	2.00
8 Cal Ripken Jr.	4.00
9 Tony Gwynn	1.50
10 Shawn Green	.75

Rookie I.P.O.

This 10-card set highlights the top young rookies on a holofoil design. Card backs are numbered with an "RI" suffix and are seeded 1:10 packs.

	NM/M
Complete Set (10):	8.00
Common Player:	.50
Inserted 1:10	
1 Josh Beckett	1.00
2 Eric Munson	.50
3 Pat Burrell	2.00
4 Alfonso Soriano	1.50
5 Rick Ankiel	.50
6 Ruben Mateo	.50
7 Mark Quinn	.50
8 Kip Wells	.50
9 Ben Petrick	.50
10 Nick Johnson	.75

Seismic Activity

This 10-card set spotlights the top power hitters in the game. The player image is in the foreground of a warp like setting with golden highlights. Card backs are numbered with an "SA" suffix and are seeded 1:40 packs. A serial numbered parallel called Richter 100 is randomly seeded and is limited to 100 serial numbered sets.

	NM/M
Complete Set (10):	45.00
Common Player:	3.00
Inserted 1:40	
Richter Parallel:	3-5X

Production 100 Sets	
1 Ken Griffey Jr.	5.00
2 Sammy Sosa	5.00
3 Derek Jeter	10.00
4 Mark McGwire	8.00
5 Manny Ramirez	3.00
6 Mike Piazza	5.00
7 Vladimir Guerrero	3.00
8 Chipper Jones	4.00
9 Alex Rodriguez	8.00
10 Jeff Bagwell	3.00

Supernaturals

This 10-card set has a warp like image of the player on the front with silver holo-foil highlights around the player image and gold foil stamping. Card backs are numbered with an "S" suffix. These were seeded 1:10 packs.

	NM/M
Complete Set (10):	15.00
Common Player:	1.00
Inserted 1:10	
1 Alex Rodriguez	3.00
2 Chipper Jones	1.75
3 Derek Jeter	4.00
4 Ivan Rodriguez	1.00
5 Ken Griffey Jr.	2.00
6 Mark McGwire	3.00
7 Mike Piazza	2.00
8 Nomar Garciaparra	2.00
9 Sammy Sosa	2.00
10 Vladimir Guerrero	1.50

Dave Winfield Auto. Memorabilia

This two-card set consists of 40 game-used helmet Winfield cards and 20 game-used ball cards.

	NM/M
Complete Set (2):	
1 Dave Winfield/Bat/20	140.00
2 Dave Winfield/ Helmet/40	125.00

2000 Fleer Showcase

The base set consists of 140 cards, including 40 Prospect Showcase subset cards. Cards 101-115 are serially numbered to 1,000 and cards 116-140 are serially numbered to 2,000. The card fronts are holo-foiled, with the player name and team stamped in gold foil. Card backs have year-by-year statistics and a small close-up photo. Five-card packs carried an SRP of $4.99.

	NM/M
Complete Set (140):	200.00
Common Player (1-100):	.25
Common (101-115):	6.00
Production 1,000 Sets	
Common (116-140):	4.00
Production 2,000 Sets	
Pack (5):	2.50
Box (24):	50.00
1 Alex Rodriguez	2.50
2 Derek Jeter	3.00
3 Jeromy Burnitz	.25
4 John Olerud	.25
5 Paul Konerko	.25
6 Johnny Damon	.40
7 Curt Schilling	.50
8 Barry Larkin	.25
9 Adrian Beltre	.40
10 Scott Rolen	.75
11 Carlos Delgado	.50
12 Pedro J. Martinez	1.00
13 Todd Helton	1.00
14 Jacque Jones	.25
15 Jeff Kent	.25
16 Darin Erstad	.65
17 Juan Encarnacion	.25
18 Roger Clemens	1.75
19 Tony Gwynn	1.50
20 Nomar Garciaparra	2.00
21 Roberto Alomar	.40
22 Matt Lawton	.25
23 Rich Aurilia	.25
24 Charles Johnson	.25
25 Jim Thome	.25
26 Eric Milton	.25
27 Barry Bonds	3.00
28 Albert Belle	.25
29 Travis Fryman	.25
30 Ken Griffey Jr.	.25
31 Phil Nevin	.25
32 Chipper Jones	1.50
33 Craig Biggio	.25
34 Mike Hampton	.25
35 Fred McGriff	.25
36 Cal Ripken Jr.	3.00
37 Manny Ramirez	.25
38 Jose Vidro	.25
39 Trevor Hoffman	.25
40 Tom Glavine	.50
41 Frank Thomas	1.00
42 Chris Widger	.25
43 J.D. Drew	.50
44 Andres Galarraga	.25
45 Pokey Reese	.25
46 Mike Piazza	2.00
47 Kevin Young	.25
48 Sean Casey	.25
49 Carlos Beltran	.60
50 Jason Kendall	.25
51 Vladimir Guerrero	1.00
52 Jermaine Dye	.25
53 Brian Giles	.25
54 Andruw Jones	1.00
55 Richard Hidalgo	.25
56 Robin Ventura	.25
57 Ivan Rodriguez	.65
58 Greg Maddux	1.50
59 Billy Wagner	.25
60 Ruben Mateo	.25
61 Troy Glaus	1.00
62 Dean Palmer	.25
63 Eric Chavez	.40
64 Edgar Martinez	.25
65 Randy Johnson	.25
66 Preston Wilson	.25
67 Orlando Hernandez	.25
68 Jim Edmonds	.25
69 Carl Everett	.25
70 Larry Walker	.25
71 Ron Belliard	.25
72 Sammy Sosa	2.00
73 Matt Williams	.25
74 Cliff Floyd	.25
75 Bernie Williams	.40
76 Fernando Tatis	.25
77 Steve Finley	.25
78 Jeff Bagwell	1.00
79 Edgardo Alfonzo	.25
80 Jose Canseco	.40
81 Magglio Ordonez	.40
82 Shawn Green	.40
83 Bobby Abreu	.25
84 Tony Batista	.25
85 Mo Vaughn	.25
86 Juan Gonzalez	1.00
87 Paul O'Neill	.25
88 Mark McGwire	2.50
89 Mark Grace	.35
90 Kevin Brown	.25
91 Ben Grieve	.25
92 Shannon Stewart	.25
93 Erubiel Durazo	.25
94 Antonio Alfonseca	.25
95 Jeff Cirillo	.25
96 Greg Vaughn	.25
97 Kerry Wood	.60
98 Geoff Jenkins	.25
99 Jason Giambi	.75
100 Rafael Palmeiro	.65
101 Rafael Furcal	6.00
102 Pablo Ozuna	6.00
103 Brad Penny	6.00
104 Mark Mulder	8.00
105 Adam Piatt	6.00

106 Mike Lamb RC	6.00
107 Kazuhiro Sasaki RC	15.00
108 Aaron McNeal RC	6.00
109 Pat Burrell	8.00
110 Rick Ankiel	6.00
111 Eric Munson	6.00
112 Josh Beckett	8.00
113 Adam Kennedy	6.00
114 Alex Escobar	6.00
115 Chad Hermansen	6.00
116 Kip Wells	4.00
117 Matt LeCroy	4.00
118 Julio Ramirez	4.00
119 Ben Petrick	4.00
120 Nick Johnson	6.00
121 Gookie Dawkins	4.00
122 Julio Zuleta RC	4.00
123 Alfonso Soriano	8.00
124 Keith McDonald RC	4.00
125 Kory DeHaan	4.00
126 Vernon Wells	6.00
127 Dernell Stenson	4.00
128 David Eckstein	4.00
129 Robert Fick	4.00
130 Cole Liniak	4.00
131 Mark Quinn	4.00
132 Eric Gagne	5.00
133 Wily Pena	4.00
134 Andy Thompson RC	4.00
135 Steve Sisco RC	4.00
136 Paul Rigdon RC	6.00
137 Rob Bell	4.00
138 Carlos Guillen	5.00
139 Jimmy Rollins	4.00
140 Jason Conti	4.00

Legacy

A parallel to the 140-card base set these feature a matte and holo-foil design and are serially numbered to 20.

	NM/M
Stars (1-100):	30-50X
Prospects (101-140):	3-6X
Production 20 Sets	

Masterpiece

Each card in 2000 Showcase was issued in a unique Masterpiece edition. The front is enhanced with gold ink while on back is printed the notice "The Only 1 Of 1 / Masterpiece."

Prospect Showcase First

A parallel of the 40-card Prospects subset. These differ from the base cards in that they have a horizontal format and are serially numbered to 500.

	NM/M
Prospects (101-140):	1-2X
Production 500 Sets	

Club 3000

This two-card set pays tribute to Lou Brock and Nolan Ryan. Each card is die-cut around the numerals 3,000 with a date displaying the day Brock or Ryan reached their 3,000 milestone. The player name is stamped in silver holo-foil. These were inserted 1:24 packs.

	NM/M
Common Player:	3.00
Inserted 1:24	
1 Lou Brock	2.00
2 Nolan Ryan	8.00

Club 3000 Memorabilia

These inserts feature actual game-used pieces of memorabilia from Nolan Ryan and Lou Brock and are serial numbered. The number produced is listed after the player name.

	NM/M
Lou Brock/Jsy/680	15.00
Lou Brock/Bat/270	25.00
Lou Brock/ Hat/Bat/Jsy/25	100.00
Nolan Ryan/Jsy/780	40.00
Nolan Ryan/Hat/65	120.00
Nolan Ryan - Bat/265	60.00
Nolan Ryan/ Bat/Jsy/100	120.00

Consummate Prose

This 15-card set has an image of a worn scroll of paper with consummate prose written on it in the background of the player image. The Showcase logo, player name and Consummate Prose are stamped in gold foil. Card backs are numbered with an "CP" suffix and are inserted 1:6 packs.

	NM/M
Complete Set (15):	20.00
Common Player:	.50
Inserted 1:6	
1 Jeff Bagwell	1.50
2 Alex Rodriguez	3.00
3 Chipper Jones	2.00
4 Derek Jeter	4.00
5 Manny Ramirez	1.50
6 Tony Gwynn	2.00
7 Sammy Sosa	2.50
8 Ivan Rodriguez	1.00
9 Greg Maddux	2.00
10 Ken Griffey Jr.	2.50
11 Rick Ankiel	.50
12 Cal Ripken Jr.	4.00
13 Pedro Martinez	1.50
14 Mike Piazza	2.50
15 Mark McGwire	3.00

Feel the Game

This set has swatches of game worn jersey embedded into the card front.

	NM/M
Common Player:	5.00
Inserted 1:72	
1 Barry Bonds	30.00
2 Gookie Dawkins	5.00
3 Darin Erstad	8.00
4 Troy Glaus	10.00
5 Scott Rolen	10.00
6 Alex Rodriguez	25.00
7 Andruw Jones	10.00
8 Robin Ventura	5.00
9 Sean Casey	5.00
10 Cal Ripken Jr.	40.00

Final Answer

These foiled inserts have a green border with the player inside a frame with question marks in the background. The card backs have trivia questions about the featured player. Card backs are numbered with a "FA" suffix. These were seeded 1:10 packs.

		NM/M
Complete Set (10):		20.00
Common Player:		1.00
Inserted 1:10		
1	Alex Rodriguez	3.00
2	Vladimir Guerrero	1.00
3	Cal Ripken Jr.	4.00
4	Sammy Sosa	2.00
5	Barry Bonds	4.00
6	Derek Jeter	4.00
7	Ken Griffey Jr.	2.00
8	Mike Piazza	2.00
9	Nomar Garciaparra	2.00
10	Mark McGwire	3.00

Fresh Ink

These autographed inserts are inserted 1:24 packs.

		NM/M
Common Player:		5.00
Inserted 1:24		
1	Rick Ankiel	20.00
2	Josh Beckett	30.00
3	Barry Bonds	200.00
4	A.J. Burnett	10.00
5	Pat Burrell	15.00
6	Ken Caminiti	8.00
7	Sean Casey	10.00
8	Jose Cruz Jr.	10.00
9	Gookie Dawkins	5.00
10	Erubiel Durazo	10.00
11	Juan Encarnacion	8.00
12	Darin Erstad	15.00
13	Rafael Furcal	15.00
14	Nomar Garciaparra	100.00
15	Jason Giambi	20.00
16	Jeremy Giambi	6.00
17	Brian Giles	15.00
18	Troy Glaus	20.00
20	Vladimir Guerrero	30.00
21	Chad Hermansen	5.00
23	Trevor Hoffman	8.00
24	Randy Johnson	60.00
25	Andruw Jones	15.00
26	Jason Kendall	8.00
27	Paul Konerko	10.00
28	Mike Lowell	10.00
29	Aaron McNeal	5.00
30	Warren Morris	5.00
31	Paul O'Neill	20.00
32	Magglio Ordonez	10.00
33	Pablo Ozuna	5.00
34	Brad Penny	8.00
35	Ben Petrick	5.00
36	Pokey Reese	5.00
37	Cal Ripken Jr.	125.00
38	Alex Rodriguez	75.00
39	Scott Rolen	30.00
40	Jose Vidro	8.00
41	Kip Wells	5.00

License to Skill

License to Skill have a rounded, die-cut top with a concentric-circles background. Silver and gold foil etching and foil stamping are used as well. Card backs are numbered with an "LS" suffix.

7	Pedro J. Martinez	1.00
8	Alex Rodriguez	3.00
9	Derek Jeter	4.00
10	Randy Johnson	1.00

Sweet Sigs

These autographed inserts have the featured players' autograph on an actual "sweet spot" from an authentic Major League baseball. These have an insertion ratio of 1:250 packs.

		NM/M
Common Player:		10.00
Inserted 1:250		
1	Nomar Garciaparra/53	150.00
2	Alex Rodriguez/67	200.00
3	Tony Gwynn	40.00
4	Roger Clemens/79	140.00
5	Scott Rolen	50.00
6	Greg Maddux	80.00
7	Jose Cruz Jr.	15.00
8	Tony Womack	10.00
9	Jay Buhner	10.00
10	Nolan Ryan	125.00

2000 Fleer Tradition

The Fleer Tradition base set consists of 450 cards including a 30-card rookies/prospects subset, 30 team cards, 10 league leaders, 6 award winners, 10 postseason recaps and 6 checklists. The card fronts have a close-up photo of the featured player as well as a small action photo surrounded by a white border. Like the fronts the card backs have a "throwback" look, which includes complete year-by-year statistics, a brief career note and vital information. 10-card packs had a SRP of $1.49.

		NM/M
Complete Set (450):		50.00
Common Player:		.10
Complete Glossy Factory Set (500):		450.00
Complete Glossy Factory Set (455):		75.00
Glossy (1-450):		1-2X
Common Glossy (451-500):		8.00
Five Glossy (451-500) per factory set.		
1,000 produced (451-500)		
Pack (10):		1.50
Wax Box:		35.00
1	AL HRs	.50
2	NL HRs	.50
3	AL RBIs	.50
4	NL RBIs	.50
5	AL Avg.	.50
6	NL Avg.	.15
7	AL Wins	.40
8	NL Wins	.40
9	AL ERA	.20
10	NL ERA	.25
11	Matt Mantei	.10
12	John Rocker	.10
13	Kyle Farnsworth	.10
14	Juan Guzman	.10
15	Manny Ramirez	.75
16	Matt Riley-P, Calvin Pickering-1B	.10
17	Tony Clark	.10
18	Brian Meadows	.10
19	Orber Moreno	.10
20	Eric Karros	.10
21	Steve Woodard	.10
22	Scott Brosius	.10
23	Gary Bennett	.10
24	Jason Wood-3B, Dave Borkowski-P	.10
25	Joe McEwing	.10
26	Juan Gonzalez	.75
27	Roy Halladay	.25

Long Gone

These inserts are die-cut around the card top to mimic the outfield dimensions of the featured players' stadium. Gold foil stamping is also used. Card backs are numbered with an "LG" suffix and have an insertion ratio of 1:20 packs.

		NM/M
Complete Set (10):		25.00
Common Player:		2.00
Inserted 1:20		
1	Sammy Sosa	4.00
2	Derek Jeter	6.00
3	Nomar Garciaparra	4.00
4	Juan Gonzalez	2.00
5	Vladimir Guerrero	2.00
6	Barry Bonds	6.00
7	Jeff Bagwell	2.00
8	Alex Rodriguez	5.00
9	Ken Griffey Jr.	4.00
10	Mark McGwire	5.00

Noise of Summer

This 10-card set has a kaleidoscope background with the insert name stamped in red foil and the logo, player name and team name stamped in gold foil. Card backs are numbered with an "NS" suffix. These were seeded 1:10 packs.

		NM/M
Complete Set (10):		15.00
Common Player:		1.00
Inserted 1:10		
1	Chipper Jones	1.50
2	Jeff Bagwell	1.00
3	Manny Ramirez	1.00
4	Mark McGwire	3.00
5	Ken Griffey Jr.	2.00
6	Mike Piazza	2.00

(Complete Set (10) above right):

		NM/M
Complete Set (10):		25.00
Common Player:		1.50
1	Vladimir Guerrero	2.00
2	Pedro J. Martinez	2.00
3	Nomar Garciaparra	4.00
4	Ivan Rodriguez	1.50
5	Mark McGwire	5.00
6	Derek Jeter	6.00
7	Ken Griffey Jr.	4.00
8	Randy Johnson	2.00
9	Sammy Sosa	4.00
10	Alex Rodriguez	5.00

28	Trevor Hoffman	.10
29	Arizona Diamondbacks	.10
30	Domingo Guzman-P RC, Wiki Gonzalez-C	.25
31	Bret Boone	.10
32	Nomar Garciaparra	2.00
33	Bo Porter	.10
34	Eddie Taubensee	.10
35	Pedro Astacio	.10
36	Derek Bell	.10
37	Jacque Jones	.10
38	Ricky Ledee	.10
39	Jeff Kent	.10
40	Matt Williams	.10
41	Alfonso Soriano-SS, D'Angelo Jimenez-3B	.75
42	B.J. Surhoff	.10
43	Denny Neagle	.10
44	Omar Vizquel	.10
45	Jeff Bagwell	.75
46	Mark Grudzielanek	.10
47	LaTroy Hawkins	.10
48	Orlando Hernandez	.10
49	Ken Griffey Jr.	2.00
50	Fernando Tatis	.10
51	Quivio Veras	.10
52	Wayne Gomes	.10
53	Rick Helling	.10
54	Shannon Stewart	.10
55	Dermal Brown-OF, Mark Quinn-OF	.20
56	Randy Johnson	1.00
57	Greg Maddux	1.50
58	Mike Cameron	.10
59	Matt Anderson	.10
60	Milwaukee Brewers	.10
61	Derek Lee	.10
62	Mike Sweeney	.10
63	Fernando Vina	.10
64	Orlando Cabrera	.20
65	Doug Glanville	.10
66	Stan Spencer	.10
67	Ray Lankford	.10
68	Kelly Dransfeldt	.10
69	Alex Gonzalez	.10
70	Russell Branyan-3B, Danny Peoples-OF	.10
71	Jim Edmonds	.10
72	Brady Anderson	.10
73	Mike Stanley	.10
74	Travis Fryman	.10
75	Carlos Febles	.10
76	Bobby Higginson	.10
77	Carlos Perez	.10
78	Steve Cox-1B, Alex Sanchez-OF	.10
79	Dustin Hermanson	.10
80	Kenny Rogers	.10
81	Miguel Tejada	.10
82	Ben Davis	.10
83	Reggie Sanders	.10
84	Eric Davis	.10
85	J.D. Drew	.45
86	Ryan Rupe	.10
87	Bobby Smith	.10
88	Jose Cruz Jr.	.10
89	Carlos Delgado	.50
90	Toronto Blue Jays	.10
91	Denny Stark-P RC, Gil Meche-P	.25
92	Randy Velarde	.10
93	Aaron Boone	.10
94	Javy Lopez	.10
95	Johnny Damon	.25
96	Jon Lieber	.10
97	Montreal Expos	.10
98	Mark Kotsay	.10
99	Luis Gonzalez	.25
100	Larry Walker	.10
101	Adrian Beltre	.25
102	Alex Ochoa	.10
103	Michael Barrett	.10
104	Tampa Bay Devil Rays	.10
105	Rey Ordonez	.10
106	Derek Jeter	3.00
107	Mike Lieberthal	.10
108	Ellis Burks	.10
109	Steve Finley	.10
110	Ryan Klesko	.10
111	Steve Avery	.10
112	Dave Veres	.10
113	Cliff Floyd	.10
114	Shane Reynolds	.10
115	Kevin Brown	.10
116	David Nilsson	.10
117	Mike Trombley	.10
118	Todd Walker	.10
119	John Olerud	.10
120	Chuck Knoblauch	.10
121	Nomar Garciaparra	2.00
122	Trot Nixon	.10
123	Erubiel Durazo	.10
124	Edwards Guzman	.10
125	Curt Schilling	.50
126	Brian Jordan	.10
127	Cleveland Indians	.10
128	Benito Santiago	.10
129	Frank Thomas	.75
130	Neifi Perez	.10
131	Alex Fernandez	.10
132	Jose Lima	.10
133	Jorge Toca-1B, Melvin Mora-OF	.10
134	Scott Karl	.10
135	Brad Radke	.10
136	Paul O'Neill	.10
137	Kris Benson	.10
138	Colorado Rockies	.10

139	Jason Phillips	.10
140	Robb Nen	.10
141	Ken Hill	.10
142	Charles Johnson	.10
143	Paul Konerko	.10
144	Dmitri Young	.10
145	Justin Thompson	.10
146	Mark Loretta	.10
147	Edgardo Alfonzo	.10
148	Armando Benitez	.10
149	Octavio Dotel	.10
150	Wade Boggs	1.50
151	Ramon Hernandez	.10
152	Freddy Garcia	.10
153	Edgar Martinez	.10
154	Ivan Rodriguez	.65
155	Kansas City Royals	.10
156	Cleatus Davidson-2B, Cristian Guzman-SS	.10
157	Andy Benes	.10
158	Todd Dunwoody	.10
159	Pedro Martinez	1.00
160	Mike Caruso	.10
161	Mike Sirotka	.10
162	Houston Astros	.10
163	Darryl Kile	.10
164	Chipper Jones	1.50
165	Carl Everett	.10
166	Geoff Jenkins	.10
167	Dan Perkins	.10
168	Andy Pettitte	.25
169	Francisco Cordova	.10
170	Jay Buhner	.10
171	Jay Bell	.10
172	Andruw Jones	.75
173	Bobby Howry	.10
174	Chris Singleton	.10
175	Todd Helton	.75
176	A.J. Burnett	.10
177	Marquis Grissom	.10
178	Eric Milton	.10
179	Los Angeles Dodgers	.10
180	Kevin Appier	.10
181	Brian Giles	.10
182	Tom Davey	.10
183	Mo Vaughn	.10
184	Jose Hernandez	.10
185	Jim Parque	.10
186	Derrick Gibson	.10
187	Bruce Aven	.10
188	Jeff Cirillo	.10
189	Doug Mientkiewicz	.10
190	Eric Chavez	.25
191	Al Martin	.10
192	Tom Glavine	.10
193	Butch Huskey	.10
194	Ray Durham	.10
195	Greg Vaughn	.10
196	Vinny Castilla	.10
197	Ken Caminiti	.10
198	Joe Mays	.10
199	Chicago White Sox	.10
200	Mariano Rivera	.20
201	Mark McGwire	2.50
202	Pat Meares	.10
203	Andres Galarraga	.10
204	Tom Gordon	.10
205	Henry Rodriguez	.10
206	Brett Tomko	.10
207	Dante Bichette	.10
208	Craig Biggio	.10
209	Matt Lawton	.10
210	Tino Martinez	.10
211	Aaron Myette-P, Josh Paul-C	.10
212	Warren Morris	.10
213	San Diego Padres	.10
214	Ramon E. Martinez	.10
215	Troy Percival	.10
216	Jason Johnson	.10
217	Carlos Lee	.10
218	Scott Williamson	.10
219	Jeff Weaver	.10
220	Ronnie Belliard	.10
221	Jason Giambi	.65
222	Ken Griffey Jr.	2.00
223	John Halama	.10
224	Brett Hinchliffe	.10
225	Wilson Alvarez	.10
226	Rolando Arrojo	.10
227	Ruben Mateo	.10
228	Rafael Palmeiro	.65
229	David Wells	.10
230	Eric Gagne-P, Jeff Williams-P	.10
231	Tim Salmon	.30
232	Mike Mussina	.50
233	Magglio Ordonez	.25
234	Ron Villone	.10
235	Antonio Alfonseca	.10
236	Jeromy Burnitz	.10
237	Ben Grieve	.10
238	Giomar Guevara	.10
239	Garret Anderson	.10
240	John Smoltz	.10
241	Mark Grace	.15
242	Cole Liniak-3B, Jose Molina-C	.10
243	Damion Easley	.10
244	Jeff Montgomery	.10
245	Kenny Lofton	.10
246	Masato Yoshii	.10
247	Philadelphia Phillies	.10
248	Raul Mondesi	.10
249	Marlon Anderson	.10
250	Shawn Green	.40
251	Sterling Hitchcock	.10

252	Randy Wolf-P, Anthony Shumaker-P	.10
253	Jeff Fassero	.10
254	Eli Marrero	.10
255	Cincinnati Reds	.10
256	Rick Ankiel-P, Adam Kennedy-2B	.10
257	Darin Erstad	.60
258	Albert Belle	.20
259	Bartolo Colon	.10
260	Bret Saberhagen	.10
261	Carlos Beltran	.50
262	Glenallen Hill	.10
263	Gregg Jefferies	.10
264	Matt Clement	.10
265	Miguel Del Toro	.10
266	Robinson Cancel-C, Kevin Barker-1B	.10
267	San Francisco Giants	.10
268	Kent Bottenfield	.10
269	Fred McGriff	.10
270	Chris Carpenter	.10
271	Atlanta Braves	.10
272	Wilton Veras-3B, Tomokazu Ohka-P RC	.50
273	Will Clark	.20
274	Troy O'Leary	.10
275	Sammy Sosa	2.00
276	Travis Lee	.15
277	Sean Casey	.25
278	Ron Gant	.10
279	Roger Clemens	1.75
280	Phil Nevin	.10
281	Mike Piazza	2.00
282	Mike Lowell	.10
283	Kevin Millwood	.10
284	Joe Nada	.10
285	Jeff Shaw	.10
286	Jason Varitek	.10
287	Harold Baines	.10
288	Gabe Kapler	.10
289	Chuck Finley	.10
290	Carl Pavano	.10
291	Brad Ausmus	.10
292	Brad Fullmer	.10
293	Boston Red Sox	.10
294	Bob Wickman	.10
295	Billy Wagner	.10
296	Shawn Estes	.10
297	Gary Sheffield	.40
298	Fernando Seguignol	.10
299	Omar Olivares	.10
300	Baltimore Orioles	.10
301	Matt Stairs	.10
302	Andy Ashby	.10
303	Todd Greene	.10
304	Jesse Garcia	.10
305	Kerry Wood	.50
306	Roberto Alomar	.40
307	New York Mets	.10
308	Dean Palmer	.10
309	Mike Hampton	.10
310	Devon White	.10
311	Chad Hermansen-OF, Mike Garcia-P	.10
312	Tim Hudson	.40
313	John Franco	.10
314	Jason Schmidt	.10
315	J.T. Snow	.10
316	Ed Sprague	.10
317	Chris Widger	.10
318	Ben Petrick-C, Luther Hackman-P RC	.25
319	Jose Mesa	.10
320	Jose Canseco	.50
321	John Wetteland	.10
322	Minnesota Twins	.10
323	Jeff DaVanon-OF RC, Brian Cooper-P	.10
324	Tony Womack	.10
325	Rod Beck	.10
326	Mickey Morandini	.10
327	Pokey Reese	.10
328	Jaret Wright	.10
329	Glen Barker	.10
330	Darren Dreifort	.10
331	Torii Hunter	.10
332	Tony Armas Jr.-P, Peter Bergeron-OF	.10
333	Hideki Irabu	.10
334	Desi Relaford	.10
335	Barry Bonds	3.00
336	Gary DiSarcina	.10
337	Gerald Williams	.10
338	John Valentin	.10
339	David Justice	.10
340	Juan Encarnacion	.10
341	Jeremy Giambi	.10
342	Chan Ho Park	.10
343	Vladimir Guerrero	1.00
344	Robin Ventura	.10
345	Bobby Abreu	.10
346	Tony Gwynn	1.50
347	Jose Jimenez	.10
348	Royce Clayton	.10
349	Kelvim Escobar	.10
350	Chicago Cubs	.10
351	Travis Dawkins-SS, Jason LaRue-C	.10
352	Barry Larkin	.10
353	Cal Ripken Jr.	3.00
353s	Cal Ripken Jr./OPS	4.00
354	Alex Rodriguez	2.50
355	Todd Stottlemyre	.10
356	Terry Adams	.10
357	Pittsburgh Pirates	.10
358	Jim Thome	.10

359	Corey Lee-P,	
	Doug Davis-P	.10
360	Moises Alou	.10
361	Todd Hollandsworth	.10
362	Marty Cordova	.10
363	David Cone	.10
364	Joe Nathan-P,	
	Wilson Delgado-SS	.10
365	Paul Byrd	.10
366	Edgar Renteria	.10
367	Rusty Greer	.10
368	David Segui	.10
369	New York Yankees	.50
370	Daryle Ward-OF/1B,	
	Carlos Hernandez-2B	.10
371	Troy Glaus	.75
372	Delino DeShields	.10
373	Jose Offerman	.10
374	Sammy Sosa	2.00
375	Sandy Alomar Jr.	.10
376	Masao Kida	.10
377	Richard Hidalgo	.10
378	Ismael Valdes	.10
379	Ugueth Urbina	.10
380	Darryl Hamilton	.10
381	John Jaha	.10
382	St. Louis Cardinals	.10
383	Scott Sauerbeck	.10
384	Russ Ortiz	.10
385	Jamie Moyer	.10
386	Dave Martinez	.10
387	Todd Zeile	.10
388	Anaheim Angels	.10
389	Rob Ryan-OF,	
	Nick Bierbrodt-P	.10
390	Rickey Henderson	.75
391	Alex Rodriguez	2.50
392	Texas Rangers	.10
393	Roberto Hernandez	.10
394	Tony Batista	.10
395	Oakland Athletics	.10
396	Randall Simon-1B,	
	David Cortes-P RC	.20
397	Gregg Olson	.10
398	Sidney Ponson	.10
399	Micah Bowie	.10
400	Mark McGwire	2.50
401	Florida Marlins	.10
402	Chad Allen	.10
403	Casey Blake-3B,	
	Vernon Wells-OF	.10
404	Pete Harnisch	.10
405	Preston Wilson	.10
406	Richie Sexson	.10
407	Rico Brogna	.10
408	Todd Hundley	.10
409	Wally Joyner	.10
410	Tom Goodwin	.10
411	Joey Hamilton	.10
412	Detroit Tigers	.10
413	Michael Tejera-P RC,	
	Ramon Castro-C	.25
414	Alex Gonzalez	.10
415	Jermaine Dye	.10
416	Jose Rosado	.10
417	Wilton Guerrero	.10
418	Rondell White	.10
419	Al Leiter	.10
420	Bernie Williams	.25
421	A.J. Hinch	.10
422	Pat Burrell	.50
423	Scott Rolen	.65
424	Jason Kendall	.10
425	Kevin Young	.10
426	Eric Owens	.10
427	Derek Jeter	1.00
428	Livan Hernandez	.10
429	Russ Davis	.10
430	Dan Wilson	.10
431	Quinton McCracken	.10
432	Homer Bush	.10
433	Seattle Mariners	.10
434	Chad Harville-P,	
	Luis Vizcaino-P	.10
435	Carlos Beltran	.45
436	Scott Williamson	.10
437	Pedro Martinez	.75
438	Randy Johnson	.75
439	Ivan Rodriguez	.60
440	Chipper Jones	.75
441	AL Division	
	(Bernie Williams)	.15
442	AL Division	
	(Pedro Martinez)	.50
443	AL Champ (Derek Jeter)	1.00
444	NL Division (Brian Jordan)	.10
445	NL Division (Todd Pratt)	.10
446	NL Champ	
	(Kevin Millwood)	.10
447	World Series	
	(Orlando Hernandez)	.10
448	World Series	
	(Derek Jeter)	1.00
449	World Series	
	(Chad Curtis)	.10
450	World Series	
	(Roger Clemens)	.75
451	Carlos Casimiro RC	8.00
452	Adam Melhuse RC	8.00
453	Adam Bernero RC	8.00
454	Dusty Allen RC	8.00
455	Chan Perry RC	8.00
56	Damian Rolls RC	8.00
57	Josh Phelps RC	10.00
58	Barry Zito RC	25.00
59	Hector Ortiz RC	8.00
60	Juan Pierre RC	15.00
61	Jose Ortiz RC	15.00

462	Chad Zerbe RC	8.00
463	Julio Zuleta RC	8.00
464	Eric Byrnes RC	25.00
465	Wilfredo Rodriguez RC	10.00
466	Wascar Serrano RC	8.00
467	Aaron McNeal RC	8.00
468	Paul Rigdon RC	8.00
469	John Snyder RC	8.00
470	J.C. Romero RC	8.00
471	Talmadge Nunnari RC	8.00
472	Mike Lamb RC	8.00
473	Ryan Kohlmeier RC	8.00
474	Rodney Lindsey RC	8.00
475	Elvis Pena RC	8.00
476	Alex Cabrera RC	10.00
477	Chris Richard RC	8.00
478	Pedro Feliz RC	10.00
479	Ross Gload RC	8.00
480	Timoniel Perez RC	8.00
481	Jason Woolf RC	8.00
482	Kenny Kelly RC	8.00
483	Sang-Hoon Lee RC	8.00
484	John Riedling RC	8.00
485	Chris Wakeland RC	8.00
486	Britt Reames RC	8.00
487	Greg LaRocca RC	8.00
488	Randy Keisler RC	8.00
489	Xavier Nady RC	20.00
490	Keith Ginter RC	8.00
491	Joey Nation RC	8.00
492	Kazuhiro Sasaki RC	8.00
493	Lesli Brea RC	8.00
494	Jace Brewer RC	8.00
495	Yohanny Valera RC	8.00
496	Adam Piatt	10.00
497	Nate Rolison	8.00
498	Aubrey Huff	10.00
499	Jason Tyner	8.00
500	Corey Patterson	10.00

Club 3000

The Club 3000 inserts are die-cut around the number 3,000, commemmorating their reaching the 3,000 hit achievement. These are seeded 1:36 packs and features George Brett, Rod Carew and Robin Yount.

		NM/M
Complete Set (3):		5.00
Common Player:		3.00
Inserted 1:36		
(1)	George Brett	4.00
(2)	Rod Carew	2.00
(3)	Robin Yount	2.00

Club 3000 Memorabilia

These are a parallel to the base version and has five different memorabilia based tiers. Level 2 (cap), Level 3 (bat), Level 4 (jersey), Level 5 (bat and jersey) and Level 6 (bat, jersey and cap). Each card is hand-numbered.

	NM/M
George Brett/Bat/250	60.00
George Brett/Hat/100	75.00
George Brett/Jsy/445	30.00
George Brett/Bat/Jsy/100	90.00
Rod Carew/Bat/225	30.00
Rod Carew/Hat/100	50.00
Rod Carew/Jsy/440	20.00
Rod Carew/Bat/Jsy/100	65.00
Robin Yount/Bat/250	40.00
Robin Yount/Hat/100	50.00
Robin Yount/Jsy/440	30.00
Robin Yount/Bat/Jsy/100	75.00

Dividends

This insert set consists of 15 cards and spotlights the top players on a horizontal format. Card fronts have silver foil stamping, a red border and are seeded 1:6 packs. They are numbered on the back with a "D" suffix.

		NM/M
Complete Set (15):		15.00
Common Player:		.50
Inserted 1:6		
1	Alex Rodriguez	2.50
2	Ben Grieve	.50
3	Cal Ripken Jr.	3.00
4	Chipper Jones	1.50
5	Derek Jeter	3.00
6	Frank Thomas	1.00
7	Jeff Bagwell	1.00
8	Sammy Sosa	2.00
9	Tony Gwynn	1.50
10	Scott Rolen	.75
11	Nomar Garciaparra	2.00
12	Mike Piazza	2.00
13	Mark McGwire	2.50
14	Ken Griffey Jr.	2.00
15	Juan Gonzalez	1.00

Fresh Ink

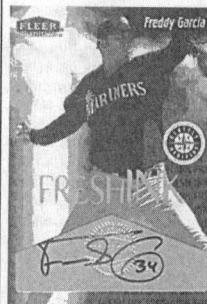

This autographed insert set consists of 38 cards on a vertical format with the autograph on the bottom third of the card below the player image. These were inserted 1:144 packs.

	NM/M
Common Player:	5.00
Inserted 1:144	
Rick Ankiel	15.00
Carlos Beltran	25.00
Pat Burrell	15.00
Miguel Cairo	5.00
Sean Casey	8.00
Will Clark	30.00
Mike Darr	5.00
J.D. Drew	10.00
Erubiel Durazo	10.00
Carlos Febles	6.00
Freddy Garcia	8.00
Greg Maddux	80.00
Jason Grilli	5.00
Vladimir Guerrero	35.00
Tony Gwynn	40.00
Jerry Hairston Jr.	8.00
Tim Hudson	15.00
John Jaha	5.00
D'Angelo Jimenez	5.00
Andruw Jones	20.00
Gabe Kapler	6.00
Cesar King	5.00
Jason LaRue	6.00
Mike Lieberthal	8.00
Pedro Martinez	50.00
Gary Matthews Jr.	5.00
Orber Moreno	5.00
Eric Munson	5.00
Rafael Palmeiro	35.00
Jim Parque	6.00
Willi Mo Pena	15.00
Cal Ripken Jr.	100.00
Alex Rodriguez	80.00
Tim Salmon	15.00
Chris Singleton	5.00
Alfonso Soriano	50.00
Ed Yarnall	5.00

Grasskickers

This 15-card set has a close-up photo of the featured player with holographic silver foil stamping. These were seeded 1:30 packs and are numbered on the back with a "GK" suffix.

		NM/M
Complete Set (15):		50.00
Common Player:		2.00
Inserted 1:30		
1	Tony Gwynn	3.00
2	Scott Rolen	2.00
3	Nomar Garciaparra	4.00
4	Mike Piazza	4.00
5	Mark McGwire	6.00
6	Frank Thomas	2.00
7	Cal Ripken Jr.	8.00

8	Chipper Jones	3.00
9	Greg Maddux	3.00
10	Ken Griffey Jr.	4.00
11	Juan Gonzalez	2.00
12	Derek Jeter	8.00
13	Sammy Sosa	2.50
14	Ken Griffey Jr.	2.00
15	Juan Gonzalez	1.00

Hall's Well

This 15-card set spotlights superstars destined for Cooperstown, featured on a transparent plastic stock with overlays of silver foil stamping. These were seeded 1:30 packs and are numbered with a "HW" suffix.

		NM/M
Complete Set (15):		50.00
Common Player:		1.50
Inserted 1:30		
1	Mark McGwire	6.00
2	Alex Rodriguez	6.00
3	Cal Ripken Jr.	8.00
4	Chipper Jones	3.00
5	Derek Jeter	8.00
6	Frank Thomas	2.00
7	Greg Maddux	3.00
8	Juan Gonzalez	2.00
9	Ken Griffey Jr.	4.00
10	Mike Piazza	4.00
11	Nomar Garciaparra	4.00
12	Sammy Sosa	4.00
13	Roger Clemens	3.50
14	Ivan Rodriguez	1.50
15	Tony Gwynn	3.00

Opening Day 2K

As part of a multi-manufacturer promotion, Fleer issued eight cards of an "Opening Day 2K" set. Packages containing some of the 32 cards in the issue were distributed by MLB teams early in the season. The cards were also available exclusively as inserts in packs sold at KMart stores early in the season. The Fleer Tradition OD2K cards have gold-foil graphic highlights on front. Backs are in the basic format of the rest of the Tradition issue, and are numbered "XX of 32/OD."

		NM/M
Complete Set (8):		6.00
Common Player:		.50
1	Cal Ripken Jr.	2.00
2	Alex Rodriguez	2.00
3	Mike Piazza	1.00
4	Jeff Bagwell	.75
5	Randy Johnson	.75
6	Jason Kendall	.50
7	Magglio Ordonez	.50
8	Carlos Delgado	.50

Ripken Collection

This 10-card set is devoted to Cal Ripken Jr. and features 10 different Fleer retro designs. These were seeded 1:30 packs.

	NM/M
Complete Set (10):	50.00
Common Card:	6.00
Inserted 1:30	

Ten-4

This 10-card insert set focuses on baseball's home run kings on a die-cut design enhanced with silver foil stamping. These were seeded 1:18 packs and are numbered on the card back with a "TF" suffix.

		NM/M
Complete Set (10):		20.00
Common Player:		2.00
Inserted 1:18		
1	Sammy Sosa	2.00
2	Nomar Garciaparra	2.00
3	Mike Piazza	2.00
4	Mark McGwire	3.00
5	Ken Griffey Jr.	2.00
6	Juan Gonzalez	1.00
7	Derek Jeter	4.00
8	Chipper Jones	1.50
9	Cal Ripken Jr.	4.00
10	Alex Rodriguez	3.00

Who To Watch

Top prospects for the 2000 season are highlighted in this 15-card set, including Rick Ankiel. They have a die-cut design with gold foil stamping. These were inserted 1:3 packs and numbered on the back with a "WW" suffix.

		NM/M
Complete Set (15):		5.00
Common Player:		.25
Inserted 1:3		
1	Rick Ankiel	.40
2	Matt Riley	.25
3	Wilton Veras	.25
4	Ben Petrick	.25
5	Chad Hermansen	.25
6	Peter Bergeron	.25
7	Mark Quinn	.25
8	Russell Branyan	.25
9	Alfonso Soriano	1.50
10	Randy Wolf	.50
11	Ben Davis	.25
12	Jeff DaVanon	.25
13	D'Angelo Jimenez	.25
14	Vernon Wells	1.00
15	Adam Kennedy	.40

Glossy Lumberjacks

	NM/M
Common Player:	8.00
One per factory set.	

Production Listed		
1	Edgardo Alfonzo/145	10.00
2	Roberto Alomar/627	10.00
3	Moises Alou/529	8.00
4	Carlos Beltran/489	8.00
7	Adrian Beltre/127	6.00
8	Barry Bonds/305	40.00
9	Pat Burrell/45	25.00
11	Sean Casey/50	15.00
12	Eric Chavez/259	10.00
13	Tony Clark/70	10.00
14	Carlos Delgado/70	20.00
16	J.D. Drew/135	10.00
17	Erubiel Durazo/70	10.00
18	Carlos Febles/120	10.00
19	Jason Giambi/220	15.00
20	Shawn Green/429	10.00
21	Vladimir Guerrero/809	15.00
22	Derek Jeter/180	50.00
23	Chipper Jones/725	25.00
24	Gabe Kapler/160	8.00
25	Paul Konerko/70	10.00
26	Mike Lieberthal/45	10.00
28	Edgar Martinez/211	10.00
29	Raul Mondesi/458	8.00
30	Warren Morris/35	10.00
31	Magglio Ordonez/190	10.00
32	Rafael Palmeiro/49	15.00
33	Pokey Reese/110	8.00
34	Cal Ripken/235	50.00
35	Alex Rodriguez/292	25.00
36	Ivan Rodriguez/602	10.00
37	Scott Rolen/502	10.00
38	Chris Singleton/68	8.00
39	Alfonso Soriano/285	15.00
40	Frank Thomas/489	10.00
41	Jim Thome/479	10.00
42	Robin Ventura/114	10.00
43	Jose Vidro/60	10.00
44	Bernie Williams/215	10.00
45	Matt Williams/152	8.00

2000 Fleer Tradition Update

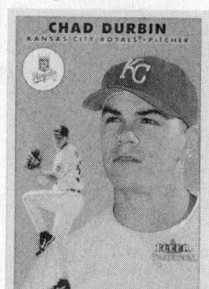

Card #50 was supposed to be Indians prospect C.C. Sabathia but it was never issued because he was not called up during the 2000 season.

		NM/M
Complete Set (150):		20.00
Common Player:		.15
1	Ken Griffey Jr. (Season Highlights)	.50
2	Cal Ripken Jr. (Season Highlights)	1.00
3	Randy Velarde (Season Highlights)	.15
4	Fred McGriff (Season Highlights)	.15
5	Derek Jeter (Season Highlights)	1.00
6	Tom Glavine (Season Highlights)	.25
7	Brent Mayne (Season Highlights)	.15
8	Alex Ochoa (Season Highlights)	.15
9	Scott Sheldon (Season Highlights)	.15
10	Randy Johnson (Season Highlights)	.35
11	Daniel Garibay RC	.15
12	Brad Fullmer	.15
13	Kazuhiro Sasaki RC	.50
14	Andy Tracy	.15
15	Bret Boone	.15
16	Chad Durbin RC	.25
17	Mark Buehrle RC	1.50
18	Julio Zuleta RC	.15
19	Jeremy Giambi	.15
20	Gene Stechschulte RC	.15
21	Lou Pote, Bengie Molina	.15
22	Darrell Einertson	.15
23	Ken Griffey Jr.	.75
24	Jeff Sparks RC, Dan Wheeler	.25
25	Aaron Fultz RC	.15
26	Derek Bell	.15

27	Rob Bell, D.T. Cromer	.15
28	Rob Fick	.15
29	Darryl Kile	.15
30	Clayton Andrews, John Bate	.15
31	Dave Veres	.15
32	Hector Mercado RC	.15
33	Willie Morales	.15
34	Kelly Wunsch, Kip Wells	.15
35	Hideki Irabu	.15
36	Sean DePaula	.15
37	Dewayne Wise, Chris Woodward	.15
38	Curt Schilling	.25
39	Mark Johnson	.15
40	Mike Cameron	.15
41	Scott Sheldon, Tom Evans	.15
42	Brett Tomko	.15
43	Johan Santana RC	15.00
44	Andy Benes	.15
45	Matt LeCroy, Mark Redman	.15
46	Ryan Klesko	.15
47	Andy Ashby	.15
48	Octavio Dotel	.15
49	Eric Byrnes RC	1.00
51	Kenny Rogers	.15
52	Ben Weber	.15
53	Matt Blank, Scott Strickland	.15
54	Tom Goodwin	.15
55	Jim Edmonds	.15
56	Derrick Turnbow RC	.25
57	Mark Mulder	.15
58	Tarrik Brock, Ruben Quevedo	.15
59	Danny Young	.15
60	Fernando Vina	.15
61	Justin Brunette RC	.15
62	Jimmy Anderson	.15
63	Reggie Sanders	.15
64	Adam Kennedy	.15
65	Jesse Garcia, B.J. Ryan	.15
66	Al Martin	.15
67	Kevin Walker	.15
68	Brad Penny	.15
69	B.J. Surhoff	.15
70	Geoff Blum, Trace Coquillette	.15
71	Jose Jimenez	.15
72	Chuck Finley	.15
73	Valerio De Los Santos, Everett Stull	.15
74	Terry Adams	.15
75	Rafael Furcal	.15
76	Mike Darr, John Roskos	.15
77	Quilvio Veras	.15
78	Armando Almanza	.15
79	Greg Vaughn	.15
80	Keith McDonald RC	.15
81	Eric Cammack	.15
82	Horacio Estrada, Ray King	.15
83	Kory DeHaan	.15
84	Kevin Hodges	.15
85	Mike Lamb RC	.25
86	Shawn Green	.40
87	Dan Reichert, Jason Rakers	.15
88	Adam Piatt	.15
89	Mike Garcia	.15
90	Rodrigo Lopez RC	1.00
91	John Olerud	.15
92	Barry Zito, Terrence Long	1.00
93	Jimmy Rollins	.25
94	Denny Neagle	.15
95	Rickey Henderson	.50
96	Adam Eaton, Buddy Carlyle	.15
97	Brian O'Connor	.15
98	Andy Thompson	.15
99	Jason Boyd	.15
100	Carlos Guillen, Joel Piniero	.15
101	Raul Gonzalez	.15
102	Brandon Kolb RC	.25
103	Jason Maxwell, Mike Lincoln	.15
104	Luis Matos RC	.50
105	Morgan Burkhart RC	.25
106	Ismael Villegas, Steve Sisco	.15
107	David Justice	.15
108	Pablo Ozuna	.15
109	Jose Canseco	.40
110	Alex Cora, Shawn Gilbert	.15
111	Will Clark	.25
112	Keith Luuloa, Eric Weaver	.15
113	Bruce Chen	.15
114	Adam Hyzdu	.15
115	Yovanny Lara, Scott Forster	.15
116	Allen McDill, Jose Macias	.15
117	Kevin Nicholson	.15
118	Israel Alcantara, Tim Young	.15
119	Juan Alvarez	.15
120	Julio Lugo, Mitch Meluskey	.15
121	B.J. Waszgis	.15
122	Jeff D'Amico, Brett Laxton	.15
123	Ricky Ledee	.15
124	Mark DeRosa, Jason Marquis	.15
125	Alex Cabrera RC	.50
126	Gary Matthews, Augie Ojeda	.15
127	Richie Sexson	.15

128	Santiago Perez, Hector Ramirez	.15
129	Rondell White	.15
130	Craig House RC	.15
131	Kevin Beirne, Jon Garland	.15
132	Wayne Franklin	.15
133	Henry Rodriguez	.15
134	Jay Payton, Jim Mann	.15
135	Ron Gant	.15
136	Paxton Crawford RC, Sang-Hoon Lee	.25
137	Kent Bottenfield	.15
138	Rocky Biddle RC	.15
139	Travis Lee	.15
140	Ryan Vogelsong	.15
141	Jason Conti, Geraldo Guzman	.15
142	Tim Drew, Mark Watson	.15
143	John Parrish RC, Chris Richard	.15
144	Javier Cardona RC, Brandon Villafuetre	.15
145	Tike Redman RC, Steve Sparks	.15
146	Brian Schneider, Matt Skrmetta	.15
147	Pasqual Coco RC, Leo Estrella	.15
148	Lorenzo Barcelo RC, Joe Crede	.15
149	Jace Brewer RC	.25
150	Milton Bradley, Tomas de la Rosa	.15

Update Mantle Pieces

Inserted 1:80 Sets

		NM/M
1	Mickey Mantle	150.00

Diamond Skills Commemorative Sheet

Utilizing the same format and card reproductions as the souvenir sheet issued in conjunction with the season-opener Cubs-Mets series in Japan, Fleer issued this commemorative sheet for distribution to participants in the 2000 Diamond Skills competition. The 10" x 9" sheets depict star cards from Fleer's 2000 Tradition set.

	NM/M
Derek Jeter, Chipper Jones, Pedro Martinez, Mike Piazza, Cal Ripken Jr., Ivan Rodriguez, Sammy Sosa, Mo Vaughn	10.00

Japan Commemorative Sheet

To commemorate the opening of the 2000 Major League Baseball season with a Cubs-Mets series in Japan, Fleer created this commemorative sheet for distribution at the opening game on March 29 (20,000) and at the Xebio Sporting Goods stores and Pro Pacific Hobby stores in Japan (5,000 each). The 10" x 9" sheets depict on front cards from Fleer's 2000 Tradition set.

	NM/M
Ivan Rodriguez, Sammy Sosa, Mo Vaughn, Derek Jeter, Chipper Jones, Pedro Martinez, Mike Piazza, Cal Ripken Jr.	20.00

Oreo

In a nationwide promotional contest in which children stacked Oreo cookies at grocery stores, a pair of hot star cards were given away as consolation prizes. Each 2-1/2" x 3-1/2" card has blue borders with a color photo at center. Jeter's card shows him stacking cookies, while Junior's card (in his new Reds uniform) shows him

holding a bag of cookies. Backs have personal information, stats, an action photo and logos of MLB, Fleer and Oreo.

		NM/M
Complete Set (2):		6.00
(1)	Ken Griffey Jr.	3.00
(2)	Derek Jeter	3.00

SportsCards Greats of the Game

The first-ever fully-licensed baseball card set to be issued in the form of a magazine insert, this set comprises the game's top players in the design of Fleer's very popular Greats of the Game issue (which depicted only former stars). The cards were issued six per month in uncut sheet form (8-1/4" x 11-1/8") in SportsCards magazine issues dated February through July 2001. The cards were only inserted in newsstand and card-shop copies. Persons who subscribed to the magazine in a special offer received the complete set in unbound format. If cut from the sheet, individual cards measure the standard 2-1/2" x 3-1/2". On front are action photos on a white background with maroon borders. Backs have player identification, licensor logos and 2000 season stats.

		NM/M
Complete Set, Sheets (6):		35.00
Complete Set, Singles (36):		25.00
Common Player:		.50
	Sheet 1, February	6.00
1	Rick Ankiel	.75
2	Jeff Bagwell	1.00
3	Barry Bonds	3.00
4	Pat Burrell	.65
5	Roger Clemens	1.50
6	Carlos Delgado	.65
	Sheet 2, March	4.00
7	J.D. Drew	.65
8	Jim Edmonds	.50
9	Darin Erstad	.65
10	Andres Galarraga	.50
11	Nomar Garciaparra	2.00
12	Jason Giambi	.75
	Sheet 3, April	6.00
13	Troy Glaus	1.00
14	Roberto Alomar	.50
15	Ken Griffey Jr.	2.00
16	Vladimir Guerrero	1.00
17	Tony Gwynn	1.25
18	Todd Helton	1.00
	Sheet 4, May	7.50
19	Derek Jeter	3.00
20	Randy Johnson	1.00
21	Chipper Jones	1.25
22	Andruw Jones	1.00
23	Greg Maddux	1.25
24	Pedro Martinez	1.00
	Sheet 5, June	10.00
25	Mark McGwire	2.50
26	Magglio Ordonez	.50
27	Mike Piazza	2.00
28	Manny Ramirez	1.00
29	Cal Ripken Jr.	2.50
30	Alex Rodriguez	2.50
	Sheet 6, July	4.00
31	Ivan Rodriguez	.65

32	Jeff Kent	.50
33	Gary Sheffield	.50
34	Sammy Sosa	2.00
35	Frank Thomas	1.00
36	Bernie Williams	.50

2000 Fleer/Twizzlers

A dozen of baseball's biggest stars were reproduced in a format only slightly different from 2000 Fleer Tradition for inclusion in packages of Twizzlers candy. The candy version features UV coating on both front and back, has a small Twizzlers logo at lower-right on back and is numbered "X of 12." Cards were included in large (26.5 oz.) packages of candy or a complete set could be obtained for $1.50 and 15 proofs of purchase from smaller packages.

		NM/M
Complete Set (12):		7.50
Common Player:		.25
1	Mark McGwire	1.50
2	Cal Ripken Jr.	2.00
3	Chipper Jones	.75
4	Bernie Williams	.35
5	Alex Rodriguez	1.50
6	Curt Schilling	.35
7	Ken Griffey Jr.	1.00
8	Sammy Sosa	1.00
9	Mike Piazza	1.00
10	Pedro Martinez	.50
11	Kenny Lofton	.25
12	Larry Walker	.25

2001 Fleer Authority

		NM/M
Complete Set (150):		265.00
Common Player:		.25
Common (101-150):		3.00
Production 2,001		
	Pack (5):	6.00
	Box (22 + 2 Graded Packs):	120.00
1	Mark Grace	.40
2	Paul Konerko	.40
3	Sean Casey	.25
4	Jim Thome	.40
5	Todd Helton	.75
6	Tony Clark	.25
7	Jeff Bagwell	.50
8	Mike Sweeney	.25
9	Eric Karros	.25
10	Richie Sexson	.25
11	Doug Mientkiewicz	.25
12	Ryan Klesko	.25
13	John Olerud	.25
14	Mark McGwire	2.00
15	Fred McGriff	.25
16	Rafael Palmeiro	.50
17	Carlos Delgado	.50
18	Roberto Alomar	.40
19	Craig Biggio	.25
20	Jose Vidro	.25
21	Edgardo Alfonzo	.25
22	Jeff Kent	.25
23	Bret Boone	.25
24	Rafael Furcal	.40
25	Nomar Garciaparra	.50
26	Barry Larkin	.40
27	Cristian Guzman	.25
28	Derek Jeter	2.50
29	Miguel Tejada	.40
30	Jimmy Rollins	.75

31	Rich Aurilia	.25
32	Alex Rodriguez	2.00
33	Cal Ripken Jr.	2.50
34	Troy Glaus	.50
35	Matt Williams	.25
36	Chipper Jones	1.00
37	Jeff Cirillo	.25
38	Robin Ventura	.25
39	Eric Chavez	.25
40	Scott Rolen	.50
41	Phil Nevin	.25
42	Mike Piazza	1.00
43	Jorge Posada	.40
44	Jason Kendall	.25
45	Ivan Rodriguez	.50
46	Frank Thomas	.75
47	Edgar Martinez	.25
48	Darin Erstad	.25
49	Tim Salmon	.25
50	Luis Gonzalez	.25
51	Andruw Jones	.50
52	Carl Everett	.25
53	Manny Ramirez	.75
54	Sammy Sosa	.75
55	Rondell White	.25
56	Magglio Ordonez	.40
57	Ken Griffey Jr.	1.50
58	Juan Gonzalez	.50
59	Larry Walker	.25
60	Bobby Higginson	.25
61	Cliff Floyd	.25
62	Preston Wilson	.25
63	Moises Alou	.40
64	Lance Berkman	.50
65	Richard Hidalgo	.25
66	Jermaine Dye	.25
67	Mark Quinn	.25
68	Shawn Green	.50
69	Gary Sheffield	.40
70	Jeromy Burnitz	.25
71	Geoff Jenkins	.25
72	Vladimir Guerrero	.75
73	Bernie Williams	.40
74	Johnny Damon	.50
75	Jason Giambi	.50
76	Bobby Abreu	.40
77	Pat Burrell	.50
78	Brian Giles	.25
79	Tony Gwynn	1.00
80	Barry Bonds	2.50
81	J.D. Drew	.40
82	Jim Edmonds	.25
83	Greg Vaughn	.25
84	Raul Mondesi	.25
85	Shannon Stewart	.25
86	Randy Johnson	.75
87	Curt Schilling	.50
88	Tom Glavine	.50
89	Greg Maddux	1.50
90	Pedro Martinez	.75
91	Kerry Wood	.50
92	David Wells	.25
93	Bartolo Colon	.25
94	Mike Hampton	.25
95	Kevin Brown	.25
96	Al Leiter	.25
97	Roger Clemens	2.00
98	Mike Mussina	.50
99	Tim Hudson	.40
100	Kazuhiro Sasaki	.25
101	Ichiro Suzuki RC	35.00
102	Albert Pujols RC	75.00
103	Drew Henson RC	5.00
104	Adam Pettyjohn	3.00
105	Adrian Hernandez RC	3.00
106	Andy Morales	3.00
107	Tsuyoshi Shinjo RC	4.00
108	Juan Uribe	3.00
109	Jack Wilson RC	5.00
110	Jason Smith RC	3.00
111	Junior Spivey RC	4.00
112	Wilson Betemit RC	4.00
113	Elpidio Guzman RC	3.00
114	Esix Snead RC	3.00
115	Winston Abreu RC	3.00
116	Jeremy Owens RC	3.00
117	Jay Gibbons RC	5.00
118	Luis Lopez	3.00
119	Ryan Freel RC	4.00
120	Rafael Soriano RC	4.00
121	Johnny Estrada RC	5.00
122	Bud Smith RC	3.00
123	Jackson Melian RC	3.00
124	Matt White RC	3.00
125	Travis Hafner RC	10.00
126	Morgan Ensberg RC	5.00
127	Endy Chavez RC	3.00
128	Bret Prinz RC	3.00
129	Juan Diaz RC	3.00
130	Erick Almonte RC	4.00
131	Rob Mackowiak RC	3.00
132	Carlos Valderrama RC	3.00
133	Wilkin Ruan RC	3.00
134	Angel Berroa RC	5.00
135	Henry Mateo RC	3.00
136	Bill Ortega	3.00
137	Billy Sylvester RC	3.00
138	Andres Torres RC	3.00
139	Nate Frese	3.00
140	Casey Fossum RC	4.00
141	Ricardo Rodriguez RC	3.00
142	Brian Roberts RC	8.00
143	Carlos Garcia RC	3.00
144	Brian Lawrence RC	4.00
145	Cory Aldridge RC	3.00
146	Mark Teixeira RC	25.00
147	Juan Cruz RC	3.00
148	Brandon Duckworth RC	3.00
149	Dewon Brazelton RC	3.00
150	Mark Prior RC	8.00

Graded

Mint:	1-1.5X
NrMt+:	.8-1X
NrMt:	.4-.6X
No Multipliers for Gem Mint.	

Prominence

Stars (1-100):	5-10X
Production 125	
SP's (101-150):	3-5X
Production 75	

Authority Figures

		NM/M
Complete Set (20):		75.00
Common Card:		2.00
1AF	Mark McGwire, Albert Pujols	8.00
2AF	Kazuhiro Sasaki, Ichiro Suzuki	8.00
3AF	Derek Jeter, Drew Henson	10.00
4AF	Ken Griffey Jr., Jackson Melian	6.00
5AF	Wilson Betemit, Chipper Jones	4.50
6AF	Jeff Bagwell, Morgan Ensberg	4.00
7AF	Cal Ripken Jr., Jay Gibbons	10.00
8AF	Mike Piazza, Tsuyoshi Shinjo	6.00
9AF	Luis Gonzalez, Junior Spivey	2.00
10AF	Barry Bonds, Carlos Valderrama	10.00
11AF	Todd Helton, Juan Uribe	4.00
12AF	Roger Clemens, Adrian Hernandez	5.00
13AF	Alex Rodriguez, Travis Hafner	8.00
14AF	Scott Rolen, Johnny Estrada	3.00
15AF	Brian Giles, Rob Mackowiak	2.00
16AF	Randy Johnson, Bret Prinz	8.00
17AF	Carlos Delgado, Luis Lopez	3.00
18AF	Manny Ramirez, Juan Diaz	3.00
19AF	Mike Sweeney, Endy Chavez	3.00
20AF	Sammy Sosa, Jaisen Randolph	6.00

Diamond Cuts

	NM/M
Common Player:	4.00
Inserted 1:10	
Rick Ankiel/Shoe	4.00
Jeff Bagwell/Jsy	8.00
Adrian Beltre/Hat	4.00
Craig Biggio/Bat	4.00
Barry Bonds/Hat	35.00
Barry Bonds/Jsy	20.00
Barry Bonds/Pants	20.00
Barry Bonds/Shoe	30.00
Barry Bonds/Wristband/100	50.00
Kevin Brown/Hat	6.00
Kevin Brown/Pants	4.00
Eric Byrnes/Bat	4.00
Sean Casey/Jsy	4.00
Eric Chavez/Hat	6.00
Chipper Jones/Jersey	10.00
Chipper Jones/Bat	10.00
Bartolo Colon/Bat	6.00
Erubiel Durazo/Bat	4.00
Ray Durham/Bat	4.00
Jim Edmonds/Hat	6.00
Jim Edmonds/Shoe	10.00
Darin Erstad/Hat	6.00
Carlos Febles/Bat	4.00
Carlos Febles/Shoe	4.00
Rafael Furcal/Hat	6.00
Juan Gonzalez/Bat Glove	10.00
Juan Gonzalez/Hat	8.00
Luis Gonzalez	8.00
Shawn Green/Bat Glv	10.00
Shawn Green/Bat	8.00
Vladimir Guerrero/Bat	8.00
Tony Gwynn/Bat	8.00
Mike Hampton/Hat	5.00
Mike Hampton/Shoe	5.00
Jerry Hairston Jr./Hat	4.00
Jason Hart/Bat	4.00
Todd Helton/Jsy	8.00
Todd Helton/Pants	8.00
Orlando Hernandez/Bat	4.00
Richard Hidalgo/Bat	4.00
Richard Hidalgo/Bat Glove	15.00
Derek Jeter/Bat	30.00
Derek Jeter/Bat Glv	60.00
Derek Jeter/Jsy	30.00
Derek Jeter/Pants	30.00
Derek Jeter/Shoe	40.00
Randy Johnson/Hat	10.00
Andruw Jones/Bat	6.00
Andruw Jones/Hat	6.00
Jason Kendall/Hat	6.00
Barry Larkin/Jersey	5.00
Matt Lawton/Hat	4.00
Mike Lieberthal/Bat Glv	6.00
Kenny Lofton/Bat	4.00
Edgar Martinez/Bat Glv	8.00
Pedro Martinez/Shoe	10.00
Raul Mondesi/Bat	4.00
Raul Mondesi/Bat Glv	6.00
Hideo Nomo/Bat	15.00
Hideo Nomo/Hat	40.00
Magglio Ordonez/Bat Glv	8.00
Magglio Ordonez/Hat	6.00
David Ortiz/Bat	4.00
Rafael Palmeiro/Bat	8.00
Rafael Palmeiro/Hat	10.00
Chan Ho Park/Hat	5.00
Mike Piazza/Bat	15.00
Mike Piazza/Jsy	15.00
Mike Piazza/Shoe	25.00
Albert Pujols/Pants	30.00
Manny Ramirez/Bat	8.00
Manny Ramirez/Bat Glv	15.00
Manny Ramirez/Hat	15.00
Cal Ripken Jr./Bat Glv	65.00
Cal Ripken Jr./Pants	25.00
Ivan Rodriguez/Bat Glv	10.00
Ivan Rodriguez/Hat	10.00
Ivan Rodriguez/Pants	8.00
Ivan Rodriguez/Shoe	10.00
Scott Rolen/Hat	4.00
Jared Sandberg/Bat	4.00
Deion Sanders/Bat	4.00
Tsuyoshi Shinjo/Wristband	10.00
Tsuyoshi Shinjo/Bat	6.00
J.T. Snow	4.00
Alfonso Soriano/Hat	20.00
Ichiro Suzuki/Bat	50.00
Ichiro Suzuki/Hat	65.00
Mike Sweeney/Hat	6.00
Miguel Tejada/Hat	6.00
Frank Thomas/Bat	8.00
Frank Thomas/Hat	10.00
Jim Thome/Bat	8.00
Larry Walker/Bat	4.00
Larry Walker/Jsy	4.00
Bernie Williams/Bat	6.00
Brian Giles/Pants	5.00

Derek Jeter Monumental Moments

			NM/M
MM4	Derek Jeter/2000		5.00
MM4AU	Derek Jeter/Auto./100		100.00

Derek Jeter Reprint Autographs

		NM/M
Production 500		
1DJRA	Derek Jeter/500	80.00

Seal of Approval

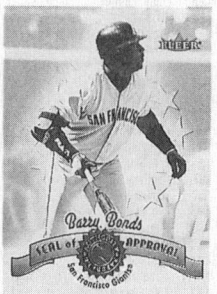

		NM/M
Complete Set (15):		45.00
Common Player:		1.50
1SA	Derek Jeter	6.00
2SA	Alex Rodriguez	5.00
3SA	Nomar Garciaparra	4.00
4SA	Cal Ripken Jr.	6.00
5SA	Mike Piazza	4.00
6SA	Mark McGwire	5.00
7SA	Tony Gwynn	3.00
8SA	Barry Bonds	6.00
9SA	Greg Maddux	3.00
10SA	Chipper Jones	3.00
11SA	Roger Clemens	3.50
12SA	Ken Griffey Jr.	4.00
13SA	Vladimir Guerrero	2.00
14SA	Sammy Sosa	4.00
15SA	Todd Helton	1.50

2001 Fleer Boston Red Sox 100th Anniversary

		NM/M
Complete Set (100):		40.00
Common Player:		.25
Pack (5):		4.00
Box (24):		125.00
1	Carl Yastrzemski	2.50
2	Mel Parnell	.25
3	Birdie Tebbetts	.25
4	Tex Hughson	.25
5	Nomar Garciaparra	4.00
6	Fred Lynn	.50
7	John Valentin	.25
8	Rico Petrocelli	.25
9	Ted Williams	3.00
10	Roger Clemens	3.00
11	Luis Aparicio	.40
12	Cy Young	1.50
13	Carlton Fisk	1.00
14	Pedro Martinez	.25
15	Joe Dobson	.25
16	Babe Ruth	5.00
17	Doc Cramer	.25
18	Pete Runnels	.25
19	Tony Conigliaro	.25
20	Bill Monbouquette	.25
21	Boo Ferriss	.25
22	Harry Hooper	.25
23	Tony Armas	.25
24	Joe Cronin	1.00
25	Rick Ferrell	.25
26	Wade Boggs	2.25
27	Don Baylor	.25
28	Jeff Reardon	.25
29	Smokey Joe Wood	.25
30	Mo Vaughn	.40
31	Walt Dropo	.25
32	Vern Stephens	.25
33	Bernie Carbo	.25
34	George Scott	.25
35	Lefty Grove	1.00
36	Dom DiMaggio	1.00
37	Dennis Eckersley	.75
38	Johnny Pesky	.25
39	Jim Lonborg	.25
40	Jimmy Piersall	.25
41	Tris Speaker	1.50
42	Frank Malzone	.25
43	Bobby Doerr	.75
44	Jimmie Foxx	2.00
45	Tony Pena	.25
46	Billy Goodman	.25
47	Jim Rice	.25
48	Reggie Smith	.25
49	Bill Buckner	.25
50	Earl Wilson	.25
51	Rick Burleson	.25
52	George Kell	.25
53	Dick Radatz	.25
54	Dwight Evans	.25
55	Luis Tiant	.25
56	Elijah "Pumpsie" Green	.25
57	Gene Conley	.25
58	Jackie Jensen	.25
59	Mike Fornieles	.25
60	Dutch Leonard	.25
61	Jake Stahl	.25
62	Don Schwall	.25
63	Jimmy Collins	.25
64	Herb Pennock	.25
65	Red Ruffing	.50
66	Carney Lansford	.25
67	Dick Stuart	.25
68	Dave Morehead	.25
69	Harry Agganis	.25
70	Lou Boudreau	.25
71	Joe Morgan	.75
72	Don Zimmer	.75
73	Tom Yawkey	.25
74	Jean Yawkey	.25
75	Origin of the Red Sox	.25
76	First Season	.25
77	World Series History	.25
78	Carl Yastrzemski (Beantown's Best)	1.00
79	Carlton Fisk (Beantown's Best)	.50
80	Dom DiMaggio (Beantown's Best)	.50
81	Wade Boggs (Beantown's Best)	.75
82	Nomar Garciaparra (Beantown's Best)	2.00
83	Pedro Martinez (Beantown's Best)	1.00
84	Ted Williams (Beantown's Best)	2.50
85	Jim Rice (Beantown's Best)	.25
86	Fred Lynn (Beantown's Best)	.25
87	Mo Vaughn (Beantown's Best)	.25
88	Bobby Doerr (Beantown's Best)	.40
89	Bernie Carbo (Beantown's Best)	.25
90	Dennis Eckersley (Beantown's Best)	.35
91	Jimmy Piersall (Beantown's Best)	.25
92	Luis Tiant (Beantown's Best)	.25
93	Jimmy Fund signage (Fenway Through the Years)	.25
94	Green Monster w/Ads (Fenway Through the Years)	.25
95	Green Monster w/All-Star logo (Fenway Through the Years)	.25
96	Ladder shot on Green Monster (Fenway Through the Years)	.25
97	Manual Scoreboard (Fenway Through the Years)	.25
98	Panoramic of Fenway (Fenway Through the Years)	.25
99	Lansdowne St. (Fenway Through the Years)	.25
100	1999 All-Star Game (Fenway Through the Years)	.25

Auto. Caps

Each box of Red Sox 100th Anniversary product includes one fitted, authentically autographed genuine MLB Red Sox cap. A certificate of authentication was included with each cap and each had a Fleer hologram attached.

	NM/M
One cap per deluxe box.	
(1) Wade Boggs	75.00
(2) Bill Buckner	30.00
(3) Bernie Carbo	30.00
(4) Roger Clemens	150.00
(6) Bobby Doerr	40.00
(7) Dennis Eckersley	50.00
(8) Dwight Evans	40.00
(10) Nomar Garciaparra	80.00
(11) Jim Lonborg	30.00
(12) Johnny Pesky	40.00
(13) Rico Petrocelli	40.00
(14) Jimmy Piersall	30.00
(15) Jim Rice	40.00
(16) Luis Tiant	40.00

BoSox Sigs

	NM/M
Common Autograph:	15.00
Inserted 1:96	
Wade Boggs	80.00
Bill Buckner	30.00
Bernie Carbo	20.00
Roger Clemens/100	200.00
Dom DiMaggio	75.00
Bobby Doerr	40.00
Dwight Evans	50.00
Carlton Fisk	80.00
Nomar Garciaparra	70.00
Jim Lonborg	20.00
Fred Lynn	40.00
Rico Petrocelli	25.00
Jim Rice	40.00
Luis Tiant	30.00
Carl Yastrzemski/200	180.00

Field the Game

A total of 7,150 exchange cards for Field the Game memorabilia cards was inserted randomly in packs. Collectors exchanging the cards received one of four types of card.

		NM/M
Complete Set (4):		75.00
(1)	Piece of Green Monster outfield wall	20.00
(2)	Piece of base from 100th anniver. game	20.00
(3)	Piece of baseball from 100th anniv. game	20.00
(4)	anniv. game	20.00

Splendid Splinters

		NM/M
Complete Set (15):		20.00
Common Player:		1.00
Inserted 1:10		
SS1	Babe Ruth	6.00
SS2	Dom DiMaggio	1.50
SS3	Carlton Fisk	2.00
SS4	Carl Yastrzemski	3.00
SS5	Nomar Garciaparra	5.00
SS6	Wade Boggs	2.50
SS7	Ted Williams	5.00
SS8	Jim Rice	1.00
SS9	Mo Vaughn	1.00
SS10	Tris Speaker	2.00
SS11	Dwight Evans	1.00
SS12	Jimmie Foxx	2.50
SS13	Bobby Doerr	1.50
SS14	Fred Lynn	1.00
SS15	Johnny Pesky	1.00

Splendid Splinters Game Bat

	NM/M
Common Player:	15.00
Inserted 1:96	
Babe Ruth/SP/100	400.00
Carl Yastrzemski	75.00
Nomar Garciaparra	30.00
Wade Boggs	25.00
Ted Williams/SP/100	200.00
Jim Rice	15.00
Dwight Evans	15.00
Jimmie Foxx/SP/100	200.00

Threads

	NM/M
Common Player:	15.00
Inserted 1:96	
Wade Boggs	25.00
Roger Clemens	50.00
Dwight Evans	15.00
Carlton Fisk/100	40.00
Pedro Martinez/100	40.00
Jim Rice	20.00
Ted Williams/100	180.00
Carl Yastrzemski	50.00
Don Zimmer	15.00

Yawkey's Heroes

		NM/M
Complete Set (20):		15.00
Common Player:		.50
Inserted 1:4		
1YH	Bobby Doerr	.75
2YH	Dom DiMaggio	1.00
3YH	Jim Rice	.50
4YH	Wade Boggs	1.50
5YH	Carlton Fisk	1.00
6YH	Nomar Garciaparra	3.00
7YH	Dennis Eckersley	1.00
8YH	Carl Yastrzemski	2.00
9YH	Ted Williams	4.00
10YH	Tony Conigliaro	.75
11YH	Tony Armas	.50
12YH	Joe Cronin	.50
13YH	Mo Vaughn	.50
14YH	Johnny Pesky	.50
15YH	Jim Lonborg	.50
16YH	Luis Tiant	.50
17YH	Tony Pena	.50
18YH	Dwight Evans	.50
19YH	Fred Lynn	.75
20YH	Jimmy Piersall	.50

2001 Fleer Cal Ripken Jr. Commemoratives

The two "commemorative cards" were produced for sale on a television home shopping program. One card is a reprint of Ripken's 1982 Fleer rookie card, with the addition of a Ripken logo at lower-right. The other is a specially designed and authentically autographed card, horizontal in format, with a game photo of Ripken at right, thre signature at left and the special logo. On back is a statement of authenticity from Fleer, along with a ghost-image portrait photo.

	NM/M
Cal Ripken Jr. (1982 Reprint)	10.00
Cal Ripken Jr. (Autograph card.)	125.00

2001 E-X

		NM/M
Complete Set (130):		100.00
Common Player:		.25
Common SP (101-130):		4.00
Production Listed		
Pack (5):		4.00
Box (24):		80.00
1	Jason Kendall	.25
2	Derek Jeter	3.00
3	Greg Vaughn	.25
4	Eric Chavez	.40
5	Nomar Garciaparra	1.00
6	Roberto Alomar	.50
7	Barry Larkin	.40
8	Matt Lawton	.25
9	Larry Walker	.25
10	Chipper Jones	1.50
11	Scott Rolen	.75
12	Carlos Lee	.40
13	Adrian Beltre	.40
14	Ben Grieve	.25
15	Mike Sweeney	.25
16	John Olerud	.25
17	Gabe Kapler	.25
18	Brian Giles	.25
19	Luis Gonzalez	.40
20	Sammy Sosa	1.00
21	Roger Clemens	1.50
22	Vladimir Guerrero	1.00
23	Ken Griffey Jr.	2.00
24	Mark McGwire	2.50
25	Orlando Hernandez	.25
26	Shannon Stewart	.25
27	Fred McGriff	.25
28	Lance Berkman	.50
29	Carlos Delgado	.75
30	Mike Piazza	2.00
31	Juan Encarnacion	.25
32	David Justice	.25
33	Greg Maddux	1.50
34	Frank Thomas	1.00
35	Jason Giambi	.75
36	Ruben Mateo	.25
37	Todd Helton	1.00
38	Jim Edmonds	.25
39	Steve Finley	.25
40	Tom Glavine	.40
41	Mo Vaughn	.25
42	Phil Nevin	.25
43	Richie Sexson	.25
44	Craig Biggio	.25
45	Kerry Wood	.50
46	Pat Burrell	.60
47	Edgar Martinez	.25
48	Jim Thome	.40
49	Jeff Bagwell	1.00
50	Bernie Williams	.45
51	Andruw Jones	.50
52	Gary Sheffield	.50
53	Johnny Damon	.50
54	Rondell White	.25
55	J.D. Drew	.50
56	Tony Batista	.25
57	Paul Konerko	.25
58	Rafael Palmeiro	.75
59	Cal Ripken Jr.	3.00
60	Darin Erstad	.50
61	Ivan Rodriguez	.75
62	Barry Bonds	3.00
63	Edgardo Alfonzo	.25
64	Ellis Burks	.25
65	Mike Lieberthal	.25
66	Robin Ventura	.25
67	Richard Hidalgo	.25
68	Magglio Ordonez	.25
69	Kazuhiro Sasaki	.25
70	Miguel Tejada	.50
71	David Wells	.25
72	Troy Glaus	.50
73	Jose Vidro	.25
74	Shawn Green	.50
75	Barry Zito	.25
76	Jermaine Dye	.25

77	Geoff Jenkins	.25
78	Jeff Kent	.25
79	Al Leiter	.25
80	Deivi Cruz	.25
81	Eric Karros	.25
82	Albert Belle	.25
83	Pedro Martinez	1.00
84	Raul Mondesi	.25
85	Preston Wilson	.25
86	Rafael Furcal	.40
87	Rick Ankiel	.50
88	Randy Johnson	1.00
89	Kevin Brown	.25
90	Sean Casey	.35
91	Mike Mussina	.25
92	Alex Rodriguez	2.50
93	Andres Galarraga	.25
94	Juan Gonzalez	.50
95	Manny Ramirez	1.00
96	Mark Grace	.35
97	Carl Everett	.25
98	Tony Gwynn	1.50
99	Mike Hampton	.25
100	Ken Caminiti	.25
101	Jason Hart/1749	4.00
102	Corey Patterson/1199	5.00
103	Timo Perez/1999	4.00
104	Marcus Giles/1999	4.00
105	Ichiro Suzuki/1999 RC	50.00
106	Aubrey Huff/1499	8.00
107	Joe Crede/1999	5.00
108	Larry Barnes/1999	4.00
109	Esix Snead/1499 RC	4.00
110	Kenny Kelly/2249	4.00
111	Justin Miller/2249	4.00
112	Jack Cust/1999	4.00
113	Xavier Nady/999	4.00
114	Eric Munson/1499	4.00
115	Elpidio Guzman/1749 RC	4.00
116	Juan Pierre/2189	4.00
117	Winston Abreu/1749 RC	4.00
118	Keith Ginter/1999	4.00
119	Jace Brewer/2699	4.00
120	Paxton Crawford/2249	4.00
121	Jason Tyner/2249	4.00
122	Tike Redman/1999	4.00
123	John Riedling/2499	4.00
124	Jose Ortiz/1499	4.00
125	Oswaldo Mairena/2499	4.00
126	Eric Byrnes/2249	6.00
127	Brian Cole/999	4.00
128	Adam Piatt/2249	4.00
129	Nate Rolison/2499	4.00
130	Keith McDonald/2249	4.00

Base Inks

Random Inserts
Derek Jeter AU/500 ... 100.00

Behind the Numbers

NM/M
Common Player: ... 5.00
Inserted 1:33

1BN	Johnny Bench	10.00
2BN	Wade Boggs	15.00
3BN	George Brett	20.00
4BN	Lou Brock	5.00
5BN	Rollie Fingers	5.00
6BN	Carlton Fisk	5.00
7BN	Reggie Jackson	10.00
8BN	Al Kaline	10.00
9BN	Willie McCovey	5.00
10BN	Paul Molitor	10.00
11BN	Eddie Murray	10.00
12BN	Jim Palmer	5.00
13BN	Ozzie Smith	15.00
14BN	Nolan Ryan	30.00
15BN	Mike Schmidt	20.00
16BN	Tom Seaver	10.00
17BN	Dave Winfield	5.00
18BN	Ted Williams	75.00
19BN	Robin Yount	10.00
20BN	Brady Anderson	5.00
21BN	Rick Ankiel	5.00
22BN	Albert Belle	5.00
23BN	Adrian Beltre	7.50
24BN	Barry Bonds	30.00
25BN	Eric Chavez	5.00
26BN	J.D. Drew	6.00
27BN	Darin Erstad	5.00
28BN	Troy Glaus	6.00
29BN	Mark Grace	5.00
30BN	Ben Grieve	5.00
31BN	Tony Gwynn	15.00
32BN	Todd Helton	10.00

34BN	Derek Jeter	30.00
35BN	Jeff Kent	5.00
36BN	Jason Kendall	5.00
37BN	Greg Maddux	15.00
38BN	John Olerud	5.00
39BN	Cal Ripken Jr.	30.00
40BN	Chipper Jones	15.00
41BN	John Smoltz	5.00
42BN	Frank Thomas	10.00
43BN	Robin Ventura	5.00
44BN	Bernie Williams	6.00

Behind the Numbers Autograph

NM/M
Quantity produced listed

2BN	Wade Boggs/26	75.00
4BN	Lou Brock/20	50.00
5BN	Rollie Fingers/34	40.00
6BN	Carlton Fisk/27	40.00
7BN	Reggie Jackson/44	80.00
10BN	Willie McCovey/44	60.00
12BN	Eddie Murray/33	75.00
13BN	Jim Palmer/22	50.00
15BN	Nolan Ryan/34	250.00
16BN	Mike Schmidt/20	200.00
17BN	Tom Seaver/41	60.00
18BN	Dave Winfield/31	60.00
20BN	Robin Yount/19	150.00
22BN	Rick Ankiel/66	40.00
23BN	Albert Belle/88	20.00
24BN	Adrian Beltre/29	25.00
25BN	Barry Bonds/25	250.00
28BN	Darin Erstad/47	40.00
29BN	Troy Glaus/25	50.00
30BN	Mark Grace/17	50.00
32BN	Tony Gwynn/19	150.00
33BN	Todd Helton/17	75.00
35BN	Jeff Kent/21	50.00
36BN	Jason Kendall/18	40.00
37BN	Greg Maddux/31	250.00
41BN	John Smoltz/29	40.00
42BN	Frank Thomas/35	75.00
44BN	Bernie Williams/51	75.00

Derek Jeter Monumental Moments

NM/M
2DJMM Derek Jeter
(Edition of 1,996.) ... 5.00
2DJMM Derek Jeter (Autographed edition of 96.) ... 80.00

Essential Credentials

NM/M
Stars (1-100): ... 3-6X
Production 299
Common (101-130): ... 10.00
Minor Stars (101-130): ... 15.00
Production 29

E-Xtra Innings

NM/M
Complete Set (10): ... 30.00
Common Player: ... 2.00
Inserted 1:20 R
1XI Mark McGwire ... 5.00

2XI	Sammy Sosa	4.00
3XI	Chipper Jones	3.00
4XI	Mike Piazza	4.00
5XI	Cal Ripken Jr.	6.00
6XI	Ken Griffey Jr.	4.00
7XI	Alex Rodriguez	5.00
8XI	Vladimir Guerrero	2.00
9XI	Nomar Garciaparra	4.00
10XI	Derek Jeter	6.00

Prospects Autograph

NM/M
Common Autograph: ... 5.00
Prod. #'s Listed

101	Jason Hart/250	5.00
102	Corey Patterson/800	10.00
103	Timoniel Perez/1000	5.00
104	Marcus Giles/500	5.00
106	Aubrey Huff/500	10.00
107	Joe Crede/500	10.00
108	Larry Barnes/500	5.00
109	Esix Snead/500	5.00
110	Kenny Kelly/250	5.00
111	Justin Miller/250	5.00
112	Jack Cust/1000	10.00
113	Xavier Nady/1000	10.00
114	Eric Munson/1500	5.00
115	Elpidio Guzman/250	5.00
116	Juan Pierre/810	5.00
117	Winston Abreu/250	5.00
118	Keith Ginter/500	5.00
119	Jace Brewer/300	5.00
120	Paxton Crawford/250	5.00
121	Jason Tyner/250	5.00
122	Tike Redman/250	5.00
123	John Riedling/500	5.00
124	Jose Ortiz/500	5.00
125	Oswaldo Mairena/500	5.00
126	Eric Byrnes/250	10.00
127	Brian Cole/2000	5.00
128	Adam Piatt/250	5.00
129	Nate Rolison/500	5.00
130	Keith McDonald/250	5.00

Wall of Fame

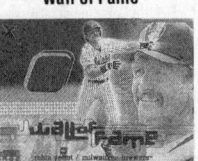

NM/M
Common Player: ... 4.00
Inserted 1:24

1WF	Robin Yount	8.00
2WF	Paul Molitor	8.00
3WF	Geoff Jenkins	4.00
4WF	Mark McGwire	15.00
5WF	Sammy Sosa	12.00
6WF	Greg Maddux	10.00
7WF	Mike Piazza	12.00
8WF	Cal Ripken Jr.	20.00
9WF	Todd Helton	8.00
10WF	Ken Griffey Jr.	12.00
11WF	Alex Rodriguez	15.00
12WF	Vladimir Guerrero	8.00
13WF	Jeff Bagwell	8.00
14WF	Ivan Rodriguez	6.00
15WF	Juan Gonzalez	8.00
16WF	Barry Bonds	20.00
17WF	Derek Jeter	20.00
18WF	Chipper Jones	10.00
19WF	Frank Thomas	8.00
20WF	Tony Gwynn	12.00
21WF	Nomar Garciaparra	12.00
22WF	Manny Ramirez	8.00
23WF	Andruw Jones	8.00
24WF	Scott Rolen	6.00
25WF	Jason Kendall	4.00
26WF	Roger Clemens	15.00
27WF	Troy Glaus	6.00
28WF	Pedro Martinez	8.00
29WF	Jason Giambi	5.00
30WF	Pat Burrell	5.00

2001 Fleer Focus

NM/M
Complete Set (240): ... 100.00
Common Player: ... .15
Common Prospect (201-224): ... 3.00
Common Prospect (225-250): ... 3.00
Pack (10): ... 2.50
Box (24): ... 50.00

1	Derek Jeter	2.00
2	Manny Ramirez	.75
3	Ken Griffey Jr.	1.50
4	Ken Caminiti	.15
5	Joe Randa	.15
6	Jason Kendall	.15
7	Ron Coomer	.15
8	Rondell White	.15
9	Tino Martinez	.25
10	Nomar Garciaparra	.50
11	Tony Batista	.15
12	Todd Stottlemyre	.15
13	Ryan Klesko	.15
14	Darin Erstad	.50
15	Todd Walker	.15
16	Al Leiter	.15
17	Carl Everett	.15
18	Bobby Abreu	.25
19	Raul Mondesi	.15
20	Vladimir Guerrero	.75
21	Mike Bordick	.15
22	Aaron Sele	.15
23	Ray Lankford	.15
24	Roger Clemens	1.00
25	Kevin Young	.15
26	Brad Radke	.15
27	Todd Hundley	.15
28	Ellis Burks	.15
29	Lee Stevens	.15
30	Eric Karros	.15
31	Darren Dreifort	.15
32	Ivan Rodriguez	.50
33	Pedro Martinez	.75
34	Travis Fryman	.15
35	Garret Anderson	.15
36	Rafael Palmeiro	.50
37	Jason Giambi	.50
38	Jeromy Burnitz	.15
39	Robin Ventura	.15
40	Derek Bell	.15
41	Carlos Guillen	.15
42	Albert Belle	.15
43	Henry Rodriguez	.15
44	Brian Jordan	.15
45	Mike Sweeney	.15
46	Ruben Rivera	.15
47	Greg Maddux	1.00
48	Corey Koskie	.15
49	Sandy Alomar Jr.	.15
50	Mike Mussina	.40
51	Tom Glavine	.40
52	Aaron Boone	.15
53	Frank Thomas	.75
54	Kenny Lofton	.15
55	Danny Graves	.15
56	Jose Valentin	.15
57	Travis Lee	.15
58	Jim Edmonds	.15
59	Jim Thome	.25
60	Steve Finley	.15
61	Shawn Green	.45
62	Lance Berkman	.40
63	Mark Quinn	.15
64	Randy Johnson	.75
65	Dmitri Young	.15
66	Andy Pettitte	.40
67	Paul O'Neill	.15
68	Gil Heredia	.15
69	Russell Branyan	.15
70	Alex Rodriguez	1.50
71	Geoff Jenkins	.15
72	Eric Chavez	.25
73	Cal Ripken Jr.	2.00
74	Mark Kotsay	.15
75	Jeff D'Amico	.15
76	Tony Womack	.15
77	Eric Milton	.15
78	Joe Girardi	.15
79	Peter Bergeron	.15
80	Miguel Tejada	.50
81	Luis Gonzalez	.25
82	Doug Glanville	.15
83	Gerald Williams	.15
84	Troy O'Leary	.15
85	Brian Giles	.15
86	Miguel Cairo	.15
87	Magglio Ordonez	.40
88	Rick Helling	.15
89	Bruce Chen	.15

90	Jason Varitek	.15
91	Mike Lieberthal	.15
92	Shawn Estes	.15
93	Rick Ankiel	.25
94	Tim Salmon	.25
95	Jacque Jones	.15
96	Johnny Damon	.50
97	Larry Walker	.15
98	Ruben Mateo	.15
99	Brad Fullmer	.15
100	Edgardo Alfonzo	.15
101	Mark Mulder	.15
102	Tony Gwynn	1.00
103	Mike Cameron	.15
104	Richie Sexson	.15
105	Barry Larkin	.25
106	Mike Piazza	1.00
107	Eric Young	.15
108	Edgar Renteria	.15
109	Todd Zeile	.15
110	Luis Castillo	.15
111	Sammy Sosa	1.00
112	David Justice	.15
113	Delino DeShields	.15
114	Mariano Rivera	.40
115	Edgar Martinez	.15
116	Ray Durham	.15
117	Brady Anderson	.15
118	Eric Owens	.15
119	Alex Gonzalez	.15
120	Jay Buhner	.15
121	Greg Vaughn	.15
122	Mike Lowell	.25
123	Marquis Grissom	.15
124	Matt Williams	.15
125	Dean Palmer	.15
126	Troy Glaus	.40
127	Bret Boone	.15
128	David Ortiz	.75
129	Glenallen Hill	.15
130	Chipper Jones	1.00
131	Tony Clark	.15
132	Terrence Long	.15
133	Chuck Finley	.15
134	Jeff Bagwell	.75
135	J.T. Snow	.15
136	Andruw Jones	.50
137	Carlos Delgado	.50
138	Mo Vaughn	.15
139	Derek Lee	.40
140	Bobby Estalella	.15
141	Kerry Wood	.50
142	Jose Vidro	.15
143	Ben Grieve	.15
144	Barry Bonds	2.00
145	Javy Lopez	.15
146	Adam Kennedy	.15
147	Jeff Cirillo	.15
148	Cliff Floyd	.15
149	Carl Pavano	.25
150	Bobby Higginson	.15
151	Kevin Brown	.15
152	Fernando Tatis	.15
153	Matt Lawton	.15
154	Damion Easley	.15
155	Curt Schilling	.40
156	Mark McGwire	1.00
157	Mark Grace	.40
158	Adrian Beltre	.40
159	Jorge Posada	.40
160	Richard Hidalgo	.15
161	Vinny Castilla	.15
162	Bernie Williams	.40
163	John Olerud	.15
164	Todd Helton	.75
165	Craig Biggio	.25
166	David Wells	.15
167	Phil Nevin	.15
168	Andres Galarraga	.15
169	Moises Alou	.25
170	Denny Neagle	.15
171	Jeffrey Hammonds	.15
172	Sean Casey	.30
173	Gary Sheffield	.40
174	Carlos Lee	.25
175	Juan Encarnacion	.15
176	Roberto Alomar	.40
177	Kenny Rogers	.15
178	Charles Johnson	.15
179	Shannon Stewart	.15
180	B.J. Surhoff	.15
181	Paul Konerko	.25
182	Jermaine Dye	.15
183	Scott Rolen	.50
184	Fred McGriff	.15
185	Juan Gonzalez	.40
186	Carlos Beltran	.40
187	Jay Payton	.15
188	Chad Hermansen	.15
189	Pat Burrell	.50
190	Omar Vizquel	.15
191	Trot Nixon	.15
192	Mike Hampton	.15
193	Kris Benson	.15
194	Gabe Kapler	.15
195	Rickey Henderson	.75
196	J.D. Drew	.45
197	Pokey Reese	.15
198	Jeff Kent	.15
199	Jose Cruz Jr.	.15
200	Preston Wilson	.15
201	Eric Munson 2,499 (Prospects)	3.00
202	Alex Cabrera 2,499 (Prospects)	3.00
203	Nate Rolison 2,499 (Prospects)	3.00

204	Julio Zuleta 2,499 (Prospects)	3.00
205	Chris Richard 2,499 (Prospects)	3.00
206	Dernell Stenson 2,499 (Prospects)	3.00
207	Aaron McNeal 2,499 (Prospects)	3.00
208	Aubrey Huff 2,999 (Prospects)	5.00
209	Mike Lamb 2,999 (Prospects)	3.00
210	Xavier Nady 2,999 (Prospects)	4.00
211	Joe Crede 2,999 (Prospects)	4.00
212	Ben Petrick 3,499 (Prospects)	3.00
213	Morgan Burkhart 3,499 (Prospects)	3.00
214	Jason Tyner 1,999 (Prospects)	3.00
215	Juan Pierre 1,999 (Prospects)	5.00
216	Adam Dunn 1,999 (Prospects)	5.00
117/217	Adam Piatt 1,999 (Prospects)	3.00
218	Eric Byrnes 1,999 (Prospects)	4.00
219	Corey Patterson 1,999 (Prospects)	4.00
220	Kenny Kelly 1,999 (Prospects)	3.00
221	Tike Redman 1,999 (Prospects)	3.00
222	Luis Matos 1,999 (Prospects)	3.00
223	Timoniel Perez 1,999 (Prospects)	3.00
224	Vernon Wells 1,999 (Prospects)	3.00
225	Barry Zito 4,999 (Prospects)	4.00
226	Adam Bernero 4,999 (Prospects)	3.00
227	Kazuhiro Sasaki 4,999 (Prospects)	3.00
228	Oswaldo Mairena 4,999 (Prospects)	3.00
229	Mark Buehrle 4,999 (Prospects)	4.00
230	Ryan Dempster 4,999 (Prospects)	3.00
231	Tim Hudson 4,999 (Prospects)	5.00
232	Scott Downs 4,999 (Prospects)	3.00
233	A.J. Burnett 4,999 (Prospects)	4.00
234	Adam Eaton 4,999 (Prospects)	3.00
235	Paxton Crawford 4,999 (Prospects)	3.00
236	Jace Brewer 3,999 (Prospects)	3.00
237	Jose Ortiz 3,999 (Prospects)	4.00
238	Rafael Furcal 3,999 (Prospects)	4.00
239	Julio Lugo 3,999 (Prospects)	3.00
240	Tomas de la Rosa 3,999 (Prospects)	3.00

Green

NM/M
Common Player: ... 1.00
Random inserts in packs.
Stated print runs listed below.

1	Derek Jeter/339	10.00
2	Manny Ramirez/351	4.00
3	Ken Griffey Jr./271	8.00
4	Ken Caminiti/303	1.00
5	Joe Randa/304	1.00
6	Jason Kendall/270	1.50
7	Ron Coomer/270	1.00
8	Rondell White/258	1.50
9	Tino Martinez/258	2.00
10	Nomar Garciaparra/372	10.00
11	Tony Batista/263	1.00
12	Todd Stottlemyre/491	1.00
13	Ryan Klesko/283	1.50
14	Darin Erstad/355	1.50
15	Todd Walker/290	1.00
16	Al Leiter/320	1.00
17	Carl Everett/300	1.00
18	Bobby Abreu/316	1.50

#	Player/Team	Price
19	Raul Mondesi/271	1.00
20	Vladimir Guerrero/345	5.00
21	Mike Bordick/285	1.00
22	Aaron Sele/451	1.00
23	Ray Lankford/253	1.00
24	Roger Clemens/370	10.00
25	Kevin Young/258	1.00
26	Brad Radke/445	1.00
27	Todd Hundley/284	1.00
28	Ellis Burks/344	1.00
29	Lee Stevens/265	1.00
30	Eric Karros/250	1.00
31	Darren Dreifort/416	1.00
32	Ivan Rodriguez/347	5.00
33	Pedro Martinez/174	5.00
34	Travis Fryman/321	1.50
35	Garret Anderson/286	1.00
36	Rafael Palmeiro/288	3.00
37	Jason Giambi/333	2.00
38	Jeromy Burnitz/232	1.00
39	Robin Ventura/232	1.50
40	Derek Bell/266	1.00
41	Carlos Guillen/257	1.00
42	Albert Belle/281	1.00
43	Henry Rodriguez/256	1.00
44	Brian Jordan/264	1.00
45	Mike Sweeney/333	1.00
46	Ruben Rivera/208	1.00
47	Greg Maddux/300	8.00
48	Corey Koskie/300	1.00
49	Sandy Alomar Jr./289	1.00
50	Mike Mussina/379	3.00
51	Tom Glavine/340	2.00
52	Aaron Boone/285	1.00
53	Frank Thomas/328	4.00
54	Kenny Lofton/278	2.00
55	Danny Graves/256	1.00
56	Jose Valentin/273	1.00
57	Travis Lee/235	1.00
58	Jim Edmonds/295	2.00
59	Jim Thome/269	4.00
60	Steve Finley/280	1.00
61	Shawn Green/269	2.00
62	Lance Berkman/297	2.00
63	Mark Quinn/294	1.00
64	Randy Johnson/264	5.00
65	Dmitri Young/303	1.00
66	Andy Pettitte/435	2.00
67	Paul O'Neill/283	1.00
68	Gil Heredia/412	1.00
69	Russell Branyan/238	1.00
70	Alex Rodriguez/316	10.00
71	Geoff Jenkins/303	1.50
72	Eric Chavez/277	2.00
73	Cal Ripken Jr./256	15.00
74	Mark Kotsay/298	1.00
75	Jeff D'Amico/266	1.00
76	Tony Womack/271	1.00
77	Eric Milton/486	1.00
78	Joe Girardi/278	1.00
79	Peter Bergeron/245	1.00
80	Miguel Tejada/275	2.00
81	Luis Gonzalez/311	2.00
82	Doug Glanville/275	1.00
83	Gerald Williams/274	1.00
84	Troy O'Leary/261	1.00
85	Brian Giles/315	2.00
86	Miguel Cairo/261	1.00
87	Magglio Ordonez/315	2.00
88	Rick Helling/448	1.00
89	Bruce Chen/329	1.00
90	Jason Varitek/248	1.00
91	Mike Lieberthal/278	1.00
92	Shawn Estes/426	1.00
93	Rick Ankiel/350	2.00
94	Tim Salmon/290	2.00
95	Jacque Jones/285	1.00
96	Johnny Damon/327	1.50
97	Larry Walker/309	2.00
98	Ruben Mateo/291	1.00
99	Brad Fullmer/295	1.00
100	Edgardo Alfonzo/324	1.00
101	Mark Mulder/544	2.00
102	Tony Gwynn/323	5.00
103	Mike Cameron/267	1.00
104	Richie Sexson/272	2.00
105	Barry Larkin/313	2.00
106	Mike Piazza/324	8.00
107	Eric Young/297	1.00
108	Edgar Renteria/278	1.00
109	Todd Zeile/268	1.00
110	Luis Castillo/334	1.00
111	Sammy Sosa/320	10.00
112	David Justice/286	1.50
113	Delino DeShields/296	1.00
114	Mariano Rivera/285	1.50
115	Edgar Martinez/324	2.00
116	Ray Durham/280	1.00
117	Brady Anderson/257	1.00
118	Eric Owens/293	1.00
119	Alex Gonzalez/252	1.00
120	Jay Buhner/253	1.00
121	Greg Vaughn/254	1.00
122	Mike Lowell/270	1.00
123	Marquis Grissom/244	1.00
124	Matt Williams/275	1.50
125	Dean Palmer/256	1.00
126	Troy Glaus/284	3.00
127	Bret Boone/251	1.50
128	David Ortiz/282	1.00
129	Glenallen Hill/293	1.00
130	Chipper Jones/311	8.00
131	Tony Clark/274	1.00
132	Terrence Long/288	1.00
133	Chuck Finley/417	1.00
134	Jeff Bagwell/310	4.00
135	J.T. Snow/284	1.00
136	Andruw Jones/303	3.00
137	Carlos Delgado/344	3.00
138	Mo Vaughn/272	1.50
139	Derek Lee/281	1.50
140	Bobby Estalella/234	1.00
141	Kerry Wood/480	3.00
142	Jose Vidro/330	1.00
143	Ben Grieve/279	1.00
144	Barry Bonds/306	12.00
145	Javy Lopez/287	2.00
146	Adam Kennedy/266	1.00
147	Jeff Cirillo/326	1.00
148	Cliff Floyd/300	1.00
149	Carl Pavano/306	1.00
150	Bobby Higginson/300	1.00
151	Kevin Brown/258	2.00
152	Fernando Tatis/253	1.00
153	Matt Lawton/305	1.00
154	Damion Easley/259	1.00
155	Curt Schilling/381	3.00
156	Mark McGwire/305	10.00
157	Mark Grace/280	2.50
158	Adrian Beltre/290	1.50
159	Jorge Posada/287	2.00
160	Richard Hidalgo/314	1.00
161	Vinny Castilla/221	1.00
162	Bernie Williams/307	3.00
163	John Olerud/285	1.50
164	Todd Helton/372	4.00
165	Craig Biggio/268	1.50
166	David Wells/411	1.00
167	Phil Nevin/303	1.00
168	Andres Galarraga/302	1.00
169	Moises Alou/355	2.00
170	Denny Neagle/452	1.00
171	Jeffrey Hammonds/335	1.00
172	Sean Casey/315	1.00
173	Gary Sheffield/325	2.00
174	Carlos Lee/301	1.00
175	Juan Encarnacion/289	1.00
176	Roberto Alomar/310	3.00
177	Kenny Rogers/455	1.00
178	Charles Johnson/304	1.00
179	Shannon Stewart/319	1.00
180	B.J. Surhoff/291	1.00
181	Paul Konerko/298	1.00
182	Jermaine Dye/321	1.00
183	Scott Rolen/298	4.00
184	Fred McGriff/277	2.00
185	Juan Gonzalez/289	4.00
186	Carlos Beltran/247	1.50
187	Jay Payton/291	1.50
188	Chad Hermansen/185	1.00
189	Pat Burrell/260	3.00
190	Omar Vizquel/287	2.00
191	Trot Nixon/276	1.00
192	Mike Hampton/314	1.00
193	Kris Benson/385	1.00
194	Gabe Kapler/302	1.00
195	Rickey Henderson/233	1.00
196	J.D. Drew/295	2.00
197	Pokey Reese/255	1.00
198	Jeff Kent/334	1.50
199	Jose Cruz Jr./242	1.00
200	Preston Wilson/264	1.00
201	Eric Munson/252	1.00
202	Alex Cabrera/263	1.00
203	Nate Rolison/77	1.00
204	Julio Zuleta/294	1.00
205	Chris Richard/265	1.00
206	Dernell Stenson/268	1.00
207	Aaron McNeal/310	1.00
208	Aubrey Huff/287	1.00
209	Mike Lamb/278	1.00
210	Joe Crede/357	2.00
211	Ben Petrick/322	1.00
212	Morgan Burkhart/288	1.00
213	Jason Tyner/226	1.00
214	Juan Pierre/310	3.00
215	Adam Dunn/281	4.00
216	Adam Piatt/299	1.00
217	Eric Byrnes/300	1.00
218	Corey Patterson/167	2.00
219	Kenny Kelly/252	1.00
220	Tike Redman/333	1.00
221	Luis Matos/225	1.00
222	Timo Perez/286	1.00
223	Vernon Wells/243	2.00
224	Barry Zito/272	3.00
225	Adam Bernero/419	1.00
226	Kazuhiro Sasaki/316	2.00
227	Oswaldo Mairena/18	5.00
228	Mark Buehrle/421	1.50
229	Ryan Dempster/366	2.00
230	Scott Downs/529	1.00
231	Tim Hudson/414	2.00
232	Scott Downs/529	1.00
233	A.J. Burnett/479	1.00
234	Adam Eaton/413	1.00
235	Paxton Crawford/341	1.00
236	Jose Ortiz/182	1.00
237	Rafael Furcal/295	2.00
238	Julio Lugo/283	1.00
239	Tomas De La Rosa/288	1.00
240	Tomas De La Rosa/288	1.00

Autographics

	NM/M
Common Player:	5.00
Inserted 1:72	

Silvers: 1-1.5X
Production 250 Sets
Golds: 1-1.5X
Production 50 Sets

Player	Price
Roberto Alomar	30.00
Rick Ankiel	20.00
Albert Belle	5.00
Adrian Beltre	15.00
Lance Berkman	25.00
Barry Bonds	150.00
Jeromy Burnitz	5.00
Pat Burrell	10.00
Sean Casey	8.00
Eric Chavez	10.00
Carlos Delgado	10.00
J.D. Drew	10.00
Jermaine Dye	10.00
Jim Edmonds	10.00
Troy Glaus	15.00
Ben Grieve	5.00
Tony Gwynn	30.00
Randy Johnson	40.00
Chipper Jones	50.00
Mike Lamb	5.00
Mike Lieberthal	5.00
Terrence Long	5.00
Greg Maddux	75.00
Edgar Martinez	15.00
Kevin Millwood	5.00
Mike Mussina	25.00
Corey Patterson	10.00
Jay Payton	8.00
Juan Pierre	8.00
Brad Radke	5.00
Scott Rolen	20.00
Gary Sheffield	15.00
Fernando Tatis	5.00
Robin Ventura	5.00
Kerry Wood	20.00

Bat Company

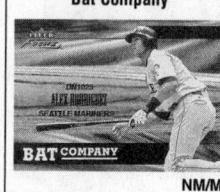

#	Player	NM/M
	Complete Set (10):	25.00
	Common Player:	1.00
	Inserted 1:24	
1	Barry Bonds	5.00
2	Mark McGwire	4.00
3	Sammy Sosa	3.00
4	Ken Griffey Jr.	3.00
5	Mike Piazza	3.00
6	Derek Jeter	5.00
7	Gary Sheffield	1.00
8	Frank Thomas	1.50
9	Chipper Jones	2.00
10	Alex Rodriguez	4.00

Big Innings

#	Player	NM/M
	Complete Set (25):	15.00
	Common Player:	.50
	Inserted 1:6	
	VIP:	5-10X
	Production 50 Sets	
1	Rick Ankiel	.50
2	Andruw Jones	1.00
3	Brian Giles	.50
4	Derek Jeter	4.00
5	Rafael Furcal	.50
6	Richie Sexson	.50
7	Jay Payton	.50
8	Carlos Delgado	.75
9	Jermaine Dye	.50
10	Darin Erstad	.75
11	Pat Burrell	.75
12	Richard Hidalgo	.50
13	Adrian Beltre	.50
14	Todd Helton	1.00
15	Vladimir Guerrero	1.00
16	Nomar Garciaparra	2.00
17	Gabe Kapler	.50
18	Carlos Lee	.50
19	J.D. Drew	.60
20	Troy Glaus	.60
21	Scott Rolen	.60
22	Alex Rodriguez	3.00
23	Magglio Ordonez	.60
24	Miguel Tejada	.60
25	Ruben Mateo	.50

Diamond Vision

#	Player	NM/M
	Complete Set (15):	25.00
	Common Player:	1.00
	Inserted 1:12	
1	Derek Jeter	4.00
2	Nomar Garciaparra	2.50

#	Player	Price
3	Cal Ripken Jr.	4.00
4	Jeff Bagwell	1.50
5	Mark McGwire	3.00
6	Ken Griffey Jr.	2.50
7	Pedro Martinez	1.50
8	Carlos Delgado	2.00
9	Chipper Jones	2.00
10	Barry Bonds	4.00
11	Mike Piazza	2.50
12	Sammy Sosa	2.50
13	Alex Rodriguez	3.00
14	Frank Thomas	1.50
15	Randy Johnson	1.50

Feel the Game

Player	NM/M
Common Player:	5.00
Inserted 1:72	
Moises Alou	6.00
Brady Anderson	5.00
Dante Bichette	5.00
Jermaine Dye	5.00
Brian Giles	5.00
Juan Gonzalez	8.00
Rickey Henderson	15.00
Javy Lopez	5.00
Tino Martinez	6.00
Phil Nevin	5.00
Matt Stairs	5.00
Shannon Stewart	5.00
Jose Vidro	5.00

ROY Collection

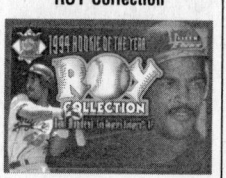

#	Player	NM/M
	Complete Set (25):	75.00
	Common Player:	2.00
	Inserted 1:24	
1	Luis Aparicio	2.00
2	Johnny Bench	3.00
3	Joe Black	2.00
4	Rod Carew	2.00
5	Orlando Cepeda	2.00
6	Carlton Fisk	2.00
7	Ben Grieve	2.00
8	Frank Howard	2.00
9	Derek Jeter	10.00
10	Fred Lynn	2.00
11	Willie Mays	8.00
12	Willie McCovey	2.00
13	Mark McGwire	8.00
14	Raul Mondesi	2.00
15	Thurman Munson	4.00
16	Eddie Murray	2.00
17	Mike Piazza	6.00
18	Cal Ripken Jr.	10.00
19	Frank Robinson	2.00
20	Jackie Robinson	8.00
21	Scott Rolen	3.00
22	Tom Seaver	2.00
23	Fernando Valenzuela	2.00
24	David Justice	2.00
25	Billy Williams	2.00

ROY Collection Memorabilia

#	Player	NM/M
	Common Player:	8.00
	Inserted 1:288	
1	Luis Aparicio/Bat	8.00
2	Johnny Bench/Jsy	15.00
3	Orlando Cepeda/Bat	8.00
4	Carlton Fisk/Jsy	10.00
5	Ben Grieve/Jsy	8.00
6	Frank Howard/Bat	8.00
7	Derek Jeter/Jsy	50.00
8	Fred Lynn/Bat	8.00
9	Willie Mays/Jsy	60.00
10	Willie McCovey/Bat	10.00
11	Mark McGwire/Ball	50.00
12	Raul Mondesi/Bat	8.00
13	Thurman Munson/Bat	30.00
14	Eddie Murray/Jsy	10.00
15	Mike Piazza/Base	15.00
16	Cal Ripken/Jsy	50.00
17	Frank Robinson/Bat	10.00
18	Jackie Robinson/Jsy	60.00
19	Scott Rolen/Bat	15.00
20	Tom Seaver/Jsy	15.00
22	David Justice/Bat	8.00

ROY Collection Signed Memorabilia

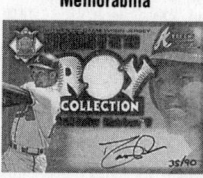

#	Player	NM/M
	Common Player:	25.00
1	Luis Aparicio/Jsy/56	40.00
2	Johnny Bench/68	85.00
3	Orlando Cepeda/58	30.00
4	Carlton Fisk/72	50.00
5	Ben Grieve/98	25.00
6	Frank Howard/60	25.00
7	Derek Jeter/96	200.00
8	Fred Lynn/75	25.00
9	Willie Mays/Jsy/51	200.00
10	Willie McCovey/Bat/59	40.00
11	Raul Mondesi/94	25.00
12	Eddie Murray/77	50.00
13	Cal Ripken/82	250.00
14	Frank Robinson/Bat/225	50.00
15	Scott Rolen/97	25.00
16	Tom Seaver/67	90.00
18	David Justice/90	25.00

2001 Fleer Futures

#	Player	NM/M
	Complete Set (220):	20.00
	Common Player:	.15
	Pack (8):	1.50
	Box (28):	30.00
1	Darin Erstad	.40
2	Manny Ramirez	.75
3	Darryl Kile	.15
4	Troy O'Leary	.15
5	Mark Quinn	.15
6	Brian Giles	.15
7	Randy Johnson	.75
8	Todd Walker	.15
9	Mike Piazza	1.50
10	Fred McGriff	.15
11	Sammy Sosa	1.00
12	Chan Ho Park	.15
13	John Rocker	.15
14	Luis Castillo	.15
15	Eric Chavez	.25
16	Carlos Delgado	.50
17	Sean Casey	.25
18	Corey Koskie	.15
19	John Olerud	.15
20	Nomar Garciaparra	.50
21	Craig Biggio	.15
22	Pat Burrell	.40
23	Bengie Molina	.15
24	Jim Thome	.15
25	Rey Ordonez	.15
26	Fernando Tatis	.15
27	Eric Young	.15
28	Eric Karros	.15
29	Adam Eaton	.15
30	Brian Jordan	.15
31	Jorge Posada	.25
32	Gabe Kapler	.15
33	Keith Foulke	.15
34	Ron Coomer	.15
35	Chipper Jones	1.00
36	Miguel Tejada	.25
37	David Wells	.15
38	Carlos Lee	.15
39	Barry Bonds	2.00
40	Derek Lee	.15
41	Tim Hudson	.25
42	Billy Koch	.15
43	Dmitri Young	.15
44	Vladimir Guerrero	.75
45	Rickey Henderson	.75
46	Jeff Bagwell	.75
47	Robert Person	.15
48	Brady Anderson	.15
49	Lance Berkman	.15
50	Mike Lieberthal	.15
51	Adam Kennedy	.15
52	Russ Branyan	.15
53	Robin Ventura	.15
54	Mark McGwire	2.00
55	Tony Gwynn	1.00
56	Matt Williams	.15
57	Jeff Cirillo	.15
58	Roger Clemens	1.25
59	Ivan Rodriguez	.50
60	Brad Radke	.15
61	Kazuhiro Sasaki	.15
62	Cal Ripken Jr.	2.50
63	Ken Caminiti	.15
64	Bobby Abreu	.15
65	Troy Glaus	.15
66	Sandy Alomar Jr.	.15
67	Jose Vidro	.15
68	Pedro Martinez	.75
69	Kevin Young	.15
70	Jay Bell	.15
71	Larry Walker	.15
72	Derek Jeter	2.50
73	Miguel Cairo	.15
74	Magglio Ordonez	.15
75	Jeromy Burnitz	.15
76	J.T. Snow	.15
77	Andres Galarraga	.15
78	Ryan Dempster	.15
79	Ken Griffey Jr.	1.50
80	Aaron Sele	.15
81	Tom Glavine	.15
82	Hideo Nomo	.50
83	Orlando Hernandez	.15
84	Tony Batista	.15
85	Aaron Boone	.15
86	Jacque Jones	.15
87	Delino DeShields	.15
88	Garret Anderson	.15
89	Fernando Seguignol	.15
90	Jim Edmonds	.15
91	Frank Thomas	.75
92	Adrian Beltre	.30
93	Ellis Burks	.15
94	Andruw Jones	.50
95	Tony Clark	.15
96	Danny Graves	.15
97	Alex Rodriguez	2.00
98	Mike Mussina	.40
99	Scott Elarton	.15
100	Jason Giambi	.50
101	Jay Payton	.15
102	Gerald Williams	.15
103	Kerry Wood	.50
104	Shawn Green	.35
105	Greg Maddux	1.00
106	Juan Encarnacion	.15
107	Bernie Williams	.30
108	Mike Lamb	.15
109	Charles Johnson	.15
110	Richie Sexson	.15
111	Jeff Kent	.15
112	Albert Belle	.15
113	Cliff Floyd	.15
114	Ben Grieve	.15
115	Tim Salmon	.25
116	Carl Pavano	.15
117	Rick Ankiel	.25
118	Dante Bichette	.15
119	Johnny Damon	.30
120	Brian Anderson	.15
121	Roberto Alomar	.40
122	Mike Hampton	.15
123	Greg Vaughn	.15
124	Carl Everett	.15
125	Moises Alou	.15
126	Jason Kendall	.15
127	Omar Vizquel	.15
128	Mark Grace	.25
129	Kevin Brown	.15
130	Phil Nevin	.15
131	Kevin Millwood	.15
132	Bobby Higginson	.15
133	Ruben Mateo	.25
134	Luis Gonzalez	.25
135	Dean Palmer	.15
136	Mariano Rivera	.25
137	Rick Helling	.15
138	Paul Konerko	.15
139	Marquis Grissom	.15
140	Robb Nen	.15
141	Javy Lopez	.15
142	Preston Wilson	.15
143	Terrence Long	.15
144	Shannon Stewart	.15
145	Barry Larkin	.25
146	Cristian Guzman	.15
147	Jay Buhner	.15
148	Jermaine Dye	.15
149	Kris Benson	.15
150	Curt Schilling	.40
151	Todd Helton	.50
152	Paul O'Neill	.15
153	Rafael Palmeiro	.50
154	Ray Durham	.15
155	Geoff Jenkins	.15
156	Livan Hernandez	.15
157	Rafael Furcal	.15
158	Juan Gonzalez	.50
159	Tino Martinez	.15
160	Raul Mondesi	.15
161	Matt Lawton	.15
162	Edgar Martinez	.25
163	Richard Hidalgo	.15
164	Scott Rolen	.50

165	Chuck Finley	.15
166	Edgardo Alfonzo	.15
167	J.D. Drew	.35
168	Trot Nixon	.15
169	Carlos Beltran	.50
170	Ryan Klesko	.15
171	Mo Vaughn	.15
172	Kenny Lofton	.15
173	Al Leiter	.15
174	Rondell White	.15
175	Mike Sweeney	.15
176	Trevor Hoffman	.15
177	Steve Finley	.15
178	Jeffrey Hammonds	.15
179	David Justice	.15
180	Gary Sheffield	.40
181	Eric Munson (Bright Futures)	.15
182	Luis Matos (Bright Futures)	.15
183	Alex Cabrera (Bright Futures)	.15
184	Randy Keisler (Bright Futures)	.15
185	Nate Rolison (Bright Futures)	.15
186	Jason Hart (Bright Futures)	.15
187	Timo Perez (Bright Futures)	.15
188	Adam Bernero (Bright Futures)	.15
189	Barry Zito (Bright Futures)	.50
190	Ryan Kohlmeier (Bright Futures)	.15
191	Joey Nation (Bright Futures)	.15
192	Oswaldo Mairena (Bright Futures)	.15
193	Aubrey Huff (Bright Futures)	.15
194	Mark Buehrle (Bright Futures)	.15
195	Jace Brewer (Bright Futures)	.15
196	Julio Zuleta (Bright Futures)	.15
197	Xavier Nady (Bright Futures)	.15
198	Vernon Wells (Bright Futures)	.25
199	Joe Crede (Bright Futures)	.15
200	Scott Downs (Bright Futures)	.15
201	Ben Petrick (Bright Futures)	.15
202	A.J. Burnett (Bright Futures)	.15
203	Esix Snead RC (Bright Futures)	.15
204	Dernell Stenson (Bright Futures)	.15
205	Jose Ortiz (Bright Futures)	.15
206	Paxton Crawford (Bright Futures)	.15
207	Jason Tyner (Bright Futures)	.15
208	Jimmy Rollins (Bright Futures)	.25
209	Juan Pierre (Bright Futures)	.25
210	Keith Ginter (Bright Futures)	.15
211	Adam Dunn (Bright Futures)	.40
212	Larry Barnes (Bright Futures)	.15
213	Adam Piatt (Bright Futures)	.15
214	Rodney Lindsey (Bright Futures)	.15
215	Eric Byrnes (Bright Futures)	.15
216	Julio Lugo (Bright Futures)	.15
217	Corey Patterson (Bright Futures)	.25
218	Reggie Taylor (Bright Futures)	.15
219	Kenny Kelly (Bright Futures)	.15
220	Tike Redman (Bright Futures)	.15

Black Gold

Production 499 Sets:	3-6X

Bases Loaded

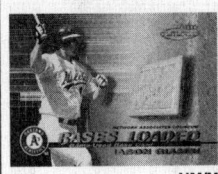

		NM/M	
Common Player:			4.00
Inserted 1:134			
BL1	Ken Griffey Jr.		10.00
BL2	Mark McGwire		12.00
BL3	Carlos Delgado		4.00
BL4	Chipper Jones		7.50
BL5	Nomar Garciaparra		12.00
BL6	Cal Ripken Jr.		15.00
BL7	Sammy Sosa		10.00
BL8	Jeff Bagwell		6.00
BL9	Vladimir Guerrero		6.00
BL10	Tony Gwynn		7.50
BL11	Frank Thomas		6.00
BL12	Mike Piazza		10.00
BL13	Jason Giambi		5.00
BL14	Troy Glaus		4.00
BL15	Pat Burrell		4.00

Bats to the Future

		NM/M
Complete Set (25):		60.00
Common Player:		1.00
Inserted 1:28		
1BF	Mike Schmidt	6.00
2BF	Carlton Fisk	3.00
3BF	Paul Molitor	3.00
4BF	Vladimir Guerrero	3.00
5BF	Dave Parker	1.00
6BF	Chipper Jones	5.00
7BF	Carlos Delgado	2.00
8BF	Tony Gwynn	5.00
9BF	Reggie Jackson	5.00
10BF	Eddie Murray	1.50
11BF	Robin Yount	3.00
12BF	Alan Trammell	1.00
13BF	Frank Thomas	3.00
14BF	Cal Ripken Jr.	8.00
15BF	Don Mattingly	6.00
16BF	Jim Rice	1.00
17BF	Juan Gonzalez	3.00
18BF	Todd Helton	3.00
19BF	George Brett	6.00
20BF	Barry Bonds	8.00
21BF	Kirk Gibson	1.00
22BF	Matt Williams	1.00
23BF	Dave Winfield	1.50
24BF	Ryne Sandberg	5.00
25BF	Ivan Rodriguez	2.00

Bats to the Future Game Bat

		NM/M
Common Player:		5.00
Inserted 1:114		
1BF	Mike Schmidt	25.00
2BF	Carlton Fisk	10.00
3BF	Paul Molitor	15.00
4BF	Vladimir Guerrero	8.00
5BF	Dave Parker	5.00
6BF	Chipper Jones	10.00
7BF	Chris Delgado	8.00
8BF	Tony Gwynn	10.00
9BF	Reggie Jackson	10.00
10BF	Eddie Murray	8.00
11BF	Robin Yount	15.00
12BF	Alan Trammell	5.00
13BF	Frank Thomas	8.00
14BF	Cal Ripken Jr.	30.00
15BF	Don Mattingly	30.00
16BF	Jim Rice	5.00
17BF	Juan Gonzalez	8.00
18BF	Todd Helton	8.00
19BF	George Brett	25.00
20BF	Barry Bonds	25.00
21BF	Kirk Gibson	5.00
22BF	Matt Williams	5.00
23BF	Dave Winfield	8.00
24BF	Ryne Sandberg	15.00
25BF	Ivan Rodriguez	8.00

Bats to the Future Game Bat Auto.

		NM/M
Common Autograph:		40.00
Production 50 Sets		

Characteristics

		NM/M
Complete Set (15):		20.00
Common Player:		.75
Inserted 1:9		
1C	Derek Jeter	4.00
2C	Mark McGwire	3.00
3C	Nomar Garciaparra	2.50
4C	Sammy Sosa	2.50
5C	Pedro Martinez	1.50
6C	Chipper Jones	2.00
7C	Cal Ripken Jr.	4.00
8C	Todd Helton	1.50
9C	Jim Edmonds	.75
10C	Ken Griffey Jr.	2.50
11C	Alex Rodriguez	3.00
12C	Mike Piazza	2.50
13C	Vladimir Guerrero	1.50
14C	Frank Thomas	1.50
15C	Carlos Delgado	1.00

Hot Commodities

		NM/M
Complete Set (10):		20.00
Common Player:		1.00
Inserted 1:14		
1HC	Mark McGwire	3.00
2HC	Ken Griffey Jr.	2.50
3HC	Derek Jeter	4.00
4HC	Cal Ripken Jr.	4.00
5HC	Chipper Jones	2.00
6HC	Barry Bonds	4.00
7HC	Mike Piazza	2.50
8HC	Sammy Sosa	2.50
9HC	Alex Rodriguez	3.00
10HC	Frank Thomas	1.00

September Call-Ups Memorabilia

		NM/M
Common Card:		4.00

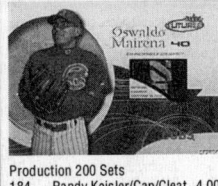

1BF	Mike Schmidt	150.00
2BF	Carlton Fisk	60.00
3BF	Paul Molitor	50.00
4BF	Vladimir Guerrero	80.00
5BF	Dave Parker	40.00
6BF	Chipper Jones	75.00
7BF	Carlos Delgado	50.00
8BF	Tony Gwynn	75.00
9BF	Reggie Jackson	70.00
10BF	Eddie Murray	70.00
11BF	Robin Yount	80.00
12BF	Alan Trammell	40.00
13BF	Frank Thomas	60.00
14BF	Cal Ripken Jr.	200.00
15BF	Don Mattingly	150.00
16BF	Jim Rice	40.00
17BF	Juan Gonzalez	60.00
18BF	Todd Helton	60.00
19BF	George Brett	150.00
20BF	Barry Bonds	150.00
21BF	Kirk Gibson	40.00
22BF	Matt Williams	40.00
23BF	Dave Winfield	60.00
24BF	Ryne Sandberg	125.00
25BF	Ivan Rodriguez	60.00

Production 200 Sets		
184	Randy Keisler/Cap/Cleat	4.00
185	Nate Rolison/Bat	4.00
187	Timoniel Perez/Bat	4.00
191	Joey Nation/Glv	4.00
192	Oswaldo Mairena/Glv	4.00
195	Jace Brewer/Bat	4.00
197	Xavier Nady/Glv	6.00
199	Joe Crede/Bat	6.00
205	Jose Ortiz/Bat	4.00
208	Jimmy Rollins/Glv	6.00
210	Keith Ginter/Bat	4.00
214	Rodney Lindsey/Bat	4.00
217	Corey Patterson/Bat	8.00
218	Reggie Taylor/Bat	4.00
219	Kenny Kelly/Bat	4.00

2001 Fleer Game Time

		NM/M
Complete Set (121):		
Common Player:		.15
Common (91-121):		3.00
Production 2,000		
Pack (5):		4.00
Box (24):		80.00
1	Derek Jeter	2.00
2	Nomar Garciaparra	.50
3	Alex Rodriguez	1.50
4	Jason Kendall	.15
5	Barry Bonds	2.00
6	David Wells	.15
7	Craig Biggio	.25
8	Adrian Beltre	.40
9	Pat Burrell	.40
10	Rafael Palmeiro	.50
11	Jim Thome	.25
12	Mike Lowell	.25
13	Trevor Hoffman	.15
14	Pokey Reese	.15
15	Juan Encarnacion	.15
16	Shawn Green	.40
17	Kerry Wood	.50
18	Richard Hidalgo	.15
19	Scott Rolen	.25
20	Jeff Kent	.25
21	Alex Gonzalez	.15
22	Matt Williams	.15
23	Mike Sweeney	.15
24	Edgar Martinez	.15
25	Sammy Sosa	.75
26	Bobby Higginson	.15
27	Kevin Brown	.15
28	Mike Lieberthal	.15
29	Pedro J. Martinez	.75
30	Jeff Weaver	.15
31	Greg Maddux	1.00
32	Mike Hampton	.15
33	Vladimir Guerrero	.75
34	Greg Vaughn	.15
35	Manny Ramirez	.75
36	Carlos Beltran	.40
37	Eric Chavez	.25
38	Troy Glaus	.50
39	Todd Helton	.50
40	Gary Sheffield	.40
41	Brady Anderson	.15
42	Juan Gonzalez	.50
43	Tim Hudson	.15
44	Kenny Lofton	.15
45	Al Leiter	.15
46	Eric Owens	.15
47	Roberto Alomar	.40
48	Preston Wilson	.15
49	Tony Gwynn	1.00
50	Cal Ripken Jr.	2.00
51	Ben Petrick	.15
52	Jason Giambi	.50
53	Ben Grieve	.15
54	Albert Belle	.15
55	Jose Vidro	.15
56	Barry Zito	.25
57	Ivan Rodriguez	.50
58	Jeff Bagwell	.50
59	Geoff Jenkins	.15
60	Roger Clemens	1.00
61	John Olerud	.15
62	Randy Johnson	.75
63	Matt Lawton	.15
64	Mark McGwire	1.50
65	Brad Radke	.15
66	Frank Thomas	.75
67	Edgardo Alfonzo	.15
68	Brian Giles	.15
69	J.T. Snow	.15
70	Carlos Delgado	.50
71	Chipper Jones	1.00
72	Mark Quinn	.15
73	Mike Mussina	.40
74	Rick Ankiel	.50
75	Rafael Furcal	.25
76	Jim Edmonds	.15
77	Vinny Castilla	.15
78	Sean Casey	.25
79	Derek Lee	.50
80	Mike Piazza	1.00
81	Warren Morris	.15
82	Tim Salmon	.25
83	Jeromy Burnitz	.15
84	Freddy Garcia	.15
85	Ken Griffey Jr.	1.00
86	Andruw Jones	.40
87	Darryl Kile	.15
88	Magglio Ordonez	.25
89	Bernie Williams	.40
90	Timo Perez	.15
91	Ichiro Suzuki RC (Next Game)	30.00
92	Larry Barnes, Darin Erstad (Next Game)	3.00
93	Jaisen Randolph RC (Next Game)	3.00
94	Paul Phillips RC (Next Game)	3.00
95	Esix Snead RC (Next Game)	3.00
96	Matt White RC (Next Game)	3.00
97	Ryan Freel RC (Next Game)	3.00
98	Winston Abreu RC (Next Game)	3.00
99	Junior Spivey RC (Next Game)	3.00
100	Randy Keisler, Roger Clemens (Next Game)	5.00
101	Brian Cole, Mike Piazza (Next Game)	4.00
102	Aubrey Huff, Chipper Jones (Next Game)	4.00
103	Corey Patterson, Sammy Sosa (Next Game)	5.00
104	Sun-Woo Kim, Pedro Martinez (Next Game)	4.00
105	Drew Henson RC (Next Game)	4.00
106	Claudio Vargas RC (Next Game)	3.00
107	Cesar Izturis, Rafael Furcal (Next Game)	3.00
108	Paxton Crawford, Pedro Martinez (Next Game)	4.00
109	Adrian Hernandez RC (Next Game)	3.00
110	Jace Brewer, Derek Jeter (Next Game)	8.00
111	Andy Morales RC (Next Game)	3.00
112	Wilson Betemit RC (Next Game)	3.00
113	Juan Diaz RC (Next Game)	3.00
114	Erick Almonte RC (Next Game)	3.00
115	Nick Punto RC (Next Game)	3.00
116	Tsuyoshi Shinjo RC (Next Game)	3.00
117	Jay Gibbons RC (Next Game)	3.00
118	Andres Torres RC (Next Game)	3.00
119	Alexis Gomez RC (Next Game)	3.00
120	Wilken Ruan RC (Next Game)	3.00
121	Albert Pujols RC (Next Game)	60.00

Next Game Extra

Cards (91-121):	2-3X
Production 200 Sets	

Famers Lumber

		NM/M
Common Player:		8.00
Production 100 Sets		
1FL	Luis Aparicio	8.00
2FL	Hank Bauer	8.00
3FL	Paul Blair	8.00
4FL	Bobby Bonds	8.00
5FL	Orlando Cepeda	8.00
6FL	Roberto Clemente	100.00
7FL	Rocky Colavito	10.00
8FL	Bucky Dent	8.00
9FL	Bill Dickey	10.00
10FL	Larry Doby	10.00
11FL	Carlton Fisk	8.00
12FL	Hank Greenberg	25.00
13FL	Elston Howard	8.00
14FL	Frank Howard	8.00
15FL	Reggie Jackson	15.00
16FL	Harmon Killebrew	20.00
17FL	Tony Lazzeri	8.00
18FL	Roger Maris	60.00
19FL	Johnny Mize	10.00
20FL	Thurman Munson	40.00
21FL	Tony Perez	10.00
22FL	Jim Rice	8.00
23FL	Phil Rizzuto	10.00
24FL	Bill Skowron	8.00
25FL	Enos Slaughter	10.00
26FL	Duke Snider	15.00
27FL	Willie Stargell	15.00
28FL	Bill Terry	8.00
29FL	Ted Williams	100.00

Famers Lumber Autograph

		NM/M
Common Player:		40.00
Production 25 Sets		
1FLS	Hank Bauer	40.00
2FLS	Bobby Bonds	50.00
3FLS	Orlando Cepeda	50.00
4FLS	Rocky Colavito	50.00
5FLS	Bucky Dent	40.00
6FLS	Larry Doby	50.00
7FLS	Carlton Fisk	65.00
8FLS	Frank Howard	40.00
9FLS	Reggie Jackson	100.00
10FLS	Harmon Killebrew	120.00
11FLS	Tony Perez	40.00
12FLS	Jim Rice	40.00
13FLS	Phil Rizzuto	60.00
14FLS	Bill Skowron	40.00
15FLS	Enos Slaughter	40.00
16FLS	Duke Snider	75.00

Derek Jeter's Monumental Moments

		NM/M
Complete Set (2):		
1JM	Derek Jeter/1996	8.00
1JMS	Derek Jeter/Auto./96	80.00

Let's Play Two!

		NM/M
Complete Set (15):		30.00
Common Card:		1.50
Inserted 1:24		
1LT	Derek Jeter, Nomar Garciaparra	4.00
2LT	Mark McGwire, Sammy Sosa	3.00
3LT	Pedro J. Martinez, Randy Johnson	1.50
4LT	Vladimir Guerrero, Carlos Delgado	1.50
5LT	Mike Piazza, Roger Clemens	2.50
6LT	Alex Rodriguez, Miguel Tejada	3.00
7LT	Troy Glaus, Chipper Jones	2.00
8LT	Derek Jeter, Alex Rodriguez	4.00
9LT	Cal Ripken Jr., Derek Jeter	4.00
10LT	Jason Giambi, Mark McGwire	3.00
11LT	Jeff Bagwell, Craig Biggio	1.50
12LT	Tom Glavine, Greg Maddux	2.00
13LT	Ken Griffey Jr., Barry Bonds	4.00
14LT	Manny Ramirez, Pedro J. Martinez	1.50
15LT	Alex Rodriguez, Ivan Rodriguez	3.00

Lumber

		NM/M
Common Player:		4.00
Inserted 1:40		
1GL	Roberto Alomar	6.00
2GL	Rick Ankiel	6.00
3GL	Adrian Beltre	4.00
4GL	Barry Bonds	25.00
5GL	Kevin Brown	4.00

7GL	Ken Caminiti	4.00
8GL	Eric Chavez	5.00
9GL	Carlos Delgado	5.00
10GL	J.D. Drew	5.00
11GL	Erubiel Durazo	4.00
12GL	Carl Everett	4.00
13GL	Rafael Furcal	5.00
14GL	Brian Giles	5.00
15GL	Juan Gonzalez	6.00
16GL	Todd Helton	5.00
18GL	Randy Johnson	10.00
19GL	Chipper Jones	10.00
20GL	Pedro J. Martinez	10.00
21GL	Tino Martinez	5.00
23GL	Cal Ripken/SP/275	40.00
24GL	Ivan Rodriguez	8.00
25GL	Frank Thomas	8.00
26GL	Jim Thome	8.00
27GL	Bernie Williams	5.00
28GL	Nomar Garciaparra	15.00

New Order

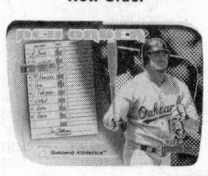

		NM/M
Complete Set (15):		30.00
Common Player:		1.50
Inserted 1:12		
1NO	Derek Jeter	6.00
2NO	Nomar Garciaparra	4.00
3NO	Alex Rodriguez	5.00
4NO	Mark McGwire	5.00
5NO	Sammy Sosa	4.00
6NO	Carlos Delgado	1.50
7NO	Troy Glaus	1.50
8NO	Jason Giambi	1.50
9NO	Mike Piazza	4.00
10NO	Todd Helton	1.50
11NO	Vladimir Guerrero	2.00
12NO	Manny Ramirez	1.50
13NO	Frank Thomas	1.50
14NO	Ken Griffey Jr.	4.00
15NO	Chipper Jones	3.00

Sticktoitness

		NM/M
Complete Set (20):		15.00
Common Player:		.50
Inserted 1:8		
1S	Derek Jeter	4.00
2S	Nomar Garciaparra	3.00
3S	Alex Rodriguez	3.00
4S	Jeff Bagwell	1.00
5S	Bernie Williams	1.00
6S	Eric Chavez	.60
7S	Richard Hidalgo	.50
8S	Ichiro Suzuki	2.00
9S	Troy Glaus	.75
10S	Magglio Ordonez	.50
11S	Corey Patterson	.50
12S	Todd Helton	1.00
13S	Jim Edmonds	.50
14S	Rafael Furcal	.50
15S	Mo Vaughn	.50
16S	Pat Burrell	.65
17S	Adrian Beltre	.60
18S	Andruw Jones	1.00
19S	Manny Ramirez	1.00
20S	Sean Casey	.65

Uniformity

		NM/M
Common Player:		4.00
Inserted 1:25		
1GU	Andres Galarraga	4.00
2GU	Barry Bonds	20.00
3GU	Ben Petrick	4.00
4GU	Brad Radke	4.00
5GU	Brian Jordan	4.00
6GU	Carlos Guillen	4.00
7GU	Fernando Seguignol	4.00
8GU	Fred McGriff	4.00
9GU	Gary Sheffield	5.00
10GU	Magglio Ordonez	15.00
11GU	Ivan Rodriguez	8.00
12GU	Jay Buhner	4.00
13GU	Jeromy Burnitz	4.00
14GU	John Olerud	4.00
15GU	Kevin Brown	4.00
16GU	Larry Walker	4.00
17GU	Magglio Ordonez	4.00
18GU	Matt Williams	4.00
19GU	Robin Ventura	4.00
20GU	Rondell White	4.00
21GU	Tony Gwynn	15.00
22GU	Troy Glaus	4.00
23GU	Vladimir Guerrero	8.00

2001 Fleer Genuine

		NM/M
Complete Set (130):		150.00
Common Player:		.25
Common (101-130):		3.00
Production 1,500		
Pack (5):		3.00
Box (24):		60.00
1	Derek Jeter	3.00
2	Nomar Garciaparra	.75
3	Alex Rodriguez	2.50
4	Frank Thomas	1.00
5	Travis Fryman	.25
6	Gary Sheffield	.40
7	Jason Giambi	.75
8	Trevor Hoffman	.25
9	Todd Helton	.75
10	Ivan Rodriguez	.75
11	Roberto Alomar	.40
12	Barry Zito	.25
13	Kevin Brown	.25
14	Shawn Green	.40
15	Kenny Lofton	.25
16	Jeff Weaver	.25
17	Geoff Jenkins	.25
18	Carlos Delgado	.50
19	Mark Grace	.40
20	Ken Griffey Jr.	2.00
21	David Justice	.25
22	Brian Giles	.25
23	Scott Williamson	.25
24	Richie Sexson	.25
25	John Olerud	.25
26	Sammy Sosa	1.00
27	Bobby Higginson	.25
28	Matt Lawton	.25
29	Vinny Castilla	.25
30	Alex S. Gonzalez	.25
31	Manny Ramirez	1.00
32	Brad Radke	.25
33	Cal Ripken Jr.	3.00
34	Richard Hidalgo	.25
35	Al Leiter	.25
36	Freddy Garcia	.25
37	Juan Encarnacion	.25
38	Corey Koskie	.25
39	Greg Vaughn	.25
40	Rafael Palmeiro	.50
41	Vladimir Guerrero	1.00
42	Troy Glaus	.50
43	Mike Hampton	.25
44	Jose Vidro	.25
45	Ryan Rupe	.25
46	Troy O'Leary	.25
47	Ben Petrick	.25
48	Mike Lieberthal	.25
49	Mike Sweeney	.25
50	Scott Rolen	.50
51	Albert Belle	.25
52	Mark Quinn	.25
53	Mike Piazza	1.50
54	Mark McGwire	1.50
55	Brady Anderson	.25
56	Carlos Beltran	.45
57	Michael Barrett	.25
58	Jason Kendall	.25
59	Jim Edmonds	.25
60	Matt Williams	.25
61	Pokey Reese	.25
62	Bernie Williams	.40
63	Barry Bonds	3.00
64	David Wells	.25
65	Chipper Jones	1.50
66	Jim Parque	.25
67	Derek Lee	.50
68	Darin Erstad	.40
69	Edgar Martinez	.40
70	Kerry Wood	.50
71	Omar Vizquel	.25
72	Jeromy Burnitz	.25
73	Warren Morris	.25
74	Rick Ankiel	.50
75	Andruw Jones	.50
76	Paul Konerko	.40
77	Mike Lowell	.40
78	Roger Clemens	1.50
79	Tim Hudson	.40
80	Rafael Furcal	.40
81	Craig Biggio	.40
82	Edgardo Alfonzo	.25
83	Pat Burrell	.50
84	Adrian Beltre	.40
85	Tony Gwynn	1.50
86	J.T. Snow	.25
87	Randy Johnson	1.00
88	Sean Casey	.25
89	Preston Wilson	.25
90	Mike Mussina	.50
91	Eric Chavez	.25
92	Tim Salmon	.25
93	Pedro Martinez	1.00
94	Darryl Kile	.25
95	Greg Maddux	1.50
96	Magglio Ordonez	.40
97	Jeff Bagwell	.50
98	Timo Perez	.25
99	Jeff Kent	.40
100	Eric Owens	.25
101	Ichiro Suzuki RC (Genuine Upside)	30.00
102	Elpidio Guzman RC (Genuine Upside)	3.00
103	Tsuyoshi Shinjo RC (Genuine Upside)	3.00
104	Travis Hafner RC (Genuine Upside)	8.00
105	Larry Barnes (Genuine Upside)	3.00
106	Jaisen Randolph RC (Genuine Upside)	3.00
107	Paul Phillips RC (Genuine Upside)	3.00
108	Erick Almonte RC (Genuine Upside)	3.00
109	Nick Punto RC (Genuine Upside)	3.00
110	Jack Wilson RC (Genuine Upside)	3.00
111	Jeremy Owens RC (Genuine Upside)	3.00
112	Esix Snead RC (Genuine Upside)	3.00
113	Jay Gibbons RC (Genuine Upside)	3.00
114	Adrian Hernandez RC (Genuine Upside)	3.00
115	Matt White RC (Genuine Upside)	3.00
116	Ryan Freel RC (Genuine Upside)	5.00
117	Martin Vargas RC (Genuine Upside)	3.00
118	Winston Abreu RC (Genuine Upside)	3.00
119	Junior Spivey RC (Genuine Upside)	3.00
120	Paxton Crawford (Genuine Upside)	3.00
121	Randy Keisler (Genuine Upside)	3.00
122	Juan Diaz RC (Genuine Upside)	3.00
123	Aaron Rowand (Genuine Upside)	4.00
124	Toby Hall (Genuine Upside)	3.00
125	Brian Cole (Genuine Upside)	3.00
126	Aubrey Huff (Genuine Upside)	4.00
127	Corey Patterson (Genuine Upside)	4.00
128	Sun-Woo Kim (Genuine Upside)	3.00
129	Jace Brewer (Genuine Upside)	3.00
130	Cesar Izturis (Genuine Upside)	3.00

@ LG (At Large)

		NM/M
Complete Set (15):		40.00
Common Player:		1.50
Inserted 1:23		
1AL	Derek Jeter	8.00
2AL	Nomar Garciaparra	5.00
3AL	Mark McGwire	5.00
4AL	Pedro Martinez	3.00
5AL	Tony Gwynn	3.00
6AL	Roger Clemens	3.00
7AL	Ivan Rodriguez	2.00
8AL	Sammy Sosa	4.00
9AL	Magglio Ordonez	4.00
10AL	Jason Giambi	2.00
11AL	Carlos Delgado	2.00
12AL	Chipper Jones	4.00
13AL	Mike Piazza	4.00
14AL	Cal Ripken Jr.	8.00
15AL	Ken Griffey Jr.	4.00

Final Cut

Final Cut cards of Ron Guidry, Don Larsen and Reggie Jackson were prepared, but not intended for release. At least a few of each have made their way into hobby channels. Because of limited numbers extant, their values cannot be determined. Some, perhaps all, of Edgar Martinez' Final Cut cards have jersey patches rather than the described glove piece.

Material Issue

	NM/M
Common Player:	4.00
Inserted 1:30	
Miguel Tejada/SP/170	6.00
Barry Bonds/SP/330	30.00
Robin Ventura	4.00
Greg Maddux	15.00
Andruw Jones/SP/135	10.00
J.D. Drew/SP/75	10.00
Chipper Jones	10.00
Tim Salmon	4.00
Edgar Martinez/SP/130	8.00
Troy Glaus	8.00
Frank Thomas	4.00
Pokey Reese	4.00
Larry Walker	4.00
Ivan Rodriguez/SP/120	10.00
Scott Rolen	8.00
Cal Ripken Jr.	30.00
Tony Gwynn	10.00
Wade Boggs	10.00
George Brett	30.00
Sean Casey	4.00
Bob Gibson	6.00
Matt Williams	6.00
Robin Yount	8.00
Ron Guidry (Not officially released.)	150.00
Reggie Jackson (Not officially released.)	250.00
Don Larsen (Not officially released.)	140.00

Genuine Coverage PLUS

	NM/M
Common Player:	5.00
Production 150 Sets	
Troy Glaus	5.00
Randy Johnson	10.00
Andruw Jones	5.00
Frank Thomas	8.00
Darin Erstad	5.00
Chipper Jones	15.00
Derek Jeter	25.00
Tony Gwynn	15.00
Barry Bonds	25.00
Cal Ripken Jr.	25.00

High Interest

		NM/M
Complete Set (15):		25.00
Common Player:		1.50
Inserted 1:23		
1HI	Derek Jeter	6.00
2HI	Nomar Garciaparra	1.50
3HI	Greg Maddux	3.00
4HI	Todd Helton	2.00
5HI	Sammy Sosa	2.50
6HI	Jeff Bagwell	1.50
7HI	Jason Giambi	1.50
8HI	Frank Thomas	2.00
9HI	Andruw Jones	1.50
10HI	Jim Edmonds	1.50
11HI	Bernie Williams	1.50
12HI	Randy Johnson	2.00
13HI	Ken Griffey Jr.	4.00
14HI	Pedro Martinez	2.00
15HI	Mark McGwire	4.00

Material Issue

	NM/M
Common Player:	5.00
Inserted 1:30	
Randy Johnson	10.00
Scott Rolen	8.00
Robin Ventura	5.00
Tony Gwynn	15.00
Troy Glaus	8.00
Kevin Millwood	5.00
Chipper Jones	15.00
Tom Glavine	8.00
Pedro Martinez/SP/60	25.00
Greg Maddux	15.00
Frank Thomas	8.00
Curt Schilling/SP/120	10.00
Edgar Martinez	5.00
Darin Erstad	5.00
J.D. Drew	5.00
Cal Ripken Jr.	30.00
Nolan Ryan	40.00
Steve Carlton	5.00

Names of the Game - Autographs

	NM/M
Common Player:	25.00
Yogi Berra	60.00
Orlando Cepeda	20.00
Rocky Colavito	60.00
Andre Dawson	20.00
Bucky Dent	20.00
Rollie Fingers	20.00
Carlton Fisk	40.00
Whitey Ford	40.00
Reggie Jackson	60.00
Randy Johnson	60.00
Chipper Jones	60.00
Harmon Killebrew	60.00
Don Mattingly	90.00
Willie McCovey	25.00
Cal Ripken Jr.	150.00
Ivan Rodriguez	40.00
Preacher Roe	35.00
Nolan Ryan	100.00
Tom Seaver	50.00
Bill Skowron	30.00
Enos Slaughter	30.00
Duke Snider	40.00

Names of the Game - Game Used

	NM/M
Common Player:	10.00
Production 50 Sets	
Yogi Berra/Bat	25.00
Orlando Cepeda/Bat	10.00
Rocky Colavito/Bat	20.00
Andre Dawson/Jsy	10.00
Bucky Dent/Bat	10.00
Rollie Fingers/Jsy	10.00
Carlton Fisk/Bat	15.00
Whitey Ford/Jsy	25.00
Jimmie Foxx/Bat	20.00
Hank Greenberg/Bat	50.00
"Catfish" Hunter/Jsy	10.00
Reggie Jackson/Jsy	
Randy Johnson/Jsy	30.00
Chipper Jones/Bat	30.00
Harmon Killebrew/Bat	25.00
Tony Lazzeri/Bat	10.00
Don Mattingly/Bat	40.00
Willie McCovey/Bat	20.00
Johnny Mize/Bat	15.00
Pee Wee Reese/Jsy	15.00
Cal Ripken Jr./Bat	60.00
Phil Rizzuto/Bat	20.00
Ivan Rodriguez/Bat	25.00
Preacher Roe/Jsy	15.00
Babe Ruth/Bat	300.00
Nolan Ryan/Jsy	50.00
Tom Seaver/Jsy	25.00
Bill Skowron/Bat	10.00
Enos Slaughter/Bat	10.00
Duke Snider/Bat	25.00
Willie Stargell/Bat	25.00
Bill Terry/Bat	10.00
Ted Williams/Bat	150.00
Hack Wilson/Bat	75.00

Pennant Aggression

		NM/M
Complete Set (10):		20.00
Inserted 1:23		
1PA	Derek Jeter	5.00
2PA	Alex Rodriguez	5.00
3PA	Nomar Garciaparra	1.50
4PA	Mark McGwire	3.00
5PA	Ken Griffey Jr.	4.00
6PA	Mike Piazza	3.00
7PA	Sammy Sosa	2.00
8PA	Barry Bonds	4.00
9PA	Chipper Jones	3.00
10PA	Pedro Martinez	2.00

Tip of the Cap

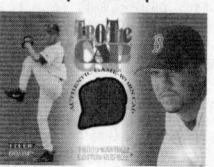

	NM/M
Common Player:	5.00
Production 150 Sets	
Barry Bonds	30.00
Eric Chavez	5.00
Shawn Green	5.00
Vladimir Guerrero	15.00
Randy Johnson	20.00
Andruw Jones	8.00
Javy Lopez	5.00
Rafael Palmeiro	10.00
Ivan Rodriguez	10.00
Miguel Tejada	8.00
Roberto Alomar	8.00
Pedro Martinez	15.00

2001 Fleer Greats of the Game

		NM/M
Complete Set (137):		50.00
Common Player:		.25
Hobby Pack (5):		10.00
Hobby Box (24):		200.00
1	Roberto Clemente	2.50
2	George "Sparky" Anderson	.25
3	Babe Ruth	4.00
4	Paul Molitor	1.00
5	Don Larsen	.25
6	Cy Young	1.00
7	Billy Martin	.50
8	Lou Brock	1.00
9	Fred Lynn	.25
10	Johnny Vander Meer	.25
11	Harmon Killebrew	1.00
12	Dave Winfield	1.00
13	Orlando Cepeda	.25
14	Johnny Mize	.75

15	Walter Johnson	1.00
16	Roy Campanella	1.00
17	Monte Irvin	.50
18	Mookie Wilson	.25
19	Elston Howard	.25
20	Walter Alston	.25
21	Rollie Fingers	.25
22	Brooks Robinson	1.00
23	Hank Greenberg	1.00
24	Maury Wills	.25
25	Rich Gossage	.25
26	Leon Day	.25
27	Jimmie Foxx	2.00
28	Alan Trammell	.50
29	Dennis Martinez	.25
30	Don Drysdale	.75
31	Bob Feller	.75
32	Jackie Robinson	3.00
33	Whitey Ford	1.00
34	Enos Slaughter	.25
35	Rod Carew	.75
36	Eddie Mathews	.25
37	Ron Cey	.25
38	Thurman Munson	1.00
39	Henry Kimbro	.25
40	Ty Cobb	3.00
41	Rocky Colavito	.50
42	Satchel Paige	1.50
43	Andre Dawson	1.00
44	Phil Rizzuto	1.00
45	Roger Maris	2.50
46	Bobby Bonds	.25
47	Joe Carter	.25
48	Christy Mathewson	.75
49	Tony Lazzeri	.25
50	Gil Hodges	.25
51	Ray Dandridge	.25
52	Gaylord Perry	.25
53	Ernie Banks	2.00
54	Lou Gehrig	3.00
55	George Kell	.25
56	Wes Parker	.25
57	Sam Jethroe	.25
58	Joe Morgan	.75
59	Steve Garvey	.50
60	Joe Torre	.75
61	Roger Craig	.25
62	Warren Spahn	1.00
63	Willie McCovey	.25
64	Cool Papa Bell	1.00
65	Frank Robinson	1.00
66	Richie Allen	.25
67	Bucky Dent	.25
68	George Foster	.25
69	Hoyt Wilhelm	.25
70	Phil Niekro	.25
71	Buck Leonard	.25
72	Preacher Roe	.25
73	Yogi Berra	1.50
74	Joe Black	.25
75	Nolan Ryan	4.00
76	Pop Lloyd	.25
77	Lester Lockett	.25
78	Paul Blair	.25
79	Ryne Sandberg	2.00
80	Bill Perkins	.25
81	Frank Howard	.25
82	Hack Wilson	1.00
83	Robin Yount	1.00
84	Harry Heilmann	.25
85	Mike Schmidt	3.00
86	Vida Blue	.25
87	George Brett	3.00
88	Juan Marichal	.50
89	Tom Seaver	1.50
90	Bill Skowron	.25
91	Don Mattingly	2.00
92	Jim Bunning	.25
93	Eddie Murray	1.00
94	Tommy Lasorda	.50
95	Pee Wee Reese	.50
96	Bill Dickey	.25
97	Ozzie Smith	1.50
98	Dale Murphy	.25
99	Artie Wilson	.25
100	Bill Terry	.25
101	Jim "Catfish" Hunter	.25
102	Don Sutton	.25
103	Luis Aparicio	.25
104	Reggie Jackson	1.50
105	Ted Radcliffe	.25
106	Carl Erskine	.25
107	Johnny Bench	2.00
108	Carl Furillo	.25
109	Stan Musial	2.00
110	Carlton Fisk	.75
111	Rube Foster	.25
112	Tony Oliva	.25
113	Hank Bauer	.25
114	Jim Rice	.25
115	Willie Mays	3.00
116	Ralph Kiner	.50
117	Al Kaline	1.00
118	Billy Williams	.25
119	Buck O'Neil	.25
120	Tony Perez	.25
121	Dave Parker	.25
122	Kirk Gibson	.25
123	Lou Piniella	.25
124	Ted Williams	4.00
125	Steve Carlton	.75
126	Dizzy Dean	.25
127	Willie Stargell	.25
128	Joe Niekro	.25
129	Lloyd Waner	.25
130	Wade Boggs	2.00
131	Wilmer Fields	.25
132	Bill Mazeroski	.50

133	Duke Snider	1.00
134	Smoky Joe Williams	.25
135	Bob Gibson	1.50
136	Jim Palmer	.75
137	Oscar Charleston	.25

Autographs

Andre Dawson *Chicago Cubs*

	NM/M
Common Player:	10.00
Inserted 1:8	
1	Richie Allen	10.00
2	George "Sparky" Anderson	10.00
3	Luis Aparicio	10.00
4	Ernie Banks/SP/250	100.00
5	Hank Bauer	10.00
6	Johnny Bench/SP/400	80.00
7	Yogi Berra/SP/500	60.00
8	Joe Black	10.00
9	Paul Blair	10.00
9a	Paul Blair/Double Signed	10.00
10	Vida Blue	10.00
11	Wade Boggs	40.00
12	Bobby Bonds	25.00
13	George Brett/SP/247	150.00
14	Lou Brock/SP/500	40.00
15	Jim Bunning	10.00
16	Rod Carew	20.00
17	Steve Carlton	25.00
18	Joe Carter	10.00
19	Orlando Cepeda	15.00
20	Ron Cey	10.00
21	Rocky Colavito	40.00
22	Roger Craig	10.00
23	Andre Dawson	15.00
24	Bucky Dent	10.00
25	Larry Doby	35.00
26	Carl Erskine	10.00
27	Bob Feller	15.00
28	Wilmer Fields	10.00
29	Rollie Fingers	10.00
30	Carlton Fisk	40.00
31	Whitey Ford	30.00
32	George Foster	10.00
33	Steve Garvey/SP/400	40.00
34	Bob Gibson	20.00
35	Kirk Gibson	20.00
36	Rich Gossage	10.00
37	Frank Howard	10.00
38	Monte Irvin	10.00
39	Reggie Jackson/SP/400	85.00
40	Sam Jethroe	10.00
41	Al Kaline	30.00
42	George Kell	15.00
43	Harmon Killebrew	30.00
44	Ralph Kiner	20.00
45	Don Larsen	15.00
46	Tommy Lasorda/SP/400	50.00
47	Lester Lockett	10.00
48	Fred Lynn	10.00
49	Juan Marichal	20.00
50	Dennis Martinez	10.00
51	Don Mattingly	75.00
52	Willie Mays/SP/100	450.00
53	Bill Mazeroski	20.00
54	Willie McCovey	20.00
55	Paul Molitor	25.00
56	Joe Morgan	10.00
57	Dale Murphy	30.00
58	Eddie Murray/SP/140	200.00
59	Stan Musial/SP/525	150.00
60	Joe Niekro	10.00
61	Phil Niekro	10.00
62	Tony Oliva	10.00
63	Buck O'Neil	40.00
64	Jim Palmer/SP/600	25.00
65	Dave Parker	10.00
66	Tony Perez	20.00
67	Gaylord Perry	10.00
68	Lou Piniella	10.00
69	Ted Radcliffe	25.00
70	Jim Rice	10.00
71	Phil Rizzuto/SP/425	50.00
72	Brooks Robinson	25.00
73	Frank Robinson	20.00
74	Preacher Roe	20.00
75	Nolan Ryan/SP/650	100.00
76	Ryne Sandberg	50.00
77	Mike Schmidt/SP/213	200.00
78	Tom Seaver	50.00
79	Bill Skowron	10.00
80	Enos Slaughter	15.00
81	Ozzie Smith	50.00
82	Duke Snider/SP/600	60.00
83	Warren Spahn	50.00

84	Willie Stargell (Redemption card only, none signed).	20.00
85	Don Sutton	10.00
86	Joe Torre/SP/500	25.00
87	Alan Trammell	15.00
88	Hoyt Wilhelm	10.00
89	Billy Williams	10.00
90	Maury Wills	10.00
91	Artie Wilson	10.00
92	Mookie Wilson	10.00
93	Dave Winfield/SP/370	50.00
94	Robin Yount/SP/400	100.00

Dodger Blues

Don Drysdale
Los Angeles Dodgers

	NM/M
Common Player:	10.00
Inserted 1:36	
(1)	Walter Alston/Jsy	10.00
(2)	Walt Alston/Uniform	10.00
(3)	Roy Campanella/Uniform/SP	100.00
(4)	Roger Craig/Jsy	10.00
(5)	Don Drysdale/Jsy	25.00
(6)	Carl Furillo/Jsy	10.00
(7)	Steve Garvey/Jsy	10.00
(8)	Gil Hodges/Uniform	20.00
(9)	Wes Parker/Bat	10.00
(10)	Wes Parker/Jsy	10.00
(11)	Pee Wee Reese/Jsy	20.00
(12)	Jackie Robinson/Uniform/SP	150.00
(13)	Preacher Roe/Jsy	20.00
(14)	Duke Snider/Bat/SP	100.00
(15)	Don Sutton/Jsy	10.00

Feel the Game Classics

	NM/M
Common Player:	5.00
Inserted 1:72	
1	Luis Aparicio/Bat	5.00
2	George Brett/Jsy	30.00
3	Lou Brock/Jsy	15.00
4	Orlando Cepeda/Bat	10.00
5	Whitey Ford/Jsy	15.00
6	Hank Greenberg/Bat	50.00
7	Elston Howard/Bat	5.00
8	"Catfish" Hunter/Jsy	8.00
9	Harmon Killebrew/Bat	15.00
10	Roger Maris/Bat	50.00
11	Eddie Mathews/Bat	15.00
12	W. McCovey/Bat/SP/200	15.00
13	Johnny Mize/Bat	5.00
14	Paul Molitor/Jsy	10.00
15	Jim Palmer/Jsy	10.00
16	Tony Perez/Bat	5.00
17	Brooks Robinson/Bat/144	25.00
18	Babe Ruth/Bat/250	200.00
19	Mike Schmidt/Jsy	25.00
20	Tom Seaver/Jsy	20.00
21	Enos Slaughter	10.00
22	Willie Stargell	10.00
23	Hack Wilson	40.00
24	Harry Heilmann	5.00

Retrospection Collection

MIKE SCHMIDT
Philadelphia Phillies

	NM/M
Complete Set (10):	20.00
Common Player:	1.00
Inserted 1:6	
1	Babe Ruth	5.00
2	Stan Musial	3.00
3	Jimmie Foxx	3.00
4	Roberto Clemente	4.00
5	Ted Williams	4.00

2001 Fleer Legacy

6	Mike Schmidt	4.00
7	Cy Young	1.50
8	Satchel Paige	2.00
9	Hank Greenberg	2.00
10	Jim Bunning	1.00

	NM/M
Complete Set (105):	
Common Player:	.50
Common (91-105):	8.00
Production 799 Sets	
Pack (5):	8.00
Box (15 + Cap):	140.00
1	Pedro J. Martinez	1.50
2	Andruw Jones	1.50
3	Mike Hampton	.50
4	Gary Sheffield	.65
5	Barry Zito	.65
6	J.D. Drew	.75
7	Charles Johnson	.50
8	David Wells	.50
9	Kazuhiro Sasaki	.50
10	Vladimir Guerrero	1.50
11	Pat Burrell	.75
12	Ruben Mateo	.50
13	Greg Maddux	2.00
14	Sean Casey	.65
15	Craig Biggio	.65
16	Bernie Williams	.65
17	Jeff Kent	.50
18	Nomar Garciaparra	1.00
19	Cal Ripken Jr.	4.00
20	Larry Walker	.50
21	Adrian Beltre	.65
22	Johnny Damon	.75
23	Rick Ankiel	.50
24	Matt Williams	.50
25	Magglio Ordonez	.50
26	Richard Hidalgo	.50
27	Robin Ventura	.50
28	Jason Kendall	.50
29	Tony Batista	.50
30	Chipper Jones	2.00
31	Jim Thome	.50
32	Kevin Brown	.50
33	Mike Mussina	.65
34	Mark McGwire	3.00
35	Darin Erstad	.75
36	Manny Ramirez	1.50
37	Bobby Higginson	.50
38	Richie Sexson	.50
39	Jason Giambi	1.00
40	Alex Rodriguez	3.00
41	Mark Grace	.65
42	Ken Griffey Jr.	2.50
43	Moises Alou	.50
44	Edgardo Alfonzo	.50
45	Phil Nevin	.50
46	Rafael Palmeiro	1.25
47	Javy Lopez	.50
48	Juan Gonzalez	1.50
49	Jermaine Dye	.50
50	Roger Clemens	2.25
51	Barry Bonds	4.00
52	Carl Everett	.50
53	Ben Sheets	.50
54	Juan Encarnacion	.50
55	Jeromy Burnitz	.50
56	Miguel Tejada	.65
57	Ben Grieve	.50
58	Randy Johnson	1.50
59	Frank Thomas	1.50
60	Preston Wilson	.50
61	Mike Piazza	2.00
62	Brian Giles	.50
63	Carlos Delgado	1.00
64	Tom Glavine	.75
65	Roberto Alomar	.65
66	Mike Sweeney	.50
67	Orlando Hernandez	.50
68	Edgar Martinez	.50
69	Tim Salmon	.75
70	Kerry Wood	1.00
71	Jack Wilson RC	3.00
72	Matt Lawton	.50
73	Scott Rolen	1.25
74	Ivan Rodriguez	1.25
75	Steve Finley	.50
76	Barry Larkin	.50
77	Jeff Bagwell	1.50
78	Derek Jeter	4.00
79	Tony Gwynn	2.00
80	Raul Mondesi	.50
81	Rafael Furcal	.50
82	Todd Helton	1.50
83	Shawn Green	.75
84	Tim Hudson	.50
85	Jim Edmonds	.50
86	Troy Glaus	1.50
87	Sammy Sosa	2.50
88	Cliff Floyd	.50
89	Jose Vidro	.50
90	Bobby Abreu	.50
91	Drew Henson/Auto. RC	15.00
92	Andy Morales/Auto. RC	8.00

93	Wilson Betemit/Auto. RC	20.00
94	Elpidio Guzman RC	8.00
95	Esix Snead RC	8.00
96	Winston Abreu RC	8.00
97	Jeremy Owens RC	8.00
99	Junior Spivey RC	10.00
100	Jaisen Randolph RC	8.00
101	Ichiro Suzuki RC	50.00
102	Albert Pujols/499 RC	150.00
102	Albert Pujols/Auto./300 RC	350.00
103	Tsuyoshi Shinjo RC	10.00
104	Jay Gibbons RC	10.00
105	Juan Uribe RC	10.00

Ultimate Legacy

Stars (1-90):	3-5X
Rookies (91-100):	.3-.75X
Rookies (101-105):	.75-1X
Production 250 Sets	

Autographed MLB Fitted Cap

	NM/M
Common Player:	25.00
Inserted one per box	
Edgardo Alfonzo	25.00
Roberto Alomar	50.00
Ernie Banks/100	125.00
Adrian Beltre	40.00
Johnny Bench/100	125.00
Lance Berkman	60.00
Yogi Berra/200	120.00
Craig Biggio	40.00
Barry Bonds	250.00
Jeromy Burnitz	25.00
Pat Burrell	40.00
Steve Carlton	40.00
Sean Casey	25.00
Orlando Cepeda	30.00
Eric Chavez	25.00
Tony Clark	25.00
Roger Clemens/100	200.00
Johnny Damon	60.00
Dom DiMaggio/200	75.00
J.D. Drew	40.00
Jermaine Dye	40.00
Darin Erstad	25.00
Carlton Fisk/150	80.00
Rafael Furcal	40.00
Nomar Garciaparra/150	120.00
Jason Giambi	50.00
Troy Glaus	40.00
Tom Glavine	60.00
Juan Gonzalez	40.00
Luis Gonzalez	30.00
Tony Gwynn	85.00
Drew Henson	25.00
Derek Jeter	250.00
Andruw Jones	40.00
David Justice	30.00
Paul Konerko	40.00
Don Mattingly	150.00
Willie McCovey	30.00
Paul Molitor	50.00
Stan Musial/200	125.00
Mike Mussina	50.00
Jim Palmer	40.00
Corey Patterson	25.00
Kirby Puckett/200	125.00
Cal Ripken/200	200.00
Brooks Robinson	60.00
Ivan Rodriguez	50.00
Scott Rolen	50.00
Nolan Ryan/150	200.00
Mike Schmidt/150	125.00
Tom Seaver/100	125.00
Ben Sheets	40.00
Ozzie Smith	100.00
Duke Snider	50.00
Miguel Tejada	50.00
Jim Thome	60.00
Matt Williams	25.00
Dave Winfield/150	75.00
Carl Yastrzemski/150	100.00
Robin Yount	100.00
Barry Zito	40.00

Hit Kings

	NM/M
Common Player:	5.00
Inserted 1:13	
Stan Musial	15.00
Barry Bonds	25.00
Corey Patterson	5.00
Shawn Green	5.00
Ralph Kiner	5.00
Troy O'Leary	5.00

Ivan Rodriguez	5.00
Jose Vidro	5.00
Carlos Beltran	8.00
Jose Canseco	5.00
Juan Encarnacion	5.00
Reggie Jackson	10.00
Ruben Mateo	5.00
Juan Pierre	5.00
Tim Salmon	5.00
Adrian Beltre	5.00
Roger Cedeno	5.00
Troy Glaus	5.00
Jason Kendall	5.00
Rick Ankiel	8.00
Andruw Jones	5.00
Jim Thome	5.00
Tony Batista	5.00
George Brett	20.00
Vladimir Guerrero	10.00
Billy Martin	5.00
Magglio Ordonez	5.00
Johnny Damon	8.00

Hit Kings Short Prints

	NM/M
Common Player:	15.00
Production 100 Sets	
Robin Yount	20.00
Scott Rolen	15.00
Johnny Bench	25.00
Steve Garvey	15.00
Joe Morgan	15.00
Frank Thomas	20.00
Eddie Mathews	20.00
Tony Gwynn	25.00
Roger Clemens	40.00
Wade Boggs	25.00

Hot Gloves

	NM/M
Inserted 1:180	
1HG	Andruw Jones	15.00
2HG	Mike Mussina	15.00
3HG	Roberto Alomar	15.00
4HG	Tony Gwynn	30.00
5HG	Bernie Williams	15.00
6HG	Ivan Rodriguez	15.00
7HG	Ken Griffey Jr.	40.00
8HG	Robin Ventura	15.00
9HG	Cal Ripken Jr.	75.00
10HG	Jeff Bagwell	50.00
11HG	Mark McGwire	50.00
12HG	Rafael Palmeiro	15.00
13HG	Scott Rolen	15.00
14HG	Barry Bonds	60.00
15HG	Greg Maddux	40.00

MLB Game Issue - Base

	NM/M
Common Player:	4.00
Inserted 1:52	
1GI	Mark McGwire	15.00
2GI	Ken Griffey Jr.	10.00
3GI	Sammy Sosa	8.00
4GI	Mike Piazza	10.00
5GI	Alex Rodriguez	15.00
6GI	Derek Jeter	20.00

#	Player	Price
7GI	Cal Ripken Jr.	20.00
8GI	Todd Helton	6.00
9GI	Tony Gwynn	8.00
10GI	Chipper Jones	10.00
11GI	Frank Thomas	6.00
12GI	Barry Bonds	20.00
13GI	Troy Glaus	4.00
14GI	Pat Burrell	4.00
15GI	Scott Rolen	5.00

MLB Game Issue - Base/Ball

	NM/M
Common Player:	10.00
Production 100 Sets	
Mark McGwire	50.00
Ken Griffey Jr.	40.00
Sammy Sosa	25.00
Mike Piazza	40.00
Alex Rodriguez	50.00
Derek Jeter	60.00
Cal Ripken Jr.	60.00
Todd Helton	15.00
Tony Gwynn	25.00
Chipper Jones	25.00
Frank Thomas	15.00
Barry Bonds	60.00
Troy Glaus	10.00
Pat Burrell	10.00
Scott Rolen	12.50

MLB Game Issue - Base/Ball/Jersey

	NM/M
Common Card:	25.00
Production 50 Sets	
Derek Jeter	100.00
Cal Ripken Jr.	100.00
Todd Helton	30.00
Tony Gwynn	50.00
Chipper Jones	50.00
Frank Thomas	30.00
Barry Bonds	100.00
Troy Glaus	25.00
Pat Burrell	25.00
Scott Rolen	30.00

Tailor Made

	NM/M
Common Player:	4.00
Inserted 1:15	
2TM Cal Ripken Jr.	40.00
3TM Orlando Cepeda	6.00
4TM Willie McCovey	6.00
5TM Dave Winfield	6.00
6TM Don Mattingly	25.00
7TM Nolan Ryan	40.00
8TM Manny Ramirez	8.00
9TM Edgardo Alfonzo	4.00
10TM Rondell White	4.00
11TM Lou Piniella	4.00
12TM Ivan Rodriguez	8.00
13TM J.D. Drew	4.00
14TM Barry Bonds	40.00
15TM Greg Maddux	15.00
16TM Rick Ankiel	6.00
17TM Carlos Delgado	8.00
18TM Kevin Brown	4.00
20TM Reggie Jackson	10.00
21TM Shawn Green	4.00
22TM Jason Kendall	4.00
23TM Rafael Palmeiro	8.00
24TM Todd Helton	8.00
25TM Curt Schilling	6.00

2001 Fleer Platinum

JEFF BAGWELL / FIRST BASE

	NM/M
Complete Set (301):	140.00

		Price
	Common Player:	.15
	Common SP (251-300):	1.00
	Inserted 1:6	
	Card #301 Production 1,500	
	Pack (10):	5.00
	Box (24):	100.00
1	Bobby Abreu	.15
2	Brad Radke	.15
3	Bill Mueller	.15
4	Adam Eaton	.15
5	Antonio Alfonseca	.15
6	Manny Ramirez	.75
7	Adam Kennedy	.15
8	Jose Valentin	.15
9	Jaret Wright	.15
10	Aramis Ramirez	.15
11	Jeff Kent	.15
12	Juan Encarnacion	.15
13	Sandy Alomar Jr.	.15
14	Joe Randa	.15
15	Darryl Kile	.15
16	Darren Dreifort	.15
17	Matt Kinney	.15
18	Pokey Reese	.15
19	Ryan Klesko	.15
20	Shawn Estes	.15
21	Moises Alou	.15
22	Edgar Renteria	.15
23	Chuck Knoblauch	.15
24	Carl Everett	.15
25	Garret Anderson	.15
26	Shane Reynolds	.15
27	Billy Koch	.15
28	Carlos Febles	.15
29	Brian Anderson	.15
30	Armando Rios	.15
31	Ryan Kohlmeier	.15
32	Steve Finley	.15
33	Brady Anderson	.15
34	Cal Ripken Jr.	2.50
35	Paul Konerko	.15
36	Chuck Finley	.15
37	Rick Ankiel	.25
38	Mariano Rivera	.25
39	Corey Koskie	.15
40	Cliff Floyd	.15
41	Kevin Appier	.15
42	Henry Rodriguez	.15
43	Mark Kotsay	.15
44	Brook Fordyce	.15
45	Brad Ausmus	.15
46	Alfonso Soriano	.50
47	Ray Lankford	.15
48	Keith Foulke	.15
49	Rich Aurilia	.15
50	Alex Rodriguez	2.00
51	Eric Byrnes	.15
52	Travis Fryman	.15
53	Jeff Bagwell	.75
54	Scott Rolen	.65
55	Matt Lawton	.15
56	Brad Fullmer	.15
57	Tony Batista	.15
58	Nate Rolison	.15
59	Carlos Lee	.15
60	Rafael Furcal	.15
61	Jay Bell	.15
62	Jimmy Rollins	.25
63	Derek Lee	.15
64	Andres Galarraga	.15
65	Derek Bell	.15
66	Tim Salmon	.25
67	Travis Lee	.15
68	Kevin Millwood	.15
69	Albert Belle	.15
70	Kazuhiro Sasaki	.15
71	Al Leiter	.15
72	Britt Reames	.15
73	Carlos Beltran	.45
74	Curt Schilling	.50
75	Curtis Leskanic	.15
76	Jeremy Giambi	.15
77	Adrian Beltre	.35
78	David Segui	.15
79	Mike Lieberthal	.15
80	Brian Giles	.15
81	Marvin Benard	.15
82	Aaron Sele	.15
83	Kenny Lofton	.15
84	Doug Glanville	.15
85	Kris Benson	.15
86	Richie Sexson	.15
87	Javy Lopez	.40
88	Doug Mientkiewicz	.15
89	Peter Bergeron	.15
90	Gary Sheffield	.40
91	Derek Lowe	.15
92	Tom Glavine	.40
93	Lance Berkman	.15
94	Chris Singleton	.15
95	Mike Lowell	.25
96	Luis Gonzalez	.30
97	Dante Bichette	.15
98	Mike Sirotka	.15
99	Julio Lugo	.15
100	Juan Gonzalez	.75
101	Craig Biggio	.15
102	Armando Benitez	.15
103	Greg Maddux	1.00
104	Mark Grace	.25
105	John Smoltz	.15
106	J.T. Snow	.15
107	Al Martin	.15
108	Danny Graves	.15
109	Barry Bonds	2.50
110	Lee Stevens	.15
111	Pedro Martinez	.75
112	Shawn Green	.40
113	Bret Boone	.15
114	Matt Stairs	.15
115	Tino Martinez	.15
116	Rusty Greer	.15
117	Mike Bordick	.15
118	Garrett Stephenson	.15
119	Edgar Martinez	.15
120	Ben Grieve	.15
121	Milton Bradley	.15
122	Aaron Boone	.15
123	Ruben Mateo	.15
124	Ken Griffey Jr.	1.50
125	Russell Branyan	.15
126	Shannon Stewart	.15
127	Fred McGriff	.15
128	Ben Petrick	.15
129	Kevin Brown	.15
130	B.J. Surhoff	.15
131	Mark McGwire	2.00
132	Carlos Guillen	.15
133	Adrian Brown	.15
134	Mike Sweeney	.15
135	Eric Milton	.15
136	Cristian Guzman	.15
137	Ellis Burks	.15
138	Fernando Tatis	.15
139	Ben Molina	.15
140	Tony Gwynn	1.00
141	Jeromy Burnitz	.15
142	Miguel Tejada	.25
143	Raul Mondesi	.15
144	Jeffrey Hammonds	.15
145	Pat Burrell	.40
146	Frank Thomas	.75
147	Eric Munson	.15
148	Mike Hampton	.15
149	Mike Cameron	.15
150	Jim Thome	.50
151	Mike Mussina	.15
152	Rick Helling	.15
153	Ken Caminiti	.15
154	John Vander Wal	.15
155	Denny Neagle	.15
156	Robb Nen	.15
157	Jose Canseco	.50
158	Mo Vaughn	.15
159	Phil Nevin	.15
160	Pat Hentgen	.15
161	Sean Casey	.25
162	Greg Vaughn	.15
163	Trot Nixon	.15
164	Roberto Hernandez	.15
165	Vinny Castilla	.15
166	Robin Ventura	.15
167	Alex Ochoa	.15
168	Orlando Hernandez	.15
169	Luis Castillo	.15
170	Quilvio Veras	.15
171	Troy O'Leary	.15
172	Livan Hernandez	.15
173	Roger Cedeno	.15
174	Jose Vidro	.15
175	John Olerud	.15
176	Richard Hidalgo	.15
177	Eric Chavez	.25
178	Fernando Vina	.15
179	Chris Stynes	.15
180	Bobby Higginson	.15
181	Bruce Chen	.15
182	Omar Vizquel	.15
183	Rey Ordonez	.15
184	Trevor Hoffman	.15
185	Jeff Cirillo	.15
186	Billy Wagner	.15
187	David Ortiz	.15
188	Tim Hudson	.40
189	Tony Clark	.15
190	Larry Walker	.15
191	Eric Owens	.15
192	Aubrey Huff	.15
193	Royce Clayton	.15
194	Todd Walker	.15
195	Rafael Palmeiro	.65
196	Todd Hundley	.15
197	Roger Clemens	1.50
198	Jeff Weaver	.15
199	Dean Palmer	.15
200	Geoff Jenkins	.15
201	Matt Clement	.15
202	David Wells	.15
203	Chan Ho Park	.15
204	Hideo Nomo	.65
205	Bartolo Colon	.15
206	John Wetteland	.15
207	Corey Patterson	.15
208	Freddy Garcia	.15
209	David Cone	.15
210	Rondell White	.15
211	Carl Pavano	.15
212	Charles Johnson	.15
213	Ron Coomer	.15
214	Matt Williams	.15
215	Jay Payton	.15
216	Nick Johnson	.15
217	Deivi Cruz	.15
218	Scott Elarton	.15
219	Neifi Perez	.15
220	Jason Isringhausen	.15
221	Jose Cruz	.15
222	Gerald Williams	.15
223	Timo Perez	.15
224	Damion Easley	.15
225	Jeff D'Amico (Photo actually Jamey Wright.)	.15
226	Preston Wilson	.15
227	Robert Person	.15
228	Jacque Jones	.15
229	Johnny Damon	.25
230	Tony Womack	.15
231	Adam Piatt	.15
232	Brian Jordan	.15
233	Ben Davis	.15
234	Kerry Wood	.50
235	Mike Piazza	1.50
236	David Justice	.15
237	Dave Veres	.15
238	Eric Young	.15
239	Juan Pierre	.15
240	Gabe Kapler	.15
241	Ryan Dempster	.15
242	Dmitri Young	.15
243	Jorge Posada	.35
244	Eric Karros	.15
245	J.D. Drew	.25
246	Todd Zeile	.15
247	Mark Quinn	.15
248	Kenny Kelly	.15
249	Jermaine Dye	.15
250	Barry Zito	.30
251	Jason Hart, Larry Barnes	1.00
252	Ichiro Suzuki RC, Elpidio Guzman	20.00
253	Tsuyoshi Shinjo RC, Brian Cole	1.00
254	John Barnes, Adrian Hernandez RC	1.00
255	Jason Tyner, Jace Brewer	1.00
256	Brian Buchanan, Luis Rivas	1.00
257	Brent Abernathy, Jose Ortiz	1.00
258	Marcus Giles, Keith Ginter	1.00
259	Tike Redman, Jaisen Randolph RC	1.00
260	Dane Sardinha, David Espinosa	1.00
261	Josh Beckett, Craig House	1.00
262	Jack Cust, Hiram Bocachica	1.00
263	Alex Escobar, Esix Snead RC	1.00
264	Chris Richard, Vernon Wells	1.00
265	Pedro Feliz, Xavier Nady	1.00
266	Brandon Inge, Joe Crede	1.00
267	Ben Sheets, Roy Oswalt	1.00
268	Drew Henson RC, Andy Morales RC	2.00
269	C.C. Sabathia, Justin Miller	1.00
270	David Eckstein, Jason Gabrowski	1.00
271	Dee Brown, Chris Wakeland	1.00
272	Junior Spivey RC, Alex Cintron	1.00
273	Elvis Pena, Juan Uribe RC	1.00
274	Carlos Pena, Jason Romano	1.00
275	Winston Abreu RC, Wilson Betemit RC	1.50
276	Jose Mieses RC, Nick Neugebauer	1.00
277	Shea Hillenbrand, Dernell Stenson	1.00
278	Jared Sandberg, Toby Hall	1.00
279	Jay Gibbons RC, Ivanon Coffie	1.00
280	Pablo Ozuna, Santiago Perez	1.00
281	Nomar Garciaparra/AS	2.00
282	Derek Jeter/AS	6.00
283	Jason Giambi/AS	2.50
284	Magglio Ordonez/AS	2.00
285	Ivan Rodriguez/AS	2.00
286	Troy Glaus/AS	1.50
287	Carlos Delgado/AS	1.50
288	Darin Erstad/AS	1.00
289	Bernie Williams/AS	1.50
290	Roberto Alomar/AS	1.50
291	Barry Larkin/AS	1.50
292	Chipper Jones/AS	2.00
293	Vladimir Guerrero/AS	2.00
294	Sammy Sosa/AS	2.50
295	Todd Helton/AS	1.50
296	Randy Johnson/AS	3.00
297	Jason Kendall/AS	1.00
298	Jim Edmonds/AS	1.50
299	Andruw Jones/AS	2.00
300	Edgardo Alfonzo/AS	1.00
301	Albert Pujols RC, Donaldo Mendez RC	80.00

Platinum Edition

Cards (1-250):	4-8X
Production 201 Sets	
SP's (251-280):	8-20X

AMERICAN LEAGUE ALL-STAR — Derek Jeter

21 / 21

SP's (281-300):	5-10X
SP Production 21 Sets	

Classic Combinations

	NM/M
Common Card:	4.00
#1-10 Numbered to 250	
11-20 Numbered to 500	
21-30 Numbered to 1,000	
31-40 Numbered to 2,000	
1CC Derek Jeter, Alex Rodriguez	20.00
2CC Willie Mays, Willie McCovey	15.00
3CC Lou Gehrig, Babe Ruth	20.00
4CC Mark McGwire, Ken Griffey Jr.	15.00
5CC Johnny Bench, Roy Campanella	10.00
6CC Ted Williams, Nomar Garciaparra	20.00
7CC Yogi Berra, Mike Piazza	15.00
8CC Ernie Banks, Sammy Sosa	12.00
9CC Nolan Ryan, Randy Johnson	25.00
10CC Roberto Clemente, Vladimir Guerrero	15.00
11CC Lou Gehrig, Stan Musial	15.00
12CC Bill Mazeroski, Roberto Clemente	10.00
13CC Ernie Banks, Alex Rodriguez	10.00
14CC Phil Rizzuto, Derek Jeter	10.00
15CC Mike Piazza, Johnny Bench	8.00
16CC Mark McGwire, Sammy Sosa	10.00
17CC Ted Williams, Tony Gwynn	12.00
18CC Eddie Mathews, Mike Schmidt	10.00
19CC Barry Bonds, Willie Mays	10.00
20CC Nolan Ryan, Pedro Martinez	15.00
21CC Barry Bonds, Ken Griffey Jr.	10.00
22CC Willie McCovey, Reggie Jackson	5.00
23CC Roberto Clemente, Sammy Sosa	8.00
24CC Willie Mays, Ernie Banks	8.00
25CC Eddie Mathews, Chipper Jones	5.00
26CC Mike Schmidt, Brooks Robinson	6.00
27CC Stan Musial, Mark McGwire	8.00
28CC Ted Williams, Roger Maris	8.00
29CC Yogi Berra, Roy Campanella	5.00
30CC Johnny Bench, Tony Perez	5.00
31CC Bill Mazeroski, Joe Carter	3.00
32CC Mike Piazza, Roy Campanella	5.00
33CC Ernie Banks, Craig Biggio	4.00
34CC Frank Thomas, Brooks Robinson	4.00
35CC Mike Schmidt, Scott Rolen	5.00
36CC Roger Maris, Mark McGwire	10.00
37CC Stan Musial, Tony Gwynn	4.00
38CC Ted Williams, Bill Terry	6.00
39CC Derek Jeter, Reggie Jackson	6.00
40CC Roger Maris, Bill Dickey	4.00

Classic Combinations Memorabilia

	NM/M
Production 25 Sets	
1 Yogi Berra, Bill Dickey	75.00
2 Yogi Berra, Roy Campanella	100.00
3 Roberto Clemente, Vladimir Guerrero	150.00
4 Eddie Mathews, Chipper Jones	80.00
5 Willie McCovey, Reggie Jackson	75.00
6 Phil Rizzuto, Derek Jeter	180.00
7 Brooks Robinson, Frank Robinson	75.00
8 Brooks Robinson, Mike Schmidt	120.00
9 Mike Schmidt, Scott Rolen	100.00
10 Ted Williams, Bill Terry	200.00
11 Ted Williams, Tony Gwynn	250.00

Grandstand Greats

	NM/M
Complete Set (20):	25.00
Common Player:	1.00
Inserted 1:12	
1GG Chipper Jones	2.00
2GG Alex Rodriguez	3.00
3GG Jeff Bagwell	1.00
4GG Troy Glaus	1.00
5GG Manny Ramirez	1.50
6GG Derek Jeter	4.00
7GG Tony Gwynn	2.00
8GG Greg Maddux	2.00
9GG Nomar Garciaparra	1.50
10GG Sammy Sosa	1.50
11GG Mike Piazza	2.00
12GG Barry Bonds	2.00
13GG Mark McGwire	2.50
14GG Vladimir Guerrero	1.50
15GG Ivan Rodriguez	1.50
16GG Ken Griffey Jr.	2.50
17GG Todd Helton	1.50
18GG Cal Ripken Jr.	4.00
19GG Pedro Martinez	1.50
20GG Frank Thomas	1.50

Nameplates

	NM/M
Common Player:	15.00
Inserted 1:12	
Cal Ripken/19	200.00
Cal Ripken/21	200.00
Cal Ripken/23	200.00
Cal Ripken/110	100.00
Randy Johnson/99	40.00
Nolan Ryan/40	200.00
Javy Lopez/49	25.00
Frank Thomas/35	40.00
Frank Thomas/75	30.00
Frank Thomas/80	30.00
Jeffrey Hammonds/135	15.00
Larry Walker/79	15.00
Larry Walker/85	15.00
Dave Winfield/80	20.00
Vladimir Guerrero/80	25.00
Vladimir Guerrero/80	25.00
Kevin Millwood/130	15.00
Mike Mussina/91	25.00
Edgar Martinez/87	25.00
Edgar Martinez/120	20.00
Scott Rolen/65	30.00
Ivan Rodriguez/177	25.00
Manny Ramirez/75	25.00
Manny Ramirez/105	25.00
J.D. Drew/170	15.00
Greg Maddux/180	50.00
Chipper Jones/95	40.00
Carlos Beltran/90	15.00
Adrian Beltre	15.00
Matt Williams/175	15.00
Curt Schilling	15.00
Pedro Martinez/120	30.00
Robin Ventura/99	15.00
Tom Glavine/125	15.00
Tony Gwynn/35	75.00
Tony Gwynn/65	40.00

Tony Gwynn/70	40.00
Troy Glaus/85	20.00
Sean Casey/21	25.00
Darin Erstad/39	25.00
Stan Musial/30	150.00

National Patch Time

	NM/M
Common Player:	4.00
Inserted 1:24 H	
Tony Gwynn	8.00
Manny Ramirez	6.00
Freddy Garcia	4.00
Rondell White	4.00
Ivan Rodriguez	5.00
Brady Anderson	4.00
Adam Piatt	4.00
Carl Everett	4.00
Magglio Ordonez	5.00
Edgardo Alfonzo	4.00
Jason Kendall	4.00
Greg Maddux	8.00
Cal Ripken Jr.	30.00
Fred McGriff	4.00
Pedro Martinez	6.00
Roger Clemens	10.00
Wade Boggs	8.00
George Brett	15.00
Ozzie Smith	8.00
Dave Winfield	6.00
Tom Seaver	6.00
Rollie Fingers	4.00
Mike Schmidt	15.00
Eddie Murray	6.00
Nolan Ryan	30.00
Jeff Cirillo	4.00
Mike Mussina	5.00

Rack Pack Autographs

	NM/M
Common Player:	5.00
Hank Aaron/1997/90	200.00
Roger Clemens/	
1998/125	100.00
Jose Cruz Jr./1997	5.00
Bob Gibson/1998/300	25.00
Ben Grieve/100	6.00
Tony Gwynn/1998/125	50.00
Wes Helms/1997	5.00
Harmon Killebrew/	
1998/300	30.00
Paul Konerko/135	20.00
Willie Mays/1997/115	125.00
Willie Mays/1998/120	125.00
Kirby Puckett/1997/105	75.00
Brooks Robinson/	
1998/40	75.00
Frank Robinson/	
1998/115	20.00
Scott Rolen/1998/150	25.00
Alex Rodriguez/	
1997/94	100.00
Alex Rodriguez/	
1998/150	75.00

Tickets

Complete Set (44):	
Common Player:	

Tickets Autographs

Complete Set (9):	
Common Player:	

20th Anniversary Reprints

	NM/M
Complete Set (18):	25.00
Common Player:	.50
Inserted 1:8	
1AR Cal Ripken Jr.	4.00
2AR Wade Boggs	1.50
3AR Ryne Sandberg	1.50
4AR Tony Gwynn	1.50
5AR Don Mattingly	3.00
6AR Roger Clemens	2.00
7AR Kirby Puckett	1.50
8AR Jose Canseco	.75
9AR Barry Bonds	1.00

10AR Ken Griffey Jr.	2.50
11AR Sammy Sosa	2.50
12AR Ivan Rodriguez	.75
13AR Jeff Bagwell	1.00
14AR J.D. Drew	.75
15AR Troy Glaus	1.00
16AR Rick Ankiel	.50
17AR Xavier Nady	.50
18AR Jose Ortiz	.50

2001 Fleer Platinum RC

	NM/M
Complete Set (300):	150.00
Common Player:	.15
Common (502-601):	1.00
Inserted 1:3 Hobby	
Pack (10):	7.00
Box (24):	140.00
302 Shawn Wooten	.15
303 Todd Walker	.15
304 Brian Buchanan	.15
305 Jim Edmonds	.25
306 Jarrod Washburn	.15
307 Jose Rijo	.15
308 Tim Raines	.15
309 Matt Morris	.15
310 Troy Glaus	.40
311 Barry Larkin	.40
312 Javier Vazquez	.15
313 Placido Polanco	.15
314 Darin Erstad	.25
315 Marty Cordova	.15
316 Vladimir Guerrero	.75
317 Kerry Robinson	.15
318 Byung-Hyun Kim	.15
319 C.C. Sabathia	.15
320 Edgardo Alfonzo	.15
321 Jason Tyner	.15
322 Reggie Sanders	.15
323 Roberto Alomar	.50
324 Matt Lawton	.15
325 Brent Abernathy	.15
326 Randy Johnson	.75
327 Todd Helton	.75
328 Andy Pettitte	.40
329 Josh Beckett	.50
330 Mark DeRosa	.15
331 Jose Ortiz	.15
332 Derek Jeter	2.00
333 Toby Hall	.15
334 Wes Helms	.15
335 Jose Macias	.15
336 Bernie Williams	.50
337 Ivan Rodriguez	.75
338 Chipper Jones	1.50
339 Brandon Inge	.15
340 Jason Giambi	.75
341 Frank Catalanotto	.15
342 Andruw Jones	.50
343 Carlos Hernandez RC	.40
344 Jermaine Dye	.15
345 Mike Lamb	.15
346 Ken Caminiti	.15
347 A.J. Burnett	.15
348 Terrence Long	.15
349 Ruben Sierra	.15
350 Marcus Giles	.15
351 Wade Miller	.15
352 Mark Mulder	.25
353 Carlos Delgado	.50
354 Chris Richard	.15
355 Daryle Ward	.15
356 Brad Penny	.15
357 Vernon Wells	.25
358 Jason Johnson	.15
359 Tim Redding	.15
360 Marlon Anderson	.15
361 Carlos Pena	.15

362 Nomar Garciaparra	.75
363 Roy Oswalt	.40
364 Todd Ritchie	.15
365 Jose Mesa	.15
366 Shea Hillenbrand	.15
367 Dee Brown	.15
368 Jason Kendall	.25
369 Vinny Castilla	.15
370 Fred McGriff	.25
371 Neifi Perez	.15
372 Xavier Nady	.15
373 Abraham Nunez	.15
374 Jon Lieber	.15
375 Paul LoDuca	.15
376 Bubba Trammell	.15
377 Brady Clark	.15
378 Joel Pineiro	.15
379 Mark Grudzielanek	.15
380 D'Angelo Jimenez	.15
381 Junior Herndon	.15
382 Magglio Ordonez	.40
383 Ben Sheets	.25
384 John Vander Wal	.15
385 Pedro Astacio	.15
386 Jose Canseco	.40
387 Jose Hernandez	.15
388 Eric Davis	.15
389 Sammy Sosa	1.00
390 Mark Buehrle	.15
391 Mark Loretta	.15
392 Andres Galarraga	.25
393 Scott Spiezio	.15
394 Joe Crede	.15
395 Luis Rivas	.15
396 David Bell	.15
397 Einar Diaz	.15
398 Adam Dunn	.75
399 A.J. Pierzynski	.15
400 Jamie Moyer	.15
401 Nick Johnson	.15
402 Freddy Garcia	4.00
403 Hideo Nomo	.40
404 Mark Mulder	.25
405 Steve Sparks	.15
406 Mariano Rivera	.25
407 Mark Buehrle,	
Mike Mussina	.25
408 Randy Johnson	.50
409 Randy Johnson	.50
410 Curt Schilling	.25
411 Matt Morris	.15
412 Greg Maddux	.75
413 Robb Nen	.15
414 Randy Johnson	.50
415 Barry Bonds	1.00
416 Jason Giambi	.40
417 Ichiro Suzuki	2.50
418 Ichiro Suzuki	2.50
419 Alex Rodriguez	1.00
420 Bret Boone	.25
421 Ichiro Suzuki	2.50
422 Alex Rodriguez	1.00
423 Jason Giambi	.40
424 Alex Rodriguez	1.00
425 Larry Walker	.25
426 Rich Aurilia	.15
427 Barry Bonds	1.00
428 Sammy Sosa	.75
429 Jimmy Rollins,	
Juan Pierre	.25
430 Sammy Sosa	.75
431 Lance Berkman	.25
432 Sammy Sosa	.75
433 Carlos Delgado	.25
434 Alex Rodriguez	1.00
435 Greg Vaughn	.15
436 Albert Pujols	10.00
437 Ichiro Suzuki	2.50
438 Barry Bonds	1.00
439 Phil Nevin	.15
440 Brian Giles	.25
441 Bobby Abreu	.25
442 Jason Giambi	.40
443 Derek Jeter	1.00
444 Mike Piazza	.75
445 Vladimir Guerrero	.50
446 Corey Koskie	.15
447 Richie Sexson	.25
448 Shawn Green	.25
449 Mike Sweeney	.15
450 Jeff Bagwell	.50
451 Cliff Floyd	.15
452 Roger Cedeno	.15
453 Todd Helton	.40
454 Juan Gonzalez	.30
455 Sean Casey	.15
456 Magglio Ordonez	.25
457 Sammy Sosa	.75
458 Manny Ramirez	.40
459 Jeff Conine	.15
460 Chipper Jones	.50
461 Luis Gonzalez	.25
462 Troy Glaus	.25
463 Ivan Rodriguez	.40
464 Luis Gonzalez, Jack Cust	.25
465 Jim Thome,	
C.C. Sabathia	.25
466 Jason Hart,	
Jason Giambi	.25
467 Jeff Bagwell, Roy Oswalt	.30
468 Sammy Sosa,	
Corey Patterson	.50
469 Mike Piazza,	
Alex Escobar	.75
470 Ken Griffey Jr.,	
Adam Dunn	.75
Roger Clemens,	
Nick Johnson	.75

471 Cliff Floyd, Josh Beckett	.15
472 Cal Ripken Jr.,	
Jerry Hairston Jr.	.75
473 Phil Nevin, Xavier Nady	.15
474 Scott Rolen,	
Jimmy Rollins	.40
475 Barry Larkin,	
David Espinosa	.25
476 Larry Walker, Jose Ortiz	.15
477 Chipper Jones,	
Marcus Giles	.40
478 Craig Biggio, Keith Ginter	.15
479 Magglio Ordonez,	
Aaron Rowand	.25
480 Alex Rodriguez,	
Carlos Pena	.75
481 Derek Jeter,	
Alfonso Soriano	.75
482 Curt Schilling	
(Post Season Glory)	.20
483-488 (Post Season Glory)	.25
489 Rudolph Giuliani	
(Post Season Glory)	.50
490 George Bush	
(Post Season Glory)	.50
491-493 (Post Season Glory)	.25
494 Derek Jeter	
(Post Season Glory)	.75
495-501 (Post Season Glory)	.25
502 Josh Fogg RC	1.00
503 Elpidio Guzman RC	1.00
504 Corky Miller RC	1.00
505 Cesar Crespo RC	1.00
506 Carlos Garcia RC	1.00
507 Carlos Valderrama RC	1.00
508 Joe Kennedy RC	1.00
509 Henry Mateo RC	1.00
510 Brandon Duckworth RC	1.00
511 Ichiro Suzuki	15.00
512 Zach Day RC	1.00
513 Ryan Freel RC	1.50
514 Brian Lawrence RC	1.00
515 Alexis Gomez RC	1.00
516 Will Ohman RC	1.00
517 Juan Diaz RC	1.00
518 Juan Moreno RC	1.00
519 Rob Mackowiak RC	1.00
520 Horacio Ramirez RC	1.50
521 Albert Pujols	75.00
522 Tsuyoshi Shinjo	1.00
523 Ryan Drese RC	1.00
524 Angel Berroa RC	1.00
525 Josh Towers RC	2.50
526 Junior Spivey	1.00
527 Greg Miller RC	1.00
528 Esix Snead RC	1.00
529 Mark Prior RC	5.00
530 Drew Henson	1.00
531 Brian Reith RC	1.00
532 Andres Torres RC	1.00
533 Casey Fossum RC	1.00
534 Wilmy Caceres RC	1.00
535 Matt White RC	1.00
536 Wilkin Ruan RC	1.00
537 Rick Bauer RC	1.00
538 Morgan Ensberg RC	1.00
539 Geronimo Gil RC	1.00
540 Dewon Brazelton RC	1.00
541 Johnny Estrada RC	1.50
542 Claudio Vargas RC	1.00
543 Donaldo Mendez RC	1.00
544 Kyle Lohse RC	2.00
545 Nate Frese RC	1.00
546 Christian Parker RC	1.00
547 Blaine Neal RC	1.00
548 Travis Hafner RC	4.00
549 Billy Sylvester RC	1.00
550 Adam Pettyjohn	1.00
551 Bill Ortega	1.00
552 Jose Acevedo RC	1.00
553 Steve Green RC	1.00
554 Jay Gibbons RC	1.00
555 Bert Snow RC	1.00
556 Erick Almonte RC	1.00
557 Jeremy Owens RC	1.00
558 Sean Douglass RC	1.00
559 Jason Smith RC	1.00
560 Ricardo Rodriguez RC	1.00
561 Mark Teixeira RC	15.00
562 Tyler Walker RC	1.00
563 Juan Uribe RC	1.50
564 Bud Smith RC	1.00
565 Angel Santos RC	1.00
566 Brandon Lyon RC	1.00
567 Eric Hinske RC	2.50
568 Nick Punto RC	1.00
569 Winston Abreu RC	1.00
570 Jason Phillips RC	1.00
571 Rafael Soriano RC	1.50
572 Wilson Betemit	1.00
573 Endy Chavez RC	1.00
574 Juan Cruz RC	1.00
575 Cory Aldridge RC	1.00
576 Adrian Hernandez	1.00
577 Brandon Larson RC	1.50
578 Bret Prinz RC	1.00
579 Jackson Melian RC	1.00
580 Dave Maurer RC	1.00
581 Jason Michaels RC	1.00
582 Travis Phelps RC	1.00
583 Cody Ransom RC	1.00
584 Benito Baez RC	1.00
585 Brian Roberts RC	1.00
586 Nate Teut RC	1.00
587 Jack Wilson RC	1.00
588 Willie Harris RC	1.00
589 Martin Vargas RC	1.00
590 Steve Torrealba RC	1.00

591 Stubby Clapp RC	1.00
592 Danny Wright RC	1.00
593 Mike Rivera RC	1.00
594 Luis Pineda RC	1.00
595 Lance Davis RC	1.00
596 Ramon Vazquez RC	1.50
597 Dustan Mohr RC	1.00
598 Troy Mattes RC	1.00
599 Grant Balfour RC	1.00
600 Jared Fernandez RC	1.00
601 Jorge Julio RC	1.00

E-X

131 Albert Pujols/499 RC	250.00
132 Bud Smith/499 RC	8.00
133 Tsuyoshi Shinjo/499 RC	8.00
134 Wilson Betemit/499 RC	10.00
135 Adrian Hernandez/	
499 RC	8.00
136 Jackson Melian/499	8.00
137 Jay Gibbons/499 RC	8.00
138 Johnny Estrada/499 RC	10.00
139 Morgan Ensberg/499 RC	8.00
140 Drew Henson/499 RC	10.00

Focus

241 Tsuyoshi Shinjo/999 RC	5.00
242 Wilson Betemit/999 RC	5.00
243 Jeremy Owens/999 RC	5.00
244 Drew Henson/999 RC	5.00
245 Albert Pujols/999 RC	100.00
246 Travis Hafner/999 RC	5.00
247 Ichiro Suzuki/999 RC	40.00
248 Elpidio Guzman/999 RC	5.00
249 Matt White/999 RC	5.00
250 Junior Spivey/999 RC	5.00

Futures

221 Drew Henson/2,499 RC	5.00
222 Johnny Estrada/2,499 RC	3.00
223 Elpidio Guzman/	
2,499 RC	3.00
224 Albert Pujols/2,499 RC	60.00
225 Wilson Betemit/2,499 RC	4.00
226 Mark Teixeira/2,499 RC	15.00
227 Tsuyoshi Shinjo/	
2,499 RC	3.00
228 Matt White/2,499 RC	3.00
229 Adrian Hernandez/	
2,499 RC	3.00
230 Ichiro Suzuki/2,499 RC	30.00

Triple Crown

301 Elpidio Guzman/	
2,999 RC	2.00
302 Drew Henson/2,999 RC	3.00
303 Bud Smith/2,999 RC	3.00
304 Carlos Valderrama/	
2,999 RC	2.00
305 Tsuyoshi Shinjo/	
2,999 RC	2.00
306 Ichiro Suzuki/2,999 RC	25.00
307 Jackson Melian/2,999	2.00
308 Morgan Ensberg/	
2,999 RC	2.00
309 Albert Pujols/2,999 RC	75.00
310 Johnny Estrada/2,999 RC	5.00

Ultra

276 Junior Spivey RC,	
Juan Uribe RC	4.00
277 Albert Pujols RC,	
Bud Smith RC	50.00
278 Ichiro Suzuki RC,	
Tsuyoshi Shinjo RC	20.00
279 Drew Henson RC,	
Jackson Melian	3.00
280 Matt White RC,	
Adrian Hernandez RC	2.00

Platinum

Cards (302-501):	4-8X
Production 201	
SP's (502-601):	
Production 21 not priced.	

Lumberjacks

	NM/M
Common Player:	4.00
Inserted 1:1 Rack Pack	
Barry Bonds	20.00
Derek Jeter	20.00
Luis Gonzalez	4.00
Mike Sweeney	4.00
Albert Pujols	15.00
Tony Gwynn	10.00
Adam Dunn	5.00
J.D. Drew	4.00
Brian Giles	4.00
Adrian Beltre	5.00
Bret Boone	4.00
Chipper Jones	10.00
Cliff Floyd	4.00
Darin Erstad	4.00
Gary Sheffield	6.00
Manny Ramirez	8.00
Mike Piazza	12.00
Todd Helton	8.00
Ivan Rodriguez	8.00
Lance Berkman	6.00
Vladimir Guerrero	8.00
Drew Henson	4.00

Cristian Guzman	4.00
Roberto Alomar	5.00
Moises Alou	4.00
Larry Walker	4.00

Lumberjacks Autographs

	NM/M
Production 100 Sets	
Barry Bonds	200.00
J.D. Drew	40.00
Adam Dunn	60.00
Luis Gonzalez	20.00
Derek Jeter	150.00
Albert Pujols	500.00
Cal Ripken Jr.	150.00
Mike Sweeney	20.00

National Patch Time

	NM/M
Common Player:	4.00
Inserted 1:24 H	
Edgardo Alfonzo	4.00
Brady Anderson	4.00
Adrian Beltre	6.00
Barry Bonds	20.00
Jeromy Burnitz	4.00
Eric Chavez	4.00
Roger Clemens	15.00
J.D. Drew	4.00
Darin Erstad	4.00
Carl Everett	4.00
Freddy Garcia	4.00
Jason Giambi	8.00
Juan Gonzalez	4.00
Mark Grace	6.00
Shawn Green	4.00
Ben Grieve	4.00
Vladimir Guerrero	8.00
Tony Gwynn	10.00
Randy Johnson	8.00
Chipper Jones	10.00
David Justice	4.00
Jeff Kent	4.00
Greg Maddux	10.00
Fred McGriff	4.00
John Olerud	4.00
Magglio Ordonez	4.00
Jorge Posada	6.00
Cal Ripken Jr.	20.00
Mariano Rivera	6.00
Ivan Rodriguez	6.00
Scott Rolen	6.00
Kazuhiro Sasaki	4.00
Aaron Sele	4.00
Gary Sheffield	6.00
John Smoltz	6.00
Frank Thomas	8.00
Mo Vaughn	4.00
Robin Ventura	4.00
Bernie Williams	6.00
Carlos Delgado	4.00
Chan Ho Park	4.00
Todd Helton	8.00
Craig Biggio	6.00
Jeff Bagwell	8.00
Paul LoDuca	4.00

Prime Numbers

	NM/M
Common Player:	8.00
Inserted 1:12 Jumbo Pack	
1PN Jeff Bagwell	15.00
2PN Cal Ripken Jr.	50.00
3PN Barry Bonds	50.00
4PN Todd Helton	15.00
5PN Derek Jeter	50.00
6PN Tony Gwynn	20.00
7PN Kazuhiro Sasaki	10.00
8PN Chan Ho Park	8.00
9PN Sean Casey	10.00
10PN Chipper Jones	20.00
11PN Pedro Martinez	15.00
12PN Mike Piazza	30.00
13PN Carlos Delgado	10.00
14PN ...	
15PN Roger Clemens	25.00

Winning Combinations

Common Card / Wood Combos

	NM/M
Common Card:	3.00

Varying quantities produced.

		NM/M
1WC	Derek Jeter, Ozzie Smith/2,000	8.00
2WC	Barry Bonds, Mark McGwire/2,000	10.00
3WC	Ichiro Suzuki, Albert Pujols/250	30.00
4WC	Ted Williams, Manny Ramirez/1,000	10.00
5WC	Tony Gwynn, Cal Ripken/250	15.00
6WC	Mike Piazza, Derek Jeter/500	10.00
7WC	Dave Winfield, Tony Gwynn/2,000	5.00
8WC	Hideo Nomo, Ichiro Suzuki/2,000	10.00
9WC	Cal Ripken, Ozzie Smith/1,000	10.00
10WC	Mark McGwire, Albert Pujols/2,000	10.00
11WC	Jeff Bagwell, Craig Biggio/1,000	3.00
12WC	Bobby Bonds, Barry Bonds/250	10.00
13WC	Ted Williams, Stan Musial/250	10.00
14WC	Babe Ruth, Reggie Jackson/500	15.00
15WC	Kazuhiro Sasaki, Ichiro Suzuki/500	10.00
16WC	Nolan Ryan, Roger Clemens/500	15.00
17WC	Roger Clemens, Derek Jeter/250	15.00
18WC	Ivan Rodriguez, Mike Piazza/1,000	6.00
19WC	Vladimir Guerrero, Sammy Sosa/2,000	6.00
20WC	Barry Bonds, Sammy Sosa/250	10.00
21WC	Roger Clemens, Greg Maddux/1,000	8.00
22WC	Juan Gonzalez, Manny Ramirez/2,000	3.00
23WC	Todd Helton, Jason Giambi/2,000	3.00
24WC	Jeff Bagwell, Lance Berkman/2,000	3.00
25WC	Mike Sweeney, George Brett/1,000	6.00
26WC	Luis Gonzalez, Babe Ruth/2,000	10.00
27WC	Bill Skowron, Don Mattingly/250	10.00
28WC	Yogi Berra, Cal Ripken/2,000	10.00
29WC	Pedro Martinez, Nomar Garciaparra/500	8.00
30WC	Ted Kluszewski, Frank Robinson/1,000	3.00
31WC	Curt Schilling, Randy Johnson/1,000	5.00
32WC	Ken Griffey Jr., Cal Ripken/500	10.00
33WC	Mike Piazza, Johnny Bench/1,000	6.00
34WC	Stan Musial, Albert Pujols/500	10.00
35WC	Jackie Robinson, Nellie Fox/500	8.00
36WC	Lefty Grove, Steve Carlton/250	5.00
37WC	Ty Cobb, Tony Gwynn/250	10.00
38WC	Albert Pujols, Frank Robinson/1,000	10.00
39WC	Ryne Sandberg, Sammy Sosa/500	10.00
40WC	Cal Ripken Jr., Lou Gehrig/250	20.00

2001 Fleer Premium

	NM/M
Complete Set (235):	
Common Player:	.15
Common SP (201-230):	3.00

Production 1,999
Cards 231-235 are redemptions.

	NM/M
Hobby Pack (8):	4.00
Hobby Box (24):	75.00

1	Cal Ripken Jr.	2.00
2	Derek Jeter	1.00
3	Edgardo Alfonzo	.15
4	Luis Castillo	.15
5	Mike Lieberthal	.15
6	Kazuhiro Sasaki	.15
7	Jeff Kent	.15
8	Eric Karros	.15
9	Tom Glavine	.40
10	Jeromy Burnitz	.15
11	Travis Fryman	.15
12	Ron Coomer	.15
13	Jeff D'Amico	.15
14	Carlos Febles	.15
15	Kevin Brown	.15
16	Deivi Cruz	.15
17	Tino Martinez	.15
18	Bobby Abreu	.15
19	Roger Clemens	1.00
20	Jeffrey Hammonds	.15
21	Peter Bergeron	.15
22	Ray Lankford	.15
23	Scott Rolen	.60
24	Jermaine Dye	.15
25	Rusty Greer	.15
26	Frank Thomas	.75
27	Jeff Bagwell	.75
28	Cliff Floyd	.15
29	Chris Singleton	.15
30	Steve Finley	.15
31	Orlando Hernandez	.15
32	Tom Goodwin	.15
33	Larry Walker	.15
34	Mike Sweeney	.15
35	Tim Hudson	.30
36	Kerry Wood	.40
37	Mike Lowell	.15
38	Andruw Jones	.75
39	Alex S. Gonzalez	.15
40	Juan Gonzalez	.75
41	J.D. Drew	.25
42	Mark McLemore	.15
43	Royce Clayton	.15
44	Paul O'Neill	.15
45	Carlos Beltran	.45
46	Phil Nevin	.15
47	Rondell White	.15
48	Gerald Williams	.15
49	Geoff Jenkins	.15
50	Marvin Benard	.15
51	Alex Rodriguez	1.50
52	Moises Alou	.15
53	Mike Lansing	.15
54	Omar Vizquel	.15
55	Eric Chavez	.30
56	Mark Quinn	.15
57	Mike Lamb	.15
58	Rick Ankiel	.25
59	Lance Berkman	.15
60	Jeff Conine	.15
61	B.J. Surhoff	.15
62	Todd Helton	.75
63	J.T. Snow	.15
64	John Vander Wal	.15
65	Johnny Damon	.25
66	Bobby Higginson	.15
67	Carlos Delgado	.40
68	Shawn Green	.35
69	Mike Redmond	.15
70	Mike Piazza	1.25
71	Adrian Beltre	.35
72	Juan Encarnacion	.15
73	Chipper Jones	1.00
74	Garret Anderson	.15
75	Paul Konerko	.15
76	Barry Larkin	.15
77	Tony Gwynn	1.00
78	Rafael Palmeiro	.60
79	Randy Johnson	.75
80	Mark Grace	.25
81	Javy Lopez	.15
82	Gabe Kapler	.15
83	Henry Rodriguez	.15
84	Raul Mondesi	.15
85	Adam Piatt	.15
86	Marquis Grissom	.15
87	Charles Johnson	.15
88	Sean Casey	.25
89	Manny Ramirez	.75
90	Curt Schilling	.40
91	Fernando Tatis	.15
92	Derek Bell	.15
93	Tony Clark	.15
94	Homer Bush	.15
95	Nomar Garciaparra	1.25
96	Vinny Castilla	.15
97	Ben Davis	.15
98	Carl Everett	.15
99	Damion Easley	.15
100	Craig Biggio	.15
101	Todd Hollandsworth	.15
102	Jay Payton	.15
103	Gary Sheffield	.35
104	Sandy Alomar Jr.	.15
105	Doug Glanville	.15
106	Barry Bonds	2.00
107	Tim Salmon	.25
108	Terrence Long	.15
109	Jorge Posada	.30
110	Jose Offerman	.15
111	Edgar Martinez	.15
112	Jeremy Giambi	.15
113	Dean Palmer	.15
114	Roberto Alomar	.35
115	Aaron Boone	.15
116	Adam Kennedy	.15
117	Joe Randa	.15
118	Jose Vidro	.15
119	Tony Batista	.15
120	Kevin Young	.15
121	Preston Wilson	.15
122	Jason Kendall	.15
123	Mark Kotsay	.15
124	Timoniel Perez	.15
125	Eric Young	.15
126	Greg Maddux	1.00
127	Richard Hidalgo	.15
128	Brian Giles	.15
129	Fred McGriff	.15
130	Troy Glaus	.75
131	Todd Walker	.15
132	Brady Anderson	.15
133	Jim Edmonds	.15
134	Ben Grieve	.15
135	Greg Vaughn	.15
136	Robin Ventura	.15
137	Sammy Sosa	1.25
138	Rich Aurilia	.15
139	Jose Valentin	.15
140	Trot Nixon	.15
141	Troy Percival	.15
142	Bernie Williams	.35
143	Warren Morris	.15
144	Jacque Jones	.15
145	Danny Bautista	.15
146	A.J. Pierzynski	.15
147	Mark McGwire	1.50
148	Rafael Furcal	.15
149	Ray Durham	.15
150	Mike Mussina	.40
151	Jay Bell	.15
152	David Wells	.15
153	Ken Caminiti	.15
154	Jim Thome	.40
155	Ivan Rodriguez	.60
156	Milton Bradley	.15
157	Ken Griffey Jr.	1.25
158	Al Leiter	.15
159	Corey Koskie	.15
160	Shannon Stewart	.15
161	Mo Vaughn	.15
162	Pedro Martinez	.15
163	Todd Hundley	.15
164	Darin Erstad	.60
165	Ruben Rivera	.15
166	Richie Sexson	.15
167	Andres Galarraga	.15
168	Darryl Kile	.15
169	Jose Cruz Jr.	.15
170	David Justice	.15
171	Vladimir Guerrero	.75
172	Jeff Cirillo	.15
173	John Olerud	.15
174	Devon White	.15
175	Ron Belliard	.15
176	Pokey Reese	.15
177	Mike Hampton	.15
178	David Ortiz	.15
179	Magglio Ordonez	.15
180	Ruben Mateo	.15
181	Carlos Lee	.15
182	Matt Williams	.15
183	Miguel Tejada	.25
184	Scott Elarton	.15
185	Bret Boone	.15
186	Pat Burrell	.40
187	Brad Radke	.15
188	Brian Jordan	.15
189	Matt Lawton	.15
190	Al Martin	.15
191	Albert Belle	.15
192	Tony Womack	.15
193	Roger Cedeno	.15
194	Travis Lee	.15
195	Dmitri Young	.15
196	Jay Buhner	.15
197	Jason Giambi	.50
198	Jason Tyner	.15
199	Ben Petrick	.15
200	Jose Canseco	.40
201	Nick Johnson RC	3.00
202	Jace Brewer	3.00
203	Ryan Freel RC	4.00
204	Jaisen Randolph RC	3.00
205	Marcus Giles RC	3.00
206	Claudio Vargas RC	3.00
207	Brian Cole	3.00
208	Scott Hodges	3.00
209	Winston Abreu RC	3.00
210	Shea Hillenbrand	3.00
211	Larry Barnes	3.00
212	Paul Phillips RC	3.00
213	Pedro Santana RC	3.00
214	Ivanon Coffie	3.00
215	Junior Spivey RC	3.00
216	Donzell McDonald	3.00
217	Vernon Wells	3.00
218	Corey Patterson	3.00
219	Sang-Hoon Lee	3.00
220	Jack Cust	4.00
221	Jason Romano	3.00
222	Jack Wilson RC	5.00
223	Adam Everett	3.00
224	Esix Snead RC	3.00
225	Jason Hart	3.00
226	Joe Lawrence	3.00
227	Brandon Inge	3.00
228	Alex Escobar	3.00
229	Abraham Nunez	3.00
230	Jared Sandberg	3.00
231	Ichiro Suzuki RC	40.00
232	Tsuyoshi Shinjo RC	5.00
233	Albert Pujols RC	75.00
234	Wilson Betemit RC	5.00
235	Drew Henson RC	5.00

Star Ruby

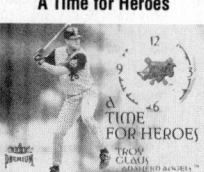

Stars (1-200):	5-10X
SPs (201-230):	.4-.8X

Production 125 Sets

Inserted 1:12
Card #17 does not exist.

Babe Ruth, Lou Gehrig	10.00
Lloyd Waner	1.00
Jimmie Foxx	3.00
Hank Greenberg	2.00
Ted Williams	8.00
Johnny Mize	2.00
Enos Slaughter	1.00
Jackie Robinson	6.00
Stan Musial	5.00
Duke Snider	3.00
Eddie Mathews	3.00
Roy Campanella	2.50
Yogi Berra	4.00
Pee Wee Reese	2.00
Phil Rizzuto	2.00
Al Kaline	4.00
Frank Howard	1.00
Roberto Clemente	8.00
Bob Gibson	3.00
Roger Maris	4.00
Don Drysdale	2.50
Maury Wills	1.00
Tom Seaver	2.50
Reggie Jackson	3.00
Johnny Bench	4.00
Carlton Fisk	2.50
Rod Carew	2.00
Steve Carlton	1.00
Mike Schmidt	6.00
Nolan Ryan	10.00
Rickey Henderson	3.00
Roger Clemens	5.00
Don Mattingly	6.00
George Brett	6.00
Greg Maddux	5.00
Cal Ripken Jr.	10.00
Chipper Jones	5.00
Barry Bonds	10.00
Ivan Rodriguez	2.50
Sammy Sosa, Mark McGwire	8.00
Ken Griffey Jr.	6.00
Tony Gwynn	4.00
Vladimir Guerrero	3.00
Shawn Green	1.00
Alex Rodriguez, Derek Jeter, Nomar Garciaparra	8.00
Pat Burrell	2.00
Rick Ankiel	1.00
Eric Chavez	1.00
Troy Glaus	2.00

A Time for Heroes

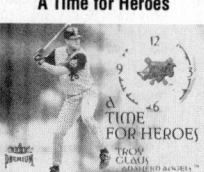

	NM/M
Complete Set (20):	25.00
Common Player:	1.00

Inserted 1:20

Darin Erstad	1.00
Alex Rodriguez	4.00
Shawn Green	1.00
Jeff Bagwell	1.50
Sammy Sosa	3.00
Derek Jeter	5.00
Nomar Garciaparra	1.50
Carlos Delgado	1.00
Pat Burrell	1.00
Tony Gwynn	2.50
Chipper Jones	2.50
Jason Giambi	1.00
Magglio Ordonez	1.00
Troy Glaus	1.00
Ivan Rodriguez	1.00
Andruw Jones	1.00
Vladimir Guerrero	2.00
Ken Griffey Jr.	3.00
J.D. Drew	1.00
Todd Helton	1.50

A Time for Heroes Memorabilia

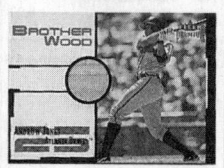

	NM/M
Common Player:	4.00

Inserted 1:82

Shawn Green	5.00
Derek Jeter	25.00
Pat Burrell	5.00
Chipper Jones	10.00
Jason Giambi	8.00
Troy Glaus	5.00
Ivan Rodriguez	6.00
Andruw Jones	8.00
J.D. Drew	4.00
Todd Helton	8.00

Brother Wood

	NM/M
Common Player:	4.00

Inserted 1:108

1BW	Vladimir Guerrero	8.00
2BW	Andruw Jones	3.00
3BW	Corey Patterson	4.00
4BW	Magglio Ordonez	5.00
5BW	Jason Giambi	4.00
6BW	Rafael Palmeiro	5.00
7BW	Eric Chavez	4.00
8BW	Pat Burrell	5.00
9BW	Adrian Beltre	5.00

Decades of Excellence

	NM/M
Complete Set (50):	140.00
Common Player:	1.00

Decades of Excellence Autograph

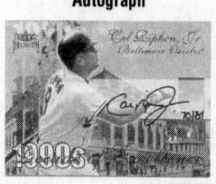

	NM/M
Common Autograph:	20.00

Production #'s listed.

1	Rick Ankiel/99	40.00
2	Johnny Bench/67	65.00
3	Barry Bonds/86	150.00
4	George Brett/73	100.00
5	Rod Carew/67	40.00
6	Steve Carlton/65	30.00
7	Eric Chavez/98	20.00
8	Carlton Fisk/69	50.00
9	Bob Gibson/59	40.00
10	Tony Gwynn/82	60.00
11	Reggie Jackson/67	50.00
12	Chipper Jones/93	65.00
13	Al Kaline/53	80.00
14	Don Mattingly/82	100.00
15	Cal Ripken Jr./82	150.00
16	Nolan Ryan/66	125.00
17	Mike Schmidt/72	80.00
18	Tom Seaver/67	50.00
19	Enos Slaughter/38	25.00
20	Maury Wills/59	20.00

Decades of Excellence Memorabilia

	NM/M
Common Player:	8.00

Inserted 1:217 H

1	Rick Ankiel/Jsy	8.00
2	Barry Bonds/Jsy	25.00
3	Pat Burrell/Jsy	8.00
4	Roy Campanella/Bat/50	50.00
5	Eric Chavez/Bat	8.00
6	Roberto Clemente/Bat/50	100.00
7	Carlton Fisk/Uni.	15.00
8	Jimmie Foxx/Bat/50	80.00
9	Shawn Green/Bat	8.00
10	Tony Gwynn/Jsy	15.00
11	Reggie Jackson/Jsy	15.00
12	Greg Maddux/Jsy	20.00
13	Roger Maris/Uni.	40.00
14	Pee Wee Reese/Jsy	8.00
15	Cal Ripken/Jsy/50	35.00
16	Ivan Rodriguez/Bat	8.00
17	Nolan Ryan/Jsy	40.00
18	Mike Schmidt/Jsy	15.00
19	Tom Seaver/Jsy	15.00
20	Duke Snider/Bat	15.00
21	Ted Williams/Jsy/50	100.00

Diamond Dominators

	NM/M
Common Player:	4.00

Inserted 1:51

1DD	Troy Glaus	5.00
2DD	Darin Erstad	4.00
3DD	J.D. Drew	4.00
4DD	Barry Bonds	20.00
5DD	Roger Clemens	15.00
6DD	Vladimir Guerrero	8.00
7DD	Tony Gwynn	10.00
8DD	Greg Maddux	15.00
9DD	Cal Ripken Jr.	25.00
10DD	Ivan Rodriguez	5.00
11DD	Frank Thomas	8.00
12DD	Bernie Williams	4.00
13DD	Jeromy Burnitz	4.00
14DD	Juan Gonzalez	4.00

Diamond Dominators Patches

	NM/M
Common Player:	15.00

Production 100 Sets

1DD	Troy Glaus	25.00
2DD	Darin Erstad	20.00
3DD	J.D. Drew	15.00
4DD	Barry Bonds	75.00
5DD	Roger Clemens	60.00
6DD	Vladimir Guerrero	25.00
7DD	Tony Gwynn	50.00
8DD	Greg Maddux	50.00
9DD	Cal Ripken Jr.	75.00
10DD	Ivan Rodriguez	20.00
11DD	Frank Thomas	25.00
12DD	Bernie Williams	20.00
13DD	Jeromy Burnitz	15.00
14DD	Juan Gonzalez	25.00

Grip It and Rip It

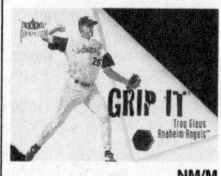

	NM/M
Complete Set (15):	10.00
Common Player:	.50

Inserted 1:6

1GRP	Roger Clemens, Derek Jeter	2.00
2GRP	Scott Rolen, Pat Burrell	.50
3GRP	Greg Maddux, Andruw Jones	1.00
4GRP	Shannon Stewart, Carlos Delgado	.50
5GRP	Shawn Estes, Barry Bonds	2.00
6GRP	Cal Eldred, Frank Thomas	.50
7GRP	Mark McGwire, Jim Edmonds	
8GRP	Jose Vidro, Vladimir Guerrero	.75
9GRP	Pedro Martinez, Nomar Garciaparra	1.50
10GRP	Tom Glavine, Chipper Jones	1.00
11GRP	Ken Griffey Jr., Sean Casey	1.00
12GRP	Jeff Bagwell, Moises Alou	.50
13GRP	Troy Glaus, Darin Erstad	.50
14GRP	Mike Piazza, Robin Ventura	1.00
15GRP	Eric Chavez, Jason Giambi	.50

Grip It and Rip It Plus

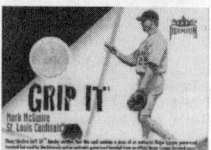

	NM/M
Common Card:	8.00

200 Base/Bat Produced
100 Ball/Bat Produced

Roger Clemens, Derek Jeter/100	50.00
Scott Rolen, Pat Burrell/200	
Greg Maddux, Andruw Jones/100	40.00
Shannon Stewart, Carlos Delgado/200	8.00
Shawn Estes, Barry Bonds/100	50.00

Cal Eldred,
Frank Thomas/200   15.00
Mark McGwire,
Jim Edmonds/100   60.00
Jose Vidro,
Vladimir Guerrero/200   15.00
Pedro Martinez,
Nomar Garciaparra/100   50.00
Tom Glavine,
Chipper Jones/200   15.00
Ken Griffey Jr.,
Sean Casey/200   20.00
Jeff Bagwell,
Moises Alou/200   10.00
Troy Glaus,
Darin Erstad/200   10.00
Mike Piazza,
Robin Ventura/100   40.00
Eric Chavez,
Jason Giambi/200   10.00

Home Field Advantage

	NM/M
Complete Set (15):	60.00
Common Player:	2.00
Inserted 1:72	
Mike Piazza	6.00
Derek Jeter	10.00
Ken Griffey Jr.	6.00
Carlos Delgado	2.00
Chipper Jones	5.00
Alex Rodriguez	8.00
Sammy Sosa	4.00
Scott Rolen	3.00
Nomar Garciaparra	5.00
Todd Helton	3.00
Vladimir Guerrero	3.00
Jeff Bagwell	3.00
Barry Bonds	10.00
Cal Ripken Jr.	10.00
Mark McGwire	8.00

Home Field Advantage Game Wall

	NM/M
Common Player:	6.00
Production 100 Sets	
Mike Piazza	15.00
Derek Jeter	25.00
Ken Griffey Jr.	15.00
Carlos Delgado	6.00
Chipper Jones	10.00
Alex Rodriguez	20.00
Sammy Sosa	10.00
Scott Rolen	8.00
Nomar Garciaparra	10.00
Todd Helton	8.00
Vladimir Guerrero	8.00
Jeff Bagwell	8.00
Barry Bonds	25.00
Cal Ripken Jr.	25.00
Mark McGwire	20.00

Derek Jeter Monumental Moments

	NM/M
Numbered to 1,995.	
Autograph numbered to 95.	
DJMM Derek Jeter	8.00
DJMM Derek Jeter/Auto./95	80.00

Solid Performers

	NM/M
Complete Set (15):	30.00
Common Player:	1.50
Inserted 1:20	
1SP Mark McGwire	4.00
2SP Alex Rodriguez	4.00
3SP Nomar Garciaparra	2.50
4SP Derek Jeter	5.00
5SP Vladimir Guerrero	1.50
6SP Todd Helton	1.50
7SP Chipper Jones	2.00
8SP Mike Piazza	2.50
9SP Ivan Rodriguez	1.50
10SP Tony Gwynn	2.00
11SP Cal Ripken Jr.	5.00
12SP Barry Bonds	5.00
13SP Jeff Bagwell	1.50
14SP Ken Griffey Jr.	2.50
15SP Sammy Sosa	2.50

Solid Performers Game Base

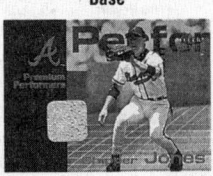

	NM/M
Common Player:	5.00
Production 150 Sets	
1SP Mark McGwire	15.00
2SP Alex Rodriguez	15.00
3SP Nomar Garciaparra	12.00
4SP Derek Jeter	20.00
5SP Vladimir Guerrero	8.00
6SP Todd Helton	8.00
7SP Chipper Jones	10.00
8SP Mike Piazza	12.00
9SP Ivan Rodriguez	8.00
10SP Tony Gwynn	10.00
11SP Cal Ripken Jr.	20.00
12SP Barry Bonds	20.00
13SP Jeff Bagwell	8.00
14SP Ken Griffey Jr.	12.00
15SP Sammy Sosa	12.00

2001 Fleer Showcase

	NM/M
Complete Set (160):	
Common Player:	.25
Common SP (116-125):	8.00
Production 500	
Common SP (126-145):	3.00
Production 1,500	
Common SP (146-160):	3.00
Production 2,000	
Pack (5):	8.00
Box (24):	160.00
1 Tony Gwynn	1.50
2 Barry Larkin	.25
3 Chan Ho Park	.25
4 Darin Erstad	.65
5 Rafael Furcal	.25
6 Roger Cedeno	.25
7 Timo Perez	.25
8 Rick Ankiel	.25
9 Pokey Reese	.25
10 Jeromy Burnitz	.25
11 Phil Nevin	.25
12 Matt Williams	.25
13 Mike Hampton	.25
14 Fernando Tatis	.25
15 Kazuhiro Sasaki	.25
16 Jim Thome	.25
17 Geoff Jenkins	.25
18 Jeff Kent	.25
19 Tom Glavine	.40
20 Dean Palmer	.25
21 Todd Zeile	.25
22 Edgar Renteria	.25
23 Andruw Jones	1.00
24 Juan Encarnacion	.25
25 Robin Ventura	.25
26 J.D. Drew	.25
27 Ray Durham	.25
28 Richard Hidalgo	.25
29 Eric Chavez	.35
30 Rafael Palmeiro	.75
31 Steve Finley	.25
32 Jeff Weaver	.25
33 Al Leiter	.25
34 Jim Edmonds	.25
35 Garret Anderson	.25
36 Larry Walker	.25
37 Jose Vidro	.25
38 Mike Cameron	.25
39 Brady Anderson	.25
40 Mike Lowell	.25
41 Bernie Williams	.35
42 Gary Sheffield	.40
43 John Smoltz	.25
44 Mike Mussina	.25
45 Greg Vaughn	.25
46 Juan Gonzalez	.75
47 Matt Lawton	.25
48 Robb Nen	.25
49 Brad Radke	.25
50 Edgar Martinez	.25
51 Mike Bordick	.25
52 Shawn Green	.40
53 Carl Everett	.40
54 Adrian Beltre	.40
55 Kerry Wood	.50
56 Kevin Brown	.25
57 Brian Giles	.25
58 Greg Maddux	1.50
59 Preston Wilson	.25
60 Orlando Hernandez	.25
61 Ben Grieve	.25
62 Jermaine Dye	.25
63 Travis Lee	.25
64 Jose Cruz Jr.	.25
65 Rondell White	.25
66 Carlos Beltran	.45
67 Scott Rolen	.75
68 Brad Fullmer	.25
69 David Wells	.25
70 Mike Sweeney	.25
71 Barry Zito	.40
72 Tony Batista	.25
73 Curt Schilling	.40
74 Jeff Cirillo	.25
75 Edgardo Alfonzo	.25
76 John Olerud	.25
77 Carlos Lee	.25
78 Moises Alou	.25
79 Tim Hudson	.35
80 Andres Galarraga	.25
81 Roberto Alomar	.45
82 Richie Sexson	.25
83 Trevor Hoffman	.25
84 Omar Vizquel	.25
85 Jacque Jones	.25
86 J.T. Snow	.25
87 Sean Casey	.25
88 Craig Biggio	.40
89 Mariano Rivera	.35
90 Rusty Greer	.25
91 Barry Bonds	3.00
92 Pedro Martinez	1.00
93 Cal Ripken Jr.	3.00
94 Pat Burrell	.50
95 Chipper Jones	1.50
96 Magglio Ordonez	.25
97 Jeff Bagwell	1.00
98 Randy Johnson	1.00
99 Frank Thomas	1.00
100 Jason Kendall	.25
101 Nomar Garciaparra (Avant Card)	6.00
102 Mark McGwire (Avant Card)	8.00
103 Troy Glaus (Avant Card)	3.00
104 Ivan Rodriguez (Avant Card)	2.50
105 Manny Ramirez (Avant Card)	3.00
106 Derek Jeter (Avant Card)	10.00
107 Alex Rodriguez (Avant Card)	8.00
108 Ken Griffey Jr. (Avant Card)	6.00
109 Todd Helton (Avant Card)	3.00
110 Sammy Sosa (Avant Card)	6.00
111 Vladimir Guerrero (Avant Card)	3.00
112 Mike Piazza (Avant Card)	6.00
113 Roger Clemens (Avant Card)	5.00
114 Jason Giambi (Avant Card)	2.50
115 Carlos Delgado (Avant Card)	2.00
116 Ichiro Suzuki RC (Rookie Avant)	75.00
117 Morgan Ensberg RC (Rookie Avant)	8.00
118 Carlos Valderrama RC (Rookie Avant)	8.00
119 Erick Almonte RC (Rookie Avant)	8.00
120 Tsuyoshi Shinjo RC (Rookie Avant)	8.00
121 Albert Pujols RC (Rookie Avant)	150.00
122 Wilson Betemit RC (Rookie Avant)	10.00
123 Adrian Hernandez RC (Rookie Avant)	8.00
124 Jackson Melian RC (Rookie Avant)	10.00
125 Drew Henson RC (Rookie Avant)	10.00
126 Paul Phillips RC	3.00
127 Esix Snead RC	3.00
128 Ryan Freel RC	4.00
129 Junior Spivey RC	3.00
130 Elpidio Guzman RC	3.00
131 Juan Diaz RC	3.00
132 Andres Torres RC	3.00
133 Jay Gibbons RC	3.00
134 Bill Ortega	3.00
135 Alexis Gomez RC	3.00
136 Wilken Ruan RC	3.00
137 Henry Mateo RC	3.00
138 Juan Uribe RC	3.00
139 Johnny Estrada RC	3.00
140 Jaisen Randolph RC	3.00
141 Eric Hinske RC	4.00
142 Jack Wilson RC	5.00
143 Cody Ransom RC	3.00
144 Nate Frese RC	3.00
145 John Grabow RC	3.00
146 Christian Parker RC	3.00
147 Brian Lawrence RC	3.00
148 Brandon Duckworth RC	3.00
149 Winston Abreu RC	4.00
150 Horacio Ramirez RC	4.00
151 Nick Maness RC	3.00
152 Blaine Neal RC	3.00
153 Billy Sylvester RC	3.00
154 David Elder RC	3.00
155 Bert Snow RC	3.00
156 Claudio Vargas RC	3.00
157 Martin Vargas RC	3.00
158 Grant Balfour RC	3.00
159 Randy Keisler RC	3.00
160 Zach Day RC	3.00

Legacy

Stars (1-100):	10-15X
Avant (101-115):	2-4X
RC's (116-125):	.75-1.5X
RC's (126-160):	1-2X
Production 50 Sets	

Autographics

	NM/M
Common Player:	5.00
Silvers:	1X
Production 250 Sets	
Golds:	1-2X
Production 50 Sets	
Roberto Alomar	25.00
Rick Ankiel	15.00
Albert Belle	8.00
Carlos Beltran	25.00
Adrian Beltre	10.00
Milton Bradley	8.00
Dee Brown	5.00
Jeromy Burnitz	5.00
Pat Burrell	15.00
Sean Casey	8.00
Joseph Crede	5.00
Jose Cruz Jr.	5.00
Ryan Dempster	5.00
J.D. Drew	15.00
Adam Dunn	15.00
Erubiel Durazo	5.00
Jermaine Dye	10.00
David Eckstein	8.00
Alex Escobar	5.00
Seth Etherton	5.00
Adam Everett	5.00
Carlos Febles	5.00
Troy Glaus	10.00
Ben Grieve	5.00
Toby Hall	5.00
Todd Helton	20.00
Shea Hillenbrand	5.00
Aubrey Huff	8.00
D'Angelo Jimenez	5.00
Paul Konerko	10.00
Mike Lamb	5.00
Matt Lawton	5.00
Derrek Lee	15.00
Mike Lieberthal	5.00
Mike Lowell	15.00
Julio Lugo	5.00
Jason Marquis	5.00
Edgar Martinez	15.00
Kevin Millwood	10.00
Eric Milton	5.00
Bengie Molina	8.00
Mike Mussina	15.00
Russ Ortiz	5.00
Corey Patterson	8.00
Jay Payton	5.00
Adam Piatt	5.00
Juan Pierre	8.00
Brad Radke	5.00
John Rocker	5.00
Alex Rodriguez	75.00
Scott Rolen	20.00
Richie Sexson	8.00
Gary Sheffield	15.00
Shannon Stewart	5.00
Miguel Tejada	25.00
Robin Ventura	5.00
Jose Vidro	5.00
Billy Wagner	8.00
Kip Wells	5.00
Rondell White	5.00
Preston Wilson	5.00
Kerry Wood	20.00
Julio Zuleta	5.00

Awards Showcase

	NM/M
Complete Set (20):	25.00
Common Player:	1.00
Inserted 1:20 Retail	
Derek Jeter	5.00
Derek Jeter	5.00
Jason Giambi	1.50
Jeff Kent	1.00
Pedro Martinez	2.00
Randy Johnson	2.00
Kazuhiro Sasaki	1.00
Rafael Furcal	1.50
Carlos Delgado	1.50
Todd Helton	2.00
Ivan Rodriguez	1.50
Darin Erstad	1.00
Bernie Williams	1.50
Greg Maddux	3.00
Jim Edmonds	1.00
Andruw Jones	1.00
Nomar Garciaparra	1.50
Todd Helton	2.00
Troy Glaus	1.50
Sammy Sosa	3.00

Awards Showcase Autographs

	NM/M
Production 25 Sets	
Johnny Bench	100.00
Yogi Berra	90.00
George Brett	200.00
Steve Carlton	60.00
Roger Clemens	150.00
Andre Dawson	40.00
Whitey Ford	80.00
Tom Glavine	50.00
Juan Gonzalez	40.00
Reggie Jackson	80.00
Randy Johnson	90.00
Chipper Jones	80.00
Harmon Killebrew	75.00
Fred Lynn	25.00
Greg Maddux	150.00
Don Mattingly	150.00
Willie McCovey	40.00
Jim Palmer	40.00
Jim Rice	25.00
Brooks Robinson	60.00
Frank Robinson	50.00
Ivan Rodriguez	50.00
Mike Schmidt	100.00
Tom Seaver	100.00

Awards Showcase Memorabilia

	NM/M
Common Player:	10.00
Production 100 Sets	
Johnny Bench	20.00
Yogi Berra	15.00
George Brett	40.00
Lou Brock	10.00
Roy Campanella	25.00
Steve Carlton	10.00
Roger Clemens	40.00
Andre Dawson	10.00
Whitey Ford	15.00
Jimmie Foxx	50.00
Kirk Gibson	10.00
Tom Glavine	10.00
Juan Gonzalez	10.00
Elston Howard	10.00
Jim "Catfish" Hunter	10.00
Reggie Jackson	20.00
Randy Johnson	15.00
Chipper Jones	15.00
Harmon Killebrew	20.00
Greg Maddux	25.00
Don Mattingly	40.00
Willie McCovey	10.00
Jim Palmer	10.00
Jim Rice	10.00
Brooks Robinson	20.00
Frank Robinson	15.00
Jackie Robinson	75.00
Ivan Rodriguez	15.00
Mike Schmidt	40.00
Tom Seaver	15.00
Willie Stargell	15.00
Ted Williams	100.00
Robin Yount	25.00

Derek Jeter's Monumental Moments

	NM/M
Production 2,000:	
MM5 Derek Jeter	8.00
Derek Jeter/Auto./100	80.00

Showcase Sticks

	NM/M
Common Player:	4.00
Inserted 1:24	
Roberto Alomar	6.00
Adrian Beltre	6.00
Pat Burrell	6.00
J.D. Drew	4.00
Juan Gonzalez	6.00
Andruw Jones	4.00
Chipper Jones	10.00
Magglio Ordonez	4.00
Ivan Rodriguez	6.00
Scott Rolen	8.00
Frank Thomas	8.00
Roger Cedeno	4.00
Shawn Green	4.00
Richard Hidalgo	4.00
Tony Clark	4.00
Preston Wilson	4.00
Barry Bonds	25.00
Rafael Furcal	6.00
Randy Johnson	8.00
Vladimir Guerrero	8.00
Al Kaline	10.00
George Kell	4.00
Jason Kendall	4.00
Carlos Delgado	5.00
Adam Piatt	4.00
Alex Gonzalez	4.00
Jorge Posada	6.00
Jose Vidro	4.00
Roger Clemens	20.00
Steve Finley	4.00
Reggie Jackson	8.00
Shannon Stewart	4.00
Rick Ankiel	4.00
Jim Thome	8.00
Tsuyoshi Shinjo	4.00
Ichiro Suzuki	25.00

Sweet Sigs

	NM/M
Common Player:	10.00
Inserted 1:24	
Prices for Lumber	
Wall:	1X
Leather:	1-1.5X
Bobby Abreu	15.00
Wilson Betemit	10.00
Russell Branyan	10.00
Pat Burrell	20.00
Eric Chavez	15.00
Rafael Furcal	15.00
Nomar Garciaparra	75.00
Juan Garciaparra	20.00
Elpidio Guzman	10.00
Drew Henson	10.00
Brandon Inge	10.00
Derek Jeter	125.00
Andruw Jones	25.00

Willie Mays	180.00
Jackson Melian	10.00
Xavier Nady	10.00
Jose Ortiz	10.00
Ben Sheets	15.00
Mike Sweeney	10.00
Miguel Tejada	25.00
Albert Pujols	400.00

2001 Fleer Tradition

ROGER CLEMENS

	NM/M
Complete Set (450):	35.00
Common Player:	.15
Comp. Factory Set (485):	100.00
Pack (10):	2.00
Box (36):	55.00

#	Player	Price
1	Andres Galarraga	.15
2	Armando Rios	.15
3	Julio Lugo	.15
4	Darryl Hamilton	.15
5	Dave Veres	.15
6	Edgardo Alfonzo	.15
7	Brook Fordyce	.15
8	Eric Karros	.15
9	Neifi Perez	.15
10	Jim Edmonds	.15
11	Barry Larkin	.25
12	Trot Nixon	.15
13	Andy Pettitte	.40
14	Jose Guillen	.15
15	David Wells	.15
16	Magglio Ordonez	.25
17	David Segui	.15
18	Juan Encarnacion	.15
19	Robert Person	.15
20	Quilvio Veras	.15
21	Mo Vaughn	.15
22	B.J. Surhoff	.15
23	Ken Caminiti	.15
24	Frank Catalanotto	.15
25	Luis Gonzalez	.25
26	Pete Harnisch	.15
27	Alex Gonzalez	.15
28	Mark Quinn	.15
29	Luis Castillo	.15
30	Rick Helling	.15
31	Barry Bonds	2.00
32	Warren Morris	.15
33	Aaron Boone	.15
34	Ricky Gutierrez	.15
35	Preston Wilson	.15
36	Erubiel Durazo	.15
37	Jermaine Dye	.25
38	John Rocker	.15
39	Mark Grudzielanek	.15
40	Pedro Martinez	.75
41	Phil Nevin	.15
42	Luis Matos	.15
43	Orlando Hernandez	.15
44	Steve Cox	.15
45	James Baldwin	.15
46	Rafael Furcal	.25
47	Todd Zeile	.15
48	Elmer Dessens	.15
49	Russell Branyan	.15
50	Juan Gonzalez	.40
51	Mac Suzuki	.15
52	Adam Kennedy	.15
53	Randy Velarde	.15
54	David Bell	.15
55	Royce Clayton	.15
56	Greg Colbrunn	.15
57	Rey Ordonez	.15
58	Kevin Millwood	.15
59	Fernando Vina	.15
60	Eddie Taubensee	.15
61	Enrique Wilson	.15
62	Jay Bell	.15
63	Brian Moehler	.15
64	Brad Fullmer	.15
65	Ben Petrick	.15
66	Orlando Cabrera	.25
67	Shane Reynolds	.15
68	Mitch Meluskey	.15
69	Jeff Shaw	.15
70	Chipper Jones	1.00
71	Tomo Ohka	.15
72	Ruben Rivera	.15
73	Mike Sirotka	.15
74	Scott Rolen	.50
75	Glendon Rusch	.15
76	Miguel Tejada	.40
77	Brady Anderson	.15
78	Bartolo Colon	.15
79	Ron Coomer	.15
80	Gary DiSarcina	.15
81	Geoff Jenkins	.15
82	Billy Koch	.15
83	Mike Lamb	.15
84	Alex Rodriguez	1.50
85	Denny Neagle	.15
86	Michael Tucker	.15
87	Edgar Renteria	.15
88	Brian Anderson	.15
89	Glenallen Hill	.15
90	Aramis Ramirez	.25
91	Rondell White	.15
92	Tony Womack	.15
93	Jeffrey Hammonds	.15
94	Freddy Garcia	.15
95	Bill Mueller	.15
96	Mike Lieberthal	.15
97	Michael Barrett	.15
98	Derrek Lee	.40
99	Bill Spiers	.15
100	Derek Lowe	.15
101	Javy Lopez	.15
102	Adrian Beltre	.40
103	Jim Parque	.15
104	Marquis Grissom	.15
105	Eric Chavez	.25
106	Todd Jones	.15
107	Eric Owens	.15
108	Roger Clemens	1.00
109	Denny Hocking	.15
110	Roberto Hernandez	.15
111	Albert Belle	.40
112	Troy Glaus	.40
113	Ivan Rodriguez	.50
114	Carlos Guillen	.15
115	Chuck Finley	.15
116	Dmitri Young	.15
117	Paul Konerko	.25
118	Damon Buford	.15
119	Fernando Tatis	.15
120	Larry Walker	.25
121	Jason Kendall	.15
122	Matt Williams	.15
123	Henry Rodriguez	.15
124	Placido Polanco	.15
125	Bobby Estalella	.15
126	Pat Burrell	.50
127	Mark Loretta	.15
128	Moises Alou	.25
129	Tino Martinez	.25
130	Milton Bradley	.15
131	Todd Hundley	.15
132	Keith Foulke	.15
133	Robert Fick	.15
134	Cristian Guzman	.15
135	Rusty Greer	.15
136	John Olerud	.15
137	Mariano Rivera	.25
138	Jeromy Burnitz	.15
139	Dave Burba	.15
140	Ken Griffey Jr.	1.50
141	Tony Gwynn	1.00
142	Carlos Delgado	.50
143	Edgar Martinez	.15
144	Ramon Hernandez	.15
145	Pedro Astacio	.15
146	Ray Lankford	.15
147	Mike Mussina	.40
148	Ray Durham	.15
149	Lee Stevens	.15
150	Jay Canizaro	.15
151	Adrian Brown	.15
152	Mike Piazza	1.00
153	Cliff Floyd	.15
154	Jose Vidro	.15
155	Jason Giambi	.50
156	Andruw Jones	.40
157	Robin Ventura	.15
158	Gary Sheffield	.40
159	Jeff D'Amico	.15
160	Chuck Knoblauch	.15
161	Roger Cedeno	.15
162	Jim Thome	.25
163	Peter Bergeron	.15
164	Kerry Wood	.50
165	Gabe Kapler	.15
166	Corey Koskie	.15
167	Doug Glanville	.15
168	Brent Mayne	.15
169	Scott Spiezio	.15
170	Steve Karsay	.15
171	Al Martin	.15
172	Fred McGriff	.15
173	Gabe White	.15
174	Alex Gonzalez	.15
175	Mike Darr	.15
176	Bengie Molina	.15
177	Ben Grieve	.15
178	Marlon Anderson	.15
179	Brian Giles	.15
180	Jose Valentin	.15
181	Brian Jordan	.15
182	Randy Johnson	.75
183	Ricky Ledee	.15
184	Russ Ortiz	.15
185	Mike Lowell	.15
186	Curtis Leskanic	.15
187	Bobby Abreu	.25
188	Derek Jeter	2.00
189	Lance Berkman	.40
190	Roberto Alomar	.40
191	Darin Erstad	.40
192	Richie Sexson	.15
193	Alex Ochoa	.15
194	Carlos Febles	.15
195	David Ortiz	.75
196	Shawn Green	.25
197	Mike Sweeney	.15
198	Vladimir Guerrero	.75
199	Jose Jimenez	.15
200	Travis Lee	.15
201	Rickey Henderson	.75
202	Bob Wickman	.15
203	Miguel Cairo	.15
204	Steve Finley	.15
205	Tony Batista	.15
206	Jamey Wright	.15
207	Terrence Long	.15
208	Trevor Hoffman	.15
209	John Vander Wal	.15
210	Greg Maddux	1.00
211	Tim Salmon	.25
212	Herbert Perry	.15
213	Marvin Benard	.15
214	Jose Offerman	.15
215	Jay Payton	.15
216	Jon Lieber	.15
217	Mark Kotsay	.15
218	Scott Brosius	.15
219	Scott Williamson	.15
220	Omar Vizquel	.15
221	Mike Hampton	.15
222	Richard Hidalgo	.15
223	Rey Sanchez	.15
224	Matt Lawton	.15
225	Bruce Chen	.15
226	Ryan Klesko	.15
227	Garret Anderson	.15
228	Kevin Brown	.15
229	Mike Cameron	.15
230	Tony Clark	.15
231	Curt Schilling	.40
232	Vinny Castilla	.15
233	Carl Pavano	.15
234	Eric Davis	.15
235	Darrin Fletcher	.15
236	Matt Stairs	.15
237	Octavio Dotel	.15
238	Mark Grace	.25
239	John Smoltz	.25
240	Matt Clement	.15
241	Ellis Burks	.15
242	Charles Johnson	.15
243	Jeff Bagwell	.50
244	Derek Bell	.15
245	Nomar Garciaparra	.50
246	Jorge Posada	.40
247	Ryan Dempster	.15
248	J.T. Snow	.15
249	Eric Young	.15
250	Daryle Ward	.15
251	Joe Randa	.15
252	Travis Fryman	.15
253	Mike Williams	.15
254	Jacque Jones	.15
255	Scott Elarton	.15
256	Mark McGwire	1.00
257	Jay Buhner	.15
258	Randy Wolf	.15
259	Sammy Sosa	.75
260	Chan Ho Park	.15
261	Damion Easley	.15
262	Rick Ankiel	.50
263	Frank Thomas	.75
264	Kris Benson	.15
265	Luis Alicea	.15
266	Jeremy Giambi	.15
267	Geoff Blum	.15
268	Joe Girardi	.15
269	Livan Hernandez	.15
270	Jeff Conine	.15
271	Danny Graves	.15
272	Craig Biggio	.25
273	Jose Canseco	.40
274	Tom Glavine	.50
275	Ruben Mateo	.15
276	Jeff Kent	.25
277	Kevin Young	.15
278	A.J. Burnett	.15
279	Dante Bichette	.15
280	Sandy Alomar Jr.	.15
281	John Wetteland	.15
282	Torii Hunter	.25
283	Jarrod Washburn	.15
284	Rich Aurilia	.15
285	Jeff Cirillo	.15
286	Fernando Seguignol	.15
287	Darren Dreifort	.15
288	Deivi Cruz	.15
289	Pokey Reese	.15
290	Garrett Stephenson	.15
291	Pat Boone	.15
292	Tim Hudson	.40
293	John Flaherty	.15
294	Shannon Stewart	.15
295	Shawn Estes	.15
296	Wilton Guerrero	.15
297	Delino DeShields	.15
298	David Justice	.15
299	Harold Baines	.15
300	Al Leiter	.15
301	Wil Cordero	.15
302	Antonio Alfonseca	.15
303	Sean Casey	.25
304	Carlos Beltran	.40
305	Brad Radke	.15
306	Jason Varitek	.25
307	Shigetosi Hasegawa	.15
308	Todd Stottlemyre	.15
309	Raul Mondesi	.15
310	Mike Bordick	.15
311	Darryl Kile	.15
312	Dean Palmer	.15
313	Johnny Damon	.50
314	Todd Helton	.75
315	Chad Hermansen	.15
316	Kevin Appier	.15
317	Greg Vaughn	.15
318	Robb Nen	.15
319	Jose Cruz Jr.	.15
320	Ron Belliard	.15
321	Bernie Williams	.40
322	Melvin Mora	.15
323	Kenny Lofton	.15
324	Armando Benitez	.15
325	Carlos Lee	.25
326	Damian Jackson	.15
327	Eric Milton	.15
328	J.D. Drew	.40
329	Byung-Hyun Kim	.15
330	Chris Stynes	.15
331	Kazuhiro Sasaki	.15
332	Troy O'Leary	.15
333	Pat Hentgen	.15
334	Brad Ausmus	.15
335	Todd Walker	.15
336	Jason Isringhausen	.15
337	Gerald Williams	.15
338	Aaron Sele	.15
339	Paul O'Neill	.25
340	Cal Ripken Jr.	2.00
341	Manny Ramirez	.75
342	Will Clark	.40
343	Mark Redman	.15
344	Bubba Trammell	.15
345	Troy Percival	.15
346	Chris Singleton	.15
347	Rafael Palmeiro	.50
348	Carl Everett	.15
349	Andy Benes	.15
350	Bobby Higginson	.15
351	Alex Cabrera (Prospects)	.15
352	Barry Zito (Prospects)	.40
353	Jace Brewer (Prospects)	.15
354	Paxton Crawford (Prospects)	.15
355	Oswaldo Mairena (Prospects)	.15
356	Joe Crede (Prospects)	.15
357	A.J. Pierzynski (Prospects)	.15
358	Daniel Garibay (Prospects)	.15
359	Jason Tyner (Prospects)	.15
360	Nate Rolison (Prospects)	.15
361	Scott Downs (Prospects)	.15
362	Keith Ginter (Prospects)	.15
363	Juan Pierre (Prospects)	.15
364	Adam Bernero (Prospects)	.15
365	Chris Richard (Prospects)	.15
366	Joey Nation (Prospects)	.15
367	Aubrey Huff (Prospects)	.15
368	Adam Eaton (Prospects)	.15
369	Jose Ortiz (Prospects)	.15
370	Eric Munson (Prospects)	.15
371	Matt Kinney (Prospects)	.15
372	Eric Byrnes (Prospects)	.40
373	Keith McDonald (Prospects)	.15
374	Matt Wise (Prospects)	.15
375	Timo Perez (Prospects)	.15
376	Julio Zuleta (Prospects)	.15
377	Jimmy Rollins (Prospects)	.50
378	Xavier Nady (Prospects)	.25
379	Ryan Kohlmeier (Prospects)	.15
380	Corey Patterson (Prospects)	.15
381	Todd Helton (League Leaders)	.40
382	Moises Alou (League Leaders)	.15
383	Vladimir Guerrero (League Leaders)	.40
384	Luis Castillo (League Leaders)	.15
385	Jeffrey Hammonds (League Leaders)	.15
386	Nomar Garciaparra (League Leaders)	.40
387	Carlos Delgado (League Leaders)	.25
388	Darin Erstad (League Leaders)	.25
389	Manny Ramirez (League Leaders)	.40
390	Mike Sweeney (League Leaders)	.15
391	Sammy Sosa (League Leaders)	.50
392	Barry Bonds (League Leaders)	1.00
393	Jeff Bagwell (League Leaders)	.40
394	Richard Hidalgo (League Leaders)	.15
395	Vladimir Guerrero (League Leaders)	.40
396	Troy Glaus (League Leaders)	.25
397	Frank Thomas (League Leaders)	.40
398	Carlos Delgado (League Leaders)	.25
399	David Justice (League Leaders)	.15
400	Jason Giambi (League Leaders)	.25
401	Randy Johnson (League Leaders)	.50
402	Kevin Brown (League Leaders)	.15
403	Greg Maddux (League Leaders)	.50
404	Al Leiter (League Leaders)	.15
405	Mike Hampton (League Leaders)	.15
406	Pedro Martinez (League Leaders)	.40
407	Roger Clemens (League Leaders)	.50
408	Mike Sirotka (League Leaders)	.15
409	Mike Mussina (League Leaders)	.25
410	Bartolo Colon (League Leaders)	.15
411	World Series Update	.15
412	World Series Update	.15
413	World Series Update	.15
414	World Series Update	.15
415	World Series Update	.15
416	World Series Update	.15
417	World Series Update	.15
418	World Series Update	.15
419	World Series Update	.15
420	World Series Update	.15
421	Atlanta Braves (Team Checklists)	.15
422	New York Mets (Team Checklists)	.15
423	Florida Marlins (Team Checklists)	.15
424	Philadelphia Phillies (Team Checklists)	.15
425	Montreal Expos (Team Checklists)	.15
426	St. Louis Cardinals (Team Checklists)	.15
427	Cincinnati Reds (Team Checklists)	.15
428	Chicago Cubs (Team Checklists)	.15
429	Milwaukee Brewers (Team Checklists)	.15
430	Houston Astros (Team Checklists)	.15
431	Pittsburgh Pirates (Team Checklists)	.15
432	San Francisco Giants (Team Checklists)	.15
433	Arizona Diamondbacks (Team Checklists)	.15
434	Los Angeles Dodgers (Team Checklists)	.15
435	Colorado Rockies (Team Checklists)	.15
436	San Diego Padres (Team Checklists)	.15
437	New York Yankees (Team Checklists)	.15
438	Boston Red Sox (Team Checklists)	.15
439	Baltimore Orioles (Team Checklists)	.15
440	Toronto Blue Jays (Team Checklists)	.15
441	Tampa Bay Devil Rays (Team Checklists)	.15
442	Chicago White Sox (Team Checklists)	.15
443	Cleveland Indians (Team Checklists)	.15
444	Detroit Tigers (Team Checklists)	.15
445	Kansas City Royals (Team Checklists)	.15
446	Minnesota Twins (Team Checklists)	.15
447	Seattle Mariners (Team Checklists)	.15
448	Oakland Athletics (Team Checklists)	.15
449	Anaheim Angels (Team Checklists)	.15
450	Texas Rangers (Team Checklists)	.15
451	Albert Pujols	50.00
452	Ichiro Suzuki RC	15.00
453	Tsuyoshi Shinjo RC	.50
454	Johnny Estrada RC	.75
455	Elpidio Guzman RC	.40
456	Adrian Hernandez RC	.25
457	Rafael Soriano RC	.75
458	Drew Henson RC	1.00
459	Juan Uribe RC	.75
460	Matt White RC	.40
461	Endy Chavez RC	.25
462	Bud Smith RC	.25
463	Morgan Ensberg RC	.50
464	Jay Gibbons RC	1.00
465	Jackson Melian RC	.25
466	Junior Spivey RC	.50
467	Juan Cruz RC	.50
468	Wilson Betemit RC	.40
469	Alexis Gomez RC	.25
470	Mark Teixeira RC	10.00
471	Erick Almonte RC	.25
472	Travis Hafner RC	4.00
473	Carlos Valderrama RC	.25
474	Brandon Duckworth RC	.50
475	Ryan Freel RC	.50
476	Wilkin Ruan RC	.25
477	Andres Torres RC	.25
478	Josh Towers RC	.50
479	Kyle Lohse RC	.50
480	Jason Michaels RC	.25
481	Alfonso Soriano RC	.50
482	C.C. Sabathia RC	.40
483	Roy Oswalt RC	.50
484	Ben Sheets RC	.25
485	Adam Dunn RC	.50

Diamond Tributes

MARK McGWIRE

DIAMOND TRIBUTES

	NM/M
Complete Set (30):	35.00
Common Player:	.50
Inserted 1:7	

#	Player	Price
1	Jackie Robinson	2.00
2	Mike Piazza	2.00
3	Alex Rodriguez	3.00
4	Barry Bonds	4.00
5	Nomar Garciaparra	1.00
6	Roger Clemens	2.00
7	Ivan Rodriguez	.75
8	Cal Ripken Jr.	4.00
9	Manny Ramirez	1.00
10	Chipper Jones	1.50
11	Barry Larkin	.50
12	Carlos Delgado	.50
13	J.D. Drew	.60
14	Carl Everett	.50
15	Todd Helton	1.00
16	Greg Maddux	2.00
17	Scott Rolen	.75
18	Troy Glaus	1.00
19	Brian Giles	.50
20	Jeff Bagwell	1.00
21	Sammy Sosa	1.50
22	Randy Johnson	1.00
23	Andruw Jones	.75
24	Ken Griffey Jr.	2.00
25	Mark McGwire	2.50
26	Derek Jeter	4.00
27	Vladimir Guerrero	1.00
28	Frank Thomas	1.00
29	Pedro Martinez	1.00
30	Bernie Williams	.50

Grass Roots

KEN GRIFFEY JR.
CINCINNATI REDS OUTFIELDER

GRASS ROOTS

	NM/M
Complete Set (15):	25.00
Common Player:	1.00
Inserted 1:18	

#	Player	Price
1	Derek Jeter	4.00
2	Greg Maddux	2.00
3	Sammy Sosa	1.50
4	Alex Rodriguez	3.00
5	Vladimir Guerrero	1.50
6	Scott Rolen	1.00
7	Frank Thomas	1.50
8	Nomar Garciaparra	1.00
9	Cal Ripken Jr.	4.00
10	Mike Piazza	2.50
11	Ivan Rodriguez	1.00
12	Chipper Jones	2.00
13	Tony Gwynn	2.00
14	Ken Griffey Jr.	2.50
15	Mark McGwire	3.00

Lumber Company

Derek Jeter

	NM/M
Complete Set (20):	25.00
Common Player:	.50
Inserted 1:12	

#	Player	Price
1	Vladimir Guerrero	1.50
2	Mo Vaughn	.50
3	Ken Griffey Jr.	2.50
4	Juan Gonzalez	1.00
5	Tony Gwynn	.50
6	Jim Edmonds	.50
7	Jason Giambi	1.00
8	Alex Rodriguez	3.00
9	Derek Jeter	4.00
10	Darin Erstad	1.00
11	Andruw Jones	4.00
12	Cal Ripken Jr.	4.00
13	Magglio Ordonez	.75
14	Nomar Garciaparra	1.50
15	Chipper Jones	1.50
16	Sean Casey	.50
17	Shawn Green	.50
18	Mike Piazza	2.50
19	Sammy Sosa	2.50
20	Barry Bonds	4.00

Season Pass

Complete Set (6):	
Common Player:	
Values Undetermined	

Stitches in Time

JACKIE ROBINSON
KANSAS CITY MONARCHS • 28
FLEER
Stitches In Time
"... in the brilliant and dazzling brand of baseball they play, they are more colorful than the leaves of autumn." - Chester L. Williams, The Pittsburgh Courier

		NM/M
Complete Set (25):		40.00
Common Player:		1.50
Inserted 1:18		
1	Henry Kimbro	1.50
2	Ernie Banks	3.00
3	James "Cool Papa" Bell	2.00
4	Joe Black	1.50
5	Roy Campanella	2.00
6	Ray Dandridge	1.50
7	Leon Day	1.50
8	Larry Doby	2.00
9	Josh Gibson	2.00
10	Elston Howard	2.00
11	Monte Irvin	2.00
12	Buck Leonard	2.00
13	Max Manning	1.50
14	Willie Mays	6.00
15	Buck O'Neil	2.00
16	Satchel Paige	3.00
17	Ted Radcliffe	2.00
18	Jackie Robinson	4.00
19	Bill Perkins	1.50
20	Andrew "Rube" Foster	2.00
21	William "Judy" Johnson	1.50
22	Oscar Charleston	1.50
23	John Henry "Pop" Lloyd	1.50
24	Artie Wilson	1.50
25	Sam Jethroe	1.50

Stitches in Time Autographs

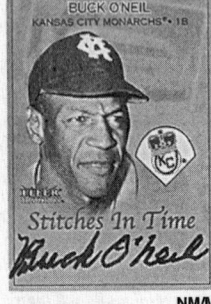

BUCK O'NEIL
KANSAS CITY MONARCHS • 18
FLEER
Stitches In Time
Buck O'Neil

		NM/M
Common Autograph:		20.00
2	Ernie Banks	60.00
4	Joe Black	25.00
11	Monte Irvin	40.00
14	Willie Mays	150.00
15	Buck O'Neil	50.00
17	Ted Radcliffe	40.00
24	Artie Wilson	20.00

Stitches in Time Game-Used

JACKIE ROBINSON
KANSAS CITY MONARCHS • 28
FLEER
Stitches In Time

		NM/M
Common Card:		25.00
5	Roy Campanella	60.00
8	Larry Doby/Bat	30.00
10	Elston Howard/Bat	30.00
14	Willie Mays/Jsy	125.00
18	Jackie Robinson/Jsy	100.00

Turn Back the Clock

		NM/M
Common Card:		8.00
Inserted 1:352		
1	Tom Glavine	10.00

2	Greg Maddux	30.00
3	Sean Casey	8.00
4	Pokey Reese	8.00
5	Jason Giambi	15.00
6	Tim Hudson	8.00
7	Larry Walker	8.00
8	Jeffrey Hammonds	8.00
9	Scott Rolen	15.00
10	Pat Burrell	10.00
11	Chipper Jones	20.00
13	Troy Glaus	15.00
14	Tony Gwynn	20.00
15	Cal Ripken Jr.	50.00
16	Tom Glavine, Greg Maddux	75.00
17	Sean Casey, Pokey Reese	30.00
18	Chipper Jones, Greg Maddux	100.00
19	Larry Walker, Jeffrey Hammonds	30.00
20	Scott Rolen, Pat Burrell	40.00
21	Jason Giambi, Tim Hudson	40.00

Warning Track

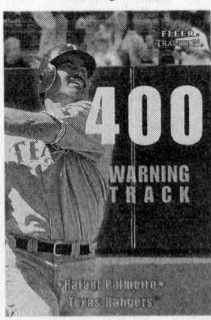

		NM/M
Complete Set (25):		120.00
Common Player:		2.00
Inserted 1:72		
1	Josh Gibson	5.00
2	Willie Mays	10.00
3	Mark McGwire	10.00
4	Barry Bonds	15.00
5	Jose Canseco	4.00
6	Ken Griffey Jr.	15.00
7	Cal Ripken Jr.	10.00
8	Rafael Palmeiro	5.00
9	Sammy Sosa	5.00
10	Juan Gonzalez	4.00
11	Frank Thomas	6.00
12	Jeff Bagwell	5.00
13	Gary Sheffield	2.50
14	Larry Walker	2.00
15	Mike Piazza	10.00
16	Larry Doby	4.00
17	Roy Campanella	5.00
18	Manny Ramirez	6.00
19	Chipper Jones	8.00
20	Alex Rodriguez	12.00
21	Ivan Rodriguez	5.00
22	Vladimir Guerrero	6.00
23	Nomar Garciaparra	4.00
24	Andres Galarraga	2.00
25	Jim Thome	2.00

2001 Fleer Tradition Milwaukee Brewers

This 10-1/2" x 7-1/2" sheet was distributed to the first 10,000 fans attending the Brewers' September 2 game at Miller Park. Eight of the team's Fleer Tradition cards are reproduced on the sheet, with a team logo at center.

	NM/M
Sheet:	12.00

2001 Fleer Triple Crown

		NM/M
Complete Set (300):		25.00
Common Player:		.15
Pack (10):		2.00
Box (24):		40.00
1	Derek Jeter	2.00
2	Vladimir Guerrero	.75
3	Henry Rodriguez	.15
4	Jason Giambi	.50
5	Nomar Garciaparra	.75
6	Jeff Kent	.15
7	Garret Anderson	.15
8	Todd Helton	.75
9	Barry Bonds	2.00
10	Preston Wilson	.15
11	Troy Glaus	.40
12	Geoff Jenkins	.15
13	Jim Edmonds	.15
14	Bobby Higginson	.15
15	Mark Quinn	.15
16	Barry Larkin	.25
17	Richie Sexson	.15
18	Fernando Tatis	.15
19	John Vander Wal	.15
20	Darin Erstad	.40
21	Shawn Green	.40
22	Scott Rolen	.50
23	Tony Batista	.15
24	Phil Nevin	.15
25	Tim Salmon	.25
26	Gary Sheffield	.35
27	Ben Grieve	.15
28	Jermaine Dye	.15
29	Andres Galarraga	.15
30	Adrian Beltre	.40
31	Rafael Palmeiro	.50
32	J.T. Snow	.15
33	Edgardo Alfonzo	.15
34	Paul Konerko	.25
35	Jim Thome	.25
36	Andruw Jones	.40
37	Mike Sweeney	.15
38	Jose Cruz Jr.	.15
39	David Ortiz	.75
40	Pat Burrell	.40
41	Chipper Jones	1.00
42	Jeff Bagwell	.50
43	Raul Mondesi	.15
44	Rondell White	.15
45	Edgar Martinez	.15
46	Cal Ripken Jr.	2.00
47	Moises Alou	.25
48	Shannon Stewart	.15
49	Tino Martinez	.25
50	Jason Kendall	.15
51	Richard Hidalgo	.15
52	Albert Belle	.15
53	Jay Payton	.15
54	Cliff Floyd	.15
55	Rusty Greer	.15
56	Matt Williams	.15
57	Sammy Sosa	1.00
58	Carl Everett	.15
59	Carlos Delgado	.50
60	Jeremy Giambi	.15
61	Jose Canseco	.40
62	David Segui	.15
63	Jose Vidro	.15
64	Matt Stairs	.15
65	Travis Fryman	.15
66	Ken Griffey Jr.	1.50
67	Mike Piazza	1.25
68	Mark McGwire	1.50
69	Craig Biggio	.25
70	Eric Chavez	.25
71	Mo Vaughn	.15
72	Matt Lawton	.15
73	Miguel Tejada	.25
74	Brian Giles	.15
75	Sean Casey	.25
76	Robin Ventura	.15
77	Ivan Rodriguez	.50
78	Dean Palmer	.15
79	Frank Thomas	.75
80	Bernie Williams	.40
81	Juan Encarnacion	.15
82	John Olerud	.15
83	Rich Aurilia	.15
84	Juan Gonzalez	.40
85	Ray Durham	.15
86	Steve Finley	.15
87	Ken Caminiti	.15
88	Roberto Alomar	.40
89	Jeromy Burnitz	.15
90	J.D. Drew	.40
91	Lance Berkman	.15
92	Gabe Kapler	.15
93	Larry Walker	.15
94	Alex Rodriguez	1.50
95	Jeffrey Hammonds	.15
96	Magglio Ordonez	.25
97	David Justice	.15
98	Eric Karros	.15
99	Manny Ramirez	.75
100	Paul O'Neill	.15
101	Ron Gant	.15
102	Erubiel Durazo	.15
103	Jason Varitek	.15
104	Chan Ho Park	.15
105	Corey Koskie	.15
106	Jeff Conine	.15
107	Kevin Tapani	.15
108	Mike Lowell	.25
109	Tim Hudson	.25
110	Bobby Abreu	.25
111	Bret Boone	.15
112	David Wells	.15
113	Brian Jordan	.15
114	Mitch Meluskey	.15
115	Terrence Long	.15
116	Matt Clement	.15
117	Fernando Vina	.15
118	Luis Alicea	.15
119	Jay Bell	.15
120	Mark Grace	.15
121	Carlos Febles	.15
122	Mark Redman	.15
123	Kevin Jordan	.15
124	Pat Meares	.15
125	Mark McLemore	.15
126	Chris Singleton	.15
127	Trot Nixon	.15
128	Carlos Beltran	.40
129	Lee Stevens	.15
130	Kris Benson	.15
131	Jay Buhner	.15
132	Greg Vaughn	.15
133	Eric Young	.15
134	Tony Womack	.15
135	Roger Cedeno	.15
136	Travis Lee	.15
137	Marvin Benard	.15
138	Aaron Sele	.15
139	Rick Ankiel	.50
140	Ruben Mateo	.15
141	Randy Johnson	.75
142	Jason Tyner	.15
143	Mike Redmond	.15
144	Ron Coomer	.15
145	Scott Elarton	.15
146	Javy Lopez	.15
147	Carlos Lee	.25
148	Tony Clark	.15
149	Roger Clemens	1.00
150	Mike Lieberthal	.15
151	Shawn Estes	.15
152	Vinny Castilla	.15
153	Alex Gonzalez	.15
154	Troy Percival	.15
155	Pokey Reese	.15
156	Todd Hollandsworth	.15
157	Marquis Grissom	.15
158	Greg Maddux	1.00
159	Dante Bichette	.15
160	Hideo Nomo	.40
161	Jacque Jones	.15
162	Kevin Young	.15
163	B.J. Surhoff	.15
164	Eddie Taubensee	.15
165	Neifi Perez	.15
166	Orlando Hernandez	.15
167	Francisco Cordova	.15
168	Miguel Cairo	.15
169	Rafael Furcal	.25
170	Sandy Alomar Jr.	.15
171	Jeff Cirillo	.15
172	A.J. Pierzynski	.15
173	Fred McGriff	.15
174	Mike Mussina	.40
175	Aaron Boone	.15
176	Nick Johnson	.15
177	Kent Bottenfield	.15
178	Felipe Crespo	.15
179	Ryan Minor	.15
180	Charles Johnson	.15
181	Damion Easley	.15
182	Michael Barrett	.15
183	Doug Glanville	.15
184	Ben Davis	.15
185	Rickey Henderson	.75
186	Edgard Clemente	.15
187	Dmitri Young	.15
188	Tom Goodwin	.15
189	Mike Hampton	.15
190	Gerald Williams	.15
191	Omar Vizquel	.15
192	Ben Petrick	.15
193	Brad Radke	.15
194	Russ Davis	.15
195	Milton Bradley	.15
196	John Parrish	.15
197	Todd Hundley	.15
198	Carl Pavano	.15
199	Bruce Chen	.15
200	Royce Clayton	.15
201	Homer Bush	.15
202	Mark Grudzielanek	.15
203	Mike Lansing	.15
204	Daryle Ward	.15
205	Jeff D'Amico	.15
206	Ray Lankford	.15
207	Curt Schilling	.40
208	Pedro Martinez	.75
209	Johnny Damon	.15
210	Al Leiter	.15
211	Ruben Rivera	.15
212	Kazuhiro Sasaki	.15
213	Will Clark	.25
214	Rick Helling	.15
215	Adam Piatt	.15
216	Joe Girardi	.15
217	A.J. Burnett	.15
218	Mike Bordick	.15
219	Mike Cameron	.15
220	Tony Gwynn	1.00
221	Deivi Cruz	.15
222	Bubba Trammell	.15
223	Scott Erickson	.15
224	Kerry Wood	.50
225	Derrek Lee	.50
226	Peter Bergeron	.15
227	Chris Gomez	.15
228	Al Martin	.15
229	Brady Anderson	.15
230	Ramon Martinez	.15
231	Darryl Kile	.15
232	Devon White	.15
233	Charlie Hayes	.15
234	Aramis Ramirez	.40
235	Mike Lamb	.15
236	Tom Glavine	.50
237	Troy O'Leary	.15
238	Joe Randa	.15
239	Dustin Hermanson	.15
240	Adam Kennedy	.15
241	Jose Valentin	.15
242	Derek Bell	.15
243	Mark Kotsay	.15
244	Ron Belliard	.15
245	Warren Morris	.15
246	Ozzie Guillen	.15
247	Andy Ashby	.15
248	Jose Offerman	.15
249	Kevin Brown	.15
250	Jorge Posada	.40
251	Alex Cabrera (Prospects)	.15
252	Chan Perry (Prospects)	.15
253	Augie Ojeda (Prospects)	.15
254	Santiago Perez (Prospects)	.15
255	Grant Roberts (Prospects)	.15
256	Dusty Allen (Prospects)	.15
257	Elvis Pena (Prospects)	.15
258	Matt Kinney (Prospects)	.15
259	Timoniel Perez (Prospects)	.15
260	Adam Eaton (Prospects)	.15
261	Geraldo Guzman (Prospects)	.15
262	Damian Rolls (Prospects)	.15
263	Alfonso Soriano (Prospects)	.50
264	Corey Patterson (Prospects)	.15
265	Juan Alvarez (Prospects)	.15
266	Shawn Gilbert (Prospects)	.15
267	Adam Bernero (Prospects)	.15
268	Ben Weber (Prospects)	.15
269	Tike Redman (Prospects)	.15
270	Willie Morales (Prospects)	.15
271	Tomas De La Rosa (Prospects)	.15
272	Rodney Lindsey (Prospects)	.15
273	Carlos Casimiro (Prospects)	.15
274	Jim Mann (Prospects)	.15
275	Pasqual Coco (Prospects)	.15
276	Julio Zuleta (Prospects)	.15
277	Damon Minor (Prospects)	.15
278	Jose Ortiz (Prospects)	.15
279	Eric Munson (Prospects)	.25
280	Andy Thompson (Prospects)	.15
281	Aubrey Huff (Prospects)	.15
282	Chris Richard (Prospects)	.15
283	Ross Gload (Prospects)	.15
284	Travis Dawkins (Prospects)	.15
285	Tim Drew (Prospects)	.15
286	Barry Zito (Prospects)	.40
287	Andy Tracy (Prospects)	.15
288	Julio Lugo (Prospects)	.15
289	Matt DeWitt (Prospects)	.15
290	Keith McDonald (Prospects)	.15
291	J.C. Romero (Prospects)	.15
292	Adam Melhuse (Prospects)	.15
293	Ryan Kohlmeier (Prospects)	.15
294	John Bale (Prospects)	.15
295	Eric Cammack (Prospects)	.15
296	Morgan Burkhart (Prospects)	.15
297	Kory DeHaan (Prospects)	.15
298	Raul Gonzalez (Prospects)	.15
299	Hector Ortiz (Prospects)	.15
300	Talmadge Nunnari (Prospects)	.15

Blue

		NM/M
Common Player:		3.00
Produced to # of 2000 HR's		
1	Derek Jeter/15	150.00
2	Vladimir Guerrero/44	25.00
3	Henry Rodriguez/20	10.00
4	Jason Giambi/43	15.00
5	Nomar Garciaparra/21	25.00
6	Jeff Kent/33	10.00
7	Garret Anderson/35	8.00
8	Todd Helton/42	15.00
9	Barry Bonds/49	40.00
10	Preston Wilson/31	8.00
11	Troy Glaus/47	10.00
12	Geoff Jenkins/34	8.00
13	Jim Edmonds/42	10.00
14	Bobby Higginson/30	3.00
15	Mark Quinn/20	5.00
16	Barry Larkin/11	15.00
17	Richie Sexson/30	10.00
18	Fernando Tatis/18	3.00
19	John Vander Wal/24	3.00
20	Darin Erstad/25	10.00
21	Shawn Green/24	10.00
22	Scott Rolen/26	15.00
23	Tony Batista/41	3.00
24	Phil Nevin/31	5.00
25	Tim Salmon/34	5.00
26	Gary Sheffield/43	8.00
27	Ben Grieve/27	5.00
28	Jermaine Dye/33	3.00
29	Andres Galarraga/28	5.00
30	Adrian Beltre/20	8.00
31	Rafael Palmeiro/39	10.00
32	J.T. Snow/19	5.00
33	Edgardo Alfonzo/25	5.00
34	Paul Konerko/21	5.00
35	Jim Thome/37	15.00
36	Andruw Jones/36	10.00
37	Mike Sweeney/29	3.00
38	Jose Cruz Jr./31	5.00
39	David Ortiz/10	8.00
40	Pat Burrell/18	15.00
41	Chipper Jones/36	15.00
42	Jeff Bagwell/47	10.00
43	Raul Mondesi/24	5.00
44	Rondell White/13	10.00
45	Edgar Martinez/37	5.00
46	Cal Ripken Jr./15	150.00
47	Moises Alou/30	5.00
48	Shannon Stewart/21	3.00
49	Tino Martinez/16	5.00
50	Jason Kendall/14	5.00
51	Richard Hidalgo/44	3.00
52	Albert Belle/23	3.00
53	Jay Payton/17	3.00
54	Cliff Floyd/22	3.00
55	Rusty Greer/8	5.00
56	Matt Williams/12	10.00
57	Sammy Sosa/50	25.00
58	Carl Everett/34	3.00
59	Carlos Delgado/41	5.00
60	Jeremy Giambi/10	5.00
61	Jose Canseco/15	10.00
62	David Segui/19	3.00
63	Jose Vidro/24	3.00
64	Matt Stairs/21	5.00
65	Travis Fryman/22	5.00
66	Ken Griffey Jr./40	15.00
67	Mike Piazza/38	15.00
68	Mark McGwire/32	20.00
69	Craig Biggio/8	10.00
70	Eric Chavez/26	10.00
71	Mo Vaughn/36	5.00
72	Matt Lawton/13	5.00
73	Miguel Tejada/30	10.00
74	Brian Giles/35	5.00
75	Sean Casey/20	5.00
76	Robin Ventura/24	5.00
77	Ivan Rodriguez/27	8.00
78	Dean Palmer/29	3.00
79	Frank Thomas/43	10.00
80	Bernie Williams/30	8.00
81	Juan Encarnacion/14	5.00
82	John Olerud/14	5.00
83	Rich Aurilia/20	3.00
84	Juan Gonzalez/22	8.00
85	Ray Durham/17	5.00
86	Steve Finley/35	3.00
87	Ken Caminiti/15	5.00
88	Roberto Alomar/19	15.00
89	Jeromy Burnitz/31	3.00
90	J.D. Drew/18	8.00
91	Lance Berkman/21	8.00
92	Gabe Kapler/14	8.00
93	Larry Walker/9	10.00
94	Alex Rodriguez/41	20.00
95	Jeffrey Hammonds/20	5.00
96	Magglio Ordonez/32	5.00
97	David Justice/41	5.00
98	Eric Karros/31	3.00
99	Manny Ramirez/38	10.00
100	Paul O'Neill/18	8.00

Green

		NM/M
Common Player:		1.00
Produced to # of 2000 RBI's		
1	Derek Jeter/73	5.00
2	Vladimir Guerrero/123	2.00
3	Henry Rodriguez/61	1.00
4	Jason Giambi/137	5.00
5	Nomar Garciaparra/96	10.00
6	Jeff Kent/125	3.00
7	Garret Anderson/117	3.00
8	Todd Helton/147	5.00
9	Barry Bonds/106	20.00
10	Preston Wilson/121	1.00
11	Troy Glaus/102	5.00
12	Geoff Jenkins/94	3.00
13	Jim Edmonds/108	4.00
14	Bobby Higginson/102	3.00
15	Mark Quinn/78	1.00
16	Barry Larkin/41	3.00
17	Richie Sexson/91	4.00
18	Fernando Tatis/64	1.00
19	John Vander Wal/94	1.00
20	Darin Erstad/100	3.00
21	Shawn Green/99	3.00
22	Scott Rolen/89	5.00
23	Tony Batista/114	1.00
24	Phil Nevin/107	1.00
25	Tim Salmon/97	3.00
26	Gary Sheffield/109	3.00
27	Ben Grieve/104	1.00
28	Jermaine Dye/118	1.00

29	Andres Galarraga/100	1.50
30	Adrian Beltre/85	1.00
31	Rafael Palmeiro/120	1.00
32	J.T. Snow/96	1.00
33	Edgardo Alfonzo/94	1.00
34	Paul Konerko/97	1.50
35	Jim Thome/106	4.00
36	Andruw Jones/104	4.00
37	Mike Sweeney/144	1.00
38	Jose Cruz Jr./76	1.00
39	David Ortiz/63	1.00
40	Pat Burrell/79	1.00
41	Chipper Jones/111	8.00
42	Jeff Bagwell/132	5.00
43	Raul Mondesi/67	2.00
44	Rondell White/61	1.50
45	Edgar Martinez/145	2.00
46	Cal Ripken Jr./56	25.00
47	Moises Alou/114	1.00
48	Shannon Stewart/69	1.00
49	Tino Martinez/91	2.00
50	Jason Kendall/58	1.00
51	Richard Hidalgo/122	1.00
52	Albert Belle/103	1.00
53	Jay Payton/62	1.00
54	Cliff Floyd/91	1.00
55	Rusty Greer/65	1.00
56	Matt Williams/47	2.00
57	Sammy Sosa/138	10.00
58	Carl Everett/108	1.00
59	Carlos Delgado/137	3.00
60	Jeremy Giambi/50	5.00
61	Jose Canseco/49	5.00
62	David Segui/103	1.00
63	Jose Vidro/97	1.00
64	Matt Stairs/81	1.00
65	Travis Fryman/106	2.00
66	Ken Griffey Jr./118	10.00
67	Mike Piazza/113	10.00
68	Mark McGwire/73	15.00
69	Craig Biggio/35	4.00
70	Eric Chavez/86	4.00
71	Mo Vaughn/117	3.00
72	Matt Lawton/88	1.00
73	Miguel Tejada/115	4.00
74	Brian Giles/123	3.00
75	Sean Casey/85	2.00
76	Robin Ventura/84	2.00
77	Ivan Rodriguez/83	5.00
78	Dean Palmer/102	1.00
79	Frank Thomas/143	5.00
80	Bernie Williams/121	4.00
81	Juan Encarnacion/72	1.00
82	John Olerud/103	3.00
83	Rich Aurilia/79	1.00
84	Juan Gonzalez/67	5.00
85	Ray Durham/75	1.00
86	Steve Finley/96	1.00
87	Ken Caminiti/45	5.00
88	Roberto Alomar/89	5.00
89	Jeromy Burnitz/98	1.00
90	J.D. Drew/57	3.00
91	Lance Berkman/67	2.00
92	Gabe Kapler/66	2.00
93	Larry Walker/51	3.00
94	Alex Rodriguez/132	15.00
95	Jeffrey Hammonds/106	1.00
96	Magglio Ordonez/126	3.00
97	David Justice/118	3.00
98	Eric Karros/106	1.00
99	Manny Ramirez/122	5.00
100	Paul O'Neill/100	2.00

Red

Common Player (1-100):
Stars: 4-8X
Produced to 2000 Bat Avg.

Autographics

NM/M
Common Autograph: 5.00
Inserted 1:72
Silvers: 1X
Production 250 Sets
Golds: 1-2X
Production 50 Sets

1	Roberto Alomar	30.00
2	Jimmy Anderson	5.00
3	Ryan Anderson	5.00
4	Rick Ankiel	15.00
5	Adrian Beltre	15.00
6	Peter Bergeron	5.00
7	Lance Berkman	15.00
8	Barry Bonds	150.00
9	Milton Bradley	8.00
10	Dee Brown	5.00
11	Roosevelt Brown	5.00
12	Pat Burrell	15.00
13	Sean Casey	8.00
14	Eric Chavez	10.00
15	Giuseppe Chiaramonte	5.00
16	Joe Crede	5.00
17	Jose Cruz Jr.	5.00
18	Carlos Delgado	10.00
19	Ryan Dempster	5.00
20	Adam Dunn	15.00
21	David Eckstein	5.00
22	Jim Edmonds	10.00
23	Troy Glaus	5.00
24	Chad Green	5.00
25	Tony Gwynn	30.00
26	Todd Helton	20.00
27	Chad Hermansen	5.00
28	Shea Hillenbrand	6.00
29	Aubrey Huff	5.00
30	Randy Johnson	40.00
31	Chipper Jones	40.00
32	Mike Lamb	5.00
33	Corey Lee	5.00
34	Steve Lomasney	5.00
35	Terrence Long	5.00
36	Julio Lugo	5.00
37	Jason Marquis	5.00
38	Bengie Molina	8.00
39	Mike Mussina	25.00
40	Pablo Ozuna	5.00
41	Corey Patterson	10.00
42	Jay Payton	6.00
43	Wily Pena	10.00
44	Josh Phelps	5.00
45	Adam Piatt	5.00
46	Matt Riley	5.00
47	Alex Rodriguez	80.00
48	Alex Sanchez	5.00
49	Gary Sheffield	15.00
50	Alfonso Soriano	40.00
51	Shannon Stewart	5.00
52	Fernando Tatis	5.00
53	Jose Vidro	5.00
54	Preston Wilson	8.00
55	Kerry Wood	25.00
56	Julio Zuleta	5.00

Crowning Achievements

NM/M
Complete Set (15): 15.00
Common Player: .50
Inserted 1:9

1	Troy Glaus	1.00
2	Mark McGwire	2.50
3	Barry Larkin, Craig Biggio	.50
4	Ken Griffey Jr.	2.00
5	Rafael Palmeiro	.75
6	Alex Rodriguez	2.50
7	Roger Clemens	1.75
8	Mike Piazza	2.00
9	Cal Ripken Jr.	3.00
10	Randy Johnson	1.00
11	Jeff Bagwell	1.00
12	Sammy Sosa	2.00
13	Greg Maddux	1.50
14	Barry Bonds	3.00
15	Fred McGriff	.50

Crowns of Gold

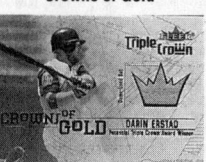

NM/M
Common Player: 4.00
Random inserts in Hobby packs.

Rick Ankiel/Jsy	4.00
Steve Carlton/Jsy	5.00
Roger Clemens/Jsy	40.00
Carlos Delgado/Bat	8.00
Darin Erstad/Bat	6.00
Jimmie Foxx/Bat	100.00
Todd Helton/Bat	10.00
Randy Johnson/Jsy	15.00
Frank Robinson/Bat	8.00
Gary Sheffield/Jsy	8.00
Frank Thomas/Bat	10.00
Ted Williams/Bat	200.00

Crowns of Gold Autograph

NM/M
Random inserts in Hobby packs.

Steve Carlton/Jsy/72	80.00
Roger Clemens/Jsy/98	150.00
Frank Robinson/Bat/66	80.00

Feel the Game

NM/M
Common Player: 4.00
Inserted 1:72
Golds: 1.5-2X
Production 50 Sets

Adrian Beltre	6.00
Dante Bichette	5.00
Roger Cedeno	4.00
Ben Davis	5.00
Carlos Delgado	6.00
J.D. Drew	5.00
Jason Giambi	6.00
Brian Giles	4.00
Juan Gonzalez	5.00
Richard Hidalgo	4.00
Chipper Jones	10.00
Eric Karros	4.00
Javy Lopez	4.00
Tino Martinez	4.00
Raul Mondesi	4.00
Phil Nevin	4.00
Chan Ho Park	4.00
Ivan Rodriguez	6.00
Shannon Stewart	4.00
Frank Thomas	8.00
Jose Vidro	4.00
Matt Williams	4.00
Preston Wilson	4.00

Future Threats

NM/M
Complete Set (15): 15.00
Common Player: .50
Inserted 1:7

1	Derek Jeter	3.00
2	Alex Rodriguez	2.50
3	Magglio Ordonez, Shawn Green	.50
4	Larry Walker	.50
5	Vladimir Guerrero	1.00
6	Nomar Garciaparra	2.00
7	Ken Griffey Jr.	2.00
8	Barry Bonds	3.00
9	Chipper Jones	1.50
10	Todd Helton	1.00
11	Ivan Rodriguez	.75
12	Jeff Bagwell	1.00
13	Frank Thomas	1.00
14	Carlos Delgado	.65
15	Mike Piazza	2.00

Glamour Boys

NM/M
Complete Set (15): 40.00
Common Player: 1.50
Inserted 1:24

1	Derek Jeter	6.00
2	Vladimir Guerrero	2.00
3	Scott Rolen, Jeff Bagwell	1.50
4	Sammy Sosa	4.00
5	Ken Griffey Jr.	4.00
6	Mark McGwire	5.00
7	Ivan Rodriguez	1.50
8	Mike Piazza	4.00
9	Nomar Garciaparra	4.00
10	Cal Ripken Jr.	6.00
11	Tony Gwynn	3.00
12	Barry Bonds	6.00
13	Randy Johnson	2.00
14	Alex Rodriguez	5.00
15	Pedro Martinez	2.00

2001 Fleer/Ritz-Oreo

In conjunction with its sponsorship of the 2001 All-Star Game in Seattle, Ritz-Oreo issued a pair of Jeter cards distributed in product packages. In standard 2-1/2" x 3-1/2" format, one card is bordered in red and pictures him batting; a blue bordered card has a picture of him throwing. Backs have biographical data with height measured in Oreos, and weight measured in Ritz, recent stats, a quote and logos of all parties involved. The cards were also available packaged with a pair of Upper Deck Griffey cards in a mail-in offer.

NM/M
Complete Set (2): 3.00
Common Card: 2.00

Derek Jeter/Btg	2.00
Derek Jeter/Throwing	2.00

2002 Fleer

NM/M
Complete Set (540): 75.00
Common Player: .15
Pack (10): 2.00
Box (24): 40.00

1	Darin Erstad	.15
2	Randy Johnson	.50
3	Chipper Jones	.50
4	Jay Gibbons	.15
5	Nomar Garciaparra	.50
6	Sammy Sosa	.50
7	Frank Thomas	.50
8	Ken Griffey Jr.	.75
9	Jim Thome	.25
10	Todd Helton	.25
11	Jeff Weaver	.15
12	Cliff Floyd	.15
13	Jeff Bagwell	.25
14	Mike Sweeney	.15
15	Adrian Beltre	.25
16	Richie Sexson	.15
17	Brad Radke	.15
18	Vladimir Guerrero	.50
19	Mike Piazza	.50
20	Derek Jeter	1.00
21	Eric Chavez	.15
22	Pat Burrell	.15
23	Brian Giles	.15
24	Trevor Hoffman	.15
25	Barry Bonds	1.00
26	Ichiro Suzuki	.75
27	Albert Pujols	1.00
28	Ben Grieve	.15
29	Alex Rodriguez	1.00
30	Carlos Delgado	.25
31	Miguel Tejada	.25
32	Todd Hollandsworth	.15
33	Marlon Anderson	.15
34	Kerry Robinson	.15
35	Chris Richard	.15
36	Jamey Wright	.15
37	Ray Lankford	.15
38	Mike Bordick	.15
39	Danny Graves	.15
40	A.J. Pierzynski	.15
41	Shannon Stewart	.15
42	Tony Armas Jr.	.15
43	Brad Ausmus	.15
44	Alfonso Soriano	.50
45	Junior Spivey	.15
46	Brent Mayne	.15
47	Jim Thome	.15
48	Dan Wilson	.15
49	Geoff Jenkins	.15
50	Kris Benson	.15
51	Rafael Furcal	.15
52	Wiki Gonzalez	.15
53	Jeff Kent	.15
54	Curt Schilling	.40
55	Ken Harvey	.15
56	Roosevelt Brown	.15
57	David Segui	.15
58	Mario Valdez	.15
59	Adam Dunn	.50
60	Bob Howry	.15
61	Michael Barrett	.15
62	Garret Anderson	.15
63	Kelvim Escobar	.15
64	Ben Grieve	.15
65	Randy Johnson	.75
66	Jose Offerman	.15
67	Jason Kendall	.15
68	Joel Pineiro	.15
69	Alex Escobar	.15
70	Chris George	.15
71	Bobby Higginson	.15
72	Nomar Garciaparra	1.50
73	Pat Burrell	.40
74	Lee Stevens	.15
75	Felipe Lopez	.15
76	Al Leiter	.15
77	Jim Edmonds	.15
78	Al Levine	.15
79	Raul Mondesi	.15
80	Jose Valentin	.15
81	Matt Clement	.15
82	Richard Hidalgo	.15
83	Jamie Moyer	.15
84	Brian Schneider	.15
85	John Franco	.15
86	Brian Buchanan	.15
87	Roy Oswalt	.25
88	Johnny Estrada	.15
89	Marcus Giles	.15
90	Carlos Valderrama	.15
91	Mark Mulder	.15
92	Mark Grace	.25
93	Andy Ashby	.15
94	Woody Williams	.15
95	Ben Petrick	.15
96	Roy Halladay	.30
97	Fred McGriff	.15
98	Shawn Green	.40
99	Todd Hundley	.15
100	Carlos Febles	.15
101	Jason Marquis	.15
102	Mike Redmond	.15
103	Shane Halter	.15
104	Trot Nixon	.15
105	Jeremy Giambi	.15
106	Carlos Delgado	.50
107	Richie Sexson	.15
108	Russ Ortiz	.15
109	David Ortiz	.25
110	Curtis Leskanic	.15
111	Jay Payton	.15
112	Travis Phelps	.15
113	J.T. Snow	.15
114	Edgar Renteria	.15
115	Freddy Garcia	.15
116	Cliff Floyd	.15
117	Charles Nagy	.15
118	Tony Batista	.15
119	Rafael Palmeiro	.65
120	Darren Dreifort	.15
121	Warren Morris	.15
122	Augie Ojeda	.15
123	Rusty Greer	.15
124	Esteban Yan	.15
125	Corey Patterson	.25
126	Matt Ginter	.15
127	Matt Lawton	.15
128	Miguel Batista	.15
129	Randy Winn	.15
130	Eric Milton	.15
131	Jack Wilson	.15
132	Sean Casey	.25
133	Mike Sweeney	.15
134	Jason Tyner	.15
135	Carlos Hernandez	.15
136	Shea Hillenbrand	.15
137	Shawn Wooten	.15
138	Peter Bergeron	.15
139	Travis Lee	.15
140	Craig Wilson	.15
141	Carlos Guillen	.15
142	Chipper Jones	1.00
143	Gabe Kapler	.15
144	Raul Ibanez	.15
145	Eric Chavez	.25
146	D'Angelo Jimenez	.15
147	Chad Hermansen	.15
148	Joe Kennedy	.15
149	Mariano Rivera	.15
150	Jeff Bagwell	.15
151	Joe McEwing	.15
152	Ronnie Belliard	.15
153	Desi Relaford	.15
154	Vinny Castilla	.15
155	Tim Hudson	.15
156	Wilton Guerrero	.15
157	Raul Casanova	.15
158	Edgardo Alfonzo	.15
159	Derrek Lee	.15
160	Phil Nevin	.15
161	Roger Clemens	1.25
162	Jason LaRue	.15
163	Brian Lawrence	.15
164	Adrian Beltre	.30
165	Troy Glaus	.75
166	Jeff Weaver	.15
167	B.J. Surhoff	.15
168	Eric Byrnes	.15
169	Mike Sirotka	.15
170	Bill Haselman	.15
171	Javier Vazquez	.15
172	Sidney Ponson	.15
173	Adam Everett	.15
174	Bubba Trammell	.15
175	Robb Nen	.15
176	Barry Larkin	.15
177	Tony Graffanino	.15
178	Rich Garces	.15
179	Juan Uribe	.15
180	Tom Glavine	.25
181	Eric Karros	.15
182	Michael Cuddyer	.15
183	Wade Miller	.15
184	Matt Williams	.15
185	Matt Morris	.15
186	Rickey Henderson	.75
187	Trevor Hoffman	.15
188	Wilson Betemit	.15
189	Steve Karsay	.15
190	Frank Catalanotto	.15
191	Jason Schmidt	.15
192	Roger Cedeno	.15
193	Magglio Ordonez	.15
194	Pat Hentgen	.15
195	Mike Lieberthal	.15
196	Andy Pettitte	.30
197	Jay Gibbons	.15
198	Rolando Arrojo	.15
199	Joe Mays	.15
200	Aubrey Huff	.15
201	Nelson Figueroa	.15
202	Paul Konerko	.25
203	Ken Griffey Jr.	1.50
204	Brandon Duckworth	.15
205	Sammy Sosa	1.50
206	Carl Everett	.15
207	Scott Rolen	.65
208	Orlando Hernandez	.15
209	Todd Helton	.75
210	Preston Wilson	.15
211	Gil Meche	.15
212	Bill Mueller	.15
213	Craig Biggio	.15
214	Dean Palmer	.15
215	Randy Wolf	.15
216	Jeff Suppan	.15
217	Jimmy Rollins	.25
218	Alexis Gomez	.15
219	Ellis Burks	.15
220	Ramon E. Martinez	.15
221	Ramiro Mendoza	.15
222	Einar Diaz	.15
223	Brent Abernathy	.15
224	Darin Erstad	.25
225	Reggie Taylor	.15
226	Jason Jennings	.15
227	Ray Durham	.15
228	John Parrish	.15
229	Kevin Young	.15
230	Xavier Nady	.15
231	Juan Cruz	.15
232	Greg Norton	.15
233	Barry Bonds	2.00
234	Kip Wells	.15
235	Paul LoDuca	.15
236	Javy Lopez	.25
237	Luis Castillo	.15
238	Tom Gordon	.15
239	Mike Mordecai	.15
240	Damian Rolls	.15
241	Julio Lugo	.15
242	Ichiro Suzuki	1.00
243	Tony Womack	.15
244	Matt Anderson	.15
245	Carlos Lee	.15
246	Alex Rodriguez	1.75
247	Bernie Williams	.30
248	Scott Sullivan	.15
249	Mike Hampton	.15
250	Orlando Cabrera	.15
251	Benito Santiago	.15
252	Steve Finley	.15
253	Dave Williams	.15
254	Adam Kennedy	.15
255	Omar Vizquel	.15
256	Garrett Stephenson	.15
257	Fernando Tatis	.15
258	Mike Piazza	1.50
259	Scott Spiezio	.15
260	Jacque Jones	.15
261	Russell Branyan	.15
262	Mark McLemore	.15
263	Mitch Meluskey	.15
264	Marlon Byrd	.15
265	Kyle Farnsworth	.15
266	Billy Sylvester	.15
267	C.C. Sabathia	.15
268	Mark Buehrle	.15
269	Geoff Blum	.15
270	Bret Prinz	.15
271	Placido Polanco	.15
272	John Olerud	.15
273	Pedro J. Martinez	.75
274	Doug Mientkiewicz	.15
275	Jason Bere	.15
276	Bud Smith	.15
277	Terrence Long	.15
278	Troy Percival	.15
279	Derek Jeter	2.00
280	Eric Owens	.15

281	Jay Bell	.15
282	Mike Cameron	.15
283	Joe Randa	.15
284	Brian Roberts	.15
285	Ryan Klesko	.15
286	Ryan Dempster	.15
287	Cristian Guzman	.15
288	Tim Salmon	.25
289	Mark Johnson	.15
290	Brian Giles	.15
291	Jon Lieber	.15
292	Fernando Vina	.15
293	Mike Mussina	.40
294	Juan Pierre	.15
295	Carlos Beltran	.40
296	Vladimir Guerrero	.75
297	Orlando Merced	.15
298	Jose Hernandez	.15
299	Mike Lamb	.15
300	David Eckstein	.15
301	Mark Loretta	.15
302	Greg Vaughn	.15
303	Jose Vidro	.15
304	Jose Ortiz	.15
305	Mark Grudzielanek	.15
306	Rob Bell	.15
307	Elmer Dessens	.15
308	Tomas Perez	.15
309	Jerry Hairston Jr.	.15
310	Mike Stanton	.15
311	Todd Walker	.15
312	Jason Varitek	.15
313	Masato Yoshii	.15
314	Ben Sheets	.15
315	Roberto Hernandez	.15
316	Eli Marrero	.15
317	Josh Beckett	.50
318	Robert Fick	.15
319	Aramis Ramirez	.15
320	Bartolo Colon	.15
321	Kenny Kelly	.15
322	Luis Gonzalez	.25
323	John Smoltz	.15
324	Homer Bush	.15
325	Kevin Millwood	.15
326	Manny Ramirez	.75
327	Armando Benitez	.15
328	Luis Alicea	.15
329	Mark Kotsay	.15
330	Felix Rodriguez	.15
331	Eddie Taubensee	.15
332	John Burkett	.15
333	Ramon Ortiz	.15
334	Daryle Ward	.15
335	Jarrod Washburn	.15
336	Benji Gil	.15
337	Mike Lowell	.15
338	Larry Walker	.15
339	Andruw Jones	.75
340	Scott Elarton	.15
341	Tony McKnight	.15
342	Frank Thomas	.50
343	Kevin Brown	.15
344	Jermaine Dye	.15
345	Luis Rivas	.15
346	Jeff Conine	.15
347	Bobby Kielty	.15
348	Jeffrey Hammonds	.15
349	Keith Foulke	.15
350	Dave Martinez	.15
351	Adam Eaton	.15
352	Brandon Inge	.15
353	Tyler Houston	.15
354	Bobby Abreu	.15
355	Ivan Rodriguez	.65
356	Doug Glanville	.15
357	Jorge Julio	.15
358	Kerry Wood	.50
359	Eric Munson	.15
360	Joe Crede	.15
361	Denny Neagle	.15
362	Vance Wilson	.15
363	Neifi Perez	.15
364	Darryl Kile	.15
365	Jose Macias	.15
366	Michael Coleman	.15
367	Erubiel Durazo	.15
368	Darrin Fletcher	.15
369	Matt White	.15
370	Marvin Benard	.15
371	Brad Penny	.15
372	Chuck Finley	.15
373	Delino DeShields	.15
374	Adrian Brown	.15
375	Corey Koskie	.15
376	Kazuhiro Sasaki	.15
377	Brent Butler	.15
378	Paul Wilson	.15
379	Scott Williamson	.15
380	Mike Young	.15
381	Toby Hall	.15
382	Shane Reynolds	.15
383	Tom Goodwin	.15
384	Seth Etherton	.15
385	Billy Wagner	.15
386	Josh Phelps	.15
387	Kyle Lohse	.15
388	Jeremy Fikac	.15
389	Jorge Posada	.30
390	Bret Boone	.15
391	Angel Berroa	.15
392	Matt Mantei	.15
393	Alex Gonzalez	.15
394	Scott Strickland	.15
395	Charles Johnson	.15
396	Ramon Hernandez	.15
397	Damian Jackson	.15
398	Albert Pujols	1.50
399	Gary Bennett	.15
400	Edgar Martinez	.15
401	Carl Pavano	.15
402	Chris Gomez	.15
403	Jaret Wright	.15
404	Lance Berkman	.15
405	Robert Person	.15
406	Brook Fordyce	.15
407	Adam Pettyjohn	.15
408	Chris Carpenter	.15
409	Rey Ordonez	.15
410	Eric Gagne	.25
411	Damion Easley	.15
412	A.J. Burnett	.15
413	Aaron Boone	.15
414	J.D. Drew	.15
415	Kelly Stinnett	.15
416	Mark Quinn	.15
417	Brad Radke	.15
418	Jose Cruz Jr.	.15
419	Greg Maddux	1.00
420	Steve Cox	.15
421	Torii Hunter	.15
422	Sandy Alomar	.15
423	Barry Zito	.40
424	Bill Hall	.15
425	Marquis Grissom	.15
426	Rich Aurilia	.15
427	Royce Clayton	.15
428	Travis Fryman	.15
429	Pablo Ozuna	.15
430	David Dellucci	.15
431	Vernon Wells	.15
432	Gregg Zaun	.15
433	Alex Gonzalez	.15
434	Hideo Nomo	.40
435	Jeromy Burnitz	.15
436	Gary Sheffield	.25
437	Tino Martinez	.15
438	Tsuyoshi Shinjo	.15
439	Chan Ho Park	.15
440	Tony Clark	.15
441	Brad Fullmer	.15
442	Jason Giambi	.50
443	Billy Koch	.15
444	Mo Vaughn	.15
445	Alex Ochoa	.15
446	Darren Lewis	.15
447	John Rocker	.15
448	Scott Hatteberg	.15
449	Brady Anderson	.15
450	Chuck Knoblauch	.15
451	Pokey Reese	.15
452	Brian Jordan	.15
453	Albie Lopez	.15
454	David Bell	.15
455	Juan Gonzalez	.75
456	Terry Adams	.15
457	Kenny Lofton	.25
458	Shawn Estes	.15
459	Josh Fogg	.15
460	Dmitri Young	.15
461	Johnny Damon	.25
462	Chris Singleton	.15
463	Ricky Ledee	.15
464	Dustin Hermanson	.15
465	Aaron Sele	.15
466	Chris Stynes	.15
467	Matt Stairs	.15
468	Kevin Appier	.15
469	Omar Daal	.15
470	Moises Alou	.15
471	Juan Encarnacion	.15
472	Robin Ventura	.15
473	Eric Hinske	.15
474	Rondell White	.15
475	Carlos Pena	.15
476	Craig Paquette	.15
477	Marty Cordova	.15
478	Brett Tomko	.15
479	Reggie Sanders	.15
480	Roberto Alomar	.15
481	Jeff Cirillo	.15
482	Todd Zeile	.15
483	John Vander Wal	.15
484	Rick Helling	.15
485	Jeff D'Amico	.15
486	David Justice	.15
487	Jason Isringhausen	.15
488	Shigetoshi Hasegawa	.15
489	Eric Young	.15
490	David Wells	.15
491	Ruben Sierra	.15
492	Aaron Cook RC	.50
493	Takahito Nomura RC	.50
494	Austin Kearns RC	.50
495	Kazuhisa Ishii RC	2.00
496	Mark Teixeira RC	.50
497	Rene Reyes RC	.50
498	Tim Spooneybarger	.15
499	Ben Broussard	.15
500	Eric Cyr RC	.25
501	Anastacio Martinez RC	.25
502	Morgan Ensberg	.15
503	Steve Kent RC	.25
504	Franklin Nunez RC	.25
505	Adam Walker RC	.25
506	Anderson Machado RC	.25
507	Ryan Drese	.15
508	Luis Ugueto RC	.25
509	Jorge Nunez RC	.25
510	Colby Lewis	.15
511	Ron Calloway RC	.50
512	Hansel Izquierdo RC	.50
513	Jason Lane	.15
514	Rafael Soriano	.15
515	Jackson Melian	.15
516	Edwin Almonte RC	.50
517	Satoru Komiyama RC	.50
518	Corey Thurman RC	.25
519	Jorge De La Rosa RC	.50
520	Victor Martinez	.15
521	Dewan Brazleton	.15
522	Marlon Byrd	.50
523	Jae Weong Seo	.15
524	Orlando Hudson	.15
525	Sean Burroughs	.15
526	Ryan Langerhans	.15
527	David Kelton	.15
528	So Taguchi RC	.50
529	Tyler Walker	.15
530	Hank Blalock	.50
531	Mark Prior	.75
532	Yankee Stadium	.50
533	Fenway Park	.50
534	Wrigley Field	.50
535	Dodger Stadium	.50
536	Camden Yards	.15
537	PacBell Park	.15
538	Jacobs Field	.15
539	SAFECO Field	.15
540	Miller Field	.15

Mini

Mini (1-540): 8-15X
Production 50 Sets
Retail Exclusive

Tiffany

Stars (1-540): 4-8X
Production 200 Sets

Barry Bonds Career Highlights

		NM/M
Complete Set (10):		40.00
Common Bonds 1-3:		3.00
Common 4-6 inserted 1:125 H.		
7-9 1:250 H		6.00
#10 1:383		6.00
1CH-3	Barry Bonds	3.00
4CH-6	Barry Bonds	4.00
7CH-10	Barry Bonds	6.00

Barry Bonds Career Highlights Autographs

No Pricing
25 Sets Produced

Barry Bonds Chasing History

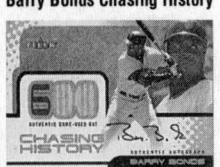

This special edition of 600 was sold exclusively via a home shopping tv program. The 3-1/2" x 2-1/2" card features on front a piece of game-used Bonds bat in the form of the two Os in "600." At right are an authentic autograph and portrait and action photos. On back is a statement of authenticity and a serial number.

	NM/M
Barry Bonds	125.00

Barry Bonds 4X MVP Super

Bonds' status as the only four-time MVP winner was marked with the issue of this home shopping channel exclusive. The 5-1/2"x3-1/2" card is serially numbered on back from within an edition of 5,000.

	NM/M
Barry Bonds	15.00

Barry Bonds 600 HR Supers

To commemorate his career 600th home run, Fleer produced a pair of jumbo-format (3-1/2" x 5") cards for sale on a TV home shopping show. One version of the card bears a facsimile autograph. A premium version, limited to 600 numbered cards, has a game-used bat chip and an authentic Bonds signature.

	NM/M
Barry Bonds (Facsimile signature.)	55.00
Barry Bonds (Autograph w/bat chip.)	250.00

Classic Cuts Autographs

		NM/M
Inserted 1:432		
LA-A	Luis Aparicio	15.00
RC-A	Ron Cey	8.00
HK-A	Harmon Killebrew	35.00
JM-A	Juan Marichal	15.00
GP-A	Gaylord Perry/SP/225	15.00
PR-A	Phil Rizzuto/SP/125	50.00
BR-A	Brooks Robinson/SP/200	40.00

Classic Cuts Game-Used

		NM/M
Common Player:		5.00
Inserted 1:24		
SA-P	Sparky Anderson/Pants	5.00
HB-B	Hank Bauer/Bat	5.00
JB-J	Johnny Bench/Jsy	15.00
PB-B	Paul Blair/Bat	5.00
WB-B	Wade Boggs/Bat/99	20.00
WB-J	Wade Boggs/Jsy	10.00
BB-B	Bobby Bonds/Bat	5.00
BB-J	Bobby Bonds/Jsy	5.00
GB-B	George Brett/Bat/250	30.00
GB-J	George Brett/Jsy/250	30.00
SC-P	Steve Carlton/Pants	6.00
OC-P	Orlando Cepeda/Pants	5.00
AD-J	Andre Dawson/Jsy	8.00
BD-B	Bill Dickey/Bat/200	20.00
LD-B	Larry Doby/Bat/250	10.00
DE-B	Dwight Evans/Bat/250	10.00
DE-J	Dwight Evans/Jsy	5.00
RF-J	Rollie Fingers/Jsy	5.00
CF-B	Carlton Fisk/Bat	10.00
CF-J	Carlton Fisk/Jsy/150	20.00
NF-B	Nellie Fox/Bat/200	20.00
SG-B	Steve Garvey/Bat	5.00
KG-B	Kirk Gibson/Bat	5.00
GH-B	Gil Hodges/Bat/200	15.00
CH-J	Jim Hunter/Jsy	10.00
BJ-J	Bo Jackson/Jsy	5.00
RJ-P	Reggie Jackson/Pants	10.00
GK-B	George Kell/Bat/150	15.00
TK-B	Ted Kluszewski/Bat/200	15.00
TK-P	Ted Kluszewski/Pants	10.00
RM-P	Roger Maris/Pants/200	60.00
EM-B	Eddie Mathews/Bat/200	50.00
DM-B	Don Mattingly/Bat/200	50.00
DM-J	Don Mattingly/Jsy	40.00
WM-J	Willie McCovey/Jsy/300	15.00
PM-B	Paul Molitor/Bat/250	25.00
JM-B	Joe Morgan/Bat/250	8.00
EM-B	Eddie Murray/Bat	10.00
EM-J	Eddie Murray/Jsy	10.00
JP-J	Jim Palmer/Jsy/273	8.00
DP-B	Dave Parker/Bat	5.00
TP-B	Tony Perez/Bat/250	10.00
TP-J	Tony Perez/Jsy	8.00
LP-P	Lou Piniella/Pants	5.00
KP-J	Kirby Puckett/Jsy	15.00
JR-B	Jim Rice/Bat/225	8.00
CR-BG	Cal Ripken Jr./Bty Glv/100	75.00
CR-FG	Cal Ripken Jr./Fld Glv/50	125.00
CR-J	Cal Ripken Jr./Jsy	35.00
CR-P	Cal Ripken Jr./Pants/200	40.00
BR-B	Brooks Robinson/Bat/250	15.00
NR-J	Nolan Ryan/Jsy	50.00
NR-P	Nolan Ryan/Pants/200	60.00
RS-B	Ryne Sandberg/Bat	25.00
OS-J	Ozzie Smith/Jsy/250	15.00
WS-B	Willie Stargell/Bat/250	15.00
JT-J	Joe Torre/Jsy/125	15.00
AT-B	Alan Trammell/Bat	10.00
EW-J	Earl Weaver/Jsy	8.00
HW-P	Hoyt Wilhelm/Pants/150	15.00
TW-B	Ted Williams/Bat	85.00
TW-P	Ted Williams/Pants	120.00
DW-B	Dave Winfield/Bat	8.00
DW-J	Dave Winfield/Jsy/231	10.00
DW-P	Dave Winfield/Pants	8.00
RY-B	Robin Yount/Bat	15.00

Classic Cuts Game Used Autographs

		NM/M
Varying quantities produced.		
LA-B	Luis Aparicio/Bat/45	25.00
BR-B	Brooks Robinson/Bat/45	80.00

Diamond Standouts

		NM/M
Complete Set (10):		40.00
Common Player:		2.00
Production 1,200 Sets		
1DS	Mike Piazza	4.00
2DS	Derek Jeter	8.00
3DS	Ken Griffey Jr.	4.00
4DS	Barry Bonds	8.00
5DS	Sammy Sosa	4.00
6DS	Alex Rodriguez	6.00
7DS	Ichiro Suzuki	8.00
8DS	Greg Maddux	3.00
9DS	Jason Giambi	2.00
10DS	Nomar Garciaparra	4.00

Golden Memories

		NM/M
Complete Set (15):		20.00
Common Player:		1.00
Inserted 1:24		
1GM	Frank Thomas	1.50
2GM	Derek Jeter	4.00
3GM	Albert Pujols	3.00
4GM	Barry Bonds	4.00
5GM	Alex Rodriguez	3.00
6GM	Randy Johnson	1.50
7GM	Jeff Bagwell	1.50
8GM	Greg Maddux	2.00
9GM	Ivan Rodriguez	1.00
10GM	Ichiro Suzuki	2.50
11GM	Mike Piazza	2.50
12GM	Pat Burrell	1.00
13GM	Rickey Henderson	1.00
14GM	Vladimir Guerrero	1.50
15GM	Sammy Sosa	2.50

Headliners

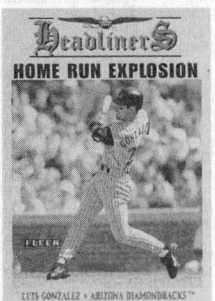

		NM/M
Complete Set (20):		10.00
Common Player:		.25
Inserted 1:8		
1HL	Randy Johnson	.75
2HL	Alex Rodriguez	1.50
3HL	Todd Helton	.75
4HL	Pedro J. Martinez	.75
5HL	Ichiro Suzuki	1.50
6HL	Vladimir Guerrero	.75
7HL	Derek Jeter	1.25
8HL	Adam Dunn	.40
9HL	Luis Gonzalez	.25
10HL	Kazuhiro Sasaki	.25
11HL	Sammy Sosa	1.25
12HL	Jason Giambi	.60
13HL	Ken Griffey Jr.	1.25
14HL	Roger Clemens	1.00
15HL	Brandon Duckworth	.25
16HL	Nomar Garciaparra	1.25
17HL	Bud Smith	.25
18HL	Juan Gonzalez	.75
19HL	Chipper Jones	1.00
20HL	Barry Bonds	2.00

Rookie Flashback

		NM/M
Complete Set (20):		6.00
Common Player:		.25
Inserted 1:3 Retail		
1RF	Bret Prinz	.25
2RF	Albert Pujols	2.00
3RF	C.C. Sabathia	.25
4RF	Ichiro Suzuki	1.50
5RF	Juan Cruz	.25
6RF	Jay Gibbons	.50
7RF	Bud Smith	.25
8RF	Johnny Estrada	.25
9RF	Roy Oswalt	.50
10RF	Tsuyoshi Shinjo	.25
11RF	Brandon Duckworth	.25
12RF	Jackson Melian	.25
13RF	Josh Beckett	1.00
14RF	Morgan Ensberg	.25
15RF	Brian Lawrence	.25
16RF	Eric Hinske	.25
17RF	Juan Uribe	.25
18RF	Matt White	.25
19RF	Junior Spivey	.25
20RF	Wilson Betemit	.25

Rookie Sensations

		NM/M
Complete Set (20):		40.00
Common Player:		2.00
Production 1,500 Sets		
1RS	Bret Prinz	2.00
2RS	Albert Pujols	10.00
3RS	C.C. Sabathia	2.00
4RS	Ichiro Suzuki	8.00
5RS	Juan Cruz	2.00
6RS	Jay Gibbons	3.00
7RS	Bud Smith	2.00
8RS	Johnny Estrada	2.00
9RS	Roy Oswalt	4.00
10RS	Tsuyoshi Shinjo	2.00
11RS	Brandon Duckworth	2.00
12RS	Jackson Melian	2.00
13RS	Josh Beckett	4.00
14RS	Morgan Ensberg	2.00
15RS	Brian Lawrence	2.00
16RS	Eric Hinske	2.00
17RS	Juan Uribe	2.00
18RS	Matt White	2.00
19RS	Junior Spivey	2.00
20RS	Wilson Betemit	2.00

Then and Now

		NM/M
Common Card:		5.00
Production 275 Sets		
1TN	Eddie Mathews, Chipper Jones	5.00
2TN	Willie McCovey, Barry Bonds	15.00
3TN	Johnny Bench, Mike Piazza	5.00
4TN	Ernie Banks, Alex Rodriguez	8.00
5TN	Rickey Henderson, Ichiro Suzuki	10.00
6TN	Tom Seaver, Roger Clemens	10.00
7TN	Juan Marichal, Pedro J. Martinez	5.00
8TN	Reggie Jackson, Derek Jeter	15.00
9TN	Nolan Ryan, Kerry Wood	20.00
10TN	Joe Morgan, Ken Griffey Jr.	10.00

2002 Fleer Authentix

	NM/M
Complete Set (170):	85.00
Common Player:	.25
Common SP (151-170):	3.00
Production 1,850	
Pack (5):	

Box (24):		60.00
1	Derek Jeter	2.00
2	Tim Hudson	.35
3	Robert Fick	.25
4	Javy Lopez	.25
5	Alfonso Soriano	.50
6	Ken Griffey Jr.	1.25
7	Rafael Palmeiro	.65
8	Bernie Williams	.35
9	Adam Dunn	.50
10	Ivan Rodriguez	.65
11	Vladimir Guerrero	.75
12	Pedro J. Martinez	.75
13	Bret Boone	.25
14	Paul LoDuca	.25
15	Tony Batista	.25
16	Barry Bonds	2.00
17	Craig Biggio	.25
18	Garret Anderson	.25
19	Mark Mulder	.25
20	Frank Thomas	.75
21	Alex Rodriguez	1.50
22	Cristian Guzman	.25
23	Sammy Sosa	1.25
24	Ichiro Suzuki	1.25
25	Carlos Beltran	.25
26	Edgardo Alfonzo	.25
27	Josh Beckett	.50
28	Eric Chavez	.40
29	Roberto Alomar	.25
30	Raul Mondesi	.25
31	Mike Piazza	1.25
32	Barry Larkin	.25
33	Ruben Sierra	.25
34	Tsuyoshi Shinjo	.25
35	Magglio Ordonez	.25
36	Ben Grieve	.25
37	Richie Sexson	.25
38	Manny Ramirez	.75
39	Jeff Kent	.25
40	Shawn Green	.40
41	Andruw Jones	.25
42	Aramis Ramirez	.25
43	Cliff Floyd	.25
44	Juan Pierre	.25
45	Jose Vidro	.25
46	Paul Konerko	.25
47	Greg Vaughn	.25
48	Geoff Jenkins	.25
49	Greg Maddux	1.00
50	Ryan Klesko	.25
51	Corey Koskie	.25
52	Nomar Garciaparra	1.25
53	Edgar Martinez	.25
54	Gary Sheffield	.40
55	Randy Johnson	.75
56	Bobby Abreu	.25
57	Mike Sweeney	.25
58	Chipper Jones	1.00
59	Brian Giles	.25
60	Charles Johnson	.25
61	Ben Sheets	.25
62	Jason Giambi	.60
63	Todd Helton	.75
64	David Eckstein	.25
65	Troy Glaus	.75
66	Sean Casey	.35
67	Gabe Kapler	.25
68	Doug Mientkiewicz	.25
69	Curt Schilling	.40
70	Pat Burrell	.40
71	Albert Pujols	1.25
72	Jermaine Dye	.25
73	Miguel Tejada	.40
74	Jim Thome	.50
75	Carlos Delgado	.40
76	Fred McGriff	.25
77	Mike Cameron	.25
78	Jeromy Burnitz	.25
79	Jay Gibbons	.25
80	Rich Aurilia	.25
81	Lance Berkman	.25
82	Brian Jordan	.25
83	Phil Nevin	.25
84	Moises Alou	.25
85	Reggie Sanders	.25
86	Scott Rolen	.65
87	Larry Walker	.25
88	Matt Williams	.25
89	Roger Clemens	1.00
90	Juan Gonzalez	.75
91	Jose Cruz Jr.	.25
92	Tino Martinez	.25
93	Kerry Wood	.65
94	Freddy Garcia	.25
95	Jeff Bagwell	.75
96	Luis Gonzalez	.35
97	Jimmy Rollins	.50
98	Bobby Higginson	.25
99	Rondell White	.25
100	Jorge Posada	.35
101	Trot Nixon	.25
102	Jason Kendall	.25
103	Preston Wilson	.25
104	Corey Patterson	.25
105	Jose Valentin	.25
106	Carlos Lee	.25
107	Chris Richard	.25
108	Todd Walker	.25
109	Ellis Burks	.25
110	Brady Anderson	.25
111	Kazuhiro Sasaki	.25
112	Roy Oswalt	.25
113	Kevin Brown	.25
114	Jeff Weaver	.25
115	Todd Hollandsworth	.25
116	Joe Crede	.25
117	Tom Glavine	.40

118	Mike Lieberthal	.25
119	Tim Salmon	.35
120	Johnny Damon	.40
121	Brad Fullmer	.25
122	Mo Vaughn	.25
123	Torii Hunter	.50
124	Jamie Moyer	.25
125	Terrence Long	.25
126	Travis Lee	.25
127	Jacque Jones	.25
128	Lee Stevens	.25
129	Russ Ortiz	.25
130	Jeremy Giambi	.25
131	Mike Mussina	.45
132	Orlando Cabrera	.25
133	Barry Zito	.40
134	Robert Person	.25
135	Andy Pettitte	.40
136	Drew Henson	.25
137	Mark Teixeira	.50
138	David Espinosa	.25
139	Orlando Hudson	.25
140	Colby Lewis	.25
141	Bill Hall	.25
142	Michael Restovich	.25
143	Angel Berroa	.40
144	Dewon Brazelton	.25
145	Joe Thurston	.25
146	Mark Prior	.50
147	Dane Sardinha	.25
148	Marlon Byrd	.25
149	Jeff Deardorff RC	.25
150	Austin Kearns	.40
151	Anderson Machado RC	5.00
152	Kazuhisa Ishii RC	8.00
153	Eric Junge RC	3.00
154	Mark Corey RC	3.00
155	So Taguchi RC	5.00
156	Jorge Padilla RC	3.00
157	Steve Kent RC	3.00
158	Jaime Cerda RC	3.00
159	Hansel Izquierdo RC	3.00
160	Rene Reyes RC	3.00
161	Jorge Nunez RC	3.00
162	Corey Thurman RC	4.00
163	Jorge Sosa RC	3.00
164	Franklin Nunez RC	3.00
165	Adam Walker RC	3.00
166	Ryan Baerlocher RC	3.00
167	Ron Calloway RC	3.00
168	Miguel Asencio RC	3.00
169	Luis Ugueto RC	3.00
170	Felix Escalona RC	3.00

Front Row

Front Row:		4-8X
Front Row SP:		1-2X
Production 150 Sets		

Second Row

Second Row:		3-5X
Second Row SP:		.75-1.5X
Production 250 Sets		

Autographed AuthenTIX

		NM/M
Common Autograph:		10.00
Inserted 1:780		
Unripped no pricing.		
Numbered to 25		
	Derek Jeter	200.00
	Mark Teixeira/25	35.00
	Brooks Robinson/145	40.00
	Ben Sheets/25	30.00
	Mark Prior	40.00
	Kazuhisa Ishii	25.00
	So Taguchi	15.00
	Dane Sardinha	10.00
	David Espinosa	10.00

Autographed Jersey AuthenTIX

		NM/M
Inserted 1:1,387		
	Derek Jeter	200.00
	Jeff Bagwell	80.00

Ballpark Classics

		NM/M
Complete Set (15):		50.00
Common Player:		1.50
Inserted 1:22		
1BC	Reggie Jackson	3.00
2BC	Don Mattingly	6.00
3BC	Duke Snider	2.00
4BC	Carlton Fisk	2.00
5BC	Cal Ripken Jr.	8.00
6BC	Willie McCovey	1.50
7BC	Robin Yount	3.00
8BC	Paul Molitor	3.00
9BC	George Brett	6.00
10BC	Ryne Sandberg	5.00
11BC	Nolan Ryan	8.00
12BC	Thurman Munson	4.00
13BC	Joe Morgan	1.50
14BC	Jim Rice	1.50
15BC	Babe Ruth	8.00

Ballpark Classics Memorabilia

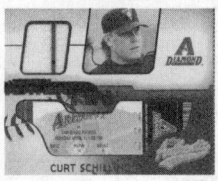

		NM/M
Common Player:		5.00
Inserted 1:83		
Golds:		2X
Production 100		
RJ	Reggie Jackson	15.00
DM	Don Mattingly	30.00
DS	Duke Snider	15.00
CF	Carlton Fisk	10.00
CR	Cal Ripken Jr.	40.00
WC	Willie McCovey	15.00
RY	Robin Yount	25.00
PM	Paul Molitor	15.00
GB	George Brett	30.00
RS	Ryne Sandberg/SP	75.00
NR	Nolan Ryan	30.00
TM	Thurman Munson/Cap/SP	50.00
JM	Joe Morgan	5.00
JR	Jim Rice	8.00
BR	Babe Ruth/Seat	150.00

Bat AuthenTIX

		NM/M
Common Player:		5.00
Inserted 1:68		
Unripped:		2-3X
Production 50		
	Pat Burrell	8.00
	Ray Durham/SP/52	5.00
	Juan Gonzalez	8.00
	Drew Henson	5.00
	Orlando Hernandez	5.00
	Hideo Nomo/SP/41	30.00
	Jimmy Rollins	5.00
	Manny Ramirez	8.00
	Bernie Williams/SP/44	10.00
	Derek Jeter/197	40.00
	Andruw Jones	8.00
	Chipper Jones/SP/37	20.00
	Barry Bonds	20.00
	Nomar Garciaparra	25.00

Jersey AuthenTIX

		NM/M
Common Player:		5.00
Inserted 1:12		
Unripped:		2-3X
Production 50		
	Barry Bonds	20.00
	Chipper Jones	12.00
	Scott Rolen/SP	12.00
	Greg Maddux	10.00
	Curt Schilling/SP	10.00
	Mike Piazza	10.00
	Nomar Garciaparra/SP	15.00
	Derek Jeter	20.00
	Luis Gonzalez/SP	8.00
	Jeff Bagwell	8.00
	Frank Thomas	8.00
	Manny Ramirez/SP	10.00
	Shawn Green	5.00
	Todd Helton	8.00
	Jim Edmonds/SP	10.00
	Paul LoDuca	5.00
	Alex Rodriguez	10.00
	Roberto Alomar	6.00
	Andruw Jones/SP	10.00
	Barry Zito	8.00
	J.D. Drew	5.00
	Magglio Ordonez	5.00
	Eric Chavez	5.00
	Darin Erstad/SP	8.00
	Freddy Garcia	5.00
	Jim Thome/SP	12.00
	Pedro J. Martinez	10.00
	Ivan Rodriguez	8.00
	Bernie Williams/SP	10.00
	Randy Johnson	8.00

Derek Jeter 1996 Autographics

		NM/M
Production 100		
	Derek Jeter	150.00

Power Alley

		NM/M
Complete Set (15):		20.00
Common Player:		.50
Inserted 1:11		
1PA	Sammy Sosa	2.00
2PA	Ken Griffey Jr.	2.00

3PA	Luis Gonzalez	.50
4PA	Alex Rodriguez	3.00
5PA	Shawn Green	.75
6PA	Barry Bonds	4.00
7PA	Todd Helton	1.00
8PA	Jim Thome	.50
9PA	Troy Glaus	1.00
10PA	Manny Ramirez	1.00
11PA	Jeff Bagwell	1.00
12PA	Jason Giambi	.75
13PA	Chipper Jones	1.50
14PA	Mike Piazza	2.00
15PA	Albert Pujols	1.50

2002 Fleer Box Score

		NM/M
Complete Set (310):		
Common Player:		.25
Common (126-150):		3.00
Production 2,499		
Complete Rising Star Set (40):		30.00
Common (151-190):		1.00
Complete Intl. Set (40):		18.00
Common (191-230):		1.00
Complete All-Star Set (40):		20.00
Common (231-270):		1.00
Comp. Cooperstown Set (40):		30.00
Common Cooperstown (271-310):		1.00
Print run for all subsets is 2,950.		
Pack (7):		5.00
Box (18 Packs + Supp. Box):		80.00
1	Derek Jeter	2.00
2	Kevin Brown	.25
3	Nomar Garciaparra	1.25
4	Mark Buehrle	.25
5	Mike Piazza	1.25
6	David Justice	.25
7	Tino Martinez	.25
8	Paul Konerko	.25
9	Larry Walker	.25
10	Ben Sheets	.25
11	Mike Cameron	.25
12	David Wells	.25
13	Barry Zito	.35
14	Pat Burrell	.45
15	Mike Mussina	.50
16	Bud Smith	.25
17	Brian Jordan	.25
18	Chris Singleton	.25
19	Daryle Ward	.25
20	Russ Ortiz	.25
21	Jason Kendall	.25
22	Kerry Wood	.65
23	Jeff Weaver	.25
24	Tony Armas	.25
25	Toby Hall	.25
26	Brian Giles	.25
27	Juan Pierre	.25
28	Ken Griffey Jr.	1.25
29	Mike Sweeney	.25
30	John Smoltz	.25
31	Sean Casey	.35
32	Jeremy Giambi	.25
33	Mike Lieberthal	.25
34	Rich Aurilia	.25
35	Matt Lawton	.25
36	Dmitri Young	.25
37	Wade Miller	.25
38	Jason Giambi	.65
39	Jeff Cirillo	.25
40	Mark Grace	.35
41	Frank Thomas	.75
42	Preston Wilson	.25
43	Brad Radke	.25
44	Greg Maddux	1.00
45	Adam Dunn	.50
46	Roy Oswalt	.35
47	Troy Glaus	.75
48	Edgar Martinez	.25
49	Billy Koch	.25
50	Chipper Jones	1.00
51	Lance Berkman	.25
52	Shannon Stewart	.25
53	Eddie Guardado	.25
54	C.C. Sabathia	.25
55	Craig Biggio	.25
56	Roger Clemens	1.00

57	Jimmy Rollins	.25
58	Carlos Delgado	.50
59	Tony Clark	.25
60	Mike Hampton	.25
61	Jeromy Burnitz	.25
62	Jorge Posada	.35
63	Todd Helton	.75
64	Richie Sexson	.25
65	Ryan Klesko	.25
66	Cliff Floyd	.25
67	Eric Milton	.25
68	Scott Rolen	.65
69	Steve Finley	.25
70	Ray Durham	.25
71	Jeff Bagwell	.75
72	Geoff Jenkins	.25
73	Jamie Moyer	.25
74	David Eckstein	.25
75	Johnny Damon	.40
76	Pokey Reese	.25
77	Mo Vaughn	.25
78	Trevor Hoffman	.25
79	Albert Pujols	1.50
80	Ben Grieve	.25
81	Matt Morris	.25
82	Aubrey Huff	.25
83	Darin Erstad	.60
84	Garret Anderson	.25
85	Jacque Jones	.25
86	Matt Anderson	.25
87	Jose Vidro	.25
88	Carlos Lee	.25
89	Jeff Suppan	.25
90	Al Leiter	.25
91	Jeff Kent	.25
92	Randy Johnson	.75
93	Moises Alou	.25
94	Bobby Higginson	.25
95	Phil Nevin	.25
96	Alex Rodriguez	1.50
97	Luis Gonzalez	.40
98	A.J. Burnett	.25
99	Torii Hunter	.25
100	Ivan Rodriguez	.60
101	Pedro J. Martinez	.75
102	Manny Ramirez	.75
103	Paul LoDuca	.25
104	Eric Chavez	.25
105	Tim Salmon	.35
106	Javier Vazquez	.25
107	Bret Boone	.25
108	Greg Vaughn	.25
109	J.D. Drew	.40
110	Jay Gibbons	.25
111	Jim Thome	.50
112	Shawn Green	.40
113	Tim Hudson	.35
114	John Olerud	.25
115	Raul Mondesi	.25
116	Curt Schilling	.50
117	Corey Patterson	.25
118	Robert Fick	.25
119	Corey Koskie	.25
120	Juan Gonzalez	.75
121	Jerry Hairston Jr.	.25
122	Gary Sheffield	.40
123	Mark Mulder	.25
124	Barry Bonds	2.00
125	Jim Edmonds	.25
126	Franklyn German RC	3.00
127	Rodrigo Rosario RC	3.00
128	Ryan Ludwick RC	3.00
129	Jorge de la Rosa RC	4.00
130	Jason Lane	3.00
131	Brian Mallette RC	3.00
132	Chris Baker RC	3.00
133	Kyle Kane RC	3.00
134	Doug DeVore RC	3.00
135	Raul Chavez RC	3.00
136	Miguel Asencio RC	3.00
137	Luis Garcia RC	3.00
138	Nick Johnson	.25
139	Michael Crudale RC	3.00
140	P.J. Bevis RC	3.00
141	Josh Hancock RC	3.00
142	Jeremy Lambert RC	3.00
143	Ben Broussard	3.00
144	John Ennis RC	3.00
145	Wilson Valdez RC	3.00
146	Eric Good RC	3.00
147	Elio Serrano RC	3.00
148	Jaime Cerda RC	3.00
149	Hank Blalock	5.00
150	Brandon Duckworth	3.00
151	Drew Henson	1.50
152	Kazuhisa Ishii RC	3.00
153	Earl Snyder RC	1.00
154	J.M. Gold	1.00
155	Satoru Komiyama RC	1.00
156	Marlon Byrd	1.00
157	So Taguchi RC	2.00
158	Eric Hinske	2.00
159	Mark Prior	3.00
160	Jorge Padilla RC	1.50
161	Rene Reyes RC	1.00
162	Jorge Nunez RC	1.00
163	Nelson Castro RC	1.00
164	Anderson Machado RC	2.00
165	Mark Teixeira	5.00
166	Orlando Hudson	1.00
167	Edwin Almonte RC	1.00
168	Luis Ugueto RC	1.00
169	Felix Escalona RC	1.00
170	Ron Calloway RC	1.00
171	Kevin Mench	1.00
172	Takahito Nomura RC	1.00
173	Sean Burroughs	1.00
174	Steve Kent RC	1.00

175	Jorge Sosa RC	1.00
176	Mike Moriarty RC	1.00
177	Carlos Pena	1.00
178	Anastacio Martinez RC	1.00
179	Reed Johnson RC	1.00
180	Juan Brito RC	1.00
181	Wilson Betemit	1.00
182	Mike Rivera	1.00
183	David Espinosa	1.00
184	Todd Donovan RC	1.00
185	Morgan Ensberg	1.00
186	Dewon Brazelton	1.00
187	Ben Howard RC	1.00
188	Austin Kearns	2.00
189	Josh Beckett	2.00
190	Brandon Backe RC	1.50
191	Ichiro Suzuki	4.00
192	Tsuyoshi Shinjo	2.00
193	Hideo Nomo	2.00
194	Kazuhiro Sasaki	1.00
195	Edgardo Alfonzo	1.00
196	Chan Ho Park	1.00
197	Carlos Hernandez	1.00
198	Byung Kim	1.00
199	Omar Vizquel	1.00
200	Freddy Garcia	1.00
201	Richard Hidalgo	1.00
202	Magglio Ordonez	2.00
203	Bobby Abreu	1.00
204	Roger Cedeno	1.00
205	Andruw Jones	2.00
206	Mariano Rivera	1.50
207	Jose Macias	1.00
208	Orlando Hernandez	1.00
209	Rafael Palmeiro	2.00
210	Danys Baez	1.00
211	Bernie Williams	1.25
212	Carlos Beltran	3.00
213	Roberto Alomar	1.50
214	Jose Cruz Jr.	1.00
215	Ryan Dempster	1.00
216	Erubiel Durazo	1.00
217	Carlos Pena	1.00
218	Sammy Sosa	4.00
219	Adrian Beltre	1.50
220	Aramis Ramirez	1.00
221	Alfonso Soriano	2.00
222	Vladimir Guerrero	2.00
223	Juan Uribe	1.00
224	Cristian Guzman	1.00
225	Manny Ramirez	3.00
226	Juan Cruz	1.00
227	Ramon Ortiz	1.00
228	Juan Encarnacion	1.00
229	Bartolo Colon	1.00
230	Miguel Tejada	1.25
231	Cal Ripken Jr.	6.00
232	Derek Jeter	6.00
233	Pedro J. Martinez	2.00
234	Roberto Alomar	1.50
235	Sandy Alomar	1.00
236	Mike Piazza	4.00
237	Jeff Conine	1.00
238	Fred McGriff	1.00
239	Kirby Puckett	3.00
240	Ken Griffey Jr.	4.00
241	Roger Clemens	3.50
242	Joe Morgan	2.00
243	Willie McCovey	1.00
244	Brooks Robinson	1.00
245	Juan Marichal	1.00
246	Todd Helton	2.00
247	Alex Rodriguez	5.00
248	Barry Bonds	6.00
249	Nomar Garciaparra	4.00
250	Jeff Bagwell	2.00
251	Kenny Lofton	1.00
252	Barry Larkin	1.00
253	Tom Glavine	1.50
254	Magglio Ordonez	1.00
255	Randy Johnson	3.00
256	Chipper Jones	3.00
257	Kevin Brown	1.00
258	Rickey Henderson	2.00
259	Greg Maddux	3.00
260	Jim Thome	2.00
261	Rafael Palmeiro	1.50
262	Frank Thomas	2.00
263	Manny Ramirez	2.00
264	Travis Fryman	1.00
265	Gary Sheffield	1.25
266	Bernie Williams	1.25
267	Matt Williams	1.00
268	Ivan Rodriguez	1.50
269	Mike Mussina	1.25
270	Larry Walker	1.00
271	Jim Palmer	1.00
272	Cal Ripken Jr.	6.00
273	Brooks Robinson	1.00
274	Bobby Doerr	1.00
275	Ernie Banks	2.00
276	Fergie Jenkins	1.00
277	Luis Aparicio	1.00
278	Hoyt Wilhelm	1.00
279	Tom Seaver	1.50
280	Joe Morgan	1.00
281	Lou Boudreau	1.00
282	Larry Doby	1.00
283	Jim Bunning	1.00
284	George Kell	1.00
285	Pee Wee Reese	1.00
286	Eddie Mathews	1.00
287	Robin Yount	2.00
288	Rod Carew	1.00
289	Monte Irvin	1.00
290	Yogi Berra	2.00
291	Whitey Ford	2.00
292	Reggie Jackson	2.00

293	Rollie Fingers	1.00
294	Jim "Catfish" Hunter	1.00
295	Richie Ashburn	1.00
296	Willie Stargell	1.00
297	Ralph Kiner	1.00
298	Orlando Cepeda	1.00
299	Juan Marichal	1.00
300	Gaylord Perry	1.00
301	Willie McCovey	1.00
302	Red Schoendienst	1.00
303	Nolan Ryan	8.00
304	Bob Gibson	1.00
305	Al Kaline	1.00
306	Harmon Killebrew	1.00
307	Stan Musial	3.00
308	Phil Rizzuto	1.00
309	Mike Schmidt	4.00
310	Enos Slaughter	1.00

Classic Miniatures

NM/M

Complete Set (40): 25.00
Stars: 1.5-3X Base Card
Production 2,950 Sets
One set per classic mini box.
First Editions: 4-8X
Production 100 Sets

Classic Miniatures Game-Used

NM/M

Common Player: 6.00
One per Classic Mini box.

Derek Jeter/Bat	20.00
Mike Piazza/Jsy	10.00
Adam Dunn/Jsy	6.00
Chipper Jones/Bat	10.00
Roger Clemens/Jsy	15.00
Alex Rodriguez/Jsy	10.00
Pedro Martinez/Jsy	10.00
Jim Thome/Bat	10.00
Curt Schilling/Jsy	8.00
Barry Bonds/Bat	20.00

First Edition

Cards (1-125): 4-8X
Cards (126-150): .5-1X
Cards (151-310): 1-2X
Production 100 Sets

All-Star Lineup

NM/M

Common Card: 15.00
1:All-Stars Box

Derek Jeter, Nomar Garciaparra, Alex Rodriguez	50.00
Joe Morgan, Willie McCovey, Brooks Robinson	15.00
Alex Rodriguez, Ivan Rodriguez, Rafael Palmeiro	20.00
Derek Jeter, Mike Mussina, Bernie Williams	35.00
Barry Bonds, Cal Ripken Jr., Frank Thomas	60.00
Cal Ripken Jr., Derek Jeter, Roberto Alomar, Pedro J. Martinez	60.00
Mike Piazza, Barry Bonds, Ken Griffey Jr., Jeff Bagwell	40.00
Roger Clemens, Greg Maddux, Randy Johnson, Pedro J. Martinez	35.00
Todd Helton, Roberto Alomar, Alex Rodriguez, Chipper Jones	25.00
Ken Griffey Jr., Barry Bonds, Larry Walker, Manny Ramirez	35.00

Amazing Greats

NM/M

Complete Set (20): 20.00
Common Player: .50
Inserted 1:5

1AG	Derek Jeter	4.00
2AG	Barry Bonds	4.00
3AG	Mike Piazza	2.50
4AG	Ivan Rodriguez	.75
5AG	Todd Helton	1.00
6AG	Nomar Garciaparra	2.50
7AG	Jim Thome	.50
8AG	Bernie Williams	.50
9AG	Kazuhiro Sasaki	.50
10AG	Torii Hunter	.50
11AG	Bret Boone	.50
12AG	Tim Hudson	.50
13AG	Randy Johnson	1.00
14AG	Rafael Palmeiro	.75
15AG	Scott Rolen	.75
16AG	Carlos Delgado	.75
17AG	Chipper Jones	2.00
18AG	Lance Berkman	.50
19AG	Frank Thomas	1.00
20AG	Greg Maddux	2.00

Amazing Greats Single Swatch

NM/M

Common Player: 5.00
Inserted 1:13
Dual Swatches: 1-2X
Inserted 1:90

Derek Jeter	20.00
Barry Bonds	20.00
Mike Piazza	10.00
Ivan Rodriguez	8.00
Nomar Garciaparra	15.00
Jim Thome/bat	10.00
Bernie Williams	8.00
Kazuhiro Sasaki	5.00
Torii Hunter	6.00
Bret Boone	5.00
Rafael Palmeiro	8.00
Scott Rolen	8.00
Carlos Delgado	8.00
Lance Berkman	5.00
Frank Thomas	8.00
Greg Maddux	10.00

Amazing Greats Patch

NM/M

Common Player: 15.00
Production 150 Sets

Derek Jeter	50.00
Barry Bonds	50.00
Mike Piazza	25.00
Ivan Rodriguez	40.00
Nomar Garciaparra	40.00
Bernie Williams	25.00
Kazuhiro Sasaki	15.00
Torii Hunter	25.00
Bret Boone	15.00
Rafael Palmeiro	25.00
Scott Rolen	25.00
Carlos Delgado	20.00
Lance Berkman	15.00
Frank Thomas	25.00
Greg Maddux	30.00

Bat Rack

NM/M

Common Card: 20.00
Production 300 Sets

1BR	Derek Jeter, Alfonso Soriano, Bernie Williams	60.00
2BR	Mike Piazza, Roberto Alomar, Mo Vaughn	30.00
3BR	Jeff Bagwell, Lance Berkman, Craig Biggio	30.00
4BR	Eric Chavez, Miguel Tejada, Carlos Pena	15.00
5BR	Alex Rodriguez, Ivan Rodriguez, Rafael Palmeiro	30.00
6BR	Chipper Jones, Gary Sheffield, Andruw Jones	20.00
7BR	Carlos Delgado, Jim Thome, Frank Thomas	20.00
8BR	Derek Jeter, Nomar Garciaparra, Alex Rodriguez	60.00
9BR	Barry Bonds, Adam Dunn, Chipper Jones	35.00
10BR	Magglio Ordonez, Juan Gonzalez, Manny Ramirez	20.00

Bat Rack Quad

NM/M

Common Card: 25.00
Production 150 Sets

Torii Hunter, Cristian Guzman, Frank Thomas, Magglio Ordonez	25.00
Alex Rodriguez, Ivan Rodriguez, Eric Chavez, Miguel Tejada	40.00
Mike Piazza, Roberto Alomar, Alfonso Soriano, Derek Jeter	80.00
Barry Bonds, Lance Berkman, Alex Rodriguez, Nomar Garciaparra	75.00
Barry Bonds, Chipper Jones, Mike Piazza, Ivan Rodriguez	75.00
Derek Jeter, Miguel Tejada, Nomar Garciaparra, Alex Rodriguez	25.00
Roberto Alomar, Mo Vaughn, Jeff Bagwell, Craig Biggio	25.00
Jim Palmer, Carlos Delgado, Jim Thome, Frank Thomas	25.00
Magglio Ordonez, Bernie Williams, Juan Gonzalez, Manny Ramirez	25.00
Chipper Jones, Adam Dunn, Jeff Bagwell, Mo Vaughn	25.00
Alex Rodriguez, Jim Palmer, Bernie Williams, Alfonso Soriano	40.00
Carlos Pena, Eric Chavez, Carlos Delgado, Juan Gonzalez	20.00

Box Score Debuts

NM/M

Complete Set (15): 40.00
Common Player: 2.50
Production 2,002 Sets

1	Hank Blalock	6.00
2	Eric Hinske	3.00
3	Kazuhisa Ishii	5.00
4	Sean Burroughs	3.00
5	Andres Torres	2.50
6	Satoru Komiyama	2.50
7	Mark Prior	10.00
8	Kevin Mench	2.50
9	Austin Kearns	3.00
10	Earl Snyder	2.50
11	Jon Rauch	2.50
12	Jason Lane	2.50
13	Ben Howard	2.50
14	Bobby Hill	2.50
15	Dennis Tankersley	2.50

Hall of Fame Material

NM/M

Common Player: 8.00
1:Cooperstown Box

Jim Palmer/Jsy	8.00
Cal Ripken Jr/Jsy	25.00
Brooks Robinson/Bat	10.00
Joe Morgan/Bat	8.00
Eddie Mathews/Bat	10.00
Robin Yount/Jsy	15.00
Reggie Jackson/Jsy	10.00
"Catfish" Hunter/Jsy	8.00
Willie McCovey/Jsy	8.00
Nolan Ryan/Jsy	30.00

Press Clippings

NM/M

Complete Set (20): 90.00
Common Player: 4.00
Inserted 1:90

1PC	Mark Mulder	4.00
2PC	Curt Schilling	6.00
3PC	Alfonso Soriano	7.50
4PC	Jeff Bagwell	7.50
5PC	J.D. Drew	5.00
6PC	Pedro J. Martinez	7.50
7PC	Bobby Abreu	4.00
8PC	Alex Rodriguez	12.00
9PC	Mike Sweeney	4.00
10PC	Carlos Pena	4.00
11PC	Josh Beckett	6.00
12PC	Roger Clemens	9.00
13PC	Manny Ramirez	7.50
14PC	Adam Dunn	6.00
15PC	Kazuhisa Ishii	4.00
16PC	Ken Griffey Jr.	10.00
17PC	Sammy Sosa	9.00
18PC	Ichiro Suzuki	9.00
19PC	Albert Pujols	15.00
20PC	Troy Glaus	7.50

Press Clippings Game-Used

NM/M

Common Player: 5.00
Inserted 1:13

Mark Mulder/Jsy	5.00
Curt Schilling/Jsy	8.00
Alfonso Soriano/Bat	10.00
Jeff Bagwell/Jsy	8.00
J.D. Drew/Jsy	5.00
Pedro Martinez/Jsy	10.00
Bobby Abreu/Jsy	5.00
Alex Rodriguez/Jsy	10.00
Mike Sweeney/Jsy	5.00
Carlos Pena/Jsy	5.00
Josh Beckett/Jsy	8.00
Manny Ramirez/Jsy	10.00
Adam Dunn/Jsy	6.00
Kazuhisa Ishii/Jsy	10.00
Ken Griffey Jr./Base	10.00
Sammy Sosa/Base	15.00
Ichiro Suzuki/Base	15.00
Albert Pujols/Base	10.00
Troy Glaus/Base	5.00

Wave of the Future

NM/M

Common Player: 4.00
1: Rising Stars Box

1WF	Drew Henson/Bat	5.00
2WF	Kazuhisa Ishii/Bat	5.00
3WF	Marlon Byrd/Jsy	4.00
4WF	So Taguchi/Bat	4.00
5WF	Jorge Padilla/Pants/75	10.00
6WF	Rene Reyes/Jsy	4.00
7WF	Mark Teixeira/100	8.00
8WF	Carlos Pena/Bat	4.00
9WF	Austin Kearns/Pants	4.00
10WF	Josh Beckett/Jsy/50	15.00

World Piece

NM/M

Common Player: 4.00
1:International Box

1WP	Ichiro Suzuki/Base	20.00
2WP	Tsuyoshi Shinjo/Bat	4.00
3WP	Hideo Nomo/Jsy	20.00
4WP	Kazuhiro Sasaki/Jsy	4.00
5WP	Chan Ho Park/Jsy	4.00
6WP	Magglio Ordonez/Jsy	6.00
7WP	Andruw Jones/Jsy	8.00
8WP	Rafael Palmeiro/Jsy	10.00
9WP	Bernie Williams/Jsy	10.00
10WP	Roberto Alomar/Bat	6.00

Adam Dunn, Lance Berkman, Jim Thome, Manny Ramirez — 25.00

2002 Fleer E-X

NM/M

Complete Set (140): .25
Common Player: .25
Common SP (101-125): 3.00
Common (126-140): 5.00
Inserted 1:24
Pack (4): 2.50
Box (24): 40.00

1	Alex Rodriguez	1.50
2	Albert Pujols	1.50
3	Ken Griffey Jr.	1.25
4	Vladimir Guerrero	.75
5	Sammy Sosa	1.25
6	Ichiro Suzuki	1.25
7	Jorge Posada	.35
8	Matt Williams	.25
9	Adrian Beltre	.40
10	Pat Burrell	.25
11	Roger Cedeno	.25
12	Tony Clark	.25
13	Steve Finley	.25
14	Rafael Furcal	.25
15	Rickey Henderson	.75
16	Richard Hidalgo	.25
17	Jason Kendall	.25
18	Tino Martinez	.25
19	Scott Rolen	.65
20	Shannon Stewart	.25
21	Jose Vidro	.25
22	Preston Wilson	.25
23	Raul Mondesi	.25
24	Lance Berkman	.25
25	Rick Ankiel	.25
26	Kevin Brown	.25
27	Jeromy Burnitz	.25
28	Jeff Cirillo	.25
29	Carl Everett	.25
30	Eric Chavez	.35
31	Freddy Garcia	.25
32	Mark Grace	.35
33	David Justice	.25
34	Fred McGriff	.25
35	Mike Mussina	.50
36	John Olerud	.25
37	Magglio Ordonez	.25
38	Curt Schilling	.50
39	Aaron Sele	.25
40	Robin Ventura	.25
41	Adam Dunn	.75
42	Jeff Bagwell	.75
43	Barry Bonds	2.00
44	Roger Clemens	1.00
45	Cliff Floyd	.25
46	Jason Giambi	.50
47	Juan Gonzalez	.75
48	Luis Gonzalez	.35
49	Cristian Guzman	.25
50	Todd Helton	.75
51	Derek Jeter	2.00
52	Rafael Palmeiro	.65
53	Mike Sweeney	.25
54	Ben Grieve	.25
55	Phil Nevin	.25
56	Mike Piazza	1.25
57	Moises Alou	.25
58	Ivan Rodriguez	.65
59	Manny Ramirez	.75
60	Brian Giles	.25
61	Jim Thome	.25
62	Larry Walker	.25
63	Bobby Abreu	.25
64	Troy Glaus	.75
65	Garret Anderson	.25
66	Roberto Alomar	.40
67	Bret Boone	.25
68	Marty Cordova	.25
69	Craig Biggio	.25
70	Omar Vizquel	.25
71	Jermaine Dye	.25
72	Darin Erstad	.60
73	Carlos Delgado	.50
74	Nomar Garciaparra	1.25
75	Greg Maddux	1.00
76	Tom Glavine	.40
77	Frank Thomas	.75
78	Shawn Green	.40
79	Bobby Higginson	.25
80	Jeff Kent	.25
81	Chuck Knoblauch	.25
82	Paul Konerko	.25
83	Carlos Lee	.25
84	Jon Lieber	.25
85	Paul LoDuca	.25
86	Mike Lowell	.25
87	Edgar Martinez	.25
88	Doug Mientkiewicz	.25
89	Pedro J. Martinez	.75
90	Randy Johnson	.75
91	Aramis Ramirez	.25
92	J.D. Drew	.40
93	Chris Richard	.25
94	Jimmy Rollins	.50
95	Ryan Klesko	.25
96	Gary Sheffield	.40
97	Chipper Jones	1.00
98	Greg Vaughn	.25
99	Mo Vaughn	.25
100	Bernie Williams	.35
101	John Foster/2,999 RC	3.00
102	Jorge De La Rosa/2,999 RC	3.00
103	Edwin Almonte/2,999 RC	3.00
104	Chris Booker/2,999 RC	3.00
105	Victor Alvarez/2,999 RC	3.00
106	Clifford Bartosh2,999 RC	3.00
107	Felix Escalona/2,999 RC	3.00
108	Corey Thurman/2,999 RC	3.00
109	Kazuhisa Ishii/2,999 RC	6.00
110	Miguel Ascencio/2,999 RC	3.00
111	P.J. Bevis/2,499 RC	3.00
112	Gustavo Chacin/2,499 RC	3.00
113	Steve Kent/2,499 RC	3.00
114	Takahito Nomura/2,499 RC	3.00
115	Adam Walker/2,499 RC	3.00
116	So Taguchi/2,499 RC	3.00
117	Reed Johnson/2,499 RC	5.00
118	Rodrigo Rosario/2,999 RC	3.00
119	Luis Martinez/2,999 RC	4.00
120	Satoru Komiyama/2,499 RC	3.00
121	Sean Burroughs/1,999	3.00
122	Hank Blalock/1,999	5.00
123	Marlon Byrd/1,999	3.00
124	Nick Johnson/1,999	3.00
125	Mark Teixeira/1,999	5.00
126	David Espinosa	3.00
127	Adrian Burnside RC	3.00
128	Mark Corey RC	3.00
129	Matt Thornton	3.00
130	Dane Sardinha	3.00
131	Juan Rivera	3.00
132	Austin Kearns	5.00
134	Ben Broussard	3.00
135	Orlando Hudson	3.00
136	Carlos Pena	3.00
137	Kenny Kelly	3.00
138	Bill Hall	3.00
139	Ron Chiavacci	3.00
140	Mark Prior	6.00

Essential Credentials Future

This insert is issued in an edition inverse to the card number, paralleling the first 125 cards in two groups. Cards #1-60 include a game-used piece; card #1 is produced in an edition of 60, while card #60 is unique, etc. Cards #61-125 are inversely numbered with 125 examples of card #61 and 61 of card #125.

NM/M

Quantity produced listed.

1	Alex Rodriguez/Jsy/60	30.00
2	Albert Pujols/Base/59	25.00
3	Ken Griffey Jr./Base/58	20.00
4	Vladimir Guerrero/Base/57	15.00
5	Sammy Sosa/Base/56	25.00
6	Ichiro Suzuki/Base/55	15.00
7	Jorge Posada/Bat/54	12.00
8	Matt Williams/Bat/53	8.00
9	Adrian Beltre/Bat/52	8.00
10	Pat Burrell/Bat/51	10.00
11	Roger Cedeno/Base/50	8.00
12	Tony Clark/Bat/49	8.00
13	Steve Finley/Bat/48	8.00
14	Rafael Furcal/Bat/47	12.00
15	Rickey Henderson/Bat/46	20.00
16	Richard Hidalgo/Bat/45	10.00
17	Jason Kendall/Bat/44	10.00
18	Tino Martinez/Bat/43	15.00
19	Scott Rolen/Bat/42	20.00
20	Shannon Stewart/Bat/41	10.00
21	Jose Vidro/Bat/40	10.00
22	Preston Wilson/Bat/39	10.00
23	Raul Mondesi/Bat/38	10.00

24	Lance Berkman/Bat/37	10.00
25	Rick Ankiel/Jsy/36	8.00
26	Kevin Brown/Jsy/35	10.00
27	Jeromy Burnitz/Bat/34	8.00
28	Jeff Cirillo/Jsy/33	8.00
29	Carl Everett/Jsy/32	8.00
30	Eric Chavez/Bat/31	10.00
31	Freddy Garcia/Jsy/30	10.00
32	Mark Grace/Jsy/29	8.00
33	David Justice/Jsy/28	15.00
34	Fred McGriff/Jsy/27	15.00
37	Magglio Ordonez/Jsy/24	8.00
38	Curt Schilling/Jsy/23	30.00
60	Jim Thome/125	8.00
61	Larry Walker/124	4.00
62	Bobby Abreu/123	4.00
63	Troy Glaus/122	6.00
64	Garret Anderson/121	4.00
65	Roberto Alomar/120	6.00
66	Bret Boone/119	4.00
67	Marty Cordova/118	4.00
68	Craig Biggio/117	4.00
69	Omar Vizquel/116	4.00
70	Jermaine Dye/115	4.00
71	Darin Erstad/114	4.00
72	Carlos Delgado/113	6.00
73	Nomar Garciaparra/112	10.00
74	Greg Maddux/111	10.00
75	Tom Glavine/110	4.00
76	Frank Thomas/109	6.00
77	Shawn Green/108	5.00
78	Bobby Higginson/107	4.00
79	Jeff Kent/106	4.00
80	Chuck Knoblauch/105	4.00
81	Paul Konerko/104	3.00
82	Carlos Lee/103	3.00
83	Jon Lieber/102	3.00
84	Paul LoDuca/101	3.00
85	Mike Lowell/100	4.00
86	Edgar Martinez/99	4.00
87	Doug Mientkiewicz/98	4.00
88	Pedro J. Martinez/97	8.00
89	Randy Johnson/96	8.00
90	Aramis Ramirez/95	4.00
91	J.D. Drew/94	4.00
92	Chris Richard/93	4.00
93	Jimmy Rollins/92	4.00
94	Ryan Klesko/91	4.00
95	Gary Sheffield/90	4.00
96	Chipper Jones/89	8.00
97	Greg Vaughn/88	3.00
98	Mo Vaughn/87	3.00
99	Bernie Williams/86	5.00
100	John Foster NT/85	3.00
101	Jorge De La Rosa NT/84	3.00
102	Edwin Almonte NT/83	3.00
103	Chris Booker NT/82	3.00
104	Victor Alvarez NT/81	3.00
105	Clifford Bartosh NT/80	3.00
106	Felix Escalona NT/79	3.00
107	Corey Thurman NT/78	3.00
108	Kazuhisa Ishii NT/77	12.00
109	Miguel Asencio NT/76	3.00
110	P.J. Bevis NT/75	3.00
111	Gustavo Chacin NT/74	3.00
112	Steve Kent NT/73	3.00
113	Takahito Nomura NT/72	3.00
114	Adam Walker NT/71	3.00
115	So Taguchi NT/70	3.00
116	Reed Johnson NT/69	6.00
117	Rodrigo Rosario NT/68	4.00
118	Luis Martinez NT/67	5.00
119	Satoru Komiyama NT/66	4.00
120	Sean Burroughs NT/65	4.00
121	Hank Blalock NT/64	6.00
122	Marlon Byrd NT/63	4.00
123	Nick Johnson NT/62	4.00
125	Mark Teixeira NT/61	6.00

Essential Credentials Now

This insert parallels the first 125 cards in E-X. Each card is in an edition equal to its card number. Cards of the first 60 players include a game-used piece.

NM/M

Quantity produced listed

19	Scott Rolen/Bat/19	45.00
22	Preston Wilson/Bat/22	15.00
24	Lance Berkman/Bat/24	20.00
25	Rick Ankiel/Jsy/25	15.00
26	Kevin Brown/Jsy/26	15.00
27	Jeromy Burnitz/Bat/27	20.00
28	Jeff Cirillo/Jsy/28	15.00
29	Carl Everett/Jsy/29	15.00
30	Eric Chavez/Bat/30	20.00

#	Player	Price
31	Freddy Garcia/Jsy/31	15.00
32	Mark Grace/Jsy/32	20.00
33	David Justice/Jsy/33	15.00
34	Fred McGriff/Jsy/34	15.00
35	Mike Mussina/Jsy/35	25.00
36	John Olerud/Jsy/36	10.00
37	Magglio Ordonez/Jsy/37	15.00
38	Curt Schilling/Jsy/38	20.00
39	Aaron Sele/Jsy/39	10.00
40	Robin Ventura/Jsy/40	15.00
41	Adam Dunn/Bat/41	15.00
42	Jeff Bagwell/Jsy/42	25.00
43	Barry Bonds/Pants/43	75.00
44	Roger Clemens/Bat/44	50.00
45	Cliff Floyd/Bat/45	10.00
46	Jason Giambi/Base/46	15.00
47	Juan Gonzalez/Base/47	15.00
48	Luis Gonzalez/Base/48	15.00
49	Cristian Guzman/Bat/49	10.00
50	Todd Helton/Base/50	15.00
51	Derek Jeter/Bat/51	60.00
52	Rafael Palmeiro/Bat/52	20.00
53	Mike Sweeney/Bat/53	10.00
54	Ben Grieve/Jsy/54	8.00
55	Phil Nevin/Bat/55	8.00
56	Mike Piazza/Base/56	40.00
57	Moises Alou/Bat/57	10.00
58	Ivan Rodriguez/Jsy/58	15.00
59	Manny Ramirez/Base/59	
60	Brian Giles/Bat/60	10.00
61	Jim Thome/61	15.00
62	Larry Walker/62	
63	Bobby Abreu/63	5.00
64	Troy Glaus/64	8.00
65	Garret Anderson/65	8.00
66	Roberto Alomar/66	8.00
67	Bret Boone/67	4.00
68	Marty Cordova/68	4.00
69	Craig Biggio/69	6.00
70	Omar Vizquel/70	4.00
71	Jermaine Dye/71	4.00
72	Darin Erstad/72	5.00
73	Carlos Delgado/73	6.00
74	Nomar Garciaparra/74	15.00
75	Greg Maddux/75	15.00
76	Tom Glavine/76	8.00
77	Frank Thomas/77	8.00
78	Shawn Green/78	6.00
79	Bobby Higginson/79	4.00
80	Jeff Kent/80	5.00
81	Chuck Knoblauch/81	4.00
82	Paul Konerko/82	5.00
83	Carlos Lee/83	5.00
84	Jon Lieber/84	5.00
85	Paul LoDuca/85	5.00
86	Mike Lowell/86	6.00
87	Edgar Martinez/87	6.00
88	Doug Mientkiewicz/88	5.00
89	Pedro J. Martinez/89	10.00
90	Randy Johnson/90	15.00
91	Aramis Ramirez/91	6.00
92	J.D. Drew/92	6.00
93	Chris Richard/93	4.00
94	Jimmy Rollins/94	10.00
95	Ryan Klesko/95	6.00
96	Gary Sheffield/96	6.00
97	Chipper Jones/97	10.00
98	Greg Vaughn/98	4.00
99	Mo Vaughn/99	4.00
100	Bernie Williams/100	6.00
101	John Foster NT/101	4.00
102	Jorge De La Rosa NT/102	4.00
103	Edwin Almonte NT/103	4.00
104	Chris Booker NT/104	4.00
105	Victor Alvarez NT/105	4.00
106	Clifford Bartosh NT/106	4.00
107	Felix Escalona NT/107	4.00
108	Corey Thurman NT/108	4.00
109	Kazuhisa Ishii NT/109	10.00
110	Miguel Asencio NT/110	4.00
111	P.J. Bevis NT/111	4.00
112	Gustavo Chacin NT/112	4.00
113	Steve Kent NT/113	4.00
114	Takahito Nomura NT/114	4.00
115	Adam Walker NT/115	4.00
116	So Taguchi NT/116	6.00
117	Reed Johnson NT/117	6.00
118	Rodrigo Rosario NT/118	4.00
119	Luis Martinez NT/119	4.00
120	Satoru Komiyama NT/120	
121	Sean Burroughs NT/121	5.00
122	Hank Blalock NT/122	6.00
123	Marlon Byrd NT/123	4.00
124	Nick Johnson NT/124	6.00
125	Mark Teixeira NT/125	6.00

Behind the Numbers

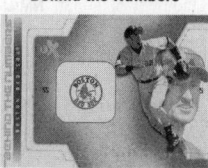

	NM/M
Complete Set (35):	75.00
Common Player:	1.00
Inserted 1:8	
1BTN	Ichiro Suzuki	5.00
2BTN	Jason Giambi	2.50

	Player	Price
3BTN	Mike Piazza	5.00
4BTN	Brian Giles	1.00
5BTN	Barry Bonds	8.00
6BTN	Pedro J. Martinez	3.00
7BTN	Nomar Garciaparra	5.00
8BTN	Randy Johnson	3.00
9BTN	Craig Biggio	1.00
10BTN	Manny Ramirez	3.00
11BTN	Mike Mussina	1.50
12BTN	Kerry Wood	2.50
13BTN	Jim Edmonds	1.00
14BTN	Ivan Rodriguez	2.50
15BTN	Jeff Bagwell	3.00
16BTN	Roger Clemens	4.50
17BTN	Chipper Jones	4.00
18BTN	Shawn Green	1.25
19BTN	Albert Pujols	6.00
20BTN	Andruw Jones	3.00
21BTN	Luis Gonzalez	1.00
22BTN	Todd Helton	3.00
23BTN	Jorge Posada	1.25
24BTN	Scott Rolen	2.50
25BTN	Ben Sheets	1.00
26BTN	Alfonso Soriano	2.50
27BTN	Greg Maddux	5.00
28BTN	Gary Sheffield	1.25
29BTN	Barry Zito	1.25
30BTN	Alex Rodriguez	6.00
31BTN	Larry Walker	1.25
32BTN	Derek Jeter	8.00
33BTN	Ken Griffey Jr.	5.00
34BTN	Vladimir Guerrero	3.00
35BTN	Sammy Sosa	5.00

Behind the Numbers Game Jersey

		NM/M
Common Player:		5.00
Inserted 1:24		
1	Jeff Bagwell	10.00
2	Craig Biggio/Pants	5.00
4	Roger Clemens	20.00
5	Jim Edmonds	5.00
6	Brian Giles	5.00
7	Luis Gonzalez	5.00
8	Shawn Green	5.00
9	Todd Helton	8.00
10	Derek Jeter/SP	30.00
11	Randy Johnson/SP	6.00
12	Andruw Jones	4.00
13	Chipper Jones	10.00
14	Greg Maddux	10.00
15	Pedro J. Martinez	10.00
16	Mike Mussina	10.00
17	Mike Piazza/Pants	10.00
18	Jorge Posada	8.00
19	Manny Ramirez	10.00
20	Alex Rodriguez	10.00
21	Ivan Rodriguez	8.00
22	Scott Rolen	8.00
23	Alfonso Soriano/SP	10.00
24	Barry Zito	5.00

Behind the Numbers Game Jersey Dual

No Pricing
Production 25 Sets

Barry Bonds 4X MVP

		NM/M
Complete Set (4):		20.00
Common Bonds:		6.00
1BB4X	Barry Bonds/1990	6.00
2BB4X	Barry Bonds/1,992	6.00
3BB4X	Barry Bonds/1,993	6.00
4BB4X	Barry Bonds/2,001	6.00

Game Essentials

		NM/M
Common Player:		5.00
	Carlos Beltran	5.00
	Kevin Brown	5.00
	Jeromy Burnitz	5.00
	Carlos Delgado	8.00
	Jason Hart/SP	8.00
	Rickey Henderson	20.00
	Drew Henson/Shoe	5.00

	Player	Price
	Drew Henson/Glv	8.00
	Derek Jeter/Shoe	40.00
	Jason Kendall	5.00
	Jeff Kent	10.00
	Barry Larkin/Glove	20.00
	Javy Lopez	8.00
	Raul Mondesi/Btg Glv	8.00
	Rafael Palmeiro	10.00
	Adam Piatt	5.00
	Brad Radke	5.00
	Cal Ripken Jr.	30.00
	Mariano Rivera	10.00
	Alex Rodriguez/Btg Glove	15.00
	Ivan Rodriguez/Shoe	10.00
	Kazuhiro Sasaki	5.00
	J.T. Snow	5.00
	Mo Vaughn	5.00
	Robin Ventura	8.00
	Jose Vidro	5.00
	Matt Williams	5.00

HardWear

		NM/M
Complete Set (10):		60.00
Common Player:		4.00
Inserted 1:72 Hobby		
1HW	Ivan Rodriguez	4.00
2HW	Mike Piazza	8.00
3HW	Derek Jeter	15.00
4HW	Barry Bonds	15.00
5HW	Todd Helton	8.00
6HW	Roberto Alomar	4.00
7HW	Albert Pujols	10.00
8HW	Ichiro Suzuki	8.00
9HW	Ken Griffey Jr.	8.00
10HW	Jason Giambi	5.00

Hit and Run

		NM/M
Complete Set (30):		50.00
Common Player:		1.00
Inserted 1:12		
1	Adam Dunn	1.00
2	Derek Jeter	6.00
3	Frank Thomas	2.00
4	Albert Pujols	5.00
5	J.D. Drew	1.00
6	Richard Hidalgo	1.00
7	John Olerud	1.00
8	Roberto Alomar	1.00
9	Pat Burrell	1.50
10	Darin Erstad	1.50
11	Mark Grace	1.00
12	Chipper Jones	3.00
13	Jose Vidro	1.00
14	Cliff Floyd	1.00
15	Mo Vaughn	1.00
16	Nomar Garciaparra	4.00
17	Ivan Rodriguez	1.50
18	Luis Gonzalez	1.00
19	Jason Giambi	1.50
20	Bernie Williams	2.00
21	Barry Bonds	6.00
22	Jose Ortiz	1.00
23	Magglio Ordonez	1.00
24	Troy Glaus	2.00
25	Alex Rodriguez	5.00
26	Ichiro Suzuki	4.00
27	Sammy Sosa	4.00
28	Ken Griffey Jr.	4.00
29	Vladimir Guerrero	2.00

Hit and Run Game Base

		NM/M
Inserted 1:120		
1	J.D. Drew	4.00
2	Adam Dunn	6.00
3	Jason Giambi	6.00
4	Troy Glaus	4.00
5	Ken Griffey Jr.	10.00
6	Vladimir Guerrero	6.00
7	Albert Pujols	15.00
8	Sammy Sosa	6.00
9	Ichiro Suzuki	15.00
10	Bernie Williams	6.00

Hit and Run Game Bat

		NM/M
Common Player:		4.00
Inserted 1:24		
1	Roberto Alomar	6.00
2	J.D. Drew	4.00
3	Darin Erstad	4.00
4	Cliff Floyd	4.00
5	Nomar Garciaparra	15.00
6	Luis Gonzalez	6.00

	Player	Price
7	Richard Hidalgo	4.00
8	Derek Jeter	25.00
9	Chipper Jones	8.00
10	John Olerud	4.00
11	Magglio Ordonez	6.00
12	Jose Ortiz	4.00
13	Mike Piazza	10.00
14	Alex Rodriguez	15.00
15	Ivan Rodriguez	8.00
16	Frank Thomas	8.00
17	Mo Vaughn	4.00
18	Jose Vidro	4.00
19	Bernie Williams	8.00

Hit and Run Game Bat and Base

		NM/M
Common Player:		10.00
Inserted 1:240		
1	Roberto Alomar	15.00
2	Barry Bonds/SP	50.00
3	Nomar Garciaparra	30.00
4	Derek Jeter	40.00
5	Chipper Jones	15.00
6	Mike Piazza	20.00
7	Alex Rodriguez	25.00
8	Mo Vaughn	10.00

Derek Jeter 4X Champ

		NM/M
Complete Set (4):		20.00
Common Jeter:		6.00
1DJFX	Derek Jeter/1,996	6.00
2DJFX	Derek Jeter/1,998	6.00
3DJFX	Derek Jeter/1,999	6.00
4DJFX	Derek Jeter/2,000	6.00

2002 Fleer Fall Classic

		NM/M
Complete Set (100):		30.00
Common Player:		.25
Common SP:		3.00
Inserted 1:18 Hobby		
Pack (5):		5.00
Box (24):		100.00
1	Rabbit Maranville	.25
2	Tris Speaker	.75
3	Harmon Killebrew	1.00
4	Lou Gehrig	2.00
5	Lou Boudreau	.25
6	Al Kaline	1.00
7	Paul Molitor	.25
7	Paul Molitor/Brewers	4.00
8	Cal Ripken Jr.	3.00
9	Yogi Berra	1.00
10	Phil Rizzuto	.75
11	Luis Aparicio	.25
11	Luis Aparicio/Orioles	4.00
12	Stan Musial	1.00
13	Mel Ott	.75
14	Larry Doby	.25
15	Ozzie Smith	1.00
16	Babe Ruth	4.00
16	Babe Ruth/Red Sox	10.00
17	Red Schoendienst	.25
17	Red Schoendienst/Cards	3.00
18	Rollie Fingers	.25
19	Thurman Munson	1.50
20	Lou Brock	.50
21	Paul O'Neill	.25
21	Paul O'Neill/Reds	.25
22	Jim Palmer	.50
23	Kirby Puckett	.50
24	Tony Perez	.25
24	Tony Perez/Phila.	3.00
25	Don Larsen	.25
26	Steve Garvey	.25
26	Steve Garvey/Padres	3.00

	Player	Price
27	Jim "Catfish" Hunter	.25
27	"Catfish" Hunter/Yanks	4.00
28	Juan Marichal	.25
29	Pee Wee Reese	.25
30	Orlando Cepeda	.25
31	Rich "Goose" Gossage	.25
32	Ray Knight	.25
33	Eddie Murray	.75
34	Nolan Ryan	3.00
35	Alan Trammell	.50
36	Grover Alexander	.75
37	Joe Carter	.25
38	Rogers Hornsby	1.00
39	Jimmie Foxx	1.50
40	Mike Schmidt	1.50
41	Eddie Mathews	.25
42	Jackie Robinson	1.50
43	Eddie Collins	.25
43	Eddie Collins/White Sox	3.00
44	Willie McCovey	.25
45	Bob Gibson	1.00
46	Keith Hernandez	.25
46	Keith Hernandez/Cards	4.00
47	Brooks Robinson	1.00
48	Mordecai Brown	.25
49	Gary Carter	.50
50	Kirk Gibson	.25
50	Kirk Gibson/Tigers	3.00
51	Johnny Mize	.25
52	Johnny Podres	.25
53	Darrell Porter	.25
54	Willie Stargell	.75
55	Lenny Dykstra	.25
55	Lenny Dykstra/Phila.	3.00
56	Christy Mathewson	.75
57	Walter Johnson	1.00
58	Whitey Ford	.75
59	Lefty Grove	.50
60	Duke Snider	.75
61	Cy Young	1.00
62	Dave Winfield	.75
62	Dave Winfield/Yanks	5.00
63	Robin Yount	1.00
64	Fred Lynn	.25
65	Ty Cobb	2.00
66	Joe Morgan	.25
67	Bill Mazeroski	.25
68	Frank Baker	.25
69	Chief Bender	.25
70	Carlton Fisk	.50
71	Jerry Coleman	.25
72	Frankie Frisch	.25
73	Wade Boggs	1.00
73	Wade Boggs/Yanks	4.00
74	Johnny Bench	1.00
75	Roger Maris	2.00
76	Roger Maris/Cards	8.00
76	Dom DiMaggio	.25
77	George Brett	3.00
78	Dave Parker	.25
78	Dave Parker/A's	3.00
79	Hank Greenberg	.25
80	Pepper Martin	.25
81	Graig Nettles	.25
81	Graig Nettles/Padres	3.00
82	Dennis Eckersley	.50
83	Donn Clendenon	.25
84	Tom Seaver	1.00
85	Honus Wagner	1.50
86	Reggie Jackson	.75
86	Reggie Jackson/A's	5.00
87	Goose Goslin	.25
87	Goose Goslin/Tigers	3.00
88	Tony Kubek	.25
89	Roy Campanella	1.00
90	Steve Carlton/Cards	4.00
91	Lou Gehrig, Mel Ott	2.00
92	Eddie Collins, Joe Morgan	.25
93	George Brett, Mike Schmidt	2.00
94	Cal Ripken Jr., Ozzie Smith	3.00
95	Thurman Munson, Johnny Bench	1.50
96	Willie Stargell, Stan Musial, Pepper Martin	1.00
97	Babe Ruth, Kirby Puckett, Reggie Jackson	3.00
98	Cy Young, Bob Gibson	1.00
99	Whitey Ford, Steve Carlton	1.00
100	Paul Molitor, Lou Brock	.50

Championship Gold

Golds:	5-10X
Gold SP's:	1-2X
Production 50 Sets	

HOF Plaque

		NM/M
Complete Set (30):		90.00
Common Player:		3.00
#'d to HOF induction year		
1HOF	Babe Ruth	8.00
2HOF	Christy Mathewson	3.00
3HOF	Honus Wagner	3.00
4HOF	Ty Cobb	5.00
5HOF	Walter Johnson	3.00
6HOF	Cy Young	4.00
7HOF	Tris Speaker	4.00
8HOF	Eddie Collins	3.00
9HOF	Lou Gehrig	6.00
10HOF	Jimmie Foxx	4.00
11HOF	Jackie Robinson	6.00
12HOF	Stan Musial	3.00
13HOF	Yogi Berra	4.00
14HOF	Duke Snider	4.00

	Player	Price
15HOF	Juan Marichal	3.00
16HOF	Luis Aparicio	3.00
17HOF	Pee Wee Reese	3.00
18HOF	Willie McCovey	3.00
19HOF	Willie Stargell	3.00
20HOF	Johnny Bench	5.00
21HOF	Joe Morgan	3.00
22HOF	Jim Palmer	3.00
23HOF	Tom Seaver	4.00
24HOF	Reggie Jackson	4.00
25HOF	Steve Carlton	3.00
26HOF	George Brett	6.00
27HOF	Nolan Ryan	4.00
28HOF	Robin Yount	4.00
29HOF	Kirby Puckett	4.00
30HOF	Ozzie Smith	4.00

MVP Collection Game-Used

		NM/M
Common Player:		5.00
Inserted 1:100		
Golds:		.75-2X
Production 100 Sets		
JB	Johnny Bench/200	20.00
DC	Donn Clendenon	5.00
RF	Rollie Fingers/200	5.00
RJOK	Reggie Jackson/50	20.00
RJNY	Reggie Jackson	10.00
RK	Ray Knight	5.00
PM	Paul Molitor/250	15.00
DP	Darrell Porter/250	5.00
BR	Brooks Robinson/250	20.00
WS	Willie Stargell/200	10.00
AT	Alan Trammell	5.00

MVP Collection Patch

		NM/M
Numbered to MVP year.		
JB	Johnny Bench/76	45.00
RF	Rollie Fingers/74	20.00
RJNY	Reggie Jackson/77	40.00
BR	Brooks Robinson/70	40.00
AT	Alan Trammell/84	30.00

October Legends

		NM/M
Common Player:		5.00
Inserted 1:48		
Golds:		.75-1.5X
Production 100 Sets		
	Joe Morgan	5.00
	Wade Boggs/60	20.00
	Keith Hernandez/100	15.00
	Robin Yount	10.00
	Eddie Murray	10.00
	Lenny Dykstra/200	8.00
	Paul O'Neill	8.00
	Red Schoendienst/210	8.00
	Pepper Martin/50	15.00
	Keith Hernandez/200	20.00
	Willie Stargell/225	12.00
	George Brett	20.00
	Dave Parker/50	20.00
	Tony Perez	5.00
	Rollie Fingers	9.00
	Gary Carter/200	10.00
	Dennis Eckersley	5.00
	Juan Marichal	8.00
	Pee Wee Reese/200	15.00
	Roger Maris	60.00
	Duke Snider/200	15.00
	Darrell Porter	5.00
	Willie McCovey/150	10.00
	Paul Molitor/150	10.00

October Legends Dual

		NM/M
Common Card:		10.00
SP's Noted		
	Rollie Fingers, Dennis Eckersley	12.00
	Keith Hernandez, Red Schoendienst	12.00
	Joe Morgan, Tony Perez	10.00
	Wade Boggs, Keith Hernandez	20.00
	Lenny Dykstra, Gary Carter	12.00
	Robin Yount, Paul Molitor/150	35.00
	Roger Maris, Paul O'Neill/200	50.00
	Duke Snider, Pee Wee Reese/200	25.00
	Juan Marichal, Willie McCovey	15.00
	George Brett, Darrell Porter/150	35.00

Willie Stargell, Dave Parker	15.00
Gary Carter, Keith Hernandez	10.00
Cal Ripken Jr., Eddie Murray/200	40.00
Cal Ripken Jr., Eddie Murray/100	50.00
Pepper Martin, Frankie Frisch	15.00

Pennant Chase

NM/M
Common Player: 10.00
Inserted 1:48 Hobby

Yogi Berra/Pants/150	20.00
Carlton Fisk/Bat	10.00
Reggie Jackson/Jsy	10.00
Fred Lynn/Bat	10.00
Thurman Munson/Bat	30.00
Wade Boggs/Jsy	10.00
Dave Winfield/Bat	10.00

Pennant Chase Dual

NM/M
Production 50 Sets

CFRJ	Carlton Fisk/Bat, Reggie Jackson/Jsy	30.00
FLTM	Fred Lynn/Bat, Thurman Munson/Bat	50.00
WBDW	Wade Boggs/Jsy, Dave Winfield/Bat	30.00

Rival Factions

NM/M
Common Card: 2.00
1-24 #'d to 1,000
25-36 #'d to 500
37-43 #'d to 50

1RF	Carlton Fisk, Thurman Munson	3.00
2RF	Frank Baker, Babe Ruth	8.00
3RF	Jimmie Foxx, Lou Gehrig	6.00
4RF	Steve Carlton, Nolan Ryan	8.00
5RF	Mordecai Brown, Honus Wagner	3.00
6RF	Frankie Frisch, Duke Snider	3.00
7RF	Ozzie Smith, Alan Trammell	3.00
8RF	Larry Doby, Jackie Robinson	5.00
9RF	Steve Garvey, Tony Perez	2.00
10RF	Johnny Bench, Willie Stargell	4.00
11RF	Ty Cobb, Eddie Collins	5.00
12RF	Reggie Jackson, Brooks Robinson	4.00
13RF	Yogi Berra, Roy Campanella	4.00
14RF	Orlando Cepeda, Willie McCovey	2.00
15RF	Al Kaline, Jim Palmer	4.00
16RF	George Brett, Kirby Puckett	6.00
17RF	Bob Gibson, Tom Seaver	4.00
18RF	Cal Ripken Jr., Robin Yount	8.00
19RF	Johnny Mize, Mel Ott	3.00
20RF	Stan Musial, Pee Wee Reese	4.00
21RF	Hank Greenburg, Lefty Grove	2.00
22RF	Dave Parker, Mike Schmidt	4.00
23RF	Bill Mazeroski, Joe Morgan	3.00
24RF	Johnny Bench, Carlton Fisk	5.00
25RF	George Brett, Mike Schmidt	8.00
26RF	Pee Wee Reese, Phil Rizzuto	4.00
27RF	Cal Ripken Jr., Alan Trammell	15.00
28RF	Tom Seaver, Jim "Catfish" Hunter	4.00
29RF	Ty Cobb, Honus Wagner	5.00
30RF	Steve Carlton, Lefty Grove	3.00
31RF	Ozzie Smith, Robin Yount	8.00
32RF	Frankie Frisch, Joe Morgan	3.00
33RF	Hank Greenberg, Jackie Robinson	5.00
34RF	Jimmie Foxx, Pepper Martin	5.00
35RF	Lou Gehrig, Cal Ripken Jr.	40.00
36RF	Ozzie Smith, Honus Wagner	40.00
37RF	Reggie Jackson, Dave Winfield	20.00
38RF	Ty Cobb, Rogers Hornsby	35.00
39RF	Babe Ruth, Roger Maris	50.00
40RF	Yogi Berra, Thurman Munson	20.00
41RF	Nolan Ryan, Tom Seaver	50.00
42RF	Joe Morgan, Jackie Robinson	20.00
43RF	Jimmie Foxx, Mel Ott	25.00

Rival Factions Game-Used Single

NM/M
Common Card: 8.00
Inserted 1:32

Carlton Fisk, Thurman Munson	25.00
Frank Baker, Babe Ruth	25.00
Jimmie Foxx, Lou Gehrig	35.00
Steve Carlton, Nolan Ryan	25.00
Frankie Frisch, Duke Snider	20.00
Ozzie Smith, Alan Trammell	15.00
Larry Doby, Jackie Robinson	15.00
Steve Garvey, Tony Perez	10.00
Johnny Bench, Willie Stargell	10.00
Reggie Jackson, Brooks Robinson	12.00
Orlando Cepeda, Willie McCovey	10.00
Al Kaline, Jim Palmer	10.00
George Brett, Kirby Puckett	25.00
Bob Gibson, Tom Seaver	20.00
Cal Ripken Jr., Robin Yount	30.00
Stan Musial, Pee Wee Reese	25.00
Hank Greenberg, Lefty Grove	20.00
Bill Mazeroski, Joe Morgan	8.00
Johnny Bench, Carlton Fisk	10.00
George Brett, Mike Schmidt	25.00
Pee Wee Reese, Phil Rizzuto	15.00
Cal Ripken Jr., Alan Trammell	35.00
Steve Carlton, Lefty Grove	15.00
Ozzie Smith, Robin Yount	15.00
Frankie Frisch, Joe Morgan	25.00
Hank Greenberg, Jackie Robinson	20.00
Jimmie Foxx, Pepper Martin	30.00
Lou Gehrig, Cal Ripken Jr.	40.00
Reggie Jackson, Dave Winfield	10.00
Babe Ruth, Roger Maris	60.00
Nolan Ryan, Tom Seaver	35.00

Rival Factions Game-Used Dual

NM/M
Common Card: 12.00

Carlton Fisk, Thurman Munson	30.00
Steve Carlton, Nolan Ryan	40.00
Frankie Frisch, Duke Snider	15.00
Ozzie Smith, Alan Trammell	25.00
Larry Doby, Jackie Robinson/75	60.00
Steve Garvey, Tony Perez	10.00
Johnny Bench, Willie Stargell	20.00
Reggie Jackson, Brooks Robinson	20.00
Orlando Cepeda, Willie McCovey/200	15.00
George Brett, Kirby Puckett	40.00
Cal Ripken Jr., Robin Yount	30.00
Johnny Bench, Carlton Fisk	20.00
Cal Ripken Jr., Alan Trammell	30.00
Jim "Catfish" Hunter, Tom Seaver	15.00
Ozzie Smith, Robin Yount	25.00
Frankie Frisch, Joe Morgan	15.00
Hank Greenberg, Jackie Robinson/50	100.00
Jimmie Foxx, Pepper Martin/200	40.00
Reggie Jackson, Dave Winfield/150	20.00
Yogi Berra, Thurman Munson	40.00
Nolan Ryan, Tom Seaver	45.00
Joe Morgan, Jackie Robinson/50	50.00

Rival Factions Dual Patch

NM/M
Production 50 Sets 12.00

Carlton Fisk, Thurman Munson	60.00
Steve Carlton, Nolan Ryan	100.00
Ozzie Smith, Alan Trammell	50.00
Steve Garvey, Tony Perez	30.00
Johnny Bench, Willie Stargell	50.00
Cal Ripken Jr., Robin Yount	125.00
Johnny Bench, Carlton Fisk	50.00
Cal Ripken Jr., Alan Trammell	100.00
Ozzie Smith, Robin Yount	60.00
Reggie Jackson, Dave Winfield	40.00

Series of Champions

NM/M
Complete Set (19): 25.00
Common Player: 1.00
Inserted 1:6

1	Yogi Berra	2.00
2	Wade Boggs	2.00
3	Dave Parker	1.00
4	Joe Carter	1.00
5	Kirk Gibson	1.00
6	Reggie Jackson	2.00
7	Tony Kubek	1.00
8	Don Larsen	1.00
9	Bill Mazeroski	1.00
10	Eddie Murray	1.50
11	Graig Nettles	1.00
12	Tony Perez	1.00
13	Phil Rizzuto	1.50
14	Mike Schmidt	2.50
15	Red Schoendienst	1.00
16	Duke Snider	2.00
17	Ty Cobb	2.50
18	Lou Gehrig	3.00
19	Babe Ruth	4.00

Series of Champions Game-Used

NM/M
Common Player: 5.00
Inserted 1:36
Golds: .75-1.5X
Production 100 Sets
Bat Knob numbered to 10 not priced.

Yogi Berra/Bat	15.00
Wade Boggs/Jsy	10.00
Dave Parker/Bat	5.00
Joe Carter/Bat	5.00
Kirk Gibson/Bat	5.00
Reggie Jackson/Bat	10.00
Tony Kubek/Bat	10.00
Eddie Murray/Bat	10.00
Graig Nettles/Bat	5.00
Tony Perez/Bat	5.00
Red Schoendienst/Jsy	5.00
Duke Snider/Bat	10.00
Babe Ruth/Bat/25	180.00

2002 Fleer Flair

NM/M
Complete Set (138):
Common Player: .25
Common (101-138): 3.00
Production 1,750
Pack (5): 4.00
Hobby Box (20): 70.00

1	Scott Rolen	.75
2	Derek Jeter	3.00
3	Sean Casey	.40
4	Hideo Nomo	.75
5	Craig Biggio	.25
6	Randy Johnson	1.00
7	J.D. Drew	.50
8	Greg Maddux	1.50
9	Paul LoDuca	.25
10	John Olerud	.25
11	Barry Larkin	.25
12	Mark Grace	.35
13	Jimmy Rollins	.50
14	Todd Helton	1.00
15	Jim Edmonds	.25
16	Roy Oswalt	.35
17	Phil Nevin	.25
18	Tim Salmon	.35
19	Magglio Ordonez	.25
20	Roger Clemens	1.75
21	Raul Mondesi	.25
22	Edgar Martinez	.25
23	Pedro J. Martinez	1.00
24	Edgardo Alfonzo	.25
25	Bernie Williams	.35
26	Gary Sheffield	.40
27	D'Angelo Jimenez	.25
28	Toby Hall	.25
29	Joe Mays	.25
30	Alfonso Soriano	.75
31	Mike Piazza	2.00
32	Lance Berkman	.25
33	Jim Thome	.25
34	Ben Sheets	.25
35	Brandon Inge	.25
36	Luis Gonzalez	.35
37	Jeff Kent	.25
38	Ben Grieve	.25
39	Carlos Delgado	.50
40	Pat Burrell	.50
41	Mark Buehrle	.25
42	Cristian Guzman	.25
43	Shawn Green	.40
44	Nomar Garciaparra	2.00
45	Carlos Beltran	.60
46	Troy Glaus	.75
47	Paul Konerko	.25
48	Moises Alou	.25
49	Kerry Wood	.75
50	Jose Vidro	.25
51	Juan Encarnacion	.25
52	Bobby Abreu	.25
53	C.C. Sabathia	.25
54	Alex Rodriguez	2.50
55	Albert Pujols	2.50
56	Bret Boone	.25
57	Orlando Hernandez	.25
58	Jason Kendall	.25
59	Tim Hudson	.40
60	Darin Erstad	.60
61	Mike Mussina	.40
62	Ken Griffey Jr.	2.00
63	Adrian Beltre	.35
64	Jeff Bagwell	1.00
65	Vladimir Guerrero	1.00
66	Mike Sweeney	.25
67	Sammy Sosa	2.00
68	Andruw Jones	.75
69	Richie Sexson	.25
70	Matt Morris	.25
71	Ivan Rodriguez	.75
72	Shannon Stewart	.25
73	Barry Bonds	3.00
74	Matt Williams	.60
75	Jason Giambi	.60
76	Brian Giles	.25
77	Cliff Floyd	.25
78	Tino Martinez	.25
79	Juan Gonzalez	1.00
80	Frank Thomas	1.00
81	Ichiro Suzuki	2.00
82	Barry Zito	.35
83	Chipper Jones	1.50
84	Adam Dunn	.75
85	Kazuhiro Sasaki	.25
86	Mark Quinn	.25
87	Rafael Palmeiro	.60
88	Jeromy Burnitz	.25
89	Curt Schilling	.50
90	Chris Richards	.25
91	Jon Leiber	.25
92	Doug Mientkiewicz	.25
93	Roberto Alomar	.40
94	Rich Aurilia	.25
95	Eric Chavez	.35
96	Larry Walker	.25
97	Manny Ramirez	1.00
98	Tony Clark	.25
99	Tsuyoshi Shinjo	.25
100	Josh Beckett	.50
101	Dewon Brazelton	3.00
102	Jeremy Lambert RC	3.00
103	Andres Torres	3.00
104	Matt Childers RC	4.00
105	Wilson Betemit	3.00
106	Willie Harris	3.00
107	Drew Henson	4.00
108	Rafael Soriano	3.00
109	Carlos Valderrama	3.00
110	Victor Martinez	6.00
111	Juan Rivera	3.00
112	Felipe Lopez	3.00
113	Brandon Duckworth	3.00
114	Jeremy Owens	3.00
115	Aaron Cook RC	3.00
116	Derrick Lewis	3.00
117	Mark Teixeira	6.00
118	Ken Harvey	5.00
119	Tim Spooneybarger	3.00
120	Bill Hall	3.00
121	Adam Pettyjohn	3.00
122	Ramon Castro	3.00
123	Marlon Byrd	4.00
124	Matt White	3.00
125	Eric Cyr RC	3.00
126	Morgan Ensberg	3.00
127	Horacio Ramirez	4.00
128	Ron Calloway RC	3.00
129	Nick Punto	3.00
130	Joe Kennedy	3.00
131	So Taguchi RC	5.00
132	Austin Kearns	4.00
133	Mark Prior	6.00
134	Kazuhisa Ishii RC	3.00
135	Steve Torrealba	3.00
136	Adam Walker RC	3.00
137	Travis Hafner	4.00
138	Zach Day	3.00

Collection

Collection (1-100): 4-6X
Production 175
Collection (101-138): 1-2X
Production 50

Hot Numbers

NM/M
Common Player: 15.00
Production 100 Sets

Manny Ramirez	30.00
Randy Johnson	30.00
Curt Schilling	25.00
Pedro J. Martinez	30.00
Nomar Garciaparra	50.00
Barry Larkin	15.00
Todd Helton	30.00
Larry Walker	15.00
Sean Casey	20.00
Jeff Bagwell	30.00
Craig Biggio	15.00
Shawn Green	20.00
Edgardo Alfonzo	15.00
Mike Piazza	50.00
Derek Jeter	75.00
Chipper Jones	40.00
Jim Edmonds	15.00
J.D. Drew	20.00
Ivan Rodriguez	25.00
Rafael Palmeiro	25.00
Alex Rodriguez	60.00
Greg Maddux	40.00
Carlos Delgado	20.00

Jersey Heights

NM/M
Common Player: 4.00
Inserted 1:18 Hobby

1JH	Edgardo Alfonzo	4.00
2JH	Jeff Bagwell	8.00
3JH	Craig Biggio	4.00
4JH	Barry Bonds	20.00
5JH	Sean Casey	4.00
6JH	Roger Clemens	15.00
7JH	Carlos Delgado	6.00
8JH	J.D. Drew	6.00
9JH	Jim Edmonds	6.00
10JH	Nomar Garciaparra	15.00
11JH	Shawn Green	5.00
12JH	Todd Helton	8.00
13JH	Derek Jeter	20.00
14JH	Randy Johnson	8.00
15JH	Chipper Jones	8.00
16JH	Barry Larkin	6.00
17JH	Greg Maddux	10.00
18JH	Pedro J. Martinez	8.00
19JH	Rafael Palmeiro	8.00
20JH	Mike Piazza	10.00
21JH	Manny Ramirez	8.00
22JH	Alex Rodriguez	15.00
23JH	Ivan Rodriguez	6.00
24JH	Curt Schilling	6.00
25JH	Larry Walker	4.00

Jersey Heights (Dual)

NM/M
Common Card: 15.00
Production 100 Sets

Randy Johnson, Curt Schilling	30.00
Pedro J. Martinez, Nomar Garciaparra	50.00
Edgardo Alfonzo, Mike Piazza	30.00
Derek Jeter, Roger Clemens	75.00
Greg Maddux, Chipper Jones	40.00
Jim Edmonds, Jeff Bagwell	20.00
Jeff Bagwell, Craig Biggio	25.00
Rafael Palmeiro, Ivan Rodriguez	25.00
Carlos Delgado, Shawn Green	15.00
Todd Helton, Larry Walker	20.00
Sean Casey, Barry Larkin	25.00
Alex Rodriguez, Manny Ramirez	40.00

Power Tools

NM/M
Common Player: 4.00
Inserted 1:19
Golds: 1-2.5X
Production 100

1PT	Roberto Alomar	6.00
2PT	Jeff Bagwell/150	8.00
3PT	Craig Biggio	4.00
4PT	Barry Bonds	15.00
5PT	Bret Boone	4.00
6PT	Pat Burrell/225	5.00
7PT	Eric Chavez	5.00
8PT	J.D. Drew/150	8.00
9PT	Jim Edmonds	6.00
10PT	Juan Gonzalez	6.00
11PT	Luis Gonzalez	4.00
12PT	Shawn Green	5.00
13PT	Derek Jeter	25.00
14PT	Doug Mientkiewicz	4.00
15PT	Magglio Ordonez	4.00
16PT	Rafael Palmeiro/100	8.00
17PT	Mike Piazza	10.00
18PT	Alex Rodriguez	15.00
19PT	Ivan Rodriguez	8.00
20PT	Scott Rolen/42	15.00
21PT	Reggie Sanders/120	6.00
22PT	Gary Sheffield	6.00
23PT	Tsuyoshi Shinjo	5.00
24PT	Miguel Tejada	6.00
25PT	Frank Thomas	8.00
26PT	Jim Thome/225	15.00
27PT	Larry Walker	6.00
28PT	Bernie Williams	6.00

Power Tools Dual

NM/M
Common Card: 10.00
Inserted 1:40
Golds: 1-2.5X
Production 50 Sets

1	Eric Chavez, Miguel Tejada	10.00
2	Barry Bonds, Tsuyoshi Shinjo	25.00
3	Jim Edmonds, J.D. Drew	15.00
4	Jeff Bagwell, Craig Biggio	15.00
5	Bernie Williams, Derek Jeter	35.00
6	Roberto Alomar, Mike Piazza	

NM/M

7 Sean Casey, Jim Thome/40   30.00
8 Pat Burrell, Scott Rolen   15.00
9 Gary Sheffield, Shawn Green   10.00
10 Ivan Rodriguez, Alex Rodriguez   15.00
11 Juan Gonzalez, Rafael Palmeiro   15.00
12 Magglio Ordonez, Frank Thomas   15.00
13 Larry Walker, Todd Helton/225   10.00
14 Luis Gonzalez, Reggie Sanders   10.00
15 Doug Mientkiewicz, Bret Boone   10.00

Sweet Swatch Autographs
NM/M
Common Player: 15.00
Quantity produced listed.
Golds: No Pricing
Production 15 Sets
Derek Jeter/375   100.00
Barry Bonds/35   200.00
Drew Henson/785   40.00
Mark Teixeira/185   40.00
Dewon Brazelton/185   15.00
Mark Prior/285   40.00
Marlon Byrd/185   15.00
Ozzie Smith/185   65.00
Ron Cey/285   20.00
Paul Molitor/85   50.00
Maury Wills/285   20.00
Dale Murphy/285   60.00
David Espinosa/485   15.00
Dane Sardinha/485   15.00
Ben Sheets/85   50.00
Tony Perez/115   30.00
Brooks Robinson/185   50.00
So Taguchi/335   30.00
Al Kaline/285   50.00
Kazuhisa Ishii/335   30.00
Albert Pujols/285   125.00
Don Mattingly/85   150.00

Sweet Swatch Game-Used
NM/M
Common Player: 8.00
1:Hobby Box
Jeff Bagwell/490   10.00
Josh Beckett/500   10.00
Darin Erstad/525   8.00
Freddy Garcia/620   8.00
Brian Giles/445   10.00
Juan Gonzalez/505   10.00
Mark Grace/795   15.00
Derek Jeter/525   40.00
Jason Kendall/990   10.00
Paul LoDuca/440   10.00
Greg Maddux/475   15.00
Magglio Ordonez/495   10.00
Rafael Palmeiro/535   10.00
Mike Piazza/1,000   15.00
Alex Rodriguez/550   25.00
Ivan Rodriguez/475   10.00
Tim Salmon/465   8.00
Kazuhiro Sasaki/770   8.00
Alfonso Soriano/775   10.00
Larry Walker/430   8.00
Ted Williams/250   125.00

Sweet Swatch Patch
NM/M
Common Player: 25.00
Random Box Topper
Jeff Bagwell/45   75.00
Josh Beckett/60   55.00
Darin Erstad/50   40.00
Freddy Garcia/50   40.00
Juan Gonzalez/55   75.00
Mark Grace/75   60.00
Jason Kendall/120   25.00
Paul LoDuca/50   35.00
Greg Maddux/50   90.00
Magglio Ordonez/50   40.00
Rafael Palmeiro/60   40.00
Mike Piazza/95   100.00
Alex Rodriguez/50   90.00
Ivan Rodriguez/50   60.00
Tim Salmon/40   50.00
Kazuhiro Sasaki/80   50.00
Alfonso Soriano/35   65.00
Larry Walker/60   40.00

2002 Fleer Focus Jersey Edition

NM/M
Complete Set (260):   60.00
Common Player: .15
Common (226-260):   1.00
Inserted 1:4
Pack (10):   2.00
Box (24):   40.00
1 Mike Piazza   1.50
2 Jason Giambi   .50
3 Jim Thome   .15
4 John Olerud   .15
5 J.D. Drew   .30
6 Richard Hidalgo   .15
7 Rusty Greer   .15
8 Tony Batista   .15
9 Omar Vizquel   .15
10 Randy Johnson   .75
11 Cristian Guzman   .15
12 Mark Grace   .25
13 Jeff Cirillo   .15
14 Mike Cameron   .15
15 Jeromy Burnitz   .15
16 Pokey Reese   .15
17 Richie Sexson   .15
18 Joe Randa   .15
19 Aramis Ramirez   .15
20 Pedro J. Martinez   .75
21 Todd Hollandsworth   .15
22 Rondell White   .15
23 Tsuyoshi Shinjo   .15
24 Melvin Mora   .15
25 Tim Hudson   .30
26 Darrin Fletcher   .15
27 Bill Mueller   .15
28 Jeff Weaver   .15
29 Tony Clark   .15
30 Tom Glavine   .40
31 Jarrod Washburn   .15
32 Greg Vaughn   .15
33 Lee Stevens   .15
34 Charles Johnson   .15
35 Lance Berkman   .15
36 Bud Smith   .15
37 Keith Foulke   .15
38 Ben Davis   .15
39 Daryle Ward   .15
40 Bernie Williams   .30
41 Dean Palmer   .15
42 Mark Mulder   .15
43 Jay Gibbons   .15
44 Brandon Duckworth   .15
45 Carlos Delgado   .40
46 Barry Zito   .25
47 Matt Morris   .15
48 J.T. Snow   .15
49 Albert Pujols   1.50
50 Brad Fullmer   .15
51 Damion Easley   .15
52 Pat Burrell   .40
53 Kevin Brown   .15
54 Todd Walker   .15
55 Rich Garces   .15
56 Carlos Pena   .15
57 Paul LoDuca   .15
58 Mike Lieberthal   .15
59 Barry Larkin   .15
60 Jon Lieber   .15
61 Jose Cruz   .15
62 Mo Vaughn   .15
63 Ivan Rodriguez   .60
64 Jorge Posada   .25
65 Magglio Ordonez   .15
66 Juan Encarnacion   .15
67 Shawn Estes   .15
68 Kevin Appier   .15
69 Jeff Bagwell   .75
70 Tim Wakefield   .15
71 Shannon Stewart   .15
72 Scott Rolen   .65
73 Bobby Higginson   .15
74 Jim Edmonds   .15
75 Adam Dunn   .50
76 Eric Chavez   .30
77 Adrian Beltre   .30
78 Jason Varitek   .15
79 Barry Bonds   2.50
80 Raul Mondesi   .15
81 Eric Karros   .15
82 Ken Griffey Jr.   1.50
83 Jermaine Dye   .15
84 Carlos Beltran   .40
85 Mark Quinn   .15
86 Terrence Long   .15
87 Shawn Green   .40
88 Nomar Garciaparra   1.50
89 Sean Casey   .25
90 Homer Bush   .15
91 Bobby Abreu   .15
92 Jamey Wright   .15
93 Tony Womack   .15
94 Larry Walker   .15
95 Doug Mientkiewicz   .15
96 Jimmy Rollins   .40
97 Brady Anderson   .15
98 Derek Jeter   2.50
99 Kevin Young   .15
100 Juan Pierre   .15
101 Edgar Martinez   .15
102 Corey Koskie   .15
103 Jeffrey Hammonds   .15
104 Luis Gonzalez   .25
105 Travis Fryman   .15
106 Kerry Wood   .50
107 Rafael Palmeiro   .60
108 Ichiro Suzuki   1.00
111 Russ Ortiz   .15
112 Jeff Kent   .15
113 Scott Erickson   .15
114 Bruce Chen   .15
115 Craig Biggio   .15
116 Robin Ventura   .15
117 Alex Rodriguez   2.00
118 Roy Oswalt   .25
119 Fred McGriff   .15
120 Juan Gonzalez   .75
121 David Justice   .15
122 Pat Hentgen   .15
123 Hideo Nomo   .65
124 Ramon Ortiz   .15
125 David Ortiz   .25
126 Phil Nevin   .15
127 Ryan Dempster   .15
128 Toby Hall   .15
129 Vladimir Guerrero   .75
130 Chipper Jones   1.00
131 Russell Branyan   .15
132 Jose Vidro   .15
133 Bubba Trammell   .15
134 Tino Martinez   .15
135 Greg Maddux   1.00
136 Derek Lee   .15
137 Troy Glaus   .75
138 Joe Crede   .15
139 Steve Cox   .15
140 Sammy Sosa   1.50
141 Corey Patterson   .15
142 Vernon Wells   .15
143 Matt Lawton   .15
144 Gabe Kapler   .15
145 Johnny Damon   .25
146 Marty Cordova   .15
147 Moises Alou   .15
148 Fernando Tatis   .15
149 Tanyon Sturtze   .15
150 Roger Clemens   1.25
151 Paul Konerko   .15
152 Chan Ho Park   .15
153 Marcus Giles   .15
154 David Eckstein   .15
155 Mike Lowell   .15
156 Preston Wilson   .15
157 John Vander Wal   .15
158 Tim Salmon   .25
159 Andy Pettitte   .35
160 Mike Mussina   .40
161 Doug Davis   .15
162 Peter Bergeron   .15
163 Rich Aurilia   .15
164 Eric Milton   .15
165 Geoff Jenkins   .15
166 Todd Helton   .75
167 Bret Boone   .15
168 Kris Benson   .15
169 Brian Anderson   .15
170 Roberto Alomar   .40
171 Javier Vazquez   .15
172 Scott Schoeneweis   .15
173 Ryan Klesko   .15
174 Jacque Jones   .15
175 Andruw Jones   .75
176 Aubrey Huff   .15
177 Mark Buehrle   .15
178 Josh Beckett   .40
179 Ben Sheets   .15
180 Curt Schilling   .40
181 C.C. Sabathia   .15
182 Denny Neagle   .15
183 Jamie Moyer   .15
184 Jason Kendall   .15
185 Dee Brown   .15
186 Frank Thomas   .75
187 Damian Rolls   .15
188 Carlos Lee   .15
189 Kevin Jarvis   .15
190 Manny Ramirez   .75
191 Cliff Floyd   .15
192 Freddy Garcia   .15
193 Orlando Cabrera   .15
194 Mike Sweeney   .15
195 Gary Sheffield   .35
196 Rafael Furcal   .15
197 Esteban Loaiza   .15
198 Mike Hampton   .15
199 Brian Giles   .15
200 Darin Erstad   .60
201 David Wells   .15
202 Kenny Lofton   .15
203 Aaron Sele   .15
204 Jason Schmidt   .15
205 Javy Lopez   .15
206 Dmitri Young   .15
207 Darryl Kile   .15
208 Matt Williams   .15
209 Joe Kennedy   .15
210 Chuck Knoblauch   .15
211 Brian Jordan   .15
212 Roberto Person   .15
213 Alex Ochoa   .15
214 Steve Finley   .15
215 Ben Petrick   .15
216 Al Leiter   .15
217 Mark Kotsay   .15
218 Miguel Tejada   .35
219 David Segui   .15
220 A.J. Burnett   .15
221 Marlon Anderson   .15
222 Wiki Gonzalez   .15
223 Jeff Suppan   .15
224 Dave Roberts   .15
225 Jose Hernandez   .15
226 Angel Berroa   1.00
227 Sean Burroughs   1.00
228 Luis Martinez RC   1.00
229 Adrian Burnside RC   1.00
230 John Ennis RC   1.00
231 Anastacio Martinez RC   1.00
232 Hank Blalock   2.00
233 Eric Hinske   1.00
234 Chris Booker RC   1.00
235 Colin Young RC   1.00
236 Mark Corey RC   1.00
237 Satoru Komiyama RC   1.00
238 So Taguchi RC   2.50
239 Elio Serrano RC   1.00
240 Reed Johnson RC   2.00
241 Jeremy Lambert RC   1.00
242 Chris Baker RC   1.00
243 Orlando Hudson RC   1.00
244 Travis Hughes RC   1.00
245 Kevin Frederick RC   1.00
246 Rodrigo Rosario RC   1.00
247 Jeremy Ward RC   1.00
248 Kazuhisa Ishii RC   4.00
249 Austin Kearns   1.00
250 Kyle Kane RC   1.00
251 Cam Esslinger RC   1.00
252 Jeff Austin RC   1.00
253 Brian Mallette RC   1.00
254 Mark Prior   4.00
255 Mark Teixeira   2.00
256 Carlos Valderrama RC   1.00
257 Jason Hart   1.00
258 Takahito Nomura RC   1.00
259 Matt Thornton   1.00
260 Marlon Byrd   1.00

Century
Cards (1-225):   6-10X
Cards (226-260):   .75-1.5X
Production 101-199

Jersey Number Parallel
(1-225) print run 26-50:   10-25X
(1-225) p/r 51-75:   8-15X
(1-225) p/r 76-99:   5-10X
Produced to player's jsy #.

Blue Chips

NM/M
Complete Set (15):   10.00
Common Player: .50
Inserted 1:6
1BC Albert Pujols   3.00
2BC Sean Burroughs   .50
3BC Vernon Wells   .50
4BC Adam Dunn   1.50
5BC Pat Burrell   1.00
6BC Juan Pierre   .50
7BC Russell Branyan   .50
8BC Carlos Pena   .50
9BC Toby Hall   .50
10BC Hank Blalock   1.00
11BC Alfonso Soriano   1.50
12BC Jimmy Rollins   .75
13BC Jose Ortiz   .50
14BC Eric Hinske   .50
15BC Nick Johnson   .50

Blue Chips Game-Used
NM/M
Inserted 1:96 Hobby
Russell Branyan/Jsy   8.00
Nick Johnson/Jsy   10.00
Patch/100   20.00

International Diamond Co.

NM/M
Complete Set (25):   25.00
Common Player: 1.00
Inserted 1:8
1 Bobby Abreu   1.00
2 Adrian Beltre   1.00
3 Jorge Posada   1.00
4 Vladimir Guerrero   3.00
5 Rafael Palmeiro   1.00
6 Sammy Sosa   4.00
7 Larry Walker   1.00
8 Manny Ramirez   3.00
9 Ichiro Suzuki   4.00
10 Jose Cruz   1.00
11 Juan Gonzalez   3.00
12 Bernie Williams   1.00
13 Ivan Rodriguez   2.00
14 Moises Alou   1.00
15 Cristian Guzman   1.00
16 Andruw Jones   3.00
17 Aramis Ramirez   1.00
18 Raul Mondesi   1.00
19 Edgar Martinez   1.00
20 Magglio Ordonez   1.00
21 Roberto Alomar   1.50
22 Chan Ho Park   1.00
23 Kazuhiro Sasaki   1.00
24 Tsuyoshi Shinjo   1.00
25 Hideo Nomo   1.00

Int. Diam. Co. Game-Used

NM/M
Common Player: 5.00
Inserted 1:144
Jorge Posada/Jsy   15.00
Rafael Palmeiro/Jsy   8.00
Manny Ramirez/Jsy   10.00
Ivan Rodriguez/Jsy   6.00
Andruw Jones/Jsy   6.00
Raul Mondesi/Jsy   5.00
Aramis Ramirez/Jsy   5.00
Edgar Martinez/Jsy   6.00
Chan Ho Park/Jsy   5.00
Kazuhiro Sasaki/Jsy   6.00
Hideo Nomo/Jsy   20.00

Int. Diam. Co. Patch
NM/M
Common Player: 15.00
Production 100
Manny Ramirez   25.00
Ivan Rodriguez   25.00
Raul Mondesi   25.00
Edgar Martinez   20.00
Chan Ho Park   20.00
Hideo Nomo   75.00

K Corps

NM/M
Complete Set (15):   20.00
Common Player: 1.00
Inserted 1:12
1KC Roger Clemens   5.00
2KC Randy Johnson   3.00
3KC Tom Glavine   1.50
4KC Josh Beckett   1.50
5KC Matt Morris   1.00
6KC Curt Schilling   1.50
7KC Greg Maddux   4.00
8KC Tim Hudson   1.50
9KC Roy Oswalt   1.50
10KC Kerry Wood   2.00
11KC Barry Zito   1.00
12KC Kevin Brown   1.00
13KC Ryan Dempster   1.00
14KC Ben Sheets   1.00
15KC Pedro J. Martinez   3.00

K Corps Game-Used
NM/M
Common Player: 5.00
Inserted 1:96
2KC Randy Johnson/Jsy   15.00
6KC Curt Schilling/Jsy   10.00
7KC Greg Maddux/Jsy   15.00
11KC Barry Zito/Jsy   8.00
12KC Kevin Brown/Jsy   5.00
15KC Pedro J. Martinez/Jsy   10.00

K Corps Patch
NM/M
Production 100
Curt Schilling   20.00

Kevin Brown   20.00
Pedro Martinez   30.00

Kings of Swing
NM/M
Complete Set (20):   80.00
Common Player: 2.00
Inserted 1:48
1KS Barry Bonds   10.00
2KS Mike Piazza   6.00
3KS Albert Pujols   8.00
4KS Todd Helton   6.00
5KS Ken Griffey Jr.   8.00
6KS Alex Rodriguez   8.00
7KS Sammy Sosa   6.00
8KS Troy Glaus   3.00
9KS Derek Jeter   10.00
10KS Ichiro Suzuki   6.00
11KS Manny Ramirez   3.00
12KS Roberto Alomar   2.00
13KS Juan Gonzalez   3.00
14KS Shawn Green   2.00
15KS Vladimir Guerrero   3.00
16KS Nomar Garciaparra   6.00
17KS Adam Dunn   2.00
18KS Jason Giambi   2.50
19KS Edgar Martinez   2.00
20KS Chipper Jones   4.00

Kings of Swing Game-Used
NM/M
Common Player: 5.00
Inserted 1:108
Mike Piazza   15.00
Todd Helton   8.00
Alex Rodriguez   15.00
Derek Jeter   30.00
Manny Ramirez   8.00
Shawn Green   5.00
Edgar Martinez   5.00
Chipper Jones   10.00

Kings of Swing Patch
NM/M
Production 100
Todd Helton   25.00
Manny Ramirez   25.00
Shawn Green   20.00
Edgar Martinez   25.00
Mike Piazza   40.00

Larger Than Life

NM/M
Common Player: 4.00
Inserted 1:240
1LL Jason Giambi   6.00
2LL Carlos Delgado   5.00
3LL Alex Rodriguez   20.00
4LL Preston Wilson   4.00
5LL Frank Thomas   9.00
6LL Nomar Garciaparra   15.00
7LL Jim Edmonds   4.00
8LL Jim Thome   4.00
9LL Barry Bonds   25.00
10LL Mo Vaughn   4.00
11LL Ichiro Suzuki   20.00
12LL Ivan Rodriguez   5.00
13LL Gary Sheffield   5.00
14LL Derek Jeter   25.00
15LL Jeff Bagwell   9.00
16LL Mike Piazza   15.00
17LL J.D. Drew   5.00
18LL Sammy Sosa   15.00
19LL Albert Pujols   20.00
20LL Luis Gonzalez   5.00

Larger Than Life Game-Used
NM/M
Common Player: 5.00
Inserted 1:144
Alex Rodriguez/Jsy   15.00
Preston Wilson/Jsy   5.00
Frank Thomas/Jsy   10.00
Jim Edmonds/Jsy   6.00
Mo Vaughn/Jsy   5.00
Ivan Rodriguez/Jsy   5.00
Derek Jeter/Jsy   25.00
Jeff Bagwell/Jsy/SP/20   25.00
Mike Piazza/Jsy   15.00
Luis Gonzalez/Jsy   5.00

Larger Than Life Patch
NM/M
Common Player: 15.00
Production 100
Preston Wilson   15.00
Frank Thomas   25.00
Jim Edmonds   15.00

Ivan Rodriguez 25.00
Mike Piazza 40.00
Luis Gonzalez 15.00

Lettermen

No Pricing
Production One Set

Materialistic Away

	NM/M
Complete Set (15):	75.00
Common Player:	4.00
Inserted 1:24	
Home:	1.5-3X
Production 50 Sets	
Away Oversized:	.5-1X
One per hobby box.	
Home Oversized:	2-4X
Production 50 Sets	

1MA	Derek Jeter	12.00
2MA	Alex Rodriguez	10.00
3MA	Mike Piazza	8.00
4MA	Ivan Rodriguez	4.00
5MA	Chipper Jones	6.00
6MA	Todd Helton	5.00
7MA	Nomar Garciaparra	8.00
8MA	Barry Bonds	12.00
9MA	Ichiro Suzuki	8.00
10MA	Ken Griffey Jr.	8.00
11MA	Jason Giambi	4.00
12MA	Sammy Sosa	8.00
13MA	Albert Pujols	10.00
14MA	Pedro J. Martinez	4.00
15MA	Vladimir Guerrero	5.00

2002 Fleer Genuine

	NM/M
Complete Set (140):	
Common Player:	.15
Common (101-140):	3.00
Production 2,002	
Pack (5):	3.00
Box (20):	50.00

1	Alex Rodriguez	2.50
2	Manny Ramirez	.75
3	Jim Thome	.15
4	Eric Milton	.15
5	Todd Helton	.75
6	Mike Mussina	.50
7	Ichiro Suzuki	1.50
8	Randy Johnson	1.00
9	Mark Mulder	.15
10	Johnny Damon	.25
11	Sean Casey	.25
12	Albert Pujols	2.50
13	Mark Grace	.25
14	Moises Alou, Mark Mulder	.15
15	Raul Mondesi, Roberto Alomar	.15
16	Cliff Floyd, Scott Rolen	.30
17	Vladimir Guerrero, Tom Glavine	.40
18	Pat Burrell, Bobby Abreu	.25
19	Ryan Klesko, Nomar Garciaparra	.50
20	Mike Hampton, Darin Erstad	.15
21	Shawn Green, Cliff Floyd	.15
22	Rich Aurilia, Tim Hudson	.15
23	Matt Morris, Jim Thome	.15
24	Curt Schilling, Nolan Ryan	1.00
25	Kevin Brown, Reggie Jackson	.25
26	Adrian Beltre, Rafael Palmeiro	.30
27	Joe Mays, Ken Griffey Jr.	.75
28	Luis Gonzalez, Sammy Sosa	.75
29	Barry Larkin, Vladimir Guerrero	.40
30	A.J. Burnett, Ichiro Suzuki	.75
31	Eric Munson	.15
32	Juan Gonzalez	.75
33	Lance Berkman	.15
34	Fred McGriff	.15
35	Paul Konerko	.15
36	Pedro J. Martinez	.75
37	Adam Dunn	.50
38	Jeromy Burnitz	.15
39	Mike Sweeney	.15
40	Bret Boone	.15
41	Ken Griffey Jr.	2.00
42	Eric Chavez	.25
43	Mark Quinn	.15
44	Roberto Alomar	.35
45	Bobby Abreu	.15
46	Bartolo Colon	.15
47	Jimmy Rollins	.25
48	Chipper Jones	1.00
49	Ben Sheets	.15
50	Freddy Garcia	.15
51	Sammy Sosa	2.00
52	Rafael Palmeiro	.65
53	Preston Wilson	.15
54	Troy Glaus	.75
55	Josh Beckett	.50
56	C.C. Sabathia	.15
57	Magglio Ordonez	.15
58	Brian Giles	.15
59	Darin Erstad	.60
60	Gary Sheffield	.35
61	Paul LoDuca	.15
62	Derek Jeter	3.00
63	Greg Maddux	1.50
64	Kerry Wood	.65
65	Toby Hall	.15
66	Barry Bonds	3.00
67	Jeff Bagwell	.75
68	Jason Kendall	.15
69	Richard Hidalgo	.15
70	J.D. Drew	.30
71	Tom Glavine	.25
72	Javier Vazquez	.15
73	Doug Mientkiewicz	.15
74	Jason Giambi	.50
75	Carlos Delgado	.40
76	Aramis Ramirez	.15
77	Torii Hunter	.15
78	Ivan Rodriguez	.65
79	Charles Johnson	.15
80	Jeff Kent	.15
81	Jacque Jones	.15
82	Larry Walker	.15
83	Cristian Guzman	.15
84	Jermaine Dye	.15
85	Roger Clemens	1.75
86	Mike Piazza	2.00
87	Craig Biggio	.15
88	Phil Nevin	.15
89	Jeff Cirillo	.15
90	Barry Zito	.25
91	Ryan Dempster	.15
92	Mark Buehrle	.15
93	Nomar Garciaparra	2.00
94	Frank Thomas	.75
95	Jim Edmonds	.15
96	Geoff Jenkins	.15
97	Scott Rolen	.65
98	Tim Hudson	.25
99	Shannon Stewart	.15
100	Richie Sexson	.15
101	Orlando Hudson	3.00
102	Doug DeVore RC	3.00
103	Rene Reyes RC	3.00
104	Steve Bechler RC	4.00
105	Jorge Nunez RC	3.00
106	Mitch Wylie RC	3.00
107	Jaime Cerda RC	3.00
108	Brandon Puffer RC	3.00
109	Tyler Yates RC	6.00
110	Bill Hall	3.00
111	Peter Zamora RC	3.00
112	Jeff Deardorff RC	3.00
113	J.J. Putz RC	3.00
114	Scotty Layfield RC	3.00
115	Brandon Backe RC	3.00
116	Andy Pratt RC	3.00
117	Mark Prior	8.00
118	Franklyn German RC	3.00
119	Todd Donovan RC	3.00
120	Franklin Nunez RC	3.00
121	Adam Walker RC	3.00
122	Ron Calloway RC	3.00
123	Tim Kalita RC	3.00
124	Kazuhisa Ishii RC	8.00
125	Mark Teixeira	5.00
126	Nate Field RC	3.00
127	Nelson Castro RC	3.00
128	So Taguchi RC	8.00
129	Marlon Byrd	3.00
130	Drew Henson	3.00
131	Kenny Kelly	3.00
132	John Ennis RC	3.00
133	Anastacio Martinez RC	3.00
134	Matt Guerrier RC	3.00
135	Tom Wilson RC	3.00
136	Ben Howard RC	3.00
137	Chris Baker RC	3.00
138	Kevin Frederick RC	3.00
159	Wilson Valdez RC	3.00
140	Austin Kearns	4.00

Bat's Incredible

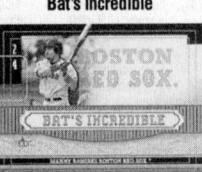

	NM/M
Complete Set (25):	60.00
Common Player:	1.50
Inserted 1:10	

1BI	Todd Helton	2.00
2BI	Chipper Jones	3.00
3BI	Luis Gonzalez	1.50
4BI	Barry Bonds	4.00
5BI	Jason Giambi	2.00
6BI	Alex Rodriguez	6.00
7BI	Manny Ramirez	4.00
8BI	Jeff Bagwell	2.00
9BI	Shawn Green	1.50
10BI	Albert Pujols	6.00
11BI	Paul LoDuca	1.50
12BI	Mike Piazza	5.00
13BI	Derek Jeter	8.00
14BI	Edgar Martinez	1.50
15BI	Juan Gonzalez	2.00
16BI	Magglio Ordonez	1.50
17BI	Jermaine Dye	1.50
18BI	Larry Walker	1.50
19BI	Phil Nevin	1.50
20BI	Ivan Rodriguez	1.50
21BI	Ichiro Suzuki	5.00
22BI	J.D. Drew	1.50
23BI	Vladimir Guerrero	2.00
24BI	Sammy Sosa	5.00
25BI	Ken Griffey Jr.	5.00

Bat's Incredible Game-Used

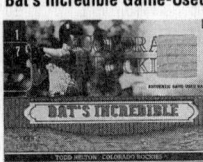

	NM/M
Common Player:	5.00
Inserted 1:20	
Todd Helton	10.00
Chipper Jones	10.00
J.D. Drew	8.00
Alex Rodriguez	15.00
Manny Ramirez	10.00
Shawn Green	6.00
Derek Jeter	20.00
Edgar Martinez	8.00
Juan Gonzalez	8.00
Jermaine Dye	5.00
Phil Nevin	5.00
Ivan Rodriguez	10.00

Genuine Ink

	NM/M
Common Autograph	15.00
Production varies	
Barry Bonds/150	150.00
Ron Cey/175	15.00
Derek Jeter/150	125.00
Al Kaline/300	60.00
Don Mattingly/50	100.00
Paul Molitor	50.00
Dale Murphy/700	40.00
Phil Rizzuto/700	30.00
Brooks Robinson/140	60.00
Maury Willis/975	15.00

Leaders

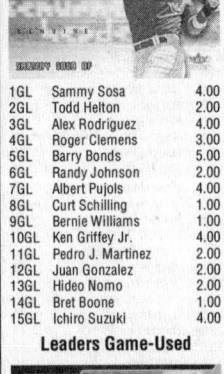

	NM/M
Complete Set (15):	25.00
Common Player:	1.00
Inserted 1:6	

1GL	Sammy Sosa	4.00
2GL	Todd Helton	2.00
3GL	Alex Rodriguez	4.00
4GL	Roger Clemens	3.00
5GL	Barry Bonds	5.00
6GL	Randy Johnson	2.00
7GL	Albert Pujols	4.00
8GL	Curt Schilling	1.00
9GL	Bernie Williams	1.00
10GL	Ken Griffey Jr.	4.00
11GL	Pedro J. Martinez	2.00
12GL	Juan Gonzalez	2.00
13GL	Hideo Nomo	2.00
14GL	Bret Boone	1.00
15GL	Ichiro Suzuki	4.00

Leaders Game-Used

	NM/M
Common Player:	8.00
Inserted 1:16	
Todd Helton	10.00
Alex Rodriguez	15.00
Roger Clemens	15.00
Barry Bonds	20.00
Randy Johnson	10.00
Curt Schilling	8.00
Bernie Williams	8.00
Pedro J. Martinez	10.00
Hideo Nomo	15.00

Names of the Game

	NM/M
Complete Set (30):	60.00
Common Player:	1.00
Inserted 1:10 H, 1:20 R	

1	Mike Piazza	5.00
2	Chipper Jones	4.00
3	Jim Edmonds	1.00
4	Barry Larkin	1.00
5	Frank Thomas	3.00
6	Manny Ramirez	3.00
7	Carlos Delgado	1.50
8	Brian Giles	1.00
9	Kerry Wood	2.00
10	Derek Jeter	8.00
11	Adam Dunn	2.00
12	Gary Sheffield	1.50
13	Luis Gonzalez	1.00
14	Mark Mulder	1.00
15	Roberto Alomar	1.50
16	Scott Rolen	2.50
17	Tom Glavine	1.50
18	Bobby Abreu	1.00
19	Nomar Garciaparra	5.00
20	Darin Erstad	2.00
21	Cliff Floyd	1.00
22	Tim Hudson	1.00
23	Jim Thome	1.00
24	Nolan Ryan	8.00
25	Reggie Jackson	3.00
26	Rafael Palmeiro	2.00
27	Ken Griffey Jr.	5.00
28	Sammy Sosa	5.00
29	Vladimir Guerrero	3.00
30	Ichiro Suzuki	5.00

Names of the Game Memorabilia

	NM/M
Common Player:	5.00
1:24 H, 1:100 R	

1	Roberto Alomar	10.00
2	Carlos Delgado	8.00
3	Jim Edmonds	8.00
4	Darin Erstad	5.00
5	Cliff Floyd	5.00
6	Nomar Garciaparra/SP/90	60.00
7	Brian Giles	5.00
8	Luis Gonzalez	5.00
9	Tim Hudson	3.00
10	Derek Jeter	30.00
11	Chipper Jones	10.00
12	Barry Larkin	8.00
13	Mark Mulder	8.00
14	Rafael Palmeiro	10.00
15	Mike Piazza	15.00
16	Manny Ramirez	8.00
17	Scott Rolen	10.00
18	Nolan Ryan	40.00
19	Jim Thome	10.00

Tip of the Cap

	NM/M
Complete Set (25):	40.00
Common Player:	.50
Inserted 1:6	

1TC	Alex Rodriguez	6.00
2TC	Derek Jeter	8.00
3TC	Kazuhiro Sasaki	.50
4TC	Barry Bonds	8.00
5TC	J.D. Drew	.75
6TC	Tsuyoshi Shinjo	.50
7TC	Alfonso Soriano	1.50
8TC	Albert Pujols	6.00
9TC	Tom Seaver	1.50
10TC	Drew Henson	.75
11TC	Dave Winfield	1.50
12TC	Carlos Delgado	1.00
13TC	Lou Boudreau	.50
14TC	Shawn Green	.75
15TC	Roger Clemens	3.00
16TC	Randy Johnson	1.50
17TC	Sammy Sosa	4.00
18TC	Rafael Palmeiro	1.25
19TC	Ken Griffey Jr.	5.00
20TC	Ichiro Suzuki	5.00
21TC	Eric Chavez	.65
22TC	Andruw Jones	1.50
23TC	Miguel Tejada	.65
24TC	Pedro J. Martinez	.50
25TC	Tim Salmon	.50

Tip of the Cap Game-Used

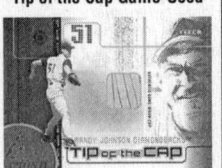

	NM/M
Common Player:	1.00
Alex Rodriguez/670	20.00
Barry Bonds/32	75.00
Tom Seaver/224	25.00
Drew Henson/361	15.00
Dave Winfield/363	15.00
Carlos Delgado/219	15.00
Lou Boudreau/303	20.00
Randy Johnson/74	30.00
Rafael Palmeiro/300	20.00
Andruw Jones/19	40.00
Miguel Tejada/225	15.00

Touch 'Em All

	NM/M
Complete Set (25):	60.00
Common Player:	1.50
Inserted 1:10	

1	Derek Jeter	8.00
2	Sammy Sosa	5.00
3	Albert Pujols	6.00
4	Vladimir Guerrero	3.00
5	Ken Griffey Jr.	5.00
6	Nomar Garciaparra	5.00
7	Luis Gonzalez	1.50
8	Barry Bonds	8.00
9	Manny Ramirez	2.50
10	Jason Giambi	2.00
11	Chipper Jones	4.00
12	Ichiro Suzuki	5.00
13	Alex Rodriguez	6.00
14	Juan Gonzalez	2.50
15	Todd Helton	2.50
16	Roberto Alomar	1.50
17	Jeff Bagwell	2.50
18	Mike Piazza	5.00
19	Gary Sheffield	1.50
20	Ivan Rodriguez	2.00
21	Frank Thomas	2.50
22	Bobby Abreu	1.50
23	J.D. Drew	1.50
24	Scott Rolen	2.00
25	Darin Erstad	1.50

Touch 'Em All Base

	NM/M
Common Player:	4.00
Production 350 Sets	
Derek Jeter	15.00
Sammy Sosa	10.00
Albert Pujols	15.00
Vladimir Guerrero	10.00
Ken Griffey Jr.	10.00
Nomar Garciaparra	10.00
Luis Gonzalez	5.00
Barry Bonds	15.00
Manny Ramirez	8.00
Jason Giambi	8.00
Chipper Jones	8.00
Ichiro Suzuki	15.00
Alex Rodriguez	10.00
Juan Gonzalez	8.00
Todd Helton	8.00
Roberto Alomar	6.00
Jeff Bagwell	8.00
Mike Piazza	10.00
Gary Sheffield	8.00
Ivan Rodriguez	8.00
Frank Thomas	8.00
Bobby Abreu	4.00
J.D. Drew	4.00
Scott Rolen	4.00
Darin Erstad	4.00

2002 Fleer Greats of the Game

Los Angeles Dodgers

	NM/M
Complete Set (100):	45.00
Common Player:	.40
Pack (5):	5.00
Box (24):	100.00

1	Cal Ripken Jr.	6.00
2	Paul Molitor	1.50
3	Roberto Clemente	4.00
4	Cy Young	1.50
5	Tris Speaker	.50
6	Lou Brock	.50
7	Fred Lynn	.40
8	Harmon Killebrew	1.50
9	Ted Williams	3.00
10	Dave Winfield	1.00
11	Orlando Cepeda	.40
12	Johnny Mize	.40
13	Walter Johnson	1.50
14	Roy Campanella	1.50
15	George Sisler	.40
16	Bo Jackson	.40
17	Rollie Fingers	.40
18	Brooks Robinson	1.50
19	Billy Williams	.40
20	Maury Wills	.40
21	Jimmie Foxx	.40
22	Alan Trammell	.40
23	Rogers Hornsby	1.50
24	Don Drysdale	1.50

#	Player	Price
25	Bob Feller	.75
26	Jackie Robinson	5.00
27	Whitey Ford	1.50
28	Enos Slaughter	.40
29	Rod Carew	1.00
30	Eddie Mathews	1.50
31	Ron Cey	.40
32	Thurman Munson	2.00
33	Ty Cobb	3.00
34	Rocky Colavito	.75
35	Satchel Paige	1.50
36	Andre Dawson	.75
37	Phil Rizzuto	.75
38	Roger Maris	3.00
39	Earl Weaver	.40
40	Joe Carter	.40
41	Christy Mathewson	1.50
42	Tony Lazzeri	.40
43	Gil Hodges	.75
44	Gaylord Perry	.40
45	Steve Carlton	1.00
46	George Kell	.40
47	Mickey Cochrane	1.00
48	Joe Morgan	.60
49	Steve Garvey	.40
50	Bob Gibson	1.50
51	Lefty Grove	.40
52	Warren Spahn	1.50
53	Willie McCovey	.75
54	Frank Robinson	1.50
55	Rich "Goose" Gossage	.40
56	Hank Bauer	.40
57	Hoyt Wilhelm	.40
58	Mel Ott	1.00
59	Preacher Roe	.75
60	Yogi Berra	1.50
61	Nolan Ryan	6.00
62	Dizzy Dean	.75
63	Ryne Sandberg	2.00
64	Frank Howard	.40
65	Hack Wilson	.40
66	Robin Yount	1.50
67	Al Kaline	1.50
68	Mike Schmidt	2.00
69	Vida Blue	.40
70	George Brett	3.00
71	Sparky Anderson	.40
72	Tom Seaver	1.50
73	Bill "Moose" Skowron	.40
74	Don Mattingly	2.50
75	Carl Yastrzemski	1.50
76	Eddie Murray	1.00
77	Jim Palmer	1.00
78	Bill Dickey	.75
79	Ozzie Smith	1.50
80	Dale Murphy	.75
81	Nap Lajoie	.40
82	Jim "Catfish" Hunter	1.00
83	Duke Snider	1.00
84	Luis Aparicio	.40
85	Reggie Jackson	1.50
86	Honus Wagner	1.50
87	Johnny Bench	2.00
88	Stan Musial	3.00
89	Carlton Fisk	.75
90	Tony Oliva	.75
91	Wade Boggs	2.00
92	Jim Rice	.40
93	Bill Mazeroski	.40
94	Ralph Kiner	.40
95	Tony Perez	.40
96	Kirby Puckett	2.00
97	Bobby Bonds	.75
98	Bill Terry	.40
99	Juan Marichal	.75
100	Hank Greenberg	1.00

Autographs

		NM/M
	Common Autograph:	10.00
	Inserted 1:24	
SA	Sparky Anderson	15.00
LA	Luis Aparicio	15.00
HB	Hank Bauer	10.00
JB	Johnny Bench	50.00
YB	Yogi Berra	40.00
PB	Paul Blair	10.00
VB	Vida Blue	15.00
WB	Wade Boggs	20.00
BB	Bobby Bonds	15.00
GB	George Brett/150	125.00
RC	Rod Carew/250	40.00
SC	Steve Carlton	25.00
JC	Joe Carter	15.00
OC	Orlando Cepeda	15.00
RC	Ron Cey	10.00
CO	Rocky Colavito	35.00
AD	Andre Dawson	15.00
BF	Bob Feller	15.00
RF	Rollie Fingers	15.00
CF	Carlton Fisk/100	65.00
WF	Whitey Ford	40.00
SG	Steve Garvey	15.00
BG	Bob Gibson/200	30.00
RG	Rich "Goose" Gossage	15.00
FH	Frank Howard	10.00
RJ	Reggie Jackson/150	70.00
AK	Al Kaline	15.00
GK	George Kell	15.00
HK	Harmon Killebrew	30.00
RK	Ralph Kiner/250	25.00
FL	Fred Lynn	15.00
JM	Juan Marichal	15.00
DM	Don Mattingly/300	75.00
BM	Bill Mazeroski/200	20.00
WM	Willie McCovey	25.00
PM	Paul Molitor	25.00
JM	Joe Morgan	15.00
MU	Dale Murphy	15.00
EM	Eddie Murray/250	70.00
SM	Stan Musial/200	70.00
TO	Tony Oliva	15.00
JP	Jim Palmer	20.00
DP	Dave Parker	10.00
TP	Tony Perez	15.00
GP	Gaylord Perry/4	60.00
KP	Kirby Puckett/250	60.00
JR	Jim Rice	15.00
CR	Cal Ripken Jr./100	180.00
PR	Phil Rizzuto/300	50.00
BR	Brooks Robinson	30.00
FR	Frank Robinson/250	50.00
PR	Preacher Roe	15.00
NR	Nolan Ryan/150	100.00
RS	Ryne Sandberg/200	75.00
MS	Mike Schmidt/150	100.00
TS	Tom Seaver/150	50.00
BS	Bill "Moose" Skowron	10.00
ES	Enos Slaughter	15.00
OS	Ozzie Smith/300	65.00
DS	Duke Snider	25.00
WS	Warren Spahn	50.00
AT	Alan Trammell	20.00
HW	Hoyt Wilhelm	15.00
BW	Billy Williams	15.00
MW	Maury Wills	15.00
DW	Dave Winfield/250	25.00
CY	Carl Yastrzemski/200	75.00
RY	Robin Yount	70.00

Dueling Duos

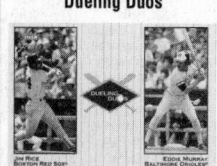

		NM/M
	Complete Set (29):	90.00
	Common Player:	2.00
	Inserted 1:6	
1DD	Johnny Bench, Carlton Fisk	4.00
2DD	Roy Campanella, Yogi Berra	5.00
3DD	Stan Musial, Ted Williams	8.00
4DD	Carl Yastrzemski, Reggie Jackson	3.00
5DD	Babe Ruth, Jimmie Foxx	8.00
6DD	Steve Carlton, Nolan Ryan	8.00
7DD	Wade Boggs, Don Mattingly	6.00
8DD	Brooks Robinson, Roger Maris	5.00
9DD	Paul Molitor, Don Mattingly	6.00
10DD	Sparky Anderson, Earl Weaver	2.00
11DD	Bob Gibson, Duke Snider	3.00
12DD	Yogi Berra, Gil Hodges	4.00
13DD	Joe Morgan, Ryne Sandberg	3.00
14DD	Tony Perez, Carl Yastrzemski	3.00
15DD	Jimmie Foxx, Bill Dickey	3.00
16DD	Ralph Kiner, Duke Snider	3.00
17DD	Nellie Fox, Rocky Colavito	2.00
18DD	Willie McCovey, Johnny Bench	3.00
19DD	Duke Snider, Eddie Mathews	4.00
20DD	Reggie Jackson, Jim Rice	3.00
21DD	Eddie Murray, Jim Rice	2.00
22DD	Paul Molitor, Dave Winfield	3.00
23DD	Robin Yount, Dave Winfield	3.00
24DD	Enos Slaughter, Ted Kluszewski	3.00
25DD	Wade Boggs, George Brett	4.00
26DD	George Brett, Eddie Murray	4.00
27DD	George Brett, Cal Ripken Jr.	8.00
28DD	Kirby Puckett, Don Mattingly	6.00
29DD	George Brett, Mike Schmidt	5.00

Dueling Duos Autograph
No Pricing
Production 25 Sets

Dueling Duos G-U Single

	NM/M
Common Card:	15.00
Inserted 1:24	
Johnny Bench, Carlton Fisk	20.00
Roy Campanella, Yogi Berra	25.00
Carl Yastrzemski, Reggie Jackson	25.00
Babe Ruth, Jimmie Foxx/75	50.00
Kirby Puckett, Don Mattingly	25.00
Steve Carlton, Nolan Ryan	80.00
Wade Boggs, Don Mattingly	25.00
Brooks Robinson, Roger Maris	25.00
Paul Molitor, Don Mattingly	25.00
Sparky Anderson, Earl Weaver	10.00
Bob Gibson, Duke Snider/200	20.00
Yogi Berra, Gil Hodges	25.00
Joe Morgan, Ryne Sandberg	25.00
Tony Perez, Carl Yastrzemski	25.00
Jimmie Foxx, Bill Dickey	20.00
Ralph Kiner, Duke Snider	20.00
Nellie Fox, Rocky Colavito	20.00
Willie McCovey, Johnny Bench	25.00
Duke Snider, Eddie Mathews	20.00
Reggie Jackson, Jim Rice	15.00
Eddie Murray, Jim Rice	15.00
Paul Molitor, Dave Winfield	15.00
Robin Yount, Dave Winfield	15.00
Enos Slaughter, Ted Kluszewski	10.00
Wade Boggs, George Brett	25.00
George Brett, Eddie Murray	20.00
George Brett, Cal Ripken Jr.	40.00

Fleer Greats of Game Dueling Duos Game-Used Dual
No Pricing
Production 25 Sets

Through the Years Level 1

	NM/M
Common Player:	10.00
Inserted 1:24	
George Brett	15.00
Reggie Jackson/A's	15.00
Reggie Jackson/Angels	15.00
Ted Williams/350	100.00
Robin Yount	20.00
Willie McCovey	15.00
Paul Molitor/Brewers	15.00
Paul Molitor/Blue Jays	15.00
Jim Palmer	15.00
Brooks Robinson	15.00
Carl Yastrzemski	25.00
Don Mattingly	25.00
Carlton Fisk/Hitting	15.00
Carlton Fisk/Fielding	15.00
Nolan Ryan	40.00
Eddie Murray	15.00
Wade Boggs	15.00
Tony Perez	10.00
Ted Kluszewski	10.00
Bo Jackson/Royals	15.00
Bo Jackson/White Sox	15.00
Johnny Bench	20.00
Jackie Robinson	65.00
Hoyt Wilhelm	10.00
Vida Blue	10.00
Dave Winfield	10.00
Frank Robinson	15.00
Jim Rice	10.00
Jim Rice	10.00
Cal Ripken/Htg	40.00
Cal Ripken/Fldg	40.00

Through the Years Level 2

	NM/M
Common Player:	25.00
Production 100 Sets	
George Brett	80.00
Reggie Jackson	30.00
Ted Williams	120.00
Robin Yount	40.00
Willie McCovey	30.00
Paul Molitor	40.00
Jim Palmer	25.00
Carl Yastrzemski	65.00
Don Mattingly	60.00
Carlton Fisk	30.00
Nolan Ryan	75.00
Eddie Murray	25.00
Wade Boggs	30.00
Ted Kluszewski	30.00
Bo Jackson/Royals	30.00
Bo Jackson/White Sox	30.00
Johnny Bench	40.00
Dave Winfield	25.00
Jim Rice	25.00
Cal Ripken Jr.	60.00
Cal Ripken Jr.	60.00

Through the Years Level 3
No Pricing
Production 25 Sets

Through Years Patch Edition

	NM/M
Common Player:	25.00
Production 100 Sets	
George Brett	80.00
Reggie Jackson/A's	30.00
Reggie Jackson/Angels	30.00
Ted Williams	120.00
Robin Yount	50.00
Willie McCovey	30.00
Paul Molitor/Brewers	40.00
Paul Molitor/Blue Jays	40.00
Jim Palmer	25.00
Carl Yastrzemski	75.00
Don Mattingly	60.00
Carlton Fisk	30.00
Carlton Fisk	30.00
Nolan Ryan	75.00
Eddie Murray	25.00
Wade Boggs	30.00
Tony Perez	25.00
Ted Kluszewski	30.00
Bo Jackson/Royals	40.00
Bo Jackson/White Sox	40.00
Johnny Bench	40.00
Dave Winfield	30.00
Frank Robinson	30.00
Jim Rice	25.00
Jim Rice	25.00
Cal Ripken Jr.	80.00
Cal Ripken Jr.	80.00

2002 Fleer Hot Prospects

#	Player	NM/M
	Complete Set (125):	
	Common Player:	.25
	Common (81-105):	8.00
	Production 1,000	
	Common (106-125):	3.00
	Production 1,500	
	Pack (5):	4.00
	Box (18):	50.00
1	Derek Jeter	3.00
2	Garret Anderson	.25
3	Scott Rolen	.75
4	Bret Boone	.25
5	Lance Berkman	.25
6	Andruw Jones	1.00
7	Ivan Rodriguez	.75
8	Bernie Williams	.35
9	Cristian Guzman	.25
10	Mo Vaughn	.25
11	Troy Glaus	1.00
12	Tim Salmon	.35
13	Jason Giambi	.65
14	Cliff Floyd	.25
15	Tim Hudson	.35
16	Curt Schilling	.40
17	Sammy Sosa	2.00
18	Alex Rodriguez	2.50
19	Chuck Knoblauch	.25
20	Jason Kendall	.25
21	Ben Sheets	.25
22	Nomar Garciaparra	.25
23	Ryan Klesko	.25
24	Greg Vaughn	.25
25	Rafael Palmeiro	.75
26	Miguel Tejada	.35
27	Shea Hillenbrand	.25
28	Jim Thome	.25
29	Randy Johnson	.25
30	Barry Larkin	.25
31	Paul LoDuca	.25
32	Pedro J. Martinez	1.00
33	Luis Gonzalez	.25
34	Carlos Delgado	.50
35	Richie Sexson	.25
36	Albert Pujols	2.25
37	Bobby Abreu	.25
38	Gary Sheffield	.40
39	Magglio Ordonez	.25
40	Eric Chavez	.35
41	Jeff Bagwell	1.00
42	Doug Mientkiewicz	.25
43	Moises Alou	.25
44	Todd Helton	1.00
45	Ichiro Suzuki	2.00
46	Jose Cruz Jr.	.25
47	Freddy Garcia	.25
48	Tino Martinez	.25
49	Roger Clemens	1.75
50	Greg Maddux	1.50
51	Mike Piazza	2.00
52	Roberto Alomar	.50
53	Adam Dunn	.50
54	Kerry Wood	.75
55	Edgar Martinez	.25
56	Ken Griffey Jr.	2.00
57	Juan Gonzalez	1.00
58	Pat Burrell	.50
59	Corey Koskie	.25
60	Jose Vidro	.25
61	Ben Grieve	.25
62	Barry Bonds	3.00
63	Raul Mondesi	.25
64	Jimmy Rollins	.50
65	Mike Sweeney	.25
66	Josh Beckett	.50
67	Chipper Jones	1.50
68	Jeff Kent	.25
69	Tony Batista	.25
70	Phil Nevin	.25
71	Brian Jordan	.25
72	Rich Aurilia	.25
73	Brian Giles	.25
74	Frank Thomas	1.00
75	Larry Walker	.25
76	Shawn Green	.40
77	Manny Ramirez	1.00
78	Craig Biggio	.25
79	Vladimir Guerrero	1.00
80	Jeromy Burnitz	.25
81	Mark Teixeira	10.00
82	Corey Thurman RC	8.00
83	Mark Prior	15.00
84	Marlon Byrd	8.00
85	Austin Kearns	10.00
86	Satoru Komiyama RC	8.00
87	So Taguchi RC	12.00
88	Jorge Padilla RC	8.00
89	Rene Reyes RC	8.00
90	Jorge Nunez RC	8.00
91	Ron Calloway RC	8.00
92	Kazuhisa Ishii RC	10.00
93	Dewon Brazelton	8.00
94	Angel Berroa	8.00
95	Felix Escalona RC	8.00
96	Sean Burroughs	8.00
97	Brandon Duckworth	8.00
98	Hank Blalock	10.00
99	Eric Hinske	8.00
100	Carlos Pena	8.00
101	Morgan Ensberg	8.00
102	Ryan Ludwick	8.00
103	Chris Snelling RC	8.00
104	Jason Lane	8.00
105	Drew Henson	10.00
106	Bobby Kielty	3.00
107	Earl Snyder RC	3.00
108	Nate Field RC	3.00
109	Juan Diaz	3.00
110	Ryan Anderson	3.00
111	Esteban German	3.00
112	Takahito Nomura RC	3.00
113	David Kelton	3.00
114	Steve Kent RC	3.00
115	Colby Lewis	3.00
116	Jason Simontacchi RC	3.00
117	Rodrigo Rosario RC	3.00
118	Ben Howard RC	3.00
119	Hansel Izquierdo RC	3.00
120	John Ennis RC	3.00
121	Anderson Machado RC	3.00
122	Luis Ugueto RC	3.00
123	Anastacio Martinez RC	3.00
124	Reed Johnson RC	6.00
125	Juan Cruz	3.00

Co-Stars

		NM/M
	Complete Set (15):	25.00
	Common Card:	1.00
	Inserted 1:6	
1CS	Barry Bonds, Alex Rodriguez	6.00
2CS	Derek Jeter, Nomar Garciaparra	5.00
3CS	Andruw Jones, Chipper Jones	3.00
4CS	Juan Gonzalez, Jim Thome	2.00
5CS	Pedro J. Martinez, Randy Johnson	2.00
6CS	Adam Dunn, Pat Burrell	1.50
7CS	Frank Thomas, Manny Ramirez	2.00
8CS	Jeff Bagwell, Lance Berkman	2.00
9CS	So Taguchi, Kazuhisa Ishii	4.00
10CS	Jimmy Rollins, Miguel Tejada	2.00
11CS	Morgan Ensberg, Carlos Pena	1.00
12CS	Adam Dunn, Austin Kearns	2.00
13CS	Vladimir Guerrero, Scott Rolen	3.00
14CS	Drew Henson, Xavier Nady	1.00
15CS	Mike Piazza, Ivan Rodriguez	4.00

Future Swatch Autograph

		NM/M
	Common Auto.	
	Production 100	
83	Mark Prior	40.00
87	So Taguchi	20.00
89	Rene Reyes	10.00
105	Drew Henson	20.00

Inside Barry Bonds

		NM/M
	Common Bonds:	15.00
1BB	Barry Bonds/Pants/1,000	20.00
2BB	Barry Bonds/Pants/900	20.00
3BB	Barry Bonds/Jsy/800	20.00
4BB	Barry Bonds/Bat/700	20.00
5BB	Barry Bonds/Base/600	15.00
6BB	Barry Bonds/Cleat/500	25.00
7BB	Barry Bonds/Glv/400	25.00
8BB	Barry Bonds/Cap/300	30.00

Jerseygraphs

		NM/M
	Common Player:	10.00
	Inserted 1:186	
DJ	Derek Jeter/108	150.00
BB	Barry Bonds/65	250.00
CJ	Chipper Jones/100	80.00
DH	Drew Henson	30.00
ST	So Taguchi/100	25.00
DE	David Espinosa	10.00
DS	Dane Sardinha	10.00
AB	Adrian Beltre/169	35.00

MLB Hot Materials

		NM/M
	Common Player:	5.00
	Inserted 1:9	
	Red Hots:	1-2X
	Production 50 Sets	
AD	Adam Dunn	8.00
AR	Alex Rodriguez	10.00
BB	Bret Boone	5.00
BB2	Barry Bonds	20.00
BD	Brandon Duckworth	5.00
BG	Brian Giles	5.00
BW	Bernie Williams	8.00
CD	Carlos Delgado	6.00
CG	Cristian Guzman	5.00
CP	Carlos Pena	8.00
CP	Corey Patterson	6.00
CS	Curt Schilling	5.00
FT	Frank Thomas	10.00
GK	Gabe Kapler	5.00
GM	Greg Maddux	6.00
GS	Gary Sheffield	6.00
IR	Ivan Rodriguez	10.00
JB	Josh Beckett	8.00
JB2	Jeff Bagwell/108	20.00
JG	Juan Gonzalez	8.00
JT	Jim Thome	10.00
JU	Juan Uribe	5.00
LB	Lance Berkman	8.00
MM	Mark Mulder	8.00
MA	Moises Alou	6.00
MP	Mike Piazza	15.00
MS	Mike Sweeney	5.00
NJ	Nick Johnson	5.00
PL	Paul LoDuca	5.00

PM	Pedro J. Martinez	10.00
RF	Rafael Furcal	5.00
RO	Roy Oswalt	5.00
RP	Rafael Palmeiro	10.00
SB	Sean Burroughs/350	10.00
SG	Shawn Green	8.00
TA	Tony Armas Jr.	5.00
TH	Torii Hunter	5.00
TM	Tino Martinez	8.00
VW	Vernon Wells	5.00
TH	Todd Helton	8.00
MO	Magglio Ordonez	8.00
FG	Freddy Garcia	5.00
ST	So Taguchi	8.00

MLB Hot Tandems

NM/M
Common Card: 10.00
Production 100 Sets
Red Hots 10 Sets No Pricing

Adam Dunn, Lance Berkman	15.00
Alex Rodriguez, Ivan Rodriguez	30.00
Bret Boone, Freddy Garcia	10.00
Barry Bonds, Kazuhisa Ishii	40.00
Brandon Duckworth, Roy Oswalt	10.00
Bernie Williams, Jorge Posada	15.00
Carlos Delgado, Vernon Wells	10.00
Cristian Guzman, Torii Hunter	10.00
Carlos Pena, Corey Patterson	10.00
Curt Schilling, Greg Maddux	25.00
Frank Thomas, Magglio Ordonez	15.00
Gabe Kapler, Rafael Palmeiro	12.00
Gary Sheffield, Rafael Furcal	10.00
Josh Beckett, Roy Oswalt	10.00
Brandon Duckworth, Josh Beckett	15.00
Jeff Bagwell, Lance Berkman	15.00
Juan Gonzalez, Rafael Palmeiro	15.00
Jim Thome, Shawn Green	15.00
Paul LoDuca, Shawn Green	10.00
Juan Uribe, Miguel Tejada	15.00
Mark Mulder, Miguel Tejada	15.00
Moises Alou, Magglio Ordonez	10.00
Jorge Posada, Mike Piazza	25.00
Mike Sweeney, Todd Helton	15.00
Carlos Pena, Nick Johnson	10.00
Curt Schilling, Pedro J. Martinez	25.00
Tony Armas Jr., Freddy Garcia	10.00
Tino Martinez, Todd Helton	15.00
Barry Bonds, Derek Jeter	60.00
Kazuhisa Ishii, Derek Jeter	40.00
Juan Uribe, Cristian Guzman	10.00
Kazuhisa Ishii, So Taguchi	20.00
Adam Dunn, Corey Patterson	15.00
Bernie Williams, Nick Johnson	10.00
Bret Boone, Torii Hunter	10.00
Greg Maddux, Pedro J. Martinez	20.00
Sean Burroughs, Drew Henson	10.00
Kazuhisa Ishii, Satoru Komiyama	20.00
Kazuhisa Ishii, Mark Prior	20.00
Hank Blalock, Austin Kearns	15.00
Hank Blalock, Mark Teixeira	15.00
Marlon Byrd, Jorge Padilla	10.00
Marlon Byrd, Austin Kearns	10.00
Gabe Kapler, Juan Gonzalez	15.00
Jeff Bagwell, Mike Piazza	25.00

We're Number One

NM/M
Complete Set (10): 35.00
Common Player: 1.50
Inserted 1:15

1WN	Derek Jeter	8.00
2WN	Barry Bonds	8.00
3WN	Ken Griffey Jr.	8.00
4WN	Roger Clemens	4.50
5WN	Alex Rodriguez	6.00
6WN	J.D. Drew	1.50
7WN	Chipper Jones	4.00
8WN	Manny Ramirez	3.00
9WN	Nomar Garciaparra	5.00
10WN	Todd Helton	3.00

We're Number One Autograph

NM/M
Common Player:
Barry Bonds/85 200.00

We're Number One Memorabilia

NM/M
Common Player: 5.00
Inserted 1:25

Derek Jeter/Jsy	25.00
Barry Bonds/Jsy	20.00
Ken Griffey Jr./Base	15.00
Alex Rodriguez/Jsy	15.00
J.D. Drew/Jsy	5.00
Chipper Jones/Jsy	10.00
Manny Ramirez/Jsy	10.00
Nomar Garciaparra/Jsy	20.00
Todd Helton/Jsy	10.00

2002 Fleer Maximum

NM/M
Complete Set (270):
Common Player: .15
Common (201-250): 5.00
Production 500
Common (251-270): .50
Inserted 1:Hobby Pack
Pack (15): 2.50
Box (16): 35.00

1	Barry Bonds	2.00
2	Alex Rodriguez	1.50
3	Jim Edmonds	.15
4	Manny Ramirez	.75
5	Jeff Bagwell	.75
6	Kazuhiro Sasaki	.15
7	Jason Giambi	.50
8	J.D. Drew	.15
9	Barry Larkin	.15
10	Chipper Jones	1.00
11	Rafael Palmeiro	.65
12	Roberto Alomar	.35
13	Randy Johnson	.75
14	Juan Gonzalez	.75
15	Gary Sheffield	.25
16	Larry Walker	.15
17	Todd Helton	.75
18	Ivan Rodriguez	.65
19	Greg Maddux	1.00
20	Mike Piazza	1.25
21	Tsuyoshi Shinjo	.15
22	Luis Gonzalez	.25
23	Pedro Martinez	.75
24	Albert Pujols	1.50
25	Jose Canseco	.35
26	Edgar Martinez	.15
27	Moises Alou	.15
28	Vladimir Guerrero	.75
29	Shawn Green	.35
30	Miguel Tejada	.25
31	Bernie Williams	.30
32	Frank Thomas	.75
33	Jim Thome	.15
34	Derek Jeter	2.00
35	Julio Lugo	.15
36	Mo Vaughn	.15
37	Steve Cox	.15
38	Brad Radke	.15
39	Brian Jordan	.15
40	Garret Anderson	.15
41	Ichiro Suzuki	1.25
42	Mike Lieberthal	.15
43	Preston Wilson	.15
44	Bud Smith	.15
45	Curt Schilling	.40
46	Eric Chavez	.25
47	Javier Vazquez	.15
48	Jose Ortiz	.15
49	Mike Sweeney	.15
50	Travis Fryman	.15
51	Brady Anderson	.15
52	Chan Ho Park	.15
53	C.C. Sabathia	.15
54	Jack Wilson	.25
55	Joe Crede	.15
56	Mike Mussina	.40
57	Sean Casey	.30
58	Bobby Abreu	.15
59	Joe Randa	.15
60	Jose Vidro	.15
61	Juan Uribe	.15
62	Mark Grace	.25
63	Matt Morris	.15
64	Omar Vizquel	.15
65	Darryl Kile	.15
66	Dee Brown	.15
67	Fernando Tatis	.15
68	Jeff Cirillo	.15
69	Johnny Damon	.25
70	Milton Bradley	.15
71	Reggie Sanders	.15
72	Al Leiter	.15
73	Andres Galarraga	.15
74	Ellis Burks	.15
75	Jermaine Dye	.15
76	Juan Pierre	.15
77	Junior Spivey	.15
78	Mark Quinn	.15
79	Ben Sheets	.15
80	Brad Fullmer	.15
81	Bubba Trammell	.15
82	Dante Bichette	.15
83	Ken Griffey Jr.	1.25
84	Paul O'Neill	.15
85	Robert Fick	.15
86	Bret Boone	.15
87	Raul Mondesi	.15
88	Josh Beckett	.40
89	Geoff Jenkins	.15
90	Ramon Ortiz	.15
91	Robin Ventura	.15
92	Tom Glavine	.30
93	Jimmy Rollins	.25
94	Jamie Moyer	.15
95	Magglio Ordonez	.15
96	Mike Lowell	.15
97	Ryan Dempster	.15
98	Scott Schoeneweis	.15
99	Todd Zeile	.15
100	A.J. Burnett	.15
101	Aaron Sele	.15
102	Cal Ripken Jr.	2.00
103	Carlos Beltran	.45
104	David Eckstein	.15
105	Jason Marquis	.15
106	Matt Lawton	.15
107	Ben Grieve	.15
108	Brian Giles	.15
109	Josh Towers	.15
110	Lance Berkman	.15
111	Sammy Sosa	1.25
112	Torii Hunter	.15
113	Aubrey Huff	.15
114	Craig Biggio	.15
115	Doug Mientkiewicz	.15
116	Fred McGriff	.15
117	Jason Johnson	.15
118	Pat Burrell	.25
119	Aaron Boone	.15
120	Carlos Delgado	.50
121	Nomar Garciaparra	1.25
122	Richie Sexson	.15
123	Russ Ortiz	.15
124	Tim Hudson	.25
125	Tony Clark	.15
126	Jeromy Burnitz	.15
127	Jose Cruz	.15
128	Juan Encarnacion	.15
129	Mark Mulder	.15
130	Mike Hampton	.15
131	Rich Aurilia	.15
132	Trot Nixon	.15
133	Greg Vaughn	.15
134	Jacque Jones	.15
135	Jason Kendall	.15
136	Jay Gibbons	.15
137	Mark Buehrle	.15
138	Richard Hidalgo	.15
139	Rondell White	.15
140	Cristian Guzman	.30
141	Andy Pettitte	.30
142	Chris Richard	.15
143	Paul LoDuca	.15
144	Phil Nevin	.15
145	Ray Durham	.15
146	Todd Walker	.15
147	Bartolo Colon	.15
148	Ben Petrick	.15
149	Freddy Garcia	.15
150	Jon Lieber	.15
151	Jose Hernandez	.15
152	Matt Williams	.15
153	Shannon Stewart	.15
154	Adrian Beltre	.30
155	Carlos Lee	.15
156	Frank Catalanotto	.15
157	Jorge Posada	.30
158	Pokey Reese	.15
159	Ryan Klesko	.15
160	Ugueth Urbina	.15
161	Adam Dunn	.50
162	Alfonso Soriano	.50
163	Ben Davis	.15
164	Paul Konerko	.25
165	Eric Karros	.25
166	Jeff Weaver	.15
167	Ruben Sierra	.15
168	Bobby Higginson	.15
169	Eric Milton	.15
170	Kerry Wood	.65
171	Roy Oswalt	.30
172	Scott Rolen	.65
173	Tim Salmon	.25
174	Aramis Ramirez	.15
175	Jason Tyner	.15
176	Juan Cruz	.15
177	Keith Foulke	.15
178	Kevin Brown	.25
179	Roger Clemens	1.00
180	Tony Batista	.15
181	Andruw Jones	.75
182	Cliff Floyd	.15
183	Darin Erstad	.25
184	Joe Mays	.15
185	Mike Cameron	.15
186	Robert Person	.15
187	Jeff Kent	.25
188	Gabe Kapler	.25
189	Jason Jennings	.15
190	Jason Varitek	.15
191	Barry Zito	.25
192	Rickey Henderson	.75
193	Tino Martinez	.25
194	Brandon Duckworth	.15
195	Corey Koskie	.15
196	Derrek Lee	.25
197	Javy Lopez	.15
198	John Olerud	.15
199	Terrance Long	.15
200	Troy Glaus	.75
201	Scott MacRae	5.00
202	Scott Chiasson	5.00
203	Bart Miadich	5.00
204	Brian Bowles	5.00
205	David Williams	5.00
206	Victor Zambrano	5.00
207	Joe Beimel	5.00
208	Scott Stewart	5.00
209	Bob File	5.00
210	Ryan Jensen	5.00
211	Jason Karnuth	5.00
212	Brandon Knight	5.00
213	Andy Shibilo RC	5.00
214	Chad Ricketts RC	5.00
215	Mark Prior	8.00
216	Chad Paronto	5.00
217	Corky Miller	5.00
218	Luis Pineda	5.00
219	Ramon Vazquez	5.00
220	Tony Cogan	5.00
221	Roy Smith	5.00
222	Mark Lukasiewicz	5.00
223	Mike Rivera	5.00
224	Brad Voyles	5.00
225	Jamie Burke RC	5.00
226	Justin Duchscherer	5.00
227	Eric Cyr RC	5.00
228	Mark Lukasiewicz	5.00
229	Marlon Byrd	5.00
230	Chris Piersoll RC	5.00
231	Ramon Vazquez	5.00
232	Tony Cogan	5.00
233	Roy Smith	5.00
234	Franklin Nunez RC	5.00
235	Corky Miller	5.00
236	Jorge Nunez RC	5.00
237	Joe Beimel	5.00
238	Eric Knott	5.00
239	Victor Zambrano	5.00
240	Jason Karnuth	5.00
241	Jason Middlebrook	5.00
242	Scott Stewart	5.00
243	Tim Spooneybarger	5.00
244	David Williams	5.00
245	Bart Miadich	5.00
246	Mike Koplove	5.00
247	Ryan Jensen	5.00
248	Jeremy Fikac	5.00
249	Bob File	5.00
250	Craig Monroe	5.00
251	Albert Pujols	2.00
252	Ichiro Suzuki	2.00
253	Nomar Garciaparra	2.00
254	Barry Bonds	3.00
255	Jason Giambi	.75
256	Derek Jeter	3.00
257	Roberto Alomar	.75
258	Roger Clemens	2.00
259	Mike Piazza	1.50
260	Vladimir Guerrero	1.00
261	Todd Helton	.75
262	Shawn Green	.50
263	Chipper Jones	1.00
264	Pedro Martinez	1.00
265	Pat Burrell	.50
266	Sammy Sosa	2.00
267	Ken Griffey Jr.	1.50
268	Cal Ripken Jr.	3.00
269	Kerry Wood	1.00
270	Alex Rodriguez	2.50

To The Max

Stars (1-200): 4-6X
Print Run 200-500
Stars (1-200): 4-8X
Print Run 121-199
Stars (1-200): 6-12X
Print Run 75-120
Stars (1-200): 10-25X
Print Run 40-75
Stars (1-200): 15-40X
Print Run 20-39
Rookies (201-250): .5-1X
Production 100
Impact (251-270): 2-4X
Production 200-400

America's Game

NM/M
Complete Set (25): 25.00
Common Player: .50
Inserted 1:10 Retail

1	Pedro Martinez	1.50
2	Miguel Tejada	.75
3	Randy Johnson	1.50
4	Barry Bonds	5.00
5	Rafael Palmeiro	1.00
6	Mike Piazza	3.00
7	Greg Maddux	2.50
8	Jeff Bagwell	1.50
9	Edgar Martinez	.50
10	Albert Pujols	4.00
11	Todd Helton	1.50
12	Chipper Jones	2.50
13	Luis Gonzalez	.50
14	Jason Giambi	1.00
15	Kazuhiro Sasaki	.50
16	Dave Winfield	1.00
17	Reggie Jackson	1.50
18	Tom Glavine	.75
19	Carlos Delgado	.75
20	Bobby Abreu	.50
21	Larry Walker	.50
22	J.D. Drew	.75
23	Alex Rodriguez	4.00
24	Frank Thomas	1.50
25	C.C. Sabathia	.50

Americas Game Jersey

NM/M
Common Player: 8.00
Inserted 1:24 H, 1:72 R

1	Jeff Bagwell	10.00
2	Craig Biggio	8.00
3	Barry Bonds	25.00
4	Carlos Delgado	8.00
5	J.D. Drew	5.00
6	Jason Giambi	10.00
7	Tom Glavine	10.00
8	Luis Gonzalez	5.00
9	Todd Helton	10.00
10	Reggie Jackson	10.00
11	Randy Johnson	10.00
12	Chipper Jones	10.00
13	Greg Maddux	10.00
14	Edgar Martinez	8.00
15	Pedro Martinez	10.00
16	Rafael Palmeiro	10.00
17	Chan Ho Park	5.00
18	Mike Piazza	10.00
19	Albert Pujols	20.00
20	Kazuhiro Sasaki	5.00
21	Miguel Tejada	5.00
22	Frank Thomas	10.00
23	Larry Walker	5.00
24	Dave Winfield	5.00

Americas Game Stars and Stripes

No Pricing
Production 25 Sets

Coverage

NM/M
Common Player: 15.00
Production 100 Sets

1	Roberto Alomar/Bat	25.00
2	Jeff Bagwell/Jsy	20.00
3	Barry Bonds/Bat	50.00
4	Jose Canseco/Bat	25.00
5	J.D. Drew/Bat	25.00
6	Jim Edmonds/Bat	25.00
7	Jason Giambi/Bat	25.00
8	Juan Gonzalez/Bat	25.00
9	Luis Gonzalez/Jsy	15.00
10	Todd Helton/Jsy	20.00
11	Randy Johnson/Jsy	40.00
12	Chipper Jones/Bat	25.00
13	Greg Maddux/Jsy	40.00
14	Pedro Martinez/Jsy	30.00
15	Rafael Palmeiro/Pants	25.00
16	Albert Pujols/Jsy	50.00
17	Manny Ramirez/Bat	20.00
18	Alex Rodriguez/Bat	30.00
19	Ivan Rodriguez/Bat	25.00
20	Kazuhiro Sasaki/Jsy	20.00
21	Gary Sheffield/Bat	20.00
22	Tsuyoshi Shinjo/Bat	15.00

Coverage Autographs

NM/M
Quantity produced listed.

1	Barry Bonds/Pants/50	200.00
2	J.D. Drew/Bat/100	25.00
3	Jim Edmonds/Bat/100	25.00
4	Drew Henson/Bat/100	25.00
5	Chipper Jones/Bat/100	50.00
6	Albert Pujols/Jsy/100	150.00
7	Gary Sheffield/Bat/100	30.00

Derek Jeter Legacy Collection

NM/M
Inserted 1:236
DJ Derek Jeter/Bat 20.00

DJ	Derek Jeter/Bat/Auto./222	150.00
DJ	Derek Jeter/Jsy	20.00
DJ	Derek Jeter/Jsy/Auto.	200.00

Maximum Power

NM/M
Common Player: 5.00
Inserted 1:24 H
Golds: 3-4X
Production 25 Sets

Luis Gonzalez	5.00
Larry Walker	5.00
Frank Thomas	10.00
Manny Ramirez	10.00
Barry Bonds	25.00
Jim Thome	10.00
Tsuyoshi Shinjo	5.00
Bernie Williams/175	25.00
Chipper Jones	10.00
Shawn Green	5.00
Juan Gonzalez	8.00
Jim Edmonds	10.00
Moises Alou	10.00
Roberto Alomar	10.00
Jose Canseco	10.00
Ivan Rodriguez	10.00
Barry Larkin/50	40.00
Mike Piazza	15.00
Gary Sheffield	8.00
J.D. Drew/200	8.00
Alex Rodriguez	15.00
Jason Giambi	10.00
Todd Helton	8.00

Maximum Power Bat

NM/M
Common Player: 5.00
Inserted 1:24 H
Golds: 3-4X
Production 25 Sets

Luis Gonzalez	5.00
Larry Walker	5.00
Frank Thomas	10.00
Manny Ramirez	10.00
Barry Bonds	25.00
Jim Thome	10.00
Tsuyoshi Shinjo	10.00
Bernie Williams/175	25.00
Chipper Jones	10.00
Shawn Green	5.00
Juan Gonzalez	8.00
Jim Edmonds	10.00
Moises Alou	10.00
Roberto Alomar	10.00
Jose Canseco	10.00
Ivan Rodriguez	10.00
Barry Larkin/50	40.00
Mike Piazza	15.00
Gary Sheffield	8.00
J.D. Drew/200	8.00
Alex Rodriguez	15.00
Jason Giambi	10.00
Todd Helton	8.00

2002 Fleer Mets All-Amazin' Team

★ JERRY KOOSMAN

To commemorate the team's 40th anniversary, Fleer produced this set of Mets greats which was given away at Shea on August 17. The cards are printed on heavy stock and feature (mostly) color poses, game-action shots and team photos on a textured-look background. The player name, uniform number and years with the Mets appear at bottom. The anniversary logo and Fleer logo are also seen on front. Backs repeat a detail from the front photo in a circle at top. There are a few sentences about the player and stats lines for his Mets days and major league career. Appropriate logos round out the design.

		NM/M
Complete Set (21):		15.00
Common Card:		.50
1	Gil Hodges	1.00
2	Keith Hernandez	.75
3	Edgardo Alfonzo	.75
4	Howard Johnson	.75
5	Bud Harrelson	.75
6	Mike Piazza	3.00
7	Mookie Wilson	.75
8	Darryl Strawberry	.75
9	Lenny Dykstra	.50
10	Tom Seaver	2.00
11	Jerry Koosman	.50
12	Roger McDowell	.50
13	John Franco	.50
14	Ed Kranepool	.50
15	Rusty Staub	.75
16	Bob Murphy (Broadcaster)	.50
17	Ralph Kiner (Broadcaster)	.50
18	1962 Team Card	1.00
19	1969 Team Card	1.00
20	1986 Team Card	1.00
---	Checklist	.10

2002 Fleer Platinum

Roger Clemens

		NM/M
Complete Set (302):		125.00
Common Player:		.15
Common (251-260):		2.00
Common (261-302):		1.50
Inserted 1:3 H, 1:6 Retail		
Hobby Pack (10):		2.00
Hobby Box (24):		35.00
Rack Box:		70.00
1	Garrett Anderson	.15
2	Randy Johnson	.65
3	Chipper Jones	.75
4	David Cone	.15
5	Corey Patterson	.15
6	Carlos Lee	.15
7	Barry Larkin	.15
8	Jim Thome	.15
9	Larry Walker	.15
10	Randall Simon	.15
11	Charles Johnson	.15
12	Richard Hidalgo	.15
13	Mark Quinn	.15
14	Paul LoDuca	.15
15	Cristian Guzman	.15
16	Orlando Cabrera	.15
17	Al Leiter	.15
18	Nick Johnson	.15
19	Eric Chavez	.25

20	Miguel Tejada	.25
21	Mike Lieberthal	.15
22	Robert Mackowiak	.15
23	Ryan Klesko	.15
24	Jeff Kent	.15
25	Edgar Martinez	.15
26	Steve Kline	.15
27	Toby Hall	.15
28	Rusty Greer	.15
29	Jose Cruz Jr.	.15
30	Darin Erstad	.50
31	Reggie Sanders	.15
32	Javy Lopez	.15
33	Carl Everett	.15
34	Sammy Sosa	1.00
35	Magglio Ordonez	.15
36	Todd Walker	.15
37	Omar Vizquel	.15
38	Matt Anderson	.15
39	Jeff Weaver	.15
40	Derrek Lee	.15
41	Julio Lugo	.15
42	Joe Randa	.15
43	Chan Ho Park	.15
44	Torii Hunter	.15
45	Vladimir Guerrero	.65
46	Rey Ordonez	.15
47	Tino Martinez	.15
48	Johnny Damon	.25
49	Barry Zito	.25
50	Robert Person	.15
51	Aramis Ramirez	.15
52	Mark Kotsay	.15
53	Jason Schmidt	.15
54	Jamie Moyer	.15
55	David Justice	.15
56	Aubrey Huff	.15
57	Rick Helling	.15
58	Carlos Delgado	.40
59	Troy Glaus	.65
60	Curt Schilling	.40
61	Greg Maddux	.75
62	Nomar Garciaparra	1.00
63	Kerry Wood	.50
64	Frank Thomas	.65
65	Dmitri Young	.15
66	Alex Ochoa	.15
67	Jose Macias	.15
68	Antonio Alfonseca	.15
69	Mike Lowell	.15
70	Wade Miller	.15
71	Mike Sweeney	.15
72	Gary Sheffield	.25
73	Corey Koskie	.15
74	Lee Stevens	.15
75	Jay Payton	.15
76	Mike Mussina	.40
77	Jermaine Dye	.15
78	Bobby Abreu	.15
79	Scott Rolen	.50
80	Todd Ritchie	.15
81	D'Angelo Jimenez	.15
82	Rob Nenn	.15
83	John Olerud	.15
84	Matt Morris	.15
85	Joe Kennedy	.15
86	Gabe Kapler	.15
87	Chris Carpenter	.15
88	David Eckstein	.15
89	Matt Williams	.15
90	John Smoltz	.15
91	Pedro J. Martinez	.65
92	Eric Young	.15
93	Jose Valentin	.15
94	Erubiel Durazo	.15
95	Jeff Cirillo	.15
96	Brandon Inge	.15
97	Josh Beckett	.40
98	Preston Wilson	.15
99	Damian Jackson	.15
100	Adrian Beltre	.25
101	Jeromy Burnitz	.15
102	Joe Mays	.15
103	Michael Barrett	.15
104	Mike Piazza	1.00
105	Brady Anderson	.15
106	Jason Giambi	.40
107	Marlon Anderson	.15
108	Jimmy Rollins	.25
109	Jack Wilson	.15
110	Brian Lawrence	.15
111	Russ Ortiz	.15
112	Kazuhiro Sasaki	.15
113	Placido Polanco	.15
114	Damian Rolls	.15
115	Rafael Palmeiro	.50
116	Brad Fullmer	.15
117	Tim Salmon	.25
118	Tony Womack	.15
119	Tony Batista	.15
120	Trot Nixon	.15
121	Mark Buehrle	.15
122	Derek Jeter	1.50
123	Ellis Burks	.15
124	Mike Hampton	.15
125	Roger Cedeno	.15
126	A.J. Burnett	.15
127	Moises Alou	.15
128	Billy Wagner	.15
129	Kevin Brown	.15
130	Jose Hernandez	.15
131	Doug Mientkiewicz	.15
132	Javier Vazquez	.15
133	Tsuyoshi Shinjo	.15
134	Andy Pettitte	.30
135	Tim Hudson	.25
136	Pat Burrell	.40
137	Brian Giles	.15

138	Kevin Young	.15
139	Xavier Nady	.15
140	J.T. Snow	.15
141	Aaron Sele	.15
142	Albert Pujols	1.25
143	Jason Tyner	.15
144	Ivan Rodriguez	.50
145	Raul Mondesi	.15
146	Matt Lawton	.15
147	Rafael Furcal	.15
148	Jeff Conine	.15
149	Hideo Nomo	.60
150	Jose Canseco	.30
151	Aaron Boone	.15
152	Bartolo Colon	.15
153	Todd Helton	.65
154	Tony Clark	.15
155	Pablo Ozuna	.15
156	Jeff Bagwell	.65
157	Carlos Beltran	.50
158	Shawn Green	.25
159	Geoff Jenkins	.15
160	Eric Milton	.15
161	Jose Vidro	.15
162	Robin Ventura	.15
163	Jorge Posada	.25
164	Terrence Long	.15
165	Brandon Duckworth	.15
166	Chad Hermansen	.15
167	Ben Davis	.15
168	Phil Nevin	.15
169	Bret Boone	.15
170	J.D. Drew	.25
171	Edgar Renteria	.15
172	Randy Winn	.15
173	Alex Rodriguez	1.50
174	Shannon Stewart	.15
175	Steve Finley	.15
176	Marcus Giles	.15
177	Jay Gibbons	.15
178	Manny Ramirez	.65
179	Ray Durham	.15
180	Sean Casey	.25
181	Travis Fryman	.15
182	Denny Neagle	.15
183	Deivi Cruz	.15
184	Luis Castillo	.15
185	Lance Berkman	.15
186	Dee Brown	.15
187	Jeff Shaw	.15
188	Mark Loretta	.15
189	David Ortiz	.25
190	Edgardo Alfonzo	.15
191	Roger Clemens	.75
192	Mariano Rivera	.25
193	Jeremy Giambi	.15
194	Johnny Estrada	.15
195	Craig Wilson	.15
196	Adam Eaton	.15
197	Rich Aurilia	.15
198	Mike Cameron	.15
199	Jim Edmonds	.15
200	Fernando Vina	.15
201	Greg Vaughn	.15
202	Mike Young	.15
203	Vernon Wells	.15
204	Luis Gonzalez	.25
205	Tom Glavine	.30
206	Chris Richard	.15
207	Jon Lieber	.15
208	Keith Foulke	.15
209	Rondell White	.15
210	Bernie Williams	.30
211	Juan Pierre	.15
212	Juan Encarnacion	.15
213	Ryan Dempster	.15
214	Tim Redding	.15
215	Jeff Suppan	.15
216	Mark Grudzielanek	.15
217	Richie Sexson	.15
218	Brad Radke	.15
219	Armando Benitez	.15
220	Orlando Hernandez	.15
221	Alfonso Soriano	.40
222	Mark Mulder	.15
223	Travis Lee	.15
224	Jason Kendall	.15
225	Trevor Hoffman	.15
226	Barry Bonds	1.50
227	Freddy Garcia	.15
228	Darryl Kile	.15
229	Ben Grieve	.15
230	Frank Catalanotto	.15
231	Ruben Sierra	.15
232	Homer Bush	.15
233	Mark Grace	.25
234	Andruw Jones	.60
235	Brian Roberts	.15
236	Fred McGriff	.15
237	Paul Konerko	.15
238	Ken Griffey Jr.	1.00
239	John Burkett	.15
240	Juan Uribe	.15
241	Bobby Higginson	.15
242	Cliff Floyd	.15
243	Craig Biggio	.25
244	Neifi Perez	.15
245	Eric Karros	.15
246	Ben Sheets	.15
247	Tony Armas Jr.	.15
248	Mo Vaughn	.15
249	David Wells	.15
250	Juan Gonzalez	.15
251	Barry Bonds	5.00
252	Sammy Sosa	3.00
253	Ken Griffey Jr.	3.00
254	Roger Clemens	4.00
255	Greg Maddux	2.50

256	Chipper Jones	1.50
257	Alex Rodriguez, Derek Jeter, Nomar Garciaparra	5.00
258	Roberto Alomar	1.50
259	Jeff Bagwell	1.50
260	Mike Piazza	3.00
261	Mark Teixeira	2.00
262	Mark Prior	2.00
263	Alex Escobar	1.50
264	C.C. Sabathia	1.50
265	Drew Henson	1.50
266	Wilson Betemit	1.50
267	Roy Oswalt	1.50
268	Adam Dunn	2.00
269	Bud Smith	1.50
270	Dewon Brazelton	1.50
271	Brandon Backe RC, Jason Standridge	1.50
272	Wilfredo Rodriguez, Carlos Hernandez	1.50
273	Geronimo Gil, Luis Rivera	1.50
274	Carlos Pena, Jovanny Cedeno	1.50
275	Austin Kearns, Ben Broussard	1.50
276	Jorge De La Rosa RC, Kenny Kelly	1.50
277	Ryan Drese, Victor Martinez	1.50
278	Joel Pinero, Nate Cornejo	1.50
279	David Kelton, Carlos Zambrano	1.50
281	Donnie Bridges, Wilkin Ruan	1.50
282	Wily Mo Pena, Brandon Claussen	2.00
283	Jason Jennings, Rene Reyes RC	1.50
284	Steve Green, Alfredo Amezaga	1.50
285	Eric Hinske, Felipe Lopez	1.50
286	Anderson Machado RC, Brad Baisley	1.50
287	Carlos Garcia, Sean Douglass	1.50
288	Pat Strange, Jae Weong Seo	1.50
289	Marcus Thames, Alex Graman	1.50
290	Matt Childers RC, Hansel Izquierdo RC	1.50
291	Ron Calloway RC, Adam Walker RC	1.50
292	J.R. House, J.J. Davis	1.50
293	Ryan Anderson, Rafael Soriano	1.50
294	Mike Bynum, Dennis Tankersley	1.50
295	Kurt Ainsworth, Carlos Valderrama	1.50
296	Billy Hall, Cristian Guerrero	1.50
297	Miguel Olivo, Danny Wright	1.50
298	Marlon Byrd, Jorge Padilla RC	1.50
299	Juan Cruz, Ben Christensen	1.50
300	Adam Johnson, Michael Restovich	1.50
301	So Taguchi RC	2.00
302	Kazuhisa Ishii RC	3.00

Edition

Stars (1-250):	4-8X
Production 202	
Cards 251-302:	No Pricing
Production 22	

Buy Back Autographs

Common Player:

Barry Bonds RC Autograph

		NM/M
73 Cards Autographed		
	Barry Bonds	400.00

Clubhouse Collection - Dual

DARIN ERSTAD • Anaheim Angels

		NM/M
Common Card:		10.00
Inserted 1:96		
	Edgardo Alfonzo	10.00
	Rick Ankiel	8.00
	Adrian Beltre	10.00
	Barry Bonds	40.00
	Sean Casey	10.00
	Eric Chavez	10.00
	Roger Clemens	30.00
	Carlos Delgado	10.00
	J.D. Drew	10.00
	Darin Erstad	10.00
	Jim Thome	20.00
	Juan Gonzalez	15.00
	Nomar Garciaparra	30.00
	Derek Jeter	40.00
	Randy Johnson	20.00

		NM/M
Andruw Jones		10.00
Johnny Damon		10.00
Paul LoDuca		10.00
Greg Maddux		20.00
Pedro J. Martinez		20.00
Magglio Ordonez		10.00
Mike Piazza		30.00
Manny Ramirez		15.00
Mariano Rivera		15.00
Ivan Rodriguez		20.00
Alex Rodriguez		25.00
Scott Rolen		20.00
Kazuhiro Sasaki		10.00
Curt Schilling		20.00
Gary Sheffield		10.00
Frank Thomas		20.00
Jim Thome		20.00
Omar Vizquel		10.00

Clubhouse Collection Memorabilia

CRAIG BIGGIO • Houston Astros

		NM/M
Common Player:		5.00
Inserted 1:32		
Edgardo Alfonzo/Jsy		5.00
Rick Ankiel/Jsy		5.00
Craig Biggio/Bat		8.00
Adrian Beltre/Jsy		5.00
Sean Casey/Jsy		8.00
Barry Bonds/Jsy		25.00
Scott Rolen/Jsy		10.00
Eric Chavez/Jsy		8.00
Roger Clemens/Jsy		25.00
Carlos Delgado/Jsy		8.00
J.D. Drew/Jsy		5.00
Darin Erstad/Jsy		5.00
Jim Thome/Bat		10.00
Juan Gonzalez/Bat		8.00
Nomar Garciaparra/Jsy		15.00
Todd Helton/Jsy		8.00
Derek Jeter/Pants		25.00
Randy Johnson/Jsy		10.00
Andruw Jones/Jsy		8.00
Tim Hudson/Jsy		5.00
Jason Kendall/Jsy		5.00
Johnny Damon/Bat		5.00
Paul LoDuca/Jsy		5.00
Greg Maddux/Jsy		10.00
Pedro Martinez/Jsy		10.00
Raul Mondesi/Bat		5.00
Magglio Ordonez/Jsy		5.00
Mike Piazza/Jsy		10.00
Manny Ramirez/Jsy		8.00
Mariano Rivera/Jsy		10.00
Ivan Rodriguez/Jsy		10.00
Alex Rodriguez/Jsy		15.00
Kazuhiro Sasaki/Jsy		5.00
Frank Thomas/Jsy		10.00
Curt Schilling/Jsy		8.00
Gary Sheffield/Bat		6.00
Omar Vizquel/Jsy		5.00

Cornerstones

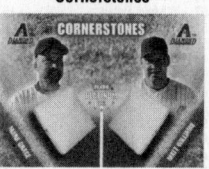

CORNERSTONES

		NM/M
Complete Set (40):		120.00
Inserted 1:12 Jumbo		
1	Bill Terry, Johnny Mize	1.50
2	Cal Ripken Jr., Eddie Murray	10.00
3	Eddie Mathews, Chipper Jones	3.00
4	Albert Pujols, George Sisler	6.00
5	Sean Casey, Tony Perez	1.50
6	Jimmie Foxx, Scott Rolen	4.00
7	Wade Boggs, George Brett	1.50
8	Rod Carew, Troy Glaus	1.50
9	Jeff Bagwell, Rafael Palmeiro	2.00
10	Willie Stargell, Pie Traynor	1.50
11	Cal Ripken Jr., Brooks Robinson	10.00
12	Tony Perez, Ted Kluszewski	1.50
13	Jason Giambi, Don Mattingly	8.00
14	Hank Greenberg, Jimmie Foxx	4.00
15	Ernie Banks, Willie McCovey	3.00
16	Jim Thome, Travis Fryman	3.00
17	Ted Kluszewski, Sean Casey	

18	Gil Hodges, Johnny Mize	3.00
19	Brooks Robinson, Boog Powell	3.00
20	Bill Terry, George Sisler	2.00
21	Wade Boggs, Don Mattingly	8.00
22	Jason Giambi, Carlos Delgado	2.50
23	Willie Stargell, Bill Madlock	2.00
24	Mark Grace, Matt Williams	2.00
25	Paul Molitor, George Brett	8.00
26	Carlos Delgado, Mo Vaughn	1.50
27	Bill Terry, Willie McCovey	1.50
28	Mike Sweeney, George Brett	8.00
29	Eddie Mathews, Ernie Banks	4.00
30	Eric Karros, Gil Hodges	1.50
31	Paul Molitor, Don Mattingly	8.00
32	Brooks Robinson, Rod Carew	3.00
33	Chipper Jones, Albert Pujols	8.00
34	Harry Heilmann, Hank Greenberg	1.50
35	Frank Thomas, Carlos Delgado	2.50
36	Jeff Bagwell, Todd Helton	2.00
37	Rafael Palmeiro, Fred McGriff	2.00
38	Cal Ripken Jr., Wade Boggs	10.00
39	Orlando Cepeda, Willie McCovey	2.00
40	John Olerud, Mark Grace	2.00

Cornerstones Memorabilia

No Pricing
Production 25 Sets

Cornerstones Numbered

		NM/M
Complete Set (40):		
#1-10: Production 250		
#11-20: Production 250		
#21-30: Production 1,000		
#31-40: Production 2,000		
1	Bill Terry, Johnny Mize	10.00
2	Cal Ripken Jr., Eddie Murray	30.00
3	Eddie Mathews, Chipper Jones	10.00
4	Albert Pujols, George Sisler	20.00
5	Sean Casey, Tony Perez	8.00
6	Jimmie Foxx, Scott Rolen	10.00
7	Wade Boggs, George Brett	20.00
8	Rod Carew, Troy Glaus	10.00
9	Jeff Bagwell, Rafael Palmeiro	10.00
10	Willie Stargell, Pie Traynor	8.00
11	Cal Ripken Jr., Brooks Robinson	20.00
12	Tony Perez, Ted Kluszewski	5.00
13	Jason Giambi, Don Mattingly	15.00
14	Hank Greenberg, Jimmie Foxx	8.00
15	Ernie Banks, Willie McCovey	8.00
16	Jim Thome, Travis Fryman	6.00
17	Ted Kluszewski, Sean Casey	5.00
18	Gil Hodges, Johnny Mize	5.00
19	Brooks Robinson, Boog Powell	8.00
20	Bill Terry, George Sisler	5.00
21	Wade Boggs, Don Mattingly	10.00
22	Jason Giambi Yanks, Carlos Delgado	3.00
23	Willie Stargell, Bill Madlock	4.00
24	Mark Grace, Matt Williams	4.00
25	Paul Molitor, George Brett	10.00
26	Carlos Delgado, Mo Vaughn	3.00
27	Bill Terry, Willie McCovey	4.00
28	Mike Sweeney, George Brett	10.00
29	Eddie Mathews, Ernie Banks	4.00
30	Eric Karros, Gil Hodges	3.00
31	Paul Molitor, Don Mattingly	8.00
32	Brooks Robinson, Rod Carew	3.00
33	Chipper Jones, Albert Pujols	6.00
34	Harry Heilmann, Hank Greenburg	3.00
35	Frank Thomas, Carlos Delgado	3.00
36	Jeff Bagwell, Todd Helton	3.00
37	Rafael Palmeiro, Fred McGriff	

38	Cal Ripken Jr., Wade Boggs	8.00
39	Orlando Cepeda, Willie McCovey	3.00
40	John Olerud, Mark Grace	3.00

Fencebusters

	NM/M
Common Player:	5.00

Rack Pack Exclusive

Derek Jeter	20.00
J.D. Drew	6.00
Brian Giles	5.00
Moises Alou	5.00
Rafael Palmeiro	6.00
Jeff Bagwell	8.00
Mike Piazza	15.00
Manny Ramirez	8.00
Tino Martinez	5.00
Jim Thome	5.00
Andruw Jones	8.00
Shawn Green	6.00
Frank Thomas	8.00
Miguel Tejada	6.00
Luis Gonzalez	5.00
Alex Rodriguez	12.50
Larry Walker	5.00
Barry Bonds	20.00
Todd Helton	8.00
Chipper Jones	10.00
Roberto Alomar	6.00
Jim Edmonds	8.00

Fencebusters Autographed

	NM/M

Numbered to 2001 HR Total.

| Barry Bonds/73 | 275.00 |

National Patch Time

	NM/M
Common Player:	20.00

Inserted 1:12 Jumbo

Barry Bonds/75	100.00
Todd Helton/110	40.00
Ivan Rodriguez/225	40.00
Kazuhiro Sasaki/310	20.00
Derek Jeter/65	100.00
Cal Ripken Jr/350	80.00
Darin Erstad/315	40.00
Jose Canseco/150	40.00
Miguel Tejada/55	35.00
Greg Maddux/775	30.00
Juan Gonzalez/50	30.00
J.D. Drew/210	25.00
Manny Ramirez/100	40.00
Pedro Martinez/45	50.00
Carlos Delgado/70	30.00
Magglio Ordonez/85	30.00
Pat Burrell/285	25.00
Adam Dunn/75	40.00
Alex Rodriguez/325	50.00

Wheelhouse

	NM/M
Complete Set (20):	40.00
Common Player:	1.00

Inserted 1:12

1WH	Derek Jeter	6.00
2WH	Barry Bonds	6.00
3WH	Luis Gonzalez	1.00
4WH	Jason Giambi	1.00
5WH	Ivan Rodriguez	1.50
6WH	Mike Piazza	4.00
7WH	Troy Glaus	1.50
8WH	Nomar Garciaparra	4.00
9WH	Juan Gonzalez	4.00
10WH	Sammy Sosa	4.00
11WH	Albert Pujols	4.00
12WH	Ken Griffey Jr.	4.00
13WH	Scott Rolen	1.00
14WH	Jeff Bagwell	4.00
15WH	Ichiro Suzuki	4.00
16WH	Todd Helton	4.00
17WH	Chipper Jones	3.00
18WH	Alex Rodriguez	4.00
19WH	Vladimir Guerrero	2.00
20WH	Manny Ramirez	2.00

2002 Fleer Premium

	NM/M
Complete Set (240):	50.00
Common Player:	.15
Common SP (201-240):	.50

Inserted 1:2

Pack (8):	2.00
Box (24):	35.00
1	Garret Anderson	.20
2	Derek Jeter	2.50

3	Ken Griffey Jr.	1.50
4	Luis Castillo	.15
5	Richie Sexson	.20
6	Mike Mussina	.40
7	Ricky Henderson	.75
8	Bud Smith	.15
9	David Eckstein	.15
10	Nomar Garciaparra	1.50
11	Barry Larkin	.20
12	Cliff Floyd	.15
13	Ben Sheets	.20
14	Jorge Posada	.30
15	Phil Nevin	.15
16	Fernando Vina	.15
17	Darin Erstad	.65
18	Shea Hillenbrand	.15
19	Todd Walker	.15
20	Charles Johnson	.15
21	Cristian Guzman	.15
22	Mariano Rivera	.30
23	Bubba Trammell	.15
24	Brent Abernathy	.15
25	Troy Glaus	.75
26	Pedro J. Martinez	.75
27	Dmitri Young	.15
28	Derrek Lee	.20
29	Torii Hunter	.20
30	Alfonso Soriano	.65
31	Rich Aurilia	.15
32	Ben Grieve	.15
33	Tim Salmon	.15
34	Trot Nixon	.15
35	Roberto Alomar	.40
36	Mike Lowell	.20
37	Jacque Jones	.15
38	Bernie Williams	.30
39	Barry Bonds	2.50
40	Toby Hall	.15
41	Mo Vaughn	.20
42	Hideo Nomo	.65
43	Travis Fryman	.15
44	Preston Wilson	.15
45	Corey Koskie	.15
46	Eric Chavez	.30
47	Andres Galarraga	.15
48	Greg Vaughn	.15
49	Shawn Wooten	.15
50	Manny Ramirez	.75
51	Juan Gonzalez	.75
52	Moises Alou	.15
53	Joe Mays	.15
54	Johnny Damon	.35
55	Jeff Kent	.20
56	Frank Catalanotto	.15
57	Steve Finley	.15
58	Jason Varitek	.15
59	Kenny Lofton	.20
60	Jeff Bagwell	.75
61	Doug Mientkiewicz	.15
62	Jermaine Dye	.15
63	John Vander Wal	.15
64	Gabe Kapler	.15
65	Luis Gonzalez	.30
66	Jon Lieber	.15
67	C.C. Sabathia	.15
68	Lance Berkman	.20
69	Eric Milton	.15
70	Jason Giambi	.50
71	Ichiro Suzuki	1.50
72	Rafael Palmeiro	.65
73	Mark Grace	.30
74	Fred McGriff	.20
75	Jim Thome	.20
76	Craig Biggio	.20
77	A.J. Pierzynski	.15
78	Ramon Hernandez	.15
79	Paul Abbott	.15
80	Alex Rodriguez	2.00
81	Randy Johnson	.75
82	Corey Patterson	.20
83	Omar Vizquel	.20
84	Richard Hidalgo	.15
85	Luis Rivas	.15
86	Tim Hudson	.30
87	Bret Boone	.20
88	Ivan Rodriguez	.60
89	Junior Spivey	.15
90	Sammy Sosa	1.50
91	Jeff Cirillo	.15
92	Roy Oswalt	.20
93	Orlando Cabrera	.15
94	Terrence Long	.15
95	Mike Cameron	.15
96	Homer Bush	.15
97	Reggie Sanders	.15
98	Rondell White	.15
99	Mike Hampton	.15
100	Carlos Beltran	.30
101	Vladimir Guerrero	.75

102	Miguel Tejada	.30
103	Freddy Garcia	.15
104	Jose Cruz Jr.	.15
105	Curt Schilling	.45
106	Kerry Wood	.65
107	Todd Helton	.75
108	Neifi Perez	.15
109	Javier Vazquez	.15
110	Barry Zito	.30
111	Edgar Martinez	.20
112	Carlos Delgado	.50
113	Matt Williams	.20
114	Eric Young	.15
115	Alex Ochoa	.15
116	Mark Quinn	.15
117	Jose Vidro	.15
118	Bobby Abreu	.20
119	David Bell	.15
120	Brad Fullmer	.15
121	Rafael Furcal	.15
122	Ray Durham	.15
123	Jose Ortiz	.15
124	Joe Randa	.15
125	Edgardo Alfonzo	.15
126	Marlon Anderson	.15
127	Jamie Moyer	.15
128	Alex Gonzalez	.15
129	Marcus Giles	.15
130	Keith Foulke	.15
131	Juan Pierre	.15
132	Mike Sweeney	.15
133	Matt Lawton	.15
134	Pat Burrell	.40
135	John Olerud	.20
136	Raul Mondesi	.20
137	Tom Glavine	.40
138	Paul Konerko	.20
139	Larry Walker	.20
140	Adrian Beltre	.35
141	Al Leiter	.20
142	Mike Lieberthal	.15
143	Kazuhiro Sasaki	.15
144	Shannon Stewart	.15
145	Andruw Jones	.75
146	Carlos Lee	.15
147	Roger Cedeno	.15
148	Kevin Brown	.20
149	Jay Payton	.15
150	Scott Rolen	.65
151	J.D. Drew	.35
152	Chipper Jones	1.00
153	Magglio Ordonez	.20
154	Tony Clark	.15
155	Shawn Green	.35
156	Mike Piazza	1.50
157	Jimmy Rollins	.25
158	Jim Edmonds	.20
159	Javy Lopez	.20
160	Chris Singleton	.15
161	Juan Encarnacion	.15
162	Eric Karros	.15
163	Tsuyoshi Shinjo	.15
164	Brian Giles	.20
165	Darryl Kile	.15
166	Greg Maddux	1.00
167	Frank Thomas	.75
168	Shane Halter	.15
169	Paul LoDuca	.15
170	Robin Ventura	.20
171	Jason Kendall	.15
172	Jason Hart	.15
173	Brady Anderson	.15
174	Jose Valentin	.15
175	Bobby Higginson	.15
176	Gary Sheffield	.40
177	Roger Clemens	1.25
178	Aramis Ramirez	.20
179	Matt Morris	.15
180	Jeff Conine	.15
181	Aaron Boone	.15
182	Jose Macias	.15
183	Jeromy Burnitz	.15
184	Carl Everett	.15
185	Trevor Hoffman	.15
186	Placido Polanco	.15
187	Jay Gibbons	.15
188	Sean Casey	.35
189	Josh Beckett	.40
190	Jeffrey Hammonds	.15
191	Chuck Knoblauch	.15
192	Ryan Klesko	.15
193	Chris Richard	.15
194	Adam Dunn	.50
195	A.J. Burnett	.15
196	Craig Biggio	.20
197	Geoff Jenkins	.25
198	Tino Martinez	.20
199	Ray Lankford	.15
200	Edgar Renteria	.20
201	Eric Cyr RC	1.00
202	Travis Phelps	.50
203	Rick Bauer	.50
204	Mark Prior	2.00
205	Wilson Betemit	.50
206	Dewon Brazelton	.50
207	Cody Ransom	.50
208	Donnie Bridges	.50
209	Justin Duchscherer	.50
210	Nate Cornejo	.50
211	Jason Romano	.50
212	Juan Cruz	.50
213	Pedro Santana	.50
214	Ryan Drese	.50
215	Bert Snow	.50
216	Nate Frese	.50
217	Rafael Soriano	.50
218	Franklin Nunez RC	.50
219	Tim Spooneybarger	.50
220	Willie Harris	.50
221	Billy Sylvester	.50

222	Carlos Hernandez	.50
223	Mark Teixeira	3.00
224	Adrian Hernandez	.50
225	Andres Torres	.50
226	Marlon Byrd	.50
227	Juan Rivera	.50
228	Adam Johnson	.50
229	Justin Kaye	.50
230	Kyle Kessel	.50
231	Horacio Ramirez	.50
232	Brandon Larson	.50
233	Luis Lopez	.50
234	Robert Mackowiak	.50
235	Henry Mateo	.50
236	Corky Miller	.50
237	Greg Miller	.50
238	Dustan Mohr	.50
239	Bill Ortega	.50
240	Billy Hall	.50

Star Ruby

| Stars (1-200): | 4-8X |
| SP's (201-240): | 1-2X |

Production 125 Sets

Diamond Stars

	NM/M
Complete Set (20):	100.00
Common Player:	2.00

Inserted 1:72

1DS	Pedro J. Martinez	4.00
2DS	Derek Jeter	15.00
3DS	Sammy Sosa	8.00
4DS	Ken Griffey Jr.	8.00
5DS	Chipper Jones	8.00
6DS	Roger Clemens	10.00
7DS	Ichiro Suzuki	8.00
8DS	Jeff Bagwell	8.00
9DS	Luis Gonzalez	2.00
10DS	Manny Ramirez	4.00
11DS	Alex Rodriguez	12.50
12DS	Kazuhiro Sasaki	2.50
13DS	Mike Piazza	8.00
14DS	Vladimir Guerrero	4.00
15DS	Randy Johnson	4.00
16DS	Ivan Rodriguez	3.00
17DS	Nomar Garciaparra	8.00
18DS	Barry Bonds	15.00
19DS	Todd Helton	4.00
20DS	Greg Maddux	8.00

Diamond Stars Autograph

	NM/M

Numbered to 100

| Derek Jeter | 125.00 |

Diamond Stars Game-Used

	NM/M
Common Player:	5.00

Inserted 1:105

Barry Bonds/Jsy	20.00
Manny Ramirez/Jsy	8.00
Ivan Rodriguez/Jsy	8.00
Kazuhiro Sasaki/Jsy	5.00
Roger Clemens	20.00
Alex Rodriguez	15.00
Derek Jeter	25.00
Chipper Jones	10.00
Todd Helton	8.00
Luis Gonzalez	8.00
Mike Piazza	10.00
Nomar Garciaparra	25.00

Diamond Stars Game-Used Premium

	NM/M

Production 75 Sets

Barry Bonds	60.00
Roger Clemens	60.00
Todd Helton	30.00
Chipper Jones	30.00
Manny Ramirez	25.00
Alex Rodriguez	30.00
Ivan Rodriguez	25.00
Luis Gonzalez	25.00
Mike Piazza	40.00
Kazuhiro Sasaki	20.00

Diamond Stars Dual Game-Used

	NM/M

Numbered to 100.

Barry Bonds	60.00
Todd Helton	20.00
Derek Jeter	60.00
Chipper Jones	30.00
Mike Piazza	35.00
Manny Ramirez	25.00
Alex Rodriguez	40.00

Diamond Stars Dual Game-Used Premium

Production 25 Sets

International Pride

	NM/M
Complete Set (15):	10.00
Common Player:	.50

Inserted 1:6

1IP	Larry Walker	.50
2IP	Albert Pujols	3.00
3IP	Juan Gonzalez	.75
4IP	Ichiro Suzuki	2.00
5IP	Rafael Palmeiro	.65
6IP	Carlos Delgado	.50
7IP	Kazuhiro Sasaki	.50
8IP	Vladimir Guerrero	.75
9IP	Bobby Abreu	.50
10IP	Ivan Rodriguez	.60
11IP	Tsuyoshi Shinjo	.50
12IP	Pedro J. Martinez	.75
13IP	Andruw Jones	.75
14IP	Sammy Sosa	2.00
15IP	Chan Ho Park	.50

International Pride Game-Used

	NM/M
Common Player:	5.00

Inserted 1:90

Carlos Delgado/Jsy	8.00
Juan Gonzalez/Jsy	8.00
Andruw Jones/Jsy	8.00
Pedro Martinez/Jsy	10.00
Rafael Palmeiro/Jsy	8.00
Chan Ho Park/Jsy	5.00
Albert Pujols/Jsy	20.00
Ivan Rodriguez/Bat	10.00
Kazuhiro Sasaki/Jsy	5.00
Tsuyoshi Shinjo/Jsy	5.00

International Pride Premium

	NM/M

Production 75 Sets | 15.00 |

Carlos Delgado	25.00
Juan Gonzalez	40.00
Andruw Jones	40.00
Pedro J. Martinez	40.00
Chan Ho Park	15.00
Ivan Rodriguez	25.00
Tsuyoshi Shinjo	15.00
Rafael Palmeiro	25.00
Albert Pujols	75.00
Kazuhiro Sasaki	15.00

Legendary Dynasties

	NM/M
Complete Set (36):	125.00
Common Player:	1.50

Inserted 1:18

| Gold: | 1X |

Production 300 Sets

1LD	Honus Wagner	4.00
2LD	Christy Mathewson	4.00
3LD	Lou Gehrig	8.00
4LD	Babe Ruth	12.00
5LD	Jimmie Foxx	4.00
6LD	Lefty Grove	2.00
7LD	Al Simmons	1.50
8LD	Bill Dickey	1.50
9LD	Stan Musial	5.00
10LD	Enos Slaughter	1.50
11LD	Johnny Mize	3.00
12LD	Yogi Berra	3.00
13LD	Whitey Ford	3.00
14LD	Jackie Robinson	8.00
15LD	Duke Snider	3.00
16LD	Roger Maris	5.00
17LD	Jim Palmer	2.00
18LD	Don Drysdale	3.00
19LD	Brooks Robinson	3.00
20LD	Rollie Fingers	1.50
21LD	Reggie Jackson	3.00
22LD	Joe Morgan	2.00
23LD	Johnny Bench	5.00
24LD	Thurman Munson	4.00
25LD	Jose Canseco	2.50
26LD	Tom Glavine	3.00
27LD	Chipper Jones	4.00
28LD	Greg Maddux	4.00
29LD	Roberto Alomar	3.00
30LD	David Cone	1.50
31LD	Jim Thome	3.00
32LD	Manny Ramirez	3.00
33LD	Roger Clemens	6.00
34LD	Derek Jeter	8.00
35LD	Bernie Williams	2.50
36LD	Alfonso Soriano	3.00

Legendary Dynasties Autographs

	NM/M

#'d to World Series Year

Johnny Bench/76	80.00
Yogi Berra/51	60.00
Reggie Jackson/73	60.00
Derek Jeter/96	125.00

Legendary Dynasties Game-Used

	NM/M
Common Player:	8.00

Inserted 1:120

Roberto Alomar/Jsy	8.00
Johnny Bench/Jsy	15.00
Yogi Berra/Bat/SP/75	8.00
Roger Clemens/Jsy	25.00
Bill Dickey/Bat	25.00
Rollie Fingers/Jsy	8.00
Reggie Jackson/Bat	25.00
Derek Jeter/Bat	30.00
Chipper Jones/Jsy	10.00
Roger Maris/Pants/SP	15.00
Johnny Mize/Bat	15.00
Joe Morgan/Bat	8.00
Thurman Munson/Bat	35.00
Jim Palmer/Jsy	10.00
Manny Ramirez/Jsy	10.00
Brooks Robinson/Bat	30.00
Jackie Robinson/SP/150	60.00
Babe Ruth/Bat	200.00
Duke Snider/Bat	30.00
Alfonso Soriano/Bat	10.00
Bernie Williams/Jsy	8.00

Legendary Dynasties Premium

	NM/M

Numbered to Highest win total.

Rollie Fingers/93	15.00
Roger Clemens/114	50.00
Roger Maris/109	70.00
Roberto Alomar/96	25.00
Reggie Jackson/93	30.00
Manny Ramirez/99	25.00
Johnny Bench/108	35.00
Jim Palmer/109	20.00
Derek Jeter/114	80.00
Alfonso Soriano/99	30.00
Chipper Jones/106	30.00
Bernie Williams/114	20.00

On Base!

	NM/M
Complete Set (30):	125.00
Common Player:	2.00

#'d to 2001 OBP

10B	Frank Thomas/316	5.00
20B	Ivan Rodriguez/347	5.00
30B	Nomar Garciaparra/352	10.00
40B	Ken Griffey Jr./365	5.00
50B	Juan Gonzalez/370	4.00
60B	Shawn Green/372	3.00
70B	Vladimir Guerrero/377	5.00
80B	Derek Jeter/377	15.00
90B	Scott Rolen/378	5.00
100B	Ichiro Suzuki/381	10.00
110B	Mike Piazza/384	10.00
120B	Bernie Williams/395	3.00
130B	Moises Alou/396	3.00
140B	Jeff Bagwell/397	4.00
150B	Alex Rodriguez/399	10.00
160B	Albert Pujols/403	10.00
170B	Manny Ramirez/405	4.00
180B	Carlos Delgado/408	4.00
190B	Jim Edmonds/410	3.00
200B	Roberto Alomar/415	4.00
210B	Jim Thome/416	4.00
220B	Gary Sheffield/417	3.00
230B	Chipper Jones/427	5.00
240B	Luis Gonzalez/429	2.00
250B	Lance Berkman/430	3.00
260B	Todd Helton/432	4.00
270B	Sammy Sosa/442	10.00
280B	Larry Walker/449	2.00
290B	Jason Giambi/477	4.00
300B	Barry Bonds/515	12.00

On Base! Game-Used

	NM/M
Common Player:	5.00

Production 100 Sets

Roberto Alomar	8.00
Moises Alou	5.00
Jeff Bagwell	8.00
Lance Berkman	5.00
Barry Bonds	20.00
Carlos Delgado	5.00

Player	Price
Jim Edmonds	6.00
Nomar Garciaparra	15.00
Jason Giambi	8.00
Juan Gonzalez	8.00
Luis Gonzalez	5.00
Shawn Green	5.00
Ken Griffey Jr.	20.00
Vladimir Guerrero	8.00
Todd Helton	8.00
Derek Jeter	25.00
Chipper Jones	10.00
Mike Piazza	15.00
Albert Pujols	20.00
Manny Ramirez	10.00
Alex Rodriguez	15.00
Ivan Rodriguez	10.00
Scott Rolen	10.00
Gary Sheffield	6.00
Sammy Sosa	20.00
Ichiro Suzuki	25.00
Frank Thomas	10.00
Jim Thome	8.00
Larry Walker	5.00
Bernie Williams	6.00

2002 Fleer Project Liberty N.Y. Mets

"New York is Getting Stronger Every Day" was the theme of this team set distributed at a promotional game in Shea Stadium. Cards feature game-action photos and symbols of the team's efforts to respond to the 9/11/01 attack. An image of the Statue of Liberty is vignetted on front of most cards. Player cards have recent stats and highlights, other cards have information on help lines and other resources.

		NM/M
	Complete Set (15):	10.00
	Common Card:	.35
1	Mets players	.35
2	Al Leiter	.75
3	Mike Piazza	3.00
4	NYPD baseball cap (Al Leiter)	.75
5	Mo Vaughn	.75
6	Roberto Alomar	1.00
7	Edgardo Alfonzo	.75
8	9-11-01 sleeve patch	.35
9	Rey Ordonez	.75
10	Roger Cedeno	.75
11	Timo Perez	.75
12	NYPD batting helmet (Mike Piazza)	1.50
13	Jeromy Burnitz	.75
14	Bobby Valentine	.75
15	U.S. flag at Shea	.35

2002 Fleer Showcase

		NM/M
	Complete Set (166):	225.00
	Common Player:	.25
	Common (126-141):	5.00
	Production 500	
	Common (141-166):	4.00
	Production 1,500	
	Pack (5):	3.00
	Box (24):	60.00
1	Albert Pujols	2.00
2	Pedro J. Martinez	.75
3	Frank Thomas	1.00
4	Gary Sheffield	.40
5	Roberto Alomar	.40
6	Luis Gonzalez	.35
7	Bobby Abreu	.25
8	Carlos Lee	.25
9	Preston Wilson	.25
10	Todd Helton	.75
11	Juan Gonzalez	.75
12	Chuck Knoblauch	.25
13	Jason Kendall	.25
14	Aaron Sele	.25
15	Greg Vaughn	.25
16	Fred McGriff	.25
17	Doug Mientkiewicz	.25
18	Richard Hidalgo	.25
19	Alfonso Soriano	.50
20	Matt Williams	.25
21	Bobby Higginson	.25
22	Mo Vaughn	.25
23	Andruw Jones	.75
24	Omar Vizquel	.25
25	Bret Boone	.25
26	Bernie Williams	.35
27	Rafael Furcal	.25
28	Jeff Bagwell	.75
29	Marty Cardova	.25
30	Lance Berkman	.25
31	Vernon Wells	.25
32	Garret Anderson	.25
33	Larry Bigbie	.25
34	Steve Finley	.25
35	Barry Bonds	3.00
36	Eric Chavez	.35
37	Tony Clark	.25
38	Roger Clemens	1.50
39	Adam Dunn	.50
40	Roger Cedeno	.25
41	Carlos Delgado	.25
42	Jermaine Dye	.25
43	Brian Jordan	.25
44	Darin Erstad	.65
45	Paul LoDuca	.25
46	Jim Edmonds	.25
47	Tom Glavine	.50
48	Cliff Floyd	.25
49	Jon Lieber	.25
50	Adrian Beltre	.40
51	Joel Pineiro	.25
52	Jim Thome	.40
53	Jimmy Rollins	.40
54	Pat Burrell	.40
55	Jeromy Burnitz	.25
56	Larry Walker	.25
57	Damon Minor	.25
58	John Olerud	.25
59	Carlos Beltran	.50
60	Vladimir Guerrero	.75
61	David Justice	.25
62	Phil Nevin	.25
63	Tino Martinez	.25
64	Curt Schilling	.75
65	Corey Patterson	.25
66	Aubrey Huff	.25
67	Mark Grace	.35
68	Rafael Palmeiro	.65
69	Jorge Posada	.25
70	Craig Biggio	.25
71	Manny Ramirez	.75
72	Mark Quinn	.25
73	Raul Mondesi	.25
74	Shawn Green	.40
75	Brian Giles	.25
76	Paul Konerko	.25
77	Troy Glaus	.75
78	Mike Mussina	.40
79	Greg Maddux	1.00
80	Edgar Martinez	.25
81	Jose Vidro	.25
82	Scott Rolen	.65
83	Ben Grieve	.25
84	Jeff Kent	.25
85	Magglio Ordonez	.25
86	Freddy Garcia	.25
87	Ivan Rodriguez	.65
88	Pokey Reese	.25
89	Shannon Stewart	.25
90	Randy Johnson	.75
91	Cristian Guzman	.25
92	Tsuyoshi Shinjo	.25
93	Steve Cox	.25
94	Mike Sweeney	.25
95	Robert Fick	.25
96	Sean Casey	.25
97	Tim Hudson	.25
98	Bud Smith	.25
99	Corey Koskie	.25
100	Richie Sexson	.25
101	Aramis Ramirez	.25
102	Barry Larkin	.25
103	Rich Aurilia	.25
104	Charles Johnson	.25
105	Ryan Klesko	.25
106	Ben Sheets	.25
107	J.D. Drew	.40
108	Jay Gibbons	.25
109	Kerry Wood	.65
110	C.C. Sabathia	.25
111	Eric Munson	.25
112	Josh Beckett	.40
113	Javier Vasquez	.25
114	Barry Zito	.35
115	Kazuhiro Sasaki	.25
116	Bubba Trammell	.25
117	Russell Branyan	.25
118	Todd Walker	.25
119	Mike Hampton	.25
120	Jeff Weaver	.25
121	Geoff Jenkins	.25
122	Edgardo Alfonzo	.25
123	Mike Lieberthal	.25
124	Mike Lowell	.25
125	Kevin Brown	.25
126	Derek Jeter	8.00
127	Ichiro Suzuki	5.00
128	Nomar Garciaparra	5.00
129	Ken Griffey Jr.	5.00
130	Jason Giambi	5.00
131	Alex Rodriguez	5.00
132	Chipper Jones	5.00
133	Mike Piazza	5.00
134	Sammy Sosa	5.00
135	Hideo Nomo	5.00
136	Kazuhisa Ishii RC	5.00
137	Satoru Komiyama RC	5.00
138	So Taguchi RC	6.00
139	Jorge Padilla RC	5.00
140	Rene Reyes RC	5.00
141	Jorge Nunez RC	5.00
142	Nelson Castro RC	4.00
143	Anderson Machado RC	4.00
144	Edwin Almonte RC	4.00
145	Luis Ugueto RC	4.00
146	Felix Escalona RC	4.00
147	Ron Calloway RC	4.00
148	Hansel Izquierdo RC	4.00
149	Mark Teixeira RC	6.00
150	Orlando Hudson RC	4.00
151	Aaron Cook RC	4.00
152	Aaron Taylor RC	4.00
153	Takahito Nomura RC	4.00
154	Matt Thornton RC	4.00
155	Mark Prior RC	8.00
156	Reed Johnson RC	4.00
157	Doug DeVore RC	4.00
158	Ben Howard RC	4.00
159	Francis Beltran RC	4.00
160	Brian Mallette RC	4.00
161	Sean Burroughs	4.00
162	Michael Restovich	4.00
163	Austin Kearns	4.00
164	Marlon Byrd	4.00
165	Hank Blalock	6.00
166	Mike Rivera	4.00

Legacy

Stars (1-125):	3-5X
Legacy (126-166):	1X
Production 175 Sets	

Baseball's Best

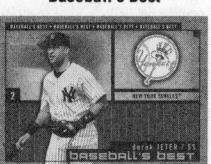

		NM/M
	Complete Set (20):	40.00
	Common Player:	1.00
	Inserted 1:8	
1	Derek Jeter	5.00
2	Barry Bonds	5.00
3	Mike Piazza	3.00
4	Alex Rodriguez	4.00
5	Pat Burrell	1.00
6	Rafael Palmeiro	1.00
7	Nomar Garciaparra	3.00
8	Todd Helton	1.50
9	Roger Clemens	2.50
10	Shawn Green	1.00
11	Chipper Jones	2.00
12	Pedro J. Martinez	1.50
13	Luis Gonzalez	1.00
14	Randy Johnson	2.00
15	Ichiro Suzuki	3.00
16	Ken Griffey Jr.	3.00
17	Vladimir Guerrero	1.50
18	Sammy Sosa	3.00
19	Jason Giambi	1.00
20	Albert Pujols	.75

Baseball's Best Memorabilia

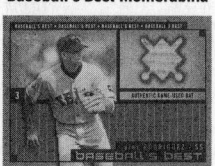

		NM/M
	Common Player:	5.00
	Inserted 1:24	
	Golds:	1-2X
	Production 100 Sets	
	Derek Jeter/Jsy	20.00
	Barry Bonds/Jsy	20.00
	Mike Piazza/Jsy	15.00
	Alex Rodriguez/Bat	15.00
	Rafael Palmeiro/Jsy	8.00
	Nomar Garciaparra/Jsy	10.00
	Todd Helton/Bat	10.00
	Roger Clemens/Jsy	15.00
	Shawn Green/Jsy	5.00
	Chipper Jones/Jsy	8.00
	Pedro Martinez/Jsy	8.00
	Luis Gonzalez/Jsy	5.00
	Randy Johnson/Jsy	10.00
	Ichiro Suzuki/Base	15.00
	Ken Griffey Jr./Base	8.00
	Vladimir Guerrero/Base	8.00
	Sammy Sosa/Base	10.00

2002 Fleer Tradition

		NM/M
	Complete Set (500):	175.00
	Jason Giambi/Base	8.00
	Albert Pujols/Base	10.00

Baseball's Best Silver Auto.

	NM/M
Serial numbered to 400.	
Derek Jeter	125.00
Barry Bonds	200.00

Baseball's Best Gold Auto.

	NM/M
Serial numbered to 100.	
Derek Jeter	150.00
Barry Bonds	225.00

Derek Jeter's Legacy Collection

		NM/M
	Complete Set (22):	80.00
	Common Jeter:	5.00
	Production 1,000 Sets	
1-22	Derek Jeter	5.00

Derek Jeter's Legacy Coll. Inserts

	NM/M
Quantity produced listed.	
Derek Jeter/Jsy/300	75.00
Derek Jeter/ Combo Jsy/175	90.00
Derek Jeter/ World Series Ball/50	100.00
Derek Jeter/Glv/425	60.00

Sweet Sigs Leather

		NM/M
	Common Player:	8.00
2	Russell Branyan/90	10.00
6	Rafael Furcal/92	15.00
8	Brandon Inge/122	8.00
10	Xavier Nady/301	8.00
11	Jose Ortiz/50	10.00
12	Ben Sheets/60	25.00
13	Mike Sweeney/103	15.00

Sweet Sigs Lumber

		NM/M
	Common Player:	5.00
1	Bobby Abreu/231	10.00
2	Russell Branyan/425	8.00
3	Pat Burrell/115	10.00
4	Sean Casey/64	20.00
5	Eric Chavez/256	10.00
6	Rafael Furcal/530	10.00
8	Brandon Inge/528	8.00
9	Jackson Melian/636	7.00
10	Xavier Nady/589	6.00
11	Jose Ortiz/515	8.00
12	Ben Sheets/458	15.00
13	Mike Sweeney/495	10.00

Sweet Sigs Wall

		NM/M
	Common Player:	8.00
1	Bobby Abreu/200	20.00
2	Russell Branyan/200	8.00
5	Eric Chavez/108	15.00
6	Rafael Furcal/207	10.00
8	Brandon Inge/187	8.00
9	Jackson Melian/146	8.00
10	Xavier Nady/286	8.00
11	Jose Ortiz/116	8.00
12	Ben Sheets/150	20.00
13	Mike Sweeney/371	10.00

2002 Fleer Tradition

	Common Player:	.15
	Common SP (1-100):	1.50
	Inserted 1:2	
	Pack (10):	2.00
	Box (36):	50.00
1	Barry Bonds	10.00
2	Cal Ripken Jr.	10.00
3	Tony Gwynn	5.00
4	Brad Radke	1.50
5	Jose Ortiz	1.50
6	Mark Mulder	1.50
7	Jon Lieber	1.50
8	John Olerud	1.50
9	Phil Nevin	1.50
10	Craig Biggio	1.50
11	Pedro Martinez	4.00
12	Fred McGriff	1.50
13	Vladimir Guerrero	4.00
14	Jason Giambi	3.00
15	Mark Kotsay	1.50
16	Bud Smith	1.50
17	Kevin Brown	1.50
18	Darin Erstad	3.00
19	Julio Franco	1.50
20	C.C. Sabathia	1.50
21	Larry Walker	1.50
22	Doug Mientkiewicz	1.50
23	Luis Gonzalez	2.00
24	Albert Pujols	8.00
25	Brian Lawrence	1.50
26	Al Leiter	1.50
27	Mike Sweeney	1.50
28	Jeff Weaver	1.50
29	Matt Morris	1.50
30	Hideo Nomo	4.00
31	Tom Glavine	2.50
32	Magglio Ordonez	1.50
33	Roberto Alomar	2.50
34	Roger Cedeno	1.50
35	Greg Vaughn	1.50
36	Chan Ho Park	1.50
37	Rich Aurilia	1.50
38	Tsuyoshi Shinjo	1.50
39	Eric Young	1.50
40	Bobby Higginson	1.50
41	Marlon Anderson	1.50
42	Mark Grace	2.00
43	Steve Cox	1.50
44	Cliff Floyd	1.50
45	Brian Roberts	1.50
46	Paul Konerko	1.50
47	Brandon Duckworth	1.50
48	Josh Beckett	2.50
49	David Ortiz	2.50
50	Geoff Jenkins	1.50
51	Ruben Sierra	1.50
52	John Franco	1.50
53	Einar Diaz	1.50
54	Luis Castillo	1.50
55	Mark Quinn	1.50
56	Shea Hillenbrand	1.50
57	Rafael Palmeiro	3.00
58	Paul O'Neill	1.50
59	Andruw Jones	4.00
60	Lance Berkman	1.50
61	Jimmy Rollins	2.00
62	Jose Hernandez	1.50
63	Rusty Greer	1.50
64	Wade Miller	1.50
65	David Eckstein	1.50
66	Jose Valentin	1.50
67	Javier Vazquez	1.50
68	Roger Clemens	6.00
69	Omar Vizquel	1.50
70	Roy Oswalt	1.50
71	Shannon Stewart	1.50
72	Byung-Hyun Kim	1.50
73	Jay Gibbons	1.50
74	Barry Larkin	1.50
75	Brian Giles	1.50
76	Andres Galarraga	1.50
77	Sammy Sosa	6.00
78	Manny Ramirez	4.00
79	Carlos Delgado	2.50
80	Jorge Posada	1.50
81	Todd Ritchie	1.50
82	Russ Ortiz	1.50
83	Brent Mayne	1.50
84	Mike Mussina	3.00
85	Raul Mondesi	1.50
86	Mark Loretta	1.50
87	Tim Raines	1.50
88	Ichiro Suzuki	6.00
89	Juan Pierre	1.50
90	Adam Dunn	2.50
91	Jason Tyner	1.50
92	Miguel Tejada	1.50
93	Elpidio Guzman	1.50
94	Freddy Garcia	1.50
95	Marcus Giles	1.50
96	Junior Spivey	1.50
97	Aramis Ramirez	1.50
98	Jose Rijo	1.50
99	Paul LoDuca	1.50
100	Mike Cameron	1.50
101	Alex Hernandez	.15
102	Benji Gil	.15
103	Benito Santiago	.15
104	Bobby Abreu	.15
105	Brad Penny	.15
106	Calvin Murray	.15
107	Chad Durbin	.15
108	Chris Singleton	.15
109	Chris Carpenter	.15
110	David Justice	.15
111	Eric Chavez	.25
112	Fernando Tatis	.15
113	Frank Castillo	.15
114	Jason LaRue	.15
115	Jim Edmonds	.15
116	Joe Kennedy	.15
117	Jose Jimenez	.15
118	Josh Towers	.15
119	Junior Herndon	.15
120	Luke Prokopec	.15
121	Mac Suzuki	.15
122	Mark DeRosa	.15
123	Marty Cordova	.15
124	Michael Tucker	.15
125	Michael Young	.15
126	Robin Ventura	.15
127	Shane Halter	.15
128	Shane Reynolds	.15
129	Tony Womack	.15
130	A.J. Pierzynski	.15
131	Aaron Rowand	.15
132	Antonio Alfonseca	.15
133	Arthur Rhodes	.15
134	Bob Wickman	.15
135	Brady Clark	.15
136	Chad Hermansen	.15
137	Marlon Byrd	.15
138	Dan Wilson	.15
139	David Cone	.15
140	Dean Palmer	.15
141	Denny Neagle	.15
142	Derek Jeter	2.50
143	Erubiel Durazo	.15
144	Felix Rodriguez	.15
145	Jason Hart	.15
146	Jay Bell	.15
147	Jeff Suppan	.15
148	Jeff Zimmerman	.15
149	Kerry Wood	.65
150	Kerry Robinson	.15
151	Kevin Appier	.15
152	Michael Barrett	.15
153	Mo Vaughn	.15
154	Rafael Furcal	.15
155	Sidney Ponson	.15
156	Terry Adams	.15
157	Tim Redding	.15
158	Toby Hall	.15
159	Aaron Sele	.15
160	Bartolo Colon	.15
161	Brad Ausmus	.15
162	Carlos Pena	.15
163	Jace Brewer	.15
164	David Wells	.15
165	David Segui	.15
166	Derek Lowe	.15
167	Derek Bell	.15
168	Jason Grabowski	.15
169	Johnny Damon	.25
170	Jose Mesa	.15
171	Juan Encarnacion	.15
172	Ken Caminiti	.15
173	Ken Griffey Jr.	1.50
174	Luis Rivas	.15
175	Mariano Rivera	.25
176	Mark Grudzielanek	.15
177	Mark McGwire	2.00
178	Mike Bordick	.15
179	Mike Hampton	.15
180	Nick Bierbrodt	.15
181	Paul Byrd	.15
182	Robb Nen	.15
183	Ryan Dempster	.15
184	Ryan Klesko	.15
185	Scott Spiezio	.15
186	Scott Strickland	.15
187	Todd Zeile	.15
188	Tom Gordon	.15
189	Troy Glaus	.75
190	Matt Williams	.15
191	Wes Helms	.15
192	Jerry Hairston Jr.	.15
193	Brook Fordyce	.15
194	Nomar Garciaparra	1.50
195	Kevin Tapani	.15
196	Mark Buehrle	.15
197	Dmitri Young	.15
198	John Rocker	.15
199	Juan Uribe	.15
200	Matt Anderson	.15
201	Alex Gonzalez	.15
202	Julio Lugo	.15
203	Roberto Hernandez	.15
204	Richie Sexson	.15
205	Corey Koskie	.15
206	Tony Armas Jr.	.15
207	Rey Ordonez	.15
208	Orlando Hernandez	.15
209	Pokey Reese	.15
210	Mike Lieberthal	.15
211	Kris Benson	.15
212	Jermaine Dye	.15
213	Livan Hernandez	.15
214	Bret Boone	.15
215	Dustin Hermanson	.15
216	Placido Polanco	.15
217	Jesus Colome	.15
218	Alex Gonzalez	.15
219	Adam Everett	.15
220	Adam Piatt	.15
221	Brad Fullmer	.15
222	Brian Buchanan	.15
223	Chipper Jones	1.00
224	Chuck Finley	.15
225	David Bell	.15
226	Jack Wilson	.25
227	Jason Bere	.15
228	Jeff Conine	.15
229	Jeff Bagwell	.75
230	Joe McEwing	.15
231	Kip Wells	.15

#	Player	Price
232	Mike Lansing	.15
233	Neifi Perez	.15
234	Omar Daal	.15
235	Reggie Sanders	.15
236	Shawn Wooten	.15
237	Shawn Chacon	.15
238	Shawn Estes	.15
239	Steve Sparks	.15
240	Steve Kline	.15
241	Tino Martinez	.15
242	Tyler Houston	.15
243	Xavier Nady	.15
244	Bengie Molina	.15
245	Ben Davis	.15
246	Casey Fossum	.15
247	Chris Stynes	.15
248	Danny Graves	.15
249	Pedro Feliz	.15
250	Darren Oliver	.15
251	Dave Veres	.15
252	Deivi Cruz	.15
253	Desi Relaford	.15
254	Devon White	.15
255	Edgar Martinez	.15
256	Eric Munson	.15
257	Eric Karros	.15
258	Homer Bush	.15
259	Jason Kendall	.15
260	Javy Lopez	.15
261	Keith Foulke	.15
262	Keith Ginter	.15
263	Nick Johnson	.15
264	Pat Burrell	.35
265	Ricky Gutierrez	.15
266	Russ Johnson	.15
267	Steve Finley	.15
268	Terrence Long	.15
269	Tony Batista	.15
270	Torii Hunter	.15
271	Vinny Castilla	.15
272	A.J. Burnett	.15
273	Adrian Beltre	.35
274	Alex Rodriguez	2.00
275	Armando Benitez	.15
276	Billy Koch	.15
277	Brady Anderson	.15
278	Brian Jordan	.15
279	Carlos Febles	.15
280	Daryle Ward	.15
281	Eli Marrero	.15
282	Garret Anderson	.15
283	Jack Cust	.15
284	Jacque Jones	.15
285	Jamie Moyer	.15
286	Jeffrey Hammonds	.15
287	Jim Thome	.15
288	Jon Garland	.15
289	Jose Offerman	.15
290	Matt Stairs	.15
291	Orlando Cabrera	.15
292	Ramiro Mendoza	.15
293	Ray Durham	.15
294	Rickey Henderson	.75
295	Rob Mackowiak	.15
296	Scott Rolen	.65
297	Tim Hudson	.25
298	Todd Helton	.75
299	Tony Clark	.15
300	B.J. Surhoff	.15
301	Bernie Williams	.30
302	Bill Mueller	.15
303	Chris Richard	.15
304	Craig Paquette	.15
305	Curt Schilling	.40
306	Damian Jackson	.15
307	Derrek Lee	.15
308	Eric Milton	.15
309	Frank Catalanotto	.15
310	J.T. Snow	.15
311	Jared Sandberg	.15
312	Jason Varitek	.15
313	Jeff Cirillo	.15
314	Jeromy Burnitz	.15
315	Joe Crede	.15
316	Joel Pineiro	.15
317	Jose Cruz Jr.	.15
318	Kevin Young	.15
319	Marquis Grissom	.15
320	Moises Alou	.15
321	Randall Simon	.15
322	Royce Clayton	.15
323	Tim Salmon	.25
324	Travis Fryman	.15
325	Travis Lee	.15
326	Vance Wilson	.15
327	Jarrod Washburn	.15
328	Ben Petrick	.15
329	Ben Grieve	.15
330	Carl Everett	.15
331	Eric Byrnes	.15
332	Doug Glanville	.15
333	Edgardo Alfonzo	.15
334	Ellis Burks	.15
335	Gabe Kapler	.15
336	Gary Sheffield	.25
337	Greg Maddux	1.00
338	J.D. Drew	.25
339	Jamey Wright	.15
340	Jeff Kent	.15
341	Jeremy Giambi	.15
342	Joe Randa	.15
343	Joe Mays	.15
344	Jose Macias	.15
345	Kazuhiro Sasaki	.15
346	Mike Kinkade	.15
347	Mike Lowell	.15
348	Randy Johnson	.75
349	Randy Wolf	.15

#	Player	Price
350	Richard Hidalgo	.15
351	Ron Coomer	.15
352	Sandy Alomar	.15
353	Sean Casey	.25
354	Trevor Hoffman	.15
355	Adam Eaton	.15
356	Alfonso Soriano	.50
357	Barry Zito	.25
358	Billy Wagner	.15
359	Brent Abernathy	.15
360	Bret Prinz	.15
361	Carlos Beltran	.40
362	Carlos Guillen	.15
363	Charles Johnson	.15
364	Cristian Guzman	.15
365	Damion Easley	.15
366	Darryl Kile	.15
367	Delino DeShields	.15
368	Eric Davis	.15
369	Frank Thomas	.75
370	Ivan Rodriguez	.65
371	Jay Payton	.15
372	Jeff D'Amico	.15
373	John Burkett	.15
374	Melvin Mora	.15
375	Ramon Ortiz	.15
376	Robert Person	.15
377	Russell Branyan	.15
378	Shawn Green	.25
379	Todd Hollandsworth	.15
380	Tony McKnight	.15
381	Trot Nixon	.15
382	Vernon Wells	.15
383	Troy Percival	.15
384	Albie Lopez	.15
385	Alex Ochoa	.15
386	Andy Pettitte	.25
387	Brandon Inge	.15
388	Bubba Trammell	.15
389	Corey Patterson	.15
390	Damian Rolls	.15
391	Dee Brown	.15
392	Edgar Renteria	.15
393	Eric Gagne	.35
394	Jason Johnson	.15
395	Jeff Nelson	.15
396	John Vander Wal	.15
397	Johnny Estrada	.15
398	Jose Canseco	.40
399	Juan Gonzalez	.75
400	Kevin Millwood	.15
401	Lee Stevens	.15
402	Matt Lawton	.15
403	Mike Lamb	.15
404	Octavio Dotel	.15
405	Ramon Hernandez	.15
406	Ruben Quevedo	.15
407	Todd Walker	.15
408	Troy O'Leary	.15
409	Wascar Serrano	.15
410	Aaron Boone	.15
411	Aubrey Huff	.15
412	Ben Sheets	.15
413	Carlos Lee	.15
414	Chuck Knoblauch	.15
415	Steve Karsay	.15
416	Dante Bichette	.15
417	David Dellucci	.15
418	Esteban Loaiza	.15
419	Fernando Vina	.15
420	Ismael Valdes	.15
421	Jason Isringhausen	.15
422	Jeff Shaw	.15
423	John Smoltz	.15
424	Jose Vidro	.15
425	Kenny Lofton	.15
426	Mark Little	.15
427	Mark McLemore	.15
428	Marvin Benard	.15
429	Mike Piazza	1.50
430	Pat Hentgen	.15
431	Preston Wilson	.15
432	Rick Helling	.15
433	Robert Fick	.15
434	Rondell White	.15
435	Adam Kennedy	.15
436	David Espinosa	.15
437	Dewon Brazelton	.15
438	Drew Henson	.25
439	Juan Cruz	.15
440	Jason Jennings	.15
441	Carlos Garcia	.15
442	Carlos Hernandez	.15
443	Wilkin Ruan	.15
444	Wilson Betemit	.15
445	Horacio Ramirez	.15
446	Danys Baez	.15
447	Abraham Nunez	.15
448	Josh Hamilton	.50
449	Chris George	.15
450	Rick Bauer	.15
451	Donnie Bridges	.15
452	Erick Almonte	.15
453	Cory Aldridge	.15
454	Ryan Drese	.15
455	Jason Romano	.15
456	Corky Miller	.15
457	Rafael Soriano	.15
458	Mark Prior	.75
459	Mark Teixeira	.50
460	Adrian Hernandez	.15
461	Tim Spooneybarger	.15
462	Bill Ortega	.15
463	D'Angelo Jimenez	.15
464	Andres Torres	.15
465	Alexis Gomez	.15
466	Angel Berroa	.15
467	Henry Mateo	.15

#	Player	Price
468	Endy Chavez	.15
469	Billy Sylvester	.15
470	Nate Frese	.15
471	Luis Gonzalez	.25
472	Barry Bonds	2.50
473	Rich Aurilia	.15
474	Albert Pujols	2.00
475	Todd Helton	.75
476	Moises Alou	.15
477	Lance Berkman	.15
478	Brian Giles	.15
479	Cliff Floyd	.15
480	Sammy Sosa	1.50
481	Shawn Green	.30
482	Jon Lieber	.15
483	Matt Morris	.15
484	Curt Schilling	.40
485	Randy Johnson	.75
486	Manny Ramirez	.75
487	Ichiro Suzuki	1.50
488	Juan Gonzalez	.75
489	Derek Jeter	2.50
490	Alex Rodriguez	2.00
491	Bret Boone	.15
492	Roberto Alomar	.30
493	Jason Giambi	.50
494	Rafael Palmeiro	.65
495	Doug Mientkiewicz	.15
496	Jim Thome	.15
497	Freddy Garcia	.15
498	Mark Buehrle	.15
499	Mark Mulder	.15
500	Roger Clemens	1.25

Heads Up

MARK McGWIRE / 1B

	NM/M
Complete Set (10):	45.00
Common Player:	1.00
Inserted 1:36	
1HU	Derek Jeter	8.00
2HU	Ichiro Suzuki	5.00
3HU	Sammy Sosa	5.00
4HU	Mike Piazza	5.00
5HU	Ken Griffey Jr.	5.00
6HU	Alex Rodriguez	6.00
7HU	Barry Bonds	8.00
8HU	Nomar Garciaparra	5.00
9HU	Mark McGwire	6.00
10HU	Cal Ripken Jr.	8.00

Diamond Tributes

Randy Johnson Pitcher #13

	NM/M
Complete Set (15):	15.00
Common Player:	.50
Inserted 1:6	
1DT	Cal Ripken Jr.	3.00
2DT	Tony Gwynn	1.00
3DT	Derek Jeter	3.00
4DT	Pedro Martinez	.75
5DT	Mark McGwire	2.50
6DT	Sammy Sosa	2.00
7DT	Barry Bonds	1.50
8DT	Roger Clemens	1.50
9DT	Mike Piazza	2.00
10DT	Alex Rodriguez	2.50
11DT	Randy Johnson	.75
12DT	Chipper Jones	1.00
13DT	Nomar Garciaparra	2.00
14DT	Ichiro Suzuki	2.00
15DT	Jason Giambi	.50

Grass Roots

DEREK JETER DEREK JETER DEREK JETER

	NM/M
Complete Set (10):	15.00
Common Player:	.75
Inserted 1:18	
1GR	Barry Bonds	2.00
2GR	Alex Rodriguez	4.00
3GR	Derek Jeter	5.00
4GR	Greg Maddux	2.50
5GR	Ivan Rodriguez	1.00
6GR	Cal Ripken Jr.	5.00
7GR	Bernie Williams	.75
8GR	Jeff Bagwell	1.50
9GR	Scott Rolen	1.00
10GR	Larry Walker	.75

Grass Roots Patch Game Worn

	NM/M
Production 50 Sets	
	Barry Bonds	100.00
	Alex Rodriguez	75.00
	Greg Maddux	50.00
	Ivan Rodriguez	25.00
	Cal Ripken Jr.	100.00
	Bernie Williams	25.00
	Jeff Bagwell	40.00
	Scott Rolen	30.00
	Larry Walker	20.00

Lumber Company

	NM/M
Complete Set (30):	40.00
Common Player:	1.00
Inserted 1:12	
1LC	Moises Alou	1.00
2LC	Luis Gonzalez	1.00
3LC	Todd Helton	2.50
4LC	Mike Piazza	4.00
5LC	J.D. Drew	1.50
6LC	Albert Pujols	5.00
7LC	Chipper Jones	3.00
8LC	Manny Ramirez	2.50
9LC	Miguel Tejada	1.00
10LC	Curt Schilling	1.50
11LC	Alex Rodriguez	5.00
12LC	Barry Larkin	1.00
13LC	Nomar Garciaparra	4.00
14LC	Cliff Floyd	1.00
15LC	Alfonso Soriano	1.50
16LC	Sean Casey	1.00
17LC	Scott Rolen	2.00
18LC	Jose Ortiz	1.00
19LC	Corey Patterson	1.00
20LC	Joe Crede	1.00
21LC	Jace Brewer	1.00
22LC	Derek Jeter	6.00
23LC	Jim Thome	1.00
24LC	Frank Thomas	2.50
25LC	Shawn Green	1.00
26LC	Drew Henson	1.00
27LC	Jimmy Rollins	1.50
28LC	Dave Justice	1.00
29LC	Roberto Alomar	1.50
30LC	Bernie Williams	1.00

Lumber Company Game-Used

	NM/M
Common Player:	5.00
Inserted 1:72	
	Moises Alou	5.00
	Luis Gonzalez	5.00
	Todd Helton	8.00
	Mike Piazza	12.00
	J.D. Drew	6.00
	Albert Pujols	15.00
	Chipper Jones	10.00
	Manny Ramirez	8.00
	Miguel Tejada	6.00
	Curt Schilling	6.00
	Alex Rodriguez	15.00
	Barry Larkin	5.00
	Nomar Garciaparra	12.00
	Cliff Floyd	5.00
	Alfonso Soriano	6.00
	Sean Casey	6.00
	Scott Rolen	8.00
	Jose Ortiz	5.00
	Corey Patterson	5.00
	Joe Crede	5.00
	Jace Brewer	5.00
	Derek Jeter	25.00
	Jim Thome	5.00
	Frank Thomas	8.00
	Shawn Green	5.00
	Drew Henson	5.00
	Jimmy Rollins	5.00
	Dave Justice	5.00
	Roberto Alomar	6.00
	Bernie Williams	5.00

This Day in History

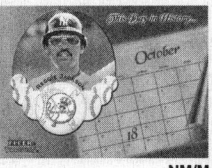

October 18

	NM/M
Complete Set (29):	120.00
Common Player:	1.50
Inserted 1:18	
1	Cal Ripken Jr.	10.00
2	Barry Bonds	10.00
3	George Brett	4.00
4	Tony Gwynn	3.00
5	Nolan Ryan	10.00
6	Reggie Jackson	3.00
7	Paul Molitor	2.00
8	Ichiro Suzuki	5.00
9	Alex Rodriguez	8.00
10	Don Mattingly	6.00
11	Sammy Sosa	5.00
12	Mark McGwire	8.00
13	Derek Jeter	10.00
14	Roger Clemens	4.00
15	Jim "Catfish" Hunter	1.50
16	Greg Maddux	3.00
17	Ken Griffey Jr.	5.00
18	Gil Hodges	1.50
19	Edgar Martinez	1.50
20	Mike Piazza	5.00
21	Jimmie Foxx	1.50
22	Albert Pujols	6.00
23	Chipper Jones	3.00
25	Jeff Bagwell	2.00
26	Nomar Garciaparra	5.00
27	Randy Johnson	2.00
28	Todd Helton	2.00
29	Ted Kluszewski	1.50
30	Ivan Rodriguez	1.75

This Day in History Autographs

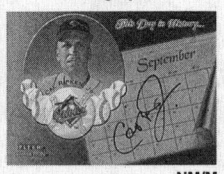

September

	NM/M
Common Player:	
3	Derek Jeter/100	100.00
4	Randy Johnson/75	50.00
5	Don Mattingly/50	90.00
7	Albert Pujols/50	200.00
8	Cal Ripken Jr./50	125.00

This Day in History Game-Used

	NM/M
Common Player:	
	Jeff Bagwell/Bat/100	15.00
	Barry Bonds/Jsy/250	40.00
	Roger Clemens/Jsy/150	30.00
	Jimmie Foxx/Bat/250	40.00
	Todd Helton/Bat/150	15.00
	Jim "Catfish" Hunter/Jsy/250	15.00
	Derek Jeter/Jsy/250	40.00
	Greg Maddux/Jsy/100	20.00
	Mike Piazza/Bat/150	20.00
	Alex Rodriguez/Hat/250	30.00

2002 Fleer Tradition Update

TINO MARTINEZ

St. Louis Cardinals #21/18

	NM/M
Complete Set (400):	75.00
Common Player:	.15
Common SP (1-100):	.50
Inserted 1:1	
Pack (10):	1.50
Box (36):	35.00
1	P.J. Bevis RC	.50
2	Michael Crudale RC	.50
3	Ben Howard RC	.75
4	Travis Driskill RC	.50
5	Reed Johnson RC	.50
6	Kyle Kane RC	.50
7	Deivis Santos	.50

#	Player	Price
8	Tim Kalita RC	.50
9	Brandon Puffer RC	.50
10	Chris Snelling RC	1.00
11	Juan Brito RC	.50
12	Tyler Yates RC	.50
13	Victor Alvarez RC	.50
14	Takahito Nomura RC	.50
15	Ron Calloway RC	.50
16	Satoru Komiyama RC	.50
17	Julius Matos RC	.50
18	Jorge Nunez RC	.50
19	Anderson Machado RC	.50
20	Scotty Layfield RC	.50
21	Aaron Cook RC	.50
22	Alex Pelaez RC	.50
23	Corey Thurman RC	.50
24	Nelson Castro RC	.50
25	Jeff Austin RC	.50
26	Felix Escalona RC	2.00
27	Luis Ugueto RC	.50
28	Jaime Cerda RC	.50
29	J.J. Trujillo RC	.50
30	Rodrigo Rosario RC	.50
31	Jorge Padilla RC	.50
32	Shawn Sedlacek RC	.50
33	Nate Field RC	.50
34	Earl Snyder RC	.75
35	Miguel Asencio RC	.50
36	Ken Huckaby RC	.50
37	Valentino Pascucci RC	.50
38	So Taguchi RC	1.00
39	Brian Mallette RC	.50
40	Kazuhisa Ishii RC	2.00
41	Matt Thornton RC	.50
42	Mark Corey	.50
43	Kirk Saarloos	.50
44	Brandon Bracke	.50
45	Hansel Izquierdo RC	.50
46	Rene Reyes RC	.50
47	Luis Garcia	.50
48	Jason Simontacchi RC	.50
49	John Ennis RC	.75
50	Franklyn German RC	.50
51	Aaron Guiel RC	.50
52	Howie Clark RC	.50
53	David Ross RC	.50
54	Walt McKeel	.50
55	Francis Beltran RC	.50
56	Barry Wesson RC	.50
57	Runelvys Hernandez RC	.50
58	Oliver Perez RC	2.00
59	Ryan Bukvich RC	.50
60	Steve Kent RC	.50
61	Julio Mateo RC	.50
62	Jason Jimenez	.50
63	Jayson Durocher RC	.75
64	Kevin Frederick RC	.50
65	Kevin Gryboski RC	.50
66	Edwin Almonte RC	.50
67	John Foster RC	.50
68	Doug DeVore RC	1.00
69	Tom Shearn RC	.50
70	Colin Young RC	.50
71	Jon Adkins RC	.50
72	Wilbert Nieves RC	.50
73	Matt Duff	.50
74	Carl Sadler RC	.50
75	Jason Kershner	.50
76	Brandon Backe RC	.50
77	Wilson Valdez RC	.50
78	Chris Baker RC	.50
79	Ryan Jamison	.50
80	Steve Bechler RC	.75
81	Allan Simpson RC	.50
82	Aaron Taylor RC	.50
83	Kevin Cash RC	.50
84	Chone Figgins RC	1.00
85	Clay Condrey RC	.50
86	Shane Nance RC	.50
87	Freddy Sanchez RC	.50
88	Jim Rushford RC	.50
89	Jeriome Robertson RC	.50
90	Trey Lunsford RC	.50
91	Cody McKay RC	.50
92	Trey Hodges RC	.50
93	Hee Seop Choi	1.00
94	Joe Borchard	.50
95	Orlando Hudson	.50
96	Carl Crawford	.50
97	Mark Prior	2.00
98	Brett Myers	.50
99	Kenny Lofton	.50
100	Cliff Floyd	.50
101	Randy Winn	.15
102	Ryan Dempster	.15
103	Josh Phelps	.15
104	Marcus Giles	.15
105	Rickey Henderson	.75
106	Jose Leon	.15
107	Tino Martinez	.15
108	Greg Norton	.15
109	Odalis Perez	.15
110	J.C. Romero	.15
111	Gary Sheffield	.35
112	Ismael Valdes	.15
113	Juan Acevedo	.15
114	Ben Broussard	.15
115	Deivi Cruz	.15
116	Geronimo Gil	.15
117	Eric Hinske	.15
118	Ted Lilly	.15
119	Quinton McCracken	.15
120	Antonio Alfonseca	.15
121	Brent Abernathy	.15
122	Johnny Damon	.25
123	Francisco Cordova	.15
124	Sterling Hitchcock	.15
125	Vladimir Nunez	.15

126	Andres Galarraga	.15
127	Timoniel Perez	.15
128	Tsuyoshi Shinjo	.15
129	Joe Girardi	.15
130	Roberto Alomar	.35
131	Ellis Burks	.15
132	Mike DeJean	.15
133	Alex Gonzalez	.15
134	Johan Santana	.35
135	Kenny Lofton	.15
136	Juan Encarnacion	.15
137	Dewon Brazelton	.15
138	Jeromy Burnitz	.15
139	Elmer Dessens	.15
140	Juan Gonzalez	.75
141	Todd Hundley	.15
142	Tomokazu Ohka	.15
143	Robin Ventura	.15
144	Rodrigo Lopez	.15
145	Ruben Sierra	.15
146	Jason Phillips	.15
147	Ryan Rupe	.15
148	Kevin Appier	.15
149	Sean Burroughs	.15
150	Masato Yoshii	.15
151	Juan Diaz	.15
152	Tony Graffanino	.15
153	Raul Ibanez	.15
154	Kevin Mench	.15
155	Pedro Astacio	.15
156	Brent Butler	.15
157	Kirk Rueter	.15
158	Eddie Guardado	.15
159	Hideki Irabu	.15
160	Wendell Magee	.15
161	Antonio Osuna	.15
162	Jose Vizcaino	.15
163	Danny Bautista	.15
164	Vinny Castilla	.15
165	Chris Singleton	.15
166	Mark Redman	.15
167	Olmedo Saenz	.15
168	Scott Erickson	.15
169	Ty Wigginton	.15
170	Jason Isringhausen	.15
171	Lou Merloni	.15
172	Chris Magruder	.15
173	Brandon Berger	.15
174	Roger Cedeno	.15
175	Kelvim Escobar	.15
176	Jose Guillen	.15
177	Damian Jackson	.15
178	Eric Owens	.15
179	Angel Berroa	.15
180	Alex Cintron	.15
181	Jeff Weaver	.15
182	Damon Minor	.15
183	Bobby Estalella	.15
184	David Justice	.15
185	Roy Halladay	.25
186	Brian Jordan	.15
187	Mike Maroth	.15
188	Pokey Reese	.15
189	Rey Sanchez	.15
190	Hank Blalock	.50
191	Jeff Cirillo	.15
192	Dmitri Young	.15
193	Carl Everett	.15
194	Joey Hamilton	.15
195	Jorge Julio	.15
196	Pablo Ozuna	.15
197	Jason Marquis	.15
198	Dustan Mohr	.15
199	Joe Borowski	.15
200	Tony Clark	.15
201	David Wells	.15
202	Josh Fogg	.15
203	Aaron Harang	.15
204	John McDonald	.15
205	John Stephens	.15
206	Chris Reitsma	.15
207	Alex Sanchez	.15
208	Milton Bradley	.15
209	Matt Clement	.15
210	Brad Fullmer	.15
211	Shigetoshi Hasegawa	.15
212	Austin Kearns	.50
213	Damaso Marte	.15
214	Vicente Padilla	.15
215	Raul Mondesi	.15
216	Russell Branyan	.15
217	Bartolo Colon	.15
218	Moises Alou	.15
219	Scott Hatteberg	.15
220	Bobby Kielty	.15
221	Kip Wells	.15
222	Scott Stewart	.15
223	Victor Martinez	.40
224	Marty Cordova	.15
225	Desi Relaford	.15
226	Reggie Sanders	.15
227	Jason Giambi	.50
228	Jimmy Haynes	.15
229	Billy Koch	.15
230	Damian Moss	.15
231	Chan Ho Park	.15
232	Cliff Floyd	.15
233	Todd Zeile	.15
234	Jeremy Giambi	.15
235	Rick Helling	.15
236	Matt Lawton	.15
237	Ramon Martinez	.15
238	Rondell White	.15
239	Scott Sullivan	.15
240	Hideo Nomo	.60
241	Todd Ritchie	.15
242	Ramon Santiago	.15
243	Jake Peavy	.15

244	Brad Wilkerson	.15
245	Reggie Taylor	.15
246	Carlos Pena	.15
247	Willis Roberts	.15
248	Jason Schmidt	.15
249	Mike Williams	.15
250	Alan Zinter	.15
251	Michael Tejera	.15
252	Dave Roberts	.15
253	Scott Schoeneweis	.15
254	Woody Williams	.15
255	John Thomson	.15
256	Ricardo Rodriguez	.15
257	Aaron Sele	.15
258	Paul Wilson	.15
259	Brett Tomko	.15
260	Kenny Rogers	.15
261	Mo Vaughn	.15
262	John Burkett	.15
263	Dennis Stark	.15
264	Ray Durham	.15
265	Scott Rolen	.65
266	Gabe Kapler	.15
267	Todd Hollandsworth	.15
268	Bud Smith	.15
269	Jay Payton	.15
270	Tyler Houston	.15
271	Brian Moehler	.15
272	David Espinosa	.15
273	Placido Polanco	.15
274	John Patterson	.15
275	Adam Hyzdu	.15
276	Albert Pujols	2.00
277	Larry Walker	.15
278	Magglio Ordonez	.15
279	Ryan Klesko	.15
280	Darin Erstad	.60
281	Jeff Kent	.15
282	Paul LoDuca	.15
283	Jim Edmonds	.15
284	Chipper Jones	1.00
285	Bernie Williams	.30
286	Pat Burrell	.40
287	Cliff Floyd	.15
288	Troy Glaus	.15
289	Brian Giles	.15
290	Jim Thome	.15
291	Greg Maddux	1.00
292	Roberto Alomar	.30
293	Jeff Bagwell	.75
294	Rafael Furcal	.15
295	Josh Beckett	.25
296	Carlos Delgado	.35
297	Ken Griffey Jr.	1.50
298	Jason Giambi	.50
299	Paul Konerko	.15
300	Mike Sweeney	.15
301	Alfonso Soriano	.50
302	Shea Hillenbrand	.15
303	Tony Batista	.15
304	Robin Ventura	.15
305	Alex Rodriguez	2.00
306	Nomar Garciaparra	1.50
307	Derek Jeter	2.50
308	Miguel Tejada	.30
309	Omar Vizquel	.15
310	Jorge Posada	.25
311	A.J. Pierzynski	.15
312	Ichiro Suzuki	1.50
313	Manny Ramirez	.75
314	Torii Hunter	.15
315	Garret Anderson	.15
316	Robert Fick	.15
317	Randy Winn	.15
318	Mark Buehrle	.15
319	Freddy Garcia	.15
320	Eddie Guardado	.15
321	Roy Halladay	.25
322	Derek Lowe	.25
323	Pedro J. Martinez	.75
324	Mariano Rivera	.25
325	Kazuhiro Sasaki	.15
326	Barry Zito	.25
327	Johnny Damon	.25
328	Ugueth Urbina	.15
329	Todd Helton	.75
330	Richie Sexson	.15
331	Jose Vidro	.15
332	Luis Castillo	.15
333	Junior Spivey	.15
334	Scott Rolen	.65
335	Mike Lowell	.15
336	Jimmy Rollins	.25
337	Jose Hernandez	.15
338	Mike Piazza	1.50
339	Benito Santiago	.15
340	Sammy Sosa	1.50
341	Barry Bonds	2.50
342	Vladimir Guerrero	.75
343	Lance Berkman	.25
344	Adam Dunn	.40
345	Shawn Green	.25
346	Luis Gonzalez	.25
347	Eric Gagne	.25
348	Tom Glavine	.30
349	Trevor Hoffman	.15
350	Randy Johnson	.75
351	Byung-Hyun Kim	.15
352	Matt Morris	.15
353	Odalis Perez	.15
354	Curt Schilling	.40
355	John Smoltz	.15
356	Mike Williams	.15
357	Andruw Jones	.25
358	Vicente Padilla	.15
359	Mike Remlinger	.15
360	Robb Nen	.15
361	Shawn Green	.25

362	Derek Jeter	2.50
363	Troy Glaus	.15
364	Ken Griffey Jr.	1.50
365	Mike Piazza	1.50
366	Jason Giambi	.50
367	Greg Maddux	1.00
368	Albert Pujols	2.00
369	Pedro J. Martinez	.75
370	Barry Zito	.25
371	Ichiro Suzuki	1.50
372	Nomar Garciaparra	1.50
373	Vladimir Guerrero	.75
374	Randy Johnson	.75
375	Barry Bonds	2.50
376	Sammy Sosa	1.50
377	Hideo Nomo	.75
378	Jeff Bagwell	.75
379	Curt Schilling	.35
380	Jim Thome	.15
381	Todd Helton	.75
382	Roger Clemens	1.25
383	Chipper Jones	1.00
384	Alex Rodriguez	2.00
385	Manny Ramirez	.40
386	Barry Bonds	2.50
387	Jim Thome	.15
388	Adam Dunn	.40
389	Alex Rodriguez	2.00
390	Shawn Green	.25
391	Jason Giambi	.50
392	Lance Berkman	.15
393	Pat Burrell	.40
394	Eric Chavez	.25
395	Mike Piazza	1.50
396	Vladimir Guerrero	.75
397	Paul Konerko	.15
398	Sammy Sosa	1.50
399	Richie Sexson	.15
400	Torii Hunter	.15

Update Glossy

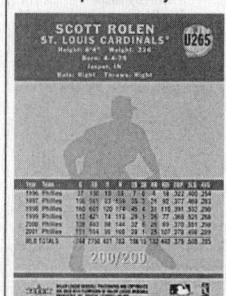

Stars (1-100):		1-2X
Cards (101-400):		4-8X
Production 200 Sets		

Update Diamond Debuts

		NM/M
Complete Set (15):		10.00
Common Player:		.50
Inserted 1:6		
1DD	Mark Prior	1.50
2DD	Eric Hinske	.50
3DD	Kazuhisa Ishii	.50
4DD	Ben Broussard	.50
5DD	Sean Burroughs	.50
6DD	Austin Kearns	1.00
7DD	Hee Seop Choi	1.00
8DD	Kirk Saarloos	.50
9DD	Orlando Hudson	.50
10DD	So Taguchi	.50
11DD	Kevin Mench	.50
12DD	Carl Crawford	.50
13DD	John Patterson	.50
14DD	Hank Blalock	1.50
15DD	Brett Myers	.50

Update Grass Patch

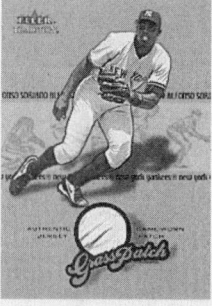

		NM/M
Common Player:		5.00
Production 150 Sets		
	Roger Clemens	25.00
	Adam Dunn	10.00
	Kazuhisa Ishii	5.00
	Barry Zito	5.00
	Alfonso Soriano	10.00
	Mark Prior	10.00
	Chipper Jones	15.00
	Randy Johnson	15.00
	Lance Berkman	5.00
	Mike Piazza	20.00
	Barry Bonds	50.00

		NM/M
		20.00
Common Player:		
Production 50 Sets		
	Alfonso Soriano	30.00
	Torii Hunter	30.00
	Andruw Jones	30.00
	Jim Edmonds	20.00
	Shawn Green	20.00
	Nomar Garciaparra	50.00
	Roberto Alomar	25.00

Update Grass Roots

		NM/M
Complete Set (10):		15.00
Common Player:		1.00
Inserted 1:24		
1GR	Alfonso Soriano	1.50
2GR	Torii Hunter	1.00
3GR	Andruw Jones	1.50
4GR	Jim Edmonds	1.00
5GR	Shawn Green	1.00
6GR	Todd Helton	1.50
7GR	Nomar Garciaparra	4.00
8GR	Roberto Alomar	1.00
9GR	Vladimir Guerrero	1.50
10GR	Ichiro Suzuki	4.00

Update Heads Up

		NM/M
Complete Set (10):		25.00
Common Player:		2.00
Inserted 1:48		
1HU	Roger Clemens	6.00
2HU	Adam Dunn	2.00
3HU	Kazuhisa Ishii	1.50
4HU	Barry Zito	1.50
5HU	Pedro J. Martinez	4.00
6HU	Alfonso Soriano	3.00
7HU	Mark Prior	2.00
8HU	Chipper Jones	5.00
9HU	Randy Johnson	4.00
10HU	Lance Berkman	1.50

Update Heads Up Game-Used

		NM/M
Common Player:		5.00
Production 150 Sets		
	Roger Clemens	25.00
	Adam Dunn	10.00
	Kazuhisa Ishii	5.00
	Barry Zito	5.00
	Alfonso Soriano	10.00
	Mark Prior	10.00
	Chipper Jones	15.00
	Randy Johnson	15.00
	Lance Berkman	10.00
	Mike Piazza	20.00
	Barry Bonds	50.00

Update New York's Finest

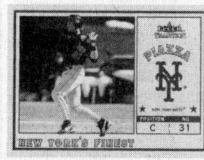

		NM/M
Complete Set (15):		60.00
Common Player:		3.00
Inserted 1:83		
1	Edgardo Alfonzo	3.00
2	Roberto Alomar	4.00
3	Jeromy Burnitz	3.00
4	Satoru Komiyama	3.00
5	Rey Ordonez	3.00
6	Mike Piazza	10.00
7	Mo Vaughn	3.00
8	Roger Clemens	10.00
9	Jason Giambi	4.00
10	Derek Jeter	15.00
11	Mike Mussina	5.00
12	Jorge Posada	3.00
13	Alfonso Soriano	7.00
14	Robin Ventura	3.00
15	Bernie Williams	4.00

Update N.Y.'s Finest Single Swatch

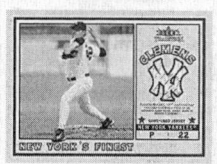

		NM/M
Common Card:		5.00
Inserted 1:112		
	Derek Jeter/Jsy, Rey Ordonez	25.00
	Alfonso Soriano/Jsy, Roberto Alomar	10.00
	Roger Clemens/Jsy, Mike Piazza	15.00
	Mike Mussina/Jsy, Mo Vaughn	8.00
	Bernie Williams/Jsy, Jeromy Burnitz	8.00
	Derek Jeter/Jsy, Satoru Komiyama	25.00
	Robin Ventura/Jsy, Edgardo Alfonzo	8.00
	Jorge Posada/Jsy, Mike Piazza	8.00
	Jason Giambi/Base, Mo Vaughn	8.00
	Alfonso Soriano/Jsy, Edgardo Alfonzo	10.00
	Derek Jeter, Rey Ordonez/Jsy	5.00
	Alfonso Soriano, Roberto Alomar/Jsy	8.00
	Roger Clemens, Mike Piazza/Jsy	15.00
	Mike Mussina, Mo Vaughn/Jsy	6.00
	Bernie Williams, Jeromy Burnitz/Jsy	5.00
	Derek Jeter, Satoru Komiyama/Bat	8.00
	Robin Ventura, Edgardo Alfonzo/Jsy	5.00
	Jorge Posada, Mike Piazza/Jsy	15.00
	Jason Giambi, Mo Vaughn/Jsy	6.00
	Alfonso Soriano, Edgardo Alfonzo/Jsy	5.00

Update N.Y.'s Finest Dual Swatch

		NM/M
Common Card:		10.00
Production 100 Sets		
	Derek Jeter, Rey Ordonez	75.00
	Alfonso Soriano, Roberto Alomar	40.00
	Roger Clemens, Mike Piazza	65.00
	Mike Mussina, Mo Vaughn	30.00
	Bernie Williams, Jeromy Burnitz	20.00
	Robin Ventura, Edgardo Alfonzo	10.00

Update Plays of the Week

		NM/M
Complete Set (30):		35.00
Common Player:		1.00
Inserted 1:12		
1PW	Troy Glaus	1.50
2PW	Andruw Jones	1.50
3PW	Curt Schilling	1.25
4PW	Manny Ramirez	1.50
5PW	Sammy Sosa	2.50
6PW	Magglio Ordonez	1.00
7PW	Ken Griffey Jr.	2.50
8PW	Jim Thome	1.00
9PW	Larry Walker	1.00
10PW	Robert Fick	1.00
11PW	Josh Beckett	1.00
12PW	Roy Oswalt	1.00
13PW	Mike Sweeney	1.00
14PW	Shawn Green	1.00
15PW	Torii Hunter	1.00
16PW	Vladimir Guerrero	1.50
17PW	Mike Piazza	2.50
18PW	Jason Giambi	1.25
19PW	Eric Chavez	1.00
20PW	Pat Burrell	1.25
21PW	Brian Giles	1.00
22PW	Ryan Klesko	1.00
23PW	Barry Bonds	5.00
24PW	Mike Cameron	1.00
25PW	Albert Pujols	4.00
26PW	Alex Rodriguez	4.00
27PW	Carlos Delgado	1.00
28PW	Richie Sexson	1.00
29PW	Jay Gibbons	1.00
30PW	Randy Winn	1.00

Update This Day in History

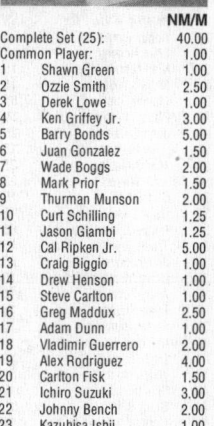

		NM/M
Complete Set (25):		40.00
Common Player:		1.00
1	Shawn Green	1.00
2	Ozzie Smith	2.50
3	Derek Lowe	1.00
4	Ken Griffey Jr.	3.00
5	Barry Bonds	5.00
6	Juan Gonzalez	1.50
7	Wade Boggs	2.00
8	Mark Prior	1.50
9	Thurman Munson	2.00
10	Curt Schilling	1.25
11	Jason Giambi	1.25
12	Cal Ripken Jr.	5.00
13	Craig Biggio	1.00
14	Drew Henson	1.00
15	Steve Carlton	1.00
16	Greg Maddux	2.50
17	Adam Dunn	1.00
18	Vladimir Guerrero	2.00
19	Alex Rodriguez	4.00
20	Carlton Fisk	1.50
21	Ichiro Suzuki	3.00
22	Johnny Bench	2.00
23	Kazuhisa Ishii	1.00
24	Derek Jeter	5.00
25	Jim Thome	1.00

Update This Day in History Auto.

		NM/M
Inserted 1:582		
	Barry Bonds/150	200.00
	Mark Prior/64	40.00
	Drew Henson	20.00
	Greg Maddux/99	150.00
	Derek Jeter	100.00

Update This Day in History Memor.

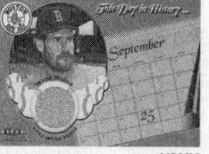

		NM/M
Common Player:		5.00
Inserted 1:24		
	Shawn Green/Jsy	5.00
	Ozzie Smith/Jsy	10.00
	Barry Bonds/Bat	15.00
	Barry Bonds/Jsy	15.00

Juan Gonzalez/Bat	6.00
Wade Boggs/Jsy	6.00
Wade Boggs/Pants	6.00
Curt Schilling/Jsy	6.00
Craig Biggio/Jsy	8.00
Adam Dunn/Jsy	8.00
Alex Rodriguez/Bat	
Alex Rodriguez/Jsy	10.00
Carlton Fisk/Bat	8.00
Kazuhisa Ishii/Bat	
Derek Jeter/Pants	20.00
Jim Thome/Jsy	8.00
Greg Maddux/Jsy	10.00

2002 Fleer Triple Crown

		NM/M
Complete Set (270):		30.00
Common Player:		.15
Pack (10):		1.50
Box (24):		30.00
1	Mo Vaughn	.15
2	Derek Jeter	2.00
3	Ken Griffey Jr.	1.25
4	Charles Johnson	.15
5	Geoff Jenkins	.15
6	Chuck Knoblauch	.15
7	Jason Kendall	.15
8	Jim Edmonds	.15
9	David Eckstein	.15
10	Carl Everett	.15
11	Barry Larkin	.15
12	Cliff Floyd	.15
13	Ben Sheets	.15
14	Jeff Conine	.15
15	Brian Giles	.15
16	Darryl Kile	.15
17	Troy Glaus	.65
18	Trot Nixon	.15
19	Jim Thome	.15
20	Preston Wilson	.15
21	Roger Clemens	1.00
22	Chad Hermansen	.15
23	Matt Morris	.15
24	Shawn Wooten	.15
25	Manny Ramirez	.65
26	Roberto Alomar	.30
27	Josh Beckett	.25
28	Jose Hernandez	.15
29	Mike Mussina	.35
30	Jack Wilson	.25
31	Bud Smith	.15
32	Garret Anderson	.15
33	Pedro J. Martinez	.65
34	Travis Fryman	.15
35	Jeff Bagwell	.65
36	Doug Mientkiewicz	.15
37	Andy Pettitte	.25
38	Ryan Klesko	.15
39	Edgar Renteria	.15
40	Mariano Rivera	.25
41	Darin Erstad	.50
42	Hideo Nomo	.50
43	Ellis Burks	.15
44	Craig Biggio	.15
45	Corey Koskie	.15
46	Jason Varitek	.15
47	Xavier Nady	.15
48	Aubrey Huff	.15
49	Tim Salmon	.25
50	Nomar Garciaparra	1.25
51	Juan Gonzalez	.65
52	Moises Alou	.15
53	A.J. Pierzynski	.15
54	Bernie Williams	.30
55	Phil Nevin	.15
56	Ben Grieve	.15
57	Mark Grace	.25
58	Mike Lansing	.15
59	Kenny Lofton	.15
60	Lance Berkman	.15
61	David Ortiz	.25
62	Jason Giambi	.40
63	Mark Kotsay	.15
64	Greg Vaughn	.15
65	Junior Spivey	.15
66	Fred McGriff	.15
67	C.C. Sabathia	.15
68	Richard Hidalgo	.15
69	Torii Hunter	.15
70	Jason Hart	.15
71	Bubba Trammell	.15
72	Jace Brewer	.15
73	Matt Williams	.15
74	Matt Stairs	.15
75	Omar Vizquel	.15
76	Daryle Ward	.15
77	Joe Mays	.15
78	Eric Chavez	.15

79	Andres Galarraga	.15
80	Rafael Palmeiro	.50
81	Steve Finley	.15
82	Eric Young	.15
83	Todd Helton	.65
84	Roy Oswalt	.25
85	Eric Milton	.15
86	Ramon Hernandez	.15
87	Jeff Kent	.15
88	Ivan Rodriguez	.50
89	Luis Gonzalez	.25
90	Corey Patterson	.15
91	Jose Ortiz	.15
92	Mike Sweeney	.15
93	Cristian Guzman	.15
94	Johnny Damon	.25
95	Barry Bonds	2.00
96	Rusty Greer	.15
97	Reggie Sanders	.15
98	Sammy Sosa	1.25
99	Jeff Cirillo	.15
100	Carlos Febles	.15
101	Jose Vidro	.15
102	Jermaine Dye	.15
103	Rich Aurilia	.15
104	Gabe Kapler	.15
105	Randy Johnson	.65
106	Rondell White	.15
107	Ben Petrick	.15
108	Joe Randa	.15
109	Fernando Tatis	.15
110	Tim Hudson	.25
111	John Olerud	.15
112	Alex Rodriguez	1.50
113	Curt Schilling	.40
114	Kerry Wood	.40
115	Alex Ochoa	.15
116	Carlos Beltran	.40
117	Vladimir Guerrero	.65
118	Mark Mulder	.15
119	Bret Boone	.15
120	Carlos Delgado	.35
121	Marcus Giles	.15
122	Paul Konerko	.15
123	Juan Pierre	.15
124	Mark Quinn	.15
125	Edgardo Alfonzo	.15
126	Barry Zito	.25
127	Dan Wilson	.15
128	Jose Cruz Jr.	.15
129	Chipper Jones	.75
130	Ray Durham	.15
131	Larry Walker	.15
132	Neifi Perez	.15
133	Robin Ventura	.15
134	Miguel Tejada	.25
135	Edgar Martinez	.15
136	Raul Mondesi	.15
137	Javy Lopez	.15
138	Jose Canseco	.25
139	Mike Hampton	.15
140	Eric Karros	.15
141	Mike Piazza	1.25
142	Travis Lee	.15
143	Ichiro Suzuki	1.25
144	Shannon Stewart	.15
145	Andruw Jones	.65
146	Frank Thomas	.65
147	Tony Clark	.15
148	Adrian Beltre	.25
149	Matt Lawton	.15
150	Marlon Anderson	.15
151	Freddy Garcia	.15
152	Brian Jordan	.15
153	Carlos Lee	.15
154	Eric Munson	.15
155	Paul LoDuca	.15
156	Jay Payton	.15
157	Scott Rolen	.50
158	Jamie Moyer	.15
159	Tom Glavine	.30
160	Magglio Ordonez	.15
161	Brandon Inge	.15
162	Shawn Green	.25
163	Tsuyoshi Shinjo	.15
164	Mike Lieberthal	.15
165	Kazuhiro Sasaki	.15
166	Greg Maddux	.75
167	Chris Singleton	.15
168	Juan Encarnacion	.15
169	Gary Sheffield	.25
170	Nick Johnson	.15
171	Bobby Abreu	.15
172	Aaron Boone	.15
173	Rafael Furcal	.15
174	Mark Buehrle	.15
175	Bobby Higginson	.15
176	Kevin Brown	.15
177	Tino Martinez	.15
178	Pat Burrell	.30
179	Fernando Vina	.15
180	Jay Gibbons	.15
181	Jose Valentin	.15
182	Derrek Lee	.15
183	Richie Sexson	.15
184	Alfonso Soriano	.50
185	Jimmy Rollins	.15
186	Albert Pujols	1.50
187	Brady Anderson	.15
188	Sean Casey	.25
189	Luis Castillo	.15
190	Jeromy Burnitz	.15
191	Jorge Posada	.25
192	Kevin Young	.15
193	Eli Marrero	.15
194	Shea Hillenbrand	.15
195	Adam Dunn	.40
196	Mike Lowell	.15

197	Jeffrey Hammonds	.15
198	David Justice	.15
199	Aramis Ramirez	.15
200	J.D. Drew	.25
201	Pedro Santana	.15
202	Endy Chavez	.15
203	Donnie Bridges	.15
204	Travis Phelps	.15
205	Drew Henson	.25
206	Angel Berroa	.15
207	George Perez	.15
208	Billy Sylvester	.15
209	Juan Cruz	.15
210	Horacio Ramirez	.15
211	J.J. Davis	.15
212	Cody Ransom	.15
213	Mark Teixeira	.50
214	Nate Frese	.15
215	Brian Rogers	.15
216	Dewon Brazelton	.15
217	Carlos Hernandez	.15
218	Juan Rivera	.15
219	Luis Lopez	.15
220	Benito Baez	.15
221	Bill Ortega	.15
222	Dustan Mohr	.15
223	Corky Miller	.15
224	Tyler Walker	.15
225	Rick Bauer	.15
226	Mark Prior	.50
227	Rafael Soriano	.15
228	Greg Miller	.15
229	Dave Williams	.15
230	Bert Snow	.15
231	Barry Bonds	1.50
232	Rickey Henderson	.50
233	Alex Rodriguez	1.25
234	Luis Gonzalez	.25
235	Derek Jeter	1.50
236	Bud Smith	.15
237	Sammy Sosa	.75
238	Jeff Bagwell	.50
239	Jim Thome	.15
240	Hideo Nomo	.50
241	Greg Maddux	.75
242	Ken Griffey Jr.	1.00
243	Curt Schilling	.25
244	Arizona Diamondbacks	.15
245	Ichiro Suzuki	.75
246	Albert Pujols	1.00
247	Ichiro Suzuki	.75
248	Barry Bonds	1.50
249	Roger Clemens	.65
250	Randy Johnson	.50
251	Todd Helton	.50
252	Rafael Palmeiro	.40
253	Mike Piazza	1.00
254	Alex Rodriguez	1.25
255	Manny Ramirez	.50
256	Ken Griffey Jr.	1.00
257	Jason Giambi	.40
258	Chipper Jones	.65
259	Larry Walker	.15
260	Sammy Sosa	.75
261	Vladimir Guerrero	.50
262	Nomar Garciaparra	.75
263	Randy Johnson	.50
264	Roger Clemens	.65
265	Ichiro Suzuki	1.00
266	Barry Bonds	1.50
267	Paul LoDuca	.15
268	Albert Pujols	1.00
269	Derek Jeter	1.50
270	Adam Dunn	.40

Batting Average Parallel

Stars:	4-8X
Numbered to 2001 batting avg.	

Home Run Parallel

Stars Print Run 50-75:	10-20X
Stars P/R 31-50:	15-25X
Stars P/R 21-30:	20-40X
Numbered to 2001 HR total.	

RBI Parallel

Stars Print Run 101-200:	4-8X
Stars P/R 76-100:	5-10X
Stars P/R 51-75:	6-12X
Stars P/R 25-50:	10-20X
Numbered to 2001 RBI total.	

Diamond Immortality

		NM/M
Complete Set (10):		25.00
Common Player:		1.00
Inserted 1:12		
1DI	Derek Jeter	5.00

2DI	Barry Bonds	5.00
3DI	Ricky Henderson	1.00
4DI	Roger Clemens	2.50
5DI	Alex Rodriguez	4.00
6DI	Albert Pujols	4.00
7DI	Nomar Garciaparra	3.00
8DI	Ichiro Suzuki	3.00
9DI	Chipper Jones	2.00
10DI	Ken Griffey Jr.	3.00

Diamond Immortality Game-Used

		NM/M
Inserted 1:129		
	Barry Bonds/Jsy	25.00
	Roger Clemens/Jsy	20.00
	Nomar Garciaparra/Jsy/SP	40.00
	Ricky Henderson/Bat	10.00
	Derek Jeter/Bat	25.00
	Chipper Jones/Bat	10.00
	Albert Pujols/Jsy	25.00
	Alex Rodriguez/Jsy	20.00

Home Run Kings

		NM/M
Complete Set (25):		100.00
Common Player:		2.00
Inserted 1:24		
1	Ted Williams	10.00
2	Todd Helton	4.00
3	Eddie Murray	2.00
4	Jeff Bagwell	4.00
5	Babe Ruth	15.00
6	Eddie Mathews	5.00
7	Alex Rodriguez	10.00
8	Juan Gonzalez	4.00
9	Chipper Jones	5.00
10	Luis Gonzalez	2.00
11	Johnny Bench	4.00
12	Frank Thomas	4.00
13	Ernie Banks	3.00
14	Jimmie Foxx	4.00
15	Ken Griffey Jr.	8.00
16	Rafael Palmeiro	3.00
17	Sammy Sosa	8.00
18	Reggie Jackson	4.00
19	Barry Bonds	10.00
20	Willie McCovey	2.00
21	Manny Ramirez	4.00
22	Larry Walker	2.00
23	Jason Giambi	4.00
24	Mike Piazza	8.00
25	Jose Canseco	2.00

Home Run Kings Autograph

		NM/M
Common Player:		
	Barry Bonds/73	300.00
	Alex Rodriguez/52	100.00

Home Run Kings Game-Used

		NM/M
Common Player:		5.00
Inserted 1:155		
	Jeff Bagwell/Jsy	10.00
	Johnny Bench/Bat/SP	10.00
	Barry Bonds/Jsy	25.00
	Jimmie Foxx/Bat	40.00
	Jason Giambi/Jsy	10.00
	Reggie Jackson/Bat	15.00
	Eddie Mathews/Bat	15.00
	Eddie Murray/Bat	10.00
	Rafael Palmeiro/Bat	10.00
	Mike Piazza/Jsy	15.00
	Manny Ramirez/Bat/SP	50.00

Todd Helton/Bat	10.00
Alex Rodriguez/Bat	15.00
Larry Walker/Bat	5.00
Ted Williams/Jsy	100.00

RBI Kings

		NM/M
Complete Set (15):		140.00
Common Player:		4.00
Inserted 1:144		
1	Sammy Sosa	15.00
2	Todd Helton	8.00
3	Albert Pujols	20.00
4	Manny Ramirez	8.00
5	Luis Gonzalez	4.00
6	Shawn Green	4.00
7	Barry Bonds	20.00
8	Ken Griffey Jr.	15.00
9	Alex Rodriguez	20.00
10	Jason Giambi	8.00
11	Jeff Bagwell	8.00
12	Vladimir Guerrero	8.00
13	Juan Gonzalez	8.00
14	Chipper Jones	8.00
15	Mike Piazza	15.00

RBI Kings Game-Used

		NM/M
Common Player:		5.00
Inserted 1:70		
	Jeff Bagwell/Jsy	10.00
	Barry Bonds/Jsy	25.00
	Jason Giambi/Jsy	15.00
	Luis Gonzalez/Bat	8.00
	Juan Gonzalez/Bat	8.00
	Shawn Green/Jsy	6.00
	Todd Helton/Jsy	8.00
	Mike Piazza/Jsy	15.00
	Albert Pujols/Bat/SP	70.00
	Manny Ramirez/Bat	8.00
	Alex Rodriguez/Shoe	25.00

Season Crowns

		NM/M
Complete Set (10):		25.00
Common Card:		2.00
Inserted 1:12		
1SC	Barry Bonds, Sammy Sosa, Larry Walker	4.00
2SC	Larry Walker, Nomar Garciaparra, Todd Helton	4.00
3SC	Sammy Sosa, Todd Helton, Manny Ramirez	4.00
4SC	Pedro J. Martinez, Derek Jeter, Cal Ripken Jr.	6.00
5SC	Jose Canseco, Barry Bonds, Alex Rodriguez	5.00
6SC	Barry Bonds, Jeff Kent, Chipper Jones	4.00
7SC	Ichiro Suzuki, Jason Giambi, Ivan Rodriguez	3.00
8SC	Curt Schilling, Tom Glavine, Pedro J. Martinez	2.00
9SC	Randy Johnson, Pedro J. Martinez, Greg Maddux	3.00
10SC	Randy Johnson, Curt Schilling, John Smoltz	2.00

Season Crowns Autograph

		NM/M
Jeter #'d to 160.		
	Derek Jeter/160	150.00
	Barry Bonds/77	250.00

Season Crowns Game-Used

		NM/M
Common Player:		5.00
Inserted 1:90		
	Barry Bonds/Jsy	25.00
	Sammy Sosa/Base	15.00
	Larry Walker/Bat	5.00
	Nomar Garciaparra/Jsy	20.00
	Todd Helton/Jsy	10.00
	Sammy Sosa/Base	15.00
	Todd Helton/Jsy	10.00
	Manny Ramirez/Jsy	10.00
	Pedro Martinez/Jsy	10.00
	Derek Jeter/Pants	25.00
	Cal Ripken Jr/Bat	60.00
	Jose Canseco/Bat	8.00
	Barry Bonds/Jsy	25.00
	Alex Rodriguez/Jsy	20.00
	Barry Bonds/Jsy	25.00
	Jeff Kent/Jsy	5.00

Ichiro Suzuki/Base	25.00
Jason Giambi/Jsy	10.00
Ivan Rodriguez/Jsy	10.00
Curt Schilling/Jsy	10.00
Tom Glavine/Jsy	10.00
Pedro Martinez/Jsy	10.00
Randy Johnson/Jsy	10.00
Pedro Martinez/Jsy	10.00
Greg Maddux/Jsy	15.00
Randy Johnson/Jsy	10.00
Curt Schilling/Jsy	10.00
John Smoltz/Jsy	5.00

Season Crowns Triple Swatch

		NM/M
Production 100 Sets		
	Barry Bonds, Sammy Sosa, Luis Gonzalez	100.00
	Larry Walker, Nomar Garciaparra, Todd Helton	40.00
	Sammy Sosa, Todd Helton, Manny Ramirez	50.00
	Barry Bonds, Jeff Kent, Chipper Jones	80.00
	Ichiro Suzuki, Jason Giambi, Ivan Rodriguez	80.00
	Curt Schilling, Tom Glavine, Pedro J. Martinez	50.00
	Randy Johnson, Pedro J. Martinez, Greg Maddux	50.00
	Randy Johnson, Curt Schilling, John Smoltz	50.00

2002 Fleer/Turn Two Foundation Derek Jeter

In conjunction with Jeter's charitable foundation, Fleer produced a three-card set that was given to youngsters entering an essay contest at after-school recreation centers in New York City. The 2-1/2" x 3-1/2" cards have pictures of Jeter on front and back and information about the contest and the foundation. Fleer reported production as 10,000 sets.

		NM/M
Complete Set (3):		13.50
Common Card:		5.00
1	Derek Jeter (Foundation's mission.)	5.00
2	Derek Jeter (W/firefighters.)	5.00
3	Derek Jeter (Stats)	5.00

2002 Fleer/Utz Yankees Starting Five

The starting rotation of the Yankees is featured on this stadium giveaway set sponsored by Utz snacks and produced by Fleer. The 3-1/2" x 2-1/2" horizontal cards have vignetted action photos. The player name is bracketed by the famed Yankee Stadium facade, with the set title in red at bottom. Backs have player biographical data, career highlights and recent stats, along with a serial number from within the edition of 25,000 sets given out to fans 14 and under on June 12. A cover card was included with the set. Autographed versions of the cards were produced for charitable purposes.

	NM/M
Complete Set (6):	7.50

#	Player	Price
	Common Player:	1.00
1	Roger Clemens	3.00
1	Roger Clemens/Auto.	100.00
2	David Wells	1.00
2	David Wells/Auto.	15.00
3	Mike Mussina	2.00
3	Mike Mussina/Auto.	15.00
4	Orlando Hernandez	1.00
4	Orlando Hernandez/Auto.	25.00
5	Andy Pettitte	1.00
5	Andy Pettitte/Auto.	15.00
--	Cover Card	.25

2003 Fleer Authentix

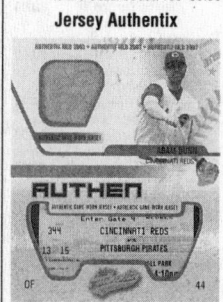

		NM/M
	Complete Set (160):	
	Common Player:	.25
	Common (111-125):	3.00
	Production 1,850	
	Common (126-160):	1.50
	Exclusive to home team boxes.	
	Pack (5):	3.00
	Box (24):	50.00
1	Derek Jeter	3.00
2	Tom Glavine	.40
3	Jason Jennings	.25
4	Craig Biggio	.25
5	Miguel Tejada	.40
6	Barry Bonds	3.00
7	Juan Gonzalez	1.00
8	Luis Gonzalez	.40
9	Johnny Damon	.40
10	Ellis Burks	.25
11	Frank Thomas	1.00
12	Richie Sexson	.25
13	Roger Clemens	1.50
14	Matt Morris	.25
15	Troy Glaus	1.00
16	Tony Batista	.25
17	Magglio Ordonez	.25
18	Jose Vidro	.25
19	Barry Zito	.40
20	Chipper Jones	1.50
21	Moises Alou	.25
22	Lance Berkman	.25
23	Jacque Jones	.25
24	Alfonso Soriano	.75
25	Sean Burroughs	.25
26	Scott Rolen	1.00
27	Mark Grace	.35
28	Manny Ramirez	1.00
29	Ken Griffey Jr.	2.00
30	Josh Beckett	.25
31	Kazuhisa Ishii	.25
32	Pat Burrell	1.00
33	Edgar Martinez	.25
34	Tim Salmon	.35
35	Raul Ibanez	.25
36	Vladimir Guerrero	1.00
37	Jermaine Dye	.25
38	Rich Aurilia	.25
39	Rafael Palmeiro	.75
40	Kerry Wood	.75
41	Omar Vizquel	.25
42	Fred McGriff	.25
43	Ben Sheets	.25
44	Bernie Williams	.40
45	Brian Giles	.25
46	Jim Edmonds	.25
47	Garret Anderson	.25
48	Pedro J. Martinez	1.00
49	Adam Dunn	.75
50	A.J. Burnett	.25
51	Eric Gagne	.25
52	Mo Vaughn	.25
53	Bobby Abreu	.25
54	Bret Boone	.25
55	Carlos Delgado	.40
56	Gary Sheffield	.40
57	Sammy Sosa	2.00
58	Jim Thome	.75
59	Jeff Bagwell	1.00
60	David Eckstein	.25
61	Jason Kendall	.25
62	Albert Pujols	2.50
63	Curt Schilling	.40
64	Nomar Garciaparra	2.00
65	Sean Casey	.35
66	Shawn Green	.40
67	Mike Piazza	2.00
68	Ichiro Suzuki	2.00
69	Eric Hinske	.25
70	Greg Maddux	1.50
71	Larry Walker	.25
72	Roy Oswalt	.40
73	Alex Rodriguez	2.50
74	Austin Kearns	.75
75	Cliff Floyd	.25
76	Kevin Brown	.25
77	Jason Giambi	.75
78	Jorge Julio	.25
79	Carlos Lee	.25
80	Mike Sweeney	.25
81	Edgardo Alfonzo	.25
82	Eric Chavez	.40
83	Andruw Jones	1.00
84	Mark Prior	.75
85	Todd Helton	1.00
86	Torii Hunter	.25
87	Ryan Klesko	.25
88	Aubrey Huff	.25
89	Randy Johnson	1.00
90	Barry Larkin	.25
91	Mike Lowell	.25
92	Jimmy Rollins	.40
93	Darin Erstad	.65
94	Jay Gibbons	.25
95	Paul Konerko	.40
96	Bobby Higginson	.25
97	Carlos Beltran	.60
98	Bartolo Colon	.25
99	Jeff Kent	.25
100	Ivan Rodriguez	.65
101	Joe Borchard	.25
102	Mark Teixeira	.50
103	Francisco Rodriguez	.25
104	Chris Snelling	.25
105	Hee Seop Choi	.25
106	Hank Blalock	.50
107	Marlon Byrd	.25
108	Michael Restovich	.25
109	Victor Martinez	.25
110	Lyle Overbay	.25
111	Brian Stokes RC	3.00
112	Josh Hall RC	3.00
113	Chris Waters RC	3.00
114	Lew Ford RC	3.00
115	Ian Ferguson RC	3.00
116	Josh Willingham RC	4.00
117	Josh Stewart RC	3.00
118	Pete LaForest RC	3.00
119	Jose Contreras RC	5.00
120	Termmel Sledge RC	3.00
121	Guillermo Quiroz RC	3.00
122	Alejandro Machado RC	3.00
123	Nook Logan RC	3.00
124	Rontrez Johnson RC	3.00
125	Hideki Matsui RC	10.00
126	Phil Rizzuto	3.00
127	Robin Ventura	1.50
128	Andy Pettitte	4.00
129	Mike Mussina	3.00
130	Mariano Rivera	3.00
131	Jeff Weaver	1.50
132	David Wells	1.50
133	Tommy Lasorda	2.00
134	Pee Wee Reese	3.00
135	Hideo Nomo	4.00
136	Adrian Beltre	2.00
137	Chin-Feng Chen	4.00
138	Odalis Perez	1.50
139	Dave Roberts	1.50
140	Bobby Doerr	3.00
141	Jason Varitek	1.50
142	Trot Nixon	1.50
143	Tim Wakefield	1.50
144	John Burkett	1.50
145	Jeremy Giambi	1.50
146	Casey Fossum	1.50
147	Phil Niekro	1.50
148	Warren Spahn	4.00
149	Rafael Furcal	2.00
150	Vinny Castilla	1.50
151	Javy Lopez	1.50
152	Jason Marquis	1.50
153	Mike Hampton	1.50
154	Gaylord Perry	1.50
155	Ruben Sierra	1.50
156	Mike Cameron	1.50
157	Freddy Garcia	1.50
158	Joel Pineiro	1.50
159	Jamie Moyer	1.50
160	Carlos Guillen	1.50

Balcony

Stars (1-110):		3-6X
SP's (111-125):		.5-1.5X
Production 250 Sets		
Club Box (1-110):		5-10X
SP's (111-125):		.75-2X
Production 100 Sets		
Standing Room Only:		No Pricing
Production 25 Sets		

Autographed Authentix

NM/M
Quantity produced listed

DJ	Derek Jeter/50	150.00
DJ	Derek Jeter/150	125.00
DJ	Derek Jeter/250	125.00
BB	Barry Bonds/50	200.00
BB	Barry Bonds/150	200.00
BB	Barry Bonds/250	200.00

Autographed Jersey Authentix

NM/M
Quantity produced listed

DJ	Derek Jeter/100	150.00
DJ	Derek Jeter/200	150.00
DJ	Derek Jeter/300	125.00
NR	Nolan Ryan/100	185.00
NR	Nolan Ryan/200	150.00
NR	Nolan Ryan/300	125.00

Ballpark Classics

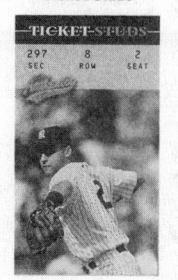

		NM/M
	Complete Set (10):	25.00
	Common Player:	1.50
	Inserted 1:12	
1	Derek Jeter	6.00
2	Randy Johnson	2.00
3	Nomar Garciaparra	4.00
4	Barry Bonds	6.00
5	Alfonso Soriano	2.00
6	Alex Rodriguez	5.00
7	Jim Thome	1.50
8	Chipper Jones	3.00
9	Mike Piazza	4.00
10	Ichiro Suzuki	4.00

Bat Authentix

		NM/M
	Common Player:	8.00
	Inserted 1:78	
	Unripped:	1.5-3X
	Production 50 Sets	
AD	Adam Dunn	8.00
NG	Nomar Garciaparra	15.00
JG	Jason Giambi	15.00
VG	Vladimir Guerrero	10.00
DJ	Derek Jeter	30.00
CJ	Chipper Jones	10.00
MR	Manny Ramirez	10.00
SS	Sammy Sosa	15.00
JT	Jim Thome	15.00

Hometown Heroes Memorabilia

		NM/M
	Common Player:	8.00
	Home Team Box Exclusive	
BB	Bret Boone/Jsy/200	8.00
KB	Kevin Brown/Jsy/150	10.00
CC	Chin-Feng Chen/Jsy/150	35.00
RC	Roger Clemens	25.00
JD	Johnny Damon/Jsy/100	8.00
FG	Freddy Garcia/Jsy/200	8.00
NG	Nomar Garciaparra	15.00
JG	Jason Giambi/Bat/300	20.00
SG	Shawn Green/Jsy/100	8.00
KI	Kazuhisa Ishii/Jsy/100	8.00
DJ	Derek Jeter	40.00
AJ	Andruw Jones/Jsy/150	10.00
CJ	Chipper Jones	15.00
GM	Greg Maddux/Jsy	15.00
EM	Edgar Martinez/Jsy/200	10.00
PM	Pedro Martinez/Jsy/100	15.00
MR	Manny Ramirez	10.00
GS	Gary Sheffield/Jsy/100	8.00
AS	Alfonso Soriano	15.00
I	Ichiro Suzuki/Base/100	30.00

Jersey Authentix

		NM/M
	Common Player:	5.00
	Inserted 1:10	
	Unripped:	1.5-3X
	Production 50 Sets	
JB	Jeff Bagwell	8.00
JB2	Josh Beckett	5.00
LB	Lance Berkman	5.00
MB	Mark Buehrle	5.00
PB	Pat Burrell	10.00
SB	Sean Burroughs	5.00
RC	Roger Clemens	15.00
CD	Carlos Delgado	5.00
AD	Adam Dunn	8.00
NG	Nomar Garciaparra	15.00
VG	Vladimir Guerrero	8.00
EH	Eric Hinske	5.00
TH	Torii Hunter	6.00
DJ	Derek Jeter	25.00
RJ	Randy Johnson	8.00
CJ	Chipper Jones	8.00
GM	Greg Maddux	15.00
MP	Mike Piazza	12.00
MR	Manny Ramirez	8.00
AR	Alex Rodriguez	12.00
AS	Alfonso Soriano	10.00
SS	Sammy Sosa	12.00
MT	Miguel Tejada	5.00
KW	Kerry Wood	8.00

Jersey Authentix Game of the Week

		NM/M
Common Card:		10.00
Inserted 1:240		
Unripped:		1.5-3X
Production 50 Sets		
Derek Jeter, Nomar Garciaparra		45.00
Mike Piazza, Sammy Sosa		25.00
Chipper Jones, Pat Burrell		20.00
Greg Maddux, Randy Johnson		20.00
Alex Rodriguez, Miguel Tejada		20.00
Adam Dunn, Lance Berkman		10.00
Torii Hunter, Alfonso Soriano		15.00
Derek Jeter, Miguel Tejada		25.00
Eric Hinske, Torii Hunter		10.00
Alfonso Soriano, Sammy Sosa		15.00

Ticket Studs

		NM/M
	Complete Set (15):	25.00
	Common Player:	1.00
	Inserted 1:6	
1TS	Curt Schilling	1.00
2TS	Greg Maddux	2.50
3TS	Torii Hunter	1.00
4TS	Mike Piazza	3.00
5TS	Pedro J. Martinez	2.00
6TS	Nomar Garciaparra	3.00
7TS	Derek Jeter	5.00
8TS	Alex Rodriguez	4.00
9TS	Alfonso Soriano	2.00
10TS	Pat Burrell	1.00
11TS	Barry Bonds	5.00
12TS	Jason Giambi	2.00
13TS	Sammy Sosa	2.50
14TS	Vladimir Guerrero	1.50
15TS	Ichiro Suzuki	3.00

2003 Fleer Avant Sample

No Pricing

2003 Fleer Avant

	NM/M
Complete Set (90):	240.00
Common Player:	.50
Common Retired SP (66-75):	5.00
Production 799	
Common Rk (76-90):	3.00
Production 699	

Pack (4):		4.00
Box (18):		60.00
1	Adam Dunn	.50
2	Barry Zito	.50
3	Preston Wilson	.50
4	Barry Bonds	4.00
5	Hank Blalock	1.00
6	Omar Vizquel	.50
7	Brian Giles	.50
8	Kerry Wood	.75
9	Miguel Tejada	.75
10	Magglio Ordonez	.50
11	Randy Johnson	1.00
12	Jeff Bagwell	1.00
13	Pat Burrell	.50
14	Jason Giambi	.75
15	Mark Prior	.75
16	Roger Clemens	2.00
17	Sammy Sosa	2.50
18	Jay Gibbons	.50
19	Torii Hunter	.50
20	Ichiro Suzuki	2.00
21	Derek Jeter	4.00
22	Tom Glavine	.50
23	Alfonso Soriano	1.00
24	Manny Ramirez	1.00
25	Frank Thomas	1.00
26	Carlos Pena	.50
27	Alex Rodriguez	3.00
28	Edgar Martinez	.50
29	Larry Walker	.50
30	Rafael Palmeiro	.75
31	Mike Piazza	2.00
32	Nomar Garciaparra	2.50
33	Lance Berkman	.50
34	Vladimir Guerrero	1.00
35	Troy Glaus	.75
36	Ivan Rodriguez	.75
37	Mark Mulder	.50
38	Curt Schilling	.75
39	Mike Sweeney	.50
40	Albert Pujols	3.00
41	Tim Hudson	.50
42	Greg Maddux	1.50
43	Shawn Green	.50
44	Scott Rolen	1.00
45	Gary Sheffield	.75
46	Richie Sexson	.75
47	Aubrey Huff	.50
48	Luis Gonzalez	.50
49	Todd Helton	1.00
50	Xavier Nady	.50
51	Juan Gonzalez	1.00
52	Pedro J. Martinez	1.00
53	Garret Anderson	.50
54	Craig Biggio	.50
55	Bret Boone	.50
56	Ken Griffey Jr.	2.00
57	Kevin Millwood	.50
58	Carlos Delgado	.75
59	Chipper Jones	1.50
60	Hideo Nomo	.50
61	Jim Edmonds	.50
62	Austin Kearns	.75
63	Jim Thome	1.00
64	Vernon Wells	.50
65	Mike Lowell	.50
66	Whitey Ford	5.00
67	Bob Gibson	5.00
68	Reggie Jackson	6.00
69	Willie McCovey	5.00
70	Phil Rizzuto	5.00
71	Al Kaline	6.00
72	Brooks Robinson	5.00
73	Nolan Ryan	15.00
74	Mike Schmidt	10.00
75	Tom Seaver	6.00
76	Hideki Matsui RC	15.00
77	Rocco Baldelli	8.00
78	Jose Contreras RC	6.00
79	Hee Seop Choi	3.00
80	Jeremy Bonderman	6.00
81	Bo Hart RC	5.00
82	Brandon Webb RC	10.00
83	Ron Calloway	3.00
84	Jesse Foppert	3.00
85	Kyle Snyder	3.00
86	Mark Teixeira	5.00
87	Jose Reyes	5.00
88	Dontrelle Willis	4.00
89	Reed Johnson	3.00
90	Rickie Weeks RC	8.00

Black/White

	NM/M
Stars (1-65):	4-6X
SP's (66-90):	1-2X
Production 199 Sets	

Autographs

		NM/M
Common Autograph:		10.00
Varying quantities produced.		
Parallel SP's:		1-1.5X
Production 75 or 150		
DJ	Derek Jeter/75	140.00
MR	Manny Ramirez/100	35.00
VW	Vernon Wells/250	10.00
HB	Hank Blalock/150	25.00
DW	Dontrelle Willis/300	30.00
AK	Al Kaline/200	35.00
BR	Brooks Robinson/300	20.00
BG	Bob Gibson/250	25.00
JR	Jose Reyes/300	25.00
BZ	Barry Zito/150	20.00
EM	Edgar Martinez/246	25.00
BH	Bo Hart/300	15.00
AH	Aubrey Huff/300	15.00
CP	Carlos Pena/150	15.00
MT	Miguel Tejada/150	20.00
ML	Mike Lowell/150	15.00
CB	Craig Biggio/250	15.00
BW	Brandon Webb/300	40.00
RB	Rocco Baldelli/250	30.00

Candid Collection

		NM/M
	Complete Set (15):	50.00
	Common Player:	2.00
	Production 500 Sets	
1CC	Derek Jeter	6.00
2CC	Mike Piazza	4.00
3CC	Albert Pujols	6.00
4CC	Randy Johnson	3.00
5CC	Alex Rodriguez	6.00
6CC	Vladimir Guerrero	3.00
7CC	Troy Glaus	2.00
8CC	Ichiro Suzuki	5.00
9CC	Barry Zito	2.00
10CC	Jim Thome	3.00
11CC	Sammy Sosa	5.00
12CC	Greg Maddux	5.00
13CC	Barry Bonds	8.00
14CC	Jason Giambi	3.00
15CC	Nomar Garciaparra	6.00

Candid Collection Memorabilia

	NM/M
Common Player:	
Production 150 Sets	
Derek Jeter	30.00
Mike Piazza	12.00
Randy Johnson	8.00
Alex Rodriguez	15.00
Barry Zito	8.00
Jim Thome	15.00
Sammy Sosa	15.00
Greg Maddux	15.00
Jason Giambi	10.00
Nomar Garciaparra	15.00

Hall of Fame

		NM/M
	Complete Set (14):	80.00
	Common Player:	6.00
	Production 299 Sets	
1	Richie Ashburn	6.00
2	Rod Carew	8.00
3	Whitey Ford	8.00
4	Bob Gibson	8.00
5	Reggie Jackson	8.00
6	Harmon Killebrew	6.00
7	Willie McCovey	6.00
8	Phil Rizzuto	8.00
9	Al Kaline	10.00
10	Brooks Robinson	8.00
11	Nolan Ryan	15.00
12	Mike Schmidt	10.00
13	Tom Seaver	8.00
14	Warren Spahn	8.00

Hall of Fame Memorabilia

	NM/M
Production 99 Sets	
Reggie Jackson	25.00
Willie McCovey	20.00
Al Kaline	35.00
Nolan Ryan	65.00
Mike Schmidt	40.00

Material

		NM/M
	Common Player:	
	Production 50 Sets	
RB	Rocco Baldelli	25.00
AR	Alex Rodriguez	25.00
AS	Alfonso Soriano	20.00
SS	Sammy Sosa	20.00
NG	Nomar Garciaparra	20.00
MT	Miguel Tejada	10.00
CJ	Chipper Jones	20.00
RJ	Randy Johnson	15.00
JT	Jim Thome	15.00
GM	Greg Maddux	25.00

JG Jason Giambi 15.00
VG Vladimir Guerrero 15.00

On Display

Complete Set (10): 50.00
Common Player: 3.00
Production 399 Sets
10D Derek Jeter 6.00
20D Barry Bonds 8.00
30D Rocco Baldelli 5.00
40D Alex Rodriguez 6.00
50D Alfonso Soriano 4.00
60D Sammy Sosa 6.00
70D Nomar Garciaparra 6.00
80D Hideki Matsui 20.00
90D Miguel Tejada 3.00
100D Chipper Jones 5.00

On Display Memorabilia

NM/M
Common Player: 5.00
Production 250 Sets
Derek Jeter 20.00
Barry Bonds 15.00
Rocco Baldelli 25.00
Alex Rodriguez 10.00
Alfonso Soriano 10.00
Sammy Sosa 12.00
Nomar Garciaparra 15.00
Hideki Matsui 40.00
Miguel Tejada 5.00
Chipper Jones 10.00

2003 Fleer Box Score

NM/M
Complete Set (245):
Common Player: .15
Common Box Score Debut (101-110): 4.00
Production 599
Common Rookie (111-125): 1.00
Inserted 1:6
Complete Rising Stars (30): 25.00
Common (126-155): 1.00
Complete All-Stars (30): 20.00
Common (156-185): .50
Comp. Intl. Road Trip (30): 20.00
Common (186-215): .50
Comp. Bronx Bombers (30): 30.00
Common (216-245): .50
Pack (7): 3.00
Box (18 + 1 Supplemental Box): 40.00
1 Troy Glaus .75
2 Derek Jeter 3.00
3 Alex Rodriguez 2.50
4 Barry Zito .40
5 Darin Erstad .60
6 Tim Hudson .40
7 Josh Beckett .15
8 Adam Dunn .60
9 Tim Salmon .25
10 Ivan Rodriguez .50
11 Mark Buehrle .15
12 Sammy Sosa 2.00
13 Vicente Padilla .15
14 Randy Johnson 1.00
15 Lance Berkman .15
16 Jim Thome .15
17 Luis Gonzalez .25
18 Craig Biggio .15
19 Cliff Floyd .15
20 Pat Burrell .50
21 Matt Morris .15
22 Torii Hunter .15
23 Curt Schilling .40
24 Paul Konerko .15
25 Jeff Bagwell .75
26 Mike Piazza 2.00
27 A.J. Burnett .15
28 Jimmy Rollins .25
29 Greg Maddux 1.50
30 Jeff Kent .15
31 Bobby Abreu .15
32 Chipper Jones 1.50
33 Mike Sweeney .15
34 Jason Kendall .15
35 Gary Sheffield .30
36 Carlos Beltran .50
37 Brian Giles .15
38 Jim Edmonds .15
39 Roger Clemens 1.75
40 Andruw Jones .75
41 Paul LoDuca .15
42 Ryan Klesko .15
43 Jay Gibbons .15
44 Shawn Green .40
45 Sean Burroughs .15
46 Magglio Ordonez .15
47 Tony Batista .15
48 J.D. Drew .45
49 Hideo Nomo .50
50 Edgardo Alfonzo .15
51 Nomar Garciaparra 2.00
52 Frank Thomas .75
53 Kazuhisa Ishii .15
54 Rich Aurilia .15
55 Shea Hillenbrand .15
56 Tom Glavine .40
57 Richie Sexson .15
58 Mo Vaughn .15
59 Barry Bonds 3.00
60 Carlos Delgado .50
61 Pedro J. Martinez 1.00
62 Jacque Jones .15
63 Edgar Martinez .15
64 Manny Ramirez .75
65 Bret Boone .15
66 Kerry Wood .50
67 Roy Oswalt .40
68 Cristian Guzman .15
69 Moises Alou .15
70 Bartolo Colon .15
71 Ichiro Suzuki 1.50
72 Jose Vidro .15
73 Scott Rolen .75
74 Mark Prior 1.00
75 Vladimir Guerrero .75
76 Albert Pujols 1.50
77 Aubrey Huff .15
78 Ken Griffey Jr. 2.00
79 Roberto Alomar .15
80 Ben Grieve .15
81 Miguel Tejada .40
82 Austin Kearns .50
83 Jason Giambi .75
84 John Olerud .15
85 Omar Vizquel .15
86 Juan Gonzalez .75
87 Larry Walker .15
88 Jorge Posada .25
89 Rafael Palmeiro .65
90 Todd Helton .75
91 Bernie Williams .30
92 Garret Anderson .15
93 Eric Hinske .15
94 Mike Lowell .15
95 Jason Jennings .15
96 Eric Chavez .30
97 Alfonso Soriano 1.00
98 David Eckstein .15
99 Bobby Higginson .15
100 Roy Halladay .15
101 Robby Hammock RC 4.00
102 Hideki Matsui RC 12.00
103 Chase Utley 4.00
104 Oscar Villarreal RC 4.00
105 Jose Contreras RC 8.00
106 Rocco Baldelli 4.00
107 Rontrez Johnson RC 4.00
108 Jeremy Bonderman 6.00
109 Shane Victorino RC 4.00
110 Ron Calloway 4.00
111 Brandon Webb RC 8.00
112 Guillermo Quiroz RC 4.00
113 Clint Barmes RC 2.00
114 Pete LaForest RC 1.00
115 Craig Brazell RC 2.00
116 Todd Wellemeyer RC 1.00
117 Bernie Castro RC 1.00
118 Alejandro Machado RC 1.50
119 Termel Sledge RC 1.00
120 Ian Ferguson RC 1.00
121 Lew Ford RC 3.00
122 Nook Logan RC 1.50
123 Mike Nicolas RC 1.00
124 Jeff Duncan RC 1.50
125 Tim Olson RC 1.00
126 Michael Hessman RC 1.00
127 Francisco Rosario RC 1.00
128 Felix Sanchez RC 1.00
129 Andrew Brown RC 1.50
130 Matt Bruback RC 2.00
131 Diegomar Markwell RC 2.00
132 Josh Willingham RC 1.50
133 Wes Obermueller RC 1.50
134 Phil Seibel RC 2.00
135 Arnie Munoz RC 1.00
136 Matt Kata RC 3.00
137 Joe Valentine RC 1.00
138 Ricardo Rodriguez RC 1.00
139 Lyle Overbay RC 2.00
140 Brian Stokes RC 1.00
141 Josh Hall RC 1.00
142 Kevin Hooper RC 1.00
143 Chien-Ming Wang RC 10.00
144 Prentice Redman RC 1.00
145 Chris Waters RC 1.50
146 Jon Leicester RC 1.00
147 Daniel Cabrera RC 3.00
148 Alfredo Gonzalez RC 1.50
149 Doug Waechter RC 1.50
150 Brandon Larson 1.00
151 Beau Kemp RC 1.50
152 Cory Stewart RC 1.00
153 Francisco Rodriguez 1.00
154 Hee Seop Choi 1.50
155 Mike Neu RC 1.00
156 Derek Jeter 3.00
157 Alex Rodriguez 2.50
158 Nomar Garciaparra 2.00
159 Barry Bonds 2.50
160 Sammy Sosa 1.50
161 Vladimir Guerrero .75
162 Roger Clemens 2.00
163 Randy Johnson 1.00
164 Greg Maddux 1.50
165 Ken Griffey Jr. 1.50
166 Mike Piazza 2.00
167 Ichiro Suzuki .75
168 Barry Larkin .50
169 Lance Berkman .50
170 Jim Thome .75
171 Jason Giambi 1.00
172 Gary Sheffield .50
173 Ivan Rodriguez .50
174 Miguel Tejada .50
175 Manny Ramirez .75
176 Mike Sweeney .50
177 Larry Walker .50
178 Jeff Bagwell .75
179 Chipper Jones 1.50
180 Craig Biggio .50
181 Curt Schilling .50
182 Pedro J. Martinez 1.00
183 Roberto Alomar .50
184 Bernie Williams .50
185 Magglio Ordonez .50
186 Jose Contreras 1.00
187 Rafael Palmeiro 1.00
188 Andruw Jones .50
189 Bartolo Colon .50
190 Vladimir Guerrero .75
191 Pedro Martinez .50
192 Albert Pujols 1.50
193 Manny Ramirez .75
194 Felix Rodriguez .50
195 Alfonso Soriano .50
196 Sammy Sosa 1.50
197 Miguel Tejada .50
198 Kazuhisa Ishii .50
199 Hideki Matsui 5.00
200 Hideo Nomo 1.00
201 Tomokazu Ohka .50
202 Kazuhiro Sasaki .50
203 Tsuyoshi Shinjo .50
204 Ichiro Suzuki 1.50
205 Vicente Padilla .50
206 Carlos Beltran .50
207 Jose Cruz Jr. .50
208 Carlos Delgado .50
209 Juan Gonzalez .75
210 Jorge Posada .50
211 Ivan Rodriguez .50
212 Hee Seop Choi .50
213 Bobby Abreu .50
214 Magglio Ordonez .50
215 Francisco Rodriguez .50
216 Juan Acevedo .50
217 Erick Almonte .50
218 Yogi Berra 1.50
219 Brandon Claussen 1.00
220 Roger Clemens 2.00
221 Jose Contreras 1.00
222 Whitey Ford 1.00
223 Jason Giambi 1.00
224 Michel Hernandez RC .50
225 Sterling Hitchcock .50
226 Jim "Catfish" Hunter .75
227 Reggie Jackson 1.50
228 Derek Jeter 3.00
229 Nick Johnson .50
230 Nick Johnson .50
231 Hideki Matsui .50
232 Raul Mondesi .50
233 Mike Mussina .75
234 Andy Pettitte
235 Jorge Posada .50
236 Mariano Rivera .50
237 Phil Rizzuto 1.00
238 Enos Slaughter 1.00
239 Alfonso Soriano 1.00
240 Robin Ventura .50
241 Chien-Ming Wang 2.00
242 Jeff Weaver .50
243 David Wells .50
244 Bernie Williams .50
245 Todd Zeile .50

First Edition

Stars (1-100): 4-8X
Rookies (101-125): 1.5-3X
Production 150 Sets

All-Star Lineup

NM/M
Common Card: 15.00
Inserted 1:All-Stars Set
Derek Jeter, Alex Rodriguez, Nomar Garciaparra, Barry Bonds, Sammy Sosa, Vladimir Guerrero 35.00
Vladimir Guerrero 15.00
Roger Clemens, Randy Johnson, Greg Maddux 30.00
Jason Giambi, Alfonso Soriano, Derek Jeter 30.00
Craig Biggio, Jeff Bagwell, Lance Berkman 20.00
Chipper Jones, Gary Sheffield, Greg Maddux 30.00
Ivan Rodriguez, Mike Piazza, Randy Johnson, Roger Clemens 40.00
Roberto Alomar, Mike Piazza, Alfonso Soriano, Jason Giambi 45.00
Jim Thome, Roberto Alomar, Alex Rodriguez, Nomar Garciaparra 40.00

Bat Rack

NM/M
Common Card: 20.00
Production 250 Sets
Derek Jeter, Alfonso Soriano, Jason Giambi, Scott Rolen, Miguel Tejada, Troy Glaus, Jim Thome, Torii Hunter, Mike Piazza 25.00
Troy Glaus, Nomar Garciaparra, Alfonso Soriano, Lance Berkman, Vladimir Guerrero, Sammy Sosa 20.00
Chipper Jones, Lance Berkman, Vladimir Guerrero 20.00
Torii Hunter, Jason Giambi, Nomar Garciaparra 25.00
Derek Jeter, Miguel Tejada, Alex Rodriguez 25.00
Scott Rolen, Sammy Sosa, Alex Rodriguez 25.00

Bat Rack Quad

NM/M
Production 50 Sets
Derek Jeter, Torii Hunter, Troy Glaus, Miguel Tejada 40.00
Derek Jeter, Mike Piazza, Nomar Garciaparra, Chipper Jones 60.00
Alex Rodriguez, Jim Thome, Sammy Sosa, Barry Bonds 50.00

Bronx Bombers Jersey

NM/M
Common Player: 4.00
Inserted 1:Bronx Bombers Set
Roger Clemens 15.00
Jason Giambi 12.00
Derek Jeter 20.00
Nick Johnson 4.00
Mike Mussina 10.00
Jorge Posada 8.00
Alfonso Soriano 10.00
Robin Ventura 5.00
Bernie Williams 8.00

Classic Minatures

NM/M
Complete Set (30): 10.00
Common Player: .25
1CM Jim Thome .40
2CM Jason Giambi .50
3CM Miguel Tejada .25

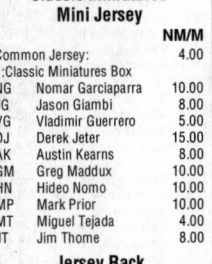

4CM Alfonso Soriano 1.00
5CM Ivan Rodriguez .40
6CM Troy Glaus .40
7CM Barry Bonds 1.00
8CM Barry Bonds 1.50
9CM Sammy Sosa 1.00
10CM Lance Berkman .25
11CM Pat Burrell .25
12CM Chipper Jones .75
13CM Shawn Green .25
14CM Manny Ramirez .50
15CM Ichiro Suzuki .50
16CM Vladimir Guerrero .50
17CM Albert Pujols .75
18CM Ken Griffey Jr. 1.00
19CM Bernie Williams .40
20CM Austin Kearns .40
21CM Randy Johnson .50
22CM Greg Maddux .75
23CM Roger Clemens 1.00
24CM Hideo Nomo .25
25CM Pedro J. Martinez .40
26CM Kerry Wood .40
27CM Mark Prior .25
28CM Derek Jeter 1.50
29CM Alex Rodriguez 1.00
30CM Nomar Garciaparra 1.00

Classic Miniatures Mini Jersey

NM/M
Common Jersey: 4.00
1:Classic Miniatures Box
NG Nomar Garciaparra 10.00
JG Jason Giambi 8.00
VG Vladimir Guerrero 5.00
DJ Derek Jeter 15.00
AK Austin Kearns 8.00
GM Greg Maddux 10.00
HN Hideo Nomo 10.00
MP Mark Prior 10.00
MT Miguel Tejada 4.00
JT Jim Thome 8.00

Jersey Rack

NM/M
Common Card: 15.00
Production 350 Sets
Derek Jeter, Alfonso Soriano, Jason Giambi 40.00
Curt Schilling, Randy Johnson, Greg Maddux 25.00
Roger Clemens, Pedro J. Martinez, Barry Zito 30.00
Alex Rodriguez, Vladimir Guerrero, Sammy Sosa 25.00
Derek Jeter, Nomar Garciaparra, Alex Rodriguez 30.00
Lance Berkman, Sammy Sosa, Torii Hunter 20.00
Vladimir Guerrero, Jim Thome, Alex Rodriguez 20.00
Derek Jeter, Miguel Tejada, Nomar Garciaparra 30.00
Alfonso Soriano, Eric Chavez, Jim Thome 20.00
Miguel Tejada, Eric Chavez, Barry Zito 15.00

Jersey Rack Quad

NM/M
Common Card:
Production 150 Sets
Derek Jeter, Alex Rodriguez, Nomar Garciaparra, Miguel Tejada 60.00
Jim Thome, Jason Giambi, Sammy Sosa, Vladimir Guerrero 50.00
Randy Johnson, Greg Maddux, Roger Clemens, Pedro J. Martinez 60.00
Curt Schilling, Vladimir Guerrero, Randy Johnson, Alex Rodriguez 40.00
Alfonso Soriano, Jim Thome, Sammy Sosa, Eric Chavez 40.00
Eric Chavez, Miguel Tejada, Barry Zito, Nomar Garciaparra 20.00

Press Clippings

NM/M
Complete Set (20): 40.00
Common Player: 1.00
Inserted 1:18
1PC Derek Jeter 6.00
2PC Nomar Garciaparra 5.00
3PC Miguel Tejada 5.00
4PC Barry Bonds 5.00
5PC Alex Rodriguez 5.00
6PC Sammy Sosa 3.00
7PC Lance Berkman 1.00
8PC Torii Hunter 1.50
9PC Troy Glaus 1.50
10PC Eric Chavez 1.00
11PC Tim Hudson 1.00
12PC Randy Johnson 2.00
13PC Mike Piazza 4.00
14PC Roberto Alomar 1.50
15PC Jim Thome 1.50
16PC Alfonso Soriano 3.00
17PC Roger Clemens 4.00
18PC Pedro J. Martinez 2.00
19PC Mark Prior 1.50
20PC Curt Schilling 1.00

Press Clippings Game-Used

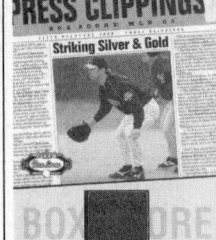

NM/M
Common Player: 4.00
Inserted 1:12
Derek Jeter 15.00
Nomar Garciaparra 15.00
Miguel Tejada 4.00
Alex Rodriguez 10.00
Sammy Sosa 12.00
Lance Berkman 4.00
Torii Hunter 6.00
Troy Glaus 5.00
Eric Chavez 4.00
Tim Hudson 4.00
Randy Johnson 8.00
Mike Piazza 12.00
Roberto Alomar 8.00
Jim Thome 10.00
Alfonso Soriano 10.00
Roger Clemens 12.00
Pedro J. Martinez 8.00
Mark Prior 8.00
Curt Schilling 8.00

Press Clippings Dual

NM/M
Complete Set (10): 35.00
Common Player: 2.00
Production 250 Sets
1 Derek Jeter, Nomar Garciaparra 8.00
2 Miguel Tejada, Barry Bonds 6.00
3 Alex Rodriguez, Sammy Sosa 6.00
4 Lance Berkman, Torii Hunter 2.00
5 Troy Glaus, Eric Chavez 2.00
6 Tim Hudson, Randy Johnson 3.00
7 Mike Piazza, Roberto Alomar 5.00
8 Jim Thome, Alfonso Soriano 4.00
9 Roger Clemens, Pedro J. Martinez 5.00
10 Mark Prior, Curt Schilling 5.00

FPress Clippings Dual Patch

	NM/M
Common Card:	25.00
Derek Jeter, Nomar Garciaparra/100	60.00
Miguel Tejada, Troy Glaus/150	25.00
Alex Rodriguez, Sammy Sosa/150	80.00
Lance Berkman, Torii Hunter/150	30.00
Troy Glaus, Eric Chavez/150	30.00
Tim Hudson, Randy Johnson/150	30.00
Mike Piazza, Roberto Alomar/150	40.00
Jim Thome, Alfonso Soriano/100	40.00
Roger Clemens, Pedro Martinez/100	50.00
Mark Prior, Curt Schilling/150	25.00

Wave of the Future

	NM/M
Common Player:	4.00
Inserted 1:Rising Stars Set	
Jeremy Bonderman/Bat	12.00
Ron Calloway/Jsy	4.00
Hee Seop Choi/Jsy	10.00
Brandon Larson/Bat	8.00
Lyle Overbay/Bat	4.00
Francisco Rodriguez/Jsy	6.00
Chase Utley/Jsy	6.00

World Piece

	NM/M
Common Player:	4.00
Inserted 1:Intl. Road Trip Set	
Vladimir Guerrero	6.00
Pedro Martinez	10.00
Sammy Sosa	12.00
Miguel Tejada	4.00
Hideo Nomo	10.00
Jose Cruz Jr.	4.00
Ivan Rodriguez	6.00
Hee Seop Choi	10.00
Francisco Rodriguez	4.00
Kazuhiro Sasaki	4.00

2003 Fleer Double Header

	NM/M
Complete Set (300):	60.00
Common Player:	.20
Common (181-300):	.40
Pack (8):	2.00
Box (20):	35.00
1 Ramon Vazquez	.20
2 Derek Jeter	2.00
3 Orlando Hudson	.20
4 Miguel Tejada	.30
5 Steve Finley	.20
6 Brad Wilkerson	.20
7 Craig Biggio	.20
8 Marlon Anderson	.20
9 Phil Nevin	.20
10 Hideo Nomo	.50
11 Barry Larkin	.20
12 Alfonso Soriano	.75
13 Rodrigo Lopez	.20
14 Paul Konerko	.25
15 Carlos Beltran	.50
16 Garret Anderson	.20
17 Kazuhisa Ishii	.20
18 Eddie Guardado	.20
19 Juan Gonzalez	.50
20 Mark Mulder	.20
21 Sammy Sosa	1.25
22 Kazuhiro Sasaki	.20
23 Jose Cruz Jr.	.20
24 Tomokazu Ohka	.20
25 Barry Bonds	2.00
26 Carlos Delgado	.50
27 Scott Rolen	.50
28 Steve Cox	.20
29 Mike Sweeney	.20

30 Ryan Klesko	.20
31 Greg Maddux	1.00
32 Derek Lowe	.20
33 David Wells	.20
34 Kerry Wood	.40
35 Randall Simon	.20
36 Ben Howard	.20
37 Jeff Suppan	.20
38 Curt Schilling	.40
39 Eric Gagne	.20
40 Raul Mondesi	.20
41 Jeffrey Hammonds	.20
42 Mo Vaughn	.20
43 Sidney Ponson	.20
44 Adam Dunn	.50
45 Pedro J. Martinez	.75
46 Jason Simontacchi	.20
47 Tom Glavine	.40
48 Torii Hunter	.20
49 Gabe Kapler	.20
50 Andy Van Hekken	.20
51 Ichiro Suzuki	1.25
52 Andruw Jones	.50
53 Bobby Abreu	.20
54 Junior Spivey	.20
55 Ray Durham	.20
56 Mark Buehrle	.20
57 Drew Henson	.20
58 Brandon Duckworth	.20
59 Robert Mackowiak	.20
60 Josh Beckett	.20
61 Chan Ho Park	.20
62 John Smoltz	.20
63 Jimmy Rollins	.40
64 Orlando Cabrera	.20
65 Johnny Damon	.20
66 Austin Kearns	.40
67 Tsuyoshi Shinjo	.20
68 Tim Hudson	.30
69 Coco Crisp	.20
70 Darin Erstad	.60
71 Jacque Jones	.20
72 Vicente Padilla	.20
73 Hee Seop Choi	.20
74 Shea Hillenbrand	.20
75 Edgardo Alfonzo	.20
76 Pat Burrell	.50
77 Ben Sheets	.20
78 Ivan Rodriguez	.40
79 Josh Phelps	.20
80 Adam Kennedy	.20
81 Eric Chavez	.30
82 Bobby Higginson	.20
83 Nomar Garciaparra	1.50
84 J.D. Drew	.30
85 Carl Crawford	.20
86 Matt Morris	.20
87 Chipper Jones	1.00
88 Luis Gonzalez	.30
89 Richie Sexson	.20
90 Eric Milton	.20
91 Andres Galarraga	.20
92 Paul LoDuca	.20
93 Mark Grace	.30
94 Ben Grieve	.20
95 Mike Lowell	.20
96 Roberto Alomar	.35
97 Wade Miller	.20
98 Sean Casey	.20
99 Roger Clemens	1.25
100 Matt Williams	.20
101 Brian Giles	.20
102 Jim Thome	.20
103 Troy Glaus	.75
104 Joe Borchard	.20
105 Vladimir Guerrero	.75
106 Kevin Mench	.20
107 Omar Vizquel	.20
108 Magglio Ordonez	.20
109 Ken Griffey Jr.	1.50
110 Mike Piazza	1.50
111 Mark Teixeira	.40
112 Jason Jennings	.20
113 Ellis Burks	.20
114 Jason Varitek	.20
115 Larry Walker	.20
116 Frank Thomas	.75
117 Ramon Ortiz	.20
118 Mark Quinn	.20
119 Preston Wilson	.20
120 Carlos Lee	.20
121 Brian Lawrence	.20
122 Tim Salmon	.20
123 Shawn Green	.30
124 Randy Johnson	.75
125 Jeff Bagwell	.75
126 C.C. Sabathia	.20
127 Bernie Williams	.35
128 Roy Oswalt	.30
129 Albert Pujols	.75
130 Reggie Sanders	.20
131 Jeff Conine	.20
132 John Olerud	.20
133 Lance Berkman	.20
134 Geoff Jenkins	.20
135 Jim Edmonds	.20
136 Todd Helton	.65
137 Jason Kendall	.20
138 Robin Ventura	.20
139 Randy Winn	.20
140 Carl Everett	.20
141 Jose Vidro	.20
142 Pokey Reese	.20
143 Edgar Renteria	.20
144 Alex Rodriguez	1.75
145 Doug Mientkiewicz	.20
146 Aramis Ramirez	.20
147 Bobby Hill	.20

148 Jorge Posada	.35
149 Sean Burroughs	.20
150 Jeff Kent	.20
151 Tino Martinez	.20
152 Mark Prior	.20
153 Brad Radke	.20
154 Al Leiter	.20
155 Eric Karros	.20
156 Manny Ramirez	.50
157 Jason Lane	.20
158 Mike Lieberthal	.20
159 Shannon Stewart	.20
160 Robert Fick	.20
161 Derrek Lee	.20
162 Jason Giambi	.50
163 Rafael Palmeiro	.65
164 Jay Payton	.20
165 Adrian Beltre	.20
166 Marlon Byrd	.20
167 Bret Boone	.20
168 Roy Halladay	.20
169 Freddy Garcia	.20
170 Rich Aurilia	.20
171 Jared Sandberg	.20
172 Paul Byrd	.20
173 Gary Sheffield	.30
174 Edgar Martinez	.20
175 Eric Hinske	.20
176 Milton Bradley	.20
177 David Eckstein	.20
178 Jay Gibbons	.20
179 Corey Patterson	.20
180 Barry Zito	.20
181-182 Darin Erstad, Troy Glaus	.50
183-184 Curt Schilling, Randy Johnson	.75
185-186 Andruw Jones, Chipper Jones	1.00
187-188 Tony Batista, Jay Gibbons	.40
189-190 Pedro Martinez, Nomar Garciaparra	1.25
191-192 Sammy Sosa, Kerry Wood	1.00
193-194 Paul Konerko, Joe Borchard	.40
195-196 Austin Kearns, Adam Dunn	.50
197-198 Omar Vizquel, Jim Thome	.50
199-200 Larry Walker, Todd Helton	.40
201-202 Josh Beckett, Luis Castillo	.40
203-204 Craig Biggio, Jeff Bagwell	.50
205-206 Paul Byrd, Mike Sweeney	.40
207-208 Adrian Beltre, Shawn Green	.40
209-210 Jose Hernandez, Richie Sexson	.40
211-212 Jacque Jones, Torii Hunter	.40
213-214 Vladimir Guerrero, Jose Vidro	.75
215-216 Edgardo Alfonzo, Mike Piazza	1.50
217-218 Roger Clemens, Derek Jeter	2.00
219-220 Eric Chavez, Miguel Tejada	.40
221-222 Marlon Byrd, Pat Burrell	.50
223-224 Jason Kendall, Brian Giles	.40
225-226 Phil Nevin, Sean Burroughs	.20
227-228 Jeff Kent, Barry Bonds	2.00
229-230 Kazuhiro Sasaki, Ichiro Suzuki	1.25
231-232 Albert Pujols, J.D. Drew	.75
233-234 Juan Gonzalez, Ivan Rodriguez	.50
235-236 Eric Hinske, Orlando Hudson	.40
237-238 Lance Berkman, Chipper Jones	1.00
239-240 Alex Rodriguez, Derek Jeter	2.00
241-242 Ichiro Suzuki, Hideo Nomo	1.25
243-244 Manny Ramirez, Bernie Williams	.50
245-246 Tom Glavine, Roger Clemens	1.00
247-248 Ken Griffey Jr., Barry Larkin	1.25
249-250 Mark Teixeira, Mark Prior	.40
251-252 Albert Pujols, Drew Henson	.75
253-254 Jason Giambi, Todd Helton	1.00
255-256 Jose Vidro, Alfonso Soriano	.75
257-258 Shea Hillenbrand, Scott Rolen	.50
259-260 Jimmy Rollins, Alex Rodriguez	2.00
261-262 Torii Hunter, Vladimir Guerrero	.75
263-264 Ichiro Suzuki, Sammy Sosa	1.25
265-266 Barry Bonds, Manny Ramirez	2.00
267-268 Mike Piazza, Jorge Posada	1.25

269-270 Robin Yount, Ozzie Smith	1.00
271-272 Josh Hancock, Freddy Sanchez	.40
273-274 Ryan Bukvich, Shawn Sedlacek	.40
275-276 Doug DeVore, Rene Reyes	.40
277-278 Hank Blalock, Travis Hafner	.50
279-280 Eric Junge, Brett Myers	.40
281-282 Brad Lidge, Jeriome Robertson	.40
283-284 Miguel Asencio, Runelvys Hernandez	.40
285-286 Fernando Rodney, Barry Wesson	.40
287-288 Victor Alvarez, David Ross	.40
289-290 Tony Torcato, Chris Snelling	.50
291-292 Kirk Saarloos, Morgan Ensberg	.40
293-294 Josh Bard, Wilbert Nieves	.40
295-296 Jung Bong, Trey Hodges	.40
297-298 Kevin Cash, Reed Johnson	.40
299-300 Chone Figgins, John Lackey	.40

Flip Card Memorabilia

KERRY WOOD
Chicago Cubs™, p
Game-Worn Jersey

	NM/M
Common Player:	4.00
Inserted 1:20	
Golds:	.75-2X
Production 100 Sets	
1 Roberto Alomar/Bat	10.00
2 Jeff Bagwell/Jsy	8.00
3 Adrian Beltre/Jsy	4.00
4 Barry Bonds/Bat/200	15.00
5 Roger Clemens/Jsy/200	12.00
6 J.D. Drew/Jsy	8.00
7 Adam Dunn/Jsy/200	10.00
8 Nomar Garciaparra/Jsy/200	15.00
9 Mark Grace/Jsy	8.00
10 Todd Helton/Jsy/200	8.00
11 Derek Jeter/Jsy/200	20.00
12 Randy Johnson/Jsy/200	10.00
13 Chipper Jones/Jsy	8.00
14 Eric Karros/Jsy	4.00
15 Barry Larkin/Jsy/200	8.00
16 Greg Maddux/Jsy/200	10.00
17 Hideo Nomo/Jsy/200	10.00
18 Kazuhisa Ishii/Jsy	6.00
19 Mike Piazza/Jsy/200	10.00
20 Jorge Posada/Jsy/200	8.00
21 Mark Prior/Jsy	5.00
22 Alex Rodriguez/Jsy	10.00
23 Kazuhiro Sasaki/Jsy/200	6.00
24 Curt Schilling/Jsy/200	8.00
25 Alfonso Soriano/Jsy	8.00
26 Miguel Tejada/Jsy	8.00
27 Jim Thome/Jsy/200	10.00
28 Robin Ventura/Jsy	4.00
29 Bernie Williams/Jsy/200	8.00
30 Kerry Wood/Jsy/200	10.00

Keystone Combination

	NM/M
Complete Set (10):	25.00
Common Card:	
Inserted 1:10	
1KC Derek Jeter, Bret Boone	6.00
2KC Miguel Tejada, Jeff Kent	1.00
3KC Nomar Garciaparra, Ray Durham	4.00
4KC Omar Vizquel, Roberto Alomar	1.00
5KC Pee Wee Reese, Joe Morgan	4.00
6KC Alex Rodriguez, Craig Biggio	5.00
7KC Orlando Hudson, Jose Vidro	1.00

8KC Phil Rizzuto, Alfonso Soriano	3.00
9KC Alex Rodriguez, Miguel Tejada	5.00
10KC Nomar Garciaparra, Derek Jeter	6.00

Keystone Combination Memorab.

	NM/M
Common Card:	4.00
Inserted 1:40	
Derek Jeter, Bret Boone/Jsy	8.00
Miguel Tejada, Jeff Kent/Jsy	4.00
N.Garciaparra/Jsy/175, Ray Durham	12.00
Omar Vizquel, Roberto Alomar/Jsy	6.00
Alex Rodriguez, Craig Biggio/Jsy	6.00
Orlando Hudson, Jose Vidro/Jsy	4.00
Phil Rizzuto, Alfonso Soriano/Jsy/75	15.00
Alex Rodriguez/Bat, Miguel Tejada	10.00
N.Garciaparra/Jsy/175, Derek Jeter	12.00
Derek Jeter/Jsy/175, Bret Boone	20.00
Derek Jeter/Jsy/175, Nomar Garciaparra	20.00
Alex Rodriguez/Jsy/200, Craig Biggio	10.00
Miguel Tejada/Jsy, Jeff Kent	8.00
Miguel Tejada/Jsy, Alex Rodriguez	8.00

Let's Play, Too!

RENE REYES • COLORADO ROCKIES™ • OF
LET'S PLAY TOO! 03

	NM/M
Complete Set (15):	8.00
Common Player:	.50
Inserted 1:5	
1LPT Chris Snelling	1.00
2LPT Kevin Mench	.50
3LPT Brett Myers	.50
4LPT Julius Matos	.50
5LPT Drew Henson	1.00
6LPT Joe Borchard	.50
7LPT Felix Escalona	.50
8LPT Kirk Saarloos	.50
9LPT Ben Howard	.50
10LPT Hee Seop Choi	1.00
11LPT Rene Reyes	.50
12LPT Josh Bard	.50
13LPT Marlon Byrd	.50
14LPT Coco Crisp	.50
15LPT Reed Johnson	.50

Matinee Idols

	NM/M
Complete Set (15):	50.00
Common Player:	2.00
Inserted 1:20	
1MI Yogi Berra	3.00
2MI Richie Ashburn	3.00
3MI Whitey Ford	3.00
4MI Eddie Mathews	3.00
5MI Jim Palmer	2.00
6MI Al Kaline	6.00
7MI Brooks Robinson	3.00
8MI Willie McCovey	3.00
9MI Billy Williams	2.00
10MI Willie Stargell	3.00
11MI Nolan Ryan	15.00
12MI Rod Carew	3.00
13MI Reggie Jackson	3.00
14MI Tom Seaver	4.00
15MI Mike Schmidt	6.00

Twin Bill

	NM/M
Complete Set (20):	45.00
Common Player:	1.00

TWIN BILL 51
Double Header
Ichiro

		NM/M
Inserted 1:10		
1a	Barry Bonds	5.00
1b	Lance Berkman	1.00
2a	Derek Jeter	6.00
2b	Alex Rodriguez	5.00
3a	Roger Clemens	3.00
3b	Pedro Martinez	2.00
4a	Roberto Alomar	1.25
4b	Chipper Jones	3.00
5a	Barry Zito	1.00
5b	Ichiro Suzuki	4.00
6a	Sammy Sosa	3.00
6b	Ken Griffey Jr.	4.00
7a	Bernie Williams	1.00
7b	Manny Ramirez	1.50
8a	Nomar Garciaparra	4.00
8b	Derek Jeter	6.00
9a	Randy Johnson	3.00
9b	Greg Maddux	3.00
10a	Albert Pujols	2.00
10b	Adam Dunn	1.50

Twin Bill Single Swatch

	NM/M
Common Player:	1.00
Barry Bonds/Cap/100	25.00
Alex Rodriguez/Cap/100	15.00
Roger Clemens/Cap/100	15.00
Pedro Martinez/Cap/100	12.00
Roberto Alomar/Cap	10.00
Barry Zito/Cap/100	15.00
Bernie Williams/Cap/100	10.00
Manny Ramirez/Cap/75	12.00
Nomar Garciaparra/Cap/100	25.00
Derek Jeter/Cap/100	30.00
Randy Johnson/Cap/100	10.00
Adam Dunn/Cap/100	12.00

Twin Bill Dual Swatch

	NM/M
Common Card:	
Production 50 Sets	
Barry Bonds, Adam Dunn	40.00
Randy Johnson, Barry Zito	35.00

2003 Fleer E-X

HANK BLALOCK

	NM/M
Complete Set (102):	125.00
Common Player:	.50
Common SP (83-102):	3.00
Pack (3):	4.00
Box (20):	60.00
1 Troy Glaus	.75
2 Darin Erstad	.75
3 Garret Anderson	.50
4 Curt Schilling	.75
5 Randy Johnson	1.00
6 Luis Gonzalez	.50
7 Greg Maddux	1.50
8 Chipper Jones	1.50
9 Andruw Jones	.50
10 Melvin Mora	.50
11 Jay Gibbons	.50
12 Nomar Garciaparra	2.00
13 Pedro J. Martinez	1.00
14 Manny Ramirez	1.00
15 Sammy Sosa	2.00
16 Kerry Wood	.75
17 Magglio Ordonez	.50
18 Frank Thomas	1.00
19 Roberto Alomar	.60
20 Barry Larkin	.50

21	Adam Dunn	1.00
22	Austin Kearns	.75
23	Omar Vizquel	.50
24	Larry Walker	.50
25	Todd Helton	1.00
26	Preston Wilson	.50
27	Dmitri Young	.50
28	Ivan Rodriguez	.75
29	Mike Lowell	.50
30	Jeff Kent	.50
31	Jeff Bagwell	1.00
32	Roy Oswalt	.75
33	Craig Biggio	.50
34	Mike Sweeney	.50
35	Carlos Beltran	.75
36	Shawn Green	.60
37	Kazuhisa Ishii	.50
38	Richie Sexson	.50
39	Torii Hunter	.50
40	Jacque Jones	.50
41	Jose Vidro	.50
42	Vladimir Guerrero	1.00
43	Mike Piazza	2.00
44	Tom Glavine	.60
45	Roger Clemens	1.75
46	Jason Giambi	.75
47	Bernie Williams	.60
48	Alfonso Soriano	1.00
49	Mike Mussina	.60
50	Barry Zito	.60
51	Miguel Tejada	.60
52	Eric Chavez	.60
53	Eric Byrnes	.50
54	Jim Thome	.50
55	Kevin Millwood	.50
56	Brian Giles	.50
57	Xavier Nady	.50
58	Barry Bonds	3.00
59	Bret Boone	.50
60	Edgar Martinez	.50
61	Kazuhiro Sasaki	.50
62	Edgar Renteria	.50
63	J.D. Drew	.50
64	Scott Rolen	1.00
65	Jim Edmonds	.50
66	Aubrey Huff	.50
67	Alex Rodriguez	2.50
68	Juan Gonzalez	1.00
69	Hank Blalock	.75
70	Mark Teixeira	.75
71	Carlos Delgado	.75
72	Vernon Wells	.50
73	Shea Hillenbrand	.50
74	Gary Sheffield	.60
75	Mark Prior	.50
76	Ken Griffey Jr.	2.00
77	Lance Berkman	.50
78	Hideo Nomo	.75
79	Derek Jeter	3.00
80	Ichiro Suzuki	2.00
81	Albert Pujols	2.50
82	Rafael Palmeiro	.75
83	Jose Reyes	4.00
84	Rocco Baldelli	3.00
85	Hee Seop Choi	3.00
86	Dontrelle Willis	3.00
87	Robby Hammock RC	3.00
88	Brandon Webb RC	10.00
89	Matt Kata RC	3.00
90	Todd Wellemeyer RC	4.00
91	Francisco Cruceta RC	3.00
92	Clint Barmes RC	4.00
93	Jeremy Bonderman	6.00
94	Dave Matranga RC	3.00
95	Ryan Wagner RC	3.00
96	Jeremy Griffiths	3.00
97	Hideki Matsui RC	15.00
98	Jose Contreras RC	6.00
99	Chien-Ming Wang RC	25.00
100	Bo Hart RC	3.00
101	Dan Haren	5.00
102	Rickie Weeks RC	5.00

Essential Credentials Now/Future

Cards serial numbered 26-50: 6-12X
Cards s/n 51-75: 4-8X
Cards s/n 76-102: 3-5X
SP's (83-102) s/n 83-102: 1-2X
Now is consecutively #'d from 1 to 102.
Future is consect. #'d from 102 to 1.

Behind the Numbers

		NM/M
Complete Set (15):		50.00
Common Player:		1.50
Inserted 1:80		
1	Derek Jeter	8.00
2	Alex Rodriguez	8.00
3	Randy Johnson	3.00
4	Chipper Jones	5.00
5	Jim Thome	3.00
6	Alfonso Soriano	4.00
7	Adam Dunn	2.00
8	Nomar Garciaparra	6.00
9	Roger Clemens	6.00
10	Gary Sheffield	1.50
11	Vladimir Guerrero	3.00
12	Greg Maddux	5.00
13	Sammy Sosa	6.00
14	Mike Piazza	5.00
15	Troy Glaus	2.00

Behind the Numbers Autograph

NM/M
No pricing due to scarcity.
Numbered to jersey number.

Behind the Numbers Game-Used

		NM/M
Common Player:		5.00
Inserted 1:10		
Patch Version:		1.5-2.5X
DJ	Derek Jeter	15.00
AR	Alex Rodriguez	10.00
RJ	Randy Johnson	8.00
CJ	Chipper Jones	8.00
JT	Jim Thome	8.00
AS	Alfonso Soriano	8.00
AD	Adam Dunn	6.00
NG	Nomar Garciaparra	10.00
RC	Roger Clemens	10.00
GS	Gary Sheffield	5.00
VG	Vladimir Guerrero	8.00
GM	Greg Maddux	8.00
SS	Sammy Sosa	8.00
MP	Mike Piazza	8.00
TG	Troy Glaus	5.00
HB	Hank Blalock	6.00
TG	Tom Glavine	5.00
BM	Brett Myers	5.00
LB	Lance Berkman	5.00
RB	Rocco Baldelli	10.00
BZ	Barry Zito	6.00
DW	Dontrelle Willis	10.00
RP	Rafael Palmeiro	6.00
RA	Roberto Alomar	6.00
MB	Marlon Byrd	5.00

Diamond Essentials

		NM/M
Common Player:		5.00
Inserted 1:480		
1DE	Randy Johnson	15.00
2DE	Ichiro Suzuki	25.00
3DE	Albert Pujols	30.00
4DE	Barry Bonds	40.00
5DE	Hideki Matsui	30.00
6DE	Derek Jeter	40.00
7DE	Chipper Jones	20.00
8DE	Sammy Sosa	25.00
9DE	Jeff Bagwell	10.00
10DE	Mike Piazza	20.00
11DE	Pedro J. Martinez	15.00
12DE	Mark Prior	20.00
13DE	Jason Giambi	10.00
14DE	Jose Reyes	5.00
15DE	Alfonso Soriano	15.00

Diamond Essentials Autograph

		NM/M
Common Player:		
Dontrelle Willis		30.00
Ryan Wagner		20.00
Rocco Baldelli		25.00
Albert Pujols		150.00

Diamond Essentials Game-Used

		NM/M
Common Player:		8.00
Same price for cards #'d 145, 245 & 345.		
Patch Versions:		1.5-2.5X
Production 55		
RJ	Randy Johnson	8.00
DJ	Derek Jeter	15.00
CJ	Chipper Jones	8.00
SS	Sammy Sosa	12.00
JB	Jeff Bagwell	8.00
MP	Mike Piazza	10.00
PM	Pedro J. Martinez	8.00
MP	Mark Prior	10.00
JG	Jason Giambi	8.00
JR	Jose Reyes	8.00

Emerald Essentials

		NM/M
Complete Set (10):		60.00
Common Player:		4.00
Inserted 1:240		
1	Austin Kearns	4.00
2	Alfonso Soriano	8.00
3	Miguel Tejada	4.00
4	Troy Glaus	4.00
5	Adam Dunn	4.00
6	Hideo Nomo	6.00
7	Kerry Wood	6.00
8	Nomar Garciaparra	15.00
9	Roger Clemens	15.00
10	Derek Jeter	15.00

Emerald Essentials Autograph

		NM/M
Common Player:		
Brandon Webb		40.00
Hank Blalock		20.00

Emerald Essentials Game-Used

		NM/M
Common Player:		4.00
Same price for levels #'d 175, 250 & 375		
Patch Versions:		1.5-2.5X
Production 60		
AK	Austin Kearns	6.00
AS	Alfonso Soriano	8.00
MT	Miguel Tejada	4.00
TG	Troy Glaus	6.00
AD	Adam Dunn	6.00
HN	Hideo Nomo	15.00
KW	Kerry Wood	8.00
NG	Nomar Garciaparra	12.00
RC	Roger Clemens	12.00
AR	Alex Rodriguez	10.00

X-tra Innings

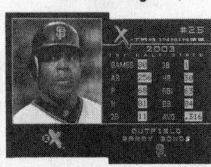

		NM/M
Complete Set (10):		25.00
Common Player:		1.00
Inserted 1:32		
1XI	Ichiro Suzuki	3.00
2XI	Albert Pujols	4.00
3XI	Barry Bonds	5.00
4XI	Jason Giambi	1.50
5XI	Pedro J. Martinez	2.00
6XI	Mark Prior	3.00
7XI	Derek Jeter	5.00
8XI	Curt Schilling	1.00
9XI	Jeff Bagwell	1.50
10XI	Alex Rodriguez	5.00

2003 Fleer Fall Classic

Complete Set (87):		30.00
Common Player:		.25
Common SP:		
Hobby Pack (5):		4.00
Hobby Box (24):		75.00
1	Rod Carew	.50
2	Bobby Doerr	.25
3	Eddie Mathews	1.00
3	Eddie Mathews/SP/Tigers	4.00
4	Tom Seaver	1.50
5	Lou Brock	.75
6	Nolan Ryan	3.00
6	Nolan Ryan/SP/Astros	10.00
7	Pee Wee Reese	.25
8	Robin Yount	.50
9	Bob Feller	.50
10	Harmon Killebrew	1.00
11	Hal Newhouser	.25
12	Al Kaline	1.00
13	Hoyt Wilhelm	.25
14	Early Wynn	.25
15	Yogi Berra	1.00
15	Yogi Berra/SP/Mets	4.00
16	Billy Williams	.25
17	Rollie Fingers	.25
18	Sparky Anderson	.25
18	Sparky Anderson/SP/Reds	3.00
19	Lou Boudreau	.25
20	Warren Spahn	1.00
21	Enos Slaughter	.25
22	Luis Aparicio	.50
23	Phil Rizzuto	.75
24	Willie McCovey	.75
25	Joe Morgan	.50
26	Alan Trammell	.75
27	Eddie Plank	.25
28	Lefty Grove	.25
29	Walter Johnson	1.00
30	Roy Campanella	1.00
31	Carlton Fisk	.75
32	Bill Dickey	.25
33	Rogers Hornsby	1.00
33	Rogers Hornsby/SP/Cubs	5.00
34	Wade Boggs	.75
35	Chick Stahl	.25
36	Don Drysdale	.75
36	Don Drysdale/SP/Dodgers	4.00
37	Jose Canseco	.75
38	Roger Maris	2.00
38	Roger Maris/SP/Yankees	8.00
39	Cal Ripken Jr.	3.00
40	Kiki Cuyler	.25
40	Kiki Cuyler/SP/Cubs	3.00
41	Hank Greenberg	.25
42	Don Larsen	.50
43	Eddie Murray	.75
43	Eddie Murray/SP/Indians	4.00
44	Jimmy Sebring	.25
45	Ozzie Smith	1.50
46	Darryl Strawberry	.75
46	Darryl Strawberry/SP/Yankees	3.00
47	Dave Parker	.25
48	Gil Hodges	.25
48	Gil Hodges/SP/Mets	3.00
49	Joe Carter	.50
50	Leo Durocher	.25
50	Leo Durocher/SP/Giants	3.00
51	Christy Mathewson	.75
52	Elston Howard	.25
53	Hughie Jennings	.25
54	Nellie Fox	.50
55	Carl Yastrzemski	1.00
56	Frank Robinson	1.00
56	Frank Robinson/SP/Reds	4.00
57	Dennis Eckersley	.25
58	Grover Alexander	.50
58	Grover Alexander/SP/Cards	4.00
59	Carl Hubbell	.25
60	Dave Winfield	.75
61	Honus Wagner	1.50
62	Duke Snider	1.00
62	Duke Snider/SP/Dodgers	5.00
63	Frankie Frisch	.25
63	Frankie Frisch/SP/Cards	3.00
64	Dizzy Dean	.75
65	Bob Gibson	1.00
66	Johnny Bench	1.50
67	Ty Cobb	2.00
68	Lou Gehrig	2.50
69	Jim "Catfish" Hunter	.50
70	Willie Stargell	.75
71	Reggie Jackson	1.00
71	Reggie Jackson/SP/Yankees	5.00
72	George Brett	2.50
73	Babe Ruth	3.00
73	Babe Ruth/SP/Yankees	10.00
74	Cy Young	1.00
75	Jim Palmer	.50
76	Mickey Lolich	.25
77	Stan Musial	1.50
78	Steve Carlton	.75
79	Roberto Clemente	2.50
80	John McGraw	.25
81	Paul Molitor	.25
82	Red Ruffing	.25
83	Connie Mack	.25
84	Mike Schmidt	2.00
85	Mickey Cochrane	.50
85	Mickey Cochrane/SP/Tigers	4.00
86	Brooks Robinson	1.00
87	Whitey Ford	1.00

Championship Gold

Cards 1-87:		3-6X
Production 50 Sets		

All-American Collection

		NM/M
Common Player:		8.00
OS	Ozzie Smith/100	20.00
TS	Tom Seaver/100	15.00
SM	Stan Musial/100	30.00
CR	Cal Ripken Jr/100	60.00
EM	Eddie Mathews/100	15.00
NR	Nolan Ryan/100	30.00
YB	Yogi Berra/100	15.00
EM	Eddie Murray/100	15.00
FR	Frank Robinson	8.00
DS	Duke Snider	8.00
RJ	Reggie Jackson	8.00
LA	Luis Aparicio/100	10.00
GH	Gil Hodges	8.00
AK	Al Kaline	8.00
BM	Bill Mazeroski/100	10.00
BR	Brooks Robinson/100	15.00
WB	Wade Boggs/100	12.00
AT	Alan Trammell/100	12.00

All American Collection Auto

		NM/M
Common Autograph:		
Varying quantities produced		
SP version #'d to 100:		1-1.5X
SP version #'d to 50:		1-2X
LA	Luis Aparicio/150	10.00
VB	Vida Blue/450	8.00
RB	Rick Burleson/250	8.00
SC	Steve Carlton/100	20.00

Bob Feller etc.

BF	Bob Feller/300	15.00
CF	Carlton Fisk/75	30.00
AL	Al Kaline/325	20.00
HK	Harmon Killebrew/150	30.00
FL	Fred Lynn/275	8.00
BM	Bill Mazeroski/75	20.00
JP	Jim Palmer/100	15.00
BR	Brooks Robinson/325	20.00
PR	Preacher Roe/450	12.00
MS	Mike Schmidt/50	60.00
BS	"Moose" Skowron/150	10.00
OS	Ozzie Smith/50	65.00
DS	Duke Snider/100	25.00
WS	Warren Spahn/75	40.00
AT	Alan Trammell/150	15.00

All Amer. Coll. Jersey Auto.

		NM/M
Production 25 Sets		
GB	George Brett	160.00
SC	Steve Carlton	50.00

Legendary Collection

		NM/M
Common Player:		
Inserted 1:Legendary Star Pack		
EM	Eddie Mathews/SP	15.00
NR	Nolan Ryan	30.00
YB	Yogi Berra	15.00
EMY	Eddie Murray	8.00
FR	Frank Robinson	6.00
DS	Duke Snider/SP	10.00
DSy	Darryl Strawberry	5.00
RJ	Reggie Jackson	8.00
RM	Roger Maris/SP	30.00
GH	Gil Hodges/SP	10.00

Pennant Aggression

		NM/M
Complete Set (20):		50.00
Common Player:		3.00
Numbered to pennant year.		
1PA	Ty Cobb/1,908	4.00
2PA	Honus Wagner/1,909	3.00
3PA	Walter Johnson/1,924	3.00
4PA	Jimmie Foxx/1,930	3.00
5PA	Frankie Frisch/1,931	3.00
6PA	Pee Wee Reese/1,947	3.00
7PA	Yogi Berra/1,951	4.00
8PA	Roy Campanella/1,953	3.00
9PA	Whitey Ford/1,961	4.00
10PA	Frank Robinson/1,966	3.00
11PA	Carl Yastrzemski/1,967	3.00
12PA	Brooks Robinson/1,970	3.00
13PA	Johnny Bench/1,972	3.00
14PA	Reggie Jackson/1,973	3.00
15PA	Jim "Catfish" Hunter/1,974	3.00
16PA	Joe Morgan/1,975	3.00
17PA	Thurman Munson/1,976	4.00
18PA	Willie Stargell/1,979	3.00
19PA	Mike Schmidt/1,980	4.00
20PA	George Brett/1,985	4.00

Pennant Aggression Game-Used

		NM/M
Common Player:		8.00
Production 100		
Patches:		1.5-2X

Production 50

YB	Yogi Berra	15.00
FB	Frank Robinson	10.00
CY	Carl Yastrzemski	20.00
BR	Brooks Robinson	15.00
JB	Johnny Bench	15.00
RJ	Reggie Jackson	12.00
CH	Jim "Catfish" Hunter	8.00
JM	Joe Morgan	8.00
TM	Thurman Munson	15.00
WS	Willie Stargell	10.00
MS	Mike Schmidt	25.00
GB	George Brett	35.00

Postseason Glory

		NM/M
Complete Set (30):		125.00
Common Player:		2.00
#1-15 Numbered to 1,500		
16-25 Numbered to 750		
26-30 Numbered to 100		
1	Carlton Fisk, Carl Yastrzemski	2.00
2	Enos Slaughter, Stan Musial	4.00
3	Reggie Jackson, Thurman Munson	4.00
4	Eddie Plank, Christy Mathewson	3.00
5	Cy Young, Jimmy Sebring	3.00
6	Yogi Berra, Whitey Ford	4.00
7	Mickey Lolich, Alan Trammell	2.00
8	Eddie Mathews, Al Schoendienst	3.00
9	Roy Campanella, Pee Wee Reese	3.00
10	Joe Carter, Bill Mazeroski	2.00
11	Brooks Robinson, Frank Robinson	3.00
12	Tom Seaver, Gil Hodges	3.00
13	Robin Yount, Paul Molitor	2.50
14	Dave Parker, Willie Stargell	2.00
15	Cal Ripken Jr., Jim Palmer	6.00
16	Babe Ruth, Whitey Ford	6.00
18	Lou Brock, Bob Gibson	4.00
19	Mike Schmidt, Brooks Robinson	5.00
20	Johnny Bench, Thurman Munson	5.00
21	Nolan Ryan, Walter Johnson	10.00
22	Don Drysdale, Duke Snider	4.00
23	Joe Carter, Paul Molitor	2.00
24	Hughie Jennings, Ty Cobb	4.00
25	Cal Ripken Jr., Eddie Murray	10.00
26	Mike Schmidt, Steve Carlton	5.00
27	Roberto Clemente, Willie Stargell	15.00
28	Jim Palmer, Nolan Ryan	25.00
29	Joe Morgan, Johnny Bench	10.00
30	Lou Gehrig, Babe Ruth	25.00

Postseason Glory Dual Game-Used

		NM/M
Production 100		
Single Jerseys:		.5X
Production 150		
	Carlton Fisk, Carl Yastrzemski	25.00
	Reggie Jackson, Thurman Munson	25.00
	Yogi Berra, Whitey Ford	30.00
	Brooks Robinson, Frank Robinson	20.00
	Robin Yount, Paul Molitor	25.00
	Dave Parker, Willie Stargell/Single/150	4.00
	Lou Brock, Bob Gibson/Single/150	10.00
	Joe Carter, Paul Molitor/Single/150	8.00
	Don Drysdale, Duke Snider	8.00
	Cal Ripken Jr., Eddie Murray	50.00

Mike Schmidt,
Steve Carlton,
Jim Palmer, Nolan Ryan 40.00
Joe Morgan,
Johnny Bench 25.00
Babe Ruth/Single/150,
Lou Gehrig 125.00

Postseason Glory Dual Patch
NM/M
Production 50
Single Patch: .5-.75X
Production 75
Carlton Fisk,
Carl Yastrzemski 70.00
Robin Yount,
Paul Molitor 50.00
Lou Brock, Bob Gibson 50.00
Cal Ripken Jr.,
Eddie Murray 120.00
Mike Schmidt,
Steve Carlton 50.00
Jim Palmer, Nolan Ryan 80.00
Joe Morgan,
Johnny Bench 50.00
Brooks Robinson,
Frank Robinson 40.00

Series Contender
NM/M
Common Player:
Inserted 1:50 Retail
Bat Knobs: No Pricing
Production 9 or 10
SK Al Kaline 15.00
BD Bill Dickey 10.00
DS Darryl Strawberry 5.00
DM Don Mattingly 30.00
PR Phil Rizzuto/SP 10.00
WM Willie McCovey/SP 10.00
HK Harmon Killebrew 25.00
CF Carlton Fisk 6.00
JC Jose Canseco 10.00

Yankee Penstripes
NM/M
Production 100
World Series Edition: No Pricing
Production 26
RJ Reggie Jackson 40.00
BSP Bill "Moose" Skowron 15.00
WB Wade Boggs 50.00
DM Don Mattingly 75.00
DW Dave Winfield 35.00

2003 Fleer Focus Jersey Edition

NM/M
Complete Set (180): 45.00
Common Player: .15
Common Prospect (161-180): .75
Inserted 1:4
Pack (7): 1.50
Box (24): 30.00
1 Derek Jeter 2.50
2 Preston Wilson .15
3 Trevor Hoffman .15
4 Moises Alou .15
5 Roberto Alomar .35
6 Tim Salmon .25
7 Mike Lowell .15
8 Barry Bonds 2.50
9 Fred McGriff .15
10 Mo Vaughn .15
11 Junior Spivey .15
12 Roy Oswalt .25
13 Ichiro Suzuki 1.50
14 Magglio Ordonez .15
15 Adam Kennedy .15
16 Randy Johnson .75
17 Carlos Beltran .50
18 John Olerud .15
19 Joe Borchard .15
20 Alfonso Soriano .75
21 Curt Schilling .15
22 Mike Sweeney .15
23 Tino Martinez .15
24 Barry Larkin .15
25 Miguel Tejada .40
26 Chipper Jones 1.00
27 Kevin Brown .15
28 J.D. Drew .15
29 Sean Casey .15
30 Bernie Williams .35
31 Troy Percival .15
32 Jeff Bagwell .75
33 Kenny Lofton .15

34 Kerry Wood .50
35 Armando Benitez .15
36 David Eckstein .15
37 Wade Miller .15
38 Edgar Martinez .15
39 Mark Prior .75
40 Mike Piazza 1.50
41 Shea Hillenbrand .15
42 Bartolo Colon .15
43 Darin Erstad .50
44 A.J. Burnett .15
45 Jeff Kent .15
46 Corey Patterson .15
47 Derek Wigginton .15
48 Troy Glaus .75
49 Josh Beckett .15
50 Brian Lawrence .15
51 Frank Thomas .75
52 Jason Giambi .60
53 Luis Gonzalez .15
54 Raul Ibanez .15
55 Kazuhiro Sasaki .15
56 Mark Buehrle .15
57 Roger Clemens 1.25
58 Matt Williams .15
59 Joe Randa .15
60 Jamie Moyer .15
61 Paul Konerko .15
62 Mike Mussina .50
63 Javy Lopez .15
64 Brian Jordan .15
65 Scott Rolen .75
66 Aaron Boone .15
67 Eric Chavez .15
68 Mark Grace .25
69 Shawn Green .25
70 Albert Pujols 1.25
71 Sammy Sosa 1.50
72 Edgardo Alfonzo .15
73 Garret Anderson .15
74 Lance Berkman .15
75 Bret Boone .15
76 Joe Crede .15
77 Al Leiter .15
78 Jarrod Washburn .15
79 Craig Biggio .15
80 Rich Aurilia .15
81 Adam Dunn .60
82 Jermaine Dye .15
83 Tom Glavine .40
84 Eric Gagne .15
85 Jared Sandberg .15
86 Jim Thome .15
87 Barry Zito .35
88 Gary Sheffield .25
89 Paul LoDuca .15
90 Matt Morris .15
91 Juan Pierre .15
92 Randy Wolf .15
93 Jay Gibbons .15
94 Brad Radke .15
95 Carlos Delgado .35
96 Carlos Pena .15
97 Brian Giles .15
98 Rodrigo Lopez .15
99 Jacque Jones .15
100 Juan Gonzalez .75
101 Randall Simon .15
102 Mike Williams .15
103 Derek Lowe .15
104 Brad Wilkerson .15
105 Eric Hinske .15
106 Luis Castillo .15
107 Phil Nevin .15
108 Manny Ramirez .75
109 Vladimir Guerrero .75
110 Roy Halladay .15
111 Ellis Burks .15
112 Bobby Abreu .15
113 Tony Batista .15
114 Richie Sexson .15
115 Rafael Palmeiro .65
116 Todd Helton .65
117 Pat Burrell .60
118 John Smoltz .15
119 Ben Sheets .15
120 Aubrey Huff .15
121 Andruw Jones .75
122 Kazuhisa Ishii .15
123 Jim Edmonds .15
124 Austin Kearns .60
125 Mark Mulder .25
126 Greg Maddux 1.00
127 Jose Hernandez .15
128 Ben Grieve .15
129 Ken Griffey Jr. 1.50
130 Tim Hudson .35
131 Jorge Julio .15
132 Torii Hunter .15
133 Ivan Rodriguez .65
134 Jason Jennings .15
135 Jason Kendall .15
136 Nomar Garciaparra 1.50
137 Michael Cuddyer .15
138 Shannon Stewart .15
139 Larry Walker .15
140 Aramis Ramirez .15
141 Johnny Damon .15
142 Orlando Cabrera .15
143 Vernon Wells .15
144 Bobby Higginson .15
145 Sean Burroughs .15
146 Pedro J. Martinez .75
147 Jose Vidro .15
148 Orlando Hudson .15
149 Robert Fick .15
150 Ryan Klesko .15
151 Kevin Millwood .15

152 Alex Sanchez .15
153 Randy Winn .15
154 Omar Vizquel .15
155 Mike Lieberthal .15
156 Marty Cordova .15
157 Cristian Guzman .15
158 Alex Rodriguez 2.00
159 C.C. Sabathia .15
160 Jimmy Rollins .25
161 Josh Willingham RC 2.00
162 Lance Niekro .15
163 Nook Logan RC .75
164 Chase Utley .75
165 Pete LaForest RC .75
166 Victor Martinez .75
167 Adam LaRoche .75
168 Ian Ferguson RC .75
169 Mark Teixeira .75
170 Chris Waters RC .75
171 Hideki Matsui RC 5.00
172 Alejandro Machado RC .75
173 Francisco Rosario RC .75
174 Terrmel Sledge RC 1.00
175 Guillermo Quiroz RC .75
176 Lew Ford RC 1.00
177 Hank Blalock .75
178 Lyle Overbay .75
179 Matt Bruback RC .75
180 Jose Contreras RC 3.00

Century Jersey Number
Stars (1-160): 5-10X
Prospects (161-180): 2-4X
Numbered to jsy number + 100.

Franchise Focus

NM/M
Complete Set (20): 15.00
Common Player: .50
Inserted 1:4
1 Troy Glaus .75
2 Randy Johnson 1.00
3 Chipper Jones 1.50
4 Nomar Garciaparra 2.00
5 Sammy Sosa 1.50
6 Ken Griffey Jr. 1.50
7 Jeff Bagwell .50
8 Mike Sweeney .50
9 Shawn Green .50
10 Torii Hunter .50
11 Vladimir Guerrero 1.00
12 Mike Piazza 2.00
13 Jason Giambi 1.00
14 Barry Zito .50
15 Pat Burrell .75
16 Barry Bonds 3.00
17 Ichiro Suzuki 1.50
18 Albert Pujols 2.50
19 Alex Rodriguez 2.50
20 Carlos Delgado .50

Home and Aways
NM/M
Common Player: 10.00
Inserted 1:288
Lance Berkman 10.00
J.D. Drew 10.00
Nomar Garciaparra 20.00
Derek Jeter 40.00
Chipper Jones 20.00
Greg Maddux 20.00
Roy Oswalt 10.00
Alex Rodriguez 30.00
Alfonso Soriano 10.00

Materialistic

NM/M
Common Player: 3.00

Inserted 1:192
Action Home: 1.5-2.5X
Production 50 Sets
Portrait Away: .75-1.5X
Inserted 1:576
Plus (Memorabilia): 1.5-2.5X
Production 250 Sets
Portrait Home: No Pricing
Production One Set
1M Greg Maddux 5.00
2M Roger Clemens 5.00
3M Nomar Garciaparra 6.00
4M Derek Jeter 10.00
5M Mike Piazza 6.00
6M Pat Burrell 3.00
7M Alfonso Soriano 5.00
8M Chipper Jones 5.00
9M Adam Dunn 3.00
10M Alex Rodriguez 8.00
11M Jason Giambi 4.00
12M Sammy Sosa 5.00
13M Albert Pujols 4.00
14M Ken Griffey Jr. 6.00
15M Ichiro Suzuki 5.00

Materialistic Flannels

Complete Set (15):
Common Player:

Materialistic Oversize

NM/M
Complete Set (16): 60.00
Common Player: 2.00
5-1/4" x 3-3/4" Box Topper
(1) Pat Burrell 2.00
(2) Roger Clemens 6.00
(3) Adam Dunn 2.00
(4) Nomar Garciaparra 4.00
(5) Jason Giambi 2.00
(6) Ken Griffey Jr. 6.00
(7) Reggie Jackson 5.00
(8) Derek Jeter 12.50
(9) Chipper Jones 5.00
(10) Greg Maddux 5.00
(11) Mike Piazza 6.00
(12) Albert Pujols 10.00
(13) Alex Rodriguez 10.00
(14) Alfonso Soriano 2.00
(15) Sammy Sosa 6.00
(16) Ichiro Suzuki 7.50

Materialistic Oversize Autographs
NM/M
Complete Set (3): 200.00
(1) Reggie Jackson/360 50.00
(2) Derek Jeter/360 100.00
(3) Chipper Jones/80 75.00

Shirtified

NM/M
Complete Set (15): 35.00
Common Player: 1.00
Inserted 1:24
1 Manny Ramirez 2.00
2 Jarrod Washburn 1.00
3 Greg Maddux 4.00
4 Austin Kearns 2.00
5 Jim Thome 2.00
6 Kazuhisa Ishii 1.00
7 Mike Piazza 5.00
8 Alfonso Soriano 3.00
9 Pat Burrell 2.00
10 Derek Jeter 8.00
11 Miguel Tejada 1.50
12 Roger Clemens 4.00
13 Alex Rodriguez 6.00
14 Barry Bonds 8.00
15 Scott Rolen 2.00

Shirtified Game-Used
NM/M
Common Player:
Inserted 1:35
Patches: 2-3X

Production 200
Manny Ramirez 8.00
Greg Maddux 12.00
Mike Piazza 15.00
Alfonso Soriano 15.00
Derek Jeter 25.00
Miguel Tejada 6.00
Roger Clemens 12.00
Alex Rodriguez 12.00

Team Colors

NM/M
Complete Set (20): 20.00
Common Player: .50
Inserted 1:12
1TC Alex Rodriguez 3.50
2TC Mark Prior 1.00
3TC Derek Jeter 4.00
4TC Curt Schilling 1.00
5TC Pat Burrell 1.00
6TC Josh Beckett .50
7TC Sean Burroughs .50
8TC Troy Glaus 1.00
9TC Torii Hunter .75
10TC Jeff Bagwell 1.00
11TC Pedro J. Martinez 1.50
12TC Mike Piazza 3.00
13TC Lance Berkman .75
14TC Nomar Garciaparra 2.50
15TC Chipper Jones 2.00
16TC Eric Chavez .75
17TC Barry Zito .75
18TC Barry Bonds 4.00
19TC Adam Dunn 1.00
20TC Randy Johnson 1.50

Team Colors Game-Used

NM/M
Common Player: 4.00
Inserted 1:28
Multi-Color: 1.5X
Production 250
Derek Jeter 25.00
Curt Schilling 5.00
Josh Beckett 4.00
Troy Glaus 8.00
Jeff Bagwell 8.00
Pedro J. Martinez 8.00
Lance Berkman 8.00
Nomar Garciaparra 10.00
Chipper Jones 12.00
Eric Chavez 6.00
Adam Dunn 8.00
Randy Johnson 8.00

2003 Fleer Genuine
NM/M
Complete Set (130): 150.00
Common Player: .25
Common Gen. Upside
(101-130): 3.00
Production 799
Pack (5): 2.00
Box (24): 40.00
1 Derek Jeter 3.00
2 Mo Vaughn .25
3 Adam Dunn .75
4 Aubrey Huff .25

5 Jacque Jones .25
6 Kerry Wood .60
7 Barry Bonds 3.00
8 Kevin Brown .25
9 Sammy Sosa 2.00
10 Ray Durham .25
11 Carlos Beltran .50
12 Tony Batista .25
13 Bobby Abreu .25
14 Craig Biggio .25
15 Gary Sheffield .45
16 Jermaine Dye .25
17 Carlos Pena .25
18 Tim Salmon .35
19 Mike Piazza 2.00
20 Moises Alou .25
21 Edgardo Alfonzo .25
22 Mike Sweeney .25
23 Jay Gibbons .25
24 Kevin Millwood .25
25 A.J. Burnett .25
26 Austin Kearns .75
27 Rafael Palmeiro .75
28 Vladimir Guerrero 1.00
29 Paul Konerko .25
30 Scott Rolen .75
31 Fred McGriff .25
32 Frank Thomas 1.00
33 John Olerud .25
34 Eric Gagne .25
35 Nomar Garciaparra 2.00
36 Ryan Klesko .25
37 Lance Berkman .25
38 Andruw Jones .75
39 Pat Burrell .60
40 Juan Encarnacion .25
41 Curt Schilling .50
42 Jason Giambi .65
43 Barry Larkin .25
44 Alex Rodriguez 2.50
45 Kazuhisa Ishii .25
46 Pedro J. Martinez 1.00
47 Sean Burroughs .25
48 Roy Oswalt .40
49 Chipper Jones 1.50
50 Barry Zito .40
51 Jeff Kent .25
52 Rodrigo Lopez .25
53 Jim Thome .40
54 Ivan Rodriguez .60
55 Luis Gonzalez .40
56 Alfonso Soriano 1.00
57 Josh Beckett .25
58 Junior Spivey .25
59 Bernie Williams .40
60 Omar Vizquel .25
61 Eric Hinske .25
62 Jose Vidro .25
63 Bartolo Colon .25
64 Jim Edmonds .25
65 Ben Sheets .25
66 Mark Prior 1.00
67 Edgar Martinez .25
68 Raul Ibanez .25
69 Darin Erstad .40
70 Roger Clemens 1.75
71 C.C. Sabathia .25
72 Carlos Delgado .50
73 Tom Glavine .40
74 Magglio Ordonez .40
75 Ichiro Suzuki 1.50
76 Johnny Damon .40
77 Brian Giles .25
78 Jeff Bagwell 1.00
79 Greg Maddux 1.50
80 Eric Chavez .40
81 Larry Walker .25
82 Randy Johnson 1.00
83 Miguel Tejada .40
84 Todd Helton .75
85 Jarrod Washburn .25
86 Troy Glaus .75
87 Ken Griffey Jr. 2.00
88 Albert Pujols 2.00
89 Torii Hunter .25
90 Joe Crede .25
91 Matt Morris .25
92 Shawn Green .40
93 Manny Ramirez 1.00
94 Jason Kendall .25
95 Preston Wilson .25
96 Garret Anderson .25
97 Cliff Floyd .25
98 Sean Casey .25
99 Juan Gonzalez .75
100 Richie Sexson .25
101 Joe Borchard 3.00
102 Josh Stewart RC 3.00

103	Francisco Rodriguez	4.00
104	Jeremy Bonderman	6.00
105	Walter Young	3.00
106	Brandon Webb RC	10.00
107	Lyle Overbay	4.00
108	Jose Contreras RC	6.00
109	Victor Martinez	4.00
110	Hideki Matsui RC	10.00
111	Brian Stokes RC	3.00
112	Daniel Cabrera RC	6.00
113	Josh Willingham RC	3.00
114	Mark Teixeira	4.00
115	Pete LaForest RC	3.00
116	Chris Waters RC	3.00
117	Chien-Ming Wang RC	30.00
118	Ian Ferguson RC	3.00
119	Rocco Baldelli	3.00
120	Terrmel Sledge RC	3.00
121	Hank Blalock	4.00
122	Alejandro Machado RC	3.00
123	Hee Seop Choi	4.00
124	Guillermo Quiroz RC	4.00
125	Chase Utley	4.00
126	Nook Logan RC	3.00
127	Josh Hall RC	3.00
128	Ryan Church	3.00
129	Lew Ford RC	4.00
130	Francisco Rosario RC	3.00

Reflection

Cards 1-100 print run 25-50: 8-15X
Cards 101-130 p/r 101-130: .5-1.5X
Cards 1-100 p/r 51-80: 4-8X
Cards 1-100 p/r 81-130: 3-5X
Ascending consecutively #'d from 1-130.
Descending consecutively #'d from 130-1.

Article Insider

NM/M
Common Player: 4.00
Inserted 1:24

Adam Dunn	5.00
Andruw Jones	6.00
Alex Rodriguez	10.00
Alfonso Soriano	8.00
Chipper Jones	8.00
Curt Schilling	5.00
Derek Jeter	15.00
Don Mattingly	25.00
Greg Maddux	10.00
Jeff Bagwell	6.00
Jason Giambi	10.00
Lance Berkman	4.00
Magglio Ordonez	4.00
Mike Piazza	10.00
Miguel Tejada	4.00
Nomar Garciaparra	15.00
Pat Burrell	4.00
Pedro J. Martinez	8.00
Randy Johnson	6.00
Shawn Green	4.00
Sammy Sosa	10.00
Troy Glaus	5.00
Torii Hunter	5.00
Todd Helton	6.00
Vladimir Guerrero	6.00

Article Insider Autograph

NM/M
Quantity produced listed.

Lance Berkman/165	25.00
Lance Berkman/100	25.00
Lance Berkman/50	40.00
Derek Jeter/100	125.00
Don Mattingly/170	85.00
Don Mattingly/100	100.00

Long Ball Threats

NM/M
Complete Set (15): 15.00
Common Card: .50
Inserted 1:8

1	Derek Jeter, Nomar Garciaparra	3.00
2	Jim Thome, Pat Burrell	1.00
3	Alex Rodriguez, Rafael Palmeiro	3.00
4	Alfonso Soriano, Hideki Matsui	3.00
5	Torii Hunter, Vladimir Guerrero	1.00
6	Mike Sweeney, Phil Nevin	.50
7	Mike Piazza, Sammy Sosa	2.00
8	Shawn Green, Jason Giambi	1.00
9	Magglio Ordonez, Andruw Jones	1.00
10	Eric Chavez, Carlos Delgado	.75
11	Manny Ramirez, Jeff Bagwell	1.00
12	Scott Rolen, Troy Glaus	1.00
13	Barry Bonds, Miguel Tejada	3.00
14	Albert Pujols, Lance Berkman	2.00
15	Chipper Jones, Todd Helton	1.50

Long Ball Threats Single Jersey

NM/M
Common Player: 3.00
Inserted 1:13

Derek Jeter/Jsy, Nomar Garciaparra	15.00
Derek Jeter, Nomar Garciaparra/Jsy	10.00
Jim Thome/Jsy, Pat Burrell	6.00
Jim Thome, Pat Burrell/Jsy	6.00
Alfonso Soriano/Jsy, Hideki Matsui	8.00
Torii Hunter/Jsy, Vladimir Guerrero	6.00
Torii Hunter, Vladimir Guerrero/Jsy	6.00
Mike Sweeney/Jsy, Phil Nevin	3.00
Mike Sweeney, Phil Nevin/Jsy	3.00
Mike Piazza/Jsy, Sammy Sosa	8.00
Mike Piazza, Sammy Sosa/Jsy	10.00
Shawn Green/Jsy, Jason Giambi	4.00
Magglio Ordonez/Jsy, Andruw Jones	4.00
Eric Chavez, Carlos Delgado/Jsy	5.00
Manny Ramirez/Jsy, Jeff Bagwell	8.00
Manny Ramirez, Jeff Bagwell/Jsy	8.00
Scott Rolen/Jsy, Troy Glaus	6.00
Scott Rolen, Troy Glaus/Jsy	6.00
Barry Bonds, Miguel Tejada/Jsy	5.00
Albert Pujols, Lance Berkman/Jsy	4.00
Chipper Jones/Jsy, Todd Helton	8.00
Chipper Jones, Todd Helton/Jsy	6.00

Long Ball Threats Dual Jersey

NM/M
Common Card: 5.00
Inserted 1:72

Derek Jeter, Nomar Garciaparra	30.00
Jim Thome, Pat Burrell	15.00
Alex Rodriguez, Rafael Palmeiro	15.00
Torii Hunter, Vladimir Guerrero	10.00
Mike Sweeney, Phil Nevin	5.00
Mike Piazza, Sammy Sosa	20.00
Magglio Ordonez, Andruw Jones	10.00
Scott Rolen, Troy Glaus	10.00
Chipper Jones, Todd Helton	12.00

Long Ball Threats Dual Patch

NM/M
#'d to combined 2002 HR total.

Derek Jeter, Nomar Garciaparra/42	80.00
Jim Thome, Pat Burrell/89	30.00
Alex Rodriguez, Rafael Palmeiro/100	50.00
Mike Piazza, Sammy Sosa/82	75.00
Shawn Green, Jason Giambi/83	40.00
Magglio Ordonez, Andruw Jones/73	40.00
Manny Ramirez, Jeff Bagwell/64	40.00
Scott Rolen, Troy Glaus/61	50.00

Tools of the Game

NM/M
Complete Set (15): 20.00
Common Player: .75
Inserted 1:20

1	Adam Dunn	1.00
2	Chipper Jones	2.00
3	Torii Hunter	.75
4	Mike Piazza	1.50
5	Hideki Matsui	8.00
6	Nomar Garciaparra	3.00
7	Derek Jeter	4.00
8	Alex Rodriguez	3.00
9	Alfonso Soriano	2.00
10	Pat Burrell	.75
11	Barry Bonds	4.00
12	Jason Giambi	1.50
13	Sammy Sosa	2.00
14	Vladimir Guerrero	1.00
15	Ichiro Suzuki	2.00

Tools of the Game 1-Piece

NM/M
Common Player:
Inserted 1:42
2-Piece: 1.5-3X
Production 250
3-Piece: 3-6X
Production 100

Adam Dunn	6.00
Mike Piazza	8.00
Derek Jeter	15.00
Alex Rodriguez	10.00
Alfonso Soriano	10.00
Jason Giambi	8.00
Sammy Sosa	10.00
Vladimir Guerrero	

2003 Fleer Hardball

NM/M
Complete Set (280): 85.00
Common Player: .15
Common (241-280): .75
Inserted 1:2 Hobby
Pack (7): 1.75
Box (24): 30.00

1	Barry Bonds	2.00
2	Derek Jeter	2.00
3	Jason Varitek	.15
4	Magglio Ordonez	.25
5	Ryan Dempster	.15
6	Adam Everett	.15
7	Paul LoDuca	.15
8	Brad Wilkerson	.15
9	Al Leiter	.15
10	Jermaine Dye	.15
11	Robert Mackowiak	.15
12	J.T. Snow	.15
13	Juan Gonzalez	.60
14	Eric Hinske	.15
15	Greg Maddux	1.00
16	Moises Alou	.15
17	Carlos Lee	.15
18	Richard Hidalgo	.15
19	Jorge Posada	.25
20	Mike Lieberthal	.15
21	Jeff Cirillo	.15
22	Corey Patterson	.15
23	C.C. Sabathia	.15
24	Brian Giles	.15
25	Edgar Martinez	.15
26	Trot Nixon	.15
27	Kerry Wood	.50
28	Austin Kearns	.40
29	Lance Berkman	.15
30	Hideo Nomo	.50
31	Brad Radke	.15
32	John Valentin	.15
33	Tim Hudson	.35
34	Aramis Ramirez	.15
35	Kevin Mench	.15
36	Kevin Appier	.15
37	Chris Richard	.15
38	Ruben Mateo	.15
39	Juan Pierre	.15
40	Nick Neugebauer	.15
41	Mike Mussina	.40
42	Rich Aurilia	.15
43	Albert Pujols	1.00
44	Carlos Delgado	.50
45	Junior Spivey	.15
46	Marcus Giles	.15
47	Johnny Damon	.15
48	Mark Prior	.50
49	Omar Vizquel	.15
50	Craig Biggio	.15
51	Chuck Knoblauch	.15
52	Eric Milton	.15
53	Jeromy Burnitz	.15
54	Jim Thome	.15
55	Steve Finley	.15
56	Kevin Millwood	.15
57	Alex Gonzalez	.15
58	Ben Broussard	.15
59	Derek Lee	.15
60	Joe Randa	.15
61	Doug Mientkiewicz	.15
62	Jason L. Phillips	.15
63	Brett Myers	.15
64	Josh Fogg	.15
65	Reggie Sanders	.15
66	Chipper Jones	1.00
67	Roosevelt Brown	.15
68	Matt Lawton	.15
69	Charles Johnson	.15
70	Mark Quinn	.15
71	Jacque Jones	.15
72	Armando Benitez	.15
73	Bobby Abreu	.15
74	Jason Kendall	.15
75	Jeff Kent	.15
76	Mark Teixeira	.50
77	Garret Anderson	.15
78	Jerry Hairston Jr.	.15
79	Tony Graffanino	.15
80	Josh Beckett	.15
81	Eric Gagne	.15
82	Fernando Tatis	.15
83	Brett Tomko	.15
84	Fernando Vina	.15
85	Rafael Palmeiro	.65
86	Luis Gonzalez	.35
87	Javy Lopez	.15
88	Shea Hillenbrand	.15
89	Hee Seop Choi	.15
90	Preston Wilson	.15
91	Neifi Perez	.15
92	Ray Lankford	.15
93	Tsuyoshi Shinjo	.15
94	Ben Grieve	.15
95	Jarrod Washburn	.15
96	Gary Sheffield	.35
97	Derek Lowe	.15
98	Tony Womack	.15
99	Milton Bradley	.15
100	Brad Penny	.15
101	Mike Sweeney	.15
102	A.J. Pierzynski	.15
103	Edgardo Alfonzo	.15
104	Marlon Byrd	.15
105	Sean Burroughs	.15
106	Kazuhiro Sasaki	.15
107	Damian Rolls	.15
108	Troy Glaus	.60
109	Rafael Furcal	.15
110	Nomar Garciaparra	1.25
111	Josh Bard	.15
112	Alex Gonzalez	.15
113	Cristian Guzman	.15
114	Roger Cedeno	.15
115	Freddy Garcia	.15
116	Travis Phelps	.15
117	Juan Cruz	.15
118	Frank Thomas	.60
119	Jaret Wright	.15
120	Carlos Beltran	.45
121	Ronnie Belliard	.15
122	Roger Clemens	1.00
123	Vicente Padilla	.15
124	Joel Pineiro	.15
125	Jared Sandberg	.15
126	Tom Glavine	.35
127	Matt Clement	.15
128	Aaron Rowand	.15
129	Alex Escobar	.15
130	Randy Wolf	.15
131	Ichiro Suzuki	1.00
132	Toby Hall	.15
133	Scott Spiezio	.15
134	Bobby Higginson	.15
135	A.J. Burnett	.15
136	Cesar Izturis	.15
137	Roberto Alomar	.40
138	Trevor Hoffman	.15
139	Edgar Renteria	.15
140	Rusty Greer	.15
141	David Eckstein	.15
142	Pedro J. Martinez	.75
143	Joe Crede	.15
144	Robert Fick	.15
145	Mike Lowell	.15
146	Brian Jordan	.15
147	Mark Mulder	.25
148	Scott Rolen	.60
149	Ivan Rodriguez	.60
150	Adam Kennedy	.15
151	Ken Griffey Jr.	1.25
152	Larry Walker	.15
153	Carlos Pena	.15
154	Geoff Jenkins	.15
155	Bartolo Colon	.15
156	Mariano Rivera	.25
157	Robb Nen	.15
158	Bret Boone	.15
159	Shannon Stewart	.15
160	Chris Singleton	.15
161	Todd Walker	.15
162	Jay Payton	.15
163	Zach Day	.15
164	Bernie Williams	.40
165	Bubba Trammell	.15
166	Matt Morris	.15
167	Jose Cruz Jr.	.15
168	Mark Grace	.40
169	Andruw Jones	.75
170	Cliff Floyd	.15
171	Antonio Alfonseca	.15
172	Jeff Bagwell	.75
173	Shawn Green	.40
174	Joe Mays	.15
175	Mike Piazza	1.25
176	Adam Piatt	.15
177	Pokey Reese	.15
178	Carl Everett	.15
179	Tim Salmon	.35
180	Rodrigo Lopez	.15
181	Brandon Inge	.15
182	Kazuhisa Ishii	.15
183	Jose Vidro	.15
184	Barry Zito	.40
185	Phil Nevin	.15
186	J.D. Drew	.35
187	Vernon Wells	.15
188	Darin Erstad	.50
189	Barry Larkin	.15
190	Jason Jennings	.15
191	Luis Castillo	.15
192	Adrian Beltre	.35
193	Tony Armas	.15
194	Terrence Long	.15
195	Mark Kotsay	.15
196	Tino Martinez	.15
197	Jayson Werth	.15
198	Eric Chavez	.25
199	Matt Williams	.15
200	Jon Lieber	.15
201	Eddie Taubensee	.15
202	Shane Reynolds	.15
203	Alex Sanchez	.15
204	Jason Giambi	.60
205	Jimmy Rollins	.15
206	Jamie Moyer	.15
207	Francisco Rodriguez	.15
208	Marty Cordova	.15
209	Aaron Boone	.15
210	Mike Hampton	.15
211	Mark Redman	.15
212	Richie Sexson	.15
213	Andy Pettitte	.40
214	Livan Hernandez	.15
215	Jason Isringhausen	.15
216	Curt Schilling	.40
217	Manny Ramirez	.75
218	Jose Valentin	.15
219	Brent Butler	.15
220	Billy Wagner	.15
221	Ben Sheets	.15
222	Jeff Weaver	.15
223	Brent Abernathy	.15
224	Jay Gibbons	.15
225	Sean Casey	.15
226	Greg Norton	.15
227	Andy Van Hekken	.15
228	Kevin Brown	.15
229	Orlando Cabrera	.15
230	Scott Hatteberg	.15
231	Ryan Klesko	.15
232	Roy Halladay	.15
233	Randy Johnson	.75
234	Mark Buehrle	.15
235	Todd Helton	.60
236	Jeffrey Hammonds	.15
237	Sidney Ponson	.15
238	Kip Wells	.15
239	John Olerud	.15
240	Aubrey Huff	.15
241	Derek Jeter	4.00
242	Barry Bonds	4.00
243	Ichiro Suzuki	2.00
244	Troy Glaus	1.00
245	Alex Rodriguez	3.00
246	Sammy Sosa	2.00
247	Lance Berkman	.75
248	Jason Giambi	2.00
249	Nomar Garciaparra	2.50
250	Miguel Tejada	.75
251	Albert Pujols	2.50
252	Mike Piazza	2.50
253	Vladimir Guerrero	1.50
254	Shawn Green	.75
255	Todd Helton	.75
256	Ken Griffey Jr.	.75
257	Torii Hunter	.75
258	Chipper Jones	2.00
259	Alfonso Soriano	1.50
260	Luis Gonzalez	1.50
261	Pedro J. Martinez	1.50
262	Tim Hudson	.75
263	Roger Clemens	2.00
264	Greg Maddux	2.00
265	Randy Johnson	1.50
266	Vinnie Chulk	.50
267	Jose Castillo	.50
268	Craig Brazell RC	1.50
269	Felix Sanchez RC	.50
270	John Webb	.50
271	Josh Hall RC	.50
272	Alexis Rios	.50
273	Phil Seibel RC	.50
274	Prentice Redman RC	.50
275	Walter Young	1.00
276	Nic Jackson	.50
277	Adam Morrissey	.50
278	Bobby Jenks	.75
279	Rodrigo Moncalvo	.50
280	Chin-Feng Chen	1.00

Gold

Gold (1-240): 2-3X
Gold (241-280): 1-2X
Inserted 1:4 Hobby

Platinum

Cards (1-240): 8-15X
Cards (241-280): 3-5X
Production 50 Sets

Discs

NM/M
Complete Set (20): 50.00
Common Player: 1.00
Inserted 1:24

1D	Derek Jeter	8.00
2D	Barry Bonds	8.00
3D	Ichiro Suzuki	4.00
4D	Sammy Sosa	4.00
5D	Nomar Garciaparra	5.00
6D	Lance Berkman	1.50
7D	Jason Giambi	4.00
8D	Mike Piazza	5.00
9D	Shawn Green	1.50
10D	Barry Zito	1.50
11D	Albert Pujols	3.00
12D	Alex Rodriguez	6.00
13D	Tim Salmon	1.00
14D	Eric Chavez	1.00
15D	Ken Griffey Jr.	4.00
16D	Alfonso Soriano	3.00
17D	Vladimir Guerrero	2.50
18D	Francisco Rodriguez	1.00
19D	Miguel Tejada	1.50
20D	Randy Johnson	2.50

On the Ball

NM/M
Complete Set (15): 20.00
Common Player: 1.00
Inserted 1:12

1	Derek Jeter	4.00
2	Barry Bonds	4.00
3	Nomar Garciaparra	2.50
4	Alfonso Soriano	1.50
5	Mike Piazza	2.50
6	Alex Rodriguez	3.00
7	Chipper Jones	1.50
8	Randy Johnson	1.50
9	Pedro J. Martinez	1.50
10	Albert Pujols	1.50
11	Vladimir Guerrero	1.50
12	Sammy Sosa	2.00
13	Ichiro Suzuki	2.00
14	Troy Glaus	1.00
15	Jason Giambi	2.00

On the Ball Memorabilia

NM/M
Common Player: 5.00
Inserted 1:18

Derek Jeter/Bat	15.00
Barry Bonds/Jsy	15.00
Nomar Garciaparra/Jsy	10.00
Alfonso Soriano/Jsy	10.00
Mike Piazza/Jsy	10.00
Alex Rodriguez/Jsy	10.00
Chipper Jones/Bat	8.00
Randy Johnson/Jsy	8.00
Pedro J. Martinez/Jsy	8.00
Troy Glaus/Jsy	8.00

Round Numbers

		NM/M
Complete Set (14):		50.00
Common Player:		3.00
Production 1,000 Sets		
1	Nolan Ryan	10.00
2	Al Kaline	6.00
3	Mike Schmidt	6.00
4	Yogi Berra	4.00
5	Brooks Robinson	4.00
6	Tom Seaver	4.00
7	Willie McCovey	3.00
8	Harmon Killebrew	4.00
9	Richie Ashburn	3.00
10	Lou Brock	3.00
11	Jim Palmer	3.00
12	Willie Stargell	4.00
13	Whitey Ford	4.00
14	Robin Yount	5.00

Round Numbers Memorabilia

		NM/M
Inserted 1:288		
	Al Kaline/Jsy	20.00
	Mike Schmidt/Jsy	15.00
	Harmon Killebrew/Bat	30.00
	Lou Brock/Jsy	30.00

Round Trippers

		NM/M
Complete Set (20):		15.00
Common Player:		.50
Inserted 1:8		
1	Alfonso Soriano	1.50
2	Alex Rodriguez	3.00
3	Lance Berkman	.75
4	Shawn Green	.75
5	Pat Burrell	1.00
6	Andruw Jones	.75
7	Garret Anderson	.50
8	Miguel Tejada	.75
9	Mike Piazza	2.50
10	Eric Chavez	.50
11	Rafael Palmeiro	.75
12	Chipper Jones	2.00
13	Manny Ramirez	1.00
14	Jeff Bagwell	1.00
15	Torii Hunter	.75
16	Nomar Garciaparra	2.50
17	Sammy Sosa	2.00
18	Vladimir Guerrero	1.50
19	Troy Glaus	1.00
20	Jason Giambi	2.00

Round Trippers Rounding First

		NM/M
Common Player:		5.00
Quantity produced listed.		
Rounding Second:		No Pricing
Production 10 Sets		
Rounding Third:		No Pricing
Production Three Sets		
	Alfonso Soriano/Jsy/228	10.00
	Alex Rodriguez/Jsy/536	12.00
	Lance Berkman/Jsy/557	5.00
	Shawn Green/Bat/249	5.00
	Pat Burrell/Bat/502	10.00
	Andruw Jones/Jsy/569	5.00
	Garret Anderson/Bat/40	20.00
	Miguel Tejada/Jsy/524	5.00

Mike Piazza/Bat/289		12.00
Eric Chavez/Jsy/572		5.00
Rafael Palmeiro/Jsy/515		6.00
Chipper Jones/Jsy/570		10.00
Manny Ramirez/Jsy/530		8.00
Jeff Bagwell/Bat/344		6.00
Nomar Garciaparra/Bat/529		12.00

Signatures

	NM/M
Bonds 600 HR Inscription:	1-1.5X
Barry Bonds/255	200.00
Derek Jeter	110.00

2003 Fleer Hot Prospects

		NM/M
Complete Set (120):		
Common Player:		.25
Common SP (81-120):		4.00
Production 1,250 unless noted.		
Pack (5):		4.00
Box (15):		50.00
1	Derek Jeter	3.00
2	Ryan Klesko	.25
3	Troy Glaus	.75
4	Jeff Kent	.40
5	Frank Thomas	.75
6	Gary Sheffield	.50
7	Jim Edmonds	.40
8	Pat Burrell	.50
9	Jacque Jones	.25
10	Jason Jennings	.25
11	Pedro J. Martinez	1.00
12	Rafael Palmeiro	.50
13	Jason Kendall	.25
14	Tom Glavine	.40
15	Josh Beckett	.50
16	Luis Gonzalez	.40
17	Edgar Martinez	.50
18	Miguel Tejada	.50
19	Fred McGriff	.40
20	Adam Dunn	.50
21	Lance Berkman	.50
22	Magglio Ordonez	.40
23	Darin Erstad	.40
24	Rich Aurilia	.25
25	Mike Piazza	1.50
26	Shawn Green	.50
27	Larry Walker	.40
28	Manny Ramirez	.75
29	Juan Gonzalez	.75
30	Eric Chavez	.50
31	Torii Hunter	.50
32	A.J. Burnett	.25
33	Sammy Sosa	1.50
34	Eric Hinske	.25
35	Brian Giles	.50
36	Mike Sweeney	.25
37	Sean Casey	.25
38	Chipper Jones	1.50
39	Scott Rolen	.75
40	Jason Giambi	1.00
41	Mo Vaughn	.25
42	Roy Oswalt	.25
43	Paul Konerko	.25
44	Tim Salmon	.40
45	Edgardo Alfonzo	.25
46	Jermaine Dye	.25
47	Ben Sheets	.25
48	Todd Helton	.75
49	Greg Maddux	1.50
50	Albert Pujols	2.00
51	Jim Thome	.75
52	Vladimir Guerrero	.75
53	Ivan Rodriguez	.50
54	Nomar Garciaparra	2.00
55	Alex Rodriguez	2.50
56	Alfonso Soriano	1.50
57	Kazuhisa Ishii	.25
58	Austin Kearns	.50
59	Curt Schilling	.50
60	Bret Boone	.40
61	Mark Prior	1.50

62	Garret Anderson	.40
63	Barry Bonds	2.50
64	Roger Clemens	2.00
65	Jeff Bagwell	.75
66	Omar Vizquel	.40
67	Jay Gibbons	.25
68	Aubrey Huff	.25
69	Bobby Abreu	.25
70	Richie Sexson	.50
71	Bobby Higginson	.25
72	Kerry Wood	.50
73	Carlos Delgado	.25
74	Sean Burroughs	.25
75	Jose Vidro	.25
76	Ken Griffey Jr.	1.50
77	Randy Johnson	1.00
78	Ichiro Suzuki	1.50
79	Barry Zito	.50
80	Carlos Beltran	.25
81	Joe Borchard	4.00
82	Mark Teixeira	5.00
83	Brandon Webb RC	15.00
84	Shane Victorino/Auto./400 RC	25.00
85	Hee Seop Choi	4.00
86	Hank Blalock	5.00
87	Brett Myers	4.00
88	Mike Ryan RC	4.00
89	Jesse Foppert	4.00
90	Lyle Overbay	4.00
91	Brian Stokes/Auto./400 RC	10.00
92	Josh Hall/Auto./400 RC	10.00
93	Chris Waters/Auto./400 RC	10.00
94	Lew Ford/Auto./400 RC	20.00
95	Ian Ferguson/Auto./500 RC	8.00
96	Josh Willingham RC	5.00
97	Josh Stewart/Auto./500 RC	8.00
98	Pete LaForest/Auto./500 RC	8.00
99	J.Contreras/Auto./Jsy/300 RC	40.00
100	Terrmel Sledge/Auto./500 RC	8.00
101	Guillermo Quiroz/Auto./500 RC	10.00
102	Alejandro Machado/Auto./500 RC	10.00
103	Nook Logan/Auto/Jsy./400 RC	10.00
104	Robby Hammock/Auto./Jsy/400 RC	10.00
105	Hideki Matsui/Auto./Base RC	15.00
106	Wilfredo Ledezma RC	4.00
107	Rocco Baldelli/Jsy	8.00
108	Oscar Villarreal RC	4.00
109	Todd Wellemeyer/Auto./400 RC	15.00
110	Michael Hessman/Auto./400 RC	8.00
111	Jeremy Bonderman/Auto./Jsy/400	25.00
112	Craig Brazell/Auto./Jsy/400 RC	10.00
113	Francisco Rosario/Auto./Jsy/400 RC	10.00
114	Jeff Duncan/Auto./Jsy/400 RC	10.00
115	Daniel Cabrera/Auto./Jsy/400 RC	25.00
116	Dontrelle Willis/Auto./Jsy/400	15.00
117	Cory Stewart/Auto./500 RC	10.00
118	Tim Olson/Auto./Jsy/400 RC	10.00
119	Chien-Ming Wang/Auto./Jsy/500 RC	200.00

Class Of...

	NM/M
Common Duo:	10.00
Inserted 1:15	
Barry Zito, Josh Beckett	10.00
Pat Burrell, J.D. Drew	12.00
Mark Prior, Mark Teixeira	15.00
Austin Kearns, Sean Burroughs	10.00
Troy Glaus, Lance Berkman	10.00
Darin Erstad, Todd Helton	10.00
Manny Ramirez, Shawn Green	10.00
Matt Morris, Kerry Wood	10.00
Nomar Garciaparra, Paul Konerko	15.00
Alex Rodriguez, Torii Hunter	20.00

Cream of the Crop

		NM/M
Complete Set (15):		35.00
Common Player:		1.50
Inserted 1:5		
1	Barry Bonds	5.00
2	Derek Jeter	5.00
3	Ichiro Suzuki	3.00
4	Nomar Garciaparra	3.00
5	Roger Clemens	3.00
6	Alex Rodriguez	4.00
7	Greg Maddux	2.50
8	Mike Piazza	2.50

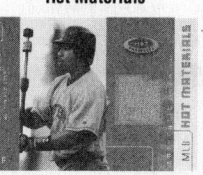

9	Sammy Sosa	2.50
10	Jason Giambi	2.00
11	Hideki Matsui	6.00
12	Albert Pujols	5.00
13	Vladimir Guerrero	1.50
14	Jim Thome	1.50
15	Pedro J. Martinez	1.50

Hot Materials

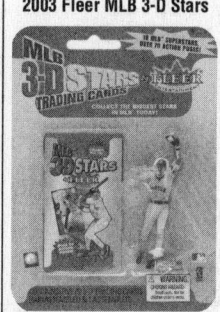

		NM/M
Common Player:		5.00
Production 499 Sets		
Red-Hots:		1-2X
Production 50		
1HM	Derek Jeter	20.00
2HM	Torii Hunter	8.00
3HM	Mark Prior	8.00
4HM	Nomar Garciaparra	15.00
5HM	Sammy Sosa	15.00
6HM	Rafael Palmeiro	6.00
7HM	Hee Seop Choi	10.00
8HM	Mark Teixeira	5.00
9HM	Mike Piazza	10.00
10HM	Pat Burrell	8.00
11HM	Jim Thome	8.00
12HM	Lance Berkman	5.00
13HM	Vladimir Guerrero	5.00
14HM	Troy Glaus	5.00
15HM	Chipper Jones	8.00
16HM	Lyle Overbay	5.00
17HM	Jason Giambi	8.00
18HM	Alex Rodriguez	10.00
19HM	Miguel Tejada	5.00
20HM	Adam Dunn	8.00
21HM	Randy Johnson	8.00
22HM	Josh Beckett	5.00
23HM	Alfonso Soriano	10.00
24HM	Greg Maddux	10.00
25HM	Shawn Green	5.00
26HM	Carlos Delgado	5.00
27HM	Todd Helton	6.00
28HM	Mike Sweeney	5.00
29HM	Manny Ramirez	6.00
30HM	Tom Glavine	6.00

Hot Tandems

	NM/M
Common Duo:	8.00
Production 100 Sets	
Red-Hots numbered to 10.	
Derek Jeter, Chipper Jones	25.00
Derek Jeter, Mike Piazza	25.00
Derek Jeter, Miguel Tejada	25.00
Torii Hunter, Lance Berkman	10.00
Mark Prior, Sammy Sosa	25.00
Sammy Sosa, Pat Burrell	20.00
Rafael Palmeiro, Mark Teixeira	10.00
Hee Seop Choi, Lyle Overbay	15.00
Alex Rodriguez, Mark Teixeira	20.00
Mike Piazza, Chipper Jones	15.00
Pat Burrell, Jim Thome	10.00
Lance Berkman, Adam Dunn	8.00
Nomar Garciaparra, Miguel Tejada	15.00
Randy Johnson, Greg Maddux	12.00
Mark Prior, Josh Beckett	10.00

Miguel Tejada, Alex Rodriguez, Jason Giambi, Jim Thome		15.00 10.00

Hot Triple Patch

		NM/M
Production 50 Sets		
Some not priced yet.		
Derek Jeter, Nomar Garciaparra, Alex Rodriguez		125.00
Mark Prior, Josh Beckett, Greg Maddux		80.00
Mike Piazza, Pat Burrell, Jim Thome		50.00
Lance Berkman, Troy Glaus, Chipper Jones, Randy Johnson, Alfonso Soriano, Shawn Green		50.00
Derek Jeter, Torii Hunter, Mark Prior		75.00
Nomar Garciaparra, Sammy Sosa, Mike Piazza		90.00
Pat Burrell, Jim Thome, Lance Berkman		40.00
Vladimir Guerrero, Troy Glaus, Chipper Jones		60.00
Alfonso Soriano, Greg Maddux, Shawn Green		60.00

Playergraphs

		NM/M
Common Player:		10.00
Production 400 Sets		
Red-Hots:		1-1.5X
Production 100		
	Hank Blalock	20.00
	Brett Myers	10.00
	Mark Prior	35.00
	Carlos Zambrano	20.00
	Mark Teixeira	20.00
	Francisco Rodriguez	15.00
	Roy Oswalt	15.00
	Xavier Nady	10.00
	Jose Reyes	25.00
	Aubrey Huff	10.00

2003 Fleer MLB 3-D Stars

Eighteen players are included in this novelty card issue from Fleer Entertainment division. Each player is printed on a 2-1/4" x 3-1/2" card that is die-cut to allow the pieces to be punched out and assembled in a variety of action poses. Each 5-5/8" x 7-3/8" blister pack contains five 3-D cards, one assembled and four unassembled. Values shown are for unpunched cards.

		NM/M
Complete Set (18):		7.50
Common Player:		.25
1	Derek Jeter	1.00
2	Barry Bonds	1.00
3	Greg Maddux	.40
4	Nomar Garciaparra	.65
5	Curt Schilling	.25
6	Jason Giambi	.50
7	Pedro Martinez	.25
8	Alfonso Soriano	.75
9	Alex Rodriguez	.75
10	Ken Griffey Jr.	.60
11	Sammy Sosa	.60
12	Albert Pujols	.50
13	Roger Clemens	.50
14	Chipper Jones	.40
15	Ichiro	.50
16	Miguel Tejada	.25
17	Mark Prior	.50
18	Mariano Rivera	.25

2003 Fleer Mystique

		NM/M
Complete Set (130):		
Common Player:		.25
Common SP (81-130):		3.00
Production 699		
Pack (4):		3.00
Box (20):		40.00
1	Alex Rodriguez	2.50
2	Derek Jeter	3.00

3	Jose Vidro	.25
4	Miguel Tejada	.40
5	Albert Pujols	2.50
6	Rocco Baldelli	.25
7	Jose Reyes	.50
8	Hideo Nomo	.75
9	Hank Blalock	.75
10	Chipper Jones	1.50
11	Barry Larkin	.25
12	Alfonso Soriano	1.00
13	Aramis Ramirez	.25
14	Darin Erstad	.65
15	Jim Edmonds	.25
16	Garret Anderson	.25
17	Todd Helton	1.00
18	Jason Kendall	.25
19	Aubrey Huff	.25
20	Troy Glaus	.75
21	Sammy Sosa	2.00
22	Roger Clemens	1.75
23	Mark Teixeira	.25
24	Barry Bonds	3.00
25	Jim Thome	.25
26	Carlos Delgado	.50
27	Vladimir Guerrero	1.00
28	Austin Kearns	.50
29	Pat Burrell	.75
30	Ken Griffey Jr.	2.00
31	Greg Maddux	1.50
32	Corey Patterson	.25
33	Larry Walker	.25
34	Kerry Wood	.65
35	Frank Thomas	1.00
36	Dontrelle Willis	.25
37	Randy Johnson	1.00
38	Curt Schilling	.40
39	Jay Gibbons	.25
40	Dmitri Young	.25
41	Edgar Martinez	.25
42	Kevin Brown	.25
43	Scott Rolen	1.00
44	Adam Dunn	.75
45	Pedro J. Martinez	.75
46	Corey Koskie	.25
47	Tom Glavine	.40
48	Torii Hunter	.40
49	Shawn Green	.40
50	Nomar Garciaparra	2.00
51	Bernie Williams	.40
52	Milton Bradley	.25
53	Jason Giambi	.75
54	Mike Lieberthal	.25
55	Jeff Bagwell	1.00
56	Carlos Pena	.25
57	Lance Berkman	.25
58	Jose Cruz Jr.	.25
59	Josh Beckett	.25
60	Mark Mulder	.40
61	Mike Piazza	2.00
62	Mark Prior	1.00
63	Sean Burroughs	.25
64	Angel Berroa	.25
65	Geoff Jenkins	.25
66	Magglio Ordonez	.25
67	Craig Biggio	.25
68	Roberto Alomar	.40
69	Hee Seop Choi	.25
70	J.D. Drew	.25
71	Richie Sexson	.25
72	Brian Giles	.25
73	Gary Sheffield	.50
74	Manny Ramirez	1.00
75	Barry Zito	.45
76	Andruw Jones	1.00
77	Ivan Rodriguez	.65
78	Ichiro Suzuki	2.00
79	Mike Sweeney	.25
80	Vernon Wells	.25
81	Craig Brazell RC	5.00
82	Wilfredo Ledezma RC	4.00
83	Josh Willingham RC	6.00
84	Chien-Ming Wang RC	35.00
85	Mike Ryan RC	3.00
86	Mike Gallo RC	3.00
87	Rickie Weeks RC	3.00
88	Brian Stokes RC	3.00
89	Humberto Quintero RC	3.00
90	Ramon Nivar RC	3.00
91	Jeremy Griffiths RC	3.00
92	Terrmel Sledge RC	4.00
93	Brandon Webb RC	20.00
94	David DeJesus RC	3.00
95	Doug Waechter RC	3.00
96	Jeremy Bonderman RC	3.00
97	Felix Sanchez RC	3.00
98	Colin Porter RC	3.00
99	Francisco Cruceta RC	3.00
100	Hideki Matsui RC	15.00

101	Chris Waters RC	5.00
102	Dan Haren RC	5.00
103	Lew Ford RC	5.00
104	Oscar Villarreal RC	3.00
105	Ryan Wagner RC	5.00
106	Prentice Redman RC	3.00
107	Josh Stewart RC	5.00
108	Carlos Mendez RC	3.00
109	Michael Hessman RC	5.00
110	Josh Hall RC	5.00
111	Daniel Garcia RC	5.00
112	Matt Kata RC	5.00
113	Michel Hernandez RC	3.00
114	Sergio Mitre RC	5.00
115	Pete LaForest RC	5.00
116	Edwin Jackson RC	6.00
117	Matt Diaz RC	5.00
118	Greg Aquino RC	3.00
119	Jose Contreras RC	8.00
120	Jeff Duncan RC	6.00
121	Richard Fischer RC	3.00
122	Todd Wellemeyer RC	6.00
123	Robby Hammock RC	5.00
124	Delmon Young RC	10.00
125	Clint Barmes RC	5.00
126	Phil Seibel RC	3.00
127	Bo Hart RC	5.00
128	Jon Leicester RC	5.00
129	Chad Gaudin RC	6.00
130	Guillermo Quiroz RC	5.00

Gold

Stars (1-80): 4-8X
Production 150
SP's (81-130): 1-2X
Production 50

Awe Pairs

Larry Walker, Colorado Rockies / Todd Helton, Colorado Rockies

		NM/M
Complete Set (20):		60.00
Common Duo:		2.00
Production 250 Sets		
Golds:		1.5X
#'d to team win total for 2003		
1	Nomar Garciaparra, Pedro J. Martinez	8.00
2	Derek Jeter, Alfonso Soriano	8.00
3	Rocco Baldelli, Aubrey Huff	2.00
4	Carlos Delgado, Vernon Wells	2.00
5	Troy Glaus, Garret Anderson	2.00
6	Ichiro Suzuki, Bret Boone	5.00
7	Alex Rodriguez, Hank Blalock	8.00
8	Chipper Jones, Andruw Jones	5.00
9	Dontrelle Willis, Mike Lowell	3.00
10	Vladimir Guerrero, Orlando Cabrera	4.00
11	Tom Glavine, Mike Piazza	5.00
12	Jim Thome, Mike Lieberthal	3.00
13	Sammy Sosa, Corey Patterson	6.00
14	Jeff Bagwell, Lance Berkman	3.00
15	Geoff Jenkins, Richie Sexson	2.00
16	Albert Pujols, Jim Edmonds	6.00
17	Todd Helton, Larry Walker	3.00
18	Paul LoDuca, Shawn Green	2.00
19	Ryan Klesko, Sean Burroughs	2.00
20	Barry Bonds, Rich Aurilia	8.00

Awe Pairs Game-Used

		NM/M
Common Duo:		10.00
Production 100 Sets		
Golds:		No Pricing

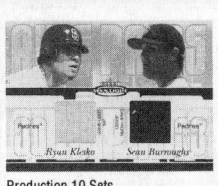

Ryan Klesko / Sean Burroughs

Production 10 Sets

	Nomar Garciaparra, Pedro J. Martinez	25.00
	Derek Jeter, Alfonso Soriano	30.00
	Rocco Baldelli, Aubrey Huff	15.00
	Carlos Delgado, Vernon Wells	10.00
	Troy Glaus, Garret Anderson	10.00
	Chipper Jones, Andruw Jones	15.00
	Dontrelle Willis, Mike Lowell	
	Vladimir Guerrero, Orlando Cabrera	10.00
	Tom Glavine, Mike Piazza	20.00
	Jim Thome, Mike Lieberthal	15.00
	Sammy Sosa, Corey Patterson	20.00
	Jeff Bagwell, Lance Berkman	15.00
	Geoff Jenkins, Richie Sexson	10.00
	Albert Pujols, Jim Edmonds	20.00
	Todd Helton, Larry Walker	10.00
	Paul LoDuca, Shawn Green	10.00
	Ryan Klesko, Sean Burroughs	10.00

Diamond Dominators

		NM/M
Complete Set (10):		50.00
Common Player:		3.00
Production 100 Sets		
1	Mike Piazza	8.00
2	Greg Maddux	8.00
3	Alfonso Soriano	5.00
4	Barry Zito	3.00
5	Alex Rodriguez	10.00
6	Roger Clemens	10.00
7	Sammy Sosa	10.00
8	Adam Dunn	3.00
9	Randy Johnson	5.00
10	Pedro J. Martinez	5.00

Diamond Dominators Gold

		NM/M
Some not priced due to scarcity.		
Numbered to jersey number.		
1DD	Mike Piazza/31	25.00
2DD	Greg Maddux/31	25.00
4DD	Barry Zito/75	5.00
8DD	Adam Dunn/44	6.00
9DD	Randy Johnson/51	8.00
10DD	Pedro Martinez/45	10.00

Diamond Dominators Game-Used

		NM/M
Common Player:		6.00
Production 75 Sets		
Golds:		No Pricing
Production 10 Sets		
RC	Roger Clemens	20.00
AD	Adam Dunn	6.00
RJ	Randy Johnson	10.00
GM	Greg Maddux	25.00
PM	Pedro Martinez	12.00
MP	Mike Piazza	15.00
AR	Alex Rodriguez	15.00
AS	Alfonso Soriano	12.00
SS	Sammy Sosa	20.00
BZ	Barry Zito	8.00

Ink Appeal Autographs

		NM/M
Common Player:		15.00
Production 50 Sets		
RB	Rocco Baldelli	40.00
HB	Hank Blalock	35.00
BH	Bo Hart	25.00
AH	Aubrey Huff	15.00
TH	Torii Hunter	20.00
CP	Corey Patterson	15.00
JR	Jose Reyes	30.00
MR	Mike Ryan	15.00
JW	Josh Willingham	15.00

Ink Appeal Gold Autographs

		NM/M
Numbered to jersey number.		
Some not priced due to scarcity.		
BH	Bo Hart/31	50.00
TH	Torii Hunter/48	20.00
MR	Mike Ryan/54	15.00
JW	Josh Willingham/70	12.00

Ink Appeal Dual Autographs

	NM/M
No pricing due to scarcity.	
Production 20 Sets	

	Golds:	No Pricing
	Production Five Sets	

Rare Finds

		NM/M
Complete Set (10):		40.00
Common Trio:		3.00
Production 250 Sets		
1	Jason Giambi, Roger Clemens, Derek Jeter	8.00
2	Randy Johnson, Curt Schilling, Brandon Webb	4.00
3	Nomar Garciaparra, Pedro J. Martinez, Manny Ramirez	8.00
4	Mark Prior, Kerry Wood, Sammy Sosa	5.00
5	Jeff Bagwell, Craig Biggio, Lance Berkman	3.00
6	Austin Kearns, Adam Dunn, Barry Larkin	3.00
7	Jim Edmonds, Scott Rolen, J.D. Drew	3.00
8	Chipper Jones, Andruw Jones, Greg Maddux	5.00
9	Barry Zito, Miguel Tejada, Mark Mulder	3.00
10	Alex Rodriguez, Mark Teixeira, Rafael Palmeiro	8.00

Rare Finds Autographs

No Pricing:	
Production 15 Sets	
Auto./Game-Used:	No Pricing
Production Five Sets	

Rare Finds Single Swatch

		NM/M
Common Player:		6.00
Production 150 Sets		
Golds:		No Pricing
Production 15 Sets		
JG	Jason Giambi, Roger Clemens, Derek Jeter	10.00
RC	Jason Giambi, Roger Clemens, Derek Jeter	15.00
DJ	Jason Giambi, Roger Clemens, Derek Jeter	20.00
RJ	Randy Johnson, Curt Schilling, Brandon Webb	8.00
BW	Randy Johnson, Curt Schilling, Brandon Webb	10.00
NG	Nomar Garciaparra, Pedro J. Martinez, Manny Ramirez	15.00
PM	Nomar Garciaparra, Pedro J. Martinez, Manny Ramirez	8.00
MP	Mark Prior, Kerry Wood, Sammy Sosa	10.00
SS	Mark Prior, Kerry Wood, Sammy Sosa	10.00
JB	Jeff Bagwell, Craig Biggio, Lance Berkman	6.00
AK	Austin Kearns, Adam Dunn, Barry Larkin	6.00
BL	Austin Kearns, Adam Dunn, Barry Larkin	6.00
SR	Jim Edmonds, Scott Rolen, J.D. Drew	10.00
JD	Jim Edmonds, Scott Rolen, J.D. Drew	10.00
CJ	Chipper Jones, Andruw Jones, Greg Maddux	10.00
GM	Chipper Jones, Andruw Jones, Greg Maddux	15.00
MT	Barry Zito, Miguel Tejada, Mark Mulder	6.00
MM	Barry Zito, Miguel Tejada, Mark Mulder	6.00
AR	Alex Rodriguez, Mark Teixeira, Rafael Palmeiro	15.00
MT	Alex Rodriguez, Mark Teixeira, Rafael Palmeiro	

Rare Finds Dual Swatch

		NM/M
Common Dual:		10.00
Production 75 Sets		
Golds:		No Pricing
Production 10 Sets		
	Jason Giambi, Roger Clemens, Derek Jeter	35.00

	Golds:	No Pricing

		NM/M
	Jason Giambi, Roger Clemens, Derek Jeter	40.00
	Randy Johnson, Curt Schilling, Brandon Webb	15.00
	Randy Johnson, Curt Schilling, Brandon Webb	10.00
	Nomar Garciaparra, Pedro J. Martinez, Manny Ramirez	20.00
	Nomar Garciaparra, Pedro J. Martinez, Manny Ramirez	
	Mark Prior, Kerry Wood, Sammy Sosa	15.00
	Mark Prior, Kerry Wood, Sammy Sosa	20.00
	Jeff Bagwell, Craig Biggio, Lance Berkman	10.00
	Austin Kearns, Adam Dunn, Barry Larkin	10.00
	Jim Edmonds, Scott Rolen, J.D. Drew	15.00
	Chipper Jones, Andruw Jones, Greg Maddux	20.00
	Chipper Jones, Andruw Jones, Greg Maddux	20.00
	Barry Zito, Miguel Tejada, Mark Mulder	10.00
	Alex Rodriguez, Mark Teixeira, Rafael Palmeiro	20.00

Rare Finds Triple Swatch

		NM/M
Golds:		No Pricing
Production 50 Sets		
Production Five Sets		
	Jason Giambi, Roger Clemens, Derek Jeter	50.00
	Randy Johnson, Curt Schilling, Brandon Webb	25.00
	Nomar Garciaparra, Pedro J. Martinez, Manny Ramirez	60.00
	Mark Prior, Kerry Wood, Sammy Sosa	40.00
	Jeff Bagwell, Craig Biggio, Lance Berkman	
	Austin Kearns, Adam Dunn, Barry Larkin	20.00
	Jim Edmonds, Scott Rolen, J.D. Drew	25.00
	Chipper Jones, Andruw Jones, Greg Maddux	40.00
	Barry Zito, Miguel Tejada, Mark Mulder	15.00
	Alex Rodriguez, Mark Teixeira, Rafael Palmeiro	40.00

Secret Weapons

		NM/M
Complete Set (10):		25.00
Common Player:		2.00
Production 250 Sets		
Golds:		1X
#'d to career batting average		
1	Hank Blalock	3.00
2	Dontrelle Willis	5.00
3	Jose Reyes	3.00
4	Bo Hart	4.00
5	Corey Patterson	4.00
6	Hideki Matsui	8.00
7	Mark Teixeira	3.00
8	Brandon Webb	3.00
9	Rocco Baldelli	3.00
10	Mark Prior	5.00

Shining Stars

Jim Thome, Philadelphia Phillies

		NM/M
Complete Set (115):		
Common Player:		.15
Common Prospect (91-115):		3.00
Production 1,500		
Pack (5):		3.00
Box (24):		50.00
1	Luis Castillo	.15
2	Derek Jeter	.75
3	Vladimir Guerrero	.75
4	Bobby Higginson	.15
5	Pat Burrell	.40
6	Ivan Rodriguez	.60

		NM/M
Complete Set (15):		50.00
Common Player:		2.00
Production 300 Sets		
1SS	Derek Jeter	8.00
2SS	Barry Bonds	8.00
3SS	Nomar Garciaparra	6.00
4SS	Austin Kearns	2.00
5SS	Vladimir Guerrero	3.00
6SS	Jim Thome	3.00
7SS	Ichiro Suzuki	5.00
8SS	Jason Giambi	3.00
9SS	Albert Pujols	8.00
10SS	Ken Griffey Jr.	5.00
11SS	Chipper Jones	5.00
12SS	Scott Rolen	3.00
13SS	Manny Ramirez	3.00
14SS	Jeff Bagwell	3.00
15SS	Torii Hunter	2.00

Shining Stars Gold

		NM/M
Numbered to career HR total.		
1SS	Derek Jeter/127	10.00
2SS	Barry Bonds/658	15.00
3SS	Nomar Garciaparra/173	10.00
4SS	Austin Kearns/28	4.00
5SS	Vladimir Guerrero/234	4.00
6SS	Jim Thome/381	3.00
7SS	Ichiro Suzuki/29	30.00
8SS	Jason Giambi/269	4.00
9SS	Albert Pujols/114	8.00
10SS	Ken Griffey Jr./481	4.00
11SS	Chipper Jones/280	5.00
12SS	Scott Rolen/192	4.00
13SS	Manny Ramirez/347	3.00
14SS	Jeff Bagwell/419	4.00
15SS	Torii Hunter/96	4.00

Shining Stars Game-Used

		NM/M
Common Player:		6.00
Production 100 Sets		
Patch:		1.5X
Production 50 Sets		
JB	Jeff Bagwell	8.00
CD	Carlos Delgado	6.00
NG	Nomar Garciaparra	15.00
JG	Jason Giambi	8.00
TH	Todd Helton	8.00
TH	Torii Hunter	8.00
DJ	Derek Jeter	20.00
AJ	Andruw Jones	6.00
CJ	Chipper Jones	10.00
AK	Austin Kearns	6.00
AP	Albert Pujols	15.00
MR	Manny Ramirez	8.00
SR	Scott Rolen	6.00
JT	Jim Thome	8.00

2003 Fleer N.Y. Mets

While the basic format of Fleer Tradition was preserved in this stadium give-away set, different photos were used than those found in regular-issue packs. Persons attending a special Baseball Card Pack promotional game received a cello-wrapped set of seven player cards and a header card.

		NM/M
Complete Set (8):		4.00
Common Player:		.25
1	Mike Piazza	3.00
2	Tom Glavine	.50
3	Cliff Floyd	.25
4	Al Leiter	.25
5	Jae Seo	.25
6	John Franco	.25
7	Ty Wigginton	.25
---	Header Card	.10

2003 Fleer Patchworks

Magglio Ordonez, Chicago White Sox

		NM/M

7	Craig Biggio	.15
8	Troy Glaus	.60
9	Barry Bonds	2.00
10	Hideo Nomo	.60
11	Barry Larkin	.35
12	Roberto Alomar	.35
13	Rodrigo Lopez	.15
14	Eric Chavez	.25
15	Shawn Green	.25
16	Joe Randa	.15
17	Mark Grace	.25
18	Jason Kendall	.15
19	Hee Seop Choi	.15
20	Luis Gonzalez	.15
21	Sammy Sosa	1.25
22	Larry Walker	.15
23	Phil Nevin	.15
24	Manny Ramirez	.75
25	Jim Thome	.75
26	Randy Johnson	.75
27	Jose Vidro	.15
28	Austin Kearns	.35
29	Mike Sweeney	.15
30	Magglio Ordonez	.15
31	Mike Piazza	1.25
32	Eric Hinske	.15
33	Alex Rodriguez	1.50
34	Kerry Wood	.60
35	Matt Morris	.15
36	Lance Berkman	.15
37	Michael Cuddyer	.15
38	Curt Schilling	.40
39	Sean Burroughs	.15
40	Ken Griffey Jr.	1.25
41	Edgardo Alfonzo	.15
42	Carlos Pena	.15
43	Adam Dunn	.75
44	Pedro J. Martinez	.75
45	Miguel Tejada	.35
46	Tom Glavine	.35
47	Torii Hunter	.15
48	Jason Giambi	.35
49	Tony Batista	.15
50	Ben Grieve	.15
51	Ichiro Suzuki	1.25
52	Bobby Abreu	.15
53	Todd Helton	.15
54	Kazuhiro Sasaki	.15
55	Nomar Garciaparra	1.25
56	Francisco Rodriguez	.15
57	Ellis Burks	.15
58	Frank Thomas	.75
59	Greg Maddux	1.00
60	Josh Beckett	.25
61	Brad Wilkerson	.15
62	Joe Borchard	.15
63	Carlos Delgado	.40
64	Alfonso Soriano	.15
65	Chipper Jones	1.00
66	J.D. Drew	.25
67	Mark Prior	.75
68	Rafael Palmeiro	.60
69	Jeff Kent	.15
70	Adrian Beltre	.25
71	Marlon Byrd	.15
72	Orlando Hudson	.15
73	Junior Spivey	.15
74	Jeff Bagwell	.75
75	Barry Zito	.15
76	Roger Clemens	1.00
77	Aubrey Huff	.15
78	Geoff Jenkins	.15
79	Andruw Jones	.75
80	Scott Rolen	.75
81	Omar Vizquel	.15
82	Darin Erstad	.50
83	Bernie Williams	.75
84	Freddy Garcia	.15
85	Richie Sexson	.15
86	Josh Phelps	.15
87	Albert Pujols	1.50
88	Aramis Ramirez	.15
89	Shea Hillenbrand	.15
90	Cristian Guzman	.15
91	Adam LaRoche	3.00
92	David Pember RC	3.00
93	Terrmel Sledge RC	3.00
94	Hideki Matsui RC	10.00
95	Nook Logan RC	3.00
96	Jose Contreras RC	4.00
97	Pete LaForest RC	3.00
98	Richard Fischer RC	3.00
99	Francisco Rosario RC	3.00
100	Josh Willingham RC	4.00
101	Alejandro Machado RC	3.00
102	Lew Ford RC	3.00
103	Joe Valentine RC	3.00
104	Guillermo Quiroz RC	3.00
105	Chien-Ming Wang RC	20.00
106	Jhonny Peralta RC	3.00
107	Shane Victorino RC	8.00
108	Prentice Redman RC	3.00
109	Matt Bruback RC	3.00
110	Lance Niekro RC	3.00
111	Travis Hughes RC	3.00
112	Nic Jackson RC	3.00
113	Hector Luna RC	4.00
114	Cliff Lee RC	3.00
115	Tim Olson RC	3.00

Star Ruby

Stars (1-90):	4-8X
Prospects (91-115):	1-30X
Production 100 Sets	

Diamond Ink

Quantity signed listed.	
Derek Jeter/210	90.00

	NM/M
Derek Jeter/101	125.00
Derek Jeter/50	175.00
Mark Prior/88	40.00
Troy Glaus/351	25.00
Mike Schmidt/194	75.00

Licensed Apparel - Jersey

	NM/M
Common Player:	4.00
Production 500 Sets	
J.D. Drew	8.00
Magglio Ordonez	6.00
Todd Helton	8.00
Paul Konerko	4.00
Shawn Green	6.00
Carlos Beltran	4.00
Kevin Brown	4.00
Shannon Stewart	4.00
Mike Mussina	8.00
Adam Dunn	10.00
Jimmy Rollins	4.00
Darin Erstad	6.00
Chipper Jones	10.00
Mike Piazza	10.00
Derek Jeter	

Licensed Apparel - Patch

	NM/M
Common Player:	10.00
Production 300 Sets	
J.D. Drew	12.00
Magglio Ordonez	15.00
Todd Helton	20.00
Paul Konerko	10.00
Shawn Green	15.00
Carlos Beltran	10.00
Kevin Brown	10.00
Shannon Stewart	10.00
Mike Mussina	15.00
Adam Dunn	20.00
Jimmy Rollins	15.00
Darin Erstad	25.00
Chipper Jones	20.00
Mike Piazza	25.00
Derek Jeter	40.00

National Pastime

	NM/M
Complete Set (25):	40.00
Common Player:	1.00
Inserted 1:12	
1NP Barry Bonds	6.00
2NP Kazuhiro Sasaki	1.00
3NP Mike Piazza	4.00
4NP Barry Zito	1.50
5NP Sammy Sosa	3.00
6NP Pedro J. Martinez	2.00
7NP Craig Biggio	1.00
8NP Rafael Palmeiro	1.50
9NP Greg Maddux	3.00
10NP Manny Ramirez	2.00
11NP Adam Dunn	1.50
12NP Omar Vizquel	1.00
13NP Hideo Nomo	1.00
14NP Alex Rodriguez	5.00
15NP Pat Burrell	1.00
16NP Nomar Garciaparra	4.00
17NP Randy Johnson	2.00
18NP Juan Gonzalez	1.50
19NP Chipper Jones	3.00
20NP Frank Thomas	1.50
21NP Vladimir Guerrero	2.00
22NP Troy Glaus	2.00
23NP Albert Pujols	3.00
24NP Ichiro Suzuki	3.00
25NP Ken Griffey Jr.	3.00

National Pastime - MLB Logo

Production One Set:

National Patchtime-Commemorative

Production 25 Sets: No Pricing

National Patchtime - Nameplate

	NM/M
Production 50 Sets	
Vladimir Guerrero	40.00
Rafael Palmeiro	25.00
Nomar Garciaparra	40.00
Greg Maddux	30.00
Sammy Sosa	60.00
Mike Piazza	35.00
Barry Zito	35.00
Hideo Nomo	50.00

Alex Rodriguez	50.00
Pat Burrell	25.00
Randy Johnson	50.00
Chipper Jones	35.00
Frank Thomas	40.00
Troy Glaus	30.00

National Patchtime - Number

	NM/M
Common Player:	15.00
Production 75 Sets	
Vladimir Guerrero	20.00
Manny Ramirez	25.00
Craig Biggio	15.00
Rafael Palmeiro	20.00
Nomar Garciaparra	40.00
Greg Maddux	25.00
Sammy Sosa	45.00
Mike Piazza	30.00
Pedro J. Martinez	25.00
Hideo Nomo	25.00
Alex Rodriguez	30.00
Pat Burrell	20.00
Randy Johnson	45.00
Chipper Jones	35.00
Frank Thomas	30.00

National Patchtime - Team Name

	NM/M
Common Player:	15.00
Production 100 Sets	
Vladimir Guerrero	15.00
Rafael Palmeiro	20.00
Nomar Garciaparra	35.00
Sammy Sosa	40.00
Mike Piazza	30.00
Barry Zito	20.00
Hideo Nomo	30.00
Alex Rodriguez	30.00
Pat Burrell	20.00
Randy Johnson	45.00
Chipper Jones	35.00
Troy Glaus	30.00
Omar Vizquel	20.00

National Patchtime - Trim

	NM/M
Common Player:	12.00
Production 200 Sets	
Vladimir Guerrero	12.00
Manny Ramirez	15.00
Rafael Palmeiro	12.00
Nomar Garciaparra	25.00
Greg Maddux	20.00
Mike Piazza	20.00
Pedro J. Martinez	20.00
Hideo Nomo	20.00
Alex Rodriguez	25.00
Chipper Jones	20.00
Frank Thomas	20.00

Numbers Game

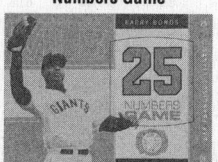

	NM/M
Complete Set (15):	30.00
Common Player:	1.00
Inserted 1:24	
1 Ichiro Suzuki	3.00
2 Derek Jeter	6.00
3 Alex Rodriguez	5.00
4 Miguel Tejada	1.00
5 Nomar Garciaparra	4.00
6 Jason Giambi	3.00
7 J.D. Drew	1.00
8 Barry Bonds	6.00
9 Alfonso Soriano	2.00
10 Jeff Bagwell	1.00
11 Barry Larkin	1.00
12 Roberto Alomar	1.00
13 Larry Walker	1.00
14 Roger Clemens	3.00
15 Ken Griffey Jr.	3.00

Numbers Game - Jersey

	NM/M
Common Player:	4.00
Inserted 1:25	
Barry Larkin	6.00
Roberto Alomar	4.00
Jeff Bagwell	8.00
Jason Giambi	8.00
Larry Walker	4.00
Derek Jeter	15.00
Alex Rodriguez	10.00
Alfonso Soriano	10.00

Roger Clemens	12.00
Miguel Tejada	4.00

Numbers Game - Patch

	NM/M
Common Player:	10.00
Production 300 Sets	
Barry Larkin	15.00
Roberto Alomar	15.00
Jeff Bagwell	25.00
Jason Giambi	15.00
Larry Walker	10.00
Derek Jeter	40.00
Alex Rodriguez	25.00
Alfonso Soriano	25.00
Roger Clemens	30.00
Miguel Tejada	10.00

Past, Present, Future

	NM/M
Complete Set (10):	40.00
Common Card:	4.00
Inserted 1:72	
1 Eddie Mathews, Rafael Palmeiro, Alex Rodriguez	5.00
2 Phil Rizzuto, Derek Jeter, Alfonso Soriano	5.00
3 Reggie Jackson, Barry Bonds, Sammy Sosa	6.00
4 Billy Williams, Sammy Sosa, Hee Seop Choi	4.00
5 Joe Morgan, Roberto Alomar, Alfonso Soriano	3.00
6 Yogi Berra, Mike Piazza, Josh Phelps	4.00
7 Nolan Ryan, Roger Clemens, Kerry Wood	6.00
8 Mike Schmidt, Scott Rolen, Eric Hinske	4.00
9 Barry Bonds, Alex Rodriguez, Alfonso Soriano	5.00
10 Yogi Berra, Derek Jeter, Hideki Matsui	

Patch, Present, Future Dual

Production 100 Sets

Patch, Present, Future Single

	NM/M
Common Player:	10.00
Production 200 Sets	
Rafael Palmeiro	15.00
Alex Rodriguez	20.00
Derek Jeter	50.00
Alfonso Soriano	50.00
Barry Bonds	50.00
Sammy Sosa	25.00
Sammy Sosa	25.00
Roberto Alomar	25.00
Mike Piazza	25.00
Alfonso Soriano	50.00
Roger Clemens	40.00
Kerry Wood	40.00
Eric Hinske	10.00
Alex Rodriguez	20.00
Alfonso Soriano	50.00
Derek Jeter	50.00

Patchworks

	NM/M
Common Player:	8.00
Production 250 Sets	
7 Frank Thomas	12.00
8 Lance Berkman	15.00
9 Kazuhiro Sasaki	15.00
10 Roy Oswalt	15.00
11 Bernie Williams	15.00
12PW Bob Abreu	15.00
14PW Greg Maddux	20.00
15PW Josh Beckett	8.00
16PW Mark Grace	20.00
17PW Eric Chavez	10.00
18PW Andruw Jones	15.00
19PW Adrian Beltre	8.00

Patchworks - Dual Color

	NM/M
Common Player:	10.00
Production 100 Sets	
Alex Rodriguez	35.00
Frank Thomas	20.00
Vladimir Guerrero	20.00
Roberto Alomar	20.00
Kerry Wood	35.00
Curt Schilling	15.00
Lance Berkman	20.00
Kazuhiro Sasaki	35.00
Roy Oswalt	20.00
Bernie Williams	25.00
Bob Abreu	10.00
Carlos Delgado	12.00
Greg Maddux	25.00
Josh Beckett	10.00
Mark Grace	15.00
Eric Chavez	15.00

Patchworks - Multi-Color

	NM/M
Common Player:	20.00
Production 50 Sets	
Alex Rodriguez	60.00
Frank Thomas	30.00
Vladimir Guerrero	35.00
Roberto Alomar	35.00
Kerry Wood	40.00
Curt Schilling	20.00
Lance Berkman	25.00
Kazuhiro Sasaki	50.00
Roy Oswalt	40.00
Bernie Williams	35.00
Bob Abreu	25.00
Carlos Delgado	20.00
Greg Maddux	35.00
Josh Beckett	20.00
Mark Grace	30.00
Eric Chavez	30.00
Andruw Jones	30.00
Adrian Beltre	20.00

2003 Fleer Platinum

	NM/M
Complete Set (250):	40.00
Common Player:	.15
Common SP (221-250):	.50
Hobby Pack (10):	1.50
Hobby Box (14 + 4 jumbo + 1 Rack):	35.00
Jumbo Pack:	3.00
Rack Pack:	5.00
1 Barry Bonds	2.50
2 Sean Casey	.25
3 Todd Walker	.15
4 Tony Batista	.15
5 Todd Zeile	.15
6 Ruben Sierra	.15
7 Jose Cruz Jr.	.15
8 Ben Grieve	.15
9 Robert Mackowiak	.15
10 Gary Sheffield	.25
11 Armando Benitez	.15
12 Tim Hudson	.25
13 Eric Milton	.15
14 Andy Pettitte	.40
15 Jeff Bagwell	.75
16 Jeff Kent	.15
17 Joe Randa	.15
18 Benito Santiago	.15
19 Russell Branyan	.15
20 Cliff Floyd	.15
21 Chris Richard	.15
22 Randy Winn	.15
23 Freddy Garcia	.15
24 Derek Lowe	.15
25 Ben Sheets	.15
26 Fred McGriff	.15
27 Bret Boone	.15
28 Jose Hernandez	.15
29 Phil Nevin	.15
30 Mike Piazza	1.50
31 Bobby Abreu	.15
32 Darin Erstad	.15
33 Andruw Jones	.75
34 Brad Wilkerson	.15
35 Brian Lawrence	.15
36 Vladimir Nunez	.15
37 Kazuhiro Sasaki	.15
38 Carlos Delgado	.45
39 Steve Cox	.15
40 Adrian Beltre	.25
41 Josh Bard	.15
42 Randall Simon	.15
43 Johnny Damon	.25
44 Ken Griffey Jr.	1.50
45 Sammy Sosa	1.00
46 Kevin Brown	.15
47 Kazuhisa Ishii	.15
48 Matt Morris	.15
49 Mark Prior	.15
50 Kip Wells	.15
51 Hee Seop Choi	.15
52 Craig Biggio	.15
53 Derek Jeter	2.50
54 Albert Pujols	1.50
55 Joe Borchard	.15
56 Robert Fick	.15
57 Jacque Jones	.15
58 Juan Pierre	.15
59 Bernie Williams	.35
60 Carlos Delgado	.15
61 Al Leiter	.15
62 Curt Schilling	.40

	NM/M
63 Carlos Pena	.15
64 Tino Martinez	.15
65 Fernando Vina	.15
66 Aaron Boone	.15
67 Michael Barrett	.15
68 Frank Thomas	.75
69 J.D. Drew	.25
70 Vladimir Guerrero	.75
71 Shannon Stewart	.15
72 Mark Buehrle	.15
73 Jamie Moyer	.15
74 Brad Radke	.15
75 Mike Williams	.15
76 Ryan Klesko	.15
77 Roberto Alomar	.35
78 Edgardo Alfonzo	.15
79 Matt Williams	.15
80 Edgar Martinez	.15
81 Shawn Green	.15
82 Kenny Lofton	.15
83 Josh Beckett	.15
84 Trevor Hoffman	.15
85 Kevin Millwood	.15
86 Odalis Perez	.15
87 Jarrod Washburn	.15
88 Jason Giambi	.60
89 Eric Young	.15
90 Barry Larkin	.15
91 Aramis Ramirez	.15
92 Ivan Rodriguez	.50
93 Steve Finley	.15
94 Brian Jordan	.15
95 Manny Ramirez	.75
96 Preston Wilson	.15
97 Rodrigo Lopez	.15
98 Ramon Ortiz	.15
99 Jim Thome	.15
100 Luis Castillo	.15
101 Alex Rodriguez	2.00
102 Jared Sandberg	.15
103 Ellis Burks	.15
104 Pat Burrell	.60
105 Brian Giles	.15
106 Mark Kotsay	.15
107 Dave Roberts	.15
108 Roy Halladay	.15
109 Chan Ho Park	.15
110 Erubiel Durazo	.15
111 Bobby Hill	.15
112 Cristian Guzman	.15
113 Troy Glaus	.60
114 Lance Berkman	.15
115 Juan Encarnacion	.15
116 Chipper Jones	1.00
117 Corey Patterson	.15
118 Vernon Wells	.15
119 Matt Clement	.15
120 Billy Koch	.15
121 Hideo Nomo	.15
122 Derrek Lee	.15
123 Todd Helton	.75
124 Sean Burroughs	.15
125 Jason Kendall	.15
126 Dmitri Young	.15
127 Adam Dunn	.60
128 Bobby Higginson	.15
129 Raul Mondesi	.15
130 Bubba Trammell	.15
131 A.J. Burnett	.15
132 Randy Johnson	.75
133 Mike Mulder	.15
134 Mariano Rivera	.25
135 Kerry Wood	.50
136 Mo Vaughn	.15
137 Jimmy Rollins	.15
138 Jose Valentin	.15
139 Brad Fullmer	.15
140 Mike Cameron	.15
141 Luis Gonzalez	.25
142 Kevin Appier	.15
143 Mike Hampton	.15
144 Pedro J. Martinez	.75
145 Javier Vazquez	.15
146 Doug Mientkiewicz	.15
147 Adam Kennedy	.15
148 Rafael Furcal	.15
149 Eric Chavez	.25
150 Mike Lieberthal	.15
151 Moises Alou	.15
152 Jermaine Dye	.15
153 Torii Hunter	.15
154 Trot Nixon	.15
155 Larry Walker	.15
156 Jorge Julio	.15
157 Mike Mussina	.40
158 Kirk Rueter	.15
159 Rafael Palmeiro	.65
160 Pokey Reese	.15
161 Miguel Tejada	.35
162 Robin Ventura	.15
163 Raul Ibanez	.15
164 Roger Cedeno	.15
165 Juan Gonzalez	.65
166 Carlos Lee	.15
167 Tim Salmon	.25
168 Orlando Hernandez	.15
169 Wade Miller	.15
170 Troy Percival	.15
171 Billy Wagner	.15
172 Jeff Conine	.15
173 Junior Spivey	.15
174 Edgar Renteria	.15
175 Scott Rolen	.65
176 Jason Varitek	.15
177 Ben Broussard	.15
178 Jeremy Giambi	.15
179 Gabe Kapler	.15
180 Armando Rios	.15

	NM/M
181 Ichiro Suzuki	2.00
182 Tom Glavine	.35
183 Greg Maddux	1.00
184 Roy Oswalt	.25
185 John Smoltz	.15
186 Eric Karros	.15
187 Alfonso Soriano	.75
188 Nomar Garciaparra	.75
189 Joe Crede	.15
190 Javy Lopez	.15
191 Carlos Beltran	.50
192 Jim Edmonds	.15
193 Geoff Jenkins	.15
194 Magglio Ordonez	.25
195 Daryle Ward	.15
196 Roger Clemens	1.25
197 Byung-Hyun Kim	.15
198 Robb Nen	.15
199 C.C. Sabathia	.15
200 Barry Zito	.35
201 Mark Grace	.25
202 Paul Konerko	.25
203 Mike Sweeney	.15
204 John Olerud	.15
205 Jose Vidro	.15
206 Ray Durham	.15
207 Omar Vizquel	.15
208 Shea Hillenbrand	.15
209 Mike Lowell	.15
210 Aubrey Huff	.15
211 Eric Hinske	.15
212 Paul LoDuca	.15
213 Jay Gibbons	.15
214 Austin Kearns	.50
215 Richie Sexson	.15
216 Garret Anderson	.15
217 Eric Gagne	.15
218 Jason Jennings	.15
219 Damian Moss	.15
220 David Eckstein	.15
221 Mark Teixeira	1.00
222 Bill Hall	.50
223 Bobby Jenks	.75
224 Adam Morrisey	.50
225 Rodrigo Rosario	.50
226 Brett Myers	.75
227 Tony Alvarez	.50
228 Willie Bloomquist	1.00
229 Ben Howard	.50
230 Nic Jackson	.50
231 Carl Crawford	.50
232 Omar Infante	.50
233 Francisco Rodriguez	1.00
234 Andy Van Hekken	.50
235 Kirk Saarloos	.50
236 Dusty Wathan RC	.75
237 Jamey Carroll	1.00
238 Jason L. Phillips	1.00
239 Jose Castillo	1.00
240 Arnaldo Munoz RC	1.00
241 Orlando Hudson	.50
242 Drew Henson	.75
243 Jason Lane	.75
244 Vinnie Chulk	1.00
245 Prentice Redman RC	1.00
246 Marlon Byrd	1.00
247 Chin-Feng Chen	1.00
248 Craig Brazell RC	1.00
249 John Webb	1.00
250 Adam LaRoche	1.00

Platinum Finish

Stars (1-220):	5-10X
SP (221-250):	2-4X
Production 100 Sets	

Barry Bonds Chasing History

	NM/M
Production 250 Sets	
Five Player card #'d to 25.	
Barry Bonds, Bobby Bonds	35.00
Barry Bonds, Roger Maris	40.00
Barry Bonds, Willie McCovey	35.00
Barry Bonds, Babe Ruth	200.00
Barry Bonds	35.00
Barry Bonds, Babe Ruth, Roger Maris, Willie McCovey, Bobby Bonds	200.00

Guts and Glory

	NM/M
Complete Set (20):	12.00
Common Player:	.40

Inserted 1:4

1GG	Jason Giambi	1.00
2GG	Alfonso Soriano	.75
3GG	Scott Rolen	.50
4GG	Ivan Rodriguez	.50
5GG	Barry Bonds	1.50
6GG	Jim Edmonds	.40
7GG	Darin Erstad	.40
8GG	Brian Giles	.40
9GG	Luis Gonzalez	.40
10GG	Adam Dunn	.50
11GG	Torii Hunter	.40
12GG	Andruw Jones	.40
13GG	Sammy Sosa	1.00
14GG	Ichiro Suzuki	1.50
15GG	Miguel Tejada	.40
16GG	Roger Clemens	1.00
17GG	Curt Schilling	.40
18GG	Nomar Garciaparra	1.50
19GG	Derek Jeter	2.00
20GG	Alex Rodriguez	1.50

Heart of the Order

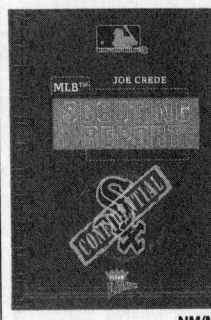

		NM/M
Complete Set (20):		20.00
Common Card:		.75
Inserted 1:12		
1	Jason Giambi, Derek Jeter, Alfonso Soriano	3.00
2	Todd Helton, Preston Wilson, Larry Walker	.75
3	Rafael Palmeiro, Alex Rodriguez, Ivan Rodriguez	3.00
4	Adam Dunn, Ken Griffey Jr., Austin Kearns	3.00
5	Jeff Bagwell, Craig Biggio, Lance Berkman	1.00
6	Eric Chavez, Miguel Tejada, Jermaine Dye	.75
7	Troy Glaus, Garrett Anderson, Darin Erstad	1.00
8	Mike Piazza, Mo Vaughn, Roberto Alomar	2.50
9	Torii Hunter, Jacque Jones, Corey Koskie	.75
10	Barry Bonds, Jeff Kent, Rich Aurilia	3.00
11	Pat Burrell, Bobby Abreu, Jimmy Rollins	1.50
12	Shawn Green, Adrian Beltre, Paul LoDuca	.75
13	Vladimir Guerrero, Brad Wilkerson, Jose Vidro	1.50
14	Chipper Jones, Andruw Jones, Gary Sheffield	2.00
15	Ichiro Suzuki, Bret Boone, Edgar Martinez	2.50
16	Albert Pujols, Scott Rolen, J.D. Drew	1.50
17	Sammy Sosa, Fred McGriff, Moises Alou	2.00
18	Nomar Garciaparra, Shea Hillenbrand, Manny Ramirez	2.50
19	Frank Thomas, Magglio Ordonez, Paul Konerko	1.00
20	Jason Kendall, Brian Giles, Aramis Ramirez	.75

Heart of the Order Memorabilia

		NM/M
Common Card:		5.00
Production 400 Sets		
	Jason Giambi, Derek Jeter, Alfonso Soriano/Jsy, Todd Helton/Jsy, Preston Wilson, Larry Walker	15.00
	Rafael Palmeiro/Jsy, Alex Rodriguez, Ivan Rodriguez	8.00
	Adam Dunn, Ken Griffey Jr., Austin Kearns/Pants	6.00
	Troy Glaus, Garrett Anderson, Darin Erstad/Jsy	12.00
	Mike Piazza/Jsy, Mo Vaughn, Roberto Alomar	8.00
	Barry Bonds, Jeff Kent/Jsy, Rich Aurilia	6.00
	Pat Burrell, Bobby Abreu, Jimmy Rollins/Jsy	6.00

	Shawn Green, Adrian Beltre/Jsy, Paul LoDuca	5.00
	Vladimir Guerrero, Brad Wilkerson, Jose Vidro/Jsy	5.00
	Chipper Jones/Jsy, Andruw Jones, Gary Sheffield	10.00
	Ichiro Suzuki, Bret Boone/Jsy, Edgar Martinez	5.00
	Albert Pujols, Scott Rolen, J.D. Drew/Jsy	8.00
	Sammy Sosa/Jsy, Fred McGriff, Moises Alou	12.00
	Nomar Garciaparra, Shea Hillenbrand, Manny Ramirez/Jsy	8.00
	Frank Thomas, Magglio Ordonez/Jsy, Paul Konerko	5.00
	Jason Kendall, Brian Giles/Bat, Aramis Ramirez	5.00

MLB Scouting Report

JOE CREDE

		NM/M
Complete Set (32):		55.00
Common Player:		1.00
Production 400 Sets		
1	Jason Giambi	3.00
2	Paul Konerko	1.00
3	Jim Thome	1.50
4	Alfonso Soriano	2.00
5	Troy Glaus	1.50
6	Eric Hinske	1.00
7	Paul LoDuca	1.00
8	Mike Piazza	4.00
9	Marlon Byrd	1.00
10	Garrett Anderson	1.00
11	Barry Bonds	5.00
12	Pat Burrell	1.50
13	Joe Crede	1.00
14	J.D. Drew	1.00
15	Ken Griffey Jr.	4.00
16	Vladimir Guerrero	2.00
17	Torii Hunter	1.00
18	Chipper Jones	3.00
19	Austin Kearns	1.00
20	Albert Pujols	2.00
21	Manny Ramirez	1.50
22	Gary Sheffield	1.50
23	Sammy Sosa	3.00
24	Ichiro Suzuki	4.00
25	Bernie Williams	1.25
26	Randy Johnson	2.00
27	Greg Maddux	3.00
28	Hideo Nomo	2.00
29	Nomar Garciaparra	4.00
30	Derek Jeter	6.00
31	Alex Rodriguez	5.00
32	Miguel Tejada	1.00

MLB Scouting Report Game-Used

		NM/M
Common Player:		6.00
Production 250 Sets		
3	Jim Thome/Jsy	10.00
4	Alfonso Soriano/Bat	10.00
8	Mike Piazza/Jsy	15.00
11	Barry Bonds/Jsy	20.00
14	J.D. Drew/Jsy	10.00
18	Chipper Jones/Jsy	10.00
19	Austin Kearns/Pants	10.00
21	Manny Ramirez/Jsy	8.00
23	Sammy Sosa/Jsy	15.00
26	Randy Johnson/Jsy	10.00
27	Greg Maddux/Jsy	10.00
28	Hideo Nomo/Jsy	20.00
30	Derek Jeter/Jsy	20.00

Nameplates

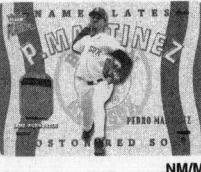

P. MARTINEZ

	NM/M
Common Player:	
Jumbo Pack Exclusive	

	Barry Larkin/97	30.00
	Kazuhiro Sasaki/82	20.00
	Greg Maddux/248	25.00
	Craig Biggio/152	25.00
	Pedro J. Martinez/244	35.00
	Barry Zito/248	25.00
	Nomar Garciaparra/258	40.00
	John Olerud/180	25.00
	Ivan Rodriguez/189	20.00
	Jeff Bagwell/121	45.00
	Chipper Jones/251	40.00
	Frank Thomas/58	45.00
	Roger Clemens/141	40.00
	Mike Piazza/200	35.00
	Mark Prior/123	25.00
	Manny Ramirez/94	30.00
	Kerry Wood/49	45.00
	Rafael Palmeiro/245	20.00
	Jimmy Rollins/74	20.00
	Barry Bonds/251	50.00
	Adam Dunn/117	25.00
	Alex Rodriguez/248	40.00
	Miguel Tejada/225	20.00
	Chin-Feng Chen/110	100.00

Portraits

NOMAR GARCIAPARRA
Platinum Portraits
BOSTON RED SOX

		NM/M
Complete Set (20):		25.00
Common Player:		.75
Inserted 1:20		
1	Josh Beckett	.75
2	Roberto Alomar	1.00
3	Alfonso Soriano	2.00
4	Mike Piazza	3.00
5	Ivan Rodriguez	2.00
6	Edgar Martinez	.75
7	Barry Bonds	4.00
8	Adam Dunn	1.25
9	Juan Gonzalez	1.00
10	Chipper Jones	2.50
11	Albert Pujols	1.50
12	Magglio Ordonez	.75
13	Shea Hillenbrand	.75
14	Larry Walker	.75
15	Pedro J. Martinez	1.50
16	Kerry Wood	1.00
17	Barry Zito	.75
18	Nomar Garciaparra	3.00
19	Derek Jeter	5.00
20	Alex Rodriguez	4.00

Portraits Game Jersey

PEDRO MARTINEZ
Platinum Portraits

	NM/M
Common Player:	5.00
Inserted 1:86	

4	Mike Piazza	10.00
5	Ivan Rodriguez	6.00
7	Barry Bonds	15.00
8	Adam Dunn	8.00
10	Chipper Jones	8.00
15	Pedro J. Martinez	8.00
16	Kerry Wood	8.00
17	Barry Zito	5.00
18	Nomar Garciaparra	6.00
19	Derek Jeter/SP/150	25.00

Portraits Game Patch

	NM/M
Common Player:	25.00
Production 100 Sets	
4	Mike Piazza	35.00
5	Ivan Rodriguez	25.00
7	Barry Bonds	40.00
8	Adam Dunn	25.00
10	Chipper Jones	25.00
15	Pedro J. Martinez	25.00
16	Kerry Wood	25.00
17	Barry Zito	25.00

18	Nomar Garciaparra	40.00
19	Derek Jeter	45.00

2003 Fleer Rookies & Greats

		NM/M
Complete Set (75):		30.00
Common Player:		.25
Pack (5):		6.00
Box (20):		100.00
1	Troy Glaus	.65
2	Gary Sheffield	.40
3	Sammy Sosa	1.00
4	Mark Prior	.50
5	Dontrelle Willis	.25
6	Shawn Green	.50
7	Vladimir Guerrero	.75
8	Jose Reyes	.50
9	Miguel Tejada	.40
10	Bret Boone	.25
11	Rocco Baldelli	.40
12	Rafael Palmeiro	.65
13	Ichiro Suzuki	1.50
14	Carlos Delgado	.25
15	Garret Anderson	.25
16	Richie Sexson	.25
17	Roger Clemens	1.75
18	Barry Zito	.40
19	Jim Thome	.25
20	Alex Rodriguez	2.50
21	Randy Johnson	.75
22	Chipper Jones	1.00
23	Kerry Wood	.60
24	Ken Griffey Jr.	1.50
25	Ivan Rodriguez	.60
26	Jeff Kent	.25
27	Todd Helton	.75
28	Jeff Bagwell	.75
29	Hideo Nomo	.60
30	Torii Hunter	.25
31	Brian Giles	.25
32	Albert Pujols	2.00
33	Vernon Wells	.25
34	Nomar Garciaparra	.75
35	Magglio Ordonez	.25
36	C.C. Sabathia	.25
37	Preston Wilson	.25
38	Mike Sweeney	.25
39	Jose Vidro	.25
40	Jason Giambi	.25
41	Derek Jeter	3.00
42	Mike Piazza	1.50
43	Rich Harden	.25
44	Jason Kendall	.25
45	Barry Bonds	3.00
46	Barry Larkin	.25
47	Dmitri Young	.25
48	Craig Biggio	.25
49	Angel Berroa	.25
50	Alfonso Soriano	.75
51	Kevin Millwood	.25
52	Edgar Martinez	.25
53	Jim Edmonds	.25
54	Curt Schilling	.40
55	Jay Gibbons	.25
56	Pedro J. Martinez	.75
57	Greg Maddux	1.00
58	Manny Ramirez	.75
59	Frank Thomas	.75
60	Adam Dunn	.60
61	Babe Ruth	2.00
62	Bob Gibson	1.00
63	Willie Stargell	.75
64	Mike Schmidt	2.00
65	Nolan Ryan	3.00
66	Tom Seaver	1.00
67	Brooks Robinson	1.00
68	Willie McCovey	.50
69	Harmon Killebrew	1.00
70	Al Kaline	1.00
71	Reggie Jackson	1.00
72	Eddie Mathews	.75
73	Ralph Kiner	.25
74	Cal Ripken Jr.	3.00
75	Phil Rizzuto	.25

Ultra

Production 1,500	
U-251	Chien-Ming Wang RC	8.00
U-252	Rickie Weeks RC	6.00
U-253	Brandon Webb RC	6.00
U-254	Hideki Matsui RC	8.00
U-255	Michael Hessman RC	4.00
U-256	Ryan Wagner RC	3.00
U-257	Matt Kata RC	3.00
U-258	Edwin Jackson RC	5.00
U-259	Jose Contreras RC	3.00
U-260	Delmon Young RC	8.00
U-261	Bo Hart RC	3.00
U-262	Jeff Duncan RC	3.00
U-263	Robby Hammock RC	2.00
U-264	Jeremy Bonderman	5.00
U-265	Clint Barmes RC	2.00

Authentix

Production 1,250	
A-161	Chien-Ming Wang RC	10.00
A-162	Rickie Weeks RC	6.00
A-163	Brandon Webb RC	6.00
A-164	Craig Brazell RC	3.00
A-165	Michael Hessman RC	3.00
A-166	Ryan Wagner RC	3.00
A-167	Matt Kata RC	4.00
A-168	Edwin Jackson RC	8.00
A-169	Mike Ryan RC	4.00
A-170	Delmon Young RC	10.00
A-171	Bo Hart RC	4.00
A-172	Jeff Duncan RC	4.00
A-173	Robby Hammock RC	3.00
A-174	Jeremy Bonderman	6.00
A-175	Clint Barmes RC	3.00

18	Nomar Garciaparra	40.00
19	Derek Jeter	45.00

Genuine

Production 1,000		
G-131	Dan Haren RC	5.00
G-132	Rickie Weeks RC	6.00
G-133	Prentice Redman RC	4.00
G-134	Craig Brazell RC	4.00
G-135	Jon Leicester RC	4.00
G-136	Ryan Wagner RC	6.00
G-137	Matt Kata RC	4.00
G-138	Edwin Jackson RC	8.00
G-139	Mike Ryan RC	5.00
G-140	Delmon Young RC	10.00
G-141	Bo Hart RC	5.00
G-142	Jeff Duncan RC	5.00
G-143	Robby Hammock RC	4.00
G-144	Michael Hessman RC	4.00
G-145	Clint Barmes RC	4.00

Showcase

Production 750		
S-136	Chien-Ming Wang RC	12.00
S-137	Rickie Weeks RC	8.00
S-138	Brandon Webb RC	8.00
S-139	Hideki Matsui RC	12.00
S-140	Michael Hessman RC	4.00
S-141	Ryan Wagner RC	6.00
S-142	Bo Hart RC	5.00
S-143	Edwin Jackson RC	8.00
S-144	Jose Contreras RC	6.00
S-145	Delmon Young RC	10.00

Flair

Production 500		
F-126	Jeff Duncan RC	6.00
F-127	Rickie Weeks RC	10.00
F-128	Brandon Webb RC	12.00
F-129	Robby Hammock RC	5.00
F-130	Jon Leicester RC	5.00
F-131	Ryan Wagner RC	7.00
F-132	Bo Hart RC	6.00
F-133	Edwin Jackson RC	10.00
F-134	Sergio Mitre RC	5.00
F-135	Delmon Young RC	15.00

Hot Prospects

Production 250		
H-120	Josh Willingham RC	10.00
H-121	Rickie Weeks RC	10.00
H-122	Prentice Redman RC	8.00
H-123	Mike Ryan RC	8.00
H-124	Oscar Villarreal RC	8.00
H-125	Ryan Wagner RC	10.00
H-126	Bo Hart RC	10.00
H-127	Edwin Jackson RC	12.00

Boyhood Idols

		NM/M
Common Player:		5.00
Production 615 Sets		
	Carlton Fisk	8.00
	Joe Carter	5.00
	Cal Ripken Jr.	20.00
	Mike Schmidt	15.00
	Robin Yount	8.00
	Joe Morgan	5.00
	Jim Palmer	5.00
	Harmon Killebrew	8.00
	Brooks Robinson	5.00
	Frank Howard	5.00
	Bill "Moose" Skowron	5.00
	Bucky Dent	5.00
	Nolan Ryan	20.00
	Don Mattingly	20.00

Boyhood Idols Auto.

		NM/M
Production 50 unless noted.		
	Carlton Fisk	30.00
	Brooks Robinson	35.00
	Bucky Dent	20.00

Dynamic Debuts

		NM/M
Complete Set (10):		10.00
Common Player:		.50
Inserted 1:10		
1DD	Rickie Weeks	4.00
2DD	Brandon Webb	1.00
3DD	Jose Reyes	4.00
4DD	Bo Hart	1.00
5DD	Dontrelle Willis	1.00
6DD	Rich Harden	1.00
7DD	Ryan Wagner	.50
8DD	Rocco Baldelli	1.00
9DD	Mark Teixeira	1.00
10DD	Hideki Matsui	3.00

Dynamic Debuts Autograph

		NM/M
Common Player:		10.00
Production 100		
	Rickie Weeks	20.00
	Jose Reyes	35.00
	Bo Hart	10.00
	Dontrelle Willis	25.00
	Ryan Wagner	10.00

Looming Large

		NM/M
Complete Set (15):		30.00
Common Player:		1.50
Production 500 Sets		
Uncommon:		1-2X
Production 150		
Rare:		No Pricing
Production 15		
1LL	Chien-Ming Wang	4.00
2LL	Rickie Weeks	5.00
3LL	Brandon Webb	3.00
4LL	Hideki Matsui	6.00
5LL	Michael Hessman	1.50

6LL	Ryan Wagner	1.50
7LL	Matt Kata	1.50
8LL	Edwin Jackson	1.50
9LL	Jose Contreras	1.50
10LL	Delmon Young	6.00
11LL	Bo Hart	3.00
12LL	Jeff Duncan	1.50
13LL	Robby Hammock	1.50
14LL	Jeremy Bonderman	1.50
15LL	Clint Barmes	1.50

The Naturals

		NM/M
Complete Set (25):		45.00
Common Player:		.50
Inserted 1:5		
Uncommons:		2-4X
Production 75 Sets		
1	Cal Ripken Jr.	5.00
2	Mike Schmidt	3.00
3	Derek Jeter	.50
4	Joe Carter	.50
5	Nomar Garciaparra	3.00
6	Frank Howard	.50
7	Al Kaline	2.00
8	Albert Pujols	4.00
9	Nolan Ryan	5.00
10	Duke Snider	1.50
11	Alex Rodriguez	4.00
12	Brooks Robinson	1.50
13	Roger Clemens	4.00
14	Sammy Sosa	3.00
15	Jim Palmer	1.00
16	Alfonso Soriano	2.00
17	Don Mattingly	3.00
18	Harmon Killebrew	1.50
19	Bob Feller	.50
20	Reggie Jackson	1.50
21	Ichiro Suzuki	2.50
22	Barry Bonds	4.00
23	Hideki Matsui	4.00
24	Willie Stargell	.50
25	Pee Wee Reese	.50

The Naturals Autograph

		NM/M
Common Player:		
Production 50		
	Joe Carter	15.00
	Bob Feller	25.00
	Frank Howard	25.00
	Al Kaline	40.00
	Harmon Killebrew	35.00
	Jim Palmer	15.00
	Cal Ripken Jr.	140.00
	Brooks Robinson	35.00
	Nolan Ryan	100.00
	Duke Snider	25.00

The Naturals Jersey Auto.

		NM/M
Common Player:		
Production 30		
	Joe Carter	25.00
	Frank Howard	25.00
	Al Kaline	60.00
	Harmon Killebrew	50.00
	Jim Palmer	25.00
	Cal Ripken Jr.	150.00
	Brooks Robinson	50.00
	Nolan Ryan	120.00
	Duke Snider	40.00

The Naturals Memorabilia

		NM/M
Common Player:		5.00
Production 250 unless noted.		
CR	Cal Ripken Jr.	30.00
MS	Mike Schmidt	15.00
DJ	Derek Jeter	20.00
JC	Joe Carter	5.00
NG	Nomar Garciaparra	15.00
FH	Frank Howard/400	5.00
AK	Al Kaline	15.00
AP	Albert Pujols	12.00
NR	Nolan Ryan/400	25.00
DS	Duke Snider	10.00
AR	Alex Rodriguez	10.00
BR	Brooks Robinson/400	10.00
RC	Roger Clemens/400	10.00
JP	Jim Palmer	8.00
AS	Alfonso Soriano	8.00
DM	Don Mattingly	20.00
HK	Harmon Killebrew/400	10.00
RJ	Reggie Jackson/400	10.00

The Naturals Patch

No Pricing	
Production 25	
Patch Autos.:	No Pricing
Production 5	

Through the Years

		NM/M
Common Duo:		10.00
Production 360		
Patches:		No Pricing
Production 25		
	Sammy Sosa, Mark Prior	10.00
	Mark Prior, Jose Reyes	10.00
	Nolan Ryan, Hank Blalock	25.00
	Roger Clemens, Chien-Ming Wang	25.00
	Jim Thome, Mike Schmidt	25.00

Alex Rodriguez,		
Mark Teixeira,		25.00
Randy Johnson,		
Brandon Webb,		15.00
Phil Rizzuto,		
Jose Reyes		15.00
Nomar Garciaparra,		
Bobby Doerr		20.00
Jason Giambi,		
Reggie Jackson		15.00
Derek Jeter,		
Phil Rizzuto		45.00
Barry Larkin,		
Joe Morgan		10.00
Harmon Killebrew,		
Torii Hunter		20.00
Willie McCovey,		
Barry Bonds		15.00
Bo Hart, Lou Brock		15.00
Jose Contreras,		
Mike Mussina		10.00
Michael Hessman,		
Chipper Jones		12.00
Steve Carlton,		
Kevin Millwood		12.00
Robin Yount,		
Scott Podsednik		20.00
Eddie Mathews,		
Chipper Jones		15.00

2003 Fleer Showcase

		NM/M
Complete Set (135):		50.00
Common Player:		.25
Common SP (106-135):		1.00
Inserted 1:4		
Pack (5):		3.00
Box (24):		60.00
1	David Eckstein	.25
2	Curt Schilling	.75
3	Jay Gibbons	.75
4	Kerry Wood	.75
5	Jeff Bagwell	.50
6	Hideo Nomo	.75
7	Tim Hudson	.40
8	J.D. Drew	.50
9	Josh Phelps	.25
10	Bartolo Colon	.25
11	Bobby Abreu	.25
12	Matt Morris	.25
13	Kazuhiro Sasaki	.25
14	Sean Burroughs	.25
15	Vicente Padilla	.25
16	Jorge Posada	.35
17	Torii Hunter	.25
18	Richie Sexson	.25
19	Lance Berkman	.25
20	Todd Helton	1.00
21	Paul Konerko	.25
22	Pedro J. Martinez	1.00
23	Rodrigo Lopez	.25
24	Gary Sheffield	.35
25	Darin Erstad	.50
26	Nomar Garciaparra	1.00
27	Adam Dunn	.75
28	Jason Giambi	.75
29	Miguel Tejada	.40
30	Chipper Jones	1.50
31	Alex Rodriguez	3.00
32	Barry Bonds	4.00
33	Roger Clemens	2.00
34	Sammy Sosa	1.50
35	Randy Johnson	1.00
36	Tim Salmon	.35
37	Shea Hillenbrand	.25
38	Larry Walker	.25
39	A.J. Burnett	.25
40	Shawn Green	.50
41	Cristian Guzman	.25
42	Bernie Williams	.35
43	Mark Mulder	.25
44	Brian Giles	.25
45	Bret Boone	.25
46	Juan Gonzalez	.75
47	Roy Halladay	.25
48	Wade Miller	.25
49	Jeff Kent	.25
50	Carlos Delgado	.50
51	Mike Lowell	.25
52	Jim Edmonds	.25
53	Ivan Rodriguez	.75
54	Aubrey Huff	.25
55	Ryan Klesko	.25
56	Paul LoDuca	.25
57	Roy Oswalt	.50
58	Omar Vizquel	.25
59	Manny Ramirez	1.00
60	Andruw Jones	1.00
61	Troy Glaus	1.00
62	Ichiro Suzuki	2.50
63	Albert Pujols	2.50
64	Derek Jeter	4.00
65	Mark Prior	1.00
66	Ken Griffey Jr.	2.50
67	Vladimir Guerrero	1.00
68	Mike Piazza	2.50
69	Alfonso Soriano	1.00
70	Greg Maddux	1.50
71	Adam Kennedy	.25
72	Junior Spivey	.25
73	Tom Glavine	.40
74	Derek Lowe	.25
75	Magglio Ordonez	.25
76	Jim Thome	.25
77	Robert Fick	.25
78	Josh Beckett	.25
79	Mike Sweeney	.25
80	Kazuhisa Ishii	.25
81	Roberto Alomar	.40
82	Barry Zito	.40
83	Pat Burrell	.65
84	Scott Rolen	1.00
85	John Olerud	.25
86	Eric Hinske	.25
87	Rafael Palmeiro	.75
88	Edgar Martinez	.25
89	Eric Chavez	.40
90	Jose Vidro	.25
91	Craig Biggio	.25
92	Rich Aurilia	.25
93	Austin Kearns	.75
94	Luis Gonzalez	.40
95	Garrett Anderson	.25
96	Yogi Berra	1.50
97	Al Kaline	1.50
98	Robin Yount	1.00
99	Reggie Jackson	1.00
100	Harmon Killebrew	1.50
101	Eddie Mathews	1.50
102	Willie McCovey	.50
103	Nolan Ryan	4.00
104	Mike Schmidt	2.50
105	Tom Seaver	1.00
106	Francisco Rodriguez	1.00
107	Carl Crawford	1.00
108	Ben Howard	1.00
109	Hank Blalock	1.00
110	Hee Seop Choi	1.00
111	Kirk Saarloos	1.00
112	Lew Ford RC	1.00
113	Andy Van Hekken	1.00
114	Drew Henson	1.50
115	Marlon Byrd	1.00
116	Jayson Werth	1.00
117	Willie Bloomquist	1.00
118	Joe Borchard	1.00
119	Mark Teixeira	2.00
120	Bobby Hill	1.00
121	Jason Lane	1.00
122	Omar Infante	1.00
123	Victor Martinez	1.50
124	Jorge Padilla	1.00
125	John Lackey	1.00
126	Anderson Machado	1.00
127	Rodrigo Rosario	1.00
128	Freddy Sanchez	1.00
129	Tony Alvarez	1.00
130	Matt Thornton	1.00
131	Joe Thurston	1.00
132	Brett Myers	1.00
133	Antonio Perez	1.00
134	Chris Snelling	1.00
135	Terrmel Sledge RC	1.00

Legacy

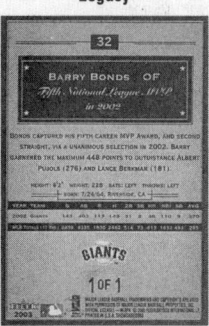

Legacy Stars (1-105):	3-6X
SP's (106-135):	1-30X
Production 150 Sets	
Masterpiece 1 of 1 also exists.	

Baseball's Best

	NM/M
Complete Set (15):	40.00
Common Player:	1.50
Inserted 1:24	

1	Curt Schilling	2.00
2	Barry Zito	2.00
3	Torii Hunter	2.00
4	Pedro J. Martinez	4.00
5	Bernie Williams	2.00
6	Magglio Ordonez	1.50
7	Alfonso Soriano	4.00
8	Hideo Nomo	2.00
9	Jason Giambi	5.00
10	Sammy Sosa	5.00
11	Vladimir Guerrero	4.00
12	Ken Griffey Jr.	5.00
13	Troy Glaus	3.00
14	Ichiro Suzuki	6.00
15	Albert Pujols	5.00

Baseball's Best Memorabilia

		NM/M
Common Player:		5.00
Inserted 1:24		
CS	Curt Schilling	6.00
BZ	Barry Zito	6.00
TH	Torii Hunter	8.00
PM	Pedro J. Martinez	10.00
BW	Bernie Williams	8.00
MO	Magglio Ordonez	8.00
AS	Alfonso Soriano	15.00
HN	Hideo Nomo	8.00
JG	Jason Giambi	15.00
SS	Sammy Sosa	15.00

Hot Gloves

		NM/M
Complete Set (10):		15.00
Common Player:		1.00
Inserted 1:8		
1	Greg Maddux	2.00
2	Ivan Rodriguez	1.00
3	Derek Jeter	4.00
4	Mike Piazza	2.50
5	Nomar Garciaparra	2.50
6	Andruw Jones	1.00
7	Scott Rolen	1.00
8	Barry Bonds	3.00
9	Roger Clemens	1.50
10	Alex Rodriguez	3.00

Hot Gloves Memorabilia

		NM/M
Common Player:		5.00
Production 350 Sets		
GM	Greg Maddux	12.00
IR	Ivan Rodriguez	5.00
DJ	Derek Jeter	25.00
MP	Mike Piazza	15.00
NG	Nomar Garciaparra	15.00
AJ	Andruw Jones	6.00
SR	Scott Rolen	15.00
BB	Barry Bonds	25.00
RC	Roger Clemens	15.00
AR	Alex Rodriguez	15.00

Sweet Sigs

		NM/M
Quantity produced listed.		
DJ	Derek Jeter/250	130.00
DJ	Derek Jeter/50/Red	185.00
BB	Barry Bonds/ 90 MVP/150	200.00
BB	Barry Bonds/ 92 MVP/100	200.00
BB	Barry Bonds/ 93 MVP/75	200.00

Sweet Stitch

		NM/M
Complete Set (10):		12.00
Common Player:		.75
Inserted 1:8		
1SS	Derek Jeter	4.00
2SS	Randy Johnson	1.50
3SS	Jeff Bagwell	1.00
4SS	Nomar Garciaparra	2.50
5SS	Roger Clemens	2.00
6SS	Todd Helton	.75
7SS	Barry Bonds	3.00
8SS	Alfonso Soriano	1.50
9SS	Miguel Tejada	.75
10SS	Mark Prior	1.50

Sweet Stitch Memorabilia

		NM/M
Varying quantities produced.		
DJ	Derek Jeter	25.00
RJ	Randy Johnson	8.00

JB	Jeff Bagwell	8.00
NG	Nomar Garciaparra	12.00
RC	Roger Clemens	12.00
TH	Todd Helton	5.00
BB	Barry Bonds	20.00
AS	Alfonso Soriano	12.00
MT	Miguel Tejada	5.00
MP	Mark Prior	10.00

FSweet Stitch Patch

		NM/M
Common Player:		20.00
DJ	Derek Jeter/50	60.00
RJ	Randy Johnson/150	40.00
JB	Jeff Bagwell/150	35.00
NG	Nomar Garciaparra/150	45.00
RC	Roger Clemens/50	45.00
TH	Todd Helton/50	30.00
BB	Barry Bonds/150	75.00
AS	Alfonso Soriano/50	40.00
MT	Miguel Tejada/150	20.00
MP	Mark Prior/150	25.00

Thundersticks

		NM/M
Complete Set (10):		12.00
Common Player:		.75
Inserted 1:8		
1TS	Adam Dunn	1.00
2TS	Alex Rodriguez	3.00
3TS	Barry Bonds	4.00
4TS	Jim Thome	1.00
5TS	Chipper Jones	2.00
6TS	Manny Ramirez	1.00
7TS	Carlos Delgado	.75
8TS	Mike Piazza	2.50
9TS	Shawn Green	.75
10TS	Pat Burrell	1.00

Thundersticks Bat

		NM/M
Common Player:		5.00
Golds:		1-2.5X
Production 99 Sets		
AD	Adam Dunn	10.00
AR	Alex Rodriguez	15.00
BB	Barry Bonds	20.00
JT	Jim Thome	8.00
CJS	Chipper Jones	8.00
MR	Manny Ramirez	8.00
SG	Shawn Green	8.00
PB	Pat Burrell	10.00

2003 Fleer Splendid Splinters

		NM/M
Complete Set (150):		
Common Player:		.20
Common Wood (91-110):		5.00
Production 499		
Common SP (111-140):		1.50
Inserted 1:6		
Common (141-150):		3.00
Production 999		
Pack (5):		3.00
Box (24):		50.00
1	David Eckstein	.20
2	Barry Larkin	.40
3	Edgardo Alfonzo	.20
4	Darin Erstad	.50
5	Ellis Burks	.20
6	Omar Vizquel	.20
7	Bartolo Colon	.20
8	Roberto Alomar	.50
9	Garret Anderson	.40
10	Al Leiter	.20
11	Tim Salmon	.20
12	Larry Walker	.40
13	Jorge Posada	.50
14	Curt Schilling	.50
15	Jason Jennings	.20
16	Jason Giambi	1.00
17	Robert Fick	.20
18	Kazuhiro Sasaki	.20
19	Bernie Williams	.50
20	Junior Spivey	.20
21	Mike Lowell	.20
22	Luis Gonzalez	.40
23	Josh Beckett	.20
24	John Smoltz	.20
25	Mike Mussina	.40
26	Gary Sheffield	.40
27	Tom Glavine	.40
28	Tim Hudson	.20
29	Austin Kearns	.75
30	Andruw Jones	.40
31	Roger Clemens	1.50
32	Mark Mulder	.20
33	Jay Gibbons	.20
34	Jeff Kent	.40
35	Barry Zito	.40
36	Rodrigo Lopez	.20
37	Jeff Bagwell	.75
38	Eric Chavez	.40
39	Pedro J. Martinez	1.00
40	Lance Berkman	.50
41	Bobby Abreu	.40
42	Wade Miller	.20
43	Bret Boone	.20
44	Vicente Padilla	.20
45	Shea Hillenbrand	.20
46	Roy Oswalt	.40
47	Pat Burrell	.75
48	Manny Ramirez	.75
49	Craig Biggio	.40
50	Randy Wolf	.20
51	Kerry Wood	.40
52	Mike Sweeney	.20
53	Brian Giles	.20
54	Kazuhisa Ishii	.20
55	Jason Kendall	.20
56	Hideo Nomo	.40
57	Josh Phelps	.20
58	Sean Burroughs	.20
59	Paul Konerko	.20
60	Shawn Green	.40
61	Ryan Klesko	.20
62	Magglio Ordonez	.40
63	Paul LoDuca	.20
64	Edgar Martinez	.20
65	J.D. Drew	.30
66	Phil Nevin	.20
67	Jim Edmonds	.40
68	Matt Morris	.40
69	Aubrey Huff	.20
70	Adam Dunn	.75
71	John Olerud	.40
72	Juan Gonzalez	.50
73	Scott Rolen	.50
74	Rafael Palmeiro	.50
75	Roy Halladay	.20
76	Kevin Brown	.20
77	Ivan Rodriguez	.50
78	Eric Hinske	.20
79	Frank Thomas	.75
80	Carlos Delgado	.40
81	Bobby Higginson	.20
82	Trevor Hoffman	.20
83	Cliff Floyd	.20
84	Derek Lowe	.20
85	Richie Sexson	.50
86	Rich Aurilia	.20
87	Sean Casey	.20
88	Cristian Guzman	.20
89	Randy Winn	.20
90	Jose Vidro	.20
91	Mark Prior	5.00
92	Derek Jeter	15.00
93	Alex Rodriguez	12.00
94	Greg Maddux	10.00
95	Troy Glaus	5.00
96	Vladimir Guerrero	8.00
97	Todd Helton	8.00
98	Albert Pujols	10.00
99	Torii Hunter	4.00
100	Mike Piazza	10.00
101	Ichiro Suzuki	10.00
102	Sammy Sosa	9.00
103	Ken Griffey Jr.	10.00
104	Nomar Garciaparra	5.00
105	Barry Bonds	10.00
106	Chipper Jones	10.00
107	Jim Thome	5.00
108	Miguel Tejada	5.00
109	Randy Johnson	8.00
110	Alfonso Soriano	8.00
111	Guillermo Quiroz RC	1.50
112	Josh Willingham RC	1.50
113	Alejandro Machado RC	1.50
114	Chris Waters RC	1.50
115	Adam LaRoche	1.50
116	Prentice Redman RC	1.50
117	Jhonny Peralta	2.50
118	Francisco Rosario RC	1.50
119	Shane Victorino RC	4.00
120	Chien-Ming Wang RC	15.00
121	Matt Bruback RC	1.50
122	Rontrez Johnson RC	1.50
123	Josh Hall RC	1.50
124	Matt Kata RC	1.50
125	Hector Luna RC	1.50
126	Josh Stewart RC	1.50
127	Craig Brazell RC	1.50
128	Tim Olson RC	1.50
129	Michel Hernandez RC	1.50
130	Michael Hessman RC	1.50
131	Clint Barmes RC	2.00
132	Justin Morneau	2.50
133	Chris Snelling	1.50
134	Bobby Jenks	1.50
135	Tim Hummel RC	1.50
136	Adam Morrissey	1.50
137	Carl Crawford	2.00
138	Garrett Atkins	1.50
139	Jung Bong	1.50
140	Ken Harvey	1.50
141	Chin-Feng Chen	1.50
142	Hee Seop Choi	1.50
143	Lance Niekro	1.50
144	Mark Teixeira	2.00
145	Nook Logan RC	1.50
146	Termmel Sledge RC	1.50
147	Lew Ford RC	1.50
148	Ian Ferguson RC	1.50
149	Hideki Matsui/499 RC	15.00
150	Jose Contreras RC	6.00

Bat Chips

		NM/M
Common Player:		4.00
Production 425 Sets		
1	Jason Giambi	8.00
2	Jeff Bagwell	8.00
3	Manny Ramirez	8.00
4	Adam Dunn	8.00
5	Derek Jeter	25.00
6	Alex Rodriguez	15.00
7	Troy Glaus	5.00
8	Mike Piazza	15.00
9	Sammy Sosa	12.00
10	Nomar Garciaparra	18.00
11	Barry Bonds	18.00
12	Jim Thome	5.00
13	Miguel Tejada	5.00
14	Alfonso Soriano	10.00
15	Ryan Klesko	4.00
16	Sean Casey	4.00
17	Bernie Williams	8.00
18	Vladimir Guerrero	8.00
19	Gary Sheffield	5.00

Family Tree

		NM/M
Complete Set (10):		10.00
Common Player:		.50
Inserted 1:8		
1	Lance Niekro, Phil Niekro	.50
2	Bob Boone, Bret Boone	.50
3	Sandy Alomar Jr., Roberto Alomar	.50
4	Ken Griffey Sr., Ken Griffey Jr.	2.00
5	Jason Giambi, Jeremy Giambi	1.50
6	Bobby Bonds, Barry Bonds	3.00
7	Tony Perez, Eduardo Perez	.50
8	Brian Giles, Marcus Giles	.50
9	Felipe Alou, Moises Alou	.75
10	Pedro J. Martinez, Ramon Martinez	1.50

Home Run Club

		NM/M
Complete Set (12):		50.00
Common Player:		2.00
Inserted 1:72		
1	Barry Bonds	10.00
2	Jason Giambi	5.00
3	Sammy Sosa	6.00
4	Jim Thome	4.00
5	Lance Berkman	2.00
6	Alfonso Soriano	5.00

#	Player	Price
7	Vladimir Guerrero	4.00
8	Shawn Green	2.00
9	Troy Glaus	3.00
10	Pat Burrell	3.00
11	Alex Rodriguez	10.00
12	Mike Piazza	8.00

Home Run Club Autographs

NM/M

Quantity produced listed.

#	Player	Price
BB1	Barry Bonds/ Black Ink/150	150.00
CR1	Cal Ripken Jr./ Black Ink/300	100.00
CR2	Cal Ripken Jr./ Blue Ink/150	125.00
CR3	Cal Ripken Jr./ Red Ink/50	200.00
DJ1	Derek Jeter/ Black Ink/400	80.00
DJ2	Derek Jeter/ Blue Ink/250	100.00
DJ3	Derek Jeter/Red Ink/50	125.00

Home Run Club Memorabilia

NM/M

Common Player: 5.00
Production 599 Sets

Player	Price
Barry Bonds/Jsy	20.00
Jason Giambi/Bat	8.00
Sammy Sosa/Jsy	12.00
Jim Thome/Bat	8.00
Lance Berkman/Bat	5.00
Alfonso Soriano/Jsy	15.00
Vladimir Guerrero/Jsy	8.00
Shawn Green/Jsy	5.00
Troy Glaus/Bat	6.00
Pat Burrell/Bat	10.00
Alex Rodriguez/Jsy	15.00
Mike Piazza/Jsy	12.00
Todd Helton/Jsy	8.00
Rafael Palmeiro/Jsy	6.00

Knot Hole Gang

NM/M

Complete Set (15): 40.00
Common Player: 1.00
Inserted 1:24

#	Player	Price
1	Derek Jeter	6.00
2	Barry Bonds	6.00
3	Sammy Sosa	3.00
4	Jason Giambi	3.00
5	Alfonso Soriano	2.00
6	Roger Clemens	3.00
7	Miguel Tejada	1.00
8	Greg Maddux	3.00
9	Randy Johnson	2.00
10	Chipper Jones	3.00
11	Nomar Garciaparra	4.00
12	Alex Rodriguez	5.00
13	Ichiro Suzuki	4.00
14	Vladimir Guerrero	2.00
15	Albert Pujols	2.00

Knot Hole Gang Game-Used

NM/M

Common Player: 4.00
Inserted 1:40

Player	Price
Derek Jeter	20.00
Barry Bonds	15.00
Sammy Sosa	10.00
Vladimir Guerrero	8.00
Alfonso Soriano	8.00
Roger Clemens	10.00
Miguel Tejada	5.00
Greg Maddux	10.00
Randy Johnson	8.00
Chipper Jones	8.00
Nomar Garciaparra	12.00
Alex Rodriguez	12.00
Magglio Ordonez	4.00
Lance Berkman	6.00

Knot Hole Gang Patch

NM/M

Common Player: 15.00
Production 99 Sets

Player	Price
Derek Jeter	45.00
Barry Bonds	45.00
Sammy Sosa	35.00
Vladimir Guerrero	25.00
Alfonso Soriano	25.00
Roger Clemens	25.00
Miguel Tejada	15.00
Greg Maddux	30.00
Randy Johnson	20.00
Chipper Jones	30.00
Nomar Garciaparra	35.00
Alex Rodriguez	35.00

Knot Hole Gang Triple

Common Player: No Pricing
Production 29 Sets

Splendid Splinters

NM/M

Complete Set (10): 15.00
Common Player: 1.00
Inserted 1:12

#	Player	Price
1	Derek Jeter	4.00
2	Barry Bonds	4.00
3	Scott Rolen	1.00
4	Nomar Garciaparra	2.50
5	Sammy Sosa	2.00
6	Alfonso Soriano	1.50
7	Alex Rodriguez	3.00
8	Mike Piazza	2.50
9	Manny Ramirez	1.00
10	Jeff Bagwell	1.00

Splendid Splinters G-U

NM/M

Common Player: 8.00
Production 349 Sets

Player	Price
Derek Jeter	20.00
Barry Bonds	20.00
Nomar Garciaparra	15.00
Sammy Sosa	10.00
Alfonso Soriano	10.00
Alex Rodriguez	12.00
Mike Piazza	12.00
Manny Ramirez	8.00
Jeff Bagwell	8.00

Splendid Splinters Dual

NM/M

Production 99 Sets

Players	Price
Derek Jeter, Alfonso Soriano	40.00
Barry Bonds, Sammy Sosa	50.00
Alex Rodriguez, Nomar Garciaparra	40.00
Mike Piazza, Jeff Bagwell	25.00

2003 Fleer Tradition

JASON GIAMBI
New York Yankees • First Base

NM/M

Complete Set (485): 150.00
Common Player: .15
Common SP (1-100): 1.00
Inserted 1:1
Hobby Pack (10): 1.50
Hobby Box (40): 40.00

#	Players	Price
1	Jarrod Washburn, Troy Glaus, Garret Anderson, Ramon Ortiz	1.50
2	Luis Gonzalez, Randy Johnson, Andruw Jones	1.50
3	Andruw Jones, Chipper Jones, Tom Glavine, Kevin Millwood	2.00
4	Tony Batista, Rodrigo Lopez	1.00
5	Manny Ramirez, Nomar Garciaparra, Derek Lowe, Pedro J. Martinez	3.00
6	Sammy Sosa, Matt Clement, Kerry Wood	3.00
7	Mark Buehrle, Magglio Ordonez, Danny Wright	1.00
8	Adam Dunn, Aaron Boone, Jimmy Haynes	1.00
9	C.C. Sabathia, Jim Thome	1.50
10	Todd Helton, Jason Jennings	.15
11	Randall Simon, Steve Sparks, Mark Redman	1.00
12	Derek Lee, Mike Lowell, A.J. Burnett	1.00
13	Lance Berkman, Roy Oswalt	1.50
14	Paul Byrd, Carlos Beltran	1.00
15	Shawn Green, Hideo Nomo	1.50
16	Richie Sexson, Ben Sheets	1.00
17	Torii Hunter, Kyle Lohse, Johan Santana	1.00
18	Vladimir Guerrero, Tomokazu Ohka, Javier Vazquez	2.00
19	Mike Piazza, Al Leiter	3.00
20	Jason Giambi, David Wells, Roger Clemens	4.00
21	Eric Chavez, Miguel Tejada, Barry Zito	1.50
22	Pat Burrell, Vicente Padilla, Randy Wolf	1.50
23	Brian Giles, Josh Fogg, Kip Wells	1.00
24	Ryan Klesko, Brian Lawrence	1.00
25	Barry Bonds, Russ Ortiz, Jason Schmidt	5.00
26	Mike Cameron, Bret Boone, Freddy Garcia	1.00
27	Albert Pujols, Matt Morris	3.00
28	Aubrey Huff, Randy Winn, Joe Kennedy, Tanyon Sturtze	1.00
29	Alex Rodriguez, Kenny Rogers, Chan Ho Park	5.00
30	Carlos Delgado, Roy Halladay	1.00
31	Greg Maddux	6.00
32	Nick Neugebauer	1.00
33	Larry Walker	1.50
34	Freddy Garcia	1.00
35	Rich Aurilia	1.00
36	Craig Wilson	1.00
37	Jeff Suppan	1.00
38	Joel Pineiro	1.00
39	Pedro Feliz	1.00
40	Bartolo Colon	1.50
41	Pete Walker	1.00
42	Mo Vaughn	1.50
43	Sidney Ponson	1.00
44	Jason Isringhausen	1.00
45	Hideki Irabu	1.00
46	Pedro J. Martinez	4.00
47	Tom Glavine	2.50
48	Matt Lawton	1.00
49	Kyle Lohse	1.00
50	Corey Patterson	1.00
51	Ichiro Suzuki	6.00
52	Wade Miller	1.00
53	Ben Diggins	1.00
54	Jayson Werth	1.00
55	Masato Yoshii	1.00
56	Mark Buehrle	1.00
57	Drew Henson	1.50
58	Dave Williams	1.00
59	Juan Rivera	1.00
60	Scott Schoeneweis	1.00
61	Josh Beckett	1.50
62	Vinny Castilla	1.00
63	Barry Zito	2.00
64	Jose Valentin	1.00
65	Jon Lieber	1.00
66	Jorge Padilla	1.00
67	Luis Aparicio	1.00
68	Boog Powell	1.00
69	Dick Radatz	1.00
70	Frank Malzone	1.00
71	Lou Brock	1.50
72	Billy Williams	1.00
73	Early Wynn	1.00
74	Jim Bunning	1.00
75	Al Kaline	5.00
76	Eddie Mathews	3.00
77	Harmon Killebrew	5.00
78	Gil Hodges	1.00
79	Duke Snider	3.00
80	Yogi Berra	4.00
81	Whitey Ford	3.00
82	Willie Stargell	1.50
83	Willie McCovey	1.50
84	Gaylord Perry	1.00
85	Red Schoendienst	1.00
86	Luis Castillo	1.00
87	Derek Jeter	8.00
88	Orlando Hudson	1.00
89	Bobby Higginson	1.00
90	Brent Butler	1.00
91	Brad Wilkerson	1.00
92	Craig Biggio	1.50
93	Marlon Anderson	1.00
94	Ty Wigginton	1.00
95	Hideo Nomo	3.00
96	Barry Larkin	2.00
97	Roberto Alomar	3.00
98	Omar Vizquel	1.50
99	Andres Galarraga	1.00
100	Shawn Green	1.50
101	Rafael Furcal	.15
102	Bill Selby	.15
103	Brent Abernathy	.15
104	Nomar Garciaparra	1.50
105	Michael Barrett	.15
106	Travis Hafner	.15
107	Carl Crawford	.15
108	Jeff Cirillo	.15
109	Mike Hampton	.15
110	Kip Wells	.15
111	Luis Alicea	.15
112	Ellis Burks	.15
113	Matt Anderson	.15
114	Carlos Beltran	.50
115	Paul LoDuca	.15
116	Lance Berkman	.15
117	Moises Alou	.15
118	Roger Cedeno	.15
119	Brad Fullmer	.15
120	Sean Burroughs	.15
121	Eric Byrnes	.15
122	Milton Bradley	.15
123	Jason Giambi	.75
124	Brook Fordyce	.15
125	Kevin Appier	.15
126	Steve Cox	.15
127	Danny Bautista	.15
128	Edgardo Alfonzo	.15
129	Matt Clement	.15
130	Robb Nen	.15
131	Roy Halladay	.15
132	Brian Jordan	.15
133	A.J. Burnett	.15
134	Aaron Cook	.15
135	Paul Byrd	.15
136	Ramon Ortiz	.15
137	Adam Hyzdu	.15
138	Rafael Soriano	.15
139	Marty Cordova	.15
140	Nelson Cruz	.15
141	Jamie Moyer	.15
142	Raul Mondesi	.15
143	Josh Bard	.15
144	Elmer Dessens	.15
145	Rickey Henderson	.75
146	Joe McEwing	.15
147	Luis Rivas	.15
148	Armando Benitez	.15
149	Keith Foulke	.15
150	Zach Day	.15
151	Troy Lunsford	.15
152	Bobby Abreu	.15
153	Juan Cruz	.15
154	Ramon Hernandez	.15
155	Brandon Duckworth	.15
156	Matt Ginter	.15
157	Robert Mackowiak	.15
158	Josh Pearce	.15
159	Marlon Byrd	.15
160	Todd Walker	.15
161	Chad Hermansen	.15
162	Felix Escalona	.15
163	Ruben Mateo	.15
164	Mark Johnson	.15
165	Juan Pierre	.15
166	Gary Sheffield	.30
167	Edgar Martinez	.15
168	Randy Winn	.15
169	Pokey Reese	.15
170	Kevin Mench	.15
171	Albert Pujols	1.50
172	J.T. Snow	.15
173	Dean Palmer	.15
174	Jay Payton	.15
175	Abraham Nunez	.15
176	Richie Sexson	.15
177	Jose Vidro	.15
178	Geoff Jenkins	.15
179	Dan Wilson	.15
180	John Olerud	.15
181	Javy Lopez	.15
182	Carl Everett	.15
183	Vernon Wells	.15
184	Juan Gonzalez	.75
185	Jorge Posada	.35
186	Mike Sweeney	.15
187	Cesar Izturis	.15
188	Jason Schmidt	.15
189	Chris Richard	.15
190	Jason Phillips	.15
191	Fred McGriff	.15
192	Shea Hillenbrand	.15
193	Ivan Rodriguez	.50
194	Mike Lowell	.15
195	Neifi Perez	.15
196	Kenny Lofton	.15
197	A.J. Pierzynski	.15
198	Larry Bigbie	.15
199	Juan Uribe	.15
200	Jeff Bagwell	.75
201	Timoniel Perez	.15
202	Jeremy Giambi	.15
203	Deivi Cruz	.15
204	Marquis Grissom	.15
205	Chipper Jones	1.00
206	Alex Gonzalez	.15
207	Steve Finley	.15
208	Ben Davis	.15
209	Mike Bordick	.15
210	Casey Fossum	.15
211	Aramis Ramirez	.15
212	Aaron Boone	.15
213	Orlando Cabrera	.15
214	Hee Seop Choi	.15
215	Jason Lane	.15
216	Todd Hollandsworth	.15
217	Rey Sanchez	.15
218	Jose Cruz Jr.	.15
219	Roosevelt Brown	.15
220	Odalis Perez	.15
221	Carlos Delgado	.40
222	Orlando Hernandez	.15
223	Adam Everett	.15
224	Adrian Beltre	.25
225	Ken Griffey Jr.	1.50
226	Brad Penny	.15
227	Carlos Lee	.15
228	J.C. Romero	.15
229	Ramon Martinez	.15
230	Matt Morris	.15
231	Ben Howard	.15
232	Damon Minor	.15
233	Jason Marquis	.15
234	Paul Wilson	.15
235	Ryan Dempster	.15
236	Jeffrey Hammonds	.15
237	Jaret Wright	.15
238	Carlos Pena	.15
239	Toby Hall	.15
240	Rick Helling	.15
241	Alex Escobar	.15
242	Trevor Hoffman	.15
243	Bernie Williams	.35
244	Jorge Julio	.15
245	Byung-Hyun Kim	.15
246	Mike Redmond	.15
247	Tony Armas	.15
248	Aaron Rowand	.15
249	Rusty Greer	.15
250	Aaron Harang	.15
251	Jeremy Fikac	.15
252	Jay Gibbons	.15
253	Brandon Puffer	.15
254	Dewayne Wise	.15
255	Chan Ho Park	.15
256	David Bell	.15
257	Kenny Rogers	.15
258	Mark Quinn	.15
259	Greg LaRocca	.15
260	Reggie Taylor	.15
261	Brett Tomko	.15
262	Jack Wilson	.15
263	Billy Wagner	.15
264	Greg Norton	.15
265	Tim Salmon	.25
266	Joe Randa	.15
267	Geronimo Gil	.15
268	Johnny Damon	.25
269	Robin Ventura	.15
270	Frank Thomas	.75
271	Terrence Long	.15
272	Mark Redman	.15
273	Mark Kotsay	.15
274	Ben Sheets	.15
275	Reggie Sanders	.15
276	Mark Grace	.25
277	Eddie Guardado	.15
278	Julio Mateo	.15
279	Bengie Molina	.15
280	Bill Hall	.15
281	Eric Chavez	.30
282	Joe Kennedy	.15
283	John Valentin	.15
284	Ray Durham	.15
285	Trot Nixon	.15
286	Rondell White	.15
287	Alex Gonzalez	.15
288	Tomas Perez	.15
289	Jared Sandberg	.15
290	Jacque Jones	.15
291	Cliff Floyd	.15
292	Ryan Klesko	.15
293	Morgan Ensberg	.15
294	Jerry Hairston Jr.	.15
295	Doug Mientkiewicz	.15
296	Darin Erstad	.50
297	Jeff Conine	.15
298	Johnny Estrada	.15
299	Mark Mulder	.15
300	Jeff Kent	.15
301	Roger Clemens	1.25
302	Endy Chavez	.15
303	Joe Crede	.15
304	J.D. Drew	.30
305	David Dellucci	.15
306	Eli Marrero	.15
307	Josh Fogg	.15
308	Mike Crudale	.15
309	Bret Boone	.15
310	Mariano Rivera	.15
311	Mike Piazza	1.50
312	Jason Jennings	.15
313	Jason Varitek	.15
314	Vicente Padilla	.15
315	Kevin Millwood	.15
316	Nick Johnson	.15
317	Shane Reynolds	.15
318	Joe Thurston	.15
319	Mike Lamb	.15
320	Aaron Sele	.15
321	Fernando Tatis	.15
322	Randy Wolf	.15
323	David Justice	.15
324	Andy Pettitte	.30
325	Freddy Sanchez	.15
326	Scott Spiezio	.15
327	Randy Johnson	.75
328	Karim Garcia	.15
329	Eric Milton	.15
330	Jermaine Dye	.15
331	Kevin Brown	.15
332	Adam Pettyjohn	.15
333	Jason Lane	.15
334	Mark Prior	.50
335	Mike Lieberthal	.15
336	Matt White	.15
337	John Patterson	.15
338	Marcus Giles	.15
339	Kazuhisa Ishii	.15
340	Willie Harris	.15
341	Travis Phelps	.15
342	Randall Simon	.15
343	Manny Ramirez	.75
344	Kerry Wood	.50
345	Shannon Stewart	.15
346	Mike Mussina	.40
347	Joe Borchard	.15
348	Tyler Walker	.15
349	Preston Wilson	.15
350	Damian Moss	.15
351	Eric Karros	.15
352	Bobby Kielty	.15
353	Jason LaRue	.15
354	Phil Nevin	.15
355	Tony Graffanino	.15
356	Antonio Alfonseca	.15
357	Eddie Taubensee	.15
358	Luis Ugueto	.15
359	Greg Vaughn	.15
360	Corey Thurman	.15
361	Omar Infante	.15
362	Alex Cintron	.15
363	Esteban Loaiza	.15
364	Tino Martinez	.15
365	David Eckstein	.15
366	David Pember RC	.15
367	Damian Rolls	.15
368	Richard Hidalgo	.15
369	Brad Radke	.15
370	Alex Sanchez	.15
371	Ben Grieve	.15
372	Brandon Inge	.15
373	Adam Piatt	.15
374	Charles Johnson	.15
375	Rafael Palmeiro	.50
376	Joe Mays	.15
377	Derrek Lee	.15
378	Fernando Vina	.15
379	Andruw Jones	.75
380	Troy Glaus	.75
381	Bobby Hill	.15
382	C.C. Sabathia	.15
383	Jose Hernandez	.15
384	Al Leiter	.15
385	Jarrod Washburn	.15
386	Cody Ransom	.15
387	Matt Stairs	.15
388	Edgar Renteria	.15
389	Tsuyoshi Shinjo	.15
390	Matt Williams	.15
391	Bubba Trammell	.15
392	Jason Kendall	.15
393	Scott Rolen	.50
394	Chuck Knoblauch	.15
395	Jimmy Rollins	.25
396	Gary Bennett	.15
397	David Wells	.15
398	Ronnie Belliard	.15
399	Austin Kearns	.50
400	Tim Hudson	.30
401	Andy Van Hekken	.15
402	Ray Lankford	.15
403	Todd Helton	.75
404	Jeff Weaver	.15
405	Gabe Kapler	.15
406	Luis Gonzalez	.40
407	Sean Casey	.15
408	Kazuhiro Sasaki	.15
409	Mark Teixeira	.50
410	Brian Giles	.15
411	Robert Fick	.15
412	Wilkin Ruan	.15
413	Jose Rijo	.15
414	Ben Broussard	.15
415	Aubrey Huff	.15
416	Magglio Ordonez	.25
417	Barry Bonds	2.00
418	Miguel Tejada	.40
419	Randy Johnson	.75
420	Barry Zito	.30
421	Jason Jennings	.15
422	Eric Hinske	.15
423	Benito Santiago	.15
424	Adam Kennedy	.15
425	Troy Glaus	.50
426	Brandon Phillips	.15
427	Jake Peavy	.15
428	Jason Romano	.15
429	Jeriome Robertson	.15
430	Aaron Guiel	.15
431	Hank Blalock	.15
432	Brad Lidge	.15
433	Francisco Rodriguez	.15
434	Jaime Cerda	.15
435	Jung Bong	.15
436	Reed Johnson	.15
437	Rene Reyes	.15
438	Chris Snelling	.15
439	Miguel Olivo	.15
440	Brian Banks	.15
441	Eric Junge	.15
442	Kirk Saarloos	.15
443	Jamey Carroll	.15
444	Josh Hancock	.15
445	Michael Restovich	.15
446	William Bloomquist	.15
447	John Lackey	.15
448	Marcus Thames	.15
449	Victor Martinez	.15
450	Brett Myers	.15
451	Wes Obermueller	.15
452	Hansel Izquierdo	.15
453	Brian Tallet	.15
454	Craig Monroe	.15
455	Doug DeVore	.15
456	John Buck	.15
457	Tony Alvarez	.15

458	Wily Mo Pena	.15
459	John Stephens	.15
460	Tony Torcato	.15
461	Adam Kennedy	.15
462	Alex Rodriguez	.15
463	Derek Lowe	.15
464	Garret Anderson	.15
465	Pat Burrell	.50
466	Eric Gagne	.15
467	Tomokazu Ohka	.15
468	Josh Phelps	.15
469	Sammy Sosa	1.50
470	Jim Thome	.15
471	Vladimir Guerrero	.75
472	Jason Simontacchi	.15
473	Adam Dunn	.50
474	Jim Edmonds	.15
475	Barry Bonds	2.00
476	Paul Konerko	.25
477	Alfonso Soriano	.75
478	Curt Schilling	.40
479	John Smoltz	.15
480	Torii Hunter	.15
481	Rodrigo Lopez	.15
482	Miguel Tejada	.35
483	Eric Hinske	.15
484	Roy Oswalt	.25
485	Junior Spivey	.15

Glossy

SP's (1-100):	1-2X
Cards (101-485):	5-10X

Production 100 Sets
Randomly inserted in Update packs.

B/W Goudey

Chicago Cubs™

	NM/M
Complete Set (25):	80.00
Common Player:	1.50

Production 1,936 Sets

Golds:	4-8X

Production 36 Sets

1BWG	Jim Thome	2.50
2BWG	Derek Jeter	10.00
3BWG	Alex Rodriguez	8.00
4BWG	Mark Prior	1.00
5BWG	Nomar Garciaparra	6.00
6BWG	Curt Schilling	2.00
7BWG	Pat Burrell	2.00
8BWG	Frank Thomas	2.50
9BWG	Roger Clemens	5.00
10BWG	Chipper Jones	5.00
11BWG	Barry Larkin	1.50
12BWG	Hideo Nomo	2.00
13BWG	Pedro J. Martinez	3.00
14BWG	Jeff Bagwell	2.50
15BWG	Greg Maddux	5.00
16BWG	Vladimir Guerrero	3.00
17BWG	Ichiro Suzuki	6.00
18BWG	Mike Piazza	8.00
19BWG	Drew Henson	1.50
20BWG	Albert Pujols	3.00
21BWG	Sammy Sosa	5.00
22BWG	Jason Giambi	5.00
23BWG	Randy Johnson	3.00
24BWG	Ken Griffey Jr.	6.00
25BWG	Barry Bonds	8.00

Checklist

	NM/M
Complete Set (18):	6.00
Common Player:	.50

Inserted 1:4

1CL-18	Derek Jeter	.50

Game-Used Parallel

FRANK THOMAS
Chicago White Sox™ - Designated Hitter

	NM/M
Common Player:	5.00

Inserted 1:35

Golds:	1-2X

Production 100 Sets

Derek Jeter/Jsy/150	35.00
Craig Biggio/Jsy	8.00
Hideo Nomo/Jsy/200	20.00
Barry Larkin/Jsy/200	10.00
Kazuhiro Sasaki/Jsy/200	10.00
Greg Maddux/Jsy	10.00
Mo Vaughn/Jsy/60	10.00
Pedro Martinez/Jsy/200	12.00
Barry Zito/Jsy	10.00
Luis Aparicio/Jsy/150	10.00
Willie Stargell/Pants/150	15.00
Nomar Garciaparra/Jsy/200	20.00
Edgardo Alfonzo/Jsy/200	8.00
John Olerud/Jsy	10.00
Juan Gonzalez/Bat/200	10.00
Jorge Posada/Bat	8.00
Shea Hillenbrand/Bat	10.00
Ivan Rodriguez/Jsy	8.00
Mike Lowell/Bat	5.00
Jeff Bagwell/Bat/200	12.00
Chipper Jones/Jsy	15.00
Jeromy Burnitz/Jsy/200	6.00
Adrian Beltre/Jsy	6.00
Robin Ventura/Jsy	8.00
Frank Thomas/Jsy	10.00
Mark Grace/Jsy	10.00
Darin Erstad/Jsy	6.00
Roger Clemens/Jsy/150	20.00
J.D. Drew/Jsy	8.00
Mike Piazza/Jsy/150	20.00
Randy Johnson/Jsy/150	12.00
Mark Prior/Jsy/200	15.00
Kazuhisa Ishii/Jsy	10.00
Manny Ramirez/Jsy/150	10.00
Kerry Wood/Jsy/200	15.00
Mike Mussina/Jsy	10.00
Eric Karros/Jsy	6.00
Rafael Palmeiro/Jsy	8.00
Andruw Jones/Bat/150	10.00
Jason Kendall/Jsy	6.00
Jimmy Rollins/Jsy	8.00
Barry Bonds/Jsy/50	40.00
Miguel Tejada/Bat/150	8.00
Jason Jennings/Jsy	6.00

Hardball Preview

	NM/M
Complete Set (10):	125.00
Common Player:	5.00

Inserted 1:400

1	Miguel Tejada	5.00
2	Derek Jeter	25.00
3	Mike Piazza	20.00
4	Barry Bonds	20.00
5	Mark Prior	4.00
6	Ichiro Suzuki	20.00
7	Alex Rodriguez	20.00
8	Nomar Garciaparra	15.00
9	Alfonso Soriano	12.00
10	Ken Griffey Jr.	15.00

Lumber Company

LUMBER COMPANY
Ichiro

	NM/M
Complete Set (30):	70.00
Common Player:	1.00

Inserted 1:10

1	Mike Piazza	6.00
2	Derek Jeter	8.00
3	Alex Rodriguez	6.00
4	Miguel Tejada	1.00
5	Nomar Garciaparra	5.00
6	Andruw Jones	1.50
7	Pat Burrell	1.50
8	Albert Pujols	3.00
9	Jeff Bagwell	2.00
10	Chipper Jones	4.00
11	Ichiro Suzuki	6.00
12	Alfonso Soriano	3.00
13	Eric Chavez	1.50
14	Brian Giles	1.00
15	Shawn Green	1.50
16	Jim Thome	2.00
17	Lance Berkman	1.50
18	Bernie Williams	1.50
19	Manny Ramirez	2.00
20	Vladimir Guerrero	3.00
21	Carlos Delgado	1.25
22	Scott Rolen	1.50
23	Sammy Sosa	4.00
24	Ken Griffey Jr.	5.00
25	Barry Bonds	6.00
26	Todd Helton	1.50
27	Jason Giambi	4.00
28	Austin Kearns	1.50
29	Jeff Kent	1.00
30	Magglio Ordonez	1.00

Lumber Company Bat

	NM/M
Common Player:	6.00

Inserted 1:108

Jeff Bagwell/200	15.00
Lance Berkman/200	10.00
Barry Bonds/150	25.00
Pat Burrell/75	25.00
Eric Chavez/125	8.00
Carlos Delgado/200	6.00
Nomar Garciaparra/200	25.00
Brian Giles/200	8.00
Shawn Green/200	8.00
Todd Helton	8.00
Derek Jeter/96	35.00
Andruw Jones	8.00
Chipper Jones	15.00
Austin Kearns/75	18.00
Jeff Kent/200	6.00
Magglio Ordonez	6.00
Mike Piazza/200	20.00
Manny Ramirez	10.00
Alex Rodriguez	15.00
Scott Rolen/80	25.00
Alfonso Soriano/200	12.00
Miguel Tejada	8.00
Jim Thome/200	12.00
Bernie Williams	8.00

Lumber Company Bat Gold

NM/M
Numbered to 2002 HR total.

Lance Berkman/42	25.00
Barry Bonds/46	70.00
Pat Burrell/37	50.00
Eric Chavez/34	20.00
Carlos Delgado/33	35.00
Nomar Garciaparra/24	60.00
Brian Giles/38	25.00
Shawn Green/42	35.00
Todd Helton/30	35.00
Derek Jeter/18	200.00
Andruw Jones/35	25.00
Chipper Jones/26	45.00
Austin Kearns/13	35.00
Jeff Kent/37	20.00
Magglio Ordonez/38	25.00
Mike Piazza/33	65.00
Alex Rodriguez/57	40.00
Miguel Tejada/34	35.00
Jim Thome/52	30.00

Milestones

MILESTONES
ROBERTO ALOMAR

	NM/M
Complete Set (25):	40.00
Common Player:	1.00

Inserted 1:5

1	Eddie Mathews	1.50
2	Rickey Henderson	1.50
3	Harmon Killebrew	1.50
4	Al Kaline	2.50
5	Willie McCovey	1.00
6	Tom Seaver	2.00
7	Reggie Jackson	2.00
8	Mike Schmidt	3.00
9	Nolan Ryan	5.00
10	Mike Piazza	4.00
11	Randy Johnson	2.00
12	Bernie Williams	1.50
13	Rafael Palmeiro	1.50
14	Juan Gonzalez	1.50
15	Ken Griffey Jr.	3.00
16	Derek Jeter	5.00
17	Roger Clemens	3.00
18	Roberto Alomar	1.50
19	Manny Ramirez	1.50
20	Luis Gonzalez	1.00
21	Barry Bonds	4.00
22	Nomar Garciaparra	3.00
23	Fred McGriff	1.00
24	Greg Maddux	2.50
25	Barry Bonds	4.00

Milestones Game-Used

PEDRO MARTINEZ
HARTFORD JERSEY

	NM/M
Common Player:	8.00

Inserted 1:143

Golds:	1-2X

Production 100 Sets

Roberto Alomar/Bat/200	8.00
Barry Bonds/600 HR/Bat/100	30.00
Barry Bonds/5 MVP/Jsy/200	25.00
Roger Clemens/Jsy/150	20.00
Nomar Garciaparra/Jsy/200	20.00
Juan Gonzalez/Bat/250	15.00
Derek Jeter/Jsy/150	35.00
Randy Johnson/Jsy/100	15.00
Greg Maddux	20.00
Fred McGriff	5.00
Rafael Palmeiro/Jsy/200	8.00
Mike Piazza/Jsy/100	20.00
Manny Ramirez/Jsy/150	10.00
Bernie Williams/Jsy/200	10.00

Standouts

ALEX RODRIGUEZ
SHORTSTOP TEXAS RANGERS™

	NM/M
Complete Set (15):	60.00
Common Player:	1.50

Inserted 1:40

1SO	Greg Maddux	5.00
2SO	Derek Jeter	10.00
3SO	Alex Rodriguez	8.00
4SO	Miguel Tejada	2.00
5SO	Nomar Garciaparra	6.00
6SO	Barry Bonds	8.00
7SO	Pat Burrell	1.50
8SO	Ken Griffey Jr.	6.00
9SO	Alfonso Soriano	4.00
10SO	Mike Piazza	8.00
11SO	Sammy Sosa	5.00
12SO	Ichiro Suzuki	6.00
13SO	Vladimir Guerrero	3.00
14SO	Roger Clemens	5.00
15SO	Adam Dunn	2.50

2003 Fleer Tradition Update

ROOKIE '03
DELMON YOUNG
Tampa Bay Devil Rays™ - Outfield

	NM/M
Complete Set (398):	175.00
Common Player:	.15
Common Rookie (286-398):	.50

Cards (286-299):
Inserted 1:4

Pack (10):	2.00
Box (32 + 25 count update box):	50.00

1	Aaron Boone	.15
2	Carl Everett	.15
3	Eduardo Perez	.15
4	Jason Michaels	.15
5	Karim Garcia	.15
6	Rainier Olmedo	.15
7	Scott Williamson	.15
8	Adam Kennedy	.15
9	Carl Pavano	.15
10	Eli Marrero	.15
11	Jason Simontacchi	.15
12	Keith Foulke	.15
13	Preston Wilson	.15
14	Scott Hatteberg	.15
15	Adam Dunn	.50
16	Carlos Baerga	.15
17	Elmer Dessens	.15
18	Javier Vazquez	.15
19	Kenny Rogers	.15
20	Quinton McCracken	.15
21	Shane Reynolds	.15
22	Adam Eaton	.15
23	Carlos Zambrano	.15
24	Enrique Wilson	.15
25	Jeff DaVanon	.15
26	Kenny Lofton	.25
27	Ramon Castro	.15
28	Shannon Stewart	.15
29	Al Martin	.15
30	Carlos Guillen	.15
31	Eric Karros	.15
32	Tim Worrell	.15
33	Kevin Millwood	.25
34	Randall Simon	.15
35	Shawn Chacon	.15
36	Alex Rodriguez	1.50
37	Casey Blake	.15
38	Eric Munson	.15
39	Jeff Kent	.25
40	Kris Benson	.15
41	Randy Winn	.15
42	Shea Hillenbrand	.15
43	Alfonso Soriano	1.00
44	Chris George	.15
45	Eric Bruntlett	.15
46	Jeromy Burnitz	.15
47	Kyle Farnsworth	.15
48	Torii Hunter	.40
49	Sidney Ponson	.15
50	Andres Galarraga	.25
51	Chris Singleton	.15
52	Eric Gagne	.25
53	Jesse Foppert	.15
54	Lance Carter	.15
55	Ray Durham	.15
56	Tanyon Sturtze	.15
57	Andy Ashby	.15
58	Cliff Floyd	.15
59	Eric Young	.15
60	Jhonny Peralta	.50
61	Livan Hernandez	.15
62	Reggie Sanders	.15
63	Tim Spooneybarger	.15
64	Angel Berroa	.15
65	Coco Crisp	.15
66	Eric Hinske	.15
67	Jim Edmonds	.25
68	Luis Matos	.15
69	Rickey Henderson	.40
70	Todd Walker	.15
71	Antonio Alfonseca	.15
72	Corey Koskie	.15
73	Erubiel Durazo	.15
74	Jim Thome	.50
75	Lyle Overbay	.15
76	Robert Fick	.15
77	Todd Hollandsworth	.15
78	Aramis Ramirez	.15
79	Cristian Guzman	.15
80	Esteban Loaiza	.15
81	Jody Gerut	.15
82	Mark Grudzielanek	.15
83	Roberto Alomar	.40
84	Todd Hundley	.15
85	Mike Hampton	.15
86	Curt Schilling	.40
87	Francisco Rodriguez	.15
88	John Lackey	.15
89	Mark Redman	.15
90	Robin Ventura	.25
91	Todd Zeile	.15
92	B.J. Surhoff	.15
93	Raul Mondesi	.15
94	Frank Catalanotto	.15
95	John Smoltz	.25
96	Mark Ellis	.15
97	Rocco Baldelli	.50
98	Todd Pratt	.15
99	Barry Bonds	2.00
100	Danny Graves	.15
101	Fred McGriff	.25
102	John Burkett	.15
103	Marquis Grissom	.15
104	Rocky Biddle	.15
105	Tom Glavine	.25
106	Bartolo Colon	.25
107	Darren Bragg	.15
108	Gabe Kapler	.15
109	John Franco	.15
110	Matt Mantei	.15
111	Rod Beck	.15
112	Tomokazu Ohka	.15
113	Ben Petrick	.15
114	Darren Dreifort	.15
115	Garret Anderson	.25
116	John Vander Wal	.15
117	Melvin Mora	.15
118	Rodrigo Lopez	.15
119	Raul Ibanez	.15
120	Benito Santiago	.15
121	David Ortiz	.15
122	Gary Bennett	.15
123	Jon Garland	.15
124	Michael Young	.15
125	Rodrigo Rosario	.15
126	Travis Lee	.15
127	Bill Mueller	.15
128	Derek Lowe	.15
129	Gil Meche	.15
130	Jose Guillen	.15
131	Miguel Cabrera	.40
132	Ron Calloway	.15
133	Troy Percival	.15
134	Billy Koch	.15
135	Dmitri Young	.15
136	Glendon Rusch	.15
137	Jose Jimenez	.15
138	Miguel Tejada	.40
139	John Thomson	.15
140	Troy O'Leary	.15
141	Bobby Kielty	.15
142	Dontrelle Willis	.50
143	Greg Myers	.15
144	Jose Vizcaino	.15
145	Mike MacDougal	.15
146	Ronnie Belliard	.15
147	Tyler Houston	.15
148	Brady Clark	.15
149	Edgardo Alfonzo	.15
150	Guillermo Mota	.15
151	Jose Lima	.15
152	Mike Williams	.15
153	Roy Oswalt	.25
154	Scott Podsednik	.25
155	Brandon Lyon	.15
156	Henry Mateo	.15
157	Jose Macias	.15
158	Mike Bordick	.15
159	Royce Clayton	.15
160	Vance Wilson	.15
161	Brent Abernathy	.15
162	Horacio Ramirez	.15
163	Jose Reyes	.50
164	Nick Punto	.15
165	Ruben Sierra	.15
166	Victor Zambrano	.15
167	Brett Tomko	.15
168	Ivan Rodriguez	.75
169	Jose Mesa	.15
170	Octavio Dotel	.15
171	Russ Ortiz	.15
172	Vladimir Guerrero	.75
173	Brian Lawrence	.15
174	Jae Weong Seo	.15
175	Jose Cruz Jr.	.15
176	Pat Burrell	.40
177	Russell Branyan	.15
178	Warren Morris	.15
179	Brian Boehringer	.15
180	Jason Johnson	.15
181	Josh Phelps	.15
182	Paul Konerko	.15
183	Ryan Franklin	.15
184	Wes Helms	.15
185	Brooks Kieschnick	.15
186	Jason Davis	.15
187	Juan Pierre	.15
188	Paul Wilson	.15
189	Sammy Sosa	1.50
190	Wil Cordero	.15
191	Byung-Hyun Kim	.15
192	Juan Encarnacion	.15
193	Placido Polanco	.15
194	Sandy Alomar	.15
195	Julio Lugo	.15
196	Junior Spivey	.15
197	Woody Williams	.15
198	Xavier Nady	.15
199	Mark Loretta	.15
200	Deivi Cruz	.15
201	Jorge Posada	.25
202	Carlos Delgado	.25
203	Alfonso Soriano	.50
204	Alex Rodriguez	1.00
205	Troy Glaus	.25
206	Garret Anderson	.15
207	Hideki Matsui	2.00
208	Ichiro Suzuki	.75
209	Esteban Loaiza	.15
210	Manny Ramirez	.25
211	Roger Clemens	.75
212	Roy Halladay	.15
213	Jason Giambi	.25
214	Edgar Martinez	.15
215	Bret Boone	.15
216	Hank Blalock	.15
217	Nomar Garciaparra	.75
218	Vernon Wells	.15
219	Melvin Mora	.15
220	Magglio Ordonez	.15
221	Mike Sweeney	.15
222	Barry Zito	.25
223	Carl Everett	.15
224	Shigetoshi Hasegawa	.15
225	Jamie Moyer	.15
226	Mark Mulder	.15
227	Eddie Guardado	.15
228	Ramon Hernandez	.15
229	Keith Foulke	.15
230	Javy Lopez	.15
231	Todd Helton	.25
232	Marcus Giles	.15
233	Edgar Renteria	.15
234	Scott Rolen	.15
235	Barry Bonds	1.00
236	Albert Pujols	.25
237	Gary Sheffield	.25
238	Jim Edmonds	.15
239	Jason Schmidt	.15
240	Mark Prior	1.00
241	Dontrelle Willis	.25
242	Kerry Wood	.25
243	Kevin Brown	.15
244	Woody Williams	.15
245	Paul LoDuca	.15
246	Richie Sexson	.15
247	Jose Vidro	.15
248	Luis Castillo	.15
249	Aaron Boone	.15
250	Mike Lowell	.15
251	Rafael Furcal	.15
252	Andruw Jones	.25
253	Preston Wilson	.15
254	John Smoltz	.15
255	Eric Gagne	.15
256	Randy Wolf	.15
257	Billy Wagner	.15
258	Luis Gonzalez	.15
259	Russ Ortiz	.15
260	Jim Thome, Pedro J. Martinez	.40
261	Alfonso Soriano, Jeff Bagwell	.50
262	Dontrelle Willis, Rocco Baldelli	.15
263	Carlos Delgado, Vladimir Guerrero	.50
264	Sammy Sosa, Magglio Ordonez	.50
265	Jason Giambi, Adam Dunn	.25
266	Mike Sweeney, Albert Pujols	.50
267	Barry Bonds, Torii Hunter	.75
268	Ichiro Suzuki, Andruw Jones	.50
269	Chipper Jones, Hank Blalock	.50
270	Mark Prior, Vernon Wells	.75
271	Nomar Garciaparra, Scott Rolen	.75

272	Alex Rodriguez, Lance Berkman	.75
273	Roger Clemens, Kerry Wood	.75
274	Derek Jeter, Jose Reyes	.75
275	Greg Maddux, Barry Zito	.50
276	Carlos Delgado	.25
277	J.D. Drew	.15
278	Barry Bonds	1.00
279	Albert Pujols	.75
280	Jim Thome	.25
281	Sammy Sosa	.75
282	Alfonso Soriano	.50
283	Hideki Matsui	1.00
284	Mike Piazza	.50
285	Vladimir Guerrero	.40
286	Rich Harden	.50
287	Chin-Hui Tsao	.50
288	Edwin Jackson RC	4.00
289	Chien-Ming Wang RC	6.00
290	Josh Willingham RC	2.00
291	Matt Kata RC	2.00
292	Jose Contreras RC	2.00
293	Chris Bootcheck	.50
294	Javier Lopez	.50
295	Delmon Young RC	8.00
296	Pedro Liriano	.50
297	Noah Lowry	.50
298	Khalil Greene	3.00
299	Rob Bowen	.50
300	Bo Hart RC	2.00
301	Beau Kemp RC	.25
302	Gerald Laird	.50
303	Miguel Ojeda RC	.40
304	Todd Wellemeyer RC	.75
305	Ryan Wagner RC	2.00
306	Jeff Duncan RC	1.50
307	Wilfredo Ledezma RC	1.50
308	Wes Obermueller	.15
309	Bernie Castro RC	.25
310	Tim Olson RC	.25
311	Colin Porter RC	.50
312	Francisco Cruceta RC	1.50
313	Guillermo Quiroz RC	1.50
314	Brian Stokes RC	.50
315	Robby Hammock RC	.50
316	Lew Ford RC	2.00
317	Todd Linden	.15
318	Mike Gallo RC	.50
319	Francisco Rosario RC	1.50
320	Rosman Garcia RC	.50
321	Felix Sanchez RC	.50
322	Chad Gaudin RC	1.00
323	Phil Seibel RC	.50
324	Jason Gilfillan RC	.50
325	Terrmel Sledge RC	.75
326	Alfredo Gonzalez RC	.50
327	Josh Stewart RC	.50
328	Jeremy Griffiths	.15
329	Cory Stewart RC	.50
330	Josh Hall RC	1.00
331	Arnie Munoz RC	.50
332	Garrett Atkins	.15
333	Neal Cotts	.15
334	Dan Haren	2.00
335	Shane Victorino RC	.50
336	David Sanders RC	.50
337	Oscar Villarreal RC	.50
338	Michael Hessman RC	.50
339	Andrew Brown RC	.50
340	Kevin Hooper	.15
341	Prentice Redman RC	.50
342	Brandon Webb RC	3.00
343	Jimmy Gobble	.15
344	Pete LaForest RC	.50
345	Chris Waters RC	.75
346	Hideki Matsui RC	8.00
347	Chris Capuano RC	1.00
348	Jon Leicester RC	.50
349	Mike Nicolas RC	.50
350	Nook Logan RC	.50
351	Craig Brazell RC	1.00
352	Aaron Looper RC	.50
353	D.J. Carrasco RC	.50
354	Clint Barmes RC	1.00
355	Doug Waechter RC	.75
356	Julio Manon RC	.50
357	Jeremy Bonderman	3.00
358	Diegomar Markwell RC	.50
359	Dave Matranga RC	.75
360	Luis Ayala RC	.50
361	Jason Stanford	.50
362	Roger Deago RC	.50
363	Geoff Geary RC	1.00
364	Edgar Gonzalez RC	.50
365	Michel Hernandez RC	.50
366	Aquilino Lopez RC	.50
367	David Manning RC	1.00
368	Carlos Mendez RC	.50
369	Matt Miller	.50
370	Micheal Nakamura RC	1.00
371	Mike Neu RC	.50
372	Ramon Nivar RC	.50
373	Kevin Ohme RC	.50
374	Alex Prieto RC	1.00
375	Stephen Randolph RC	.50
376	Brian Sweeney RC	1.00
377	Matt Diaz RC	.50
378	Alexis Rios	.15
379	Daniel Cabrera RC	.50
380	Fernando Cabrera RC	.50
381	David DeJesus RC	.50
382	Mike Ryan RC	1.00
383	Rick Roberts RC	.50
384	Seung Jun Song	.50
385	Rickie Weeks RC	5.00
386	Humberto Quintero RC	.50
387	Alexis Rios	.15

388	Aaron Miles RC	2.00
389	Tom Gregorio RC	.50
390	Anthony Ferrari RC	.75
391	Kevin Correia RC	.75
392	Rafael Betancourt RC	.75
393	Rett Johnson RC	.50
394	Richard Fischer RC	.50
395	Greg Aquino RC	.50
396	Daniel Garcia RC	1.00
397	Sergio Mitre RC	1.00
398	Edwin Almonte	.15

Update Glossy

ELI MARRERO
Cardinals® - Outfield

Stars (1-285): 5-10X
Rookies (286-398): .5-1.5X
Production 100 Sets

Update Diamond Debuts

		NM/M
Complete Set (25):		40.00
Common Player:		1.00
Inserted 1:10		
1	Dontrelle Willis	4.00
2	Bo Hart	1.00
3	Jose Reyes	4.00
4	Chin-Hui Tsao	1.00
5	Brandon Webb	3.00
6	Rich Harden	2.00
7	Jesse Foppert	1.00
8	Rocco Baldelli	2.00
9	Hideki Matsui	5.00
10	Ron Calloway	1.00
11	Jeremy Bonderman	1.50
12	Mark Teixeira	3.00
13	Ryan Wagner	2.00
14	Jose Contreras	2.00
15	Miguel Cabrera	4.00
16	Lew Ford	1.00
17	Jeff Duncan	1.50
18	Matt Kata	1.00
19	Jeremy Griffiths	1.00
20	Todd Wellemeyer	1.00
21	Robby Hammock	1.00
22	Dave Matranga	1.00
23	Laynce Nix	1.00
24	Jhonny Peralta	1.00
25	Oscar Villarreal	1.00

Long GONE!

		NM/M
Complete Set (20):		60.00
Common Player:		2.00
Quantity produced listed.		
1	Barry Bonds/475	8.00
2	Jason Giambi/440	2.00
3	Albert Pujols/452	6.00
4	Chipper Jones/420	4.00
5	Manny Ramirez/430	2.00
6	Sammy Sosa/536	5.00

7	Alfonso Soriano/440	3.00
8	Alex Rodriguez/430	6.00
9	Jim Thome/445	3.00
10	Vladimir Guerrero/502	3.00
11	Austin Kearns/430	2.00
12	Jeff Bagwell/420	2.00
13	Andruw Jones/430	2.00
14	Carlos Delgado/451	2.00
15	Nomar Garciaparra/440	6.00
16	Adam Dunn/464	3.00
17	Mike Piazza/450	4.00
18	Derek Jeter/410	4.00
19	Ken Griffey Jr./420	4.00
20	Hank Blalock/424	2.00

Update Milestones

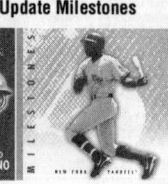

ALFONSO SORIANO

		NM/M
Complete Set (20):		25.00
Common Player:		1.00
Inserted 1:8		
1	Roger Clemens	3.00
2	Rafael Palmeiro	1.00
3	Jeff Bagwell	1.00
4	Barry Bonds	4.00
5	Sammy Sosa	2.50
6	Albert Pujols	3.00
7	Ichiro Suzuki	2.00
8	Alfonso Soriano	1.00
9	Alex Rodriguez	3.00
10	Randy Johnson	1.50
11	Manny Ramirez	1.00
12	Chipper Jones	2.00
13	Todd Helton	1.00
14	Ken Griffey Jr.	2.00
15	Jim Thome	1.00
16	Frank Thomas	1.00
17	Pedro J. Martinez	1.50
18	Hideo Nomo	1.00
19	Jason Schmidt	1.00
20	Carlos Delgado	1.00

Update Milestones Memorabilia

		NM/M
Common Player:		5.00
Inserted 1:20		
Golds:		1-2X
Production 100 Sets		
	Roger Clemens	15.00
	Rafael Palmeiro	5.00
	Jeff Bagwell	8.00
	Sammy Sosa	10.00
	Alfonso Soriano	10.00
	Alex Rodriguez	10.00
	Randy Johnson	8.00
	Manny Ramirez	8.00
	Chipper Jones	8.00
	Todd Helton	6.00
	Jim Thome	8.00
	Frank Thomas	8.00
	Pedro J. Martinez	8.00
	Hideo Nomo	8.00
	Jason Schmidt	8.00
	Carlos Delgado	5.00

Update Milestones Memorabilia Gold

Complete Set (16):
Common Player:

Update Throwback Threads

AL LEITER

		NM/M
Common Player:		4.00
Inserted 1:64		
	Kevin Millwood	6.00
	Vladimir Guerrero	8.00
	Troy Glaus	6.00
	Mike Piazza	10.00
	Al Leiter	4.00

Update Throwback Threads Dual

		NM/M
Production 100 Sets		
	Vladimir Guerrero, Troy Glaus	15.00
	Mike Piazza, Al Leiter	15.00

Update Throwback Threads Patch

		NM/M
Common Player:		10.00
Production 100 Sets		
	Kevin Millwood	15.00
	Vladimir Guerrero	20.00
	Troy Glaus	15.00

	Mike Piazza	25.00
	Al Leiter	10.00

Update Turn Back the Clock

		NM/M
Complete Set (10):		75.00
Common Player:		4.00
Inserted 1:160		
1	Yogi Berra	8.00
2	Mike Schmidt	15.00
3	Tom Seaver	6.00
4	Reggie Jackson	5.00
5	Pee Wee Reese	4.00
6	Phil Rizzuto	4.00
7	Jim Palmer	4.00
8	Robin Yount	5.00
9	Nolan Ryan	20.00
10	Al Kaline	10.00

2003 Fleer/Cub Foods

OMAR VIZQUEL

INDIANS® / SS

In an unusual 2" x 2-3/4" format, these cards were distributed in 24-can cubes of soda, reportedly only at Cub Foods stores in the Upper Midwest. Fronts have player portraits over team logos on a white background. Cub Foods and Pepsi logos are at bottom. Backs have personal data, recent stats, career highlights and a team logo.

		NM/M
Complete Set (10):		7.50
Common Player:		.50
1	Ichiro	2.00
2	Kerry Wood	.75
3	Mike Piazza	1.00
4	Randy Johnson	.75
5	Magglio Ordonez	.50
6	Brad Radke	.50
7	Omar Vizquel	.50
8	Ben Sheets	.50
9	Barry Zito	.50
10	Ken Griffey Jr.	1.00

2003 Fleer/Pepsi-Cola

No Pricing

2004 Fleer America's National Pastime

		NM/M
Common Player (1-60):		.25
Minor Stars (1-60):		.60
Unlisted Stars (1-60):		.75
Common Card (61-90):		3.00
Production 699 Sets		
Pack (5):		10.00
Box (10):		100.00

1	Hideki Matsui	2.50
2	Khalil Greene	1.00
3	Pedro J. Martinez	1.00
4	Sammy Sosa	2.00
5	Mark Teixeira	.40
6	Orlando Cabrera	.25
7	Scott Podsednik	.25
8	Miguel Tejada	.60
9	Andruw Jones	.75
10	Manny Ramirez	.75
11	Jose Reyes	.25
12	Bobby Abreu	.40
13	Alex Rodriguez	2.50
14	Ivan Rodriguez	.60
15	Jason Schmidt	.40
16	Mike Piazza	1.50
17	Eric Chavez	.40
18	Mark Prior	1.50
19	Adam Dunn	.60
20	Richard Hidalgo	.25
21	Todd Helton	.75
22	Rocco Baldelli	.60
23	Roy Oswalt	.40
24	Angel Berroa	.25
25	Jason Giambi	1.00
26	Jim Thome	1.00
27	Javy Lopez	.40
28	Derek Jeter	3.00
29	Tom Glavine	.40
30	Magglio Ordonez	.40
31	Austin Kearns	.60
32	Scott Rolen	1.00
33	Miguel Cabrera	.75
34	Vernon Wells	.40
35	Frank Thomas	.75
36	Jeff Bagwell	.75
37	Shannon Stewart	.25
38	Richie Sexson	.60
39	Hideo Nomo	.40
40	Nomar Garciaparra	2.50
41	C.C. Sabathia	.25
42	Albert Pujols	2.50
43	Barry Zito	.60
44	Hank Blalock	.60
45	Carlos Delgado	.75
46	Greg Maddux	1.50
47	Randy Johnson	1.00
48	Josh Beckett	.75
49	Kerry Wood	.75
50	Roger Clemens	1.50
51	Garret Anderson	.40
52	Ichiro Suzuki	2.00
53	Kip Wells	.25
54	Vladimir Guerrero	1.00
55	Shawn Green	.40
56	Chipper Jones	1.50
57	Aubrey Huff	.25
58	Ken Griffey Jr.	1.50
59	Torii Hunter	.60
60	Alfonso Soriano	1.00
61	Chris Shelton RC	8.00
62	Graham Koonce	4.00
63	Kazuo Matsui RC	8.00
64	Alfredo Simon RC	4.00
65	Mike Gosling	3.00
66	Mike Rouse	4.00
67	Mariano Gomez RC	3.00
68	Justin Leone RC	4.00
69	Jose Capellan RC	3.00
70	Donald Kelly RC	4.00
71	Merkin Valdez RC	4.00
72	Greg Dobbs RC	4.00
73	Shingo Takatsu RC	4.00
74	Chris Aguila RC	3.00
75	Jerome Gamble RC	3.00
76	Onil Joseph RC	4.00
77	Ramon Ramirez RC	4.00
78	Angel Chavez RC	3.00
79	Hector Gimenez RC	3.00
80	Ivan Ochoa RC	4.00
81	Aarom Baldiris RC	4.00
82	Akinori Otsuka RC	3.00
83	Ruddy Yan RC	3.00
84	Jerry Gil RC	3.00
85	Shawn Hill RC	3.00
86	John Gall RC	4.00
87	Jason Bartlett RC	4.00
88	Jorge Sequea RC	4.00
89	Luis Gonzalez RC	4.00
90	Sean Henn	3.00

Red

VLADIMIR GUERRERO / ANAHEIM ANGELS®

	NM/M
(1-60):	1-4X
(61-90):	.75-1.25X
Production 150 Sets	

White

MARK TEIXEIRA / TEXAS RANGERS®

(1-60):	2X-6X
(61-90):	.75X-2X
Production 50 Sets	

Blue

No Pricing
Production One Set

American Flag Box Topper

No Pricing
Numbered to indicated quantity.

American GAME

	NM/M
Common Player:	1.00
Inserted 1:10 (Hobby)	
Inserted 1:12 (Retail)	
1	Greg Maddux	2.50
2	Randy Johnson	2.00
3	Roger Clemens	4.00
4	Mark Prior	3.00
5	Mike Piazza	2.50
6	Alex Rodriguez	4.00
7	Adam Dunn	1.00
8	Jim Thome	2.00
9	Derek Jeter	5.00
10	Scott Rolen	2.00
11	Nomar Garciaparra	4.00
12	Kerry Wood	1.50
13	Chipper Jones	2.50
14	Frank Thomas	1.50
15	Jeff Bagwell	1.50

American Game Retired - Dual

Numbered between 10 & 25.
No Pricing

American Game Retired - Single

Numbered between 6 & 31.
No Pricing

American GAME - Jersey

		NM/M
Common Player:		8.00
Inserted 1:96		
Patch #'d between 25 & 50:		2-6X
Patch #'d less than 25:		No Pricing
Masterpiece:		No Pricing
Production One Set		
JB	Jeff Bagwell/50	8.00
RCL	Roger Clemens/47	10.00
AD	Adam Dunn/30	8.00
DJ	Derek Jeter/10	15.00
RJO	Randy Johnson/42	8.00
CJ	Chipper Jones/37	10.00
GM	Greg Maddux/46	12.00
MP	Mike Piazza/29	10.00
MPR	Mark Prior/45	10.00
AR	Alex Rodriguez/13	15.00
SR	Scott Rolen/49	8.00
FT	Frank Thomas/35	8.00
JT	Jim Thome/47	8.00
KW	Kerry Wood/43	8.00

History in the Making

HISTORY IN THE MAKING

		NM/M
Common Player:		.75
Inserted 1:5 (Hobby)		
Inserted 1:4 (Retail)		
1	Pedro J. Martinez	1.50
2	Alex Rodriguez	3.00
3	Sammy Sosa	2.50
4	Mike Piazza	2.00
5	Jason Giambi	1.50

6	Jim Thome	1.50
7	Derek Jeter	4.00
8	Hideo Nomo	.75
9	Nomar Garciaparra	3.00
10	Albert Pujols	3.00
11	Greg Maddux	2.00
12	Randy Johnson	1.50
13	Roger Clemens	2.00
14	Ichiro Suzuki	2.50
15	Vladimir Guerrero	1.50
16	Chipper Jones	2.00
17	Ken Griffey Jr.	2.00
18	Manny Ramirez	1.00
19	Ivan Rodriguez	.75
20	Mark Prior	2.00
21	Austin Kearns	.75
22	Alfonso Soriano	1.50
23	Barry Zito	.75
24	Josh Beckett	1.00
25	Angel Berroa	.75
26	Jose Reyes	.75
27	Adam Dunn	.75
28	Todd Helton	1.00
29	Hank Blalock	.75
30	Kazuo Matsui	6.00

History in the Making - Jersey

NM/M
Common Player: 5.00
Inserted 1:36
Patch: 2-6X
Numbered between 20 & 50.
Masterpiece: No Pricing
Production One Set

JB	Josh Beckett/45	8.00
AB	Angel Berroa/20	5.00
MB	Hank Blalock/48	8.00
RC	Roger Clemens/26	10.00
AD	Adam Dunn/49	8.00
JG	Jason Giambi/24	8.00
VG	Vladimir Guerrero/50	8.00
TH	Todd Helton/32	8.00
DJ	Derek Jeter/22	15.00
RJ	Randy Johnson/38	8.00
CJ	Chipper Jones/48	10.00
AK	Austin Kearns/41	8.00
GM	Greg Maddux/47	12.00
PM	Pedro J. Martinez/45	8.00
KM	Kazuo Matsui/20	20.00
HN	Hideo Nomo/50	5.00
MP	Mike Piazza/42	10.00
MPR	Mark Prior/49	10.00
AP	Albert Pujols/46	15.00
MR	Manny Ramirez/46	8.00
JR	Jose Reyes/37	5.00
AR	Alex Rodriguez/21	15.00
IR	Ivan Rodriguez/43	8.00
AS	Alfonso Soriano/48	8.00
SS	Sammy Sosa/39	12.00
JT	Jim Thome/49	8.00
BZ	Barry Zito/44	8.00

History in the Making Dual Swatch

No Pricing
Production Five Sets

National Treasures

NM/M
Common Card: 3.00
Production 500 Sets
Gold: Numbered to notable year.
#75-99: 1-30X
#25-74: 1-5X
Less than 25: No Pricing

2NT	Kenesaw Landis	3.00
5NT	Leo Durocher	3.00
9NT	Peter Gammons	3.00
10NT	Ernie Harwell	3.00
11NT	Billy Martin	4.00
12NT	John McGraw	3.00
13NT	Red Barber	3.00
15NT	Casey Stengel	3.00
16NT	Sparky Anderson	3.00
17NT	Harry Caray	4.00
18NT	Ban Johnson	3.00
20NT	Ralph Kiner	3.00

National Treasures - Red

NM/M
	Peter Gammons/50	20.00
	Ernie Harwell/50	20.00
	Ralph Kiner/50	20.00

National Treasures - White

NM/M
	Ernie Harwell/30	15.00

National Treasures - Blue

No Pricing

National Treasures - Masterpiece

No Pricing

Signature Swing - Red

NM/M
Numbered to indicated quantity.
Carlos Beltran/109	25.00
Lance Berkman/98	25.00
Hank Blalock/109	20.00
George Brett/42	120.00
Sean Casey/108	15.00
Eric Chavez/85	20.00
Bucky Dent/35	20.00
David Eckstein/76	15.00
Carlton Fisk/51	40.00
Lew Ford/109	20.00
Jay Gibbons/33	20.00
Luis Gonzalez/109	10.00
Chipper Jones/88	40.00
Al Kaline/43	50.00
Javy Lopez/65	20.00
Don Mattingly/73	50.00
Bill Mazeroski/56	30.00
Stan Musial/36	60.00
Jim Palmer/25	25.00
Dave Parker/79	15.00
Mike Piazza/31	125.00
Albert Pujols/76	150.00
Gary Sheffield/26	60.00
Bill "Moose" Skowron/69	15.00
Warren Spahn/106	40.00
Alan Trammell/89	15.00

Signature Swing - White

NM/M
Numbered to indicated quantity.
Carlos Beltran/29	25.00
Lance Berkman/42	30.00
Hank Blalock/30	30.00
George Brett/30	120.00
Joe Carter/35	20.00
Sean Casey/35	25.00
Eric Chavez/34	25.00
Jim Edmonds/42	20.00
Carlton Fisk/37	40.00
Jay Gibbons/28	20.00
Luis Gonzalez/57	20.00
Vladimir Guerrero/44	30.00
Frank Howard/48	15.00
Aubrey Huff/34	15.00
Chipper Jones/45	50.00
Al Kaline/29	50.00
Javy Lopez/43	20.00
Edgar Martinez/37	30.00
Don Mattingly/35	80.00
Stan Musial/39	60.00
Rafael Palmeiro/47	50.00
Dave Parker/34	15.00
Mike Piazza/40	125.00
Albert Pujols/43	175.00
Cal Ripken Jr./25	200.00
Ivan Rodriguez/35	50.00
Scott Rolen/28	80.00
Gary Sheffield/43	60.00
Bill "Moose" Skowron/28	20.00
Frank Thomas/43	80.00
Alan Trammell/28	20.00

Signature Swing - Blue

NM/M
Numbered to indicated quantity.
Sean Casey/37	40.00
Adam Dunn/31	20.00
David Eckstein/44	15.00
Jim Edmonds/37	20.00
Lew Ford/44	40.00
Bill Mazeroski/39	50.00
Jim Palmer/44	25.00
Dave Parker/29	15.00
Scott Podsednik/38	20.00
Warren Spahn/26	50.00

Signature Swing - Gold

NM/M
Numbered to indicated quantity.
Carlos Beltran/176	25.00
Lance Berkman/173	20.00
Hank Blalock/265	15.00
Joe Carter/95	12.00
Sean Casey/169	12.00
Eric Chavez/138	15.00
David Eckstein/161	10.00
Carlton Fisk/36	40.00
Lew Ford/183	20.00
Luis Gonzalez/61	15.00
Frank Howard/60	20.00
Derek Jeter/35	125.00
Chipper Jones/116	40.00
Al Kaline/79	30.00
Javy Lopez/220	15.00
Edgar Martinez/85	20.00

	Bill Mazeroski/61	25.00
	Jim Palmer/33	25.00
	Dave Parker/57	15.00
	Mike Piazza/64	100.00
	Albert Pujols/110	125.00
	Gary Sheffield/25	60.00
	Warren Spahn/188	30.00
	Alan Trammell/138	10.00

Signature Swing - Masterpiece

No Pricing

Signs of the Future - Red

NM/M
Numbered to indicated quantity.
Aarom Baldiris/64	10.00
Jeremy Bonderman/120	10.00
A.J. Burnett/58	20.00
Miguel Cabrera/133	25.00
Bobby Crosby/114	20.00
Adam Everett/106	10.00
Luis Gonzalez/132	12.00
Mike Gosling/132	10.00
Khalil Greene/121	50.00
Rich Harden/133	15.00
Sean Henn/128	10.00
Koyie Hill/58	12.00
Edwin Jackson/52	15.00
Graham Koonce/55	10.00
Josh Labandeira/55	8.00
Adam LaRoche/124	12.00
Justin Leone/68	20.00
Micheal Nakamura/133	10.00
Bubba Nelson/99	10.00
Jose Reyes/93	25.00
Mike Rouse/124	8.00
Alfredo Simon/112	10.00
Ryan Wagner/98	12.00
Kerry Wood/55	30.00
Kevin Youkilis/133	10.00

Signs of the Future - White

NM/M
Numbered to indicated quantity.
Garrett Atkins/25	15.00
Miguel Cabrera/34	40.00
Bobby Crosby/52	30.00
Adam Everett/36	15.00
Luis Gonzalez/52	15.00
Mike Gosling/41	12.00
Khalil Greene/52	80.00
Rich Harden/52	20.00
Sean Henn/48	12.00
Koyie Hill/27	15.00
Tim Hudson/28	15.00
Adam LaRoche/50	12.00
Micheal Nakamura/33	15.00
Jose Reyes/52	30.00
Alexis Rios/39	15.00
Mike Rouse/40	10.00
Alfredo Simon/28	15.00
Ryan Wagner/46	15.00
Kevin Youkilis/52	25.00

Signs of the Future - Blue

NM/M
Numbered to indicated quantity.
Javier Vazquez/98	15.00
Kerry Wood/98	25.00

Signs of the Future - Gold

NM/M
Numbered to indicated quantity.
Jeremy Bonderman/300	8.00
Miguel Cabrera/300	20.00
Bobby Crosby/299	20.00
Adam Everett/285	10.00
Luis Gonzalez/264	8.00
Mike Gosling/195	8.00
Khalil Greene/300	50.00
Rich Harden/304	10.00
Sean Henn/300	8.00
Koyie Hill/340	8.00
Ryan Howard/53	60.00
Tim Hudson/72	12.00
Adam LaRoche/78	8.00
Micheal Nakamura/231	8.00
Alexis Rios/45	15.00
Alfredo Simon/258	8.00
Javier Vazquez/21	20.00
Ryan Wagner/251	10.00
Dontrelle Willis/47	40.00
Kevin Youkilis/317	15.00

1959 Fleer Ted Williams Reprint Set

NM/M
Ted Williams Card (1-81): 6.00
Production 406 Sets
Masterpiece: No Pricing
Production One Set
1-80 Ted Williams 6.00

Ted Williams Reprint Game-Used

No Pricing
Production Nine Sets

2004 Fleer Authentix

NM/M
Complete Set (130):
Common Player: .25
Common SP (101-130): 2.50
Production 999
Pack (5): 4.00
Box (24): 80.00

1	Albert Pujols	2.50
2	Derek Jeter	3.00
3	Jody Gerut	.40
4	Mark Teixeira	.40
5	Tom Glavine	.40
6	Kerry Wood	1.00
7	Ichiro Suzuki	1.50
8	Jose Vidro	.25
9	Mark Prior	1.50
10	Jim Edmonds	.50
11	Richie Sexson	.50
12	Jay Gibbons	.25
13	Jason Kendall	.25
14	Lance Berkman	.50
15	Andruw Jones	.75
16	Jim Thome	1.00
17	Josh Beckett	.50
18	Troy Glaus	.50
19	Jason Giambi	1.00
20	Sammy Sosa	2.00
21	Bret Boone	.40
22	Eric Gagne	.40
23	Nomar Garciaparra	2.00
24	Geoff Jenkins	.25
25	Ivan Rodriguez	.50
26	Preston Wilson	.25
27	Alex Rodriguez	2.50
28	Jorge Posada	.50
29	Ken Griffey Jr.	1.50
30	Rocco Baldelli	.50
31	Shannon Stewart	.25
32	Frank Thomas	.75
33	Edgar Renteria	.25
34	Torii Hunter	.50
35	Corey Patterson	.25
36	Edgar Martinez	.40
37	Jeff Bagwell	.75
38	Greg Maddux	1.50
39	Mike Lieberthal	.25
40	Craig Biggio	.40
41	Randy Johnson	1.00
42	Marlon Byrd	.25
43	Jay Payton	.25
44	Carlos Delgado	.75
45	Scott Podsednik	.25
46	Pedro J. Martinez	1.00
47	Carlos Beltran	.40
48	Mike Sweeney	.25
49	Gary Sheffield	.50
50	Pat Burrell	.40
51	Shawn Green	.40
52	Tony Batista	.25
53	Brian Giles	.40
54	Roy Oswalt	.40
55	Brandon Webb	.40
56	Miguel Tejada	.40
57	Miguel Cabrera	.75
58	Luis Gonzalez	.40
59	Billy Wagner	.25
60	Craig Monroe	.25
61	Vernon Wells	.40
62	Bernie Williams	.50
63	Austin Kearns	.40
64	Aubrey Huff	.25
65	Mike Piazza	1.50
66	Magglio Ordonez	.50
67	Bo Hart	.25
68	Hideo Nomo	.50
69	Curt Schilling	.50
70	Barry Zito	.50
71	Todd Helton	.75
72	Roy Halladay	.50
73	Alfonso Soriano	1.00
74	Roberto Alomar	.50
75	Scott Rolen	1.00
76	Manny Ramirez	.75
77	Sean Burroughs	.25
78	Angel Berroa	.40
79	Javy Lopez	.40
80	Reggie Sanders	.25
81	Juan Pierre	.25
82	Chipper Jones	1.50
83	Bobby Abreu	.40
84	Dontrelle Willis	.50
85	Tim Salmon	.40
86	Eric Chavez	.40
87	Adam Dunn	.75
88	Rafael Palmeiro	.75
89	Hideki Matsui	2.50

90	Esteban Loaiza	.25
91	Darin Erstad	.25
92	Vladimir Guerrero	1.00
93	David Ortiz	.50
94	Jason Schmidt	.40
95	Dmitri Young	.25
96	Garret Anderson	.50
97	Mark Mulder	.25
98	Omar Vizquel	.25
99	Hank Blalock	.50
100	Jose Reyes	.25
101	Rickie Weeks	8.00
102	Chad Gaudin	2.50
103	Ryan Wagner	2.50
104	Koyie Hill	2.50
105	Rich Harden	2.50
106	Edwin Jackson	4.00
107	Khalil Greene	3.00
108	Chien-Ming Wang	3.00
109	Matt Kata	2.50
110	Chin-Hui Tsao	2.50
111	Dan Haren	2.50
112	Delmon Young	8.00
113	Mike Hessman	2.50
114	Bobby Crosby	2.50
115	Cory Sullivan **RC**	2.50
116	Brandon Watson	2.50
117	Aaron Miles	2.50
118	Jonny Gomes	2.50
119	Graham Koonce	2.50
120	Shawn Hill **RC**	2.50
121	Garrett Atkins	2.50
122	John Gall **RC**	2.50
123	Chad Bentz **RC**	2.50
124	Alfredo Simon **RC**	2.50
125	Josh Labandeira **RC**	3.00
126	Ryan Howard	2.50
127	Jason Bartlett **RC**	2.50
128	Dallas McPherson	2.50
129	Greg Dobbs **RC**	2.50
130	Jerry Gil **RC**	2.50

Balcony

Stars (1-100):	4-8X
SP's (101-130):	1-2X
Production 100 Sets	

Club Box

Stars (1-100):	10-15X
SP's (101-130):	2-4X
Production 25 Sets	

Standing Room Only

No Pricing
Production Five Sets

Autographed Authentix

NM/M
Common Autograph: 15.00
Production 75
Championship: No Pricing
Production 25
Rocco Baldelli	40.00
Angel Berroa	15.00
Marlon Byrd	15.00
Miguel Cabrera	40.00
Eric Gagne	40.00
Roy Halladay	20.00
Trot Nixon	35.00
Juan Pierre	15.00
Albert Pujols	120.00
Vernon Wells	20.00

Ballpark Classics

NM/M
Complete Set (10): 15.00
Common Player: 1.00
Inserted 1:12
1BC	Nomar Garciaparra	3.00
2BC	Alfonso Soriano	1.50
3BC	Chipper Jones	1.50
4BC	Jason Giambi	3.00
5BC	Jason Giambi	1.00
6BC	Mark Prior	2.00
7BC	Sammy Sosa	2.50
8BC	Derek Jeter	4.00
9BC	Greg Maddux	2.00
10BC	Alex Rodriguez	3.00

Ballpark Classics Game-Used

NM/M
Common Player: 8.00
Inserted 1:37
Nomar Garciaparra	10.00
Jason Giambi	8.00
Derek Jeter	15.00
Chipper Jones	8.00
Greg Maddux	10.00
Mark Prior	10.00
Albert Pujols	15.00
Alex Rodriguez	10.00
Alfonso Soriano	8.00
Sammy Sosa	12.00

Jersey Authentix Autograph

NM/M
Common Autograph: 15.00

Jersey Authentix Game of the Week

NM/M
Common Duo: 10.00
Inserted 1:120
Unripped: 1-1.5X
Production 50
1	Dontrelle Willis, Kerry Wood	20.00
2	Miguel Cabrera, Mark Teixeira	15.00
3	Nomar Garciaparra, Alfonso Soriano	15.00
4	Jim Thome, Ivan Rodriguez	10.00
5	Josh Beckett, Mark Prior	15.00
6	Alex Rodriguez, Derek Jeter	35.00
7	Jeff Bagwell, Austin Kearns	15.00
8	Jason Giambi, Barry Zito	10.00
9	Jose Reyes, Juan Pierre	10.00
10	Chipper Jones, Albert Pujols	20.00

Jersey Authentix Ripped

NM/M
Common Player: 4.00
Inserted 1:16
Unripped: 2-3X
Production 50 Sets
All-Star Unripped: No Pricing
Production One Set
Jeff Bagwell	8.00
Josh Beckett	6.00
Miguel Cabrera	8.00
Hee Seop Choi	4.00
Nomar Garciaparra	10.00
Jason Giambi	8.00
Torii Hunter	5.00
Derek Jeter	15.00
Randy Johnson	8.00
Chipper Jones	8.00
Austin Kearns	6.00
Greg Maddux	8.00
Juan Pierre	4.00
Mark Prior	10.00
Albert Pujols	15.00
Jose Reyes	8.00
Alex Rodriguez	10.00
Ivan Rodriguez	6.00
Alfonso Soriano	8.00
Sammy Sosa	12.00
Mark Teixeira	6.00
Jim Thome	8.00
Dontrelle Willis	6.00
Kerry Wood	8.00
Barry Zito	6.00

Ticket for Four

NM/M
Common Quad Jersey: 20.00
Production 100 Sets
1	Dontrelle Willis, Josh Beckett, Mark Prior, Kerry Wood	20.00
2	Nomar Garciaparra, Alex Rodriguez, Derek Jeter, Jose Reyes	50.00
3	Jason Giambi, Jim Thome, Mark Teixeira, Jeff Bagwell	25.00
5	Chipper Jones, Albert Pujols, Sammy Sosa, Torii Hunter	40.00
6	Greg Maddux, Randy Johnson, Kerry Wood, Barry Zito	20.00
7	Nomar Garciaparra, Alfonso Soriano, Chipper Jones, Albert Pujols	40.00
8	Sammy Sosa, Derek Jeter, Alex Rodriguez, Jim Thome	
9	Mark Prior, Greg Maddux, Austin Kearns, Ivan Rodriguez	15.00
10	Jason Giambi, Randy Johnson, Jeff Bagwell, Torii Hunter	20.00

Ticket Studs

		NM/M
Complete Set (15):		20.00
Common Player:		.75
Inserted 1:6		
1TS	Nomar Garciaparra	3.00
2TS	Josh Beckett	1.00
3TS	Derek Jeter	4.00
4TS	Mark Prior	2.00
5TS	Albert Pujols	3.00
6TS	Alfonso Soriano	1.50
7TS	Jim Thome	1.50
8TS	Ichiro Suzuki	2.00
9TS	Hideki Matsui	3.00
10TS	Dontrelle Willis	.75
11TS	Mike Schmidt	2.00
12TS	Nolan Ryan	4.00
13TS	Reggie Jackson	1.00
14TS	Tom Seaver	1.00
15TS	Brooks Robinson	1.00

2004 Fleer Classic Clippings

		NM/M
Common Player (1-75):		.25
Minor Stars (1-75):		.40
Unlisted Stars (1-75):		.60
Common Player (76-110):		5.00
Production 500 Sets		
Pack (5):		5.00
Box (18):		90.00
1	Juan Pierre	.25
2	Derek Jeter	3.00
3	Jose Reyes	.40
4	Eric Chavez	.40
5	Alex Rodriguez	2.50
6	Mark Prior	2.00
7	Carlos Beltran	.40
8	Ichiro Suzuki	2.00
9	Shawn Green	.40
10	Richie Sexson	.60
11	Andruw Jones	.75
12	Geoff Jenkins	.40
13	Luis Gonzalez	.40
14	Garret Anderson	.40
15	Adam Dunn	.60
16	Nomar Garciaparra	2.50
17	Albert Pujols	2.50
18	Jeff Bagwell	.75
19	Rocco Baldelli	.60
20	Preston Wilson	.25
21	Gary Sheffield	.60
22	Magglio Ordonez	.40
23	Kerry Wood	.75
24	Manny Ramirez	.75
25	Randy Johnson	1.00
26	Ken Griffey Jr.	1.50
27	Rafael Palmeiro	.60
28	Vernon Wells	.25
29	Mike Piazza	1.50
30	Hank Blalock	.75
31	Miguel Cabrera	.75
32	Jason Giambi	.60
33	Troy Glaus	.60
34	Angel Berroa	.25
35	Greg Maddux	1.50
36	Lance Berkman	.40
37	Austin Kearns	.60
38	Hideo Nomo	.40
39	Sammy Sosa	2.00
40	Jose Vidro	.25
41	Curt Schilling	.60
42	Melvin Mora	.25
43	Scott Podsednik	.40
44	Dontrelle Willis	.40
45	Roy Halladay	.40
46	Hideki Matsui	2.50

47	Tom Glavine	.40
48	Torii Hunter	.60
49	Chipper Jones	1.50
50	Barry Zito	.60
51	Vladimir Guerrero	1.00
52	Jim Thome	1.00
53	Shannon Stewart	.25
54	Miguel Tejada	.60
55	Roy Oswalt	.40
56	Jason Kendall	.40
57	Brian Giles	.40
58	Jason Schmidt	.40
59	Pedro J. Martinez	1.00
60	Bret Boone	.40
61	Josh Beckett	.75
62	Scott Rolen	1.00
63	Aubrey Huff	.25
64	Pat Burrell	.40
65	Mark Teixeira	.40
66	Alfonso Soriano	1.00
67	Carlos Delgado	.75
68	Ivan Rodriguez	.60
69	Brandon Webb	.25
70	Eric Gagne	.40
71	Frank Thomas	.75
72	Jody Gerut	.25
73	Todd Helton	.75
74	Andy Pettitte	.60
75	Roger Clemens	1.50
76	Rickie Weeks	6.00
77	Chien-Hui Wang	8.00
78	Edwin Jackson	6.00
79	Dallas McPherson	8.00
80	John Gall RC	5.00
81	Ryan Wagner	6.00
82	Clint Barmes	8.00
83	Khalil Greene	6.00
84	Chin-Hui Tsao	6.00
85	Alexis Rios	6.00
86	Merkin Valdez RC	5.00
87	Aarom Baldiris RC	5.00
88	Onil Joseph RC	5.00
89	Ruddy Yan RC	5.00
90	Chad Bentz RC	5.00
91	Shawn Hill RC	5.00
92	Delmon Young	8.00
93	Hector Gimenez RC	5.00
94	William Bergolla RC	5.00
95	Ronny Cedeno RC	5.00
96	Angel Chavez RC	5.00
97	Justin Leone RC	5.00
98	Ivan Ochoa RC	5.00
99	Ian Snell RC	10.00
100	Rich Harden	6.00
101	Joe Mauer	10.00
102	Akinori Otsuka RC	10.00
103	Bobby Crosby	6.00
104	Garrett Atkins	5.00
105	Dan Haren	5.00
106	Koyie Hill	5.00
107	Kazuo Matsui RC	20.00
108	Adam LaRoche	5.00
109	Terrmel Sledge	5.00
110	Shingo Takatsu RC	5.00

First Edition

(1-75):	1-5X
(76-110):	.5-1.25X
Production 150 Sets	

All-Star Lineup Triple Jersey Silver

		NM/M
Common Card:		15.00
Production 75 Sets		
Gold Triple Patch:		2-4X
Production 25 Sets		
No Gold Card For ASL-SMA		
S/C/G	Alfonso Soriano, Roger Clemens, Jason Giambi	25.00
R/G/R	Alex Rodriguez, Nomar Garciaparra, Manny Ramirez	25.00
W/P/W	Kerry Wood, Mark Prior, Dontrelle Willis	25.00
S/P/W	Gary Sheffield, Albert Pujols, Preston Wilson	20.00
C/H/R	Luis Castillo, Todd Helton, Scott Rolen	15.00
D/S/G	Carlos Delgado, Alfonso Soriano, Troy Glaus	15.00
W/D/H	Vernon Wells, Carlos Delgado, Roy Halladay	15.00
S/M/A	Ichiro Suzuki, Hideki Matsui, Garret Anderson	30.00
R/R/P	Edgar Renteria, Scott Rolen, Albert Pujols	50.00
S/J/L	Gary Sheffield, Andruw Jones, Javy Lopez	15.00
C/Z/H	Roger Clemens, Barry Zito, Roy Halladay	20.00
C/W/L	Luis Castillo, Dontrelle Willis, Mike Lowell	10.00
O/B/G	Magglio Ordonez, Hank Blalock, Troy Glaus	15.00
G/R/G	Nomar Garciaparra, Alex Rodriguez, Troy Glaus	15.00
H/S/P	Todd Helton, Richie Sexson, Albert Pujols	20.00

Bat Rack (3 Bat) - Green

		NM/M
Common Card:		10.00
Production 175 Sets		
Red:		.5-1.5X
Production 50 Sets		
Gold:		1-2X
Production 25 Sets		
	Derek Jeter, Alex Rodriguez, Gary Sheffield	40.00
	Sammy Sosa, Derek Lee, Mark Prior	25.00
	Miguel Cabrera, Juan Pierre, Josh Beckett	15.00
	Nomar Garciaparra, Manny Ramirez, Curt Schilling	20.00
	Alfonso Soriano, Hank Blalock, Mark Teixeira	15.00
	Mike Piazza, Jose Reyes, Kazuo Matsui	15.00
	Richie Sexson, Brandon Webb, Roberto Alomar	10.00
	Mark Prior, Josh Beckett, Curt Schilling	15.00
	Carlos Delgado, Aubrey Huff, Carlos Delgado	10.00
	Jeff Bagwell, Jim Thome, Todd Helton	15.00
	Gary Sheffield, Manny Ramirez, Rocco Baldelli	10.00
	Troy Glaus, Scott Rolen, Hank Blalock	15.00
	Roberto Alomar, Jose Reyes, Alfonso Soriano	15.00
	Alex Rodriguez, Miguel Tejada, Miguel Cabrera	15.00
	Vladimir Guerrero, Juan Pierre, Chipper Jones	15.00
	Jason Giambi, Jim Thome, Todd Helton	15.00
	Vladimir Guerrero, Albert Pujols, Sammy Sosa	25.00
	Derek Jeter, Hideki Matsui, Nomar Garciaparra	40.00

Bat Rack (4 bat) - Green

		NM/M
Common Card:		15.00
Production 75 Sets		
Red:		1-2X
Production 25 Sets		
Gold:		No Pricing
Production 10 Sets		
	Derek Jeter, Alex Rodriguez, Gary Sheffield	50.00
	Jason Giambi, Sammy Sosa, Mark Prior, Miguel Cabrera, Josh Beckett	30.00
	Derek Jeter, Alex Rodriguez, Kazuo Matsui, Nomar Garciaparra	60.00
	Juan Pierre, Gary Sheffield, Miguel Cabrera, Rocco Baldelli	15.00
	Jim Thome, Jeff Bagwell, Mark Teixeira, Carlos Delgado	20.00
	Albert Pujols, Mark Prior, Alex Rodriguez, Curt Schilling	40.00
	Todd Helton, Jose Reyes, Kazuo Matsui, Scott Rolen	40.00
	Sammy Sosa, Vladimir Guerrero, Jim Edmonds, Chipper Jones	25.00
	Alfonso Soriano, Roberto Alomar, Hank Blalock, Troy Glaus	15.00
	Rocco Baldelli, Chipper Jones, Juan Pierre, Manny Ramirez	20.00

Jersey Rack (3 Jersey)-Blue

		NM/M
Common Card:		15.00
Production 225 Sets		
Bronze Jersey:		.5-1.25X

	Jim Thome, Jeff Bagwell, Todd Helton, Derek Lee	20.00
	Curt Schilling, Nomar Garciaparra, Brandon Webb, Richie Sexson	25.00
	Mike Piazza, Jose Reyes, Albert Pujols, Scott Rolen	30.00
	Vladimir Guerrero, Miguel Tejada, Jason Giambi, Mike Piazza	25.00
	Jeff Bagwell, Derek Lee, Aubrey Huff, Carlos Delgado	20.00

Bat Rack Autographs-Bronze

		NM/M
Common Player:		12.00
Production 75 Sets		
	Roberto Alomar	40.00
	Josh Beckett	40.00
	Hank Blalock	30.00
	Miguel Cabrera	40.00
	Jim Edmonds	30.00
	Aubrey Huff	12.00
	Edgar Martinez	20.00
	Jose Reyes	25.00
	Gary Sheffield	30.00
	Mark Teixeira	20.00

Classic Clippings

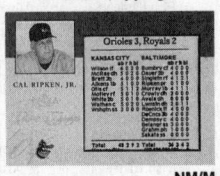

		NM/M
Common Player (1-20):		4.00
Production 750 Sets		
Common Player (21-25):		8.00
Production 100 Sets		
1CC	Nolan Ryan	15.00
2CC	Mike Schmidt	6.00
3CC	Cal Ripken Jr.	10.00
4CC	Don Mattingly	8.00
5CC	Roger Clemens	5.00
6CC	Randy Johnson	4.00
7CC	Mark Prior	3.00
8CC	Jim Thome	4.00
9CC	Sammy Sosa	5.00
10CC	Pedro J. Martinez	4.00
11CC	Chipper Jones	4.00
12CC	Vladimir Guerrero	5.00
13CC	Albert Pujols	6.00
14CC	Ichiro Suzuki	8.00
15CC	Derek Jeter	10.00
16CC	Alex Rodriguez	8.00
17CC	Greg Maddux	5.00
18CC	Nomar Garciaparra	6.00
19CC	Mike Piazza	6.00
20CC	Ken Griffey Jr.	8.00
21CC	Pie Traynor	8.00
22CC	Bill Dickey	8.00
23CC	George Sisler	10.00
24CC	Ted Williams	20.00
25CC	Enos Slaughter	8.00

C.C. Signature Edition

		NM/M
Common Player:		15.00
Production 50 Sets		
Masterpiece:		No Pricing
Production One Set		
1	Nolan Ryan	125.00
2	Mike Schmidt	75.00
3	Cal Ripken Jr.	175.00
4	Don Mattingly	75.00
5	Albert Pujols	125.00
6	Randy Johnson	60.00
7	Khalil Greene	40.00
8	Rickie Weeks	25.00
9	Edwin Jackson	25.00
10	Rich Harden	15.00
16	Vladimir Guerrero	40.00
17	Mark Prior	40.00

Production 99 Sets

Silver Jersey:	.75-1.5X
Production to player's jersey no.	
Patch Pack Gold:	No Pricing
Production 125 Sets	
	Derek Jeter, Alex Rodriguez, Jason Giambi	50.00
	Sammy Sosa, Kerry Wood, Mark Prior	25.00
	Miguel Cabrera, Dontrelle Willis	
	Josh Beckett	15.00
	Nomar Garciaparra, Pedro J. Martinez	
	Curt Schilling	15.00
	Alex Rodriguez, Derek Jeter, Nomar Garciaparra	40.00
	Mike Piazza, Ivan Rodriguez, Javy Lopez	20.00
	Roger Clemens, Mark Prior, Josh Beckett	20.00
	Roger Clemens, Andy Pettitte, Roy Oswalt	40.00
	Dontrelle Willis, Kerry Wood, Curt Schilling	20.00
	Albert Pujols, Sammy Sosa, Manny Ramirez	20.00
	Rocco Baldelli, Miguel Cabrera, Albert Pujols	20.00
	Barry Zito, Tim Hudson, Mark Mulder	15.00
	Randy Johnson, Richie Sexson, Brandon Webb	15.00
	Dontrelle Willis, Brandon Webb, Angel Berroa	15.00
	Carlos Delgado, Miguel Tejada, Alfonso Soriano	15.00

Jersey Rack Auto. - Bronze

		NM/M
Common Player:		12.00
Production 149 Sets		
Silver Jersey:		.5-1.5X
Production 50 Sets		
Patch Rack Gold:		No Pricing
Production To Player's Jersey No.		
	Garret Anderson	15.00
	Garrett Atkins	12.00
	Rocco Baldelli	20.00
	Josh Beckett	20.00
	Angel Berroa	15.00
	Marlon Byrd	12.00
	Miguel Cabrera	40.00
	Carlos Delgado	20.00
	Jody Gerut	12.00
	Roy Halladay	15.00
	Dan Haren	12.00
	Torii Hunter	15.00
	Edwin Jackson	20.00
	Barry Larkin	40.00
	Mark Mulder	15.00
	Mike Mussina	30.00
	Andy Pettitte	40.00
	Albert Pujols	120.00
	Ivan Rodriguez	50.00
	Scott Rolen	50.00
	Ryan Wagner	12.00
	Brandon Webb	15.00
	Dontrelle Willis	20.00
	Kerry Wood	30.00

Phenom Lineup Auto. - Red

		NM/M
Common Card:		10.00
Production 150 Sets		
Silver: .5-1.25X		
Production 99 Sets		
Gold:		.5-1.5X
Production 50 Sets		
Cards contain autograph of the first player listed.		
	Ryan Howard, Jim Thome, Todd Helton	10.00
	John Gall, Albert Pujols, Scott Rolen	10.00
	Jose Reyes, Kazuo Matsui, Rickie Weeks	10.00
	Hank Blalock, Troy Glaus, Alex Rodriguez	10.00
	Rich Harden, Roy Halladay, Barry Zito	10.00
	Alexis Rios, Carlos Delgado, Vernon Wells	10.00
	Laynce Nix, Alex Rodriguez, Garret Anderson	10.00
	Khalil Greene, Edgar Renteria, Mike Lowell	25.00
	Dontrelle Willis, Mark Prior, Kerry Wood	15.00
	Rickie Weeks, Luis Castillo, Jose Reyes	15.00

	Dallas McPherson, Troy Glaus, Garret Anderson	15.00
	Chien-Ming Wang, Hideki Matsui, Jason Giambi	20.00
	Scott Podsednik, Albert Pujols, Andruw Jones	15.00
	Bobby Crosby, Nomar Garciaparra, Alex Rodriguez	18.00
	Ryan Wagner, Dontrelle Willis, Mark Prior	8.00
	Delmon Young, Ichiro Suzuki, Hideki Matsui	30.00
	Grady Sizemore, Manny Ramirez, Garret Anderson	20.00
	Adam LaRoche, Albert Pujols, Jim Thome	10.00
	Edwin Jackson, Mark Prior, Kerry Wood	10.00
	Miguel Cabrera, Luis Castillo, Mike Lowell	40.00
	Merkin Valdez, Edwin Jackson, Dontrelle Willis	10.00
	Angel Berroa, Nomar Garciaparra, Alex Rodriguez	10.00

Press Clippings

		NM/M
Common Player:		1.25
Inserted 1:6		
1PC	Josh Beckett	1.75
2PC	Albert Pujols	4.00
3PC	Derek Jeter	5.00
4PC	Alex Rodriguez	5.00
5PC	Jim Thome	2.00
6PC	Angel Berroa	1.00
7PC	Dontrelle Willis	1.25
8PC	Roy Halladay	1.25
9PC	Kerry Wood	1.75
10PC	Mark Prior	3.00
11PC	Roger Clemens	3.00
12PC	Hideki Matsui	4.00
13PC	Ichiro Suzuki	3.50
14PC	Eric Gagne	1.25
15PC	Miguel Cabrera	1.75
16PC	Nomar Garciaparra	4.00
17PC	Hank Blalock	1.25
18PC	Chipper Jones	3.00
19PC	Sammy Sosa	3.50
20PC	Alfonso Soriano	2.00

Press Proof Black

(1-100):	No Pricing
Production One Set	

Press Proof Cyan

(1-100):	No Pricing
Production One Set	

Press Proof Magenta

(1-100):	No Pricing
Production One Set	

Press Proof Yellow

(1-100):	No Pricing
Production One Set	

2004 Fleer EX

	NM/M
Common Player (1-40):	1.50
Minor Stars (1-40):	2.00
Unlisted Stars (1-40):	2.50
Common Player (41-65):	5.00
Production 500 Sets	
Die-Cuts (41-65):	.75-1.25X
First 150 seq. #'d cards are die-cut.	
1	Vladimir Guerrero	3.50
2	Randy Johnson	3.50
3	Chipper Jones	4.00
4	Miguel Tejada	2.50
5	Pedro J. Martinez	3.50

#	Player	Price
6	Nomar Garciaparra	6.00
7	Sammy Sosa	5.00
8	Greg Maddux	4.00
9	Frank Thomas	3.00
10	Ken Griffey Jr.	4.00
11	Omar Vizquel	2.00
12	Todd Helton	3.00
13	Ivan Rodriguez	2.50
14	Miguel Cabrera	3.00
15	Dontrelle Willis	2.00
16	Jeff Bagwell	3.00
17	Roger Clemens	4.00
18	Carlos Beltran	2.00
19	Hideo Nomo	2.00
20	Scott Podsednik	1.50
21	Torii Hunter	2.50
22	Jose Vidro	1.50
23	Mike Piazza	4.00
24	Hideki Matsui	6.00
25	Alex Rodriguez	6.00
26	Derek Jeter	8.00
27	Tim Hudson	2.00
28	Jim Thome	3.50
29	Craig Wilson	1.50
30	Brian Giles	2.00
31	Jason Schmidt	2.00
32	Ichiro Suzuki	5.00
33	Scott Rolen	3.50
34	Albert Pujols	6.00
35	Rocco Baldelli	2.50
36	Alfonso Soriano	3.50
37	Carlos Delgado	3.00
38	Curt Schilling	2.50
39	Mark Prior	4.00
40	Josh Beckett	3.00
41	Merkin Valdez **RC**	5.00
42	Akinori Otsuka **RC**	8.00
43	Ian Snell **RC**	8.00
44	Kazuo Matsui **RC**	10.00
45	Jason Bartlett **RC**	8.00
46	Dennis Sarfate **RC**	5.00
47	Sean Henn **RC**	5.00
48	David Aardsma **RC**	5.00
49	Casey Kotchman **RC**	8.00
50	John Gall **RC**	5.00
51	William Bergolla **RC**	5.00
52	Angel Chavez **RC**	5.00
53	Hector Gimenez **RC**	5.00
54	Aarom Baldiris **RC**	5.00
55	Justin Leone **RC**	8.00
56	Onil Joseph **RC**	5.00
57	Freddy Guzman **RC**	5.00
58	Andres Blanco **RC**	5.00
59	Greg Dobbs **RC**	5.00
60	Joe Mauer	5.00
61	Luis Gonzalez **RC**	8.00
62	Chris Saenz **RC**	5.00
63	Zack Greinke	5.00
64	Jose Capellan **RC**	8.00
65	Brad Halsey **RC**	5.00

Essential Credentials Future

Cards 1-25:	.75-2X
Cards 26-40:	2-4X
Cards 41-65:	No Pricing
Production 65 - 1 Sets	

Essential Credentials Now

Cards 51-65:	1-2X
Cards 41-50:	1.25-2.25X
Cards 25-40:	3-5X
Cards 1-24:	No Pricing
Production 65 - 1 Sets	

Check Mates

NM/M

Production 1 or 25 Sets
1 Albert Pujols,
Stan Musial/25 .... 500.00

2	Eddie Murray, Rafael Palmeiro/25	200.00
4	Ernie Banks, Ryne Sandberg/25	300.00
9	Manny Ramirez, Pedro J. Martinez/25	300.00
10	Wade Boggs, Tony Gwynn/25	175.00
11	Reggie Jackson, Don Mattingly/25	200.00
14	Robin Yount, Kirby Puckett/25	150.00

Classic ConnEXions Doubles

No Pricing
Production 22 Sets
Emerald: No Pricing
Production One Set

Classic ConnEXions Triples

No Pricing
Production 13 Sets
Emerald: No Pricing
Production One Set

Clearly Authentics Signature Black Jersey

NM/M

Sequentially #'d to varying quantities.
Burgundy Buttons: No Pricing
Production 6 Sets
Emerald MLB Logo: No Pricing
Production One Set

Josh Beckett/50	30.00
Hank Blalock/50	50.00
Miguel Cabrera/50	30.00
Roger Clemens/50	150.00
J.D. Drew/50	30.00
Troy Glaus/50	25.00
Vladimir Guerrero/50	50.00
Todd Helton/50	40.00
Chipper Jones/50	60.00
Roy Oswalt/49	50.00
Rafael Palmeiro/43	60.00
Albert Pujols/50	225.00
Manny Ramirez/50	60.00
Mariano Rivera/50	80.00
Gary Sheffield/50	50.00
Frank Thomas/50	60.00
Bernie Williams/42	75.00
Dontrelle Willis/50	25.00
Kerry Wood/34	50.00

Clearly Authentics Black Patch

NM/M

Common Player: 10.00
Production 75 Sets

Jeff Bagwell	20.00
Rocco Baldelli	15.00
Josh Beckett	20.00
Lance Berkman	15.00
Hank Blalock	15.00
Pat Burrell	15.00
Miguel Cabrera	20.00
Rod Carew	30.00
Roger Clemens	30.00
Adam Dunn	15.00
Eric Gagne	15.00
Jason Giambi	25.00
Brian Giles	15.00
Troy Glaus	15.00
Shawn Green	15.00
Vladimir Guerrero	25.00
Tony Gwynn	30.00
Todd Helton	20.00
Rickey Henderson	30.00
Tim Hudson	15.00
Torii Hunter	15.00
Randy Johnson	25.00
Andruw Jones	20.00
Chipper Jones	30.00
Greg Maddux	30.00
Pedro J. Martinez	25.00
Hideki Matsui	40.00
Kazuo Matsui	40.00
Don Mattingly	40.00
Paul Molitor	30.00
Eddie Murray	50.00
Hideo Nomo	15.00
Magglio Ordonez	15.00
Rafael Palmeiro	20.00
Mike Piazza	30.00
Mark Prior	30.00
Albert Pujols	40.00
Manny Ramirez	20.00
Cal Ripken Jr.	75.00
Alex Rodriguez	40.00
Ivan Rodriguez	15.00
Scott Rolen	25.00
Curt Schilling	15.00
Ozzie Smith	25.00
Alfonso Soriano	25.00
Sammy Sosa	35.00
Mark Teixeira	15.00
Miguel Tejada	15.00
Frank Thomas	20.00

Jim Thome		25.00
Rickie Weeks		15.00
Dontrelle Willis		15.00
Kerry Wood		20.00
Barry Zito		15.00

Clearly Authentics Bronze Patch/Jersey

.75-1.5X Black Patch Version
Production 35 Sets

Clearly Authentics Burgundy Triple Patch

No Pricing
Production 13 Sets

Clearly Authentics - Double MLB Logo

No Pricing
Production One Set

Clearly Authentics Pewter

Sequentially #'d to varying quantities.

Clearly Authentics Pewter Patch/Bat

.75-1.5X Black Patch Version
Production 44 Sets

Clearly Authentics Royal Patch/Bat/Jersey

No Pricing
Production Eight Sets

Clearly Authentics Signature Tan Patch

Sequentially #'d to varying quantities.

Clearly Authentics Tan Double Patch

No Pricing
Production 22 Sets

Clearly Authentics Tan Double Patches

No Pricing
Production 22 Sets

Clearly Authentics Turquoise Nameplate

No Pricing
Sequentially #'d to varying quantities.

ConnEXions

NM/M

Production 25 or 50 Sets

6	Casey Kotchman, Joe Mauer/50	100.00
7	Shannon Stewart, Torii Hunter/25	90.00
9	Johnny Damon, Trot Nixon/25	90.00
10	Carlos Lee, Magglio Ordonez/25	30.00
12	Scott Podsednik, Lyle Overbay/25	60.00
13	Barry Zito, Tim Hudson/25	125.00
14	Bucky Dent, Mike Torrez/50	40.00
15	Brian Giles, Marcus Giles/25	60.00
17	Dontrelle Willis, Miguel Cabrera/25	60.00
18	Michael Young, Khalil Greene/50	80.00
19	Mark Teixeira, Hank Blalock/25	100.00

Double Barrel

No Pricing
Production One Set

Signings of the Times Best Year

NM/M

Sequentially #'d to player's best year.
Emerald: .... No Pricing

Jim Thome		25.00
Rickie Weeks		15.00
Dontrelle Willis		15.00
Kerry Wood		20.00
Barry Zito		15.00

Clearly Authentics Bronze Patch/Jersey

Ernie Banks/58/Bat	60.00
Johnny Bench/72/Jsy	60.00
Wade Boggs/87/Bat	40.00
George Brett/80/Jsy	80.00
Jose Canseco/88/Jsy	30.00
Will Clark/91/Jsy	40.00
Tony Gwynn/94/Jsy	50.00
Rickey Henderson/90/Jsy	75.00
Bo Jackson/89/Jsy	60.00
Don Mattingly/85/Jsy	80.00
Eddie Murray/83/Jsy	60.00
Stan Musial/48/Bat	75.00
Nolan Ryan/73/Jsy	150.00
Ryne Sandberg/90/Bat	60.00
Mike Schmidt/80/Jsy	80.00
Tom Seaver/69/Jsy	75.00
Ozzie Smith/87/Jsy	60.00
Duke Snider/55/Bat	50.00
Carl Yastrzemski/67/Bat	60.00

Signings of the Times Debut Year

NM/M

Sequentially #'d to player's debut year.

Ernie Banks/53/Bat	60.00
Johnny Bench/67/Jsy	60.00
Yogi Berra/46/Bat	60.00
Wade Boggs/82/Bat	40.00
Jose Canseco/85/Jsy	30.00
Will Clark/86/Jsy	40.00
Tony Gwynn/82/Jsy	50.00
Rickey Henderson/79/Jsy	75.00
Bo Jackson/86/Jsy	60.00
Reggie Jackson/67/Jsy	50.00
Don Mattingly/82/Jsy	80.00
Eddie Murray/77/Jsy	60.00
Stan Musial/41/Bat	75.00
Kirby Puckett/84/Bat	50.00
Nolan Ryan/66/Jsy	150.00
Ryne Sandberg/81/Bat	60.00
Deion Sanders/89/Jsy	40.00
Mike Schmidt/72/Jsy	80.00
Ozzie Smith/78/Jsy	50.00
Duke Snider/47/Bat	50.00
Carl Yastrzemski/61/Bat	75.00
Robin Yount/74/Jsy	40.00

Signings of the Times HOF Year

NM/M

Sequentially #'d to player's HOF year.

Ernie Banks/77/Bat	60.00
Johnny Bench/89/Jsy	60.00
Yogi Berra/72/Bat	50.00
George Brett/99/Jsy	80.00
Reggie Jackson/93/Jsy	50.00
Stan Musial/69/Bat	75.00
Mike Schmidt/95/Jsy	75.00
Tom Seaver/92/Jsy	50.00
Duke Snider/80/Bat	30.00
Carl Yastrzemski/89/Bat	60.00

Signings of the Times Pewter

NM/M

Sequentially #'d to varying quantities.

Wade Boggs/32/Bat	50.00
Jose Canseco/27/Jsy	75.00
Rickey Henderson/32/Jsy	50.00
Bo Jackson/60/Jsy	50.00
Don Mattingly/33/Jsy	80.00
Eddie Murray/50/Bat	80.00
Stan Musial/51/Bat	80.00
Kirby Puckett/31/Bat	50.00
Ryne Sandberg/28/Bat	60.00
Ozzie Smith/36/Jsy	80.00

2004 Fleer Flair

NM/M

Common Player (1-60):	1.00
Minor Star (1-60):	1.25
Unlisted Star (1-60):	1.75
Common Rookie (61-82):	5.00
Rookie Production 799 Sets	
Collection Row (1-60):	1-30X
Collection Row (61-82):	.5-2X
Row 1 Production 125 Sets	
Collection Row 2:	No Pricing
Production One Set	
Box (1):	100.00

1	Brandon Webb	1.00
2	Todd Helton	2.00
3	Jeff Bagwell	2.00

4	Shawn Green	1.25
5	Vladimir Guerrero	3.00
6	Tom Glavine	1.25
7	Jason Giambi	3.00
8	Barry Zito	1.75
9	Jason Kendall	1.25
10	Carlos Delgado	2.00
11	Curt Schilling	1.75
12	Ken Griffey Jr.	3.50
13	Mike Piazza	3.50
14	Alfonso Soriano	3.00
15	Albert Pujols	5.00
16	Chipper Jones	3.50
17	Alex Rodriguez	5.00
18	Miguel Tejada	1.75
19	Pedro J. Martinez	3.00
20	Mark Prior	4.00
21	Magglio Ordonez	1.25
22	Scott Podsednik	1.75
23	Shannon Stewart	1.00
24	Rocco Baldelli	1.75
25	Darin Erstad	1.25
26	Omar Vizquel	1.00
27	Angel Berroa	1.00
28	Jose Vidro	1.00
29	Rich Harden	1.00
30	Andruw Jones	2.00
31	Troy Glaus	1.75
32	Sammy Sosa	4.00
33	Dontrelle Willis	1.25
34	Ivan Rodriguez	1.75
35	Nomar Garciaparra	5.00
36	Josh Beckett	2.00
37	Jose Reyes	1.00
38	Scott Rolen	3.00
39	Greg Maddux	3.50
40	Andy Pettitte	1.75
41	Jason Schmidt	1.25
42	Edgar Martinez	1.25
43	Manny Ramirez	2.00
44	Torii Hunter	1.75
45	Mark Teixeira	1.25
46	Hideo Nomo	1.00
47	Brian Giles	1.25
48	Adam Dunn	1.75
49	Fernando Vina	1.00
50	Hideki Matsui	4.00
51	Jim Thome	3.00
52	Hank Blalock	1.75
53	Miguel Cabrera	2.00
54	Randy Johnson	3.00
55	Javy Lopez	1.25
56	Frank Thomas	2.00
57	Roger Clemens	3.50
58	Marlon Byrd	1.00
59	Derek Jeter	6.00
60	Ichiro Suzuki	4.00
61	Kazuo Matsui **RC**	25.00
62	Chad Bentz **RC**	8.00
63	Greg Dobbs **RC**	5.00
64	John Gall **RC**	5.00
65	Cory Sullivan **RC**	5.00
66	Hector Gimenez **RC**	5.00
67	Graham Koonce	5.00
68	Jason Bartlett **RC**	5.00
69	Angel Chavez **RC**	5.00
70	Ronny Cedeno **RC**	5.00
71	Donald Kelly **RC**	5.00
72	Ivan Ochoa **RC**	5.00
73	Ruddy Yan **RC**	5.00
74	Mike Gosling	5.00
75	Alfredo Simon **RC**	5.00
76	Jerome Gamble **RC**	5.00
77	Chris Aguila **RC**	5.00
78	Mike Rouse	5.00
79	Justin Leone **RC**	5.00
80	Merkin Valdez **RC**	5.00
81	Aarom Baldiris **RC**	5.00
82	Chris Shelton **RC**	10.00

Autograph Collection

NM/M

Common Player:	10.00
Production between 65-200 Sets	
Crown:	.5-1X
Production 100 Sets	
Parchment:	1-1.75X
Production 25 Sets	
Platinum:	No Pricing
Production 10 Sets	
Masterpiece:	No Pricing
Production One Set	

Garrett Atkins/195	15.00
Rocco Baldelli/180	25.00
Aarom Baldiris/180	10.00
Jason Bartlett/95	15.00
Josh Beckett/65	40.00
Angel Berroa/178	15.00

Miguel Cabrera/172	40.00
Bobby Crosby/87	30.00
Jim Edmonds/73	25.00
John Gall/94	30.00
Khalil Greene/40	195.00
Dan Haren/195	15.00
Ryan Howard/185	75.00
Edwin Jackson/183	15.00
Andruw Jones/163	25.00
Graham Koonce/175	10.00
Josh Labandeira/166	10.00
Adam LaRoche/280	15.00
Justin Leone/180	15.00
Ryan Meaux/180	15.00
Mike Mussina/69	50.00
Micheal Nakamura/180	10.00
Bubba Nelson/185	10.00
Corey Patterson/172	15.00
Juan Pierre/94	15.00
Scott Podsednik/96	25.00
Mark Prior/60	60.00
Alexis Rios/185	20.00
Michael Rouse/195	10.00
Chris Shelton/170	30.00
Grady Sizemore/197	30.00
Merkin Valdez/179	10.00
Javier Vazquez/187	30.00
Ryan Wagner/175	15.00
Chien-Ming Wang/178	50.00
Brandon Webb/122	15.00
Rickie Weeks/169	20.00
Dontrelle Willis/73	30.00
Kerry Wood/73	40.00
Delmon Young/177	25.00

Cuts and Glory

NM/M

Common Player:	25.00
Production 100 Sets	
Silver:	.75-1.25X
Production 50 Sets	
Gold:	No Pricing
Production 15 Sets	
Platinum:	No Pricing
Production Three Sets	
Masterpiece:	No Pricing
Production One Set	

Garret Anderson	30.00
Hank Blalock	25.00
Marlon Byrd	25.00
Carlos Delgado	30.00
Adam Dunn	40.00
Eric Gagne	40.00
Luis Gonzalez	25.00
Vladimir Guerrero	50.00
Ricky Henderson	100.00
Torii Hunter	25.00
Randy Johnson	60.00
Chipper Jones	25.00
Austin Kearns	25.00
Greg Maddux	75.00
Edgar Martinez	40.00
Magglio Ordonez	25.00
Albert Pujols	150.00
Jose Reyes	30.00
Scott Rolen	40.00
Mark Teixeira	25.00
Frank Thomas	75.00

Diamond Cuts Game-Used Blue

NM/M

Common Player:	5.00
Production 250 Sets	
Blue Die-Cut:	1-30X
Production 25 Sets	
Red:	.5-1.25X
Production 175 Sets	
Red Die-Cut:	No Pricing
Production 18 Sets	
Pewter:	.5-1.5X
Production 125 Sets	
Pewter Die-Cut:	No Pricing
Production 13 Sets	
Copper:	.5-1.5X
Production 75 Sets	
Die-Cut Copper:	No Pricing
Production Eight Sets	
Silver:	.5-1.5X
Production 50 Sets	
Silver Die-Cut:	No Pricing
Production Five Sets	
Gold:	1-5X
Numbered to player's jersey No.	
Gold Die-Cut:	No Pricing
Production Three Sets	
Platinum:	2-5X
Numbered to 2003 HR/Win total.	
Platinum Die-Cut:	No Pricing

Production One Set		
Purple:		No Pricing
Production One Set		
JB	Josh Beckett	8.00
HB	Hank Blalock	5.00
RC	Roger Clemens	10.00
NG	Nomar Garciaparra	12.00
DJ	Derek Jeter	15.00
AJ	Andruw Jones	8.00
CJ	Chipper Jones	8.00
PM	Pedro J. Martinez	8.00
HM	Hideki Matsui	12.00
ANP	Andy Pettitte	8.00
MIP	Mike Piazza	8.00
MAP	Mark Prior	8.00
ALP	Albert Pujols	12.00
JR	Jose Reyes	5.00
SR	Scott Rolen	8.00
SS	Curt Schilling	5.00
SS	Sammy Sosa	10.00
IS	Ichiro Suzuki	10.00
MT	Mark Teixeira	5.00
DW	Dontrelle Willis	5.00

Dual Patch
No Pricing
Production 10 Sets

Hot Numbers
Game-Used Blue

	NM/M
Common Player:	5.00
Production 250 Sets	
Blue Die-Cut:	1X-3X
Production 25 Sets	
Red:	.5X-1.25X
Production 175 Sets	
Red Die-Cut:	No Pricing
Production 18 Sets	
Pewter:	.5X-1.5X
Production 125 Sets	
Pewter Die-Cut:	No Pricing
Production 13 Sets	
Copper:	.5X-1.5X
Production 75 Sets	
Die-Cut Copper:	No Pricing
Production Eight Sets	
Silver:	.5X-1.5X
Production 50 Sets	
Silver Die-Cut:	No Pricing
Production Five Sets	
Gold:	1X-5X
Numbered to player's jersey no.	
Gold Die-Cut:	No Pricing
Production Three Sets	
Platinum:	2X-5X
Numbered to 2003 HR/Win total.	
Platinum Die-Cut:	No Pricing
Production One Set	
Purple:	No Pricing
Production One Set	
	Jeff Bagwell	8.00
	Rocco Baldelli	5.00
	Josh Beckett	8.00
	Hank Blalock	5.00
	Nomar Garciaparra	12.00
	Jason Giambi	8.00
	Troy Glaus	5.00
	Tom Glavine	5.00
	Vladimir Guerrero	8.00
	Todd Helton	8.00
	Derek Jeter	15.00
	Randy Johnson	8.00
	Chipper Jones	8.00
	Barry Larkin	5.00
	Greg Maddux	8.00
	Pedro J. Martinez	8.00
	Mike Mussina	5.00
	Hideo Nomo	5.00
	Mike Piazza	8.00
	Mark Prior	8.00
	Albert Pujols	12.00
	Manny Ramirez	8.00
	Alex Rodriguez	12.00
	Curt Schilling	5.00
	Sammy Sosa	10.00
	Mark Teixeira	5.00
	Frank Thomas	8.00
	Jim Thome	8.00
	Brandon Webb	5.00
	Kerry Wood	8.00

Lettermen
No Pricing
Numbered to number of letters in player's last name.

Power Tools
Game-Used Blue

	NM/M
Common Player:	5.00
Production 250 Sets	
Blue Die-Cut:	1X-3X
Production 25 Sets	
Red:	.5X-1.25X
Production 175 Sets	
Red Die-Cut:	No Pricing

Production 18 Sets		
Pewter:		.5X-1.5X
Production 125 Sets		
Pewter Die-Cut:		No Pricing
Production 13 Sets		
Copper:		.5X-1.5X
Production 75 Sets		
Die-Cut Copper:		No Pricing
Production Eight Sets		
Silver:		.5X-1.5X
Production 50 Sets		
Silver Die-Cut:		No Pricing
Production Five Sets		
Gold:		1X-5X
Numbered to player's jersey no.		
Gold Die-Cut:		No Pricing
Production Three Sets		
Platinum:		2X-5X
Platinum Die-Cut No Pricing		
Production One Set		
Purple:		No Pricing
Production One Set		
	Rocco Baldelli	5.00
	Adam Dunn	5.00
	Nomar Garciaparra	12.00
	Jason Giambi	8.00
	Vladimir Guerrero	8.00
	Derek Jeter	15.00
	Chipper Jones	8.00
	Mike Piazza	10.00
	Jorge Posada	8.00
	Albert Pujols	12.00
	Manny Ramirez	8.00
	Alex Rodriguez	12.00
	Alfonso Soriano	8.00
	Sammy Sosa	10.00
	Jim Thome	8.00

SIGnificant Cuts

		NM/M
Serially Numbered		
RA	Roberto Alomar/50	60.00
JB2	Johnny Bench/25	100.00
VC	Vince Carter/200	50.00
TC	Ty Cobb	2,650
DE	Dennis Eckersley/75	30.00
RH	Roy Halladay/50	40.00
BL	Barry Larkin/75	30.00
PM	Paul Molitor/75	50.00
AP1	Andy Pettitte/50	40.00
JR	Jose Reyes/25	40.00
MR	Mariano Rivera/50	75.00
IR	Ivan Rodriguez/50	50.00
NR	Nolan Ryan/25	200.00
MS	Mike Schmidt/25	125.00
GS	Gary Sheffield/50	50.00

2004 Fleer Genuine Insider

	NM/M
Common Player (1-90):	.25
Minor Stars:	.40
Unlisted Stars:	.60
Common Rookie Insider	
(91-100):	4.00
Production 499 Sets	
Common Upside (101-120):	4.00
Production 799 Sets	
Common Mini Rookie:	4.00
Production 350 Sets	
Pack (5):	4.00
Box (18):	75.00
1	Troy Glaus	.60
2	Eric Chavez	.40
3	Lance Berkman	.40
4	Pedro J. Martinez	.60
5	Jim Edmonds	.40
6	Tom Glavine	.40
7	Ken Griffey Jr.	1.50
8	Vernon Wells	.40
9	Hideki Matsui	2.50
10	Jeff Bagwell	.75
11	Rafael Palmeiro	.40
12	Edgar Martinez	.40
13	Bernie Williams	.60
14	Josh Beckett	.75
15	Javy Lopez	.40
16	Ichiro Suzuki	2.00

17	Scott Podsednik	.40
18	Sammy Sosa	2.00
19	Mark Teixeira	.40
20	Jorge Posada	.60
21	Miguel Cabrera	.75
22	Chipper Jones	1.50
23	Sean Burroughs	.25
24	Dmitri Young	.25
25	Brandon Webb	.25
26	Bobby Abreu	.40
27	Hideo Nomo	.40
28	Frank Thomas	.75
29	Alex Rodriguez	2.50
30	Derek Jeter	3.00
31	Todd Helton	.75
32	Andruw Jones	.75
33	Jason Kendall	.40
34	Eric Gagne	.40
35	Omar Vizquel	.40
36	Vladimir Guerrero	1.00
37	Jim Thome	1.00
38	Mike Sweeney	.25
39	Manny Ramirez	.75
40	Scott Rolen	.40
41	Jose Vidro	.25
42	Adam Dunn	.60
43	Garret Anderson	.40
44	Mike Lieberthal	.25
45	Roy Oswalt	.40
46	Geoff Jenkins	.40
47	Magglio Ordonez	.40
48	Hank Blalock	.60
49	Barry Zito	.60
50	Dontrelle Willis	.40
51	Greg Maddux	1.50
52	Brian Giles	.40
53	Shawn Green	.40
54	Carlos Lee	.25
55	Carlos Delgado	.75
56	Alfonso Soriano	1.00
57	Angel Berroa	.25
58	Kerry Wood	.75
59	Rocco Baldelli	.60
60	Gary Sheffield	.60
61	Ivan Rodriguez	.60
62	Richie Sexson	.40
63	Marlon Byrd	.25
64	Carlos Beltran	.40
65	Mark Prior	2.00
66	Aubrey Huff	.25
67	Jason Giambi	1.00
68	Curt Schilling	.60
69	Reggie Sanders	.25
70	Mike Piazza	1.50
71	Craig Monroe	.25
72	Randy Johnson	1.00
73	Pat Burrell	.40
74	Craig Biggio	.40
75	Nomar Garciaparra	2.50
76	Albert Pujols	2.50
77	Jose Reyes	.25
78	Preston Wilson	.25
79	Miguel Tejada	.60
80	Bret Boone	.40
81	Shannon Stewart	.25
82	Jody Gerut	.25
83	Tim Salmon	.25
84	Tim Hudson	.40
85	Juan Pierre	.40
86	Jay Gibbons	.40
87	Jason Schmidt	.40
88	Torii Hunter	.60
89	Austin Kearns	.25
90	Roy Halladay	.40
91	John Gall RC	8.00
92	Hideki Matsui RC	25.00
93	Merkin Valdez RC	4.00
94	William Bergolla RC	8.00
95	Angel Chavez RC	4.00
96	Hector Gimenez RC	4.00
97	Aarom Baldiris RC	4.00
98	Justin Leone RC	6.00
99	Onil Joseph RC	4.00
100	Freddy Guzman RC	4.00
101	Rickie Weeks	5.00
102	Chad Bentz RC	5.00
103	Bobby Crosby	6.00
104	Dallas McPherson	5.00
105	Brandon Watson	4.00
106	Garrett Atkins	4.00
107	Graham Koonce	4.00
108	Chien-Ming Wang	4.00
109	Jonny Gomes	4.00
110	Edwin Jackson	4.00
111	Alfredo Simon RC	5.00
112	Delmon Young	6.00
113	Angel Guzman	4.00
114	Ryan Howard	4.00
115	Scott Hairston	10.00
116	Edwin Encarnacion	4.00
117	Byron Gettis	4.00
118	Kevin Youkilis	8.00
119	Grady Sizemore	4.00
120	Corey Hart	4.00
121	Greg Dobbs RC	4.00
122	Jerry Gil RC	4.00
123	Shawn Hill RC	4.00
124	John Labandeira RC	4.00
125	Jason Bartlett RC	4.00
126	Ronny Cedeno RC	4.00
127	Donald Kelly RC	8.00
128	Ivan Ochoa RC	4.00
129	Mariano Gomez RC	5.00
130	Ruddy Yan RC	5.00

Genuine Reflection

(1-90):	.5-2X

(101-120):	.5-1.25X
Production 99 Sets	

Autograph Insider

	NM/M
Common Player:	10.00
Production as indicated.	
RA	Roberto Alomar/150	30.00
MB	Marlon Byrd/550	10.00
MC	Miguel Cabrera/250	40.00
DE	David Eckstein/350	10.00
JG	Jody Gerut/550	10.00
JG2	Jay Gibbons/350	10.00
OH	Orlando Hudson/550	15.00
AH	Aubrey Huff/550	10.00
AK	Austin Kearns/350	10.00
MO	Magglio Ordonez/250	20.00
RP	Rafael Palmeiro/150	50.00
SP	Scott Podsednik/550	15.00
JR	Jose Reyes/350	25.00
MR	Mariano Rivera/160	60.00
IR	Ivan Rodriguez/150	40.00
JR2	Jimmy Rollins/350	15.00
JS	Jason Schmidt/300	300.00
JS2	John Smoltz/150	30.00
MT	Mark Teixeira/350	20.00
BW	Brandon Webb/450	10.00

Autograph Insider - Ball
No Pricing
Production 10 Sets

Autograph Insider - Bat

	NM/M
Common Card:	20.00
Production 50 Sets	
RA	Roberto Alomar	40.00
MB	Marlon Byrd	20.00
MC	Miguel Cabrera	60.00
DE	David Eckstein	30.00
JG	Jody Gerut	25.00
JG2	Jay Gibbons	20.00
OH	Orlando Hudson	20.00
AH	Aubrey Huff	25.00
AK	Austin Kearns	20.00
RP	Rafael Palmeiro	50.00
SP	Scott Podsednik	25.00
JR	Jose Reyes	35.00
IR	Ivan Rodriguez	50.00
JR2	Jimmy Rollins	30.00
MT	Mark Teixeira	25.00

Autograph Insider-Cut Sigs
No Pricing

Autograph Insider - Jersey

	NM/M
Common Player:	10.00
Production 100 Sets	
RA	Roberto Alomar	30.00
MB	Marlon Byrd	10.00
MC	Miguel Cabrera	40.00
DE	David Eckstein	15.00
JG	Jody Gerut	25.00
JG2	Jay Gibbons	20.00
OH	Orlando Hudson	10.00
AH	Aubrey Huff	10.00
AK	Austin Kearns	20.00
MO	Magglio Ordonez	40.00
RP	Rafael Palmeiro	50.00
SP	Scott Podsednik	25.00
AP	Albert Pujols	100.00
JR	Jose Reyes	35.00
MR	Mariano Rivera	75.00
IR	Ivan Rodriguez	50.00
JR2	Jimmy Rollins	20.00
JS	Jason Schmidt	20.00
JS2	John Smoltz	50.00
MT	Mark Teixeira	25.00
BW	Brandon Webb	10.00

Classic Confrontations

	NM/M
Common Card:	3.00
Inserted 1:18	
1CC	Mike Piazza, Roger Clemens	4.00
2CC	Pedro J. Martinez, Derek Jeter	6.00
3CC	Randy Johnson, Jeff Bagwell	3.00
4CC	Mark Prior, Albert Pujols	4.00
5CC	Josh Beckett, Sammy Sosa	4.00
6CC	Eric Gagne, Hank Blalock	3.00
7CC	Mariano Rivera, Nomar Garciaparra	5.00
8CC	Chipper Jones, Curt Schilling	4.00
9CC	Kerry Wood, Jim Edmonds	3.00
10CC	Barry Zito, Alfonso Soriano	3.00
11CC	Randy Johnson, Ken Griffey Jr.	4.00
12CC	Derek Jeter, John Smoltz	6.00
13CC	Roy Oswalt, Ken Griffey Jr.	4.00
14CC	Dontrelle Willis, Hideki Matsui	4.00
15CC	Hideo Nomo, Ichiro Suzuki	4.00

Cl. Confrontations Jersey

	NM/M
Common Card:	5.00
Production 400 Sets	
JB	Jeff Bagwell w/Randy Johnson	6.00
JB2	Josh Beckett w/Sammy Sosa	6.00
HB	Hank Blalock w/Eric Gagne	8.00
RC	Roger Clemens w/Mike Piazza	15.00
JE	Jim Edmonds w/Kerry Wood	5.00
EG	Eric Gagne w/Hank Blalock	5.00
NG	Nomar Garciaparra w/Mariano Rivera	8.00
DJ	Derek Jeter w/Pedro J. Martinez	15.00
RJ1	Randy Johnson w/Jeff Bagwell	8.00
RJ2	Randy Johnson w/Ken Griffey Jr.	8.00
CJ	Chipper Jones w/Curt Schilling	8.00
PM	Pedro J. Martinez w/Derek Jeter	10.00
HN	Hideo Nomo w/Ichiro Suzuki	12.00
RO	Roy Oswalt w/Ken Griffey Jr.	5.00
MP	Mike Piazza w/Roger Clemens	8.00
MP2	Mark Prior w/Albert Pujols	8.00
AP	Albert Pujols w/Mark Prior	12.00
MR	Mariano Rivera w/Nomar Garciaparra	8.00
CS	Curt Schilling w/Chipper Jones	5.00
JS	John Smoltz w/Derek Jeter	5.00
AS	Alfonso Soriano w/Barry Zito	8.00
SS	Sammy Sosa w/Josh Beckett	8.00
DW	Dontrelle Willis w/Matsui	5.00
KW	Kerry Wood w/Jim Edmonds	8.00
BZ	Barry Zito w/Alfonso Soriano	5.00

Classic Conf. Dual Jersey

	NM/M
Common Card:	12.00
Production 100 Sets	
Dual Patch	No Pricing
Production 10 Sets	
	Barry Zito, Alfonso Soriano	12.00
	Curt Schilling, Chipper Jones	12.00
	Eric Gagne, Hank Blalock	12.00
	Josh Beckett, Sammy Sosa	12.00
	Kerry Wood, Jim Edmonds	15.00
	Mark Prior, Albert Pujols	15.00
	Mike Piazza, Roger Clemens	15.00
	Mariano Rivera, Nomar Garciaparra	20.00

Pedro J. Martinez, Derek Jeter		20.00
Randy Johnson, Jeff Bagwell		12.00

Gen. Article Insider-Jersey

	NM/M
Common Player:	5.00
Production 250 Sets	
Bat:	.75-1.25X
Production 100 Sets	
Jersey/Bat:	.75-1.5X
Production 50 Sets	
Jersey Tags:	No Pricing
Production Five Sets	
RB	Rocco Baldelli	5.00
LB	Lance Berkman	5.00
HB	Hank Blalock	5.00
MC	Miguel Cabrera	8.00
CD	Carlos Delgado	6.00
AD	Adam Dunn	5.00
NG	Nomar Garciaparra	12.00
JG	Jason Giambi	6.00
TG	Troy Glaus	5.00
VG	Vladimir Guerrero	8.00
TH	Todd Helton	8.00
DJ	Derek Jeter	18.00
CJ	Chipper Jones	8.00
MO	Magglio Ordonez	5.00
RP	Rafael Palmeiro	5.00
MP	Mike Piazza	8.00
AP	Albert Pujols	12.00
MR	Manny Ramirez	6.00
JR	Jose Reyes	6.00
AR	Alex Rodriguez	15.00
CS	Gary Sheffield	6.00
AS	Alfonso Soriano	6.00
SS	Sammy Sosa	10.00
MT	Mark Teixeira	5.00
JT	Jim Thome	6.00

Tools of the Game

	NM/M
Common Player:	1.00
Inserted 1:6	
1TG	Jason Giambi	1.50
2TG	Torii Hunter	1.00
3TG	Derek Jeter	4.00
4TG	Nomar Garciaparra	3.00
5TG	Albert Pujols	3.00
6TG	Jim Thome	1.50
7TG	Alex Rodriguez	3.00
8TG	Chipper Jones	2.00
9TG	Sammy Sosa	2.50
10TG	Jose Reyes	1.50
11TG	Pedro J. Martinez	1.50
12TG	Greg Maddux	2.00
13TG	Randy Johnson	1.50
14TG	Curt Schilling	1.00
15TG	Mark Prior	2.00
16TG	Ichiro Suzuki	2.50
17TG	Hideki Matsui	3.00
18TG	Kazuo Matsui	2.00
19TG	Ken Griffey Jr.	2.00
20TG	Josh Beckett	2.00

Tools of Game-Game Jersey

	NM/M
Common Player:	5.00
Production 250 Sets	
Jersey/Bat:	.75-2X
Production 125	
Jersey/Bat/Cap:	1-2.5X
Production 75	
NG	Nomar Garciaparra	12.00
JG	Jason Giambi	8.00
TH	Torii Hunter	5.00
DJ	Derek Jeter	15.00
RJ	Randy Johnson	6.00
CJ	Chipper Jones	8.00
GM	Greg Maddux	8.00
PM	Pedro J. Martinez	6.00
MP	Mark Prior	10.00
AP	Albert Pujols	8.00
JR	Jose Reyes	8.00
AR	Alex Rodriguez	15.00
CS	Curt Schilling	5.00
SS	Sammy Sosa	10.00
JT	Jim Thome	5.00

2004 Fleer Greats of the Game

		NM/M
Common Player:		.40
Minor Stars:		.75
Pack (5):		10.00
Box (15):		130.00
1	Lou Gehrig	4.00
2	Ty Cobb	3.00
3	Dizzy Dean	1.50
4	Jimmie Foxx	1.50
5	Hank Greenberg	1.00
6	Babe Ruth	6.00
7	Honus Wagner	1.50
8	Mickey Cochrane	1.50
9	Pepper Martin	.40
10	Charlie Gehringer	.75
11	Carl Hubbell	.40
12	Bill Terry	.40
13	Mel Ott	.75
14	Bill Dickey	1.50
15	Ted Williams	6.00
16	Roger Maris	3.00
17	Thurman Munson	2.00
18	Phil Rizzuto	2.00
19	Stan Musial	3.00
20	Duke Snider	2.50
21	Reggie Jackson	1.50
22	Don Mattingly	1.50
23	Vida Blue	.75
24	Harmon Killebrew	1.50
25	Lou Brock	.75
26	Al Kaline	1.00
27	Dave Parker	.40
28	Nolan Ryan	6.00
29	Jim Rice	.40
30	Paul Molitor	2.00
31	Dwight Evans	.40
32	Brooks Robinson	1.50
33	Jose Canseco	.40
34	Alan Trammell	.40
35	Johnny Bench	2.00
36	Carlton Fisk	1.00
37	Jim Palmer	1.50
38	George Brett	2.00
39	Mike Schmidt	2.00
40	Tony Perez	.75
41	Paul Blair	.40
42	Fred Lynn	.40
43	Carl Yastrzemski	1.50
44	Steve Carlton	1.00
45	Dennis Eckersley	1.50
46	Tom Seaver	1.50
47	Juan Marichal	.75
48	Tony Gwynn	2.00
49	Bill "Moose" Skowron	.75
50	Bob Gibson	1.50
51	Luis Tiant	.75
52	Eddie Murray	1.00
53	Frank Robinson	2.00
54	Rocky Colavito	.75
55	Bobby Shantz	.40
56	Ernie Banks	2.00
57	Rod Carew	1.00
58	Gorman Thomas	.40
59	Bernie Carbo	.40
60	Joe Rudi	.40
61	Graig Nettles	.75
62	Ron Guidry	.75
63	Whitey Ford	1.50
64	George Kell	1.00
65	Cal Ripken Jr.	6.00
66	Willie McCovey	1.00
67	Bo Jackson	1.00
68	Kirby Puckett	2.00
69	Ted Kluszewski	.75
70	Johnny Podres	.40
71	Davey Lopes	.40
72	Chris Short	.40
73	Jeff Torborg	.40
74	Bill Freehan	.40
75	Frank Tanana	.40
76	Jack Morris	.75
77	Rick Dempsey	.40
78	Yogi Berra	1.50
79	Tim McCarver	.40
80	Rusty Staub	.40
81	Tony Lazzeri	.40
82	Al Rosen	.40
83	Willie McGee	.75
84	Preacher Roe	.75
85	Dave Kingman	.40
86	Luis Aparicio	1.00
87	John Kruk	.40
88	Bing Miller	.40
89	Joe Charboneau	.40
90	Mark Fidrych	.40

91	Jim "Catfish" Hunter	2.00
92	Nap Lajoie	2.00
93	Eddie Murray	2.00
94	Johnny Pesky	1.00
95	Tom Seaver	2.00
96	Frank Robinson	2.00
97	Enos Slaughter	1.00
98	Cecil Travis	.40
99	Robin Yount	2.00
100	Don Zimmer	.75
101	Babe Herman	.40
102	Ron Santo	.40
103	Willie Stargell	2.00
105	Jimmy Piersall	.75
106	Johnny Sain	.40
107	Joe Pepitone	.75
108	Ryne Sandberg	3.00
109	Jim Thorpe	3.00
110	Steve Garvey	1.50
111	Ray Knight	.75
112	Fernando Valenzuela	1.00
113	Will Clark	1.00
114	Tony Kubek	.75
115	Jim Bouton	.40
116	Jerry Koosman	.75
117	Steve Carlton	3.00
118	Richie Ashburn	.75
119	Roberto Clemente	6.00
120	Paul O'Neill	.40
121	Reggie Jackson	3.00
122	Andre Dawson	1.50
123	Hoyt Wilhelm	1.50
124	Dale Murphy	1.50
125	Dwight Gooden	1.50
126	Roger Maris	1.00
127	Bill Mazeroski	1.00
128	Don Newcombe	.75
129	Robin Roberts	.75
130	Duke Snider	2.00
131	Eddie Mathews	3.00
132	Wade Boggs	2.00
133	Rollie Fingers	1.50
134	Frankie Frisch	.40
135	Billy Williams	.75
136	Rod Carew	1.50
137	Dom DiMaggio	.75
138	Orel Hershiser	.40
139	Gary Carter	1.00
140	Keith Hernandez	.75
141	Bob Lemon	.75
142	Nolan Ryan	6.00
143	Ozzie Smith	1.50
144	Rick Sutcliffe	.40
145	Carlton Fisk	1.50

Blue

Cards 81-145	
Cards #'d to 51-96:	3-5X
Cards #'d to 26-50:	5-10X
Cards #'d to less than 25:	No Pricing

Announcing Greats

		NM/M
Common Card:		6.00
Inserted 1:12 Retail		
1AG	Harry Kalas, Mike Schmidt	8.00
2AG	Vin Scully, Steve Garvey	12.00
3AG	Harry Caray, Ryne Sandberg	12.00
4AG	Ned Martin, Carlton Fisk	6.00
5AG	Ernie Harwell, Kirk Gibson	6.00
6AG	Ken Harrelson, Carl Yastrzemski	8.00
7AG	Don Mattingly, Phil Rizzuto	10.00
8AG	Yogi Berra, Mel Allen	10.00
9AG	Jonathan Miller, Cal Ripken Jr.	10.00
10AG	Marty Brennaman, Johnny Bench	10.00

Announcing Greats Autographs

		NM/M
Sequentially #'d between 1 & 50.		
	Ken Harrelson, Carl Yastrzemski/50	75.00
	Phil Rizzuto, Don Mattingly/26	225.00
	Johnny Bench, Marty Brennaman/50	60.00

Battery Mates

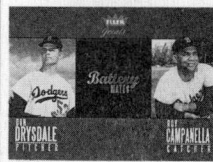

		NM/M
Common Card:		5.00
Serially Numbered		
1BM	Steve Carlton, Tim McCarver/1972	5.00
2BM	Don Drysdale, Roy Campanella/1957	5.00
3BM	Tom Seaver, Johnny Bench/1979	8.00
4BM	Whitey Ford, Yogi Berra/1956	8.00

5BM	Ron Guidry, Thurman Munson/1978	8.00
6BM	Nolan Ryan, Jeff Torborg/1973	10.00
7BM	Denny McLain, Bill Freehan/1968	5.00
8BM	Lefty Gomez, Bill Dickey/1934	5.00
9BM	Jim Palmer, Rick Dempsey/1977	5.00
10BM	Luis Tiant, Carlton Fisk	5.00

Single Panel: Battery Mates

		NM/M
Common Card:		15.00
Serially Numbered		
TM	Steve Carlton, Tim McCarver/72	30.00
TS-JB	Tom Seaver, Johnny Bench/79	60.00
WF-YB	Whitey Ford, Yogi Berra/56	40.00
RG-TM	Ron Guidry, Thurman Munson/78	25.00
NR-JT	Nolan Ryan, Jeff Torborg/73	15.00
DM-BF	Denny McLain, Bill Freehan/68	60.00
JP-RD	Jim Palmer, Rick Dempsey/77	25.00

Dual Panel: Battery Mates

No Pricing
Production 10 Sets

Comparison Cuts: Dual Cut

No Pricing
Production One Set

Forever

		NM/M
Common Player:		4.00
Sequentially #'d to player's rookie year		
1	Fernando Valenzuela/1980	4.00
2	Steve Garvey/1969	4.00
3	Zach Wheat/1909	4.00
4	Orel Hershiser/1983	4.00
5	Duke Snider/1947	6.00
6	Jim Rice/1974	5.00
7	Carlton Fisk/1969	6.00
8	Wade Boggs/1982	6.00
9	Ted Williams/1939	10.00
10	Carl Yastrzemski/1961	8.00
11	Dom DiMaggio/1940	4.00
12	Ron Santo/1960	4.00
13	Billy Williams/1959	5.00
14	Ryne Sandberg/1981	8.00
15	Ernie Banks/1953	8.00
16	Gabby Hartnett/1922	4.00
17	Hack Wilson/1923	4.00
18	Dwight Gooden/1984	5.00
19	Ray Knight/1974	4.00
20	Tom Seaver/1967	8.00
21	Nolan Ryan/1966	10.00
22	Keith Hernandez/1974	5.00
23	Darryl Strawberry/1983	5.00
24	Bob Gibson/1959	8.00
25	Pepper Martin/1928	4.00
26	Stan Musial/1941	8.00
27	Frankie Frisch/1919	4.00
28	Steve Carlton/1965	8.00
29	Ozzie Smith/1978	6.00

Forever Game-Used Jersey

		NM/M
Common Player:		10.00
Production 149 Sets		
Jersey:		.75-1.5X
Production 99 Sets		
Patch Number:		1-2X
Production 49 Sets		
Patch Logo:		No Pricing
Production 10 Sets		
EB	Ernie Banks	20.00
WB	Wade Boggs	12.00
SC	Steve Carlton	12.00
DD	Dom DiMaggio	20.00
CF	Carlton Fisk	15.00
SG	Steve Garvey	10.00
BG	Bob Gibson	15.00
DG	Dwight Gooden	10.00
KH	Keith Hernandez	10.00
OH	Orel Hershiser	10.00
RK	Ray Knight	10.00
SM	Stan Musial	30.00
JR	Jim Rice	12.00

		NM/M
NR	Nolan Ryan	50.00
RS	Ryne Sandberg	25.00
RST	Ron Santo	10.00
TS	Tom Seaver	15.00
OS	Ozzie Smith	15.00
DS	Darryl Strawberry	12.00
FV	Fernando Valenzuela	10.00
BW	Billy Williams	10.00
TW	Ted Williams	75.00
CY	Carl Yastrzemski	20.00

Gold Border Autographs

		NM/M
Common Player:		10.00
Randomly Inserted		
	Ernie Banks	60.00
	Johnny Bench	50.00
	Yogi Berra	60.00
	Paul Blair	10.00
	Vida Blue	10.00
	George Brett	125.00
	Lou Brock	20.00
	Jose Canseco	30.00
	Bernie Carbo	10.00
	Rod Carew	30.00
	Steve Carlton	30.00
	Rocky Colavito	100.00
	Rick Dempsey	15.00
	Dennis Eckersley	50.00
	Dwight Evans	15.00
	Carlton Fisk	40.00
	Whitey Ford	40.00
	Bill Freehan	10.00
	Bob Gibson	25.00
	Ron Guidry	20.00
	Tony Gwynn	50.00
	Bo Jackson	50.00
	Reggie Jackson	100.00
	Al Kaline	25.00
	George Kell	15.00
	Harmon Killebrew	30.00
	Davey Lopes	10.00
	Fred Lynn	10.00
	Juan Marichal	20.00
	Don Mattingly	80.00
	Tim McCarver	15.00
	Willie McCovey	40.00
	Paul Molitor	40.00
	Jack Morris	15.00
	Eddie Murray	80.00
	Stan Musial	100.00
	Graig Nettles	15.00
	Jim Palmer	20.00
	Dave Parker	10.00
	Tony Perez	30.00
	Johnny Podres	10.00
	Kirby Puckett	80.00
	Jim Rice	20.00
	Cal Ripken Jr.	150.00
	Phil Rizzuto	40.00
	Brooks Robinson	20.00
	Frank Robinson	30.00
	Joe Rudi	10.00
	Nolan Ryan	150.00
	Mike Schmidt	60.00
	Tom Seaver	80.00
	Bobby Shantz	10.00
	Bill "Moose" Skowron	10.00
	Duke Snider	30.00
	Rusty Staub	10.00
	Frank Tanana	10.00
	Gorman Thomas	10.00
	Luis Tiant	10.00
	Jeff Torborg	10.00
	Alan Trammell	10.00
	Carl Yastrzemski	60.00

Gold Border Auto. Series 2

		NM/M
Common Player:		4.00
Serially Numbered		
1GOT	Harmon Killebrew/1961	4.00
2GOT	Johnny Bench/1974	5.00
3GOT	George Brett/1980	8.00
4GOT	Tony Gwynn/1987	5.00
5GOT	Paul Molitor/1987	4.00
6GOT	Don Mattingly/1986	8.00
7GOT	Reggie Jackson/1980	8.00
8GOT	Carlton Fisk/1985	5.00
9GOT	Cal Ripken Jr./1983	10.00
10GOT	Brooks Robinson/1964	4.00
11GOT	Bill "Moose" Skowron/1960	4.00
12GOT	Lou Brock/1974	5.00
13GOT	Don Drysdale/1962	4.00
14GOT	Tony Gwynn/1997	4.00

		NM/M
Common Player:		15.00
Inserted 1:75		
LA	Luis Aparicio	20.00
WB	Wade Boggs	40.00
JBO	Jim Bouton	15.00
RC2	Rod Carew/Twins	40.00
SC2	Steve Carlton/Cards	30.00
GC	Gary Carter	15.00
JCH	Joe Charboneau	15.00
WC	Will Clark	40.00
DC	David Cone	40.00
AD	Andre Dawson	20.00
DD	Dom DiMaggio	50.00
RF	Rollie Fingers	15.00
CF2	Carlton Fisk/White Sox	40.00
SG	Steve Garvey	15.00
DG	Dwight Gooden	20.00
KH	Keith Hernandez	15.00
OH	Orel Hershiser	15.00
RJ2	Reggie Jackson/Angels	60.00
DK	Dave Kingman	15.00
RK	Ray Knight	15.00
JK	Jerry Koosman	20.00
JKR	John Kruk	15.00
TK	Tony Kubek	25.00
BM	Bill Mazeroski	30.00
WMG	Willie McGee	25.00
PM2	Paul Molitor/Jays	40.00
DMU	Dale Murphy	25.00
DN	Don Newcombe	15.00
PO	Paul O'Neill	30.00
JPP	Joe Pepitone	15.00
JPS	Johnny Pesky	25.00
JPI	Jimmy Piersall	20.00
RR	Robin Roberts	25.00
FR2	Frank Robinson/O's	20.00
PRO	Preacher Roe	15.00
AR	Al Rosen	10.00
NR2	Nolan Ryan/Angels	120.00
RS	Ryne Sandberg	75.00
DS	Deion Sanders	30.00
RST	Ron Santo	20.00
TS2	Tom Seaver/Reds	75.00
OS	Ozzie Smith	40.00
DS2	Duke Snider	40.00
BW	Billy Williams	20.00
RY	Robin Yount	40.00
DZ	Don Zimmer	25.00

Personality Cuts

No Pricing
Production One Set

Personality Cuts Series 2

No Pricing
Production One or Two Sets

Single Cuts: Etched in Time

		NM/M
No Pricing		
ET-RC	Roberto Clemente/1 (7/04 Auction)	6,100

Etched In Time Series 2

		NM/M
Sequentially #'d to indicated quantity.		
Cards 25 or less:		No Pricing
EA	Ethan Allen/75	150.00
EAV	Earl Averill/50	125.00
DC	Dolph Camilli/40	250.00
BH	Babe Herman/35	250.00
HK	Harvey Kuenn/32	120.00
SM	Sal Maglie/40	100.00
ER	Edd Roush/95	100.00
PR	Pee Runnels/35	200.00
CS	Chris Short/30	120.00

The Glory of Their Time

		NM/M
Common Player:		4.00
Serially Numbered		
1GOT	Harmon Killebrew/1961	4.00
2GOT	Johnny Bench/1974	5.00
3GOT	George Brett/1980	8.00
4GOT	Tony Gwynn/1987	5.00
5GOT	Paul Molitor/1987	4.00
6GOT	Don Mattingly/1986	8.00
7GOT	Reggie Jackson/1980	8.00
8GOT	Carlton Fisk/1985	5.00
9GOT	Cal Ripken Jr./1983	10.00
10GOT	Brooks Robinson/1964	4.00
11GOT	Bill "Moose" Skowron/1960	4.00
12GOT	Lou Brock/1974	5.00
13GOT	Don Drysdale/1962	4.00
14GOT	Tony Gwynn/1997	4.00
15GOT	Tony Gwynn/1997	4.00
16GOT	Mike Schmidt/1980	8.00
17GOT	Carl Yastrzemski/1967	8.00
18GOT	Babe Ruth/1927	10.00
19GOT	Nolan Ryan/1989	10.00
20GOT	Yogi Berra/1950	8.00
21GOT	Al Kaline/1955	5.00
22GOT	Ty Cobb/1911	5.00
23GOT	Duke Snider/1955	5.00
24GOT	Stan Musial/1948	8.00
25GOT	Jose Canseco/1988	5.00
26GOT	Rocky Colavito/1958	5.00
27GOT	Dave Winfield/1979	4.00
28GOT	Nolan Ryan/1982	8.00
29GOT	Thurman Munson/1977	8.00
30GOT	Jackie Robinson/1949	8.00
31GOT	Kirby Puckett/1988	8.00
32GOT	Ted Kluszewski/1954	5.00
33GOT	Warren Spahn/1953	5.00
34GOT	Willie McCovey/1969	4.00
35GOT	Phil Rizzuto/1950	5.00

The Glory/Time: Game-Used

		NM/M
Common Player:		10.00
Production 250 Sets		
Hobby Only		
Gold:		1.5-2X
Retail Only (Not Numbered)		
No Rizzuto Retail Version		
JB	Johnny Bench/Jsy	15.00
YB	Yogi Berra/Pants	15.00
GB	George Brett/Jsy	15.00
LB	Lou Brock/Jsy	15.00
JC1	Jose Canseco/Jsy	10.00
JC2	Jose Canseco/Bat	10.00
RC	Rocky Colavito/Bat	25.00
DD	Don Drysdale/Jsy	15.00
CF1	Carlton Fisk/Jsy	10.00
CF2	Carlton Fisk/Bat	10.00
TG1	Tony Gwynn/Jsy	10.00
TG2	Tony Gwynn/Jsy	10.00
RJ	Reggie Jackson/Pants	20.00
AK	Al Kaline/Pants	15.00
HK	Harmon Killebrew/Bat	10.00
TK	Ted Kluszewski/Pants	15.00
DM	Don Mattingly/Pants	20.00
WM	Willie McCovey/Pants	15.00
PM	Paul Molitor/Jsy	15.00
TM	Thurman Munson/Pants	15.00
EM	Eddie Murray/Jsy	15.00
KP	Kirby Puckett/Bat	20.00
CR	Cal Ripken Jr./Jsy	25.00
PR	Phil Rizzuto/Pants	15.00
BR	Brooks Robinson/Jsy	15.00
NR1	Nolan Ryan/Jsy	20.00
NR2	Nolan Ryan/Bat	20.00
MS	Mike Schmidt/Jsy	15.00
MS	Bill "Moose" Skowron/Pants	15.00
WS	Warren Spahn/Jsy	20.00
DW	Dave Winfield/Jsy	20.00
CY	Carl Yastrzemski/Jsy	20.00

The Glory/Time: G-U Patch

No Pricing
Production 25 Sets

Yankee Clippings

		NM/M
Common Player:		25.00
Inserted 1:45		
YB	Yogi Berra	60.00
WB	Wade Boggs	40.00
RJ	Reggie Jackson	40.00
LG	Roger Maris	400.00
DM	Don Mattingly	100.00
PO	Paul O'Neill	30.00
PR	Phil Rizzuto	325.00
BS	Bill "Moose" Skowron	25.00

Yankee Clippings Autographs

No Pricing
Sequentially #'d between 3 & 26.

2004 Fleer Hot Prospects Draft Edition

	NM/M
Common Player (1-60):	.25
Minor Stars (1-60):	.40
Unlisted Stars (1-60):	.60
Common Rookie (61-70):	3.00
Common Rookie (71-120):	15.00
Production 1,000 Sets	
Cards 112 & 113 do not exist.	
Production 299 Sets	
Pack (5):	7.00
Box (15):	100.00

1	Miguel Tejada	.50
2	Jose Vidro	.25
3	Hideki Matsui	2.00
4	Roger Clemens	2.50
5	Craig Wilson	.25
6	Bobby Crosby	.25
7	Pat Burrell	.40
8	Mike Sweeney	.25
9	Craig Biggio	.40
10	Scott Rolen	1.00
11	Roy Halladay	.40
12	Lyle Overbay	.25
13	Rocco Baldelli	.50
14	Mike Piazza	1.50
15	Rafael Palmeiro	.75
16	Hank Blalock	.50
17	Sammy Sosa	1.50
18	Dontrelle Willis	.40
19	Alfonso Soriano	1.00
20	Gary Sheffield	.75
21	Jim Thome	1.00
22	Ivan Rodriguez	.75
23	Adam Dunn	.50
24	Kerry Wood	.50
25	Khalil Greene	.50
26	Richie Sexson	.50
27	Nomar Garciaparra	.75
28	Andruw Jones	.75
29	Tom Glavine	.40
30	Carlos Beltran	.75
31	Chipper Jones	1.00
32	Jeff Bagwell	.75
33	Tim Hudson	.40
34	Alex Rodriguez	2.00
35	Omar Vizquel	.40
36	Albert Pujols	2.50
37	Frank Thomas	.75
38	Ben Sheets	.40
39	Jason Schmidt	.40
40	Miguel Cabrera	.75
41	Carlos Delgado	.75
42	Ichiro Suzuki	2.00
43	Curt Schilling	.75
44	Todd Helton	.75
45	Ken Griffey Jr.	1.50
46	Mark Prior	.75
47	Vladimir Guerrero	1.00
48	Pedro Martinez	1.00
49	Manny Ramirez	1.00
50	Joe Mauer	.50
51	Jorge Posada	.50
52	Troy Glaus	.50
53	Randy Johnson	1.00
54	Adrian Beltre	.40
55	Eric Gagne	.40
56	Josh Beckett	.50
57	Jason Giambi	.75
58	Barry Zito	.50
59	Lance Berkman	.50
60	Derek Jeter	3.00
61	Kazuo Matsui RC	5.00
62	Jason Bartlett RC	5.00
63	John Gall RC	3.00
64	Chris Saenz RC	3.00
65	Merkin Valdez RC	3.00
66	Akinori Otsuka RC	3.00
67	Joey Gathright RC	5.00
68	Brad Halsey RC	5.00
69	David Aardsma	3.00
70	Scott Kazmir	10.00
71	Matt Bush/AU RC	15.00
72	John Bowker/AU RC	30.00
73	Mike Ferris/AU RC	10.00
74	Brian Bixler/AU RC	15.00
75	Scott Elbert/AU RC	20.00
76	Josh Fields/AU RC	30.00
77	Bill Bray/AU RC	30.00
78	Greg Golson/AU RC	30.00
79	Neil Walker/AU RC	30.00
80	Phillip Hughes/AU	100.00
81	Chris Nelson/AU RC	15.00
82	Mark Rogers/AU RC	20.00
83	Trevor Plouffe/AU RC	20.00
84	Christian Garcia/AU RC	15.00
85	Thomas Diamond/ AU RC	10.00
86	B.J. Szymanski/AU RC	15.00
87	Richie Robnett/AU RC	15.00
88	Seth Smith/AU RC	25.00
89	Kyle Waldrop/AU RC	15.00
90	Curtis Thigpen/AU RC	15.00
91	J.P. Howell/AU RC	15.00
92	Blake DeWitt/AU RC	35.00
93	Taylor Tankersley/ AU RC	10.00
94	Zach Jackson/AU RC	15.00
95	Justin Orenduff/AU RC	15.00
96	Tyler Lumsden/AU RC	15.00

97	Danny Putnam RC	20.00
98	Jon Poterson/AU RC	20.00
99	Matt Fox/AU RC	15.00
100	Gio Gonzalez/AU RC	35.00
101	Huston Street/AU RC	15.00
102	Jay Rainville/AU RC	15.00
103	Matt Durkin/AU RC	15.00
104	Brett Smith/AU RC	15.00
105	Justin Hoyman/AU RC	15.00
106	Erick San Pedro/AU RC	15.00
107	Jeff Marquez/AU RC	15.00
108	Hunter Pence/AU RC	120.00
109	Dustin Pedroia/AU RC	125.00
110	Kurt Suzuki/AU RC	20.00
111	Billy Buckner/AU RC	10.00
114	J.C. Holt/AU RC	10.00
115	Homer Bailey/AU RC	35.00
116	David Purcey/AU RC	15.00
117	Jeremy Sowers/AU RC	20.00
118	Chris Lambert/AU RC	10.00
119	Eric Hurley/AU RC	40.00
120	Grant Johnson/AU RC	10.00

Red Hot
Veterans (1-60):	2-4X
Rookies (61-70):	1-2X
Production 150	
Rookies (71-120):	No Pricing
Production 25 Sets	

White Hot
Cards (1-120):	No Pricing
Production One Set	

Alumni Ink
No Pricing	
Production 15 Sets	
Red Hot:	No Pricing
Production Five Sets	
White Hot:	No Pricing
Production One Set	

Double Team Auto. Patch Red Hot
No Pricing	
Production 22 Sets	
White Hot:	No Pricing
Production One Set	

Double Team Jersey
	NM/M
Common Player:	10.00
Production 100 Sets	
Red Hot:	No Pricing
Production 25 Sets	
White Hot:	No Pricing
Production One Set	
Patch:	.75-1.5X
Production 50 Sets	
Patch Red Hot:	No Pricing
Production 10 Sets	
Patch White Hot:	No Pricing
Production One Set	

CB	Carlos Beltran	15.00
RCA	Rod Carew	20.00
RCL	Roger Clemens	20.00
JG	Jason Giambi	12.00
TG	Tom Glavine	10.00
VG	Vladimir Guerrero	15.00
RH	Rickey Henderson	20.00
RJ	Reggie Jackson	25.00
GM	Greg Maddux	15.00
PM	Pedro Martinez	15.00
EM	Eddie Murray	20.00
HN	Hideo Nomo	15.00
RP	Rafael Palmeiro	12.00
MP	Mike Piazza	20.00
MR	Manny Ramirez	15.00
IR	Ivan Rodriguez	10.00
SR	Scott Rolen	15.00
NR	Nolan Ryan	50.00
AS	Alfonso Soriano	12.00
MT	Miguel Tejada	10.00

Draft Rewind

	NM/M
Common Player:	2.00
Inserted 1:5	

1	Joe Mauer	2.00
2	Derek Jeter	6.00
3	Chipper Jones	3.50
4	Greg Maddux	3.50
5	Alex Rodriguez	5.00
6	Nomar Garciaparra	3.00
7	Curt Schilling	3.00
8	Kerry Wood	3.00
9	Troy Glaus	3.00
10	Pat Burrell	2.00
11	Mark Mulder	3.00
12	Josh Beckett	3.00
13	Barry Zito	3.00
14	Mark Prior	4.00
15	Rickie Weeks	3.00
16	Khalil Greene	3.00
17	Ken Griffey Jr.	3.50
18	Gary Sheffield	3.00
19	Todd Helton	3.00
20	Barry Larkin	3.00

21	Kevin Brown	2.00
22	Frank Thomas	3.00
23	Manny Ramirez	3.00
24	Roger Clemens	5.00
25	Lance Berkman	2.00
26	Randy Johnson	3.00
27	Jason Giambi	3.00
28	Ben Sheets	2.00
29	Scott Rolen	3.00
30	Tom Glavine	2.00

Draft Rewind Jersey
	NM/M
Common Player:	8.00
Sequentially #'d to indicated quantity.	
Red Hot:	No Pricing
Production 10 Sets	
White Hot:	No Pricing
Production One Set	
Patch	
Cards #'d 41-68:	.75-1.5X
Cards #'d 29 or less:	No Pricing
Patch Red Hot:	No Pricing
Production Five Sets	
Patch White Hot:	No Pricing
Production One Set	

RB	Rocco Baldelli/119	8.00
JB	Josh Beckett/102	10.00
LB	Lance Berkman/116	8.00
KB	Kevin Brown/104	8.00
PB	Pat Burrell/101	8.00
EC	Eric Chavez/110	8.00
RC	Roger Clemens/119	15.00
JG	Jason Giambi/158	8.00
TG	Troy Glaus/103	8.00
TG	Tom Glavine/147	8.00
KG	Khalil Greene/113	15.00
ZG	Zack Greinke/106	8.00
TH	Todd Helton/108	10.00
RJ	Randy Johnson/136	10.00
CJ	Chipper Jones/101	12.00
CK	Casey Kotchman/113	8.00
BL	Barry Larkin/104	10.00
GM	Greg Maddux/131	12.00
JM	Joe Mauer/101	10.00
MM	Mark Mulder/102	8.00
MP	Mark Prior/102	8.00
MR	Manny Ramirez/113	10.00
SR	Scott Rolen/146	10.00
CS	Curt Schilling/139	8.00
BS	Ben Sheets/110	8.00
GS	Gary Sheffield/106	8.00
FT	Frank Thomas/107	15.00
RW	Rickie Weeks/102	8.00
KW	Kerry Wood/104	10.00
BZ	Barry Zito/109	8.00

Hot Tandems
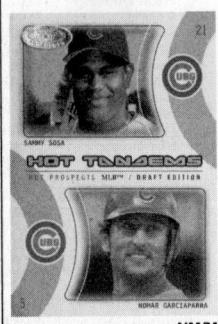

	NM/M
Common Card:	3.00
Inserted 1:15	

1HT	Mark Prior, Greg Maddux	4.00
2HT	Jim Thome, Pat Burrell	3.50
3HT	Ken Griffey Jr., Adam Dunn	4.00
4HT	Mike Piazza, Tom Glavine	4.00
5HT	Alex Rodriguez, Derek Jeter	10.00
6HT	Roger Clemens, Andy Pettitte	6.00
7HT	Hideki Matsui, Jason Giambi	6.00
8HT	Hank Blalock, Alfonso Soriano	3.50
9HT	Manny Ramirez, David Ortiz	3.50
10HT	Miguel Cabrera, Dontrelle Willis	3.50
11HT	Hideki Matsui, Ichiro Suzuki	6.00
12HT	Albert Pujols, Scott Rolen	6.00
13HT	Curt Schilling, Pedro J. Martinez	3.50
14HT	Nomar Garciaparra, Sammy Sosa	
15HT	Kazuo Matsui, Derek Jeter	8.00

MLB Hot Materials
	NM/M
Common Player:	5.00
Production 325 Sets	
Red Hot:	1-2X
Production 50 Sets	
White Hot Patch:	No Pricing
Production One Set	

LB	Lance Berkman/Jsy	5.00
HB	Hank Blalock/Jsy	6.00
MC	Miguel Cabrera/Jsy	8.00
RC	Roger Clemens/Jsy	12.00
CD	Carlos Delgado/Jsy	6.00
JD	J.D. Drew/Jsy	6.00
AD	Adam Dunn/Jsy	6.00
JE	Jim Edmonds/Jsy	5.00
EG	Eric Gagne/Jsy	6.00
VG	Vladimir Guerrero/Jsy	8.00
THE	Todd Helton/Jsy	8.00
THU	Tim Hudson/Jsy	5.00
THN	Torii Hunter/Jsy	6.00
RJ	Randy Johnson/Jsy	8.00
AJ	Andruw Jones/Jsy	6.00
CJ	Chipper Jones/Jsy	8.00
HM	Hideki Matsui/Jsy	20.00
KM	Kazuo Matsui/Jsy	10.00
JM	Joe Mauer/Jsy	8.00
MM	Mike Mussina/Jsy	6.00
HN	Hideo Nomo/Jsy	8.00
LO	Lyle Overbay/Jsy	5.00
APE	Andy Pettitte/Jsy	6.00
MPI	Mike Piazza/Jsy	8.00
JP	Jorge Posada/Jsy	6.00
MPR	Mark Prior/Jsy	8.00
APU	Albert Pujols/Jsy	12.00
MR	Manny Ramirez/Jsy	8.00
IR	Ivan Rodriguez/Jsy	6.00
CS	Curt Schilling/Jsy	8.00
JS	Jason Schmidt/Jsy	5.00
AS	Alfonso Soriano/Jsy	8.00
SS	Sammy Sosa/Jsy	10.00
MTX	Mark Teixeira/Jsy	6.00
MTJ	Miguel Tejada/Jsy	5.00
FT	Frank Thomas/Jsy	8.00
JT	Jim Thome/Jsy	8.00
DW	Dontrelle Willis/Jsy	5.00
KW	Kerry Wood/Jsy	5.00

Past, Present, Future Triple Auto.
	NM/M
Production 33 Sets	
Red Hot:	No Pricing
Production Three Sets	
White Hot:	No Pricing
Production One Set	

Matt Durkin, Mookie Wilson, Mike Piazza	150.00
Hideo Nomo, Scott Elbert, Kirk Gibson	250.00
Josh Fields, Carlton Fisk, Ryan Meaux	80.00
Greg Golson, Steve Carlton, Jim Thome	100.00
Jack Wilson, Neil Walker, Ralph Kiner	80.00
Ryne Sandberg, Mark Prior, Grant Johnson	250.00
Homer Bailey, Johnny Bench, Adam Dunn	250.00
Albert Pujols, Chris Lambert, Stan Musial	300.00
Richie Robnett, Reggie Jackson, Eric Chavez	80.00
Dustin Pedroia, Bill Buckner, Manny Ramirez	60.00

2004 Fleer InScribed

	NM/M
Common Player (1-75):	.25
Minor Stars (1-75):	.40
Unlisted Stars (1-75):	.60
Common Player (76-85):	3.00
Production 1,000 Sets	
Numbered to 750	3.00
Not all 750 of each card not released.	
Pack (5):	10.00
Box (12):	85.00

1	Vladimir Guerrero	1.00
2	Bartolo Colon	.40
3	Troy Glaus	.60
4	Richie Sexson	.60
5	Randy Johnson	1.00
6	Luis Gonzalez	.40
7	J.D. Drew	.40
8	Chipper Jones	1.50
9	Andruw Jones	.75
10	Melvin Mora	.25
11	Miguel Tejada	.60
12	Curt Schilling	.60
13	Pedro J. Martinez	1.00
14	Nomar Garciaparra	2.50
15	Kerry Wood	.75
16	Mark Prior	2.00
17	Sammy Sosa	2.00

Red
No Pricing	
Production Five Sets	

Gold
Veterans (1-75):	2-5X
Rookies (76-100):	.75-2X
Production 199 Sets	

Autographs Silver
	NM/M
Common Player:	10.00
Numbered to indicated quantity.	
Red:	No Pricing
Production 25 Sets	
Purple:	.5-2X
Numbered to jersey number.	

RB	Rocco Baldelli/34	25.00
CB	Carlos Beltran/296	25.00
JB	Jeremy Bonderman/287	10.00
EC	Eric Chavez/322	15.00
EG	Eric Gagne/57	40.00
BG	Brian Giles/134	15.00
LG	Luis Gonzalez/55	15.00
RHL	Roy Halladay/139	10.00
RHR	Rich Harden/235	10.00
TH	Trevor Hoffman/174	15.00
BL	Barry Larkin/140	20.00
JL	Javy Lopez/257	15.00
WM	Wade Miller/195	15.00
TN	Trot Nixon/318	15.00
LO	Lyle Overbay/240	10.00
SP	Scott Podsednik/280	10.00
BR	Brad Radke/168	15.00

Facsimile Signature Gold
Current (1-75):	3-5X
Retired (76-85):	1-2X
Rookies (86-100):	.75-1.5X
Production 199 Sets	

Award Winners
	NM/M
Common Player:	
Production 150 Sets	

1	Alex Rodriguez	10.00
2	Eric Gagne	3.00
3	Miguel Tejada	4.00
4	Roy Halladay	3.00
5	Randy Johnson	5.00
6	Barry Zito	4.00
7	Chipper Jones	5.00
8	Ivan Rodriguez	4.00
9	Pedro J. Martinez	5.00
10	Barry Larkin	3.00
11	Dontrelle Willis	3.00
12	Angel Berroa	3.00
13	Kerry Wood	5.00
14	Albert Pujols	8.00
15	Hideo Nomo	3.00

Award Winners Jersey Silver
	NM/M
Common Player:	
Production 175 Sets	
Copper:	.75-1.5X
Production 99 Sets	
Purple:	1-30X
Production 49 Sets	

AB	Angel Berroa	5.00
EG	Eric Gagne	8.00
RH	Roy Halladay	8.00
RJ	Randy Johnson	10.00
CJ	Chipper Jones	10.00
BL	Barry Larkin	10.00
PM	Pedro J. Martinez	10.00
HN	Hideo Nomo	8.00
AP	Albert Pujols	15.00
IR	Ivan Rodriguez	8.00
MT	Miguel Tejada	8.00
DW	Dontrelle Willis	5.00
KW	Kerry Wood	10.00
BZ	Barry Zito	8.00

Award Winners Autographs
	NM/M
Common Player:	15.00
Numbered to Award Year.	
All cards not released for some cards.	

AB	Angel Berroa/103	15.00
RH	Roy Halladay/102	20.00
BL	Barry Larkin 95/50	30.00
DW	Dontrelle Willis/103	25.00

Induction Ceremony
	NM/M
Common Player:	6.00
Numbered to Year of Induction.	

1	Carlton Fisk/100	8.00
2	Tony Perez/100	6.00
3	Nolan Ryan/99	20.00
4	Robin Yount/99	10.00
5	Orlando Cepeda/99	8.00
6	Bill Mazeroski/101	8.00
7	Larry Doby/98	6.00
8	Phil Niekro/97	6.00
9	Jim Bunning/96	6.00
10	Sparky Anderson/100	6.00
11	Phil Rizzuto/94	8.00
12	Rollie Fingers/92	6.00
13	Hal Newhouser/92	6.00
14	Rod Carew/91	8.00
15	Reggie Jackson/93	8.00
16	Tom Seaver/92	8.00
17	Bob Gibson/81	6.00
18	Jim Palmer/90	6.00
19	Joe Morgan/90	6.00
20	Al Kaline/80	10.00

Induction Ceremony Auto. Bronze
	NM/M
Common Player:	20.00
Numbered to 50	
Silver:	No Pricing
Production 15 Sets	
Gold:	No Pricing
Production Five Sets	

JB	Jim Bunning	20.00
OC	Orlando Cepeda/40	20.00
RF	Rollie Fingers	20.00

Autographs Silver (continued column)
18	Frank Thomas	.75
19	Magglio Ordonez	.40
20	Sean Casey	.25
21	Ken Griffey Jr.	1.50
22	Adam Dunn	.60
23	Jody Gerut	.25
24	Omar Vizquel	.25
25	Todd Helton	.75
26	Vinny Castilla	.25
27	Alex Sanchez	.25
28	Ivan Rodriguez	.60
29	Dontrelle Willis	.40
30	Josh Beckett	.75
31	Miguel Cabrera	.75
32	Roger Clemens	1.50
33	Andy Pettitte	.60
34	Jeff Bagwell	.75
35	Ken Harvey	.25
36	Carlos Beltran	.60
37	Shawn Green	.40
38	Hideo Nomo	.40
39	Scott Podsednik	.25
40	Ben Sheets	.40
41	Torii Hunter	.60
42	Jacque Jones	.25
43	Jose Vidro	.25
44	Mike Piazza	1.50
45	Tom Glavine	.40
46	Derek Jeter	3.00
47	Alex Rodriguez	2.50
48	Jason Giambi	1.00
49	Hideki Matsui	3.00
50	Eric Chavez	.40
51	Barry Zito	.60
52	Tim Hudson	.40
53	Mark Mulder	.40
54	Jim Thome	1.00
55	Pat Burrell	.40
56	Chase Utley	.40
57	Jason Kendall	.40
58	Jack Wilson	.25
59	Khalil Greene	.75
60	Brian Giles	.40
61	Jason Schmidt	.40
62	Marquis Grissom	.25
63	Ichiro Suzuki	2.00
64	Bret Boone	.40
65	Albert Pujols	2.50
66	Scott Rolen	1.00
67	Jim Edmonds	.40
68	Tino Martinez	.25
69	Rocco Baldelli	.60
70	Alfonso Soriano	1.00
71	Michael Young	.25
72	Hank Blalock	.40
73	Roy Halladay	.40
74	Carlos Delgado	.75
75	Vernon Wells	.40
76	Johnny Bench	5.00
77	Reggie Jackson	5.00
78	Al Kaline	3.00
79	Nolan Ryan	10.00
80	Tom Seaver	5.00
81	Robin Yount	6.00
82	Mike Schmidt	5.00
83	Jim Palmer	3.00
84	Harmon Killebrew	3.00
85	Joe Morgan	3.00
86	Kazuo Matsui RC	5.00
87	Luis Gonzalez RC	5.00
88	Yadier Molina RC	4.00
89	Jon Knott RC	5.00
90	Kevin Youkilis	5.00
91	Chris Saenz RC	3.00
92	Andres Blanco RC	3.00
93	David Aardsma	3.00
94	Merkin Valdez RC	3.00
95	Jason Bartlett RC	3.00
96	John Gall RC	3.00
97	Zack Greinke	3.00
98	Scott Hairston	3.00
99	Matt Holliday	4.00
100	Casey Kotchman	5.00

CF	Carlton Fisk	30.00
BG	Bob Gibson	40.00
AK	Al Kaline	50.00
TP	Tony Perez	30.00

Induction Ceremony Material Silver

NM/M

Common Player: 10.00
Numbered (two-digit) to induction year.
Masterpiece: No Pricing
Production One Set

SA	Sparky Anderson/100	10.00
RC	Rod Carew/91	15.00
OC	Orlando Cepeda/99	10.00
LD	Larry Doby/98	20.00
RF	Rollie Fingers/92	10.00
CF	Carlton Fisk/100	15.00
RJ	Reggie Jackson/93	10.00
AK	Al Kaline/80	20.00
BM	Bill Mazeroski/101	10.00
JM	Joe Morgan/90	10.00
PN	Phil Niekro/97	10.00
JP	Jim Palmer/90	10.00
TP	Tony Perez/100	15.00
PR	Phil Rizzuto/94	20.00
NR	Nolan Ryan/99	25.00
TS	Tom Seaver/92	10.00
RY	Robin Yount/99	10.00

Names of the Game

NM/M

Common Player: 2.00
Production 299 Sets

1	Nomar Garciaparra	8.00
2	Randy Johnson	3.00
3	Hideki Matsui	8.00
4	Frank Thomas	2.00
5	Ivan Rodriguez	2.00
6	Roger Clemens	5.00
7	Chipper Jones	5.00
8	Dontrelle Willis	2.00
9	Luis Gonzalez	2.00
10	Alex Rodriguez	8.00
11	Eric Gagne	2.00
12	Juan Gonzalez	2.00
13	Hideo Nomo	2.00
14	Sean Casey	2.00
15	Greg Maddux	5.00
16	Cal Ripken Jr.	15.00
17	Carl Yastrzemski	5.00
18	Tony Perez	3.00
19	Joe Morgan	3.00
20	Carlton Fisk	3.00
21	Willie McCovey	5.00
22	Al Kaline	5.00
23	Dennis Eckersley	3.00
24	Ted Williams	10.00
25	Willie Stargell	5.00
26	Rollie Fingers	3.00
27	Yogi Berra	2.00
28	Reggie Jackson	5.00
29	Harmon Killebrew	5.00
30	Nolan Ryan	10.00

Names of the Game Autograph Silver

NM/M

Common Player: 15.00
Stated Production 99 Sets
All 99 not released for some cards.
Gold: No Pricing
Stated Production 25 Sets
All 25 not released for some cards.

SC	Sean Casey	20.00
DE	Dennis Eckersley/90	25.00
RF	Rollie Fingers/90	15.00
CF	Carlton Fisk/50	30.00
LG	Luis Gonzalez/75	15.00
CJ	Chipper Jones/40	40.00
AK	Al Kaline/90	15.00
DW	Dontrelle Willis	25.00

Names of the Game Material Copper

NM/M

Common Player: 5.00
Production 250 Sets
Gold: .5-1.25X
Production 150 Sets
Red: .75-1.5X
Production 79 Sets
Purple: 1-2X
Production 33 Sets

YB	Yogi Berra	10.00

SC	Sean Casey	5.00
RC	Roger Clemens	10.00
DE	Dennis Eckersley	8.00
RF	Rollie Fingers	8.00
CF	Carlton Fisk	8.00
EG	Eric Gagne	10.00
JG	Juan Gonzalez	5.00
LG	Luis Gonzalez	5.00
RJA	Reggie Jackson	10.00
RJO	Randy Johnson	8.00
CJ	Chipper Jones	8.00
AK	Al Kaline	10.00
HK	Harmon Killebrew	10.00
GM	Greg Maddux	10.00
HM	Hideki Matsui	15.00
WM	Willie McCovey	10.00
JM	Joe Morgan	8.00
HN	Hideo Nomo	5.00
TP	Tony Perez	8.00
CR	Cal Ripken Jr.	30.00
IR	Ivan Rodriguez	5.00
NR	Nolan Ryan	20.00
WS	Willie Stargell	10.00
FT	Frank Thomas	5.00
TW	Ted Williams	25.00
DW	Dontrelle Willis	5.00
CY	Carl Yastrzemski	10.00

Rookie Autographs Notation

NM/M

Common Player: 15.00
Stated Production 750 Sets
75 Notation Cards for each player

87	Luis A. Gonzalez 4/6/04	15.00
89	Jon Knott 5/30/04	15.00
90	Kevin Youkilis 5/15/04	20.00
91	Chris Saenz 4/24/04	15.00
92	Andres Blanco 4/17/04	15.00
94	Merkin Valdez Jr. Giants	20.00
95	Jason Bartlett Go Twins	20.00
96B	John Gall Go Cards/50	20.00
98	Scott Hairston 5/17/04	15.00
100	Casey Kotchman 5/9/04	25.00

2004 Fleer L.A. Dodgers

Persons attending April 11 (#1-7), May 30 (#8-14) and July 10 (#15-21) special Baseball Card Pack promotional games received a cello-wrapped series of seven Tradition cards and a checklist card. Fronts have game-action photos with blue borders. Backs have major/minor league stats.

NM/M

Complete Set (22): 7.50
Common Player: .25

1	Hideo Nomo	1.50
2	Paul LoDuca	.50
3	Alex Cora	.25
4	Paul Shuey	.25
5	Juan Encarnacion	.25
6	Steve Colyer	.25
7	Joe Thurston	.25
8	Shawn Green	.35
9	Edwin Jackson	.50
10	Dave Roberts	.25
11	Guillermo Mota	.25
12	Jolbert Cabrera	.25
13	Darren Dreifort	.25
14	David Ross	.25
15	Eric Gagne	.35
16	Adrian Beltre	.35
17	Cesar Izturis	.25
18	Robin Ventura	.25
19	Wilson Alvarez	.25
20	Bubba Trammell	.25
21	Wilkin Ruan	.25
---	Checklist	.25

2004 Fleer Legacy

NM/M

Common Player (1-60): 1.50
Minor Stars (1-60): 2.00
Unlisted Stars (1-60): 2.50

Common Rookie (61-75): 4.00
Production 599 Sets
Box (1 Pack, 1 Autographed Baseball): 150.00

1	Angel Berroa	1.50
2	Derek Jeter	8.00
3	Jody Gerut	1.50
4	Curt Schilling	2.50
5	Khalil Greene	3.00
6	Manny Ramirez	3.00
7	Rocco Baldelli	2.50
8	Sammy Sosa	5.00
9	Shawn Green	2.00
10	Austin Kearns	2.50
11	Frank Thomas	3.00
12	Alfonso Soriano	4.00
13	Alex Rodriguez	6.00
14	Carlos Delgado	4.00
15	Chipper Jones	4.00
16	Edgar Martinez	2.00
17	Ivan Rodriguez	2.50
18	Mark Prior	4.00
19	Mike Piazza	4.00
20	Orlando Cabrera	1.50
21	Adam Dunn	2.50
22	Andruw Jones	3.00
23	Eric Chavez	2.00
24	Mark Teixeira	2.00
25	Scott Podsednik	1.50
26	Torii Hunter	2.50
27	Miguel Cabrera	3.00
28	Hideki Matsui	6.00
29	Jose Reyes	1.50
30	Vladimir Guerrero	3.00
31	Albert Pujols	6.00
32	Greg Maddux	3.00
33	Jason Giambi	3.00
34	Randy Johnson	3.00
35	Roger Clemens	6.00
36	Casey Kotchman	2.00
37	Ken Griffey Jr.	4.00
38	Todd Helton	3.00
39	Javy Lopez	1.50
40	Jim Thome	3.00
41	Josh Beckett	3.00
42	Kerry Wood	3.00
43	Scott Rolen	3.00
44	Pat Burrell	2.00
45	Pedro J. Martinez	3.00
46	Barry Zito	2.50
47	Hank Blalock	2.50
48	Hideo Nomo	4.00
49	Jeff Bagwell	3.00
50	Magglio Ordonez	2.00
51	Ichiro Suzuki	5.00
52	Joe Mauer	2.00
53	Richie Sexson	2.50
54	Shannon Stewart	1.50
55	Craig Wilson	1.50
56	Miguel Tejada	2.50
57	Sean Casey	1.50
58	Tom Glavine	2.00
59	Jason Schmidt	2.00
60	Nomar Garciaparra	6.00
61	Kazuo Matsui RC	8.00
62	Justin Leone RC	4.00
63	Merkin Valdez RC	6.00
64	Shingo Takatsu RC	6.00
65	Andres Blanco RC	4.00
66	Angel Chavez RC	4.00
67	Hector Gimenez RC	4.00
68	Akinori Otsuka RC	4.00
69	Jason Bartlett RC	4.00
70	Luis Gonzalez RC	4.00
71	Sean Henn	4.00
72	Mike Rouse	4.00
73	Chris Aguila RC	4.00
74	Aarom Baldiris RC	4.00
75	Jerry Gil RC	4.00

Gold Legacy

NM/M

Veterans (1-60): 2-4X
Rookies (61-75): .75-1.5X
Production 50 Sets

Ultimate Legacy

NM/M

No Pricing
Production One Set

Franchise Legacy Patch

NM/M

Common Player: 10.00
Production 99 Sets
Patch 50: .5-1.5X
Production 50 Sets
Patch 25: No Pricing
Production 25 Sets
Masterpiece: No Pricing
Production One Set

JBA	Jeff Bagwell	15.00
JBE	Josh Beckett	15.00
RC	Roger Clemens	25.00
VG	Vladimir Guerrero	15.00
RJ	Randy Johnson	20.00
CJ	Chipper Jones	20.00
JL	Javy Lopez	10.00
GM	Greg Maddux	30.00
PM	Pedro Martinez	15.00
HM	Hideki Matsui	60.00
KM	Kazuo Matsui	20.00
DM	Don Mattingly	40.00
HN	Hideo Nomo	20.00
MP	Mike Piazza	30.00
MPR	Mark Prior	10.00
AP	Albert Pujols	50.00
CR	Cal Ripken Jr.	60.00
IR	Ivan Rodriguez	15.00
NR	Nolan Ryan	50.00
SS	Sammy Sosa	30.00
MT	Miguel Tejada	10.00
JT	Jim Thome	15.00
KW	Kerry Wood	15.00

Franchise Dual Patch

No Pricing
Sequentially #'d between 5 & 31.

Franchise Legacy Quad Patch

No Pricing
Sequentially #'d between 2 & 22.

Hit Kings Patch Silver

NM/M

Common Player: 15.00
Production 99 Sets
Gold: .5-1.5X
Production 50 Sets
Masterpiece: No Pricing
Production One Set

JB	Jeff Bagwell	15.00
LB	Lance Berkman	15.00
HB	Hank Blalock	20.00
MC	Miguel Cabrera	20.00
CD	Carlos Delgado	20.00
AD	Adam Dunn	30.00
JG	Jason Giambi	15.00
VG	Vladimir Guerrero	20.00
CJ	Chipper Jones	20.00
AK	Austin Kearns	15.00
HM	Hideki Matsui	50.00
MP	Mike Piazza	25.00
AP	Albert Pujols	50.00
MR	Manny Ramirez	25.00
SR	Scott Rolen	20.00
MS	Mike Schmidt	40.00
RS	Richie Sexson	15.00
GS	Gary Sheffield	20.00
SS	Sammy Sosa	20.00
MT	Mark Teixeira	15.00
FT	Frank Thomas	15.00
JT	Jim Thome	25.00

Hit Kings Dual Patch

No Pricing
Sequentially numbered between 7 & 21.

2004 Fleer Kaz Matsui Special Edition

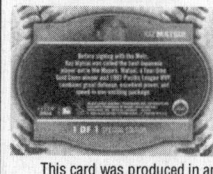

This card was produced in an edition of 25,000. It was available to customers presenting a sheet of the Fleer/N.Y. Post Mets cards at any Mets Team Store and purchasing a Fleer pack. The back is labeled "1 OF 1 SPECIAL EDITION."

NM/M

1	Kaz Matsui	3.00

2004 Fleer National Trading Card Day

As part of its participation in NTCD on April 3, Fleer issued a foil pack with four baseball player cards, two football and three basketball, plus a header. Only the baseball players are listed here. Fronts have game-action photos on a ghosted background; backs have recent stats and biographical data. The NTCD logo appears on both sides.

NM/M

Unopened Pack: 3.00
Common Player: .25

1	Derek Jeter	.50
2	Alex Rodriguez	.50
3	Nomar Garciaparra	.35
4	Jose Reyes	.25

2004 Fleer N.Y. Mets

Persons attending a special Baseball Card Pack promotional game received a cello-wrapped set of seven player cards and a header card. Fronts have game-action photos on a blue graph background. Backs have portrait and action photos and career highlights.

NM/M

Complete Set (8): 4.00
Common Player: .50

1	Mike Cameron	.50
2	Cliff Floyd	.50
3	Al Leiter	.50
4	Kaz Matsui	1.00
5	Mike Piazza	1.00
6	Jose Reyes	1.00
7	Shea Stadium	.50
---	Checklist	.05

2004 Fleer Patchworks

NM/M

Common Player (1-90): .15
Minor Stars: .40
Unlisted Stars: .60
Common Rookie (91-110): 2.00
Minor Rookies: 3.00
Unlisted Rookies: 5.00
Production 799 Sets
Pack (5): 4.00
Box (18): 70.00

1	Kerry Wood	1.00
2	Brian Giles	.40
3	Tino Martinez	.15
4	Mark Mulder	.40
5	Andy Pettitte	.60
6	Gary Sheffield	.60
7	Mark Teixeira	.40
8	Garret Anderson	.40
9	Craig Biggio	.40
10	Alfonso Soriano	1.50
11	Bret Boone	.40
12	Mike Piazza	2.00
13	Todd Helton	1.00
14	Jay Gibbons	.40
15	Eric Chavez	.40
16	Andruw Jones	1.00
17	Adam Dunn	.40
18	Corey Koskie	.15
19	Rafael Palmeiro	1.00
20	Ivan Rodriguez	.60
21	Tom Glavine	.40
22	Luis Gonzalez	.40
23	Miguel Tejada	.60
24	Jose Vidro	.15
25	Richie Sexson	.60
26	Roy Halladay	.40
27	Vladimir Guerrero	1.50
28	Randy Johnson	.40
29	Vernon Wells	.40
30	Pat Burrell	.40
31	Jason Schmidt	.40
32	Casey Blake	.15
33	Greg Maddux	2.00
34	Mike Lowell	.15
35	Hideo Nomo	.40
36	Carlos Delgado	1.00
37	Dontrelle Willis	.40
38	Shawn Green	.40
39	Pedro Martinez	1.50
40	Josh Beckett	1.00
41	Eric Gagne	.40
42	Manny Ramirez	1.00
43	Jim Edmonds	.40
44	Curt Schilling	.60
45	Mike Sweeney	.15
46	Albert Pujols	3.00
47	Nomar Garciaparra	3.00
48	Alex Rodriguez	3.00
49	Angel Berroa	.15
50	Jim Thome	1.50
51	Edgardo Alfonzo	.15
52	Jeremy Bonderman	.15
53	Miguel Cabrera	1.00
54	Bobby Higginson	.15
55	John Smoltz	.40
56	Jason Kendall	.40
57	Torii Hunter	.60
58	Troy Glaus	.60
59	Rafael Furcal	.40
60	Austin Kearns	.60
61	Esteban Loaiza	.15
62	Darin Erstad	.40
63	Jose Reyes	.15
64	Preston Wilson	.15
65	Rocco Baldelli	.60
66	Barry Zito	.60
67	Ken Griffey Jr.	2.00
68	Frank Thomas	1.00
69	Roger Clemens	2.00
70	Brett Myers	.15
71	Billy Wagner	.15
72	Scott Podsednik	.15
73	Jody Gerut	.15
74	Bartolo Colon	.40
75	Jeff Bagwell	1.00
76	Jason Giambi	1.50
77	Edgar Martinez	.40
78	Chipper Jones	2.00
79	Jason Bay	.15
80	Doug Mientkiewicz	.15
81	Hank Blalock	.60
82	Sammy Sosa	2.00
83	Derek Jeter	4.00
84	Ichiro Suzuki	2.00
85	Ben Sheets	.40
86	Magglio Ordonez	.40
87	Carlos Beltran	.40
88	Mark Prior	2.00
89	Sean Burroughs	.15
90	Tim Hudson	.40
91	Hector Gimenez RC	5.00
92	Khalil Greene RC	5.00
93	Rickie Weeks RC	5.00
94	Delmon Young	10.00
95	Donald Kelly RC	3.00
96	Chad Bentz RC	3.00
97	Greg Dobbs RC	3.00
98	John Gall RC	3.00
99	Cory Sullivan RC	3.00
100	Kazuo Matsui RC	8.00
101	Graham Koonce	3.00
102	Jason Bartlett RC	5.00
103	Angel Chavez RC	3.00
104	Ronny Cedeno RC	3.00
105	Jerry Gil RC	3.00
106	Ivan Ochoa RC	3.00
107	Ruddy Yan RC	4.00
108	Mike Gosling	2.00
109	Alfredo Simon RC	2.00
110	Koyie Hill RC	2.00

Ruby

Ruby (1-90): 3-10X
Ruby (91-110): .5-2X
Production 50 Sets

Autoworks

NM/M

Common Player: 10.00
Inserted 1:54
Parallel: .5-1.25X
Production 100 Sets
Patch
Production 10 Sets

1	Garret Anderson/145	15.00
2	Josh Beckett/148	30.00
3	Angel Berroa/145	20.00
4	Eric Gagne/193	20.00
5	Jody Gerut/376	10.00
6	Roy Halladay/286	10.00
7	Mark Mulder/190	15.00
8	Andy Pettitte/148	30.00
9	Scott Podsednik/146	20.00
10	Albert Pujols/193	120.00
11	Grady Sizemore/263	25.00
12	Miguel Tejada/164	20.00

By The Numbers

NM/M

Common Player: 3.00

Inserted 1:24		
Patch:		3-8X
Production 100 Sets		
1	Albert Pujols	8.00
2	Derek Jeter	10.00
3	Mike Piazza	6.00
4	Nomar Garciaparra	8.00
5	Eric Gagne	4.00
6	Sammy Sosa	6.00
7	Josh Beckett	4.00
8	Vladimir Guerrero	5.00
9	Jose Reyes	3.00
10	Bret Boone	3.00
11	Alex Rodriguez	8.00
12	Randy Johnson	6.00
13	Chipper Jones	6.00
14	Tim Hudson	4.00
15	Rocco Baldelli	4.00

Game-Used Level 1

		NM/M
Common Player:		6.00
Production 200 Sets		
Level 2:		1-1.5X
Production 100 Sets		
Patch:		1-2X
Production 50 Sets		
1	Albert Pujols	15.00
2	Andy Pettitte	6.00
3	Dontrelle Willis	6.00
4	Mike Piazza	10.00
5	Barry Zito	6.00
6	Troy Glaus	6.00
7	Carlos Delgado	8.00
8	Torii Hunter	6.00
9	Roy Halladay	6.00
10	Andruw Jones	8.00
11	Garret Anderson	6.00
12	Larry Walker	6.00
13	Shawn Green	6.00
14	Bernie Williams	6.00
15	Alfonso Soriano	10.00
16	Bret Boone	6.00
17	Hank Blalock	6.00
18	Jose Reyes	6.00
19	Mark Prior	10.00

Licensed Apparel

		NM/M
Common Player:		5.00
Production 300 Sets		
Team Name:		1-2X
Production 150 Sets		
Number:		1-2X
Production 100 Sets		
Nameplate:		1-30X
Production 50 Sets		
Jersey Tags:		
Production 10 Sets		
MLB Logo		
Production One Set		
1	Albert Pujols	15.00
2	Derek Jeter	18.00
3	Alex Rodriguez	15.00
4	Jim Thome	8.00
5	Mike Piazza	10.00
6	Dontrelle Willis	5.00
7	Torii Hunter	5.00
8	Tim Hudson	5.00
9	Sammy Sosa	12.00
10	Troy Glaus	5.00
11	Andruw Jones	8.00
12	Austin Kearns	5.00
13	Jeff Bagwell	8.00
14	Mark Prior	10.00
15	Bret Boone	5.00

National Pastime

		NM/M
Common Player:		5.00
Production 250 Sets		
Jersey:		1-1.5X
Production 350 Sets		
Gold Jersey:		1-2X
Production 200 Sets		
Patch:		1-30X
Production 100 Sets		
1	Albert Pujols	15.00

2	Alex Rodriguez	15.00
3	Derek Jeter	18.00
4	Nomar Garciaparra	15.00
5	Jim Thome	8.00
6	Chipper Jones	10.00
7	Mark Prior	10.00
8	Ichiro Suzuki	12.00
9	Jeff Bagwell	6.00
10	Troy Glaus	5.00
11	Randy Johnson	8.00
12	Sammy Sosa	12.00
13	Austin Kearns	5.00
14	Miguel Cabrera	6.00
15	Vladimir Guerrero	8.00

Stitches In Time

		NM/M
Common Player:		2.00
Inserted 1:12		
Jersey:		
Production 350 Sets		
Patch:		
Production 150 Sets		
1	Albert Pujols	5.00
2	Alex Rodriguez	5.00
3	Derek Jeter	6.00
4	Nomar Garciaparra	5.00
5	Jim Thome	3.00
6	Chipper Jones	3.00
7	Mark Prior	4.00
8	Eric Gagne	2.00
9	Jeff Bagwell	3.00
10	Troy Glaus	2.00
11	Randy Johnson	3.00
12	Sammy Sosa	4.00
13	Austin Kearns	2.00
14	Miguel Cabrera	3.00
15	Vladimir Guerrero	3.00
16	Mike Piazza	3.00
17	Jason Giambi	3.00
18	Tim Hudson	2.00
19	Carlos Delgado	3.00
20	Rocco Baldelli	2.00
21	Ichiro Suzuki	4.00
22	Barry Zito	2.00
23	Pedro Martinez	3.00
24	Torii Hunter	2.00
25	Andruw Jones	3.00

2004 Fleer Platinum

Vladimir Guerrero
MONTREAL EXPOS™ • OUTFIELD

		NM/M
Complete Set (200):		35.00
Common Player:		.15
Common SP (136-151):		.50
Inserted 1:3		
Pack (7):		2.00
Jumbo Pack (20):		5.00
Box (18 + 4 Jumbo):		55.00
1	Luis Castillo	.15
2	Preston Wilson	.15
3	Johan Santana	.15
4	Fred McGriff	.25
5	Albert Pujols	1.50
6	Reggie Sanders	.15
7	Ivan Rodriguez	.40
8	Roy Halladay	.25
9	Brian Giles	.25
10	Bernie Williams	.40
11	Barry Larkin	.25
12	Marlon Anderson	.15
13	Ramon Ortiz	.15
14	Luis Matos	.15
15	Esteban Loaiza	.15
16	Orlando Cabrera	.15
17	Jamie Moyer	.15
18	Tino Martinez	.15
19	Josh Beckett	.50
20	Derek Jeter	2.00

21	Derek Lowe	.15
22	Jack Wilson	.15
23	Bret Boone	.25
24	Matt Morris	.15
25	Javier Vazquez	.25
26	Joe Crede	.15
27	Jose Vidro	.15
28	Mike Piazza	1.00
29	Curt Schilling	.40
30	Alex Rodriguez	1.50
31	John Olerud	.25
32	Dontrelle Willis	.25
33	Larry Walker	.25
34	Joe Randa	.15
35	Paul LoDuca	.15
36	Marlon Byrd	.15
37	Bo Hart	.15
38	Rafael Palmeiro	.50
39	Garret Anderson	.40
40	Tom Glavine	.25
41	Ichiro Suzuki	1.25
42	Derek Lee	.25
43	Lance Berkman	.25
44	Nomar Garciaparra	1.50
45	Mike Sweeney	.25
46	A.J. Burnett	.15
47	Sean Casey	.15
48	Eric Gagne	.25
49	Joel Pineiro	.15
50	Russ Ortiz	.15
51	Placido Polanco	.15
52	Sammy Sosa	1.25
53	Mark Teixeira	.25
54	Randy Wolf	.15
55	Vladimir Guerrero	.75
56	Tim Hudson	.25
57	Lew Ford	.15
58	Carlos Delgado	.50
59	Darin Erstad	.25
60	Mike Lieberthal	.15
61	Craig Biggio	.25
62	Ryan Klesko	.25
63	C.C. Sabathia	.15
64	Carlos Lee	.15
65	Al Leiter	.15
66	Brandon Webb	.15
67	Jacque Jones	.15
68	Kerry Wood	.50
69	Omar Vizquel	.15
70	Jeremy Bonderman	.15
71	Kevin Brown	.25
72	Richie Sexson	.40
73	Zach Day	.15
74	Mike Mussina	.40
75	Sidney Ponson	.15
76	Andruw Jones	.50
77	Woody Williams	.15
78	Kazuhiro Sasaki	.15
79	Matt Clement	.15
80	Shea Hillenbrand	.15
81	Bartolo Colon	.25
82	Ken Griffey Jr.	1.00
83	Todd Helton	.50
84	Dmitri Young	.15
85	Richard Hidalgo	.15
86	Carlos Beltran	.25
87	Brad Wilkerson	.15
88	Andy Pettitte	.40
89	Miguel Tejada	.25
90	Edgar Martinez	.25
91	Vernon Wells	.25
92	Magglio Ordonez	.25
93	Tony Batista	.15
94	Jose Reyes	.15
95	Matt Stairs	.15
96	Manny Ramirez	.50
97	Carlos Pena	.15
98	A.J. Pierzynski	.15
99	Jim Thome	.75
100	Aubrey Huff	.15
101	Roberto Alomar	.40
102	Luis Gonzalez	.25
103	Chipper Jones	1.00
104	Jay Gibbons	.25
105	Adam Dunn	.40
106	Jay Payton	.15
107	Scott Podsednik	.40
108	Roy Oswalt	.25
109	Milton Bradley	.25
110	Shawn Green	.25
111	Ryan Wagner	.15
112	Eric Chavez	.25
113	Pat Burrell	.25
114	Frank Thomas	.50
115	Jason Kendall	.25
116	Jake Peavy	.15
117	Mike Cameron	.15
118	Jim Edmonds	.25
119	Hank Blalock	.40
120	Troy Glaus	.40
121	Jeff Kent	.25
122	Jason Schmidt	.25
123	Corey Patterson	.25
124	Austin Kearns	.40
125	Edwin Jackson	.25
126	Alfonso Soriano	.75
127	Bobby Abreu	.25
128	Scott Rolen	.75
129	Jeff Bagwell	.50
130	Shannon Stewart	.15
131	Rich Aurilia	.15
132	Ty Wigginton	.15
133	Randy Johnson	.75
134	Rocco Baldelli	.40
135	Hideo Nomo	.25
136	Greg Maddux	2.00
137	Johnny Damon	1.50
138	Mark Prior	.75

139	Corey Koskie	.50
140	Miguel Cabrera	1.50
141	Hideki Matsui	2.00
142	Jose Cruz	.50
143	Barry Zito	.50
144	Javy Lopez	.50
145	Jason Varitek	1.00
146	Moises Alou	1.00
147	Torii Hunter	1.00
148	Juan Encarnacion	.50
149	Jorge Posada	1.00
150	Marquis Grissom	1.00
151	Rich Harden	1.00
152	Gary Sheffield	4.00
153	Pedro J. Martinez	5.00
154	Brad Radke	3.00
155	Mike Lowell	3.00
156	Jason Giambi	4.00
157	Mark Mulder	4.00
158	Ben Weber	.15
159	Mark DeRosa	.15
160	Melvin Mora	.15
161	Bill Mueller	.15
162	Jon Garland	.15
163	Jody Gerut	.15
164	Javier Lopez	.15
165	Craig Monroe	.15
166	Juan Pierre	.15
167	Morgan Ensberg	.15
168	Angel Berroa	.15
169	Geoff Jenkins	.25
170	Matt LeCroy	.15
171	Livan Hernandez	.15
172	Jason L. Phillips	.15
173	Mariano Rivera	.25
174	Erubiel Durazo	.15
175	Jason Michaels	.15
176	Kip Wells	.15
177	Ray Durham	.15
178	Randy Winn	.15
179	Edgar Renteria	.15
180	Carl Crawford	.15
181	Laynce Nix	.15
182	Greg Myers	.15
183	Delmon Young, Chad Gaudin	1.00
184	Humberto Quintero, Bernie Castro	.50
185	Craig Brazell, Daniel Garcia	.50
186	Ryan Wing, Francisco Cruceta	.50
187	William Bergolla RC, Josh Hall	.50
188	Clint Barmes, Garrett Atkins	.50
189	Chris Bootcheck, Richard Fischer	.50
190	Edgar Gonzalez, Matt Kata	.50
191	Andrew Brown, Koyie Hill	.50
192	John Gall RC, Dan Haren	.50
193	Chad Bentz RC, Luis Ayala	.50
194	Hector Gimenez RC, Eric Bruntlett	.50
195	Boof Bonser, Rob Bowen	.50
196	Chris Snelling, Rett Johnson	.50
197	Rickie Weeks, Adam Morrissey	1.00
198	Noah Lowry, Todd Linden	.50
199	Chris Waters, Brett Evert	.50
200	Jorge DePaula, Chien-Ming Wang	.50

Finish

Barry Zito
OAKLAND ATHLETICS™ • PITCHER

		NM/M
Stars (1-200):		4-6X
Production 100 Sets		

Big Signs

		NM/M
Complete Set (15):		25.00
Common Player:		.75
Inserted 1:9		
1	Albert Pujols	3.00
2	Derek Jeter	4.00
3	Mike Piazza	2.00
4	Jason Giambi	1.50
5	Ichiro Suzuki	2.50
6	Nomar Garciaparra	3.00
7	Mark Prior	2.00
8	Randy Johnson	1.50
9	Greg Maddux	2.00
10	Sammy Sosa	2.50
11	Ken Griffey Jr.	2.00
12	Dontrelle Willis	.75

RANGERS
RODRIGUEZ

13	Alex Rodriguez	3.00
14	Chipper Jones	2.00
15	Hank Blalock	.75

Big Signs Autographs

		NM/M
Production 100		
	Hank Blalock	25.00
	Albert Pujols	150.00
	Dontrelle Willis	25.00

Classic Combinations

		NM/M
Complete Set (10):		50.00
Common Player:		3.00
Inserted 1:108		
1	Ivan Rodriguez, Mike Piazza	6.00
2	Alex Rodriguez, Sammy Sosa	8.00
3	Dontrelle Willis, Angel Berroa	3.00
4	Nomar Garciaparra, Derek Jeter	10.00
5	Ichiro Suzuki, Hideo Nomo	6.00
6	Josh Beckett, Kerry Wood	4.00
7	Albert Pujols, Carlos Delgado	8.00
8	Alfonso Soriano, Joe Morgan	4.00
9	Jason Giambi, Reggie Jackson	4.00
10	Nolan Ryan, Tom Seaver	10.00

Clubhouse Memorabilia

		NM/M
Common Player:		5.00
Inserted 1:24		
	Rocco Baldelli	5.00
	Josh Beckett	8.00
	Hank Blalock	5.00
	Nomar Garciaparra	12.00
	Jason Giambi	8.00
	Vladimir Guerrero	8.00
	Todd Helton	6.00
	Torii Hunter	5.00
	Derek Jeter	15.00
	Chipper Jones	8.00
	Austin Kearns	6.00
	Greg Maddux	10.00
	Hideo Nomo	8.00
	Mike Piazza	8.00
	Mark Prior	10.00
	Albert Pujols	12.00
	Alex Rodriguez	10.00
	Richie Sexson	5.00
	Alfonso Soriano	6.00
	Sammy Sosa	12.00
	Miguel Tejada	5.00
	Jim Thome	8.00
	Dontrelle Willis	8.00

Clubhouse Memorabilia Dual

		NM/M
Common Player:		10.00
Production 50 Sets		
	Hank Blalock	15.00
	Nomar Garciaparra	30.00
	Jason Giambi	15.00
	Vladimir Guerrero	20.00
	Todd Helton	20.00
	Torii Hunter	15.00
	Derek Jeter	35.00
	Chipper Jones	15.00
	Austin Kearns	10.00
	Greg Maddux	30.00
	Hideo Nomo	25.00
	Mark Prior	20.00
	Albert Pujols	30.00
	Alex Rodriguez	25.00
	Sammy Sosa	20.00
	Jim Thome	20.00

Nameplates

		NM/M
Common Player:		8.00
Inserted 1:4 Jumbo		
Varying quantities produced.		

Mets
NAME PLATES
JOSE REYES

1	Austin Kearns	10.00
2	Juan Pierre	10.00
3	Albert Pujols	30.00
4	Manny Ramirez	15.00
5	Kerry Wood	20.00
6	Alex Rodriguez	20.00
7	Barry Zito	10.00
8	Hee Seop Choi	8.00
9	Kevin Brown	10.00
10	Jose Reyes	15.00
11	Marlon Byrd	10.00
12	Nomar Garciaparra	20.00
13	Josh Beckett	15.00
14	Hideo Nomo	15.00
15	Randy Johnson	15.00
16	Hank Blalock	12.00
17	Tom Glavine/25	25.00
18	Luis Castillo	8.00
19	Mark Teixeira	12.00
20	Gary Sheffield	10.00
21	Richie Sexson	10.00
22	Miguel Cabrera	20.00
23	Sammy Sosa	25.00
24	Curt Schilling	10.00
25	Chipper Jones	20.00

Portraits

CUBS
Platinum Portraits
MARK PRIOR

		NM/M
Complete Set (10):		25.00
Common Player:		1.50
Inserted 1:18		
1	Jason Giambi	1.50
2	Nomar Garciaparra	4.00
3	Vladimir Guerrero	1.50
4	Mark Prior	3.00
5	Jim Thome	1.50
6	Derek Jeter	5.00
7	Sammy Sosa	3.00
8	Alex Rodriguez	4.00
9	Greg Maddux	2.50
10	Albert Pujols	4.00

Portraits Jersey

		NM/M
Common Player:		8.00
Inserted 1:48		
	Nomar Garciaparra	15.00
	Jason Giambi	8.00
	Vladimir Guerrero	8.00
	Derek Jeter	15.00
	Greg Maddux	8.00
	Mark Prior	6.00
	Albert Pujols	15.00
	Alex Rodriguez	10.00
	Sammy Sosa	12.00
	Jim Thome	8.00

Portraits Patch

		NM/M
Common Player:		10.00
Production 100 Sets		
	Nomar Garciaparra	20.00
	Jason Giambi	10.00
	Vladimir Guerrero	10.00
	Derek Jeter	25.00
	Mark Prior	20.00
	Albert Pujols	30.00
	Alex Rodriguez	15.00
	Sammy Sosa	20.00
	Jim Thome	12.00

Scouting Report

		NM/M
Complete Set (15):		35.00
Common Player:		1.50
Production 400 Sets		
1	Josh Beckett	2.00
2	Todd Helton	2.00

3	Rocco Baldelli	2.00
4	Pedro J. Martinez	3.00
5	Jeff Bagwell	2.00
6	Mark Prior	4.00
7	Ichiro Suzuki	4.00
8	Barry Zito	2.00
9	Manny Ramirez	2.00
10	Miguel Cabrera	2.00
11	Richie Sexson	1.50
12	Hideki Matsui	8.00
13	Magglio Ordonez	1.50
14	Brandon Webb	1.50
15	Kerry Wood	2.00

Scouting Report Memorabilia

	NM/M
Common Player:	6.00
Production 250 Sets	
Jeff Bagwell	8.00
Rocco Baldelli	8.00
Josh Beckett	8.00
Todd Helton	6.00
Pedro J. Martinez	8.00
Mark Prior	10.00
Manny Ramirez	6.00
Brandon Webb	8.00
Kerry Wood	8.00

2004 Fleer Showcase

	NM/M
Complete Set (130):	.25
Common Player:	.25
Common SP (101-130):	1.00
Inserted 1:6	
Pack (5):	4.50
Box (24):	90.00

1	Corey Patterson	.25
2	Ken Griffey Jr.	1.50
3	Preston Wilson	.40
4	Juan Pierre	.25
5	Jose Reyes	.50
6	Jason Schmidt	.40
7	Rocco Baldelli	.50
8	Carlos Delgado	.75
9	Hideki Matsui	2.50
10	Nomar Garciaparra	2.00
11	Brian Giles	.40
12	Darin Erstad	.40
13	Larry Walker	.50
14	Bernie Williams	.50
15	Laynce Nix	.50
16	Manny Ramirez	.75
17	Magglio Ordonez	.50
18	Khalil Greene	.25
19	Jim Edmonds	.40
20	Troy Glaus	.50
21	Curt Schilling	.50
22	Chipper Jones	1.50
23	Sammy Sosa	2.00
24	Frank Thomas	.75
25	Todd Helton	.75
26	Craig Biggio	.40
27	Shannon Stewart	.40
28	Mark Mulder	.40
29	Mike Lieberthal	.25
30	Reggie Sanders	.25
31	Edgar Martinez	.25
32	Bo Hart	.25
33	Mark Teixeira	.40
34	Jay Gibbons	.25
35	Roberto Alomar	.50
36	Kip Wells	.25
37	J.D. Drew	.40
38	Jason Varitek	.25
39	Craig Monroe	.25
40	Roy Oswalt	.40
41	Edgardo Alfonzo	.25
42	Roy Halladay	.50
43	Gary Sheffield	.50
44	Lance Berkman	.50
45	Torii Hunter	.50
46	Vladimir Guerrero	1.00
47	Marlon Byrd	.25
48	Austin Kearns	.50
49	Angel Berroa	.25
50	Geoff Jenkins	.50
51	Aubrey Huff	.25

52	Dontrelle Willis	.50
53	Tony Batista	.25
54	Shawn Green	.40
55	Jason Kendall	.25
56	Garret Anderson	.50
57	Andruw Jones	.75
58	Dmitri Young	.25
59	Richie Sexson	.50
60	Jorge Posada	.50
61	Bobby Abreu	.40
62	Vernon Wells	.40
63	Javy Lopez	.40
64	Josh Beckett	.75
65	Eric Chavez	.40
66	Tim Salmon	.40
67	Brandon Webb	.40
68	Pedro J. Martinez	1.00
69	Kerry Wood	1.00
70	Jose Vidro	.25
71	Alfonso Soriano	1.00
72	Barry Zito	.50
73	Sean Burroughs	.25
74	Jamie Moyer	.25
75	Luis Gonzalez	.40
76	Adam Dunn	.50
77	Mike Piazza	1.50
78	Pat Burrell	.50
79	Scott Rolen	1.00
80	Milton Bradley	.25
81	Mike Sweeney	.50
82	Hank Blalock	.50
83	Esteban Loaiza	.25
84	Hideo Nomo	.50
85	Derek Jeter	3.00
86	Albert Pujols	2.50
87	Greg Maddux	1.50
88	Mark Prior	1.50
89	Mike Lowell	.25
90	Jeff Bagwell	.75
91	Scott Podsednik	.50
92	Tom Glavine	.50
93	Jason Giambi	1.00
94	Jim Thome	1.00
95	Ichiro Suzuki	2.00
96	Randy Johnson	1.00
97	Omar Vizquel	.25
98	Ivan Rodriguez	.50
99	Miguel Tejada	.50
100	Alex Rodriguez	2.50
101	Rickie Weeks	3.00
102	Chad Gaudin	1.00
103	Rich Harden	1.00
104	Edwin Jackson	1.50
105	Chien-Ming Wang	1.00
106	Matt Kata	1.00
107	Delmon Young	3.00
108	Ryan Wagner	1.00
109	Jeff Duncan	1.00
110	Prentice Redman	1.00
111	Clint Barmes	1.00
112	Jeremy Guthrie	1.00
113	Brian Stokes	1.00
114	David DeJesus	1.00
115	Felix Sanchez	1.00
116	Josh Stewart	1.00
117	Daniel Garcia	1.00
118	Jon Leicester	1.00
119	Francisco Cruceta	1.00
120	Oscar Villarreal	1.00
121	Michael Hessman	1.00
122	Michel Hernandez	1.00
123	Richard Fischer	1.00
124	Robby Hammock	1.00
125	Guillermo Quiroz	1.00
126	Craig Brazell	1.00
127	Wilfredo Ledezma	1.00
128	Josh Willingham	1.00
129	Ramon Nivar	1.00
130	Matt Diaz	1.00

Legacy

Stars (1-100):	4-8X
SP's (101-130):	1-30X
Production 99 Sets	

Masterpiece

	01/01

No Pricing	
Production One Set	

Albert Pujols Legacy Collection

	NM/M
Complete Set (10):	60.00
Common Pujols:	8.00
Production 1,000 Sets	
1 Albert Pujols	8.00
2 Albert Pujols	8.00

3	Albert Pujols	8.00
4	Albert Pujols	8.00
5	Albert Pujols	8.00
6	Albert Pujols	8.00
7	Albert Pujols	8.00
8	Albert Pujols	8.00
9	Albert Pujols	8.00
10	Albert Pujols	8.00

Albert Pujols Legacy Coll. Auto.
Varying quantities produced.
No Pricing

Albert Pujols Legacy Coll. Jersey

	NM/M
Varying quantities produced.	
3 Albert Pujols/30	40.00
4 Albert Pujols/40	30.00
5 Albert Pujols/50	30.00
6 Albert Pujols/60	30.00
7 Albert Pujols/70	25.00
8 Albert Pujols/80	25.00
9 Albert Pujols/90	25.00
10 Albert Pujols/100	25.00

Baseball's Best

	NM/M
Complete Set (15):	20.00
Common Player:	.75
Inserted 1:24	
1 Derek Jeter	4.00
2 Mark Prior	2.00
3 Mike Piazza	2.50
4 Jeff Bagwell	1.00
5 Kerry Wood	1.00
6 Ivan Rodriguez	1.00
7 Albert Pujols	3.00
8 Jim Thome	1.50
9 Sammy Sosa	2.50
10 Vladimir Guerrero	1.50
11 Eric Gagne	.75
12 Randy Johnson	1.50
13 Todd Helton	1.00
14 Chipper Jones	1.00
15 Alex Rodriguez	4.00

Baseball's Best Memorabilia

	NM/M
Common Player:	5.00
Inserted 1:72	
Parallel 150:	.75-1.5X
Production 150	
Parallel 50:	1.5-2X
Patch Versions:	2-4X
Production 50	
Derek Jeter	15.00
Mark Prior	10.00
Mike Piazza	10.00
Jeff Bagwell	8.00
Kerry Wood	8.00
Ivan Rodriguez	5.00
Albert Pujols	15.00
Jim Thome	8.00
Sammy Sosa	10.00
Vladimir Guerrero	8.00
Eric Gagne	8.00
Randy Johnson	8.00
Todd Helton	8.00
Chipper Jones	8.00
Alex Rodriguez	10.00

Grace

	NM/M
Complete Set (20):	20.00
Common Player:	.75
Inserted 1:12	
1 Kerry Wood	1.50
2 Derek Jeter	4.00
3 Nomar Garciaparra	3.00
4 Mike Piazza	2.50
5 Mark Prior	2.00
6 Jose Reyes	1.00
7 Dontrelle Willis	.75
8 Pedro J. Martinez	1.50
9 Tim Hudson	.75
10 Troy Glaus	.75
11 Hank Blalock	1.00
12 Albert Pujols	3.00
13 Juan Pierre	.75
14 Angel Berroa	.75
15 Rocco Baldelli	1.00
16 Carlos Delgado	1.00
17 Manny Ramirez	1.00
18 Alex Rodriguez	3.00
19 Andruw Jones	1.00
20 Luis Gonzalez	.75

Grace Memorabilia

	NM/M
Common Player:	5.00
Inserted 1:48	
Parallel 150:	1-1.5X
Production 150	
Patch:	1.5-2.5X
Production 50	
Derek Jeter	15.00
Nomar Garciaparra	10.00
Mike Piazza	10.00
Mark Prior	9.00
Dontrelle Willis	5.00
Pedro J. Martinez	8.00
Albert Pujols	15.00
Rocco Baldelli	8.00
Manny Ramirez	8.00
Alex Rodriguez	10.00

Hot Gloves

	NM/M
Common Player:	8.00
Inserted 1:288	
1 Derek Jeter	40.00
2 Nomar Garciaparra	30.00
3 Alex Rodriguez	30.00
4 Chipper Jones	15.00
5 Torii Hunter	8.00
6 Ichiro Suzuki	35.00
7 Mark Prior	15.00
8 Vladimir Guerrero	15.00
9 Albert Pujols	30.00
10 Ivan Rodriguez	10.00
11 Hideki Matsui	30.00
12 Sammy Sosa	25.00
13 Jim Thome	15.00
14 Rocco Baldelli	10.00
15 Jeff Bagwell	10.00

Hot Gloves Memorabilia

	NM/M
Common Player:	20.00
All jerseys unless noted.	
Production 50 Sets	
Derek Jeter	60.00
Nomar Garciaparra	50.00
Alex Rodriguez	40.00
Chipper Jones	40.00
Ichiro Suzuki/Base	65.00
Mark Prior	25.00
Vladimir Guerrero	30.00
Albert Pujols	50.00
Ivan Rodriguez	20.00
Hideki Matsui/Base	60.00
Sammy Sosa	40.00
Jim Thome	20.00
Rocco Baldelli	20.00
Jeff Bagwell	20.00

Sweet Sigs

	NM/M
Common Player:	6.00
Inserted 1:24	
Sweet Sigs Game-Used:	No Pricing
Production 5	
Hank Blalock/824	20.00
Taylor Bucholz/Redemp.	6.00
John Gall/Redemp.	8.00
Bo Hart/667	15.00
Torii Hunter/294	9.00
Austin Kearns/224	20.00
Wilfredo Ledezma/376	6.00
Mike Lowell/44	15.00
Corey Patterson/176	15.00
Carlos Pena/48	15.00
Albert Pujols/Redemp.	120.00
Jose Reyes/115	40.00
Scott Rolen/200	25.00
Michael Ryan/288	12.00
Miguel Tejada/52	20.00
Ryan Wagner/Redemp.	10.00
Brandon Webb/1,000	15.00
Rickie Weeks/416	15.00
Josh Willingham/180	15.00
Dontrelle Willis/26	60.00
Delmon Young/1,000	25.00
Barry Zito/248	25.00

2004 Fleer Sweet Sigs

	NM/M
Common Player (1-75):	.20
Minor Stars (1-75):	.40

Unlisted Star (1-75):		.60
Common Future Sig-cess		
(76-100):		3.00
Future Sig-cess Production 999 Sets		
Pack (6):		5.00
Box (12):		80.00
1	Manny Ramirez	1.00
2	Frank Thomas	1.00
3	Josh Beckett	1.00
4	Shawn Green	.40
5	Tom Glavine	.40
6	Marquis Grissom	.20
7	Nomar Garciaparra	3.00
8	Magglio Ordonez	.40
9	Alex Rodriguez	3.00
10	Chipper Jones	2.00
11	Jody Gerut	.40
12	Dontrelle Willis	.40
13	Lance Berkman	.40
14	Jose Vidro	.20
15	Barry Zito	.60
16	Jason Kendall	.20
17	Scott Rolen	1.50
18	Troy Glaus	.60
19	Brandon Webb	.20
20	Tim Hudson	.40
21	Shannon Stewart	.20
22	Darin Erstad	.40
23	Curt Schilling	.60
24	Bret Boone	.40
25	Richie Sexson	.60
26	Hideki Matsui	3.00
27	Albert Pujols	3.00
28	Greg Maddux	2.00
29	Austin Kearns	.60
30	Todd Helton	1.00
31	Miguel Cabrera	1.00
32	Jeff Bagwell	.60
33	Marlon Byrd	.20
34	Ichiro Suzuki	2.50
35	Rocco Baldelli	.60
36	Garret Anderson	.40
37	Javy Lopez	.40
38	Kerry Wood	1.00
39	Adam Dunn	.60
40	Geoff Jenkins	.20
41	Derek Jeter	4.00
42	Rich Harden	.20
43	Alfonso Soriano	1.50
44	Ken Griffey Jr.	.60
45	Ivan Rodriguez	.60
46	Pedro J. Martinez	.60
47	Andy Pettitte	.60
48	Gary Sheffield	.20
49	Brian Giles	.40
50	Carlos Delgado	1.00
51	Mike Piazza	1.50
52	Hank Blalock	.60
53	Roger Clemens	.20
54	Scott Podsednik	.20
55	Torii Hunter	.40
56	Jose Reyes	.20
57	Jim Thome	1.50
58	Jason Schmidt	.40
59	Jose Cruz	.20
60	Mark Teixeira	.40
61	Randy Johnson	1.50
62	Miguel Tejada	.60
63	Sammy Sosa	2.50
64	Larry Walker	.40
65	Carl Everett	.20
66	Luis Castillo	.20
67	Jason Giambi	1.50
68	Mike Sweeney	.20
69	Andruw Jones	.40
70	Vladimir Guerrero	1.50
71	J.D. Drew	.40
72	Mark Prior	2.00
73	Angel Berroa	.20
74	Hideo Nomo	.40
75	Roy Halladay	.40
76	Gm Gall RC	3.00
77	Angel Chavez RC	3.00
78	Alfredo Simon RC	3.00
79	Merkin Valdez RC	3.00
80	Chad Bentz RC	3.00
81	Justin Leone RC	6.00
82	Mike Rouse RC	3.00
83	Aarom Baldiris RC	3.00
84	Chris Shelton RC	8.00
85	Akinori Otsuka RC	6.00
86	Ruddy Yan RC	3.00
87	Ramon Ramirez RC	3.00
88	Hector Gimenez RC	6.00
89	Mike Gosling RC	3.00
90	Greg Dobbs RC	3.00
91	Kazuo Matsui RC	8.00
92	Donald Kelly RC	6.00
93	Shingo Takatsu RC	6.00
94	Ivan Ochoa RC	5.00
95	Chris Aguila RC	5.00
96	Jason Bartlett RC	3.00
97	Graham Koonce RC	5.00
98	Ronny Cedeno RC	3.00
99	Jerome Gamble RC	3.00
100	Onil Joseph RC	3.00

Black
(1-100):	No Pricing
Production Five Sets	

Gold

(1-75):	1-5X
(76-100):	.5-2X
Production 99 Sets	

Ballpark Heroes

	NM/M
Common Player:	1.25
Inserted 1:6	
1 Rocco Baldelli	1.75
2 Adam Dunn	1.75
3 Nomar Garciaparra	5.00
4 Ken Griffey Jr.	3.50
5 Vladimir Guerrero	3.00
6 Torii Hunter	1.75
7 Andruw Jones	2.00
8 Mike Piazza	3.50
9 Alfonso Soriano	3.00
10 Frank Thomas	2.00
11 Dontrelle Willis	1.25
12 Barry Zito	1.75
13 Javy Lopez	1.25
14 Miguel Cabrera	2.00
15 Kazuo Matsui	3.50
16 Josh Beckett	2.00
17 Derek Jeter	6.00
18 Greg Maddux	3.50
19 Pedro J. Martinez	3.00
20 Hideo Nomo	1.25
21 Mark Prior	4.00
22 Albert Pujols	5.00
23 Alex Rodriguez	5.00
24 Scott Rolen	3.00
25 Ichiro Suzuki	4.00

Ballpark Heroes Duals
No Pricing
Sequentially Numbered

Ballpark Heroes Quad

		NM/M
Sequentially Numbered		
1	Josh Beckett, Greg Maddux, Pedro J. Martinez, Mark Prior/42	150.00
2	Dontrelle Willis, Kazuo Matsui, Miguel Cabrera, Rocco Baldelli/24	75.00
4	Dontrelle Willis, Josh Beckett, Derek Jeter, Alex Rodriguez/32	150.00
5	Albert Pujols, Vladimir Guerrero, Mike Piazza, Alex Rodriguez/37	150.00

Ballpark Heroes Black Patch

	NM/M
Sequentially Numbered	
MP Mike Piazza/31	50.00

Ballpark Heroes Copper Jersey

	NM/M
Common Player:	5.00
Production 110 Sets	
Gold Patch:	1-30X
Production 50 Sets	
Masterpiece Version:	No Pricing
Production One Set	
RB Rocco Baldelli/110	5.00
MC Miguel Cabrera/110	6.00
AD Adam Dunn/110	5.00
VG Vladimir Guerrero/110	8.00

GM	Greg Maddux/110	10.00
PM	Pedro J. Martinez/110	8.00
HN	Hideo Nomo/110	5.00
MP	Mike Piazza/110	10.00
AP	Albert Pujols/110	15.00
SR	Scott Rolen/110	8.00
AS	Alfonso Soriano/110	8.00
FT	Frank Thomas/110	6.00
DW	Dontrelle Willis/110	5.00
BZ	Barry Zito/110	5.00

Ballpark Heroes Silver Jersey

NM/M
Common Player: 4.00
Sequentially Numbered

RB	Rocco Baldelli/250	4.00
MC	Miguel Cabrera/196	5.00
AD	Adam Dunn/215	4.00
VG	Vladimir Guerrero/200	6.00
GM	Greg Maddux/224	8.00
PM	Pedro J. Martinez/239	6.00
HN	Hideo Nomo/210	4.00
MP	Mike Piazza/163	8.00
AP	Albert Pujols/199	12.00
SR	Scott Rolen/221	6.00
AS	Alfonso Soriano/235	6.00
FT	Frank Thomas/242	5.00
DW	Dontrelle Willis/186	4.00
BZ	Barry Zito/195	4.00

Sweet Sigs Copper

NM/M
Common Player: 10.00
Sequentially Numbered
Gold: .75-1.5X
Production 30 Sets
Hideo Nomo #'d to 10.
No Roger Clemens or Ted Williams.
Gold card.
Masterpiece: No Pricing
Production One Set

GA	Garret Anderson/100	20.00
RB	Rocco Baldelli/75	25.00
JB	Josh Beckett/75	30.00
CB	Carlos Beltran/75	20.00
LB	Lance Berkman/75	20.00
AB	Angel Berroa/75	20.00
JB	Jeremy Bonderman/150	15.00
MC	Miguel Cabrera/150	30.00
MC	Mike Cameron/150	20.00
RC	Roger Clemens/52	400.00
CC	Carl Crawford/150	15.00
JD	Johnny Damon/100	30.00
JD	J.D. Drew/98	40.00
DE	Dennis Eckersley/75	40.00
AE	Adam Everett/150	10.00
JF	Julio Franco/150	30.00
LG	Luis Gonzalez/150	15.00
KG	Khalil Greene/150	40.00
VG	Vladimir Guerrero/75	75.00
TH	Torii Hunter/150	25.00
EJ	Edwin Jackson/75	15.00
RJ	Randy Johnson/28	150.00
CJ	Chipper Jones/50	100.00
MK	Matt Kata/150	10.00
BL	Barry Larkin/50	50.00
CL	Carlos Lee/150	15.00
AL	Al Leiter/75	25.00
KL	Kenny Lofton/50	50.00
JL	Javy Lopez/75	25.00
GM	Greg Maddux/50	75.00
PM	Pedro J. Martinez/75	125.00
JM	Joe Mauer/150	40.00
WM	Wade Miller/150	20.00
KM	Kevin Millwood/100	15.00
PM	Paul Molitor/75	40.00
SM	Stan Musial/25	80.00
MM	Mike Mussina/50	40.00
LN	Lance Niekro/75	10.00
JO	John Olerud/75	30.00
MO	Magglio Ordonez/150	20.00
RO	Russ Ortiz/150	15.00
RO	Roy Oswalt/150	20.00
AO	Akinori Otsuka/150	20.00
BP	Brad Penny/150	10.00
AP	Andy Pettitte/50	40.00
MP	Mike Piazza/50	120.00
AP	Albert Pujols/73	300.00
BR	Brad Radke/100	20.00
JR	Jose Reyes/163	30.00
AR	Alexis Rios/150	15.00
NR	Nolan Ryan/50	300.00
CS	C.C. Sabathia/150	20.00
TS	Tim Salmon/100	40.00
DS	Deion Sanders/150	50.00
JS	Johan Santana/150	80.00
MS	Mike Schmidt/50	60.00
SS	Shannon Stewart/75	30.00
FT	Frank Thomas/75	75.00
JV	Jason Varitek/75	20.00
TW	Tim Wakefield/150	30.00
VW	Vernon Wells/150	20.00
BW	Bernie Williams/50	80.00
DW	Dontrelle Willis/150	20.00
KW	Kerry Wood/75	60.00
CY	Carl Yastrzemski/50	100.00
BZ	Barry Zito/44	30.00

Sweet Sigs Jersey Number

NM/M
No. 3-25: 1-30X Copper
No. 26-57: .75-1.5X Copper
Numbered to player's jersey #.
No Hideo Nomo card.

MC	Mike Cameron/44	30.00

Sweet Stitches Black Patch

NM/M
Sequentially Numbered

SS-GM	Greg Maddux/32	25.00

Sweet Stitches Copper Jersey

NM/M
Common Player: 5.00
Production 125 Sets
Gold Patch: 1-30X
Production 50 Sets
Masterpiece: No Pricing
Production One Set

HB	Hank Blalock/125	5.00
MC	Miguel Cabrera/125	8.00
RC	Roger Clemens/125	8.00
JG	Jason Giambi/125	8.00
VG	Vladimir Guerrero/125	8.00
AJ	Andruw Jones/125	10.00
GM	Greg Maddux/125	8.00
MO	Magglio Ordonez/125	5.00
MP	Mike Piazza/125	8.00
MP	Mark Prior/125	8.00
AP	Albert Pujols/125	15.00
MR	Manny Ramirez/125	8.00
JR	Jose Reyes/125	8.00
SR	Scott Rolen/125	8.00
GS	Gary Sheffield/125	8.00
AS	Alfonso Soriano/125	8.00
SS	Sammy Sosa/125	10.00
MT	Mark Teixeira/125	5.00
MT	Miguel Tejada/125	8.00
FT	Frank Thomas/125	8.00
JT	Jim Thome/125	8.00
KW	Kerry Wood/125	8.00

Sweet Stitches Silver Jersey

NM/M
Common Player: 5.00
Sequentially Numbered

HB	Hank Blalock/166	5.00
MC	Miguel Cabrera/169	8.00
RC	Roger Clemens/165	8.00
JG	Jason Giambi/125	8.00
VG	Vladimir Guerrero/172	8.00
AJ	Andruw Jones/175	8.00
GM	Greg Maddux/156	8.00
MO	Magglio Ordonez/113	5.00
MP	Mike Piazza/174	8.00
MP	Mark Prior/172	8.00
AP	Albert Pujols/170	12.00
MR	Manny Ramirez/163	8.00
JR	Jose Reyes/171	8.00
SR	Scott Rolen/166	8.00
GS	Gary Sheffield/88	8.00
AS	Alfonso Soriano/162	8.00
SS	Sammy Sosa/158	10.00
MT	Mark Teixeira/158	5.00
MT	Miguel Tejada/162	8.00
FT	Frank Thomas/159	8.00
JT	Jim Thome/8	8.00
KW	Kerry Wood/134	8.00

Sweet Stitches Quad Patches

NM/M
Sequentially Numbered
No pricing for quantities less than 25.

4	Andruw Jones/31, Miguel Cabrera/31, Albert Pujols/31, Sammy Sosa/31	80.00
10	Greg Maddux/33, Sammy Sosa/33, Mark Prior/33, Kerry Wood/33	150.00

Sweet Swing

NM/M
Common Player: 2.50
Inserted 1:12

1SS	Sammy Sosa	5.00
2SS	Vladimir Guerrero	3.50
3SS	Jason Giambi	3.50
4SS	Chipper Jones	4.00
5SS	Alfonso Soriano	3.50
6SS	Manny Ramirez	3.00
7SS	Todd Helton	3.00
8SS	Alex Rodriguez	6.00
9SS	Albert Pujols	6.00
10SS	Jeff Bagwell	3.00
11SS	Mike Piazza	4.00
12SS	Hank Blalock	2.50
13SS	Jim Thome	3.50
14SS	Carlos Delgado	3.00
15SS	Nomar Garciaparra	6.00

Sweet Swing Black Bat/Patch

Numbered to most home runs.

Sweet Swing Copper Jersey

NM/M
Common Player: 4.00
Production 200 Sets
Gold Bat/Jersey: 1.5-4X
Production 50 Sets
Masterpiece Bat/Patch
Production One Set

HB	Hank Blalock/200	4.00
JG	Jason Giambi/200	6.00
VG	Vladimir Guerrero/200	6.00
CJ	Chipper Jones/200	8.00
MP	Mike Piazza/200	8.00
AP	Albert Pujols/200	12.00
MR	Manny Ramirez/200	5.00
AR	Alex Rodriguez/200	12.00
AS	Alfonso Soriano/200	6.00
SS	Sammy Sosa/200	10.00
JT	Jim Thome/200	6.00

Sweet Swing Silver Bat

NM/M
Common Player: 5.00
Sequentially Numbered

JG	Jason Giambi/247	6.00
VG	Vladimir Guerrero/250	6.00
CJ	Chipper Jones/235	8.00
MP	Mike Piazza/231	8.00
AP	Albert Pujols/237	12.00
MR	Manny Ramirez/224	5.00
AR	Alex Rodriguez/213	12.00
AS	Alfonso Soriano/216	6.00
SS	Sammy Sosa/221	10.00
JT	Jim Thome/245	6.00

Sweet Swing Quad

NM/M
Sequentially Numbered

1	Jason Giambi, Alex Rodriguez, Jeff Bagwell, Manny Ramirez/35	80.00
3	Mike Piazza, Alfonso Soriano, Todd Helton, Hank Blalock/32	125.00

2004 Fleer Tradition

NM/M
Complete Set (500): 100.00
Common Player: .15
Common SP (401-500): .25
Pack (10): 1.75
Hobby Box (36): 50.00

1	Juan Pierre	.15
2	Josh Beckett	.50
3	Ivan Rodriguez	.50
4	Miguel Cabrera	.50
5	Dontrelle Willis	.25
6	Derek Jeter	2.00
7	Jason Giambi	.75
8	Bernie Williams	.40
9	Alfonso Soriano	.75
10	Hideki Matsui	2.00
11	Garret Anderson, Ramon Ortiz, John Lackey	.15
12	Luis Gonzalez, Brandon Webb, Curt Schilling	.25
13	Javy Lopez, Gary Sheffield, Russ Ortiz	.25
14	Tony Batista, Jay Gibbons, Sidney Ponson, Jason Johnson	.15
15	Manny Ramirez, Nomar Garciaparra, Derek Lowe, Pedro J. Martinez	.50
16	Sammy Sosa, Mark Prior, Kerry Wood	.75
17	Frank Thomas, Carlos Lee, Esteban Loaiza	.25
18	Adam Dunn, Sean Casey, Chris Reitsma, Paul Wilson	.25
19	Jody Gerut, C.C. Sabathia	.15
20	Preston Wilson, Darren Oliver, Jason Jennings	.15
21	Dmitri Young, Mike Maroth, Jeremy Bonderman	.15
22	Mike Lowell, Dontrelle Willis, Josh Beckett	.25
23	Jeff Bagwell, Jeriome Robertson, Wade Miller	.25
24	Carlos Beltran, Darrell May	.15
25	Adrian Beltre, Shawn Green, Hideo Nomo, Kevin Brown	.15
26	Richie Sexson, Ben Sheets	.15
27	Torii Hunter, Brad Radke, Johan Santana	.15
28	Vladimir Guerrero, Orlando Cabrera, Livan Hernandez, Javier Vazquez	.25
29	Cliff Floyd, Ty Wigginton, Steve Trachsel, Al Leiter	.15
30	Jason Giambi, Andy Pettitte, Mike Mussina	.15
31	Eric Chavez, Miguel Tejada, Tim Hudson	.25
32	Jim Thome, Randy Wolf	.15
33	Reggie Sanders, Josh Fogg, Kip Wells	.15
34	Ryan Klesko, Mark Loretta, Jake Peavy	.15
35	Jose Cruz, Edgardo Alfonzo, Jason Schmidt	.15
36	Bret Boone, Jamie Moyer, Joel Pineiro	.15
37	Albert Pujols, Woody Williams	.75
38	Aubrey Huff, Victor Zambrano	.15
39	Alex Rodriguez, John Thomson	.75
40	Carlos Delgado, Roy Halladay	.25
41	Greg Maddux	1.00
42	Ben Grieve	.15
43	Darin Erstad	.25
44	Ruben Sierra	.15
45	Byung-Hyun Kim	.15
46	Freddy Garcia	.15
47	Richard Hidalgo	.15
48	Tike Redman	.15
49	Kevin Millwood	.25
50	Marquis Grissom	.15
51	Jae Weong Seo	.15
52	Wil Cordero	.15
53	LaTroy Hawkins	.15
54	Jolbert Cabrera	.15
55	Kevin Appier	.15
56	John Lackey	.15
57	Garret Anderson	.25
58	R.A. Dickey	.15
59	David Segui	.15
60	Erubiel Durazo	.15
61	Bobby Abreu	.25
62	Travis Hafner	.15
63	Victor Zambrano	.15
64	Randy Johnson	.75
65	Bernie Williams	.40
66	J.T. Snow	.15
67	Sammy Sosa	1.50
68	Al Leiter	.15
69	Jason Jennings	.15
70	Matt Morris	.15
71	Mike Hampton	.15
72	Juan Encarnacion	.15
73	Alex Gonzalez	.15
74	Bartolo Colon	.25
75	Brett Myers	.15
76	Michael Young	.15
77	Ichiro Suzuki	1.50
78	Jason Johnson	.15
79	Brad Ausmus	.15
80	Ted Lilly	.15
81	Ken Griffey Jr.	1.00
82	Chone Figgins	.15
83	Edgar Martinez	.15
84	Adam Eaton	.15
85	Ken Harvey	.15
86	Francisco Rodriguez	.15
87	Bill Mueller	.15
88	Mike Maroth	.15
89	Charles Johnson	.15
90	Jhonny Peralta	.15
91	Kip Wells	.15
92	Cesar Izturis	.15
93	Matt Clement	.15
94	Lyle Overbay	.15
95	Kirk Rueter	.15
96	Cristian Guzman	.15
97	Garrett Stephenson	.15
98	Lance Berkman	.25
99	Brett Tomko	.15
100	Chris Stynes	.15
101	Nate Cornejo	.15
102	Aaron Rowand	.15
103	Javier Vazquez	.15
104	Jason Kendall	.25
105	Mark Redman	.15
106	Benito Santiago	.15
107	C.C. Sabathia	.15
108	David Wells	.15
109	Mark Ellis	.15
110	Casey Blake	.15
111	Sean Burroughs	.15
112	Carlos Beltran	.25
113	Ramon Hernandez	.15
114	Eric Hinske	.15
115	Luis Gonzalez	.25
116	Jarrod Washburn	.15
117	Ronnie Belliard	.15
118	Troy Percival	.15
119	Jose Valentine	.15
120	Chase Utley	.40
121	Odalis Perez	.15
122	Steve Finley	.15
123	Bret Boone	.25
124	Jeff Conine	.15
125	Jason Fogg	.15
126	Neifi Perez	.15
127	Ben Sheets	.25
128	Randy Winn	.15
129	Matt Stairs	.15
130	Carlos Delgado	.50
131	Morgan Ensberg	.15
132	Vinny Castilla	.15
133	Matt Mantei	.15
134	Alex Rodriguez	1.50
135	Matthew LeCroy	.15
136	Woody Williams	.15
137	Frank Catalanotto	.15
138	Rondell White	.15
139	Scott Rolen	.75
140	Cliff Floyd	.15
141	Chipper Jones	.75
142	Robin Ventura	.15
143	Mariano Rivera	.25
144	Brady Clark	.15
145	Ramon Ortiz	.15
146	Omar Infante	.15
147	Mike Matheny	.15
148	Pedro J. Martinez	.75
149	Carlos Baerga	.15
150	Shannon Stewart	.15
151	Travis Lee	.15
152	Eric Byrnes	.15
153	Rafael Furcal	.25
154	B.J. Surhoff	.15
155	Zach Day	.15
156	Marlon Anderson	.15
157	Mark Hendrickson	.15
158	Mike Mussina	.50
159	Randall Simon	.15
160	Jeff DaVanon	.15
161	Joel Pineiro	.15
162	Vernon Wells	.25
163	Adam Kennedy	.15
164	Trot Nixon	.15
165	Rodrigo Lopez	.15
166	Curt Schilling	.50
167	Horacio Ramirez	.15
168	Gerald Laird	.15
169	Magglio Ordonez	.25
170	Scott Schoeneweis	.15
171	Andruw Jones	.50
172	Tino Martinez	.25
173	Moises Alou	.25
174	Kelvim Escobar	.15
175	Xavier Nady	.15
176	Ramon Martinez	.15
177	Pat Hentgen	.15
178	Austin Kearns	.40
179	D'Angelo Jimenez	.15
180	Deivi Cruz	.15
181	John Smoltz	.25
182	Toby Hall	.15
183	Mark Buehrle	.15
184	Howie Clark	.15
185	David Ortiz	.15
186	Raul Mondesi	.15
187	Milton Bradley	.15
188	Jorge Julio	.15
189	Victor Martinez	.15
190	Gabe Kapler	.15
191	Julio Franco	.15
192	Ryan Freel	.15
193	Brad Fullmer	.15
194	Joe Borowski	.15
195	Darren Oliver	.15
196	Jason Varitek	.15
197	Greg Myers	.15
198	Eric Munson	.15
199	Tim Wakefield	.15
200	Kyle Farnsworth	.15
201	John Vander Wal	.15
202	Alex Escobar	.15
203	Sean Casey	.15
204	John Thomson	.15
205	Carlos Zambrano	.15
206	Kenny Lofton	.15
207	Marcus Giles	.15
208	Wade Miller	.15
209	Geoff Blum	.15
210	Jason LaRue	.15
211	Omar Vizquel	.25
212	Carlos Pena	.15
213	Adam Dunn	.40
214	Oscar Villarreal	.15
215	Paul Konerko	.15
216	Hideo Nomo	.40
217	Mike Sweeney	.15
218	Coco Crisp	.15
219	Shawn Chacon	.15
220	Brook Fordyce	.15
221	Josh Beckett	.50
222	Paul Wilson	.15
223	Josh Towers	.15
224	Geoff Jenkins	.25
225	Shawn Green	.25
226	Derek Lee	.15
227	Karim Garcia	.15
228	Preston Wilson	.15
229	Dane Sardinha	.15
230	Aramis Ramirez	.15
231	Doug Mientkiewicz	.15
232	Jay Gibbons	.15
233	Adam Everett	.15
234	Brooks Kieschnick	.15
235	Dmitri Young	.15
236	Brad Penny	.15
237	Todd Zeile	.15
238	Eric Gagne	.25
239	Esteban Loaiza	.15
240	Billy Wagner	.15
241	Nomar Garciaparra	1.50
242	Desi Relaford	.15
243	Luis Rivas	.15
244	Andy Pettitte	.40
245	Ty Wigginton	.15
246	Edgar Gonzalez	.15
247	Brian Anderson	.15
248	Richie Sexson	.40
249	Russell Branyan	.15
250	Jose Guillen	.15
251	Chin-Hui Tsao	.15
252	Jose Hernandez	.15
253	Kevin Brown	.25
254	Pete LaForest	.15
255	Adrian Beltre	.15
256	Jacque Jones	.15
257	Jimmy Rollins	.25
258	Brandon Phillips	.15
259	Derek Jeter	2.00
260	Carl Everett	.15
261	Wes Helms	.15
262	Kyle Lohse	.15
263	Jason L. Phillips	.15
264	Jake Peavy	.15
265	Orlando Hernandez	.15
266	Keith Foulke	.15
267	Brad Wilkerson	.15
268	Corey Koskie	.15
269	Josh Hall	.15
270	Bobby Higginson	.15
271	Andres Galarraga	.15
272	Alfonso Soriano	.75
273	Carlos Rivera	.15
274	Steve Trachsel	.15
275	David Bell	.15
276	Endy Chavez	.15
277	Jay Payton	.15
278	Mark Mulder	.25
279	Terrence Long	.15
280	A.J. Burnett	.15
281	Pokey Reese	.15
282	Phil Nevin	.15
283	Jose Contreras	.25
284	Jim Thome	.75
285	Pat Burrell	.40
286	Luis Castillo	.15
287	Juan Uribe	.15
288	Raul Ibanez	.25
289	Sidney Ponson	.15
290	Shane Hattebarg	.15
291	Jack Wilson	.15
292	Reggie Sanders	.15
293	Brian Giles	.25
294	Craig Biggio	.25
295	Kazuhisa Ishii	.15
296	Jim Edmonds	.25
297	Trevor Hoffman	.15
298	Ray Durham	.15
299	Mike Lieberthal	.15
300	Todd Worrell	.15
301	Chris George	.15
302	Jamie Moyer	.15
303	Mike Cameron	.15
304	Matt Kinney	.15
305	Aubrey Huff	.15
306	Brian Lawrence	.15
307	Carlos Guillen	.15
308	J.D. Drew	.15
309	Paul LoDuca	.15
310	Tim Salmon	.15
311	Jason Schmidt	.15
312	A.J. Pierzynski	.15
313	Lance Carter	.15
314	Julio Lugo	.15
315	Johan Santana	.25
316	Laynce Nix	.15
317	John Olerud	.25
318	Robb Quinlan	.15
319	Scott Spiezio	.15
320	Tony Clark	.15
321	Jose Vidro	.15
322	Shea Hillenbrand	.15
323	Doug Glanville	.15
324	Orlando Palmeiro	.15
325	Juan Gonzalez	.40
326	Jason Giambi	.75
327	Junior Spivey	.15
328	Tom Glavine	.25
329	Reed Johnson	.15
330	David Eckstein	.15
331	Damian Jackson	.15
332	Orlando Hudson	.15
333	Barry Zito	.40
334	Robert Fick	.15
335	Aaron Boone	.15
336	Rafael Palmeiro	.50
337	Bobby Kielty	.15
338	Tony Batista	.15
339	Ryan Dempster	.15

#	Player	Price
340	Derek Lowe	.25
341	Alex Cintron	.15
342	Jermaine Dye	.15
343	John Burkett	.15
344	Javy Lopez	.25
345	Eric Karros	.15
346	Corey Patterson	.25
347	Josh Phelps	.15
348	Ryan Klesko	.25
349	Craig Wilson	.15
350	Brian Roberts	.15
351	Roberto Alomar	.40
352	Frank Thomas	.40
353	Gary Sheffield	.40
354	Alex Gonzalez	.15
355	Jose Cruz	.15
356	Jerome Williams	.15
357	Mark Kotsay	.15
358	Chris Reitsma	.15
359	Carlos Lee	.15
360	Todd Helton	.50
361	Gil Meche	.15
362	Ryan Franklin	.15
363	Josh Bard	.15
364	Juan Pierre	.15
365	Barry Larkin	.25
366	Edgar Renteria	.15
367	Alex Sanchez	.15
368	Jeff Bagwell	.50
369	Ben Broussard	.15
370	Chan Ho Park	.15
371	Darrell May	.15
372	Roy Oswalt	.25
373	Craig Monroe	.15
374	Fred McGriff	.25
375	Bengie Molina	.15
376	Aaron Guiel	.15
377	Jeriome Robertson	.15
378	Kenny Rogers	.15
379	Colby Lewis	.15
380	Jeromy Burnitz	.15
381	Orlando Cabrera	.15
382	Joe Randa	.15
383	Miguel Batista	.15
384	Brad Radke	.15
385	Jason Giambi	.75
386	Vladimir Guerrero	.75
387	Melvin Mora	.15
388	Royce Clayton	.15
389	Danny Garcia	.15
390	Manny Ramirez	.50
391	Dave McCarty	.15
392	Mark Grudzielanek	.15
393	Mike Piazza	1.00
394	Jorge Posada	.40
395	Tim Hudson	.25
396	Placido Polanco	.15
397	Mark Loretta	.15
398	Jesse Foppert	.15
399	Albert Pujols	1.50
400	Jeremi Gonzalez	.15
401	Paul Bako	.25
402	Luis Matos	.25
403	Johnny Damon	.50
404	Kerry Wood	1.00
405	Joe Crede	.25
406	Jason Davis	.25
407	Larry Walker	.50
408	Ivan Rodriguez	1.00
409	Nick Johnson	.25
410	Jose Lima	.25
411	Brian Jordan	.25
412	Eddie Guardado	.25
413	Ron Calloway	.25
414	Aaron Heilman	.25
415	Eric Chavez	.50
416	Randy Wolf	.25
417	Jason Bay	.25
418	Edgardo Alfonzo	.25
419	Kazuhiro Sasaki	.25
420	Eduardo Perez	.25
421	Carl Crawford	.25
422	Troy Glaus	1.00
423	Joaquin Benoit	.25
424	Russ Ortiz	.25
425	Larry Bigbie	.25
426	Todd Walker	.25
427	Kris Benson	.25
428	Sandy Alomar	.25
429	Jody Gerut	.25
430	Rene Reyes	.25
431	Mike Lowell	.25
432	Jeff Kent	.25
433	Mike MacDougal	.25
434	Dave Roberts	.25
435	Torii Hunter	.75
436	Tomokazu Ohka	.25
437	Jeremy Griffiths	.25
438	Miguel Tejada	.75
439	Vicente Padilla	.25
440	Bobby Hill	.25
441	Rich Aurilia	.25
442	Shigetoshi Hasegawa	.25
443	So Taguchi	.25
444	Damian Rolls	.25
445	Roy Halladay	.75
446	Rocco Baldelli	.75
447	Dontrelle Willis	.75
448	Mark Prior	2.00
449	Jason Lane	.25
450	Angel Berroa	.25
451	Jose Reyes	.75
452	Ryan Wagner	.25
453	Marlon Byrd	.25
454	Hee Seop Choi	.25
455	Brandon Webb	.50
456	Bo Hart	.75
457	Hank Blalock	1.00
458	Mark Teixeira	.75
459	Hideki Matsui	4.00
460	Scott Podsednik	.25
461	Miguel Cabrera	1.00
462	Josh Beckett	1.00
463	Mariano Rivera	.50
464	Ivan Rodriguez	1.00
465	Alex Rodriguez	3.00
466	Albert Pujols	3.00
467	Roy Halladay	.75
468	Eric Gagne	.50
469	Angel Berroa	.25
470	Dontrelle Willis	.50
471	Chris Bootcheck, Tom Gregorio, Richard Fischer	.25
472	Matt Kata, Tim Olson, Robby Hammock	.25
473	Michael Hessman, Chris Waters, Humberto Quintero	.25
474	Carlos Mendez, Daniel Cabrera, Jeremy Guthrie	.25
475	Edwin Almonte, Phil Seibel, Felix Sanchez	.25
476	Todd Wellemeyer, Jon Leicester, Sergio Mitre	.25
477	Josh Stewart, Neal Cotts, Aaron Miles	.25
478	Termel Sledge, Josh Hall, Brandon Claussen	.25
479	Francisco Cruceta, Jason Stanford, Rafael Betancourt	.25
480	Javier Lopez, Garrett Atkins, Clint Barmes	.25
481	Wilfredo Ledezma, Nook Logan, Jeremy Bonderman	.25
482	Josh Willingham, Kevin Hooper, Rick Roberts	.25
483	Colin Porter, Mike Gallo, Dave Matranga	.25
484	David DeJesus, Jason Gilfillan, Jimmy Gobble	.25
485	Koyie Hill, Alfredo Gonzalez, Andrew Brown	.25
486	Rickie Weeks, Pedro Liriano, Wes Obermueller	1.00
487	Alex Prieto, Mike Ryan, Lew Ford	.25
488	Julio Manon, Luis Ayala, Seung Jun Song	.25
489	Jeff Duncan, Prentice Redman, Craig Brazell	.25
490	Chien-Ming Wang, Michel Hernandez, Mike Gonzalez	.25
491	Rich Harden, Mike Neu, Geoff Geary	.25
492	Diegomar Markwell, Chad Gaudin, David Sanders	.25
493	Beau Kemp, Micheal Nakamura, D.J. Carrasco	.25
494	Khalil Greene, Miguel Ojeda, Bernie Castro	.25
495	Noah Lowry, Todd Linden, Kevin Correia	.25
496	Aaron Looper, Brian Sweeney, Rett Johnson	.25
497	Bo Hart, Dan Haren, Kevin Ohme	.50
498	Delmon Young, Doug Waechter, Matt Diaz	1.00
499	Gerald Laird, Rosman Garcia, Ramon Nivar	.25
500	Alexis Rios, Guillermo Quiroz, Francisco Rosario	.25

Career Tributes

		NM/M
Complete Set (10):		30.00
Common Player:		3.00

Numbered to last season.
Die-Cuts: 2-3X
#'d to last two digits of last season

1CT	Mike Schmidt/1,989	5.00
2CT	Nolan Ryan/1,993	6.00
3CT	Tom Seaver/1,986	4.00
4CT	Reggie Jackson/1,987	3.00
5CT	Bob Gibson/1,975	4.00
6CT	Harmon Killebrew/1,975	4.00
7CT	Phil Rizzuto/1,956	3.00
8CT	Lou Brock/1,979	3.00
9CT	Eddie Mathews/1,968	3.00
10CT	Al Kaline/1,974	4.00

Diamond Tributes

		NM/M
Complete Set (20):		18.00
Common Player:		.50

Inserted 1:6

1DT	Derek Jeter	3.00
2DT	Chipper Jones	1.50
3DT	Vladimir Guerrero	1.00
4DT	Kerry Wood	.75
5DT	Jim Thome	1.00
6DT	Nomar Garciaparra	2.00

7DT	Alex Rodriguez	3.00
8DT	Mike Piazza	1.50
9DT	Jason Giambi	1.00
10DT	Barry Zito	.50
11DT	Dontrelle Willis	.50
12DT	Albert Pujols	2.50
13DT	Todd Helton	.75
14DT	Richie Sexson	.50
15DT	Randy Johnson	1.00
16DT	Pedro J. Martinez	1.00
17DT	Josh Beckett	.75
18DT	Manny Ramirez	.75
19DT	Roy Halladay	.75
20DT	Mark Prior	1.50

Diamond Tributes Game-Used

	NM/M
Common Player:	5.00

Inserted 1:36
Patch Versions: 2-3X
Production 50 Sets

Josh Beckett	8.00
Nomar Garciaparra	8.00
Jason Giambi	8.00
Vladimir Guerrero	8.00
Roy Halladay	5.00
Todd Helton	8.00
Derek Jeter	15.00
Randy Johnson	8.00
Chipper Jones	8.00
Pedro J. Martinez	10.00
Mike Piazza	8.00
Mark Prior	10.00
Albert Pujols	15.00
Manny Ramirez	8.00
Alex Rodriguez	10.00
Richie Sexson	6.00
Jim Thome	8.00
Dontrelle Willis	8.00
Kerry Wood	8.00
Barry Zito	8.00

Retrospection Collection

	NM/M
Complete Set (10):	60.00
Common Player:	4.00

Inserted 1:360

1RC	Rickie Weeks	8.00
2RC	Delmon Young	12.00
3RC	Torii Hunter	5.00
4RC	Aubrey Huff	6.00
5RC	Rocco Baldelli	6.00
6RC	Mike Lowell	4.00
7RC	Dontrelle Willis	8.00
8RC	Albert Pujols	10.00
9RC	Bo Hart	4.00
10RC	Brandon Webb	4.00

Retrospection Collection Autograph

	NM/M
Common Autograph:	10.00

Production 60

Hank Blalock	25.00
Bo Hart	25.00
Aubrey Huff	10.00
Torii Hunter	30.00
Austin Kearns	20.00
Corey Patterson	25.00
Albert Pujols	75.00
Jose Reyes	25.00
Scott Rolen	30.00
Mike Ryan	15.00
Ryan Wagner	20.00
Brandon Webb	20.00
Rickie Weeks	25.00

Josh Willingham	20.00
Dontrelle Willis	35.00
Delmon Young	50.00

Retrospective Collection Dual Auto.

No Pricing
Production 19 Sets

Standouts Game-Used

	NM/M
Common Player:	4.00

Inserted 1:41

Rocco Baldelli	8.00
Angel Berroa	5.00
Hank Blalock	6.00
Marlon Byrd	5.00
Miguel Cabrera	8.00
Hee Seop Choi	4.00
Bo Hart	8.00
Jose Reyes	6.00
Mark Teixeira	8.00
Brandon Webb	5.00
Dontrelle Willis	6.00

Standouts Game-Used Gold

Numbered to player's age.

This Day in History

	NM/M
Complete Set (15):	12.00
Common Player:	.50

Inserted 1:18

1	Josh Beckett	1.00
2	Carlos Delgado	1.00
3	Javy Lopez	.50
4	Greg Maddux	2.00
5	Rafael Palmeiro	1.00
6	Sammy Sosa	2.50
7	Jeff Bagwell	1.00
8	Frank Thomas	1.00
9	Kevin Millwood	.50
10	Jose Reyes	.75
11	Rafael Furcal	.50
12	Alfonso Soriano	1.50
13	Eric Gagne	.50
14	Hideki Matsui	4.00
15	Hank Blalock	.75

This Day in History Memorabilia

	NM/M
Common Player:	5.00

Inserted 1:288

Jeff Bagwell	8.00
Carlos Delgado	8.00
Javy Lopez	5.00
Greg Maddux	15.00
Rafael Palmeiro	8.00
Alfonso Soriano	5.00
Sammy Sosa	12.00
Frank Thomas	8.00

This Day/ History Dual Memorabilia

	NM/M
Production 25 Sets	
Frank Thomas, Jeff Bagwell	25.00

2004 Fleer/N.Y. Daily News Yankees

Ten popular Yankees stars are featured on this promotional issue. The April 25 Sunday Daily News included a nine-card sheet produced in an edition of 1.1 million. The 7-1/2" x 12" sheet has nine standard-size player cards. Fronts have game-action photos on a dark blue background. Backs are in blue and black on white, presenting personal data and stats. A 10th card, Alex Rodriguez, in a special

edition of 50,000 was available at the Yankees Clubhouse Store with the purchase of a Fleer product and a coupon found in the newspaper. Cards on the sheet are not perforated and must be hand-cut to seperate.

	NM/M
Uncut Sheet:	2.00
Alex Rodriguez:	7.50

2004 Fleer/N.Y. Post Mets

The opening day lineup of the N.Y. Mets was featured in this promotional issue. The April 19 issue of the Post included a nine-card sheet produced in an edition of 800,000. The 7-1/2" x 12" sheet has nine standard-size player cards. Fronts have game-action photos superimposed on a background resembling the team's jersey. Backs are in team colors and reproduce part of the photo while presenting personal data, stats and career highlights. A 10th card, a Kaz Matsui special edition of 25,000 was available with the purchase of a Fleer product at Mets Team Store outlets. Cards on the sheet are not perforated and must be hand-cut to seperate.

	NM/M
Complete Sheet:	2.00

2005 Fleer

	NM/M
Common Player (1-50):	1.00
Minor Stars (1-50):	1.25
Unlisted Stars (1-50):	1.75
Common Class '05 (51-80):	3.00
Minor Class '05 (51-80):	4.00
Production 699 Sets	
Common Veteran (81-90):	3.00
Production 699 Sets	
Box (1):	90.00

1	Curt Schilling	1.75
2	Jim Thome	3.00
3	Miguel Cabrera	2.00
4	Randy Johnson	3.50
5	David Ortiz	1.75
6	Vladimir Guerrero	3.00
7	Nomar Garciaparra	2.00
8	Ivan Rodriguez	1.75
9	Jason Schmidt	1.25
10	Khalil Greene	2.00
11	Jose Vidro	1.00
12	Lyle Overbay	1.00
13	Todd Helton	1.75
14	Vernon Wells	1.25
15	B.J. Upton	1.75
16	Hideki Matsui	5.00
17	Pedro Martinez	3.00
18	Victor Martinez	1.00
19	Adam Dunn	1.75
20	Andruw Jones	2.00
21	Jeff Bagwell	1.75
22	Mike Sweeney	1.00
23	Mike Piazza	3.50
24	Ben Sheets	1.25
25	Adrian Beltre	1.25
26	Chipper Jones	3.50
27	Greg Maddux	3.50
28	Manny Ramirez	2.00
29	Roger Clemens	5.00
30	Johan Santana	1.25
31	Derek Jeter	6.00
32	Jason Bay	1.00
33	Ken Griffey Jr.	3.50
34	Miguel Tejada	1.75
35	Richie Sexson	1.75
36	Scott Rolen	3.00
37	Alfonso Soriano	3.00
38	Ichiro Suzuki	4.00
39	Sammy Sosa	4.00
40	Barry Zito	1.75
41	Kazuo Matsui	3.00
42	Mark Teixeira	1.25
43	Carlos Beltran	1.75
44	Mark Prior	4.00
45	Travis Hafner	1.00
46	Alex Rodriguez	5.00
47	Lew Ford	1.00
48	Albert Pujols	5.00
49	Frank Thomas	2.00
50	Juan Pierre	1.00
51	David Aardsma	5.00
52	J.D. Durbin	3.00
53	Zack Greinke	4.00
54	Dioner Navarro	4.00
55	Edwin Encarnacion	4.00
56	Luis Hernandez RC	4.00
57	Jeff Baker	4.00
58	Victor Diaz	5.00
59	Joey Gathright	3.00
60	Casey Kotchman	4.00
61	David Wright	5.00
62	Jon Knott	4.00
63	Charlton Jimerson	4.00
64	Nick Swisher	5.00
65	Ryan Raburn	3.00
66	Josh Kroeger	3.00
67	Kelly Johnson	4.00
68	Justin Verlander RC	6.00
69	Taylor Buchholz	3.00
70	Ubaldo Jimenez RC	10.00
71	Russ Adams	4.00
72	Ronny Cedeno	4.00
73	Bobby Jenks	5.00
74	Dan Meyer	4.00
75	Jeff Francis	3.00
76	Scott Kazmir	5.00
77	Sean Burnett	3.00
78	Jose Lopez	4.00
79	Andres Blanco	3.00
80	Gavin Floyd	4.00
81	Tom Seaver	3.00
82	Steve Carlton	4.00
83	Al Kaline	4.00
84	Cal Ripken Jr.	10.00
85	Willie McCovey	5.00
86	Johnny Bench	4.00
87	Nolan Ryan	10.00
88	Mike Schmidt	4.00
89	Carlton Fisk	3.00
90	Don Mattingly	4.00

Row 1

Stars (1-50):	
Class of '05 (51-80):	.5-2X
Veterans:	.5-2X
Production 100 Sets	

Row 2

| Cards 1-90: | No Pricing |
| Production One Set | |

Cuts and Glory Jersey

	NM/M
Common Card:	15.00
Production 100 Sets	
Patch:	2-4X
Production 50 Sets	
Jersey and Patch:	No Pricing
Production 15 Sets	
Masterpiece Logo:	No Pricing
Production One Set	
JB	Johnny Bench	60.00
CC	Carl Crawford	20.00
JL	Javy Lopez	20.00
JP	Josh Phelps	15.00
BS	Ben Sheets	20.00
SS	Shannon Stewart	20.00

Cust and Glory Dual Patch

Production 35 Sets

Diamond Cuts Jersey

	NM/M
Common Player:	5.00
Production 150 Sets	
Die-Cut:	.75-1.5X
Production 75 Sets	
Patch:	1-30X
Production 50 Sets	
Super Patch:	No Pricing
Production 20 Sets	
Die-Cut Patch:	No Pricing
Production 10 Sets	
MLB Logo Masterpiece:	No Pricing
Production One Set	
JB	Jeff Bagwell	8.00
CB	Carlos Beltran	6.00
HB	Hank Blalock	4.00
MC	Miguel Cabrera	8.00
RC	Roger Clemens	12.00
AD	Adam Dunn	6.00
VG	Vladimir Guerrero	8.00

TH	Todd Helton	8.00
RJ	Randy Johnson	8.00
AJ	Andruw Jones	8.00
CJ	Chipper Jones	8.00
AK	Austin Kearns	6.00
PM	Pedro Martinez	8.00
VM	Victor Martinez	5.00
HM	Hideki Matsui	15.00
HN	Hideo Nomo	8.00
DO	David Ortiz	6.00
MP	Mike Piazza	8.00
MP2	Mark Prior	8.00
AP	Albert Pujols	12.00
MR	Manny Ramirez	8.00
SR	Scott Rolen	6.00
CS	Curt Schilling	6.00
GS	Gary Sheffield	6.00
AS	Alfonso Soriano	8.00
SS	Sammy Sosa	10.00
MT	Mark Teixeira	5.00
JT	Jim Thome	8.00
BU	B.J. Upton	5.00
KW	Kerry Wood	8.00

Diamond Cuts Dual Jersey
NM/M
Common Card: 8.00
Production 99 Sets
Die-Cut: .5-1.5X
Production 50 Sets
Patch: No Pricing
Production 15 Sets
Patch Die-Cut: No Pricing
Production Five Sets

BC	Jeff Bagwell, Roger Clemens	15.00
BM	Carlos Beltran, Pedro Martinez	10.00
BS	Hank Blalock, Alfonso Soriano	10.00
CH	Miguel Cabrera, Todd Helton	10.00
DK	Adam Dunn, Austin Kearns	8.00
JJ	Chipper Jones, Andruw Jones	12.00
JS	Randy Johnson, Curt Schilling	10.00
MS	Hideki Matsui, Gary Sheffield	20.00
MT	Victor Martinez, Mark Teixeira	8.00
NU	Hideo Nomo, B.J. Upton	10.00
OR	David Ortiz, Manny Ramirez	10.00
PR	Albert Pujols, Scott Rolen	15.00
PT	Mike Piazza, Jim Thome	12.00
PW	Mark Prior, Kerry Wood	10.00
SG	Sammy Sosa, Vladimir Guerrero	15.00

Dynasty Cornerstones Signatures
NM/M
Sequentially Numbered

JB	Jeremy Bonderman/75	20.00
DG	Dwight Gooden/25	30.00
DO	David Ortiz/75	40.00

Dynasty Cornerstones Dual Signatures
NM/M
Sequentially Numbered

Dynasty Foundations Dual Player Jersey
NM/M
Common Card: 10.00
Production 150 Sets
Patch: 1-30X
Production 50 Sets

BO	Miguel Tejada, Javy Lopez	15.00
BR	Manny Ramirez, David Ortiz	10.00
CI	Victor Martinez, Travis Hafner	10.00
CR1	Adam Dunn, Austin Kearns	12.00
CR2	Todd Helton, Preston Wilson	12.00
FM	Miguel Cabrera, Juan Pierre	10.00
HA	Jeff Bagwell, Lance Berkman	12.00
LA	Vladimir Guerrero, Garret Anderson	12.00
MT	Johan Santana, Torii Hunter	12.00
NM	Mike Piazza, Tom Glavine	10.00
OA	Barry Zito, Eric Chavez	10.00
PP	Jim Thome, Bobby Abreu	10.00
SC	Scott Rolen, Albert Pujols	25.00
TD	B.J. Upton, Scott Kazmir	10.00
TR	Mark Teixeira, Michael Young	10.00

Dynasty Foundations Three Player Jersey
NM/M
Common Card: 15.00
Production 99 Sets

	Patch:	No Pricing
	Production 25 Sets	
CR1	Adam Dunn, Austin Kearns, Joe Morgan	15.00
FM	Miguel Cabrera, Josh Beckett, Juan Pierre	15.00
HA	Jeff Bagwell, Lance Berkman, Roger Clemens	40.00
LA	Vladimir Guerrero, Garret Anderson, Darin Erstad	20.00
MT	Johan Santana, Torii Hunter, Shannon Stewart	15.00
NM	Mike Piazza, Pedro Martinez, Tom Glavine	20.00
SC	Scott Rolen, Albert Pujols, Jim Edmonds	40.00
TR	Alfonso Soriano, Mark Teixeira, Michael Young	15.00

Dynasty Foundations Four Player Jersey
NM/M
Production 40 Sets
Patch: No Pricing
Production 15 Sets

NM	Mike Piazza, Nolan Ryan, Pedro Martinez, Tom Glavine	100.00

Dynasty Foundations Five Player Jersey
NM/M
No Pricing
Production 25 Sets
Patch: No Pricing
Production Nine Sets
MLB Logo Masterpiece: No Pricing
Production One Set

Head of the Class Triple Player Jersey
NM/M
Common Card: 15.00
Numbered to Debut Year.
No pricing for quantities three or less.
Patch: 1-30X
Production 33 Sets
MLB Logo Masterpiece: No Pricing
Production One Set

AGJ	Bobby Abreu, Vladimir Guerrero, Andruw Jones/96	20.00
BGB	Carlos Beltran, Troy Glaus, Adrian Beltre/98	15.00
BTR	Jeff Bagwell, Jim Thome, Ivan Rodriguez/91	15.00
GBH	Eric Gagne, A.J. Burnett, Tim Hudson/99	15.00
JDR	Chipper Jones, Carlos Delgado, Manny Ramirez/93	20.00
OHS	David Ortiz, Torii Hunter, Richie Sexson/97	15.00
SNP	Jason Schmidt, Hideo Nomo, Andy Pettitte/95	15.00

Letterman
Sequentially numbered between 4-8.
No Pricing

Significant Signings Blue
NM/M
Common Player: 10.00
Sequentially #'d to indicated quantity.
Silver Die-Cut: 1-30X
Cards #'d 50 or less: .25-1X
Production 50 Sets
Gold Jersey: No Pricing
Production 25 Sets
Patch: No Pricing
Production 15 Sets
Masterpiece Jersey Tag: No Pricing
Production One Set

JB	Jason Bay/250	15.00
AB	Adrian Beltre/30	50.00
MC	Miguel Cabrera/250	20.00
SC	Steve Carlton/59	30.00
BC	Bobby Crosby/93	15.00
GF	Gavin Floyd/221	10.00
LF	Lew Ford/230	10.00
ZG	Zack Greinke/250	15.00
TH	Travis Hafner/250	10.00
SK	Scott Kazmir/250	10.00
CK	Casey Kotchman/250	10.00
PM	Pedro Martinez/101	40.00
VM	Victor Martinez/224	10.00
DM	Don Mattingly/103	40.00
JM	Justin Morneau/225	25.00
JR	Jeremy Reed/250	40.00
NR	Nolan Ryan/92	100.00
BU	B.J. Upton/250	10.00
KW	Kerry Wood/200	25.00
DW	David Wright/250	40.00

Significant Dual
NM/M
Common Player: 30.00
Production 40 Sets
Dual Jersey: No Pricing
Production 15 Sets
Dual Patch: No Pricing
Production Five Sets

BR	Adrian Beltre, Jeremy Reed	60.00
CF	Steve Carlton, Gavin Floyd	40.00
FM	Lew Ford, Justin Morneau	40.00
MH	Victor Martinez, Travis Hafner	30.00
SR	Mike Schmidt, Cal Ripken Jr.	250.00

Dynasty Foundations
NM/M
Common Card: 6.00
Production 500 Sets

1DF	Rod Carew, Nolan Ryan, Vladimir Guerrero, Garret Anderson, Darin Erstad	8.00
2DF	Cal Ripken Jr., Brooks Robinson, Miguel Tejada, Javy Lopez, Jim Palmer	15.00
3DF	Ted Williams, Manny Ramirez, Johnny Damon, Carl Yastrzemski, David Ortiz	15.00
4DF	Ryne Sandberg, Sammy Sosa, Ernie Banks, Greg Maddux, Mark Prior	8.00
5DF	Adam Dunn, Johnny Bench, Tony Perez, Austin Kearns, Joe Morgan	8.00
6DF	Victor Martinez, Travis Hafner, Bob Feller, C.C. Sabathia, Larry Doby	6.00
7DF	Aaron Miles, Matt Holliday, Todd Helton, Garrett Atkins, Preston Wilson	6.00
8DF	Miguel Cabrera, Dontrelle Willis, Juan Pierre, Al Leiter, Josh Beckett	6.00
9DF	Lance Berkman, Jeff Bagwell, Craig Biggio, Roger Clemens, Roy Oswalt	8.00
10DF	Ben Sheets, Lyle Overbay, Robin Yount, Geoff Jenkins, Paul Molitor	6.00
11DF	Johan Santana, Shannon Stewart, Harmon Killebrew, Torii Hunter, Lee Ford	6.00
12DF	Tom Glavine, Mike Piazza, Tom Seaver, Nolan Ryan, Pedro Martinez	8.00
13DF	Eric Chavez, Reggie Jackson, Bobby Crosby, Dennis Eckersley, Barry Zito	6.00
14DF	Jim Thome, Bobby Abreu, Gavin Floyd, Robin Roberts, Mike Schmidt	6.00
15DF	Craig Wilson, Willie Stargell, Bill Mazeroski, Jason Bay, Jack Wilson	6.00
16DF	Willie McCovey, Jason Schmidt, Juan Marichal, Orlando Cepeda, Ray Durham	6.00
17DF	Scott Rolen, Mark Mulder, Albert Pujols, Jim Edmonds, Stan Musial	10.00
18DF	Rocco Baldelli, Scott Kazmir, Aubrey Huff, B.J. Upton, Carl Crawford	6.00
19DF	Alfonso Soriano, Mark Teixeira, Hank Blalock, Nolan Ryan, Michael Young	10.00
20DF	Alexis Rios, Paul Molitor, Roy Halladay, Vernon Wells, Orlando Hudson	6.00

2005 Fleer America's National Pastime
NM/M
Common Player (1-50): .25
Minor Stars (1-50): .40
Unlisted Stars (1-50): .60
Common Player (51-70): 3.00
Production 699 Sets
Common Player (71-80): 3.00
Production 699 Sets
Pack (5): 7.00
Box (10): 60.00

1	Khalil Greene	.75
2	Pedro Martinez	1.00
3	Mark Teixeira	.40
4	Jim Thome	.60
5	Jack Wilson	.25
6	Johan Santana	.40
7	Jason Bay	.25
8	Adam Dunn	.25
9	Lyle Overbay	.25
10	Jason Schmidt	.40
11	Jeremy Reed	.40
12	J.D. Drew	.40
13	Ken Griffey Jr.	1.50
14	Sammy Sosa	2.00
15	Hank Blalock	.25
16	Victor Martinez	.25
17	Randy Johnson	1.00
18	Vernon Wells	.25
19	Todd Helton	.75
20	Javy Lopez	.60
21	Kazuo Matsui	.60
22	Ben Sheets	.40
23	Brad Wilkerson	.25
24	Miguel Cabrera	.75
25	Mike Sweeney	.25
26	Roger Clemens	2.50
27	Chipper Jones	1.50
28	Hideki Matsui	2.50
29	Manny Ramirez	.75
30	Scott Rolen	1.00
31	Lance Berkman	.40
32	Jim Edmonds	.40
33	Derek Jeter	3.00
34	B.J. Upton	.40
35	Carlos Delgado	.75
36	Ichiro Suzuki	2.00
37	Nomar Garciaparra	2.50
38	Albert Pujols	2.50
39	Ivan Rodriguez	.60
40	Gary Sheffield	.60
41	Alfonso Soriano	1.00
42	Carlos Beltran	.60
43	Magglio Ordonez	.40
44	Alex Rodriguez	2.50
45	Curt Schilling	.60
46	Greg Maddux	1.50
47	Vladimir Guerrero	1.00
48	Mike Piazza	1.50
49	Miguel Tejada	.60
50	Adrian Beltre	.40
51	Scott Kazmir	5.00
52	Gavin Floyd	4.00
53	Zack Greinke	4.00
54	David Wright	5.00
55	David Aardsma	4.00
56	Ryan Raburn	3.00
57	Joey Gathright	3.00
58	J.D. Durbin	3.00
59	Sean Burnett	3.00
60	Jose Lopez	3.00
61	Nick Swisher	3.00
62	Bobby Jenks	3.00
63	Kelly A. Johnson	3.00
64	Ronny Cedeno	4.00
65	Edwin Encarnacion	3.00
66	Jeff Baker	3.00
67	Taylor Buchholz	3.00
68	Justin Verlander RC	5.00
69	Luis Hernandez RC	5.00
70	Mike Schmidt	5.00
71	Al Kaline	3.00
72	Yogi Berra	4.00
73	Robin Yount	4.00
74	Nolan Ryan	6.00
75	Johnny Bench	5.00
76	Eddie Murray	5.00
77	Tom Seaver	4.00
78	Willie McCovey	3.00
79	Cal Ripken Jr.	6.00

Blue Foil
NM/M
No Pricing
Production One Set

Red Foil
NM/M
Cards 1-50: 1-30X
Cards 51-70: .75-1.5X
Cards 71-80: .75-1.5X
Production 150 Sets

White Foil
NM/M
Cards 1-50 #'d to 41-57: 2-6X
Cards 1-50 #'d to 26-40: 4-8X
Cards 1-50 #'d 25 or less: No Pricing
Cards 71-80 #'d to 26-44: 1-30X
Cards 71-80 #'d 25 or less: No Pricing
Numbered to player's jersey number.

Beltway Baseball
NM/M
Common Card: 6.00
Production 202 Sets

1	Ed Delahanty	8.00
2	Benjamin Harrison	8.00
3	William Howard Taft	8.00
4	Clark Griffith	6.00
5	Bobby Burke	8.00
6	Roy Seivers	8.00
7	Tom Cheney	8.00
8	Woodrow Wilson	8.00
9	Franklin D. Roosevelt	8.00
10	John F. Kennedy	10.00
11	Frank Howard	8.00
12	Griffith Stadium	10.00
13	RFK Stadium	8.00
14	All-Star Game	6.00
15	Ted Williams	15.00
16	Harmon Killebrew	12.00
17	Jeff Burroughs	8.00
18	All-Star Game	6.00
19	Unveiling the Nationals	10.00
20	New Logo	8.00

First Name Bases Auto. Gold
NM/M
Cards #'d 25 or less: No Pricing
Sequentially #'d to indicated quantity.

AB	Adrian Beltre/96	25.00
MCAM	Mike Cameron/126	15.00
SH	Shea Hillenbrand/99	15.00
JL	Javy Lopez/73	15.00
AP	Albert Pujols/73	200.00
MT	Mark Teixeira/147	25.00
JV	Justin Verlander/149	20.00

First Name Bases Auto. Red
NM/M
Cards #'d 25 or less: No Pricing
Sequentially #'d to indicated quantity.

MCAM	Mike Cameron/90	15.00
BL	Barry Larkin/27	40.00
MT	Mark Teixeira/95	30.00
JV	Justin Verlander/99	20.00

First Name Bases Auto. Silver
NM/M
Sequentially #'d to indicated quantity.
Blue: No Pricing
Production One Set

MCAM	Mike Cameron/375	10.00
SH	Shea Hillenbrand/316	10.00
JL	Javy Lopez/158	15.00
MT	Mark Teixeira/225	10.00
JV	Justin Verlander/401	15.00

First Name Bases Auto. White
NM/M
Cards #'d 25 or less: No Pricing
Sequentially #'d to indicated quantity.

AB	Adrian Beltre/48	25.00

Grand Old Gamers
NM/M
Common Player: .75
Inserted 1:5

1	Pedro Martinez	1.50
2	Jim Thome	1.50
3	Ken Griffey Jr.	2.00
4	Sammy Sosa	2.50
5	Hank Blalock	1.00
6	Randy Johnson	1.50
7	Roger Clemens	3.00
8	Chipper Jones	2.00
9	Hideki Matsui	3.00
10	Manny Ramirez	1.25
11	Derek Jeter	4.00
12	Ichiro Suzuki	2.50
13	Nomar Garciaparra	3.00
14	Albert Pujols	3.00
15	Gary Sheffield	1.00
16	Alfonso Soriano	1.50
17	Alex Rodriguez	3.00
18	Curt Schilling	1.00
19	Vladimir Guerrero	1.50
20	Mike Piazza	2.00
21	Greg Maddux	2.00
22	Frank Thomas	1.25
23	Adrian Beltre	.75
24	Barry Larkin	.75
25	Todd Helton	1.25
26	Kerry Wood	1.25
27	Kazuo Matsui	1.00
28	Scott Rolen	1.50
29	Ivan Rodriguez	1.00
30	Miguel Tejada	1.00
31	Mark Teixeira	.75
32	Rafael Palmeiro	.75
33	Andruw Jones	1.25
34	Carlos Beltran	1.00
35	Jeff Bagwell	1.25

Grand Old Gamers Jersey
NM/M
Common Player: 6.00
Inserted 1:36 Retail

JB	Jeff Bagwell	8.00
CB	Carlos Beltran	8.00
AB	Adrian Beltre	8.00
HB	Hank Blalock	8.00
RC	Roger Clemens/SP/50	15.00
VG	Vladimir Guerrero	8.00
TH	Todd Helton	8.00
RJ	Randy Johnson	8.00
AJ	Andruw Jones	8.00
CJ	Chipper Jones	8.00
BL	Barry Larkin	6.00
GM	Greg Maddux/SP/75	12.00
PM	Pedro Martinez	8.00
HM	Hideki Matsui/SP/50	15.00
KM	Kazuo Matsui	8.00
RP	Rafael Palmeiro	8.00
MP	Mike Piazza	8.00
AP	Albert Pujols	12.00
MR	Manny Ramirez	8.00
IR	Ivan Rodriguez	8.00
SR	Scott Rolen	8.00
CS	Curt Schilling	8.00
GS	Gary Sheffield	8.00
AS	Alfonso Soriano	8.00
SS	Sammy Sosa	12.00
MT	Mark Teixeira	8.00
FT	Frank Thomas	8.00
JT	Jim Thome	8.00
KW	Kerry Wood	8.00

Grand Old Gamers Patch Blue
NM/M
Numbered to player's jersey number.
Cards numbered 25 or less: No Pricing
Masterpiece: No Pricing
Production One Set

VG	Vladimir Guerrero/27	25.00
RJ	Randy Johnson/51	20.00
GM	Greg Maddux/31	25.00
PM	Pedro Martinez/45	20.00
HM	Hideki Matsui/50	50.00
MP	Mike Piazza/31	25.00
SR	Scott Rolen/17	15.00
CS	Curt Schilling/38	15.00
FT	Frank Thomas/35	15.00
KW	Kerry Wood/34	20.00

Grand Old Gamers Dual Patch
NM/M
Cards #'d to 25 or less: No Pricing
Production 5-33 Sets

Ivan Rodriguez, Mike Piazza/31	75.00
Hank Blalock, Mark Teixeira/33	30.00

Historical Record
NM/M
Common Card: 2.00
Inserted 1:6

1	Ichiro Suzuki/2004	2.50
2	Greg Maddux/2004	2.00
3	Alex Rodriguez/1998	3.00
4	Mike Piazza/2004	2.00
5	Nolan Ryan/1991	5.00
6	Albert Pujols/2001	3.00
7	Mike Schmidt/1987	4.00
8	Randy Johnson/2004	2.00
9	Sammy Sosa/2003	2.50
10	Cal Ripken Jr./1996	5.00
11	Roger Clemens/2004	3.00
12	Hideki Matsui/2003	3.00
13	Hideo Nomo/1994	3.00
14	Gene Autry/1961	2.00
15	Walter O'Malley/1944	2.00

Historical Record Jersey
NM/M
Common Player: 6.00
Inserted 1:96 Retail

RC	Roger Clemens	10.00
RJ	Randy Johnson	8.00
GM	Greg Maddux	8.00
HM	Hideki Matsui	12.00
HN	Hideo Nomo	6.00
MP	Mike Piazza	8.00
AP	Albert Pujols	10.00
CR	Cal Ripken Jr.	30.00
NRO	Nolan Ryan	20.00
MS	Mike Schmidt	25.00
SS	Sammy Sosa	10.00

Hist. Record Patch Blue
No Pricing
Numbered to player's jersey number.
Masterpiece: No Pricing
Production One Set

Historical Record Dual Patc
No Pricing
Production 8-25 Sets

Sign. Swings Bat Red
NM/M
Common Player: 20.00
Production 30-99 Sets

BAY	Jason Bay/99	20.00
JB	Johnny Bench/42	80.00
LB	Lance Berkman/99	20.00
CC	Carl Crawford/99	20.00
LF	Lew Ford/76	20.00
CK	Casey Kotchman/99	20.00
BR	Brooks Robinson/64	40.00
MS	Mike Schmidt/30	100.00
SS	Shannon Stewart/99	20.00
DW	David Wright/99	60.00

Sign. Swings Jersey White
NM/M
Production 3-29 Sets
Cards #'d less than 25: No Pricing

LB	Lance Berkman/29	30.00
CC	Carl Crawford/29	30.00
JP	Josh Phelps/27	15.00

Sign. Swings Patch Blue
NM/M
Numbered to player's jersey number.
Cards #'d less than 25: No Pricing
Masterpiece: No Pricing
Production One Set

BAY	Jason Bay/38	60.00
JP	Josh Phelps/45	20.00

Sign. Swings Silver
NM/M
Common Player: 10.00
Gold: .75-1.5X
Sequentially #'d between 50 & 199.

BAY	Jason Bay	20.00
CC	Carl Crawford	10.00
AE	Adam Everett	10.00
CF	Chone Figgins	10.00
LF	Lew Ford	10.00
JG	Joey Gathright	10.00
KG	Khalil Greene	30.00
TH	Travis Hafner	10.00
AH	Aubrey Huff	10.00
CK	Casey Kotchman	10.00
VAL	Val Majewski	10.00
JM	Joe Mauer	25.00
DM	Dallas McPherson	15.00
JMO	Justin Morneau	40.00
WMP	Wily Mo Pena	25.00
JP	Josh Phelps	10.00
RR	Ryan Raburn	10.00
SS	Shannon Stewart	10.00
NS	Nick Swisher	15.00
BJU	B.J. Upton	15.00
CU	Chase Utley	20.00
DW	David Wright	50.00
MY	Michael Young	10.00

2005 Fleer Authentix
NM/M
Common Player (1-100): .25
Minor Stars (1-100): .40
Unlisted Stars (1-100): .60
Common Player Autograph (101-125):

David Aardsma

Minor Stars Autograph

(101-125):		15.00
Production 250 Sets		
Pack (5):		3.00
Box (24):		60.00
1	Albert Pujols	2.50
2	Bernie Williams	.60
3	Vinny Castilla	.25
4	Rocco Baldelli	.60
5	Mike Piazza	1.50
6	Sean Casey	.25
7	Oliver Perez	.25
8	Tony Batista	.25
9	Paul Konerko	.25
10	Scott Rolen	1.00
11	Justin Morneau	.25
12	Nomar Garciaparra	2.50
13	Lance Berkman	.40
14	Mike Sweeney	.25
15	Miguel Tejada	.75
16	Craig Wilson	.25
17	Craig Biggio	.40
18	Shea Hillenbrand	.25
19	Mark Mulder	.40
20	Juan Pierre	.25
21	Troy Glaus	.60
22	Eric Chavez	.40
23	Jeromy Burnitz	.25
24	Carl Crawford	.75
25	Kazuo Matsui	.75
26	Ivan Rodriguez	.60
27	Aubrey Huff	.25
28	Derek Jeter	3.00
29	Casey Blake	.25
30	Mark Teixeira	.40
31	Brad Wilkerson	.25
32	Austin Kearns	.60
33	Jim Edmonds	.40
34	Johan Santana	.40
35	Kerry Wood	.75
36	Ichiro Suzuki	2.00
37	Lyle Overbay	.25
38	Melvin Mora	.25
39	Jason Bay	.25
40	Jake Westbrook	.25
41	Andruw Jones	.75
42	Chase Utley	.50
43	Carl Pavano	.25
44	Luis Gonzalez	.40
45	Bobby Crosby	.25
46	Carlos Guillen	.25
47	Carlos Delgado	.75
48	Alex Rodriguez	2.50
49	Todd Helton	.75
50	Michael Young	.25
51	Geoff Jenkins	.40
52	Pedro Martinez	1.00
53	Brian Giles	.40
54	Ken Harvey	.25
55	Johnny Estrada	.25
56	Billy Wagner	.25
57	Roger Clemens	2.50
58	Chipper Jones	1.50
59	Jim Thome	1.00
60	Miguel Cabrera	.75
61	Vladimir Guerrero	1.00
62	Gary Sheffield	.60
63	Travis Hafner	.25
64	Alfonso Soriano	1.00
65	Richard Hidalgo	.25
66	Adam Dunn	.60
67	Garret Anderson	.40
68	Lew Ford	.25
69	Mark Prior	1.50
70	Bret Boone	.40
71	Ben Sheets	.40
72	David Ortiz	.60
73	Mark Loretta	.25
74	Eric Gagne	.25
75	Curt Schilling	.60
76	Jason Schmidt	.40
77	Adrian Beltre	.40
78	Javy Lopez	.25
79	Jack Wilson	.25
80	Carlos Beltran	.60
81	J.D. Drew	.40
82	Bobby Abreu	.40
83	Jeff Bagwell	.75
84	Randy Johnson	1.00
85	Tim Hudson	.40
86	Carlos Pena	.25
87	Vernon Wells	.40
88	Tom Glavine	.40
89	Victor Martinez	.25
90	Hank Blalock	.60
91	Jose Vidro	.25
92	Magglio Ordonez	.40
93	Jake Peavy	.25

94	Torii Hunter	.60
95	Sammy Sosa	2.00
96	Hideki Matsui	2.50
97	Shawn Green	.40
98	Manny Ramirez	.75
99	Khalil Greene	.75
100	Jason Marquis	.25
101	B.J. Upton/Auto.	20.00
102	Scott Kazmir/Auto.	20.00
103	Gavin Floyd/Auto.	20.00
104	Jeff Francis/Auto.	20.00
105	Russ Adams/ Auto. Exch.	10.00
106	Zack Greinke/Auto.	15.00
107	David Wright/Auto.	60.00
108	David Aardsma/Auto.	20.00
109	Josh Kroeger/Auto.	10.00
110	Ryan Raburn/Auto.	30.00
111	Jason Kubel/Auto.	10.00
112	Casey Kotchman/Auto.	20.00
113	Joey Gathright/Auto.	15.00
114	Jon Knott/Auto.	10.00
115	J.D. Durbin/Auto.	25.00
116	Andres Blanco/Auto.	10.00
117	Charlton Jimerson/ Auto.	10.00
118	Sean Burnett/Auto.	15.00
119	Joe Mauer/Auto.	30.00
120	Justin Verlander/ Auto. RC	30.00
121	Mike Gosling/Auto.	10.00
122	Jeff Keppinger/Auto.	10.00
123	David Krynzel/Auto.	10.00
124	Jose Lopez/Auto.	15.00
125	Ruben Gotay/Auto.	15.00

General Admission

Cards 1-100:		1-2.5X
Cards 101-125:		.75-1.5X
Production 100 Sets		

Autographed General Admission

		NM/M
Common Player:		15.00
Production 100 Sets		
Mezzanine:		1-2X
Production 40 Sets		
Club Box:		No Pricing
Production Five Sets		
Standing Room Only:		No Pricing
Production One Set		
JB	Jason Bay	15.00
JE	Johnny Estrada	15.00
CF	Chone Figgins	20.00
LF	Lew Ford	15.00
KG	Khalil Greene	50.00
TH	Travis Hafner	15.00
JM	Justin Morneau	40.00
JS	Johan Santana	25.00
BS	Ben Sheets	20.00
CU	Chase Utley	20.00
JW	Jack Wilson	15.00

Mezzanine

Cards 1-100:		1-30X
Cards 101-125:		.75-2X
Production 75 Sets		

Club Box

Cards 1-100:		1-3.25X
Cards 101-125:		1-2X
Production 50 Sets		

Standing Room Only

Cards 1-125:		No Pricing
Production 10 Sets		

Hot Ticket

		NM/M
Common Player:		2.00
Inserted 1:12		
1	Derek Jeter	6.00
2	Roger Clemens	5.00
3	Vladimir Guerrero	3.00
4	Manny Ramirez	5.00
5	Alex Rodriguez	5.00
6	Albert Pujols	5.00
7	Mike Piazza	3.50
8	Hideki Matsui	5.00
9	Sammy Sosa	4.00
10	Chipper Jones	3.50

Hot Ticket Jersey

		NM/M
Common Player:		8.00
Inserted 1:87		
Patch		
Cards #'d to 55:		1-30X
Cards #'d to 27:		2-4X
Cards #'d to 25 or less:		No Pricing
Sequentially #'d to player's jersey #.		
MLB Logo:		No Pricing
Production One Set		
RC	Roger Clemens	15.00
VG	Vladimir Guerrero	8.00
CJ	Chipper Jones	10.00
HM	Hideki Matsui	25.00
MP	Mike Piazza	10.00
AP	Albert Pujols	20.00
MR	Manny Ramirez	8.00
SS	Sammy Sosa	12.00

Jersey Game of the Week

		NM/M
Common Player:		10.00
Sequentially #'d between 10 & 200.		
No pricing for cards #'d to 20 or less.		
Patch:		No Pricing
Production 10 Sets		
BR	Carlos Beltran, Scott Rolen/120	15.00
BT	Tony Batista, Miguel Tejada/170	10.00
CG	Eric Chavez, Troy Glaus/150	12.00
CJ	Roger Clemens, Randy Johnson/70	15.00
CJ2	Miguel Cabrera, Chipper Jones/90	12.00
CP	Carl Crawford, Juan Pierre/190	10.00
DT	Adam Dunn, Jim Thome/110	20.00
GG	Shawn Green, Vladimir Guerrero/180	12.00
GS	Vladimir Guerrero, Alfonso Soriano/100	15.00
KG	Scott Kazmir, Zack Greinke/80	10.00
MM	Kazuo Matsui, Hideki Matsui/30	100.00
MM2	Joe Mauer, Victor Martinez/130	10.00
MR	Pedro Martinez, Mariano Rivera/60	12.00
OP	David Ortiz, Albert Pujols/200	15.00
OS	Magglio Ordonez, Sammy Sosa/160	15.00
RH	Manny Ramirez, Torii Hunter/140	10.00
SS	Johan Santana, Curt Schilling/40	30.00
WO	Kerry Wood, Roy Oswalt/50	30.00

Jersey General Admission

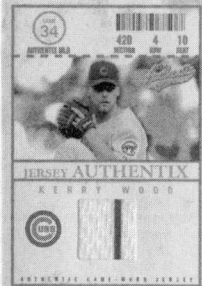

		NM/M
Production 40 Sets		
Mezzanine:		No Pricing
Production 10 Sets		
Club Box:		No Pricing
Production Five Sets		
Standing Room Only		
Production One Set		
CF	Chone Figgins	25.00
MP	Mike Piazza	150.00
CR	Cal Ripken Jr.	400.00
MS	Mike Schmidt	150.00
JT	Jim Thome	80.00

Showstoppers

		NM/M
Common Player:		2.00
Inserted 1:8		
1	Nomar Garciaparra	4.00
2	Ichiro Suzuki	3.50
3	Ken Griffey Jr.	3.00
4	Alex Rodriguez	4.00
5	Albert Pujols	5.00
6	Derek Jeter	5.00
7	Roger Clemens	4.00

LB	Lance Berkman	5.00
HB	Hank Blalock	5.00
MC	Miguel Cabrera	5.00
RC	Roger Clemens	12.00
AD	Adam Dunn	5.00
EG	Eric Gagne	5.00
KG	Khalil Greene	10.00
VG	Vladimir Guerrero	8.00
TH	Todd Helton	8.00
RJ	Randy Johnson	8.00
CJ	Chipper Jones	8.00
PM	Pedro Martinez	8.00
HM	Hideki Matsui	20.00
KM	Kazuo Matsui	10.00
JM	Joe Mauer	8.00
HN	Hideo Nomo	8.00
DO	David Ortiz	10.00
MP	Mike Piazza	15.00
AP	Albert Pujols	15.00
MR	Manny Ramirez	8.00
MR2	Mariano Rivera	5.00
IR	Ivan Rodriguez	5.00
SR	Scott Rolen	8.00
JS	Johan Santana	5.00
CS	Curt Schilling	5.00
GS	Gary Sheffield	5.00
AS	Alfonso Soriano	4.00
SS	Sammy Sosa	10.00
JT	Jim Thome	8.00
BU	B.J. Upton	8.00
BW	Bernie Williams	5.00
KW	Kerry Wood	5.00
DW	David Wright	15.00

Auto. Jersey General Admission

		NM/M
Common Player:		20.00
Production 75 Sets		
Mezzanine:		No Pricing
Production 15 Sets		
Club Box:		No Pricing
Production Five Sets		
Standing Room Only:		No Pricing
Production One Set		
JB	Jason Bay	20.00
MC	Miguel Cabrera	30.00
JE	Johnny Estrada	20.00
CF	Chone Figgins	25.00
LF	Lew Ford	20.00
KG	Khalil Greene	60.00
TH	Travis Hafner	20.00
JM	Justin Morneau	50.00
JS	Johan Santana	20.00
MS	Mike Schmidt	75.00
BS	Ben Sheets	25.00
CU	Chase Utley	25.00
JW	Jack Wilson	20.00

Auto. Patch General Admission

		NM/M
Production 40 Sets		
Mezzanine		No Pricing
Production 10 Sets		
Club Box:		No Pricing
Production Five Sets		
Standing Room Only		
Production One Set		
Patch General Admission:		2-4X
Production 75 Sets		
Patch Mezzanine:		No Pricing
Production 15 Sets		
Patch Club Box:		No Pricing
Production Five Sets		
Patch Standing Room Only:	No Pricing
Production One Set		
CB	Carlos Beltran	10.00
AB	Adrian Beltre	5.00

8	Randy Johnson	2.50
9	Hideo Nomo	2.00
10	Jim Thome	2.50
11	Mike Piazza	3.00
12	Hideki Matsui	4.00
13	Sammy Sosa	3.50
14	Kerry Wood	2.00
15	Eric Gagne	2.00

Teammate Trios

		NM/M
Common Card:		12.00
Production 75 Sets		
Hometown 1:		2-3X
Production 25 Sets		
Hometown 2:		No Pricing
Production Five Sets		
BR	David Ortiz, Manny Ramirez, Pedro Martinez	25.00
NY	Hideki Matsui, Bernie Williams, Gary Sheffield	30.00
AB	J.D. Drew, Chipper Jones, Andruw Jones	15.00
CC	Sammy Sosa, Mark Prior, Nomar Garciaparra	15.00
CI	Victor Martinez, Travis Hafner, Casey Blake	12.00
HA	Lance Berkman, Roger Clemens, Carlos Beltran	25.00
MT	Johan Santana, Torii Hunter, Corey Koskie	12.00
WN	Tony Batista, Jose Vidro, Brad Wilkerson	12.00
NM	Mike Piazza, David Wright, Kazuo Matsui	40.00
OA	Barry Zito, Tim Hudson, Mark Mulder	12.00
PP	Bobby Abreu, Jim Thome, Pat Burrell	15.00
SC	Scott Rolen, Albert Pujols, Jim Edmonds	30.00
TD	Scott Kazmir, Rocco Baldelli, B.J. Upton	15.00
TR	Hank Blalock, Mark Teixeira, Alfonso Soriano	15.00
LD	Shawn Green, Adrian Beltre, Steve Finley	15.00

2005 Fleer Classic Clippings

		NM/M
Common Player (1-75):		.25
Minor Stars (1-75):		.40
Unlisted Stars (1-75):		.60
Common Legends (76-105):		2.00
Production 999 Sets		
Common Player (106-125):		3.00
Inserted 1:6		
1	Frank Thomas	.75
2	Vladimir Guerrero	1.00
3	Ken Griffey Jr.	1.50
4	Derek Jeter	3.00
5	Rafael Palmeiro	.75
6	Adrian Beltre	.40
7	Khalil Greene	.40
8	Richie Sexson	.60
9	Roger Clemens	2.50
10	Mike Piazza	1.50
11	Chipper Jones	1.50
12	Juan Pierre	.40
13	Todd Helton	.75
14	Ben Sheets	.40
15	John Smoltz	.40
16	Steve Finley	.25
17	Jim Thome	1.00
18	Vernon Wells	.40
19	Melvin Mora	.40
20	Dontrelle Willis	.40
21	Eric Gagne	.40
22	Craig Wilson	.25
23	Curt Schilling	.60
24	Justin Morneau	.40
25	Jason Schmidt	.40
26	Kerry Wood	.60
27	Ivan Rodriguez	.60
28	Rocco Baldelli	.60
29	Mark Prior	2.00
30	Josh Beckett	.75
31	Scott Rolen	1.00
32	Nomar Garciaparra	2.50
33	Carl Crawford	.25
34	Paul Konerko	.40
35	Miguel Cabrera	.75
36	Hank Blalock	.60
37	Sammy Sosa	2.00
38	Jim Edmonds	.40
39	David Ortiz	.60
40	Lance Berkman	.40
41	Ichiro Suzuki	2.00
42	Adam Dunn	.60
43	Carlos Guillen	.25
44	Alfonso Soriano	1.00
45	Victor Martinez	.25
46	Torii Hunter	.60
47	Kazuo Matsui	.60
48	Andruw Jones	.75
49	Matt Holliday	.50
50	Eric Chavez	.40
51	Randy Johnson	1.00
52	Lew Ford	.25
53	Hideki Matsui	2.50
54	Manny Ramirez	.75
55	Mark Teixeira	.40
56	Jose Vidro	.25
57	Mike Sweeney	.25
58	Jack Wilson	.25

59	Greg Maddux	1.50
60	Tony Batista	.25
61	Albert Pujols	2.50
62	Miguel Tejada	.60
63	Carlos Beltran	.60
64	Bobby Abreu	.40
65	Carlos Delgado	.75
66	Travis Hafner	.25
67	Scott Podsednik	.25
68	Gary Sheffield	.60
69	Johan Santana	.40
70	Barry Zito	.40
71	Pedro Martinez	1.00
72	Brian Giles	.40
73	Garret Anderson	.40
74	Jeff Bagwell	.75
75	Alex Rodriguez	2.50
76	Johnny Bench	4.00
77	Yogi Berra	3.00
78	Lou Brock	3.00
79	Rod Carew	3.00
80	Orlando Cepeda	2.00
81	Carlton Fisk	5.00
82	Bob Gibson	3.00
83	Reggie Jackson	5.00
84	Al Kaline	4.00
85	Harmon Killebrew	3.00
86	Ralph Kiner	2.00
87	Willie McCovey	2.00
88	Eddie Murray	4.00
89	Phil Rizzuto	4.00
90	Brooks Robinson	3.00
91	Nolan Ryan	4.00
92	Mike Schmidt	4.00
93	Tom Seaver	3.00
94	Willie Stargell	2.00
95	Rollie Fingers	2.00
96	Dennis Eckersley	2.00
97	Enos Slaughter	2.00
98	Jim Palmer	3.00
99	Warren Spahn	3.00
100	Joe Morgan	2.00
101	Richie Ashburn	3.00
102	Robin Yount	3.00
103	Bob Feller	3.00
104	Pee Wee Reese	2.00
105	Eddie Mathews	3.00
106	David Wright	6.00
107	David Aardsma	3.00
108	B.J. Upton	3.00
109	Scott Kazmir	4.00
110	Gavin Floyd	3.00
111	Jeff Francis	3.00
112	Dioner Navarro	3.00
113	Zack Greinke	3.00
114	Nick Swisher	5.00
115	Josh Kroeger	3.00
116	Ryan Raburn	3.00
117	Victor Diaz	4.00
118	Casey Kotchman	4.00
119	Joey Gathright	3.00
120	Jon Knott	3.00
121	J.D. Durbin	3.00
122	Andres Blanco	3.00
123	Charlton Jimerson	3.00
124	Russ Adams	3.00
125	Justin Verlander RC	5.00

First Edition

(1-75):		2-5X
(76-105):		1-1.5X
(106-125):		1-2X
Production 150 Sets		

Final Edition

No Pricing
Production One Set

Bat Rack Quad Blue

		NM/M
Inserted 1:118		
Silver:		No Pricing
Production 10 Sets		
Purple:		No Pricing
Production One Set		
	Gary Sheffield, Vladimir Guerrero, Manny Ramirez, Sammy Sosa	20.00
	Manny Ramirez, Wade Boggs, Carl Yastrzemski, Bobby Doerr	40.00
	Kirby Puckett, Jacque Jones, Harmon Killebrew, Torii Hunter	40.00
	Brandon Webb, Randy Johnson, Curt Schilling, Roger Clemens	40.00
	Willie Stargell, Bill Madlock, Bill Mazeroski, Roberto Clemente	100.00
	Al Kaline, Tony Gwynn, Frank Howard, Rocky Colavito	50.00
	Jose Reyes, Gary Carter, Mike Piazza, Kazuo Matsui	25.00
	Bobby Abreu, Adam Dunn, Rocco Baldelli, Hideki Matsui	30.00
	Jim Thome, Albert Pujols, Jeff Bagwell, Todd Helton	40.00
	Hank Blalock, Miguel Tejada, Troy Glaus, Ivan Rodriguez	25.00

Carlos Delgado,
Jason Giambi,
Rafael Palmeiro,
Mark Teixeira 25.00

Classic Clippings
NM/M
Common Player: 3.00
Gold: 2-5X
Production 51-95 Sets
1	Nolan Ryan/1991	6.00
2	Cal Ripken Jr./1995	8.00
3	Joe Carter/1993	3.00
4	Bucky Dent/1978	3.00
5	Kirk Gibson/1988	3.00
6	Reggie Jackson/1977	5.00
7	Carlton Fisk/1975	4.00
8	Bobby Thomson/1951	3.00
9	Bill Mazeroski/1960	3.00
10	Don Larsen/1956	3.00

Cut of History Single Autograph Blue
NM/M
Common Player: 20.00
Inserted 1:161
Silver: No Pricing
Production 25 Sets
Purple: No Pricing
Production One Set
JB	Johnny Bench	50.00
BB	Bill Buckner	20.00
BF	Bob Feller	20.00
KG	Kirk Gibson	20.00
DG	Dwight Gooden	30.00
DL	Don Larsen	20.00
DM	Don Mattingly	50.00
JP	Jim Palmer	30.00
BR	Brooks Robinson	40.00
DS	Darryl Strawberry	25.00
MW	Mookie Wilson	20.00

Cut of History Dual Autograph Blue
NM/M
Production 49 Sets
Silver: No Pricing
Production 22 Sets
Purple: No Pricing
Production One Set
GE	Kirk Gibson, Dennis Eckersley	50.00
GS	Dwight Gooden, Darryl Strawberry	40.00
WB	Mookie Wilson, Bill Buckner	40.00

Cut of History Triple Autograph Blue

No Pricing
Production 15 Sets
Silver: No Pricing
Production Five Sets
Purple: No Pricing
Production One Set

Cut of History Single Jersey Blue
NM/M
Common Player: 6.00
Inserted 1:21
Silver Patch: No Pricing
Production 25 Sets
Purple Patch: No Pricing
Production One Set
SA	Sparky Anderson	6.00
JB	Johnny Bench	15.00
OC	Orlando Cepeda	8.00
CF	Carlton Fisk	10.00
BG	Bob Gibson	8.00
DG	Dwight Gooden	6.00
RJ	Reggie Jackson	12.00
DM	Don Mattingly	15.00
WM	Willie McCovey	6.00
JM	Joe Morgan/SP/82	8.00
EM	Eddie Murray	10.00
CR	Cal Ripken Jr.	20.00
BR	Brooks Robinson	8.00
NR	Nolan Ryan	20.00
MS	Mike Schmidt	12.00
TS	Tom Seaver	10.00
OS	Ozzie Smith	15.00
WS	Willie Stargell	10.00
DS	Darryl Strawberry	6.00
CY	Carl Yastrzemski	6.00

Cut of History Dual Jersey Blue
NM/M
Common Card: 15.00
Inserted 1:112
Silver Patch: No Pricing
Production 15 Sets
Purple Patch: No Pricing
Production One Set

BF	Johnny Bench, Carlton Fisk	20.00
BS	Lou Brock, Mike Schmidt	25.00
CM	Orlando Cepeda, Willie McCovey	15.00
GS	Dwight Gooden, Darryl Strawberry	15.00
JY	Reggie Jackson, Carl Yastrzemski	20.00
RS	Cal Ripken Jr., Ozzie Smith	30.00
RS	Nolan Ryan, Tom Seaver	30.00
SJ	Willie Stargell, Reggie Jackson	20.00

Cut of History Triple Jersey Blue
NM/M
Inserted 1:67
Silver Patch: No Pricing
Production 25 Sets
Purple Patch: No Pricing
Production One Set
ACW	Hank Aaron, Roberto Clemente, Ted Williams	160.00
BSG	Lou Brock, Kirk Gibson, Ozzie Smith	50.00
JKM	Reggie Jackson, Harmon Killebrew, Willie McCovey	40.00
MMC	Eddie Murray, Orlando Cepeda, Willie McCovey	25.00
MRS	Don Mattingly, Cal Ripken Jr., Mike Schmidt	75.00
OJM	Paul O'Neill, Don Mattingly, Reggie Jackson	50.00
RCJ	Nolan Ryan, Roger Clemens, Randy Johnson	50.00

Diamond Signings Single Blue
NM/M
Inserted 1:29
Silver: No Pricing
Production 25 Sets
Purple: No Pricing
Production One Set
JB	Jason Bay	20.00
AB	Andres Blanco	15.00
CF	Chone Figgins	15.00
GF	Gavin Floyd	15.00
KG	Khalil Greene/150	25.00
ZG	Zack Greinke	15.00
TH	Travis Hafner	10.00
CJ	Charlton Jimerson	10.00
SK	Scott Kazmir	20.00
CK	Casey Kotchman	10.00
BL	Brad Lidge/97	40.00
JM	Justin Morneau/98	25.00
DN	Dioner Navarro	10.00
JP	Jake Peavy	20.00
NS	Nick Swisher	15.00
BU	B.J. Upton	15.00
JV	Justin Verlander/150	35.00
DW	David Wright/97	50.00

Diamond Signings Dual Blue
NM/M
Production 49 Sets
Silver: No Pricing
Production 22 Sets
Purple: No Pricing
Production One Set
BC	Jason Bay, B. Crosby Exch	30.00
FU	Gavin Floyd, Chase Utley	40.00

Diamond Signings Triple Blue
NM/M
Sequentially Numbered
Silver: No Pricing
Production Five Sets
Purple: No Pricing
Production One Set
Khalil Greene, B.J. Upton, Bobby Crosby/99	50.00
Justin Verlander, Gavin Floyd, Scott Kazmir/99	75.00
Nick Swisher, Charlton Jimerson, Chone Figgins/99	30.00
Casey Kotchman, Justin Morneau, Jason Bay/86	40.00

Jersey Rack Dual Jersey Blue
NM/M
Common Card: 10.00
Inserted 1:100
Silver Patch: No Pricing
Production 25 Sets
Purple Patch: No Pricing
Production One Set
BW	Josh Beckett, Kerry Wood	10.00
CJ	Miguel Cabrera, Andruw Jones	12.00
DB	Adam Dunn, Lance Berkman	10.00
GS	Vladimir Guerrero, Sammy Sosa	15.00
GT	Khalil Greene, Miguel Tejada	10.00
HB	Todd Helton, Jeff Bagwell	10.00
HE	Torii Hunter, Jim Edmonds	10.00
JC	Randy Johnson, Roger Clemens	20.00
JW	Chipper Jones, David Wright	15.00
MM	Hideki Matsui, Kazuo Matsui	25.00
OG	David Ortiz, Jason Giambi	12.00
RB	Scott Rolen, Adrian Beltre	12.00
RS	Manny Ramirez, Gary Sheffield	12.00
SG	John Smoltz, Eric Gagne	10.00
SM	Jason Schmidt, Pedro Martinez	12.00
SM1	Alfonso Soriano, Kazuo Matsui	10.00
SP	Curt Schilling, Mark Prior	8.00
TP	Jim Thome, Mike Piazza	12.00
WS	Dontrelle Willis, Johan Santana	12.00

Jersey Rack Triple Jersey Blue
NM/M
Common Card: 12.00
Inserted 1:54
Silver Patch: No Pricing
Production 25 Sets
Purple Patch: No Pricing
Production One Set
CJS	Roger Clemens, Randy Johnson, Jason Schmidt	20.00
CSJ	Roger Clemens, Curt Schilling, Randy Johnson	20.00
EHJ	Jim Edmonds, Torii Hunter, Andruw Jones	12.00
GRS	Vladimir Guerrero, Manny Ramirez, Gary Sheffield	15.00
GSR	Eric Gagne, John Smoltz, Mariano Rivera	15.00
HSB	Todd Helton, Alfonso Soriano, Adrian Beltre	12.00
MGT	Kazuo Matsui, Khalil Greene, Miguel Tejada	15.00
MRG	Hideki Matsui, Mariano Rivera, Jason Giambi	25.00
ORM	David Ortiz, Manny Ramirez, Pedro Martinez	15.00
PRE	Albert Pujols, Scott Rolen, Jim Edmonds	25.00
PTB	Albert Pujols, Jim Thome, Jeff Bagwell	20.00
RBJ	Scott Rolen, Adrian Beltre, Chipper Jones	15.00
SDC	Sammy Sosa, Adam Dunn, Miguel Cabrera	12.00
SJJ	John Smoltz, Chipper Jones, Andruw Jones	20.00
SPB	Jason Schmidt, Mark Prior, Josh Beckett	10.00
STB	Sammy Sosa, Miguel Tejada, Adrian Beltre	15.00
WPM	David Wright, Mike Piazza, Kazuo Matsui	20.00
WSW	Dontrelle Willis, Johan Santana, Kerry Wood	15.00

Press Clippings
NM/M
Common Player: 2.00
Inserted 1:6
Gold: No Pricing
Production Four Sets
1	Ichiro Suzuki	4.00
2	Manny Ramirez	2.00
3	Albert Pujols	5.00
4	David Ortiz	2.00
5	Greg Maddux	3.00
6	Ken Griffey Jr.	3.00
7	Vladimir Guerrero	3.00
8	Randy Johnson	3.00
9	Johan Santana	2.00
10	Roger Clemens	5.00
11	Bobby Crosby	2.00
12	Jason Bay	2.00

2005 Fleer Patchworks

NM/M
Complete Set (100):
Common (1-70): .40
Common (71-90): 1.50
Production 499 Sets
Common (91-100): 2.00
Production 999 Sets
Pack (5): 4.00
Box (18): 60.00
1	Bobby Abreu	.50
2	Miguel Cabrera	1.00
3	J.D. Drew	.40
4	Justin Morneau	.40
5	David Ortiz	1.00
6	Ivan Rodriguez	.75
7	Jason Schmidt	.40
8	Frank Thomas	.75
9	Travis Hafner	.50
10	Curt Schilling	1.00
11	Jim Edmonds	.75
12	Randy Johnson	1.00
13	Jose Vidro	.40
14	Vernon Wells	.40
15	Lance Berkman	.50
16	Khalil Greene	.50
17	Andruw Jones	.75
18	Mark Prior	.75
19	Mark Teixeira	.75
20	Jack Wilson	.40
21	Adrian Beltre	.50
22	Lew Ford	.40
23	Shawn Green	.50
24	Juan Pierre	.40
25	Alfonso Soriano	.75
26	Mike Sweeney	.40
27	Chipper Jones	1.00
28	Javy Lopez	.40
29	Victor Martinez	.40
30	Kazuo Matsui	.40
31	Bernie Williams	.50
32	Kerry Wood	.50
33	Barry Zito	.50
34	Austin Kearns	.40
35	Todd Helton	.75
36	B.J. Upton	.40
37	Jeff Bagwell	.75
38	Pedro Martinez	1.00
39	Lyle Overbay	.40
40	Ichiro Suzuki	2.00
41	Jason Bay	.50
42	Bobby Crosby	.50
43	Vladimir Guerrero	1.00
44	Richie Sexson	.50
45	Johan Santana	1.00
46	Magglio Ordonez	.40
47	Derek Jeter	3.00
48	Eric Gagne	.40
49	Albert Pujols	3.00
50	Jim Thome	.75
51	Hideki Matsui	2.00
52	Torii Hunter	.40
53	Greg Maddux	2.00
54	Michael Young	.40
55	Carlos Beltran	.75
56	Carl Crawford	.50
57	Adam Dunn	.75
58	Nomar Garciaparra	1.00
59	Mike Piazza	1.00
60	Alex Rodriguez	3.00
61	Scott Rolen	.50
62	Ben Sheets	.50
63	Sammy Sosa	1.00
64	Hank Blalock	.50
65	Carlos Delgado	.50
66	Ken Griffey Jr.	2.00
67	Manny Ramirez	1.00
68	Miguel Tejada	.75
69	Roger Clemens	3.00
70	Gary Sheffield	.75
71	Jon Knott	1.50
72	Ryan Raburn	1.50
73	Zack Greinke	1.50
74	David Aardsma	1.50
75	Justin Verlander RC	4.00
76	Andres Blanco	1.50
77	David Wright	4.00
78	Jeff Baker	1.50
79	Charlton Jimerson	1.50
80	Sean Burnett	1.50
81	Joey Gathright	1.50
82	Victor Diaz	1.50
83	Scott Kazmir	1.50
84	Edwin Encarnacion	1.50
85	J.D. Durbin	1.50
86	Nick Swisher	1.50
87	Casey Kotchman	1.50
88	Gavin Floyd	1.50
89	Josh Kroeger	1.50
90	Taylor Buchholz	1.50
91	Reggie Jackson	2.00
92	Nolan Ryan	6.00
93	Eddie Murray	2.00
94	Carlton Fisk	2.00
95	Mike Schmidt	4.00
96	Joe Morgan	2.00
97	Rod Carew	2.00
98	Harmon Killebrew	2.00
99	Tom Seaver	3.00
100	Brooks Robinson	3.00

Gold
Gold (1-70): 3-6X
Gold (71-100): 1-2X
Production 99 Sets

Autoworks Silver
NM/M
Production 99 Sets
RB	Rocco Baldelli	12.00
JB	Jason Bay	20.00
JBO	Jeremy Bonderman	15.00
SB	Sean Burnett	8.00
MC	Miguel Cabrera	25.00
MCA	Mike Cameron	12.00
CC	Carl Crawford	15.00
JD	J.D. Durbin	8.00
LF	Lew Ford	10.00
ZG	Zack Greinke	15.00
TH	Travis Hafner	15.00
BL	Brad Lidge	15.00
VM	Victor Martinez	15.00
JM	Justin Morneau	20.00
JP	Josh Phelps	10.00
BS	Ben Sheets	15.00
BU	B.J. Upton	15.00
JV	Justin Verlander	20.00
DW	David Wright	60.00

Autoworks Gold
NM/M
Production 49 Sets
HA	Hank Aaron	250.00
RB	Rocco Baldelli	15.00
EB	Ernie Banks	50.00
JB	Jason Bay	20.00
LB	Lance Berkman	20.00
JBO	Jeremy Bonderman	20.00
SB	Sean Burnett	10.00
MC	Miguel Cabrera	30.00
MCA	Mike Cameron	12.00
CC	Carl Crawford	20.00
JD	J.D. Durbin	10.00
GF	Gavin Floyd	10.00
LF	Lew Ford	10.00
ZG	Zack Greinke	20.00
TH	Travis Hafner	20.00
BL	Brad Lidge	20.00
VM	Victor Martinez	20.00
JM	Justin Morneau	25.00
JP	Josh Phelps	10.00
BS	Ben Sheets	20.00
BU	B.J. Upton	20.00
DW	David Wright	60.00
MY	Michael Young	15.00

Autoworks Copper
NM/M
Production 75-250
Masterpiece: No Pricing
Production One Set
RB	Rocco Baldelli/100	12.00
JB	Jason Bay/150	20.00
JBO	Jeremy Bonderman/100	15.00
SB	Sean Burnett/100	8.00
MC	Miguel Cabrera/75	25.00
CC	Carl Crawford/175	15.00
JD	J.D. Durbin/100	10.00
ZG	Zack Greinke/200	15.00
TH	Travis Hafner/150	15.00
BL	Brad Lidge/75	15.00
VM	Victor Martinez/100	15.00
JM	Justin Morneau/175	20.00
BU	B.J. Upton/150	15.00
JV	Justin Verlander/100	15.00
DW	David Wright/250	50.00

Autoworks Dual
Production 25 Sets

Autoworks Quad
Production 10 Sets

By the Numbers

BY THE NUMBERS
ADRIAN BELTRE / SEATTLE MARINERS

NM/M
Common Player: 1.00
Inserted 1:18
1	Roy Oswalt	1.00
2	Hideki Matsui	3.00
3	Curt Schilling	1.50
4	Mike Piazza	2.00
5	Alex Rodriguez	4.00
6	Vladimir Guerrero	1.50
7	Victor Martinez	1.00
8	Adrian Beltre	1.00
9	Johnny Estrada	1.00
10	Ken Griffey Jr.	3.00
11	Sammy Sosa	2.00
12	Ichiro Suzuki	3.00
13	Roger Clemens	4.00
14	David Ortiz	1.50
15	Johan Santana	1.50
16	Pedro Martinez	1.50
17	Austin Kearns	1.00
18	Randy Johnson	1.50
19	Nomar Garciaparra	1.50
20	Albert Pujols	4.00

By the Numbers Jersey
NM/M
Common Player: 4.00
AB	Adrian Beltre	4.00
RC	Roger Clemens/SP	10.00
JE	Johnny Estrada	4.00
VG	Vladimir Guerrero/SP	8.00
RJ	Randy Johnson	8.00
PM	Pedro Martinez	8.00
HM	Hideki Matsui	20.00
RO	Roy Oswalt	4.00
AP	Albert Pujols	15.00
JS	Johan Santana	8.00
CS	Curt Schilling	8.00
SS	Sammy Sosa	8.00

By the Numbers Jersey Die Cut
NM/M
Production 199 Sets
Jersey Tag: No Pricing
Production One Set
AB	Adrian Beltre	4.00
RC	Roger Clemens	10.00
JE	Johnny Estrada	4.00
VG	Vladimir Guerrero	8.00
RJ	Randy Johnson	8.00
AK	Austin Kearns	4.00
PM	Pedro Martinez	8.00
HM	Hideki Matsui	20.00
DO	David Ortiz	8.00
RO	Roy Oswalt	8.00
MP	Mike Piazza/116	10.00
AP	Albert Pujols	15.00
JS	Johan Santana	8.00
CS	Curt Schilling	8.00
SS	Sammy Sosa	8.00

By the Numbers Patch
NM/M
Production 99 Sets
Patch Die-Cut: No Pricing
Production 25 Sets
AB	Adrian Beltre	10.00
JE	Johnny Estrada	8.00
VG	Vladimir Guerrero	15.00
AK	Austin Kearns/78	10.00
HM	Hideki Matsui	30.00
DO	David Ortiz/46	15.00
RO	Roy Oswalt	15.00
MP	Mike Piazza	20.00
AP	Albert Pujols	30.00
JS	Johan Santana	15.00
CS	Curt Schilling	15.00
SS	Sammy Sosa	20.00

By the Numbers Patch Autographs
No Pricing
Production 25 Sets

Heart of the Team

NM/M
Inserted 1:108
1	Braves/Marlins	8.00
2	Red Sox/Yankees	15.00
3	Cardinals/Astros	10.00
4	Angels/A's	8.00
5	Phillies/Mets	8.00
6	Twins/White Sox	10.00
7	Reds/Cubs	10.00
8	Mariners/Rangers	8.00
9	Orioles/Nationals	8.00
10	Blue Jays/Devil Rays	8.00

Heart of the Team Jersey
Production 199 Sets
Patch: No Pricing
Production 15 Sets

Jersey
NM/M
Common Player: 4.00
JB	Josh Beckett	4.00
TH	Torii Hunter	4.00
MARK	Mark Prior	8.00
MR	Manny Ramirez	8.00
GS	Gary Sheffield	6.00
AS	Alfonso Soriano	6.00
SS	Shannon Stewart	4.00
BW	Bernie Williams	6.00
DW	Dontrelle Willis	4.00
KW	Kerry Wood	4.00
DWR	David Wright	15.00
MY	Michael Young	4.00

Dual Jersey
NM/M
Common Duo: 6.00
Die-Cut: 1.5X

Production 199 Sets		
Dual MLB Logo:	No Pricing	
Production One Set		
Dual Patch:	No Pricing	
Production 25 Sets		
Dual Patch Die-Cut:	No Pricing	
Production 15 Sets		
DWJB	Dontrelle Willis, Josh Beckett	6.00
DWMP	David Wright, Mike Piazza	15.00
GSBW	Gary Sheffield, Bernie Williams/SP	8.00
KWMP	Kerry Wood, Mark Prior/SP	
MRDO	Manny Ramirez, David Ortiz	15.00
MYAS	Michael Young, Alfonso Soriano	8.00
SSTH	Shannon Stewart, Torii Hunter	6.00

Patch

		NM/M
Production 99 Sets		
Die-Cut:		1-1.5X
Production 49 Sets		
JB	Josh Beckett	8.00
TH	Torii Hunter	10.00
DO	David Ortiz/51	20.00
MIKE	Mike Piazza	20.00
MARK	Mark Prior	15.00
MR	Manny Ramirez	20.00
AS	Alfonso Soriano/73	12.00
SS	Shannon Stewart	10.00
BW	Bernie Williams	12.00
DW	Dontrelle Willis	15.00
KW	Kerry Wood	12.00
DWR	David Wright	35.00
MY	Michael Young	10.00

Property of

		NM/M
Common Player:		1.00
Inserted 1:6		
1	Vladimir Guerrero	1.50
2	Luis Gonzalez	1.00
3	Chipper Jones	1.50
4	Miguel Tejada	1.50
5	David Ortiz	1.50
6	Kerry Wood	1.00
7	Frank Thomas	1.00
8	Adam Dunn	1.00
9	Victor Martinez	1.00
10	Todd Helton	1.00
11	Ivan Rodriguez	1.50
12	Miguel Cabrera	1.50
13	Jeff Bagwell	1.50
14	Mike Sweeney	1.00
15	Eric Gagne	1.00
16	Lyle Overbay	1.00
17	Johan Santana	1.50
18	Mike Piazza	2.00
19	Derek Jeter	5.00
20	Bobby Crosby	1.00
21	Jim Thome	1.50
22	Jason Bay	1.00
23	Khalil Greene	1.00
24	Jason Schmidt	1.00
25	Ichiro Suzuki	3.00
26	Albert Pujols	5.00
27	B.J. Upton	1.00
28	Hank Blalock	1.00
29	Vernon Wells	1.00
30	Jose Vidro	1.00

Property of Jersey

		NM/M
JB	Jeff Bagwell	6.00
JBA	Jason Bay	4.00
HB	Hank Blalock	4.00
MC	Miguel Cabrera	8.00
EG	Eric Gagne	4.00
LG	Luis Gonzalez	4.00
VG	Vladimir Guerrero/SP	8.00
CJ	Chipper Jones	8.00
AP	Albert Pujols	15.00
IR	Ivan Rodriguez	6.00
JS	Johan Santana/SP	8.00
JSC	Jason Schmidt	4.00
MT	Miguel Tejada	6.00
FT	Frank Thomas	6.00
JT	Jim Thome	6.00
BU	B.J. Upton	4.00
VW	Vernon Wells	4.00
KW	Kerry Wood	4.00

Property of Jersey Die Cut

		NM/M
Production 199 Sets		
MLB Logo:	No Pricing	
Production One Set		
JB	Jeff Bagwell	6.00
JBA	Jason Bay	4.00
HB	Hank Blalock	4.00
MC	Miguel Cabrera	8.00
EG	Eric Gagne	4.00
LG	Luis Gonzalez	4.00
KG	Khalil Greene	4.00
VG	Vladimir Guerrero	8.00
CJ	Chipper Jones	8.00
DO	David Ortiz	8.00
LO	Lyle Overbay/86 UER	4.00
MP	Mike Piazza	8.00
AP	Albert Pujols	15.00
IR	Ivan Rodriguez	6.00
JS	Johan Santana	6.00

JSC	Jason Schmidt	4.00
MT	Miguel Tejada	6.00
FT	Frank Thomas	6.00
JT	Jim Thome	6.00
BU	B.J. Upton	4.00
VW	Vernon Wells	4.00
KW	Kerry Wood	4.00

Property of Patch

	NM/M
Production 99 Sets	
Die-Cut:	No Pricing
Production 25 Sets	
Nameplate:	1-2X
Production 49 Sets	
JB	Jeff Bagwell	15.00
JBA	Jason Bay/84	10.00
HB	Hank Blalock	12.00
MC	Miguel Cabrera	15.00
AD	Adam Dunn/42	10.00
EG	Eric Gagne	10.00
LG	Luis Gonzalez	10.00
KG	Khalil Greene	10.00
VG	Vladimir Guerrero	15.00
CJ	Chipper Jones	15.00
DO	David Ortiz/45	20.00
MP	Mike Piazza	20.00
AP	Albert Pujols	30.00
IR	Ivan Rodriguez	15.00
JS	Johan Santana	15.00
JSC	Jason Schmidt	12.00
MS	Mike Sweeney/77	15.00
MT	Miguel Tejada	15.00
JT	Jim Thome	15.00
BU	B.J. Upton	10.00
VW	Vernon Wells/30	15.00
KW	Kerry Wood/89	15.00

2005 Fleer Platinum

		NM/M
Common Players (1-100):		.25
Minor Players (1-100):		.40
Unlisted Stars (1-100):		.50
Common Players (101-125):		3.00
Production 1,000 Sets		
Pack (5):		2.00
Box (24):		40.00
1	Nomar Garciaparra	1.50
2	Matt Holliday	.50
3	Rickie Weeks	.25
4	Jim Thome	.75
5	Roy Halladay	.40
6	Paul Konerko	.25
7	Lance Berkman	.40
8	Ichiro Suzuki	1.25
9	Kerry Wood	.60
10	Lew Ford	.25
11	Omar Vizquel	.40
12	Manny Ramirez	.60
13	Carlos Beltran	.50
14	Lyle Overbay	.40
15	Billy Wagner	.40
16	Jose Vidro	.25
17	Vladimir Guerrero	.75
18	Miguel Tejada	.50
19	Alex Rodriguez	1.50
20	Rocco Baldelli	.40
21	David Ortiz	.50
22	Victor Martinez	.25
23	Shawn Green	.25
24	Jason Bay	.25
25	Pedro Martinez	.75
26	Travis Hafner	.40
27	Eric Gagne	.40
28	Jack Wilson	.25
29	Ivan Rodriguez	.50
30	Jody Gerut	.25
31	Adrian Beltre	.40
32	Craig Wilson	.25
33	J.D. Drew	.40
34	Craig Biggio	.40
35	Mark Mulder	.40
36	Mark Teixeira	.50
37	Melvin Mora	.25
38	Ken Griffey Jr.	1.00
39	Mike Sweeney	.25
40	Khalil Greene	.60
41	Rafael Palmeiro	.50
42	Austin Kearns	.50
43	Garret Anderson	.40
44	Trevor Hoffman	.25
45	Andruw Jones	.60
46	Adam Dunn	.50
47	Angel Berroa	.25
48	Ryan Klesko	.25
49	Sean Casey	.25
50	Kazuo Matsui	.50
51	Jim Edmonds	.40

52	Magglio Ordonez	.40
53	Tom Glavine	.40
54	Larry Walker	.40
55	Johnny Estrada	.25
56	Brad Lidge	.25
57	Barry Zito	.50
58	Michael Young	.40
59	Chipper Jones	1.00
60	Andy Pettitte	.50
61	Eric Chavez	.40
62	Carlos Delgado	.60
63	David Eckstein	.25
64	Dmitri Young	.25
65	Mike Piazza	1.00
66	Albert Pujols	1.50
67	Luis Gonzalez	.40
68	Hideki Matsui	1.50
69	Gary Sheffield	.50
70	Carl Crawford	.50
71	Curt Schilling	.50
72	Todd Helton	.50
73	Ben Sheets	.40
74	Bobby Abreu	.40
75	Jose Guillen	.25
76	Richie Sexson	.25
77	Miguel Cabrera	.60
78	Bernie Williams	.50
79	Aubrey Huff	.40
80	John Smoltz	.40
81	Jeff Bagwell	.60
82	Tim Hudson	.40
83	Alfonso Soriano	.75
84	Freddy Garcia	.40
85	Johan Santana	.40
86	Bret Boone	.25
87	Troy Glaus	.50
88	Carlos Guillen	.25
89	Derek Jeter	2.00
90	Scott Rolen	.75
91	Sammy Sosa	1.25
92	Jacque Jones	.25
93	Jason Schmidt	.40
94	Randy Johnson	.75
95	Dontrelle Willis	.40
96	Mariano Rivera	.40
97	Hank Blalock	.25
98	Mark Prior	1.50
99	Torii Hunter	.50
100	Roger Clemens	1.50
101	David Wright	6.00
102	Justin Morneau	4.00
103	Scott Kazmir	4.00
104	Gavin Floyd	3.00
105	Justin Verlander RC	4.00
106	Zack Greinke	4.00
107	David Aardsma	3.00
108	Ryan Raburn	3.00
109	Joey Gathright	3.00
110	J.D. Durbin	3.00
111	Sean Burnett	3.00
112	Jose Lopez	5.00
113	Nick Swisher	4.00
114	Bobby Jenks	4.00
115	Kelly Johnson	8.00
116	B.J. Upton	5.00
117	Ronny Cedeno	3.00
118	Edwin Encarnacion	3.00
119	Jeff Baker	3.00
120	Taylor Buchholz	3.00
121	Livan Hernandez RC	4.00
122	Dioner Navarro	4.00
123	Victor Diaz	4.00
124	Jon Knott	4.00
125	Russ Adams	3.00

Finish

Cards 1-100:		3-6X
Cards 101-125:		.75-1.25X
Production 199 Sets		

Extreme

Cards 1-125:		No Pricing
Production 20 Sets		

Autograph Die Cuts

		NM/M
Numbered to indicated quantities.		
1	Lew Ford/99	10.00
3	Jason Bay/50	15.00
4	Travis Hafner/99	15.00
6	Brad Lidge/99	30.00
7	Michael Young/99	15.00
8	David Eckstein/99	20.00
9	Carl Crawford/50	15.00
10	Miguel Cabrera/50	25.00
11	David Wright/50	50.00
13	Scott Kazmir/99	15.00
12	Gavin Floyd/99	10.00
15	Justin Verlander/99	10.00
18	Joey Gathright/50	10.00

Decade of Excellence

		NM/M
Common Player:		2.00
Inserted 1:199		
1	Albert Pujols	8.00
2	Derek Jeter	8.00
3	Randy Johnson	4.00
4	Ichiro Suzuki	5.00
5	Alex Rodriguez	6.00
6	Mike Piazza	4.00
7	Greg Maddux	5.00
8	Curt Schilling	3.00
9	Frank Thomas	3.00
10	Torii Hunter	3.00
11	Al Kaline	6.00
12	Travis Hafner	2.00
13	Ivan Rodriguez	3.00

14	Rafael Palmeiro	3.00
15	Mike Schmidt	8.00
16	Johnny Bench	8.00
17	Jim Edmonds	2.00
18	Pedro Martinez	4.00
19	Robin Yount	6.00
20	Sammy Sosa	5.00

Decade of Excellence Jersey Silver

		NM/M
Common Player:		5.00
Inserted 1:54		
Gold:		.75-1.25X
Production 99 Sets		
Patch Platinum:	No Pricing	
Production 10 Sets		
JB	Johnny Bench	15.00
JE	Jim Edmonds	8.00
TF	Travis Hafner	5.00
TH	Torii Hunter	5.00
RJ	Randy Johnson	8.00
AK	Al Kaline	10.00
GM	Greg Maddux	8.00
PM	Pedro Martinez	8.00
RP	Rafael Palmeiro	8.00
MP	Mike Piazza	8.00
AP	Albert Pujols	12.00
IR	Ivan Rodriguez	5.00
CS	Curt Schilling	5.00
MS	Mike Schmidt	15.00
SS	Sammy Sosa	10.00
FT	Frank Thomas	8.00
RY	Robin Yount	10.00

Decade of Ex. Auto. Jersey Platinum

No Pricing	
Production Five Sets	

Diamond Dominators

		NM/M
Common Player:		2.00
Inserted 1:12 Retail		
1	Albert Pujols	6.00
2	Curt Schilling	3.00
3	Adrian Beltre	3.00
4	Randy Johnson	4.00
5	Ivan Rodriguez	3.00
6	Mike Piazza	4.00
7	Chipper Jones	4.00
8	Sammy Sosa	5.00
9	Tim Hudson	2.00
10	Rocco Baldelli	4.00
11	Alfonso Soriano	4.00
12	David Ortiz	3.00
13	Mariano Rivera	3.00
14	Kazuo Matsui	3.00
15	Khalil Greene	3.00
16	Eric Gagne	2.00
17	Vladimir Guerrero	4.00
18	Jason Giambi	4.00
19	Scott Rolen	4.00
20	Miguel Cabrera	3.00

Diamond Dominators Jersey Silver

		NM/M
Common Player:		
Inserted 1:45		
Gold:		.75-1.25X
Production 199 Sets (Hobby)		
Red:		.5-1X
Inserted 1:50 (Retail)		
RB	Rocco Baldelli	5.00
AB	Adrian Beltre	5.00
MC	Miguel Cabrera	8.00
EG	Eric Gagne	5.00
JG	Jason Giambi	8.00
KG	Khalil Greene	8.00
VG	Vladimir Guerrero	8.00
TH	Tim Hudson	5.00
RJ	Randy Johnson	8.00
CJ	Chipper Jones	4.00
KM	Kazuo Matsui	5.00
DO	David Ortiz	5.00
MP	Mike Piazza	8.00
AP	Albert Pujols	12.00
IR	Ivan Rodriguez	5.00
SR	Scott Rolen	5.00
CS	Curt Schilling	5.00
AS	Alfonso Soriano	5.00
SS	Sammy Sosa	10.00

Diamond Dominators Metal

		NM/M
Common Player:		2.00
Inserted 1:18 Hobby		
1	Albert Pujols	6.00
2	Curt Schilling	3.00
3	Adrian Beltre	3.00
4	Randy Johnson	4.00
5	Ivan Rodriguez	3.00
6	Mike Piazza	4.00
7	Chipper Jones	4.00
8	Sammy Sosa	5.00
9	Tim Hudson	2.00
10	Rocco Baldelli	4.00
11	Alfonso Soriano	4.00
12	David Ortiz	3.00
13	Kazuo Matsui	3.00
14	Khalil Greene	3.00
15	Eric Gagne	2.00
16	Vladimir Guerrero	4.00
17	Jason Giambi	4.00
18	Scott Rolen	4.00
19	Miguel Cabrera	3.00

Diamond Dominators Metal Autograph

No Pricing	
Production 10 Sets	

Diamond Dominators Metal Patch

		NM/M
1-2X Diamond Dominators Jersey Silver		
Sequentially #'d to 30.		
HA	Hank Aaron	100.00

Lumberjacks

		NM/M
Common Player:		.75
Inserted 1:6		
Bat Silver:		2-3X
Inserted 1:9		
Bat Gold:		2-4X
Production 250 Sets		
Bat Patch:	No Pricing	
Production 20 Sets		
1	Albert Pujols	2.50
2	Jim Thome	1.25
3	Andruw Jones	1.00
4	Kazuo Matsui	.75
5	Adam Dunn	.75
6	Bernie Williams	.75
7	Hank Blalock	.75
8	Bobby Abreu	.75
9	Rocco Baldelli	.75
10	Jacque Jones	.75
11	Mark Teixeira	.75
12	Ichiro Suzuki	2.00
13	Gary Sheffield	.75
14	Sean Casey	.75
15	Carl Crawford	.75

Lumberjacks Autograph Platinum

No Pricing	
Production 20 Sets	

Nameplates Patch Platinum

No Pricing	
Production 25 Sets	
Masterpiece:	No Pricing
Production One Set	

Nameplates Dual Patch Platinum

No Pricing	
Production 25 Sets	
Masterpiece:	No Pricing
Production One Set	

Nameplates Patch Autograph Platinum

No Pricing	
Production 25 Sets	

Nameplates Dual Patch Auto. Platinum

No Pricing	
Production One Set	

2005 Fleer Showcase

		NM/M
Common Player (1-100):		.25
Minor Stars (1-100):		.40
Unlisted Stars (1-100):		.60
Common Showcasing Talent (101-110):		2.00
Inserted 1:5		
Common Showcasing History (111-135):		.40
Inserted 1:20		
Pack (5):		3.00
Box (20):		50.00
1	Albert Pujols	2.50
2	Rocco Baldelli	.60
3	Bernie Williams	.60
4	Shawn Green	.40
5	Garret Anderson	.40
6	Paul Konerko	.25
7	Mike Sweeney	.25

8	Jim Thome	1.00
9	Mark Teixeira	.40
10	Mark Prior	2.00
11	Angel Berroa	.25
12	Barry Zito	.60
13	Carlos Delgado	.75
14	Troy Glaus	.60
15	Travis Hafner	.25
16	Lyle Overbay	.60
17	David Ortiz	.60
18	Ivan Rodriguez	.60
19	Jack Wilson	.25
20	Jason Schmidt	.40
21	Mike Piazza	1.50
22	David Eckstein	.40
23	Ben Sheets	.40
24	Randy Johnson	1.00
25	Jacque Jones	.25
26	Jody Gerut	.25
27	Kris Benson	.25
28	Luis Gonzalez	.40
29	Victor Martinez	.25
30	Torii Hunter	.60
31	Gary Sheffield	.60
32	Miguel Tejada	.60
33	Dontrelle Willis	.60
34	Bret Boone	.25
35	Hideki Matsui	.60
36	Shea Hillenbrand	.25
37	Wily Mo Pena	.25
38	Johan Santana	.40
39	Derek Jeter	3.00
40	Chipper Jones	1.50
41	Sean Casey	.25
42	Corey Koskie	.25
43	Alex Rodriguez	2.50
44	Andruw Jones	.75
45	Austin Kearns	.60
46	Jose Vidro	.25
47	Adam Dunn	.60
48	Adrian Beltre	.40
49	Bobby Abreu	.40
50	Michael Young	.40
51	Freddy Garcia	.25
52	Eric Gagne	.40
53	Chase Utley	.50
54	Alfonso Soriano	1.00
55	Nick Johnson	.25
56	Johnny Estrada	.25
57	Jeff Bagwell	.60
58	Randy Winn	.25
59	Roy Halladay	.40
60	J.D. Drew	.40
61	Craig Biggio	.40
62	Scott Rolen	1.00
63	Nomar Garciaparra	2.50
64	Matt Holliday	.50
65	Billy Wagner	.25
66	Carl Crawford	.25
67	Pedro J. Martinez	1.00
68	Jeremy Bonderman	.25
69	Jason Bay	.25
70	A.J. Pierzynski	.25
71	Vladimir Guerrero	1.00
72	Rickie Weeks	.60
73	Mark Loretta	.25
74	Todd Helton	.75
75	Manny Ramirez	.75
76	Carlos Guillen	.25
77	Khalil Greene	.75
78	Javy Lopez	.40
79	Josh Beckett	.75
80	Ichiro Suzuki	2.00
81	Magglio Ordonez	.40
82	Ken Harvey	.25
83	Mark Mulder	.40
84	Hank Blalock	.60
85	Richard Hidalgo	.25
86	Curt Schilling	.60
87	Jeromy Burnitz	.25
88	Craig Wilson	.25
89	Aubrey Huff	.25
90	Kerry Wood	.75
91	Andy Pettitte	.60
92	Tim Hudson	.40
93	Jim Edmonds	.40
94	Melvin Mora	.25
95	Miguel Cabrera	.75
96	Trevor Hoffman	.25
97	J.T. Snow	.25
98	Sammy Sosa	2.00
99	Roger Clemens	2.50
100	Eric Chavez	4.00
101	B.J. Upton	5.00
102	Gavin Floyd	3.00
103	Casey Kotchman	3.00
104	David Wright	5.00
105	Dioner Navarro	3.00
106	Scott Kazmir	3.00
107	Andres Blanco	2.00
108	Joey Gathright	2.00
109	Jon Knott	2.00
110	Charlton Jimerson	2.00
111	Larry Doby	.75
112	Reggie Jackson	2.00
113	Enos Slaughter	.60
114	Bill "Moose" Skowron	.60
115	Duke Snider	.75
116	Harmon Killebrew	1.00
117	Willie McCovey	.75
118	Rollie Fingers	1.00
119	Preacher Roe	.40
120	Carlton Fisk	.60
121	Andre Dawson	.60
122	Orlando Cepeda	.60
123	Bucky Dent	.25
124	Cal Ripken Jr.	1.50
125	Nolan Ryan	3.00

126	Tony Perez	.60
127	Mike Schmidt	1.50
128	Johnny Bench	1.50
129	Sparky Anderson	.40
130	Ted Williams	2.50
131	Al Kaline	.75
132	Carl Yastrzemski	1.00
133	Eddie Murray	.75
134	Roberto Clemente	1.50
135	Yogi Berra	1.50

Masterpiece Legacy
Cards (1-135): No Pricing
Production One Set

Masterpiece Showpiece Patch
Cards (1-135): No Pricing
Production One Set
Autograph Patch: No Pricing
Production One Set
Patch Showdown: No Pricing
Production One Set
Patch Showtime: No Pricing
Production One Set

Autographed Legacy

		NM/M
Common Player:		15.00
Sequentially Numbered		
8	Jim Thome/34	60.00
10	Mark Prior/43	30.00
12	Barry Zito/45	35.00
18	Ivan Rodriguez/217	40.00
19	Jack Wilson/298	15.00
20	Jason Schmidt/127	15.00
21	Mike Piazza/26	100.00
22	David Eckstein/40	35.00
23	Ben Sheets/427	15.00
40	Chipper Jones/41	60.00
45	Austin Kearns/460	10.00
47	Adam Dunn/52	35.00
48	Adrian Beltre/180	15.00
50	Michael Young/80	15.00
52	Eric Gagne/310	15.00
53	Chase Utley/446	25.00
59	Roy Halladay/99	15.00
68	Jeremy Bonderman/97	20.00
72	Rickie Weeks/453	15.00
75	Manny Ramirez/31	75.00
77	Khalil Greene/299	25.00
88	Craig Wilson/40	20.00
89	Aubrey Huff/453	15.00
90	Kerry Wood/28	25.00
92	Tim Hudson/183	25.00
95	Miguel Cabrera/32	35.00
99	Roger Clemens/64	100.00
100	Eric Chavez/204	15.00
103	Casey Kotchman/454	15.00
104	David Wright/298	40.00
106	Scott Kazmir/458	20.00
107	Andres Blanco/23	15.00
109	Jon Knott/402	10.00
114	Bill "Moose" Skowron/64	20.00
119	Preacher Roe/304	20.00
120	Carlton Fisk/86	30.00
123	Bucky Dent/99	15.00
135	Yogi Berra/25	75.00

Showdown
Cards (1-135): No Pricing
Production 15 Sets
Masterpiece: No Pricing
Production One Set

Showtime

	NM/M
Veterans (1-100):	3-6X
Showcasing Talent (101-110):	2-4X
Showcasing History (111-135):	1-30X
Production 99 Sets	
Masterpiece:	No Pricing
Production One Set	

Measures of Greatness

	NM/M
Common Player:	.75
Inserted 1:5	
Jersey Red:	2-4X

		NM/M
Common Player:		1.00
Inserted 1:15		
Jersey Red:		1-30X
Production 610 Sets		
Patch:		2-5X
Production 50 Sets		
Masterpiece:		No Pricing
Production One Set		
1	Kazuo Matsui	5.00
2	Johan Santana	1.50
3	Khalil Greene	2.00
4	Dontrelle Willis	1.50
5	Mark Teixeira	1.50
6	Travis Hafner	1.00
7	Jason Bay	1.50
8	Angel Berroa	1.00
9	Miguel Cabrera	2.00
10	Joe Mauer	1.50
11	Adam Dunn	2.00
12	B.J. Upton	3.00
13	Victor Martinez	1.00
14	Michael Young	1.00
15	David Wright	3.00

2005 Fleer Tradition

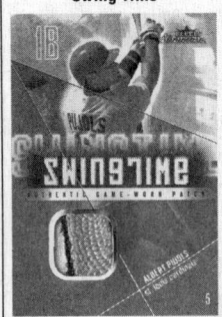

		NM/M
Common Player (1-300):		.15
Minor Stars (1-300):		.25
Unlisted Stars (1-300):		.40
Common Card (301-330):		3.00
Unlisted Card (301-330):		4.00
Inserted 1:2		
Common Player (331-350):		.15
Minor Stars (331-350):		.25
Unlisted Stars (331-350):		.40
Cards 1-12; 331-350 Inserted 1:2		
Pack (10):		1.25
Box (36):		35.00
1	Johan Santana, Curt Schilling, Jake Westbrook	.40
2	Ben Sheets, Jake Peavy, Randy Johnson	.75
3	Johan Santana, Bartolo Colon, Curt Schilling	.40
4	Carl Pavano, Roy Oswalt, Roger Clemens	1.50
5	Johan Santana, Pedro Martinez, Curt Schilling	.75
6	Jason Schmidt, Randy Johnson, Ben Sheets	.75
7	Melvin Mora, Vladimir Guerrero, Ichiro Suzuki	1.25
8	Adrian Beltre, Todd Helton, Mark Loretta	.50
9	Manny Ramirez, Paul Konerko, David Ortiz	.50
10	Albert Pujols, Adrian Beltre, Adam Dunn	1.50
11	David Ortiz, Manny Ramirez, Miguel Tejada	.50
12	Albert Pujols, Vinny Castilla, Scott Rolen	1.50
13	Jason Bay	.15
14	Greg Maddux	1.00
15	Melvin Mora	.15
16	Matt Stairs	.15
17	Scott Podsednik	.25
18	Bartolo Colon	.25
19	Roger Clemens	1.50
20	Eric Hinske	.15
21	Johnny Estrada	.15
22	Brett Tomko	.15
23	John Buck	.15
24	Nomar Garciaparra	1.50
25	Milton Bradley	.25
26	Craig Biggio	.25
27	Kyle Denney	.50
28	Brad Penny	.15
29	Todd Helton	.50
30	Luis Gonzalez	.25
31	Bill Hall	.15
32	Ruben Sierra	.15
33	Zack Greinke	.25
34	Sandy Alomar Jr.	.15
35	Jason Giambi	.75
36	Ben Sheets	.25
37	Edgardo Alfonzo	.15
38	Kenny Rogers	.15
39	Coco Crisp	.15
40	Randy Choate	.50
41	Braden Looper	.15
42	Adam Dunn	.40

		NM/M
43	Adam Eaton	.15
44	Luis Castillo	.25
45	Casey Fossum	.15
46	Mike Piazza	1.00
47	Juan Pierre	.15
48	Doug Davis	.15
49	Manny Ramirez	.50
50	Travis Hafner	.15
51	Jack Wilson	.15
52	Mike Maroth	.15
53	Ken Harvey	.15
54	Brooks Kieschnick	.15
55	Brad Fullmer	.15
56	Octavio Dotel	.15
57	Mike Matheny	.15
58	Andruw Jones	.50
59	Alfonso Soriano	.75
60	Royce Clayton	.15
61	Jon Garland	.15
62	John Mabry	.15
63	Rafael Palmeiro	.25
64	Garrett Atkins	.15
65	Brian Meadows	.15
66	Tony Armas Jr.	.15
67	Toby Hall	.15
68	Carlos Baerga	.15
69	Barry Larkin	.25
70	Jody Gerut	.15
71	Brent Mayne	.15
72	Shigetoshi Hasegawa	.15
73	Jose Cruz Jr.	.15
74	Dan Wilson	.15
75	Sidney Ponson	.15
76	Jason Jennings	.15
77	A.J. Burnett	.15
78	Tony Batista	.15
79	Kris Benson	.15
80	Sean Burroughs	.15
81	Eric Young	.15
82	Casey Kotchman	.40
83	Derrek Lee	.25
84	Mariano Rivera	.25
85	Julio Franco	.15
86	Corey Patterson	.15
87	Carlos Beltran	.40
88	Trevor Hoffman	.15
89	Danny Garcia	.15
90	Marco Scutaro	.15
91	Marquis Grissom	.15
92	Aubrey Huff	.15
93	Tony Womack	.15
94	Placido Polanco	.15
95	Bengie Molina	.15
96	Roger Cedeno	.15
97	Geoff Jenkins	.25
98	Kip Wells	.15
99	Derek Jeter	2.00
100	Omar Infante	.15
101	Phil Nevin	.15
102	Edgar Renteria	.15
103	B.J. Surhoff	.15
104	David DeJesus	.15
105	Raul Ibanez	.15
106	Hank Blalock	.40
107	Shawn Estes	.15
108	Wily Mo Pena	.15
109	Shawn Green	.25
110	David Wright	.50
111	Kenny Lofton	.15
112	Matt Clement	.15
113	Cesar Izturis	.15
114	John Lackey	.15
115	Torii Hunter	.40
116	Charles Johnson	.15
117	Ray Durham	.15
118	Luke Hudson	.15
119	Jeremy Bonderman	.15
120	Sean Casey	.15
121	Johnny Damon	.25
122	Eric Milton	.15
123	Shea Hillenbrand	.15
124	Jim Edmonds	.25
125	Jim Edmonds	.25
126	Javier Vazquez	.15
127	Jon Adkins	.15
128	Mike Lowell	.15
129	Khalil Greene	.50
130	Quinton McCracken	.15
131	Edgar Martinez	.25
132	Matt Lawton	.15
133	Jeff Weaver	.15
134	Marlon Byrd	.15
135	John Smoltz	.25
136	Grady Sizemore	.25
137	Brian Roberts	.15
138	Dee Brown	.15
139	Joel Pineiro	.15
140	David Dellucci	.15
141	Bobby Higginson	.15
142	Ryan Madson	.15
143	Scott Hatteberg	.15
144	Gregg Zaun	.15
145	Brian Jordan	.15
146	Jason Isringhausen	.15
147	Vinnie Chulk	.15
148	Al Leiter	.15
149	Pedro Martinez	.25
150	Carlos Guillen	.15
151	Randy Wolf	.15
152	Vernon Wells	.25
153	Barry Zito	.25
154	Pedro Feliz	.15
155	Omar Vizquel	.15
156	Chone Figgins	.15
157	David Ortiz	.40
158	Sun-Woo Kim RC	1.00
159	Adam Kennedy	.15
160	Carlos Lee	.15

161	Rick Ankiel	.25
162	Roy Oswalt	.25
163	Armando Benitez	.15
164	Erubiel Durazo	.15
165	Adam Hyzdu	.15
166	Esteban Yan	.15
167	Victor Santos	.15
168	Kevin Millwood	.15
169	Andy Pettitte	.60
170	Mike Cameron	.15
171	Scott Rolen	.75
172	Trot Nixon	.15
173	Eric Munson	.15
174	Roy Halladay	.25
175	Juan Encarnacion	.15
176	Eric Chavez	.25
177	Terrmel Sledge	.15
178	Jason Schmidt	.25
179	Endy Chavez	.15
180	Carlos Zambrano	.15
181	Carlos Delgado	.50
182	Dewon Brazelton	.15
183	J.D. Drew	.25
184	Orlando Cabrera	.15
185	Craig Wilson	.15
186	Chin-Hui Tsao	.15
187	Jolbert Cabrera	.15
188	Rod Barajas	.15
189	Craig Monroe	.15
190	Dave Berg	.15
191	Carlos Silva	.15
192	Eric Gagne	.25
193	Marcus Giles	.15
194	Nick Johnson	.15
195	Kelvim Escobar	.15
196	Wade Miller	.15
197	David Bell	.15
198	Rondell White	.15
199	Brian Giles	.25
200	Jeromy Burnitz	.15
201	Carl Pavano	.15
202	Alex Rios	.15
203	Ryan Freel	.15
204	R.A. Dickey	.15
205	Miguel Cairo	.15
206	Kerry Wood	.50
207	C.C. Sabathia	.15
208	Jaime Cerda	.15
209	Jerome Williams	.15
210	Ryan Wagner	.15
211	Javy Lopez	.25
212	Tike Redman	.15
213	Richie Sexson	.40
214	Shannon Stewart	.15
215	Ben Davis	.15
216	Jeff Bagwell	.50
217	David Wells	.15
218	Justin Leone	.15
219	Brad Radke	.15
220	Ramon Santiago	.15
221	Richard Hidalgo	.15
222	Aaron Miles	.15
223	Mark Loretta	.15
224	Aaron Boone	.15
225	Steve Trachsel	.15
226	Geoff Blum	.15
227	Shingo Takatsu	.15
228	Kevin Youkilis	.15
229	Laynce Nix	.15
230	Daniel Cabrera	.15
231	Kyle Lohse	.15
232	Todd Pratt	.15
233	Reed Johnson	.15
234	Lance Berkman	.25
235	Hideki Matsui	1.50
236	Randy Winn	.15
237	Joe Randa	.15
238	Bob Howry	.15
239	Jason LaRue	.15
240	Jose Valentin	.15
241	Livan Hernandez	.15
242	Jamie Moyer	.15
243	Garret Anderson	.25
244	Brad Ausmus	.15
245	Russell Branyan	.15
246	Paul Wilson	.15
247	Tim Wakefield	.15
248	Roberto Alomar	.40
249	Kazuhisa Ishii	.15
250	Tino Martinez	.25
251	Tomokazu Ohka	.15
252	Mark Redman	.15
253	Paul Byrd	.15
254	Greg Aquino	.15
255	Adrian Beltre	.25
256	Ricky Ledee	.15
257	Josh Fogg	.15
258	Derek Lowe	.15
259	Lew Ford	.15
260	Bobby Crosby	.15
261	Jim Thome	.75
262	Jaret Wright	.15
263	Chin-Feng Chen	.15
264	Troy Glaus	.40
265	Jorge Sosa	.15
266	Mike Lamb	.15
267	Russ Ortiz	.15
268	Reggie Sanders	.15
269	Orlando Hudson	.15
270	Rodrigo Lopez	.15
271	Jose Vidro	.15
272	Akinori Otsuka	.15
273	Victor Martinez	.15
274	Carl Crawford	.25
275	Roberto Novoa	.25
276	Brian Lawrence	.15
277	Angel Berroa	.15
278	Josh Beckett	.50

279	Lyle Overbay	.15
280	Dustin Hermanson	.15
281	Jeff Conine	.15
282	Mark Prior	1.00
283	Kevin Brown	.25
284	Magglio Ordonez	.25
285	Dontrelle Willis	.25
286	Dallas McPherson	.25
287	Rafael Furcal	.25
288	Ty Wigginton	.15
289	Moises Alou	.15
290	A.J. Pierzynski	.15
291	Todd Walker	.15
292	Hideo Nomo	.15
293	Larry Walker	.25
294	Choo Freeman	.15
295	Eduardo Perez	.15
296	Miguel Tejada	.40
297	Corey Koskie	.15
298	Jermaine Dye	.15
299	John Riedling	.15
300	John Olerud	.25
301	Tim Bittner, Jake Woods, Bobby Jenks	5.00
302	Josh Kroeger, Casey Daigle, Brandon Medders	5.00
303	Kelly Johnson, Charles Thomas, Dan Meyer	4.00
304	Eddy Rodriguez, Ryan Hannaman, John Maine	6.00
305	Anastacio Martinez, Jerome Gamble, Lenny Dinardo	8.00
306	Ronny Cedeno, Carlos Vasquez, Renyel Pinto	6.00
307	Arnie Munoz, Ryan Wing, Felix Diaz	6.00
308	William Bergolla, Ray Olmedo RC, Edwin Encarnacion	4.00
309	Mariano Gomez, Ivan Ochoa, Kazuhito Tadano	4.00
310	Toby Miller RC, Jeff Baker, Matt Holliday	6.00
311	Preston Larrison, Curtis Granderson, Ryan Raburn	8.00
312	Josh Wilson, Logan Kensing, Kevin Cave	5.00
313	Hector Gimenez, Willy Taveras, Taylor Buchholz	3.00
314	Ruben Gotay, Brian Bass, Andres Blanco	4.00
315	Joel Hanrahan, Willy Aybar, Yhency Brazoban	3.00
316	David Krynzel, Ben Hendrickson, Corey Hart	3.00
317	Colby Miller, Jason Kubel, J.D. Durban	3.00
318	Maicer Izturis, Chad Cordero, Brandon Watson	3.00
319	Victor Diaz, Aarom Baldiris, Wayne Lydon	8.00
320	Edwardo Sierra, Dioner Navarro, Sean Henn	3.00
321	Nick Swisher, Joe Blanton, Dan Johnson	6.00
322	Ryan Howard, Gavin Floyd, Keith Bucktrot	6.00
323	Ryan Doumit, Sean Burnett, Bobby Bradley	6.00
324	Justin Germano, Rusty Tucker, Freddy Guzman	6.00
325	David Aardsma, Justin Knoedler, Alfredo Simon	4.00
326	Jose Lopez, Rene Rivera, Cha Sueng Baek	4.00
327	Yadier Molina, Evan Rust, Adam Wainwright	4.00
328	Jorge Cantu, Scott Kazmir, B.J. Upton	5.00
329	Adrian Gonzalez, Ramon Nivar, Jason Bourgeois	6.00
330	Russ Adams, Dustin McGowan, Gustavo Chacin	8.00
331	Alfonso Soriano	.75
332	Albert Pujols	1.50
333	David Ortiz	.40
334	Manny Ramirez	.50
335	Jason Bay	.15
336	Bobby Crosby	.15
337	Roger Clemens	1.50
338	Johan Santana	.75
339	Jim Thome	.75
340	Vladimir Guerrero	.75
341	David Ortiz	.40
342	Alex Rodriguez	1.50
343	Albert Pujols	1.50
344	Carlos Beltran	.40
345	Johnny Damon	.75
346	Scott Rolen	.75
347	Larry Walker	.40
348	Curt Schilling	.40
349	Pedro Martinez	.75
350	David Ortiz	.40

Gray Backs
Cards 13-300: .75-1.5X

Swing Time

		NM/M
Common Player:		2.50
Inserted 1:45		
Jersey Red:		1-30X
Production 610 Sets		
Patch:		2-5X
Production 50 Sets		
Masterpiece:		No Pricing
Production One Set		
1	Ivan Rodriguez	2.50
2	Gary Sheffield	2.50
3	Bernie Williams	2.50
4	Vladimir Guerrero	3.50
5	Jim Edmonds	2.50
6	Manny Ramirez	3.00
7	Todd Helton	3.00
8	Hank Blalock	2.50
9	Hideki Matsui	6.00
10	David Ortiz	2.50
11	Albert Pujols	6.00
12	Miguel Tejada	2.50
13	Miguel Cabrera	3.00
14	Alex Rodriguez	6.00
15	Ichiro Suzuki	5.00

Timepiece Extreme
No Pricing
Production One Set

Timepiece Ink
No Pricing
Production 10 Sets

Timepiece Teammates
No Pricing
Production One Set

Timepiece Unique
No Pricing
Production Five Sets

Wave of the Future

Cards 1-10; 301-350: .5-1.25X
Inserted 1:2

Club 3,000/500/300

Inserted 1:360

		NM/M
1	Ernie Banks/500	30.00
2	Stan Musial/3,000	40.00
3	Steve Carlton/3,000	15.00
4	Greg Maddux/300	15.00
5	Dave Winfield/3,000	15.00
6	Rafael Palmeiro/500	15.00
7	Rickey Henderson/	
	3,000	15.00
8	Roger Clemens/3,000	30.00
9	Don Sutton/300	10.00
10	George Brett/3,000	25.00
11	Reggie Jackson/500	20.00
12	Wade Boggs/3,000	20.00
13	Bob Gibson/3,000	20.00
14	Eddie Murray/3,000	20.00
15	Tom Seaver/3,000	20.00
16	Willie McCovey/500	20.00
17	Rod Carew/3,000	20.00
18	Fergie Jenkins/300	15.00
19	Phil Niekro/300	10.00
20	Frank Robinson/500	10.00

Cooperstown Tribute

	NM/M
Common Player:	4.00

Sequentially #'d to HOF Induction Year.
Gold: .5-1X
Inserted 1:24
Jersey: 1-2X
Inserted 1:200
There are 20 total jersey cards for Joe Morgan & Yogi Berra.
Patch: No Pricing
Production 10 Sets

1	Mike Schmidt/1995	5.00
2	Al Kaline/1980	4.00
3	Yogi Berra/1972	4.00
4	Robin Yount/1999	4.00
5	Joe Morgan/1990	4.00
6	Willie Stargell/1988	4.00
7	Harmon Killebrew/1984	5.00
8	Nolan Ryan/1999	10.00
9	Carlton Fisk/2000	5.00
10	Johnny Bench/1989	6.00

Diamond Tributes

	NM/M
Common Player:	2.00

Inserted 1:6

1	Albert Pujols	5.00
2	Alex Rodriguez	5.00
3	Ken Griffey Jr.	3.50
4	Sammy Sosa	4.00
5	Chipper Jones	3.50
6	Johan Santana	2.00
7	Roger Clemens	5.00
8	Pedro Martinez	3.00
9	Jim Thome	3.00
10	Greg Maddux	3.50
11	Alfonso Soriano	3.00
12	Derek Jeter	6.00
13	Randy Johnson	3.00
14	Miguel Cabrera	2.00
15	Adrian Beltre	2.00
16	Ivan Rodriguez	2.00
17	Manny Ramirez	2.00
18	Mark Teixeira	2.00
19	Adam Dunn	2.00
20	Scott Rolen	3.00
21	Mike Piazza	3.50
22	J.D. Drew	2.00
23	Hideki Matsui	5.00
24	Nomar Garciaparra	4.00
25	Kazuo Matsui	3.00

Diamond Tribute Jersey

	NM/M
Common Player:	6.00

Inserted 1:30
Patch: 1-30X
Production 50 Sets

AB	Adrian Beltre/Bat	6.00
RC	Roger Clemens/Jsy	12.00
JD	J.D. Drew/Bat	6.00
NG	Nomar Garciaparra/Bat	12.00
RJ	Randy Johnson/Jsy	6.00
CJ	Chipper Jones/Bat	10.00
GM	Greg Maddux/Jsy	10.00
PM	Pedro Martinez/Jsy	8.00
HM	Hideki Matsui/Bat	15.00
KM	Kazuo Matsui/Bat	8.00

Diamond Tributes

MP	Mike Piazza/Bat	10.00
AP	Albert Pujols/Bat	15.00
MR	Manny Ramirez/Bat	6.00
JS	Johan Santana/Jsy	8.00
AS	Alfonso Soriano/Bat	8.00
SS	Sammy Sosa/Bat	10.00
MT	Mark Teixeira/Bat	8.00
JT	Jim Thome/Bat	8.00

Diamond Tributes Dual Patch

	NM/M
Common Player:	75.00

Production 50 Sets

APSR	Albert Pujols, Scott Rolen	100.00
ASMT	Alfonso Soriano, Mark Teixeira	75.00
CJJD	Chipper Jones, J.D. Drew	80.00
HMKM	Hideki Matsui, Kazuo Matsui	125.00
JTAB	Jim Thome, Adrian Beltre	75.00
MPIR	Mike Piazza, Ivan Rodriguez	75.00
PMMR	Pedro Martinez, Manny Ramirez	120.00
RCJS	Roger Clemens, Johan Santana	100.00
RJGM	Randy Johnson, Greg Maddux	75.00
SSMC	Miguel Cabrera, Sammy Sosa	80.00

Standouts

	NM/M
Common Player:	3.50

Inserted 1:18

1	Albert Pujols	6.00
2	Ichiro Suzuki	5.00
3	Derek Jeter	8.00
4	Randy Johnson	3.50
5	Greg Maddux	4.00
6	Hideki Matsui	6.00
7	Mike Piazza	4.00
8	Vladimir Guerrero	3.50
9	Sammy Sosa	5.00
10	Jim Thome	3.50
11	Chipper Jones	4.00
12	Alex Rodriguez	6.00
13	Roger Clemens	6.00
14	Nomar Garciaparra	6.00
15	Lance Berkman	3.50

Standouts Jersey

	NM/M
Common Player:	10.00

Inserted 1:18
Patch: 1-30X
Production 50 Sets

LB	Lance Berkman	6.00
RC	Roger Clemens	18.00
VG	Vladimir Guerrero	10.00
RJ	Randy Johnson	10.00
CJ	Chipper Jones	12.00
GM	Greg Maddux	12.00
HM	Hideki Matsui	20.00
MP	Mike Piazza	12.00
AP	Albert Pujols	18.00
SS	Sammy Sosa	12.00
JT	Jim Thome	10.00

2006 Fleer

	NM/M
Complete Set (400):	40.00
Complete Factory Set (430):	50.00

#'s 401-430 available in Factory Set

	Common Player:	.15
	Pack (10):	1.50
	Box (36):	40.00
1	Adam Kennedy	.15
2	Bartolo Colon	.25
3	Bengie Molina	.15
4	Chone Figgins	.15
5	Dallas McPherson	.15
6	Darin Erstad	.15
7	Francisco Rodriguez	.25
8	Garret Anderson	.25
9	Jarrod Washburn	.15
10	John Lackey	.15
11	Orlando Cabrera	.15
12	Ryan Theriot RC	.50
13	Steve Finley	.15
14	Vladimir Guerrero	.75
15	Adam Everett	.15
16	Andy Pettitte	.40
17	Charlton Jimerson	.15
18	Brad Lidge	.15
19	Chris Burke	.15
20	Craig Biggio	.25
21	Jason Lane	.15
22	Jeff Bagwell	.40
23	Lance Berkman	.50
24	Morgan Ensberg	.25
25	Roger Clemens	2.00
26	Roy Oswalt	.25
27	Willy Taveras	.25
28	Barry Zito	.25
29	Bobby Crosby	.25
30	Bobby Kielty	.15
31	Dan Johnson	.15
32	Danny Haren	.15
33	Eric Chavez	.25
34	Huston Street	.25
35	Jason Kendall	.15
36	Jay Payton	.15
37	Joe Blanton	.15
38	Mark Kotsay	.15
39	Nick Swisher	.25
40	Rich Harden	.25
41	Ron Flores RC	.15
42	Alex Rios	.15
43	John-Ford Griffin RC	.15
44	David Bush	.15
45	Eric Hinske	.15
46	Frank Catalanotto	.15
47	Gustavo Chacin	.15
48	Josh Towers	.15
49	Miguel Batista	.15
50	Orlando Hudson	.15
51	Roy Halladay	.25
52	Shea Hillenbrand	.15
53	Shaun Marcum RC	.15
54	Vernon Wells	.25
55	Adam LaRoche	.15
56	Andruw Jones	.50
57	Chipper Jones	.40
58	Anthony Lerew RC	.15
59	Jeff Francoeur	.25
60	John Smoltz	.40
61	Johnny Estrada	.15
62	Julio Franco	.15
63	Joey Devine RC	1.00
64	Marcus Giles	.15
65	Mike Hampton	.15
66	Rafael Furcal	.25
67	Chuck James RC	.25
68	Tim Hudson	.25
69	Ben Sheets	.25
70	Bill Hall	.15
71	Brady Clark	.15
72	Carlos Lee	.25
73	Chris Capuano	.15
74	Nelson Cruz RC	.15
75	Derrick Turnbow	.15
76	Doug Davis	.15
77	Geoff Jenkins	.15
78	J.J. Hardy	.15
79	Lyle Overbay	.15
80	Prince Fielder RC	1.00
81	Rickie Weeks	.25
82	Albert Pujols	2.00
83	Chris Carpenter	.25
84	David Eckstein	.15
85	Jason Isringhausen	.15
86	Tyler Johnson RC	.15
87	Adam Wainwright RC	.15
88	Jim Edmonds	.25
89	Chris Duncan	.15
90	Mark Grudzielanek	.15
91	Mark Mulder	.25
92	Matt Morris	.15
93	Reggie Sanders	.15
94	Scott Rolen	.50

95	Yadier Molina	.15
96	Aramis Ramirez	.40
97	Carlos Zambrano	.25
98	Corey Patterson	.15
99	Derrek Lee	.50
100	Glendon Rusch	.15
101	Greg Maddux	1.00
102	Jeromy Burnitz	.15
103	Kerry Wood	.25
104	Mark Prior	.50
105	Michael Barrett	.15
106	Geovany Soto RC	.25
107	Nomar Garciaparra	.50
108	Ryan Dempster	.15
109	Todd Walker	.15
110	Alex Gonzalez	.15
111	Aubrey Huff	.15
112	Victor Diaz	.15
113	Carl Crawford	.25
114	Danys Baez	.15
115	Joey Gathright	.15
116	Jonny Gomes	.25
117	Jorge Cantu	.15
118	Julio Lugo	.15
119	Rocco Baldelli	.15
120	Scott Kazmir	.15
121	Toby Hall	.15
122	Tim Corcoran RC	.40
123	Alex Cintron	.15
124	Brandon Webb	.15
125	Chad Tracy	.15
126	Dustin Nippert RC	.15
127	Claudio Vargas	.15
128	Craig Counsell	.15
129	Javier Vazquez	.15
130	Jose Valverde	.15
131	Luis Gonzalez	.15
132	Royce Clayton	.15
133	Russ Ortiz	.15
134	Shawn Green	.15
135	Tony Clark	.15
136	Troy Glaus	.25
137	Brad Penny	.15
138	Cesar Izturis	.15
139	Derek Lowe	.15
140	Eric Gagne	.15
141	Hee Seop Choi	.15
142	J.D. Drew	.15
143	Jason Phillips	.15
144	Jayson Werth	.15
145	Jeff Kent	.25
146	Jeff Weaver	.15
147	Milton Bradley	.15
148	Odalis Perez	.15
149	Hong-Chih Kuo	.15
150	Brian Myrow RC	.25
151	Armando Benitez	.15
152	Edgardo Alfonzo	.15
153	J.T. Snow	.15
154	Jason Schmidt	.15
155	Lance Niekro	.15
156	Doug Clark	.15
157	Daniel Ortmeier RC	.15
158	Moises Alou	.25
159	Noah Lowry	.15
160	Omar Vizquel	.25
161	Pedro Feliz	.15
162	Randy Winn	.15
163	Jeremy Accardo RC	.15
164	Aaron Boone	.15
165	Ryan Garko RC	.15
166	C.C. Sabathia	.15
167	Casey Blake	.15
168	Cliff Lee	.15
169	Coco Crisp	.15
170	Grady Sizemore	.40
171	Jake Westbrook	.15
172	Jhonny Peralta	.15
173	Kevin Millwood	.15
174	Scott Elarton	.15
175	Travis Hafner	.50
176	Victor Martinez	.25
177	Aaron Beltre	.15
178	Eddie Guardado	.15
179	Felix Hernandez	.40
180	Gil Meche	.15
181	Ichiro Suzuki	1.50
182	Jamie Moyer	.15
183	Jeremy Reed	.15
184	Jaime Bubela RC	.15
185	Raul Ibanez	.15
186	Richie Sexson	.40
187	Ryan Franklin	.15
188	Jeff Harris RC	.15
189	A.J. Burnett	.15
190	Josh Wilson RC	.15
191	Josh Johnson RC	.15
192	Carlos Delgado	.40
193	Dontrelle Willis	.25
194	Bernie Castro	.15
195	Josh Beckett	.25
196	Juan Encarnacion	.15
197	Juan Pierre	.15
198	Robert Andino RC	.25
199	Miguel Cabrera	.75
200	Ryan Jorgensen RC	.25
201	Paul LoDuca	.15
202	Todd Jones	.15
203	Braden Looper	.15
204	Carlos Beltran	.50
205	Cliff Floyd	.15
206	David Wright	1.00
207	Doug Mientkiewicz	.15
208	Jae Weong Seo	.15
209	Jose Reyes	.50
210	Anderson Hernandez RC	.15
211	Juan Cairo	.15
212	Mike Cameron	.15

213	Mike Piazza	.50
214	Pedro Martinez	.75
215	Tom Glavine	.25
216	Tim Hamulack	.15
217	Brad Wilkerson	.15
218	Darrell Rasner RC	.15
219	Chad Cordero	.15
220	Cristian Guzman	.15
221	Jason Bergmann RC	.50
222	John Patterson	.15
223	Jose Guillen	.15
224	Jose Vidro	.15
225	Livan Hernandez	.15
226	Nick Johnson	.15
227	Preston Wilson	.15
228	Ryan Zimmerman RC	.25
229	Vinny Castilla	.15
230	B.J. Ryan	.15
231	B.J. Surhoff	.15
232	Brian Roberts	.25
233	Walter Young	.15
234	Daniel Cabrera	.15
235	Erik Bedard	.15
236	Javy Lopez	.15
237	Jay Gibbons	.15
238	Luis Matos	.15
239	Melvin Mora	.25
240	Miguel Tejada	.50
241	Rafael Palmeiro	.25
242	Alejandro Freire RC	.25
243	Sammy Sosa	.75
244	Adam Eaton	.15
245	Brian Giles	.25
246	Brian Lawrence	.15
247	Dave Roberts	.15
248	Jake Peavy	.15
249	Khalil Greene	.15
250	Mark Loretta	.15
251	Ramon Hernandez	.15
252	Ryan Klesko	.15
253	Trevor Hoffman	.15
254	Woody Williams	.15
255	Craig Breslow RC	.25
256	Billy Wagner	.15
257	Bobby Abreu	.25
258	Brett Myers	.15
259	Chase Utley	.50
260	David Bell	.15
261	Jim Thome	.50
262	Jimmy Rollins	.40
263	Jon Lieber	.15
264	Danny Sandoval RC	.25
265	Mike Lieberthal	.15
266	Pat Burrell	.25
267	Randy Wolf	.15
268	Ryan Howard	1.00
269	J.J. Furmaniak RC	.15
270	Ronny Paulino RC	.15
271	Craig Wilson	.15
272	Bryan Bullington	.15
273	Jack Wilson	.15
274	Jason Bay	.25
275	Matt Capps RC	.15
276	Oliver Perez	.15
277	Robert Mackowiak	.15
278	Tom Gorzelanny RC	.15
279	Zachary Duke	.15
280	Alfonso Soriano	.50
281	Chris Young	.15
282	David Dellucci	.15
283	Francisco Cordero	.15
284	Jason Botts RC	.15
285	Hank Blalock	.25
286	Josh Rupe	.15
287	Kevin Mench	.15
288	Laynce Nix	.15
289	Mark Teixeira	.50
290	Michael Young	.25
291	Richard Hidalgo	.15
292	Scott Feldman RC	.15
293	Bill Mueller	.15
294	Hanley Ramirez RC	.40
295	Curt Schilling	.75
296	David Ortiz	.75
297	Alejandro Machado	.15
298	Edgar Renteria	.25
299	Jason Varitek	.40
300	Johnny Damon	.75
301	Keith Foulke	.15
302	Manny Ramirez	.75
303	Matt Clement	.15
304	Craig Hansen RC	2.00
305	Tim Wakefield	.15
306	Trot Nixon	.15
307	Aaron Harang	.15
308	Adam Dunn	.50
309	Austin Kearns	.25
310	Brandon Claussen	.15
311	Chris Booker	.15
312	Edwin Encarnacion	.15
313	Chris Denorfia RC	.15
314	Felipe Lopez	.15
315	Miguel Perez RC	.15
316	Ken Griffey Jr.	1.50
317	Ryan Freel	.15
318	Sean Casey	.15
319	Wily Mo Pena	.15
320	Mike Esposito	.15
321	Aaron Miles	.15
322	Brad Hawpe	.15
323	Brian Fuentes	.15
324	Clint Barmes	.15
325	Cory Sullivan	.15
326	Garrett Atkins	.15
327	J.D. Closser	.15
328	Jeff Francis	.15
329	Luis Gonzalez	.15
330	Matt Holliday	.25

331	Todd Helton	.50
332	Angel Berroa	.15
333	David DeJesus	.15
334	Emil Brown	.15
335	Jeremy Affeldt	.15
336	Chris Demaria RC	.50
337	Mark Teahen	.15
338	Matt Stairs	.15
339	Steve Stemle RC	.25
340	Mike Sweeney	.15
341	Runelvys Hernandez	.15
342	Jonah Bayliss RC	.25
343	Zack Greinke	.15
344	Brandon Inge	.15
345	Carlos Guillen	.15
346	Carlos Pena	.15
347	Chris Shelton	.25
348	Craig Monroe	.15
349	Dmitri Young	.15
350	Ivan Rodriguez	.40
351	Jeremy Bonderman	.15
352	Magglio Ordonez	.25
353	Mark Woodyard RC	.15
354	Omar Infante	.15
355	Placido Polanco	.15
356	Rondell White	.15
357	Brad Radke	.15
358	Carlos Silva	.15
359	Jacque Jones	.15
360	Joe Mauer	.25
361	Chris Heintz RC	.25
362	Joe Nathan	.15
363	Johan Santana	.50
364	Justin Morneau	.25
365	Francisco Liriano RC	.50
366	Travis Bowyer	.15
367	Michael Cuddyer	.15
368	Scott Baker	.15
369	Shannon Stewart	.15
370	Torii Hunter	.25
371	A.J. Pierzynski	.15
372	Aaron Rowand	.15
373	Carl Everett	.15
374	Dustin Hermanson	.15
375	Frank Thomas	.40
376	Freddy Garcia	.15
377	Jermaine Dye	.15
378	Joe Crede	.15
379	Jon Garland	.15
380	Jose Contreras	.15
381	Juan Uribe	.15
382	Mark Buehrle	.25
383	Orlando Hernandez	.25
384	Paul Konerko	.25
385	Scott Podsednik	.15
386	Tadahito Iguchi	.25
387	Alex Rodriguez	2.00
388	Bernie Williams	.25
389	Chien-Ming Wang	.40
390	Derek Jeter	2.00
391	Gary Sheffield	.40
392	Hideki Matsui	1.00
393	Jason Giambi	.40
394	Jorge Posada	.25
395	Michael Vento	.15
396	Mariano Rivera	.25
397	Mike Mussina	.25
398	Randy Johnson	.75
399	Robinson Cano	.25
400	Tino Martinez	.25
401	Alay Soler RC	.40
402	Boof Bonser RC	.40
403	Cole Hamels RC	1.50
404	Ian Kinsler RC	.40
405	Jason Kubel RC	.40
406	Joel Zumaya RC	1.00
407	Jonathan Papelbon RC	2.50
408	Jered Weaver RC	2.50
409	Kendry Morales RC	1.00
410	Lastings Milledge RC	1.00
411	Matthew Kemp RC	1.00
412	Taylor Buchholz RC	.40
413	Andre Ethier RC	2.50
414	Dan Uggla RC	1.00
415	Jeremy Sowers RC	.40
416	Chad Billingsley RC	.75
417	Josh Barfield RC	.40
418	Matt Cain RC	.75
419	Fausto Carmona RC	.40
420	Josh Willingham RC	.40
421	Jeremy Hermida RC	.75
422	Conor Jackson RC	.75
423	Dave Gassner RC	.40
424	Brian Bannister RC	.40
425	Fernando Nieve RC	.40
426	Justin Verlander RC	2.50
427	Scott Olsen RC	.40
428	Takashi Saito RC	.50
429	Willie Eyre RC	.40
430	Travis Ishikawa RC	.40

Top 40

	NM/M
Common Player:	.50

Inserted 2:1 Fat Pack

1	Ken Griffey Jr.	3.00
2	Derek Jeter	4.00
3	Albert Pujols	4.00
4	Alex Rodriguez	3.00
5	Vladimir Guerrero	1.50
6	Roger Clemens	3.00
7	Derrek Lee	1.00
8	David Ortiz	1.50
9	Miguel Cabrera	1.50
10	Bobby Abreu	.50
11	Mark Teixeira	1.00
12	Johan Santana	1.50
13	Hideki Matsui	2.50

		NM/M
14	Ichiro Suzuki	3.00
15	Andruw Jones	1.00
16	Eric Chavez	.50
17	Roy Oswalt	.75
18	Curt Schilling	1.00
19	Randy Johnson	1.50
20	Ivan Rodriguez	1.00
21	Chipper Jones	1.50
22	Mark Prior	.75
23	Jason Bay	.75
24	Pedro Martinez	1.50
25	David Wright	2.50
26	Carlos Beltran	1.00
27	Jim Edmonds	.75
28	Chris Carpenter	.75
29	Roy Halladay	.75
30	Jake Peavy	1.00
31	Paul Konerko	.75
32	Travis Hafner	.75
33	Barry Zito	.50
34	Miguel Tejada	.75
35	Josh Beckett	1.00
36	Todd Helton	1.00
37	Dontrelle Willis	.50
38	Manny Ramirez	1.50
39	Mariano Rivera	1.00
40	Jeff Kent	.50

Glossy

Glossy: 2-3X
Inserted 1:12

Glossy Gold

Glossy Gold: 4-8X
Inserted 1:144

Autographics

Inserted 1:432

		NM/M
AN	Garret Anderson	15.00
GA	Garrett Atkins	15.00
JB	Joe Blanton	10.00
EC	Eric Chavez	15.00
KG	Ken Griffey Jr.	75.00
TI	Tadahito Iguchi	40.00
CS	Chris Shelton	10.00
NS	Nick Swisher	15.00
KY	Kevin Youkilis	20.00

Award Winners

		NM/M
Complete Set (6):		5.00
Common Player:		.50
1	Albert Pujols	3.00
2	Alex Rodriguez	3.00
3	Chris Carpenter	.50
4	Bartolo Colon	.50
5	Ryan Howard	1.00
6	Huston Street	.50

Fabrics

Inserted 1:36

		NM/M
BA	Bobby Abreu	6.00
CB	Carlos Beltran	8.00
MC	Miguel Cabrera	8.00
EC	Eric Chavez	4.00
RC	Roger Clemens	15.00
JD	Johnny Damon	8.00
JE	Jim Edmonds	6.00
EG	Eric Gagne	4.00
LG	Luis Gonzalez	4.00
GR	Khalil Greene	4.00
KG	Ken Griffey Jr.	15.00
VG	Vladimir Guerrero	8.00
RH	Roy Halladay	4.00
TH	Todd Helton	6.00
DJ	Derek Jeter	20.00
RJ	Randy Johnson	8.00
AJ	Andruw Jones	6.00
CJ	Chipper Jones	8.00
DL	Derek Lee	8.00
GM	Greg Maddux	15.00
PM	Pedro Martinez	8.00
JM	Joe Mauer	4.00
DO	David Ortiz	8.00
JP	Jake Peavy	6.00
MP	Mark Prior	6.00

		NM/M
AP	Albert Pujols	20.00
AR	Aramis Ramirez	6.00
MR	Manny Ramirez	8.00
IR	Ivan Rodriguez	6.00
SR	Scott Rolen	8.00
JS	Johan Santana	8.00
CS	Curt Schilling	8.00
GS	Gary Sheffield/SP	10.00
SM	John Smoltz	8.00
AS	Alfonso Soriano	6.00
MT	Mark Teixeira	8.00
TE	Miguel Tejada	6.00
JT	Jim Thome	6.00
RW	Rickie Weeks	4.00
DW	Dontrelle Willis/SP	8.00
WR	David Wright	12.00
MY	Michael Young	4.00

Lumber Company

MARK TEIXEIRA • 1B

		NM/M
1	Adam Dunn	1.00
2	Albert Pujols	3.00
3	Alex Rodriguez	3.00
4	Alfonso Soriano	.75
5	Andruw Jones	.75
6	Aramis Ramirez	.75
7	Bobby Abreu	.75
8	Carlos Delgado	.75
9	Carlos Lee	.50
10	David Ortiz	1.00
11	David Wright	1.50
12	Derek Lee	1.00
13	Eric Chavez	.50
14	Gary Sheffield	.75
15	Jeff Kent	.50
16	Ken Griffey Jr.	2.00
17	Manny Ramirez	1.00
18	Mark Teixeira	1.00
19	Miguel Cabrera	1.00
20	Miguel Tejada	.75
21	Paul Konerko	.75
22	Richie Sexson	.50
23	Todd Helton	.75
24	Troy Glaus	.50
25	Vladimir Guerrero	1.00

Smoke 'n Heat

SMOKE 'n HEAT

		NM/M
1	Carlos Zambrano	.50
2	Chris Carpenter	.50
3	Curt Schilling	1.00
4	Dontrelle Willis	.50
5	Felix Hernandez	1.00
6	Jake Peavy	.75
7	Johan Santana	1.00
8	John Smoltz	.75
9	Mark Prior	.75
10	Pedro Martinez	1.00
11	Randy Johnson	1.00
12	Roger Clemens	3.00
13	Roy Halladay	.50
14	Roy Oswalt	.50
15	Scott Kazmir	.75

Smooth Leather

		NM/M
Complete Set (14):		10.00
Common Player:		.50
1	Alex Rodriguez	3.00
2	Andruw Jones	1.00
3	Derek Jeter	3.00
4	Derek Lee	1.00
5	Eric Chavez	.50
6	Greg Maddux	2.00
7	Ichiro Suzuki	2.00
8	Ivan Rodriguez	.75
9	Jim Edmonds	.75
10	Mike Mussina	.75

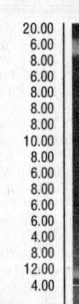

ICHIRO
MARINERS • OF

		NM/M
11	Omar Vizquel	.50
12	Scott Rolen	1.00
13	Todd Helton	.75
14	Torii Hunter	.50

Stars of Tomorrow

		NM/M
Complete Set (10):		5.00
Common Player:		.50
Inserted 1:10		
1	David Wright	1.50
2	Ryan Howard	1.00
3	Felix Hernandez	1.00
4	Jeff Francoeur	.50
5	Joe Mauer	.50
6	Mark Prior	.75
7	Mark Teixeira	1.00
8	Miguel Cabrera	1.00
9	Prince Fielder RC	1.00
10	Rickie Weeks	.50

Team Fleer

Inserted 1:Case

		NM/M
1	Albert Pujols	40.00
2	Alex Rodriguez	30.00
3	Alfonso Soriano	10.00
4	Andruw Jones	10.00
5	Bobby Abreu	10.00
6	David Ortiz	15.00
7	David Wright	25.00
8	Eric Gagne	10.00
9	Ichiro Suzuki	30.00
10	Jason Varitek	15.00
11	Jeff Kent	8.00
12	Johan Santana	15.00
13	Jose Reyes	15.00
14	Manny Ramirez	10.00
15	Mariano Rivera	10.00
16	Miguel Cabrera	15.00
17	Miguel Tejada	10.00
18	Mike Piazza	15.00
19	Roger Clemens	30.00
20	Torii Hunter	8.00

Team Leaders

		NM/M
Complete Set (30):		15.00
Common Player:		.50
1	Troy Glaus, Brandon Webb	.50
2	John Smoltz, Andruw Jones	.44
3	Miguel Tejada, Erik Bedard	.50
4	David Ortiz, Curt Schilling	.75
5	Derek Lee, Mark Prior	.75
6	Mark Buehrle, Paul Konerko	.50
7	Ken Griffey Jr., Aaron Harang	1.50
8	Cliff Lee, Travis Hafner	.50
9	Todd Helton, Jeff Francis	.50
10	Jeremy Bonderman, Ivan Rodriguez	.50
11	Miguel Cabrera, Dontrelle Willis	.75
12	Lance Berkman, Roger Clemens	2.00
13	Mike Sweeney, Zack Greinke	.50
14	Derek Lowe, Jeff Kent	.50
15	Carlos Lee, Ben Sheets	.50
16	Johan Santana, Torii Hunter	.50
17	Pedro Martinez, David Wright	1.00
18	Derek Jeter, Randy Johnson	2.00
19	Barry Zito, Eric Chavez	.50

		NM/M
20	Bobby Abreu, Brett Myers	.50
21	Jason Bay, Zachary Duke	.50
22	Jake Peavy, Brian Giles	.50
23	Moises Alou, Jason Schmidt	.50
24	Felix Hernandez, Ichiro Suzuki	1.00
25	Chris Carpenter, Albert Pujols	2.00
26	Scott Kazmir, Carl Crawford	.50
27	Mark Teixeira, Kenny Rogers	.50
28	Vernon Wells, Roy Halladay	.50
29	Livan Hernandez, Jose Guillen	.50
30	Bartolo Colon, Vladimir Guerrero	.50

2006 Fleer Greats of the Game

Kirby Puckett
MINNESOTA TWINS

		NM/M
Complete Set (100):		35.00
Common Player:		.40
Pack (5):		8.00
Box (15):		100.00
1	Al Kaline	1.50
2	Alan Trammell	.50
3	Andre Dawson	.75
4	Barry Larkin	.75
5	Bill Buckner	.40
6	Bill Freehan	.40
7	Bill Madlock	.40
8	Bill Mazeroski	.40
9	Billy Williams	.50
10	Bo Jackson	1.00
11	Bob Feller	.50
12	Bob Gibson	.50
13	Bobby Doerr	.40
14	Bobby Murcer	.50
15	Boog Powell	.40
16	Brooks Robinson	1.50
17	Bruce Sutter	.40
18	Bucky Dent	.40
19	Cal Ripken Jr.	4.00
20	Rico Petrocelli	.40
21	Carlton Fisk	.75
22	Chris Chambliss	.40
23	Dave Concepcion	.40
24	Dave Parker	.50
25	Dave Winfield	1.00
26	David Cone	.50
27	Denny McLain	.50
28	Don Mattingly	3.00
29	Don Newcombe	.50
30	Don Sutton	.50
31	Dusty Baker	.50
32	Dwight Evans	.50
33	Eric Davis	.50
34	Ernie Banks	2.00
35	Fergie Jenkins	.75
36	Frank Robinson	1.00
37	Fred Lynn	.40
38	Fred McGriff	.40
39	Andre Thornton	.40
40	Garry Maddox	.40
41	Gary Matthews	.40
42	Gaylord Perry	.40
43	George Foster	.40
44	George Kell	.40
45	Graig Nettles	.40
46	Greg Luzinski	.40
47	Harmon Killebrew	1.50
48	Jack Clark	.50
49	Jack Morris	.50
50	Jim Palmer	.75
51	Jim Rice	.50
52	Joe Morgan	.75
53	John Kruk	.50
54	Johnny Bench	2.00
55	Jose Canseco	.75
56	Kirby Puckett	2.00
57	Kirk Gibson	.50
58	Lee Mazzilli	.50
59	Lou Brock	.75
60	Lou Piniella	.50
61	Luis Aparicio	.50
62	Luis Tiant	.50
63	Mark Fidrych	.50
64	Mark Grace	.75
65	Maury Wills	.50
66	Mike Schmidt	2.00
67	Nolan Ryan	4.00
68	Ozzie Smith	1.00
69	Paul Molitor	1.00
70	Paul O'Neill	.50

		NM/M
71	Phil Niekro	.50
72	Ralph Kiner	.75
73	Randy Hundley	.40
74	Red Schoendienst	.50
75	Reggie Jackson	1.00
76	Robin Yount	1.00
77	Rod Carew	.75
78	Rollie Fingers	.50
79	Ron Cey	.50
80	Ron Guidry	.50
81	Ron Santo	.75
82	Rusty Staub	.40
83	Ryne Sandberg	2.00
84	Sparky Lyle	.40
85	Stan Musial	2.00
86	Steve Carlton	.75
87	Steve Garvey	.50
88	Steve Sax	.40
89	Tommy Herr	.40
90	Tim McCarver	.40
91	Tim Raines	.50
92	Tom Seaver	1.00
93	Tony Gwynn	1.00
94	Tony Perez	.50
95	Wade Boggs	.75
96	Whitey Ford	1.00
97	Will Clark	.75
98	Willie Horton	.40
99	Willie McCovey	1.00
100	Yogi Berra	1.50

Copper

Copper: 2-4X
Production 299 Sets

Pewter

Pewter: 2X
Inserted 1:15

AUTOGRAPHics

Inserted 1:180
Cards are not serial numbered.

		NM/M
LA	Luis Aparicio/25	20.00
LB	Lou Brock/25	25.00
RC	Rod Carew/25	30.00
SC	Steve Carlton/50	25.00
WC	Will Clark/25	40.00
AD	Andre Dawson/99	25.00
BF	Bob Feller/50	30.00
GF	George Foster/50	20.00
SG	Steve Garvey/50	25.00
BG	Bob Gibson/25	40.00
KG	Kirk Gibson/25	25.00
MG	Mark Grace/50	30.00
RG	Ron Guidry/99	50.00
BJ	Bo Jackson/75	75.00
FJ	Fergie Jenkins/25	30.00
AK	Al Kaline/50	35.00
HK	Harmon Killebrew/25	40.00
BL	Barry Larkin/50	40.00
BI	Bill Mazeroski/25	35.00
FM	Fred McGriff/99	30.00
PM	Paul Molitor/25	25.00
JM	Joe Morgan/25	35.00
BM	Bobby Murcer/99	30.00
DN	Don Newcombe/99	15.00
PN	Phil Niekro/50	20.00
JP	Jim Palmer/99	20.00
DP	Dave Parker/99	20.00
TP	Tony Perez/99	30.00
JR	Jim Rice/99	20.00
BR	Brooks Robinson/99	40.00
RS	Ron Santo/99	30.00
OS	Ozzie Smith/25	60.00
BS	Bruce Sutter/50	15.00
SU	Don Sutton/50	20.00
BW	Billy Williams/25	25.00
MW	Maury Wills/99	20.00

Bat Barrel Auto.

No Pricing
Production 1-5

Cardinals Greats

		NM/M
Complete Set (10):		8.00
LB	Lou Brock	1.00
SC	Steve Carlton	.50
DD	Dizzy Dean	1.00
BG	Bob Gibson	1.00
TH	Tommy Herr	.25
RH	Rogers Hornsby	1.00
TM	Tim McCarver	.50
SM	Stan Musial	2.00
RS	Red Schoendienst	.50
OS	Ozzie Smith	1.00

Cubs Greats

		NM/M
Complete Set (10):		8.00
EB	Ernie Banks	2.00
AD	Andre Dawson	1.00
MG	Mark Grace	.50
RH	Randy Hundley	.50
FJ	Fergie Jenkins	.50
GM	Gary Mathews	.50

		NM/M
SA	Ryne Sandberg	2.00
RS	Ron Santo	1.00
BS	Bruce Sutter	.50
BW	Billy Williams	.50

Decade Greats

		NM/M
Complete Set (30):		20.00
EA	Earl Averill	.50
RO	Rod Carew	1.00
SC	Steve Carlton	.75
CC	Chris Chambliss	.50
JC	Jack Clark	.50
WC	Will Clark	1.00
RC	Roberto Clemente	3.00
MC	Mickey Cochrane	.50
BF	Bob Feller	1.00
TG	Tony Gwynn	1.00
BJ	Bo Jackson	1.00
JK	John Kruk	.50
BI	Bill Madlock	.50
EM	Eddie Mathews	1.00
BM	Bill Mazeroski	.50
WM	Willie McCovey	1.00
JM	Johnny Mize	.50
PM	Paul Molitor	1.00
MO	Mel Ott	1.00
DP	Dave Parker	.50
KP	Kirby Puckett	1.00
TR	Tim Raines	.50
CR	Cal Ripken Jr.	3.00
BR	Brooks Robinson	1.00
NR	Nolan Ryan	2.00
TS	Tom Seaver	1.00
MS	Mike Schmidt	1.00
WS	Willie Stargell	1.00
PT	Paul Traynor	.50
RY	Robin Yount	1.00

Dodgers Greats

		NM/M
Complete Set (10):		6.00
DB	Dusty Baker	.50
CA	Roy Campanella	1.00
RC	Ron Cey	.50
DD	Don Drysdale	1.00
SG	Steve Garvey	.50
PR	Pee Wee Reese	.50
JR	Jackie Robinson	2.00
SS	Steve Sax	.50
DS	Don Sutton	.50
MW	Maury Wills	.50

Nickname Greats

		NM/M
LA	Luis Aparicio	.50
SB	Steve Balboni	.50
DB	Don Baylor	.50
BE	Steve Bedrosian	.50
JB	Jim Bouton	.50
TB	Tom Brunansky	.50
RB	Rick Burleson	.50
RC	Ron Cey	.50
CH	Joe Charboneau	.50
JC	Jack Clark	.50
WC	Will Clark	1.00
DD	Darren Daulton	.50
DE	Dwight Evans	.50
BF	Bob Feller	.50
SF	Sid Fernandez	.50
MF	Mark Fidrych	.50
CF	Carlton Fisk	.75
DF	Dan Ford	.50
GF	George Foster	.50
AG	Andres Galarraga	.50
RG	Ron Guidry	.50

MH	Mike Hargrove	.50
KH	Ken Harrelson	.50
TH	Tom Henke	.50
HE	Tommy Herr	.50
BH	Burt Hooton	.50
AH	Al Hrabosky	.50
GH	Glenn Hubbard	.50
HJ	Howard Johnson	.50
JJ	Jay Johnstone	.50
ML	Mike LaValliere	.50
BL	Bill Lee	.50
SL	Sparky Lyle	.50
GM	Garry Maddox	.50
BM	Bill Madlock	.50
MZ	Dennis Martinez	.50
MA	Gary Matthews	.50
DM	Don Mattingly	2.00
LM	Lee Mazzilli	.50
WM	Willie McCovey	1.00
SM	Sam McDowell	.50
JM	John Montefusco	.50
DP	Dave Parker	.50
JP	Joe Pepitone	.50
LP	Lou Piniella	.50
RA	Doug Rader	.50
TR	Tim Raines	.50
RR	Rick Reuschel	.50
DR	Dave Righetti	.50
MR	Mickey Rivers	.50
FR	Frank Robinson	1.00
GS	George Scott	.50
JS	John Shelby	.50
FS	Fred Stanley	.50
RS	Rusty Staub	.50
AT	Andre Thornton	.50
ST	Steve Trout	.50
EV	Ellis Valentine	.50
MW	Mitch Williams	.50
JW	Jimmy Wynn	.50

Red Sox Greats
NM/M
	Complete Set (10):	8.00
WB	Wade Boggs	1.00
BD	Bobby Doerr	.50
DE	Dwight Evans	.50
CF	Carlton Fisk	1.00
JF	Jimmie Foxx	2.00
FL	Fred Lynn	.50
RP	Rico Petrocelli	.50
JR	Jim Rice	.75
LT	Luis Tiant	.50
TW	Ted Williams	2.00

Reds Greats
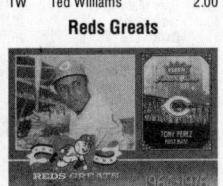
NM/M
	Complete Set (10):	8.00
JB	Johnny Bench	1.50
DC	Dave Concepcion	.50
ED	Eric Davis	.50
GF	George Foster	.50
KG	Ken Griffey Sr.	.50
BL	Barry Larkin	1.00
JM	Joe Morgan	1.00
TP	Tony Perez	1.00
FR	Frank Robinson	1.00
TS	Tom Seaver	1.00

Tigers Greats

NM/M
	Complete Set (10):	6.00
TC	Ty Cobb	2.00
MF	Mark Fidrych	.50
BF	Bill Freehan	.50
KG	Kirk Gibson	1.00
WH	Willie Horton	.50
AK	Al Kaline	1.00
GK	George Kell	.50
DM	Denny McLain	1.00
JM	Jack Morris	.50
AT	Alan Trammell	.50

Yankee Clippings

NM/M
	Complete Set (10):	12.00
YB	Yogi Berra	1.50

JD	Joe DiMaggio	2.00
WF	Whitey Ford	1.00
RG	Ron Guidry	.50
RJ	Reggie Jackson	1.00
DM	Don Mattingly	2.00
TM	Thurman Munson	1.50
BM	Bobby Murcer	.50
GN	Graig Nettles	.50
BR	Babe Ruth	3.00

Autographs
NM/M
	Common Autograph:	10.00
1	Al Kaline	25.00
2	Alan Trammell	15.00
3	Andre Dawson	20.00
4	Barry Larkin	35.00
5	Bill Buckner	12.00
6	Bill Freehan	12.00
7	Bill Madlock	15.00
8	Bill Mazeroski	35.00
9	Billy Williams	20.00
10	Bo Jackson	60.00
11	Bob Feller	25.00
12	Bob Gibson	40.00
13	Bobby Doerr	20.00
14	Bobby Murcer	15.00
15	Boog Powell	15.00
16	Brooks Robinson	25.00
17	Bruce Sutter	15.00
18	Bucky Dent	10.00
19	Cal Ripken Jr./SP	140.00
20	Rico Petrocelli	10.00
21	Carlton Fisk	30.00
22	Chris Chambliss	15.00
23	Dave Concepcion	15.00
24	Dave Parker	20.00
25	Dave Winfield	30.00
26	David Cone	15.00
27	Denny McLain	20.00
28	Don Mattingly	60.00
29	Don Newcombe	20.00
30	Don Sutton	15.00
31	Dusty Baker	25.00
32	Dwight Evans	20.00
33	Eric Davis	20.00
34	Ernie Banks	75.00
35	Fergie Jenkins	20.00
36	Frank Robinson	30.00
37	Fred Lynn	15.00
38	Fred McGriff	25.00
39	Andre Thornton	10.00
40	Garry Maddox	20.00
41	Gary Matthews	10.00
42	Gaylord Perry	15.00
43	George Foster	15.00
44	George Kell	15.00
45	Graig Nettles	20.00
46	Greg Luzinski	15.00
47	Harmon Killebrew	35.00
48	Jack Clark/SP/50	35.00
49	Jack Morris	15.00
50	Jim Palmer	20.00
51	Jim Rice	20.00
52	Joe Morgan	25.00
53	John Kruk	20.00
54	Johnny Bench	60.00
56	Kirby Puckett	100.00
57	Kirk Gibson	20.00
58	Lee Mazzilli	15.00
59	Lou Brock	30.00
60	Lou Piniella	15.00
61	Luis Aparicio	15.00
62	Luis Tiant	15.00
63	Mark Fidrych	25.00
64	Mark Grace	25.00
65	Maury Wills	20.00
66	Mike Schmidt	50.00
67	Nolan Ryan/SP/50	100.00
68	Ozzie Smith	40.00
69	Paul Molitor	25.00
70	Paul O'Neill	25.00
71	Phil Niekro	20.00
72	Ralph Kiner	20.00
73	Randy Hundley	15.00
74	Red Schoendienst	20.00
75	Reggie Jackson	35.00
76	Robin Yount	50.00
77	Rod Carew	25.00
78	Rollie Fingers	20.00
79	Ron Cey	10.00
80	Ron Guidry/SP	50.00
81	Ron Santo	20.00
82	Ryne Sandberg	50.00
83	Ryne Sandberg/SP	50.00
84	Sparky Lyle	15.00
85	Stan Musial	65.00
86	Steve Carlton	25.00
87	Steve Garvey	25.00
88	Steve Sax	10.00
89	Tommy Herr	15.00
90	Tim McCarver	20.00
91	Tim Raines/SP	20.00
92	Tom Seaver	50.00
93	Tony Gwynn	40.00
94	Tony Perez	25.00
95	Wade Boggs	25.00
96	Whitey Ford	50.00
97	Will Clark/SP	35.00
98	Willie Horton	15.00
99	Willie McCovey	35.00
100	Yogi Berra	60.00

Cardinals Greats Mem Auto
NM/M
Production 30 Sets
LB	Lou Brock	50.00
SC	Steve Carlton	35.00
BG	Bob Gibson	60.00

TH	Tommy Herr	20.00
TM	Tim McCarver	30.00
SM	Stan Musial	75.00
RS	Red Schoendienst	30.00
OS	Ozzie Smith	50.00

Cardinals Greats Auto.
NM/M
Production 30 Sets
LB	Lou Brock	40.00
SC	Steve Carlton	30.00
BG	Bob Gibson	50.00
TH	Tommy Herr	20.00
TM	Tim McCarver	30.00
SM	Stan Musial	75.00
RS	Red Schoendienst	25.00
OS	Ozzie Smith	50.00

Cardinals Greats Mem.
NM/M
	Common Player:	5.00
LB	Lou Brock	5.00
SC	Steve Carlton	5.00
DD	Dizzy Dean/SP	50.00
BG	Bob Gibson	15.00
TH	Tommy Herr	5.00
RH	Rogers Hornsby	40.00
TM	Tim McCarver	5.00
SM	Stan Musial	20.00
RS	Red Schoendienst	10.00
OS	Ozzie Smith	15.00

Cubs Greats Mem. Auto.
NM/M
Production 30 Sets
EB	Ernie Banks	60.00
AD	Andre Dawson	30.00
FJ	Fergie Jenkins	25.00
GM	Gary Matthews	25.00
SA	Ryne Sandberg	60.00
RS	Ron Santo	40.00
BS	Bruce Sutter	25.00
BW	Billy Williams	30.00

Cubs Greats Autograph
NM/M
Production 30 Sets
EB	Ernie Banks	60.00
AD	Andre Dawson	30.00
MG	Mark Grace	30.00
FJ	Fergie Jenkins	25.00
GM	Gary Matthews	25.00
SA	Ryne Sandberg	60.00
RS	Ron Santo	40.00
BS	Bruce Sutter	30.00
BW	Billy Williams	30.00

Cubs Greats Memorabilia
NM/M
EB	Ernie Banks	20.00
AD	Andre Dawson	8.00
MG	Mark Grace	8.00
FJ	Fergie Jenkins	8.00
GM	Gary Matthews	15.00
SA	Ryne Sandberg	15.00
RS	Ron Santo	10.00
BS	Brian Sutter	5.00
BW	Billy Williams	8.00

Decade Greats Mem. Auto.
NM/M
Production 30 Sets
RO	Rod Carew	35.00
SC	Steve Carlton	35.00
CC	Chris Chambliss	25.00
JC	Jack Clark	25.00
WC	Will Clark	30.00
BF	Bob Feller	50.00
TG	Tony Gwynn	60.00
BJ	Bo Jackson	65.00
JK	John Kruk	25.00
BI	Bill Madlock	20.00
BM	Bill Mazeroski	35.00
WM	Willie McCovey	40.00
PM	Paul Molitor	35.00
DP	Dave Parker	20.00
KP	Kirby Puckett	100.00
TR	Tim Raines	20.00
CR	Cal Ripken Jr.	150.00
BR	Brooks Robinson	40.00
NR	Nolan Ryan	100.00
MS	Mike Schmidt	75.00
TS	Tom Seaver	50.00
RY	Robin Yount	50.00

Decade Greats Autograph
NM/M
Production 30 Sets
RO	Rod Carew	35.00
SC	Steve Carlton	35.00
CC	Chris Chambliss	25.00
JC	Jack Clark	25.00
WC	Will Clark	30.00
BF	Bob Feller	50.00
TG	Tony Gwynn	60.00
BJ	Bo Jackson	65.00
JK	John Kruk	25.00

BI	Bill Madlock	20.00
BM	Bill Mazeroski	35.00
WM	Willie McCovey	40.00
PM	Paul Molitor	35.00
DP	Dave Parker	20.00
KP	Kirby Puckett	100.00
TR	Tim Raines	20.00
CR	Cal Ripken Jr.	150.00
BR	Brooks Robinson	40.00
NR	Nolan Ryan	100.00
MS	Mike Schmidt	75.00
TS	Tom Seaver	50.00
RY	Robin Yount	50.00

Decade Greats Memorabilia

NM/M
	Common Player:	5.00
EA	Earl Averill	20.00
RO	Rod Carew	8.00
SC	Steve Carlton	5.00
CC	Chris Chambliss	5.00
JC	Jack Clark	5.00
WC	Will Clark	8.00
RC	Roberto Clemente	60.00
BF	Bob Feller	15.00
BJ	Bo Jackson	15.00
JK	John Kruk	8.00
BI	Bill Madlock	5.00
EM	Eddie Matthews	10.00
BM	Bill Mazeroski	8.00
WM	Willie McCovey	10.00
JM	Johnny Mize	15.00
PM	Paul Molitor	15.00
MO	Mel Ott/SP	50.00
DP	Dave Parker	5.00
KP	Kirby Puckett	15.00
TR	Tim Raines	5.00
CR	Cal Ripken Jr.	20.00
BR	Brooks Robinson	8.00
NR	Nolan Ryan	15.00
MS	Mike Schmidt	20.00
TS	Tom Seaver	10.00
WS	Willie Stargell	15.00
RY	Robin Yount	8.00

Dodgers Greats Mem. Auto.
NM/M
Production 30 Sets
DB	Dusty Baker	40.00
RC	Ron Cey	30.00
SG	Steve Garvey	35.00
SS	Steve Sax	20.00
DS	Don Sutton	35.00
MW	Maury Wills	35.00

Dodgers Greats Autograph
NM/M
Production 30 Sets
DB	Dusty Baker	40.00
RC	Ron Cey	30.00
SG	Steve Garvey	35.00
SS	Steve Sax	25.00
DS	Don Sutton	35.00
MW	Maury Wills	35.00

Dodgers Greats Mem.
NM/M
	Common Player:	5.00
DB	Dusty Baker	8.00
CA	Roy Campanella	35.00
RC	Ron Cey	5.00
DD	Don Drysdale	25.00
SG	Steve Garvey	8.00
PR	Pee Wee Reese	10.00
JR	Jackie Robinson	40.00
SS	Steve Sax	5.00
DS	Don Sutton	5.00
MW	Maury Wills	5.00

Nickname Greats Autograph
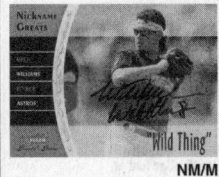
"Wild Thing"
NM/M
SB	Steve Balboni	15.00
BE	Steve Bedrosian	15.00
JB	Jim Bouton	35.00
TB	Tom Brunansky	15.00
RB	Rick Burleson	15.00
CH	Joe Charboneau	20.00
JC	Jack Clark	20.00
WC	Will Clark	30.00
DD	Darren Daulton	20.00
DE	Dwight Evans	20.00
BF	Bob Feller	50.00
SF	Sid Fernandez	15.00
MF	Mark Fidrych	35.00
CF	Carlton Fisk	50.00
DF	Dan Ford	15.00
GF	George Foster	20.00

RG	Ron Guidry	40.00
MH	Mike Hargrove	20.00
TH	Tom Henke	15.00
HE	Tommy Herr	15.00
BH	Burt Hooton	15.00
AH	Al Hrabosky	15.00
GH	Glenn Hubbard	15.00
HJ	Howard Johnson	25.00
JJ	Jay Johnstone	20.00
ML	Mike LaValliere	20.00
BL	Bill Lee	20.00
SL	Sparky Lyle	15.00
GM	Garry Maddox	20.00
BM	Bill Madlock	15.00
MZ	Dennis Martinez	15.00
MA	Gary Matthews	15.00
LM	Lee Mazzilli	20.00
WM	Willie McCovey	50.00
SM	Sam McDowell	20.00
JM	John Montefusco	20.00
DP	Dave Parker	20.00
JP	Joe Pepitone	20.00
LP	Lou Piniella	25.00
RA	Doug Rader	15.00
TR	Tim Raines	15.00
RR	Rick Reuschel	20.00
DR	Dave Righetti	20.00
MR	Mickey Rivers	20.00
FR	Frank Robinson	50.00
GS	George Scott	20.00
JS	John Shelby	15.00
FS	Fred Stanley	20.00
RS	Rusty Staub	15.00
AT	Andre Thornton	15.00
ST	Steve Trout	20.00
EV	Ellis Valentine	15.00
MW	Mitch Williams	15.00
JW	Jimmy Wynn	15.00

Red Sox Greats Mem. Auto.
NM/M
Production 30 Sets
WB	Wade Boggs	50.00
BD	Bobby Doerr	20.00
DE	Dwight Evans	25.00
CF	Carlton Fisk	35.00
FL	Fred Lynn	20.00
RP	Rico Petrocelli	25.00
JR	Jim Rice	25.00
LT	Luis Tiant	25.00

Red Sox Greats Autograph
NM/M
Production 30 Sets
WB	Wade Boggs	50.00
BD	Bobby Doerr	20.00
DE	Dwight Evans	25.00
CF	Carlton Fisk	35.00
FL	Fred Lynn	20.00
RP	Rico Petrocelli	25.00
JR	Jim Rice	25.00
LT	Luis Tiant	25.00
TW	Ted Williams	50.00

Red Sox Greats Mem.
NM/M
WB	Wade Boggs	10.00
BD	Bobby Doerr	8.00
DE	Dwight Evans	5.00
CF	Carlton Fisk	8.00
JF	Jimmie Foxx	50.00
FL	Fred Lynn	5.00
RP	Rico Petrocelli	5.00
JR	Jim Rice	8.00
LT	Luis Tiant	5.00
TW	Ted Williams	50.00

Reds Greats Mem. Auto.
NM/M
Production 30 Sets
JB	Johnny Bench	65.00
DC	Dave Concepcion	25.00
ED	Eric Davis	30.00
GF	George Foster	25.00
KG	Ken Griffey Sr.	30.00
BL	Barry Larkin	40.00
JM	Joe Morgan	40.00
TP	Tony Perez	40.00
FR	Frank Robinson	40.00
TS	Tom Seaver	50.00

Reds Greats Autograph
NM/M
Production 30 Sets
JB	Johnny Bench	65.00
DC	Dave Concepcion	25.00
ED	Eric Davis	30.00
GF	George Foster	25.00
KG	Ken Griffey Sr.	30.00
BL	Barry Larkin	40.00
JM	Joe Morgan	40.00
TP	Tony Perez	40.00
FR	Frank Robinson	40.00
TS	Tom Seaver	50.00

Reds Greats Memorabilia
NM/M
	Common Player:	5.00
JB	Johnny Bench	15.00
DC	Dave Concepcion	5.00
ED	Eric Davis	10.00
GF	George Foster	5.00
KG	Ken Griffey Sr.	8.00
BL	Barry Larkin	8.00
JM	Joe Morgan	10.00
TP	Tony Perez	8.00
FR	Frank Robinson	10.00
TS	Tom Seaver	10.00

Tigers Greats Mem. Auto.
NM/M
Production 30 Sets
MF	Mark Fidrych	35.00
BF	Bill Freehan	30.00
KG	Kirk Gibson	35.00
WH	Willie Horton	20.00
AK	Al Kaline	50.00
GK	George Kell	40.00
JM	Jack Morris	25.00
AT	Alan Trammell	35.00

Tigers Greats Autograph
NM/M
Production 30 Sets
MF	Mark Fidrych	35.00
BF	Bill Freehan	30.00
KG	Kirk Gibson	35.00
WH	Willie Horton	20.00
AK	Al Kaline	50.00
GK	George Kell	40.00
DM	Denny McLain	35.00
JM	Jack Morris	25.00
AT	Alan Trammell	35.00

Tigers Greats Memorabilia
NM/M
	Common Player:	5.00
TC	Ty Cobb	85.00
MF	Mark Fidrych	10.00
BF	Bill Freehan	5.00
KG	Kirk Gibson	5.00
WH	Willie Horton	5.00
AK	Al Kaline	12.00
GK	George Kell	8.00
JM	Jack Morris	5.00
AT	Alan Trammell	5.00

Yankee Clippings Mem Auto
NM/M
Production 30 Sets
YB	Yogi Berra	80.00
WF	Whitey Ford	60.00
RG	Ron Guidry	65.00
RJ	Reggie Jackson	50.00
DM	Don Mattingly	100.00
BM	Bobby Murcer	25.00
GN	Graig Nettles	40.00

Yankee Clippings Auto.
NM/M
Production 30 Sets
YB	Yogi Berra	80.00
WF	Whitey Ford	60.00
RG	Ron Guidry	65.00
RJ	Reggie Jackson	50.00
DM	Don Mattingly	100.00
BM	Bobby Murcer	25.00
GN	Graig Nettles	40.00

Yankee Clippings Mem.

NM/M
	Common Player:	8.00
YB	Yogi Berra	25.00
JD	Joe DiMaggio	75.00
WF	Whitey Ford	15.00
RG	Ron Guidry	15.00
RJ	Reggie Jackson	12.00
DM	Don Mattingly	15.00
TM	Thurman Munson	20.00
BM	Bobby Murcer	10.00
GN	Graig Nettles	8.00
BR	Babe Ruth	200.00

2006 Fleer Tradition

BONDERMAN

NM/M
	Complete Set (200):	35.00
	Common Player:	.15
	Hobby Pack (10):	1.50
	Hobby Box (36):	50.00
1	Andruw Jones	.50
2	Chipper Jones	.75
3	John Smoltz	.25
4	Tim Hudson	.25
5	Joey Devine RC	.25
6	Chuck James RC	.25
7	Alay Soler RC	.50

#	Player	Price
8	Conor Jackson RC	.25
9	Luis Gonzalez	.15
10	Brandon Webb	.15
11	Chad Tracy	.15
12	Orlando Hudson	.15
13	Shawn Green	.15
14	Vladimir Guerrero	.75
15	Bartolo Colon	.15
16	Chone Figgins	.15
17	Garret Anderson	.15
18	Francisco Rodriguez	.15
19	Casey Kotchman	.15
20	Lance Berkman	.25
21	Craig Biggio	.25
22	Andy Pettitte	.25
23	Morgan Ensberg	.15
24	Brad Lidge	.15
25	Jered Weaver RC	1.00
26	Roy Oswalt	.25
27	Eric Chavez	.25
28	Rich Harden	.15
29	Cole Hamels RC	.25
30	Huston Street	.15
31	Bobby Crosby	.15
32	Nick Swisher	.25
33	Vernon Wells	.25
34	Roy Halladay	.25
35	A.J. Burnett	.15
36	Troy Glaus	.25
37	B.J. Ryan	.15
38	Bengie Molina	.15
39	Alex Rios	.15
40	Prince Fielder RC	2.00
41	Jose Capellan RC	.25
42	Rickie Weeks	.15
43	Ben Sheets	.25
44	Carlos Lee	.25
45	J.J. Hardy	.15
46	Albert Pujols	2.00
47	Skip Schumaker RC	.25
48	Adam Wainwright RC	.25
49	Jim Edmonds	.25
50	Scott Rolen	.50
51	Chris Carpenter	.25
52	David Eckstein	.15
53	Derrek Lee	.50
54	Jon Lester RC	3.00
55	Mark Prior	.40
56	Aramis Ramirez	.25
57	Juan Pierre	.15
58	Greg Maddux	1.50
59	Michael Barrett	.15
60	Carl Crawford	.15
61	Scott Kazmir	.25
62	Jorge Cantu	.15
63	Jonny Gomes	.15
64	Julio Lugo	.15
65	Aubrey Huff	.15
66	Jeff Kent	.25
67	Nomar Garciaparra	.50
68	Rafael Furcal	.15
69	Tim Hamulack RC	.25
70	Chad Billingsley RC	.25
71	Hong-Chih Kuo RC	.25
72	J.D. Drew	.15
73	Moises Alou	.25
74	Randy Winn	.15
75	Jason Schmidt	.25
76	Jeremy Accardo RC	.25
77	Matt Cain RC	.50
78	Joel Zumaya RC	.50
79	Travis Hafner	.50
80	Victor Martinez	.25
81	Grady Sizemore	.40
82	C.C. Sabathia	.15
83	Jhonny Peralta	.15
84	Jason Michaels	.15
85	Jeremy Sowers RC	.25
86	Ichiro Suzuki	1.50
87	Richie Sexson	.25
88	Adrian Beltre	.25
89	Felix Hernandez	.25
90	Kenji Johjima RC	2.00
91	Jeff Harris RC	.25
92	Taylor Buchholz RC	.25
93	Miguel Cabrera	.75
94	Dontrelle Willis	.25
95	Jeremy Hermida RC	.25
96	Mike Jacobs RC	.25
97	Josh Johnson RC	.25
98	Hanley Ramirez RC	.40
99	Josh Willingham RC	.25
100	Dan Uggla RC	1.00
101	David Wright	1.00
102	Jose Reyes	.50
103	Pedro Martinez	.75
104	Carlos Beltran	.50
105	Carlos Delgado	.40
106	Billy Wagner	.25
107	Lastings Milledge RC	.50
108	Alfonso Soriano	.75
109	Jose Vidro	.15
110	Livan Hernandez	.15
111	Matthew Kemp RC	.25
112	Brandon Watson RC	.15
113	Ryan Zimmerman RC	2.00
114	Miguel Tejada	.50
115	Ramon Hernandez	.15
116	Brian Roberts	.25
117	Melvin Mora	.15
118	Erik Bedard	.15
119	Jay Gibbons	.15
120	Aaron Rakers RC	.25
121	Jake Peavy	.25
122	Brian Giles	.25
123	Khalil Greene	.15
124	Trevor Hoffman	.25
125	Josh Barfield RC	.25

#	Player	Price
126	Ben Johnson RC	.25
127	Ryan Howard	1.50
128	Bobby Abreu	.25
129	Chase Utley	.50
130	Pat Burrell	.25
131	Jimmy Rollins	.50
132	Brett Myers	.25
133	Mike Thompson RC	.25
134	Jason Bay	.40
135	Oliver Perez	.15
136	Matt Capps RC	.25
137	Paul Maholm RC	.25
138	Nate McLouth RC	.25
139	John Van Benschoten RC	.25
140	Mark Teixeira	.50
141	Michael Young	.25
142	Hank Blalock	.25
143	Kevin Millwood	.25
144	Laynce Nix	.15
145	Francisco Cordero	.15
146	Ian Kinsler RC	.25
147	David Ortiz	.75
148	Manny Ramirez	.75
149	Jason Varitek	.75
150	Curt Schilling	.75
151	Josh Beckett	.25
152	Coco Crisp	.15
153	Jonathan Papelbon RC	2.00
154	Ken Griffey Jr.	1.50
155	Adam Dunn	.50
156	Felipe Lopez	.15
157	Bronson Arroyo	.15
158	Ryan Freel	.15
159	Chris Denorfia RC	.25
160	Todd Helton	.50
161	Garrett Atkins	.15
162	Matt Holliday	.25
163	Clint Barmes	.15
164	Kendry Morales RC	.25
165	Ryan Shealy RC	.25
166	Josh Wilson RC	.25
167	Reggie Sanders	.15
168	Angel Berroa	.15
169	Mike Sweeney	.15
170	Mark Grudzielanek	.15
171	Jeremy Affeldt	.15
172	Steve Stemle RC	.50
173	Justin Verlander RC	2.00
174	Ivan Rodriguez	.50
175	Chris Shelton	.15
176	Jeremy Bonderman	.25
177	Magglio Ordonez	.15
178	Carlos Guillen	.15
179	Placido Polanco	.15
180	Johan Santana	.75
181	Torii Hunter	.25
182	Joe Nathan	.15
183	Joe Mauer	.50
184	David Gassner RC	.25
185	Jason Kubel RC	.25
186	Francisco Liriano RC	1.50
187	Jim Thome	.50
188	Paul Konerko	.40
189	Scott Podsednik	.25
190	Tadahito Iguchi	.15
191	A.J. Pierzynski	.15
192	Jose Contreras	.15
193	Brian Anderson RC	.25
194	Hideki Matsui	1.50
195	Wilbert Nieves RC	.25
196	Alex Rodriguez	1.00
197	Gary Sheffield	.25
198	Randy Johnson	.25
199	Johnny Damon	.40
200	Derek Jeter	1.00

Griffey Jr. 1989 Fleer Buyback Auto.
NM/M

Production 50
Ken Griffey Jr. 250.00

Black & White

B&W (1-200): 2-3X

Printing Plates
No Pricing
Production one set per color.

Sepia Tone
Sepia (1-200): 2-3X

1934 Goudey Greats
NM/M

Common Player: 2.00
GG-1	Andruw Jones	5.00
GG-2	Chipper Jones	8.00
GG-3	John Smoltz	4.00

GG-4	Tim Hudson	3.00
GG-5	Conor Jackson	2.00
GG-6	Luis Gonzalez	2.00
GG-7	Brandon Webb	3.00
GG-8	Vladimir Guerrero	8.00
GG-9	Bartolo Colon	2.00
GG-10	Lance Berkman	3.00
GG-11	Craig Biggio	4.00
GG-12	Andy Pettitte	3.00
GG-13	Morgan Ensberg	2.00
GG-14	Roy Oswalt	3.00
GG-15	Eric Chavez	3.00
GG-16	Rich Harden	3.00
GG-17	Huston Street	3.00
GG-18	Vernon Wells	3.00
GG-19	Roy Halladay	3.00
GG-20	Troy Glaus	3.00
GG-21	Prince Fielder	10.00
GG-22	Rickie Weeks	3.00
GG-23	Ben Sheets	3.00
GG-24	Carlos Lee	3.00
GG-25	Albert Pujols	20.00
GG-26	Jim Edmonds	4.00
GG-27	Scott Rolen	8.00
GG-28	Chris Carpenter	5.00
GG-29	Derrek Lee	5.00
GG-30	Mark Prior	5.00
GG-31	Greg Maddux	15.00
GG-32	Carl Crawford	4.00
GG-33	Scott Kazmir	3.00
GG-34	Jorge Cantu	2.00
GG-35	Jeff Kent	3.00
GG-36	Nomar Garciaparra	8.00
GG-37	J.D. Drew	2.00
GG-38	Randy Winn	2.00
GG-39	Jason Schmidt	3.00
GG-40	Travis Hafner	5.00
GG-41	Victor Martinez	3.00
GG-42	Grady Sizemore	4.00
GG-43	Jhonny Peralta	2.00
GG-44	Ichiro Suzuki	15.00
GG-45	Richie Sexson	4.00
GG-46	Felix Hernandez	4.00
GG-47	Kenji Johjima	8.00
GG-48	Miguel Cabrera	8.00
GG-49	Dontrelle Willis	4.00
GG-50	Josh Willingham	2.00
GG-51	David Wright	15.00
GG-52	Jose Reyes	5.00
GG-53	Pedro Martinez	8.00
GG-54	Carlos Beltran	5.00
GG-55	Alfonso Soriano	8.00
GG-56	Ryan Zimmerman	8.00
GG-57	Miguel Tejada	4.00
GG-58	Brian Roberts	2.00
GG-59	Jake Peavy	3.00
GG-60	Brian Giles	2.00
GG-61	Khalil Greene	2.00
GG-62	Ryan Howard	15.00
GG-63	Bobby Abreu	4.00
GG-64	Chase Utley	5.00
GG-65	Jimmy Rollins	5.00
GG-66	Jason Bay	4.00
GG-67	Mark Teixeira	5.00
GG-68	Michael Young	3.00
GG-69	Hank Blalock	3.00
GG-70	David Ortiz	8.00
GG-71	Manny Ramirez	8.00
GG-72	Curt Schilling	8.00
GG-73	Josh Beckett	3.00
GG-74	Jonathan Papelbon	10.00
GG-75	Ken Griffey Jr.	15.00
GG-76	Adam Dunn	5.00
GG-77	Todd Helton	4.00
GG-78	Garrett Atkins	2.00
GG-79	Matt Holliday	2.00
GG-80	Reggie Sanders	2.00
GG-81	Justin Verlander	10.00
GG-82	Ivan Rodriguez	5.00
GG-83	Chris Shelton	2.00
GG-84	Jeremy Bonderman	3.00
GG-85	Magglio Ordonez	3.00
GG-86	Johan Santana	6.00
GG-87	Torii Hunter	3.00
GG-88	Joe Nathan	2.00
GG-89	Joe Mauer	5.00
GG-90	Francisco Liriano	5.00
GG-91	Jim Thome	4.00
GG-92	Paul Konerko	4.00
GG-93	Scott Podsednik	2.00
GG-94	Tadahito Iguchi	4.00
GG-95	A.J. Pierzynski	2.00
GG-96	Hideki Matsui	12.00
GG-97	Alex Rodriguez	20.00
GG-98	Gary Sheffield	4.00
GG-99	Derek Jeter	25.00
GG-100	Jason Giambi	4.00

Blue Chip Prospects
NM/M

Common Player: .50

BC-1	Ryan Zimmerman	3.00
BC-2	Conor Jackson	.75
BC-3	Jonathan Papelbon	3.00
BC-4	Justin Verlander	3.00
BC-5	Jeremy Hermida	.75
BC-6	Josh Willingham	.50
BC-7	Hanley Ramirez	1.00
BC-8	Prince Fielder	3.00
BC-9	Francisco Liriano	2.00
BC-10	Lastings Milledge	2.00
BC-11	Jon Lester	2.00
BC-12	Matt Cain	1.50
BC-13	Adam Wainwright	.75
BC-14	Chuck James	1.00
BC-15	Kenji Johjima	.75
BC-16	Josh Johnson	.75
BC-17	Jason Kubel	.50
BC-18	Brian Anderson	.50
BC-19	Cole Hamels	2.00
BC-20	Mike Jacobs	.50
BC-21	Jered Weaver	3.00
BC-22	Kendry Morales	.50
BC-23	Alay Soler	.50
BC-24	Chris Denorfia	.50
BC-25	Chad Billingsley	1.00

Diamond Tribute

NM/M
Common Player: .50
DT-1	Derek Jeter	3.00
DT-2	Ken Griffey Jr.	3.00
DT-3	Vladimir Guerrero	1.50
DT-4	Albert Pujols	3.00
DT-5	Derrek Lee	1.00
DT-6	David Ortiz	1.50
DT-7	Miguel Tejada	1.00
DT-8	Jim Thome	1.00
DT-9	Travis Hafner	1.00
DT-10	Grady Sizemore	1.00
DT-11	Chris Shelton	.50
DT-12	Dontrelle Willis	1.00
DT-13	Craig Biggio	1.00
DT-14	Roy Oswalt	1.00
DT-15	Prince Fielder	2.00
DT-16	David Wright	2.50
DT-17	Jose Reyes	1.00
DT-18	Hideki Matsui	2.00
DT-19	Rich Harden	.75
DT-20	Bobby Abreu	.75
DT-21	Jason Bay	1.00
DT-22	Jake Peavy	.75
DT-23	Felix Hernandez	.75
DT-24	Carl Crawford	.75
DT-25	Vernon Wells	.75

Grass Roots

NM/M
Common Player: .50

GR-1	Ken Griffey Jr.	2.50
GR-2	Albert Pujols	3.00
GR-3	Derek Jeter	3.00
GR-4	Derrek Lee	1.00
GR-5	Vladimir Guerrero	1.00
GR-6	Andruw Jones	1.00
GR-7	Manny Ramirez	1.00
GR-8	Johan Santana	1.00
GR-9	Victor Martinez	.75
GR-10	Todd Helton	1.00
GR-11	Ivan Rodriguez	1.00
GR-12	Miguel Cabrera	1.00
GR-13	Lance Berkman	.75
GR-14	Bartolo Colon	.50
GR-15	Jeff Kent	.50
GR-16	Carlos Lee	.75
GR-17	Torii Hunter	.50
GR-18	Carlos Beltran	1.00
GR-19	Alex Rodriguez	3.00
GR-20	Randy Johnson	1.00
GR-21	Eric Chavez	.50
GR-22	Ryan Howard	2.50
GR-23	Ichiro Suzuki	2.00
GR-24	Chris Carpenter	1.00
GR-25	Mark Teixeira	1.00

Signature Tradition
NM/M

Inserted 1:1,269 Hobby
CH	Craig Hansen	35.00
JM	Joe Mauer/SP	30.00

Traditional Threads

NM/M
Common Player: 4.00
JB	Josh Barfield	4.00
BA	Jason Bay	6.00
EB	Erik Bedard	4.00
HB	Hank Blalock	4.00
SC	Sean Casey	4.00
JD	Johnny Damon	8.00
ZD	Zachary Duke	4.00
PF	Prince Fielder	15.00
CF	Chone Figgins	4.00
BG	Brian Giles	4.00
MG	Marcus Giles	4.00
GR	Khalil Greene	4.00
KG	Ken Griffey Jr.	15.00
VG	Vladimir Guerrero	8.00
JH	Jeremy Hermida	4.00
FH	Felix Hernandez	6.00
LH	Livan Hernandez	4.00
GJ	Geoff Jenkins	4.00
DJ	Derek Jeter	20.00
CK	Casey Kotchman/SP	4.00
CL	Carlos Lee	6.00
DL	Derrek Lee	6.00
JL	Javy Lopez	4.00
GM	Greg Maddux	10.00
MM	Melvin Mora	4.00
DO	David Ortiz	6.00
RO	Roy Oswalt	6.00
JP	Jake Peavy	6.00
AP	Albert Pujols	20.00
AR	Aramis Ramirez	4.00
AS	Alfonso Soriano	8.00
BR	Brian Roberts	6.00
BS	Ben Sheets	6.00
TE	Mark Teixeira	8.00
MT	Miguel Tejada	6.00
JV	Jose Vidro	4.00
OV	Omar Vizquel	6.00
RW	Rickie Weeks	6.00
MY	Michael Young	6.00
CZ	Carlos Zambrano	4.00
RZ	Ryan Zimmerman	8.00

Triple Crown Contenders
NM/M

Common Player: .75
TC-1	Albert Pujols	3.00
TC-2	Derek Lee	.75
TC-3	Manny Ramirez	1.00
TC-4	David Ortiz	.75
TC-5	Mark Teixeira	.75
TC-6	Alex Rodriguez	3.00
TC-7	Andruw Jones	.75
TC-8	Todd Helton	.75
TC-9	Vladimir Guerrero	1.00
TC-10	Miguel Cabrera	1.00
TC-11	Hideki Matsui	2.00
TC-12	Travis Hafner	.75
TC-13	David Wright	2.00
TC-14	Ken Griffey Jr.	2.50
TC-15	Jason Bay	.75

2007 Fleer
NM/M

Complete Set (400): 75.00
Common Player: .15
Hobby Pack (10): 1.50
Hobby Box (36): 50.00
Rack Pack (52): 4.50
Rack Box (18): 75.00

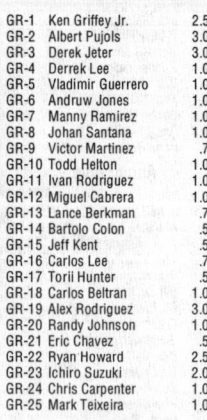

#	Player	Price
1	Chad Cordero	.15
2	Alfonso Soriano	.50
3	Nick Johnson	.15
4	Austin Kearns	.15
5	Ramon Ortiz	.15
6	Brian Schneider	.15
7	Ryan Zimmerman	.40
8	Jose Vidro	.15
9	Felipe Lopez	.15
10	Cristian Guzman	.15
11	B.J. Ryan	.15
12	Alex Rios	.25
13	Vernon Wells	.25
14	Roy Halladay	.25
15	A.J. Burnett	.15
16	Lyle Overbay	.15
17	Troy Glaus	.25
18	Bengie Molina	.15
19	Gustavo Chacin	.15
20	Aaron Hill	.15
21	Vicente Padilla	.15
22	Kevin Millwood	.15
23	Akinori Otsuka	.15
24	Adam Eaton	.15
25	Hank Blalock	.25
26	Mark Teixeira	.40
27	Michael Young	.25
28	Mark DeRosa	.15
29	Gary Matthews	.15
30	Ian Kinsler	.15
31	Carlos Lee	.25
32	James Shields	.15
33	Scott Kazmir	.25
34	Carl Crawford	.25
35	Jonny Gomes	.15
36	Tim Corcoran	.15
37	B.J. Upton	.25
38	Rocco Baldelli	.25
39	Jae Weong Seo	.15
40	Jorge Cantu	.15
41	Ty Wigginton	.15
42	Chris Carpenter	.25
43	Albert Pujols	1.50
44	Scott Rolen	.50
45	Jim Edmonds	.40
46	Jason Isringhausen	.15
47	Yadier Molina	.15
48	Adam Wainwright	.15
49	Mark Mulder	.15
50	Jason Marquis	.15
51	Juan Encarnacion	.15
52	Aaron Miles	.15
53	Ichiro Suzuki	1.00
54	Felix Hernandez	.40
55	Kenji Johjima	.25
56	Richie Sexson	.40
57	Yuniesky Betancourt	.15
58	J.J. Putz	.15
59	Jarrod Washburn	.15
60	Ben Broussard	.15
61	Adrian Beltre	.25
62	Raul Ibanez	.15
63	Jose Lopez	.15
64	Matt Cain	.25
65	Noah Lowry	.15
66	Jason Schmidt	.25
67	Pedro Feliz	.15
68	Matt Morris	.15
69	Ray Durham	.15
70	Steve Finley	.15
71	Randy Winn	.15
72	Moises Alou	.15
73	Eliezer Alfonzo	.15
74	Armando Benitez	.15
75	Omar Vizquel	.25
76	Chris Young	.25
77	Adrian Gonzalez	.25
78	Khalil Greene	.15
79	Mike Piazza	.25
80	Josh Barfield	.25
81	Brian Giles	.25
82	Jake Peavy	.25
83	Trevor Hoffman	.25
84	Mike Cameron	.15
85	Dave Roberts	.15
86	David Wells	.15
87	Zachary Duke	.15
88	Ian Snell	.15
89	Jason Bay	.40
90	Freddy Sanchez	.15
91	Jack Wilson	.15
92	Tom Gorzelanny	.15
93	Chris Duffy	.15

#	Player	Price	#	Player	Price
94	Jose Castillo	.15	212	Mike Jacobs	.15
95	Matt Capps	.15	213	Kenny Rogers	.15
96	Mike Gonzalez	.15	214	Justin Verlander	.40
97	Chase Utley	.50	215	Ivan Rodriguez	.40
98	Jimmy Rollins	.50	216	Magglio Ordonez	.25
99	Aaron Rowand	.15	217	Todd Jones	.15
100	Ryan Howard	1.00	218	Joel Zumaya	.40
101	Cole Hamels	.50	219	Jeremy Bonderman	.40
102	Pat Burrell	.25	220	Nate Robertson	.15
103	Shane Victorino	.15	221	Brandon Inge	.15
104	Jamie Moyer	.15	222	Craig Monroe	.15
105	Mike Lieberthal	.15	223	Carlos Guillen	.15
106	Tom Gordon	.15	224	Jeff Francis	.15
107	Brett Myers	.15	225	Brian Fuentes	.15
108	Nick Swisher	.25	226	Todd Helton	.25
109	Barry Zito	.25	227	Matt Holliday	.25
110	Jason Kendall	.15	228	Garrett Atkins	.15
111	Milton Bradley	.25	229	Clint Barmes	.15
112	Bobby Crosby	.15	230	Jason Jennings	.15
113	Huston Street	.25	231	Aaron Cook	.15
114	Eric Chavez	.25	232	Brad Hawpe	.15
115	Frank Thomas	.40	233	Cory Sullivan	.15
116	Danny Haren	.25	234	Aaron Boone	.15
117	Jay Payton	.15	235	C.C. Sabathia	.25
118	Randy Johnson	.50	236	Grady Sizemore	.50
119	Mike Mussina	.40	237	Travis Hafner	.25
120	Bobby Abreu	.40	238	Jhonny Peralta	.15
121	Jason Giambi	.40	239	Jake Westbrook	.15
122	Derek Jeter	1.50	240	Jeremy Sowers	.15
123	Alex Rodriguez	1.50	241	Andy Marte	.15
124	Jorge Posada	.40	242	Victor Martinez	.25
125	Robinson Cano	.40	243	Jason Michaels	.15
126	Mariano Rivera	.40	244	Cliff Lee	.15
127	Chien-Ming Wang	.40	245	Bronson Arroyo	.15
128	Hideki Matsui	1.00	246	Aaron Harang	.15
129	Gary Sheffield	.40	247	Ken Griffey Jr.	1.00
130	Lastings Milledge	.25	248	Adam Dunn	.40
131	Tom Glavine	.25	249	Rich Aurilia	.15
132	Billy Wagner	.25	250	Eric Milton	.15
133	Pedro Martinez	.50	251	David Ross	.15
134	Paul LoDuca	.15	252	Brandon Phillips	.15
135	Carlos Delgado	.25	253	Ryan Freel	.15
136	Carlos Beltran	.40	254	Eddie Guardado	.15
137	David Wright	.50	255	Jose Contreras	.15
138	Jose Reyes	.50	256	Freddy Garcia	.15
139	Julio Franco	.15	257	Jon Garland	.15
140	Michael Cuddyer	.15	258	Mark Buehrle	.25
141	Justin Morneau	.40	259	Bobby Jenks	.15
142	Johan Santana	.25	260	Paul Konerko	.25
143	Francisco Liriano	.25	261	Jermaine Dye	.15
144	Joe Mauer	.25	262	Joe Crede	.15
145	Torii Hunter	.25	263	Jim Thome	.25
146	Luis Castillo	.15	264	Javier Vazquez	.15
147	Joe Nathan	.25	265	A.J. Pierzynski	.15
148	Carlos Silva	.15	266	Tadahito Iguchi	.25
149	Boof Bonser	.15	267	Carlos Zambrano	.25
150	Ben Sheets	.25	268	Derrek Lee	.40
151	Prince Fielder	.50	269	Aramis Ramirez	.40
152	Bill Hall	.25	270	Ryan Theriot	.15
153	Rickie Weeks	.25	271	Juan Pierre	.25
154	Geoff Jenkins	.15	272	Rich Hill	.15
155	Kevin Mench	.15	273	Ryan Dempster	.15
156	Francisco Cordero	.15	274	Jacque Jones	.15
157	Chris Capuano	.15	275	Mark Prior	.25
158	Brady Clark	.15	276	Kerry Wood	.25
159	Tony Gwynn Jr.	.15	277	Josh Beckett	.25
160	Chad Billingsley	.25	278	David Ortiz	.50
161	Russell Martin	.25	279	Kevin Youkilis	.15
162	Wilson Betemit	.15	280	Jason Varitek	.40
163	Nomar Garciaparra	.25	281	Manny Ramirez	.50
164	Kenny Lofton	.15	282	Curt Schilling	.50
165	Rafael Furcal	.15	283	Jon Lester	.25
166	Julio Lugo	.15	284	Jonathan Papelbon	.50
167	Brad Penny	.15	285	Alex Gonzalez	.15
168	Jeff Kent	.25	286	Mike Lowell	.25
169	Greg Maddux	1.00	287	Kyle Snyder	.15
170	Derek Lowe	.15	288	Miguel Tejada	.40
171	Andre Ethier	.25	289	Erik Bedard	.25
172	Chone Figgins	.15	290	Ramon Hernandez	.15
173	Francisco Rodriguez	.25	291	Melvin Mora	.15
174	Garret Anderson	.15	292	Nicholas Markakis	.25
175	Orlando Cabrera	.15	293	Brian Roberts	.25
176	Adam Kennedy	.15	294	Corey Patterson	.15
177	John Lackey	.25	295	Kris Benson	.15
178	Vladimir Guerrero	.50	296	Jay Gibbons	.15
179	Bartolo Colon	.25	297	Rodrigo Lopez	.15
180	Jered Weaver	.25	298	Chris Ray	.15
181	Juan Rivera	.15	299	Andruw Jones	.50
182	Howie Kendrick	.25	300	Brian McCann	.40
183	Ervin Santana	.25	301	Jeff Francoeur	.25
184	Mark Redman	.15	302	Chuck James	.25
185	David DeJesus	.15	303	John Smoltz	.40
186	Joey Gathright	.15	304	Bob Wickman	.15
187	Mike Sweeney	.15	305	Edgar Renteria	.25
188	Mark Teahen	.15	306	Adam LaRoche	.25
189	Angel Berroa	.15	307	Marcus Giles	.15
190	Ambiorix Burgos	.15	308	Tim Hudson	.25
191	Luke Hudson	.15	309	Chipper Jones	.50
192	Mark Grudzielanek	.15	310	Miguel Batista	.15
193	Roger Clemens	1.50	311	Claudio Vargas	.15
194	Willy Taveras	.15	312	Brandon Webb	.25
195	Craig Biggio	.25	313	Luis Gonzalez	.15
196	Andy Pettitte	.15	314	Livan Hernandez	.15
197	Roy Oswalt	.40	315	Stephen Drew	.25
198	Lance Berkman	.25	316	Johnny Estrada	.15
199	Morgan Ensberg	.25	317	Orlando Hudson	.15
200	Brad Lidge	.15	318	Conor Jackson	.25
201	Chris Burke	.15	319	Chad Tracy	.25
202	Miguel Cabrera	.50	320	Carlos Quentin	.25
203	Dontrelle Willis	.25	321	Alvin Colina **RC**	.50
204	Josh Johnson	.15	322	Miguel Montero **(RC)**	.25
205	Ricky Nolasco	.15	323	Jeff Fiorentino **(RC)**	.25
206	Dan Uggla	.15	324	Jeff Baker **(RC)**	.25
207	Jeremy Hermida	.15	325	Brian Burres **(RC)**	.25
208	Scott Olsen	.25	326	David Murphy **(RC)**	.25
209	Josh Willingham	.15	327	Francisco Cruceta **(RC)**	.25
210	Joe Borowski	.15	328	Beltran Perez **(RC)**	.25
211	Hanley Ramirez	.40	329	Scott Moore **(RC)**	.25

#	Player	Price
330	Sean Henn **(RC)**	.25
331	Ryan Sweeney **(RC)**	.25
332	Josh Fields **(RC)**	.25
333	Jerry Owens **(RC)**	.25
334	Vinny Rottino **(RC)**	.25
335	Kevin Kouzmanoff **(RC)**	.50
336	Alexi Casilla **RC**	.25
337	Justin Hampson **(RC)**	.25
338	Troy Tulowitzki **(RC)**	.50
339	Jose Garcia **RC**	.50
340	Andrew Miller **RC**	1.00
341	Glen Perkins **(RC)**	.25
342	Ubaldo Jimenez **(RC)**	2.50
343	Doug Slaten **RC**	.25
344	Angel Sanchez **RC**	.50
345	Mitch Maier **RC**	.25
346	Ryan Braun **(RC)**	.50
347	Joselo Diaz **(RC)**	.25
348	Delwyn Young **(RC)**	.25
349	Kevin Hooper **(RC)**	.25
350	Dennis Sarfate **(RC)**	.25
351	Andy Cannizaro **RC**	.50
352	Devern Hansack **RC**	.75
353	Michael Bourn **(RC)**	.25
354	Carlos Maldonado **(RC)**	.25
355	Shane Youman **RC**	.50
356	Philip Humber **(RC)**	.50
357	Hector Gimenez **(RC)**	.25
358	Fred Lewis **(RC)**	.25
359	Ryan Feierabend **(RC)**	.25
360	Juan Morillo **(RC)**	.25
361	Travis Chick **(RC)**	.25
362	Oswaldo Navarro **RC**	.25
363	Cesar Jimenez **RC**	.50
364	Brian Stokes **(RC)**	.25
365	Delmon Young **(RC)**	.50
366	Juan Salas **(RC)**	.25
367	Shawn Riggans **(RC)**	.25
368	Adam Lind **(RC)**	.50
369	Joaquin Arias **(RC)**	.25
370	Eric Stults **RC**	.50
371	Brandon Webb	.50
372	John Smoltz	.50
373	Miguel Tejada	.50
374	David Ortiz	1.00
375	Carlos Zambrano	.50
376	Jermaine Dye	.50
377	Ken Griffey Jr.	1.50
378	Victor Martinez	.25
379	Todd Helton	.50
380	Ivan Rodriguez	.50
381	Miguel Cabrera	.50
382	Lance Berkman	.25
383	Mike Sweeney	.25
384	Vladimir Guerrero	.50
385	Derek Lowe	.25
386	Bill Hall	.25
387	Johan Santana	.75
388	Carlos Beltran	.75
389	Derek Jeter	2.00
390	Nick Swisher	.50
391	Ryan Howard	1.50
392	Jason Bay	.50
393	Trevor Hoffman	.25
394	Omar Vizquel	.25
395	Ichiro Suzuki	1.00
396	Albert Pujols	2.00
397	Carl Crawford	.50
398	Mark Teixeira	.50
399	Roy Halladay	.25
400	Ryan Zimmerman	.50

Printing Plates

No Pricing
Production one set per color.

Mini Die-Cuts

Mini:		1.5-2X
Inserted 1:2		
Mini Gold:		No Pricing
Inserted 1:576		

Autographics

Inserted 1:720

Crowning Achievement

		NM/M
Common Player:		.50
Inserted 1:5		
AP	Albert Pujols	3.00
BZ	Barry Zito	.50
CD	Carlos Delgado	.75
CS	Curt Schilling	.75
DJ	Derek Jeter	3.00
DO	David Ortiz	1.00
FT	Frank Thomas	.75
GM	Greg Maddux	2.00
IS	Ichiro Suzuki	2.00
JS	Johan Santana	.75
JT	Jim Thome	.75
KG	Ken Griffey Jr.	2.00
MC	Miguel Cabrera	1.00
MP	Mike Piazza	1.00
MR	Manny Ramirez	1.00
PM	Pedro Martinez	1.00
RC	Roger Clemens	2.50
RH	Ryan Howard	2.00
TG	Tom Glavine	.75
TH	Trevor Hoffman	.50

Fresh Ink

		NM/M
Inserted 1:720		
BB	Brandon Backe	15.00
BW	Brian Wilson	20.00
CB	Clint Barmes	15.00
CC	Craig Counsell	20.00
GQ	Guillermo Quiroz	15.00
JB	Joe Blanton	15.00
JV	John Van Benschoten	10.00
LN	Leo Nunez	15.00
MM	Matt Murton	25.00
SR	Saul Rivera	15.00

Genuine Coverage

		NM/M
Inserted 1:720		
AP	Albert Pujols	25.00
AS	Alfonso Soriano	20.00
BR	Brian Roberts	15.00
DW	Dontrelle Willis	8.00
ES	Johnny Estrada	8.00
JB	Josh Beckett	15.00
JE	Jim Edmonds	15.00
JM	Justin Morneau	15.00
JT	Jim Thome	15.00
LB	Lance Berkman	10.00
RC	Robinson Cano	20.00
SM	John Smoltz	15.00
VG	Vladimir Guerrero	15.00

In the Zone

		NM/M
Common Player:		1.00
Inserted 1:10		
AJ	Andruw Jones	1.00
AP	Albert Pujols	3.00
AR	Alex Rodriguez	2.50
DO	David Ortiz	1.50
DW	David Wright	1.50
KG	Ken Griffey Jr.	2.00
MC	Miguel Cabrera	1.00
MT	Mark Teixeira	1.00
RH	Ryan Howard	2.00
VG	Vladimir Guerrero	1.00

Perfect 10

		NM/M
Common Player:		.50
Inserted 1:5		
CC	Carl Crawford	.75
DO	David Ortiz	1.50
DJ	Derek Jeter	3.00
IR	Ivan Rodriguez	.75
JD	Jermaine Dye	.50
JS	Johan Santana	1.00
MM	Mike Mussina	.75
MY	Michael Young	.75
RH	Roy Halladay	.50
VG	Vladimir Guerrero	1.00
AP	Albert Pujols	3.00
AS	Alfonso Soriano	1.00

		NM/M
Common Player:		.50
Inserted 1:1		
BB	Boof Bonser	.50
CB	Chad Billingsley	1.00
CH	Cole Hamels	1.50
CJ	Conor Jackson	.75
DU	Dan Uggla	.50
FL	Francisco Liriano	1.00
HR	Hanley Ramirez	1.00
IK	Ian Kinsler	1.00
JB	Josh Barfield	.75
JE	Jeremy Hermida	.50
JH	Josh Johnson	.50
JL	Jon Lester	.75
JP	Jonathan Papelbon	2.00
JS	Jeremy Sowers	.50
JV	Justin Verlander	2.00
JW	Jered Weaver	1.00
KJ	Kenji Johjima	.75
LO	James Loney	.75
MK	Matthew Kemp	.75
NM	Nicholas Markakis	1.00
PF	Prince Fielder	1.50
RG	Matt Garza	1.00
RN	Ricky Nolasco	.50
RZ	Ryan Zimmerman	2.00
SO	Scott Olsen	.75

Rookie Sensations

(Common Player: .50, Inserted 1:1)

Soaring Stars

		NM/M
Common Player:		.50
Inserted 1:2 Rack Packs		
AD	Adam Dunn	.75
AJ	Andruw Jones	1.00
AL	Alex Rodriguez	2.50
AP	Albert Pujols	3.00
AR	Alex Rios	1.00
AS	Alfonso Soriano	1.00
BW	Brandon Webb	.50
BZ	Barry Zito	.50
CB	Carlos Beltran	1.00
CJ	Chipper Jones	1.00
CU	Chase Utley	1.00
DA	Johnny Damon	1.00
DJ	Derek Jeter	3.00
DL	Derrek Lee	1.00
DO	David Ortiz	1.50
DW	David Wright	1.50
HA	Roy Halladay	.50
IR	Ivan Rodriguez	.75
IS	Ichiro Suzuki	2.00
JB	Jason Bay	.75
JD	Jermaine Dye	.50
JG	Jon Garland	.50
JM	Joe Mauer	.75
JS	Johan Santana	1.00
JV	Justin Verlander	1.00
KG	Ken Griffey Jr.	2.00
LB	Lance Berkman	.75
MC	Miguel Cabrera	1.00
MP	Mike Piazza	1.50
MR	Manny Ramirez	1.00
MT	Mark Teixeira	1.00
NG	Nomar Garciaparra	.75
PF	Prince Fielder	1.00
PM	Pedro Martinez	1.00
RH	Ryan Howard	2.00

RI	Mariano Rivera	.75
RO	Roy Oswalt	.75
TE	Miguel Tejada	.75
TG	Tom Glavine	.75
TH	Travis Hafner	.75
VG	Vladimir Guerrero	1.00
WI	Dontrelle Willis	.75

Year in Review

		NM/M
Common Player:		.50
Inserted 1:5		
AP	Albert Pujols	3.00
AR	Alex Rodriguez	2.50
AS	Alfonso Soriano	1.00
BA	Bobby Abreu	1.00
CU	Chase Utley	1.00
DJ	Derek Jeter	3.00
DO	David Ortiz	1.00
FL	Francisco Liriano	.75
FS	Freddy Sanchez	.50
HO	Ryan Howard	2.00
JD	Jermaine Dye	.50
JM	Joe Mauer	.75
JR	Jose Reyes	1.00
JV	Justin Verlander	1.00
JW	Jered Weaver	1.00
KG	Ken Griffey Jr.	2.00
MD	Mark DeRosa	.50
MO	Justin Morneau	1.00
RH	Roy Halladay	.50
TH	Travis Hafner	.75

1992 Flopps Promos

Prior to the 1992 season, Pro Set announced plans to produce a set of 66 cards parodying contemporary baseball-Stars and teams. The name "Flopps" was used instead of Pro Set, which does not appear anywhere on the cards. While the announced checklist included players such as Craig Piggio, George Brat and Cal Ripped-One, only five promo cards were produced before the Players Union complained and the idea was dropped. Pro Set didn't want to offend the union at the time because they were attempting to get a baseball card license. Cards pictured caricatures of the players on front and funny biographies on back, all in color in the standard 2-1/2" x 3-1/2" format.

		NM/M
Complete Set (5):		6.00
Common Player:		.50
(1)	Barry Bones	4.00
(2)	Wade Bugs	2.50
(3)	Ken Groovy, Jr.	3.00
(4)	Stickey Henderson	1.50
(5)	Lance Perishable	.50

1993 Florida Agriculture Dept. Braves/Marlins

A pair of eight-card team panels of the Atlanta Braves and Florida Marlins was issued by the Florida Department of Agriculture and Consumer Services to promote the state's fruit and vegetable products. Individual cards show the player posing - sometimes comically - with one of the state's agricultural products. The photos are bordered in team colors and have a "Fresh 2 U" logo in the upper-left consisting of a fruit or vegetable superimposed on a ball diamond and crossed bats. Backs have the player's name, uniform number, and a short career summary at top. In center is a baseball with the result of an at-bat. In the bottom panel is a statistic about one of the state's crops. A card number is at top. Individual cards measure the standard 2-1/2" x 3-1/2", with the eight-card perforated sheets measuring 10" x 7". The card sheets were distributed during the Sunshine State Games in Tallahassee.

		NM/M
Complete Set (16):		18.00
Common Player:		1.00
Atlanta Braves Team Set:		10.00
1	Team Logo Card	1.00
2	Steve Avery	1.00
3	Jeff Blauser	1.00
4	Sid Bream	1.00
5	Tom Glavine	4.00
6	Mark Lemke	1.00
7	Greg Olson	1.00
8	Terry Pendleton	1.00
Florida Marlins Team Set:		9.00
1	Team Logo Card	1.00
2	Billy the Marlin (Mascot)	1.00
3	Ryan Bowen	1.00
4	Benito Santiago	1.00
5	Richie Lewis	1.00
6	Bret Barbarie	1.00
7	Rich Renteria	1.00
8	Jeff Conine	1.00

1987 Red Foley Stickers

Individual player stickers were inserted in sheets within the pages of "Red Foley's Best Baseball Book Ever." The 8-1/2" x 11", 96-page softbound book offered games, quizzes and trivia, with a space to put each sticker. Individual stickers measure about 1-3/8" x 1-3/4". Stickers have color photos on front with a number in the white border at bottom. Player identification does not appear on the sticker. Cover price of the book in 1987 was about $7.

		NM/M
Complete Book:		9.00
Complete Sticker Set (130):		7.50
Common Player:		.05
1	Julio Franco	.05
2	Willie Randolph	.05
3	Jesse Barfield	.05
4	Mike Witt	.05
5	Orel Hershiser	.05
6	Dwight Gooden	.05
7	Dan Quisenberry	.05
8	Vince Coleman	.05
9	Rich Gossage	.05
10	Kirk Gibson	.05
11	Joaquin Andujar	.05
12	Dave Concepcion	.05
13	Andre Dawson	.25
14	Tippy Martinez	.05
15	Bob James	.05

16	Ryne Sandberg	1.00
17	Bob Knepper	.05
18	Bob Stanley	.05
19	Jim Presley	.05
20	Greg Gross	.05
21	Bob Horner	.05
22	Paul Molitor	.75
23	Kirby Puckett	1.00
24	Scott Garrelts	.05
25	Tony Pena	.05
26	Charlie Hough	.05
27	Joe Carter	.05
28	Dave Winfield	.75
29	Tony Fernandez	.05
30	Bobby Grich	.05
31	Mike Marshall	.05
32	Keith Hernandez	.05
33	Dennis Leonard	.05
34	John Tudor	.05
35	Kevin McReynolds	.05
36	Lance Parrish	.05
37	Carney Lansford	.05
38	Buddy Bell	.05
39	Tim Raines	.05
40	Mike Boddicker	.05
41	Carlton Fisk	.75
42	Lee Smith	.05
43	Glenn Davis	.05
44	Jim Rice	.25
45	Mark Langston	.05
46	Mike Schmidt	1.50
47	Dale Murphy	.45
48	Cecil Cooper	.05
49	Kent Hrbek	.05
50	Will Clark	.10
51	Johnny Ray	.05
52	Darrell Porter	.05
53	Brook Jacoby	.05
54	Ron Guidry	.05
55	Lloyd Moseby	.05
56	Donnie Moore	.05
57	Fernando Valenzuela	.05
58	Darryl Strawberry	.50
59	Hal McRae	.05
60	Tommy Herr	.05
61	Steve Garvey	.35
62	Alan Trammell	.05
63	Jose Canseco	.50
64	Pete Rose	1.75
65	Jeff Reardon	.05
66	Eddie Murray	.75
67	Ozzie Guillen	.05
68	Jody Davis	.05
69	Bill Doran	.05
70	Roger Clemens	1.25
71	Alvin Davis	.05
72	Von Hayes	.05
73	Zane Smith	.05
74	Ted Higuera	.05
75	Tom Brunansky	.05
76	Chili Davis	.05
77	R.J. Reynolds	.05
78	Oddibe McDowell	.05
79	Brett Butler	.05
80	Rickey Henderson	.75
81	Dave Steib	.05
82	Wally Joyner	.05
83	Pedro Guerrero	.05
84	Jesse Orosco	.05
85	Steve Balboni	.05
86	Willie McGee	.05
87	Graig Nettles	.05
88	Lou Whitaker	.05
89	Jay Howell	.05
90	Dave Parker	.05
91	Hubie Brooks	.05
92	Rick Dempsey	.05
93	Neil Allen	.05
94	Shawon Dunston	.05
95	Jose Cruz	.05
96	Wade Boggs	1.00
97	Danny Tartabull	.05
98	Steve Bedrosian	.05
99	Ken Oberkfell	.05
100	Ben Oglivie	.05
101	Bert Blyleven	.05
102	Jeff Leonard	.05
103	Rick Rhoden	.05
104	Larry Parrish	.05
105	Tony Bernazard	.05
106	Don Mattingly	1.50
107	Willie Upshaw	.05
108	Reggie Jackson	1.00
109	Bill Madlock	.05
110	Gary Carter	.75
111	George Brett	1.50
112	Ozzie Smith	1.00
113	Tony Gwynn	1.00
114	Jack Morris	.05
115	Dave Kingman	.05
116	John Franco	.05
117	Tim Wallach	.05
118	Cal Ripken Jr.	2.00
119	Harold Baines	.05
120	Leon Durham	.05
121	Nolan Ryan	2.00
122	Dennis (Oil Can) Boyd	.05
123	Matt Young	.05
124	Shane Rawley	.05
125	Bruce Sutter	.65
126	Robin Yount	.75
127	Frank Viola	.05
128	Vida Blue	.05
129	Rick Reuschel	.05
130	Pete Incaviglia	.05

1988 Red Foley Stickers

Identical in format to the previous year's issues, the 104 player and 26 team logo stickers in this set were bound into a 96-page, 8-1/2" x 11" softbound book titled "Red Foley's Best Baseball Book Ever." Each 1-3/8" x 1-3/4" sticker could be placed in the book as an answer to trivia questions, quizzes, games, etc. Stickers have color player photos with a number in the white border at bottom. There is no player identification on the stickers. Original issue price was about $8.

		NM/M
Complete Book:		9.00
Complete Sticker Set (130):		6.00
Common Player:		.05
1	Mike Aldrete	.05
2	Andy Ashby	.05
3	Harold Baines	.05
4	Floyd Bannister	.05
5	Buddy Bell	.05
6	George Bell	.05
7	Barry Bonds	2.00
8	Scott Bradley	.05
9	Bob Brower	.05
10	Ellis Burks	.05
11	Casey Candaele	.05
12	Jack Clark	.05
13	Roger Clemens	1.25
14	Kal Daniels	.05
15	Eric Davis	.05
16	Mike Davis	.05
17	Andre Dawson	.25
18	Rob Deer	.05
19	Brian Downing	.05
20	Doug Drabek	.05
21	Dwight Evans	.05
22	Sid Fernandez	.05
23	Carlton Fisk	.75
24	Scott Fletcher	.05
25	Julio Franco	.05
26	Gary Gaetti	.05
27	Ken Gerhardt	.05
28	Ken Griffey	.05
29	Pedro Guerrero	.05
30	Billy Hatcher	.05
31	Mike Heath	.05
32	Neal Heaton	.05
33	Tom Henke	.05
34	Larry Herndon	.05
35	Brian Holton	.05
36	Glenn Hubbard	.05
37	Bruce Hurst	.05
38	Bo Jackson	.10
39	Michael Jackson	.05
40	Howard Johnson	.05
41	Wally Joyner	.05
42	Jimmy Key	.05
43	Ray Knight	.05
44	John Kruk	.05
45	Mike Krukow	.05
46	Mark Langston	.05
47	Gene Larkin	.05
48	Jeff Leonard	.05
49	Bill Long	.05
50	Fred Lynn	.05
51	Dave Magadan	.05
52	Joe Magrane	.05
53	Don Mattingly	1.50
54	Fred McGriff	.05
55	Mark McGwire	1.75
56	Kevin McReynolds	.05
57	Dave Meads	.05
58	Keith Moreland	.05
59	Dale Murphy	.30
60	Juan Nieves	.05
61	Paul Noce	.05
62	Matt Nokes	.05
63	Pete O'Brien	.05
64	Paul O'Neill	.05
65	Lance Parrish	.05
66	Larry Parrish	.05
67	Tony Pena	.05
68	Terry Pendleton	.05
69	Ken Phelps	.05
70	Dan Plesac	.05
71	Luis Polonia	.05
72	Kirby Puckett	1.00
73	Jeff Reardon	.05
74	Rick Rhoden	.05
75	Dave Righetti	.05
76	Cal Ripken Jr.	2.00
77	Bret Saberhagen	.05

78	Benito Santiago	.05
79	Mike Schmidt	1.50
80	Dick Schofield	.05
81	Mike Scott	.05
82	John Smiley	.05
83	Cory Snyder	.05
84	Franklin Stubbs	.05
85	B.J. Surhoff	.05
86	Rick Sutcliffe	.05
87	Pat Tabler	.05
88	Jose Tartabull (Danny)	.05
89	Garry Templeton	.05
90	Walt Terrell	.05
91	Andre Thornton	.05
92	Andy Van Slyke	.05
93	Ozzie Virgil	.05
94	Tim Wallach	.05
95	Gary Ward	.05
96	Mark Wasinger	.05
97	Mitch Webster	.05
98	Bob Welch	.05
99	Devon White	.05
100	Frank White	.05
101	Ed Whitson	.05
102	Bill Wilkinson	.05
103	Glenn Wilson	.05
104	Curt Young	.05
105	Braves Logo	.05
106	Phillies Logo	.05
107	Padres Logo	.05
108	Giants Logo	.05
109	Orioles Logo	.05
110	Tigers Logo	.05
111	Pirates Logo	.05
112	Royals Logo	.05
113	Astros Logo	.05
114	Indians Logo	.05
115	Brewers Logo	.05
116	Cardinals Logo	.05
117	White Sox Logo	.05
118	Blue Jays Logo	.05
119	Red Sox Logo	.05
120	Athletics Logo	.05
121	Cubs Logo	.05
122	Mariners Logo	.05
123	Rangers Logo	.05
124	Dodgers Logo	.05
125	Yankees Logo	.05
126	Mets Logo	.05
127	Twins Logo	.05
128	Expos Logo	.05
129	Angels Logo	.05
130	Reds Logo	.05

1989 Red Foley Stickers

In its third consecutive year of publication, "Red Foley's Best Baseball Book Ever" retained its 96-page softbound 8-1/2" x 11" format of trivia, quizzes and games to be illustrated by placing one of 130 player stickers in the book. Individual stickers are 1-3/8" x 1-3/4" and feature color photos with a white border. Sticker number appears in the bottom-right. There is no player identification on the sticker. Original price of the book was about $8.

		NM/M
Complete Book:		9.00
Complete Sticker Set (130):		7.50
Common Player:		.05
1	Doyle Alexander	.05
2	Luis Alicea	.05
3	Roberto Alomar	.15
4	Andy Ashby	.05
5	Floyd Bannister	.05
6	Jesse Barfield	.05
7	George Bell	.05
8	Wade Boggs	1.00
9	Barry Bonds	2.00
10	Bobby Bonilla	.05
11	Chris Bosio	.05
12	George Brett	1.50
13	Hubie Brooks	.05
14	Tom Brunansky	.05
15	Tim Burke	.05
16	Ivan Calderon	.05
17	Tom Candiotti	.05
18	Jose Canseco	.50
19	Gary Carter	.75
20	Joe Carter	.05
21	Jack Clark	.05
22	Will Clark	.10
23	Roger Clemens	1.25
24	David Cone	.05

25	Ed Correa	.05
27	Kal Daniels	.05
28	Al Davis	.05
29	Chili Davis	.05
30	Eric Davis	.05
31	Glen Davis	.05
32	Jody Davis	.05
33	Mark Davis	.05
34	Andre Dawson	.25
35	Rob Deer	.05
36	Jose DeLeon	.05
37	Bo Diaz	.05
38	Bill Doran	.05
39	Shawon Dunston	.05
40	Dennis Eckersley	.60
41	Dwight Evans	.05
42	Tony Fernandez	.05
43	Brian Fisher	.05
44	Carlton Fisk	.75
45	Mike Flanagan	.05
46	John Franco	.05
47	Gary Gaetti	.05
48	Andres Galarraga	.05
49	Scott Garrelts	.05
50	Kirk Gibson	.05
51	Dan Gladden	.05
52	Dwight Gooden	.05
53	Pedro Guerrero	.05
54	Ozzie Guillen	.05
55	Tony Gwynn	1.00
56	Mel Hall	.05
57	Von Hayes	.05
58	Keith Hernandez	.05
59	Orel Hershiser	.05
60	Ted Higuera	.05
61	Charlie Hough	.05
62	Jack Howell	.05
63	Kent Hrbek	.05
64	Pete Incaviglia	.05
65	Bo Jackson	.10
66	Brook Jacoby	.05
67	Chris James	.05
68	Lance Johnson	.05
69	Wally Joyner	.05
70	John Kruk	.05
71	Mike LaCoss	.05
72	Mark Langston	.05
73	Carney Lansford	.05
74	Barry Larkin	.05
75	Mike LaValliere	.05
76	Jose Lind	.05
77	Fred Lynn	.05
78	Greg Maddux	1.00
79	Candy Maldonado	.05
80	Don Mattingly	1.50
81	Mark McGwire	1.75
82	Paul Molitor	.75
83	Jack Morris	.05
84	Lloyd Moseby	.05
85	Dale Murphy	.30
86	Eddie Murray	.75
87	Matt Nokes	.05
88	Pete O'Brien	.05
89	Rafael Palmeiro	.65
90	Melido Perez	.05
91	Gerald Perry	.05
92	Tim Raines	.05
93	Willie Randolph	.05
94	Johnny Ray	.05
95	Jeff Reardon	.05
96	Jody Reed	.05
97	Harold Reynolds	.05
98	Dave Righetti	.05
99	Billy Ripken	.05
100	Cal Ripken Jr.	2.00
101	Nolan Ryan	2.00
102	Juan Samuel	.05
103	Benito Santiago	.05
104	Steve Sax	.05
105	Mike Schmidt	1.50
106	Rick Schu	.05
107	Mike Scott	.05
108	Kevin Seitzer	.05
109	Ruben Sierra	.05
110	Lee Smith	.05
111	Ozzie Smith	1.00
112	Zane Smith	.05
113	Dave Stewart	.05
114	Darryl Strawberry	.05
115	Bruce Sutter	.65
116	Bill Swift	.05
117	Greg Swindell	.05
118	Frank Tanana	.05
119	Danny Tartabull	.05
120	Milt Thompson	.05
121	Rob Thompson	.05
122	Alan Trammell	.05
123	John Tudor	.05
124	Fernando Valenzuela	.05
125	Dave Valle	.05
126	Frank Viola	.05
127	Ozzie Virgil	.05
128	Tim Wallach	.05
129	Dave Winfield	.75
130	Mike Witt	.05
131	Robin Yount	.75

1990 Red Foley Stickers

In its fourth consecutive year of publication, "Red Foley's Best Baseball Book Ever" retained its 96-page softbound 8-1/2" x 11" format of trivia, quizzes and games to be illustrated by placing one of 104 player or 26 team logo stickers in the book. Individual stickers are 1-3/8" x 1-3/4" and

feature color photos with a white border. Sticker number appears in the bottom-right. There is no player identification on the sticker.

		NM/M
Complete Book:		9.00
Complete Sticker Set (130):		7.00
Common Player:		.05
1	Allan Anderson	.05
2	Scott Bailes	.05
3	Jeff Ballard	.05
4	Jesse Barfield	.05
5	Bert Blyleven	.05
6	Wade Boggs	1.00
7	Barry Bonds	2.00
8	Chris Bosio	.05
9	George Brett	1.50
10	Tim Burke	.05
11	Ellis Burks	.05
12	Brett Butler	.05
13	Ivan Calderon	.05
14	Jose Canseco	.50
15	Joe Carter	.05
16	Jack Clark	.05
17	Will Clark	.10
18	Roger Clemens	1.25
19	Vince Coleman	.05
20	Eric Davis	.05
21	Glenn Davis	.05
22	Mark Davis	.05
23	Andre Dawson	.25
24	Rob Deer	.05
25	Jose DeLeon	.05
26	Jim Deshaies	.05
27	Doug Drabek	.05
28	Lenny Dykstra	.05
29	Dennis Eckersley	.65
30	Steve Farr	.05
31	Tony Fernandez	.05
32	Carlton Fisk	.75
33	John Franco	.05
34	Julio Franco	.05
35	Andres Galarraga	.05
36	Tom Glavine	.25
37	Dwight Gooden	.05
38	Mark Grace	.10
39	Mike Greenwell	.05
40	Ken Griffey Jr.	1.25
41	Kelly Gruber	.05
42	Pedro Guerrero	.05
43	Tony Gwynn	1.00
44	Bryan Harvey	.05
45	Von Hayes	.05
46	Willie Hernandez	.05
47	Tommy Herr	.05
48	Orel Hershiser	.05
49	Jay Howell	.05
50	Kent Hrbek	.05
51	Bo Jackson	.10
52	Steve Jeltz	.05
53	Jimmy Key	.05
54	Ron Kittle	.05
55	Mark Langston	.05
56	Carney Lansford	.05
57	Barry Larkin	.05
58	Jeffrey Leonard	.05
59	Don Mattingly	1.50
60	Fred McGriff	.05
61	Mark McGwire	1.75
62	Kevin McReynolds	.05
63	Randy Myers	.05
64	Kevin Mitchell	.05
65	Paul Molitor	.75
66	Mike Morgan	.05
67	Dale Murphy	.30
68	Eddie Murray	.75
69	Matt Nokes	.05
70	Greg Olson	.05
71	Paul O'Neill	.05
72	Rafael Palmeiro	.65
73	Lance Parrish	.05
74	Dan Plesac	.05
75	Kirby Puckett	1.00
76	Jeff Reardon	.05
77	Rick Reuschel	.05
78	Cal Ripken Jr.	2.00
79	Dave Righetti	.05
80	Jeff Russell	.05
81	Nolan Ryan	2.00
82	Benito Santiago	.05
83	Steve Sax	.05
84	Mike Schooler	.05
85	Mike Scott	.05
86	Kevin Seitzer	.05
87	Dave Smith	.05
88	Lonnie Smith	.05

89	Ozzie Smith	1.00
90	John Smoltz	.05
91	Cory Snyder	.05
92	Darryl Strawberry	.05
93	Greg Swindell	.05
94	Mickey Tettleton	.05
95	Bobby Thigpen	.05
96	Alan Trammell	.05
97	Dave Valle	.05
98	Andy Van Slyke	.05
99	Tim Wallach	.05
100	Jerome Walton	.05
101	Lou Whitaker	.05
102	Devon White	.05
103	Mitch Williams	.05
104	Glen Wilson	.05
105	Indians Logo	.05
106	Rangers Logo	.05
107	Reds Logo	.05
108	Orioles Logo	.05
109	Red Sox Logo	.05
110	White Sox Logo	.05
111	Dodgers Logo	.05
112	Tigers Logo	.05
113	Mariners Logo	.05
114	Blue Jays Logo	.05
115	Expos Logo	.05
116	Pirates Logo	.05
117	Astros Logo	.05
118	Cardinals Logo	.05
119	Padres Logo	.05
120	Angels Logo	.05
121	Yankees Logo	.05
122	Cubs Logo	.05
123	Brewers Logo	.05
124	Twins Logo	.05
125	Giants Logo	.05
126	Royals Logo	.05
127	A's Logo	.05
128	Mets Logo	.05
129	Phillies Logo	.05
130	Braves Logo	.05

1991 Red Foley Stickers

In its fifth consecutive year of publication, "Red Foley's Best Baseball Book Ever" retained its 96-page softbound 8-1/2" x 11" format of trivia, quizzes and games to be illustrated by placing one of 112 regular player or 18 All-Star (#113-130) stickers in the book. Individual stickers are 1-3/8" x 1-3/4" and feature color photos with a white border. Sticker number appears in the bottom-right. There is no player identification on the sticker.

		NM/M
Complete Book:		10.00
Comlete Sticker Set (130):		8.00
Common Player:		.05
1	Jim Abbott	.05
2	Rick Aguilera	.05
3	Roberto Alomar	.30
4	Rob Dibble	.05
5	Wally Backman	.05
6	Harold Baines	.05
7	Steve Bedrosian	.05
8	Craig Biggio	.05
9	Wade Boggs	1.00
10	Bobby Bonilla	.05
11	George Brett	1.25
12	Greg Brock	.05
13	Hubie Brooks	.05
14	Tom Brunansky	.05
15	Tim Burke	.05
16	Tom Candiotti	.05
17	Jose Canseco	.50
18	Jack Clark	.05
19	Will Clark	.10
20	Roger Clemens	1.25
21	Vince Coleman	.05
22	Kal Daniels	.05
23	Glenn Davis	.05
24	Mark Davis	.05
25	Andre Dawson	.25
26	Rob Deer	.05
27	Delino DeShields	.05
28	Doug Drabek	.05
29	Shawon Dunston	.05
30	Lenny Dykstra	.05
31	Dennis Eckersley	.35
32	Kevin Elster	.05
33	Tony Fernandez	.05
34	Cecil Fielder	.05
35	Chuck Finley	.05
36	Carlton Fisk	.75

37	Greg Gagne	.05
38	Ron Gant	.05
39	Dan Gladden	.05
40	Dwight Gooden	.05
41	Ken Griffey Jr.	1.50
42	Kelly Gruber	.05
43	Pedro Guerrero	.05
44	Ozzie Guillen	.05
45	Pete Harnisch	.05
46	Billy Hatcher	.05
47	Von Hayes	.05
48	Rickey Henderson	.75
49	Mike Henneman	.05
50	Kent Hrbek	.05
51	Pete Incaviglia	.05
52	Howard Johnson	.05
53	Randy Johnson	.75
54	Doug Jones	.05
55	Ricky Jordan	.05
56	Wally Joyner	.05
57	Roberto Kelly	.05
58	Barry Larkin	.05
59	Craig Lefferts	.05
60	Candy Maldonado	.05
61	Don Mattingly	1.25
62	Oddibe McDowell	.05
63	Roger McDowell	.05
64	Willie McGee	.05
65	Fred McGriff	.05
66	Kevin Mitchell	.05
67	Mike Morgan	.05
68	Eddie Murray	.75
69	Gregg Olson	.05
70	Joe Orsulak	.05
71	Dan Petry	.05
72	Dan Plesac	.05
73	Jim Presley	.05
74	Kirby Puckett	1.00
75	Tim Raines	.05
76	Jeff Reardon	.05
77	Dave Righetti	.05
78	Cal Ripken Jr.	2.00
79	Nolan Ryan	2.00
80	Bret Saberhagen	.05
81	Chris Sabo	.05
82	Ryne Sandberg	1.00
83	Benito Santiago	.05
84	Steve Sax	.05
85	Mike Schooler	.05
86	Mike Scott	.05
87	Ruben Sierra	.05
88	Cory Snyder	.05
89	Dave Steib	.05
90	Dave Stewart	.05
91	Kurt Stillwell	.05
92	Bobby Thigpen	.05
93	Alan Trammell	.05
94	John Tudor	.05
95	Dave Valle	.05
96	Andy Van Slyke	.05
97	Robin Ventura	.05
98	Frank Viola	.05
99	Tim Wallach	.05
100	Matt Williams	.40
101	Mitch Williams	.05
102	Dave Winfield	.75
103	Eric Yelding	.05
104	Robin Yount	.75
105	Steve Avery	.05
106	Travis Fryman	.05
107	Juan Gonzalez	.40
108	Todd Hundley	.05
109	Ben McDonald	.05
110	Jose Offerman	.05
111	Frank Thomas	.75
112	Bernie Williams	.10
113	Sandy Alomar Jr.	.05
114	Jack Armstrong	.05
115	Wade Boggs	.40
116	Jose Canseco	.25
117	Will Clark	.10
118	Andre Dawson	.05
119	Lenny Dykstra	.05
120	Ken Griffey Jr.	.65
121	Rickey Henderson	.40
122	Mark McGwire	1.75
123	Kevin Mitchell	.05
124	Cal Ripken Jr.	1.00
125	Chris Sabo	.05
126	Ryne Sandberg	.50
127	Steve Sax	.05
128	Mike Scoscia	.05
129	Ozzie Smith	.50
130	Bob Welch	.05

1992 Red Foley Stickers

The format was unchanged when "Red Foley's Best Baseball Book Ever" was published in 1992.

The 96-page, 8-1/2" x 11" softcover book features 96 pages of quizzes, trivia and games, along with 130 player stickers (#105-130 are All-Star stickers) to be placed on the proper pages. Single stickers measure 1-3/8" x 1-3/4" and have color photos with a white border. A sticker number is in the bottom-right. No player identification appears on the stickers. Issue price of the book was about $9.

		NM/M
Complete Book:		12.00
Complete Sticker Set (130):		10.00
Common Player:		.05
1	Jim Abbott	.05
2	Roberto Alomar	.15
3	Sandy Alomar Jr.	.05
4	Eric Anthony	.05
5	Kevin Appier	.05
6	Jack Armstrong	.05
7	Steve Avery	.05
8	Carlos Baerga	.05
9	Scott Bankhead	.05
10	George Bell	.05
11	Albert Belle	.05
12	Andy Benes	.05
13	Craig Biggio	.05
14	Wade Boggs	1.00
15	Barry Bonds	2.00
16	Bobby Bonilla	.05
17	Sid Bream	.05
18	George Brett	1.25
19	Hubie Brooks	.05
20	Ellis Burks	.05
21	Brett Butler	.05
22	Jose Canseco	.40
23	Joe Carter	.05
24	Jack Clark	.05
25	Will Clark	.10
26	Roger Clemens	1.25
27	Vince Coleman	.05
28	Eric Davis	.05
29	Glenn Davis	.05
30	Andre Dawson	.25
31	Rob Deer	.05
32	Delino DeShields	.05
33	Lenny Dykstra	.05
34	Scott Erickson	.05
35	Cecil Fielder	.05
36	Carlton Fisk	.75
37	Travis Fryman	.05
38	Greg Gagne	.05
39	Juan Gonzalez	.40
40	Tommy Greene	.05
41	Ken Griffey Jr.	1.50
42	Kent Hrbek	.05
43	Kelly Gruber	.05
44	Tony Gwynn	1.00
45	Dave Henderson	.05
46	Rickey Henderson	.75
47	Orel Hershiser	.05
48	Marquis Grissom	.05
49	Howard Johnson	.05
50	Felix Jose	.05
51	Wally Joyner	.05
52	David Justice	.05
53	Roberto Kelly	.05
54	Ray Lankford	.05
55	Barry Larkin	.05
56	Mark Lewis	.05
57	Kevin Maas	.05
58	Greg Maddux	1.00
59	Dennis Martinez	.05
60	Edgar Martinez	.05
61	Don Mattingly	1.50
62	Ben McDonald	.05
63	Jack McDowell	.05
64	Willie McGee	.05
65	Fred McGriff	.05
66	Brian McRae	.05
67	Mark McGwire	1.75
68	Kevin Mitchell	.05
69	Terry Mulholland	.05
70	Dale Murphy	.25
71	Eddie Murray	.75
72	John Olerud	.05
73	Rafael Palmeiro	.65
74	Terry Pendleton	.05
75	Luis Polonia	.05
76	Mark Portugal	.05
77	Kirby Puckett	1.00
78	Tim Raines	.05
79	Harold Reynolds	.05
80	Billy Ripken	.05
81	Cal Ripken Jr.	2.00
82	Nolan Ryan	2.00
83	Chris Sabo	.05
84	Ryne Sandberg	1.00
85	Benito Santiago	.05
86	Kevin Seitzer	.05
87	Gary Sheffield	.30
88	Ruben Sierra	.05
89	John Smiley	.05
90	Ozzie Smith	1.00
91	Darryl Strawberry	.05
92	B.J. Surhoff	.05
93	Frank Thomas	.75
94	Alan Trammell	.05
95	Andy Van Slyke	.05
96	Greg Vaughn	.05
97	Frank Viola	.05
98	Tim Wallach	.05
99	Matt Williams	.05

100	Dave Winfield	.75
101	Mike Witt	.05
102	Eric Yelding	.05
103	Robin Yount	.75
104	Todd Zeile	.05
105	Roberto Alomar	.10
106	Sandy Alomar Jr.	.05
107	Wade Boggs	.50
108	Bobby Bonilla	.05
109	Ivan Calderon	.05
110	Will Clark	.05
111	Andre Dawson	.05
112	Cecil Fielder	.05
113	Carlton Fisk	.30
114	Tom Glavine	.25
115	Ken Griffey Jr.	.65
116	Tony Gwynn	.50
117	Dave Henderson	.05
118	Rickey Henderson	.30
119	Felix Jose	.05
120	Jimmy Key	.05
121	Tony LaRussa	.05
122	Jack Morris	.05
123	Lou Piniella	.05
124	Cal Ripken Jr.	1.00
125	Chris Sabo	.05
126	Juan Samuel	.05
127	Ryne Sandberg	.50
128	Benito Santiago	.05
129	Ozzie Smith	.50
130	Danny Tartabull	.05

1993 Red Foley Stickers

The format was unchanged when "Red Foley's Best Baseball Book Ever" was published in 1993. The 96-page, 8-1/2" x 11" softcover book features 96 pages of quizzes, trivia and games, along with 130 player stickers (#105-130 are All-Star stickers) to be placed on the proper pages. Single stickers measure 1-3/8" x 1-3/4" and have color photos with a white border. A sticker number is in the bottom-right. No player identification appears on the stickers.

		NM/M
Complete Book:		10.00
Complete Sticker Set (130):		9.00
Common Player:		.05
1	Jim Abbott	.05
2	Roberto Alomar	.15
3	Sandy Alomar Jr.	.05
4	Steve Avery	.05
5	Jeff Bagwell	.75
6	Harold Baines	.05
7	Bret Barberie	.05
8	Derek Bell	.05
9	Jay Bell	.05
10	Albert Belle	.05
11	Andy Benes	.05
12	Craig Biggio	.05
13	Wade Boggs	1.00
14	Barry Bonds	2.00
15	Bobby Bonilla	.05
16	Jose Canseco	.40
17	Joe Carter	.05
18	Wes Chamberlain	.05
19	Will Clark	.10
20	Roger Clemens	1.25
21	Milt Cuyler	.05
22	Eric Davis	.05
23	Delino DeShields	.05
24	Rob Dibble	.05
25	Doug Drabek	.05
26	Shawon Dunston	.05
27	Lenny Dykstra	.05
28	Scott Erickson	.05
29	Cecil Fielder	.05
30	Steve Finley	.05
31	Tom Glavine	.25
32	Dwight Gooden	.05
33	Mark Grace	.10
34	Ken Griffey Jr.	1.50
35	Marquis Grissom	.05
36	Kelly Gruber	.05
37	Mark Gubicza	.05
38	Tony Gwynn	1.00
39	Mel Hall	.05
40	Pete Harnisch	.05
41	Brian Harper	.05
42	Bryan Harvey	.05
43	Rickey Henderson	.75
44	Orel Hershiser	.05

45	Gregg Jefferies	.05
46	Howard Johnson	.05
47	Felix Jose	.05
48	Wally Joyner	.05
49	David Justice	.05
50	Roberto Kelly	.05
51	Chuck Knoblauch	.05
52	John Kruk	.05
53	Barry Larkin	.05
54	Kenny Lofton	.05
55	Greg Maddux	1.00
56	Dennis Martinez	.05
57	Edgar Martinez	.05
58	Tino Martinez	.05
59	Don Mattingly	1.25
60	Jack McDowell	.05
61	Willie McGee	.05
62	Fred McGriff	.05
63	Mark McGwire	1.75
64	Brian McRae	.05
65	Randy Milligan	.05
66	Kevin Mitchell	.05
67	Paul Molitor	.75
68	Dale Murphy	.25
69	Mike Mussina	.40
70	Charles Nagy	.05
71	Gregg Olson	.05
72	Rafael Palmeiro	.65
73	Dean Palmer	.05
74	Phil Plantier	.05
75	Luis Polonia	.05
76	Kirby Puckett	1.00
77	Tim Raines	.05
78	Cal Ripken Jr.	2.00
79	Bip Roberts	.05
80	Ivan Rodriguez	.65
81	Nolan Ryan	2.00
82	Bret Saberhagen	.05
83	Ryne Sandberg	1.00
84	Deion Sanders	.10
85	Reggie Sanders	.05
86	Benito Santiago	.05
87	Mike Scoscia	.05
88	Lee Smith	.05
89	Ozzie Smith	1.00
90	Lee Stevens	.05
91	Darryl Strawberry	.05
92	B.J. Surhoff	.05
93	Danny Tartabull	.05
94	Mickey Tettleton	.05
95	Frank Thomas	.75
96	Robby Thompson	.05
97	Alan Trammell	.05
98	Greg Vaughn	.05
99	Mo Vaughn	.05
100	Andy Van Slyke	.05
101	Robin Ventura	.05
102	Matt Williams	.05
103	Robin Yount	.75
104	Todd Zeile	.05
105	Roberto Alomar	.15
106	Sandy Alomar Jr.	.05
107	Wade Boggs	.50
108	Kevin Brown	.05
109	Joe Carter	.05
110	Will Clark	.05
111	Bobby Cox	.05
112	Dennis Eckersley	.40
113	Tony Fernandez	.05
114	Tom Glavine	.05
115	Ken Griffey Jr.	.65
116	Tony Gwynn	.50
117	Tom Kelly	.05
118	John Kruk	.05
119	Fred McGriff	.05
120	Mark McGwire	.75
121	Kirby Puckett	.50
122	Cal Ripken Jr.	1.00
123	Bip Roberts	.05
124	Ivan Rodriguez	.20
125	Gary Sheffield	.25
126	Ruben Sierra	.05
127	Ozzie Smith	.50
128	Andy Van Slyke	.05
129	Robin Ventura	.05
130	Larry Walker	.05

1994 Red Foley

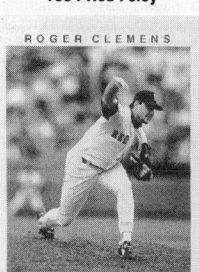

ROGER CLEMENS

SUPERSTAR

Beginning in 1994, major changes were seen in "Red Foley's Best Baseball Book Ever." The book remained in 8-1/2" x 11" format, but was downsized to 64 pages. The previous years' stickers were replaced with four nine-card sheets of perforated baseball cards. When separated from the sheets, cards measure

the standard 2-1/2" x 3-1/2". The unnumbered cards appear in two types. "Superstar" cards feature a single player in a color action photo on front. "Team Leaders" cards have two teammates on front. Red and black printing on backs give personal data and career highlights. Original retail cost of the book was $8.95.

	NM/M
Complete Book:	15.00
Complete Set (36):	12.00
Common Card:	.25
(1) Barry Bonds	2.00
(2) Joe Carter	.25
(3) Roger Clemens	1.25
(4) Juan Gonzalez	.60
(5) Ken Griffey Jr.	1.50
(6) Fred McGriff	.25
(7) Jose Rijo	.25
(8) Ryne Sandberg	1.00
(9) Angels (Tim Salmon, Mark Langston)	.25
(10) Astros (Jeff Bagwell, Doug Drabek)	.50
(11) Athletics (Mark McGwire, Dennis Eckersley)	.75
(12) Blue Jays (Roberto Alomar, John Olerud)	.30
(13) Braves (Greg Maddux, Tom Glavine)	.60
(14) Brewers (Robin Yount, Cal Eldred)	.50
(15) Cardinals (Ray Lankford, Ozzie Smith)	.60
(16) Cubs (Mark Grace, Randy Myers)	.30
(17) Dodgers (Mike Piazza, Orel Hershiser)	.65
(18) Expos (Larry Walker, Marquis Grissom)	.25
(19) Giants (Will Clark, Matt Williams)	.25
(20) Indians (Albert Belle, Carlos Baerga)	.25
(21) Mariners (Jay Buhner, Randy Johnson)	.40
(22) Marlins (Gary Sheffield, Bryan Harvey)	.25
(23) Mets (Bobby Bonilla, Dwight Gooden)	.25
(24) Orioles (Cal Ripken Jr., Mike Mussina)	1.00
(25) Padres (Andy Benes, Tony Gwynn)	.60
(26) Phillies (John Kruk, Tommy Greene)	.25
(27) Pirates (Jay Bell, Andy Van Slyke)	.25
(28) Rangers (Jose Canseco, Kevin Brown)	.35
(29) Reds (Barry Larkin, Reggie Sanders)	.25
(30) Red Sox (Mo Vaughn, Frank Viola)	.25
(31) Rockies (Charlie Hayes, Andres Galarraga)	.25
(32) Royals (Brian McRae, David Cone)	.25
(33) Tigers (Cecil Fielder, Mike Henneman)	.25
(34) Twins (Kirby Puckett, Rick Aguilera)	.60
(35) White Sox (Frank Thomas, Jack McDowell)	.50
(36) Yankees (Don Mattingly, Jim Abbott)	.75

1995 Red Foley

The Red Foley book of children's games, quizzes, trivia and other baseball related entertainment reprised its 1994 format for 1995. The 36 perforated insert cards, 2-1/2" x 3-1/2", were again divided into single-player "Superstar" and two-player "Team Leaders" types. Designs were identical to the previous year, with color action photos on front and career highlights on back. The unnumbered cards are checklisted here in alphabetical order by type.

	NM/M
Complete Book:	15.00
Complete Set (36):	12.00
Common Card:	.25
(1) Barry Bonds	2.00
(2) Joe Carter	.25
(3) Roger Clemens	1.00
(4) Juan Gonzalez	.60
(5) Ken Griffey Jr.	1.50
(6) Fred McGriff	.25
(7) Cal Ripken Jr.	2.00
(8) Frank Thomas	.75
(9) Angels (Tim Salmon, Steve Finley)	.35
(10) Astros (Jeff Bagwell, Craig Biggio)	.50
(11) Athletics (Mark McGwire, Dennis Eckersley)	.75
(12) Blue Jays (Roberto Alomar, John Olerud)	.35
(13) Braves (Greg Maddux, David Justice)	.60
(14) Brewers (Cal Eldred, Dave Nillson)	.25
(15) Cardinals (Ozzie Smith, Gregg Jefferies)	.25
(16) Cubs (Mark Grace, Randy Myers)	.35
(17) Dodgers (Mike Piazza, Orel Hershiser)	.65
(18) Expos (Larry Walker, Ken Hill)	.25
(19) Giants (Matt Williams, Rod Beck)	.25
(20) Indians (Albert Belle, Carlos Baerga)	.25
(21) Mariners (Jay Buhner, Randy Johnson)	.25
(22) Marlins (Gary Sheffield, Benito Santiago)	.25
(23) Mets (Bret Saberhagen, Bobby Bonilla)	.25
(24) Orioles (Rafael Palmeiro, Mike Mussina)	.40
(25) Padres (Tony Gwynn, Andy Benes)	.60
(26) Phillies (John Kruk, Lenny Dykstra)	.25
(27) Pirates (Andy Van Slyke, Al Martin)	.25
(28) Rangers (Jose Canseco, Will Clark)	.25
(29) Reds (Barry Larkin, Jose Rijo)	.25
(30) Red Sox (Mo Vaughn, Aaron Sele)	.25
(31) Rockies (Andres Galarraga, Dante Bichette)	.25
(32) Royals (Brian McRae, David Cone)	.25
(33) Tigers (Cecil Fielder, Travis Fryman)	.25
(34) Twins (Kirby Puckett, Rick Aguilera)	.60
(35) White Sox (Robin Ventura, Wilson Alvarez)	.25
(36) Yankees (Don Mattingly, Jimmy Key)	.65

1996 Red Foley

WALLY JOYNER

FIRST BASE

The Red Foley book of children's games, quizzes, trivia and other baseball related entertainment changed little for its 1996 edition. The number of cards was decreased to 32 and the size to a 2" x 2-3/4" perforated format. Only single-player cards were produced. Designs were nearly identical to the previous year, with color action photos on front and career highlights on back. The unnumbered cards are checklisted here in alphabetical order.

	NM/M
Complete Book:	12.00
Complete Set (32):	9.00
Common Player:	.25
(1) Roberto Alomar	.30
(2) Moises Alou	.25
(3) Carlos Baerga	.25
(4) Jay Bell	.25
(5) Craig Biggio	.25
(6) Barry Bonds	1.50
(7) Jeff Conine	.25
(8) Lenny Dykstra	.25
(9) Cecil Fielder	.25
(10) Ken Griffey Jr.	1.00
(11a) Tony Gwynn (Red)	.75
(11b) Tony Gwynn (Purple)	.75
(12) Rickey Henderson	.65
(13) Wally Joyner	.25
(14) Barry Larkin	.25
(15) Mark McGwire	1.25
(16) Eddie Murray	.65
(17) Rafael Palmeiro	.50
(18) Mike Piazza	1.00
(19) Greg Maddux	.75
(20) Paul O'Neill	.25
(21) Kirby Puckett	.75
(22) Bill Pulsipher	.25
(23) Cal Ripken Jr.	1.50
(24) Ivan Rodriguez	.50
(25) Kenny Rogers	.25
(26) Tim Salmon	.30
(27) Kevin Seitzer	.25
(28) Ozzie Smith	.75
(29) Sammy Sosa	.90
(30) Frank Thomas	.65
(31) Mo Vaughn	.25
(32) Larry Walker	.25

1988 Foot Locker Slam Fest

Two baseball players are among the athletes pictured in this Foot Locker set issued in conjunction with the shoe store chain's Slam Fest competition. Cards were given away at local stores. The 2-1/2" x 3-1/2" cards have color player portrait photos on a semi-gloss front. All athletes are pictured in Slam Dunk basketball jerseys. A sponsor's banner is at top; the chain's referee logo at lower-left. Backs are printed in blue with information about the televised competition and the player's career.

	NM/M
Complete Set (9):	6.00
Common Player:	.50
(1) Carl Banks (Football)	.50
(2) Mike Conley/SP (Track)	.50
(3) Thomas Hearns (Boxing)	2.00
(4) Bo Jackson	2.00
(5) Keith Jackson (Football)	.50
(6) Karch Kiraly (Volleyball)	.50
(7) Ricky Sanders (Football)	.50
(8) Dwight Stones (Track)	.50
(9) Devon White	1.00

1989 Foot Locker Slam Fest

VINCE COLEMAN

One baseball player is among the athletes pictured in this Foot Locker set issued in conjunction with the shoe store chain's Slam Fest competition. Cards were given away at local stores. The 2-1/2" x 3-1/2" cards have color player portrait photos on a semi-gloss front. All athletes are pictured in Slam Dunk basketball jerseys. A sponsor's banner is at top. Backs have information about the televised competition and the player's career.

	NM/M
Complete Set (10):	3.00
Common Player:	.35
1 Mike Conley (Track)	.40
2 Keith Jackson (Football)	.75
3 Vince Coleman	1.00
4 Eric Dickerson (Football)	2.00
5 Steve Timmons (Volleyball)	.40
6 Matt Biondi (Swimming)	.50
7 Carl Lewis (Track)	.75
8 Mike Quick (Football)	.50
9 Mike Powell (Track)	.50
10 Checklist	.05

1991 Foot Locker Slam Fest

A number of baseball players were included among the various current and former athletes in this set of three 10-card series produced in conjunction with the sporting gear retailer's Slam Fest

Limited Edition

BARRY BONDS

charity event. Players are pictured in color on the 2-1/2" x 3-1/2" cards wearing Nike basketball uniforms.

	NM/M
Complete Set (30):	5.00
Common Player:	.03
1-1 Ken Griffey Jr.	1.50
1-2 Delino DeShields	1.00
1-3 Barry Bonds	4.00
1-4 Jack Armstrong	.10
1-5 Dave Justice	.25
1-6 Deion Sanders	.50
1-7 Michael Dean Perry (Football)	.10
1-8 Tim Brown (Football)	.10
1-9 Mike Conley (Track)	.10
1-10 Mike Powell (Track)	.10
10-1 Wilt Chamberlain (Basketball)	1.00
10-2 Carl Ramsey (Basketball)	.10
10-3 Bobby Jones (Basketball)	.10
10-4 John Havlicek (Basketball)	.10
10-5 Calvin Murphy (Basketball)	.10
10-6 Nate Thurmond (Basketball)	.10
10-7 John Havlicek (Basketball)	.10
10-8 Checklist Series 1	.05
10-9 Checklist Series 2	.05
10-10 Checklist Series 3	.05
20-1 Jerry Lucas (Basketball)	.10
20-2 Bo Jackson	.25
20-3 Elvin Hayes (Basketball)	.10
20-4 Thomas Hearns (Boxing)	.10
20-5 Matt Biondi (Swimming)	.10
20-6 Earl Monroe (Basketball)	.10
20-7 Eric Dickerson (Football)	.50
20-8 Carl Lewis (Track)	.25
20-9 Wilt and Company (Basketball)	.10
20-10 TV Schedule	.05

1989 Foxes Holsum Super Stars Discs

(See 1989 Holsum for checklist and price guide. Ditributed in Carolinas.)

1981 Franchise 1966 Baltimore Orioles

One of the lesser-known producers of collectors' issues in the early 1980s was "The Franchise." Most of their card sets featured subjects of special interest to their home (Maryland) area. This set, for example, features the 1966 Baltimore Orioles World Champions. In 2-1/2" x 3-1/2" size, cards have black-and-white player photos on front surrounded by orange borders. Black-and-white backs are somewhat in the style of 1953 Bowman, with personal data, career highlights and 1966/Lifetime stats.

	NM/M
Complete Set (32):	13.50
Common Player:	.50
1 World Champs 1966	.50
2 Team Photo	.50
3 Luis Aparicio	2.50
4 Steve Barber	.50
5 Hank Bauer	.50
6 Paul Blair	.50
7 Curt Blefary	.50
8 Sam Bowens	.50
9 Gene Brabender	.50
10 Harry Brecheen	.50
11 Wally Bunker	.50
12 Moe Drabowsky	.50
13 Andy Etchebarren	.50
14 Eddie Fisher	.50
15 Dick Hall	.50
16 Larry Haney	.50
17 Woody Held	.50
18 Billy Hunter	.50
19 Bob Johnson	.50
20 Dave Johnson	.50
21 Sherman Lollar	.50
22 Dave McNally	.50
23 John Miller	.50
24 Stu Miller	.50
25 Jim Palmer	2.50
26 Boog Powell	1.50
27 Brooks Robinson	3.00
28 Frank Robinson	3.00
29 Vic Roznovsky	.50
30 Russ Snyder	.50
31 Eddie Watt	.50
32 Gene Woodling	.50

1983 Franchise Brooks Robinson

This collectors' issue was produced by a Maryland company which specialized in sets of local interest. Cards detail the career of the Hall of Famer. Fronts of the 2-1/2" x 3-1/2" cards have a black-and-white photo with orange graphics. Backs are printed in black, white and orange and provide a title and details about the front photo.

	NM/M
Complete Set (40):	35.00
Common Card:	1.00
1 Professional record	1.00
2 Youngest on team	1.00
3 All-state performer	1.00
4 Teen-ager in Texas	1.00
5 First spring training	1.00
6 Another uniform	1.00
7 First solid infield	1.00
8 Celebration time	1.00
9 Instinctive baserunner	1.00
10 Wedding day	1.00
11 First business partner	1.00
12 Second solid infield	1.00
13 Two Baltimore heroes	1.00
14 Enjoying the kids	1.00
15 Playing every game	1.00
16 Upsetting the Yankees	1.00
17 Tag out at third	1.00
18 Getting net results	1.00
19 The future MVPs	1.50
20 The original Rocky	1.00
21 Bauer's gloveman	1.00
22 World Series infield	1.00
23 Orioles' power parade	1.00
24 All-star trio	1.50
25 Lethal lumber	1.00
26 Belanger joins infield	1.00
27 Respect for Oliva	1.00
28 Out of Harm's way	1.00
29 Master trader	1.00
30 Eastern Shore visit	1.00
31 Gloves of gold	1.00
32 Ripping the Reds	1.00
33 Rappin' with Willie	2.00
34 Using the body	1.00
35 Getting the umps' attention	1.00
36 Respect from teammate	1.00
37 Touch of class	1.00
38 Bubble never burst	1.00
39 Honored by Yankees	1.00
40 Two greats at third	1.00

2002 Franz Bread Seattle Mariners

This team set was produced by Upper Deck and issued regionally with individually cello-wrapped cards inserted into loaves of bread. The cards have game-action photos which are borderless at top and sides. In a wide white strip at bottom are the team name, player name, po-

sition and uniform number and a Franz logo. In the upper corners are UD and Mariners 25th Anniversary logos. Backs have a portrait photo, a few words about the player, previous season's stats and various logos and copyright information.

	NM/M
Complete Set (16):	10.00
Common Player:	.50
1 Ichiro	5.00
2 Edgar Martinez	1.00
3 John Olerud	.75
4 Bret Boone	.75
5 Jeff Cirillo	.50
6 Carlos Guillen	.50
7 Mike Cameron	.50
8 Ruben Sierra	.50
9 Ben Davis	.50
10 Freddy Garcia	.50
11 Kazuhiro Sasaki	1.00
12 Jamie Moyer	.50
13 James Baldwin	.50
14 Jeff Nelson	.50
15 Dan Wilson	.50
16 Mark McLemore	.50

1987 French/Bray Orioles

The Baltimore Orioles and French Bray, Inc. issued a baseball card set to be handed out to fans in attendance at Memorial Stadium on July. 26th. Thirty perforated, detachable cards were printed within a three-panel fold-out piece measuring 9-1/2" x 11-1/4". The card fronts feature full-color player photos surrounded by an orange border. The French/Bray logo appears on the card front. The backs are of simple design, containing only the player's name, uniform number, position and professional record.

	NM/M
Complete Set, Panel:	45.00
Complete Set, Singles (30):	40.00
Common Player:	1.00
2 Alan Wiggins	1.00
3 Bill Ripken	1.00
4 Floyd Rayford	1.00
7 Cal Ripken, Sr.	1.00
8 Cal Ripken, Jr.	25.00
9 Jim Dwyer	1.00
10 Terry Crowley	1.00
12 Terry Kennedy	1.00
16 Scott McGregor	1.00
18 Larry Sheets	1.00
19 Fred Lynn	1.00
20 Frank Robinson	4.00
24 Dave Schmidt	1.00
25 Ray Knight	1.00
28 Lee Lacy	1.00
31 Mark Wiley	1.00
33 Mark Williamson	1.00
33 Eddie Murray	12.50
38 Ken Gerhart	1.00
39 Ken Dixon	1.00
40 Jimmy Williams	1.00
42 Mike Griffin	1.00
43 Mike Young	1.00
44 Elrod Hendricks	1.00
45 Eric Bell	1.00
46 Mike Flanagan	1.00
47 Tom Niedenfuer	1.00
52 Mike Boddicker	1.00
54 John Habyan	1.00
57 Tony Arnold	1.00

1988 French/Bray Orioles

French-Bray sponsored a full-color brochure that was distributed to fans during an in-stadium promotion. A blue and orange front cover features inset photos of the Orioles in action on the upper left in a filmstrip motif. To the right is the Orioles logo and their 1988 slogan, "You Gotta Be There" above a baseball glove and ball. The 3-panel foldout measures approximately 9-1/2" x 11-1/4" and includes a team photo on the inside cover, with two perforated pages of individual cards featuring players, coaches and the team manager. Individual cards measure 2-1/4" x 3-1/8", with close-ups framed in white with an orange accent line. The player name and sponsor logo are printed beneath the photo. The black-and-white backs are numbered by player uniform and provide career stats. Additional copies of the brochure were made available from the Orioles Baseball Store following the free giveaway.

	NM/M
Complete Set, Panel:	70.00
Complete Set, Singles (31):	60.00
Common Player:	1.00
2 Don Buford	1.00
6 Joe Orsulak	1.00
7 Bill Ripken	1.00
8 Cal Ripken, Jr.	40.00
9 Jim Dwyer	1.00
10 Terry Crowley	1.00
12 Mike Morgan	1.00
14 Mickey Tettleton	1.00
15 Terry Kennedy	1.00
17 Pete Stanicek	1.00
18 Larry Sheets	1.00
19 Fred Lynn	1.00
21 Frank Robinson	5.00
23 Ozzie Peraza	1.00
24 Dave Schmidt	1.00
25 Rich Schu	1.00
28 Jim Traber	1.00
31 Herm Starrette	1.00
33 Eddie Murray	15.00
37 Jeff Ballard	1.00
38 Ken Gerhart	1.00
41 Minnie Mendoza	1.00
41 Don Aase	1.00
44 Elrod Hendricks	1.00
46 John Hart	1.00
48 Jose Bautista	1.00
49 Tom Niedenfuer	1.00
52 Mike Boddicker	1.00
53 Jay Tibbs	1.00
88 Rene Gonzales	1.00
--- Team Photo	5.00

1989 French/Bray Orioles

This 32-card team set was co-sponsored by French-Bray and the Wilcox Walter Furlong Paper Co., and was distributed as an in-stadium promotion to fans attending the May 12 game. Smaller than standard size, the cards measure 2-1/4" x 3" and feature a full-color player photo with number, name and position below. The backs, done in black-and-white, include brief player data and complete major and minor league stats.

		NM/M
Complete Set (32):		20.00
Common Player:		.50
3	Bill Ripken	.50
6	Joe Orsulak	.50
7	Cal Ripken, Sr.	.50
8	Cal Ripken, Jr.	15.00
9	Brady Anderson	1.50
10	Steve Finley	.50
11	Craig Worthington	.50
12	Mike Devereaux	.50
14	Mickey Tettleton	.50
14	Randy Milligan	.50
16	Phil Bradley	.50
18	Bob Milacki	.50
19	Larry Sheets	.50
20	Frank Robinson	4.50
21	Mark Thurmond	.50
23	Kevin Hickey	.50
24	Dave Schmidt	.50
28	Jim Traber	.50
29	Jeff Ballard	.50
30	Gregg Olson	.50
31	Al Jackson	.50
32	Mark Williamson	.50
36	Bob Melvin	.50
37	Brian Holton	.50
40	Tom McCraw	.50
42	Pete Harnisch	.50
43	Fransisco Melendez	.50
44	Elrod Hendricks	.50
46	Johnny Oates	.50
48	Jose Bautista	.50
88	Rene Gonzales	.50
---	Sponsor's Card	.50

1992 French's Mustard

In 1992 French's gave away a promotional card with the purchase of its mustard products. Each of the cards displays photographs of two players. The cards, which have team insignias airbrushed out, feature a green border, color photos and the players' statistics on the back.

		NM/M
Complete Set (18):		4.00
Common Card:		.10
1	Jeff Bagwell,	
	Chuck Knoblauch	.50
2	Roger Clemens,	
	Tom Glavine	.65
3	Julio Franco,	
	Terry Pendleton	.10
4	Howard Johnson,	
	Jose Canseco	.35
5	John Smiley,	
	Scott Erickson	.10
6	Bryan Harvey, Lee Smith	.10
7	Kirby Puckett,	
	Barry Bonds	1.00
8	Robin Ventura,	
	Matt Williams	1.00
9	Tony Pena, Tom Pagnozzi	.10
10	Benito Santiago,	
	Sandy Alomar, Jr.	.10
11	Don Mattingly, Will Clark	.75
12	Ryne Sandberg,	
	Roberto Alomar	.60
13	Cal Ripken, Jr.,	
	Ozzie Smith	1.00
14	Wade Boggs, Chris Sabo	.60
15	Ken Griffey Jr.,	
	David Justice	.75
16	Joe Carter, Tony Gwynn	.60
17	Rickey Henderson,	
	Darryl Strawberry	.50
18	Jack Morris, Steve Avery	.10

2003 French's Mustard N.Y. Yankees

This six-card set sponsored by Yankee Stadium's long-time condiments concessionaire was distributed to fans 14 and under. Produced by Donruss, the standard-sized cards have game-action photos on front with the sponsor's ad message at bottom. Backs have player personal data, career highlights and career stats.

		NM/M
Complete Set (6):		5.00
Common Player:		.25
1	Derek Jeter	4.00
2	Alfonso Soriano	1.00
3	Jorge Posada	.25

4	Jose Contreras	.50
5	Jeff Weaver	.25
6	Steve Karsay	.25
--	Header Card	.05

1983 Fritsch One-Year Winners

Larry Fritsch Cards continued its series of collector's issues under the banner of "One-Year Winners" with a 64-card color issue in 1983. Most of the player photos featured are unused Topps pictures. As in previous issues, the set features players with short major league careers, few of whom appear on any contemporary baseball card. In the style of 1966 Topps cards, the set has large player photos bordered in white with a diagonal blue strip in an upper corner containing the initials OYW. A blue strip beneath the photo has the player name in black. Backs are in red, black and white with personal data, stats and career highlights.

		NM/M
Complete Set (64):		35.00
Common Player:		2.00
55	Don Prince	2.00
56	Tom Gramly	2.00
57	Roy Heiser	2.00
58	Hank Izquierdo	2.00
59	Rex Johnston	2.00
60	Jack Damaska	2.00
61	John Flavin	2.00
62	John Glenn	2.00
63	Stan Johnson	2.00
64	Don Choate	2.00
65	Bill Kern	2.00
66	Dick Luebke	2.00
68	Glen Clark	2.00
68	Lamar Jacobs	2.00
69	Rick Herrscher	2.00
70	Jim McManus	2.00
71	Len Church	2.00
72	Larry Stubing	2.00
73	Cal Emery	2.00
74	Lee Gregory	2.00
75	Mike Page	2.00
76	Benny Valenzuela	2.00
77	John Papa	2.00
78	Jim Stump	2.00
79	Brian McCall	2.00
80	Al Kenders	2.00
81	Corky Withrow	2.00
82	Verle Tiefenthaler	2.00
83	Dave Wissman	2.00
84	Tom Fletcher	2.00
85	Dale Willis	2.00
86	Larry Foster	2.00
87	Johnnie Seale	2.00
88	Jim Lehew	2.00
89	Charlie Shoemaker	2.00
90	Don Arlick	2.00
91	George Gerberman	2.00
92	John Pregenzer	2.00
93	Merlin Nippert	2.00
94	Steve Demeter	2.00
95	John Paciorek	2.00
96	Larry Loughlin	2.00
97	Alan Brice	2.00
98	Chet Boak	2.00
99	Alan Koch	2.00
100	Dan Thomas	2.00
101	Elder White	2.00

102	Jim Snyder	2.00
103	Ted Schreiber	2.00
104	Evans Killeen	2.00
105	Ray Daviault	2.00
106	Larry Foss	2.00
107	Wayne Graham	2.00
108	Santiago Rosario	2.00
109	Bob Sprout	2.00
110	Tom Hughes	2.00
111	Em Lindbeck	2.00
112	Ray Blemker	2.00
113	Shaun Fitzmaurice	2.00
114	Ron Stillwell	2.00
115	Carl Thomas	2.00
116	Mike DeGerick	2.00
117	Jay Dahl	2.00
118	Al Lary	2.00

1983 Fritsch 1953 Boston/Milwaukee Braves

This collectors' issue commemorates the 30th anniversary of the move of the Boston Braves to Milwaukee. The black-and-white photos on the front of the cards (bordered in blue) were taken in spring training, with players still wearing Boston caps. Card backs have personal data and detailed career highlights. Cards measure about 2-5/8" x 3-3/4", which was the standard prior to 1957.

		NM/M
Complete Set (33):		8.00
Common Player:		.25
1	Joe Adcock	.35
2	John Antonelli	.35
3	Billy Bruton	.25
4	Bob Buhl	.25
5	Lew Burdette	.35
6	Paul Burris	.25
7	Dave Cole	.25
8	Johnny Cooney	.25
9	Walker Cooper	.25
10	Del Crandall	.35
11	George Crowe	.25
12	Jack Dittmer	.25
13	Dick Donovan	.25
14	Sid Gordon	.25
15	Virgil Jester	.25
16	Ernie Johnson	.25
17	Dave Jolly	.25
18	Billy Klaus	.25
19	Don Liddle	.25
20	Johnny Logan	.25
21	Luis Marquez	.25
21s	Luis Marquez	
	(Sample overprint.)	.25
22	Eddie Mathews	1.00
22s	Eddie Mathews	
	(Sample overprint.)	.25
23	Andy Pafko	.35
24	Jim Pendleton	.25
25	Ebba St. Claire	.25
26	Sibby Sisti	.25
27	Warren Spahn	1.00
28	Max Surkont	.25
29	Bob Thorpe	.25
30	Murray Wall	.25
31	Bucky Walters	.25
32	Jim Wilson	.25
33	1953 Braves Team	.25

1986 Fritsch Negro League BaseAll-Stars

One of the most comprehensive collectors' issues to feature the stars of the Negro Leagues, the

Fritsch set features black-and-white photos of varying quality; most of the photos are contemporary with the players' careers from the 1920s into the 1950s, with a few of the segregated leagues' earlier pioneers also included. Fronts are highlighted with red graphics. Backs are printed in blue and present a brief summary of the player's career and a list of the teams on which he played. Cards are in standard 2-1/2" x 3-1/2" format.

		NM/M
Complete Set (119):		15.00
Common Player:		.10
1	Buck Leonard	.15
2	Ted Page	.10
3	Cool Papa Bell	.15
4	Oscar Charleston,	
	Josh Gibson, Ted Page,	
	Judy Johnson	.15
5	Judy Johnson	.15
6	Monte Irvin	.15
7	Ray Dandridge	.15
8	Oscar Charleston	.15
9	Josh Gibson	.15
10	Satchel Paige	.25
10s	Satchel Paige	
	(SAMPLE on back.)	2.50
11	Jackie Robinson	.50
12	Piper Davis	.10
13	Josh Johnson	.10
14	Lou Dials	.15
15	Andy Porter	.10
16	Pop Lloyd	.15
17	Andy Watts	.10
18	Rube Foster	.15
19	Martin Dihigo	.15
20	Lou Dials	.15
21	Satchel Paige	.25
22	Crush Holloway	.10
23	Josh Gibson	.15
24	Oscar Charleston	.15
25	Jackie Robinson	.50
26	Larry Brown	.15
27	Hilton Smith	.15
28	Moses Fleetwood Walker	.15
29	Jimmie Crutchfield	.10
30	Josh Gibson	.15
30s	Josh Gibson	
	(SAMPLE on back.)	2.00
31	Josh Gibson	.15
32	Bullet Rogan	.10
33	Clint Thomas	.10
34	Rats Henderson	.10
35	Pat Scantlebury	.10
36	Sidney Morton	.10
37	Larry Kimbrough	.10
38	Sam Jethroe	.10
39	Normal "Tweed" Webb	.10
40	Mahlon Duckett	.10
41	Andy Anderson	.10
42	Buster Haywood	.10
43	Bob Trice	.10
44	Bus Clarkson	.10
45	Buck O'Neil	.15
46	Jim Zapp	.10
47	Piper Davis	.10
48	Ed Steel	.10
49	Bob Boyd	.10
50	Marlin Carter	.10
51	George Giles	.10
52	Bill Byrd	.10
53	Art Pennington	.10
54	Max Manning	.10
55	Ron Teasley	.10
56	Ziggy Marcell	.10
57	Bill Cash	.10
58	Joe Scott	.10
59	Joe Fillmore	.10
60	Bob Thurman	.10
61	Larry Kimbrough	.10
62	Verdell Mathis	.10
63	Josh Johnson	.10
64	Double Duty Radcliffe	.15
65	William Bobby Robinson	.10
66	Bingo DeMoss	.15
67	John Beckwith	.10
68	Bill Jackman	.10
69	Bill Drake	.10
70	Charles Grant	.15
71	Willie Wells	.25
72	Jose Fernandez	.10
73	Isidro Fabri	.10
74	Frank Austin	.10
75	Richard Lundy	.10
76	Junior Gilliam	.15
77	John Donaldson	.10
78	Herb Dixon	.10
79	Slim Jones	.10
80	Sam Jones	.10
81	Dave Hoskins	.10
82	Jerry Benjamin	.10
83	Luke Easter	.10
84	Ramon Herrera	.10
85	Matthew Carlisle	.10
86	Smoky Joe Williams	.25
87	Marv Williams	.10
88	William Yancey	.10
89	Monte Irvin	.15
89s	Monte Irvin	
	(SAMPLE on back.)	1.00
90	Cool Papa Bell	.25
91	Biz Mackey	.25
92	Harry Simpson	.10

93	Lazario Salazar	.10
94	Bill Perkins	.10
95	Johnny Davis	.10
96	Jelly Jackson	.10
97	Sam Bankhead	.10
98	Hank Thompson	.10
99	William Bell	.10
100	Cliff Bell	.10
101	Dave Barnhill	.10
102	Dan Bankhead	.10
103	Lloyd Bassett	.10
104	Newt Allen	.10
105	George Jefferson	.10
106	Pat Paterson	.10
107	Goose Tatum	.15
108	Dave Malarcher	.10
109	Home Run Johnson	.10
110	Bill Monroe	.10
111	Sammy Hughes	.10
112	Dick Redding	.10
113	Fats Jenkins	.10
114	Jimmie Lyons	.10
115	Mule Suttles	.15
116	Ted Trent	.10
117	George Sweatt	.10
118	Frank Duncan	.10
119	Checklist	.05

1991 Front Row Ken Griffey Jr.

Production of this collectors' set and related promo cards was reported at 25,000 sets each. Cards trace the three-year career of Junior in photos, stats, highlights and biographic details. Fronts have various posed and color action photos, complete with team logos, and a white border. Horizontal backs are printed in black on a light blue background. Promo cards have a large "PROMO" printed on a baseball at center. Size is 2-1/2" x 3-1/2".

		NM/M
Complete Set (10):		2.00
Complete Promo Set (5):		1.00
Common Card:		.25
Common Promo:		.25
1	Ken Griffey Jr./AS	.25
1	Ken Griffey Jr./AS (Promo)	.25
2	Ken Griffey Jr.	
	(The Breakdown)	.25
2	Ken Griffey Jr.	
	(The Breakdown)(Promo)	.25
3	Ken Griffey Jr. (Homers)	.25
3	Ken Griffey Jr.	
	(Homers)(Promo)	.25
4	Ken Griffey Jr. (Gold Glv)	.25
4	Ken Griffey Jr.	
	(Gold Glv)(Promo)	.25
5	Ken Griffey Jr. (Drafted)	.25
5	Ken Griffey Jr.	
	(Drafted)(Promo)	.25
6	Ken Griffey Jr.	
	(Up Close and Personal)	.25
7	Ken Griffey Jr.	
	(Background)	.25
8	Ken Griffey Jr.	
	(The Majors)	.25
9	Ken Griffey Jr.	
	(Career Highlights)	.25
10	Ken Griffey Jr.	
	(The American League)	.25

1992-95 Front Row All-Time Great Series

BUCK LEONARD

Some of baseball's greatest living former stars were featured in this run of five-card sets. Originally intended to encompass 100 players, the issue was cut considerably short. Each single-player set contains five cards featuring black-and-white and/or color photos on front. Backs have a photo in the background, overprinted with statistical, biographical or career information. Major league uniform logos have been removed from photos for lack of licensing by MLB. Each set was issued in an edition of 25,000, with an illustrated, numbered certificate of authenticity included. Each set was also produced with the top card authentically autographed. The Perry and Spahn sets were issued some time after the first 37 players. Sets are checklisted here alphabetically; single cards are not listed because the cards are usually sold only as sets.

		NM/M
Common Player Set:		.25
(1)	Hank Aaron (5-card set)	1.00
(1a)	Hank Aaron/Auto.	40.00
(2)	Ernie Banks (5-card set)	.75
(2a)	Ernie Banks/Auto.	15.00
(3)	Al Barlick (5-card set)	.25
(3a)	Al Barlick/Auto.	25.00
(4)	Johnny Bench (5-card set)	.75
(4a)	Johnny Bench/Auto.)	20.00
(5)	Yogi Berra (5-card set)	.75
(5a)	Yogi Berra/Auto.	20.00
(6)	Lou Boudreau (5-card set)	.25
(6a)	Lou Boudreau/Auto.	16.00
(7)	Lou Brock (5-card set)	.25
(7a)	Lou Brock/Auto.	12.50
(8)	Roy Campanella	
	(5-card set)	.75
(8a)	Roy Campanella/Auto.	150.00
(9)	Rod Carew (5-card set)	.35
(9a)	Rod Carew/Auto.	20.00
(10)	Ray Dandridge	
	(5-card set)	.25
(10a)	Ray Dandridge/Auto.	17.50
(11)	Bobby Doerr (5-card set)	.25
(11a)	Bobby Doerr/Auto.	12.50
(12)	Rick Ferrell (5-card set)	.25
(12a)	Rick Ferrell/Auto.	30.00
(13)	Rollie Fingers (5-card set)	.25
(13a)	Rollie Fingers/Auto.	12.50
(14)	Whitey Ford (5-card set)	.50
(14a)	Whitey Ford/Auto.	22.50
(15)	George Foster (5-card set)	.25
(15a)	George Foster/Auto.	10.00
(16)	Catfish Hunter (5-card set)	.25
(16a)	Catfish Hunter/Auto.	15.00
(17)	Monte Irvin (5-card set)	.25
(17a)	Monte Irvin/Auto.	5.00
(18)	Al Kaline (5-card set)	.50
(18a)	Al Kaline/Auto.15.00(19)	
	George Kell (5-card set)	.25
(19a)	George Kell/Auto.	12.50
(20)	Ralph Kiner (5-card set)	.25
(20a)	Ralph Kiner/Auto.	30.00
(21)	Don Larsen (5-card set)	.25
(21a)	Don Larsen/Auto.	15.00
(22)	Bob Lemon (5-card set)	.25
(22a)	Bob Lemon/Auto.	25.00
(23)	Buck Leonard (5-card set)	.25
(23a)	Buck Leonard/Auto.	22.50
(23p)	Buck Leonard	
	("PROMO" on back.)	1.00
(24)	Juan Marichal (5-card set)	.35
(24a)	Juan Marichal/Auto.	15.00
(25)	Joe Morgan (5-card set)	.25
(25a)	Joe Morgan/Auto.	25.00
(26)	Stan Musial (5-card set)	.50
(26a)	Stan Musial/Auto.	40.00
(27)	Hal Newhouser	
	(5-card set)	.25
(27a)	Hal Newhouser/Auto.	15.00
(28)	Jim Palmer (5-card set)	.35
(28a)	Jim Palmer/Auto.	12.50
(29)	Tony Perez (5-card set)	.25
(29a)	Tony Perez/Auto.	12.50
(30)	Gaylord Perry (5-card set)	.25
(30a)	Gaylord Perry/Auto.	12.50
(31)	Pee Wee Reese	
	(5-card set)	.35
(32a)	Pee Wee Reese/Auto.	40.00
(32a)	Phil Rizzuto (5-card set)	.50
(32a)	Phil Rizzuto/Auto.	20.00
(33)	Brooks Robinson	
	(5-card set)	.35
(33a)	Brooks Robinson/Auto.	12.50
(34)	Frank Robinson	
	(5-card set)	.35
(34a)	Frank Robinson/Auto.	15.00
(35)	Red Schoendienst	
	(5-card set)	.25
(35a)	Red Schoendienst/Auto.	40.00
(36)	Tom Seaver (5-card set)	.35
(36a)	Tom Seaver/Auto.	17.50
(37)	Warren Spahn (5-card set)	.50
(37a)	Warren Spahn/Auto.	30.00
(38)	Willie Stargell (5-card set)	.25
(38a)	Willie Stargell/Auto.	15.00

(39)	Carl Yastrzemski (5-card set)	.35
(39a)	Carl Yastrzemski/Auto.	30.00

1992 Front Row Club House Series Ken Griffey, Jr.

Ten cards tracing the life and career of Ken Griffey Jr. comprise this collectors' issue. Cards are standard 2-1/2" x 3-1/2" with borderless color action and posed photos. Uniform logos have been removed from the photos since the set is not licensed by MLB. A Club House Series logo is on front at bottom-right. Horizontal backs have a color photo of Griffey ghosted in the background. Printed over that are personal data, career highlights and stats.

		NM/M
Complete Set (10):		1.00
Common Player:		.15
1	Ken Griffey Jr. (Background)	.15
2	Ken Griffey Jr. (Drafted)	.15
3	Ken Griffey Jr. (The Majors)	.15
4	Ken Griffey Jr. (The Breakdown)	.15
5	Ken Griffey Jr. (The American League)	.15
6	Ken Griffey Jr./AS	.15
7	Ken Griffey Jr. (Gold Glv)	.15
8	Ken Griffey Jr. (Homers)	.15
9	Ken Griffey Jr. (Career Highlights)	.15
10	Ken Griffey Jr. (A Closer Look)	.15

1992 Front Row Ken Griffey Jr. Holograms

This set of collectors' edition cards was produced in an issue of 50,000, with each set including a numbered certificate of authenticity. In standard 2-1/2" x 3-1/2" size, the cards have a borderless hologram picture on front. Conventionally printed backs have a color photo of the player and a few sentences about his career. Team logos have been removed from the pictures because the cards were not licensed by MLB.

		NM/M
Complete Set (3):		3.00
Common Card:		1.00
1	Ken Griffey Jr. (Making History)	1.00
2	Ken Griffey Jr. (Rewriting the Record Book)	1.00
3	Ken Griffey Jr. (Turning Up Gold)	1.00

1992 Front Row Ken Griffey Jr. Pure Gold

This set of collectors' edition cards was produced in an issue of 20,000, with each set including a numbered certificate of authenticity. In standard 2-1/2" x 3-1/2" size,

the cards have wide gold-foil borders on front. Backs have stats or a few sentences about his career. Team logos have been removed from the pictures because the cards were not licensed by MLB.

		NM/M
Complete Set (3):		3.00
Uncut Strip:		5.00
Common Card:		1.00
1	Ken Griffey Jr. (Gold Glv)	1.00
2	Ken Griffey Jr. (Background)	1.00
3	Ken Griffey Jr. (Drafted)	1.00

1992 Front Row Holograms

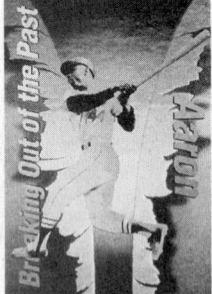

The "career" seasons of three Hall of Famers are remembered in this series of cards. In standard 2-1/2" x 3-1/2" format, fronts have a borderless hologram featuring a vintage action photo. Conventionally printed backs have a color photo, a recap and stats from the named season, and a foil holographic serial number tag designating the card's place in an edition of 100,000 each.

		NM/M
Complete Set (3):		1.50
Common Player:		.50
(1)	Hank Aaron	.70
(2)	Roy Campanella	.50
(3)	Tom Seaver	.50

1992 Front Row Pure Gold

Each of these 2-1/2" x 3-1/2" cards features 23-K gold borders on front, surrounding a color action photo on which uniform details have been airbrushed away. Backs have player information.

		NM/M
Complete Set (6):		15.00
Common Player:		3.00
(1)	Hank Aaron	3.00
(2)	Roy Campanella	3.00
(3)	Tom Seaver	3.00
	Frank Thomas Strip (3):	10.00
(4)	Frank Thomas/Btg	3.00
(5)	Frank Thomas/Standing	3.00
(6)	Frank Thomas/Fldg	3.00

1992 Front Row Frank Thomas

Budding super slugger Frank Thomas is featured in this collectors' issue. The 2-1/2" x 3-1/2"

cards have color photos on front, from which team logos have been airbrushed because the set was licensed only by the player, and not by MLB. Horizontally formatted backs have a second color photo along with a headline and a few sentences about his career to that point. The set was released in an edition of 30,000 and each was sold with a serial-numbered certificate of authenticity.

		NM/M
Complete Set (7):		3.00
Common Card:		.50
Autographed (# to 4,000):		15.00
1	Frank Thomas (A Good Start)	.50
nno	Frank Thomas (A Good Start-promo overprint on back.)	.50
2	Frank Thomas (Multi-Talented)	.50
3	Frank Thomas (Auburn Career)	.50
4	Frank Thomas (Accomplishments)	.50
5	Frank Thomas (Individual Honors)	.50
6	Frank Thomas (Minor League Stats)	.50
7	Frank Thomas (Major League Stats)	.50

1993 Front Row Gold Collection

Five borderless color photos (uniform logos removed) of Rollie Fingers are featured on the cards in this set. At bottom in a dark green stripe is the player name and, at left, the Front Row logo and the word "PREMIUM." Vertically at left is "The Gold Collection." All front printing is in gold foil. Backs have dark green borders with a ghost-image action photo and a few sentences about the player. A baseball at top carries the legend, "All Time Great / Series." Production was reported as 5,000 sets.

		NM/M
Complete Set (5):		2.00
Common Card:		.50
1-5	Rollie Fingers	.50

1999 FroZsnack's High-Screamers Lids

These 3-1/4" plastic lids were found on ice cream snacks sold at ballparks and possibly other outlets. A player photo with uniform logos covered is featured at center with personal data and 1998 stats on the side. The player name is in a banner at top, his team, position and career highlights are in a banner at bottom.

		NM/M
Complete Set (40):		30.00
Common Player:		.75
(1)	Roberto Alomar	.75
(2)	Jeff Bagwell	1.25
(3)	Albert Belle	.75
(4)	Dante Bichette	.75
(5)	Craig Biggio	.75
(6)	Barry Bonds	2.50
(7)	Kevin Brown	.75
(8)	Jose Canseco	1.00
(9)	Vinny Castilla	.75
(10)	Tony Clark	.75
(11)	Francisco Cordova	.75
(12)	Eric Davis	.75
(13)	Nomar Garciaparra	1.75
(14)	Tom Glavine	1.00
(15)	Ben Grieve	.75
(16)	Ken Griffey Jr.	2.00
(17)	Tony Gwynn	1.50
(18)	Rickey Henderson	1.25
(19)	Livan Hernandez	.75
(20)	Derek Jeter	2.50
(21)	Jason Kendall	.75
(22)	Randy Johnson	1.25
(23)	Barry Larkin	.75
(24)	Greg Maddux	1.50
(25)	Tino Martinez	.75
(26)	Mark McGwire	2.25
(27)	Robb Nen	.75
(28)	Mike Piazza	2.00
(29)	Manny Ramirez	1.25
(30)	Cal Ripken Jr.	2.50
(31)	Alex Rodriguez	2.25
(32)	Scott Rolen	1.00
(33)	Sammy Sosa	1.75
(34)	Frank Thomas	1.25
(35)	Greg Vaughn	.75
(36)	Fernando Vina	.75
(37)	Omar Vizquel	.75
(38)	Larry Walker	.75
(39)	Matt Williams	.75
(40)	Kerry Wood	1.00

1998 Fruit Roll-Ups All-Stars

Perforated panels of eight small (1-1/2" x 2") cards bearing the Topps logo were found on 38-count boxes of Fruit Roll-Ups snacks early in the 1998 season. The blank-back cards are printed on a 6" x 4" panel which can be removed from the box back. The front of the box pictures Rodriguez, Thomas and McGwire.

		NM/M
Complete Box:		5.00
Complete Panel:		4.00
Complete Set, Singles (8):		3.50
Common Player:		.50
(1)	Tony Gwynn	1.00
(2)	Derek Jeter	1.50
(3)	Kenny Lofton	.50
(4)	Mark McGwire	1.25
(5)	Mike Piazza	1.25
(6)	Cal Ripken Jr.	1.50
(7)	Ivan Rodriguez	.65
(8)	Frank Thomas	.75

1985 Fun Food Buttons

Fun Foods of Little Silver, N.J., issued a set of 133 full-color metal pins in 1985. The buttons, which are 1-1/4" in diameter and have a "safety pin" back, have bright borders which correspond to the player's team colors. The button backs are numbered and contain the player's 1984 batting or earned run average. The buttons were available as complete sets through hobby dealers and were also distributed in packs of three through retail stores. Cardboard 1-1/2" x 1-1/2" square proofs of the buttons' fronts are also seen in the hobby; their value is 2-3X that of the corresponding button, with production reported to be only 2,000 cardboard proofs.

		NM/M
Complete Set (133):		20.00
Common Player:		.10
Wax Pack (3):		.50
Wax Box (36):		9.00

1	Dave Winfield	1.00
2	Lance Parrish	.10
3	Gary Carter	1.00
4	Pete Rose	2.00
5	Jim Rice	.35
6	George Brett	1.75
7	Fernando Valenzuela	.10
8	Darryl Strawberry	.10
9	Steve Garvey	.45
10	Rollie Fingers	.75
11	Mike Schmidt	1.75
12	Kent Tekulve	.10
13	Ryne Sandberg	1.50
14	Bruce Sutter	.75
15	Tom Seaver	1.00
16	Reggie Jackson	1.50
17	Rickey Henderson	1.00
18	Mark Langston	.10
19	Jack Clark	.10
20	Willie Randolph	.10
21	Kirk Gibson	.10
22	Andre Dawson	.35
23	Dave Concepcion	.10
24	Tony Armas	.10
25	Dan Quisenberry	.10
26	Pedro Guerrero	.10
27	Dwight Gooden	.10
28	Tony Gwynn	1.50
29	Robin Yount	1.00
30	Steve Carlton	1.00
31	Bill Madlock	.10
32	Rick Sutcliffe	.10
33	Willie McGee	.10
34	Greg Luzinski	.10
35	Rod Carew	1.00
36	Dave Kingman	.10
37	Alvin Davis	.10
38	Chili Davis	.10
39	Don Baylor	.10
40	Alan Trammell	.10
41	Tim Raines	.10
42	Cesar Cedeno	.10
43	Wade Boggs	1.50
44	Frank White	.10
45	Steve Sax	.10
46	George Foster	.10
47	Terry Kennedy	.10
48	Cecil Cooper	.10
49	John Denny	.10
50	John Candelaria	.10
51	Jody Davis	.10
52	George Hendrick	.10
53	Ron Kittle	.10
54	Fred Lynn	.10
55	Carney Lansford	.10
56	Gorman Thomas	.10
57	Manny Trillo	.10
58	Steve Kemp	.10
59	Jack Morris	.10
60	Dan Petry	.10
61	Mario Soto	.10
62	Dwight Evans	.10
63	Hal McRae	.10
64	Mike Marshall	.10
65	Mookie Wilson	.10
66	Graig Nettles	.10
67	Ben Oglivie	.10
68	Juan Samuel	.10
69	Johnny Ray	.10
70	Gary Matthews	.10
71	Ozzie Smith	1.50
72	Carlton Fisk	1.00
73	Doug DeCinces	.10
74	Joe Morgan	1.00
75	Dave Stieb	.10
76	Buddy Bell	.10
77	Don Mattingly	1.75
78	Lou Whitaker	.10
79	Willie Hernandez	.10
80	Dave Parker	.10
81	Bob Stanley	.10
82	Willie Wilson	.10
83	Orel Hershiser	.10
84	Rusty Staub	.10
85	Goose Gossage	.10
86	Don Sutton	.75
87	Al Holland	.10
88	Tony Pena	.10
89	Ron Cey	.10
90	Joaquin Andujar	.10
91	LaMarr Hoyt	.10
92	Tommy John	.10
93	Dwayne Murphy	.10
94	Willie Upshaw	.10
95	Gary Ward	.10
96	Ron Guidry	.10
97	Chet Lemon	.10
98	Aurelio Lopez	.10
99	Tony Perez	.75
100	Bill Buckner	.10
101	Mike Hargrove	.10
102	Scott McGregor	.10
103	Dale Murphy	.50
104	Keith Hernandez	.10
105	Paul Molitor	1.00
106	Bert Blyleven	.10
107	Leon Durham	.10
108	Lee Smith	.10
109	Nolan Ryan	3.00
110	Harold Baines	.10
111	Kent Hrbek	.10
112	Ron Davis	.10
113	George Bell	.10
114	Charlie Hough	.10
115	Phil Niekro	.75
116	Dave Righetti	.10
117	Darrell Evans	.10
118	Cal Ripken, Jr.	3.00
119	Eddie Murray	1.00
120	Storm Davis	.10
121	Mike Boddicker	.10
122	Bob Horner	.10
123	Chris Chambliss	.10
124	Ted Simmons	.10
125	Andre Thornton	.10
126	Larry Bowa	.10
127	Bob Dernier	.10
128	Joe Niekro	.10
129	Jose Cruz	.10
130	Tom Brunansky	.10
131a	Garry Gaetti	50.00
131b	Gary Gaetti	.10
132	Lloyd Moseby	.10
133	Frank Tanana	.10

G

1982 Renata Galasso 20 Years of Met Baseball

The original New York Mets team of 1962 is featured on this 20-year anniversary set. The 2-1/2" x 3-1/2" cards have black-and-white photos with blue borders. The player name and position is in orange at bottom. Backs repeat the team colors with blue and orange printing on white cardboard. Card and uniform numbers appear in the top corners, there is a career summary, 1962 and career stats and a trivia question. Production was reported as 2,500 sets.

		NM/M
Complete Set (30):		10.00
Common Player:		.50
1	Marv Throneberry	.75
2	Richie Ashburn	2.00
3	Charlie Neal	.50
4	Cliff Cook	.50
5	Elio Chacon	.50
6	Chris Cannizzaro	.50
7	Jim Hickman	.50
8	Rod Kanehl	.50
9	Gene Woodling	.50
10	Gil Hodges	2.00
11	Al Jackson	.50
12	Sammy Taylor	.50
13	Felix Mantilla	.50
14	Ken MacKenzie	.50
15	Craig Anderson	.50
16	Bob Moorhead	.50
17	Joe Christopher	.50
18	Bob Miller	.50
19	Frank Thomas	.75
20	Vinegar Bend Mizell	.50
21	Bill Hunter	.50
22	Roger Craig	.50
23	Jay Hook	.50
24	Meet The Mets (Team card.)	.75
25	Choo Choo Coleman	.50
26	Casey Stengel	2.00
28	Solly Hemus	.50
29	Rogers Hornsby	2.00
31	Red Ruffing	.50
32	George Weiss	.50

1983 Renata Galasso 1933 All-Stars

The premiere All-Star Game in 1933 is commemorated in this 50th anniversary collectors' issue. In standard 2-1/2" x 3-1/2" format (though not uniformly cut to exact size), the cards feature black-and-white portrait photos on front. Many of the National League All-Stars are pictured in their special NL uniforms. In the wide white border at bottom is the player's name, position and league. Backs are printed in red, white and blue with a large Galasso ad and a short career summary; there is little mention of the 1933 All-Star Game. Two

CHUCK KLEIN
OUTFIELDER – NATIONAL LEAGUE

unnumbered cards issued with the set have N.L. and A.L. team photos on front and blue-tone backs showing A-S managers Connie Mack and John McGraw "choosing up sides."

		NM/M
Complete Set (45):		15.00
Common Player:		1.00
1	Tony Cuccinello	1.00
2	Lon Warenke (Warneke)	1.00
3	Hal Schumacher	1.00
4	Wally Berger	1.00
5	Lefty O'Doul	1.00
6	Chuck Klein	1.00
7	Chick Hafey	1.00
8	Jimmie Wilson	1.00
9	John McGraw	1.00
10	Max Carey	1.00
11	Bill McKechnie	1.00
12	Dick Bartell	1.00
13	Bill Hallahan	1.00
14	Woody English	1.00
15	Paul Waner	1.00
16	Carl Hubbell	1.50
17	Frank Frisch	1.00
18	Gabby Hartnett	1.00
19	Pie Traynor	1.00
20	Bill Terry	1.00
21	Pepper Martin	1.00
22	Earl Averill	1.00
23	Jimmy Dykes	1.00
24	Charlie Gehringer	1.50
25	Rich Ferrell (Rick)	1.00
26	Joe Cronin	1.00
27	Ben Chapman	1.00
28	Eddie Rommel	1.00
29	Lefty Grove	1.50
30	Connie Mack	1.00
31	Babe Ruth	5.00
32	Sam West	1.00
33	Tony Lazzeri	1.00
34	Al Simmons	1.00
35	Wes Ferrell	1.00
36	Bill Dickey	1.00
37	General Crowder	1.00
38	Oral Hildebrand	1.00
39	Lefty Gomez	1.00
40	Jimmie Foxx	1.50
41	Art Fletcher	1.00
42	Eddie Collins	1.00
43	Lou Gehrig	3.00
(44)	1933 N.L. All-Star Team	2.00
(45)	1933 A.L. All-Star Team	2.00

1983 Renata Galasso 1969 Seattle Pilots

JIM BOUTON
PITCHER

The one-year American League franchise in Seattle is recalled with this collectors' issue. Full-color photos of the peripatetic Pilots are framed in team-color blue and gold on a beige background in standard 2-1/2" x 3-1/2" size. Backs are printed in red and blue on white and feature a career summary and 1969 stats. For some players, this represents their only baseball card appearance and for many more, it is their only card in a Pilots' uniform. Many of the sets were originally sold with the #1 Jim Bouton card personally autographed.

		NM/M
Complete Set (43):		15.00
Common Player:		.50
1	Jim Bouton	2.00
1(a)	Jim Bouton/Auto.	15.00
2	Joe Schultz	.50
3	Bill Edgerton	.70
4	Gary Timberlake	.70
5	Dick Baney	.50
6	Mike G. Marshall	1.00
7	Jim Gosger	.50
8	Mike Hegan	.50
9	Steve Hovley	.50
10	Don Mincher	.50
11	Miguel Fuentes	.50
12	Charlie Bates	.50
13	John O'Donoghue	.50
14	Tommy Davis	.75
15	Jerry McNertney	.50
16	Rich Rollins	.50
17	Fred Talbot	.50
18	John Gelnar	.50
19	Bob Locker	.50
20	Frank Crosetti	.75
21	Sal Maglie	.75
22	Sibby Sisti	.50
23	Ron Plaza	.50
24	Federico Velazquez	.50
25	Diego Segui	.50
26	Steve Barber	.50
27	Jack Aker	.50
28	Marty Pattin	.50
29	Ray Oyler	.50
30	Danny Walton	.75
31	Merritt Ranew	.50
32	John Donaldson	.50
33	Greg Goossen	.50
34	Gary Bell	.50
35	Jim Pagliaroni	.50
36	Mike Ferraro	.50
37	Tommy Harper	.75
38	John Morris	.50
39	Larry Haney	.50
40	Ron Clark	.50
41	Steve Whitaker	.50
42	Wayne Comer	.50
43	Gene Brabender	.50

1984 Renata Galasso Baseball Collector Series

Some of baseball's best are presented in this glossy-front black-and-white, 2-3/8" x 3-1/2", collectors' set patterned after the 1953 Bowmans. Backs are in red and black with a career summary and lifetime stats.

		NM/M
Complete Set (20):		15.00
Common Player:		.50
1	Roberto Clemente	1.50
2	Duke Snider	.75
3	Sandy Koufax	1.50
4	Carl Hubbell	.50
5	Ty Cobb	1.00
6	Willie Mays	1.50
7	Jackie Robinson	1.50
8	Joe DiMaggio	3.00
9	Stan Musial	1.00
10	Pie Traynor	.50
11	Yogi Berra	.75
12	Babe Ruth	3.00
13	Brooks Robinson	.50
14	Walter Johnson	.50
15	Ted Williams	1.50
16	Bill Dickey	.50
17	Lou Gehrig	2.00
18	Hank Aaron	1.50
19	Eddie Mathews	.50
20	Mickey Mantle	5.00

Hall of Fame Art Card Series

Painting on these 2-7/8" x 5" deckle-edge cards are by Ron Lewis and depict Hall of Famers induction between 1936-46. There are no graphics or player identification on the front. Backs are printed in red and black and have player personal data, career highlights and lifetime stats within a decorative shield.

	NM/M
Complete Set (45):	15.00
Common Player:	.50
1	Ty Cobb	3.00
2	Babe Ruth	5.00
3	Walter Johnson	1.50
4	Christy Mathewson	1.50
5	Honus Wagner	1.50
6	Napoleon Lajoie	.75
7	Tris Speaker	.75
8	Cy Young	1.50
9	Morgan Bulkeley	.50
10	Ban Johnson	.50
11	John McGraw	.50
12	Connie Mack	.50
13	George Wright	.50
14	Grover Alexander	1.00
15	Alexander Cartwright	.50
16	Henry Chadwick	.50
17	Eddie Collins	.50
18	Lou Gehrig	4.00
19	Willie Keeler	.50
20	George Sisler	.50
21	Cap Anson	.50
22	Charles Comiskey	.50
23	Candy Cummings	.50
24	Buck Ewing	.50
25	Charlie Radbourne	.50
26	A.G. Spalding	.50
27	Roger (Rogers) Hornsby	.75
28	Kenesaw M. Landis	.50
29	Roger Bresnahan	.50
30	Dan Brouthers	.50
31	Fred Clarke	.50
32	Jimmy Collins	.50
33	Ed Delahanty	.50
34	Hugh Duffy	.50
35	Mike "King" Kelly	.50
36	Hughie Jennings	.50
37	Jim O'Rourke	.50
38	Wilbert Robinson	.50
39	Jesse Burkett	.50
40	Frank Chance	.50
41	Jack Chesbro	.50
42	Johnny Evers	.50
43	Joe Tinker	.50
44	Eddie Plank	.50
45	Checklist	

Reggie Jackson

This collectors' issue chronicling the career of "Mr. October" was produced in two sizes - the standard 2-1/2" x 3-1/2" and the Topps' "mini" format of 2-1/4" x 3-1/8". Both sizes share the same design of a color or black-and-white photo on a blue border with "Reggie 44" at bottom, along with a photo of his classic swing. Backs have statistical data, career summary or part of a puzzle showing all of Jackson's Topps cards to that point. The full-size set was limited to 10,000, with 500 featuring a genuine autograph on card #1; the mini set was issued in an edition of 5,000.

	NM/M
Complete Standard-Size Set (30):	7.50
Complete Set w/Auto. #1:	45.00

Willie Mays Story

Complete Mini Set (30):	10.00
Common Card:	.40

Color and black-and-white photos from the Hall of Famer's career and off-field life are featured in this collectors' set. Each photo is surrounded with a red frame and white border. Many of the photos will be familiar to collectors as having earlier appeared on Topps cards. Backs of the first 45 cards are in red, black and white, with biographical information or a description of the front photo. Backs of cards #46-90 can be assembled into a full-color puzzle of Mays' baseball cards from Topps, Bowman and others. Card #1 in each set is authentically autographed by Mays. Retail price at issue was $20.

	NM/M
Complete Set (90):	35.00
Common Card:	.50

1927 N.Y. Yankees

Paintings by Ron Lewis adorn this collectors' issue honoring what may have been been baseball's best team ever. The 2-1/2" x 3-1/2" cards have blue borders with the player's name in a banner at bottom. Backs have typical player data plus 1927 and career stats. The set was originally issued at about $5.

		NM/M
Complete Set (30):		18.00
Common Player:		.50
1	Lou Gehrig	5.00
2	Babe Ruth	7.50
3	Earle Combs	1.00
4	Ed Barrow	.50
5	Bob Shawkey	.50
6	Bob Meusel	.50
7	Urban Shocker	.50
8	Ben Paschal	.50
9	John Grabowski	.50
10	Jacob Ruppert	.50
11	Herb Pennock	1.00
12	Miller Huggins	1.00
13	Wilcy Moore	.50
14	Walter Beall	.50
15	Cedric Durst	.50
16	Tony Lazzeri	1.00
17	Mark Koenig	.50
18	Waite Hoyt	1.00
19	Myles Thomas	.50
20	Joe Dugan	.50
21	Art Fletcher	.50
22	Charlie O'Leary	.50
23	Ray Morehart	.50
24	Benny Bengough	.50
25	Pat Collins	.50
26	Dutch Reuther (Ruether)	.50
27	George Pipgras	.50
28	Mike Gazella	.50
29	Julian Wera	.50
30	Joe Giard	.50

1985 Renata Galasso Dwight Gooden

	NM/M
Complete Set (30):	6.00
Single Card:	.50

1986 Renata Galasso 1961 Yankees Black-and-White

Illustrating one of the problems with collectors' issues, a person holding one of these cards might assume it is of 1961 or 1962 vintage because there is no date of actual is-

This collectors' issue was produced by Brooklyn dealer Renata Galasso as one of several to capitalize on Gooden's early fame. Card #1 features a Ron Lewis painting of Gooden, the others feature color photos from his boyhood and early career. (Card #16 pictures him shaking hands with Henry Aaron.) Photos are surrounded on front with a border of blue squares. A pink "DR. K" logo is at bottom-right. Backs are inblue and white and feature a question and answer session with the pitcher, stats, or part of a nine-piece puzzle. Five thousand sets were produced, with 500 of them featuring Gooden's autograph on Card #1. Issue price was about $11.

	NM/M
Complete Set (30):	4.00
Complete Autographed Set:	15.00
Single Card:	.15

1986 Renata Galasso Dwight Gooden

Dr. K's Cy Young Season in 1985 is recalled in this collectors' set. Numbered from 31-60, picking up where the 1985 set had left off, the series share a similar format. Fronts have black-and-white or color photos surrounded by a frame of blue dots and larger orange squares. A blue "Dr. K" appears in the lower-right corner. Backs are in blue and orange on white and narrate the 1985 season. The final nine cards in the set have pieces forming a puzzle picture of Gooden.

	NM/M
Complete Set (30):	4.00
Single Card:	.15

Don Mattingly

The life and career of the Yankees superstar is traced in this collectors' issue. The 2-1/2" x 3-1/2" cards have a mix of black-and-white and color photos on a white background with blue pinstripes. A yellow circle in a bottom corner of each card front has "THE HIT MAN" in red. Backs are printed in blue, with 21 of them featuring a question-and-answer format and nine forming a puzzle picture of Mattingly.

	NM/M
Complete Set (30):	6.00
Single Card:	.50

sue, which occurred around 1986, anywhere on the cards. In a format similar to Topps' 1961 cards, this set features large black-and-white player photos on a 2-1/2" x 3-1/2" glossy stock. The player name and position are in a pair of color bars at bottom. Backs are in red and black and have personal data, season and career stats, a 1961 season summary and a trivia question. Reported production was 2,500.

ROGER MARIS OUTFIELDER

		NM/M
Complete Set (30):		20.00
Common Player:		.50
1	Roger Maris	3.00
2	Bobby Richardson	.75
3	Tony Kubek	.75
4	Elston Howard	.75
5	Bill Skowron	.75
6	Clete Boyer	.50
7	Mickey Mantle	7.50
8	Yogi Berra	2.00
9	Johnny Blanchard	.50
10	Hector Lopez	.50
11	Whitey Ford	2.00
12	Ralph Terry	.50
13	Bill Stafford	.50
14	Bud Daley	.50
15	Billy Gardner	.50
16	Jim Coates	.50
17	Luis Arroyo	.50
18	Tex Clevenger	.50
19	Bob Cerv	.50
20	Art Ditmar	.50
21	Bob Turley	.50
22	Joe DeMaestri	.50
23	Rollie Sheldon	.50
24	Earl Torgeson	.50
25	Hal Reniff	.50
26	Ralph Houk	.50
27	Jim Hegan	.50
28	Johnny Sain	.60
29	Frank Crosetti	.50
30	Wally Moses	.50

1961 Yankees Color

MICKEY MANTLE Outfielder

The World Champion N.Y. Yankees of 1961 are remembered in this collectors' set. The 2-1/2" x 3-1/2" cards borrow the design of Topps' 1961 issue, with a large color photo at top and red and yellow boxes below with player name and position in contrasting color. Backs are printed in blue and red with a few biographical details, 1961 and career stats and a career summary.

		NM/M
Complete Set (37):		15.00
Common Player:		.25
1	Roger Maris	3.00
2	Yogi Berra	1.50
3	Whitey Ford	1.50
4	Hector Lopez	.25
5	Bob Turley	.25
6	Frank Crosetti	.25
7	Bob Cerv	.25
8	Jack Reed	.25
9	Luis Arroyo	.25
10	Danny McDevitt	.25
11	Duke Maas	.25
12	Jesse Gonder	.25

13	Ralph Terry	.25
14	Deron Johnson	.25
15	Johnny Blanchard	.25
16	Bill Stafford	.25
17	Earl Torgeson	.25
18	Tony Kubek	.40
19	Rollie Sheldon	.25
20	Tex Clevenger	.25
21	Art Ditmar	.25
22	Bud Daley	.25
23	Jim Coates	.25
24	Al Downing	.25
25	Johnny Sain	.25
26	Jim Hegan	.25
27	Wally Moses	.25
28	Ralph Houk	.25
29	Bill Skowron	.40
30	Bobby Richardson	.40
31	Johnny James	.25
32	Hal Reniff	.25
33	Mickey Mantle	6.00
34	Clete Boyer	.25
35	Elston Howard	.35
36	Joe DeMaestri	.25
37	Billy Gardner	.25

1983 Gardner's Brewers

PETE VUCKOVICH
BREWERS P

Topps produced in 1983 for Gardner's Bakery of Madison Wis., a 22-card set featuring the American League champion Milwaukee Brewers. The cards, which measure 2-1/2" x 3-1/2", have colorful fronts which contain the player's name, team and position plus the Brewers and Gardner's logos. The card backs are identical to the regular Topps issue but are numbered 1-22. The cards were inserted in specially marked packages of Gardner's bread products and were susceptible to grease stains.

		NM/M
Complete Set (22):		8.00
Common Player:		.25
1	Harvey Kuenn	.25
2	Dwight Bernard	.25
3	Mark Brouhard	.25
4	Mike Caldwell	.25
5	Cecil Cooper	.25
6	Marshall Edwards	.25
7	Rollie Fingers	1.00
8	Jim Gantner	.25
9	Moose Haas	.25
10	Bob McClure	.25
11	Paul Molitor	4.00
12	Don Money	.25
13	Charlie Moore	.25
14	Ben Oglivie	.25
15	Ed Romero	.25
16	Ted Simmons	.25
17	Jim Slaton	.25
18	Don Sutton	1.00
19	Gorman Thomas	.25
20	Pete Vuckovich	.25
21	Ned Yost	.25
22	Robin Yount	4.00

1984 Gardner's Brewers

DON SUTTON P
1984 SERIES II

For the second straight year, Gardner's Bakery inserted baseball cards featuring the Milwaukee Brewers with its bread products. The 22-card set, entitled "1984 Series II," have multi-colored fronts that include the Brewers and Gardner's logos. The card backs are identical to the regular 1984 Topps issue except for the 1-22 numbering system. The Topps-produced cards are the standard 2-1/2" x 3-1/2" size. The cards are sometimes found with grease stains, resulting from contact with the bread.

		NM/M
Complete Set (22):		5.00
Common Player:		.25
1	Rene Lachemann	.25
2	Mark Brouhard	.25
3	Mike Caldwell	.25
4	Bobby Clark	.25
5	Cecil Cooper	.25
6	Rollie Fingers	.50
7	Jim Gantner	.25
8	Moose Haas	.25
9	Roy Howell	.25
10	Pete Ladd	.25
11	Rick Manning	.25
12	Bob McClure	.25
13	Paul Molitor	3.00
14	Charlie Moore	.25
15	Ben Oglivie	.25
16	Ed Romero	.25
17	Ted Simmons	.25
18	Jim Sundberg	.25
19	Don Sutton	.50
20	Tom Tellmann	.25
21	Pete Vuckovich	.25
22	Robin Yount	3.00

1985 Gardner's Brewers

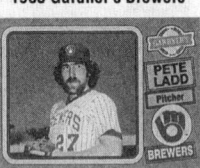

PETE LADD
Pitcher
BREWERS

Gardner's Bakery issued a 22-card set featuring the Milwaukee Brewers for the third consecutive year in 1985. The set was produced by Topps and is designed in a horizontal format. The card fronts feature color photos inside blue, red and yellow frames. The player's name and position are placed in orange boxes to the right of the photo and are accompanied by the Brewers and Gardner's logos. The card backs are identical to the regular 1985 Topps set but are blue rather than green and are numbered 1-22. The cards, which were inserted in specially marked bread products, are often found with grease stains.

		NM/M
Complete Set (22):		5.00
Common Player:		.25
1	George Bamberger	.25
2	Mark Brouhard	.25
3	Bob Clark	.25
4	Jaime Cocanower	.25
5	Cecil Cooper	.25
6	Rollie Fingers	.50
7	Jim Gantner	.25
8	Moose Haas	.25
9	Dion James	.25
10	Pete Ladd	.25
11	Rick Manning	.25
12	Bob McClure	.25
13	Paul Molitor	3.00
14	Charlie Moore	.25
15	Ben Oglivie	.25
16	Chuck Porter	.25
17	Ed Romero	.25
18	Bill Schroeder	.25
19	Ted Simmons	.25
20	Tom Tellmann	.25
21	Pete Vuckovich	.25
22	Robin Yount	3.00

1989 Gardner's Brewers

ROBIN YOUNT
MILWAUKEE BREWERS OUTFIELD

Returning after a three-year hiatus, Gardner's Bread of Madison, Wis., issued a 15-card Milwaukee Brewers set in 1989. The blue and white-bordered cards are the standard size and feature posed portrait photos with all Brewer logos airbrushed from the players' caps. The Gardner's logo appears at the top of the card, while the player's name is below the photo. The set, which was produced in conjunction with Mike Schechter Associates, was issued with loaves of bread or packages of buns, one card per bread.

		NM/M
Complete Set (15):		5.00
Common Player:		.25
1	Paul Molitor	2.50
2	Robin Yount	2.50
3	Jim Gantner	.25
4	Rob Deer	.25
5	B.J. Surhoff	.25
6	Dale Sveum	.25
7	Ted Higuera	.25
8	Dan Plesac	.25
9	Bill Wegman	.25
10	Juan Nieves	.25
11	Greg Brock	.25
12	Glenn Braggs	.25
13	Joey Meyer	.25
14	Ernest Riles	.25
15	Don August	.25

1986 Gatorade Cubs

CHICAGO CUBS
(19) MANNY TRILLO, IF

Gatorade sponsored this set which was given away at the July 17, 1986, Cubs game. Cards measure 2-7/8" x 4-1/4" and feature color photos inside red and white frames. The Cubs logo appears at the top of the card. Backs include statistical information and the Gatorade logo. This set marked the fifth consecutive year the Cubs had held a baseball card giveaway promotion.

		NM/M
Complete Set (28):		12.00
Common Player:		.25
4	Gene Michael	.25
6	Keith Moreland	.25
7	Jody Davis	.25
10	Leon Durham	.25
11	Ron Cey	.25
12	Shawon Dunston	.25
15	Davey Lopes	.25
16	Terry Francona	.25
18	Steve Christmas	.25
19	Manny Trillo	.25
20	Bob Dernier	.25
21	Scott Sanderson	.25
22	Jerry Mumphrey	.25
23	Ryne Sandberg	9.00
27	Thad Bosley	.25
28	Chris Speier	.25
29	Steve Lake	.25
31	Ray Fontenot	.25
34	Steve Trout	.25
36	Gary Matthews	.25
39	George Frazier	.25
43	Rick Sutcliffe	.35
46	Dennis Eckersley	1.50
46	Lee Smith	.35
48	Jay Baller	.25
49	Jamie Moyer	.25
50	Guy Hoffman	.25
---	The Coaching Staff (Ruben Amaro, Billy Connors, Johnny Oates, John Vukovich, Billy Williams)	.25

1987 Gatorade Indians

For the second year in a row, the Indians gave out a perforated set of baseball cards to fans attending the Team Photo/Baseball Card Day promotion. Sponsored by Gatorade, the individual cards measure 2-1/2" x 3-1/8". Fronts contain a color photo surrounded by a red frame inside a white border. The player's name, uniform number and the Gatorade logo are also on front. Backs are printed in black, blue and red and carry a facsimile autograph and the player's stats.

		NM/M
Complete Set, Foldout:		6.00
Complete Set, Singles (31):		6.00
Common Player:		.25
2	Brett Butler	.25
6	Tony Bernazard	.25
8	Andy Allanson	.25
8	Pat Corrales	.25
8	Carmen Castillo	.25
11	Pat Tabler	.25
12	Jamie Easterly	.25
12	Dave Clark	.25
13	Ernie Camacho	.25
14	Julio Franco	.35
17	Junior Noboa	.25
18	Ken Schrom	.25
20	Otis Nixon	.25
21	Greg Swindell	.25
22	Frank Wills	.25
23	Chris Bando	.25
24	Rick Dempsey	.25
26	Brook Jacoby	.25
27	Mel Hall	.25
28	Cory Snyder	.25
29	Andre Thornton	.35
30	Joe Carter	.75
35	Phil Niekro	.75
36	Ed Vande Berg	.25
42	Rich Yett	.25
43	Scott Bailes	.25
46	Doug Jones	.25
49	Tom Candiotti	.25
54	Tom Waddell	.25
---	Manager and Coaching Staff (Jack Aker, Bobby Bonds, Pat Corrales, Doc Edwards, Johnny Goryl)	.25
---	Team Photo	.25

1988 Gatorade Indians

(52) JOHN FARRELL, P
COMPLIMENTS OF Gatorade

This three-panel foldout was sponsored by Gatorade for distribution during an in-stadium giveaway. The cover includes four game-action photos. One panel of the 9-1/2" x 11-1/4" glossy color foldout features a team photo (with checklist), two panels consist of 30 perforated baseball cards (2-1/4" x 3") featuring team members. Posed portrait photos are framed in red on a white background. The player's name and uniform number are printed below the photo. Backs are printed in red, blue and black. A facsimile autograph appears at the top-right of the card back, opposite the player uniform number, name and position. Both major and minor league stats are listed.

		NM/M
Complete Set, Foldout:		5.00
Complete Set, Singles (31):		5.00
Common Player:		.25
2	Tom Spencer	.25
6	Andy Allanson	.25
8	Luis Issac	.25
9	Carmen Castillo	.25
10	Pat Tabler	.25
11	Doug Jones	.25
15	Julio Franco	.50
16	Ron Washington	.25
16	Jay Bell	.75
17	Bill Laskey	.25
20	Willie Upshaw	.25
21	Greg Swindell	.25
23	Chris Bando	.25
25	Dave Clark	.25
26	Brook Jacoby	.25
27	Mel Hall	.25
28	Cory Snyder	.25
30	Joe Carter	.75
31	Dan Schatzeder	.25
32	Doc Edwards	.25
33	Ron Kittle	.25
42	Mark Wiley	.25
42	Rich Yett	.25
43	Scott Bailes	.25
46	Johnny Goryl	.25
47	Jeff Kaiser	.25
49	Tom Candiotti	.25
50	Jeff Dedmon	.25
52	John Farrell	.25
---	Team Photo	2.00

1993 Gatorade Detroit Tigers

ALAN TRAMMELL

Color action photos are featured on these oversized (2-7/8" x 4-1/4") cards. The pictures are framed in team-color navy and orange pinstripes with a white border. Player name is in white in a navy border below the photo, with the position printed in orange at bottom. A large team logo appears in the upper-right corner. Backs are printed in orange and black and include a Gatorade logo, player identification and stats. Cards are listed here by uniform number.

		NM/M
Complete Set (28):		4.00
Common Player:		.25
1	Lou Whitaker	.75
3	Alan Trammell	1.00
4	Tony Phillips	.25
7	Scott Livingstone	.25
9	Skeeter Barnes	.25
14	Sparky Anderson	.75
15	Gary Thurman	.25
16	David Wells	.25
18	David Haas	.25
19	Chad Kreuter	.25
20	Mickey Tettleton	.25
21	Mike Moore	.25
22	Milt Cuyler	.25
23a	Kirk Gibson	.50
23b	Mark Leiter	.50
27	Travis Fryman	.50
27	Kurt Knudsen	.25
28	Rob Deer	.25
30	Bill Krueger	.25
32	Dan Gladden	.25
36	Bill Gullickson	.25
38	Bob MacDonald	.25
39	Mike Henneman	.25
44	Buddy Groom	.25
44	John Doherty	.25
45	Cecil Fielder	.50
49	Tom Bolton	.25
---	Coaches (Dick Tracewksi, Billy Muffett, Larry Herndon, Gene Roof, Dan Whitmer)	.25

1995 Gatorade Cubs

SHAWON DUNSTON-12
INFIELDER

Fans attending the August 24 game at Wrigley Field received a set of oversized (2-7/8" x 4-1/4") cards of the Chicago Cubs, sponsored by Gatorade. Cards feature a color action photo at top, with the player's name, position and uniform number in a blue box at bottom. Backs have a small black-and-white portrait photo, complete minor and major league stats and the team and sponsor logos. Cards are checklisted here by player uniform number.

		NM/M
Complete Set (27):		5.00
Common Player:		.25
5	Jim Riggleman	.25
9	Scott Servais	.25
10	Scott Bullett	.25
11	Rey Sanchez	.25
12	Shawon Dunston	.25
16	Turk Wendell	.25
17	Anthony Young	.25
18	Mark Grace	.50
19	Jose Hernandez	.25
20	Howard Johnson	.25
23	Sammy Sosa	4.00
25	Luis Gonzalez	.50
27	Todd Zeile	.25
28	Randy Myers	.25
29	Jose Guzman	.25
30	Ozzie Timmons	.25
32	Kevin Foster	.25
38	Jaime Navarro	.25
46	Steve Trachsel	.25
47	Mike Perez	.25
49	Frank Castillo	.25
52	Jim Bullinger	.25
53	Chris Nabholz	.25
55	Larry Casian	.25
56	Brian McRae	.25
57	Rich Garces	.25
---	Cubs Coaches (Dave Bialas, Fergie Jenkins, Tony Muser, Max Oliveras, Dan Radison, Billy Williams)	.25

1997 Gatorade Cubs

This postcard-size set was a stadium give-away. Fronts have game-action photos on a green ivy background. Backs have player data and stats. The set is arranged here alphabetically.

		NM/M
Complete Set (26):		8.00
Common Player:		.25
(1)	Terry Adams	.25
(2)	Kent Bottenfield	.25
(3)	Brant Brown	.25
(4)	Dave Clark	.25
(5)	Shawon Dunston	.25
(6)	Kevin Foster	.25
(7)	Doug Glanville	.25
(8)	Jeremi Gonzalez	.25
(9)	Mark Grace	.50
(10)	Dave Hansen	.25
(11)	Jose Hernandez	.25
(12)	Tyler Houston	.25
(13)	Brian McRae	.25
(14)	Kevin Orie	.25
(15)	Bob Patterson	.25
(16)	Jim Riggleman	.25
(17)	Mel Rojas	.25
(18)	Rey Sanchez	.25
(19)	Ryne Sandberg	4.00
(20)	Scott Servais	.25
(21)	Sammy Sosa	4.00
(22)	Kevin Tapani	.25
(23)	Ramon Tatis	.25
(24)	Steve Traschel	.25
(25)	Turk Wendell	.25
(26)	Cubs Coaches (Rick Kranitz, Jeff Pentland, Mako Oliveras, Dan Radison, Phil Regan, Billy Williams)	.25

1985 General Mills Stickers

OZZIE SMITH   DAVE WINFIELD

General Mills of Canada inserted a panel of two cellophane-wrapped baseball stickers in each box of Cheerios in 1985. The full-color sticker panels, measuring 2-3/8" x 3-3/4", are blank-backed and unnumbered and contain the player's name, team and position in both English and French. The General Mills logo appears at the top of each sticker. All team insignia on the players' uniforms and caps have been airbrushed off.

	NM/M
Complete Panel Set (15):	10.00

Complete Singles Set (26):		7.00
Common Panel:		.50
Common Player:		.25
Panel (1)		1.25
(1)	Gary Carter	.50
(2)	Tom Brunansky	.25
Panel (2)		1.25
(1)	Gary Carter	.50
(3)	Dave Steib	.25
Panel (3)		1.00
(4)	Andre Dawson	.35
(5)	Alvin Davis	.25
Panel (4)		1.00
(4)	Andre Dawson	.35
(3)	Dave Steib	.25
Panel (5)		1.00
(6)	Steve Garvey	.35
(7)	Buddy Bell	.25
Panel (6)		1.25
(6)	Steve Garvey	.35
(8)	Jim Rice	.30
Panel (7)		1.00
(9)	Jeff Leonard	.25
(10)	Eddie Murray	.50
Panel (8)		1.50
(11)	Dale Murphy	.35
(12)	Robin Yount	.50
Panel (9)		1.50
(13)	Terry Puhl	.25
(14)	Reggie Jackson	.60
Panel (10)		.50
(15)	Johnny Ray	.25
(16)	Lou Whitaker	.25
Panel (11)		1.00
(17)	Ryne Sandberg	.75
(18)	Mike Hargrove	.25
Panel (12)		2.00
(19)	Mike Schmidt	.75
(20)	George Brett	.75
Panel (13)		2.00
(21)	Ozzie Smith	.60
(22)	Dave Winfield	.75
Panel (14)		1.25
(23)	Mario Soto	.25
(24)	Carlton Fisk	.50
Panel (15)		1.00
(25)	Fernando Valenzuela	.25
(26)	Dwayne Murphy	.25

1986 General Mills Booklets

In 1986, General Mills of Canada inserted six different "Baseball Players Booklets" in specially marked boxes of Cheerios. Ten different players are featured in each booklet, with statistics for the 1985 season in both English and French. The booklet, when opened fully, measures 3-3/4" x 15". Also included in the booklet is a contest sponsored by Petro-Canada service stations to win a day with a major league player at his 1987 spring training site in Florida. Team insignias have been airbrushed off the players' uniforms and caps.

		NM/M
Complete Set (6):		12.50
Common Booklet:		1.25
1	A.L. East (Wade Boggs, Kirk Gibson, Rickey Henderson, Don Mattingly, Jack Morris, Lance Parrish, Jim Rice, Dave Righetti, Cal Ripken, Lou Whitaker)	4.00
2	A.L. West (Harold Baines, Phil Bradley, George Brett, Carlton Fisk, Ozzie Guillen, Kent Hrbek, Reggie Jackson, Dan Quisenberry, Bret Saberhagen, Frank White)	2.50
3	Toronto Blue Jays (Jesse Barfield, George Bell, Bill Caudill, Tony Fernandez, Damaso Garcia, Lloyd Moseby, Rance Mulliniks, Dave Stieb, Willie Upshaw, Ernie Whitt)	2.00
4	N.L. East (Gary Carter, Jack Clark, George Foster, Dwight Gooden, Gary Matthews, Willie McGee,	

	Ryne Sandberg, Mike Schmidt, Lee Smith, Ozzie Smith)	2.50
5	N.L. West (Dave Concepcion, Pedro Guerrero, Terry Kennedy, Dale Murphy, Graig Nettles, Dave Parker, Tony Perez, Steve Sax, Bruce Sutter, Fernando Valenzuela)	1.25
6	Montreal Expos (Hubie Brooks, Andre Dawson, Mike Fitzgerald, Vance Law, Tim Raines, Jeff Reardon, Bryn Smith, Jason Thompson, Tim Wallach, Mitch Webster)	2.00

1987 General Mills Booklets

For a second straight year, General Mills of Canada inserted one of six different "Baseball Super-Stars Booklets" in specially marked boxes of Cheerios and Honey Nut Cheerios cereal. Each booklet contains ten full-color photos for a total of 60 players. The booklets, when completely unfolded, measure 15" x 3-3/4". Written in both English and French, the set was produced by Mike Schechter and Associates. All team insignias have been airbrushed off the photos.

		NM/M
Complete Set (6):		9.00
Common Booklet:		2.00
1	Toronto Blue Jays (Jesse Barfield, George Bell, Tony Fernandez, Kelly Gruber, Tom Henke, Jimmy Key, Lloyd Moseby, Dave Stieb, Willie Upshaw, Ernie Whitt)	2.00
2	A.L. East (Wade Boggs, Roger Clemens, Kirk Gibson, Rickey Henderson, Don Mattingly, Jack Morris, Eddie Murray, Pat Tabler, Dave Winfield, Robin Yount)	4.00
3	A.L. West (Phil Bradley, George Brett, Jose Canseco, Carlton Fisk, Reggie Jackson, Wally Joyner, Kirk McCaskill, Larry Parrish, Kirby Puckett, Dan Quisenberry)	2.50
4	Montreal Expos (Hubie Brooks, Mike Fitzgerald, Andres Galarraga, Vance Law, Andy McGaffigan, Bryn Smith, Jason Thompson, Tim Wallach, Mitch Webster, Floyd Youmans)	2.00
5	N.L. East (Gary Carter, Dwight Gooden, Keith Hernandez, Willie McGee, Tim Raines, R.J. Reynolds, Ryne Sandberg, Mike Schmidt, Ozzie Smith, Darryl Strawberry)	2.50
6	N.L. West (Kevin Bass, Chili Davis, Bill Doran, Pedro Guerrero, Tony Gwynn, Dale Murphy, Dave Parker, Steve Sax, Mike Scott, Fernando Valenzuela)	2.00

1990 Giant Eagle Roberto Clemente Stickers

The Giant Eagle food stores around Pittsburgh issued a collectors' poster and set of 18 stickers circa 1990. Each of the 2-1/2" x 3-1/2" stickers features one of Roberto Clemente's regular-issue Topps cards 1955-72. The stickers were originally issued in strips of three.

Backs are blank. The issue was almost certainly not authorized by Topps or the Clemente estate.

	NM/M
Complete Set, Strips (6):	20.00
Common Sticker:	2.00
Poster:	16.00

1981 Granny Goose Potato Chips A's

The 1981 Granny Goose set features the Oakland A's. The 2-1/2" x 3-1/2" cards were issued in bags of potato chips and are sometimes found with grease stains. The cards have full color fronts with the graphics done in the team's green and yellow colors. The backs contain the A's logo and a short player biography. The Revering card was withdrawn from the set shortly after he was traded and is in shorter supply than the rest of the cards in the set. The cards are numbered in the checklist that follows by the player's uniform number.

		NM/M
Complete Set (15):		100.00
Common Player:		2.00
1	Billy Martin	8.00
2	Mike Heath	2.00
5	Jeff Newman	2.00
8	Mitchell Page	2.00
8	Rob Picciolo	2.00
10	Wayne Gross	2.00
13	Dave Revering	40.00
17	Mike Norris	2.00
20	Tony Armas	2.00
21	Dwayne Murphy	2.00
22	Rick Langford	2.00
27	Matt Keough	2.00
35	Rickey Henderson	35.00
39	Dave McKay	2.00
54	Steve McCatty	2.00

1982 Granny Goose Potato Chips A's

Granny Goose repeated its promotion from the previous year and issued another set featuring the Oakland A's. The 2-1/2" x 3-1/2" cards

were distributed in two fashions - in bags of potato chips and at Fan Appreciation Day at Oakland-Alameda Coliseum. The cards are identical in design to the 1981 set and can be distinguished from it by the date on the copyright on the bottom of the card reverse. The cards are numbered in the checklist that follows by the player's uniform number.

		NM/M
Complete Set (15):		7.50
Common Player:		.50
1	Billy Martin	1.00
2	Mike Heath	.50
5	Jeff Newman	.50
8	Rob Picciolo	.50
10	Wayne Gross	.50
14	Fred Stanley	.50
15	Davey Lopes	.50
17	Mike Norris	.50
20	Tony Armas	.50
21	Dwayne Murphy	.50
22	Rick Langford	.50
27	Matt Keough	.50
35	Rickey Henderson	6.00
44	Cliff Johnson, Jr.	.50
54	Steve McCatty	.50

1982 Granny Goose Signature Set

The cards from this very scarce 15-card set are identical to the regular Granny Goose cards, but contain a facsimile autograph on the front. The cards were initially intended as special prize-redemption inserts from Granny Goose potato chips, but were never released in any quantity.

		NM/M
Complete Set (15):		125.00
Common Player:		5.00
1	Billy Martin	30.00
2	Mike Heath	5.00
5	Jeff Newman	5.00
8	Rob Picciolo	5.00
10	Wayne Gross	5.00
14	Fred Stanley	5.00
15	Davey Lopes	7.50
17	Mike Norris	5.00
20	Tony Armas	5.00
21	Dwayne Murphy	5.00
22	Rick Langford	5.00
27	Matt Keough	5.00
35	Rickey Henderson	45.00
44	Cliff Johnson, Jr.	5.00
54	Steve McCatty	5.00

1983 Granny Goose Potato Chips A's

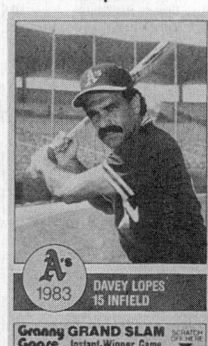

For the third consecutive year, Granny Goose issued a set of baseball cards featuring the Oakland A's. The cards were issued with or without a detachable coupon found at the bottom of each card. Issued in bags of potato chips were the

coupon cards, which contain a scratch-off section offering prizes. The cards without the coupon section were given away to fans at Oakland-Alameda Coliseum on July 3, 1983. Cards with the detachable coupon command a 50 per cent premium over the coupon-less variety. The cards in the following checklist are numbered by the player's uniform number.

		NM/M
Complete Set (15):		8.00
Common Player:		.50
2	Mike Heath	.50
4	Carney Lansford	.50
10	Wayne Gross	.50
14	Steve Boros	.50
15	Davey Lopes	.50
16	Mike Davis	.50
17	Mike Norris	.50
21	Dwayne Murphy	.50
27	Rick Langford	.50
27	Matt Keough	.50
31	Tom Underwood	.50
33	Dave Beard	.50
35	Rickey Henderson	6.00
39	Tom Burgmeier	.50
54	Steve McCatty	.50

1999 GTE Tampa Bay Devil Rays

This team set was a stadium giveaway. Fronts have game-action color photos. On back are complete minor and major league stats along with team and sponsor logos.

		NM/M
Complete Set (30):		10.00
Common Player:		.25
1	Scott Aldred	.25
2	Wilson Alvarez	.25
3	Rolando Arrojo	.25
4	Wade Boggs	3.00
5	Miguel Cairo	.25
6	Jose Canseco	2.00
7	Coaches (Orlando Gomez, Billy Hatcher, Frank Howard, Greg Riddoch, Leon Roberts, Rick Williams)	.25
8	Mike DiFelice	.25
9	John Flaherty	.25
10	Roberto Hernandez	.25
11	David Lamb	.25
12	Aaron Ledesma	.25
13	Albie Lopez	.25
14	Dave Martinez	.25
15	Quinton McCracken	.35
16	Fred McGriff	.35
17	Herbert Perry	.25
18	Bryan Rekar	.25
19	Larry Rothschild	.25
20	Ryan Rupe	.25
21	Julio Santana	.25
22	Tony Saunders	.25
23	Paul Sorrento	.25
24	Kevin Stocker	.25
25	Rick White	.25
26	Randy Winn	.25
27	Bobby Witt	.25
28	Esteban Yan	.25
---	Literacy Champion (Quinton McCracken)	.25
---	Sponsor's Card	.25

H

1981-89 Hall of Fame Metallic Plaque-Cards

Between 1981-89, the National Baseball Hall of Fame & Museum issued a set of metallic baseball cards reproducing the plaques of the baseball greats inducted. The plaques are pictured on 2-1/2" x 3-1/2" blank-backed gold anodized aluminum. Every detail of the plaque is fully and faithfully reproduced. The set was

sold in series through the Hall of Fame's gift shop. The series was discontinued for economic reasons in 1989. Only 1,000 plaques of each player were produced. Values are, to some extent, based not only on player popularity, but on year of issue; later plaques tend to be more expensive because fewer were sold.

		NM/M
Complete Set (204):		550.00
Common Player:		3.00
(1)	Hank Aaron/1983	20.00
(2)	Grover Alexander/1982	5.00
(3)	Walter Alston/1984	4.00
(4)	Cap Anson/1981	4.00
(5)	Luis Aparicio/1984	6.50
(6)	Luke Appling/1982	3.50
(7)	Earl Averill/1983	4.00
(8)	"Home Run" Baker/1983	3.00
(9)	David Bancroft/1982	3.00
(10)	Ernie Banks/1982	8.00
(11)	Al Barlick/1989	4.50
(12)	Ed Barrow/1982	3.00
(13)	Jacob Beckley/1982	3.00
(14)	Cool Papa Bell/1982	6.00
(15)	Johnny Bench/1989	15.00
(16)	"Chief" Bender/1982	3.50
(17)	Yogi Berra/1982	12.00
(18)	Jim Bottomley/1981	4.00
(19)	Lou Boudreau/1982	3.00
(20)	Roger Bresnahan/1982	3.00
(21)	Lou Brock/1986	12.00
(22)	Dan Brouthers/1982	3.00
(23)	Mordecai Brown/1981	4.00
(24)	Morgan Burkeley/1981	3.00
(25)	Jesse Burkett/1982	3.00
(26)	Roy Campanella/1981	12.50
(27)	Max Carey/1982	4.00
(28)	Alexander Cartwright/1981	3.00
(29)	Henry Chadwick/1982	3.00
(30)	Frank Chance/1981	4.50
(31)	Happy Chandler/1983	3.00
(32)	Oscar Charleston/1982	4.00
(33)	Jack Chesbro/1982	3.50
(34)	Fred Clarke/1983	3.00
(35)	John Clarkson/1982	3.00
(36)	Roberto Clemente/1982	30.00
(37)	Ty Cobb/1981	30.00
(38)	Mickey Cochrane/1983	5.00
(39)	Eddie Collins/1981	3.00
(40)	James Collins/1982	3.00
(41)	Earle Combs/1983	3.00
(42)	Charles Comiskey/1982	3.00
(43)	Jocko Conlan/1981	3.00
(44)	Thomas Connolly/1982	3.00
(45)	Roger Connor/1982	3.00
(46)	Stan Coveleski/1982	3.00
(47)	Sam Crawford/1983	3.50
(48)	Joe Cronin/1981	5.00
(49)	Candy Cummings/1982	3.00
(50)	Kiki Cuyler/1983	4.00
(51)	Ray Dandridge (1989)	6.00
(52)	Dizzy Dean/1983	10.00
(53)	Ed Delahanty/1981	3.00
(54)	Bill Dickey/1981	5.00
(55)	Martin Dihigo/1982	6.50
(56)	Joe DiMaggio/1983	35.00
(57)	Bobby Doerr/1986	4.00
(58)	Don Drysdale/1984	10.00
(59)	Hugh Duffy/1982	3.00
(60)	Bill Evans/1983	3.00
(61)	John Evers/1982	4.50
(62)	Buck Ewing/1981	3.00
(63)	Urban Faber/1983	3.00
(64)	Bob Feller/1981	6.50
(65)	Rick Ferrell/1984	4.00
(66)	Elmer Flick/1982	3.00
(67)	Whitey Ford/1983	10.00
(68)	Rube Foster/1983	3.00
(69)	Jimmie Foxx/1982	7.50
(70)	Ford Frick/1982	3.00
(71)	Frank Frisch/1982	3.00
(72)	Pud Galvin/1982	3.00
(73)	Lou Gehrig/1982	35.00
(74)	Charles Gehringer/1982	6.50
(75)	Bob Gibson/1982	6.50
(76)	Josh Gibson/1981	6.50
(77)	Warren Giles/1983	3.00
(78)	Lefty Gomez/1981	4.00
(79)	Goose Goslin/1982	4.00
(80)	Hank Greenberg/1981	8.00
(81)	Clark Griffith/1982	3.00
(82)	Burleigh Grimes/1982	3.00
(83)	Lefty Grove/1981	4.50

(84)	Chick Hafey/1982	3.00
(85)	Pop Haines/1982	3.00
(86)	William Hamilton/1982	3.00
(87)	William Harridge/1982	4.00
(88)	Bucky Harris/1982	4.00
(89)	Gabby Hartnett/1982	3.50
(90)	Harry Heilmann/1983	3.00
(91)	Bill Herman/1982	3.00
(92)	Harry Hooper/1982	3.00
(93)	Rogers Hornsby/1981	8.00
(94)	Schoolboy Hoyt/1983	3.00
(95)	Cal Hubbard/1982	3.00
(96)	Carl Hubbell/1981	3.50
(97)	Miller Huggins/1982	3.50
(98)	Catfish Hunter/1989	6.00
(99)	Monte Irvin/1981	3.50
(100)	Travis Jackson/1983	3.00
(101)	Hugh Jennings/1983	3.00
(102)	Ban Johnson/1981	3.00
(103)	Judy Johnson/1981	3.00
(104)	Walter Johnson/1982	10.00
(105)	Addie Joss/1981	3.00
(106)	Al Kaline/1981	8.00
(107)	Timothy Keefe/1983	3.00
(108)	Willie Keeler/1982	4.00
(109)	George Kell/1984	4.00
(110)	Joe Kelley/1983	3.00
(111)	Highpockets Kelly (?)	3.00
(112)	King Kelly/1981	4.00
(113)	Harmon Killebrew/1984	6.50
(114)	Ralph Kiner/1982	4.00
(115)	Chuck Klein/1983	4.00
(116)	Bill Klem/1981	3.00
(117)	Sandy Koufax/1982	25.00
(118)	Nap Lajoie/1982	3.00
(119)	Kenesaw Landis/1981	3.00
(120)	Buck Leonard/1982	3.50
(121)	Bob Lemon/1981	3.00
(122)	Fred Lindstrom/1982	3.00
(123)	Pop Lloyd/1981	3.00
(124)	Ernie Lombardi/1986	4.50
(125)	Al Lopez/1981	3.00
(126)	Ted Lyons/1983	4.00
(127)	Connie Mack/1981	4.00
(128)	Larry MacPhail/1983	3.00
(129)	Mickey Mantle/1983	40.00
(130)	Heinie Manush/1981	3.00
(131)	Rabbit Maranville/1981	4.00
(132)	Juan Marichal/1984	5.00
(133)	Rube Marquard/1983	3.50
(134)	Eddie Mathews/1983	3.50
(135)	Christy Mathewson/ 1981	10.00
(136)	Willie Mays/1981	20.00
(137)	Joe McCarthy/1983	3.00
(138)	Thomas McCarthy/1983	3.00
(139)	Willie McCovey/1986	3.50
(140)	Iron Man McGinnity/ 1982	3.00
(141)	John McGraw/1982	3.00
(142)	Bill McKechnie/1982	3.00
(143)	Joe Medwick/1983	3.00
(144)	Johnny Mize/1982	3.00
(145)	Stan Musial/1981	15.00
(146)	Kid Nichols/1983	4.00
(147)	James O'Rourke/1982	3.00
(148)	Mel Ott/1981	4.00
(149)	Satchel Paige/1981	12.50
(150)	Herb Pennock/1983	3.00
(151)	Eddie Plank/1982	3.00
(152)	Hoss Radbourne/1983	3.00
(153)	Pee Wee Reese/1984	3.50
(154)	Sam Rice/1983	3.00
(155)	Branch Rickey/1981	3.00
(156)	Eppa Rixey/1983	3.00
(157)	Robin Roberts/1982	5.00
(158)	Brooks Robinson/1984	6.00
(159)	Frank Robinson/1983	6.50
(160)	Jackie Robinson/1981	20.00
(161)	Wilbert Robinson/1982	3.50
(162)	Edd Roush/1982	3.00
(163)	Red Ruffing/1982	4.00
(164)	Amos Rusie/1983	3.00
(165)	Babe Ruth/1981	40.00
(166)	Ray Schalk/1982	3.00
(167)	Red Schoendienst/1989	8.00
(168)	Joe Sewell/1982	3.00
(169)	Al Simmons/1982	5.00
(170)	George Sisler/1981	3.00
(171)	Enos Slaughter/1986	8.00
(172)	Duke Snider/1981	8.00
(173)	Warren Spahn/1982	8.00
(174)	Al Spalding/1982	4.00
(175)	Tris Speaker/1982	6.50
(176)	Willie Stargell/1989	3.00
(177)	Casey Stengel/1981	6.50
(178)	Bill Terry/1981	3.00
(179)	Sam Thompson/1983	3.00
(180)	Joe Tinker/1982	6.00
(181)	Pie Traynor/1982	4.00
(182)	Dazzy Vance/1983	4.00
(183)	Arky Vaughan/1986	3.00
(184)	Rube Waddell/1983	4.00
(185)	Honus Wagner/1982	15.00
(186)	Roderick Wallace/1982	3.00
(187)	Ed Walsh/1982	3.00
(188)	Lloyd Waner/1981	4.00
(189)	Paul Waner/1981	5.00
(190)	John Ward/1982	3.00
(191)	George Weiss/1983	3.00
(192)	Mickey Welch/1983	3.00
(193)	Zack Wheat/1982	4.00
(194)	Hoyt Wilhelm/1985	6.50
(195)	Billy Williams/1989	8.00
(196)	Ted Williams/1981	27.50
(197)	Hack Wilson/1982	4.00
(198)	George Wright/1982	3.00
(199)	Harry Wright/1983	3.00

(200)	Early Wynn/1982	4.00
(201)	Carl Yastrzemski/1989	12.00
(202)	Tom Yawkey/1982	3.00
(203)	Cy Young/1981	10.00
(204)	Ross Youngs/1982	3.00

2001 Hall of Fame Postcards

Colorized artist's renderings of 19th Century Old Judge cabinet cards are the basis for this set of postcards produced for the Hall of Fame by R.F. Ball, who produced a similar set of lithographs in 1987. The postcards are 5" x 7" and have the central color painting bordered in black. Postcard-format backs have a few words about the player. The cards were produced in a serial-numbered edition of 2,000 each, packaged with a like-numbered checklist. Issue price at the Hall of Fame's gift shop was $12.95. A 21-1/2" x 38" uncut poster of the cards was sold for $49.95.

		NM/M
Complete Set (10):		13.00
Common Player:		1.50
1	Cap Anson	2.00
2	Dan Brouthers	1.50
3	John Clarkson	1.50
4	Ed Delahanty	1.50
5	Buck Ewing	1.50
6	Tim Keefe	1.50
7	Mike Kelly	2.00
8	Kid Nichols	1.50
9	Jim O'Rourke	1.50
10	Sam Thompson	1.50

2005 Hall of Fame Education Program

Each of the National Baseball Hall of Fame's educational programs is featured on a card in this special issue. Cards were issued in two 10-card cello packs.

		NM/M
Complete Set (20):		7.50
Common Card:		.50
(1)	Header Card	.05
(2)	American History (Joe Jackson)	1.50
(3)	Artifacts and Education (The Doubleday Ball)	.50
(4)	Civil Rights (Satchel Paige)	.75
(5)	Cultural Diversity (Jim Thorpe)	1.00
(6)	Economics (T206 Honus Wagner)	.50
(7)	Fine Art (Babe Ruth painting.)	.50
(8)	Leadership (Jackie Robinson)	.50
(9)	Popular Culture (Ichiro Suzuki bobblehead.)	.50
(10)	Women's History (Mickey Maguire)	.50
(11)	Header Card	.05
(12)	Artifacts and Education (Roberto Clemente artifacts.)	.50
(13)	Character Education (Lou Gehrig)	.75
(14)	Communication Arts (Dizzy Dean)	.50
(15)	Geography (1958 N.Y. Yankees)	.50
(16)	Industrial Technology (Roger Bresnahan)	.50
(17)	Labor History (John Montgomery Ward)	.50
(18)	Mathematics (Hank Aaron)	.75
(19)	Science (Ozzie Smith)	.50
(20)	Special Abilities (Pete Gray)	.75

1995 Baseball's Hall of Famers Creating History

This boxed set of large-format (2-7/8" x 4-1/2") round-cornered cards was designated "Flash-Pack / Knowledge in a Nutshell." It was described as the the first in a series. Card fronts feature borderless black-and-white or color photos with no player identification or other graphics. Black-and-white backs identify the player, provide a career summary and date of selection to the Hall of Fame. The un-numbered cards are listed here alphabetically. The boxed set originally retailed for $9.95.

		NM/M
Complete Set (36):		20.00
Common Player:		.50
(1)	Cap Anson	.50
(2)	Ernie Banks	2.00
(3)	Edward G. Barrow	.50
(4)	Roger Bresnahan	.50
(5)	Lou Brock	1.00
(6)	Roy Campanella	2.00
(7)	Alexander Cartwright	.50
(8)	Henry Chadwick	.50
(9)	Oscar Charleston	.50
(10)	Jack Chesbro	.50
(11)	Roberto Clemente	4.00
(12)	Charles Comiskey	.50
(13)	Candy Cummings	.50
(14)	Andrew "Rube" Foster	.50
(15)	Ford Frick	.50
(16)	Josh Gibson	1.00
(17)	Burleigh Grimes	.50
(18)	Cal Hubbard	.50
(19)	Carl Hubbell	.50
(20)	Willie Keeler	.50
(21)	Bill Klem	.50
(22)	Kenesaw M. Landis	.50
(23)	Larry MacPhail	.75
(24)	Juan Marichal	.50
(25)	Willie Mays	3.00
(26)	John McGraw	.50
(27)	Stan Musial	2.00
(28)	Charles Radbourne	.50
(29)	Branch Rickey	.50
(30)	Robin Roberts	1.00
(31)	Brooks Robinson	1.00
(32)	Warren Spahn	1.00
(33)	Albert Spalding	.50
(34)	Willie Stargell	1.00
(35)	Rube Waddell	.50
(36)	Harry Wright	.50

1998 Hamburger Helper Home Run Heroes

Eight top sluggers are featured in this box-back set from Hamburger Helper. The 2-1/2" x 3-1/2" cards are printed on the backs of various flavors of the skillet meal boxes. Unlike many similar issues these are fully licensed by Major League Baseball, as well as the Players Association, and the player photos have uniform logos. Also unusual is that the cards have a printed back in black-and-white offering personal data, career highlights and stats.

		NM/M
Complete Set, Boxes (8):		15.00
Complete Set, Singles (8):		15.00
Common Player:		.50
1	Mark McGwire	3.00
2	Rafael Palmeiro	1.25
3	Tino Martinez	.50
4	Barry Bonds	4.00
5	Larry Walker	.50
6	Juan Gonzalez	1.25
7	Mike Piazza	2.00
8	Frank Thomas	1.50

1988 Hardee's/Coke Conlon

Regionally issued in a promotion sponsored by Hardee's restaurants and Coca-Cola, this six-card set features the photos of Charles Martin Conlon and is closely related to the Sporting News-Wide World Conlon issues of the time. The cards feature sepia photos on front and career stats and summary on back. The unnumbered cards are checklisted here alphabetically.

		NM/M
Complete Set (6):		3.00
Common Player:		.40
(1)	Cool Papa Bell	.40
(2)	Ty Cobb	1.25
(3)	Lou Gehrig	1.50
(4)	Connie Mack	.40
(5)	Casey Stengel	.40
(6)	Rube Waddell	.40

1996 Hebrew National Detroit Tigers

One of the team's hot dog concessionaires sponsored a set of Tiger cards given away at the September 1 game. Originally intended to be 28 cards, only 26 were issued due to late-season trades. Cards are in a larger than normal 2-7/8" x 4-1/4" format with game-action photo on front. Down one side in team colors are the player name and position, with the stalking tiger logo at bottom. Backs have a large light blue gothic "D" in the background with player personal data and major/minor league stats and team/sponsor logos.

	NM/M
Complete Set (26):	12.00
Common Player:	.50

1	Kimera Bartee	.50
2	Jose Lima	.50
3	Tony Clark	.50
5	Travis Fryman	.50
7	Bobby Higginson	.50
8	Greg Keagle	.50
9	Mark Lewis	.50
10	Richie Lewis	.50
11	Felipe Lira	.50
12	Mike Myers	.50
13	Melvin Nieves	.50
14	Alan Trammell	1.00
15	Tom Urbani	.50
16	Brian Williams	.50
17	Eddie Williams	.50
18	Curtis Pride	.50
19	Mark Parent	.50
20	Raul Casanova	.50
21	Omar Olivares	.50
22	Gregg Olson	.50
23	Justin Thompson	.50
24	Brad Ausmus	.50
25	Andujar Cedeno	.50
26	Buddy Bell	.50
27	Paws (Mascot)	.50
28	Detroit Tigers Coaches (Glenn Ezell, Terry Francona, Larry Herndon, Fred Kendall, John (Jon) Matlack, Ron Oester)	.50

1997 Hebrew National Detroit Tigers

The hot dog concessionaire at Tiger Stadium produced a second annual team set in 1997, giving the cards away at the June 22 game. Cards feature borderless color action photos on front, with a tiny black-and-white portrait photo at bottom-right. Backs are printed in blue and yellow and have player data, complete major and minor league stats and the team and sponsor logos.

	NM/M
Complete Set (28):	12.00
Common Player:	.50

1	Jose Bautista	.50
2	Willie Blair	.50
3	Doug Brocail	.50
4	Raul Casanova	.50
5	Tony Clark	.50
6	Deivi Cruz	.50
7	John Cummings	.50
8	Damion Easley	.50
9	Travis Fryman	.50
11	Bobby Higginson	.50
11	Brian Hunter	.50
12	Todd Johnson	.50
13	Todd Jones	.50
14	Felipe Lira	.50
15	Dan Miceli	.50
16	Brian Moehler	.50
17	Mike Myers	.50
18	Phil Nevin	.50
19	Melvin Nieves	.50
20	Omar Oliveras	.50
21	Curtis Pride	.50
22	A.J. Sager	.50
23	Justin Thompson	.50
24	Matt Walbeck	.50
25	Jody Reed	.50
26	Bob Hamelin	.50
27	Buddy Bell	.50
28	Tigers Coaches (Rick Adair, Larry Herndon, Perry Hill, Fred Kendall, Larry Parrish, Jerry White)	.50

2005 Helmar Brewing Co.

These cards were inserted three per foil pack in packages of snack foods from a Michigan company. The product was sold only in parts of Michigan, Ohio and Pennsylvania. Fronts have color artwork. Besides major leaguers, Negro Leagues and Japanese Leagues players, the set included House of David players, wrestlers and boxers. The 1-5/8" x 2-3/4" cards are printed on thick cardboard. Backs

have a scratch-off circle for prize redemptions. No checklist was ever issued for the unnumbered cards, so it is possible additions to this list may be forthcoming. Gaps have been left in the assigned numbering for that reason.

		NM/M
Common Player:		.50
(1)	Frank "Home Run" Baker	1.00
(2)	Moe Berg	2.50
(3)	Mordecai Brown	1.00
(4)	Slim Caldwell	.50
(5)	Ray Chapman	1.00
(6)	Kiki Cuyler	.50
(7)	Bill Donovan	.50
(8)	Johnny "The Crab" Evers	1.00
(9)	Happy Felsch	1.00
(10)	Elmer Flick	.50
(11)	Chick Gandil	1.00
(12)	Sy Gragg (Gregg)	.50
(13)	Miller Huggins	.50
(14)	Joe Jackson (Chicago)	2.50
(15)	Joe Jackson (Cleveland)	2.50
(16)	Hughie Jennings	.50
(17)	Davy Jones	.50
(18)	Jimmy McAleer	.50
(19)	John McGraw	1.00
(20)	Herb Pennock	.50
(21)	Eppa Rixey	.50
(22)	Billy Rogell	.50
(23)	Rube Waddell	.50
(24)	Buck Weaver	1.50
(25)	Ross Youngs	.50
(30)	Joe Hauser	1.00
(31)	Walter Ball	.50
(32)	James "Cool Papa" Bell	1.00
(33)	Dennis Biddle	.50
(34)	Sherwood Brewer	.50
(35)	Jim Cobbin	.50
(36)	Jimmie Crutchfield	.50
(37)	Leon (Pepper) Daniels	.50
(38)	Martin DiHigo	1.00
(39)	Rube Foster	1.00
(40)	Arthur Hamilton	.50
(41)	Pete Hill	1.00
(42)	Dave Malarcher	.50
(43)	"Double Duty" Radcliffe	.50
(44)	Turkey Stearns (Stearnes)	.50
(45)	Moses Walker	1.00
(48)	George Anderson	.50
(49)	Barnstorming Team	.50
(51)	Lloyd Dalager	.50
(52)	Eddie Deal	.50
(53)	Judge Dewhurst	.50
(54)	David Harrison	.50
(55)	Jesse Lee Tally	.50
(56)	John Tucker	.50
(57)	Percy Walker	.50
(58)	Kaoru Betto	.50
(59)	Sadayushi Fujimoto	.50
(60)	Taketoshi Goto	.50
(61)	Tetsuhara Kawakami	1.00
(62)	Tokuji Iida	.50
(63)	Jiro Noguchi	.50
(64)	Tokyo Team (Tetsuhara Kawakami, Shigeru Chiba, Noboru Aota, Jiro Noguchi)	

1998 Hershey's Baltimore Orioles

This team set was a stadium giveaway at a late-season game. The 2-1/2" x 3-1/2" cards have portrait or game-action photos bordered in black. An orange stripe vertically at left has the player name. Backs have a red border around complete major and minor league stats. Team and Hershey's logos are at bottom.

	NM/M
Complete Set (25):	15.00
Common Player:	.50
(1) Roberto Alomar	.75
(2) Brady Anderson	.75
(3) Harold Baines	.75
(4) Rich Becker	.50
(5) Armando Benitez	.50
(6) Mike Bordick	.50
(7) Eric Davis	.60
(8) Doug Drabek	.50
(9) Scott Erickson	.50
(10) Chris Hoiles	.50
(11) Doug Johns	.50
(12) Scott Kamieniecki	.50
(13) Jimmy Key	.50
(14) Alan Mills	.50
(15) Mike Mussina	2.00
(16) Jesse Orosco	.50
(17) Rafael Palmeiro	2.00
(18) Sidney Ponson	.50
(19) Jeff Reboulet	.50
(20) Arthur Rhodes	.50
(21) Cal Ripken	4.00
(22) Pete Smith	.50
(23) B.J. Surhoff	.50
(24) Lenny Webster	.50
(25) Orioles Coaches (Carlos Bernhardt, Rick Down, Mike Flanagan, Elrod Hendricks, Eddie Murray, Sam Perlozzo)	.50

1993 Highland Mint Mint-Cards

The Highland Mint produced replicas of several Topps rookie cards and other prominent cards in bronze and silver. Limited to 1,000 in silver and 5,000 in bronze, the company produced cards of many current stars along with a replica of Brooks Robinson's 1957 rookie card. The cards carried a suggested retail price of $235 for the silver and $50 for the bronze. Cards measure 2-1/2" x 3-1/2" and are 1/10" thick. Each Mint-Card has a serial number engraved on the edge and is sold in a heavy lucite holder, packaged with a certificate of authenticity in a plastic book-style folder.

	NM/M
Common Player, Silver:	70.00
Common Player, Bronze:	12.50
(1s) Brooks Robinson (1957 Topps, silver edition of 796)	110.00
(1b) Brooks Robinson (1957 Topps, bronze edition of 2,043)	20.00
(2s) Dave Winfield (1974 Topps, silver edition of 266)	200.00
(2b) Dave Winfield (1974 Topps, bronze edition of 1,216)	20.00
(3s) George Brett (1975 Topps, silver edition of 999)	100.00
(3b) George Brett (1975 Topps, bronze edition of 3,560)	20.00
(4s) Robin Yount (1975 Topps, silver edition of 349)	110.00
(4b) Robin Yount (1975 Topps, bronze edition of 1,564)	40.00
(5s) Ozzie Smith (1979 Topps, silver edition of 211)	245.00
(5b) Ozzie Smith (1979 Topps, bronze edition of 1,088)	35.00
(6s) Don Mattingly (1984 Topps, silver edition of 414)	75.00
(6b) Don Mattingly (1984 Topps, bronze edition of 1,550)	40.00

	NM/M
(7s) Roger Clemens (1985 Topps, silver edition of 432)	140.00
(7b) Roger Clemens (1985 Topps, bronze edition of 1,789)	25.00
(8s) Kirby Puckett (1985 Topps, silver edition of 359)	85.00
(8b) Kirby Puckett (1985 Topps, bronze edition of 1,723)	20.00
(9s) Barry Bonds (1986 Topps Traded, silver edition of 596)	125.00
(9b) Barry Bonds (1986 Topps Traded, bronze edition of 2,677)	50.00
(10s) Will Clark (1986 Topps Traded, silver edition of 150)	225.00
(10b) Will Clark (1986 Topps Traded, bronze edition of 1,0444)	20.00
(11s) Roberto Alomar (1988 Topps Traded, silver edition of 214)	90.00
(11b) Roberto Alomar (1988 Topps Traded, bronze edition of 928)	20.00
(12s) Juan Gonzalez (1990 Topps, silver edition of 365)	65.00
(12b) Juan Gonzalez (1990 Topps, bronze edition of 1,899)	15.00
(13s) Ken Griffey Jr. (1992 Topps, silver edition of 1,000)	100.00
(13b) Ken Griffey Jr. (1992 Topps, bronze edition of 5,000)	15.00
(13g) Ken Griffey Jr. (1992 Topps, gold edition of 500)	200.00
(14s) Cal Ripken, Jr. (1992 Topps, silver edition of 1,000)	100.00
(14b) Cal Ripken, Jr. (1992 Topps, bronze edition of 4,065)	15.00
(15s) Nolan Ryan (1992 Topps, silver edition of 999)	150.00
(15b) Nolan Ryan (1992 Topps, bronze edition of 5,000)	25.00
(16s) Ryne Sandberg (1992 Topps, silver edition of 430)	145.00
(16b) Ryne Sandberg (1992 Topps, bronze edition of 1,932)	15.00
(17s) Frank Thomas (1992 Topps, silver edition of 1,000)	85.00
(17b) Frank Thomas (1992 Topps, bronze edition of 5,000)	12.50
(17g) Frank Thomas (1992 Topps, gold edition of 500)	150.00

1994 Highland Mint Mint-Cards

In 1994 the Highland Mint continued its production of Mint-Cards, licensed metal replicas of Topps baseball, football and hockey cards. Maximum production of baseball players in the series was reduced to 750 in silver and halved to 2,500 in bronze. Suggested retail prices remained at $235 and $50, respectively. Once again cards were produced in the same 2-1/2" x 3-1/2" format as original Topps cards and were minted to a thickness of 1/10", with a serial number engraved on the edge. Mint-cards were sold in a heavy lucite holder, packaged with a certificate of authenticity in a plastic book-style holder. In mid-year, the company announced it was ceasing production of Topps-replica baseball cards and that henceforth all baseball Mint-Cards would reproduce the designs of Pinnacle brand cards.

	NM/M
Common Player, Silver:	50.00
Common Player, Bronze:	12.00
Common Player, Gold:	200.00
(1a) Ernie Banks (1954 Topps, silver edition of 437)	65.00
(1b) Ernie Banks (1954 Topps, bronze edition of 920)	25.00
(2a) Carl Yastrzemski (1960 Topps, silver edition of 500)	75.00

	NM/M
(2b) Carl Yastrzemski (1960 Topps, bronze edition of 1,072)	30.00
(3a) Johnny Bench (1969 Topps, silver edition of 500)	75.00
(3b) Johnny Bench (1969 Topps, bronze edition of 1,384)	22.50
(4a) Mike Schmidt (1974 Topps, silver edition of 500)	75.00
(4b) Mike Schmidt (1974 Topps, bronze edition of 1,641)	20.00
(5a) Paul Molitor (1979 Topps, silver edition of 260)	175.00
(5b) Paul Molitor (1979 Topps, bronze edition of 639)	17.50
(6a) Deion Sanders (1989 Topps, silver edition of 187)	60.00
(6b) Deion Sanders (1989 Topps, bronze edition of 668)	12.50
(7a) Dave Justice (1990 Topps, silver edition of 265)	75.00
(7b) Dave Justice (1990 Topps, bronze edition of 1,396)	12.50
(8a) Jeff Bagwell (1992 Pinnacle, silver edition of 750)	50.00
(8b) Jeff Bagwell (1992 Pinnacle, bronze edition of 2,500)	15.00
(9a) Greg Maddux (1992 Pinnacle, silver edition of 750)	175.00
(9b) Greg Maddux (1992 Pinnacle, bronze edition of 2,500)	20.00
(10a) Mike Piazza (1992 Topps, silver edition of 750)	75.00
(10b) Mike Piazza (1992 Topps, bronze edition of 2,500)	20.00
(10c) Mike Piazza (1992 Topps, gold edition of 374)	300.00
(12a) Nolan Ryan (1992 Pinnacle Then and Now, silver edition of 1,000)	75.00
(12b) Nolan Ryan (1992 Pinnacle Then and Now, bronze edition of 5,000)	15.00
(12c) Nolan Ryan (1992 Pinnacle Then & Now, gold edition 500)	200.00
(13a) Tim Salmon (1993 Topps, silver edition of 264)	110.00
(13b) Tim Salmon (1993 Topps, bronze edition of 768)	10.00

1995 Highland Mint Mint-Cards

For 1995, the Highland Mint continued its series of precious-metal editions of cards in all major team sports. The 2-1/2" x 3-1/2" cards contain 4-1/4 oz. of bronze or silver or 24-K gold plating on silver. Each Mint-card is sold in a heavy plastic holder within a numbered album and with a certificate of authenticity. Only the firm's baseball cards are listed here.

	NM/M
38b Michael Jordan (Upper Deck Rare Air, bronze, edition of 5,000.)	15.00
38s Michael Jordan (Upper Deck Rare Air, silver, edition of 1,000.)	100.00
38g Michael Jordan (Upper Deck Rare Air, gold, edition of 500.)	300.00
Mickey Mantle (1992 Pinnacle, bronze edition of 1,000)	20.00
Mickey Mantle (1992 Pinnacle, silver edition of 1,000)	75.00
Mickey Mantle (1992 Pinnacle, gold edition of 500)	300.00

1992 High 5 Decals

This issue of peelable, reusable "decals" was sold in both team sets and superstar panels. Each $2.99 panel contains five player decals and a team logo decal. The backing paper has a color 5" x 7" photo of a superstar that can be cut out and framed. Overall dimensions of the decal sheet are

7-1/2" x 7". The unnumbered decals are checklisted here in alphabetical order within team.

	NM/M
Complete Set (156):	30.00
Common Player:	.25
(1) Baltimore Orioles Logo	.25
(2) Mike Devereaux	.25
(3) Ben McDonald	.25
(4) Gregg Olson	.25
(5) Joe Orsulak	.25
(6) Cal Ripken Jr.	3.00
(7) Boston Red Sox Logo	.25
(8) Wade Boggs	2.00
(9) Roger Clemens	2.25
(10) Phil Plantier	.25
(11) Jeff Reardon	.25
(12) Mo Vaughn	.25
(13) California Angels Logo	.25
(14) Jim Abbott	.25
(15) Chuck Finley	.25
(16) Bryan Harvey	.25
(17) Mark Langston	.25
(18) Dave Winfield	1.50
(19) Chicago White Sox Logo	.25
(20) Carlton Fisk	1.50
(21) Jack McDowell	.25
(22) Bobby Thigpen	.25
(23) Frank Thomas	1.50
(24) Robin Ventura	.25
(25) Cleveland Indians Logo	.25
(26) Sandy Alomar Jr.	.25
(27) Carlos Baerga	.25
(28) Albert Belle	.25
(29) Alex Cole	.25
(30) Charles Nagy	.25
(31) Detroit Tigers Logo	.25
(32) Cecil Fielder	.25
(33) Travis Fryman	.25
(34) Tony Phillips	.25
(35) Alan Trammell	.25
(36) Lou Whitaker	.25
(37) Kansas City Royals Logo	.25
(38) George Brett	2.50
(39) Jim Eisenreich	.25
(40) Brian McRae	.25
(41) Jeff Montgomery	.25
(42) Bret Saberhagen	.25
(43) Milwaukee Brewers Logo	.25
(44) Chris Bosio	.25
(45) Paul Molitor	1.50
(46) B.J. Surhoff	.25
(47) Greg Vaughn	.25
(48) Robin Yount	1.50
(49) Minnesota Twins Logo	.25
(50) Rick Aguilera	.25
(51) Scott Erickson	.25
(52) Kent Hrbek	.25
(53) Kirby Puckett	2.00
(54) Kevin Tapani	.25
(55) New York Yankees Logo	.25
(56) Mel Hall	.25
(57) Roberto Kelly	.25
(58) Kevin Maas	.25
(59) Don Mattingly	2.50
(60) Steve Sax	.25
(61) Oakland A's Logo	.25
(62) Harold Baines	.25
(63) Jose Canseco	.75
(64) Dennis Eckersley	1.25
(65) Dave Henderson	.25
(66) Rickey Henderson	1.50
(67) Seattle Mariners Logo	.25
(68) Jay Buhner	.25
(69) Ken Griffey Jr.	2.75
(70) Randy Johnson	1.50
(71) Edgar Martinez	.25
(72) Harold Reynolds	.25
(73) Texas Rangers Logo	.25
(74) Julio Franco	.25
(75) Juan Gonzalez	1.25
(76) Rafael Palmeiro	1.25
(77) Nolan Ryan	3.00
(77p) Nolan Ryan (Prototype)	6.50
(78) Ruben Sierra	.25
(79) Toronto Blue Jays Logo	.25
(80) Roberto Alomar	.50
(81) Joe Carter	.25
(82) Kelly Gruber	.25
(83) John Olerud	.25
(84) Devon White	.25
(85) Atlanta Braves Logo	.25
(86) Steve Avery	.25
(87) Ron Gant	.25
(88) Tom Glavine	.40
(89) David Justice	.25
(90) Terry Pendleton	.25
(91) Chicago Cubs Logo	.25
(92) George Bell	.25
(93) Andre Dawson	.30
(94) Mark Grace	.25
(95) Greg Maddux	2.00
(96) Ryne Sandberg	2.00

	NM/M
(97) Cincinnati Reds Logo	.25
(98) Eric Davis	.25
(99) Barry Larkin	.25
(100) Hal Morris	.25
(101) Jose Rijo	.25
(102) Chris Sabo	.25
(103) Houston Astros Logo	.25
(104) Jeff Bagwell	1.50
(105) Craig Biggio	.25
(106) Ken Caminiti	.25
(107) Luis Gonzalez	.50
(108) Pete Harnisch	.25
(109) Los Angeles Dodgers Logo	.25
(110) Brett Butler	.25
(111) Lenny Harris	.25
(112) Ramon Martinez	.25
(113) Eddie Murray	1.50
(114) Darryl Strawberry	.25
(115) Montreal Expos Logo	.25
(116) Ivan Calderon	.25
(117) Delino DeShields	.25
(118) Marquis Grissom	.25
(119) Dennis Martinez	.25
(120) Larry Walker	.25
(121) New York Mets Logo	.25
(122) David Cone	.25
(123) Dwight Gooden	.25
(124) Gregg Jefferies	.25
(125) Howard Johnson	.25
(126) Kevin McReynolds	.25
(127) Philadelphia Phillies Logo	.25
(128) Wes Chamberlain	.25
(129) Lenny Dykstra	.25
(130) John Kruk	.25
(131) Terry Mulholland	.25
(132) Mitch Williams	.25
(133) Pittsburgh Pirates Logo	.25
(134) Barry Bonds	3.00
(135) Doug Drabek	.25
(136) John Smiley	.25
(137) Zane Smith	.25
(138) Andy Van Slyke	.25
(139) St. Louis Cardinals Logo	.25
(140) Felix Jose	.25
(141) Ray Lankford	.25
(142) Lee Smith	.25
(143) Ozzie Smith	2.00
(144) Todd Zeile	.25
(145) San Diego Padres Logo	.25
(146) Tony Fernandez	.25
(147) Tony Gwynn	2.00
(148) Bruce Hurst	.25
(149) Fred McGriff	.25
(150) Gary Sheffield	.25
(151) San Francisco Giants Logo	.25
(152) Will Clark	.30
(152p) Will Clark (Prototype)	1.50
(153) Willie McGee	.25
(154) Kevin Mitchell	.25
(155) Robby Thompson	.25
(156) Matt Williams	.25

1989 Hills Team MVP's

This high-gloss, boxed set of superstars was produced by Topps for the Hills department store chain. The words "Hills Team MVP's" appear above the player photos, while the player's name and team are printed below. The front of the card carries a red, white and blue color scheme with yellow and gold accents. The horizontal backs include player data set against a green playing field background.

	NM/M
Complete Set (33):	4.00
Common Player:	.10
1 Harold Baines	.10
2 Wade Boggs	.75
3 George Brett	1.00
4 Tom Brunansky	.10
5 Jose Canseco	.35
6 Joe Carter	.10
7 Will Clark	.15
8 Roger Clemens	.85
9 Dave Cone	.10
10 Glenn Davis	.10
11 Andre Dawson	.25
12 Dennis Eckersley	.40
13 Andres Galarraga	.10
14 Kirk Gibson	.10
15 Mike Greenwell	.10
16 Tony Gwynn	.75
17 Orel Hershiser	.10

18 Danny Jackson	.10
19 Mark Langston	.10
20 Fred McGriff	.10
21 Dale Murphy	.25
22 Eddie Murray	.50
23 Kirby Puckett	.75
24 Johnny Ray	.10
25 Juan Samuel	.10
26 Ruben Sierra	.10
27 Dave Stewart	.10
28 Darryl Strawberry	.10
29 Alan Trammell	.10
30 Andy Van Slyke	.10
31 Frank Viola	.10
32 Dave Winfield	.50
33 Robin Yount	.50

1990 Hills Hit Men

The 33 slugging percentage leaders are featured in this high-gloss boxed set. The cards were produced by Topps for the Hills department store chain. Fronts feature "Hit Men" in a bat design above the photo. The player's name appears on a band below the photo. Horizontal backs feature a breakdown of the player's slugging percentage and also display career statistics.

	NM/M
Complete Set (33):	5.00
Common Player:	.10
1 Eric Davis	.10
2 Will Clark	.15
3 Don Mattingly	.75
4 Darryl Strawberry	.10
5 Kevin Mitchell	.10
6 Pedro Guerrero	.10
7 Jose Canseco	.35
8 Jim Rice	.15
9 Danny Tartabull	.10
10 George Brett	.75
11 Kent Hrbek	.10
12 George Bell	.10
13 Eddie Murray	.50
14 Fred Lynn	.10
15 Andre Dawson	.25
16 Dale Murphy	.15
17 Dave Winfield	.50
18 Jack Clark	.10
19 Wade Boggs	.65
20 Ruben Sierra	.10
21 Dave Parker	.10
22 Glenn Davis	.10
23 Dwight Evans	.10
24 Jesse Barfield	.10
25 Kirk Gibson	.10
26 Alvin Davis	.10
27 Kirby Puckett	.65
28 Joe Carter	.10
29 Carlton Fisk	.50
30 Harold Baines	.10
31 Andres Galarraga	.10
32 Cal Ripken, Jr.	1.50
33 Howard Johnson	.10

1993 Hills Pirates Kids Club

Stars of the Eastern Division N.L. champions are picutred on this 12-card issue. The set was issued in the form of a perforated 10" x 10-1/2" panel. Fronts have player action photos with orange frames, white borders and a team logo. Black-and-white backs have a player portrait, personal data and stats, and the Hills Pirates Kids Club logo. Cards are numbered by uniform number.

		NM/M
Complete Set, Sheet:		7.00
Complete Set, Singles (12):		6.00
Common Player:		.50
6	Orlando Merced	.50
7	Jeff King	.50
10	Jim Leyland	.50
14	Tom Prince	.50
23	Lloyd McClendon	.50
26	Steve Cooke	.50
28	Al Martin	.50
32	Denny Neagle	.50
36	Kevin Young	.50
45	John Candelaria	.50
50	Stan Belinda	.50
55	Blas Minor	.50

Hillshire Farm Home Run Heroes

Via a special offer on packages of Hillshire Farm meats, collectors could order an autographed card of several star sluggers of the 1960s. Cards were available by sending in a package coupon and $4 for handling. The 2-1/2" x 3-1/2" cards have color player photos on which uniform logos have been removed. Borders are black and enhanced with gold foil. Black and gold backs offer lifetime stats and career highlights.

		NM/M
Complete Set (4):		30.00
Common Player:		7.50
(1)	Ernie Banks	10.00
(2)	Harmon Killebrew	7.50
(3)	Frank Robinson	7.50
(4)	Willie Stargell	12.00

1988 Historic Limited Editions Brooklyn Dodgers

This set of Brooklyn Dodgers postcards features the artwork of Susan Rini, combining on most cards a player portrait and an action pose with Ebbets Field as the background. Fronts of the 5-1/2" x 3-1/2" cards have the artwork at left, bordered in bright blue. In the wide right border, the team name and logo, and the player name, are printed in white. Postcard-style backs are printed in blue. The cards were issued in three series of 12 each, but are checklisted here in alphabetical order. Two different cards each exist for Erskine and Lavagetto. Production of the series was limited to 5,000 sets; 2,000 sets were produced with a low-gloss finish to facilitate autographing, while the remaining 3,000 sets were high-gloss. Either sold for $20 at time of issue. Two hundred uncut sheets of each series were sold for $30 apiece. A special album was also made available.

		NM/M
Complete Set (36):		10.00
Common Player:		.50
(1)	Cal Abrams	.50
(2)	Sandy Amoros	.50
(3)	Red Barber (Announcer)	.50
(4)	Ralph Branca	.50
(5)	Chuck Connors	.75
(6)	Roger Craig	.50
(7)	Roy Campanella	1.50
(8)	Don Drysdale	1.00
(9)	Leo Durocher	.50
(10)	Carl Erskine	.50
(11)	Carl Erskine	.50
(12)	Carl Furillo	.50
(13)	Gene Hermanski	.50
(14)	Gil Hodges	1.00
(15)	Clyde King	.50
(16)	Clem Labine	.50
(17)	Tommy Lasorda	.75
(18)	Cookie Lavagetto	.50
(19)	Cookie Lavagetto	.50
(20)	Larry MacPhail (GM)	.50
(21)	Sal Maglie	.50
(22)	Eddie Miksis	.50
(23)	Don Newcombe	.60
(24)	Walter O'Malley (Owner)	.50
(25)	Mickey Owen	.50
(26)	Andy Pafko	.50
(27)	Johnny Podres	.50
(28)	Pee Wee Reese	1.00
(29)	Preacher Roe	.50
(30)	Jackie Robinson	2.50
(31)	George Shuba	.50
(32)	Duke Snider	1.50
(33)	Red Barber, Leo Durocher	.50
(34)	Jackie Robinson, Branch Rickey	1.00
(35)	Ebbets Field	.50
(36)	Dodgers Sym-Phony Band	.50

Historic Limited Editions Lou Gehrig Postcards

This set of postcards combines portrait and action art with a Yankee Stadium backdrop in paintings by Susan Rini. The art is set towards the top of the 3-1/2" x 5-1/2" cards which have a pinstripe background, player name beneath the art and team name and logo at bottom. Horizontal backs are postcard-style and printed in blue with appropriate credit lines, copyright notice and logos. Original price was $10 per set, with uncut sheets available for $15.

		NM/M
Complete Set (8):		6.00
Common Card:		1.00

Don Mattingly Series 1

One of the most popular Yankees of the past 25 years is honored on this set of postcards. The 3-1/2" x 5-1/2" cards feature the artwork of Susan Rini on each card. Mattingly is shown in portrait and action art on most of the cards, though sometimes the picture of another Yankee great takes the place of the action picture. Background on the front is white with blue pinstripes. Postcard-style backs are printed in blue and announce an edition of 5,000 sets. Price at issue was about $10, with uncut sheets of the cards available for $24.

Negro Leagues Postcards

WILLIE WELLS

NEGRO LEAGUE

Both well-known and obscure players of the segregated Negro Leagues are included in this series of color postcards. Fronts of the 3-1/2" x 5-1/2" cards have portrait and action paintings of the players on a peach-colored background. Postcard-style backs are printed in blue and indicate a limit of 5,000 sets were produced. An edition of 200 uncut sheets was also produced.

		NM/M
Complete Set (12):		7.00
Common Player:		.50
Uncut Sheet:		10.00
1	Monte Irvin	1.00
2	Martin Dihigo	.85
3	Clint Thomas	.50
4	Buster Haywood	.50
5	George Giles	.50
6	Isidro Fabri	.50
7	James (Cool Papa) Bell	.65
8	Josh Gibson	1.50
9	Lou Dials	.50
10	Willie Wells	.75
11	Walter (Buck) Leonard	.75
12	Jose Fernandez	.50

1990 Historic Limited Editions Roberto Clemente

ROBERTO CLEMENTE

PITTSBURGH PIRATES

This set of 3-1/2" x 5-1/2" postcards details the career of the Pirates outfielder. Background of each card is beige. At top is an approximately 3" x 3-1/2" color painting of Clemente in both portrait and action poses, created by sports artist Susan Rini. Player and team name, and team logo are at bottom. Postcard-style backs are printed in blue with appropriate credit lines and copyright data. Production was reported at 5,000 sets.

		NM/M
Complete Set (12):		12.50
Common Card:		1.50

Thurman Munson Postcards

The late, great Yankees catcher is memorialized in this set of color postcards from sports artist Susan Rini. Fronts of the 3-1/2" x 5-1/2" cards have a combination portrait/action painting toward the top, on a background of pinstripes. Player and team names and the Yankees logo are at bottom. Horizontal backs are in postcard style, printed in blue with appropriate licensing, copyright

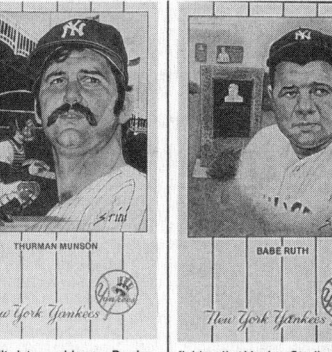

THURMAN MUNSON

New York Yankees

BABE RUTH

New York Yankees

and credit data, and logos. Production was limited to 5,000 sets and 200 complete-set uncut sheets.

		NM/M
Complete Set (12):		10.00
Common Card:		1.25
Uncut Sheet:		55.00
1-12	Thurman Munson	1.25

Nolan Ryan Series 1

NOLAN RYAN

Texas Rangers

The Mets and Rangers years are graphically depicted on this set of postcards in combined portrait and action paintings by sports artist Susan Rini. The 3-1/2" x 5-1/2" cards have a light blue background on front, with the player and team name, and the team logo at bottom. Postcard-style backs are printed in blue and offer copyright and licensing information, along with a notice that the set is limited to an edition of 10,000.

		NM/M
Complete Set (12):		10.00
Common Card:		1.00

Nolan Ryan Series 2

NOLAN RYAN

Astros

The Astros and Angels years are graphically depicted on this set of postcards in combined portrait and action paintings by sports artist Susan Rini. The 3-1/2" x 5-1/2" cards have a beige background on front, with the player and team name, and the team logo at bottom. Postcard-style backs are printed in blue and offer copyright and licensing information, along with a notice that the set is limited to an edition of 10,000.

		NM/M
Complete Set (12):		10.00
Common Card:		1.00

Yankees Monuments

Those honored with plaques in Monument Park behind the center

field wall at Yankee Stadium are presented in this series of postcards. On a pinstriped background, the fronts of the 3-1/2" x 5-1/2" cards have a portrait of the person with his plaque in the background, the work of Susan Rini. The team name and logo are at bottom. Postcard-style backs are printed in blue with various copyright and creator notices, MLB logo and an indication that the cards were produced in an edition of 5,000. At time of issue, complete sets sold for about $10; uncut sheets were available for $20.

		NM/M
Complete Set (12):		12.00
Common Player:		.70
1	Lou Gehrig	2.25
2	Babe Ruth	3.00
3	Thurman Munson	1.50
4	Elston Howard	.70
5	Phil Rizzuto	.70
6	Mickey Mantle	4.50
7	Bill Dickey	.70
8	Lefty Gomez	.70
9	Pope Paul VI	2.25
10	Jacob Ruppert	.70
11	Roger Maris	2.25
12	Joe DiMaggio	3.00

1969 Mets Postcards

This set commemorates the Amazin' Mets World Championship team of 1969. The 5-1/2" x 3-1/2" cards have bright blue front borders. At left is a portrait/action painting of the players by sports artist Susan Rini. Postcard-style backs are printed in blue with copyright and credit data, card number, logos, etc. The issue was limited to 5,000 sets and originally sold for about $20. Uncut sheets were available for $25.

		NM/M
Complete Set (36):		11.00
Common Player:		.50
1	Championship Trophy	.50
2	Shea Stadium	.50
3	Tommie Agee	.50
4	Ken Boswell	.50
5	Ed Charles	.50
6	Don Cardwell	.50
7	Donn Clendenon	.65
8	Jack DiLauro	.50
9	Duffy Dyer	.50
10	Wayne Garrett	.50
11	Jerry Grote	.50
12	Rod Gaspar	.50
13	Gary Gentry	.50
14	Bud Harrelson	.65
15	Gil Hodges	1.00
16	Cleon Jones	.65
17	Ed Kranepool	.65
18	Cal Koonce	.50
19	Jerry Koosman	.65
20	Jim McAndrew	.50
21	Tug McGraw	.75
22	J.C. Martin	.50
23	Bob Pfeil	.50
24	Nolan Ryan	4.00
25	Ron Swoboda	.50
26	Tom Seaver	1.50
27	Art Shamsky	.50
28	Ron Taylor	.50
29	Al Weis	.50
30	Joe Pignatano	.50
31	Eddie Yost	.50
32	Ralph Kiner (Announcer)	.50
33	Bob Murphy (Writer)	.50

34	Lindsey Nelson (Announcer)	.50
35	Yogi Berra	1.00
36	Rube Walker	.50

1991 Historic Limited Editions Brooklyn Dodgers

Three additional series of 12-card player postcard sets in 1991 were issued as a follow-up to the company's debut issue of 1988. Identical in format, the 5-1/2" x 3-1/2" cards have a Dodger blue background on front. At the left end is artwork by Susan Rini combining portrait and action pictures of the player against a background of Ebbets Field. Player and team identification are in white at right. Postcard backs are printed in blue with credits, copyright data, logos and series and card numbers.

		NM/M
Complete Set (36):		20.00
Common Player:		.50
SERIES 2		5.00
1	Charley Dressen	.50
2	John Roseboro	.50
3	Eddie Stanky	.50
4	Goody Rosen	.50
5	Ed Head	.50
6	Dick Williams	.50
7	Clarence (Bud) Podbielan	.50
8	Erv Palica	.50
9	Augie Galan	.50
10	Billy Loes	.50
11	Billy Cox	.50
12	Phil Phifer	.50
SERIES 3		5.00
1	Joe Black	.75
2	Jack Banta	.50
3	Whitlow Wyatt	.50
4	Gino Cimoli	.50
5	Dolph Camilli (Dolf)	.50
6	Dan Bankhead	.50
7	Henry Behrman	.50
8	Pete Reiser	.50
9	Chris Van Cuyk	.50
10	James (Junior) Gilliam	.75
11	Don Zimmer	.75
12	Ed Roebuck	.50
SERIES 4		5.00
1	Billy Herman	.50
2	Rube Walker	.50
3	Tommy Brown	.50
4	Charlie Neal	.50
5	Kirby Higbe	.50
6	Bruce Edwards	.50
7	Joe Hatten	.50
8	Rex Barney	.50
9	Al Gionfriddo	.50
10	Luis Olmo	.50
11	Dixie Walker	.50
12	Walter Alston	1.00

Don Mattingly Series 2

DON MATTINGLY

New York Yankees

Two years after the release of the first series, another 12 Mattingly postcards were issued. The 3-1/2" x 5-1/2" cards feature the artwork of Susan Rini on each card. Mattingly is shown in portrait and action art on each of the cards. Background on the front is white with blue pinstripes. Postcard-style backs are printed in blue and announce an edition of 5,000 sets. Price at issue was about $10, with uncut sheets of the cards available for $24.

		NM/M
Complete Set (12):		6.00
Common Card:		.50
1-12	Don Mattingly	.50

1961 Yankees Postcards

Three series of 12 postcards each were issued to commemorate the '61 Yanks. All cards are 5-1/2" x 3-1/2", with a pinstriped border design. At left front are combination portrait/action paintings by Susan Rini. Team name and logo are at right, along with player identification. Backs are printed in blue, in postcard style, with copyright, credits, logos, etc.

		NM/M
Complete Set (36):		16.00
Common Player:		.25
SERIES 1		3.00
1	Yogi Berra	1.00
2	Tom Tresh	.45
3	Bill Skowron	.45
4	Al Downing	.25
5	Jim Coates	.25
6	Luis Arroyo	.25
7	Johnny Blanchard	.25
8	Hector Lopez	.25
9	Tony Kubek	.50
10	Ralph Houk	.25
11	Bobby Richardson	.50
12	Clete Boyer	.35
SERIES 2		8.00
1	Roger Maris	6.00
2	Jesse Gonder	.25
3	Danny McDevitt	.25
4	Leroy Thomas	.25
5	Billy Gardner	.25
6	Ralph Terry	.25
7	Hal Reniff	.25
8	Earl Torgeson	.25
9	Art Ditmar	.25
10	Jack Reed	.25
11	Johnny James	.25
12	Elston Howard	.75
SERIES 3		6.00
1	Mickey Mantle	5.00
2	Deron Johnson	.25
3	Bob Hale	.25
4	Bill Stafford	.25
5	Duke Maas	.25
6	Bob Cerv	.25
7	Roland Sheldon	.25
8	Ryne Duren	.35
9	Bob Turley	.25
10	Whitey Ford	1.00
11	Bud Daley	.25
12	Joe DeMaestri	.25

1989 Holsum/Schafer's Super Stars Discs

This version of the 1989 MSA bakeries disc set was issued in Canada by Ben's bakeries. The discs are nearly identical to the other regional variations except for the appearance of a red "Schafer's" logo at top.

		NM/M
Complete Set (20):		9.00
Common Player:		.25
1	Wally Joyner	.25
2	Wade Boggs	1.00
3	Ozzie Smith	1.00
4	Don Mattingly	1.25
5	Jose Canseco	.50
6	Tony Gwynn	1.00
7	Eric Davis	.25
8	Kirby Puckett	1.00
9	Kevin Seitzer	.25
10	Darryl Strawberry	.25
11	Gregg Jefferies	.25
12	Mark Grace	.25
13	Matt Nokes	.25
14	Mark McGwire	2.00
15	Don Mattingly	1.25
16	Roger Clemens	1.25
17	Frank Viola	.25
18	Orel Hershiser	.25
19	Dave Cone	.25
20	Kirk Gibson	.25

1989 Holsum Bakeries Super Stars Discs

This set of 2-3/4" diameter discs was manufactured by Mike Schechter Associates for Holsum bakeries' inclusion in various bread brands. Because the cards are licensed only by the Players Association and not MLB, the player photos have been airbrushed to remove cap and uniform logos. Cards feature white borders with red, yellow and blue decorations. Backs are printed in dark blue and include a few 1988 and career stats and some player vitals. The set was distributed in Michigan.

		NM/M
Complete Set (20):		12.00
Common Player:		.50
1	Wally Joyner	.50
2	Wade Boggs	2.00
3	Ozzie Smith	2.00
4	Don Mattingly	2.50
5	Jose Canseco	1.00
6	Tony Gwynn	.50
7	Eric Davis	.50
8	Kirby Puckett	2.00
9	Kevin Seitzer	.50
10	Darryl Strawberry	.50
11	Gregg Jefferies	.50
12	Mark Grace	.50
13	Matt Nokes	.50
14	Mark McGwire	3.00
15	Bobby Bonilla	.50
16	Roger Clemens	2.50
17	Frank Viola	.50
18	Orel Hershiser	.50
19	Dave Cone	.50
20	Kirk Gibson	.50

1990 Holsum Bakeries Super Stars Discs

Players in this disc set are featured in round portrait photos on which uniform logos have been painted over for lack of a license from Major League Baseball (the set is licensed by the Players Union and bears their logo on back). Most of the front border on these 2-3/4" diameter discs is in red, with yellow stars and white baseballs around the portrait and the bakery's logo at top. A yellow banner beneath the photo has the "Superstars" logo. At bottom, in the white portion of the border, the player's name is presented in red, with his team and position in blue. Backs are printed in blue and include 1989 and career stats, a few biographical details, the card number and appropriate copyrights.

		NM/M
Complete Set (20):		4.00
Common Player:		.25
1	George Bell	.25
2	Tim Raines	.25
3	Tom Henke	.25
4	Andres Galarraga	.25
5	Bret Saberhagen	.25
6	Mark Davis	.25
7	Robin Yount	.75
8	Rickey Henderson	.75
9	Kevin Mitchell	.25
10	Howard Johnson	.25
11	Will Clark	.30
12	Orel Hershiser	.25
13	Fred McGriff	.25
14	Dave Stewart	.25
15	Vince Coleman	.25
16	Steve Sax	.25
17	Kirby Puckett	1.00
18	Tony Gwynn	1.00
19	Jerome Walton	.25
20	Gregg Olson	.25

1991 Holsum Bakeries Super Stars Discs

Similar to the previous year's issue, the 20 discs in the 1991 bakery set feature a color player photo (uniform logos airbrushed off) at center, with a wide white border to the edge of the 2-3/4" diameter

cardboard. The player's name appears in a yellow stripe at bottom, along with his team and position. Backs are printed in dark blue and include a few stats from the previous season. The issue was distributed in Canada for Ben's Bakeries.

		NM/M
Complete Set (20):		45.00
Common Player:		.75
1	Darryl Strawberry	.75
2	Eric Davis	.75
3	Tim Wallach	.75
4	Kevin Mitchell	.75
5	Tony Gwynn	4.50
6	Ryne Sandberg	4.50
7	Doug Drabek	.75
8	Randy Myers	.75
9	Ken Griffey Jr.	6.50
10	Alan Trammell	.75
11	Ken Griffey Sr.	.75
12	Rickey Henderson	3.00
13	Roger Clemens	5.50
14	Bob Welch	.75
15	Kelly Gruber	.75
16	Mark McGwire	7.50
17	Cecil Fielder	.75
18	Dave Steib	.75
19	Nolan Ryan	9.00
20	Cal Ripken, Jr.	9.00

1983 Homeplate Sports Cards Al Kaline Story

Commemorating Al Kaline's 30th anniversary with the Detroit Tigers, this set chronicles his life and career. The 2-1/2" x 3-1/2" cards have either black-and-white front photos with orange borders or color photos with black borders. Backs reverse the color scheme and provide details about the photo on front. The first card in each set has been personally autographed by Kaline.

		NM/M
Complete Set (73):		15.00
Common Card:		.25
1a	30 Years a Tiger/Auto.	12.00
1b	I'd play baseball for nothing	.25
2	Sandlot days in Baltimore	.25
3	MVP trophy winner	.25
4	Learning the ropes	.25
5	Working for a living	.25
6	Pleasing a young fan	.25
7	Al and Louise - the newlyweds	.25
8	Al and Pat Mullin	.25
9	How Al does it #1	.25
10	How Al does it #2	.25
11	Silver Bat for the Champ	.25
12	Al and George Stark	.25
13	Al watches Gordie Howe swing a bat	2.00
14	Kaline and Mantle - Batting Champs	1.00
15	Kaline	.25
16	Martin, Kaline, Kuenn, Mantle, Ford	.50
17	Crossing the plate	.25
18	1959 All-Star Game (W/Bill Skowron.)	.25
19	Cash, Colavito, Kaline	.25
20	Kaline slides under Nellie Fox	.25
21	One of many awards	.25
22	Kaline, Jim Campbell, Norm Cash - 1962	.25
23	Costly catch - 1962	.25
24	Jim Bunning, Al, Norm Cash in Japan	.25
25	Perfect form	.25
26	Ernie Harwell, Al, George Kell	.25
27	Life isn't always easy	.25
28	Al, Michael and Mark Kaline	.25
29	Al and Charlie Dressen - 1965	.25
30	George Kell and Al - Fielding masters	.25
31	Al and Hal Newhouser	.25
32	Michael, Louise, Al and Mark Kaline	.25
33	Al, Charlie Gehringer, Bill Freehan	.25
34	Rapping a hit in 1967	.25
35	Veteran rivals Mantle and Kaline	1.00
36	Al homers against Boston - 1968	.25
37	1968 World Series homer	.25
38	Premier fielder	.25
39	All-Time All-Stars (W/Hank Greenberg, etc.)	.50
40	Part of the game	.25
41	Family portrait	.25
42	Spring training tribute	.25
43	Billy Martin and Al	.25
44	First $100,000 Tiger	.25
45	On deck - 1972	.25
46	A close call	.25
47	On deck in Baltimore - 1974	.25
48	Hit number 3,000 - 1974	.25
49	April 17, 1955 - 3 Homers	.25
50	All-Star Game record	.25
51	1968 Series action - Cepeda	.25
52	Celebrating 1968	.25
53	Al Kaline Day	.25
54	3,000 Hit Day	.25
55	Thank you - Sept. 29, 1974	.25
56	Silver salute - Sept. 29, 1974	.25
57	Al and Kell - a new career	.25
58	Voices of the Tigers	.25
59	Tiger record setter	.25
60	1970 AL All-Star team	.25
61	Pat Mullin and Al	.25
62	Al and Lolich - Aug., 1980	.25
63	Hall of Fame plaque	.25
64	Al and Bowie Kuhn - Aug. 4, 1980	.25
65	Al and parents - Aug., 1980	.25
66	Fame	.25
67	"The Man" and the Boy (W/Stan Musial.)	.50
68	Two Kids - Ted Williams and Kaline	.50
69	Master glovemen (W/Brooks Robinson.)	.45
70	Coach and Pupil - Al and Pat Underwood	.25
71	Kaline career records	.25
72	A Tiger Forever	.25

1990 Homers Cookies Pittsburgh Pirates

This set of 4" x 6" color cards was a stadium giveaway. Fronts have borderless game-action photos. Backs are in black, white and green and have player biographical data, major and minor league stats, career highlights and a sponsor's logo.

		NM/M
Complete Set (31):		20.00
Common Player:		.50
(1)	Wally Backman	.50
(2)	Doug Bair	.50
(3)	Jay Bell	.50
(4)	Rafael Belliard	.50
(5)	Barry Bonds	8.00
(6)	Bobby Bonilla	.50
(7)	Sid Bream	.50
(8)	Jose Cangelosi	.50
(9)	Rich Donnelly	.50
(10)	Doug Drabek	.50
(11)	Billy Hatcher	.50
(12)	Neal Heaton	.50
(13)	Jeff King	.50

1991 Homers Cookies

One Hall of Famer's card was inserted in each box of Homers Cookies. The cards measure 2-1/2" x 3-1/2" and feature sepia-toned photos. The card backs feature lifetime statistics and career highlights. The cards are also numbered on the back and a checklist is featured on the back of each card.

		NM/M
Complete Set (9):		5.00
Common Player:		.50
1	Babe Ruth	2.00
2	Satchel Paige	.75
3	Lefty Gomez	.50
4	Ty Cobb	1.00
5	Cy Young	.50
6	Bob Feller	.50
7	Roberto Clemente	2.00
8	Dizzy Dean	.50
9	Lou Gehrig	1.50

1999 Homers Cookies

Former stars are featured in this set of cards inserted into specially marked boxes of cookies (suggested retail about $1). The 2-1/2" x 3-1/2" cards have color player photos (without logos) with a white border. At top is player identification, at bottom is is a red stripe with "HOMERS." Horizontal backs have a cartoon, career data, biographical information and a checklist.

		NM/M
Complete Set (9):		7.50
Common Player:		1.00
1	Vida Blue	1.00
2	Orlando Cepeda	1.00
3	Darrell Evans	1.00
4	Harmon Killebrew	1.00
5	Dave Kingman	1.00
6	Eddie Murray	1.50
7	Frank Robinson	1.50
8	Willie Stargell	1.00
9	Carl Yastrzemski	1.50

1985 Hostess Braves

After a five-year hiatus, Hostess returned to the production of baseball cards in 1985 with an Atlanta Braves team set. The 22 cards in the set were printed by Topps and

(14)	Bob Kipper	.50
(15)	Randy Kramer	.50
(16)	Gene Lamont	.50
(17)	Bill Landrum	.50
(18)	Mike LaValliere	.50
(19)	Jim Leyland	.50
(20)	Jose Lind	.50
(21)	Milt May	.50
(22)	Ray Miller	.50
(23)	Ted Power	.50
(24)	Gary Redus	.50
(25)	R.J. Reynolds	.50
(26)	Tommy Sandt	.50
(27)	Don Slaught	.50
(28)	John Smiley	.50
(29)	Walt Terrell	.50
(30)	Andy Van Slyke	.50
(31)	Bob Walk	.50

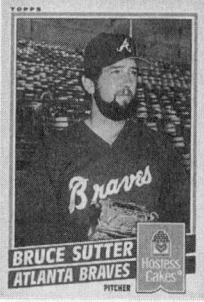

inserted into packages of snack cake products, three cello-wrapped player cards and a header card per box. The 2-1/2" x 3-1/2" cards share a common back design with the regular-issue Topps cards of 1985.

		NM/M
Complete Set (22):		4.00
Common Player:		.35
1	Eddie Haas	.35
2	Len Barker	.35
3	Steve Bedrosian	.35
4	Bruce Benedict	.35
5	Rick Camp	.35
6	Rick Cerone	.35
7	Chris Chambliss	.35
8	Terry Forster	.35
9	Gene Garber	.35
10	Albert Hall	.35
11	Bob Horner	.50
12	Glenn Hubbard	.35
13	Brad Komminsk	.35
14	Rick Mahler	.35
15	Craig McMurtry	.35
16	Dale Murphy	3.00
17	Ken Oberkfell	.35
18	Pascual Perez	.35
19	Gerald Perry	.35
20	Rafael Ramirez	.35
21	Bruce Sutter	2.50
22	Claudell Washington	.35
---	Header Card	.05

1987 Hostess Stickers

Hostess of Canada issued a 30-card set of stickers in specially marked bags of potato chips. One sticker, measuring 1-3/4" x 1-3/8" in size, was found in each bag. The stickers have full-color fronts with the player's name appearing in black type in a white band. The Hostess logo and the sticker number are also included on the fronts. The backs are written in both English and French and contain the player's name, position and team.

		NM/M
Complete Set (30):		12.00
Common Player:		.25
1	Jesse Barfield	.25
2	Ernie Whitt	.25
3	George Bell	.25
4	Hubie Brooks	.25
5	Tim Wallach	.25
6	Floyd Youmans	.25
7	Dale Murphy	.50
8	Ryne Sandberg	2.25
9	Eric Davis	.25
10	Mike Scott	.25
11	Fernando Valenzuela	.25
12	Gary Carter	1.50
13	Mike Schmidt	2.50
14	Tony Pena	.25
15	Ozzie Smith	2.00
16	Tony Gwynn	2.00
17	Mike Krukow	.25
18	Eddie Murray	1.50
19	Wade Boggs	2.00
20	Wally Joyner	.25
21	Harold Baines	.25
22	Brook Jacoby	.25
23	Lou Whitaker	.25
24	George Brett	2.50
25	Robin Yount	1.50
26	Kirby Puckett	2.00

27	Don Mattingly	2.50
28	Jose Canseco	.75
29	Phil Bradley	.25
30	Pete O'Brien	.25

1988 Hostess Potato Chips Expos/Blue Jays

The Expos and Blue Jays are showcased in this set of 24 discs (1-1/2" diameter). Full-color portraits are framed in white, surrounded by red stars. A yellow-banner "1988 Collectors Edition" label is printed (English and French) beneath the photo, followed by the player's name in black. Numbered disc backs are bilingual, blue and white, and include player name and stats. This set was distributed inside Hostess potato chip packages sold in Canada.

		NM/M
Complete Panel Set (12):		6.50
Complete Singles Set (24):		4.50
Common Panel:		.50
Common Player:		.35
Panel 1		
1	Mitch Webster	.35
20	Lloyd Moseby	.35
Panel 2		.50
2	Tim Burke	.35
23	Tom Henke	.35
Panel 3		.50
3	Tom Foley	.35
13	Jim Clancy	.35
Panel 4		.50
4	Herm Winningham	.35
14	Rance Mulliniks	.35
Panel 5		.75
5	Hubie Brooks	.35
24	Jimmy Key	.35
Panel 6		.75
6	Mike Fitzgerald	.35
17	Dave Steib	.35
Panel 7		1.50
7	Tim Wallach	.35
15	Fred McGriff	.50
Panel 8		1.50
8	Andres Galarraga	.45
21	Tony Fernandez	.35
Panel 9		.50
9	Floyd Youmans	.35
18	Mark Eichhorn	.35
Panel 10		.50
10	Neal Heaton	.35
19	Jesse Barfield	.35
Panel 11		1.00
11	Tim Raines	.45
16	Ernie Whitt	.35
Panel 12		.75
12	Casey Candaele	.35
22	George Bell	.35

1990 Hostess Blue Jays Highlight Stickers

Team history highlights through the 1980 season are featured in this set of stickers. The set was produced in strips of three 2-1/4" x 3-1/4" stickers, some oriented horizontally, some vertically. Fronts have color photos with a light blue box beneath containing the highlight printed in both English and French. Black-and-white Hostess and team logos are at

the left and right, respectively. Backs are blank. The set is checklisted here alphabetically based on the title of the sticker at top or left of the strip.

		NM/M
Complete Set (18):		15.00
Common Sticker:		.50
Panel 1		2.00
(1)	First AL East Pennant (Dave Steib)	.50
(2)	Killer Bees Born (George Bell, Lloyd Moseby, Jesse Barfield)	1.00
(3)	AL Home Run Champ (Jesse Barfield)	1.00
Panel 2		3.00
(4)	First Home Run in Skydome (Fred McGriff)	1.50
(5)	Club Save Leader (Tom Henke)	.50
(6)	Three Winning Openers in a Row (Jimmy Key)	1.00
Panel 3		2.00
(7)	First 100 Wins (Jim Clancy)	.50
(8)	ML Home Run Record (Ernie Whitt)	.50
(9)	AL East Champs Again (Tom Henke)	.50
Panel 4		2.00
(10)	Home Run on First Pitch (Junior Felix)	.50
(11)	Almost Perfect (Dave Steib)	.50
(12)	First Game at Skydome	.50
Panel 5		2.00
(13)	Most Double Plays (Damaso Garcia)	.50
(14)	M.V.P. (George Bell)	.50
(15)	Hits the Cycle (Kelly Gruber)	.50
Panel 6		2.00
(16)	Stolen Bases (Dave Collins)	.50
(17)	Gold Glove Winners (Jesse Barfield, Tony Fernandez)	.50
(18)	Goodbye to Exhibition Stadium	.50

1993 Hostess Twinkies

The Continental Baking Co., makers of Hostess Twinkies and cupcakes, returned to the baseball card market in 1993 with a 32-card set issued in two series. The promotion began around opening day with the first series; the second series was made available after the All-Star break. The cards were packaged in multi-packs with cupcakes that look like baseballs, with three cards in a box of eight cupcakes.

		NM/M
Complete Set (32):		4.00
Common Player:		.10
Uncut Sheet:		9.00
1	Andy Van Slyke	.10
2	Ryne Sandberg	.65
3	Bobby Bonilla	.10
4	John Kruk	.10
5	Ray Lankford	.10
6	Gary Sheffield	.25
7	Darryl Strawberry	.10
8	Barry Larkin	.10
9	Terry Pendleton	.10
10	Jose Canseco	.40
11	Dennis Eckersley	.50
12	Brian McRae	.10
13	Frank Thomas	.60
14	Roberto Alomar	.25
15	Cecil Fielder	.10
16	Carlos Baerga	.15
17	Will Clark	.25
18	Andres Galarraga	.60
19	Jeff Bagwell	.60
20	Brett Butler	.10
21	Benito Santiago	.10
22	Tom Glavine	.25
23	Rickey Henderson	.60
24	Wally Joyner	.10
25	Ken Griffey Jr.	.85
26	Cal Ripken Jr.	1.00
27	Roger Clemens	.75

28	Don Mattingly	.75
29	Kirby Puckett	.65
30	Larry Walker	.10
31	Jack McDowell	.10
32	Pat Listach	.10

1986 Houston Astros Police

Astros #34 NOLAN RYAN PITCHER

This full-color police safety set was issued by the Houston Police Department and sponsored by Kool-Aid. The set was distributed at the Astrodome on June 14, when 15,000 sets of the first 12 cards were given away. The balance of the set was distributed throughout the summer by police. The cards feature player photos on the fronts and a safety tip on the back. The cards measure 4-1/8" x 2-5/8".

		NM/M
Complete Set (26):		4.00
Common Player:		.25
1	Jim Pankovits	.25
2	Nolan Ryan	3.00
3	Mike Scott	.25
4	Kevin Bass	.25
5	Bill Doran	.25
6	Hal Lanier	.25
7	Denny Walling	.25
8	Alan Ashby	.25
9	Phil Garner	.25
10	Charlie Kerfeld	.25
11	Dave Smith	.25
12	Jose Cruz	.25
13	Craig Reynolds	.25
14	Mark Bailey	.25
15	Bob Knepper	.25
16	Julio Solano	.25
17	Dickie Thon	.25
18	Mike Madden	.25
19	Jeff Calhoun	.25
20	Tony Walker	.25
21	Terry Puhl	.25
22	Glenn Davis	.25
23	Billy Hatcher	.25
24	Jim Deshaies	.25
25	Frank DiPino	.25
26	Coaching Staff (Yogi Berra, Matt Galante, Denis Menke, Les Moss, Gene Tenace)	.25

1987 Houston Astros Police

Astros #27 GLENN DAVIS INFIELDER

The 1987 Astros safety set was produced through the combined efforts of the team, Deer Park Hospital and Sportsmedia Presentations. Cards #1-12 were handed out to youngsters 14 and under at the Astrodome on July 14. The balance of the distribution was handled by Deer Park Hospital. The cards, which measure 2-5/8" x 4-1/8", contain full-color photos. The backs offer a brief team/player history and a "Tips From The Dugout" anti-drug message.

		NM/M
Complete Set (26):		5.00
Common Player:		.25
1	Larry Andersen	.25

2	Mark Bailey	.25
3	Jose Cruz	.25
4	Danny Darwin	.25
5	Bill Doran	.25
6	Billy Hatcher	.25
7	Hal Lanier	.25
8	Davey Lopes	.25
9	Dave Meads	.25
10	Craig Reynolds	.25
11	Mike Scott	.25
12	Denny Walling	.25
13	Aurelio Lopez	.25
14	Dickie Thon	.25
15	Terry Puhl	.25
16	Nolan Ryan	4.00
17	Dave Smith	.25
18	Julio Solano	.25
19	Jim Deshaies	.25
20	Bob Knepper	.25
21	Alan Ashby	.25
22	Kevin Bass	.25
23	Glenn Davis	.25
24	Phil Garner	.25
25	Jim Pankovits	.25
26	Coaching Staff (Yogi Berra, Matt Galante, Denis Menke, Les Moss, Gene Tenace)	.25

1988 Houston Astros Police

Astros #27 GLENN DAVIS INFIELDER

This set of full-color cards highlighting the Houston Astros was produced by the team, in conjunction with Deer Park Hospital and Sportsmedia Promotions for distribution to fans 14 years and younger at a ballpark giveaway. The 2-5/8" x 4-1/8" cards feature full-color player photos framed by a narrow blue border with an orange player/team name block below the photo. Blue-and-white backs have orange borders with player information, career highlights and anti-drug tips.

		NM/M
Complete Set (26):		5.00
Common Player:		.25
1	Juan Agosto	.25
2	Larry Andersen	.25
3	Joaquin Andujar	.25
4	Alan Ashby	.25
5	Mark Bailey	.25
6	Kevin Bass	.25
7	Danny Darwin	.25
8	Glenn Davis	.25
9	Jim Deshaies	.25
10	Bill Doran	.25
11	Billy Hatcher	.25
12	Jeff Heathcock	.25
13	Steve Henderson	.25
14	Chuck Jackson	.25
15	Bob Knepper	.25
16	Jim Pankovits	.25
17	Terry Puhl	.25
18	Rafael Ramirez	.25
19	Craig Reynolds	.25
20	Nolan Ryan	4.00
21	Mike Scott	.25
22	Dave Smith	.25
23	Denny Walling	.25
24	Gerald Young	.25
25	Hal Lanier	.25
26	Coaching Staff (Yogi Berra, Gene Clines, Matt Galante, Marc Hill, Denis Menke, Les Moss)	.25

2005 Houston Astros Card Deck

This stadium giveaway was sponsored by Academy Sports+ Outdoors. Cards are 2-1/2" x 3-1/2" with rounded corners. Backs have a baseball in the background with team and sponsor's logos. Fronts have game-action photos. Many players have two cards in the deck, most with the same photo.

		NM/M
Complete Set (56):		12.00
Common Player:		.25
AS	Roger Clemens	3.00

Roger Clemens
HOUSTON ASTROS · 2005 SEASON
A ♠

2S	Russ Springer	.25
3S	Chad Harville	.25
4S	Brad Lidge	.35
5S	Jeff Bagwell	1.00
6S	Jason Lane	.25
7S	Luke Scott	.25
8S	Brad Lidge	.25
9S	Roger Clemens	3.00
JS	Jason Lane	.25
JS	Luke Scott	.25
QS	Minute Maid Park	.25
KS	Jeff Bagwell	1.00
AD	Roy Oswalt	.50
2D	Brad Ausmus	.25
3D	Russ Springer	.25
4D	Raul Chavez	.25
5D	Morgan Ensberg	.25
6D	Brandon Duckworth	.25
7D	Orlando Palmeiro	.25
8D	Brandon Duckworth	.25
9D	Roy Oswalt	.50
10D	Orlando Palmeiro	.25
JD	Morgan Ensberg	.25
QD	Minute Maid Park	.25
KD	Brad Ausmus	.25
AC	Brandon Backe	.25
2C	Chris Burke	.25
3C	Dan Wheeler	.25
4C	Eric Bruntlett	.25
5C	Jose Vizcaino	.25
6C	Dan Wheeler	.25
7C	Craig Biggio	.50
8C	Willy Taveras	.25
9C	Brandon Backe	.25
10C	Jose Vizcaino	.25
JC	Willy Taveras	.25
QC	Minute Maid Park	.25
KC	Craig Biggio	.50
AH	Andy Pettitte	.35
2H	Raul Chavez	.25
3H	Chad Qualls	.25
4H	John Franco	.25
5H	Mike Lamb	.25
6H	Adam Everett	.25
7H	John Franco	.25
8H	Lance Berkman	.50
9H	Andy Pettitte	.35
10H	Mike Lamb	.25
JH	Adam Everett	.25
QH	Minute Maid Park	.25
KH	Lance Berkman	.50
---	Phil Garner	.25
---	Phil Garner	.25
---	NL Wild Cardb 04	.05
---	NL Wild Card 04	.05

1989 Houston Colt .45s Fire Safety

The expansion Houston Colt .45s of 1962 are featured in this 1989 fire safety issue. The 2-1/2" x 3-1/2" cards have sepia player photos on front, with blue pistol frames and team logo, an orange name banner and brown Smokey logo. Backs are in black-and-white with a fire prevention cartoon, Forest Service logos and the player name, position and uniform number. Cards numbers are at upper-right.

		NM/M
Complete Set (29):		12.50
Common Player:		.50
1	Bob Bruce	.50
2	Al Cicotte	.50

3	Dave Giusti	.50
4	Jim Golden	.50
5	Ken Johnson	.50
6	Tom Borland	.50
7	Bobby Shantz	.50
8	Dick Farrell	.50
9	Jim Umbricht	.50
10	Hal Woodshick	.50
11	Merritt Ranew	.50
12	Hal Smith	.50
13	Jim Campbell	.50
14	Norm Larker	.75
15	Joe Amalfitano	.50
16	Bob Aspromonte	.75
17	Bob Lillis	.50
18	Dick Gernert	.50
19	Don Buddin	.50
20	Pidge Browne	.50
21	Von McDaniel	.50
22	Don Taussig	.50
23	Al Spangler	.50
24	Al Heist	.50
25	Jim Pendleton	.50
26	Johnny Weekly	.50
27	Harry Craft	.50
28	.45s Coaches (Lum Harris, Bobby Bragan, Jim Busby, Cot Deal, Jim Adair)	.50
29	Team Photo	.50

1993 Hoyle Legends of Baseball

SATCHEL PAIGE

Specially marked decks of Hoyle playing cards contained one of nine Hall of Famer's cards. In the 2-1/2" x 3-1/2" round-cornered poker-size format, the cards have oft-seen black-and-white photos on a glossy front. Backs have a facsimile autograph, biographical data, some stats and career highlights.

		NM/M
Complete Set (9):		12.00
Common Player:		1.00
(1)	Ty Cobb	2.00
(2)	Dizzy Dean	1.00
(3)	Lou Gehrig	2.00
(4)	Walter Johnson	1.00
(5)	Satchel Paige	1.00
(6)	Babe Ruth	3.00
(7)	Casey Stengel	1.00
(8)	Honus Wagner	1.50
(9)	Cy Young	1.00

1993 Humpty Dumpty

The Canadian potato chip company Humpty Dumpty issued a 50-card set of miniature cards in 1993. The UV coated cards measure 1-7/16" x 1-15/16", with a full-bleed color photo on the front along with the team logo. The backs have three-year statistics and biographical information about the player, along with appropriate product and baseball logos and a card number. Besides being packed one per bag in chips, the complete set was also available via a mail-in offer with a plastic album.

		NM/M
Complete Set (50):		10.00
Complete Set, W/Album:		15.00
Common Player:		

1	Cal Ripken, Jr.	3.00
2	Mike Mussina	.50
3	Roger Clemens	2.25
4	Chuck Finley	.25
5	Sandy Alomar	.25
6	Frank Thomas	1.00
7	Robin Ventura	.25
8	Cecil Fielder	.25
9	George Brett	2.00
10	Cal Eldred	.25
11	Kirby Puckett	1.50
12	Dave Winfield	1.00
13	Jim Abbott	.25
14	Rickey Henderson	1.00
15	Ken Griffey Jr.	2.50
16	Nolan Ryan	3.00
17	Ivan Rodriguez	.75
18	Paul Molitor	1.00
19	John Olerud	.25
20	Joe Carter	.25
21	Jack Morris	.25
22	Roberto Alomar	.40
23	Pat Borders	.25
24	Devon White	.25
25	Juan Guzman	.25
26	Steve Avery	.25
27	John Smoltz	.25
28	Mark Grace	.25
29	Jose Rijo	.25
30	Dave Nied	.25
31	Benito Santiago	.25
32	Jeff Bagwell	1.00
33	Tim Wallach	.25
34	Eric Karros	.25
35	Delino DeShields	.25
36	Wilfredo Cordero	.25
37	Marquis Grissom	.25
38a	Ken Hill (Weight: 1915)	.50
38b	Ken Hill (Weight: 195)	.25
39	Moises Alou	.25
40	Chris Nabholz	.25
41	Dennis Martinez	.25
42	Larry Walker	.25
43	Bobby Bonilla	.25
44	Lenny Dykstra	.25
45	Tim Wakefield	.25
46	Andy Van Slyke	.25
47	Tony Gwynn	1.50
48	Fred McGriff	.25
49	Barry Bonds	3.00
50	Ozzie Smith	1.50
---	Checklist	.10

1982 Hygrade Expos

Gary Carter 8

This Montreal Expos team set was the object of intense collector speculation when it was first issued. Single cello-wrapped cards were included in packages of Hygrade luncheon meat in the province of Quebec only. A mail-in offer for the complete set appeared later in the season. It remains a relatively scarce issue today. The 2" x 3" cards are printed on heavy paper, with round corners. Backs are printed in French, and contain an offer for an album to house the set.

		NM/M
Complete Set (24):		15.00
Common Player:		1.00
Album:		5.00
0	Al Oliver	2.00
4	Chris Speier	1.00
5	John Milner	1.00
6	Jim Fanning	1.00
8	Gary Carter	7.50
10	Andre Dawson	5.00
11	Frank Tavaras (Taveras)	1.00
17	Terry Francona	1.00
17	Tim Blackwell	1.00
18	Jerry White	1.00
20	Bob James	1.00
21	Scott Sanderson	1.00
24	Brad Mills	1.00
29	Tim Wallach	1.00
30	Tim Raines	3.00
32	Bill Gullickson	1.00
35	Woodie Fryman	1.00
38	Bryn Smith	1.00
41	Jeff Reardon	1.00
42	Dan Norman	1.00
45	Steve Rogers	1.00
48	Ray Burris	1.00

49	Warren Cromartie	1.00
53	Charlie Lea	1.00

1987 Hygrade Baseball's All-Time Greats

(See "Baseball's All-Time Greats" for checklist and values.)

I

1994 Innovative Confections Sucker Savers

These 2-3/8" diameter discs were included in a plastic snap-top lollipop holder. A yellow strip which intersects the red border at the top contains the player name and team, while a yellow diamond graphic surrounds the player photo. Produced by Michael Schechter Assoc., the discs are licensed by the Players Union but not MLB, so team uniform logos are airbrushed off the photos. Backs are printed in blue and have 1993 and career stats. Square "proof" versions are common in the hobby and carry little or no premium.

		NM/M
Complete Set (20):		25.00
Common Player:		1.00
1	Rickey Henderson	2.00
2	Ken Caminiti	1.00
3	Terry Pendleton	1.00
4	Tim Raines	1.00
5	Joe Carter	1.00
6	Benito Santiago	1.00
7	Jim Abbott	1.00
8	Ozzie Smith	2.50
9	Don Slaught	1.00
10	Tony Gwynn	2.50
11	Mark Langston	1.00
12	Darryl Strawberry	1.00
13	David Justice	1.00
14	Cecil Fielder	1.00
15	Cal Ripken Jr.	4.00
16	Jeff Bagwell	2.00
17	Mike Piazza	3.00
18	Bobby Bonilla	1.00
19	Barry Bonds	4.00
20	Roger Clemens	2.75

1995 International Playing Cards Toronto Blue Jays

For a second year the Canadian affiliate of the U.S. Playing Card Co. issued a team set of Blue Jays. Fronts have color portrait and action photos - up to three for popular players - with player identification and traditional playing card suit and value indicators in opposite corners. Backs have a large team logo. Cards are in 2-1/2" x 3-1/2" round-cornered format and were sold in a colorful flip-top box.

		NM/M
Complete Set (56):		4.00
Common Player:		.05
AC	John Olerud	.15
2C	Pat Hentgen	.05
3C	Juan Guzman	.05
4C	Cecil Fielder	.10
5C	Roberto Alomar	.25
6C	Joe Carter	.10
7C	Mark Eichhorn	.05
8C	Carlos Delgado	.75
9C	Tom Candiotti	.05
10C	Dave Stewart	.10
JC	Tony Fernandez	.05
QC	Pat Borders	.05
KC	Dave Winfield	1.00
AS	Paul Molitor	1.00
2S	Todd Stottlemyre	.10
3S	Rickey Henderson	1.00
4S	Tom Henke	.05
5S	Fred McGriff	.10
6S	Devon White	.10
7S	Duane Ward	.05
8S	David Wells	.10
9S	David Cone	.10
10S	Mike Timlin	.05
JS	Ed Sprague	.05
QS	Jack Morris	.05
KS	Jimmy Key	.05
AH	Roberto Alomar	.35
2H	Candy Maldonado	.05
3H	Mike Timlin	.05
4H	Ed Sprague	.05
5H	Pat Borders	.05
6H	Jimmy Key	.05
7H	Paul Molitor	1.00
8H	Candy Maldonado	.05
9H	Danny Cox	.05

top-center and sponsors' logos along the bottom. The set was sold in a colorful cardboard box.

		NM/M
Complete Set (55):		4.00
Common Player:		.05
AC	John Olerud	.15
2C	Al Leiter	.05
3C	Dave Stewart	.10
4C	Pat Borders	.05
5C	Devon White	.05
6C	Joe Carter	.10
7C	Roberto Alomar	.35
8C	Woody Williams	.05
9C	Eddie Zosky	.05
10C	Willie Canate	.05
JC	Danny Cox	.05
QC	Todd Stottlemyre	.10
KC	Ed Sprague	.05
AS	Paul Molitor	1.00
2S	Michael Timlin	.05
3S	Randy Knorr	.05
4S	Pat Hentgen	.05
5S	Darnell Coles	.05
6S	Juan Guzman	.05
7S	Roberto Alomar	.35
8S	Joe Carter	.10
9S	Scott Brow	.05
10S	Dick Schofield	.05
JS	Rob Butler	.05
QS	Tony Castillo	.05
KS	Duane Ward	.05
AH	Joe Carter	.10
2H	Woody Williams	.05
3H	Danny Cox	.05
4H	Todd Stottlemyre	.10
5H	Ed Sprague	.05
6H	John Olerud	.15
7H	Paul Molitor	1.00
8H	Scott Brow	.05
9H	Pat Hentgen	.05
10H	Al Leiter	.05
JH	Dave Stewart	.05
QH	Pat Borders	.05
KH	Devon White	.10
AD	Roberto Alomar	.35
2D	Eddie Zosky	.05
3D	Rob Butler	.05
4D	Tony Castillo	.05
5D	Duane Ward	.05
6D	Paul Molitor	1.00
7D	John Olerud	.15
8D	Carlos Delgado	.75
9D	Michael Timlin	.05
10D	Randy Knorr	.05
JD	Pat Hentgen	.05
QD	Darnell Coles	.05
KD	Juan Guzman	.05
Joker	Team Name	.05
Joker	A.L. Logo	.05
---	Checklist	.05

J

1984 Jarvis Press Rangers

BILLY SAMPLE OF

For its second annual "Baseball Card Day" game promotional set, the Rangers picked up a new sponsor, Jarvis Press of Dallas. The 30 cards in the set include 27 players, the manager, trainer and a group card of the coaches. Cards measure 2-3/8" x 3-1/2". Color game-action photos make up the card fronts. Backs, printed in black and white, include a portrait photo of the player. A source close to the promotion indicated 10,000 sets were produced.

		NM/M
Complete Set (30):		4.00
Common Player:		.35
1	Bill Stein	.35
2	Alan Bannister	.35
4	Wayne Tolleson	.35
5	Billy Sample	.35
6	Bobby Jones	.35
7	Ned Yost	.35
8	Pete O'Brien	.35
11	Doug Rader	.35
12	Tommy Dunbar	.35
14	Jim Anderson	.35
15	Larry Parrish	.35
16	Mike Mason	.35
17	Mickey Rivers	.35
19	Curtis Wilkerson	.35
20	Jeff Kunkel	.35
21	Odell Jones	.35
24	Dave Schmidt	.35
25	Buddy Bell	.35
26	George Wright	.35
28	Frank Tanana	.35
30	Marv Foley	.35
31	Dave Stewart	.50
32	Gary Ward	.35
36	Dickie Noles	.35
43	Donnie Scott	.35
44	Danny Darwin	.35
49	Charlie Hough	.35
53	Joey McLaughlin	.35
	Coaching Staff (Rich Donnelly, Glenn Ezell, Merv Rettenmund, Dick Such, Wayne Terwilliger)	.35
---	Trainer (Bill Zeigler)	.35

1986 Jays Potato Chips

One of a handful of round baseball cards produced for inclusion in boxes of potato chips on a regional basis in 1986, the Jays set of 2-7/8" discs is believed to be the scarcest of the type. The 20 cards in the issue include the most popular Milwaukee Brewers and Chicago Cubs and White Sox players; the set having been distributed in the southern Wisconsin- northern Illi-

10H	Todd Stottlemyre	.05
JH	Rickey Henderson	1.00
QH	Tom Henke	.05
KH	Cecil Fielder	.10
AD	Joe Carter	.10
2D	Duane Ward	.05
3D	Dave Stewart	.10
4D	Tony Fernandez	.05
5D	Jack Morris	.05
6D	Dave Winfield	1.00
7D	John Olerud	.15
8D	Manny Lee	.05
9D	Pat Hentgen	.05
10D	Randy Knorr	.05
JD	Juan Guzman	.05
QD	Fred McGriff	.10
KD	Devon White	.10
---	Toronto Blue Jays	.05
---	Team Logo Card	.05
---	A.L. Logo Card	.05
---	Checklist	.05

nois area. Like many contemporary sets produced by Mike Schechter Associates, the '86 Jays cards feature player photos on which the team logos have been airbrushed off the caps.

		NM/M
Complete Set (20):		17.50
Common Player:		.50
(1)	Harold Baines	.50
(2)	Cecil Cooper	.50
(3)	Jody Davis	.50
(4)	Bob Dernier	.50
(5)	Richard Dotson	.50
(6)	Shawon Dunston	.50
(7)	Carlton Fisk	3.00
(8)	Jim Gantner	.50
(9)	Ozzie Guillen	.50
(10)	Teddy Higuera	.50
(11)	Ron Kittle	.50
(12)	Paul Molitor	3.00
(13)	Keith Moreland	.50
(14)	Ernie Riles	.50
(15)	Ryne Sandberg	6.00
(16)	Tom Seaver	3.00
(17)	Lee Smith	.50
(18)	Rick Sutcliffe	.50
(19)	Greg Walker	.50
(20)	Robin Yount	3.00

1984 Jewel Food Chicago Cubs/White Sox

Similar in format to previous issues by the Midwestern food company, these 16-piece sets of Chicago's National and American League teams are printed on 6" x 9" paper. Fronts feature a chest-to-cap color player photo with a black facsimile autograph. A logo and copyright notice by the Players Association is at upper-left. Backs are blank. Cards were distributed four per week with the purchase of specific sale products.

		NM/M
Complete Cubs Set (16):		12.00
Complete White Sox Set (16):		12.50
Common Player:		.50
(1)	Larry Bowa	.50
(2)	Ron Cey	.50
(3)	Jody Davis	.50
(4)	Bob Dernier	.50
(5)	Leon Durham	.50
(6)	Dennis Eckersley	2.50
(7)	Richie Hebner	.50
(8)	Gary Matthews	.50
(9)	Keith Moreland	.50
(10)	Ryne Sandberg	6.00
(11)	Scott Sanderson	.50
(12)	Lee Smith	.75
(13)	Tom Stoddard	.50
(14)	Rick Sutcliffe	.50
(15)	Steve Trout	.50
(16)	Gary Woods	.50
(1)	Harold Baines	.50
(2)	Alan Bannister	.50
(3)	Julio Cruz	.50
(4)	Richard Dotson	.50
(5)	Jerry Dybzinski	.50
(6)	Carlton Fisk	4.00
(7)	Scott Fletcher	.50
(8)	LaMarr Hoyt	.50
(9)	Ron Kittle	.50
(10)	Rudy Law	.50
(11)	Vance Law	.50
(12)	Greg Luzinski	.50
(13)	Tom Paciorek	.50

(14)	Tom Seaver	4.00
(15)	Mike Squires	.50
(16)	Greg Walker	.50

2003 Jewish Major Leaguers

Art Shamsky

Produced by Fleer for the American Jewish Historical Society, this set is a first-ever compilation of cards of every American Jew who played in Major League Baseball between 1871 and the All-Star break of 2003. Cards are standard 2-1/2" x 3-1/2", uv-coated on both front and back. Fronts have color or black-and-white photos, bordered in black. Backs have personal data, a career summary, an indication of what other baseball cards the player appeared on and photo/text credits. The issue was sold only as a complete boxed set with an initial price of about $100. A more limited silver-stamped version was available for $200.

		NM/M
Complete Set (149):		100.00
Common Player:		.75
Silver Edition:		3X
1	Sandy Koufax	15.00
2	Harry Danning	.75
3	Hank Greenberg	7.50
4	Andy Cohen	.75
5	Al Rosen	2.50
6	Buddy Myer	.75
7	Sid Gordon	.75
8	Shawn Green	3.00
9	Morrie Arnovich	.75
10	"Lip" Pike	2.00
11	Nate Berkenstock	.75
12	Jacob Pike (?)	.75
13	Jake Goodman	.75
14	Ike Samuls' 1895 St. Louis Team	.75
15	Leo Fishel	.75
16	Bill Cristall	.75
17	Harry Kane	.75
18	Barney Pelty	.75
19	Moxie Manuel	.75
20	Phil Cooney	.75
21	Guy Zinn	.75
22	Ed Mensor	.75
23	Erskine Mayer	.75
24	Henry Bostick	.75
25	Sam Mayer	.75
26	Sammy Bohne	.75
27	Jake Pitler	.75
28	Bob Berman	.75
29	Eddie Corey	.75
30	Jesse Baker	.75
31	Al Schacht	.75
32	Sam Fishburn	.75
33	Reuben Ewing	.75
34	Heinie Scheer	.75
35	Lou Rosenberg	.75
36	Moe Berg	7.50
37	Joe Bennett	.75
38	Moe Solomon	.75
39	Happy Foreman	.75
40	Simon Rosenthal	.75
41	Ike Danning	.75
42	Jonah Goldman	.75
43	Ed Wineapple	.75
44	Jimmie Reese	.75
45	Harry Rosenberg	.75
46	Jim Levey	.75
47	Alta Cohen	.75
48	Max Rosenfeld	.75
49	Lou Brower	.75
50	Izzy Goldstein	.75
51	Milt Galatzer	.75
52	Phil Weintraub	.75
53	Cy Malis	.75
54	Syd Cohen	.75
55	Fred Sington	.75
56	Harry Eisenstat	.75
57	Chick Starr	.75
58	Goody Rosen	.75
59	Harry Chozen	.75
60	Eddie Feinberg	.75
61	Sam Nahem	.75
62	Dick Conger	.75
63	Murray Franklin	.75
64	Harry Feldman	.75
65	Harry Shuman	.75

66	Eddie Turchin	.75
67	Cy Block	.75
68	Hal Schacker	.75
69	Mike Schemer	.75
70	Herb Karpel	.75
71	Bud Swartz	.75
72	Mickey Rutner	.75
73	Marv Rotblatt	.75
74	Joe Ginsberg	.75
75	Cal Abrams	.75
76	Saul Rogovin	.75
77	Sid Schacht	.75
78	Lou Limmer	.75
79	Duke Markell	.75
80	Al Richter	.75
81	Al Federoff	.75
82	Herb Gorman	.75
83	Moe Savransky	.75
84	Hy Cohen	.75
85	Al Silvera	.75
86	Barry Latman	.75
87	Ed Mayer	.75
88	Larry Sherry	1.00
89	Don Taussig	.75
90	Norm Sherry	1.00
91	Randy Cardinal	.75
92	Alan Koch	.75
93	Larry Yellen	.75
94	Steve Hertz	.75
95	Art Shamsky	.75
96	Richie Scheinblum	.75
97	Greg Goossen	.75
98	Norm Miller	.75
99	Ken Holtzman	.75
100	Mike Epstein	.75
101	Ron Blomberg	.75
102	Lloyd Allen	.75
103	Dave Roberts	.75
104	Elliott Maddox	.75
105	Steve Stone	2.00
106	Steve Yeager	.75
107	Skip Jutze	.75
108	Dick Sharon	.75
109	Jeff Newman	.75
110	Ross Baumgarten	.75
111	Jeff Stember	.75
112	Steve Ratzer	.75
113	Bob Tufts	.75
114	Larry Rothschild	.75
115	Mark Gilbert	.75
116	Steve Rosenberg	.75
117	Roger Samuels	.75
118	Steve Wapnick	.75
119	Scott Radinsky	.75
120	Ruben Amaro, Jr.	.75
121	Wayne Rosenthal	.75
122	Eddie Zosky	.75
123	Jesse Levis	.75
124	Brad Ausmus	.75
125	Eric Helfand	.75
126	Mike Lieberthal	2.00
127	Andrew Lorraine	.75
128	Brian Kowitz	.75
129	Brian Bark	.75
130	Mike Milchin	.75
131	Al Levine	.75
132	Micah Franklin	.75
133	Mike Saipe	.75
134	Keith Glauber	.75
135	Gabe Kapler	2.00
136	Scott Schoeneweis	.75
137	David Newhan	.75
138	Jason Marquis	.75
139	Frank Charles	.75
140	Tony Cogan	.75
141	Justin Wayne	.75
142	Matt Ford	.75
---	Career Batting Leaders	.10
---	Career Pitching Leaders	.10
---	Alphabetical Listing A-M	.10
---	Alphabetical Listing M-Z	.10
---	Header Card/Credits	.05
---	Credits	.05
149	George Brace (Photographer)	.25

Jewish Major Leaguers Update Edition

Solomon Israel

Produced by the American Jewish Historical Society, this set updates the premiere edition of 2003. Cards are standard 2-1/2" x 3-1/2". Fronts have color or black-and-white photos, bordered in blue. Backs have personal data, a career summary, and photo/text credits. Ther update includes players who debuted after 2003, as well as female players, minor leaguers and many specialty cards.

		NM/M
Complete Set (55):		40.00
Common Player:		.50
(1)	Header Card	.50
(2)	All-time Roster, A-F	.50
(3)	All-time Roster, G-Rad	.50
(4)	All-time Roster, Rat-Z	.50
(5)	Career Leaders: Batting	.50
(6)	Career Leaders: Pitching	.50
7	Shawn Green	.75
8	Brad Ausmus	.75
9	Mike Lieberthal	.75
10	Al Levine	.75
11	Scott Schoeneweis	.75
12	Jason Marquis	.75
13	Gabe Kapler	.75
14	John Grabow	.75
15	Kevin Youkilis	.75
16	Adam Stern	.75
17	Craig Breslow	.75
18	Adam Greenberg	.75
19	Scott Feldman	.75
20	Prospects (Aaron Rifkin, Scott Schneider, Tony Schrager, Jeff Pickler)	.75
21	1901 Giants Team (Jacob Livingston)	.50
22	Jacob Atz	.75
23	Lefty Weinert	.75
24	Lou Boudreau	1.50
25	Bob Davis	.75
26	Jose Bautista	.75
27	Sam Nahem	.50
28	Thelma Eisen	.50
29	Anita Foss	.50
30	Blanche Schachter	.50
31	Margaret Wigiser (SP)(Withdrawn)	.50
31A	Error! (Replacement)	.50
32	Cy Block	.50
33	Harry Danning	.50
34	Lipman Pike	1.50
35	Abe Yager	.50
36	Barney Dreyfuss	.50
37	Dolly Stark	.50
38	Hank Greenberg	1.50
39	Allen Roth	.50
40	Mel Allen	.75
41	Ron Blomberg	.50
42	Richie Scheinblum	.50
43	Allan H. "Bud" Selig	.75
44	Israel's National Baseball Team	.50
45	Marvin Miller, Donald Fehr	.50
46	Moe Berg, Heinie Scheer	.75
47	Saul Rogovin, Lou Limmer, Joe Ginsberg	.50
48	"The Cooperstown Eight"	.50
49	Half a "Minyan": 1946 Giants	.50
50	Clown Princes (Al Schacht, Max Patkin)	.50
51	Mickey Rutner, Lou Limmer	.50
52	Jake Levy, Hal Saltzman	.50
53	Solomon Israel	.50
54	Marty Abramowitz	.50
55	Gabe Kapler, Adam Stern, Kevin Youkilis	.50

1986 Jiffy Pop/MSA Promos

This 20-card set was produced by Mike Schecter Associates in 1986 to provide attendees at a restaruant and food trade show with examples of his card promotions. The promos have the same fronts as the 1986 Jiffy Pop discs on a 2-7/8" diameter format. The backs have an advertisement for MSA's services. Like the regular issues, the uniform logos have been airbrushed from the discs due to lack of a license from Major League Baseball (the issue is licensed by the Players Union). The unnumbered promo discs are checklisted here alphabetically.

		NM/M
Complete Set (20):		175.00
Common Player:		4.00
(1)	Wade Boggs	10.00
(2)	George Brett	15.00
(3)	Gary Carter	10.00
(4)	Steve Garvey	6.00
(5)	Dwight Gooden	4.00
(6)	Reggie Jackson	12.50
(7)	Don Mattingly	15.00
(8)	Willie McGee	4.00
(9)	Dale Murphy	4.00
(10)	Eddie Murray	10.00
(11)	Lance Parrish	4.00
(12)	Jim Rice	6.00
(13)	Cal Ripken, Jr.	25.00
(14)	Pete Rose	20.00
(15)	Nolan Ryan	25.00
(16)	Ryne Sandberg	12.50
(17)	Mike Schmidt	15.00
(18)	Fernando Valenzuela	4.00
(19)	Dave Winfield	10.00
(20)	Robin Yount	10.00

1986 Jiffy Pop

DAVE WINFIELD — OUTFIELDER-NEW YORK YANKEES

One of the scarcer of the 1986 regionals, the Jiffy Pop discs were inserted in packages of heat-and-eat popcorn. A production of Mike Schechter Associates, the 2-7/8" diameter discs feature 20 popular stars, many in the same pictures found in other '86 regionals. Like other MSA issues, caps have had the team logos erased, allowing Jiffy Pop to avoid paying a licensing fee to the teams. Backs have a few biographical details and stats.

		NM/M
Complete Set (20):		15.00
Common Player:		.50
1	Jim Rice	.65
2	Wade Boggs	1.00
3	Lance Parrish	.50
4	George Brett	2.00
5	Robin Yount	1.00
6	Don Mattingly	2.00
7	Dave Winfield	1.00
8	Reggie Jackson	1.50
9	Cal Ripken	3.50
10	Eddie Murray	1.00
11	Pete Rose	2.50
12	Ryne Sandberg	1.50
13	Nolan Ryan	3.50
14	Fernando Valenzuela	.50
15	Willie McGee	.50
16	Dale Murphy	.75
17	Mike Schmidt	2.00
18	Steve Garvey	.50
19	Gary Carter	1.00
20	Dwight Gooden	.50

1987 Jiffy Pop

JIM RICE

For a second year, Jiffy Pop inserted player discs in its packages of popcorn. The full-color discs measure 2-7/8" in diameter and were produced by Mike Schechter Associates. Titled "2nd Annual Collectors' Edition," the card fronts feature player photos with all team insignias airbrushed away. Information on the backs of the discs is printed in bright red on white stock. Die-cut 16-1/4" x 14" press sheets containing all 20 discs were available via a mail-in offer.

		NM/M
Complete Set (20):		20.00
Uncut Sheet:		25.00
Common Player:		.75
1	Ryne Sandberg	2.00
2	Dale Murphy	1.25
3	Jack Morris	.75
4	Keith Hernandez	.75
5	George Brett	2.50
6	Don Mattingly	2.50
7	Ozzie Smith	2.00
8	Cal Ripken, Jr.	3.50
9	Dwight Gooden	.75
10	Pedro Guerrero	.75
11	Lou Whitaker	.75
12	Roger Clemens	2.50
13	Lance Parrish	.75
14	Rickey Henderson	2.00
15	Fernando Valenzuela	.75
16	Mike Schmidt	2.50
17	Darryl Strawberry	.75
18	Mike Scott	.75
19	Jim Rice	1.00
20	Wade Boggs	2.00

1988 Jiffy Pop

BUDDY BELL — CINCINNATI REDS

This 20-disc set is the third Jiffy Pop issue spotlighting leading players. Discs are 2-1/2" in diameter with a semi-gloss finish and feature full-color closeups on white stock. Team logos have been airbrushed off the player's caps. Fronts have a curved label "3rd Annual Collector's Edition." Disc backs are white, with dark blue lettering, and contain player information, stats and disc number. An uncut sheet (16" x 14-1/2") with all 20 discs was available in a mail-in redemption offer.

		NM/M
Complete Set (20):		9.00
Uncut Sheet:		10.00
Common Player:		.35
1	Buddy Bell	.35
2	Wade Boggs	1.25
3	Gary Carter	1.25
4	Jack Clark	.35
5	Will Clark	.45
6	Roger Clemens	2.00
7	Vince Coleman	.35
8	Andre Dawson	.50
9	Keith Hernandez	.35
10	Kent Hrbek	.35
11	Wally Joyner	.35
12	Paul Molitor	1.25
13	Eddie Murray	1.25
14	Tim Raines	.35
15	Bret Saberhagen	.35
16	Alan Trammell	.35
17	Ozzie Virgil	.35
18	Tim Wallach	.35
19	Dave Winfield	1.25
20	Robin Yount	1.25

Ronnie Joyner St. Louis Browns Heads-Up

JIM DELSING

Though there is nothing on the cards themselves to identify their origins, this set is the work of sports artist Ronnie Joyner, produced in co-operation with the St. Louis Browns Historical Society. They approximate the 1938 Goudey Heads-Up format in 2-1/2" x 2-7/8" size with sepia portraits and orange backgrounds. Backs have a vintage look with player personal data, a career summary and trivia question. Cards were sold as complete sets.

		NM/M
Complete Set (20):		10.00
Common Player:		.50
1	Hank Arft	.50
2	Ellis Clary	.50
3	Jim Delsing	.50
4	Ned Garver	.65
5	Don Gutteridge	.50
6	Red Hayworth	.50
7	Bill Jennings	.50
8	Dick Kryhoski	.50
9	Don Lenhardt	.50
10	Bob Mahoney	.50
11	Frank Mancuso	.50
12	Babe Martin	.50
13	Ed Mickelson	.50
14	J.W. Porter	.50
15	Roy Sievers	.75
16	Virgil Trucks	.65
17	Al Widmar	.50
18	Jerry Witte	.50
19	Arthur Richman (Number One Fan)	.50
20	Stan Musial (Cross Town Rival)	5.00

2003 Ronnie Joyner 1953 St. Louis Browns

MIRANDA — SHORTSTOP — 1953 ST. LOUIS BROWNS

Though there is nothing on the cards themselves to identify their origins, or even that they do not actually date from 1953, this set is the work of sports artist Ronnie Joyner, who produced two other Brownies sets in previous years in co-operation with the St. Louis Browns Historical Society. The cards are in the modern 2-1/2" x 3-1/2" format with colorful fronts featuring Joyner portraits of the players and cartoon-style names. Backs have a vintage look with player personal data, a cartoon about the player, a career summary and 1953 and lifetime stats. Cards were sold as complete sets.

		NM/M
Complete Set (40):		15.00
Common Player:		.50
1	Satchel Paige	5.00
2	Les Moss	.50
3	Roy Sievers	.65
4	Bobby Young	.50
5	Marlin Stuart	.50
6	Billy Hunter	.50
7	Don Lenhardt	.50
8	Johnny Groth	.50
9	Vic Wertz	.50
10	Don Larsen	1.00
11	Clint Courtney	.50
12	Dick Kryhoski	.50
13	Neil Berry	.50
14	Bob Cain	.50
15	Willie Miranda	.50
16	Hank Edwards	.50
17	Dick Kokos	.50
18	Jim Pisoni	.50
19	Harry Brecheen	.65
20	Browns 1953 Season Summary	.50
21	Checklist	.50
22	Lou Kretlow	.50
23	Babe Martin	.50
24	Ed Mickelson	.50
25	Frank Kellert	.50
26	Virgil Trucks	.65
27	Dick Littlefield	.50
28	Jim Dyck	.50
29	Mike Blyzka	.50
30	Bob Habenicht	.75
31	Max Lanier	.50
32	Bob Elliott	.50
33	Duane Pillette	.50
34	Johnny Lipon	.50
35	Bob Turley	.65
36	Vern Stephens	.50
37	Hal White	.50
38	Dixie Upright	.75
39	Bobo Holloman	.50
40	Marty Marion	.50

1990 Jumbo Sunflower Seeds

The 1990 "Autograph Series" of 24 cards came in packages of sunflower seeds and were produced by Mike Schecter Associates for Stagi & Scriven Farms Inc. The cards were found in specially-marked packages of Jumbo California Sunflower Seeds, three cards per package. Standard size with MLB logos airbrushed out, the cards are blue with a white frame. The numbered backs contain yearly statistics and biographical information along with a facsimile autograph.

PEDRO GUERRERO — ST. LOUIS CARDINALS - FIRST BASE

		NM/M
Complete Set (24):		10.00
Common Player:		.25
(1)	Kevin Mitchell	.25
(2)	Ken Griffey Jr.	1.75
(3)	Howard Johnson	.25
(4)	Bo Jackson	.35
(5)	Kirby Puckett	1.25
(6)	Robin Yount	1.00
(7)	Dave Stieb	.25
(8)	Don Mattingly	1.50
(9)	Barry Bonds	2.00
(10)	Pedro Guerrero	.25
(11)	Tony Gwynn	1.25
(12)	Von Hayes	.25
(13)	Rickey Henderson	1.00
(14)	Tim Raines	.25
(15)	Alan Trammell	.25
(16)	Dave Stewart	.25
(17)	Will Clark	.35
(18)	Roger Clemens	1.50
(19)	Wally Joyner	.25
(20)	Ryne Sandberg	1.25
(21)	Eric Davis	.25
(22)	Mike Scott	.25
(23)	Cal Ripken, Jr.	2.00
(24)	Eddie Murray	1.00

1991 Jumbo Sunflower Seeds

LEN DYKSTRA — PHILADELPHIA PHILLIES - OUTFIELD

In its second year of baseball card production, Jumbo California Sunflower Seeds maintained the same basic format for its cards. Player photos, with uniform logos airbrushed away, in a white frame surrounded by a red border with yellow pinstripe. At top left is the issuer's logo; above the photo in white is "Autograph Series II." A facsimile autograph is printed over the photo. Beneath the picture are the player's name, team and position. Backs are printed in red and include major league stats and a career summary.

		NM/M
Complete Set (24):		7.50
Common Player:		.25
1	Ozzie Smith	1.00
2	Wade Boggs	1.00
3	Bobby Bonilla	.25
4	George Brett	1.25
5	Kal Daniels	.25
6	Glenn Davis	.25
7	Chuck Finley	.25
8	Cecil Fielder	.25
9	Len Dykstra	.25
10	Dwight Gooden	.25
11	Ken Griffey Jr.	1.50
12	Kelly Gruber	.25
13	Kent Hrbek	.25
14	Andre Dawson	.35
15	Dave Justice	.25
16	Barry Larkin	.25
17	Ben McDonald	.25
18	Mark McGwire	1.75
19	Roberto Alomar	.25
20	Nolan Ryan	2.00
21	Sandy Alomar, Jr.	.25
22	Bobby Thigpen	.25
23	Tim Wallach	.25
24	Mitch Williams	.25

1992 Jumbo Sunflower Seeds

Jumbo Sunflower Seeds
Autograph Series III

HOWARD JOHNSON
NEW YORK METS • THIRD BASE • SHORTSTOP

The basic format used in 1990-91 was returned for 1992 when Michael Schecter Associates produced another 24-card set for inclusion in packages of Jumbo Sunflower Seeds (the "California" identifier was dropped in 1992). Cards feature a player photo on which the uniform logos have been eliminated. Across the photo in black is a facsimile autograph. Around the photo are borders of, successively, white, blue, yellow and white. In the upper-left corner is the issuer's logo. "Autograph Series III" appears in red at upper-right. Beneath the picture, the player's name is printed in red, with his team and position in white. Backs are printed in blue, with major league stats and a career summary, along with a few personal data and the appropriate logos.

		NM/M
Complete Set (24):		6.00
Common Player:		.25
1	Jeff Reardon	.25
2	Bill Gullickson	.25
3	Todd Zeile	.25
4	Terry Mulholland	.25
5	Kirby Puckett	1.00
6	Howard Johnson	.25
7	Terry Pendleton	.25
8	Will Clark	.35
9	Cal Ripken, Jr.	2.00
10	Chris Sabo	.25
11	Jim Abbott	.25
12	Joe Carter	.25
13	Paul Molitor	.75
14	Ken Griffey Jr.	1.50
15	Randy Johnson	.75
16	Bobby Bonilla	.25
17	John Smiley	.25
18	Jose Canseco	.50
19	Tom Glavine	.50
20	Darryl Strawberry	.25
21	Brett Butler	.25
22	Devon White	.25
23	Scott Erickson	.25
24	Willie McGee	.25

K

1987 Kahn's Reds

(44) ERIC DAVIS, OF

After a nearly 20-year layoff, Kahn's Wieners sponsored a baseball card set in 1987. The hot dog concessionaire sponsored a Reds team set that was distributed to fans attending the August 2 game at Riverfront Stadium. Cards are the standard 2-1/2" x 3-1/2" size. The fronts offer a full-color player photo bordered in red and white. Backs carry the Kahn's logo, a portrait photo of the player and career stats.

		NM/M
Complete Set (26):		9.00
Common Player:		.25
6	Bo Diaz	.25
10	Terry Francona	.25
11	Kurt Stillwell	.25
12	Nick Esasky	.25
13	Dave Concepcion	.25
16	Barry Larkin	3.00
16	Ron Oester	.25
21	Paul O'Neill	1.00
23	Lloyd McClendon	.25
25	Buddy Bell	.25
35	Kal Daniels	.25
29	Tracy Jones	.25
30	Guy Hoffman	.25
31	John Franco	.25
32	Tom Browning	.25
35	Ron Robinson	.25
34	Bill Gullickson	.25
35	Pat Pacillo	.25
39	Dave Parker	.25
43	Bill Landrum	.25
44	Eric Davis	.50
46	Rob Murphy	.25
47	Frank Williams	.25
48	Ted Power	.25
---	Pete Rose (Manager)	3.00
---	Reds Coaches (Scott Breeden, Billy DeMars, Tommy Helms, Bruce Kimm, Jim Lett, Tony Perez)	.25

1988 Kahn's Mets

DAVID CONE 44

PITCHER

Approximately 50,000 Mets fans received this complimentary card set during a ballpark promotion sponsored by Kahn's Wieners. Twenty-five players are featured in the set, along with manager Davey Johnson, four coaches and a team photo. Card fronts have a dark blue border with an orange rectangle framing the color player photo; players' uniform numbers are printed in white in the upper-right corner, beside the team logo. Backs are black-and-white with red accents. In addition to player acquisition date, birthday and residence, a paragraph-style career summary is included. Cards measure 2-1/2" x 3-1/2".

		NM/M
Complete Set (31):		4.00
Common Player:		.25
1	Mookie Wilson	.25
2	Mackey Sasser	.25
3	Bud Harrelson	.25
4	Lenny Dykstra	.35
5	Davey Johnson	.25
6	Wally Backman	.25
8	Gary Carter	3.00
11	Tim Teufel	.25
12	Ron Darling	.25
13	Lee Mazzilli	.25
14	Rick Aguilera	.25
16	Dwight Gooden	.50
17	Keith Hernandez	.35
18	Darryl Strawberry	.50
19	Bob Ojeda	.25
20	Howard Johnson	.30
21	Kevin Elster	.25
22	Kevin McReynolds	.25
26	Terry Leach	.25
28	Bill Robinson	.25
29	Dave Magadan	.25
30	Mel Stottlemyre	.25
31	Gene Walter	.25
33	Barry Lyons	.25
34	Sam Perlozzo	.25
42	Roger McDowell	.25
44	David Cone	.50
49	Randy Myers	.25
50	Sid Fernandez	.25
52	Greg Pavlick	.25
---	Team Photo	.25

Reds

This 26-card team set was a giveaway during the Aug. 14, 1988 Cincinnati Reds game. The glossy cards (2-1/2" x 3-1/2") feature color action photos inside red and white

(17) CHRIS SABO, IF

borders. The Reds logo, player uniform number, name and position are printed below the photo. The backs are black and white, with small player close-ups and career stats. A promotional 25-cent coupon for Kahn's Wieners was included with each set.

		NM/M
Complete Set (26):		6.00
Common Player:		.25
6	Bo Diaz	.25
8	Terry McGriff	.25
9	Eddie Milner	.25
10	Leon Durham	.25
11	Barry Larkin	.50
12	Nick Esasky	.25
13	Dave Concepcion	.25
14	Pete Rose	3.00
15	Jeff Treadway	.25
17	Chris Sabo	.30
20	Danny Jackson	.25
21	Paul O'Neill	.30
27	Dave Collins	.25
27	Jose Rijo	.25
29	Kal Daniels	.25
29	Tracy Jones	.25
31	Lloyd McClendon	.25
31	John Franco	.25
32	Tom Browning	.25
33	Ron Robinson	.25
40	Jack Armstrong	.25
44	Eric Davis	.30
46	Rob Murphy	.25
47	Frank Williams	.25
48	Tim Birtsas	.25
---	Coaches (Danny Breeden, Tommy Helms, Bruce Kimm, Jim Lett, Lee May, Tony Perez)	.25

1989 Kahn's Cooperstown Collection

COOPERSTOWN COLLECTION

JOHNNY BENCH

This 11-player card set was available through a mail-in offer. One dollar and three proofs of purchase from Hillshire Farms were needed to obtain the set. The card fronts feature paintings of recent Hall of Fame inductees. A coupon card was also included with each set.

		NM/M
Complete Set (11):		3.00
Common Player:		.50
(1)	Cool Papa Bell	.50
(2)	Johnny Bench	.75
(3)	Lou Brock	.60
(4)	Whitey Ford	.75
(5)	Bob Gibson	.65
(6)	Billy Herman	.65
(7)	Harmon Killebrew	.65
(8)	Eddie Mathews	.65
(9)	Brooks Robinson	.65
(10)	Willie Stargell	.65
(11)	Carl Yastrzemski	.75

1989 Kahn's Mets

This team set was sponsored by Kahn's Wieners and given to fans attending the July 6 game at Shea Stadium. Standard-size cards feature a color photo surrounded by a blue and orange border with the player's name and uniform

Mookie Wilson 1

NEW YORK Mets OF

number across the top. Backs include the Kahn's logo, along with player information and complete Major League stats. Four update cards were later added to the set.

		NM/M
Complete Set (35):		4.00
Common Player:		.20
1	Mookie Wilson	.25
2	Mackey Sasser	.20
3	Bud Harrelson	.20
4	Davey Johnson	.20
7	Juan Samuel	.20
8	Gary Carter	1.00
9	Gregg Jefferies	.50
11	Tim Teufel	.20
12	Ron Darling	.20
13	Lee Mazzilli	.20
16	Dwight Gooden	.30
17	Keith Hernandez	.20
18	Darryl Strawberry	.20
19	Bob Ojeda	.20
20	Howard Johnson	.20
21	Kevin Elster	.20
22	Kevin McReynolds	.20
28	Bill Robinson	.20
29	Dave Magadan	.20
30	Mel Stottlemyre	.20
32	Mark Carreon	.20
33	Barry Lyons	.20
34	Sam Perlozzo	.20
38	Rick Aguilera	.20
44	David Cone	.50
46	Dave West	.20
48	Randy Myers	.20
49	Don Aase	.20
50	Sid Fernandez	.20
52	Greg Pavlick	.20
---	Team Card	.20
13	Jeff Musselman	.50
25	Keith Miller	.50
28	Frank Viola	.50
40	Jeff Innis	.50

Reds

ROB DIBBLE 49

PITCHER

This team set, sponsored by Kahn's Wieners, was distributed to fans attending the August 6 Reds game at Riverfront Stadium. The standard-size, red-bordered cards feature action photos with the player's name in the upper-left corner, his uniform number in the upper-right and the Reds logo in the middle. Backs include a black-and-white portrait, player data and complete major and minor league stats. The Kahn's logo appears in the upper-right corner of the back.

		NM/M
Complete Set (26):		6.00
Common Player:		.20
6	Bo Diaz	.20
7	Lenny Harris	.25
11	Barry Larkin	.50
13	Joel Youngblood	.20
14	Pete Rose	3.00
16	Ron Oester	.20
17	Chris Sabo	.20
20	Danny Jackson	.20
21	Paul O'Neill	.40
25	Todd Benzinger	.20
27	Jose Rijo	.20
28	Kal Daniels	.20

29	Herm Winningham	.20
30	Ken Griffey	.25
31	John Franco	.25
32	Tom Browning	.20
33	Ron Robinson	.20
34	Jeff Reed	.20
36	Rolando Roomes	.20
37	Norm Charlton	.20
42	Rick Mahler	.20
43	Kent Tekulve	.20
44	Eric Davis	.30
48	Tim Birtsas	.20
49	Rob Dibble	.25
---	Coaches (Danny Breeden, Dave Bristol, Tommy Helms, Jim Lett, Lee May, Tony Perez)	.20

1990 Kahn's Mets

Mets

DAVID CONE 44

For the third consecutive year, Kahn's issued a team set of Mets baseball cards. The sets were distrubted at Shea Stadium on May 3, prior to the Mets/Reds game. Cards feature blue and orange (team colors) graphics and are numbered according to uniform number. Two coupon cards were also included with each set.

		NM/M
Complete Set (34):		3.00
Common Player:		.20
1	Lou Thornton	.20
2	Mackey Sasser	.20
3	Bud Harrelson	.20
4	Mike Cubbage	.20
5	Davey Johnson	.20
6	Mike Marshall	.20
9	Gregg Jefferies	.50
10	Dave Magadan	.20
11	Tim Teufel	.20
13	Jeff Musselman	.20
15	Ron Darling	.20
16	Dwight Gooden	.30
18	Darryl Strawberry	.30
19	Bob Ojeda	.20
20	Howard Johnson	.20
21	Kevin Elster	.20
22	Kevin McReynolds	.20
25	Keith Miller	.20
26	Alejandro Pena	.20
27	Tom O'Malley	.20
29	Frank Viola	.20
30	Mel Stottlemyre	.20
31	John Franco	.20
32	Doc Edwards	.20
33	Barry Lyons	.20
35	Orlando Mercado	.20
40	Jeff Innis	.20
44	David Cone	.35
45	Mark Carreon	.20
47	Wally Whitehurst	.20
48	Julio Machado	.20
50	Sid Fernandez	.20
52	Greg Pavlick	.20
---	Team Card	.20

Reds

CINCINNATI REDS

(44) Eric Davis, OF

This team set marks the fourth consecutive year in which Kahn's released a modern Reds issue. The cards feature color photos, red and white borders and the player's name, number, and postion on the card front. The flip sides feature bio-

graphical information, statistics, a posed photo and the Kahn's logo. The set is numbered by uniform.

		NM/M
Complete Set (27):		4.00
Common Player:		.25
7	Mariano Duncan	.25
9	Joe Oliver	.25
10	Luis Quinones	.25
11	Barry Larkin	.50
15	Glenn Braggs	.25
16	Ron Oester	.25
17	Chris Sabo	.25
20	Danny Jackson	.25
21	Paul O'Neill	.40
22	Billy Hatcher	.25
23	Hal Morris	.25
25	Todd Benzinger	.25
27	Jose Rijo	.25
28	Randy Myers	.25
29	Herm Winningham	.25
30	Ken Griffey	.25
32	Tom Browning	.25
34	Jeff Reed	.25
37	Norm Charlton	.25
40	Jack Armstrong	.25
41	Lou Pinella	.30
42	Rick Mahler	.25
43	Tim Layana	.25
44	Eric Davis	.35
48	Tim Birtsas	.25
49	Rob Dibble	.25
---	Coaches (Jackie Moore, Tony Perez, Sam Perlozzo, Larry Rothschild, Stan Williams)	.25

1991 Kahn's Mets

Mets

Howard Johnson 20 IF

Kahn's kept its tradition in 1991 with the release of this set featuring members of the New York Mets. Cards measure 2 1/2" x 3 1/2" and the fronts feature a pinstripe design. The backs are printed horizontally and feature complete statistics. The cards are numbered according to uniform number. The complete set was distributed at a 1991 home game.

		NM/M
Complete Set (33):		4.00
Common Player:		.20
1	Vince Coleman	.20
2	Mackey Sasser	.20
3	Bud Harrelson	.20
4	Mike Cubbage	.20
5	Charlie O'Brien	.20
7	Hubie Brooks	.20
8	Daryl Boston	.20
9	Gregg Jefferies	.30
10	Dave Magadan	.20
11	Tim Teufel	.20
13	Rick Cerone	.20
15	Ron Darling	.20
16	Dwight Gooden	.30
17	David Cone	.50
20	Howard Johnson	.20
21	Kevin Elster	.20
22	Kevin McReynolds	.20
25	Keith Miller	.20
26	Alejandro Pena	.20
28	Tom Herr	.20
29	Frank Viola	.20
30	Mel Stottlemyre	.20
31	John Franco	.20
32	Doc Edwards	.20
40	Jeff Innis	.20
43	Doug Simons	.20
45	Mark Carreon	.20
47	Wally Whitehurst	.20
48	Pete Schourek	.20
50	Sid Fernandez	.20
51	Tom Spencer	.20
52	Greg Pavlick	.20
---	Team Card	.20

Reds

The World Champion Cincinnati Reds are showcased in this 28-card set. The card fronts feature small color action photos on white stock. Backs feature statistics, biographical information and the Kahn's logo. A special card of team mascot Schottzie is included in this set.

		NM/M
Complete Set (28):		4.00
Common Player:		.25
7	Mariano Duncan	.25
9	Joe Oliver	.25
10	Luis Quinones	.25
11	Barry Larkin	.50
15	Glenn Braggs	.25
17	Chris Sabo	.25
19	Bill Doran	.25
21	Paul O'Neill	.30
22	Billy Hatcher	.25
23	Hal Morris	.25
25	Todd Benzinger	.25
27	Jose Rijo	.25
28	Randy Myers	.25
29	Herm Winningham	.25
32	Tom Browning	.25
34	Jeff Reed	.25
36	Don Carman	.25
37	Norm Charlton	.25
40	Jack Armstrong	.25
41	Lou Piniella	.30
44	Eric Davis	.30
45	Chris Hammond	.25
47	Scott Scudder	.25
48	Ted Power	.25
49	Rob Dibble	.25
57	Freddie Benavides	.25
---	Schottzie (Mascot)	.25
----	Coaches (Jackie Moore, Tony Perez, Sam Perlozzo, Larry Rothschild, Stan Williams)	.25

1992 Kahn's Mets

A Mets' blue border surrounds the game-action photos in this team set. Backs are horizontally formatted and present full major league stats and the '92 Mets team slogan, "Hardball is Back." A baseball on front carries the uniform number by which the set is checklisted here. Cents-offs coupons for Kahn's hot dogs and corn dogs were packaged with the set when it was distributed at a home game, but are not considered part of the set.

		NM/M
Complete Set (33):		4.00
Common Player:		.20
1	Vince Coleman	.20
2	Mackey Sasser	.20
3	Junior Noboa	.20
4	Mike Cubbage	.20
6	Daryl Boston	.20
8	Dave Gallagher	.20
9	Todd Hundley	.35
10	Jeff Torborg	.20
11	Dick Schofield	.20
12	Willie Randolph	.20
15	Kevin Elster	.20
16	Dwight Gooden	.40
17	David Cone	.40
18	Bret Saberhagen	.35
19	Anthony Young	.20
20	Howard Johnson	.25
22	Charlie O'Brien	.20
25	Bobby Bonilla	.25
26	Barry Foote	.20
27	Tom McCraw	.20

28	Dave LaRoche	.20
29	Dave Magadan	.20
30	Mel Stottlemyre	.20
31	John Franco	.20
32	Bill Pecota	.20
33	Eddie Murray	1.00
40	Jeff Innis	.20
44	Tim Burke	.20
45	Paul Gibson	.20
47	Wally Whitehurst	.20
50	Sid Fernandez	.20
51	John Stephenson	.20
---	Mets Team	.20

Reds

(37) NORM CHARLTON P

This 27-card set (two coupon cards distributed with the team set are not considered part of the set) was given to fans at a promotional home date. The 2-1/2" x 3-1/2" cards have a red border with the team name at top and player name at bottom in white. The player's uniform number and position in black flank his name. A team logo appears in the lower-left corner of the photo. Backs are printed in red and black and have complete pro stats, a few biographical details and the logo of the Riverfront Stadium hot dog concessionaire. The checklist presented here is in order of uniform number.

		NM/M
Complete Set (27):		4.00
Common Player:		.25
2	Schottzie (Mascot)	.25
9	Joe Oliver	.25
10	Bip Roberts	.25
11	Barry Larkin	.45
12	Freddie Benavides	.25
15	Glenn Braggs	.25
16	Reggie Sanders	.25
17	Chris Sabo	.25
19	Bill Doran	.25
21	Paul O'Neill	.35
23	Hal Morris	.25
25	Scott Bankhead	.25
26	Darnell Coles	.25
27	Jose Rijo	.25
28	Scott Ruskin	.25
30	Greg Swindell	.25
32	Dave Martinez	.25
31	Tim Belcher	.25
32	Tom Browning	.25
34	Jeff Reed	.25
37	Norm Charlton	.25
38	Troy Afenir	.25
41	Lou Piniella	.30
43	Chris Hammond	.25
48	Dwayne Henry	.25
49	Rob Dibble	.25
---	Coaches (Jackie Moore, John McLaren, Sam Perlozzo, Tony Perez, Larry Rothschild)	.25

1993 Kahn's Mets

1F EDDIE MURRAY 33

The Mets distributed the 1993 Kahn's team set to fans on May 23 at Shea Stadium. Cards feature color photos and a white border. The Mets logo is at the bottom center and the player's name, position and uniform number at the top. Backs include ca-

reer statistics and biography inside a red border. Also included in the set is a team photo card and a title card which features the New York skyline and the stadium. Apparently not all cards, such as those of coaches, were issued in all sets.

		NM/M
Complete Set (36):		7.50
Common Player:		.25
4	Tony Fernandez	.25
4	Mike Cubbage	.50
6	Joe Orsulak	.25
7	Jeff McKnight	.25
8	Dave Gallagher	.25
9	Todd Hundley	.50
10	Jeff Torborg	.50
11	Vince Coleman	.50
12	Jeff Kent	1.00
16	Dwight Gooden	.25
18	Bret Saberhagen	.35
19	Anthony Young	.25
20	Howard Johnson	.25
21	Darren Reed	.25
22	Charlie O'Brien	.25
23	Tim Bogar	.25
25	Bobby Bonilla	.30
26	Barry Foote	.50
27	Tom McCraw	.50
28	Dave LaRoche	.50
29	Frank Tanana	.50
30	Mel Stottlemyre	.50
31	John Franco	.25
33	Eddie Murray	1.50
34	Chico Walker	.25
40	Jeff Innis	.25
47	Ryan Thompson	.25
47	Mike Draper	.25
48	Pete Schourek	.25
50	Sid Fernandez	.25
51	Mike Maddux	.25
---	John Stephenson	.50
---	Team Photo	.25
---	Header Card	.10
---	Corn Dog Coupon	.05
---	Hot Dog Coupon	.05

Reds

BIP ROBERTS

Kahn's produced a Reds team set which was given away to fans at Riverfront Stadium on August 1. The cards, organized by player's uniform number, show a photo of the player on the front with the player's name at the top and the Reds logo in the lower corner, surrounded by a pinstripe border. Card backs have the player's lifetime statistics and biography. Card #2 in the set portrays team owner Marge Schott and her dog Schottzie II. Coupon cards good for discounts on packages of Kahn's hot dogs and corn dogs were packaged with the set but are not considered part of the set.

		NM/M
Complete Set (28):		6.00
Common Player:		.25
2	Schottzie (Mascot) (Marge Schott)	.25
7	Kevin Mitchell	.25
8	Juan Samuel	.25
9	Joe Oliver	.25
10	Bip Roberts	.25
11	Barry Larkin	.40
15	Davey Johnson	.25
16	Reggie Sanders	.25
17	Chris Sabo	.25
19	Randy Milligan	.25
20	Jeff Branson	.25
23	Hal Morris	.25
25	Greg Cadaret	.25
27	Jose Rijo	.25
30	Bobby Kelly	.25
31	Tim Belcher	.25
32	Tom Browning	.25
40	Tim Pugh	.25
41	Jeff Reardon	.25
42	Gary Varsho	.25
43	Bill Landrum	.25
46	Jacob Brumfield	.25
49	Rob Dibble	.25
53	Kevin Wickander	.25

57	John Smiley	.25
59	Bobby Ayala	.25
---	Coaches (Jose Cardenal, Don Gullett, Ray Knight, Bobby Valentine, Dave Miley)	.25
---	Broadcasters (Marty Brennaman, Joe Nuxhall)	.25

Reds

RON GANT OUTFIELDER

Distributed at a promotional game and sponsored by the hot dog concessionaire at Riverfront Stadium this was the eighth consecutive Reds team set produced by Kahn's. Cards feature a player action photo with a red stripe superimposed near the left border. The stripe contains the player name and position at top and the team logo at bottom. Backs are printed in red and black and include full minor and major league stats. Cards are numbered by uniform number printed on back.

		NM/M
Complete Set (31):		4.00
Common Player:		.20
2	Schottzie (Mascot)	.20
4	Jacob Brumfield	.20
7	Kevin Mitchell	.20
9	Joe Oliver	.20
10	Eddie Taubensee	.20
11	Barry Larkin	.35
12	Deion Sanders	.50
15	Davey Johnson	.20
16	Reggie Sanders	.20
19	Jerome Walton	.20
20	Jeff Branson	.20
21	Tony Fernandez	.20
23	Thomas Howard	.20
23	Hal Morris	.20
27	Jose Rijo	.20
29	Lenny Harris	.20
29	Brett Boone	.50
31	Chuck McElroy	.20
32	Tom Browning	.20
33	Brian Dorsett	.20
38	Erik Hanson	.20
40	Tim Pugh	.20
44	John Roper	.20
46	Jeff Brantley	.20
46	Pete Schourek	.20
47	Johnny Ruffin	.20
49	Rob Dibble	.20
55	Tim Fortugno	.20
57	John Smiley	.20
58	Hector Carrasco	.20
---	Reds Coaching Staff (Bob Boone, Don Gullett, Grant Jackson, Ray Knight, Joel Youngblood)	.20

1995 Kahn's Mets

BUTLER

Game-action photos are featured in this edition of the annual tradition of cards sponsored by the Mets hot dog concessionaire. In standard 2-1/2" x 3-1/2" format the cards have a gray background with navy pinstripes. The player's name, uniform number and position are in team colors of blue and orange at bottom. Backs are in red, black and

white with personal data, previous-year or career stats and team and sponsor logos. The cards are checklisted here by uniform number.

		NM/M
Complete Set (36):		4.00
Common Player:		.25
4	Ricky Otero	.25
6	Mike Cubbage	.25
7	Chris Jones	.25
9	Joe Orsulak	.25
7	Bobby Wine	.25
8	Steve Swisher	.25
9	Todd Hundley	.30
10	Tom McCraw	.25
11	Aaron Ledesma	.25
12	Jeff Kent	.75
13	Edgardo Alfonzo	.60
16	Jose Vizcaino	.25
17	Bret Saberhagen	.35
18	Jeff Barry	.25
19	Bill Spiers	.25
20	Ryan Thompson	.25
21	Bill Pulsipher	.25
22	Brett Butler	.25
23	Tim Bogar	.25
25	Bobby Bonilla	.25
26	Rico Brogna	.25
27	Pete Harnisch	.25
29	Bobby Jones	.25
31	John Franco	.25
32	Kelly Stinnett	.25
34	Blas Minor	.25
38	Doug Henry	.25
38	Dave Mlicki	.25
40	Eric Gunderson	.25
42	Jason Isringhausen	.25
45	Jerry DiPoto	.25
52	Dallas Green	.25
52	Greg Pavlick	.25
55	Frank Howard	.25
---	50-Cent Hot Dog Coupon	.05
---	50-Cent Corn Dog Coupon	.05

Reds

CINCINNATI REDS 1995

RON GANT • OUTFIELDER

This team set continues the tradition of baseball card sponsorship by Kahn's Meats. The set was given away at the August 6 game. Team name and the year are printed in the white border above the photo; the player's name and position are in white in a red strip at bottom. A Reds logo appears in the upper-right corner of the photo, with the player's uniform number below in white. Backs have complete minor and major league stats, along with a few biographical details and the Reds and Kahn's logos. The checklist is presented here by uniform number. Two Kahn's coupons were included in each cello-wrapped set.

		NM/M
Complete Set (34):		4.50
Common Player:		.15
02	Schottzie (02)	.15
6	Ron Gant	.30
8	Damon Berryhill	.15
9	Eric Anthony	.15
10	Eddie Taubensee	.15
11	Barry Larkin	.40
12	Willie Greene	.15
15	Davey Johnson	.15
16	Reggie Sanders	.15
17	Mark Lewis	.15
18	Benito Santiago	.15
19	Jerome Walton	.15
20	Jeff Branson	.15
23	Thomas Howard	.15
23	Hal Morris	.15
26	Johnny Ruffin	.15
27	Jose Rijo	.15
29	Lenny Harris	.15
29	Bret Boone	.40
30	Brian Hunter	.15
31	Chuck McElroy	.15
32	Kevin Jarvis	.15
37	Xavier Hernandez	.15
40	Tim Pugh	.15
41	Brad Pennington	.15
42	Mike Jackson	.15

44	John Roper	.15
45	Jeff Brantley	.15
46	Pete Schourek	.15
49	C.J. Nitkowski	.15
57	John Smiley	.15
58	Hector Carrasco	.15
---	Reds Coaches (Ray Knight, Don Gullett, Grant Jackson, Hal McRae, Joel Youngblood)	.15

1996 Kahn's Mets

ROBERT PERSON Mets 29

This team set was handed out to attendees at the August 3 game at Shea Stadium. Sponsored by the Mets' hot dog concessionaire, the set features the players, coaches and manager in color action photos. Borders are in dark shades and include a Mets logo at lower-right. The player name and uniform number are in white. Backs are in black, red and white with personal data, 1995 stats and sponsors logos. The uniform number is repeated at lower-left. Cards are checklisted here in alphabetical order. The set was distributed cello-wrapped with two 50-cent hot dogs coupons.

		NM/M
Complete Set (32):		5.00
Common Player:		.25
(1)	Edgardo Alfonzo	.25
(2)	Tim Bogar	.25
(3)	Rico Brogna	.25
(4)	Paul Byrd	.25
(5)	Mark Clark	.25
(6)	Mike Cubbage	.25
(7)	Jerry Dipoto	.25
(8)	Carl Everett	.25
(9)	John Franco	.25
(10)	Bernard Gilkey	.25
(11)	Dallas Green	.25
(12)	Pete Harnisch	.25
(13)	Doug Henry	.25
(14)	Frank Howard	.25
(15)	Todd Hundley	.25
(16)	Butch Huskey	.25
(17)	Jason Isringhausen	.25
(18)	Lance Johnson	.25
(19)	Bobby Jones	.25
(20)	Chris Jones	.25
(21)	Brent Mayne	.25
(22)	Tom McCraw	.25
(23)	Dave Mlicki	.25
(24)	Alex Ochoa	.25
(25)	Rey Ordonez	.25
(26)	Greg Pavlick	.25
(27)	Robert Person	.25
(28)	Bill Pulsipher	.25
(29)	Steve Swisher	.25
(30)	Andy Tomberlin	.25
(31)	Paul Wilson	.25
(32)	Bobby Wine	.25

Reds

29 BRET BOONE INFIELDER

1996 CINCINNATI REDS

The players, manager, coaches and mascot are once again featured in a Cincinnati Reds team set sponsored by the team's hot dog concessionaire and given away to fans at the August 4 game. The 2-1/2" x 3-1/2" cards have color game-action photos on front. A red stripe at top has the team logo, player name, position and uniform number. A stripe beneath the photo has team name and year. Backs are printed in black and red on white and include personal data and complete major and minor league stats. Cards are checklisted here by uniform number.

		NM/M
Complete Set (34):		5.00
Common Player:		.25
02	Schottzie (Mascot)	.25
7	Curtis Goodwin	.25
9a	Eric Anthony	.25
9b	Joe Oliver	.25
10	Eddie Taubensee	.25
11	Barry Larkin	.45
12	Willie Greene	.25
15	Mike Kelly	.25
16	Reggie Sanders	.25
17	Chris Sabo	.25
18	Eric Owens	.25
20	Jeff Branson	.25
21	Mark Portugal	.25
22	Thomas Howard	.25
23	Hal Morris	.25
25	Ray Knight	.25
26	Johnny Ruffin	.25
27	Jose Rijo	.25
28	Lenny Harris	.25
29	Bret Boone	.50
30	Eduardo Perez	.25
32	Kevin Jarvis	.25
34	Dave Burba	.25
36	Scott Service	.25
41	Jeff Shaw	.25
42	Roger Salkeld	.25
44	Eric Davis	.30
45	Jeff Brantley	.25
46	Pete Schourek	.25
57	John Smiley	.25
63	Hector Carrasco	.25
69	Tim Belk	.25
---	Coaches (Marc Bombard, Don Gullett, Tom Hume, Jim Lett, Hal McRae)	.25
---	Bernie Stowe (Equipment Manager)	.25

Reds

This team set was given away to fans at the August 3 game, sponsored by the Reds' hot dog concessionaire. The 2-1/2" x 3-1/2" cards have game action player photos at right and the player's name, position and uniform number in a two-toned red stripe vertically at left. Backs are printed in red and black and include complete major and minor league stats. Cards are listed here according to uniform number.

		NM/M
Complete Set (34):		5.00
Common Player:		.25
00	Curtis Goodwin	.25
02	Schottzie (Mascot)	.25
3	Pokey Reese	.25
4	Brook Fordyce	.25
7	Joe Oliver	.25
8	Terry Pendleton	.25
10	Eddie Taubensee	.25
11	Barry Larkin	.35
12	Willie Greene	.25
15	Mike Kelly	.25
16	Reggie Sanders	.25
17	Aaron Boone	.50
20	Jeff Branson	.25
21	Deion Sanders	.35
23	Hal Morris	.25
25	Ray Knight	.25
27	Jose Rijo	.25
28	Lenny Harris	.25
29	Bret Boone	.50
32	Steve Gibralter	.25
34	Dave Burba	.25
36	Mike Morgan	.25
38	Stan Belinda	.25
38	Kent Mercker	.25
40	Eduardo Perez	.25
42	Brett Tomko	.25
41	Jeff Shaw	.25
46	Mike Remlinger	.25
45	Jeff Brantley	.25
46	Pete Schourek	.25
56	Scott Sullivan	.25
57	John Smiley	.25
67	Felix Rodriguez	.25
---	Ken Griffey Sr., Don Gullett, Tom Hume, Denis Menke, Joel Youngblood	.25

Reds

For the 12th consecutive year, the Reds hot dog concessionaire issued a team set, given away at an August 9 promotional game. The 2-1/2" x 3-1/2" cards have game-action photos at right, borderless at top, bottom and right. At left is a vertical red stripe with player name and uniform number. Horizontal backs have player data and complete major and minor league stats overprinted on a Kahn's logo. Backs are printed in red, black and white.

		NM/M
Complete Set (34):		5.00
Common Player:		.25
3	Pokey Reese	.25
4	Damian Jackson	.25
6	Brook Fordyce	.25
9	Pat Watkins	.25
10	Ed Taubensee	.25
11	Barry Larkin	.35
12	Willie Greene	.25
15	Jack McKeon	.25
16	Reggie Sanders	.25
17	Aaron Boone	.25
21	Sean Casey	.75
22	Jon Nunnally	.25
23	Chris Stynes	.25
25	Dmitri Young	.25
26	Steve Cooke	.25
28	Paul Konerko	.75
29	Bret Boone	.50
31	Scott Sullivan	.25
32	Danny Graves	.25
33	John Hudek	.25
34	Mike Frank	.25
36	Gabe White	.25
37	Stan Belinda	.25
38	Pete Harnisch	.25
39	Eduardo Perez	.25
40	Brett Tomko	.25
43	Mike Remlinger	.25
44	Scott Winchester	.25
46	Melvin Nieves	.25
48	Rick Krivda	.25
53	Todd Williams	.25
58	Steve Parris	.25
---	Reds Coaches (Harry Dunlop, Ken Griffey, Don Gullett, Tom Hume, Ron Oester)	.25
02	Schottzie (Mascot)	.25

Reds

Distribution of a Kahn's team set for the Reds attained its 13th annual celebration July 31 when the cards were handed out to fans at Cinergy Field. Cards have player action photos which are borderless at top and right. At left is a ragged-edged red strip with player identification. Team identification is in a red strip at bottom. Backs are in red and black on white with a large Kahn's logo ghosted at center. Player data and complete professional stats are provided. Cards are checklisted here by uniform number.

		NM/M
Complete Set (34):		5.00
Common Player:		.25
02	Schottzie (Mascot)	.25
3	Pokey Reese	.25
4	Jeffrey Hammonds	.25
9	Hal Morris	.25
10	Eddie Taubensee	.25
11	Barry Larkin	.35
12	Chris Stynes	.25
15	Denny Neagle	.25
17	Aaron Boone	.25
21	Sean Casey	.50
23	Greg Vaughn	.25
25	Dmitri Young	.25
26	Jason LaRue	.25
28	Mark Lewis	.25
29	Brian Johnson	.25
31	Jack McKeon	.25
32	Danny Graves	.25
34	Steve Avery	.25
37	Michael Tucker	.25
36	Gabe White	.25
38	Stan Belinda	.25
38	Pete Harnisch	.25
40	Brett Tomko	.25
41	Ron Villone	.25
43	Mark Wohlers	.25
46	Mike Cameron	.25
46	Jason Bere	.25
48	Scott Williamson	.25
49	Dennis Reyes	.25
56	Scott Sullivan	.25
58	Steve Parris	.25
---	Marty Brennaman, Joe Nuxhall (Broadcasters)	.25
---	Ken Griffey Sr., Ron Oester, Denis Menke, Dave Collins (Reds Coaches)	.25

Reds

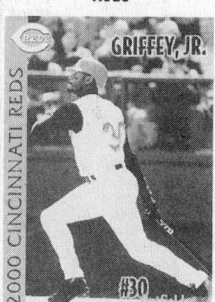

Some 42,500 sets of Reds cards were distributed to fans at the July 22 game at Cinergy Field. Sponsored for the 14th consecutive year by Kahn's meats, the cards do not have a Kahn's logo. Fronts have game action photos with the team logo at top-left, the player name at top-right, his position and uniform number at lower-right and "2000 Cincinnati Reds" vertically in a red stripe at left. Backs have a ghosted team logo, player data and stats. The checklist here is presented by uniform number.

		NM/M
Complete Set (34):		5.00
Common Player:		.25
3	Pokey Reese	.25
4	Chris Stynes	.25
6	Benito Santiago	.25
8	Alex Ochoa	.25
9	Dante Bichette	.25
10	Eddie Taubensee	.25
11	Barry Larkin	.45
12	Juan Castro	.25
15	Denny Neagle	.25
17	Aaron Boone	.25
21	Sean Casey	.65
23	Hal Morris	.25
25	Dmitri Young	.25
29	Rob Bell	.25
30	Ken Griffey Jr.	3.00
31	Jack McKeon	.25
32	Danny Graves	.25
34	Michael Tucker	.25
36	Manny Aybar	.25
38	Pete Harnisch	.25
41	Ron Villone	.25
43	Osvaldo Fernandez	.25
48	Elmer Dessens	.25
48	Scott Williamson	.25
49	Dennis Reyes	.25
56	Scott Sullivan	.25
58	Steve Parris	.25
---	Coaching Staff (Ken Griffey Sr., Denis Menke, Ron Oester, Dave Collins)	.25
---	Coaching Staff (Don Gullett, Harry Dunlop, Tom Hume, Mark Berry)	.25
---	Marty Brennaman, Joe Nuxhall (Broadcasters)	.25
---	Red (Mascot)	.25
---	Kahnlee (Mascot)	.25
---	Coupon	.05
---	Coupon	.05

2001 Kahn's Reds

This team set was distributed to fans attending the August 11 game at Cinergy Field. The 2-1/2" x 3-1/2" cards have borderless game-action photos on front. Backs have brief biographical data along with minor and major league stats. The set is checklisted here by uniform number which appears on both front and back.

		NM/M
Complete Set (33):		7.50
Common Player:		.25
3	Pokey Reese	.25
9	Bob Boone	.35
11	Barry Larkin	.45
12	Juan Castro	.25
17	Aaron Boone	.25
21	Sean Casey	.50
22	Brady Clark	.25
23	Jason LaRue	.25
25	Dmitri Young	.25
28	Ruben Rivera	.25
29	Jose Acevedo	.25
30	Ken Griffey Jr.	3.00
31	Kelly Stinnett	.25
32	Danny Graves	.25
34	Michael Tucker	.25
38	Pete Harnisch	.25
41	Chris Reitsma	.25
43	Osvaldo Fernandez	.25
45	Adam Dunn	3.00
46	Elmer Dessens	.25
47	John Riedling	.25
48	Scott Williamson	.25
49	Dennys Reyes	.25
52	Hector Mercado	.25
53	Jim Brower	.25
54	Bill Selby	.25
56	Scott Sullivan	.25
57	Chris Nichting	.25
59	Lance Davis	.25
---	Coaches (Don Gullett, Mark Berry, Tom Hume)	.25
---	Coaches (Ken Griffey Sr., Ron Oester, Tim Foli, Bill Doran)	.25
---	Broadcasters (Marty Brennaman, Joe Nuxhall)	.25
---	Mr. Red (Mascot)	.25

2002 Kahn's Reds

Team sets sponsored by the Reds' hot dog concessionaire were given to fans attending the August 16 game at Cinergy Field. The 2-1/2" x 3-1/2" cards have game-action photos that are borderless at top, bottom and right. At left is a vertical blue stripe with the date, team name and a 1970-2002 Riverfront Stadium logo. The player name is at bottom-right in black and red; his uniform number is in red at top-right. Horizontal backs are printed in red and black and have personal data and complete professional stats, overprinted on a large Kahn's logo.

		NM/M
Complete Set (33):		10.00
Common Player:		.25
(1)	Aaron Boone	.25
(2)	Bob Boone	.35
(3)	Russell Branyan	.25
(4)	Sean Casey	.50
(5)	Juan Castro	.25
(6)	Bruce Chen	.25
(7)	Ryan Dempster	.25
(8)	Elmer Dessens	.25
(9)	Adam Dunn	3.00
(10)	Jared Fernandez	.25
(11)	Danny Graves	.25
(12)	Ken Griffey Jr.	3.00
(13)	Joey Hamilton	.25
(14)	Jimmy Haynes	.25
(15)	Austin Kearns	1.50
(16)	Barry Larkin	.35
(17)	Jason LaRue	.25
(18)	Corky Miller	.25
(19)	Luis Pineda	.25
(20)	Chris Reitsma	.25
(21)	John Riedling	.25
(22)	Jose Rijo	.25
(23)	Jose Silva	.25
(24)	Kelly Stinnett	.25
(25)	Scott Sullivan	.25
(26)	Reggie Taylor	.25
(27)	Todd Walker	.25
(28)	Gabe White	.25
(29)	Scott Williamson	.25
(30)	Coaching Staff (Jim Lefebvre, Ray Knight, Tim Foli, Jose Cardenal)	.25
(31)	Coaching Staff (Don Gullett, Tom Hume, Mark Berry)	.25
(32)	Marty Brennaman, Joe Nuxhall (Broadcasters)	.25
(33)	Riverfront Stadium	.25

2003 Kahn's Cincinnati Reds

Team sets sponsored by the Reds' hot dog concessionaire were given to fans attending the August 15 game at Cinergy Field. The 2-1/2" x 3-9/16" cards have game-action photos that are borderless at top and right. At left is a vertical black stripe with the team name. At bottom-left is a Great American Ball Park inaugural season logo. The player name and uniform number are at bottom in white on black. Horizontal backs are printed in red, yellow and black and have personal data and complete professional stats, along with a color Kahn's logo.

		NM/M
Complete Set (28):		7.50
Common Player:		.25
(1)	Aaron Boone	.50
(2)	Bob Boone	.50
(3)	Russell Branyan	.25
(4)	Sean Casey	.50
(5)	Juan Castro	.25
(6)	Coaching Staff (Tom Robson, Tim Foli, Ray Knight, Jose Cardenal)	.25
(7)	Coaching Staff (Don Gullett, Tom Hume, Mark Berry)	.25
(8)	Ryan Dempster	.25
(9)	Adam Dunn	1.00
(10)	Danny Graves	.25
(11)	Ken Griffey Jr.	3.00
(12)	Jose Guillen	.25
(13)	Jimmy Haynes	.25
(14)	Felix Heredia	.25
(15)	Austin Kearns	.75
(16)	Barry Larkin	.35
(17)	Jason LaRue	.25
(18)	Kent Mercker	.25
(19)	Wily Mo Pena	.25
(20)	Brian Reith	.25
(21)	Chris Reitsma	.25
(22)	John Riedling	.25
(23)	Kelly Stinnett	.25
(24)	Scott Sullivan	.25
(25)	Reggie Taylor	.25
(26)	Gabe White	.25
(27)	Scott Williamson	.25
(28)	Paul Wilson	.25

2004 Kahn's Cincinnati Reds

This set, sponsored by the Reds' hot dog concessionaire, was given to fans attending the Auugust 15 game at Great American Ball Park. The 2-1/2" x 3-1/2" cards have game-action photos that are borderless at top, left and right. At left is a vertical black stripe with the

team name. At bottom-left is a team logo. The player name, position and uniform number are at bottom in white on black or red. Horizontal backs are printed in red, yellow and black and have personal data and complete professional stats, along with a color Kahn's logo.

		NM/M
Complete Set (29):		7.50
Common Player:		.25
3	D'Angelo Jimenez	.25
6	Ryan Freel	.35
9	Juan Castro	.25
11	Barry Larkin	.35
12	Dave Miley	.25
16	Cory Lidle	.25
16	Brandon Larson	.25
17	Javier Valentin	.25
21	Sean Casey	.50
23	Jason Larue	.25
26	John Vander Wal	.25
26	Wily Mo Pena	.25
29	Austin Kearns	.50
29	Jose Acevedo	.25
30	Ken Griffey Jr.	3.00
32	Danny Graves	.25
34	Brandon Claussen	.25
36	Gabe White	.25
38	Ryan Wagner	.40
39	Aaron Harang	.25
40	Paul Wilson	.25
44	Adam Dunn	1.50
45	Todd Van Poppel	.25
46	John Riedling	.25
52	Phil Norton	.25
60	Tim Hummel	.25
---	Mark Berry, Chris Chambliss, Don Gullett, Tom Hume	.25
---	Coaching Staff (Jerry Narron, Randy Whisler, Mike Stefanski, Mark Mann)	.25

2005 Kahn's Cincinnati Reds

This set, sponsored by the Reds' hot dog concessionaire, was given to fans attending the August 7 game at Great American Ball Park. The 2-1/2" x 3-1/2" cards have game-action photos that are borderless at top, left and right. At bottom, are a team logo, player name, position and uniform number. Horizontal backs are printed in red, yellow and black and have personal data and complete professional stats, along with a color Kahn's logo.

		NM/M
Complete Set (28):		10.00
Common Player:		.25
2	Felipe Lopez	.25
6	Ryan Freel	.25
9	Jacob Cruz	.25
12	Edwin Encarnacion	.50
16	Joe Randa	.25
17	Javier Valentin	.25
21	Sean Casey	.60
22	Eric Milton	.25
23	Jason LaRue	.25
24	David Weathers	.25
26	Wily Mo Pena	.25
28	Austin Kearns	.25
30	Ken Griffey Jr.	3.00
31	Matt Belisle	.25
33	Rich Aurilia	.25
34	Brandon Claussen	.25
37	Ramon Ortiz	.25
38	Ryan Wagner	.25
39	Aaron Harang	.25
40	Paul Wilson	.25
41	Jerry Narron	.25

44	Adam Dunn	1.00
50	Kent Mercker	.25
54	Luke Hudson	.25
56	Todd Coffey	.25
57	Randy Keisler	.25
77	Ben Weber	.25
---	Coaching Staff (Mark Berry, Chris Chambliss, Tom Hume, John Moses, Vern Ruhle, Randy Whisler)	.25

1981 Kansas City Royals Police

CLINT HURDLE
Outfielder
6'-3"
195 lbs.

Ten of the most popular Royals players are featured in this 2-1/2" x 4-1/8" set. Card fronts feature full-color photos with player name, position, facsimile autograph and team logo. Backs include player statistics, a tip from the Royals and list the four sponsoring organizations. The set was issued by the Ft. Myers, Fla., Police Department near the Royals' spring training headquarters.

		NM/M
Complete Set (10):		20.00
Common Player:		1.00
(1)	Willie Mays Aikens	1.00
(2)	George Brett	15.00
(3)	Rich Gale	1.00
(4)	Clint Hurdle	1.00
(5)	Dennis Leonard	1.00
(6)	Hal McRae	1.00
(7)	Amos Otis	1.00
(8)	U.L. Washington	1.00
(9)	Frank White	1.00
(10)	Willie Wilson	1.50

1983 Kansas City Royals Police

JOHN WATHAN
Catcher
6' 2"
205 lbs.

After skipping the 1982 season, the Ft. Myers, Fla., Police Department issued a Royals safety set in 1983 that is almost identical to their 1981 set. Cards are again 2-1/2" x 4-1/8" and include just 10 players. Cards are unnumbered, with vertical fronts and horizontal backs. Fronts have team logos, player name and position and facsimile autographs. Backs list the four sponsoring organizations, a "Tip from the Royals" and a "Kids and Cops Fact" about each player.

		NM/M
Complete Set (10):		15.00
Common Player:		.50
(1)	Willie Mays Aikens	.50
(2)	George Brett	13.50
(3)	Dennis Leonard	.50
(4)	Hal McRae	.50
(5)	Amos Otis	.50
(6)	Dan Quisenberry	.50
(7)	U.L. Washington	.50
(8)	John Wathan	.50
(9)	Frank White	.50
(10)	Willie Wilson	.75

1983 Kansas City Royals Fire Safety

BO JACKSON

This set featuring full-color player caricatures by K.K. Goodale was produced for an in-stadium promotion August 14. The 3" x 5" cards depict players, manager and coaches in action poses against a white background with a Royals logo at upper-left, opposite the Smokey Bear logo. Backs are black-and-white and contain brief player data and a Smokey cartoon.

		NM/M
Complete Set (28):		7.50
Common Player:		.25
1	John Wathan	.25
2	Coaches (Frank Funk, Adrian Garrett, Mike Lum, Ed Napolean, Bob Schaefer, Jim Schaefer)	.25
3	Willie Wilson	.35
4	Danny Tartabull	.25
5	Bo Jackson	1.50
6	Gary Thurman	.25
7	Jerry Don Gleaton	.25
8	Floyd Bannister	.25
9	Buddy Black	.25
10	Steve Farr	.25
11	Gene Garber	.25
12	Mark Gubicza	.25
13	Charlie Liebrandt	.25
14	Ted Power	.25
15	Dan Quisenberry	.25
16	Bret Saberhagen	.35
17	Mike Macfarlane	.25
18	Scotti Madison	.25
19	Jamie Quirk	.25
20	George Brett	5.00
21	Kevin Seitzer	.25
22	Bill Pecota	.25
23	Kurt Stillwell	.25
24	Brad Wellman	.25
25	Frank White	.25
26	Jim Eisenreich	.25
27	Smokey Bear	.10
---	Checklist	.10

1991 Kansas City Royals Police

#16 Bo Jackson

Bo Jackson's release by the Royals in spring training caused his card to be withdrawn from distribution with the other 26 cards in this set. The 2-5/8" x 4-1/8" cards feature a color action photo on front, with the team name in royal blue and the player name and uniform number in black in the bottom border. Backs are printed in blue on white and feature a large cartoon safety message at center, career stats and bio at top, and the logos of the set's sponsors, Kansas City Life Insurance Co., and the Metro Chiefs and Sheriffs Assn., at bot-

tom. Complete sets were distributed in a white paper envelope with team and sponsor logos.

		NM/M
Complete Set (27):		5.00
Common Player:		.10
1	Kurt Stillwell	.10
3	Terry Shumpert	.10
4	Danny Tartabull	.10
5	George Brett	3.00
8	Jim Eisenreich	.10
12	John Wathan	.10
14	Storm Davis	.10
15	Mike MacFarlane	.10
16	Bo Jackson	3.00
18	Bret Saberhagen	.25
21	Jeff Montgomery	.10
23	Mark Gubicza	.10
25	Gary Thurman	.10
27	Luis Aquino	.10
28	Steve Crawford	.10
32	Kirk Gibson	.15
30	Bill Pecota	.10
34	Kevin Seitzer	.15
36	Tom Gordon	.10
38	Andy McGaffigan	.10
48	Mark Davis	.10
52	Mike Boddicker	.10
55	Kevin Appier	.15
56	Brian McRae	.25
---	Royals Coaches (Pat Dobson, Adrian Garrett)	.10
---	Royals Coaches (Glenn Ezell, Lynn Jones, Bob Schaefer)	.10
---	Header Card - Royals Stadium	.10

1992 Kansas City Royals Police

Royals   #5   George Brett

Sponsored by K.C. Life Insurance and distributed by the Metropolitan Chiefs and Sheriffs Association, this 27-card set was distributed at a promotional game. Though they are checklisted, it is rumored that the cards of Kevin Seitzer (traded) and Kirk Gibson (released) were withdrawn early in the promotion, though both names appear on the checklist. The cards are numbered to match the player's uniform numbers. Cards are in the popular police-set format of 2-5/8" x 4-1/8" with white borders around color action photos. Backs have player data, stats, a fire safety message and sponsor's information.

		NM/M
Complete Set (27):		5.00
Common Player:		.25
2	Bob Melvin	.25
3	Terry Shumpert	.25
5	George Brett	3.00
8	Jim Eisenreich	.25
11	Gregg Jefferies	.35
12	Hal McRae	.25
14	Wally Joyner	.35
13	David Howard	.25
15	Mike MacFarlane	.25
16	Keith Miller	.25
21	Jeff Montgomery	.25
22	Kevin McReynolds	.25
23	Mark Gubicza	.25
24	Brent Mayne	.25
25	Gary Thomas	.25
27	Luis Aquino	.25
29	Chris Gwynn	.25
30	Kirk Gibson	.35
34	Kevin Seitzer	.25
36	Tom Gordon	.25
37	Joel Johnson	.25
48	Mark Davis	.25
52	Mike Boddicker	.25
55	Kevin Appier	.25
56	Brian McRae	.25
57	Mike Magnante	.25

1993 Kansas City Royals Police

GEORGE BRETT
INF/DH • 5

One of the longest-running police/fire safety issues continued in 1993 with a set marking the team's 25th anniversary season. The 2-5/8" x 4" cards have a light blue border, a color photo at center, and an anniversary logo at lower-left and the player's name, position and uniform number at lower-right. All typography is in royal blue. Backs are printed in blue on white and feature career stats and highlights, a few biographical notes and a large safety message. Logos of the set's sponsors, Kansas City Life Insurance and the Metro Police Chiefs and Sheriffs Assn. are featured at bottom.

		NM/M
Complete Set (27):		4.00
Common Player:		.15
5	George Brett	3.00
7	Greg Gagne	.15
9	Craig Wilson	.15
11	Hal McRae	.15
12	Wally Joyner	.25
13	Jose Lind	.15
14	Chris Gwynn	.15
15	Mike MacFarlane	.15
16	Keith Miller	.15
17	David Cone	.25
19	Curtis Wilkerson	.15
21	Jeff Montgomery	.15
22	Kevin McReynolds	.15
23	Mark Gubicza	.15
24	Brent Mayne	.15
28	Luis Aquino	.15
33	Chris Haney	.15
34	Felix Jose	.15
35	Hipolito Pichardo	.15
36	Tom Gordon	.15
37	Mark Gardner	.15
40	Kevin Koslofski	.15
52	Mike Boddicker	.15
55	Kevin Appier	.15
56	Brian McRae	.15
---	Royals Coaches (Steve Boros, Glenn Ezell, Guy Hansen, Bruce Kison, Lee May)	.15

1994 Kansas City Royals Police

Gary Gaetti
3rd Base

The team's long run of police/fire safety issues continued in 1994. The 2-5/8" x 4" cards have a pale yellow background with vertical light blue stripe, a color photo at center, team logo at top and the player's name, position and uniform number at bottom. Backs are printed in blue on white and feature career stats and highlights, a few biograph-

ical notes and a large safety message. Logos of the set's sponsors, Kansas City Life Insurance and the Metro Police Chiefs and Sheriffs Assn. are featured at bottom.

		NM/M
Complete Set (27):		8.00
Common Player:		.25
3	Bob Hamelin	.25
4	David Howard	.25
7	Greg Gagne	.25
8	Gary Gaetti	.25
11	Hal McRae	.25
12	Wally Joyner	.25
13	Jose Lind	.25
15	Mike MacFarlane	.25
16	Keith Miller	.25
21	Jeff Montgomery	.25
22	David Cone	.25
23	Mark Gubicza	.25
24	Brent Mayne	.25
29	Vince Coleman	.25
33	Chris Haney	.25
34	Felix Jose	.25
35	Hipolito Pichardo	.25
36	Tom Gordon	.25
40	Kevin Koslofski	.25
41	Billy Brewer	.25
42	Dave Henderson	.25
50	Stan Belinda	.25
55	Kevin Appier	.25
56	Brian McRae	.25
'94	Royals Coaches (Steve Boros, Glenn Ezell, Bruce Kison, Lee May, Jamie Quirk)	.25
---	George Brett (Royals Hall of Fame)	3.00
---	Frank White (Royals Hall of Fame)	.50

1995 Kansas City Royals Police

In 1995, the Royals safety set was sponsored by Kansas City Life Insurance Co., and distributed by law enforcement agencies in the greater Kansas City area. The cards measure about 2-5/8" x 4" and feature action photos on front. The team name is scripted at bottom with logo and the player's last name and "1995" are vertically at right. Backs have a few vital data, a career stats line, a safety message and sponsor's logo. Cards are listed here in alphabetical order.

		NM/M
Complete Set (12):		4.00
Common Player:		.50
(1)	Kevin Appier	.50
(2)	Bob Boone	.65
(3)	Vince Coleman	.50
(4)	Gary Gaetti	.50
(5)	Greg Gagne	.50
(6)	Tom Gordon	.50
(7)	Mark Gubicza	.50
(8)	Chris Haney	.50
(9)	Wally Joyner	.65
(10)	Brent Mayne	.50
(11)	Jeff Montgomery	.50
(12)	Hipolito Pichardo	.50

1996 Kansas City Royals Police

Nunnally • 22

The 1997 Royals safety set issue is a 23-card presentation given to young fans at a promotional game. The 2-5/8" x 4" cards have game-action color photo bordered in white. Backs are in blue on white with a few personal data, career highlights and record, a cartoon safety message and the logo of sponsoring Kansas City Life Insurance, which provided the cards for distribution by the Metropolitan Chiefs and Sheriffs Assn. Cards are checklisted here alphabetically.

1997 Kansas City Royals Police

In 1996 the Royals returned to safety set issue with this 27-card presentation given to fans 14 and under at the April 20 game. The 2-5/8" x 4" cards have game-action color photo in white. Backs are in blue on white with a few personal data, career highlights and record, a cartoon safety message and the logo of sponsoring Kansas City Life Insurance, which provided the cards for distribution by the Metropolitan Chiefs and Sheriffs Assn. Cards are checklisted here by uniform number.

		NM/M
Complete Set (27):		4.00
Common Player:		.25
1	Bip Roberts	.25
3	Bob Hamelin	.25
4	Keith Lockhart	.25
6	David Howard	.25
8	Bob Boone	.45
12	Mike Macfarlane	.25
16	Joe Randa	.25
17	Kevin Appier	.25
18	Johnny Damon	1.50
21	Jeff Montgomery	.25
22	Jon Nunnally	.25
23	Mark Gubicza	.25
24	Terry Clark	.25
25	Les Norman	.25
28	Rusty Meacham	.25
30	Jose Offerman	.25
31	Michael Tucker	.25
33	Chris Haney	.25
35	Hipolito Pichardo	.25
37	Rick Huisman	.25
39	Jim Converse	.25
41	Tim Belcher	.25
42	Tom Goodwin	.25
44	Joe Vitiello	.25
45	Jason Jacome	.25
50	Melvin Bunch	.25
57	Mike Magnante	.25

1997 Kansas City Royals Police

In 1996 the Royals returned to safety set issue with this 27-card presentation given to fans 14 and under at the April 20 game. The 2-5/8" x 4" cards have game-action color photo in white. Backs are in blue on white with a few personal data, career highlights and record, a cartoon safety message and the logo of sponsoring Kansas City Life Insurance, which provided the cards for distribution by the Metropolitan Chiefs and Sheriffs Assn. Cards are checklisted here by uniform number.

		NM/M
Complete Set (23):		4.00
Common Player:		.25
(1)	Kevin Appier	.25
(2)	Tim Belcher	.25
(3)	Jay Bell	.25
(4)	Jaime Bluma	.25
(5)	Bob Boone	.50
(6)	Johnny Damon	1.50
(7)	Chili Davis	.25
(8)	Tom Goodwin	.25
(9)	Chris Haney	.25
(10)	David Howard	.25
(11)	Rick Huisman	.25
(12)	Jason Jacome	.25
(13)	Jeff King	.25
(14)	Mike Macfarlane	.25
(15)	Jeff Montgomery	.25
(16)	Jose Offerman	.25
(17)	Craig Paquette	.25
(18)	Hipolito Pichardo	.25
(19)	Bip Roberts	.25
(20)	Jose Rosado	.25
(21)	Sluggerrr (Mascot)	.25
(22)	Mike Sweeney	.25
(23)	Joe Vitiello	.25

1998 Kansas City Royals Police

Johnny Damon • 18

In 1998 the Royals issued this safety set to fans 14 and under at a promotional game. The 2-5/8" x 4" cards have game-action color photo bordered in white. Backs are in blue on white with a few bits of personal data, a cartoon safety message and the logo of sponsoring Kansas City Life Insurance, which provided the cards for distribution by the Metropolitan Chiefs and Sheriffs Assn. Cards are checklisted here by uniform number.

		NM/M
Complete Set (26):		4.00
Common Player:		.25
2	Jed Hansen	.25
4	Shane Halter	.25
7	Jeff King	.35
14	Felix Martinez	.25
15	Mike Macfarlane	.25
16	Dean Palmer	.25
17	Kevin Appier	.25
18	Johnny Damon	1.50
19	Jeff Conine	.50
21	Jeff Montgomery	.25
22	Larry Sutton	.25
23	Hal Morris	.25
27	Jermaine Dye	.25
27	Joe Vitiello	.25
29	Mike Sweeney	.25
32	Jose Offerman	.25
33	Chris Haney	.25
37	Hipolito Pichardo	.25
40	Tony Muser	.25
41	Tim Belcher	.25
43	Roderick Myers	.25
47	Brian Bevil	.25
50	Jose Rosado	.25
53	Glendon Rusch	.25
56	Matt Whisenant	.25
	Sluggerrr (Mascot)	.25

2000 Kansas City Royals Police

The Royals issued this safety set to the first 10,000 fans 14 and under at an April 30 promotional game. The 2-5/8" x 4" cards have game-action color photo bordered in white. Backs are in blue on white with a few bits of personal data, a cartoon safety message and the logo of sponsoring Kansas City Life Insurance, which provided the cards for distribution by the Metropolitan Chiefs and Sheriffs Assn. Cards are checklisted here by uniform number.

		NM/M
Complete Set (25):		4.00
Common Player:		.25
1	Rey Sanchez	.25
3	Carlos Febles	.50
4	Ray Holbert	.25
6	Todd Dunwoody	.25
12	Jeff Reboulet	.25
14	Mark Quinn	.25
15	Carlos Beltran	3.00
16	Joe Randa	.25
18	Johnny Damon	1.00
19	Brian Johnson	.25
24	Jermaine Dye	.25
28	Jay Witasick	.25
29	Mike Sweeney	.25
33	Chad Durbin	.25
34	Blake Stein	.25
37	Jeff Suppan	.25
38	Scott Pose	.25
40	Tony Muser	.25
41	Dan Reichert	.25
44	Jose Santiago	.25
48	Jerry Spradlin	.25
49	Chris Fussell	.25
50	Jose Rosado	.25
52	Ricky Bottalico	.25
	Sluggerrr (Mascot)	.25

1993 Kansas City Star Royals All-Time Team

On the occasion of the team's 25th anniversary the Kansas City Star newspaper issued a sheet honoring the All-Time Team. The 10-3/8" x 14-3/8" sheet is perforated to allow separation of the individual 2-1/2" x 3-1/2" cards. Fronts have color photos at center with royal blue borders at the sides and gold at top and bottom. A Royals 25th anniversary logo is at lower-right. Backs are printed in black and blue on white with a career

summary and the player's K.C. stats. The unnumbered cards are checklisted here alphabetically.

		NM/M
Uncut Sheet:		12.00
Complete Set (16):		10.00
Common Player:		.50
(1)	George Brett	6.00
(2)	Steve Busby	.50
(3)	Al Cowens	.50
(4)	Dick Howser	.50
(5)	Dennis Leonard	.50
(6)	John Mayberry	.50
(7)	Hal McRae	.75
(8)	Amos Otis	.50
(9)	Fred Patek	.50
(10)	Darrell Porter	.50
(11)	Dan Quisenberry	.75
(12)	Bret Saberhagen	1.00
(13)	Paul Splittorff	.50
(14)	Frank White	.75
(15)	Willie Wilson	1.00
(16)	25th Anniversary Logo	.50

2001 Kansas City Royals Police

The Royals issued this safety set to fans attending a promotional game. The 2-5/8" x 4" cards have a game-action color photo on front. The same photo is enlarged, posterized and rendered in blue as a background. A gold stripe at left and top has player identification. Backs have a few bits of personal data, a cartoon safety message and the logo of sponsoring Kansas City Life Insurance, which provided the cards for distribution by the Metropolitan Chiefs and Sheriffs Assn. Cards are checklisted here alphabetically.

		NM/M
Complete Set (27):		4.00
Common Player:		.25
(1)	Luis Alicea	.25
(2)	Carlos Beltran	2.00
(3)	Dee Brown	.25
(4)	Chad Durbin	.25
(5)	Jermaine Dye	.25
(6)	Carlos Febles	.40
(7)	Doug Henry	.25
(8)	Roberto Hernandez	.25
(9)	Dave McCarty	.25
(10)	Brian Meadows	.25
(11)	Scott Mullen	.25
(12)	Tony Muser	.25
(13)	Luis Ordaz	.25
(14)	Hector Ortiz	.25
(15)	Mark Quinn	.25
(16)	Joe Randa	.25
(17)	Dan Reichert	.25
(18)	Jose Rosado	.25
(19)	Rey Sanchez	.25
(20)	Jose Santiago	.25
(21)	Blake Stein	.25
(22)	Jeff Suppan	.25
(23)	Mac Suzuki	.25
(24)	Mike Sweeney	.25
(25)	Kris Wilson	.25
(26)	Gregg Zaun	.25
(27)	Slugger (Mascot)	.25

2002 Kansas City Royals Police

This safety set was a stadium give-away to fans attending an early-season promotional game. The 2-5/8" x 4" cards have a game-action color photo on front, with the background rendered in blue and an arc of blue at left. Backs have a few bits of personal data, a cartoon, safety message and the logo of sponsoring Kansas City Life Insurance, which provided the cards for distribution by the Metropolitan Chiefs and Sheriffs Assn. Cards are checklisted here alphabetically.

		NM/M
Complete Set (26):		4.00
Common Player:		.25
(1)	Luis Alicea	.25
(2)	Cory Bailey	.25
(3)	Carlos Beltran	2.00
(4)	Dee Brown	.25
(5)	Paul Byrd	.25
(6)	Chad Durbin	.25
(7)	Carlos Febles	.50
(8)	Jason Grimsley	.25
(9)	Roberto Hernandez	.25
(10)	A.J. Hinch	.25
(11)	Raul Ibanez	.25
(12)	Chuck Knoblauch	.25
(13)	Darrell May	.25
(14)	Brent Mayne	.25
(15)	Dave McCarty	.25
(16)	Tony Muser	.25
(17)	Neifi Perez	.25
(18)	Mark Quinn	.25
(19)	Joe Randa	.35
(20)	Dan Reichert	.25
(21)	Donnie Sadler	.25
(22)	Slugger (Mascot)	.25
(23)	Blake Stein	.25
(24)	Jeff Suppan	.25
(25)	Mike Sweeney	.50
(26)	Michael Tucker	.25

2003 Kansas City Royals Police

The Royals issued this safety set to fans attending an early-season promotional game. The 2-5/8" x 4" cards have a game-action color photo on front. Backs have a few bits of personal data, a cartoon safety message and the logo of sponsoring Kansas City Life Insurance, which provided the cards for distribution by the Metropolitan Chiefs and Sheriffs Assn. Cards are checklisted here by uniform number.

		NM/M
Complete Set (27):		6.00
Common Player:		.50
2	Brent Mayne	.50
3	Carlos Febles	.50
6	Angel Berroa	1.00
6	Tony Pena	.50
12	Desi Relaford	.50
15	Carlos Beltran	2.00

16	Joe Randa	.50
18	Raul Ibanez	.50
24	Michael Tucker	.50
26	Mike DiFelice	.50
28	Ken Harvey	.50
29	Mike Sweeney	.60
30	Brandon Berger	.50
31	Albie Lopez	.50
32	Chris George	.50
33	James Baldwin	.50
34	Darrell May	.50
35	Ryan Bukvich	.50
38	Jason Grimsley	.50
40	Runelvys Hernandez	.50
45	Aaron Guiel	.50
48	Jeremy Affeldt	.50
51	Kris Wilson	.50
53	Miguel Asencio	.50
54	Mike MacDougal	.50
57	Scott Mullen	.50
---	Sluggerrr (Mascot)	.50

2004 Kansas City Royals Police

The Royals issued this safety set to fans attending an early-season promotional game. The 2-5/8" x 4" cards have a game-action color photo on front, on a dot-matrix background. Backs have a few bits of personal data, a cartoon, safety message and the logo of sponsoring Kansas City Life Insurance, which provided the cards for distribution by the Metropolitan Chiefs and Sheriffs Assn. Cards are checklisted here by uniform number.

		NM/M
Complete Set (26):		4.00
Common Player:		.25
(1)	Luis Alicea	.25
(2)	Cory Bailey	.25
(3)	Carlos Beltran	2.00
(4)	Dee Brown	.25
(5)	Paul Byrd	.25
(6)	Chad Durbin	.25
(7)	Carlos Febles	.50
(8)	Jason Grimsley	.25
(9)	Roberto Hernandez	.25
(10)	A.J. Hinch	.25
(11)	Raul Ibanez	.25
(12)	Chuck Knoblauch	.25
(13)	Darrell May	.25
(14)	Brent Mayne	.25
(15)	Dave McCarty	.25
(16)	Tony Muser	.25
(17)	Neifi Perez	.25
(18)	Mark Quinn	.25
(19)	Joe Randa	.35
(20)	Dan Reichert	.25
(21)	Donnie Sadler	.25
(22)	Slugger (Mascot)	.25
(23)	Blake Stein	.25
(24)	Jeff Suppan	.25
(25)	Mike Sweeney	.50
(26)	Michael Tucker	.25

1985 Kas Potato Chips Discs

The Royals issued this safety set to fans attending an early-season promotional game. The 2-5/8" x 4" cards have a game-action color photo on front, on a marbled background. Backs are printed in blue and have a few bits of personal data, a cartoon, safety message and the logo of sponsoring Kansas City Life Insurance, which provided the cards for distribution by the Metropolitan Chiefs and Sheriffs Assn. Cards are checklisted here by uniform number.

		NM/M
Complete Set (27):		10.00
Common Player:		.50
00	Sluggerrr (Mascot)	.50
4	Angel Berroa	1.00
6	Tony Pena	.50
9	David DeJesus	.50
11	Matt Stairs	.50
12	Desi Relaford	.50
14	Tony Graffanino	.50
15	Carlos Beltran	2.00
16	Joe Randa	.50
18	Kelly Stinnett	.50
19	Brian Anderson	.50
22	Juan Gonzalez	1.00
24	Rich Thompson	.50
28	Ken Harvey	.50
29	Mike Sweeney	.65
30	Benito Santiago	.50
33	Curtis Leskanic	.50
34	Darrell May	.50
38	Jason Grimsley	.50
41	Jimmy Gobble	.50
45	Aaron Guiel	.50
47	Scott Sullivan	.50
48	Jeremy Affeldt	.50
54	Mike MacDougal	.50
55	Kevin Appier	.50
59	D.J. Carrasco	.50
61	Jaime Cerda	.50

2005 Kansas City Royals Police

		NM/M
Complete Set (27):		8.00
Common Player:		.50
00	Sluggerrr (Mascot)	.50
3	John Buck	.50
3	Terrence Long	.50
4	Angel Berroa	.75
6	Tony Pena	.50
9	David DeJesus	.50
11	Eli Marrero	.50
12	Matt Stairs	.50
14	Tony Graffanino	.50
19	Brian Anderson	.50
23	Zack Greinke	1.50
24	Mark Teahen	.50
27	Denny Bautista	.50
28	Ken Harvey	.50
29	Mike Sweeney	.65
30	Ruben Gotay	.50
33	Jose Lima	.50
40	Runelvys Hernandez	.50
41	Jimmy Gobble	.50
45	Aaron Guiel	.50
46	Mike Wood	.50
48	Jeremy Affeldt	.50
51	Andy Sisco	.50
54	Mike MacDougal	.50
56	Jaime Cerda	.50
57	Nate Field	.50
58	Shawn Camp	.50

1985 Kas Potato Chips Discs

One of a pair of nearly identical (see Kitty Clover) sets issued by midwestern potato chip companies, this issue features top stars of the day on 2-3/4" cardboard discs. The discs have a player portrait at center, with uniform logos airbrushed away because the producer was licensed only by the MLB Players Association and not Major League Baseball. The player's name, team and position are printed in a white diamond around the photo. The sponsor's logo is in the orange border. Backs are in black-and-white and have a few biographical data, a 1984 stats line and a Snack Time logo. The unnumbered discs are checklisted here in alphabetical order. Square versions of the discs, which have been cut from press sheets are known within the hobby and carry a small premium. KAS was based in St. Louis.

		NM/M
Complete Set (20):		75.00
Common Player:		1.50
(1)	Steve Carlton	4.50
(2)	Jack Clark	1.50
(3)	Rich Gossage	1.50
(4)	Tony Gwynn	7.50
(5)	Bob Horner	1.50
(6)	Keith Hernandez	1.50
(7)	Kent Hrbek	1.50
(8)	Willie McGee	1.50
(9)	Dan Quisenberry	1.50
(10)	Cal Ripken Jr.	20.00
(11)	Ryne Sandberg	7.50
(12)	Mike Schmidt	12.50
(13)	Tom Seaver	5.00
(14)	Ozzie Smith	7.50
(15)	Rick Sutcliffe	1.50
(16)	Bruce Sutter	4.00
(17)	Alan Trammell	1.50
(18)	Fernando Valenzuela	1.50
(19)	Willie Wilson	1.50
(20)	Dave Winfield	4.50

1986 Kas Potato Chips Cardinals

One of several of 2-7/8" round baseball card discs created by Mike Schecter Associates for inclusion in packages of potato chips, the 20-card Kas set features players of the defending National League Champion St. Louis Cardinals. Fronts feature color photos on which the team logos have been removed from the caps by airbrushing the photos' uniform logos. Card backs have minimal personal data and 1985 stats.

		NM/M
Complete Set (20):		16.00
Common Player:		.50
1	Vince Coleman	1.00
2	Ken Dayley	.50
3	Tito Landrum	.50
4	Steve Braun	.50
5	Danny Cox	.50
6	Bob Forsch	.50
7	Ozzie Smith	9.00
8	Brian Harper	.50
9	Jack Clark	.50
10	Todd Worrell	.50
11	Joaquin Andujar	.50
12	Tom Nieto	.50
13	Kurt Kepshire	.50
14	Terry Pendleton	.50
15	Tom Herr	.50
16	Darrell Porter	.50
17	John Tudor	.50
18	Jeff Lahti	.50
19	Andy Van Slyke	1.00
20	Willie McGee	1.00

1986 Kay Bee Young Superstars

One of the most-widely distributed of the specialty boxed sets of 1986, the Kay Bee toy store chain set of "Young Superstars of Baseball" was produced by Topps. The 2-1/2" x 3-1/2" cards are printed on white stock with a glossy surface finish. Backs, printed in red and black, are strongly reminiscent of the 1971 Topps cards. While the set concentrated on "young" stars of the game, few of the year's top rookies were included.

		NM/M
Complete Set (33):		2.00
Common Player:		.05
1	Rick Aguilera	.05
2	Chris Brown	.05
3	Tom Browning	.05
4	Tom Brunansky	.05
5	Vince Coleman	.05
6	Ron Darling	.05
7	Alvin Davis	.05
8	Mariano Duncan	.05
9	Shawon Dunston	.05
10	Sid Fernandez	.05
11	Tony Fernandez	.05
12	Brian Fisher	.05
13	John Franco	.05
14	Julio Franco	.05
15	Dwight Gooden	.05
16	Ozzie Guillen	.05
17	Tony Gwynn	.75
18	Jimmy Key	.05
19	Don Mattingly	1.50
20	Oddibe McDowell	.05
21	Roger McDowell	.05
22	Dan Pasqua	.05

23	Terry Pendleton	.05
24	Jim Presley	.05
25	Kirby Puckett	.75
26	Earnie Riles	.05
27	Bret Saberhagen	.05
28	Mark Salas	.05
29	Juan Samuel	.05
30	Jeff Stone	.05
31	Darryl Strawberry	.05
32	Andy Van Slyke	.05
33	Frank Viola	.05

logo. Backs feature player closeups in a horizontal layout in blue ink on a green and white background. Backs are numbered and carry biographical information, career data and major league batting stats.

	NM/M
Complete Set (33):	3.00
Common Player:	.05

1987 Kay Bee Superstars of Baseball

For a second year, Topps produced a boxed set for the Kay Bee toy store chain. Called "Superstars of Baseball," cards in the set measure 2-1/2" x 3-1/2". The glossy-coated fronts carry a color player photo plus the Kay Bee logo. Backs, reminiscent of those found in the 1971 Topps set, offer a black-and-white portrait of the player along with his name, postion, personal information, playing record and a brief biography.

	NM/M
Complete Set (33):	3.00
Common Player:	.05

1	George Bell	.05
2	Wade Boggs	.65
3	Jose Canseco	.30
4	Joe Carter	.05
5	Jack Clark	.05
6	Alvin Davis	.05
7	Eric Davis	.05
8	Andre Dawson	.25
9	Darrell Evans	.05
10	Dwight Evans	.05
11	Gary Gaetti	.05
12	Pedro Guerrero	.05
13	Tony Gwynn	.65
14	Howard Johnson	.05
15	Wally Joyner	.05
16	Don Mattingly	.75
17	Willie McGee	.05
18	Mark McGwire	.85
19	Paul Molitor	.50
20	Dale Murphy	.25
21	Dave Parker	.05
22	Lance Parrish	.05
23	Kirby Puckett	.65
24	Tim Raines	.05
25	Cal Ripken, Jr.	1.00
26	Juan Samuel	.05
27	Mike Schmidt	.75
28	Ruben Sierra	.05
29	Darryl Strawberry	.05
30	Danny Tartabull	.05
31	Alan Trammell	.05
32	Tim Wallach	.05
33	Dave Winfield	.50

1988 Kay Bee Team Leaders

This boxed edition of 44 player and six team logo cards was produced by Fleer for distribution by Kay Bee toy stores nationwide. Color player photos are framed in black against a bright red border. "Fleer Team Leaders 1988" and Kay Bee logos appear on the front. Backs, (red, white and pink) repeat the Team Leaders logo, followed by stats, personal data, team and MLB logos. The player's name, card number and position are listed on the lower border. The set includes six team logo sticker cards that feature black-and-white stadium photos on the backs.

	NM/M
Complete Set (44):	3.00
Common Player:	.05

1	George Bell	.05
2	Wade Boggs	.65
3	Jose Canseco	.40
4	Will Clark	.10
5	Roger Clemens	.75
6	Eric Davis	.05
7	Andre Dawson	.25
8	Julio Franco	.05
9	Andres Galarraga	.05
10	Dwight Gooden	.05
11	Tony Gwynn	.65
12	Tom Henke	.05
13	Orel Hershiser	.05
14	Kent Hrbek	.05
15	Ted Higuera	.05
16	Wally Joyner	.05
17	Jimmy Key	.05
18	Mark Langston	.05
19	Don Mattingly	.75
20	Willie McGee	.05
21	Mark McGwire	.65
22	Paul Molitor	.50
23	Jack Morris	.05
24	Dale Murphy	.25
25	Larry Parrish	.05
26	Kirby Puckett	.65
27	Tim Raines	.05
28	Jeff Reardon	.05
29	Dave Righetti	.05
30	Cal Ripken, Jr.	1.00
31	Don Robinson	.05
32	Bret Saberhagen	.05
33	Juan Samuel	.05
34	Mike Schmidt	.75
35	Mike Scott	.05
36	Kevin Seitzer	.05
37	Dave Smith	.05
38	Ozzie Smith	.65
39	Zane Smith	.05
40	Darryl Strawberry	.05
41	Rick Sutcliffe	.05
42	Bobby Thigpen	.05
43	Alan Trammell	.05
44	Andy Van Slyke	.05

1988 Kay Bee Superstars of Baseball

This boxed set was produced by Topps for exclusive distribution via Kay Bee toy stores nationwide. Card fronts are super glossy and feature color player action photos below a bright red and yellow player name banner. Photos are framed in green above a large, cartoon-style Kay Bee

1989 Kay Bee Superstars of Baseball

The top stars of baseball are featured in this boxed set produced by Topps for the Kay Bee Toy store chain. The glossy, standard-size cards display the Kay Bee logo below the player photo on the front. The top of the card is headlined "Superstars of Baseball," with the player's name underneath. Backs include a small black-and-white player photo and personal data.

	NM/M
Complete Set (33):	4.00
Common Player:	.05

1	Doyle Alexander	.05
2	Bert Blyleven	.05
3	Wade Boggs	.65
4	George Brett	.75
5	John Candelaria	.05
6	Gary Carter	.50
7	Vince Coleman	.05
8	Andre Dawson	.25
9	Dennis Eckersley	.40
10	Darrell Evans	.05
11	Dwight Evans	.05
12	Carlton Fisk	.05
13	Ken Griffey	.05
14	Tony Gwynn	.65
15	Rickey Henderson	.50
16	Keith Hernandez	.05
17	Charlie Hough	.05
18	Don Mattingly	.75
19	Jack Morris	.05
20	Dale Murphy	.25
21	Eddie Murray	.50
22	Dave Parker	.05
23	Kirby Puckett	.65
24	Tim Raines	.05
25	Rick Reuschel	.05
26	Jerry Reuss	.05
27	Jim Rice	.15
28	Nolan Ryan	1.00
29	Ozzie Smith	.65
30	Frank Tanana	.05
31	Willie Wilson	.05
32	Dave Winfield	.50
33	Robin Yount	.50

1990 Kay Bee Kings

This boxed set was the fifth annual issue produced by Topps for the Kay Bee toy store chain. The 2-1/2" x 3-1/2" cards feature color action photos on the front and complete statistics on the flip sides. The cards are numbered alphabetically.

1993 Keebler Texas Rangers

Over a series of eight home dates in Arlington Stadium's final season, the Keebler baking company along with a group of rotating co-sponsors produced and distributed a team set featuring "all players, manager and coaches who have ever appeared in a Rangers game." Besides the player cards there were checklists, team photo cards, team-leader cards, logo cards and other specials. The cards were made up into 8-1/2" x 11" booklets, with the cards perforated for removal. Series 2 and 3 booklets had 72 cards; the other series had 54 cards each. Single cards measure 2-1/2" x 3-1/2". Sepia-toned player portraits are featured with red frames. A blue banner at top has the team name. The player name is printed in black in the white bottom border. The Keebler logo is at the photo's lower-left, while the player's position is in a baseball diamond diagram at lower-right. Backs are printed in black, include a few biographical details and the player's Rangers' and major league career stats. The Keebler logo is repeated on the back, along with the logo of the co-sponsor of that particular series. A total of 42,000 of the first series booklets were distributed; 35,000 each of the other seven series were produced.

	NM/M
Complete Set (468):	35.00
Common Player:	.10

1	Ted Williams	5.00
2	Larry Biittner	.10
3	Rich Billings	.10
4	Dick Bosman	.10
5	Pete Broberg	.10
6	Jeff Burroughs	.10
7	Casey Cox	.10
8	Jim Driscoll	.10
9	Jan Dukes	.10
10	Bill Fahey	.10
11	Ted Ford	.10
12	Bill Gogolewski	.10
13	Tom Grieve	.10
14	Rich Hand	.10
15	Toby Harrah	.25
16	Vic Harris	.10
17	Rich Hinton	.10
18	Frank Howard	.25
19	Gerry Janeski	.10
20	Dalton Jones	.10
21	Hal King	.10
22	Ted Kubiak	.10
23	Steve Lawson	.10
24	Paul Lindblad	.10
25	Joe Lovitto	.10
26	Elliott Maddox	.10
27	Marty Martinez	.10
28	Jim Mason	.10
29	Don Mincher	.10
30	Dave Nelson	.10
31	Jim Panther	.10
32	Mike Paul	.10
33	Horacio Pina	.10
34	Tom Ragland	.10
35	Lenny Randle	.10
36	Jim Roland	.10
37	Jim Shellenback	.10
38	Don Stanhouse	.10
39	Ken Suarez	.10
40	Joe Camacho	.10
41	Nellie Fox	2.00
42	Sid Hudson	.10
43	George Susce	.10
44	Wayne Terwilliger	.10
45	Darrel Akerfelds	.10
46	Doyle Alexander	.10
47	Gerald Alexander	.10
48	Brian Allard	.10
49	Lloyd Allen	.10
50	Sandy Alomar	.10
51	Wilson Alvarez	.10
52	Jim Anderson	.10
53	Scott Anderson	.10
54	Brad Arnsberg	.10
55	Tucker Ashford	.10
56	Doug Ault	.10
57	Bob Babcock	.10
58	Mike Bacsik	.10
59	Harold Baines	.10
60	Alan Bannister	.10
61	Floyd Bannister	.10
62	John Barfield	.10
63	Len Barker	.10
64	Steve Barr	.10
65	Randy Bass	.10
66	Lew Beasley	.10
67	Kevin Belcher	.10
68	Buddy Bell	.10
69	Juan Beniquez	.10
70	Kurt Bevacqua	.10
71	Jim Bibby	.10
72	Joe Bitker	.10
73	Larvell Blanks	.10
74	Bert Blyleven	.25
75	Terry Bogener	.10
76	Tommy Boggs	.10
77	Dan Boitano	.10
78	Bobby Bonds	.25
79	Thad Bosley	.10
80	Dennis Boyd	.10
81	Nelson Briles	.10
82	Ed Brinkman	.10
83	Bob Brower	.10
84	Jackie Brown	.10
85	Larry Brown	.10
86	Jerry Browne	.10
87	Glenn Brummer	.10
88	Kevin Buckley	.10
89	Steve Buechele	.10
90	Ray Burris	.10
91	John Butcher	.10
92	Bert Campaneris	.10
93	Mike Campbell	.10
94	John Cangelosi	.10
95	Nick Capra	.10
96	Leo Cardenas	.10
97	Don Carman	.10
98	Rico Carty	.10
99	Don Castle	.10
100	Jose Cecena	.10
101	Dave Chalk	.10
102	Scott Chiamparino	.10
103	Ken Clay	.10
104	Reggie Cleveland	.10
105	Gene Clines	.10
106	David Clyde	.10
107	Cris Colon	.10
108	Merrill Combs	.10
109	Steve Comer	.10
110	Glen Cook	.10
111	Scott Coolbaugh	.10
112	Pat Corrales	.10
113	Edwin Correa	.10
114	Larry Cox	.10
115	Keith Creel	.10
116	Victor Cruz	.10
117	Mike Cubbage	.10
118	Bobby Cuellar	.10
119	Danny Darwin	.10
120	Jack Daugherty	.10
121	Doug Davis	.10
122	Odie Davis	.10
123	Willie Davis	.10
124	Bucky Dent	.10
125	Adrian Devine	.10
126	Mario Diaz	.10
127	Rich Donnelly	.10
128	Brian Downing	.10
129	Tommy Dunbar	.10
130	Steve Dunning	.10
131	Dan Duran	.10
132	Don Durham	.10
133	Dick Egan	.10
134	Dock Ellis	.10
135	John Ellis	.10
136	Mike Epstein	.10
137	Cecil Espy	.10
138	Chuck Estrada	.10
139	Glenn Ezell	.10
140	Hector Fajardo	.10
141	Monty Fariss	.10
142	Ed Farmer	.10
143	Jim Farr	.10
144	Joe Ferguson	.10
145	Ed Figueroa	.10
146	Steve Fireovid	.10
147	Scott Fletcher	.10
148	Doug Flynn	.10
149	Marv Foley	.10
150	Tim Foli	.10
151	Tony Fossas	.10
152	Steve Foucault	.10
153	Art Fowler	.10
154	Jim Fregosi	.10
155	Pepe Frias	.10
156	Oscar Gamble	.10
157	Barbaro Garbey	.10
158	Dick Gernert	.10
159	Jim Gideon	.10
160	Jerry Don Gleaton	.10
161	Orlando Gomez	.10
162	Rich Gossage	.25
163	Gary Gray	.10
164	Gary Green	.10
165	John Grubb	.10
166	Cecilio Guante	.10
167	Jose Guzman	.10
168	Drew Hall	.10
169	Bill Hands	.10
170	Steve Hargan	.10
171	Mike Hargrove	.10
172	Toby Harrah	.10
173	Bud Harrelson	.10
174	Donald Harris	.10
175	Greg Harris	.10
176	Mike Hart	.10
177	Bill Haselman	.10
178	Ray Hayward	.10
179	Tommy Helms	.10
180	Ken Henderson	.10
181	Rick Henninger	.10
182	Dwayne Henry	.10
183	Jose Hernandez	.10
184	Whitey Herzog	.10
185	Chuck Hiller	.10
186	Joe Hoerner	.10
187	Guy Hoffman	.10
188	Gary Holle	.10
189	Rick Honeycutt	.10
190	Burt Hooton	.10
191	John Hoover	.10
192	Willie Horton	.10
193	Dave Hostetler	.10
194	Charlie Hough	.10
195	Tom House	.10
196	Art Howe	.10
197	Steve Howe	.10
198	Roy Howell	.10
199	Charles Hudson	.10
200	Billy Hunter	.10
201	Pete Incaviglia	.25
202	Mike Jeffcoat	.10
203	Ferguson Jenkins	2.00
204	Alex Johnson	.10
205	Bobby Johnson	.10
206	Cliff Johnson	.10
207	Darrell Johnson	.10
208	John Henry Johnson	.10
209	Lamar Johnson	.10
210	Bobby Jones	.10
211	Odell Jones	.10
212	Mike Jorgensen	.10
213	Don Kainer	.10
214	Mike Kekich	.10
215	Steve Kemp	.10
216	Jim Kern	.10
217	Paul Kilgus	.10
218	Ed Kirkpatrick	.10
219	Darold Knowles	.10
220	Fred Koenig	.10
221	Jim Kremmel	.10
222	Chad Kreuter	.10
223	Jeff Kunkel	.10
224	Bob Lacey	.10
225	Al Lachowicz	.10
226	Joe Lahoud	.10
227	Rick Leach	.10
228	Danny Leon	.10
229	Dennis Lewallyn	.10
230	Rick Lisi	.10
231	Davey Lopes	.10
232	John Lowenstein	.10
233	Mike Loynd	.10
234	Frank Lucchesi	.10
235	Sparky Lyle	.10
236	Pete Mackanin	.10
237	Bill Madlock	.25
238	Greg Mahlberg	.10
239	Mickey Mahler	.10
240	Bob Malloy	.10
241	Ramon Manon	.10
242	Fred Manrique	.10
243	Barry Manuel	.10
244	Mike Marshall	.10
245	Billy Martin	.50
246	Mike Mason	.10
247	Terry Mathews	.10
248	Jon Matlack	.10
249	Rob Maurer	.10
250	Dave May	.10

#	Player	Price
251	Scott May	.10
252	Lee Mazzilli	.10
253	Larry McCall	.10
254	Lance McCullers	.10
255	Oddibe McDowell	.10
256	Russ McGinnis	.10
257	Joey McLaughlin	.10
258	Craig McMurtry	.10
259	Doc Medich	.10
260	Dave Meier	.10
261	Mario Mendoza	.10
262	Orlando Mercado	.10
263	Mark Mercer	.10
264	Ron Meridith	.10
265	Jim Merritt	.10
266	Gary Mielke	.10
267	Eddie Miller	.10
268	Paul Mirabella	.10
269	Dave Moates	.10
270	Dale Mohorcic	.10
271	Willie Montanez	.10
272	Tommy Moore	.10
273	Roger Moret	.10
274	Jamie Moyer	.10
275	Dale Murray	.10
276	Al Newman	.10
277	Dickie Noles	.10
278	Eric Nolte	.10
279	Nelson Norman	.10
280	Jim Norris	.10
281	Edwin Nunez	.10
282	Pete O'Brien	.10
283	Al Oliver	.25
284	Tom O'Malley	.10
285	Tom Paciorek	.10
286	Ken Pape	.10
287	Mark Parent	.10
288	Larry Parrish	.10
289	Gaylord Perry	2.00
290	Stan Perzanowski	.10
291	Fritz Peterson	.10
292	Mark Petkovsek	.10
293	Gary Pettis	.10
294	Jim Piersall	.25
295	John Poloni	.10
296	Jim Poole	.10
297	Tom Poquette	.10
298	Darrell Porter	.10
299	Ron Pruitt	.10
300	Greg Pryor	.10
301	Luis Pujols	.10
302	Pat Putnam	.10
303	Doug Rader	.10
304	Dave Rajsich	.10
305	Kevin Reimer	.10
306	Merv Rettenmund	.10
307	Mike Richardt	.10
308	Mickey Rivers	.10
309	Dave Roberts	.10
310	Leon Roberts	.10
311	Jeff Robinson	.10
312	Tom Robson	.10
313	Wayne Rosenthal	.10
314	Dave Rozema	.10
315	Jeff Russell	.10
316	Connie Ryan	.10
317	Billy Sample	.10
318	Jim Schaffer	.10
319	Calvin Schiraldi	.10
320	Dave Schmidt	.10
321	Donnie Scott	.10
322	Tony Scruggs	.10
323	Bob Sebra	.10
324	Larry See	.10
325	Sonny Siebert	.10
326	Ruben Sierra	.10
327	Charlie Silvera	.10
328	Duke Sims	.10
329	Bill Singer	.10
330	Craig Skok	.10
331	Don Slaught	.10
332	Roy Smalley	.10
333	Dan Smith	.10
334	Keith Smith	.10
335	Mike Smithson	.10
336	Eric Soderholm	.10
337	Sammy Sosa	4.00
338	Jim Spencer	.10
339	Dick Such	.10
340	Eddie Stanky	.10
341	Mike Stanley	.10
342	Rusty Staub	.35
343	James Steels	.10
344	Bill Stein	.10
345	Rick Stelmaszek	.10
346	Ray Stephens	.10
347	Dave Stewart	.10
348	Jeff Stone	.10
349	Bill Sudakis	.10
350	Jim Sundberg	.10
351	Rich Surhoff	.10
352	Greg Tabor	.10
353	Frank Tanana	.10
354	Jeff Terpko	.10
355	Stan Thomas	.10
356	Bobby Thompson	.10
357	Danny Thompson	.10
358	Dickie Thon	.10
359	Dave Tobik	.10
360	Wayne Tolleson	.10
361	Cesar Tovar	.10
362	Jim Umbarger	.10
363	Bobby Valentine	.10
364	Ellis Valentine	.10
365	Ed Vande Berg	.10
366	Dewayne Vaughn	.10
367	Mark Wagner	.10
368	Rick Waits	.10

#	Player	Price
369	Duane Walker	.10
370	Mike Wallace	.10
371	Denny Walling	.10
372	Danny Walton	.10
373	Gary Ward	.10
374	Claudell Washington	.10
375	Larue Wasington	.10
376	Chris Welsh	.10
377	Don Werner	.10
378	Len Whitehouse	.10
379	Del Wilber	.10
380	Curtis Wilkerson	.10
381	Matt Williams	.10
382	Mitch Williams	.10
383	Bump Wills	.10
384	Paul Wilmet	.10
385	Steve Wilson	.10
386	Bobby Witt	.10
387	Clyde Wright	.10
388	George Wright	.10
389	Ricky Wright	.10
390	Ned Yost	.10
391	Don Zimmer	.10
392	Richie Zisk	.10
393	Kevin Kennedy	.10
394	Steve Balboni	.10
395	Brian Bohanon	.10
396	Jeff Bronkey	.10
397	Kevin Brown	.10
398	Todd Burns	.10
399	Jose Canseco	.75
400	Cris Carpenter	.10
401	Doug Dascenzo	.10
402	Butch Davis	.10
403	Steve Dreyer	.10
404	Rob Ducey	.10
405	Julio Franco	.10
406	Jeff Frye	.10
407	Benji Gil	.10
408	Juan Gonzalez	3.00
409	Tom Henke	.10
410	David Hulse	.10
411	Jeff Huson	.10
412	Chris James	.10
413	Manuel Lee	.10
414	Craig Lefferts	.10
415	Charlie Leibrandt	.10
416	Gene Nelson	.10
417	Robb Nen	.10
418	Darren Oliver	.10
419	Rafael Palmeiro	2.00
420	Dean Palmer	.10
421	Bob Patterson	.10
422	Roger Pavlik	.10
423	Dan Peltier	.10
424	Geno Petralli	.10
425	Gary Redus	.10
426	Rick Reed	.10
427	Bill Ripken	.10
428	Ivan Rodriguez	3.00
429	Kenny Rogers	.10
430	John Russell	.10
431	Nolan Ryan	6.00
432	Mike Schooler	.10
433	Jon Shave	.10
434	Doug Strange	.10
435	Matt Whiteside	.10
436	Mickey Hatcher	.10
437	Perry Hill	.10
438	Jackie Moore	.10
439	Dave Oliver	.10
440	Claude Osteen	.10
441	Willie Upshaw	.10
442	Checklist 1-112	.10
443	Checklist 113-224	.10
444	Checklist 225-336	.10
445	Checklist 337-446	.10
446	Arlington Stadium	.10

Los Angeles Dodgers

In a promotion similar to those of Mother's Cookies in the past, Keebler sponsored a kids' trading card day August 15 distributing 28-card packs to fans 14 and under. Each pack contained 21 different cards and seven duplicates to trade in an effort to complete the set. The 2-1/2" x 3-1/2" cards have borderless player photos on front with a Dodgers logo and team-color red and blue stripes at bottom in which the player's name appears.

Color backs have a team logo, a Keebler's elf logo and a few bits of player biographical data.

NM/M

Complete Set (28): 10.00
Common Player: .50

#	Player	Price
1	Davey Johnson	.50
2	Eric Karros	.50
3	Gary Sheffield	.75
4	Raul Mondesi	.50
5	Kevin Brown	.60
6	Mark Grudzielanek	.50
7	Todd Hollandsworth	.50
8	Todd Hundley	.50
9	Jeff Shaw	.50
10	Pedro Borbon	.50
11	Chan Ho Park	.75
12	Jose Vizcaino	.50
13	Devon White	.50
14	Darren Dreifort	.50
15	Onan Masaoka	.50
16	Dave Hansen	.50
17	Adrian Beltre	1.50
18	Ismael Valdes	.50
19	Alan Mills	.50
20	Eric Young	.50
21	Mike Maddux	.50
22	Carlos Perez	.50
23	Tripp Cromer	.50
24	Jamie Arnold	.50
25	Angel Pena	.50
26	Trenidad Hubbard	.50
27	Doug Bochtler	.50
28	Coaches/Checklist (Rick Dempsey, Rich Down, Glenn Hoffman, Manny Mota, Claude Osteen, John Shelby, Jim Tracy)	.50

San Diego Padres

In a promotion similar to those of Mother's Cookies in the past, Keebler sponsored a kids' trading card day August 1 distributing 28-card packs to fans 14 and under. Each pack contained 21 different cards and seven duplicates to trade in an effort to complete the set. The 2-1/2" x 3-1/2" cards have borderless player photos on front with a Padres logo and team-color orange and blue stripes at bottom in which the player's name appears. Color backs have a Padres 1969-1999 logo, a Keebler's elf logo and a few bits of player biographical data.

NM/M

Complete Set (28): 10.00
Common Player: .50

#	Player	Price
1	Bruce Bochy	.50
2	Tony Gwynn	4.00
3	Wally Joyner	.50
4	Sterling Hitchcock	.50
5	Jim Leyritz	.50
6	Trevor Hoffman	.75
7	Quilvio Veras	.50
8	Dave Magadan	.50
9	Andy Ashby	.50
10	Damian Jackson	.50
11	Dan Miceli	.50
12	Reggie Sanders	.50
13	Chris Gomez	.50
14	Ruben Rivera	.50
15	Greg Myers	.50
16	Ed Vosberg	.50
17	John Vander Wal	.50
18	Donne Wall	.50
19	Eric Owens	.50
20	Brian Boehringer	.50
21	Woody Williams	.50
22	Matt Clement	.50
23	Carlos Reyes	.50
24	Stan Spencer	.50
25	George Arias	.50
26	Carlos Almanzar	.50
27	Phil Nevin	.50
28	Greg Booker, Tim Flannery, Davey Lopes, Rob Picciolo, Merv Rettenmund, Dave Smith (Padres Coaches)	.50

S.F. Giants

In a promotion similar to those of Mother's Cookies in the past, Keebler sponsored a kids' trading card day distributing 28-card packs to fans 14 and under. Each pack contained 21 different cards and seven duplicates to trade in an effort to complete the set. The 2-1/2" x 3-1/2" cards have borderless player photos on front with a farewell to Candlestick Park logo and team-color orange and black stripes at bottom in which the player's name appears. Color backs have a Keebler's elf logo and a few bits of player biographical data.

NM/M

Complete Set (28): 12.50
Common Player: .50

#	Player	Price
1	Dusty Baker	.50
2	Barry Bonds	7.50
3	Jeff Kent	.75
4	Robb Nen	.50
5	Bill Mueller	.50
6	Russ Ortiz	.50
7	Ellis Burks	.50
8	Marvin Benard	.50
9	Kirk Rueter	.50
10	J.T. Snow	.50
11	Stan Javier	.50
12	Chris Brock	.50
13	Charlie Hayes	.50
14	Joe Nathan	.50
15	Rich Rodriguez	.50
16	Brent Mayne	.50
17	Shawn Estes	.50
18	Rich Aurilia	.50
19	Mark Gardner	.50
20	Scott Servais	.50
21	John Johnstone	.50
22	Felix Rodriguez	.50
23	Armando Rios	.50
24	Alan Embree	.50
25	F.P. Santangelo	.50
26	Jerry Spradlin	.50
27	Lon Simmons (Broadcaster)	.50
28	Giants Coaches (Carlos Alfonso, Gene Clines, Sonny Jackson, Juan Lopez, Ron Perranoski, Ron Wotus)	.50

2000 Keebler Arizona Diamondbacks

Keebler cookies sponsored a kids' trading card day, distributing 28-card packs to fans 14 and under. Each pack contained 21 different cards and seven duplicates to trade in an effort to complete the set. Round-cornered cards have borderless portrait photos with a stripe at bottom featuring player identification and team logo. Backs have player data, uniform number, biographical information and Keebler's logo.

NM/M

Complete Set (28): 10.00
Common Player: .50

#	Player	Price
1	Buck Showalter	.50
2	Randy Johnson	3.00
3	Luis Gonzalez	.65
4	Todd Stottlemyre	.50
5	Matt Williams	.75
6	Curt Schilling	1.50
7	Jay Bell	.50
8	Steve Finley	.50
9	Brian Anderson	.50
10	Tony Womack	.50
11	Mike Morgan	.50
12	Damian Miller	.50
13	Greg Swindell	.50
14	Greg Colbrunn	.50
15	Dan Plesac	.50
16	Craig Counsell	.50
17	Russ Springer	.50
18	Kelly Stinnett	.50
19	Alex Cabrera	.50
20	Matt Mantei	.50
21	Danny Klassen	.50

#	Player	Price
22	Hanley Frias	.50
23	Byung-Hyun Kim	.50
24	Jason Conti	.50
25	Danny Bautista	.50
26	Erubiel Durazo	.50
27	Armando Reynoso	.50
28	Coaches/Checklist	.50

L.A. Dodgers

Keebler cookies sponsored a kids' trading card day August 20, distributing 28-card packs to fans 14 and under. Each pack contained 21 different cards and seven duplicates to trade in an effort to complete the set. Round-cornered cards have borderless portrait photos with a red stripe at bottom featuring player identification and team logo. Backs have player data, uniform number, biographical information and Keebler's logo.

NM/M

Complete Set (28): 10.00
Common Player: .50

#	Player	Price
1	Davey Johnson	.50
2	Eric Karros	.50
3	Gary Sheffield	.75
4	Kevin Brown	.60
5	Shawn Green	2.50
6	Mark Grudzielanek	.50
7	Todd Hollandsworth	.50
8	Todd Hundley	.50
9	Jeff Shaw	.50
10	Adrian Beltre	1.00
11	Chan Ho Park	.60
12	Jose Vizcaino	.50
13	Devon White	.50
14	Darren Dreifort	.50
15	Onan Masaoka	.50
16	Dave Hansen	.50
17	Kevin Elster	.50
18	Antonio Osuna	.50
19	Geronimo Berroa	.50
20	Orel Hershiser	.65
21	Chad Kreuter	.50
22	Carlos Perez	.50
23	F.P. Santangelo	.50
24	Terry Adams	.50
25	Alex Cora	.50
26	Matt Herges	.50
27	Mike Fetters	.50
28	Coaches/Checklist (Rick Dempsey, Claude Osteen, Rick Down, Manny Mota, Jim Tracy, Glenn Hoffman, John Shelby)	.50

San Diego Padres

Keebler cookies sponsored a kids' trading card day July 16 distributing 28-card packs to fans 14 and under. Each pack contained 21 different cards and seven duplicates to trade in an effort to complete the set. Fronts of the round-cornered 2-1/2" x 3-1/2" cards have posed photos with team-color orange and blue bars at bottom with player name and team logo. Backs have player ID, jersey number and team logo.

NM/M

Complete Set (28): 10.00

#	Player	Price
	Common Player:	.50
1	Bruce Bochy	.50
2	Tony Gwynn	4.00
3	Ryan Klesko	.50
4	Sterling Hitchcock	.50
5	Al Martin	.50
6	Trevor Hoffman	.75
7	Bret Boone	.65
8	Dave Magadan	.50
9	Steve Montgomery	.50
10	Damian Jackson	.50
11	Woody Williams	.50
12	Wiki Gonzalez	.50
13	Chris Gomez	.50
14	Ruben Rivera	.50
15	Ed Sprague	.50
16	Carlton Loewer	.50
17	Kory DeHaan	.50
18	Donne Wall	.50
19	Eric Owens	.50
20	Brian Boehringer	.50
21	Phil Nevin	.50
22	Matt Clement	.50
23	Brian Meadows	.50
24	Vincente Palacios	.50
25	Carlos Hernandez	.50
26	Carlos Almanzar	.50
27	Kevin Walker	.50
28	Coaches/Checklist (Greg Booker, Tim Flannery, Ben Ogilvie, Rob Picciolo, Dave Smith, Alan Trammell)	.50

S.F. Giants

Keebler cookies sponsored a trading card day August 6, distributing 25,000 28-card packs to fans. Each pack contained 21 different cards and seven duplicates to trade in an effort to complete the set.

NM/M

Complete Set (28): 10.00
Common Player: .50

#	Player	Price
1	Dusty Baker	.50
2	Barry Bonds	5.00
3	Jeff Kent	.75
4	Robb Nen	.50
5	J.T. Snow	.50
6	Russ Ortiz	.50
7	Ellis Burks	.50
8	Bill Mueller	.50
9	Shawn Estes	.50
10	Marvin Benard	.50
11	Kirk Rueter	.50
12	Bobby Estalella	.50
13	Livan Hernandez	.50
14	Rich Aurilia	.50
15	Alan Embree	.50
16	Armando Rios	.50
17	Felix Rodriguez	.50
18	Doug Mirabelli	.50
19	John Johnstone	.50
20	Russ Davis	.50
21	Joe Nathan	.50
22	Aaron Fultz	.50
23	Felipe Crespo	.50
24	Mark Gardner	.50
25	Ramon Martinez	.50
26	Calvin Murray	.50
27	Carlos Alfonso	.50
28	Giants Coaches (Gene Clines, Sonny Jackson, Juan Lopez, Dave Righetti, Robby Thompson, Ron Wotus)	.50

Seattle Mariners

Keebler cookies sponsored a trading card day at a home game August 13, distributing 20,000 28-card packs to fans. Each pack contained 21 different cards and seven duplicates to trade in an effort to complete the set. Cards are 2-1/2" x 3-1/2" with rounded corners. Fronts have borderless posed photos with a team logo at lower-left and the player name in white in a dark blue strip. Backs have a color Keebler logo and basic player information.

NM/M

Complete Set (28): 15.00
Common Player: .50

#	Player	Price
1	Lou Piniella	.50
2	Alex Rodriguez	6.00
3	Jamie Moyer	.50
4	Edgar Martinez	.50
5	Kazuhiro Sasaki	.75
6	Jay Buhner	.50
7	Rickey Henderson	2.50
8	John Olerud	.50
9	Aaron Sele	.50
10	Charles Gipson	.50
11	Arthur Rhodes	.50
12	Dan Wilson	.50
13	Jose Mesa	.50
14	Mike Cameron	.50
15	John Halama	.50
16	Mark McLemore	.50
17	Brett Tomko	.50
18	Tom Lampkin	.50
19	Freddy Garcia	.50
20	John Mabry	.50

21 Paul Abbott .50
22 Stan Javier .50
23 Gil Meche .50
24 David Bell .50
25 Frankie Rodriguez .50
26 Raul Ibanez .50
27 Jose Paniagua .50
28 Coaches/Checklist .50

2001 Keebler Arizona Diamondbacks

Keebler cookies sponsored a trading card day on July 29, distributing 20,000 28-card packs to fans. Each pack contained 21 different cards and seven duplicates to trade in an effort to complete the set. Round-cornered cards have borderless portrait photos with a stripe at bottom featuring player name and team logo. Backs have player data, uniform number, biographical information and Keebler's logo.

		NM/M
Complete Set (28):		10.00
Common Player:		.50
1	Bob Brenly	.50
2	Randy Johnson	3.00
3	Luis Gonzalez	.60
4	Curt Schilling	1.50
5	Matt Williams	.65
6	Todd Stottlemyre	.50
7	Jay Bell	.50
8	Steve Finley	.50
9	Mark Grace	.60
10	Brian Anderson	.50
11	Tony Womack	.50
12	Damian Miller	.50
13	Russ Springer	.50
14	Greg Colbrunn	.50
15	Craig Counsell	.50
16	Greg Swindell	.50
17	Reggie Sanders	.50
18	Matt Mantei	.50
19	Danny Bautista	.50
20	Mike Morgan	.50
21	Erubiel Durazo	.50
22	Troy Brohawn	.50
23	Byung-Hyun Kim	.50
24	David Dellucci	.50
25	Robert Ellis	.50
26	Rod Barajas	.50
27	Armando Reynoso	.50
28	Coaches/Checklist (Bob Melvin, Dwayne Murphy, Eddie Rodriguez, Glenn Sherlock, Chris Speier, Bob Welch)	.50

2001 Keebler L.A. Dodgers

Keebler cookies sponsored a kids' trading card day, on August 19, distributing 28-card packs to fans 14 and under. Each pack contained 21 different cards and seven duplicates to trade in an effort to complete the set. Round-cornered cards have borderless portrait photos with a stripe at bottom featuring player name and team logo. Backs have player data, uniform number, biographical information and Keebler's logo.

		NM/M
Complete Set (28):		10.00
Common Player:		.50
1	Jim Tracy	.50
2	Eric Karros	.50
3	Shawn Green	2.00
4	Kevin Brown	.60
5	Gary Sheffield	.75
6	Mark Grudzielanek	.50
7	Darren Dreifort	.50
8	Dave Hansen	.50
9	Jeff Shaw	.50
10	Chad Kreuter	.50
11	Chan Ho Park	1.00
12	Adrian Beltre	1.00
13	Marquis Grissom	.50
14	Alex Cora	.50
15	Tom Goodwin	.50
16	Gregg Olson	.50
17	Andy Ashby	.50
18	Paul LoDuca	.60
19	Luke Prokopec	.50
20	Mike Fetters	.50
21	Giovanni Carrara	.50
22	Chris Donnels	.50
23	Matt Herges	.50
24	Jeff Reboulet	.50
25	Terry Adams	.50
26	Hiram Bocachica	.50
27	Jesse Orosco	.50
28	Dodgers coaches/checklist (Travis Barbary, Jack Clark, Jim Colborn, Glenn Hoffman, Jim Lett, Manny Mota, Jim Riggleman, John Shelby)	.50

2001 Keebler San Diego Padres

Keebler cookies sponsored a kids' trading card day July 22, distributing 15,000 28-card packs to fans 14 and under. Each pack contained 21 different cards and seven duplicates to trade in an effort to complete the set. Fronts of the round-cornered 2-1/2" x 3-1/2" cards have posed photos with a dark blue bar at bottom with player name and team logo. Backs have player data, jersey number and color team and sponsor's logos.

		NM/M
Complete Set (28):		10.00
Common Player:		.50
1	Bruce Bochy	.50
2	Tony Gwynn	4.00
3	Trevor Hoffman	.60
4	Rickey Henderson	2.00
5	Ryan Klesko	.50
6	Phil Nevin	.50
7	Ben Davis	.50
8	Woody Williams	.50
9	Chris Gomez	.50
10	Dave Magadan	.50
11	Wiki Gonzalez	.50
12	Bobby J. Jones	.50
13	Damian Jackson	.50
14	Kevin Jarvis	.50
15	Bubba Trammell	.50
16	Kevin Walker	.50
17	Mark Kotsay	.50
18	Alex Arias	.50
19	Jay Witasick	.50
20	Mike Darr	.50
21	Adam Eaton	.75
22	Wascar Serrano	.50
23	Jose Nunez	.50
24	Brian Tollberg	.50
25	Donaldo Mendez	.50
26	Tom Davey	.50
27	Rodney Myers	.50
28	Coaches/Checklist (Greg Booker, Duane Espy, Tim Flannery, Rob Picciolo, Dave Smith, Alan Trammell)	.50

2001 Keebler San Francisco Giants

Keebler cookies sponsored a trading card day, on September 2, distributing 28-card packs to the first 25,000 fans. Each pack contained 20 different cards and eight duplicates to trade in an effort to complete the set.

		NM/M
Complete Set (28):		10.00
Common Player:		.50
1	Dusty Baker	.50
2	Jeff Kent	.75
3	Barry Bonds	6.00
4	Robb Nen	.50
5	J.T. Snow	.50
6	Russ Ortiz	.50
7	Rich Aurilia	.50
8	Benito Santiago	.50
9	Shawn Estes	.50
10	Marvin Benard	.50
11	Kirk Reuter	.50
12	Calvin Murray	.50
13	Livan Hernandez	.50
14	Eric Davis	.50
15	Aaron Fultz	.50
16	Armando Rios	.50
17	Felix Rodriguez	.50
18	Shawon Dunston	.50
19	Mark Gardner	.50
20	Ramon Martinez	.50
21	Pedro Feliz	.50
22	Chad Zerbe	.50
23	Felipe Crespo	.50
24	Tim Worrell	.50
25	Edwards Guzman	.50
26	Ryan Vogelsong	.50
27	Brian Boehringer	.50
28	Coaches/Checklist (Carlos Alfonso, Gene Clines, Sonny Jackson, Juan Lopez, Dave Righetti, Robby Thompson, Ron Wotus)	.50

2001 Keebler Seattle Mariners

Keebler cookies sponsored a kids' trading card day at Safeco Field July 15, distributing 20,000 28-card packs to fans. Each pack contained 21 different cards and seven duplicates to trade in an effort to complete the set. Cards are 2-1/2" x 3-1/2" with rounded corners. Fronts have borderless posed photos with a team logo at lower-left and the player name in white in a dark blue strip. Backs have a color Keebler logo and basic player information.

		NM/M
Complete Set (28):		10.00
Common Player:		.50
1	Lou Piniella	.50
2	Edgar Martinez	.75
3	Mike Cameron	.50
4	Jamie Moyer	.50
5	Ichiro Suzuki	6.00
6	Jay Buhner	.50
7	Kazuhiro Sasaki	.50
8	John Olerud	.50
9	Aaron Sele	.50
10	Bret Boone	.65
11	Arthur Rhodes	.50
12	Al Martin	.50
13	Jeff Nelson	.50
14	Dan Wilson	.50
15	John Halama	.50
16	Stan Javier	.50
17	Brett Tomko	.50
18	Carlos Guillen	.50
19	Freddy Garcia	.50
20	David Bell	.50
21	Paul Abbott	.50
22	Mark McLemore	.50
23	Tom Lampkin	.50
24	Charles Gipson	.50
25	Ryan Franklin	.50
26	Anthony Sanders	.50
27	Jose Paniagua	.50
28	Coaches/Checklist (Lee Elia, John McLaren, John Moses, Dave Myers, Gerald Perry, Bryan Price, Matt Sinatro)	.50

2002 Keebler Arizona Diamondbacks

Keebler cookies sponsored a kids' trading card day July 28, distributing 20,000 28-card packs to fans 14 and under. Each pack contained 20 different cards and eight duplicates to trade in an effort to complete the set. Fronts of the round-cornered 2-1/2" x 3-1/2" cards have posed photos with a purple stripe at bottom with player name and team logo. Color-printed backs have player data, jersey number and team and sponsor's logos.

		NM/M
Complete Set (28):		10.00
Common Player:		.50
1	Dusty Baker	.50
2	Jeff Kent	.75
3	Barry Bonds	6.00
4	Robb Nen	.50
5	J.T. Snow	.50
6	Russ Ortiz	.50
7	Rich Aurilia	.50
8	Benito Santiago	.50
9	Shawn Estes	.50
10	Marvin Benard	.50
11	Kirk Reuter	.50
12	Calvin Murray	.50
13	Livan Hernandez	.50
14	Eric Davis	.50
15	Aaron Fultz	.50
16	Armando Rios	.50
17	Felix Rodriguez	.50
18	Shawon Dunston	.50
19	Mark Gardner	.50
20	Ramon Martinez	.50
21	Pedro Feliz	.50
22	Chad Zerbe	.50
23	Felipe Crespo	.50
24	Tim Worrell	.50
25	Edwards Guzman	.50
26	Ryan Vogelsong	.50
27	Brian Boehringer	.50
28	Coaches/Checklist (Carlos Alfonso, Gene Clines, Sonny Jackson, Juan Lopez, Dave Righetti, Robby Thompson, Ron Wotus)	.50

2001 Keebler Seattle Mariners

Keebler cookies sponsored a kids' trading card day at Safeco Field July 15, distributing 20,000 28-card packs to fans. Each pack contained 21 different cards and seven duplicates to trade in an effort to complete the set. Cards are 2-1/2" x 3-1/2" with rounded corners. Fronts have borderless posed photos with a team logo at lower-left and the player name in white in a dark blue strip. Backs have a color Keebler logo and basic player information.

		NM/M
Complete Set (28):		10.00
Common Player:		.50
1	Lou Piniella	.50
2	Edgar Martinez	.50
3	Mike Cameron	.50
4	Jamie Moyer	.50
5	Ichiro Suzuki	6.00
6	Jay Buhner	.50
7	Kazuhiro Sasaki	.50
8	John Olerud	.50
9	Aaron Sele	.50
10	Bret Boone	.65
11	Arthur Rhodes	.50
12	Al Martin	.50
13	Jeff Nelson	.50
14	Dan Wilson	.50
15	John Halama	.50
16	Stan Javier	.50
17	Brett Tomko	.50
18	Carlos Guillen	.50
19	Freddy Garcia	.50
20	David Bell	.50
21	Paul Abbott	.50
22	Mark McLemore	.50
23	Tom Lampkin	.50
24	Charles Gipson	.50
25	Ryan Franklin	.50
26	Anthony Sanders	.50
27	Jose Paniagua	.50
28	Coaches/Checklist (Lee Elia, John McLaren, John Moses, Dave Myers, Gerald Perry, Bryan Price, Matt Sinatro)	.50

2002 Keebler L.A. Dodgers

Keebler cookies sponsored a kids' trading card day in August, distributing 28-card packs to fans 14 and under. Each pack contained 20 different cards and eight duplicates to trade in an effort to complete the set. Fronts of the round-cornered 2-1/2" x 3-1/2" cards have posed photos with a red stripe at bottom with player name and team logo. Color-printed backs have player data, jersey number and team and sponsor's logos.

		NM/M
Complete Set (28):		10.00
Common Player:		.50
1	Jim Tracy	.50
2	Eric Karros	.50
3	Shawn Green	1.50
4	Kevin Brown	.65
5	Paul LoDuca	.65
6	Mark Grudzielanek	.50
7	Brian Jordan	.50
8	Kazuhiro Ishii	1.00
9	Hideo Nomo	1.50
10	Dave Hansen	.50
11	Chad Kreuter	.50
12	Adrian Beltre	1.00
13	Marquis Grissom	.50
14	Eric Gagne	.65
15	Odalis Perez	.50
16	Dave Roberts	.50
17	Omar Daal	.50
18	Alex Cora	.50
19	Andy Ashby	.50
20	Hiram Bocachica	.50
21	Darren Dreifort	.50
22	Jesse Orosco	.50
23	Cesar Izturis	.50
24	Terry Mulholland	.50
25	Jeff Reboulet	.50
26	Paul Quantrill	.50
27	Giovanni Carrara	.50
28	Checklist/Coaches (Robert Flippo, Jack Clark, Jim Colborn, Glenn Hoffman, Jim Lett, Manny Mota, Jim Riggleman, John Shelby)	.50

2002 Keebler San Diego Padres

Keebler cookies sponsored a kids' trading card day July 21, distributing 28-card packs to fans 14 and under. Each pack contained 21 different cards and seven duplicates to trade in an effort to complete the set. Fronts of the round-cornered 2-1/2" x 3-1/2" cards have posed photos with an orange and dark blue stripe at bottom with player name and team logo. Color-printed backs have player data, jersey number and color team and sponsor's logos.

		NM/M
Complete Set (28):		7.50
Common Player:		.50
1	Bruce Bochy	.50
2	Trevor Hoffman	.60
3	Sean Burroughs	1.50
4	Ryan Klesko	.50
5	Phil Nevin	.50
6	Kevin Jarvis	.50
7	Ron Gant	.50
8	Ramon Vazquez	.50
9	Alan Embree	.50
10	Wiki Gonzalez	.50
11	Bobby J. Jones	.50
12	Mark Kotsay	.50
13	Brett Tomko	.50
14	Bubba Trammell	.50
15	Tom Lampkin	.50
16	Steve Reed	.50
17	Deivi Cruz	.50
18	Brian Tollberg	.50
19	Trenidad Hubbard	.50
20	Jose Nunez	.50
21	Ray Lankford	.50
22	Kevin Walker	.50
23	Dennis Tankersley	.50
24	Jeremy Fikac	.50
25	D'Angelo Jimenez	.50
26	Brian Lawrence	.50
27	Adam Eaton	.50
28	Coaches/Checklist (Greg Booker, Darrel Akerfelds, Duane Espy, Tim Flannery, Rob Picciolo, Alan Trammell)	.50

2002 Keebler San Francisco Giants

Keebler cookies sponsored a kids' trading card day August 25, distributing 28-card packs to fans 14 and under. Each pack contained 21 different cards and seven duplicates to trade in an effort to complete the set. Fronts of the round-cornered 2-1/2" x 3-1/2" cards have posed photos with an orange and dark black stripe at bottom with player name and team logo.

Color-printed backs have player data, jersey number and team and sponsor's logos.

		NM/M
Complete Set (28):		10.00
Common Player:		.50
1	Dusty Baker	.50
2	Barry Bonds	6.00
3	Jeff Kent	.75
4	Robb Nen	.50
5	J.T. Snow	.50
6	Russ Ortiz	.50
7	Rich Aurilia	.50
8	Marvin Benard	.50
9	Kirk Reuter	.50
10	Benito Santiago	.50
11	Jason Schmidt	.50
12	Reggie Sanders	.50
13	Livan Hernandez	.50
14	Tsuyoshi Shinjo	.50
15	Aaron Fultz	.50
16	Ramon Martinez	.50
17	Felix Rodriguez	.50
18	Shawon Dunston	.50
19	Tim Worrell	.50
20	David Bell	.50
21	Pedro Feliz	.50
22	Chad Zerbe	.50
23	Damon Minor	.50
24	Yorvit Torrealba	.50
25	Jay Witasick	.50
26	Ryan Jensen	.50
27	Jason Christiansen	.50
28	Coaches/Checklist (Carlos Alfonso, Gene Clines, Sonny Jackson, Joe Lefebvre, Juan Lopez, Dave Righetti, Ron Wotus)	.50

2002 Keebler Seattle Mariners

Keebler cookies sponsored a kids' trading card day August 4, distributing 28-card packs to fans 14 and under. Each pack contained 21 different cards and seven duplicates to trade in an effort to complete the set. Fronts of the round-cornered 2-1/2" x 3-1/2" cards have posed photos with a dark blue strip at bottom with player name and team logo. Color-printed backs have player data, jersey number and color team and sponsor's logos.

		NM/M
Complete Set (28):		10.00
Common Player:		.50
1	Lou Piniella	.50
2	Ichiro Suzuki	5.00
3	Edgar Martinez	.50
4	Jamie Moyer	.50
5	Mike Cameron	.50
6	Bret Boone	.75
7	Kazuhiro Sasaki	.65
8	Mark McLemore	.50
9	John Olerud	.50
10	Arthur Rhodes	.50
11	Ruben Sierra	.50
12	Freddy Garcia	.50
13	Dan Wilson	.50
14	Jeff Nelson	.50
15	John Halama	.50
16	Carlos Guillen	.50
17	Ben Davis	.50

18	James Baldwin	.50
19	Jeff Cirillo	.50
20	Shigetoshi Hasegawa	.50
21	Paul Abbott	.50
22	Desi Relaford	.50
23	Ryan Franklin	.50
24	Luis Ugueto	.50
25	Charles Gipson	.50
26	Joel Pineiro	.50
27	Rafael Soriano	.50
28	M's coaches	.50

2003 Keebler Arizona Diamondbacks

Keebler cookies sponsored a kids' trading card day July 27, distributing 20,000 28-card packs to fans 14 and under. Each pack contained 20 different cards and eight duplicates to trade in an effort to complete the set. Fronts of the round-cornered 2-1/2" x 3-1/2" cards have posed photos with a purple stripe at bottom with player name and team logo. Color-printed backs have player data, jersey number and team and sponsor's logos.

		NM/M
Complete Set (28):		12.00
Common Player:		.50
1	Bob Brenly	.50
2	Luis Gonzalez	.60
3	Randy Johnson	3.00
4	Curt Schilling	1.50
5	Danny Bautista	.50
6	Matt Mantei	.50
7	Craig Counsell	.50
8	Steve Finley	.50
9	Mark Grace	.60
10	Alex Cintron	.50
11	Tony Womack	.50
12	Chad Moeller	.50
13	Shea Hillenbrand	.50
14	Miguel Batista	.50
15	David Dellucci	.50
16	Elmer Dessens	.50
17	Lyle Overbay	.75
18	Mike Myers	.50
19	Quinton McCracken	.50
20	Rod Barajas	.50
21	Junior Spivey	.50
22	Stephen Randolph	.50
23	Carlos Baerga	.50
24	Mike Koplove	.50
25	Brandon Webb	1.00
26	Oscar Villarreal	.50
27	Bret Prinz	.50
28	Coaches/Checklist	
	(Mark Davis, Chuck Kniffin,	
	Dwayne Murphy,	
	Eddie Rodriguez,	
	Glenn Sherlock,	
	Robin Yount)	.50

2003 Keebler L.A. Dodgers

Keebler cookies sponsored a kids' trading card night August 24, distributing 20,000 28-card packs to fans 14 and under. Each pack contained 20 different cards and eight duplicates to trade in an effort to complete the set. Fronts of the round-cornered 2-1/2" x 3-1/2" cards have posed photos with an

orange stripe at bottom with player name and team logo. Color-printed backs have player data, jersey number and team and sponsor's logos.

		NM/M
Complete Set (28):		7.50
Common Player:		.50
1	Jim Tracy	.50
2	Shawn Green	1.00
3	Paul LoDuca	.60
4	Kevin Brown	.60
5	Adrian Beltre	1.00
6	Eric Gagne	.50
7	Brian Jordan	.50
8	Kazuhisa Ishii	.50
9	Fred McGriff	.50
10	Dave Roberts	.50
11	Hideo Nomo	1.00
12	Alex Cora	.50
13	Paul Quantrill	.50
14	Darren Dreifort	.50
15	Odalis Perez	.50
16	Cesar Izturis	.50
17	Todd Hundley	.50
18	Daryle Ward	.50
19	Paul Shuey	.50
20	Guillermo Mota	.50
21	Andy Ashby	.50
22	Tom Martin	.50
23	Jason Romano	.50
24	Jolbert Cabrera	.50
25	Mike Kinkade	.50
26	Ron Coomer	.50
27	David Ross	.50
28	Coaches	.50

2003 Keebler San Diego Padres

Keebler cookies sponsored a kids' trading card day distributing 28-card packs to fans 14 and under. Each pack contained 21 different cards and seven duplicates to trade in an effort to complete the set. Fronts of the round-cornered 2-1/2" x 3-1/2" cards have posed photos with an orange and dark blue stripe at bottom with player name and team logo. Color-printed backs have player data, jersey number and color team and sponsor's logos.

		NM/M
Complete Set (28):		5.00
Common Player:		.50
1	Bruce Bochy	.50
2	Trevor Hoffman	.50
3	Phil Nevin	.50
4	Ryan Klesko	.50
5	Sean Burroughs	.75
6	Brian Lawrence	.50
7	Rondell White	.50
8	Ramon Vazquez	.50
9	Mark Kotsay	.50
10	Dave Hansen	.50
11	Jaret Wright	.50
12	Gary Bennett	.50
13	Brandon Villafuerte	.50
14	Lou Merloni	.50
15	Jesse Orosco	.50
16	Keith Lockhart	.50
17	Kevin Walker	.50
18	Mark Loretta	.50
19	Kevin Jarvis	.50
20	Xavier Nady	.50
21	Jake Peavy	.50
22	Mike Matthews	.50
23	Brian Buchanan	.50
24	Luther Hackman	.50
25	Adam Eaton	.50
26	Matt Herges	.50
27	Jay Witasick	.50
28	Coaches/Checklist	
	(Darrel Akerfelds,	
	Darren Balsley, Davey Lopes,	
	Dave Magadan, Mark Merila,	
	Tony Muser, Rob Picciolo)	.50

2003 Keebler S.F. Giants

Keebler cookies sponsored a kids' trading card day August 10, distributing 28-card packs to fans 14 and under. Each pack contained 21 different cards and seven duplicates to trade in an effort to com-

plete the set. Fronts of the round-cornered 2-1/2" x 3-1/2" cards have posed photos with an orange stripe at bottom with player name and team logo. Color-printed backs have player data, jersey number and color team and sponsor's logos.

		NM/M
Complete Set (28):		10.00
Common Player:		.50
1	Felipe Alou	.50
2	Barry Bonds	4.00
3	Rich Aurilia	.50
4	Robb Nen	.50
5	J.T. Snow	.50
6	Kirk Reuter	.50
7	Benito Santiago	.50
8	Jose Cruz Jr.	.50
9	Damian Moss	.50
10	Ray Durham	.50
11	Jason Schmidt	.50
12	Marquis Grissom	.50
13	Kurt Ainsworth	.50
14	Andres Galarraga	.50
15	Scott Eyre	.50
16	Yorvit Torrealba	.50
17	Felix Rodriguez	.50
18	Edgardo Alfonzo	.50
19	Tim Worrell	.50
20	Pedro Feliz	.50
21	Jesse Foppert	.50
22	Chad Zerbe	.50
23	Neifi Perez	.50
24	Jason Christiansen	.50
25	Marvin Benard	.50
26	Jim Brower	.50
27	Joe Nathan	.50
28	Coaches (Carlos Alfonzo,	
	Mark Gardner, Gene Glynn,	
	Bill Hayes, Joe Lefebvre,	
	Luis Pujols, Dave Righetti,	
	Ron Wotus)	.50

2003 Keebler Seattle Mariners

Keebler cookies sponsored a kids' trading card day July 13, distributing 28-card packs to fans 14 and under. Each pack contained 21 different cards and seven duplicates to trade in an effort to complete the set. Fronts of the round-cornered 2-1/2" x 3-1/2" cards have posed photos with a dark blue stripe at bottom with player name and team logo. Color-printed backs have player data, jersey number and color team and sponsor's logos.

		NM/M
Complete Set (28):		10.00
Common Player:		.50
1	Bob Melvin	.50
2	Ichiro Suzuki	4.00
3	Edgar Martinez	.50
4	Jamie Moyer	.50
5	Mike Cameron	.50
6	Bret Boone	.75
7	Kazuhiro Sasaki	.60
8	John Olerud	.50
9	Mark McLemore	.50
10	Arthur Rhodes	.50
11	Randy Winn	.50
12	Freddy Garcia	.50

13	Dan Wilson	.50
14	Jeff Nelson	.50
15	Carlos Guillen	.50
16	Ryan Franklin	.50
17	Ben Davis	.50
18	Joel Pineiro	.50
19	Jeff Cirillo	.50
20	Shigetoshi Hasegawa	.50
21	Greg Colbrunn	.50
22	John Mabry	.50
23	Julio Mateo	.50
24	Willie Bloomquist	.75
25	Gil Meche	.50
26	Giovanni Carrara	.50
27	Chris Snelling	.50
28	M's Coaches	.50

1986 Keller's Butter Phillies

It's a good thing the Keller's Butter set of six Philadelphia Phillies players is downright unattractive or their value would be sky high. One card was printed on each one pound package of butter. The 2-1/2" x 2-3/4" cards feature crude drawings of the players, the backs are blank.

		NM/M
Complete Set (6):		15.00
Common Player:		1.00
(1)	Steve Carlton	4.00
(2)	Von Hayes	1.00
(3)	Gary Redus	1.00
(4)	Juan Samuel	1.00
(5)	Mike Schmidt	8.00
(6)	Glenn Wilson	1.00

1981 Kellogg's

"Bigger" is the word to best describe Kellogg's 1981 card set. Not only were the cards themselves larger than ever before at 2-1/2" x 3-1/2", but the size of the set was increased to 66, the largest since the 75-card issues of 1970-71. The '81 Kellogg's set was available only as complete sets by mail. It is thought that the wider format of the 1981s may help prevent the problems of curling and cracking from which other years of Kellogg's issues suffer.

		NM/M
Complete Set (66):		15.00
Common Player:		.50
1	George Foster	.50
2	Jim Palmer	1.50
3	Reggie Jackson	2.50
4	Al Oliver	.50
5	Mike Schmidt	3.00
6	Nolan Ryan	7.50
7	Bucky Dent	.50
8	George Brett	3.00
9	Jim Rice	.75
10	Steve Garvey	.75
11	Willie Stargell	1.50
12	Phil Niekro	1.00
13	Dave Parker	.50
14	Cesar Cedeno	.50
15	Don Baylor	.50
16	J.R. Richard	.50
17	Tony Perez	1.00
18	Eddie Murray	1.50
19	Chet Lemon	.50
20	Ben Oglivie	.50
21	Dave Winfield	1.50
22	Joe Morgan	1.50
23	Vida Blue	.50
24	Willie Wilson	.50
25	Steve Henderson	.50

26	Rod Carew	1.50
27	Garry Templeton	.50
28	Dave Concepcion	.50
29	Davey Lopes	.50
30	Ken Landreaux	.50
31	Keith Hernandez	.50
32	Cecil Cooper	.50
33	Rickey Henderson	3.00
34	Frank White	.50
35	George Hendrick	.50
36	Reggie Smith	.50
37	Tug McGraw	.50
38	Tom Seaver	1.50
39	Ken Singleton	.50
40	Fred Lynn	.50
41	Rich "Goose" Gossage	.50
42	Terry Puhl	.50
43	Larry Bowa	.50
44	Phil Garner	.50
45	Ron Guidry	.50
46	Lee Mazzilli	.50
47	Dave Kingman	.50
48	Carl Yastrzemski	2.00
49	Rick Burleson	.50
50	Steve Carlton	1.50
51	Alan Trammell	.75
52	Tommy John	.50
53	Paul Molitor	1.50
54	Joe Charboneau	1.00
55	Rick Langford	.50
56	Bruce Sutter	1.00
57	Robin Yount	1.50
58	Steve Stone	.50
59	Larry Gura	.50
60	Mike Flanagan	.50
61	Bob Horner	.50
62	Bruce Bochte	.50
63	Pete Rose	6.00
64	Buddy Bell	.50
65	Johnny Bench	2.00
66	Mike Hargrove	.50

1982 Kellogg's

For the second straight year in 1982, Kellogg's cards were not inserted into cereal boxes, but had to be obtained by sending cash and box tops to the company for complete sets. The '82 cards were downsized both in number of cards in the set - 64 - and in physical dimensions, 2-1/8" x 3-1/4".

		NM/M
Complete Set (64):		15.00
Common Player:		.25
1	Richie Zisk	.25
2	Bill Buckner	.25
3	George Brett	3.00
4	Rickey Henderson	1.50
5	Jack Morris	.25
6	Ozzie Smith	2.00
7	Rollie Fingers	1.00
8	Tom Seaver	2.00
9	Fernando Valenzuela	.25
10	Hubie Brooks	.25
11	Nolan Ryan	7.50
12	Dave Winfield	1.50
13	Bob Horner	.25
14	Reggie Jackson	2.50
15	Burt Hooton	.25
16	Mike Schmidt	3.00
17	Bruce Sutter	.50
18	Pete Rose	6.00
19	Dave Kingman	.25
20	Neil Allen	.25
21	Don Sutton	1.00
22	Dave Concepcion	.25
23	Keith Hernandez	.25
24	Gary Carter	1.50
25	Carlton Fisk	1.50
26	Ron Guidry	.25
27	Steve Carlton	1.50
28	Robin Yount	1.50
29	John Castino	.25
30	Johnny Bench	2.00
31	Bob Knepper	.25
32	Rich "Goose" Gossage	.25
33	Buddy Bell	.25
34	Art Howe	.25
35	Tony Armas	.25
36	Phil Niekro	1.00
37	Len Barker	.25
38	Bobby Grich	.25
39	Steve Kemp	.25
40	Kirk Gibson	.25

41	Carney Lansford	.25
42	Jim Palmer	1.50
43	Carl Yastrzemski	2.00
44	Rick Burleson	.25
45	Dwight Evans	.25
46	Ron Cey	.25
47	Steve Garvey	.50
48	Dave Parker	.25
49	Mike Easler	.25
50	Dusty Baker	.25
51	Rod Carew	1.50
52	Chris Chambliss	.25
53	Tim Raines	.50
54	Chet Lemon	.25
55	Bill Madlock	.25
56	George Foster	.25
57	Dwayne Murphy	.25
58	Ken Singleton	.25
59	Mike Norris	.25
60	Cecil Cooper	.25
61	Al Oliver	.25
62	Willie Wilson	.25
63	Vida Blue	.25
64	Eddie Murray	1.50

1983 Kellogg's

In its 14th consecutive year of baseball card issue, Kellogg's returned to the policy of inserting single cards into cereal boxes, as well as offering complete sets by a mail-in box top redemption offer. The 3-D cards themselves returned to a narrow 1-7/8" x 3-1/4" format, while the set size was reduced to 60 cards.

		NM/M
Complete Set (60):		15.00
Common Player:		.40
1	Rod Carew	1.50
2	Rollie Fingers	1.00
3	Reggie Jackson	2.50
4	George Brett	3.00
5	Hal McRae	.40
6	Pete Rose	6.00
7	Fernando Valenzuela	.40
8	Rickey Henderson	1.50
9	Carl Yastrzemski	2.00
10	Rich "Goose" Gossage	.40
11	Eddie Murray	1.50
12	Buddy Bell	.40
13	Jim Rice	.60
14	Robin Yount	1.50
15	Dave Winfield	1.50
16	Harold Baines	.40
17	Garry Templeton	.40
18	Bill Madlock	.40
19	Pete Vuckovich	.40
20	Pedro Guerrero	.40
21	Ozzie Smith	2.00
22	George Foster	.40
23	Willie Wilson	.40
24	Johnny Ray	.40
25	George Hendrick	.40
26	Andre Thornton	.40
27	Leon Durham	.40
28	Cecil Cooper	.40
29	Don Baylor	.40
30	Lonnie Smith	.40
31	Nolan Ryan	7.50
32	Dan Quisenberry (Quisenberry)	.40
33	Len Barker	.40
34	Neil Allen	.40
35	Jack Morris	.40
36	Dave Stieb	.40
37	Bruce Sutter	1.00
38	Jim Sundberg	.40
39	Jim Palmer	1.50
40	Lance Parrish	.40
41	Floyd Bannister	.40
42	Larry Gura	.40
43	Britt Burns	.40
44	Toby Harrah	.40
45	Steve Carlton	1.50
46	Greg Minton	.40
47	Gorman Thomas	.40
48	Jack Clark	.40
49	Keith Hernandez	.40
50	Greg Luzinski	.40
51	Fred Lynn	.40
52	Dale Murphy	.75
53	Kent Hrbek	.40
54	Bob Horner	.40

55	Gary Carter	1.50
56	Carlton Fisk	1.50
57	Dave Concepcion	.40
58	Mike Schmidt	3.00
59	Bill Buckner	.40
60	Bobby Grich	.40

1991 Kellogg's Baseball Greats

Six Hall of Famers are featured on the backs of 7- and 12-ounce Corn Flakes boxes. The photos are designed to be cut out and assembled as a stand-up figure. A career summary also appears on the box back.

		NM/M
Complete Set (6):		12.00
Common Player:		2.00
(1)	Hank Aaron	4.00
(2)	Ernie Banks	2.50
(3)	Yogi Berra	2.50
(4)	Lou Brock	2.00
(5)	Steve Carlton	2.00
(6)	Bob Gibson	2.00

1991 Kellogg's Leyendas

These bilingual (English/Spanish) cards honoring past Hispanic stars were inserted in several brands of Kellogg's cereal in selected geographic areas. Fronts have an action player photo, while backs have a black-and-white portrait photo, biographical details, career stats and highlights.

		NM/M
Complete Set (11):		9.00
Common Player:		.50
(1)	Bert Campaneris	.50
(2)	Rod Carew	1.00
(3)	Rico Carty	.50
(4)	Cesar Cedeno	.50
(5)	Orlando Cepeda	1.00
(6)	Roberto Clemente	6.00
(7)	Mike Cuellar	.50
(8)	Ed Figueroa	.50
(9)	Minnie Minoso	.75
(10)	Manny Sanguillen	.50
(11)	Header card	.25

1991 Kellogg's 3-D

In 1991, specially-marked packages of Kellogg's Corn Flakes included 3-D baseball cards, resuming a tradition that began in 1970 and continued without interruption until 1983. In the 1991 edition, there are 15 cards to collect, featuring many of the greatest living retired stars in the game. Most of the players are in the Hall of Fame. The card fronts show two pictures of the player, while the backs include career highlights and a portrait. The cards are 2-1/2" x 3-5/16", numbered and were made by Sportflics. A complete set was available via a mail-in offer for $4.95 plus proofs of purchase.

		NM/M
Complete Set (15):		4.50
Common Player:		.25
1	Gaylord Perry	.25
2	Hank Aaron	1.00
3	Willie Mays	1.00
4	Ernie Banks	.75
5	Bob Gibson	.50
6	Harmon Killebrew	.50
7	Rollie Fingers	.25
8	Steve Carlton	.50
9	Billy Williams	.25
10	Lou Brock	.25
11	Yogi Berra	.75
12	Warren Spahn	.50
13	Boog Powell	.25
14	Don Baylor	.25
15	Ralph Kiner	.25

1992 Kellogg's 3-D

Kellogg's cereal company created a 10-card 1992 All-Star set of retired stars, with one card inserted in specially-marked boxes of corn flakes, and complete sets available by mail. The cards, produced by Sportflics, feature two sequential action images on each front. Red, white and blue designs comprise the border, with yellow bands above and beneath the photo. On back is a black-and-white portrait photo, plus a career summary, a few stats, and the logos of the cereal company, the Major League Baseball Players Alumni and Sportflics. As in the previous year, cards are slightly longer, at 2-1/2" x 2-5/16", than standard size. Also available by mail was a large, colorful cardboard display in which the cards could be placed.

		NM/M
Complete Set (10):		2.00
Common Player:		.25
1	Willie Stargell	.50
2	Tony Perez	.50
3	Jim Palmer	.50
4	Rod Carew	.50
5	Tom Seaver	.65
6	Phil Niekro	.50
7	Bill Madlock	.25
8	Jim Rice	.35
9	Dan Quisenberry	.25
10	Mike Schmidt	1.00

3-D Canadian

Very similar in format to the American version, 3-D cards of 10 basebAll-Stars of the past were found in packages of Kellogg's Frosted Flakes. Backs of the Canadi-

---

an cards are printed in both English and French, which left no room for a card number, so the checklist provided here is alphabetical.

		NM/M
Complete Set (10):		8.00
Common Player:		.75
(1)	Rod Carew	1.00
(2)	Bill Madlock	.75
(3)	Phil Niekro	1.00
(4)	Jim Palmer	1.00
(5)	Tony Perez	1.00
(6)	Dan Quisenberry	.75
(7)	Jim Rice	.75
(8)	Mike Schmidt	3.00
(9)	Tom Seaver	1.50
(10)	Willie Stargell	1.00

1994 Kellogg's Clemente Collection

To commemorate the life and career of its greatest sports hero, special boxes of Kellogg's Corn Flakes sold in Puerto Rico for a time in 1994 contained one of three special cards in a cello pack. The 2-1/2" x 3-1/2" cards have color photos on front bordered in bright colors. A home plate design at top-left reads: "Kellogg's Clemente Coleccion Classico." Black-and-white backs are printed in Spanish, have personal data, career stats, highlights and a portrait photo.

		NM/M
Complete Set (3):		35.00
Common Card:		12.50
1	Roberto Clemente (Bat on shoulder.)	12.50
2	Roberto Clemente/Running (Black helmet.)	12.50
3	Roberto Clemente/Running (Yyellow helmet.)	12.50

1987 Key Food Discs

(See 1987 Super Stars Discs for checklist and price guide.)

1988 Key Food Discs

(See 1988 Super Stars Discs for checklist and price guide.)

1988 King-B

Created by Mike Schechter Associates, this set consists of 24 numbered discs, 2-3/4" in diameter. The cards were inserted in specially marked 7/16 ounce tubs of Jerky Stuff. Fronts feature full-color photos surrounded by a blue border. The King-B logo appears in the upper left portion of the disc. Backs are printed in blue on white stock and carry player personal and playing

---

information. Team insignias have been airbrushed from the players' caps and jerseys.

		NM/M
Complete Set (24):		15.00
Common Player:		.50
Uncut Sheet:		20.00
1	Mike Schmidt	1.50
2	Dale Murphy	.65
3	Kirby Puckett	1.00
4	Ozzie Smith	1.00
5	Tony Gwynn	1.00
6	Mark McGwire	2.50
7	George Brett	1.50
8	Darryl Strawberry	.50
9	Wally Joyner	.50
10	Cory Snyder	.50
11	Barry Bonds	3.00
12	Darrell Evans	.50
13	Mike Scott	.50
14	Andre Dawson	.65
15	Don Mattingly	1.50
16	Candy Maldonado	.50
17	Alvin Davis	.50
18	Carlton Fisk	.75
19	Fernando Valenzuela	.50
20	Roger Clemens	1.50
21	Larry Parrish	.50
22	Eric Davis	.50
23	Paul Molitor	.75
24	Cal Ripken, Jr.	3.00

1989 King-B

The second King-B set created by Mike Schechter Associates again consists of 24 circular baseball cards measuring 2-3/4" in diameter. The cards were inserted into specially-marked tubs of "Jerky Stuff." Fronts feature full-color photos bordered in red. The King-B logo appears in the upper left portion of the disc. Like the 1988 set, the team insignias have airbrushed from uniforms and caps. The backs are printed in red and display personal information and stats.

		NM/M
Complete Set (24):		15.00
Common Player:		.50
1	Kirk Gibson	.50
2	Eddie Murray	1.50
3	Wade Boggs	2.00
4	Mark McGwire	3.00
5	Ryne Sandberg	2.00
6	Ozzie Guillen	.50
7	Chris Sabo	.50
8	Joe Carter	.50
9	Alan Trammell	.50
10	Nolan Ryan	4.00
11	Bo Jackson	.75
12	Orel Hershiser	.50
13	Robin Yount	1.50
14	Frank Viola	.50
15	Darryl Strawberry	.50
16	Dave Winfield	1.50
17	Jose Canseco	.75
18	Von Hayes	.50
19	Andy Van Slyke	.50
20	Pedro Guerrero	.50
21	Tony Gwynn	2.00
22	Will Clark	.50
23	Danny Jackson	.50
24	Pete Incaviglia	.50

1990 King-B

King-B meat products offered baseball player discs inside specially-marked packages in 1990, the third year in a row the company inserted the discs with shredded beef jerky. Each disc measures 2-3/4" across and uses full-color pictures on the front. The backs have bio-

---

graphical information and statistics. Team insignias have been airbrushed from caps and uniforms. As in the first two years of the promotion, there are 24 cards in the set.

		NM/M
Complete Set (24):		8.00
Common Player:		.50
1	Mike Scott	.50
2	Kevin Mitchell	.50
3	Tony Gwynn	.75
4	Ozzie Smith	.75
5	Kirk Gibson	.50
6	Tim Raines	.50
7	Von Hayes	.50
8	Bobby Bonilla	.50
9	Wade Boggs	.75
10	Chris Sabo	.50
11	Dale Murphy	.65
12	Cory Snyder	.50
13	Fred McGriff	.50
14	Don Mattingly	1.00
15	Jerome Walton	.50
16	Ken Griffey Jr.	2.50
17	Bo Jackson	.65
18	Robin Yount	.65
19	Rickey Henderson	.65
20	Jim Abbott	.50
21	Kirby Puckett	.75
22	Nolan Ryan	3.00
23	Gregg Olson	.50
24	Lou Whitaker	.50

1991 King-B

The 1991 release of baseball player discs in cans of shredded beef snack was labeled "Fourth Annual Collectors' Edition." Once again the discs are 2-3/8" in diameter and feature player photos on which uniform logos have been removed for lack of an MLB license. Front border is in green; backs are printed in blue and include 1990 and major league cumulative stats. One player from each major league team is included in the set.

		NM/M
Complete Set (24):		15.00
Common Player:		.50
1	Willie McGee	.50
2	Kevin Seitzer	.50
3	Kevin Maas	.50
4	Ben McDonald	.50
5	Rickey Henderson	1.00
6	Ken Griffey Jr.	2.00
7	John Olerud	.50
8	Dwight Gooden	.50
9	Ruben Sierra	.50
10	Luis Polonia	.50
11	Wade Boggs	1.50
12	Ramon Martinez	.50
13	Craig Biggio	.50
14	Cecil Fielder	.50
15	Will Clark	.50
16	Matt Williams	.50
17	Sandy Alomar Jr.	.50
18	David Justice	.50
19	Ryne Sandberg	1.50
20	Benito Santiago	.50
21	Barry Bonds	3.00
22	Carlton Fisk	1.00
23	Kirby Puckett	1.50
24	Jose Rijo	.50

1992 King-B

Labeled the "Fifth Annual Collectors' Edition," the 1992 King-B discs were again packaged in plastic containers of shredded beef snack. The 2-3/8" diameter discs have a color player portrait at center. Uniform logos have been removed from the photos for lack of

---

an MLB licensing agreement. The player's name and team are in white in a blue banner above his photo. Backs are printed in blue and include previous year and career stats along with a few biographical details and appropriate logos.

		NM/M
Complete Set (24):		15.00
Common Player:		.50
1	Terry Pendleton	.50
2	Chris Sabo	.50
3	Frank Thomas	1.00
4	Todd Zeile	.50
5	Bobby Bonilla	.50
6	Howard Johnson	.50
7	Nolan Ryan	3.00
8	Ken Griffey Jr.	2.00
9	Roger Clemens	1.75
10	Tony Gwynn	1.50
11	Steve Avery	.50
12	Cal Ripken Jr.	3.00
13	Danny Tartabull	.50
14	Paul Molitor	1.00
15	Willie McGee	.50
16	Wade Boggs	1.50
17	Cecil Fielder	.50
18	Jack Morris	.50
19	Ryne Sandberg	1.50
20	Kirby Puckett	1.50
21	Craig Biggio	.50
22	Harold Baines	.50
23	Scott Erickson	.50
24	Joe Carter	.50

1993 King-B

The sixth annual edition of baseball player discs inserted into packages of King-B meat snacks followed the format of previous issues. Measuring 2-3/8" in diameter, the cards have a photo (with uniform logos airbrushed away) in a yellow baseball diamond design at center. The disc is bordered in black. Backs are printed in red and contain 1992 and career stats.

		NM/M
Complete Set (24):		9.00
Common Player:		.50
1	Barry Bonds	2.00
2	Ken Griffey Jr.	1.50
3	Cal Ripken, Jr.	2.00
4	Frank Thomas	.75
5	Steve Avery	.50
6	Benito Santiago	.50
7	Luis Polonia	.50
8	Jose Rijo	.50
9	George Brett	1.25
10	Darren Daulton	.50
11	Cecil Fielder	.50
12	Ozzie Smith	1.00
13	Joe Carter	.50
14	Dwight Gooden	.50
15	Tom Henke	.50
16	Brett Butler	.50
17	Nolan Ryan	2.00
18	Sandy Alomar, Jr.	.50
19	Tom Glavine	.60
20	Rafael Palmeiro	.75
21	Roger Clemens	1.25
22	Ryne Sandberg	1.00
23	Doug Drabek	.50
24	Chuck Knoblauch	.50

1994 King-B

King-B once again created and inserted discs of 24 major league stars with its products in 1994. The entire set was also available in uncut sheet form which was found in each case. Discs measure 2-3/8" diameter and have a broad purple border with yellow and white typography surrounding the player photo at center. A black glove holds a King-B logo at bottom. Uniform logos have been airbrushed from the photos. Backs are printed in purple and include 1993 and career stats.

		NM/M
Complete Set (24):		6.00
Common Player:		.50
1	Fred McGriff	.50
2	Paul Molitor	.75
3	Jack McDowell	.50
4	Darren Daulton	.50
5	Wade Boggs	1.00
6	Ken Griffey Jr.	2.00
7	Tim Salmon	.50
8	Dennis Eckersley	.65
9	Albert Belle	.50
10	Travis Fryman	.50
11	Chris Hoiles	.50
12	Kirby Puckett	1.00
13	John Olerud	.50
14	Frank Thomas	.75
15	Lenny Dykstra	.50
16	Andres Galarraga	.50
17	Barry Larkin	.50
18	Greg Maddux	1.00
19	Mike Piazza	1.50
20	Roberto Alomar	.50
21	Robin Ventura	.50
22	Ryne Sandberg	1.00
23	Andy Van Slyke	.50
24	Barry Bonds	3.00

1995 King-B

A wood-grain background distinguishes the eighth annual baseball disc issue packaged inside shredded beef snack tins. Because they are licensed only by the Players Association, and not MLB, cards in the set have had team logos removed from the color player photos at the center of the 2-3/8" diameter discs. Backs are printed in red and have a few personal bits of data, previous season and career stats and the logos of King-B and the MLBPA.

		NM/M
Complete Set (24):		15.00
Common Player:		.35
1	Roberto Alomar	.35
2	Jeff Bagwell	.75
3	Wade Boggs	1.50
4	Barry Bonds	3.00
5	Joe Carter	.35
6	Mariano Duncan	.35
7	Lenny Dykstra	.35
8	Andres Galarraga	.35
9	Matt Williams	.35
10	Raul Mondesi	.35
11	Ken Griffey Jr.	2.00
12	Gregg Jefferies	.35
13	Fred McGriff	.35
14	Paul Molitor	.75
15	Dave Justice	.35
16	Mike Piazza	1.75
17	Kirby Puckett	1.50
18	Cal Ripken Jr.	3.00
19	Ivan Rodriguez	.65
20	Ozzie Smith	1.50
21	Gary Sheffield	.50
22	Frank Thomas	.75
23	Greg Maddux	1.50
24	Jimmy Key	.35
	("JIIMY" on back.)	

1996 King-B

The "9th Annual Collectors Edition" of King-B discs once again features player photos on which uniform insignia have been airbrushed away. The cards are li-

censed by Michael Schechter Associates only with the Players Union, not MLB, and so cannot display team logos. The 2-5/8" cardboard discs are packaged in plastic cannisters of shredded dried meat. Fronts have the 1996 date at left in a black and gold pinstriped area. The backs are in black and white with 1995 and career stats, along with a few vital data and appropriate logos and copyright information.

		NM/M
Complete Set (24):		15.00
Common Player:		.50
1	Roger Clemens	1.75
2	Mo Vaughn	.50
3	Dante Bichette	.50
4	Jeff Bagwell	1.00
5	Randy Johnson	1.00
6	Ken Griffey Jr.	2.00
7	Kirby Puckett	1.50
8	Orel Hershiser	.50
9	Albert Belle	.50
10	Tony Gwynn	1.50
11	Tom Glavine	.65
12	Jim Abbott	.50
13	Andres Galarraga	.50
14	Frank Thomas	1.00
15	Barry Larkin	.50
16	Mike Piazza	1.75
17	Matt Williams	.50
18	Greg Maddux	1.50
19	Hideo Nomo	.50
20	Roberto Alomar	.50
21	Ivan Rodriguez	.75
22	Cal Ripken Jr.	3.00
23	Barry Bonds	3.00
24	Mark McGwire	2.50

1997 King-B

The shredded beef product issued its 10th Anniversary set of player discs in 1997. The discs are packed inside the plastic canisters of the snack food and measure 2-3/8" in diameter. The '97 discs have a player action photo on front against a gold and black marbled background. Backs are in black-and-white and repeat the photo in the background, along with a few stats and personal data, logos and a disc number. One player from each team is represented in the checklist.

		NM/M
Complete Set (28):		15.00
Common Player:		.50
1	Brady Anderson	.50
2	Barry Bonds	3.00
3	Travis Fryman	.50
4	Rey Ordonez	.50
5	Kenny Lofton	.50
6	Mark McGwire	2.50
7	Jeff Bagwell	1.00
8	Roger Clemens	1.75
9	Juan Gonzalez	.75
10	Mike Piazza	1.75
11	Tim Salmon	.50
12	Jeff Montgomery	.50
13	Joe Carter	.50
14	David Cone	.50
15	Frank Thomas	1.00
16	Mickey Morandini	.50
17	Ray Lankford	.50
18	Pedro Martinez	1.00
19	Tom Glavine	.65
20	Chuck Knoblauch	.50
21	Dan Wilson	.50
22	Gary Sheffield	.65
23	Dante Bichette	.50
24	Al Martin	.50
25	Barry Larkin	.50
26	Ryne Sandberg	1.50
27	Steve Finley	.50
28	Matt Mieske	.50

1998 King-B

Except for the expansion teams, each Major League team has one player in this issue of player discs which were packed inside plastic canisters of the snack food. The cards measure 2-3/8" in diameter with a color player action photo on front

(uniform logos have been removed). Backs have a few stats and personal data, logos plus a disc number.

		NM/M
Complete Set (28):		12.50
Common Player:		.50
1	Brady Anderson	.50
2	Barry Bonds	3.00
3	Tony Clark	.50
4	Rey Ordonez	.50
5	Travis Fryman	.50
6	Jason Giambi	.75
7	Jeff Bagwell	1.00
8	Tim Naehring	.50
9	Juan Gonzalez	.75
10	Mike Piazza	1.50
11	Tim Salmon	.50
12	Jeff Montgomery	.50
13	Tom Glavine	.65
14	Chuck Knoblauch	.50
15	Dan Wilson	.50
16	Gary Sheffield	.65
17	Dante Bichette	.50
18	Al Martin	.50
19	Roger Clemens	1.50
20	David Cone	.50
21	Frank Thomas	1.00
22	Mike Lieberthal	.50
23	Ray Lankford	.50
24	Rondell White	.50
25	Barry Larkin	.50
26	Matt Mieske	.50
27	Steve Finley	.50
28	Fernando Vina	.50

1999 King-B

The shredded beef product issued its 12th set of cardboard player discs in 1999. The discs are packed inside plastic canisters of the snack food and measure 2-3/8" in diameter. The cards have a color player action photo on front. Uniform logos are removed and team names are nowhere to be seen on the cards. Backs repeat the front photo in black-and-white in the background, along with a few stats and personal data, logos and a disc number. One player from each team is represented in the checklist.

		NM/M
Complete Set (30):		15.00
Common Player:		.50
1	Brady Anderson	.50
2	Barry Bonds	3.00
3	Scott Rolen	.75
4	Tony Clark	.50
5	Jeff Bagwell	1.00
6	Roberto Alomar	.50
7	Mark Kotsay	.50
8	Juan Gonzalez	.75
9	Tim Salmon	.50
10	Tom Glavine	.65
11	Frank Thomas	1.00
12	Dan Wilson	.50
13	Dante Bichette	.50
14	Mickey Morandini	.50
15	Fred McGriff	.50
16	Andy Benes	.50
17	Jeff Montgomery	.50
18	Pedro Martinez	1.00
19	Barry Larkin	.50
20	Carlos Delgado	.75
21	Mike Myers	.50
22	Ray Lankford	.50
23	Brad Radke	.50
24	Al Martin	.50
25	Raul Mondesi	.50
26	Ugueth Urbina	.50
27	Derek Jeter	3.00
28	Ben Grieve	.50
29	Mike Piazza	1.75
30	Wally Joyner	.50

2000 King-B

The shredded beef product issued its 13th annual set of cardboard player discs in 2000. The discs are packed inside plastic canisters of the snack food and measure 2-3/8" in diameter. The cards have a color player action photo on front. Uniform logos are removed and team names are nowhere to be seen on the cards. Backs have a black-and-white portrait photo, along with a few stats and personal data, logos and a disc number. One player from each team is represented in the checklist.

		NM/M
Complete Set (30):		15.00
Common Player:		.50
1	Nomar Garciaparra	1.50
2	Larry Walker	.50
3	Manny Ramirez	.75
4	Carlos Beltran	.65
5	Mark McGwire	2.00
6	Jeromy Burnitz	.50
7	Carlos Delgado	.60
8	Tom Glavine	.65
9	Shawn Green	.60
10	Mark Kotsay	.50
11	Warren Morris	.50
12	Fred McGriff	.50
13	Brady Anderson	.50
14	Jeff Bagwell	.75
15	Tony Clark	.50
16	Ben Grieve	.50
17	Vladimir Guerrero	.75
18	Tony Gwynn	1.00
19	Derek Jeter	3.00
20	Barry Larkin	.50
21	Rafael Palmeiro	.65
22	Mike Piazza	1.50
23	Brad Radke	.50
24	Scott Rolen	.65
25	Tim Salmon	.50
26	Frank Thomas	.50
27	Mark Grace	.50
28	Jeff Kent	.50
29	Dan Wilson	.50
30	Jay Bell	.50

2001 King B

The cardboard discs for the shredded-beef snack's 14th annual issue were produced by Playoff, whose logo is among those appearing on back. The 2-3/8" diameter discs have a color action photo and black-and-white portrait on a pinstriped ball diamond background on front. Backs have another black-and-white portrait photo, along with 2000 and career stats and a few biographical bits. All photos have had team logos removed. Each disc is numbered "1 of 30" on back, so the checklist presented here is in alphabetical order.

		NM/M
Complete Set (30):		15.00
Common Player:		.50
(1)	Brady Anderson	.50
(2)	Jeff Bagwell	.75
(3)	Jay Bell	.50
(4)	Carlos Beltran	.65
(5)	Jeromy Burnitz	.50
(6)	Tony Clark	.50
(7)	Carlos Delgado	.60
(8)	Nomar Garciaparra	1.50
(9)	Tom Glavine	.50
(10)	Mark Grace	.50
(11)	Shawn Green	.60
(12)	Ben Grieve	.50
(13)	Vladimir Guerrero	.75
(14)	Tony Gwynn	1.00

2000 King-B

(15)	Derek Jeter	2.50
(16)	Jeff Kent	.50
(17)	Mark Kotsay	.50
(18)	Barry Larkin	.50
(19)	Fred McGriff	.50
(20)	Mark McGwire	2.00
(21)	Warren Morris	.50
(22)	Rafael Palmeiro	.65
(23)	Mike Piazza	1.50
(24)	Brad Radke	.50
(25)	Manny Ramirez	.75
(26)	Scott Rolen	.65
(27)	Tim Salmon	.50
(28)	Frank Thomas	.75
(29)	Larry Walker	.50
(30)	Dan Wilson	.50

2001 King B League Legends

For the first time in its 14 years of producing cardboard player discs as a premium with its beef snacks, King B produced a set in 2001 featuring non-current players. Issued one per package of King B jerky, the 2-3/8" diameter discs have a color portrait (with uniform logos removed) on front, against a ballpark photo background. Backs are in white and green and have a baseball design background with player data and a repeat of the "League Legends" logo.

		NM/M
Complete Set (18):		12.00
Common Player:		.50
1	Frank Robinson	1.00
2	Steve Carlton	1.00
3	Harmon Killebrew	1.00
4	Frank Torre	.50
5	Rollie Fingers	.50
6	Robin Roberts	1.00
7	Ernie Banks	1.50
8	Steve Sax	.50
9	Duke Snider	1.50
10	Gaylord Perry	.50
11	Andre Dawson	.50
12	Dave Kingman	.50
13	Reggie Jackson	2.00
14	Willie McCovey	1.00
15	Gary Carter	.50
16	Orlando Cepeda	.50
17	Willie Randolph	.50
18	Bob Gibson	1.00

2002 King B

For the shredded-beef snack's 15th annual issue, Donruss produced the 2-3/8" diameter discs. Fronts have a large "15" over which is printed a color action photo. Backs have a portrait photo, along with 2001 and career stats and a few biographical bits. All photos have had team logos removed.

		NM/M
Complete Set (28):		12.50
Common Player:		.50
1	Randy Johnson	.75
2	Curt Schilling	.65
3	Chipper Jones	1.00
4	Greg Maddux	1.00
5	John Burkett	.50
6	Manny Ramirez	.75
7	Barry Larkin	.50
8	Roberto Alomar	.50
9	Chuck Finley	.50
10	Jim Thome	.65
11	Juan Gonzalez	.65
12	Larry Walker	.50
13	Charles Johnson	.50
14	Moises Alou	.50
15	Gary Sheffield	.65
16	Chan Ho Park	.50
17	Vladimir Guerrero	.75
18	Roger Clemens	1.25

19	Mariano Rivera	.60
20	Jason Giambi	.65
21	Rich Aurilia	.50
22	Jeff Kent	.50
23	Edgar Martinez	.50
24	Kazuhiro Sasaki	.50
25	Bret Boone	.50
26	John Olerud	.50
27	Greg Vaughn	.50
28	Ivan Rodriguez	.65

1985 Kitty Clover Potato Chips Discs

One of a pair of nearly identical (see KAS) sets issued by midwestern potato chip companies, this issue features top stars of the day on 2-3/4" cardboard discs. The discs have a player portrait at center, with uniform logos airbrushed away because the producer was licensed only by the Players Association and not Major League Baseball. The player's name, team and position are printed in a white diamond around the photo. The sponsor's logo is in the yellow border. Backs are in black-and-white and have a few biographical data, a 1984 stats line and a Snack Time logo. The unnumbered discs are checklisted here in alphabetical order. Square versions of the discs, which have been cut from press sheets are known within the hobby and carry a small premium. Kitty Clover was based in Omaha.

		NM/M
Complete Set (20):		60.00
Common Player:		1.50
(1)	Steve Carlton	6.00
(2)	Jack Clark	1.50
(3)	Rich Gossage	1.50
(4)	Tony Gwynn	7.50
(5)	Bob Horner	1.50
(6)	Keith Hernandez	1.50
(7)	Kent Hrbek	1.50
(8)	Willie McGee	1.50
(9)	Dan Quisenberry	1.50
(10)	Cal Ripken Jr.	25.00
(11)	Ryne Sandberg	7.50
(12)	Mike Schmidt	20.00
(13)	Tom Seaver	6.00
(14)	Ozzie Smith	7.50
(15)	Rick Sutcliffe	1.50
(16)	Bruce Sutter	4.00
(17)	Alan Trammell	1.50
(18)	Fernando Valenzuela	1.50
(19)	Willie Wilson	1.50
(20)	Dave Winfield	6.00

1986 Kitty Clover Potato Chips Royals

Twenty players of the 1985 World's Champion Kansas City Royals are featured in a round card set inserted into packages of potato chips in the K.C. area. The 2-7/8" discs were similar to other contemporary snack issues produced by Mike Schechter Associates in that team logos have been airbrushed off the players' caps. The photos of some of the players can be found on other regional issues of 1986.

		NM/M
Complete Set (20):		15.00
Common Player:		.75
1	Lonnie Smith	.75
2	Buddy Biancalana	.75
3	Bret Saberhagen	1.00
4	Hal McRae	.75

5	Onix Concepcion	.75
6	Jorge Orta	.75
7	Bud Black	.75
8	Dan Quisenberry	.75
9	Dane Iorg	.75
10	Charlie Leibrandt	.75
11	Pat Sheridan	.75
12	John Wathan	.75
13	Frank White	.75
14	Darryl Motley	.75
15	Willie Wilson	1.00
16	Danny Jackson	.75
17	Steve Balboni	.75
18	Jim Sundberg	.75
19	Mark Gubicza	.75
20	George Brett	6.00

1996 Klosterman Baking Big Red Machine

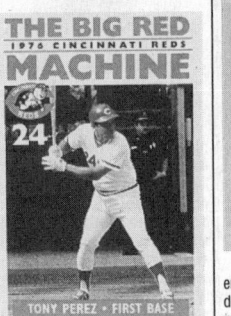

Twenty years after The Big Red Machine captured the World's Championship, the 1976 Cincinnati Reds were honored on a card set issued by this Queen City bakery. One card was included with each 20-oz. loaf of bread during the run of the promotion. Cards are 2-3/8" x 3-1/2". Fronts feature color game-action photos with a large headline above and the player's name and position in white on a red strip at bottom. The Reds logo is in an upper corner of the photo, with the player's uniform number beneath. Backs have career summary and stats for the 1976 season and M.L. career, along with sponsors' logos and copyright information.

		NM/M
Complete Set (10):		10.00
Common Player:		.50
5	Johnny Bench	4.00
8	Joe Morgan	1.50
10	Sparky Anderson	1.00
13	Dave Concepcion	.50
15	George Foster	.50
20	Cesar Geronimo	.50
24	Tony Perez	1.00
30	Ken Griffey	.50
35	Don Gullett	.50
----	The Big Four (Tony Perez, Johnny Bench, Joe Morgan, Pete Rose)	3.00

2000 Klosterman Bakery Big Red Machine

The 25th anniversary of Cincinnati's 1975 World Series championship is marked with this issue by a regional bakery. The cards are printed on thin stock in a 2-3/8" x 3-1/2" format. Fronts have vintage game-action photos with red borders and a Big Red Machine 25th anniversary logo. Backs recap the player's 1975 season in words and stats. The cards were distributed singly in loaves of bread. The unnumbered cards are listed here in alphabetical order.

The first of what became dozens of boxed sets specially produced for retail chain stores by the major card producers, the 1982 K-Mart set has enjoyed little collector popularity. The theme of the set is Most Valuable Players and selected record- breaking performances in the 1962-1981 seasons. The design used miniature reproductions of Topps cards of the era, except in a few cases where designs had to be created because original cards were never issued (1962 Maury Wills, 1975 Fred Lynn). Originally sold for about $2 per boxed set of 44, large quantities were bought up by speculators who got burned when over-production and lack of demand caused the set to drop as low as 10¢. The 2-1/2" x 3-1/2" cards were printed by Topps.

		NM/M
Complete Set (44):		3.00
Common Player:		.10
1	Mickey Mantle	2.00
2	Maury Wills	.10
3	Elston Howard	.10
4	Sandy Koufax	.50
5	Brooks Robinson	.10
6	Ken Boyer	.10
7	Zoilo Versalles	.10
8	Willie Mays	.50
9	Frank Robinson	.50
10	Bob Clemente	.50
11	Carl Yastrzemski	.25
12	Orlando Cepeda	.10
13	Denny McLain	.10
14	Bob Gibson	.10
15	Harmon Killebrew	.02
16	Willie McCovey	.10
17	Boog Powell	.10
18	Johnny Bench	.10
19	Vida Blue	.10
20	Joe Torre	.10
21	Rich Allen	.10
22	Johnny Bench	.10
23	Reggie Jackson	.25
24	Pete Rose	.45
25	Jeff Burroughs	.10
26	Steve Garvey	.10
27	Fred Lynn	.10
28	Joe Morgan	.10
29	Thurman Munson	.10
30	Joe Morgan	.10
31	Rod Carew	.10
32	George Foster	.10
33	Jim Rice	.10
34	Dave Parker	.10
35	Don Baylor	.10
36	Keith Hernandez	.10
37	Willie Stargell	.10
38	George Brett	.50
39	Mike Schmidt	.50
40	Rollie Fingers	.10
41	Mike Schmidt	.50
42	Don Drysdale	.10
43	Hank Aaron	.50
44	Pete Rose	.45

1987 K-Mart

Produced by Topps for K-Mart, the 1987 K-Mart set was distributed by the department stores to celebrate their 25th anniversary. Entitled "Baseball's Stars of the Decades," the 33-card set was issued in a spe-

ROGER MARIS

cial cardboard box with one stick of bubblegum. Fronts feature a full-color photo set diagonally against a red background. The backs contain career highlights plus pitching or batting statistics for the decade in which the player enjoyed his greatest success. Cards are the standard 2-1/2" x 3-1/2".

		NM/M
Complete Set (33):		3.00
Common Player:		.10
1	Hank Aaron	.60
2	Roberto Clemente	.75
3	Bob Gibson	.10
4	Harmon Killebrew	.10
5	Mickey Mantle	2.00
6	Juan Marichal	.10
7	Roger Maris	.25
8	Willie Mays	.60
9	Brooks Robinson	.10
10	Frank Robinson	.10
11	Carl Yastrzemski	.25
12	Johnny Bench	.10
13	Lou Brock	.10
14	Rod Carew	.10
15	Steve Carlton	.10
16	Reggie Jackson	.25
17	Jim Palmer	.10
18	Jim Rice	.10
19	Pete Rose	.60
20	Nolan Ryan	.75
21	Tom Seaver	.10
22	Willie Stargell	.10
23	Wade Boggs	.25
24	George Brett	.50
25	Gary Carter	.10
26	Dwight Gooden	.10
27	Rickey Henderson	.10
28	Don Mattingly	.50
29	Dale Murphy	.10
30	Eddie Murray	.10
31	Mike Schmidt	.50
32	Darryl Strawberry	.10
33	Fernando Valenzuela	.10

1988 K-Mart

ROBIN YOUNT

This 33-card boxed set, titled "Memorable Moments," was produced by Topps for distribution via K-Mart. The 1988 cards are standard-size with red, white and blue borders and a super glossy coating. Numbered card backs are printed in red and blue on white and highlight special events in the featured players' careers. The set was marketed in a bright yellow and green checklist box (gum included).

		NM/M
Complete Set (33):		2.00
Common Player:		.10
1	George Bell	.10
2	Wade Boggs	.45
3	George Brett	.50
4	Jose Canseco	.25
5	Jack Clark	.10
6	Will Clark	.10
7	Roger Clemens	.10
8	Vince Coleman	.10
9	Andre Dawson	.15
10	Dwight Gooden	.10
11	Pedro Guerrero	.10
12	Tony Gwynn	.45

13	Rickey Henderson	.35
14	Keith Hernandez	.10
15	Don Mattingly	.50
16	Mark McGwire	.75
17	Paul Molitor	.35
18	Dale Murphy	.15
19	Tim Raines	.10
20	Dave Righetti	.10
21	Cal Ripken, Jr.	1.00
22	Pete Rose	.60
23	Nolan Ryan	1.00
24	Benny Santiago	.10
25	Mike Schmidt	.50
26	Mike Scott	.10
27	Kevin Seitzer	.10
28	Ozzie Smith	.45
29	Darryl Strawberry	.10
30	Rick Sutcliffe	.10
31	Fernando Valenzuela	.10
32	Todd Worrell	.10
33	Robin Yount	.35

1989 K-Mart

DreamTeam — KIRBY PUCKETT

This 33-card, glossy set was produced by Topps for K-Mart, where it was sold in stores nationwide. The standard-size cards feature mostly action shots on the front, and include the Topps "Dream Team" logo at the top, with the K-Mart logo in the lower right corner. The first 11 cards in the set picture the top rookies of 1988, while the next 11 picture the top A.L. rookies of the '80s, and the final 11 cards highlight the top N.L. rookies of the decade.

		NM/M
Complete Set (33):		2.00
Common Player:		.10
1	Mark Grace	.10
2	Ron Gant	.10
3	Chris Sabo	.10
4	Walt Weiss	.10
5	Jay Buhner	.10
6	Cecil Espy	.10
7	Dave Gallagher	.10
8	Damon Berryhill	.10
9	Tim Belcher	.10
10	Paul Gibson	.10
11	Gregg Jefferies	.10
12	Don Mattingly	.75
13	Harold Reynolds	.10
14	Wade Boggs	.50
15	Cal Ripken, Jr.	1.00
16	Kirby Puckett	.60
17	George Bell	.10
18	Jose Canseco	.25
19	Terry Steinbach	.10
20	Roger Clemens	.65
21	Mark Langston	.10
22	Harold Baines	.10
23	Will Clark	.10
24	Ryne Sandberg	.60
25	Tim Wallach	.10
26	Shawon Dunston	.10
27	Tim Raines	.10
28	Darryl Strawberry	.10
29	Tony Gwynn	.60
30	Tony Pena	.10
31	Doc Gooden	.10
32	Fernando Valenzuela	.10
33	Pedro Guerrero	.10

1990 K-Mart

This 33-card glossy set was produced by Topps for K-Mart, where it was available nationwide. The set is subtitled "Superstars" and features 16 A.L. players, 16 N.L. stars and a managers' card featuring both Tony LaRussa and Roger Craig. A special Superstars logo is featured on the card fronts. The 1990 issue marks the fourth consecutive year that Topps has produced a set in cooperation with K-Mart.

		NM/M
Complete Set (33):		3.00
Common Player:		.10
1	Will Clark	.10
2	Ryne Sandberg	.50
3	Howard Johnson	.10

RICKEY HENDERSON — OF

4	Ozzie Smith	.50
5	Tony Gwynn	.50
6	Kevin Mitchell	.10
7	Jerome Walton	.10
8	Craig Biggio	.10
9	Mike Scott	.10
10	Dwight Gooden	.10
11	Sid Fernandez	.10
12	Joe Magrane	.10
13	Jay Howell	.10
14	Mark Davis	.10
15	Pedro Guerrero	.10
16	Glenn Davis	.10
17	Don Mattingly	.65
18	Julio Franco	.10
19	Wade Boggs	.50
20	Cal Ripken, Jr.	1.00
21	Jose Canseco	.25
22	Kirby Puckett	.50
23	Rickey Henderson	.35
24	Mickey Tettleton	.10
25	Nolan Ryan	1.00
26	Bret Saberhagen	.10
27	Jeff Ballard	.10
28	Chuck Finley	.10
29	Dennis Eckersley	.30
30	Dan Plesac	.10
31	Fred McGriff	.10
32	Mark McGwire	.75
33	Managers (Tony LaRussa, Roger Craig)	.10

1988 Kodak White Sox

These blank-back large format (8" x 12") cards feature borderless color action photos of team stars, overprinted with team and sponsor logos and a facsimile autograph. At top is a line of type with the card number and a "1988 Kodak Collectible Series" title.

		NM/M
Complete Set (5):		10.00
Common Player:		2.00
1	Ozzie Guillen	2.00
2	Carlton Fisk	4.00
3	Rick Horton	2.00
4	Ivan Calderon	2.00
5	Harold Baines	2.00

1989 Kodak White Sox

1989 Kodak Collectible Series #1 — Greg Walker, First Baseman

A series of six collectible pictures was given to fans over the course of the 1989 season. Sponsored by Kodak and Osco drug stores, the 8" x 12" sheets combine pictures of a current White Sox star with those of two former stars who played the same position. Ads for the sponsors appear on the photos' fronts, while there is a modicum of information about the former stars accompanying their portraits, including the years they played for the Sox.

		NM/M
Complete Set (6):		10.00
Common Card:		2.00
1	Greg Walker, Dick Allen, Ted Kluszewski	2.50
2	Steve Lyons, Eddie Collins, Nellie Fox	2.50
3	Carlton Fisk, Sherm Lollar, Ray Schalk	2.50

ROGER MARIS — OF (*K mart 1962 ◆ 1987 25th ANNIVERSARY COLLECTORS' EDITION*)

4	Harold Baines, Minnie Minoso, Jim Landis	2.00
5	Bobby Thigpen, Gerry Staley, Hoyt Wilhelm	2.00
6	Ozzie Guillen, Luke Appling, Luis Aparicio	2.00

1990 Kodak White Sox

1990 Kodak Collectible Series #5 — Scott Fletcher, Second Baseman

Again utilizing a large format (7" x 11") with borderless color action photos, the "1990 Kodak Collectible Series" features top stars of the South Siders. Player name and position, along with team and sponsor's logos, are superimposed over the photo, along with the title line and card number. The blank-back cards were distributed over the course of the season at various home games.

		NM/M
Complete Set (6):		10.00
Common Player:		2.00
1	Carlton Fisk	4.00
2	Melido Perez	2.00
3	Ozzie Guillen	2.00
4	Ron Kittle	2.00
5	Scott Fletcher	2.00
6	Comiskey Park	2.00

1991 Kodak White Sox

FRANK THOMAS — 35

For a fourth year in a row, Kodak sponsored a White Sox team set in 1991. Fronts feature a full-bleed color action photo with the player's name and uniform number at the bottom and a commemorative logo for new Comiskey Park's inaugural season at top. Black-and-white backs have a few stats, personal details and career highlights along with the Kodak logo.

		NM/M
Complete Set (30):		24.00
Common Player:		.50
1	Lance Johnson	.50
6	Matt Merullo	.50
7	Scott Fletcher	.50
8	Bo Jackson	1.50
10	Jeff Torborg	.50
13	Ozzie Guillen	.50
14	Craig Grebeck	.50
20	Ron Karkovice	.50
21	Joey Cora	.50
22	Donn Pall	.50
23	Robin Ventura	1.00
25	Sammy Sosa	10.00
27	Greg Hibbard	.50
28	Cory Snyder	.50
29	Jack McDowell	.50
30	Tim Raines	.50
31	Scott Radinsky	.50
32	Alex Fernandez	.50
33	Melido Perez	.50
34	Ken Patterson	.50
35	Frank Thomas	5.00
37	Bobby Thigpen	.50
44	Dan Pasqua	.50
45	Wayne Edwards	.50
49	Charlie Hough	.50
50	Brian Drahman	.50

1982 K-Mart

		NM/M
Complete Set (10):		5.00
Common Player:		.50
(1)	Sparky Anderson	.65
(2)	Johnny Bench	1.00
(3)	Jack Billingham	.50
(4)	Dave Concepcion	.50
(5)	George Foster	.50
(6)	Cesar Geronimo	.50
(7)	Ken Griffey	.50
(8)	Joe Morgan	.75
(9)	Tony Perez	.65
(10)	Pete Rose, Joe Morgan, Johnny Bench	1.00

1982 K-Mart

HANK AARON — MVP SERIES — 1974 HIGHLIGHT (K mart 20th Anniversary 1962-1982)

72	Carlton Fisk	3.00
---	White Sox Coaches	
	(Terry Bevington,	
	Sammy Ellis, Barry Foote,	
	Walt Hriniak, Dave Laroche,	
	Joe Nossek,	
	John Stephenson)	.50
---	Co-captains (Ozzie Guillen,	
	Carlton Fisk)	.50
---	No. 1 Draft Choices	
	(Alex Fernandez,	
	Jack McDowell,	
	Frank Thomas,	
	Robin Ventura)	1.00

1992 Kodak White Sox

With the theme of "Good Guys Wear Black," this set depicts the Chicago southsiders in photos featuring the team's Sunday-best black uniform jerseys. Photos on the cards are full-bleed with the GGWB logo in the upper-left corner of each card. At bottom is a black strip with the player's last name and uniform number. On back are the player's 1991 and career stats, a few biographical details, a trivia question and Kodak logo. At 2-5/8" x 3-1/2", the cards are slightly wider than current standard.

		NM/M
Complete Set (30):		10.00
Common Player:		.25
1	Lance Johnson	.25
5	Matt Merullo	.25
7	Steve Sax	.25
12	Mike Huff	.25
13	Ozzie Guillen	.25
14	Craig Grebeck	.25
20	Ron Karkovice	.25
21	George Bell	.25
22	Donn Pall	.25
23	Robin Ventura	.50
24	Warren Newson	.25
25	Kirk McCaskill	.25
27	Greg Hibbard	.25
28	Joey Cora	.25
29	Jack McDowell	.25
30	Tim Raines	.25
31	Scott Radinsky	.25
32	Alex Fernandez	.25
33	Gene Lamont	.25
34	Terry Leach	.25
35	Frank Thomas	4.00
37	Bobby Thigpen	.25
39	Roberto Hernandez	.25
40	Wilson Alvarez	.25
44	Dan Pasqua	.25
45	Shawn Abner	.25
49	Charlie Hough	.25
72	Carlton Fisk	2.50
00	Waldo (Cartoon mascot.)	.25
---	Mike Squires,	
	Terry Bevington,	
	Gene Lamont, Joe Nossek,	
	Jackie Brown, Walt Hriniak,	
	Doug Mansolino,	
	Dave Huppert.	.25

1993 Kodak White Sox

Kodak produced a White Sox set of 30 cards in 1993 that was given away prior to the July 23 game between Chicago and Milwaukee. The full color cards are slightly over-

sized at 2-5/8" x 3-1/2" and are printed on a very heavy card stock. The photo on the front is full bleed, with the White Sox logo appearing in the upper corner and a metallic blue stripe at the card bottom displaying the player's uniform number, name and position. The backs are white with gray borders and a Kodak logo, with year and career statistics and biographical information. The cards are unnumbered.

		NM/M
Complete Set (30):		10.00
Common Player:		.25
1	Lance Johnson	.25
7	Steve Sax	.25
8	Bo Jackson	.75
10	Mike LaValliere	.25
12	Mike Huff	.25
13	Ozzie Guillen	.25
14	Craig Grebeck	.25
20	Ron Karkovice	.25
21	George Bell	.25
22	Donn Pall	.25
23	Robin Ventura	.50
25	Kirk McCaskill	.25
28	Ellis Burks	.25
28	Joey Cora	.25
29	Jack McDowell	.25
30	Tim Raines	.25
31	Scott Radinsky	.25
32	Alex Fernandez	.25
33	Gene Lamont	.25
34	Terry Leach	.25
35	Frank Thomas	4.00
37	Bobby Thigpen	.25
39	Roberto Hernandez	.25
40	Wilson Alvarez	.25
44	Rod Bolton	.25
44	Dan Pasqua	.25
45	Chuck Cary	.25
49	Jeff Schwartz	.25
51	Jason Bere	.25
---	1993 Coaching Staff	
	(Gene Lamont, Jackie Brown,	
	Terry Bevington, Joe Nossek,	
	Walt Hriniak,	
	Doug Mansolino,	
	Dewey Robinson,	
	Jose Antigua)	.25

1994 Kodak White Sox

Slightly wider than standard cards, at 2-5/8" x 3-1/2" cards, this team set features borderless game-action photos on front with a silver facsimile autograph. Backs are bordered in silver and have a few stats, player personal data, career highlights and logos of the team and sponsor.

		NM/M
Complete Set (30):		12.00
Common Player:		.50
(1)	Wilson Alvarez	.50
(2)	Paul Assenmacher	.50
(3)	Jason Bere	.50
(4)	Dennis Cook	.50
(5)	Joey Cora	.50
(6)	Jose DeLeon	.50
(7)	Alex Fernandez	.50
(8)	Julio Franco	.50
(9)	Craig Grebeck	.50
(10)	Ozzie Guillen	.50
(11)	Joe Hall	.50
(12)	Roberto Hernandez	.50
(13)	Dann Howitt	.50
(14)	Darrin Jackson	.50
(15)	Dane Johnson	.50
(16)	Lance Johnson	.50
(17)	Ron Karkovice	.50
(18)	Gene Lamont	.50
(19)	Mike LaValliere	.50
(20)	Norberto Martin	.50
(21)	Kirk McCaskill	.50
(22)	Jack McDowell	.50
(23)	Warren Newson	.50
(24)	Dan Pasqua	.50
(25)	Tim Raines	.50
(26)	Scott Sanderson	.50
(27)	Frank Thomas	4.00
(28)	Robin Ventura	.50
(29)	Bob Zupcic	.50
(30)	Coaches (Terry Bevington,	
	Jackie Brown, Roly de Armas,	
	Walt Hriniak, Gene Lamont,	
	Doug Mansolino, Joe Nossek,	
	Rick Peterson)	.50

1995 Kodak Pittsburgh Pirates

This 13-1/2" x 20-1/4" perforated sheet containing 30 player and staff cards and sponsor advertising was issued to persons attending a July 23 promotional game. Individual cards measure 2-1/4" x 3-1/4". Player photos at center are flanked by the team name in gold with the player name in yellow in a red banner above. Backs are in black-and-white with just a few biographical notes

and team and sponsor logos. The unnumbered cards are checklisted here alphabetically.

		NM/M
Complete Set, Sheet:		6.00
Complete Set, Singles (30):		6.00
Common Player:		.25
(1)	Rich Aude	.25
(2)	Jay Bell	.50
(3)	Jacob Brumfield	.25
(4)	Jason Christiansen	.25
(5)	Dave Clark	.25
(6)	Steve Cooke	.25
(7)	Midre Cummings	.25
(8)	Mike Dyer	.25
(9)	Angelo Encarnacion	.25
(10)	Carlos Garcia	.25
(11)	Freddy Garcia	.25
(12)	Jim Gott	.25
(13)	Mark Johnson	.25
(14)	Jeff King	.25
(15)	Jim Leyland	.25
(16)	Jon Lieber	.25
(17)	Nelson Liriano	.25
(18)	Esteban Loaiza	.25
(19)	Al Martin	.25
(20)	Jeff McCurry	.25
(21)	Orlando Merced	.25
(22)	Dan Miceli	.25
(23)	Denny Neagle	.25
(24)	Mark Parent	.25
(25)	Steve Pegues	.25
(26)	Dan Plesac	.25
(27)	Don Slaught	.25
(28)	Paul Wagner	.25
(29)	Rick White	.25
(30)	Gary Wilson	.25

1995 Kodak White Sox

Fans attending the July 21 game at Comiskey Park received a cello-wrapped 30-card team set. Fronts of the 2-5/8" x 3-1/2" cards have color player photos that are borderless at top and sides. At bottom the player's name appears in black-and-white. Backs are in black-and-white and feature the sponsor's logo and the team's 95-year anniversary logo. There are also a few biographical details, 1994 and career stats and a player trivia question. Cards are numbered by player uniform number.

		NM/M
Complete Set (30):		9.00
Common Player:		.15
1	Lance Johnson	.15
5	Ray Durham	.30
7	Norberto Martin	.15
8	Mike Devereaux	.15
10	Mike Lavalliere	.15
12	Craig Grebeck	.15
13	Ozzie Guillen	.15
14	Dave Martinez	.15
15	Kirk McCaskill	.15
18	Terry Bevington	.15
20	Ron Karkovice	.15
23	Robin Ventura	.15
24	Warren Newson	.15
25	Jim Abbott	.15
26	Brian Keyser	.15
29	John Kruk	.15
30	Tim Raines	.15

31	Scott Radinsky	.15
32	Alex Fernandez	.15
35	Frank Thomas	4.00
39	Roberto Hernandez	.15
40	Wilson Alvarez	.15
46	Jason Bere	.15
48	Jose DeLeon	.15
49	Rob Dibble	.15
51	Tim Fortugno	.15
---	Frank Thomas	
	(1995 All-Star)	2.00
---	White Sox Coaching Staff	
	(Terry Bevington,	
	Don Cooper, Roly DeArmas,	
	Walt Hriniak, Ron Jackson,	
	Doug Mansolino, Joe Nossek,	
	Mark Salas)	.15
---	Trainers (Herm Schneider,	
	Mark Anderson)	.15
---	Director of Conditioning	
	(Steve Odgers)	.15

1985 Kondritz Vince Coleman

The debut season of 1985 N.L. Rookie of the Year Vince Coleman is traced in this 20-card set issued by Illinois dealer Kondritz Trading Cards. Fronts of the 2-1/2" x 3-1/2" cards have player posed or action photos surrounded by a wide red border. Backs are in black-and-white with a few sentences about Coleman, a card number, large "Invincible" and copyright data. Sets were originally sold for about $10.

	NM/M
Complete Set (20):	5.00
Common Card:	.25

1986 Kondritz Ozzie Smith

The career of future Hall of Fame Cardinals shortstop Ozzie Smith is traced in this 20-card set issued by Illinois dealer Kondritz Trading Cards. Fronts of the 2-1/2" x 3-1/2" cards have player posed or action photos surrounded by a wide red border. Backs are in black-and-white with a few sentences about Smith, a card number, a large "THE WIZARD" and copyright data. Sets were originally sold for about $10.

	NM/M
Complete Set (20):	20.00
Common Card:	1.50
1-20 Ozzie Smith	1.50

1987 Kraft Home Plate Heroes

Kraft Foods issued a 48-card set on specially marked packages of macaroni & cheese dinners. Titled "Home Plate Heroes," 24 two-card panels measuring 3-1/2" x 7-1/8" make up the set. Individual cards measure 2-1/4" x 3-1/2". The blank-backed cards feature fronts with full-color photos, although all team insignias have been erased. In conjunction with the card set, Kraft offered a contest to "Win A Day With A Major

Leaguer." Mike Schechter Associates produced the set for Kraft. A total of 120 different panel combinations (five with each player) can be found.

		NM/M
Complete Set, Panels:		20.00
Complete Set, Singles (48):		16.00
Common Player:		.25
1	Eddie Murray	.50
2	Dale Murphy	.40
3	Cal Ripken, Jr.	1.00
4	Mike Scott	.25
5	Jim Rice	.35
6	Jody Davis	.25
7	Wade Boggs	.60
8	Ryne Sandberg	.60
9	Wally Joyner	.25
10	Eric Davis	.25
11	Ozzie Guillen	.25
12	Tony Pena	.25
13	Harold Baines	.25
14	Johnny Ray	.25
15	Joe Carter	.35
16	Ozzie Smith	.60
17	Cory Snyder	.25
18	Vince Coleman	.25
19	Kirk Gibson	.25
20	Steve Garvey	.35
21	George Brett	.75
22	John Tudor	.25
23	Robin Yount	.50
24	Von Hayes	.25
25	Kent Hrbek	.25
26	Darryl Strawberry	.25
27	Kirby Puckett	.60
28	Ron Darling	.25
29	Don Mattingly	.75
30	Mike Schmidt	.75
31	Rickey Henderson	.50
32	Fernando Valenzuela	.25
33	Dave Winfield	.50
34	Pete Rose	.85
35	Jose Canseco	.40
36	Glenn Davis	.25
37	Alvin Davis	.25
38	Steve Sax	.25
39	Pete Incaviglia	.25
40	Jeff Reardon	.25
41	Jesse Barfield	.25
42	Hubie Brooks	.25
43	George Bell	.25
44	Tony Gwynn	.50
45	Roger Clemens	.65
46	Chili Davis	.25
47	Mike Witt	.25
48	Nolan Ryan	1.00

1993 Kraft Pop-Up Action

Kraft released a set of Pop-Up Action baseball cards in 1993 that was available in specially-marked packages of Kraft Singles. The cards are similar to the 1992 Canadian Post Cereal cards with a pop-up tab. The set is made up of 15 players each from the American and National Leagues.

		NM/M
Complete Set (30):		12.00
Common Player:		.35

31	Scott Radinsky	.15
32	Alex Fernandez	.15
35	Frank Thomas	4.00
39	Roberto Hernandez	.15
40	Wilson Alvarez	.15
46	Jason Bere	.15
48	Jose DeLeon	.15
49	Rob Dibble	.15
51	Tim Fortugno	.15

American League
(1)	Jim Abbott	.35
(2)	Roberto Alomar	.35
(3)	Sandy Alomar Jr.	.35
(4)	George Brett	.75
(5)	Roger Clemens	.75
(6)	Dennis Eckersley	.50
(7)	Cecil Fielder	.35
(8)	Ken Griffey Jr.	1.00
(9)	Don Mattingly	.75
(10)	Mark McGwire	1.50
(11)	Kirby Puckett	.65
(12)	Cal Ripken, Jr.	2.00
(13)	Nolan Ryan	2.00
(14)	Robin Ventura	.35
(15)	Robin Yount	.60

National League
(1)	Bobby Bonilla	.35
(2)	Ken Caminiti	.35
(3)	Will Clark	.35
(4)	Darren Daulton	.35
(5)	Doug Drabek	.35
(6)	Delino DeShields	.35
(7)	Tom Glavine	.45
(8)	Tony Gwynn	.65
(9)	Orel Hershiser	.35
(10)	Barry Larkin	.35
(11)	Terry Pendleton	.35
(12)	Ryne Sandberg	.65
(13)	Gary Sheffield	.50
(14)	Lee Smith	.35
(15)	Andy Van Slyke	.35

1994 Kraft Pop-Ups

Kraft offered a 30-card set in 1994 featuring major stars in a pop-up format. The cards show the players in action shots front and back, with the front picture "popping up." Kraft Singles consumers could find one 2-1/2" x 3-3/8" card in each package of cheese, with 15 players from each league. The cards were licensed by the Major League Baseball Players Association, but not by Major League Baseball, so the team logos were airbrushed from player's caps and uniforms. Through an on-pack and in-store mail-in offer, collectors could order complete sets of the cards for $1.95 per league (15 cards), plus the appropriate proofs of purchase. In a somewhat unusual move, officials of Kraft USA announced that the print run would be eight million cards, which works out to about 266,000 sets.

		NM/M
Complete Set (30):		7.50
Common Player:		.25
1	Carlos Baerga	.25
2	Dennis Eckersley	.50
3	Cecil Fielder	.25
4	Juan Gonzalez	.50
5	Ken Griffey Jr.	1.00
6	Mark Langston	.25
7	Brian McRae	.25
8	Paul Molitor	.60
9	Kirby Puckett	.75
10	Cal Ripken Jr.	1.50
11	Danny Tartabull	.25
12	Frank Thomas	.60
13	Greg Vaughn	.25
14	Mo Vaughn	.25
15	Dave Winfield	.60
16	Jeff Bagwell	.60
17	Barry Bonds	1.50
18	Bobby Bonilla	.25
19	Delino DeShields	.25
20	Lenny Dykstra	.25
21	Andres Galarraga	.25
22	Tom Glavine	.25
23	Mark Grace	.25
24	Tony Gwynn	.75
25	David Justice	.60
26	Barry Larkin	.25
27	Mike Piazza	.90
28	Gary Sheffield	.40
29	Ozzie Smith	.75
30	Andy Van Slyke	.25

1995 Kraft Singles Superstars

Once again incorporating a pop-up center action figure, these cards were available both in packages of cheese slices and via a mail-in offer. The 2-1/2" x 3-1/2" cards have a second player photo in the center which is revealed by pushing down the hinged front and back of the card, creating a stand. All photos have had uniform logos removed. A baseball design is at the bottom of each player photo. Back of the card has abbreviated stats and career highlights. The back of the pop-up figure has a paragraph about the player titled, "What Singles Him Out." Besides being packaged with cheese, the cards were available by sending in proofs of purchase and $1.95 for each 15-player A.L. or N.L. set.

		NM/M
Complete Set (30):		7.50
Common Player:		.25
1	Roberto Alomar	.25
2	Joe Carter	.25
3	Cecil Fielder	.25
4	Juan Gonzalez	.50
5	Ken Griffey Jr.	1.25
6	Jimmy Key	.25
7	Chuck Knoblauch	.25
8	Kenny Lofton	.25
9	Mike Mussina	.40
10	Paul O'Neill	.25
11	Kirby Puckett	.75
12	Cal Ripken Jr.	1.50
13	Ivan Rodriguez	.50
14	Frank Thomas	.60
15	Mo Vaughn	.25
16	Moises Alou	.25
17	Jeff Bagwell	.60
18	Barry Bonds	1.50
19	Jeff Conine	.25
20	Lenny Dykstra	.25
21	Andres Galarraga	.25
22	Tony Gwynn	.75
23	Gregg Jefferies	.25
24	Barry Larkin	.25
25	Greg Maddux	.75
26	Mike Piazza	1.00
27	Bret Saberhagen	.25
28	Ozzie Smith	.75
29	Sammy Sosa	1.00
30	Matt Williams	.25

1994 KVTU-TV San Francisco Giants

This short set was sponsored by the Giants' television broadcasting partner. Eight of the team's top names are featured on the 2-1/2" x 3-1/2" cards. Fronts have action photos framed in orange and brown with white borders. Black-and-white backs have a few career highlights and the TV station's logo.

		NM/M
Complete Set (9):		12.00
Common Player:		1.00
(1)	Dusty Baker	1.00

(2)	Rod Beck	1.00
(3)	Barry Bonds	7.50
(4)	Bobby Bonds	1.00
(5)	John Burkett	1.00
(6)	Billy Swift	1.00
(7)	Robby Thompson	1.00
(8)	Matt Williams	1.00
(9)	Header Card	.50

L

1981 L.A. Dodgers Police

TOM LASORDA
No. 2 - Manager
LAPD SALUTES THE 1981
Dodgers

Similar in format to the previous year's set, the Dodgers 1981 police set grew to 32 cards due to the acquisitions of Ken Landreaux and Dave Stewart shortly before printing of the sets. These two cards may even have been added after the initial printing run, making them slightly more difficult to obtain. The full-color cards are again 2-13/16" x 4-1/8", with a safety tip on the card back. Each card front has the line "LAPD Salutes the 1981 Dodgers."

		NM/M
Complete Set (32):		6.00
Common Player:		.25
2	Tom Lasorda	.50
3	Rudy Law	.25
6	Steve Garvey	3.00
7	Steve Yeager	.25
8	Reggie Smith	.25
10	Ron Cey	.25
12	Dusty Baker	.35
13	Joe Ferguson	.25
15	Mike Scioscia	.25
15	Davey Lopes	.25
16	Rick Monday	.25
18	Bill Russell	.25
21	Jay Johnstone	.25
26	Don Stanhouse	.25
27	Joe Beckwith	.25
28	Pete Guerrero	.25
30	Derrel Thomas	.25
34	Fernando Valenzuela	1.50
35	Bob Welch	.25
36	Pepe Frias	.25
37	Robert Castillo	.25
38	Dave Goltz	.25
41	Jerry Reuss	.25
43	Rick Sutcliffe	.25
44a	Mickey Hatcher	.25
44b	Ken Landreaux	1.25
46	Burt Hooton	.25
48	Dave Stewart	1.50
51	Terry Forster	.25
57	Steve Howe	.25
---	Coaching Staff (Monty Basgall, Mark Cresse, Tom Lasorda, Manny Mota, Danny Ozark, Ron Perranoski)	.25
---	Team Photo/Checklist	.25

1982 L.A. Dodgers Police

FERNANDO VALENZUELA No. 34
The Los Angeles Police Department
presents the World Champion
Dodgers

Again issued in the same 2-13/16" x 4-1/8" size of the '80 and '81 sets, the 1982 Los Angeles set

commemorates the team's 1981 World Championship. In addition to the 26 cards numbered by uniform for players and manager Tom Lasorda, there are four unnumbered cards which feature the team winning the division, league and World Series titles, plus one of the World Series trophy. The full-color card photos are once again vivid portraits on a clean white card stock. Card backs offer brief biographies and stadium information in addition to a safety tip.

		NM/M
Complete Set (30):		5.00
Common Player:		.25
2	Tom Lasorda	.50
6	Steve Garvey	2.00
7	Steve Yeager	.25
8	Mark Belanger	.25
10	Ron Cey	.25
12	Dusty Baker	.35
14	Mike Scioscia	.25
16	Rick Monday	.25
18	Bill Russell	.25
21	Jay Johnstone	.25
26	Alejandro Pena	.25
28	Pedro Guerrero	.25
30	Derrel Thomas	.25
31	Jorge Orta	.25
34	Fernando Valenzuela	.75
38	Bob Welch	.25
38	Dave Goltz	.25
40	Ron Roenicke	.25
41	Jerry Reuss	.25
44	Ken Landreaux	.25
46	Burt Hooton	.25
48	Dave Stewart	.35
49	Tom Niedenfuer	.25
51	Terry Forster	.25
52	Steve Sax	.35
57	Steve Howe	.25
---	Division Championship	.25
---	League Championship	.25
---	World Series Championship	.25
---	Trophy Card/Checklist	.25

1983 L.A. Dodgers Police

FERNANDO VALENZUELA 34
1983
Dodgers

While these full-color cards remained 2-13/16" x 4-1/8" and card fronts were similar to those of previous years, the card backs are quite different. Card backs are in a horizontal design for the first time, and include a small head portrait photo of the player in the upper left corner. Fairly complete player statistics are included but there is no safety tip. The 30 cards are numbered by uniform number, with an unnumbered coaches card also included. Fronts include the year, team logo, player name and number.

		NM/M
Complete Set (30):		6.00
Common Player:		.25
2	Tom Lasorda	.50
3	Steve Sax	.25
5	Mike Marshall	.25
7	Steve Yeager	.25
12	Dusty Baker	.35
14	Mike Scioscia	.25
16	Rick Monday	.25
18	Greg Brock	.25
18	Bill Russell	.25
20	Candy Maldonado	.25
21	Ricky Wright	.25
22	Mark Bradley	.25
23	Dave Sax	.25
26	Alejandro Pena	.25
27	Joe Beckwith	.25
28	Pedro Guerrero	.25
30	Derrel Thomas	.25
34	Fernando Valenzuela	.75
35	Bob Welch	.25
38	Pat Zachry	.25
40	Ron Roenicke	.25
41	Jerry Reuss	.25
43	Jose Morales	.25
44	Ken Landreaux	.25

46	Burt Hooton	.25
47	Larry White	.25
48	Dave Stewart	.35
57	Tom Niedenfuer	.25
57	Steve Howe	.25
---	Coaches Card (Joe Amalfitano, Monty Basgall, Mark Cresse, Manny Mota, Ron Perranoski)	.25

1984 L.A. Dodgers Fire Safety

Unlike the California Angels and San Diego Padres sets issued in conjunction with the Forestry Service in 1984, the Los Angeles Dodgers set contains only three players, pictured on much larger 5" x 7" cards. Each player is pictured with Smokey in a forest scene on the full-color fronts. Backs of the unnumbered cards have brief biographical information and lifetime statistics. The cards were distributed at a Dodgers home game.

		NM/M
Complete Set (4):		7.00
Common Player:		2.50
(1)	Ken Landreaux	2.50
(2)	Tom Niedenfuer	2.50
(3)	Steve Sax	2.50
(4)	Smokey Bear	.50

1984 L.A. Dodgers Police

Dodgers
MIKE MARSHALL 1984 5

This was the fifth yearly effort of the Dodgers and the Los Angeles Police Department. There are 30 cards in the set, which remains 2-13/16" x 4-1/8". Card fronts are designed somewhat differently than previous years, with more posed photos, bolder player names and numbers and a different team logo. Card backs again feature a small portrait photo in the upper left corner, along with brief biographical information and an anti-drug tip. Card backs are in Dodger blue. Cards are numbered by uniform number, with an unnumbered coaches card also included.

		NM/M
Complete Set (30):		4.00
Common Player:		.25
2	Tom Lasorda	.50
3	Steve Sax	.25
5	Mike Marshall	.25
7	Steve Yeager	.25
9	Greg Brock	.25
10	Dave Anderson	.25
14	Mike Scioscia	.25
16	Rick Monday	.25
17	Rafael Landestoy	.25
18	Bill Russell	.25
20	Candy Maldonado	.25
21	Bob Bailor	.25
25	German Rivera	.25
26	Alejandro Pena	.25
27	Carlos Diaz	.25
28	Pedro Guerrero	.25
31	Jack Fimple	.25
34	Fernando Valenzuela	.75
35	Bob Welch	.25

38	Pat Zachry	.25
40	Rick Honeycutt	.25
41	Jerry Reuss	.25
43	Jose Morales	.25
44	Ken Landreaux	.25
44	Terry Whitfield	.25
46	Burt Hooton	.25
49	Tom Niedenfuer	.25
49	Orel Hershiser	3.00
56	Richard Rodas	.25
---	Coaches Card (Joe Amalfitano, Monty Basgall, Mark Cresse, Manny Mota, Ron Perranoski)	.25

1986 L.A. Dodgers Police

Dodgers 1986
MIKE MARSHALL 5

After skipping the 1985 season, the Los Angeles Dodgers once again issued baseball cards related to police safety. The 1986 set features 30 full-color glossy cards measuring 2-1/4" x 4-1/8", numbered according to player uniforms. The backs feature brief player data and a safety tip from the Los Angeles Police Department. The sets were given away May 18 during Baseball Card Day at Dodger Stadium.

		NM/M
Complete Set (30):		4.00
Common Player:		.20
2	Tom Lasorda	.40
3	Steve Sax	.20
5	Mike Marshall	.20
8	Greg Brock	.20
10	Dave Anderson	.20
12	Bill Madlock	.20
14	Mike Scioscia	.20
17	Len Matuszek	.20
18	Bill Russell	.20
22	Franklin Stubbs	.20
23	Enos Cabell	.20
26	Mariano Duncan	.20
26	Alejandro Pena	.20
27	Carlos Diaz	.20
28	Pedro Guerrero	.20
29	Alex Trevino	.20
31	Ed Vande Berg	.20
34	Fernando Valenzuela	.50
35	Bob Welch	.20
40	Rick Honeycutt	.20
41	Jerry Reuss	.20
44	Ken Howell	.20
44	Ken Landreaux	.20
45	Terry Whitfield	.20
48	Dennis Powell	.20
49	Tom Niedenfuer	.20
51	Reggie Williams	.20
55	Orel Hershiser	.50
---	Team Photo/Checklist	.20
---	Coaching Staff (Joe Amalfitano, Monty Basgall, Mark Cresse, Ben Hines, Don McMahon, Manny Mota, Ron Perranoski)	.20

1987 L.A. Dodgers All-Stars Fire Safety

25 Years of Dodger All-Stars

This fire safety set features "25 Years of Dodger All-Stars." The cards, which measure 2-1/2" x 3-3/4",

were given out to fans 14 and younger at the September 18 game at Dodgers Stadium. Fronts have full-color photos set in the shape of Dodger Stadium and have attractive silver borders. Backs carry the player's All-Star Game record plus a fire prevention message. Many of the photos used in the set were from team-issued picture packs sold by the Dodgers in the past.

		NM/M
Complete Set (40):		7.50
Common Player:		.25
(1)	Walt Alston	.45
(2)	Dusty Baker	.30
(3)	Jim Brewer	.25
(4)	Ron Cey	.25
(5)	Tommy Davis	.25
(6)	Willie Davis	.25
(7)	Don Drysdale	2.00
(8)	Steve Garvey	1.50
(9)	Bill Grabarkewitz	.25
(10)	Pedro Guerrero	.25
(11)	Tom Haller	.25
(12)	Orel Hershiser	.45
(13)	Burt Hooton	.25
(14)	Steve Howe	.25
(15)	Tommy John	.30
(16)	Sandy Koufax	5.00
(17)	Tom Lasorda	.45
(18)	Jim Lefebvre	.25
(19)	Davey Lopes	.25
(20)	Mike Marshall/Outfielder	.25
(21)	Mike Marshall/Pitcher	.25
(22)	Andy Messersmith	.25
(23)	Rick Monday	.25
(24)	Manny Mota	.25
(25)	Claude Osteen	.25
(26)	Johnny Podres	.30
(27)	Phil Regan	.25
(28)	Jerry Reuss	.25
(29)	Rick Rhoden	.25
(30)	John Roseboro	.25
(31)	Bill Russell	.25
(32)	Steve Sax	.25
(33)	Bill Singer	.25
(34)	Reggie Smith	.25
(35)	Don Sutton	1.00
(36)	Fernando Valenzuela	.50
(37)	Bob Welch	.25
(38)	Maury Wills	.45
(39)	Jim Wynn	.25
(40)	Logo Card/Checklist	.10

Police

JOSE GONZALEZ 47

Producing a police set for the seventh time in eight years, the 1987 edition contains 30 cards which measure 2-13/16" x 4-1/8". The set includes a special Dodger Stadium 25th Anniversary card. The card fronts contain a full-color photo plus the Dodger Stadium 25th Anniversary logo. The photos are a mix of action and posed shots. The backs contain personal player data plus a police safety tip. The cards were given out April 24th at Dodger Stadium and were distributed by the Los Angeles police department at a rate of two cards per week.

		NM/M
Complete Set (30):		4.00
Common Player:		.20
2	Tom Lasorda	.50
3	Steve Sax	.25
5	Mike Marshall	.25
10	Dave Anderson	.25
12	Bill Madlock	.25
14	Mike Scioscia	.25
15	Gilberto Reyes	.25
17	Len Matuszek	.25
21	Reggie Williams	.25
22	Franklin Stubbs	.25
23	Tim Leary	.25
25	Mariano Duncan	.25
26	Alejandro Pena	.25
27	Pedro Guerrero	.25
29	Alex Trevino	.25
33	Jeff Hamilton	.25
34	Fernando Valenzuela	.50

35	Bob Welch	.25
36	Matt Young	.25
40	Rick Honeycutt	.25
41	Jerry Reuss	.25
43	Ken Howell	.25
44	Ken Landreaux	.25
46	Ralph Bryant	.25
47	Jose Gonzalez	.25
49	Tom Niedenfuer	.25
51	Brian Holton	.25
55	Orel Hershiser	.60
---	Coaching Staff	
	(Joe Amalfitano, Mark Cresse,	
	Tom Lasorda, Don McMahon,	
	Manny Mota, Ron Perranoski,	
	Bill Russell)	.25
---	Dodger Stadium/Checklist	.25

1988 L.A. Dodgers Fire Safety

Record-breaking Dodgers from the past three decades are featured on this perforated sheet. Individual cards measure 2-1/2" x 4" and are printed on a light blue background in a design similar to the previous year's All-Star set. Black-and-white card backs contain the player name, a summary of the player's record-breaking performance and a reproduction of one of a number of Smokey Bear fire prevention posters printed during the 1950s-1980s. The sheets were distributed to fans in Dodger Stadium.

		NM/M
	Complete Set, Foldout:	9.00
	Complete Set, Singles (32):	7.50
	Common Player:	.25
1	Walter Alston	.30
2	John Roseboro	.25
3	Frank Howard	.30
4	Sandy Koufax	5.00
5	Manny Mota	.25
6	Record Pitchers	
	(Sandy Koufax, Jerry Reuss,	
	Bill Singer)	.35
7	Maury Wills	.30
8	Tommy Davis	.25
9	Phil Regan	.25
10	Wes Parker	.25
11	Don Drysdale	1.50
12	Willie Davis	.25
13	Bill Russell	.25
14	Jim Brewer	.25
15	Record Fielders (Ron Cey,	
	Steve Garvey, Davey Lopes,	
	Bill Russell)	.25
16	Mike Marshall/Pitcher	.25
17	Steve Garvey	.75
18	Davey Lopes	.25
19	Burt Hooton	.25
20	Jim Wynn	.25
21	Record Hitters (Dusty Baker,	
	Ron Cey, Steve Garvey,	
	Reggie Smith)	.25
22	Dusty Baker	.30
23	Tom Lasorda	.25
24	Fernando Valenzuela	.50
25	Steve Sax	.25
26	Dodger Stadium	.25
27	Ron Cey	.25
28	Pedro Guerrero	.25
29	Mike Marshall/Outfielder	.25
30	Don Sutton	.75
---	Logo Card/Checklist	.10
---	Smokey Bear	.10

Police

The Los Angeles Police Department sponsored this 30-card set (2-3/4" x 4-1/8") for use in a local crime prevention promotion. The sets include an unnumbered manager/coaches photo and three double-photo cards. The double cards feature posed closeups; the rest are action photos. The card fronts have white borders, with the team logo lower right and a bold black player

DON SUTTON 20

name lower left. Card backs are black and white with a small close-up photo of the player, followed by personal and career info, a crime prevention tip and a LAPD badge logo. Card numbers refer to players' uniform numbers (the double-photo cards carry two numbers on both front and back).

		NM/M
	Complete Set (30):	6.00
	Common Player:	.15
2	Tom Lasorda	.30
3	Steve Sax	.15
7	Mike Marshall	.15
9	Alfredo Griffin	.15
10	Dave Anderson	.15
12	Danny Heep	.15
14	Mike Scioscia	.15
17/21	Tito Landrum,	
	Len Matuszek	.15
20	Don Sutton	.60
22	Franklin Stubbs	.15
23	Kirk Gibson	.40
25	Mariano Duncan	.15
26	Alejandro Pena	.15
27/52	Tim Crews,	
	Mike Sharperson	.25
28	Pedro Guerrero	.15
29	Alex Trevino	.15
31	John Shelby	.15
33	Jeff Hamilton	.15
34	Fernando Valenzuela	.50
37	Mike Davis	.15
41	Brad Havens	.15
43	Ken Howell	.15
47	Jesse Orosco	.15
49/57	Tim Belcher,	
	Shawn Hillegas	.15
50	Jay Howell	.15
51	Brian Holton	.15
54	Tim Leary	.15
55	Orel Hershiser	.40
---	Manager/Coaches	
	(Joe Amalfitano, Steve Boros,	
	Mark Cresse, Joe Ferguson,	
	Tom Lasorda, Manny Mota,	
	Ron Perranoski,	
	Bill Russell)	.15

1989 L.A. Dodgers Greats Fire Safety

The largest baseball card set ever issued in conjunction with the U.S. Forest Service's Smokey the Bear fire prevention campaign was this 104-card issue featuring great players of the Brooklyn and L.A. Dodgers. Issued on perforated sheets, individual cards measure 2-1/2" x 3-1/2". White-bordered fronts have a sepia-toned photo of the player, with Dodger blue rules on the top and sides. Beneath the photo is a baseball-and-banner logo, "A Century of Dodger Greats." The player's name is beneath the ball with Smokey at left and the team logo at right. Backs

are printed in blue, feature career stats and highlights and include a Smokey fire safety cartoon.

		NM/M
	Complete Set (104):	20.00
	Common Player:	.10
1	Tommy Lasorda,	
	Walter Alston,	
	Burt Shotton	.50
3	David Bancroft	.10
3	Dan Brouthers	.10
4	Roy Campanella	2.00
5	Max Carey	.10
6	Hazen "Kiki" Cuyler	.10
7	Don Drysdale	1.00
8	Burleigh Grimes	.10
9	Billy Herman	.10
10	Waite Hoyt	.10
11	Hughie Jennings	.10
12	Willie Keeler	.10
13	Joseph Kelley	.10
14	George Kelly	.10
15	Sandy Koufax	3.00
16	Heinie Manush	.10
17	Juan Marichal	.75
18	Walter Maranville	.10
19	Rube Marquard	.10
20	Thomas McCarthy	.10
21	Joseph McGinnity	.10
22	Joe Medwick	.10
23	Pee Wee Reese	2.00
24	Frank Robinson	1.00
25	Jackie Robinson	3.50
26	Babe Ruth	4.00
27	Duke Snider	2.00
28	Casey Stengel	.10
29	Dazzy Vance	.10
30	Arky Vaughan	.10
31	Mike Scioscia	.10
32	Lloyd Waner, Paul Waner	.10
33	John Monte Ward	.10
34	Zack Wheat	.10
35	Hoyt Wilhelm	.10
36	Hack Wilson	.10
37	Tony Cuccinello	.10
38	Al Lopez	.10
39	Leo Durocher	.25
40	Cookie Lavagetto	.10
41	Babe Phelps	.10
42	Dolf Camilli	.10
43	Whit Wyatt	.10
44	Mickey Owen	.10
45	Van Mungo	.10
46	Pete Coscarart	.10
47	Pete Reiser	.10
48	Augie Galan	.10
49	Dixie Walker	.10
50	Kirby Higbe	.10
51	Ralph Branca	.10
52	Bruce Edwards	.10
53	Eddie Stanky	.10
54	Gil Hodges	1.50
55	Don Newcombe	.50
56	Preacher Roe	.25
57	Willie Randolph	.50
58	Carl Furillo	.50
59	Charles Dressen	.10
60	Carl Erskine	.25
61	Clem Labine	.15
62	Gino Cimoli	.10
63	Johnny Podres	.25
64	Johnny Roseboro	.15
65	Wally Moon	.10
66	Charlie Neal	.10
67	Norm Larker	.10
68	Stan Williams	.10
69	Maury Wills	.20
70	Tommy Davis	.15
71	Jim Lefebvre	.10
72	Phil Regan	.10
73	Claude Osteen	.10
74	Tom Haller	.10
75	Bill Singer	.10
76	Bill Grabarkewitz	.10
77	Willie Davis	.15
78	Don Sutton	.50
79	Jim Brewer	.10
80	Manny Mota	.10
81	Bill Russell	.10
82	Ron Cey	.10
83	Steve Garvey	.50
84	Mike G. Marshall	.10
85	Andy Messersmith	.10
86	Jimmy Wynn	.10
87	Rick Rhoden	.10
88	Reggie Smith	.15
89	Jay Howell	.10
90	Rick Monday	.15
91	Tommy John	.15
92	Bob Welch	.10
93	Dusty Baker	.20
94	Pedro Guerrero	.10
95	Burt Hooton	.10
96	Davey Lopes	.10
97	Fernando Valenzuela	.20
98	Steve Howe	.10
99	Steve Sax	.10
100	Orel Hershiser	.40
101	Mike A. Marshall	.10
102	Wilbert Robinson	.10
103	Fred Lindstrom	.10
104	Ernie Lombardi	.10

Police

MIKE SCIOSCIA 14

The Los Angeles Dodgers and the L.A. Police Department teamed up in 1989 to produce a 30-card police set. The cards, which measure 4-1/4" x 2-5/8", feature color action photos with the player's name and uniform number below. The Dodgers logo and "1989" appear in the upper left. The backs include player information plus a safety message.

		NM/M
	Complete Set (30):	3.00
	Common Player:	.15
2	Tom Lasorda	.30
3	Jeff Hamilton	.15
7	Mike Marshall	.15
9	Alfredo Griffin	.15
10	Dave Anderson	.15
12	Willie Randolph	.15
14	Mike Scioscia	.15
17	Rick Dempsey	.15
20	Mike Davis	.15
21	Tracy Woodson	.15
22	Franklin Stubbs	.15
23	Kirk Gibson	.30
25	Mariano Duncan	.15
26	Alejandro Pena	.15
27	Mike Sharperson	.15
29	Ricky Horton	.15
30	John Tudor	.15
31	John Shelby	.15
33	Eddie Murray	2.00
34	Fernando Valenzuela	.35
36	Mike Morgan	.15
48	Ramon Martinez	.35
49	Tim Belcher	.15
50	Jay Howell	.15
52	Tim Crews	.15
54	Tim Leary	.15
55	Orel Hershiser	.35
57	Ray Searage	.15
---	Dodger Coaches	
	(Joe Amalfitano, Mark Cresse,	
	Joe Ferguson, Ben Hines,	
	Tommy Lasorda,	
	Manny Mota, Ron Perranoski,	
	Bill Russell)	.15

1990 L.A. Dodgers Police

CENTENNIAL CELEBRATION

HUBIE BROOKS 21

This set honors the centennial celebration of the Los Angeles Dodgers. A special 100 Anniversary logo appears on the card fronts. The cards measure 2-3/4" x 4-1/4" and feature full-color photos. The card backs are printed horizontally and contain a special safety tip or anti-drug message along with player information. The L.A.P.D. logo is featured on the bottom of the card back.

		NM/M
	Complete Set (30):	3.00
	Common Player:	.15
2	Tommy Lasorda	.30
3	Jeff Hamilton	.15
9	Alfredo Griffin	.15
10	Mickey Hatcher	.15
11	Juan Samuel	.15
12	Willie Randolph	.15
14	Mike Scioscia	.15

15	Chris Gwynn	.15
17	Rick Dempsey	.15
21	Hubie Brooks	.15
22	Franklin Stubbs	.15
23	Kirk Gibson	.25
27	Mike Sharperson	.15
28	Kal Daniels	.15
29	Lenny Harris	.15
31	John Shelby	.15
33	Eddie Murray	2.00
34	Fernando Valenzuela	.40
35	Jim Gott	.15
36	Mike Morgan	.15
38	Jose Gonzalez	.15
46	Mike Hartley	.15
48	Ramon Martinez	.15
49	Tim Belcher	.15
50	Jay Howell	.15
52	Tim Crews	.15
55	Orel Hershiser	.25
57	John Wetteland	.15
59	Ray Searage	.15
---	Dodgers Coaches	
	(Joe Amalfitano, Mark Cresse,	
	Joe Ferguson, Ben Hines,	
	Tommy Lasorda,	
	Manny Mota, Ron Perranoski,	
	Bill Russell)	.15

1991 L.A. Dodgers Police

EDDIE MURRAY 33

One of the longest-running police/fire safety sets continued in 1991 with this 30-card set. Players are featured in color action photos set in a tombstone shape against a white background. The date is in a banner at top with the player name, team logo and uniform number at bottom. All typography is printed in Dodger blue. Backs are printed in black-and-white and include biographical data, an anti-drug message and an LAPD badge. Cards measure 2-13/16" x 4-1/8".

		NM/M
	Complete Set (30):	4.00
	Common Player:	.15
3	Jeff Hamilton	.15
7	Stan Javier	.15
9	Alfredo Griffin	.15
10	Juan Samuel	.15
12	Gary Carter	1.50
14	Mike Scioscia	.15
15	Chris Gwynn	.15
17	Bob Ojeda	.15
22	Brett Butler	.15
25	Dennis Cook	.15
27	Mike Sharperson	.15
28	Kal Daniels	.15
29	Lenny Harris	.15
30	Jose Offerman	.15
31	Jim Neidlinger	.15
33	Eddie Murray	1.50
35	Jim Gott	.15
36	Mike Morgan	.15
38	Jose Gonzalez	.15
40	Barry Lyons	.15
44	Darryl Strawberry	.45
46	Kevin Gross	.15
48	Mike Hartley	.15
48	Ramon Martinez	.15
49	Tim Belcher	.15
50	Jay Howell	.15
52	Tim Crews	.15
54	John Candelaria	.15
55	Orel Hershiser	.35
---	Dodgers Coaches (Ben Hines,	
	Ron Perranoski, Mark Cresse,	
	Manny Mota,	
	Tommy Lasorda,	
	Joe Amalfitano,	
	Joe Ferguson, Bill Russell)	.15

1992 L.A. Dodgers Police

The 1992 Dodgers Police set consists of 30 cards numbered to correspond to the player's uniform number. The set includes a card of manager Tommy Lasorda and Dodgers coaches. They were given out at promotional dates at Dodger Stadium.

		NM/M
	Complete Set (30):	4.00

ERIC KARROS

	Common Player:	.25
2	Tommy Lasorda	.35
3	Jeff Hamilton	.25
7	Stan Javier	.25
10	Juan Samuel	.25
14	Mike Scioscia	.25
15	Dave Hansen	.25
17	Bob Ojeda	.25
22	Mitch Webster	.25
22	Brett Butler	.25
23	Eric Karros	.50
27	Mike Sharperson	.25
28	Kal Daniels	.25
29	Lenny Harris	.25
30	Jose Offerman	.25
31	Roger McDowell	.25
33	Eric Davis	.25
35	Jim Gott	.25
36	Todd Benzinger	.25
38	Steve Wilson	.25
41	Carlos Hernandez	.25
44	Darryl Strawberry	.35
46	Kevin Gross	.25
48	Ramon Martinez	.25
49	Tom Candiotti	.25
50	Jay Howell	.25
52	Tim Crews	.25
54	John Candelaria	.25
55	Orel Hershiser	.40
57	Kip Gross	.25
---	Coaches (Joe Amalfitano,	
	Mark Cresse, Joe Ferguson,	
	Ben Hines, Tommy Lasorda,	
	Manny Mota, Ron Perranoski,	
	Ron Roenicke)	.25

1993 L.A. Dodgers Police

LANCE PARRISH

The 1993 Los Angeles Dodgers Police Set consisted of 29 cards, including cards of manager Tommy Lasorda and his coaches. The fronts of the cards have a photo surrounded by a blue border, with the Dodgers logo and the player's name on the bottom. The set is not numbered, but the player's uniform number does appear on the front of the cards.

		NM/M
	Complete Set (29):	6.00
	Common Player:	.25
2	Tommy Lasorda	.35
3	Jody Reed	.25
5	Dave Hansen	.25
12	Lance Parrish	.25
17	Roger McDowell	.25
20	Mitch Webster	.25
22	Brett Butler	.25
23	Eric Karros	.25
25	Tim Wallach	.25
26	Henry Rodriguez	.25
27	Mike Sharperson	.25
29	Cory Snyder	.25
29	Lenny Harris	.25
30	Jose Offerman	.25
31	Mike Piazza	3.00
33	Eric Davis	.25
35	Jim Gott	.25
38	Todd Worrell	.25
41	Carlos Hernandez	.25
45	Pedro Martinez	2.00
46	Kevin Gross	.25
47	Tom Goodwin	.25
48	Ramon Martinez	.25
49	Tom Candiotti	.25
50	Steve Wilson	.25
55	Orel Hershiser	.45

56	Pedro Astacio	.25
57	Kip Gross	.25
---	Coaches (Joe Amalfitano, Mark Cresse, Joe Ferguson, Ben Hines, Tommy Lasorda, Manny Mota, Ron Perranoski, Ron Roenicke)	.25

1994 L.A. Dodgers Police

This 30-card set was distributed to all fans attending the Dodgers May 27 home game. Cards were produced in the form of a perforated sheet. Fronts have mostly game-action photos surrounded by a Dodger-blue border. The player's uniform number is in red in a baseball in the upper-left corner. At bottom is the team logo and the player's name in black on a yellow strip. Backs are in black on white, have a few career and biographical notes and an anti-drug message from the L.A.P.D. and the D.A.R.E. program. When removed from the sheet, cards measure the standard 2-1/2" x 3-1/2". They are checklisted here by uniform number.

		NM/M
Uncut Sheet:		6.00
Complete Set (30):		5.00
Common Player:		.25
2	Tommy Lasorda	.35
5	Dave Hansen	.25
7	Billy Ashley	.25
10	Chris Gwynn	.25
12	Jeff Treadway	.25
14	Delino DeShields	.25
15	Tom Prince	.25
17	Roger McDowell	.25
20	Mitch Webster	.25
21	Rafael Bournigal	.25
22	Brett Butler	.25
23	Eric Karros	.25
26	Carlos Hernandez	.25
28	Cory Snyder	.25
29	Tim Wallach	.25
30	Jose Offerman	.25
31	Mike Piazza	2.50
35	Jim Gott	.25
37	Darren Dreifort	.25
38	Todd Worrell	.25
40	Henry Rodriguez	.25
43	Raul Mondesi	.50
46	Kevin Gross	.25
47	Garey Wayne	.25
48	Ramon Martinez	.25
49	Tom Candiotti	.25
55	Orel Hershiser	.35
56	Pedro Astacio	.75
61	Chan Ho Park	.75
---	Coaches (Mark Cresse, Manny Mota, Bill Russell, Reggie Smith, Joe Ferguson, Ron Perranoski, Tommy Lasorda, Joe Amalfitano)	.25

1995 L.A. Dodgers Limited Edition

This special high-tech set of Brooklyn/Los Angeles Dodgers rookie of the year winners between 1947-94 was given to Dodger season ticket purchasers prior to the strike-shortened 1995 baseball season. Produced in a technique similar to Topps Finest, the cards have on front metallic backgrounds in red, green, blue or purple. A color player action photo is featured. Faux granite strips at bottom have the player's name and year of his ROY award in gold. Backs have a color portrait photo in a gold frame with career stats and highlights and a few personal details. The primary front background color is repeated on the back. A header card printed in blue on white linen-texture paper accompanies the set.

		NM/M
Complete Set (14):		50.00
Common Player:		2.00
1	Jackie Robinson	15.00
2	Don Newcombe	4.00
3	Joe Black	4.00
4	Jim Gilliam	4.00
5	Frank Howard	4.00
6	Jim Lefebvre	2.00
7	Ted Sizemore	2.00
8	Rick Sutcliffe	3.00
9	Steve Howe	3.00
10	Fernando Valenzuela	5.00
11	Steve Sax	3.00
12	Eric Karros	3.00
13	Mike Piazza	15.00
14	Raul Mondesi	3.00
---	Header Card	.10

1995 L.A. Dodgers Police

Action photos of the L.A. Dodgers are featured on this 30-card safety set which was given away to some 40,000 fans attending an early-season game. The set was produced as a perforated sheet measuring 14-13/16" x 17-1/2", with individual cards measuring 2-1/2" x 3-1/2". Fronts feature a Dodger-blue border with the player name in black in a yellow stripe at bottom. The player's uniform number is in red in a baseball in the upper-right. Backs are in black-and-white and have a few player biographical details along with an anti-drug safety message and the logos of the LAPD and D.A.R.E.

		NM/M
Uncut Sheet:		6.00
Complete Set (30):		6.00
Common Player:		.25
2	Tommy Lasorda	.35
3	Eddie Pye	.25
5	Dave Hansen	.25
7	Billy Ashley	.25
12	Jeff Treadway	.25
14	Delino DeShields	.25
16	Hideo Nomo	2.00
21	Rafael Bournigal	.25
23	Eric Karros	.25
25	Ron Coomer	.25
26	Carlos Hernandez	.25
28	Todd Hollandsworth	.25
29	Tim Wallach	.25
30	Jose Offerman	.25
31	Mike Piazza	2.00
38	Todd Worrell	.25
40	Henry Rodriguez	.25
43	Raul Mondesi	.35
45	Al Osuna	.25
48	Ramon Martinez	.25
49	Tom Candiotti	.25
50	Antonio Osuna	.25
52	Greg Hansell	.25
54	Omar Daal	.25
57	Rudy Seanez	.25
61	Ismael Valdes	.25
66	Todd Williams	.25
---	Coaches (Mark Cresse, Manny Mota, Bill Russell, Reggie Smith, Tommy Lasorda, Joe Amalfitano, Dave Wallace, Ralph Avila)	.25

1996 L.A. Dodgers Police

For the 16th time in 17 years (they skipped 1985), the Dodgers issued a safety set to fans attending the April 11 game. As in recent years, the set was issued in the form of a perforated 30-card sheet. Each card measures just under 2-1/2" wide and is 3-1/2" tall; sheet dimensions are 14-7/8" x 17-1/2". Game-action photos are bordered in Dodger blue with the uniform number in red at upper-left. Backs are in black-and-white with a few vital stats and an anti-drug abuse, anti-gang message from D.A.R.E.

		NM/M
Uncut Sheet:		6.50
Complete Set (30):		6.00
Common Player:		.10
2	Tommy Lasorda	.25
3	Chad Fonville	.10
5	Dave Hansen	.10
7	Greg Gagne	.10
8	Karim Garcia	.25
13	Antonio Osuna	.10
14	Delino DeShields	.10
16	Hideo Nomo	2.00
20	Mike Blowers	.10
21	Billy Ashley	.10
22	Brett Butler	.10
23	Eric Karros	.10
25	Mike Busch	.10
26	Carlos Hernandez	.10
27	Roger Cedeno	.10
28	Todd Hollandsworth	.10
29	Milt Thompson	.10
31	Mike Piazza	2.00
33	Garey Ingram	.10
38	Todd Worrell	.10
41	John Cummings	.10
43	Raul Mondesi	.10
44	Mark Guthrie	.10
48	Ramon Martinez	.10
49	Tom Candiotti	.10
51	Joey Eischen	.10
52	Darren Hall	.10
56	Pedro Astacio	.10
59	Ismael Valdes	.10
---	Dodgers Coaches (Joe Amalfitano, Mark Cresse, Tommy Lasorda, Manny Mota, Bill Russell, Reggie Smith, Dave Wallace)	.10

Rookies of the Year

This card was inserted into a die-cut space in the 1996 holiday greetings card sent out by the L.A. Dodgers. In 2-1/2" x 3-1/2 format it features portrait photos of the 1992-96 National League Rookies of the Year - all Dodgers. Overall background of the front is green. Back has information on previous Dodgers ROYs and the rookie season stats of the 1992-96 winners.

	NM/M
Dodger Rookies of the Year: (Eric Karros/1992, Mike Piazza/1993, Raul Mondesi/1994, Hideo Nomo/1995, Todd Hollandsworth/1996)	15.00

1997 L.A. Dodgers Fan Appreciation Days

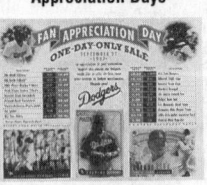

Fans attending the September 21 game were given this 11" x 8-1/2" sheet announcing a one-day sale of Dodgers souvenirs. At bottom are three differently styled cards of some of the team's most popular players. All are in color and standard 2-1/2" x 3-1/2" size, perforated for easy separation from the sheet. Card backs are in black-and-white with drawings of the players in the upper-left, biographical data and trivia. Cards are numbered by uniform number.

		NM/M
Complete Sheet:		6.00
Complete Set, Singles (3):		6.00
16	Hideo Nomo	3.00
31	Mike Piazza	4.00
61	Chan Ho Park	1.50

Police

Action photos of the 1997 Dodgers are featured on this set distributed at the April 23 game to nearly 30,500 fans. The 14-3/4" x 17-1/2" sheet has 30 cards, perforated on two, three or four sides, depending on position on the sheet. Individual cards measure 2-1/2" x 3-1/2". A central photo is surrounded with a white border. A ball with the player's uniform number in red is at top-left. At bottom is the team logo and player name. Backs are in black-and-white with biographical notes, an anti-drug message from each player and the logos of LAPD and DARE. Cards are checklisted here by uniform number.

		NM/M
Uncut Sheet:		7.00
Complete Set (30):		6.00
Common Player:		.20
3	Chad Fonville	.20
5	Chip Hale	.20
7	Greg Gagne	.20
12	Karim Garcia	.20
13	Anthony Osuna	.20
15	Tom Prince	.20
16	Hideo Nomo	1.50
18	Bill Russell	.20
21	Billy Ashley	.20
22	Brett Butler	.20
23	Eric Karros	.20
25	Juan Castro	.20
27	Todd Zeile	.20
28	Todd Hollandsworth	.20
30	Wilton Guerrero	.20
31	Mike Piazza	2.50
35	Wayne Kirby	.20
36	Scott Radinsky	.20
37	Darren Dreifort	.20
38	Todd Worrell	.20
43	Raul Mondesi	.20
44	Mark Guthrie	.20
46	Nelson Liriano	.20
48	Ramon Martinez	.20
52	Tom Candiotti	.20
52	Darren Hall	.20
56	Pedro Astacio	.20
59	Ismael Valdes	.20
61	Chan Ho Park	.20
---	Coaches (Mark Cresse, Manny Mota, Mike Scioscia, Reggie Smith, Dave Wallace)	.20

1998 L.A. Dodgers Fan Appreciation Days

Fans attending the Dodgers' final homestand were given this 11" x 8-1/2" sheet announcing a sale of Dodgers souvenirs. At bottom are three cards of some of the team's most popular players. All are in color and standard 2-1/2" x 3-1/2" size, perforated for easy separation from the sheet. Card backs are in black-and-white with personal data, a facsimile autograph and trivia. Cards are numbered by uniform number.

		NM/M
Complete Sheet:		6.00
Complete Set (3):		4.00
Common Player:		2.00
10	Gary Sheffield	2.50
23	Eric Karros	2.00
43	Raul Mondesi	2.00

Police

Repeating the format used in recent years, a 30-card perforated sheet, the Dodgers issued their annual D.A.R.E. drug-awareness set in April. Individual cards are the standard 2-1/2" x 3-1/2" on the 15" x 17-1/2" sheet. Fronts have action photos with blue borders. A baseball at top-left has the player's uniform number, by which the set is checklisted here.

		NM/M
Uncut Sheet:		7.00
Complete Set (30):		6.00
Common Player:		.25
7	Paul Konerko	.50
12	Jose Vizcaino	.25
12	Mike Devereaux	.25
13	Antonio Osuna	.25
15	Tom Prince	.25
16	Hideo Nomo	2.00
18	Bill Russell	.25
22	Thomas Howard	.25
23	Eric Karros	.25
25	Juan Castro	.25
26	Eric Young	.25
27	Todd Zeile	.25
28	Todd Hollandsworth	.25
30	Wilton Guerrero	.25
31	Mike Piazza	3.00
36	Scott Radinsky	.25
37	Darren Dreifort	.25
40	Matt Luke	.25
41	Tripp Cromer	.25
43	Raul Mondesi	.25
44	Mark Guthrie	.25
45	Roger Cedeno	.25
47	Jim Bruske	.25
47	Trenidad Hubbard	.25
48	Ramon Martinez	.25
49	Frank Lankford	.25
52	Darren Hall	.25
59	Ismael Valdes	.25
61	Chan Ho Park	.25
---	Joe Amalfitano, Mark Cresse, Glenn Gregson, Manny Mota, Mike Scioscia, Reggie Smith	.25

Record Breakers

This set of motion cards was distributed one per month to members of the Dodgers Kids Clubhouse when they attended a game. The 3-1/2" x 2-1/2" cards have a borderless front with an action scene viewed by changing the angle of the card. The team logo appears in an upper corner. Backs repeat the logo and have personal data and details of the record performance. The cards are unnumbered. Distribution of the Nomo and Piazza cards was cut short when those players were traded in mid-season.

		NM/M
Complete Set (5):		17.50
Common Player:		2.00
(1)	Ramon Martinez	2.00
(2)	Raul Mondesi/Action	2.00
(3)	Raul Mondesi/Portrait (Membership card.)	2.00
(4)	Hideo Nomo	6.00
(5)	Mike Piazza	7.50

1999 L.A. Dodgers Concession Stand Cards

During the first five home games of the 1999 season, fans visiting the concession stands at Dodgers Stadium could receive a free player card. Fronts have color action photos on a white background with blue borders. The player's first name is printed at bottom, and a catchword at top. Backs are horizontal in black-and-white with a portrait photo career highlights and personal data, plus team and Dodger Stadium logos.

		NM/M
Complete Set (5):		4.00
Common Player:		1.00
1	Kevin Brown	1.50
2	Chan Ho Park	1.00
3	Ismael Valdes	1.00
4	Carlos Perez	1.00
5	Darren Dreifort	1.00

Fan Appreciation Days

Fans attending the Dodgers' final homestand were given this 11" x 8-1/2" sheet announcing special sales of Dodgers souvenirs. At bottom are three cards of some of the team's most popular players. All are in color and standard 2-1/2" x 3-1/2" size, perforated for easy separation from the sheet. The card fronts are in the style of 1953 Topps while backs are in black-and-white 1951-Bowman format with personal data, and a career summary.

	NM/M
Complete Sheet:	5.00
Complete Set (3):	4.00

1   Adrian Beltre   2.00
2   Kevin Brown   1.00
3   Eric Karros   1.00

Library Card

As part of a promotion to draw youngsters to the library to receive a free baseball bat, these sheets were given away at a promotional game at Dodger Stadium. The 8-1/2" x 4-3/4" sheet has a standard-size card perforated for easy removal. Front has an action photo. On back is another photo overprinted with stats.

		NM/M
(1)	Eric Karros	3.00

Police

PAUL LODUCA

Repeating the format used in recent years, a 30-card perforated sheet, the Dodgers issued their annual D.A.R.E. drug-awareness set in April. Individual cards are the standard 2-1/2" x 3-1/2" on the 15" x 17-1/2" sheet. Fronts have action photos with blue borders. A baseball at top-left has the player's uniform number, by which the set is checklisted here. Backs are in black-and-white with LAPD and D.A.R.E. logos, player data and a safety message.

		NM/M
Uncut Sheet:		7.00
Complete Set (30):		6.00
Common Player:		.25
5	Jose Vizcaino	.25
7	Tripp Cromer	.25
8	Mark Grudzielanek	.25
10	Todd Hundley	.25
10	Gary Sheffield	.75
13	Antonio Osuna	.25
14	Adam Riggs	.25
15	Davey Johnson	.25
17	Paul LoDuca	.75
17	Juan Castro	.25
21	Eric Young	.25
22	Devon White	.25
23	Eric Karros	.25
25	Dave Hansen	.25
27	Kevin Brown	.45
28	Todd Hollandsworth	.25
29	Adrian Beltre	2.00
33	Carlos Perez	.25
37	Darren Dreifort	.25
41	Jeff Shaw	.25
43	Raul Mondesi	.25
46	Rick Wilkins	.25
48	Jacob Brumfield	.25
55	Pedro Borbon	.25
56	Onan Masaoka	.25
59	Ismael Valdes	.25
61	Chan Ho Park	.20
63	Angel Pena	.25
75	Alan Mills	.25
	Coaches (Rick Dempsey, Rick Down, Glenn Hoffman, Charlie Hough, Manny Mota, John Shelby, Jim Tracy)	.25

2000 L.A. Dodgers Fan Appreciation Days

Fans attending late-season Dodgers' games were given this 11" x 8-1/2" sheet announcing special sales of Dodgers souvenirs. At bottom are three cards of some of the team's most popular players. All are in color and standard 2-1/2" x 3-1/2" perforated for easy separation

Shawn Green

from the sheet. Card fronts have portrait and action photos while backs have 1/3 of a color team photo.

		NM/M
Complete Sheet:		5.00
Complete Set (3):		4.00
10	Gary Sheffield	1.00
15	Shawn Green	2.00
23	Eric Karros	1.00

Library Cards

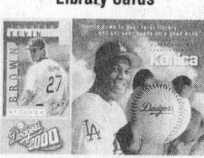

As part of a promotion to draw youngsters to the library to receive a free baseball, this sheet was given away at a promotional game at Dodger Stadium. The 8-1/2" x 4-3/4" sheet has a standard-size card perforated for easy removal. Front has both portrait and action photos. On back is another photo overprinted with stats.

		NM/M
Complete Set (2):		4.00
Common Player:		2.00
(1)	Kevin Brown	2.00
(2)	Gary Sheffield	2.00

Police

SHAWN GREEN

Repeating the format used in recent years, a 30-card 14-7/8" x 17-1/2" perforated sheet, the Dodgers issued their annual D.A.R.E. drug-awareness set in April. Individual cards are the standard 2-1/2" x 3-1/2". Fronts have game-action photos with blue borders. A baseball at top-left has the player's uniform number, by which the set is checklisted here. Backs are in black-and-white with LAPD and D.A.R.E. logos, player data and a safety message.

		NM/M
Uncut Sheet:		7.00
Complete Set (30):		6.00
Common Player:		.25
3	Alex Cora	.25
5	Jose Vizcaino	.25
8	Mark Grudzielanek	.25
10	Todd Hundley	.25
10	Gary Sheffield	.75
13	Antonio Osuna	.25
14	F.P. Santangelo	.25
15	Shawn Green	1.00
16	Paul LoDuca	.75
21	Chad Kreuter	.25
23	Devon White	.25
23	Eric Karros	.25
25	Dave Hansen	.25
27	Kevin Brown	.60
28	Todd Hollandsworth	.25
29	Adrian Beltre	1.00
30	Gregg Olson	.25
33	Carlos Perez	.25
36	Angel Pena	.25
37	Darren Dreifort	.25
40	Onan Masaoka	.25
41	Jeff Shaw	.25
43	Kevin Elster	.25
48	Eric Gagne	.75
51	Terry Adams	.25
55	Orel Hershiser	.50
56	Mike Fetters	.25
61	Chan Ho Park	.25
75	Alan Mills	.25
	Coaches (Rick Down, Glenn Hoffman, Davey Johnson, Manny Mota, Claude Osteen, John Shelby, Jim Tracy)	.25

2001 L.A. Dodgers Fan Appreciation Days

PAUL LODUCA

Fans attending late-season Dodgers' games were given this 8-1/2" x 11" tri-fold sheet announcing special sales of Dodgers souvenirs. At bottom are three cards of some of the team's most popular players. All are in color and standard 2-1/2" x 3-1/2" size, perforated for easy separation from the sheet. Card fronts action photos set on an embossed steel design background. Backs have a color portrait photo along with 2000 and 2001 highlights and stats.

		NM/M
Complete Sheet:		4.00
Complete Set (3):		3.00
1	Paul LoDuca	1.50
2	Chan Ho Park	1.00
3	Gary Sheffield	1.00

2001 L.A. Dodgers Police

ANDY ASHBY

All fans attending the April 29 game at Dodger Stadium received the team's annual police-sponsored drug awareness safety set. The 30-card set was produced in the format of a 14-3/4" x 17-1/2" perforated sheet. Virtually identical in design to previous years' issues, there is no 2001 identifier on the cards. Fronts have game-action photos bordered in blue with the uniform number in a baseball at top-left. Black-and-white backs have some personal data, an anti-drug message and sponsors' logos.

		NM/M
Uncut Sheet:		9.00
Complete Set (30):		6.00
Common Player:		.25
3	Alex Cora	.25
8	Mark Grudzielanek	.25
9	Marquis Grissom	.25
10	Gary Sheffield	.75
13	Jeff Reboulet	.25
15	Shawn Green	1.00
16	Paul LoDuca	.75
18	Tim Bogar	.25
21	Chad Kreuter	.25
23	Eric Karros	.25
25	Dave Hansen	.25
27	Kevin Brown	.60
28	Tom Goodwin	.25
29	Adrian Beltre	1.00
30	Gregg Olson	.25
36	Angel Pena	.25
37	Darren Dreifort	.25
38	Eric Gagne	.50
40	Onan Masaoka	.25
41	Jeff Shaw	.25
43	Andy Ashby	.25
45	Jose Antonio Nunez	.25
46	Hiram Bocachica	.25
47	Bruce Aven	.25
49	Matt Herges	.25
50	Chris Donnels	.25
51	Terry Adams	.25
56	Mike Fetters	.25
61	Chan Ho Park	.25
	Coaches (Travis Barbary, Jack Clark, Jim Colborn, Glenn Hoffman, Jim Lett, Manny Mota, Jim Riggleman, John Shelby, Jim Tracy)	.25

2002 L.A. Dodgers Police

KAZUHISA ISHII

Once again in 2002, at the April 21 game, children 14 and under received the team's annual police-sponsored drug awareness safety set, produced in the format of a 14-7/8" x 17-1/2" perforated sheet. Virtually identical in design to previous years' issues, there is no 2002 identifier on the cards. Fronts have game-action photos bordered in blue with the uniform number in a baseball at top-left. Black-and-white backs have some personal data, an anti-drug message and sponsors' logos.

		NM/M
Uncut Sheet:		10.00
Complete Set (30):		8.00
Common Player:		.25
3	Cesar Izturis	.25
7	Jeff Branson	.25
8	Mark Grudzielanek	.25
9	Marquis Grissom	.25
10	Hideo Nomo	1.50
13	Alex Cora	.25
14	Jeff Reboulet	.25
15	Shawn Green	1.00
16	Paul LoDuca	.75
17	Kazuhisa Ishii	1.50
21	Chad Kreuter	.25
23	Eric Karros	.25
25	Dave Hansen	.25
26	Hiram Bocachica	.25
27	Kevin Brown	.60
29	Adrian Beltre	1.00
30	Dave Roberts	.35
33	Brian Jordan	.25
36	Omar Daal	.25
38	Darren Dreifort	.25
38	Eric Gagne	.60
41	Odalis Perez	.25
43	Andy Ashby	.25
44	Phil Hiatt	.25
46	Terry Mulholland	.25
46	Paul Quantrill	.25
47	Jesse Orosco	.25
47	Giovanni Carrara	.25
74	Mike Kinkade	.35
---	Manager & Coaches (Jack Clark, Jim Colborn, Rob Flippo, Glenn Hoffman, Jim Lett, Manny Mota, Jim Riggleman, John Shelby, Jim Tracy)	.25

2003 L.A. Dodgers Fan Appreciation Days

Fans attending late-season Dodgers' games were given this 8-1/2" x 11" tri-fold sheet announcing special sales of Dodgers souvenirs. At bottom are three cards of some of the team's most popular players. All are in color and standard 2-1/2" x 3-1/2" size, perforated for easy separation from the sheet. Card fronts action photos and player-themed pen-

nants. Black-and-white backs have another photo along with personal data and highlights.

		NM/M
Complete Sheet:		6.00
Complete Set (3):		5.00
10	Hideo Nomo	2.50
16	Paul Lo Duca	1.50
38	Eric Gagne	1.50

Police

MIKE KINKADE

At the April 20 game, children 14 and under received the team's annual police-sponsored drug awareness safety set, produced in the format of a 14-3/4" x 17-3/4" perforated sheet. Virtually identical in design to previous years' issues, there is no 2002 identifier on the cards. Fronts have game-action photos bordered in blue with the uniform number in a baseball at top-left. Black-and-white backs have some personal data, an anti-drug message and sponsors' logos.

		NM/M
Uncut Sheet:		10.00
Complete Set (30):		9.00
Common Player:		.25
3	Cesar Izturis	.25
6	Jolbert Cabrera	.25
8	Mike Kinkade	.35
8	Ron Coomer	.25
10	Todd Hundley	.25
10	Hideo Nomo	1.50
13	Alex Cora	.25
15	Shawn Green	1.00
16	Paul LoDuca	.50
17	Kazuhisa Ishii	.25
26	Wilkin Ruan	.25
27	Kevin Brown	.45
28	Fred McGriff	.25
29	Adrian Beltre	1.00
30	Dave Roberts	.25
33	Brian Jordan	.25
36	Daryle Ward	.25
37	Darren Dreifort	.25
38	Eric Gagne	.60
40	David Ross	.25
41	Chad Hermansen	.25
43	Andy Ashby	.25
44	Paul Shuey	.25
45	Odalis Perez	.25
46	Paul Quantrill	.25
52	Chin-Feng Chen	.75
57	Troy Brohawn	.25
57	Victor Alvarez	.25
59	Guillermo Mota	.25
---	Manager & Coaches (Jack Clark, Jim Colborn, Rob Flippo, Glenn Hoffman, Jim Lett, Manny Mota, Jim Riggleman, John Shelby, Jim Tracy)	.25

2005 L.A./Brooklyn Dodgers Medallion Collection

A set of 21 commemorative medallions was sponsored by the Los Angeles Newspaper Group in this promotion. Coupons found in the newspapers between June 6-29 could be redeemed at convenience stores (along with $2.99) for that

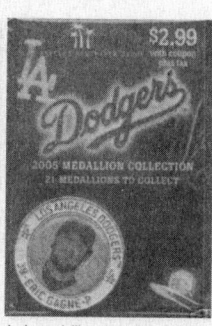

day's medallion. Larger and thicker than a quarter, the 1-3/16" diameter medals are struck in bronze (Brooklyn players) or nickel (current players) and have on their fronts an enameled portrait photo. A team logo dominates the back. A colorful, photo-filled album is available to house the pieces. The medals are listed here alphabetically.

		NM/M
Complete Set (21):		75.00
Common Player:		3.00
Album:		3.00
(1)	Wilson Alvarez	3.00
(2)	Milton Bradley	3.00
(3)	Yhency Brazoban	3.00
(4)	Roy Campanella	6.00
(5)	Hee Seop Choi	3.50
(6)	J.D. Drew	3.50
(7)	Eric Gagne	4.50
(8)	Cesar Izturis	3.00
(9)	Jeff Kent	4.50
(10)	Tommy Lasorda	3.00
(11)	Derek Lowe	3.00
(12)	Don Newcombe	3.00
(13)	Brad Penny	3.00
(14)	Odalis Perez	3.00
(15)	Jason Phillips	3.00
(16)	Jackie Robinson	10.00
(17)	Duke Snider	6.00
(18)	Jose Valentin	3.00
(19)	Jeff Weaver	3.00
(20)	Jayson Werth	3.00
(21)	50th Anniversary 1955 World Champions	3.00

1997 LaSalle Bank Ryne Sandberg

This card was part of a souvenir tribute distributed to more than 30,000 persons attending Ryne Sandberg's final game at Wrigley Field on September 20. A commemorative program and this card marked Ryno's 15 years as a Chicago Cub. The 2-1/2" x 3-1/2" card is printed on heavy, UV-coated cardboard. The front features a borderless color action photo. On the full-color back are portrait and action photos, career highlights and stats through September 14.

	NM/M
Ryne Sandberg	7.50

1985 Leaf-Donruss

In an attempt to share in the Canadian baseball card market, Donruss issued a 264-card version of its regular set to be sold in Canada. Fronts of the 2-1/2" x 3-1/2" cards are virtually identical to the regular '85 Donruss cards of the same players, except that a green stylized leaf has been added to the logo in the upper-left. On back, player biographies have been rewritten to accomodate both English and French versions, and new card numbers have been assigned. The

KENT HRBEK 1B

264 cards in this shortened set concentrate on star-caliber players, as well as those of Canada's two major league teams. A special two-card subset, "Canadian Greats," featured paintings of Dave Stieb and Tim Raines. The Leaf-Donruss cards were widely distributed in the U.S. through hobby dealers.

NM/M
Complete Set (264): 35.00
Common Player: .05
Wax Pack (12): 2.50
Wax Box (36): 75.00

1 Ryne Sandberg/DK 1.25
2 Doug DeCinces/DK .05
3 Rich Dotson/DK .05
4 Bert Blyleven/DK .05
5 Lou Whitaker/DK .05
6 Dan Quisenberry/DK .05
7 Don Mattingly/DK 2.00
8 Carney Lansford/DK .05
9 Frank Tanana/DK .05
10 Willie Upshaw/DK .05
11 Claudell Washington/DK .05
12 Mike Marshall/DK .05
13 Joaquin Andujar/DK .05
14 Cal Ripken, Jr./DK 5.00
15 Jim Rice/DK .25
16 Don Sutton/DK .60
17 Frank Viola/DK .05
18 Alvin Davis/DK .05
19 Mario Soto/DK .05
20 Jose Cruz/DK .05
21 Charlie Lea/DK .05
22 Jesse Orosco/DK .05
23 Juan Samuel/DK .05
24 Tony Pena/DK .05
25 Tony Gwynn/DK 1.25
26 Bob Brenly/DK .05
27 Steve Kiefer/RR .05
28 Joe Morgan .60
29 Luis Leal .05
30 Dan Gladden .05
31 Shane Rawley .05
32 Mark Clear .05
33 Terry Kennedy .05
34 Hal McRae .05
35 Mickey Rivers .05
36 Tom Brunansky .05
37 LaMarr Hoyt .05
38 Orel Hershiser 1.00
39 Chris Bando .05
40 Lee Lacy .05
41 Lance Parrish .05
42 George Foster .05
43 Kevin McReynolds .05
44 Robin Yount .60
45 Craig McMurtry .05
46 Mike Witt .05
47 Gary Redus .05
48 Dennis Rasmussen .05
49 Gary Woods .05
50 Phil Bradley .05
51 Steve Bedrosian .05
52 Duane Walker .05
53 Geoff Zahn .05
54 Dave Stieb .05
55 Pascual Perez .05
56 Mark Langston .25
57 Bob Dernier .05
58 Joe Cowley .05
59 Dan Schatzeder .05
60 Ozzie Smith 1.25
61 Bob Knepper .05
62 Keith Hernandez .05
63 Rick Rhoden .05
64 Alejandro Pena .05
65 Damaso Garcia .05
66 Chili Davis .05
67 Al Oliver .05
68 Alan Wiggins .05
69 Darryl Motley .05
70 Gary Ward .05
71 John Butcher .05
72 Scott McGregor .05
73 Bruce Hurst .05
74 Dwayne Murphy .05
75 Greg Luzinski .05
76 Pat Tabler .05
77 Chet Lemon .05
78 Jim Sundberg .05
79 Wally Backman .05
80 Terry Puhl .05
81 Storm Davis .05
82 Jim Wohlford .05
83 Willie Randolph .05
84 Ron Cey .05
85 Jim Beattie .05
86 Rafael Ramirez .05
87 Cesar Cedeno .05
88 Bobby Grich .05
89 Jason Thompson .05
90 Steve Sax .05
91 Tony Fernandez .15
92 Jeff Leonard .05
93 Von Hayes .05
94 Steve Garvey .30
95 Steve Balboni .05
96 Larry Parrish .05
97 Tim Teufel .05
98 Sammy Stewart .05
99 Roger Clemens 30.00
100 Steve Kemp .05
101 Tom Seaver 1.00
102 Andre Thornton .05
103 Kirk Gibson .05
104 Ted Simmons .05
105 David Palmer .05
106 Roy Lee Jackson .05
107 Kirby Puckett 4.00
108 Charlie Hough .05
109 Mike Boddicker .05
110 Willie Wilson .05
111 Tim Lollar .05
112 Tony Armas .05
113 Steve Carlton .60
114 Gary Lavelle .05
115 Cliff Johnson .05
116 Ray Burris .05
117 Rudy Law .05
118 Mike Scioscia .05
119 Kent Tekulve .05
120 George Vukovich .05
121 Barbaro Garbey .05
122 Mookie Wilson .05
123 Ben Oglivie .05
124 Jerry Mumphrey .05
125 Willie McGee .05
126 Jeff Reardon .05
127 Dave Winfield 1.00
128 Lee Smith .10
129 Ken Phelps .05
130 Rick Camp .05
131 Dave Concepcion .05
132 Rod Carew .60
133 Andre Dawson .25
134 Doyle Alexander .05
135 Miguel Dilone .05
136 Jim Gott .05
137 Eric Show .05
138 Phil Niekro .45
139 Rick Sutcliffe .05
140 Two For The Title
(Don Mattingly,
Dave Winfield) 3.00
141 Ken Oberkfell .05
142 Jack Morris .05
143 Lloyd Moseby .05
144 Pete Rose 2.00
145 Gary Gaetti .05
146 Don Baylor .05
147 Bobby Meacham .05
148 Frank White .05
149 Mark Thurmond .05
150 Dwight Evans .05
151 Al Holland .05
152 Joel Youngblood .05
153 Rance Mulliniks .05
154 Bill Caudill .05
155 Carlton Fisk .60
156 Rick Honeycutt .05
157 John Candelaria .05
158 Alan Trammell .05
159 Darryl Strawberry .05
160 Aurelio Lopez .05
161 Enos Cabell .05
162 Dion James .05
163 Bruce Sutter .75
164 Razor Shines .05
165 Butch Wynegar .05
166 Rich Bordi .05
167 Spike Owen .05
168 Chris Chambliss .05
169 Dave Parker .05
170 Reggie Jackson 1.00
171 Bryn Smith .05
172 Dave Collins .05
173 Dave Engle .05
174 Buddy Bell .05
175 Mike Flanagan .05
176 George Brett 1.50
177 Graig Nettles .05
178 Jerry Koosman .05
179 Wade Boggs 1.25
180 Jody Davis .05
181 Ernie Whitt .05
182 Dave Kingman .05
183 Vance Law .05
184 Fernando Valenzuela .05
185 Bill Madlock .05
186 Brett Butler .05
187 Doug Sisk .05
188 Dan Petry .05
189 Joe Niekro .05
190 Rollie Fingers .45
191 David Green .05
192 Steve Rogers .05
193 Ken Griffey .05
194 Scott Sanderson .05
195 Barry Bonnell .05
196 Bruce Benedict .05
197 Keith Moreland .05
198 Fred Lynn .05
199 Tim Wallach .20
200 Kent Hrbek .05
201 Pete O'Brien .05
202 Bud Black .05
203 Eddie Murray .60
204 Goose Gossage .05
205 Mike Schmidt 1.50
206 Mike Easler .05
207 Jack Clark .05
208 Rickey Henderson 1.00
209 Jesse Barfield .15
210 Ron Kittle .05
211 Pedro Guerrero .05
212 Johnny Ray .05
213 Julio Franco .05
214 Hubie Brooks .05
215 Darrell Evans .05
216 Nolan Ryan 5.00
217 Jim Gantner .05
218 Tim Raines .20
219 Dave Righetti .05
220 Gary Matthews .05
221 Jack Perconte .05
222 Dale Murphy .30
223 Brian Downing .05
224 Mickey Hatcher .05
225 Lonnie Smith .05
226 Jorge Orta .05
227 Milt Wilcox .05
228 John Denny .05
229 Marty Barrett .05
230 Alfredo Griffin .05
231 Harold Baines .05
232 Bill Russell .05
233 Marvell Wynne .05
234 Dwight Gooden .50
235 Willie Hernandez .05
236 Bill Gullickson .05
237 Ron Guidry .05
238 Leon Durham .05
239 Al Cowens .05
240 Bob Horner .05
241 Gary Carter 1.00
242 Glenn Hubbard .05
243 Steve Trout .05
244 Jay Howell .05
245 Terry Francona .05
246 Cecil Cooper .05
247 Larry McWilliams .05
248 George Bell .15
249 Larry Herndon .05
250 Ozzie Virgil .05
251 Dave Stieb
(Canadian Great) .50
252 Tim Raines
(Canadian Great) 2.00
253 Ricky Horton .05
254 Bill Buckner .05
255 Dan Driessen .05
256 Ron Darling .05
257 Doug Flynn .05
258 Darrell Porter .05
259 George Hendrick .05
653 Lou Gehrig Puzzle Card .05
---- Checklist 1-26 DK .05
---- Checklist 27-102 .05
---- Checklist 103-178 .05
---- Checklist 179-259 .05

1986 Leaf

ANDRES GALARRAGA 1B

For its second Canadian card set the Donruss name was removed from the front of the company's 264-card issue, identifying the cards as "Leaf '86." Again concentrating on big-name stars and players from the Expos and Blue Jays, the 264-card set feature a design identical to the 1986 Donruss cards. Backs were altered to allow the publication of career highlights in both English and French, and card numbers were changed. The "Canadian Greats" cards in the 1986 Leaf set, painted portraits rather than photos, were Jesse Barfield and Jeff Reardon. Besides being sold in its intended market in Canada, the set was widely distributed in the U.S. through hobby vendors.

NM/M
Complete Set (264): 12.00
Common Player: .05
Wax Pack: 1.00
Wax Box (36): 20.00

1 Kirk Gibson/DK .05
2 Goose Gossage/DK .05
3 Willie McGee/DK .05
4 George Bell/DK .10
5 Tony Armas/DK .05
6 Chili Davis/DK .05
7 Cecil Cooper/DK .05
8 Mike Boddicker/DK .05
9 Davey Lopes/DK .05
10 Bill Doran/DK .05
11 Bret Saberhagen/DK .05
12 Brett Butler/DK .05
13 Harold Baines/DK .05
14 Mike Davis/DK .05
15 Tony Perez/DK .35
16 Willie Randolph/DK .05
17 Bob Boone/DK .05
18 Orel Hershiser/DK .05
19 Johnny Ray/DK .05
20 Gary Ward/DK .05
21 Rick Mahler/DK .05
22 Phil Bradley/DK .05
23 Jerry Koosman/DK .05
24 Tom Brunansky/DK .05
25 Andre Dawson/DK .35
26 Dwight Gooden/DK .05
27 Andres Galarraga/RR 2.00
28 Fred McGriff/RR 4.00
29 Dave Shipanoff/RR .05
30 Danny Jackson .05
31 Robin Yount .50
32 Mike Fitzgerald .05
33 Lou Whitaker .05
34 Alfredo Griffin .05
35 "Oil Can" Boyd .05
36 Ron Guidry .05
37 Rickey Henderson .75
38 Jack Morris .05
39 Brian Downing .05
40 Mike Marshall .05
41 Tony Gwynn 1.00
42 George Brett 1.25
43 Jim Gantner .05
44 Hubie Brooks .05
45 Tony Fernandez .10
46 Oddibe McDowell .05
47 Ozzie Smith 1.00
48 Ken Griffey .05
49 Jose Cruz .05
50 Mariano Duncan .05
51 Mike Schmidt 1.25
52 Pat Tabler .05
53 Pete Rose 1.50
54 Frank White .05
55 Carney Lansford .05
56 Steve Garvey .15
57 Vance Law .05
58 Tony Pena .05
59 Wayne Tolleson .05
60 Dale Murphy .20
61 LaMarr Hoyt .05
62 Ryne Sandberg 1.00
63 Gary Carter 1.00
64 Lee Smith .05
65 Alvin Davis .05
66 Edwin Nunez .05
67 Kent Hrbek .05
68 Dave Stieb .05
69 Kirby Puckett 1.00
70 Paul Molitor .75
71 Glenn Hubbard .05
72 Lloyd Moseby .05
73 Mike Smithson .05
74 Jeff Leonard .05
75 Danny Darwin .05
76 Kevin McReynolds .05
77 Bill Buckner .05
78 Ron Oester .05
79 Tommy Herr .05
80 Mike Pagliarulo .05
81 Ron Romanick .05
82 Brook Jacoby .05
83 Eddie Murray .50
84 Gary Pettis .05
85 Chet Lemon .05
86 Toby Harrah .05
87 Mike Scioscia .05
88 Bert Blyleven .05
89 Dave Righetti .05
90 Bob Knepper .05
91 Fernando Valenzuela .05
92 Dave Dravecky .05
93 Julio Franco .05
94 Keith Moreland .05
95 Darryl Motley .05
96 Jack Clark .05
97 Tim Wallach .05
98 Steve Balboni .05
99 Steve Brown .05
100 Jay Howell .05
101 Alan Trammell .05
102 Willie Hernandez .05
103 Don Mattingly 1.25
104 Lee Lacy .05
105 Pedro Guerrero .05
106 Willie Wilson .05
107 Craig Reynolds .05
108 Tim Raines .15
109 Shane Rawley .05
110 Larry Parrish .05
111 Eric Show .05
112 Mike Witt .05
113 Dennis Eckersley .35
114 Mike Moore .05
115 Vince Coleman .05
116 Damaso Garcia .05
117 Steve Carlton .50
118 Floyd Bannister .05
119 Mario Soto .05
120 Fred Lynn .05
121 Bob Horner .05
122 Rick Sutcliffe .05
123 Walt Terrell .05
124 Keith Hernandez .05
125 Dave Winfield .75
126 Frank Viola .05
127 Dwight Evans .05
128 Willie Upshaw .05
129 Andre Thornton .05
130 Donnie Moore .05
131 Darryl Strawberry .05
132 Nolan Ryan 2.00
133 Garry Templeton .05
134 John Tudor .05
135 Dave Parker .05
136 Larry McWilliams .05
137 Terry Pendleton .05
138 Terry Puhl .05
139 Bob Dernier .05
140 Ozzie Guillen .05
141 Jim Clancy .05
142 Cal Ripken, Jr. 2.00
143 Mickey Hatcher .05
144 Dan Petry .05
145 Rich Gedman .05
146 Jim Rice .10
147 Butch Wynegar .05
148 Donnie Hill .05
149 Jim Sundberg .05
150 Joe Hesketh .05
151 Chris Codiroli .05
152 Charlie Hough .05
153 Herman Winningham .05
154 Dave Rozema .05
155 Don Slaught .05
156 Juan Beniquez .05
157 Ted Higuera .05
158 Andy Hawkins .05
159 Don Robinson .05
160 Glenn Wilson .05
161 Earnest Riles .05
162 Nick Esasky .05
163 Carlton Fisk .50
164 Claudell Washington .05
165 Scott McGregor .05
166 Nate Snell .05
167 Ted Simmons .05
168 Wade Boggs 1.00
169 Marty Barrett .05
170 Bud Black .05
171 Charlie Leibrandt .05
172 Charlie Lea .05
173 Reggie Jackson .50
174 Bryn Smith .05
175 Glenn Davis .05
176 Von Hayes .05
177 Danny Cox .05
178 Sam Khalifa .05
179 Tom Browning .05
180 Scott Garrelts .05
181 Shawon Dunston .05
182 Doyle Alexander .05
183 Jim Presley .05
184 Al Cowens .05
185 Mark Salas .05
186 Tom Niedenfuer .05
187 Dave Henderson .05
188 Lonnie Smith .05
189 Bruce Bochte .05
190 Leon Durham .05
191 Terry Francona .05
192 Bruce Sutter .75
193 Steve Crawford .05
194 Bob Brenly .05
195 Dan Pasqua .05
196 Juan Samuel .05
197 Floyd Rayford .05
198 Tim Burke .05
199 Ben Oglivie .05
200 Don Carman .05
201 Lance Parrish .05
202 Terry Forster .05
203 Neal Heaton .05
204 Ivan Calderon .05
205 Jorge Orta .05
206 Tom Henke .05
207 Rick Reuschel .05
208 Dan Quisenberry .05
209 Ty-Breaking Hit
(Pete Rose) .25
210 Floyd Youmans .05
211 Tom Filer .05
212 R.J. Reynolds .05
213 Gorman Thomas .05
214 Canadian Great (Jeff Reardon
(Canadian Great)) .45
215 Chris Brown .05
216 Rick Aguilera .05
217 Ernie Whitt .05
218 Joe Orsulak .05
219 Jimmy Key .05
220 Atlee Hammaker .05
221 Ron Darling .05
222 Zane Smith .05
223 Bob Welch .05
224 Reid Nichols .05
225 Fleet Feet (Vince Coleman,
Willie McGee) .10
226 Mark Gubicza .05
227 Tim Birtsas .05
228 Mike Hargrove .05
229 Randy St. Claire .05
230 Larry Herndon .05
231 Dusty Baker .05
232 Mookie Wilson .05
233 Jeff Lahti .05
234 Tom Seaver .50
235 Mike Scott .05
236 Don Sutton .35
237 * Roy Smalley .05
238 Bill Madlock .05
239 Charles Hudson .05
240 John Franco .05
241 Frank Tanana .05
242 Sid Fernandez .05
243 Knuckle Brothers
(Joe Niekro, Phil Niekro) .10
244 Dennis Lamp .05
245 Gene Nelson .05
246 Terry Harper .05
247 Vida Blue .05
248 Roger McDowell .05
249 Tony Bernazard .05
250 Cliff Johnson .05
251 Hal McRae .05
252 Garth Iorg .05
253 Mitch Webster .05
254 Jesse Barfield
(Canadian Great) .35
255 Dan Driessen .05
256 Mike Brown .05
257 Ron Kittle .05
258 Bo Diaz .05
259 Hank Aaron Puzzle Card .05
260 Pete Rose
(King of Kings) 1.50
---- Checklist 1-26 DK .05
---- Checklist 27-106 .05
---- Checklist 107-186 .05
---- Checklist 187-260 .05

1987 Leaf

MARK McGWIRE 3B

For the third consecutive season, Leaf-Donruss issued a Canadian baseball card set. These cards are nearly identical to the American set except for the name "Leaf" which appears on the front in place of "Donruss." The set contains 264 cards, each measuring 2-1/2" x 3-1/2", with a special emphasis being placed on players from the Montreal and Toronto teams. Backs feature career highlights in both English and French. As in the previous years, two "Canadian Greats" cards appear in the set. These painted portraits feature Mark Eichhorn and Floyd Youmans.

NM/M
Unopened Factory Set (264): 25.00
Complete Set (264): 17.50
Common Player: .05
Wax Pack: 1.50
Wax Box (36): 30.00

1 Wally Joyner/DK .05
2 Roger Clemens/DK 1.00
3 Dale Murphy/DK .15
4 Darryl Strawberry/DK .05
5 Ozzie Smith/DK .65
6 Jose Canseco/DK .40
7 Charlie Hough/DK .05
8 Brook Jacoby/DK .05
9 Fred Lynn/DK .05
10 Rick Rhoden/DK .05
11 Chris Brown/DK .05
12 Von Hayes/DK .05
13 Jack Morris/DK .10
14 Kevin McReynolds/DK .05
15 George Brett/DK .75
16 Ted Higuera/DK .05
17 Hubie Brooks/DK .05
18 Mike Scioscia/DK .05
19 Kirby Puckett/DK .65
20 Dave Winfield/DK .75
21 Lloyd Moseby/DK .10
22 Eric Davis/DK .05
23 Jim Presley/DK .05
24 Keith Moreland/DK .05
25 Greg Walker/DK .05
26 Steve Sax/DK .05
27 Checklist 1-27 .05
28 B.J. Surhoff/RR .05
29 Randy Myers/RR .05
30 Ken Gerhart/RR .05
31 Benito Santiago/RR .05
32 Greg Swindell/RR .05
33 Mike Birkbeck/RR .05
34 Terry Steinbach/RR .05
35 Bo Jackson/RR .25

#	Player	Price	#	Player	Price
36	Greg Maddux/RR	2.00	152	Gary Pettis	.05
37	Jim Lindeman/RR	.05	153	Don Sutton	.30
38	Devon White/RR	.75	154	Jim Presley	.05
39	Eric Bell/RR	.05	155	Checklist 28-105	.05
40	Will Fraser/RR	.05	156	Dale Sveum	.05
41	Jerry Browne/RR	.05	157	Cory Snyder	.05
42	Chris James/RR	.05	158	Jeff Sellers	.05
43	Rafael Palmeiro/RR	1.00	159	Denny Walling	.05
44	Pat Dodson/RR	.05	160	Danny Cox	.05
45	Duane Ward/RR	.05	161	Bob Forsch	.05
46	Mark McGwire/RR	4.00	162	Joaquin Andujar	.05
47	Bruce Fields/RR (Photo actually Darnell Coles.)		163	Roberto Clemente Puzzle Card	.10
48	Jody Davis	.05	164	Paul Assenmacher	.05
49	Roger McDowell	.05	165	Marty Barrett	.05
50	Jose Guzman	.05	166	Ray Knight	.05
51	Oddibe McDowell	.05	167	Rafael Santana	.05
52	Harold Baines	.05	168	Bruce Ruffin	.05
53	Dave Righetti	.05	169	Buddy Bell	.05
54	Moose Haas	.05	170	Ken Oberkfell	.05
55	Mark Langston	.05	171	Ken Mitchell	.05
56	Kirby Puckett	.65	172	Gene Garber	.05
57	Dwight Evans	.05	173	Canadian Greats (Mark Eichhorn)	.15
58	Willie Randolph	.05	174	Don Carman	.05
59	Wally Backman	.05	175	Jesse Orosco	.05
60	Bryn Smith	.05	176	Mookie Wilson	.05
61	Tim Wallach	.05	177	Gary Ward	.05
62	Joe Hesketh	.05	178	John Franco	.05
63	Garry Templeton	.05	179	Eric Davis	.05
64	Rob Thompson	.05	180	Walt Terrell	.05
65	Canadian Greats (Floyd Youmans)	.10	181	Phil Niekro	.30
66	Ernest Riles	.05	182	Pat Tabler	.05
67	Robin Yount	.50	183	Brett Butler	.05
68	Darryl Strawberry	.05	184	George Bell	.10
69	Ernie Whitt	.05	185	Pete Incaviglia	.05
70	Dave Winfield	.65	186	Pete O'Brien	.05
71	Paul Molitor	.75	187	Jimmy Key	.05
72	Dave Stieb	.05	188	Frank White	.05
73	Tom Henke	.05	189	Mike Pagliarulo	.05
74	Frank Viola	.05	190	Roger Clemens	1.00
75	Scott Garretts	.05	191	Rickey Henderson	.75
76	Mike Boddicker	.05	192	Mike Easler	.05
77	Keith Moreland	.05	193	Wade Boggs	.75
78	Lou Whitaker	.05	194	Vince Coleman	.05
79	Dave Parker	.05	195	Charlie Kerfeld	.05
80	Lee Smith	.05	196	Dickie Thon	.05
81	Tom Candiotti	.05	197	Bill Doran	.05
82	Greg Harris	.05	198	Alfredo Griffin	.05
83	Fred Lynn	.05	199	Carlton Fisk	.50
84	Dwight Gooden	.05	200	Phil Bradley	.05
85	Ron Darling	.05	201	Reggie Jackson	.65
86	Mike Krukow	.05	202	Bob Boone	.05
87	Spike Owen	.05	203	Steve Sax	.05
88	Len Dykstra	.05	204	Tom Niedenfuer	.05
89	Rick Aguilera	.05	205	Tim Burke	.05
90	Jim Clancy	.05	206	Floyd Youmans	.05
91	Joe Johnson	.05	207	Jay Tibbs	.05
92	Damaso Garcia	.05	208	Chili Davis	.05
93	Sid Fernandez	.05	209	Larry Parrish	.05
94	Bob Ojeda	.05	210	John Cerutti	.05
95	Ted Higuera	.05	211	Kevin Bass	.05
96	George Brett	.75	212	Andre Dawson	.25
97	Willie Wilson	.05	213	Bob Sebra	.05
98	Cal Ripken	1.50	214	Kevin McReynolds	.05
99	Kent Hrbek	.05	215	Jim Morrison	.05
100	Bert Blyleven	.05	216	Candy Maldonado	.05
101	Ron Guidry	.05	217	John Kruk	.05
102	Andy Allanson	.05	218	Todd Worrell	.05
103	Dave Henderson	.05	219	Barry Bonds	10.00
104	Kirk Gibson	.05	220	Andy McGaffigan	.05
105	Lloyd Moseby	.05	221	Andres Galarraga	.10
106	Tony Fernandez	.05	222	Mike Fitzgerald	.05
107	Lance Parrish	.05	223	Kirk McCaskill	.05
108	Ozzie Smith	.75	224	Dave Smith	.05
109	Gary Carter	.75	225	Ruben Sierra	.05
110	Eddie Murray	.50	226	Scott Fletcher	.05
111	Mike Witt	.05	227	Chet Lemon	.05
112	Bobby Witt	.05	228	Dan Petry	.05
113	Willie McGee	.05	229	Mark Eichhorn	.05
114	Steve Garvey	.10	230	Cecil Cooper	.05
115	Glenn Davis	.05	231	Willie Upshaw	.05
116	Jose Cruz	.05	232	Don Baylor	.05
117	Ozzie Guillen	.05	233	Keith Hernandez	.05
118	Alvin Davis	.05	234	Ryne Sandberg	.75
119	Jose Rijo	.05	235	Tony Gwynn	.65
120	Bill Madlock	.05	236	Chris Brown	.05
121	Tommy Herr	.05	237	Pedro Guerrero	.05
122	Mike Schmidt	.75	238	Mark Gubicza	.05
123	Mike Scioscia	.05	239	Sid Bream	.05
124	Terry Pendleton	.05	240	Joe Cowley	.05
125	Leon Durham	.05	241	Bill Buckner	.05
126	Alan Trammell	.05	242	John Candelaria	.05
127	Jesse Barfield	.05	243	Scott McGregor	.05
128	Shawon Dunston	.05	244	Tom Brunansky	.05
129	Pete Rose	1.25	245	Gary Gaetti	.05
130	Von Hayes	.05	246	Orel Hershiser	.05
131	Julio Franco	.05	247	Jim Rice	.10
132	Juan Samuel	.05	248	Oil Can Boyd	.05
133	Joe Carter	.10	249	Bob Knepper	.05
134	Brook Jacoby	.05	250	Danny Tartabull	.05
135	Jack Morris	.05	251	John Cangelosi	.05
136	Bob Horner	.05	252	Wally Joyner	.05
137	Calvin Schiraldi	.05	253	Bruce Hurst	.05
138	Tom Browning	.05	254	Rich Gedman	.05
139	Shane Rawley	.05	255	Jim Deshaies	.05
140	Mario Soto	.05	256	Tony Pena	.05
141	Dale Murphy	.15	257	Nolan Ryan	1.50
142	Hubie Brooks	.05	258	Mike Scott	.05
143	Jeff Reardon	.05	259	Checklist 106-183	.05
144	Will Clark	.15	260	Dennis Rasmussen	.05
145	Ed Correa	.05	261	Bret Saberhagen	.05
146	Glenn Wilson	.05	262	Steve Balboni	.05
147	Johnny Ray	.05	263	Tom Seaver	.50
148	Fernando Valenzuela	.05	264	Checklist 184-264	.05
149	Tim Raines	.10			
150	Don Mattingly	.75			
151	Jose Canseco	.40			

1987 Leaf Candy City Team

Leaf produced this set as part of its endorsement for the Special Olympics. Twelve cards feature Baseball Hall of Famers. The cards measure 2-1/2" x 3-1/2" and are numbered H1-H12. The remaining six cards in the set are numbered S1-S6 and feature unnamed Special Olympics champions. All cards feature the artwork of Dick Perez. The cards were available through a mail-in offer advertised at special store displays. Only the baseball-related subjects are listed in the checklist.

		NM/M
Complete Set (12):		3.00
Common Player:		.15
H1	Mickey Mantle	1.00
H2	Yogi Berra	.35
H3	Roy Campanella	.35
H4	Stan Musial	.50
H5	Ted Williams	.60
H6	Duke Snider	.35
H7	Hank Aaron	.60
H8	Pee Wee Reese	.35
H9	Brooks Robinson	.25
H10	Al Kaline	.25
H11	Willie McCovey	.25
H12	Cool Papa Bell	.15

1988 Leaf

This 264-card set features color player photos from among the 1988 Donruss 660-card standard issue, with emphasis on players from Montreal and Toronto. A border of red, blue and black stripes duplicates the design of the Donruss set, with the exception of a "Leaf '88" logo in the upper-left corner that replaces the Donruss logo. Two special Canadian Greats cards are included in this set: Perez-Steele portraits of Tim Wallach and George Bell. The set also includes the portrait-style Diamond Kings cards (the set's first 26 cards, one for each team). The DK's carry the Donruss logo above the gold DK banner. All card backs are bilingual (French/English), numbered, and printed in black on white stock with a light blue border. This set was sold in 10-card wax packs with one triple-piece puzzle card per pack and was distributed via larger hobby and retail shops in the U.S. and Canada.

		NM/M
Complete Set (264):		6.00
Common Player:		.05
Wax Pack (15):		.50
Wax Box (36):		9.00
1	Mark McGwire/DK	1.25
2	Tim Raines/DK	.20
3	Benito Santiago/DK	.05
4	Alan Trammell/DK	.05
5	Danny Tartabull/DK	.05
6	Ron Darling/DK	.05
7	Paul Molitor/DK	.75
8	Devon White/DK	.20
9	Andre Dawson/DK	.25

#	Player	Price	#	Player	Price
10	Julio Franco/DK	.05	128	Vince Coleman	.05
11	Scott Fletcher/DK	.05	129	Bryn Smith	.05
12	Tony Fernandez/DK	.10	130	Lance Parrish	.05
13	Shane Rawley /DK	.05	131	Willie Upshaw	.05
14	Kal Daniels/DK	.05	132	Pete O'Brien	.05
15	Jack Clark/DK	.05	133	Tony Fernandez	.10
16	Dwight Evans/DK	.05	134	Billy Ripken	.05
17	Tommy John/DK	.05	135	Len Dykstra	.05
18	Andy Van Slyke/DK	.05	136	Kirk Gibson	.05
19	Gary Gaetti/DK	.05	137	Kevin Bass	.05
20	Mark Langston/DK	.05	138	Jose Canseco	.50
21	Will Clark/DK	.15	139	Kent Hrbek	.05
22	Glenn Hubbard/DK	.05	140	Lloyd Moseby	.05
23	Billy Hatcher/DK	.05	141	Marty Barrett	.05
24	Bob Welch/DK	.05	142	Carmelo Martinez	.05
25	Ivan Calderon/DK	.05	143	Tom Foley	.05
26	Cal Ripken, Jr./DK	1.50	144	Kirby Puckett	.75
27	Checklist 1-27	.05	145	Rickey Henderson	.75
28	Mackey Sasser/RR	.05	146	Juan Samuel	.05
29	Jeff Treadway/RR	.05	147	Pete Incaviglia	.05
30	Mike Campbell/RR	.05	148	Greg Brock	.05
31	Lance Johnson/RR	.05	149	Eric Davis	.05
32	Nelson Liriano/RR	.05	150	Kal Daniels	.05
33	Shawn Abner/RR	.05	151	Bob Boone	.05
34	Roberto Alomar/RR	2.50	152	John Cerutti	.05
35	Shawn Hillegas/RR	.05	153	Mike Greenwell	.05
36	Joey Meyer/RR	.05	154	Oddibe McDowell	.05
37	Kevin Elster/RR	.05	155	Scott Fletcher	.05
38	Jose Lind/RR	.05	156	Gary Carter	.75
39	Kirt Manwaring/RR	.05	157	Harold Baines	.05
40	Mark Grace/RR	.75	158	Greg Swindell	.05
41	Jody Reed/RR	.05	159	Mark McLemore	.05
42	John Farrell/RR	.05	160	Keith Moreland	.05
43	Al Leiter/RR	.25	161	Jim Gantner	.05
44	Gary Thurman/RR	.05	162	Willie Randolph	.05
45	Vincente Palacios/RR	.05	163	Fred Lynn	.05
46	Eddie Williams/RR	.05	164	B.J. Surhoff	.05
47	Jack McDowell/RR	.20	165	Ken Griffey	.05
48	Dwight Gooden	.05	166	Chet Lemon	.05
49	Mike Witt	.05	167	Alan Trammell	.05
50	Wally Joyner	.05	168	Paul Molitor	.75
51	Brook Jacoby	.05	169	Lou Whitaker	.05
52	Bert Blyleven	.05	170	Will Clark	.10
53	Ted Higuera	.05	171	Dwight Evans	.05
54	Mike Scott	.05	172	Eddie Murray	.50
55	Jose Guzman	.05	173	Darrell Evans	.05
56	Roger Clemens	1.25	174	Ellis Burks	.05
57	Dave Righetti	.05	175	Ivan Calderon	.05
58	Benito Santiago	.05	176	John Kruk	.05
59	Ozzie Guillen	.05	177	Don Mattingly	1.00
60	Matt Nokes	.05	178	Dick Schofield	.05
61	Fernando Valenzuela	.05	179	Bruce Hurst	.05
62	Orel Hershiser	.05	180	Ron Guidry	.05
63	Sid Fernandez	.05	181	Jack Clark	.05
64	Ozzie Virgil	.05	182	Franklin Stubbs	.05
65	Wade Boggs	.50	183	Bill Doran	.05
66	Floyd Youmans	.05	184	Joe Carter	.05
67	Jimmy Key	.05	185	Steve Sax	.05
68	Bret Saberhagen	.05	186	Glenn Davis	.05
69	Jody Davis	.05	187	Bo Jackson	.10
70	Shawon Dunston	.05	188	Bobby Bonilla	.05
71	Julio Franco	.05	189	Willie Wilson	.05
72	Danny Cox	.05	190	Danny Tartabull	.05
73	Jim Clancy	.05	191	Bo Diaz	.05
74	Mark Eichhorn	.05	192	Buddy Bell	.05
75	Scott Bradley	.05	193	Tim Wallach	.05
76	Charlie Liebrandt	.05	194	Mark McGwire	1.25
77	Nolan Ryan	1.50	195	Carney Lansford	.05
78	Ron Darling	.05	196	Alvin Davis	.05
79	John Franco	.05	197	Von Hayes	.05
80	Dave Stieb	.05	198	Mitch Webster	.05
81	Mike Fitzgerald	.05	199	Casey Candaele	.05
82	Steve Bedrosian	.05	200	Gary Gaetti	.05
83	Dale Murphy	.05	201	Tommy Herr	.05
84	Tim Burke	.05	202	Wally Backman	.05
85	Jack Morris	.05	203	Brian Downing	.05
86	Greg Walker	.05	204	Rance Mulliniks	.05
87	Kevin Mitchell	.05	205	Craig Reynolds	.05
88	Doug Drabek	.05	206	Ruben Sierra	.05
89	Charlie Hough	.05	207	Ryne Sandberg	.75
90	Tony Gwynn	.05	208	Carlton Fisk	.50
91	Rick Sutcliffe	.05	209	Checklist 28-107	.05
92	Shane Rawley	.05	210	Gerald Young	.05
93	George Brett	1.00	211	MVP (Tim Raines)	.25
94	Frank Viola	.05	212	John Tudor	.05
95	Tony Pena	.05	213	Canadian Greats (George Bell)	.60
96	Jim Deshaies	.05	214	MVP (George Bell)	.25
97	Mike Scioscia	.05	215	Jim Rice	.10
98	Rick Rhoden	.05	216	Gerald Perry	.05
99	Terry Kennedy	.05	217	Dave Stewart	.05
100	Cal Ripken	1.50	218	Jose Uribe	.05
101	Pedro Guerrero	.05	219	Rick Rueschel	.05
102	Andy Van Slyke	.05	220	Darryl Strawberry	.05
103	Willie McGee	.05	221	Chris Brown	.05
104	Mike Kingery	.05	223	Lee Mazzilli	.05
105	Kevin Seitzer	.05	224	Denny Walling	.05
106	Robin Yount	.50	225	Jesse Barfield	.05
107	Tracy Jones	.05	226	Barry Larkin	.05
108	Dave Magadan	.05	227	Harold Reynolds	.05
109	Mel Hall	.05	228	Kevin McReynolds	.05
110	Billy Hatcher	.05	229	Todd Worrell	.05
111	Todd Benzinger	.05	230	Tommy John	.05
112	Mike LaValliere	.05	231	Rick Aguilera	.05
113	Barry Bonds	1.50	232	Bill Madlock	.05
114	Tim Raines	.20	233	Roy Smalley	.05
115	Ozzie Smith	.05	234	Jeff Musselman	.05
116	Dave Winfield	.75	235	Mike Dunne	.05
117	Keith Hernandez	.05	236	Jerry Browne	.05
118	Jeffrey Leonard	.05	237	Sam Horn	.05
119	Larry Parrish	.05	238	Howard Johnson	.05
120	Rob Thompson	.05	239	Candy Maldonado	.05
121	Andres Galarraga	.15	240	Nick Esasky	.05
122	Mickey Hatcher	.05	241	Geno Petralli	.05
123	Mark Langston	.05	242	Herm Winningham	.05
124	Mike Schmidt	1.00	243	Roger McDowell	.05
125	Cory Snyder	.05	244	Brian Fisher	.05
126	Andre Dawson	.15	245	John Marzano	.05
127	Devon White	.15			

#	Player	Price
246	Terry Pendleton	.05
247	Rick Leach	.05
248	Pascual Perez	.05
249	Mookie Wilson	.05
250	Ernie Whitt	.05
251	Ron Kittle	.05
252	Oil Can Boyd	.05
253	Jim Gott	.05
254	George Bell	.10
255	Canadian Greats (Tim Wallach)	.60
256	Luis Polonia	.05
257	Hubie Brooks	.05
258	Mickey Brantley	.05
259	Gregg Jefferies	.25
260	Johnny Ray	.05
261	Checklist 108-187	.05
262	Dennis Martinez	.05
263	Stan Musial Puzzle Card	.05
264	Checklist 188-264	.05

1989 Leaf Blue Chip Cards

Unknown until 2001, these cards are a variation of the 1989 Donruss Grand Slammers insert set and share the back design with that issue. Instead of the GS logo in the lower-left corner of the photo, these cards have a black, white and blue logo reading "Blue Chip / CARDS / Leaf." The Blue Chip cards are printed on heavier stock and have a blue background on the back. Why they were produced is not apparently not distributed is not known. It is presumed, though not confirmed, that all 12 Grand Slammers cards can also be found in the Blue Chip version.

		NM/M
Complete Set (12):		1,200
Common Player:		60.00
1	Jose Canseco	125.00
2	Mike Marshall	60.00
3	Walt Weiss	60.00
4	Kevin McReynolds	60.00
5	Mike Greenwell	60.00
6	Dave Winfield	150.00
7	Mark McGwire	400.00
8	Keith Hernandez	75.00
9	Franklin Stubbs	60.00
10	Danny Tartabull	60.00
11	Jesse Barfield	60.00
12	Ellis Burks	60.00

1990 Leaf Previews

JOE CARTER OF

This 12-card set was produced for dealer distribution to introduce Leaf as Donruss' premium-quality brand in mid-1990. Cards have the same format as the regular-issue versions with metallic silver ink highlights on front and back. The preview cards have a white undertype on back over the stats and career highlights. It reads "Special Preview Card."

		NM/M
Complete Set (12):		275.00
Common Player:		12.50
1	Steve Sax	12.50
2	Joe Carter	12.50
3	Dennis Eckersley	20.00

#	Player	Price
4	Ken Griffey Jr.	200.00
5	Barry Larkin	12.50
6	Mark Langston	12.50
7	Eric Anthony	12.50
8	Robin Ventura	12.50
9	Greg Vaughn	12.50
10	Bobby Bonilla	12.50
11	Gary Gaetti	12.50
12	Ozzie Smith	75.00

1990 Leaf

BOB TEWKSBURY P

This 528-card set was issued in two 264-card series. The cards were printed on heavy quality stock and both the card fronts and backs have full color player photos. Cards also have an ultra-glossy finish on both the fronts and backs. A high-tech foil Hall of Fame puzzle features former Yankee great Yogi Berra.

	NM/M
Complete Set (528):	75.00
Series 1 (264):	50.00
Series 2 (264):	25.00
Common Player:	.10
Series 1 Foil Pack (15):	4.00
Series 1 Foil Box (36):	80.00
Series 2 Foil Pack (15):	2.50
Series 2 Foil Box (36):	60.00

#	Player	Price
1	Introductory Card	.10
2	Mike Henneman	.10
3	Steve Bedrosian	.10
4	Mike Scott	.10
5	Allan Anderson	.10
6	Rick Sutcliffe	.10
7	Gregg Olson	.10
8	Kevin Elster	.10
9	Pete O'Brien	.10
10	Carlton Fisk	1.00
11	Joe Magrane	.10
12	Roger Clemens	2.50
13	Tom Glavine	.35
14	Tom Gordon	.10
15	Todd Benzinger	.10
16	Hubie Brooks	.10
17	Roberto Kelly	.10
18	Barry Larkin	.10
19	Mike Boddicker	.10
20	Roger McDowell	.10
21	Nolan Ryan	5.00
22	John Farrell	.10
23	Bruce Hurst	.10
24	Wally Joyner	.10
25	Greg Maddux	2.00
26	Chris Bosio	.10
27	John Cerutti	.10
28	Tim Burke	.10
29	Dennis Eckersley	.75
30	Glenn Davis	.10
31	Jim Abbott	.10
32	Mike LaValliere	.10
33	Andres Thomas	.10
34	Lou Whitaker	.10
35	Alvin Davis	.10
36	Melido Perez	.10
37	Craig Biggio	.10
38	Rick Aguilera	.10
39	Pete Harnisch	.10
40	David Cone	.10
41	Scott Garrelts	.10
42	Jay Howell	.10
43	Eric King	.10
44	Pedro Guerrero	.10
45	Mike Bielecki	.10
46	Bob Boone	.10
47	Kevin Brown	.10
48	Jerry Browne	.10
49	Mike Scioscia	.10
50	Chuck Cary	.10
51	Wade Boggs	2.00
52	Von Hayes	.10
53	Tony Fernandez	.10
54	Dennis Martinez	.10
55	Tom Candiotti	.10
56	Andy Benes	.10
57	Rob Dibble	.10
58	Chuck Crim	.10
59	John Smoltz	.10
60	Mike Heath	.10
61	Kevin Gross	.10
62	Mark McGwire	3.50
63	Bert Blyleven	.10
64	Bob Walk	.10
65	Mickey Tettleton	.10
66	Sid Fernandez	.10
67	Terry Kennedy	.10
68	Fernando Valenzuela	.10
69	Don Mattingly	2.50
70	Paul O'Neill	.10
71	Robin Yount	1.00
72	Bret Saberhagen	.10
73	Geno Petralli	.10
74	Brook Jacoby	.10
75	Roberto Alomar	.25
76	Devon White	.10
77	Jose Lind	.10
78	Pat Combs	.10
79	Dave Steib	.10
80	Tim Wallach	.10
81	Dave Stewart	.10
82	Eric Anthony RC	.10
83	Randy Bush	.10
84	Checklist	.10
85	Jaime Navarro	.10
86	Tommy Gregg	.10
87	Frank Tanana	.10
88	Omar Vizquel	.10
89	Ivan Calderon	.10
90	Vince Coleman	.10
91	Barry Bonds	5.00
92	Randy Milligan	.10
93	Frank Viola	.10
94	Matt Williams	.10
95	Alfredo Griffin	.10
96	Steve Sax	.10
97	Gary Gaetti	.10
98	Ryne Sandberg	2.00
99	Danny Tartabull	.10
100	Rafael Palmeiro	1.00
101	Jesse Orosco	.10
102	Garry Templeton	.10
103	Frank DiPino	.10
104	Tony Pena	.10
105	Dickie Thon	.10
106	Kelly Gruber	.10
107	Marquis Grissom RC	2.00
108	Jose Canseco	.60
109	Mike Blowers	.10
110	Tom Browning	.10
111	Greg Vaughn	.10
112	Oddibe McDowell	.10
113	Gary Ward	.10
114	Jay Buhner	.10
115	Eric Show	.10
116	Bryan Harvey	.10
117	Andy Van Slyke	.10
118	Jeff Ballard	.10
119	Barry Lyons	.10
120	Kevin Mitchell	.10
121	Mike Gallego	.10
122	Dave Smith	.10
123	Kirby Puckett	2.00
124	Jerome Walton	.10
125	Bo Jackson	.20
126	Harold Baines	.10
127	Scott Bankhead	.10
128	Ozzie Guillen	.10
129	Jose Oquendo	.10
130	John Dopson	.10
131	Charlie Hayes	.10
132	Fred McGriff	.10
133	Chet Lemon	.10
134	Gary Carter	1.00
135	Rafael Ramirez	.10
136	Shane Mack	.10
137	Mark Grace	.10
138	Phil Bradley	.10
139	Dwight Gooden	.10
140	Harold Reynolds	.10
141	Scott Fletcher	.10
142	Ozzie Smith	2.00
143	Mike Greenwell	.10
144	Pete Smith	.10
145	Mark Gubicza	.10
146	Chris Sabo	.10
147	Ramon Martinez	.10
148	Tim Leary	.10
149	Randy Myers	.10
150	Jody Reed	.10
151	Bruce Ruffin	.10
152	Jeff Russell	.10
153	Doug Jones	.10
154	Tony Gwynn	2.00
155	Mark Langston	.10
156	Mitch Williams	.10
157	Gary Sheffield	.60
158	Tom Henke	.10
159	Oil Can Boyd	.10
160	Rickey Henderson	1.00
161	Bill Doran	.10
162	Chuck Finley	.10
163	Jeff King	.10
164	Nick Esasky	.10
165	Cecil Fielder	.10
166	Dave Valle	.10
167	Robin Ventura	.10
168	Jim Deshaies	.10
169	Juan Berenguer	.10
170	Craig Worthington	.10
171	Gregg Jefferies	.10
172	Will Clark	.10
173	Kirk Gibson	.10
174	Checklist	.10
175	Bobby Thigpen	.10
176	John Tudor	.10
177	Andre Dawson	.35
178	George Brett	2.50
179	Steve Buechele	.10
180	Albert Belle	.10
181	Eddie Murray	1.00
182	Bob Geren	.10
183	Rob Murphy	.10
184	Tom Herr	.10
185	George Bell	.10
186	Spike Owen	.10
187	Cory Snyder	.10
188	Fred Lynn	.10
189	Eric Davis	.10
190	Dave Parker	.10
191	Jeff Blauser	.10
192	Matt Nokes	.10
193	Delino DeShields RC	.50
194	Scott Sanderson	.10
195	Lance Parrish	.10
196	Bobby Bonilla	.10
197	Cal Ripken, Jr.	5.00
198	Kevin McReynolds	.10
199	Robby Thompson	.10
200	Tim Belcher	.10
201	Jesse Barfield	.10
202	Mariano Duncan	.10
203	Bill Spiers	.10
204	Frank White	.10
205	Julio Franco	.10
206	Greg Swindell	.10
207	Benito Santiago	.10
208	Johnny Ray	.10
209	Gary Redus	.10
210	Jeff Parrett	.10
211	Jimmy Key	.10
212	Tim Raines	.10
213	Carney Lansford	.10
214	Gerald Young	.10
215	Gene Larkin	.10
216	Dan Plesac	.10
217	Lonnie Smith	.10
218	Alan Trammell	.10
219	Jeffrey Leonard	.10
220	Sammy Sosa RC	20.00
221	Todd Zeile	.10
222	Bill Landrum	.10
223	Mike Devereaux	.10
224	Mike Marshall	.10
225	Jose Uribe	.10
226	Juan Samuel	.10
227	Mel Hall	.10
228	Kent Hrbek	.10
229	Shawon Dunston	.10
230	Kevin Seitzer	.10
231	Pete Incaviglia	.10
232	Sandy Alomar	.10
233	Bip Roberts	.10
234	Scott Terry	.10
235	Dwight Evans	.10
236	Ricky Jordan	.10
237	John Olerud RC	5.00
238	Zane Smith	.10
239	Walt Weiss	.10
240	Alvaro Espinoza	.10
241	Billy Hatcher	.10
242	Paul Molitor	1.00
243	Dale Murphy	.30
244	Dave Bergman	.10
245	Ken Griffey Jr.	3.00
246	Ed Whitson	.10
247	Kirk McCaskill	.10
248	Jay Bell	.10
249	Ben McDonald RC	.50
250	Darryl Strawberry	.10
251	Brett Butler	.10
252	Terry Steinbach	.10
253	Ken Caminiti	.10
254	Dan Gladden	.10
255	Dwight Smith	.10
256	Kurt Stillwell	.10
257	Ruben Sierra	.10
258	Mike Schooler	.10
259	Lance Johnson	.10
260	Terry Pendleton	.10
261	Ellis Burks	.10
262	Len Dykstra	.10
263	Mookie Wilson	.10
264	Checklist (Nolan Ryan)	.10
265	Nolan Ryan (No-Hit King)	2.00
266	Brian DuBois	.10
267	Don Robinson	.10
268	Glenn Wilson	.10
269	Kevin Tapani RC	.25
270	Marvell Wynne	.10
271	Billy Ripken	.10
272	Howard Johnson	.10
273	Brian Holman	.10
274	Dan Pasqua	.10
275	Ken Dayley	.10
276	Jeff Reardon	.10
277	Jim Presley	.10
278	Jim Eisenreich	.10
279	Danny Jackson	.10
280	Orel Hershiser	.10
281	Andy Hawkins	.10
282	Jose Rijo	.10
283	Luis Rivera	.10
284	John Kruk	.10
285	Jeff Huson	.10
286	Joel Skinner	.10
287	Jack Clark	.10
288	Chili Davis	.10
289	Joe Girardi	.10
290	B.J. Surhoff	.10
291	Luis Sojo	.10
292	Tom Foley	.10
293	Mike Moore	.10
294	Ken Oberkfell	.10
295	Luis Polonia	.10
296	Doug Drabek	.10
297	Dave Justice RC	2.00
298	Paul Gibson	.10
299	Edgar Martinez	.10
300	Frank Thomas RC	20.00
301	Eric Yelding	.10
302	Greg Gagne	.10
303	Brad Komminsk	.10
304	Ron Darling	.10
305	Kevin Bass	.10
306	Jeff Hamilton	.10
307	Ron Karkovice	.10
308	Milt Thompson	.10
309	Mike Harkey	.10
310	Mel Stottlemyre	.10
311	Kenny Rogers	.10
312	Mitch Webster	.10
313	Kal Daniels	.10
314	Matt Nokes	.10
315	Dennis Lamp	.10
316	Ken Howell	.10
317	Glenallen Hill	.10
318	Dave Martinez	.10
319	Chris James	.10
320	Mike Pagliarulo	.10
321	Hal Morris	.10
322	Rob Deer	.10
323	Greg Olson	.10
324	Tony Phillips	.10
325	Larry Walker RC	8.00
326	Ron Hassey	.10
327	Jack Howell	.10
328	John Smiley	.10
329	Steve Finley	.10
330	Dave Magadan	.10
331	Greg Litton	.10
332	Mickey Hatcher	.10
333	Lee Guetterman	.10
334	Norm Charlton	.10
335	Edgar Diaz	.10
336	Willie Wilson	.10
337	Bobby Witt	.10
338	Candy Maldonado	.10
339	Craig Lefferts	.10
340	Dante Bichette	.10
341	Wally Backman	.10
342	Dennis Cook	.10
343	Pat Borders	.10
344	Wallace Johnson	.10
345	Willie Randolph	.10
346	Danny Darwin	.10
347	Al Newman	.10
348	Mark Knudson	.10
349	Joe Boever	.10
350	Larry Sheets	.10
351	Mike Jackson	.10
352	Wayne Edwards	.10
353	Bernard Gilkey RC	.50
354	Don Slaught	.10
355	Joe Orsulak	.10
356	John Franco	.10
357	Jeff Brantley	.10
358	Mike Morgan	.10
359	Deion Sanders	.10
360	Terry Leach	.10
361	Les Lancaster	.10
362	Storm Davis	.10
363	Scott Coolbaugh	.10
364	Checklist	.10
365	Cecilio Guante	.10
366	Joey Cora	.10
367	Willie McGee	.10
368	Jerry Reed	.10
369	Darren Daulton	.10
370	Manny Lee	.10
371	Mark Gardner	.10
372	Rick Honeycutt	.10
373	Steve Balboni	.10
374	Jack Armstrong	.10
375	Charlie O'Brien	.10
376	Ron Gant	.10
377	Lloyd Moseby	.10
378	Gene Harris	.10
379	Joe Carter	.10
380	Scott Bailes	.10
381	R.J. Reynolds	.10
382	Bob Melvin	.10
383	Tim Teufel	.10
384	John Burkett	.10
385	Felix Jose	.10
386	Larry Andersen	.10
387	David West	.10
388	Luis Salazar	.10
389	Mike Macfarlane	.10
390	Charlie Hough	.10
391	Greg Briley	.10
392	Donn Pall	.10
393	Bryn Smith	.10
394	Carlos Quintana	.10
395	Steve Lake	.10
396	Mark Whiten RC	.15
397	Edwin Nunez	.10
398	Rick Parker	.10
399	Mark Portugal	.10
400	Roy Smith	.10
401	Hector Villanueva	.10
402	Bob Milacki	.10
403	Alejandro Pena	.10
404	Scott Bradley	.10
405	Ron Kittle	.10
406	Bob Tewksbury	.10
407	Wes Gardner	.10
408	Ernie Whitt	.10
409	Terry Shumpert	.10
410	Tim Layana	.10
411	Chris Gwynn	.10
412	Jeff Robinson	.10
413	Scott Scudder	.10
414	Kevin Romine	.10
415	Jose DeJesus	.10
416	Mike Jeffcoat	.10
417	Rudy Seanez	.10
418	Mike Dunne	.10
419	Dick Schofield	.10
420	Steve Wilson	.10
421	Bill Krueger	.10
422	Junior Felix	.10
423	Drew Hall	.10
424	Curt Young	.10
425	Franklin Stubbs	.10
426	Dave Winfield	1.00
427	Rick Reed	.10
428	Charlie Leibrandt	.10
429	Jeff Robinson	.10
430	Erik Hanson	.10
431	Barry Jones	.10
432	Alex Trevino	.10
433	John Moses	.10
434	Dave Johnson	.10
435	Mackey Sasser	.10
436	Rick Leach	.10
437	Lenny Harris	.10
438	Carlos Martinez	.10
439	Rex Hudler	.10
440	Domingo Ramos	.10
441	Gerald Perry	.10
442	John Russell	.10
443	Carlos Baerga RC	.50
444	Checklist	.10
445	Stan Javier	.10
446	Kevin Maas RC	.10
447	Tom Brunansky	.10
448	Carmelo Martinez	.10
449	Willie Blair RC	.10
450	Andres Galarraga	.10
451	Bud Black	.10
452	Greg Harris	.10
453	Joe Oliver	.10
454	Greg Brock	.10
455	Jeff Treadway	.10
456	Lance McCullers	.10
457	Dave Schmidt	.10
458	Todd Burns	.10
459	Max Venable	.10
460	Neal Heaton	.10
461	Mark Williamson	.10
462	Keith Miller	.10
463	Mike LaCoss	.10
464	Jose Offerman RC	.25
465	Jim Leyritz RC	.50
466	Glenn Braggs	.10
467	Ron Robinson	.10
468	Mark Davis	.10
469	Gary Pettis	.10
470	Keith Hernandez	.10
471	Dennis Rasmussen	.10
472	Mark Eichhorn	.10
473	Ted Power	.10
474	Terry Mulholland	.10
475	Todd Stottlemyre	.10
476	Jerry Goff	.10
477	Gene Nelson	.10
478	Rich Gedman	.10
479	Brian Harper	.10
480	Mike Felder	.10
481	Steve Avery	.10
482	Jack Morris	.10
483	Randy Johnson	1.00
484	Scott Radinsky	.10
485	Jose DeLeon	.10
486	Stan Belinda RC	.10
487	Brian Holton	.10
488	Mark Carreon	.10
489	Trevor Wilson	.10
490	Mike Sharperson	.10
491	Alan Mills RC	.10
492	John Candelaria	.10
493	Paul Assenmacher	.10
494	Steve Crawford	.10
495	Brad Arnsberg	.10
496	Sergio Valdez	.10
497	Mark Parent	.10
498	Tom Pagnozzi	.10
499	Greg Harris	.10
500	Randy Ready	.10
501	Duane Ward	.10
502	Nelson Santovenia	.10
503	Joe Klink	.10
504	Eric Plunk	.10
505	Jeff Reed	.10
506	Ted Higuera	.10
507	Joe Hesketh	.10
508	Dan Petry	.10
509	Jerald Clark	.10
510	John Orton RC	.10
511	Scott Ruskin	.10
512	Chris Hoiles RC	.50
513	Daryl Boston	.10
514	Francisco Oliveras	.10
515	Ozzie Canseco	.10
516	Xavier Hernandez RC	.10
517	Fred Manrique	.10
518	Shawn Boskie	.10
519	Jeff Montgomery	.10
520	Jack Daugherty	.10
521	Keith Comstock	.10
522	Greg Hibbard RC	.10
523	Lee Smith	.10
524	Dana Kiecker	.10
525	Darrel Akerfelds	.10
526	Greg Myers	.10
527	Checklist	.10

RYNE SANDBERG 2B

tion, "1991 PREVIEW CARD" in white print beneath the statistics and career information on the back.

	NM/M
Complete Set (26):	20.00
Common Player:	.50

#	Player	Price
1	Dave Justice	.50
2	Ryne Sandberg	1.50
3	Barry Larkin	.50
4	Craig Biggio	.50
5	Ramon Martinez	.50
6	Tim Wallach	.50
7	Dwight Gooden	.50
8	Len Dykstra	.50
9	Barry Bonds	4.00
10	Ray Lankford	.50
11	Tony Gwynn	1.50
12	Will Clark	.60
13	Leo Gomez	.50
14	Wade Boggs	1.50
15	Chuck Finley	.50
16	Carlton Fisk	1.00
17	Sandy Alomar, Jr.	.50
18	Cecil Fielder	.50
19	Bo Jackson	.75
20	Paul Molitor	.50
21	Kirby Puckett	1.50
22	Don Mattingly	2.00
23	Rickey Henderson	1.50
24	Tino Martinez	.50
25	Nolan Ryan	4.00
26	Dave Steib	.50

1991 Leaf

JOHN OLERUD 1B

Silver borders and black insets surround the color action photos on the 1991 Leaf cards. The set was once again released in two series. Series 1 consists of cards 1-264. Card backs feature an additional player photo, biographical information, statistics and career highlights. The 1991 issue is not considered as scarce as the 1990 release.

	NM/M
Complete Set (528):	8.00
Common Player:	.05
Series 1 or 2 Pack (15):	.50
Series 1 or 2 Box (36):	12.50

#	Player	Price
1	The Leaf Card	.05
2	Kurt Stillwell	.05
3	Bobby Witt	.05
4	Tony Phillips	.05
5	Scott Garrelts	.05
6	Greg Swindell	.05
7	Billy Ripken	.05
8	Dave Martinez	.05
9	Kelly Gruber	.05
10	Juan Samuel	.05
11	Brian Holman	.05
12	Craig Biggio	.05
13	Lonnie Smith	.05
14	Ron Robinson	.05
15	Mike LaValliere	.05
16	Mark Davis	.05
17	Jack Daugherty	.05
18	Mike Henneman	.05
19	Mike Greenwell	.05
20	Dave Magadan	.05
21	Mark Williamson	.05
22	Marquis Grissom	.05
23	Pat Borders	.05
24	Mike Scioscia	.05
25	Shawon Dunston	.05
26	Randy Bush	.05

1991 Leaf Previews

Cello packs of four cards previewing the 1991 Leaf set were included in each 1991 Donruss hobby factory set. The cards are identical in format to the regular 1991 Leafs, except there is a nota-

No.	Player	Price
27	John Smoltz	.05
28	Chuck Crim	.05
29	Don Slaught	.05
30	Mike Macfarlane	.05
31	Wally Joyner	.05
32	Pat Combs	.05
33	Tony Pena	.05
34	Howard Johnson	.05
35	Leo Gomez	.05
36	Spike Owen	.05
37	Eric Davis	.05
38	Roberto Kelly	.05
39	Jerome Walton	.05
40	Shane Mack	.05
41	Kent Mercker	.05
42	B.J. Surhoff	.05
43	Jerry Browne	.05
44	Lee Smith	.05
45	Chuck Finley	.05
46	Terry Mulholland	.05
47	Tom Bolton	.05
48	Tom Herr	.05
49	Jim Deshaies	.05
50	Walt Weiss	.05
51	Hal Morris	.05
52	Lee Guetterman	.05
53	Paul Assenmacher	.05
54	Brian Harper	.05
55	Paul Gibson	.05
56	John Burkett	.05
57	Doug Jones	.05
58	Jose Oquendo	.05
59	Dick Schofield	.05
60	Dickie Thon	.05
61	Ramon Martinez	.05
62	Jay Buhner	.05
63	Mark Portugal	.05
64	Bob Welch	.05
65	Chris Sabo	.05
66	Chuck Cary	.05
67	Mark Langston	.05
68	Joe Boever	.05
69	Jody Reed	.05
70	Alejandro Pena	.05
71	Jeff King	.05
72	Tom Pagnozzi	.05
73	Joe Oliver	.05
74	Mike Witt	.05
75	Hector Villanueva	.05
76	Dan Gladden	.05
77	Dave Justice	.05
78	Mike Gallego	.05
79	Tom Candiotti	.05
80	Ozzie Smith	.60
81	Luis Polonia	.05
82	Randy Ready	.05
83	Greg Harris	.05
84	Checklist (Dave Justice)	.05
85	Kevin Mitchell	.05
86	Mark McLemore	.05
87	Terry Steinbach	.05
88	Tom Browning	.05
89	Matt Nokes	.05
90	Mike Harkey	.05
91	Omar Vizquel	.05
92	Dave Bergman	.05
93	Matt Williams	.05
94	Steve Olin	.05
95	Craig Wilson	.05
96	Dave Stieb	.05
97	Ruben Sierra	.05
98	Jay Howell	.05
99	Scott Bradley	.05
100	Eric Yelding	.05
101	Rickey Henderson	.45
102	Jeff Reed	.05
103	Jimmy Key	.05
104	Terry Shumpert	.05
105	Kenny Rogers	.05
106	Cecil Fielder	.05
107	Robby Thompson	.05
108	Alex Cole	.05
109	Randy Milligan	.05
110	Andres Galarraga	.05
111	Bill Spiers	.05
112	Kal Daniels	.05
113	Henry Cotto	.05
114	Casy Candaele	.05
115	Jeff Blauser	.05
116	Robin Yount	.45
117	Ben McDonald	.05
118	Bret Saberhagen	.05
119	Juan Gonzalez	.35
120	Lou Whitaker	.05
121	Ellis Burks	.05
122	Charlie O'Brien	.05
123	John Smiley	.05
124	Tim Burke	.05
125	John Olerud	.05
126	Eddie Murray	.45
127	Greg Maddux	.60
128	Kevin Tapani	.05
129	Ron Gant	.05
130	Jay Bell	.05
131	Chris Hoiles	.05
132	Tom Gordon	.05
133	Kevin Seitzer	.05
134	Jeff Huson	.05
135	Jerry Don Gleaton	.05
136	Jeff Brantley	.05
137	Felix Fermin	.05
138	Mike Devereaux	.05
139	Delino DeShields	.05
140	David Wells	.05
141	Tim Crews	.05
142	Erik Hanson	.05
143	Mark Davidson	.05
144	Tommy Gregg	.05
145	Jim Gantner	.05
146	Jose Lind	.05
147	Danny Tartabull	.05
148	Geno Petralli	.05
149	Travis Fryman	.05
150	Tim Naehring	.05
151	Kevin McReynolds	.05
152	Joe Orsulak	.05
153	Steve Frey	.05
154	Duane Ward	.05
155	Stan Javier	.05
156	Damon Berryhill	.05
157	Gene Larkin	.05
158	Greg Olson	.05
159	Mark Knudson	.05
160	Carmelo Martinez	.05
161	Storm Davis	.05
162	Jim Abbott	.05
163	Len Dykstra	.05
164	Tom Brunansky	.05
165	Dwight Gooden	.05
166	Jose Mesa	.05
167	Oil Can Boyd	.05
168	Barry Larkin	.05
169	Scott Sanderson	.05
170	Mark Grace	.05
171	Mark Guthrie	.05
172	Tom Glavine	.15
173	Gary Sheffield	.30
174	Checklist (Roger Clemens)	.25
175	Chris James	.05
176	Milt Thompson	.05
177	Donnie Hill	.05
178	Wes Chamberlain	.05
179	John Marzano	.05
180	Frank Viola	.05
181	Eric Anthony	.05
182	Jose Canseco	.30
183	Scott Scudder	.05
184	Dave Eiland	.05
185	Luis Salazar	.05
186	Pedro Munoz	.05
187	Steve Searcy	.05
188	Don Robinson	.05
189	Sandy Alomar	.05
190	Jose DeLeon	.05
191	John Orton	.05
192	Darren Daulton	.05
193	Mike Morgan	.05
194	Greg Briley	.05
195	Karl Rhodes	.05
196	Harold Baines	.05
197	Bill Doran	.05
198	Alvaro Espinoza	.05
199	Kirk McCaskill	.05
200	Jose DeJesus	.05
201	Jack Clark	.05
202	Daryl Boston	.05
203	Randy Tomlin	.05
204	Pedro Guerrero	.05
205	Billy Hatcher	.05
206	Tim Leary	.05
207	Ryne Sandberg	.60
208	Kirby Puckett	.60
209	Charlie Leibrandt	.05
210	Rick Honeycutt	.05
211	Joel Skinner	.05
212	Rex Hudler	.05
213	Bryan Harvey	.05
214	Charlie Hayes	.05
215	Matt Young	.05
216	Terry Kennedy	.05
217	Carl Nichols	.05
218	Mike Moore	.05
219	Paul O'Neill	.05
220	Steve Sax	.05
221	Shawn Boskie	.05
222	Rich DeLucia	.05
223	Lloyd Moseby	.05
224	Mike Kingery	.05
225	Carlos Baerga	.05
226	Bryn Smith	.05
227	Todd Stottlemyre	.05
228	Julio Franco	.05
229	Jim Gott	.05
230	Mike Schooler	.05
231	Steve Finley	.05
232	Dave Henderson	.05
233	Luis Quinones	.05
234	Mark Whiten	.05
235	Brian McRae	.05
236	Rich Gossage	.05
237	Rob Deer	.05
238	Will Clark	.10
239	Albert Belle	.05
240	Bob Melvin	.05
241	Larry Walker	.05
242	Dante Bichette	.05
243	Orel Hershiser	.05
244	Pete O'Brien	.05
245	Pete Harnisch	.05
246	Jeff Treadway	.05
247	Julio Machado	.05
248	Dave Johnson	.05
249	Kirk Gibson	.05
250	Kevin Brown	.05
251	Milt Cuyler	.05
252	Jeff Reardon	.05
253	David Cone	.05
254	Gary Redus	.05
255	Junior Noboa	.05
256	Greg Myers	.05
257	Dennis Cook	.05
258	Joe Girardi	.05
259	Allan Anderson	.05
260	Paul Marak	.05
261	Barry Bonds	2.00
262	Juan Bell	.05
263	Russ Morman	.05
264	Checklist (George Brett)	.25
265	Jerald Clark	.05
266	Dwight Evans	.05
267	Roberto Alomar	.15
268	Danny Jackson	.05
269	Brian Downing	.05
270	John Cerutti	.05
271	Robin Ventura	.05
272	Gerald Perry	.05
273	Wade Boggs	.60
274	Dennis Martinez	.05
275	Andy Benes	.05
276	Tony Fossas	.05
277	Franklin Stubbs	.05
278	John Kruk	.05
279	Kevin Gross	.05
280	Von Hayes	.05
281	Frank Thomas	.45
282	Rob Dibble	.05
283	Mel Hall	.05
284	Rick Mahler	.05
285	Dennis Eckersley	.35
286	Bernard Gilkey	.05
287	Dan Plesac	.05
288	Jason Grimsley	.05
289	Mark Lewis	.05
290	Tony Gwynn	.60
291	Jeff Russell	.05
292	Curt Schilling	.25
293	Pascual Perez	.05
294	Jack Morris	.05
295	Hubie Brooks	.05
296	Alex Fernandez	.05
297	Harold Reynolds	.05
298	Craig Worthington	.05
299	Willie Wilson	.05
300	Mike Maddux	.05
301	Dave Righetti	.05
302	Paul Molitor	.45
303	Gary Gaetti	.05
304	Terry Pendleton	.05
305	Kevin Elster	.05
306	Scott Fletcher	.05
307	Jeff Robinson	.05
308	Jesse Barfield	.05
309	Mike LaCoss	.05
310	Andy Van Slyke	.05
311	Glenallen Hill	.05
312	Bud Black	.05
313	Kent Hrbek	.05
314	Tim Teufel	.05
315	Tony Fernandez	.05
316	Beau Allred	.05
317	Curtis Wilkerson	.05
318	Bill Sampen	.05
319	Randy Johnson	.45
320	Mike Heath	.05
321	Sammy Sosa	1.00
322	Mickey Tettleton	.05
323	Jose Vizcaino	.05
324	John Candelaria	.05
325	David Howard	.05
326	Jose Rijo	.05
327	Todd Zeile	.05
328	Gene Nelson	.05
329	Dwayne Henry	.05
330	Mike Boddicker	.05
331	Ozzie Guillen	.05
332	Sam Horn	.05
333	Wally Whitehurst	.05
334	Dave Parker	.05
335	George Brett	.75
336	Bobby Thigpen	.05
337	Ed Whitson	.05
338	Ivan Calderon	.05
339	Mike Pagliarulo	.05
340	Jack McDowell	.05
341	Dana Kiecker	.05
342	Fred McGriff	.05
343	Mark Lee	.05
344	Alfredo Griffin	.05
345	Scott Bankhead	.05
346	Darrin Jackson	.05
347	Rafael Palmeiro	.35
348	Steve Farr	.05
349	Hensley Meulens	.05
350	Danny Cox	.05
351	Alan Trammell	.05
352	Edwin Nunez	.05
353	Joe Carter	.05
354	Eric Show	.05
355	Vance Law	.05
356	Jeff Gray	.05
357	Bobby Bonilla	.05
358	Ernest Riles	.05
359	Ron Hassey	.05
360	Willie McGee	.05
361	Mackey Sasser	.05
362	Glenn Braggs	.05
363	Mario Diaz	.05
364	Checklist (Barry Bonds)	.35
365	Kevin Bass	.05
366	Pete Incaviglia	.05
367	Luis Sojo	.05
368	Lance Parrish	.05
369	Mark Leonard	.05
370	Heathcliff Slocumb	.05
371	Jimmy Jones	.05
372	Ken Griffey Jr.	1.00
373	Chris Hammond	.05
374	Chili Davis	.05
375	Joey Cora	.05
376	Ken Hill	.05
377	Darryl Strawberry	.05
378	Ron Darling	.05
379	Sid Bream	.05
380	Bill Swift	.05
381	Shawn Abner	.05
382	Eric King	.05
383	Mickey Morandini	.05
384	Carlton Fisk	.45
385	Steve Lake	.05
386	Mike Jeffcoat	.05
387	Darren Holmes	.05
388	Tim Wallach	.05
389	George Bell	.05
390	Craig Lefferts	.05
391	Ernie Whitt	.05
392	Felix Jose	.05
393	Kevin Maas	.05
394	Devon White	.05
395	Otis Nixon	.05
396	Chuck Knoblauch	.05
397	Scott Coolbaugh	.05
398	Glenn Davis	.05
399	Manny Lee	.05
400	Andre Dawson	.20
401	Scott Chiamparino	.05
402	Bill Gullickson	.05
403	Lance Johnson	.05
404	Juan Agosto	.05
405	Danny Darwin	.05
406	Barry Jones	.05
407	Larry Andersen	.05
408	Luis Rivera	.05
409	Jaime Navarro	.05
410	Roger McDowell	.05
411	Brett Butler	.05
412	Dale Murphy	.15
413	Tim Raines	.05
414	Norm Charlton	.05
415	Greg Cadaret	.05
416	Chris Nabholz	.05
417	Dave Stewart	.05
418	Rich Gedman	.05
419	Willie Randolph	.05
420	Mitch Williams	.05
421	Brook Jacoby	.05
422	Greg Harris	.05
423	Nolan Ryan	2.00
424	Dave Rohde	.05
425	Don Mattingly	.75
426	Greg Gagne	.05
427	Vince Coleman	.05
428	Dan Pasqua	.05
429	Alvin Davis	.05
430	Cal Ripken, Jr.	2.00
431	Jamie Quirk	.05
432	Benito Santiago	.05
433	Jose Uribe	.05
434	Candy Maldonado	.05
435	Junior Felix	.05
436	Deion Sanders	.05
437	John Franco	.05
438	Greg Hibbard	.05
439	Floyd Bannister	.05
440	Steve Howe	.05
441	Steve Decker	.05
442	Vicente Palacios	.05
443	Pat Tabler	.05
444	Checklist (Darryl Strawberry)	.05
445	Mike Felder	.05
446	Al Newman	.05
447	Chris Donnels	.05
448	Rich Rodriguez	.05
449	Turner Ward	.05
450	Bob Walk	.05
451	Gilberto Reyes	.05
452	Mike Jackson	.05
453	Rafael Belliard	.05
454	Wayne Edwards	.05
455	Andy Allanson	.05
456	Dave Smith	.05
457	Gary Carter	.45
458	Warren Cromartie	.05
459	Jack Armstrong	.05
460	Bob Tewksbury	.05
461	Joe Klink	.05
462	Xavier Hernandez	.05
463	Scott Radinsky	.05
464	Jeff Robinson	.05
465	Gregg Jefferies	.05
466	Denny Neagle	.05
467	Carmelo Martinez	.05
468	Donn Pall	.05
469	Bruce Hurst	.05
470	Eric Bullock	.05
471	Rick Aguilera	.05
472	Charlie Hough	.05
473	Carlos Quintana	.05
474	Marty Barrett	.05
475	Kevin Brown	.05
476	Bobby Ojeda	.05
477	Edgar Martinez	.05
478	Bip Roberts	.05
479	Mike Flanagan	.05
480	John Habyan	.05
481	Larry Casian	.05
482	Wally Backman	.05
483	Doug Dascenzo	.05
484	Rick Dempsey	.05
485	Ed Sprague	.05
486	Steve Chitren	.05
487	Mark McGwire	1.50
488	Roger Clemens	.75
489	Orlando Merced	.05
490	Rene Gonzales	.05
491	Mike Stanton	.05
492	Al Osuna	.05
493	Rick Cerone	.05
494	Mariano Duncan	.05
495	Zane Smith	.05
496	John Morris	.05
497	Frank Tanana	.05
498	Junior Ortiz	.05
499	Dave Winfield	.45
500	Gary Varsho	.05
501	Chico Walker	.05
502	Ken Caminiti	.05
503	Ken Griffey Sr.	.05
504	Randy Myers	.05
505	Steve Bedrosian	.05
506	Cory Snyder	.05
507	Cris Carpenter	.05
508	Tim Belcher	.05
509	Jeff Hamilton	.05
510	Steve Avery	.05
511	Dave Valle	.05
512	Tom Lampkin	.05
513	Shawn Hillegas	.05
514	Reggie Jefferson	.05
515	Ron Karkovice	.05
516	Doug Drabek	.05
517	Tom Henke	.05
518	Chris Bosio	.05
519	Gregg Olson	.05
520	Bob Scanlan	.05
521	Alonzo Powell	.05
522	Jeff Ballard	.05
523	Ray Lankford	.05
524	Tommy Greene	.05
525	Mike Timlin	.05
526	Juan Berenguer	.05
527	Scott Erickson	.05
528	Checklist (Sandy Alomar Jr.)	.05

1992 Leaf Previews

FRED McGRIFF 1B — PADRES

In a format identical to the regular-issue 1992 Leaf cards, this 26-card preview set was issued as a bonus in packs of four cards in each 1992 Donruss hobby factory set.

		NM/M
Complete Set (26):		15.00
Common Player:		.25
1	Steve Avery	.25
2	Ryne Sandberg	1.00
3	Chris Sabo	.25
4	Jeff Bagwell	.75
5	Darryl Strawberry	.25
6	Bret Barberie	.25
7	Howard Johnson	.25
8	John Kruk	.25
9	Andy Van Slyke	.25
10	Felix Jose	.25
11	Fred McGriff	.25
12	Will Clark	.35
13	Cal Ripken, Jr.	3.00
14	Phil Plantier	.25
15	Lee Stevens	.25
16	Frank Thomas	.75
17	Mark Whiten	.25
18	Cecil Fielder	.25
19	George Brett	1.50
20	Robin Yount	.75
21	Scott Erickson	.25
22	Don Mattingly	1.50
23	Jose Canseco	.50
24	Ken Griffey Jr.	2.00
25	Nolan Ryan	3.00
26	Joe Carter	.25

Gold Rookies

MO VAUGHN 1B

Special gold rookie and gold bonus cards were randomly inserted in 1991 Leaf packs. Backs have a design similar to the regular-issue cards, but have gold, rather than silver background. Fronts have gold-foil highlights. Card numbers of the issued version have a "BC" prefix, but there is a much rarer second version of the Series 1 cards, which carry card numbers between 265-276.

		NM/M
Complete Set (26):		10.00
Common Player:		.10
1	Scott Leius	.10
2	Luis Gonzalez	.40
3	Wil Cordero	.10
4	Gary Scott	.10
5	Willie Banks	.10
6	Arthur Rhodes	.10
7	Mo Vaughn	.25
8	Henry Rodriguez	.10
9	Todd Van Poppel	.10
10	Reggie Sanders	.10
11	Rico Brogna	.10
12	Mike Mussina	2.00
13	Kirk Dressendorfer	.10
14	Jeff Bagwell	6.00
15	Pete Schourek	.10
16	Wade Taylor	.10
17	Pat Kelly	.10
18	Tim Costo	.10
19	Roger Salkeld	.10
20	Andujar Cedeno	.10
21	Ryan Klesko	.10
22	Mike Huff	.10
23	Anthony Young	.10
24	Eddie Zosky	.10
25	Nolan Ryan (7th no-hitter)	.50
26	Rickey Henderson (Record Steal)	.25
	Plooey (Babe Ruth)	.01
265	Scott Leius	4.00
266	Luis Gonzalez	6.00
267	Wil Cordero	4.00
268	Gary Scott	4.00
269	Willie Banks	4.00
270	Arthur Rhodes	4.00
271	Mo Vaughn	10.00
272	Henry Rodriguez	4.00
273	Todd Van Poppel	4.00
274	Reggie Sanders	4.00
275	Rico Brogna	4.00
276	Mike Mussina	30.00

1992 Leaf

TRAVIS FRYMAN 3B

Two 264-card series comprise this 528-card set. The cards feature action photos on both the front and the back. Silver borders surround the photo on the card front. Each leaf card was also produced in a gold foil version. One gold card was issued per pack and a complete Leaf Gold Edition set can be assembled. Traded players and free agents are shown in uniform with their new teams.

		NM/M
Complete Set (528):		7.50
Common Player:		.05
Series 1 or 2 Pack:		.40
Series 1 or 2 Wax Box:		7.50
1	Jim Abbott	.05
2	Cal Eldred	.05
3	Bud Black	.05
4	Dave Howard	.05
5	Luis Sojo	.05
6	Gary Scott	.05
7	Joe Oliver	.05
8	Chris Gardner	.05
9	Sandy Alomar	.05
10	Greg Harris	.05
11	Doug Drabek	.05
12	Darryl Hamilton	.05
13	Mike Mussina	.30
14	Kevin Tapani	.05
15	Ron Gant	.05
16	Mark McGwire	1.00
17	Robin Ventura	.05
18	Pedro Guerrero	.05
19	Roger Clemens	.65
20	Steve Farr	.05

#	Player	Price
21	Frank Tanana	.05
22	Joe Hesketh	.05
23	Erik Hanson	.05
24	Greg Cadaret	.05
25	Rex Hudler	.05
26	Mark Grace	.05
27	Kelly Gruber	.05
28	Jeff Bagwell	.45
29	Darryl Strawberry	.05
30	Dave Smith	.05
31	Kevin Appier	.05
32	Steve Chitren	.05
33	Kevin Gross	.05
34	Rick Aguilera	.05
35	Juan Guzman	.05
36	Joe Orsulak	.05
37	Tim Raines	.05
38	Harold Reynolds	.05
39	Charlie Hough	.05
40	Tony Phillips	.05
41	Nolan Ryan	1.50
42	Vince Coleman	.05
43	Andy Van Slyke	.05
44	Tim Burke	.05
45	Luis Polonia	.05
46	Tom Browning	.05
47	Willie McGee	.05
48	Gary DiSarcina	.05
49	Mark Lewis	.05
50	Phil Plantier	.05
51	Doug Dascenzo	.05
52	Cal Ripken, Jr.	1.50
53	Pedro Munoz	.05
54	Carlos Hernandez	.05
55	Jerald Clark	.05
56	Jeff Brantley	.05
57	Don Mattingly	.65
58	Roger McDowell	.05
59	Steve Avery	.05
60	John Olerud	.05
61	Bill Gullickson	.05
62	Juan Gonzalez	.30
63	Felix Jose	.05
64	Robin Yount	.45
65	Greg Briley	.05
66	Steve Finley	.05
67	Checklist	.05
68	Tom Gordon	.05
69	Rob Dibble	.05
70	Glenallen Hill	.05
71	Calvin Jones	.05
72	Joe Girardi	.05
73	Barry Larkin	.05
74	Andy Benes	.05
75	Milt Cuyler	.05
76	Kevin Bass	.05
77	Pete Harnisch	.05
78	Wilson Alvarez	.05
79	Mike Devereaux	.05
80	Doug Henry	.05
81	Orel Hershiser	.05
82	Shane Mack	.05
83	Mike Macfarlane	.05
84	Thomas Howard	.05
85	Alex Fernandez	.05
86	Reggie Jefferson	.05
87	Leo Gomez	.05
88	Mel Hall	.05
89	Mike Greenwell	.05
90	Jeff Russell	.05
91	Steve Buechele	.05
92	David Cone	.05
93	Kevin Reimer	.05
94	Mark Lemke	.05
95	Bob Tewksbury	.05
96	Zane Smith	.05
97	Mark Eichhorn	.05
98	Kirby Puckett	.60
99	Paul O'Neill	.05
100	Dennis Eckersley	.35
101	Duane Ward	.05
102	Matt Nokes	.05
103	Mo Vaughn	.05
104	Pat Kelly	.05
105	Ron Karkovice	.05
106	Bill Spiers	.05
107	Gary Gaetti	.05
108	Mackey Sasser	.05
109	Robby Thompson	.05
110	Marvin Freeman	.05
111	Jimmy Key	.05
112	Dwight Gooden	.05
113	Charlie Leibrandt	.05
114	Devon White	.05
115	Charles Nagy	.05
116	Rickey Henderson	.45
117	Paul Assenmacher	.05
118	Junior Felix	.05
119	Julio Franco	.05
120	Norm Charlton	.05
121	Scott Servais	.05
122	Gerald Perry	.05
123	Brian McRae	.05
124	Don Slaught	.05
125	Juan Samuel	.05
126	Harold Baines	.05
127	Scott Livingstone	.05
128	Jay Buhner	.05
129	Darrin Jackson	.05
130	Luis Mercedes	.05
131	Brian Harper	.05
132	Howard Johnson	.05
133	Checklist	.05
134	Dante Bichette	.05
135	Dave Righetti	.05
136	Jeff Montgomery	.05
137	Joe Grahe	.05
138	Delino DeShields	.05
139	Jose Rijo	.05
140	Ken Caminiti	.05
141	Steve Olin	.05
142	Kurt Stillwell	.05
143	Jay Bell	.05
144	Jaime Navarro	.05
145	Ben McDonald	.05
146	Greg Gagne	.05
147	Jeff Blauser	.05
148	Carney Lansford	.05
149	Ozzie Guillen	.05
150	Milt Thompson	.05
151	Jeff Reardon	.05
152	Scott Sanderson	.05
153	Cecil Fielder	.05
154	Greg Harris	.05
155	Rich DeLucia	.05
156	Roberto Kelly	.05
157	Bryn Smith	.05
158	Chuck McElroy	.05
159	Tom Henke	.05
160	Luis Gonzalez	.25
161	Steve Wilson	.05
162	Shawn Boskie	.05
163	Mark Davis	.05
164	Mike Moore	.05
165	Mike Scioscia	.05
166	Scott Erickson	.05
167	Todd Stottlemyre	.05
168	Alvin Davis	.05
169	Greg Hibbard	.05
170	David Valle	.05
171	Dave Winfield	.45
172	Alan Trammell	.05
173	Kenny Rogers	.05
174	John Franco	.05
175	Jose Lind	.05
176	Pete Schourek	.05
177	Von Hayes	.05
178	Chris Hammond	.05
179	John Burkett	.05
180	Dickie Thon	.05
181	Joel Skinner	.05
182	Scott Cooper	.05
183	Andre Dawson	.25
184	Billy Ripken	.05
185	Kevin Mitchell	.05
186	Brett Butler	.05
187	Tony Fernandez	.05
188	Cory Snyder	.05
189	John Habyan	.05
190	Dennis Martinez	.05
191	John Smoltz	.05
192	Greg Myers	.05
193	Rob Deer	.05
194	Ivan Rodriguez	.05
195	Ray Lankford	.05
196	Bill Wegman	.05
197	Edgar Martinez	.05
198	Darryl Kile	.05
199	Checklist	.05
200	Brent Mayne	.05
201	Larry Walker	.05
202	Carlos Baerga	.05
203	Russ Swan	.05
204	Mike Morgan	.05
205	Hal Morris	.05
206	Tony Gwynn	.60
207	Mark Leiter	.05
208	Kirt Manwaring	.05
209	Al Osuna	.05
210	Bobby Thigpen	.05
211	Chris Hoiles	.05
212	B.J. Surhoff	.05
213	Lenny Harris	.05
214	Scott Leius	.05
215	Gregg Jefferies	.05
216	Bruce Hurst	.05
217	Steve Sax	.05
218	Dave Otto	.05
219	Sam Horn	.05
220	Charlie Hayes	.05
221	Frank Viola	.05
222	Jose Guzman	.05
223	Gary Redus	.05
224	Dave Gallagher	.05
225	Dean Palmer	.05
226	Greg Olson	.05
227	Jose DeLeon	.05
228	Mike LaValliere	.05
229	Mark Langston	.05
230	Chuck Knoblauch	.05
231	Bill Doran	.05
232	Dave Henderson	.05
233	Roberto Alomar	.20
234	Scott Fletcher	.05
235	Tim Naehring	.05
236	Mike Gallego	.05
237	Lance Johnson	.05
238	Paul Molitor	.05
239	Dan Gladden	.05
240	Willie Randolph	.05
241	Will Clark	.10
242	Sid Bream	.05
243	Derek Bell	.05
244	Bill Pecota	.05
245	Terry Pendleton	.05
246	Randy Ready	.05
247	Jack Armstrong	.05
248	Todd Van Poppel	.05
249	Shawon Dunston	.05
250	Bobby Rose	.05
251	Jeff Huson	.05
252	Bip Roberts	.05
253	Doug Jones	.05
254	Lee Smith	.05
255	George Brett	.65
256	Randy Tomlin	.05
257	Todd Benzinger	.05
258	Dave Stewart	.05
259	Mark Carreon	.05
260	Pete O'Brien	.05
261	Tim Teufel	.05
262	Bob Milacki	.05
263	Mark Guthrie	.05
264	Darrin Fletcher	.05
265	Omar Vizquel	.05
266	Chris Bosio	.05
267	Jose Canseco	.30
268	Mike Boddicker	.05
269	Lance Parrish	.05
270	Jose Vizcaino	.05
271	Chris Sabo	.05
272	Royce Clayton	.05
273	Marquis Grissom	.05
274	Fred McGriff	.05
275	Barry Bonds	1.50
276	Greg Vaughn	.05
277	Gregg Olson	.05
278	Dave Hollins	.05
279	Tom Glavine	.25
280	Bryan Hickerson	.05
281	Scott Radinsky	.05
282	Omar Olivares	.05
283	Ivan Calderon	.05
284	Kevin Maas	.05
285	Mickey Tettleton	.05
286	Wade Boggs	.60
287	Stan Belinda	.05
288	Bret Barberie	.05
289	Jose Oquendo	.05
290	Frank Castillo	.05
291	Dave Stieb	.05
292	Tommy Greene	.05
293	Eric Karros	.05
294	Greg Maddux	.60
295	Jim Eisenreich	.05
296	Rafael Palmeiro	.35
297	Ramon Martinez	.05
298	Tim Wallach	.05
299	Jim Thome	.45
300	Chito Martinez	.05
301	Mitch Williams	.05
302	Randy Johnson	.45
303	Carlton Fisk	.45
304	Travis Fryman	.05
305	Bobby Witt	.05
306	Dave Magadan	.05
307	Alex Cole	.05
308	Bobby Bonilla	.05
309	Bryan Harvey	.05
310	Rafael Belliard	.05
311	Mariano Duncan	.05
312	Chuck Crim	.05
313	John Kruk	.05
314	Ellis Burks	.05
315	Craig Biggio	.05
316	Glenn Davis	.05
317	Ryne Sandberg	.60
318	Mike Sharperson	.05
319	Rich Rodriguez	.05
320	Lee Guetterman	.05
321	Benito Santiago	.05
322	Jose Offerman	.05
323	Tony Pena	.05
324	Pat Borders	.05
325	Mike Henneman	.05
326	Kevin Brown	.05
327	Chris Nabholz	.05
328	Franklin Stubbs	.05
329	Tino Martinez	.05
330	Mickey Morandini	.05
331	Checklist	.05
332	Mark Gubicza	.05
333	Bill Landrum	.05
334	Mark Whiten	.05
335	Darren Daulton	.05
336	Rick Wilkins	.05
337	Brian Jordan RC	.25
338	Kevin Ward	.05
339	Ruben Amaro	.05
340	Trevor Wilson	.05
341	Andujar Cedeno	.05
342	Michael Huff	.05
343	Brady Anderson	.05
344	Craig Grebeck	.05
345	Bobby Ojeda	.05
346	Mike Pagliarulo	.05
347	Terry Shumpert	.05
348	Dann Bilardello	.05
349	Frank Thomas	.45
350	Albert Belle	.05
351	Jose Mesa	.05
352	Rich Monteleone	.05
353	Bob Walk	.05
354	Monty Fariss	.05
355	Luis Rivera	.05
356	Anthony Young	.05
357	Geno Petralli	.05
358	Otis Nixon	.05
359	Tom Pagnozzi	.05
360	Reggie Sanders	.05
361	Lee Stevens	.05
362	Kent Hrbek	.05
363	Orlando Merced	.05
364	Mike Bordick	.05
365	Dion James	.05
366	Jack Clark	.05
367	Mike Stanley	.05
368	Randy Velarde	.05
369	Dan Pasqua	.05
370	Pat Listach	.05
371	Mike Fitzgerald	.05
372	Tom Foley	.05
373	Matt Williams	.05
374	Brian Hunter	.05
375	Joe Carter	.05
376	Bret Saberhagen	.05
377	Mike Stanton	.05
378	Hubie Brooks	.05
379	Eric Bell	.05
380	Walt Weiss	.05
381	Danny Jackson	.05
382	Manuel Lee	.05
383	Ruben Sierra	.05
384	Greg Swindell	.05
385	Ryan Bowen	.05
386	Kevin Ritz	.05
387	Curtis Wilkerson	.05
388	Gary Varsho	.05
389	Dave Hansen	.05
390	Bob Welch	.05
391	Lou Whitaker	.05
392	Ken Griffey Jr.	.75
393	Mike Maddux	.05
394	Arthur Rhodes	.05
395	Chili Davis	.05
396	Eddie Murray	.45
397	Checklist	.05
398	Dave Cochrane	.05
399	Kevin Seitzer	.05
400	Ozzie Smith	.60
401	Paul Sorrento	.05
402	Les Lancaster	.05
403	Junior Noboa	.05
404	Dave Justice	.05
405	Andy Ashby	.05
406	Danny Tartabull	.05
407	Bill Swift	.05
408	Craig Lefferts	.05
409	Tom Candiotti	.05
410	Lance Blankenship	.05
411	Jeff Tackett	.05
412	Sammy Sosa	.65
413	Jody Reed	.05
414	Bruce Ruffin	.05
415	Gene Larkin	.05
416	John Vanderwal	.05
417	Tim Belcher	.05
418	Steve Frey	.05
419	Dick Schofield	.05
420	Jeff King	.05
421	Kim Batiste	.05
422	Jack McDowell	.05
423	Damon Berryhill	.05
424	Gary Wayne	.05
425	Jack Morris	.05
426	Moises Alou	.05
427	Mark McLemore	.05
428	Juan Guerrero	.05
429	Scott Scudder	.05
430	Eric Davis	.05
431	Joe Slusarski	.05
432	Todd Zeile	.05
433	Dwayne Henry	.05
434	Cliff Brantley	.05
435	Butch Henry	.05
436	Todd Worrell	.05
437	Bob Scanlan	.05
438	Wally Joyner	.05
439	John Flaherty	.05
440	Brian Downing	.05
441	Darren Lewis	.05
442	Gary Carter	.45
443	Wally Ritchie	.05
444	Chris Jones	.05
445	Jeff Kent	.05
446	Gary Sheffield	.30
447	Ron Darling	.05
448	Deion Sanders	.05
449	Andres Galarraga	.05
450	Chuck Finley	.05
451	Derek Lilliquist	.05
452	Carl Willis	.05
453	Wes Chamberlain	.05
454	Roger Mason	.05
455	Spike Owen	.05
456	Thomas Howard	.05
457	Dave Martinez	.05
458	Pete Incaviglia	.05
459	Keith Miller	.05
460	Mike Fetters	.05
461	Paul Gibson	.05
462	George Bell	.05
463	Checklist	.05
464	Terry Mulholland	.05
465	Storm Davis	.05
466	Gary Pettis	.05
467	Randy Bush	.05
468	Ken Hill	.05
469	Rheal Cormier	.05
470	Andy Stankiewicz	.05
471	Dave Burba	.05
472	Henry Cotto	.05
473	Dale Sveum	.05
474	Rich Gossage	.05
475	William Suero	.05
476	Doug Strange	.05
477	Bill Krueger	.05
478	John Wetteland	.05
479	Melido Perez	.05
480	Lonnie Smith	.05
481	Mike Jackson	.05
482	Mike Gardiner	.05
483	David Wells	.05
484	Barry Jones	.05
485	Scott Bankhead	.05
486	Terry Leach	.05
487	Vince Horsman	.05
488	Dave Eiland	.05
489	Alejandro Pena	.05
490	Julio Valera	.05
491	Joe Boever	.05
492	Paul Miller	.05
493	Arci Cianfrocco RC	.05
494	Dave Fleming	.05
495	Kyle Abbott	.05
496	Chad Kreuter	.05
497	Chris James	.05
498	Donnie Hill	.05
499	Jacob Brumfield	.05
500	Ricky Bones	.05
501	Terry Steinbach	.05
502	Bernard Gilkey	.05
503	Dennis Cook	.05
504	Len Dykstra	.05
505	Mike Bielecki	.05
506	Bob Kipper	.05
507	Jose Melendez	.05
508	Rick Sutcliffe	.05
509	Ken Patterson	.05
510	Andy Allanson	.05
511	Al Newman	.05
512	Mark Gardner	.05
513	Jeff Schaefer	.05
514	Jim McNamara	.05
515	Peter Hoy	.05
516	Curt Schilling	.30
517	Kirk McCaskill	.05
518	Chris Gwynn	.05
519	Sid Fernandez	.05
520	Jeff Parrett	.05
521	Scott Ruskin	.05
522	Kevin McReynolds	.05
523	Rick Cerone	.05
524	Jesse Orosco	.05
525	Troy Afenir	.05
526	John Smiley	.05
527	Dale Murphy	.25
528	Leaf Set Card	.05

JOSE VIZCAINO IF

	NM/M
Complete Set (528):	35.00
Common Player:	.10
Stars/Rookies:	3X

Gold Rookies

PAT MAHOMES RHP

Two dozen of the major leagues' most promising players are featured in this insert set. Cards 1-12 were randomly included in Series 1 foil packs, while cards 13-24 were in Series 2 packs. Cards, numbered with a BC prefix, are standard size and enhanced with gold foil.

		NM/M
Complete Set (24):		4.00
Common Player:		.25
Jumbo:		1.5X
1	Chad Curtis	.25
2	Brent Gates	.25
3	Pedro Martinez	3.00
4	Kenny Lofton	.35
5	Turk Wendell	.25
6	Mark Hutton	.25
7	Todd Hundley	.25
8	Matt Stairs	.25
9	Ed Taubensee	.25
10	David Nied	.25
11	Salomon Torres	.25
12	Bret Boone	.50
13	John Ruffin	.25
14	Ed Martel	.25
15	Rick Trlicek	.25
16	Raul Mondesi	.50
17	Pat Mahomes	.25
18	Dan Wilson	.25
19	Donovan Osborne	.25
20	Dave Silvestri	.25
21	Gary DiSarcina	.25
22	Denny Neagle	.25
23	Steve Hosey	.25
24	John Doherty	.25

1993 Leaf Promo

This unmarked promo of company spokesman Frank Thomas can be distinguished from the issued version of his card #195 by the presence of the Franklin logo on the batting glove he wears. The logo was airbrushed away from the issued card.

		NM/M
195	Frank Thomas	10.00

1993 Leaf

Leaf issued this set in three series: two 220-card series and a 110-card update set. Card fronts have full-bleed action photos and players' names stamped in gold foil. Color-coded slate corners are used to differentiate teams. Backs have player photos against cityscapes or landmarks from the team's home city, a holographic embossed team logo and 1992 career statistics. Players from the National League's expansion teams, the Colorado Rockies and Florida Marlins, along with the Cincinnati Reds, California Angels and Seattle Mariners were featured in

Gold Previews

CHRIS SABO 3B

In the same format as the chase cards which would be included in the regular 1992 Leaf packs, this preview set was produced for distribution to the Donruss dealer network. Cards feature the same black borders and gold highlights as the regular-issue Leaf Gold cards, but are numbered "X of 33" on the back.

		NM/M
Complete Set (33):		30.00
Common Player:		.50
1	Steve Avery	.50
2	Ryne Sandberg	2.00
3	Chris Sabo	.50
4	Jeff Bagwell	1.50
5	Darryl Strawberry	.50
6	Bret Barberie	.50
7	Howard Johnson	.50
8	John Kruk	.50
9	Andy Van Slyke	.50
10	Felix Jose	.50
11	Fred McGriff	.50
12	Will Clark	.60
13	Cal Ripken, Jr.	4.00
14	Phil Plantier	.50
15	Lee Stevens	.50
16	Frank Thomas	1.50
17	Mark Whiten	.50
18	Cecil Fielder	.50
19	George Brett	2.50
20	Robin Yount	1.50
21	Scott Erickson	.50
22	Don Mattingly	2.50
23	Jose Canseco	1.00
24	Ken Griffey Jr.	3.00
25	Nolan Ryan	4.00
26	Joe Carter	.50
27	Deion Sanders	.50
28	Dean Palmer	.50
29	Andy Benes	.50
30	Gary DiSarcina	.50
31	Chris Hoiles	.50
32	Mark McGwire	3.00
33	Reggie Sanders	.50

Gold Edition

This set is a parallel version of Leaf's regular 1992 set. Card fronts do not have silver borders like the regular cards do; black borders and gold foil highlights are seen instead. A Gold Edition card was inserted in each 15-card 1992 Leaf foil pack.

Series II packs so they could be pictured in their new uniforms. The Update series included a specially numbered "DW" insert card honoring Dave Winfield's 3,000-hit landmark, plus 3,500 special Frank Thomas autographed cards.

	NM/M
Complete Set (550):	12.50
Common Player:	.05
Series 1 or 2 Pack (14):	.65
Series 1 or 2 Box (36):	12.50
Update Pack (14):	1.50
Update Box (36):	25.00

#	Player	Price
1	Ben McDonald	.05
2	Sid Fernandez	.05
3	Juan Guzman	.05
4	Curt Schilling	.40
5	Ivan Rodriguez	.65
6	Don Slaught	.05
7	Terry Steinbach	.05
8	Todd Zeile	.05
9	Andy Stankiewicz	.05
10	Tim Teufel	.05
11	Marvin Freeman	.05
12	Jim Austin	.05
13	Bob Scanlan	.05
14	Rusty Meacham	.05
15	Casey Candaele	.05
16	Travis Fryman	.05
17	Jose Offerman	.05
18	Albert Belle	.05
19	John Vander Wahl (Vander Wal)	.05
20	Dan Pasqua	.05
21	Frank Viola	.05
22	Terry Mulholland	.05
23	Gregg Olson	.05
24	Randy Tomlin	.05
25	Todd Stottlemyre	.05
26	Jose Oquendo	.05
27	Julio Franco	.05
28	Tony Gwynn	1.00
29	Ruben Sierra	.05
30	Robby Thompson	.05
31	Jim Bullinger	.05
32	Rick Aguilera	.05
33	Scott Servais	.05
34	Cal Eldred	.05
35	Mike Piazza	1.50
36	Brent Mayne	.05
37	Wil Cordero	.05
38	Milt Cuyler	.05
39	Howard Johnson	.05
40	Kenny Lofton	.05
41	Alex Fernandez	.05
42	Denny Neagle	.05
43	Tony Pena	.05
44	Bob Tewksbury	.05
45	Glenn Davis	.05
46	Fred McGriff	.05
47	John Olerud	.05
48	Steve Hosey	.05
49	Rafael Palmeiro	.65
50	Dave Justice	.05
51	Pete Harnisch	.05
52	Sam Militello	.05
53	Orel Hershiser	.05
54	Pat Mahomes	.05
55	Greg Colbrunn	.05
56	Greg Vaughn	.05
57	Vince Coleman	.05
58	Brian McRae	.05
59	Len Dykstra	.05
60	Dan Gladden	.05
61	Ted Power	.05
62	Donovan Osborne	.05
63	Ron Karkovice	.05
64	Frank Seminara	.05
65	Bob Zupcic	.05
66	Kirt Manwaring	.05
67	Mike Devereaux	.05
68	Mark Lemke	.05
69	Devon White	.05
70	Sammy Sosa	1.25
71	Pedro Astacio	.05
72	Dennis Eckersley	.60
73	Chris Nabholz	.05
74	Melido Perez	.05
75	Todd Hundley	.05
76	Kent Hrbek	.05
77	Mickey Morandini	.05
78	Tim McIntosh	.05
79	Andy Van Slyke	.05
80	Kevin McReynolds	.05
81	Mike Henneman	.05
82	Greg Harris	.05
83	Sandy Alomar Jr.	.05
84	Mike Jackson	.05
85	Ozzie Guillen	.05
86	Jeff Blauser	.05
87	John Valentin	.05
88	Rey Sanchez	.05
89	Rick Sutcliffe	.05
90	Luis Gonzalez	.25
91	Jeff Fassero	.05
92	Kenny Rogers	.05
93	Bret Saberhagen	.05
94	Bob Welch	.05
95	Darren Daulton	.05
96	Mike Gallego	.05
97	Orlando Merced	.05
98	Chuck Knoblauch	.05
99	Bernard Gilkey	.05
100	Billy Ashley	.05
101	Kevin Appier	.05
102	Jeff Brantley	.05
103	Bill Gullickson	.05
104	John Smoltz	.05
105	Paul Sorrento	.05
106	Steve Buechele	.05
107	Steve Sax	.05
108	Andujar Cedeno	.05
109	Billy Hatcher	.05
110	Checklist	.05
111	Alan Mills	.05
112	John Franco	.05
113	Jack Morris	.05
114	Mitch Williams	.05
115	Nolan Ryan	2.50
116	Jay Bell	.05
117	Mike Bordick	.05
118	Geronimo Pena	.05
119	Danny Tartabull	.05
120	Checklist	.05
121	Steve Avery	.05
122	Ricky Bones	.05
123	Mike Morgan	.05
124	Jeff Montgomery	.05
125	Jeff Bagwell	.75
126	Tony Phillips	.05
127	Lenny Harris	.05
128	Glenallen Hill	.05
129	Marquis Grissom	.05
130	Gerald Williams (Photo, stats actually Bernie Williams.)	.20
131	Greg Harris	.05
132	Tommy Greene	.05
133	Chris Hoiles	.05
134	Bob Walk	.05
135	Duane Ward	.05
136	Tom Pagnozzi	.05
137	Jeff Huson	.05
138	Kurt Stillwell	.05
139	Dave Henderson	.05
140	Darrin Jackson	.05
141	Frank Castillo	.05
142	Scott Erickson	.05
143	Darryl Kile	.05
144	Bill Wegman	.05
145	Steve Wilson	.05
146	George Brett	1.25
147	Moises Alou	.05
148	Lou Whitaker	.05
149	Chico Walker	.05
150	Jerry Browne	.05
151	Kirk McCaskill	.05
152	Zane Smith	.05
153	Matt Young	.05
154	Lee Smith	.05
155	Leo Gomez	.05
156	Dan Walters	.05
157	Pat Borders	.05
158	Matt Williams	.05
159	Dean Palmer	.05
160	John Patterson	.05
161	Doug Jones	.05
162	John Habyan	.05
163	Pedro Martinez	.75
164	Carl Willis	.05
165	Darrin Fletcher	.05
166	B.J. Surhoff	.05
167	Eddie Murray	.75
168	Keith Miller	.05
169	Ricky Jordan	.05
170	Juan Gonzalez	.65
171	Charles Nagy	.05
172	Mark Clark	.05
173	Bobby Thigpen	.05
174	Tim Scott	.05
175	Scott Cooper	.05
176	Royce Clayton	.05
177	Brady Anderson	.05
178	Sid Bream	.05
179	Derek Bell	.05
180	Otis Nixon	.05
181	Kevin Gross	.05
182	Ron Darling	.05
183	John Wetteland	.05
184	Mike Stanley	.05
185	Jeff Kent	.05
186	Brian Harper	.05
187	Mariano Duncan	.05
188	Robin Yount	.75
189	Al Martin	.05
190	Eddie Zosky	.05
191	Mike Munoz	.05
192	Andy Benes	.20
193	Dennis Cook	.05
194	Bill Swift	.05
195	Frank Thomas	.75
196	Damon Berryhill	.05
197	Mike Greenwell	.05
198	Mark Grace	.05
199	Darryl Hamilton	.05
200	Derrick May	.05
201	Ken Hill	.05
202	Kevin Brown	.05
203	Dwight Gooden	.05
204	Bobby Witt	.05
205	Juan Bell	.05
206	Kevin Maas	.05
207	Jeff King	.05
208	Scott Leius	.05
209	Rheal Cormier	.05
210	Darryl Strawberry	.05
211	Tom Gordon	.05
212	Bud Black	.05
213	Mickey Tettleton	.05
214	Pete Smith	.05
215	Felix Fermin	.05
216	Rick Wilkins	.05
217	George Bell	.05
218	Eric Anthony	.05
219	Pedro Munoz	.05
220	Checklist	.05
221	Lance Blankenship	.05
222	Deion Sanders	.10
223	Craig Biggio	.05
224	Ryne Sandberg	1.00
225	Ron Gant	.05
226	Tom Brunansky	.05
227	Chad Curtis	.05
228	Joe Carter	.05
229	Brian Jordan	.05
230	Brett Butler	.05
231	Frank Bolick	.05
232	Rod Beck	.05
233	Carlos Baerga	.05
234	Eric Karros	.05
235	Jack Armstrong	.05
236	Bobby Bonilla	.05
237	Don Mattingly	1.25
238	Jeff Gardner	.05
239	Dave Hollins	.05
240	Steve Cooke	.05
241	Jose Canseco	.35
242	Ivan Calderon	.05
243	Tim Belcher	.05
244	Freddie Benavides	.05
245	Roberto Alomar	.25
246	Rob Deer	.05
247	Will Clark	.10
248	Mike Felder	.05
249	Harold Baines	.05
250	David Cone	.05
251	Mark Guthrie	.05
252	Ellis Burks	.05
253	Jim Abbott	.05
254	Chili Davis	.05
255	Chris Bosio	.05
256	Bret Barberie	.05
257	Hal Morris	.05
258	Dante Bichette	.05
259	Storm Davis	.05
260	Gary DiSarcina	.05
261	Ken Caminiti	.05
262	Paul Molitor	.75
263	Joe Oliver	.05
264	Pat Listach	.05
265	Gregg Jefferies	.05
266	Jose Guzman	.05
267	Eric Davis	.05
268	Delino DeShields	.05
269	Barry Bonds	2.50
270	Mike Bielecki	.05
271	Jay Buhner	.05
272	Scott Pose RC	.05
273	Tony Fernandez	.05
274	Chito Martinez	.05
275	Phil Plantier	.05
276	Pete Incaviglia	.05
277	Carlos Garcia	.05
278	Tom Henke	.05
279	Roger Clemens	1.25
280	Rob Dibble	.05
281	Daryl Boston	.05
282	Greg Gagne	.05
283	Cecil Fielder	.05
284	Carlton Fisk	.75
285	Wade Boggs	1.00
286	Damion Easley	.05
287	Norm Charlton	.05
288	Jeff Conine	.05
289	Roberto Kelly	.05
290	Jerald Clark	.05
291	Rickey Henderson	.75
292	Chuck Finley	.05
293	Doug Drabek	.05
294	Dave Stewart	.05
295	Tom Glavine	.35
296	Jaime Navarro	.05
297	Ray Lankford	.05
298	Greg Hibbard	.05
299	Jody Reed	.05
300	Dennis Martinez	.05
301	Dave Martinez	.05
302	Reggie Jefferson	.05
303	John Cummings RC	.05
304	Orestes Destrade	.05
305	Mike Maddux	.05
306	David Segui	.05
307	Gary Sheffield	.35
308	Danny Jackson	.05
309	Criag Lefferts	.05
310	Andre Dawson	.20
311	Barry Larkin	.05
312	Alex Cole	.05
313	Mark Gardner	.05
314	Kirk Gibson	.05
315	Shane Mack	.05
316	Bo Jackson	.10
317	Jimmy Key	.05
318	Greg Myers	.05
319	Ken Griffey Jr.	1.50
320	Monty Fariss	.05
321	Kevin Mitchell	.05
322	Andres Galarraga	.05
323	Mark McGwire	2.00
324	Mark Langston	.05
325	Steve Finley	.05
326	Greg Maddux	1.00
327	Dave Nilsson	.05
328	Ozzie Smith	1.00
329	Candy Maldonado	.05
330	Checklist	.05
331	Tim Pugh RC	.05
332	Joe Girardi	.05
333	Junior Felix	.05
334	Greg Swindell	.05
335	Ramon Martinez	.05
336	Sean Berry	.05
337	Joe Orsulak	.05
338	Wes Chamberlain	.05
339	Stan Belinda	.05
340	Checklist	.05
341	Bruce Hurst	.05
342	John Burkett	.05
343	Mike Mussina	.40
344	Scott Fletcher	.05
345	Rene Gonzales	.05
346	Roberto Hernandez	.05
347	Carlos Martinez	.05
348	Bill Krueger	.05
349	Felix Jose	.05
350	John Jaha	.05
351	Willie Banks	.05
352	Matt Nokes	.05
353	Kevin Seitzer	.05
354	Erik Hanson	.05
355	David Hulse RC	.05
356	Domingo Martinez RC	.05
357	Greg Olson	.05
358	Randy Myers	.05
359	Tom Browning	.05
360	Charlie Hayes	.05
361	Bryan Harvey	.05
362	Eddie Taubensee	.05
363	Tim Wallach	.05
364	Mel Rojas	.05
365	Frank Tanana	.05
366	John Kruk	.05
367	Tim Laker RC	.05
368	Rich Rodriguez	.05
369	Darren Lewis	.05
370	Harold Reynolds	.05
371	Jose Melendez	.05
372	Joe Grahe	.05
373	Lance Johnson	.05
374	Jose Mesa	.05
375	Scott Livingstone	.05
376	Wally Joyner	.05
377	Kevin Reimer	.05
378	Kirby Puckett	1.00
379	Paul O'Neill	.05
380	Randy Johnson	.75
381	Manuel Lee	.05
382	Dick Schofield	.05
383	Darren Holmes	.05
384	Charlie Hough	.05
385	John Orton	.05
386	Edgar Martinez	.05
387	Terry Pendleton	.05
388	Dan Plesac	.05
389	Jeff Reardon	.05
390	David Nied	.05
391	Dave Magadan	.05
392	Larry Walker	.05
393	Ben Rivera	.05
394	Lonnie Smith	.05
395	Craig Shipley	.05
396	Willie McGee	.05
397	Arthur Rhodes	.05
398	Mike Stanton	.05
399	Luis Polonia	.05
400	Jack McDowell	.05
401	Mike Moore	.05
402	Jose Lind	.05
403	Bill Spiers	.05
404	Kevin Tapani	.05
405	Spike Owen	.05
406	Tino Martinez	.05
407	Charlie Leibrandt	.05
408	Ed Sprague	.05
409	Bryn Smith	.05
410	Benito Santiago	.05
411	Jose Rijo	.05
412	Pete O'Brien	.05
413	Willie Wilson	.05
414	Bip Roberts	.05
415	Eric Young	.05
416	Walt Weiss	.05
417	Milt Thompson	.05
418	Chris Sabo	.05
419	Scott Sanderson	.05
420	Tim Raines	.05
421	Alan Trammell	.05
422	Mike Macfarlane	.05
423	Dave Winfield	.05
424	Bob Wickman	.05
425	David Valle	.05
426	Gary Redus	.05
427	Turner Ward	.05
428	Reggie Sanders	.05
429	Todd Worrell	.05
430	Julio Valera	.05
431	Cal Ripken, Jr.	2.50
432	Mo Vaughn	.05
433	John Smiley	.05
434	Omar Vizquel	.05
435	Billy Ripken	.05
436	Cory Snyder	.05
437	Carlos Quintana	.05
438	Omar Olivares	.05
439	Robin Ventura	.05
440	Checklist	.05
441	Kevin Higgins	.05
442	Carlos Hernandez	.05
443	Dan Peltier	.05
444	Derek Lilliquist	.05
445	Tim Salmon	.05
446	Sherman Obando RC	.05
447	Pat Kelly	.05
448	Todd Van Poppel	.05
449	Mark Whiten	.05
450	Checklist	.05
451	Pat Meares	.05
452	Tony Tarasco RC	.05
453	Chris Gwynn	.05
454	Armando Reynoso	.05
455	Danny Darwin	.05
456	Willie Greene	.05
457	Mike Blowers	.05
458	Kevin Roberson RC	.05
459	Graeme Lloyd RC	.05
460	David West	.05
461	Joey Cora	.05
462	Alex Arias	.05
463	Chad Kreuter	.05
464	Mike Lansing	.05
465	Mike Timlin	.05
466	Paul Wagner	.05
467	Mark Portugal	.05
468	Jim Leyritz	.05
469	Ryan Klesko	.05
470	Mario Diaz	.05
471	Guillermo Velasquez	.05
472	Fernando Valenzuela	.05
473	Raul Mondesi	.05
474	Mike Pagliarulo	.05
475	Chris Hammond	.05
476	Torey Lovullo	.05
477	Trevor Wilson	.05
478	Marcos Armas RC	.05
479	Dave Gallagher	.05
480	Jeff Treadway	.05
481	Jeff Branson	.05
482	Dickie Thon	.05
483	Eduardo Perez	.05
484	David Wells	.05
485	Brian Williams	.05
486	Domingo Cedeno	.05
487	Tom Candiotti	.05
488	Steve Frey	.05
489	Greg McMichael	.05
490	Marc Newfield	.05
491	Larry Andersen	.05
492	Damon Buford	.05
493	Ricky Gutierrez	.05
494	Jeff Russell	.05
495	Vinny Castilla	.05
496	Wilson Alvarez	.05
497	Scott Bullett	.05
498	Larry Casian	.05
499	Jose Vizcaino	.05
500	J.T. Snow RC	.75
501	Bryan Hickerson	.05
502	Jeremy Hernandez	.05
503	Jeromy Burnitz	.05
504	Steve Farr	.05
505	J. Owens	.05
506	Craig Paquette	.05
507	Jim Eisenreich	.05
508	Matt Whiteside	.05
509	Luis Aquino	.05
510	Mike LaValliere	.05
511	Jim Gott	.05
512	Mark McLemore	.05
513	Randy Milligan	.05
514	Gary Gaetti	.05
515	Lou Frazier	.05
516	Rich Amaral	.05
517	Gene Harris	.05
518	Aaron Sele	.05
519	Mark Wohlers	.05
520	Scott Kamieniecki	.05
521	Kent Mercker	.05
522	Jim Deshaies	.05
523	Kevin Stocker	.05
524	Jason Bere	.05
525	Tim Bogar	.05
526	Brad Pennington	.05
527	Curt Leskanic RC	.05
528	Wayne Kirby	.05
529	Tim Costo	.05
530	Doug Henry	.05
531	Trevor Hoffman	.05
532	Kelly Gruber	.05
533	Mike Harkey	.05
534	John Doherty	.05
535	Erik Pappas	.05
536	Brent Gates	.05
537	Roger McDowell	.05
538	Chris Haney	.05
539	Blas Minor	.05
540	Pat Hentgen	.05
541	Chuck Carr	.05
542	Doug Strange	.05
543	Xavier Hernandez	.05
544	Paul Quantrill	.05
545	Anthony Young	.05
546	Bret Boone	.05
547	Dwight Smith	.05
548	Bobby Munoz	.05
549	Russ Springer	.05
550	Roger Pavlik	.05
----	Dave Winfield (3,000 Hits)	2.00

Fasttrack

This 20-card insert set was released in two series; cards 1-10 were randomly included in Leaf Series I retail packs, while 11-20 were in Series II packs. Card fronts and backs are similar with a player photo and a diagonal white strip with "on the Fasttrack" printed in black and red. Fronts have the gold embossed Leaf logo, backs have the silver holographic team logo.

	NM/M
Complete Set (20):	15.00
Common Player:	.60
1	Frank Thomas	3.00
2	Tim Wakefield	.60
3	Kenny Lofton	.60
4	Mike Mussina	1.00
5	Juan Gonzalez	2.50
6	Chuck Knoblauch	.60
7	Eric Karros	.60
8	Ray Lankford	.60
9	Juan Guzman	.60
10	Pat Listach	.60
11	Carlos Baerga	.60
12	Felix Jose	.60
13	Steve Avery	.60
14	Robin Ventura	.60
15	Ivan Rodriguez	2.50
16	Cal Eldred	.60
17	Jeff Bagwell	3.00
18	Dave Justice	.60
19	Travis Fryman	.60
20	Marquis Grissom	.60

Gold All-Stars

Cards 1-10 in this insert set were randomly inserted one per Leaf Series I jumbo packs, while cards 11-20 were in Series II jumbo packs. Cards feature two players per card, one on each side. Only one side is numbered, but both sides have gold foil.

	NM/M
Complete Set (20):	15.00
Common Player:	.25
1	Ivan Rodriguez, Darren Daulton	.75
2	Don Mattingly, Fred McGriff	1.50
3	Cecil Fielder, Jeff Bagwell	.75
4	Carlos Baerga, Ryne Sandberg	1.00
5	Chuck Knoblauch, Delino DeShields	.25
6	Robin Ventura, Terry Pendleton	.25
7	Ken Griffey Jr., Andy Van Slyke	2.00
8	Joe Carter, Dave Justice	.25
9	Jose Canseco, Tony Gwynn	1.00
10	Dennis Eckersley, Rob Dibble	.60
11	Mark McGwire, Will Clark	2.50
12	Frank Thomas, Mark Grace	.75
13	Roberto Alomar, Craig Biggio	.50
14	Barry Larkin, Cal Ripken, Jr.	3.00

15	Gary Sheffield, Edgar Martinez	.50
16	Juan Gonzalez, Barry Bonds	3.00
17	Kirby Puckett, Marquis Grissom	1.00
18	Jim Abbott, Tom Glavine	.40
19	Nolan Ryan, Greg Maddux	3.00
20	Roger Clemens, Doug Drabek	1.50

Gold Rookies

These cards, numbered 1 of 20 etc., feature 1993 rookies and were randomly inserted into hobby foil packs, 10 players per series. Card fronts feature action photos, while the backs show a player photo against a landmark from his team's city. Jumbo versions in 3-1/2" x 5" format were produced as special retail box toppers, in a numbered edition of 5,000 each.

		NM/M
Complete Set (20):		5.00
Common Player:		.25
1	Kevin Young	.25
2	Wil Cordero	.25
3	Mark Kiefer	.25
4	Gerald Williams	.25
5	Brandon Wilson	.25
6	Greg Gohr	.25
7	Ryan Thompson	.25
8	Tim Wakefield	.25
9	Troy Neel	.25
10	Tim Salmon	.50
11	Kevin Rogers	.25
12	Rod Bolton	.25
13	Ken Ryan	.25
14	Phil Hiatt	.25
15	Rene Arocha	.25
16	Nigel Wilson	.25
17	J.T. Snow	.50
18	Benji Gil	.25
19	Chipper Jones	3.00
20	Darrell Sherman	.25

Heading for the Hall

Ten players on the way to the Baseball Hall of Fame are featured in this insert set. Series I Leaf packs had cards 1-5 randomly included; Series II packs had cards 6-10.

		NM/M
Complete Set (10):		10.00
Common Player:		1.00
1	Nolan Ryan	2.50
2	Tony Gwynn	1.00
3	Robin Yount	1.00
4	Eddie Murray	1.00
5	Cal Ripken, Jr.	2.50
6	Roger Clemens	2.00
7	George Brett	2.00
8	Ryne Sandberg	1.00
9	Kirby Puckett	1.00
10	Ozzie Smith	1.00

Frank Thomas

Leaf signed Frank Thomas as its spokesman for 1993, and honored him with a 10-card insert set. Cards 1-5 were randomly included in Series I packs; cards 6-10 were in Series II packs. A large "Frank"

logo in a holographic foil stamp is featured on each card front along with a one-word character trait. On back is a color portrait photo of Thomas superimposed on a Chicago skyline. A paragraph on back describes how the character trait on front applies to Thomas.

		NM/M
Complete Set (10):		4.50
Common Card:		.75
Autographed Card:		30.00
1	Aggressive (Frank Thomas)	.75
2	Serious (Frank Thomas)	.75
3	Intense (Frank Thomas)	.75
4	Confident (Frank Thomas)	.75
5	Assertive (Frank Thomas)	.75
6	Power (Frank Thomas)	.75
7	Control (Frank Thomas)	.75
8	Strength (Frank Thomas)	.75
9	Concentration (Frank Thomas)	.75
10	Preparation (Frank Thomas)	.75

Update Gold All-Stars

These 10 cards, featuring 20 all-stars, were randomly inserted in Leaf Update packs. Each card features two players, one on each side. Cards are distinguished from the regular Gold All-Stars by indicating on the front the card is number X of 10, with a tiny white "Update" in the red stripe above the card number.

		NM/M
Complete Set (10):		7.50
Common Player:		.25
1	Mark Langston, Terry Mulholland	.25
2	Ivan Rodriguez, Darren Daulton	.50
3	John Olerud, John Kruk	.25
4	Roberto Alomar, Ryne Sandberg	1.00
5	Wade Boggs, Gary Sheffield	.75
6	Cal Ripken, Jr., Barry Larkin	3.00
7	Kirby Puckett, Barry Bonds	2.50
8	Marquis Grissom, Ken Griffey Jr.	2.00
9	Joe Carter, Dave Justice	.25
10	Mark Grace, Paul Molitor	.75

Update Gold Rookies

These five cards were randomly inserted in Leaf Update packs. Cards are similiar in design to the regular Gold Rookies cards, except the logo on the back indicates they are from the Update series. Jumbo 3-1/2" x 5" versions were produced as special retail box toppers in a numbered edition of 5,000 each.

		NM/M
Complete Set (5):		3.50
Common Player:		.25
Jumbos:		1.5X
1	Allen Watson	.25
2	Jeffrey Hammonds	.25

3	David McCarty	.25
4	Mike Piazza	3.00
5	Roberto Mejia	.25

Update Frank Thomas Autograph

This card was a random insert in '93 Leaf Update packs and features a genuine Frank Thomas autograph on front. Unlike the other cards in the set, this has a silver-gray border on front and back. Front has a gold-foil seal in upper-left. Back has a photo of Thomas in his batting follow-through. At bottom on back is a white strip bearing the card's individual serial number from an edition of 3,500.

		NM/M
FT	Frank Thomas	35.00

Update Frank Thomas Super

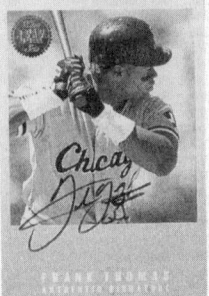

This 10-card insert set features Leaf's 1993 spokesman, Frank Thomas. Cards, which measure 5" x 7", were included one per every Leaf Update foil box and are identical to the inserts found in Series I and II except in size. Cards are individually numbered. Thomas autographed 3,500 cards.

		NM/M
Complete Set (10):		17.50
Common Card:		2.00
1	Aggressive (Frank Thomas)	2.00
2	Serious (Frank Thomas)	2.00
3	Intense (Frank Thomas)	2.00
4	Confident (Frank Thomas)	2.00
5	Assertive (Frank Thomas)	2.00
6	Power (Frank Thomas)	2.00
7	Control (Frank Thomas)	2.00
8	Strength (Frank Thomas)	2.00
9	Concentration (Frank Thomas)	2.00
10	Preparation (Frank Thomas)	2.00

1994 Leaf Promos

Identical in format to the regular issue, this nine-card set was produced as a preview for the 1994 Leaf cards. The only differences on the promo cards are a large, black "Promotional Sample" notice overprinted diagonally on both the front and back of the cards. Instead of the regular card numbers, the promos are numbered "X of 9" at top to the left of the team logo hologram.

		NM/M
Complete Set (9):		7.50
Common Player:		.25
1	Roberto Alomar	.75
2	Darren Daulton	.25
3	Ken Griffey Jr.	2.00
4	David Justice	.25
5	Don Mattingly	1.50
6	Mike Piazza	2.00
7	Cal Ripken, Jr.	3.00
8	Ryne Sandberg	1.25
9	Frank Thomas	1.00

1994 Leaf

Donruss returned its premium-brand Leaf set in 1994 with an announced 25 percent production cut from the previous season - fewer than 20,000 20-box cases of each 220-card series. Game-action photos dominate the fronts of the cards, borderless at the top and sides. At bottom are team color-coded faux-marble borders with the player's name (last name in gold foil) and team. Backs have a background of the player's home stadium with another action photo superimposed. In a ticket-stub device at upper-left is a portrait photo and a few personal numbers. Previous season and career stats are in white stripes at bottom. The team logo is presented in holographic foil at upper-right. To feature 1994's new stadiums and uniforms, cards of the Indians, Rangers, Brewers and Astros were included only in the second series. Seven different types of insert cards were produced and distributed among the various types of Leaf packaging.

		NM/M
Complete Set (440):		10.00
Common Player:		.05
Series 1 or 2 Pack (12):		.75
Series 1 or 2 Box (36):		12.50
1	Cal Ripken, Jr.	2.50
2	Tony Tarasco	.05
3	Joe Girardi	.05
4	Bernie Williams	.20
5	Chad Kreuter	.05
6	Troy Neel	.05
7	Tom Pagnozzi	.05
8	Kirk Rueter	.05
9	Chris Bosio	.05
10	Dwight Gooden	.05
11	Mariano Duncan	.05
12	Jay Bell	.05
13	Lance Johnson	.05
14	Richie Lewis	.05
15	Dave Martinez	.05
16	Orel Hershiser	.05
17	Rob Butler	.05
18	Glenallen Hill	.05
19	Chad Curtis	.05
20	Mike Stanton	.05
21	Tim Wallach	.05
22	Milt Thompson	.05
23	Kevin Young	.05
24	John Smiley	.05
25	Jeff Montgomery	.05
26	Robin Ventura	.05
27	Scott Lydy	.05
28	Todd Stottlemyre	.05
29	Mark Whiten	.05
30	Robby Thompson	.05
31	Bobby Bonilla	.05
32	Andy Ashby	.05
33	Greg Myers	.05
34	Billy Hatcher	.05
35	Brad Holman	.05
36	Mark McLemore	.05
37	Scott Sanders	.05
38	Jim Abbott	.05
39	David Wells	.05
40	Roberto Kelly	.05
41	Jeff Conine	.05
42	Sean Berry	.05
43	Mark Grace	.05
44	Eric Young	.05
45	Rick Aguilera	.05
46	Chipper Jones	1.00
47	Mel Rojas	.05
48	Ryan Thompson	.05
49	Al Martin	.05
50	Cecil Fielder	.05
51	Pat Kelly	.05
52	Kevin Tapani	.05
53	Tim Costo	.05
54	Dave Hollins	.05
55	Kirt Manwaring	.05
56	Gregg Jefferies	.05
57	Ron Darling	.05
58	Bill Haselman	.05
59	Phil Plantier	.05
60	Frank Viola	.05
61	Todd Zeile	.05
62	Bret Barberie	.05
63	Roberto Mejia	.05
64	Chuck Knoblauch	.05
65	Jose Lind	.05
66	Brady Anderson	.05
67	Ruben Sierra	.05
68	Jose Vizcaino	.05
69	Joe Grahe	.05
70	Kevin Appier	.05
71	Wilson Alvarez	.05
72	Tom Candiotti	.05
73	John Burkett	.05
74	Anthony Young	.05
75	Scott Cooper	.05
76	Nigel Wilson	.05
77	John Valentin	.05
78	Dave McCarty	.05
79	Archi Cianfrocco	.05
80	Lou Whitaker	.05
81	Dante Bichette	.05
82	Mark Dewey	.05
83	Danny Jackson	.05
84	Harold Baines	.05
85	Todd Benzinger	.05
86	Damion Easley	.05
87	Danny Cox	.05
88	Jose Bautista	.05
89	Mike Lansing	.05
90	Phil Hiatt	.05
91	Tim Pugh	.05
92	Tino Martinez	.05
93	Raul Mondesi	.05
94	Greg Maddux	1.00
95	Al Leiter	.05
96	Benito Santiago	.05
97	Len Dykstra	.05
98	Sammy Sosa	1.25
99	Tim Bogar	.05
100	Checklist	.05
101	Deion Sanders	.10
102	Bobby Witt	.05
103	Wil Cordero	.05
104	Rich Amaral	.05
105	Mike Mussina	.50
106	Reggie Sanders	.05
107	Ozzie Guillen	.05
108	Paul O'Neill	.05
109	Tim Salmon	.05
110	Rheal Cormier	.05
111	Billy Ashley	.05
112	Jeff Kent	.05
113	Derek Bell	.05
114	Danny Darwin	.05
115	Chip Hale	.05
116	Tim Raines	.05
117	Ed Sprague	.05
118	Darrin Fletcher	.05
119	Darren Holmes	.05
120	Alan Trammell	.05
121	Don Mattingly	1.25
122	Greg Gagne	.05
123	Jose Offerman	.05
124	Joe Orsulak	.05
125	Jack McDowell	.05
126	Barry Larkin	.05
127	Ben McDonald	.05
128	Mike Bordick	.05
129	Devon White	.05
130	Mike Perez	.05
131	Jay Buhner	.05
132	Phil Leftwich	.05
133	Tommy Greene	.05
134	Charlie Hayes	.05
135	Don Slaught	.05
136	Mike Gallego	.05
137	Dave Winfield	.75
138	Steve Avery	.05
139	Derrick May	.05
140	Bryan Harvey	.05
141	Wally Joyner	.05
142	Andre Dawson	.20
143	Andy Benes	.05
144	John Franco	.05
145	Jeff King	.05
146	Joe Oliver	.05
147	Bill Gullickson	.05
148	Armando Reynoso	.05
149	Dave Fleming	.05
150	Checklist	.05
151	Todd Van Poppel	.05
152	Bernard Gilkey	.05
153	Kevin Gross	.05
154	Mike Devereaux	.05
155	Tim Wakefield	.05
156	Andres Galarraga	.05
157	Pat Meares	.05
158	Jim Leyritz	.05
159	Mike Macfarlane	.05
160	Tony Phillips	.05
161	Brent Gates	.05
162	Mark Langston	.05
163	Allen Watson	.05
164	Randy Johnson	.75
165	Doug Brocail	.05
166	Rob Dibble	.05
167	Roberto Hernandez	.05
168	Felix Jose	.05
169	Steve Cooke	.05
170	Darren Daulton	.05
171	Eric Karros	.05
172	Geronimo Pena	.05
173	Gary DiSarcina	.05
174	Marquis Grissom	.05
175	Joey Cora	.05
176	Jim Eisenreich	.05
177	Brad Pennington	.05
178	Terry Steinbach	.05
179	Pat Borders	.05
180	Steve Buechele	.05
181	Jeff Fassero	.05
182	Mike Greenwell	.05
183	Mike Henneman	.05
184	Ron Karkovice	.05
185	Pat Hentgen	.05
186	Jose Guzman	.05
187	Brett Butler	.05
188	Charlie Hough	.05
189	Terry Pendleton	.05
190	Melido Perez	.05
191	Orestes Destrade	.05
192	Mike Morgan	.05
193	Joe Carter	.05
194	Jeff Blauser	.05
195	Chris Hoiles	.05
196	Ricky Gutierrez	.05
197	Mike Moore	.05
198	Carl Willis	.05
199	Aaron Sele	.05
200	Checklist	.05
201	Tim Naehring	.05
202	Scott Livingstone	.05
203	Luis Alicea	.05
204	Torey Lovullo RC	.05
205	Jim Gott	.05
206	Bob Wickman	.05
207	Greg McMichael	.05
208	Scott Brosius	.05
209	Chris Gwynn	.05
210	Steve Sax	.05
211	Dick Schofield	.05
212	Robb Nen	.05
213	Ben Rivera	.05
214	Vinny Castilla	.05
215	Jamie Moyer	.05
216	Wally Whitehurst	.05
217	Frank Castillo	.05
218	Mike Blowers	.05
219	Tim Scott	.05
220	Paul Wagner	.05
221	Jeff Bagwell	.75
222	Ricky Bones	.05
223	Sandy Alomar Jr.	.05
224	Rod Beck	.05
225	Roberto Alomar	.20
226	Jack Armstrong	.05
227	Scott Erickson	.05
228	Rene Arocha	.05
229	Eric Anthony	.05
230	Jeromy Burnitz	.05
231	Kevin Brown	.05
232	Tim Belcher	.05
233	Bret Boone	.05
234	Dennis Eckersley	.60
235	Tom Glavine	.30
236	Craig Biggio	.05
237	Pedro Astacio	.05
238	Ryan Bowen	.05
239	Brad Ausmus	.05
240	Vince Coleman	.05
241	Jason Bere	.05
242	Ellis Burks	.05
243	Wes Chamberlain	.05
244	Ken Caminiti	.05
245	Willie Banks	.05
246	Sid Fernandez	.05
247	Carlos Baerga	.05
248	Carlos Garcia	.05

249	Jose Canseco	.50
250	Alex Diaz	.05
251	Albert Belle	.05
252	Moises Alou	.05
253	Bobby Ayala	.05
254	Tony Gwynn	1.00
255	Roger Clemens	1.25
256	Eric Davis	.05
257	Wade Boggs	1.00
258	Chili Davis	.05
259	Rickey Henderson	.75
260	Andujar Cedeno	.05
261	Cris Carpenter	.05
262	Juan Guzman	.05
263	Dave Justice	.05
264	Barry Bonds	2.50
265	Pete Incaviglia	.05
266	Tony Fernandez	.05
267	Cal Eldred	.05
268	Alex Fernandez	.05
269	Kent Hrbek	.05
270	Steve Farr	.05
271	Doug Drabek	.05
272	Brian Jordan	.05
273	Xavier Hernandez	.05
274	David Cone	.05
275	Brian Hunter	.05
276	Mike Harkey	.05
277	Delino DeShields	.05
278	David Hulse	.05
279	Mickey Tettleton	.05
280	Kevin McReynolds	.05
281	Darryl Hamilton	.05
282	Ken Hill	.05
283	Wayne Kirby	.05
284	Chris Hammond	.05
285	Mo Vaughn	.05
286	Ryan Klesko	.10
287	Rick Wilkins	.05
288	Bill Swift	.05
289	Rafael Palmeiro	.65
290	Brian Harper	.05
291	Chris Turner	.05
292	Luis Gonzalez	.25
293	Kenny Rogers	.05
294	Kirby Puckett	1.00
295	Mike Stanley	.05
296	Carlos Reyes	.05
297	Charles Nagy	.05
298	Reggie Jefferson	.05
299	Bip Roberts	.05
300	Darrin Jackson	.05
301	Mike Jackson	.05
302	Dave Nilsson	.05
303	Ramon Martinez	.05
304	Bobby Jones	.05
305	Johnny Ruffin	.05
306	Brian McRae	.05
307	Bo Jackson	.10
308	Dave Stewart	.05
309	John Smoltz	.05
310	Dennis Martinez	.05
311	Dean Palmer	.05
312	David Nied	.05
313	Eddie Murray	.75
314	Darryl Kile	.05
315	Rick Sutcliffe	.05
316	Shawon Dunston	.05
317	John Jaha	.05
318	Salomon Torres	.05
319	Gary Sheffield	.45
320	Curt Schilling	.30
321	Greg Vaughn	.05
322	Jay Howell	.05
323	Todd Hundley	.05
324	Chris Sabo	.05
325	Stan Javier	.05
326	Willie Greene	.05
327	Hipolito Pichardo	.05
328	Doug Strange	.05
329	Dan Wilson	.05
330	Checklist	.05
331	Omar Vizquel	.05
332	Scott Servais	.05
333	Bob Tewksbury	.05
334	Matt Williams	.05
335	Tom Foley	.05
336	Jeff Russell	.05
337	Scott Leius	.05
338	Ivan Rodriguez	.65
339	Kevin Seitzer	.05
340	Jose Rijo	.05
341	Eduardo Perez	.05
342	Kirk Gibson	.05
343	Randy Milligan	.05
344	Edgar Martinez	.05
345	Fred McGriff	.05
346	Kurt Abbott	.05
347	John Kruk	.05
348	Mike Felder	.05
349	Dave Staton	.05
350	Kenny Lofton	.05
351	Graeme Lloyd	.05
352	David Segui	.05
353	Danny Tartabull	.05
354	Bob Welch	.05
355	Duane Ward	.05
356	Tuffy Rhodes	.05
357	Lee Smith	.05
358	Chris James	.05
359	Walt Weiss	.05
360	Pedro Munoz	.05
361	Paul Sorrento	.05
362	Todd Worrell	.05
363	Bob Hamelin	.05
364	Julio Franco	.05
365	Roberto Petagine	.05
366	Willie McGee	.05

367	Pedro Martinez	.75
368	Ken Griffey Jr.	1.50
369	B.J. Surhoff	.05
370	Kevin Mitchell	.05
371	John Doherty	.05
372	Manuel Lee	.05
373	Terry Mulholland	.05
374	Zane Smith	.05
375	Otis Nixon	.05
376	Jody Reed	.05
377	Doug Jones	.05
378	John Olerud	.05
379	Greg Swindell	.05
380	Checklist	.05
381	Royce Clayton	.05
382	Jim Thome	.65
383	Steve Finley	.05
384	Ray Lankford	.05
385	Henry Rodriguez	.05
386	Dave Magadan	.05
387	Gary Redus	.05
388	Orlando Merced	.05
389	Tom Gordon	.05
390	Luis Polonia	.05
391	Mark McGwire	2.00
392	Mark Lemke	.05
393	Doug Henry	.05
394	Chuck Finley	.05
395	Paul Molitor	.75
396	Randy Myers	.05
397	Larry Walker	.05
398	Pete Harnisch	.05
399	Darren Lewis	.05
400	Frank Thomas	.75
401	Jack Morris	.05
402	Greg Hibbard	.05
403	Jeffrey Hammonds	.05
404	Will Clark	.10
405	Travis Fryman	.05
406	Scott Sanderson	.05
407	Gene Harris	.05
408	Chuck Carr	.05
409	Ozzie Smith	1.00
410	Kent Mercker	.05
411	Andy Van Slyke	.05
412	Jimmy Key	.05
413	Pat Mahomes	.05
414	John Wetteland	.05
415	Todd Jones	.05
416	Greg Harris	.05
417	Kevin Stocker	.05
418	Juan Gonzalez	.65
419	Pete Smith	.05
420	Pat Listach	.05
421	Trevor Hoffman	.05
422	Scott Fletcher	.05
423	Mark Lewis	.05
424	Mickey Morandini	.05
425	Ryne Sandberg	1.00
426	Erik Hanson	.05
427	Gary Gaetti	.05
428	Harold Reynolds	.05
429	Mark Portugal	.05
430	Dave Valle	.05
431	Mitch Williams	.05
432	Howard Johnson	.05
433	Hal Morris	.05
434	Tom Henke	.05
435	Shane Mack	.05
436	Mike Piazza	1.50
437	Bret Saberhagen	.05
438	Jose Mesa	.05
439	Jaime Navarro	.05
440	Checklist	.05

Clean-Up Crew

The number four spot in the line-up is featured on this 12-card insert set (six per series) found only in magazine distributor packaging. Fronts are gold-foil enhanced; backs feature an action photo set against a background of a lineup card on which the player is pencilled into the #4 spot. His 1993 stats when batting clean-up are presented.

		NM/M
	Complete Set (12):	8.00
	Common Player:	1.00
1	Larry Walker	1.00
2	Andres Galarraga	1.00
3	Dave Hollins	1.00
4	Bobby Bonilla	1.00
5	Cecil Fielder	1.00
6	Danny Tartabull	1.00
7	Juan Gonzalez	2.00

Gamers

Leaf jumbo packs are the exclusive venue for the six cards of this insert set which were issued in each series.

		NM/M
	Complete Set (12):	30.00
	Common Player:	1.00
1	Ken Griffey Jr.	6.00
2	Len Dykstra	1.00
3	Juan Gonzalez	4.00
4	Don Mattingly	6.00
5	Dave Justice	1.00
6	Mark Grace	1.00
7	Frank Thomas	4.00
8	Barry Bonds	7.50
9	Kirby Puckett	4.50
10	Will Clark	1.00
11	John Kruk	1.00
12	Mike Piazza	6.00

Gold Rookies

A gold-foil rendered stadium background and huge black "94 Gold Leaf Rookie" serve as a backdrop for a player photo in these insert cards found at the rate of about one per 18 foil packs. The player's name and team are in silver at bottom. Horizontal backs have a ghosted action photo of the player in the background. A portrait photo is in the upper-right corner, above some personal data and stats. Cards are numbered "X of 20."

		NM/M
	Complete Set (20):	6.00
	Common Player:	.25
1	Javier Lopez	.25
2	Rondell White	.25
3	Butch Huskey	.25
4	Midre Cummings	.25
5	Scott Ruffcorn	.25
6	Manny Ramirez	3.50
7	Danny Bautista	.25
8	Russ Davis	.25
9	Steve Karsay	.25
10	Carlos Delgado	2.50
11	Bob Hamelin	.25
12	Marcus Moore	.25
13	Miguel Jimenez	.25
14	Matt Walbeck	.25
15	James Mouton	.25
16	Rich Becker	.25
17	Brian Anderson	.25
18	Cliff Floyd	.25
19	Steve Trachsel	.25
20	Hector Carrasco	.25

Gold Stars

The "Cadillac" of 1994 Leaf inserts, this 15-card series (#1-8 in Series 1; 9-15 in Series 2) is found on average of one card per 90 packs. The edition of 10,000 of each player's card is serially numbered. Fronts feature a rather small photo in a diamond-shaped frame

8	Joe Carter	1.00
9	Fred McGriff	1.00
10	Matt Williams	1.00
11	Albert Belle	1.00
12	Harold Baines	1.00

against a green marble-look background. The border, facsimile autograph and several other graphic elements are presented in prismatic foil. The back repeats the basic front design with a few sentences about the player and a serial number strip at bottom.

		NM/M
	Complete Set (15):	60.00
	Common Player:	3.00
1	Roberto Alomar	4.00
2	Barry Bonds	12.00
3	Dave Justice	3.00
4	Ken Griffey Jr.	9.00
5	Len Dykstra	3.00
6	Don Mattingly	7.50
7	Andres Galarraga	3.00
8	Greg Maddux	6.00
9	Carlos Baerga	3.00
10	Paul Molitor	5.00
11	Frank Thomas	5.00
12	John Olerud	4.00
13	Juan Gonzalez	3.00
14	Fred McGriff	3.00
15	Jack McDowell	3.00

MVP Contenders

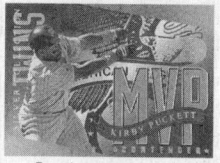

Found on an average of about once per 36-pack foil box, these inserts were produced in an edition of 10,000 each. Cards found in packs were marked "Silver Collection" on the horizontal fronts, and featured a silver-foil Leaf seal and other enhancements. Persons holding cards of the players selected as N.L. and A.L. MVPs could trade in their Contender card for an individually numbered 5" x 7" card of Leaf spokesman Frank Thomas and be entered in a drawing for one of 5,000 Gold Collection MVP Contender 28-card sets. Winning cards were punch-cancelled and returned to the winner along with his prize.

		NM/M
	Complete Set, Silver (30):	20.00
	Complete Set, Gold (30):	40.00
	Common Player, Silver:	.25
	Common Player, Gold:	.50
	AMERICAN LEAGUE	2.00
1a	Albert Belle/Silver	.25
1b	Albert Belle/Gold	.50
2a	Jose Canseco/Silver	1.25
2b	Jose Canseco/Gold	2.50
3a	Joe Carter/Silver	.25
3b	Joe Carter/Gold	.50
4a	Will Clark/Silver	.35
4b	Will Clark/Gold	.60
5a	Cecil Fielder/Silver	.25
5b	Cecil Fielder/Gold	.50
6a	Juan Gonzalez/Silver	1.50
6b	Juan Gonzalez/Gold	2.50
7a	Ken Griffey Jr./Silver	4.00
7b	Ken Griffey Jr./Gold	7.50
8a	Paul Molitor/Silver	2.00
8b	Paul Molitor/Gold	4.00
9a	Rafael Palmeiro/Silver	1.00
9b	Rafael Palmeiro/Gold	2.00
10a	Kirby Puckett/Silver	2.50
10b	Kirby Puckett/Gold	5.00
11a	Cal Ripken, Jr./Silver	7.50
11b	Cal Ripken, Jr./Gold	12.50
12a	Frank Thomas/Silver	2.00
12b	Frank Thomas/Gold	4.00
13a	Mo Vaughn/Silver	.25
13b	Mo Vaughn/Gold	.50
14a	Carlos Baerga/Silver	.25
14b	Carlos Baerga/Gold	.50
15	AL Bonus Card/Silver	.25
	NATIONAL LEAGUE	.60
1a	Gary Sheffield/Silver	.35

1b	Gary Sheffield/Gold	.65
2a	Jeff Bagwell/Silver	2.00
2b	Jeff Bagwell/Gold	4.00
3a	Dante Bichette/Silver	.25
3b	Dante Bichette/Gold	.50
4a	Barry Bonds/Silver	2.50
4b	Barry Bonds/Gold	12.50
5a	Darren Daulton/Silver	.25
5b	Darren Daulton/Gold	.50
6a	Andres Galarraga/Silver	.25
6b	Andres Galarraga/Gold	.50
7a	Gregg Jefferies/Silver	.25
7b	Gregg Jefferies/Gold	.50
8a	Dave Justice (Silver)	.25
8b	Dave Justice/Gold	.50
9a	Ray Lankford/Silver	.25
9b	Ray Lankford/Gold	.50
10a	Fred McGriff/Silver	.25
10b	Fred McGriff/Gold	.50
11a	Barry Larkin/Silver	.25
11b	Barry Larkin/Gold	.50
12a	Mike Piazza/Silver	4.00
12b	Mike Piazza/Gold	7.50
13a	Deion Sanders/Silver	.25
13b	Deion Sanders/Gold	.50
14a	Matt Williams/Silver	.25
14b	Matt Williams/Gold	.50
15	NL Bonus Card/Silver	.25

Power Brokers

This insert set was unique to Leaf Series 2 and features top sluggers. Horizontal fronts have a player photo at left, depicting his power stroke. A fireworks display is featured in the large letters of "POWER" at top. Other gold and silver foil highlights are featured on the black background. Backs have pie charts showing home run facts along with another player photo and a few stats. Stated odds of finding a Power Brokers insert card were one per dozen packs, on average.

		NM/M
	Complete Set (10):	8.00
	Common Player:	.40
1	Frank Thomas	.75
2	Dave Justice	.40
3	Barry Bonds	3.00
4	Juan Gonzalez	.65
5	Ken Griffey Jr.	2.00
6	Mike Piazza	2.00
7	Cecil Fielder	.40
8	Fred McGriff	.40
9	Joe Carter	.40
10	Albert Belle	.40

Slide Show

A new level of high-tech insert card production values was reached with the creation of Leaf's "Slide Show" cards, featuring a printed acetate center sandwiched between cardboard front and back. The see-through portion of the card is bordered in white to give it the appearance of a slide. The player's name, location and date of the photo are printed on the front of the "slide," with the card number on back. The pseudo-slide is bordered in black (Series 1) or white (Series 2), with a blue "Slide Show" logo at bottom and a silver-foil Leaf logo. Backs of the Slide Show inserts have a few sentences about the featured player from Frank Thomas, Leaf's official spokesman again in 1994. The first five cards were re-

leased in Series 1; cards 6-10 in Series 2. Stated odds of finding a Slide Show insert are one per 54 packs.

		NM/M
	Complete Set (10):	9.00
	Common Player:	.25
1	Frank Thomas	1.00
2	Mike Piazza	2.00
3	Darren Daulton	.25
4	Ryne Sandberg	1.50
5	Roberto Alomar	.50
6	Barry Bonds	3.00
7	Juan Gonzalez	.75
8	Tim Salmon	.25
9	Ken Griffey Jr.	2.00
10	Dave Justice	.25

Statistical Standouts

Significant statistical achievements of the 1993 season are marked in this insert set found in both retail and hobby packs at a rate of about once every 12 packs. Fronts feature player action photos set against a foil background of silver at right and a team color at left. A gold embossed Leaf seal is at upper-left. Backs are bordered in the complementary team color at right, silver at left and have a vertical player photo along with the statistical achievement. Cards are numbered "X-10."

		NM/M
	Complete Set (10):	10.00
	Common Player:	.40
1	Frank Thomas	.75
2	Barry Bonds	2.50
3	Juan Gonzalez	.65
4	Mike Piazza	2.00
5	Greg Maddux	1.00
6	Ken Griffey Jr.	2.00
7	Joe Carter	.40
8	Dave Winfield	.75
9	Tony Gwynn	1.00
10	Cal Ripken, Jr.	2.50

Frank Thomas Super

An edition of 20,000 super-size versions of Frank Thomas' 1994 Leaf card was produced for inclusion in Series II hobby boxes as a bonus. Except for its 5" x 7" format and a white strip on back bearing a serial number, the card is identical to the normal-size issue.

		NM/M
400	Frank Thomas	5.00

5th Anniversary

The card which insured the success of the Leaf brand name when it was re-introduced in 1990, the Frank Thomas rookie card, was re-issued in a 5th anniversary commemorative form as an insert in the 1994 set. On the chase card, silver foil rays emanate from the White Sox logo at lower-left, while a silver-foil 5th anniversary logo at upper-right replaces the Leaf script on the 1990 version.

FRANK THOMAS 1B

The card back carries a 1994 copyright. The Thomas anniversary card is found on average of once every 36 Series I hobby packs.

		NM/M
300	Frank Thomas	2.50

1994 Leaf/Limited Promo

A single, unlabeled promo card was issued by Leaf to preview its Limited brand. The front is printed on a matte finish background as opposed to the shiny silver of the issued versions, but is otherwise identical. On back there are subtle differences in the cropping of the background photo, and a Total Bases stat is provided instead of Slugging Percentage as on the issued card. The principal difference is the use of card number 1 on the promo; the issued card is #24.

		NM/M
1	Frank Thomas	100.00

1994 Leaf/Limited

Joe Girardi

Leaf Limited is a 160-card super-premium set printed on the highest quality board stock ever used by Donruss. Production was limited to 3,000 20-box case equivalents, making this the most limited product up to that point from Donruss. Fronts feature silver holographic Spectra Tech foiling and a silhouetted player action photo over full silver foil. The team name and logo in silver and player name in black are at the bottom of the card. Leaf Limited appears in silver at the top. Backs are dull gray with a quote from a baseball personality and a player picture in the top-right corner.

		NM/M
Complete Set (160):		35.00
Common Player:		.25
Pack (5):		2.50
Wax Box (20):		40.00
1	Jeffrey Hammonds	.25
2	Ben McDonald	.25
3	Mike Mussina	.75

4	Rafael Palmeiro	1.50
5	Cal Ripken, Jr.	6.00
6	Lee Smith	.25
7	Roger Clemens	3.00
8	Scott Cooper	.25
9	Andre Dawson	.40
10	Mike Greenwell	.25
11	Aaron Sele	.25
12	Mo Vaughn	.25
13	Brian Anderson RC	.25
14	Chad Curtis	.25
15	Chili Davis	.25
16	Gary DiSarcina	.25
17	Mark Langston	.25
18	Tim Salmon	.25
19	Wilson Alvarez	.25
20	Jason Bere	.25
21	Julio Franco	.25
22	Jack McDowell	.25
23	Tim Raines	.25
24	Frank Thomas	2.00
25	Robin Ventura	.25
26	Carlos Baerga	.25
27	Albert Belle	.25
28	Kenny Lofton	.25
29	Eddie Murray	2.00
30	Manny Ramirez	2.00
31	Cecil Fielder	.25
32	Travis Fryman	.25
33	Mickey Tettleton	.25
34	Alan Trammell	.25
35	Lou Whitaker	.25
36	David Cone	.25
37	Gary Gaetti	.25
38	Greg Gagne	.25
39	Bob Hamelin	.25
40	Wally Joyner	.25
41	Brian McRae	.25
42	Ricky Bones	.25
43	Brian Harper	.25
44	John Jaha	.25
45	Pat Listach	.25
46	Dave Nilsson	.25
47	Greg Vaughn	.25
48	Kent Hrbek	.25
49	Chuck Knoblauch	.25
50	Shane Mack	.25
51	Kirby Puckett	2.50
52	Dave Winfield	2.00
53	Jim Abbott	.25
54	Wade Boggs	2.50
55	Jimmy Key	.25
56	Don Mattingly	3.00
57	Paul O'Neill	.25
58	Danny Tartabull	.25
59	Dennis Eckersley	1.50
60	Rickey Henderson	2.00
61	Mark McGwire	5.00
62	Troy Neel	.25
63	Ruben Sierra	.25
64	Eric Anthony	.25
65	Jay Buhner	.25
66	Ken Griffey Jr.	4.00
67	Randy Johnson	2.00
68	Edgar Martinez	.25
69	Tino Martinez	.25
70	Jose Canseco	.75
71	Will Clark	.35
72	Juan Gonzalez	1.50
73	Dean Palmer	.25
74	Ivan Rodriguez	1.50
75	Roberto Alomar	.40
76	Joe Carter	.25
77	Carlos Delgado	1.00
78	Paul Molitor	2.00
79	John Olerud	.25
80	Devon White	.25
81	Steve Avery	.25
82	Tom Glavine	.50
83	Dave Justice	.25
84	Roberto Kelly	.25
85	Ryan Klesko	.25
86	Javier Lopez	.25
87	Greg Maddux	2.50
88	Fred McGriff	.25
89	Shawon Dunston	.25
90	Mark Grace	.25
91	Derrick May	.25
92	Sammy Sosa	3.00
93	Rick Wilkins	.25
94	Bret Boone	.25
95	Barry Larkin	.25
96	Kevin Mitchell	.25
97	Hal Morris	.25
98	Deion Sanders	.25
99	Reggie Sanders	.25
100	Dante Bichette	.25
101	Ellis Burks	.25
102	Andres Galarraga	.25
103	Joe Girardi	.25
104	Charlie Hayes	.25
105	Chuck Carr	.25
106	Jeff Conine	.25
107	Bryan Harvey	.25
108	Benito Santiago	.25
109	Gary Sheffield	.60
110	Jeff Bagwell	.25
111	Craig Biggio	.25
112	Ken Caminiti	.25
113	Andujar Cedeno	.25
114	Doug Drabek	.25
115	Luis Gonzalez	.40
116	Brett Butler	.25
117	Delino DeShields	.25
118	Eric Karros	.25
119	Raul Mondesi	.25
120	Mike Piazza	4.00
121	Henry Rodriguez	.25

122	Tim Wallach	.25
123	Moises Alou	.25
124	Cliff Floyd	.25
125	Marquis Grissom	.25
126	Ken Hill	.25
127	Larry Walker	.25
128	John Wetteland	.25
129	Bobby Bonilla	.25
130	John Franco	.25
131	Jeff Kent	.25
132	Bret Saberhagen	.25
133	Ryan Thompson	.25
134	Darren Daulton	.25
135	Mariano Duncan	.25
136	Len Dykstra	.25
137	Danny Jackson	.25
138	John Kruk	.25
139	Jay Bell	.25
140	Jeff King	.25
141	Al Martin	.25
142	Orlando Merced	.25
143	Andy Van Slyke	.25
144	Bernard Gilkey	.25
145	Gregg Jefferies	.25
146	Ray Lankford	.25
147	Ozzie Smith	2.50
148	Mark Whiten	.25
149	Todd Zeile	.25
150	Derek Bell	.25
151	Andy Benes	.25
152	Tony Gwynn	2.50
153	Phil Plantier	.25
154	Bip Roberts	.25
155	Rod Beck	.25
156	Barry Bonds	6.00
157	John Burkett	.25
158	Royce Clayton	.25
159	Bill Swift	.25
160	Matt Williams	.25

Gold

Mariano Duncan

Leaf Limited Gold was an 18-card insert set randomly packed into Leaf Limited. All cards are individually numbered and feature the starting lineups at each position in both the National League and American League for the 1994 All-Star Game. There were only 10,000 cards of each player produced in this insert set.

		NM/M
Complete Set (18):		20.00
Common Player:		.25
1	Frank Thomas	1.50
2	Gregg Jefferies	.25
3	Roberto Alomar	.50
4	Mariano Duncan	.25
5	Wade Boggs	2.00
6	Matt Williams	.25
7	Cal Ripken, Jr.	4.00
8	Ozzie Smith	2.00
9	Kirby Puckett	2.00
10	Barry Bonds	4.00
11	Ken Griffey Jr.	3.00
12	Tony Gwynn	2.00
13	Joe Carter	.25
14	Dave Justice	.25
15	Ivan Rodriguez	1.25
16	Mike Piazza	3.00
17	Jimmy Key	.25
18	Greg Maddux	2.00

Rookies

LOS ANGELES DODGERS

Similar in format to the super-premium Leaf Limited issue, this separate issue features 80 of base-

ball's brightest young talents. Total production was reported as 30,000 serial numbered 20-pack foil boxes.

		NM/M
Complete Set (80):		17.50
Common Player:		.25
Pack (5):		3.00
Box (20):		60.00
1	Charles Johnson	.25
2	Rico Brogna	.25
3	Melvin Nieves	.25
4	Rich Becker	.25
5	Russ Davis	.25
6	Matt Mieske	.25
7	Paul Shuey	.25
8	Hector Carrasco	.25
9	J.R. Phillips	.25
10	Scott Ruffcorn	.25
11	Kurt Abbott	.25
12	Danny Bautista	.25
13	Rick White	.25
14	Steve Dunn	.25
15	Joe Ausanio	.25
16	Salomon Torres	.25
17	Rick Bottalico	.25
18	Johnny Ruffin	.25
19	Kevin Foster	.25
20	W. Van Landingham RC	.25
21	Troy O'Leary	.25
22	Mark Acre	.25
23	Norberto Martin	.25
24	Jason Jacome RC	.25
25	Steve Trachsel	.25
26	Denny Hocking	.25
27	Mike Lieberthal	.25
28	Gerald Williams	.25
29	John Mabry	.25
30	Greg Blosser	.25
31	Carl Everett	.25
32	Steve Karsay	.25
33	Jose Valentin	.25
34	Jon Lieber	.25
35	Chris Gomez	.25
36	Jesus Tavarez	.25
37	Tony Longmire	.25
38	Luis Lopez	.25
39	Matt Walbeck	.25
40	Rikkert Faneyte	.25
41	Shane Reynolds	.25
42	Joey Hamilton	.25
43	Ismael Valdes	.25
44	Danny Miceli	.25
45	Darren Bragg	.25
46	Alex Gonzalez	.25
47	Rick Helling	.25
48	Jose Oliva	.25
49	Jim Edmonds	4.00
50	Miguel Jimenez	.25
51	Tony Eusebio	.25
52	Shawn Green	4.00
53	Billy Ashley	.25
54	Rondell White	.25
55	Cory Bailey	.25
56	Tim Davis	.25
57	John Hudek	.25
58	Darren Hall	.25
59	Darren Dreifort	.25
60	Mike Kelly	.25
61	Marcus Moore	.25
62	Garret Anderson	.25
63	Brian Hunter	.25
64	Mark Smith	.25
65	Garey Ingram	.25
66	Rusty Greer RC	.25
67	Marc Newfield	.25
68	Gar Finnvold	.25
69	Paul Spoljaric	.25
70	Ray McDavid	.25
71	Orlando Miller	.25
72	Jorge Fabregas	.25
73	Ray Holbert	.25
74	Armando Benitez	.25
75	Ernie Young	.25
76	James Mouton	.25
77	Robert Perez RC	.25
78	Chan Ho Park RC	1.00
79	Roger Salkeld	.25
80	Tony Tarasco	.25

Rookies Rookie Phenoms

Alex Rodriguez

Similar in format to the other Leaf Limited cards for 1994, these Phenom inserts feature gold-foil background and graphics, rather

than silver. Each card is numbered from within an edition of 5,000 of each player.

		NM/M
Complete Set (10):		260.00
Common Player:		1.00
Production 5,000 Sets		
1	Raul Mondesi	1.00
2	Bob Hamelin	1.00
3	Midre Cummings	1.00
4	Carlos Delgado	8.00
5	Cliff Floyd	1.00
6	Jeffrey Hammonds	1.00
7	Ryan Klesko	1.00
8	Javier Lopez	1.00
9	Manny Ramirez	10.00
10	Alex Rodriguez	250.00

1995 Leaf Promos

The lack of a "Sample" or "Promotional Card" notice makes these promos difficult to spot. They can be detected by the placement of the Registered symbol farther down and to the right compared to regular-issue cards. Also the thin line inside the gold-foil stamping enclosing the Leaf logo and inner "95" diamond is missing on the promos.

		NM/M
Complete Set (9):		35.00
Common Player:		2.00
1	Frank Thomas	4.00
10	Joe Carter	2.00
28	Matt Williams	2.00
60	Wade Boggs	6.00
60	Raul Mondesi	2.00
115	Greg Maddux	6.00
119	Jeff Bagwell	4.00
134	Cal Ripken Jr.	12.00
183	Kirby Puckett	6.00

1995 Leaf

CARDINALS Bobby Bonilla

Two series of 200 basic cards each, plus numerous insert sets, are featured in 1995 Leaf. The basic card design has a borderless action photo on front, with a small portrait photo printed at upper-left on holographic silver foil. The team name is printed in the same foil in large letters down the left side. A script rendition of the player's name is at bottom-right, with the Leaf logo under the portrait photo; both elements are in gold foil. Backs have a couple more player photos. The card number is in white in a silver-foil seal at upper-right. Previous season and career stats are at lower-left. Several of the insert sets are unique to various package configurations, while others are found in all types of packs.

		NM/M
Complete Set (400):		12.50
Common Player:		.05
Series 1 or 2 Pack (12):		.75
Series 1 or 2 Wax Box (36):		15.00
1	Frank Thomas	.75
2	Carlos Garcia	.05
3	Todd Hundley	.05
4	Damion Easley	.05
5	Roberto Mejia	.05
6	John Mabry	.05
7	Aaron Sele	.05
8	Kenny Lofton	.05
9	John Doherty	.05
10	Joe Carter	.05
11	Mike Lansing	.05
12	John Valentin	.05
13	Ismael Valdes	.05
14	Dave McCarty	.05
15	Melvin Nieves	.05
16	Bobby Jones	.05
17	Trevor Hoffman	.05
18	John Smoltz	.05
19	Leo Gomez	.05
20	Roger Pavlik	.05
21	Dean Palmer	.05
22	Rickey Henderson	.75

23	Eddie Taubensee	.05
24	Damon Buford	.05
25	Mark Wohlers	.05
26	Jim Edmonds	.05
27	Wilson Alvarez	.05
28	Matt Williams	.05
29	Jeff Montgomery	.05
30	Shawon Dunston	.05
31	Tom Pagnozzi	.05
32	Jose Lind	.05
33	Royce Clayton	.05
34	Cal Eldred	.05
35	Chris Gomez	.05
36	Henry Rodriguez	.05
37	Dave Fleming	.05
38	Jon Lieber	.05
39	Scott Servais	.05
40	Wade Boggs	1.00
41	John Olerud	.05
42	Eddie Williams	.05
43	Paul Sorrento	.05
44	Ron Karkovice	.05
45	Kevin Foster	.05
46	Miguel Jimenez	.05
47	Reggie Sanders	.05
48	Rondell White	.05
49	Scott Leius	.05
50	Jose Valentin	.05
51	William Van Landingham	.05
52	Denny Hocking	.05
53	Jeff Fassero	.05
54	Chris Hoiles	.05
55	Walt Weiss	.05
56	Geronimo Berroa	.05
57	Rich Rowland	.05
58	Dave Weathers	.05
59	Sterling Hitchcock	.05
60	Raul Mondesi	.05
61	Rusty Greer	.05
62	Dave Justice	.05
63	Cecil Fielder	.05
64	Brian Jordan	.05
65	Mike Lieberthal	.05
66	Rick Aguilera	.05
67	Chuck Finley	.05
68	Andy Ashby	.05
69	Alex Fernandez	.05
70	Ed Sprague	.05
71	Steve Buechele	.05
72	Willie Greene	.05
73	Dave Nilsson	.05
74	Bret Saberhagen	.05
75	Jimmy Key	.05
76	Darren Lewis	.05
77	Steve Cooke	.05
78	Kirk Gibson	.05
79	Ray Lankford	.05
80	Paul O'Neill	.05
81	Mike Bordick	.05
82	Wes Chamberlain	.05
83	Rico Brogna	.05
84	Kevin Appier	.05
85	Juan Guzman	.05
86	Kevin Seitzer	.05
87	Mickey Morandini	.05
88	Pedro Martinez	.75
89	Matt Mieske	.05
90	Tino Martinez	.05
91	Paul Shuey	.05
92	Bip Roberts	.05
93	Chili Davis	.05
94	Deion Sanders	.05
95	Darrell Whitmore	.05
96	Joe Orsulak	.05
97	Bret Boone	.05
98	Kent Mercker	.05
99	Scott Livingstone	.05
100	Brady Anderson	.05
101	James Mouton	.05
102	Jose Rijo	.05
103	Bobby Munoz	.05
104	Ramon Martinez	.05
105	Bernie Williams	.10
106	Troy Neel	.05
107	Ivan Rodriguez	.65
108	Salomon Torres	.05
109	Johnny Ruffin	.05
110	Darryl Kile	.05
111	Bobby Ayala	.05
112	Ron Darling	.05
113	Jose Lima	.05
114	Joey Hamilton	.05
115	Greg Maddux	1.00
116	Greg Colbrunn	.05
117	Ozzie Guillen	.05
118	Brian Anderson	.05
119	Jeff Bagwell	.75
120	Pat Listach	.05
121	Sandy Alomar	.05
122	Jose Vizcaino	.05
123	Rick Helling	.05
124	Allen Watson	.05
125	Pedro Munoz	.05
126	Craig Biggio	.05
127	Kevin Stocker	.05
128	Wil Cordero	.05
129	Rafael Palmeiro	.65
130	Gar Finnvold	.05
131	Darren Hall	.05
132	Heath Slocumb	.05
133	Darrin Fletcher	.05
134	Cal Ripken Jr.	2.50
135	Dante Bichette	.05
136	Don Slaught	.05
137	Pedro Astacio	.05
138	Ryan Thompson	.05
139	Greg Gohr	.05
140	Javier Lopez	.05

141	Lenny Dykstra	.05	259	Marvin Freeman	.05	377	Roberto Kelly	.05
142	Pat Rapp	.05	260	Jose Offerman	.05	378	Chris Hammond	.05
143	Mark Kiefer	.05	261	Greg Vaughn	.05	379	Mike Macfarlane	.05
144	Greg Gagne	.05	262	David Segui	.05	380	J.R. Phillips	.05
145	Eduardo Perez	.05	263	Geronimo Pena	.05	381	Luis Alicea	.05
146	Felix Fermin	.05	264	Tim Salmon	.35	382	Bret Barberie	.05
147	Jeff Frye	.05	265	Eddie Murray	.75	383	Tom Goodwin	.05
148	Terry Steinbach	.05	266	Mariano Duncan	.05	384	Mark Whiten	.05
149	Jim Eisenreich	.05	267	Hideo Nomo RC	2.50	385	Jeffrey Hammonds	.05
150	Brad Ausmus	.05	268	Derek Bell	.05	386	Omar Vizquel	.05
151	Randy Myers	.05	269	Mo Vaughn	.05	387	Mike Mussina	.35
152	Rick White	.05	270	Jeff King	.05	388	Rickey Bones	.05
153	Mark Portugal	.05	271	Edgar Martinez	.05	389	Steve Ontiveros	.05
154	Delino DeShields	.05	272	Sammy Sosa	1.25	390	Jeff Blauser	.05
155	Scott Cooper	.05	273	Scott Ruffcorn	.05	391	Jose Canseco	.35
156	Pat Hentgen	.05	274	Darren Daulton	.05	392	Bob Tewksbury	.05
157	Mark Gubicza	.05	275	John Jaha	.05	393	Jacob Brumfield	.05
158	Carlos Baerga	.05	276	Andres Galarraga	.05	394	Doug Jones	.05
159	Joe Girardi	.05	277	Mark Grace	.05	395	Ken Hill	.05
160	Rey Sanchez	.05	278	Mike Moore	.05	396	Pat Borders	.05
161	Todd Jones	.05	279	Barry Bonds	2.50	397	Carl Everett	.05
162	Luis Polonia	.05	280	Manny Ramirez	.75	398	Gregg Jefferies	.05
163	Steve Trachsel	.05	281	Ellis Burks	.05	399	Jack McDowell	.05
164	Roberto Hernandez	.05	282	Greg Swindell	.05	400	Denny Neagle	.05
165	John Patterson	.05	283	Barry Larkin	.05			
166	Rene Arocha	.05	284	Albert Belle	.05			
167	Will Clark	.10	285	Shawn Green	.35			
168	Jim Leyritz	.05	286	John Roper	.05			
169	Todd Van Poppel	.05	287	Scott Erickson	.05			
170	Robb Nen	.05	288	Moises Alou	.05			
171	Midre Cummings	.05	289	Mike Blowers	.05			
172	Jay Buhner	.05	290	Brent Gates	.05			
173	Kevin Tapani	.05	291	Sean Berry	.05			
174	Mark Lemke	.05	292	Mike Stanley	.05			
175	Marcus Moore	.05	293	Jeff Conine	.05			
176	Wayne Kirby	.05	294	Tim Wallach	.05			
177	Rich Amaral	.05	295	Bobby Bonilla	.05			
178	Lou Whitaker	.05	296	Bruce Ruffin	.05			
179	Jay Bell	.05	297	Chad Curtis	.05			
180	Rick Wilkins	.05	298	Mike Greenwell	.05			
181	Paul Molitor	.75	299	Tony Gwynn	1.00			
182	Gary Sheffield	.35	300	Russ Davis	.05			
183	Kirby Puckett	1.00	301	Danny Jackson	.05			
184	Cliff Floyd	.05	302	Pete Harnisch	.05			
185	Darren Oliver	.05	303	Don Mattingly	1.25			
186	Tim Naehring	.05	304	Rheal Cormier	.05			
187	John Hudek	.05	305	Larry Walker	.05			
188	Eric Young	.05	306	Hector Carrasco	.05			
189	Roger Salkeld	.05	307	Jason Jacome	.05			
190	Kirt Manwaring	.05	308	Phil Plantier	.05			
191	Kurt Abbott	.05	309	Harold Baines	.05			
192	David Nied	.05	310	Mitch Williams	.05			
193	Todd Zeile	.05	311	Charles Nagy	.05			
194	Wally Joyner	.05	312	Ken Caminiti	.05			
195	Dennis Martinez	.05	313	Alex Rodriguez	2.00			
196	Billy Ashley	.05	314	Chris Sabo	.05			
197	Ben McDonald	.05	315	Gary Gaetti	.05			
198	Bob Hamelin	.05	316	Andre Dawson	.05			
199	Chris Turner	.05	317	Mark Clark	.05			
200	Lance Johnson	.05	318	Vince Coleman	.05			
201	Willie Banks	.05	319	Brad Clontz	.05			
202	Juan Gonzalez	.50	320	Steve Finley	.05			
203	Scott Sanders	.05	321	Doug Drabek	.05			
204	Scott Brosius	.05	322	Mark McLemore	.05			
205	Curt Schilling	.25	323	Stan Javier	.05			
206	Alex Gonzalez	.05	324	Ron Gant	.05			
207	Travis Fryman	.05	325	Charlie Hayes	.05			
208	Tim Raines	.05	326	Carlos Delgado	.50			
209	Steve Avery	.05	327	Ricky Bottalico	.05			
210	Hal Morris	.05	328	Rod Beck	.05			
211	Ken Griffey Jr.	1.50	329	Mark Acre	.05			
212	Ozzie Smith	1.00	330	Chris Bosio	.05			
213	Chuck Carr	.05	331	Tony Phillips	.05			
214	Ryan Klesko	.05	332	Garret Anderson	.05			
215	Robin Ventura	.05	333	Pat Meares	.05			
216	Luis Gonzalez	.20	334	Todd Worrell	.05			
217	Ken Ryan	.05	335	Marquis Grissom	.05			
218	Mike Piazza	1.50	336	Brent Mayne	.05			
219	Matt Walbeck	.05	337	Lee Tinsley	.05			
220	Jeff Kent	.05	338	Terry Pendleton	.05			
221	Orlando Miller	.05	339	David Cone	.05			
222	Kenny Rogers	.05	340	Tony Fernandez	.05			
223	J.T. Snow	.05	341	Jim Bullinger	.05			
224	Alan Trammell	.05	342	Armando Benitez	.05			
225	John Franco	.05	343	John Smiley	.05			
226	Gerald Williams	.05	344	Dan Miceli	.05			
227	Andy Benes	.05	345	Charles Johnson	.05			
228	Dan Wilson	.05	346	Lee Smith	.05			
229	Dave Hollins	.05	347	Brian McRae	.05			
230	Vinny Castilla	.05	348	Jim Thome	.65			
231	Devon White	.05	349	Jose Oliva	.05			
232	Fred McGriff	.05	350	Terry Mulholland	.05			
233	Quilvio Veras	.05	351	Tom Henke	.05			
234	Tom Candiotti	.05	352	Dennis Eckersley	.65			
235	Jason Bere	.05	353	Sid Fernandez	.05			
236	Mark Langston	.05	354	Paul Wagner	.05			
237	Mel Rojas	.05	355	John Dettmer	.05			
238	Chuck Knoblauch	.05	356	John Wetteland	.05			
239	Bernard Gilkey	.05	357	John Burkett	.05			
240	Mark McGwire	2.00	358	Marty Cordova	.05			
241	Kirk Rueter	.05	359	Norm Charlton	.05			
242	Pat Kelly	.05	360	Mike Devereaux	.05			
243	Ruben Sierra	.05	361	Alex Cole	.05			
244	Randy Johnson	.75	362	Brett Butler	.05			
245	Shane Reynolds	.05	363	Mickey Tettleton	.05			
246	Danny Tartabull	.05	364	Al Martin	.05			
247	Darryl Hamilton	.05	365	Tony Tarasco	.05			
248	Danny Bautista	.05	366	Pat Mahomes	.05			
249	Tom Gordon	.05	367	Gary DiSarcina	.05			
250	Tom Glavine	.25	368	Bill Swift	.05			
251	Orlando Merced	.05	369	Chipper Jones	1.00			
252	Eric Karros	.05	370	Orel Hershiser	.05			
253	Benji Gil	.05	371	Kevin Gross	.05			
254	Sean Bergman	.05	372	Dave Winfield	.75			
255	Roger Clemens	1.25	373	Andujar Cedeno	.05			
256	Roberto Alomar	.20	374	Jim Abbott	.05			
257	Benito Santiago	.05	375	Glenallen Hill	.05			
258	Robby Thompson	.05	376	Otis Nixon	.05			

Checklists

Honoring the major 1994 award winners in the American (Series I) and National (Series II) Leagues, checklists for the 1995 Leaf set are not numbered among the regular issue. Horizontal cards have a player action photo at left with his name and team in gold foil at bottom. The award is printed vertically at left with the checklist beginning on the right. Backs continue the checklist on a graduated purple background with the checklist number in a silver-foil seal at top-right.

		NM/M
Complete Set (8):		1.50
Common Player:		.25
1	Checklist 1-67 (Bob Hamelin) (Rookie of the Year)	.25
2	Checklist 68-134 (David Cone (Cy Young))	
3	Checklist 135-200 (Frank Thomas (MVP))	.45
4	Series II inserts checklist (Paul O'Neill) (Batting title.)	.25
5	Checklist 201-267 (Raul Mondesi) (Rookie of the Year)	.25
6	Checklist 268-334 (Greg Maddux) (Cy Young)	
7	Checklist 335-400 (Jeff Bagwell (MVP))	.45
8	Series 2 inserts checklist (Tony Gwynn) (Batting title.)	.50

Cornerstones

Cornerstones, six of the best first baseman-third baseman combos in baseball, is a six-card insert series found, on average, once every 18 packs in Series I Leaf. Card fronts are horizontally oriented and have a silver prismatic border and player names. Player defensive action photos are set against a background resembling their team logo chiseled into a stone block. Backs have player batting photos at each end with offensive and defensive stats from 1994, and a few words about the duo.

		NM/M
Complete Set (6):		3.50
Common Player:		.40
1	Frank Thomas, Robin Ventura	.75
2	Cecil Fielder, Travis Fryman	.40
3	Don Mattingly, Wade Boggs	2.00
4	Jeff Bagwell, Ken Caminiti	.75
5	Will Clark, Dean Palmer	.40
6	J.R. Phillips, Matt Williams	.40

Gold Stars

Once again the toughest pull among the Leaf inserts are the Gold Leaf Stars found in both series. Found on average of one card per 90-270 packs, depending on pack card count, each of these chase cards is numbered on back in an edition of 10,000. Cards have fronts printed on metallic foil with the player name at top, the series title at bottom and a vertical stars and stripe device at right all printed in gold foil. A die-cut star appears at bottom-left. Backs are conventionally printed with another player photo and a few sentences about the star. The serial number is in gold foil in a white strip at top.

		NM/M
Complete Set (14):		35.00
Common Player:		1.00
1	Jeff Bagwell	2.50
2	Albert Belle	1.00
3	Tony Gwynn	3.50
4	Ken Griffey Jr.	4.50
5	Barry Bonds	6.00
6	Don Mattingly	4.00
7	Raul Mondesi	1.00
8	Joe Carter	1.00
9	Greg Maddux	3.50
10	Frank Thomas	2.50
11	Mike Piazza	4.50
12	Jose Canseco	1.50
13	Kirby Puckett	3.50
14	Matt Williams	1.00

Gold Rookies

Every other pack of Series I Leaf Series I is seeded with a Gold Leaf Rookie card. Fronts have a largely white background with a large player photo at left-center and a smaller picture in a rectangle at upper-right. A team-color stripe is at left, with a smaller gray stripe is at top-right. The team name is printed in large gray letters across the center of the card, with the player name in a team color beneath that and above the gold-foil Leaf logo at lower-left. "Gold Leaf Rookies" is printed in gold foil down the right side. Backs repeat the team-color motif with a large action photo of the player in a single color and a smaller color portrait. Full career stats are at bottom.

		NM/M
Complete Set (16):		3.00
Common Player:		.10
1	Alex Rodriguez	2.50
2	Garret Anderson	.10
3	Shawn Green	.50
4	Armando Benitez	.10
5	Darren Dreifort	.10
6	Orlando Miller	.10
7	Jose Oliva	.10
8	Ricky Bottalico	.10
9	Charles Johnson	.10
10	Brian Hunter	.10

Great Gloves

While the stated emphasis is on fielding prowess in this Series II chase set, players who don't also swing a big stick are ignored. Found as frequently as one per two packs, cards have a detail photo of a glove at left, with an action photo at right. The player name in the Great Gloves logo at bottom-right is in gold foil, as are the Leaf logo at top-left and the team name vertically at right. Backs repeat the glove photo and series logo as background for another player photo and a few words and stats about the player's defense.

		NM/M
Complete Set (16):		3.00
Common Player:		.15
1	Jeff Bagwell	.35
2	Roberto Alomar	.20
3	Barry Bonds	1.00
4	Wade Boggs	.45
5	Andres Galarraga	.15
6	Ken Griffey Jr.	.60
7	Marquis Grissom	.15
8	Kenny Lofton	.15
9	Barry Larkin	.15
10	Don Mattingly	.50
11	Greg Maddux	.45
12	Kirby Puckett	.45
13	Ozzie Smith	.45
14	Cal Ripken Jr.	1.00
15	Matt Williams	.15
16	Ivan Rodriguez	.30

Heading For The Hall

Series 2 hobby packs were the home of this scarce (one per 75 packs, average) chase set. Eight players deemed to be sure shots for Cooperstown are pictured in a semblance of the famed tombstone-shaped plaque they will someday adorn at the Hall of Fame; in fact the cards are die-cut to that shape. Backs have a sepia-toned photo, career stats and a serial number placing the card within an edition of 5,000.

		NM/M
Complete Set (8):		50.00
Common Player:		4.50
1	Frank Thomas	4.50
2	Ken Griffey Jr.	9.00
3	Jeff Bagwell	4.50
4	Barry Bonds	15.00
5	Kirby Puckett	6.00
6	Cal Ripken Jr.	15.00
7	Tony Gwynn	6.00
8	Paul Molitor	4.50

11	Ray McDavid	.10
12	Chan Ho Park	.10
13	Mike Kelly	.10
14	Cory Bailey	.10
15	Alex Gonzalez	.10
16	Andrew Lorraine	.10

Slideshow

The hold-to-light technology which Leaf debuted with its 1994 Slideshow inserts continued in 1995 with a cross-series concept. The same eight players are featured on these cards in both Series 1 and 2. Each card has three clear photos at center, between the spokes of a silver-foil wheel. When both the player's cards are placed side-by-side, the six-picture see-through photo device is complete. Slideshow inserts are found on average of just over one per box among all types of pack configurations. Cards were issued with a peelable plastic protector on the front.

		NM/M
Complete Set (16):		35.00
Complete Series 1 (1a-8a):		20.00
Complete Series 2 (1b-8b):		20.00
Same CL and prices for both series.		
Common Player:		1.50
1a	Raul Mondesi	1.50
1b	Raul Mondesi	1.50
2a	Frank Thomas	3.00
2b	Frank Thomas	3.00
3a	Fred McGriff	1.50
3b	Fred McGriff	1.50
4a	Cal Ripken Jr.	6.00
4b	Cal Ripken Jr.	6.00
5a	Jeff Bagwell	3.00
5b	Jeff Bagwell	3.00
6a	Will Clark	1.50
6b	Will Clark	1.50
7a	Matt Williams	1.50
7b	Matt Williams	1.50
8a	Ken Griffey Jr.	4.50
8b	Ken Griffey Jr.	4.50

Statistical Standouts

Embossed red stitches on the large baseball background make the Statistical Standouts chase cards stand out among the inserts in Series 1 hobby packs (one per 70, average). The leather surface of the ball is also lightly textured, as is the player action photo at center. Printed in gold foil on front are the series name at top, the player's facsimile autograph at lower-center and the Leaf logo and team name at bottom. Backs have a graduated black background with a large team logo at bottom, and a circular player portrait at center. A few words explain why the player's stats stand out among his peers. Each card is serially numbered on back to 5,000. A promo card version of each was issued without the specific serial number on back and with the upper-right corner cut off.

		NM/M
Complete Set (9):		90.00
Common Player:		3.00
Promos: 25-50 Percent		
1	Joe Carter	3.00
2	Ken Griffey Jr.	25.00
3	Don Mattingly	15.00
4	Fred McGriff	3.00
5	Paul Molitor	8.00
6	Kirby Puckett	12.00
7	Cal Ripken Jr.	30.00
8	Frank Thomas	8.00
9	Matt Williams	3.00

Special Edition Jumbos

As a dealer incentive, each case of 1995 Leaf Series I cards contained one of two 3" x 5" jumbos. Similar in format to the players' regular Leaf cards, each is individually serially numbered within an edition of 5,000.

		NM/M
Complete Set (2):		7.00
1	Frank Thomas	3.00
2	Barry Bonds	5.00

Frank Thomas

The Big Hurt's six seasons in the major leagues are chronicled in this flashy insert set. Silver and gold foil squares are the background for a photo of Thomas on front. Backs repeat the motif with standard print technology and another photo, along with a few words about Thomas' season. The Frank Thomas inserts are found in all types of Series II packs, with odds varying from one in 42 packs to one in 14 packs, depending on card count per pack.

		NM/M
Complete Set (6):		7.50
Common Card:		1.50
1	The Rookie	1.50
2	Sophomore Stardom	1.50
3	Super Star	1.50
4	AL MVP	1.50
5	Back-To-Back	1.50
6	The Big Hurt	1.50

300 Club

Issued in both Series I and II Leaf, but only in the retail and magazine packs, at a rate of one per 12-30 packs, depending on pack configuration, 300 Club inserts feature the 18 active players with lifetime .300+ batting averages in a minimum of 1,000 AB. Fronts have color player photos with a large white "300" in the background and "club" in gold foil near the bottom. The player name is in gold foil in an arc above the silver Leaf logo at bottom-center. Large embossed silver triangles in each bottom corner have the team name and player position (left) and career BA (right). Backs have another player photo and highlight his place on the list of .300+ batters.

		NM/M
Complete Set (18):		12.50
Common Player:		.25
1	Frank Thomas	1.00
2	Paul Molitor	1.00
3	Mike Piazza	3.00
4	Moises Alou	.25
5	Mike Greenwell	.25
6	Will Clark	.25
7	Hal Morris	.25
8	Edgar Martinez	.25
9	Carlos Baerga	.25
10	Ken Griffey Jr.	3.00
11	Wade Boggs	1.50
12	Jeff Bagwell	1.00
13	Tony Gwynn	1.50
14	John Kruk	.25
15	Don Mattingly	2.00
16	Mark Grace	.25
17	Kirby Puckett	1.50
18	Kenny Lofton	.25

1995 Leaf/Limited

Issued in two series of 96 basic cards each, plus inserts, Leaf Limited was a hobby-only product limited to 90,000 numbered 20-pack boxes. Five-card packs had a suggested retail price of $4.99. Fronts of the basic cards have a player action photo on a background of silver holographic foil highlighted with team colors and a gold-foil Leaf Limited logo. Horizontal-format backs have two more player photos, career stats and holographic foil team logos and card numbers.

		NM/M
Complete Set (192):		20.00
Common Player:		.10
Series 1 or 2 Pack (5):		2.00
Series 1 or 2 Wax Box (20):		30.00
1	Frank Thomas	.75
2	Geronimo Berroa	.10
3	Tony Phillips	.10
4	Roberto Alomar	.25
5	Steve Avery	.10
6	Darryl Hamilton	.10
7	Scott Cooper	.10
8	Mark Grace	.10
9	Billy Ashley	.10
10	Wil Cordero	.10
11	Barry Bonds	5.00
12	Kenny Lofton	.10
13	Jay Buhner	.10
14	Alex Rodriguez	3.00
15	Bobby Bonilla	.10
16	Brady Anderson	.10
17	Ken Caminiti	.10
18	Charlie Hayes	.10
19	Jay Bell	.10
20	Will Clark	.15
21	Jose Canseco	.35
22	Bret Boone	.10
23	Dante Bichette	.10
24	Kevin Appier	.10
25	Chad Curtis	.10
26	Marty Cordova	.10
27	Jason Bere	.10
28	Jimmy Key	.10
29	Rickey Henderson	.75
30	Tim Salmon	.10
31	Joe Carter	.10
32	Tom Glavine	.35
33	Pat Listach	.10
34	Brian Jordan	.10
35	Brian McRae	.10
36	Eric Karros	.10
37	Pedro Martinez	.75
38	Royce Clayton	.10
39	Eddie Murray	.75
40	Randy Johnson	.75
41	Jeff Conine	.10
42	Brett Butler	.10
43	Jeffrey Hammonds	.10
44	Andujar Cedeno	.10
45	Dave Hollins	.10
46	Jeff King	.10
47	Benji Gil	.10
48	Roger Clemens	2.00
49	Barry Larkin	.10
50	Joe Girardi	.10
51	Bob Hamelin	.10
52	Travis Fryman	.10
53	Chuck Knoblauch	.10
54	Ray Durham	.10
55	Don Mattingly	2.00
56	Ruben Sierra	.10
57	J.T. Snow	.10
58	Derek Bell	.10
59	David Cone	.10
60	Marquis Grissom	.10
61	Kevin Seitzer	.10
62	Ozzie Smith	1.50
63	Rick Wilkins	.10
64	Hideo Nomo RC	3.00
65	Tony Tarasco	.10
66	Manny Ramirez	.75
67	Charles Johnson	.10
68	Craig Biggio	.10
69	Bobby Jones	.10
70	Mike Mussina	.60
71	Alex Gonzalez	.10
72	Gregg Jefferies	.10
73	Rusty Greer	.10
74	Mike Greenwell	.10
75	Hal Morris	.10
76	Paul O'Neill	.10
77	Luis Gonzalez	.25
78	Chipper Jones	1.50
79	Mike Piazza	2.50
80	Rondell White	.10
81	Glenallen Hill	.10
82	Shawn Green	.50
83	Bernie Williams	.10
84	Jim Thome	.65
85	Terry Pendleton	.10
86	Rafael Palmeiro	.65
87	Tony Gwynn	1.50
88	Mickey Tettleton	.10
89	John Valentin	.10
90	Deion Sanders	.10
91	Larry Walker	.10
92	Michael Tucker	.10
93	Alan Trammell	.10
94	Tim Raines	.10
95	Dave Justice	.10
96	Tino Martinez	.10
97	Cal Ripken Jr.	5.00
98	Deion Sanders	.10
99	Darren Daulton	.10
100	Paul Molitor	.75
101	Randy Myers	.10
102	Wally Joyner	.10
103	Carlos Perez	.10
104	Brian Hunter	.10
105	Wade Boggs	1.50
106	Bobby Higginson RC	.50
107	Jeff Kent	.10
108	Jose Offerman	.10
109	Dennis Eckersley	.65
110	Dave Nilsson	.10
111	Chuck Finley	.10
112	Devon White	.10
113	Bip Roberts	.10
114	Ramon Martinez	.10
115	Greg Maddux	1.50
116	Curtis Goodwin	.10
117	John Jaha	.10
118	Ken Griffey Jr.	2.50
119	Geronimo Pena	.10
120	Shawon Dunston	.10
121	Ariel Prieto	.10
122	Kirby Puckett	1.50
123	Carlos Baerga	.10
124	Todd Hundley	.10
125	Tim Naehring	.10
126	Gary Sheffield	.45
127	Dean Palmer	.10
128	Rondell White	.10
129	Greg Gagne	.10
130	Jose Rijo	.10
131	Ivan Rodriguez	.65
132	Jeff Bagwell	.75
133	Greg Vaughn	.10
134	Chili Davis	.10
135	Al Martin	.10
136	Kenny Rogers	.10
137	Aaron Sele	.10
138	Raul Mondesi	.10
139	Cecil Fielder	.10
140	Tim Wallach	.10
141	Andres Galarraga	.10
142	Lou Whitaker	.10
143	Jack McDowell	.10
144	Matt Williams	.10
145	Ryan Klesko	.10
146	Carlos Garcia	.10
147	Albert Belle	.10
148	Ryan Thompson	.10
149	Roberto Kelly	.10
150	Edgar Martinez	.10
151	Robby Thompson	.10
152	Mo Vaughn	.10
153	Todd Zeile	.10
154	Harold Baines	.10
155	Phil Plantier	.10
156	Mike Stanley	.10
157	Ed Sprague	.10
158	Moises Alou	.10
159	Quilvio Veras	.10
160	Reggie Sanders	.10
161	Delino DeShields	.10
162	Rico Brogna	.10
163	Greg Colbrunn	.10
164	Steve Finley	.10
165	Orlando Merced	.10
166	Mark McGwire	3.00
167	Garret Anderson	.10
168	Paul Sorrento	.10
169	Mark Langston	.10
170	Danny Tartabull	.10
171	Vinny Castilla	.10
172	Javier Lopez	.10
173	Bret Saberhagen	.10
174	Eddie Williams	.10
175	Scott Leius	.10
176	Juan Gonzalez	.50
177	Gary Gaetti	.10
178	Jim Edmonds	.10
179	John Olerud	.10
180	Lenny Dykstra	.10
181	Ray Lankford	.10
182	Ron Gant	.10
183	Doug Drabek	.10
184	Fred McGriff	.10
185	Andy Benes	.10
186	Kurt Abbott	.10
187	Bernard Gilkey	.10
188	Sammy Sosa	2.00
189	Lee Smith	.10
190	Dennis Martinez	.10
191	Ozzie Guillen	.10
192	Robin Ventura	.10

Bat Patrol

Yet another insert of the game's top veteran hitters was featured as chase cards in Series 2 Leaf Limited. The cards have player action photos on front with large silver-foil "BAT / PATROL" lettering at lower-left. Backs are printed on a silver background and include career stats plus another color player photo. The cards were seeded at the rate of one per pack.

		NM/M
Complete Set (24):		7.50
Common Player:		.15
1	Frank Thomas	.75
2	Tony Gwynn	1.00
3	Wade Boggs	1.00
4	Larry Walker	.25
5	Ken Griffey Jr.	1.50
6	Jeff Bagwell	.75
7	Manny Ramirez	.75
8	Mark Grace	.25
9	Kenny Lofton	.15
10	Mike Piazza	1.50
11	Will Clark	.25
12	Mo Vaughn	.25
13	Carlos Baerga	.15
14	Rafael Palmeiro	.65
15	Barry Bonds	2.50
16	Kirby Puckett	1.00
17	Roberto Alomar	.35
18	Barry Larkin	.25
19	Eddie Murray	.75
20	Tim Salmon	.25
21	Don Mattingly	1.25
22	Fred McGriff	.15
23	Albert Belle	.25
24	Dante Bichette	.15

Gold

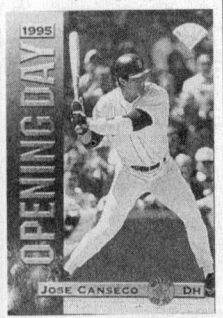

Seeded one per pack in Series I only, this insert set follows the format of the basic Leaf Limited cards, but is distinguished by the presence of gold, rather than silver, holographic foil.

		NM/M
Complete Set (24):		10.00
Common Player:		.25
1	Frank Thomas	.60
2	Jeff Bagwell	.60
3	Raul Mondesi	.25
4	Barry Bonds	1.50
5	Albert Belle	.25
6	Ken Griffey Jr.	1.00
7	Cal Ripkin (Ripken) Jr.	1.50
8	Will Clark	.25
9	Jose Canseco	.45
10	Larry Walker	.25
11	Kirby Puckett	.75
12	Don Mattingly	1.00
13	Tim Salmon	.25
14	Roberto Alomar	.35
15	Greg Maddux	.75
16	Mike Piazza	1.00
17	Matt Williams	.25
18	Kenny Lofton	.25
19	Alex Rodriguez (Rodriquez)	1.25
20	Tony Gwynn	.75
21	Mo Vaughn	.25
22	Chipper Jones	.75
23	Manny Ramirez	.60
24	Deion Sanders	.25

Lumberjacks

Lumberjacks inserts are found in both Series 1 and 2 Limited at a rate of one per 23 packs on average (less than one per box). Fronts are printed on woodgrain veneer with a large team logo behind a batting action photo of the game's top sluggers. Backs have another photo against a background of tree trunks. A white stripe at bottom carries each card's unique serial number within an edition of 5,000.

		NM/M
Complete Set (16):		55.00
Common Player:		2.00
1	Albert Belle	2.00
2	Barry Bonds	12.00
3	Juan Gonzalez	3.50
4	Ken Griffey Jr.	7.50
5	Fred McGriff	2.00
6	Mike Piazza	7.50
7	Kirby Puckett	6.00
8	Mo Vaughn	2.00
9	Frank Thomas	4.50
10	Jeff Bagwell	4.50
11	Matt Williams	2.00
12	Jose Canseco	3.00
13	Raul Mondesi	2.00
14	Manny Ramirez	4.50
15	Cecil Fielder	2.00
16	Cal Ripken Jr.	12.00

Opening Day

Issued in celebration of the 1995's season's delayed debut, this set was only available via a mail-in offer for $2 and eight wrappers. Cards were advertised as featuring front and back photos shot on opening day. Fronts have a player photo bordered on the left with a vertical "1995 Opening Day" stripe featuring exploding fireworks at the bottom. The player's name and position appear in a silver-foil strip at bottom; a silver-foil Leaf logo is at upper-right. Backs have a player action photo set against a background of exploding fireworks and a re-cap of the player's 1995 Opening Day performance.

		NM/M
Complete Set (8):		6.00
Common Player:		.25
1	Frank Thomas	.50
2	Jeff Bagwell	.50
3	Barry Bonds	2.00
5	Ken Griffey Jr.	1.00
6	Mike Piazza	1.00
7	Cal Ripken Jr.	2.00
8	Jose Canseco	.35
	Larry Walker	.25

1996 Leaf

Reverting to a single-series issue of 220 basic cards, plus numerous insert set bells and whistles, this was the final Leaf set under Donruss' ownership. Regular cards offer large action photos on front and back with a side and bottom border subdued through darkening (front) or lightening (back). Fronts feature silver prismatic-foil graphic highlights while the back includes a circular portrait photo with vital data around. Leaf was sold in both hobby and retail versions, each with some unique inserts. Basic unit was the 12-card foil pack, with suggested retail of $2.49.

		NM/M
Complete Set (220):		10.00
Common Player:		.05
Complete Gold Set (220):		100.00
Common Golds:		1.00
Gold Press Proofs:		15X
Complete Silver Set (220):		50.00
Common Silvers:		.50
Silver Press Proofs:		6X
Complete Bronze Set (220):		40.00
Common Bronze:		.25
Bronze Press Proofs:		4X
Pack (12):		1.00
Wax Box (30):		25.00
1	John Smoltz	.05
2	Dennis Eckersley	.60
3	Delino DeShields	.05
4	Cliff Floyd	.05
5	Chuck Finley	.05
6	Cecil Fielder	.05
7	Tim Naehring	.05
8	Carlos Perez	.05
9	Brad Ausmus	.05
10	Matt Lawton RC	.15
11	Alan Trammell	.05
12	Steve Finley	.05
13	Paul O'Neill	.05
14	Gary Sheffield	.40
15	Mark McGwire	1.50
16	Bernie Williams	.05
17	Jeff Montgomery	.05
18	Chan Ho Park	.05
19	Greg Vaughn	.05
20	Jeff Kent	.05
21	Cal Ripken Jr.	2.00
22	Charles Johnson	.05
23	Eric Karros	.05
24	Alex Rodriguez	1.50
25	Chris Snopek	.05
26	Jason Isringhausen	.05
27	Chili Davis	.05
28	Chipper Jones	.75
29	Bret Saberhagen	.05
30	Tony Clark	.05
31	Marty Cordova	.05
32	Dwayne Hosey	.05
33	Fred McGriff	.05
34	Deion Sanders	.05
35	Orlando Merced	.05
36	Brady Anderson	.05
37	Ray Lankford	.05
38	Manny Ramirez	.05
39	Alex Fernandez	.05

40	Greg Colbrunn	.05
41	Ken Griffey Jr.	1.00
42	Mickey Morandini	.05
43	Chuck Knoblauch	.05
44	Quinton McCracken	.05
45	Tim Salmon	.05
46	Jose Mesa	.05
47	Marquis Grissom	.05
48	Checklist	.05
49	Raul Mondesi	.05
50	Mark Grudzielanek	.05
51	Ray Durham	.05
52	Matt Williams	.05
53	Bob Hamelin	.05
54	Lenny Dykstra	.05
55	Jeff King	.05
56	LaTroy Hawkins	.05
57	Terry Pendleton	.05
58	Kevin Stocker	.05
59	Ozzie Timmons	.05
60	David Justice	.05
61	Ricky Bottalico	.05
62	Andy Ashby	.05
63	Larry Walker	.05
64	Jose Canseco	.40
65	Bret Boone	.05
66	Shawn Green	.35
67	Chad Curtis	.05
68	Travis Fryman	.05
69	Roger Clemens	1.00
70	David Bell	.05
71	Rusty Greer	.05
72	Bob Higginson	.05
73	Joey Hamilton	.05
74	Kevin Seitzer	.05
75	Julian Tavarez	.05
76	Troy Percival	.05
77	Kirby Puckett	.75
78	Barry Bonds	2.00
79	Michael Tucker	.05
80	Paul Molitor	.65
81	Carlos Garcia	.05
82	Johnny Damon	.35
83	Mike Hampton	.05
84	Ariel Prieto	.05
85	Tony Tarasco	.05
86	Pete Schourek	.05
87	Tom Glavine	.30
88	Rondell White	.05
89	Jim Edmonds	.05
90	Robby Thompson	.05
91	Wade Boggs	.75
92	Pedro Martinez	.65
93	Gregg Jefferies	.05
94	Albert Belle	.05
95	Benji Gil	.05
96	Denny Neagle	.05
97	Mark Langston	.05
98	Sandy Alomar	.05
99	Tony Gwynn	.75
100	Todd Hundley	.05
101	Dante Bichette	.05
102	Eddie Murray	.65
103	Lyle Mouton	.05
104	John Jaha	.05
105	Checklist	.05
106	Jon Nunnally	.05
107	Juan Gonzalez	.50
108	Kevin Appier	.05
109	Brian McRae	.05
110	Lee Smith	.05
111	Tim Wakefield	.05
112	Sammy Sosa	1.00
113	Jay Buhner	.05
114	Garret Anderson	.05
115	Edgar Martinez	.05
116	Edgardo Alfonzo	.05
117	Billy Ashley	.05
118	Joe Carter	.05
119	Javy Lopez	.05
120	Bobby Bonilla	.05
121	Ken Caminiti	.05
122	Barry Larkin	.05
123	Shannon Stewart	.05
124	Orel Hershiser	.05
125	Jeff Conine	.05
126	Mark Grace	.05
127	Kenny Lofton	.05
128	Luis Gonzalez	.25
129	Rico Brogna	.05
130	Mo Vaughn	.05
131	Brad Radke	.05
132	Jose Herrera	.05
133	Rick Aguilera	.05
134	Gary DiSarcina	.05
135	Andres Galarraga	.05
136	Carl Everett	.05
137	Steve Avery	.05
138	Vinny Castilla	.05
139	Dennis Martinez	.05
140	John Wetteland	.05
141	Alex Gonzalez	.05
142	Brian Jordan	.05
143	Todd Hollandsworth	.05
144	Terrell Wade	.05
145	Wilson Alvarez	.05
146	Reggie Sanders	.05
147	Will Clark	.05
148	Hideo Nomo	.50
149	J.T. Snow	.05
150	Frank Thomas	.65
151	Ivan Rodriguez	.60
152	Jay Bell	.05
153	Checklist	.05
154	David Cone	.05
155	Roberto Alomar	.20
156	Carlos Delgado	.40
157	Carlos Baerga	.05

158	Geronimo Berroa	.05
159	Joe Vitiello	.05
160	Terry Steinbach	.05
161	Doug Drabek	.05
162	David Segui	.05
163	Ozzie Smith	.75
164	Kurt Abbott	.05
165	Randy Johnson	.65
166	John Valentin	.05
167	Mickey Tettleton	.05
168	Ruben Sierra	.05
169	Jim Thome	.60
170	Mike Greenwell	.05
171	Quilvio Veras	.05
172	Robin Ventura	.05
173	Bill Pulsipher	.05
174	Rafael Palmeiro	.60
175	Hal Morris	.05
176	Ryan Klesko	.05
177	Eric Young	.05
178	Shane Andrews	.05
179	Brian Hunter	.05
180	Brett Butler	.05
181	John Olerud	.05
182	Moises Alou	.05
183	Glenallen Hill	.05
184	Ismael Valdes	.05
185	Andy Pettitte	.25
186	Yamil Benitez	.05
187	Jason Bere	.05
188	Dean Palmer	.05
189	Jimmy Haynes	.05
190	Trevor Hoffman	.05
191	Mike Mussina	.40
192	Greg Maddux	.75
193	Ozzie Guillen	.05
194	Pat Listach	.05
195	Derek Bell	.05
196	Darren Daulton	.05
197	John Mabry	.05
198	Ramon Martinez	.05
199	Jeff Bagwell	.65
200	Mike Piazza	1.00
201	Al Martin	.05
202	Aaron Sele	.05
203	Ed Sprague	.05
204	Rod Beck	.05
205	Checklist	.05
206	Mike Lansing	.05
207	Craig Biggio	.05
208	Jeffrey Hammonds	.05
209	Dave Nilsson	.05
210	Checklist, Inserts (Dante Bichette, Albert Belle)	.05
211	Derek Jeter	2.00
212	Alan Benes	.05
213	Jason Schmidt	.05
214	Alex Ochoa	.05
215	Ruben Rivera	.05
216	Roger Cedeno	.05
217	Jeff Suppan	.05
218	Billy Wagner	.05
219	Mark Loretta	.05
220	Karim Garcia	.10

Press Proofs

Carrying the parallel edition concept to its inevitable next level, '96 Leaf offered the Press Proof insert cards in three degrees of scarcity, each highlighted with appropriate holographic foil. At the top of the line are Gold Press Proofs in an edition of only 500 of each card. Silver and Bronze versions were produced in editions of 1,000 and 2,000, respectively. Press Proofs are inserted into both hobby and retail packs at an average rate of one card per 10 packs.

	NM/M
Complete Set, Gold (220):	200.00
Complete Set, Silver (220):	100.00
Complete Set, Bronze (220):	75.00
Common Player, Gold:	1.00
Common Player, Silver:	.50
Common Player, Bronze:	.25

All-Star MVP Contenders

A surprise insert in Leaf boxes was this interactive redemption issue. Twenty leading candidates for MVP honors at the 1996 All-Star Game in Philadelphia were present-

ed in a silver-foil highlighted horizontal format. The player's league logo serves as a background to the color action photo on front. Backs have details of the redemption offer which expired Aug. 15, 1996. The first 5,000 persons who sent in the Mike Piazza card for redemption received a gold version of the set and had their Piazza card punch-cancelled and returned.

		NM/M
Complete Set (20):		12.50
Common Card:		.25
Golds:		1.5X
1	Frank Thomas	.75
2	Mike Piazza	1.50
2c	Mike Piazza (Redeemed and punch-cancelled.)	1.00
3	Sammy Sosa	1.50
4	Cal Ripken Jr.	2.00
5	Jeff Bagwell	.75
6	Reggie Sanders	.25
7	Mo Vaughn	.25
8	Tony Gwynn	1.00
9	Dante Bichette	.25
10	Tim Salmon	.25
11	Chipper Jones	1.00
12	Kenny Lofton	.25
13	Manny Ramirez	.75
14	Barry Bonds	2.00
15	Raul Mondesi	.25
16	Kirby Puckett	1.00
17	Albert Belle	.25
18	Ken Griffey Jr.	1.50
19	Greg Maddux	1.00
20	Bonus Card	.10

Gold Leaf Stars

A vignetted background of embossed gold metallic cardboard and a Gold Leaf Stars logo in 22-K gold foil are featured on this limited (2,500 of each) edition insert. Backs include a second color photo of the player and a serial number from within the edition. Gold Leaf Stars were included in both hobby and retail packaging, with an average insertion rate of one per 210 packs.

		NM/M
Complete Set (15):		125.00
Common Player:		3.00
1	Frank Thomas	9.00
2	Dante Bichette	3.00
3	Sammy Sosa	15.00
4	Ken Griffey Jr.	15.00
5	Mike Piazza	15.00
6	Tim Salmon	3.00
7	Hideo Nomo	6.00
8	Cal Ripken Jr.	20.00
9	Chipper Jones	12.00
10	Albert Belle	3.00
11	Tony Gwynn	12.00
12	Mo Vaughn	3.00
13	Barry Larkin	3.00
14	Manny Ramirez	9.00
15	Greg Maddux	12.00

Hats Off

The most technically innovative inserts of 1996 have to be the Hats Off series exclusive to Leaf retail packs. Front player photos are on a background that is both flocked to simulate the cloth of a baseball cap, plus enhanced with a stiched team logo. The graphics are all in raised textured gold foil. Backs are conventionally printed and in-

clude a gold-foil serial number placing each card within an edition of 5,000 per player.

		NM/M
Complete Set (8):		30.00
Common Player:		3.00
1	Cal Ripken Jr.	12.00
2	Barry Larkin	3.00
3	Frank Thomas	4.50
4	Mo Vaughn	3.00
5	Ken Griffey Jr.	7.50
6	Hideo Nomo	4.00
7	Albert Belle	3.00
8	Greg Maddux	6.00

Picture Perfect

Leaf calls the glossy central area of these inserts "pearlized foil," which allows the player action photo to stand out in contrast to the actual wood veneer background. Gold-foil highlights complete the design. Backs are conventionally printed and include a gold-foil serial number from within the edition of 5,000 of each player's card. Cards #1-6 are hobby-only inserts, while #7-12 are found in retail packs. Average insertion rate is one per 140 packs. A promo version of each card was also issued.

		NM/M
Complete Set (12):		22.50
Common Player:		1.00
Promos:		2X
1	Frank Thomas	2.00
2	Cal Ripken Jr.	5.00
3	Greg Maddux	2.50
4	Manny Ramirez	2.00
5	Chipper Jones	2.50
6	Tony Gwynn	2.50
7	Ken Griffey Jr.	3.00
8	Albert Belle	1.00
9	Jeff Bagwell	2.00
10	Mike Piazza	3.00
11	Mo Vaughn	1.00
12	Barry Bonds	5.00

Statistical Standouts

The feel of leather complements the game-used baseball background on these hobby-only inserts featuring the game's top names. Backs offer statistical data

and a gold-foil serial number placing the card within an edition of 2,500 for each player. Average insertion rate is one per 210 packs.

		NM/M
Complete Set (8):		60.00
Common Player:		3.00
1	Cal Ripken Jr.	20.00
2	Tony Gwynn	10.00
3	Frank Thomas	7.50
4	Ken Griffey Jr.	13.50
5	Hideo Nomo	6.00
6	Greg Maddux	10.00
7	Albert Belle	3.00
8	Chipper Jones	10.00

Frank Thomas' Greatest Hits

Die-cut plastic with a background of prismatic foil to simulate a segment of a compact disc is the format for this insert issue chronicling the career-to-date of Frank Thomas. Backs include a few stats and a portrait photo, plus a gold-foil serial number from within an edition of 5,000. Cards #1-4 are found only in hobby packs; cards #5-7 are exclusive to retail packs (average insertion rate one per 210 packs) and card #8 could be had only through a wrapper redemption.

		NM/M
Complete Set (8):		12.50
Common Card:		2.00
1	1990	2.00
2	1991	2.00
3	1992	2.00
4	1993	2.00
5	1994	2.00
6	1995	2.00
7	Career	2.00
8	MVP	2.00

Total Bases

Total-base leaders from 1991-95 are featured in this hobby-only insert set. Card fronts are printed on textured canvas to simulate a base. Fronts are highlighted with gold foil. Backs have stats ranking the player in this category plus a gold-foil serial number from an edition of 5,000 of each player. Total Bases inserts are seeded at an average rate of one per 72 packs. Each player can also be found in a promo card version, marked as such on each side.

		NM/M
Complete Set (12):		25.00
Common Player:		1.00
Promos:		2X
1	Frank Thomas	2.50
2	Albert Belle	1.00
3	Rafael Palmeiro	2.00
4	Barry Bonds	6.00
5	Kirby Puckett	3.00
6	Joe Carter	1.00
7	Paul Molitor	2.50
8	Fred McGriff	1.00
9	Ken Griffey Jr.	4.00

10	Carlos Baerga	1.00
11	Juan Gonzalez	2.00
12	Cal Ripken Jr.	6.00

1996 Leaf/Limited

Leaf Limited contains 90 of the top rookies and stars. There is also a 100-card Limited Gold parallel set which includes the 90 base cards, plus 10 Limited Rookies inserts. The gold parallel cards are seeded one per 11 packs. Regular Limited Rookies inserts were seeded one per seven packs. Other insert sets were two versions of Lumberjacks and Pennant Craze.

	NM/M
Complete Set (90):	15.00
Common Player:	.10
Gold Set (90):	50.00
Gold Stars/Rookies:	3X
Pack (5):	1.50
Wax Box (14):	20.00

1	Ivan Rodriguez	.60
2	Roger Clemens	1.50
3	Gary Sheffield	.40
4	Tino Martinez	.10
5	Sammy Sosa	1.50
6	Reggie Sanders	.10
7	Ray Lankford	.10
8	Manny Ramirez	.75
9	Jeff Bagwell	.75
10	Greg Maddux	1.00
11	Ken Griffey Jr.	1.50
12	Rondell White	.10
13	Mike Piazza	1.50
14	Marc Newfield	.10
15	Cal Ripken Jr.	3.00
16	Carlos Delgado	.40
17	Tim Salmon	.10
18	Andres Galarraga	.10
19	Chuck Knoblauch	.10
20	Matt Williams	.10
21	Mark McGwire	2.00
22	Ben McDonald	.10
23	Frank Thomas	.75
24	Johnny Damon	.35
25	Gregg Jefferies	.10
26	Travis Fryman	.10
27	Chipper Jones	1.00
28	David Cone	.10
29	Kenny Lofton	.10
30	Mike Mussina	.30
31	Alex Rodriguez	2.00
32	Carlos Baerga	.10
33	Brian Hunter	.10
34	Juan Gonzalez	.60
35	Bernie Williams	.10
36	Wally Joyner	.10
37	Fred McGriff	.10
38	Randy Johnson	.75
39	Marty Cordova	.10
40	Garret Anderson	.10
41	Albert Belle	.10
42	Edgar Martinez	.10
43	Barry Larkin	.10
44	Paul O'Neill	.10
45	Cecil Fielder	.10
46	Rusty Greer	.10
47	Mo Vaughn	.10
48	Dante Bichette	.10
49	Ryan Klesko	.10
50	Roberto Alomar	.25
51	Raul Mondesi	.10
52	Robin Ventura	.10
53	Tony Gwynn	1.00
54	Mark Grace	.10
55	Jim Thome	.60
56	Jason Giambi	.50
57	Tom Glavine	.25
58	Jim Edmonds	.10
59	Pedro Martinez	.75
60	Charles Johnson	.10
61	Wade Boggs	1.00
62	Orlando Merced	.10
63	Craig Biggio	.10
64	Brady Anderson	.10
65	Hideo Nomo	.60
66	Ozzie Smith	1.00
67	Eddie Murray	.75
68	Will Clark	.15
69	Jay Buhner	.10
70	Kirby Puckett	1.00
71	Barry Bonds	3.00
72	Ray Durham	.10

73	Sterling Hitchcock	.10
74	John Smoltz	.10
75	Andre Dawson	.35
76	Joe Carter	.10
77	Ryne Sandberg	1.00
78	Rickey Henderson	.75
79	Brian Jordan	.10
80	Greg Vaughn	.10
81	Andy Pettitte	.25
82	Dean Palmer	.10
83	Paul Molitor	.75
84	Rafael Palmeiro	.60
85	Henry Rodriguez	.10
86	Larry Walker	.10
87	Ismael Valdes	.10
88	Derek Bell	.10
89	J.T. Snow	.10
90	Jack McDowell	.10

Lumberjacks

Lumberjacks inserts returned to Leaf Limited, but the 1996 versions feature an improved maple stock that puts wood grains on both sides of the card. Ten different Lumberjacks are available in two different versions. Regular versions are serial numbered to 5,000, while a special black-bordered Limited Edition version is numbered to 500. Each Lumberjacks card was also produced in a promo card version, appropriately marked on each side.

		NM/M
Complete Set (10):		40.00
Common Player:		1.50
Lumberjack Blacks (500):		2X
Promos:		2X
1	Ken Griffey Jr.	5.00
2	Sammy Sosa	5.00
3	Cal Ripken Jr.	7.50
4	Frank Thomas	3.00
5	Alex Rodriguez	6.00
6	Mo Vaughn	1.50
7	Chipper Jones	5.00
8	Mike Piazza	5.00
9	Jeff Bagwell	3.00
10	Mark McGwire	6.00

Pennant Craze

Each card in this insert set is sequentially numbered to 2,500 in silver foil on the back. The top-front of the cards have a die-cut pennant shape and is felt-textured. Appropriately marked promotional versions of each card can also be found.

		NM/M
Complete Set (10):		20.00
Common Player:		1.00
Promos:		2X
1	Juan Gonzalez	1.25
2	Cal Ripken Jr.	4.00
3	Frank Thomas	1.50
4	Ken Griffey Jr.	2.50
5	Albert Belle	1.00
6	Greg Maddux	2.00
7	Paul Molitor	1.50
8	Alex Rodriguez	3.00
9	Barry Bonds	4.00
10	Chipper Jones	2.00

Rookies

There are two versions of this 1996 Limited insert set. The cards are reprinted as part of a Limited Gold parallel set, which also includes the regular issue's 90 cards. The gold cards are seeded one per every 11 packs. The top young players are also

featured on regular Limited Rookies inserts; these versions are seeded one per every seven packs.

		NM/M
Complete Set (10):		7.50
Common Player:		.50
Limited Gold:		3X
1	Alex Ochoa	.50
2	Darin Erstad	.50
3	Ruben Rivera	.50
4	Derek Jeter	5.00
5	Jermaine Dye	.50
6	Jason Kendall	.50
7	Mike Grace	.50
8	Andruw Jones	2.50
9	Rey Ordonez	.50
10	George Arias	.50

1996 Leaf/Preferred

Leaf Preferred consists of 150 cards, a Press Proof parallel set and three insert sets, one of which has its own parallel set, too. While no individual odds are given for insert sets, the overall odds of getting an insert card are one per 10 packs. The Press Proof inserts replace the silver foil name and strip down the left side of the card with gold foil. Press Proof parallels were limited to 250 sets. Another insert set, Silver Leaf Steel, has a card seeded one per pack. This insert set is paralleled by a Gold Leaf Steel set, which appears in much more limited numbers. The two other insert sets are Steel Power and Staremaster.

		NM/M
Complete Set (150):		15.00
Common Player:		.05
Press Proofs:		12X
Pack (6):		1.00
Wax Box (24):		20.00
1	Ken Griffey Jr.	1.25
2	Rico Brogna	.05
3	Gregg Jefferies	.05
4	Reggie Sanders	.05
5	Manny Ramirez	.75
6	Shawn Green	.40
7	Tino Martinez	.05
8	Jeff Bagwell	.75
9	Marc Newfield	.05
10	Ray Lankford	.05
11	Jay Bell	.05
12	Greg Maddux	1.00
13	Frank Thomas	.75
14	Travis Fryman	.05
15	Mark McGwire	1.50
16	Chuck Knoblauch	.05
17	Sammy Sosa	1.25
18	Matt Williams	.05
19	Roger Clemens	1.25
20	Rondell White	.05
21	Ivan Rodriguez	.65
22	Cal Ripken Jr.	2.00
23	Ben McDonald	.05
24	Kenny Lofton	.05
25	Mike Piazza	1.25
26	David Cone	.05
27	Gary Sheffield	.40
28	Tim Salmon	.05
29	Andres Galarraga	.05
30	Johnny Damon	.35
31	Ozzie Smith	1.00

32	Carlos Baerga	.05
33	Raul Mondesi	.05
34	Moises Alou	.05
35	Alex Rodriguez	1.50
36	Mike Mussina	.40
37	Jason Isringhausen	.05
38	Barry Larkin	.05
39	Bernie Williams	.05
40	Chipper Jones	1.00
41	Joey Hamilton	.05
42	Charles Johnson	.05
43	Juan Gonzalez	.50
44	Greg Vaughn	.05
45	Robin Ventura	.05
46	Albert Belle	.05
47	Rafael Palmeiro	.65
48	Brian Hunter	.05
49	Mo Vaughn	.05
50	Paul O'Neill	.05
51	Mark Grace	.05
52	Randy Johnson	.75
53	Pedro Martinez	.75
54	Marty Cordova	.05
55	Garret Anderson	.05
56	Joe Carter	.05
57	Jim Thome	.60
58	Edgardo Alfonzo	.05
59	Dante Bichette	.05
60	Darryl Hamilton	.05
61	Roberto Alomar	.20
62	Fred McGriff	.05
63	Kirby Puckett	1.00
64	Hideo Nomo	.60
65	Alex Fernandez	.05
66	Ryan Klesko	.05
67	Wade Boggs	1.00
68	Eddie Murray	.75
69	Eric Karros	.05
70	Jim Edmonds	.05
71	Edgar Martinez	.05
72	Andy Pettitte	.30
73	Mark Grudzielanek	.05
74	Tom Glavine	.25
75	Ken Caminiti	.05
76	Will Clark	.10
77	Craig Biggio	.05
78	Brady Anderson	.05
79	Tony Gwynn	1.00
80	Larry Walker	.05
81	Brian Jordan	.05
82	Lenny Dykstra	.05
83	Butch Huskey	.05
84	Jack McDowell	.05
85	Cecil Fielder	.05
86	Jose Canseco	.40
87	Jason Giambi	.50
88	Rickey Henderson	.75
89	Kevin Seitzer	.05
90	Carlos Delgado	.40
91	Ryne Sandberg	1.00
92	Dwight Gooden	.05
93	Michael Tucker	.05
94	Barry Bonds	2.00
95	Eric Young	.05
96	Dean Palmer	.05
97	Henry Rodriguez	.05
98	John Mabry	.05
99	J.T. Snow	.05
100	Andre Dawson	.25
101	Ismael Valdes	.05
102	Charles Nagy	.05
103	Jay Buhner	.05
104	Derek Bell	.05
105	Paul Molitor	.75
106	Hal Morris	.05
107	Ray Durham	.05
108	Bernard Gilkey	.05
109	John Valentin	.05
110	Melvin Nieves	.05
111	John Smoltz	.05
112	Terrell Wade	.05
113	Chad Mottola	.05
114	Tony Clark	.05
115	John Wasdin	.05
116	Derek Jeter	2.00
117	Rey Ordonez	.05
118	Jason Thompson	.05
119	Robin Jennings **RC**	.05
120	Rocky Coppinger **RC**	.05
121	Billy Wagner	.05
122	Steve Gibralter	.05
123	Jermaine Dye	.05
124	Jason Kendall	.05
125	Mike Grace **RC**	.05
126	Jason Schmidt	.05
127	Paul Wilson	.05
128	Alan Benes	.05
129	Justin Thompson	.05
130	Brooks Kieschnick	.05
131	George Arias	.05
132	Osvaldo Fernandez **RC**	.20
133	Todd Hollandsworth	.05
134	Eric Owens	.05
135	Chan Ho Park	.05
136	Mark Loretta	.05
137	Ruben Rivera	.05
138	Jeff Suppan	.05
139	Ugueth Urbina	.05
140	LaTroy Hawkins	.05
141	Chris Snopek	.05
142	Edgar Renteria	.05
143	Raul Casanova	.05
144	Jose Herrera	.05
145	Matt Lawton **RC**	.05
146	Ralph Milliard **RC**	.05
147	Checklist (Frank Thomas)	.05
148	Checklist (Jeff Bagwell)	.05
149	Checklist (Ken Griffey Jr.)	.05
150	Checklist (Mike Piazza)	.05

Press Proofs

Inserted at a rate of about one per 48 packs, Press Proof parallels of the 150 cards in Leaf Preferred are identifiable only by the use of gold foil, rather than silver, on the card fronts, and gold ink on back. The cards are not otherwise marked or numbered. It is believed the issue was limited to 250-500 of each card.

	NM/M
Complete Set (150):	100.00
Common Player:	.50
Stars/Rookies:	12X

Leaf Steel Promos

Each of the 77 gold cards in the Preferred Steel set can also be found in gold, silver and bronze promo card versions. The samples differ from the issued versions only in an overprint diagonally on the back which reads "PROMOTIONAL CARD." This parallel promo edition represents one of the largest promo card issues of the mid-1990s. Cards were reportedly distributed to dealers on the basis of one gold promo per three-case order. The silver and bronze versions were reportedly never officially released, though examples have found their way into the market in some quantity.

		NM/M
Complete Gold Set (77):		625.00
Common Gold Player:		4.00
Silver: Values Undetermined		
Bronze: Values Undetermined		
1	Frank Thomas	15.00
2	Paul Molitor	15.00
3	Kenny Lofton	4.00
4	Travis Fryman	4.00
5	Jeff Conine	4.00
6	Barry Bonds	50.00
7	Gregg Jefferies	4.00
8	Alex Rodriguez	40.00
9	Wade Boggs	20.00
10	David Justice	4.00
11	Hideo Nomo	12.50
12	Roberto Alomar	6.00
13	Todd Hollandsworth	4.00
14	Mark McGwire	40.00
15	Rafael Palmeiro	12.50
16	Will Clark	4.00
17	Cal Ripken Jr.	50.00
18	Derek Bell	4.00
19	Gary Sheffield	7.50
20	Juan Gonzalez	12.50
21	Garret Anderson	4.00
22	Mo Vaughn	4.00
23	Robin Ventura	4.00
24	Carlos Baerga	4.00
25	Tim Salmon	4.00
26	Matt Williams	4.00
27	Fred McGriff	4.00
28	Rondell White	4.00
29	Ray Lankford	4.00
30	Lenny Dykstra	4.00
31	J.T. Snow	4.00
32	Sammy Sosa	25.00
33	Chipper Jones	20.00
34	Bobby Bonilla	4.00
35	Paul Wilson	4.00

36	Darren Daulton	4.00
37	Larry Walker	4.00
38	Raul Mondesi	4.00
39	Jeff Bagwell	15.00
40	Derek Jeter	50.00
41	Kirby Puckett	20.00
42	Jason Isringhausen	4.00
43	Vinny Castilla	4.00
44	Jim Edmonds	4.00
45	Ron Gant	4.00
46	Carlos Delgado	7.50
47	Jose Canseco	7.50
48	Tony Gwynn	20.00
49	Mike Mussina	7.50
50	Charles Johnson	4.00
51	Mike Piazza	25.00
52	Ken Griffey Jr.	25.00
53	Greg Maddux	20.00
54	Mark Grace	4.00
55	Ryan Klesko	4.00
56	Dennis Eckersley	12.50
57	Rickey Henderson	15.00
58	Michael Tucker	4.00
59	Joe Carter	4.00
60	Randy Johnson	15.00
61	Brian Jordan	4.00
62	Shawn Green	7.50
63	Roger Clemens	22.50
64	Andres Galarraga	4.00
65	Johnny Damon	7.50
66	Ryne Sandberg	20.00
67	Alan Benes	4.00
68	Albert Belle	4.00
69	Barry Larkin	4.00
70	Marty Cordova	4.00
71	Dante Bichette	4.00
72	Craig Biggio	4.00
73	Reggie Sanders	4.00
74	Moises Alou	4.00
75	Chuck Knoblauch	4.00
76	Cecil Fielder	4.00
77	Manny Ramirez	15.00

Leaf Steel

This 77-card insert set has two versions - a silver one and a much more limited gold one. A Silver Leaf Steel card is included in every pack; the parallel versions appear about one per 24 packs.

		NM/M
Complete Set (77):		25.00
Common Player:		.15
Gold:		2X
1	Frank Thomas	1.00
2	Paul Molitor	1.00
3	Kenny Lofton	.15
4	Travis Fryman	.15
5	Jeff Conine	.15
6	Barry Bonds	3.00
7	Gregg Jefferies	.15
8	Alex Rodriguez	2.50
9	Wade Boggs	1.50
10	David Justice	.75
11	Hideo Nomo	.75
12	Roberto Alomar	.30
13	Todd Hollandsworth	.15
14	Mark McGwire	2.50
15	Rafael Palmeiro	.15
16	Will Clark	.25
17	Cal Ripken Jr.	3.00
18	Derek Bell	.15
19	Gary Sheffield	.15
20	Juan Gonzalez	.65
21	Garret Anderson	.15
22	Mo Vaughn	.15
23	Robin Ventura	.15
24	Carlos Baerga	.15
25	Tim Salmon	.15
26	Matt Williams	.15
27	Fred McGriff	.15
28	Rondell White	.15
29	Ray Lankford	.15
30	Lenny Dykstra	.15
31	J.T. Snow	.15
32	Sammy Sosa	2.00
33	Chipper Jones	1.50
34	Bobby Bonilla	.15
35	Paul Wilson	.15
36	Darren Daulton	.15
37	Larry Walker	.15
38	Raul Mondesi	.15
39	Jeff Bagwell	1.00
40	Derek Jeter	3.00
41	Kirby Puckett	1.50
42	Jason Isringhausen	.15
43	Vinny Castilla	.15

44	Jim Edmonds	.15
45	Ron Gant	.15
46	Carlos Delgado	.50
47	Jose Canseco	.40
48	Tony Gwynn	1.50
49	Mike Mussina	.50
50	Charles Johnson	.15
51	Mike Piazza	2.00
52	Ken Griffey Jr.	2.00
53	Greg Maddux	1.50
54	Mark Grace	.15
55	Ryan Klesko	.15
56	Dennis Eckersley	.75
57	Rickey Henderson	1.00
58	Michael Tucker	.15
59	Joe Carter	.15
60	Randy Johnson	1.00
61	Brian Jordan	.15
62	Shawn Green	.50
63	Roger Clemens	2.00
64	Andres Galarraga	.15
65	Johnny Damon	.40
66	Ryne Sandberg	1.50
67	Alan Benes	.15
68	Albert Belle	.15
69	Barry Larkin	.15
70	Marty Cordova	.15
71	Dante Bichette	.15
72	Craig Biggio	.15
73	Reggie Sanders	.15
74	Moises Alou	.15
75	Chuck Knoblauch	.15
76	Cecil Fielder	.15
77	Manny Ramirez	1.00

Staremaster

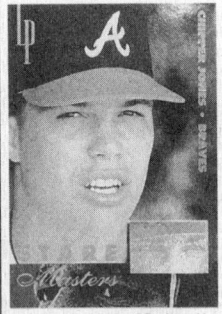

These 1996 Leaf Preferred inserts provide a photographic tribute to the stares of 12 top players. Each card is printed on silver holographic card stock and is numbered up to 2,500.

		NM/M
Complete Set (12):		50.00
Common Player:		3.00
1	Chipper Jones	5.00
2	Alex Rodriguez	7.50
3	Derek Jeter	10.00
4	Tony Gwynn	5.00
5	Frank Thomas	4.00
6	Ken Griffey Jr.	6.00
7	Cal Ripken Jr.	10.00
8	Greg Maddux	5.00
9	Albert Belle	3.00
10	Barry Bonds	10.00
11	Jeff Bagwell	4.00
12	Mike Piazza	6.00

Steel Power

This eight-card Leaf Steel insert set combines micro-etched foil with interior die-cutting to honor the game's top power hitters. Each insert card carries a serial number up to 5,000.

		NM/M
Complete Set (8):		17.50
Common Player:		1.00
1	Albert Belle	1.00
2	Mo Vaughn	1.00
3	Ken Griffey Jr.	3.50
4	Cal Ripken Jr.	5.00
5	Mike Piazza	3.50
6	Barry Bonds	5.00
7	Jeff Bagwell	2.50
8	Frank Thomas	2.50

1996 Leaf/Signature Series

The base set which rode along with the autographed cards of more than 250 Major League players in Leaf's Signature Series (at least one authentic signature is guaranteed in every pack) features action photos with silver-foil highlights. Horizontal backs have a large photo along with a few stats and bits of personal data. One out of every 48 packs is a super pack containing nothing but autographed cards. The 150-card base set is paralleled in Gold and Platinum Press Proof insert sets. The gold version is seeded one per 12 packs in Series 1 and one per eight in the Extended Series. Platinums were issued in an edition of 150 of each of the 150 cards and are found only in the Extended Series at the rate of one per 24 packs. Four-card packs of Leaf Signature Series carried a suggested retail price at issue of $9.99.

	NM/M
Complete Set (150):	30.00
Complete 1st Series (100):	20.00
Complete Extended Series (50):	10.00
Common Player:	.05
Gold PP Stars/Rookies:	8X
Platinum PP Stars/Rookies:	20X
Pack (4):	5.00
Wax Box (12):	50.00

		NM/M
1	Mike Piazza	1.25
2	Juan Gonzalez	.65
3	Greg Maddux	1.00
4	Marc Newfield	1.00
5	Wade Boggs	.05
6	Ray Lankford	.05
7	Frank Thomas	.75
8	Rico Brogna	.05
9	Tim Salmon	.05
10	Ken Griffey Jr.	1.25
11	Manny Ramirez	.75
12	Cecil Fielder	.05
13	Gregg Jefferies	.05
14	Rondell White	.05
15	Cal Ripken Jr.	2.00
16	Alex Rodriguez	1.50
17	Bernie Williams	.05
18	Andres Galarraga	.05
19	Mike Mussina	.50
20	Chuck Knoblauch	.05
21	Joe Carter	.05
22	Jeff Bagwell	.75
23	Mark McGwire	1.50
24	Sammy Sosa	1.00
25	Reggie Sanders	.05
26	Chipper Jones	1.00
27	Jeff Cirillo	.05
28	Roger Clemens	1.25
29	Craig Biggio	.05
30	Gary Sheffield	.45
31	Paul O'Neill	.05
32	Johnny Damon	.35
33	Jason Isringhausen	.05
34	Jay Bell	.05
35	Henry Rodriguez	.05
36	Matt Williams	.05
37	Randy Johnson	.75
38	Fred McGriff	.05
39	Jason Giambi	.60
40	Ivan Rodriguez	.65
41	Raul Mondesi	.05
42	Barry Larkin	.05
43	Ryan Klesko	.05
44	Joey Hamilton	.05
45	Todd Hundley	.05
46	Jim Edmonds	.05
47	Dante Bichette	.05
48	Roberto Alomar	.20
49	Mark Grace	.05
50	Brady Anderson	.05
51	Hideo Nomo	.65
52	Ozzie Smith	1.00
53	Robin Ventura	.05
54	Andy Pettitte	.35
55	Kenny Lofton	.05
56	John Mabry	.05
57	Paul Molitor	.75
58	Rey Ordonez	.05
59	Albert Belle	.05

60	Charles Johnson	.05
61	Edgar Martinez	.05
62	Derek Bell	.05
63	Carlos Delgado	.50
64	Raul Casanova	.05
65	Ismael Valdes	.05
66	J.T. Snow	.05
67	Derek Jeter	2.00
68	Jason Kendall	.05
69	John Smoltz	.05
70	Chad Mottola	.05
71	Jim Thome	.60
72	Will Clark	.10
73	Mo Vaughn	.05
74	John Wasdin	.05
75	Rafael Palmeiro	.65
76	Mark Grudzielanek	.05
77	Larry Walker	.05
78	Alan Benes	.05
79	Michael Tucker	.05
80	Billy Wagner	.05
81	Paul Wilson	.05
82	Greg Vaughn	.05
83	Dean Palmer	.05
84	Ryne Sandberg	1.00
85	Eric Young	.05
86	Jay Buhner	.05
87	Tony Clark	.05
88	Jermaine Dye	.05
89	Barry Bonds	2.00
90	Ugueth Urbina	.05
91	Charles Nagy	.05
92	Ruben Rivera	.05
93	Todd Hollandsworth	.05
94	Darin Erstad RC	1.50
95	Brooks Kieschnick	.05
96	Edgar Renteria	.05
97	Lenny Dykstra	.05
98	Tony Gwynn	1.00
99	Kirby Puckett	1.00
100	Checklist	.05
101	Andruw Jones	.75
102	Alex Ochoa	.05
103	David Cone	.05
104	Rusty Greer	.05
105	Jose Canseco	.45
106	Ken Caminiti	.05
107	Mariano Rivera	.15
108	Ron Gant	.05
109	Darryl Strawberry	.05
110	Vladimir Guerrero	.75
111	George Arias	.05
112	Jeff Conine	.05
113	Bobby Higginson	.05
114	Eric Karros	.05
115	Brian Hunter	.05
116	Eddie Murray	.75
117	Todd Walker	.05
118	Chan Ho Park	.05
119	John Jaha	.05
120	David Justice	.05
121	Makoto Suzuki	.05
122	Scott Rolen	.65
123	Tino Martinez	.05
124	Kimera Bartee	.05
125	Garret Anderson	.05
126	Brian Jordan	.05
127	Andre Dawson	.30
128	Javier Lopez	.05
129	Bill Pulsipher	.05
130	Dwight Gooden	.05
131	Al Martin	.05
132	Terrell Wade	.05
133	Steve Gibralter	.05
134	Tom Glavine	.35
135	Kevin Appier	.05
136	Tim Raines	.05
137	Curtis Pride	.05
138	Todd Greene	.05
139	Bobby Bonilla	.05
140	Trey Beamon	.05
141	Marty Cordova	.05
142	Rickey Henderson	.75
143	Ellis Burks	.05
144	Dennis Eckersley	.65
145	Kevin Brown	.05
146	Carlos Baerga	.05
147	Brett Butler	.05
148	Marquis Grissom	.05
149	Karim Garcia	.05
150	Checklist	.05

Press Proofs

The 150-card base set of Leaf/Signature was paralleled in a pair of Press Proof versions. Identical in format to the regular issue, the Press Proofs have an embossed gold- or platinum-foil oval seal at left and "PRESS PROOF" vertically at right in the same color foil. Backs are identical to the regular version. Gold Press Proofs were inserted one per 12 packs of Extended Series 1 and one per eight packs of Extended. Platinum Proofs are found only in Extended Series packs, at an average rate of one per 24. Total production of Platinum Press proofs was 150 of each card.

	NM/M
Common Gold:	2.00
Gold Stars:	8X
Common Platinum:	4.00
Platinum Stars:	20X

Autographs Promos

To introduce its Autograph Series, Leaf sent dealers one of two promo card versions of the Frank Thomas card. Most received a card with a pre-printed facsimile autograph, duly noted in small type beneath the signature. Others (500) received a genuine Frank Thomas autograph on their promo. All of the cards are marked "PROMOTIONAL CARD" diagonally on both front and back.

	NM/M
Frank Thomas (Facsimile signature.)	4.00
Frank Thomas (Genuine autograph.)	50.00

Autographs

Every pack of 1996 Leaf Signature Series includes at least one authentically signed card from one of over 250 players. There were 240 players who signed three versions in these quantities: 500 Gold, 1,000 Silver and 3,500 Bronze. There are also short-printed autographs for 10 players in quantities of 100 Gold, 200 Silver and 700 Bronze. The short-printed players are designated with an "SP" in the checklist. Cards are numbered alphabetically in the checklist since the autographed cards are unnumbered. Each major leaguer signed a notarized affidavit to guarantee each signature was authentic. Series 1 cards of Carlos Delgado, Brian Hunter, Phil Plantier, Jim Thome, Terrell Wade and Ernie Young were signed too late for inclusion in Series 1 packs, and were inserted with Extended. No Bronze cards of Thome were signed.

	NM/M
Common Bronze Player:	4.00
Silver:	1.5X
Gold:	2X
SPs: 100 Gold, 200 Silver, 700 Bronze	

(1)	Kurt Abbott	4.00
(2)	Juan Acevedo	4.00
(3)	Terry Adams	4.00
(4)	Manny Alexander	4.00
(5)	Roberto Alomar/SP	35.00
(6)	Moises Alou	12.00
(7)	Wilson Alvarez	4.00
(8)	Garret Anderson	10.00
(9)	Shane Andrews	4.00
(10)	Andy Ashby	4.00
(11)	Pedro Astacio	4.00
(12)	Brad Ausmus	4.00
(13)	Bobby Ayala	4.00
(14)	Carlos Baerga	4.00
(15)	Harold Baines	10.00
(16)	Jason Bates	4.00
(17)	Allen Battle	4.00
(18)	Rich Becker	4.00
(19)	David Bell	4.00
(20)	Rafael Belliard	4.00
(21)	Andy Benes	4.00
(22)	Armando Benitez	4.00
(23)	Jason Bere	4.00
(24)	Geronimo Berroa	4.00
(25)	Willie Blair	4.00
(26)	Mike Blowers	4.00
(27)	Wade Boggs/SP	50.00
(28)	Ricky Bones	4.00
(29)	Mike Bordick	4.00
(30)	Toby Borland	4.00
(31)	Ricky Bottalico	4.00
(32)	Darren Bragg	4.00
(33)	Jeff Branson	4.00
(34)	Tilson Brito	4.00
(35)	Rico Brogna	4.00
(36)	Scott Brosius	7.50
(37)	Damon Buford	4.00
(38)	Mike Busby	4.00
(39)	Tom Candiotti	4.00
(40)	Frank Castillo	4.00
(41)	Andujar Cedeno	4.00
(42)	Domingo Cedeno	4.00
(43)	Roger Cedeno	4.00
(44)	Norm Charlton	4.00
(45)	Jeff Cirillo	4.00
(46)	Will Clark	10.00
(47)	Jeff Conine	4.00
(48)	Steve Cooke	4.00
(49)	Joey Cora	4.00
(50)	Marty Cordova	4.00
(51)	Rheal Cormier	4.00
(52)	Felipe Crespo	4.00
(53)	Chad Curtis	4.00
(54)	Johnny Damon	15.00
(55)	Russ Davis	4.00
(56)	Andre Dawson	10.00
(57a)	Carlos Delgado (Black autograph.)	15.00
(57b)	Carlos Delgado (Blue autograph.)	15.00
(58)	Doug Drabek	4.00
(59)	Darren Dreifort	4.00
(60)	Shawon Dunston	4.00
(61)	Ray Durham	4.00
(62)	Jim Edmonds	12.00
(63)	Joey Eischen	4.00
(64)	Jim Eisenreich	4.00
(65)	Sal Fasano	4.00
(66)	Jeff Fassero	4.00
(67)	Alex Fernandez	4.00
(68)	Darrin Fletcher	4.00
(69)	Chad Fonville	4.00
(70)	Kevin Foster	4.00
(71)	John Franco	4.00
(72)	Julio Franco	10.00
(73)	Marvin Freeman	4.00
(74)	Travis Fryman	4.00
(75)	Gary Gaetti	4.00
(76)	Carlos Garcia	4.00
(77)	Jason Giambi	10.00
(78)	Benji Gil	4.00
(79)	Greg Gohr	4.00
(80)	Chris Gomez	4.00
(81)	Leo Gomez	4.00
(82)	Tom Goodwin	4.00
(83)	Mike Grace	4.00
(84)	Mike Greenwell	6.00
(85)	Rusty Greer	4.00
(86)	Mark Grudzielanek	4.00
(87)	Mark Gubicza	4.00
(88)	Juan Guzman	4.00
(89)	Darryl Hamilton	4.00
(90)	Joey Hamilton	4.00
(91)	Chris Hammond	4.00
(92)	Mike Hampton	7.50
(93)	Chris Haney	4.00
(94)	Todd Haney	4.00
(95)	Erik Hanson	4.00
(96)	Pete Harnisch	4.00
(97)	LaTroy Hawkins	4.00
(98)	Charlie Hayes	4.00
(99)	Jimmy Haynes	4.00
(100)	Roberto Hernandez	4.00
(101)	Bobby Higginson	4.00
(102)	Glenallen Hill	4.00
(103)	Ken Hill	4.00
(104)	Sterling Hitchcock	4.00
(105)	Trevor Hoffman	10.00
(106)	Dave Hollins	4.00
(107)	Dwayne Hosey	4.00
(108)	Thomas Howard	4.00
(109)	Steve Howe	6.00
(110)	John Hudek	4.00
(111)	Rex Hudler	4.00
(112)	Brian Hunter	4.00
(113)	Butch Huskey	4.00
(114)	Mark Hutton	4.00
(115)	Jason Jacome	4.00
(116)	John Jaha	4.00
(117)	Reggie Jefferson	4.00
(118)	Derek Jeter/SP	150.00

(119)	Bobby Jones	4.00
(120)	Todd Jones	4.00
(121)	Brian Jordan	5.00
(122)	Kevin Jordan	4.00
(123)	Jeff Juden	4.00
(124)	Ron Karkovice	4.00
(125)	Roberto Kelly	4.00
(126)	Mark Kiefer	4.00
(127)	Brooks Kieschnick	4.00
(128)	Jeff King	4.00
(129)	Mike Lansing	4.00
(130)	Matt Lawton	7.50
(131)	Al Leiter	6.00
(132)	Mark Leiter	4.00
(133)	Curtis Leskanic	4.00
(134)	Darren Lewis	4.00
(135)	Mark Lewis	4.00
(136)	Felipe Lira	4.00
(137)	Pat Listach	4.00
(138)	Keith Lockhart	4.00
(139)	Kenny Lofton/SP	25.00
(140)	John Mabry	4.00
(141)	Mike Macfarlane	4.00
(142)	Kirt Manwaring	4.00
(143)	Al Martin	4.00
(144)	Norberto Martin	4.00
(145)	Dennis Martinez	5.00
(146)	Pedro Martinez	40.00
(147)	Sandy Martinez	4.00
(148)	Mike Matheny	4.00
(149)	T.J. Mathews	4.00
(150)	David McCarty	4.00
(151)	Ben McDonald	4.00
(152)	Pat Meares	4.00
(153)	Orlando Merced	4.00
(154)	Jose Mesa	4.00
(155)	Matt Mieske	4.00
(156)	Orlando Miller	4.00
(157)	Mike Mimbs	4.00
(158)	Paul Molitor/SP	40.00
(159)	Raul Mondesi/SP	20.00
(160)	Jeff Montgomery	4.00
(161)	Mickey Morandini	4.00
(162)	Lyle Mouton	4.00
(163)	James Mouton	4.00
(164)	Jamie Moyer	4.00
(165)	Rodney Myers	4.00
(166)	Denny Neagle	4.00
(167)	Robb Nen	4.00
(168)	Marc Newfield	4.00
(169)	Dave Nilsson	4.00
(170)	Jon Nunnally	4.00
(171)	Chad Ogea	4.00
(172)	Troy O'Leary	4.00
(173)	Rey Ordonez	4.00
(174)	Jayhawk Owens	4.00
(175)	Tom Pagnozzi	4.00
(176)	Dean Palmer	4.00
(177)	Roger Pavlik	4.00
(178)	Troy Percival	4.00
(179)	Carlos Perez	4.00
(180)	Robert Perez	4.00
(181)	Andy Pettitte	30.00
(182)	Phil Plantier	4.00
(183)	Mike Potts	4.00
(184)	Curtis Pride	4.00
(185)	Ariel Prieto	4.00
(186)	Bill Pulsipher	4.00
(187)	Brad Radke	4.00
(188)	Manny Ramirez/SP	35.00
(189)	Joe Randa	4.00
(190)	Pat Rapp	4.00
(191)	Bryan Rekar	4.00
(192)	Shane Reynolds	4.00
(193)	Arthur Rhodes	4.00
(194)	Mariano Rivera	45.00
(195a)	Alex Rodriguez/SP (Black autograph.)	120.00
(195b)	Alex Rodriguez/SP (Blue autograph.)	120.00
(196)	Frank Rodriguez	4.00
(197)	Mel Rojas	4.00
(198)	Ken Ryan	4.00
(199)	Bret Saberhagen	4.00
(200)	Tim Salmon	5.00
(201)	Rey Sanchez	4.00
(202)	Scott Sanders	4.00
(203)	Steve Scarsone	4.00
(204)	Curt Schilling	25.00
(205)	Jason Schmidt	20.00
(206)	David Segui	4.00
(207)	Kevin Seitzer	4.00
(208)	Scott Servais	4.00
(209)	Don Slaught	4.00
(210)	Zane Smith	4.00
(211)	Paul Sorrento	4.00
(212)	Scott Stahoviak	4.00
(213)	Mike Stanley	4.00
(214)	Terry Steinbach	4.00
(215)	Kevin Stocker	4.00
(216)	Jeff Suppan	4.00
(217)	Bill Swift	4.00
(218)	Greg Swindell	4.00
(219)	Kevin Tapani	4.00
(220)	Danny Tartabull	4.00
(221)	Julian Tavarez	4.00
(222a)	Frank Thomas/SP (Blue autograph.)	40.00
(222b)	Frank Thomas/SP (Black autograph.)	40.00
(223)	Jim Thome/SP/Silver	40.00
(224)	Ozzie Timmons	4.00
(225a)	Michael Tucker (Black autograph.)	4.00
(225b)	Michael Tucker (Blue autograph.)	4.00
(226)	Ismael Valdez	4.00
(227)	Jose Valentin	4.00

(228)	Todd Van Poppel	4.00
(229)	Mo Vaughn/SP	15.00
(230)	Quilvio Veras	4.00
(231)	Fernando Vina	4.00
(232)	Joe Vitiello	4.00
(233)	Jose Vizcaino	4.00
(234)	Omar Vizquel	12.00
(235)	Terrell Wade	4.00
(236)	Paul Wagner	4.00
(237)	Matt Walbeck	4.00
(238)	Jerome Walton	4.00
(239)	Turner Ward	4.00
(240)	Allen Watson	4.00
(241)	David Weathers	4.00
(242)	Walt Weiss	4.00
(244)	Turk Wendell	4.00
(243)	Rondell White	5.00
(245)	Brian Williams	4.00
(246)	George Williams	4.00
(247)	Paul Wilson	4.00
(248)	Bobby Witt	4.00
(249)	Bob Wolcott	4.00
(250)	Eric Young	4.00
(251)	Ernie Young	4.00
(252)	Gregg Zaun	4.00
---	Frank Thomas (Auto. jumbo edition of 1,500.)	25.00

1996 Leaf/Signature Series Extended Autographs

Signature Series Extended Autograph cards comprise 30 short-printed stars and top prospects, and 187 other major leaguers. Most players signed 5,000 cards each, while other signees' totals are listed in parentheses. Signature cards for Alex Rodriguez, Juan Gonzalez and Andruw Jones were only available through mail-in redemption. Autographed cards were a different design from Series 1 and were seeded two per pack in Extended. The unnumbered cards are checklisted here in alphabetical order.

	NM/M
Common Player:	4.00
Extended Pack:	20.00
Extended Box:	150.00

(1)	Scott Aldred	4.00
(2)	Mike Aldrete	4.00
(3)	Rich Amaral	4.00
(4)	Alex Arias	4.00
(5)	Paul Assenmacher	4.00
(6)	Roger Bailey	4.00
(7)	Erik Bennett	4.00
(8)	Sean Bergman	4.00
(9)	Doug Bochtler	4.00
(10)	Tim Bogar	4.00
(11)	Pat Borders	4.00
(12)	Pedro Borbon	4.00
(13)	Shawn Boskie	4.00
(14)	Rafael Bournigal	4.00
(15)	Mark Brandenburg	4.00
(16)	John Briscoe	4.00
(17)	Jorge Brito	4.00
(18)	Doug Brocail	4.00
(19)	Jay Buhner/SP/1,000	17.50
(20)	Scott Bullett	4.00
(21)	Dave Burba	4.00
(22)	Ken Caminiti/SP/1,000	25.00
(23)	John Cangelosi	4.00
(24)	Cris Carpenter	4.00
(25)	Chuck Carr	4.00
(26)	Larry Casian	4.00
(27)	Tony Castillo	4.00
(28)	Jason Christiansen	4.00
(29)	Archi Cianfrocco	4.00
(30)	Mark Clark	4.00
(31)	Terry Clark	4.00
(32)	Roger Clemens/SP/1,000	150.00
(33)	Jim Converse	4.00
(34)	Dennis Cook	4.00
(35)	Francisco Cordova	4.00
(36)	Jim Corsi	4.00
(37)	Tim Crabtree	4.00
(38)	Doug Creek/SP/1,950	8.00
(39)	John Cummings	4.00
(40)	Omar Daal	4.00
(41)	Rich DeLucia	4.00
(42)	Mark Dewey	4.00
(43)	Alex Diaz	4.00
(44)	Jermaine Dye/SP/2,500	12.00
(45)	Ken Edenfield	4.00

#	Player	Price
(46)	Mark Eichhorn	4.00
(47)	John Ericks	4.00
(48)	Darin Erstad	10.00
(49)	Alvaro Espinoza	4.00
(50)	Jorge Fabregas	4.00
(51)	Mike Fetters	4.00
(52)	John Flaherty	4.00
(53)	Bryce Florie	4.00
(54)	Tony Fossas	4.00
(55)	Lou Frazier	4.00
(56)	Mike Gallego	4.00
(57)	Karim Garcia/SP/2,500	6.00
(58)	Jason Giambi	12.00
(59)	Ed Giovanola	4.00
(60)	Tom Glavine/SP/1,250	40.00
(61)	Juan Gonzalez/SP/1,000	30.00
(61)	Juan Gonzalez (Redemption card.)	5.00
(62)	Craig Grebeck	4.00
(63)	Buddy Groom	4.00
(64)	Kevin Gross	4.00
(65)	Eddie Guardado	4.00
(66)	Mark Guthrie	4.00
(67)	Tony Gwynn/SP/1,000	60.00
(68)	Chip Hale	4.00
(69)	Darren Hall	4.00
(70)	Lee Hancock	4.00
(71)	Dave Hansen	4.00
(72)	Bryan Harvey	4.00
(73)	Bill Haselman	4.00
(74)	Mike Henneman	4.00
(75)	Doug Henry	4.00
(76)	Gil Heredia	4.00
(77)	Carlos Hernandez	4.00
(78)	Jose Hernandez	4.00
(79)	Darren Holmes	4.00
(80)	Mark Holzemer	4.00
(81)	Rick Honeycutt	4.00
(82)	Chris Hook	4.00
(83)	Chris Howard	4.00
(84)	Jack Howell	4.00
(85)	David Hulse	4.00
(86)	Edwin Hurtado	4.00
(87)	Jeff Huson	4.00
(88)	Mike James	4.00
(89)	Derek Jeter/SP/1,000	160.00
(90)	Brian Johnson	4.00
(91)	Randy Johnson/SP/1,000	125.00
(92)	Mark Johnson	4.00
(93)	Andruw Jones/SP/2,000	30.00
(93)	Andruw Jones (Redemption card.)	5.00
(94)	Chris Jones	4.00
(95)	Ricky Jordan	4.00
(96)	Matt Karchner	4.00
(97)	Scott Karl	4.00
(98)	Jason Kendall/SP/2,500	10.00
(99)	Brian Keyser	4.00
(100)	Mike Kingery	4.00
(101)	Wayne Kirby	4.00
(102)	Ryan Klesko/SP/1,000	17.50
(103)	Chuck Knoblauch/SP/1,000	15.00
(104)	Chad Kreuter	4.00
(105)	Tom Lampkin	4.00
(106)	Scott Leius	4.00
(107)	Jon Lieber	4.00
(108)	Nelson Liriano	4.00
(109)	Scott Livingstone	4.00
(110)	Graeme Lloyd	4.00
(111)	Kenny Lofton/SP/1,000	10.00
(112)	Luis Lopez	4.00
(113)	Torey Lovullo	4.00
(114)	Greg Maddux/SP/500	250.00
(115)	Mike Maddux	4.00
(116)	Dave Magadan	4.00
(117)	Mike Magnante	4.00
(118)	Joe Magrane	4.00
(119)	Pat Mahomes	4.00
(120)	Matt Mantei	4.00
(121)	John Marzano	4.00
(122)	Terry Matthews	4.00
(123)	Chuck McElroy	4.00
(124)	Fred McGriff/SP/1,000	35.00
(125)	Mark McLemore	4.00
(126)	Greg McMichael	4.00
(127)	Blas Minor	4.00
(128)	Dave Mlicki	4.00
(129)	Mike Mohler	4.00
(130)	Paul Molitor /SP/1,000	25.00
(131)	Steve Montgomery	4.00
(132)	Mike Mordecai	4.00
(133)	Mike Morgan	4.00
(134)	Mike Munoz	4.00
(135)	Greg Myers	4.00
(136)	Jimmy Myers	4.00
(137)	Mike Myers	4.00
(138)	Bob Natal	4.00
(139)	Dan Naulty	4.00
(140)	Jeff Nelson	4.00
(141)	Warren Newson	4.00
(142)	Chris Nichting	4.00
(143)	Melvin Nieves	4.00
(144)	Charlie O'Brien	4.00
(145)	Alex Ochoa	4.00
(146)	Omar Olivares	4.00
(147)	Joe Oliver	4.00
(148)	Lance Painter	4.00
(149)	Rafael Palmeiro/SP/2,000	35.00
(150)	Mark Parent	4.00
(151)	Steve Parris/SP/1,800	7.50
(152)	Bob Patterson	4.00
(153)	Tony Pena	7.50
(154)	Eddie Perez	4.00
(155)	Yorkis Perez	4.00
(156)	Robert Person	4.00
(157)	Mark Petkovsek	4.00
(158)	Andy Pettitte/SP/1,000	60.00
(159)	J.R. Phillips	4.00
(160)	Hipolito Pichardo	4.00
(161)	Eric Plunk	4.00
(162)	Jimmy Poole	4.00
(163)	Kirby Puckett/SP/1,000	80.00
(164)	Paul Quantrill	4.00
(165)	Tom Quinlan	4.00
(166)	Jeff Reboulet	4.00
(167)	Jeff Reed	4.00
(168)	Steve Reed	4.00
(169)	Carlos Reyes	4.00
(170)	Bill Risley	4.00
(171)	Kevin Ritz	4.00
(172)	Kevin Roberson	4.00
(173)	Rich Robertson	4.00
(174)	Alex Rodriguez/SP/500	180.00
(174)	Alex Rodriguez (Redemption card.)	15.00
(175)	Ivan Rodriguez/SP/1,250	40.00
(176)	Bruce Ruffin	4.00
(177)	Juan Samuel	4.00
(178)	Tim Scott	4.00
(179)	Kevin Sefcik	4.00
(180)	Jeff Shaw	4.00
(181)	Danny Sheaffer	4.00
(182)	Craig Shipley	4.00
(183)	Dave Silvestri	4.00
(184)	Aaron Small	4.00
(185)	John Smoltz/SP/1,000	90.00
(186)	Luis Sojo	4.00
(187)	Sammy Sosa/SP/1,000	160.00
(188)	Steve Sparks	4.00
(189)	Tim Spehr	4.00
(190)	Russ Springer	4.00
(191)	Matt Stairs	4.00
(192)	Andy Stankiewicz	4.00
(193)	Mike Stanton	4.00
(194)	Kelly Stinnett	4.00
(195)	Doug Strange	4.00
(196)	Mark Sweeney	4.00
(197)	Jeff Tabaka	4.00
(198)	Jesus Tavarez	4.00
(199)	Frank Thomas/SP/1,000	45.00
(200)	Larry Thomas	4.00
(201)	Mark Thompson	4.00
(202)	Mike Timlin	4.00
(203)	Steve Trachsel	4.00
(204)	Tom Urbani	4.00
(205)	Julio Valera	4.00
(206)	Dave Valle	4.00
(207)	William Van Landingham	4.00
(208)	Mo Vaughn/SP/1,000	10.00
(209)	Dave Veres	4.00
(210)	Ed Vosberg	4.00
(211)	Don Wengert	4.00
(212)	Matt Whiteside	4.00
(213)	Bob Wickman	4.00
(214)	Matt Williams/SP/1,250	12.00
(215)	Mike Williams	4.00
(216)	Woody Williams	4.00
(217)	Craig Worthington	4.00
	Frank Thomas (Auto. jumbo edition of 1,500.)	30.00

Extended Autographs - Century Marks

Century Marks represent the first 100 autographs by the 30 short-printed stars and prospects, plus Alex Ochoa. These are designated with a blue holographic foil "Century Marks" logo. Cards of Gonzalez, Jeter, Andruw Jones, Palmeiro and Alex Rodriguez were available only via mail-in redemption cards.

		NM/M
	Common Player:	15.00
(1)	Jay Buhner	30.00
(2)	Ken Caminiti	30.00
(3)	Roger Clemens	250.00
(4)	Jermaine Dye	30.00
(5)	Darin Erstad	45.00
(6)	Karim Garcia	30.00
(7)	Jason Giambi	75.00
(8)	Tom Glavine	90.00
(9)	Juan Gonzalez	90.00
(9)	Juan Gonzalez (Redemption card.)	7.50
(10)	Tony Gwynn	150.00
(11)	Derek Jeter	350.00
(11)	Derek Jeter (Redemption card.)	15.00
(12)	Randy Johnson	185.00
(13)	Andruw Jones	150.00
(13)	Andruw Jones (Redemption card.)	7.50
(14)	Jason Kendall	30.00
(15)	Ryan Klesko	30.00
(16)	Chuck Knoblauch	30.00
(17)	Kenny Lofton	30.00
(18)	Greg Maddux	200.00
(19)	Fred McGriff	30.00
(20)	Paul Molitor	110.00
(21)	Alex Ochoa	15.00
(22)	Rafael Palmeiro	110.00
(22)	Rafael Palmeiro (Redemption card.)	7.50
(23)	Andy Pettitte	75.00
(24)	Kirby Puckett	185.00
(25)	Alex Rodriguez	350.00
(25)	Alex Rodriguez (Redemption card.)	15.00
(26)	Ivan Rodriguez	100.00
(27)	John Smoltz	100.00
(28)	Sammy Sosa	350.00
(29)	Frank Thomas	135.00
(30)	Mo Vaughn	30.00
(31)	Matt Williams	30.00

Frank Thomas The Big Heart

In one of several specialty card charitable endeavors, Frank Thomas and Leaf teamed up to issue this set as a fund raiser for "The Big Hurt's" charitable foundation. Each of the cards was available in an edition limited to 3,500 each for a $20 donation. Cards are standard 2-1/2" x 3-1/2" with posed photos on front and "THE BIG HEART," a play on his nickname. Backs have information on the foundation.

		NM/M
	Complete Set (4):	35.00
	Common Card:	10.00
(1)	Frank Thomas (Bat on shoulder.)	10.00
(2)	Frank Thomas (Holding glove.)	10.00
(3)	Frank Thomas (Horizontal)	10.00
(4)	Frank Thomas (Seated)	10.00

1997 Leaf

Leaf produced a 400-card set in two series in 1997. The cards feature a gray border with the player photo vignetted at center. The player's name, team and a Leaf logo are displayed at bottom in silver foil. A team logo is in the upper-right corner. Besides the base cards, 10-card packs retailing for $2.99 could contain one of the following inserts: Banner Season, Dress for Success, Get-A-Grip, Knot-hole Gang, Statistical Standouts, Fractal Matrix or Fractal Matrix Die-cut.

		NM/M
	Complete Set (400):	25.00
	Common Player:	.05
	Jackie Robinson 1948 Leaf Reprint:	10.00
	Series 1 Pack (12):	2.00
	Series 1 Wax Box (18):	30.00
	Series 2 Pack (12):	1.50
	Series 2 Wax Box (24):	30.00

#	Player	Price
1	Wade Boggs	1.50
2	Brian McRae	.05
3	Jeff D'Amico	.05
4	George Arias	.05
5	Billy Wagner	.05
6	Ray Lankford	.05
7	Will Clark	.10
8	Edgar Renteria	.05
9	Alex Ochoa	.05
10	Roberto Hernandez	.05
11	Joe Carter	.05
12	Gregg Jefferies	.05
13	Mark Grace	.05
14	Roberto Alomar	.10
15	Joe Randa	.05
16	Alex Rodriguez	2.50
17	Tony Gwynn	1.50
18	Steve Gibralter	.05
19	Scott Stahoviak	.05
20	Matt Williams	.05
21	Quinton McCracken	.05
22	Ugueth Urbina	.05
23	Jermaine Allensworth	.05
24	Paul Molitor	.75
25	Carlos Delgado	.50
26	Bob Abreu	.05
27	John Jaha	.05
28	Rusty Greer	.05
29	Kimera Bartee	.05
30	Ruben Rivera	.05
31	Jason Kendall	.05
32	Lance Johnson	.05
33	Robin Ventura	.05
34	Kevin Appier	.05
35	John Mabry	.05
36	Ricky Otero	.05
37	Mike Lansing	.05
38	Mark McGwire	2.50
39	Tim Naehring	.05
40	Tom Glavine	.30
41	Rey Ordonez	.05
42	Tony Clark	.05
43	Rafael Palmeiro	.65
44	Pedro Martinez	.75
45	Keith Lockhart	.05
46	Dan Wilson	.05
47	John Wetteland	.05
48	Chan Ho Park	.05
49	Gary Sheffield	.40
50	Shawn Estes	.05
51	Royce Clayton	.05
52	Jaime Navarro	.05
53	Raul Casanova	.05
54	Jeff Bagwell	1.00
55	Barry Larkin	.05
56	Charles Nagy	.05
57	Ken Caminiti	.05
58	Todd Hollandsworth	.05
59	Pat Hentgen	.05
60	Jose Valentin	.05
61	Frank Rodriguez	.05
62	Mickey Tettleton	.05
63	Marty Cordova	.05
64	Cecil Fielder	.05
65	Barry Bonds	3.00
66	Scott Servais	.05
67	Ernie Young	.05
68	Wilson Alvarez	.05
69	Mike Grace	.05
70	Shane Reynolds	.05
71	Henry Rodriguez	.05
72	Eric Karros	.05
73	Mark Langston	.05
74	Scott Karl	.05
75	Trevor Hoffman	.05
76	Orel Hershiser	.05
77	John Smoltz	.05
78	Raul Mondesi	.05
79	Jeff Brantley	.05
80	Donne Wall	.05
81	Joey Cora	.05
82	Mel Rojas	.05
83	Chad Mottola	.05
84	Omar Vizquel	.05
85	Greg Maddux	1.50
86	Jamey Wright	.05
87	Chuck Finley	.05
88	Brady Anderson	.05
89	Alex Gonzalez	.05
90	Andy Benes	.05
91	Reggie Jefferson	.05
92	Paul O'Neill	.05
93	Javier Lopez	.05
94	Mark Grudzielanek	.05
95	Marc Newfield	.05
96	Kevin Ritz	.05
97	Fred McGriff	.05
98	Dwight Gooden	.05
99	Hideo Nomo	.65
100	Steve Finley	.05
101	Juan Gonzalez	.65
102	Jay Buhner	.05
103	Paul Wilson	.05
104	Alan Benes	.05
105	Manny Ramirez	1.00
106	Kevin Elster	.05
107	Frank Thomas	1.00
108	Orlando Miller	.05
109	Ramon Martinez	.05
110	Kenny Lofton	.05
111	Bernie Williams	.05
112	Robby Thompson	.05
113	Bernard Gilkey	.05
114	Ray Durham	.05
115	Jeff Cirillo	.05
116	Brian Jordan	.05
117	Rich Becker	.05
118	Al Leiter	.05
119	Mark Johnson	.05
120	Ellis Burks	.05
121	Sammy Sosa	2.00
122	Willie Greene	.05
123	Michael Tucker	.05
124	Eddie Murray	.75
125	Joey Hamilton	.05
126	Antonio Osuna	.05
127	Bobby Higginson	.05
128	Tomas Perez	.05
129	Tim Salmon	.05
130	Mark Wohlers	.05
131	Charles Johnson	.05
132	Randy Johnson	.75
133	Brooks Kieschnick	.05
134	Al Martin	.05
135	Dante Bichette	.05
136	Andy Pettitte	.30
137	Jason Giambi	.60
138	James Baldwin	.05
139	Ben McDonald	.05
140	Shawn Green	.35
141	Geronimo Berroa	.05
142	Jose Offerman	.05
143	Curtis Pride	.05
144	Terrell Wade	.05
145	Ismael Valdes	.05
146	Mike Mussina	.40
147	Mariano Rivera	.15
148	Ken Hill	.05
149	Darin Erstad	.25
150	Jay Bell	.05
151	Mo Vaughn	.05
152	Ozzie Smith	1.50
153	Jose Mesa	.05
154	Osvaldo Fernandez	.05
155	Vinny Castilla	.05
156	Jason Isringhausen	.05
157	B.J. Surhoff	.05
158	Robert Perez	.05
159	Ron Coomer	.05
160	Darren Oliver	.05
161	Mike Mohler	.05
162	Russ Davis	.05
163	Bret Boone	.05
164	Ricky Bottalico	.05
165	Derek Jeter	3.00
166	Orlando Merced	.05
167	John Valentin	.05
168	Andruw Jones	1.00
169	Angel Echevarria	.05
170	Todd Walker	.05
171	Desi Relaford	.05
172	Trey Beamon	.05
173	Brian Giles RC	.75
174	Scott Rolen	.60
175	Shannon Stewart	.05
176	Dmitri Young	.05
177	Justin Thompson	.05
178	Trot Nixon	.05
179	Josh Booty	.05
180	Robin Jennings	.05
181	Marvin Benard	.05
182	Luis Castillo	.05
183	Wendell Magee	.05
184	Vladimir Guerrero	1.00
185	Nomar Garciaparra	2.00
186	Ryan Hancock	.05
187	Mike Cameron	.05
188	Cal Ripken Jr. (Legacy)	1.50
189	Chipper Jones (Legacy)	.75
190	Albert Belle (Legacy)	.05
191	Mike Piazza (Legacy)	1.00
192	Chuck Knoblauch (Legacy)	.05
193	Ken Griffey Jr. (Legacy)	1.00
194	Ivan Rodriguez (Legacy)	.30
195	Jose Canseco (Legacy)	.25
196	Ryne Sandberg (Legacy)	.30
197	Jim Thome (Legacy)	.30
198	Andy Pettitte (Checklist)	.05
199	Andruw Jones (Checklist)	.50
200	Derek Jeter (Checklist)	1.50
201	Chipper Jones	1.50
202	Albert Belle	.05
203	Mike Piazza	2.00
204	Ken Griffey Jr.	2.00
205	Ryne Sandberg	1.50
206	Jose Canseco	.40
207	Chili Davis	.05
208	Roger Clemens	2.00
209	Deion Sanders	.05
210	Darryl Hamilton	.05
211	Jermaine Dye	.05
212	Matt Williams	.05
213	Kevin Elster	.05
214	John Wetteland	.05
215	Garret Anderson	.05
216	Kevin Brown	.05
217	Matt Lawton	.05
218	Cal Ripken Jr.	3.00
219	Moises Alou	.05
220	Chuck Knoblauch	.05
221	Ivan Rodriguez	.65
222	Travis Fryman	.05
223	Jim Thome	.65
224	Eddie Murray	.75
225	Eric Young	.05
226	Ron Gant	.05
227	Tony Phillips	.05
228	Reggie Sanders	.05
229	Johnny Damon	.35
230	Bill Pulsipher	.05
231	Jim Edmonds	.05
232	Melvin Nieves	.05
233	Ryan Klesko	.05
234	David Cone	.05
235	Derek Bell	.05
236	Julio Franco	.05
237	Juan Guzman	.05
238	Larry Walker	.05
239	Delino DeShields	.05
240	Troy Percival	.05
241	Andres Galarraga	.05
242	Rondell White	.05
243	John Burkett	.05
244	J.T. Snow	.05
245	Alex Fernandez	.05
246	Edgar Martinez	.05
247	Craig Biggio	.05
248	Todd Hundley	.05
249	Jimmy Key	.05
250	Cliff Floyd	.05
251	Jeff Conine	.05
252	Curt Schilling	.35
253	Jeff King	.05
254	Tino Martinez	.05
255	Carlos Baerga	.05
256	Jeff Fassero	.05
257	Dean Palmer	.05
258	Robb Nen	.05
259	Sandy Alomar Jr.	.05
260	Carlos Perez	.05
261	Rickey Henderson	.75
262	Bobby Bonilla	.05
263	Darren Daulton	.05
264	Jim Leyritz	.05
265	Dennis Martinez	.05
266	Butch Huskey	.05
267	Joe Vitiello	.05
268	Steve Trachsel	.05
269	Glenallen Hill	.05
270	Terry Steinbach	.05
271	Mark McLemore	.05
272	Devon White	.05
273	Jeff Kent	.05
274	Tim Raines	.05
275	Carlos Garcia	.05
276	Hal Morris	.05
277	Gary Gaetti	.05
278	John Olerud	.05
279	Wally Joyner	.05
280	Brian Hunter	.05
281	Steve Karsay	.05
282	Denny Neagle	.05
283	Jose Herrera	.05
284	Todd Stottlemyre	.05
285	Bip Roberts	.05
286	Kevin Seitzer	.05
287	Benji Gil	.05
288	Dennis Eckersley	.65
289	Brad Ausmus	.05
290	Otis Nixon	.05
291	Darryl Strawberry	.05
292	Marquis Grissom	.05
293	Darryl Kile	.05
294	Quilvio Veras	.05
295	Tom Goodwin	.05
296	Benito Santiago	.05
297	Mike Bordick	.05
298	Roberto Kelly	.05
299	David Justice	.05
300	Carl Everett	.05
301	Mark Whiten	.05
302	Aaron Sele	.05
303	Darren Dreifort	.05
304	Bobby Jones	.05
305	Fernando Vina	.05
306	Ed Sprague	.05
307	Andy Ashby	.05
308	Tony Fernandez	.05
309	Roger Pavlik	.05
310	Mark Clark	.05
311	Mariano Duncan	.05
312	Tyler Houston	.05
313	Eric Davis	.05
314	Greg Vaughn	.05
315	David Segui	.05
316	Dave Nilsson	.05
317	F.P. Santangelo	.05
318	Wilton Guerrero	.05
319	Jose Guillen	.05
320	Kevin Orie	.05
321	Derrek Lee	.05
322	Bubba Trammell RC	.50
323	Pokey Reese	.05
324	Hideki Irabu RC	.50
325	Scott Spiezio	.05
326	Bartolo Colon	.05
327	Damon Mashore	.05
328	Ryan McGuire	.05
329	Chris Carpenter	.05
330	Jose Cruz Jr. RC	.50
331	Todd Greene	.05
332	Brian Moehler	.05
333	Mike Sweeney	.05
334	Neifi Perez	.05
335	Matt Morris	.05
336	Marvin Benard	.05
337	Karim Garcia	.05
338	Jason Dickson	.05
339	Brant Brown	.05
340	Jeff Suppan	.05
341	Deivi Cruz RC	.25
342	Antone Williamson	.05
343	Curtis Goodwin	.05
344	Brooks Kieschnick	.05
345	Tony Womack RC	.25
346	Rudy Pemberton	.05
347	Todd Dunwoody	.05
348	Frank Thomas (Legacy)	.50
349	Andruw Jones (Legacy)	.50
350	Alex Rodriguez (Legacy)	1.25
351	Greg Maddux (Legacy)	.75
352	Jeff Bagwell (Legacy)	.50
353	Juan Gonzalez (Legacy)	.35
354	Barry Bonds (Legacy)	1.50
355	Mark McGwire (Legacy)	1.25
356	Tony Gwynn (Legacy)	.75
357	Gary Sheffield (Legacy)	.25
358	Derek Jeter (Legacy)	1.50
359	Manny Ramirez (Legacy)	.50
360	Hideo Nomo (Legacy)	.30
361	Sammy Sosa (Legacy)	1.00
362	Paul Molitor (Legacy)	.40
363	Kenny Lofton (Legacy)	.25
364	Eddie Murray (Legacy)	.40
365	Barry Larkin (Legacy)	.25
366	Roger Clemens (Legacy)	1.00
367	John Smoltz (Legacy)	.25
368	Alex Rodriguez (Gamers)	1.50
369	Frank Thomas (Gamers)	.40
370	Cal Ripken Jr. (Gamers)	1.50

371	Ken Griffey Jr. (Gamers)	1.50
372	Greg Maddux (Gamers)	1.00
373	Mike Piazza (Gamers)	1.25
374	Chipper Jones (Gamers)	1.00
375	Albert Belle (Gamers)	.05
376	Chuck Knoblauch (Gamers)	.05
377	Brady Anderson (Gamers)	.05
378	David Justice (Gamers)	.05
379	Randy Johnson (Gamers)	.40
380	Wade Boggs (Gamers)	.75
381	Kevin Brown (Gamers)	.05
382	Tom Glavine (Gamers)	.05
383	Raul Mondesi (Gamers)	.05
384	Ivan Rodriguez (Gamers)	.30
385	Larry Walker (Gamers)	.05
386	Bernie Williams (Gamers)	.05
387	Rusty Greer (Gamers)	.05
388	Rafael Palmeiro (Gamers)	.05
389	Matt Williams (Gamers)	.05
390	Eric Young (Gamers)	.05
391	Fred McGriff (Gamers)	.05
392	Ken Caminiti (Gamers)	.05
393	Roberto Alomar (Gamers)	.05
394	Brian Jordan (Gamers)	.05
395	Mark Grace (Gamers)	.05
396	Jim Edmonds (Gamers)	.05
397	Deion Sanders (Gamers)	.05
398	Checklist (Vladimir Guerrero)	.50
399	Checklist (Darin Erstad)	.10
400	Checklist (Nomar Garciaparra)	1.00

Fractal Matrix

Leaf introduced Fractal Matrix inserts, a 400-card parallel set broken down into three colors and three unique die-cuts. One "fracture" breaks the insert set down by foil background color (80 Gold, 120 Silver and 200 Bronze). A second fracture breaks those cards down into X, Y and Z "axis" variations. There are no markings on the cards to segregate the X, Y and Z groups, though that information was printed on the box bottoms. No production numbers or insert ratios were released for either fracture. Each player is available in only one color/axis combination. The incredibly convoluted nature of the issue insured that virtually nobody understood the concept, putting a damper on collector interest.

		NM/M
	Common Bronze:	.35
	Common Silver:	.50
	Common Gold:	1.25
1	Wade Boggs G/Y	8.00
2	Brian McRae B/Y	.35
3	Jeff D'Amico B/Y	.35
4	George Arias S/Y	.35
5	Billy Wagner S/Y	.50
6	Ray Lankford B/Z	.50
7	Will Clark S/Y	.60
8	Edgar Renteria S/Y	.50
9	Alex Ochoa S/Y	.35
10	Roberto Hernandez B/X	.35
11	Joe Carter S/X	.35
12	Gregg Jefferies B/Y	.35
13	Mark Grace B/X	.35
14	Roberto Alomar G/Y	2.00
15	Joe Randa B/X	.35
16	Alex Rodriguez G/Z	10.00
17	Tony Gwynn G/Z	6.00
18	Steve Gibralter B/Y	.35
19	Scott Stahoviak B/X	.35
20	Matt Williams S/Z	.50
21	Quinton McCracken B/Y	.35
22	Ugueth Urbina B/X	.35
23	Jermaine Allensworth S/X	.35
24	Paul Molitor G/X	5.00
25	Carlos Delgado S/Y	1.00
26	Bob Abreu S/Y	.50
27	John Jaha S/Y	.35
28	Rusty Greer S/Z	.50
29	Kimera Bartee B/X	.35
30	Ruben Rivera S/Y	.35
31	Jason Kendall S/Y	.50
32	Lance Johnson B/X	.35
33	Robin Ventura B/Y	.35
34	Kevin Appier S/X	.50
35	John Mabry S/Y	.50
36	Ricky Otero B/X	.35
37	Mike Lansing B/X	.35
38	Mark McGwire G/Z	10.00
39	Tim Naehring B/X	.35
40	Tom Glavine S/Z	1.00
41	Rey Ordonez S/Y	.50
42	Tony Clark S/Y	.50
43	Rafael Palmeiro S/Z	2.00
44	Pedro Martinez B/X	2.00
45	Keith Lockhart B/X	.35
46	Dan Wilson B/X	.35
47	John Wetteland B/Y	.35
48	Chan Ho Park B/X	.35
49	Gary Sheffield G/Z	3.00
50	Shawn Estes B/X	.35
51	Royce Clayton B/X	.35
52	Jaime Navarro B/X	.35
53	Raul Casanova B/X	.35
54	Jeff Bagwell G/Z	5.00
55	Barry Larkin G/X	1.25
56	Charles Nagy B/Y	.35
57	Ken Caminiti B/X	1.25
58	Todd Hollandsworth S/Z	.50
59	Pat Hentgen S/X	.50
60	Jose Valentin B/X	.35
61	Frank Rodriguez B/X	.35
62	Mickey Tettleton B/X	.35
63	Marty Cordova S/X	1.25
64	Cecil Fielder S/X	.50
65	Barry Bonds G/Z	13.50
66	Scott Servais B/X	.35
67	Ernie Young B/X	.35
68	Wilson Alvarez B/X	.35
69	Mike Grace B/X	.35
70	Shane Reynolds S/X	.35
71	Henry Rodriguez S/Y	.50
72	Eric Karros B/X	.35
73	Mark Langston B/X	.35
74	Scott Karl B/X	.35
75	Trevor Hoffman B/X	.35
76	Orel Hershiser S/X	.35
77	John Smoltz S/Y	1.50
78	Raul Mondesi G/Z	1.25
79	Jeff Brantley B/X	.35
80	Donne Wall B/X	.35
81	Joey Cora B/X	.35
82	Mel Rojas B/X	.35
83	Chad Mottola B/X	.35
84	Omar Vizquel B/X	.35
85	Greg Maddux G/Z	6.00
86	Jamey Wright B/Y	.50
87	Chuck Finley B/X	.35
88	Brady Anderson G/Y	1.25
89	Alex Gonzalez S/X	.50
90	Andy Benes B/X	.35
91	Reggie Jefferson B/X	.35
92	Paul O'Neill B/X	.35
93	Javier Lopez S/X	.50
94	Mark Grudzielanek S/X	.50
95	Marc Newfield B/X	.35
96	Kevin Ritz B/X	.35
97	Fred McGriff G/Y	1.25
98	Dwight Gooden S/X	.50
99	Hideo Nomo B/X	.35
100	Steve Finley B/X	.35
101	Juan Gonzalez G/Z	4.00
102	Jay Buhner S/Z	.50
103	Paul Wilson S/Y	.50
104	Alan Benes B/Y	.35
105	Manny Ramirez G/X	5.00
106	Kevin Elster B/X	.35
107	Frank Thomas G/Z	5.00
108	Orlando Miller B/X	.35
109	Ramon Martinez B/X	.35
110	Kenny Lofton G/X	1.25
111	Bernie Williams G/Y	1.25
112	Robby Thompson B/X	.35
113	Bernard Gilkey B/X	.35
114	Ray Durham B/X	.35
115	Jeff Cirillo S/Z	.35
116	Brian Jordan G/Z	1.25
117	Rich Becker S/Y	.50
118	Al Leiter B/X	.35
119	Mark Johnson B/X	.35
120	Ellis Burks B/Y	.35
121	Sammy Sosa G/Z	7.50
122	Willie Greene B/X	.35
123	Michael Tucker B/X	.35
124	Eddie Murray G/Y	6.00
125	Joey Hamilton B/X	.35
126	Antonio Osuna B/X	.35
127	Bobby Higginson B/X	.35
128	Tomas Perez B/X	.35
129	Tim Salmon G/Z	1.25
130	Mark Wohlers B/X	.35
131	Charles Johnson S/X	.50
132	Randy Johnson S/Y	2.00
133	Brooks Kieschnick S/X	.35
134	Al Martin S/Y	.50
135	Dante Bichette B/X	.35
136	Andy Pettitte G/Z	2.00
137	Jason Giambi G/Y	4.00
138	James Baldwin S/X	.50
139	Ben McDonald B/X	.35
140	Shawn Green S/X	1.00
141	Geronimo Berroa B/X	.35
142	Jose Offerman B/X	.35
143	Curtis Pride B/X	.35
144	Terrell Wade B/X	.35
145	Ismael Valdes S/X	.50
146	Mike Mussina S/X	1.25
147	Mariano Rivera S/X	.75
148	Ken Hill B/X	.35
149	Darin Erstad G/Z	4.00
150	Jay Bell B/X	.35
151	Mo Vaughn G/Z	1.25
152	Ozzie Smith G/Y	8.00
153	Jose Mesa B/X	.35
154	Osvaldo Fernandez B/X	.35
155	Vinny Castilla B/Y	.35
156	Jason Isringhausen S/Y	.50
157	B.J. Surhoff B/X	.35
158	Robert Perez B/X	.35
159	Ron Coomer B/X	.35
160	Darren Oliver B/X	.35
161	Mike Mohler B/X	.35
162	Russ Davis B/X	.35
163	Bret Boone B/X	.35
164	Ricky Bottalico B/X	.35
165	Derek Jeter B/X	13.50
166	Orlando Merced B/X	.35
167	John Valentin B/X	.35
168	Andruw Jones G/Z	5.00
169	Angel Echevarria B/X	.35
170	Todd Walker G/Z	1.25
171	Desi Relaford B/Y	.35
172	Trey Beamon S/X	.50
173	Brian Giles B/Y	.50
174	Scott Rolen S/Z	3.50
175	Shannon Stewart S/Z	.50
176	Dmitri Young G/Z	1.25
177	Justin Thompson B/X	.35
178	Trot Nixon S/Y	.50
179	Josh Booty S/Y	.50
180	Robin Jennings B/X	.35
181	Marvin Benard B/X	.35
182	Luis Castillo B/X	.35
183	Wendell Magee B/X	.35
184	Vladimir Guerrero G/X	5.00
185	Nomar Garciaparra G/X	12.50
186	Ryan Hancock B/X	.35
187	Mike Cameron B/X	.50
188	Cal Ripken Jr. B/X (Legacy)	5.00
189	Chipper Jones S/Z (Legacy)	4.00
190	Albert Belle S/Z (Legacy)	1.00
191	Mike Piazza B/Z (Legacy)	4.00
192	Chuck Knoblauch S/Y (Legacy)	.50
193	Ken Griffey Jr. B/Z (Legacy)	3.50
194	Ivan Rodriguez G/Z (Legacy)	4.00
195	Jose Canseco S/Z (Legacy)	1.25
196	Ryne Sandberg S/X (Legacy)	3.00
197	Jim Thome G/Y (Legacy)	1.50
198	Checklist (Andy Pettitte B/Y)	.75
199	Checklist (Andruw Jones B/Y)	2.00
200	Checklist (Derek Jeter S/Y)	2.00
201	Chipper Jones G/X	10.00
202	Albert Belle G/Y	.50
203	Mike Piazza G/X	12.00
204	Ken Griffey Jr. G/X	15.00
205	Ryne Sandberg G/X	6.00
206	Jose Canseco S/Y	.75
207	Chili Davis B/X	.35
208	Roger Clemens G/Z	6.50
209	Deion Sanders G/Z	1.50
210	Darryl Hamilton B/X	.35
211	Jermaine Dye S/X	.50
212	Matt Williams B/X	1.25
213	Kevin Elster B/X	.35
214	John Wetteland S/X	.50
215	Garret Anderson G/Z	1.25
216	Kevin Brown G/Y	1.25
217	Matt Lawton S/Y	.50
218	Cal Ripken Jr. G/X	16.50
219	Moises Alou G/X	1.25
220	Chuck Knoblauch B/X	1.25
221	Ivan Rodriguez G/Y	5.50
222	Travis Fryman B/Y	.35
223	Jim Thome G/Z	2.00
224	Eddie Murray S/Z	3.00
225	Eric Young G/Z	1.25
226	Ron Gant S/X	.50
227	Tony Phillips B/X	.35
228	Reggie Sanders B/Y	.35
229	Johnny Damon S/Z	1.00
230	Bill Pulsipher B/X	.35
231	Jim Edmonds B/X	1.25
232	Melvin Nieves B/X	.35
233	Ryan Klesko B/Z	1.25
234	David Cone S/X	.50
235	Derek Bell B/Y	.35
236	Julio Franco S/Y	.50
237	Juan Guzman B/X	.35
238	Larry Walker B/X	1.25
239	Delino DeShields B/X	.35
240	Troy Percival B/X	.35
241	Andres Galarraga G/Z	1.25
242	Rondell White B/Z	1.25
243	John Burkett B/X	.35
244	J.T. Snow B/Y	.35
245	Alex Fernandez S/Y	.50
246	Edgar Martinez G/Z	1.25
247	Craig Biggio G/Z	1.25
248	Todd Hundley G/Z	1.25
249	Jimmy Key S/Y	.50
250	Cliff Floyd B/Y	.50
251	Jeff Conine B/X	.35
252	Curt Schilling B/X	.65
253	Jeff King B/X	.35
254	Tino Martinez S/Y	1.25
255	Carlos Baerga S/Y	.50
256	Jeff Fassero B/X	.35
257	Dean Palmer S/Y	.50
258	Robb Nen B/X	.35
259	Sandy Alomar Jr. S/Y	.50
260	Carlos Perez B/X	.35
261	Rickey Henderson S/Y	2.00
262	Bobby Bonilla S/Y	.50
263	Darren Daulton B/X	.35
264	Jim Leyritz B/X	.35
265	Dennis Martinez B/X	.35
266	Butch Huskey B/X	.35
267	Joe Vitiello B/X	.50
268	Steve Trachsel B/X	.35
269	Glenallen Hill B/X	.35
270	Terry Steinbach B/X	.35
271	Mark McLemore B/X	.35
272	Devon White B/X	.35
273	Jeff Kent B/X	.35
274	Tim Raines B/X	.35
275	Carlos Garcia B/X	.35
276	Hal Morris B/X	.35
277	Gary Gaetti B/X	.35
278	John Olerud S/Y	.50
279	Wally Joyner B/X	.35
280	Brian Hunter S/X	.50
281	Steve Karsay B/X	.35
282	Denny Neagle S/X	.50
283	Jose Herrera B/X	.35
284	Todd Stottlemyre B/X	.35
285	Bip Roberts S/X	.50
286	Kevin Seitzer B/X	.35
287	Benji Gil B/X	.35
288	Dennis Eckersley S/X	.50
289	Brad Ausmus B/X	.35
290	Otis Nixon B/X	.35
291	Darryl Strawberry B/X	.35
292	Marquis Grissom S/Y	.50
293	Darryl Kile B/X	.35
294	Quilvio Veras B/X	.35
295	Tom Goodwin B/X	.35
296	Benito Santiago B/X	.35
297	Mike Bordick B/X	.35
298	Roberto Kelly B/X	.35
299	David Justice G/X	1.25
300	Carl Everett B/X	.35
301	Mark Whiten B/X	.35
302	Aaron Sele B/X	.35
303	Darren Dreifort B/X	.45
304	Bobby Jones B/X	.35
305	Fernando Vina B/X	.35
306	Ed Sprague B/X	.35
307	Andy Ashby S/X	.50
308	Tony Fernandez B/X	.35
309	Roger Pavlik B/X	.35
310	Mark Clark B/X	.35
311	Mariano Duncan B/X	.35
312	Tyler Houston B/X	.35
313	Eric Davis S/Y	.50
314	Greg Vaughn B/Y	.35
315	David Segui S/Y	.50
316	Dave Nilsson S/X	.50
317	F.P. Santangelo S/X	.50
318	Wilton Guerrero B/X	1.25
319	Jose Guillen G/Z	1.25
320	Kevin Orie S/Y	.50
321	Derrek Lee G/Z	2.50
322	Bubba Trammell S/Y	.50
323	Pokey Reese G/Z	1.25
324	Hideki Irabu G/X	1.25
325	Scott Spiezio S/Z	.50
326	Bartolo Colon G/Z	1.25
327	Damon Mashore S/X	.50
328	Ryan McGuire S/Y	.50
329	Chris Carpenter B/X	.35
330	Jose Cruz, Jr. G/X	1.25
331	Todd Greene S/Z	.50
332	Brian Moehler B/X	.35
333	Mike Sweeney B/X	.35
334	Neifi Perez G/Z	1.25
335	Matt Morris S/Y	.50
336	Marvin Benard B/X	.35
337	Karim Garcia S/Y	.75
338	Jason Dickson S/Y	.50
339	Brant Brown S/Y	.50
340	Jeff Suppan S/Z	.50
341	Deivi Cruz B/X	.35
342	Antone Williamson G/Z	1.25
343	Curtis Goodwin B/X	.35
344	Brooks Kieschnick S/X	.50
345	Tony Womack B/X	.35
346	Rudy Pemberton B/X	.35
347	Todd Dunwoody B/X	.35
348	Frank Thomas S/X (Legacy)	2.25
349	Andruw Jones S/X (Legacy)	2.00
350	Alex Rodriguez B/Y (Legacy)	4.00
351	Greg Maddux S/Y (Legacy)	3.00
352	Jeff Bagwell B/Y (Legacy)	2.25
353	Juan Gonzalez S/Y (Legacy)	1.50
354	Barry Bonds S/Y (Legacy)	5.00
355	Mark McGwire S/Y (Legacy)	4.00
356	Tony Gwynn S/Y (Legacy)	3.00
357	Gary Sheffield S/Y (Legacy)	.75
358	Derek Jeter S/X (Legacy)	4.00
359	Manny Ramirez S/Y (Legacy)	2.00
360	Hideo Nomo B/X (Legacy)	4.00
361	Sammy Sosa B/X (Legacy)	3.50
362	Paul Molitor S/Z (Legacy)	3.00
363	Kenny Lofton S/Y (Legacy)	.35
364	Eddie Murray B/X (Legacy)	2.00
365	Barry Larkin S/Z (Legacy)	.50
366	Roger Clemens S/Y (Legacy)	3.50
367	John Smoltz B/Z (Legacy)	.35
368	Alex Rodriguez S/X (Gamers)	3.25
369	Frank Thomas B/X (Gamers)	2.25
370	Cal Ripken Jr. B/X (Gamers)	4.00
371	Ken Griffey Jr. S/Y (Gamers)	3.25
372	Greg Maddux B/X (Gamers)	3.00
373	Mike Piazza S/X (Gamers)	3.00
374	Chipper Jones B/X (Gamers)	3.00
375	Albert Belle B/X (Gamers)	.50
376	Chuck Knoblauch B/X (Gamers)	.35
377	Brady Anderson B/Z (Gamers)	.35
378	David Justice S/X (Gamers)	.50
379	Randy Johnson B/Z (Gamers)	2.00
380	Wade Boggs B/X (Gamers)	3.00
381	Kevin Brown B/X (Gamers)	.35
382	Tom Glavine S/X (Gamers)	3.00
383	Raul Mondesi S/X (Gamers)	.50
384	Ivan Rodriguez S/X (Gamers)	1.25
385	Larry Walker B/Y (Gamers)	.50
386	Bernie Williams B/X (Gamers)	.45
387	Rusty Greer G/Y (Gamers)	1.25
388	Rafael Palmeiro G/X (Gamers)	4.50
389	Matt Williams B/X (Gamers)	.35
390	Eric Young B/X (Gamers)	.35
391	Fred McGriff B/X (Gamers)	.35
392	Ken Caminiti B/X (Gamers)	.35
393	Roberto Alomar B/Z (Gamers)	.75
394	Brian Jordan B/X (Gamers)	.35
395	Mark Grace G/Z (Gamers)	1.25
396	Jim Edmonds B/X (Gamers)	.35
397	Deion Sanders B/X (Gamers)	.50
398	Checklist (Vladimir Guerrero S/Z)	1.25
399	Checklist (Darin Erstad S/Y)	1.00
400	Checklist (Nomar Garciaparra S/Z)	2.00

Fractal Matrix Die-Cut

A second parallel set to the Leaf product, the Fractal Matrix Die-Cuts offer three different die-cut designs with three colors for each. The Axis-X die-cuts comprise 200 players (150 Bronze, 40 Silver and 10 Gold), the Axis-Y die-cuts has 120 players (60 Silver, 40 Bronze, 20 Gold), and the Axis-Z die-cuts consist of 80 players (50 Gold, 20 Silver, 10 Bronze). Odds of finding any of these inserts are 1:6 packs. Each player is issued in only one color/cut combination.

		NM/M
	Common X- or Y-Axis:	.75
	Common Z-Axis:	1.25
1	Wade Boggs G/Y	6.00
2	Brian McRae B/Y	.75
3	Jeff D'Amico B/Y	.75
4	George Arias S/Y	.75
5	Billy Wagner S/Y	.75
6	Ray Lankford B/Z	1.25
7	Will Clark S/Y	.75
8	Edgar Renteria S/Y	.75
9	Alex Ochoa S/Y	.75
11	Joe Carter S/Y	.75
12	Gregg Jefferies B/Y	.75
13	Mark Grace S/Y	.75
14	Roberto Alomar G/Y	1.50
15	Joe Randa B/X	.75
16	Alex Rodriguez G/Z	12.50
17	Tony Gwynn G/Z	7.50
18	Steve Gibralter B/Y	.75
19	Scott Stahoviak B/X	.75
20	Matt Williams S/Z	1.25
21	Quinton McCracken B/Y	.75
22	Ugueth Urbina B/X	.75
23	Jermaine Allensworth S/X	.75
24	Paul Molitor G/X	5.00
25	Carlos Delgado S/Y	2.00
26	Bob Abreu S/Y	.75
27	John Jaha S/Y	.75
28	Rusty Greer S/Z	1.25
29	Kimera Bartee B/X	.75
30	Ruben Rivera S/Y	.75
31	Jason Kendall S/Y	.75
32	Lance Johnson B/X	.75
33	Robin Ventura B/Y	.75
34	Kevin Appier S/Y	.75
35	John Mabry S/Y	.75
36	Ricky Otero B/X	.75
37	Mike Lansing B/X	.75
38	Mark McGwire G/Z	12.50
39	Tim Naehring B/X	.75
40	Tom Glavine S/Z	3.00
41	Rey Ordonez S/Y	.75
42	Tony Clark S/Y	.75
43	Rafael Palmeiro S/Z	4.00
44	Pedro Martinez B/X	5.00
45	Keith Lockhart B/X	.75
46	Dan Wilson B/X	.75
47	John Wetteland B/Y	.75
48	Chan Ho Park B/X	.75
49	Gary Sheffield G/Z	2.50
50	Shawn Estes B/X	.75
51	Royce Clayton B/X	.75
52	Jaime Navarro B/X	.75
53	Raul Casanova B/X	.75
54	Jeff Bagwell G/Z	6.00
55	Barry Larkin G/X	.75
56	Charles Nagy B/Y	.75
57	Ken Caminiti B/X	.75
58	Todd Hollandsworth S/Z	1.25
59	Pat Hentgen S/X	.75
60	Jose Valentin B/X	.75
61	Frank Rodriguez B/X	.75
62	Mickey Tettleton B/X	.75
63	Marty Cordova S/X	.75
64	Cecil Fielder S/X	.75
65	Barry Bonds G/Z	15.00
66	Scott Servais B/X	.75
67	Ernie Young B/X	.75
68	Wilson Alvarez B/X	.75
69	Mike Grace B/X	.75
70	Shane Reynolds S/X	.75
71	Henry Rodriguez S/Y	.75
72	Eric Karros B/X	.75
73	Mark Langston B/X	.75
74	Scott Karl B/X	.75
75	Trevor Hoffman B/X	.75
76	Orel Hershiser S/X	.75
77	John Smoltz G/Y	.75
78	Raul Mondesi G/Z	1.25
79	Jeff Brantley B/X	.75
80	Donne Wall B/X	.75
81	Joey Cora B/X	.75
82	Mel Rojas B/X	.75
83	Chad Mottola B/X	.75
84	Omar Vizquel B/X	.75
85	Greg Maddux G/Z	7.50
86	Jamey Wright S/Y	.75
87	Chuck Finley B/X	.75
88	Brady Anderson B/X	.75
89	Alex Gonzalez S/X	.75
90	Andy Benes B/X	.75
91	Reggie Jefferson B/X	.75
92	Paul O'Neill B/Y	.75
93	Javier Lopez S/X	.75
94	Mark Grudzielanek S/X	.75
95	Marc Newfield B/X	.75
96	Kevin Ritz B/X	.75
97	Fred McGriff G/Y	.75
98	Dwight Gooden S/X	.75
99	Hideo Nomo B/X	4.00
100	Steve Finley B/X	.75
101	Juan Gonzalez G/Z	4.00
102	Jay Buhner S/Z	1.25
103	Paul Wilson S/Y	.75
104	Alan Benes B/Y	.75
105	Manny Ramirez G/X	6.00
106	Kevin Elster B/X	.75
107	Frank Thomas G/Z	6.00
108	Orlando Miller B/X	.75
109	Ramon Martinez B/X	.75
110	Kenny Lofton G/X	1.25
111	Bernie Williams G/Y	.75
112	Robby Thompson B/X	.75
113	Bernard Gilkey B/X	.75
114	Ray Durham B/X	.75
115	Jeff Cirillo S/Z	1.25
116	Brian Jordan G/Z	1.25
117	Rich Becker S/Y	.75
118	Al Leiter B/X	.75
119	Mark Johnson B/X	.75
120	Ellis Burks B/Y	.75
121	Sammy Sosa G/Z	9.00
122	Willie Greene B/X	.75
123	Michael Tucker B/X	.75
124	Eddie Murray G/Y	5.00
125	Joey Hamilton B/X	.75
126	Antonio Osuna B/X	.75
127	Bobby Higginson S/Y	.75

#	Player	Price
128	Tomas Perez B/X	.75
129	Tim Salmon G/Z	1.25
130	Mark Wohlers B/X	.75
131	Charles Johnson S/X	.75
132	Randy Johnson S/Y	5.00
133	Brooks Kieschnick S/X	.75
134	Al Martin S/Y	.75
135	Dante Bichette B/X	.75
136	Andy Pettitte G/Z	3.00
137	Jason Giambi G/Y	.75
138	James Baldwin S/X	.75
139	Ben McDonald B/X	.75
140	Shawn Green B/X	1.25
141	Geronimo Berroa B/Y	.75
142	Jose Offerman B/X	.75
143	Curtis Pride B/X	.75
144	Terrell Wade B/X	.75
145	Ismael Valdes S/X	.75
146	Mike Mussina S/Y	2.00
147	Mariano Rivera S/X	1.00
148	Ken Hill B/Y	.75
149	Darin Erstad G/Z	2.50
150	Jay Bell B/X	.75
151	Mo Vaughn G/Z	1.25
152	Ozzie Smith G/Y	6.00
153	Jose Mesa B/X	.75
154	Osvaldo Fernandez B/X	.75
155	Vinny Castilla B/Y	.75
156	Jason Isringhausen S/Y	.75
157	B.J. Surhoff B/X	.75
158	Robert Perez B/X	.75
159	Ron Coomer B/X	.75
160	Darren Oliver B/X	.75
161	Mike Mohler B/X	.75
162	Russ Davis B/X	.75
163	Bret Boone B/X	.75
164	Ricky Bottalico B/X	.75
165	Derek Jeter G/Z	15.00
166	Orlando Merced B/X	.75
167	John Valentin B/X	.75
168	Andruw Jones B/X	6.00
169	Angel Echevarria B/X	.75
170	Todd Walker G/Z	1.25
171	Desi Relaford B/Y	.75
172	Trey Beamon S/X	.75
173	Brian Giles S/Y	.75
174	Scott Rolen G/Z	4.00
175	Shannon Stewart S/Z	1.25
176	Dmitri Young S/Y	1.25
177	Justin Thompson B/X	.75
178	Trot Nixon S/Y	1.00
179	Josh Booty S/Y	.75
180	Robin Jennings B/X	.75
181	Marvin Benard B/X	.75
182	Luis Castillo B/Y	.75
183	Wendell Magee B/X	.75
184	Vladimir Guerrero G/X	5.00
185	Nomar Garciaparra G/X	7.50
186	Ryan Hancock B/X	.75
187	Mike Cameron S/X	.75
188	Cal Ripken Jr. B/Z (Legacy)	15.00
189	Chipper Jones S/Z (Legacy)	7.50
190	Albert Belle B/X (Legacy)	1.25
191	Mike Piazza B/Z (Legacy)	12.50
192	Chuck Knoblauch S/Y (Legacy)	.75
193	Ken Griffey Jr. B/Z (Legacy)	10.00
194	Ivan Rodriguez G/Z (Legacy)	5.00
195	Jose Canseco B/X (Legacy)	1.50
196	Ryne Sandberg S/X (Legacy)	5.00
197	Jim Thome G/Y (Legacy)	.75
198	Checklist (Andy Pettitte B/Y)	1.00
199	Checklist (Andruw Jones B/Y)	5.00
200	Checklist (Derek Jeter S/Y)	7.50
201	Chipper Jones G/X	6.00
202	Albert Belle B/X	.75
203	Mike Piazza G/Y	10.00
204	Ken Griffey Jr. G/X	7.50
205	Ryne Sandberg G/Z	6.00
206	Jose Canseco S/Y	1.50
207	Chili Davis B/X	.75
208	Roger Clemens G/Z	9.00
209	Deion Sanders S/Y	1.50
210	Darryl Hamilton B/X	.75
211	Jermaine Dye S/X	.75
212	Matt Williams G/Y	.75
213	Kevin Elster B/X	.75
214	John Wetteland S/X	.75
215	Garret Anderson G/Z	1.25
216	Kevin Brown S/Y	.75
217	Matt Lawton S/Y	.75
218	Cal Ripken Jr. G/X	12.50
219	Moises Alou G/Y	.75
220	Chuck Knoblauch G/Z	1.25
221	Ivan Rodriguez G/Z	4.00
222	Travis Fryman B/Y	.75
223	Jim Thome S/Z	2.50
224	Eddie Murray S/Z	6.00
225	Eric Young G/Y	1.25
226	Ron Gant S/X	.75
227	Tony Phillips B/X	.75
228	Reggie Sanders B/Y	.75
229	Johnny Damon S/Z	1.25
230	Bill Pulsipher B/X	.75
231	Jim Edmonds G/Z	1.25
232	Melvin Nieves B/X	.75
233	Ryan Klesko G/Z	1.25
234	David Cone S/X	.75
235	Derek Bell B/Y	.75
236	Julio Franco S/X	.75
237	Juan Guzman B/X	.75
238	Larry Walker B/X	1.25
239	Delino DeShields B/X	.75
240	Troy Percival B/Y	.75
241	Andres Galarraga G/Z	1.25
242	Rondell White G/Z	1.25
243	John Burkett B/X	.75
244	J.T. Snow B/Y	.75
245	Alex Fernandez S/Y	.75
246	Edgar Martinez G/Z	1.25
247	Craig Biggio G/Z	1.25
248	Todd Hundley G/Y	.75
249	Jimmy Key S/X	.75
250	Cliff Floyd B/Y	.75
251	Jeff Conine B/Y	.75
252	Curt Schilling B/X	1.50
253	Jeff King B/X	.75
254	Tino Martinez G/Z	1.25
255	Carlos Baerga B/Y	.75
256	Jeff Fassero B/Y	.75
257	Dean Palmer S/Y	.75
258	Robb Nen B/X	.75
259	Sandy Alomar Jr. S/Y	.75
260	Carlos Perez B/X	.75
261	Rickey Henderson S/Y	5.00
262	Bobby Bonilla B/X	.75
263	Darren Daulton B/X	.75
264	Jim Leyritz B/X	.75
265	Dennis Martinez B/X	.75
266	Butch Huskey B/X	.75
267	Joe Vitiello S/Y	.75
268	Steve Trachsel B/X	.75
269	Glenallen Hill B/X	.75
270	Terry Steinbach B/X	.75
271	Mark McLemore B/X	.75
272	Devon White B/X	.75
273	Jeff Kent B/X	.75
274	Tim Raines B/X	.75
275	Carlos Garcia B/X	.75
276	Hal Morris B/X	.75
277	Gary Gaetti B/X	.75
278	John Olerud B/X	.75
279	Wally Joyner B/X	.75
280	Brian Hunter S/Y	.75
281	Steve Karsay B/X	.75
282	Denny Neagle S/X	.75
283	Jose Herrera B/X	.75
284	Todd Stottlemyre B/X	.75
285	Bip Roberts S/X	.75
286	Kevin Seitzer B/X	.75
287	Benji Gil B/X	.75
288	Dennis Eckersley S/X	.75
289	Brad Ausmus B/X	.75
290	Otis Nixon B/X	.75
291	Darryl Strawberry B/X	.75
292	Marquis Grissom S/Y	.75
293	Darryl Kile B/X	.75
294	Quilvio Veras B/X	.75
295	Tom Goodwin B/X	.75
296	Benito Santiago B/X	.75
297	Mike Bordick B/X	.75
298	Roberto Kelly B/X	.75
299	David Justice G/Z	1.25
300	Carl Everett B/X	.75
301	Mark Whiten B/X	.75
302	Aaron Sele B/X	.75
303	Darren Dreifort B/X	.75
304	Bobby Jones B/X	.75
305	Fernando Vina B/X	.75
306	Ed Sprague B/X	.75
307	Andy Ashby S/X	.75
308	Tony Fernandez B/X	.75
309	Roger Pavlik B/X	.75
310	Mark Clark B/X	.75
311	Mariano Duncan B/X	.75
312	Tyler Houston B/X	.75
313	Eric Davis S/Y	.75
314	Greg Vaughn B/Y	.75
315	David Segui S/Y	.75
316	Dave Nilsson S/X	.75
317	F.P. Santangelo S/X	.75
318	Wilton Guerrero G/Z	1.25
319	Jose Guillen S/Y	1.25
320	Kevin Orie S/Y	.75
321	Derrek Lee G/Z	2.50
322	Bubba Trammell S/Y	1.25
323	Pokey Reese G/Z	1.25
324	Hideki Irabu G/X	.75
325	Scott Spiezio G/Z	1.25
326	Bartolo Colon G/Z	1.25
327	Damon Mashore S/Y	.75
328	Ryan McGuire S/Y	.75
329	Chris Carpenter S/Y	.75
330	Jose Cruz, Jr. G/X	.75
331	Todd Greene S/Z	1.25
332	Brian Moehler B/X	.75
333	Mike Sweeney B/Y	.75
334	Neifi Perez G/Z	1.25
335	Matt Morris S/Y	.75
336	Marvin Benard B/Y	.75
337	Karim Garcia S/Z	1.25
338	Jason Dickson S/Y	.75
339	Brant Brown S/Y	.75
340	Jeff Suppan S/Z	1.25
341	Deivi Cruz B/Y	.75
342	Antone Williamson B/X	.75
343	Curtis Goodwin B/X	.75
344	Brooks Kieschnick S/Y	.75
345	Tony Womack B/X	.75
346	Rudy Pemberton B/X	.75
347	Todd Dunwoody B/X	.75
348	Frank Thomas (Legacy)	5.00
349	Andruw Jones S/X (Legacy)	5.00
350	Alex Rodriguez B/Y (Legacy)	10.00
351	Greg Maddux S/Y (Legacy)	6.00
352	Jeff Bagwell B/Y (Legacy)	5.00
353	Juan Gonzalez S/Y (Legacy)	4.00
354	Barry Bonds B/Y (Legacy)	12.50
355	Mark McGwire B/Y (Legacy)	10.00
356	Tony Gwynn B/Y (Legacy)	6.00
357	Gary Sheffield B/X (Legacy)	1.50
358	Derek Jeter S/X (Legacy)	12.50
359	Manny Ramirez S/Y (Legacy)	5.00
360	Hideo Nomo G/Z (Legacy)	4.00
361	Sammy Sosa B/X (Legacy)	6.50
362	Paul Molitor S/Z (Legacy)	6.00
363	Kenny Lofton B/Y (Legacy)	.75
364	Eddie Murray B/X (Legacy)	5.00
365	Barry Larkin S/Z (Legacy)	1.25
366	Roger Clemens S/Y (Legacy)	6.50
367	John Smoltz B/Z (Legacy)	1.25
368	Alex Rodriguez S/X (Gamers)	10.00
369	Frank Thomas B/X (Gamers)	5.00
370	Cal Ripken Jr. S/Y (Gamers)	12.50
371	Ken Griffey Jr. S/Y (Gamers)	7.50
372	Greg Maddux B/X (Gamers)	6.00
373	Mike Piazza S/X (Gamers)	10.00
374	Chipper Jones B/Y (Gamers)	6.00
375	Albert Belle B/X (Gamers)	.75
376	Chuck Knoblauch B/X (Gamers)	.75
377	Brady Anderson B/Z (Gamers)	1.25
378	David Justice S/X (Gamers)	.75
379	Randy Johnson B/X (Gamers)	6.00
380	Wade Boggs B/X (Gamers)	6.00
381	Kevin Brown B/X (Gamers)	.75
382	Tom Glavine G/Y (Gamers)	2.00
383	Raul Mondesi S/X (Gamers)	.75
384	Ivan Rodriguez S/X (Gamers)	4.00
385	Larry Walker B/X (Gamers)	.75
386	Bernie Williams B/Z (Gamers)	1.25
387	Rusty Greer G/Y (Gamers)	.75
388	Rafael Palmeiro G/Y (Gamers)	4.00
389	Matt Williams B/X (Gamers)	.75
390	Eric Young B/X (Gamers)	.75
391	Fred McGriff B/X (Gamers)	.75
392	Ken Caminiti B/X (Gamers)	.75
393	Roberto Alomar B/Z (Gamers)	2.00
394	Brian Jordan B/X (Gamers)	.75
395	Mark Grace G/Z (Gamers)	1.25
396	Jim Edmonds S/Y (Gamers)	.75
397	Deion Sanders S/Y (Gamers)	.75
398	Checklist (Vladimir Guerrero S/Z)	3.00
399	Checklist (Darin Erstad S/Y)	1.00
400	Checklist (Nomar Garciaparra S/Z)	4.00

Banner Season

Banner Season was a 15-card insert set that was die-cut and printed on a canvas card stock. Only 2,500 individually numbered sets were produced, with cards only found in pre-priced packs.

		NM/M
Complete Set (15):		30.00
Common Player:		.50
1	Jeff Bagwell	2.50
2	Ken Griffey Jr.	5.00
3	Juan Gonzalez	1.50
4	Frank Thomas	2.50
5	Alex Rodriguez	6.00
6	Kenny Lofton	.50
7	Chuck Knoblauch	.50
8	Mo Vaughn	.50
9	Chipper Jones	4.00
10	Ken Caminiti	.50
11	Craig Biggio	.50
12	John Smoltz	.50
13	Pat Hentgen	.50
14	Derek Jeter	7.50
15	Todd Hollandsworth	.50

Dress for Success

Exclusive to retail packs was an insert called Dress for Success. It included 18 players printed on nylon and flocking card stock. Dress for Success was limited to 3,500 individually numbered sets.

		NM/M
Complete Set (18):		17.50
Common Player:		.25
1	Greg Maddux	1.50
2	Cal Ripken Jr.	3.00
3	Albert Belle	.25
4	Frank Thomas	1.00
5	Dante Bichette	.25
6	Gary Sheffield	.50
7	Jeff Bagwell	1.00
8	Mike Piazza	2.00
9	Mark McGwire	2.25
10	Ken Caminiti	.25
11	Alex Rodriguez	2.50
12	Ken Griffey Jr.	2.00
13	Juan Gonzalez	.75
14	Brian Jordan	.25
15	Mo Vaughn	.25
16	Ivan Rodriguez	.25
17	Andruw Jones	1.00
18	Chipper Jones	1.50

Get-A-Grip

Get a Grip included 16 double-sided cards, with a star hitter on one side and a star pitcher on the other. The card slated the two stars against each other and explained how the hitter would hit against the pitcher, while featuring the pitcher's top pitch. This insert was printed on silver foilboard with the right side die-cut, and limited to 3,500 numbered sets found only in hobby packs.

		NM/M
Complete Set (16):		30.00
Common Card:		1.00
1	Ken Griffey Jr., Greg Maddux	3.00
2	John Smoltz, Frank Thomas	1.50
3	Mike Piazza, Andy Pettitte	3.00
4	Randy Johnson, Chipper Jones	2.50
5	Tom Glavine, Alex Rodriguez	
6	Pat Hentgen, Jeff Bagwell	1.50
7	Kevin Brown, Juan Gonzalez	1.25
8	Barry Bonds, Mike Mussina	
9	Hideo Nomo, Albert Belle	1.25
10	Troy Percival, Andruw Jones	1.50
11	Roger Clemens, Brian Jordan	3.00
12	Paul Wilson, Ivan Rodriguez	1.25
13	Andy Benes, Mo Vaughn	1.00
14	Al Leiter, Derek Jeter	5.00
15	Bill Pulsipher, Cal Ripken Jr.	5.00
16	Mariano Rivera, Ken Caminiti	1.00

Knot-Hole Gang

Knot-Hole Gang pictures 12 hitters viewed through a wood picket fence. Cards are die-cut along the top of the fence and printed on a wood stock. Production was limited to 5,000 numbered sets. A "SAMPLE" marked promo card exists for each.

		NM/M
Complete Set (12):		18.00
Common Player:		.50
Promos:		2X
1	Chuck Knoblauch	.50
2	Ken Griffey Jr.	3.50
3	Frank Thomas	1.50
4	Tony Gwynn	2.50
5	Mike Piazza	3.50
6	Jeff Bagwell	1.50
7	Rusty Greer	.50
8	Cal Ripken Jr.	5.00
9	Chipper Jones	2.50
10	Ryan Klesko	.50
11	Barry Larkin	.50
12	Paul Molitor	1.50

Leagues of the Nation

A 15-card insert set featuring a double-sided die-cut design. The players on each card represent matchups from the initial rounds of interleague play. Cards were numbered to 2,500 and feature a flocked texture.

		NM/M
Complete Set (15):		60.00
Common Card:		1.50
1	Juan Gonzalez, Barry Bonds	10.00
2	Cal Ripken Jr., Chipper Jones	10.00
3	Mark McGwire, Ken Caminiti	7.00
4	Derek Jeter, Kenny Lofton	10.00
5	Ivan Rodriguez, Mike Piazza	6.00
6	Ken Griffey Jr., Larry Walker	6.00
7	Frank Thomas, Sammy Sosa	5.00
8	Paul Molitor, Barry Larkin	3.00
9	Albert Belle, Deion Sanders	1.50
10	Matt Williams, Jeff Bagwell	3.00
11	Mo Vaughn, Gary Sheffield	1.50
12	Alex Rodriguez, Tony Gwynn	7.50
13	Tino Martinez, Scott Rolen	2.00
14	Darin Erstad, Wilton Guerrero	2.00
15	Tony Clark, Vladimir Guerrero	3.00

Statistical Standouts

Statistical Standouts were limited to only 1,000 individually numbered sets. Inserts were printed on leather and die-cut. The set included 15 top stars who excelled beyond their competition in many statistical categories.

		NM/M
Complete Set (15):		175.00
Common Player:		4.00
1	Albert Belle	4.00
2	Juan Gonzalez	9.00
3	Ken Griffey Jr.	20.00
4	Alex Rodriguez	25.00
5	Frank Thomas	12.00
6	Chipper Jones	15.00
7	Greg Maddux	15.00
8	Mike Piazza	20.00
9	Cal Ripken Jr.	30.00
10	Mark McGwire	25.00
11	Barry Bonds	30.00
12	Derek Jeter	30.00
13	Ken Caminiti	4.00
14	John Smoltz	4.00
15	Paul Molitor	12.00

Thomas Collection

This six-card insert from Series 2 features pieces of various game-used Frank Thomas items built into the texture of each card. Jerseys, bats, hats, batting gloves and sweatbands are all featured on the various cards, which are numbered to 100 each.

		NM/M
Complete Set (6):		360.00
Common Card:		60.00
1	Frank Thomas/Hat	60.00
2	Frank Thomas/Home Jsy	80.00
3	Frank Thomas/Btg Glv	60.00
4	Frank Thomas/Bat	60.00
5	Frank Thomas/Sweatband	60.00
6	Frank Thomas/Away Jsy	80.00

Warning Track

A 12-card insert printed on embossed canvas depicting players who are known for making tough catches. Cards were numbered to 3,500.

22kt Gold Stars

	NM/M
Complete Set (18):	40.00
Common Player:	1.00
1 Ken Griffey Jr.	6.00
2 Albert Belle	1.00
3 Barry Bonds	7.50
4 Andruw Jones	4.00
5 Kenny Lofton	1.00
6 Tony Gwynn	5.00
7 Manny Ramirez	4.00
8 Rusty Greer	1.00
9 Bernie Williams	1.00
10 Gary Sheffield	2.00
11 Juan Gonzalez	2.50
12 Raul Mondesi	1.00
13 Brady Anderson	1.00
14 Rondell White	1.00
15 Sammy Sosa	6.00
16 Deion Sanders	1.00
17 David Justice	1.00
18 Jim Edmonds	1.00

A 36-card insert from Series II Leaf, each card features a special 22-K. gold foil embossed stamp on front which is printed on gold foil cardboard. Horizontal backs have a portrait photo on a dark background and are serially numbered to a limit of 2,500 each.

	NM/M
Complete Set (36):	115.00
Common Player:	1.00
1 Frank Thomas	4.00
2 Alex Rodriguez	8.00
3 Ken Griffey Jr.	6.50
4 Andruw Jones	4.00
5 Chipper Jones	6.00
6 Jeff Bagwell	4.00
7 Derek Jeter	10.00
8 Deion Sanders	1.00
9 Ivan Rodriguez	3.50
10 Juan Gonzalez	3.00
11 Greg Maddux	5.50
12 Andy Pettitte	2.50
13 Roger Clemens	4.00
14 Hideo Nomo	3.00
15 Tony Gwynn	5.50
16 Barry Bonds	10.00
17 Kenny Lofton	1.00
18 Paul Molitor	4.00
19 Jim Thome	3.00
20 Albert Belle	1.00
21 Cal Ripken Jr.	10.00
22 Mark McGwire	8.00
23 Barry Larkin	1.00
24 Mike Piazza	6.50
25 Darin Erstad	2.00
26 Chuck Knoblauch	1.00
27 Vladimir Guerrero	4.00
28 Tony Clark	1.00
29 Scott Rolen	1.00
30 Nomar Garciaparra	6.50
31 Eric Young	1.00
32 Ryne Sandberg	5.50
33 Roberto Alomar	2.00
34 Eddie Murray	4.00
35 Rafael Palmeiro	3.50
36 Jose Guillen	1.00

1998 Leaf

The 50th Anniversary edition of Leaf Baseball consists of a 200-card base set with three subsets, three parallels and four inserts. The base set has 148 regular cards, a 10-card Curtain Calls subset, Gold Leaf Stars subset (20 cards), Gold Leaf Rookies subset (20 cards) and three checklists. The subsets cards #148-197 are short-printed in relation to the rest of the set. Card #42 does not exist because Leaf retired the number in honor of Jackie Robinson. The base set was paralleled in Fractal Matrix, Fractal Matrix Die-Cuts and Fractal Diamond Axis. Inserts include Crusade, Heading for the Hall, State Representatives and Statistical Standouts.

	NM/M
Complete Set (200):	40.00
Common Player:	.05
Common SP (#148-197):	.40
Pack (10):	2.00
Wax Box (24):	40.00
1 Rusty Greer	.05
2 Tino Martinez	.05
3 Bobby Bonilla	.05
4 Jason Giambi	.50
5 Matt Morris	.05
6 Craig Counsell	.05
7 Reggie Jefferson	.05
8 Brian Rose	.05
9 Ruben Rivera	.05
10 Shawn Estes	.05
11 Tony Gwynn	1.00
12 Jeff Abbott	.05
13 Jose Cruz Jr.	.05
14 Francisco Cordova	.05
15 Ryan Klesko	.05
16 Tim Salmon	.05
17 Brett Tomko	.05
18 Matt Williams	.05
19 Joe Carter	.05
20 Harold Baines	.05
21 Gary Sheffield	.50
22 Charles Johnson	.05
23 Aaron Boone	.05
24 Eddie Murray	.75
25 Matt Stairs	.05
26 David Cone	.05
27 Jon Nunnally	.05
28 Chris Stynes	.05
29 Enrique Wilson	.05
30 Randy Johnson	.75
31 Garret Anderson	.05
32 Manny Ramirez	.05
33 Jeff Suppan	.05
34 Rickey Henderson	.05
35 Scott Spiezio	.05
36 Rondell White	.05
37 Todd Greene	.05
38 Delino DeShields	.05
39 Kevin Brown	.05
40 Chili Davis	.05
41 Jimmy Key	.05
43 Mike Mussina	.40
44 Joe Randa	.05
45 Chan Ho Park	.05
46 Brad Radke	.05
47 Geronimo Berroa	.05
48 Wade Boggs	1.00
49 Kevin Appier	.05
50 Moises Alou	.05
51 David Justice	.05
52 Ivan Rodriguez	.65
53 J.T. Snow	.05
54 Brian Giles	.05
55 Will Clark	.10
56 Justin Thompson	.05
57 Javier Lopez	.05
58 Hideki Irabu	.05
59 Mark Grudzielanek	.05
60 Abraham Nunez	.05
61 Todd Hollandsworth	.05
62 Jay Bell	.05
63 Nomar Garciaparra	1.25
64 Vinny Castilla	.05
65 Lou Collier	.05
66 Kevin Orie	.05
67 John Valentin	.05
68 Robin Ventura	.05
69 Denny Neagle	.05
70 Tony Womack	.05
71 Dennis Reyes	.05
72 Wally Joyner	.05
73 Kevin Brown	.05
74 Ray Durham	.05
75 Mike Cameron	.05
76 Dante Bichette	.05
77 Jose Guillen	.50
78 Carlos Delgado	.05
79 Paul Molitor	.75
80 Jason Kendall	.05
81 Mark Belhorn	.05
82 Damian Jackson	.05
83 Bill Mueller	.05
84 Kevin Young	.05
85 Curt Schilling	.25
86 Jeffrey Hammonds	.05
87 Sandy Alomar Jr.	.05
88 Bartolo Colon	.05
89 Wilton Guerrero	.05
90 Bernie Williams	.05
91 Deion Sanders	.05
92 Mike Piazza	1.25
93 Butch Huskey	.05
94 Edgardo Alfonzo	.05
95 Alan Benes	.05
96 Craig Biggio	.05
97 Mark Grace	.05
98 Shawn Green	.25
99 Derrek Lee	.05
100 Ken Griffey Jr.	1.25
101 Tim Raines	.05
102 Pokey Reese	.05
103 Lee Stevens	.05
104 Shannon Stewart	.05
105 John Smoltz	.05
106 Frank Thomas	.75
107 Jeff Fassero	.05
108 Jay Buhner	.05
109 Jose Canseco	.50
110 Omar Vizquel	.05
111 Travis Fryman	.05
112 Dave Nilsson	.05
113 John Olerud	.05
114 Larry Walker	.05
115 Jim Edmonds	.05
116 Bobby Higginson	.05
117 Todd Hundley	.05
118 Paul O'Neill	.05
119 Bip Roberts	.05
120 Ismael Valdes	.05
121 Pedro Martinez	.75
122 Jeff Cirillo	.05
123 Andy Benes	.05
124 Bobby Jones	.05
125 Brian Hunter	.05
126 Darryl Kile	.05
127 Pat Hentgen	.05
128 Marquis Grissom	.05
129 Eric Davis	.05
130 Chipper Jones	1.00
131 Edgar Martinez	.05
132 Andy Pettitte	.20
133 Cal Ripken Jr.	2.00
134 Scott Rolen	.65
135 Ron Coomer	.05
136 Luis Castillo	.05
137 Fred McGriff	.05
138 Neifi Perez	.05
139 Eric Karros	.05
140 Alex Fernandez	.05
141 Jason Dickson	.05
142 Lance Johnson	.05
143 Ray Lankford	.05
144 Sammy Sosa	1.25
145 Eric Young	.05
146 Bubba Trammell	.05
147 Todd Walker	.05
148 Mo Vaughn/CC	.40
149 Jeff Bagwell/CC	1.00
150 Kenny Lofton/CC	.40
151 Raul Mondesi/CC	.40
152 Mike Piazza/CC	2.00
153 Chipper Jones/CC	1.50
154 Larry Walker/CC	.40
155 Greg Maddux/CC	1.50
156 Ken Griffey Jr./CC	2.00
157 Frank Thomas/CC	1.00
158 Darin Erstad/GLS	.75
159 Roberto Alomar/GLS	.60
160 Albert Belle/GLS	.40
161 Jim Thome/GLS	.75
162 Tony Clark/GLS	.40
163 Chuck Knoblauch/GLS	.40
164 Derek Jeter/GLS	3.00
165 Alex Rodriguez/GLS	2.50
166 Tony Gwynn/GLS	1.50
167 Roger Clemens/GLS	2.00
168 Barry Larkin/GLS	.40
169 Andres Galarraga/GLS	.40
170 Vladimir Guerrero/GLS	.60
171 Mark McGwire/GLS	2.50
172 Barry Bonds/GLS	3.00
173 Juan Gonzalez/GLS	.75
174 Andruw Jones/GLS	1.00
175 Paul Molitor/GLS	.40
176 Hideo Nomo/GLS	.75
177 Cal Ripken Jr./GLS	3.00
178 Brad Fullmer/GLR	.40
179 Jaret Wright/GLR	.40
180 Bobby Estalella/GLR	.40
181 Ben Grieve/GLR	.40
182 Paul Konerko/GLR	.60
183 David Ortiz/GLR	.75
184 Todd Helton/GLR	1.00
185 Juan Encarnacion/GLR	.40
186 Miguel Tejada/GLR	.60
187 Jacob Cruz/GLR	.40
188 Mark Kotsay/GLR	.40
189 Fernando Tatis/GLR	.40
190 Ricky Ledee/GLR	.40
191 Richard Hidalgo/GLR	.40
192 Richie Sexson/GLR	.40
193 Luis Ordaz/GLR	.40
194 Eli Marrero/GLR	.40
195 Livan Hernandez/GLR	.40
196 Homer Bush/GLR	.40
197 Raul Ibanez/GLR	.40
198 Checklist (Nomar Garciaparra)	.60
199 Checklist (Scott Rolen)	.30
200 Checklist (Jose Cruz Jr.)	.05
201 Al Martin	.05

Crusade

Thirty cards from the cross-brand Crusade insert appear in 1998 Leaf. The cards had Green (250 sets), Purple (100 sets) and Red (25 sets) versions. Forty Crusade cards were in 1998 Donruss and 30 each in 1998 Donruss Update and Leaf Rookies & Stars.

tives" or "Provincial Powers" is printed at the top with the player's name at the bottom. This set is sequentially numbered to 5,000.

	NM/M
Complete Set (30):	400.00
Common Player:	6.00
Purples:	3X
Reds:	12X
3 Jim Edmonds	7.50
4 Darin Erstad	7.50
11 Mike Mussina	15.00
18 Albert Belle	6.00
19 Manny Ramirez	25.00
24 Jim Thome	20.00
26 Bubba Trammell	6.00
26 Bobby Higginson	6.00
28 Paul Molitor	25.00
30 Todd Walker	6.00
34 Andy Pettitte	10.00
35 Wade Boggs	30.00
40 Alex Rodriguez	60.00
41 Randy Johnson	25.00
46 Ivan Rodriguez	20.00
48 Roger Clemens	40.00
54 John Smoltz	6.00
56 Andruw Jones	25.00
58 Javier Lopez	6.00
59 Fred McGriff	6.00
64 Pokey Reese	6.00
66 Andres Galarraga	6.00
70 Eric Young	6.00
73 Moises Alou	6.00
76 Ben Grieve	6.00
91 Mike Piazza	50.00
95 Jason Kendall	6.00
95 Alan Benes	6.00
97 Tony Gwynn	30.00
98 Ken Caminiti	6.00

Heading for the Hall

This 20-card insert features players destined for the Hall of Fame. The set is sequentially numbered to 3,500. Each card is also found in a "SAMPLE" marked edition with no serial number.

	NM/M
Complete Set (20):	35.00
Common Player:	.75
Samples:	1X
1 Roberto Alomar	1.00
2 Jeff Bagwell	1.50
3 Albert Belle	.75
4 Wade Boggs	2.00
5 Barry Bonds	5.00
6 Roger Clemens	2.50
7 Juan Gonzalez	1.50
8 Ken Griffey Jr.	3.00
9 Tony Gwynn	2.00
10 Barry Larkin	.75
11 Kenny Lofton	.75
12 Greg Maddux	2.00
13 Mark McGwire	4.00
14 Paul Molitor	1.50
15 Eddie Murray	1.50
16 Mike Piazza	3.00
17 Cal Ripken Jr.	5.00
18 Ivan Rodriguez	1.25
19 Ryne Sandberg	2.00
20 Frank Thomas	1.50

State Representatives/ Provincial Powers

This 30-card insert features top players. The background has a picture of the state or, in the case of Canadian teams, the province in which he plays. "State Representa-

	NM/M
Complete Set (30):	40.00
Common Player:	.50
1 Ken Griffey Jr.	3.00
2 Frank Thomas	2.00
3 Alex Rodriguez	4.00
4 Cal Ripken Jr.	5.00
5 Chipper Jones	2.50
6 Andruw Jones	2.00
7 Scott Rolen	1.50
8 Nomar Garciaparra	3.00
9 Tim Salmon	.50
10 Manny Ramirez	.50
11 Jose Cruz Jr.	.50
12 Vladimir Guerrero	2.00
13 Tino Martinez	.50
14 Larry Walker	.50
15 Mo Vaughn	.50
16 Jim Thome	1.50
17 Tony Clark	.50
18 Derek Jeter	5.00
19 Juan Gonzalez	1.00
20 Jeff Bagwell	2.00
21 Ivan Rodriguez	1.50
22 Mark McGwire	4.00
23 David Justice	.50
24 Chuck Knoblauch	.50
25 Andy Pettitte	.75
26 Raul Mondesi	.50
27 Randy Johnson	2.00
28 Greg Maddux	2.50
29 Bernie Williams	.50
30 Rusty Greer	.50

Statistical Standouts

This 24-card insert features players with impressive statistics. The cards have a horizontal layout and the feel of leather. The background has a ball and glove with the player's facsimile signature on the ball. Statistical Standouts is numbered to 2,500. A parallel die-cut version of each card comprises the first 250 numbered cards.

	NM/M
Complete Set (24):	55.00
Common Player:	1.00
Die-Cuts:	2X
1 Frank Thomas	2.50
2 Ken Griffey Jr.	4.00
3 Alex Rodriguez	5.00
4 Mike Piazza	4.00
5 Greg Maddux	3.00
6 Cal Ripken Jr.	6.00
7 Chipper Jones	3.00
8 Juan Gonzalez	2.00
9 Jeff Bagwell	2.50
10 Mark McGwire	5.00
11 Tony Gwynn	3.00
12 Mo Vaughn	1.00
13 Nomar Garciaparra	4.00
14 Jose Cruz Jr.	1.00
15 Vladimir Guerrero	2.50
16 Scott Rolen	2.00
17 Andy Pettitte	1.50
18 Randy Johnson	2.50
19 Larry Walker	1.00
20 Kenny Lofton	1.00
21 Tony Clark	1.00
22 David Justice	1.00
23 Derek Jeter	6.00
24 Barry Bonds	6.00

Fractal Foundation

Fractal Foundation is a stand-alone product but it parallels the 1998 Leaf set. It contains the Curtain Calls, Gold Leaf Stars and Gold Leaf Rookies subsets and is miss-

ing card #42 which Leaf retired in honor of Jackie Robinson. The set was printed on foil board and each card is numbered to 3,999. The set is paralleled in Fractal Materials, Fractal Materials Die-Cuts and Fractal Materials Z2 Axis.

	NM/M
Complete Set (200):	60.00
Common Player:	.20
Semistars:	.60
Unlisted Stars:	1.00
Pack (3):	2.00
Wax Box (18):	35.00
1 Rusty Greer	.20
2 Tino Martinez	.20
3 Bobby Bonilla	.20
4 Jason Giambi	.60
5 Matt Morris	.20
6 Craig Counsell	.20
7 Reggie Jefferson	.20
8 Brian Rose	.20
9 Ruben Rivera	.20
10 Shawn Estes	.20
11 Tony Gwynn	1.50
12 Jeff Abbott	.20
13 Jose Cruz Jr.	.20
14 Francisco Cordova	.20
15 Ryan Klesko	.20
16 Tim Salmon	.20
17 Brett Tomko	.20
18 Matt Williams	.20
19 Joe Carter	.20
20 Harold Baines	.20
21 Gary Sheffield	.50
22 Charles Johnson	.20
23 Aaron Boone	.20
24 Eddie Murray	1.00
25 Matt Stairs	.20
26 David Cone	.20
27 Jon Nunnally	.20
28 Chris Stynes	.20
29 Enrique Wilson	.20
30 Randy Johnson	1.00
31 Garret Anderson	.20
32 Manny Ramirez	1.00
33 Jeff Suppan	.20
34 Rickey Henderson	1.00
35 Scott Spiezio	.20
36 Rondell White	.20
37 Todd Greene	.20
38 Delino DeShields	.20
39 Kevin Brown	.20
40 Chili Davis	.20
41 Jimmy Key	.20
43 Mike Mussina	.40
44 Joe Randa	.20
45 Chan Ho Park	.20
46 Brad Radke	.20
47 Geronimo Berroa	.20
48 Wade Boggs	1.50
49 Kevin Appier	.20
50 Moises Alou	.20
51 David Justice	.20
52 Ivan Rodriguez	.75
53 J.T. Snow	.20
54 Brian Giles	.20
55 Will Clark	.20
56 Justin Thompson	.20
57 Javier Lopez	.20
58 Hideki Irabu	.20
59 Mark Grudzielanek	.20
60 Abraham Nunez	.20
61 Todd Hollandsworth	.20
62 Jay Bell	.20
63 Nomar Garciaparra	1.75
64 Vinny Castilla	.20
65 Lou Collier	.20
66 Kevin Orie	.20
67 John Valentin	.20
68 Robin Ventura	.20
69 Denny Neagle	.20
70 Tony Womack	.20
71 Dennis Reyes	.20
72 Wally Joyner	.20
73 Kevin Brown	.20
74 Ray Durham	.20
75 Mike Cameron	.20
76 Dante Bichette	.20
77 Jose Guillen	.50
78 Carlos Delgado	.20
79 Paul Molitor	1.00
80 Jason Kendall	.20
81 Mark Belhorn	.20
82 Damian Jackson	.20
83 Bill Mueller	.20

84 Kevin Young .20
85 Curt Schilling .40
86 Jeffrey Hammonds .20
87 Sandy Alomar Jr. .20
88 Bartolo Colon .20
89 Wilton Guerrero .20
90 Bernie Williams .20
91 Deion Sanders .20
92 Mike Piazza 2.00
93 Butch Huskey .20
94 Edgardo Alfonzo .20
95 Alan Benes .20
96 Craig Biggio .20
97 Mark Grace .40
98 Shawn Green .40
99 Derrek Lee .50
100 Ken Griffey Jr. 2.00
101 Tim Raines .20
102 Pokey Reese .20
103 Lee Stevens .20
104 Shannon Stewart .20
105 John Smoltz .20
106 Frank Thomas 1.00
107 Jeff Fassero .20
108 Jay Buhner .20
109 Jose Canseco .40
110 Omar Vizquel .20
111 Travis Fryman .20
112 Dave Nilsson .20
113 John Olerud .20
114 Larry Walker .20
115 Jim Edmonds .20
116 Bobby Higginson .20
117 Todd Hundley .20
118 Paul O'Neill .20
119 Bip Roberts .20
120 Ismael Valdes .20
121 Pedro Martinez 1.00
122 Jeff Cirillo .20
123 Andy Benes .20
124 Bobby Jones .20
125 Brian Hunter .20
126 Darryl Kile .20
127 Pat Hentgen .20
128 Marquis Grissom .20
129 Eric Davis .20
130 Chipper Jones 1.50
131 Edgar Martinez .20
132 Andy Pettitte .35
133 Cal Ripken Jr. 3.00
134 Scott Rolen .75
135 Ron Coomer .20
136 Luis Castillo .20
137 Fred McGriff .20
138 Neifi Perez .20
139 Eric Karros .20
140 Alex Fernandez/CC .20
141 Jason Dickson .20
142 Lance Johnson .20
143 Ray Lankford .20
144 Sammy Sosa 1.75
145 Eric Young .20
146 Bubba Trammell .20
147 Todd Walker .20
148 Mo Vaughn/CC .20
149 Jeff Bagwell/CC 1.00
150 Kenny Lofton/CC .20
151 Raul Mondesi/CC .20
152 Mike Piazza/CC 2.00
153 Chipper Jones/CC 1.50
154 Larry Walker/CC .20
155 Greg Maddux/CC 1.50
156 Ken Griffey Jr./CC 2.00
157 Frank Thomasv 1.00
158 Darin Erstad/GLS .50
159 Roberto Alomar/GLS .40
160 Albert Belle/GLS .20
161 Jim Thome/GLS .75
162 Tony Clark/GLS .20
163 Chuck Knoblauch/GLS .20
164 Derek Jeterv 3.00
165 Alex Rodriguez/GLS 2.50
166 Tony Gwynn/GLS 1.50
167 Roger Clemens/GLS 1.75
168 Barry Larkinv .20
169 Andres Galarraga/GLS .20
170 Vladimir Guerrero/GLS 1.00
171 Mark McGwire/GLS 2.50
172 Barry Bonds/GLS 3.00
173 Juan Gonzalez/GLS .75
174 Andruw Jones/GLS 1.00
175 Paul Molitor/GLS 1.00
176 Hideo Nomo/GLS .75
177 Cal Ripken Jr./GLS 3.00
178 Brad Fullmer/GLR .20
179 Jaret Wright/GLR .20
180 Bobby Estalella/GLR .20
181 Ben Grieve/GLR .20
182 Paul Konerko/GLR .40
183 David Ortiz/GLR .75
184 Todd Helton/GLR 1.00
185 Juan Encarnacion/GLR .20
186 Miguel Tejada/GLR .40
187 Jacob Cruz/GLR .20
188 Mark Kotsay/GLR .20
189 Fernando Tatis/GLR .20
190 Ricky Ledee/GLR .20
191 Richard Hidalgo/GLR .20
192 Richie Sexson/GLR .20
193 Luis Ordaz/GLR .20
194 Eli Marrero/GLR .20
195 Livan Hernandez/GLR .20
196 Homer Bush/GLR .20
197 Raul Ibanez/GLR .20
198 Checklist
  (Nomar Garciaparra) 1.00
199 Checklist (Scott Rolen) .30
200 Checklist (Jose Cruz Jr.) .20

1998 Leaf Fractal Materials Samples

Each of the 50 Leather cards in Fractal Materials can be found in a sample version, prominently marked as such on back.

NM/M
Complete Set (50): 100.00
Common Player: 2.00
5 Matt Morris 2.00
9 Ruben Rivera 2.00
10 Shawn Estes 2.00
15 Ryan Klesko 2.00
17 Brett Tomko 2.00
22 Charles Johnson 2.00
33 Jeff Suppan 2.00
36 Rondell White 2.00
39 Kevin Brown 2.00
53 J.T. Snow 2.00
55 Will Clark 2.00
58 Hideki Irabu 2.00
66 Kevin Orie 2.00
70 Tony Womack 2.00
71 Dennis Reyes 2.00
76 Dante Bichette 3.50
78 Carlos Delgado 2.00
81 Mark Belhorn 2.00
87 Sandy Alomar Jr. 2.00
89 Wilton Guerrero 2.00
93 Butch Huskey 2.00
94 Edgardo Alfonzo 2.00
95 Alan Benes 2.00
97 Mark Grace 2.00
98 Shawn Green 3.00
99 Derrek Lee 2.00
105 John Smoltz 2.00
108 Jay Buhner 2.00
109 Jose Canseco 3.50
116 Bobby Higginson 2.00
117 Todd Hundley 2.00
136 Luis Castillo 2.00
137 Fred McGriff 2.00
138 Neifi Perez 2.00
146 Bubba Trammell 2.00
147 Todd Walker 2.00
158 Darin Erstad/GLS 3.50
160 Albert Belle/GLS 2.00
161 Jim Thome/GLS 4.00
162 Tony Clark/GLS 2.00
163 Chuck Knoblauch/GLS 2.00
170 Vladimir Guerrero/GLS 5.00
172 Barry Bonds/GLS 10.00
189 Fernando Tatis/GLR 2.00
194 Eli Marrero/GLR 2.00
195 Livan Hernandez/GLR 2.00
201 Al Martin 2.00

1998 Leaf Fractal Materials

The Fractal Materials set fully parallels Fractal Foundations. Each of the inserts is sequentially numbered. The 200 card chase set was printed on four different materials: 100 plastic cards (numbered to 3,250), 50 leather (1,000), 30 nylon (500) and 20 wood (250). These parallels were inserted one per pack of Fractal Foundations. Each of the Leather cards can be found in a sample version marked as such on back.

NM/M
Complete Set (200): 375.00
Complete Plastic Set (100): 65.00
Common Plastic (3,250): .35
Complete Leather Set (50): 55.00
Common Leather (1,000): .75
Complete Nylon Set (30): 60.00
Common Nylon (500): 1.25
Complete Wood Set (20): 200.00
Common Wood (250): 5.00
Wax Box: 120.00
1 Rusty Greer/N 1.25
2 Tino Martinez/W 5.00
3 Bobby Bonilla/N 1.25
4 Jason Giambi/N 4.00
5 Matt Morris/L .75
6 Craig Counsell/P .35
7 Reggie Jefferson/P .35
8 Brian Rose/P .35
9 Ruben Rivera/L .75
10 Shawn Estes/L .75
11 Tony Gwynn/W 20.00
12 Jeff Abbott/P .35
13 Jose Cruz Jr./W 5.00
14 Francisco Cordova/P .35
15 Ryan Klesko/L .75
16 Tim Salmon/W 5.00
17 Brett Tomko/L .75
18 Matt Williams/N 1.25
19 Joe Carter/P .35
20 Harold Baines/P .35
21 Gary Sheffield/N 2.50
22 Charles Johnson/L .75
23 Aaron Boone/P .35
24 Eddie Murray/N 5.00
25 Matt Stairs/P .35
26 David Cone/P .35
27 Jon Nunnally/P .35
28 Chris Stynes/P .35
29 Enrique Wilson/P .35
30 Randy Johnson/W 15.00
31 Garret Anderson/N 1.25
32 Manny Ramirez/W 15.00
33 Jeff Suppan/L .75
34 Rickey Henderson/N 5.00
35 Scott Spiezio/P .35
36 Rondell White/L .75
37 Todd Greene/N 1.25
38 Delino DeShields/P .35
39 Kevin Brown/L .75
40 Chili Davis/P .35
41 Jimmy Key/P .35
42 Mike Mussina/N 4.00
43 Joe Randa/P .35
44 Chan Ho Park/N 1.25
45 Brad Radke/P .35
46 Geronimo Berroa/P .35
47 Wade Boggs/N 6.00
48 Kevin Appier/P .35
49 Moises Alou/N 1.25
50 David Justice/N 1.25
51 Ivan Rodriguez/W 12.50
52 J.T. Snow/L .75
53 Brian Giles/P .35
54 Will Clark/L .75
55 Justin Thompson/N 1.25
56 Javier Lopez/P .35
57 Hideki Irabu/L .75
58 Mark Grudzielanek/P .35
59 Abraham Nunez/P .35
60 Todd Hollandsworth/P .35
61 Jay Bell/P .35
62 Nomar Garciaparra/W 20.00
63 Vinny Castilla/P .35
64 Lou Collier/P .35
65 Kevin Orie/P .75
66 John Valentin/P .35
67 Robin Ventura/P .35
68 Denny Neagle/P .35
69 Tony Womack/L .75
70 Dennis Reyes/P .35
71 Wally Joyner/P .35
72 Kevin Brown/P .35
73 Ray Durham/P .35
74 Mike Cameron/N 1.25
75 Dante Bichette/L .75
76 Jose Guillen/L 1.25
77 Carlos Delgado/L 1.50
78 Paul Molitor/W 15.00
79 Jason Kendall/P .35
80 Mark Belhorn/P .35
81 Damian Jackson/P .35
82 Bill Mueller/P .35
83 Kevin Young/P .35
84 Curt Schilling/P .60
85 Jeffrey Hammonds/P .35
86 Sandy Alomar Jr./L .75
87 Bartolo Colon/P .35
88 Wilton Guerrero/L .75
89 Bernie Williams/N 1.25
90 Deion Sanders/N 1.25
91 Mike Piazza/W 25.00
92 Butch Huskey/L .75
93 Edgardo Alfonzo/N .75
94 Alan Benes/L .75
95 Craig Biggio/N 1.25
96 Mark Grace/L .75
97 Shawn Green/L 1.25
98 Derrek Lee/L 2.00
99 Ken Griffey Jr./W 25.00
100 Tim Raines/P .35
101 Pokey Reese/P .35
102 Lee Stevens/P .35
103 Shannon Stewart/N 1.25
104 John Smoltz/P .75
105 Frank Thomas/W 15.00
107 Jeff Fassero/P .35

108 Jay Buhner/L .75
109 Jose Canseco/L 1.50
110 Omar Vizquel/P .35
111 Travis Fryman/P .35
112 Dave Nilsson/P .35
113 John Olerud/P .35
114 Larry Walker/W 5.00
115 Jim Edmonds/N 1.25
116 Bobby Higginson/P .75
117 Todd Hundley/L .75
118 Paul O'Neill/P .35
119 Bip Roberts/P .35
120 Ismael Valdes/P .35
121 Pedro Martinez/N 5.00
122 Jeff Cirillo/P .35
123 Andy Benes/P .35
124 Bobby Jones/P .35
125 Brian Hunter/P .35
126 Darryl Kile/P .35
127 Pat Hentgen/P .35
128 Marquis Grissom/P .35
129 Eric Davis/P .35
130 Chipper Jones/W 20.00
131 Edgar Martinez/N 1.25
132 Andy Pettitte/N 10.00
133 Cal Ripken Jr./W 35.00
134 Scott Rolen/W 12.50
135 Ron Coomer/P .35
136 Luis Castillo/L .75
137 Fred McGrift/L .75
138 Neifi Perez/L .75
139 Eric Karros/P .35
140 Alex Fernandez/P .35
141 Jason Dickson/P .35
142 Lance Johnson/P .35
143 Ray Lankford/P .35
144 Sammy Sosa/W 7.00
145 Eric Young/P .35
146 Bubba Trammell/L .75
147 Todd Walker/L .75
148 Mo Vaughn/P/CC .35
149 Jeff Bagwell/P/CC 3.00
150 Kenny Lofton/P/CC .35
151 Raul Mondesi/P/CC .35
152 Mike Piazza/P/CC 5.00
153 Chipper Jones/P/CC 4.00
154 Larry Walker/P/CC .35
155 Greg Maddux/P/CC 4.00
156 Ken Griffey Jr./P/CC 5.00
157 Frank Thomas/P/CC 3.00
158 Darin Erstad/L/GLS 2.00
159 Roberto Alomar/P/GLS .65
160 Albert Belle/L/GLS .75
161 Jim Thome/L/GLS 2.00
162 Tony Clark/L/GLS .75
163 Chuck Knoblauch/L/GLS .75
164 Derek Jeter/P/GLS 7.50
165 Alex Rodriguez/P/GLS 6.00
166 Tony Gwynn/P/GLS 4.00
167 Roger Clemens/L/GLS 5.00
168 Barry Larkin/P/GLS .35
169 Andres Galarraga/L/GLS .35
170 Vladimir Guerrero/L/GLS 4.00
171 Mark McGwire/L/GLS 6.00
172 Barry Bonds/P/GLS 7.50
173 Juan Gonzalez/P/GLS 2.00
174 Andruw Jones/P/GLS 3.00
175 Paul Molitor/P/GLS 3.00
176 Hideo Nomo/P/GLS 2.00
177 Cal Ripken Jr./P/GLS 7.50
178 Brad Fullmer/P/GLR .35
179 Jaret Wright/N/GLR 1.25
180 Bobby Estalella/P/GLR .35
181 Ben Grieve/W/GLR 5.00
182 Paul Konerko/W/GLR 6.00
183 David Ortiz/N/GLR 2.50
184 Todd Helton/W/GLR 10.00
185 Juan Encarnacion/N/GLR 1.25
186 Miguel Tejada/N/GLR 1.50
187 Jacob Cruz/P/GLR .35
188 Mark Kotsay/N/GLR 1.25
189 Fernando Tatis/L/GLR .75
190 Ricky Ledee/P/GLR .35
191 Richard Hidalgo/P/GLR .35
192 Richie Sexson/P/GLR .35
193 Luis Ordaz/P/GLR .35
194 Eli Marrero/L/GLR .75
195 Livan Hernandez/L/GLR .75
196 Homer Bush/P/GLR .35
197 Raul Ibanez/P/GLR .35
198 Checklist
  (Nomar Garciaparra) 3.00
199 Checklist (Scott Rolen/P) .40
200 Checklist (Jose Cruz Jr./P) .35
201 Al Martin/L .75

Fractal Materials Die-Cut

This parallel set adds a die-cut to the Fractal Materials set. The first 200 of 75 plastic, 15 leather, 5 nylon and 5 wood cards have an x-axis die-cut. The first 100 of 20 plastic, 25 leather, 10 nylon and 5 wood cards have a y-axis die-cut. The first 50 of 5 plastic, 10 leather, 15 nylon and 10 wood cards have a z-axis die-cut. The serial numbers on the backs of the die-cut cards are meaningless because they were printed prior to the die-cut fracture. This compounds the confusion engendered among collectors which has had a significant dampening effect on demand and, thus, market values.

NM/M
Common X (200 of each): 1.50
Common Y (100): 3.00
Common Z (50): 6.00
1 Rusty Greer/Z 6.00
2 Tino Martinez/Y 3.00
3 Bobby Bonilla/Y 3.00
4 Jason Giambi/Z 20.00
5 Matt Morris/Y 3.00
6 Craig Counsell/X 1.50
7 Reggie Jefferson/X 1.50
8 Brian Rose/X 1.50
9 Ruben Rivera/X 3.00
10 Shawn Estes/Y 3.00
11 Tony Gwynn/X 12.50
12 Jeff Abbott/X 3.00
13 Jose Cruz Jr./Z 6.00
14 Francisco Cordova/Y 3.00
15 Ryan Klesko/Y 1.50
16 Tim Salmon/Y 3.00
17 Brett Tomko/Y 3.00
18 Matt Williams/X 3.00
19 Joe Carter/X 1.50
20 Harold Baines/X 1.50
21 Gary Sheffield/Z 12.00
22 Charles Johnson/X 3.00
23 Aaron Boone/X 1.50
24 Eddie Murray/Y 10.00
25 Matt Stairs/X 1.50
26 David Cone/X 1.50
27 Jon Nunnally/X 1.50
28 Chris Stynes/X 1.50
29 Enrique Wilson/Y 3.00
30 Randy Johnson/Y 10.00
31 Garret Anderson/Y 3.00
32 Manny Ramirez/Y 10.00
33 Jeff Suppan/Y 3.00
34 Rickey Henderson/Y 10.00
35 Scott Spiezio/Y 3.00
36 Rondell White/Y 3.00
37 Todd Greene/Y 6.00
38 Delino DeShields/Y 3.00
39 Kevin Brown/X 1.50
40 Chili Davis/X 1.50
41 Jimmy Key/X 1.50
42 Mike Mussina/Z 20.00
43 Joe Randa/X 1.50
44 Chan Ho Park/Y 3.00
45 Brad Radke/X 1.50
46 Geronimo Berroa/X 1.50
47 Wade Boggs/X 12.50
48 Kevin Appier/X 1.50
49 Moises Alou/X 1.50
50 David Justice/X 6.00
51 Ivan Rodriguez/X 7.50
52 J.T. Snow/X 1.50
53 Brian Giles/X 1.50
54 Will Clark/X 1.50
55 Justin Thompson/X 3.00
56 Javier Lopez/X 3.00
57 Hideki Irabu/X 1.50
58 Mark Grudzielanek/X 1.50
59 Abraham Nunez/Z 6.00
60 Todd Hollandsworth/X 1.50
61 Jay Bell/X 1.50
62 Nomar Garciaparra/Z 45.00
63 Vinny Castilla/Y 3.00
64 Lou Collier/Y 1.50
65 Kevin Orie/X 1.50
66 John Valentin/X 1.50
67 Robin Ventura/X 1.50
68 Denny Neagle/X 1.50
69 Tony Womack/X 1.50
70 Dennis Reyes/Y 3.00
71 Wally Joyner/X 1.50
72 Kevin Brown/X 1.50
73 Ray Durham/X 1.50
74 Mike Cameron/N 3.00
75 Dante Bichette/X 1.50
76 Jose Guillen/X 6.00
77 Carlos Delgado/X 5.00
78 Paul Molitor/X 10.00
79 Jason Kendall/X 1.50
80 Mark Belhorn/X 1.50
81 Damian Jackson/X 3.00
82 Bill Mueller/X 1.50
83 Kevin Young/X 1.50
84 Curt Schilling/X 3.00
85 Jeffrey Hammonds/X 1.50
86 Sandy Alomar Jr./X 3.00
87 Bartolo Colon/X 3.00
88 Wilton Guerrero/X 1.50
89 Bernie Williams/Z 6.00
90 Deion Sanders/Y 3.00
91 Mike Piazza/Z 55.00
92 Butch Huskey/X 1.50
93 Edgardo Alfonzo/Y 3.00
94 Edgardo Alfonzo/Y 3.00

95 Alan Benes/Z 6.00
96 Craig Biggio/X 1.50
97 Mark Grace/X 3.00
98 Shawn Green/Y 5.00
99 Derrek Lee/Y 6.00
100 Ken Griffey Jr./Z 55.00
101 Tim Raines/Y 1.50
102 Pokey Reese/Y 3.00
103 Lee Stevens/Y 1.50
104 Shannon Stewart/X 3.00
105 John Smoltz/Y 3.00
106 Frank Thomas/Z 30.00
107 Jeff Fassero/Y 3.00
108 Jay Buhner/Y 3.00
109 Jose Canseco/X 3.00
110 Omar Vizquel/X 1.50
111 Travis Fryman/X 1.50
112 Dave Nilsson/X 1.50
113 John Olerud/X 1.50
114 Larry Walker/X 1.50
115 Jim Edmonds/Z 6.00
116 Bobby Higginson/Y 1.50
117 Todd Hundley/X 6.00
118 Paul O'Neill/X 1.50
119 Bip Roberts/X 1.50
120 Ismael Valdes/X 1.50
121 Pedro Martinez/Y 10.00
122 Jeff Cirillo/X 1.50
123 Andy Benes/X 1.50
124 Bobby Jones/X 1.50
125 Brian Hunter/X 1.50
126 Darryl Kile/X 1.50
127 Pat Hentgen/X 1.50
128 Marquis Grissom/X 1.50
129 Eric Davis/X 1.50
130 Chipper Jones/Z 45.00
131 Edgar Martinez/Y 6.00
132 Andy Pettitte/Y 6.00
133 Cal Ripken Jr./Z 75.00
134 Scott Rolen/X 7.50
135 Ron Coomer/X 1.50
136 Luis Castillo/X 1.50
137 Fred McGriff/X 1.50
138 Neifi Perez/Y 3.00
139 Eric Karros/X 1.50
140 Alex Fernandez/X 1.50
141 Jason Dickson/X 1.50
142 Lance Johnson/X 1.50
143 Ray Lankford/X 3.00
144 Sammy Sosa/Y 17.50
145 Eric Young/Y 1.50
146 Bubba Trammell/Z 6.00
147 Todd Walker/Z 6.00
148 Mo Vaughn/X /CC 6.00
149 Jeff Bagwell/X/CC 10.00
150 Kenny Lofton/X/CC 6.00
151 Raul Mondesi/X/CC 1.50
152 Mike Piazza/X/CC 15.00
153 Chipper Jones/X/CC 12.50
154 Larry Walker/X/CC 1.50
155 Greg Maddux/X/CC 12.50
156 Ken Griffey Jr./X/CC 15.00
157 Frank Thomas/X/CC 10.00
158 Darin Erstad/Y/GLS 4.00
159 Roberto Alomar/X/GLS 2.00
160 Albert Belle/X/GLS 1.50
161 Jim Thome/X/GLS 6.00
162 Tony Clark/Z/GLS 1.50
163 Chuck Knoblauch/Z/GLS 6.00
164 Derek Jeter/X/GLS 25.00
165 Alex Rodriguez/Y/GLS 30.00
166 Tony Gwynn/X/GLS 12.50
167 Roger Clemens/Y/GLS 17.50
168 Barry Larkin/Y/GLS 3.00
169 Andres Galarraga/Y/GLS 3.00
170 Vladimir Guerrero/Y/GLS 10.00
171 Mark McGwire/Z/GLS 65.00
172 Barry Bonds/Y/GLS 35.00
173 Juan Gonzalez/Z/GLS 7.50
174 Andruw Jones/X/GLS 10.00
175 Paul Molitor/X/GLS 10.00
176 Hideo Nomo/Z/GLS 25.00
177 Cal Ripken Jr./X/GLS 25.00
178 Brad Fullmer/Z/GLR 6.00
179 Jaret Wright/Z/GLR 6.00
180 Bobby Estalella/Y/GLR 3.00
181 Ben Grieve/Z/GLR 7.50
182 Paul Konerko/Z/GLR 7.50
183 David Ortiz/Z/GLR 10.00
184 Todd Helton/Z/GLR 20.00
185 Juan Encarnacion/Z/GLR 6.00
186 Miguel Tejada/Z/GLR 12.00
187 Jacob Cruz/X/GLR 1.50
188 Mark Kotsay/Z/GLR 6.00
189 Fernando Tatis/Y/GLR 3.00
190 Ricky Ledee/X/GLR 1.50
191 Richard Hidalgo/Z/GLR 1.50
192 Richie Sexson/Z/GLR 1.50
193 Luis Ordaz/Z/GLR 1.50
194 Eli Marrero/Z/GLR 6.00
195 Livan Hernandez/Z/GLR 6.00
196 Homer Bush/X/GLR 1.50
197 Raul Ibanez/X/GLR 1.50
198 Checklist
  (Nomar Garciaparra/X) 7.50
199 Checklist (Scott Rolen/Z) 7.50
200 Checklist
  (Jose Cruz Jr./X) 3.00
201 Al Martin/X 3.00

Fractal Materials Z2 Axis

This 200-card set parallels Leaf Fractal Materials and was numbered to 20 sets.

Common Player: 10.00
Z2 Stars: 10X
Production 20 Sets

Fractal Matrix

Fractal Matrix is a parallel insert set to 1998 Leaf. Cards have a metallic finish, with 100 done in bronze, 60 in silver and 40 in gold, and each color having some cards in X, Y and Z axis. Stated print runs are: Bronze: X - 1,600; Y - 1,800; Z - 1,900. Silver: X - 600; Y - 800; Z - 900. Gold: X - 100; Y - 300; Z - 400. Each player is found only in a single color/axis combination.

		NM/M
Complete Set (200):		250.00
Common Bronze:		.25
Common Silver:		.75
Common Gold:		2.00

No.	Player	Price
1	Rusty Greer G/Z	2.00
2	Tino Martinez G/Z	2.00
3	Bobby Bonilla S/Y	.75
4	Jason Giambi S/Y	1.25
5	Matt Morris S/Y	.75
6	Craig Counsell S/Y	.25
7	Reggie Jefferson B/X	.25
8	Brian Rose S/Y	.75
9	Ruben Rivera B/X	.25
10	Shawn Estes S/Y	.75
11	Tony Gwynn G/Z	10.00
12	Jeff Abbott B/Y	.25
13	Jose Cruz Jr. G/Z	2.00
14	Francisco Cordova B/X	.25
15	Ryan Klesko B/X	.25
16	Tim Salmon G/Y	2.00
17	Brett Tomko B/X	.25
18	Matt Williams S/Y	.75
19	Joe Carter B/X	.25
20	Harold Baines B/X	.25
21	Gary Sheffield S/Z	1.25
22	Charles Johnson S/X	.75
23	Aaron Boone B/X	.25
24	Eddie Murray G/Y	7.50
25	Matt Stairs B/X	.25
26	David Cone B/X	.25
27	Jon Nunnally B/X	.25
28	Chris Stynes B/X	.25
29	Enrique Wilson B/Y	.25
30	Randy Johnson S/Z	2.00
31	Garret Anderson S/Y	.75
32	Manny Ramirez G/Z	7.50
33	Jeff Suppan S/X	.25
34	Rickey Henderson B/X	1.00
35	Scott Spiezio B/X	.25
36	Rondell White S/Y	.75
37	Todd Greene S/Z	.25
38	Delino DeShields B/X	.25
39	Kevin Brown S/X	.75
40	Chili Davis B/X	.25
41	Jimmy Key B/X	.25
42	Mike Mussina G/Y	5.00
43	Joe Randa B/X	.25
44	Chan Ho Park S/Z	.75
45	Brad Radke B/X	.25
46	Geronimo Berroa B/X	.25
47	Wade Boggs S/Z	2.50
48	Kevin Appier B/X	.25
49	Moises Alou S/Y	.75
50	David Justice G/Y	2.00
51	Ivan Rodriguez G/Z	6.00
52	J.T. Snow B/X	.25
53	Brian Giles B/X	.25
55	Will Clark B/Y	.25
56	Justin Thompson S/Y	.75
57	Javier Lopez S/X	.75
58	Hideki Irabu B/Z	.25
59	Mark Grudzielanek B/X	.25
60	Abraham Nunez S/X	.75
61	Todd Hollandsworth B/X	.25
62	Jay Bell B/X	.25
63	Nomar Garciaparra G/Z	10.00
64	Vinny Castilla B/Y	.25
65	Lou Collier B/Y	.25
66	Kevin Orie S/X	.75
67	John Valentin B/X	.25
68	Robin Ventura B/X	.25
69	Denny Neagle B/X	.25
70	Tony Womack S/Y	.75
71	Dennis Reyes B/Y	.25
72	Wally Joyner B/X	.25
73	Kevin Brown B/X	.25
74	Ray Durham B/X	.25
75	Mike Cameron S/Z	.75
76	Dante Bichette B/X	.25
77	Jose Guillen B/Y	2.00
78	Carlos Delgado B/Y	.50
79	Paul Molitor G/Z	7.50
80	Jason Kendall B/X	.25
81	Mark Belhorn B/X	.25
82	Damian Jackson B/X	.25
83	Bill Mueller B/X	.25
84	Kevin Young B/X	.25
85	Curt Schilling B/X	.40
86	Jeffrey Hammonds B/X	.25
87	Sandy Alomar Jr. S/Y	.75
88	Bartolo Colon B/Y	.50
89	Wilton Guerrero B/Y	.25
90	Bernie Williams B/X	2.00
91	Deion Sanders S/Y	.75
92	Mike Piazza G/X	12.50
93	Butch Huskey B/X	.25
94	Edgardo Alfonso S/X	.75
95	Alan Benes S/Y	.75
96	Craig Biggio S/Y	.75
97	Mark Grace S/Y	.75
98	Shawn Green S/Y	1.50
99	Derrek Lee S/Y	2.00
100	Ken Griffey Jr. G/Z	12.50
101	Tim Raines B/X	.25
102	Pokey Reese S/X	.25
103	Lee Stevens B/X	.25
104	Shannon Stewart S/Y	.75
105	John Smoltz S/Y	.75
106	Frank Thomas G/X	7.50
107	Jeff Fassero B/X	.25
108	Jay Buhner B/Y	.25
109	Jose Canseco B/X	.50
110	Omar Vizquel B/X	.25
111	Travis Fryman B/X	.25
112	Dave Nilsson B/X	.25
113	John Olerud B/X	.25
114	Larry Walker G/Z	2.00
115	Jim Edmonds B/X	.75
116	Bobby Higginson S/X	.75
117	Todd Hundley S/Y	.75
118	Paul O'Neill B/X	.25
119	Bip Roberts B/X	.25
120	Ismael Valdes B/X	.25
121	Pedro Martinez S/Y	2.00
122	Jeff Cirillo B/X	.25
123	Andy Benes B/X	.25
124	Bobby Jones B/X	.25
125	Brian Hunter B/X	.25
126	Darryl Kile B/X	.25
127	Pat Hentgen B/X	.25
128	Marquis Grissom B/X	.25
129	Eric Davis B/X	.25
130	Chipper Jones G/Z	10.00
131	Edgar Martinez S/Z	.75
132	Andy Pettitte G/Z	3.00
133	Cal Ripken Jr. G/X	20.00
134	Scott Rolen G/Z	6.00
135	Ron Coomer B/X	.25
136	Luis Castillo B/Y	.25
137	Fred McGriff B/Y	.75
138	Neifi Perez S/Y	.75
139	Eric Karros B/X	.25
140	Alex Fernandez B/X	.25
141	Jason Dickson B/X	.25
142	Lance Johnson B/X	.25
143	Ray Lankford B/Y	.25
144	Sammy Sosa G/Y	10.00
145	Eric Young B/Y	.25
146	Bubba Trammell S/Y	.75
147	Todd Walker S/Y	.75
148	Mo Vaughn S/X/CC	.75
149	Jeff Bagwell S/X/CC	2.00
150	Kenny Lofton S/X/CC	.75
151	Raul Mondesi S/X/CC	.75
152	Mike Piazza S/X/CC	4.00
153	Chipper Jones S/X/CC	3.00
154	Larry Walker S/X/CC	.75
155	Greg Maddux S/X/CC	3.00
156	Ken Griffey Jr. S/X/CC	4.00
157	Frank Thomas S/X/CC	2.00
158	Darin Erstad B/Z/GLS	.50
159	Roberto Alomar B/Y/GLS	.35
160	Albert Belle G/Y/GLS	.25
161	Jim Thome G/Y/GLS	4.00
162	Tony Clark G/Y/GLS	2.00
163	Chuck Knoblauch B/Y/GLS	.25
164	Derek Jeter G/Z/GLS	20.00
165	Alex Rodriguez G/Z/GLS	15.00
166	Tony Gwynn B/X/GLS	1.25
167	Roger Clemens G/Z/GLS	12.00
168	Barry Larkin B/Y/GLS	.25
169	Andres Galarraga B/Y/GLS	.25
170	Vladimir Guerrero G/Z/GLS	7.50
171	Mark McGwire B/Z/GLS	2.00
172	Barry Bonds B/Z/GLS	3.00
173	Juan Gonzalez G/Z/GLS	4.00
174	Andruw Jones G/Z/GLS	7.50
175	Paul Molitor B/X	1.00
176	Hideo Nomo B/Z/GLS	.75
177	Cal Ripken Jr. B/X/GLS	2.25
178	Brad Fullmer S/Z/GLR	.75
179	Jaret Wright G/Z/GLS	.75
180	Bobby Estabella B/Y/GLR	.25
181	Ben Grieve G/X/GLR	2.00
182	Paul Konerko G/Z/GLR	3.00
183	David Ortiz G/Z/GLR	6.00
184	Todd Helton G/Z/GLR	5.00
185	Juan Encarnacion G/Z/GLR	2.00
186	Miguel Tejada G/Z/GLR	4.00
187	Jacob Cruz B/Y/GLR	.25
188	Mark Kotsay B/Z/GLR	2.00
189	Fernando Tatis S/Z/GLR	.75
190	Ricky Ledee S/Y/GLR	.75
191	Richard Hidalgo S/Y/GLR	.75
192	Richie Sexson S/Y/GLR	.75
193	Luis Ordaz B/X/GLR	.25
194	Eli Marrero S/Z/GLR	.75
195	Livan Hernandez S/Z/GLR	.75
196	Homer Bush B/X/GLR	.25
197	Raul Ibanez B/X/GLR	.25
198	Checklist (Nomar Garciaparra B/X)	.75
199	Checklist (Scott Rolen B/X)	.35
200	Checklist (Jose Cruz Jr. B/X)	.25
201	Al Martin B/X	.25

Fractal Matrix Die-Cut

This parallel set adds a die-cut to the Fractal Matrix set. Three different die-cut versions were created: X-axis, Y-axis and Z-axis. An X-axis die-cut was added to 75 bronze, 20 silver and 5 gold cards. A Y-axis die-cut was added to 20 bronze, 30 silver and 10 gold cards. Of the 40 Z-axis cards, 5 are bronze, 10 silver and 25 gold. Stated print runs were 400 of each X-axis card; 200 Y and 100 Z.

		NM/M
Complete Set (200):		950.00
Common X-Axis:		2.00
Common Y-Axis:		3.00
Common Z-Axis:		5.00

No.	Player	Price
1	Rusty Greer G/Z	5.00
2	Tino Martinez G/Z	5.00
3	Bobby Bonilla S/Y	3.00
4	Jason Giambi S/Y	7.50
5	Matt Morris S/Y	3.00
6	Craig Counsell S/Y	2.00
7	Reggie Jefferson B/X	2.00
8	Brian Rose S/Y	3.00
9	Ruben Rivera B/X	2.00
10	Shawn Estes S/Y	3.00
11	Tony Gwynn G/Z	35.00
12	Jeff Abbott B/Y	3.00
13	Jose Cruz Jr. G/Z	5.00
14	Francisco Cordova B/X	2.00
15	Ryan Klesko B/X	3.00
16	Tim Salmon G/Y	4.00
17	Brett Tomko B/X	2.00
18	Matt Williams S/Y	3.00
19	Joe Carter B/X	2.00
20	Harold Baines B/X	2.00
21	Gary Sheffield S/Z	15.00
22	Charles Johnson S/X	2.00
23	Aaron Boone B/X	2.00
24	Eddie Murray G/Y	10.00
25	Matt Stairs B/X	2.00
26	David Cone B/X	2.00
27	Jon Nunnally B/X	2.00
28	Chris Stynes B/X	2.00
29	Enrique Wilson B/Y	2.00
30	Randy Johnson S/Z	30.00
31	Garret Anderson S/Y	3.00
32	Manny Ramirez G/Z	30.00
33	Jeff Suppan S/X	2.00
34	Rickey Henderson B/X	6.00
35	Scott Spiezio B/X	2.00
36	Rondell White S/Y	3.00
37	Todd Greene S/Z	5.00
38	Delino DeShields B/X	2.00
39	Kevin Brown S/X	2.00
40	Chili Davis B/X	2.00
41	Jimmy Key B/X	2.00
42	Mike Mussina G/Y	7.50
43	Joe Randa B/X	2.00
45	Chan Ho Park S/Z	5.00
46	Brad Radke B/X	2.00
47	Geronimo Berroa B/X	2.00
48	Wade Boggs B/X	12.00
49	Kevin Appier B/X	2.00
50	Moises Alou S/Y	3.00
51	David Justice G/Y	3.00
52	Ivan Rodriguez G/Z	25.00
53	J.T. Snow B/X	2.00
54	Brian Giles B/X	2.00
55	Will Clark B/Y	3.00
56	Justin Thompson S/Y	3.00
57	Javier Lopez S/X	2.00
58	Hideki Irabu B/Z	5.00
59	Mark Grudzielanek B/X	2.00
60	Abraham Nunez S/X	3.00
61	Todd Hollandsworth B/X	2.00
62	Jay Bell B/X	2.00
63	Nomar Garciaparra G/Z	40.00
64	Vinny Castilla B/Y	3.00
65	Lou Collier B/Y	3.00
66	Kevin Orie S/X	2.00
67	John Valentin B/X	2.00
68	Robin Ventura B/X	2.00
69	Denny Neagle B/X	2.00
70	Tony Womack S/Y	3.00
71	Dennis Reyes B/Y	3.00
72	Wally Joyner B/X	2.00
73	Kevin Brown B/X	3.00
74	Ray Durham B/X	2.00
75	Mike Cameron S/Z	2.00
76	Dante Bichette B/X	2.00
77	Jose Guillen B/Y	2.00
78	Carlos Delgado B/Y	3.00
79	Paul Molitor G/Z	30.00
80	Jason Kendall B/X	2.00
81	Mark Belhorn B/X	2.00
82	Damian Jackson B/X	2.00
83	Bill Mueller B/X	2.00
84	Kevin Young B/X	2.00
85	Curt Schilling B/X	3.00
86	Jeffrey Hammonds B/X	2.00
87	Sandy Alomar Jr. S/Y	3.00
88	Bartolo Colon B/Y	3.00
89	Wilton Guerrero B/Y	3.00
90	Bernie Williams B/X	4.00
91	Deion Sanders S/Y	3.00
92	Mike Piazza G/X	20.00
93	Butch Huskey B/X	2.00
94	Edgardo Alfonso S/X	2.00
95	Alan Benes S/Y	3.00
96	Craig Biggio S/Y	3.00
97	Mark Grace S/Y	4.00
98	Shawn Green S/Y	5.00
99	Derrek Lee S/Y	5.00
100	Ken Griffey Jr. G/Z	40.00
101	Tim Raines B/X	2.00
102	Pokey Reese S/X	2.00
103	Lee Stevens B/X	2.00
104	Shannon Stewart S/Y	3.00
105	John Smoltz S/Y	3.00
106	Frank Thomas G/X	6.00
107	Jeff Fassero B/X	2.00
108	Jay Buhner B/Y	3.00
109	Jose Canseco B/X	4.50
110	Omar Vizquel B/X	2.00
111	Travis Fryman B/X	2.00
112	Dave Nilsson B/X	2.00
113	John Olerud B/X	2.00
114	Larry Walker G/Z	5.00
115	Jim Edmonds B/X	3.00
116	Bobby Higginson S/X	2.00
117	Todd Hundley S/Y	2.00
118	Paul O'Neill B/X	2.00
119	Bip Roberts B/X	2.00
120	Ismael Valdes B/X	2.00
121	Pedro Martinez S/Y	10.00
122	Jeff Cirillo B/X	2.00
123	Andy Benes B/X	2.00
124	Bobby Jones B/X	2.00
125	Brian Hunter B/X	2.00
126	Darryl Kile B/X	2.00
127	Pat Hentgen B/X	2.00
128	Marquis Grissom B/X	2.00
129	Eric Davis B/X	2.00
130	Chipper Jones G/Z	35.00
131	Edgar Martinez S/Z	3.00
132	Andy Pettitte G/Z	3.00
133	Cal Ripken Jr. G/X	25.00
134	Scott Rolen G/Z	25.00
135	Ron Coomer B/X	2.00
136	Luis Castillo B/Y	3.00
137	Fred McGriff B/Y	3.00
138	Neifi Perez S/Y	3.00
139	Eric Karros B/X	2.00
140	Alex Fernandez B/X	2.00
141	Jason Dickson B/X	2.00
142	Lance Johnson B/X	2.00
143	Ray Lankford B/Y	3.00
144	Sammy Sosa G/Y	20.00
145	Eric Young B/Y	3.00
146	Bubba Trammell S/Y	3.00
147	Todd Walker S/Y	3.00
148	Mo Vaughn S/X/CC	3.00
149	Jeff Bagwell S/X/CC	6.00
150	Kenny Lofton S/X/CC	2.00
151	Raul Mondesi S/X/CC	2.00
152	Mike Piazza S/X/CC	20.00
153	Chipper Jones S/X/CC	10.00
154	Larry Walker S/X/CC	3.00
155	Greg Maddux S/X/CC	10.00
156	Ken Griffey Jr. S/X/CC	15.00
157	Frank Thomas S/X/CC	6.00
158	Darin Erstad B/Z/GLS	3.00
159	Roberto Alomar B/Y/GLS	4.00
160	Albert Belle G/Y/GLS	3.50
161	Jim Thome G/Y/GLS	4.00
162	Tony Clark G/Y/GLS	3.00
163	Chuck Knoblauch B/Y/GLS	3.00
164	Derek Jeter G/Z/GLS	50.00
165	Alex Rodriguez G/Z/GLS	45.00
166	Tony Gwynn B/X/GLS	10.00
167	Roger Clemens G/Z/GLS	37.50
168	Barry Larkin B/Y/GLS	3.00
169	Andres Galarraga B/Y/GLS	3.00
170	Vladimir Guerrero G/Z/GLS	30.00
171	Mark McGwire B/Z/GLS	45.00
172	Barry Bonds B/Z/GLS	50.00
173	Juan Gonzalez G/Z/GLS	30.00
174	Andruw Jones G/Z/GLS	30.00
175	Paul Molitor B/X/GLS	6.00
176	Hideo Nomo B/Z/GLS	30.00
177	Cal Ripken Jr. B/X/GLS	20.00
178	Brad Fullmer S/Z/GLS	3.00
179	Jaret Wright G/Z/GLS	3.00
180	Bobby Estabella B/Y/GLS	3.00
181	Ben Grieve G/X/GLS	3.00
182	Paul Konerko G/Z/GLS	6.00
183	David Ortiz G/Z/GLS	7.50
184	Todd Helton G/X/GLS	6.00
185	Juan Encarnacion G/Z/GLS	5.00
186	Miguel Tejada G/Z/GLS	10.00
187	Jacob Cruz B/Y/GLS	3.00
188	Mark Kotsay G/Z/GLS	5.00
189	Fernando Tatis S/Z/GLS	5.00
190	Ricky Ledee S/Y/GLS	3.00
191	Richard Hidalgo S/Y/GLS	3.00
192	Richie Sexson S/Y/GLR	3.00
193	Luis Ordaz B/X/GLR	2.00
194	Eli Marrero S/Z/GLR	5.00
195	Livan Hernandez S/Z/GLR	5.00
196	Homer Bush B/X/GLR	2.00
197	Raul Ibanez B/X/GLR	2.00
198	Checklist (Nomar Garciaparra B/X)	5.00
199	Checklist (Scott Rolen B/X)	2.00
200	Checklist (Jose Cruz Jr. B/X)	2.00
201	Al Martin B/X	2.00

Fractal Matrix Diamond Axis

Production of this blue-foil finished top-shelf parallel within the 1998 Leaf set was limited to 50 serially numbered examples of each card.

	NM/M
Common Player:	7.50
Stars/Rookies:	20X
SP (148-177):	12X

1998 Leaf Limited Star Factor Sample

This sample card was intended to preview the 1998 Leaf Limited issue which was never released due to Pinnacle's bankruptcy. The card is printed with a refractive foil background and hundreds of embossed stars front and back. The back has a large "SAMPLE" overprint and is numbered "000."

		NM/M
000	Frank Thomas	4.00

1998 Leaf Rookies & Stars

This 339-card set consists of three subsets: Power Tools, Lineup Card and Rookies. Fronts feature full-bleed photos and silver-foil graphics. Backs have complete year-by-year statistics and a small photo. The base set has short-printed base cards, numbers 131-230, 301-339, which are seeded 1:2 packs. Rookies and Stars has two parallels to the base set: True Blue and Longevity. True Blue's feature blue foil stamping and are each numbered "1 0f 500" on the card back. Longevity's are printed on a full-foiled card front with gold foil stamping and limited to 50 serially numbered sets.

	NM/M
Complete Set (339):	200.00
Common Player:	.10
Common SP (131-230):	.20
Common SP (301-339):	.50
Inserted 1:2	
True Blues:	12X
SP True Blues:	2X
Production 500 Sets	
Longevitys:	50X
SP Longevitys:	15X
Production 50 Sets	
Pack (9):	7.50
Wax Box (24):	150.00

No.	Player	Price
1	Andy Pettitte	.30
2	Roberto Alomar	.20
3	Randy Johnson	.75
4	Manny Ramirez	.75
5	Paul Molitor	.75
6	Mike Mussina	.50
7	Jim Thome	.65
8	Tino Martinez	.10
9	Gary Sheffield	.50
10	Chuck Knoblauch	.10
11	Bernie Williams	.10
12	Tim Salmon	.10
13	Sammy Sosa	1.25
14	Wade Boggs	1.00
15	Andres Galarraga	.10
16	Pedro Martinez	.75
17	David Justice	.10
18	Chan Ho Park	.10
19	Jay Buhner	.10
20	Ryan Klesko	.10
21	Barry Larkin	.15
22	Will Clark	.15
23	Raul Mondesi	.10
24	Rickey Henderson	.75
25	Jim Edmonds	.10
26	Ken Griffey Jr.	1.25
27	Frank Thomas	.75
28	Cal Ripken Jr.	2.00
29	Alex Rodriguez	1.50
30	Mike Piazza	1.25
31	Greg Maddux	1.00
32	Chipper Jones	1.00
33	Tony Gwynn	1.00
34	Derek Jeter	2.00
35	Jeff Bagwell	.75
36	Juan Gonzalez	.50
37	Nomar Garciaparra	1.00
38	Andruw Jones	.75
39	Hideo Nomo	.60
40	Roger Clemens	1.25
41	Mark McGwire	1.50
42	Scott Rolen	.60
43	Vladimir Guerrero	.75
44	Barry Bonds	2.00
45	Darin Erstad	.25
46	Albert Belle	.10
47	Kenny Lofton	.10
48	Mo Vaughn	.10
49	Ivan Rodriguez	.60
50	Jose Cruz Jr.	.10
51	Tony Clark	.10
52	Larry Walker	.10
53	Mark Grace	.10
54	Edgar Martinez	.10
55	Fred McGriff	.10
56	Rafael Palmeiro	.60
57	Matt Williams	.10
58	Craig Biggio	.10
59	Ken Caminiti	.10
60	Jose Canseco	.40
61	Brady Anderson	.10
62	Moises Alou	.10

63	Justin Thompson	.10
64	John Smoltz	.10
65	Carlos Delgado	.50
66	J.T. Snow	.10
67	Jason Giambi	.50
68	Garret Anderson	.10
69	Rondell White	.10
70	Eric Karros	.10
71	Javier Lopez	.10
72	Pat Hentgen	.10
73	Dante Bichette	.10
74	Charles Johnson	.10
75	Tom Glavine	.30
76	Rusty Greer	.10
77	Travis Fryman	.10
78	Todd Hundley	.10
79	Ray Lankford	.10
80	Denny Neagle	.10
81	Henry Rodriguez	.10
82	Sandy Alomar Jr.	.10
83	Robin Ventura	.10
84	John Olerud	.10
85	Omar Vizquel	.10
86	Darren Dreifort	.10
87	Kevin Brown	.10
88	Curt Schilling	.35
89	Francisco Cordova	.10
90	Brad Radke	.10
91	David Cone	.10
92	Paul O'Neill	.10
93	Vinny Castilla	.10
94	Marquis Grissom	.10
95	Brian Hunter	.10
96	Kevin Appier	.10
97	Bobby Bonilla	.10
98	Eric Young	.10
99	Jason Kendall	.10
100	Shawn Green	.40
101	Edgardo Alfonzo	.10
102	Alan Benes	.10
103	Bobby Higginson	.10
104	Todd Greene	.10
105	Jose Guillen	.15
106	Neifi Perez	.10
107	Edgar Renteria	.10
108	Chris Stynes	.10
109	Todd Walker	.10
110	Brian Jordan	.10
111	Joe Carter	.10
112	Ellis Burks	.10
113	Brett Tomko	.10
114	Mike Cameron	.10
115	Shannon Stewart	.10
116	Kevin Orie	.10
117	Brian Giles	.10
118	Hideki Irabu	.10
119	Delino DeShields	.10
120	David Segui	.10
121	Dustin Hermanson	.10
122	Kevin Young	.10
123	Jay Bell	.10
124	Doug Glanville	.10
125	John Roskos RC	.10
126	Damon Hollins RC	.10
127	Matt Stairs	.10
128	Cliff Floyd	.10
129	Derek Bell	.10
130	Darryl Strawberry	.10
131	Ken Griffey Jr. (Power Tools)	1.25
132	Tim Salmon (Power Tools)	.20
133	Manny Ramirez (Power Tools)	.75
134	Paul Konerko (Power Tools)	.30
135	Frank Thomas (Power Tools)	.75
136	Todd Helton (Power Tools)	.75
137	Larry Walker (Power Tools)	.20
138	Mo Vaughn (Power Tools)	.20
139	Travis Lee (Power Tools)	.20
140	Ivan Rodriguez (Power Tools)	.60
141	Ben Grieve (Power Tools)	.20
142	Brad Fullmer (Power Tools)	.20
143	Alex Rodriguez (Power Tools)	1.50
144	Mike Piazza (Power Tools)	1.25
145	Greg Maddux (Power Tools)	1.00
146	Chipper Jones (Power Tools)	1.00
147	Kenny Lofton (Power Tools)	.20
148	Albert Belle (Power Tools)	.20
149	Barry Bonds (Power Tools)	2.00
150	Vladimir Guerrero (Power Tools)	.75
151	Tony Gwynn (Power Tools)	1.00
152	Derek Jeter (Power Tools)	2.00
153	Jeff Bagwell (Power Tools)	.75
154	Juan Gonzalez (Power Tools)	.60
155	Nomar Garciaparra (Power Tools)	1.00
156	Andruw Jones (Power Tools)	.75
157	Hideo Nomo (Power Tools)	.60
158	Roger Clemens (Power Tools)	1.25
159	Mark McGwire (Power Tools)	1.50
160	Scott Rolen (Power Tools)	.60
161	Travis Lee (Team Line-Up)	.20
162	Ben Grieve (Team Line-Up)	.20
163	Jose Guillen (Team Line-Up)	.20
164	John Olerud (Team Line-Up)	.20
165	Kevin Appier (Team Line-Up)	.20
166	Marquis Grissom (Team Line-Up)	.20
167	Rusty Greer (Team Line-Up)	.20
168	Ken Caminiti (Team Line-Up)	.20
169	Craig Biggio (Team Line-Up)	.20
170	Ken Griffey Jr. (Team Line-Up)	1.25
171	Larry Walker (Team Line-Up)	.20
172	Barry Larkin (Team Line-Up)	.20
173	Andres Galarraga (Team Line-Up)	.20
174	Wade Boggs (Team Line-Up)	1.00
175	Sammy Sosa (Team Line-Up)	1.25
176	Mike Piazza (Team Line-Up)	1.50
177	Jim Thome (Team Line-Up)	.60
178	Paul Molitor (Team Line-Up)	.75
179	Tony Clark (Team Line-Up)	.20
180	Jose Cruz Jr. (Team Line-Up)	.20
181	Darin Erstad (Team Line-Up)	.25
182	Barry Bonds (Team Line-Up)	2.00
183	Vladimir Guerrero (Team Line-Up)	.75
184	Scott Rolen	.60
185	Mark McGwire (Team Line-Up)	1.50
186	Nomar Garciaparra (Team Line-Up)	1.00
187	Gary Sheffield (Team Line-Up)	.50
188	Cal Ripken Jr. (Team Line-Up)	2.00
189	Frank Thomas (Team Line-Up)	.75
190	Andy Petitte (Team Line-Up)	.30
191	Paul Konerko	.35
192	Todd Helton	1.50
193	Mark Kotsay	.20
194	Brad Fullmer	.20
195	Kevin Millwood RC	8.00
196	David Ortiz	3.00
197	Kerry Wood	1.50
198	Miguel Tejada	.40
199	Fernando Tatis	.20
200	Jaret Wright	.20
201	Ben Grieve	.20
202	Travis Lee	.20
203	Wes Helms	.20
204	Geoff Jenkins	.20
205	Russell Branyan	.20
206	Esteban Yan RC	.20
207	Ben Ford RC	.20
208	Rich Butler RC	.75
209	Ryan Jackson RC	.50
210	A.J. Hinch	.20
211	Magglio Ordonez RC	25.00
212	David Dellucci RC	.50
213	Billy McMillon	.20
214	Mike Lowell RC	10.00
215	Todd Erdos RC	.20
216	Carlos Mendoza RC	.25
217	Frank Catalanotto RC	.75
218	Julio Ramirez RC	.20
219	John Halama RC	.50
220	Wilson Delgado RC	.20
221	Mike Judd RC	.20
222	Rolando Arrojo RC	1.00
223	Jason LaRue RC	.50
224	Manny Aybar RC	.50
225	Jorge Velandia RC	.20
226	Mike Kinkade RC	.75
227	Carlos Lee RC	15.00
228	Bobby Hughes RC	.20
229	Ryan Christenson RC	.50
230	Masato Yoshii RC	1.00
231	Richard Hidalgo	.10
232	Rafael Medina	.10
233	Damian Jackson	.10
234	Derek Lowe	.15
235	Mario Valdez	.10
236	Eli Marrero	.10
237	Juan Encarnacion	.10
238	Livan Hernandez	.10
239	Bruce Chen	.10
240	Eric Milton	.10
241	Jason Varitek	.10
242	Scott Elarton	.10
243	Manuel Barrios RC	.10
244	Mike Caruso	.10
245	Tom Evans	.10
246	Pat Cline	.10
247	Matt Clement	.15
248	Karim Garcia	.15
249	Richie Sexson	.10
250	Sidney Ponson	.10
251	Randall Simon	.10
252	Tony Saunders	.10
253	Javier Valentin	.10
254	Danny Clyburn	.10
255	Michael Coleman	.10
256	Hanley Frias RC	.10
257	Miguel Cairo	.10
258	Rob Stanifer RC	.10
259	Lou Collier	.10
260	Abraham Nunez	.10
261	Ricky Ledee	.10
262	Carl Pavano	.10
263	Derrek Lee	.50
264	Jeff Abbott	.10
265	Bob Abreu	.10
266	Bartolo Colon	.10
267	Mike Drumright	.10
268	Daryle Ward	.10
269	Gabe Alvarez	.10
270	Josh Booty	.10
271	Damian Moss	.10
272	Brian Rose	.10
273	Jarrod Washburn	.10
274	Bobby Estalella	.10
275	Enrique Wilson	.10
276	Derrick Gibson	.10
277	Ken Cloude	.10
278	Kevin Witt	.10
279	Donnie Sadler	.10
280	Sean Casey	.20
281	Jacob Cruz	.10
282	Ron Wright	.10
283	Jeremi Gonzalez	.10
284	Desi Relaford	.10
285	Bobby Smith	.10
286	Javier Vazquez	.10
287	Steve Woodard RC	.20
288	Greg Norton	.10
289	Cliff Politte	.10
290	Felix Heredia	.10
291	Braden Looper	.10
292	Felix Martinez	.10
293	Brian Meadows	.10
294	Edwin Diaz	.10
295	Pat Watkins	.10
296	Marc Pisciotta RC	.10
297	Rick Gorecki	.10
298	DaRond Stovall	.10
299	Andy Larkin	.10
300	Felix Rodriguez	.10
301	Blake Stein	.50
302	John Rocker RC	1.00
303	Justin Baughman RC	.50
304	Jesus Sanchez RC	.50
305	Randy Winn	.50
306	Lou Merloni	.50
307	Jim Parque RC	1.00
308	Dennis Reyes	.50
309	Orlando Hernandez RC	10.00
310	Jason Johnson	.50
311	Torii Hunter	1.00
312	Mike Piazza	2.50
313	Mike Frank RC	.50
314	Troy Glaus RC	60.00
315	Jin Cho RC	.75
316	Ruben Mateo RC	1.00
317	Ryan Minor RC	1.00
318	Aramis Ramirez RC	.75
319	Adrian Beltre	1.00
320	Matt Anderson RC	1.00
321	Gabe Kapler RC	2.00
322	Jeremy Giambi RC	1.00
323	Carlos Beltran RC	1.00
324	Dermal Brown	.50
325	Ben Davis	.50
326	Eric Chavez	1.50
327	Bob Howry RC	1.00
328	Roy Halladay	1.00
329	George Lombard	.50
330	Michael Barrett	1.00
331	Fernando Seguignol RC	1.00
332	J.D. Drew RC	20.00
333	Odalis Perez RC	4.00
334	Alex Cora RC	1.00
335	Placido Polanco RC	8.00
336	Armando Rios RC	.50
337	Sammy Sosa (HR Commemorative)	3.00
338	Mark McGwire (HR Commemorative)	4.00
339	Sammy Sosa, Mark McGwire (Checklist)	4.00

Longevity

	NM/M
Common Player:	3.00
Stars:	50X
SP Stars (131-230):	15X
SP Stars (301-339):	5X

True Blue

This parallel edition of the Rookies & Stars base set is labeled at top-back "1 of 500." The parallels feature blue foil graphic highlights on front with TRUE BLUE at top.

	NM/M
Common Player:	1.00
Stars:	12X
SP Stars (131-230; 301-339):	2X

Cross Training

This 10-card insert set highlights players who excel at multiple aspects of the game. Card fronts are full-foiled and sequentially numbered on the card back to 1,000.

		NM/M
Complete Set (10):		30.00
Common Player:		1.50
Production 1,000 Sets		
1	Kenny Lofton	1.50
2	Ken Griffey Jr.	5.00
3	Alex Rodriguez	6.00
4	Greg Maddux	4.00
5	Barry Bonds	7.50
6	Ivan Rodriguez	2.50
7	Chipper Jones	4.00
8	Jeff Bagwell	3.00
9	Nomar Garciaparra	4.00
10	Derek Jeter	7.50

Crusade

This 30-card set is a continuation of this cross-brand insert. Cards are printed on a holographic green foil front and limited to 250 serial numbered sets. Two parallels are also randomly seeded: Purple and Red. Purples have purple holographic foil fronts and limited to 100 serial numbered sets. Reds are printed on red holographic foil fronts and limited to 25 serial numbered sets.

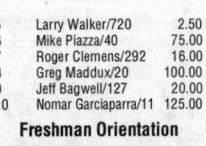

		NM/M
Complete Green Set (30):		225.00
Common Player:		7.50
Production 250 Sets		
Purples (100 Sets):		3X
Reds (25 Sets):		10X
101	Richard Hidalgo	7.50
102	Paul Konerko	15.00
103	Miguel Tejada	15.00
104	Fernando Tatis	7.50
105	Travis Lee	7.50
106	Wes Helms	7.50
107	Rich Butler	7.50
108	Mark Kotsay	7.50
109	Eli Marrero	7.50
110	David Ortiz	15.00
111	Juan Encarnacion	7.50
112	Jaret Wright	7.50
113	Livan Hernandez	7.50
114	Ron Wright	7.50
115	Ryan Christenson	7.50
116	Eric Milton	7.50
117	Brad Fullmer	7.50
118	Karim Garcia	10.00
119	Abraham Nunez	7.50
120	Ricky Ledee	7.50
121	Carl Pavano	7.50
122	Derek Lee	15.00
123	A.J. Hinch	7.50
124	Brian Rose	7.50
125	Bobby Estalella	7.50
126	Kevin Millwood	10.00
127	Kerry Wood	30.00
128	Sean Casey	12.50
129	Russell Branyan	7.50
130	Magglio Ordonez	20.00

Leaf Rookies & Stars Extreme Measures

These inserts are printed on a full-foiled card front. Each card highlights an outstanding statistic for the featured player and is sequentially numbered to 1,000, minus the number of die-cut versions produced for each.

		NM/M
Complete Set (10):		50.00
Common Player:		3.00
1	Ken Griffey Jr./944	7.50
2	Frank Thomas/653	5.00
3	Tony Gwynn/628	6.00
4	Mark McGwire/902	9.00
5	Larry Walker/280	3.00
6	Mike Piazza/960	7.50
7	Roger Clemens/708	5.00
8	Greg Maddux/980	5.00
9	Jeff Bagwell/873	4.50
10	Nomar Garciaparra/989	6.50

Leaf Rookies & Stars Extreme Measures Die-Cuts

Each card highlights an outstanding statistic for each featured player, is die-cut and serially numbered to the limit of the particular statistic as shown.

		NM/M
Complete Set (10):		375.00
Common Player:		2.50
1	Ken Griffey Jr./56	65.00
2	Frank Thomas/347	11.00
3	Tony Gwynn/372	13.50
4	Mark McGwire/58	80.00

5	Larry Walker/720	2.50
6	Mike Piazza/40	75.00
7	Roger Clemens/292	16.00
8	Greg Maddux/20	100.00
9	Jeff Bagwell/127	20.00
10	Nomar Garciaparra/11	125.00

Freshman Orientation

Card fronts are printed on holographic foil with silver foil stamping and feature top prospects. Card backs highlight the date of the featured player's Major League debut, have a small photo and are serially numbered to 5,000 sets. Each card was also issued in an appropriately labeled sample version.

		NM/M
Complete Set (20):		20.00
Common Player:		.75
Production 5,000 Sets		
Samples:		1X
1	Todd Helton	4.00
2	Ben Grieve	.75
3	Travis Lee	.75
4	Paul Konerko	1.50
5	Jaret Wright	.75
6	Livan Hernandez	.75
7	Brad Fullmer	.75
8	Carl Pavano	.75
9	Richard Hidalgo	.75
10	Miguel Tejada	1.50
11	Mark Kotsay	.75
12	David Ortiz	1.50
13	Juan Encarnacion	.75
14	Fernando Tatis	.75
15	Kevin Millwood	1.50
16	Kerry Wood	2.50
17	Magglio Ordonez	1.50
18	Derek Lee	1.50
19	Jose Cruz Jr.	.75
20	A.J. Hinch	.75

Great American Heroes

Card fronts are stamped with a holographic silver foil and done on a horizontal format. Card backs have a photo and are serially numbered to 2,500. Each card was also produced in an appropriately marked sample version.

		NM/M
Complete Set (20):		35.00
Common Player:		.75
Production 2,500 Sets		
Samples:		1X
1	Frank Thomas	1.75
2	Cal Ripken Jr.	5.00
3	Ken Griffey Jr.	3.00
4	Alex Rodriguez	4.00
5	Greg Maddux	2.25
6	Mike Piazza	3.00
7	Chipper Jones	3.00
8	Tony Gwynn	2.25
9	Jeff Bagwell	1.75
10	Juan Gonzalez	1.25
11	Hideo Nomo	1.25
12	Roger Clemens	2.50
13	Mark McGwire	4.00
14	Barry Bonds	5.00
15	Kenny Lofton	.75
16	Larry Walker	.75
17	Paul Molitor	1.75
18	Wade Boggs	2.25
19	Barry Larkin	.75
20	Andres Galarraga	.75

Greatest Hits

These inserts feature holographic silver foil stamping on the card front done on a horizontal format. Card backs have a photo and are serially numbered to 2,500.

Longevity

Only 50 sets of this parallel edition were issued. Each card is serially numbered on back. Fronts are printed with gold foil background and have LONGEVITY printed at top. Special Longevity holographic 1 of 1 cards exist, but cannot be priced due to rarity.

	NM/M
Complete Set (20):	30.00
Common Player:	.50
Production 2,500 Sets	
1 Ken Griffey Jr.	2.50
2 Frank Thomas	1.50
3 Cal Ripken Jr.	4.00
4 Alex Rodriguez	3.00
5 Ben Grieve	.50
6 Mike Piazza	2.50
7 Chipper Jones	2.00
8 Tony Gwynn	2.00
9 Derek Jeter	4.00
10 Jeff Bagwell	1.50
11 Tino Martinez	.50
12 Juan Gonzalez	.75
13 Nomar Garciaparra	2.00
14 Mark McGwire	3.00
15 Scott Rolen	.75
16 David Justice	.50
17 Darin Erstad	.75
18 Mo Vaughn	.50
19 Ivan Rodriguez	1.00
20 Travis Lee	.50

Home Run Derby

This 20-card set spotlights the top home run hitters on a bronze full-foiled card front. Card backs have a portrait photo and are serially numbered to 2,500.

	NM/M
Complete Set (20):	30.00
Common Player:	.75
Production 2,500 Sets	
1 Tino Martinez	.75
2 Jim Thome	1.25
3 Larry Walker	.75
4 Tony Clark	.75
5 Jose Cruz Jr.	.75
6 Barry Bonds	5.00
7 Scott Rolen	1.00
8 Paul Konerko	1.25
9 Travis Lee	1.25
10 Todd Helton	1.25
11 Mark McGwire	4.00
12 Andruw Jones	1.50
13 Nomar Garciaparra	2.50
14 Juan Gonzalez	1.00
15 Jeff Bagwell	1.50
16 Chipper Jones	2.50
17 Mike Piazza	3.00
18 Frank Thomas	3.00
19 Ken Griffey Jr.	3.00
20 Albert Belle	.75

ML Hard Drives

Card fronts are stamped with silver holographic foil. Card backs detail to which field (left, center and right) the featured player hit each of his singles, doubles, triples and home runs. Each card is serially numbered to 2,500. Each card was also produced in an appropriately marked sample version.

	NM/M
Complete Set (20):	30.00
Common Player:	.75
Production 2,500 Sets	
Samples:	1X
1 Jeff Bagwell	1.50
2 Juan Gonzalez	1.00
3 Nomar Garciaparra	2.00
4 Ken Griffey Jr.	3.00
5 Frank Thomas	1.50
6 Cal Ripken Jr.	4.50
7 Alex Rodriguez	3.50
8 Mike Piazza	3.00
9 Chipper Jones	2.00
10 Tony Gwynn	2.00
11 Derek Jeter	4.50
12 Mo Vaughn	.75
13 Ben Grieve	.75
14 Manny Ramirez	1.50
15 Vladimir Guerrero	1.50
16 Scott Rolen	1.00
17 Darin Erstad	.75
18 Kenny Lofton	.75
19 Brad Fullmer	.75
20 David Justice	.75

MVPs

Ivan Rodriguez

This 20-card set is printed on a full silver-foil card stock and sequentially numbered to 5,000. The first 500 of each card is treated with a "Pennant Edition" logo and unique color coating.

	NM/M
Complete Set (20):	35.00
Common Player:	.50
Production 4,500 Sets	
Pennant Editions:	2X
Production 500 Sets	
1 Frank Thomas	2.00
2 Chuck Knoblauch	.50
3 Cal Ripken Jr.	5.00
4 Alex Rodriguez	4.00
5 Ivan Rodriguez	1.50
6 Albert Belle	.50
7 Ken Griffey Jr.	3.00
8 Juan Gonzalez	1.50
9 Roger Clemens	2.75
10 Mo Vaughn	.50
11 Jeff Bagwell	2.00
12 Craig Biggio	.50
13 Chipper Jones	2.50
14 Barry Larkin	.50
15 Mike Piazza	3.00
16 Barry Bonds	5.00
17 Andruw Jones	2.00
18 Tony Gwynn	2.50
19 Greg Maddux	2.50
20 Mark McGwire	4.00

Standing Ovation

Barry Bonds • Giants
1993: Barry Bonds Grabs Third MVP

Card fronts are stamped with silver holographic foil and card backs have a small photo of the featured player and are serially numbered to 5,000. Each card was also produced in an appropriately labeled sample version.

	NM/M
Complete Set (10):	12.50
Common Player:	.75
Production 5,000 Sets	
Samples:	1X
1 Barry Bonds	3.00
2 Mark McGwire	2.50
3 Ken Griffey Jr.	2.00
4 Frank Thomas	1.00
5 Tony Gwynn	1.50
6 Cal Ripken Jr.	3.00
7 Greg Maddux	1.50
8 Roger Clemens	1.75
9 Paul Molitor	1.00
10 Ivan Rodriguez	.75

Ticket Masters

Card fronts are printed on a full-foiled card stock with silver foil stamping and have a photo of one of the two players featured from the same team. Card backs have a photo of the other featured player and are serially numbered to 2,500. The first 250 of each card are die-cut.

	NM/M
Complete Set (20):	32.50
Common Card:	.50
Production 2,250 Sets	
Die-Cuts:	1.5X
Production 250 Sets	
1 Ken Griffey Jr., Alex Rodriguez	4.00
2 Frank Thomas, Albert Belle	1.50
3 Cal Ripken Jr., Roberto Alomar	5.00
4 Greg Maddux, Chipper Jones	2.00
5 Tony Gwynn, Ken Caminiti	2.00
6 Derek Jeter, Andy Pettitte	5.00
7 Jeff Bagwell, Craig Biggio	1.50
8 Juan Gonzalez, Ivan Rodriguez	1.25
9 Nomar Garciaparra, Mo Vaughn	2.00
10 Vladimir Guerrero, Brad Fullmer	1.50
11 Andruw Jones, Andres Galarraga	1.50
12 Tino Martinez, Chuck Knoblauch	.50
13 Raul Mondesi, Paul Konerko	.75
14 Roger Clemens, Jose Cruz Jr.	2.25
15 Mark McGwire, Brian Jordan	4.00
16 Kenny Lofton, Manny Ramirez	1.50
17 Larry Walker, Todd Helton	1.25
18 Darin Erstad, Tim Salmon	.75
19 Travis Lee, Matt Williams	.50
20 Ben Grieve, Jason Giambi	1.00

2001 Leaf Certified Materials

Derek Jeter

	NM/M
Complete Set (160):	
Common Player:	.40
Common SP (111-160):	10.00
Production 200	
Pack (5):	15.00
Box (5):	160.00
1 Alex Rodriguez	5.00
2 Barry Bonds	6.00
3 Cal Ripken Jr.	6.00
4 Chipper Jones	3.00
5 Derek Jeter	6.00
6 Troy Glaus	1.50
7 Frank Thomas	2.00
8 Greg Maddux	4.00
9 Ivan Rodriguez	2.00
10 Jeff Bagwell	2.00
11 Eric Karros	.40
12 Todd Helton	2.00
13 Ken Griffey Jr.	4.00
14 Manny Ramirez	2.00
15 Mark McGwire	4.00
16 Mike Piazza	4.00
17 Nomar Garciaparra	1.50
18 Pedro Martinez	2.00
19 Randy Johnson	2.00
20 Rick Ankiel	1.50
21 Rickey Henderson	1.50
22 Roger Clemens	3.00
23 Sammy Sosa	2.50
24 Tony Gwynn	3.00
25 Vladimir Guerrero	2.00
26 Kazuhiro Sasaki	.40
27 Roberto Alomar	.75
28 Barry Zito	.40
29 Pat Burrell	1.00
30 Harold Baines	.40
31 Carlos Delgado	1.00
32 J.D. Drew	1.00
33 Jim Edmonds	.60
34 Darin Erstad	.50
35 Jason Giambi	1.00
36 Tom Glavine	1.50
37 Juan Gonzalez	1.00
38 Mark Grace	.75
39 Shawn Green	.75
40 Tim Hudson	.75
41 Andruw Jones	.75
42 Jeff Kent	.75
43 Barry Larkin	.75
44 Rafael Furcal	.75
45 Mike Mussina	1.00
46 Hideo Nomo	.75
47 Rafael Palmeiro	1.00
48 Scott Rolen	1.00
49 Gary Sheffield	1.00
50 Bernie Williams	.75
51 Bobby Abreu	.75
52 Edgardo Alfonzo	.40
53 Edgar Martinez	.40
54 Magglio Ordonez	.75
55 Kerry Wood	1.00
56 Adrian Beltre	.75
57 Lance Berkman	1.00
58 Kevin Brown	.40
59 Sean Casey	.60
60 Eric Chavez	.60
61 Bartolo Colon	.40
62 Johnny Damon	1.50
63 Jermaine Dye	.40
64 Juan Encarnacion	.40
65 Carl Everett	.40
66 Brian Giles	.40
67 Mike Hampton	.40
68 Richard Hidalgo	.40
69 Geoff Jenkins	.40
70 Jacque Jones	.40
71 Jason Kendall	.40
72 Ryan Klesko	.40
73 Chan Ho Park	.40
74 Richie Sexson	.40
75 Mike Sweeney	.40
76 Fernando Tatis	.40
77 Miguel Tejada	1.00
78 Jose Vidro	.40
79 Larry Walker	.40
80 Preston Wilson	.40
81 Craig Biggio	.75
82 Fred McGriff	.40
83 Jim Thome	1.50
84 Garret Anderson	.40
85 Russell Branyan	.40
86 Tony Batista	.40
87 Terrence Long	.40
88 Deion Sanders	.40
89 Rusty Greer	.40
90 Orlando Hernandez	.40
91 Gabe Kapler	.40
92 Paul Konerko	.75
93 Carlos Lee	.75
94 Kenny Lofton	.40
95 Raul Mondesi	.40
96 Jorge Posada	.75
97 Tim Salmon	.40
98 Greg Vaughn	.40
99 Mo Vaughn	.40
100 Omar Vizquel	.40
101 Ray Durham	.40
102 Jeff Cirillo	.40
103 Dean Palmer	.40
104 Ryan Dempster	.40
105 Carlos Beltran	1.00
106 Timo Perez	.40
107 Robin Ventura	.40
108 Andy Pettitte	.75
109 Aramis Ramirez	1.00
110 Phil Nevin	.40
111 Alex Escobar	10.00
112 Johnny Estrada RC	15.00
113 Pedro Feliz	10.00
114 Nate Frese RC	10.00
115 Joe Kennedy RC	10.00
116 Brandon Larson RC	10.00
117 Alexis Gomez RC	10.00
118 Jason Hart	10.00
119 Jason Michaels RC	10.00
120 Marcus Giles	10.00
121 Christian Parker RC	10.00
122 Jackson Melian RC	10.00
123 Donaldo Mendez RC	10.00
124 Adrian Hernandez RC	10.00
125 Bud Smith RC	20.00
126 Jose Mieses RC	10.00
127 Roy Oswalt	10.00
128 Eric Munson	10.00
129 Xavier Nady RC	10.00
130 Horacio Ramirez RC	10.00
131 Abraham Nunez	10.00
132 Jose Ortiz	10.00
133 Jeremy Owens RC	10.00
134 Claudio Vargas RC	10.00
135 Ricardo Rodriguez RC	10.00
136 Aubrey Huff	10.00
137 Ben Sheets	10.00
138 Adam Dunn	15.00
139 Andres Torres RC	10.00
140 Elpidio Guzman RC	10.00
141 Jay Gibbons RC	10.00
142 Wilkin Ruan RC	10.00
143 Tsuyoshi Shinjo RC	10.00
144 Alfonso Soriano	15.00
145 Josh Towers RC	10.00
146 Ichiro Suzuki RC	140.00
147 Juan Uribe RC	10.00
148 Joe Crede	20.00
149 Carlos Valderrama RC	10.00
150 Matt White RC	10.00
151 Dee Brown	10.00
152 Juan Cruz RC	10.00
153 Cory Aldridge RC	10.00
154 Wilmy Caceres	10.00
155 Josh Beckett	15.00
156 Wilson Betemit RC	15.00
157 Corey Patterson	10.00
158 Albert Pujols RC	200.00
159 Rafael Soriano RC	10.00
160 Jack Wilson RC	15.00

Mirror Red/Gold

Mike Piazza

These randomly inserted parallels of both the base low-numbers and the short-printed Rookie Freshman Fabric high-numbers are printed on "holographic dual-sided metallized film board" with appropriate color tinting and foil highlights. Mirror red cards are individually serial numbered to 75; golds to 25. All of the mirror red SPs can be found autographed except Kennedy, Melian, Munson, Shinjo and Ichiro. Because no information was released about the number of each autographed, values cannot be attributed.

	NM/M
Common Mirror Red (1-110):	2.00
Stars (1-110):	3-5X
Common Mirror Red (111-160):	6.00
Stars (111-160):	1-2X
Production 75	
Mirror Gold:	6-8X
Production 25	

Fabric of the Game

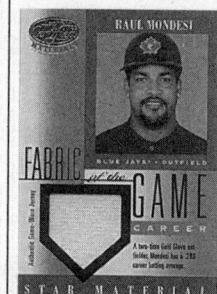

Raul Mondesi

	NM/M
Common Player:	5.00
1 Lou Gehrig/184	200.00
1 Lou Gehrig/23	375.00
2 Babe Ruth/136	250.00
2 Babe Ruth/60	400.00
3 Stan Musial/177	40.00
3 Stan Musial/39	100.00
4 Nolan Ryan	40.00
4 Nolan Ryan/61	60.00
4 Nolan Ryan/34	80.00
5 Roberto Clemente/166	100.00
5 Roberto Clemente/29	250.00
6 Al Kaline/137	25.00
7 Brooks Robinson	20.00
7 Brooks Robinson/68	30.00
8 Mel Ott	25.00
8 Mel Ott/72	50.00
9 Dave Winfield/88	15.00
10 Eddie Mathews/115	25.00
10 Eddie Mathews/72	40.00
11 Ernie Banks/50	40.00
11 Ernie Banks/47	40.00
12 Frank Robinson	15.00
13 George Brett/137	40.00
14 Hank Aaron	40.00
14 Hank Aaron/98	50.00
14 Hank Aaron/47	100.00
15 Harmon Killebrew	25.00
15 Harmon Killebrew/49	50.00
16 Joe Morgan	15.00
16 Joe Morgan/96	15.00
17 Johnny Bench	20.00
17 Johnny Bench/68	30.00
18 Kirby Puckett/134	40.00
19 Mike Schmidt	40.00
19 Mike Schmidt/59	60.00
20 Phil Rizzuto/149	15.00
21 Reggie Jackson	15.00
21 Reggie Jackson/44	30.00
22 Catfish Hunter	15.00
22 Catfish Hunter/42	25.00
23 Rod Carew/92	20.00
23 Rod Carew/100	20.00
24 Bob Feller	15.00
24 Bob Feller/44	30.00
25 Lou Brock	10.00
25 Lou Brock/141	15.00
26 Tom Seaver	15.00
26 Tom Seaver/61	30.00
27 Paul Molitor	15.00
27 Paul Molitor/114	25.00
28 Willie McCovey/126	15.00
29 Yogi Berra	20.00
29 Yogi Berra/49	40.00
30 Don Drysdale	15.00
30 Don Drysdale/49	30.00
31 Duke Snider	20.00
31 Duke Snider/99	30.00
33 Orlando Cepeda/46	20.00
34 Casey Stengel	10.00
34 Casey Stengel/103	15.00
35 Robin Yount	20.00
35 Robin Yount/126	40.00
36 Eddie Murray	15.00
36 Eddie Murray/35	40.00
37 Jim Palmer	10.00
38 Juan Marichal	10.00
38 Juan Marichal/52	20.00
39 Willie Stargell	15.00
39 Willie Stargell/55	20.00
40 Ted Williams	150.00
40 Ted Williams/71	100.00
40 Ted Williams/43	150.00
41 Cal Ripken Jr.	30.00
41 Cal Ripken/75	50.00
41 Cal Ripken/277	40.00
42 Vladimir Guerrero/322	15.00
42 Vladimir Guerrero/44	25.00
43 Greg Maddux	15.00
43 Greg Maddux/240	20.00
44 Barry Bonds	30.00
44 Barry Bonds/49	75.00
44 Barry Bonds/289	30.00
45 Pedro Martinez	15.00
45 Pedro Martinez/268	15.00
46 Ivan Rodriguez	10.00
46 Ivan Rodriguez/304	15.00
47 Roger Maris	50.00
47 Roger Maris/275	50.00
48 Randy Johnson	15.00
48 Randy Johnson/179	25.00
49 Roger Clemens	20.00
49 Roger Clemens/260	20.00
50 Todd Helton	10.00
50 Todd Helton/334	10.00
51 Tony Gwynn	15.00
51 Tony Gwynn/119	20.00
51 Tony Gwynn/134	20.00
52 Troy Glaus	8.00
52 Troy Glaus/47	15.00
52 Troy Glaus/256	8.00
53 Phil Niekro	8.00
53 Phil Niekro/245	10.00
54 Don Sutton	8.00
54 Don Sutton/178	10.00
55 Frank Thomas	10.00
55 Frank Thomas/321	15.00
56 Jeff Bagwell	10.00
56 Jeff Bagwell/305	15.00
57 Rickey Henderson	10.00
57 Rickey Henderson/282	15.00
58 Darin Erstad/301	8.00
59 Andruw Jones	10.00
59 Andruw Jones/272	15.00
60 Roberto Alomar	10.00
60 Roberto Alomar/120	15.00
60 Roberto Alomar/170	15.00
61 Mike Piazza	20.00
61 Mike Piazza/328	20.00
62 Chipper Jones	15.00
62 Chipper Jones/189	15.00
63 Shawn Green	8.00
63 Shawn Green/143	8.00
64 Don Mattingly	50.00
64 Don Mattingly/145	50.00
64 Don Mattingly/222	40.00
65 Rafael Palmeiro	10.00
66 Wade Boggs	15.00
66 Wade Boggs/116	15.00
66 Wade Boggs/89	20.00
67 Hoyt Wilhelm	8.00
67 Hoyt Wilhelm/143	8.00
68 Andre Dawson	8.00
68 Andre Dawson/49	15.00
68 Andre Dawson/314	15.00
69 Ryne Sandberg	30.00
69 Ryne Sandberg/282	35.00
70 Nomar Garciaparra/333	25.00
71 Tom Glavine	10.00
71 Tom Glavine/208	10.00

#	Player	Price
71	Tom Glavine/247	10.00
72	Magglio Ordonez	8.00
72	Magglio Ordonez/301	8.00
73	Magglio Ordonez/126	10.00
73	Bernie Williams	10.00
73	Bernie Williams/304	15.00
74	Jim Edmonds	8.00
74	Jim Edmonds/108	10.00
74	Jim Edmonds/291	10.00
75	Hideo Nomo	20.00
75	Hideo Nomo/69	30.00
76	Barry Larkin	8.00
76	Barry Larkin/300	10.00
77	Scott Rolen	8.00
77	Scott Rolen/284	10.00
78	Miguel Tejada	8.00
78	Miguel Tejada/253	10.00
79	Freddy Garcia	5.00
79	Freddy Garcia/170	5.00
79	Freddy Garcia/249	5.00
80	Edgar Martinez	8.00
80	Edgar Martinez/320	10.00
81	Edgardo Alfonzo	5.00
81	Edgardo Alfonzo/108	5.00
81	Edgardo Alfonzo/296	5.00
82	Steve Garvey	8.00
82	Steve Garvey/272	8.00
83	Larry Walker	5.00
83	Larry Walker/311	5.00
83	Larry Walker/49	5.00
84	A.J. Burnett	5.00
84	A.J. Burnett/90	8.00
85	Richie Sexson	8.00
85	Richie Sexson/242	8.00
85	Richie Sexson/116	8.00
86	Mark Mulder	8.00
86	Mark Mulder/88	10.00
87	Kerry Wood	5.00
87	Kerry Wood/233	10.00
88	Sean Casey	5.00
88	Sean Casey/312	5.00
89	Jermaine Dye	5.00
89	Jermaine Dye/118	5.00
89	Jermaine Dye/286	5.00
90	Kevin Brown	5.00
90	Kevin Brown/170	5.00
90	Kevin Brown/257	5.00
91	Craig Biggio	5.00
91	Craig Biggio/88	8.00
91	Craig Biggio/291	5.00
92	Mike Sweeney	5.00
92	Mike Sweeney/302	5.00
92	Mike Sweeney/144	5.00
93	Jim Thome	10.00
93	Jim Thome/233	10.00
93	Jim Thome/40	20.00
94	Al Leiter	5.00
94	Al Leiter/247	5.00
94	Al Leiter/106	5.00
95	Barry Zito	8.00
95	Barry Zito/272	8.00
95	Barry Zito/78	15.00
96	Rafael Furcal	5.00
96	Rafael Furcal/295	5.00
97	J.D. Drew	5.00
97	J.D. Drew/276	5.00
98	Andres Galarraga	5.00
98	Andres Galarraga/150	5.00
98	Andres Galarraga/291	5.00
99	Kazuhiro Sasaki	5.00
99	Kazuhiro Sasaki/266	5.00
100	Chan Ho Park	5.00
100	Chan Ho Park/65	5.00
100	Chan Ho Park/217	5.00
101	Eric Milton	5.00
101	Eric Milton/163	5.00
102	Carlos Lee	5.00
102	Carlos Lee/297	5.00
103	Preston Wilson	5.00
103	Preston Wilson/266	5.00
104	Adrian Beltre	5.00
104	Adrian Beltre/85	5.00
104	Adrian Beltre/272	5.00
105	Luis Gonzalez	5.00
105	Luis Gonzalez/281	5.00
105	Luis Gonzalez/114	5.00
106	Kenny Lofton	5.00
106	Kenny Lofton/306	5.00
107	Shannon Stewart	5.00
107	Shannon Stewart/297	5.00
108	Javy Lopez	5.00
108	Javy Lopez/290	5.00
108	Javy Lopez/106	5.00
109	Raul Mondesi	5.00
109	Raul Mondesi/286	5.00
110	Mark Grace	10.00
110	Mark Grace/51	20.00
110	Mark Grace/308	15.00
111	Curt Schilling	8.00
111	Curt Schilling/235	8.00
111	Curt Schilling/110	10.00
112	Cliff Floyd	5.00
112	Cliff Floyd/275	5.00
113	Moises Alou	5.00
113	Moises Alou/124	5.00
113	Moises Alou/303	5.00
114	Aaron Sele	5.00
114	Aaron Sele/92	5.00
115	Jose Cruz Jr.	5.00
115	Jose Cruz Jr/245	5.00
116	John Olerud	5.00
116	John Olerud/186	5.00
116	John Olerud/107	5.00
117	Jose Vidro	5.00
117	Jose Vidro/296	5.00
118	John Smoltz	5.00
118	John Smoltz/334	5.00

2001 Leaf Limited

NM/M

Complete Set (375):		
Common Player:		.75
Common Lumberjack (151-200):		5.00
#'d to 100, 250 or 500		
Common Rk (201-300):		5.00
Production 1,500		
Common Auto.(301-325):		10.00
Production 1,000		
Pack (3):		8.00
Box (18):		125.00

#	Player	Price
1	Curt Schilling	1.50
2	Craig Biggio	1.00
3	Brian Giles	.75
4	Scott Brosius	.75
5	Barry Larkin	1.00
6	Bartolo Colon	.75
7	John Olerud	.75
8	Cal Ripken Jr.	6.00
9	Moises Alou	.75
10	Barry Zito	.75
11	Ken Griffey Jr.	4.00
12	Garret Anderson	.75
13	Andy Pettitte	1.00
14	Jim Edmonds	1.00
15	Tom Glavine	1.50
16	Jose Canseco	1.00
17	Fred McGriff	.75
18	Robin Ventura	.75
19	Tony Gwynn	3.00
20	Jeff Cirillo	.75
21	Brad Radke	.75
22	Ellis Burks	.75
23	Scott Rolen	1.50
24	Rickey Henderson	1.50
25	Edgar Martinez	.75
26	Kerry Wood	1.00
27	Al Leiter	.75
28	Jose Cruz Jr.	.75
29	Sean Casey	.75
30	Eric Chavez	.75
31	Jarrod Washburn	.75
32	Gary Sheffield	1.00
33	Jermaine Dye	.75
34	Bernie Williams	1.00
35	Tony Armas Jr.	.75
36	Carlos Beltran	1.50
37	Geoff Jenkins	.75
38	Shawn Green	.75
39	Ryan Klesko	.75
40	Richie Sexson	.75
41	Pat Burrell	1.00
42	J.D. Drew	.75
43	Larry Walker	.75
44	Andres Galarraga	.75
45	Tino Martinez	.75
46	Rafael Furcal	1.00
47	Cristian Guzman	.75
48	Omar Vizquel	.75
49	Bret Boone	.75
50	Wade Miller	.75
51	Eric Milton	.75
52	Gabe Kapler	.75
53	Johnny Damon	1.50
54	Shannon Stewart	.75
55	Kenny Lofton	.75
56	Raul Mondesi	.75
57	Jorge Posada	1.00
58	Mark Grace	1.00
59	Robert Fick	.75
60	Phil Nevin	.75
61	Mike Mussina	1.00
62	Joe Mays	.75
63	Todd Helton	1.50
64	Tim Hudson	1.00
65	Manny Ramirez	2.00
66	Sammy Sosa	3.00
67	Darin Erstad	.75
68	Roberto Alomar	1.50
69	Jeff Bagwell	1.50
70	Mark McGwire	4.00
71	Jason Giambi	1.00
72	Cliff Floyd	.75
73	Barry Bonds	5.00
74	Juan Gonzalez	1.00
75	Jeremy Giambi	.75
76	Carlos Lee	1.00
77	Randy Johnson	2.00
78	Frank Thomas	2.00
79	Carlos Delgado	1.00
80	Pedro Martinez	2.00
81	Rusty Greer	.75
82	Brian Jordan	.75
83	Vladimir Guerrero	2.00
84	Mike Sweeney	.75
85	Jose Vidro	.75
86	Paul LoDuca	.75
87	Matt Morris	.75
88	Adrian Beltre	.75
89	Aramis Ramirez	1.50
90	Derek Jeter	6.00
91	Rich Aurilia	.75
92	Freddy Garcia	.75
93	Preston Wilson	.75
94	Greg Maddux	4.00
95	Miguel Tejada	1.00
96	Luis Gonzalez	.75
97	Torii Hunter	1.00
98	Nomar Garciaparra	1.50
99	Jamie Moyer	.75
100	Javier Vazquez	.75
101	Ben Grieve	.75
102	Mike Piazza	4.00
103	Paul O'Neill	1.00
104	Terrence Long	.75
105	Charles Johnson	.75
106	Rafael Palmeiro	1.00
107	David Cone	.75
108	Alex Rodriguez	4.00
109	John Burkett	.75
110	Chipper Jones	3.00
111	Ryan Dempster	.75
112	Bobby Abreu	1.00
113	Brad Fullmer	.75
114	Kazuhiro Sasaki	.75
115	Mariano Rivera	1.00
116	Edgardo Alfonzo	.75
117	Ray Durham	.75
118	Richard Hidalgo	.75
119	Jeff Weaver	.75
120	Paul Konerko	1.00
121	Jon Lieber	.75
122	Mike Hampton	.75
123	Mike Cameron	.75
124	Kevin Brown	.75
125	Doug Mientkiewicz	.75
126	Jim Thome	1.00
127	Corey Koskie	.75
128	Trot Nixon	.75
129	Darryl Kile	.75
130	Ivan Rodriguez	1.50
131	Carl Everett	.75
132	Jeff Kent	.75
133	Rondell White	.75
134	Chan Ho Park	.75
135	Robert Person	.75
136	Troy Glaus	1.00
137	Aaron Sele	.75
138	Roger Clemens	3.00
139	Tony Clark	.75
140	Mark Buehrle	.75
141	David Justice	.75
142	Magglio Ordonez	1.00
143	Bobby Higginson	.75
144	Hideo Nomo	1.00
145	Tim Salmon	.75
146	Mark Mulder	.75
147	Troy Percival	.75
148	Lance Berkman	1.50
149	Russ Ortiz	.75
150	Andruw Jones	1.00
151	Mike Piazza	15.00
152	Manny Ramirez	10.00
153	Bernie Williams	8.00
154	Nomar Garciaparra	8.00
155	Andres Galarraga	5.00
156	Kenny Lofton	5.00
157	Scott Rolen	8.00
158	Jim Thome	5.00
159	Darin Erstad	5.00
160	Garret Anderson	5.00
161	Andruw Jones	8.00
162	Juan Gonzalez	8.00
163	Rafael Palmeiro	8.00
164	Magglio Ordonez	8.00
165	Jeff Bagwell	8.00
166	Eric Chavez	5.00
167	Brian Giles	5.00
168	Adrian Beltre	5.00
169	Tony Gwynn	15.00
170	Shawn Green	5.00
171	Todd Helton	8.00
172	Troy Glaus	8.00
173	Lance Berkman	10.00
174	Ivan Rodriguez	8.00
175	Sean Casey	5.00
176	Aramis Ramirez	8.00
177	J.D. Drew	5.00
178	Barry Bonds	25.00
179	Barry Larkin	8.00
180	Cal Ripken Jr.	40.00
181	Frank Thomas	8.00
182	Craig Biggio	5.00
183	Carlos Lee	5.00
184	Chipper Jones	10.00
185	Miguel Tejada	8.00
186	Jose Vidro	5.00
187	Terrence Long	5.00
188	Moises Alou	5.00
189	Trot Nixon	5.00
190	Shannon Stewart	5.00
191	Ryan Klesko	5.00
192	Carlos Beltran	10.00
193	Vladimir Guerrero	5.00
194	Edgar Martinez	5.00
195	Luis Gonzalez	5.00
196	Richard Hidalgo	5.00
197	Roberto Alomar	6.00
198	Mike Sweeney	5.00
199	Bobby Abreu	8.00
200	Cliff Floyd	5.00
201	Jackson Melian RC	5.00
202	Jason Jennings	5.00
203	Toby Hall	5.00
204	Jason Karnuth RC	5.00
205	Jason Smith RC	5.00
206	Mike Maroth RC	5.00
207	Sean Douglass RC	5.00
208	Adam Johnson	5.00
209	Luke Hudson RC	5.00
210	Nick Maness RC	5.00
211	Les Walrond RC	5.00
212	Travis Phelps RC	5.00
213	Carlos Garcia RC	5.00
214	Bill Ortega RC	5.00
215	Gene Altman RC	5.00
216	Nate Frese RC	5.00
217	Bob File RC	5.00
218	Steve Green RC	5.00
219	Kris Keller RC	5.00
220	Matt White RC	5.00
221	Nate Teut RC	5.00
222	Nick Johnson RC	5.00
223	Jeremy Fikac RC	5.00
224	Abraham Nunez RC	5.00
225	Mike Penney RC	5.00
226	Roy Smith RC	5.00
227	Tim Christman RC	5.00
228	Carlos Pena RC	5.00
229	Joe Beimel RC	5.00
230	Mike Koplove RC	5.00
231	Scott MacRae RC	5.00
232	Kyle Lohse RC	8.00
233	Jerrod Riggan RC	5.00
234	Scott Podsednik RC	10.00
235	Winston Abreu RC	5.00
236	Ryan Freel RC	5.00
237	Ken Vining RC	5.00
238	Bret Prinz RC	5.00
239	Paul Phillips RC	5.00
240	Josh Fogg RC	5.00
241	Saul Rivera RC	5.00
242	Esix Snead RC	5.00
243	John Grabow RC	5.00
244	Tony Cogan RC	5.00
245	Pedro Santana RC	5.00
246	Jack Cust RC	5.00
247	Joe Crede RC	8.00
248	Juan Moreno RC	5.00
249	Kevin Joseph RC	5.00
250	Scott Stewart RC	5.00
251	Rob Mackowiak RC	5.00
252	Luis Pineda RC	5.00
253	Bert Snow RC	5.00
254	Dustan Mohr RC	5.00
255	Justin Kaye RC	5.00
256	Chad Paronto RC	5.00
257	Nick Punto RC	5.00
258	Brian Roberts RC	15.00
259	Eric Hinske RC	8.00
260	Victor Zambrano RC	5.00
261	Juan Pena RC	5.00
262	Rick Bauer RC	5.00
263	Jorge Julio RC	5.00
264	Craig Monroe RC	5.00
265	Stubby Clapp RC	5.00
266	Martin Vargas RC	5.00
267	Josue Perez RC	5.00
268	Cody Ransom RC	5.00
269	Will Ohman RC	5.00
270	Juan Diaz RC	5.00
271	Ramon Vazquez RC	5.00
272	Grant Balfour RC	5.00
273	Ryan Jensen RC	5.00
274	Benito Baez RC	5.00
275	Angel Santos RC	5.00
276	Brian Reith RC	5.00
277	Brandon Lyon RC	5.00
278	Erik Hiljus RC	5.00
279	Brandon Knight RC	5.00
280	Jose Acevedo RC	5.00
281	Cesar Crespo RC	5.00
282	Kevin Olsen RC	5.00
283	Duaner Sanchez RC	5.00
284	Endy Chavez RC	5.00
285	Blaine Neal RC	5.00
286	Brett Jodie RC	5.00
287	Brad Voyles RC	5.00
288	Doug Nickle RC	5.00
289	Junior Spivey RC	5.00
290	Henry Mateo RC	5.00
291	Xavier Nady RC	5.00
292	Lance Davis RC	5.00
293	Willie Harris RC	5.00
294	Mark Lukasiewicz RC	5.00
295	Ryan Drese RC	5.00
296	Morgan Ensberg RC	5.00
297	Jose Mieses RC	5.00
298	Jason Michaels RC	5.00
299	Kris Foster RC	5.00
300	Justin Duchscherer RC	10.00
301	Elpidio Guzman RC	5.00
302	Cory Aldridge RC	5.00
303	Angel Berroa RC	10.00
304	Travis Hafner RC	40.00
305	Horacio Ramirez RC	10.00
306	Juan Uribe RC	10.00
307	Mark Prior RC	40.00
308	Brandon Larson RC	10.00
309	Nick Neugebauer RC	10.00
310	Zach Day RC	10.00
311	Jeremy Owens RC	10.00
312	Dewon Brazelton RC	10.00
313	Brandon Duckworth RC	10.00
314	Adrian Hernandez RC	10.00
315	Mark Teixeira RC	100.00
316	Brian Rogers RC	10.00
317	David Brous RC	10.00
318	Geronimo Gil RC	10.00
319	Erick Almonte RC	10.00
320	Claudio Vargas RC	10.00
321	Wilkin Ruan RC	10.00
322	David Williams RC	10.00
323	Alexis Gomez RC	10.00
324	Mike Rivera RC	10.00
325	Brandon Berger RC	10.00
326	Keith Ginter	10.00
327	Brandon Inge/700	10.00
328	Brent Abernathy/700	10.00
329	Billy Sylvester/700 RC	10.00
330	Bart Miadich/500 RC	10.00
331	Tsuyoshi Shinjo/500 RC	10.00
332	Eric Valent	10.00
333	Dee Brown/500	10.00
334	Andres Torres/125 RC	10.00
335	Timo Perez/700	10.00
336	Cesar Izturis/500	10.00
337	Pedro Feliz	10.00
338	Jason Hart/200	10.00
339	Greg Miller/700 RC	10.00
340	Eric Munson/700	10.00
341	Aubrey Huff/450	10.00
342	Wilmy Caceres/700 RC	10.00
343	Alex Escobar/650	10.00
344	Brian Lawrence/700 RC	10.00
345	Adam Pettyjohn/650 RC	10.00
346	Donaldo Mendez/700 RC	10.00
347	Carlos Valderrama RC	10.00
348	Christian Parker/650 RC	10.00
349	Corky Miller/500 RC	10.00
350	Michael Cuddyer/500	10.00
351	Adam Dunn/500	10.00
352	Josh Beckett/650	10.00
353	Juan Cruz/500 RC	10.00
354	Ben Sheets/400	10.00
355	Roy Oswalt/650	20.00
356	Rafael Soriano/650 RC	10.00
357	Ricardo Rodriguez/650 RC	10.00
358	Jimmy Rollins/300	20.00
359	C.C. Sabathia	10.00
360	Bud Smith/500 RC	10.00
361	Jose Ortiz	10.00
362	Marcus Giles/400	10.00
363	Jack Wilson RC	10.00
364	Wilson Betemit/100 RC	15.00
365	Corey Patterson/500 RC	10.00
366	Jay Gibbons/Spikes/125 RC	20.00
367	Albert Pujols/250 RC	200.00
368	Joe Kennedy RC	10.00
369	Alfonso Soriano/Hat/100	30.00
370	Delvin James/650 RC	10.00
371	Josh Towers/500 RC	10.00
372	Jeremy Affeldt/650 RC	10.00
373	Tim Redding/500	10.00
374	Ichiro Suzuki/100 RC	400.00
375	Johnny Estrada/100	20.00

2001 Leaf Rookies & Stars Samples

Each January 2002 issue of Beckett Baseball Card Monthly included a sample 2002 Leaf R&S card rubber-cemented inside. The cards differ from the issued version only in the appearance on back of a (usually) silver-foil "SAMPLE" notation. Some cards were produced with the overprint in gold-foil, in much more limited quantities. The number of different players' cards involved in the promotion is unknown.

NM/M

Common Player:	.10
Stars:	1.5-2X
Gold:	20X

2001 Leaf Rookies & Stars

NM/M

Complete Set (300):		
Common Player:		.15
Common (101-200):		1.50
Inserted 1:4		
Common (201-300):		4.00
Inserted 1:24		
Pack (5):		5.00
Box (24):		100.00

#	Player	Price
1	Alex Rodriguez	1.50
2	Derek Jeter	.75
3	Aramis Ramirez	.25
4	Cliff Floyd	.15
5	Nomar Garciaparra	.75
6	Craig Biggio	.25
7	Ivan Rodriguez	.50
8	Cal Ripken Jr.	3.00
9	Fred McGriff	.15
10	Chipper Jones	1.50
11	Roberto Alomar	.40
12	Moises Alou	.25
13	Freddy Garcia	.15
14	Bobby Abreu	.40
15	Shawn Green	.25
16	Jason Giambi	.50
17	Todd Helton	.50
18	Robert Fick	.15
19	Tony Gwynn	1.00
20	Luis Gonzalez	.25
21	Sean Casey	.25
22	Roger Clemens	1.00
23	Brian Giles	.15
24	Manny Ramirez	1.00
25	Barry Bonds	3.00
26	Richard Hidalgo	.15
27	Vladimir Guerrero	1.00
28	Kevin Brown	.15
29	Mike Sweeney	.15
30	Ken Griffey Jr.	1.50
31	Mike Piazza	1.50
32	Richie Sexson	.15
33	Matt Morris	.15
34	Jorge Posada	.40
35	Eric Chavez	.25
36	Mark Buehrle	.15
37	Jeff Bagwell	.50
38	Curt Schilling	.25
39	Bartolo Colon	.15
40	Mark Quinn	.15
41	Tony Clark	.15
42	Brad Radke	.15
43	Gary Sheffield	.25
44	Doug Mientkiewicz	.15
45	Pedro Martinez	.25
46	Carlos Lee	.25
47	Troy Glaus	.50
48	Preston Wilson	.15
49	Phil Nevin	.15
50	Chan Ho Park	.15
51	Randy Johnson	.75
52	Jermaine Dye	.15
53	Terrence Long	.15
54	Joe Mays	.15
55	Scott Rolen	.50
56	Miguel Tejada	.25
57	Jim Thome	.40
58	Jose Vidro	.15
59	Gabe Kapler	.15
60	Darin Erstad	.25
61	Jim Edmonds	.25
62	Jarrod Washburn	.15
63	Tom Glavine	.50
64	Adrian Beltre	.15
65	Sammy Sosa	.75
66	Juan Gonzalez	.40
67	Rafael Furcal	.40
68	Mike Mussina	.50
69	Mark McGwire	1.50
70	Ryan Klesko	.15
71	Raul Mondesi	.15
72	Trot Nixon	.15
73	Barry Larkin	.25
74	Rafael Palmeiro	.25
75	Mark Mulder	.25
76	Carlos Delgado	.25
77	Mike Hampton	.15
78	Carl Everett	.15
79	Paul Konerko	.25
80	Larry Walker	.40
81	Kerry Wood	.40
82	Frank Thomas	1.00
83	Andruw Jones	.40
84	Eric Milton	.15
85	Ben Grieve	.15
86	Carlos Beltran	.50
87	Tim Hudson	.25
88	Hideo Nomo	.15
89	Greg Maddux	1.50
90	Edgar Martinez	.50
91	Lance Berkman	.50
92	Pat Burrell	.40
93	Jeff Kent	.25
94	Magglio Ordonez	.40
95	Cristian Guzman	.15
96	Jose Canseco	.40
97	J.D. Drew	.40
98	Bernie Williams	.40
99	Kazuhiro Sasaki	.15
100	Rickey Henderson	.75
101	Wilson Guzman RC	1.50
102	Nick Neugebauer RC	1.50
103	Lance Davis RC	1.50
104	Felipe Lopez	1.50
105	Toby Hall	1.50
106	Jack Cust	1.50
107	Jason Kamuth	1.50
108	Bart Miadich RC	1.50
109	Brian Roberts RC	8.00
110	Brandon Larson RC	1.50
111	Sean Douglass RC	1.50
112	Joe Crede	3.00
113	Tim Redding	1.50
114	Adam Johnson	1.50
115	Marcus Giles	1.50
116	Jose Ortiz	1.50
117	Jose Mieses RC	1.50
118	Nick Maness RC	1.50
119	Les Walrond RC	1.50
120	Travis Phelps RC	1.50
121	Troy Mattes RC	1.50
122	Carlos Garcia	1.50
123	Bill Ortega	1.50
124	Gene Altman RC	1.50
125	Nate Frese	1.50

#	Player	Price
126	Alfonso Soriano	2.00
127	Jose Nunez	1.50
128	Bob File RC	1.50
129	Dan Wright	1.50
130	Nick Johnson	1.50
131	Brent Abernathy	1.50
132	Steve Green RC	1.50
133	Billy Sylvester RC	1.50
134	Scott MacRae RC	1.50
135	Kris Keller RC	1.50
136	Scott Stewart RC	1.50
137	Henry Mateo RC	1.50
138	Timoniel Perez	1.50
139	Nate Teut RC	1.50
140	Jason Michaels RC	1.50
141	Junior Spivey RC	2.00
142	Carlos Pena	1.50
143	Wilmy Caceres RC	1.50
144	David Lundquist	1.50
145	Jack Wilson RC	2.00
146	Jeremy Fikac RC	1.50
147	Alex Escobar	1.50
148	Abraham Nunez	1.50
149	Xavier Nady	2.00
150	Michael Cuddyer	1.50
151	Greg Miller RC	1.50
152	Eric Munson	1.50
153	Aubrey Huff	1.50
154	Tim Christman RC	1.50
155	Erick Almonte RC	1.50
156	Mike Penny	1.50
157	Delvin James RC	1.50
158	Ben Sheets	1.50
159	Jason Hart	1.50
160	Jose Acevedo RC	1.50
161	Will Ohman RC	1.50
162	Erik Hiljus RC	1.50
163	Juan Moreno RC	1.50
164	Mike Koplove RC	1.50
165	Pedro Santana RC	1.50
166	Jimmy Rollins	3.00
167	Matt White RC	1.50
168	Cesar Crespo RC	1.50
169	Carlos Hernandez	1.50
170	Chris George	1.50
171	Brad Voyles RC	1.50
172	Luis Pineda RC	1.50
173	Carlos Zambrano	2.00
174	Nate Comejo	1.50
175	Jason Smith RC	1.50
176	Craig Monroe RC	1.50
177	Cody Ransom RC	1.50
178	John Grabow RC	1.50
179	Pedro Feliz	1.50
180	Jeremy Owens RC	1.50
181	Kurt Ainsworth	1.50
182	Luis Lopez	1.50
183	Stubby Clapp RC	1.50
184	Ryan Freel RC	2.00
185	Duaner Sanchez RC	1.50
186	Jason Jennings	1.50
187	Kyle Lohse RC	3.00
188	Jerrod Riggan RC	1.50
189	Joe Beimel RC	1.50
190	Nick Punto RC	1.50
191	Willie Harris RC	1.50
192	Ryan Jensen RC	1.50
193	Adam Pettyjohn RC	1.50
194	Donaldo Mendez RC	1.50
195	Bret Prinz RC	1.50
196	Paul Phillips RC	1.50
197	Brian Lawrence RC	1.50
198	Cesar Izturis	1.50
199	Blaine Neal RC	1.50
200	Josh Fogg RC	1.50
201	Josh Towers RC	4.00
202	Tim Spooneybarger RC	4.00
203	Mike Rivera RC	4.00
204	Juan Cruz RC	4.00
205	Albert Pujols RC	200.00
206	Josh Beckett	6.00
207	Roy Oswalt	4.00
208	Elpidio Guzman RC	4.00
209	Horacio Ramirez RC	4.00
210	Corey Patterson	4.00
211	Geronimo Gil RC	4.00
212	Jay Gibbons RC	4.00
213	Orlando Woodwards	4.00
214	David Espinosa	4.00
215	Angel Berroa RC	4.00
216	Brandon Duckworth RC	4.00
217	Brian Reith RC	4.00
218	David Brous RC	4.00
219	Bud Smith RC	4.00
220	Ramon Vazquez RC	4.00
221	Mark Teixeira RC	35.00
222	Justin Atchley RC	4.00
223	Tony Cogan RC	4.00
224	Grant Balfour RC	4.00
225	Ricardo Rodriguez RC	4.00
226	Brian Rogers RC	4.00
227	Adam Dunn	6.00
228	Wilson Betemit RC	6.00
229	Juan Diaz RC	4.00
230	Jackson Melian RC	4.00
231	Claudio Vargas RC	4.00
232	Wilkin Ruan RC	4.00
233	Justin Duchscherer RC	8.00
234	Kevin Olsen RC	4.00
235	Tony Fiore	4.00
236	Jeremy Affeldt RC	4.00
237	Mike Maroth RC	4.00
238	C.C. Sabathia	6.00
239	Cory Aldridge RC	4.00
240	Zach Day RC	6.00
241	Brett Jodie RC	4.00
242	Winston Abreu RC	4.00
243	Travis Hafner RC	10.00

#	Player	Price
244	Joe Kennedy RC	4.00
245	Rick Bauer RC	4.00
246	Mike Young	6.00
247	Ken Vining RC	4.00
248	Doug Nickle RC	4.00
249	Pablo Ozuno	4.00
250	Dustan Mohr RC	4.00
251	Ichiro Suzuki RC	30.00
252	Ryan Drese RC	4.00
253	Morgan Ensberg RC	4.00
254	George Perez RC	4.00
255	Roy Smith RC	4.00
256	Juan Uribe RC	4.00
257	Dewon Brazelton RC	4.00
258	Endy Chavez RC	4.00
259	Kris Foster RC	4.00
260	Eric Knott RC	4.00
261	Corky Miller RC	4.00
262	Larry Bigbie	4.00
263	Andres Torres RC	4.00
264	Adrian Hernandez RC	4.00
265	Johnny Estrada RC	4.00
266	David Williams RC	4.00
267	Steve Lomasney	4.00
268	Victor Zambrano RC	4.00
269	Keith Ginter	4.00
270	Casey Fossum RC	4.00
271	Josue Perez RC	4.00
272	Josh Phelps	4.00
273	Mark Prior RC	6.00
274	Brandon Berger RC	4.00
275	Scott Podsednik RC	6.00
276	Jorge Julio RC	4.00
277	Esix Snead RC	4.00
278	Brandon Knight RC	4.00
279	Saul Rivera RC	4.00
280	Benito Baez RC	4.00
281	Robert Mackowiak RC	4.00
282	Eric Hinske RC	8.00
283	Juan Rivera	4.00
284	Kevin Joseph RC	4.00
285	Juan Pena	4.00
286	Brandon Lyon RC	4.00
287	Adam Everett	4.00
288	Eric Valent	4.00
289	Ken Harvey	4.00
290	Bert Snow RC	4.00
291	Wily Mo Pena	4.00
292	Rafael Soriano RC	4.00
293	Carlos Valderrama RC	4.00
294	Christian Parker RC	4.00
295	Tsuyoshi Shinjo RC	4.00
296	Martin Vargas RC	4.00
297	Luke Hudson RC	4.00
298	Dee Brown	4.00
299	Alexis Gomez RC	4.00
300	Angel Santos RC	4.00

Longevity

Stars (1-100): 10-20X
Production 50
#'s 101-300 Production 25

Autographs

		NM/M
Common Player:		8.00
107	Jason Karnuth	8.00
110	Brandon Larson/100	8.00
117	Jose Mieses	8.00
118	Nick Maness	8.00
119	Les Walrond	8.00
122	Carlos Garcia	8.00
123	Bill Ortega	8.00
124	Gene Altman	8.00
125	Nate Frese	8.00
130	Nick Johnson/100	10.00
133	Billy Sylvester	8.00
135	Kris Keller	8.00
139	Nate Teut	8.00

#	Player	Price
140	Jason Michaels	8.00
143	Wilmy Caceres	8.00
145	Jack Wilson/100	15.00
151	Greg Miller	8.00
155	Erick Almonte	8.00
156	Mike Penney	8.00
157	Delvin James	8.00
161	Will Ohman	8.00
167	Matt White	8.00
180	Jeremy Owens	8.00
184	Ryan Freel	10.00
185	Duaner Sanchez	8.00
193	Adam Pettyjohn/100	8.00
194	Donaldo Mendez/100	8.00
196	Paul Phillips	8.00
197	Brian Lawrence/100	8.00
199	Blaine Neal	8.00
201	Josh Towers/100	8.00
203	Michael Rivera	8.00
204	Juan Cruz/100	10.00
207	Roy Oswalt/50	50.00
208	Elpidio Guzman/100	8.00
209	Horacio Ramirez	10.00
210	Corey Patterson/SP	15.00
211	Geronimo Gil	8.00
212	Jay Gibbons/100	10.00
213	Orlando Woodards	8.00
215	Angel Berroa/100	8.00
216	Brandon Duckworth/100	8.00
218	David Brous	8.00
219	Bud Smith/50	8.00
221	Mark Teixeira/100	200.00
223	Tony Cogan	8.00
225	Ricardo Rodriguez	8.00
226	Brian Rogers	8.00
227	Adam Dunn/50	40.00
228	Wilson Betemit/100	30.00
231	Claudio Vargas	8.00
232	Wilkin Ruan	8.00
234	Kevin Olsen	8.00
236	Jeremy Affeldt	8.00
237	Mike Maroth	8.00
238	C.C. Sabathia/50	40.00
239	Cory Aldridge	8.00
240	Zach Day	8.00
243	Travis Hafner	30.00
244	Joe Kennedy/100	8.00
254	George Perez	8.00
256	Juan Uribe	10.00
257	Dewon Brazelton/100	10.00
261	Corky Miller/100	8.00
263	Andres Torres/100	8.00
265	Johnny Estrada/100	10.00
266	David Williams	10.00
270	Casey Fossum	8.00
273	Mark Prior/100	15.00
274	Brandon Berger	8.00
277	Esix Snead	8.00
282	Eric Hinske	10.00
292	Rafael Soriano	10.00
293	Carlos Valderrama	8.00
299	Alexis Gomez	8.00

Dress For Success

		NM/M
Common Player:		8.00
Inserted 1:96		
Prime Cuts:		2X
Numbered to 50 each.		
1	Cal Ripken Jr.	40.00
2	Mike Piazza	25.00
3	Barry Bonds	40.00
4	Frank Thomas	15.00
5	Nomar Garciaparra	10.00
6	Richie Sexson	8.00
7	Brian Giles	8.00
8	Todd Helton	15.00
9	Ivan Rodriguez	10.00
10	Andruw Jones	10.00
11	Juan Gonzalez	15.00
12	Vladimir Guerrero	15.00
13	Greg Maddux	25.00
14	Tony Gwynn	20.00
15	Randy Johnson	15.00
16	Jeff Bagwell	15.00
17	Kerry Wood	10.00
18	Roberto Alomar	8.00
19	Chipper Jones	20.00
20	Pedro Martinez	15.00
21	Shawn Green	8.00
22	Magglio Ordonez	10.00
23	Darin Erstad	8.00
24	Rafael Palmeiro	15.00
25	Edgar Martinez	8.00

Dress For Success Autographs

Values Undetermined

Freshman Orientation

		NM/M
Common Player:		8.00
Inserted 1:96		
Class Officers:		2X
Numbered to 50 each.		
1	Adam Dunn	15.00
2	Josh Towers	8.00
3	Vernon Wells	10.00
4	Corey Patterson	10.00
6	Ben Sheets	8.00
7	Pedro Feliz	8.00
8	Keith Ginter	8.00
9	Luis Rivas	8.00
10	Andres Torres	8.00
11	Carlos Valderrama	8.00
12	Brandon Inge	8.00
13	Jay Gibbons	15.00
14	Cesar Izturis	8.00
15	Marcus Giles	8.00
16	Tsuyoshi Shinjo	12.00
17	Eric Valent	8.00
18	David Espinosa	8.00
19	Aubrey Huff	8.00
20	Wilmy Caceres	8.00
21	Bud Smith	8.00
22	Ricardo Rodriguez	8.00
23	Wes Helms	8.00
24	Jason Hart	8.00
25	Dee Brown	8.00

Freshman Orientation Auto.

Values Undetermined

Great American Treasures

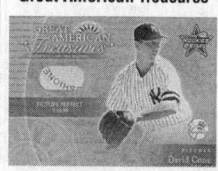

		NM/M
Inserted 1:1,120		
1	Barry Bonds/Jsy	100.00
2	Magglio Ordonez/Bat	40.00
3	Derek Jeter/Ball	150.00
4	Nolan Ryan/Ball	600.00
5	Sammy Sosa/Ball	125.00
6	Tom Glavine/Jsy	50.00
7	Ivan Rodriguez/Bat	30.00
8	Pedro Martinez/Ball	100.00
9	Mark McGwire/Ball	250.00
10	Ted Williams/Ball	350.00
11	Ryne Sandberg/Bat	60.00
12	Barry Bonds/Ball	300.00
13	Hideo Nomo/Ball	450.00
14	Roger Maris/Ball	300.00
15	Ty Cobb/Ball	300.00
16	Harmon Killebrew/Bat	150.00
17	Magglio Ordonez/Cap	30.00
18	Wade Boggs/Bat	40.00
19	Hank Aaron/Cap	400.00
20	David Cone/Ball	100.00

Great American Treasures Auto.

		NM/M
Common Player:		8.00
Inserted 1:96		
Prime Cuts:		2X
Numbered to 50 each.		
GT-6	Tom Glavine	
	96 WS Jsy	125.00
GT-11	Ryne Sandberg	
	91 AS Bat	300.00
GT-16	Harmon Killebrew	
	570 HR Bat	200.00
GT-18	Wade Boggs WS Bat	150.00

Player's Collection

		NM/M
Singles #'d to 100.		
1	Tony Gwynn/Bat	30.00
2	Tony Gwynn/Jsy	30.00
3	Tony Gwynn/Pants	30.00
4	Tony Gwynn/Shoe	30.00
6	Cal Ripken/Jsy	75.00
7	Cal Ripken/Bat	75.00
8	Cal Ripken/Glove	75.00
9	Cal Ripken/Jsy	75.00
11	Barry Bonds/Jsy	60.00
12	Barry Bonds/Shoe	60.00
13	Barry Bonds/Pants	60.00
14	Barry Bonds/Bat	60.00

Player's Collection Auto.

No Pricing

Slideshow

		NM/M
Common Player:		10.00
Production 100 Sets		
View Masters:		1.5X
Numbered to 25 each.		
1	Cal Ripken Jr.	40.00
2	Chipper Jones	20.00
3	Jeff Bagwell	15.00
4	Larry Walker	10.00
5	Greg Maddux	25.00
6	Ivan Rodriguez	15.00
7	Andruw Jones	15.00
8	Lance Berkman	10.00
9	Luis Gonzalez	10.00
10	Tony Gwynn	25.00
11	Troy Glaus	15.00
12	Todd Helton	20.00
13	Roberto Alomar	10.00
14	Barry Bonds	40.00
15	Vladimir Guerrero	20.00
16	Sean Casey	10.00
17	Curt Schilling	15.00
18	Frank Thomas	20.00
19	Pedro Martinez	20.00
20	Juan Gonzalez	15.00
21	Randy Johnson	20.00
22	Kerry Wood	10.00
23	Mike Sweeney	10.00
24	Magglio Ordonez	10.00
25	Kazuhiro Sasaki	10.00
26	Manny Ramirez	20.00
27	Roger Clemens	25.00
28	Albert Pujols	120.00
29	Hideo Nomo	25.00
30	Miguel Tejada	10.00

Slideshow Autographs

No Pricing

Statistical Standouts

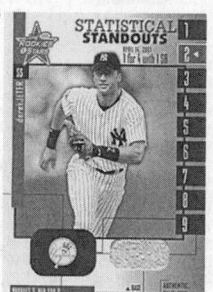

		NM/M
Common Player:		5.00
Inserted 1:96		
1	Ichiro Suzuki	35.00
2	Barry Bonds	40.00
3	Ivan Rodriguez	10.00
4	Jeff Bagwell	10.00
5	Vladimir Guerrero	10.00
6	Mike Sweeney	5.00
7	Miguel Tejada	5.00
8	Mike Piazza	30.00
9	Darin Erstad	5.00
10	Alex Rodriguez	35.00
11	Jason Giambi	25.00
12	Cal Ripken Jr.	40.00
13	Albert Pujols	35.00
14	Carlos Delgado	8.00
15	Rafael Palmeiro	5.00
16	Lance Berkman	5.00
17	Luis Gonzalez	5.00
18	Sammy Sosa	30.00
19	Andruw Jones	5.00
20	Derek Jeter	40.00
21	Edgar Martinez	5.00
22	Troy Glaus	10.00
23	Magglio Ordonez	5.00
24	Mark McGwire	35.00
25	Manny Ramirez	10.00

Statistical Standouts Auto.

No Pricing

Triple Threads

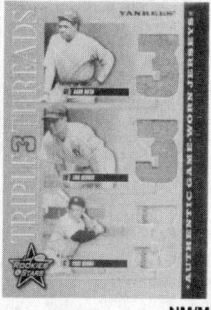

		NM/M
Common Card:		50.00
Numbered to 100.		
TT-1	Pedro Martinez, Manny Ramirez, Nomar Garciaparra	75.00
TT-2	Frank Robinson, Cal Ripken Jr., Brooks Robinson	120.00
TT-3	Yogi Berra, Lou Gehrig, Babe Ruth	500.00
TT-4	Andre Dawson, Ryne Sandberg, Ernie Banks	120.00
TT-5	Warren Spahn, Hank Aaron, Eddie Mathews	150.00
TT-6	Greg Maddux, Chipper Jones, Andruw Jones	75.00
TT-7	Nolan Ryan, Ivan Rodriguez, Juan Gonzalez	100.00
TT-8	Lance Berkman, Jeff Bagwell, Craig Biggio	50.00
TT-9	Rod Carew, Harmon Killebrew, Kirby Puckett	75.00
TT-10	Luis Gonzalez, Curt Schilling, Randy Johnson	60.00

2002 Leaf Samples

Each April 2002 issue of Beckett Baseball Card Monthly included a sample Leaf card rubber-cemented inside. The cards differ from the issued version only in the appearance on back of a (usually) silver-foil "SAMPLE" notation. Some cards were produced with the back overprint in gold-foil in much more limited quantities. The number of different players' cards involved in the promotion is unknown.

	NM/M
Common Player:	.10
Stars:	1.5-2X
Gold:	20X

2002 Leaf

		NM/M
Complete Set (1-200):		80.00
Common Player:		.15
Common (151-200):		1.50
Inserted 1:6		
Pack (4):		1.50
Box (24):		30.00
1	Tim Salmon	.25

#	Player	Price
2	Troy Glaus	.65
3	Curt Schilling	.40
4	Luis Gonzalez	.25
5	Mark Grace	.25
6	Matt Williams	.15
7	Randy Johnson	.40
8	Tom Glavine	.40
9	Brady Anderson	.15
10	Hideo Nomo	.65
11	Pedro Martinez	.65
12	Corey Patterson	.15
13	Paul Konerko	.25
14	Jon Lieber	.15
15	Carlos Lee	.15
16	Magglio Ordonez	.15
17	Adam Dunn	.40
18	Ken Griffey Jr.	1.00
19	C.C. Sabathia	.15
20	Jim Thome	.50
21	Juan Gonzalez	.65
22	Kenny Lofton	.15
23	Juan Encarnacion	.15
24	Tony Clark	.15
25	A.J. Burnett	.15
26	Josh Beckett	.25
27	Lance Berkman	.15
28	Eric Karros	.15
29	Shawn Green	.30
30	Brad Radke	.15
31	Joe Mays	.15
32	Javier Vazquez	.15
33	Alfonso Soriano	.50
34	Jorge Posada	.25
35	Eric Chavez	.25
36	Mark Mulder	.25
37	Miguel Tejada	.25
38	Tim Hudson	.25
39	Bobby Abreu	.15
40	Pat Burrell	.40
41	Ryan Klesko	.15
43	John Olerud	.15
44	Ellis Burks	.15
45	Mike Cameron	.15
46	Jim Edmonds	.15
47	Ben Grieve	.15
48	Carlos Pena	.15
49	Alex Rodriguez	1.50
50	Raul Mondesi	.15
51	Billy Koch	.15
52	Manny Ramirez	.65
53	Darin Erstad	.25
54	Troy Percival	.15
55	Andruw Jones	.65
56	Chipper Jones	.75
57	David Segui	.15
58	Chris Stynes	.15
59	Trot Nixon	.15
60	Sammy Sosa	1.00
61	Kerry Wood	.50
62	Frank Thomas	.65
63	Barry Larkin	.15
64	Bartolo Colon	.15
65	Kazuhiro Sasaki	.15
66	Roberto Alomar	.35
67	Mike Hampton	.15
68	Roger Cedeno	.15
69	Cliff Floyd	.15
70	Mike Lowell	.15
71	Billy Wagner	.15
72	Craig Biggio	.25
73	Jeff Bagwell	.65
74	Carlos Beltran	.50
75	Mark Quinn	.15
76	Mike Sweeney	.15
77	Gary Sheffield	.15
78	Kevin Brown	.15
79	Paul LoDuca	.15
80	Ben Sheets	.15
81	Jeromy Burnitz	.15
82	Richie Sexson	.15
83	Corey Koskie	.15
84	Eric Milton	.15
85	Jose Vidro	.15
86	Mike Piazza	1.00
87	Robin Ventura	.15
88	Andy Pettitte	.25
89	Mike Mussina	.40
90	Orlando Hernandez	.15
91	Roger Clemens	.85
92	Barry Zito	.25
93	Jermaine Dye	.15
94	Jimmy Rollins	.25
95	Jason Kendall	.15
96	Rickey Henderson	.65
97	Andres Galarraga	.15
98	Bret Boone	.15
99	Freddy Garcia	.15
100	J.D. Drew	.25
101	Jose Cruz Jr.	.15
102	Greg Maddux	.75
103	Javy Lopez	.15
104	Nomar Garciaparra	1.00
105	Fred McGriff	.15
106	Keith Foulke	.15
107	Ray Durham	.15
108	Sean Casey	.25
109	Todd Walker	.15
110	Omar Vizquel	.15
111	Travis Fryman	.15
112	Larry Walker	.25
113	Todd Helton	.65
114	Bobby Higginson	.15
115	Charles Johnson	.15
116	Moises Alou	.15
117	Richard Hidalgo	.15
118	Roy Oswalt	.25
119	Neifi Perez	.15
120	Adrian Beltre	.30

#	Player	Price
121	Chan Ho Park	.15
122	Geoff Jenkins	.15
123	Doug Mientkiewicz	.15
124	Torii Hunter	.15
125	Vladimir Guerrero	.65
126	Matt Lawton	.15
127	Tsuyoshi Shinjo	.15
128	Bernie Williams	.40
129	Derek Jeter	2.00
130	Mariano Rivera	.25
131	Tino Martinez	.15
132	Jason Giambi	.45
133	Scott Rolen	.50
134	Brian Giles	.15
135	Phil Nevin	.15
136	Trevor Hoffman	.15
137	Barry Bonds	2.00
138	Jeff Kent	.15
139	Shannon Stewart	.15
140	Shawn Estes	.15
141	Edgar Martinez	.15
142	Ichiro Suzuki	1.00
143	Albert Pujols	1.50
144	Bud Smith	.15
145	Matt Morris	.15
146	Frank Catalanotto	.15
147	Gabe Kapler	.15
148	Ivan Rodriguez	.45
149	Rafael Palmeiro	.45
150	Carlos Delgado	.40
151	Marlon Byrd	2.00
152	Alex Herrera	1.50
153	Brandon Backe RC	2.00
154	Jorge De La Rosa RC	1.50
155	Corky Miller	1.50
156	Dennis Tankersley	1.50
157	Kyle Kane RC	2.00
158	Justin Duchscherer	1.50
159	Brian Mallette RC	1.50
160	Eric Hinske	1.50
161	Jason Lane	1.50
162	Hee Seop Choi	3.00
163	Juan Cruz	1.50
164	Rodrigo Rosario RC	1.50
165	Matt Guerrier	1.50
166	Anderson Machado RC	1.50
167	Geronimo Gil	1.50
168	Dewon Brazelton	1.50
169	Mark Prior	4.00
170	Bill Hall	1.50
171	Jorge Padilla RC	2.00
172	Josh Pearce	1.50
173	Allan Simpson RC	2.00
174	Doug DeVore RC	2.00
175	Morgan Ensberg	1.50
176	Angel Berroa	1.50
177	Steve Bechler RC	2.00
178	Antonio Perez	1.50
179	Mark Teixeira	3.00
180	Mark Ellis	1.50
181	Michael Cuddyer	1.50
182	Mike Rivera	1.50
183	Raul Chavez RC	2.00
184	Juan Pena	1.50
185	Austin Kearns	2.00
186	Ryan Ludwick	1.50
187	Ed Rogers	1.50
188	Wilson Betemit	1.50
189	Nick Neugebauer	1.50
190	Tom Shearn RC	1.50
191	Eric Cyr RC	2.00
192	Victor Martinez	1.50
193	Brandon Berger	1.50
194	Erik Bedard	1.50
195	Franklin German RC	2.00
196	Joe Thurston	1.50
197	John Buck	1.50
198	Jeff Deardorff RC	2.00
199	Ryan Jamison RC	2.00
200	Alfredo Amezaga	1.50
201	So Taguchi/500 RC	6.00
202	Kazuhisa Ishii/250 RC	8.00

Lineage

Set	Price
1999 Lineage (1-50):	2-5X
Inserted 1:12	
2000 Lineage (51-100):	2-5X
Inserted 1:12	
2001 Lineage (101-150):	2-5X
Inserted 1:12	
Silver Holofoils:	8-15X
Production 100	

Press Proof Blue

	Price
Stars (1-150):	5-10X
Inserted 1:24 Retail	

Press Proof Red

	Price
Stars (1-150):	4-6X
Inserted 1:12 Retail	

Autograph

Quantity produced listed.

Burn n' Turn

		NM/M
Complete Set (10):		50.00
Common Player:		4.00
Inserted 1:96		
1	Fernando Vina, Edgar Renteria	4.00
2	Alex Rodriguez, Mike Young	10.00
3	Derek Jeter, Alfonso Soriano	15.00
4	Carlos Guillen, Bret Boone	4.00
5	Jose Vidro, Orlando Cabrera	4.00
6	Barry Larkin, Todd Walker	4.00
7	Carlos Febles, Neifi Perez	4.00
8	Jeff Kent, Rich Aurilia	4.00
9	Craig Biggio, Julio Lugo	5.00
10	Miguel Tejada, Mark Ellis	4.00

Clean Up Crew

		NM/M
Complete Set (15):		90.00
Common Player:		4.00
Inserted 1:192		
1	Barry Bonds	20.00
2	Sammy Sosa	12.00
3	Luis Gonzalez	4.00
4	Richie Sexson	4.00
5	Jim Thome	6.00
6	Chipper Jones	6.00
7	Alex Rodriguez	15.00
8	Troy Glaus	5.00
9	Rafael Palmeiro	5.00
10	Lance Berkman	4.00
11	Mike Piazza	12.00
12	Jason Giambi	5.00
13	Todd Helton	6.00
14	Shawn Green	5.00
15	Carlos Delgado	5.00

Clubhouse Signatures Bronze

		NM/M
Common Player:		5.00
(1)	Wilson Betemit/150	6.00
(2)	Marlon Byrd/200	6.00
(3)	Joe Crede/200	8.00
(4)	Andre Dawson/100	30.00
(5)	J.D. Drew/25	35.00
(6)	Adam Dunn/200	25.00
(7)	Jermaine Dye/125	10.00
(8)	Mark Ellis/300	5.00
(9)	Johnny Estrada/250	8.00
(10)	Bob Feller/250	15.00
(11)	Robert Fick/300	5.00
(12)	Steve Garvey/200	15.00
(13)	Austin Kearns/300	10.00
(14)	Jason Lane/250	5.00
(15)	Paul LoDuca/300	8.00
(16)	Terrence Long/250	5.00
(17)	Edgar Martinez/50	30.00
(18)	Don Mattingly/25	100.00
(19)	Joe Mays/200	6.00
(20)	Mark Mulder/50	25.00
(21)	Xavier Nady/200	8.00
(22)	Roy Oswalt/300	10.00
(23)	Aramis Ramirez/300	15.00
(24)	Tim Redding/300	5.00
(25)	Phil Rizzuto/25	45.00
(26)	Ryne Sandberg/25	100.00
(27)	Ron Santo/300	5.00
(28)	Bud Smith/200	5.00
(29)	Ozzie Smith/25	85.00
(30)	Alfonso Soriano/75	30.00
(31)	Alan Trammell/75	10.00
(32)	Billy Williams/150	10.00
(33)	Barry Zito/100	25.00

Clubhouse Signatures Silver

		NM/M
Common Player:		10.00
(1)	Rich Aurilia/100	15.00
(2)	Wilson Betemit/100	15.00
(3)	Marlon Byrd/100	15.00
(4)	Sean Casey/50	20.00
(5)	Eric Chavez/100	20.00

Clubhouse Signatures Gold

		NM/M
Common Player:		15.00
Numbered to 25.		
(1)	Rich Aurilia	15.00
(2)	Josh Beckett	60.00
(3)	Wilson Betemit	15.00
(4)	Marlon Byrd	15.00
(5)	Sean Casey	25.00
(6)	Eric Chavez	30.00
(7)	Roger Clemens	150.00
(8)	Joe Crede	50.00
(9)	Andre Dawson	40.00
(10)	J.D. Drew	40.00
(11)	Adam Dunn	65.00
(12)	Jermaine Dye	20.00
(13)	Mark Ellis	15.00
(14)	Johnny Estrada	20.00
(15)	Bob Feller	45.00
(16)	Robert Fick	15.00
(17)	Steve Garvey	40.00
(18)	Luis Gonzalez	35.00
(19)	Vladimir Guerrero	75.00
(20)	Todd Helton	50.00
(21)	Orel Hershiser	35.00
(22)	Austin Kearns	50.00
(23)	Jason Lane	15.00
(24)	Paul LoDuca	25.00
(25)	Terrence Long	15.00
(26)	Edgar Martinez	30.00
(27)	Don Mattingly	125.00
(28)	Joe Mays	25.00
(29)	Mark Mulder	40.00
(30)	Xavier Nady	20.00
(31)	Roy Oswalt	30.00
(32)	Chan Ho Park	15.00
(33)	Kirby Puckett	125.00
(34)	Aramis Ramirez	40.00
(35)	Tim Redding	15.00
(36)	Cal Ripken Jr.	225.00
(37)	Phil Rizzuto	60.00
(38)	Ryne Sandberg	125.00
(39)	Ron Santo	65.00
(40)	Mike Schmidt	90.00
(41)	Bud Smith	20.00
(42)	Ozzie Smith	100.00
(43)	Alfonso Soriano	80.00
(44)	Miguel Tejada	30.00
(45)	Alan Trammell	25.00
(46)	Javier Vazquez	20.00
(47)	Billy Williams	35.00
(48)	Barry Zito	50.00

Cornerstones

		NM/M
Production 50 Sets		
Some not priced yet.		
1	Andruw Jones, Chipper Jones	40.00
4	Curt Schilling, Randy Johnson	40.00
6	Larry Walker, Todd Helton	25.00
7	Carlos Delgado, Shannon Stewart	25.00
10	Bernie Williams, Roger Clemens	60.00

Future 500 Club

		NM/M
Complete Set (10):		40.00
Common Player:		2.00
Inserted 1:64		
1	Sammy Sosa	8.00

#	Player	Price
(6)	Roger Clemens/25	150.00
(7)	Joe Crede/50	20.00
(8)	Andre Dawson/100	30.00
(9)	Adam Dunn/75	40.00
(10)	Jermaine Dye/100	15.00
(11)	Mark Ellis/100	15.00
(12)	Johnny Estrada/100	15.00
(13)	Bob Feller/100	15.00
(14)	Robert Fick/100	15.00
(15)	Steve Garvey/100	20.00
(16)	Vladimir Guerrero/25	60.00
(17)	Todd Helton/25	50.00
(18)	Austin Kearns/100	20.00
(19)	Jason Lane/100	15.00
(20)	Paul LoDuca/100	15.00
(21)	Terrence Long/100	15.00
(22)	Edgar Martinez/100	25.00
(23)	Joe Mays/50	20.00
(24)	Mark Mulder/100	30.00
(25)	Xavier Nady/100	10.00
(26)	Roy Oswalt/100	15.00
(27)	Aramis Ramirez/100	20.00
(28)	Tim Redding/100	15.00
(29)	Cal Ripken Jr./25	225.00
(30)	Phil Rizzuto/25	50.00
(31)	Ron Santo/100	40.00
(32)	Mike Schmidt/75	75.00
(33)	Bud Smith/100	10.00
(34)	Miguel Tejada/100	30.00
(35)	Javier Vazquez/100	15.00
(36)	Billy Williams/100	20.00
(37)	Barry Zito/100	30.00

Game Collection

		NM/M
Common Player:		5.00
Inserted 1:62 R		
SP's Indicated		
AB B	Adrian Beltre/Bat	5.00
AD BG	Adam Dunn/Btg Glv/25	25.00
AG B	Andres Galarraga/Bat	5.00
AJ B	Andruw Jones/Bat/300	8.00
BG B	Brian Giles/Bat	5.00
BH B	Bobby Higginson/Bat	5.00
BS H	Ben Sheets/Hat/25	35.00
BW S	Bernie Williams/Shoe/25	30.00
BZ FG	Barry Zito/Fldg Glv/25	25.00
CB B	Carlos Beltran/Bat	8.00
CBl B	Craig Biggio/Bat	6.00
CF B	Carlton Fisk/Bat	10.00
CK B	Chuck Knoblauch/Bat	5.00
CP S	Corey Patterson/Shoe/25	25.00
EM B	Eddie Murray/Bat/250	15.00
GJ P	Geoff Jenkins/Pants	5.00
IR BG	Ivan Rodriguez/Btg Glv/25	30.00
JB B	Jeff Bagwell/Bat/100	15.00
JD H	Johnny Damon/Hat/25	25.00
JE B	Juan Encarnacion/Bat	5.00
JG B	Juan Gonzalez/Bat	8.00
KL B	Kenny Lofton/Bat	5.00
KW S	Kerry Wood/Shoe/25	40.00
LB BG	Lance Berkman/Btg Glv/25	25.00
LW B	Larry Walker/Bat/50	15.00
MB BG	Marlon Byrd/Btg Glv/25	20.00
MG B	Mark Grace/Bat/200	8.00
MM FG	Mike Mussina/Fldg Glv/25	55.00
MO B	Magglio Ordonez/Bat/150	6.00
MP B	Mike Piazza/Bat/100	15.00
PB B	Pat Burrell/Bat/100	15.00
RA B	Roberto Alomar/Bat	8.00
RD B	Ray Durham/Bat	5.00
RG B	Rusty Greer/Bat	5.00
RJ FG	Randy Johnson/Fldg Glv	80.00
RP B	Rafael Palmeiro/Bat	10.00
RP BG	Rafael Palmeiro/Btg Glv/25)	30.00
RV B	Robin Ventura/Bat	5.00
SC B	Sean Casey/Bat	5.00
SR B	Scott Rolen/Bat/250	15.00
SS H	Shannon Stewart/Hat/25	20.00
TC B	Tony Clark/Bat	5.00
TG BG	Tony Gwynn/Btg Glv/25	90.00
TH B	Todd Helton/Bat	10.00
TN B	Trot Nixon/Bat	5.00
WB B	Wade Boggs/Bat	5.00

Gold Leaf Rookies

		NM/M
Complete Set (10):		20.00
Common Player:		2.00
Inserted 1:24		
1	Josh Beckett	4.00
2	Marlon Byrd	2.00
3	Dennis Tankersley	2.00
4	Jason Lane	2.00
5	Dewon Brazelton	2.00
6	Mark Prior	4.00
7	Bill Hall	2.00
8	Angel Berroa	2.00
9	Mark Teixeira	4.00
10	John Buck	2.00

Heading for the Hall Autographs

		NM/M
Common Player:		25.00
Production 50 each.		
1	Greg Maddux	125.00
2	Ozzie Smith	100.00
3	Andre Dawson	40.00
4	Dennis Eckersley	45.00
5	Roberto Alomar	25.00

#	Player	Price
2	Mike Piazza	8.00
3	Alex Rodriguez	10.00
4	Chipper Jones	6.00
5	Jeff Bagwell	4.00
6	Carlos Delgado	2.00
7	Shawn Green	2.00
8	Ken Griffey Jr.	8.00
9	Rafael Palmeiro	3.00
10	Vladimir Guerrero	4.00

Heading for the Hall

#	Player	Price
6	Cal Ripken Jr.	200.00
7	Roger Clemens	150.00
8	Tony Gwynn	100.00
9	Alex Rodriguez	150.00
10	Jeff Bagwell	40.00

League of Nations

		NM/M
Complete Set (10):		20.00
Common Player:		2.00
Inserted 1:60		
1	Ichiro Suzuki	8.00
2	Tsuyoshi Shinjo	2.00
3	Chan Ho Park	2.00
4	Larry Walker	2.00
5	Andruw Jones	4.00
6	Hideo Nomo	4.00
7	Byung-Hyun Kim	2.00
8	Sun-Woo Kim	2.00
9	Orlando Hernandez	2.00
10	Luke Prokopec	2.00

Retired Numbers

#'d to jersey number.
No Pricing

Rookie Reprints

		NM/M
Complete Set (6):		35.00
Common Player:		3.00
#'d to year of issue		
1	Roger Clemens/1,985	10.00
2	Kirby Puckett/1,985	9.00
3	Andres Galarraga/1,986	3.00
4	Fred McGriff/1,986	3.00
5	Sammy Sosa/1,990	8.00
6	Frank Thomas/1,990	8.00

Shirt Off My Back

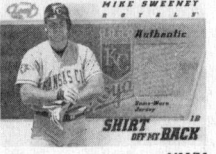

		NM/M
Common Player:		5.00
Inserted 1:29		
Patch Variations:		2-4X
RA	Roberto Alomar	8.00
JB	Jeff Bagwell/SP	20.00
MB	Michael Barrett	5.00
CB	Carlos Beltran	15.00
LB	Lance Berkman	5.00
GB	George Brett/SP	50.00
KB	Kevin Brown	5.00
MB	Mark Buehrle	5.00
AB	A.J. Burnett	5.00
JBU	Jeromy Burnitz	5.00
CD	Carlos Delgado	8.00
RD	Ryan Dempster	5.00
DE	Darin Erstad/SP	15.00
CF	Cliff Floyd	5.00
FG	Freddy Garcia/SP	8.00
NG	Nomar Garciaparra/SP	40.00
TGL	Troy Glaus/SP	20.00
TGL	Tom Glavine	8.00
LG	Luis Gonzalez	5.00
TG	Tony Gwynn	25.00
MH	Mike Hampton	5.00
TH	Todd Helton	20.00
THU	Tim Hudson	5.00
BJA	Bo Jackson/SP	25.00
RJ	Randy Johnson	20.00
CJ	Chipper Jones/SP	30.00
AK	Al Kaline/SP	50.00
EK	Eric Karros	5.00
BL	Barry Larkin	5.00
CL	Carlos Lee	5.00
JL	Javy Lopez	5.00
GM	Greg Maddux/SP	30.00
EM	Edgar Martinez/SP	8.00
PM	Pedro Martinez/SP	

Code	Player	Price
DM	Don Mattingly/SP	50.00
KM	Kevin Millwood	5.00
HN	Hideo Nomo/SP	25.00
JO	John Olerud	5.00
MO	Magglio Ordonez	5.00
RP	Rafael Palmeiro	10.00
CHP	Chan Ho Park/SP	8.00
TP	Troy Percival	5.00
AP	Andy Pettitte/SP	12.00
MP	Mike Piazza	30.00
KP	Kirby Puckett	25.00
BR	Brad Radke	5.00
MR	Manny Ramirez	5.00
CR	Cal Ripken Jr./SP/50	100.00
AR	Alex Rodriguez	35.00
SR	Scott Rolen/SP	15.00
KS	Kazuhiro Sasaki/SP	8.00
CS	Curt Schilling/SP	15.00
RS	Richie Sexson	5.00
TS	Tsuyoshi Shinjo/SP	8.00
JS	John Smoltz	5.00
MS	Mike Sweeney	5.00
MT	Miguel Tejada	6.00
LW	Larry Walker/SP	8.00
MW	Matt Williams	5.00
DW	Dave Winfield/SP	20.00

2002 Leaf Certified Samples

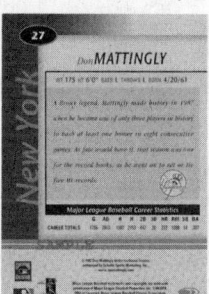

Each October 2002 issue of Beckett Baseball Card Monthly included a sample Leaf Certified card rubber-cemented inside. The cards differ from the issued version only in the appearance on back of a (usually) silver-foil "SAMPLE" notation. Some cards were produced with the back overprint in gold foil in much more limited quantities. The number of different players' cards involved in the promotion is unknown.

	NM/M
Common Player:	.10
Stars:	1.5X
Gold:	20X

2002 Leaf Certified

	NM/M
Complete Set (200):	—
Common Player:	.50
Common (151-200):	5.00
Production 500	
Pack (5):	6.00
Box (16):	75.00
1 Alex Rodriguez	4.00
2 Luis Gonzalez	.65
3 Javier Vazquez	.50
4 Juan Uribe	.50
5 Ben Sheets	.50
6 George Brett	4.00
7 Magglio Ordonez	.50
8 Randy Johnson	1.00
9 Joe Kennedy	.50
10 Richie Sexson	.50
11 Larry Walker	.50
12 Lance Berkman	.50
13 Jose Cruz Jr.	.50
14 Doug Davis	.50
15 Cliff Floyd	.50
16 Ryan Klesko	.50
17 Troy Glaus	1.00
18 Robert Person	.50
19 Bartolo Colon	.50
20 Adam Dunn	.75
21 Kevin Brown	.50
22 John Smoltz	.50
23 Edgar Martinez	.50
24 Eric Karros	.50
25 Tony Gwynn	2.00
26 Mark Mulder	.50
27 Don Mattingly	4.00
28 Brandon Duckworth	.50
29 C.C. Sabathia	.50
30 Nomar Garciaparra	3.00
31 Adam Johnson	.50
32 Miguel Tejada	.65
33 Ryne Sandberg	2.00
34 Roger Clemens	2.50
35 Edgardo Alfonzo	.50
36 Jason Jennings	.50
37 Todd Helton	1.00
38 Nolan Ryan	5.00
39 Paul LoDuca	.50
40 Cal Ripken Jr.	5.00
41 Terrence Long	.50
42 Mike Sweeney	.50
43 Carlos Lee	.50
44 Ben Grieve	.50
45 Tony Armas Jr.	.50
46 Joe Mays	.50
47 Jeff Kent	.50
48 Andy Pettitte	.65
49 Kirby Puckett	2.00
50 Aramis Ramirez	.50
51 Tim Redding	.50
52 Freddy Garcia	.50
53 Javy Lopez	.50
54 Mike Schmidt	4.00
55 Wade Miller	.50
56 Ramon Ortiz	.50
57 Ray Durham	.50
58 J.D. Drew	.75
59 Bret Boone	.50
60 Mark Buehrle	.50
61 Geoff Jenkins	.50
62 Greg Maddux	2.00
63 Mark Grace	.65
64 Toby Hall	.50
65 A.J. Burnett	.50
66 Bernie Williams	.65
67 Roy Oswalt	.65
68 Shannon Stewart	.50
69 Barry Zito	.65
70 Juan Pierre	.50
71 Preston Wilson	.50
72 Rafael Furcal	.50
73 Sean Casey	.65
74 John Olerud	.50
75 Paul Konerko	.75
76 Vernon Wells	.50
77 Juan Gonzalez	1.00
78 Ellis Burks	.50
79 Jim Edmonds	.75
80 Robert Fick	.50
81 Michael Cuddyer	.50
82 Tim Hudson	.65
83 Phil Nevin	.50
84 Curt Schilling	.75
85 Jeff Bagwell	1.00
86 Raul Mondesi	.50
87 Bud Smith	.50
88 Omar Vizquel	.50
89 Vladimir Guerrero	1.00
90 Garret Anderson	.50
91 Mike Piazza	3.00
92 Josh Beckett	.65
93 Carlos Delgado	1.00
94 Kazuhiro Sasaki	.50
95 Chipper Jones	2.00
96 Jacque Jones	.50
97 Pedro J. Martinez	1.00
98 Marcus Giles	.50
99 Craig Biggio	.50
100 Orlando Cabrera	.50
101 Al Leiter	.50
102 Michael Barrett	.50
103 Hideo Nomo	1.00
104 Mike Mussina	.75
105 Jeremy Giambi	.50
106 Cristian Guzman	.50
107 Frank Thomas	1.00
108 Carlos Beltran	.50
109 Jorge Posada	.65
110 Roberto Alomar	.65
111 Bobby Abreu	.50
112 Robin Ventura	.50
113 Pat Burrell	.50
114 Kenny Lofton	.50
115 Adrian Beltre	.50
116 Gary Sheffield	.75
117 Jermaine Dye	.50
118 Manny Ramirez	1.00
119 Brian Giles	.50
120 Tsuyoshi Shinjo	.50
121 Rafael Palmeiro	.85
122 Mo Vaughn	.50
123 Kerry Wood	.75
124 Moises Alou	.50
125 Rickey Henderson	1.00
126 Corey Patterson	.50
127 Jim Thome	1.00
128 Richard Hidalgo	.50
129 Darin Erstad	.50
130 Johnny Damon	.75
131 Juan Encarnacion	.50
132 Scott Rolen	1.00
133 Tom Glavine	.75
134 Ivan Rodriguez	.85
135 Jay Gibbons	.50
136 Trot Nixon	.50
137 Nick Neugebauer	.50
138 Barry Larkin	.50
139 Andruw Jones	1.00
140 Shawn Green	.75
141 Jose Vidro	.50
142 Derek Jeter	5.00
143 Ichiro Suzuki	3.00
144 Ken Griffey Jr.	3.00
145 Barry Bonds	5.00
146 Albert Pujols	4.00
147 Sammy Sosa	3.00
148 Jason Giambi	.75
149 Alfonso Soriano	.75
150 Drew Henson/Bat	8.00
151 Luis Garcia/Bat	5.00
152 Geronimo Gil/Jsy	5.00
153 Corky Miller/Jsy	5.00
154 Mike Rivera/Bat	5.00
155 Mark Ellis/Jsy	5.00
156 Josh Pearce/Bat	5.00
157 Ryan Ludwick/Bat	5.00
158 So Taguchi/Bat RC	12.00
159 Cody Ransom/Jsy	5.00
160 Jeff Deardorff/Bat RC	5.00
161 Franklyn German/Bat RC	5.00
162 Ed Rogers/Jsy	5.00
163 Eric Cyr/Jsy RC	5.00
164 Victor Alvarez/Jsy RC	15.00
165 Victor Martinez/Jsy	15.00
166 Brandon Berger/Jsy	5.00
167 Juan Diaz/Jsy	5.00
168 Kevin Frederick/Jsy RC	5.00
169 Earl Snyder/Bat RC	5.00
170 Morgan Ensberg/Bat	5.00
171 Ryan Jamison/Jsy RC	5.00
172 Rodrigo Rosario/Jsy RC	5.00
173 Willie Harris/Jsy	5.00
174 Ramon Vazquez/Bat	5.00
175 Kazuhisa Ishii/Bat RC	12.00
176 Hank Blalock/Jsy	10.00
177 Mark Prior/Bat	8.00
178 Dewon Brazelton/Jsy	5.00
179 Doug DeVore/Jsy RC	5.00
180 Jorge Padilla/Bat	5.00
181 Mark Teixeira/Bat	10.00
182 Orlando Hudson/Bat	5.00
183 John Buck/Jsy	5.00
184 Erik Bedard/Jsy	5.00
185 Allan Simpson/Jsy RC	5.00
186 Travis Hafner/Jsy	10.00
187 Jason Lane/Jsy	5.00
188 Marlon Byrd/Jsy	5.00
189 Joe Thurston/Jsy	5.00
190 Brandon Backe/Jsy RC	5.00
191 Josh Phelps/Jsy	5.00
192 Bill Hall/Bat	5.00
193 Chris Snelling/Bat RC	8.00
194 Austin Kearns/Bat	8.00
195 Antonio Perez/Bat	5.00
196 Angel Berroa/Bat	6.00
197 Anderson Machado/Jsy RC	5.00
198 Alfredo Amezaga/Jsy	5.00
199 Eric Hinske/Bat	8.00

Mirror Red

	NM/M
Common (1-200):	5.00
Cards (151-200):	.5-1X base
Production 150 Sets	
Mirror Blues (1-200):	.5-1.5X
Production 75 Sets	
Mirror Golds not priced.	
Production 25 Sets	
Mirror Emerald five sets produced.	
Mirror Black one set produced.	
1 Alex Rodriguez/Jsy	25.00
2 Luis Gonzalez/Jsy	5.00
3 Javier Vazquez/Bat	5.00
4 Juan Uribe/Jsy	5.00
5 Ben Sheets/Jsy	5.00
6 George Brett/Jsy	40.00
7 Magglio Ordonez/Jsy	8.00
8 Randy Johnson/Jsy	15.00
9 Joe Kennedy/Jsy	5.00
10 Richie Sexson/Jsy	10.00
11 Larry Walker/Jsy	8.00
12 Lance Berkman/Jsy	8.00
13 Jose Cruz Jr./Jsy	5.00
14 Doug Davis/Jsy	5.00
15 Cliff Floyd/Jsy	5.00
16 Ryan Klesko/Jsy	5.00
17 Troy Glaus/Jsy	10.00
18 Robert Person/Bat	5.00
19 Bartolo Colon/Jsy	5.00
20 Adam Dunn/Jsy	15.00
21 Kevin Brown/Jsy	8.00
22 John Smoltz/Jsy	8.00
23 Edgar Martinez/Jsy	8.00
24 Eric Karros/Jsy	5.00
25 Tony Gwynn/Jsy	20.00
26 Mark Mulder/Jsy	8.00
27 Don Mattingly/Jsy	40.00
28 Brandon Duckworth/Jsy	5.00
29 C.C. Sabathia/Jsy	5.00
30 Nomar Garciaparra/Jsy	20.00
31 Adam Johnson/Jsy	5.00
32 Miguel Tejada/Jsy	8.00
33 Ryne Sandberg/Jsy	40.00
34 Roger Clemens/Jsy	25.00
35 Edgardo Alfonzo/Jsy	5.00
36 Jason Jennings/Jsy	5.00
37 Todd Helton/Jsy	10.00
38 Nolan Ryan/Jsy	60.00
39 Paul LoDuca/Jsy	5.00
40 Cal Ripken Jr/Jsy	55.00
41 Terrence Long/Jsy	5.00
42 Mike Sweeney/Jsy	5.00
43 Carlos Lee/Jsy	5.00
44 Ben Grieve/Jsy	5.00
45 Tony Armas Jr./Jsy	5.00
46 Joe Mays/Jsy	5.00
47 Jeff Kent/Jsy	8.00
48 Andy Pettitte/Jsy	8.00
49 Kirby Puckett/Jsy	15.00
50 Aramis Ramirez/Jsy	8.00
51 Tim Redding/Jsy	5.00
52 Freddy Garcia/Jsy	5.00
53 Javy Lopez/Jsy	6.00
54 Mike Schmidt/Jsy	35.00
55 Wade Miller/Jsy	5.00
56 Ramon Ortiz/Jsy	5.00
57 Ray Durham/Jsy	5.00
58 J.D. Drew/Jsy	5.00
59 Bret Boone/Jsy	5.00
60 Mark Buehrle/Jsy	5.00
61 Geoff Jenkins/Jsy	5.00
62 Greg Maddux/Jsy	20.00
63 Mark Grace/Jsy	10.00
64 Toby Hall/Jsy	5.00
65 A.J. Burnett/Jsy	5.00
66 Bernie Williams/Jsy	8.00
67 Roy Oswalt/Jsy	5.00
68 Shannon Stewart/Jsy	5.00
69 Barry Zito/Jsy	8.00
70 Juan Pierre/Jsy	5.00
71 Preston Wilson/Jsy	5.00
72 Rafael Furcal/Jsy	5.00
73 Sean Casey/Jsy	5.00
74 John Olerud/Jsy	5.00
75 Paul Konerko/Jsy	5.00
76 Vernon Wells/Jsy	5.00
77 Juan Gonzalez/Jsy	8.00
78 Ellis Burks/Jsy	5.00
79 Jim Edmonds/Jsy	8.00
80 Robert Fick/Jsy	5.00
81 Michael Cuddyer/Jsy	5.00
82 Tim Hudson/Jsy	5.00
83 Phil Nevin/Jsy	5.00
84 Curt Schilling/Jsy	8.00
85 Juan Cruz/Jsy	5.00
86 Jeff Bagwell/Jsy	10.00
87 Raul Mondesi/Jsy	5.00
88 Bud Smith/Jsy	5.00
89 Omar Vizquel/Jsy	5.00
90 Vladimir Guerrero/Jsy	20.00
91 Garret Anderson/Jsy	8.00
92 Mike Piazza/Jsy	15.00
93 Josh Beckett/Jsy	8.00
94 Carlos Delgado/Jsy	8.00
95 Kazuhiro Sasaki/Jsy	5.00
96 Chipper Jones/Jsy	10.00
97 Jacque Jones/Jsy	5.00
98 Pedro Martinez/Jsy	15.00
99 Marcus Giles/Jsy	5.00
100 Craig Biggio/Jsy	6.00
101 Orlando Cabrera/Jsy	5.00
102 Al Leiter/Jsy	5.00
103 Michael Barrett/Jsy	5.00
104 Hideo Nomo/Jsy	15.00
105 Mike Mussina/Jsy	12.00
106 Jeremy Giambi/Jsy	5.00
107 Cristian Guzman/Bat	5.00
108 Frank Thomas/Jsy	10.00
109 Carlos Beltran/Bat	8.00
110 Jorge Posada/Bat	5.00
111 Roberto Alomar/Bat	12.00
112 Bobby Abreu/Bat	5.00
113 Robin Ventura/Bat	10.00
114 Pat Burrell/Bat	18.00
115 Kenny Lofton/Bat	5.00
116 Adrian Beltre/Bat	8.00
117 Gary Sheffield/Bat	5.00
118 Jermaine Dye/Bat	5.00
119 Brian Giles/Bat	5.00
120 Manny Ramirez/Bat	8.00
121 Tsuyoshi Shinjo/Jsy	5.00
122 Rafael Palmeiro/Jsy	10.00
123 Mo Vaughn/Bat	5.00
124 Kerry Wood/Bat	15.00
125 Moises Alou/Bat	5.00
126 Rickey Henderson/Bat	15.00
127 Corey Patterson/Bat	8.00
128 Jim Thome/Bat	15.00
129 Richard Hidalgo/Bat	5.00
130 Darin Erstad/Jsy	5.00
131 Johnny Damon/Bat	5.00
132 Juan Encarnacion/Bat	5.00
133 Scott Rolen/Bat	10.00
134 Tom Glavine/Bat	10.00
135 Ivan Rodriguez/Bat	10.00
136 Jay Gibbons/Bat	5.00
137 Trot Nixon/Bat	5.00
138 Nick Neugebauer/Bat	5.00
139 Barry Larkin/Jsy	10.00
140 Andruw Jones/Bat	8.00
141 Shawn Green/Bat	8.00
142 Jose Vidro/Jsy	5.00
143 Derek Jeter/Base	25.00
144 Ichiro Suzuki/Base	20.00
145 Ken Griffey Jr./Base	15.00
146 Barry Bonds/Base	20.00
147 Albert Pujols/Base	15.00
148 Sammy Sosa/Base	15.00
149 Jason Giambi/Base	8.00
150 Alfonso Soriano/Jsy	10.00
151 Drew Henson/Bat	5.00
152 Luis Garcia/Bat	5.00
153 Geronimo Gil/Jsy	5.00
154 Corky Miller/Jsy	5.00
155 Mike Rivera/Jsy	5.00
156 Mark Ellis/Jsy	5.00
157 Josh Pearce/Bat	5.00
158 Ryan Ludwick/Bat	5.00
159 So Taguchi/Bat	12.00
160 Cody Ransom/Jsy	5.00
161 Jeff Deardorff/Bat	5.00
162 Franklyn German/Bat	5.00
163 Ed Rogers/Jsy	5.00
164 Eric Cyr/Jsy	5.00
165 Victor Alvarez/Jsy	5.00
166 Victor Martinez/Jsy	10.00
167 Brandon Berger/Jsy	5.00
168 Juan Diaz/Jsy	5.00
169 Kevin Frederick/Jsy	5.00
170 Earl Snyder/Bat	5.00
171 Morgan Ensberg/Bat	5.00
172 Ryan Jamison/Jsy	5.00
173 Rodrigo Rosario/Jsy	5.00
174 Willie Harris/Bat	5.00
175 Ramon Vazquez/Bat	5.00
176 Kazuhisa Ishii/Bat	15.00
177 Hank Blalock/Jsy	10.00
178 Mark Prior/Bat	10.00
179 Dewon Brazelton/Jsy	5.00
180 Doug DeVore/Jsy	5.00
181 Jorge Padilla/Bat	5.00
182 Mark Teixeira/Jsy	10.00
183 Orlando Hudson/Bat	5.00
184 John Buck/Jsy	5.00
185 Erik Bedard/Jsy	5.00
186 Allan Simpson/Jsy	5.00
187 Travis Hafner/Jsy	5.00
188 Jason Lane/Jsy	5.00
189 Marlon Byrd/Jsy	5.00
190 Joe Thurston/Jsy	5.00
191 Brandon Backe/Jsy	5.00
192 Josh Phelps/Jsy	5.00
193 Bill Hall/Jsy	5.00
194 Chris Snelling/Bat	5.00
195 Austin Kearns/Jsy	8.00
196 Antonio Perez/Bat	5.00
197 Angel Berroa/Bat	6.00
198 Anderson Machado/Jsy	5.00
199 Alfredo Amezaga/Jsy	5.00
200 Eric Hinske/Bat	6.00

All Certified Team

	NM/M
Complete Set (25):	75.00
Common Player:	1.50
Inserted 1:17	
Mirror Blues:	2-4X
Production 50 Sets	
Mirror Reds:	1.5-3X
Production 75 Sets	
Golds not priced 25 sets produced.	
1 Ichiro Suzuki	5.00
2 Alex Rodriguez	6.00
3 Sammy Sosa	5.00
4 Jeff Bagwell	3.00
5 Greg Maddux	4.00
6 Todd Helton	3.00
7 Nomar Garciaparra	3.00
8 Ken Griffey Jr.	3.00
9 Roger Clemens	4.50
10 Adam Dunn	2.00
11 Chipper Jones	3.00
12 Hideo Nomo	3.00
13 Lance Berkman	1.50
14 Barry Bonds	8.00
15 Manny Ramirez	3.00
16 Jason Giambi	3.00
17 Rickey Henderson	3.00
18 Randy Johnson	3.00
19 Derek Jeter	8.00
20 Kazuhisa Ishii	1.50
21 Frank Thomas	3.00
22 Mike Piazza	3.00
23 Albert Pujols	6.00
24 Pedro J. Martinez	3.00
25 Vladimir Guerrero	3.00

Certified Skills

	NM/M
Complete Set (20):	65.00
Common Player:	2.00
Inserted 1:17	

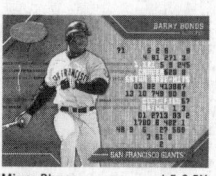

	NM/M
Mirror Blues:	1.5-2.5X
Production 75 Sets	
Mirror Reds:	1-2X
Production 150 Sets	
Mirror Golds not priced 25 sets.	
1 Barry Bonds	8.00
2 Greg Maddux	4.00
3 Rickey Henderson	2.00
4 Ichiro Suzuki	2.00
5 Pedro J. Martinez	2.00
6 Kazuhisa Ishii	1.50
7 Alex Rodriguez	6.00
8 Mike Piazza	3.00
9 Sammy Sosa	5.00
10 Derek Jeter	8.00
11 Albert Pujols	6.00
12 Roger Clemens	4.50
13 Mark Prior	1.50
14 Chipper Jones	3.00
15 Ken Griffey Jr.	2.00
16 Frank Thomas	2.00
17 Randy Johnson	2.00
18 Vladimir Guerrero	2.00
19 Nomar Garciaparra	5.00
20 Jeff Bagwell	2.00

Fabric of the Game

	NM/M
Common Player:	
1 Bobby Doerr/37	20.00
2 Ozzie Smith/78	40.00
3 Pee Wee Reese/40	35.00
4 Tommy Lasorda/80	8.00
4 Tommy Lasorda/54	15.00
4 Tommy Lasorda/50	15.00
5 Red Schoendienst/45	20.00
7 Harmon Killebrew/54	35.00
8 Roger Maris A's/57	75.00
10 Mel Ott/26	75.00
11 Paul Molitor/100	20.00
11 Paul Molitor/78	20.00
11 Paul Molitor/50	30.00
12 Duke Snider/47	25.00
13 Brooks Robinson/55	40.00
14 George Brett/40	75.00
14 George Brett/73	50.00
15 Johnny Bench/80	20.00
15 Johnny Bench/67	30.00
15 Johnny Bench/50	30.00
16 Lou Boudreau/38	20.00
17 Stan Musial/41	60.00
18 Al Kaline/53	30.00
19 Steve Garvey/100	8.00
19 Steve Garvey/69	15.00
19 Steve Garvey/45	15.00
20 Nomar Garciaparra/100	25.00
20 Nomar Garciaparra/96	25.00
20 Nomar Garciaparra/50	35.00
21 Joe Morgan/80	15.00
21 Joe Morgan/63	20.00
21 Joe Morgan/50	20.00
22 Willie Stargell/62	25.00
23 Andre Dawson/80	15.00
23 Andre Dawson/76	15.00
23 Andre Dawson/50	20.00
24 Gary Carter/100	10.00
24 Gary Carter/74	20.00
24 Gary Carter/50	20.00
27 Reggie Jackson A's/67	30.00
27 Phil Rizzuto/41	30.00
28 Luis Aparicio/56	20.00
29 Robin Yount/80	30.00
29 Robin Yount/74	30.00
29 Robin Yount/50	40.00
30 Tony Gwynn/100	20.00
30 Tony Gwynn/82	20.00
30 Tony Gwynn/50	30.00
31 Ernie Banks/53	40.00
32 Joe Torre/55	15.00
32 Joe Torre/60	15.00
33 Bo Jackson/100	20.00
33 Bo Jackson/86	25.00
33 Bo Jackson/50	50.00
34 Alfonso Soriano/80	15.00
34 Alfonso Soriano/99	15.00
34 Alfonso Soriano/50	20.00
35 Cal Ripken Jr./80	60.00
35 Cal Ripken Jr./81	60.00
35 Cal Ripken Jr./50	60.00
36 Miguel Tejada/100	10.00
36 Miguel Tejada/97	10.00
36 Miguel Tejada/50	20.00
37 Alex Rodriguez M's/100	20.00
37 Alex Rodriguez M's/94	20.00
37 Alex Rodriguez M's/50	35.00
38 Mike Schmidt/80	40.00
38 Mike Schmidt/72	40.00

#	Player	Price
38	Mike Schmidt/50	50.00
39	Lou Brock/61	25.00
40	Don Sutton/80	8.00
40	Don Sutton/66	10.00
40	Don Sutton/50	15.00
41	Roberto Clemente/55	125.00
42	Jim Palmer/65	20.00
43	Don Mattingly/40	75.00
43	Don Mattingly/82	50.00
44	Ryne Sandberg/40	60.00
44	Ryne Sandberg/81	40.00
45	Early Wynn/39	20.00
46	Mike Piazza Dodgers/100	20.00
46	Mike Piazza Dodgers/92	20.00
46	Mike Piazza Dodgers/31	25.00
46	Mike Piazza Dodgers/50	25.00
47	Wade Boggs/100	15.00
47	Wade Boggs/82	15.00
47	Wade Boggs/26	40.00
47	Wade Boggs/45	30.00
48	Jim "Catfish" Hunter/65	25.00
48	Jim "Catfish" Hunter/27	40.00
49	Juan Marichal/60	20.00
49	Juan Marichal/27	40.00
50	Carlton Fisk Red Sox/80	25.00
50	Carlton Fisk Red Sox/69	40.00
50	Carlton Fisk Red Sox/27	50.00
50	Carlton Fisk Red Sox/50	30.00
51	Curt Schilling/100	15.00
51	Curt Schilling/88	15.00
51	Curt Schilling/38	25.00
51	Curt Schilling/50	20.00
52	Rod Carew Angels/80	15.00
52	Rod Carew Angels/67	25.00
52	Rod Carew Angels/50	20.00
53	Rod Carew Twins/67	25.00
54	Joe Carter/100	8.00
54	Joe Carter/83	8.00
54	Joe Carter/29	15.00
54	Joe Carter/50	10.00
55	Nolan Ryan Angels/66	60.00
56	Orlando Cepeda/80	8.00
56	Orlando Cepeda/55	10.00
56	Orlando Cepeda/50	15.00
57	Dave Winfield/80	15.00
57	Dave Winfield/73	20.00
57	Dave Winfield/31	30.00
57	Dave Winfield/50	20.00
58	Hoyt Wilhelm/80	8.00
58	Hoyt Wilhelm/31	15.00
58	Hoyt Wilhelm/50	10.00
59	Steve Carlton/80	15.00
59	Steve Carlton/65	20.00
59	Steve Carlton/32	30.00
59	Steve Carlton/50	20.00
60	Eddie Murray/100	15.00
60	Eddie Murray/77	15.00
60	Eddie Murray/33	30.00
60	Eddie Murray/50	20.00
61	Nolan Ryan Rangers/40	75.00
61	Nolan Ryan Rangers/66	60.00
61	Nolan Ryan Rangers/34	75.00
62	Nolan Ryan Astros/40	75.00
62	Nolan Ryan Astros/66	60.00
62	Nolan Ryan Astros/34	75.00
63	Kirby Puckett/40	40.00
63	Kirby Puckett/84	20.00
63	Kirby Puckett/34	40.00
64	Yogi Berra/46	40.00
64	Yogi Berra/35	40.00
65	Phil Niekro/80	8.00
65	Phil Niekro/64	10.00
65	Phil Niekro/35	10.00
65	Phil Niekro/50	10.00
66	Gaylord Perry/80	8.00
66	Gaylord Perry/62	10.00
66	Gaylord Perry/36	15.00
66	Gaylord Perry/50	10.00
67	Pedro Martinez Expos/100	15.00
67	Pedro Martinez Expos/92	15.00
67	Pedro Martinez Expos/45	25.00
67	Pedro Martinez Expos/50	15.00
68	Alex Rodriguez Rgr/100	20.00
68	Alex Rodriguez Rgr/94	20.00
68	Alex Rodriguez Rgr/50	30.00
69	Dave Parker/100	8.00
69	Dave Parker/73	10.00
69	Dave Parker/39	15.00
69	Dave Parker/50	10.00
70	Darin Erstad/100	8.00
70	Darin Erstad/96	8.00
70	Darin Erstad/50	15.00
71	Eddie Matthews/52	30.00
71	Eddie Matthews/41	30.00
72	Tom Seaver Mets/67	30.00
72	Tom Seaver Mets/41	40.00
73	Tom Seaver Reds/67	30.00
73	Tom Seaver Reds/41	40.00
74	Jackie Robinson/47	100.00
74	Jackie Robinson/42	100.00
75	Randy Johnson M's/80	15.00
75	Randy Johnson M's/88	15.00
75	Randy Johnson M's/31	25.00
75	Randy Johnson M's/50	25.00
76	Reggie Jackson Yanks/57	30.00
76	Reggie Jackson Yanks/44	40.00
77	Reggie Jackson Angels/80	20.00

#	Player	Price
77	Reggie Jackson Angels/67	30.00
77	Reggie Jackson Angels/44	40.00
77	Reggie Jackson Angels/50	40.00
78	Willie McCovey/80	10.00
78	Willie McCovey/59	15.00
78	Willie McCovey/44	20.00
78	Willie McCovey/50	15.00
79	Eric Davis/100	5.00
79	Eric Davis/84	5.00
79	Eric Davis/34	10.00
79	Eric Davis/50	8.00
80	Carlos Delgado/95	6.00
80	Carlos Delgado/93	6.00
81	Dale Murphy/100	20.00
81	Dale Murphy/76	20.00
81	Dale Murphy/50	30.00
82	Brian Giles/100	5.00
82	Brian Giles/95	5.00
82	Brian Giles/50	8.00
83	Kazuhiro Sasaki/100	8.00
83	Kazuhiro Sasaki/100	5.00
83	Kazuhiro Sasaki/50	10.00
84	Phil Nevin/100	5.00
84	Phil Nevin/95	5.00
84	Phil Nevin/50	8.00
85	Frank Thomas/80	15.00
85	Frank Thomas/90	15.00
85	Frank Thomas/35	25.00
85	Frank Thomas/50	15.00
86	Raul Mondesi/100	5.00
86	Raul Mondesi/93	5.00
86	Raul Mondesi/43	8.00
86	Raul Mondesi/50	8.00
87	Don Drysdale/56	25.00
87	Don Drysdale/53	25.00
88	Gary Sheffield/100	6.00
88	Gary Sheffield/88	6.00
88	Gary Sheffield/50	10.00
89	Andy Pettitte/100	12.00
89	Andy Pettitte/95	15.00
89	Andy Pettitte/46	30.00
89	Andy Pettitte/50	20.00
90	Lance Berkman/45	20.00
90	Lance Berkman/99	10.00
91	Paul LoDuca/100	5.00
91	Paul LoDuca/98	5.00
91	Paul LoDuca/50	8.00
92	Kevin Brown/86	5.00
92	Kevin Brown/27	15.00
93	Jim Thome/100	15.00
93	Jim Thome/91	15.00
93	Jim Thome/50	25.00
94	Mike Sweeney/100	5.00
94	Mike Sweeney/95	15.00
94	Mike Sweeney/29	15.00
94	Mike Sweeney/50	10.00
95	Pedro J. Martinez Red Sox/100	15.00
95	Pedro J. Martinez Red Sox/92	15.00
95	Pedro J. Martinez Red Sox/45	25.00
95	Pedro J. Martinez Red Sox/50	25.00
96	Cliff Floyd/100	5.00
96	Cliff Floyd/93	5.00
96	Cliff Floyd/30	15.00
96	Cliff Floyd/50	10.00
97	Larry Walker/100	8.00
97	Larry Walker/89	8.00
97	Larry Walker/33	30.00
97	Larry Walker/50	10.00
98	Ivan Rodriguez/100	10.00
98	Ivan Rodriguez/91	10.00
98	Ivan Rodriguez/50	20.00
99	Aramis Ramirez/100	8.00
99	Aramis Ramirez/98	8.00
99	Aramis Ramirez/50	12.00
100	Roberto Alomar/100	10.00
100	Roberto Alomar/88	10.00
100	Roberto Alomar/50	15.00
101	Ben Sheets/100	8.00
101	Ben Sheets/101	8.00
101	Ben Sheets/50	15.00
102	Adam Dunn/101	20.00
102	Adam Dunn/39	40.00
103	Hideo Nomo/100	30.00
104	C.C. Sabathia/50	10.00
104	C.C. Sabathia/101	5.00
104	C.C. Sabathia/52	10.00
104	C.C. Sabathia/50	10.00
105	Rickey Henderson A's/100	20.00
105	Rickey Henderson A's/79	20.00
105	Rickey Henderson A's/30	50.00
105	Rickey Henderson A's/50	30.00
106	Carlton Fisk White Sox/80	20.00
106	Carlton Fisk White Sox/69	30.00
106	Carlton Fisk White Sox/72	15.00
106	Carlton Fisk White Sox/50	30.00
107	Chan Ho Park/100	5.00
107	Chan Ho Park/94	5.00
107	Chan Ho Park/61	8.00
107	Chan Ho Park/50	8.00
108	Mike Mussina/100	15.00
108	Mike Mussina/35	50.00
108	Mike Mussina/50	30.00

#	Player	Price
109	Mark Mulder/100	8.00
109	Mark Mulder/101	5.00
109	Mark Mulder/20	20.00
109	Mark Mulder/35	20.00
110	Tsuyoshi Shinjo/100	5.00
110	Tsuyoshi Shinjo/101	5.00
110	Tsuyoshi Shinjo/30	15.00
111	Pat Burrell/100	10.00
111	Pat Burrell/100	10.00
111	Pat Burrell/50	15.00
112	Edgar Martinez/100	10.00
112	Edgar Martinez/87	10.00
112	Edgar Martinez/50	15.00
113	Barry Larkin/100	10.00
113	Barry Larkin/86	10.00
113	Barry Larkin/50	15.00
114	Jeff Kent/100	6.00
114	Jeff Kent/92	6.00
114	Jeff Kent/50	8.00
115	Chipper Jones/100	15.00
115	Chipper Jones/93	15.00
115	Chipper Jones/50	30.00
116	Magglio Ordonez/100	8.00
116	Magglio Ordonez/97	8.00
116	Magglio Ordonez/30	20.00
116	Magglio Ordonez/50	15.00
117	Jim Edmonds/100	8.00
117	Jim Edmonds/93	8.00
117	Jim Edmonds/50	15.00
118	Andruw Jones/100	10.00
118	Andruw Jones/96	10.00
118	Andruw Jones/45	20.00
119	Jose Canseco/100	15.00
119	Jose Canseco/85	15.00
119	Jose Canseco/50	20.00
120	Manny Ramirez/100	15.00
120	Manny Ramirez/93	10.00
120	Manny Ramirez/50	20.00
121	Sean Casey/100	10.00
121	Sean Casey/97	10.00
121	Sean Casey/50	15.00
122	Bret Boone/100	6.00
122	Bret Boone/92	6.00
122	Bret Boone/29	15.00
122	Bret Boone/50	10.00
123	Tim Hudson/100	8.00
123	Tim Hudson/99	8.00
123	Tim Hudson/50	15.00
124	Craig Biggio/100	10.00
124	Craig Biggio/88	10.00
124	Craig Biggio/50	15.00
125	Mike Piazza Mets/100	20.00
125	Mike Piazza Mets/92	20.00
125	Mike Piazza Mets/31	40.00
125	Mike Piazza Mets/51	25.00
126	Jack Morris/100	5.00
126	Jack Morris/77	5.00
126	Jack Morris/47	10.00
127	Roy Oswalt/100	8.00
127	Roy Oswalt/101	8.00
127	Roy Oswalt/39	15.00
127	Roy Oswalt/50	15.00
128	Shawn Green/100	8.00
128	Shawn Green/93	8.00
128	Shawn Green/50	15.00
129	Carlos Beltran/100	8.00
129	Carlos Beltran/98	8.00
129	Carlos Beltran/50	10.00
130	Todd Helton/100	10.00
130	Todd Helton/97	15.00
130	Todd Helton/50	20.00
131	Barry Zito/75	15.00
131	Barry Zito/100	15.00
131	Damian Moss/15	15.00
131	Barry Zito/30	30.00
132	J.D. Drew/100	15.00
132	J.D. Drew/98	15.00
132	J.D. Drew/50	20.00
133	Mark Grace/100	10.00
133	Mark Grace/88	8.00
133	Mark Grace/50	15.00
134	Rickey Henderson Mets/100	20.00
134	Rickey Henderson Mets/79	20.00
134	Rickey Henderson Mets/50	30.00
135	Greg Maddux/100	20.00
135	Greg Maddux/86	20.00
135	Greg Maddux/50	30.00
136	Garret Anderson/100	8.00
136	Garret Anderson/94	8.00
136	Garret Anderson/50	15.00
137	Rafael Palmeiro/100	15.00
137	Rafael Palmeiro/86	15.00
137	Rafael Palmeiro/50	20.00
138	Luis Gonzalez/100	10.00
138	Luis Gonzalez/90	8.00
138	Luis Gonzalez/45	15.00
139	Nick Johnson/100	5.00
139	Nick Johnson/101	5.00
139	Nick Johnson/26	20.00
139	Nick Johnson/50	10.00
140	Vladimir Guerrero/80	15.00
140	Vladimir Guerrero/96	15.00
140	Vladimir Guerrero/50	25.00
141	Mark Buehrle/100	5.00
141	Mark Buehrle/56	5.00
142	Troy Glaus/100	15.00
142	Troy Glaus/98	10.00
142	Troy Glaus/50	25.00
143	Juan Gonzalez/100	10.00
143	Juan Gonzalez/89	10.00
143	Juan Gonzalez/50	15.00
144	Kerry Wood/100	15.00
144	Kerry Wood/98	15.00
144	Kerry Wood/34	40.00
144	Kerry Wood/50	30.00

#	Player	Price
145	Roger Clemens/80	25.00
145	Roger Clemens/84	25.00
145	Roger Clemens/50	40.00
146	Bob Abreu/100	8.00
146	Bob Abreu/96	8.00
146	Bob Abreu/53	15.00
146	Bob Abreu/50	15.00
147	Bernie Williams/95	15.00
147	Bernie Williams/91	10.00
147	Bernie Williams/51	20.00
148	Tom Glavine/100	10.00
148	Tom Glavine/87	10.00
148	Tom Glavine/47	25.00
148	Tom Glavine/50	25.00
149	Jorge Posada/100	10.00
149	Jorge Posada/95	10.00
149	Jorge Posada/50	25.00
150	Randy Johnson D'Backs/80	15.00
150	Randy Johnson D'Backs/88	15.00
150	Randy Johnson D'Backs/51	30.00
150	Randy Johnson D'Backs/50	30.00

2002 Leaf Rookies & Stars Samples

Each December 2002 issue of Beckett Baseball Card Monthly included a sample Leaf R&S card rubber-cemented inside. The cards differ from the issued version only in the appearance on back of a (usually) silver-foil "SAMPLE" notation. Some cards were produced with the back overprint in gold foil in much more limited quantities. The number of different players' cards involved in the promotion is unknown.

	NM/M
Common Player:	.10
Stars:	1.5-2X
Gold:	20X

2002 Leaf Rookies & Stars

MIKE PIAZZA

	NM/M
Complete Set (400):	
Common Player:	.15
Common SP (1-300):	.75
Common (301-400):	.40
Inserted 1:2	
Pack (6):	1.50
Box (24):	30.00
1 Darin Erstad	.25
2 Garret Anderson	.15
3 Troy Glaus	.40
4 David Eckstein	.15
5 Adam Kennedy	.15
6 Kevin Appier	.15
6 Kevin Appier/SP/Mets	.75
6 Kevin Appier/SP/Royals	.75
7 Jarrod Washburn	.15
8 David Segui	.15
9 Jay Gibbons	.15
10 Tony Batista	.15
11 Scott Erickson	.15
12 Jeff Conine	.15
13 Melvin Mora	.15
14 Shea Hillenbrand	.15
15 Manny Ramirez	.65
15 Manny Ramirez/SP/Indians	2.00
16 Pedro J. Martinez	.65

#	Player	Price
16	Pedro J. Martinez SP/Dodgers	2.50
16	Pedro J. Martinez/SP/Expos	2.50
17	Nomar Garciaparra	1.00
18	Rickey Henderson	.65
18	Rickey Henderson/SP/Angels	3.00
18	Rickey Henderson/SP/A's	3.00
18	Rickey Henderson/SP/Blue Jays	3.00
18	Rickey Henderson/SP/M's	3.00
18	Rickey Henderson/SP/Mets	3.00
18	Rickey Henderson/SP/Padres	3.00
18	Rickey Henderson/SP/Yankees	3.00
19	Johnny Damon	.25
19	Johnny Damon/SP/A's	1.00
19	Johnny Damon/SP/Royals	1.00
20	Trot Nixon	.15
21	Derek Lowe	.15
22	Jason Varitek	.15
23	Tim Wakefield	.15
24	Frank Thomas	.65
25	Kenny Lofton	.15
25	Kenny Lofton/SP/Indians	.75
26	Magglio Ordonez	.15
27	Ray Durham	.15
28	Mark Buehrle	.15
29	Paul Konerko	.25
29	Paul Konerko/SP/Dodgers	1.00
29	Paul Konerko/SP/Reds	1.00
30	Jose Valentin	.15
31	C.C. Sabathia	.15
32	Ellis Burks	.15
32	Ellis Burks/SP/Giants	.75
32	Ellis Burks/SP/Red Sox	.75
32	Ellis Burks/SP/Rockies	.75
33	Omar Vizquel	.15
33	Omar Vizquel/SP/Mariners	1.00
34	Jim Thome	.15
35	Matt Lawton	.15
36	Travis Fryman	.15
36	Travis Fryman/SP/Tigers	.75
37	Robert Fick	.15
38	Bobby Higginson	.15
39	Steve Sparks	.15
40	Mike Rivera	.15
41	Wendell Magee	.15
42	Randall Simon	.15
43	Carlos Pena	.15
43	Carlos Pena/SP/A's	.75
43	Carlos Pena/SP/Rangers	.75
44	Mike Sweeney	.15
45	Chuck Knoblauch	.15
46	Carlos Beltran	.50
47	Joe Randa	.15
48	Paul Byrd	.15
49	Mac Suzuki	.15
50	Torii Hunter	.25
51	Jacque Jones	.15
52	David Ortiz	.35
53	Corey Koskie	.15
54	Brad Radke	.15
55	Doug Mientkiewicz	.15
56	A.J. Pierzynski	.15
57	Dustan Mohr	.15
58	Derek Jeter	2.00
59	Bernie Williams	.30
60	Roger Clemens	.85
60	Roger Clemens/SP/Blue Jays	4.00
60	Roger Clemens/SP/Red Sox	4.00
61	Mike Mussina	.40
61	Mike Mussina/SP/Orioles	1.50
62	Jorge Posada	.50
63	Alfonso Soriano	.50
64	Jason Giambi	.15
64	Jason Giambi/SP/A's	2.50
65	Robin Ventura	.15
65	Robin Ventura/SP/Mets	.75
65	Robin Ventura/SP/White Sox	.75
66	Andy Pettitte	.25
67	David Wells	.15
67	David Wells/SP/Blue Jays	.75
67	David Wells/SP/Tigers	.75
68	Nick Johnson	.15
69	Jeff Weaver	.15
69	Jeff Weaver/SP/Tigers	.15
70	Raul Mondesi	.15
70	Raul Mondesi/SP/Blue Jays	.75
70	Raul Mondesi/SP/Dodgers	.75
71	Tim Hudson	.25
72	Barry Zito	.25
73	Mark Mulder	.25
74	Miguel Tejada	.25
75	Eric Chavez	.25
76	Billy Koch	.15
77	Billy Koch/SP/Blue Jays	.75
78	Jermaine Dye	.15
78	Jermaine Dye/SP/Royals	.75
79	Scott Hatteberg	.15
79	Ichiro Suzuki	1.00
80	Edgar Martinez	.15
81	Mike Cameron	.15
81	Mike Cameron/SP/White Sox	.75
82	John Olerud	.15

#	Player	Price
82	John Olerud/SP/Blue Jays	.75
82	John Olerud/SP/Mets	.15
83	Bret Boone	.15
84	Dan Wilson	.15
85	Freddy Garcia	.15
86	Jamie Moyer	.15
87	Carlos Guillen	.15
88	Ruben Sierra	.15
89	Kazuhiro Sasaki	.15
90	Mark McLemore	.15
91	Ben Grieve	.15
92	Aubrey Huff	.15
93	Steve Cox	.15
94	Toby Hall	.15
95	Randy Winn	.15
96	Brent Abernathy	.15
97	Chan Ho Park	.15
97	Chan Ho Park/SP/Dodgers	.75
98	Alex Rodriguez	1.50
98	Alex Rodriguez/SP/Mariners	4.00
99	Juan Gonzalez	.40
99	Juan Gonzalez/SP/Indians	1.50
99	Juan Gonzalez/SP/Tigers	1.50
100	Rafael Palmeiro	.60
100	Rafael Palmeiro/SP/Cubs	1.00
100	Rafael Palmeiro/SP/Orioles	1.00
101	Ivan Rodriguez	.50
102	Rusty Greer	.15
103	Kenny Rogers	.15
103	Kenny Rogers/SP/A's	.15
103	Kenny Rogers/SP/Yankees	.75
104	Hank Blalock	.40
105	Mark Teixeira	.25
106	Carlos Delgado	.15
107	Shannon Stewart	.15
108	Eric Hinske	.25
109	Roy Halladay	.25
110	Felipe Lopez	.15
111	Vernon Wells	.25
112	Curt Schilling	.40
112	Curt Schilling/SP/Phillies	1.50
113	Randy Johnson	.65
113	Randy Johnson/SP/Astros	3.00
113	Randy Johnson/SP/Expos	3.00
113	Randy Johnson/SP/Mariners	3.00
114	Luis Gonzalez	.25
114	Luis Gonzalez/SP/Astros	1.00
114	Luis Gonzalez/SP/Cubs	1.00
115	Mark Grace	.25
115	Mark Grace/SP/Cubs	1.50
116	Junior Spivey	.15
117	Tony Womack	.15
118	Matt Williams	.15
118	Matt Williams/SP/Giants	1.00
118	Matt Williams/SP/Indians	1.00
119	Danny Bautista	.15
120	Byung-Hyun Kim	.15
121	Craig Counsell	.15
122	Greg Maddux	.75
122	Greg Maddux/SP/Cubs	4.00
123	Tom Glavine	.25
124	John Smoltz	.15
124	John Smoltz/SP/Tigers	.75
125	Chipper Jones	.75
126	Gary Sheffield	.25
127	Andruw Jones	.25
128	Vinny Castilla	.15
129	Damian Moss	.15
130	Rafael Furcal	.15
131	Kerry Wood	.50
132	Fred McGriff	.15
132	Fred McGriff/SP/Blue Jays	1.00
132	Fred McGriff/SP/Braves	1.00
132	Fred McGriff/SP/Devil Rays	1.00
132	Fred McGriff/SP/Padres	1.00
133	Sammy Sosa	1.00
133	Sammy Sosa/SP/Rangers	4.00
133	Sammy Sosa/SP/White Sox	4.00
134	Alex Gonzalez	.15
135	Corey Patterson	.15
136	Moises Alou	.15
137	Mark Prior	.50
138	Jon Lieber	.15
139	Matt Clement	.15
140	Ken Griffey Jr.	1.00
140	Ken Griffey Jr./SP/Mariners	4.00
141	Barry Larkin	.15
142	Adam Dunn	.40
143	Sean Casey	.15
143	Sean Casey/SP/Indians	.75
144	Jose Rijo	.15
145	Elmer Dessens	.15
146	Austin Kearns	.15
147	Corky Miller	.15
148	Todd Walker	.15
148	Todd Walker/SP/Rockies	.75
148	Todd Walker/SP/Expos	.75
149	Chris Reitsma	.15
150	Ryan Dempster	.15
151	Larry Walker	.25
152	Todd Helton	.25
153	Juan Uribe	.15
154	Juan Pierre	.15
155	Mike Hampton	.15
156	Todd Zeile	.15
157	Josh Beckett	.25
158	Mike Lowell	.15

158	Mike Lowell/SP/Yankees	.75
159	Derrek Lee	.15
160	A.J. Burnett	.15
161	Luis Castillo	.15
162	Tim Raines	.15
163	Preston Wilson	.15
164	Juan Encarnacion	.15
165	Jeff Bagwell	.65
166	Craig Biggio	.15
167	Lance Berkman	.15
168	Wade Miller	.15
169	Roy Oswalt	.25
170	Richard Hidalgo	.15
171	Carlos Hernandez	.15
172	Daryle Ward	.15
173	Shawn Green	.30
173	Shawn Green/	
	SP/Blue Jays	1.00
174	Adrian Beltre	.35
175	Paul LoDuca	.15
176	Eric Karros	.15
177	Kevin Brown	.15
178	Hideo Nomo	.65
178	Hideo Nomo/SP/Brewers	1.50
178	Hideo Nomo/SP/Mets	1.50
178	Hideo Nomo/SP/Red Sox	1.50
178	Hideo Nomo/SP/Tigers	1.50
179	Odalis Perez	.15
180	Eric Gagne	.35
181	Brian Jordan	.15
182	Cesar Izturis	.15
183	Geoff Jenkins	.15
184	Richie Sexson	.15
184	Richie Sexson/	
	SP/Indians	1.00
185	Jose Hernandez	.15
186	Ben Sheets	.15
187	Ruben Quevedo	.15
188	Jeffrey Hammonds	.15
189	Alex Sanchez	.15
190	Vladimir Guerrero	.65
191	Jose Vidro	.15
192	Orlando Cabrera	.15
193	Michael Barrett	.15
194	Javier Vazquez	.15
195	Tony Armas Jr.	.15
196	Andres Galarraga	.15
197	Tomokazu Ohka	.15
198	Bartolo Colon	.15
198	Bartolo Colon/SP/Indians	.75
199	Cliff Floyd	.15
199	Cliff Floyd/SP/Marlins	.75
200	Mike Piazza	1.00
200	Mike Piazza/SP/Dodgers	4.00
200	Mike Piazza/SP/Marlins	4.00
201	Jeromy Burnitz	.15
202	Roberto Alomar	.35
202	Roberto Alomar/	
	SP/Blue Jays	1.50
202	Roberto Alomar/	
	SP/Indians	1.50
202	Roberto Alomar/	
	SP/Orioles	1.50
202	Roberto Alomar/	
	SP/Padres	1.50
203	Mo Vaughn	.15
203	Mo Vaughn/SP/Angels	1.00
203	Mo Vaughn/SP/Red Sox	1.00
204	Al Leiter	.15
204	Al Leiter/SP/Blue Jays	.75
205	Pedro Astacio	.15
206	Edgardo Alfonzo	.15
207	Armando Benitez	.15
208	Scott Rolen	.50
209	Pat Burrell	.35
210	Bobby Abreu	.15
210	Bobby Abreu/SP/Astros	1.00
211	Mike Lieberthal	.15
212	Brandon Duckworth	.15
213	Jimmy Rollins	.40
214	Jeremy Giambi	.15
215	Vicente Padilla	.15
216	Travis Lee	.15
217	Jason Kendall	.15
218	Brian Giles	.15
218	Brian Giles/SP/Indians	1.00
219	Aramis Ramirez	.15
220	Pokey Reese	.15
221	Kip Wells	.15
222	Josh Fogg	.15
222	Josh Fogg/SP/White Sox	.75
223	Mike Williams	.15
224	Ryan Klesko	.15
224	Ryan Klesko/SP/Braves	.75
225	Phil Nevin	.15
225	Phil Nevin/SP/Tigers	.75
226	Brian Lawrence	.15
227	Mark Kotsay	.15
228	Brett Tomko	.15
229	Trevor Hoffman	.15
229	Trevor Hoffman/	
	SP/Marlins	.75
230	Barry Bonds	2.00
230	Barry Bonds/SP/Pirates	6.00
231	Jeff Kent	.15
231	Jeff Kent/SP/Blue Jays	1.00
232	Rich Aurilia	.15
233	Tsuyoshi Shinjo	.15
233	Tsuyoshi Shinjo/SP/Mets	1.00
234	Benito Santiago	.15
234	Benito Santiago/	
	SP/Padres	.75
235	Kirk Rueter	.15
236	Kurt Ainsworth	.15
237	Livan Hernandez	.15
238	Russ Ortiz	.15
239	David Bell	.15
240	Jason Schmidt	.15

241	Reggie Sanders	.15
242	Jim Edmonds	.25
242	Jim Edmonds/SP/Angels	1.00
243	J.D. Drew	.25
244	Albert Pujols	1.50
245	Fernando Vina	.15
246	Tino Martinez	.15
246	Tino Martinez/	
	SP/Mariners	1.00
246	Tino Martinez/	
	SP/Yankees	1.00
247	Edgar Renteria	.15
248	Matt Morris	.15
249	Woody Williams	.15
250	Jason Isringhausen	.15
250	Jason Isringhausen/	
	SP/A's	.75
251	Cal Ripken Jr.	2.00
252	Cal Ripken Jr.	2.00
253	Cal Ripken Jr.	2.00
254	Cal Ripken Jr.	2.00
255	Ryne Sandberg	.75
256	Don Mattingly	1.00
257	Don Mattingly	1.00
258	Roger Clemens	.85
259	Roger Clemens	.85
260	Roger Clemens	.85
261	Roger Clemens	.85
262	Roger Clemens	.85
263	Roger Clemens	.85
264	Roger Clemens	.85
265	Rickey Henderson	.65
266	Rickey Henderson	.65
267	Jose Canseco	.40
268	Barry Bonds	2.00
269	Barry Bonds	2.00
270	Barry Bonds	2.00
271	Barry Bonds	2.00
272	Jeff Bagwell	.65
273	Kirby Puckett	.75
274	Kirby Puckett	.75
275	Greg Maddux	.75
276	Greg Maddux	.75
277	Greg Maddux	.75
278	Greg Maddux	.75
279	Ken Griffey Jr.	1.00
280	Mike Piazza	1.00
281	Kirby Puckett	.75
282	Mike Piazza	1.00
283	Frank Thomas	.65
284	Hideo Nomo	.65
285	Randy Johnson	.65
286	Juan Gonzalez	.65
287	Derek Jeter	2.00
288	Derek Jeter	2.00
289	Derek Jeter	2.00
290	Nomar Garciaparra	1.00
291	Pedro J. Martinez	.65
292	Kerry Wood	.50
293	Sammy Sosa	1.00
294	Chipper Jones	.75
295	Ivan Rodriguez	.50
296	Ivan Rodriguez	.50
297	Albert Pujols	1.50
298	Ichiro Suzuki	1.00
299	Ichiro Suzuki	1.00
300	Ichiro Suzuki	1.00
301	So Taguchi RC	1.00
302	Kazuhisa Ishii RC	2.00
303	Jeremy Lambert RC	.50
304	Sean Burroughs	.40
305	P.J. Bevis RC	.50
306	Jon Rauch	.40
307	Scotty Layfield RC	.50
308	Miguel Ascencio	.50
309	Franklyn German RC	.50
310	Luis Ugueto RC	.50
311	Jorge Sosa RC	.50
312	Felix Escalona RC	.50
313	Jose Valverde RC	.50
314	Jeremy Ward RC	.50
315	Kevin Gryboski RC	.50
316	Francis Beltran RC	.50
317	Joe Thurston	.40
318	Cliff Lee RC	3.00
319	Takahito Nomura RC	.50
320	Bill Hall	.40
321	Marlon Byrd	.50
322	Andy Shibilo RC	.50
323	Edwin Almonte RC	.50
324	Brandon Backe RC	.40
325	Chone Figgins RC	1.50
326	Brian Mallette RC	.50
327	Rodrigo Rosario RC	.50
328	Anderson Machado RC	.50
329	Jorge Padilla RC	.50
330	Allan Simpson RC	.50
331	Doug DeVore RC	.50
332	Drew Henson	.50
333	Raul Chavez RC	.50
334	Tom Shearn RC	.50
335	Ben Howard RC	.50
336	Chris Baker RC	.50
337	Travis Hughes RC	.50
338	Kevin Mench	.40
339	Brian Tallet RC	.40
340	Mike Moriarty RC	.50
341	Corey Thurman RC	.50
342	Terry Pearson RC	.50
343	Steve Kent RC	.50
344	Satoru Komiyama RC	.50
345	Jason Lane	.40
346	Freddy Sanchez RC	.50
347	Brandon Puffer RC	.50
348	Clay Condrey RC	.50
349	Rene Reyes RC	.50
350	Hee Seop Choi	.50
351	Rodrigo Lopez RC	.40

352	Colin Young RC	.50
353	Jason Simontacchi RC	.50
354	Oliver Perez RC	2.00
355	Kirk Saarloos RC	.50
356	Marcus Thames RC	.40
357	Jeff Austin RC	.50
358	Justin Kaye RC	.40
359	Julio Mateo RC	.50
360	Mike Smith RC	.50
361	Chris Snelling RC	.75
362	Dennis Tankersley RC	.40
363	Runelvys Hernandez RC	.50
364	Aaron Cook RC	.50
365	Joe Borchard RC	.50
366	Earl Snyder RC	.50
367	Shane Nance RC	.50
368	Aaron Guiel RC	.50
369	Steve Bechler RC	.50
370	Tim Kalita RC	.50
371	Shawn Sedlacek RC	.50
372	Eric Good RC	.50
373	Eric Junge RC	.50
374	Matt Thornton RC	.40
375	Travis Driskill RC	.50
376	Mitch Wylie RC	.50
377	John Ennis RC	.50
378	Reed Johnson RC	.75
379	Juan Brito RC	.50
380	Ron Calloway RC	.50
381	Adrian Burnside RC	.50
382	Josh Bard RC	.50
383	Matt Childers RC	.50
384	Gustavo Chacin RC	.50
385	Luis Martinez RC	.50
386	Trey Hodges RC	.50
387	Hansel Izquierdo RC	.50
388	Jeriome Robertson RC	.50
389	Victor Alvarez RC	.50
390	David Ross RC	.40
391	Ron Chiavacci RC	.40
392	Adam Walker RC	.50
393	Mike Gonzalez RC	.50
394	John Foster RC	.50
395	Kyle Kane RC	.50
396	Cam Esslinger RC	.50
397	Kevin Frederick RC	.50
398	Franklin Nunez RC	.50
399	Todd Donovan RC	.50
400	Kevin Cash RC	.50

Longevity

Travis Fryman

Stars (1-300):	5-10X
SP's (1-300):	1-30X
Production 100	
Rookies (301-400):	No Pricing
Production 25	

BLC Homers

Common Player:		20.00
Production 25 Sets		
1-3	Luis Gonzalez	20.00
4-11	Todd Helton	35.00
12-14	Jim Thome	35.00
15-19	Rafael Palmeiro	30.00
20-22	Troy Glaus	35.00
23-25	Gary Sheffield	20.00
26-30	Mike Piazza	50.00

Dress For Success

Common Player:		8.00
Production 250 Sets		
Prime Cuts: No Pricing		
Production 25 Sets		
1	Mike Piazza	25.00
2	Cal Ripken Jr.	40.00

3	Carlos Delgado	8.00
4	Chipper Jones	20.00
5	Bernie Williams	8.00
6	Carlos Beltran	10.00
7	Curt Schilling	10.00
8	Greg Maddux	20.00
9	Ivan Rodriguez	12.00
10	Alex Rodriguez	20.00
11	Roger Clemens	20.00
12	Todd Helton	15.00
13	Jim Edmonds	8.00
14	Manny Ramirez	15.00
15	Mark Buehrle	8.00

Freshman Orientation

	NM/M
Common Player:	5.00
Inserted 1:142	
Class Officer Parallel:	1.5X
Production 50 Sets	

1	Andres Torres/Bat	8.00
2	Mark Ellis/Jsy	8.00
3	Erik Bedard/Bat	8.00
4	Delvin James/Jsy	5.00
5	Austin Kearns/Bat	10.00
6	Josh Pearce/Bat	5.00
7	Rafael Soriano/Jsy	8.00
8	Jason Lane/Bat	5.00
9	Mark Prior/Jsy	15.00
10	Alfredo Amezaga/Bat	5.00
11	Ryan Ludwick/Bat	5.00
12	So Taguchi/Bat	10.00
13	Duaner Sanchez/Bat	5.00
14	Kazuhisa Ishii/Jsy	15.00
15	Zach Day/Jsy	8.00
16	Eric Cyr/Bat	5.00
17	Francis Beltran/Jsy	5.00
18	Joe Borchard/Jsy	10.00
19	Jeremy Affeldt/Shoe	5.00
20	Alexis Gomez/Jsy	5.00

Great American Signings

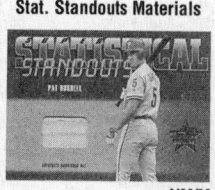

Rickey Henderson

	NM/M
Common Autograph:	5.00
Inserted 1:56	

Brent Abernathy/175	5.00
Brandon Backe/175	5.00
Chris Baker/175	5.00
Francis Beltran/175	5.00
Raul Chavez/175	5.00
Doug DeVore/175	5.00
Felix Escalona/100	8.00
Franklyn German/175	5.00
Jay Gibbons/150	10.00
Bill Hall/175	5.00
Drew Henson/50	15.00
Eric Hinske/175	8.00
Ben Howard/175	5.00
Aubrey Huff/175	8.00
Travis Hughes/175	5.00
Cesar Izturis/175	8.00
Nick Johnson/175	8.00
Austin Kearns/75	15.00
Satoru Komiyama/75	20.00
Jason Lane/150	8.00
Brian Lawrence/175	5.00
Anderson Machado/175	5.00
Roy Oswalt/100	20.00
Jorge Padilla/175	5.00
Oliver Perez/175	10.00
Rene Reyes/175	5.00
Mike Rivera/175	5.00
Rodrigo Rosario/175	5.00
Tom Shearn/175	5.00
Chris Snelling/175	10.00
Mac Suzuki/100	30.00
So Taguchi/50	15.00
Dennis Tankersley/175	8.00
Corey Thurman/175	5.00
Luis Ugueto/175	5.00
Kip Wells/175	5.00

Statistical Standouts

	NM/M
Complete Set (50):	120.00
Common Player:	1.50
Inserted 1:12	

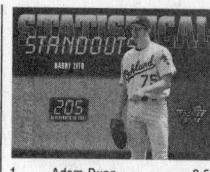

Barry Zito

1	Adam Dunn	2.50
2	Alex Rodriguez	8.00
3	Andruw Jones	4.00
4	Brian Giles	1.50
5	Chipper Jones	5.00
6	Cliff Floyd	1.50
7	Craig Biggio	1.50
8	Frank Thomas	4.00
9	Fred McGriff	1.50
10	Garret Anderson	1.50
11	Greg Maddux	5.00
12	Luis Gonzalez	1.50
13	Magglio Ordonez	1.50
14	Ivan Rodriguez	3.00
15	Ken Griffey Jr.	6.00
16	Ichiro Suzuki	6.00
17	Jason Giambi	2.50
18	Derek Jeter	10.00
19	Sammy Sosa	6.00
20	Albert Pujols	8.00
21	J.D. Drew	1.50
22	Jeff Bagwell	4.00
23	Jim Edmonds	1.50
24	Jose Vidro	1.50
25	Juan Encarnacion	1.50
26	Kerry Wood	3.00
27	Al Leiter	1.50
28	Curt Schilling	2.50
29	Manny Ramirez	4.00
30	Lance Berkman	1.50
31	Miguel Tejada	1.50
32	Mike Piazza	6.00
33	Nomar Garciaparra	6.00
34	Omar Vizquel	1.50
35	Pat Burrell	2.00
36	Paul Konerko	1.50
37	Rafael Palmeiro	3.00
38	Randy Johnson	4.00
39	Richie Sexson	1.50
40	Roger Clemens	5.50
41	Shawn Green	2.00
42	Todd Helton	4.00
43	Tom Glavine	1.50
44	Troy Glaus	4.00
45	Vladimir Guerrero	4.00
46	Mike Sweeney	1.50
47	Alfonso Soriano	3.00
48	Barry Zito	1.50
49	John Smoltz	1.50
50	Ellis Burks	1.50

Stat. Standouts Materials

Pat Burrell

	NM/M
Common Player:	5.00
Inserted 1:69	
Super Materials:	2-3X
Production 25 Sets	

1	Adam Dunn/Bat/200	8.00
2	Alex Rodriguez/Bat/200	15.00
3	Andruw Jones/Bat/200	10.00
4	Brian Giles/Bat	8.00
5	Chipper Jones/Bat/200	15.00
6	Cliff Floyd/Jsy	5.00
7	Craig Biggio/Jsy	8.00
8	Frank Thomas/Jsy/125	12.00
9	Fred McGriff/Bat	10.00
10	Garret Anderson/Bat	8.00
11	Greg Maddux/Jsy/200	20.00
12	Luis Gonzalez/Jsy	8.00
13	Magglio Ordonez/	
	Bat/150	10.00
14	Ivan Rodriguez/Jsy/100	15.00
15	Ken Griffey Jr./	
	Base/100	30.00
16	Ichiro Suzuki/Base/100	30.00
17	Jason Giambi/Base	10.00
18	Derek Jeter/Base/100	25.00
19	Sammy Sosa/Base/100	15.00
20	Albert Pujols/Base/100	15.00
21	J.D. Drew/Bat/150	8.00
22	Jeff Bagwell/Jsy/150	15.00
23	Jim Edmonds/Bat	8.00
24	Jose Vidro/Bat	5.00
25	Juan Encarnacion/Bat	5.00
26	Kerry Wood/Jsy/200	15.00
27	Al Leiter/Jsy	8.00
28	Curt Schilling/Jsy/225	12.00
29	Manny Ramirez/Bat/150	15.00
30	Lance Berkman/Bat/150	12.00
31	Miguel Tejada/Jsy	10.00
32	Mike Piazza/Bat/200	20.00
33	Nomar Garciaparra/	
	Bat/200	20.00
34	Omar Vizquel/Jsy	8.00
35	Pat Burrell/Bat	10.00
36	Paul Konerko/Jsy	6.00
37	Rafael Palmeiro/Bat	10.00

38	Randy Johnson/Jsy/200	15.00
39	Richie Sexson/Jsy	10.00
40	Roger Clemens/Jsy/200	10.00
41	Shawn Green/Jsy	10.00
42	Todd Helton/Jsy/175	15.00
43	Tom Glavine/Jsy/125	10.00
44	Troy Glaus/Jsy	10.00
45	Vladimir Guerrero/Jsy	15.00
46	Mike Sweeney/Bat	5.00
47	Alfonso Soriano/	
	Jsy/200	15.00
48	Barry Zito/Jsy/100	8.00
49	John Smoltz/Jsy	5.00
50	Ellis Burks/Jsy	5.00

Triple Threats

	NM/M
Common Card:	25.00
Production 100 Sets	

1	Reggie Jackson, Alfonso Soriano, Don Mattingly	80.00
2	Alex Rodriguez, Rafael Palmeiro, Ivan Rodriguez	30.00
3	Mike Piazza, Gary Carter, Rickey Henderson	40.00
4	Dale Murphy, Andruw Jones, Chipper Jones	40.00
5	Mike Schmidt, Steve Carlton, Scott Rolen	85.00
6	Rickey Henderson	40.00
7	Johnny Bench, Joe Morgan, Tom Seaver	50.00
8	Randy Johnson, Pedro J. Martinez, Vladimir Guerrero	35.00
9	Nolan Ryan, Rod Carew, Troy Glaus	75.00
10	Lou Brock, J.D. Drew, Stan Musial	65.00

View Masters

	NM/M
Common Player:	10.00
Production 100 Sets	
Slideshows:	No Pricing
Production 25 Sets	

1	Carlos Delgado	12.00
2	Todd Helton	20.00
3	Tony Gwynn	25.00
4	Bernie Williams	10.00
5	Luis Gonzalez	10.00
6	Larry Walker	10.00
7	Troy Glaus	20.00
8	Alfonso Soriano	15.00
9	Curt Schilling	12.00
10	Chipper Jones	25.00
11	Vladimir Guerrero	20.00
12	Adam Dunn	15.00
13	Rickey Henderson	20.00
14	Miguel Tejada	10.00
15	Kazuhisa Ishii	10.00
16	Greg Maddux	25.00
17	Pedro J. Martinez	20.00
18	Nomar Garciaparra	30.00
19	Mike Piazza	30.00
20	Lance Berkman	10.00

Leaf Samples

Each March 2003 issue of Beckett Baseball Card Monthly and April issue of Beckett Vintage Sports Collectibles included a sample Leaf card rubber-cemented inside. The cards differ from the issued version only in the appearance on back of a (usually) silver-foil "SAMPLE" notation. Some cards were produced with the back overprint in gold-foil in much more limited quantities. The number of different players' cards involved in the promotion is unknown.

	NM/M
Common Player:	.10
Stars:	1.5-2X
Gold:	20X

2003 Leaf

		NM/M
Complete Set (320):		40.00
Common Player:		.15
Pack (10):		1.50
Box (24):		30.00
1	Brad Fullmer	.15
2	Darin Erstad	.25
3	David Eckstein	.15
4	Garret Anderson	.15
5	Jarrod Washburn	.15
6	Kevin Appier	.15
7	Tim Salmon	.25
8	Troy Glaus	.75
9	Troy Percival	.15
10	Buddy Groom	.15
11	Jay Gibbons	.15
12	Jeff Conine	.15
13	Marty Cordova	.15
14	Melvin Mora	.15
15	Rodrigo Lopez	.15
16	Tony Batista	.15
17	Jorge Julio	.15
18	Cliff Floyd	.15
19	Derek Lowe	.15
20	Jason Varitek	.15
21	Johnny Damon	.25
22	Manny Ramirez	.75
23	Nomar Garciaparra	1.25
24	Pedro J. Martinez	.75
25	Rickey Henderson	.75
26	Shea Hillenbrand	.15
27	Trot Nixon	.15
28	Carlos Lee	.15
29	Frank Thomas	.75
30	Jose Valentin	.15
31	Magglio Ordonez	.15
32	Mark Buehrle	.15
33	Paul Konerko	.25
34	C.C. Sabathia	.15
35	Danys Baez	.15
36	Ellis Burks	.15
37	Jim Thome	.75
38	Omar Vizquel	.15
39	Ricky Gutierrez	.15
40	Travis Fryman	.15
41	Bobby Higginson	.15
42	Carlos Pena	.15
43	Juan Acevedo	.15
44	Mark Redman	.15
45	Randall Simon	.15
46	Robert Fick	.15
47	Steve Sparks	.15
48	Carlos Beltran	.50
49	Joe Randa	.15
50	Michael Tucker	.15
51	Mike Sweeney	.15
52	Paul Byrd	.15
53	Raul Ibanez	.15
54	Runelvys Hernandez	.15
55	A.J. Pierzynski	.15
56	Brad Radke	.15
57	Corey Koskie	.15
58	Cristian Guzman	.15
59	David Ortiz	.50
60	Doug Mientkiewicz	.15
61	Dustan Mohr	.15
62	Eddie Guardado	.15
63	Jacque Jones	.15
64	Torii Hunter	.15
65	Alfonso Soriano	.50
66	Andy Pettitte	.35
67	Bernie Williams	.30
68	David Wells	.15
69	Derek Jeter	2.00
70	Jason Giambi	.40
71	Jeff Weaver	.15
72	Jorge Posada	.25
73	Mike Mussina	.30
74	Nick Johnson	.15
75	Raul Mondesi	.15
76	Robin Ventura	.15
77	Roger Clemens	1.00
78	Barry Zito	.25
79	Billy Koch	.15
80	David Justice	.15
81	Eric Chavez	.25
82	Jermaine Dye	.15
83	Mark Mulder	.15
84	Miguel Tejada	.30
85	Ray Durham	.15
86	Scott Hatteberg	.15
87	Ted Lilly	.15

88	Tim Hudson	.25
89	Bret Boone	.15
90	Carlos Guillen	.15
91	Chris Snelling	.15
92	Dan Wilson	.15
93	Edgar Martinez	.15
94	Freddy Garcia	.15
95	Ichiro Suzuki	1.25
96	Jamie Moyer	.15
97	Joel Pineiro	.15
98	John Olerud	.15
99	Mark McLemore	.15
100	Mike Cameron	.15
101	Kazuhiro Sasaki	.15
102	Aubrey Huff	.15
103	Ben Grieve	.15
104	Joe Kennedy	.15
105	Paul Wilson	.15
106	Randy Winn	.15
107	Steve Cox	.15
108	Alex Rodriguez	1.50
109	Chan Ho Park	.15
110	Hank Blalock	.50
111	Herbert Perry	.15
112	Ivan Rodriguez	.65
113	Juan Gonzalez	.75
114	Kenny Rogers	.15
115	Kevin Mench	.15
116	Rafael Palmeiro	.65
117	Carlos Delgado	.40
118	Eric Hinske	.15
119	Jose Cruz	.15
120	Josh Phelps	.15
121	Roy Halladay	.25
122	Shannon Stewart	.15
123	Vernon Wells	.15
124	Curt Schilling	.40
125	Junior Spivey	.15
126	Luis Gonzalez	.25
127	Mark Grace	.25
128	Randy Johnson	.75
129	Steve Finley	.15
130	Tony Womack	.15
131	Andruw Jones	.75
132	Chipper Jones	1.00
133	Gary Sheffield	.30
134	Greg Maddux	1.00
135	John Smoltz	.25
136	Kevin Millwood	.15
137	Rafael Furcal	.15
138	Tom Glavine	.40
139	Alex Gonzalez	.15
140	Corey Patterson	.15
141	Fred McGriff	.15
142	Jon Lieber	.15
143	Kerry Wood	.65
144	Mark Prior	.75
145	Matt Clement	.15
146	Moises Alou	.15
147	Sammy Sosa	1.25
148	Aaron Boone	.15
149	Adam Dunn	.50
150	Austin Kearns	.15
151	Barry Larkin	.25
152	Danny Graves	.15
153	Elmer Dessens	.15
154	Ken Griffey Jr.	1.25
155	Sean Casey	.25
156	Todd Walker	.15
157	Gabe Kapler	.15
158	Jason Jennings	.15
159	Jay Payton	.15
160	Larry Walker	.25
161	Mike Hampton	.15
162	Todd Helton	.75
163	Todd Zeile	.15
164	A.J. Burnett	.15
165	Derrek Lee	.15
166	Josh Beckett	.50
167	Juan Encarnacion	.15
168	Luis Castillo	.15
169	Mike Lowell	.15
170	Preston Wilson	.15
171	Billy Wagner	.15
172	Craig Biggio	.25
173	Daryle Ward	.15
174	Jeff Bagwell	.75
175	Lance Berkman	.75
176	Octavio Dotel	.15
177	Richard Hidalgo	.15
178	Roy Oswalt	.25
179	Adrian Beltre	.40
180	Eric Gagne	.40
181	Eric Karros	.15
182	Hideo Nomo	.65
183	Kazuhisa Ishii	.15
184	Kevin Brown	.15
185	Mark Grudzielanek	.15
186	Odalis Perez	.15
187	Paul LoDuca	.15
188	Shawn Green	.40
189	Alex Sanchez	.15
190	Ben Sheets	.15
191	Jeffrey Hammonds	.15
192	Jose Hernandez	.15
193	Takahito Nomura	.15
194	Richie Sexson	.15
195	Andres Galarraga	.15
196	Bartolo Colon	.15
197	Brad Wilkerson	.15
198	Javier Vazquez	.15
199	Jose Vidro	.15
200	Michael Barrett	.15
201	Tomokazu Ohka	.15
202	Vladimir Guerrero	.75
203	Al Leiter	.15
204	Armando Benitez	.15
205	Edgardo Alfonzo	.15

206	Mike Piazza	1.25
207	Mo Vaughn	.15
208	Pedro Astacio	.15
209	Roberto Alomar	.35
210	Roger Cedeno	.15
211	Timoniel Perez	.15
212	Bobby Abreu	.15
213	Jimmy Rollins	.15
214	Mike Lieberthal	.15
215	Pat Burrell	.25
216	Randy Wolf	.15
217	Travis Lee	.15
218	Vicente Padilla	.15
219	Aramis Ramirez	.15
220	Brian Giles	.15
221	Craig Wilson	.15
222	Jason Kendall	.15
223	Josh Fogg	.15
224	Kevin Young	.15
225	Kip Wells	.15
226	Mike Williams	.15
227	Brett Tomko	.15
228	Brian Lawrence	.15
229	Mark Kotsay	.15
230	Oliver Perez	.15
231	Phil Nevin	.15
232	Ryan Klesko	.15
233	Sean Burroughs	.15
234	Trevor Hoffman	.15
235	Barry Bonds	2.00
236	Benito Santiago	.15
237	Jeff Kent	.15
238	Kirk Rueter	.15
239	Livan Hernandez	.15
240	Kenny Lofton	.15
241	Rich Aurilia	.15
242	Russ Ortiz	.15
243	Albert Pujols	1.50
244	Edgar Renteria	.15
245	J.D. Drew	.40
246	Jason Isringhausen	.15
247	Jim Edmonds	.40
248	Matt Morris	.15
249	Tino Martinez	.15
250	Scott Rolen	.75
251	Curt Schilling	.25
252	Ivan Rodriguez	.35
253	Mike Piazza	.75
254	Sammy Sosa	.75
255	Matt Williams	.15
256	Frank Thomas	.25
257	Barry Bonds	1.00
258	Roger Clemens	.65
259	Rickey Henderson	.25
260	Ken Griffey Jr.	.60
261	Greg Maddux	.50
262	Randy Johnson	.40
263	Jeff Bagwell	.25
264	Roberto Alomar	.15
265	Tom Glavine	.25
266	Juan Gonzalez	.25
267	Mark Grace	.25
268	Mike Mussina	.25
269	Ryan Klesko	.15
270	Fred McGriff	.15
271	Joe Borchard	.15
272	Chris Snelling	.15
273	Brian Tallet	.15
274	Cliff Lee	.25
275	Freddy Sanchez	.15
276	Chone Figgins	.15
277	Kevin Cash	.15
278	Josh Bard	.15
279	Jeriome Robertson	.15
280	Jeremy Hill	.15
281	Shane Nance	.15
282	Jeff Baker	.15
283	Trey Hodges	.15
284	Eric Eckenstahler	.15
285	Jim Rushford	.15
286	Carlos Rivera	.15
287	Josh Bonifay	.15
288	Garrett Atkins	.15
289	Nic Jackson	.15
290	Corwin Malone	.15
291	Jimmy Gobble	.15
292	Josh Wilson	.15
293	Clint Barmes RC	.50
294	Jon Adkins	.15
295	Tim Kalita	.15
296	Nelson Castro	.15
297	Colin Young	.15
298	Adrian Burnside	.15
299	Luis Martinez	.15
300	Terrmel Sledge RC	.50
301	Todd Donovan	.15
302	Jeremy Ward	.15
303	Wilson Valdez	.15
304	Jose Contreras RC	.75
305	Marshall McDougall	.15
306	Mitch Wylie	.15
307	Ron Calloway	.15
308	Jose Valverde	.15
309	Jason Davis	.15
310	Scotty Layfield	.15
311	Matt Thornton	.15
312	Adam Walker	.15
313	Gustavo Chacin	.15
314	Ron Chiavacci	.15
315	Wilbert Nieves	.15
316	Clifford Bartosh	.15
317	Mike Gonzalez	.15
318	Jeremy Guthrie	.15
319	Eric Junge	.15
320	Ben Kozlowski	.15

Green

No Pricing
Production 25 Sets

Blue Press Proofs

Stars: 8-15X
Production 50 Sets

Red Press Proofs

Stars: 3-5X
Inserted 1:12

Clean Up Crew

		NM/M
Complete Set (10):		30.00
Common Card:		1.50
Inserted 1:49		
1	Alex Rodriguez, Rafael Palmeiro, Ivan Rodriguez	6.00
2	Nomar Garciaparra, Manny Ramirez, Cliff Floyd	5.00
3	Jason Giambi, Bernie Williams, Jorge Posada	4.00
4	Rich Aurilia, Jeff Kent, Barry Bonds	6.00
5	Larry Walker, Todd Helton, Jay Payton	1.50
6	Lance Berkman, Jeff Bagwell, Daryle Ward	2.00
7	Scott Rolen, Albert Pujols, Jim Edmonds	5.00
8	Gary Sheffield, Chipper Jones, Andruw Jones	4.00
9	Miguel Tejada, Eric Chavez, Jermaine Dye	1.50
10	Sammy Sosa, Moises Alou, Fred McGriff	4.00

Clean Up Crew Memorabilia

		NM/M
Production 50 Sets		
1	Alex Rodriguez, Rafael Palmeiro, Ivan Rodriguez	30.00
2	Nomar Garciaparra, Manny Ramirez, Cliff Floyd	25.00
3	Jason Giambi, Bernie Williams, Jorge Posada	25.00
4	Rich Aurilia, Jeff Kent, Barry Bonds	35.00
5	Larry Walker, Todd Helton, Jay Payton	20.00
6	Lance Berkman, Jeff Bagwell, Daryle Ward	25.00
7	Scott Rolen, Albert Pujols, Jim Edmonds	40.00
8	Gary Sheffield, Chipper Jones, Andruw Jones	30.00
9	Miguel Tejada, Eric Chavez, Jermaine Dye	20.00
10	Sammy Sosa, Moises Alou, Fred McGriff	30.00

Clubhouse Signatures Bronze

	NM/M
Common Bronze Auto.:	8.00
Inserted 1:300	
Silvers:	1-2X
Production 100 Sets	
Golds:	No Pricing
Production 25 Sets	
Edwin Almonte	8.00
Jeff Baker	10.00
Josh Bard	10.00
Angel Berroa	8.00
Joe Crede/SP/25	
Andre Dawson/SP/50	25.00
Bobby Doerr/SP/100	20.00
Dwight "Doc" Gooden	25.00
Drew Henson/SP/50	
Eric Hinske	10.00
Torii Hunter/SP/75	35.00
Omar Infante	8.00

	NM/M
Brian Lawrence	8.00
Kevin Mench	8.00
Jack Morris/SP/100	15.00
Franklin Nunez	8.00
Magglio Ordonez/SP/50	25.00
Corey Patterson/SP/100	15.00
Jhonny Peralta	20.00
J.C. Romero	10.00
Chris Snelling/SP/100	10.00
Alfonso Soriano/SP/25	40.00
Brian Tallet/SP/100	8.00

Game Collection

		NM/M
Common Player:		8.00
Production 150 Sets		
1	Miguel Tejada/Cap	
2	Shannon Stewart/Cap	6.00
3	Mike Schmidt/Jkt	40.00
4	Nolan Ryan/Jkt	75.00
5	Rafael Palmeiro/Glv	15.00
6	Andruw Jones/Shoe	10.00
7	Bernie Williams/Shoe	15.00
8	Ivan Rodriguez/Shoe	10.00
9	Lance Berkman/Shoe	10.00
10	Magglio Ordonez/Shoe	10.00
11	Roy Oswalt/Glove	10.00
12	Andy Pettitte/Shoe	10.00
13	Vladimir Guerrero/Glv	30.00
14	Jason Jennings/Glv	8.00
15	Mike Sweeney/Shoe	8.00
16	Joe Borchard/Shoe	10.00
17	Mark Prior/Shoe	10.00
18	Gary Carter/Jkt	10.00
19	Austin Kearns/Glv	10.00
20	Ryan Klesko/Glv	10.00

Gold Leaf Rookies

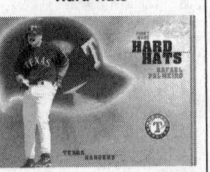

	NM/M
Complete Set (10):	10.00
Common Player:	1.00
Inserted 1:24	
Mirror Golds:	10-20X
Production 25 Sets	
1	Joe Borchard	1.00
2	Chone Figgins	1.00
3	Alexis Gomez	1.00
4	Chris Snelling	1.00
5	Cliff Lee	1.00
6	Victor Martinez	2.00
7	Hee Seop Choi	1.50
8	Michael Restovich	1.00
9	Anderson Machado	1.00
10	Drew Henson	2.00

Hard Hats

	NM/M
Complete Set (12):	15.00
Common Player:	1.00
Inserted 1:13	
1	Alex Rodriguez	4.00
2	Bernie Williams	1.00
3	Ivan Rodriguez	1.25
4	Jeff Bagwell	1.50
5	Rafael Furcal	1.00
6	Rafael Palmeiro	1.50
7	Tony Gwynn	2.00
8	Vladimir Guerrero	1.50
9	Adrian Beltre	1.00
10	Shawn Green	1.00
11	Andruw Jones	1.50
12	George Brett	4.00

Hard Hats Batting Helmets

	NM/M
Common Player:	15.00
Production 100 Sets	
1	Alex Rodriguez	50.00
2	Bernie Williams	35.00
3	Ivan Rodriguez	30.00
4	Jeff Bagwell	40.00
5	Rafael Furcal	15.00
6	Rafael Palmeiro	35.00
7	Tony Gwynn	35.00
8	Vladimir Guerrero	35.00
9	Adrian Beltre	20.00
10	Shawn Green	20.00
11	Andruw Jones	20.00
12	George Brett	100.00

Home / Away

	NM/M
Complete Set (20):	40.00
Common Player:	1.00
Home Inserted 1:34	
1	Andruw Jones/Home	1.50
2	Cal Ripken Jr./Home	6.00
3	Edgar Martinez/Home	1.00
4	Jim Thome/Home	1.50
5	Larry Walker/Home	1.00
6	Nomar Garciaparra/Home	4.00
7	Mark Prior/Home	1.00
8	Mike Piazza/Home	4.00
9	Vladimir Guerrero/Home	1.50
10	Chipper Jones/Home	3.00
Away Inserted 1:34		
1	Andruw Jones	1.50
2	Cal Ripken Jr.	6.00
3	Edgar Martinez	1.00
4	Jim Thome	2.00
5	Larry Walker	1.00
6	Nomar Garciaparra	4.00
7	Mark Prior	1.00
8	Mike Piazza	4.00
9	Vladimir Guerrero	2.00
10	Chipper Jones	3.00

Home / Away Memorabilia

	NM/M
Common Player:	6.00
Home Production 250	
1	Andruw Jones/Home	8.00
2	Cal Ripken Jr./Home	45.00
3	Edgar Martinez/Home	8.00
4	Jim Thome/Home	10.00
5	Larry Walker/Home	8.00
6	Nomar Garciaparra/Home	20.00
7	Mark Prior/Home	10.00
8	Mike Piazza/Home	15.00
9	Vladimir Guerrero/Home	12.00
10	Chipper Jones/Home	15.00
Away Production 250		
1	Andruw Jones	8.00
2	Cal Ripken Jr.	45.00
3	Edgar Martinez	8.00
4	Jim Thome	10.00
5	Larry Walker	6.00
6	Nomar Garciaparra	20.00
7	Mark Prior	15.00
8	Mike Piazza	15.00
9	Vladimir Guerrero	12.00
10	Chipper Jones	15.00

Maple & Ash

	NM/M
Common Player:	6.00
Production 400 Sets	
1	Jorge Posada	8.00
2	Mike Piazza	12.00
3	Alex Rodriguez	15.00
4	Jeff Bagwell	10.00
5	Joe Borchard	6.00
6	Miguel Tejada	6.00
7	Adam Dunn	8.00
8	Jim Thome	8.00
9	Lance Berkman	6.00
10	Torii Hunter	6.00
11	Carlos Delgado	6.00
12	Reggie Jackson	10.00
13	Juan Gonzalez	6.00
14	Vladimir Guerrero	10.00
15	Richie Sexson	6.00

Number Off My Back

	NM/M
Production 50 Sets	

#	Player	Price
1	Carlos Delgado	15.00
2	Don Mattingly	100.00
3	Todd Helton	30.00
4	Vernon Wells	10.00
5	Bernie Williams	20.00
6	Luis Gonzalez	20.00
7	Kerry Wood	30.00
8	Eric Chavez	10.00
9	Shawn Green	15.00
10	Roy Oswalt	15.00
11	Nomar Garciaparra	40.00
12	Robin Yount	60.00
13	Troy Glaus	20.00
14	C.C. Sabathia	10.00
15	Alex Rodriguez	50.00
16	Mark Mulder	10.00
17	Will Clark	60.00
18	Alfonso Soriano	30.00
19	Andy Pettitte	20.00
20	Curt Schilling	25.00

Shirt Off My Back

		NM/M
Common Player:		5.00
Production 500 Sets		
Number Off My Back:		2-4X
Production 50 Sets		
1	Carlos Delgado	6.00
2	Don Mattingly	25.00
3	Todd Helton	10.00
4	Vernon Wells	5.00
5	Bernie Williams	6.00
6	Luis Gonzalez	6.00
7	Kerry Wood	6.00
8	Eric Chavez	6.00
9	Shawn Green	6.00
10	Roy Oswalt	6.00
11	Nomar Garciaparra	12.00
12	Robin Yount	15.00
13	Troy Glaus	8.00
14	C.C. Sabathia	5.00
15	Alex Rodriguez	15.00
16	Mark Mulder	5.00
17	Will Clark	10.00
18	Alfonso Soriano	10.00
19	Andy Pettitte	8.00
20	Curt Schilling	8.00

Slick Leather

		NM/M
Complete Set (15):		20.00
Common Player:		1.00
Inserted 1:21		
1	Omar Vizquel	1.00
2	Roberto Alomar	1.50
3	Ivan Rodriguez	2.00
4	Greg Maddux	3.00
5	Scott Rolen	2.00
6	Todd Helton	2.00
7	Andruw Jones	2.00
8	Jim Edmonds	1.50
9	Barry Bonds	6.00
10	Eric Chavez	1.00
11	Ichiro Suzuki	5.00
12	Mike Mussina	1.50
13	John Olerud	1.00
14	Torii Hunter	1.00
15	Larry Walker	1.00

60

		NM/M
Complete Set (50):		80.00
Common Player:		.75
Inserted 1:8		
Foil Parallels:		3-5X
Production 60 Sets		
1	Troy Glaus	3.00
2	Curt Schilling	2.00
3	Randy Johnson	3.00
4	Andruw Jones	3.00
5	Chipper Jones	4.00
6	Greg Maddux	4.00
7	Tom Glavine	1.00
8	Manny Ramirez	3.00
9	Nomar Garciaparra	5.00
10	Pedro J. Martinez	3.00
11	Rickey Henderson	3.00

SHAWN GREEN
OUTFIELD—LOS ANGELES DODGERS

12	Sammy Sosa	5.00
13	Frank Thomas	3.00
14	Magglio Ordonez	.75
15	Mark Buehrle	.75
16	Adam Dunn	1.50
17	Ken Griffey Jr.	5.00
18	Jim Thome	2.00
19	Omar Vizquel	.75
20	Larry Walker	.75
21	Todd Helton	3.00
22	Lance Berkman	.75
23	Roy Oswalt	.75
24	Mike Sweeney	.75
25	Hideo Nomo	3.00
26	Kazuhisa Ishii	1.00
27	Shawn Green	1.00
28	Torii Hunter	.75
29	Vladimir Guerrero	3.00
30	Mike Piazza	3.00
31	Alfonso Soriano	3.00
32	Bernie Williams	3.00
33	Derek Jeter	8.00
34	Jason Giambi	2.00
35	Roger Clemens	4.00
36	Barry Zito	.75
37	Miguel Tejada	.75
38	Pat Burrell	1.00
39	Ryan Klesko	.75
40	Barry Bonds	8.00
41	Jeff Kent	.75
42	Ichiro Suzuki	5.00
43	John Olerud	.75
44	Albert Pujols	5.00
45	Jim Edmonds	1.00
46	Scott Rolen	2.50
47	Alex Rodriguez	6.00
48	Ivan Rodriguez	2.50
49	Rafael Palmeiro	2.50
50	Roy Halladay	.75

2003 Leaf Certified Materials Samples

Each September 2003 issue of Beckett Baseball Card Monthly included a sample Leaf Certified Materials card rubber-cemented inside. The cards differ from the issued version only in the appearance on back of a (usually) silver-foil "SAMPLE" notation. Some cards were produced with the back overprint in gold-foil in much more limited quantities. The number of different players' cards involved in the promotion is unknown.

		NM/M
Common Player:		.10
Stars:		1.5X
Gold:		20X

2003 Leaf Certified Materials

		NM/M
Complete Set (250):		
Common Player:		.50
Common SP Auto. (206-250):		
Production 400 unless noted.		
Mirror Red Auto. SP's (06-250): 1-1.5X		
Production 100		
Mirror Blue Auto. SP's (206-250): 1-2X		
Production 50		
Mirror Gold Autos.		
(206-250):		No Pricing
Production 25		
Pack (5):		20.00
Box (10):		150.00
1	Troy Glaus	1.00

2	Alfredo Amezaga	.50
3	Garret Anderson	.50
4	Nolan Ryan	6.00
5	Darin Erstad	.75
6	Junior Spivey	.50
7	Randy Johnson	2.00
8	Curt Schilling	1.50
9	Luis Gonzalez	.75
10	Steve Finley	.50
11	Matt Williams	.75
12	Greg Maddux	3.00
13	Chipper Jones	2.00
14	Gary Sheffield	1.00
15	Adam LaRoche	.50
16	Andruw Jones	1.00
17	Robert Fick	.50
18	John Smoltz	1.00
19	Javy Lopez	.75
20	Jay Gibbons	.50
21	Geronimo Gil	.50
22	Cal Ripken Jr.	6.00
23	Nomar Garciaparra	4.00
24	Pedro J. Martinez	2.00
25	Freddy Sanchez	.50
26	Rickey Henderson	1.00
27	Manny Ramirez	.50
28	Casey Fossum	.50
29	Sammy Sosa	2.00
30	Kerry Wood	1.00
31	Corey Patterson	1.00
32	Nic Jackson	.50
33	Mark Prior	1.50
34	Juan Cruz	.50
35	Steve Smyth	.50
36	Magglio Ordonez	.75
37	Joe Borchard	.50
38	Frank Thomas	1.50
39	Mark Buehrle	.50
40	Joe Crede	.50
41	Carlos Lee	.50
42	Paul Konerko	.50
43	Adam Dunn	1.50
44	Corky Miller	.50
45	Brandon Larson	.50
46	Ken Griffey Jr.	3.00
47	Barry Larkin	1.00
48	Sean Casey	.50
49	Wily Mo Pena	1.00
50	Austin Kearns	.75
51	Victor Martinez	.50
52	Brian Tallet	.50
53	Cliff Lee	.50
54	Jeremy Guthrie	.50
55	C.C. Sabathia	.50
56	Ricardo Rodriguez	.50
57	Omar Vizquel	1.00
58	Travis Hafner	.50
59	Todd Helton	1.50
60	Jason Jennings	.50
61	Jeff Baker	.50
62	Larry Walker	1.00
63	Travis Chapman	.50
64	Mike Maroth	.50
65	Josh Beckett	1.00
66	Ivan Rodriguez	1.50
67	Brad Penny	.50
68	A.J. Burnett	.50
69	Craig Biggio	.50
70	Roy Oswalt	1.00
71	Jason Lane	.50
72	Nolan Ryan	6.00
73	Wade Miller	.50
74	Richard Hidalgo	.50
75	Jeff Bagwell	1.50
76	Lance Berkman	1.00
77	Rodrigo Rosario	.50
78	Jeff Kent	1.00
79	John Buck	.50
80	Angel Berroa	.50
81	Mike Sweeney	.50
82	Mac Suzuki	.50
83	Alexis Gomez	.50
84	Carlos Beltran	1.50
85	Runelvys Hernandez	.50
86	Hideo Nomo	1.00
87	Paul LoDuca	.50
88	Cesar Izturis	.50
89	Kazuhisa Ishii	.50
90	Shawn Green	.50
91	Joe Thurston	.50
92	Adrian Beltre	.50
93	Kevin Brown	.50
94	Richie Sexson	.50
95	Ben Sheets	.50
96	Takahito Nomura	.50
97	Geoff Jenkins	.50
98	Bill Hall	.50
99	Torii Hunter	1.00

100	A.J. Pierzynski	.50
101	Michael Cuddyer	.50
102	Jose Morban	.50
103	Brad Radke	.50
104	Jacque Jones	.50
105	Eric Milton	.50
106	Joe Mays	.50
107	Adam Johnson	.50
108	Javier Vazquez	.50
109	Vladimir Guerrero	2.00
110	Jose Vidro	.50
111	Michael Barrett	.50
112	Orlando Cabrera	.50
113	Tom Glavine	1.00
114	Roberto Alomar	1.00
115	Tsuyoshi Shinjo	.50
116	Cliff Floyd	.50
117	Mike Piazza	3.00
118	Al Leiter	.50
119	Don Mattingly	4.00
120	Roger Clemens	4.00
121	Derek Jeter	6.00
122	Alfonso Soriano	2.00
123	Drew Henson	.50
124	Brandon Claussen	.50
125	Christian Parker	.50
126	Jason Giambi	1.00
127	Mike Mussina	1.00
128	Bernie Williams	1.00
129	Jason Anderson	.50
130	Nick Johnson	.50
131	Jorge Posada	1.00
132	Andy Pettitte	1.00
133	Barry Zito	1.00
134	Miguel Tejada	1.00
135	Eric Chavez	1.00
136	Tim Hudson	1.00
137	Mark Mulder	.75
138	Terrence Long	.50
139	Mark Ellis	.50
140	Jim Thome	1.50
141	Pat Burrell	.75
142	Marlon Byrd	.50
143	Bobby Abreu	.75
144	Brandon Duckworth	.50
145	Robert Person	.50
146	Anderson Machado	.50
147	Aramis Ramirez	1.00
148	Jack Wilson	.50
149	Carlos Rivera	.50
150	Jose Castillo	.50
151	Walter Young	.50
152	Brian Giles	.75
153	Jason Kendall	.50
154	Ryan Klesko	.75
155	Mike Rivera	.50
156	Sean Burroughs	.50
157	Brian Lawrence	.50
158	Xavier Nady	.50
159	Dennis Tankersley	.50
160	Phil Nevin	.50
161	Barry Bonds	6.00
162	Kenny Lofton	.50
163	Rich Aurilia	.50
164	Ichiro Suzuki	4.00
165	Edgar Martinez	.75
166	Chris Snelling	.50
167	Rafael Soriano	.50
168	John Olerud	.75
169	Bret Boone	.50
170	Freddy Garcia	.50
171	Aaron Sele	.50
172	Kazuhiro Sasaki	.50
173	Albert Pujols	4.00
174	Scott Rolen	2.00
175	So Taguchi	.50
176	Jim Edmonds	1.00
177	Edgar Renteria	1.00
178	J.D. Drew	1.00
179	Antonio Perez	.50
180	Dewon Brazelton	.50
181	Aubrey Huff	.50
182	Toby Hall	.50
183	Ben Grieve	.50
184	Joe Kennedy	.50
185	Alex Rodriguez	5.00
186	Rafael Palmeiro	1.50
187	Hank Blalock	1.50
188	Mark Teixeira	1.00
189	Juan Gonzalez	1.50
190	Kevin Mench	.50
191	Nolan Ryan	6.00
192	Doug Davis	.50
193	Eric Hinske	.50
194	Vinnie Chulk	.50
195	Alexis Rios	.50
196	Carlos Delgado	1.00
197	Shannon Stewart	.50
198	Josh Phelps	.50
199	Vernon Wells	.75
200	Roy Halladay	.75
201	Babe Ruth	8.00
202	Lou Gehrig	8.00
203	Jackie Robinson	6.00
204	Ty Cobb	5.00
205	Thurman Munson	4.00
206	Prentice Redman RC	5.00
207	Craig Brazell RC	5.00
208	Nook Logan RC	5.00
209	Hong-Chih Kuo RC	75.00
210	Matt Kata RC	5.00
211	Chien-Ming Wang RC	150.00
212	Alejandro Machado RC	5.00
213	Michael Hessman RC	5.00
214	Francisco Rosario RC	5.00
215	Pedro Liriano RC	5.00
216	Jeremy Bonderman RC	25.00
217	Oscar Villarreal RC	8.00

218	Arnie Munoz RC	5.00
219	Tim Olson RC	5.00
220	Jose Contreras/100 RC	40.00
221	Francisco Cruceta RC	5.00
222	John Webb	5.00
223	Phil Seibel RC	5.00
224	Aaron Looper RC	5.00
225	Brian Stokes RC	5.00
226	Guillermo Quiroz RC	8.00
227	Fernando Cabrera RC	5.00
228	Josh Hall RC	5.00
229	Diegomar Markwell RC	5.00
230	Andrew Brown RC	5.00
231	Doug Waechter RC	5.00
232	Felix Sanchez RC	5.00
233	Gerardo Garcia RC	5.00
234	Matt Bruback RC	5.00
235	Michel Hernandez RC	5.00
236	Rett Johnson RC	5.00
237	Ryan Cameron RC	5.00
238	Rob Hammock RC	5.00
239	Clint Barmes RC	10.00
240	Brandon Webb RC	40.00
241	Jon Leicester RC	5.00
242	Shane Bazzell RC	5.00
243	Joe Valentine RC	5.00
244	Josh Stewart RC	5.00
245	Pete LaForest RC	5.00
246	Shane Victorino RC	25.00
247	Terrmel Sledge RC	5.00
248	Lew Ford RC	8.00
249	Todd Wellemeyer RC	10.00
250	Hideki Matsui/ No Auto. RC	15.00

Mirror Red

Stars (1-205):		2-5X
SP's (206-250):		.2-.4X
Production 100 Sets		
Mirror Blues (1-205):		4-10X
SP's (206-250):		.3-.5X
Production 50 Sets		
Mirror Golds:		No Pricing
Production 25 Sets		
Mirror Emeralds:		No Pricing
Production Five Sets		
Mirror Blacks: One Set Produced		

Mirror Red Materials

		NM/M
Common Player:		4.00
Production 250 unless noted.		
Mirror Red SP's (206-250):		.5X
Mirror Blues:		1-1.5X
Production 100		
Mirror Golds:		No Pricing
Production 25 Sets		
Mirror Emeralds:		No Pricing
Production Five Sets		
Mirror Blacks: One Set Produced		
1	Troy Glaus	6.00
2	Alfredo Amezaga	4.00
3	Garret Anderson	4.00
4	Nolan Ryan/35	65.00
5	Darin Erstad	5.00
6	Junior Spivey	4.00
7	Randy Johnson	5.00
8	Curt Schilling	8.00
9	Luis Gonzalez	5.00
10	Steve Finley	4.00
11	Matt Williams	4.00
12	Greg Maddux	10.00
13	Chipper Jones	8.00
14	Gary Sheffield/125	6.00
15	Adam LaRoche	4.00
16	Andruw Jones	6.00
17	Robert Fick	4.00
18	John Smoltz	6.00
19	Javy Lopez	6.00

20	Jay Gibbons	4.00
21	Geronimo Gil	4.00
22	Cal Ripken Jr./35	75.00
23	Nomar Garciaparra	15.00
24	Pedro J. Martinez	10.00
25	Freddy Sanchez	4.00
26	Rickey Henderson	10.00
27	Manny Ramirez	8.00
28	Casey Fossum	4.00
29	Sammy Sosa	15.00
30	Kerry Wood	10.00
31	Corey Patterson	4.00
32	Nic Jackson	4.00
33	Mark Prior	8.00
34	Juan Cruz	4.00
35	Steve Smyth	4.00
36	Magglio Ordonez	6.00
37	Joe Borchard	4.00
38	Frank Thomas	10.00
39	Mark Buehrle	5.00
40	Joe Crede/100	8.00
41	Carlos Lee	4.00
42	Paul Konerko	4.00
43	Adam Dunn	8.00
44	Brandon Larson/150	4.00
46	Ken Griffey Jr.	12.00
47	Barry Larkin	8.00
48	Sean Casey	6.00
49	Wily Mo Pena	6.00
50	Austin Kearns	6.00
51	Victor Martinez/100	8.00
55	C.C. Sabathia	4.00
56	Ricardo Rodriguez	4.00
57	Omar Vizquel	6.00
58	Travis Hafner	6.00
59	Todd Helton	8.00
60	Jason Jennings	4.00
62	Larry Walker	6.00
63	Travis Chapman	4.00
64	Mike Maroth	4.00
65	Josh Beckett	6.00
66	Ivan Rodriguez	8.00
67	Brad Penny	4.00
68	A.J. Burnett	6.00
69	Craig Biggio	6.00
70	Roy Oswalt	6.00
71	Jason Lane	4.00
72	Nolan Ryan/35	65.00
73	Wade Miller	5.00
74	Richard Hidalgo	4.00
75	Jeff Bagwell	10.00
76	Lance Berkman	6.00
77	Rodrigo Rosario	4.00
78	Jeff Kent	6.00
79	John Buck	4.00
80	Angel Berroa	4.00
81	Mike Sweeney	6.00
84	Carlos Beltran	8.00
86	Hideo Nomo	15.00
87	Paul LoDuca	6.00
88	Cesar Izturis	4.00
89	Kazuhisa Ishii	5.00
90	Shawn Green	6.00
91	Joe Thurston	6.00
92	Adrian Beltre	6.00
93	Kevin Brown	6.00
94	Richie Sexson	6.00
95	Ben Sheets	5.00
97	Geoff Jenkins	5.00
98	Bill Hall	4.00
99	Torii Hunter	8.00
101	Michael Cuddyer	4.00
102	Jose Morban	4.00
103	Brad Radke	6.00
104	Jacque Jones	4.00
105	Eric Milton	4.00
106	Joe Mays	5.00
107	Adam Johnson	4.00
108	Javier Vazquez	4.00
109	Vladimir Guerrero	10.00
110	Jose Vidro	4.00
111	Michael Barrett/50	6.00
112	Orlando Cabrera	5.00
113	Tom Glavine	8.00
114	Roberto Alomar	10.00
115	Tsuyoshi Shinjo	4.00
116	Cliff Floyd	5.00
117	Mike Piazza	10.00
118	Al Leiter	4.00
119	Don Mattingly/35	60.00
120	Roger Clemens	25.00
121	Derek Jeter	20.00
122	Alfonso Soriano	8.00
123	Drew Henson	6.00
124	Brandon Claussen/50	10.00
125	Christian Parker	4.00
126	Jason Giambi	6.00
127	Mike Mussina	10.00
128	Bernie Williams	8.00
130	Nick Johnson	4.00
131	Jorge Posada	6.00
132	Andy Pettitte	10.00
133	Barry Zito	6.00
134	Miguel Tejada	6.00
135	Eric Chavez	6.00
136	Tim Hudson	6.00
137	Mark Mulder	6.00
138	Terrence Long	4.00
139	Mark Ellis	4.00
140	Jim Thome	8.00
141	Pat Burrell	6.00
142	Marlon Byrd	6.00
143	Bobby Abreu	6.00
144	Brandon Duckworth	4.00
145	Robert Person	4.00
146	Anderson Machado	4.00
147	Aramis Ramirez	4.00
148	Jack Wilson	4.00

150 Jose Castillo 4.00
151 Walter Young 4.00
152 Brian Giles 6.00
153 Jason Kendall 5.00
155 Mike Rivera 4.00
157 Brian Lawrence 4.00
158 Xavier Nady/60 8.00
159 Dennis Tankersley 4.00
160 Phil Nevin 4.00
161 Barry Bonds 20.00
162 Kenny Lofton 6.00
163 Rich Aurilia 4.00
164 Ichiro Suzuki 25.00
165 Edgar Martinez/100 8.00
166 Chris Snelling 4.00
167 Rafael Soriano 4.00
168 John Olerud 4.00
169 Bret Boone 5.00
170 Freddy Garcia 4.00
171 Aaron Sele 4.00
172 Kazuhiro Sasaki 4.00
173 Albert Pujols 25.00
174 Scott Rolen 10.00
175 So Taguchi 4.00
176 Jim Edmonds 6.00
177 Edgar Renteria 8.00
178 J.D. Drew 6.00
179 Antonio Perez 4.00
180 Dewon Brazelton 4.00
181 Aubrey Huff/50 8.00
182 Toby Hall 4.00
183 Ben Grieve 4.00
184 Joe Kennedy 4.00
185 Alex Rodriguez 15.00
186 Rafael Palmeiro 8.00
187 Hank Blalock 8.00
188 Mark Teixeira 8.00
189 Juan Gonzalez 8.00
190 Kevin Mench 4.00
191 Nolan Ryan/35 65.00
192 Doug Davis 4.00
193 Eric Hinske 8.00
196 Carlos Delgado 6.00
197 Shannon Stewart 5.00
198 Josh Phelps 4.00
199 Vernon Wells 5.00
200 Roy Halladay 4.00

Mirror Red Signatures

NM/M
Common Player:
Production 100 unless noted.
Mirror Blues: 1-1.5X
Production 50
Mirror Golds: 1.5-2X
Production 25 Sets
Mirror Emeralds: No Pricing
Production Five Sets
Mirror Blacks: One Set Produced
2 Alfredo Amezaga 6.00
15 Adam LaRoche 10.00
17 Robert Fick/15 20.00
20 Jay Gibbons 10.00
21 Geronimo Gil/15 15.00
25 Freddy Sanchez 10.00
28 Casey Fossum/50 10.00
32 Nic Jackson 10.00
34 Juan Cruz/15 15.00
35 Steve Smyth/94 8.00
37 Joe Borchard/50 15.00
39 Mark Buehrle/50 20.00
40 Joe Crede/30 15.00
45 Brandon Larson 10.00
49 Wily Mo Pena 15.00
51 Victor Martinez/50 25.00
53 Cliff Lee/50 20.00
54 Jeremy Guthrie/50 15.00
56 Ricardo Rodriguez 8.00
60 Jason Jennings/50 12.00
61 Jeff Baker/50 8.00
63 Travis Chapman 10.00
64 Mike Maroth 10.00
70 Roy Oswalt/50 20.00
71 Jason Lane 10.00
73 Wade Miller/50 15.00
77 Rodrigo Rosario 10.00
80 Angel Berroa/50 15.00
85 Runelvys Hernandez 10.00
88 Cesar Izturis 6.00
91 Joe Thurston 8.00
98 Bill Hall 10.00
102 Jose Morban 10.00
107 Adam Johnson/50 10.00
117 Mike Piazza/20 150.00
124 Brandon Claussen/60 15.00
125 Christian Parker/50 10.00
127 Jason Anderson 10.00
138 Terrence Long/50 15.00

142 Marlon Byrd 10.00
144 Brandon Duckworth/50 10.00
145 Robert Person/50 8.00
146 Anderson Machado 8.00
149 Carlos Rivera 8.00
150 Jose Castillo 8.00
151 Walter Young 8.00
155 Mike Rivera 8.00
157 Brian Lawrence 8.00
166 Chris Snelling 10.00
167 Rafael Soriano 12.00
179 Antonio Perez/50 8.00
180 Dewon Brazelton/50 8.00
181 Aubrey Huff/50 8.00
182 Toby Hall 10.00
184 Joe Kennedy/50 8.00
187 Hank Blalock/50 25.00
188 Mark Teixeira/50 40.00
190 Kevin Mench 10.00
193 Eric Hinske 15.00
194 Vinnie Chulk 8.00
195 Alexis Rios 25.00

Fabric of the Game

NM/M 4.00
Common Player:
Quantity produced listed.
1BA Bobby Doerr/50 15.00
1JY Bobby Doerr/39 15.00
1PS Bobby Doerr/50 15.00
2BA Ozzie Smith/100 25.00
2IN Ozzie Smith/50 30.00
2JY Ozzie Smith/88 20.00
2PS Ozzie Smith/50 30.00
3DY Pee Wee Reese/32 30.00
3JY Pee Wee Reese/58 15.00
4BA Jeff Bagwell/100 10.00
4DY Jeff Bagwell/65 10.00
4IN Jeff Bagwell/50 12.00
4JY Jeff Bagwell/98 15.00
4PS Jeff Bagwell/50 12.00
5BA Tommy Lasorda/100 8.00
5DY Tommy Lasorda/58 10.00
5JY Tommy Lasorda/84 8.00
5PS Tommy Lasorda/50 10.00
6JY Red Schoendienst/55 10.00
7DY Harmon Killebrew/50 15.00
7IN Harmon Killebrew/61 15.00
7IN Harmon Killebrew/50 15.00
7JY Harmon Killebrew/71 15.00
7PS Harmon Killebrew/50 15.00
8DY Roger Maris/55 40.00
8JY Roger Maris/58 40.00
8PS Roger Maris/50 40.00
9BA Alex Rodriguez/100 15.00
9DY Alex Rodriguez/77 15.00
9IN Alex Rodriguez/50 15.00
9JY Alex Rodriguez/99 15.00
9PS Alex Rodriguez/50 15.00
10BA Alex Rodriguez/100 15.00
10DY Alex Rodriguez/72 15.00
10IN Alex Rodriguez/50 15.00
10JY Alex Rodriguez/101 15.00
10PS Alex Rodriguez/50 15.00
11BA Dale Murphy/50 15.00
11DY Dale Murphy/66 15.00
11IN Dale Murphy/50 15.00
11JY Dale Murphy/85 15.00
11PS Dale Murphy/50 15.00
12BA Alan Trammell/100 15.00
12IN Alan Trammell/50 15.00
12JY Alan Trammell/90 10.00
12PS Alan Trammell/50 10.00
13BA Babe Ruth/10 250.00
13DY Babe Ruth/13 250.00
13IN Babe Ruth/50 250.00
13JY Babe Ruth/30 200.00
13PS Babe Ruth/10 250.00
14JY Lou Gehrig/38 200.00
15JY Babe Ruth/30 250.00
16JY Mel Ott/46 30.00
17BA Paul Molitor/50 15.00
17DY Paul Molitor/70 15.00
17IN Paul Molitor/50 15.00
17JY Paul Molitor/84 15.00
17PS Paul Molitor/50 15.00
18DY Duke Snider/58 15.00
18JY Duke Snider/62 15.00
19BA Miguel Tejada/50 10.00
19DY Miguel Tejada/68 8.00
19IN Miguel Tejada/50 10.00
19JY Miguel Tejada/99 5.00
19PS Miguel Tejada/50 10.00
20JY Lou Gehrig/38 200.00
21DY Brooks Robinson/54 15.00
21JY Brooks Robinson/66 15.00
22BA George Brett/50 30.00
22DY George Brett/69 25.00
22IN George Brett/50 30.00
22JY George Brett/91 25.00
22PS George Brett/50 30.00
23BA Johnny Bench/50 15.00
23DY Johnny Bench/59 15.00
23IN Johnny Bench/50 15.00
23JY Johnny Bench/81 15.00
23PS Johnny Bench/50 15.00
24JY Lou Boudreau/48 15.00

25BA Nomar Garciaparra/100 20.00
25IN Nomar Garciaparra/50 25.00
25JY Nomar Garciaparra/100 20.00
25PS Nomar Garciaparra/50 25.00
26BA Tsuyoshi Shinjo/50 8.00
26DY Tsuyoshi Shinjo/62 8.00
26JY Tsuyoshi Shinjo/50 5.00
27BA Pat Burrell/100 8.00
27DY Pat Burrell/46 10.00
27JY Pat Burrell/101 8.00
28BA Albert Pujols/100 20.00
28IN Albert Pujols/50 20.00
28JY Albert Pujols/101 20.00
28PS Albert Pujols/50 20.00
29JY Stan Musial/43 30.00
30JY Al Kaline/64 15.00
31BA Ivan Rodriguez/100 8.00
31DY Ivan Rodriguez/72 8.00
31IN Ivan Rodriguez/50 10.00
31JY Ivan Rodriguez/101 5.00
32BA Craig Biggio/100 6.00
32DY Craig Biggio/65 8.00
32JY Craig Biggio/101 6.00
32PS Craig Biggio/50 10.00
33DY Joe Morgan/59 10.00
33JY Joe Morgan/74 10.00
34BA Willie Stargell/50 15.00
34JY Willie Stargell/68 15.00
34PS Willie Stargell/50 15.00
35BA Andre Dawson/100 8.00
35IN Andre Dawson/87 8.00
35JY Andre Dawson/50 8.00
35PS Andre Dawson/50 10.00
36BA Gary Carter/100 10.00
36DY Gary Carter/62 10.00
36IN Gary Carter/50 10.00
36JY Gary Carter/85 8.00
36PS Gary Carter/50 10.00
37BA Cal Ripken Jr./50 50.00
37DY Cal Ripken Jr./54 50.00
37IN Cal Ripken Jr./50 50.00
37JY Cal Ripken Jr./101 40.00
37PS Cal Ripken Jr./50 50.00
38JY Enos Slaughter/53 20.00
39BA Reggie Jackson/50 15.00
39DY Reggie Jackson/68 15.00
39JY Reggie Jackson/75 15.00
39PS Reggie Jackson/50 15.00
40JY Phil Rizzuto/47 15.00
41BA Chipper Jones/100 15.00
41DY Chipper Jones/66 15.00
41IN Chipper Jones/101 10.00
41JY Chipper Jones/50 15.00
41PS Chipper Jones/50 15.00
42BA Hideo Nomo/100 10.00
42DY Hideo Nomo/58 15.00
42IN Hideo Nomo/50 10.00
42JY Hideo Nomo/95 10.00
42PS Hideo Nomo/50 15.00
43JY Luis Aparicio/69 10.00
44BA Hideo Nomo/100 10.00
44IN Hideo Nomo/50 15.00
44JY Hideo Nomo/101 10.00
44PS Hideo Nomo/50 15.00
45BA Edgar Martinez/100 8.00
45DY Edgar Martinez/77 8.00
45JY Edgar Martinez/100 8.00
45PS Edgar Martinez/50 8.00
46BA Barry Larkin/100 6.00
46DY Barry Larkin/59 10.00
46JY Barry Larkin/50 6.00
46PS Barry Larkin/50 10.00
47BA Alfonso Soriano/100 15.00
47IN Alfonso Soriano/50 15.00
47JY Alfonso Soriano/102 10.00
47PS Alfonso Soriano/50 15.00
48DY Wade Boggs/98 8.00
48IN Wade Boggs/50 10.00
48JY Wade Boggs/99 8.00
48PS Wade Boggs/50 10.00
49BA Wade Boggs/100 8.00
49IN Wade Boggs/94 8.00
49PS Wade Boggs/50 15.00
50JY Ernie Banks/68 15.00
51BA Joe Torre/50 10.00
51DY Joe Torre/66 10.00
51IN Joe Torre/50 10.00
51JY Joe Torre/66 10.00
51PS Joe Torre/50 10.00
52BA Tim Hudson/100 4.00
52DY Tim Hudson/68 6.00
52JY Tim Hudson/101 4.00
52PS Tim Hudson/50 6.00
53BA Shawn Green/100 4.00
53DY Shawn Green/58 6.00
53JY Shawn Green/102 4.00
53PS Shawn Green/50 6.00
54BA Carlos Beltran/100 6.00
54DY Carlos Beltran/69 6.00
54JY Carlos Beltran/101 6.00
54PS Carlos Beltran/50 8.00
55BA Bo Jackson/50 15.00
55DY Bo Jackson/69 10.00
55JY Bo Jackson/90 10.00
55PS Bo Jackson/50 15.00
56BA Hal Newhouser/50 8.00
56JY Hal Newhouser/55 8.00
56PS Hal Newhouser/50 8.00
57BA Jason Giambi/100 6.00
57DY Jason Giambi/68 6.00
57IN Jason Giambi/50 8.00
57JY Jason Giambi/101 6.00
57PS Jason Giambi/50 8.00
58BA Lance Berkman/100 6.00

58DY Lance Berkman/65 8.00
58IN Lance Berkman/50 8.00
58JY Lance Berkman/102 8.00
58PS Lance Berkman/50 8.00
59BA Todd Helton/100 8.00
59DY Todd Helton/93 6.00
59IN Todd Helton/50 8.00
59JY Todd Helton/50 8.00
59PS Todd Helton/50 8.00
60BA Mark Grace/50 8.00
60JY Mark Grace/95 8.00
60PS Mark Grace/50 15.00
61BA Fred Lynn/100 6.00
61JY Fred Lynn/75 8.00
61PS Fred Lynn/50 8.00
62JY Bob Feller/52 15.00
63BA Robin Yount/100 20.00
63DY Robin Yount/70 20.00
63JY Robin Yount/50 20.00
63PS Robin Yount/50 25.00
64BA Tony Gwynn/100 15.00
64DY Tony Gwynn/69 20.00
64IN Tony Gwynn/50 20.00
64JY Tony Gwynn/99 25.00
64PS Tony Gwynn/50 20.00
65BA Tony Gwynn/100 15.00
65DY Tony Gwynn/69 15.00
65IN Tony Gwynn/50 15.00
65JY Tony Gwynn/99 15.00
65PS Tony Gwynn/50 15.00
66DY Frank Robinson/54 10.00
66JY Frank Robinson/70 10.00
67BA Mike Schmidt/50 20.00
67DY Mike Schmidt/46 20.00
67IN Mike Schmidt/50 20.00
67JY Mike Schmidt/81 20.00
67PS Mike Schmidt/50 20.00
68JY Lou Brock/66 15.00
69BA Don Sutton/50 8.00
69DY Don Sutton/58 8.00
69JY Don Sutton/72 8.00
70BA Mark Mulder/100 4.00
70DY Mark Mulder/68 6.00
70IN Mark Mulder/101 4.00
70PS Mark Mulder/50 6.00
71BA Luis Gonzalez/100 4.00
71DY Luis Gonzalez/98 4.00
71JY Luis Gonzalez/101 4.00
71PS Luis Gonzalez/50 6.00
72BA Jorge Posada/100 6.00
72JY Jorge Posada/101 6.00
72PS Jorge Posada/50 8.00
73BA Sammy Sosa/50 20.00
73IN Sammy Sosa/50 25.00
73JY Sammy Sosa/101 20.00
73PS Sammy Sosa/50 25.00
74BA Roberto Alomar/100 6.00
74DY Roberto Alomar/62 10.00
74JY Roberto Alomar/102 8.00
74PS Roberto Alomar/50 6.00
75JY Roberto Clemente/69 80.00
76BA Jeff Kent/100 4.00
76DY Jeff Kent/58 6.00
76JY Jeff Kent/101 4.00
76PS Jeff Kent/50 6.00
77DY Sean Casey/59 8.00
77JY Sean Casey/100 4.00
78BA Roger Clemens/50 25.00
78IN Roger Clemens/50 25.00
78JY Roger Clemens/95 20.00
78PS Roger Clemens/50 25.00
79DY Warren Spahn/53 15.00
79JY Warren Spahn/58 15.00
80BA Roger Clemens/100 20.00
80IN Roger Clemens/50 25.00
80JY Roger Clemens/102 25.00
80PS Roger Clemens/50 25.00
81BA Jim Palmer/50 10.00
81DY Jim Palmer/54 10.00
81JY Jim Palmer/69 10.00
81PS Jim Palmer/50 10.00
82BA Juan Gonzalez/100 10.00
82JY Juan Gonzalez/101 10.00
82PS Juan Gonzalez/50 10.00
83BA Will Clark/100 15.00
83DY Will Clark/58 15.00
83JY Will Clark/88 15.00
84BA Don Mattingly/50 25.00
84IN Don Mattingly/50 25.00
84JY Don Mattingly/93 25.00
84PS Don Mattingly/50 25.00
85BA Ryne Sandberg/40 30.00
85IN Ryne Sandberg/50 30.00
85JY Ryne Sandberg/85 30.00
85PS Ryne Sandberg/50 30.00
86JY Early Wynn/55 8.00
87BA Manny Ramirez/50 10.00
87JY Manny Ramirez/102 6.00
87PS Manny Ramirez/50 10.00
88BA Rickey Henderson/100 10.00
88DY Rickey Henderson/62 15.00
88IN Rickey Henderson/50 10.00
88JY Rickey Henderson/99 15.00
88PS Rickey Henderson/50 15.00
89BA Rickey Henderson/100 10.00
89DY Rickey Henderson/69 10.00
89PS Rickey Henderson/50 15.00
90BA Jason Giambi/50 10.00
90IN Jason Giambi/50 10.00
90JY Jason Giambi/102 8.00
90PS Jason Giambi/50 10.00
91BA Carlos Delgado/50 6.00
91DY Carlos Delgado/68 6.00
91JY Carlos Delgado/100 4.00
91PS Carlos Delgado/50 8.00
92BA Jim Thome/50 8.00
92JY Jim Thome/102 10.00

92PS Jim Thome/50 10.00
93BA Andruw Jones/100 6.00
93DY Andruw Jones/66 8.00
93JY Andruw Jones/101 6.00
93PS Andruw Jones/50 8.00
94BA Rafael Palmeiro/100 8.00
94DY Rafael Palmeiro/72 8.00
94JY Rafael Palmeiro/102 8.00
94PS Rafael Palmeiro/50 8.00
95BA Troy Glaus/100 6.00
95DY Troy Glaus/97 6.00
95IN Troy Glaus/50 6.00
95JY Troy Glaus/100 6.00
95PS Troy Glaus/50 8.00
96BA Wade Boggs/50 10.00
96IN Wade Boggs/50 10.00
96JN Wade Boggs/26 25.00
96JY Wade Boggs/86 8.00
96PS Wade Boggs/50 10.00
97BA Jim "Catfish" Hunter/50 10.00
97DY Jim "Catfish" Hunter/68 10.00
97JN Jim "Catfish" Hunter/27 15.00
97JY Jim "Catfish" Hunter/68 10.00
97PS Jim "Catfish" Hunter/50 10.00
98BA Juan Marichal/50 10.00
98DY Juan Marichal/58 10.00
98JY Juan Marichal/67 10.00
98PS Juan Marichal/50 10.00
99BA Carlton Fisk/50 15.00
99IN Carlton Fisk/27 25.00
99JY Carlton Fisk/50 10.00
99PS Carlton Fisk/50 15.00
100BA Vladimir Guerrero/100 8.00
100DY Vladimir Guerrero/69 15.00
100IN Vladimir Guerrero/27 30.00
100JY Vladimir Guerrero/101 8.00
100PS Vladimir Guerrero/50 10.00
101BA Rod Carew/100 10.00
101DY Rod Carew/65 15.00
101JN Rod Carew/29 20.00
101JY Rod Carew/85 10.00
101PS Rod Carew/50 10.00
102BA Rod Carew/100 10.00
102DY Rod Carew/61 15.00
102JN Rod Carew/29 20.00
102JY Rod Carew/71 10.00
102PS Rod Carew/50 15.00
103BA Joe Carter/50 6.00
103DY Joe Carter/77 8.00
103JN Joe Carter/29 15.00
103JY Joe Carter/94 6.00
104BA Mike Sweeney/100 4.00
104DY Mike Sweeney/69 6.00
104JN Mike Sweeney/29 15.00
104JY Mike Sweeney/101 4.00
104PS Mike Sweeney/50 6.00
105DY Nolan Ryan/65 40.00
105JN Nolan Ryan/50 50.00
105JY Nolan Ryan/70 50.00
105PS Nolan Ryan/50 40.00
106BA Orlando Cepeda/50 8.00
106DY Orlando Cepeda/58 8.00
106IN Orlando Cepeda/30 15.00
106JN Orlando Cepeda/30 15.00
106JY Orlando Cepeda/50 8.00
106PS Orlando Cepeda/65 8.00
107BA Magglio Ordonez/100 4.00
107DY Magglio Ordonez/30 15.00
107JY Magglio Ordonez/100 4.00
107PS Magglio Ordonez/50 8.00
108BA Hoyt Wilhelm/50 8.00
108IN Hoyt Wilhelm/31 15.00
108JY Hoyt Wilhelm/68 8.00
108PS Hoyt Wilhelm/50 8.00
109BA Mike Piazza/50 15.00
109DY Mike Piazza/62 20.00
109IN Mike Piazza/31 30.00
109JY Mike Piazza/50 15.00
109PS Mike Piazza/50 20.00
110BA Greg Maddux/100 10.00
110DY Greg Maddux/66 15.00
110IN Greg Maddux/50 15.00
110JN Greg Maddux/31 30.00
110JY Greg Maddux/102 15.00
110PS Greg Maddux/50 15.00
111BA Mark Prior/100 8.00
111IN Mark Prior/50 10.00
111JY Mark Prior/102 8.00
111PS Mark Prior/50 10.00
112BA Torii Hunter/100 6.00
112DY Torii Hunter/61 8.00
112IN Torii Hunter/50 10.00
112JN Torii Hunter/48 10.00
112JY Torii Hunter/101 6.00
112PS Torii Hunter/50 8.00
113BA Steve Carlton/50 8.00
113DY Steve Carlton/46 15.00
113IN Steve Carlton/50 10.00
113JN Steve Carlton/31 15.00
113JY Steve Carlton/81 8.00
113PS Steve Carlton/50 10.00
114BA Jose Canseco/50 10.00
114DY Jose Canseco/68 10.00
114IN Jose Canseco/50 10.00
114JN Jose Canseco/33 15.00
114JY Jose Canseco/89 10.00
114PS Jose Canseco/50 15.00
115BA Nolan Ryan/50 30.00
115DY Nolan Ryan/72 30.00
115IN Nolan Ryan/50 30.00
115JN Nolan Ryan/34 40.00

115JY Nolan Ryan/90 30.00
115PS Nolan Ryan/50 30.00
116BA Nolan Ryan/50 30.00
116DY Nolan Ryan/65 30.00
116JN Nolan Ryan/34 40.00
116JY Nolan Ryan/84 30.00
116PS Nolan Ryan/50 30.00
118BA Kerry Wood/50 10.00
118JN Kerry Wood/34 25.00
118JY Kerry Wood/101 10.00
118PS Kerry Wood/50 15.00
119BA Mike Mussina/50 10.00
119JN Mike Mussina/35 25.00
119JY Mike Mussina/101 10.00
119PS Mike Mussina/50 15.00
120JN Yogi Berra/35 25.00
120JY Yogi Berra/47 25.00
121JY Thurman Munson/79 15.00
122BA Frank Thomas/100 8.00
122JN Frank Thomas/35 15.00
122JY Frank Thomas/94 8.00
122PS Frank Thomas/50 8.00
123BA Rickey Henderson/50 15.00
123DY Rickey Henderson/68 10.00
123JN Rickey Henderson/35 20.00
123JY Rickey Henderson/80 10.00
123PS Rickey Henderson/50 15.00
124BA Mike Mussina/100 6.00
124DY Mike Mussina/54 10.00
124JN Mike Mussina/35 20.00
124JY Mike Mussina/97 8.00
124PS Mike Mussina/50 10.00
125BA Gaylord Perry/100 6.00
125DY Gaylord Perry/77 6.00
125JN Gaylord Perry/36 10.00
125JY Gaylord Perry/82 6.00
125PS Gaylord Perry/50 8.00
126BA Nick Johnson/100 4.00
126JN Nick Johnson/36 6.00
126JY Nick Johnson/50 4.00
126PS Nick Johnson/50 8.00
127BA Curt Schilling/100 8.00
127DY Curt Schilling/98 8.00
127JN Curt Schilling/38 15.00
127JY Curt Schilling/102 8.00
127PS Curt Schilling/50 6.00
128BA Dave Parker/100 6.00
128JN Dave Parker/39 10.00
128JY Dave Parker/80 8.00
128PS Dave Parker/50 8.00
129DY Eddie Mathews/53 15.00
129JN Eddie Mathews/41 25.00
129JY Eddie Mathews/59 20.00
130DY Tom Seaver/62 15.00
130JN Tom Seaver/41 20.00
130JY Tom Seaver/69 15.00
131DY Tom Seaver/59 15.00
131JN Tom Seaver/41 25.00
131JY Tom Seaver/78 15.00
132JN Jackie Robinson/42 80.00
132JY Jackie Robinson/52 60.00
133BA Reggie Jackson/100 15.00
133DY Reggie Jackson/65 15.00
133IN Reggie Jackson/50 10.00
133JN Reggie Jackson/44 20.00
133JY Reggie Jackson/80 10.00
133PS Reggie Jackson/50 15.00
134BA Willie McCovey/100 8.00
134DY Willie McCovey/58 10.00
134JN Willie McCovey/44 10.00
134JY Willie McCovey/77 8.00
134PS Willie McCovey/50 10.00
135BA Eric Davis/100 6.00
135DY Eric Davis/59 8.00
135JN Eddie Davis/44 10.00
135JY Eric Davis/89 6.00
135PS Eric Davis/50 8.00
136BA Adam Dunn/100 8.00
136DY Adam Dunn/59 10.00
136JN Adam Dunn/44 15.00
136JY Adam Dunn/102 8.00
136PS Adam Dunn/50 10.00
137BA Roy Oswalt/100 4.00
137DY Roy Oswalt/65 6.00
137IN Roy Oswalt/50 6.00
137JY Roy Oswalt/102 4.00
137PS Roy Oswalt/50 6.00
138BA Pedro J. Martinez/50 15.00
138DY Pedro J. Martinez/50 15.00
138JN Pedro J. Martinez/45 20.00
138JY Pedro J. Martinez/95 15.00
138PS Pedro J. Martinez/50 15.00
139BA Pedro Martinez/100 8.00
139IN Pedro Martinez/50 10.00
139JN Pedro J. Martinez/45 10.00
139JY Pedro J. Martinez/102 8.00
139PS Pedro J. Martinez/50 8.00
140BA Andy Pettitte/50 6.00
140DY Andy Pettitte/46 8.00
140JY Andy Pettitte/97 8.00
140PS Andy Pettitte/50 8.00
141BA Jack Morris/100 6.00
141IN Jack Morris/50 8.00
141JN Jack Morris/47 8.00
141JY Jack Morris/85 6.00
141PS Jack Morris/50 8.00
142BA Tom Glavine/100 6.00
142DY Tom Glavine/66 10.00
142IN Tom Glavine/47 15.00
142JY Tom Glavine/50 10.00
142PS Tom Glavine/50 10.00
143BA Randy Johnson/50 15.00
143DY Randy Johnson/77 15.00
143IN Randy Johnson/50 15.00
143JN Randy Johnson/51 15.00
143JY Randy Johnson/98 10.00
143PS Randy Johnson/50 15.00

144BA	Bernie Williams/100	8.00
144IN	Bernie Williams/50	10.00
144JN	Bernie Williams/51	10.00
144JY	Bernie Williams/100	8.00
144PS	Bernie Williams/50	10.00
145BA	Randy Johnson/50	15.00
145DY	Randy Johnson/98	10.00
145IN	Randy Johnson/50	15.00
145JN	Randy Johnson/51	15.00
145JY	Randy Johnson/102	15.00
145PS	Randy Johnson/50	15.00
146DY	Don Drysdale/58	10.00
146JN	Don Drysdale/53	10.00
146JY	Don Drysdale/64	10.00
147BA	Mark Buehrle/100	4.00
147JN	Mark Buehrle/56	6.00
147JY	Mark Buehrle/101	6.00
147PS	Mark Buehrle/50	6.00
148BA	Chan Ho Park/100	4.00
148DY	Chan Ho Park/58	6.00
148JN	Chan Ho Park/61	6.00
148JY	Chan Ho Park/101	4.00
148PS	Chan Ho Park/50	6.00
149BA	Carlton Fisk/100	8.00
149IN	Carlton Fisk/50	15.00
149JN	Carlton Fisk/72	15.00
149JY	Carlton Fisk/92	15.00
149PS	Carlton Fisk/50	15.00
150BA	Barry Zito/100	6.00
150DY	Barry Zito/68	8.00
150JN	Barry Zito/75	8.00
150JY	Barry Zito/101	6.00
150PS	Barry Zito/50	8.00

2003 Leaf Limited

		NM/M
Complete Set (170):		
Common Player (1-151):		1.50
Production 999		
Common (152-170):		4.00
Production 399		
Common Auto. Memor.		
(171-200):		15.00
Production 99		
Common Auto. (171-200):		8.00
Pack (4):		75.00
Box (4):		250.00
1	Derek Jeter	6.00
2	Eric Chavez	1.50
3	Alex Rodriguez	5.00
4	Miguel Tejada	1.50
5	Nomar Garciaparra	4.00
6	Jeff Bagwell	3.00
7	Jim Thome	2.00
8	Pat Burrell	1.50
9	Albert Pujols	5.00
10	Juan Gonzalez	3.00
11	Shawn Green	1.50
12	Craig Biggio	1.50
13	Chipper Jones	3.00
14	Hideo Nomo	2.00
15	Vernon Wells	1.50
16	Gary Sheffield	2.00
17	Barry Larkin	1.50
18	Josh Beckett	1.50
19	Edgar Martinez	1.50
20	Ivan Rodriguez	2.00
21	Jeff Kent	1.50
22	Roberto Alomar	1.50
23	Alfonso Soriano	3.00
24	Jim Thome	2.00
25	Juan Gonzalez	3.00
26	Carlos Beltran	2.00
27	Shawn Green	1.50
28	Tim Hudson	1.50
29	Deion Sanders	1.50
30	Rafael Palmeiro	2.00
31	Todd Helton	3.00
32	Lance Berkman	1.50
33	Mike Mussina	2.00
34	Kazuhisa Ishii	1.50
35	Bill Mueller	1.50
36	Miguel Tejada	1.50
37	Juan Gonzalez	2.00
38	Roberto Alomar	1.50
39	Roberto Alomar	1.50
40	Luis Gonzalez	1.50
41	Jorge Posada	1.50
42	Mark Mulder	1.50
43	Sammy Sosa	4.00
44	Mark Prior	2.00
45	Roger Clemens	4.00
46	Tom Glavine	1.50
47	Mark Teixeira	1.50
48	Manny Ramirez	2.00
49	Frank Thomas	2.00
50	Troy Glaus	3.00
51	Andruw Jones	3.00

52	Jason Giambi	2.00
53	Jim Thome	2.00
54	Barry Bonds	6.00
55	Rafael Palmeiro	2.00
56	Edgar Martinez	1.50
57	Vladimir Guerrero	3.00
58	Roberto Alomar	1.50
59	Mike Sweeney	1.50
60	Magglio Ordonez	1.50
61	Ken Griffey Jr.	4.00
62	Craig Biggio	1.50
63	Greg Maddux	4.00
64	Mike Piazza	4.00
65	Tom Glavine	1.50
66	Kerry Wood	2.00
67	Frank Thomas	3.00
68	Mike Mussina	1.50
69	Nick Johnson	1.50
70	Bernie Williams	1.50
71	Scott Rolen	2.00
72	Curt Schilling	2.00
73	Adam Dunn	2.00
74	Roy Oswalt	1.50
75	Pedro J. Martinez	3.00
76	Tom Glavine	1.50
77	Torii Hunter	1.50
78	Austin Kearns	1.50
79	Randy Johnson	3.00
80	Bernie Williams	1.50
81	Ichiro Suzuki	4.00
82	Kerry Wood	2.00
83	Kazuhisa Ishii	1.50
84	Randy Johnson	1.50
85	Nick Johnson	1.50
86	Josh Beckett	1.50
87	Curt Schilling	2.00
88	Mike Mussina	2.00
89	Pedro J. Martinez	3.00
90	Barry Zito	1.50
91	Jim Edmonds	1.50
92-96	Rickey Henderson	3.00
97	Randy Johnson	3.00
98	Mark Grace	1.50
99	Pedro J. Martinez	3.00
100	Hee Seop Choi	1.50
101	Ivan Rodriguez	2.00
102	Jeff Kent	1.50
103	Hideo Nomo	3.00
104	Hideo Nomo	3.00
105	Mike Piazza	4.00
106	Tom Glavine	1.50
107	Roberto Alomar	1.50
108	Roger Clemens	5.00
109	Jason Giambi	2.00
110	Jim Thome	2.00
111	Alex Rodriguez	5.00
112	Juan Gonzalez	2.00
113	Torii Hunter	1.50
114	Roy Oswalt	1.50
115	Curt Schilling	2.00
116	Magglio Ordonez	1.50
117	Rafael Palmeiro	2.00
118	Andruw Jones	3.00
119	Manny Ramirez	3.00
120	Mark Teixeira	1.50
121	Mark Mulder	1.50
122	Garret Anderson	1.50
123	Tim Hudson	1.50
124	Todd Helton	3.00
125	Troy Glaus	3.00
126	Derek Jeter	6.00
127	Barry Bonds	6.00
128	Greg Maddux	4.00
129	Roger Clemens	5.00
130	Nomar Garciaparra	4.00
131	Mike Piazza	4.00
132	Alex Rodriguez	5.00
133	Ichiro Suzuki	4.00
134	Randy Johnson	3.00
135	Sammy Sosa	4.00
136	Ken Griffey Jr.	4.00
137	Alfonso Soriano	3.00
138	Jason Giambi	2.00
139	Albert Pujols	5.00
140	Chipper Jones	3.00
141	Adam Dunn	2.00
142	Pedro J. Martinez	3.00
143	Vladimir Guerrero	3.00
144	Mark Prior	2.00
145	Barry Zito	1.50
146	Jeff Bagwell	3.00
147	Lance Berkman	1.50
148	Shawn Green	1.50
149	Jason Giambi	2.00
150	Randy Johnson	3.00
151	Alex Rodriguez	5.00
152	Babe Ruth	10.00
153	Ty Cobb	6.00
154	Jackie Robinson	6.00
155	Lou Gehrig	8.00
156	Thurman Munson	6.00
157	Roberto Clemente	5.00
158	Nolan Ryan	10.00
159	Nolan Ryan	10.00
160	Nolan Ryan	10.00
161	Cal Ripken Jr.	10.00
162	Don Mattingly	8.00
163	Stan Musial	6.00
164	Tony Gwynn	3.00
165	Yogi Berra	3.00
166	Johnny Bench	5.00
167	Mike Schmidt	8.00
168	George Brett	8.00
169	Ryne Sandberg	4.00
170	Ernie Banks	5.00
171	J. Bonderman/Auto./Jsy	40.00
172	Jose Contreras/	
	Auto. **RC**	40.00

173	Chien-Ming Wang/	
	Auto. **RC**	200.00
174	Hideki Matsui/Base **RC**	40.00
175	Hong-Chih Kuo/	
	Auto./Bat **RC**	120.00
176	Brandon Webb/	
	Auto./Bat **RC**	50.00
177	Richard Fischer/Auto.	8.00
178	Robby Hammock/	
	Auto./Bat	10.00
179	Todd Wellemeyer/	
	Auto./.49 **RC**	20.00
180	Prentice Redman/	
	Auto./Bat **RC**	10.00
181	Nook Logan/Auto. **RC**	10.00
182	Craig Brazell/Auto. **RC**	10.00
183	Tim Olson/Auto./Bat **RC**	10.00
184	Matt Kata/Auto./Bat **RC**	10.00
185	A. Machado/Auto.	8.00
186	Michael Hessman/	
	Auto. **RC**	10.00
187	Oscar Villarreal/Auto. **RC**	8.00
188	Guillermo Quiroz/	
	Auto./Bat **RC**	10.00
189	Michel Hernandez/	
	Auto. **RC**	10.00
190	Clint Barmes/	
	Auto./Bat **RC**	20.00
191	Pete LaForest/	
	Auto./Bat **RC**	10.00
192	Adam Loewen/Auto. **RC**	10.00
193	Terrmel Sledge/	
	Auto./Bat **RC**	10.00
194	Lew Ford/Auto./Bat **RC**	10.00
195	Todd Wellemeyer/	
	Auto./.49 **RC**	20.00
196	Clint Barmes/	
	Auto./Bat **RC**	20.00
197	J. Bonderman/Auto./Jsy	40.00
198	Brandon Webb/	
	Auto./Jsy **RC**	50.00
199	Hideki Matsui/Base **RC**	30.00
200	Jose Contreras/	
	Auto. **RC**	40.00

Silver Spotlight

Silvers (1-170):	1-2X
Production 100	
Silver Auto. Memor. (171-200):	1X
Silver Memor. (171-200):	1X
Silver Auto:	1X
Production 29 to 50	

Gold Spotlight

Golds (1-151):	2-4X
Golds (152-170):	1.5-3X
Production 50	
Golds (171-200):	No Pricing
Production 10 to 25	

Jersey Numbers

		NM/M
Common Player:		
Production 5-100		
Some not priced due to scarcity.		
2	Rod Carew/50	20.00
3	Nolan Ryan/50	40.00
8	Reggie Jackson/50	30.00
5	Brooks Robinson/50	25.00
5	Frank Robinson/50	20.00
6	Cal Ripken Jr./100	40.00
7	Carlton Fisk/50	15.00
8	Roger Clemens/100	15.00
10	Lou Boudreau/50	10.00
11	Bob Feller/50	30.00
14	Alan Trammell/50	10.00
14	Harmon Killebrew/50	20.00
16	Rod Carew/50	20.00
16	Kirby Puckett/50	20.00
19	Yogi Berra/50	30.00
20	Thurman Munson/50	30.00
21	Don Mattingly/100	25.00
26	Alex Rodriguez/100	10.00
26	Randy Johnson/50	10.00
27	Nolan Ryan/100	30.00
28	Dale Murphy/50	20.00
29	Warren Spahn/50	20.00
30	Eddie Mathews/50	25.00
32	Ryne Sandberg/100	30.00
32	Johnny Bench/50	30.00
34	Joe Morgan/50	10.00
35	Randy Johnson/50	10.00
36	Nolan Ryan/100	30.00
37	Pee Wee Reese/50	15.00
38	Duke Snider/25	25.00
39	Jackie Robinson/25	65.00
40	Robin Yount/50	30.00
41	Paul Molitor/50	20.00

42	Pedro Martinez/50	10.00
43	Randy Johnson/50	10.00
44	Tom Seaver/50	25.00
45	Gary Carter/50	10.00
46	Mike Schmidt/50	30.00
47	Steve Carlton/50	10.00
48	Willie Stargell/50	20.00
50	Ozzie Smith/50	35.00
51	Stan Musial/100	30.00
52	Enos Slaughter/50	10.00
53	Orlando Cepeda/50	10.00
54	Willie McCovey/50	15.00
57	Harmon Killebrew/, Rod Carew/50	50.00
58	Harmon Killebrew/, Kirby Puckett/50	50.00
68	Thurman Munson/, Yogi Berra/25	50.00
69	Don Mattingly/, Yogi Berra/25	60.00
71	Dale Murphy/, Warren Spahn/25	50.00
72	Dale Murphy/, Eddie Mathews/25	45.00
73	Eddie Mathews/, Warren Spahn/25	60.00
74	Joe Morgan/, Johnny Bench/25	40.00
75	Duke Snider/, Pee Wee Reese/25	40.00
78	Paul Molitor/, Robin Yount/25	75.00
81	Ozzie Smith/, Stan Musial/25	60.00
82	Enos Slaughter/, Stan Musial/25	60.00
83	Orlando Cepeda/, Willie McCovey/25	40.00
84	Nolan Ryan/, Reggie Jackson/25	60.00
90	Alex Rodriguez/, Randy Johnson/25	25.00
91	Pedro J. Martinez/, Randy Johnson/25	35.00
94	Reggie Jackson/25	60.00
95	Nolan Ryan/25	60.00
96	Nolan Ryan/25	60.00
97	Nolan Ryan/25	60.00
98	Nolan Ryan/25	60.00
99	Cal Ripken Jr./, Rafael Palmeiro/25	90.00
100	Dale Murphy/, Deion Sanders/25	50.00

Jersey Numbers Retired

		NM/M
Many not priced due to scarcity.		
1	Rod Carew/29	30.00
2	Nolan Ryan/30	50.00
5	Frank Robinson/20	20.00
7	Carlton Fisk/27	30.00
9	Carlton Fisk/27	15.00
16	Kirby Puckett/34	35.00
21	Don Mattingly/23	50.00
27	Nolan Ryan/34	50.00
30	Eddie Mathews/41	20.00
36	Nolan Ryan/34	50.00
39	Jackie Robinson/42	50.00
44	Tom Seaver/41	20.00
46	Mike Schmidt/20	50.00
47	Steve Carlton/32	15.00
49	Roberto Clemente/21	100.00
50	Orlando Cepeda/25	15.00
54	Willie McCovey/44	30.00

Leather

		NM/M
Common Player:		
Production 10-25		
Golds:		No Pricing
Production 5-10		
Leather & Lace:		No Pricing
Production 10		
Leather & Lace Gold:		No Pricing
Production 5		
1	Alex Rodriguez/25	40.00
2	Chipper Jones/25	30.00
3	Jimmie Foxx/25	65.00
4	Kirby Puckett/25	25.00
5	Mike Schmidt/25	65.00
6	Roger Clemens/25	45.00
8	Tony Gwynn/25	20.00
10	Vladimir Guerrero/25	25.00
11	Adam Dunn/25	20.00
12	Andruw Jones/25	25.00
13	Curt Schilling/25	20.00
14	Randy Johnson/25	25.00
15	Mark Prior/25	40.00

Lineups - Bats

		NM/M
Common Player:		
Production 25-50		
1	Paul Molitor/, Robin Yount/50	35.00
2	Bernie Williams/, Don Mattingly/50	40.00
4	Derek Jeter/, Hideki Matsui/50	60.00
5	Andre Dawson/, Ryne Sandberg/50	40.00
6	Bo Jackson/, George Brett/50	40.00
7	Jose Canseco/, Reggie Jackson/25	40.00
8	Mark Grace/, Ryne Sandberg/50	40.00

9	Jose Canseco/, Rickey Henderson/50	30.00
10	Hideo Nomo/, Mike Piazza/50	30.00

Lineups - Buttons

		NM/M
Production One Set		

Lineups - Jerseys

		NM/M
Production 5-50		
1	Paul Molitor/, Robin Yount/50	35.00
2	Bernie Williams/, Don Mattingly/50	40.00
3	Hee Seop Choi/, Sammy Sosa/50	30.00
4	Derek Jeter/, Hideki Matsui/50/Base	30.00
5	Andre Dawson/, Ryne Sandberg/50	35.00
6	Bo Jackson/, George Brett/50	50.00
8	Jose Canseco/, Reggie Jackson/50	25.00
9	Jose Canseco/, Rickey Henderson/50	25.00
10	Hideo Nomo/, Mike Piazza/25	25.00

Lineups Tag Team

No Pricing
Production 5

Lumberjacks

		NM/M
Some not priced due to scarcity.		
Production 1-25		
Black:		No Pricing
Production 1-5		
Silver:		No Pricing
Production 1-10		
1	Babe Ruth/25	200.00
2	Lou Gehrig/25	150.00
3	Roberto Clemente/25	120.00
4	Stan Musial/25	40.00
5	Rogers Hornsby/25	50.00
6	Don Mattingly/25	50.00
7	Rickey Henderson/25	20.00
8	Cal Ripken Jr./25	75.00
9	Yogi Berra/25	30.00
10	Reggie Jackson/25	35.00
11	George Brett/25	60.00
12	Mel Ott/25	40.00
13	Roger Maris/25	60.00
14	Ryne Sandberg/25	50.00
16	Richie Ashburn/25	40.00
17	Mike Schmidt/25	60.00
18	Tony Gwynn/25	25.00
19	Ty Cobb/25	110.00
20	Thurman Munson/25	35.00
21	Jimmie Foxx/25	60.00
22	Duke Snider/25	25.00
24	Alex Rodriguez/25	30.00
25	Nomar Garciaparra/25	30.00
26	Hideki Matsui/25/Base	50.00
27	Ichiro Suzuki/25/Base	50.00
28	Barry Bonds/25/Base	35.00
29	Mike Piazza/25	30.00
30	Alfonso Soriano/25	25.00
31	Al Kaline/25	30.00
33	Dale Murphy/25	30.00
34	Orlando Cepeda/25	30.00
35	Willie McCovey/25	30.00
37	Brooks Robinson/25	30.00

Lumberjacks - Barrel

		NM/M
1/1 except where indicated.		
No pricing due to scarcity.		
21	Jimmie Foxx	
	(7/05 Auction)	1,525

Lumberjacks - Jerseys

		NM/M
Production 1-25		
Black:		No Pricing
Production 1-5		
Silver:		No Pricing
Production 1-10		
4	Stan Musial/25	40.00
6	Don Mattingly/25	30.00
8	Cal Ripken Jr./25	80.00
9	Yogi Berra/25	25.00
11	George Brett/25	60.00
12	Mel Ott/25	40.00
14	Ryne Sandberg/25	50.00
15	Eddie Mathews/25	25.00
17	Mike Schmidt/25	50.00
18	Tony Gwynn/25	25.00
20	Thurman Munson/25	25.00
22	Duke Snider/25	20.00
24	Alex Rodriguez/25	30.00
25	Nomar Garciaparra/25	30.00
26	Hideki Matsui/25/Ball	50.00
27	Ichiro Suzuki/25/Ball	40.00
28	Barry Bonds/25/Ball	40.00
29	Mike Piazza/25	25.00
30	Alfonso Soriano/25	25.00
32	Harmon Killebrew/25	25.00
33	Dale Murphy/25	25.00
34	Orlando Cepeda/25	15.00
35	Willie McCovey/25	30.00
36	Willie Stargell/25	30.00
37	Brooks Robinson/25	20.00

Lumberjacks - Jerseys/Bats

		NM/M
Some not priced due to scarcity.		
Black:		No Pricing
Production 1-5		
Silver:		No Pricing
Production 1-10		
4	Stan Musial/25	60.00
6	Don Mattingly/25	75.00
8	Cal Ripken Jr./25	140.00
9	Yogi Berra/25	30.00
11	George Brett/25	80.00
13	Roger Maris/25	100.00
14	Ryne Sandberg/25	65.00
15	Eddie Mathews/25	40.00
17	Mike Schmidt/25	65.00
18	Tony Gwynn/25	40.00
20	Thurman Munson/25	40.00
24	Alex Rodriguez/25	40.00
25	Nomar Garciaparra/25	40.00
26	Hideki Matsui/25/ Base/Ball	65.00
27	Ichiro Suzuki/25/ Base/Ball	60.00
28	Barry Bonds/25/ Base/Ball	100.00
29	Mike Piazza/25	40.00
30	Alfonso Soriano/25	25.00
33	Dale Murphy/25	40.00
35	Willie McCovey/25	35.00
36	Willie Stargell/25	30.00
37	Brooks Robinson/25	30.00

Lumberjacks Combos

		NM/M
Production 1-25		
Black:		No Pricing
Production 1-5		
Silver:		No Pricing
Production 1-10		
38	Hideki Matsui/, Ichiro Suzuki/25/Base	80.00
40	Don Mattingly/, Lou Gehrig/25	240.00
41	Thurman Munson/, Yogi Berra/25	50.00
42	Mike Schmidt/, Richie Ashburn/25	60.00
43	Rogers Hornsby/, Stan Musial/25	80.00
44	Don Mattingly/, Roger Maris/25	100.00

Lumberjacks Combos - Jerseys

		NM/M
Production 1-25		
Some not priced due to scarcity.		
Black:		No Pricing
Production 1-5		
Silver:		No Pricing
Production 1-10		
38	Hideki Matsui/, Ichiro Suzuki/25/Ball	100.00
41	Thurman Munson/, Yogi Berra/25	60.00

Lumberjacks Combos - Jerseys/Bats

		NM/M
Production 1-25		
Some not priced due to scarcity.		
Black:		No Pricing
Production 1-5		
Silver:		No Pricing
Production 1-10		
38	Hideki Matsui/, Ichiro Suzuki/25/Ball	100.00
41	Thurman Munson/, Yogi Berra/25	50.00
42	Mike Schmidt/, Richie Ashburn/25	60.00

Material Monikers Bats

		NM/M
Production 1-25		
No pricing for many, due to scarcity.		
2	Eric Chavez/25	35.00
12	Craig Biggio/25	40.00
15	Vernon Wells/25	30.00
19	Edgar Martinez/25	50.00
26	Carlos Beltran/25	40.00
28	Tim Hudson/25	40.00
44	Mark Prior/25	50.00
47	Mark Teixeira/25	40.00
69	Nick Johnson/25	25.00

73	Adam Dunn/25	40.00
74	Roy Oswalt/25	30.00
77	Torii Hunter/25	30.00
85	Nick Johnson/25	25.00
113	Torii Hunter/25	30.00
114	Roy Oswalt/25	30.00
120	Mark Teixeira/25	25.00

Material Monikers Jerseys

NM/M

Common Player:

2	Eric Chavez/25	25.00
4	Miguel Tejada/25	35.00
12	Craig Biggio/25	35.00
15	Vernon Wells/25	25.00
19	Edgar Martinez/25	40.00
26	Carlos Beltran/25	50.00
28	Tim Hudson/25	25.00
44	Mark Prior/25	25.00
47	Mark Teixeira/25	30.00
69	Nick Johnson/25	40.00
73	Adam Dunn/25	40.00
74	Roy Oswalt/25	25.00
77	Torii Hunter/25	25.00
85	Nick Johnson/25	20.00
113	Torii Hunter/25	25.00
114	Roy Oswalt/25	25.00
120	Mark Teixeira/25	25.00

Material Monikers Jersey Numbers

NM/M

Production 1-25
Many not priced due to scarcity.

2	Eric Chavez/25	25.00
4	Miguel Tejada/25	30.00
12	Craig Biggio/25	35.00
15	Vernon Wells/25	20.00
19	Edgar Martinez/25	30.00
26	Carlos Beltran/25	50.00
28	Tim Hudson/25	25.00
44	Mark Prior/25	40.00
47	Mark Teixeira/25	40.00
69	Nick Johnson/25	15.00
73	Adam Dunn/25	40.00
74	Roy Oswalt/25	20.00
77	Torii Hunter/25	25.00
85	Nick Johnson/25	15.00
113	Torii Hunter/25	25.00
114	Roy Oswalt/25	20.00
120	Mark Teixeira/25	40.00

Material Monikers Jersey Position

NM/M

Production 1-25
Many not priced due to scarcity.

2	Eric Chavez/25	25.00
4	Miguel Tejada/25	30.00
12	Craig Biggio/25	35.00
15	Vernon Wells/25	20.00
19	Edgar Martinez/25	40.00
26	Carlos Beltran/25	50.00
28	Tim Hudson/25	25.00
29	Deion Sanders/25	50.00
44	Mark Prior/25	40.00
47	Mark Teixeira/25	40.00
69	Nick Johnson/25	20.00
73	Adam Dunn/25	40.00
74	Roy Oswalt/25	25.00
77	Torii Hunter/25	25.00
85	Nick Johnson/25	20.00
113	Torii Hunter/25	25.00
114	Roy Oswalt/25	25.00
120	Mark Teixeira/25	40.00

Player Threads

NM/M

Production 5-50
Some not priced due to scarcity.
Primes: No Pricing
Production 5-10

1	Roger Clemens/50	15.00
2	Alex Rodriguez/50	15.00
3	Pedro Martinez/50	10.00
4	Randy Johnson/50	10.00
7	Curt Schilling/50	8.00
8	Nolan Ryan/50	35.00
9	Hideo Nomo/50	12.00
10	Mike Piazza/50	15.00
11	Rickey Henderson/50	15.00
12	Ivan Rodriguez/50	10.00
13	Gary Sheffield/50	8.00
14	Jeff Kent/50	8.00
15	Roberto Alomar/50	10.00
16	Rafael Palmeiro/50	8.00
17	Juan Gonzalez/50	8.00
18	Shawn Green/50	8.00
19	Jason Giambi/50	8.00
20	Jim Thome/50	10.00
21	Scott Rolen/50	12.00
22	Mike Mussina/50	10.00
23	Tom Glavine/50	8.00
24	Sammy Sosa/50	10.00

layer Threads Double

NM/M

Production 5-50
Some not priced due to scarcity.
Double Primes: No Pricing
Production 5-10

1	Roger Clemens/50	25.00
2	Alex Rodriguez/50	25.00
3	Pedro Martinez/50	20.00
4	Randy Johnson/50	15.00
7	Curt Schilling/50	10.00
7	Nolan Ryan/50	50.00

8	Hideo Nomo/50	20.00
9	Mike Piazza/50	25.00
11	Rickey Henderson/50	20.00
12	Ivan Rodriguez/50	15.00
13	Gary Sheffield/50	10.00
14	Jeff Kent/50	10.00
15	Roberto Alomar/50	15.00
16	Rafael Palmeiro/50	15.00
18	Juan Gonzalez/50	15.00
18	Shawn Green/50	15.00
19	Jason Giambi/50	15.00
20	Jim Thome/50	15.00
21	Scott Rolen/50	20.00
22	Mike Mussina/50	15.00
23	Tom Glavine/50	15.00
24	Sammy Sosa/50	25.00

Player Threads Triple

NM/M

Production 50
Some not priced due to scarcity.
Triple Primes: No Pricing
Production 5-10

4	Randy Johnson/50	20.00
7	Nolan Ryan/50	75.00
8	Hideo Nomo/50	60.00
11	Rickey Henderson/50	30.00
13	Gary Sheffield/50	15.00
14	Jeff Kent/50	15.00
15	Roberto Alomar/50	25.00

Swatch

Complete Set (40):
Common Player:

Team Threads

NM/M

Production 10-50
Some not priced due to scarcity.
Primes: No Pricing
Production 5-10

26	Alex Rodriguez, Nolan Ryan/50	50.00
27	Hideo Nomo, Mike Piazza/50	20.00
28	Cal Ripken Jr., Mike Mussina/50	50.00
29	Hideo Nomo, Kazuhisa Ishii/50	15.00
30	Nolan Ryan, Randy Johnson/50	40.00

Team Trademarks Autographs

NM/M

Some not priced due to scarcity.

1	Alan Trammell/25	40.00
3	Jim Palmer/25	30.00
6	Gary Carter/25	40.00
6	Andre Dawson/25	30.00
8	Dale Murphy/25	50.00
10	Bobby Doerr/25	35.00
11	Brooks Robinson/25	50.00
12	Eric Davis/25	35.00
13	Fred Lynn/25	30.00
14	Jack Morris/25	25.00
15	Al Kaline/25	60.00
17	Deion Sanders/25	50.00
18	Luis Aparicio/25	35.00
20	Phil Rizzuto/25	40.00
24	Will Clark/25	70.00

Team Trademarks Jersey Autograph

NM/M

Some not priced due to scarcity.

12	Eric Davis/44	30.00
15	Jack Morris/47	25.00
23	Rod Carew/29	50.00
25	Willie McCovey/44	25.00
31	Nolan Ryan/34	140.00
31	Rod Carew/29	50.00
32	Nolan Ryan/34	140.00
34	Nolan Ryan/30	140.00
37	Greg Maddux/31	150.00

Team Trademarks Threads Jersey Number

NM/M

Some not priced due to scarcity.
Primes: 1-1.5X
Production 1-25
Some not priced due to scarcity.

3	Jim Palmer/22	20.00
12	Eric Davis/44	8.00
15	Jack Morris/47	8.00
17	Deion Sanders/24	25.00
19	Orlando Cepeda/30	10.00
23	Rod Carew/29	20.00
24	Will Clark/22	50.00
25	Willie McCovey/44	10.00
31	Nolan Ryan/34	50.00
31	Rod Carew/29	20.00
32	Nolan Ryan/34	50.00
34	Nolan Ryan/30	50.00
37	Greg Maddux/31	30.00

Threads

NM/M

Common Player: 8.00
Varying quantities produced.

1	Derek Jeter/Base/50	20.00
2	Eric Chavez/25	15.00
3	Alex Rodriguez/100	15.00
4	Miguel Tejada/50	8.00
5	Nomar Garciaparra/100	15.00
6	Jeff Bagwell/50	10.00
7	Jim Thome/50	10.00
8	Pat Burrell/25	10.00
9	Albert Pujols/100	20.00
10	Juan Gonzalez/25	20.00
11	Shawn Green/50	10.00
12	Craig Biggio/25	10.00
13	Chipper Jones/25	8.00
14	Hideo Nomo/100	12.00
15	Vernon Wells/25	10.00
16	Gary Sheffield/25	10.00
17	Barry Larkin/25	15.00
18	Josh Beckett/25	15.00
19	Edgar Martinez/25	15.00
20	Ivan Rodriguez/25	20.00
21	Jeff Kent/25	10.00
22	Roberto Alomar/25	15.00
23	Alfonso Soriano/100	8.00
24	Jim Thome/50	10.00
25	Juan Gonzalez/25	15.00
26	Carlos Beltran/25	20.00
27	Shawn Green/50	8.00
28	Tim Hudson/25	10.00
29	Deion Sanders/25	20.00
30	Rafael Palmeiro/25	20.00
31	Todd Helton/25	10.00
32	Lance Berkman/25	10.00
33	Mike Mussina/50	10.00
34	Kazuhisa Ishii/50	8.00
35	Pat Burrell/25	10.00
36	Miguel Tejada/50	8.00
37	Juan Gonzalez/25	15.00
38	Roberto Alomar/25	15.00
39	Roberto Alomar/25	15.00
40	Luis Gonzalez/25	10.00
41	Jorge Posada/25	15.00
42	Mark Mulder/25	10.00
43	Sammy Sosa/25	15.00
44	Mark Prior/50	15.00
45	Roger Clemens/100	15.00
46	Tom Glavine/25	15.00
47	Mark Teixeira/25	10.00
48	Manny Ramirez/50	12.00
49	Frank Thomas/25	15.00
50	Troy Glaus/50	8.00
51	Andruw Jones/50	8.00
52	Jason Giambi/100	8.00
53	Jim Thome/50	10.00
54	Barry Bonds/50/Base	25.00
55	Rafael Palmeiro/25	15.00
56	Edgar Martinez/25	10.00
57	Vladimir Guerrero/50	15.00
58	Roberto Alomar/25	15.00
59	Mike Sweeney/25	10.00
60	Magglio Ordonez/25	10.00
61	Craig Biggio/25	10.00
63	Greg Maddux/25	10.00
64	Mike Piazza/100	15.00
65	Tom Glavine/25	15.00
66	Kerry Wood/25	20.00
67	Frank Thomas/25	20.00
68	Mike Mussina/50	10.00
69	Nick Johnson/25	8.00
70	Bernie Williams/100	10.00
71	Scott Rolen/25	20.00
72	Curt Schilling/25	10.00
73	Adam Dunn/25	15.00
74	Roy Oswalt/25	10.00
75	Pedro Martinez/25	15.00
77	Tom Glavine/25	15.00
77	Torii Hunter/25	10.00
79	Austin Kearns/25	10.00
79	Randy Johnson/100	8.00
81	Bernie Williams/50	8.00
81	Ichiro Suzuki/50	25.00
82	Kerry Wood/25	20.00
83	Kazuhisa Ishii/50	8.00
84	Randy Johnson/50	8.00
86	Nick Johnson/25	8.00
87	Josh Beckett/25	10.00
87	Curt Schilling/25	10.00
88	Mike Mussina/50	10.00
89	Pedro Martinez/25	15.00
91	Barry Zito/75	8.00
91	Jim Edmonds/100	6.00
92	Rickey Henderson/100	20.00
93	Rickey Henderson/50	12.00
94	Rickey Henderson/50	12.00
95	Rickey Henderson/50	12.00
96	Rickey Henderson/50	12.00
97	Randy Johnson/50	8.00
98	Mark Grace/50	10.00
99	Pedro Martinez/25	15.00
100	Hee Seop Choi/25	8.00
101	Ivan Rodriguez/25	15.00
102	Jeff Kent/25	10.00
104	Hideo Nomo/25	15.00
105	Mike Piazza/100	15.00
106	Tom Glavine/25	15.00

107	Roberto Alomar/25	15.00
108	Roger Clemens/100	10.00
109	Jason Giambi/25	10.00
110	Jim Thome/25	15.00
111	Alex Rodriguez/100	10.00
112	Juan Gonzalez/25	10.00
113	Torii Hunter/25	10.00
114	Roy Oswalt/25	10.00
115	Curt Schilling/25	15.00
116	Magglio Ordonez/25	10.00
117	Rafael Palmeiro/25	15.00
118	Andruw Jones/50	8.00
119	Manny Ramirez/50	12.00
120	Mark Teixeira/25	10.00
121	Mark Mulder/25	10.00
123	Tim Hudson/25	10.00
124	Todd Helton/50	10.00
125	Troy Glaus/50	6.00
126	Derek Jeter/Base/50	20.00
127	Barry Bonds/Base/50	25.00
128	Greg Maddux/100	10.00
129	Roger Clemens/100	10.00
130	Nomar Garciaparra/100	10.00
131	Mike Piazza/100	15.00
132	Alex Rodriguez/100	10.00
133	Ichiro Suzuki/Base	25.00
134	Randy Johnson/100	8.00
136	Sammy Sosa/100	15.00
137	Alfonso Soriano/100	8.00
138	Jason Giambi/100	6.00
139	Albert Pujols/100	20.00
140	Chipper Jones/25	20.00
141	Adam Dunn/50	8.00
142	Pedro Martinez/50	10.00
143	Vladimir Guerrero/50	10.00
144	Mark Prior/50	15.00
145	Barry Zito/50	8.00
146	Jeff Bagwell/50	12.00
147	Lance Berkman/ Socks/25	10.00
148	Shawn Green/25	10.00
149	Jason Giambi/25	10.00
150	Randy Johnson/25	20.00
151	Alex Rodriguez/100	10.00
153	Ty Cobb/100	100.00
154	Jackie Robinson/50	25.00
156	Thurman Munson/100	15.00
158	Nolan Ryan/100	30.00
159	Nolan Ryan/100	30.00
160	Nolan Ryan/100	30.00
161	Cal Ripken Jr./100	60.00
162	Don Mattingly/100	25.00
163	Stan Musial/100	25.00
164	Tony Gwynn/100	12.00
165	Yogi Berra/100	12.00
166	Johnny Bench/100	12.00
167	Mike Schmidt/100	25.00
168	George Brett/100	30.00
169	Ryne Sandberg/100	25.00
170	Ernie Banks/50	30.00

Threads Button Up

Production 2-6
No Pricing

Threads Double

NM/M

Common Player:
Production 5 to 25
Some not priced due to scarcity.
Primes: No Pricing
Production 1 to 10

3	Alex Rodriguez/25	40.00
4	Miguel Tejada/25	25.00
10	Juan Gonzalez/25	20.00
12	Craig Biggio/25	25.00
14	Hideo Nomo/25	40.00
15	Vernon Wells/25	15.00
26	Carlos Beltran/25	25.00
28	Tim Hudson/25	20.00
31	Todd Helton/25	25.00
32	Lance Berkman/25	15.00
34	Kazuhisa Ishii/25	20.00
37	Juan Gonzalez/25	20.00
43	Sammy Sosa/25	50.00
44	Mark Prior/25	25.00
51	Andruw Jones/25	20.00
54	Barry Bonds/25	60.00
55	Rafael Palmeiro/25	30.00
60	Magglio Ordonez/25	20.00
73	Adam Dunn/25	20.00
75	Pedro Martinez/25	30.00
78	Austin Kearns/25	20.00
81	Ichiro Suzuki/25	60.00
90	Barry Zito/25	20.00
94	Rickey Henderson/25	25.00
101	Ivan Rodriguez/25	25.00
109	Jason Giambi/25	25.00
116	Magglio Ordonez/25	20.00
117	Rafael Palmeiro/25	30.00
118	Andruw Jones/25	20.00
120	Mark Teixeira/25	20.00
123	Tim Hudson/25	20.00
124	Todd Helton/25	25.00
127	Barry Bonds/25	50.00
132	Alex Rodriguez/25	40.00
133	Ichiro Suzuki/25	60.00
135	Sammy Sosa/25	50.00
141	Adam Dunn/25	30.00
142	Pedro Martinez/25	35.00
144	Mark Prior/25	40.00
146	Jeff Bagwell/25	30.00
147	Lance Berkman/25	15.00
149	Jason Giambi/25	20.00
158	Nolan Ryan/25	80.00

162	Don Mattingly/25	65.00
164	Tony Gwynn/25	40.00
165	Mike Schmidt/25	65.00
168	George Brett/25	75.00
169	Ryne Sandberg/25	65.00

Threads Number

NM/M

Common Player:

7	Jim Thome/25	20.00
18	Josh Beckett/61	10.00
24	Jim Thome/25	20.00
29	Deion Sanders/21	35.00
30	Rafael Palmeiro/20	20.00
33	Mike Mussina/35	15.00
40	Luis Gonzalez/20	15.00
41	Jorge Posada/20	25.00
42	Mark Mulder/20	15.00
43	Sammy Sosa/21	50.00
44	Mark Prior/22	25.00
45	Roger Clemens/22	50.00
46	Tom Glavine/47	8.00
47	Mark Teixeira/23	15.00
48	Manny Ramirez/24	30.00
49	Frank Thomas/35	15.00
50	Troy Glaus/35	10.00
51	Andruw Jones/25	15.00
52	Jason Giambi/52	10.00
53	Jim Thome/25	15.00
55	Rafael Palmeiro/25	20.00
57	Vladimir Guerrero/27	20.00
59	Mike Sweeney/22	10.00
60	Magglio Ordonez/30	10.00
63	Greg Maddux/25	25.00
64	Mike Piazza/31	30.00
65	Tom Glavine/47	8.00
66	Kerry Wood/52	15.00
67	Frank Thomas/35	15.00
68	Mike Mussina/35	15.00
69	Nick Johnson/36	8.00
70	Bernie Williams/51	10.00
71	Scott Rolen/27	20.00
72	Curt Schilling/38	10.00
73	Adam Dunn/44	8.00
74	Roy Oswalt/44	6.00
75	Pedro Martinez/45	10.00
76	Tom Glavine/47	8.00
77	Torii Hunter/48	8.00
79	Austin Kearns/28	10.00
79	Randy Johnson/51	10.00
80	Bernie Williams/51	10.00
82	Kerry Wood/34	20.00
84	Randy Johnson/51	10.00
85	Nick Johnson/36	8.00
86	Josh Beckett/61	10.00
87	Curt Schilling/38	10.00
88	Mike Mussina/35	10.00
89	Pedro Martinez/45	10.00
91	Barry Zito/75	8.00
93	Rickey Henderson/24	25.00
94	Rickey Henderson/35	25.00
95	Rickey Henderson/24	25.00
96	Rickey Henderson/24	25.00
97	Randy Johnson/51	10.00
99	Pedro Martinez/45	10.00
105	Mike Piazza/31	30.00
106	Tom Glavine/47	8.00
108	Roger Clemens/21	50.00
110	Jim Thome/25	15.00
112	Juan Gonzalez/22	20.00
113	Torii Hunter/48	8.00
114	Roy Oswalt/44	6.00
115	Curt Schilling/38	10.00
116	Magglio Ordonez/30	8.00
117	Rafael Palmeiro/25	20.00
118	Andruw Jones/25	10.00
119	Manny Ramirez/24	25.00
120	Mark Teixeira/23	25.00
121	Mark Mulder/20	15.00
125	Troy Glaus/25	12.00
128	Greg Maddux/31	25.00
129	Roger Clemens/22	50.00
131	Mike Piazza/31	30.00
134	Randy Johnson/51	12.00
135	Sammy Sosa/21	50.00
138	Jason Giambi/25	10.00
141	Adam Dunn/44	8.00
142	Pedro Martinez/45	10.00
143	Vladimir Guerrero/27	20.00
144	Mark Prior/22	25.00
145	Barry Zito/75	8.00
150	Randy Johnson/51	10.00
154	Jackie Robinson/42	50.00
157	Roberto Clemente/21	140.00
158	Nolan Ryan/34	50.00
159	Nolan Ryan/34	50.00
160	Nolan Ryan/34	50.00
162	Don Mattingly/23	50.00
165	Yogi Berra/42	15.00
167	Mike Schmidt/20	60.00
169	Ryne Sandberg/23	60.00

Threads Position

NM/M

Common (2-151):	8.00
#'s 2-151	
Production 25	
#'s 152-170	
Production 5-25	
Primes:	1-1.5X
Production 25 for #'s 2-151.	

2	Eric Chavez	8.00
3	Alex Rodriguez	25.00
4	Miguel Tejada	
5	Nomar Garciaparra	30.00
6	Jeff Bagwell	15.00
7	Jim Thome	15.00
8	Pat Burrell	10.00

9	Albert Pujols	35.00
10	Juan Gonzalez	10.00
11	Shawn Green	10.00
12	Craig Biggio	8.00
13	Chipper Jones	25.00
14	Hideo Nomo	30.00
15	Vernon Wells	8.00
16	Gary Sheffield	10.00
17	Barry Larkin	10.00
18	Josh Beckett	15.00
19	Edgar Martinez	15.00
20	Ivan Rodriguez	15.00
21	Jeff Kent	8.00
22	Roberto Alomar	15.00
23	Alfonso Soriano	20.00
25	Juan Gonzalez	15.00
26	Carlos Beltran	8.00
27	Shawn Green	10.00
28	Tim Hudson	10.00
29	Deion Sanders	30.00
30	Rafael Palmeiro	15.00
31	Todd Helton	15.00
32	Lance Berkman	10.00
33	Mike Mussina	15.00
34	Kazuhisa Ishii	10.00
35	Pat Burrell	10.00
36	Miguel Tejada	15.00
37	Juan Gonzalez	15.00
38	Roberto Alomar	15.00
39	Roberto Alomar	15.00
40	Luis Gonzalez	15.00
41	Jorge Posada	15.00
42	Mark Mulder	10.00
43	Sammy Sosa	40.00
44	Mark Prior	25.00
45	Roger Clemens	40.00
46	Tom Glavine	15.00
47	Mark Teixeira	10.00
48	Manny Ramirez	15.00
49	Frank Thomas	15.00
50	Troy Glaus	15.00
51	Andruw Jones	15.00
52	Jason Giambi	15.00
53	Jim Thome	15.00
55	Rafael Palmeiro	15.00
56	Edgar Martinez	15.00
57	Vladimir Guerrero	15.00
58	Roberto Alomar	15.00
60	Magglio Ordonez	10.00
62	Craig Biggio	15.00
63	Greg Maddux	30.00
64	Mike Piazza	25.00
66	Kerry Wood	15.00
67	Frank Thomas	15.00
68	Mike Mussina	15.00
69	Nick Johnson	15.00
70	Bernie Williams	15.00
71	Scott Rolen	15.00
72	Curt Schilling	15.00
73	Adam Dunn	15.00
74	Roy Oswalt	8.00
75	Pedro J. Martinez	15.00
76	Tom Glavine	15.00
77	Torii Hunter	15.00
78	Austin Kearns	15.00
79	Randy Johnson	15.00
80	Bernie Williams	15.00
82	Kerry Wood	15.00
83	Kazuhisa Ishii	10.00
84	Randy Johnson	15.00
85	Nick Johnson	15.00
86	Josh Beckett	15.00
87	Curt Schilling	15.00
88	Mike Mussina	15.00
89	Pedro J. Martinez	15.00
90	Barry Zito	15.00
91	Jim Edmonds	15.00
93	Rickey Henderson	25.00
94	Rickey Henderson	25.00
95	Rickey Henderson	25.00
96	Rickey Henderson	25.00
97	Randy Johnson	15.00
98	Mark Grace	15.00
99	Pedro J. Martinez	15.00
100	Hee Seop Choi	10.00
101	Ivan Rodriguez	15.00
102	Jeff Kent	15.00
104	Hideo Nomo	30.00
105	Mike Piazza	25.00
106	Tom Glavine	15.00
107	Roberto Alomar	15.00
108	Roger Clemens	40.00
109	Jason Giambi	15.00
110	Jim Thome	15.00
111	Alex Rodriguez	25.00
112	Juan Gonzalez	15.00
113	Torii Hunter	10.00
114	Roy Oswalt	10.00
115	Curt Schilling	15.00
116	Magglio Ordonez	10.00
117	Rafael Palmeiro	15.00
118	Andruw Jones	15.00
119	Manny Ramirez	15.00
120	Mark Teixeira	15.00
121	Mark Mulder	10.00
123	Tim Hudson	10.00
124	Todd Helton	15.00
125	Troy Glaus	15.00
128	Greg Maddux	30.00
129	Roger Clemens	40.00
130	Nomar Garciaparra	25.00
131	Mike Piazza	25.00
132	Alex Rodriguez	25.00
134	Randy Johnson	15.00
135	Sammy Sosa	40.00
137	Alfonso Soriano	15.00
138	Jason Giambi	15.00

#	Player	Price
139	Albert Pujols	35.00
140	Chipper Jones	25.00
141	Adam Dunn	15.00
142	Pedro J. Martinez	15.00
143	Vladimir Guerrero	15.00
144	Mark Prior	25.00
145	Barry Zito	15.00
146	Jeff Bagwell	15.00
147	Lance Berkman	15.00
148	Shawn Green	10.00
149	Jason Giambi	15.00
150	Randy Johnson	15.00
151	Alex Rodriguez	25.00
153	Ty Cobb	125.00
156	Thurman Munson	30.00
158	Nolan Ryan	50.00
159	Nolan Ryan	50.00
160	Nolan Ryan	50.00
161	Cal Ripken Jr.	85.00
162	Don Mattingly	60.00
163	Stan Musial	60.00
164	Tony Gwynn	30.00
165	Yogi Berra	30.00
168	George Brett	60.00
169	Ryne Sandberg	60.00

Timber

NM/M
Common Player: 10.00
Production 25 Sets

#	Player	Price
2	Eric Chavez	10.00
3	Alex Rodriguez	25.00
4	Miguel Tejada	10.00
5	Nomar Garciaparra	30.00
6	Jeff Bagwell	15.00
7	Jim Thome	15.00
8	Pat Burrell	15.00
9	Albert Pujols	35.00
10	Juan Gonzalez	15.00
11	Shawn Green	10.00
12	Craig Biggio	10.00
13	Chipper Jones	25.00
14	Hideo Nomo	30.00
15	Vernon Wells	10.00
16	Gary Sheffield	10.00
17	Barry Larkin	15.00
18	Josh Beckett	15.00
19	Edgar Martinez	15.00
20	Ivan Rodriguez	15.00
21	Jeff Kent	15.00
22	Roberto Alomar	15.00
23	Alfonso Soriano	20.00
24	Jim Thome	15.00
25	Juan Gonzalez	15.00
26	Carlos Beltran	10.00
27	Shawn Green	15.00
28	Tim Hudson	15.00
30	Rafael Palmeiro	15.00
31	Todd Helton	15.00
32	Lance Berkman	15.00
33	Mike Mussina	15.00
34	Kazuhisa Ishii	10.00
35	Pat Burrell	15.00
36	Miguel Tejada	15.00
37	Juan Gonzalez	15.00
38	Roberto Alomar	15.00
39	Roberto Alomar	15.00
40	Luis Gonzalez	10.00
41	Jorge Posada	15.00
42	Mark Mulder	10.00
43	Sammy Sosa	40.00
44	Mark Prior	25.00
45	Roger Clemens	40.00
46	Tom Glavine	15.00
47	Mark Teixeira	15.00
48	Manny Ramirez	15.00
49	Frank Thomas	15.00
50	Troy Glaus	10.00
51	Andruw Jones	15.00
52	Jason Giambi	15.00
53	Jim Thome	15.00
55	Rafael Palmeiro	15.00
56	Edgar Martinez	15.00
57	Vladimir Guerrero	15.00
58	Roberto Alomar	15.00
59	Mike Sweeney	10.00
60	Magglio Ordonez	10.00
62	Craig Biggio	15.00
63	Greg Maddux	30.00
64	Mike Piazza	25.00
65	Tom Glavine	15.00
66	Kerry Wood	15.00
67	Frank Thomas	15.00
68	Mike Mussina	15.00
69	Nick Johnson	10.00
70	Bernie Williams	15.00
71	Scott Rolen	15.00
72	Curt Schilling	15.00
73	Adam Dunn	15.00
74	Roy Oswalt	10.00
75	Pedro J. Martinez	15.00
76	Tom Glavine	15.00
77	Torii Hunter	15.00
78	Austin Kearns	15.00
79	Randy Johnson	15.00
80	Bernie Williams	15.00
82	Kerry Wood	15.00
83	Kazuhisa Ishii	10.00
84	Randy Johnson	15.00
85	Nick Johnson	10.00
86	Josh Beckett	15.00
87	Curt Schilling	15.00
88	Mike Mussina	15.00
89	Pedro J. Martinez	15.00
90	Barry Zito	15.00
91	Jim Edmonds	10.00
92-96	Rickey Henderson	15.00
97	Randy Johnson	15.00
98	Mark Grace	15.00
99	Pedro J. Martinez	15.00
101	Ivan Rodriguez	15.00
102	Jeff Kent	10.00
103	Hideo Nomo	30.00
104	Hideo Nomo	30.00
105	Mike Piazza	25.00
106	Tom Glavine	15.00
107	Roberto Alomar	15.00
108	Roger Clemens	40.00
109	Jason Giambi	15.00
110	Jim Thome	15.00
111	Alex Rodriguez	25.00
112	Juan Gonzalez	15.00
113	Torii Hunter	15.00
114	Roy Oswalt	10.00
115	Curt Schilling	15.00
116	Magglio Ordonez	10.00
117	Rafael Palmeiro	15.00
118	Andruw Jones	15.00
119	Manny Ramirez	15.00
120	Mark Teixeira	15.00
121	Mark Mulder	15.00
122	Garret Anderson	10.00
123	Tim Hudson	10.00
124	Todd Helton	15.00
125	Troy Glaus	10.00
128	Greg Maddux	30.00
129	Roger Clemens	40.00
130	Nomar Garciaparra	30.00
131	Mike Piazza	25.00
132	Alex Rodriguez	25.00
134	Randy Johnson	15.00
135	Sammy Sosa	40.00
137	Alfonso Soriano	20.00
138	Jason Giambi	15.00
139	Albert Pujols	35.00
140	Chipper Jones	25.00
141	Adam Dunn	15.00
142	Pedro J. Martinez	15.00
143	Vladimir Guerrero	15.00
144	Mark Prior	15.00
146	Jeff Bagwell	15.00
147	Lance Berkman	10.00
148	Shawn Green	10.00
149	Jason Giambi	15.00
150	Randy Johnson	15.00
151	Alex Rodriguez	25.00
152	Babe Ruth	180.00
153	Ty Cobb	125.00
155	Lou Gehrig	150.00
156	Thurman Munson	15.00
157	Roberto Clemente	140.00
158	Nolan Ryan	50.00
159	Nolan Ryan	50.00
160	Nolan Ryan	50.00
161	Cal Ripken Jr.	85.00
162	Don Mattingly	60.00
163	Stan Musial	60.00
164	Tony Gwynn	30.00
165	Yogi Berra	30.00
166	Johnny Bench	35.00
167	Mike Schmidt	60.00
168	George Brett	60.00
169	Ryne Sandberg	60.00
170	Ernie Banks/1	10.00

TNT

NM/M
Production 25 unless noted.
Some cards not priced due to scarcity.
Primes: 1X
Production 1-25
No pricing production 15 or less.

#	Player	Price
2	Eric Chavez	15.00
3	Alex Rodriguez	45.00
4	Miguel Tejada	15.00
5	Nomar Garciaparra	45.00
6	Jeff Bagwell	25.00
7	Jim Thome	30.00
8	Pat Burrell	30.00
9	Albert Pujols	60.00
10	Juan Gonzalez	25.00
11	Shawn Green	15.00
12	Craig Biggio	15.00
13	Chipper Jones	40.00
14	Hideo Nomo	50.00
15	Vernon Wells	15.00
16	Gary Sheffield	25.00
17	Barry Larkin	20.00
18	Josh Beckett	25.00
19	Edgar Martinez	15.00
20	Ivan Rodriguez	20.00
21	Jeff Kent	15.00
22	Roberto Alomar	15.00
23	Alfonso Soriano	30.00
24	Jim Thome	30.00
25	Juan Gonzalez	25.00
26	Carlos Beltran	15.00
27	Shawn Green	15.00
28	Tim Hudson	20.00
30	Rafael Palmeiro	20.00
31	Todd Helton	20.00
32	Lance Berkman	20.00
33	Mike Mussina	25.00
34	Kazuhisa Ishii	10.00
35	Pat Burrell	30.00
37	Juan Gonzalez	25.00
38	Roberto Alomar	20.00
39	Roberto Alomar	20.00
40	Luis Gonzalez	15.00
41	Jorge Posada	25.00
42	Mark Mulder	40.00
44	Mark Prior	25.00
45	Roger Clemens	50.00
46	Tom Glavine	20.00
47	Mark Teixeira	20.00
48	Manny Ramirez	20.00
49	Frank Thomas	35.00
50	Troy Glaus	15.00
51	Andruw Jones	20.00
52	Jason Giambi	15.00
53	Jim Thome	30.00
55	Rafael Palmeiro	25.00
56	Edgar Martinez	30.00
57	Vladimir Guerrero	30.00
60	Magglio Ordonez	15.00
62	Craig Biggio	20.00
63	Greg Maddux	40.00
65	Tom Glavine	15.00
66	Kerry Wood	30.00
67	Frank Thomas	35.00
68	Mike Mussina	25.00
69	Nick Johnson	15.00
70	Bernie Williams	15.00
71	Scott Rolen	30.00
72	Curt Schilling	20.00
73	Adam Dunn	25.00
74	Roy Oswalt	15.00
75	Pedro J. Martinez	35.00
76	Tom Glavine	20.00
77	Torii Hunter	15.00
78	Austin Kearns	15.00
79	Randy Johnson	30.00
80	Bernie Williams	15.00
82	Kerry Wood	30.00
83	Kazuhisa Ishii	10.00
84	Randy Johnson	30.00
85	Nick Johnson	15.00
86	Josh Beckett	20.00
87	Curt Schilling	25.00
88	Mike Mussina	25.00
89	Pedro J. Martinez	35.00
90	Barry Zito	15.00
91	Jim Edmonds	20.00
92-96	Rickey Henderson	50.00
97	Randy Johnson	30.00
98	Mark Grace	25.00
99	Pedro J. Martinez	35.00
101	Ivan Rodriguez	20.00
102	Jeff Kent	10.00
103	Hideo Nomo	40.00
104	Hideo Nomo	40.00
105	Mike Piazza	40.00
106	Tom Glavine	25.00
107	Roberto Alomar	25.00
108	Roger Clemens	50.00
109	Jason Giambi	25.00
110	Jim Thome	35.00
111	Alex Rodriguez	45.00
112	Juan Gonzalez	25.00
113	Torii Hunter	15.00
114	Roy Oswalt	15.00
115	Curt Schilling	25.00
116	Magglio Ordonez	15.00
117	Rafael Palmeiro	25.00
118	Andruw Jones	25.00
119	Manny Ramirez	30.00
120	Mark Teixeira	25.00
121	Mark Mulder	20.00
124	Todd Helton	20.00
125	Troy Glaus	15.00
128	Greg Maddux	40.00
129	Roger Clemens	50.00
130	Nomar Garciaparra	40.00
131	Mike Piazza	40.00
132	Alex Rodriguez	45.00
134	Randy Johnson	30.00
135	Sammy Sosa	40.00
137	Alfonso Soriano	20.00
138	Jason Giambi	20.00
139	Albert Pujols	60.00
140	Chipper Jones	30.00
141	Adam Dunn	25.00
142	Pedro J. Martinez	35.00
143	Vladimir Guerrero	30.00
144	Mark Prior	30.00
145	Barry Zito	15.00
146	Jeff Bagwell	20.00
147	Lance Berkman	20.00
148	Shawn Green	15.00
149	Jason Giambi	15.00
150	Randy Johnson	40.00
151	Alex Rodriguez	40.00
156	Thurman Munson	50.00
158	Nolan Ryan	65.00
159	Nolan Ryan	65.00
160	Nolan Ryan	65.00
161	Cal Ripken Jr.	100.00
162	Don Mattingly	65.00
163	Stan Musial	65.00
164	Tony Gwynn	40.00
165	Yogi Berra	40.00
166	Johnny Bench	40.00
167	Mike Schmidt	65.00
168	George Brett	75.00
169	Ryne Sandberg	65.00

7th Inning Stretch

NM/M
Production 50 unless noted.

#	Player	Price
1	Alex Rodriguez	20.00
3	Sammy Sosa	25.00
4	Juan Gonzalez	10.00
5	Albert Pujols	30.00
6	Chipper Jones	15.00
7	Alfonso Soriano/40	15.00
8	Jim Thome	15.00
9	Mike Piazza	20.00
10	Rafael Palmeiro	15.00

2004 Leaf

Barry ZITO

NM/M
Complete Set (300): 50.00
Common Player: .15
Common (202-301): .25
Second Edition (1-301): 1X
Pack (8): 5.00
Box (24): 90.00

#	Player	Price
1	Darin Erstad	.25
2	Garret Anderson	.25
3	Jarrod Washburn	.15
4	Kevin Appier	.15
5	Tim Salmon	.25
6	Troy Glaus	.40
7	Troy Percival	.15
8	Jason Johnson	.15
9	Jay Gibbons	.25
10	Melvin Mora	.15
11	Sidney Ponson	.15
12	Tony Batista	.15
13	Derek Lowe	.25
14	Robert Person	.15
15	Manny Ramirez	.50
16	Nomar Garciaparra	1.50
17	Pedro J. Martinez	.75
18	Jorge de la Rosa	.15
19	Bartolo Colon	.25
20	Carlos Lee	.15
21	Esteban Loaiza	.15
22	Frank Thomas	.50
23	Joe Crede	.15
24	Magglio Ordonez	.25
25	Ryan Ludwick	.15
26	Luis Garcia	.15
27	Brandon Phillips	.15
28	C.C. Sabathia	.15
29	Jhonny Peralta	.15
30	Josh Bard	.15
31	Omar Vizquel	.25
32	Fernando Rodney	.15
33	Mike Maroth	.15
34	Bobby Higginson	.15
35	Omar Infante	.15
36	Dmitri Young	.15
37	Eric Munson	.15
38	Jeremy Bonderman	.15
39	Carlos Beltran	.25
40	Jeremy Affeldt	.15
41	Dee Brown	.15
42	Mike Sweeney	.15
43	Brent Abernathy	.15
44	Runelvys Hernandez	.15
45	A.J. Pierzynski	.15
46	Corey Koskie	.15
47	Cristian Guzman	.15
48	Jacque Jones	.15
49	Kenny Rogers	.15
50	J.C. Romero	.15
51	Torii Hunter	.40
52	Alfonso Soriano	.75
53	Bernie Williams	.50
54	David Wells	.15
55	Derek Jeter	2.00
56	Hideki Matsui	1.50
57	Jason Giambi	.75
58	Jorge Posada	.40
59	Jose Contreras	.25
60	Mike Mussina	.50
61	Nick Johnson	.15
62	Roger Clemens	1.50
63	Barry Zito	.40
64	Justin Duchscherer	.15
65	Eric Chavez	.25
66	Erubiel Durazo	.15
67	Miguel Tejada	.40
68	Mark Mulder	.25
70	Terrence Long	.15
71	Tim Hudson	.25
72	Bret Boone	.25
73	Dan Wilson	.15
74	Edgar Martinez	.25
75	Freddy Garcia	.15
76	Rafael Soriano	.15
77	Ichiro Suzuki	1.25
78	Jamie Moyer	.15
79	John Olerud	.15
80	Kazuhiro Sasaki	.15
81	Aubrey Huff	.15
82	Carl Crawford	.25
83	Joe Kennedy	.15
84	Rocco Baldelli	.15
85	Toby Hall	.15
86	Alex Rodriguez	1.50
87	Kevin Mench	.15
88	Hank Blalock	.25
89	Juan Gonzalez	.50
90	Mark Teixeira	.50
91	Rafael Palmeiro	.25
92	Carlos Delgado	.50
93	Eric Hinske	.15
94	Josh Phelps	.15
95	Brian Bowles	.15
96	Roy Halladay	.40
97	Shannon Stewart	.15
98	Vernon Wells	.25
99	Curt Schilling	.40
100	Junior Spivey	.15
101	Luis Gonzalez	.25
102	Lyle Overbay	.15
103	Mark Grace	.40
104	Randy Johnson	.75
105	Shea Hillenbrand	.15
106	Andruw Jones	.50
107	Chipper Jones	.75
108	Gary Sheffield	.40
109	Greg Maddux	1.00
110	Javy Lopez	.25
111	John Smoltz	.25
112	Marcus Giles	.15
113	Rafael Furcal	.25
114	Corey Patterson	.15
115	Juan Cruz	.15
116	Kerry Wood	.50
117	Mark Prior	1.00
118	Moises Alou	.25
119	Sammy Sosa	1.00
120	Aaron Boone	.15
121	Adam Dunn	.25
122	Austin Kearns	.50
123	Barry Larkin	.40
124	Ken Griffey Jr.	1.00
125	Brian Reith	.15
126	Wily Mo Pena	.15
127	Jason Jennings	.15
128	Jay Payton	.15
129	Larry Walker	.25
130	Preston Wilson	.15
131	Todd Helton	.50
132	Dontrelle Willis	.40
133	Ivan Rodriguez	.50
134	Josh Beckett	.50
135	Juan Encarnacion	.15
136	Mike Lowell	.15
137	Craig Biggio	.25
138	Jeff Bagwell	.50
139	Jeff Kent	.25
140	Lance Berkman	.25
141	Richard Hidalgo	.15
142	Roy Oswalt	.25
143	Eric Gagne	.25
144	Fred McGriff	.25
145	Hideo Nomo	.40
146	Kazuhisa Ishii	.15
147	Kevin Brown	.25
148	Paul LoDuca	.15
149	Shawn Green	.25
150	Ben Sheets	.25
151	Geoff Jenkins	.15
152	Rey Sanchez	.15
153	Richie Sexson	.40
155	Wes Helms	.15
156	Shane Nance	.15
157	Fernando Tatis	.15
158	Javier Vazquez	.15
159	Jose Vidro	.15
160	Orlando Cabrera	.15
161	Henry Mateo	.15
162	Vladimir Guerrero	.75
163	Zach Day	.15
164	Edwin Almonte	.15
165	Al Leiter	.15
166	Cliff Floyd	.15
167	Jae Weong Seo	.15
168	Mike Piazza	1.00
169	Roberto Alomar	.50
170	Tom Glavine	.25
171	Bobby Abreu	.25
172	Brandon Duckworth	.15
173	Jim Thome	.75
174	Kevin Millwood	.25
175	Pat Burrell	.25
176	Aramis Ramirez	.15
177	Jack Wilson	.15
178	Brian Giles	.25
179	Jason Kendall	.15
180	Kenny Lofton	.15
181	Kip Wells	.15
182	Kris Benson	.15
183	Albert Pujols	1.50
184	J.D. Drew	.15
185	Jim Edmonds	.15
186	Matt Morris	.15
187	Scott Rolen	.75
188	Woody Williams	.15
189	Brian Lawrence	.15
190	Ryan Klesko	.25
191	Sean Burroughs	.15
192	Xavier Nady	.15
193	Dennis Tankersley	.15
194	Donaldo Mendez	.15
195	Barry Bonds	2.00
196	Benito Santiago	.15
197	Edgardo Alfonzo	.15
198	Cody Ransom	.15
199	Jason Schmidt	.15
200	Rich Aurilia	.15
201	Ken Harvey	.15
202	Adam Loewen	.25
203	Alfredo Gonzalez	.25
204	Arnie Munoz	.25
205	Andrew Brown	.25
206	Josh Hall	.25
207	Josh Stewart	.25
208	Clint Barmes	.25
209	Brandon Webb	.25
210	Chien-Ming Wang	.40
211	Edgar Gonzalez	.25
212	Alejandro Machado	.25
213	Jeremy Griffiths	.25
214	Craig Brazell	.25
215	Daniel Cabrera	.25
216	Fernando Cabrera	.25
217	Termel Sledge	.25
218	Rob Hammock	.25
219	Francisco Rosario	.25
220	Francisco Cruceta	.25
221	Rett Johnson	.25
222	Guillermo Quiroz	.25
223	Hong-Chih Kuo	.25
224	Ian Ferguson	.25
225	Tim Olson	.25
226	Todd Wellemeyer	.25
227	Rich Fischer	.25
228	Phil Seibel	.25
229	Joe Valentine	.25
230	Matt Kata	.25
231	Michael Hessman	.25
232	Michel Hernandez	.25
233	Doug Waechter	.25
234	Prentice Redman	.25
235	Nook Logan	.25
236	Oscar Villarreal	.25
237	Pete LaForest	.25
238	Matt Bruback	.25
239	Josh Willingham	.25
240	Greg Aquino	.25
241	Lew Ford	.25
242	Jeff Duncan	.25
243	Chris Waters	.25
244	Miguel Ojeda	.25
245	Rosman Garcia	.25
246	Felix Sanchez	.25
247	Jon Leicester	.25
248	Roger Deago	.25
249	Mike Ryan	.25
250	Chris Capuano	.25
251	Matt White	.25
252	Bernie Williams	.50
253	Chipper Jones	1.00
254	Chipper Jones	1.00
255	Greg Maddux	1.50
256	Sammy Sosa	2.00
257	Mike Mussina	.75
258	Tim Salmon	.50
259	Barry Larkin	.50
260	Randy Johnson	1.00
261	Jeff Bagwell	.75
262	Roberto Alomar	.50
263	Tom Glavine	.50
264	Roger Clemens	2.50
265	Barry Bonds	3.00
266	Ivan Rodriguez	.75
267	Pedro J. Martinez	1.00
268	Ken Griffey Jr.	1.50
269	Jim Thome	.75
270	Frank Thomas	.75
271	Mike Piazza	1.50
272	Troy Glaus	.40
273	Melvin Mora	.25
274	Nomar Garciaparra	2.00
275	Magglio Ordonez	.40
276	Omar Vizquel	.40
277	Dmitri Young	.25
278	Mike Sweeney	.25
279	Torii Hunter	.50
280	Derek Jeter	2.00
281	Barry Zito	.50
282	Ichiro Suzuki	1.50
283	Rocco Baldelli	.50
284	Alex Rodriguez	2.00
285	Carlos Delgado	.50
286	Randy Johnson	.75
287	Greg Maddux	1.00
288	Sammy Sosa	1.50
289	Ken Griffey Jr.	1.00
290	Todd Helton	.50
291	Ivan Rodriguez	.50
292	Jeff Bagwell	.50
293	Hideo Nomo	.50
294	Richie Sexson	.50
295	Vladimir Guerrero	.75
296	Mike Piazza	1.00
297	Jim Thome	.75
298	Jason Kendall	.25
299	Albert Pujols	1.50
300	Ryan Klesko	.40
301	Barry Bonds	2.00

Black Press Proof

Stars (1-301): 5-10X
Production 50 Sets
Hot Pack Exclusive

Blue Press Proof

Josh BECKETT

4	Albert Pujols	4.00
5	Jason Giambi	1.50
6	Chipper Jones	2.00
7	Vladimir Guerrero	1.50
8	Mike Piazza	2.50
9	Nomar Garciaparra	3.00
10	Austin Kearns	1.00

Stars (1-301): 4-8X
Production 100 Sets

Gold Press Proof

Cards (1-301): 12-25X
Production 25 Sets

Red Press Proof

Curt SCHILLING

Stars (1-301): 1-2X
Inserted 1:8

Autographs

Jorge DE LA ROSA

		NM/M
	Common Autograph	6.00
14	Robert Person	6.00
18	Jorge De La Rosa	6.00
25	Ryan Ludwick	10.00
26	Luis Garcia	6.00
29	Jhonny Peralta	6.00
30	Josh Bard	6.00
32	Fernando Rodney	6.00
33	Mike Maroth	6.00
35	Omar Infante	6.00
41	Dee Brown	6.00
44	Brent Abernathy/SP	10.00
51	J.C. Romero	6.00
65	Justin Duchscherer	10.00
70	Terrence Long/SP	15.00
76	Rafael Soriano	8.00
85	Toby Hall/SP	10.00
87	Kevin Mench	6.00
95	Brian Bowles	6.00
115	Juan Cruz	6.00
125	Brian Reith	6.00
126	Wily Mo Pena	8.00
127	Jason Jennings	6.00
155	Shane Nance	6.00
160	Henry Mateo/SP	8.00
163	Edwin Almonte	6.00
171	Brandon Duckworth	6.00
176	Jack Wilson	6.00
180	Kip Wells	6.00
188	Clifford Bartosh	6.00
189	Brian Lawrence	6.00
193	Dennis Tankersley	6.00
194	Donaldo Mendez	6.00
198	Cody Ransom/SP	8.00
247	Jon Leicester/SP	8.00

Away

		NM/M
	Complete Set (10):	20.00
	Common Player:	1.00
	Inserted 1:35	
1	Greg Maddux	2.50
2	Sammy Sosa	3.00
3	Alex Rodriguez	4.00

Away Jersey

SAMMY SOSA

		NM/M
	Common Player:	5.00
	Inserted 1:119	
	Prime:	1.5-2X
	Production 50	
1	Greg Maddux	8.00
2	Sammy Sosa	12.00
3	Alex Rodriguez	10.00
4	Albert Pujols	15.00
5	Jason Giambi	8.00
6	Chipper Jones	8.00
7	Vladimir Guerrero	8.00
8	Mike Piazza	10.00
9	Nomar Garciaparra	12.00
10	Austin Kearns	6.00

Clean Up Crew

		NM/M
	Complete Set (10):	20.00
	Common Player:	1.00
	Inserted 1:49	
1	Sammy Sosa, Moises Alou, Hee Seop Choi	3.00
2	Jason Giambi, Alfonso Soriano, Hideki Matsui	5.00
3	Vernon Wells, Carlos Delgado, Josh Phelps	1.00
4	Alex Rodriguez, Juan Gonzalez, Hank Blalock	4.00
5	Gary Sheffield, Andruw Jones, Chipper Jones	2.50
6	Ken Griffey Jr., Austin Kearns, Aaron Boone	3.00
7	Albert Pujols, Jim Edmonds, Scott Rolen	4.00
8	Jeff Bagwell, Jeff Kent, Lance Berkman	1.50
9	Todd Helton, Preston Wilson, Larry Walker	1.50
10	Miguel Tejada, Erubiel Durazo, Eric Chavez	1.00

Clean Up Crew Materials

		NM/M
	Common Card:	15.00
	Production 50 Sets	
1	Sammy Sosa, Moises Alou, Hee Seop Choi	35.00
2	Jason Giambi, Alfonso Soriano, Hideki Matsui	60.00
3	Vernon Wells, Carlos Delgado, Josh Phelps	15.00
4	Alex Rodriguez, Juan Gonzalez, Hank Blalock	35.00
5	Gary Sheffield, Andruw Jones, Chipper Jones	20.00
6	Ken Griffey Jr., Austin Kearns, Aaron Boone	25.00
7	Albert Pujols, Jim Edmonds, Scott Rolen	40.00
8	Jeff Bagwell, Jeff Kent, Lance Berkman	25.00
9	Todd Helton, Preston Wilson, Larry Walker	20.00
10	Miguel Tejada, Erubiel Durazo, Eric Chavez	15.00

Cornerstones

		NM/M
	Complete Set (10):	20.00
	Common Player:	1.00
	Inserted 1:78	
1	Alex Rodriguez, Hank Blalock	4.00
2	Kerry Wood, Mark Prior	3.00
3	Roger Clemens, Alfonso Soriano	4.00
4	Nomar Garciaparra, Manny Ramirez	4.00

5	Austin Kearns, Adam Dunn	1.00
6	Tom Glavine, Mike Piazza	2.50
7	Andruw Jones, Chipper Jones	2.50
8	Albert Pujols, Scott Rolen	4.00
9	Curt Schilling, Randy Johnson	2.00
10	Hideo Nomo, Kazuhisa Ishii	1.00

Cornerstones Materials

		NM/M
	Common Duo:	15.00
	Production 50 Sets	
1	Alex Rodriguez, Hank Blalock	25.00
2	Kerry Wood, Mark Prior	40.00
3	Roger Clemens, Alfonso Soriano	40.00
4	Nomar Garciaparra, Manny Ramirez	30.00
5	Austin Kearns, Adam Dunn	15.00
6	Andruw Jones, Chipper Jones	20.00
7	Albert Pujols, Scott Rolen	40.00
8	Curt Schilling, Randy Johnson	20.00
9	Hideo Nomo, Kazuhisa Ishii	20.00

Exhibits

		NM/M
	Common Player:	2.50
	Production 66 Sets	
	Variations #'d to 63:	1X
	Variations #'d to 46:	1X
	Variations #'d 21 to 27:	1.5X
1	Adam Dunn	2.50
2	Albert Pujols	8.00
3	Alex Rodriguez	8.00
4	Alfonso Soriano	4.00
5	Andruw Jones	3.00
6	Barry Bonds	10.00
7	Barry Larkin	2.50
8	Barry Zito	2.50
9	Cal Ripken Jr.	10.00
10	Chipper Jones	5.00
11	Dale Murphy	2.50
12	Derek Jeter	10.00
13	Don Mattingly	8.00
14	Ernie Banks	5.00
15	Frank Thomas	4.00
16	George Brett	6.00
17	Greg Maddux	5.00
18	Hank Blalock	2.50
19	Hideo Nomo	2.50
20	Ichiro Suzuki	6.00
21	Jason Giambi	3.00
22	Jim Thome	4.00
23	Juan Gonzalez	2.50
24	Ken Griffey Jr.	5.00
25	Kirby Puckett	4.00
26	Mark Prior	5.00
27	Mike Mussina	2.50
28	Mike Piazza	5.00
29	Mike Schmidt	6.00
30	Nolan Ryan	8.00
31	Nolan Ryan	8.00
32	Nolan Ryan	8.00
33	Nomar Garciaparra	8.00
34	Ozzie Smith	2.50
35	Pedro J. Martinez	4.00
36	Randy Johnson	3.00
37	Reggie Jackson	2.50
38	Reggie Jackson	2.50
39	Rickey Henderson	2.50
40	Roberto Alomar	2.50
41	Roberto Clemente	8.00
42	Rod Carew	3.00
43	Roger Clemens	8.00
44	Sammy Sosa	6.00
45	Stan Musial	6.00
46	Tom Glavine	2.50
47	Tom Seaver	4.00
48	Tony Gwynn	4.00
49	Vladimir Guerrero	4.00
50	Yogi Berra	4.00

Gamers

		NM/M
	Complete Set (20):	40.00
	Common Player:	1.00
	Quantum:	2-4X
	Production 100 Sets	

1	Albert Pujols	4.00
2	Alex Rodriguez	4.00
3	Alfonso Soriano	1.50
4	Barry Bonds	5.00
5	Barry Zito	1.00
6	Chipper Jones	2.00
7	Derek Jeter	5.00
8	Greg Maddux	2.50
9	Ichiro Suzuki	3.00
10	Jason Giambi	1.50
11	Jeff Bagwell	1.50
12	Ken Griffey Jr.	2.50
13	Manny Ramirez	1.50
14	Mark Prior	3.00
15	Mike Piazza	2.50
16	Nomar Garciaparra	3.00
17	Pedro J. Martinez	2.00
18	Randy Johnson	2.00
19	Roger Clemens	2.00
20	Sammy Sosa	3.00

Gold Leaf Rookies

GOLD LEAF ROOKIES

		NM/M
	Complete Set (10):	6.00
	Common Player:	.50
	Inserted 1:23	
	Mirror Gold:	No Pricing
	Production 25 Sets	
1	Adam Loewen	2.00
2	Rickie Weeks	5.00
3	Khalil Greene	.50
4	Chad Tracy	.50
5	Alexis Rios	.50
6	Craig Brazell	.50
7	Clint Barmes	.50
8	Pete LaForest	.50
9	Alfredo Gonzalez	.50
10	Arnie Munoz	.50

Home

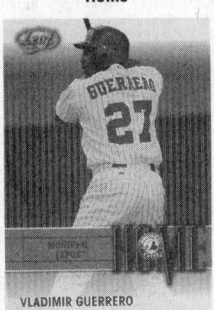

VLADIMIR GUERRERO

		NM/M
	Complete Set (10):	20.00
	Common Player:	1.00
	Inserted 1:35	
1	Greg Maddux	2.50
2	Sammy Sosa	3.00
3	Alex Rodriguez	4.00
4	Albert Pujols	4.00
5	Jason Giambi	1.50
6	Chipper Jones	2.00
7	Vladimir Guerrero	1.50
8	Mike Piazza	2.50
9	Nomar Garciaparra	3.00
10	Austin Kearns	1.00

Home Jersey

		NM/M
	Common Player:	5.00
	Inserted 1:119	
	Primes:	1.5-2X
	Production 50	
1	Greg Maddux	8.00
2	Sammy Sosa	12.00
3	Alex Rodriguez	10.00
4	Albert Pujols	15.00
5	Jason Giambi	8.00
6	Chipper Jones	8.00
7	Vladimir Guerrero	8.00
8	Mike Piazza	10.00
9	Nomar Garciaparra	12.00
10	Austin Kearns	5.00

Limited Previews

		NM/M
	Common Player:	2.00
	Production 999 Sets	
	Silver:	1-2X
	Production 100 Sets	

(Checklist continued)

1	Albert Pujols	4.00
2	Alex Rodriguez	4.00
3	Alfonso Soriano	1.50
4	Barry Bonds	5.00
5	Barry Zito	1.00
6	Chipper Jones	2.00
7	Derek Jeter	5.00
8	Greg Maddux	2.50
9	Ichiro Suzuki	3.00
10	Jason Giambi	1.50
11	Jeff Bagwell	1.50
12	Ken Griffey Jr.	2.50
13	Manny Ramirez	1.50
14	Mark Prior	3.00
15	Mike Piazza	2.50
16	Nomar Garciaparra	3.00
17	Pedro J. Martinez	2.00
18	Randy Johnson	2.00
19	Roger Clemens	2.00
20	Sammy Sosa	3.00

MVP Winners

		NM/M
	Complete Set (20):	50.00
	Common Player:	1.00
	Gold:	1-2X
	Production 500 Sets	
1	Stan Musial - 1948 NL	3.00
2	Ernie Banks - 1958 NL	2.00
3	Roberto Clemente/1966 NL	4.00
4	George Brett/1980 AL	4.00
5	Mike Schmidt/1980 NL	4.00
6	Cal Ripken Jr./1983 AL	5.00
7	Dale Murphy/1983 NL	1.50
8	Ryne Sandberg/1984 NL	3.00
9	Don Mattingly/1985 AL	3.00
10	Roger Clemens/1986 AL	4.00
11	Rickey Henderson/1990 AL	1.00
12	Cal Ripken Jr./1991 AL	5.00
13	Barry Bonds/1992 NL	5.00
14	Barry Bonds/1993 NL	5.00
15	Frank Thomas/1994 AL	1.50
16	Ken Griffey Jr./1997 AL	2.50
17	Sammy Sosa/1998 NL	3.00
18	Chipper Jones/1999 NL	2.00
19	Jason Giambi/2000 AL	1.50
20	Ichiro Suzuki/2001 AL	3.00

Picture Perfect

		NM/M
	Complete Set (15):	25.00
	Common Player:	1.00
	Inserted 1:37	
1	Albert Pujols	5.00
2	Alex Rodriguez	5.00
3	Alfonso Soriano	2.00
4	Austin Kearns	1.00
5	Carlos Delgado	1.50
6	Chipper Jones	2.50
7	Hank Blalock	1.50
8	Jason Giambi	2.00
9	Jeff Bagwell	1.50
10	Jim Thome	2.00
11	Manny Ramirez	1.50
12	Mike Piazza	3.00
13	Nomar Garciaparra	4.00
14	Sammy Sosa	4.00
15	Todd Helton	1.50

Picture Perfect Materials

		NM/M
	Common Player:	6.00
	Inserted 1:437	
1	Albert Pujols	15.00
2	Alex Rodriguez	10.00
3	Alfonso Soriano	8.00
4	Austin Kearns	6.00
5	Carlos Delgado	6.00
6	Chipper Jones	8.00
7	Hank Blalock	6.00
8	Jason Giambi	8.00
9	Jeff Bagwell	8.00
10	Jim Thome	10.00

Gold:

		2-3X
	Production 50 Sets	
1	Derek Jeter	8.00
2	Barry Zito	2.00
3	Ichiro Suzuki	8.00
4	Pedro J. Martinez	3.00
5	Alfonso Soriano	3.00
6	Alex Rodriguez	6.00
7	Greg Maddux	4.00
8	Mike Piazza	4.00
9	Mark Prior	2.00
10	Albert Pujols	8.00
11	Jason Giambi	1.50
12	Ken Griffey Jr.	4.00
13	Nomar Garciaparra	4.00
14	Randy Johnson	3.00
15	Jason Giambi	2.00
16	Barry Bonds	8.00
17	Manny Ramirez	4.00
18	Chipper Jones	3.00
19	Jeff Bagwell	2.00
20	Roger Clemens	6.00

Recollection Autographs

All are 1990 Leaf cards.

Shirt Off My Back

		NM/M
	Common Player:	4.00
	Inserted 1:47	
1	Shawn Green	4.00
2	Andruw Jones	6.00
3	Ivan Rodriguez	6.00
4	Hideo Nomo	6.00
5	Don Mattingly	20.00
6	Mark Prior	10.00
7	Alfonso Soriano	6.00
8	Richie Sexson	5.00
9	Vernon Wells	4.00
10	Nomar Garciaparra	8.00
11	Jason Giambi	6.00
12	Austin Kearns	5.00
13	Chipper Jones	6.00
14	Rickey Henderson	6.00
15	Alex Rodriguez	12.00
16	Garret Anderson	4.00
17	Vladimir Guerrero	4.00
18	Sammy Sosa	10.00
19	Mike Piazza	8.00
20	David Wells	4.00
21	Scott Rolen	6.00
22	Adam Dunn	5.00
23	Carlos Delgado	5.00
24	Greg Maddux	8.00
25	Hank Blalock	5.00

Shirt Off My Back Team Logo Patch

		NM/M
	Common Player:	10.00
	Autographs:	No Pricing
	Production Five Sets	
	Jersey Number Patch:	.75-1X
	Production 50 Sets	
	Sosa #'d to 42.	
	Jersey Number Patch Auto:	No Pricing
	Production Five Sets	
1	Shawn Green/41	15.00
2	Andruw Jones/75	15.00
3	Ivan Rodriguez/75	15.00
4	Hideo Nomo/74	20.00
6	Mark Prior/46	20.00
7	Alfonso Soriano/28	25.00
8	Richie Sexson/38	15.00
9	Vernon Wells/74	15.00
10	Nomar Garciaparra/75	25.00
11	Jason Giambi/26	20.00
12	Austin Kearns/32	10.00
13	Chipper Jones/75	20.00
14	Rickey Henderson/40	20.00
15	Alex Rodriguez/75	30.00
16	Garret Anderson/71	10.00
17	Vladimir Guerrero/55	20.00
18	Sammy Sosa/39	25.00
19	Mike Piazza/75	20.00
20	David Wells/74	10.00
21	Scott Rolen/29	30.00
22	Adam Dunn/32	15.00
23	Carlos Delgado/56	15.00
24	Greg Maddux/75	20.00
25	Hank Blalock/62	15.00

Sunday Dress

		NM/M
	Complete Set (10):	10.00
	Common Player:	.75
	Inserted 1:17	
1	Frank Thomas	1.00
2	Barry Zito	.75
3	Mike Piazza	2.00
4	Mark Prior	2.00
5	Jeff Bagwell	1.00
6	Roy Oswalt	.75
7	Todd Helton	1.00
8	Magglio Ordonez	.75
9	Alex Rodriguez	3.00
10	Manny Ramirez	1.00

Sunday Dress Jersey

		NM/M
	Common Player:	5.00
	Inserted 1:119	
	Prime Jersey:	1-1.5X
	Production 100 Sets	
1	Frank Thomas	8.00
2	Barry Zito	6.00
3	Mike Piazza	10.00
4	Mark Prior	10.00
5	Jeff Bagwell	8.00
6	Roy Oswalt	5.00
7	Todd Helton	8.00
8	Magglio Ordonez	6.00
9	Alex Rodriguez	10.00
10	Manny Ramirez	6.00

2004 Leaf Certified Cuts

NM/M

Complete Set (300):
Common Player (1-200): .75
Common (201-250): 2.00
Production 599
Common (251-300): 5.00
Production 499
Auto. Production 99-499
Pack (5): 20.00
Box (10): 160.00

#	Player	NM/M
1	Vladimir Guerrero	1.50
2	Garret Anderson	.75
3	John Lackey	.75
4	Bartolo Colon	.75
5	Troy Glaus	.75
6	Tim Salmon	.75
7	Shea Hillenbrand	.75
8	Brandon Webb	.75
9	Roberto Alomar	.75
10	Randy Johnson	2.00
11	Alex Cintron	.75
12	Richie Sexson	.75
13	Luis Gonzalez	.75
14	Adam LaRoche	.75
15	Rafael Furcal	.75
16	Chipper Jones	2.00
17	Marcus Giles	.75
18	Andruw Jones	1.00
19	Russ Ortiz	.75
20	Rafael Palmeiro	1.00
21	Melvin Mora	.75
22	Luis Matos	.75
23	Jay Gibbons	.75
24	Adam Loewen	.75
25	Larry Bigbie	.75
26	Rodrigo Lopez	.75
27	Javy Lopez	.75
28	Miguel Tejada	1.00
29	Trot Nixon	.75
30	Curt Schilling	1.00
31	Jason Varitek	1.00
32	Manny Ramirez	1.00
33	Keith Foulke	.75
34	Derek Lowe	.75
35	Pedro J. Martinez	1.50
36	Nomar Garciaparra	2.50
37	Bill Mueller	.75
38	Johnny Damon	.75
39	David Ortiz	1.50
40	Mark Prior	1.00
41	Kerry Wood	1.50
42	Sammy Sosa	2.50
43	Derek Lee	.75
44	Greg Maddux	2.00
45	Aramis Ramirez	.75
46	Matt Clement	.75
47	Carlos Zambrano	.75
48	Todd Walker	.75
49	Moises Alou	.75
50	Corey Patterson	.75
51	Frank Thomas	1.00
52	Magglio Ordonez	.75
53	Carlos Lee	.75
54	Mark Buehrle	.75
55	Esteban Loaiza	.75
56	Joe Crede	.75
57	Paul Konerko	.75
58	Adam Dunn	1.00
59	Austin Kearns	.75
60	Barry Larkin	.75
61	Ryan Wagner	.75
62	Danny Graves	.75
63	Sean Casey	.75
64	Ken Griffey Jr.	2.00
65	Jody Gerut	.75
66	Cliff Lee	.75
67	Victor Martinez	.75
68	C.C. Sabathia	.75
69	Omar Vizquel	.75
70	Travis Hafner	.75
71	Todd Helton	1.00
72	Preston Wilson	.75
73	Jeromy Burnitz	.75
74	Larry Walker	.75
75	Ivan Rodriguez	1.00
76	Rondell White	.75
77	Miguel Cabrera	1.50
78	Luis Castillo	.75
79	Josh Beckett	.75
80	Mike Lowell	.75
81	Dontrelle Willis	.75
82	Brad Penny	.75
83	Hee Seop Choi	.75
84	Juan Pierre	.75
85	Andy Pettitte	.75
86	Jeff Bagwell	1.00
87	Roy Oswalt	.75
88	Lance Berkman	.75
89	Morgan Ensberg	.75
90	Craig Biggio	.75
91	Octavio Dotel	.75
92	Wade Miller	.75
93	Jeff Kent	.75
94	Richard Hidalgo	.75
95	Roger Clemens	3.00
96	Carlos Beltran	1.00
97	Angel Berroa	.75
98	Jeremy Affeldt	.75
99	Juan Gonzalez	.75
100	Mike Sweeney	.75
101	Kazuhisa Ishii	.75
102	Shawn Green	.75
103	Milton Bradley	.75
104	Paul LoDuca	.75
105	Hideo Nomo	.75
106	Eric Gagne	.75
107	Adrian Beltre	.75
108	Scott Podsednik	.75
109	Rickie Weeks	.75
110	Ben Sheets	.75
111	Geoff Jenkins	.75
112	Jacque Jones	.75
113	Johan Santana	1.00
114	Shannon Stewart	.75
115	Corey Koskie	.75
116	Lew Ford	.75
117	Torii Hunter	.75
118	Chad Cordero	.75
119	Orlando Cabrera	.75
120	Jose Vidro	.75
121	Nick Johnson	.75
122	Brad Wilkerson	.75
123	Mike Piazza	2.00
124	Jae Weong Seo	.75
125	Jose Reyes	.75
126	Tom Glavine	.75
127	Jorge Posada	.75
128	Gary Sheffield	1.00
129	Bernie Williams	1.00
130	Mike Mussina	1.00
131	Mariano Rivera	.75
132	Bubba Crosby	.75
133	Kevin Brown	.75
134	Javier Vazquez	.75
135	Jason Giambi	.75
136	Derek Jeter	4.00
137	Alex Rodriguez	4.00
138	Hideki Matsui	3.00
139	Mark Mulder	.75
140	Jermaine Dye	.75
141	Tim Hudson	.75
142	Barry Zito	.75
143	Eric Chavez	.75
144	Bobby Crosby	.75
145	Eric Byrnes	.75
146	Marlon Byrd	.75
147	Billy Wagner	.75
148	Mike Lieberthal	.75
149	Jimmy Rollins	1.00
150	Jim Thome	1.50
151	Bobby Abreu	.75
152	Pat Burrell	.75
153	Jose Castillo	.75
154	Craig Wilson	.75
155	Jason Bay	.75
156	Jason Kendall	.75
157	Raul Mondesi	.75
158	Jay Payton	.75
159	Trevor Hoffman	.75
160	Jake Peavy	.75
161	Sean Burroughs	.75
162	Phil Nevin	.75
163	Brian Giles	.75
164	Ryan Klesko	.75
165	Todd Linden	.75
166	Jerome Williams	.75
167	Jason Schmidt	1.00
168	Ray Durham	.75
169	Marquis Grissom	.75
170	Shigetoshi Hasegawa	.75
171	Edgar Martinez	.75
172	Freddy Garcia	.75
173	Bret Boone	.75
174	Raul Ibanez	.75
175	Ichiro Suzuki	3.00
176	Randy Winn	.75
177	Scott Rolen	1.50
178	Jim Edmonds	.75
179	Albert Pujols	3.00
180	Matt Morris	.75
181	Edgar Renteria	.75
182	Aubrey Huff	.75
183	Delmon Young	.75
184	Dewon Brazelton	.75
185	Rocco Baldelli	.75
186	Carl Crawford	.75
187	Mark Teixeira	.75
188	Hank Blalock	1.00
189	Michael Young	.75
190	Laynce Nix	.75
191	Alfonso Soriano	1.50
192	Kevin Mench	.75
193	Adrian Gonzalez	.75
194	Alexis Rios	.75
195	Roy Halladay	.75
196	Vernon Wells	.75
197	Carlos Delgado	.75
198	Bill Hall	.75
199	Jose Guillen	.75
200	Jeremy Bonderman	.75
201	Roger Clemens/SP	6.00
202	Alex Rodriguez/SP	6.00
203	Greg Maddux/SP	4.00
204	Miguel Tejada/SP	2.00
205	Alfonso Soriano/SP	3.00
206	Andy Pettitte/SP	2.00
207	Curt Schilling/SP	2.00
208	Gary Sheffield/SP	2.00
209	Ivan Rodriguez/SP	2.00
210	Jim Thome/SP	2.00
211	Mike Mussina/SP	3.00
212	Mike Piazza/SP	4.00
213	Randy Johnson/SP	3.00
214	Roger Clemens/SP	6.00
215	Sammy Sosa/SP	4.00
216	Alex Rodriguez/SP	6.00
217	Randy Johnson/SP	3.00
218	Vladimir Guerrero/SP	3.00
219	Rafael Palmeiro/SP	2.00
220	Manny Ramirez/SP	2.00
221	Mike Piazza/SP	4.00
222	Cal Ripken Jr.	10.00
223	Ted Williams	8.00
224	Duke Snider	2.00
225	Ernie Banks	4.00
226	Ryne Sandberg	8.00
227	Mark Grace	2.00
228	Andre Dawson	2.00
229	Bob Feller	2.00
230	Bob Feller	6.00
231	George Brett	8.00
232	Bo Jackson	3.00
233	Robin Yount	4.00
234	Harmon Killebrew	4.00
235	Gary Carter	2.00
236	Don Mattingly	8.00
237	Phil Rizzuto	2.00
238	Babe Ruth	8.00
239	Lou Gehrig	8.00
240	Reggie Jackson	3.00
241	Rickey Henderson	3.00
242	Mike Schmidt	8.00
243	Roberto Clemente	8.00
244	Tony Gwynn	3.00
245	Will Clark	3.00
246	Lou Brock	2.00
247	Bob Gibson	3.00
248	Stan Musial	5.00
249	Nolan Ryan	10.00
250	Dale Murphy	2.00
251	Aarom Baldiris/ Auto./499 RC	8.00
252	Akinori Otsuka/ Auto./99 RC	40.00
253	Andres Blanco/ Auto./499 RC	8.00
254	Angel Chavez/ Auto./499 RC	5.00
255	Carlos Hines/ Auto./199 RC	8.00
256	Carlos Vasquez/ Auto./499 RC	10.00
257	Casey Daigle/499 RC	10.00
258	Chris Oxspring/ Auto./499 RC	8.00
259	Colby Miller/ Auto./499 RC	5.00
260	David Crouthers/ Auto./199	8.00
261	Donald Kelly/ Auto./499 RC	5.00
262	Eddy Rodriguez/ Auto./499 RC	10.00
263	Edwardo Sierra/ Auto./299 RC	8.00
264	Edwin Moreno/ Auto./499 RC	10.00
265	Fernando Nieve/ Auto./499 RC	5.00
266	Freddy Guzman/ Auto./499 RC	5.00
267	Greg Dobbs/ Auto./499 RC	5.00
268	Brad Halsey/ Auto./499 RC	5.00
269	Hector Gimenez/ Auto./499 RC	5.00
270	Ivan Ochoa/Auto./499 RC	5.00
271	Jake Woods/Auto./499	8.00
272	Jamie Brown/ Auto./499 RC	5.00
273	Jason Bartlett/ Auto./499 RC	8.00
274	Jason Szuminski/ Auto./499 RC	5.00
275	John Gall/499 RC	5.00
276	Jorge Vasquez/ Auto./499 RC	5.00
277	Josh Labandeira/ Auto./499 RC	8.00
278	Justin Hampson/ Auto./499 RC	5.00
279	Kazuo Matsui/499 RC	15.00
280	Kevin Cave/Auto./499 RC	8.00
281	Lance Cormier/ Auto./499 RC	5.00
282	Lincoln Holdzkom/ Auto./199 RC	8.00
283	Merkin Valdez/ Auto./199 RC	15.00
284	Mike Wuertz/ Auto./199 RC	8.00
285	Mike Johnston/ Auto./499 RC	5.00
286	Mike Rouse/Auto./329	8.00
287	Onil Joseph/ Auto./499 RC	5.00
288	Phil Stockman/ Auto./499 RC	5.00
289	Roberto Novoa/ Auto./499 RC	8.00
290	Ronald Belisario/ Auto./499 RC	5.00
291	Ronny Cedeno/ Auto./499 RC	5.00
292	Ryan Meaux/ Auto./499 RC	5.00
293	Scott Proctor/499 RC	5.00
294	Sean Henn/Auto./499	10.00
295	Shawn Camp/ Auto./499 RC	5.00
296	Shawn Hill/Auto./499 RC	5.00
297	Shingo Takatsu/ Auto./99 RC	15.00
298	Tim Bittner/Auto./199 RC	8.00
299	William Bergolla/499 RC	5.00
300	Yadier Molina/ Auto./499 RC	25.00

Marble Black
No Pricing
Production One Set

Marble Blue
Blue 1-200:	3-5X
Blue 201-250:	2-3X
Blue 251-300:	.5-1X

Production 50 Sets

Marble Emerald
No Pricing
Production Five Sets

Marble Gold
Gold 1-200:	6-8X
Gold 201-250:	2-4X
Gold 251-300:	No Pricing

Production 25 Sets

Marble Red
Red 1-200:	2-3X
Red 201-250:	1-2X
Red 251-300:	.4-1X

Production 100 Sets

Check Signature Blue
NM/M
Quantity produced listed.

#	Player	NM/M
1	Al Kaline/22	60.00
2	Andre Dawson/22	25.00
22	Duke Snider/20	40.00
31	George Kell/60	35.00

Check Signature Green
No Pricing
Production 1-15

Check Signature Red
No Pricing

Check Signature Material Blue

NM/M
Quantity produced listed.

#	Player	NM/M
1	Al Kaline/Bat/50	50.00
2	Andre Dawson/Jsy/50	20.00
4	Bob Gibson/Hat/50	30.00
5	Bobby Doerr/Jsy/50	20.00
6	Brooks Robinson/ Bat/50	50.00
7	Cal Ripken Jr./Jsy/50	200.00
8	Cal Ripken Jr./Jsy/25	200.00
9	Cal Ripken Jr./Bat/25	200.00
10	Cal Ripken Jr./Jkt/25	200.00
13	Carlton Fisk/Jkt/35	40.00
14	Carlton Fisk/Jsy/35	40.00
16	Dale Murphy/Jsy/50	50.00
17	Dale Murphy/Jsy/50	30.00
18	Don Mattingly/Jsy/25	80.00
19	Don Mattingly/ Gray/25	80.00
20	Don Mattingly/Jkt/25	80.00
21	Don Mattingly/Jkt/25	80.00
22	Duke Snider/Pants/100	40.00
23	Ozzie Smith/Jsy/40	60.00
24	Ozzie Smith/Jsy/40	60.00
25	Ozzie Smith/Bat/40	60.00
26	Frank Robinson/Bat/30	30.00
27	George Brett/ White Jsy/30	80.00
28	George Brett/ Blue Jsy/30	80.00
29	George Brett/Bat/30	80.00
32	Hal Newhouser/Jsy/15	30.00
33	Harmon Killebrew/ Shoe/35	60.00
34	Harmon Killebrew/ Bat/35	60.00
38	Kirby Puckett/Fld Glv/25	60.00
39	Kirby Puckett/Bat/25	60.00
40	Lou Boudreau/Jsy/15	100.00
41	Lou Brock/Jsy/50	30.00
44	Luis Aparicio/Pants/50	20.00
44	Mark Grace/Fld Glv/30	30.00
46	Mike Schmidt/ Fld Glv/25	80.00
48	Mike Schmidt/Jsy/25	80.00
48	Mike Schmidt/Jkt/25	80.00
49	Mike Schmidt/Bat/25	80.00
50	Nolan Ryan/ Astros Jkt/30	150.00
51	Nolan Ryan/ Rgr Pants/30	150.00
52	Nolan Ryan/ Angels Jkt/30	150.00
53	Paul Molitor/Bat/50	35.00
57	Red Schoendienst/ Bat/50	20.00
63	Ron Santo/Bat/25	40.00
65	Ryne Sandberg/Jsy/50	65.00
67	Stan Musial/ White Jsy/30	80.00
68	Stan Musial/ Gray Jsy/30	
69	Stan Musial/Bat/30	80.00
70	Steve Carlton/Pants/25	40.00
73	Steve Carlton/Jsy/25	40.00
73	Tony Gwynn/ White Jsy/50	50.00
74	Tony Gwynn/ Navy Jsy/50	50.00
77	Whitey Ford/Pants/50	30.00
78	Will Clark/Jsy/50	50.00
79	Will Clark/Bat/50	50.00

Check Signature Material Green
NM/M
Quantity produced listed.

#	Player	NM/M
1	Al Kaline/Bat/33	65.00
3	Andre Dawson/Jsy/33	25.00
4	Bob Gibson/Hat/15	25.00
6	Brooks Robinson/ Bat/15	80.00
22	Duke Snider/Pants/25	50.00
26	Frank Robinson/Bat/15	50.00
41	Lou Brock/Jsy/15	50.00
43	Luis Aparicio/Pants/15	30.00
44	Mark Grace/Fld Glv/15	40.00
53	Paul Molitor/Jsy/15	40.00
77	Whitey Ford/Pants/15	75.00

Check Signature Material Red
NM/M
Quantity produced listed.

#	Player	NM/M
4	Bob Gibson/Hat/25	50.00
5	Bobby Doerr/Jsy/25	30.00
6	Brooks Robinson/ Bat/25	65.00
13	Carlton Fisk/Jkt/25	50.00
14	Carlton Fisk/Jsy/25	50.00
17	Dale Murphy/Jsy/25	40.00
22	Duke Snider/Pants/50	40.00
26	Frank Robinson/Bat/25	40.00
27	George Brett/Jsy/15	100.00
28	George Brett/Jsy/15	100.00
29	George Brett/Bat/15	100.00
33	Harmon Killebrew/ Shoe/25	65.00
34	Harmon Killebrew/ Bat/25	65.00
41	Lou Brock/Jsy/25	40.00
43	Luis Aparicio/Pants/25	25.00
44	Mark Grace/Fld Glve/25	40.00
53	Paul Molitor/Bat/25	40.00
57	Red Schoendienst/ Bat/25	25.00
65	Ryne Sandberg/Jsy/25	75.00
73	Tony Gwynn/Jsy/25	70.00
74	Tony Gwynn/Jsy/25	70.00
77	Whitey Ford/Pants/25	60.00
78	Will Clark/Jsy/25	40.00
79	Will Clark/Bat/25	40.00

Hall of Fame Souvenirs

NM/M
Quantity produced listed.

#	Player	NM/M
1	Ernie Banks/84	8.00
2	Stan Musial/93	15.00
3	Nolan Ryan/99	25.00
4	Duke Snider/87	8.00
5	Bob Feller/94	8.00
6	George Brett/98	20.00
7	Robin Yount/78	15.00
8	Harmon Killebrew/83	10.00
9	Gary Carter/78	4.00
10	Phil Rizzuto/75	8.00
11	Reggie Jackson/94	8.00
12	Mike Schmidt/97	8.00
13	Lou Brock/80	6.00
14	Bob Gibson/84	8.00
15	Bobby Doerr/86	4.00
16	Tony Perez/77	4.00
17	Whitey Ford/78	4.00
18	Juan Marichal/84	4.00
19	Monte Irvin/75	4.00
20	Fergie Jenkins/75	4.00
21	Ralph Kiner/75	4.00
22	Eddie Murray/85	10.00
23	George Kell/75	4.00
24	Hoyt Wilhelm/84	4.00
25	Carlton Fisk/80	6.00
26	Rod Carew/91	4.00
27	Frank Robinson/89	6.00
28	Gaylord Perry/77	4.00
29	Red Schoendienst/75	4.00
30	Brooks Robinson/92	8.00
31	Al Kaline/88	10.00
32	Orlando Cepeda/75	4.00
33	Steve Carlton/96	4.00
34	Luis Aparicio/85	4.00
35	Warren Spahn/83	8.00
36	Kirby Puckett/82	10.00
37	Phil Niekro/80	4.00
38	Jim Bunning/75	4.00
39	Tom Seaver/99	8.00
40	Paul Molitor/85	8.00
41	Johnny Bench/96	8.00
42	Don Sutton/82	4.00
43	Robin Roberts/87	6.00
44	Jim Palmer/93	8.00
45	Joe Morgan/82	4.00
46	Roberto Clemente/93	25.00
47	Lou Gehrig/100	10.00
48	Babe Ruth/95	20.00
49	Ty Cobb/98	10.00
50	Ted Williams/94	20.00

Hall of Fame Souvenirs Sign.
NM/M
Quantity produced listed.

#	Player	NM/M
3	Nolan Ryan/34	150.00
4	Duke Snider/50	30.00
5	Bob Feller/50	30.00
8	Harmon Killebrew/25	50.00
9	Gary Carter/50	15.00
10	Phil Rizzuto/50	25.00
12	Mike Schmidt/20	60.00
13	Lou Brock/50	25.00
14	Bob Gibson/45	25.00
15	Bobby Doerr/50	15.00
16	Tony Perez/50	15.00
17	Whitey Ford/16	40.00
18	Juan Marichal/50	15.00
19	Monte Irvin/50	25.00
20	Fergie Jenkins/75	15.00
21	Ralph Kiner/25	25.00
22	Eddie Murray/33	60.00
23	George Kell/50	15.00
24	Hoyt Wilhelm/49	15.00
25	Carlton Fisk/27	30.00
26	Rod Carew/29	30.00
29	Gaylord Perry/50	15.00
30	Red Schoendienst/50	15.00
31	Al Kaline/50	40.00
32	Orlando Cepeda/50	15.00
33	Steve Carlton/50	25.00
34	Luis Aparicio/50	15.00
35	Warren Spahn/21	50.00
36	Kirby Puckett/34	50.00
37	Phil Niekro/50	15.00
38	Jim Bunning/50	15.00
40	Paul Molitor/50	30.00
42	Don Sutton/50	15.00
43	Robin Roberts/50	15.00
44	Jim Palmer/22	20.00
45	Joe Morgan/25	20.00

HOF Souvenirs Material
NM/M
Production 25 Sets

#	Player	NM/M
1	Ernie Banks/Jsy	30.00
2	Stan Musial/Jsy	50.00
3	Nolan Ryan/Jsy	60.00
4	Duke Snider/Pants	20.00
5	Bob Feller/Jsy	20.00
6	George Brett/Jsy	20.00
7	Robin Yount/Jsy	40.00
8	Harmon Killebrew/Jsy	25.00
9	Gary Carter/Jkt	15.00
10	Phil Rizzuto/Pants	20.00
11	Reggie Jackson/Jsy	25.00
12	Mike Schmidt/Jsy	20.00
13	Lou Brock/Jsy	20.00
14	Bob Gibson/Jsy	20.00
15	Bobby Doerr/Jsy	15.00
16	Tony Perez/Bat	10.00
17	Whitey Ford/Pants	20.00
18	Juan Marichal/Jsy	15.00
20	Fergie Jenkins/Pants	10.00
21	Ralph Kiner/Bat	25.00
24	Hoyt Wilhelm/Jsy	25.00
25	Carlton Fisk/Jsy	20.00
26	Rod Carew/Jsy	20.00
28	Frank Robinson/Jsy	15.00
29	Red Schoendienst/Jsy	15.00
30	Brooks Robinson/Bat	30.00
31	Al Kaline/Pants	30.00
32	Orlando Cepeda/Bat	15.00
33	Steve Carlton/Pants	15.00
34	Luis Aparicio/Pants	15.00
35	Warren Spahn/Pants	25.00
36	Kirby Puckett/Jsy	25.00
37	Phil Niekro/Jsy	10.00
39	Tom Seaver/Jsy	20.00
40	Paul Molitor/Bat	20.00
41	Johnny Bench/Jsy	25.00
42	Don Sutton/Jsy	15.00
44	Robin Roberts/Hat	15.00
45	Jim Palmer/Jsy	15.00
46	Joe Morgan/Jsy	15.00
47	Roberto Clemente/Jsy	40.00
48	Lou Gehrig/Pants	150.00
49	Babe Ruth/Pants	275.00
50	Ty Cobb/Pants	150.00
	Ted Williams/Jsy	125.00

HOF Souvenirs Sign. Material
NM/M
Quantity produced listed

#	Player	NM/M
3	Nolan Ryan/Jsy/34	180.00
5	Bob Feller/Jsy/19	50.00
12	Mike Schmidt/Jsy/20	50.00
13	Lou Brock/Jsy/20	40.00
14	Bob Gibson/Jsy/45	30.00
16	Tony Perez/Bat/24	25.00
17	Whitey Ford/Pants/16	50.00

18	Juan Marichal/Jsy/27	30.00
20	Fergie Jenkins/Pants/31	30.00
22	Eddie Murray/Jsy/33	85.00
25	Carlton Fisk/Jsy/27	50.00
26	Rod Carew/Jsy/29	50.00
32	Orlando Cepeda/Bat/32	40.00
33	Steve Carlton/Pants/32	40.00
35	Warren Spahn/Pants/21	75.00
36	Kirby Puckett/Jsy/34	65.00
37	Phil Niekro/Jsy/35	25.00
42	Don Sutton/Jsy/40	40.00
43	Robin Roberts/Hat/36	25.00
44	Jim Palmer/Jsy/22	30.00
45	Joe Morgan/Jsy/16	35.00

K-Force

Quantity produced listed. NM/M
1	Nolan Ryan/500	8.00
2	Steve Carlton/500	2.00
3	Roger Clemens/500	6.00
4	Randy Johnson/500	3.00
5	Bert Blyleven/500	1.50
6	Tom Seaver/500	3.00
7	Don Sutton/500	1.50
8	Gaylord Perry/500	1.50
9	Phil Niekro/500	1.50
10	Fergie Jenkins/500	1.50
11	Bob Gibson/500	3.00
12	Nolan Ryan/383	8.00
13	Randy Johnson/308	3.00
14	Bob Feller/348	3.00
15	Curt Schilling/319	3.00
16	Pedro J. Martinez/313	3.00
17	Dwight Gooden/276	1.50
18	John Smoltz/276	2.00
19	Curt Schilling/316	3.00
20	Randy Johnson/319	3.00
21	Pedro Martinez/305	3.00
22	Roger Clemens/291	6.00
23	Roger Clemens/292	6.00
24	Tom Seaver/289	3.00
25	Hal Newhouser/275	2.00
26	Jim Bunning/201	2.00
27	Robin Roberts/198	3.00
28	Warren Spahn/191	4.00
29	Jack Morris/232	2.00
30	Nolan Ryan/270	8.00
31	Hideo Nomo/236	3.00
32	Barry Zito/205	2.00
33	Mike Mussina/214	3.00
34	Roy Oswalt/208	2.00
35	Mark Prior/245	3.00
36	Kerry Wood/266	4.00
37	Roy Halladay/204	2.00
38	Esteban Loaiza/207	1.50
39	Whitey Ford/94	6.00
40	Bob Gibson/17	12.00
41	Ben Sheets/18	8.00
42	Hoyt Wilhelm/139	3.00
43	Satchel Paige/91	10.00
44	Burleigh Grimes/136	3.00
45	Mark Prior, Kerry Wood/500	3.00
46	Nolan Ryan, Roger Clemens/500	10.00
47	Steve Carlton, Randy Johnson/500	3.00
48	Nolan Ryan, Roger Clemens/500	8.00
49	Nolan Ryan, Steve Carlton/500	8.00
50	Kerry Wood, Roger Clemens/20	30.00

K-Force Material
NM/M
Quantity produced listed.
1	Nolan Ryan/Jsy/100	25.00
2	Steve Carlton/Jsy/32	12.00
3	Roger Clemens/Jsy/25	25.00
4	Randy Johnson/Jsy/51	15.00
5	Bert Blyleven/Jsy/28	10.00
7	Tom Seaver/Jsy/25	25.00
8	Gaylord Perry/Jsy/36	8.00
9	Phil Niekro/Jsy/35	8.00
10	Fergie Jenkins/Pants/31	10.00
11	Bob Gibson/Jsy/45	15.00
12	Nolan Ryan/Jkt/100	25.00
13	Randy Johnson/Jsy/25	15.00
14	Bob Feller/Jsy/25	20.00
15	Curt Schilling/Jsy/25	12.00
16	Pedro J. Martinez/Jsy/45	15.00
17	Dwight Gooden/Jsy/25	10.00
18	John Smoltz/Jsy/25	15.00
19	Curt Schilling/Jsy/25	12.00

20	Randy Johnson/Jsy/51	15.00
21	Pedro Martinez/Jsy/45	15.00
22	Roger Clemens/Jsy/100	15.00
25	Hal Newhouser/Jsy/45	15.00
28	Warren Spahn/Jsy/50	15.00
29	Jack Morris/Jsy/47	8.00
30	Nolan Ryan/Jkt/100	25.00
31	Hideo Nomo/Jsy/25	20.00
32	Barry Zito/Jsy/25	10.00
33	Mike Mussina/Jsy/25	20.00
34	Roy Oswalt/Jsy/44	6.00
35	Mark Prior/Jsy/50	20.00
36	Kerry Wood/Jsy/34	20.00
39	Whitey Ford/Jsy/50	15.00
40	Bob Gibson/Jsy/50	10.00
41	Ben Sheets/Jsy/100	10.00
43	Satchel Paige/Jsy/100	60.00
44	Burleigh Grimes/Pants/100	75.00
45	Mark Prior, Kerry Wood/Pants/50	15.00
46	Nolan Ryan, Roger Clemens/Jsy/50	40.00
47	Steve Carlton, Randy Johnson/Jsy/25	40.00
48	Nolan Ryan, Roger Clemens/Jsy/50	40.00
49	Nolan Ryan, Carlton Fisk/Pants/50	35.00
50	Kerry Wood/Jsy, Roger Clemens/Jsy/50	25.00

K-Force Signature
NM/M
2	Steve Carlton/50	30.00
5	Bert Blyleven/50	15.00
7	Don Sutton/50	15.00
8	Gaylord Perry/50	15.00
9	Phil Niekro/50	25.00
14	Bob Feller/50	30.00
17	Dwight Gooden/50	20.00
26	Jim Bunning/50	25.00
27	Robin Roberts/50	20.00
29	Jack Morris/50	15.00
34	Roy Oswalt/50	15.00
38	Esteban Loaiza/50	10.00

K-Force Signature Material

NM/M
1	Nolan Ryan/Jsy/34	150.00
2	Steve Carlton/Jsy/32	50.00
5	Bert Blyleven/Jsy/28	25.00
8	Gaylord Perry/Jsy/25	25.00
9	Phil Niekro/Jsy/35	40.00
10	Fergie Jenkins/Pants/31	25.00
11	Bob Gibson/Jsy/45	40.00
14	Bob Feller/Jsy/19	50.00
17	Dwight Gooden/Jsy/16	30.00
28	Warren Spahn/Jsy/21	65.00
29	Jack Morris/Jsy/47	20.00
30	Nolan Ryan/Jsy/34	150.00
34	Roy Oswalt/Jsy/44	20.00
36	Kerry Wood/Jsy/34	50.00
37	Roy Halladay/Jsy/32	15.00
39	Whitey Ford/Jsy/16	50.00
40	Bob Gibson/Jsy/45	30.00

Marble Material Black
No Pricing
Production One Set

Marble Material Blue Number
NM/M
Quanity produced listed.
1	Vladimir Guerrero/Jsy/27	25.00
2	Garret Anderson/Jsy/16	15.00
5	Troy Glaus/Jsy/25	10.00
6	Tim Salmon/Jsy/15	20.00
8	Brandon Webb/Jsy/55	5.00
10	Randy Johnson/Jsy/51	12.00
13	Luis Gonzalez/Jsy/20	10.00
18	Marcus Giles/Jsy/22	10.00
19	Andruw Jones/Jsy/25	10.00
20	Rafael Palmeiro/Jsy/25	15.00
22	Luis Matos/Jsy/32	10.00
23	Jay Gibbons/Jsy/31	15.00
25	Rodrigo Lopez/Jsy/19	15.00
27	Javy Lopez/Jsy/18	15.00
30	Curt Schilling/Jsy/38	12.00
31	Jason Varitek/Jsy/33	10.00
32	Manny Ramirez/Jsy/24	20.00
35	Pedro Martinez/Jsy/45	15.00
37	David Ortiz/Jsy/34	20.00
38	Mark Prior/Jsy/22	15.00
41	Kerry Wood/Pants/34	20.00
42	Sammy Sosa/Jsy/21	30.00
43	Greg Maddux/Jsy/31	25.00
45	Aramis Ramirez/Jsy/16	15.00
49	Moises Alou/Jsy/18	15.00
51	Frank Thomas/Jsy/35	20.00

Next Column

52	Magglio Ordonez/Jsy/30	10.00
53	Carlos Lee/Jsy/45	5.00
54	Mark Buehrle/Jsy/56	5.00
58	Adam Dunn/Jsy/44	12.00
63	Austin Kearns/Jsy/28	10.00
66	Sean Casey/Jsy/21	10.00
67	Cliff Lee/Jsy/34	10.00
68	Victor Martinez/Jsy/41	8.00
70	C.C. Sabathia/Jsy/52	5.00
71	Travis Hafner/Jsy/48	8.00
72	Todd Helton/Jsy/17	20.00
73	Preston Wilson/Jsy/44	5.00
74	Jeromy Burnitz/Jsy/35	5.00
77	Larry Walker/Jsy/33	10.00
79	Miguel Cabrera/Jsy/24	20.00
81	Josh Beckett/Jsy/21	12.00
82	Dontrelle Willis/Jsy/35	10.00
85	Brad Penny/Jsy/31	8.00
87	Andy Pettitte/Jsy/21	15.00
88	Roy Oswalt/Jsy/44	5.00
95	Lance Berkman/Jsy/17	10.00
99	Roger Clemens/Jsy/22	25.00
100	Mike Sweeney/Jsy/29	10.00
101	Kazuhisa Ishii/Jsy/17	15.00
107	Adrian Beltre/Jsy/29	15.00
113	Johan Santana/Jsy/57	15.00
117	Shannon Stewart/Jsy/23	10.00
119	Torii Hunter/Jsy/48	5.00
123	Orlando Cabrera/Jsy/18	20.00
124	Mike Piazza/Jsy/31	30.00
127	Jae Weong/Seo Jsy/26	10.00
128	Tom Glavine/Jsy/47	10.00
129	Jorge Posada/Jsy/20	15.00
131	Bernie Williams/Jsy/51	10.00
133	Mike Mussina/Jsy/35	15.00
135	Mariano Rivera/Jsy/42	10.00
138	Jason Giambi/Jsy/25	15.00
139	Hideki Matsui/Jsy/55	40.00
145	Mark Mulder/Jsy/40	10.00
146	Barry Zito/Jsy/75	5.00
148	Marlon Byrd/Jsy/29	10.00
150	Jim Thome/Jsy/25	25.00
151	Bobby Abreu/Jsy/53	5.00
154	Craig Wilson/Jsy/36	5.00
161	Sean Burroughs/Jsy/32	10.00
163	Brian Giles/Jsy/24	8.00
166	Ryan Klesko/Jsy/30	8.00
166	Jerome Williams/Jsy/57	5.00
172	Freddy Garcia/Jsy/34	8.00
177	Scott Rolen/Jsy/27	20.00
178	Jim Edmonds/Jsy/15	15.00
180	Matt Morris/Jsy/35	5.00
181	Edgar Renteria/Jsy/15	15.00
182	Aubrey Huff/Jsy/19	10.00
184	Dewon Brazelton/Jsy/45	5.00
187	Mark Teixeira/Jsy/33	15.00
192	Kevin Mench/Jsy/28	8.00
195	Roy Halladay/Jsy/32	5.00
197	Carlos Delgado/Jsy/25	10.00
200	Jeremy Bonderman/Jsy/38	5.00
201	Roger Clemens/Jsy/22	30.00
203	Greg Maddux/Jsy/31	25.00
206	Andy Pettitte/Jsy/46	15.00
207	Curt Schilling/Jsy/38	12.00
210	Jim Thome/Jsy/25	25.00
211	Mike Mussina/Jsy/35	15.00
212	Mike Piazza/Jsy/31	30.00
213	Randy Johnson/Jsy/51	15.00
214	Roger Clemens/Jsy/21	30.00
215	Sammy Sosa/Jsy/21	30.00
217	Randy Johnson/Jsy/51	15.00
219	Vladimir Guerrero/Jsy/27	25.00
219	Rafael Palmeiro/Jsy/25	15.00
221	Mike Piazza/Jsy/25	30.00
226	Ryne Sandberg/Jsy/23	40.00
227	Mark Grace/Jsy/17	25.00
229	Bob Feller/Jsy/19	20.00
232	Bo Jackson/Jsy/16	40.00
233	Robin Yount/Jsy/19	40.00
236	Don Mattingly/Jsy/23	40.00
241	Rickey Henderson/Jsy/35	25.00
242	Mike Schmidt/Jsy/20	40.00
243	Roberto Clemente/Jsy/21	100.00
245	Will Clark/Jsy/22	30.00
246	Lou Brock/Jsy/20	20.00
247	Bob Gibson/Jsy/45	15.00
249	Nolan Ryan/Jsy/34	40.00

Marble Material Emerald Prime
No Pricing
Production Five Sets

Marble Material Red Position
NM/M
Quantity produced listed.
1	Vladimir Guerrero/Jsy/100	10.00
2	Garret Anderson/Jsy/100	4.00
5	Troy Glaus/Jsy/75	4.00
6	Tim Salmon/Jsy/75	6.00
10	Randy Johnson/Jsy/100	8.00
13	Luis Gonzalez/Jsy/100	4.00
15	Rafael Furcal/Jsy/100	4.00
16	Chipper Jones/Jsy/100	8.00
18	Marcus Giles/Jsy/100	4.00
19	Andruw Jones/Jsy/100	6.00
20	Rafael Palmeiro/Jsy/100	6.00
21	Melvin Mora/Jsy/100	4.00
22	Luis Matos/Jsy/50	4.00

Next Column

23	Jay Gibbons/Jsy/100	4.00
25	Larry Bigbie/Jsy/50	6.00
26	Rodrigo Lopez/Jsy/50	6.00
27	Javy Lopez/Jsy/50	12.00
28	Miguel Tejada/Jsy/100	6.00
30	Curt Schilling/Jsy/100	8.00
31	Jason Varitek/Jsy/100	4.00
34	Manny Ramirez/Jsy/100	8.00
35	Pedro J. Martinez/Jsy/100	10.00
39	David Ortiz/Jsy/100	8.00
40	Mark Prior/Jsy/100	8.00
41	Kerry Wood/Pants/100	10.00
42	Sammy Sosa/Jsy/100	10.00
43	Greg Maddux/Jsy/100	15.00
45	Aramis Ramirez/Jsy/100	4.00
51	Frank Thomas/Jsy/100	8.00
52	Magglio Ordonez/Jsy/100	4.00
53	Carlos Lee/Jsy/100	4.00
54	Mark Buehrle/Jsy/100	4.00
57	Paul Konerko/Jsy/50	6.00
58	Adam Dunn/Jsy/100	8.00
59	Austin Kearns/Jsy/100	6.00
65	Barry Larkin/Jsy/100	6.00
65	Jody Gerut/Jsy/100	4.00
67	Cliff Lee/Jsy/100	4.00
67	Victor Martinez/Jsy/100	6.00
69	C.C. Sabathia/Jsy/100	4.00
69	Omar Vizquel/Jsy/100	4.00
70	Travis Hafner/Jsy/100	4.00
71	Todd Helton/Jsy/100	8.00
72	Preston Wilson/Jsy/100	4.00
72	Ivan Rodriguez/Jsy/50	10.00
77	Miguel Cabrera/Jsy/100	8.00
77	Josh Beckett/Jsy/100	6.00
81	Dontrelle Willis/Jsy/100	8.00
82	Brad Penny/Jsy/100	4.00
86	Jeff Bagwell/Jsy/100	8.00
87	Roy Oswalt/Jsy/100	4.00
88	Lance Berkman/Jsy/100	4.00
89	Morgan Ensberg/Jsy/100	4.00
90	Craig Biggio/Jsy/100	6.00
93	Jeff Kent/Jsy/100	4.00
94	Richard Hidalgo/Pants/100	4.00
95	Roger Clemens/Jsy/25	30.00
96	Carlos Beltran/Jsy/100	6.00
97	Angel Berroa/Pants/100	4.00
100	Mike Sweeney/Jsy/100	4.00
101	Kazuhisa Ishii/Jsy/100	6.00
102	Shawn Green/Jsy/100	4.00
104	Paul LoDuca/Jsy/100	4.00
107	Hideo Nomo/Jsy/100	8.00
107	Adrian Beltre/Jsy/100	4.00
111	Ben Sheets/Jsy/100	6.00
111	Geoff Jenkins/Jsy/100	4.00
112	Jacque Jones/Jsy/100	4.00
113	Johan Santana/Jsy/100	8.00
114	Shannon Stewart/Jsy/100	4.00
117	Torii Hunter/Jsy/75	4.00
123	Mike Piazza/Jsy/100	10.00
125	Jose Reyes/Jsy/75	4.00
125	Tom Glavine/Jsy/75	6.00
127	Jorge Posada/Jsy/100	8.00
129	Bernie Williams/Jsy/100	6.00
130	Mike Mussina/Jsy/25	20.00
131	Mariano Rivera/Jsy/100	8.00
139	Hideki Matsui/Jsy/100	25.00
145	Mark Mulder/Jsy/100	4.00
143	Barry Zito/Jsy/100	4.00
146	Eric Chavez/Jsy/100	6.00
148	Marlon Byrd/Jsy/100	4.00
150	Jim Thome/Jsy/100	8.00
151	Bobby Abreu/Jsy/100	4.00
152	Pat Burrell/Jsy/100	4.00
154	Craig Wilson/Jsy/100	4.00
156	Jason Kendall/Jsy/100	4.00
161	Sean Burroughs/Jsy/100	4.00
164	Ryan Klesko/Jsy/100	4.00
166	Jerome Williams/Jsy/25	10.00
171	Edgar Renteria/Jsy/100	6.00
172	Freddy Garcia/Jsy/100	4.00
177	Scott Rolen/Jsy/100	10.00
178	Jim Edmonds/Jsy/100	6.00
179	Albert Pujols/Jsy/100	20.00
180	Matt Morris/Jsy/75	4.00
181	Edgar Renteria/Jsy/25	10.00
182	Aubrey Huff/Jsy/100	4.00
185	Rocco Baldelli/Jsy/100	4.00
186	Carl Crawford/Jsy/100	4.00
187	Mark Teixeira/Jsy/100	8.00
188	Hank Blalock/Jsy/100	8.00
191	Alfonso Soriano/Jsy/100	8.00
192	Kevin Mench/Jsy/100	4.00
195	Roy Halladay/Jsy/100	4.00
196	Vernon Wells/Jsy/100	4.00
197	Carlos Delgado/Jsy/100	4.00
200	Jeremy Bonderman/Jsy/100	4.00
201	Roger Clemens/Jsy/100	10.00
202	Alex Rodriguez/Jsy/100	10.00
203	Greg Maddux/Jsy/100	15.00
204	Miguel Tejada/Jsy/100	4.00
205	Alfonso Soriano/Jsy/100	8.00
206	Andy Pettitte/Jsy/100	6.00
207	Curt Schilling/Jsy/100	8.00
208	Gary Sheffield/Jsy/100	6.00
209	Ivan Rodriguez/Jsy/100	4.00
210	Jim Thome/Jsy/100	8.00
211	Mike Mussina/Jsy/100	6.00
212	Mike Piazza/Jsy/100	10.00
213	Randy Johnson/Jsy/100	10.00
215	Sammy Sosa/Jsy/100	10.00
216	Alex Rodriguez/Jsy/100	10.00
217	Randy Johnson/Jsy/100	8.00

Next Column

218	Vladimir Guerrero/Jsy/100	8.00
219	Rafael Palmeiro/Jsy/100	6.00
221	Mike Piazza/Jsy/100	10.00
222	Cal Ripken Jr./Jsy/50	50.00
223	Ted Williams/Jsy/100	100.00
226	Ernie Banks/Jsy/50	15.00
226	Ryne Sandberg/Jsy/100	15.00
227	Mark Grace/Jsy/25	20.00
228	Andre Dawson/Jsy/100	8.00
229	Bob Feller/Jsy/25	20.00
231	George Brett/Jsy/100	15.00
232	Bo Jackson/Jsy/100	10.00
233	Robin Yount/Jsy/100	12.00
234	Harmon Killebrew/Jsy/25	25.00
235	Gary Carter/Jkt/100	6.00
236	Don Mattingly/Jsy/100	15.00
237	Phil Rizzuto/Pants/25	20.00
238	Babe Ruth/Pants/50	200.00
239	Lou Gehrig/Pants/50	150.00
240	Reggie Jackson/Jsy/100	8.00
241	Rickey Henderson/Jsy/100	10.00
242	Mike Schmidt/Jsy/25	25.00
243	Roberto Clemente/Jsy/50	75.00
244	Tony Gwynn/Jsy/100	10.00
245	Will Clark/Jsy/100	10.00
246	Lou Brock/Jsy/25	20.00
247	Bob Gibson/Jsy/25	20.00
248	Stan Musial/Jsy/25	60.00
249	Nolan Ryan/Jsy/50	40.00
250	Dale Murphy/Jsy/100	10.00

Marble Signature Black
No Pricing
Production One Set

Marble Signature Blue
NM/M
Quantity produced listed
2	Garret Anderson/75	20.00
3	John Lackey/75	15.00
7	Shea Hillenbrand/75	15.00
8	Brandon Webb/75	10.00
11	Alex Cintron/75	10.00
14	Adam LaRoche/75	15.00
15	Rafael Furcal/75	20.00
17	Marcus Giles/75	10.00
19	Russ Ortiz/75	10.00
21	Melvin Mora/75	15.00
22	Luis Matos/75	10.00
23	Jay Gibbons/75	15.00
24	Adam Loewen/50	10.00
25	Larry Bigbie/75	15.00
26	Rodrigo Lopez/75	10.00
29	Trot Nixon/75	35.00
32	Keith Foulke/75	8.00
39	David Ortiz/50	40.00
40	Mark Prior/25	40.00
41	Kerry Wood/25	50.00
43	Derrek Lee/25	30.00
45	Aramis Ramirez/25	20.00
46	Matt Clement/25	15.00
47	Carlos Zambrano/35	35.00
48	Todd Walker/75	10.00
52	Magglio Ordonez/25	20.00
53	Carlos Lee/75	15.00
54	Mark Buehrle/50	15.00
55	Esteban Loaiza/25	15.00
58	Adam Dunn/25	40.00
61	Austin Kearns/25	20.00
63	Sean Casey/25	25.00
65	Jody Gerut/75	8.00
66	Cliff Lee/75	10.00
67	Victor Martinez/75	20.00
68	C.C. Sabathia/75	15.00
70	Travis Hafner/75	15.00
72	Preston Wilson/75	15.00
77	Miguel Cabrera/50	35.00
80	Mike Lowell/25	20.00
82	Brad Penny/75	15.00
87	Roy Oswalt/75	15.00
89	Morgan Ensberg/75	12.00
90	Craig Biggio/25	30.00
91	Octavio Dotel/75	15.00
92	Wade Miller/75	10.00
96	Carlos Beltran/50	50.00
97	Angel Berroa/50	10.00
98	Jeremy Affeldt/75	10.00
103	Milton Bradley/75	15.00
104	Paul LoDuca/75	15.00
108	Scott Podsednik/75	15.00
109	Rickie Weeks/25	20.00
112	Jacque Jones/75	10.00
113	Johan Santana/50	50.00
114	Shannon Stewart/75	15.00
116	Lew Ford/75	15.00
117	Torii Hunter/25	25.00
118	Chad Cordero/75	10.00
119	Orlando Cabrera/75	20.00
120	Jose Vidro/50	15.00
125	Jose Reyes/75	30.00
132	Bubba Crosby/75	10.00
139	Mark Mulder/25	25.00
140	Jermaine Dye/75	10.00
144	Bobby Crosby/75	40.00
145	Eric Byrnes/75	10.00
146	Marlon Byrd/75	10.00
148	Mike Lieberthal/75	15.00
153	Jose Castillo/75	10.00
154	Craig Wilson/75	10.00
155	Jason Bay/75	25.00
158	Jay Payton/75	10.00
161	Sean Burroughs/25	15.00
165	Todd Linden/75	8.00

Next Column

170	Shigetoshi Hasegawa/50	40.00
171	Edgar Martinez/50	40.00
174	Raul Ibanez/75	10.00
177	Scott Rolen/50	35.00
182	Aubrey Huff/75	10.00
183	Delmon Young/25	20.00
184	Dewon Brazelton/75	10.00
186	Carl Crawford/75	20.00
187	Mark Teixeira/25	40.00
188	Hank Blalock/50	25.00
189	Michael Young/75	15.00
190	Laynce Nix/75	15.00
191	Alfonso Soriano/25	50.00
193	Adrian Gonzalez/75	10.00
194	Alexis Rios/75	20.00
196	Vernon Wells/50	15.00
198	Bill Hall/75	15.00
199	Jose Guillen/75	15.00
200	Jeremy Bonderman/75	8.00
222	Cal Ripken Jr./25	150.00
224	Duke Snider/35	35.00
228	Andre Dawson/50	20.00
229	Bob Feller/50	30.00
235	Gary Carter/25	25.00
237	Phil Rizzuto/25	40.00
245	Will Clark/75	20.00
246	Lou Brock/25	35.00
247	Bob Gibson/25	40.00
248	Stan Musial/25	75.00
249	Nolan Ryan/25	150.00
250	Dale Murphy/50	30.00
251	Aaron Baldiris/75	10.00
252	Akinori Otsuka/25	15.00
253	Andres Blanco/75	10.00
254	Angel Chavez/75	8.00
255	Carlos Hines/75	8.00
256	Carlos Vasquez/75	12.00
258	Chris Oxspring/75	8.00
259	Colby Miller/75	8.00
261	Donald Kelly/75	8.00
262	Eddy Rodriguez/75	8.00
263	Edwardo Sierra/65	10.00
264	Edwin Moreno/75	12.00
265	Fernando Nieve/75	8.00
266	Freddy Guzman/75	8.00
267	Greg Dobbs/75	8.00
268	Brad Halsey/75	8.00
269	Hector Gimenez/75	8.00
270	Ivan Ochoa/75	8.00
271	Jake Woods/75	10.00
272	Jamie Brown/75	8.00
273	Jason Bartlett/75	15.00
274	Jason Szuminski/75	8.00
275	John Gall/75	8.00
276	Jorge Vasquez/75	8.00
277	Josh Labandeira/75	8.00
278	Justin Hampson/75	8.00
280	Kevin Cave/75	10.00
281	Lance Cormier/75	8.00
283	Merkin Valdez/75	15.00
284	Mike Wuertz/75	8.00
285	Mike Johnston/75	8.00
287	Onil Joseph/75	8.00
288	Phil Stockman/75	8.00
289	Roberto Novoa/75	10.00
290	Ronald Belisario/75	8.00
291	Ronny Cedeno/75	8.00
292	Ryan Meaux/75	8.00
293	Scott Proctor/75	10.00
295	Shawn Camp/75	8.00
296	Shawn Hill/75	8.00
297	Shingo Takatsu/25	60.00
299	William Bergolla/75	8.00
300	Yadier Molina/75	25.00

Marble Signature Emerald
No Pricing
Production 1-5

Marble Signature Gold
No Pricing
Production 1-25

Marble Sig. Mat. Gold Number
NM/M
Quantity produced listed.
1	Vladimir Guerrero/Jsy/27	60.00
8	Brandon Webb/Jsy/55	10.00
18	Andruw Jones/Jsy/25	40.00
22	Luis Matos/Jsy/32	15.00
23	Jay Gibbons/Jsy/31	15.00
32	Manny Ramirez/Jsy/24	75.00
39	David Ortiz/Jsy/34	50.00
40	Mark Prior/Jsy/22	50.00
41	Kerry Wood/Pants/34	50.00
42	Sammy Sosa/Jsy/21	150.00
44	Greg Maddux/Jsy/31	50.00
51	Frank Thomas/Jsy/35	50.00
52	Magglio Ordonez/Jsy/30	25.00
53	Carlos Lee/Jsy/45	20.00
54	Mark Buehrle/Jsy/56	20.00
58	Adam Dunn/Jsy/44	40.00
59	Austin Kearns/Jsy/28	20.00
67	Cliff Lee/Jsy/34	20.00
67	Victor Martinez/Jsy/41	20.00
68	C.C. Sabathia/Jsy/52	20.00
70	Travis Hafner/Jsy/48	20.00
71	Todd Helton/Jsy/17	60.00
72	Preston Wilson/Jsy/44	20.00
81	Dontrelle Willis/Jsy/35	30.00
82	Brad Penny/Jsy/31	15.00
85	Andy Pettitte/Jsy/21	40.00
104	Paul LoDuca/Jsy/16	35.00
113	Johan Santana/Jsy/57	25.00

#	Player	Price
114	Shannon Stewart/Jsy/23	25.00
117	Torii Hunter/Jsy/48	20.00
119	Orlando Cabrera/Jsy/18	30.00
123	Mike Piazza/Jsy/31	100.00
124	Jae Weong/Seo Jsy/26	20.00
127	Jorge Posada/Jsy/20	40.00
130	Mike Mussina/Jsy/35	45.00
139	Mark Mulder/Jsy/20	25.00
141	Tim Hudson/Jsy/15	30.00
146	Marlon Byrd/Jsy/29	15.00
177	Scott Rolen/Jsy/27	50.00
182	Aubrey Huff/Jsy/19	30.00
184	Dewon Brazelton/Jsy/45	15.00
187	Mark Teixeira/Jsy/23	50.00
195	Roy Halladay/Jsy/32	15.00
200	Jeremy Bonderman/Jsy/38	10.00
236	Don Mattingly/Jsy/23	85.00
240	Reggie Jackson/Jsy/44	50.00
241	Rickey Henderson/Jsy/35	50.00
242	Mike Schmidt/Pants/20	100.00
244	Tony Gwynn/Jsy/19	75.00
245	Will Clark/Jsy/22	50.00
246	Lou Brock/Jsy/30	40.00
247	Bob Gibson/Jsy/45	40.00
249	Nolan Ryan/Jsy/34	150.00

Marble Sig. Material Gold Position

NM/M
Quantity produced listed.

#	Player	Price
2	Garret Anderson/Jsy/50	20.00
8	Brandon Webb/Jsy/50	15.00
15	Rafael Furcal/Jsy/50	30.00
17	Marcus Giles/Jsy/50	20.00
21	Melvin Mora/Jsy/50	15.00
23	Luis Matos/Jsy/50	15.00
25	Jay Gibbons/Jsy/50	15.00
26	Larry Bigbie/Jsy/50	15.00
26	Rodrigo Lopez/Jsy/50	10.00
45	Aramis Ramirez/Jsy/50	30.00
53	Carlos Lee/Jsy/50	15.00
54	Mark Buehrle/Jsy/50	20.00
58	Austin Kearns/Jsy/50	20.00
65	Jody Gerut/Jsy/50	10.00
67	Cliff Lee/Jsy/50	20.00
67	Victor Martinez/Jsy/50	25.00
68	C.C. Sabathia/Jsy/50	20.00
72	Travis Hafner/Jsy/50	20.00
72	Preston Wilson/Jsy/50	15.00
82	Brad Penny/Jsy/50	10.00
89	Morgan Ensberg/Jsy/50	10.00
96	Carlos Beltran/Jsy/50	50.00
97	Angel Berroa/Pants/50	15.00
104	Paul LoDuca/Jsy/25	25.00
112	Jacque Jones/Jsy/50	50.00
113	Johan Santana/Jsy/50	50.00
114	Shannon Stewart/Jsy/50	20.00
117	Torii Hunter/Jsy/25	25.00
119	Orlando Cabrera/Jsy/50	20.00
120	Jose Vidro/Jsy/50	15.00
139	Mark Mulder/Jsy/25	25.00
146	Marlon Byrd/Jsy/50	15.00
154	Craig Wilson/Jsy/50	15.00
161	Sean Burroughs/Jsy/50	15.00
171	Edgar Martinez/Jsy/25	50.00
182	Aubrey Huff/Jsy/50	20.00
186	Carl Crawford/Jsy/50	30.00
187	Hank Blalock/Jsy/25	50.00
200	Jeremy Bonderman/Jsy/50	10.00
228	Andre Dawson/Jsy/50	20.00
229	Bob Feller/Jsy/50	35.00
234	Harmon Killebrew/Jsy/25	65.00

Marble Signature Red

NM/M
Quantity produced listed

#	Player	Price
2	Garret Anderson/100	20.00
3	John Lackey/100	15.00
7	Shea Hillenbrand/100	15.00
8	Brandon Webb/100	15.00
11	Alex Cintron/100	10.00
14	Adam LaRoche/100	15.00
15	Rafael Furcal/50	20.00
17	Marcus Giles/100	15.00
19	Russ Ortiz/100	10.00
21	Melvin Mora/100	15.00
23	Luis Matos/100	15.00
25	Jay Gibbons/100	15.00
26	Larry Bigbie/100	15.00
26	Rodrigo Lopez/100	15.00
29	Trot Nixon/50	35.00
32	Keith Foulke/100	8.00
39	David Ortiz/50	40.00
42	Mark Prior/25	40.00
43	Derrek Lee/50	25.00
45	Aramis Ramirez/100	20.00
46	Matt Clement/25	15.00
47	Carlos Zambrano/100	35.00
48	Todd Walker/100	10.00
53	Carlos Lee/100	15.00
54	Mark Buehrle/50	15.00
55	Esteban Loaiza/100	10.00
58	Adam Dunn/25	40.00
59	Austin Kearns/25	20.00
63	Sean Casey/25	25.00
65	Jody Gerut/100	8.00
66	Cliff Lee/100	15.00
67	Victor Martinez/100	20.00
68	C.C. Sabathia/100	15.00
70	Travis Hafner/100	15.00
72	Preston Wilson/100	15.00
77	Miguel Cabrera/50	35.00
80	Mike Lowell/25	20.00
82	Brad Penny/100	10.00
89	Morgan Ensberg/100	10.00
90	Craig Biggio/25	30.00
91	Octavio Dotel/100	15.00
92	Wade Miller/100	10.00
96	Carlos Beltran/50	50.00
97	Angel Berroa/50	10.00
98	Jeremy Affeldt/100	15.00
103	Milton Bradley/100	15.00
104	Paul LoDuca/50	15.00
108	Scott Podsednik/100	15.00
109	Rickie Weeks/25	20.00
112	Jacque Jones/100	15.00
113	Johan Santana/50	50.00
114	Shannon Stewart/50	15.00
116	Lew Ford/100	15.00
117	Torii Hunter/25	25.00
118	Chad Cordero/100	10.00
119	Orlando Cabrera/100	20.00
120	Jose Vidro/50	15.00
132	Bubba Crosby/100	10.00
139	Mark Mulder/25	25.00
140	Jermaine Dye/100	10.00
144	Bobby Crosby/100	40.00
145	Eric Byrnes/100	10.00
146	Marlon Byrd/100	10.00
148	Mike Lieberthal/100	15.00
153	Jose Castillo/100	15.00
155	Jason Bay/100	25.00
158	Jay Payton/100	10.00
161	Sean Burroughs/25	15.00
165	Todd Linden/100	8.00
170	Shigetoshi Hasegawa/50	40.00
171	Edgar Martinez/25	40.00
174	Raul Ibanez/100	10.00
177	Scott Rolen/50	35.00
182	Aubrey Huff/100	10.00
183	Delmon Young/25	20.00
184	Dewon Brazelton/100	10.00
186	Carl Crawford/100	20.00
187	Mark Teixeira/50	40.00
189	Hank Blalock/50	25.00
189	Michael Young/100	15.00
190	Laynce Nix/100	15.00
191	Alfonso Soriano/25	50.00
193	Adrian Gonzalez/100	15.00
194	Alexis Rios/100	20.00
196	Vernon Wells/50	15.00
199	Bill Hall/100	10.00
199	Jose Guillen/100	10.00
200	Jeremy Bonderman/100	10.00
222	Cal Ripken Jr./25	150.00
224	Duke Snider/25	40.00
228	Andre Dawson/100	20.00
229	Bob Feller/100	25.00
235	Gary Carter/25	20.00
237	Phil Rizzuto/25	40.00
245	Will Clark/25	50.00
247	Bob Gibson/25	40.00
248	Stan Musial/25	75.00
249	Nolan Ryan/25	150.00
250	Dale Murphy/50	30.00
251	Aarom Baldiris/100	10.00
252	Akinori Otsuka/25	10.00
253	Andres Blanco/100	10.00
254	Angel Chavez/100	8.00
255	Carlos Hines/100	8.00
256	Carlos Vasquez/100	12.00
258	Chris Oxspring/100	10.00
259	Colby Miller/100	8.00
260	David Crouthers/50	8.00
261	Donald Kelly/100	8.00
262	Eddy Rodriguez/100	8.00
263	Edwardo Sierra/100	10.00
264	Edwin Moreno/100	8.00
266	Freddy Guzman/100	8.00
267	Greg Dobbs/100	8.00
268	Brad Halsey/100	8.00
269	Hector Gimenez/100	8.00
270	Ivan Ochoa/100	8.00
271	Jake Woods/100	10.00
272	Jamie Brown/100	8.00
273	Jason Bartlett/100	15.00
274	Jason Szuminski/100	8.00
275	John Gall/100	10.00
277	Jorge Vasquez/100	8.00
280	Kevin Cave/100	10.00
281	Lance Cormier/100	8.00
283	Merkin Valdez/100	15.00
284	Mike Wuertz/100	10.00
285	Mike Johnston/100	8.00
288	Onil Joseph/100	8.00
288	Phil Stockman/100	10.00
290	Roberto Novoa/100	10.00
291	Ronny Cedeno/100	8.00
292	Ryan Meaux/100	8.00
293	Scott Proctor/100	10.00
295	Shawn Camp/100	8.00
298	Shingo Takatsu/25	60.00
299	William Bergolla/100	8.00
300	Yadier Molina/100	25.00

Stars

NM/M
Production 599 Sets

#	Player	Price
1	Ryne Sandberg	6.00
2	Mark Prior	2.00
3	Andre Dawson	2.00
4	Don Mattingly	6.00
5	Vladimir Guerrero	3.00
6	Garret Anderson	2.00
7	Dale Murphy	2.00

#	Player	Price
8	Cal Ripken Jr.	10.00
9	Mark Grace	3.00
10	Kerry Wood	3.00
11	Frank Thomas	2.00
12	Magglio Ordonez	2.00
13	Adam Dunn	3.00
14	Preston Wilson	2.00
15	Bo Jackson	3.00
16	Carlos Beltran	3.00
17	Tony Gwynn	4.00
18	Will Clark	3.00
19	Edgar Martinez	2.00
20	Scott Rolen	3.00
21	Alfonso Soriano	3.00
22	Randy Johnson	3.00
23	Chipper Jones	3.00
24	Andruw Jones	2.00
25	Javy Lopez	2.00
26	Curt Schilling	3.00
27	Manny Ramirez	3.00
28	Sammy Sosa	4.00
29	Greg Maddux	3.00
30	Todd Helton	3.00
31	Jeff Bagwell	3.00
32	Shawn Green	3.00
33	Mike Piazza	5.00
34	Jorge Posada	2.00
35	Gary Sheffield	3.00
36	Mike Mussina	3.00
37	Miguel Cabrera	4.00
38	Rickey Henderson	3.00
39	Albert Pujols	4.00
40	Vernon Wells	2.00
41	Fred Lynn	2.00
42	Alan Trammell	2.00
43	Lenny Dykstra	2.00
44	Dwight Gooden	2.00
45	Keith Hernandez	2.00
46	Luis Tiant	2.00
47	Orel Hershiser	2.00
48	George Foster	2.00
49	Darryl Strawberry	2.00
50	Marty Marion	2.00

Stars Signature

NM/M
Quantity produced listed.

#	Player	Price
3	Andre Dawson/50	20.00
5	Don Mattingly/25	65.00
6	Garret Anderson/20	20.00
7	Dale Murphy/50	30.00
12	Magglio Ordonez/25	20.00
13	Adam Dunn/25	40.00
14	Preston Wilson/50	15.00
16	Carlos Beltran/50	40.00
18	Will Clark/25	40.00
19	Edgar Martinez/25	40.00
20	Scott Rolen/25	40.00
37	Miguel Cabrera/50	40.00
40	Vernon Wells/25	20.00
41	Fred Lynn/50	10.00
42	Alan Trammell/50	20.00
43	Lenny Dykstra/50	20.00
44	Dwight Gooden/50	20.00
45	Keith Hernandez/50	20.00
46	Luis Tiant/50	15.00
47	Orel Hershiser/25	25.00
48	George Foster/50	10.00
49	Darryl Strawberry/50	20.00

Stars Signature Jersey

NM/M
Quantity produced listed

#	Player	Price
1	Ryne Sandberg/23	75.00
2	Mark Prior/22	40.00
4	Don Mattingly/25	40.00
5	Vladimir Guerrero/27	60.00
6	Garret Anderson/16	35.00
8	Mark Grace/17	50.00
9	Kerry Wood/34	35.00
11	Frank Thomas/35	50.00
12	Magglio Ordonez/30	25.00
13	Adam Dunn/44	35.00
14	Preston Wilson/44	20.00
15	Bo Jackson/15	125.00
16	Carlos Beltran/15	75.00
17	Tony Gwynn/19	75.00
18	Will Clark/22	65.00
20	Scott Rolen/27	60.00
24	Andruw Jones/45	40.00
29	Sammy Sosa/21	150.00
29	Greg Maddux/33	100.00
34	Todd Helton/17	50.00
34	Jorge Posada/20	50.00
37	Miguel Cabrera/24	50.00
41	Fred Lynn/19	20.00
45	Keith Hernandez/37	20.00
46	Luis Tiant/25	25.00
48	George Foster/15	25.00
49	Darryl Strawberry/18	35.00
50	Marty Marion/25	20.00

2004 Leaf Certified Materials

NM/M

Item	Price
Complete Set (300):	
Common Player:	.50
Common (201-211):	.50
Common (212-240):	4.00
Production 500	
Common Auto. (241-300):	8.00
Pack (5):	10.00
Box (10):	85.00

#	Player	Price
1	A.J. Burnett	.50
2	Adam Dunn	1.00
3	Adam LaRoche	.50
4	Adam Loewen	.50
5	Adrian Beltre	.75
6	Al Leiter	.50
7	Albert Pujols	3.00
8	Alex Rodriguez	3.00
9	Alexis Rios	.50
10	Alfonso Soriano	1.50
11	Andruw Jones	1.00
12	Andy Pettitte	.75
13	Angel Berroa	.50
14	Aramis Ramirez	.75
15	Aubrey Huff	.50
16	Austin Kearns	.75
17	Barry Larkin	.75
18	Barry Zito	.75
19	Ben Sheets	.75
20	Bernie Williams	.75
21	Bobby Abreu	.75
22	Brad Penny	.50
23	Brad Wilkerson	.50
24	Brandon Webb	.50
25	Brendan Harris	.50
26	Bret Boone	.50
27	Brett Myers	.50
28	Bubba Crosby	.50
29	Brian Giles	.75
30	Chad Cordero	.50
31	Bubba Nelson	.50
32	Byron Gettis	.50
33	C.C. Sabathia	.50
34	Carl Crawford	.50
35	Carl Everett	.50
36	Carlos Beltran	.75
37	Carlos Delgado	.75
38	Carlos Lee	.50
39	Chad Gaudin	.50
40	Cliff Lee	.50
41	Chipper Jones	1.50
42	Cliff Floyd	.50
43	Clint Barmes	.50
44	Corey Patterson	.75
45	Craig Biggio	.75
46	Curt Schilling	1.00
47	Dan Haren	.50
48	Darin Erstad	.75
49	David Ortiz	1.00
50	Delmon Young	.50
51	Derek Jeter	4.00
52	Dewon Brazelton	.50
53	Dontrelle Willis	.75
54	Edgar Martinez	.75
55	Edgar Renteria	.75
56	Edwin Almonte	.50
57	Edwin Jackson	.50
58	Eric Chavez	.75
59	Eric Hinske	.50
60	Eric Munson	.50
61	Erubiel Durazo	.50
62	Frank Thomas	1.00
63	Fred McGriff	.75
64	Freddy Garcia	.50
65	Garret Anderson	.75
66	Garrett Atkins	.50
67	Gary Sheffield	.75
68	Geoff Jenkins	.50
69	Greg Maddux	2.00
70	Hank Blalock	.50
71	Hee Seop Choi	.50
72	Hideki Matsui	2.50
73	Hideo Nomo	.75
74	Craig Wilson	.50
75	Ichiro Suzuki	2.50
76	Ivan Rodriguez	1.00
77	J.D. Drew	.50
78	John Lackey	.50
79	Jacque Jones	.50
80	Jae Weong Seo	.50
81	Jamie Moyer	.50
82	Jason Giambi	1.00
83	Jason Jennings	.50
84	Jason Kendall	.50
85	Melvin Mora	.50
86	Jason Varitek	.75
87	Javier Vazquez	.75
88	Javy Lopez	.75
89	Jay Gibbons	.50
90	Jay Payton	.50
91	Jeff Bagwell	1.00
92	Jeff Baker	.50
93	Jeff Kent	.50
94	Jeremy Bonderman	.50
95	Milton Bradley	.50
96	Jerome Williams	.50
97	Jim Edmonds	.75
98	Jim Thome	1.50
99	Jody Gerut	.50
100	Joe Borchard	.50
101	Joe Crede	.50
102	Johan Santana	.50
103	John Olerud	.50
104	John Smoltz	.75
105	Johnny Damon	.75
107	Jorge Posada	.75
108	Jose Castillo	.50
109	Jose Reyes	.75
109	Jose Vidro	.50
110	Josh Beckett	1.00
111	Josh Phelps	.50
112	Juan Encarnacion	.50
113	Juan Gonzalez	1.00
114	Junior Spivey	.50
115	Kazuhisa Ishii	.50
116	Kenny Lofton	.75
117	Kerry Wood	1.50
118	Kevin Millwood	.50
119	Kevin Youkilis	.50
120	Lance Berkman	.50
121	Larry Bigbie	.50
122	Larry Walker	.75
123	Luis Castillo	.50
124	Luis Gonzalez	.50
125	Luis Matos	.50
126	Lyle Overbay	.50
127	Magglio Ordonez	.50
128	Manny Ramirez	1.00
129	Marcus Giles	.50
130	Mariano Rivera	.75
131	Mark Buehrle	.50
132	Mark Mulder	.75
133	Mark Prior	1.00
134	Mark Teixeira	.75
135	Marlon Byrd	.50
136	Matt Morris	.50
137	Miguel Cabrera	1.00
138	Mike Lowell	.50
139	Mike Mussina	.75
140	Mike Piazza	2.00
141	Mike Sweeney	.50
142	Morgan Ensberg	.50
143	Nick Johnson	.50
144	Nomar Garciaparra	2.00
145	Omar Vizquel	.50
146	Orlando Cabrera	.50
147	Orlando Hudson	.50
148	Pat Burrell	.50
149	Paul Konerko	.50
150	Paul LoDuca	.50
151	Pedro J. Martinez	1.50
152	Jermaine Dye	.50
153	Preston Wilson	.50
154	Rafael Furcal	.50
155	Rafael Palmeiro	1.00
156	Randy Johnson	1.50
157	Rich Aurilia	.50
158	Rich Harden	.50
159	Richard Hidalgo	.50
160	Richie Sexson	.75
161	Rickie Weeks	.75
162	Roberto Alomar	.75
163	Rocco Baldelli	.50
164	Roger Clemens	3.00
165	Roy Halladay	.50
166	Roy Oswalt	.75
167	Ryan Howard	1.50
168	Ryan Klesko	.50
169	Rodrigo Lopez	.50
170	Sammy Sosa	2.50
171	Scott Podsednik	.50
172	Scott Rolen	1.50
173	Sean Burroughs	.50
174	Sean Casey	.50
175	Shannon Stewart	.50
176	Shawn Green	.75
177	Shea Hillenbrand	.50
178	Shigetoshi Hasegawa	.50
179	Steve Finley	.50
180	Tim Hudson	.75
181	Todd Helton	1.00
182	Tom Glavine	.75
183	Torii Hunter	.75
184	Trot Nixon	.50
185	Troy Glaus	.75
186	Vernon Wells	.75
187	Victor Martinez	.75
188	Vladimir Guerrero	1.50
189	Wade Miller	.50
190	Brandon Larson	.50
191	Travis Hafner	.75
192	Tim Salmon	.75
193	Tim Redding	.50
194	Runelvys Hernandez	.50
195	Ramon Nivar	.50
196	Moises Alou	.75
197	Michael Young	.50
198	Laynce Nix	.50
199	Tino Martinez	.50
200	Randall Simon	.50
201	Roger Clemens/SP	8.00
202	Greg Maddux/SP	8.00
203	Vladimir Guerrero/SP	6.00
204	Miguel Tejada/SP	4.00
205	Kevin Brown/SP	4.00
206	Jason Giambi/SP	5.00
207	Curt Schilling/SP	5.00
208	Alex Rodriguez/SP	8.00
209	Alfonso Soriano/SP	6.00
210	Ivan Rodriguez/SP	6.00
211	Rafael Palmeiro/SP	6.00
212	Gary Carter/SP	4.00
213	Duke Snider/SP	5.00
214	Whitey Ford/SP	4.00
215	Bob Feller/SP	4.00
216	Reggie Jackson/SP	5.00
217	Ryne Sandberg/SP	10.00
218	Dale Murphy/SP	4.00
219	Tony Gwynn/SP	6.00
220	Don Mattingly/SP	10.00
221	Mike Schmidt/SP	8.00
222	Rickey Henderson/SP	5.00
223	Cal Ripken Jr./SP	20.00
224	Nolan Ryan/SP	15.00
225	George Brett/SP	10.00
226	Bob Gibson/SP	5.00
227	Lou Brock/SP	4.00
228	Andre Dawson/SP	4.00
229	Rod Carew/SP	4.00
230	Wade Boggs/SP	4.00
231	Roberto Clemente/SP	12.00
232	Roy Campanella/SP	5.00
233	Babe Ruth/SP	15.00
234	Lou Gehrig/SP	10.00
235	Ty Cobb/SP	8.00
236	Roger Maris/SP	6.00
237	Satchel Paige/SP	6.00
238	Ernie Banks/SP	6.00
239	Ted Williams/SP	10.00
240	Stan Musial/SP	6.00
241	Hector Gimenez/Auto./500 RC	8.00
242	Justin Germano/Auto./500 RC	8.00
243	Ian Snell/Auto./500 RC	12.00
244	Graham Koonce/Auto./500	8.00
245	Jose Capellan/Auto./500 RC	10.00
246	Onil Joseph/Auto./500 RC	8.00
247	Shingo Takatsu/Auto./200 RC	15.00
248	Carlos Hines/Auto./500 RC	8.00
249	Lincoln Holdzkom/Auto./500 RC	8.00
250	Mike Gosling/Auto./500	8.00
251	Edwardo Sierra/Auto./500 RC	10.00
252	Renyel Pinto/Auto./500 RC	10.00
253	Merkin Valdez/Auto./500 RC	10.00
254	Angel Chavez/Auto./500 RC	8.00
255	Ivan Ochoa/Auto./1,000 RC	8.00
256	Greg Dobbs/Auto./500	8.00
257	William Bergolla/Auto./500 RC	8.00
258	Aarom Baldiris/Auto./500 RC	10.00
259	Kazuo Matsui/500 RC	8.00
260	Carlos Vasquez/Auto./500	8.00
261	Freddy Guzman/Auto./500 RC	8.00
262	Akinori Otsuka/Auto./200 RC	15.00
263	Mariano Gomez/Auto./200 RC	8.00
264	Nick Regilio/Auto./500 RC	8.00
265	Jamie Brown/Auto./500 RC	8.00
266	Shawn Hill/Auto./500 RC	8.00
267	Roberto Novoa/Auto./500 RC	8.00
268	Sean Henn/Auto./500	10.00
269	Ramon Ramirez/Auto./500 RC	8.00
270	Ronny Cedeno/Auto./1,000 RC	8.00
271	Ryan Wing/Auto./400	8.00
272	Ruddy Yan/Auto./500 RC	8.00
273	Fernando Nieve/Auto./500 RC	8.00
274	Rusty Tucker/Auto./500 RC	8.00
275	Jason Bartlett/Auto./500 RC	15.00
276	Mike Rouse/Auto./500	8.00
277	Dennis Sarfate/Auto./500	8.00
278	Cory Sullivan/Auto./500 RC	8.00
279	Casey Daigle/Auto./250 RC	8.00
280	Chris Shelton/Auto./400 RC	15.00
281	Jesse Harper/Auto./500 RC	8.00
282	Mike Wuertz/Auto./500 RC	10.00
283	Tim Bausher/Auto./400 RC	8.00

284	Jorge Sequea/Auto./500 **RC**	8.00
285	Josh Labandeira/Auto./500 **RC**	10.00
286	Justin Leone/Auto./500 **RC**	10.00
287	Tim Bittner/Auto./500 **RC**	8.00
288	Andres Blanco/Auto./500 **RC**	8.00
289	Kevin Cave/Auto./1,000 **RC**	8.00
290	Mike Johnston/Auto./1,000 **RC**	8.00
291	Jason Szuminski/Auto./500 **RC**	8.00
292	Shawn Camp/500 **RC**	8.00
293	Colby Miller/Auto./500 **RC**	8.00
294	Jake Woods/Auto./500	8.00
295	Ryan Meaux/Auto./500 **RC**	8.00
296	Donald Kelly/Auto./500 **RC**	8.00
297	Edwin Moreno/Auto./500 **RC**	8.00
298	Phil Stockman/Auto./500 **RC**	8.00
299	Jorge Vasquez/500 **RC**	8.00
300	Kazuhito Tadano/Auto./500 **RC**	15.00

Fabric of the Game

		NM/M
Common Player:		6.00
Quantity produced listed.		
AL/NL:		.75-1.5X
Production 1-100		
Jersey Number:		.75-2X
Production 1-72		
Position:		.75-2X
Production 1-100		
Prime:		No Pricing
Production One Set		
Game Reward:		.75-2X
Production 1-50		
Jersey Year:		.75-2X
Production 1-99		
Game Stats:		.75-2X
Production 1-66		

No Pricing production 20 or less.

n	Ozzie Smith/Jsy/100	20.00
2	Al Kaline/Pants/100	15.00
3	Alan Trammell/Jsy/100	10.00
4	Albert Pujols/Jsy/100	20.00
5	Alex Rodriguez/Jsy/100	12.00
6	Alex Rodriguez/Jsy/100	12.00
7	Andre Dawson/Jsy/100	8.00
8	Andre Dawson/Pants/100	8.00
11	Billy Williams/Jsy/100	10.00
12	Bo Jackson/Jsy/100	20.00
13	Bob Feller/Jsy/50	15.00
14	Bob Gibson/Jsy/50	15.00
15	Bobby Doerr/Jsy/100	8.00
16	Brooks Robinson/Jsy/25	25.00
17	Cal Ripken Jr./Jsy/100	30.00
18	Carl Yastrzemski/Jsy/100	20.00
19	Carlton Fisk/Jsy/100	10.00
20	Dale Murphy/Jsy/100	12.00
21	Darryl Strawberry/Pants/100	10.00
22	Darryl Strawberry/Jsy/100	10.00
23	Dave Parker/Jsy/100	10.00
24	Dave Parker/Jsy/100	10.00
25	Dave Winfield/Jsy/50	10.00
26	Dave Winfield/Jsy/100	10.00
27	Deion Sanders/Jsy/25	25.00
28	Derek Jeter/Jsy/100	20.00
29	Don Drysdale/Jsy/100	15.00
30	Don Mattingly/Jsy/100	20.00
31	Don Mattingly/Jkt/100	20.00
32	Don Sutton/Jsy/100	8.00
33	Duke Snider/Jsy/100	12.00
34	Dwight Gooden/Jsy/100	8.00
35	Early Wynn/Jsy/100	10.00
36	Eddie Mathews/Jsy/50	20.00
37	Eddie Murray/Jsy/100	15.00
38	Eddie Murray/Jsy/100	15.00
39	Enos Slaughter/Jsy/100	10.00
40	Eric Davis/Jsy/50	10.00
41	Ernie Banks/Jsy/100	15.00
42	Fergie Jenkins/Pants/100	10.00
43	Frank Robinson/Jsy/100	10.00
45	Gary Carter/Jsy/25	15.00
46	Gaylord Perry/Jsy/25	15.00
47	George Brett/White Jsy/100	20.00
48	George Foster/Jsy/100	8.00
49	Hal Newhouser/Jsy/100	8.00
50	Harmon Killebrew/Jsy/25	30.00
51	Harmon Killebrew/Pants/25	30.00
52	Harold Baines/Jsy/100	10.00
53	Hoyt Wilhelm/Jsy/100	10.00
54	Jack Morris/Jsy/100	8.00
56	Jim "Catfish" Hunter/Jsy/100	8.00
57	Jim Palmer/Jsy/100	10.00
58	Jim Rice/Jsy/100	8.00
59	Joe Carter/Jsy/100	8.00
60	Joe Morgan/Jsy/100	8.00
61	Tommy Lasorda/Jsy/100	8.00
62	Johnny Mize/Pants/100	12.00
63	Johnny Bench/Jsy/100	15.00
64	Jose Canseco/Jsy/100	8.00
65	Juan Marichal/Jsy/100	10.00
66	Kirby Puckett/Jsy/100	15.00
67	Lou Boudreau/Jsy/100	10.00
68	Lou Brock/Jsy/100	10.00
71	Luis Aparicio/Jsy/100	10.00
72	Luis Aparicio/Pants/100	10.00
73	Mariano Rivera/Jsy/100	10.00
74	Mark Grace/Jsy/100	12.00
75	Mark Prior/Jsy/100	8.00
76	Mel Ott/Jsy/25	60.00
77	Mel Ott/Pants/25	60.00
78	Mike Schmidt/Jsy/100	20.00
79	Mike Schmidt/Pants/100	20.00
80	Mike Schmidt/Jkt/100	20.00
81	Nolan Ryan/Angels Jsy/100	25.00
82	Nolan Ryan/Angels Jkt/100	25.00
83	Nolan Ryan/Astros Jsy/100	25.00
84	Nolan Ryan/Astros Jkt/100	25.00
85	Nolan Ryan/Rgr Jsy/100	25.00
86	Nolan Ryan/Rgr Pants/100	25.00
88	Ozzie Smith/Jsy/100	15.00
89	Paul Molitor/Jsy/100	12.00
90	Pee Wee Reese/Jsy/100	15.00
91	Phil Niekro/Jsy/100	8.00
92	Phil Rizzuto/Jsy/100	15.00
93	Phil Rizzuto/Pants/100	15.00
94	Red Schoendienst/Jsy/100	10.00
95	Reggie Jackson/Jkt/100	15.00
96	Reggie Jackson/Jsy/100	15.00
97	Richie Ashburn/Jsy/100	20.00
98	Rickey Henderson/Jsy/50	15.00
99	Roberto Clemente/Jsy/50	75.00
100	Robin Yount/Jsy/100	15.00
101	Rod Carew/Jsy/100	10.00
102	Rod Carew/Pants/100	10.00
103	Rod Carew/Jkt/100	10.00
104	Rod Carew/Jsy/100	10.00
105	Roger Clemens/Jsy/100	15.00
106	Roger Clemens/Jsy/100	15.00
107	Roger Maris/Jsy/100	30.00
108	Roger Maris/Pants/100	30.00
109	Roger Maris/Jsy/100	30.00
110	Roy Campanella/Pants/100	15.00
111	Ryne Sandberg/Jsy/100	25.00
112	Stan Musial/Jsy/50	30.00
113	Steve Carlton/Jsy/100	10.00
114	Ted Williams/Jsy/100	75.00
115	Ted Williams/Jkt/100	75.00
116	Thurman Munson/Jsy/100	25.00
117	Thurman Munson/Pants/100	25.00
118	Tony Gwynn/Jsy/100	15.00
119	Wade Boggs/Jsy/100	10.00
120	Wade Boggs/Jsy/100	10.00
121	Warren Spahn/Jsy/100	15.00
122	Warren Spahn/Pants/100	15.00
123	Whitey Ford/Jsy/100	15.00
124	Whitey Ford/Pants/100	15.00
125	Will Clark/Jsy/100	10.00
126	Willie McCovey/Jsy/100	10.00
127	Willie Stargell/Jsy/100	15.00
128	Yogi Berra/Jsy/100	35.00
129	Frankie Frisch/Jkt/100	15.00
130	Marty Marion/Jsy/100	15.00
131	Tommy John/Pants/100	8.00
132	Chipper Jones/Jsy/100	10.00
133	Sammy Sosa/Jsy/100	15.00
134	Rickey Henderson/Jsy/100	10.00
135	Mike Piazza/Jsy/100	12.00
136	Mike Piazza/Jsy/100	12.00
137	Nomar Garciaparra/Jsy/100	15.00
138	Hideo Nomo/Jsy/100	10.00
139	Hideo Nomo/Jsy/100	10.00
140	Randy Johnson/Jsy/100	10.00
141	Randy Johnson/Jsy/100	10.00
142	Randy Johnson/Jsy/100	10.00
143	Jason Giambi/Jsy/100	6.00
144	Jason Giambi/Jsy/100	6.00
145	Curt Schilling/Jsy/100	6.00
146	Dennis Eckersley/Jsy/100	10.00
147	Carlton Fisk/Jsy/25	30.00
148	Tom Seaver/Jsy/25	30.00
149	Joe Torre/Jsy/100	10.00
150	Pedro Martinez/Jsy/100	10.00
151	Albert Pujols/Jsy/100	20.00
152	Andre Dawson/Jsy/50	8.00
153	Bert Blyleven/Jsy/100	10.00
154	Bo Jackson/Jsy/100	15.00
155	Cal Ripken Jr./Pants/100	35.00
156	Carlton Fisk/Jsy/100	10.00
157	Curt Schilling/Jsy/100	6.00
158	Darryl Strawberry/Jsy/100	8.00
159	Dave Concepcion/Jsy/100	8.00
160	Dwight Evans/Jsy/100	8.00
161	Ernie Banks/Pants/100	15.00
163	Gary Carter/Pants/100	8.00
164	Gary Sheffield/Jsy/100	6.00
165	George Brett/Jsy/100	20.00
166	Greg Maddux/Jsy/100	10.00
167	Ivan Rodriguez/Jsy/100	10.00
168	Joe Morgan/Jsy/100	10.00
169	Jose Canseco/Jsy/100	8.00
170	Juan Gonzalez/Jsy/100	8.00
171	Juan Gonzalez/Jsy/100	8.00
172	Keith Hernandez/Jsy/100	10.00
173	Ken Boyer/Jsy/100	20.00
174	Kerry Wood/Jsy/100	10.00
175	Lee Smith/Jsy/100	8.00
176	Luis Tiant/Jsy/100	8.00
177	Manny Ramirez/Jsy/100	8.00
178	Mark Grace/Jsy/100	12.00
179	Matt Williams/Jsy/100	8.00
180	Miguel Tejada/Jsy/100	6.00
181	Mike Mussina/Jsy/100	10.00
182	Mike Piazza/Jsy/100	12.00
183	Nomar Garciaparra/Jsy/100	15.00
184	Pedro Martinez/Jsy/100	10.00
185	Rafael Palmeiro/Jsy/100	8.00
186	Reggie Jackson/Pants/100	12.00
187	Rickey Henderson/Jsy/100	10.00
188	Rickey Henderson/Pants/100	10.00
189	Rickey Henderson/Jsy/100	10.00
190	Sammy Sosa/Jsy/100	15.00
191	Satchel Paige/Jsy/100	60.00
192	Shawn Green/Jsy/100	6.00
193	Stan Musial/Jsy/50	35.00
194	Steve Carlton/Jsy/100	10.00
195	Steve Garvey/Jsy/100	8.00
196	Tom Seaver/Jsy/100	12.00
197	Tony Gwynn/Pants/100	12.00
198	Vladimir Guerrero/Jsy/100	10.00
199	Wade Boggs/Jsy/100	10.00
200	Willie Stargell/Jsy/100	10.00

Fabric of the Game Auto.

No Pricing		
Production 1-10		
AL/NL Auto:		No Pricing
Production 1-25		
Jersey Number Auto.:		No Pricing
Production 1-8		
Jersey Year Auto.:		No Pricing
Production 1-8		
Position Auto.:		No Pricing
Production 1-8		
Reward Auto.:		No Pricing
Production 1-8		
Stats Auto.:		No Pricing
Production 1-8		

Mirror Black

No Pricing	
Production One Set	

Mirror Blue

Stars (1-200):	3-5X
Mirror Blue (201-240):	1-2X
Auto. (201-240):	3X
No Auto. (241-300):	1X
Production 50 Sets	

Mirror Emerald

No Pricing	
Production Five Sets	

Mirror Gold

Mirror Gold (1-200):	4-8X
Mirror Gold (201-240):	1.5-2X
Mirror Gold (241-300):	No Pricing
Production 25 Sets	

Mirror Red

Mirror Red (1-200):	2-4X
Mirror Red (201-240):	.5-1X
Mirror Red (241-300):	.5X
Production 100 Sets	

Mirror White

Mirror White (1-200):	2-4X
Mirror White (201-240):	.5-1X
Mirror White (241-300):	.5X
Production 100 Sets	

Mirror Autograph Black

No Pricing	
Production One Set	

Mirror Autograph Blue

Mirror Auto. Blue:	.5-1.5X Red Auto.
Production 1-100	
No pricing 25 or less.	

Mirror Autograph Emerald

No Pricing	
Production 1-5	

Mirror Autograph Gold

No Pricing	
Production 1-25	

Mirror Autograph Red

		NM/M
Quantity produced listed.		
3	Adam LaRoche/250	8.00
4	Adam Loewen/250	8.00
8	Alexis Rios/250	15.00
10	Alfonso Soriano/250	50.00
11	Andruw Jones/25	25.00
12	Andy Pettitte/25	35.00
13	Angel Berroa/100	10.00
14	Aramis Ramirez/100	25.00
15	Aubrey Huff/250	10.00
16	Austin Kearns/200	12.00
21	Barry Larkin/25	40.00
22	Brad Penny/25	15.00
24	Brandon Webb/250	8.00
25	Brendan Harris/50	10.00
27	Brett Myers/100	8.00
29	Bubba Crosby/250	8.00
30	Chad Cordero/250	8.00
31	Bubba Nelson/250	8.00
32	Byron Gettis/250	8.00
36	Carlos Beltran/100	25.00
38	Carlos Lee/250	10.00
39	Chad Gaudin/100	8.00
42	Cliff Lee/250	15.00
43	Clint Barmes/100	8.00
47	Dan Haren/250	8.00
49	David Ortiz/250	40.00
50	Delmon Young/250	25.00
52	Dewon Brazelton/250	8.00
53	Dontrelle Willis/100	20.00
56	Edwin Almonte/250	8.00
57	Edwin Jackson/250	8.00
58	Eric Chavez/25	30.00
62	Frank Thomas/50	50.00
65	Garret Anderson/250	15.00
66	Gary Sheffield/250	30.00
70	Hank Blalock/100	30.00
74	Craig Wilson/100	10.00
78	John Lackey/250	8.00
79	Jacque Jones/250	8.00
85	Jae Weong Seo/100	15.00
87	Melvin Mora/250	15.00
88	Jason Varitek/100	40.00
89	Jay Gibbons/250	8.00
90	Jay Payton/250	8.00
91	Jeff Bagwell/50	50.00
92	Jeff Baker/25	20.00
96	Jerome Williams/100	15.00
97	Jim Edmonds/25	35.00
99	Jody Gerut/250	10.00
100	Joe Borchard/250	10.00
101	Joe Crede/50	15.00
102	Johan Santana/250	25.00
106	Jorge Posada/250	50.00
107	Jose Castillo/250	8.00
109	Jose Vidro/250	8.00
110	Josh Beckett/250	50.00
113	Juan Gonzalez/25	40.00
114	Junior Spivey/25	15.00
117	Kerry Wood/50	50.00
119	Kevin Youkilis/250	10.00
120	Lance Berkman/25	30.00
121	Larry Bigbie/250	12.00
123	Luis Castillo/25	15.00
125	Luis Matos/250	8.00
127	Magglio Ordonez/250	15.00
129	Marcus Giles/250	12.00
131	Mark Buehrle/250	12.00
132	Mark Mulder/250	20.00
133	Mark Prior/100	40.00
134	Mark Teixeira/100	25.00
135	Marlon Byrd/250	8.00
137	Miguel Cabrera/250	30.00
140	Mike Piazza/125	125.00
142	Morgan Ensberg/250	8.00
146	Orlando Cabrera/25	20.00
150	Paul LoDuca/25	25.00
152	Jermaine Dye/250	10.00
153	Preston Wilson/250	10.00
154	Rafael Furcal/100	12.00
157	Rich Aurilia/100	10.00
158	Rich Harden/203	15.00
166	Roy Halladay/50	35.00
166	Roy Oswalt/50	40.00
167	Ryan Howard/100	80.00
169	Rodrigo Lopez/250	8.00
170	Sammy Sosa/250	50.00
171	Scott Podsednik/250	15.00
172	Scott Rolen/100	40.00
175	Shannon Stewart/100	8.00
176	Shawn Green/250	30.00
177	Shea Hillenbrand/250	10.00
178	Shigetoshi Hasegawa/250	40.00
179	Steve Finley/100	20.00
183	Torii Hunter/250	15.00
184	Trot Nixon/250	20.00
187	Victor Martinez/250	20.00
189	Vladimir Guerrero/50	75.00
190	Brandon Larson/200	10.00
191	Travis Hafner/250	15.00
197	Michael Young/250	15.00
212	Gary Carter/250	15.00
213	Duke Snider/250	25.00
214	Whitey Ford/50	40.00
215	Bob Feller /250	20.00
216	Reggie Jackson/50	50.00
217	Ryne Sandberg/60	60.00
218	Dale Murphy/50	30.00
219	Tony Gwynn/50	50.00
220	Don Mattingly/50	75.00
221	Mike Schmidt/50	75.00
222	Rickey Henderson/50	50.00
223	Cal Ripken Jr./50	180.00
224	Nolan Ryan/50	100.00
225	George Brett/50	75.00
226	Bob Gibson/100	25.00
227	Lou Brock/100	25.00
228	Andre Dawson/250	15.00
229	Rod Carew/250	25.00
230	Wade Boggs/50	25.00
238	Ernie Banks/50	60.00
240	Stan Musial/50	60.00
241	Hector Gimenez/200	8.00
242	Justin Germano/100	8.00
243	Ian Snell/100	25.00
244	Graham Koonce/200	8.00
245	Jose Capellan/100	40.00
246	Onil Joseph/200	8.00
247	Shingo Takatsu/50	50.00
248	Carlos Hines/200	8.00
249	Lincoln Holdzkom/100	8.00
250	Mike Gosling/100	10.00
251	Edwardo Sierra/200	8.00
252	Renyel Pinto/100	10.00
253	Merkin Valdez/200	12.00
254	Angel Chavez/200	8.00
255	Ivan Ochoa/200	8.00
257	William Bergolla/200	8.00
258	Aarom Baldiris/100	8.00
260	Carlos Vasquez/200	8.00
261	Freddy Guzman/200	8.00
262	Akinori Otsuka/50	50.00
264	Nick Regilio/200	8.00
266	Shawn Hill/200	8.00
268	Sean Henn/200	10.00
269	Ramon Ramirez/200	8.00
270	Ronny Cedeno/200	8.00
273	Fernando Nieve/200	8.00
274	Rusty Tucker/200	8.00
275	Jason Bartlett/200	8.00
276	Mike Rouse/200	8.00
277	Dennis Sarfate/200	8.00
278	Cory Sullivan/200	8.00
282	Mike Wuertz/200	8.00
284	Jorge Sequea/250	8.00
287	Tim Bittner/250	8.00
288	Andres Blanco/200	12.00
289	Kevin Cave/100	8.00
290	Mike Johnston/100	8.00
293	Colby Miller/100	8.00
294	Jake Woods/100	10.00
295	Ryan Meaux/100	8.00
296	Donald Kelly/100	8.00
297	Edwin Moreno/100	8.00
298	Phil Stockman/100	8.00

Mirror Autograph White

White Auto. (1-240):	.75-1.5X Red Auto
White Auto.(241-300):	.5-1X Red Auto
Production 1-100	
No pricing 25 or less.	

Mirror Bat Blue

		NM/M
Blue Bat:		1-1.5X Red Price
Production 25-100		
Cards listed don't have a red version.		
217	Ryne Sandberg/50	40.00
219	Tony Gwynn/50	20.00
221	Mike Schmidt/25	25.00
223	Cal Ripken Jr./50	50.00
224	Nolan Ryan/50	35.00
225	George Brett/50	30.00

Mirror Bat Gold

		NM/M
Gold Bat:		1.5-3X Red Price
Production 25 Sets		
Cards listed don't have a red version.		
69	Greg Maddux	25.00
217	Ryne Sandberg	50.00
219	Tony Gwynn	30.00
221	Mike Schmidt	40.00
223	Cal Ripken Jr.	90.00
224	Nolan Ryan	60.00
225	George Brett	40.00
231	Roberto Clemente	90.00
233	Babe Ruth	200.00
234	Lou Gehrig	150.00
235	Ty Cobb	125.00
236	Roger Maris	40.00
239	Ted Williams	80.00

Mirror Bat Red

		NM/M
Common Player:		4.00
Quantity produced listed		
Black:		No Pricing
Production One Set		

Emerald:

		No Pricing
Production Five Sets		
2	Adam Dunn/150	6.00
3	Adam LaRoche/150	4.00
5	Adrian Beltre/150	4.00
7	Albert Pujols/150	15.00
9	Alex Rodriguez/250	10.00
9	Alexis Rios/150	4.00
10	Alfonso Soriano/150	8.00
11	Andruw Jones/150	8.00
12	Andy Pettitte/150	6.00
13	Angel Berroa/150	4.00
15	Aubrey Huff/150	4.00
16	Austin Kearns/150	4.00
17	Barry Larkin/150	6.00
19	Bernie Williams/150	6.00
21	Bobby Abreu/150	6.00
24	Brandon Webb/150	4.00
25	Brendan Harris/250	4.00
26	Bret Boone/150	4.00
29	Brian Giles/250	4.00
35	Carl Everett/250	4.00
36	Carlos Beltran/150	6.00
37	Carlos Delgado/150	6.00
38	Carlos Lee/150	4.00
41	Chipper Jones/150	8.00
42	Cliff Floyd/250	4.00
43	Clint Barmes/250	4.00
44	Corey Patterson/250	6.00
45	Craig Biggio/150	6.00
47	Dan Haren/150	4.00
48	Darin Erstad/150	4.00
49	David Ortiz/250	8.00
50	Delmon Young/250	4.00
51	Derek Jeter/150	20.00
54	Edgar Martinez/150	6.00
55	Edgar Renteria/150	4.00
59	Eric Hinske/150	4.00
60	Eric Munson/250	4.00
61	Erubiel Durazo/250	4.00
62	Frank Thomas/150	8.00
63	Fred McGriff/150	4.00
65	Garret Anderson/150	6.00
67	Gary Sheffield/250	6.00
68	Geoff Jenkins/150	4.00
70	Hank Blalock/150	4.00
71	Hee Seop Choi/150	4.00
73	Hideo Nomo/150	8.00
76	Ivan Rodriguez /250	4.00
77	J.D. Drew/250	6.00
79	Jacque Jones/150	4.00
82	Jason Giambi/150	6.00
83	Jason Jennings/150	4.00
86	Jason Varitek/150	6.00
88	Javy Lopez/250	4.00
89	Jay Gibbons/150	4.00
91	Jeff Bagwell/150	8.00
92	Jeff Baker/250	4.00
93	Jeff Kent/150	4.00
97	Jim Edmonds/150	6.00
98	Jim Thome/150	8.00
100	Joe Borchard/150	4.00
101	Joe Crede/250	4.00
103	John Olerud/150	4.00
105	Johnny Damon/250	4.00
106	Jorge Posada/150	6.00
107	Jose Castillo/150	4.00
108	Jose Reyes/150	6.00
109	Jose Vidro/150	4.00
110	Josh Beckett/150	6.00
111	Josh Phelps/150	4.00
112	Juan Encarnacion/250	4.00
113	Juan Gonzalez/250	6.00
114	Junior Spivey/150	4.00
115	Kazuhisa Ishii/150	4.00
116	Kenny Lofton/250	4.00
117	Kerry Wood/150	8.00
119	Kevin Youkilis/250	4.00
120	Lance Berkman/150	6.00
122	Larry Walker/150	6.00
123	Luis Castillo/150	4.00
124	Luis Gonzalez/150	6.00
126	Lyle Overbay/250	4.00
127	Magglio Ordonez/150	6.00
128	Manny Ramirez/150	8.00
129	Marcus Giles/150	4.00
131	Mark Buehrle/150	4.00
132	Mark Mulder/150	6.00
133	Mark Prior/150	8.00
134	Mark Teixeira/150	8.00
135	Marlon Byrd/150	4.00
137	Miguel Cabrera/150	8.00
138	Mike Lowell/150	4.00
141	Mike Piazza/150	10.00
143	Mike Sweeney/150	4.00
144	Nomar Garciaparra/150	10.00
145	Omar Vizquel/150	4.00
146	Orlando Cabrera/150	4.00
147	Orlando Hudson/150	4.00
148	Pat Burrell/150	4.00
149	Paul Konerko/150	4.00
150	Paul LoDuca/150	4.00
152	Jermaine Dye/250	4.00
153	Preston Wilson/150	4.00
154	Rafael Furcal/150	4.00
155	Rafael Palmeiro/150	8.00
157	Rich Aurilia/150	4.00
159	Richard Hidalgo/150	4.00
160	Richie Sexson/250	6.00
161	Rickie Weeks/250	6.00
162	Roberto Alomar/250	4.00
163	Rocco Baldelli/150	4.00
164	Roger Clemens/250	12.00
168	Ryan Klesko/150	4.00
170	Sammy Sosa/150	12.00
174	Sean Casey/250	4.00
175	Shannon Stewart/150	4.00

#	Player	Price
176	Shawn Green/150	4.00
181	Todd Helton/150	8.00
183	Torii Hunter/150	6.00
184	Trot Nixon/150	6.00
185	Troy Glaus/150	6.00
186	Vernon Wells/150	4.00
187	Victor Martinez/250	4.00
188	Vladimir Guerrero/250	4.00
189	Wade Miller/250	4.00
190	Brandon Larson/175	4.00
191	Travis Hafner/150	4.00
192	Tim Salmon/150	4.00
195	Ramon Nivar/150	4.00
196	Moises Alou/250	6.00
197	Michael Young/250	4.00
198	Laynce Nix/150	4.00
199	Tino Martinez/250	4.00
200	Randall Simon/250	4.00
201	Roger Clemens/150	12.00
203	Vladimir Guerrero/150	8.00
204	Miguel Tejada/150	6.00
206	Jason Giambi/150	6.00
208	Alex Rodriguez/150	10.00
209	Alfonso Soriano/150	8.00
210	Ivan Rodriguez/150	8.00
211	Rafael Palmeiro/150	8.00
212	Gary Carter/150	6.00
216	Reggie Jackson/150	10.00
220	Don Mattingly/150	20.00
222	Rickey Henderson/150	6.00
227	Lou Brock/150	6.00
228	Andre Dawson/150	6.00
229	Rod Carew /150	8.00
230	Wade Boggs/150	6.00
240	Stan Musial/100	25.00

Mirror Bat White

NM/M
White Bat: .75-1X Red Price
Production 25-200
Cards listed don't have a red version.

219	Tony Gwynn/100	15.00
221	Mike Schmidt/100	20.00
223	Cal Ripken Jr./100	40.00
224	Nolan Ryan/100	30.00
225	George Brett/100	30.00
231	Roberto Clemente/50	65.00
233	Babe Ruth/25	200.00
234	Lou Gehrig/25	150.00
235	Ty Cobb/25	125.00
236	Roger Maris/25	40.00
239	Ted Williams/25	80.00

Mirror Combo Red

NM/M
Common (2-211): 6.00
Production 250
Common (212-239): 8.00
Production 50-250
Black Prime: No Pricing
Production One Set

2	Adam Dunn/Bat-Jsy	8.00
5	Adrian Beltre/Bat-Jsy	6.00
7	Albert Pujols/Bat-Jsy	25.00
11	Andruw Jones/Bat-Jsy	8.00
13	Angel Berroa/Bat-Pants	6.00
15	Aubrey Huff/Bat-Jsy	6.00
16	Austin Kearns/Bat-Jsy	8.00
17	Barry Larkin/Bat-Jsy	8.00
18	Barry Zito/Bat-Jsy	6.00
19	Ben Sheets/Bat-Jsy	6.00
20	Bernie Williams/Bat-Jsy	10.00
21	Bobby Abreu/Bat-Jsy	6.00
22	Brad Penny/Bat-Jsy	6.00
24	Brandon Webb/Bat-Jsy	6.00
26	Bret Boone/Bat-Jsy	6.00
36	Carlos Beltran/Bat-Jsy	8.00
37	Carlos Delgado/Bat-Jsy	8.00
38	Carlos Lee/Bat-Jsy	6.00
41	Chipper Jones/Bat-Jsy	10.00
45	Craig Biggio/Bat-Pants	6.00
47	Dan Haren/Bat-Jsy	6.00
51	Derek Jeter/Bat-Jsy	30.00
52	Dewon Brazelton/Glv-Jsy	6.00
54	Edgar Martinez/Bat-Jsy	8.00
55	Edgar Renteria/Bat-Jsy	6.00
56	Eric Chavez/Bat-Jsy	8.00
59	Eric Hinske/Bat-Jsy	6.00
62	Frank Thomas/Bat-Jsy	10.00
63	Fred McGriff/Bat-Jsy	6.00
65	Garret Anderson/Bat-Jsy	8.00
68	Geoff Jenkins/Bat-Jsy	6.00
70	Hank Blalock/Bat-Jsy	10.00
72	Hideo Nomo/Bat-Jsy	10.00
76	Jacque Jones/Bat-Jsy	6.00
82	Jason Giambi/Bat-Jsy	10.00
83	Jason Jennings/Bat-Jsy	6.00
86	Jason Varitek/Bat-Jsy	10.00

89	Jay Gibbons/Bat-Jsy	6.00
91	Jeff Bagwell/Bat-Jsy	10.00
93	Jeff Kent/Bat-Jsy	6.00
97	Jim Edmonds/Bat-Jsy	8.00
98	Jim Thome/Bat-Jsy	10.00
100	Joe Borchard/Bat-Jsy	6.00
103	John Olerud/Bat-Jsy	6.00
106	Jorge Posada/Bat-Jsy	8.00
108	Jose Reyes/Bat-Jsy	8.00
109	Jose Vidro/Bat-Jsy	6.00
110	Josh Beckett/Bat-Jsy	8.00
111	Josh Phelps/Bat-Jsy	6.00
115	Kazuhisa Ishii/Bat-Jsy	6.00
117	Kerry Wood/Bat-Jsy	12.00
120	Lance Berkman/Bat-Jsy	6.00
122	Larry Walker/Bat-Jsy	6.00
123	Luis Castillo/Bat-Jsy	6.00
124	Luis Gonzalez/Bat-Jsy	6.00
127	Magglio Ordonez/Bat-Jsy	6.00
128	Manny Ramirez/Bat-Jsy	10.00
131	Mark Buehrle/Bat-Jsy	6.00
132	Mark Mulder/Bat-Jsy	8.00
133	Mark Prior/Bat-Jsy	8.00
134	Mark Teixeira/Bat-Jsy	8.00
135	Marlon Byrd/Bat-Jsy	6.00
138	Mike Lowell/Bat-Jsy	6.00
140	Mike Piazza/Bat-Jsy	12.00
141	Mike Sweeney/Bat-Jsy	6.00
142	Morgan Ensberg/Bat-Jsy	6.00
144	Nomar Garciaparra/Bat-Jsy	12.00
145	Omar Vizquel/Bat-Jsy	6.00
147	Orlando Hudson/Bat-Jsy	6.00
148	Pat Burrell/Bat-Jsy	6.00
149	Paul Konerko/Bat-Jsy	6.00
150	Paul LoDuca/Bat-Jsy	6.00
151	Pedro J. Martinez/Bat-Jsy	10.00
153	Preston Wilson/Bat-Jsy	6.00
154	Rafael Furcal/Bat-Jsy	6.00
155	Rafael Palmeiro/Bat-Jsy	10.00
156	Randy Johnson/Bat-Jsy	12.00
159	Richard Hidalgo/Bat-Pants	6.00
163	Rocco Baldelli/Bat-Jsy	6.00
166	Roy Oswalt/Bat-Jsy	6.00
168	Ryan Klesko/Bat-Jsy	6.00
170	Sammy Sosa/Bat-Jsy	15.00
172	Scott Rolen/Bat-Jsy	10.00
175	Shannon Stewart/Bat-Jsy	6.00
176	Shawn Green/Bat-Jsy	6.00
180	Tim Hudson/Bat-Jsy	8.00
181	Todd Helton/Bat-Jsy	10.00
182	Tom Glavine/Bat-Jsy	8.00
183	Torii Hunter/Bat-Jsy	8.00
184	Trot Nixon/Bat-Jsy	8.00
185	Troy Glaus/Bat-Jsy	8.00
186	Vernon Wells/Bat-Jsy	6.00
191	Travis Hafner/Bat-Jsy	8.00
192	Tim Salmon/Bat-Jsy	6.00
195	Ramon Nivar/Bat-Jsy	6.00
201	Roger Clemens/Bat-Jsy	15.00
203	Vladimir Guerrero/Bat-Jsy	12.00
204	Miguel Tejada/Bat-Jsy	8.00
206	Jason Giambi/Bat-Jsy	8.00
207	Curt Schilling/Bat-Jsy	8.00
208	Alex Rodriguez/Bat-Jsy	12.00
209	Alfonso Soriano/Bat-Jsy	10.00
210	Ivan Rodriguez/Bat-Jsy	10.00
211	Rafael Palmeiro/Bat-Jsy	10.00
212	Gary Carter/Bat-Pants/250	8.00
216	Reggie Jackson/Bat-Jsy/250	12.00
217	Ryne Sandberg/Bat-Jsy/250	25.00
218	Dale Murphy/Bat-Jsy/250	10.00
219	Tony Gwynn/Bat-Jsy/250	12.00
220	Don Mattingly/Bat-Jsy/250	25.00
221	Mike Schmidt/Bat-Pants/250	25.00
222	Rickey Henderson/Bat-Jsy/250	10.00
223	Cal Ripken Jr./Bat-Jsy/250	35.00
224	Nolan Ryan/Bat-Jsy/250	35.00
225	George Brett/Bat-Jsy/250	25.00
227	Lou Brock/Bat-Jsy/250	8.00
228	Andre Dawson/Bat-Jsy/250	8.00
229	Rod Carew/Bat-Jkt/250	10.00
230	Wade Boggs/Bat-Jsy/250	8.00
231	Roberto Clemente/Bat-Jsy/100	100.00
232	Roy Campanella/Bat-Pants/100	15.00
233	Babe Ruth/Bat-Jsy/50	350.00
234	Lou Gehrig/Bat-Jsy/50	200.00
235	Ty Cobb/Bat-Pants/50	200.00
236	Roger Maris/Bat-Pants/100	50.00
238	Ernie Banks/Bat-Pants/100	15.00
239	Ted Williams/Bat-Jkt/100	85.00

Mirror Fabric Blue

NM/M
Blue: 1-1.5X Red Price
Production 25-100
Cards listed don't have red version.

217	Ryne Sandberg/100	25.00
219	Tony Gwynn/100	15.00
220	Don Mattingly/100	25.00
221	Mike Schmidt/100	20.00
223	Cal Ripken Jr./100	35.00
224	Nolan Ryan/100	25.00
225	George Brett/100	15.00
231	Roberto Clemente/25	90.00
233	Babe Ruth/25	240.00
235	Lou Gehrig/25	150.00
235	Ty Cobb/25	140.00
236	Roger Maris/25	50.00
237	Satchel Paige/25	90.00
239	Ted Williams/25	90.00

Mirror Fabric Gold

NM/M
Gold: 2-3X Red Price
Production 10-25
No pricing 20 or less.
Cards listed don't have red version.

217	Ryne Sandberg/25	45.00
219	Tony Gwynn/25	30.00
220	Don Mattingly/25	60.00
221	Mike Schmidt/25	40.00
223	Cal Ripken Jr./25	90.00
224	Nolan Ryan/25	60.00
225	George Brett/25	50.00

Mirror Fabric Red

NM/M
Common Player: 4.00
Quantity produced listed.

1	A.J. Burnett/250	4.00
2	Adam Dunn/250	6.00
5	Adrian Beltre/150	6.00
6	Al Leiter/250	4.00
7	Albert Pujols/Jsy/150	15.00
11	Andruw Jones/150	6.00
13	Angel Berroa/Pants/150	4.00
15	Aubrey Huff/150	4.00
16	Austin Kearns/Jsy/150	4.00
17	Barry Larkin/Jsy/150	6.00
18	Barry Zito/Jsy/150	5.00
19	Ben Sheets/Jsy/150	4.00
20	Bernie Williams/Jsy/150	6.00
21	Bobby Abreu/Jsy/150	4.00
22	Brad Penny/Jsy/150	4.00
27	Brett Myers/Jsy/150	4.00
33	C.C. Sabathia/Jsy/250	4.00
34	Carl Crawford/Jsy/250	6.00
36	Carlos Beltran/Jsy/150	6.00
38	Carlos Lee/150	4.00
39	Chad Gaudin/Jsy/250	4.00
41	Chipper Jones/Jsy/150	8.00
45	Craig Biggio/Pants/150	4.00
47	Dan Haren/Jsy/250	4.00
48	Darin Erstad/Jsy/250	4.00
51	Derek Jeter/Jsy/250	20.00
53	Dontrelle Willis/Jsy/250	6.00
54	Edgar Martinez/Jsy/150	6.00
55	Edgar Renteria/Jsy/150	4.00
58	Eric Chavez/Jsy/150	4.00
59	Eric Hinske/Jsy/150	4.00
62	Frank Thomas/Jsy/150	8.00
64	Freddy Garcia/Jsy/250	4.00
66	Garrett Atkins/Jsy/250	4.00
68	Geoff Jenkins/Jsy/150	4.00
70	Hank Blalock/Jsy/150	6.00
72	Hideki Matsui/Base/150	15.00
73	Hideo Nomo/Jsy/150	4.00
75	Ichiro Suzuki/Base/150	15.00
79	Jacque Jones/Jsy/150	4.00
81	Jamie Moyer/Jsy/250	4.00
82	Jason Giambi/Jsy/150	6.00
83	Jason Jennings/Jsy/150	4.00
84	Jason Kendall/Jsy/250	4.00
86	Jason Varitek/Jsy/150	6.00
89	Jay Gibbons/Jsy/150	4.00
91	Jeff Bagwell/Jsy/150	8.00
93	Jeff Kent/Jsy/150	4.00
96	Jerome Williams/Jsy/250	4.00
97	Jim Edmonds/Jsy/150	6.00
98	Jim Thome/Jsy/150	8.00
102	Jose Santana/Jsy/250	4.00
103	John Olerud/Jsy/150	4.00
104	John Smoltz/Jsy/250	6.00
108	Jose Reyes/Jsy/150	8.00
109	Jose Vidro/Jsy/150	4.00
110	Josh Beckett/Jsy/150	6.00
111	Josh Phelps/Jsy/150	4.00
115	Kazuhisa Ishii/Jsy/150	4.00

117	Kerry Wood/Jsy/150	8.00
118	Kevin Millwood/Jsy/250	4.00
120	Lance Berkman/Jsy/150	4.00
121	Larry Bigbie/Jsy/250	4.00
122	Larry Walker/Jsy/150	4.00
123	Luis Castillo/Jsy/150	4.00
124	Luis Gonzalez/Jsy/150	4.00
130	Mariano Rivera/Jsy/250	6.00
131	Mark Buehrle/Jsy/150	4.00
133	Mark Prior/Jsy/150	8.00
135	Marlon Byrd/Jsy/150	4.00
139	Matt Morris/Jsy/250	4.00
140	Mike Piazza/Jsy/150	10.00
141	Mike Sweeney/Jsy/150	4.00
142	Morgan Ensberg/Jsy/150	4.00
144	Nomar Garciaparra/Jsy/150	10.00
145	Omar Vizquel/Jsy/150	4.00
147	Orlando Hudson/Jsy/150	4.00
148	Pat Burrell/Jsy/150	4.00
151	Pedro J. Martinez/Jsy/150	8.00
153	Preston Wilson/Jsy/150	4.00
154	Rafael Furcal/Jsy/150	4.00
157	Randy Johnson/Jsy/150	8.00
158	Rich Harden/Jsy/150	4.00
159	Richard Hidalgo/Pants/150	4.00
163	Rocco Baldelli/Jsy/150	4.00
165	Roy Halladay/Jsy/250	4.00
168	Ryan Klesko/Jsy/150	4.00
172	Sammy Sosa/Jsy/150	12.00
172	Scott Rolen/Jsy/150	8.00
175	Sean Burroughs/Jsy/250	4.00
175	Shannon Stewart/Jsy/150	4.00
176	Shawn Green/Jsy/150	4.00
179	Steve Finley/Jsy/250	4.00
180	Tim Hudson/Jsy/150	6.00
181	Todd Helton/Jsy/150	8.00
182	Tom Glavine/Jsy/150	6.00
185	Troy Glaus/Jsy/150	6.00
186	Vernon Wells/Jsy/150	4.00
191	Travis Hafner/Jsy/150	6.00
192	Tim Salmon/Jsy/150	4.00
193	Tim Redding/Jsy/250	4.00
194	Runelvys Hernandez/Jsy/250	4.00
195	Ramon Nivar/Jsy/150	4.00
201	Roger Clemens/Jsy/150	15.00
202	Greg Maddux/Jsy/250	10.00
203	Vladimir Guerrero/Jsy/150	8.00
204	Miguel Tejada/Jsy/150	6.00
205	Kevin Brown/Jsy/250	4.00
206	Jason Giambi/Jsy/150	6.00
207	Curt Schilling/Jsy/150	6.00
208	Alex Rodriguez/Jsy/150	10.00
209	Alfonso Soriano/Jsy/150	6.00
210	Ivan Rodriguez/Jsy/150	8.00
212	Gary Carter/Pants/150	4.00
225	Bob Gibson/Jsy/250	10.00
237	Satchel Paige/Jsy/100	50.00

Mirror Fabric White

NM/M
White: .5-1.5X Red Price
Production 25-200
Cards listed don't have red version.

217	Ryne Sandberg/25	45.00
219	Tony Gwynn/25	25.00
220	Don Mattingly/25	50.00
221	Mike Schmidt/25	40.00
223	Cal Ripken Jr./25	90.00
224	Nolan Ryan/25	60.00
225	George Brett/25	50.00
231	Roberto Clemente/25	90.00
233	Babe Ruth/25	240.00
234	Lou Gehrig/25	150.00
235	Ty Cobb/25	140.00
236	Roger Maris/25	50.00
237	Satchel Paige/25	90.00
239	Ted Williams/25	100.00

2004 Leaf Limited

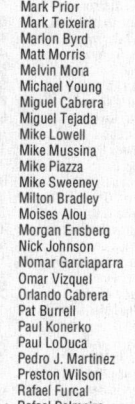

NM/M
Complete Set (275):
Common Player (1-200): 1.50
Common SP (201-229): 3.00
Production 499
Common SP (251-275): 10.00
Production 99
Pack (4): 60.00
Box (4): 200.00

1	Adam Dunn	4.00
2	Adrian Beltre	2.00

3	Albert Pujols	6.00
4	Alex Rodriguez	6.00
5	Alfonso Soriano	2.50
6	Andruw Jones	1.50
7	Andy Pettitte	1.50
8	Angel Berroa	1.50
9	Aramis Ramirez	1.50
10	Aubrey Huff	1.50
11	Aubrey Huff	1.50
12	Barry Larkin	1.50
13	Barry Zito	1.50
14	Bartolo Colon	1.50
15	Ben Sheets	1.50
16	Bernie Williams	1.50
17	Bobby Abreu	1.50
18	Brandon Webb	1.50
19	Brian Giles	1.50
20	C.C. Sabathia	1.50
21	Carlos Beltran	2.00
22	Carlos Delgado	1.50
23	Chipper Jones	3.00
24	Craig Biggio	1.50
25	Curt Schilling	3.00
26	Darin Erstad	1.50
27	Delmon Young	1.50
28	Derek Jeter	6.00
29	Derek Lee	1.50
30	Dontrelle Willis	1.50
31	Edgar Renteria	1.50
32	Eric Chavez	1.50
33	Esteban Loaiza	1.50
34	Frank Thomas	2.00
35	Fred McGriff	1.50
36	Garret Anderson	1.50
37	Gary Sheffield	1.50
38	Geoff Jenkins	1.50
39	Greg Maddux	3.00
40	Hank Blalock	2.00
41	Hideki Matsui	5.00
42	Hideo Nomo	1.50
43	Ichiro Suzuki	5.00
44	Ivan Rodriguez	2.00
45	J.D. Drew	1.50
46	Jacque Jones	1.50
47	Jae Weong Seo	1.50
48	Jake Peavy	1.50
49	Jamie Moyer	1.50
50	Jason Giambi	1.50
51	Jason Kendall	1.50
52	Jason Schmidt	1.50
53	Jason Varitek	1.50
54	Javier Vazquez	1.50
55	Javy Lopez	1.50
56	Jay Gibbons	1.50
57	Jay Payton	1.50
58	Jeff Bagwell	1.50
59	Jeff Kent	1.50
60	Jeremy Bonderman	1.50
61	Jermaine Dye	1.50
62	Jeromy Burnitz	1.50
63	Jim Edmonds	2.00
64	Jim Thome	1.50
65	Jimmy Rollins	1.50
66	Jody Gerut	1.50
67	Johan Santana	2.00
68	John Olerud	1.50
69	John Smoltz	1.50
70	Johnny Damon	2.00
71	Jorge Posada	1.50
72	Jose Contreras	1.50
73	Jose Reyes	1.50
74	Jose Vidro	1.50
75	Josh Beckett	1.50
76	Juan Gonzalez	1.50
77	Juan Pierre	1.50
78	Junior Spivey	1.50
79	Kazuhisa Ishii	1.50
80	Keith Foulke	1.50
81	Ken Griffey Jr.	3.00
82	Ken Harvey	1.50
83	Kenny Rogers	1.50
84	Kerry Wood	2.50
85	Kevin Brown	1.50
86	Kevin Millwood	1.50
87	Kip Wells	1.50
88	Lance Berkman	1.50
89	Larry Bigbie	1.50
90	Larry Walker	1.50
91	Laynce Nix	1.50
92	Luis Castillo	1.50
93	Luis Gonzalez	1.50
94	Luis Matos	1.50
95	Lyle Overbay	1.50
96	Magglio Ordonez	1.50
97	Manny Ramirez	2.00
98	Marcus Giles	1.50
99	Mark Buehrle	1.50
100	Mark Mulder	1.50

101	Mark Prior	2.00
102	Mark Teixeira	1.50
103	Marlon Byrd	1.50
104	Matt Morris	1.50
105	Melvin Mora	1.50
106	Michael Young	1.50
107	Miguel Cabrera	3.00
108	Miguel Tejada	2.00
109	Mike Lowell	1.50
110	Mike Mussina	2.00
111	Mike Piazza	4.00
112	Mike Sweeney	1.50
113	Milton Bradley	1.50
114	Moises Alou	1.50
115	Morgan Ensberg	1.50
116	Nick Johnson	1.50
117	Nomar Garciaparra	4.00
118	Omar Vizquel	1.50
119	Orlando Cabrera	1.50
120	Pat Burrell	1.50
121	Paul Konerko	1.50
122	Paul LoDuca	1.50
123	Pedro J. Martinez	3.00
124	Preston Wilson	1.50
125	Rafael Furcal	1.50
126	Rafael Palmeiro	2.00
127	Randy Johnson	3.00
128	Rich Harden	1.50
129	Richard Hidalgo	1.50
130	Richie Sexson	1.50
131	Rickie Weeks	1.50
132	Roberto Alomar	1.50
133	Robin Ventura	1.50
134	Rocco Baldelli	1.50
135	Roger Clemens	6.00
136	Roy Halladay	1.50
137	Roy Oswalt	1.50
138	Russ Ortiz	1.50
139	Ryan Klesko	1.50
140	Sammy Sosa	5.00
141	Scott Podsednik	1.50
142	Scott Rolen	3.00
143	Sean Burroughs	1.50
144	Sean Casey	1.50
145	Shannon Stewart	1.50
146	Shawn Green	1.50
147	Shigetoshi Hasegawa	1.50
148	Sidney Ponson	1.50
149	Steve Finley	1.50
150	Tim Hudson	1.50
151	Tim Salmon	1.50
152	Tino Martinez	1.50
153	Todd Helton	2.00
154	Tom Glavine	2.00
155	Torii Hunter	1.50
156	Trot Nixon	1.50
157	Troy Glaus	1.50
158	Vernon Wells	1.50
159	Victor Martinez	1.50
160	Vinny Castilla	1.50
161	Vladimir Guerrero	3.00
162	Alex Rodriguez	6.00
163	Alfonso Soriano	2.50
164	Andy Pettitte	1.50
165	Curt Schilling	3.00
166	Gary Sheffield	1.50
167	Greg Maddux	3.00
168	Hideo Nomo	1.50
169	Ivan Rodriguez	2.00
170	Jason Giambi	1.50
171	Jim Thome	2.00
172	Juan Gonzalez	2.00
173	Ken Griffey Jr.	3.00
174	Kevin Brown	1.50
175	Manny Ramirez	2.00
176	Miguel Tejada	2.00
177	Mike Mussina	1.50
178	Mike Piazza	4.00
179	Pedro Martinez	3.00
180	Rafael Palmeiro	2.00
181	Randy Johnson	3.00
182	Roger Clemens	6.00
183	Scott Rolen	3.00
184	Shawn Green	1.50
185	Tom Glavine	1.50
186	Vladimir Guerrero	3.00
187	Alex Rodriguez	6.00
188	Mike Piazza	4.00
189	Randy Johnson	3.00
190	Roger Clemens	6.00
191	Albert Pujols	6.00
192	Barry Zito	1.50
193	Chipper Jones	3.00
194	Garret Anderson	1.50
195	Jeff Bagwell	2.00
196	Josh Beckett	1.50
197	Magglio Ordonez	1.50
198	Mark Prior	2.00
199	Sammy Sosa	5.00
200	Todd Helton	2.00
201	Andre Dawson	3.00
202	Babe Ruth	8.00
203	Bob Feller	4.00
204	Bob Gibson	4.00
205	Bobby Doerr	3.00
206	Cal Ripken Jr.	10.00
207	Dale Murphy	4.00
208	Don Mattingly	8.00
209	Gary Carter	3.00
210	George Brett	8.00
211	Jackie Robinson	5.00
212	Lou Brock	4.00
213	Lou Gehrig	6.00
214	Mark Grace	4.00
215	Maury Wills	3.00
216	Mike Schmidt	8.00
217	Nolan Ryan	8.00
218	Orel Hershiser	3.00

#	Player	Value
219	Paul Molitor	4.00
220	Roberto Clemente	8.00
221	Rod Carew	4.00
222	Roy Campanella	4.00
223	Ryne Sandberg	8.00
224	Stan Musial	8.00
225	Ted Williams	8.00
226	Tony Gwynn	6.00
227	Ty Cobb	5.00
228	Whitey Ford	4.00
229	Yogi Berra	4.00
230	Carlos Beltran	3.00
231	David Ortiz	3.00
232	David Ortiz	3.00
233	Carlos Zambrano	1.50
234	Carlos Lee	1.50
235	Travis Hafner	1.50
236	Brad Penny	1.50
237	Wade Miller	1.50
238	Edgar Martinez	1.50
239	Carl Crawford	1.50
240	Roy Oswalt	1.50
241	Kazuo Matsui	8.00
242	Carlos Beltran	3.00
243	Carlos Beltran	3.00
244	Miguel Cabrera	2.00
245	Scott Rolen	3.00
246	Hank Blalock	2.00
247	Vernon Wells	1.50
248	Adam Dunn	2.00
249	Preston Wilson	1.50
250	Victor Martinez	1.50
251	Aarom Baldiris RC	10.00
252	Akinori Otsuka RC	15.00
253	Andres Blanco RC	10.00
254	Brad Halsey RC	10.00
255	Joey Gathright RC	10.00
256	Colby Miller RC	10.00
257	Fernando Nieve RC	15.00
258	Freddy Guzman RC	15.00
259	Hector Gimenez RC	10.00
260	Jake Woods RC	10.00
261	Jason Bartlett RC	10.00
262	John Gall RC	15.00
263	Jose Capellan RC	10.00
264	Josh Labandeira RC	10.00
265	Justin Germano RC	10.00
266	Kazuhito Tadano RC	15.00
267	Lance Cormier RC	10.00
268	Merkin Valdez RC	20.00
269	Mike Gosling	10.00
270	Ramon Ramirez RC	10.00
271	Rusty Tucker RC	10.00
272	Shawn Hill RC	10.00
273	Shingo Takatsu RC	40.00
274	William Bergolla RC	10.00
275	Yadier Molina RC	25.00

Bronze Spotlight

Bronze: 1-2X
Production 100 Sets

Silver Spotlight

Silver (1-250): 2-3X
Production 50 Sets

Gold Spotlight

Golds (1-250): 3-5X
Production 25 Sets

Platinum Spotlight

No Pricing
Production One Set

Barrels

No Pricing
Production 1-5

Cuts

NM/M
Quantity produced listed.

#	Player	Value
1	Nolan Ryan/100	125.00
2	Bob Gibson/100	40.00
3	Harmon Killebrew/100	40.00
4	Duke Snider/100	30.00
5	George Brett/100	75.00
6	Stan Musial/100	80.00
7	Alan Trammell/100	20.00
8	Cal Ripken Jr./100	180.00
9	Steve Carlton/100	40.00
10	Phil Rizzuto/100	30.00
11	Mark Prior/100	40.00
12	Will Clark/100	40.00
13	Lou Brock/100	30.00
14	Ozzie Smith/100	30.00
15	Bob Feller/100	30.00
16	Gary Carter/50	25.00
17	Al Kaline/100	40.00
18	Brooks Robinson/100	40.00
19	Tony Gwynn/100	50.00
20	Mike Schmidt/100	75.00
21	Ralph Kiner/50	40.00
22	Jim Palmer/50	40.00
23	Don Mattingly/100	75.00
24	Paul Molitor/50	40.00
25	Dale Murphy/100	30.00

Cuts Gold

NM/M

#	Player	Value
1	Nolan Ryan/34	200.00
2	Bob Gibson/45	40.00
3	Steve Carlton/32	50.00
11	Mark Prior/22	60.00
12	Will Clark/22	65.00
14	Lou Brock/20	50.00
15	Bob Feller/28	50.00
19	Tony Gwynn/19	100.00
20	Mike Schmidt/20	100.00
22	Jim Palmer/22	50.00
23	Don Mattingly/23	100.00

Legends Material Number

NM/M
Quantity produced listed.

#	Player	Value
1	Al Kaline/Pants/50	15.00
2	Babe Ruth/Pants/50	160.00
3	Bob Feller/Jsy/50	10.00
4	Bob Gibson/Jsy/50	10.00
6	Burleigh Grimes/Pants/100	40.00
7	Carl Yastrzemski/Jsy/100	15.00
8	Harmon Killebrew/Jsy/25	25.00
9	Hoyt Wilhelm/Jsy/50	5.00
10	Johnny Mize/Pants/100	10.00
11	Ernie Banks/Pants/50	15.00
12	Lou Brock/Jsy/50	10.00
13	Luis Aparicio/Pants/100	10.00
14	Pee Wee Reese/Jsy/50	10.00
15	Reggie Jackson/Jsy/100	10.00
16	Red Schoendienst/Jsy/50	8.00
17	Roberto Clemente/Jsy/25	80.00
18	Roger Maris/Pants/100	25.00
19	Stan Musial/Jsy/100	20.00
20	Ted Williams/Jsy/50	75.00
21	Ty Cobb/Pants/50	80.00
22	Warren Spahn/Jsy/100	10.00
23	Whitey Ford/Pants/100	10.00
24	Yogi Berra/Jsy/50	15.00
25	Satchel Paige/CO Jsy/100	50.00

Legends Material Autographs Number

NM/M
Quanity produced listed.

#	Player	Value
1	Al Kaline/Pants/50	50.00
3	Bob Feller/Jsy/50	30.00
4	Bob Gibson/Jsy/50	30.00
7	Carl Yastrzemski/Jsy/25	80.00
8	Harmon Killebrew/Jsy/50	65.00
9	Hoyt Wilhelm/Jsy/25	40.00
12	Lou Brock/Jsy/50	30.00
13	Luis Aparicio/Jsy/50	20.00
15	Reggie Jackson/Jsy/50	50.00
16	Red Schoendienst/Jsy/50	30.00
19	Stan Musial/Jsy/50	75.00
23	Whitey Ford/Pants/50	50.00
24	Yogi Berra/Jsy/25	75.00

Legends Material Position

NM/M
Quantity produced listed.

#	Player	Value
1	Al Kaline/Pants/50	15.00
2	Babe Ruth/Pants/50	160.00
3	Bob Feller/Jsy/50	10.00
6	Bob Gibson/Jsy/50	10.00
6	Burleigh Grimes/Pants/100	40.00
7	Carl Yastrzemski/Jsy/100	15.00
8	Harmon Killebrew/Jsy/25	25.00
9	Hoyt Wilhelm/Jsy/50	5.00
10	Johnny Mize/Pants/100	10.00
11	Ernie Banks/Pants/50	15.00
12	Lou Brock/Jsy/50	10.00
13	Luis Aparicio/Pants/100	5.00
14	Pee Wee Reese/Jsy/50	10.00
15	Reggie Jackson/Jsy/100	10.00
16	Red Schoendienst/Jsy/50	8.00
17	Roberto Clemente/Jsy/25	80.00
18	Roger Maris/Pants/100	25.00
19	Stan Musial/Jsy/100	20.00
20	Ted Williams/Jsy/50	75.00
21	Ty Cobb/Jsy/50	80.00
22	Warren Spahn/Jsy/100	10.00
23	Whitey Ford/Pants/50	50.00
24	Yogi Berra/Jsy/25	75.00

Legends Material Autographs Position

NM/M
Quantity produced listed.

#	Player	Value
1	Al Kaline/Pants/50	50.00
3	Bob Feller/Jsy/50	30.00
4	Bob Gibson/Jsy/50	30.00
7	Carl Yastrzemski/Jsy/50	80.00
8	Harmon Killebrew/Jsy/25	65.00
12	Hoyt Wilhelm/Jsy/25	40.00
12	Lou Brock/Jsy/50	30.00
13	Luis Aparicio/Pants/50	20.00
15	Reggie Jackson/Jsy/50	50.00
16	Red Schoendienst/Jsy/50	30.00
19	Stan Musial/Jsy/50	75.00
23	Whitey Ford/Pants/25	50.00
24	Yogi Berra/Jsy/25	75.00

Lumberjacks

NM/M
Common Player: 2.00
Quantity produced listed.
Black: 1-30X
Production 16-100

#	Player	Value
1	Al Kaline/399	4.00
2	Albert Pujols/114	15.00
3	Andre Dawson/438	3.00
4	Babe Ruth/714	8.00
5	Bo Jackson/141	5.00
6	Bobby Doerr/223	3.00
7	Brooks Robinson/268	4.00
8	Cal Ripken Jr./431	10.00
9	Carlton Fisk/376	2.00
10	Dale Murphy/398	2.00
11	Darryl Strawberry/335	2.00
12	Don Mattingly/222	6.00
13	Duke Snider/407	3.00
14	Eddie Mathews/512	3.00
15	Eddie Murray/504	3.00
16	Frank Robinson/586	3.00
17	Frank Thomas/418	3.00
18	Gary Carter/324	2.00
19	George Brett/317	6.00
20	Harmon Killebrew/573	4.00
22	Lou Gehrig/493	5.00
23	Mark Grace/173	5.00
24	Mike Piazza/358	4.00
25	Mike Schmidt/548	5.00
26	Orlando Cepeda/379	2.00
27	Rafael Palmeiro/528	2.00
28	Ralph Kiner/369	2.00
29	Reggie Jackson/563	3.00
30	Rickey Henderson/297	3.00
31	Roger Maris/275	5.00
32	Ryne Sandberg/282	4.00
33	Sammy Sosa/539	4.00
34	Scott Rolen/192	4.00
35	Stan Musial/475	4.00
36	Ted Williams/521	6.00
37	Thurman Munson/113	5.00
38	Vladimir Guerrero/234	4.00
39	Willie McCovey/521	2.00
40	Willie Stargell/475	2.00
41	Roberto Clemente, Stan Musial	6.00
42	Cal Ripken Jr., Ernie Banks	10.00
43	Babe Ruth, Lou Gehrig	8.00
44	George Brett, Mike Schmidt	8.00
45	Frank Robinson, Jackie Robinson	4.00
46	Don Mattingly, Roger Maris	8.00
47	Nomar Garciaparra, Ted Williams	8.00
48	Johnny Bench, Mike Piazza	8.00
49	Reggie Jackson, Sammy Sosa	4.00
50	Mel Ott, Willie McCovey	4.00

Lumberjacks Autographs

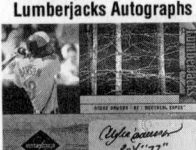

NM/M
Quantity produced listed.

#	Player	Value
1	Al Kaline/100	30.00
3	Andre Dawson/100	15.00
5	Bo Jackson/25	60.00
6	Bobby Doerr/100	20.00
7	Brooks Robinson/50	20.00
8	Cal Ripken Jr./25	180.00
9	Carlton Fisk/25	30.00
10	Dale Murphy/100	20.00
11	Darryl Strawberry/100	15.00
12	Don Mattingly/25	70.00
13	Duke Snider/100	20.00
16	Frank Robinson/100	20.00
17	Frank Thomas/50	50.00
18	Gary Carter/100	15.00
19	George Brett/25	70.00
20	Harmon Killebrew/100	40.00
23	Mark Grace/25	40.00
25	Mike Schmidt/50	65.00
28	Ralph Kiner/100	20.00
29	Reggie Jackson/25	50.00
30	Rickey Henderson/25	50.00
32	Ryne Sandberg/25	90.00
34	Scott Rolen/25	40.00
35	Stan Musial/50	65.00
39	Willie McCovey/50	30.00

Lumberjacks Autographs Bat

NM/M
Quantity produced listed.

#	Player	Value
1	Al Kaline/100	40.00
3	Andre Dawson/50	20.00
5	Bo Jackson/25	70.00
6	Bobby Doerr/50	25.00
7	Brooks Robinson/50	60.00
8	Cal Ripken Jr./25	200.00
9	Carlton Fisk/25	40.00
10	Dale Murphy/100	25.00
11	Darryl Strawberry/25	25.00
12	Don Mattingly/25	80.00
17	Frank Thomas/25	70.00
18	Gary Carter/50	20.00
19	George Brett/50	80.00
22	Harmon Killebrew/50	50.00
23	Mark Grace/17	50.00
25	Mike Schmidt/25	80.00
28	Ralph Kiner/100	25.00
29	Reggie Jackson/25	60.00
32	Ryne Sandberg/25	90.00
34	Scott Rolen/25	50.00
35	Stan Musial/50	75.00
39	Willie McCovey/25	40.00

Lumberjacks Autographs Jersey

NM/M
Quantity produced listed.

#	Player	Value
1	Al Kaline Pants/100	40.00
3	Andre Dawson/50	20.00
5	Bo Jackson/25	70.00
6	Bobby Doerr/100	15.00
7	Brooks Robinson/25	75.00
8	Cal Ripken Jr./25	200.00
9	Carlton Fisk/50	30.00
10	Dale Murphy/100	25.00
11	Darryl Strawberry/Pants/25	25.00
12	Don Mattingly/25	80.00
15	Eddie Murray/25	70.00
16	Frank Robinson/30	30.00
17	Frank Thomas/25	70.00
18	Gary Carter/50	20.00
19	George Brett/50	80.00
20	Harmon Killebrew/25	60.00
23	Mark Grace/17	50.00
25	Mike Schmidt/50	80.00
26	Orlando Cepeda/Pants/50	20.00
29	Reggie Jackson/25	60.00
32	Ryne Sandberg/50	90.00
34	Scott Rolen/25	50.00
35	Stan Musial/50	75.00
39	Willie McCovey/25	40.00

Lumberjacks Barrel

Quantity produced listed.
No Pricing
Production 1-5

Lumberjacks Bat

NM/M
Quantity produced listed.

#	Player	Value
1	Al Kaline/100	15.00
2	Albert Pujols/100	15.00
3	Andre Dawson/25	15.00
4	Babe Ruth/100	125.00
5	Bo Jackson/100	15.00
6	Bobby Doerr/25	12.00
7	Brooks Robinson/25	20.00
8	Cal Ripken Jr./100	40.00
9	Carlton Fisk/100	10.00
10	Dale Murphy/50	15.00
11	Darryl Strawberry/100	15.00
12	Don Mattingly/100	20.00
14	Eddie Mathews/100	10.00
15	Eddie Murray/100	15.00
16	Frank Robinson/100	8.00
17	Frank Thomas/25	20.00
18	Gary Carter/50	10.00
19	George Brett/100	20.00
20	Harmon Killebrew/100	15.00
21	Hideki Matsui/100	25.00
22	Lou Gehrig/100	100.00
23	Mark Grace/25	15.00
25	Mike Piazza/100	15.00
26	Orlando Cepeda/50	8.00
27	Rafael Palmeiro/100	8.00
28	Ralph Kiner/100	10.00
29	Reggie Jackson/100	10.00
30	Rickey Henderson/100	15.00
31	Roger Maris/100	25.00
32	Ryne Sandberg/100	15.00
33	Sammy Sosa/100	10.00
34	Scott Rolen/25	15.00
35	Stan Musial/100	25.00
36	Ted Williams/50	50.00
37	Thurman Munson/100	20.00
38	Vladimir Guerrero/25	15.00
39	Willie McCovey/50	10.00
40	Willie Stargell/50	8.00
41	Roberto Clemente, Stan Musial/50	85.00
42	Cal Ripken Jr., Ernie Banks/50	100.00
43	Babe Ruth, Lou Gehrig/25	250.00
44	George Brett, Mike Schmidt/50	50.00
46	Don Mattingly, Roger Maris/50	40.00
47	Nomar Garciaparra, Ted Williams/100	75.00
48	Johnny Bench, Mike Piazza/25	35.00
49	Reggie Jackson, Sammy Sosa/50	20.00
50	Mel Ott, Willie McCovey/100	40.00

Lumberjacks Jersey

NM/M
Quantity produced listed.

#	Player	Value
1	Al Kaline/Pants/50	20.00
2	Albert Pujols/25	15.00
3	Andre Dawson/25	15.00
4	Babe Ruth/25	300.00
5	Bo Jackson/100	10.00
6	Bobby Doerr/100	5.00
7	Brooks Robinson/50	30.00
8	Cal Ripken Jr./100	40.00
9	Carlton Fisk/100	10.00
10	Dale Murphy/100	10.00
11	Darryl Strawberry/Pants/100	8.00
12	Don Mattingly/100	20.00
14	Eddie Mathews/100	10.00
15	Eddie Murray/50	20.00
16	Frank Robinson/100	10.00
17	Frank Thomas/100	15.00
18	Gary Carter/50	10.00
19	George Brett/100	20.00
20	Harmon Killebrew/25	30.00
21	Hideki Matsui/100	15.00
22	Lou Gehrig/25	180.00
23	Mark Grace/100	8.00
24	Mike Piazza/100	10.00
25	Mike Schmidt/100	15.00
26	Orlando Cepeda/Pants/100	5.00
29	Rafael Palmeiro/100	10.00
30	Reggie Jackson/100	10.00
31	Rickey Henderson/100	10.00
32	Roger Maris/100	25.00
33	Ryne Sandberg/100	15.00
34	Sammy Sosa/100	10.00
35	Scott Rolen/50	10.00
36	Stan Musial/50	30.00
37	Ted Williams/100	50.00
38	Thurman Munson/100	20.00
39	Vladimir Guerrero/100	10.00
41	Willie McCovey/100	10.00
42	Willie Stargell/100	8.00
43	Roberto Clemente, Stan Musial/100	120.00
44	Cal Ripken Jr., Ernie Banks/Pants/100	65.00
45	George Brett, Mike Schmidt/Jkt/100	30.00
46	Frank Robinson, Jackie Robinson/25	30.00
47	Don Mattingly, Roger Maris/Pants/100	25.00
48	Johnny Bench, Mike Piazza/100	10.00
49	Reggie Jackson, Sammy Sosa/100	15.00
50	Mel Ott Pants, Willie McCovey/25	80.00

Lumberjacks Combos

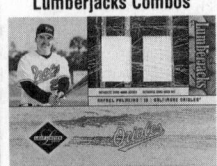

NM/M
Quantity produced listed

#	Player	Value
1	Al Kaline/Bat-Pants/100	20.00
2	Albert Pujols/Bat-Jsy/100	20.00
3	Andre Dawson/Bat-Jsy/50	15.00
4	Babe Ruth/Bat-Jsy/25	400.00
5	Bo Jackson/Bat-Jsy/25	40.00
6	Bobby Doerr/Bat-Jsy/25	12.00
7	Brooks Robinson/Bat-Jsy/25	40.00
8	Cal Ripken Jr./Bat-Jsy/100	
9	Carlton Fisk/Bat-Jsy/50	15.00
10	Dale Murphy/Bat-Jsy/100	15.00
11	Darryl Strawberry/Bat-Pants/25	15.00
12	Don Mattingly/Bat-Jsy/100	25.00
14	Eddie Mathews/Bat-Jsy/100	15.00
15	Eddie Murray/Bat-Jsy/50	20.00
16	Frank Robinson/Bat-Jsy/100	8.00
17	Frank Thomas/Bat-Jsy/50	20.00
18	Gary Carter/Bat-Jsy/50	10.00
19	George Brett/Bat-Jsy/100	25.00
20	Harmon Killebrew/Bat-Jsy/100	15.00
21	Hideki Matsui/Bat-Jsy/100	25.00
22	Lou Gehrig/Bat-Jsy/100	100.00
23	Mark Grace/Bat-Jsy/15	15.00
24	Mike Piazza/Bat-Jsy/100	15.00
25	Mike Schmidt/Bat-Jsy/100	15.00
26	Orlando Cepeda/Bat-Jsy/50	8.00
27	Rafael Palmeiro/Bat-Jsy/100	10.00
28	Ralph Kiner/Bat-Jsy/100	10.00
29	Reggie Jackson/Bat-Jsy/100	10.00
30	Rickey Henderson/Bat-Jsy/100	15.00
31	Roger Maris/Bat-Jsy/100	25.00
32	Ryne Sandberg/Bat-Jsy/100	15.00
33	Sammy Sosa/Bat-Jsy/100	10.00

Matching Numbers

NM/M
Quantity produced listed.
Prime: No Pricing
Production One Set

#	Player	Value
1	Bobby Doerr/Jsy, Pee Wee Reese/Jsy/100	10.00
2	Lou Gehrig/Pants, Mel Ott/Jsy/100	160.00
3	Albert Pujols/Jsy, George Brett/Jsy/100	30.00
4	Cal Ripken Jr./Jsy, Carl Yastrzemski/Jsy/100	50.00
5	Dwight Gooden/Jsy, Whitey Ford/Pants/50	15.00
6	Mark Grace/Jsy, Todd Helton/Jsy/25	25.00
7	Robin Yount/Jsy, Tony Gwynn/Jsy/50	40.00
8	Frank Robinson/Jsy, Mike Schmidt/Jsy/100	25.00
9	Roberto Clemente/Jsy, Sammy Sosa/Jsy/100	75.00
10	Roger Clemens/Jsy, Warren Spahn/Pant/100	25.00
11	Mark Prior/Jsy, Roger Clemens/Jsy	15.00
12	Don Mattingly/Jkt, Ryne Sandberg/Jsy/100	30.00
13	Billy Williams/Jsy, Wade Boggs/Jsy/100	10.00
14	Jim "Catfish" Hunter/Jsy, Juan Marichal/Jsy/50	10.00
15	Fergie Jenkins/Pants, Greg Maddux/Jsy/50	20.00
16	Kerry Wood/Pants, Nolan Ryan/Jsy	35.00
17	Rickey Henderson/Jsy, Roger Maris/Pants/100	40.00
18	Dontrelle Willis/Jsy, Mike Mussina/Jsy/100	15.00
19	Reggie Jackson/Jsy, Willie McCovey/Jsy/100	15.00
20	Bob Gibson/Jsy, Pedro Martinez/Jsy/50	15.00
21	Duke Snider/Jsy, Paul Molitor/Jsy/100	10.00
22	Johnny Bench/Jsy, Lou Boudreau/Jsy/100	15.00
23	Andre Dawson/Jsy, Chipper Jones/Jsy/100	15.00
24	Ernie Banks/Jsy, Boyer/Jsy/100	15.00
25	Manny Ramirez/Jsy, Rickey Henderson/Jsy/100	15.00

26 Carlton Fisk/Jsy,
Scott Rolen/Jsy/100 15.00
27 Nolan Ryan/Jsy,
Orlando Cepeda/Pnt/100 25.00
28 Roy Halladay/Jsy,
Steve Carlton/Jsy/100 8.00
29 Eddie Mathews/Jsy,
Tom Seaver/Jsy/100 15.00
30 Brandon Webb/Jsy,
Orel Hershiser/Jsy/100 10.00

Moniker Bat

NM/M
Quanity produced listed.

1 Adam Dunn/50 30.00
5 Alfonso Soriano/25 50.00
6 Andruw Jones/25 40.00
8 Angel Berroa/25 15.00
9 Aramis Ramirez/25 25.00
10 Aubrey Huff/25 25.00
15 Ben Sheets/25 25.00
21 Carlos Beltran/50 40.00
24 Craig Biggio/25 40.00
27 Delmon Young/50 25.00
30 Dontrelle Willis/25 30.00
31 Edgar Renteria/25 25.00
34 Frank Thomas/25 70.00
35 Fred McGriff/25 15.00
36 Garret Anderson/50 20.00
37 Gary Sheffield/25 40.00
40 Hank Blalock/50 35.00
61 Jermaine Dye/25 25.00
71 Jorge Posada/25 50.00
84 Kerry Wood/25 50.00
88 Lance Berkman/25 40.00
96 Mark Mulder/50 20.00
101 Mark Prior/50 40.00
102 Mark Teixeira/25 40.00
106 Michael Young/50 15.00
107 Miguel Cabrera/40 40.00
109 Mike Lowell/25 25.00
122 Paul LoDuca/25 25.00
124 Preston Wilson/25 20.00
131 Rickie Weeks/25 20.00
137 Roy Oswalt/25 20.00
144 Sean Casey/50 20.00
145 Shannon Stewart/25 25.00
155 Torii Hunter/25 25.00
156 Trot Nixon/25 25.00
159 Victor Martinez/25 20.00
163 Alfonso Soriano/25 50.00
166 Gary Sheffield/25 35.00
194 Garret Anderson/50 20.00
198 Mark Prior/50 40.00
201 Andre Dawson/50 20.00
205 Bobby Doerr/25 25.00
207 Dale Murphy/100 25.00
208 Don Mattingly/50 75.00
209 Gary Carter/100 15.00
212 Lou Brock/50 30.00
214 Mark Grace/25 30.00
216 Mike Schmidt/50 75.00
217 Nolan Ryan/50 150.00
219 Paul Molitor/50 30.00
221 Rod Carew/50 35.00
223 Ryne Sandberg/50 80.00
224 Stan Musial/50 75.00
226 Tony Gwynn/50 50.00
230 Carlos Beltran/50 40.00
231 David Ortiz/50 60.00
232 David Ortiz/50 60.00
234 Carlos Lee/50 20.00
235 Travis Hafner/25 25.00
238 Edgar Martinez/25 40.00
240 Roy Oswalt/25 25.00
242 Carlos Beltran/50 45.00
243 Carlos Beltran/50 45.00
244 Miguel Cabrera/50 40.00
247 Hank Blalock/50 35.00
247 Vernon Wells/50 20.00
248 Adam Dunn/50 35.00
249 Preston Wilson/25 25.00
250 Victor Martinez/25 20.00

Moniker Bronze

NM/M
Quanity produced listed.
Silver: .5-1.5X
Production 1-50
No pricing 15 or less.
Platinum: No Pricing
Production One Set

1 Adam Dunn/50 30.00
3 Albert Pujols/50 180.00
5 Alfonso Soriano/100 30.00
6 Andruw Jones/50 30.00
9 Angel Berroa/25 15.00
11 Austin Kearns/50 20.00
18 Brandon Webb/21 15.00
21 Carlos Beltran/50 40.00
23 Chipper Jones/25 65.00
24 Craig Biggio/5 40.00
30 Dontrelle Willis/25 30.00
31 Edgar Renteria/25 25.00
34 Frank Thomas/50 60.00
36 Garret Anderson/50 20.00
37 Gary Sheffield/50 25.00
39 Greg Maddux/25 85.00
40 Hank Blalock/50 35.00
46 Jacque Jones/25 25.00
51 Jeff Bagwell/25 75.00
71 Jorge Posada/50 50.00
76 Juan Gonzalez/25 30.00
79 Kazuhisa Ishii/25 35.00
84 Kerry Wood/50 50.00
88 Lance Berkman/50 30.00
98 Marcus Giles/25 25.00
100 Mark Mulder/100 15.00
101 Mark Prior/50 15.00
102 Mark Teixeira/50 30.00
106 Michael Young/25 15.00
107 Miguel Cabrera/50 30.00
109 Mike Lowell/25 25.00
122 Paul LoDuca/25 25.00
131 Rickie Weeks/25 20.00
137 Roy Oswalt/10 25.00
140 Sammy Sosa/25 85.00
142 Scott Rolen/25 60.00
144 Sean Casey/25 25.00
145 Shannon Stewart/25 25.00
153 Todd Helton/25 40.00
155 Torii Hunter/50 25.00
156 Trot Nixon/25 25.00
158 Vernon Wells/25 25.00
163 Alfonso Soriano/100 30.00
166 Gary Sheffield/10 25.00
167 Greg Maddux/5 80.00
172 Juan Gonzalez/25 40.00
183 Scott Rolen/25 50.00
191 Albert Pujols/5 180.00
193 Chipper Jones/5 65.00
194 Garret Anderson/10 25.00
195 Jeff Bagwell/25 75.00
198 Mark Prior/50 40.00
199 Sammy Sosa/25 80.00
200 Todd Helton/25 40.00
201 Andre Dawson/100 15.00
203 Bob Feller/100 25.00
204 Bob Gibson/100 25.00
205 Bobby Doerr/100 15.00
206 Cal Ripken Jr./25 180.00
207 Dale Murphy/25 25.00
208 Don Mattingly/25 60.00
209 Gary Carter/100 15.00
210 George Brett/25 75.00
212 Lou Brock/100 20.00
214 Mark Grace/100 20.00
215 Maury Wills/100 15.00
216 Mike Schmidt/100 60.00
217 Nolan Ryan/25 120.00
218 Orel Hershiser/25 40.00
219 Paul Molitor/25 25.00
221 Rod Carew/100 20.00
223 Ryne Sandberg/100 50.00
224 Stan Musial/100 60.00
226 Tony Gwynn/100 40.00
230 Carlos Beltran/50 45.00
231 David Ortiz/50 60.00
232 David Ortiz/50 60.00
233 Carlos Zambrano/25 30.00
234 Carlos Lee/25 20.00
238 Edgar Martinez/25 40.00
240 Roy Oswalt/50 20.00
242 Carlos Beltran/50 40.00
243 Carlos Beltran/50 40.00
244 Miguel Cabrera/50 40.00
245 Scott Rolen/25 50.00
246 Hank Blalock/50 35.00
247 Vernon Wells/25 25.00
248 Adam Dunn/50 35.00

Moniker Gold

NM/M
Quanity produced listed.

5 Alfonso Soriano/25 40.00
21 Carlos Beltran/25 50.00
100 Mark Mulder/25 25.00
163 Alfonso Soriano/25 40.00
201 Andre Dawson/25 20.00
203 Bob Feller/25 35.00
204 Bob Gibson/25 40.00
205 Bobby Doerr/25 25.00
207 Dale Murphy/25 40.00
208 Don Mattingly/25 90.00
209 Gary Carter/25 25.00
212 Lou Brock/25 30.00
214 Mark Grace/25 30.00
215 Maury Wills/25 25.00
216 Mike Schmidt/25 85.00
217 Nolan Ryan/25 150.00
219 Paul Molitor/25 40.00
221 Rod Carew/25 35.00
223 Ryne Sandberg/25 75.00
224 Stan Musial/25 100.00
226 Tony Gwynn/25 50.00

Moniker Jersey Number

Moniker Jersey

NM/M
Quanity produced listed.
Prime: No Pricing
Production One Set

1 Adam Dunn/50 30.00
5 Alfonso Soriano/25 40.00
6 Andruw Jones/25 40.00
9 Angel Berroa Pants/25 15.00
9 Aramis Ramirez/25 25.00
10 Aubrey Huff/25 25.00
11 Austin Kearns/25 25.00
15 Ben Sheets/25 25.00
18 Brandon Webb/25 15.00
20 C.C. Sabathia/25 25.00
21 Carlos Beltran/50 40.00
23 Chipper Jones/25 65.00
24 Craig Biggio/25 40.00
30 Dontrelle Willis/25 30.00
32 Eric Chavez/20 20.00
35 Fred McGriff/25 15.00
36 Garret Anderson/50 20.00
40 Hank Blalock/50 35.00
46 Jacque Jones/25 25.00
63 Jim Edmonds/25 40.00
66 Jody Gerut/25 15.00
67 Johan Santana/25 40.00
71 Jorge Posada/25 50.00
74 Jose Vidro/25 15.00
84 Kerry Wood/25 50.00
88 Lance Berkman/25 40.00
89 Larry Bigbie/25 20.00
98 Marcus Giles/25 25.00
99 Mark Buehrle/25 25.00
100 Mark Mulder/75 15.00
101 Mark Prior/50 40.00
102 Mark Teixeira/25 40.00
105 Melvin Mora/25 25.00
107 Miguel Cabrera/38 40.00
109 Mike Lowell/25 25.00
115 Morgan Ensberg/25 15.00
122 Paul LoDuca/25 25.00
124 Preston Wilson/25 20.00
137 Roy Oswalt/25 25.00
142 Scott Rolen/50 50.00
143 Sean Burroughs/25 25.00
144 Sean Casey/25 25.00
145 Shannon Stewart/25 25.00
149 Steve Finley/25 25.00
153 Todd Helton/25 40.00
154 Tom Glavine/25 40.00
155 Torii Hunter/25 25.00
156 Trot Nixon/25 25.00
158 Vernon Wells/50 20.00
159 Victor Martinez/50 40.00
163 Alfonso Soriano/50 40.00
166 Gary Sheffield/25 40.00
172 Juan Gonzalez/25 40.00
183 Scott Rolen/50 40.00
185 Tom Glavine/25 40.00
193 Chipper Jones/25 65.00
194 Garret Anderson/50 20.00
200 Todd Helton/25 40.00
201 Andre Dawson/50 25.00
204 Bob Gibson/25 30.00
205 Bobby Doerr/50 20.00
207 Dale Murphy/100 25.00
208 Don Mattingly/50 70.00
209 Gary Carter/100 15.00
216 Mike Schmidt/75 25.00
217 Nolan Ryan/120 120.00
218 Orel Hershiser/50 30.00
219 Paul Molitor/50 30.00
221 Rod Carew/50 30.00
223 Ryne Sandberg/25 100.00
224 Stan Musial/25 100.00
226 Tony Gwynn/100 40.00
228 Whitey Ford Pants/25 40.00
229 Yogi Berra/25 75.00
230 Carlos Beltran/50 40.00
231 David Ortiz/50 60.00
232 David Ortiz/50 60.00
234 Carlos Lee/50 20.00
235 Travis Hafner/25 25.00
236 Brad Penny/15 15.00
237 Wade Miller/25 15.00
238 Edgar Martinez/50 40.00
239 Carl Crawford/25 25.00
240 Roy Oswalt/25 25.00
242 Carlos Beltran/50 45.00
243 Carlos Beltran/50 45.00
244 Miguel Cabrera/50 40.00
245 Scott Rolen/50 40.00
246 Hank Blalock/50 35.00
247 Vernon Wells/50 20.00
248 Adam Dunn/50 35.00
249 Preston Wilson/25 25.00

Moniker Jersey Number (continued)

NM/M
Quanity produced listed.
Prime: No Pricing
Production One Set

5 Adam Dunn/50 30.00
5 Alfonso Soriano/50 40.00
6 Andruw Jones/25 40.00
9 Angel Berroa Pants/25 15.00
9 Aramis Ramirez/25 25.00
10 Aubrey Huff/25 25.00
11 Austin Kearns/25 25.00
15 Ben Sheets/25 25.00
18 Brandon Webb/25 15.00
20 C.C. Sabathia/25 25.00
23 Carlos Beltran/50 40.00
23 Chipper Jones/25 65.00
24 Craig Biggio/25 40.00
30 Dontrelle Willis/25 30.00
34 Frank Thomas/25 70.00
35 Fred McGriff/25 15.00
40 Hank Blalock/25 35.00
46 Jacque Jones/25 25.00
63 Jim Edmonds/25 40.00
66 Jody Gerut/25 15.00
67 Johan Santana/25 40.00
71 Jorge Posada/25 50.00
74 Jose Vidro/25 15.00
84 Kerry Wood/25 50.00
88 Lance Berkman/25 40.00
90 Larry Walker/25 20.00
98 Marcus Giles/25 25.00
99 Mark Buehrle/25 25.00
100 Mark Mulder/75 15.00
101 Mark Prior/40 40.00
102 Mark Teixeira/25 40.00
105 Melvin Mora/25 25.00
109 Miguel Cabrera/50 30.00
109 Mike Lowell/25 25.00
115 Morgan Ensberg/25 15.00
122 Paul LoDuca/25 25.00
124 Preston Wilson/25 20.00
137 Roy Oswalt/25 25.00
140 Sammy Sosa/25 120.00
142 Scott Rolen/50 50.00
143 Sean Burroughs/25 25.00
149 Steve Finley/25 25.00
153 Todd Helton/25 40.00
154 Tom Glavine/25 40.00
155 Torii Hunter/25 25.00
156 Trot Nixon/25 25.00
158 Vernon Wells/50 20.00
159 Victor Martinez/50 40.00
163 Alfonso Soriano/50 40.00
166 Gary Sheffield/25 40.00
172 Juan Gonzalez/25 40.00
183 Scott Rolen/50 40.00
185 Tom Glavine/25 40.00
193 Chipper Jones/25 65.00
194 Garret Anderson/50 20.00
199 Sammy Sosa/25 120.00
201 Andre Dawson/25 40.00
204 Bob Gibson/25 40.00
205 Bobby Doerr/25 20.00
207 Dale Murphy/100 25.00
208 Don Mattingly/50 70.00
209 Gary Carter/100 15.00
216 Mike Schmidt/75 75.00
217 Nolan Ryan/120 120.00
218 Orel Hershiser/50 30.00
219 Paul Molitor/50 30.00
221 Rod Carew/50 30.00
223 Ryne Sandberg/25 100.00
224 Stan Musial/25 100.00
226 Tony Gwynn/100 40.00
228 Whitey Ford/Pants/25 40.00
229 Yogi Berra/25 75.00
230 Carlos Beltran/50 40.00
231 David Ortiz/50 60.00
232 David Ortiz/50 60.00
234 Carlos Lee/50 20.00
235 Travis Hafner/25 25.00
236 Brad Penny/15 15.00
237 Wade Miller/25 15.00
238 Edgar Martinez/50 40.00
239 Carl Crawford/25 25.00
240 Roy Oswalt/25 25.00
242 Carlos Beltran/50 45.00
243 Carlos Beltran/50 45.00
244 Miguel Cabrera/50 40.00
245 Scott Rolen/50 40.00
246 Hank Blalock/50 35.00
247 Vernon Wells/50 20.00
248 Adam Dunn/50 35.00
249 Preston Wilson/25 25.00
250 Victor Martinez/50 20.00

Player Threads Jersey Number

NM/M
Quantity produced listed.
Prime: No Pricing
Production One Set

1 Mike Piazza/100 10.00
3 Nolan Ryan/Jkt/100 20.00
4 Reggie Jackson/100 10.00
6 Wade Boggs/50 10.00
6 Steve Carlton/Pants/100 5.00
7 Ivan Rodriguez/50 10.00
8 Pedro Martinez/50 12.00
10 Rickey Henderson/Pants/100 10.00
11 Randy Johnson/50 10.00
12 Curt Schilling/25 20.00
13 Roger Maris/50 50.00
14 Sammy Sosa/100 10.00
15 Gary Carter/Pants/50 8.00
16 Gary Sheffield/25 10.00
17 Eddie Murray/50 15.00
18 Hideo Nomo/50 10.00
19 Rafael Palmeiro/50 8.00
20 Andre Dawson/50 8.00

Player Threads Double

NM/M
Quantity produced listed.

1 Mike Piazza/100 15.00
2 Roger Clemens/100 20.00
3 Nolan Ryan/100 30.00
4 Reggie Jackson/100 10.00
5 Wade Boggs/100 10.00
6 Steve Carlton/100 10.00
7 Ivan Rodriguez/100 10.00
8 Pedro Martinez/100 10.00
9 Rickey Henderson/50 25.00
10 Rickey Henderson/100 10.00
11 Randy Johnson/100 20.00
12 Curt Schilling/100 10.00
13 Roger Maris/100 25.00
14 Sammy Sosa/100 15.00
15 Gary Carter/100 10.00
16 Gary Sheffield/50 10.00
17 Eddie Murray/50 20.00
18 Hideo Nomo/50 15.00
19 Rafael Palmeiro/100 10.00
20 Andre Dawson/50 10.00

Player Threads Triple

NM/M
Quantity produced listed

1 Mike Piazza/25 30.00
2 Roger Clemens/25 50.00
3 Nolan Ryan/25 70.00
4 Reggie Jackson/25 40.00
5 Wade Boggs/25 30.00
6 Steve Carlton/25 25.00
7 Ivan Rodriguez/25 30.00
8 Pedro Martinez/25 30.00
10 Rickey Henderson/25 50.00
14 Curt Schilling/25 30.00
13 Roger Maris/25 120.00
14 Sammy Sosa/25 40.00
15 Gary Carter/25 20.00
17 Eddie Murray/25 25.00
18 Hideo Nomo/25 30.00
19 Rafael Palmeiro/25 20.00
20 Andre Dawson/25 20.00

Team Threads Jersey Number

NM/M
Common Card: 15.00
Production 100 Sets
Prime: No Pricing
Production One Set

1 Stan Musial, Albert Pujols 40.00
2 Cal Ripken Jr./Jkt, Mike Mussina 40.00
3 Carlton Fisk, Roger Clemens 25.00
4 Dale Murphy, Chipper Jones 15.00
5 Tony Gwynn, Dave Winfield 25.00
6 Don Mattingly, Hideki Matsui 50.00
7 Lou Boudreau, Early Wynn 15.00
8 Ernie Banks, Sammy Sosa 30.00
9 Nolan Ryan/Jkt, Jeff Bagwell 50.00
10 Mike Schmidt, Jim Thome 25.00

Team Trademarks

NM/M
Common Player: 5.00
Production 100 Sets
Gold: No Pricing
Production 10 Sets

1 Bob Gibson 8.00
2 Cal Ripken Jr. 30.00
3 Carl Yastrzemski 10.00
4 Dale Murphy 8.00
5 Gary Carter 5.00
6 George Brett 15.00
7 Tom Seaver 8.00
8 Kerry Wood 8.00
9 Lou Brock 8.00
10 Luis Aparicio 5.00
11 Mike Piazza 10.00
12 Nolan Ryan 15.00
13 Nolan Ryan 8.00
14 Randy Johnson 8.00
15 Reggie Jackson 8.00
16 Ricky Henderson 8.00
17 Robin Yount 10.00
18 Rod Carew 8.00
19 Ryne Sandberg 15.00
20 Steve Carlton 5.00
21 Steve Garvey 5.00
22 Johnny Bench 8.00
23 Tony Gwynn 10.00
24 Whitey Ford 8.00
25 Will Clark 8.00

Team Trademarks Autographs

NM/M
Quantity produced listed.

1 Bob Gibson/100 20.00
2 Cal Ripken Jr./150 150.00
3 Carl Yastrzemski/100 60.00
4 Dale Murphy/100 10.00
5 Gary Carter/100 15.00
6 George Brett/25 65.00
7 Tom Seaver/25 30.00
8 Kerry Wood/25 40.00
9 Lou Brock/100 20.00
10 Luis Aparicio/100 15.00
11 Nolan Ryan Astros/25 100.00
13 Nolan Ryan Rgr/100 100.00
15 Reggie Jackson/50 50.00
17 Robin Yount/50 30.00
18 Rod Carew/50 25.00
19 Ryne Sandberg/25 65.00
20 Steve Carlton/100 20.00
21 Steve Garvey/50 15.00
22 Johnny Bench/25 50.00
23 Tom Seaver/25 30.00
24 Whitey Ford/25 30.00
25 Will Clark/34 50.00

Team Trademarks Jersey Number

NM/M
Quantity produced listed.
Prime: No Pricing
Production One Set

1 Bob Gibson/100 10.00
2 Cal Ripken Jr./Pants/25 40.00
3 Carl Yastrzemski/100 15.00
4 Dale Murphy/100 10.00
5 Gary Carter/100 5.00
6 George Brett/100 15.00
7 Tom Seaver/100 10.00
8 Kerry Wood/Pants/50 10.00
9 Lou Brock/100 5.00
10 Luis Aparicio/Pants/100 5.00
11 Mike Piazza/50 15.00
12 Nolan Ryan/Astros/100 20.00
13 Nolan Ryan/Rgr/100 10.00
15 Reggie Jackson/Pants/100 8.00
16 Ricky Henderson/100 8.00
17 Robin Yount/100 8.00
18 Rod Carew/Jkt/100 8.00
19 Ryne Sandberg/100 15.00
22 Steve Carlton/100 5.00
23 Tony Gwynn/100 10.00
24 Whitey Ford/100 10.00
25 Will Clark/50 15.00

Team Trademarks Auto. Jersey Numbers

NM/M
Quantity produced listed.
Prime: No Pricing
Production One Set

1 Bob Gibson/100 25.00
2 Cal Ripken Jr./Pants/25 200.00
3 Carl Yastrzemski/25 75.00
4 Dale Murphy/100 25.00
5 Gary Carter/100 15.00
6 George Brett/100 80.00
7 Tom Seaver/25 65.00
8 Kerry Wood/Pants/50 50.00
9 Lou Brock/100 25.00
11 Luis Aparicio/Pants/100 5.00
12 Nolan Ryan/Astros/25 120.00
13 Nolan Ryan/Rgr/25 120.00
15 Reggie Jackson/Pants/25 60.00
17 Robin Yount/25 75.00
18 Rod Carew/Jkt/50 30.00
19 Ryne Sandberg/25 65.00
20 Steve Carlton/50 50.00
22 Johnny Bench/50 50.00
23 Tony Gwynn/50 30.00
24 Whitey Ford/50 30.00
25 Will Clark/84 40.00

Threads Jersey

NM/M
Quantity produced listed.
Prime: No Pricing
Production One Set
Button: No Pricing
Production 1-6

1 Adam Dunn/50 15.00
3 Albert Pujols/50 15.00
5 Alfonso Soriano/25 15.00
6 Andruw Jones/25 10.00
11 Austin Kearns/25 10.00
12 Barry Larkin/25 15.00
13 Barry Zito/25 8.00
16 Bernie Williams/50 8.00
21 Carlos Beltran/25 8.00
22 Carlos Delgado/25 8.00
23 Chipper Jones/25 15.00
24 Craig Biggio/25 15.00
27 Curt Schilling/25 20.00
30 Dontrelle Willis/25 15.00
31 Edgar Renteria/25 10.00
32 Eric Chavez/25 8.00
34 Frank Thomas/25 20.00
36 Garret Anderson/25 8.00
39 Greg Maddux/50 15.00
40 Hank Blalock/25 10.00

41 Hideki Matsui/50 40.00
42 Hideo Nomo/50 10.00
44 Ivan Rodriguez/25 15.00
50 Jason Giambi/50 5.00
55 Javy Lopez/25
58 Jeff Bagwell/50 10.00
59 Jeff Kent/50 5.00
63 Jim Edmonds/25 10.00
64 Jim Thome/50 10.00
69 John Smoltz/25 15.00
71 Jorge Posada/25 15.00
75 Josh Beckett/25 10.00
76 Juan Gonzalez/25 15.00
84 Kerry Wood/50 12.00
88 Lance Berkman/50 5.00
90 Larry Walker/25 15.00
93 Luis Gonzalez/25 8.00
96 Magglio Ordonez/25 8.00
97 Manny Ramirez/50 10.00
100 Mark Mulder/25 10.00
101 Mark Prior/25 8.00
107 Miguel Cabrera/25 10.00
108 Miguel Tejada/25 10.00
110 Mike Mussina/50 15.00
111 Mike Piazza/50 15.00
112 Mike Sweeney/25 10.00
123 Pedro J. Martinez/50 12.00
126 Rafael Palmeiro/25 15.00
127 Randy Johnson/25 20.00
137 Roy Oswalt/25 10.00
140 Sammy Sosa/50 15.00
142 Scott Rolen/25 20.00
146 Shawn Green/25 8.00
150 Tim Hudson/25 10.00
153 Todd Helton/25 10.00
154 Tom Glavine/25 10.00
155 Torii Hunter/25 10.00
157 Troy Glaus/25 8.00
158 Vernon Wells/25 8.00
161 Vladimir Guerrero/25 20.00
162 Alex Rodriguez/100 10.00
163 Alfonso Soriano/25 10.00
164 Andy Pettitte/25 15.00
165 Curt Schilling/25 10.00
166 Gary Sheffield/25 10.00
167 Greg Maddux/50 15.00
168 Hideo Nomo/25 20.00
169 Ivan Rodriguez/50 12.00
170 Jason Giambi/25 8.00
172 Juan Gonzalez/25 15.00
174 Kevin Brown/25 8.00
176 Miguel Tejada/25 10.00
177 Mike Mussina/50 10.00
178 Mike Piazza/25 25.00
179 Pedro Martinez/25 20.00
180 Rafael Palmeiro/25 15.00
181 Randy Johnson/50 10.00
182 Roger Clemens/100 10.00
183 Scott Rolen/25 20.00
184 Shawn Green/25 8.00
185 Tom Glavine/25 15.00
186 Vladimir Guerrero/25 20.00
187 Alex Rodriguez/100 10.00
189 Randy Johnson/100 10.00
190 Roger Clemens/100 10.00
191 Albert Pujols/25 20.00
192 Barry Zito/25 10.00
193 Chipper Jones/50 10.00
194 Garret Anderson/25 10.00
195 Jeff Bagwell/50 10.00
196 Josh Beckett/25 10.00
197 Magglio Ordonez/25 10.00
198 Mark Prior/50 8.00
199 Sammy Sosa/25 15.00
200 Todd Helton/50 10.00
201 Andre Dawson/25 5.00
202 Babe Ruth/25 350.00
203 Bob Feller/25 20.00
205 Bobby Doerr/50 8.00
206 Cal Ripken Jr./100 40.00
207 Dale Murphy/100 10.00
208 Don Mattingly/50 25.00
209 Gary Carter/50 8.00
210 George Brett/100 15.00
211 Jackie Robinson/50 40.00
212 Lou Brock/25 20.00
213 Lou Gehrig/25 140.00
214 Mark Grace/25 15.00
215 Maury Wills/50 5.00
216 Mike Schmidt/100 15.00
217 Nolan Ryan/100 20.00
218 Orel Hershiser/25 15.00
219 Paul Molitor/50 10.00
220 Roberto Clemente/25 80.00
221 Rod Carew/100 10.00
222 Roy Campanella/Pants/50 15.00
223 Ryne Sandberg/50 25.00
224 Stan Musial/50 40.00
225 Ted Williams/50 75.00
226 Tony Gwynn/100 10.00
227 Ty Cobb Pants/100 75.00
228 Whitey Ford/Pants/25 20.00
229 Yogi Berra/25 25.00
231 Carlos Beltran/25 15.00
232 David Ortiz/25 20.00
238 Edgar Martinez/25 10.00
240 Roy Oswalt/25 10.00
242 Carlos Beltran/25 15.00
243 Carlos Beltran/25 15.00
244 Miguel Cabrera/25 15.00
245 Scott Rolen/25 20.00
246 Hank Blalock/25 12.00
247 Vernon Wells/25 8.00
248 Adam Dunn/25 15.00

Threads Jersey Number

NM/M
Quanity produced listed.
Prime: No Pricing
Production One Set
MLB Logo: No Pricing
Production One Set

1 Adam Dunn/25 15.00
3 Albert Pujols/25 20.00
5 Alfonso Soriano/25 15.00
6 Andruw Jones/25 10.00
11 Austin Kearns/25 8.00
12 Barry Larkin/25 15.00
13 Barry Zito/25 8.00
16 Bernie Williams/50 10.00
21 Carlos Beltran/25 15.00
22 Carlos Delgado/25 8.00
23 Chipper Jones/50 10.00
25 Curt Schilling/25 20.00
30 Dontrelle Willis/25 8.00
31 Edgar Renteria/25 8.00
32 Eric Chavez/25 8.00
34 Frank Thomas/25 15.00
36 Garret Anderson/25 10.00
38 Greg Maddux/50 15.00
40 Hank Blalock/25 12.00
41 Hideki Matsui/50 40.00
42 Hideo Nomo/25 10.00
44 Ivan Rodriguez/25 20.00
50 Jason Giambi/25 5.00
55 Javy Lopez/25 8.00
58 Jeff Bagwell/50 10.00
59 Jeff Kent/25 10.00
63 Jim Edmonds/25 10.00
64 Jim Thome/25 15.00
69 John Smoltz/25 15.00
71 Jorge Posada/25 15.00
75 Josh Beckett/25 10.00
84 Kerry Wood/50 12.00
90 Lance Berkman/25 5.00
93 Larry Walker/25 10.00
96 Luis Gonzalez/25 8.00
97 Magglio Ordonez/25 8.00
97 Manny Ramirez/25 12.00
100 Mark Mulder/25 10.00
101 Mark Prior/25 8.00
107 Miguel Cabrera/25 15.00
108 Miguel Tejada/25 10.00
110 Mike Mussina/25 10.00
111 Mike Piazza/50 15.00
112 Mike Sweeney/25 10.00
123 Pedro J. Martinez/25 12.00
126 Rafael Palmeiro/25 15.00
127 Randy Johnson/25 20.00
137 Roy Oswalt/25 10.00
140 Sammy Sosa/25 15.00
142 Scott Rolen/25 20.00
146 Shawn Green/25 8.00
150 Tim Hudson/25 10.00
153 Todd Helton/50 10.00
154 Tom Glavine/25 15.00
155 Torii Hunter/25 10.00
157 Troy Glaus/25 8.00
158 Vernon Wells/25 8.00
161 Vladimir Guerrero/25 20.00
162 Alex Rodriguez/100 10.00
163 Alfonso Soriano/25 10.00
164 Andy Pettitte/25 15.00
165 Curt Schilling/25 10.00
166 Gary Sheffield/25 10.00
167 Greg Maddux/50 15.00
168 Hideo Nomo/25 20.00
169 Ivan Rodriguez/25 12.00
170 Jason Giambi/25 8.00
172 Juan Gonzalez/25 12.00
174 Kevin Brown/25 8.00
176 Miguel Tejada/25 10.00
177 Mike Mussina/50 10.00
178 Mike Piazza/25 25.00
179 Pedro Martinez/25 20.00
180 Rafael Palmeiro/25 15.00
181 Randy Johnson/25 20.00
182 Roger Clemens/25 10.00
183 Scott Rolen/25 20.00
184 Shawn Green/25 8.00
185 Tom Glavine/25 15.00
186 Vladimir Guerrero/25 20.00
187 Alex Rodriguez/100 10.00
189 Randy Johnson/100 10.00
190 Roger Clemens/100 10.00
191 Albert Pujols/25 20.00
192 Barry Zito/25 8.00
193 Chipper Jones/50 10.00
194 Garret Anderson/25 10.00
195 Jeff Bagwell/25 10.00
196 Josh Beckett/25 10.00
197 Magglio Ordonez/25 8.00
198 Mark Prior/25 10.00
199 Sammy Sosa/25 15.00
200 Todd Helton/50 10.00
201 Andre Dawson/25 10.00
202 Babe Ruth/25 300.00
203 Bob Feller/25 20.00
205 Bobby Doerr/25 8.00
206 Cal Ripken Jr./100 40.00
207 Dale Murphy/50 10.00
208 Don Mattingly/50 25.00
209 Gary Carter/50 8.00
210 George Brett/100 15.00
211 Jackie Robinson/100 40.00
212 Lou Brock/25 20.00
213 Lou Gehrig/25 150.00
214 Mark Grace/25 8.00
215 Maury Wills/50 8.00
216 Mike Schmidt/100 15.00
217 Nolan Ryan/100 20.00
218 Orel Hershiser/25 15.00
219 Paul Molitor/25 20.00
220 Roberto Clemente/25 80.00
221 Rod Carew/100 10.00
222 Roy Campanella/Pants/50 15.00
223 Ryne Sandberg/50 25.00
224 Stan Musial/50 40.00
225 Ted Williams/50 75.00
226 Tony Gwynn/100 10.00
227 Ty Cobb/Pants/100 60.00
228 Whitey Ford/Pants/25 20.00
229 Yogi Berra/25 25.00
231 Carlos Beltran/25 15.00
232 David Ortiz/25 20.00
238 Edgar Martinez/25 10.00
240 Roy Oswalt H/25 10.00
242 Carlos Beltran/25 15.00
244 Miguel Cabrera/25 15.00
245 Scott Rolen/25 20.00
246 Hank Blalock/25 10.00
248 Adam Dunn/25 15.00

Timber

NM/M
Quanity produced listed.

1 Adam Dunn/25 15.00
4 Alex Rodriguez/100 10.00
5 Alfonso Soriano/25 15.00
6 Andruw Jones/25 10.00
7 Andy Pettitte/25 15.00
11 Austin Kearns/25 8.00
12 Barry Larkin/25 15.00
13 Barry Zito/25 8.00
16 Bernie Williams/25 12.00
21 Carlos Beltran/25 15.00
22 Carlos Delgado/25 10.00
23 Chipper Jones/25 20.00
24 Craig Biggio/25 12.00
25 Curt Schilling/25 20.00
30 Dontrelle Willis/25 8.00
32 Eric Chavez/25 8.00
34 Frank Thomas/25 20.00
35 Fred McGriff/25 12.00
36 Garret Anderson/25 8.00
37 Gary Sheffield/25 10.00
38 Greg Maddux/25 25.00
40 Hank Blalock/25 10.00
41 Hideki Matsui/25 60.00
42 Hideo Nomo/25 20.00
44 Ivan Rodriguez/25 20.00
50 Jason Giambi/25 8.00
55 Javy Lopez/25 8.00
58 Jeff Bagwell/25 15.00
59 Jeff Kent/25 8.00
63 Jim Edmonds/25 10.00
64 Jim Thome/25 20.00
71 Jorge Posada/25 15.00
75 Josh Beckett/25 10.00
76 Juan Gonzalez/25 15.00
84 Kerry Wood/25 20.00
85 Kevin Brown/25 8.00
88 Lance Berkman/25 8.00
90 Larry Walker/25 8.00
93 Luis Gonzalez/25 8.00
96 Magglio Ordonez/25 8.00
97 Manny Ramirez/25 15.00
100 Mark Mulder/25 8.00
101 Mark Prior/25 15.00
102 Mark Teixeira/25 10.00
106 Michael Young/25 10.00
107 Miguel Cabrera/25 15.00
108 Miguel Tejada/25 10.00
109 Mike Lowell/25 8.00
110 Mike Mussina/25 15.00
111 Mike Piazza/25 25.00
112 Mike Sweeney/25 8.00
116 Nick Johnson/25 8.00
117 Nomar Garciaparra/25 20.00
122 Paul LoDuca/25 8.00
123 Pedro J. Martinez/25 20.00
126 Rafael Palmeiro/25 15.00
127 Randy Johnson/25 20.00
130 Richie Sexson/25 10.00
134 Rocco Baldelli/25 8.00
135 Roger Clemens/25 25.00
137 Roy Oswalt/25 8.00
140 Sammy Sosa/50 15.00
142 Scott Rolen/25 20.00
146 Shawn Green/25 8.00
150 Tim Hudson/25 8.00
153 Todd Helton/25 15.00
154 Tom Glavine/25 15.00
155 Torii Hunter/25 8.00
156 Trot Nixon/25 8.00
157 Troy Glaus/25 8.00
158 Vernon Wells/25 8.00
161 Vladimir Guerrero/25 20.00
162 Alex Rodriguez/100 10.00
163 Alfonso Soriano/25 10.00
164 Andy Pettitte/25 15.00
165 Curt Schilling/25 10.00
166 Gary Sheffield/25 10.00
167 Greg Maddux/25 15.00
168 Hideo Nomo/25 15.00
169 Ivan Rodriguez/25 15.00
170 Jason Giambi/25 15.00
171 Jim Thome/25 15.00
172 Juan Gonzalez/25 12.00
174 Kevin Brown/25 8.00
175 Manny Ramirez/25 15.00
176 Miguel Tejada/25 10.00
177 Mike Mussina/25 15.00
178 Mike Piazza/25 25.00
179 Pedro Martinez/25 20.00
180 Rafael Palmeiro/25 15.00
181 Randy Johnson/25 20.00
182 Roger Clemens/25 25.00
183 Scott Rolen/25 20.00
184 Shawn Green/25 8.00
185 Tom Glavine/25 15.00
186 Vladimir Guerrero/25 20.00
187 Alex Rodriguez/100 10.00
188 Mike Piazza/25 25.00
189 Randy Johnson/25 20.00
190 Roger Clemens/25 25.00
191 Albert Pujols/25 20.00
192 Barry Zito/25 8.00
193 Chipper Jones/25 20.00
194 Garret Anderson/25 8.00
195 Jeff Bagwell/25 15.00
196 Josh Beckett/25 8.00
197 Magglio Ordonez/25 8.00
198 Mark Prior/25 15.00
199 Sammy Sosa/50 15.00
200 Todd Helton/25 15.00
201 Andre Dawson/25 8.00
202 Babe Ruth/25 120.00
207 Dale Murphy/50 15.00
208 Don Mattingly/50 25.00
209 Gary Carter/50 10.00
210 George Brett/50 25.00
212 Lou Brock/25 15.00
213 Lou Gehrig/100 100.00
214 Mark Grace/25 15.00
216 Mike Schmidt/50 25.00
217 Nolan Ryan/25 30.00
218 Paul Molitor/50 10.00
220 Roberto Clemente/100 75.00
221 Rod Carew/25 10.00
222 Roy Campanella/100 10.00
223 Ryne Sandberg/25 25.00
224 Stan Musial/100 20.00
225 Ted Williams/100 50.00
226 Tony Gwynn/25 20.00
227 Ty Cobb/100 75.00
229 Yogi Berra/100 10.00
230 Carlos Beltran/25 15.00
231 David Ortiz/25 20.00
232 David Ortiz/25 20.00
238 Edgar Martinez/25 15.00
240 Roy Oswalt/25 10.00
242 Carlos Beltran/25 15.00
243 Carlos Beltran/25 15.00
244 Miguel Cabrera/25 15.00
245 Scott Rolen/25 20.00
246 Hank Blalock/25 10.00
248 Adam Dunn/25 15.00

TNT

NM/M
Quanity produced listed.
Prime: No Pricing
Production One Set

1 Adam Dunn/Bat-Jsy/50 10.00
2 Albert Pujols/Bat-Jsy/100 15.00
5 Alfonso Soriano/Bat-Jsy/100 10.00
6 Andruw Jones/Bat-Jsy/50 8.00
11 Austin Kearns/Bat-Jsy/25 20.00
12 Barry Larkin/Bat-Jsy/25 20.00
13 Barry Zito/Bat-Jsy/50 5.00
16 Bernie Williams/Bat-Jsy/50 10.00
21 Carlos Beltran/Bat-Jsy/50 10.00
22 Carlos Delgado/Bat-Jsy/50 5.00
23 Chipper Jones/Bat-Jsy/50 15.00
24 Craig Biggio/Bat-Jsy/50 8.00
25 Curt Schilling/Bat-Jsy/25 25.00
32 Eric Chavez/Bat-Jsy/25 10.00
34 Frank Thomas/Bat-Jsy/50
36 Garret Anderson/Bat-Jsy/50 15.00
39 Greg Maddux/Bat-Jsy/50 15.00
40 Hank Blalock/Bat-Jsy/50 8.00
41 Hideki Matsui/Bat-Jsy/50 50.00
42 Hideo Nomo/Bat-Jsy/50 8.00
44 Ivan Rodriguez/Bat-Jsy/50 20.00
50 Jason Giambi/Bat-Jsy/50 8.00
55 Javy Lopez/Bat-Jsy/100 8.00
58 Jeff Bagwell/Bat-Jsy/50 10.00
59 Jeff Kent/Bat-Jsy/100 10.00
63 Jim Edmonds/Bat-Jsy
64 Jim Thome/Bat-Jsy/25 15.00
71 Jorge Posada/Bat-Jsy/50 20.00
75 Josh Beckett/Bat-Jsy/50 10.00
76 Juan Gonzalez/Bat-Jsy/50 20.00
84 Kerry Wood/Bat-Jsy/50 15.00
88 Lance Berkman/Bat-Jsy/50 5.00
90 Larry Walker/Bat-Jsy/50 8.00
93 Luis Gonzalez/Bat-Jsy/50
96 Magglio Ordonez/Bat-Jsy/50 10.00
97 Manny Ramirez/Bat-Jsy/50
100 Mark Mulder/Bat-Jsy/25 10.00
101 Mark Prior/Bat-Jsy/50 10.00
102 Mark Teixeira/Bat-Jsy/20 20.00
107 Miguel Cabrera/Bat-Jsy/20 20.00
108 Miguel Tejada/Bat-Jsy 10.00
109 Mike Lowell/Bat-Jsy 10.00
110 Mike Mussina/Bat-Jsy
111 Mike Piazza/Bat-Jsy/50 20.00
112 Mike Sweeney/Bat-Jsy 10.00
123 Pedro J. Martinez/Bat-Jsy 15.00
126 Rafael Palmeiro/Bat-Jsy 20.00
127 Randy Johnson/Bat-Jsy 15.00
137 Roy Oswalt/Bat-Jsy/25 10.00
140 Sammy Sosa/Bat-Jsy 20.00
142 Scott Rolen/Bat-Jsy/25 25.00
146 Shawn Green/Bat-Jsy 10.00
150 Tim Hudson/Bat-Jsy/25 10.00
153 Todd Helton/Bat-Jsy/50 10.00
154 Tom Glavine/Bat-Jsy/25 20.00
155 Torii Hunter/Bat-Jsy/25 10.00
157 Troy Glaus/Bat-Jsy/25 10.00
158 Vernon Wells/Bat-Jsy 10.00
161 Vladimir Guerrero/Bat-Jsy 25.00
162 Alex Rodriguez/Bat-Jsy 10.00
163 Alfonso Soriano/Bat-Jsy 10.00
164 Andy Pettitte/Bat-Jsy 20.00
165 Curt Schilling/Bat-Jsy
166 Gary Sheffield/Bat-Jsy 20.00
167 Greg Maddux/Bat-Jsy 20.00
168 Hideo Nomo/Bat-Jsy 20.00
169 Ivan Rodriguez/Bat-Jsy 15.00
170 Jason Giambi/Bat-Jsy 15.00
172 Juan Gonzalez/Bat-Jsy 15.00
174 Kevin Brown/Bat-Jsy 10.00
176 Miguel Tejada/Bat-Jsy 10.00
177 Mike Mussina/Bat-Jsy
178 Mike Piazza/Bat-Jsy/50 20.00
179 Pedro Martinez/Bat-Jsy
180 Rafael Palmeiro/Bat-Jsy 15.00
181 Randy Johnson/Bat-Jsy 15.00
182 Roger Clemens/Bat-Jsy/100 10.00
183 Scott Rolen/Bat-Jsy/25 25.00
184 Shawn Green/Bat-Jsy
185 Tom Glavine/Bat-Jsy/25 20.00
186 Vladimir Guerrero/Bat-Jsy
187 Alex Rodriguez/Bat-Jsy/100 10.00
189 Randy Johnson/Bat-Jsy 15.00
190 Roger Clemens/Bat-Jsy/100 10.00
191 Albert Pujols/Bat-Jsy/25 25.00
192 Barry Zito/Bat-Jsy/25 10.00
193 Chipper Jones/Bat-Jsy .15.00
194 Garret Anderson/Bat-Jsy 10.00
195 Jeff Bagwell/Bat-Jsy/50 10.00
196 Josh Beckett/Bat-Jsy/25 10.00
197 Magglio Ordonez/Bat-Jsy 10.00
198 Mark Prior/Bat-Jsy/50 10.00
199 Sammy Sosa/Bat-Jsy 20.00
200 Todd Helton/Bat-Jsy/25 10.00
201 Andre Dawson/Bat-Jsy 8.00
202 Babe Ruth/Bat-Jsy/25 425.00
206 Cal Ripken Jr./Bat-Jsy/100 60.00
207 Dale Murphy/Bat-Jsy 10.00
208 Don Mattingly/Bat-Jsy 20.00
209 Gary Carter/Bat-Jsy/50 20.00
210 George Brett/Bat-Jsy 20.00
212 Lou Brock/Bat-Jsy/25 20.00
213 Lou Gehrig/Bat-Jsy/25 250.00
214 Mark Grace/Bat-Jsy/25 20.00
216 Mike Schmidt/Bat-Jsy 30.00
217 Nolan Ryan/Bat-Jsy/100 25.00
219 Paul Molitor/Bat-Jsy 20.00
221 Rod Carew/Bat-Jsy/25 15.00
222 Roy Campanella/Bat-Pants/25 20.00
223 Ryne Sandberg/Bat-Jsy 30.00
224 Stan Musial/Bat-Jsy/25 50.00
225 Ted Williams/Bat-Jsy/50 100.00
226 Tony Gwynn/Bat-Jsy/100 15.00
227 Ty Cobb/Bat-Pants/50 120.00
230 Carlos Beltran/Bat-Jsy/25 20.00
231 David Ortiz/Bat-Jsy/25 25.00
232 David Ortiz/Bat-Jsy/25 25.00
238 Edgar Martinez/Bat-Jsy/25 15.00
240 Roy Oswalt/Bat-Jsy/25 10.00
242 Carlos Beltran/Bat-Jsy/25 20.00
243 Carlos Beltran/Bat-Jsy/25 20.00
244 Miguel Cabrera/Bat-Jsy/25 20.00
245 Scott Rolen/Bat-Jsy/25 20.00
246 Hank Blalock/Bat-Jsy/25 10.00
247 Vernon Wells/Bat-Jsy/25 10.00
248 Adam Dunn/Bat-Jsy/25 20.00

2005 Leaf

NM/M
Complete Set (300):
Common Player (1-200): .15
Common SP (201-250): 1.00
Inserted 1:3
Common SP (251-300): 1.00
#251-270 Inserted 1:6
271-300 Inserted 1:4
Hobby Pack (8): 4.00
Hobby Box (24): 80.00

1 Bartolo Colon .25
2 Casey Kotchman .15
3 Chone Figgins .15
4 Darin Erstad .25
5 Francisco Rodriguez .25
6 Garret Anderson .25
7 Jarrod Washburn .15
8 Troy Glaus .25
9 Vladimir Guerrero .50
10 Brandon Webb .15
11 Casey Fossum .15
12 Luis Gonzalez .25
13 Randy Johnson .50
14 Richie Sexson .25
15 Andruw Jones .25
16 Chipper Jones .25
17 J.D. Drew .25
18 John Smoltz .25
19 Johnny Estrada .15
20 Marcus Giles .15
21 Rafael Furcal .25
22 Russ Ortiz .15
23 Javy Lopez .25
24 Jay Gibbons .15
25 Melvin Mora .15
26 Miguel Tejada .40
27 Rafael Palmeiro .40
28 Sidney Ponson .15
29 Bill Mueller .15
30 Curt Schilling .40
31 David Ortiz .50
32 Doug Mientkiewicz .15
33 Jason Varitek .25
34 Johnny Damon .40
35 Manny Ramirez .50
36 Pedro J. Martinez .50
37 Trot Nixon .15
38 Aramis Ramirez .25
39 Corey Patterson .15
40 Derrek Lee .25
41 Greg Maddux .75
42 Kerry Wood .50
43 Mark Prior .50
44 Moises Alou .25
45 Nomar Garciaparra 1.00
46 Sammy Sosa 1.00
47 Carlos Lee .15
48 Kip Wells .15
49 Magglio Ordonez .25
50 Mark Buehrle .15
51 Paul Konerko .25
52 Roberto Alomar .25
53 Adam Dunn .40
54 Austin Kearns .25
55 Barry Larkin .25
56 Danny Graves .15
57 Ken Griffey Jr. 1.00
58 Sean Casey .15
59 C.C. Sabathia .15
60 Cliff Lee .15
61 Jody Gerut .15
62 Omar Vizquel .15

#	Player	Price		#	Player	Price
63	Travis Hafner	.15		182	Jeff Suppan	.15
64	Victor Martinez	.25		183	Jim Edmonds	.25
65	Charles Johnson	.15		184	Scott Rolen	.50
66	Jason Jennings	.15		185	Woody Williams	.15
67	Jeromy Burnitz	.15		186	Aubrey Huff	.15
68	Preston Wilson	.15		187	Carl Crawford	.15
69	Todd Helton	.40		188	Dewon Brazelton	.15
70	Bobby Higginson	.15		189	Jose Cruz Jr.	.15
71	Dmitri Young	.15		190	Rocco Baldelli	.25
72	Eric Munson	.15		191	Alfonso Soriano	.40
73	Ivan Rodriguez	.40		192	Hank Blalock	.40
74	Jeremy Bonderman	.15		193	Kenny Rogers	.15
75	Rondell White	.15		194	Laynce Nix	.15
76	A.J. Burnett	.15		195	Mark Teixeira	.25
77	Carl Pavano	.15		196	Michael Young	.15
78	Dontrelle Willis	.25		197	Alexis Rios	.15
79	Hee Seop Choi	.15		198	Carlos Delgado	.25
80	Josh Beckett	.25		199	Roy Halladay	.15
81	Juan Pierre	.15		200	Vernon Wells	.15
82	Miguel Cabrera	.50		201	Josh Kroeger	1.00
83	Mike Lowell	.15		202	Angel Guzman	1.00
84	Paul LoDuca	.15		203	Brad Halsey	1.00
85	Andy Pettitte	.25		204	Bucky Jacobsen	1.00
86	Carlos Beltran	.40		205	Carlos Hines	1.00
87	Craig Biggio	.25		206	Carlos Vasquez	1.00
88	Jeff Bagwell	.40		207	Billy Traber	1.00
89	Jeff Kent	.25		208	Bubba Crosby	1.00
90	Lance Berkman	.25		209	Chris Oxspring	1.00
91	Roger Clemens	1.50		210	Chris Shelton	1.00
92	Roy Oswalt	.25		211	Colby Miller	1.00
93	Andres Blanco	.15		212	David Crouthers	1.00
94	Jeremy Affeldt	.15		213	Dennis Sarfate	1.00
95	Juan Gonzalez	.25		214	Donald Kelly	1.00
96	Ken Harvey	.15		215	Edwardo Sierra	1.00
97	Mike Sweeney	.15		216	Edwin Moreno	1.00
98	Zack Greinke	.15		217	Fernando Nieve	1.00
99	Adrian Beltre	.25		218	Freddy Guzman	1.00
100	Brad Penny	.15		219	Greg Dobbs	1.00
101	Eric Gagne	.25		220	Hector Gimenez	1.00
102	Kazuhisa Ishii	.15		221	Andy Green	1.00
103	Milton Bradley	.15		222	Jason Bartlett	1.00
104	Shawn Green	.25		223	Jerry Gil	1.00
105	Steve Finley	.15		224	Jesse Crain	2.00
106	Ben Sheets	.25		225	Joey Gathright	1.00
107	Bill Hall	.15		226	John Gall	1.00
108	Danny Kolb	.15		227	Jorge Sequea	1.00
109	Geoff Jenkins	.15		228	Jorge Vasquez	1.00
110	Junior Spivey	.15		229	Josh Labandeira	1.00
111	Lyle Overbay	.15		230	Justin Leone	1.00
112	Scott Podsednik	.15		231	Lance Cormier	1.00
113	A.J. Pierzynski	.15		232	Lincoln Holdzkom	1.00
114	Brad Radke	.15		233	Miguel Olivo	1.00
115	Corey Koskie	.15		234	Mike Rouse	1.00
116	Jacque Jones	.15		235	Onil Joseph	1.00
117	Joe Mauer	.50		236	Phil Stockman	1.00
118	Joe Nathan	.15		237	Ramon Ramirez	1.00
119	Shannon Stewart	.15		238	Robb Quinlan	1.00
120	Torii Hunter	.25		239	Roberto Novoa	1.00
121	Brad Wilkerson	.15		240	Ronald Belisario	1.00
122	Jeff Fassero	.15		241	Ronny Cedeno	1.00
123	Jose Vidro	.15		242	Ruddy Yan	1.00
124	Livan Hernandez	.15		243	Ryan Meaux	1.00
125	Nick Johnson	.15		244	Ryan Wing	1.00
126	Al Leiter	.15		245	Scott Proctor	1.00
127	Jose Reyes	.25		246	Sean Henn	1.00
128	Kazuo Matsui	.25		247	Tim Bausher	1.00
129	Mike Cameron	.15		248	Tim Bittner	1.00
130	Mike Piazza	1.00		249	William Bergolla	1.00
131	Richard Hidalgo	.15		250	Yadier Molina	1.00
132	Tom Glavine	.25		251	Bernie Williams	1.00
133	Alex Rodriguez	1.50		252	Craig Biggio	1.00
134	Bernie Williams	.25		253	Chipper Jones	2.00
135	Derek Jeter	1.50		254	Greg Maddux	3.00
136	Gary Sheffield	.40		255	Sammy Sosa	3.00
137	Jason Giambi	.25		256	Mike Mussina	1.50
138	Javier Vazquez	.25		257	Tim Salmon	1.00
139	Jorge Posada	.25		258	Barry Larkin	1.00
140	Kevin Brown	.15		259	Randy Johnson	2.00
141	Mariano Rivera	.25		260	Jeff Bagwell	1.50
142	Mike Mussina	.25		261	Roberto Alomar	1.50
143	Barry Zito	.25		262	Tom Glavine	1.00
144	Bobby Crosby	.25		263	Roger Clemens	4.00
145	Eric Chavez	.25		264	Alex Rodriguez	4.00
146	Erubiel Durazo	.15		265	Ivan Rodriguez	1.50
147	Jermaine Dye	.15		266	Pedro J. Martinez	2.00
148	Mark Mulder	.25		267	Ken Griffey Jr.	3.00
149	Tim Hudson	.25		268	Jim Thome	2.00
150	Bobby Abreu	.25		269	Frank Thomas	1.50
151	Eric Milton	.15		270	Mike Piazza	3.00
152	Jim Thome	.50		271	Garret Anderson	1.00
153	Kevin Millwood	.15		272	Luis Gonzalez	1.00
154	Mike Lieberthal	.15		273	John Smoltz	1.00
155	Pat Burrell	.25		274	Rafael Palmeiro	1.50
156	Randy Wolf	.15		275	Curt Schilling	1.50
157	Craig Wilson	.15		276	Mark Prior	1.50
158	Jack Wilson	.15		277	Magglio Ordonez	1.00
159	Jason Bay	.25		278	Adam Dunn	1.50
160	Jason Kendall	.15		279	Travis Hafner	1.00
161	Kris Benson	.15		280	Jeromy Burnitz	1.00
162	Brian Giles	.15		281	Carlos Guillen	1.00
163	Jake Peavy	.25		282	Dontrelle Willis	1.50
164	Jay Payton	.15		283	Carlos Beltran	1.50
165	Khalil Greene	.15		284	Zack Greinke	1.00
166	Mark Loretta	.15		285	Adrian Beltre	1.00
167	Ryan Klesko	.15		286	Ben Sheets	1.00
168	Sean Burroughs	.15		287	Johan Santana	1.00
169	David Aardsma	.15		288	Livan Hernandez	1.00
170	Edgardo Alfonzo	.15		289	Kazuo Matsui	1.00
171	Jason Schmidt	.25		290	Derek Jeter	4.00
172	Merkin Valdez	.15		291	Tim Hudson	1.00
173	Ray Durham	.15		292	Eric Milton	1.00
174	Bret Boone	.15		293	Jason Kendall	1.00
175	Dan Wilson	.15		294	Jake Peavy	1.00
176	Ichiro Suzuki	1.25		295	Ray Durham	1.00
177	Jamie Moyer	.15		296	Ichiro Suzuki	3.00
178	Rich Aurilia	.15		297	Scott Rolen	2.00
179	Albert Pujols	1.50		298	Carl Crawford	1.00
180	Edgar Renteria	.25		299	Hank Blalock	1.50
181	Jason Isringhausen	.15		300	Roy Halladay	1.00

Press Proofs Blue

Blue (1-200):	5-10X
Blue (201-250):	1-2X
Blue (251-300):	2-4X
Production 75 Sets	

Press Proofs Gold

Gold (1-200):	10-20X
Gold (201-250):	2-4X
Blue (251-300):	4-8X
Production 25 Sets	

Press Proofs Red

Red (1-200):	2-4X
Red (201-250):	.5-1X
Red (251-300):	1-2X
Inserted 1:8	

Alternate Threads

	NM/M
Complete Set (25):	30.00
Common Player:	1.00
Inserted 1:18	
Holo:	1-2X
Production 150 Sets	
Holo Die-Cut:	2-4X
Production 50 Sets	

#	Player	Price
1	Adam Dunn	1.50
2	C.C. Sabathia	1.00
3	Curt Schilling	1.50
4	Dontrelle Willis	1.00
5	Greg Maddux	3.00
6	Hank Blalock	1.50
7	Ichiro Suzuki	4.00
8	Jeff Bagwell	1.50
9	Ken Griffey Jr.	3.00
10	Ken Harvey	1.00
11	Magglio Ordonez	1.00
12	Mark Mulder	1.00
13	Mark Teixeira	1.00
14	Michael Young	1.00
15	Miguel Tejada	1.50
16	Mike Piazza	4.00
17	Pedro Martinez	2.00
18	Randy Johnson	2.00
19	Roger Clemens	6.00
20	Sammy Sosa	4.00
21	Tim Hudson	1.00
22	Todd Helton	1.50
23	Torii Hunter	1.00
24	Travis Hafner	1.00
25	Vernon Wells	1.00

Autographs

	NM/M
Common Autograph:	5.00

#	Player	Price
201	Josh Kroeger	5.00
202	Angel Guzman	10.00
203	Brad Halsey	5.00
204	Bucky Jacobsen	10.00
205	Carlos Hines	5.00
207	Bill Tucker	5.00
208	Bubba Crosby	10.00
210	Chris Shelton	10.00
211	Colby Miller	5.00
212	David Crouthers	5.00
217	Fernando Nieve	10.00
220	Hector Gimenez	5.00
221	Andy Green	5.00
222	Jason Bartlett	5.00
227	Jorge Sequea/84	10.00
228	Jorge Vasquez	8.00
232	Lincoln Holdzkom	8.00
233	Miguel Olivo	8.00
234	Mike Rouse	8.00
236	Phil Stockman	8.00
237	Ramon Ramirez	8.00
242	Ruddy Yan	5.00
245	Scott Proctor	8.00
247	Tim Bausher	8.00
249	William Bergolla	10.00

Autographs Blue

No Pricing
Production 15-25
Golds: No Pricing

Autographs Red

#	Player	NM/M
	Common Autograph:	
3	Chone Figgins/100	8.00
19	Johnny Estrada/100	15.00
24	Jay Gibbons/100	10.00
47	Carlos Lee/100	10.00
56	Danny Graves/100	8.00
60	Cliff Lee/100	10.00
63	Travis Hafner/50	15.00
74	Jeremy Bonderman/100	10.00
94	Jeremy Affeldt/100	8.00
96	Ken Harvey/100	8.00
103	Milton Bradley/100	10.00
111	Lyle Overbay/50	15.00
118	Joe Nathan/100	8.00
144	Bobby Crosby/100	25.00
154	Mike Lieberthal/50	15.00
157	Craig Wilson/100	15.00
158	Jack Wilson/100	12.00
163	Jake Peavy/50	15.00
172	Merkin Valdez/100	8.00
187	Jeff Suppan/100	8.00
188	Carl Crawford/50	15.00
190	Dewon Brazelton/50	10.00
194	Laynce Nix/100	8.00
201	Josh Kroeger/100	8.00
202	Angel Guzman/100	8.00
203	Brad Halsey/100	8.00
204	Bucky Jacobsen/100	10.00
205	Carlos Hines/100	8.00
207	Billy Traber/100	8.00
208	Bubba Crosby/100	10.00
210	Chris Shelton/100	8.00
211	Colby Miller/100	8.00
212	David Crouthers/100	8.00
217	Fernando Nieve/100	10.00
218	Freddy Guzman/100	8.00
220	Hector Gimenez/100	8.00
221	Andy Green/100	8.00
222	Jason Bartlett/100	8.00
224	Josh Crain/100	15.00
227	Jorge Sequea/84	10.00
228	Jorge Vasquez/100	8.00
233	Miguel Olivo/100	8.00
234	Mike Rouse/100	8.00
236	Phil Stockman/100	10.00
237	Ramon Ramirez/100	8.00
238	Robb Quinlan/100	8.00
241	Ronny Cedeno/65	10.00
242	Ruddy Yan/100	8.00
243	Ryan Meaux/93	8.00
247	Tim Bausher/100	8.00
249	William Bergolla/100	10.00
250	Yadier Molina/100	15.00

Certified Materials Preview

	NM/M
Complete Set (15):	25.00
Common Player:	1.50
Inserted 1:21	
Blue:	2-3X
Production 100 Sets	
Gold:	4-8X
Production 25 Sets	
Red:	1-2X
Production 200 Sets	

#	Player	Price
1	Albert Pujols	4.00
2	Alex Rodriguez	3.00
3	Alfonso Soriano	1.50
4	Curt Schilling	1.50
5	Derek Jeter	4.00
6	Greg Maddux	2.00
7	Ichiro Suzuki	3.00
8	Jim Thome	1.50
9	Ken Griffey Jr.	2.00
10	Manny Ramirez	1.50
11	Mark Prior	1.50
12	Randy Johnson	1.50
13	Roger Clemens	2.00
14	Sammy Sosa	2.50
15	Vladimir Guerrero	1.50

Clean Up Crew

	NM/M
Complete Set (15):	45.00
Common Card:	
Inserted 1:49	
Die-Cut:	1X
Production 250 Sets	

#	Players	Price
1	Albert Pujols, Jim Edmonds, Scott Rolen	6.00
2	Melvin Mora, Miguel Tejada, Rafael Palmeiro	3.00
3	Alfonso Soriano, Michael Young, Hank Blalock	3.00
4	Gary Sheffield, Alex Rodriguez, Hideki Matsui	3.00
5	Moises Alou, Sammy Sosa, Nomar Garciaparra	5.00
6	Paul LoDuca, Mike Lowell, Miguel Cabrera	3.00
7	Carlos Beltran, Lance Berkman, Jeff Bagwell	3.00
8	Paul Konerko, Magglio Ordonez, Frank Thomas	5.00
9	Sean Casey, Ken Griffey Jr., Adam Dunn	5.00
10	Vladimir Guerrero, Garret Anderson, Troy Glaus	3.00
11	Joe Morgan, Johnny Bench, Tony Perez	3.00
12	Keith Hernandez, Darryl Strawberry, Gary Carter	2.00
13	Jim Rice, Carl Yastrzemski, Dwight Evans	5.00
14	Ryne Sandberg, Andre Dawson, Mark Grace	6.00
15	Cal Ripken Jr., Eddie Murray, Rafael Palmeiro	10.00

Cornerstones

	NM/M
Complete Set (20):	50.00
Common Card:	1.50
Inserted 1:37	

#	Players	Price
1	Albert Pujols, Scott Rolen	6.00
2	Hideki Matsui, Jorge Posada	5.00
3	Nomar Garciaparra, Sammy Sosa	4.00
4	David Ortiz, Manny Ramirez	3.00
5	Miguel Cabrera, Mike Lowell	3.00
6	Hank Blalock, Mark Teixeira	2.00
7	Chipper Jones, J.D. Drew	3.00
8	Craig Biggio, Jeff Bagwell	3.00
9	Kazuo Matsui, Mike Piazza	3.00
10	Shawn Green, Adrian Beltre	1.50
11	Bobby Abreu, Jim Thome	3.00
12	Mike Schmidt, Steve Carlton	6.00
13	Cal Ripken Jr., Eddie Murray	10.00
14	Carl Yastrzemski, Dwight Evans	5.00
15	Joe Morgan, Johnny Bench	3.00
16	Dale Murphy, Phil Niekro	2.00
17	Alan Trammell, Kirk Gibson	2.00
18	Jose Canseco, Rickey Henderson	3.00
19	Paul Molitor, Robin Yount	4.00
20	Bo Jackson, George Brett	6.00

Cornerstones Bats

	NM/M
Common Dual Bat:	8.00

#	Players	Price
1	Albert Pujols, Scott Rolen	20.00
2	Hideki Matsui, Jorge Posada	35.00
3	Sammy Sosa, Nomar Garciaparra	15.00
4	Manny Ramirez, David Ortiz	20.00
5	Miguel Cabrera, Mike Lowell	10.00
6	Hank Blalock, Mark Teixeira	10.00
7	Chipper Jones, J.D. Drew	15.00
8	Craig Biggio, Jeff Bagwell	10.00
9	Mike Piazza, Kazuo Matsui	15.00
10	Shawn Green, Adrian Beltre	8.00

Cornerstones Jerseys

	NM/M
Common Dual Jersey:	8.00

#	Players	Price
1	Albert Pujols, Scott Rolen	20.00
2	Hideki Matsui, Jorge Posada	35.00
4	Manny Ramirez, David Ortiz	20.00
5	Miguel Cabrera, Mike Lowell	10.00
6	Hank Blalock, Mark Teixeira	10.00
8	Craig Biggio, Jeff Bagwell	10.00
9	Mike Piazza, Kazuo Matsui	15.00
10	Shawn Green, Adrian Beltre	8.00

Cy Young Winners

	NM/M
Complete Set (15):	30.00
Common Player:	1.50
Inserted 1:31	
Gold:	1X
Production 350 Sets	
Gold Die-Cut:	1.5-2X
Production 100 Sets	

#	Player	Price
1	Warren Spahn	3.00
2	Whitey Ford	3.00
3	Bob Gibson	3.00
4	Tom Seaver	3.00
5	Steve Carlton	2.00
6	Jim Palmer	2.00
7	Rollie Fingers	1.50
8	Dwight Gooden	1.50
9	Roger Clemens	6.00
10	Orel Hershiser	1.50
11	Greg Maddux	4.00
12	Dennis Eckersley	1.50
13	Randy Johnson	3.00
14	Pedro Martinez	3.00
15	Eric Gagne	2.00

Game Collection

	NM/M
Inserted 1:118	

#	Player	Price
1	Cal Ripken Jr./Bat	30.00
2	Carl Crawford/Jsy	5.00
3	Dale Murphy/Bat	20.00
4	Don Mattingly/Bat	25.00
5	George Brett/Jsy	25.00
6	Victor Martinez/Bat	8.00
7	Sean Casey/Bat	5.00
8	Torii Hunter/Bat	5.00
10	Magglio Ordonez/Bat	5.00
11	Lance Berkman/Bat	5.00
11	Mike Schmidt/Bat	25.00
12	Nolan Ryan/Jkt	40.00
13	Paul LoDuca/Bat	5.00
14	Preston Wilson/Bat	5.00
15	Rod Carew/Jkt	10.00
16	Reggie Jackson/Bat	10.00
17	Ivan Rodriguez/Bat	8.00
18	Larry Walker/Cards Bat	10.00
19	Miguel Tejada/Bat	10.00
20	Vladimir Guerrero/Bat	10.00

Game Collection Autograph

	NM/M
Production 5-200	

#	Player	Price
2	Carl Crawford/Jsy/200	15.00
5	Victor Martinez/Bat/200	20.00
7	Sean Casey/Bat/200	8.00
9	Torii Hunter/Bat/50	25.00
13	Paul LoDuca/Bat/100	20.00

Gamers

	NM/M
Complete Set (15):	20.00
Common Player:	1.00
Inserted 1:13	
Quantum:	2-3X
Production 175 Sets	
Quantum Die-Cut:	3-5X
Production 50 Sets	

GAMERS

1	Albert Pujols	4.00
2	Alex Rodriguez	3.00
3	Alfonso Soriano	1.50
4	Chipper Jones	1.50
5	Derek Jeter	4.00
6	Greg Maddux	2.00
7	Ichiro Suzuki	3.00
8	Jim Thome	1.50
9	Ken Griffey Jr.	2.00
10	Lance Berkman	1.00
11	Miguel Tejada	1.00
12	Mike Piazza	2.50
13	Roger Clemens	4.00
14	Scott Rolen	1.50
15	Vladimir Guerrero	1.50

Gold Rookies

Complete Set (10): 15.00
Common Player: 2.00
Inserted 1:24
Mirror: 3-5X
Production 25 Sets

1	Dennis Sarfate	2.00
2	Donnie Kelly	2.00
3	Eddy Rodriguez	2.00
4	Edwin Moreno	2.00
5	Greg Dobbs	2.00
6	Josh Labandeira	2.00
7	Kevin Cave	2.00
8	Mariano Gomez	2.00
9	Ronald Belisario	2.00
10	Ruddy Yan	2.00

Gold Rookies Autograph

Common Autograph:
Mirror: No Pricing
Production 25 Sets

1	Dennis Sarfate	10.00
2	Donnie Kelly	8.00
5	Greg Dobbs	8.00
6	Kevin Cave	10.00
9	Ronald Belisario	8.00
10	Ruddy Yan	8.00

Gold Stars

Complete Set (20): 40.00
Common Player: .75
Inserted 1:27
Mirror: 4-6X
Production 25 Sets

1	Albert Pujols	4.00
2	Ichiro Suzuki	3.00
3	Derek Jeter	4.00
4	Alex Rodriguez	3.00
5	Scott Rolen	1.50
6	Randy Johnson	1.50
7	Roger Clemens	4.00
8	Greg Maddux	2.00
9	Alfonso Soriano	1.50
10	Mark Mulder	.75
11	Sammy Sosa	3.00
12	Mike Piazza	3.00
13	Rafael Palmeiro	.75
14	Ivan Rodriguez	.75
15	Miguel Cabrera	.75
16	Stan Musial	3.00
17	Nolan Ryan	6.00
18	Don Mattingly	4.00
19	George Brett	4.00
20	Cal Ripken Jr.	6.00

Home/Road

MIGUEL CABRERA

NM/M
Common Player: 1.00
Inserted 1:22
Home & Road price is identical.

1H	Albert Pujols/H	4.00
1R	Albert Pujols/R	4.00
2H	Alfonso Soriano/H	1.50
2R	Alfonso Soriano/R	1.50
3H	Carlos Beltran/H	1.00
3R	Carlos Beltran/R	1.00
4H	Chipper Jones/H	1.50
4R	Chipper Jones/R	1.50
5H	Frank Thomas/H	1.50
5R	Frank Thomas/R	1.50
6H	Hank Blalock/H	1.00
6R	Hank Blalock/R	1.00
7H	Ivan Rodriguez/H	1.50
7R	Ivan Rodriguez/R	1.50
8H	Manny Ramirez/H	1.50
8R	Manny Ramirez/R	1.50
9H	Mark Prior/H	1.50
9R	Mark Prior/R	1.50
10H	Miguel Cabrera/H	1.50
10R	Miguel Cabrera/R	1.50
11H	Miguel Tejada/H	1.00
11R	Miguel Tejada/R	1.00
12H	Mike Piazza/H	2.50
12R	Mike Piazza/R	2.50
13H	Roger Clemens/H	4.00
13R	Roger Clemens/R	4.00
14H	Todd Helton/H	1.50
14R	Todd Helton/R	1.50
15H	Vladimir Guerrero/H	1.50
15R	Vladimir Guerrero/R	1.50

Home/Road Jersey

NM/M
Common Player:

1H	Albert Pujols/H	20.00
1R	Albert Pujols/R	20.00
2H	Alfonso Soriano/H	8.00
3H	Carlos Beltran/H	8.00
3R	Carlos Beltran/R	8.00
4R	Chipper Jones/R	8.00
5H	Frank Thomas/H	8.00
5R	Frank Thomas/R	8.00
6H	Hank Blalock/H	8.00
7H	Ivan Rodriguez/H	8.00
7R	Ivan Rodriguez/R	8.00
8R	Manny Ramirez/R	8.00
9H	Mark Prior/H	8.00
11H	Miguel Tejada/H	5.00
11R	Miguel Tejada/R	5.00
12H	Mike Mussina	12.00
13H	Roger Clemens/H	15.00
13R	Roger Clemens/R	15.00
14H	Todd Helton/H	8.00
14R	Todd Helton/R	8.00
15H	Vladimir Guerrero/H	8.00

Patch Off My Back

NM/M
Common Patch: 15.00
Production 50 Sets

1	Adam Dunn	25.00
2	Aubrey Huff	15.00
3	Austin Kearns	15.00
4	Bobby Crosby	25.00
5	C.C. Sabathia	15.00
7	David Ortiz	25.00
8	Dewon Brazelton	15.00
9	Edgar Martinez	20.00
10	Frankie Francisco	15.00
11	Garret Anderson	20.00
12	Hideki Matsui	50.00
13	Hideo Nomo	20.00
14	Jack Wilson	15.00
15	Javy Lopez	15.00
16	Jay Gibbons	15.00
17	Jim Edmonds	20.00
18	Jody Gerut	15.00
19	Joey Gathright	15.00
20	Johan Santana	20.00
21	Jose Reyes	15.00
22	Jose Vidro	15.00
23	Lance Berkman	15.00
24	Mariano Rivera	20.00
25	Mark Teixeira	20.00
26	Michael Young	15.00
27	Mike Cameron	15.00
28	Mike Sweeney	15.00
29	Omar Vizquel	15.00
30	Preston Wilson	15.00
31	Rocco Baldelli	15.00
32	Scott Rolen	25.00
33	Sean Burroughs	15.00
34	Sean Casey	15.00
35	Tim Hudson	20.00
36	Torii Hunter	20.00
37	Trevor Hoffman	20.00
38	Troy Glaus	20.00
39	Vernon Wells	15.00
40	Victor Martinez	20.00

Patch Off My Back Autograph

NM/M
Production 10-75

2	Aubrey Huff/50	35.00
3	Bobby Crosby/75	50.00
5	C.C. Sabathia/75	30.00
7	David Ortiz/50	100.00
8	Dewon Brazelton/75	25.00
14	Jack Wilson/75	30.00
16	Jay Gibbons/50	25.00
18	Jody Gerut/75	20.00
20	Johan Santana/50	60.00
22	Jose Vidro/75	25.00
26	Michael Young/75	35.00
33	Sean Burroughs/25	25.00
40	Victor Martinez/75	35.00

Picture Perfect

Picture Perfect — MARK PRIOR

NM/M
Complete Set (20): 30.00
Common Player: 1.00
Inserted 1:20
Die-Cut: 2-3X
Production 100 Sets

1	Albert Pujols	4.00
2	Alex Rodriguez	3.00
3	Alfonso Soriano	1.50
4	Derek Jeter	4.00
5	Greg Maddux	2.00
6	Hideki Matsui	3.00
7	Ichiro Suzuki	3.00
8	Ivan Rodriguez	1.50
9	Jim Thome	1.50
10	Mark Mulder	1.00
11	Mark Prior	1.00
12	Miguel Tejada	1.00
13	Mike Mussina	1.00
14	Mike Piazza	2.50
15	Nomar Garciaparra	2.50
16	Randy Johnson	1.50
17	Roger Clemens	4.00
18	Sammy Sosa	3.00
19	Scott Rolen	1.50
20	Vladimir Guerrero	1.50

Recollection Autographs

No Pricing
Production 1-29

Shirt Off My Back

NM/M
Common Player: 5.00
Inserted 1:48

1	Adam Dunn	15.00
4	Bobby Crosby	15.00
5	C.C. Sabathia	8.00
6	David Ortiz	15.00
8	Dewon Brazelton	5.00
10	Edgar Martinez	5.00
11	Frankie Francisco	5.00
12	Garret Anderson	5.00
13	Hideki Matsui	25.00
14	Hideo Nomo	5.00
15	Jack Wilson	5.00
16	Javy Lopez	8.00
16	Jay Gibbons	5.00
17	Jim Edmonds	15.00
18	Jody Gerut/SP	5.00
19	Joey Gathright	5.00
20	Johan Santana	10.00
21	Jose Reyes	5.00
22	Jose Vidro	5.00
23	Lance Berkman	5.00
25	Mark Teixeira	5.00
26	Michael Young	5.00
27	Mike Cameron	5.00
28	Mike Sweeney	5.00
29	Omar Vizquel	8.00
30	Preston Wilson	5.00
31	Rocco Baldelli	8.00
32	Scott Rolen	10.00
33	Sean Burroughs	5.00
34	Sean Casey	5.00
35	Tim Hudson	5.00
36	Torii Hunter	5.00
37	Trevor Hoffman	5.00
38	Troy Glaus	5.00
39	Vernon Wells	5.00
40	Victor Martinez	8.00

Sportscasters 70 Green

Baseball — Steve Carlton

NM/M
Common Player: 2.00
Production 70 Sets
Variations #'d 35-65: 1X
Variations #'d 20-30: 1.5X
No pricing 15 or less.

1	Adam Dunn	3.00
2	Al Kaline	5.00
3	Albert Pujols	8.00
4	Alex Rodriguez	8.00
5	Alfonso Soriano	3.00
6	Bob Gibson	3.00
7	Cal Ripken Jr.	25.00
8	Carl Yastrzemski	8.00
9	Dale Murphy	3.00
10	Derek Jeter	10.00
11	Don Mattingly	10.00
12	Duke Snider	4.00
13	Eric Gagne	3.00
14	Ernie Banks	6.00
15	Frank Robinson	3.00
16	George Brett	10.00
17	Greg Maddux	6.00
18	Harmon Killebrew	5.00
19	Ichiro Suzuki	8.00
20	Ivan Rodriguez	4.00
21	Jim Edmonds	2.00
22	Jim Palmer	3.00
23	Jim Thome	4.00
24	Johnny Bench	5.00
25	Ken Griffey Jr.	6.00
26	Larry Walker	3.00
27	Mark Mulder	2.00
28	Mark Prior	4.00
29	Miguel Tejada	3.00
30	Mike Mussina	3.00
31	Mike Piazza	6.00
32	Mike Schmidt	10.00
33	Nolan Ryan	15.00
34	Nomar Garciaparra	4.00
35	Pedro Martinez	4.00
36	Rafael Palmeiro	3.00
37	Randy Johnson	3.00
38	Reggie Jackson	3.00
39	Rickey Henderson	4.00
40	Roberto Clemente	15.00
41	Rod Carew	3.00
42	Roger Clemens	6.00
43	Ryne Sandberg	4.00
44	Sammy Sosa	6.00
45	Stan Musial	8.00
46	Steve Carlton	2.00
47	Tony Gwynn	5.00
48	Vladimir Guerrero	4.00
49	Warren Spahn	4.00
50	Willie McCovey	3.00

4 Star Staffs

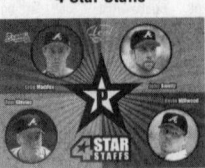

NM/M
Common Card: 2.00
Inserted 1:48
Die-Cut: 1X
Production 250 Sets

1	Greg Maddux, John Smoltz, Kevin Millwood, Tom Glavine	4.00
2	A.J. Burnett, Carl Pavano, Dontrelle Willis, Josh Beckett	2.00
3	Andy Pettitte, David Wells, Mike Mussina, Roger Clemens	6.00
4	Carlos Zambrano, Greg Maddux, Kerry Wood, Mark Prior	4.00
5	Andy Pettitte, Mariano Rivera, Mike Mussina, Roger Clemens	4.00
6	Curt Schilling, Derek Lowe, Pedro J. Martinez, Tim Wakefield	4.00
7	Barry Zito, Mark Mulder, Rich Harden, Tim Hudson	2.00
8	Brandon Webb, Byung-Hyun Kim, Curt Schilling, Randy Johnson	3.00
9	Jamie Moyer, Kenny Rogers, Kevin Brown, Nolan Ryan	8.00
10	Kelvim Escobar, Roger Clemens, Roy Halladay, Woody Williams	6.00
11	Andy Pettitte, Roger Clemens, Roy Oswalt, Wade Miller	6.00
12	Barry Zito, Billy Koch, Mark Mulder, Tim Hudson	2.00
13	Eric Gagne, Hideo Nomo, Kazuhisa Ishii, Kevin Brown	3.00
14	Greg Maddux, Jason Schmidt, John Smoltz, Tom Glavine	6.00
15	Derek Lowe, Hideo Nomo, Pedro Martinez, Tim Wakefield	4.00

2005 Leaf Century

JOHAN SANTANA

NM/M
Complete Set (200): 40.00
Common Player: .25
Pack (5): 12.00
Box (10): 100.00

1	Brian Roberts	.25
2	Derek Jeter	2.00
3	Harmon Killebrew	.50
4	Angel Berroa	.25
5	George Brett	2.00
6	Stan Musial	1.50
7	Ivan Rodriguez	.50
8	Cal Ripken Jr.	3.00
9	Hank Blalock	.50
10	Miguel Tejada	.50
11	Barry Larkin	.40
12	Alfonso Soriano	.75
13	Alex Rodriguez	2.00
14	Paul Konerko	.25
15	Jim Edmonds	.40
16	Garret Anderson	.40
17	Todd Helton	.50
18	Moises Alou	.40
19	Tony Gwynn	.75
20	Mike Schmidt	2.00
21	Sammy Sosa	1.25
22	Roger Clemens	2.00
23	Tony Perez	.25
24	Manny Ramirez	.75
25	Jim Thome	.75
26	Chase Utley	.40
27	Scott Rolen	.75
28	Austin Kearns	.25
29	John Smoltz	.40
30	Ken Griffey Jr.	1.00
31	Mike Piazza	1.00
32	Steve Carlton	.50
33	Larry Walker	.40
34	Nolan Ryan	2.50
35	Mike Mussina	.40
36	Joe Nathan	.25
37	Kenny Rogers	.25
38	Eric Gagne	.40
39	Brett Myers	.25
40	Rich Harden	.25
41	Victor Martinez	.40
42	Mariano Rivera	.40
43	Dennis Eckersley	.50
44	Roy Oswalt	.25
45	Pedro Martinez	.75
46	Jason Bay	.40
47	Tom Glavine	.40
48	Torii Hunter	.25
49	Larry Bigbie	.25
50	Nomar Garciaparra	1.50
51	Ichiro Suzuki	1.50
52	C.C. Sabathia	.25
53	Bobby Abreu	.40
54	Doug Mientkiewicz	.25
55	Hideki Matsui	1.50
56	Mark Buehrle	.25
57	Johan Santana	.50
58	Johnny Damon	.75
59	Edgar Martinez	.40
60	Preston Wilson	.25
61	Livan Hernandez	.25
62	Eric Chavez	.25
63	Lyle Overbay	.40
64	Jason Schmidt	.50
65	Cliff Lee	.25
66	Shingo Takatsu	.25
67	Jeff Bagwell	.50
68	Danny Graves	.25
69	Kip Wells	.25
70	Steve Finley	.25
71	Lew Ford	.25
72	Chone Figgins	.25
73	Delmon Young	.40
74	Esteban Loaiza	.25
75	Barry Zito	.40
76	Carlos Delgado	.40
77	Joe Mauer	.50
78	Ryan Wagner	.25
79	John Lackey	.25
80	Adrian Beltre	.40
81	Vernon Wells	.25
82	Sean Burroughs	.25
83	Francisco Cordero	.25
84	Carlos Guillen	.25
85	Eric Byrnes	.25
86	Jose Reyes	.40
87	Rocco Baldelli	.40
88	Josh Beckett	.40
89	Casey Kotchman	.25
90	Scott Podsednik	.25
91	Mike Sweeney	.25
92	Khalil Greene	.50
93	Trot Nixon	.25
94	Chad Cordero	.25
95	Derek Lowe	.25
96	Jason Giambi	.40
97	Jose Guillen	.25
98	Craig Biggio	.40
99	Pat Burrell	.40
100	Kazuo Matsui	.25
101	Rafael Furcal	.25
102	Jack Wilson	.25
103	Edgar Renteria	.50
104	Carlos Beltran	.75
105	Albert Pujols	2.00
106	Melvin Mora	.25
107	J.D. Drew	.40
108	Andre Dawson	.50
109	Jody Gerut	.25
110	Michael Young	.25
111	Gary Sheffield	.50
112	Wade Boggs	.50
113	Carl Crawford	.25
114	Paul LoDuca	.25
115	Tim Hudson	.40
116	Aramis Ramirez	.40
117	Lance Berkman	.40
118	Javy Lopez	.40
119	Robin Yount	1.00
120	Mark Mulder	.25
121	Sean Casey	.25
122	Will Clark	.50
123	Don Mattingly	2.00
124	Miguel Cabrera	.75
125	Rafael Palmeiro	.50
126	David Ortiz	.75
127	Vladimir Guerrero	.75
128	Ken Harvey	.25
129	Rod Carew	.50
130	Magglio Ordonez	.25
131	Greg Maddux	1.00
132	Roy Halladay	.25
133	Javier Vazquez	.25
134	Kerry Wood	.75
135	Frank Thomas	.50
136	Tom Gordon	.25
137	Jake Peavy	.25
138	Curt Schilling	.75
139	Dewon Brazelton	.25
140	Jae Weong Seo	.25
141	Danny Kolb	.25
142	Jeff Kent	.40
143	Juan Encarnacion	.25
144	Adam Dunn	.50
145	Carlos Lee	.25
146	Matt Clement	.25
147	Guillermo Mota	.25
148	Travis Hafner	.25
149	Brad Wilkerson	.25
150	Eric Milton	.25
151	Randy Johnson	.75
152	Joe Crede	.25
153	Mark Kotsay	.25
154	Jason Varitek	.40
155	David Wright	.75
156	Brad Penny	.25
157	Francisco Rodriguez	.25
158	Gary Carter	.50
159	Adrian Gonzalez	.25
160	Derrek Lee	.40
161	Mark Prior	.50
162	Carlos Zambrano	.25
163	Bobby Crosby	.40

164 Jermaine Dye .25
165 Kris Benson .25
166 Dontrelle Willis .40
167 Dallas McPherson .40
168 Johnny Estrada .40
169 Milton Bradley .25
170 Shannon Stewart .25
171 Ben Sheets .40
172 Richard Hidalgo .25
173 Laynce Nix .25
174 B.J. Upton .50
175 Craig Wilson .25
176 Hideo Nomo .40
177 Troy Glaus .42
178 Akinori Otsuka .25
179 Rickie Weeks .40
180 Mike Lowell .40
181 Marcus Giles .25
182 Randy Wolf .25
183 A.J. Burnett .25
184 Aubrey Huff .25
185 Billy Ripken .25
186 Octavio Dotel .25
187 Kazuhisa Ishii .25
188 Mark Teixeira .50
189 Todd Walker .25
190 Dale Murphy .50
191 Alexis Rios .25
192 Reggie Sanders .25
193 Orlando Cabrera .40
194 Shawn Green .40
195 Andy Pettitte .25
196 Chipper Jones .75
197 Jose Vidro .25
198 Jacque Jones .25
199 Brian Giles .25
200 Andruw Jones .40

Post Marks Silver

Silvers: 3-6X
Production 100 Sets

Post Marks Gold

Golds: 4-8X
Production 50 Sets

Post Marks Platinum

No Pricing
Production One Set

Air Mail Bat

NM/M
Production 50-250
1 Babe Ruth/50 150.00
2 Frank Robinson/250 12.00
3 Harmon Killebrew/100 20.00
4 Sammy Sosa/100 10.00
5 Reggie Jackson/250 15.00
6 Mike Schmidt/100 20.00
7 Rafael Palmeiro/100 8.00
8 Ted Williams/50 80.00
9 Willie McCovey/250 10.00
10 Ernie Banks/100 20.00

Air Mail Bat Signature

NM/M
Production 1-25
2 Frank Robinson/25 40.00
3 Harmon Killebrew/25 60.00
9 Willie McCovey/25 35.00

Material Bat

NM/M
Common Player: 5.00
3 Harmon Killebrew/250 12.00
4 Angel Berroa/50 5.00
5 George Brett/250 15.00
8 Stan Musial/250 15.00
9 Ivan Rodriguez/100 8.00

8 Cal Ripken Jr./250 25.00
9 Hank Blalock/100 8.00
10 Miguel Tejada/100 6.00
11 Barry Larkin/100 6.00
12 Alfonso Soriano/100 8.00
14 Paul Konerko/50 5.00
15 Jim Edmonds/100 5.00
16 Garret Anderson/100 5.00
17 Todd Helton/100 8.00
18 Moises Alou/100 5.00
19 Tony Gwynn/250 10.00
20 Mike Schmidt/100 15.00
21 Sammy Sosa/100 10.00
22 Roger Clemens/100 15.00
23 Tony Perez/100 8.00
24 Manny Ramirez/100 10.00
25 Jim Thome/100 12.00
27 Scott Rolen/100 10.00
31 Austin Kearns/50 5.00
31 Mike Piazza/100 12.00
32 Steve Carlton/100 8.00
33 Larry Walker/100 8.00
34 Nolan Ryan/250 20.00
41 Mike Mussina/100 8.00
41 Victor Martinez/50 5.00
45 Roy Oswalt/100 5.00
45 Pedro Martinez/100 6.00
47 Tom Glavine/100 6.00
48 Torii Hunter/100 6.00
50 Nomar Garciaparra/100 15.00
53 Bobby Abreu/25 10.00
54 Doug Mientkiewicz/50 5.00
55 Hideki Matsui/100 25.00
56 Mark Buehrle/100 5.00
58 Johnny Damon/100 12.00
59 Edgar Martinez/100 6.00
60 Preston Wilson/50 5.00
62 Eric Chavez/100 5.00
63 Lyle Overbay/100 5.00
67 Jeff Bagwell/100 8.00
71 Lew Ford/50 5.00
73 Delmon Young/100 8.00
75 Barry Zito/100 5.00
76 Carlos Delgado/100 8.00
80 Adrian Beltre/100 8.00
81 Vernon Wells/100 5.00
86 Jose Reyes/100 8.00
87 Rocco Baldelli/100 5.00
88 Josh Beckett/100 5.00
91 Mike Sweeney/100 5.00
93 Trot Nixon/50 5.00
96 Jason Giambi/100 5.00
98 Craig Biggio/100 5.00
99 Pat Burrell/50 8.00
100 Kazuo Matsui/50 5.00
101 Rafael Furcal/50 6.00
102 Jack Wilson/50 8.00
103 Edgar Renteria/100 8.00
104 Carlos Beltran/100 8.00
105 Albert Pujols/50 15.00
106 Melvin Mora/50 5.00
107 J.D. Drew/50 6.00
108 Andre Dawson/250 5.00
109 Jody Gerut/50 6.00
110 Michael Young/250 5.00
111 Gary Sheffield/100 6.00
112 Wade Boggs/250 5.00
114 Paul LoDuca/100 10.00
115 Tim Hudson/100 5.00
116 Aramis Ramirez/250 5.00
117 Lance Berkman/250 5.00
118 Javy Lopez/100 5.00
119 Robin Yount/100 10.00
120 Mark Mulder/100 5.00
121 Sean Casey/100 5.00
122 Will Clark/250 5.00
123 Don Mattingly/250 15.00
124 Miguel Cabrera/100 12.00
125 Rafael Palmeiro/250 8.00
126 David Ortiz/250 12.00
127 Vladimir Guerrero/250 8.00
128 Ken Harvey/250 5.00
129 Rod Carew/250 8.00
130 Magglio Ordonez/250 5.00
131 Greg Maddux/100 10.00
134 Kerry Wood/100 8.00
135 Frank Thomas/100 8.00
138 Curt Schilling/100 5.00
142 Jeff Kent/250 5.00
143 Juan Encarnacion/50 5.00
144 Adam Dunn/250 8.00
145 Carlos Lee/250 5.00
148 Travis Hafner/50 6.00
149 Brad Wilkerson/50 5.00
151 Randy Johnson/100 10.00
152 Joe Crede/50 5.00
154 Jason Varitek/250 10.00
156 Brad Penny/50 5.00
158 Gary Carter/250 5.00
160 Derrek Lee/250 5.00
161 Mark Prior/250 8.00
164 Jermaine Dye/50 5.00
166 Dontrelle Willis/50 5.00
168 Johnny Estrada/50 6.00
170 Shannon Stewart/100 5.00
171 Ben Sheets/50 5.00
172 Richard Hidalgo/50 5.00
173 Laynce Nix/50 5.00
174 B.J. Upton/50 8.00
175 Craig Wilson/100 5.00
176 Hideo Nomo/100 8.00
177 Troy Glaus/25 5.00
179 Rickie Weeks/25 5.00
180 Mike Lowell/100 5.00
183 A.J. Burnett/50 5.00
184 Aubrey Huff/50 5.00
187 Kazuhisa Ishii/50 5.00
188 Mark Teixeira/250 5.00

190 Dale Murphy/250 8.00
191 Alexis Rios/50 5.00
193 Orlando Cabrera/50 6.00
194 Shawn Green/250 5.00
195 Andy Pettitte/100 6.00
196 Chipper Jones/100 5.00
197 Jose Vidro/250 5.00
198 Jacque Jones/100 5.00
199 Brian Giles/100 5.00
200 Andruw Jones/250 5.00

Material Fabric Number

NM/M
Common Player: 5.00
20 Mike Schmidt/Jsy/20 50.00
21 Sammy Sosa/Jsy/21 20.00
22 Roger Clemens/Jsy/22 40.00
23 Tony Perez/Jsy/24 15.00
24 Manny Ramirez/Jsy/24 20.00
25 Jim Thome/Jsy/25 20.00
27 Scott Rolen/Jsy/27 20.00
28 Austin Kearns/Jsy/28 15.00
29 John Smoltz/Jsy/29 15.00
31 Mike Piazza/Jsy/31 25.00
32 Steve Carlton/Pants/32 15.00
34 Nolan Ryan/Jsy/34 15.00
35 Mike Mussina/Jsy/35 15.00
39 Brett Myers/Jsy/39 8.00
41 Victor Martinez/Jsy/41 8.00
42 Mariano Rivera/Jsy/42 15.00
43 Dennis Eckersley/Jsy/43 10.00
44 Roy Oswalt/Jsy/44 8.00
45 Pedro Martinez/Jsy/45 10.00
47 Tom Glavine/Jsy/47 10.00
48 Torii Hunter/Jsy/48 8.00
52 C.C. Sabathia/Jsy/52 8.00
53 Bobby Abreu/Jsy/53 8.00
55 Hideki Matsui/Jsy/55 35.00
56 Mark Buehrle/Jsy/56 8.00
57 Johan Santana/Jsy/57 15.00
60 Preston Wilson/Jsy/44 8.00
61 Livan Hernandez/Jsy/61 5.00
65 Cliff Lee/Jsy/34 5.00
71 Lew Ford/Jsy/20 10.00
75 Barry Zito/Jsy/75 5.00
76 Carlos Delgado/Jsy/25 10.00
78 Ryan Wagner/Jsy/38 5.00
80 Adrian Beltre/Jsy/29 15.00
82 Sean Burroughs/Jsy/32 8.00
83 Francisco Cordero/Jsy/31 8.00
85 Eric Byrnes/Jsy/22 8.00
91 Mike Sweeney/Jsy/29 8.00
96 Jason Giambi/Jsy/25 10.00
100 Kazuo Matsui/Jsy/25 12.00
118 Javy Lopez/Jsy/18 15.00
119 Robin Yount/Jsy/19 30.00
120 Mark Mulder/Jsy/12 12.00
121 Sean Casey/Jsy/21 12.00
122 Will Clark/Jsy/22 12.00
123 Don Mattingly/Pants/23 40.00
124 Miguel Cabrera/Jsy/24 20.00
125 Rafael Palmeiro/Jsy/15 20.00
126 David Ortiz/Jsy/34 20.00
127 Vladimir Guerrero/Jsy/27 20.00
128 Ken Harvey/Jsy/28 10.00
129 Rod Carew/Jsy/29 15.00
130 Magglio Ordonez/Jsy/30 10.00
131 Greg Maddux/Jsy/31 25.00
132 Roy Halladay/Jsy/32 10.00
134 Kerry Wood/Jsy/34 12.00
135 Frank Thomas/Jsy/35 20.00
138 Curt Schilling/Jsy/34 10.00
139 Dewon Brazelton/Jsy/45 5.00
140 Jae Weong/Seo/Jsy/40 5.00
141 Danny Kolb/Jsy/41 5.00
144 Adam Dunn/Jsy/44 15.00
145 Carlos Lee/Jsy/45 5.00
146 Matt Clement/Jsy/30 10.00
148 Travis Hafner/Jsy/48 8.00
151 Randy Johnson/Pants/51 5.00
154 Jason Varitek/Jsy/33 20.00
157 Francisco Rodriguez/Jsy/57 5.00
162 Carlos Zambrano/Jsy/38 8.00
164 Jermaine Dye/Jsy/24 10.00
166 Dontrelle Willis/Jsy/35 12.00
168 Johnny Estrada/Jsy/23 10.00
170 Shannon Stewart/Jsy/23 10.00
175 Craig Wilson/Jsy/36 8.00
177 Troy Glaus/Jsy/25 15.00
180 Mike Lowell/Jsy/19 8.00
183 A.J. Burnett/Jsy/34 10.00
188 Mark Teixeira/Jsy/23 15.00
195 Andy Pettitte/Jsy/21 8.00
200 Andruw Jones/Jsy/200 8.00

Material Fabric Position

NM/M
Common Player: 4.00
Prime: No Pricing
Production One Set
1 Brian Roberts/Jsy/250 4.00
3 Harmon Killebrew/Jsy/250 12.00
4 Angel Berroa/Jsy/250 4.00
5 George Brett/Jsy/250 15.00
6 Stan Musial/Pants/250 15.00
7 Ivan Rodriguez/Jsy/250 6.00
8 Cal Ripken Jr./Jkt/250 25.00
9 Hank Blalock/Jsy/250 4.00
10 Miguel Tejada/Jsy/250 4.00
11 Barry Larkin/Jsy/100 6.00

12 Alfonso Soriano/Jsy/250 4.00
14 Paul Konerko/Jsy/250 4.00
15 Jim Edmonds/Jsy/250 4.00
16 Garret Anderson/Jsy/250 4.00
17 Todd Helton/Jsy/250 6.00
19 Tony Gwynn/Jsy/250 10.00
20 Mike Schmidt/Jsy/250 15.00
21 Sammy Sosa/Jsy/250 10.00
22 Roger Clemens/Jsy/250 12.00
23 Tony Perez/Jsy/250 8.00
24 Manny Ramirez/Jsy/250 8.00
25 Jim Thome/Jsy/250 8.00
27 Scott Rolen/Jsy/250 8.00
28 Austin Kearns/Jsy/250 4.00
29 John Smoltz/Jsy/250 4.00
31 Mike Piazza/Jsy/250 10.00
32 Steve Carlton/Pants/250 8.00
34 Nolan Ryan/Jsy/250 20.00
35 Mike Mussina/Jsy/250 6.00
39 Brett Myers/Jsy/250 4.00
41 Victor Martinez/Jsy/250 4.00
42 Mariano Rivera/Jsy/250 8.00
43 Dennis Eckersley/Jsy/250 6.00
44 Roy Oswalt/Jsy/250 6.00
45 Pedro Martinez/Jsy/250 8.00
46 Jason Bay/Jsy/250 4.00
47 Tom Glavine/Jsy/250 6.00
48 Torii Hunter/Jsy/250 4.00
49 Larry Bigbie/Jsy/250 4.00
52 C.C. Sabathia/Jsy/250 4.00
53 Bobby Abreu/Jsy/250 4.00
55 Hideki Matsui/Jsy/250 20.00
56 Mark Buehrle/Jsy/250 4.00
57 Johan Santana/Jsy/250 6.00
59 Edgar Martinez/Jsy/250 6.00
60 Preston Wilson/Jsy/250 4.00
61 Livan Hernandez/Jsy/250 4.00
62 Eric Chavez/Jsy/250 6.00
63 Lyle Overbay/Jsy/250 6.00
65 Cliff Lee/Jsy/250 6.00
67 Jeff Bagwell/Jsy/250 8.00
71 Lew Ford/Jsy/250 4.00
72 Chone Figgins/Jsy/250 4.00
75 Barry Zito/Jsy/250 4.00
76 Carlos Delgado/Jsy/250 4.00
78 Ryan Wagner/Jsy/250 4.00
80 Adrian Beltre/Jsy/250 8.00
81 Vernon Wells/Jsy/250 4.00
82 Sean Burroughs/Jsy/250 4.00
83 Francisco Cordero/Jsy/250 4.00
85 Eric Byrnes/Jsy/250 10.00
86 Jose Reyes/Jsy/250 4.00
87 Rocco Baldelli/Jsy/250 4.00
88 Josh Beckett/Jsy/250 4.00
89 Scott Podsednik/Jsy/250 4.00
91 Mike Sweeney/Jsy/250 4.00
93 Trot Nixon/Jsy/250 4.00
96 Jason Giambi/Jsy/250 4.00
98 Craig Biggio/Jsy/250 6.00
99 Pat Burrell/Jsy/250 4.00
100 Kazuo Matsui/Jsy/250 4.00
101 Rafael Furcal/Jsy/250 4.00
102 Jack Wilson/Jsy/250 4.00
103 Edgar Renteria/Jsy/250 4.00
104 Carlos Beltran/Jsy/250 6.00
105 Albert Pujols/Jsy/250 15.00
106 Melvin Mora/Jsy/100 4.00
108 Andre Dawson/Jsy/250 4.00
109 Jody Gerut/Jsy/250 4.00
110 Michael Young/Jsy/250 4.00
111 Gary Sheffield/Jsy/250 4.00
112 Wade Boggs/Jsy/100 8.00
113 Carl Crawford/Jsy/250 4.00
115 Tim Hudson/Jsy/250 4.00
116 Aramis Ramirez/Jsy/250 4.00
117 Lance Berkman/Jsy/250 4.00
118 Javy Lopez/Jsy/250 4.00
119 Robin Yount/Jsy/250 10.00
120 Mark Mulder/Jsy/250 4.00
121 Sean Casey/Jsy/250 4.00
122 Will Clark/Jsy/250 6.00
123 Don Mattingly/Pants/250 15.00
124 Miguel Cabrera/Jsy/250 8.00
125 Rafael Palmeiro/Jsy/250 8.00
126 David Ortiz/Jsy/250 8.00
127 Vladimir Guerrero/Jsy/250 8.00
128 Ken Harvey/Jsy/250 4.00
129 Rod Carew/Jsy/250 8.00
130 Magglio Ordonez/Jsy/250 4.00
131 Greg Maddux/Jsy/100 10.00
132 Roy Halladay/Jsy/250 4.00
134 Kerry Wood/Jsy/250 6.00
135 Frank Thomas/Jsy/250 8.00

138 Curt Schilling/Jsy/250 8.00
139 Dewon Brazelton/Jsy/100 4.00
140 Jae Weong/Seo/Jsy/100 4.00
141 Danny Kolb/Jsy/100 4.00
142 Jeff Kent/Jsy/100 6.00
144 Adam Dunn/Jsy/250 4.00
146 Carlos Lee/Jsy/250 4.00
146 Matt Clement/Jsy/250 4.00
148 Travis Hafner/Jsy/250 4.00
151 Randy Johnson/Pants/250 8.00
157 Francisco Rodriguez/Jsy/100 4.00
158 Gary Carter/Jsy/250 4.00
162 Carlos Zambrano/Jsy/100 6.00
163 Bobby Crosby/Jsy/250 8.00
164 Jermaine Dye/Jsy/100 4.00
166 Dontrelle Willis/Jsy/250 4.00
168 Johnny Estrada/Jsy/100 4.00
170 Shannon Stewart/Jsy/100 4.00
171 Ben Sheets/Jsy/100 4.00
173 Laynce Nix/Jsy/100 4.00
175 Craig Wilson/Jsy/100 4.00
176 Hideo Nomo/Jsy/100 8.00
177 Troy Glaus/Jsy/250 4.00
180 Mike Lowell/Jsy/250 4.00
183 A.J. Burnett/Jsy/250 4.00
187 Kazuhisa Ishii/Jsy/250 4.00
188 Mark Teixeira/Jsy/250 6.00
190 Dale Murphy/Jsy/250 6.00
194 Shawn Green/Jsy/250 4.00
196 Andy Pettitte/Jsy/250 6.00
197 Chipper Jones/Jsy/250 8.00
197 Jose Vidro/Jsy/100 4.00
198 Jacque Jones/Jsy/250 4.00
200 Andruw Jones/Jsy/250 4.00

Pennant Patches

NM/M
Production 5-25
1 Ozzie Smith/25 40.00
2 Keith Hernandez/25 20.00
3 Rickey Henderson/25 30.00
4 Paul Molitor/25 25.00
5 George Brett/25 50.00
6 Steve Garvey/25 20.00
7 Randy Johnson/25 25.00
8 Cal Ripken Jr./25 90.00
9 Darryl Strawberry/25 20.00
11 Chipper Jones/25 30.00
12 Steve Carlton/25 20.00
13 Orel Hershiser/25 20.00
14 Carlton Fisk/25 25.00
15 Dave Parker/25 20.00
15 Rollie Fingers/25 20.00
16 Dwight Gooden/25 20.00
19 Dontrelle Willis/25 15.00
19 Dave Righetti/25 15.00

Pennant Patches Signature

NM/M
Production 5-25
2 Keith Hernandez/25 40.00
5 Steve Garvey/25 35.00
9 Darryl Strawberry/25 40.00
12 Steve Carlton/25 35.00
15 Rollie Fingers/25 35.00
16 Dwight Gooden/25 40.00

Shirts

NM/M
Production 25-100
1 Rod Carew/100 10.00
2 Red Schoendienst/50 8.00
3 Harmon Killebrew/50 20.00
4 Joe Cronin/50 35.00
5 Early Wynn/50 8.00
6 Gaylord Perry/100 8.00
7 Willie McCovey/100 10.00
8 Carl Yastrzemski/100 20.00
9 Reggie Jackson/100 20.00
10 Duke Snider/50 15.00
11 Luis Aparicio/50 10.00
12 Bob Gibson/50 15.00
13 Maury Wills/50 15.00
14 Ernie Banks/50 20.00
15 Enos Slaughter/100 10.00
16 Whitey Ford/50 15.00
17 Warren Spahn/100 15.00
18 Roger Maris/100 35.00
19 Hal Newhouser/100 10.00
20 Marty Marion/25 12.00

Shirts Signature

NM/M
Production 5-50
Prime: No Pricing
Production One Set
2 Red Schoendienst/50 15.00
6 Gaylord Perry/50 20.00
7 Willie McCovey/50 30.00
11 Luis Aparicio/50 20.00
13 Maury Wills/50 20.00

Signature Post Marks Gold

NM/M
Production 1-50
36 Joe Nathan/50 15.00
39 Brett Myers/50 12.00
40 Rich Harden/50 15.00
49 Larry Bigbie/50 15.00
61 Livan Hernandez/50 15.00
63 Lyle Overbay/50 15.00

65 Cliff Lee/50 15.00
68 Danny Graves/25 20.00
71 Lew Ford/50 15.00
72 Chone Figgins/50 20.00
78 Esteban Loaiza/50 20.00
78 Ryan Wagner/50 10.00
79 John Lackey/50 15.00
83 Francisco Cordero/25 20.00
89 Eric Byrnes/50 20.00
90 Casey Kotchman/50 25.00
90 Scott Podsednik/50 15.00
94 Chad Cordero/25 15.00
97 Jose Guillen/25 20.00
102 Jack Wilson/50 15.00
106 Melvin Mora/25 20.00
109 Jody Gerut/50 15.00
128 Ken Harvey/50 10.00
136 Tom Gordon/50 10.00
137 Jake Peavy/25 25.00
139 Dewon Brazelton/50 10.00
140 Jae Weong Seo/25 10.00
141 Danny Kolb/50 15.00
145 Carlos Lee/25 20.00
147 Guillermo Mota/50 10.00
148 Travis Hafner/25 20.00
156 Brad Penny/50 10.00
159 Adrian Gonzalez/50 15.00
163 Bobby Crosby/25 30.00
164 Jermaine Dye/25 20.00
168 Johnny Estrada/25 25.00
169 Milton Bradley/25 20.00
170 Shannon Stewart/25 15.00
173 Laynce Nix/25 20.00
175 Craig Wilson/50 15.00
181 Randy Wolf/50 15.00
184 Aubrey Huff/25 20.00
185 Billy Ripken/25 10.00
186 Octavio Dotel/50 15.00
189 Todd Walker/25 20.00
191 Alexis Rios/50 15.00
198 Jacque Jones/25 15.00

Signature Post Marks Silver

NM/M
Production 1-250
Platinum: No Pricing
Production One Set
1 Brian Roberts/250 8.00
4 Angel Berroa/25 15.00
36 Joe Nathan/250 15.00
39 Brett Myers/250 8.00
40 Rich Harden/100 15.00
49 Larry Bigbie/250 10.00
52 C.C. Sabathia/25 20.00
56 Mark Buehrle/50 10.00
61 Livan Hernandez/100 10.00
63 Lyle Overbay/100 10.00
65 Cliff Lee/50 10.00
68 Danny Graves/250 10.00
71 Lew Ford/250 10.00
72 Chone Figgins/250 10.00
78 Esteban Loaiza/250 10.00
78 Ryan Wagner/250 10.00
79 John Lackey/250 10.00
82 Sean Burroughs/250 15.00
83 Francisco Cordero/100 8.00
89 Eric Byrnes/100 10.00
90 Casey Kotchman/250 20.00
90 Scott Podsednik/250 10.00
93 Trot Nixon/25 25.00
94 Chad Cordero/250 8.00
97 Jose Guillen/250 10.00
102 Jack Wilson/250 10.00
106 Melvin Mora/100 10.00
108 Andre Dawson/25 25.00
109 Jody Gerut/250 8.00
116 Aramis Ramirez/25 25.00
128 Ken Harvey/250 8.00
136 Tom Gordon/250 20.00
137 Jake Peavy/250 10.00
139 Dewon Brazelton/250 8.00
140 Jae Weong Seo/100 10.00
141 Danny Kolb/250 12.00
145 Carlos Lee/100 12.00
147 Guillermo Mota/250 8.00
148 Travis Hafner/100 15.00
155 David Wright/25 80.00
156 Brad Penny/50 10.00
157 Francisco Rodriguez/100 15.00
159 Adrian Gonzalez/250 15.00
160 Derrek Lee/25 30.00
162 Carlos Zambrano/25 25.00
163 Bobby Crosby/25 25.00
164 Jermaine Dye/25 20.00
168 Johnny Estrada/200 15.00
169 Milton Bradley/50 15.00
170 Shannon Stewart/50 10.00
173 Laynce Nix/250 10.00
175 Craig Wilson/100 12.00
181 Marcus Giles/25 20.00
182 Randy Wolf/250 12.00
184 Aubrey Huff/100 10.00
185 Billy Ripken/25 8.00
186 Octavio Dotel/50 15.00
189 Todd Walker/50 15.00
191 Alexis Rios/200 15.00
193 Orlando Cabrera/50 20.00
197 Jose Vidro/25 15.00
198 Jacque Jones/100 10.00

Stamps Centennial Autograph

NM/M
Production 1-40
2 Red Schoendienst/39 40.00

6 Bob Feller/39 40.00
11 Dwight Evans/39 30.00
15 Whitey Ford/27 50.00
22 Tony Perez/24 40.00
24 Billy Williams/39 30.00
25 Juan Marichal/39 30.00
27 Maury Wills/39 25.00
28 Fergie Jenkins/39 30.00
29 Steve Carlton/39 30.00
30 Dale Murphy/39 50.00
32 Gaylord Perry/39 25.00
33 Fred Lynn/39 30.00
35 Ron Guidry/39 40.00
38 Jack Morris/39 25.00
39 Torii Hunter/39 25.00
40 Andre Dawson/39 30.00
41 Dave Righetti/39 20.00
43 Lou Brock/20 40.00
46 Sean Casey/21 40.00
48 Ralph Kiner/39 30.00
50 Jim Rice/39 35.00
51 Duke Snider/25 50.00
56 Harold Baines/39 25.00
57 Bobby Doerr/59 30.00
59 Monte Irvin/39 35.00
61 Alan Trammell/40 25.00
62 Al Kaline/39 50.00
64 Bert Blyleven/39 25.00
65 Miguel Cabrera/39 30.00
69 Luis Tiant/39 25.00
69 Michael Young/39 25.00
70 Tony Oliva/39 35.00
71 Mark Mulder/25

Stamps Legendary Fields Autograph
NM/M
Production 1-34
11 Dwight Evans/34 30.00
22 Tony Perez/34 35.00
24 Billy Williams/34 30.00
28 Fergie Jenkins/34 30.00
29 Steve Carlton/34 30.00
33 Fred Lynn/34 30.00
35 Ron Guidry/34 50.00
38 Jack Morris/34 25.00
40 Andre Dawson/34 30.00
41 Dave Righetti/34 20.00
48 Ralph Kiner/34 30.00
50 Jim Rice/34 35.00
52 Harold Baines/34 25.00
57 Bobby Doerr/34 30.00
59 Monte Irvin/34 35.00
66 Luis Tiant/23 30.00

Stamps Masterpiece Signature Centennial
No Pricing
Production 1-2

Stamps Material Centennial
NM/M
Production 1-39
1 Pee Wee Reese/Bat/39 20.00
3 Babe Ruth/Jsy/39 275.00
4 George Brett/Jsy/39 40.00
5 Stan Musial/Bat/39 40.00
6 Bob Feller/Pants/39 15.00
7 Cal Ripken Jr./Pants/39 100.00
8 Ted Williams/Jsy/39 100.00
11 Dwight Evans/Jsy/39 25.00
12 Dave Concepcion/Jsy/39 20.00
13 Ernie Banks/Jsy/39 25.00
14 Pedro J. Martinez/Jsy/39 20.00
16 Scott Rolen/Jsy/39 25.00
17 Tony Gwynn/Jsy/39 40.00
18 Mike Schmidt/Jsy/39 60.00
19 Roberto Clemente/Hat/21 200.00
20 Roger Clemens/Jsy/39 35.00
21 Don Mattingly/Jsy/39 50.00
22 Tony Perez/Bat/39 15.00
23 Roger Maris/Jsy/39 75.00
24 Billy Williams/Jsy/39 15.00
25 Juan Marichal/Pants/39 20.00
26 Hank Blalock/Jsy/39 15.00
27 Maury Wills/Jsy/39 15.00
28 Fergie Jenkins/Pants/39 20.00
29 Steve Carlton/Jsy/39 15.00
30 Dale Murphy/Jsy/39 20.00
31 Kerry Wood/Jsy/39 20.00
32 Gaylord Perry/Jsy/39 15.00
33 Fred Lynn/Jsy/39 20.00
34 Tom Seaver/Jsy/39 20.00
36 Reggie Jackson/Pants/39 25.00
37 Bob Gibson/Jsy/39 20.00
38 Jack Morris/Jsy/39 20.00
39 Torii Hunter/Jsy/39 15.00
40 Andre Dawson/Jsy/39 20.00
42 Dave Righetti/Jsy/39 20.00
42 Hideki Matsui/Pants/39 65.00
43 Lou Brock/Jkt/39 25.00
45 Yogi Berra/Jsy/39 30.00
45 Frankie Frisch/Jkt/39 25.00
46 Sean Casey/Jsy/39 15.00
47 Sammy Sosa/Jsy/39 30.00
48 Ralph Kiner/Bat/39 30.00
49 Hoyt Wilhelm/Jsy/39 15.00
50 Jim Rice/Jsy/39 20.00
51 Duke Snider/Pants/39 25.00
52 Harold Baines/Jsy/39 20.00
53 Willie Stargell/Jsy/39 20.00
54 Johnny Bench/Pants/39 25.00
55 Carlton Fisk/Jsy/39 25.00
56 Jim Palmer/Jsy/39 20.00
57 Bobby Doerr/Jsy/39 25.00
58 Mark Prior/Jsy/39 30.00
60 Lou Boudreau/Jsy/39 25.00
61 Alan Trammell/Bat/39 25.00
62 Al Kaline/Bat/39 25.00
63 Warren Spahn/Pants/39 30.00
64 Bert Blyleven/Jsy/39 25.00
65 Miguel Cabrera/Jsy/39 20.00
66 Luis Tiant/Jsy/39 15.00
67 Harmon Killebrew/Jsy/39 30.00
68 Richie Ashburn/Pants/39 25.00
69 Michael Young/Jsy/39 15.00
70 Tony Oliva/Jsy/39 20.00
71 Mark Mulder/Jsy/39 15.00
72 Nolan Ryan/Jsy/39 75.00
73 Willie McCovey/Jsy/39 20.00
74 Kirk Gibson/Jsy/39 20.00
75 Carl Yastrzemski/Pants/39 40.00

Stamps Material Centennial Autograph
NM/M
Production 1-39
2 Red Schoendienst/Jsy/39 40.00
6 Bob Feller/Pants/39 30.00
11 Dwight Evans/Jsy/39 30.00
22 Tony Perez/Bat/24 40.00
24 Billy Williams/Jsy/39 35.00
25 Juan Marichal/Pants/39 30.00
27 Maury Wills/Jsy/39 30.00
28 Fergie Jenkins/Pants/39 35.00
29 Steve Carlton/Jsy/39 30.00
30 Dale Murphy/Jsy/39 30.00
32 Gaylord Perry/Jsy/39 30.00
33 Fred Lynn/Jsy/39 30.00
37 Bob Gibson/Jsy/39 40.00
38 Jack Morris/Jsy/39 25.00
40 Andre Dawson/Jsy/39 35.00
43 Lou Brock/Jkt/39 30.00
46 Sean Casey/Jsy/39 30.00
48 Ralph Kiner/Jsy/39 30.00
50 Jim Rice/Jsy/39 30.00
51 Duke Snider/Pants/39 50.00
52 Harold Baines/Jsy/39 25.00
56 Jim Palmer/22 25.00
57 Bobby Doerr/Jsy/39 35.00
61 Alan Trammell/Bat/39 30.00
62 Al Kaline/Bat/39 50.00
64 Bert Blyleven/Jsy/39 25.00
65 Miguel Cabrera/Jsy/39 30.00
66 Luis Tiant/Jsy/39 25.00
67 Harmon Killebrew/Jsy/39 60.00
70 Tony Oliva/Jsy/39 35.00
71 Mark Mulder/Jsy/39 40.00
74 Kirk Gibson/Jsy/39 30.00

Stamps Material Legendary Fields
NM/M
Production 1-34
1 Pee Wee Reese/Bat/34 30.00
11 Dwight Evans/Jsy/34 25.00
12 Dave Concepcion/Jsy/34 20.00
13 Ernie Banks/Jsy/34 40.00
14 Pedro J. Martinez/Jsy/34 25.00
15 Whitey Ford/Jsy/34 35.00
19 Roberto Clemente/Hat/21 200.00
21 Don Mattingly/Jsy/34 50.00
22 Tony Perez/34 20.00
23 Roger Maris/34 85.00
24 Billy Williams/Jsy/34 30.00
28 Fergie Jenkins/Pants/34 20.00
29 Steve Carlton/Jsy/34 25.00
31 Kerry Wood/Jsy/34 20.00
33 Fred Lynn/Jsy/34 20.00
36 Reggie Jackson/Pants/34 25.00
38 Jack Morris/Jsy/34 25.00
40 Andre Dawson/Jsy/34 20.00
41 Dave Righetti/Jsy/34 20.00
42 Hideki Matsui/Pants/34 80.00
45 Yogi Berra/Jsy/34 40.00
47 Sammy Sosa/Jsy/34 40.00
48 Ralph Kiner/Bat/34 30.00
49 Hoyt Wilhelm/Jsy/34 15.00
50 Jim Rice/Jsy/34 20.00
51 Duke Snider/Pants/34 40.00
52 Harold Baines/Jsy/34 15.00
53 Willie Stargell/Jsy/34 30.00
54 Johnny Bench/Pants/34 40.00
55 Carlton Fisk/Jsy/34 25.00
57 Bobby Doerr/Jsy/34 25.00
58 Mark Prior/Jsy/34 25.00
61 Alan Trammell/Bat/34 30.00
62 Al Kaline/Bat/34 40.00
66 Luis Tiant/Jsy/34 25.00
74 Kirk Gibson/Jsy/34 30.00
75 Carl Yastrzemski/Pants/34 50.00

Stamps Material Legendary Fields Auto.
NM/M
Production 1-34
11 Dwight Evans/Jsy/34 30.00
22 Tony Perez/Bat/34 40.00
24 Billy Williams/Jsy/34 30.00
28 Fergie Jenkins/Jsy/34 35.00
29 Steve Carlton/Jsy/34 30.00
33 Fred Lynn/Jsy/34 30.00
38 Jack Morris/Jsy/34 30.00
40 Andre Dawson/Jsy/34 30.00
41 Dave Righetti/Jsy/34 20.00
50 Jim Rice/Jsy/33 40.00
66 Luis Tiant/Jsy/23 35.00
74 Kirk Gibson/Jsy/23 30.00

Stamps Material Legendary Players 20
NM/M
Complete Set (2):
19 Roberto Clemente/Hat/21 200.00

Stamps Material Legendary Players 33
NM/M
Complete Set (2):
19 Roberto Clemente/Hat/21 200.00

Stamps Material Olympic
NM/M
Production 1-92
1 Pee Wee Reese/Bat/92 15.00
4 George Brett/Jsy/92 30.00
5 Stan Musial/Bat/92 30.00
6 Bob Feller/Pants/92 15.00
7 Cal Ripken Jr./Pants/92 60.00
11 Dwight Evans/Jsy/92 20.00
13 Ernie Banks/Jsy/92 25.00
14 Pedro J. Martinez/Jsy/45 20.00
16 Scott Rolen/Jsy/27 30.00
17 Tony Gwynn/Jsy/92 40.00
18 Mike Schmidt/Jsy/92 40.00
19 Roberto Clemente/Hat/21 200.00
20 Roger Clemens/Jsy/92 30.00
21 Don Mattingly/Jsy/23 40.00
22 Tony Perez/Bat/24 30.00
24 Billy Williams/Jsy/26 15.00
25 Juan Marichal/Pants/92 15.00
26 Hank Blalock/Jsy/92 15.00
27 Maury Wills/Jsy/30 20.00
28 Fergie Jenkins/Pants/92 15.00
29 Steve Carlton/Jsy/92 15.00
30 Dale Murphy/Jsy/92 15.00
31 Kerry Wood/Jsy/92 15.00
32 Gaylord Perry/Jsy/92 15.00
33 Fred Lynn/Jsy/92 15.00
34 Tom Seaver/Bat/92 20.00
36 Reggie Jackson/Pants/44 20.00
37 Bob Gibson/Jsy/45 20.00
38 Jack Morris/Jsy/92 15.00
39 Torii Hunter/Jsy/48 15.00
40 Andre Dawson/Jsy/69 15.00
41 Dave Righetti/Jsy/92 15.00
42 Hideki Matsui/Pants/92 40.00
43 Lou Brock/Jkt/92 15.00
44 Yogi Berra/Bat/92 20.00
45 Frankie Frisch/Jkt/92 15.00
46 Sean Casey/Jsy/21 25.00
47 Sammy Sosa/Jsy/92 25.00
48 Ralph Kiner/Bat/92 15.00
49 Hoyt Wilhelm/Jsy/92 15.00
50 Jim Rice/Jsy/92 20.00
51 Duke Snider/Jsy/92 25.00
52 Harold Baines/Jsy/92 15.00
53 Willie Stargell/Jsy/92 20.00
54 Johnny Bench/Pants/92 25.00
55 Carlton Fisk/Jsy/92 25.00
56 Jim Palmer/Jsy/92 15.00
57 Bobby Doerr/Jsy/92 20.00
58 Mark Prior/Jsy/92 20.00
60 Lou Boudreau/Jsy/92 25.00
61 Alan Trammell/Bat/92 15.00
62 Al Kaline Bat/92 20.00
63 Warren Spahn/Pants/92 25.00
65 Miguel Cabrera/Jsy/92 20.00
66 Luis Tiant/Jsy/92 20.00
67 Harmon Killebrew/Jsy/92 30.00
68 Richie Ashburn/Pants/92 20.00
70 Tony Oliva/Jsy/92 15.00
72 Mark Mulder/Jsy/92 20.00
72 Nolan Ryan/Jsy/30 100.00
73 Willie McCovey/Jsy/92 20.00
74 Kirk Gibson/Jsy/92 15.00
75 Carl Yastrzemski/Pants/92 30.00

Stamps Material Olympic Autograph
NM/M
Production 1-29
6 Bob Feller/Pants/29 45.00
11 Dwight Evans/Jsy/29 35.00
22 Tony Perez/29 40.00
24 Billy Williams/Jsy/29 35.00
25 Juan Marichal/Pants/29 35.00
27 Maury Wills/Jsy/29 30.00
28 Fergie Jenkins/Pants/29 35.00
29 Steve Carlton/Jsy/29 35.00
30 Dale Murphy/Jsy/29 50.00
32 Gaylord Perry/Jsy/29 40.00
33 Fred Lynn/Jsy/29 35.00
37 Bob Gibson/Jsy/29 40.00
38 Jack Morris/Jsy/29 35.00
40 Andre Dawson/Jsy/25 40.00

Stamps Material Pro Ball
NM/M
Production 1-69
1 Pee Wee Reese/Bat/69 20.00
4 George Brett/Jsy/69 40.00
5 Stan Musial/Bat/69 30.00
6 Bob Feller/Pants/69 15.00
7 Cal Ripken Jr./Pants/69 60.00
11 Dwight Evans/Jsy/69 30.00
13 Ernie Banks/Jsy/69 25.00
14 Pedro J. Martinez/Jsy/45 25.00
16 Scott Rolen/Jsy/27 40.00
17 Tony Gwynn/Jsy/35 40.00
18 Mike Schmidt/Jsy/69 60.00
19 Roberto Clemente/Hat/21 200.00
20 Roger Clemens/Jsy/69 30.00
21 Don Mattingly/Jsy/23 50.00
22 Tony Perez/Bat/24 20.00
24 Billy Williams/Jsy/69 15.00
25 Juan Marichal/Pants/69 15.00
26 Hank Blalock/Jsy/69 15.00
27 Maury Wills/Jsy/69 15.00
28 Fergie Jenkins/Pants/69 20.00
29 Steve Carlton/Jsy/69 15.00
30 Dale Murphy/Jsy/69 15.00
31 Kerry Wood/Jsy/69 15.00
32 Gaylord Perry/Jsy/69 15.00
33 Fred Lynn/Jsy/69 15.00
34 Tom Seaver/Bat/69 20.00
36 Reggie Jackson/Pants/69 15.00
37 Bob Gibson/Jsy/45 25.00
38 Jack Morris/Jsy/69 15.00
39 Torii Hunter/Jsy/48 15.00
40 Andre Dawson/Jsy/69 15.00
41 Dave Righetti/Jsy/69 15.00
42 Hideki Matsui/Pants/69 40.00
43 Lou Brock/Jkt/69 15.00
44 Yogi Berra/Bat/69 20.00
45 Frankie Frisch/Jkt/69 20.00
46 Sean Casey/Jsy/69 15.00
47 Sammy Sosa/Jsy/69 15.00
48 Ralph Kiner/Bat/69 15.00
49 Hoyt Wilhelm/Jsy/69 15.00
50 Jim Rice/Jsy/69 12.00
51 Duke Snider/Pants/69 15.00
52 Harold Baines/Jsy/69 15.00
53 Willie Stargell/Jsy/69 15.00
54 Johnny Bench/Pants/69 20.00
55 Carlton Fisk/Jsy/72 15.00
56 Jim Palmer/Jsy/69 15.00
57 Bobby Doerr/Jsy/69 15.00
58 Mark Prior/Jsy/69 20.00
60 Lou Boudreau/Jsy/69 25.00
61 Alan Trammell/Bat/69 15.00
62 Al Kaline/Bat/69 20.00
63 Warren Spahn/Pants/69 25.00
65 Miguel Cabrera/Jsy/69 20.00
66 Luis Tiant/Jsy/69 15.00
67 Harmon Killebrew/Jsy/69 35.00
68 Richie Ashburn/Pants/69 20.00
69 Michael Young/Jsy/69 15.00
70 Tony Oliva/Jsy/69 20.00
72 Mark Mulder/Jsy/20 25.00
72 Nolan Ryan/Jsy/69 60.00
73 Willie McCovey/Jsy/69 25.00
74 Kirk Gibson/Jsy/69 15.00
75 Carl Yastrzemski/Pants/69 30.00

Stamps Material Pro Ball Autograph
NM/M
Production 1-69
6 Bob Feller/Pants/69 30.00
11 Dwight Evans/Jsy/24 30.00
22 Tony Perez/Bat/24 40.00
24 Billy Williams/Jsy/26 35.00
25 Juan Marichal/Pants/27 35.00
27 Maury Wills/Jsy/69 30.00
28 Fergie Jenkins/Pants/69 25.00
29 Steve Carlton/Jsy/69 30.00
30 Dale Murphy/Jsy/69 40.00
33 Fred Lynn/Jsy/69 25.00
37 Bob Gibson/Jsy/45 35.00
43 Lou Brock/Jkt/20 40.00
46 Sean Casey/Jsy/21 40.00
57 Bobby Doerr/Jsy/48 30.00
65 Miguel Cabrera/Jsy/24 50.00
66 Luis Tiant/Jsy/23 40.00
71 Mark Mulder/Jsy/20 30.00
74 Kirk Gibson/Jsy/23 30.00

Stamps Material USA Flag
NM/M
Production 1-100
1 Pee Wee Reese/Bat/100 15.00
4 George Brett/Jsy/100 40.00
5 Stan Musial/Bat/100 25.00
6 Bob Feller/Pants/100 15.00
7 Cal Ripken Jr./Pants/100 65.00
11 Dwight Evans/Jsy/24 35.00
13 Ernie Banks/Jsy/100 30.00
14 Pedro J. Martinez/Jsy/45 25.00
16 Scott Rolen/Jsy/27 40.00
17 Tony Gwynn/Jsy/100 50.00
18 Mike Schmidt/Jsy/100 50.00
19 Roberto Clemente/Hat/21 200.00
20 Roger Clemens/Jsy/100 25.00
21 Don Mattingly/Jsy/100 30.00
22 Tony Perez/Bat/100 15.00
24 Billy Williams/Jsy/100 15.00
25 Juan Marichal/Pants/100 15.00
26 Hank Blalock/Jsy/100 15.00
27 Maury Wills/Jsy/100 15.00
28 Fergie Jenkins/Pants/100 15.00
29 Steve Carlton/Jsy/100 15.00
30 Dale Murphy/Jsy/100 15.00
31 Kerry Wood/Jsy/100 20.00
32 Gaylord Perry/Jsy/100 10.00
33 Fred Lynn/Jsy/100 15.00
36 Reggie Jackson/Pants/44 20.00
37 Bob Gibson/Jsy/100 25.00
38 Jack Morris/Jsy/100 10.00
39 Torii Hunter/Jsy/48 15.00
40 Andre Dawson 15.00
42 Dave Righetti/Jsy/100 10.00
42 Hideki Matsui/Pants/100 40.00
43 Lou Brock/Jsy/100 15.00
44 Yogi Berra/Bat/100 20.00
45 Frankie Frisch/Jkt/100 15.00
46 Sean Casey/Jsy/100 10.00
47 Sammy Sosa/Jsy/100 15.00
48 Ralph Kiner/Bat/100 15.00
49 Hoyt Wilhelm/Jsy/100 10.00
51 Duke Snider/Pants/100 15.00
52 Harold Baines/Jsy/100 10.00
53 Willie Stargell/Jsy/100 15.00
54 Johnny Bench/Pants/100
55 Carlton Fisk/Jsy/72 15.00
56 Jim Palmer/Jsy/100 15.00
57 Bobby Doerr/Jsy/100 15.00
58 Mark Prior/Jsy/100 20.00
62 Al Kaline/Bat/100 15.00
63 Warren Spahn/Pants/100 20.00
64 Bert Blyleven/Jsy/28 20.00
65 Miguel Cabrera/Jsy/24 25.00
66 Luis Tiant/Jsy/23 20.00
67 Harmon Killebrew/Jsy/100 30.00
68 Richie Ashburn/Pants/100 15.00
70 Tony Oliva/Jsy/100 15.00
72 Mark Mulder/Jsy/100 25.00
72 Nolan Ryan/Jsy/100 50.00
73 Willie McCovey/Jsy/44 25.00
74 Kirk Gibson/Jsy/100 10.00
75 Carl Yastrzemski/Pants/100 25.00

Stamps Material USA Flag Autograph
NM/M
Production 1-37
2 Red Schoendienst/Jsy/37 40.00
6 Bob Feller/Pants/8 40.00
11 Dwight Evans/Jsy/37 30.00
22 Tony Perez/Bat/37 35.00
24 Billy Williams/Jsy/37 30.00
25 Juan Marichal/Pants/37 30.00
27 Maury Wills/Jsy/37 25.00
28 Fergie Jenkins/Pants/37 30.00
29 Steve Carlton/Jsy/37 30.00
30 Dale Murphy/Jsy/37 50.00
32 Gaylord Perry/Jsy/37 30.00
33 Fred Lynn/37 40.00
37 Bob Gibson/Jsy/37 40.00
38 Jack Morris/Jsy/37 25.00
41 Dave Righetti/Jsy/37 20.00
43 Lou Brock/Jkt/37 30.00
46 Sean Casey/Jsy/37 30.00
48 Ralph Kiner/Bat/37 30.00
50 Jim Rice/Jsy/37 30.00
51 Duke Snider/Pants/37 40.00
52 Harold Baines/Jsy/37 25.00
56 Jim Palmer/37 40.00
57 Bobby Doerr/Jsy/37 40.00
61 Alan Trammell/Bat/37 40.00
62 Al Kaline/Jsy/37 50.00
64 Bert Blyleven/Jsy/37 25.00
65 Miguel Cabrera/Jsy/24 25.00
66 Luis Tiant/Jsy/23 25.00
67 Harmon Killebrew/Jsy/37 60.00
70 Tony Oliva/Jsy/37 30.00
72 Mark Mulder/Jsy/37 30.00
74 Kirk Gibson/Jsy/23 30.00

Stamps Olympic Autograph
NM/M
Production 1-92
2 Red Schoendienst/92 25.00
6 Bob Feller/92 25.00
11 Dwight Evans/92 20.00
22 Tony Perez/92 25.00
24 Billy Williams/26 35.00
25 Juan Marichal/27 35.00
27 Maury Wills/92 30.00
28 Fergie Jenkins/92 25.00
29 Steve Carlton/92 20.00
30 Dale Murphy/92 30.00
32 Gaylord Perry/92 20.00
33 Fred Lynn/92 20.00
35 Ron Guidry/48 35.00
38 Jack Morris/48 20.00
39 Torii Hunter/48 20.00
40 Andre Dawson/92 25.00
43 Lou Brock/20 40.00
46 Sean Casey/21 20.00
50 Jim Rice/92 25.00
52 Harold Baines/92 20.00
56 Jim Palmer/22 50.00
57 Bobby Doerr/92 40.00
59 Monte Irvin/92 40.00
61 Alan Trammell/92 25.00
62 Al Kaline/92 40.00
64 Bert Blyleven/92 20.00
65 Miguel Cabrera/24 60.00
66 Luis Tiant/92 20.00
70 Tony Oliva/91 20.00
71 Mark Mulder/20 40.00

Stamps Pro Ball Autograph
NM/M
Production 1-69
6 Bob Feller/69 30.00
11 Dwight Evans/69 25.00
22 Tony Perez/69 35.00
24 Billy Williams/26 35.00
25 Juan Marichal/27 35.00
27 Maury Wills/69 20.00
28 Fergie Jenkins/69 25.00
29 Steve Carlton/69 20.00
30 Dale Murphy/69 40.00
32 Gaylord Perry/69 20.00
33 Fred Lynn/69 25.00
35 Ron Guidry/49 40.00
38 Jack Morris/69 20.00
39 Torii Hunter/48 25.00
43 Lou Brock/20 40.00
46 Sean Casey/21 40.00
57 Bobby Doerr/69 30.00
59 Monte Irvin/69 40.00
64 Bert Blyleven/28 25.00
65 Miguel Cabrera/24 50.00
66 Luis Tiant/69 20.00
71 Mark Mulder/20 40.00

Stamps USA Flag Autograph
NM/M
Production 1-100
2 Red Schoendienst/100 25.00
6 Bob Feller/24 30.00
11 Dwight Evans/24 35.00
22 Tony Perez/24 40.00
24 Billy Williams/26 35.00
25 Juan Marichal/27 35.00
27 Maury Wills/100 20.00
28 Fergie Jenkins/100 25.00
29 Steve Carlton/100 20.00
30 Dale Murphy/100 30.00
32 Gaylord Perry/100 20.00
33 Fred Lynn/100 20.00
35 Ron Guidry/49 35.00
38 Jack Morris/100 25.00
39 Torii Hunter/48 25.00
43 Lou Brock/20 40.00
46 Sean Casey/21 25.00
48 Ralph Kiner/100 25.00
51 Duke Snider/25 45.00
52 Harold Baines/100 20.00
56 Jim Palmer/22 50.00
57 Bobby Doerr/100 40.00
59 Monte Irvin/100 40.00
61 Alan Trammell/100 40.00
62 Al Kaline/100 40.00
64 Bert Blyleven/100 25.00
65 Miguel Cabrera/24 60.00
66 Luis Tiant/100 20.00
70 Tony Oliva/100 30.00
71 Mark Mulder/20 40.00

Timeline Threads Jersey Number
NM/M
Production 1-43
6 Orlando Cepeda/Pants/30 10.00
9 Tony Perez/Jsy/15 15.00
11 Tommy John/Jsy/25 15.00
15 Carlton Fisk/Jsy/27 20.00
17 Bert Blyleven/Jsy/28 15.00
20 Lou Brock/Jsy/20 20.00
21 Sammy Sosa/Jsy/21 20.00
22 Roger Clemens/Jsy/22 40.00
23 Don Mattingly/Jsy/23 40.00
 Rickey Henderson/Jsy/35 15.00
26 Wade Boggs/Jsy/26 20.00
29 Jim "Catfish" Hunter/Jsy/29 15.00
30 Maury Wills/Jsy/30 15.00
31 Hoyt Wilhelm/Jsy/31 10.00
34 Eddie Murray/Pants/34 50.00
35 Nolan Ryan/Jsy/35 50.00
35 Phil Niekro/Jsy/35 15.00
38 Curt Schilling/Jsy/38 15.00
39 Sandy Koufax/Jsy/39 500.00
40 Don Sutton/Jsy/40 15.00
41 Randy Johnson/Jsy/51 15.00
 Dennis Eckersley/Jsy/43 10.00
44 Frank Thomas/Jsy/35 20.00
45 Mike Mussina/Jsy/45 15.00

#	Player	Price
46	Greg Maddux/Jsy/31	25.00
47	Jim Palmer/Pants/22	15.00
49	Mike Piazza/Jsy/31	25.00

Timeline Threads Number Autograph
Production 1-19
Position Autograph: No Pricing
Production 1-19
Prime: No Pricing
Production One Set

Timeline Threads Position

#	Player	NM/M
	Common Player:	4.00
1	Bobby Doerr/Jsy/39	10.00
2	Burleigh Grimes/Pants/26	50.00
3	Babe Ruth/Pants/30	200.00
4	Joe Cronin/Pants/38	20.00
5	Johnny Bench/Pants/71	15.00
6	Orlando Cepeda/Pants/62	8.00
7	Ivan Rodriguez/Jsy/103	8.00
8	Cal Ripken Jr./Jsy/78	40.00
9	Tony Perez/Jsy/78	8.00
10	Andre Dawson/Jsy/86	8.00
11	Tommy John/Jsy/86	8.00
12	Alfonso Soriano/Jsy/102	8.00
13	Ozzie Smith/Jsy/78	8.00
14	Ernie Banks/Jsy/70	15.00
15	Carlton Fisk/Jsy/80	8.00
16	Bo Jackson/Jsy/89	10.00
17	Bert Blyleven/Jsy/83	4.00
18	Darryl Strawberry/Jsy/88	6.00
19	Bob Feller/Pants/36	8.00
20	Lou Brock/Jsy/74	8.00
21	Sammy Sosa/Jsy/103	12.00
22	Roger Clemens/Jsy/101	15.00
23	Don Mattingly/Jsy/94	20.00
24	Rickey Henderson/Jsy/83	10.00
25	Albert Pujols/Jsy/103	15.00
26	Wade Boggs/Jsy/87	8.00
27	Joe Morgan/Jsy/82	8.00
28	Gary Carter/Jsy/86	8.00
29	Jim "Catfish" Hunter/Jsy/78	6.00
30	Maury Wills/Jsy/65	4.00
31	Hoyt Wilhelm/Jsy/68	4.00
32	Matt Williams/Jsy/95	4.00
33	Eddie Murray/Pants/88	8.00
34	Nolan Ryan/Jsy/90	25.00
35	Phil Niekro/Jsy/80	6.00
36	Paul Molitor/Jsy/96	10.00
37	Dale Murphy/Jsy/83	8.00
38	Curt Schilling/Jsy/99	8.00
39	Fred Lynn/Jsy/75	4.00
40	Sandy Koufax/Jsy/64	260.00
41	Don Sutton/Jsy/76	4.00
42	Randy Johnson/Jsy/98	8.00
43	Dennis Eckersley/Jsy/97	6.00
44	Frank Thomas/Jsy/94	8.00
45	Mike Mussina/Jsy/100	6.00
46	Greg Maddux/Jsy/100	10.00
47	Jim Palmer/Pants/76	8.00
48	Harmon Killebrew/Jsy/62	20.00
49	Mike Piazza/Jsy/99	10.00
50	Billy Martin/Jsy/83	15.00

2005 Leaf Certified Materials

#	Player	NM/M
	Complete Set (250):	
	Common Player:	.50
	Common Auto. (201-250):	6.00
	Production 499 unless noted.	
	Hobby Pack (5):	10.00
	Hobby Box (10):	80.00
1	A.J. Burnett	.50
2	Adam Dunn	.75
3	Adrian Beltre	.75
4	Bret Boone	.50
5	Albert Pujols	2.50
6	Alex Rodriguez	2.50
7	Alfonso Soriano	1.00
8	Andruw Jones	1.00
9	Andy Pettitte	.75
10	Aramis Ramirez	.75
11	Aubrey Huff	.50
12	Austin Kearns	.50
13	B.J. Upton	.75
14	Brandon Webb	.50
15	Barry Zito	.50
16	Tim Salmon	.50
17	Bobby Abreu	.50
18	Bobby Crosby	.50
19	Brad Penny	.50
20	Preston Wilson	.50
21	C.C. Sabathia	.50
22	Carl Crawford	.50
23	Keith Foulke	.50
24	Carlos Beltran	.75
25	Casey Kotchman	.50
26	Chipper Jones	1.00
27	Chone Figgins	.50
28	Craig Biggio	.75
29	Craig Wilson	.50
30	Curt Schilling	1.00
31	Danny Kolb	.50
32	David Ortiz	1.00
33	Orlando Hudson	.50
34	David Wright	1.50
35	Derek Jeter	2.50
36	Jake Peavy	.75
37	Derrek Lee	.75
38	Dontrelle Willis	.75
39	Edgar Renteria	.50
40	Angel Berroa	.50
41	Eric Chavez	.50
42	Akinori Otsuka	.50
43	Francisco Rodriguez	.50
44	Garret Anderson	.50
45	Gary Sheffield	.75
46	Greg Maddux	1.50
47	Hideki Matsui	2.00
48	Hideo Nomo	.75
49	Ichiro Suzuki	2.00
50	Ivan Rodriguez	.75
51	J.D. Drew	.50
52	J.T. Snow	.50
53	Jack Wilson	.50
54	Jamie Moyer	.50
55	Jason Bay	.50
56	Jason Giambi	.75
57	Trot Nixon	.50
58	Jason Schmidt	.50
59	Jason Varitek	.50
60	Roy Oswalt	.50
61	Javy Lopez	.50
62	Eric Byrnes	.50
63	Jeff Bagwell	.75
64	Jeff Kent	.50
65	Jeff Suppan	.50
66	Jeremy Bonderman	.50
67	Jermaine Dye	.50
68	Kazuhito Tadano	.50
69	Jim Edmonds	.75
70	Jim Thome	.75
71	Johan Santana	1.00
72	John Smoltz	.75
73	Johnny Damon	1.00
74	Johnny Estrada	.50
75	Brett Myers	.50
76	Jose Guillen	.50
77	Jose Vidro	.50
78	Josh Beckett	.50
79	Edwin Jackson	.50
80	Raul Ibanez	.50
81	Rich Harden	.50
82	Justin Morneau	.75
83	Kazuhisa Ishii	.50
84	Kazuo Matsui	.50
85	Ken Griffey Jr.	1.50
86	Ken Harvey	.50
87	Frank Thomas	.75
88	Kerry Wood	.75
89	Wade Miller	.50
90	Kevin Millwood	.50
91	Jeremy Affeldt	.50
92	Francisco Cordero	.50
93	Lance Berkman	.50
94	Larry Walker	.50
95	Laynce Nix	.50
96	Luis Gonzalez	.50
97	Lyle Overbay	.50
98	Carlos Zambrano	.75
99	Manny Ramirez	1.00
100	Marcus Giles	.50
101	Mark Buehrle	.50
102	Mark Loretta	.50
103	Mark Mulder	.50
104	Mark Prior	1.00
105	Mark Teixeira	.75
106	Marlon Byrd	.50
107	Rafael Furcal	.50
108	Melvin Mora	.50
109	Michael Young	.75
110	Miguel Cabrera	1.00
111	Miguel Tejada	.75
112	Mike Lowell	.50
113	Mike Mussina	.75
114	Mike Piazza	1.50
115	Moises Alou	.50
116	Livan Hernandez	.50
117	Nomar Garciaparra	1.50
118	Omar Vizquel	.50
119	Orlando Cabrera	.50
120	Pat Burrell	.50
121	Paul Konerko	.50
122	Paul LoDuca	.50
123	Pedro Martinez	1.00
124	Rafael Palmeiro	.75
125	Randy Johnson	1.00
126	Richard Hidalgo	.50
127	Richie Sexson	.50
128	Magglio Ordonez	.50
129	Roger Clemens	2.50
130	Russ Ortiz	.50
131	Sammy Sosa	1.50
132	Scott Podsednik	.50
133	Scott Rolen	1.00
134	Sean Burroughs	.50
135	Sean Casey	.50
136	Shawn Green	.50
137	Jorge Posada	.75
138	Roy Halladay	.50
139	Steve Finley	.50
140	Tim Hudson	.75
141	Todd Helton	.75
142	Tom Glavine	.75
143	Torii Hunter	.50
144	Travis Hafner	.75
145	Trevor Hoffman	.50
146	Troy Glaus	.50
147	Vernon Wells	.50
148	Victor Martinez	.50
149	Vladimir Guerrero	1.00
150	Sammy Sosa	1.50
151	Hank Blalock	.75
152	Danny Graves	.50
153	Rocco Baldelli	.50
154	Carlos Delgado	.50
155	Bubba Nelson	.50
156	Kevin Youkilis	.50
157	Jacque Jones	.50
158	Mike Lieberthal	.50
159	Ben Sheets	.50
160	Lew Ford	.50
161	Ervin Santana	.50
162	Jody Gerut	.50
163	Nick Johnson	.50
164	Brian Roberts	.50
165	Joe Nathan	.50
166	Mike Sweeney	.50
167	Ryan Wagner	.50
168	David Dellucci	.50
169	Jae Weong Seo	.50
170	Tom Gordon	.50
171	Carlos Lee	.50
172	Octavio Dotel	.50
173	Jose Castillo	.50
174	Troy Percival	.50
175	Carlos Delgado	.50
176	Curt Schilling	1.00
177	David Ortiz	1.00
178	Greg Maddux	1.50
179	Ivan Rodriguez	.75
180	Jeff Kent	.50
181	Larry Walker	.50
182	Miguel Tejada	.75
183	Pedro J. Martinez	1.00
184	Rafael Palmeiro	.75
185	Roger Clemens	2.50
186	Shawn Green	.50
187	Tim Hudson	.75
188	Tom Glavine	.75
189	Troy Glaus	.50
190	Vladimir Guerrero	1.00
191	Cal Ripken Jr.	4.00
192	Don Mattingly	2.00
193	George Brett	2.00
194	Harmon Killebrew	1.50
195	Mike Schmidt	2.00
196	Nolan Ryan	3.00
197	Stan Musial	2.00
198	Tony Gwynn	1.00
199	Wade Boggs	1.00
200	Willie Mays	2.00
201	Ambiorix Concepcion/Auto. RC	10.00
202	Agustin Montero/Auto. RC	8.00
203	Carlos Ruiz/Auto. RC	10.00
204	Casey Rogowski/Auto. RC	6.00
205	Chris Resop/Auto. RC	8.00
206	Chris Roberson/Auto. RC	8.00
207	Colter Bean RC	2.00
208	Danny Rueckel/Auto. RC	6.00
209	David Gassner/Auto. RC	6.00
210	Devon Lowery/Auto. RC	8.00
211	Norihiro Nakamura/Auto./115 RC	20.00
212	Erick Threets/Auto./299 RC	6.00
213	Garrett Jones/Auto./299 RC	15.00
214	Geovany Soto/Auto. RC	40.00
215	Jared Gothreaux/Auto. RC	6.00
216	Jason Hammel/Auto./299 RC	10.00
217	Jeff Miller/Auto./299 RC	6.00
218	Jeff Niemann/Auto. RC	20.00
219	Huston Street	2.00
220	John Hattig Jr./Auto. RC	6.00
221	Justin Verlander/Auto./299 RC	50.00
222	Justin Wechsler/Auto. RC	6.00
223	Luke Scott/Auto. RC	20.00
224	Mark McLemore/Auto. RC	8.00
225	Mark Woodyard/Auto./299 RC	6.00
226	Matt Lindstrom/Auto./299 RC	8.00
227	Miguel Negron/Auto. RC	6.00
228	Mike Morse/Auto. RC	10.00
229	Nate McLouth/Auto. RC	12.00
230	Paulino Reynoso/Auto./299 RC	6.00
231	Philip Humber/Auto./299 RC	15.00
232	Tony Pena/Auto. RC	6.00
233	Randy Messenger/Auto. RC	6.00
234	Raul Tablado/Auto. RC	8.00
235	Russel Rohlicek/Auto. RC	6.00
236	Ryan Speier/Auto. RC	8.00
237	Scott Munter/Auto. RC	8.00
238	Sean Thompson/Auto. RC	6.00
239	Sean Tracey/Auto./299 RC	6.00
240	Marcos Carvajal RC	1.50
241	Travis Bowyer/Auto. RC	10.00
242	Ubaldo Jimenez/Auto. RC	125.00
243	Wladimir Balentien/Auto. RC	15.00
244	Eude Brito RC	8.00
245	Ambiorix Burgos RC	2.00
246	Tadahito Iguchi RC	5.00
247	Dae-Sung Koo RC	1.00
248	Chris Seddon RC	8.00
249	Keiichi Yabu/Auto. RC	15.00
250	Yuniesky Betancourt/Auto. RC	25.00

Cuts Blue

#	Player	NM/M
	Production 1-80	
3	Willie Mays/26	150.00
7	Jim Palmer/50	25.00
12	Steve Carlton/50	25.00
15	Maury Wills/80	8.00
20	Dale Murphy/50	30.00

Cuts Green

#	Player	NM/M
	Production 3-50	
7	Jim Palmer/50	25.00
12	Steve Carlton/50	25.00
15	Maury Wills/80	20.00
20	Dale Murphy/50	30.00

Cuts Red

#	Player	NM/M
	Production 1-60	
7	Jim Palmer/50	25.00
12	Steve Carlton/50	25.00
15	Maury Wills/60	20.00
20	Dale Murphy/50	30.00

Cuts Materials Blue

#	Player	NM/M
	Production 4-43	
3	Hank Aaron/Bat/43	275.00
5	Willie Mays/Grace/43	175.00
7	Sandy Koufax/Jsy/32	400.00
8	Nolan Ryan/Jsy/34	200.00
9	Rod Carew/Jsy/29	25.00
10	Ryne Sandberg/Jsy/23	120.00
12	Steve Carlton/Pants/32	25.00
14	Mike Schmidt/Jsy/20	65.00
19	Don Mattingly/Jsy/23	75.00

Cuts Materials Green

#	Player	NM/M
	Production 4-32	
3	Willie Mays/Pants/24	175.00
9	Rod Carew/Jsy/29	25.00
10	Ryne Sandberg/Jsy/23	120.00
12	Steve Carlton/Pants/32	25.00
14	Mike Schmidt/Jsy/20	65.00

Cuts Materials Red

#	Player	NM/M
	Production 4-32	
3	Willie Mays/Pants/24	175.00
9	Rod Carew/Jsy/29	25.00
10	Ryne Sandberg/Jsy/23	120.00
12	Steve Carlton/Pants/32	25.00
14	Mike Schmidt/Jsy/20	65.00

Fabric of the Game

#	Player	NM/M
	Common Player:	
	Production 5-100	
1	Al Oliver/Jsy/50	6.00
2	Alan Trammell/Jsy/100	6.00
3	Andres Galarraga/Jsy/100	4.00
4	Andres Galarraga/Jsy/100	4.00
6	Babe Ruth/Pants/25	240.00
7	Billy Martin/Pants/100	4.00
8	Billy Williams/Jsy/50	6.00
9	Bo Jackson/Jsy/100	10.00
10	Bo Jackson/Jsy/100	10.00
12	Bob Gibson/Jsy/25	12.00
13	Bobby Doerr/Jsy/100	10.00
14	Burleigh Grimes/Pants/25	50.00
15	Cal Ripken Jr./Jsy/30	30.00
16	Cal Ripken Jr./Jsy/30	30.00
17	Carl Yastrzemski/Pants/50	15.00
18	Carlton Fisk/Jkt/50	10.00
19	Jim "Catfish" Hunter/Pants/50	8.00
20	Darryl Strawberry/Jsy/25	8.00
21	Darryl Strawberry/Jsy/100	4.00
22	Dave Concepcion/Jsy/50	6.00
23	Dave Righetti/Jsy/50	6.00
24	Dave Winfield/Pants/100	8.00
25	David Cone/Jsy/100	4.00
26	David Justice/Jsy/100	4.00
27	Deion Sanders/Jsy/50	8.00
28	Deion Sanders/Jsy/50	8.00
30	Dennis Eckersley/Pants/50	6.00
31	Don Mattingly/Jsy/100	15.00
32	Don Sutton/Jsy/25	8.00
33	Don Sutton/Jsy/50	8.00
37	Dwight Gooden/Jsy/100	6.00
38	Eddie Murray/Jsy/25	15.00
39	Eddie Murray/Pants/50	10.00
40	Edgar Martinez/Jsy/100	4.00
41	Ernie Banks/Jsy/25	15.00
42	Fergie Jenkins/Jsy/50	8.00
43	Frankie Frisch/Jkt/50	20.00
44	Fred Lynn/Jsy/50	6.00
45	Fred McGriff/Jsy/100	6.00
46	Gary Carter/Jsy/50	6.00
47	Gary Carter/Jsy/50	6.00
48	Gaylord Perry/Jsy/50	6.00
49	Gaylord Perry/Jsy/50	6.00
50	George Brett/Jsy/25	25.00
51	Hal Newhouser/Jsy/50	8.00
54	Harmon Killebrew/Jsy/25	15.00
55	Harmon Killebrew/Jsy/50	12.00
56	Harold Baines/Jsy/50	8.00
57	Hoyt Wilhelm/Jsy/100	6.00
58	Jack Morris/Jsy/100	4.00
59	Jim Thorpe/Jsy/25	300.00
60	Jose Cruz/Jsy/100	4.00
61	Jim Rice/Jsy/50	6.00
62	Joe Cronin/Jsy/50	15.00
63	Joe Cronin/Pants/100	15.00
64	Joe Morgan/Jsy/50	8.00
65	Joe Torre/Jsy/50	10.00
66	John Kruk/Jsy/100	4.00
67	Johnny Bench/Jsy/50	10.00
68	Juan Marichal/Jsy/100	6.00
71	Kirk Gibson/Jsy/100	4.00
72	Lee Smith/Jsy/100	4.00
73	Lenny Dykstra/Jsy/100	6.00
74	Lou Boudreau/Jsy/25	15.00
75	Luis Aparicio/Jsy/50	6.00
76	Luis Tiant/Pants/100	4.00
77	Mark Grace/Jsy/50	8.00
78	Hoyt Wilhelm/Jsy/100	6.00
79	Matt Williams/Jsy/100	4.00
80	Matt Williams/Jsy/50	6.00
82	Nolan Ryan/Jsy/20	20.00
84	Nolan Ryan/Jsy/50	25.00
85	Nolan Ryan/Jsy/25	25.00
86	Orlando Cepeda/Jsy/50	8.00
87	Ozzie Smith/Jsy/25	15.00
88	Paul Molitor/Jsy/50	8.00
89	Paul Molitor/Jsy/50	8.00
90	Paul Molitor/Jsy/50	8.00
91	Phil Niekro/Jsy/50	8.00
92	Reggie Jackson/Pants/100	8.00
93	Reggie Jackson/Jkt/100	8.00
94	Reggie Jackson/Jsy/50	8.00
95	Reggie Jackson/Jsy/50	8.00
96	Rickey Henderson/Jkt/100	10.00
97	Rickey Henderson/Jsy/100	10.00
98	Rickey Henderson/Jsy/100	10.00
99	Rickey Henderson/Jsy/100	10.00
100	Rickey Henderson/Jsy/50	10.00
101	Rickey Henderson/Pants/50	10.00
102	Robin Ventura/Jsy/100	6.00
103	Robin Ventura/Jsy/100	6.00
104	Robin Yount/Jsy/100	12.00
105	Rod Carew/Jsy/100	8.00
106	Rod Carew/Jsy/100	8.00
107	Roger Maris/Pants/50	40.00
108	Ron Cey/Jsy/50	6.00
109	Ron Guidry/Jsy/100	6.00
110	Ryne Sandberg/Jsy/50	15.00
111	Sandy Koufax/Jsy/25	180.00
112	Stan Musial/Jsy/25	25.00
113	Stan Musial/Pants/25	25.00
114	Steve Garvey/Jsy/100	8.00
115	Ted Williams/Jkt/50	50.00
116	Ted Williams/Jkt/50	50.00
117	Tom Seaver/Jsy/100	10.00
118	Tom Seaver/Jsy/100	10.00
119	Tommy John/Jsy/100	4.00
120	Tommy John/Jsy/100	4.00
121	Tommy Lasorda/Jsy/100	6.00
122	Tony Gwynn/Jsy/100	8.00
123	Tony Gwynn/Pants/100	10.00
124	Tony Perez/Jsy/100	8.00
125	Wade Boggs/Jsy/100	8.00
126	Warren Spahn/Jsy/25	15.00
127	Whitey Ford/Jsy/25	15.00
128	Will Clark/Jsy/50	8.00
129	Willie Mays/Pants/50	40.00
130	Willie McCovey/Pants/100	10.00
131	Roger Clemens/Jsy/50	15.00
132	Roger Clemens/Jsy/50	15.00
133	Roger Clemens/Jsy/50	15.00
134	Randy Johnson/Jsy/50	8.00
135	Randy Johnson/Jsy/50	8.00
136	Cal Ripken Jr./Jsy/50	30.00
137	Don Mattingly/Jsy/100	15.00
138	George Brett/Jsy/25	20.00
139	Harmon Killebrew/Jsy/25	15.00
140	Mike Schmidt/Jsy/50	25.00
141	Nolan Ryan/Jkt/25	25.00
143	Tony Gwynn/Jsy/100	10.00
144	Wade Boggs/Jsy/50	10.00
145	Willie Mays/Jsy/50	50.00
146	Hideo Nomo/Jsy/100	4.00
147	Dale Murphy/Jsy/100	4.00
148	Dale Murphy/Jsy/100	4.00
149	Bo Jackson/Jsy/50	12.00
151	Darryl Strawberry/Jsy/50	6.00
152	Deion Sanders/Jsy/50	8.00
153	Dennis Eckersley/Jsy/50	8.00
155	Dwight Gooden/Jsy/100	6.00
156	Edgar Martinez/Jsy/100	4.00
158	Lou Brock/Jsy/50	8.00
159	Albert Pujols/Jsy/50	20.00
160	Tom Glavine/Jsy/100	6.00
161	Hideki Matsui/Pants/50	20.00
162	Babe Ruth/Pants, Jim Thorpe/Jsy/25	500.00
164	Ted Williams/Jkt, Bob Gibson/Jsy/25	50.00
165	Whitey Ford/Jsy, Sandy Koufax/Jsy/25	150.00
166	Roger Maris/Pants, Don Mattingly/Jsy/25	50.00
167	Nolan Ryan/Jsy, Tom Seaver/Jsy/50	25.00
168	Cal Ripken Jr./Jsy, George Brett/Jsy/100	40.00
169	Ryne Sandberg/Jsy, Mike Schmidt/Jsy/50	30.00
170	Tony Gwynn/Jsy, Wade Boggs/Jsy/50	15.00
172	Carlton Fisk/Jsy, Johnny Bench/Pants/50	15.00
	Reggie Jackson/Pants, Darryl Strawberry/Jsy/50	10.00
173	Robin Yount/Jsy, Paul Molitor/Jsy/50	15.00
174	Warren Spahn/Pants, Juan Marichal/Jsy/50	15.00
175	Bo Jackson/Jsy, Deion Sanders/Pants/100	15.00
176	Tony Gwynn/Jsy, Rickey Henderson/Jsy/100	15.00
177	Hideki Matsui/Jsy, Jim Edmonds/Jsy/100	20.00
178	Rickey Henderson/Jsy, Lou Brock/Jsy/100	15.00
179	Roger Clemens/Jsy, Albert Pujols/Jsy/100	25.00
180	Hideo Nomo/Jsy, Kazuhisa Ishii/Jsy/100	12.00

Fabric of the Game Auto.
No Pricing
Production One Set

Fabric of the Game Jersey Number

#	Player	NM/M
	Production 1-72	
8	Billy Williams/Jsy/26	8.00
18	Carlton Fisk/Jkt/72	8.00
19	Jim "Catfish" Hunter/Pants/29	10.00
20	Darryl Strawberry/Jsy/36	6.00
21	Darryl Strawberry/Jsy/44	6.00
24	Dave Winfield/Pants/31	10.00
25	David Cone/Jsy/44	8.00
26	David Justice/Jsy/23	10.00
27	Deion Sanders/Jsy/21	12.00
28	Deion Sanders/Jsy/21	12.00
29	Dennis Eckersley/Jsy/43	6.00
30	Dennis Eckersley/Pants/43	8.00
36	Dwight Evans/Jsy/24	10.00
38	Eddie Murray/Jsy/33	15.00
39	Eddie Murray/Pants/33	15.00
42	Fergie Jenkins/Jsy/31	8.00
45	Fred McGriff/Jsy/29	8.00
48	Gaylord Perry/Jsy/36	8.00
49	Gaylord Perry/Jsy/36	8.00
52	Hank Aaron/Jsy/44	40.00
53	Hank Aaron/Jsy/44	40.00
57	Hoyt Wilhelm/Jsy/31	8.00
58	Jack Morris/Jsy/47	4.00
60	Jose Cruz/Jsy/25	6.00
66	John Kruk/Jsy/25	8.00
68	Juan Marichal/Pants/27	10.00
71	Kirk Gibson/Jsy/23	10.00
72	Lee Smith/Jsy/47	10.00
76	Luis Tiant/Pants/23	8.00
81	Hoyt Wilhelm/Jsy/31	8.00
82	Nolan Ryan/Jsy/34	25.00
83	Nolan Ryan/Jsy/34	25.00

84	Nolan Ryan/Jsy/30	25.00
85	Nolan Ryan/Jsy/30	25.00
86	Orlando Cepeda/Pants/30	10.00
91	Phil Niekro/Jsy/35	8.00
92	Reggie Jackson/Pants/44	10.00
93	Reggie Jackson/Jkt/44	10.00
94	Reggie Jackson/Jsy/44	10.00
95	Reggie Jackson/Jsy/44	10.00
96	Rickey Henderson/Jkt/24	12.00
97	Rickey Henderson/Jsy/25	12.00
98	Rickey Henderson/Jsy/35	12.00
99	Rickey Henderson/Jsy/35	12.00
100	Rickey Henderson/Pants/24	12.00
101	Rickey Henderson/Pants/24	12.00
105	Rod Carew/Jsy/29	15.00
106	Rod Carew/Jsy/29	15.00
109	Ron Guidry/Pants/49	8.00
110	Ryne Sandberg/Jsy/23	35.00
111	Sandy Koufax/Jsy/32	180.00
117	Tom Seaver/Jsy/41	10.00
118	Tom Seaver/Pants/41	10.00
119	Tommy John/Jsy	8.00
120	Tommy John/Pants	8.00
124	Tony Perez/Jsy/24	10.00
125	Wade Boggs/Jsy/26	10.00
129	Willie Mays/Pants/24	50.00
130	Willie McCovey/Pants/44	10.00
131	Roger Clemens/Jsy/22	20.00
132	Roger Clemens/Jsy/22	20.00
133	Roger Clemens/Jsy/21	20.00
134	Randy Johnson/Jsy/51	10.00
135	Randy Johnson/Jsy/51	10.00
137	Don Mattingly/Jsy/23	20.00
144	Wade Boggs/Jsy/26	10.00
145	Willie Mays/Jsy/24	50.00
150	Darryl Strawberry/Jsy/44	6.00
153	Dennis Eckersley/Jsy/43	8.00
159	Tom Glavine/Jsy/47	10.00
160	Hideki Matsui/Jsy/55	20.00
166	Nolan Ryan/Jsy, Tom Seaver/Jsy/25	25.00
167	Cal Ripken Jr./Jsy, George Brett/Jsy/50	50.00
168	Ryne Sandberg/Jsy, Mike Schmidt/Jsy/25	35.00
169	Tony Gwynn/Jsy, Wade Boggs/Jsy/15	15.00
170	Carlton Fisk/Jsy, Johnny Bench/Pants/25	20.00
172	Reggie Jackson/Pants, Darryl Strawberry/Jsy/50	10.00
173	Robin Yount/Jsy, Paul Molitor/Jsy/25	20.00
174	Warren Spahn/Jsy, Juan Marichal/Jsy/25	20.00
175	Bo Jackson/Jsy, Deion Sanders/Pants/50	15.00
176	Tony Gwynn/Jsy, Rickey Henderson/Jsy/50	20.00
177	Hideki Matsui/Jsy, Jim Edmonds/Jsy/50	20.00
178	Rickey Henderson/Pants, Lou Brock/Jsy/50	20.00
179	Roger Clemens/Jsy, Albert Pujols/Jsy/50	25.00
180	Hideo Nomo/Jsy, Kazuhisa Ishii/Jsy/50	15.00

Fabric of the Game Position

NM/M

Production 3-100

1	Al Oliver/Jsy/50	6.00
2	Alan Trammell/Jsy/25	8.00
3	Andres Galarraga/Jsy/25	8.00
4	Andres Galarraga/Jsy/25	8.00
7	Billy Martin/Pants/50	15.00
8	Billy Williams/Jsy/25	8.00
9	Bo Jackson/Jsy/25	12.00
10	Bo Jackson/Jsy/25	12.00
13	Bobby Doerr/Pants/25	12.00
14	Burleigh Grimes/Pants/25	50.00
15	Cal Ripken Jr./Jsy/25	35.00
16	Cal Ripken Jr./Jsy/25	35.00
17	Carl Yastrzemski/Pants/25	15.00
18	Carlton Fisk/Jkt/25	12.00
19	Jim "Catfish" Hunter/Pants/100	8.00
20	Darryl Strawberry/Jsy/25	8.00
21	Darryl Strawberry/Jsy/25	8.00
22	Dave Concepcion/Jsy/25	6.00
23	Dave Righetti/Jsy/25	8.00
24	Dave Winfield/Pants/25	10.00
25	David Cone/Jsy/50	4.00
26	David Justice/Jsy/100	4.00
27	Deion Sanders/Jsy/50	8.00
28	Deion Sanders/Jsy/50	8.00
29	Dennis Eckersley/Jsy/50	8.00
30	Dennis Eckersley/Pants/50	8.00
36	Don Sutton/Jsy/50	
37	Dwight Gooden/Jsy/100	6.00
40	Edgar Martinez/Jsy/25	4.00
42	Fergie Jenkins/Jsy/25	10.00
43	Frankie Frisch/Jkt/100	15.00
44	Fred Lynn/Jsy/50	4.00

45	Fred McGriff/Jsy/100	6.00
46	Gary Carter/Jsy/50	6.00
47	Gary Carter/Jsy/25	8.00
48	Gaylord Perry/Jsy/50	6.00
49	Gaylord Perry/Jsy/50	8.00
54	Harmon Killebrew/Jsy/25	15.00
56	Harold Baines/Jsy/100	8.00
57	Hoyt Wilhelm/Jsy/100	8.00
61	Jose Cruz/Jsy/100	4.00
63	Jim Rice/Jsy/50	8.00
64	Joe Cronin/Pants/50	15.00
65	Joe Morgan/Jsy/50	10.00
66	John Kruk/Jsy/50	10.00
67	Johnny Bench/Pants/25	12.00
68	Juan Marichal/Pants/25	10.00
71	Kirk Gibson/Jsy/50	4.00
72	Lee Smith/Jsy/50	4.00
73	Lenny Dykstra/Jsy/50	6.00
75	Luis Aparicio/Jsy/25	8.00
76	Luis Tiant/Pants/25	6.00
77	Mark Grace/Jsy/50	10.00
78	Hoyt Wilhelm/Jsy/50	8.00
79	Matt Williams/Jsy/50	8.00
84	Nolan Ryan/Jsy/25	25.00
85	Nolan Ryan/Jsy/25	25.00
86	Orlando Cepeda/Pants/50	8.00
87	Ozzie Smith/Pants/25	15.00
88	Paul Molitor/Jsy/50	8.00
89	Paul Molitor/Jsy/50	8.00
90	Paul Molitor/Pants/25	10.00
91	Phil Niekro/Jsy/50	8.00
92	Reggie Jackson/Pants/50	10.00
93	Reggie Jackson/Jkt/25	10.00
94	Reggie Jackson/Jsy/25	10.00
95	Reggie Jackson/Jsy/25	10.00
96	Rickey Henderson/Jkt/100	10.00
97	Rickey Henderson/Jsy/50	10.00
99	Rickey Henderson/Jsy/25	12.00
100	Rickey Henderson/Pants/25	12.00
101	Rickey Henderson/Pants/50	10.00
102	Robin Ventura/Jsy/50	6.00
103	Robin Ventura/Jsy/50	6.00
104	Robin Yount/Jsy/50	15.00
105	Rod Carew/Jsy/50	10.00
106	Rod Carew/Jsy/50	10.00
107	Roger Maris/Pants/50	50.00
109	Ron Guidry/Pants/50	8.00
110	Ryne Sandberg/Jsy/50	15.00
111	Sandy Koufax/Jsy/25	180.00
112	Stan Musial/Jsy/25	25.00
113	Stan Musial/Pants/25	25.00
114	Steve Garvey/Jsy/25	8.00
115	Ted Williams/Jkt/50	50.00
118	Tom Seaver/Pants/50	10.00
119	Tommy John/Jsy	4.00
120	Tommy John/Pants/50	4.00
121	Tommy Lasorda/Jsy/50	6.00
122	Tony Gwynn/Jsy/50	10.00
123	Tony Gwynn/Pants/50	8.00
124	Tony Perez/Jsy/50	8.00
125	Wade Boggs/Jsy/50	10.00
129	Willie Mays/Pants/25	50.00
130	Willie McCovey/Pants/50	10.00
131	Roger Clemens/Jsy/25	20.00
132	Roger Clemens/Jsy/50	15.00
133	Roger Clemens/Jsy/50	15.00
134	Randy Johnson/Jsy/50	8.00
135	Randy Johnson/Jsy/50	8.00
136	Cal Ripken Jr./Jsy/50	30.00
137	Don Mattingly/Jsy/25	20.00
138	George Brett/Jsy/25	20.00
139	Harmon Killebrew/Jsy/25	15.00
140	Mike Schmidt/Jsy/25	20.00
143	Tony Gwynn/Jsy/50	10.00
144	Wade Boggs/Jsy/50	10.00
145	Willie Mays/Jsy/50	50.00
146	Hideo Nomo/Jsy/50	6.00
147	Dale Murphy/Jsy/50	10.00
148	Dale Murphy/Jsy/50	10.00
149	Bo Jackson/Jsy/50	12.00
150	Darryl Strawberry/Jsy/50	8.00
152	Deion Sanders/Jsy/50	8.00
153	Dennis Eckersley/Jsy/50	8.00
154	Dwight Gooden/Jsy/50	6.00
155	Edgar Martinez/Jsy/50	4.00
156	Lou Brock/Jsy/50	8.00
157	Steve Carlton/Jsy/50	6.00
158	Albert Pujols/Jsy/50	20.00
159	Tom Glavine/Jsy/25	8.00
160	Hideki Matsui/Jsy/50	20.00
161	Babe Ruth/Pants, Jim Thorpe/Jsy/25	500.00
162	Ted Williams/Jkt, Stan Musial/Jsy/50	50.00
164	Whitey Ford/Jsy, Sandy Koufax/Jsy/25	150.00
165	Roger Maris/Pants, Don Mattingly/Jsy/50	50.00
166	Nolan Ryan/Jsy, Tom Seaver/Jsy/100	25.00
167	Cal Ripken Jr./Jsy, George Brett/Jsy/100	40.00
168	Ryne Sandberg/Jsy, Mike Schmidt/Jsy/50	30.00
169	Tony Gwynn/Jsy, Wade Boggs/Jsy/50	15.00

170	Carlton Fisk/Jsy, Johnny Bench/Pants/25	20.00
172	Reggie Jackson/Pants, Darryl Strawberry/Jsy/50	10.00
173	Robin Yount/Jsy, Paul Molitor/Jsy/25	20.00
174	Warren Spahn/Pants, Juan Marichal/Jsy/25	20.00
175	Bo Jackson/Jsy, Deion Sanders/Pants/50	15.00
176	Tony Gwynn/Jsy, Rickey Henderson/Jsy/50	20.00
177	Hideki Matsui/Jsy, Jim Edmonds/Jsy/50	20.00
178	Rickey Henderson/Pants, Lou Brock/Jsy/50	20.00
179	Roger Clemens/Jsy, Albert Pujols/Jsy/50	25.00
180	Hideo Nomo/Jsy, Kazuhisa Ishii/Jsy/50	15.00

Fabric of the Game Reward

NM/M

Production 3-50

1	Al Oliver/Jsy/50	6.00
2	Alan Trammell/Jsy/50	8.00
3	Andres Galarraga/Jsy/50	6.00
4	Andres Galarraga/Jsy/50	6.00
7	Billy Martin/Pants/50	15.00
9	Bo Jackson/Jsy/50	12.00
10	Bo Jackson/Jsy/50	12.00
13	Bobby Doerr/Pants/50	12.00
17	Carl Yastrzemski/Pants/25	15.00
19	Jim "Catfish" Hunter/Pants/50	8.00
21	Darryl Strawberry/Jsy/50	6.00
23	Dave Righetti/Jsy/25	8.00
44	Fred Lynn/Jsy/50	4.00
46	Gary Carter/Jsy/50	6.00
47	Gary Carter/Jsy/25	8.00
48	Gaylord Perry/Jsy/50	6.00
49	Gaylord Perry/Jsy/50	8.00
52	Hal Newhouser/Jsy/25	8.00
58	Jack Morris/Jsy/50	6.00
61	Jim Rice/Jsy/50	8.00
62	Joe Cronin/Jsy/25	20.00
63	Joe Cronin/Pants/25	20.00
64	Joe Morgan/Jsy/50	10.00
66	John Kruk/Jsy/50	10.00
68	Juan Marichal/Pants/25	10.00
71	Kirk Gibson/Jsy/50	4.00
72	Lee Smith/Jsy/50	4.00
75	Luis Aparicio/Jsy/25	8.00
76	Luis Tiant/Pants/25	6.00
78	Hoyt Wilhelm/Jsy/50	10.00
79	Matt Williams/Jsy/25	8.00
82	Nolan Ryan/Jsy/25	25.00
85	Nolan Ryan/Jsy/25	25.00
86	Orlando Cepeda/Pants/25	10.00
87	Ozzie Smith/Pants/25	15.00
88	Paul Molitor/Jsy/50	8.00
89	Paul Molitor/Jsy/50	8.00
90	Paul Molitor/Jsy/50	10.00
91	Phil Niekro/Jsy/25	8.00
92	Reggie Jackson/Pants/50	10.00
93	Reggie Jackson/Jkt/25	10.00
95	Reggie Jackson/Jsy/25	10.00
96	Rickey Henderson/Jkt/50	10.00
97	Rickey Henderson/Jsy/50	10.00
99	Rickey Henderson/Jsy/25	12.00
102	Robin Ventura/Jsy/50	6.00
103	Robin Ventura/Jsy/50	6.00
104	Robin Yount/Jsy/50	12.00
105	Rod Carew/Jsy/50	10.00
106	Rod Carew/Jsy/50	10.00
108	Ron Cey/Jsy/50	8.00
109	Ron Guidry/Pants/50	8.00
110	Ryne Sandberg/Jsy/50	15.00
111	Sandy Koufax/Jsy/50	180.00
113	Stan Musial/Jsy/25	25.00
114	Steve Garvey/Jsy/8	8.00
115	Ted Williams/Jkt/50	50.00
118	Tom Seaver/Pants/50	10.00
119	Tommy John/Jsy	4.00
120	Tommy John/Pants/50	4.00
121	Tommy Lasorda/Jsy/50	6.00
122	Tony Gwynn/Jsy/50	10.00
123	Tony Gwynn/Pants/50	8.00
124	Tony Perez/Jsy/50	8.00
125	Wade Boggs/Jsy/50	10.00
126	Warren Spahn/Jsy/25	12.00
128	Will Clark/Jsy/50	8.00
129	Willie Mays/Pants/25	50.00
130	Willie McCovey/Pants/50	10.00
131	Roger Clemens/Jsy/25	20.00
132	Roger Clemens/Jsy/50	15.00
133	Roger Clemens/Jsy/50	15.00
134	Randy Johnson/Jsy/50	8.00
135	Randy Johnson/Jsy/50	8.00
136	Cal Ripken Jr./Jsy/50	30.00
137	Don Mattingly/Jsy/50	20.00
138	George Brett/Jsy/25	20.00
139	Harmon Killebrew/Jsy/25	15.00
140	Mike Schmidt/Jsy/25	20.00
143	Tony Gwynn/Jsy/25	10.00
144	Wade Boggs/Jsy/50	10.00
145	Willie Mays/Jsy/50	50.00
146	Hideo Nomo/Jsy/50	6.00

147	Dale Murphy/Jsy/50	10.00
148	Dale Murphy/Jsy/50	10.00
150	Darryl Strawberry/Jsy/50	8.00
151	Deion Sanders/Jsy/50	8.00
152	Deion Sanders/Pants/50	8.00
153	Dennis Eckersley/Jsy/50	8.00
154	Dwight Gooden/Jsy/50	6.00
155	Edgar Martinez/Jsy/50	4.00
156	Lou Brock/Jsy/50	8.00
157	Steve Carlton/Jsy/50	6.00
158	Albert Pujols/Jsy/50	20.00
159	Tom Glavine/Jsy/50	8.00
160	Hideki Matsui/Pants/50	20.00
161	Babe Ruth/Pants, Jim Thorpe/Jsy/25	500.00
162	Ted Williams/Jkt, Stan Musial/Jsy/50	50.00
163	Willie Mays/Jsy, Bob Gibson/Jsy/50	50.00
164	Whitey Ford/Jsy, Sandy Koufax/Jsy/25	150.00
165	Roger Maris/Pants, Don Mattingly/Jsy/50	50.00
166	Nolan Ryan/Jsy, Tom Seaver/Jsy/25	25.00
167	Cal Ripken Jr./Jsy, George Brett/Jsy/50	40.00
168	Ryne Sandberg/Jsy, Mike Schmidt/Jsy/50	30.00
169	Tony Gwynn/Jsy, Wade Boggs/Jsy/50	15.00
170	Carlton Fisk/Jsy, Johnny Bench/Pants/25	20.00
172	Reggie Jackson/Pants, Darryl Strawberry/Jsy/50	10.00
173	Robin Yount/Jsy, Paul Molitor/Jsy/25	20.00
174	Warren Spahn/Pants, Juan Marichal/Jsy/25	20.00
175	Bo Jackson/Jsy, Deion Sanders/Pants/50	15.00
176	Tony Gwynn/Jsy, Rickey Henderson/Jsy/50	20.00
177	Hideki Matsui/Jsy, Jim Edmonds/Jsy/50	20.00
178	Rickey Henderson/Pants, Lou Brock/Jsy/50	20.00
179	Roger Clemens/Jsy, Albert Pujols/Jsy/50	25.00
180	Hideo Nomo/Jsy, Kazuhisa Ishii/Jsy/50	15.00

Fabric of the Game Stats

NM/M

Production 3-75

1	Al Oliver/Jsy/75	6.00
3	Andres Galarraga/Jsy/75	6.00
4	Andres Galarraga/Jsy/75	6.00
7	Billy Martin/Pants/75	15.00
8	Billy Williams/Jsy/75	6.00
9	Bo Jackson/Jsy/75	10.00
10	Bo Jackson/Jsy/75	10.00
13	Bobby Doerr/Jsy/75	12.00
14	Burleigh Grimes/Pants/75	50.00
15	Cal Ripken Jr./Jsy/75	30.00
16	Cal Ripken Jr./Jsy/75	30.00
17	Carl Yastrzemski/Pants/75	15.00
18	Carlton Fisk/Jkt/75	10.00
19	Jim "Catfish" Hunter/Pants/75	8.00
21	Darryl Strawberry/Jsy/75	6.00
22	Dave Concepcion/Jsy/75	4.00
23	Dave Righetti/Jsy/75	8.00
24	Dave Winfield/Pants/75	8.00
25	David Cone/Jsy/75	4.00
26	David Justice/Jsy/75	4.00
27	Deion Sanders/Jsy/75	8.00
28	Deion Sanders/Jsy/75	8.00
29	Dennis Eckersley/Jsy/75	8.00
30	Dennis Eckersley/Pants/75	8.00
39	Eddie Murray/Pants/75	12.00
40	Edgar Martinez/Jsy/75	4.00
43	Frankie Frisch/Jkt/75	15.00
44	Fred Lynn/Jsy/75	4.00
45	Fred McGriff/Jsy/75	6.00
46	Gary Carter/Jsy/75	6.00
47	Gary Carter/Jsy/25	8.00
48	Gaylord Perry/Jsy/75	6.00
49	Gaylord Perry/Jsy/75	8.00
52	Hal Newhouser/Jsy/75	10.00
54	Harmon Killebrew/Jsy/25	15.00
55	Harmon Killebrew/Jsy/50	12.00
56	Harold Baines/Jsy/50	8.00
57	Hoyt Wilhelm/Jsy/75	8.00
62	Joe Cronin/Jsy/75	20.00
63	Joe Cronin/Pants/75	20.00
65	Joe Morgan/Jsy/75	10.00
66	John Kruk/Jsy/75	10.00
71	Kirk Gibson/Jsy/75	4.00
72	Lee Smith/Jsy/75	4.00
73	Lenny Dykstra/Jsy/75	6.00
75	Luis Aparicio/Jsy/25	8.00
76	Luis Tiant/Pants/25	6.00
78	Hoyt Wilhelm/Jsy/75	8.00
79	Matt Williams/Jsy/75	8.00
82	Nolan Ryan/Jsy/25	25.00
85	Nolan Ryan/Jsy/25	25.00
86	Orlando Cepeda/Pants/25	10.00
87	Ozzie Smith/Pants/25	15.00
88	Paul Molitor/Jsy/50	8.00

89	Paul Molitor/Jsy/50	8.00
90	Paul Molitor/Pants/25	10.00
91	Phil Niekro/Jsy/50	8.00
92	Reggie Jackson/Pants/50	10.00
93	Reggie Jackson/Jkt/25	10.00
94	Reggie Jackson/Jsy/75	10.00
95	Reggie Jackson/Jsy/75	10.00
96	Rickey Henderson/Jkt/75	10.00
97	Rickey Henderson/Jsy/75	10.00
98	Rickey Henderson/Jsy/50	10.00
101	Rickey Henderson/Pants/75	10.00
102	Robin Ventura/Jsy/50	6.00
103	Robin Ventura/Jsy/75	6.00
104	Robin Yount/Jsy/75	12.00
105	Rod Carew/Jsy/75	8.00
106	Rod Carew/Jsy/75	8.00
107	Roger Maris/Pants/75	40.00
108	Ron Cey/Jsy/75	8.00
109	Ron Guidry/Pants/50	8.00
111	Sandy Koufax/Jsy/75	180.00
113	Stan Musial/Jsy/75	25.00
114	Steve Garvey/Jsy/75	8.00
115	Ted Williams/Jkt/25	50.00
117	Tom Seaver/Jsy/75	10.00
118	Tom Seaver/Jsy/75	10.00
119	Tommy John/Jsy/25	4.00
120	Tommy John/Pants/75	6.00
121	Tommy Lasorda/Jsy/75	6.00
124	Tony Perez/Jsy/75	8.00
125	Wade Boggs/Jsy/75	10.00
126	Warren Spahn/Jsy/75	12.00
128	Will Clark/Jsy/50	8.00
129	Willie Mays/Pants/25	50.00
130	Willie McCovey/Pants/75	10.00
131	Roger Clemens/Jsy/25	20.00
140	Mike Schmidt/Jsy/25	20.00
144	Wade Boggs/Jsy/50	10.00
145	Willie Mays/Jsy/25	25.00
146	Hideo Nomo/Jsy/75	10.00
147	Dale Murphy/Jsy/75	10.00
148	Dale Murphy/Jsy/75	10.00
153	Dennis Eckersley/Jsy/75	8.00
154	Dwight Gooden/Jsy/75	6.00
155	Edgar Martinez/Jsy/75	4.00
156	Lou Brock/Jsy/75	8.00
157	Steve Carlton/Pants/75	6.00
159	Tom Glavine/Jsy/75	8.00
160	Hideki Matsui/Jsy/75	20.00
161	Babe Ruth/Pants, Jim Thorpe/Jsy/25	500.00
162	Ted Williams/Jkt, Stan Musial/Jsy/25	50.00
163	Willie Mays/Jsy, Bob Gibson/Jsy/25	50.00
164	Whitey Ford/Jsy, Sandy Koufax/Jsy/25	150.00
165	Roger Maris/Pants, Don Mattingly/Jsy/25	50.00
166	Nolan Ryan/Jsy, Tom Seaver/Jsy/25	25.00
167	Cal Ripken Jr./Jsy, George Brett/Jsy/25	40.00
168	Ryne Sandberg/Jsy, Mike Schmidt/Jsy/25	30.00
169	Tony Gwynn/Jsy, Wade Boggs/Jsy/15	15.00
170	Carlton Fisk/Jsy, Johnny Bench/Pants/25	20.00
172	Reggie Jackson/Pants, Darryl Strawberry/Jsy/50	10.00
173	Robin Yount/Jsy, Paul Molitor/Jsy/25	20.00
174	Warren Spahn/Pants, Juan Marichal/Jsy/25	20.00
175	Bo Jackson/Jsy, Deion Sanders/Pants/50	15.00
176	Tony Gwynn/Jsy, Rickey Henderson/Jsy/50	20.00
177	Hideki Matsui/Jsy, Jim Edmonds/Jsy/50	20.00
178	Rickey Henderson/Pants, Lou Brock/Jsy/50	20.00
179	Roger Clemens/Jsy, Albert Pujols/Jsy/25	25.00
180	Hideo Nomo/Jsy, Kazuhisa Ishii/Jsy/50	15.00

Gold Team

NM/M

Complete Set (25):		
Common Player:		1.00
Inserted 1:7		
Mirror:		2-3X
1	Albert Pujols	4.00
2	Alex Rodriguez	3.00
3	Carlos Beltran	1.50
4	Chipper Jones	1.50
5	Curt Schilling	1.50
6	Derek Jeter	4.00
7	Greg Maddux	2.50
8	Hank Blalock	1.00
10	Ivan Rodriguez	1.00
11	Jim Thome	1.00
12	Ken Griffey Jr.	3.00
13	Lyle Overbay	1.00
14	Manny Ramirez	1.50
15	Mark Mulder	1.00
16	Mark Prior	1.50
17	Michael Young	1.00

18	Miguel Cabrera	1.50
19	Mike Piazza	2.00
20	Pedro Martinez	1.50
21	Randy Johnson	1.50
22	Roger Clemens	4.00
23	Sammy Sosa	2.00
24	Tim Hudson	1.00
25	Todd Helton	1.50

Gold Team Autograph

No Pricing
Production 5-10

Gold Team Jersey Number

NM/M

Production 100-250

1	Albert Pujols/100	20.00
3	Carlos Beltran/200	5.00
4	Chipper Jones/100	8.00
5	Curt Schilling/250	8.00
7	Greg Maddux/100	10.00
8	Hank Blalock/250	4.00
10	Ivan Rodriguez/120	6.00
11	Jim Thome/250	4.00
13	Lyle Overbay/250	4.00
14	Manny Ramirez/250	8.00
15	Mark Mulder/250	4.00
16	Mark Prior/100	4.00
17	Michael Young/250	4.00
18	Miguel Cabrera/100	8.00
19	Mike Piazza/250	10.00
20	Pedro Martinez/100	8.00
21	Randy Johnson/250	8.00
22	Roger Clemens/250	10.00
23	Sammy Sosa/250	8.00
24	Tim Hudson/100	4.00
25	Todd Helton/100	6.00

Mirror Red

Mirror Red (1-200):	2-4X
Auto. (201-250):	.4X
No Auto. (201-250):	1X
Production 100 Sets	

Mirror White

Mirror White (1-200):	2-4X
Auto. (201-250): .4X	
No Auto. (201-250):	1X
Production 100 Sets	

Mirror Blue

Mirror Blue (1-200):	3-6X
Auto. (201-250):	.5X
No Auto. (201-250):	1-2X
Production 50 Sets	

Mirror Gold

Mirror Gold (1-200):	5-10X
Mirror Gol (201-250):	No Pricing
Production 25 Sets	

Mirror Emerald

No Pricing
Production Five Sets

Mirror Black

No Pricing
Production One Set

Mirror Autograph Red

NM/M

Production 1-250

16	Tim Salmon/25	30.00
18	Bobby Crosby/50	25.00
25	Casey Kotchman/50	12.00
33	Orlando Hudson/250	8.00
53	Jack Wilson/50	12.00
62	Eric Byrnes/50	10.00
66	Jeremy Bonderman/50	15.00
67	Jermaine Dye/50	15.00
78	Kazuhito Tadano/100	12.00
79	Edwin Jackson/50	12.00
80	Raul Ibanez/50	12.00
86	Ken Harvey/250	8.00
89	Wade Miller/250	10.00
92	Jeremy Affeldt/250	8.00
94	Francisco Cordero/25	15.00
95	Laynce Nix/100	8.00
106	Marlon Byrd/250	8.00
155	Bubba Nelson/250	6.00
159	Kevin Youkilis/50	20.00
160	Lew Ford/50	15.00
161	Ervin Santana/250	10.00
162	Jody Gerut/50	15.00
164	Brian Roberts/250	30.00
167	Ryan Wagner/50	10.00
168	David Dellucci/50	15.00
169	Jae Weong Seo/25	15.00

173 Jose Castillo/250 10.00
202 Agustin Montero/99 10.00
211 Norihiro Nakamura/99 50.00
212 Erick Threets/49 15.00
218 Jeff Niemann/49 25.00
221 Justin Verlander/49 40.00
223 Luke Scott/99 30.00
229 Nate McLouth/25 20.00
230 Paulino Reynoso/49 10.00
231 Philip Humber/25 25.00
234 Raul Tablado/99 12.00
239 Sean Tracey/49 10.00
243 Wladimir Balentien/99 10.00

Mirror Autograph White
NM/M
Production 1-50
18 Bobby Crosby/25 25.00
19 Brad Penny/25 15.00
2 Casey Kotchman/25 15.00
33 Orlando Hudson/25 8.00
53 Jack Wilson/25 15.00
62 Eric Byrnes/25 12.00
68 Jermaine Dye/25 15.00
68 Kazuhito Tadano/50 15.00
79 Edwin Jackson/25 10.00
80 Raul Ibanez/25 15.00
81 Rich Harden/50 15.00
86 Ken Harvey/25 8.00
89 Wade Miller/50 12.00
91 Jeremy Affeldt/50 10.00
95 Laynce Nix/50 10.00
106 Marlon Byrd/50 8.00
156 Bubba Nelson/50 8.00
156 Kevin Youkilis/25 25.00
160 Lew Ford/25 15.00
161 Ervin Santana/50 12.00
165 Jody Gerut/25 15.00
165 Joe Nathan/25 20.00
167 Ryan Wagner/25 10.00
167 David Dellucci/25 20.00
173 Jose Castillo/50 12.00
202 Agustin Montero/49 12.00
211 Norihiro Nakamura/49 60.00
212 Erick Threets/49 10.00
218 Jeff Niemann/49 25.00
221 Justin Verlander/49 40.00
221 Luke Scott/49 40.00
229 Nate McLouth/49 25.00
230 Paulino Reynoso/49 10.00
231 Philip Humber/49 25.00
234 Raul Tablado/49 15.00
239 Sean Tracey/49 10.00
243 Wladimir Balentien/49 15.00

Mirror Autograph Blue
NM/M
Production 1-100
Black: No Pricing
Production One Set
Emerald: No Pricing
Production 1-5
18 Bobby Crosby/25 25.00
25 Casey Kotchman/25 15.00
33 Orlando Hudson/100 10.00
53 Jack Wilson/25 15.00
62 Eric Byrnes/25 12.00
66 Jeremy Bonderman/25 20.00
67 Jermaine Dye/25 15.00
68 Kazuhito Tadano/25 15.00
79 Edwin Jackson/100 8.00
80 Raul Ibanez/25 8.00
86 Ken Harvey/100 8.00
89 Wade Miller/100 8.00
91 Jeremy Affeldt/100 8.00
95 Laynce Nix/50 8.00
106 Marlon Byrd/100 8.00
156 Bubba Nelson/100 8.00
156 Kevin Youkilis/25 25.00
160 Lew Ford/25 15.00
161 Ervin Santana/100 14.00
165 Joe Nathan/25 20.00
167 Ryan Wagner/25 10.00
167 David Dellucci/25 20.00
169 Jae Weong Seo/25 15.00
173 Jose Castillo/100 10.00
221 Luke Scott/49 30.00
229 Nate McLouth/49 20.00
234 Raul Tablado/49 10.00
243 Wladimir Balentien/49 15.00

Mirror Autograph Gold
NM/M
Production 1-25
2 Adam Dunn/25 35.00
4 Aubrey Huff/25 15.00
12 Austin Kearns/25 15.00
12 B.J. Upton/25 15.00
14 Brandon Webb/25 15.00
16 Tim Salmon/25 30.00
18 Bobby Crosby/25 15.00
19 Brad Penny/25 15.00
23 C.C. Sabathia/25 15.00
23 Keith Foulke/25 25.00
27 Casey Kotchman/25 15.00
27 Chone Figgins/25 12.00
29 Craig Wilson/25 10.00
31 Danny Kolb/25 10.00
33 Orlando Hudson/25 10.00
34 David Wright/25 70.00
36 Jake Peavy/25 35.00
37 Derek Lee/25 40.00
39 Edgar Renteria/25 10.00
40 Angel Berroa/25 10.00
41 Eric Chavez/25 20.00
41 Akinori Otsuka/25 25.00
43 Francisco Rodriguez/25 25.00
43 Garret Anderson/25 20.00

53 Jack Wilson/25 15.00
54 Jamie Moyer/25 15.00
55 Jason Bay/25 25.00
55 Trot Nixon/25 20.00
60 Roy Oswalt/25 25.00
62 Eric Byrnes/25 12.00
63 Jeff Bagwell/25 40.00
65 Jeff Suppan/25 15.00
66 Jeremy Bonderman/25 20.00
67 Jermaine Dye/25 15.00
68 Kazuhito Tadano/25 15.00
75 Brett Myers/25 20.00
76 Jose Guillen/25 15.00
77 Jose Vidro/25 15.00
79 Edwin Jackson/25 10.00
80 Raul Ibanez/25 15.00
81 Rich Harden/25 20.00
86 Ken Harvey/25 10.00
89 Wade Miller/25 15.00
91 Jeremy Affeldt/25 12.00
92 Francisco Cordero/25 15.00
95 Laynce Nix/25 12.00
97 Lyle Overbay/25 15.00
98 Carlos Zambrano/25 30.00
101 Mark Buehrle/25 25.00
102 Mark Loretta/25 15.00
105 Marlon Byrd/25 10.00
107 Rafael Furcal/25 25.00
109 Michael Young/25 25.00
128 Miguel Cabrera/25 40.00
128 Magglio Ordonez/25 15.00
134 Sean Burroughs/25 15.00
135 Sean Casey/25 15.00
139 Steve Finley/25 15.00
143 Torii Hunter/25 20.00
144 Travis Hafner/25 20.00
147 Vernon Wells/25 15.00
152 Danny Graves/25 12.00
155 Bubba Nelson/25 10.00
156 Kevin Youkilis/25 25.00
157 Jacque Jones/25 15.00
158 Mike Lieberthal/25 15.00
160 Lew Ford/25 15.00
161 Ervin Santana/25 15.00
162 Jody Gerut/25 15.00
163 Nick Johnson/25 20.00
164 Brian Roberts/25 30.00
165 Joe Nathan/25 20.00
167 Ryan Wagner/25 10.00
167 David Dellucci/25 20.00
169 Jae Weong Seo/25 15.00
170 Tom Gordon/25 15.00
171 Carlos Lee/25 20.00
172 Octavio Dotel/25 12.00
173 Jose Castillo/25 15.00
174 Troy Percival/25 15.00
194 Harmon Killebrew/25 40.00

Mirror Bat Red
NM/M
Production 100-250
Gold: 1-2X
Production 25 Sets
2 Adam Dunn/250 6.00
5 Albert Pujols/250 15.00
8 Andruw Jones/250 6.00
11 Aubrey Huff/250 4.00
12 B.J. Upton/250 6.00
14 Brandon Webb/100 4.00
16 Tim Salmon/250 4.00
25 Casey Kotchman/250 4.00
26 Chipper Jones/250 6.00
28 Craig Biggio/50 6.00
29 Craig Wilson/250 4.00
34 David Wright/250 10.00
38 Dontrelle Willis/250 4.00
44 Garret Anderson/250 4.00
45 Gary Sheffield/250 6.00
59 Jason Varitek/250 4.00
61 Javy Lopez/250 4.00
63 Jeff Bagwell/250 6.00
77 Jose Vidro/250 4.00
93 Lance Berkman/250 4.00
99 Manny Ramirez/250 8.00
105 Mark Teixeira/250 6.00
109 Michael Young/250 4.00
110 Miguel Cabrera/250 8.00
111 Miguel Tejada/250 6.00
121 Paul Konerko/250 4.00
124 Rafael Palmeiro/250 6.00
128 Magglio Ordonez/250 4.00
136 Shawn Green/250 4.00
141 Todd Helton/250 6.00
142 Tom Glavine/250 4.00
143 Torii Hunter/200 4.00
148 Victor Martinez/250 4.00
149 Vladimir Guerrero/250 8.00
150 Sammy Sosa/250 8.00
153 Rocco Baldelli/250 4.00
160 Lew Ford/250 4.00
166 Mike Sweeney/100 4.00
184 Rafael Palmeiro/100 6.00
188 Tom Glavine/250 4.00
190 Vladimir Guerrero/250 8.00

Mirror Bat White
NM/M
Production 75-250
2 Adam Dunn/1 6.00
5 Albert Pujols/1 20.00
7 Alfonso Soriano/1 6.00
11 Aubrey Huff/10 4.00
12 Austin Kearns/5 6.00
12 B.J. Upton/5 6.00
14 Brandon Webb/50 4.00
25 Casey Kotchman/250 6.00
26 Chipper Jones/100 6.00
28 Craig Biggio/100 6.00

29 Craig Wilson/250 10.00
34 David Wright/100 6.00
37 Derek Lee/250 6.00
38 Dontrelle Willis/100 4.00
44 Garret Anderson/100 6.00
45 Gary Sheffield/100 6.00
59 Jason Varitek/100 4.00
61 Javy Lopez/100 4.00
63 Jeff Bagwell/100 4.00
77 Jose Vidro/100 4.00
88 Kerry Wood/100 4.00
93 Lance Berkman/100 6.00
94 Larry Walker/100 4.00
99 Manny Ramirez/250 6.00
105 Mark Teixeira/250 8.00
109 Michael Young/250 8.00
110 Miguel Cabrera/250 8.00
111 Miguel Tejada/250 4.00
121 Paul Konerko/75 6.00
124 Rafael Palmeiro/75 6.00
128 Magglio Ordonez/100 4.00
136 Shawn Green/100 4.00
141 Todd Helton/100 6.00
142 Tom Glavine/100 4.00
143 Torii Hunter/100 4.00
148 Victor Martinez/100 4.00
149 Vladimir Guerrero/100 8.00
150 Sammy Sosa/100 8.00
153 Rocco Baldelli/100 4.00
184 Rafael Palmeiro/100 6.00
188 Tom Glavine/100 4.00
190 Vladimir Guerrero/100 8.00

Mirror Bat Blue
NM/M
Production 75-100
Black: No Pricing
Production One Set
Emerald: No Pricing
Production Five Sets
2 Adam Dunn/100 6.00
5 Albert Pujols/100 20.00
8 Andruw Jones/100 8.00
11 Aubrey Huff/100 4.00
14 B.J. Upton/100 4.00
14 Brandon Webb/100 4.00
16 Tim Salmon/100 4.00
25 Casey Kotchman/100 4.00
26 Chipper Jones/100 6.00
32 David Ortiz/100 10.00
37 Derek Lee/100 8.00
38 Dontrelle Willis/100 6.00
44 Garret Anderson/100 4.00
45 Gary Sheffield/100 6.00
59 Jason Varitek/100 4.00
61 Javy Lopez/100 4.00
63 Jeff Bagwell/100 6.00
77 Jose Vidro/100 4.00
93 Lance Berkman/100 4.00
99 Manny Ramirez/100 8.00
105 Mark Teixeira/100 8.00
109 Michael Young/100 4.00
110 Miguel Cabrera/5 8.00
111 Miguel Tejada/100 8.00
117 Nomar Garciaparra/100 8.00
121 Paul Konerko/100 4.00
124 Rafael Palmeiro/100 6.00
128 Magglio Ordonez/100 6.00
136 Shawn Green/100 4.00
141 Todd Helton/100 6.00
142 Tom Glavine/100 4.00
143 Torii Hunter/100 4.00
144 Travis Hafner/100 4.00
148 Victor Martinez/100 4.00
149 Vladimir Guerrero/100 8.00
150 Sammy Sosa/100 8.00
153 Rocco Baldelli/100 4.00
160 Lew Ford/100 4.00
166 Mike Sweeney/75 4.00
184 Rafael Palmeiro/100 6.00
188 Tom Glavine/100 4.00
190 Vladimir Guerrero/100 8.00

Mirror Fabric Red
NM/M
Production 100-250
Gold: 1-2X
Production 25 Sets
2 Adam Dunn/Jsy/250 6.00
5 Albert Pujols/Jsy/250 15.00
7 Alfonso Soriano/Jsy/250 6.00
8 Andruw Jones/Jsy/250 6.00
11 Aramis Ramirez/Jsy/250 4.00
11 Aubrey Huff/Jsy/250 4.00
12 B.J. Upton/Jsy/250 6.00
14 Brandon Webb/Pants/100 4.00
15 Barry Zito/Jsy/250 4.00
17 Bobby Abreu/Jsy/250 4.00
25 Preston Wilson/Jsy/250 4.00
25 Casey Kotchman/Jsy/250 4.00
26 Chipper Jones/Jsy/250 8.00
28 Craig Biggio/Jsy/250 4.00
32 Curt Schilling/Jsy/250 8.00
37 David Ortiz/Jsy/250 8.00
37 Derek Lee/Jsy/250 8.00
38 Dontrelle Willis/Jsy/225 4.00
41 Eric Chavez/Jsy/250 4.00
43 Francisco Rodriguez/Jsy/250 4.00
44 Garret Anderson/Jsy/250 4.00
45 Gary Sheffield/Jsy/250 4.00
46 Greg Maddux/Jsy/250 10.00
47 Hideki Matsui/Jsy/100 15.00
48 Hideo Nomo/Jsy/250 6.00
50 Ivan Rodriguez/Jsy/250 4.00
57 Trot Nixon/Jsy/250 4.00

60 Roy Oswalt/Jsy/250 4.00
61 Javy Lopez/Jsy/250 4.00
63 Jeff Bagwell/Jsy/250 6.00
69 Jim Edmonds/Jsy/250 6.00
70 Jim Thome/Jsy/250 6.00
71 Johan Santana/Jsy/250 6.00
82 Justin Morneau/Jsy/250 6.00
84 Kazuo Matsui/Jsy/250 4.00
87 Frank Thomas/Jsy/250 6.00
88 Kerry Wood/Jsy/250 4.00
92 Francisco Cordero/Jsy/250 4.00
93 Lance Berkman/Jsy/250 6.00
94 Larry Walker/Jsy/250 6.00
96 Luis Gonzalez/Jsy/250 4.00
97 Lyle Overbay/Jsy/250 4.00
98 Carlos Zambrano/Jsy/250 4.00
99 Manny Ramirez/Jsy/250 8.00
104 Mark Prior/Jsy/250 6.00
109 Michael Young/Jsy/250 4.00
110 Miguel Cabrera/Jsy/250 8.00
111 Miguel Tejada/Jsy/250 4.00
114 Mike Piazza/Jsy/250 6.00
121 Paul Konerko/Jsy/250 4.00
124 Rafael Palmeiro/Jsy/75 6.00
129 Roger Clemens/Jsy/250 10.00
131 Sammy Sosa/Jsy/100 8.00
133 Scott Rolen/Jsy/250 4.00
135 Sean Casey/Jsy/250 4.00
138 Roy Halladay/Jsy/250 4.00
141 Todd Helton/Jsy/250 6.00
144 Travis Hafner/Jsy/250 4.00
147 Vernon Wells/Jsy/250 4.00
148 Victor Martinez/Jsy/250 4.00
149 Vladimir Guerrero/Jsy/250 8.00
153 Rocco Baldelli/Jsy/250 4.00
159 Ben Sheets/Jsy/250 4.00
160 Lew Ford/Jsy/250 4.00
166 Mike Sweeney/Jsy/250 4.00
178 Greg Maddux/Jsy/250 10.00
179 Ivan Rodriguez/Jsy/250 4.00
183 Pedro J. Martinez/Jsy/250 8.00
184 Rafael Palmeiro/Jsy/250 6.00
185 Roger Clemens/Jsy/250 10.00
188 Tom Glavine/Jsy/250 4.00
190 Vladimir Guerrero/Jsy/100 8.00

Mirror Fabric White
NM/M
Production 50-250
2 Adam Dunn/Jsy/100 6.00
5 Albert Pujols/Jsy/100 15.00
7 Alfonso Soriano/Jsy/100 6.00
8 Andruw Jones/Jsy/100 6.00
11 Aramis Ramirez/Jsy/100 6.00
11 Aubrey Huff/Jsy/150 4.00
15 Barry Zito/Jsy/100 4.00
26 Chipper Jones/Pants/250 4.00
28 Craig Biggio/Pants/250 4.00
30 Curt Schilling/Jsy/100 8.00
32 David Ortiz/Jsy/100 8.00
34 David Wright/Jsy/100 10.00
38 Dontrelle Willis/Jsy/50 6.00
41 Eric Chavez/Jsy/100 4.00
44 Garret Anderson/Jsy/100 4.00
45 Gary Sheffield/Jsy/50 6.00
46 Greg Maddux/Jsy/250 6.00
47 Hideki Matsui/Pants/100 15.00
48 Hideo Nomo/Jsy/100 6.00
57 Trot Nixon/Jsy/100 4.00
60 Roy Oswalt/Jsy/25 4.00
63 Jeff Bagwell/Jsy/100 6.00
69 Jim Edmonds/Jsy/100 6.00
70 Jim Thome/Jsy/100 6.00
71 Johan Santana/Jsy/100 6.00
82 Josh Beckett/Jsy/100 4.00
82 Justin Morneau/Jsy/100 6.00
84 Kazuo Matsui/Jsy/50 4.00
88 Kerry Wood/Jsy/50 6.00
93 Lance Berkman/Jsy/100 6.00
94 Larry Walker/Jsy/100 6.00
95 Laynce Nix/Jsy/100 4.00
96 Luis Gonzalez/Jsy/100 4.00
98 Carlos Zambrano/Jsy/100 6.00
99 Manny Ramirez/Jsy/100 8.00
104 Mark Prior/Jsy/100 8.00
109 Michael Young/Jsy/100 4.00
110 Miguel Cabrera/Jsy/150 8.00
111 Miguel Tejada/Jsy/100 4.00
113 Mike Mussina/Jsy/100 4.00
114 Mike Piazza/Jsy/100 8.00
121 Paul Konerko/Jsy/150 4.00
124 Rafael Palmeiro/Jsy/50 6.00
129 Roger Clemens/Jsy/100 10.00
131 Sammy Sosa/Jsy/150 8.00
133 Scott Rolen/Jsy/100 4.00
135 Sean Casey/Jsy/100 4.00
138 Roy Halladay/Jsy/100 4.00
141 Todd Helton/Jsy/100 6.00
144 Travis Hafner/Jsy/100 4.00
147 Vernon Wells/Jsy/100 4.00
148 Victor Martinez/Jsy/100 4.00
149 Vladimir Guerrero/Jsy/100 8.00
151 Hank Blalock/Jsy/100 4.00
159 Ben Sheets/Jsy/100 4.00
166 Mike Sweeney/Jsy/100 4.00
178 Greg Maddux/Jsy/200 10.00
179 Ivan Rodriguez/Jsy/100 4.00
184 Rafael Palmeiro/Jsy/100 6.00
185 Roger Clemens/Jsy/100 10.00
188 Tom Glavine/Jsy/250 4.00

Mirror Fabric Blue
NM/M
Production 50-100
Black: No Pricing
Production One Set
Emerald: No Pricing
Production Five Sets
2 Adam Dunn/Jsy/100 6.00
5 Albert Pujols/Jsy/100 15.00
7 Alfonso Soriano/Jsy/100 6.00
8 Andruw Jones/Jsy/100 6.00
10 Aramis Ramirez/Jsy/100 4.00
11 Aubrey Huff/Jsy/100 4.00
13 B.J. Upton/Jsy/100 4.00
14 Brandon Webb/Pants/100 4.00
15 Barry Zito/Jsy/100 4.00
17 Bobby Abreu/Jsy/100 4.00
18 Bobby Crosby/Jsy/50 4.00
25 Casey Kotchman/Jsy/100 4.00
26 Chipper Jones/Jsy/100 8.00
28 Craig Biggio/Jsy/100 4.00
30 Curt Schilling/Jsy/100 8.00
32 David Ortiz/Jsy/100 8.00
37 Derek Lee/Jsy/100 8.00
38 Dontrelle Willis/Jsy/100 6.00
41 Eric Chavez/Jsy/100 4.00
43 Francisco Rodriguez/Jsy/100 4.00
46 Greg Maddux/Jsy/100 10.00
47 Hideki Matsui/Pants/100 15.00
48 Hideo Nomo/Jsy/100 6.00
50 Ivan Rodriguez/Jsy/100 6.00
57 Trot Nixon/Jsy/100 4.00
60 Roy Oswalt/Jsy/50 4.00
61 Javy Lopez/Jsy/100 6.00
63 Jeff Bagwell/Jsy/100 6.00
69 Jim Edmonds/Jsy/100 6.00
70 Jim Thome/Jsy/100 6.00
71 Johan Santana/Jsy/100 6.00
73 Johnny Damon/Jsy/100 6.00
78 Josh Beckett/Jsy/100 4.00
82 Justin Morneau/Jsy/100 6.00
84 Kazuo Matsui/Jsy/50 4.00
87 Frank Thomas/Jsy/100 6.00
88 Kerry Wood/Jsy/100 6.00
92 Francisco Cordero/Jsy/100 4.00
93 Lance Berkman/Jsy/100 4.00
94 Larry Walker/Jsy/100 6.00
96 Luis Gonzalez/Jsy/100 4.00
97 Lyle Overbay/Jsy/100 4.00
98 Carlos Zambrano/Jsy/100 6.00
99 Manny Ramirez/Jsy/100 8.00
104 Mark Prior/Jsy/100 8.00
109 Michael Young/Jsy/100 8.00
110 Miguel Cabrera/Jsy/100 8.00
111 Miguel Tejada/Jsy/100 8.00
113 Mike Mussina/Jsy/50 6.00
114 Mike Piazza/Jsy/100 8.00
121 Paul Konerko/Jsy/100 4.00
124 Rafael Palmeiro/Jsy/100 6.00
129 Roger Clemens/Jsy/100 10.00
131 Sammy Sosa/Jsy/100 8.00
133 Scott Rolen/Jsy/100 4.00
135 Sean Casey/Jsy/100 4.00
138 Roy Halladay/Jsy/100 4.00
141 Todd Helton/Jsy/100 6.00
144 Travis Hafner/Jsy/100 4.00
147 Vernon Wells/Jsy/100 4.00
148 Victor Martinez/Jsy/100 4.00
149 Vladimir Guerrero/Jsy/100 8.00
151 Hank Blalock/Jsy/100 4.00
153 Rocco Baldelli/Jsy/100 4.00
159 Ben Sheets/Jsy/100 4.00
160 Lew Ford/Jsy/100 4.00
166 Mike Sweeney/Jsy/100 4.00
178 Greg Maddux/Jsy/100 10.00
179 Ivan Rodriguez/Jsy/100 4.00
183 Pedro J. Martinez/Jsy/100 8.00
184 Rafael Palmeiro/Jsy/Pants/100 8.00
190 Vladimir Guerrero/Jsy/100 8.00

Skills
NM/M
Common: 1.50
Inserted 1:7
Mirror: 2X-3X
1 Andy Pettitte 1.50
2 Barry Zito 1.50
3 Bobby Crosby 2.00
4 Brandon Webb 1.50
5 Craig Biggio 2.00
6 David Ortiz 3.00
7 Dontrelle Willis 2.00
8 Francisco Rodriguez 1.50
9 Gary Sheffield 2.00
10 Jack Wilson 1.50
12 Jason Bay 2.00
13 Jeff Bagwell 2.00
13 Jim Edmonds 2.00
14 Josh Beckett 1.50
15 Kerry Wood 2.00
16 Lance Berkman 1.50
17 Mark Buehrle 1.50
18 Mark Teixeira 2.00
19 Miguel Tejada 2.00
20 Paul Konerko 1.50

21 Scott Rolen 2.00
22 Sean Burroughs 1.50
23 Vernon Wells 1.50
24 Victor Martinez 1.50
25 Vladimir Guerrero 3.00

Skills Autographs
NM/M
Production 5-25
3 Bobby Crosby/25 25.00
11 Jason Bay/25 25.00

Skills Jersey Position
NM/M
Production 100-250
Prime: No Pricing
Production 5-25
1 Andy Pettitte/250 4.00
2 Barry Zito/250 4.00
3 Bobby Crosby/250 6.00
4 Brandon Webb/Pants/250 4.00
5 Craig Biggio/250 4.00
6 David Ortiz/250 4.00
7 Dontrelle Willis/100 4.00
8 Francisco Rodriguez/250 4.00
9 Gary Sheffield/250 6.00
10 Jack Wilson/250 4.00
11 Jason Bay/250 6.00
12 Jeff Bagwell/250 6.00
13 Jim Edmonds/250 6.00
14 Josh Beckett/250 4.00
15 Kerry Wood/50 6.00
16 Lance Berkman/250 4.00
17 Mark Buehrle/150 4.00
19 Miguel Tejada/250 8.00
20 Paul Konerko/100 6.00
21 Scott Rolen/100 6.00
22 Sean Burroughs/100 4.00
23 Vernon Wells/100 4.00
24 Victor Martinez/250 4.00
25 Vladimir Guerrero/250 8.00

2005 Leaf Limited

NM/M
Complete Set (205):
Common Player (1-150): 1.00
Common (151-175, 197): 4.00
Production 699
Common Auto. (176-196),
(198-200): 12.00
Production 99
Pack (4): 70.00
1 Roger Clemens 5.00
2 Roger Clemens 5.00
3 Ichiro Suzuki 4.00
4 Ichiro Suzuki 4.00
5 Todd Helton 1.50
6 Todd Helton 1.50
7 Vladimir Guerrero 2.00
8 Vladimir Guerrero 2.00
9 Miguel Cabrera 2.00
10 Miguel Cabrera 2.00
11 Albert Pujols 5.00
12 Albert Pujols 5.00
13 Mark Prior 1.50
14 Mark Prior 1.50
15 Chipper Jones 2.00
16 Chipper Jones 2.00
17 Jeff Bagwell 1.50
18 Jeff Bagwell 1.50
19 Kerry Wood 1.00
20 Kerry Wood 1.00
21 Gary Sheffield 1.50
22 Carl Crawford 1.50
23 Mariano Rivera 1.50
24 Curt Schilling 2.00
25 Ben Sheets 1.00
26 Jimmy Rollins 1.00
27 Melvin Mora 1.00
28 Corey Patterson 1.00
29 Rafael Furcal 1.00
30 Jim Thome 1.50
31 Derek Jeter 5.00
32 Jake Peavy 1.50
33 Francisco Cordero 1.00
34 Aramis Ramirez 1.00
35 Javy Lopez 1.00
36 Aaron Rowand 1.00
37 Jason Bay 1.00
38 Michael Young 1.00
39 Ivan Rodriguez 1.50
40 Joe Nathan 1.00
41 Oliver Perez 1.00
42 Adam Dunn 1.50
43 Eric Chavez 1.00
44 Pedro Martinez 2.00

#	Player	Price
45	Roy Oswalt	1.00
46	Carlos Delgado	1.00
47	Jeff Kent	1.00
48	Johnny Damon	2.00
49	Edgar Renteria	1.00
50	Mark Buehrle	1.00
51	Carl Pavano	1.00
52	J.D. Drew	1.00
53	Hank Blalock	1.00
54	Moises Alou	1.00
55	Brad Radke	1.00
56	Brad Wilkerson	1.00
57	Sean Casey	1.00
58	Mike Lowell	1.00
59	Octavio Dotel	1.00
60	Francisco Rodriguez	1.00
61	Jose Guillen	1.00
62	Greg Maddux	3.00
63	A.J. Burnett	1.00
64	Chris Carpenter	1.50
65	Jose Reyes	1.50
66	Travis Hafner	1.50
67	Rich Harden	1.00
68	Bret Boone	1.00
69	Scott Podsednik	1.00
70	Andruw Jones	1.50
71	Milton Bradley	1.00
72	Zack Greinke	1.00
73	Torii Hunter	1.00
74	Paul Konerko	1.50
75	David Wells	1.00
76	Tim Hudson	1.50
77	Sammy Sosa	2.50
78	Jason Varitek	1.50
79	Lance Berkman	1.50
80	Justin Morneau	1.50
81	Troy Glaus	1.00
82	Jose Vidro	1.00
83	Joe Mauer	1.50
84	Josh Beckett	1.00
85	Craig Biggio	1.00
86	Luis Gonzalez	1.00
87	Larry Walker	1.00
88	Barry Zito	1.00
89	Jacque Jones	1.00
90	Lyle Overbay	1.00
91	Roy Halladay	1.50
92	Orlando Cabrera	1.00
93	Magglio Ordonez	1.00
94	Mike Sweeney	1.00
95	Rafael Palmeiro	1.50
96	Brandon Webb	1.00
97	Preston Wilson	1.00
98	Shannon Stewart	1.00
99	Trot Nixon	1.00
100	Mike Piazza	2.50
101	Dontrelle Willis	1.50
102	Ken Griffey Jr.	3.00
103	Andy Pettitte	1.00
104	Kazuo Matsui	1.00
105	Bobby Crosby	1.00
106	Shawn Green	1.00
107	Alfonso Soriano	2.00
108	Carlos Zambrano	1.00
109	Keith Foulke	1.00
110	Aubrey Huff	1.00
111	Adrian Beltre	1.00
112	Mark Teixeira	1.50
113	Randy Johnson	2.00
114	Miguel Tejada	1.50
115	Alex Rodriguez	4.00
116	Carlos Beltran	1.50
117	Bobby Abreu	1.50
118	Johan Santana	1.50
119	Manny Ramirez	2.00
120	Juan Pierre	1.00
121	Scott Rolen	1.50
122	Livan Hernandez	1.00
123	Carlos Lee	1.00
124	Derrek Lee	1.00
125	Brian Giles	1.00
126	Nomar Garciaparra	2.00
127	John Smoltz	1.50
128	Jim Edmonds	1.50
129	Bartolo Colon	1.00
130	Garret Anderson	1.00
131	Austin Kearns	1.00
132	Shingo Takatsu	1.00
133	Omar Vizquel	1.00
134	Tom Glavine	1.00
135	Mark Mulder	1.50
136	Bernie Williams	1.00
137	Richie Sexson	1.00
138	Mike Mussina	1.50
139	Mark Loretta	1.00
140	Vernon Wells	1.00
141	David Wright	3.00
142	Marcus Giles	1.00
143	David Ortiz	2.00
144	Victor Martinez	1.00
145	Hideki Matsui	4.00
146	C.C. Sabathia	1.00
147	Angel Berroa	1.00
148	Troy Percival	1.00
149	Paul LoDuca	1.00
150	Jorge Posada	1.50
151	Willie Mays	8.00
152	Ryne Sandberg	8.00
153	Rickey Henderson	4.00
154	Ted Williams	10.00
155	Roberto Clemente	10.00
156	George Brett	8.00
157	Whitey Ford	4.00
158	Duke Snider	5.00
159	Don Mattingly	10.00
160	Bob Gibson	4.00
161	Hank Aaron	8.00
162	Al Kaline	6.00

#	Player	Price
163	Nolan Ryan	10.00
164	Stan Musial	6.00
165	George Kell	4.00
166	Harmon Killebrew	6.00
167	Cal Ripken Jr.	15.00
168	Babe Ruth	10.00
169	Roger Clemens/SP	8.00
170	Curt Schilling/SP	4.00
171	Rafael Palmeiro/SP	4.00
172	Randy Johnson/SP	5.00
173	Mike Piazza/SP	5.00
174	Greg Maddux/SP	6.00
175	Sammy Sosa/SP	5.00
176	Hayden Penn/Auto. RC	15.00
177	Ambiorix Concepcion/ Auto. RC	15.00
178	Casey Rogowski/ Auto. RC	15.00
179	Prince Fielder/Auto.	80.00
180	Geovany Soto/Auto. RC	40.00
181	Wladimir Balentien/ Auto. RC	20.00
182	Jason Hammel/ Auto. RC	15.00
183	Keiichi Yabu/Auto. RC	25.00
184	Brandon McCarthy/ Auto. RC	15.00
185	Ubaldo Jimenez/ Auto. RC	125.00
186	Keiichi Yabu/Auto. RC	25.00
187	Miguel Negron/ Auto. RC	15.00
188	Mike Morse/Auto. RC	25.00
189	Nate McLouth/Auto. RC	20.00
190	Norihiro Nakamura/ Auto. RC	15.00
191	Bill McCarthy/Auto. RC	15.00
192	Tony Pena/Auto. RC	12.00
193	Ambiorix Concepcion/ Auto. RC	15.00
194	Raul Tablado/Auto. RC	15.00
195	Hayden Penn/Auto. RC	15.00
196	Sean Thompson/ Auto. RC	15.00
197	Tadahito Iguchi/ RC	15.00
198	Ubaldo Jimenez/ Auto. RC	125.00
199	Wladimir Balentien/ Auto. RC	20.00
200	Prince Fielder/Auto.	80.00
201	Philip Humber/ Auto./99 RC	25.00
202	Jeff Niemann/ Auto./95 RC	40.00
203	Justin Verlander/ Auto./70 RC	75.00
205	Yuniesky Betancourt/ Auto./99 RC	30.00

Bronze Spotlight

Bronze (1-150):	1-1.5X
Bronze (151-175):	1X
Bronze (176-200):	.25X
Production 99 Sets	

Silver Spotlight

Silver (1-150):	1-2X
Silver (151-175):	1-1.5X
Silver (176-200):	.25X
Production 50 Sets	

Gold Spotlight

Gold (1-150):	2-4X
Gold (151-175):	2-3X
Production 25 Sets	
Gold (176-205):	No Pricing
Production 5-25	

Platinum Spotlight

No Pricing
Production One Set

Cuts Silver

NM/M
Production 7-99
Platinum: No Pricing
Production One Set

1	Orlando Cepeda/30	35.00
2	Hank Aaron/34	275.00
3	Willie Mays/24	175.00
4	Sandy Koufax/32	400.00
5	Cal Ripken Jr./32	150.00
6	Nolan Ryan/34	120.00
7	Jim Palmer/22	30.00
8	Tony Gwynn/19	60.00
9	Rod Carew/29	40.00
10	Ryne Sandberg/23	70.00
11	Stan Musial/28	70.00
12	Steve Carlton/32	30.00
14	Mike Schmidt/20	60.00
15	Harmon Killebrew/25	40.00
17	Duke Snider/53	50.00
18	Don Mattingly/25	50.00
19	Dale Murphy/25	25.00
21	Juan Marichal/99	25.00
22	Greg Maddux/37	50.00
24	Paul Molitor/25	35.00
26	Wade Boggs/26	40.00
27	Mark Prior/27	30.00
28	Al Kaline/28	40.00

Cuts Gold

Production 3-30

Legends

NM/M
Common Player:
Production 50 Sets
Foil: No Pricing

1	Billy Martin	4.00
2	Bobby Doerr	3.00
3	Carlton Fisk	4.00
4	Harmon Killebrew	5.00
5	Duke Snider	5.00
6	George Brett	6.00
7	Johnny Bench	5.00
8	Lou Boudreau	3.00
9	Brooks Robinson	4.00
10	Al Kaline	4.00
11	Stan Musial	5.00
12	Burleigh Grimes	3.00
13	Cal Ripken Jr.	10.00
14	Carl Yastrzemski	6.00
15	Willie Stargell	3.00
16	Yogi Berra	4.00
17	Enos Slaughter	3.00
18	Phil Rizzuto	3.00
19	Luis Aparicio	3.00
20	Ernie Banks	5.00
21	Hal Newhouser	3.00
22	Whitey Ford	4.00
23	Tony Gwynn	4.00
24	Bob Feller	4.00
25	Don Sutton	3.00
26	Lou Brock	3.00
27	Jim Palmer	3.00
28	Billy Williams	2.00
29	Juan Marichal	3.00
30	Rod Carew	3.00
31	Jim "Catfish" Hunter	2.00
32	Maury Wills	2.00
33	Joe Cronin	2.00
34	Fergie Jenkins	2.00
35	Sandy Koufax	5.00
36	Steve Carlton	3.00
37	Eddie Murray	3.00
38	Roger Maris	4.00
39	Gaylord Perry	2.00
40	Bob Gibson	3.00
41	Tom Seaver	3.00
42	Dennis Eckersley	2.00
43	Reggie Jackson	3.00
44	Willie McCovey	3.00
45	Willie Mays	6.00
46	Willie Mays	6.00
47	Rickey Henderson	3.00
48	Rickey Henderson	3.00
49	Nolan Ryan	6.00
50	Nolan Ryan	6.00

Legends Jersey Number

NM/M
Production 1-45

3	Carlton Fisk/50	10.00
25	Don Sutton/20	8.00
26	Lou Brock/20	10.00
27	Jim Palmer/22	8.00
28	Billy Williams/26	8.00
29	Juan Marichal/27	8.00
30	Rod Carew/29	10.00
31	Jim "Catfish" Hunter/ Pants/29	8.00
34	Fergie Jenkins/31	8.00
35	Sandy Koufax/32	250.00
36	Steve Carlton/32	8.00
37	Eddie Murray/33	6.00
39	Gaylord Perry/36	6.00
40	Bob Gibson/45	10.00
41	Tom Seaver/41	10.00
42	Dennis Eckersley/45	6.00
43	Reggie Jackson/Pants/44	8.00
44	Willie McCovey/44	10.00
45	Willie Mays/24	40.00
46	Willie Mays/24	40.00
49	Nolan Ryan/30	25.00
50	Nolan Ryan/30	25.00

Legends Jersey Number Prime

NM/M
Production 1-45

3	Carlton Fisk/50	10.00
25	Don Sutton/20	8.00
26	Lou Brock/20	10.00
27	Jim Palmer/22	8.00
28	Billy Williams/26	8.00
29	Juan Marichal/27	8.00
30	Rod Carew/29	10.00
31	Jim "Catfish" Hunter/ Pants/29	8.00
34	Fergie Jenkins/31	8.00
35	Sandy Koufax/32	250.00
36	Steve Carlton/32	8.00
37	Eddie Murray/33	12.00
39	Gaylord Perry/36	6.00
40	Bob Gibson/45	10.00
41	Tom Seaver/41	10.00
42	Dennis Eckersley/45	6.00
43	Reggie Jackson/Pants/44	8.00
44	Willie McCovey/44	10.00
45	Willie Mays/24	40.00
46	Willie Mays/24	40.00
49	Nolan Ryan/30	25.00
50	Nolan Ryan/30	25.00

Legends Signature

NM/M
Production 2-50

2	Bobby Doerr/50	15.00
4	Harmon Killebrew/50	30.00
5	Duke Snider/50	25.00
9	Brooks Robinson/50	25.00
10	Al Kaline/50	40.00
18	Phil Rizzuto/50	35.00

#	Player	Price
19	Luis Aparicio/50	20.00
24	Bob Feller/50	25.00
25	Don Sutton/50	15.00
26	Lou Brock/50	30.00
27	Jim Palmer/50	20.00
28	Billy Williams/25	25.00
29	Juan Marichal/50	25.00
30	Rod Carew/25	35.00
32	Maury Wills/50	15.00
34	Fergie Jenkins/50	15.00
36	Steve Carlton/50	25.00
39	Gaylord Perry/50	15.00
40	Bob Gibson/25	40.00
42	Dennis Eckersley/50	20.00

Legends Signature Jersey Number

NM/M
Production 5-30

2	Bobby Doerr/Pants/25	25.00
4	Harmon Killebrew/25	40.00
11	Stan Musial/25	65.00
13	Cal Ripken Jr./25	150.00
18	Phil Rizzuto/Pants/25	40.00
19	Luis Aparicio/25	25.00
23	Tony Gwynn/25	40.00
25	Don Sutton/20	20.00
27	Jim Palmer/22	25.00
34	Fergie Jenkins/25	20.00
36	Steve Carlton/25	30.00
39	Gaylord Perry/25	20.00
40	Bob Gibson/25	40.00
42	Dennis Eckersley/25	25.00
44	Willie McCovey/25	40.00
46	Willie Mays/24	160.00
49	Nolan Ryan/30	90.00
50	Nolan Ryan/30	90.00

Legends Signature Jersey Number Prime

NM/M
Production 5-30

2	Bobby Doerr/Pants/25	25.00
4	Harmon Killebrew/25	40.00
11	Stan Musial/25	65.00
13	Cal Ripken Jr./25	150.00
18	Phil Rizzuto/Pants/25	40.00
19	Luis Aparicio/25	25.00
23	Tony Gwynn/25	40.00
25	Don Sutton/20	20.00
27	Jim Palmer/22	25.00
34	Fergie Jenkins/25	20.00
36	Steve Carlton/25	30.00
39	Gaylord Perry/25	20.00
40	Bob Gibson/25	40.00
42	Dennis Eckersley/25	25.00
44	Willie McCovey/25	40.00
46	Willie Mays/24	160.00
49	Nolan Ryan/30	90.00
50	Nolan Ryan/30	90.00

Lettermen

NM/M
Production 4-21

DU-H	Dale Murphy H/20	150.00
DU-M	Dale Murphy M/20	150.00
DU-P	Dale Murphy P/20	150.00
DU-R	Dale Murphy R/20	150.00
DU-U	Dale Murphy U/20	150.00
DU-Y	Dale Murphy Y/20	150.00
NR-A	Nolan Ryan A/21	200.00
NR-N	Nolan Ryan N/21	200.00
NR-R	Nolan Ryan R/21	200.00
NR-Y	Nolan Ryan Y/21	200.00

Lumberjacks

NM/M
Common Player:
Production 50 Sets
Foil: No Pricing

1	Al Kaline	4.00
2	Albert Pujols	8.00
3	Andre Dawson	3.00
4	Babe Ruth	8.00
5	Cal Ripken Jr.	15.00
6	Chipper Jones	4.00
7	Dale Murphy	3.00
8	Dave Winfield	3.00
9	Don Mattingly	8.00
10	Duke Snider	4.00
11	Eddie Murray	3.00
12	Frank Robinson	4.00
13	Frank Thomas	4.00
14	Gary Carter	3.00
15	Hack Wilson	3.00
16	Hank Aaron	10.00
17	Harmon Killebrew	4.00
18	Joe Morgan	3.00
19	Johnny Bench	4.00
20	Kirby Puckett	4.00
21	Kirk Gibson	3.00
22	Manny Ramirez	4.00
23	Mark Grace	3.00
24	Mike Piazza	5.00
25	Mike Schmidt	6.00
26	Orlando Cepeda	3.00
27	Paul Molitor	3.00
28	Rafael Palmeiro	4.00
29	Ralph Kiner	4.00
30	Reggie Jackson	4.00
31	Richie Ashburn	3.00
32	Rickey Henderson	4.00
33	Robin Yount	5.00
34	Rod Carew	4.00
35	Ryne Sandberg	4.00

#	Player	Price
36	Stan Musial	5.00
37	Ted Williams	8.00
38	Tony Gwynn	4.00
40	Vladimir Guerrero	4.00
41	Willie Mays	8.00
43	George Brett, Bo Jackson	8.00
44	John Kruk, Jim Thome	3.00
45	Willie Mays, Jim Thorpe	8.00
46	Wade Boggs, Johnny Damon	4.00
47	M. Williams, W. Clark	3.00
48	Willie Stargell, D. Parker	4.00

Legends (continued)

41	Ernie Banks, Bernie Williams	6.00
42	Ted Williams, Joe Cronin	10.00
43	George Brett, Bo Jackson	8.00
44	John Kruk, Jim Thome	3.00
45	Willie Mays, Jim Thorpe	8.00
46	Wade Boggs, Johnny Damon	4.00
47	M. Williams, W. Clark	3.00
48	Willie Stargell, D. Parker	4.00
50	Ichiro Suzuki, Edgar Martinez	6.00
	Carl Yastrzemski, Carlton Fisk	6.00

Lumberjacks Barrel

No Pricing
Production 1-5

Lumberjacks Bat

NM/M
Production 1-50

1	Al Kaline/50	10.00
4	Babe Ruth/25	180.00
8	Dave Winfield/25	10.00
11	Eddie Murray/25	15.00
12	Frank Robinson/50	15.00
14	Gary Carter/25	10.00
15	Hack Wilson/50	40.00
16	Hank Aaron/40	40.00
18	Joe Morgan/25	8.00
19	Johnny Bench/25	10.00
20	Kirby Puckett/50	10.00
24	Mike Schmidt/50	15.00
26	Orlando Cepeda/25	8.00
27	Paul Molitor/50	8.00
29	Ralph Kiner/25	15.00
31	Richie Ashburn/25	15.00
33	Robin Yount/25	20.00
35	Ryne Sandberg/25	20.00
36	Stan Musial/50	40.00
37	Ted Williams/50	40.00
39	Willie Mays/30	30.00
43	George Brett, Bo Jackson/50	25.00
47	M. Williams, W. Clark/50	15.00
48	Willie Stargell, D. Parker/50	15.00

Lumberjacks Combos

NM/M
Production 1-50

2	Albert Pujols/Bat-Jsy/50	30.00
5	Cal Ripken Jr./ Bat-Jsy/50	35.00
6	Chipper Jones/ Bat-Jsy/50	15.00
7	Dale Murphy/Bat-Jsy/50	12.00
8	Dave Winfield/ Bat-Pants/50	8.00
11	Eddie Murray/ Bat-Jsy/50	20.00
13	Frank Thomas/ Bat-Jsy/50	15.00
16	Hank Aaron/Bat-Jsy/50	60.00
19	Johnny Bench/ Bat-Jsy/50	15.00
20	Kirby Puckett/ Bat-Jsy/50	15.00
21	Kirk Gibson/Bat-Jsy/50	8.00
22	Manny Ramirez/ Bat-Jsy/50	12.00
23	Mark Grace/Bat-Jsy/50	12.00
24	Mike Piazza/Bat-Jsy/50	15.00
25	Mike Schmidt/ Bat-Jsy/50	25.00
26	Orlando Cepeda/ Bat-Pants/50	8.00
27	Paul Molitor/Bat-Jsy/50	12.00
31	Richie Ashburn/ Bat-Jsy/50	15.00
33	Robin Yount/Bat-Jsy/50	15.00
34	Stan Musial/Bat-Jsy/50	35.00
40	Willie Mays/Bat-Jsy/50	50.00

Lumberjacks Combos Prime

NM/M
Production 1-50

2	Albert Pujols/Bat-Jsy/50	35.00
3	Andre Dawson/ Bat-Jsy/50	8.00
5	Cal Ripken Jr./ Bat-Jsy/50	50.00
6	Chipper Jones/ Bat-Jsy/50	15.00
11	Eddie Murray/ Bat-Jsy/50	25.00
12	Frank Robinson/ Bat-Jsy/50	12.00
13	Frank Thomas/ Bat-Jsy/50	15.00
14	Gary Carter/Bat-Jsy/50	10.00
18	Joe Morgan/Bat-Jsy/25	15.00
21	Kirk Gibson/Bat-Jsy/50	8.00
22	Manny Ramirez/ Bat-Jsy/50	20.00
24	Mike Piazza/Bat-Jsy/50	15.00
28	Rafael Palmeiro/ Bat-Jsy/50	12.00

Lumberjacks Jersey

NM/M
Production 1-50

4	Babe Ruth/25	250.00
8	Dave Winfield/Pants/50	6.00
10	Duke Snider/Pants/50	10.00
11	Eddie Murray/25	15.00
14	Gary Carter/50	5.00
16	Hank Aaron/25	40.00
19	Johnny Bench/25	15.00
20	Kirby Puckett/25	15.00
27	Paul Molitor/50	8.00
30	Reggie Jackson/50	20.00
31	Richie Ashburn/50	10.00
33	Robin Yount/50	12.00
35	Ryne Sandberg/50	12.00
36	Stan Musial/25	50.00
37	Ted Williams/25	50.00
39	Willie Mays/25	35.00
41	Ernie Banks, Bernie Williams/25	30.00
42	Ted Williams, Joe Cronin/25	60.00
43	George Brett, Bo Jackson/50	30.00
44	John Kruk, Jim Thome/25	20.00
45	Willie Mays, Jim Thorpe/25	200.00
46	Wade Boggs, Johnny Damon/50	20.00
47	M. Williams, W. Clark/50	20.00
48	Willie Stargell, D. Parker/25	25.00

Lumberjacks Jersey Prime

NM/M
Production 1-50

4	Babe Ruth/25	250.00
8	Dave Winfield/Pants/50	6.00
10	Duke Snider/Pants/50	10.00
11	Eddie Murray/25	15.00
14	Gary Carter/50	5.00
16	Hank Aaron/25	40.00
19	Johnny Bench/25	15.00
20	Kirby Puckett/25	15.00
27	Paul Molitor/50	8.00
30	Reggie Jackson/50	10.00
31	Richie Ashburn/50	10.00
33	Robin Yount/50	12.00
35	Ryne Sandberg/50	12.00
36	Stan Musial/25	25.00
37	Ted Williams/50	50.00
39	Willie Mays/25	35.00
41	Ernie Banks, Bernie Williams/25	30.00
42	Ted Williams, Joe Cronin/25	60.00
43	George Brett, Bo Jackson/50	30.00
44	John Kruk, Jim Thome/25	20.00
45	Willie Mays, Jim Thorpe/25	200.00
46	Wade Boggs, Johnny Damon/50	20.00
47	M. Williams, W. Clark/50	20.00
48	Willie Stargell, D. Parker/25	25.00

Lumberjacks Signature

NM/M
Production 1-50

1	Al Kaline/50	40.00
4	Andre Dawson/25	20.00
5	Cal Ripken Jr./21	120.00
7	Dale Murphy/50	25.00
9	Don Mattingly/50	50.00
10	Duke Snider/25	25.00
12	Frank Robinson/50	30.00
13	Frank Thomas/50	50.00
14	Gary Carter/50	20.00
17	Harmon Killebrew/50	35.00
18	Joe Morgan/25	25.00
19	Johnny Bench/50	40.00
20	Kirby Puckett/25	40.00
24	Mark Grace/25	35.00
25	Mike Schmidt/50	40.00
27	Paul Molitor/50	30.00
29	Ralph Kiner/50	30.00
34	Rod Carew/50	25.00
35	Ryne Sandberg/50	40.00
36	Stan Musial/50	50.00
37	Tony Gwynn/25	50.00
40	Willie Mays/25	140.00

Lumberjacks Signature Bat

NM/M
Production 1-100

1	Al Kaline/50	40.00
4	Andre Dawson/100	14.00
5	Cal Ripken Jr./25	140.00
7	Dale Murphy/100	25.00
9	Don Mattingly/50	50.00
12	Frank Robinson/100	35.00
13	Frank Thomas/50	50.00
14	Gary Carter/25	25.00
18	Joe Morgan/25	25.00
19	Johnny Bench/50	50.00

#	Player	Price
21	Kirk Gibson/25	25.00
23	Mark Grace/25	40.00
26	Orlando Cepeda/100	20.00
27	Paul Molitor/25	40.00
29	Ralph Kiner/100	30.00
33	Robin Yount/25	30.00
34	Rod Carew/25	40.00
36	Stan Musial/25	65.00
38	Tony Gwynn/50	40.00

Lumberjacks Signature Jersey

NM/M — Production 1-100

#	Player	Price
3	Andre Dawson/100	20.00
5	Cal Ripken Jr./25	140.00
7	Dale Murphy/100	25.00
9	Don Mattingly/50	30.00
10	Duke Snider/Pants/50	30.00
13	Frank Thomas/25	
14	Gary Carter/50	25.00
17	Harmon Killebrew/25	40.00
19	Johnny Bench/25	
23	Mark Grace/25	40.00
27	Paul Molitor/25	40.00
30	Reggie Jackson/25	40.00
33	Robin Yount/50	50.00
38	Tony Gwynn/50	40.00

Lumberjacks Signature Jersey Prime

NM/M — Production 1-100

#	Player	Price
3	Andre Dawson/100	20.00
5	Cal Ripken Jr./25	140.00
7	Dale Murphy/100	25.00
9	Don Mattingly/50	
10	Duke Snider/Pants/50	30.00
13	Frank Thomas/25	
14	Gary Carter/50	25.00
17	Harmon Killebrew/25	40.00
19	Johnny Bench/25	
23	Mark Grace/25	40.00
27	Paul Molitor/25	40.00
30	Reggie Jackson/25	40.00
33	Robin Yount/50	50.00
38	Tony Gwynn/50	40.00

Lumberjacks Signature Combos

NM/M — Production 1-100

#	Player	Price
3	Andre Dawson/Bat-Jsy/100	20.00
5	Cal Ripken Jr./Bat-Jsy/25	140.00
7	Dale Murphy/Bat-Jsy/100	25.00
9	Don Mattingly/at-Jsy/50	50.00
13	Frank Thomas/Bat-Jsy/25	50.00
14	Gary Carter/Bat-Jsy/25	25.00
23	Mark Grace/Bat-Jsy/25	40.00
38	Tony Gwynn/Bat-Jsy/25	45.00

Lumberjacks Signature Combos Prime

Production 1-25

Leaf Limited Matching Numbers

NM/M — Production 5-50 — Prime: No Pricing — Production 1-5

#	Player	Price
1	Ted Williams, Roger Maris/25	160.00
2	Nolan Ryan, Kerry Wood/50	35.00
3	Cal Ripken Jr., Gary Carter/50	40.00
5	Johnny Bench, Albert Pujols/25	40.00
6	Roger Clemens, W. Clark/50	35.00
7	Willie McCovey, Reggie Jackson/25	20.00
9	Ryne Sandberg, Don Mattingly/50	35.00
	Duke Snider, Joe Cronin/25	25.00

Monikers Bronze

NM/M — Production 1-100

#	Player	Price
9	Miguel Cabrera/100	25.00
10	Miguel Cabrera/100	25.00
13	Mark Prior/50	35.00
14	Mark Prior/50	35.00
25	Ben Sheets/50	15.00
27	Melvin Mora/50	15.00
29	Rafael Furcal/50	20.00
32	Jake Peavy/25	25.00
33	Francisco Cordero/25	15.00
38	Michael Young/25	15.00
40	Joe Nathan/25	20.00
43	Eric Chavez/25	25.00
45	Roy Oswalt/25	25.00
49	Edgar Renteria/25	
57	Mark Buehrle/25	30.00
57	Sean Casey/50	15.00
60	Octavio Dotel/25	
60	Francisco Rodriguez/25	30.00
61	Jose Guillen/25	20.00
66	Travis Hafner/25	15.00
67	Rich Harden/50	15.00
71	Milton Bradley/25	15.00
73	Torii Hunter/25	25.00
74	Paul Konerko/50	30.00
76	Tim Hudson/25	25.00
80	Justin Morneau/100	25.00
82	Jose Vidro/25	15.00
84	Josh Beckett/25	30.00
85	Craig Biggio/25	30.00
89	Jacque Jones/25	15.00
91	Roy Halladay/50	
93	Magglio Ordonez/100	15.00
96	Brandon Webb/50	15.00
97	Preston Wilson/50	15.00
98	Shannon Stewart/50	10.00
99	Trot Nixon/50	20.00
105	Bobby Crosby/40	15.00
107	Alfonso Soriano/25	30.00
108	Carlos Zambrano/25	25.00
109	Keith Foulke/25	30.00
110	Aubrey Huff/50	15.00
112	Mark Teixeira/100	25.00
116	Carlos Beltran/25	30.00
118	Johan Santana/100	30.00
121	Scott Rolen/25	
123	Carlos Lee/50	
124	Derrek Lee/50	25.00
130	Garret Anderson/100	15.00
131	Austin Kearns/100	
133	Omar Vizquel/25	20.00
135	Mark Mulder/50	20.00
139	Mark Loretta/25	
141	David Wright/50	60.00
144	Victor Martinez/25	20.00
151	Willie Mays/25	175.00
152	Ryne Sandberg/50	50.00
158	Duke Snider/50	
159	Don Mattingly/25	50.00
160	Bob Gibson/50	50.00
162	Al Kaline/25	
163	Nolan Ryan/50	80.00
164	Stan Musial/50	
165	George Kell/50	15.00
166	Harmon Killebrew/50	30.00
167	Cal Ripken Jr./25	120.00
176	Hayden Penn/50	20.00
177	Ambiorix Concepcion/50	15.00
179	Prince Fielder/50	60.00
181	Wladimir Balentien/50	15.00
182	Jason Hammel/50	15.00
183	Keiichi Yabu/50	
184	Brandon McCarthy/50	12.00
185	Ubaldo Jimenez/50	40.00
186	Keiichi Yabu/50	
187	Miguel Negron/50	
188	Mike Morse/50	30.00
189	Nate McLouth/50	25.00
190	Norihiro Nakamura/50	
191	Brandon McCarthy/50	12.00
192	Tony Pena/50	10.00
193	Ambiorix Concepcion/50	15.00
194	Raul Tablado/50	
195	Hayden Penn/50	15.00
196	Sean Thompson/50	12.00
198	Ubaldo Jimenez/50	40.00
199	Wladimir Balentien/50	15.00
200	Prince Fielder/50	60.00

Monikers Silver

NM/M — Production 1-50

#	Player	Price
9	Miguel Cabrera/50	30.00
10	Miguel Cabrera/50	30.00
13	Mark Prior/25	40.00
14	Mark Prior/25	40.00
25	Ben Sheets/50	20.00
27	Melvin Mora/25	20.00
29	Rafael Furcal/25	20.00
32	Jake Peavy/50	25.00
33	Francisco Cordero/25	15.00
38	Michael Young/25	20.00
40	Joe Nathan/25	20.00
43	Eric Chavez/25	25.00
45	Roy Oswalt/25	30.00
49	Edgar Renteria/25	25.00
57	Mark Buehrle/25	30.00
57	Sean Casey/25	20.00
60	Octavio Dotel/25	12.00
60	Francisco Rodriguez/25	30.00
61	Jose Guillen/25	20.00
66	Travis Hafner/50	15.00
71	Rich Harden/50	15.00
80	Milton Bradley/50	15.00
89	Justin Morneau/50	15.00
93	Jacque Jones/25	15.00
96	Magglio Ordonez/50	15.00
97	Brandon Webb/25	20.00
98	Preston Wilson/25	20.00
105	Shannon Stewart/25	
108	Trot Nixon/25	25.00
105	Bobby Crosby/29	
108	Carlos Zambrano/25	25.00
109	Keith Foulke/25	30.00
110	Aubrey Huff/25	
112	Mark Teixeira/50	35.00
118	Johan Santana/50	
123	Carlos Lee/50	20.00
130	Garret Anderson/50	
131	Austin Kearns/25	15.00
133	Omar Vizquel/25	20.00
135	Mark Mulder/25	20.00
139	Mark Loretta/25	20.00
141	David Wright/25	70.00
144	Victor Martinez/25	15.00
151	Willie Mays/25	175.00
152	Ryne Sandberg/50	50.00
158	Duke Snider/25	30.00
159	Don Mattingly/25	50.00
162	Al Kaline/25	35.00
163	Nolan Ryan/25	80.00
164	Stan Musial/50	60.00
165	George Kell/50	15.00
166	Harmon Killebrew/25	40.00
167	Cal Ripken Jr./25	120.00

Monikers Material Bat Bronze

NM/M — Production 1-100 — Platinum: No Pricing — Production One Set

#	Player	Price
9	Miguel Cabrera/50	35.00
10	Miguel Cabrera/50	35.00
13	Mark Prior/25	40.00
14	Mark Prior/25	40.00
29	Rafael Furcal/75	15.00
34	Aramis Ramirez/100	20.00
37	Jason Bay/100	20.00
38	Michael Young/100	20.00
43	Eric Chavez/50	20.00
45	Roy Oswalt/50	25.00
50	Mark Buehrle/50	20.00
57	Sean Casey/25	15.00
66	Travis Hafner/100	15.00
73	Torii Hunter/50	20.00
74	Paul Konerko/50	30.00
80	Justin Morneau/100	25.00
82	Jose Vidro/100	15.00
85	Craig Biggio/50	30.00
93	Magglio Ordonez/50	20.00
97	Preston Wilson/50	15.00
98	Shannon Stewart/50	10.00
107	Alfonso Soriano/25	30.00
110	Aubrey Huff/100	12.00
111	Adrian Beltre/50	20.00
112	Mark Teixeira/50	30.00
116	Carlos Beltran/50	30.00
121	Scott Rolen/50	15.00
123	Carlos Lee/100	15.00
124	Derrek Lee/100	25.00
130	Garret Anderson/100	15.00
131	Austin Kearns/50	15.00
140	Vernon Wells/50	15.00
141	David Wright/50	70.00
143	David Ortiz/50	50.00
144	Victor Martinez/100	15.00
147	Angel Berroa/100	15.00

Monikers Material Button Gold

No Pricing — Platinum: No Pricing — Production One Set

Monikers Mat. Jersey Number Silver

NM/M — Production 1-75 — Prime Platinum: No Pricing — Production One Set

#	Player	Price
9	Miguel Cabrera/50	35.00
10	Miguel Cabrera/50	35.00
13	Mark Prior/25	40.00
25	Ben Sheets/Pants/50	20.00
34	Francisco Cordero/25	15.00
38	Aramis Ramirez/75	
43	Michael Young/25	25.00
45	Eric Chavez/75	
57	Roy Oswalt/75	25.00
60	Sean Casey/75	15.00
66	Francisco Rodriguez/75	25.00
70	Travis Hafner/50	15.00
85	Andruw Jones/25	40.00
89	Craig Biggio/25	30.00
90	Jacque Jones/25	15.00
98	Lyle Overbay/75	10.00
99	Shannon Stewart/75	10.00
101	Trot Nixon/25	35.00
107	Dontrelle Willis/24	30.00
112	Alfonso Soriano/25	30.00
117	Mark Teixeira/50	30.00
121	Bobby Abreu/25	30.00
124	Scott Rolen/25	30.00
128	Derrek Lee/25	25.00
130	Jim Edmonds/35	35.00
131	Garret Anderson/25	15.00
140	Austin Kearns/25	15.00
141	Vernon Wells/75	15.00
143	David Wright/75	70.00
144	David Ortiz/75	50.00
152	Victor Martinez/100	15.00
158	Ryne Sandberg/50	40.00
159	Duke Snider/25	30.00
160	Don Mattingly/60	60.00
164	Bob Gibson/50	30.00
166	Nolan Ryan/25	100.00
167	Stan Musial/25	80.00
	Harmon Killebrew/50	
	Cal Ripken Jr./25	140.00

Monikers Material Jersey Prime Gold

NM/M — Production 1-100 — Platinum: No Pricing — Production One Set

#	Player	Price
9	Miguel Cabrera/50	40.00
10	Miguel Cabrera/50	40.00
13	Mark Prior/50	50.00
14	Mark Prior/50	50.00
25	Ben Sheets/50	25.00
34	Aramis Ramirez/100	25.00
38	Michael Young/100	25.00
43	Eric Chavez/25	25.00
45	Roy Oswalt/100	30.00
57	Sean Casey/30	15.00
60	Francisco Rodriguez/75	25.00
66	Travis Hafner/100	25.00
66	Andruw Jones/50	40.00
84	Josh Beckett/25	30.00
85	Barry Zito/30	25.00
89	Jacque Jones/50	15.00
98	Shannon Stewart/75	15.00
112	Alfonso Soriano/40	40.00
117	Mark Teixeira/20	50.00
117	Bobby Abreu/25	25.00
128	Scott Rolen/25	35.00
128	Jim Edmonds/25	40.00
131	Garret Anderson/25	20.00
131	Austin Kearns/75	20.00
152	Vernon Wells/50	20.00
159	Ryne Sandberg/25	75.00
160	Don Mattingly/25	85.00
163	Bob Gibson/25	50.00
167	Nolan Ryan/25	120.00
	Cal Ripken Jr./25	175.00

Team Trademarks

NM/M — Common Player: 3.00 — Production 50 Sets — Foil: No Pricing — Production 10 Sets

#	Player	Price
1	Ryne Sandberg	8.00
2	George Brett	8.00
3	Steve Carlton	3.00
4	Reggie Jackson	4.00
5	Edgar Martinez	3.00
6	Barry Larkin	4.00
7	Ozzie Smith	6.00
8	Carlton Fisk	4.00
9	Wade Boggs	5.00
10	Will Clark	4.00
11	Nolan Ryan	8.00
12	Gary Carter	3.00
13	Don Mattingly	5.00
14	Willie Stargell	4.00
15	Don Sutton	3.00
16	Kirk Gibson	3.00
17	Kirby Puckett	5.00
18	Dale Murphy	4.00
19	Rickey Henderson	
20	Willie Mays	8.00
21	Cal Ripken Jr.	10.00
22	Paul Molitor	4.00
23	Tony Gwynn	5.00
24	Andre Dawson	3.00
25	Bob Feller	4.00
26	Alan Trammell	3.00
27	Dave Parker	3.00
28	Dave Righetti	3.00
29	Dwight Gooden	3.00
30	Harold Baines	3.00
31	Jack Morris	3.00
32	John Kruk	3.00
33	Lee Smith	3.00
34	Lenny Dykstra	3.00
35	Luis Tiant	3.00
36	Matt Williams	3.00
37	Ron Guidry	3.00
38	Tony Oliva	3.00

Team Trademarks Jersey Number

NM/M — Production 1-50

#	Player	Price
1	Ryne Sandberg/23	20.00
2	Steve Carlton/Pants/32	8.00
4	Reggie Jackson/44	
8	Carlton Fisk/50	8.00
9	Wade Boggs/26	10.00
11	Nolan Ryan/Pants/34	25.00
20	Willie Mays/24	

Team Trademarks Jersey Number Prime

NM/M

#	Player	Price
1	Ryne Sandberg/50	25.00
2	George Brett/50	25.00
3	Steve Carlton/50	10.00
4	Reggie Jackson/50	15.00
5	Edgar Martinez/50	15.00
6	Barry Larkin/50	15.00
7	Ozzie Smith/50	20.00
8	Carlton Fisk/50	15.00
9	Wade Boggs/50	15.00
10	Will Clark/50	15.00
11	Nolan Ryan/50	25.00
12	Gary Carter/50	12.00
13	Don Mattingly/40	25.00
14	Willie Stargell/50	15.00
15	Don Sutton/25	12.00
16	Kirk Gibson/50	12.00
18	Dale Murphy/50	15.00
19	Rickey Henderson/50	15.00
21	Cal Ripken Jr./25	50.00
23	Tony Gwynn/50	20.00
24	Andre Dawson/25	15.00
26	Alan Trammell/25	12.00
27	Dave Parker/25	
29	Dwight Gooden/25	15.00
30	Harold Baines/25	15.00
31	Jack Morris/47	10.00
32	John Kruk/25	15.00
33	Lee Smith/47	10.00
34	Lenny Dykstra/25	15.00
36	Matt Williams/25	10.00
38	Tony Oliva/26	15.00

Team Trademarks Signature

NM/M — Production 5-50

#	Player	Price
1	Ryne Sandberg/50	50.00
2	Steve Carlton/25	25.00
4	Reggie Jackson/50	30.00
6	Edgar Martinez/50	20.00
7	Barry Larkin/50	25.00
9	Ozzie Smith/50	35.00
8	Carlton Fisk/50	25.00
9	Wade Boggs/25	35.00
10	Will Clark/50	25.00
11	Nolan Ryan/50	75.00
12	Gary Carter/50	15.00
13	Don Mattingly/25	50.00
15	Don Sutton/50	12.00
16	Kirk Gibson/50	20.00
17	Kirby Puckett/50	40.00
18	Dale Murphy/100	20.00
20	Willie Mays/50	160.00
21	Cal Ripken Jr./50	90.00
22	Paul Molitor/25	25.00
23	Tony Gwynn/50	40.00
24	Andre Dawson/100	15.00
25	Bob Feller/50	20.00
26	Alan Trammell/25	25.00
27	Dave Parker/50	15.00
28	Dave Righetti/25	15.00
29	Dwight Gooden/50	15.00
30	Harold Baines/50	15.00
31	Jack Morris/50	12.00
32	John Kruk/25	20.00
33	Lee Smith/50	15.00
34	Lenny Dykstra/50	20.00
35	Luis Tiant/50	15.00
36	Matt Williams/50	20.00
37	Ron Guidry/25	15.00
38	Tony Oliva/50	15.00

Team Trademarks Sign. Jersey Number

NM/M — Production 1-72

#	Player	Price
4	Reggie Jackson/44	50.00
8	Carlton Fisk/72	35.00
9	Wade Boggs/26	50.00
11	Nolan Ryan/Pants/34	90.00
17	Kirby Puckett/34	60.00
27	Dave Parker/39	25.00
31	Jack Morris/47	20.00
33	Lee Smith/47	20.00
	Ron Guidry/Pants/49	20.00

Team Trade. Sig. Jersey Number Prime

NM/M

#	Player	Price
3	Steve Carlton/25	30.00
24	Andre Dawson/25	30.00
	Dave Parker/39	
31	Jack Morris/47	20.00
33	Lee Smith/47	25.00
38	Tony Oliva/26	35.00

Threads Button

No Pricing — Production 1-7

Threads Jersey Number

NM/M — Production 1-50 — Logo: No Pricing — Production One Set

#	Player	Price
152	Ryne Sandberg/50	15.00
154	Ted Williams/60	60.00
157	Whitey Ford/50	12.00
158	Duke Snider/50	12.00
164	Stan Musial/25	25.00
166	Harmon Killebrew/50	20.00

Threads Jersey Prime

NM/M — Production 5-100

#	Player	Price
1	Roger Clemens/25	25.00
5	Todd Helton/100	10.00
6	Todd Helton/100	10.00
8	Vladimir Guerrero/100	12.00
9	Vladimir Guerrero/Jkt/30	20.00
9	Miguel Cabrera/100	10.00
10	Miguel Cabrera/100	10.00
12	Albert Pujols/50	30.00
13	Mark Prior/100	10.00
14	Mark Prior/100	10.00
15	Chipper Jones/100	10.00
17	Chipper Jones/100	10.00
18	Jeff Bagwell/50	8.00
18	Jeff Bagwell/100	8.00
19	Kerry Wood/100	8.00
22	Carl Crawford/100	8.00
25	Mariano Rivera/60	12.00
25	Ben Sheets/50	8.00
28	Melvin Mora/25	10.00
28	Corey Patterson/50	5.00
29	Rafael Furcal/100	5.00
30	Jim Thome/100	8.00
34	Aramis Ramirez/100	5.00
	Javy Lopez/25	
38	Michael Young/100	5.00
42	Ivan Rodriguez/100	8.00
42	Adam Dunn/100	8.00
43	Eric Chavez/100	5.00
45	Roy Oswalt/100	5.00
48	Johnny Damon/50	15.00
50	Mark Buehrle/50	8.00
53	Hank Blalock/100	5.00
55	Brad Radke/50	5.00
57	Sean Casey/50	5.00
58	Mike Lowell/100	5.00
60	Francisco Rodriguez/100	5.00
62	Greg Maddux/25	25.00
63	A.J. Burnett/100	5.00
66	Travis Hafner/100	5.00
68	Bret Boone/100	5.00
70	Andruw Jones/100	10.00
73	Torii Hunter/100	8.00
74	Paul Konerko/100	8.00
79	Lance Berkman/100	10.00
80	Justin Morneau/100	10.00
82	Jose Vidro/100	5.00
84	Josh Beckett/100	5.00
86	Luis Gonzalez/100	5.00
88	Barry Zito/100	5.00
91	Roy Halladay/100	5.00
94	Mike Sweeney/100	5.00
95	Rafael Palmeiro/100	8.00
97	Preston Wilson/100	5.00
98	Shannon Stewart/50	8.00
99	Trot Nixon/25	8.00
100	Mike Piazza/100	12.00
101	Dontrelle Willis/50	10.00
103	Andy Pettitte/100	10.00
104	Kazuo Matsui/100	5.00
107	Alfonso Soriano/100	8.00
110	Aubrey Huff/100	5.00
111	Adrian Beltre/100	5.00
112	Mark Teixeira/60	10.00
114	Miguel Tejada/100	5.00
117	Bobby Abreu/100	5.00
119	Manny Ramirez/60	15.00
121	Scott Rolen/100	10.00
124	Derrek Lee/100	10.00
127	John Smoltz/100	8.00
128	Jim Edmonds/100	8.00
130	Garret Anderson/60	8.00
131	Austin Kearns/100	5.00
135	Mike Mussina/50	8.00
140	Vernon Wells/100	5.00
141	David Wright/100	25.00
142	Marcus Giles/100	5.00
144	Victor Martinez/100	5.00
145	Hideki Matsui/100	40.00
146	C.C. Sabathia/100	5.00
147	Jorge Posada/75	10.00
152	Ryne Sandberg/50	25.00
153	Rickey Henderson/25	20.00
156	George Brett/50	25.00
158	Don Mattingly/50	25.00
160	Bob Gibson/25	20.00
163	Hank Aaron/25	75.00
167	Nolan Ryan/25	25.00
167	Cal Ripken Jr./25	30.00
169	Roger Clemens/50	20.00
170	Curt Schilling/100	8.00
171	Rafael Palmeiro/100	8.00
173	Mike Piazza/100	12.00
174	Greg Maddux/100	15.00
175	Sammy Sosa/100	15.00

Timber Barrel

No Pricing — Production 1-3

TNT

NM/M — Production 1-50 — Prime: .50X-1.5X — Production 5-100

#	Player	Price
7	Vladimir Guerrero/Bat-Jsy/50	15.00
10	Miguel Cabrera/Bat-Jsy/50	12.00
11	Albert Pujols/Bat-Jsy/50	25.00
12	Albert Pujols/Bat-Jsy/50	25.00
13	Mark Prior/Bat-Jsy/50	8.00
14	Mark Prior/Bat-Jsy/50	8.00
15	Chipper Jones/Bat-Jsy/50	12.00
16	Chipper Jones/Bat-Jsy/50	12.00
39	Ivan Rodriguez/Bat-Jsy/50	12.00
42	Adam Dunn/Bat-Jsy/50	5.00
62	Greg Maddux/Bat-Jsy/50	20.00
100	Mike Piazza/Bat-Jsy/50	12.00
107	Alfonso Soriano/Bat-Jsy/50	12.00
112	Mark Teixeira/Bat-Jsy/50	10.00
119	Manny Ramirez/Bat-Jsy/50	12.00
124	Scott Rolen/Bat-Jsy/50	10.00
124	Derrek Lee/Bat-Jsy/50	8.00
143	David Ortiz/Bat-Jsy/50	15.00
151	Willie Mays/Bat-Jsy/50	50.00
153	Rickey Henderson/Bat-Jsy/50	15.00
154	Ted Williams/Bat-Jsy/50	20.00
161	Hank Aaron/Bat-Jsy/50	25.00
163	Nolan Ryan/Bat-Jsy/50	25.00
165	Stan Musial/Bat-Jsy/50	30.00
166	Harmon Killebrew/Bat-Jsy/50	20.00
167	Cal Ripken Jr./Bat-Jsy/50	30.00
169	Roger Clemens/Bat-Jsy/50	15.00
171	Rafael Palmeiro/Bat-Jsy/50	10.00
172	Randy Johnson/Bat-Jsy/50	15.00
174	Greg Maddux/Bat-Jsy/50	15.00
175	Sammy Sosa/Bat-Jsy/50	15.00

1996 Legends of the Negro Leagues Playing Cards

This set of playing cards depicting ballplayers of the pre-integration Negro Leagues was issued as a fundraiser by the International Society of Athletes in conjunction with a reunion of the players. In standard playing card finish and round-corner format, the cards have black-and-white photos at center. Backs are in black with gold printing. Size is 2-1/2" x 3-1/2". The deck's queens feature notable females of the Negro Leagues and the sponsor.

		NM/M
Complete Set (56):		10.00
Common Player:		.15
AS	Satchel Paige	1.00
2S	James "Joe" Greene	.15
3S	James "Red" Moore	.15
4S	Othello "Chico" Renfroe	.15
5S	William "Judy" Johnson	.25
6S	Willie "The Devil" Wells	.25
7S	Gene Benson	.15
8S	Willard "Sunnie" Brown	.25
9S	Martin Dihigo	.25
10S	Don Newcombe	.25
JS	Ray "Hooks" Dandridge	.25
QS	Billie Harden	.15
KS	Roy "Campy" Campanella	.75
AD	Jack "Jackie" Robinson	2.00
2D	Sam Haynes	.15
3D	Bob "The Rope" Boyd	.20
4D	William "Bonnie" Serrell	.15
5D	Orestes "Minnie" Minoso	.20
6D	Pop Lloyd	.25
7D	Art "Superman" Pennington	.15
8D	Francisco "Pancho" Coimbre	.15
9D	Sam "Jet" Jethroe	.20
10D	Joe Black	.25
JD	Monte Irvin	.25
QD	Effa "Effie" Manley	.25
KD	Henry "Hank" Aaron	1.50
AC	Joshua "Josh" Gibson	.25
2C	William "Bill" Cash	.15
3C	Francis "Fran" Matthews	.15
4C	Fred "Leap" Bankhead	.15
5C	Alex Radcliffe	.15
6C	Authur "Artie" Wilson (Arthur)	.20
7C	James "Jim" Zapp	.15
8C	Henry "Kimmie" Kimbro	.15
9C	Chester "Chet" Brewer	.15
10C	Verdell "Lefty" Mathis	.15
JC	James "Junior" Gilliam	.25
QC	Marcenia "Toni" Stone	.15
KC	Willie Mays	1.50
AH	James "Cool Papa" Bell	.25
2H	Samuel "Harriston" Hairston	.20
3H	John "Buck" O'Neil	.15
4H	Lorenzo "Piper" Davis	.15
5H	Parnell Woods	.15
6H	Thomas "Pee Wee" Butts	.15
7H	Oscar Charleston	.25
8H	Lawrence "Larry" Doby	1.00
9H	Hilton Smith	.25
10H	Leon Day	.25
JH	Walter "Buck" Leonard	.25
QH	Pamela Pryor-Fuller	.25
KH	Ernest "Ernie" Banks	.75
---	Joker (Ted "Double Duty" Radcliffe)	.25
---	Super Joker (Andrew "Rube" Foster)	.25
---	Wilmer "Red" Fields	.15
---	Clifford "Connie" Johnson	.15

2001 Legends European Tour

This two-play, four-card set was issued in conjunction with the 8th annual Baseball Legends European Tour which made a goodwill swing through 11 military bases in Germany in June. Cards feature borderless vintage color photos on front. Team logos have been airbrushed away. A Legends tour logo appears in one corner. Backs have

career stats and highlights and some of the tour sponsor's logos. The cards were given away at autograph sessions, baseball clinics, softball games and other events.

		NM/M
Complete Set (4):		10.00
Common Player:		2.00
(1)	Vida Blue (Green jersey)	3.00
(2)	Vida Blue (Yellow jersey)	3.00
(3)	Manny Sanguillen/Btg	2.00
(4)	Manny Sanguillen/ Catching	2.00

1998 Lemon Chill Chicago White Sox

In standard 2-1/2" x 3-1/2" format, this team set was a stadium giveaway. Fronts feature game-action photos with a stylized flame-like effect at left and bottom. The team logo is at lower-left, with the player name at bottom right. Backs have player personal data, stats, career highlights and a large sponsor's logo. The cards are checklisted here in alphabetical order.

		NM/M
Complete Set (30):		12.00
Common Player:		.50
(1)	Jeff Abbott	.50
(2)	Mark Anderson (Trainer), Steve Odgers (Strength Coach), Mark Salas, Herm Schneider (Trainer)	.50
(3)	James Baldwin	.50
(4)	Albert Belle	.50
(5)	Mike Cameron	.50
(6)	Mike Caruso	.50
(7)	Carlos Castillo	.50
(8)	Nardi Contreras, Von Joshua	.50
(9)	Wil Cordero	.50
(10)	Ray Durham	.50
(11)	Scott Eyre	.50
(12)	Keith Foulke	.50
(13)	Bob Howry	.50
(14)	Wallace Johnson, Bryan Little	.50
(15)	Matt Karchner	.50
(16)	Chad Kreuter	.50
(17)	Art Kusnyer, Joe Nossek	.50
(18)	Jerry Manuel	.50
(19)	Jaime Navarro	.50
(20)	Greg Norton	.50
(21)	Charlie O'Brien	.50
(22)	Magglio Ordonez	2.00
(23)	Jim Parque	.50
(24)	Bill Simas	.50
(25)	Mike Sirotka	.50
(26)	Chris Snopek	.50
(27)	John Snyder	.50
(28)	Frank Thomas	4.00
(29)	Robin Ventura	.50
(30)	Bryan Ward	.50

1999 Lemon Chill Chicago White Sox

In standard 2-1/2" x 3-1/2" format, this team set was a stadium giveaway. Fronts feature game-action photos on a borderless ghost-photo background with the team

motto, "The Kids Can Play" and logo at lower-left, with the player name at top-left in red. Backs have a red duotone photo, '98 stats, uniform and card numbers and a large sponsor's logo. A five-card 1959 World Series commemorative subset was also included.

		NM/M
Complete Set (33):		10.00
Common Player:		.25
1	Brook Fordyce	.25
2	Carlos Lee	.50
3	Greg Norton	.25
4	John Snyder	.25
5	Craig Wilson	.25
6	Chris Singleton	.25
7	Liu Rodriguez	.25
8	Magglio Ordonez	1.00
9	Mike Sirotka	.25
10	Jaime Navarro	.25
11	Mark Johnson	.25
12	Jim Parque	.25
13	Jeff Liefer	.25
14	Mike Caruso	.25
15	Ray Durham	.25
16	Bob Howry	.25
17	James Baldwin	.25
18	Jerry Manuel	.25
19	Bill Simas	.25
20	Frank Thomas	2.00
21	Bryan Ward	.25
22	Scott Eyre	.25
23	Paul Konerko	1.00
24	Sean Lowe	.25
25	Keith Foulke	.25
---	Von Joshua, Nardi Contreras	.25
---	Joe Nossek, Art Kusnyer	.25
---	Herm Schneider (Trainer), Steve Odgers (Conditioning), Mark Salas (Bullpen), Mark Anderson (Trainer)	.25
1 of 5	1959 World Series Recap	.25
2 of 5	Billy Pierce	.25
3 of 5	Jim Landis	.25
4 of 5	Al Smith	.25
5 of 5	Al Lopez	.25

2000 Lemon Chill Chicago White Sox

The first 20,000 fans through the gates of Comiskey Park on July 16 received this team set. On front a color action photo stands out from the black-and-white background and is vignetted with black borders. The player name is in purple at bottom. A black-and-white portrait photo is featured on back along with player data, 1999 stats and the sponsor's logo.

		NM/M
Complete Set (31):		10.00
Common Player:		.35
1	James Baldwin	.35
2	Herbert Perry	.35
3	Keith Foulke	.35
4	Tony Graffanino	.35
5	Kip Wells	.35
6	Mark Johnson	.35
7	Chris Singleton	.35
8	Ray Durham	.35
9	Jose Valentin	.35
10	Kevin Beirne	.35
11	Paul Konerko	1.00
12	Greg Norton	.35
13	Bill Simas	.35
14	Jeff Abbott	.35
15	Frank Thomas	3.00
16	Mike Sirotka	.35
17	Brook Fordyce	.35
18	Cal Eldred	.35
19	Bob Howry	.35
20	Jerry Manuel	.35
21	Kelly Wunsch	.35
22	Bryan Little, Wallace Johnson	.35
23	Joe Nossek, Art Kusnyer	.35
24	Jim Parque	.35
25	Carlos Lee	.50
26	Von Joshua, Nardi Contreras	.35
27	Sean Lowe	.35
28	Magglio Ordonez	1.00
29	Jesus Pena	.35
30	Craig Wilson	.35
31	Mark Anderson, Herm Schneider, Man Soo Lee, Steve Odgers	.35

1989 Lennox/HSE Astros

Astros #4 Craig Biggio Catcher

Formatted similar to a police/fire safety set, this Astros team issue is sponsored instead by a furnace company and the team's cable TV outlet. Cards measure 2-5/8" x 4-1/8" and feature portrait photos on front with orange and black team color pinstripes. Backs have biographical data, career summary and sponsors' logos.

		NM/M
Complete Set (26):		10.00
Common Player:		.25
1	Billy Hatcher	.25
2	Greg Gross	.25
3	Rick Rhoden	.25
4	Mike Scott	.25
5	Kevin Bass	.25
6	Alex Trevino	.25
7	Jim Clancy	.25
8	Bill Doran	.25
9	Dan Schatzeder	.25
10	Bob Knepper	.25
11	Jim Deshaies	.25
12	Eric Yelding	.25
13	Danny Darwin	.25
14	Coaches	.25
15	Craig Reynolds	.25
16	Rafael Ramirez	.25
17	Juan Agosto	.25
18	Larry Andersen	.25
19	Dave Smith	.25
20	Gerald Young	.25
21	Ken Caminiti	.25
22	Terry Puhl	.25
23	Bob Forsch	.25
24	Craig Biggio	6.00
25	Art Howe	.25
26	Glenn Davis	.25

1990 Lennox/HSE Astros

Ken Oberkfell #10 - Infielder

For a second straight year Lennox, the furnace people, and HSE, the Astros cable TV outlet, sponsored a team set in an oversize

(3-1/2" x 5") format on thin, semi-gloss stock. Fronts feature color player portrait photos, backs have a few biographical notes and logos for all parties. Cards are checklisted here by uniform numbers which appear on front and back.

		NM/M
Complete Set (29):		15.00
Common Player:		.50
1	Casey Candaele	.50
6	David Rohde	.50
7	Craig Biggio	5.00
9	Alex Trevino	.50
10	Ken Oberkfell	.50
11	Ken Caminiti	.50
12	Glenn Wilson	.50
13	Gerald Young	.50
15	Eric Yelding	.50
16	Rafael Ramirez	.50
18	Art Howe	.50
19	Bill Doran	.50
20	Dan Schatzeder	.50
21	Terry Puhl	.50
22	Mark Davidson	.50
23	Eric Anthony	.50
24	Franklin Stubbs	.50
27	Glenn Davis	.50
31	Xavier Hernandez	.50
33	Mike Scott	.50
36	Bill Gullickson	.50
38	Jim Clancy	.50
39	Jose Cano	.50
43	Jim Deshaies	.50
44	Danny Darwin	.50
45	Dave Smith	.50
47	Larry Andersen	.50
49	Juan Agosto	.50
51	Mark Portugal	.50

1990 Ron Lewis 1961 N.Y. Yankees

The World's Champion 1961 N.Y. Yankees are featured in this set of cards by sports artist Ron Lewis. The 42-card set contains cards of individual players, coaches and the manager, plus a team picture. The 3-1/2" x 5-1/2" cards were sold only in a complete boxed set edition of 10,000. Cards have oil painted portraits of the players set against a blue background. The card borders are pinstriped in dark blue. At bottom is a blank panel for autographing. Backs are printed in red and blue and have personal data, career summary, 1961 and career stats.

		NM/M
Complete Boxed Set (42):		10.00
Common Player:		.25
1	1961 N.Y. Yankees Team	3.00
2	Bobby Richardson	.75
3	Roger Maris	2.00
4	Elston Howard	.75
5	Bill Skowron	.60
6	Clete Boyer	.50
7	Mickey Mantle	4.00
8	Yogi Berra	1.00
9	Johnny Blanchard	.50
10	Hector Lopez	.50
11	Whitey Ford	1.00
12	Ralph Terry	.50
13	Bill Stafford	.50
14	Bud Daley	.50
15	Billy Gardner	.50
16	Jim Coates	.50
17	Luis Arroyo	.50
18	Tex Clevenger	.50
19	Bob Cerv	.50
20	Art Ditmar	.50
21	Bob Turley	.50
22	Joe DeMaestri	.50
23	Rollie Sheldon	.50
24	Earl Torgeson	.50
25	Hal Reniff	.50
26	Ralph Houk	.50
27	Johnny James	.50
28	Bob Hale	.50
29	Danny McDevitt	.50
30	Duke Maas	.50
31	Jim Hegan	.50
32	Wally Moses	.50
33	Frank Crosetti	.50
34	Lee Thomas	.50
35	Al Downing	.50
36	Jack Reed	.50
37	Ryne Duren	.50
38	Tom Tresh	.50
39	Johnny Sain	.50
40	Jesse Gonder	.50
41	Deron Johnson	.50
42	Tony Kubek	.60

1991 Ron Lewis Negro Leagues Postcards

Willie Mays

The 1991 Negro League Living Legends Postcard Set features paintings by artist Ron Lewis. Cards measure 3-1/2" x 5-1/2" and are stamped with a number within the 10,000 sets produced. Between each player's image and the player's name at the bottom of the card, is ample space for an autograph. The set, originally sold for $27, was created as a fund raiser for the Negro League Baseball Players Association. Two hundred uncut sheets were offered at $100 each.

		NM/M
Complete Set (30):		30.00
Common Player:		.75
1	George Giles	.75
2	Bill Cash	.75
3	Bob Harvey	.75
4	Lyman Bostock Sr.	.90
5	Ray Dandridge	2.50
6	Leon Day	2.00
7	Verdell "Lefty" Mathis	.75
8	Jimmie Crutchfield	.75
9	Clyde McNeal	.75
10	Bill Wright	.75
11	Mahlon Duckett	.75
12	William "Bobby" Robinson	.75
13	Max Manning	.75
14	Armando Vazquez	.75
15	Jehosie Heard	.75
16	Quincy Trouppe	.90
17	Wilmer Fields	.75
18	Lonnie Blair	.75
19	Garnett Blair	.75
20	Monte Irvin	2.50
21	Willie Mays	7.50
22	Buck Leonard	4.00
23	Frank Evans	.75
24	Josh Gibson Jr.	5.00
25	Ted "Double Duty" Radcliffe	1.50
26	Josh Johnson	.75
27	Gene Benson	.75
28	Lester Lockett	.75
29	Cowan "Bubba" Hyde	.75
30	Rufus Lewis	.75

1994 Ron Lewis Negro Leagues Postcards

BUCK O'NEIL

A second series of postcards honoring players of the Negro Leagues was produced by artist Ron Lewis in September 1994. In this set, more emphasis was placed on multi-player cards. Many of the cards also feature detailed backgrounds of street scenes with vintage vehicles, old-time stadiums, etc. Cards measure 3-1/2" x 5-1/2" and have a wide front border with the player(s) name printed at bottom and space above for autographing. Postcard backs are printed in black and include a few career stats, a card number and the card's position among the limited edition of 10,000.

		NM/M
Complete Set (32):		25.00
Common Card:		1.00
1	Willie Mays, Ernie Banks, Hank Aaron	4.00
1p	2-1/2"	2.00
2	Bill Wright, Lester Lockett, Lyman Bostock, Sr.	1.00
3	Josh Gibson, Josh Gibson Jr., Buck Leonard	2.50
4	Max Manning, Monte Irvin, Leon Day	1.50
5	Armando Vazquez, Minnie Minoso, Martin Dihigo	1.50
6	Ted "Double Duty" Radcliffe	1.50
7	Bill Owens, Turkey Stearnes, Bobby Robinson	1.00
8	Wilmer Fields, Edsall Walker, Josh Johnson	1.00
9	Artie Wilson, Lionel Hampton	1.50
10	Earl Taborn	1.00
11	Barney "Bonnie" Serrell	1.00
12	Rodolfo "Rudy" Fernandez	1.00
13	Willie Pope	1.00
14	Ray Noble	1.00
15	Jim "Fireball" Cohen	1.00
16	Henry Kimbro	1.00
17	Charlie Biot	1.00
18	Al Wilmore	1.00
19	Sam Jethroe	1.50
20	Tommy Sampson	1.00
21	Charlie Rivera	1.00
22	Claro Duany	1.00
23	Russell Awkard	1.00
24	Art "Superman" Pennington	1.00
25	Wilmer Harris	1.00
26	Napoleon "Nap" Gulley	1.00
27	Emilio Navarro	1.00
28	Andy Porter	1.00
29	Willie Grace	1.00
30	Red Moore	1.00
31	Buck O'Neill	2.00
32	Stanley Glenn	1.00

1996 Liberty Satellite Sports

This business-to-business promotion for a cable sports network content provider features on card fronts the logo of different cable networks. Space on back is shared by player data and stats and information about a local cable network.

		NM/M
Complete Set (21):		125.00
Common Player:		2.00
1	Cal Ripken Jr.	40.00
2	Paul O'Neill	2.00
3	Mo Vaughn	2.00
4	Travis Fryman	2.00
5	Brian Jordan	2.00
6	Ken Griffey Jr.	20.00
7	Craig Biggio	2.00
8	Chili Davis	2.00
9	Greg Maddux	15.00
10	Gary Sheffield	4.00
11	Frank Thomas	10.00
12	Barry Larkin	2.00
13	John Franco	2.00
14	Albert Belle	2.00
15	Mark McGwire	20.00
16	Barry Bonds	40.00
17	Lenny Dykstra	2.00
(18)	Mickey Lopez	2.00
(19)	Tim Salmon	2.00
(20)	Matt Williams	2.00
(21)	Header Card	.35

1992 Lime Rock Griffey Baseball Holograms

This set of three hologram cards features the Griffey family of pro players. Each card carries a "GRIFFEY BASEBALL" headline at top, with a large central action photo of one of the family and his facsimile autograph. The backs have a color photo, career highlights and stats. The cards were issued in several different versions as noted below.

	NM/M
Complete Set, Holograms (3):	3.00
Complete Set, Gold Holograms (3):	10.00
Complete Set, Autographed (3):	35.00
Complete Set, Blank-backed Promos (3):	6.00
Three-card strip, edition of 5,000:	6.50
1 Ken Griffey Sr. (Silver hologram, edition of 250,000.)	.50
1 Ken Griffey Sr. (Gold hologram, edition of 1,000.)	1.50
1 Ken Griffey Sr. (Auto. edition of 2,500.)	5.00
1 Ken Griffey Sr. (Blank-back promo, edition of 750.)	1.50
2 Ken Griffey Jr./Silver	2.50
2 Ken Griffey Jr./Gold	9.00
2 Ken Griffey Jr./Auto.	30.00
2 Ken Griffey Jr. (Promo)	9.00
3 Craig Griffey/Silver	.50
3 Craig Griffey/Gold	1.50
3 Craig Griffey/Auto.	2.00
3 Craig Griffey (Promo)	1.50

1991 Line Drive

This set of "old-timers" includes many Hall of Famers, as well as stars who had played into the late 1980s. In standard 2-1/2" x 3-1/2", the cards have color or sepia photos framed in blue and bordered in white. Horizontal backs have biographical and career notes and stats.

		NM/M
Complete Set (50):		6.00
Common Player:		.10
1	Don Drysdale	.25
2	Joe Torre	.15
3	Bob Gibson	.25
4	Bobby Richardson	.25
5	Ron Santo	.25
6	Eric Soderholm	.10
7	Yogi Berra	.35
8	Steve Garvey	.15
9	Steve Carlton	.25
10	Toby Harrah	.10
11	Luis Tiant	.10
12	Earl Weaver	.10
13	Bill Mazeroski	.25
14	Don Baylor	.10
15	Lew Burdette	.10
16	Jim Lonborg	.10
17	Jerry Grote	.10
18	Ernie Banks	.35
19	Doug DeCinces	.10
20	Jimmy Piersall	.10
21	Ken Holtzman	.10
22	Manny Mota	.10
23	Alvin Dark	.10
24	Lou Brock	.25
25	Ralph Houk	.15
26	Graig Nettles	.15
27	Bill White	.25
28	Billy Williams	.25
29	Willie Horton	.10
30	Tommie Agee	.10
31	Rico Petrocelli	.10
32	Julio Cruz	.10
33	Robin Roberts	.25
34	Dave Johnson	.10
35	Wilbur Wood	.10
36	Cesar Cedeno	.10
37	George Foster	.10
38	Thurman Munson	.25
39	Roberto Clemente	2.00
40	Eddie Mathews	.25
41	Harmon Killebrew	.25
42	Monte Irvin	.25
43	Bob Feller	2.00
44	Jimmie Foxx	1.00
45	Walter Johnson	1.00
46	Casey Stengel	.25
47	Satchel Paige	1.00
48	Ty Cobb	2.00
49	Mickey Cochrane	.25
50	Dizzy Dean	.35

1991 Line Drive Mickey Mantle

This 20-card set was part of a collector's kit featuring the Yankees superstar. Fronts of the 2-1/2" x 3-1/2" cards have sepia or color poses or action photos. The player's name appears in white in a blue panel at bottom. Red striping seperates the graphics from the white border. The Line Drive logo appears in an upper corner. Backs are printed in red and blue and feature a facsimile autograph, a few sentences about Mantle's career, manufacturer's and licensor's logos, and a card number. The same basic cards were included in a Collectors Marketing Corp. (see CMC) in 1989, lacking the Line Drive logo on front and the Impel logo and 1991 dates on back.

	NM/M
Complete Set (20):	15.00
Common Card:	2.00
1-20 Mickey Mantle	2.00

1991 Line Drive Don Mattingly

This 20-card set was part of a collectors kit featuring the Yankees' star. Fronts of the 2-1/2" x 3-1/2" cards have color poses or action photos. The player's name appears in white in a blue panel at bottom along with the Line Drive logo in red and white. Backs are printed in red and blue and feature a facsimile autograph, a few sentences about Mattingly's career, manufacturer's and licensor's logos, and a card number.

	NM/M
Complete Set (20):	3.00
Common Card:	.15
1-20 Don Mattingly	.25

1991 Line Drive Ryne Sandberg

This 20-card set was part of a collectors kit featuring the Cubs Hall of Fame second baseman. Fronts of the 2-1/2" x 3-1/2" cards have color poses or action photos. The player's name appears in blue and red in the white border above the photo. Backs are printed in red and blue and feature a few sentences about Sandberg's career, along with manufacturer's and licensor's logos, and a card number.

	NM/M
Complete Set (20):	10.00
Common Card:	.50
1-20 Ryne Sandberg	.50

1986 Lite Beer Astros

This regional set of the Houston Astros was sponsored by Lite Beer and given away in a special stadium promotion. The 4-1/2" x 6-3/4" cards feature full-color photos surrounded by a wide, white border. Diagonal color bands of yellow, orange, red and purple extend throught the upper-right and lower-left corners of the card, which also displays the Astros' 25th Anniversary logo and the Lite Beer logo in opposite corners. The backs include player information and statistics.

		NM/M
Complete Set (22):		25.00
Common Player:		1.00
3	Phil Garner	1.00
6	Mark Bailey	1.00
10	Dickie Thon	1.00
11	Frank DiPino	1.00
12	Craig Reynolds	1.00
14	Alan Ashby	1.00
17	Kevin Bass	1.00
19	Bill Doran	1.00
20	Jim Pankovits	1.00
21	Terry Puhl	1.00
22	Hal Lanier	1.00
25	Jose Cruz	1.00
27	Glenn Davis	1.00
28	Billy Hatcher	1.00
29	Denny Walling	1.00
33	Mike Scott	1.00
34	Nolan Ryan	15.00
37	Charlie Kerfeld	1.00
39	Bob Knepper	1.00
43	Jim Deshaies	1.00
45	Dave Smith	1.00
53	Mike Madden	1.00

Rangers

This postcard-size (approximately 4" x 6") set of Texas Rangers cards was sponsored by Lite Beer and was available by mail directly from the team. Fronts feature full-color photos surrounded by a wide, white border with the player's name, uniform number and postion appearing below. The Rangers logo

is displayed in the lower-left corner, while the Lite Beer logo is in the lower-right. Backs offer personal information and stats.

		NM/M
Complete Set (28):		20.00
Common Player:		1.00
0	Oddibe McDowell	1.00
1	Scott Fletcher	1.00
4	Bobby Valentine	1.00
4	Don Slaught	1.00
5	Pete Incaviglia	2.00
5	Pete O'Brien	1.00
10	Art Howe	1.00
11	Toby Harrah	1.00
12	Geno Petralli	1.00
13	Joe Ferguson	1.00
14	Tim Foli	1.00
15	Larry Parrish	1.00
16	Mike Mason	1.00
17	Darrell Porter	1.00
18	Ed Correa	1.00
19	Curtis Wilkerson	1.00
22	Steve Buechele	1.00
23	Jose Guzman	1.00
24	Ricky Wright	1.00
27	Greg Harris	1.00
31	Tom Robson	1.00
32	Gary Ward	1.00
35	Tom House	1.00
44	Tom Paciorek	1.00
45	Dwayne Henry	1.00
48	Bobby Witt	1.00
49	Charlie Hough	1.00
---	Arlington Stadium	1.00

1994 Lite Beer Milwaukee Brewers

The 1994 baseball strike interrupted the issue of this four-series commemorative set advertised as including "Every Player in the Brewers Twenty-Five Year History." The set was produced in four booklets of 94 cards each. Individual 2-1/2" x 3-1/2" cards were perforated for easy detachment from the 13" x 7" booklets. Cards feature black-and-white player photos against a gold border. A blue, green and gold Brewers 25th anniversary logo is in the upper-left corner on front. Half of the cards (Series I, II) have a Lite beer logo at top, while half (Series III, IV) have a Miller Genuine Draft logo. Backs are in black-and-white and include a few biographical bits, a line of career stats, the years played with the Brewers and team and brewery logos. Books I and II were issued as planned to adults attending the April 24 and June 26, 1994 games. The Series IV book, containing 10 special cards honoring the Brewers 25th Anniversary Team, was given away at a June 1995 game and Book III was distributed in August of 1995. Individual cards are un-numbered and are presented here

in alphabetical order within series. Cards of Bobby Clark, Tom Edens, Ken McMullen and Danny Walton, which appear in Series I or III are repeated in Series IV.

		NM/M
Complete Set, Booklets (4):		30.00
Complete Set, Singles (376):		24.00
Common Player:		.10
Series I		
	Complete Book:	10.00
(1)	Hank Aaron	5.00
(2)	Jim Adduci	.10
(3)	Jay Aldrich	.10
(4)	Andy Allanson	.10
(5)	Dave Baldwin	.10
(6)	Sal Bando	.10
(7)	Len Barker	.10
(8)	Kevin Bass	.10
(9)	Ken Berry	.10
(10)	George Canale	.10
(11)	Tom Candiotti	.10
(12)	Mike Capel	.10
(13)	Bobby Darwin	.10
(14)	Danny Darwin	.10
(15)	Brock Davis	.10
(16)	Dick Davis	.10
(17)	Jamie Easterley	.10
(18)	Tom Edens	.10
(19)	Marshall Edwards	.10
(20)	Cal Eldred	.10
(21)	Bob Ellis	.10
(22)	Ed Farmer	.10
(23)	Mike Felder	.10
(24)	John Felske	.10
(25)	Mike Ferraro	.10
(26)	Mike Fetters	.10
(27)	Danny Frisella	.10
(28)	Bob Galasso	.10
(29)	Jim Gantner	.10
(30)	Pedro Garcia	.10
(31)	Bob Gardner	.10
(32)	John Gelnar	.10
(33)	Moose Haas	.10
(34)	Darryl Hamilton	.10
(35)	Larry Haney	.10
(36)	Jim Hannan	.10
(37)	Bob Hansen	.10
(38)	Mike Ignasiak	.10
(39)	John Jaha	.10
(40)	Dion James	.10
(41)	Deron Johnson	.10
(42)	John Henry Johnson	.10
(43)	Tim Johnson	.10
(44)	Rickey Keeton	.10
(45)	John Kennedy	.10
(46)	Jim Kern	.10
(47)	Pete Ladd	.10
(48)	Joe Lahoud	.10
(49)	Tom Lampkin	.10
(50)	Dave LaPoint	.10
(51)	George Lauzerique	.10
(52)	Julio Machado	.10
(53)	Alex Madrid	.10
(54)	Candy Maldonado	.10
(55)	Carlos Maldonado	.10
(56)	Rick Manning	.10
(57)	Jaime Navarro	.10
(58)	Ray Newman	.10
(59)	Juan Nieves	.10
(60)	Dave Nilsson	.10
(61)	Charlie O'Brien	.10
(62)	Syd O'Brien	.10
(63)	John O'Donoghue	.10
(64)	Jim Paciorek	.10
(65)	Dave Parker	.10
(66)	Bill Parsons	.10
(67)	Marty Pattin	.10
(68)	Jamie Quirk	.10
(69)	Willie Randolph	.10
(70)	Paul Ratliff	.10
(71)	Lance Rautzhan	.10
(72)	Randy Ready	.10
(73)	Ray Sadecki	.10
(74)	Lenn Sakata	.10
(75)	Ken Sanders	.10
(76)	Ted Savage	.10
(77)	Dick Schofield	.10
(78)	Jim Tatum	.10
(79)	Chuck Taylor	.10
(80)	Tom Tellmann	.10
(81)	Frank Tepedino	.10
(82)	Sandy Valdespino	.10
(83)	Jose Valentin	.10
(84)	Greg Vaughn	.10
(85)	Carlos Velazquez	.10
(86)	Rick Waits	.10
(87)	Danny Walton	.10
(88)	Floyd Weaver	.10
(89)	Bill Wegman	.10
(90)	Floyd Wicker	.10
(91)	Al Yates	.10
(92)	Ned Yost	.10
(93)	Mike Young	.10
(94)	Robin Yount	3.00
Series II		
	Complete Book:	8.00
(95)	Hank Allen	.10
(96)	Felipe Alou	.25
(97)	Max Alvis	.10
(98)	Larry Anderson	.10
(99)	Rick Auerbach	.10
(100)	Don August	.10
(101)	Billy Bates	.10
(102)	Gary Beare	.10
(103)	Larry Bearnarth	.10

(104) Andy Beene	.10	(220) Terry Francona	.10
(105) Jerry Bell	.10	(221) Tito Francona	.10
(106) Juan Bell	.10	(222) LaVel Freeman	.10
(107) Dwight Bernard	.10	(223) Brian Giles	.10
(108) Bernie Carbo	.10	(224) Bob Heise	.10
(109) Jose Cardenal	.10	(225) Doug Henry	.10
(110) Matias Carrillo	.10	(226) Mike Hershberger	.10
(111) Juan Castillo	.10	(227) Teddy Higuera	.10
(112) Bill Castro	.10	(228) Sam Hinds	.10
(113) Rick Cerone	.10	(229) Fred Holdsworth	.10
(114) Rob Deer	.10	(230) Darren Holmes	.10
(115) Rick Dempsey	.10	(231) Paul Householder	.10
(116) Alex Diaz	.10	(232) Odell Jones	.10
(117) Dick Ellsworth	.10	(233) Brad Komminsk	.10
(118) Narciso Elvira	.10	(234) Andy Kosco	.10
(119) Tom Filer	.10	(235) Lew Krausse	.10
(120) Rollie Fingers	.75	(236) Ray Krawczyk	.10
(121) Scott Fletcher	.10	(237) Bill Krueger	.10
(122) John Flinn	.10	(238) Ted Kubiak	.10
(123) Rich Folkers	.10	(239) Jack Lind	.10
(124) Tony Fossas	.10	(240) Frank Linzy	.10
(125) Chris George	.10	(241) Pat Listach	.10
(126) Bob L. Gibson	.10	(242) Graeme Lloyd	.10
(127) Gus Gil	.10	(243) Bob Locker	.10
(128) Tommy Harper	.10	(244) Skip Lockwood	.10
(129) Vic Harris	.10	(245) Ken McMullen	.10
(130) Paul Hartzell	.10	(246) Jerry McNertney	.10
(131) Tom Hausman	.10	(247) Doc Medich	.10
(132) Neal Heaton	.10	(248) Bob Meyer	.10
(133) Mike Hegan	.10	(249) Joey Meyer	.10
(134) Jack Heidemann	.10	(250) Matt Mieske	.10
(135) Doug Jones	.10	(251) Roger Miller	.10
(136) Mark Kiefer	.10	(252) Paul Mirabella	.10
(137) Steve Kiefer	.10	(253) Angel Miranda	.10
(138) Ed Kirkpatrick	.10	(254) Bobby Mitchell	.10
(139) Joe Kmak	.10	(255) Paul Mitchell	.10
(140) Mark Knudson	.10	(256) Paul Molitor	3.00
(141) Kevin Kobel	.10	(257) Rafael Novoa	.10
(142) Pete Koegel	.10	(258) Jesse Orosco	.10
(143) Jack Lazorko	.10	(259) Carlos Ponce	.10
(144) Tim Leary	.10	(260) Chuck Porter	.10
(145) Mark Lee	.10	(261) Darrell Porter	.10
(146) Jeffrey Leonard	.10	(262) Billy Jo Robidoux	.10
(147) Randy Lerch	.10	(263) Ron Robinson	.10
(148) Brad Lesley	.10	(264) Eduardo Rodriguez	.10
(149) Sixto Lezcano	.10	(265) Ellie Rodriguez	.10
(150) Josias Manzanillo	.10	(266) Rich Rollins	.10
(151) Buck Martinez	.10	(267) Ed Romero	.10
(152) Tom Matchick	.10	(268) Gary Sheffield	1.00
(153) Davey May	.10	(269) Bob Sheldon	.10
(154) Matt Maysey	.10	(270) Chris Short	.10
(155) Bob McClure	.10	(271) Bob Skube	.10
(156) Tim McIntosh	.10	(272) Jim Slaton	.10
(157) Tim Nordbrook	.10	(273) Bernie Smith	.10
(158) Ben Oglivie	.10	(274) Russ Snyder	.10
(159) Jim Olander	.10	(275) Lary Sorensen	.10
(160) Troy O'Leary	.10	(276) Billy Spiers	.10
(161) Roberto Pena	.10	(277) Ed Sprague	.10
(162) Jeff Peterek	.10	(278) Dickie Thon	.10
(163) Ray Peters	.10	(279) Bill Travers	.10
(164) Rob Picciolo	.10	(280) Pete Vuckovich	.10
(165) John Poff	.10	(281) Clyde Wright	.10
(166) Gus Polidor	.10	(282) Jeff Yurak	.10
(167) Dan Plesac	.10	**Series IV**	
(168) Kevin Reimer	.10	Complete Book:	8.00
(169) Andy Replogle	.10	(283) Joe Azcue	.10
(170) Jerry Reuss	.10	(284) Mike Boddicker	.10
(171) Archie Reynolds	.10	(285) Ken Brett	.10
(172) Bob Reynolds	.10	(286) John Briggs	.10
(173) Ken Reynolds	.10	(287) Pete Broberg	.10
(174) Tommie Reynolds	.10	(288) Greg Brock	.10
(175) Ernest Riles	.10	(289) Jeff Bronkey	.10
(176) Bill Schroeder	.10	(290) Mark Brouhard	.10
(177) George Scott	.15	(291) Kevin Brown	.10
(178) Ray Searage	.10	(292) Ollie Brown	.10
(179) Bob Sebra	.10	(293) Bruce Brubaker	.10
(180) Kevin Seitzer	.10	(294) Tom Brunansky	.10
(181) Dick Selma	.10	(295) Steve Brye	.10
(182) Bill Sharp	.10	(296) Bob Burda	.10
(183) Ron Theobald	.10	(297) Ray Burris	.10
(184) Dan Thomas	.10	(298) Jeff Cirillo	.10
(185) Gorman Thomas	.15	(299) Bobby Clark	.10
(186) Randy Veres	.10	(300) Bob Coluccio	.10
(187) Bill Voss	.10	(301) Wayne Comer	.10
(188) Jim Wohlford	.10	(302) Billy Conigliaro	.10
Series III		(303) Cecil Cooper (25th Anniversary Team)	.10
Complete Book:	8.00	(304) Barry Cort	.10
(189) Jerry Augustine	.10	(305) Chuck Crim	.10
(190) James Austin	.10	(306) Lafayette Currence	.10
(191) Rick Austin	.10	(307) Kiki Diaz	.10
(192) Kurt Bevacqua	.10	(308) Bill Doran	.10
(193) Tom Bianco	.10	(309) Al Downing	.10
(194) Dante Bichette	.10	(310) Tom Edens	.10
(195) Mike Birkbeck	.10	(311) Andy Etchebarren	.10
(196) Dan Boitano	.10	(312) Rollie Fingers (25th)	.50
(197) Bobby Bolin	.10	(313) Jim Gantner (25th)	.10
(198) Mark Bomback	.10	(314) Greg Goossen	.10
(199) Ricky Bones	.10	(315) Brian Harper	.10
(200) Chris Bosio	.10	(316) Larry Hisle	.10
(201) Thad Bosley	.10	(317) Steve Hovley	.10
(202) Steve Bowling	.10	(318) Wilbur Howard	.10
(203) Gene Brabender	.10	(319) Roy Howell	.10
(204) Glenn Braggs	.10	(320) Bob Humphreys	.10
(205) Mike Caldwell	.10	(321) Jim Hunter	.10
(206) Billy Champion	.10	(322) Dave Huppert	.10
(207) Mark Ciardi	.10	(323) Von Joshua	.10
(208) Bobby Clark	.10	(324) Art Kusnyer	.10
(209) Ron Clark	.10	(325) Doug Loman	.10
(210) Mark Clear	.10	(326) Jim Lonborg	.10
(211) Reggie Cleveland	.10	(327) Marcelino Lopez	.10
(212) Bryan Clutterbuck	.10	(328) Willie Lozado	.10
(213) Jaime Cocanower	.10	(329) Mike Matheny	.10
(214) Jim Colborn	.10	(330) Ken McMullen	.10
(215) Cecil Cooper	.15	(331) Jose Mercedes	.10
(216) Edgar Diaz	.10	(332) Paul Molitor (25th)	1.50
(217) Frank DiPino	.10	(333) Don Money	.10
(218) Dave Engle	.10	(334) Don Money (25th)	.10
(219) Ray Fosse	.10		

(335) Charlie Moore	.10
(336) Donnie Moore	.10
(337) John Morris	.10
(338) Curt Motton	.10
(339) Willie Mueller	.10
(340) Tom Murphy	.10
(341) Tony Muser	.10
(342) Edwin Nunez	.10
(343) Ben Oglivie (25th)	.10
(344) Pat Osborn (Osburn)	.10
(345) Dennis Powell	.10
(346) Jody Reed	.10
(347) Phil Roof	.10
(348) Jimmy Rosario	.10
(349) Bruce Ruffin	.10
(350) Gary Ryerson	.10
(351) Bob Scanlan	.10
(352) Ted Simmons	.10
(353) Ted Simmons (25th)	.10
(354) Duane Singleton	.10
(355) Steve Stanicek	.10
(356) Fred Stanley	.10
(357) Dave Stapleton	.10
(358) Randy Stein	.10
(359) Earl Stephenson	.10
(360) Franklin Stubbs	.10
(361) William Suero	.10
(362) Jim Sundberg	.10
(363) B.J. Surhoff	.10
(364) Gary Sutherland	.10
(365) Don Sutton	.50
(366) Dale Sveum	.10
(367) Gorman Thomas (25th)	.10
(368) Wayne Twitchell	.10
(369) Dave Valle	.10
(370) Greg Vaughn (25th)	.10
(371) John Vukovich	.10
(372) Danny Walton	.10
(373) Turner Ward	.10
(374) Rick Wrona	.10
(375) Jim Wynn	.10
(376) Robin Yount (25th)	1.50

1990 Little Big Leaguers

This set was issued on a series of five nine-card perforated panels at the back of a book titled, "little BIG LEAGUERS / Amazing Boyhood Stories of Today's BasebAll-Stars." The 96 text pages of the book offer inspiring boyhood baseball tales as well as childhood and major league photos of the players. The tear-out cards measure 2-1/2" x 3-1/2" and are perforated on all four sides. Fronts have a black-and-white childhood photo of the player, nearly all in baseball uniform. The player's name is in white in a red strip at top, with the set name at bottom. Backs have the same red strips. At center in black-and-white are biographical data and career highlights. The unnumbered cards are checklisted here alphabetically.

	NM/M
Complete Set, Book:	6.00
Complete Set (45):	6.00
Common Player:	.25
(1) Todd Benzinger	.25
(2) Bud Black	.25
(3) Wade Boggs	.75
(4) Chris Bosio	.25
(5) George Brett	2.00
(6) Brett Butler	.10
(7) Jose Canseco	.65
(8) Gary Carter	.75
(9) Joe Carter	.25
(10) Eric Davis	.25
(11) Glenn Davis	.25
(12) Storm Davis	.25
(13) Kevin Elster	.10
(14) Tony Fernandez	.25
(15) John Franco	.25
(16) Gary Gaetti	.25
(17) Mark Gubicza	.25
(18) Tony Gwynn	1.00
(19) Bruce Hurst	.25
(20) Bo Jackson	.60
(21) Bob Kipper	.25
(22) Ron Kittle	.25
(23) Carney Lansford	.25
(24) Jeffrey Leonard	.25
(25) Mike A. Marshall	.25
(26) Lloyd McClendon	.25
(27) Andy McGaffigan	.25
(28) Keith Moreland	.25
(29) Lloyd Moseby	.25
(30) Dale Murphy	.50
(31) Pete O'Brien	.25
(32) Mike Pagliarulo	.25
(33) Tim Raines	.25
(34) Dennis Rasmussen	.25
(35) Harold Reynolds	.25
(36) Billy Ripken	.25
(37) Nolan Ryan	3.00
(38) Steve Sax	.25
(39) Ozzie Smith	1.00
(40) Jim Sundberg	.25
(41) Rick Sutcliffe	.25
(42) Dave Valle	.25
(43) Andy Van Slyke	.25
(44) Glenn Wilson	.25
(45) Todd Worrell	.25

1991 Little Big Leaguers

This set was issued on a series of five nine-card perforated panels at the back of a book titled, "little BIG LEAGUERS / Amazing Boyhood Stories of Today's BasebAll-Stars." The 96 text pages of the book offer inspiring boyhood baseball tales as well as childhood and major league photos of the players. The tear-out cards measure 2-1/2" x 3-1/2" and are perforated on all four sides. Fronts have a black-and-white childhood photo of the player, nearly all in baseball uniform. The player's name is in white in a green strip at top, with the set name at bottom. Backs have the same green strips. At center in black-and-white are biographical data and career highlights. The unnumbered cards are checklisted here alphabetically.

	NM/M
Complete Book:	6.00
Complete Set (45):	6.00
Common Player:	.25
(1) Jim Abbott	.25
(2) Jesse Barfield	.25
(3) Kevin Bass	.25
(4) Craig Biggio	.25
(5) Phil Bradley	.25
(6) Jeff Brantley	.25
(7) Tom Brunansky	.25
(8) Ken Caminiti	.25
(9) Will Clark	.35
(10) Vince Coleman	.25
(11) David Cone	.25
(12) Alvin Davis	.25
(13) Andre Dawson	.50
(14) Bill Doran	.25
(15) Nick Esasky	.25
(16) Dwight Gooden	.25
(17) Tom Gordon	.25
(18) Ken Griffey Jr.	2.50
(19) Kevin Gross	.25
(20) Kelly Gruber	.25
(21) Lee Guetterman	.25
(22) Terry Kennedy	.25
(23) John Kruk	.25
(24) Bill Landrum	.25
(25) Mark Langston	.25
(26) Barry Larkin	.25
(27) Dave Magadan	.25
(28) Don Mattingly	2.00
(29) Mark McGwire	3.00
(30) Kevin Mitchell	.25
(31) Bob Ojeda	.25
(32) Gregg Olson	.25
(33) Terry Pendleton	.25
(34) Ted Power	.25
(35) Kirby Puckett	1.50
(36) Terry Puhl	.25
(37) Bret Saberhagen	.25
(38) Chris Sabo	.25
(39) Kevin Seitzer	.25
(40) Don Slaught	.25
(41) Lonnie Smith	.25
(42) Darryl Strawberry	.25
(43) Mickey Tettleton	.25
(44) Bobby Thigpen	.25
(45) Frank White	.25

2005 Los Angeles Angels Card Deck

This stadium giveaway was sponsored by ValleyCrest Companies, a golf course design firm. Cards are 2-1/4" x 3-7/16" with rounded corners. Red backs have team and sponsor's logos. Each player appears four times in the deck, with an identical portrait photo on the same value card in each suit. Two wild cards complete the boxed set.

		NM/M
Complete Set (54):		10.00
Common Player:		.25
2	Adam Kennedy	.25
3	Darin Erstad	.25
4	Kelvim Escobar	.25
5	Bengie Molina	.25
6	Orlando Cabrera	.25
7	Garret Anderson	.25
8	Steve Finley	.25
9	Bartolo Colon	.25
10	Francisco Rodriguez	.25
J	Chone Figgins	.25
Q	Rally Money (Mascot)	.25
K	Mike Scioscia	.25
A	Vladimir Guerrero	.50
WC	Mascot (Brendan Donnelly)	.25
WC	Mascot (Brendan Donnelly)	.25

1981-93 Louisville Slugger

Hillerich & Bradsby, makers of Louisville Slugger bats and gloves, produced these cards to be attached to the company's baseball gloves. A small round hole is punched in the upper-left corner of each standard-size card to enable them to be attached to the gloves. Undamaged cards are hard to find. All cards follow the same basic design - bright blue and green borders, player name and position above the full-color photo (with autograph overprint), yellow Louisville Slugger logo across the bottom border. Beneath the logo are the words "Member Louisville Slugger Bat & Glove Advisory Staff." The card backs are blue and green and include the player name, short biography and a list of personal records and information. Cards were printed with a glossy finish through 1987, when a flat finish was adopted as production moved from Taiwan to the Philippines.

	NM/M
Common Player:	2.00
(1) Steve Garvey/Dodgers	5.00
(2) Graig Nettles/Yankees	4.00
(1) Pedro Guerrero/Dodgers	.25
(2) Fred Lynn/Angels	2.00
(1) Ray Knight/Astros	5.00
(2) Ray Knight/Mets	4.00
(3) Graig Nettles/Padres	3.25
(1) Steve Garvey/Padres	3.25
(2) Gary Matthews/Cubs	2.00
(1) Orel Hershiser/Dodgers	2.00
(2) Rick Rhoden/Pirates	2.00
(1) Eric Davis/Reds	2.00
(2) Eric Davis/Reds	2.00
(3) Steve Garvey/Padres	4.00
(3) Orel Hershiser/Dodgers	2.00
(4) Mike Pagliarulo/Yankees	2.00
(2) Orel Hershiser/Dodgers	2.00
(1) Orel Hershiser/Dodgers	2.00
(1) Andy Van Slyke/Pirates	2.00
(3) Lou Whitaker/Tigers	3.00
(1) Wade Boggs/Red Sox	5.00
(1) Eric Davis/Dodgers	3.00
(2) Jack McDowell/White Sox	2.00

1990s Louisville Slugger TPX Advisory Staff

This series of cards issued sometime, or over a period of time, in the 1990s depicts members of Hillerich & Bradsby's Pro Advisory Staff for its TPX line-up of baseball equipment. Cards are in standard 2-1/2" x 3-1/2" format with game-action or posed color photos and a facsimile autograph on front. Backs picture a bat, glove and bat bag.

	NM/M
Common Player:	3.00
(1) Brett Butler/Dodgers	3.00
(2) Bobby Jones/Mets	3.00
(3) Reggie Sanders/Reds	3.00
(4) Todd Stottlemyre/Cardinals	3.00
(5) Robin Ventura/White Sox	3.00

1992 Lykes Braves Team Photo Set

When Lykes Meats was awarded the Braves hot dog contract for 1992 they continued the previous years' baseball card promotions, including this early-May team photo/player card panel. Three 9-1/2" x 10-1/2" panels feature a team photo and 30 player cards. The cards have player portraits against a blue background in a tombstone shape. A blue ball at lower-left has the player's uniform number, while his name is in white in a red strip beneath the photo. Red logos of the team and hot dog vendor are at bottom. Backs are printed in red and dark blue and feature full stats, player data and a facsimile autograph. These cards are much more common than the Lykes singles distributed later in the season. The checklist here is alphabetized.

	NM/M
Complete Foldout Set:	6.00
Common Player:	.15
(1) Steve Avery	.15
(2) Rafael Belliard	.15
(3) Juan Berenguer	.15
(4) Damon Berryhill	.15
(5) Mike Bielecki	.15
(6) Jeff Blauser	.15
(7) Sid Bream	.15
(8) Francisco Cabrera	.15
(9) Bobby Cox	.15
(10) Nick Esasky	.15
(11) Marvin Freeman	.15
(12) Ron Gant	.15
(13) Tom Glavine	1.00
(14) Tommy Gregg	.15
(15) Brian Hunter	.15
(16) David Justice	.15
(17) Charlie Leibrandt	.15
(18) Mark Lemke	.15
(19) Kent Mercker	.15
(20) Otis Nixon	.15
(21) Greg Olson	.15
(22) Alejandro Pena	.15
(23) Terry Pendleton	.25
(24) Deion Sanders	.25
(25) Lonnie Smith	.15
(26) John Smoltz	1.00
(27) Mike Stanton	.15

(28)	Jeff Treadway	.15
(29)	Jerry Willard	.15
(30)	Mark Wohlers	.15
(31)	Team Photo	.50

1992 Lykes Braves

Though Braves players no longer appeared at an autograph booth on card giveaway days in 1992, the team's hot dog vendor continued to offer small groups of cards to kids attending Tuesday home games. This distribution makes assembling complete sets very challenging. In standard 2-1/2" x 3-1/2" size, the cards have a player photo border in, successively, white, dark blue, red and white. A red-and-blue Lykes logo is at lower-right. Above is a blue ball with the year of issue, and the team and player name printed in white. Backs are in black with the player's uniform number, full minor and major league stats, and biographical vitae.

		NM/M
Complete Set (37):		12.00
Common Player:		.25
(1)	Steve Avery	.25
(2)	Jim Beauchamp	.25
(3)	Rafael Belliard	.25
(4)	Juan Berenguer	.25
(5)	Damon Berryhill	.25
(6)	Mike Bielecki	.25
(7)	Jeff Blauser	.25
(8)	Sid Bream	.25
(9)	Francisco Cabrera	.25
(10)	Pat Corrales	.25
(11)	Bobby Cox	.25
(12)	Marvin Freeman	.25
(13)	Ron Gant	.40
(14)	Tom Glavine	1.50
(15)	Tommy Gregg	.25
(16)	Brian Hunter	.25
(17)	Clarence Jones	.25
(18)	David Justice	.75
(19)	Charlie Leibrandt	.25
(20)	Mark Lemke	.25
(21)	Leo Mazzone	.25
(22)	Kent Mercker	.25
(23)	Otis Nixon	.25
(24)	Greg Olson	.25
(25)	Alejandro Pena	.25
(26)	Terry Pendleton	.25
(27)	Deion Sanders	.50
(28)	Lonnie Smith	.25
(29)	John Smoltz	1.50
(30)	Mike Stanton	.25
(31)	Jeff Treadway	.25
(32)	Jerry Willard	.25
(33)	Jimy Williams	.25
(34)	Mark Wohlers	.25
(35)	Ned Yost	.25
(36)	Homer the Brave (Mascot)	.25
(37)	Rally (Mascot)	.25

1993 Lykes Braves

Each Tuesday home game during the 1993 season, three player cards were distributed to youngsters, sponsored by the team's hot dog vendor. This style of distribution makes collecting a complete 38-card set very challenging. Stan-

dard 2-1/2" x 3-1/2" size cards have a player portrait photo against a blue background. The card's front border is a darker blue separated from the photo by a yellow stripe. Red-white-and-blue team and vendor logos appear at the corners and the player's name and position are in white at lower-left. Backs are printed in black with complete career stats, biographical data and sponsors' logos. The unnumbered cards are checklisted here alphabetically. The final Tuesday's handouts, Lopez, McGriff and Tarasco have slightly different back printing and are somewhat scarcer than other cards.

		NM/M
Complete Set (38):		20.00
Common Player:		.50
(1)	Steve Avery	.50
(2)	Jim Beauchamp	.50
(3)	Steve Bedrosian	.50
(4)	Rafael Belliard	.50
(5)	Damon Berryhill	.50
(6)	Jeff Blauser	.50
(7)	Sid Bream	.50
(8)	Francisco Cabrera	.50
(9)	Pat Corrales	.50
(10)	Bobby Cox	.50
(11)	Marvin Freeman	.50
(12)	Ron Gant	.50
(13)	Tom Glavine	1.50
(14)	Jay Howell	.50
(15)	Brian Hunter	.50
(16)	Clarence Jones	.50
(17)	David Justice	.60
(18)	Mark Lemke	.50
(19)	Javier Lopez	1.00
(20)	Greg Maddux	2.50
(21)	Leo Mazzone	.50
(22)	Fred McGriff	1.00
(23)	Greg McMichael	.50
(24)	Kent Mercker	.50
(25)	Otis Nixon	.50
(26)	Greg Olson	.50
(27)	Bill Pecota	.50
(28)	Terry Pendleton	.50
(29)	Deion Sanders	1.00
(30)	Pete Smith	.50
(31)	John Smoltz	1.50
(32)	Mike Stanton	.50
(33)	Tony Tarasco	1.00
(34)	Jimy Williams	.50
(35)	Mark Wohlers	.50
(36)	Ned Yost	.50
(37)	Homer the Brave (Mascot)	.50
(38)	Rally (Mascot)	.50

Team Photo Set

The Atlanta Braves offered a perforated, uncut sheet team set in 1992 that was handed out in an early season game. The set, sponsored by Lykes, includes 30 cards and a team photo and carries the player's name and uniform number on the front of the card along with the Braves and Lykes logos. The backs contain the player's biography, career statistics and a facsimile autograph. The first card of Fred McGriff as a Brave appears in this promotional set issued later in the season than in previous years. The 30 individual player cards also include Ryan Klesko, who was not in the single-card season-long giveaways. Three 9-1/2" x 10-1/2" panels comprise this issue, with each of the player cards perforated at the edges. Also for the first time in 1992, the same photos were used for the team sheet and single card promotions. Single cards measure 2-1/4" x 3-1/2" and are checklisted alphabetically here.

		NM/M
Complete Foldout Set:		5.00
Common Player:		.15
(1)	Steve Avery	.15
(2)	Steve Bedrosian	.15
(3)	Rafael Belliard	.15
(4)	Damon Berryhill	.15
(5)	Jeff Blauser	.15
(6)	Sid Bream	.15
(7)	Francisco Cabrera	.15
(8)	Bobby Cox	.15
(9)	Marvin Freeman	.15
(10)	Ron Gant	.15
(11)	Tom Glavine	1.00
(12)	Jay Howell	.15
(13)	Brian Hunter	.15
(14)	David Justice	.25
(15)	Ryan Klesko	.15
(16)	Mark Lemke	.15
(17)	Greg Maddux	2.00
(18)	Fred McGriff	.25

1994 Lykes Braves

While 34 cards were printed, only 27 were publicly released prior to the beginning of the 1994 baseball strike. Sponsored by the Braves' stadium hot dog concessionaire, the cards were given away at the rate of three per Tuesday home game. Because of the strike, the cards of Cox, Hill, Chipper Jones, Mike Kelly, Klesko, McGriff and Sanders were not officially released and are scarcer than the other 27. Card fronts feature a chest-to-cap player portrait photo set against a blue background with an orange border and vertical blue stripe at right bearing the player's name. Backs are printed in black-and-white and have full major and minor league stats along with a few biographical details. There is no card or uniform number on the cards. They are presented here alphabetically.

		NM/M
Complete Set (34):		40.00
Common Player:		.25
(1)	Steve Avery	.25
(2)	Jim Beauchamp	.25
(3)	Steve Bedrosian	.25
(4)	Rafael Belliard	.25
(5)	Mike Bielecki	.25
(6)	Jeff Blauser	.25
(7)	Pat Corrales	.25
(8)	Bobby Cox	2.00
(9)	Dave Gallagher	.25
(10)	Tom Glavine	1.50
(11)	Milt Hill	2.00
(12)	Chipper Jones	10.00
(13)	Clarence Jones	.25
(14)	David Justice	.50
(15)	Mike Kelly	2.00
(16)	Ryan Klesko	6.00
(17)	Mark Lemke	.25
(18)	Javy Lopez	.25
(19)	Greg Maddux	3.00
(20)	Leo Mazzone	.25
(21)	Greg McMichael	.25
(22)	Fred McGriff	6.00
(23)	Kent Mercker	.25
(24)	Charlie O'Brien	.25
(25)	Gregg Olson	.25
(26)	Bill Pecota	.25
(27)	Terry Pendleton	.25
(28)	Deion Sanders	6.00
(29)	John Smoltz	1.50
(30)	Mike Stanton	.25
(31)	Tony Tarasco	.25
(32)	Jimy Williams	.25
(33)	Mark Wohlers	.25
(34)	Ned Yost	.25

1994 Lykes Braves Team Photo Set

Few of these team photo/player card sets have found their way into the hobby because they were intended for distribution at the August 14 Sunday home game which fell after the beginning of the 1994 baseball strike. As in past years, the set was produced as a fold-out containing a team photo and 35 player cards. Unlike previous editions, however, the player cards are identical in format to the single cards given away during the season, except that they are printed in red and

1987 M & M's (top right photo)

(19)	Greg McMichael	.15
(20)	Kent Mercker	.15
(21)	Otis Nixon	.15
(22)	Greg Olson	.15
(23)	Bill Pecota	.15
(24)	Terry Pendleton	.15
(25)	Deion Sanders	.25
(26)	Pete Smith	.15
(27)	John Smoltz	1.00
(28)	Mike Stanton	.15
(29)	Tony Tarasco	.15
(30)	Mark Wohlers	.15
(31)	Team Photo	.50

blue on the back and are slightly smaller, at 2-1/8" x 3-1/8". The cards are checklisted here alphabeitcally.

		NM/M
Complete Foldout Set:		17.50
Common Player:		.25
(1)	Steve Avery	.25
(2)	Jim Beauchamp	.25
(3)	Steve Bedrosian	.25
(4)	Rafael Belliard	.25
(5)	Mike Bielecki	.25
(6)	Jeff Blauser	.25
(7)	Pat Corrales	.25
(8)	Bobby Cox	.25
(9)	Dave Gallagher	.25
(10)	Tom Glavine	1.50
(11)	Chipper Jones	3.50
(12)	Clarence Jones	.25
(13)	David Justice	.50
(14)	Mike Kelly	.25
(15)	Roberto Kelly	.25
(16)	Ryan Klesko	.25
(17)	Mark Lemke	.25
(18)	Javy Lopez	.25
(19)	Greg Maddux	3.50
(20)	Leo Mazzone	.25
(21)	Fred McGriff	.25
(22)	Kent Mercker	.25
(23)	Mike Mordecai	.25
(24)	Charlie O'Brien	.25
(25)	Jose Oliva	.25
(26)	Gregg Olson	.25
(27)	Bill Pecota	.25
(28)	Terry Pendleton	.25
(29)	John Smoltz	1.50
(30)	Mike Stanton	.25
(31)	Tony Tarasco	.25
(32)	Jimy Williams	.25
(33)	Mark Wohlers	.25
(34)	Ned Yost	.25
(35)	Team Photo	.50

1995 Lykes Braves

For the only time since Atlanta's hot dog concessionaires began issuing cards in 1989, the team honored past, as well as current players, as part of its 30th anniversary celebration. The cards were distributed at Tuesday home games, usually three at a time, making assembly of a complete set difficult. Thus, this checklist may or may not be complete. Fronts have game-action photos with a black strip at bottom bearing the player name. A 30th anniversary logo is at top, the sponsor's logo appears over a baseball in a lower corner. Black-and-white backs have player personal data and career record.

		NM/M
Complete Set (30):		10.00
Common Player:		.25
(1)	Hank Aaron	2.50
(2)	Steve Avery	.25
(3)	Steve Bedrosian	.25
(4)	Jeff Blauser	.25
(5)	Sid Bream	.25
(6)	Francisco Cabrera	.25
(7)	Chris Chambliss	.25
(8)	Bobby Cox	.25

1987 M & M's (fourth column top)

(9)	Ron Gant	.25
(10)	Tom Glavine	1.50
(11)	Marquis Grissom	.25
(12)	Bob Horner	.25
(13)	Glenn Hubbard	.25
(14)	Chipper Jones	2.00
(15)	David Justice	.25
(16)	Ryan Klesko	.25
(17)	Mark Lemke	.25
(18)	Javy Lopez	.25
(19)	Greg Maddux	2.00
(20)	Fred McGriff	.25
(21)	Kent Mercker	.25
(22)	Dale Murphy	1.50
(23)	Phil Niekro	.40
(24)	Otis Nixon	.25
(25)	Charlie O'Brien	.25
(26)	Greg Olson	.25
(27)	Pascual Perez	.25
(28)	Lonnie Smith	.25
(29)	John Smoltz	1.50
(30)	Mark Wohlers	.25

Team Photo Set

Once again this promotional giveaway by the team's hot dog concessionaire took the form of a three-panel cardboard poster. Overall 10-3/4" x 28", the foldout features a color team photo at top and 30 individual player portrait cards below. Each card is 2-1/8" x 3-1/8" and perforated for separation. Backs are printed in red, white and blue with a few stats and vital data, along with team and sponsor logos. The unnumbered cards are checklisted here alphabetically.

		NM/M
Complete Foldout Set:		8.00
Common Player:		.10
(1)	Steve Avery	.10
(2)	Jim Beauchamp	.10
(3)	Rafael Belliard	.10
(4)	Jeff Blauser	.10
(5)	Pedro Borbon	.10
(6)	Brad Clontz	.10
(7)	Pat Corrales	.10
(8)	Bobby Cox	.10
(9)	Tom Glavine	.75
(10)	Marquis Grissom	.10
(11)	Chipper Jones	2.00
(12)	Clarence Jones	.10
(13)	David Justice	.25
(14)	Mike Kelly	.10
(15)	Ryan Klesko	.10
(16)	Mark Lemke	.10
(17)	Javier Lopez	.10
(18)	Greg Maddux	1.50
(19)	Leo Mazzone	.10
(20)	Fred McGriff	.10
(21)	Greg McMichael	.10
(22)	Kent Mercker	.10
(23)	Mike Mordecai	.10
(24)	Charlie O'Brien	.10
(25)	Jason Schmidt	.10
(26)	Dwight Smith	.10
(27)	John Smoltz	.75
(28)	Jimy Williams	.10
(29)	Mark Wohlers	.10
(30)	Ned Yost	.10
(31)	Team Photo	.10

1996 Lykes Braves Team Photo Set

The Braves offered a perforated, four-panel 10-3/4" x 31-1/4" uncut sheet team set in 1996 that was handed out to children 12 and under at an early season game. The set was sponsored by Lykes, the team's hot dog concessionaire. There are 35 individual player and staff portrait cards in 2-1/8" x 3-1/8" format, and a 10-3/4" x 9-1/2" team photo panel. Each card carries the player's name, position and uniform number on the front, along with the Lykes logo. Black, white and blue backs contain biographical data, 1995 and career major and minor league statistics and team and sponsor logos. The cards are checklisted alphabetically here.

		NM/M
Complete Foldout Set:		8.00
Common Player:		.10
(1)	Steve Avery	.10
(2)	Danny Bautista	.10
(3)	Jim Beauchamp	.10
(4)	Rafael Belliard	.10
(5)	Mike Bielecki	.10
(6)	Jeff Blauser	.10
(7)	Pedro Borbon	.10
(8)	Brad Clontz	.10
(9)	Pat Corrales	.10
(10)	Bobby Cox	.10
(11)	Jermaine Dye	.10
(12)	Frank Fultz	.10
(13)	Tom Glavine	1.25
(14)	Marquis Grissom	.10
(15)	Chipper Jones	3.00
(16)	Clarence Jones	.10
(17)	David Justice	.25
(18)	Ryan Klesko	.10
(19)	Mark Lemke	.10
(20)	Javy Lopez	.10
(21)	Greg Maddux	2.50
(22)	Leo Mazzone	.10
(23)	Fred McGriff	.10
(24)	Greg McMichael	.10
(25)	Mike Mordecai	.10
(26)	Eddie Perez	.10
(27)	Jason Schmidt	.10
(28)	Dwight Smith	.10
(29)	John Smoltz	1.25
(30)	Terrell Wade	.10
(31)	Jerome Walton	.10
(32)	Mark Whiten	.10
(33)	Jimy Williams	.10
(34)	Mark Wohlers	.10
(35)	Ned Yost	.10
(36)	Team Photo	.50

M

1987 M & M's

The M&M's "Star Lineup" set consists of 12 two-card panels inserted in specially marked packages of large M&M's candy. The two-card panels measure 5" x 3-1/2" with individual cards measuring 2-1/2" x 3-1/2" in size. The full-color photos are enclosed by a wavy blue frame and a white border. Card backs are printed in red ink on white stock and carry the player's career statistics and highlights. All team insignias have been airbrushed away. The set was designed and produced by Mike Schechter and Associates.

		NM/M
Complete Panel Set (12):		5.00
Complete Singles Set (24):		4.00
Common Panel:		1.00
Common Single Player:		.25
PANEL 1		
1	Wally Joyner	.10
2	Tony Pena	.10
PANEL 2		1.25
3	Mike Schmidt	.50
4	Ryne Sandberg	.40
PANEL 3		.65
5	Wade Boggs	.40
6	Jack Morris	.10
PANEL 4		.65
7	Roger Clemens	.45
8	Harold Baines	.10
PANEL 5		.60
9	Dale Murphy	.25

10	Jose Canseco	.20

PANEL 6

		.75
11	Don Mattingly	.45
12	Gary Carter	.35

PANEL 7

		2.00
13	Cal Ripken Jr.	1.00
14	George Brett	.50

PANEL 8

		.65
15	Kirby Puckett	.40
16	Joe Carter	.10

PANEL 9

		.25
17	Mike Witt	.10
18	Mike Scott	.10

PANEL 10

		.45
19	Fernando Valenzuela	.15
20	Steve Garvey	.15

PANEL 11

		1.50
21	Steve Sax	.10
22	Nolan Ryan	1.00

PANEL 12

		1.25
23	Tony Gwynn	.40
24	Ozzie Smith	.40

2005 Major League Baseball Superstars Medallions

Coupons in USA Today between July 11 and August 19 allowed collectors to purchase these medallions on a one-per-day basis for $2.99 at 7-Eleven, SuperAmerica and Speedway convenience stores.

		NM/M
Complete Set (30):		100.00
Common Player:		3.00
(1)	Roger Clemens	6.00
(2)	Ichiro Suzuki	7.50
(3)	Derek Jeter	8.00
(4)	Curt Schilling	3.00
(5)	Albert Pujols	8.00
(6)	Randy Johnson	3.00
(7)	Ivan Rodriguez	3.00
(8)	Eric Gagne	3.00
(9)	Kerry Wood	3.00
(10)	Ben Sheets	3.00
(11)	John Smoltz	3.00
(12)	Vladimir Guerrero	3.00
(13)	Torii Hunter	3.00
(14)	David Ortiz	3.00
(15)	Carlos Delgado	3.00
(16)	Scott Rolen	3.00
(17)	Jason Schmidt	3.00
(18)	Sammy Sosa	3.00
(19)	Carlos Beltran	3.00
(20)	Luis Gonzalez	3.00
(21)	Ken Griffey Jr.	4.50
(22)	Todd Helton	3.00
(23)	Alfonso Soriano	3.00
(24)	Pedro Martinez	3.00
(25)	Jim Thome	3.00
(26)	Manny Ramirez	3.00
(27)	Johan Santana	3.00
(28)	Eric Chavez	3.00
(29)	Mark Prior	3.00
(30)	Alex Rodriguez	7.50

1997-2002 Major League Dad

To promote responsible fatherhood the California Department of Child Support Services issued a series of cards picturing big league players and their children. Issued in a variety of designs, all have the phrase "Major League Dad" on front.

		NM/M
Complete Set (10):		20.00
Common Player:		2.00
(1)	Garret Anderson/2000	2.00
(2)	Marvin Benard/2000	2.00

(3)	Mike Fetters/1998	2.00
(4)	Mark Gardner/1998	2.00
(5)	Wally Joyner	2.00
(6)	Chad Kreuter	2.00
(7)	Tim Salmon	2.00
(8)	Jeff Shaw/2000	2.00
(9)	Matt Stairs/2000	2.00
(10)	Greg Vaughn/1998	2.00

1988 Mickey Mantle's Restaurant

To promote the grand opening of Mickey Mantle's restaurant in New York City, this promotional card was issued by an Oklahoma public relations firm to members of the media. In round-cornered 2-1/2" x 3-1/2" format on thin, semi-gloss cardboard, the front has a posed color photo of Mantle. The back has details of the restaurant opening and a design reminiscent of the Yankee Stadium facade, printed in white on a dark blue background.

	NM/M
Mickey Mantle	7.50

1989 Marathon Cubs

(12) SHAWON DUNSTON   INFIELDER

This colorful 25-card Cubs team set was sponsored by Marathon and was distributed as a stadium promotion to fans attending the Aug. 10, 1989, game at Chicago's Wrigley Field. The oversize (2-3/4" x 4-1/4") feature an action photo inside a diagonal box on the card front, with the Chicago Cubs logo at the top and the player's uniform number, name and position along the bottom. The backs include a small black-and-white photo, player data and the Cubs and Marathon logos.

		NM/M
Complete Set (25):		12.00
Common Player:		.50
2	Vance Law	.50
4	Don Zimmer	.50
7	Joe Girardi	.50
8	Andre Dawson	2.50
9	Damon Berryhill	.50
10	Lloyd McClendon	.50
15	Domingo Ramos	.50
17	Mark Grace	.75
18	Dwight Smith	.50
19	Curt Wilkerson	.50
20	Jerome Walton	.50
21	Scott Sanderson	.50
23	Ryne Sandberg	6.50
28	Mitch Williams	.50
31	Greg Maddux	6.00
33	Calvin Schiraldi	.50
33	Mitch Webster	.50
36	Mike Bielecki	.50
39	Paul Kilgus	.50
40	Rick Sutcliffe	.50
41	Jeff Pico	.50
44	Steve Wilson	.50
50	Les Lancaster	.50
---	Coaches (Joe Altobelli, Chuck Cottier, Larry Cox, Jose Martinez, Dick Pole)	.50

1989 Marathon Tigers

(39) MIKE HENNEMAN—P

Marathon sponsored this giveaway set for a 1989 Tigers home game. The oversized cards feature thin white stock and full-color player photos. The cards are numbered according to uniform number.

		NM/M
Complete Set (28):		9.00
Common Player:		.50
1	Lou Whitaker	.75
3	Alan Trammell	1.00
8	Mike Heath	.50
9	Fred Lynn	.50
10	Keith Moreland	.50
11	Sparky Anderson	.75
12	Mike Brumley	.50
14	Dave Bergman	.50
15	Pat Sheridan	.50
17	Al Pedrique	.50
18	Ramon Pena	.50
19	Doyle Alexander	.50
22	Guillermo Hernandez	.50
23	Torey Lovullo	.50
24	Gary Pettis	.50
25	Ken Williams	.50
26	Frank Tanana	.50
27	Charles Hudson	.50
32	Gary Ward	.50
33	Matt Nokes	.50
34	Chet Lemon	.50
35	Rick Schu	.50
36	Frank Williams	.50
39	Mike Henneman	.50
44	Jeff Robinson	.50
47	Jack Morris	.50
48	Paul Gibson	.50
---	Coaches (Billy Consolo, Alex Grammas, Billy Muffett, Vada Pinson, Dick Tracewksi)	.50

1990 Marathon Cubs

NO. 4
DON ZIMMER • MANAGER

Marathon sponsored its second consecutive Chicago Cubs team set. The oversized cards feature thin white stock and full-color photos. The cards are numbered according to uniform number, and were distributed at a Cubs home game.

		NM/M
Complete Set (28):		6.00
Common Player:		.25
4	Don Zimmer	.35
7	Joe Girardi	.25
8	Andre Dawson	1.50
10	Lloyd McClendon	.25
11	Luis Salazar	.25
12	Shawon Dunston	.25
15	Domingo Ramos	.25
17	Mark Grace	.35
18	Dwight Smith	.25
19	Curtis Wilkerson	.25
20	Jerome Walton	.25
22	Mike Harkey	.25
23	Ryne Sandberg	4.50
25	Marvell Wynne	.25
28	Mitch Williams	.25
29	Doug Dascenzo	.25
30	Dave Clark	.25
31	Greg Maddux	4.00
32	Hector Villanueva	.25
36	Mike Bielecki	.25

37	Bill Long	.25
40	Rick Sutcliffe	.25
41	Jeff Pico	.25
44	Steve Wilson	.25
45	Paul Assenmacher	.25
47	Shawn Boskie	.25
50	Les Lancaster	.25
---	Coaches (Joe Altobelli, Chuck Cottier, Jose Martinez, Dick Pole, Phil Roof)	.25

1991 Marathon Cubs

GREG MADDUX
PITCHER

Marathon Oil once again sponsored a set featuring the Chicago Cubs. This 28-card release features oversized cards measuring 2-7/8" x 4-1/4". The card fronts feature full-color action photos. The flip sides feature complete statistics. The cards are numbered according to uniform number. This number appears on both the front and back of the card.

		NM/M
Complete Set (28):		12.50
Common Player:		.50
7	Joe Girardi	.50
8	Andre Dawson	2.50
9	Damon Berryhill	.50
10	Luis Salazar	.50
11	George Bell	.50
12	Shawon Dunston	.50
16	Jose Vizcaino	.50
17	Mark Grace	.65
18	Dwight Smith	.50
19	Hector Villanueva	.50
20	Jerome Walton	.50
22	Mike Harkey	.50
23	Ryne Sandberg	6.50
24	Chico Walker	.50
29	Doug Dascenzo	.50
30	Bob Scanlan	.50
31	Greg Maddux	6.00
32	Danny Jackson	.50
35	Chuck McElroy	.50
36	Mike Bielecki	.50
40	Rick Sutcliffe	.50
41	Jim Essian	.50
42	Dave Smith	.50
45	Paul Assenmacher	.50
47	Shawn Boskie	.50
50	Les Lancaster	.50
51	Heathcliff Slocumb	.50
---	Coaches (Joe Altobelli, Billy Connors, Chuck Cottier, Jose Martinez, Phil Roof, Richie Zisk)	.50

1992 Marathon Cubs

SAMMY SOSA
1 9 9 2

The fourth consecutive year of a Cubs team set sponsored by Marathon Oil consists of 28 cards, including manager Jim Lefebvre and his coaching staff. The set was originally given away at the July 10, 1993 game at Wrigley Field. Cards are checklisted here by uniform number.

		NM/M
Complete Set (28):		9.00
Common Player:		.25
1	Doug Strange	.30
2	Frank Castillo	.30
5	Jim Lefebvre	.30

6	Rey Sanchez	.30
7	Joe Girardi	.30
8	Andre Dawson	.75
12	Luis Salazar	.30
12	Shawon Dunston	.30
16	Jose Vazcaino	.30
17	Mark Grace	.45
18	Dwight Smith	.30
19	Hector Villanueva	.30
20	Jerome Walton	.30
21	Sammy Sosa	3.50
23	Ryne Sandberg	3.50
27	Derrick May	.30
29	Doug Dascenzo	.30
30	Bob Scanlan	.30
31	Greg Maddux	3.00
32	Danny Jackson	.30
34	Ken Patterson	.30
35	Chuck McElroy	.30
36	Mike Morgan	.30
38	Jeff Robinson	.30
42	Dave Smith	.30
45	Paul Assenmacher	.30
47	Shawn Boskie	.30
---	Coaches (Tom Treblehorn, Jose Martinez, Billy Williams, Sammy Ellis, Chuck Cottier, Billy Connprs)	.30

1993 Marathon Cubs

ASSENMACHER

The Cubs distributed the 1993 Marathon Oil set on July 28 in a game against the Padres. The cards, measuring an oversized 4-1/4" x 2-7/8", are unnumbered, with uniform numbers appearing on the back. The cards have a vertical blue stripe down the right side with the player's last name in large, white letters. Backs carry complete major and minor league statistics. There are 27 cards in the set. The checklist is presented here by uniform number.

		NM/M
Complete Set (27):		7.50
Common Player:		.25
2	Rick Wilkins	.25
5	Jim Lefebvre	.25
6	Willie Wilson	.25
10	Steve Lake	.25
11	Rey Sanchez	.25
16	Jose Vizcaino	.25
17	Mark Grace	.35
18	Dwight Smith	.25
20	Eric Yelding	.25
21	Sammy Sosa	3.50
22	Mike Harkey	.25
23	Ryne Sandberg	3.50
24	Steve Buechele	.25
25	Candy Maldonado	.25
27	Derrick May	.25
28	Randy Myers	.25
29	Jose Guzman	.25
30	Bob Scanlan	.25
32	Dan Plesac	.25
36	Mike Morgan	.25
37	Greg Hibbard	.25
38	Jose Bautista	.25
45	Paul Assenmacher	.25
49	Frank Castillo	.25
53	Doug Jennings	.25
---	Coaches (Billy Williams, Jose Martinez, Billy Connors, Tony Muser)	.25
---	Coaches (Dan Simonds, Tom Treblehorn, Chuck Cottier)	.25

2004 Maryland Lottery Golden Ticket Baltimore Orioles

In conjunction with the 50th anniversary of the Baltimore Orioles, the Maryland Lottery issued a set of baseball cards depicting great moments and players from the past. They were issued in a four-card foil pack with the purchase of a $10 Golden Ticket scratch-off card. Cards #1-45 were reported issued in quantities of 50,000 to 100,000 each. The team highlight

DON BAYLOR

cards, #45-48 were issued in an edition of 25,000 each. Fifteen thousand of the Ripken Ironman card #49 were produced. Card #50, Babe Ruth (shown on a 1914 Orioles minor league baseball card), was produced in an edition of 10,000. The first 100 persons turning in a complete set won $1,000 and an Orioles prize package. Cards are in the standard 2-1/2" x 3-1/2" format, printed on thin cardboard UV-coated on both sides.

		NM/M
Complete Set (50):		40.00
Common Player:		.50
1	Luis Aparicio	.75
2	Steve Barber	.50
3	Don Baylor	.50
4	Mark Belanger	.50
5	Mike Boddicker	.50
6	Don Buford	.50
7	Al Bumbry	.50
8	Mike Cuellar	.50
9	Rich Dauer	.50
10	Storm Davis	.50
11	Doug DeCinces	.50
12	Pat Dobson	.50
13	Moe Drabowsky	.50
14	Andy Etchebarren	.50
15	Bobby Grich	.50
16	George Kell	.50
17	Tito Landrum	.50
18	Lee MacPhail	.50
19	Tippy Martinez	.50
20	Scott McGregor	.50
21	Dave McNally	.50
22	Milt Pappas	.50
23	Paul Richards	.50
24	Gary Roenicke	.50
25	Dave Schmidt	.50
26	Steve Stone	.50
27	Gus Triandos	.50
28	Gene Woodling	.50
29	Terry Crowley	.50
30	Elrod Hendricks	.50
31	Memorial Stadium	.50
32	Orioles Park	.50
33	Rex Barney	.50
34	Rick Dempsey	.50
35	Mike Flanagan	.50
36	Jim Gentile	.50
37	Reggie Jackson	2.00
38	Frank Robinson	2.00
39	Chuck Thompson	.50
40	Earl Weaver	.50
41	Opening Day 1954	.50
42	Brady Anderson	.65
43	Boog Powell	2.00
44	Brooks Robinson	2.00
45	Jim Palmer	1.50
46	1966 World Series	7.50
47	1970 World Series	7.50
48	1983 World Series	7.50
49	2131 Ironman Breaks Record	7.50
50	Babe Ruth	15.00
---	Checklist/Rules	.10

1988 Master Bread Twins

KENT HRBEK
MINNESOTA TWINS

This set of 12 cardboard discs (2-3/4" diameter) features full-color photos of Minnesota Twins team members. Fronts have a bright blue background with red, yellow and black printing. The player photo (with team logos airbrushed off) is centered beneath a "Master Is Good Bread" headliner and a vivid yellow player/team name banner. Backs are black-and-white with five stars printed above the player's name, team, personal data, disc number, stats and "1988 Collector's Edition" banner. The discs were printed in Canada and marketed exclusively in Minnesota in packages of Master Bread, one disc per loaf. Squares cut from sheets are known in the hobby, valued about 50 percent of the issued version.

		NM/M
Complete Set (12):		12.00
Common Player:		1.00
1	Bert Blyleven	1.00
2	Frank Viola	1.00
3	Juan Berenguer	1.00
4	Jeff Reardon	1.00
5	Tim Laudner	1.00
6	Steve Lombardozzi	1.00
7	Randy Bush	1.00
8	Kirby Puckett	5.00
9	Gary Gaetti	1.00
10	Kent Hrbek	1.00
11	Greg Gagne	1.00
12	Tom Brunansky	1.00

1989 Master Bread

For a second year Master Bread packages in the Twin Cities area contained a baseball player disc in 1989. The 2-3/4" discs are in the familiar Mike Schechter Associates format and, unlike the '88 set, featured American League players other than Twins. The issue is among the scarcer of the MSA disc issues. Fronts are trimmed in yellow banners and blue stars. Backs are in blue and have a few stats and player data, along with a disc number.

		NM/M
Complete Set (12):		20.00
Common Player:		1.00
1	Frank Viola	1.00
2	Kirby Puckett	4.00
3	Gary Gaetti	1.00
4	Alan Trammell	1.00
5	Wade Boggs	4.00
6	Don Mattingly	5.00
7	Wally Joyner	1.00
8	Paul Molitor	3.50
9	George Brett	5.00
10	Jose Canseco	2.00
11	Julio Franco	1.00
12	Cal Ripken Jr.	7.50

1989 MasterCard Masters of the Game

The reason for issue and method of distribution for this set is not known. The issue was in the form of a 7-1/2" x 10-1/2" sheet on thin cardboard, picturing eight Hall of Famers around a title card. If cut from the unperforated sheet, single cards measure the standard 2-1/2" x 3-1/2". Fronts have familiar black-and-white photos with a gold border. Backs are in black, white and red with a repeat of the Masters of the Game logo, a few biographical details, lifetime stats and an MLB licensee logo. The unnumbered cards are checklisted here in alphabetical order.

		NM/M
Uncut Sheet:		6.00
Complete Set (9):		6.00
Common Player:		1.00
(1)	Ty Cobb	1.50
(2)	Lou Gehrig	1.50
(3)	Rogers Hornsby	1.00
(4)	Christy Mathewson	1.00
(5)	Satchel Paige	1.00
(6)	Babe Ruth	2.00
(7)	Casey Stengel	1.00
(8)	Cy Young	1.00
(9)	Title Card	.05

1985 Thom McAn Discs

One of the more obscure 1985 issues, this 47-card set of "Pro Player Discs" was issued by Thom McAn as a promotion for its "Jox" tennis shoes, which are advertised on the back of the cards. The discs, which measure 2-3/4" in diameter, feature black-and-white player photos against a background of either gold, yellow, red, pink, green or blue. Although not included in the "official" checklist released by the company, cards of George Brett have also been reported. Many of the Latin players' discs are quite scarce and are believed to have been issued in more limited quantities in Hispanic communities. The discs are unnumbered and checklisted here alphabetically.

		NM/M
Complete Set (47):		50.00
Common Player:		1.00
(1)	Benny Ayala	1.25
(2)	Buddy Bell	1.00
(3)	Juan Beniquez	1.25
(4)	Tony Bernazard	1.25
(5)	Mike Boddicker	1.00
(6)	George Brett	9.00
(7)	Bill Buckner	1.00
(8)	Rod Carew	6.00
(9)	Steve Carlton	6.00
(10)	Caesar Cedeno (Cesar)	1.00
(11)	Onix Concepcion	1.00
(12)	Cecil Cooper	1.00
(13)	Al Cowens	1.00
(14)	Jose Cruz	1.25
(15)	Ivan DeJesus	1.25
(16)	Luis DeLeon	1.25
(17)	Rich Gossage	1.00
(18)	Pedro Guerrero	1.00
(19)	Ron Guidry	1.00
(20)	Tony Gwynn	7.50
(21)	Mike Hargrove	1.00
(22)	Keith Hernandez	1.25
(23)	Bob Horner	1.00
(24)	Kent Hrbek	1.00
(25)	Rick Langford	1.00
(26)	Jeff Leonard	1.00
(27)	Willie McGee	1.00
(28)	Jack Morris	1.00
(29)	Jesse Orosco	1.25
(30)	Junior Ortiz	1.25
(31)	Terry Puhl	1.00
(32)	Dan Quisenberry	1.00
(33)	Johnny Ray	1.00
(34)	Cal Ripken	12.00
(35)	Ed Romero	1.00
(36)	Ryne Sandberg	7.50
(37)	Mike Schmidt	9.00
(38)	Tom Seaver	6.00
(39)	Rick Sutcliffe	1.00
(40)	Bruce Sutter	4.50
(41)	Alan Trammell	1.00
(42)	Fernando Valenzuela	2.00
(43)	Ozzie Virgil	1.25
(44)	Greg Walker	1.00
(45)	Willie Wilson	1.00
(46)	Dave Winfield	6.00
(47)	Geoff Zahn	1.00

1990 McDonald's

This 25-card set was released exclusively at 11 McDonald's restaurants in Idaho and eastern Oregon. Four cards were given with a large fries-soda purchase. Production was reported as 4,000 each. The cards have front borders of graduated purple shades around a game-action photo. Backs are similar in format to regular 1990 Score cards and include a portrait photo. The McDonald's

logo appears on front and back. Fifteen World Series trivia cards were part of the promotion.

		NM/M
Complete Set (25):		50.00
Common Player:		1.25
Trivia Card:		.60
1	Will Clark	1.25
2	Sandy Alomar, Jr.	1.25
3	Julio Franco	1.25
4	Carlton Fisk	5.00
5	Rickey Henderson	5.00
6	Matt Williams	1.25
7	John Franco	1.25
8	Ryne Sandberg	6.00
9	Kelly Gruber	1.25
10	Andre Dawson	3.00
11	Barry Bonds	12.00
12	Gary Sheffield	3.00
13	Ramon Martinez	1.25
14	Len Dykstra	1.25
15	Benito Santiago	1.25
16	Cecil Fielder	1.25
17	John Olerud	1.25
18	Roger Clemens	7.50
19	George Brett	10.00
20	George Bell	1.25
21	Ozzie Guillen	1.25
22	Steve Sax	1.25
23	Dave Stewart	1.25
24	Ozzie Smith	6.00
25	Robin Yount	5.00

1991 McDonald's Cleveland Indians

Distributed only at northern Ohio area McDonalds, this set features the players, coaches and manager of the Indians on an over-size (2-7/8" x 4-1/4") format. Color photos on front are framed in white and red with a white border all around. In the upper-left corner is a "Tribe Kids Fan Club" logo, while the McDonald's logo appears at lower-right. The player's uniform number, name and position are in black at lower-left. Backs are printed in black and have complete major and minor league statistics.

		NM/M
Complete Set (30):		5.00
Common Player:		.25
1	John McNamara	.25
2	Alex Cole	.25
3	Joel Skinner	.25
5	Jose Escobar	.25
6	Chris James	.25
8	Albert Belle	.50
9	Carlos Baerga	.25
11	Doug Jones	.25
12	Jerry Browne	.25
14	Sandy Alomar	.25
16	Felix Fermin	.25
20	Turner Ward	.25
21	Greg Swindell	.25
23	Mitch Webster	.25
26	Brook Jacoby	.25
27	Dave Otto	.25
30	Steve Olin	.25
37	Beau Allred	.25
38	Shawn Hillegas	.25
40	Eric King	.25
41	Charles Nagy	.25
44	Mike Huff	.25
45	Jeff Manto	.25
46	Bruce Egloff	.25
47	Jesse Orosco	.25
49	Mike Walker	.25
52	Tom Candiotti	.25
53	John Farrell	.25
54	Rod Nichols	.25
---	Coaches (Billy Williams, Jose Morales, Rich Dauer, Mike Hargrove, Luis Isaac, Mark Wiley)	

1992 McDonald's Baseball's Best

Sold in five-card cello packs with a food purchase at McDonald's stores in New York, New Jersey and Connecticut, this 44-card set was produced by Topps and carries the Topps logo, along with the Golden Arches, on front and back. Player photos on front are framed in yellow, surrounded by a black border. A red and blue "Baseball's Best" logo appears at top-right of the photo. Above that is a gold-foil stripe announcing "Limited Edition." At lower-right is another gold-foil stripe with the McDonald's logo and the player's name embossed thereon. On cards #34-44, which were distributed one per pack, there is an additional gold embossed "Rookie" shield at upper-left. Backs have a red border with a yellow stat box at center framed in white.

		NM/M
Complete Set (44):		6.00
Common Player:		.10
1	Cecil Fielder	.10
2	Benito Santiago	.10
3	Rickey Henderson	.60
4	Roberto Alomar	.20
5	Ryne Sandberg	.75
6	George Brett	1.25
7	Terry Pendleton	.10
8	Ken Griffey Jr.	1.25
9	Bobby Bonilla	.10
10	Roger Clemens	1.00
11	Ozzie Smith	.75
12	Barry Bonds	1.50
13	Cal Ripken, Jr.	1.50
14	Ron Gant	.10
15	Carlton Fisk	.60
16	Steve Avery	.10
17	Robin Yount	.60
18	Will Clark	.10
19	Kirby Puckett	.75
20	Jim Abbott	.10
21	Barry Larkin	.10
22	Jose Canseco	.45
23	Howard Johnson	.10
24	Nolan Ryan	1.50
25	Frank Thomas	.60
26	Danny Tartabull	.10
27	Julio Franco	.10
28	David Justice	.10
29	Joe Carter	.10
30	Dale Murphy	.35
31	Andre Dawson	.25
32	Dwight Gooden	.10
33	Bo Jackson	.20
34	Jeff Bagwell	.60
35	Chuck Knoblauch	.10
36	Derek Bell	.10
37	Jim Thome	.10
38	Royce Clayton	.10
39	Ryan Klesko	.10
40	Chito Martinez	.10
41	Ivan Rodriguez	.50
42	Todd Hundley	.10
43	Eric Karros	.10
44	Todd Van Poppel	.10

Cardinals

Pacific Trading Cards and McDonald's combined in 1992 to produce this 55-card (plus checklist) team set for the benefit of Ronald McDonald Children's Charities on the occasion of the St. Louis Cardinals' 100th anniversary. Sets were sold

initially for $1.49. Cards are standard 2-1/2" x 3-1/2" size and UV coated on each side. There is a sepia-toned or color photo on both front and back; generally an action photo on front and a portrait on back. Player selection is largely weighted to the last half of the 20th Century, with only a few cards of players pre-dating the Gashouse Gang era. The front design is completed with a Cardinals anniversary logo in the upper-left corner, a McDonald's logo at lower-right and gold stripes top and bottom. The player's name and position appear in red at the bottom of the photo. Besides the portrait photo, backs have a career summary stats for the player's Cardinals year and major league career and all appropriate logos.

		NM/M
Complete Set (55):		6.00
Common Player:		.10
1	Jim Bottomley	.15
2	Rip Collins	.15
3	Johnny Mize	.25
4	Rogers Hornsby	.25
5	Miller Huggins	.10
6	Marty Marion	.25
7	Frank Frisch	.25
8	Whitey Kurowski	.10
9	Joe Medwick	.10
10	Terry Moore	.10
11	Chick Hafey	.10
12	Pepper Martin	.25
13	Bob O'Farrell	.10
14	Walker Cooper	.10
15	Dizzy Dean	.50
16	Grover Cleveland Alexander	.25
17	Jesse Haines	.10
18	Bill Hallahan	.10
19	Mort Cooper	.10
20	Burleigh Grimes	.10
21	Red Schoendienst	.25
22	Stan Musial	3.00
23	Enos Slaughter	.25
24	Keith Hernandez	.25
25	Bill White	.25
26	Orlando Cepeda	.25
27	Julian Javier	.10
28	Dick Groat	.10
29	Ken Boyer	.20
30	Lou Brock	.50
31	Mike Shannon	.25
32	Curt Flood	.25
33	Joe Cunningham	.10
34	Reggie Smith	.10
35	Ted Simmons	.10
36	Tim McCarver	.25
37	Tom Herr	.10
38	Ozzie Smith	2.00
39	Joe Torre	.45
40	Terry Pendleton	.20
41	Ken Reitz	.10
42	Vince Coleman	.25
43	Willie McGee	.25
44	Bake McBride	.10
45	George Hendrick	.10
46	Bob Gibson	1.00
47	Whitey Herzog	.10
48	Harry Brecheen	.10
49	Howard Pollet	.10
50	John Tudor	.10
51	Bob Forsch	.10
52	Bruce Sutter	.50
53	Lee Smith	.15
54	Todd Worrell	.10
55	Al Hrabosky	.10
---	Checklist	.02

Ken Griffey, Jr. Pin/Cards

This set of three card-pin combinations saw limited distribution in the Northwestern U.S., with sales benefitting the Ronald McDonald Children's Charities. Cards measure 2-1/2" x 3-1/2" and have the same color photo of Ken Griffey, Jr. on the front. Fronts also have a McDonald's logo and facsimile autograph. Uniform logos have been

removed from the player's photo. Backs have a description of the charity and the logo "Griffey's Golden Moments," along with a 1992 Alrak Enterprises copyright. The pins were fastened through the cardboard of the card, leaving each with a hole. Prices quoted are for card/pin combinations.

		NM/M
Complete Set (3):		7.50
Common Card/Pin:		2.50
1-3	Ken Griffey Jr.	2.50

MVP

McDonald's restaurants in Ontario released a 26-card All-Star baseball card set in 1992 featuring many of the top players in the game. The cards were sold at Canadian McDonald's in packs of four with the purchase of a meal. Additionally, the company offered a six-card Toronto Blue Jays subset. The cards were produced by Donruss.

		NM/M
Complete Set (33):		8.00
Common Player:		.25
1	Cal Ripken, Jr.	1.50
2	Frank Thomas	.65
3	George Brett	1.00
4	Roberto Kelly	.25
5	Nolan Ryan	1.50
6	Ryne Sandberg	.75
7	Darryl Strawberry	.25
8	Len Dykstra	.25
9	Fred McGriff	.25
10	Roger Clemens	.85
11	Sandy Alomar Jr.	.25
12	Robin Yount	.65
13	Jose Canseco	.45
14	Jimmy Key	.25
15	Barry Larkin	.25
16	Dennis Martinez	.25
17	Andy Van Slyke	.25
18	Will Clark	.25
19	Mark Langston	.25
20	Cecil Fielder	.25
21	Kirby Puckett	.75
22	Ken Griffey Jr.	1.00
23	David Justice	.25
24	Jeff Bagwell	.65
25	Howard Johnson	.25
26	Ozzie Smith	.75
1	Roberto Alomar	.35
2	Joe Carter	.25
3	Kelly Gruber	.25
4	Jack Morris	.25
5	Tom Henke	.25
6	Devon White	.25

WUAB Cleveland Indians

These larger-than-standard (2-7/8" x 4-1/4") cards were given to members of the Tribe Kids Fan Club, sponsored by McDonald's and television station WUAB, whose logos appear on front and back, respectively. Cards have poses or game photos with red frames, white borders and a row of vertical blue diamonds on front. Horizontally formatted backs are in

Jack ARMSTRONG 77

black-and-white with complete career stats. Cards are listed here in order of the uniform numbers which appear on front.

		NM/M
Complete Set (30):		6.00
Common Player:		.25
0	Junior Ortiz	.25
1	Glenallen Hill	.25
4	Alex Cole	.25
4	Bob Skinner	.25
7	Kenny Lofton	.40
8	Albert Belle	.35
9	Carlos Baerga	.25
10	Mark Lewis	.25
11	Paul Sorrento	.25
15	Sandy Alomar Jr.	.25
16	Felix Fermin	.25
20	Tony Perezchica	.25
21	Mike Hargrove	.25
23	Mark Whiten	.25
25	Jim Thome	2.50
26	Brook Jacoby	.25
27	Dave Otto	.25
28	Derek Lilliquist	.25
31	Steve Olin	.25
33	Thomas Howard	.25
36	Brad Arnsberg	.25
39	Dennis Cook	.25
41	Charles Nagy	.25
44	Reggie Jefferson	.25
47	Scott Scudder	.25
48	Ted Power	.25
54	Rod Nichols	.25
63	Eric Bell	.25
77	Jack Armstrong	.25
---	The Coaches (Rick Adair, Ken Bolek, Dom Chiti, Ron Clark, Jose Morales, Dave Nelson, Jeff Newman)	.25

Cy Young

This pair of cards honoring a local hero was issued by McDonald's of Tuscarawas and Coshocton Counties in Ohio. A blue border card shows Young at bat and measures about 3-1/2" x 6". A red-bordered card has a commonly seen pitching pose and is about 3-3/4" x 5-15/16". A banner in front of crossed bats on front has his birth and death dates with a pair of McDonald's logos near the bottom. Backs are identical with biographical and statistical information.

		NM/M
Complete Set (2):		5.00
(1)	Cy Young/Btg	3.00
(2)	Cy Young/Pitching	3.00

1993 McDonald's Blue Jays

JACK MORRIS

This 36-card set was produced by Donruss and distributed by McDonald's of Canada. The set features two distinct styles of cards. The first 26 are "Great Moments" cards which feature team highlights of the 1985-1992 seasons. These cards have gold-foil embossed on front with a team logo/Great Moments seal. Backs

have a description of the highlight. Cards #27-35 are individual player cards. They feature full-bleed color action photos on front. Backs have a second photo and recent stats. All cards have the McDonald's and Donruss logos on front. The 36th card in the set is a header card with a checklist on back.

		NM/M
Complete Set (36):		5.00
Common Card:		.15
1	First Title/1985 (Doyle Alexander)	.15
2	Home Run King/1986 (Jesse Barfield)	.15
3	Major League Home Run Record/1987 (Fred McGriff)	.15
4	Opening Bell/1988 (George Bell)	.35
5	First Cycle/1989 (Kelly Gruber)	.15
6	Unbelievable Comeback - 1989 (Ernie Whitt)	.15
7	Winners Again/1989 (Tom Henke)	.15
8	First No-Hitter/1990 (Dave Stieb)	.15
9	First 20-Gamer (Jack Morris)	.15
10	FANtastic/1992	.15
11	Sudden Impact/1992 (Pat Borders, Mark McGwire)	.50
12	The Turning Point/1992 (Roberto Alomar)	.35
13	On to Atlanta/1992 (Candy Maldonado)	.15
14	Instant Hero/1992 (Ed Sprague)	.15
15	Old Friends/1992 (Cito Gaston, Bobby Cox)	.15
16	The Catch/1992 (Devon White)	.15
17	Near Triple Play/1992 (Kelly Gruber, Deion Sanders)	.15
18	Winning Welcome/1992 (Roberto Alomar)	.35
19	Winning Slide/1992 (Kelly Gruber)	.15
20	Final Farewell/1992 (Jimmy Key)	.15
21	Winning RBI/1992 (Devon White, Candy Maldonado)	.15
22	Clincher/1992 (Joe Carter)	.35
23	World Champions/1992	.15
24	Trophy Presentation/1992 (Cito Gaston, Bobby Brown)	.15
25	MVP - 1992 (Pat Borders)	.15
26	Heroes' Welcome/1992 (Roberto Alomar)	.35
	PLAYER CARDS	.15
27	John Olerud	.35
28	Roberto Alomar	.40
29	Ed Sprague	.15
30	Dick Schofield	.15
31	Devon White	.15
32	Joe Carter	.35
33	Darrin Jackson	.15
34	Pat Borders	.15
35	Paul Molitor	1.00
36	Checklist	.05

Expos

DAVE CASH

Top players and manager's from the team's 25 years were featured in a 33-card set produced by Donruss and distributed by Canadian McDonald's outlets. Card fronts feature a full-color borderless photo with the McDonald's and Donruss logos at top. A blue strip at bottom contains the player name and uniform number. At lower-left is an embossed silver-foil 25th anniversary logo. Fronts of the 2-1/2" x 3-1/2" cards are UV coated. Backs are printed in English and French and include a career summary and the player's

stats while with the Expos. Appropriate sponsor, team and licensor logos also appear. Autographed cards of Expos manager Felipe Alou were randomly packaged.

		NM/M
Complete Set (33):		12.00
Common Player:		.25
1	Moises Alou	.75
2	Andre Dawson	1.50
3	Delino DeShields	.25
4	Andres Galarraga	.50
5	Marquis Grissom	.50
6	Tim Raines	.50
7	Larry Walker	1.00
8	Tim Wallach	.25
9	Ken Hill	.25
10	Dennis Martinez	.35
11	Jeff Reardon	.25
12	Gary Carter	4.00
13	Dave Cash	.25
14	Warren Cromartie	.25
15	Mack Jones	.25
16	Al Oliver	.35
17	Larry Parrish	.25
18	Rodney Scott	.25
19	Ken Singleton	.25
20	Rusty Staub	.35
21	Ellis Valentine	.25
22	Woody Fryman	.25
23	Charlie Lea	.25
24	Bill Lee	.25
25	Mike G. Marshall	.25
26	Claude Raymond	.25
27	Steve Renko	.25
28	Steve Rogers	.25
29	Bill Stoneman	.25
30	Gene Mauch	.25
31	Felipe Alou	.45
31a	Felipe Alou/Auto.	20.00
32	Buck Rodgers	.25
33	Checklist	.05

1997 McDonald's N.Y. Yankees

Three popular Yankees stars of the 1996 World Championship team are featured in this issue which raised funds for Ronald McDonald House Charities. The 2-1/2" x 3-1/2" cards have color action photos on front with dark blue borders, a facsimile autograph and McDonald's logo. Uniform and cap logos have been removed from the photos. Backs are printed in blue with a cartoon of Ronald McDonald in baseball gear, a few biographical details about the player and some information about the charity.

		NM/M
Complete Set (3):		10.00
Common Player:		4.00
(1)	Dwight Gooden	4.00
(2)	Tino Martinez	4.00
(3)	Andy Pettitte	4.00

1998 McDonald's Arizona Diamondbacks

Travis Lee

Marking the team's first year in the National League, this card set was given away to children 14 and under at an August 14 promotional

game. In standard 2-1/2 x 3-1/2 format, the cards feature color portrait photos. Team and sponsor logos are in the left corners, with player identification in a green stripe at bottom. Backs have a desert scene background over which is printed personal data and professional stats. At bottom is a "Diamondbacks' Fact." Cards are listed here according to uniform number appearing on front.

		NM/M
Complete Set (24):		7.50
Common Player:		.50
5	Andy Stankiewicz	.50
6	Andy Fox	.50
9	Matt Williams	.75
10	Tony Batista	.50
11	Buck Showalter	.50
12	Jorge Fabregas	.50
15	Brent Brede	.50
19	Travis Lee	1.00
20	Willie Blair	.50
22	Jeff Suppan	.50
23	Devon White	.50
24	Karim Garcia	.75
25	David Dellucci	.50
26	Damian Miller	.50
30	Gregg Olson	.50
33	Jay Bell	.50
34	Brian Anderson	.50
35	Kelly Stinnett	.50
36	Clint Sodowsky	.50
37	Omar Daal	.50
40	Joel Adamson	.50
43	Andy Benes	.50
43	Yamil Benitez	.50
47	Felix Rodriguez	.50

1999 McDonald's St. Louis Cardinals

A late-season promotion at McDonald's restaurants in the St. Louis area offered six-card packs of Upper Deck Cardinal cards at $2.49, or $1.99 with a purchase. Cards are in the basic style of UD's 1999 MVP issue, but lack the silver-foil highlights on front. Backs are also nearly identical, but include a McDonald's logo at bottom-right. Both front and back photos on the McDonald's cards differ from those used on UD MVP. Each foil pack contains four of the 15 player cards, plus two of the special Mark McGwire Milestone inserts. Checklist cards are a one-in-nine pack insert.

		NM/M
Complete Set (16):		4.00
Common Player:		.15
1	J.D. Drew	1.00
2	Jose Jiminez	.15
3	Mark McGwire	1.50
4	Fernando Tatis	.15
5	Edgar Renteria	.15
6	Ray Lankford	.15
7	Willie McGee	.15
8	Ricky Bottalico	.15
9	Eli Marrero	.15
10	Kent Bottenfield	.15
11	Eric Davis	.15
12	Darren Bragg	.15
13	Joe McEwing	.15
14	Shawon Dunston	.15
15	Darren Oliver	.15
---	Checklist	.05

1999 McDonald's Mark McGwire Milestones

A late-season promotion at McDonald's restaurants in the St. Louis area offered six-card packs of Upper Deck Cardinal cards at $2.49, or $1.99 with a purchase. Each foil pack contains four of the 15 player cards, plus two special Mark McGwire Milestone inserts. Horizontally formatted, the Milestones inserts have an action photo of McGwire on a silver metallic-foil background with red, blue and black high-tech graphic designs. The cards mark one of McGwire's important home runs of 1998. Backs have a portrait photo and recount some of his career highlights. A McDonald's logo appears in the lower-right corner.

		NM/M
Complete Set (9):		7.00
Common Card:		1.00
M1	Mark McGwire/#50	1.00
M2	Mark McGwire/#60	1.00
M3	Mark McGwire/#61	1.00
M4	Mark McGwire/#62	1.50
M5	Mark McGwire/#63	1.00
M6	Mark McGwire/#67	1.00
M7	Mark McGwire/#68	1.00
M8	Mark McGwire/#69	1.00
M9	Mark McGwire/#70	1.50

2000 McDonald's Negro League Baseball

DENNIS "BOSE" BIDDLE

A set of 10 cards of former Negro Leagues ballplayers was issued by McDonald's in Milwaukee. The 2-1/2" x 3-1/2" cards have black-and-white oval photos at center, bordered in blue. A color logo reading "Yesterday's / Negro League Baseball / Players Wall of Fame" appears at top. A red starburst has the card number at upper-right. Below the photo are the McDonald's logo, the player's name and the years he was active in the Negro League. The red-on-white backs have biographical and career information and stats. Cards originally sold in one-card packs for 99 cents, or the set of 10 for about $9.

		NM/M
Complete Set (10):		20.00
Common Player:		2.00
1	William "Bobby" Robinson	2.00
2	Mamie "Peanut" Johnson	2.00
3	Carl Long	2.00
4	John "Mule" Miles	2.00
5	Sherwood Brewer	2.00
6	Ira McKnight	2.00
7	Gordon Hopkins	2.00
8	Johnny Washington	2.00
9	Jim Robinson	2.00
10	Dennis "Bose" Biddle	2.00

St. Louis Cardinals Coin/Cards

A late-season promotion at McDonald's restaurants in the St. Louis area offered six-card packs of Upper Deck Cardinal cards at $2.49, or $1.99 with a purchase.

A series of promotional games during the season, the Cardinals distributed these coin/cards. Wrapped in cellophane was a 2-1/2" x 4" card and a 39mm (about 1-1/2") bronze medallion. The card was horizontally perforated so it could be separated into a 2-1/2" x 2" player card and two 2-1/2" x 1" coupons. The player card has a game action photo on front. On back is the player name and career highlights. The coupons are for $1 off a McDonald's meal and for a free soft drink at Shell gas stations. Coins have the team logo on front, a player image roughly the same as pictured on the card, and the player uniform number. Back of the coin has the team and sponsor logos and the date the coin was distributed.

		NM/M
Complete Set (4):		20.00
Common Player:		4.00
1	Willie McGee (May 13)	4.00
2	Fernando Vina (June 24)	4.00
3	Jim Edmonds (July 9)	6.00
4	Mark McGwire (September 3)	8.00

2003 McDonald's N.Y. Yankees

Beginning July 28, and extending until 8.75 million cards were given away, these Upper Deck-produced cards were available at 600+ McDonald's in the metro New York area with the purchase of a special Yankees-themed Happy Meal. Cards were issued in either singly in a cello pack, or in a pack with a scratch-off game card. Fronts have an action photo with a large ghost-image team logo behind. Also on front are the Yankees' 100th anniversary logo and logos of UD and McDonald's. Backs have another player photo, stats, personal data and the logos.

		NM/M
Complete Set (24):		8.00
Common Player:		.25
1	Juan Acevedo	.25
2	Roger Clemens	1.50
3	John Flaherty	.25
4	Jason Giambi	.50
5	Chris Hammond	.25
6	Sterling Hitchcock	.25
7	Derek Jeter	2.50
8	Nick Johnson	.25
9	Steve Karsay	.25
10	Hideki Matsui	1.50
11	Raul Mondesi	.25
12	Mike Mussina	.35
13	Antonio Osuna	.25
14	Andy Pettitte	.35
15	Jorge Posada	.35
16	Mariano Rivera	.35
17	Alfonso Soriano	.50
18	Bubba Trammell	.25
19	Robin Ventura	.25
20	Jeff Weaver	.25
21	David Wells	.25
22	Bernie Williams	.35
23	Enrique Wilson	.25
24	Todd Zeile	.25

2004 McDonald's Philadelphia Phillies

A two-card pack was given away with each Extra Value Meal purchase at Philly area McDonald's in July. Production of 170,000 of each card was reported. Upper Deck created the cards for the promotion.

		NM/M
Complete Set (27):		6.00
Common Player:		.50
1	Jim Thome	

		NM/M
2	Placido Polanco	.50
3	Jimmy Rollins	1.00
4	David Bell	.50
5	Bobby Abreu	.50
6	Pat Burrell	1.00
7	Marlon Byrd	.50
8	Mike Lieberthal	.75
9	Kevin Millwood	.50
10	Randy Wolf	.50
11	Vicente Padilla	.50
12	Eric Milton	.50
13	Brett Myers	.50
14	Billy Wagner	.50
15	Tim Worrell	.50
16	Rheal Cormier	.50
17	Roberto Hernandez	.50
18	Ryan Madson	.50
19	Amaury Telemaco	.50
20	Tomas Perez	.50
21	Shawn Wooten	.50
22	Doug Glanville	.50
23	Ricky Ledee	.50
24	Jason Michaels	.50
25	Todd Pratt	.50
26	Larry Bowa	.50
27	Citizens Bank Park/ Checklist	.50

1992 MCI Ambassadors

Issued in conjunction with the MCI-sponsored Ambassadors of Baseball World Tour of overseas military bases, this set features retired players who participated in the tour. Cards feature color photos with a white border, a color tour logo in the lower-left and a banner across the upper-left reading, "Support MWR With MCI." The player's name and position appear in the bottom border. Horizontally oriented backs have career stats and highlights and the logos of MCI and the Major League Baseball Players Alumni in black-and-white.

		NM/M
Complete Set (16):		35.00
Common Player:		2.00
1	Earl Weaver	3.00
2	Steve Garvey	6.00
3	Doug Flynn	2.00
4	Bert Campaneris	2.00
5	Bill Madlock	2.00
6	Graig Nettles	2.00
7	Dave Kingman	3.00
8	Paul Blair	2.00
9	Jeff Burroughs	2.00
10	Rick Waits	2.00
11	Elias Sosa	2.00
12	Tug McGraw	2.00
13	Ferguson Jenkins (Photo)	4.00
14	Bob Feller	6.00
---	Ferguson Jenkins (Art)	4.00
---	Header Card	.50

1993 MCI Ambassadors

The Major League Baseball Players Alumni Association produced a set of 13 former players who were featured in 1993's MCI Ambassadors of Baseball World Tour. The card set was available free to military personnel who completed an MCI

application. The tour of military bases worldwide included appearances by the players at base exchanges, clinics for dependent children and a softball game against base all-stars. The cards feature a photo of the player on the front with logos from the Ambassador tour and MCI in opposite corners.

		NM/M
Complete Set (14):		20.00
Common Player:		1.25
1	Vida Blue	1.25
2	Paul Blair	1.25
3	Mudcat Grant	1.25
4	Phil Niekro	2.00
5	Bob Feller	3.00
6	Joe Charboneau	2.00
7	Joe Rudi	1.25
8	Catfish Hunter	2.00
9	Manny Sanguillen	1.25
10	Harmon Killebrew	3.00
11	Al Oliver	1.25
12	Bob Dernier	1.25
13	Graig Nettles, Sparky Lyle	1.75
---	Header Card	.10

1994 MCI Ambassadors

Once again in 1994, the old-timers' tour of overseas military bases sponsored by MCI spawned a card set. The '94 set is similar to previous years' issues except that color player photos have had the uniform logos airbrushed away. MCI and tour logos appear in color on the front; backs are in black-and-white and contain career data and highlights along with MCI and Major League Baseball Players Alumni logos. Besides 11 numbered cards, there are four unnumbered cards in the 1994 set which include a pair honoring major leaguers who served in the military during World War II.

		NM/M
Complete Set (15):		30.00
Common Player:		2.00
1	Sparky Lyle	2.00
2	John Stearns	2.00
3	Bobby Thomson	3.00
4	Jimmy Wynn	2.00
5	Ferguson Jenkins	4.00
6	Tug McGraw	2.00
7	Paul Blair	2.00
8	Ron LeFlore	2.00
9	Manny Sanguillen	2.00
10	Doug Flynn	2.00
11	Bill North	2.00
---	Manny Sanguillen (Signing autographs.)	2.00
---	Doug Flynn (Instructing children.)	2.00
---	American Leaguers in WWII	2.00
---	National Leaguers in WWII	2.00

1995 MCI Ambassadors

For a fourth year, Major League Baseball, the Players' Union and the long distance phone provider issued a card set in conjunction with its series of softball games at military bases. Approximately 2,000 sets were issued. The 2-1/2" x 3-1/2" cards have player photos on front with MCI and the baseball tour logos in opposite corners. Backs have biographical and career information about the retired stars.

		NM/M
Complete Set (16):		30.00
Common Player:		2.00
1	Vida Blue	2.00
2	Bert Campaneris	2.00
3	Tug McGraw	2.00
4	Doug Flynn	2.00
5	Paul Blair	2.00
6	Harmon Killebrew	5.00
7	Sparky Lyle	2.00
8	Steve Garvey	4.00
9	Bert Blyleven	2.00
10	Omar Moreno	2.00
11	Bill Lee	2.00
12	Maury Wills	2.00
13	Dave Parker	2.00
14	Luis Aparicio	5.00
15	Brooks Robinson	5.00
16	George Foster	2.00

1996 MCI Ambassadors

This set of former players cards was issued in conjunction with a tour of overseas U.S. military bases by members of the Major League Baseball Players Alumni Association. Players taking part in the tour are featured on the card fronts in photos contemporary with their major league days. Backs have career summaries and stats along with sponsors logos. The cards were virtually all distributed overseas.

		NM/M
Complete Set (8):		30.00
Common Player:		5.00
(1)	Tommy Davis	6.00
(2)	Darrell Evans	6.00
(3)	Jay Howell	5.00
(4)	John Montefusco	6.00
(5)	Graig Nettles	6.00
(6)	Jim Sundberg	5.00
(7)	Header card	.50
(8)	American Airlines Sponsor Card	.50

1991 MDA All-Stars

Though the Muscular Dystrophy Association isn't mentioned on the player cards, it was the beneficiary of this set produced by Smith-Kline Beecham. Card fronts feature color photos of the players during their active careers. Because the set was not licensed by MLB, team uniform logos have been airbrushed off the photos. Black-and-white backs have a recent portrait photo of the player, along with biographical and

career data. The set was available by mail for $3.99 plus proofs of purchase from Tums antacid.

		NM/M
Complete Set (20):		15.00
Common Player:		.50
1	Steve Carlton	1.00
2	Ted Simmons	.50
3	Willie Stargell	1.00
4	Bill Mazeroski	1.00
5	Ron Santo	.75
6	Dave Concepcion	.50
7	Bobby Bonds	.50
8	George Foster	.50
9	Billy Williams	1.00
10	Whitey Ford	2.00
11	Yogi Berra	2.00
12	Boog Powell	.60
13	Davey Johnson	.50
14	Brooks Robinson	1.00
15	Jim Fregosi	.50
16	Harmon Killebrew	1.00
17	Ted Williams	3.00
18	Al Kaline	1.00
---	MDA Fact Card (Brooks Robinson)	.50
---	Header Card	.25

1992 MVP for MDA

The Muscular Dystrophy Association was the beneficiary of this set sponsored by SmithKline Beecham. Card fronts feature color photos of the players during their active careers. Because the set was not licensed by MLB, team uniform logos have been airbrushed off the photos. Black-and-white backs have a portrait photo of the player, along with biographical and career data. A vinyl album to house the set was included in the mail-in offer.

		NM/M
Complete Set (20):		9.00
Common Player:		1.00
Album:		4.50
1	Yogi Berra	2.00
2	Dick Groat	1.00
3	Maury Wills	1.00
4	Brooks Robinson	1.50
5	Orlando Cepeda	1.00
6	Harmon Killebrew	1.50
7	Boog Powell	1.00
8	Vida Blue	1.00
9	Jeff Burroughs	1.00
10	George Foster	1.00
11	Rod Carew	1.50
12	Jim Rice	1.00
13	Don Baylor	1.00
14	Willie Stargell	1.50
15	Rollie Fingers	1.00
16	Ray Knight	1.00
17	History of the MVP	.25
18	MVP Trivia	.25
19	Harmon Killebrew (W/1992 MDA Poster Child.)	1.00
20	MLB Players Assn. Alumni Info	.25

1986 Meadow Gold Blank Backs

This was the second set to be distributed by Meadow Gold Dairy (Beatrice Foods) in 1986. It was issued on Double Play ice cream cartons, one card per package. Full-color player photos have team logos and insignias airbrushed away. This 16-card set is very similar to the Meadow Gold popsicle set, but the photos are different in some instances. The cards measure 2-3/8" x 3-1/2". The Willie McGee card is reportedly tougher to find than other cards in the set.

		NM/M
Complete Singles Set (16):		20.00
Complete Carton Set (16):		22.50
Common Player:		.75
(1)	George Brett	2.50
(2)	Wade Boggs	2.00

(3)	Carlton Fisk	1.50
(4)	Steve Garvey	1.00
(5)	Dwight Gooden	.75
(6)	Pedro Guerrero	.75
(7)	Reggie Jackson	2.50
(8)	Don Mattingly	2.50
(9)	Willie McGee	.75
(10)	Dale Murphy	1.00
(11)	Cal Ripken, Jr.	3.00
(12)	Pete Rose	3.00
(13)	Ryne Sandberg	2.00
(14)	Mike Schmidt	2.50
(15)	Fernando Valenzuela	.75
(16)	Dave Winfield	1.50

Statistic Backs

DON MATTINGLY
NEW YORK YANKEES   INFIELD

Beatrice Foods produced this set of 20 cards on specially marked boxes of Meadow Gold Double Play popsicles, fudgesicles and bubble gum coolers. They came in two-card panels and have full-color player pictures with player name, team and position printed below the photo. Card backs are printed in red ink and feature player career highlights. The cards measure 2-3/8" x 3-1/2" and were distributed in the West and Midwest. It is considered one of the toughest 1986 regional sets to complete.

		NM/M
Complete Panel Set (10):		10.00
Complete Singles Set (20):		10.00
Common Panel:		1.00
Common Single:		.30
PANEL 1		2.00
1	George Brett	1.50
2	Fernando Valenzuela	.30
PANEL 2		1.00
3	Dwight Gooden	.30
4	Dale Murphy	.75
PANEL 3		3.50
5	Don Mattingly	1.50
6	Reggie Jackson	1.50
PANEL 4		3.00
7	Dave Winfield	1.00
8	Pete Rose	2.00
PANEL 5		1.50
9	Wade Boggs	1.25
10	Willie McGee	.30
PANEL 6		5.00
11	Cal Ripkin (Ripken)	3.00
12	Ryne Sandberg	1.25
PANEL 7		1.50
13	Carlton Fisk	1.00
14	Jim Rice	.50
PANEL 8		2.50
15	Steve Garvey	.50
16	Mike Schmidt	1.50
PANEL 9		1.00
17	Bruce Sutter	.75
18	Pedro Guerrero	.30
PANEL 10		1.00
19	Rick Sutcliff (Sutcliffe)	.30
20	Rich Gossage	.30

Milk

DWIGHT GOODEN
NEW YORK METS   PITCHER

The third set from Meadow Gold from 1986 came on milk cartons; on pint, quart and half-gallon size containers. The cards measure 2-1/2" x 3-1/2" and feature drawings instead of photographs. Different dairies distributed the cards in various colors of ink. The cards

can be found printed in red, brown or black ink. The crude drawings have prevented this rare set from being higher in price.

		NM/M
Complete Set (11):		75.00
Common Player:		3.50
(1)	Wade Boggs	9.00
(2)	George Brett	12.00
(3)	Steve Carlton	7.50
(4)	Dwight Gooden	3.50
(5)	Willie McGee	3.50
(6)	Dale Murphy	6.00
(7)	Cal Ripken, Jr.	17.50
(8)	Pete Rose	15.00
(9)	Ryne Sandberg	9.00
(10)	Mike Schmidt	12.00
(11)	Fernando Valenzuela	3.50

1992 Megacards Babe Ruth Prototypes

THE BAMBINO – THE MAN
LOU GEHRIG APPRECIATION DAY; JULY 4TH.

Basically identical to the regularly issued versions, these sample cards were distributed to hobby dealers to introduce Megacards Babe Ruth Collection. Most of the prototypes have different card numbers than those in the regular set, and all carry a large gray diagonal "PROTOTYPE" on back.

		NM/M
Complete Set (9):		7.50
Common Card:		1.00
14	Year in Review/1921 (Babe Ruth)	1.00
31	World Series/1916 (Babe Ruth)	1.00
75	Place in History/1928 (Babe Ruth)	1.00
106	Career Highlights/1927 (Babe Ruth)	1.00
124	Trivia/1926 (Babe Ruth)	1.00
129	Sultan of Swat/1925 (Babe Ruth)	1.00
134	Being Remembered/1948 - George Bush (Babe Ruth)	1.00
138	Being Remembered/1923 - Grantland Rice (Babe Ruth)	1.00
154	The Bambino - The Man (Babe Ruth, Lou Gehrig)	1.25

1992 Megacards Babe Ruth

YEAR IN REVIEW   1922
SUSPENDED FOR FIRST 39 GAMES

This 165-card set chronicles the life and times of Babe Ruth. The set was produced by Megacards and is officially entitled "The Babe Ruth Collection." The cards feature classic black and white photos with black borders and captions below the photo. The card backs feature coordinating statistics and information.

		NM/M
Complete Set (165):		15.00
Complete Set, Tin:		20.00
Common Card:		.10
Wax Box (48):		20.00
1	Lifetime Pitching Statistics	.10
2	Lifetime Batting Statistics	.10
3	Lifetime - World Series Pitching	.10

4	Lifetime World Series Batting	.10
5	22-9 Record in the Minors	.10
6	2-1 Record First Year in the Majors	.10
7	Won 17 of his Last 21 Decisions	.10
8	Led League with 1.75 ERA and 9 Shutouts	.10
9	Defeats Walter Johnson for 6th Time	.10
10	Doubles as Pitcher and a Regular	.10
11	First Season in the Outfield	.10
12	Sold to Yankees for $100,000	.10
13	The Best Year Any Batter Ever Had	.10
14	Suspended for First 38 Games	.10
15	Wins American League MVP	.10
16	Wins Only Batting Title - .378	.10
17	The "Million Dollar Stomachache"	.10
18	Bats .372 with a .737 Slugging Average	.10
19	The Best Baseball Team in History	.20
20	Tops 50 Home Runs - 4th Time	.10
21	Clubs 500th Home Run	.10
22	Bam Bams Nine in a Week	.10
23	.700 Slugging Average for 9th Time	.10
24	Blasts Over 40 Homers for 11th Time	.10
25	Over 100 RBIs for 13th Time	.10
26	Tops 2,000 Career Walks	.10
27	Babe Retires	.10
28	Babe Coaches the Dodgers	.10
29	The Babe in Retirement	.10
30	1915 World Series - Warms Bench	.10
31	1916 World Series - Hurls 14-Inning Win	.10
32	1918 World Series - Scoreless Innings	.10
33	1921 World Series - Yankees' First	.10
34	1922 World Series - Back to the Farm	.10
35	1923 World Series - First Championship	.10
36	1926 World Series - 4 HR in Losing Cause	.15
37	1927 World Series - Destroy Bucs in Four	.15
38	1928 World Series - .625 BA and 1.375 SA	.10
39	1932 World Series - Yanks Sweep Cubs	.15
40	Lifetime - 2,056 Walks	.10
41	First to Fan 1,000 Times	.10
42	Lifetime - 2,174 Runs Scored	.15
43	Lifetime - 5,793 Total Bases	.15
44	Lifetime - 1,356 Extra-Base Hits	.10
45	Lifetime - 714 Home Runs	.10
46	Lifetime - 16 Grand Slams	.10
47	Lifetime - 8.5 Home Run Percentage	.15
48	Lifetime - Most Games, 2 or More HR	.10
49	Lifetime - 11 Seasons with 40+ HRs	.10
50	Lifetime - 2,211 RBIs	.15
51	Lifetime - .342 Batting Average	.15
52	Lifetime - .690 Slugging Average	.15
53	Season - Nine Shutouts	.10
54	Season - 170 Walks	.10
55	Season - 177 Runs Scored	.20
56	Season - .545 On-Base Percentage	.10
57	Season - 457 Total Bases	.15
58	Season - 119 Extra-Base Hits	.15
59	Season - 171 Runs Batted In	.15
60	Season - 60 Home Runs	.10
61	Season - 11.8 Home Run Percentage	.15
62	Season - .847 Slugging Average	.15
63	World Series 3-0 Record	.10
64	World Series - 0.87 ERA	.10
65	World Series - 33 Walks	.10
66	World Series - 37 Runs	.10
67	World Series - 96 Total Bases	.10
68	World Series - 15 Home Runs	.10
69	World Series - 33 RBIs	.10
70	World Series - .744 Slugging Average	.20
71	1914 - First Major League Victory	.10
72	1915 - First Major League Home Run	.10

73	1916 - Babe Derails "Big Train"	.10
74	1919 - Leads League in Fielding	.10
75	1919 First Home Run Record	.10
76	1920 - Babe Becomes a Yankee	.10
77	1923 - First Home Run in Yankee Stadium	.10
78	1923 - American League MVP	.10
79	1924 - Wins Only Batting Title	.15
80	1926 - Hits 3 Home Runs in Series Game	.10
81	1927 - Babe and Lou Smack 107 Home Runs (Lou Gehrig)	.20
82	1927 - The Babe's 60th Home Run	.20
83	1928 - Three HR in World Series Game	.10
84	1932 - Early "Called Shots" by the Bam	.10
85	1932 - The "Called Shot" - The Legend	.10
86	1932 - The "Called Shot" - The Believers	.10
87	1932 - The "Called Shot" - The Doubters	.10
88	1932 - The "Called Shot" - Babe's View	.10
89	1933 - First HR in an All-Star Game	.15
90	1933 - Last Time on the Mound	.10
91	1934 - Babe Hits 700th Home Run	.10
92	1934 - The Babe in Japan	.10
93	1935 - Last Major League Homers	.10
94	1939 - Inaugurated into Hall of Fame	.10
95	1942 - Faces Johnson Again in Exhibition	.10
96	1947 - Babe Ruth Day	.10
97	1948 - Babe's Farewell	.25
98	A Perfect Punch	.10
99	Yankees Best Base Thief	.10
100	Hub Pruett: Babe Buster	.10
101	Babe Caught Stealing, Ends 1926 Series	.10
102	Never Won a Triple Crown	.10
103	Babe Used a 54-Ounce Bat	.10
104	Babe Bats Righty	.10
105	Babe's Greatness	.10
106	The Babe's Best	.10
107	Outslugged Entire Teams	.10
108	First to Hit 30, 40, 50 and 60 Home Runs	.10
109	The Pitkin Study	.10
110	First to Put the Ball Into Orbit	.10
111	Afraid to Kill Somebody	.10
112	The Wonder Years: 1926-31	.10
113	Hit .422 With 7 Homers on Opening Days	.10
114	Babe at Bat	.10
115	"Greatest Ballplayer the Game Has Known"	.10
116	The Babe's Early Childhood	.10
117	St. Mary's Industrial School	.10
118	Babe and Brother Matthias	.10
119	The Babe's Nicknames	.10
120	Babe's First Wife, Helen	.10
121	Babe's Second Wife, Claire	.10
122	Lou Gehrig Appreciation Day	.20
123	Babe's Friendship With Herb Pennock	.10
124	The Babe and Miller Huggins	.10
125	The Babe and Ty Cobb	.15
126	Babe and Walter Johnson	.15
127	Baseball's Biggest Drawing Card	.10
128	Babe's Barnstorming	.10
129	Costly Confrontation	.10
130	He Often Played Hurt	.10
131	Babe's Big Bucks	.10
132	Want to be a Manager	.10
133	The Babe on the Links	.10
134	Babe in the Movies	.10
135	Babe Contributes to War Effort	.10
136	The Babe - Peace Negotiator	.10
137	Everyone Loved the Babe	.10
138	He Brought Children Joy	.10
139	He Always Had Time for Kids	.10
140	The Johnny Sylvester Story	.10
141	Moving with the Great Babe Ruth	.10
142	Babe Ruth and the American Dream	.10
143	Being Remembered - Bill James	.10
144	Being Remembered - Bill James	.10
145	Being Remembered - Bill James	.10
146	Being Remembered - Mel Allen	.10

147	Being Remembered - Mel Allen	.10
148	Being Remembered - Wes Ferrell	.10
149	Being Remembered - George Bush	.50
150	Being Remembered - Ethan Allen	.20
151	Being Remembered - Daughter Dorothy	.10
152	Being Remembered - Daughter Julia	.10
153	Being Remembered - Daughter Julia	.10
154	Being Remembered - Mark Koenig	.10
155	Being Remembered - Donald Honig	.10
156	Being Remembered - L. Waner, Waite Hoyt	.10
157	Being Remembered - Waite Hoyt	.10
158	Being Remembered - Bill Dickey	.10
159	Being Remembered - Bob Meusel	.10
160	Being Remembered - Jim Chapman	.10
161	Being Remembered - Christy Walsh	.10
162	Being Remembered - The Babe Passes Away	.10
163	Being Remembered - Grantland Rice	.10
164	Checklist 1-83	.10
165	Checklist 84-165	.10

1995 Megacards Ken Griffey, Jr. MegaCaps

Three different "MegaCaps" picturing Ken Griffey, Jr., were prepared for insertion into blister packs containing full sets of the Ken Griffey Jr. Wish List Collection. Each of the 1-5/8" diameter cardboard discs has a color photo of Junior on front. Backs have trademark information. Reported print run for each of the three versions was 34,000.

		NM/M
Complete Set:		1.50
Common Cap:		.50
1	Ken Griffey Jr.	.50
2	Ken Griffey Jr.	.50
3	Ken Griffey Jr.	.50

1995 Megacards Ken Griffey, Jr. Wish List

Sold only as a complete set in a clam-shell plastic blister pack, this set has two areas of focus. The first 14 cards details Griffey's hopes for his baseball career and his life; the second 11 cards feature projections on Junior's possible career stats based on numbers generated by baseball statistician Bill James. Each card has a different action photo of Griffey on the front. Backs have a smaller version of the front photo in the upper-right corner, and a muted background photo of Griffey at bat. Card fronts are gold-foil enhanced. Packed with each set was one of three "MegaCaps" with Griffey's picture. With a reported print run of 100,000 sets, the issue sold for about $10 re-

tail, with part of the purchase price going to the Make a Wish Foundation for seriously ill children.

		NM/M
Complete Set (27):		7.50
Common Card:		.50
1	Introduction (Ken Griffey Jr.)	.50
2	Make-A-Wish Foundation (Ken Griffey Jr.)	.50
3	To Make Dreams Come True (Ken Griffey Jr.)	.50
4	To Play With Dad (Ken Griffey, Sr.))	.50
5	"The Best I Can Be" (Ken Griffey Jr.)	.50
6	To Make the Majors (Ken Griffey Jr.)	.50
7	To Play for a Winner (Ken Griffey Jr.)	.50
8	To Assist B.A.T. (Ken Griffey Jr.)	.50
9	To Enrich Inner-City Baseball (Ken Griffey Jr.)	.50
10	A Lot to Live For (Ken Griffey Jr.)	.50
11	To Be an All-Around Player (Ken Griffey Jr.)	.50
12	To Be #1 in the Draft (Ken Griffey Jr.)	.50
13	To Win the Gold (Ken Griffey Jr.)	.50
14	Most Home Runs by Father/Son (Ken Griffey Jr. (W/Ken Griffey, Sr.))	.50
15	The Field of Possibilities (Ken Griffey Jr.)	.50
16	The Griffey Forecast (Ken Griffey Jr.)	.50
17	3,598 Career Games (Ken Griffey Jr.)	.50
18	2,361 Career Runs (Ken Griffey Jr.)	.50
19	3,947 Career Hits (Ken Griffey Jr.)	.50
20	777 Career Doubles (Ken Griffey Jr.)	.50
21	699 Career Home Runs (Ken Griffey Jr.)	.50
22	2,234 Career RBIs (Ken Griffey Jr.)	.50
23	1,541 Career Extra Base Hits (Ken Griffey Jr.)	.50
24	40 or More Home Runs 5 Times (Ken Griffey Jr.)	.50
25	28 Career Grand Slams (Ken Griffey Jr.)	.50
---	Contest Card	.05
---	Merchandise Order Card	.05

1995 Megacards Babe Ruth 100th Anniversary

Marking the centennial of Babe Ruth's birth, Megacards issued this 25-card set chronicling the life and career of baseball's all-time greatest player. Most of the cards feature on front black-and-white photos of Ruth, although there are several colorized pictures scattered through the set. Fronts have gold-foil frames, captions and Ruth Centennial logo. Reverses have a background photo of Ruth's classic swing and a detailed vignette pertinent to the card's theme. The Babe Ruth 100th Anniversary Collection set was sold in a plastic clam-shell package containing one of three Babe Ruth "Megacaps." The edition was limited to 100,000 sets.

		NM/M
Complete Set (27):		5.00
Common Card:		.25
1	Baseball's Greatest Ever? (Babe Ruth)	.25
2	60 Home Run Club (Babe Ruth)	.25
3	No Slugger Comes Close (Babe Ruth (With Jimmie Foxx, Lou Gehrig, Al Simmons.))	.25
4	History's Most Frequent Home Run Threat (Babe Ruth)	.25
5	He Knew the Way Home (Babe Ruth)	.25
6	He Didn't Leave Them Stranded (Babe Ruth (With Lou Gehrig.))	.25
7	50 Home Run King (Babe Ruth)	.25
8	Long Ball Legend (Babe Ruth)	.25
9	.342 Plus Power (Babe Ruth (With Lloyd Waner, Paul Waner, Lou Gehrig.))	.25
10	No One Hit 'Em More Often (Babe Ruth)	.25
11	Greatest Pitching Prospect (Babe Ruth (Colorized, Red Sox pitcher.))	.25
12	Career Year (Babe Ruth (Colorized, fishing with Lou Gehrig.))	.25
13	Mr. Yankee (Babe Ruth (With Lou Gehrig; Don Mattingly superimposed.))	.50
14	Babe and "The Kid" (Babe Ruth (Ken Griffey, Jr., superimposed.))	.50
15	Everyone Loved the Babe (Babe Ruth)	.25
16	The Babe Played Hurt (Babe Ruth)	.25
17	He Did It His Way (Babe Ruth)	.25
18	The Rewards of Greatness (Babe Ruth)	.25
19	Babe and Today's Rules (Babe Ruth)	.25
20	Babe in Today's Ballparks (Babe Ruth)	.25
21	Babe and Today's Best (Babe Ruth (Colorized, Ken Griffey Jr. superimposed.))	.75
22	Babe vs. Today's Pitching (Babe Ruth)	.25
23	The Babe and Father Time (Babe Ruth)	.25
24	How He Changed the Game (Babe Ruth (Colorized, with Dizzy Dean, Frank Frisch, Mickey Cochrane, Schoolboy Rowe.))	.25
25	Will There Be Another Babe? (Babe Ruth)	.25
---	Sweepstakes Card	.05
---	Babe Ruth Merchandise Order Card	.05

Babe Ruth MegaCaps

One of three different 1-5/8" "MegaCaps" picturing Babe Ruth was packaged in each set of Babe Ruth 100th Anniversary Collection cards. The discs feature a photo of Ruth on front and trademark information on the back. Each cap was produced in an edition of 34,000.

		NM/M
Complete Set (3):		1.50
Common Cap:		.50
1	Babe Ruth	.50
2	Babe Ruth	.50
3	Babe Ruth	.50

1994 Mellon Bank Phillies

This set sponsored by "The Official Bank of the Phillies" was issued in the form of a perforated fold-out, with individual cards in the standard 2-1/2" x 3-1/2" size. One panel is a 12-1/2" x 7" team photo. Fronts have game-action photos with a border of red pinstripes on white. The team name is in a box at top, the player name is in a banner at bottom. On back are personal data, stats and career highlights, along with the logos of the team, the sponsor and MLB's 125th Anniversary.

		NM/M
Foldout:		12.00
Complete Set, Singles (26):		8.00
Common Player:		.50
(1)	Larry Anderson	.50
(2)	Kim Batiste	.50
(3)	Shawn Boskie	.50
(4)	Darren Daulton	.75
(5)	Mariano Duncan	.50
(6)	Lenny Dykstra	.75
(7)	Jim Eisenreich	.50
(8)	Tommy Greene	.50
(9)	Dave Hollins	.50
(10)	Pete Incaviglia	.50
(11)	Danny Jackson	.50
(12)	Doug Jones	.50
(13)	Ricky Jordan	.50
(14)	John Kruk	.75
(15)	Tony Longmire	.50
(16)	Mickey Morandini	.50
(17)	Bobby Munoz	.50
(18)	Todd Pratt	.50
(19)	Paul Quantrill, Billy Hatcher	.50
(20)	Curt Schilling	1.50
(21)	Heathcliff Slocumb	.50
(22)	Kevin Stocker	.50
(23)	Milt Thompson	.50
(24)	David West	.50
(25)	Mike Williams	.50
(26)	Team photo	2.00

1995 Mellon Bank Phillies

Dave Gallagher

This set was issued in the form of a perforated fold-out, with individual cards in the standard 2-1/2" x 3-1/2" size. Fronts have game-action photos with a border of red pinstripes on white. The team name is in a box at top, the player name is in a banner at bottom. On back are personal data and stats, along with the logos of the team, the sponsor and the Phillies "Silver Season." The unnumbered cards are checklisted here alphabetically.

		NM/M
Foldout:		10.00
Complete Set, Singles (25):		8.00
Common Player:		.50
(1)	Kyle Abbott	.50
(2)	Toby Borland	.50
(3)	Ricky Bottalico	.50
(4)	Norm Charlton	.50
(5)	Darren Daulton	.75
(6)	Mariano Duncan	.50
(7)	Lenny Dykstra	.75
(8)	Jim Eisenreich	.50
(9)	Dave Gallagher	.50
(10)	Tyler Green	.50
(11)	Gene Harris	.50
(12)	Charlie Hayes	.50
(13)	Dave Hollins	.50
(14)	Gregg Jefferies	.50
(15)	Tony Longmire	.50
(16)	Michael Mimbs	.50
(17)	Mickey Morandini	.50
(18)	Paul Quantrill	.50
(19)	Randy Ready	.50
(20)	Curt Schilling	1.50
(21)	Heathcliff Slocumb	.50
(22)	Kevin Stocker	.50
(23)	Gary Varsho	.50
(24)	Lenny Webster	.50
(25)	David West	.50

2003 Merrick Mint Laser Line Gold Cards

These 2-1/2" x 3-1/2" cards are produced from 23-K gold foil in an intaglio printing process which gives them an engraved look and feel. Because the set is licensed only by the Player's Association, and not MLB, team logos and nicknames are not shown. Fronts have a portrait photo and facsimile autograph. Backs have information on the production process. The unnumbered cards are checklisted here alphabetically. Cards were issued in an acrylic case at an original price of about $15.

		NM/M
Complete Set (17):		75.00
Common Player:		3.00
(1)	Roger Clemens	5.00
(2)	Nomar Garciaparra	5.00
(3)	Ken Griffey Jr.	6.00
(4)	Vladimir Guerrero	4.00
(5)	Derek Jeter	10.00
(6)	Randy Johnson	4.00
(7)	Pedro Martinez	4.00
(8)	Hideki Matsui	4.00
(9)	Mike Piazza	6.00
(10)	Mark Prior	3.00
(11)	Albert Pujols	8.00
(12)	Alex Rodriguez	8.00
(13)	Alfonso Soriano	3.00
(14)	Sammy Sosa	5.00
(15)	Ichiro Suzuki	4.00
(16)	Jim Thome	3.00
(17)	Dontrelle Willis	3.00

2003 Merrick Mint N.Y. Yankees Stickers/Cards

To commemorate the 100th anniversary of the N.Y. Yankees, this set of stickers and cards was produced. Each player is represented on a self-adhesive 1-3/8" x 1-7/8" sticker and a 3-1/2" x 2-1/2" blank-backed card on which the sticker could be placed. Stickers were issued in sheets of nine or 16, and cards on perforated sheets of four or nine. The stickers have portrait photos, a facsimile autograph and uniform number. Cards have an action photo and facsimile autograph. Because the issued was licensed only by the Players Union and not MLB, uniform logos have been excised and the team nickname "Yankees" is nowhere to be seen. The issue was sold in sheets in either 5" x 7" or 8" x 10" format.

		NM/M
Set 8x10 Sheets (2):		7.00
Set 5x7 Sheets (4):		6.00
Complete Set Stickers (17):		2.00
Common Sticker:		.25
Complete Set Cards (17):		5.00
Common Card:		.50
1	Derek Jeter	1.00
6	Joe Torre	.25
12	Alfonso Soriano	.25
18	Jeff Weaver	.25
19	Robin Ventura	.25
20	Jorge Posada	.25
22	Jason Giambi	.50
25	Roger Clemens	.75
33	David Wells	.25
35	Mike Mussina	.35
36	Nick Johnson	.25
42	Mariano Rivera	.35
43	Raul Mondesi	.25
46	Andy Pettitte	.35
51	Bernie Williams	.25
55	Hideki Matsui	.50
---	100th Anniversary Logo	.25
2	Derek Jeter	2.00
6	Joe Torre	.50
12	Alfonso Soriano	.75
18	Jeff Weaver	.50
19	Robin Ventura	.50
20	Jorge Posada	.50
22	Jason Giambi	.75
25	Roger Clemens	1.00
33	David Wells	.50
35	Mike Mussina	.60
36	Nick Johnson	.50
42	Mariano Rivera	.60
43	Raul Mondesi	.50
46	Andy Pettitte	.60
51	Bernie Williams	.50
55	Hideki Matsui	.75
---	100th Anniversary Logo	.25

Stickers/Cards

This issue comprises several types of collectibles in one cellobagged package. Each pack consists of nine self-adhesive 1-1/2" x 2" stickers, nine 3-1/2" x 2-1/2" blank-backed cards on which the sticker could be placed, one 2-1/2" x 5" "Colossal" sticker and one of seven 2-1/2" x 1-7/8" "Rookie Star" sticker of Hideki Matsui. The stickers have color portrait and black-and-white game action photos and a facsimile autograph. Cards have a color version of the action photo. Because the issued was licensed only by the Players Union and not MLB, uniform logos have been excised and team nicknames are nowhere to be seen.

		NM/M
Complete Set, Sheets (7):		20.00
Common Player Sticker + Card:		.50
Package 1		5.00
(C1)	Derek Jeter (Colossal)	1.00
RS1	Hideki Matsui/Btg (Rookie Star) (One hand visible.))	.50
(1)	Barry Bonds (Facing his right.)	1.50
(2)	Roger Clemens/DP	.75
(3)	Ken Griffey Jr./TP	.75
(4)	Randy Johnson	.65
(5)	Pedro Martinez/DP	.60
(6)	Mike Piazza/DP	.75
(7)	Mark Prior	.50
(8)	Sammy Sosa/DP	.75
(9)	Ichiro/DP	.75
Package 2		3.50
(C2)	Alex Rodriguez (Colossal)	.75
(RS2)	Hideki Matsui/Btg (Rookie Star) (No hands visible.)	.50
(10)	Barry Bonds/DP (Arms up.)	1.00
(11)	Pat Burrell	.50
(12)	Jose Contreras	.50
(13)	Jim Edmonds	.50
(14)	Todd Helton	.65
(15)	Austin Kearns	.50
(16)	Greg Maddux	.75
(17)	Sammy Sosa/DP	.75
(18)	Mike Sweeney	.50
Package 3		3.75
(C3)	Nomar Garciaparra (Colossal)	.50
(RS3)	Hideki Matsui/Throwing (Rookie Star)	.50
(19)	Jeff Bagwell	.65
(20)	Barry Bonds/DP (Arms up.)	1.00
(21)	Ken Griffey Jr./TP	.75
(22)	Rafael Palmeiro	.60
(23)	Albert Pujols	1.25
(24)	Alfonso Soriano	.50
(25)	Miguel Tedaja (Tejada)	.50
(26)	Larry Walker	.50
(27)	Dontrelle Willis	.50
Package 4		3.25
(C4)	Sammy Sosa (Colossal)	.50
(RS4)	Hideki Matsui (Rookie Star)(Thumb up.)	.50
(28)	Roger Clemen/DP	.75
(29)	Adam Dunn	.50
(30)	Vladimir Guerrero	.65
(31)	Torii Hunter	.50
(32)	Pedro Martinez/DP	.60
(33)	Magglio Ordonez	.50
(34)	Mike Piazza/DP	1.00
(35)	Ivan Rodriguez	.60
(36)	John Smoltz	.50
	Package 5	3.50
(C5)	Barry Bonds (Colossal)	1.00
(RS5)	Hideki Matsui/Fldg (Rookie Star)(Running.)	.50
(37)	Lance Berkman	.50
(38)	Eric Chavez	.50
(39)	Troy Glaus	.50
(40)	Shawn Green	.50
(41)	Andruw Jones	.65
(42)	Manny Ramirez	.65
(43)	Curt Schilling	.50
(44)	Ichiro/DP	1.00
(45)	Bernie Williams	.50
Package 6		3.75
(C6)	Mike Piazza (Colossal)	.50
(RS6)	Hideki Matsui/Fldg (Rookie Star)(Standing.)	.50
(46)	Garret Anderson	.50
(47)	Rocco Baldelli	.50
(48)	Nomar Garciaparra	1.00
(49)	Juan Gonzalez	.50
(50)	Ken Griffey Jr./TP	.75
(51)	Derek Jeter	1.50
(52)	Gary Sheffield	.50
(53)	Frank Thomas	.65
(54)	Jim Thome	.65
Package 7		3.25
(C7)	Ichiro (Colossal)	.50
(RS7)	Hideki Matsui/Btg (Rookie Star)(Both hands visible.)	.50
(55)	Carlos Delgado	.50
(56)	Jason Giambi	.60
(57)	Tom Glavine	.50
(58)	Luis Gonzalez	.50
(59)	Chipper Jones	.75
(60)	Mike Mussina	.50
(61)	Alex Rodriguez	1.25
(62)	Scott Rolen	.60
(63)	Barry Zito	.50

1993 Metallic Images Cooperstown Collection

This set of retired players is produced of durable, embossed metal with rolled edges. Limited to 49,900, it came packaged in a collectors' tin with a numbered certificate of authenticity. The cards feature full-color photos on the front and back and statistics on the reverse. Half of the players in the set are members of the Hall of Fame.

		NM/M
Complete Set (20):		5.00
Common Player:		.10
1	Hank Aaron	1.50
2	Vida Blue	.10
3	Yogi Berra	.50
4	Bobby Bonds	.10
5	Lou Brock	.20
6	Lew Burdette	.10
7	Rod Carew	.20
8	Rocky Colavito	.20
9	George Foster	.10
10	Bob Gibson	.20
11	Mickey Lolich	.10
12	Willie Mays	1.50
13	Johnny Mize	.20
14	Don Newcombe	.15
15	Gaylord Perry	.20
16	Boog Powell	.15
17	Bill Skowron	.15
18	Warren Spahn	.35
19	Willie Stargell	.20
20	Luis Tiant	.10
P1	Willie Mays	1.25

1995 Metallic Images Babe Ruth

This five-card set of metal cards honors Babe Ruth in the 100th anniversary of his birth. The cards are 2-5/8" x 3-9/16" and featured gold-toned rolled edges. Fronts have familiar sepia-toned photos of the Babe with colorized back-

grounds. "Cooperstown Collection" logos appear on front and back. Backs have an overall background of a ghost-image picture of Ruth at bat, along with a small sepia portrait photo, career summary and, on some cards, a few stats. The set was issued in a black embossed tin box, with cards in a cello wrapper.

		NM/M
Complete Boxed Set (5):		5.00
Common Card:		1.00
1	Babe Ruth (Batting follow-through.)	1.00
2	Babe Ruth (Seated with bat on shoulders.)	1.00
3	Babe Ruth (Batting follow-through.)	1.00
4	Babe Ruth (Standing behind 10 bats.)	1.00
5	Babe Ruth (Batting follow-through.)	1.00

Impressions Willie Mays

As part of its Cooperstown Collection series of embossed metal cards, this set traces Willie Mays' career. The set was originally marketed by Avon cosmetics and sold in a lithographed steel box with pictures of Mays on the top and sides. Each of the cards inside was sealed in a cellophane wrapper. Cards measure about 2-5/8" x 3-5/8" and feature monochrome or color photos lithographed on steel. Borders and other design details are embossed. A second photo of Mays is on back, along with a few sentences about his life and career.

		NM/M
Complete Boxed Set (5):		4.00
Common Card:		1.00
1	Willie Mays (Negro Leagues)	1.00
2	Willie Mays (Minor Leagues)	1.00
3	Willie Mays (Rookie Year)	1.00
4	Willie Mays (New York Mets)	1.00
5	Willie Mays (Willie, Mickey, and the Duke)	1.00

1996 Metallic Impressions Ken Griffey, Jr.

This set of metal cards was sold in a lithographed steel box with pictures of Griffey on the top and sides. Each of the cards inside was sealed in a cellophane wrapper. Cards measure about 2-5/8" x 3-5/8" and feature color photos lithographed on steel. Borders and other design details are embossed. Two more photos of Griffey are on back, along with a few sentences about his life and career.

		NM/M
Complete Boxed Set (5):		3.00
Common Card:		1.00
1	Ken Griffey Jr. (At bat.)	1.00
2	Ken Griffey Jr./Throwing	1.00
3	Ken Griffey Jr./Running	1.00
4	Ken Griffey Jr./Fldg	1.00
5	Ken Griffey Jr./Swinging	1.00

Iron Men of Baseball

Originally sold by Avon, this set of embossed metal cards was sold in a lithographed steel box with player pictures on the top and sides. Each of the cards inside was sealed in in a cellophane wrapper. Cards measure about 2-5/8" x 3-5/8" and feature black-and-white or color photos lithographed on steel. Borders and other design details are embossed. A pair of photos is on back, along with details of each player's consecutive games streak.

		NM/M
Complete Boxed Set (5):		6.00
Common Player:		1.50
1	Lou Gehrig	1.50
2	Lou Gehrig	1.50
3	Cal Ripken Jr.	1.50
4	Cal Ripken Jr.	1.50
5	Lou Gehrig, Cal Ripken Jr.	1.50

Cal Ripken, Jr.

Two versions of this set were produced, a five-card set (#1-5) and a 10-card set (#1-10). Highlights of Cal Ripken's career are presented on these metallic baseball cards. Each 2-5/8" x 3-5/8" card has a color photo at center, surrounded by team-colored borders. Embossed at the bottom is a script version of Ripken's name with an oriole atop. In the lower-right corner is a metallic-looking home plate with "Iron Oriole." Backs repeat some of the front graphics and have identical portrait and action photos of Ripken and the magic number "2131" in lights at top. A paragraph at bottom describes a career milestone or highlight. The sets were sold in embossed lithographed metal boxes. The 10-card set is accompanied by a serial numbered certificate from an edition of 29,950.

		NM/M
Complete Boxed Set (10):		7.50
Complete Boxed Set (5):		4.00
Common Card:		1.00
1	Cal Ripken Jr. (Major League debut.)	1.00
2	Cal Ripken Jr. (1982 - Opening Day 3B)	1.00
3	Cal Ripken Jr. (Streak begins.)	1.00
4	Cal Ripken Jr. (Rookie of the Year)	1.00
5	Cal Ripken Jr. (1983)	1.00
6	Cal Ripken Jr. (Consecutive innings streak.)	1.00
7	Cal Ripken Jr. (1991 MVP)	1.00
8	Cal Ripken Jr. (Gold Glover)	1.00
9	Cal Ripken Jr. (Game 2,130.)	1.00
10	Cal Ripken Jr. (Game 2,131.)	1.00

1996 Metallic Impressions 1936 Hall of Fame Electees

As part of its Cooperstown Collection series of embossed metal cards, this set was released in the 60th anniversary year of the first Hall of Fame selections. The set was sold in a lithographed steel box with player pictures on the top and sides. Each of the cards inside was sealed in a cellophane wrapper. Cards measure about 2-5/8" x 3-5/8" and feature black-and-white photos lithographed on steel. Borders and other design details are embossed. A black-and-white photo is on back, along with "Peak Performance" stats and a career summary. Sets were originally sold through Avon.

		NM/M
Complete Boxed Set (5):		4.50
Common Player:		1.00
1	Babe Ruth	2.00
2	Ty Cobb	1.50
3	Christy Mathewson	1.00
4	Walter Johnson	1.00
5	Honus Wagner	1.00

1997 Metallic Impressions Jackie Robinson

As part of its Cooperstown Collection series of embossed metal cards, this set was released in the 50th anniversary year of Jackie Robinson's entry into the major leagues. The set was sold in a lithographed steel box with pictures of Robinson on the top and sides. Each of the cards inside was sealed in a cellophane wrapper. Cards measure about 2-5/8" x 3-5/8" and feature monochrome or color photos lithographed on steel. Borders and other design details are embossed. A black-and-white photo of Robinson is on back, along with a few sentences about his life and career.

		NM/M
Complete Boxed Set (5):		5.00
Common Card:		1.25
1	Jackie Robinson (Thigh-to-cap portrait.)	1.25
2	Jackie Robinson (Chest-to-cap portrait.)	1.25
3	Jackie Robinson/Btg (Color)	1.25
4	Jackie Robinson/Fldg	1.25
5	Jackie Robinson/Btg (B/w)	1.2

1996 Metal Universe Sample Sheet

To introduce its premiere edition of Metal Universe baseball cards, Fleer sent a nine-card sample sheet to dealers. The 8" x 11" sheet has a black border on each side of each card. The cards are identical in format to the issued version, printed on etched foil and overprinted "PROMOTIONAL SAMPLE" in gold diagonally on front and back.

	NM/M
Complete Sheet:	10.00

1996 Metal Universe

One of the most unusual baseball card issues of its era, Fleer's Metal Universe set is distinguished by its colored, textured metallic-foil backgrounds created by comic book illustrators. The effects range from gaudy to grotesque. Glossy player action photos are featured on front, with a steel-colored metallic strip at bottom carrying set and player ID. Conventionally printed backs have a heavy-metal theme with a color player portrait and a few stats and personal data around. The issue was sold in hobby and retail packaging with the basic eight-card pack at a suggested retail price of $2.49. Several insert sets were included, along with a platinum parallel edition of the player cards.

		NM/M
Complete Set (250):		17.50
Common Player:		.10
Platinum Set (250):		75.00
Common Platinum:		.25
Platinums:		5X
Pack (8):		1.50
Wax Box (24):		17.50
1	Roberto Alomar	.20
2	Brady Anderson	.10
3	Bobby Bonilla	.10
4	Chris Holles	.10
5	Ben McDonald	.10
6	Mike Mussina	.40
7	Randy Myers	.10
8	Rafael Palmeiro	.60
9	Cal Ripken Jr.	2.50
10	B.J. Surhoff	.10
11	Luis Alicea	.10
12	Jose Canseco	.50
13	Roger Clemens	1.25
14	Wil Cordero	.10
15	Tom Gordon	.10
16	Mike Greenwell	.10
17	Tim Naehring	.10
18	Troy O'Leary	.10
19	Mike Stanley	.10
20	John Valentin	.10
21	Mo Vaughn	.10
22	Tim Wakefield	.10
23	Garret Anderson	.10
24	Chili Davis	.10
25	Gary DiSarcina	.10
26	Jim Edmonds	.10
27	Chuck Finley	.10
28	Todd Greene	.10
29	Mark Langston	.10
30	Troy Percival	.10
31	Tony Phillips	.10
32	Tim Salmon	.10
33	Lee Smith	.10
34	J.T. Snow	.10
35	Ray Durham	.10
36	Alex Fernandez	.10
37	Ozzie Guillen	.10
38	Roberto Hernandez	.10
39	Lyle Mouton	.10
40	Frank Thomas	.75
41	Robin Ventura	.10
42	Sandy Alomar	.10
43	Carlos Baerga	.10
44	Albert Belle	.10
45	Orel Hershiser	.10
46	Kenny Lofton	.10
47	Dennis Martinez	.10
48	Jack McDowell	.10
49	Jose Mesa	.10
50	Eddie Murray	.75
51	Charles Nagy	.10
52	Manny Ramirez	.75
53	Julian Tavarez	.10
54	Jim Thome	.60
55	Omar Vizquel	.10
56	Chad Curtis	.10
57	Cecil Fielder	.10
58	John Flaherty	.10
59	Travis Fryman	.10
60	Chris Gomez	.10
61	Felipe Lira	.10
62	Kevin Appier	.10
63	Johnny Damon	.35
64	Tom Goodwin	.10
65	Mark Gubicza	.10
66	Jeff Montgomery	.10
67	Jon Nunnally	.10
68	Ricky Bones	.10
69	Jeff Cirillo	.10
70	John Jaha	.10
71	Dave Nilsson	.10
72	Joe Oliver	.10
73	Kevin Seitzer	.10
74	Greg Vaughn	.10
75	Marty Cordova	.10
76	Chuck Knoblauch	.10
77	Pat Meares	.10
78	Paul Molitor	.75
79	Pedro Munoz	.10

80	Kirby Puckett	1.00
81	Brad Radke	.10
82	Scott Stahoviak	.10
83	Matt Walbeck	.10
84	Wade Boggs	1.00
85	David Cone	.10
86	Joe Girardi	.10
87	Derek Jeter	2.50
88	Jim Leyritz	.10
89	Tino Martinez	.10
90	Don Mattingly	1.50
91	Paul O'Neill	.10
92	Andy Pettitte	.25
93	Tim Raines	.10
94	Kenny Rogers	.10
95	Ruben Sierra	.10
96	John Wetteland	.10
97	Bernie Williams	.10
98	Geronimo Berroa	.10
99	Dennis Eckersley	.65
100	Brent Gates	.10
101	Mark McGwire	2.00
102	Steve Ontiveros	.10
103	Terry Steinbach	.10
104	Jay Buhner	.10
105	Vince Coleman	.10
106	Joey Cora	.10
107	Ken Griffey Jr.	1.50
108	Randy Johnson	.75
109	Edgar Martinez	.10
110	Alex Rodriguez	2.00
111	Paul Sorrento	.10
112	Will Clark	.10
113	Juan Gonzalez	.50
114	Rusty Greer	.10
115	Dean Palmer	.10
116	Ivan Rodriguez	.65
117	Mickey Tettleton	.10
118	Joe Carter	.10
119	Alex Gonzalez	.10
120	Shawn Green	.30
121	Erik Hanson	.10
122	Pat Hentgen	.10
123	Sandy Martinez RC	.10
124	Otis Nixon	.10
125	John Olerud	.10
126	Steve Avery	.10
127	Tom Glavine	.40
128	Marquis Grissom	.10
129	Chipper Jones	1.00
130	David Justice	.10
131	Ryan Klesko	.10
132	Mark Lemke	.10
133	Javier Lopez	.10
134	Greg Maddux	1.00
135	Fred McGriff	.10
136	John Smoltz	.10
137	Mark Wohlers	.10
138	Frank Castillo	.10
139	Shawon Dunston	.10
140	Luis Gonzalez	.20
141	Mark Grace	.10
142	Brian McRae	.10
143	Jaime Navarro	.10
144	Rey Sanchez	.10
145	Ryne Sandberg	1.00
146	Sammy Sosa	1.25
147	Bret Boone	.10
148	Curtis Goodwin	.10
149	Barry Larkin	.10
150	Hal Morris	.10
151	Reggie Sanders	.10
152	Pete Schourek	.10
153	John Smiley	.10
154	Dante Bichette	.10
155	Vinny Castilla	.10
156	Andres Galarraga	.10
157	Bret Saberhagen	.10
158	Bill Swift	.10
159	Larry Walker	.10
160	Walt Weiss	.10
161	Kurt Abbott	.10
162	John Burkett	.10
163	Greg Colbrunn	.10
164	Jeff Conine	.10
165	Chris Hammond	.10
166	Charles Johnson	.10
167	Al Leiter	.10
168	Pat Rapp	.10
169	Gary Sheffield	.40
170	Quilvio Veras	.10
171	Devon White	.10
172	Jeff Bagwell	.75
173	Derek Bell	.10
174	Sean Berry	.10
175	Craig Biggio	.10
176	Doug Drabek	.10
177	Tony Eusebio	.10
178	Brian Hunter	.10
179	Orlando Miller	.10
180	Shane Reynolds	.10
181	Mike Blowers	.10
182	Roger Cedeno	.10
183	Eric Karros	.10
184	Ramon Martinez	.10
185	Raul Mondesi	.10
186	Hideo Nomo	.60
187	Mike Piazza	1.50
188	Moises Alou	.10
189	Yamil Benitez	.10
190	Darrin Fletcher	.10
191	Cliff Floyd	.10
192	Pedro Martinez	.75
193	Carlos Perez	.10
194	David Segui	.10
195	Tony Tarasco	.10
196	Rondell White	.10
197	Edgardo Alfonzo	.10

198	Rico Brogna	.10
199	Carl Everett	.10
200	Todd Hundley	.10
201	Jason Isringhausen	.10
202	Lance Johnson	.10
203	Bobby Jones	.10
204	Jeff Kent	.10
205	Bill Pulsipher	.10
206	Jose Vizcaino	.10
207	Ricky Bottalico	.10
208	Darren Daulton	.10
209	Lenny Dykstra	.10
210	Jim Eisenreich	.10
211	Gregg Jefferies	.10
212	Mickey Morandini	.10
213	Heathcliff Slocumb	.10
214	Jay Bell	.10
215	Carlos Garcia	.10
216	Jeff King	.10
217	Al Martin	.10
218	Orlando Merced	.10
219	Dan Miceli	.10
220	Denny Neagle	.10
221	Andy Benes	.10
222	Royce Clayton	.10
223	Gary Gaetti	.10
224	Ron Gant	.10
225	Bernard Gilkey	.10
226	Brian Jordan	.10
227	Ray Lankford	.10
228	John Mabry	.10
229	Ozzie Smith	1.00
230	Todd Stottlemyre	.10
231	Andy Ashby	.10
232	Brad Ausmus	.10
233	Ken Caminiti	.10
234	Steve Finley	.10
235	Tony Gwynn	1.00
236	Joey Hamilton	.10
237	Rickey Henderson	.75
238	Trevor Hoffman	.10
239	Wally Joyner	.10
240	Rod Beck	.10
241	Barry Bonds	2.50
242	Glenallen Hill	.10
243	Stan Javier	.10
244	Mark Leiter	.10
245	Deion Sanders	.10
246	William VanLandingham	.10
247	Matt Williams	.10
248	Checklist	.10
249	Checklist	.10
250	Checklist	.10

Platinum Edition

One of the eight cards in each pack of Fleer Metal baseball is a Platinum Edition parallel insert. Each of the 247 player cards (no checklists) in this special version has the textured foil background rendered only in silver. The second line of the logo/ID strip at bottom also identifies the card as part of the Platinum Edition.

		NM/M
Complete Set (247):		75.00
Common Player:		.25
Stars:		5X

Heavy Metal

Some of the game's biggest hitters are included in this insert set. Action photos of players at bat are set on a silver-foil background on front. Backs have a close-up photo

down one side, with praise for the player's power potential down the other. The Heavy Metal inserts can be expected to turn up at an average rate of one per eight packs.

		NM/M
Complete Set (10):		5.00
Common Player:		.35
1	Albert Belle	.35
2	Barry Bonds	1.50
3	Juan Gonzalez	.50
4	Ken Griffey Jr.	1.00
5	Mark McGwire	1.25
6	Mike Piazza	1.00
7	Sammy Sosa	.90
8	Frank Thomas	.60
9	Mo Vaughn	.35
10	Matt Williams	.35

Mining for Gold

Available only in retail packs, at an average rate of one per dozen packs, the Mining for Gold insert series focuses on 1995's top rookies. Fronts have player action photos frame and backgrounded with several different gold tones in etched metal foil. Backs are conventionally printed, carrying on the same format with a portrait photo and a few words about the player.

		NM/M
Complete Set (12):		12.50
Common Player:		.75
1	Yamil Benitez	.75
2	Marty Cordova	.75
3	Shawn Green	2.00
4	Todd Greene	.75
5	Brian Hunter	.75
6	Derek Jeter	7.50
7	Charles Johnson	.75
8	Chipper Jones	3.50
9	Hideo Nomo	2.50
10	Alex Ochoa	.75
11	Andy Pettitte	1.00
12	Quilvio Veras	.75

Mother Lode

Medieval designs rendered in textured silver-foil on a plain white background are the setting for the color player photos in this hobby-only insert. Backs also have a silver and white background along with another player photo and some kind words about his skills. The cards are found at an average rate of one per 12 packs.

		NM/M
Complete Set (12):		15.00
Common Player:		.75
1	Barry Bonds	4.50
2	Jim Edmonds	.75
3	Ken Griffey Jr.	3.50
4	Kenny Lofton	.75
5	Raul Mondesi	.75
6	Rafael Palmeiro	1.50
7	Manny Ramirez	2.00
8	Cal Ripken Jr.	4.50
9	Tim Salmon	.75
10	Ryne Sandberg	3.00
11	Frank Thomas	2.00
12	Matt Williams	.75

Platinum Portraits

Close-up color photos on a plain metallic-foil background are featured in this insert set. The checklist is heavy in rookie and sophomore players, who are featured in an action photo on back, with a few career details. Platinum Portraits inserts are found in every fourth pack, on average.

		NM/M
Complete Set (10):		4.00
Common Player:		.40
1	Garret Anderson	.40
2	Marty Cordova	.40
3	Jim Edmonds	.40
4	Jason Isringhausen	.40
5	Chipper Jones	2.25
6	Ryan Klesko	.40
7	Hideo Nomo	1.00
8	Carlos Perez	.40
9	Manny Ramirez	1.50
10	Rondell White	.40

1996 Metal Universe Titanium

A huge purple-highlighted silver baseball in a star-studded night sky is the background for the action photos of the game's biggest names in this insert series. Backs have a second, more up-close, photo and a few words about the player. Titanium inserts are found in Metal Universe packs at an average rate of one per 24 packs.

		NM/M
Complete Set (10):		15.00
Common Player:		.50
1	Albert Belle	.50
2	Barry Bonds	4.00
3	Ken Griffey Jr.	2.50
4	Tony Gwynn	1.50
5	Greg Maddux	1.50
6	Mike Piazza	2.50
7	Cal Ripken Jr.	4.00
8	Frank Thomas	1.00
9	Mo Vaughn	.50
10	Matt Williams	.50

1997 Metal Universe

Metal Universe Baseball arrived in a 250-card set, including three checklists. Each card is printed on 100-percent etched foil with "comic book" art full-bleed backgrounds, with the player's name, team, position and the Metal Universe logo near the bottom of the card. Backs contain another player photo and key statistics. Metal Universe sold in eight-card packs and contained six differ-

ent insert sets. They included: Blast Furnace, Magnetic Field, Mining for Gold, Mother Lode, Platinum Portraits and Titanium.

		NM/M
Complete Set (250):		17.50
Common Player:		.10
Pack (8):		1.50
Wax Box (24):		18.00
1	Roberto Alomar	.20
2	Brady Anderson	.10
3	Rocky Coppinger	.10
4	Chris Hoiles	.10
5	Eddie Murray	.60
6	Mike Mussina	.40
7	Rafael Palmeiro	.50
8	Cal Ripken Jr.	2.00
9	B.J. Surhoff	.10
10	Brant Brown	.10
11	Mark Grace	.10
12	Brian McRae	.10
13	Jaime Navarro	.10
14	Ryne Sandberg	.75
15	Sammy Sosa	1.00
16	Amaury Telemaco	.10
17	Steve Trachsel	.10
18	Darren Bragg	.10
19	Jose Canseco	.40
20	Roger Clemens	1.00
21	Nomar Garciaparra	1.00
22	Tom Gordon	.10
23	Tim Naehring	.10
24	Mike Stanley	.10
25	John Valentin	.10
26	Mo Vaughn	.10
27	Jermaine Dye	.10
28	Tom Glavine	.30
29	Marquis Grissom	.10
30	Andruw Jones	.60
31	Chipper Jones	.75
32	Ryan Klesko	.10
33	Greg Maddux	.75
34	Fred McGriff	.10
35	John Smoltz	.10
36	Garret Anderson	.10
37	George Arias	.10
38	Gary DiSarcina	.10
39	Jim Edmonds	.10
40	Darin Erstad	.25
41	Chuck Finley	.10
42	Troy Percival	.10
43	Tim Salmon	.10
44	Bret Boone	.10
45	Jeff Brantley	.10
46	Eric Davis	.10
47	Barry Larkin	.10
48	Hal Morris	.10
49	Mark Portugal	.10
50	Reggie Sanders	.10
51	John Smiley	.10
52	Wilson Alvarez	.10
53	Harold Baines	.10
54	James Baldwin	.10
55	Albert Belle	.10
56	Mike Cameron	.10
57	Ray Durham	.10
58	Alex Fernandez	.10
59	Roberto Hernandez	.10
60	Tony Phillips	.10
61	Frank Thomas	.60
62	Robin Ventura	.10
63	Jeff Cirillo	.10
64	Jeff D'Amico	.10
65	John Jaha	.10
66	Scott Karl	.10
67	Ben McDonald	.10
68	Marc Newfield	.10
69	Dave Nilsson	.10
70	Jose Valentin	.10
71	Dante Bichette	.10
72	Ellis Burks	.10
73	Vinny Castilla	.10
74	Andres Galarraga	.10
75	Kevin Ritz	.10
76	Larry Walker	.10
77	Walt Weiss	.10
78	Jamey Wright	.10
79	Eric Young	.10
80	Julio Franco	.10
81	Orel Hershiser	.10
82	Kenny Lofton	.10
83	Jack McDowell	.10
84	Jose Mesa	.10
85	Charles Nagy	.10
86	Manny Ramirez	.60
87	Jim Thome	.50
88	Omar Vizquel	.10
89	Matt Williams	.10
90	Kevin Appier	.10
91	Johnny Damon	.35
92	Chili Davis	.10
93	Tom Goodwin	.10
94	Keith Lockhart	.10
95	Jeff Montgomery	.10
96	Craig Paquette	.10
97	Jose Rosado	.10
98	Michael Tucker	.10
99	Wilton Guerrero	.10
100	Todd Hollandsworth	.10
101	Eric Karros	.10
102	Ramon Martinez	.10
103	Raul Mondesi	.10
104	Hideo Nomo	.60
105	Mike Piazza	1.25
106	Ismael Valdes	.10
107	Todd Worrell	.10

108	Tony Clark	.10
109	Travis Fryman	.10
110	Bob Higginson	.10
111	Mark Lewis	.10
112	Melvin Nieves	.10
113	Justin Thompson	.10
114	Wade Boggs	.75
115	David Cone	.10
116	Cecil Fielder	.10
117	Dwight Gooden	.10
118	Derek Jeter	2.00
119	Tino Martinez	.10
120	Paul O'Neill	.10
121	Andy Pettitte	.20
122	Mariano Rivera	.20
123	Darryl Strawberry	.10
124	John Wetteland	.10
125	Bernie Williams	.10
126	Tony Batista	.10
127	Geronimo Berroa	.10
128	Scott Brosius	.10
129	Jason Giambi	.50
130	Jose Herrera	.10
131	Mark McGwire	1.50
132	John Wasdin	.10
133	Bob Abreu	.10
134	Jeff Bagwell	.60
135	Derek Bell	.10
136	Craig Biggio	.10
137	Brian Hunter	.10
138	Darryl Kile	.10
139	Orlando Miller	.10
140	Shane Reynolds	.10
141	Billy Wagner	.10
142	Donne Wall	.10
143	Jay Buhner	.10
144	Jeff Fassero	.10
145	Ken Griffey Jr.	1.25
146	Sterling Hitchcock	.10
147	Randy Johnson	.60
148	Edgar Martinez	.10
149	Alex Rodriguez	1.50
149p	Alex Rodriguez/OPS	1.50
150	Paul Sorrento	.10
151	Dan Wilson	.10
152	Moises Alou	.10
153	Darrin Fletcher	.10
154	Cliff Floyd	.10
155	Mark Grudzielanek	.10
156	Vladimir Guerrero	.60
157	Mike Lansing	.10
158	Pedro Martinez	.60
159	Henry Rodriguez	.10
160	Rondell White	.10
161	Will Clark	.10
162	Juan Gonzalez	.50
163	Rusty Greer	.10
164	Ken Hill	.10
165	Mark McLemore	.10
166	Dean Palmer	.10
167	Roger Pavlik	.10
168	Ivan Rodriguez	.50
169	Mickey Tettleton	.10
170	Bobby Bonilla	.10
171	Kevin Brown	.10
172	Greg Colbrunn	.10
173	Jeff Conine	.10
174	Jim Eisenreich	.10
175	Charles Johnson	.10
176	Al Leiter	.10
177	Robb Nen	.10
178	Edgar Renteria	.10
179	Gary Sheffield	.40
180	Devon White	.10
181	Joe Carter	.10
182	Carlos Delgado	.40
183	Alex Gonzalez	.10
184	Shawn Green	.35
185	Juan Guzman	.10
186	Pat Hentgen	.10
187	Orlando Merced	.10
188	John Olerud	.10
189	Robert Perez	.10
190	Ed Sprague	.10
191	Mark Clark	.10
192	John Franco	.10
193	Bernard Gilkey	.10
194	Todd Hundley	.10
195	Lance Johnson	.10
196	Bobby Jones	.10
197	Alex Ochoa	.10
198	Rey Ordonez	.10
199	Paul Wilson	.10
200	Ricky Bottalico	.10
201	Gregg Jefferies	.10
202	Wendell Magee Jr.	.10
203	Mickey Morandini	.10
204	Ricky Otero	.10
205	Scott Rolen	.50
206	Benito Santiago	.10
207	Curt Schilling	.25
208	Rich Becker	.10
209	Marty Cordova	.10
210	Chuck Knoblauch	.10
211	Pat Meares	.10
212	Paul Molitor	.60
213	Frank Rodriguez	.10
214	Terry Steinbach	.10
215	Todd Walker	.10
216	Andy Ashby	.10
217	Ken Caminiti	.10
218	Steve Finley	.10
219	Tony Gwynn	.75
220	Joey Hamilton	.10
221	Rickey Henderson	.60
222	Trevor Hoffman	.10
223	Wally Joyner	.10
224	Scott Sanders	.10

225	Fernando Valenzuela	.10
226	Greg Vaughn	.10
227	Alan Benes	.10
228	Andy Benes	.10
229	Dennis Eckersley	.50
230	Ron Gant	.10
231	Brian Jordan	.10
232	Ray Lankford	.10
233	John Mabry	.10
234	Tom Pagnozzi	.10
235	Todd Stottlemyre	.10
236	Jermaine Allensworth	.10
237	Francisco Cordova	.10
238	Jason Kendall	.10
239	Jeff King	.10
240	Al Martin	.10
241	Rod Beck	.10
242	Barry Bonds	2.00
243	Shawn Estes	.10
244	Mark Gardner	.10
245	Glenallen Hill	.10
246	Bill Mueller	.10
247	J.T. Snow	.10
248	Checklist	.10
249	Checklist	.10
250	Checklist	.10

Blast Furnace

Blast Furnace inserts were found only in hobby packs, at a rate of one per 48 packs. The 12-card set was printed on a red-tinted plastic, with the words "Blast Furnace" near the bottom in gold foil with a fire-like border.

		NM/M
Complete Set (12):		40.00
Common Player:		1.50
1	Jeff Bagwell	4.00
2	Albert Belle	1.50
3	Barry Bonds	7.50
4	Andres Galarraga	1.50
5	Juan Gonzalez	2.50
6	Ken Griffey Jr.	5.00
7	Todd Hundley	1.50
8	Mark McGwire	6.00
9	Mike Piazza	5.00
10	Alex Rodriguez	6.00
11	Frank Thomas	4.00
12	Mo Vaughn	1.50

Emerald Autograph Redemption

Six different young stars were featured in this insert, which was found every 480 hobby packs of Metal Universe. The cards are similar to regular-issue cards, but have green foil highlights. Redemption cards are numbered AU1-AU6. The redemption period expired Jan. 15, 1998.

		NM/M
Complete Set (6):		10.00
Common Player:		1.00
1	Darin Erstad	1.50
2	Todd Hollandsworth	1.00
3	Alex Ochoa	1.00
4	Alex Rodriguez	7.50
5	Scott Rolen	1.50
6	Todd Walker	1.00

Emerald Autographs

Six different young stars were featured in this insert, which was found every 480 hobby packs of Metal Universe. The cards are similar to regular-issue cards, but have a green foil finish and autograph on the front. Redemption cards are numbered AU1-AU6, the autographed cards have a notation on back, "Certified Emerald Autograph Card."

		NM/M
Complete Set (6):		75.00
Common Autograph:		4.00
1	Darin Erstad	6.00
2	Todd Hollandsworth	4.00
3	Alex Ochoa	4.00
4	Alex Rodriguez	60.00
5	Scott Rolen	10.00
6	Todd Walker	4.00

Magnetic Field

Magnetic Field inserts are printed in a horizontal format with prismatic foil backgrounds. This 10-card insert was found every 12 packs of Metal Universe.

		NM/M
Complete Set (10):		15.00
Common Player:		.75
1	Roberto Alomar	.75
2	Jeff Bagwell	1.25
3	Barry Bonds	3.00
4	Ken Griffey Jr.	2.00
5	Derek Jeter	3.00
6	Kenny Lofton	.75
7	Edgar Renteria	.75
8	Cal Ripken Jr.	3.00
9	Alex Rodriguez	2.50
10	Matt Williams	.75

Mining for Gold

Mining for Gold was a 10-card insert that featured some of baseball's brightest stars on a die-cut "ingot" design with pearlized gold coating. This insert was found every nine packs.

		NM/M
Complete Set (10):		12.00
Common Player:		.75
1	Bob Abreu	.75
2	Kevin Brown	.75
3	Nomar Garciaparra	3.50
4	Vladimir Guerrero	3.00
5	Wilton Guerrero	.75
6	Andruw Jones	3.00
7	Curt Lyons	.75
8	Neifi Perez	.75
9	Scott Rolen	2.00
10	Todd Walker	.75

Mother Lode

Mother lode was the most difficult insert out of Metal Universe with a one per 288 pack insertion ratio. Each card in this 10-card inert was printed on etched foil with a plant-type monument in back of the player.

		NM/M
Complete Set (12):		80.00
Common Player:		2.00
1	Roberto Alomar	2.50
2	Jeff Bagwell	6.00
3	Barry Bonds	15.00
4	Ken Griffey Jr.	10.00
5	Andruw Jones	6.00
6	Chipper Jones	8.00
7	Kenny Lofton	2.00
8	Mike Piazza	10.00
9	Cal Ripken Jr.	15.00
10	Alex Rodriguez	12.50
11	Frank Thomas	6.00
12	Matt Williams	2.00

Platinum Portraits

Each card in the Platinum Portraits insert is printed on a background of platinum-colored etched foil. The 10-card set includes some of the top prospects and rising stars in baseball, and is included every 36 packs.

		NM/M
Complete Set (10):		10.00
Common Player:		.60
1	James Baldwin	.60
2	Jermaine Dye	.60
3	Todd Hollandsworth	.60
4	Derek Jeter	5.00
5	Chipper Jones	2.00
6	Jason Kendall	.60
7	Rey Ordonez	.60
8	Andy Pettitte	1.00
9	Edgar Renteria	.60
10	Alex Rodriguez	3.25

Titanium

These retail exclusive inserts include 10 cards and were found every 24 packs. Each card is die-cut on the top-left and bottom-right corner with a silver foil background. Titanium includes some of the most popular players in baseball on cards that are also embossed.

		NM/M
Complete Set (10):		24.00
Common Player:		1.50
1	Jeff Bagwell	2.00
2	Albert Belle	1.50
3	Ken Griffey Jr.	3.00
4	Chipper Jones	2.50
5	Greg Maddux	2.50
6	Mark McGwire	4.00
7	Mike Piazza	3.00
8	Cal Ripken Jr.	5.00
9	Alex Rodriguez	4.00
10	Frank Thomas	2.00

1998 Metal Universe

This 220-card single series release captured players over a foil etched, art background that related in some way to them or the city they played in. Metal Universe included a 15-card Hardball Galaxy subset and dealers and media were given an Alex Rodriguez promo card that was identical the base card except for the words "Promotional Sample" written across the back. The set arrived with a parallel called Precious Metal Gems, and included the following insert sets: All-Galactic Team, Diamond Heroes, Platinum Portraits, Titanium and Universal Language.

		NM/M
Complete Set (220):		15.00
Common Player:		.10
Pack (8):		1.50
Wax Box (24):		20.00
1	Jose Cruz Jr.	.10
2	Jeff Abbott	.10
3	Rafael Palmeiro	.65
4	Ivan Rodriguez	.65
5	Jaret Wright	.10
6	Derek Bell	.10
7	Chuck Finley	.10
8	Travis Fryman	.10
9	Randy Johnson	.75
10	Derrek Lee	.50
11	Bernie Williams	.10
12	Carlos Baerga	.10
13	Ricky Bottalico	.10
14	Ellis Burks	.10
15	Russ Davis	.10
16	Nomar Garciaparra	1.00
17	Joey Hamilton	.10
18	Jason Kendall	.10
19	Darryl Kile	.10
20	Edgardo Alfonzo	.10
21	Moises Alou	.10
22	Bobby Bonilla	.10
23	Jim Edmonds	.10
24	Jose Guillen	.10
25	Chuck Knoblauch	.10
26	Javy Lopez	.10
27	Billy Wagner	.10
28	Kevin Appier	.10
29	Joe Carter	.10
30	Todd Dunwoody	.10
31	Gary Gaetti	.10
32	Juan Gonzalez	.60
33	Jeffrey Hammonds	.10
34	Roberto Hernandez	.10
35	Dave Nilsson	.10
36	Manny Ramirez	.75
37	Robin Ventura	.10
38	Rondell White	.10
39	Vinny Castilla	.10
40	Will Clark	.10
41	Scott Hatteberg	.10
42	Russ Johnson	.10
43	Ricky Ledee	.10
44	Kenny Lofton	.10
45	Paul Molitor	.75
46	Justin Thompson	.10
47	Craig Biggio	.10
48	Damion Easley	.10
49	Brad Radke	.10
50	Ben Grieve	.10
51	Mark Bellhorn	.10
52	Henry Blanco RC	.10
53	Mariano Rivera	.20
54	Reggie Sanders	.10
55	Paul Sorrento	.10
56	Terry Steinbach	.10
57	Mo Vaughn	.10
58	Brady Anderson	.10
59	Tom Glavine	.40

60	Sammy Sosa	1.25
61	Larry Walker	.10
62	Rod Beck	.10
63	Jose Canseco	.45
64	Steve Finley	.10
65	Pedro Martinez	.75
66	John Olerud	.10
67	Scott Rolen	.60
68	Ismael Valdes	.10
69	Andrew Vessel	.10
70	Mark Grudzielanek	.10
71	Eric Karros	.10
72	Jeff Shaw	.10
73	Lou Collier	.10
74	Edgar Martinez	.10
75	Vladimir Guerrero	.75
76	Paul Konerko	.25
77	Kevin Orie	.10
78	Kevin Polcovich	.10
79	Brett Tomko	.10
80	Jeff Bagwell	.75
81	Barry Bonds	2.50
82	David Justice	.10
83	Hideo Nomo	.60
84	Ryne Sandberg	1.00
85	Shannon Stewart	.10
86	Derek Wallace	.10
87	Tony Womack	.10
88	Jason Giambi	.50
89	Mark Grace	.10
90	Pat Hentgen	.10
91	Raul Mondesi	.10
92	Matt Morris	.10
93	Matt Perisho	.10
94	Tim Salmon	.10
95	Jeremi Gonzalez	.10
96	Shawn Green	.25
97	Todd Greene	.10
98	Ruben Rivera	.10
99	Deion Sanders	.10
100	Alex Rodriguez	2.00
101	Will Cunnane	.10
102	Ray Lankford	.10
103	Ryan McGuire	.10
104	Charles Nagy	.10
105	Rey Ordonez	.10
106	Mike Piazza	1.50
107	Tony Saunders	.10
108	Curt Schilling	.25
109	Fernando Tatis	.10
110	Mark McGwire	2.00
111	David Dellucci RC	.10
112	Garret Anderson	.10
113	Shane Bowers	.10
114	David Cone	.10
115	Jeff King	.10
116	Matt Williams	.10
117	Aaron Boone	.10
118	Dennis Eckersley	.65
119	Livan Hernandez	.10
120	Richard Hidalgo	.10
121	Bobby Higginson	.10
122	Tino Martinez	.10
123	Tim Naehring	.10
124	Jose Vidro	.10
125	John Wetteland	.10
126	Jay Bell	.10
127	Albert Belle	.10
128	Marty Cordova	.10
129	Chili Davis	.10
130	Jason Dickson	.10
131	Rusty Greer	.10
132	Hideki Irabu	.10
133	Greg Maddux	1.00
134	Billy Taylor	.10
135	Jim Thome	.60
136	Gerald Williams	.10
137	Jeff Cirillo	.10
138	Delino DeShields	.10
139	Andres Galarraga	.10
140	Willie Greene	.10
141	John Jaha	.10
142	Charles Johnson	.10
143	Ryan Klesko	.10
144	Paul O'Neill	.10
145	Robinson Checo	.10
146	Roberto Alomar	.20
147	Wilson Alvarez	.10
148	Bobby Jones	.10
149	Raul Casanova	.10
150	Andruw Jones	.75
151	Mike Lansing	.10
152	Mickey Morandini	.10
153	Neifi Perez	.10
154	Pokey Reese	.10
155	Edgar Renteria	.10
156	Eric Young	.10
157	Darin Erstad	.20
158	Kelvim Escobar	.10
159	Carl Everett	.10
160	Tom Gordon	.10
161	Ken Griffey Jr.	1.50
162	Al Martin	.10
163	Bubba Trammell	.10
164	Carlos Delgado	.30
165	Kevin Brown	.10
166	Ken Caminiti	.10
167	Roger Clemens	1.25
168	Ron Gant	.10
169	Jeff Kent	.10
170	Mike Mussina	.40
171	Dean Palmer	.10
172	Henry Rodriguez	.10
173	Matt Stairs	.10
174	Jay Buhner	.10
175	Frank Thomas	.75
176	Mike Cameron	.10
177	Johnny Damon	.35

178	Tony Gwynn	1.00
179	John Smoltz	.10
180	B.J. Surhoff	.10
181	Antone Williamson	.10
182	Alan Benes	.10
183	Jeromy Burnitz	.10
184	Tony Clark	.10
185	Shawn Estes	.10
186	Todd Helton	.65
187	Todd Hundley	.10
188	Chipper Jones	1.00
189	Mark Kotsay	.10
190	Barry Larkin	.10
191	Mike Lieberthal	.10
192	Andy Pettitte	.25
193	Gary Sheffield	.35
194	Jeff Suppan	.10
195	Mark Wohlers	.10
196	Dante Bichette	.10
197	Trevor Hoffman	.10
198	J.T. Snow	.10
199	Derek Jeter	2.50
200	Cal Ripken Jr.	2.50
201	Steve Woodard RC	.25
202	Ray Durham	.10
203	Barry Bonds (Hardball Galaxy)	1.50
204	Tony Clark (Hardball Galaxy)	.10
205	Roger Clemens (Hardball Galaxy)	.65
206	Ken Griffey Jr. (Hardball Galaxy)	.75
207	Tony Gwynn (Hardball Galaxy)	.50
208	Derek Jeter (Hardball Galaxy)	1.50
209	Randy Johnson (Hardball Galaxy)	.40
210	Mark McGwire (Hardball Galaxy)	1.00
211	Hideo Nomo (Hardball Galaxy)	.30
212	Mike Piazza (Hardball Galaxy)	.75
213	Cal Ripken Jr. (Hardball Galaxy)	1.50
214	Alex Rodriguez (Hardball Galaxy)	1.00
215	Frank Thomas (Hardball Galaxy)	.40
216	Mo Vaughn (Hardball Galaxy)	.10
217	Larry Walker (Hardball Galaxy)	.10
218	Checklist (Ken Griffey Jr.)	.50
219	Checklist (Alex Rodriguez)	.60
220	Checklist (Frank Thomas)	.30

Precious Metal Gems

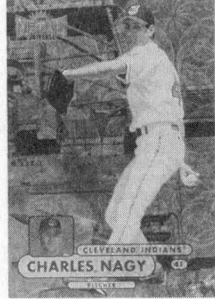

Precious Metal Gems includes 217 (no checklists) player cards from Metal Universe and are serial numbered to 50 sets. Because there were five Ultimate Metal Gems redemption cards (good for a complete set of Metal Gems) available, only serial numbers 1-45 were found in packs (46-50 were held back for the exchange program).

	NM/M
Common Player:	3.00
Stars:	25X
Production 50 Sets	

All-Galactic Team

This 18-card insert captures players over a planet holofoil background. Cards were inserted one per 192 packs.

		NM/M
Complete Set (18):		140.00
Common Player:		3.00
Inserted 1:192		
1	Ken Griffey Jr.	12.50
2	Frank Thomas	7.50
3	Chipper Jones	10.00
4	Albert Belle	3.00
5	Juan Gonzalez	5.00
6	Jeff Bagwell	7.50
7	Andruw Jones	7.50

8	Cal Ripken Jr.	20.00
9	Derek Jeter	20.00
10	Nomar Garciaparra	10.00
11	Darin Erstad	4.00
12	Greg Maddux	10.00
13	Alex Rodriguez	15.00
14	Mike Piazza	12.50
15	Vladimir Guerrero	15.00
16	Jose Cruz Jr.	3.00
17	Mark McGwire	15.00
18	Scott Rolen	5.00

Diamond Heroes

Diamond Heroes displayed six players in a comic book setting. This insert was seeded one per 18 packs and contained a foil etched image of a Marvel comic in the background.

		NM/M
Complete Set (6):		8.00
Common Player:		.50
Inserted 1:18		
1	Ken Griffey Jr.	2.00
2	Frank Thomas	1.50
3	Andruw Jones	1.50
4	Alex Rodriguez	2.50
5	Jose Cruz Jr.	.50
6	Cal Ripken Jr.	3.00

Platinum Portraits

This 12-card insert set featured color portraits of top players highlighted with a platinum-colored etched foil frame over it. Platinum Portraits are seeded one per 360 packs of Metal Universe.

		NM/M
Complete Set (12):		90.00
Common Player:		4.00
Inserted 1:360		
1	Ken Griffey Jr.	12.00
2	Frank Thomas	7.50
3	Chipper Jones	10.00
4	Jose Cruz Jr.	4.00
5	Andruw Jones	7.50
6	Cal Ripken Jr.	17.50
7	Derek Jeter	17.50
8	Darin Erstad	4.00
9	Greg Maddux	9.00
10	Alex Rodriguez	15.00
11	Mike Piazza	12.00
12	Vladimir Guerrero	7.50

Titanium

This die-cut 15-card insert contained color photos printed on embossed, sculpted cards on etched foil. Titanium inserts were seeded one per 96 packs.

	NM/M
Complete Set (15):	50.00
Common Player:	2.00
Inserted 1:96	

1	Ken Griffey Jr.	5.00
2	Frank Thomas	3.00
3	Chipper Jones	4.00
4	Jose Cruz Jr.	2.00
5	Juan Gonzalez	2.50
6	Scott Rolen	2.50
7	Andruw Jones	3.00
8	Cal Ripken Jr.	7.50
9	Derek Jeter	7.50
10	Nomar Garciaparra	4.00
11	Darin Erstad	2.50
12	Greg Maddux	4.00
13	Alex Rodriguez	6.00
14	Mike Piazza	5.00
15	Vladimir Guerrero	3.00

Universal Language

This 20-card insert features illustration and copy done in the player's native language. Cards were die-cut and inserted one per six packs.

		NM/M
Complete Set (20):		16.00
Common Player:		.40
Inserted 1:6		
1	Ken Griffey Jr.	1.25
2	Frank Thomas	.75
3	Chipper Jones	1.00
4	Albert Belle	.40
5	Juan Gonzalez	.60
6	Jeff Bagwell	.75
7	Andruw Jones	.75
8	Cal Ripken Jr.	2.00
9	Derek Jeter	2.00
10	Nomar Garciaparra	1.00
11	Darin Erstad	.50
12	Greg Maddux	1.00
13	Alex Rodriguez	1.50
14	Mike Piazza	1.25
15	Vladimir Guerrero	.75
16	Jose Cruz Jr.	.40
17	Hideo Nomo	.60
18	Kenny Lofton	.40
19	Tony Gwynn	1.00
20	Scott Rolen	.60

	NM/M
Complete Sheet:	7.50
Complete Autographed Sheet:	60.00

1999 Metal Universe

The 300-card base set offers 232 player cards and three subsets: Building Blocks, M.L.P.D. and Caught on the Fly. Base cards feature an action photo framed in an etched-foil and metallic, embossed name plate. Packs consist of eight cards with an S.R.P. of $2.69. There are two parallels, Precious Metal Gems and Gem Masters. Metal Gems are numbered to 50 with gold-foil etching. Gem Masters are limited to only one set, with silver foil etching and serial numbered "one of one."

	NM/M
Complete Set (300):	15.00
Common Player:	.10
Pack (8):	1.00
Wax Box (24):	20.00
1	Mark McGwire	1.50
2	Jim Edmonds	.10
3	Travis Fryman	.10
4	Tom Gordon	.10
5	Jeff Bagwell	.65
6	Rico Brogna	.10
7	Tom Evans	.10
8	John Franco	.10
9	Juan Gonzalez	.50
10	Paul Molitor	.65
11	Roberto Alomar	.20
12	Mike Hampton	.10
13	Orel Hershiser	.10
14	Todd Stottlemyre	.10
15	Robin Ventura	.10
16	Todd Walker	.10
17	Bernie Williams	.10
18	Shawn Estes	.10
19	Richie Sexson	.10
20	Kevin Millwood	.10
21	David Ortiz	.50
22	Mariano Rivera	.15
23	Ivan Rodriguez	.60
24	Mike Sirotka	.10
25	David Justice	.10
26	Carl Pavano	.10
27	Albert Belle	.10
28	Will Clark	.10
29	Jose Cruz Jr.	.10
30	Trevor Hoffman	.10
31	Dean Palmer	.10
32	Edgar Renteria	.10
33	David Segui	.10
34	B.J. Surhoff	.10
35	Miguel Tejada	.15
36	Bob Wickman	.10
37	Charles Johnson	.10
38	Andruw Jones	.65
39	Mike Lieberthal	.10
40	Eli Marrero	.10
41	Neifi Perez	.10
42	Jim Thome	.50

43	Barry Bonds	2.00
44	Carlos Delgado	.30
45	Chuck Finley	.10
46	Brian Meadows	.10
47	Tony Gwynn	.75
48	Jose Offerman	.10
49	Cal Ripken Jr.	2.00
50	Alex Rodriguez	1.50
51	Esteban Yan	.10
52	Matt Stairs	.10
53	Fernando Vina	.10
54	Rondell White	.10
55	Kerry Wood	.30
56	Dmitri Young	.10
57	Ken Caminiti	.10
58	Alex Gonzalez	.10
59	Matt Mantei	.10
60	Tino Martinez	.10
61	Hal Morris	.10
62	Rafael Palmeiro	.60
63	Troy Percival	.10
64	Bobby Smith	.10
65	Ed Sprague	.10
66	Brett Tomko	.10
67	Steve Trachsel	.10
68	Ugueth Urbina	.10
69	Jose Valentin	.10
70	Kevin Brown	.10
71	Shawn Green	.30
72	Dustin Hermanson	.10
73	Livan Hernandez	.10
74	Geoff Jenkins	.10
75	Jeff King	.10
76	Chuck Knoblauch	.10
77	Edgar Martinez	.10
78	Fred McGriff	.10
79	Mike Mussina	.40
80	Dave Nilsson	.10
81	Kenny Rogers	.10
82	Tim Salmon	.10
83	Reggie Sanders	.10
84	Wilson Alvarez	.10
85	Rod Beck	.10
86	Jose Guillen	.10
87	Bob Higginson	.10
88	Gregg Olson	.10
89	Jeff Shaw	.10
90	Masato Yoshii	.10
91	Todd Helton	.50
92	David Dellucci	.10
93	Johnny Damon	.35
94	Cliff Floyd	.10
95	Ken Griffey Jr.	1.00
96	Juan Guzman	.10
97	Derek Jeter	2.00
98	Barry Larkin	.10
99	Quinton McCracken	.10
100	Sammy Sosa	.85
101	Kevin Young	.10
102	Jay Bell	.10
103	Jay Buhner	.10
104	Jeff Conine	.10
105	Ryan Jackson	.10
106	Sidney Ponson	.10
107	Jeromy Burnitz	.10
108	Roberto Hernandez	.10
109	A.J. Hinch	.10
110	Hideki Irabu	.10
111	Paul Konerko	.20
112	Henry Rodriguez	.10
113	Shannon Stewart	.10
114	Tony Womack	.10
115	Wilton Guerrero	.10
116	Andy Benes	.10
117	Jeff Cirillo	.10
118	Chili Davis	.10
119	Eric Davis	.10
120	Vladimir Guerrero	.65
121	Dennis Reyes	.10
122	Rickey Henderson	.65
123	Mickey Morandini	.10
124	Jason Schmidt	.10
125	J.T. Snow	.10
126	Justin Thompson	.10
127	Billy Wagner	.10
128	Armando Benitez	.10
129	Sean Casey	.15
130	Brad Fullmer	.10
131	Ben Grieve	.10
132	Robb Nen	.10
133	Shane Reynolds	.10
134	Todd Zeile	.10
135	Brady Anderson	.10
136	Aaron Boone	.10
137	Orlando Cabrera	.10
138	Jason Giambi	.50
139	Randy Johnson	.65
140	Jeff Kent	.10
141	John Wetteland	.10
142	Rolando Arrojo	.10
143	Scott Brosius	.10
144	Mark Grace	.10
145	Jason Kendall	.10
146	Travis Lee	.10
147	Gary Sheffield	.40
148	David Cone	.10
149	Jose Hernandez	.10
150	Todd Jones	.10
151	Al Martin	.10
152	Ismael Valdes	.10
153	Wade Boggs	.75
154	Garret Anderson	.10
155	Bobby Bonilla	.10
156	Darryl Kile	.10
157	Ryan Klesko	.10
158	Tim Wakefield	.10
159	Kenny Lofton	.10
160	Jose Canseco	.40

161	Doug Glanville	.10
162	Todd Hundley	.10
163	Brian Jordan	.10
164	Steve Finley	.10
165	Tom Glavine	.25
166	Al Leiter	.10
167	Raul Mondesi	.10
168	Desi Relaford	.10
169	Bret Saberhagen	.10
170	Omar Vizquel	.10
171	Larry Walker	.10
172	Bobby Abreu	.10
173	Moises Alou	.10
174	Mike Caruso	.10
175	Royce Clayton	.10
176	Bartolo Colon	.10
177	Marty Cordova	.10
178	Darin Erstad	.30
179	Nomar Garciaparra	.75
180	Andy Ashby	.10
181	Dan Wilson	.10
182	Larry Sutton	.10
183	Tony Clark	.10
184	Andres Galarraga	.10
185	Ray Durham	.10
186	Hideo Nomo	.60
187	Steve Woodard	.10
188	Scott Rolen	.35
189	Mike Stanley	.10
190	Jaret Wright	.10
191	Vinny Castilla	.10
192	Jason Christiansen	.10
193	Paul Bako	.10
194	Carlos Perez	.10
195	Mike Piazza	1.00
196	Fernando Tatis	.10
197	Mo Vaughn	.10
198	Devon White	.10
199	Ricky Gutierrez	.10
200	Charlie Hayes	.10
201	Brad Radke	.10
202	Rick Helling	.10
203	John Smoltz	.10
204	Frank Thomas	.65
205	David Wells	.10
206	Roger Clemens	.85
207	Mark Grudzielanek	.10
208	Chipper Jones	.75
209	Ray Lankford	.10
210	Pedro Martinez	.65
211	Manny Ramirez	.65
212	Greg Vaughn	.10
213	Craig Biggio	.10
214	Rusty Greer	.10
215	Greg Maddux	.75
216	Rick Aguilera	.10
217	Andy Pettitte	.20
218	Dante Bichette	.10
219	Damion Easley	.10
220	Matt Morris	.10
221	John Olerud	.10
222	Chan Ho Park	.10
223	Curt Schilling	.25
224	John Valentin	.10
225	Matt Williams	.10
226	Ellis Burks	.10
227	Tom Goodwin	.10
228	Javy Lopez	.10
229	Eric Milton	.10
230	Paul O'Neill	.10
231	Magglio Ordonez	.15
232	Derrek Lee	.10
233	Ken Griffey Jr. (Caught on the Fly)	.60
234	Randy Johnson (Caught on the Fly)	.30
235	Alex Rodriguez (Caught on the Fly)	.75
236	Darin Erstad (Caught on the Fly)	.15
237	Juan Gonzalez (Caught on the Fly)	.20
238	Derek Jeter (Caught on the Fly)	1.00
239	Tony Gwynn (Caught on the Fly)	.40
240	Kerry Wood (Caught on the Fly)	.20
241	Cal Ripken Jr. (Caught on the Fly)	1.00
242	Sammy Sosa (Caught on the Fly)	.50
243	Greg Maddux (Caught on the Fly)	.40
244	Mark McGwire (Caught on the Fly)	.75
245	Chipper Jones (Caught on the Fly)	.40
246	Barry Bonds (Caught on the Fly)	1.00
247	Ben Grieve (Caught on the Fly)	
248	Ben Davis (Building Blocks)	
249	Robert Fick (Building Blocks)	.10
250	Carlos Guillen (Building Blocks)	.10
251	Mike Frank (Building Blocks)	
252	Ryan Minor (Building Blocks)	.10
253	Troy Glaus (Building Blocks)	.65
254	Matt Anderson (Building Blocks)	
255	Josh Booty (Building Blocks)	

Precious Metal Gems

(continued on 1999 Metal Universe)

1999 Metal Universe Sample Sheet

To introduce its annual issue of embossed cards this six-card sheet of Metal Universe samples was issued. The 5" x 10-1/2" sheet has five regular cards and an example of the Building Blocks insert set. Cards on the sheet are virtually identical to the issued versions except they have the word "SAMPLE" on back in place of card numbers. At the February Hawaii trade show, 325 sheets with a special gold seal, serial numbered and autographed by J.D. Drew were distributed to attendees.

256 Gabe Alvarez (Building Blocks) .10
257 Gabe Kapler (Building Blocks) .10
258 Enrique Wilson (Building Blocks) .10
259 Alex Gonzalez (Building Blocks) .10
260 Preston Wilson (Building Blocks) .10
261 Eric Chavez (Building Blocks) .20
262 Adrian Beltre (Building Blocks) .30
263 Corey Koskie (Building Blocks) .10
264 Robert Machado RC (Building Blocks) .10
265 Orlando Hernandez (Building Blocks) .10
266 Matt Clement (Building Blocks) .10
267 Luis Ordaz (Building Blocks) .10
268 Jeremy Giambi (Building Blocks) .10
269 J.D. Drew (Building Blocks) .50
269a J.D. Drew (Building Blocks "Sample" autographed edition of 35.) 30.00
270 Cliff Politte (Building Blocks) .10
271 Carlton Loewer (Building Blocks) .10
272 Aramis Ramirez (Building Blocks) .10
273 Ken Griffey Jr. (M.L.P.D.) .60
274 Randy Johnson (M.L.P.D.) .30
275 Alex Rodriguez (M.L.P.D.) .75
276 Darin Erstad (M.L.P.D.) .20
277 Scott Rolen (M.L.P.D.) .25
278 Juan Gonzalez (M.L.P.D.) .20
279 Jeff Bagwell (M.L.P.D.) .30
280 Mike Piazza (M.L.P.D.) .65
281 Derek Jeter (M.L.P.D.) 1.00
282 Travis Lee (M.L.P.D.) .10
283 Tony Gwynn (M.L.P.D.) .40
284 Kerry Wood (M.L.P.D.) .20
285 Albert Belle (M.L.P.D.) .10
286 Sammy Sosa (M.L.P.D.) .50
287 Mo Vaughn (M.L.P.D.) .10
288 Nomar Garciaparra (M.L.P.D.) .45
289 Frank Thomas (M.L.P.D.) .30
290 Cal Ripken Jr. (M.L.P.D.) 1.00
291 Greg Maddux (M.L.P.D.) .40
292 Chipper Jones (M.L.P.D.) .40
293 Ben Grieve (M.L.P.D.) .10
294 Andruw Jones (M.L.P.D.) .30
295 Mark McGwire (M.L.P.D.) .75
296 Roger Clemens (M.L.P.D.) .50
297 Barry Bonds (M.L.P.D.) 1.00
298 Ken Griffey Jr.-Checklist (M.L.P.D.) .60
299 Kerry Wood-Checklist (M.L.P.D.) .10
300 Alex Rodriguez-Checklist (M.L.P.D.) .75

Precious Metal Gems

A 300-card parallel of the base set, these cards feature gold-foil etching and are inserted exclusively in hobby packs. Each card is serially numbered to 50. A Gem Master 1 of 1 parallel was also issued, but is too rare to value.

NM/M
Common Player: 3.00
Stars: 25X
Gem Master 1 of 1: (Value Undetermined)

Boyz With The Wood

The top hitters in the game are featured on these folded cards with four sides. These are inserted 1:18.

NM/M
Complete Set (15): 17.50
Common Player: .60
Inserted 1:18
1 Ken Griffey Jr. 2.00
2 Frank Thomas 1.00
3 Jeff Bagwell 1.00

4 Juan Gonzalez .75
5 Mark McGwire 2.50
6 Scott Rolen .60
7 Travis Lee .60
8 Tony Gwynn 2.00
9 Mike Piazza 2.00
10 Chipper Jones 2.00
11 Nomar Garciaparra 2.00
12 Derek Jeter 3.00
13 Cal Ripken Jr. 3.00
14 Andruw Jones 1.00
15 Alex Rodriguez 2.50

Diamond Soul

Utilizing lenticular technology these inserts showcase a soulful "galactic" design. The set consists of 15 cards which are seeded at 1:72 packs.

NM/M
Complete Set (15): 60.00
Common Player: 1.50
Inserted 1:72
1 Cal Ripken Jr. 12.00
2 Alex Rodriguez 9.00
3 Chipper Jones 6.00
4 Derek Jeter 12.00
5 Frank Thomas 4.00
6 Greg Maddux 6.00
7 Juan Gonzalez 3.00
8 Ken Griffey Jr. 7.50
9 Kerry Wood 3.00
10 Mark McGwire 9.00
11 Mike Piazza 7.50
12 Nomar Garciaparra 6.00
13 Scott Rolen 2.50
14 Tony Gwynn 6.00
15 Travis Lee 1.50

Linchpins

This 10-card set features a laser die-cut background and highlights key players who hold their teams together on the field and in the clubhouse. These are seeded 1:360 packs.

NM/M
Complete Set (10): 75.00
Common Player: 5.00
Inserted 1:360
1 Mike Piazza 10.00
2 Mark McGwire 12.50
3 Kerry Wood 5.00
4 Ken Griffey Jr. 10.00
5 Greg Maddux 7.50
6 Frank Thomas 6.00
7 Derek Jeter 15.00
8 Chipper Jones 7.50
9 Cal Ripken Jr. 15.00
10 Alex Rodriguez 12.50

Neophytes

This 15-card insert set showcases young stars like J.D. Drew and Troy Glaus. The cards feature silver foil stamping on a horizontal format, found on an average of 1:6 packs.

NM/M
Complete Set (15): 7.50
Common Player: .35
Inserted 1:6
1 Troy Glaus 3.00
2 Travis Lee .75
3 Scott Elarton .35
4 Ricky Ledee .35
5 Richard Hidalgo .35
6 J.D. Drew 1.50
7 Paul Konerko .75
8 Orlando Hernandez .75
9 Mike Caruso .35
10 Mike Frank .35
11 Miguel Tejada .50
12 Matt Anderson .35
13 Kerry Wood 1.00
14 Gabe Alvarez .35
15 Adrian Beltre .50

Planet Metal

These die-cut cards feature a metallic view of the planet behind pop-out action photography. The 15-card set features the top players in the game and are seeded 1:36 packs.

NM/M
Complete Set (15): 45.00
Common Player: 1.50
Inserted 1:36
1 Alex Rodriguez 9.00
2 Andruw Jones 3.50
3 Cal Ripken Jr. 12.00
4 Chipper Jones 5.00
5 Darin Erstad 2.00
6 Derek Jeter 12.00
7 Frank Thomas 3.50
8 Travis Lee 1.50
9 Scott Rolen 2.50
10 Nomar Garciaparra 5.00
11 Mike Piazza 6.50
12 Mark McGwire 9.00
13 Ken Griffey Jr. 6.50
14 Juan Gonzalez 2.50
15 Jeff Bagwell 3.50

2000 Metal

NM/M
Complete Set (250): 20.00
Common Player: .10
Common Prospect (201-250): .50
Inserted 1:2
Pack (10): 1.50
Wax Box (28): 25.00
1 Tony Gwynn 1.00
2 Derek Jeter 2.50
3 Johnny Damon .35
4 Javy Lopez .10
5 Preston Wilson .10
6 Derek Bell .10
7 Richie Sexson .10
8 Vinny Castilla .10
9 Billy Wagner .10
10 Carlos Beltran .50
11 Chris Singleton .10
12 Nomar Garciaparra 1.00
13 Carlos Febles .10
14 Jason Varitek .10
15 Luis Gonzalez .20
16 Jon Lieber .10
17 Mo Vaughn .10
18 Dave Burba .10
19 Brady Anderson .10
20 Carlos Lee .20
21 Chuck Finley .10
22 Alex Gonzalez .10
23 Matt Williams .10
24 Chipper Jones 1.00
25 Pokey Reese .10
26 Todd Helton .65
27 Mike Mussina .40
28 Butch Huskey .10
29 Jeff Bagwell .75
30 Juan Encarnacion .10
31 A.J. Burnett .10
32 Micah Bowie .10
33 Brian Jordan .10
34 Scott Erickson .10
35 Sean Casey .25
36 John Smoltz .10
37 Edgard Clemente .10
38 Mike Hampton .10
39 Tom Glavine .35
40 Albert Belle .10
41 Jim Thome .60
42 Jermaine Dye .10
43 Sammy Sosa 1.25
44 Pedro Martinez .75
45 Paul Konerko .20
46 Damion Easley .10
47 Cal Ripken Jr. 2.50
48 Jose Lima .10
49 Mike Lowell .10
50 Randy Johnson .75
51 Dean Palmer .10
52 Tim Salmon .10
53 Kevin Millwood .10
54 Mark Grace .10
55 Aaron Boone .10
56 Omar Vizquel .10
57 Moises Alou .10
58 Travis Fryman .10
59 Erubiel Durazo .10
60 Carl Everett .10
61 Charles Johnson .10
62 Trot Nixon .10
63 Andres Galarraga .10
64 Magglio Ordonez .10
65 Pedro Astacio .10
66 Roberto Alomar .20
67 Pete Harnisch .10
68 Scott Williamson .10
69 Alex Fernandez .10
70 Robin Ventura .10
71 Chad Allen .10
72 Darin Erstad .20
73 Ron Coomer .10
74 Ellis Burks .10
75 Kent Bottenfield .10
76 Ken Griffey Jr. 1.50
77 Mike Piazza 1.50
78 Jorge Posada .20
79 Dante Bichette .10
80 Adrian Beltre .25
81 Andruw Jones .75
82 Wilson Alvarez .10
83 Edgardo Alfonzo .10
84 Brian Giles .10
85 Gary Sheffield .25
86 Matt Stairs .10
87 Bret Boone .10
88 Kenny Rogers .10
89 Barry Bonds 2.50
90 Scott Rolen .60
91 Edgar Renteria .10
92 Larry Walker .10
93 Roger Cedeno .10
94 Kevin Brown .10
95 Lee Stevens .10
96 Brad Radke .10
97 Andy Pettitte .25
98 Bobby Higginson .10
99 Eric Chavez .25
100 Alex Rodriguez 2.00
100s Alex Rodriguez/OPS 2.00
101 Shannon Stewart .10
102 Ryan Rupe .10
103 Freddy Garcia .10
104 John Jaha .10
105 Greg Maddux 1.00
106 Hideki Irabu .10
107 Rey Ordonez .10
108 Troy O'Leary .10
109 Frank Thomas .75
110 Corey Koskie .10
111 Bernie Williams .10
112 Barry Larkin .10
113 Kevin Appier .10
114 Curt Schilling .35
115 Bartolo Colon .10
116 Edgar Martinez .10
117 Ray Lankford .10
118 Todd Walker .10
119 John Wetteland .10
120 David Nilsson .10
121 Tino Martinez .10
122 Phil Nevin .10
123 Ben Grieve .10
124 Ron Gant .10
125 Jeff Kent .10
126 Rick Helling .10
127 Russ Ortiz .10
128 Troy Glaus .65
129 Chan Ho Park .10
130 Jeromy Burnitz .10
131 Aaron Sele .10
132 Mike Sirotka .10
133 Brad Ausmus .10
134 Jose Rosado .10
135 Mariano Rivera .25
136 Jason Giambi .50
137 Mike Lieberthal .10
138 Chris Carpenter .10
139 Henry Rodriguez .10
140 Mike Sweeney .10
141 Vladimir Guerrero .75
142 Charles Nagy .10
143 Jason Kendall .10
144 Matt Lawton .10
145 Michael Barrett .10
146 David Cone .10
147 Bobby Abreu .10
148 Fernando Tatis .10
149 Jose Canseco .40
150 Craig Biggio .10
151 Matt Mantei .10
152 Jacque Jones .10
153 John Halama .10
154 Trevor Hoffman .10
155 Rondell White .10
156 Reggie Sanders .10
157 Steve Finley .10
158 Roberto Hernandez .10
159 Geoff Jenkins .10
160 Chris Widger .10
161 Orel Hershiser .10
162 Tim Hudson .20
163 Kris Benson .10
164 Kevin Young .10
165 Rafael Palmeiro .60
166 David Wells .10
167 Ben Davis .10
168 Jamie Moyer .10
169 Randy Wolf .10
170 Jeff Cirillo .10
171 Warren Morris .10
172 Billy Koch .10
173 Marquis Grissom .10
174 Geoff Blum .10
175 Octavio Dotel .10
176 Orlando Hernandez .20
177 J.D. Drew .30
178 Carlos Delgado .40
179 Sterling Hitchcock .10
180 Shawn Green .25
181 Tony Clark .10
182 Joe McEwing .10
183 Fred McGriff .10
184 Tony Batista .10
185 Al Leiter .10
186 Roger Clemens 1.25
187 Al Martin .10
188 Eric Milton .10
189 Bobby Smith .10
190 Rusty Greer .10
191 Shawn Estes .10
192 Ken Caminiti .10
193 Eric Karros .10
194 Manny Ramirez .75
195 Jim Edmonds .10
196 Paul O'Neill .10
197 Rico Brogna .10
198 Ivan Rodriguez .60
199 Doug Glanville .10
200 Mark McGwire 2.00
201 Mark Quinn (Prospect) .50
202 Norm Hutchins (Prospect) .50
203 Ramon Ortiz (Prospect) .50
204 Brett Laxton (Prospect) .50
205 Jimmy Anderson (Prospect) .50
206 Calvin Murray (Prospect) .50
207 Wilton Veras (Prospect) .50
208 Chad Hermansen (Prospect) .50
209 Nick Johnson (Prospect) .50
210 Kevin Barker (Prospect) .50
211 Casey Blake (Prospect) .50
212 Chad Meyers (Prospect) .50
213 Kip Wells (Prospect) .50
214 Eric Munson (Prospect) .50
215 Lance Berkman (Prospect) .50
216 Wily Pena (Prospect) .50
217 Gary Matthews Jr. (Prospect) .50
218 Travis Dawkins (Prospect) .50
219 Josh Beckett (Prospect) .50
220 Tony Armas Jr. (Prospect) .50
221 Alfonso Soriano (Prospect) 1.00
222 Pat Burrell (Prospect) 1.00
223 Danys Baez RC (Prospect) .50
224 Adam Kennedy (Prospect) .50
225 Ruben Mateo (Prospect) .50
226 Vernon Wells (Prospect) .75
227 Brian Cooper (Prospect) .50
228 Jeff DaVanon RC (Prospect) .50
229 Glen Barker (Prospect) .50
230 Robinson Cancel (Prospect) .50
231 D'Angelo Jimenez (Prospect) .50
232 Adam Piatt (Prospect) .50
233 Buddy Carlyle (Prospect) .50
234 Chad Hutchinson (Prospect) .50
235 Matt Riley (Prospect) .50
236 Cole Liniak (Prospect) .50
237 Ben Petrick (Prospect) .50
238 Peter Bergeron (Prospect) .50
239 Cesar King (Prospect) .50
240 Aaron Myette (Prospect) .50
241 Eric Gagne (Prospect) .60
242 Joe Nathan (Prospect) .50
243 Bruce Chen (Prospect) .50
244 Rob Bell (Prospect) .50
245 Juan Sosa RC (Prospect) .60
246 Julio Ramirez (Prospect) .50
247 Wade Miller (Prospect) .50
248 Trace Coquillette RC (Prospect) .50
249 Robert Ramsay (Prospect) .50
250 Rick Ankiel (Prospect) .50

Emerald

A green tone at the top 1/4 of the card fronts, and a small circled "E" at top-right on back differentiate these parallels from the regular-issue cards. The first 200 cards in the set are found in this version about one every four packs. The odds double for the Prospects cards (#201-250) that were short-printed in the regular version as well.

NM/M
Complete Set (250): 100.00
Common Player: .25
Stars: 2.5X
Inserted 1:4
Prospects (201-250): 2.5X
Inserted 1:8

Fusion

NM/M
Complete Set (15): 12.50
Common Player: .50
Inserted 1:4
1 Ken Griffey Jr., Alex Rodriguez 2.00
2 Mark McGwire, Rick Ankiel 2.00
3 Scott Rolen, Curt Schilling .50
4 Pedro Martinez, Nomar Garciaparra 1.25
5 Carlos Beltran, Carlos Febles .60
6 Sammy Sosa, Mark Grace 1.50
7 Vladimir Guerrero, Ugueth Urbina 1.00
8 Roger Clemens, Derek Jeter 3.00
9 Jeff Bagwell, Craig Biggio 1.00
10 Chipper Jones, Andruw Jones 1.50
11 Cal Ripken Jr., Mike Mussina 2.50
12 Manny Ramirez, Roberto Alomar 1.00
13 Sean Casey, Barry Larkin .50
14 Ivan Rodriguez, Rafael Palmeiro .75
15 Mike Piazza, Robin Ventura 1.50

Autographics

NM/M
Common Player: 4.00
Bobby Abreu 8.00
Chad Allen 4.00
Marlon Anderson 4.00
Rick Ankiel 10.00
Glen Barker 4.00
Rob Bell 4.00
Mark Bellhorn 5.00
Peter Bergeron 4.00

Lance Berkman		8.00
Wade Boggs		25.00
Barry Bonds		150.00
Kent Bottenfield		4.00
Pat Burrell		10.00
Miguel Cairo		4.00
Mike Cameron		6.00
Chris Carpenter		6.00
Roger Cedeno		4.00
Mike Darr		6.00
Einar Diaz		4.00
J.D. Drew		15.00
Erubiel Durazo		6.00
Ray Durham		6.00
Damion Easley		4.00
Scott Elarton		4.00
Jeremy Giambi		4.00
Doug Glanville		4.00
Shawn Green		10.00
Jerry Hairston Jr.		4.00
Bob Howry		4.00
Norm Hutchins		4.00
Randy Johnson		40.00
Jacque Jones		4.00
Gabe Kapler		6.00
Cesar King		4.00
Mark Kotsay		4.00
Cole Liniak		4.00
Greg Maddux		50.00
Pedro Martinez		30.00
Ruben Mateo		4.00
Warren Morris		4.00
Heath Murray		4.00
Joe Nathan		4.00
Jim Parque		4.00
Angel Pena		4.00
Cal Ripken Jr.		100.00
Alex Rodriguez		60.00
Ryan Rupe		4.00
Randall Simon		4.00
Chris Singleton		4.00
Mike Sweeney		6.00
Wilton Veras		4.00
Scott Williamson		4.00
Randy Wolf		6.00
Tony Womack		6.00

Base Shredders

		NM/M
Complete Set (18):		160.00
Common Player:		5.00
Inserted 1:288		
(1)	Roberto Alomar	7.50
(2)	Michael Barrett	5.00
(3)	Tony Clark	5.00
(4)	Ben Davis	5.00
(5)	Erubiel Durazo	5.00
(6)	Troy Glaus	12.50
(7)	Ben Grieve	5.00
(8)	Vladimir Guerrero	15.00
(9)	Tony Gwynn	25.00
(10)	Todd Helton	12.50
(11)	Eric Munson	5.00
(12)	Rafael Palmeiro	10.00
(13)	Manny Ramirez	20.00
(14)	Ivan Rodriguez	10.00
(15)	Miguel Tejada	7.50
(16)	Mo Vaughn	5.00
(17)	Larry Walker	5.00
(18)	Matt Williams	5.00

Heavy Metal

		NM/M
Complete Set (10):		15.00
Common Player:		1.50
Inserted 1:20		
1	Sammy Sosa	2.25
2	Mark McGwire	3.00
3	Ken Griffey Jr.	2.50

4	Mike Piazza	2.50
5	Nomar Garciaparra	2.00
6	Alex Rodriguez	3.00
7	Manny Ramirez	1.50
8	Jeff Bagwell	1.50
9	Chipper Jones	2.00
10	Vladimir Guerrero	1.50

Hit Machines

		NM/M
Complete Set (10):		20.00
Common Player:		1.00
Inserted 1:20		
1	Ken Griffey Jr.	3.00
2	Mark McGwire	4.00
3	Frank Thomas	1.50
4	Tony Gwynn	2.00
5	Rafael Palmeiro	1.25
6	Bernie Williams	1.00
7	Derek Jeter	6.00
8	Sammy Sosa	2.50
9	Mike Piazza	3.00
10	Chipper Jones	2.00

Platinum Portraits

		NM/M
Complete Set (10):		6.00
Common Player:		.25
Inserted 1:8		
1	Carlos Beltran	.50
2	Vladimir Guerrero	.75
3	Manny Ramirez	.75
4	Ivan Rodriguez	.65
5	Sean Casey	.40
6	Alex Rodriguez	1.50
7	Derek Jeter	2.00
8	Nomar Garciaparra	1.00
9	Vernon Wells	.25
10	Shawn Green	.50

Talent Show

		NM/M
Complete Set (15):		6.00
Common Player:		.30
Inserted 1:4		
1	Rick Ankiel	.50
2	Matt Riley	.30
3	Chad Hermansen	.30
4	Ruben Mateo	.30
5	Eric Munson	.30
6	Alfonso Soriano	1.50
7	Wilton Veras	.30
8	Vernon Wells	.75
9	Erubiel Durazo	.30
10	Pat Burrell	.50
11	Ben Davis	.30
12	A.J. Burnett	.30
13	Peter Bergeron	.30

14	Mark Quinn	.30
15	Ben Petrick	.30

1993 Metz Bakeries

Paul Molitor
Toronto Blue Jays

Metz Baking Co. of Sioux City, Iowa, produced this set utilizing drawings of players rather than photos. The company also made available uncut sheets of the sets via a mail-in offer. Cards have either a yellow background with blue pinstripes or a blue background with yellow pinstripes. Players are shown in a red, white and black porthole at center. Backs are printed in black-and-white with complete major and minor league stats. Because the cards are licensed only by the Players Union and not Major League Baseball, the player paintings omit uniform logos. The unnumbered cards are checklisted here in alphabetical order. A special collectors tin to house the set was also available.

		NM/M
Complete Set (40):		35.00
Common Player:		.75
(1)	Dante Bichette	.75
(2)	Wade Boggs	2.00
(3)	Barry Bonds	4.00
(4)	Bobby Bonilla	.75
(5)	Jose Canseco	1.00
(6)	Joe Carter	.75
(7)	Will Clark	.75
(8)	Roger Clemens	2.25
(9)	Doug Drabek	.75
(10)	Shawon Dunston	.75
(11)	Dennis Eckersley	1.25
(12)	Cecil Fielder	.75
(13)	Carlton Fisk	1.50
(14)	Andres Galarraga	.75
(15)	Kirk Gibson	.75
(16)	Dwight Gooden	.75
(17)	Mark Grace	.75
(18)	Ken Griffey Jr.	2.50
(19)	Tony Gwynn	2.00
(20)	Rickey Henderson	1.50
(21)	Kent Hrbek	.75
(22)	Howard Johnson	.75
(23)	Wally Joyner	.75
(24)	Dave Justice	.75
(25)	Barry Larkin	.75
(26)	Don Mattingly	2.50
(27)	Jack McDowell	.75
(28)	Paul Molitor	1.50
(29)	Terry Pendleton	.75
(30)	Kirby Puckett	2.00
(31)	Cal Ripken, Jr.	4.00
(32)	Nolan Ryan	4.00
(33)	Ryne Sandberg	2.00
(34)	Ozzie Smith	2.00
(35)	Darryl Strawberry	.75
(36)	Danny Tartabull	.75
(37)	Mickey Tettleton	.75
(38)	Alan Trammell	.75
(39)	Andy Van Slyke	.75
(40)	Dave Winfield	1.50

1993 Milk Bone Super Stars

Milk Bone Flavor Snacks and Dog Treats issued a 20-card Super Stars set in 1993 in a format comprable to the NFL Pro Line cards.

Mark McGwire 1B
Ellis & Sam

The cards show the player at home with his dog, with the player shown in an action photo in the lower left corner of the card. The card backs have the player's stats and biography, along with information about the pet and a quote from the player about his dog. The cards were available, two at a time, in specially-marked packages of the company's products. The set also could be obtained through the mail by following instructions on the boxes.

		NM/M
Complete Set (20):		12.50
Common Player:		.50
(1)	Paul Molitor	1.00
(2)	Tom Glavine	.65
(3)	Barry Larkin	.50
(4)	Mark McGwire	2.50
(5)	Bill Swift	.50
(6)	Ken Caminiti	.50
(7)	Will Clark	.50
(8)	Rafael Palmeiro	.50
(9)	Matt Young	.50
(10)	Todd Zeile	.50
(11)	Wally Joyner	.50
(12)	Cal Ripken Jr.	3.50
(13)	Tom Foley	.50
(14)	Ben McDonald	.50
(15)	Larry Walker	.50
(16)	Rob Dibble	.50
(17)	Brett Butler	.50
(18)	Joe Girardi	.50
(19)	Brady Anderson	.50
(20)	Craig Biggio	.50

1989 Milk Duds Pittsburgh Pirates

John SMILEY
PIRATES

This set of Pirates photocards carries on its backs advertising for various brands of Leaf candies, principally Milk Duds. The 3-3/8" x 5-1/2" cards have color portrait photo on front with the player's name near the bottom and a team logo at bottom center. Backs have a few vital statistics, candy advertising and/or free ticket or contest offers. The cards are numbered by uniform number, but are listed here in alphabetical order.

		NM/M
Complete Set (38):		20.00
Common Player:		.75
(1)	Pirate Parrot (Mascot)	.75
(2)	Rafael Belliard	.75
(3)	Dann Bilardello	.75
(4)	Barry Bonds	9.00
(5)	Sid Bream	.75
(6)	Bobby Bonilla	1.00
(7)	John Cangelosi	.75
(8)	Benny Distefano	.75
(9)	Rich Donnelly	.75
(10)	Doug Drabek	.75
(11)	Brian Fisher	.75
(12)	Miguel Garcia	.75
(13)	Jim Gott	.75
(14)	Neal Heaton	.75
(15)	Bruce Kimm	.75

(16)	Jeff King	1.00
(17)	Bob Kipper	.75
(18)	Randy Kramer	.75
(19)	Gene Lamont	.75
(20)	Bill Landrum	.75
(21)	Mike LaValliere	.75
(22)	Jim Leyland	.75
(23)	Jose Lind	.75
(24)	Morris Madden	.75
(25)	Milt May	.75
(26)	Ray Miller	.75
(27)	Junior Ortiz	.75
(28)	Tom Prince	.75
(29)	Rey Quinones	.75
(30)	Gary Redus	.75
(31)	R.J. Reynolds	.75
(32)	Jeff Robinson	.75
(33)	Tommy Sandt	.75
(34)	John Smiley	.75
(35)	Dorn Taylor	.75
(36)	Andy Van Slyke	1.00
(37)	Bob Walk	.75
(38)	Glenn Wilson	.75

1997 Milk Mustache Trading Cards

MILK
ALEX RODRIGUEZ

shortstop SEATTLE MARINERS

Sponsored by the National Fluid Milk Processor Promotion Board (really), this nine-card panel was an advertising insert in the October 1997 issue of Sports Illustrated for Kids. The perforated panel measures about 7-1/2" x 10-1/2", with each card measuring the standard 2-1/2" x 3-1/2" and perforated on two, three or four sides, depending on its placement on the sheet. Player portrait photos are set on a silver-look background. Cap and uniform logos have been eliminated and a milk moustache added. "MILK" appears in white in a purple stripe at the top of each player's card. Backs have a baseball tip and a milk tip ascribed to each player.

		NM/M
Complete Sheet:		5.00
Complete Set (9):		5.00
Common Player:		.25
1	Alex Rodriguez	2.50
2	Nomar Garciaparra	1.00
3	Andy Pettitte	.35
4	Darin Erstad	.45
5	Jason Kendall	.25
6	Vladimir Guerrero	1.00
7	Scott Rolen	.60
8	Tony Clark	.25
--	Header Card	.05

1990 Miller Beer Milwaukee Brewers

Miller
with Cuts

GARY SHEFFIELD
INFIELD

This 32-card set was given away with an album to adults attending an August Brewers game. Cards are standard 2-1/2" x 3-1/2" and feature borderless color photos above gold and black bottom stripes. The beer company's logo is featured in the upper-right corner, with the team logo at lower-left. Black-and-white backs feature

player stats. The set has been checklisted below in alphabetical order. Cards are not numbered.

		NM/M
Complete Set w/Album (32):		10.00
Common Player:		.25
(1)	Chris Bosio	.25
(2)	Greg Brock	.25
(3)	Chuck Crim	.25
(4)	Rob Deer	.25
(5)	Edgar Diaz	.25
(6)	Tom Edens	.25
(7)	Mike Felder	.25
(8)	Tom Filer	.25
(9)	Jim Gantner	.25
(10)	Darryl Hamilton	.25
(11)	Teddy Higuera	.25
(12)	Mark Knudson	.25
(13)	Bill Krueger	.25
(14)	Paul Mirabella	.25
(15)	Paul Molitor	4.00
(16)	Jaime Navarro	.25
(17)	Charlie O'Brien	.25
(18)	Dave Parker	.25
(19)	Dan Plesac	.25
(20)	Dennis Powell	.25
(21)	Ron Robinson	.25
(22)	Bob Sebra	.25
(23)	Gary Sheffield	2.00
(24)	Bill Spiers	.25
(25)	B.J. Surhoff	.25
(26)	Dale Sveum	.25
(27)	Tom Trebelhorn	.25
(28)	Greg Vaughn	.25
(29)	Randy Veres	.25
(30)	Bill Wegman	.25
(31)	Robin Yount	4.00
(32)	Coaches (Don Baylor, Ray Burris, Duffy Dyer, Andy Etchebarren, Larry Haney)	.25

1991 Miller Beer Milwaukee Brewers

'91 BREWERS

PAUL MOLITOR • IF
Miller High Life

The Miller High Life Brewing Co., in conjunction with the Milwaukee Brewers, sponsored a 32-card limited edition baseball card set in 1991. The set, which features 30 cards of Brewer players plus additional cards of manager Tom Trebelhorn and his coaching staff, employs a home plate window for the front photo, with the player's name and words "Miller High Life" along the bottom of the card. Complete major and minor league stats are printed on the black-and-white backs, which also include sponsors' logos.

		NM/M
Complete Set w/Album (32):		10.00
Common Player:		.25
(1)	Don August	.25
(2)	James Austin	.25
(3)	Dante Bichette	.35
(4)	Chris Bosio	.25
(5)	Kevin Brown	.25
(6)	Chuck Crim	.25
(7)	Rick Dempsey	.25
(8)	Jim Gantner	.25
(9)	Darryl Hamilton	.25
(10)	Teddy Higuera	.25
(11)	Darren Holmes	.25
(12)	Jim Hunter	.25
(13)	Mark Knudson	.25
(14)	Mark Lee	.25
(15)	Julio Machado	.25
(16)	Candy Maldonado	.25
(17)	Paul Molitor	4.00
(18)	Jaime Navarro	.25
(19)	Edwin Nunez	.25
(20)	Dan Plesac	.25
(21)	Willie Randolph	.25
(22)	Ron Robinson	.25
(23)	Gary Sheffield	1.00
(24)	Bill Spiers	.25
(25)	Franklin Stubbs	.25
(26)	B.J. Surhoff	.25
(27)	Dale Sveum	.25
(28)	Tom Trebelhorn	.25
(29)	Greg Vaughn	.25
(30)	Bill Wegman	.25
(31)	Robin Yount	.25

1994 Miller Genuine Draft Milwaukee Brewers

(See 1994 Lite Beer Milwaukee Brewers.)

1984 Milton Bradley

In 1984 Milton Bradley printed their baseball game cards in full-color and adopted the standard baseball card size of 2-1/2" x 3-1/2". A total of 30 cards were in the set. The card fronts show the player photos with the team insignias and logos airbrushed away. The game is called Championship Baseball. Card backs varied in style; some had player statistics plus game information, and others only game information.

		NM/M
Complete Boxed Set:		12.00
Complete Card Set (30):		7.50
Common Player:		.25
(1)	Wade Boggs	.75
(2)	George Brett	1.50
(3)	Rod Carew	.50
(4)	Steve Carlton	.50
(5)	Gary Carter	.50
(6)	Dave Concepcion	.25
(7)	Cecil Cooper	.25
(8)	Andre Dawson	.40
(9)	Carlton Fisk	.50
(10)	Steve Garvey	.40
(11)	Pedro Guerrero	.25
(12)	Ron Guidry	.25
(13)	Rickey Henderson	.50
(14)	Reggie Jackson	1.50
(15)	Ron Kittle	.25
(16)	Bill Madlock	.25
(17)	Dale Murphy	.40
(18)	Al Oliver	.25
(19)	Darrell Porter	.25
(20)	Cal Ripken, Jr.	2.50
(21)	Pete Rose	1.50
(22)	Steve Sax	.25
(23)	Mike Schmidt	1.50
(24)	Ted Simmons	.25
(25)	Ozzie Smith	.75
(26)	Dave Stieb	.25
(27)	Fernando Valenzuela	.25
(28)	Lou Whitaker	.25
(29)	Dave Winfield	.50
(30)	Robin Yount	.50

1982 Milwaukee Brewers Police

ROBIN YOUNT
No. 19 — Shortstop
New Berlin Police Department
Salutes The 1982
Milwaukee Brewers

The inaugural Milwaukee Brewers police set contains 30 cards in a 2-13/16" x 4-1/8" format. There are 26 players included in the set, which is numbered by player uniform number. Unnumbered cards were also issued for general manager Harry Dalton, manager Buck Rodgers, the coaches and a team card with checklist. The full-color photos are especially attractive, printed on the cards' crisp white stock. A number of Wisconsin law enforcement agencies distributed the cards and credit lines on the card fronts were changed accordingly.

		NM/M
Complete Set (30):		6.00
Common Player:		.25
4	Paul Molitor	3.00
5	Ned Yost	.25
7	Don Money	.25
8	Rob Picciolo	.25
10	Bob McClure	.25
11	Ed Romero	.25
13	Roy Howell	.25
15	Cecil Cooper	.25
16	Marshall Edwards	.25
17	Jim Gantner	.25
19	Robin Yount	3.00
20	Gorman Thomas	.25
21	Don Sutton	1.00
22	Charlie Moore	.25
23	Ted Simmons	.25
24	Ben Oglivie	.25
26	Bob Skube	.25
27	Pete Ladd	.25
28	Jamie Easterly	.25
30	Moose Haas	.25
32	Harvey Kuenn	.25
34	Rollie Fingers	1.00
40	Bob L. Gibson	.25
41	Jim Slaton	.25
43	Tom Tellmann	.25
46	Jerry Augustine	.25

		NM/M
Complete Set (30):		12.00
Common Player:		.25
4	Paul Molitor	4.00
5	Ned Yost	.25
7	Don Money	.25
9	Larry Hisle	.25
10	Bob McClure	.25
11	Ed Romero	.25
13	Roy Howell	.25
15	Cecil Cooper	.25
17	Jim Gantner	.25
19	Robin Yount	4.00
20	Gorman Thomas	.25
22	Charlie Moore	.25
23	Ted Simmons	.25
24	Ben Oglivie	.25
26	Kevin Bass	.25
28	Jamie Easterly	.25
29	Mark Brouhard	.25
30	Moose Haas	.25
34	Rollie Fingers	2.00
35	Randy Lerch	.25
37	Buck Rodgers	.25
41	Jim Slaton	.25
45	Doug Jones	.25
46	Jerry Augustine	.25
47	Dwight Bernard	.25
48	Mike Caldwell	.25
50	Pete Vuckovich	.25
---	Team Photo/Checklist	.25
---	Harry Dalton (General Mgr.)	.25
---	Coaches Card (Pat Dobson, Larry Haney, Ron Hansen, Cal McLish, Buck Rogers, Harry Warner)	.25

1983 Milwaukee Brewers Police

16 MARSHALL EDWARDS — OF
The Milwaukee Police Department
Presents The 1983
Milwaukee Brewers

Similar to 1982, a number of issuer variations exist for the 1983 Brewers police set, as law enforcement agencies throughout the state distributed the set with their own credit lines on the cards. At least 28 variations are known to exist, with those issued by smaller agencies being scarcest. Prices quoted below are for the most common variations, generally the Milwaukee Police Department and a few small-town departments whose entire supply of police cards seem to have fallen into dealers' hands. Some specialists are willing to pay a premium for the scarcer departments' issues. The 30, 2-13/16" x 4-1/8" cards include 29 players and coaches, along with a team card (with a checklist back). The team card and group coaches' card are unnumbered, while the others are numbered by uniform number.

		NM/M
Complete Set (30):		6.00
Common Player:		.25
2	Randy Ready	.15
4	Paul Molitor	2.50
9	Jim Sundberg	.15
9	Rene Lachemann	.15
10	Bob McClure	.15
11	Ed Romero	.15
13	Roy Howell	.15
14	Dion James	.15
15	Cecil Cooper	.15
17	Jim Gantner	.15
19	Robin Yount	2.50
20	Don Sutton	1.00
21	Bill Schroeder	.15
22	Charlie Moore	.15
23	Ted Simmons	.15
24	Ben Oglivie	.15
25	Bobby Clark	.15
27	Pete Ladd	.15
28	Rick Manning	.15
29	Mark Brouhard	.15
30	Moose Haas	.15
34	Rollie Fingers	1.00
42	Tom Tellmann	.15
43	Chuck Porter	.15
46	Jerry Augustine	.15
47	Jaime Cocanower	.15
48	Mike Caldwell	.15
50	Pete Vuckovich	.15
---	Team Photo/Checklist	.15
---	Coaches Card (Pat Dobson, Dave Garcia, Larry Haney, Tom Trebelhorn)	.15

1984 Milwaukee Brewers Police

20 DON SUTTON — P
The Winneconne Police Department
Presents The 1984
MILWAUKEE BREWERS

The king of the variations again in 1984, the Milwaukee Brewers set has been found with 57 different police agencies' credit lines on the front of the cards. Once again, law enforcement agencies statewide participated in distributing the sets. Some departments also include a badge of the participating agency on the card backs. The full-color cards measure 22-13/16" x 4-1/8". There are 28 numbered player and manager cards, along with an unnumbered coaches card and a team card. Player names, uniform numbers and positions are listed on each card front. Prices listed are for the most common variety (Milwaukee Police Department); sets issued by smaller departments may be worth a premium to specialists. Reported print runs varied from 120,000 sets for the Milwaukee P.D., to just 500 sets for the community of Verona.

		NM/M
Complete Set (30):		6.00
Common Player:		.15
2	Randy Ready	.15
4	Paul Molitor	2.50
7	Doug Loman	.15
9	Paul Householder	.15
10	Bob McClure	.15
11	Ed Romero	.15
14	Dion James	.15
17	Cecil Cooper	.15
17	Jim Gantner	.15
18	Danny Darwin	.15
19	Robin Yount	2.50
21	Bill Schroeder	.15
23	Charlie Moore	.15
23	Ted Simmons	.15
24	Ben Oglivie	.15
26	Brian Giles	.15
27	Pete Ladd	.15
28	Rick Manning	.15
29	Mark Brouhard	.15
30	Moose Haas	.15
31	George Bamberger	.15
34	Rollie Fingers	1.00
40	Bob L. Gibson	.15
41	Ray Searage	.15
47	Jaime Cocanower	.15
48	Ray Burris	.15
49	Ted Higuera	.15
50	Pete Vuckovich	.15
---	Coaches Card (Andy Etchebarren, Larry Haney, Frank Howard, Tony Muser, Herm Starrette)	.15
---	Team Photo	.15

1986 Milwaukee Brewers Police

45 Rob Deer OF
The Fond du Lac Police Dept., KFIZ Radio,
and National Exchange Bank & Trust
present the 1986
Milwaukee Brewers

The Milwaukee Brewers, in conjunction with the Milwaukee Police Department, WTMJ Radio and Kinney Shoes, produced this attractive police safety set of 30 cards. The cards measure 2-13/16" x 4-1/2". A thin black border encloses a full-color player photo on the front. The card backs give a safety tip and promos for the sponsor. The cards were distributed throughout the state of Wisconsin by numerous police departments; those of the smaller departments generally being scarcer than those issued in the big cities. Prices quoted below are for the most common departments' issues.

		NM/M
Complete Set (30):		4.00
Common Player:		.15
1	Ernest Riles	.15
2	Randy Ready	.15
3	Juan Castillo	.15
4	Paul Molitor	2.00
7	Paul Householder	.15
10	Bob McClure	.15
11	Rick Cerone	.15

The Brewers changed the size of their annual police set in 1985, but almost imperceptibly. The full-color cards are 2-3/4" x 4-1/8", a slight 1/16" narrower than the four previous efforts. Player and team name on the card fronts are much bolder than in previous years. Once again, numerous area police groups distributed the sets, leading to nearly 60 variations, as each agency put their own credit line on the cards. Card backs include the Brewers logo, a safety tip and, in some cases, a badge of the participating law enforcement group. There are 27 numbered player cards (by uniform number) and three unnumbered cards - team roster, coaches and a newspaper carrier card. Prices are for the most common departments.

		NM/M
Complete Set (30):		6.00
Common Player:		.15
2	Randy Ready	.15
4	Paul Molitor	2.50
5	Doug Loman	.15
7	Paul Householder	.15
10	Bob McClure	.15
14	Dion James	.15
17	Cecil Cooper	.15
17	Jim Gantner	.15
18	Danny Darwin	.15
19	Robin Yount	2.50
21	Bill Schroeder	.15
22	Charlie Moore	.15
23	Ted Simmons	.15
24	Ben Oglivie	.15
26	Brian Giles	.15
27	Pete Ladd	.15
28	Rick Manning	.15
29	Mark Brouhard	.15
30	Moose Haas	.15
31	George Bamberger	.15
34	Rollie Fingers	1.00
40	Bob L. Gibson	.15
41	Ray Searage	.15
47	Jaime Cocanower	.15
48	Ray Burris	.15
49	Ted Higuera	.15
50	Pete Vuckovich	.15
---	Coaches Card (Andy Etchebarren, Larry Haney, Frank Howard, Tony Muser, Herm Starrette)	.15
---	Team Photo	.15

1985 Milwaukee Brewers Police

49 Ted Higuera P
The Milwaukee Police Department
and The Milwaukee Journal
present the 1985
Milwaukee Brewers

		NM/M
Complete Set (30):		4.00
Common Player:		.15
1	Ernest Riles	.15
2	Randy Ready	.15
3	Juan Castillo	.15
4	Paul Molitor	2.00
7	Paul Householder	.15
10	Bob McClure	.15
11	Rick Cerone	.15

13	Billy Jo Robidoux	.15
16	Cecil Cooper	.15
16	Mike Felder	.15
17	Jim Gantner	.15
18	Danny Darwin	.15
19	Robin Yount	2.00
20	Juan Nieves	.15
21	Bill Schroeder	.15
22	Charlie Moore	.15
24	Ben Oglivie	.15
26	Mark Clear	.15
28	Rick Manning	.15
32	George Bamberger	.15
37	Dan Plesac	.15
39	Tim Leary	.15
41	Ray Searage	.15
43	Chuck Porter	.15
45	Rob Deer	.15
46	Bill Wegman	.15
47	Jamie Cocanower	.15
49	Ted Higuera	.15
---	Coaches Card (Andy Etchebarren, Larry Haney, Frank Howard, Tony Muser, Herm Starrette)	.15
---	Team Photo/Roster	.15

1987 Milwaukee Brewers Police

5 B.J. Surhoff C
The Milwaukee Police Department
Kinney Shoes and WTMJ Radio
present the 1987
Milwaukee Brewers

The Milwaukee Brewers issued a safety set in 1987 for the sixth consecutive year. As in the past, many local police departments throughout Wisconsin participated in the giveaway program. The Milwaukee version was sponsored by Kinney Shoe Stores and WTMJ Radio and was handed out to youngsters attending the Baseball Card Day at County Stadium on May 9th. The cards, which measure 2-1/4" x 4-1/8", feature full-color photos plus a safety tip on the backs. Chris Bosio can be found with a uniform number of 26 or 29. The card was corrected to #29 in later printings.

		NM/M
Complete Set (30):		5.00
Common Player:		.15
1	Ernest Riles	.15
2	Edgar Diaz	.15
3	Juan Castillo	.15
4	Paul Molitor	2.00
5	B.J. Surhoff	.15
7	Dale Sveum	.15
9	Greg Brock	.15
13	Billy Jo Robidoux	.15
14	Jim Paciorek	.15
15	Cecil Cooper	.15
16	Mike Felder	.15
17	Jim Gantner	.15
19	Robin Yount	2.00
20	Juan Nieves	.15
21	Bill Schroeder	.15
24	Mark Clear	.15
26a	Glenn Braggs	.15
26b	Chris Bosio	.30
28	Rick Manning	.15
29	Chris Bosio	.30
32	Chuck Crim	.15
34	Mark Ciardi	.15
37	Dan Plesac	.15
38	John Henry Johnson	.15
42	Mike Birbeck	.15
42	Tom Trebelhorn	.15
43	Rob Deer	.15
46	Bill Wegman	.15
49	Ted Higuera	.15
---	Coaches Card (Andy Etchebarren, Larry Haney, Chuck Hartenstein, Dave Hilton, Tony Muser)	.15
---	Team Photo	.15

1988 Milwaukee Brewers Police

This 30-card set is the 7th annual issue sponsored by the Milwaukee Police Department for local distribution during a crime preven-

3 Juan Castillo 1F
The Marathon County Sheriff's Dept. and
Brickner Chrysler Center Inc.
2925 Grand Avenue, Wausau, WI 54401
present the 1988
Milwaukee Brewers

tion promotion. The full-color card fronts (2-3/4" x 4-1/8") feature the same design as the 1987 set with white borders and a black frame outlining the player photo and name. Sponsor credits and the team name are listed below the photo. The vertical card backs are blue on white with messages from the player and sponsors. Two group photos - one of the team's five coaches and one of the team (with a checklist back) - are unnumbered and printed horizontally. Card numbers refer to the players' uniform numbers.

		NM/M
Complete Set (30):		4.00
Common Player:		.15
1	Ernest Riles	.15
3	Juan Castillo	.15
4	Paul Molitor	2.00
5	B.J. Surhoff	.15
7	Dale Sveum	.15
9	Greg Brock	.15
11	Charlie O'Brien	.15
14	Jim Adduci	.15
16	Mike Felder	.15
17	Jim Gantner	.15
19	Robin Yount	2.00
20	Juan Nieves	.15
21	Bill Schroeder	.15
23	Joey Meyer	.15
25	Mark Clear	.15
26	Glenn Braggs	.15
29	Odell Jones	.15
29	Chris Bosio	.15
30	Steve Kiefer	.15
32	Chuck Crim	.15
34	Jay Aldrich	.15
37	Dan Plesac	.15
40	Mike Birkbeck	.15
42	Tom Trebelhorn	.15
43	Dave Stapleton	.15
45	Rob Deer	.15
46	Bill Wegman	.15
49	Ted Higuera	.15
---	Coaches Card (Andy Etchebarren, Larry Haney, Chuck Hartenstein, Dave Hilton, Tony Muser)	.15
---	Team Photo	.15

1989 Milwaukee Brewers Police

30 Terry Francona OF
Iola; Manawa & Marion Police Depts.
and Wisconsin Power and Light
present the 1989
Milwaukee Brewers

The Milwaukee Brewers, in conjunction with various corporate and civic sponsors, issued a 30-card police set in 1989, the eighth consecutive police set issued by the club. Some 95 law enforcement agencies in Wisconsin participated in the program, each releasing their own version of the same set. The cards measure 2-13/16" x 4-1/8" and feature full-color action photos with the player's name, uniform number and position below, along with the sponsoring agencies. The backs include the traditional safety messages. The cards were distributed in complete sets at a stadium promotion and also handed out individually over the course of the summer by uniformed police officers in various Wisconsin cities and counties.

		NM/M
Complete Set (30):		5.00
Common Player:		.15
1	Gary Sheffield	2.00
4	Paul Molitor	1.50
5	B.J. Surhoff	.15
6	Bill Spiers	.15
7	Dale Sveum	.15
9	Greg Brock	.15
14	Gus Polidor	.15
16	Mike Felder	.15
17	Jim Gantner	.15
19	Robin Yount	1.50
20	Juan Nieves	.15
22	Charlie O'Brien	.15
23	Joey Meyer	.15
25	Dave Engle	.15
26	Glenn Braggs	.15
27	Paul Mirabella	.15
29	Chris Bosio	.15
30	Terry Francona	.15
32	Chuck Crim	.15
37	Dan Plesac	.15
40	Mike Birkbeck	.15
41	Mark Knudson	.15
42	Tom Trebelhorn	.15
45	Rob Deer	.15
46	Bill Wegman	.15
48	Bryan Clutterbuck	.15
49	Teddy Higuera	.15
---	Team Photo	.15
---	Coaching Staff	.15

Yearbook Cards

4
Paul Molitor
Infielder

Included in the team's special 20th anniversary edition yearbook was a set of 18 player cards stapled into the center of the book. Printed on a 16-1/2" x 11" cardboard sheet, there are nine cards per page, perforated on two, three or four sides, depending on sheet position. Cards have a pale yellow background. A blue and bright yellow 20th Anniversary team logo appears in the lower-right corner with the player's uniform number, name and position stacked at left in black. All but one of the photos are game-action shots. Backs are printed in black and include complete major and minor league stats. Cards are checklisted here by uniform number.

		NM/M
Complete Set, Singles (18):		8.00
Complete Yearbook:		10.00
Common Player:		.25
1	Gary Sheffield	2.00
4	Paul Molitor	4.00
5	B.J. Surhoff	.25
7	Dale Sveum	.25
9	Greg Brock	.25
17	Jim Gantner	.25
19	Robin Yount	4.00
20	Juan Nieves	.25
26	Glenn Braggs	.25
29	Chris Bosio	.25
32	Chuck Crim	.25
37	Dan Plesac	.25
38	Don August	.25
40	Mike Birkbeck	.25
42	Tom Trebelhorn	.25
45	Rob Deer	.25
46	Bill Wegman	.25
49	Teddy Higuera	.25

1990 Milwaukee Brewers Police

Blue borders are featured on the front of the 1990 Brewer Police/Fire Safety set. The cards are numbered according to uniform number and public service messages appear on the card backs.

4
Paul Molitor IF
The Chilton Police Department
Chilton Food Mart & Valley Bank-Chilton
present the 1990
Milwaukee Brewers

The 2-13/16" x 4-1/8" cards were distributed by various Wisconsin police departments.

		NM/M
Complete Set (30):		4.00
Common Player:		.15
2	Eddie Diaz	.15
4	Paul Molitor	1.50
6	B.J. Surhoff	.15
7	Bill Spiers	.15
7	Dale Sveum	.15
9	Greg Brock	.15
11	Gary Sheffield	.75
14	Gus Polidor	.15
16	Mike Felder	.15
17	Jim Gantner	.15
19	Robin Yount	1.50
22	Charlie O'Brien	.15
23	Greg Vaughn	.15
26	Glenn Braggs	.15
27	Paul Mirabella	.15
28	Tom Filer	.15
29	Chris Bosio	.15
31	Jaime Navarro	.15
32	Chuck Crim	.15
34	Billy Bates	.15
36	Tony Fossas	.15
37	Dan Plesac	.15
38	Don August	.15
39	Dave Parker	.15
41	Mark Knudson	.15
42	Tom Trebelhorn	.15
45	Rob Deer	.15
49	Ted Higuera	.15
---	Coaches (Don Baylor, Ray Burris, Duffy Dyer, Larry Haney, Andy Etchebarren)	.15
---	Team photo/roster card	.15

Yearbook Cards

Ted Higuera
P 49

Brewers

Printed on cardboard stock and stapled into the center of the team's 1990 yearbook was a set of 18 cards. The sheet is 16-1/2" x 11" overall. Each page has nine 2-5/8" x 3-1/2" cards perforated on two, three or four sides, depending on sheet position. Above-left and below-right of the color player poses are yellow triangles with blue pinstripes. The team's scrip logo is in the same team colors in the lower-left of the photo. The player's name, position abbreviation and uniform number are in yellow in the upper-right corner. The backs are printed in blue and include complete major and minor league stats. The checklist is presented here by uniform number.

		NM/M
Complete Set, Singles (18):		8.00
Complete Yearbook:		10.00
Common Player:		.25
4	Paul Molitor	4.00
6	B.J. Surhoff	.25
7	Bill Spiers	.25
7	Dale Sveum	.25
9	Greg Brock	.25
17	Jim Gantner	.25
19	Robin Yount	4.00
26	Glenn Braggs	.25

		NM/M
28	Tom Filer	.25
29	Chris Bosio	.25
31	Jaime Navarro	.25
32	Chuck Crim	.25
37	Dan Plesac	.25
38	Don August	.25
39	Dave Parker	.25
42	Tom Trebelhorn	.25
45	Rob Deer	.25
49	Ted Higuera	.25

1991 Milwaukee Brewers Police

JIM GANTNER • IF

Presented by
The Elm Grove Police Department
& Kartavus Landscape Mgmt., Inc. **1991**

The Milwaukee Brewers are featured on a 1991 team set sponsored by several Milwaukee area police departments and Delicious Brand Cookies and Crackers. The 30-card set is in full color with light gray border on the front and the backs are unnumbered and contain safety tips from the players.

		NM/M
Complete Set (30):		4.00
Common Player:		.25
(1)	Robin Yount	1.50
(2)	Rick Dempsey	.25
(3)	Jamie Navarro	.25
(4)	Darryl Hamilton	.25
(5)	Bill Spiers	.25
(6)	Dante Bichette	.25
(7)	Dan Plesac	.25
(8)	Don August	.25
(9)	Willie Randolph	.25
(10)	Franklin Stubbs	.25
(11)	Julio Machado	.25
(12)	Greg Vaughn	.25
(13)	Chris Bosio	.25
(14)	Mark Knudson	.25
(15)	Paul Molitor	1.50
(16)	Kevin Brown	.25
(17)	Ron Robinson	.25
(18)	Bill Wegman	.25
(19)	Teddy Higuera	.25
(20)	Mark Lee	.25
(21)	B.J. Surhoff	.25
(22)	Candy Maldonado	.25
(23)	Chuck Crim	.25
(24)	Dale Sveum	.25
(25)	Jim Gantner	.25
(26)	Greg Brock	.25
(27)	Gary Sheffield	.75
(28)	Edwin Nunez	.25
(29)	Tom Trebelhorn	.25
(30)	Coaches (Don Baylor, Ray Burris, Duffy Dyer, Andy Etchebarren, Larry Haney, Fred Stanley)	.25

1992 Milwaukee Brewers Police

BREWERS '92

DANTE BICHETTE • OF

Presented by
The Waukesha Police Department
& Waukesha Sports Cards

The 1992 Milwaukee Brewers Police set consists of 30-cards in the standard, 2-1/2" x 3-1/2" format. The yellow-bordered cards were produced by Delicious Brand Cookies and Crackers and distributed by local Wisconsin police departments in co-operation with the Brewers.

		NM/M
Complete Set (30):		4.00
Common Player:		.15
(1)	Andy Allanson	.15
(2)	James Austin	.15

		NM/M
(3)	Dante Bichette	.15
(4)	Ricky Bones	.15
(5)	Chris Bosio	.15
(6)	Mike Fetters	.15
(7)	Scott Fletcher	.15
(8)	Jim Gantner	.15
(9)	Phil Garner	.15
(10)	Darryl Hamilton	.15
(11)	Doug Henry	.15
(12)	Teddy Higuera	.15
(13)	Pat Listach	.15
(14)	Jamie Navarro	.15
(15)	Edwin Nunez	.15
(16)	Tim McIntosh	.15
(17)	Paul Molitor	1.50
(18)	Jesse Orosco	.15
(19)	Dan Plesac	.15
(20)	Ron Robinson	.15
(21)	Bruce Ruffin	.15
(22)	Kevin Seitzer	.15
(23)	Bill Spiers	.15
(24)	Franklin Stubbs	.15
(25)	William Suero	.15
(26)	B.J. Surhoff	.15
(27)	Greg Vaughn	.15
(28)	Bill Wegman	.15
(29)	Robin Yount	1.50
(30)	Coaches (Bill Castro, Duffy Dyer, Mike Easler, Tim Foli, Don Rowe)	.15

1993 Milwaukee Brewers Police

DICKIE THON • IF

Presented by
Brown County Sheriff's Dept.

The 1993 Milwaukee Brewers Police set included 30 cards with a graduated blue border. The left side has a '93 Brewers flag along the border in yellow, with the player's name in the upper right corner in white. The backs, which are white with black print, feature quotes from the player pictured. The cards are not numbered and the set also includes a card commemorating Robin Yount's 3,000th hit.

		NM/M
Complete Set (30):		3.00
Common Player:		.15
(1)	Bernie Brewer (Mascot)	.15
(2)	Phil Garner	.15
(3)	Yount's 3,000th Hit (Robin Yount)	1.00
(4)	Mark Kiefer	.15
(5)	Bill Spiers	.15
(6)	John Jaha	.15
(7)	Bill Wegman	.15
(8)	Ted Higuera	.15
(9)	Greg Vaughn	.15
(10)	Kevin Reimer	.15
(11)	Doug Henry	.15
(12)	William Suero	.15
(13)	Dave Nilsson	.15
(14)	James Austin	.15
(15)	Mike Fetters	.15
(16)	Ricky Bones	.15
(17)	Jaime Navarro	.15
(18)	Jesse Orosco	.15
(19)	Darryl Hamilton	.15
(20)	Cal Eldred	.15
(21)	Tim McIntosh	.15
(22)	Dickie Thon	.15
(23)	Graeme Lloyd	.15
(24)	Pat Listach	.15
(25)	Joe Kmak	.15
(26)	Alex Diaz	.15
(27)	Robin Yount	1.50
(28)	Tom Brunansky	.15
(29)	B.J. Surhoff	.15
(30)	Bill Doran	.15

1994 Milwaukee Brewers Police

All youngsters attending the April 23 Brewers game received this 30-card set sponsored by Pick'n Save supermarkets and Snickers candy bar, whose logos appear on both front and back. Cards featured posed player photos in their new 25th anniversary uniforms, against a lime green fabric backdrop or game action photos. Two green bars surround the

TURNER WARD 27

'94 BREWERS
Presented by
The Milwaukee Police Department

photos. Navy blue bars above and below the photo have the player's name, team and uniform number. A 25th anniversary logo is at lower-right. The name of one of the many Wisconsin police agencies which distributed the cards is printed in black at bottom. Backs are printed in black-on-white and feature full major and minor league stats. The traditional safety message or anti-drug warning is not included on this issue. Cards are checklisted here by uniform number. Cards are in the 2-1/2" x 3-1/2" format.

		NM/M
Complete Set (30):		3.00
Common Player:		.25
2	Jose Valentin	.25
3	Phil Garner	.25
8	B.J. Surhoff	.25
9	Jody Reed	.25
9	Bill Spiers	.25
11	Dave Nilsson	.25
12	Brian Harper	.25
16	Pat Listach	.25
18	Tom Brunansky	.25
20	Kevin Seitzer	.25
21	Cal Eldred	.25
23	Greg Vaughn	.25
24	Darryl Hamilton	.25
25	Ricky Bones	.25
27	Turner Ward	.25
28	Doug Henry	.25
29	Jeff Bronkey	.25
30	Matt Mieske	.25
31	Jaime Navarro	.25
32	John Jaha	.25
36	Mike Fetters	.25
37	Graeme Lloyd	.25
39	Bob Scanlan	.25
40	Mike Ignasiak	.25
43	Mark Kiefer	.25
46	Bill Wegman	.25
47	Jesse Orosco	.25
49	Teddy Higuera	.25
63	Jeff D'Amico, Kelly Wunsch	.25
---	Bernie Brewer (Mascot)	.25

1995 Milwaukee Brewers Police

Presented by
The Milwaukee Police Department

Some of the finest portrait photos seen on modern baseball cards are combined with game-action shots in the annual Brewers police set, sponsored by Old Fashioned Foods (makers of Squeeze Cheese). The 2-1/2" x 3-1/2" cards feature forest green borders with the player and team name, and uniform number in white on a deep blue band beneath. A tan panel at bottom has the name of the Milwaukee P.D. Many of the cards are presented in horizontal format. Backs are in black-and-white and include career stats and a safety tip. Cards are checklisted here according to uniform number.

		NM/M
Complete Set (33):		3.00
Common Player:		.25
1	Fernando Vina	.25
2	Jose Valentin	.25
3	Phil Garner	.25
8	B.J. Surhoff	.25
9	Joe Oliver	.25

1996 Milwaukee Brewers Police

Dave Nilsson

Milwaukee Brewers
Baseball Club

Metallic gold borders are featured on the Brewers' 14th annual safety set issued June 16 as a stadium giveaway. Cards are a mix of horizontal and vertical design with a large color photo at left. In a gold strip at right is the team logotype, player name, position and uniform number. Backs are in black-and-white with a safety message from the pictured player and the team logo. No sponsoring company or police agency is mentioned on the card. A special card in the set illustrates the proposed new Brewers stadium. Cards are listed here by uniform number.

		NM/M
Complete Set (30):		3.00
Common Player:		.15
1	Fernando Vina	.15
2	Jose Valentin	.15
3	Phil Garner	.15
4	Pat Listach	.15
8	Mark Loretta	.15
14	Dave Nilsson	.15
15	David Hulse	.15
16	Jesse Levis	.15
20	Kevin Seitzer	.15
21	Cal Eldred	.15
22	Mike Matheny	.15
23	Greg Vaughn	.15
24	Chuckie Carr	.15
25	Ricky Bones	.15
26	Jeff Cirillo	.15
27	Turner Ward	.15
30	Matt Mieske	.15
32	John Jaha	.15
36	Mike Fetters	.15
37	Graeme Lloyd	.15
38	Angel Miranda	.15
40	Ben McDonald	.15
42	Scott Karl	.15
44	Marshall Boze	.15
49	Mike Potts	.15
50	Steve Sparks	.15
51	Ramon Garcia	.15
52	Kevin Wickander	.15
---	Brewers Coaches	.15
---	Miller Park	.15

1997 Milwaukee Brewers Police

One of the more attractive safety sets of recent years, the 1997 Brewers team issue features action photos of each player in the stan-

---

(center-right column, "Turner Ward" card listing)

		NM/M
10	Brewers Coaches (Bill Castro, Duffy Dyer, Tim Foli, Lamar Johnson, Don Rowe)	.25
11	Dave Nilsson	.25
12	Derrick May	.25
15	Dave Hulse	.25
16	Pat Listach	.25
20	Kevin Seitzer	.25
21	Cal Eldred	.25
22	Mike Matheny, Jeff Cirillo	.25
23	Greg Vaughn	.25
24	Darryl Hamilton	.25
25	Ricky Bones	.25
27	Turner Ward	.25
29	Jeff Bronkey	.25
30	Matt Mieske	.25
32	John Jaha	.25
36	Mike Fetters	.25
37	Graeme Lloyd	.25
38	Angel Miranda	.25
39	Bob Scanlan	.25
40	Michael Ignasiak	.25
41	Jose Mercedes, Mark Kiefer	.25
42	Scott Karl, Al Reyes, Steve Sparks	.25
46	Bill Wegman	.25
---	Bob Uecker (Announcer)	1.50
---	Charlie the Mouse (Sponsor)	.05
---	Iris the Cow (Sponsor)	.05
---	Squeezasaurus (Sponsor)	.05
---	Squeeze Cheese (Coupon)	.05

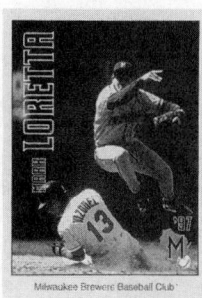

Milwaukee Brewers Baseball Club

dard 2-1/2" x 3-1/2" format. Down one side of the photo is the player's name in outline type. A team logo is at bottom-right. Backs are in black-and-white with a few bits of personal data and a cartoon figure presenting a safety tip for youngsters. The set was distributed to children attending the May 30 game at County Stadium. The checklist here is arranged by uniform number.

		NM/M
Complete Set (30):		3.00
Common Player:		.25
1	Fernando Vina	.25
2	Jose Valentin	.25
3	Phil Garner	.25
8	Mark Loretta	.25
9	Tim Unroe	.25
10	Marc Newfield	.25
13	Jeff D'Amico	.25
14	Dave Nillson	.25
15	Jeff Huson	.25
16	Jesse Levis	.25
20	Jeromy Burnitz	.50
21	Cal Eldred	.25
22	Mike Matheny	.25
24	Chuckie Carr	.25
25	Angel Miranda	.25
26	Jeff Cirillo	.25
27	Bob Wickman	.25
29	Gerald Williams	.25
30	Matt Mieske	.25
32	John Jaha	.25
36	Mike Fetters	.25
39	Bryce Florie	.25
40	Ben McDonald	.25
41	Jose Mercedes	.25
42a	Scott Karl	.25
42b	Jackie Robinson (Tribute)	2.00
43	Doug Jones	.25
49	Ron Villone	.25
51	Eddy Diaz	.25
---	Coaches (Chris Bando, Bill Castro, Jim Gantner, Lamar Johnson, Don Rowe)	.25

1998 Milwaukee Brewers Diamond Celebration

MICHAEL HARRISON
COMMUNITY SERVICE AWARD

Persons attending a January 30 banquet in Milwaukee received a set of these cards highlighting the team's award winners for 1997. The set was sponsored by the Milwaukee Metropolitan Association of Commerce; their logo appears on the back. Fronts have color photos centered on a white background. The players are pictured in action, the staff in portraits. "Diamond Celebration" and the name are in script. The banquet date and specific honor also appear on front. Backs are in black-and-white with season highlights. The unnumbered cards are checklisted here alphabetically.

		NM/M
Complete Set (10):		15.00
Common Card:		.50
(1)	Hank Aaron	6.00
(2)	Jeromy Burnitz	2.00
(3)	Jeff Cirillo	2.00

(4)	Dick Hackett (Staff)	.50
(5)	Bill Haig (Staff)	.50
(6)	John Jaha	1.00
(7)	Doug Jones (MV Pitcher)	1.00
(8)	Doug Jones (MVP)	1.00
(9)	Bob Uecker (MC)	3.00
(10)	Bob Wickman	1.00

Police

For 1998, the Brewers cable television outlet sponsored the team's annual safety set, given away to kids at the June 21 game. Card fronts have player action photos vignetted on a close-up baseball background. Team and sponsor logos appear in opposite corners. Backs have a few bits of player data, a safety tip, sponsor's logo and uniform number.

		NM/M
Complete Set (30):		3.00
Common Player:		.25
1	Fernando Vina	.25
2	Jose Valentin	.25
3	Phil Garner	.25
7	Geoff Jenkins	.60
7	Dave Nillson	.25
8	Mark Loretta	.25
9	Marquis Grissom	.25
10	Marc Newfield	.25
13	Jeff D'Amico	.25
14	Jeff Juden	.25
16	Jesse Levis	.25
20	Jeromy Burnitz	.50
21	Cal Eldred	.25
22	Mike Matheny	.25
24	Darrin Jackson	.25
26	Jeff Cirillo	.25
27	Bob Wickman	.25
28	Mike Myers	.25
30	Bob Hamelin	.25
32	John Jaha	.25
33/39	Bobby Hughes, Eric Owens	.25
37	Steve Woodard	.25
40	Chad Fox	.25
41	Jose Mercedes	.25
42	Scott Karl	.25
43	Doug Jones	.25
46	Paul Wagner	.25
47	Al Reyes	.25
48/30	Brad Woodall, Bronswell Patrick	.25
---	Coaches (Chris Bando, Bill Castro, Lamar Johnson, Doug Mansolino, Don Rowe, Joel Youngblood)	.25

1999 Milwaukee Brewers Diamond Celebration

Robin Yount
Hall of Famer

Persons attending a January 22 banquet in Milwaukee received a set of these cards highlighting the team's award winners for 1997. The set was sponsored by the Milwaukee Metropolitan Association of Commerce, whose logo appears on the back. Fronts have color photos. The players are pictured in action, the staff in portraits. "Diamond Celebration" and team logo are at left. The specific honor also appears on front. Backs are in

black-and-white with season highlights. The unnumbered cards are checklisted here alphabetically.

		NM/M
Complete Set (11):		15.00
Common Player:		.50
(1)	Bob Betts (P.A. Announcer)	.50
(2)	Jeromy Burnitz (HR Champ)	2.00
(3)	Jeromy Burnitz (MVP)	2.00
(4)	Jeff Cirillo	1.00
(5)	Peter Gammons (Writer)	.50
(6)	Mark Loretta (Manager's award.)	1.00
(7)	Mark Loretta (Community service.)	1.00
(8)	Bud Selig (Owner)	.50
(9)	Bob Wickman	1.00
(10)	Steve Woodard	1.00
(11)	Robin Yount	6.00

Police

Presented by:
Midwest Sports Channel
and The Milwaukee Brewers

The regional cable station which carries Brewers games was the principal sponsor of the team's safety set given to fans on May 29. Cards feature color player poses against a sepia background showing Milwaukee County Stadium throughout the course of its 46-year history. Sponsor and team logos are in various corners on front along with the player's name and uniform number. Backs have a few bits of personal data, a safety message and an ad from the sponsor. Cards are checklisted here in order of uniform number.

		NM/M
Complete Set (30):		3.00
Common Player:		.25
1	Fernando Vina	.25
2	Jose Valentin	.25
3	Phil Garner	.25
5	Geoff Jenkins	.60
7	Sean Berry	.25
8	Mark Loretta	.25
9	Marquis Grissom	.25
14	David Nillson	.25
16	Lou Collier	.25
20	Jeromy Burnitz	.25
21	Cal Eldred	.25
22/48	Rich Becker, Steve Falteisek	.25
23	Brian Banks	.25
24	Alex Ochoa	.25
25	Jim Abbott	.35
26	Jeff Cirillo	.25
27	Bob Wickman	.25
28	Mike Myers	.25
31	Bobby Hughes	.25
37	Steve Woodard	.25
38	Eric Plunk	.25
40	Chad Fox	.25
42	Scott Karl	.25
46	Bill Pulsipher	.25
47	Al Reyes	.25
49	David Weathers	.25
52	Rafael Roque	.25
58	Valerio de los Santos	.25
---	Coaches (Bill Campbell, Bill Castro, Ron Jackson, Jim Lefebvre, Doug Mansolino, Bob Melvin)	.25
---	Milwaukee County Stadium	.25

2000 Milwaukee Brewers Diamond Celebration

Winners of various annual awards by the Milwaukee Brewers are featured in this standard-size card set which was issued at the team's Diamond Celebration dinner on January 21. A large portrait photo is featured along the left or right edge on front. Down the other side is player identification and the name of the

26
Jeff Cirillo
Brewers
January 21 · 2000

award won. Backs have season highlights. The unnumbered cards are checklisted here alphabetically.

		NM/M
Complete Set (10):		15.00
Common Player:		.50
(1)	Kevin Barker	1.50
(2)	Ron Belliard	1.50
(3)	Jeromy Burnitz (HR Champ)	2.50
(4)	Jeromy Burnitz (MVP)	2.50
(5)	Jeff Cirillo	1.50
(6)	Marquis Grissom	1.50
(7)	Geoff Jenkins	3.00
(8)	Tim Kurkjian	.50
(9)	Dean Taylor, Davey Lopes	.50
(10)	Bob Wickman	.50

Police

Presented by:
Midwest Sports Channel and The Milwaukee Brewers

In its third season of sponsoring the team's safety set, the Brewers' cable franchisee offered the cards to the first 10,000 youngsters at a May promotional game. Other sets were distributed by police agencies. Card fronts have the players posed in their dark blue jerseys against a black background lit by a colorful Milwaukee Brewers neon sign. In a lower corner are the sponsor's logo, player name and uniform number. A Time-Warner Cable logo is in the white border at bottom. Backs have player identification and a safety message. Cards are checklisted here by uniform number.

		NM/M
Complete Set (30):		3.00
Common Player:		.25
00	Curtis Leskanic	.25
1	Luis Lopez	.25
2	Tyler Houston	.25
5	Geoff Jenkins	.50
7	Sean Berry	.25
8	Mark Loretta	.25
9	Marquis Grissom	.25
10	Ron Belliard	.25
12	Henry Blanco	.25
14	Charlie Hayes	.25
18	Jose Hernandez	.25
20	Jeromy Burnitz	.45
22	Kevin Barker	.25
24	James Mouton	.25
27	Bob Wickman	.25
28	Valerio de los Santos	.25
30	Davey Lopes	.25
31	Everett Stull	.25
33	Lyle Mouton	.25
37	Steve Woodard	.25
40	Jaime Navarro	.25
41	Matt Williams	.25
47	Jason Bere	.25
49	David Weathers	.25
51	Jimmy Haynes	.25
53	Juan Acevedo	.25
59	John Snyder	.25
88	Jim Bruske	.25
---	Coaches (Jerry Royster, Rod Carew, Bill Castro, Bob Apodaca, Chris Speier, Gary Allenson)	.25
---	Matt Vasgersian, Bill Schroeder (Broadcasters)	.25

2000 Milwaukee Journal Sentinel 1970s Brewers

ALL-DECADE TEAM
1970's

MILWAUKEE
JOURNAL SENTINEL

As selected by fan balloting, an All-Decade team of 1970s Milwaukee Brewers is honored on this set of cards given to fans at a promotional game in July. The standard 2-1/2" x 3-1/2" cards have borderless game-action photos on front with a gold-foil diamond naming the player, his position and uniform number. Backs have a team logo, player personal data, stats and career highlights. The unnumbered cards are checklisted here in alphabetical order.

		NM/M
Complete Set (13):		12.00
Common Player:		.50
(1)	Hank Aaron	6.00
(2)	George Bamberger	.50
(3)	Mike Caldwell	.50
(4)	Cecil Cooper	.75
(5)	Tommy Harper	.50
(6)	Larry Hisle	.50
(7)	Sixto Lezcano	.50
(8)	Don Money	.50
(9)	Charlie Moore	.50
(10)	Ken Sanders	.50
(11)	Jim Slaton	.50
(12)	Gorman Thomas	.50
(13)	Robin Yount	4.00

1980s Brewers

ALL-DECADE TEAM
1980's

MILWAUKEE
JOURNAL SENTINEL

As selected by fan balloting, an All-Decade team of 1980s Milwaukee Brewers is honored on this set of cards given to fans at a promotional game August 11. The standard 2-1/2" x 3-1/2" cards have game-action photos on front with a gold-foil diamond naming the player, his position and uniform number. The newspaper sponsor's logo is at bottom. Backs have a team logo, player personal data, stats and career highlights. The unnumbered cards are checklisted here in alphabetical order.

		NM/M
Complete Set (13):		12.00
Common Player:		.50
(1)	Mike Caldwell	.50
(2)	Cecil Cooper	.50
(3)	Rollie Fingers	.75
(4)	Jim Gantner	.50
(5)	Harvey Kuenn	.50
(6)	Paul Molitor (DH)	3.00
(7)	Paul Molitor (3B)	3.00
(8)	Ben Oglivie	.50
(9)	Ted Simmons	.50
(10)	Gorman Thomas	.50
(11)	Pete Vuckovich	.50
(12)	Robin Yount (OF)	3.00
(13)	Robin Yount (SS)	3.00

1990s Brewers

As selected by fan balloting, an All-Decade team of 1990s Milwaukee Brewers is honored on this

set of cards given to fans at a promotional game September 8. The standard 2-1/2" x 3-1/2" cards have game-action photos on front with a gold-foil diamond naming the player, his position and uniform number. The newspaper sponsor's logo is at bottom. Backs have a team logo, player personal data, stats and career highlights. The unnumbered cards are checklisted here in alphabetical order.

		NM/M
Complete Set (13):		9.00
Common Player:		.50
(1)	Chris Bosio	.50
(2)	Jeromy Burnitz	1.00
(3)	Jeff Cirillo	.50
(4)	Phil Garner	.50
(5)	John Jaha	.50
(6)	Geoff Jenkins	2.00
(7)	David Nillson	.50
(8)	B.J. Surhoff	.50
(9)	Jose Valentin	.50
(10)	Fernando Vina	.50
(11)	Bill Wegman	.50
(12)	Bob Wickman	.50
(13)	Robin Yount	3.00

2001 Milwaukee Brewers Diamond Celebration

29

MICHAEL HARRISON
COMMUNITY SERVICE AWARD
ROD CAREW

Winners of various annual awards by the Milwaukee Brewers are featured in this standard-size card set which was issued at the team's Diamond Celebration dinner on January 19. Fronts have a large portrait photo along the left or right edge side. Down the other side is player identification and the name of the award won. Backs have season highlights and the Miller Park logo. The unnumbered cards are checklisted here alphabetically.

		NM/M
Complete Set (9):		20.00
Common Player:		2.00
(1)	Rod Carew (Community Service Award)	3.00
(2)	Jeff D'Amico (Most Valuable Pitcher)	2.00
(3)	Geoff Jenkins (Harvey Kuenn Award)	2.50
(4)	Geoff Jenkins (Home Run Leader)	2.50
(5)	Geoff Jenkins (MVP)	2.50
(6)	Tommy Lasorda/SP (Bud Selig Award)	5.00
(7)	Curtis Leskanic (Newcomer of the Year)	2.00
(8)	Richie Sexson (Manager's Award)	2.00
(9)	Ben Sheets (Minor League Player/Year)	4.00

2001 Milwaukee Brewers Police

2
Tyler Houston
INFIELDER

FOX
SPORTS NET

Presented by:
FOX SPORTS NET and THE MILWAUKEE BREWERS

This team set was given to youngsters attending a special promotional game. The 2-1/2" x 3-1/2" cards have close-up player portraits over a large logo in one of several colors. Also appearing in the photo area are Miller Park and Fox Sports Net logos and the player's name, position and uniform number. There is a white border, at the bottom of which is sponsor credits. Backs have a safety or character-building message from the player. Sets were also distributed locally by more than six dozen Wisconsin police agencies.

		NM/M
Complete Set (30):		4.00
Common Player:		.25
1	Luis Lopez	.25
5	Tyler Houston	.25
5	Geoff Jenkins	.50
7	Tony Fernandez	.25
8	Mark Loretta	.25
10	Ronnie Belliard	.25
11	Richie Sexson	.50
12	Henry Blanco	.25
13	Jeff D'Amico	.25
15	Ben Sheets	.50
18	Jose Hernandez	.25
20	Jeromy Burnitz	.50
21	Jamey Wright	.25
22	Devon White	.35
23	Mark Leiter	.25
24	James Mouton	.25
25	Raul Casanova	.25
30	Davey Lopes	.25
31	Paul Rigdon	.25
33	Will Cunnane	.25
39	Angel Echevarria	.25
40	Chad Fox	.25
41	Jeffrey Hammonds	.25
46	Ray King	.25
48	Mike DeJean	.25
49	David Weathers	.25
51	Jimmy Haynes	.25
00	Curtis Leskanic	.25
---	Brewers Coaches (Bob Apodaca, Gary Allenson, Rod Carew, Bill Castro, Jerry Royster, Luis Salazar)	.25
---	Bill Schroeder, Matt Vasgersian	.25

2002 Milwaukee Brewers Diamond Celebration

Winners of various annual awards by the Milwaukee Brewers are featured in this 2-1/2" x 3-1/2" card set which was issued at the team's Diamond Celebration dinner on January 25. Fronts have a photo set against a solid colored background on which the last name is ghosted vertically. An identification strip is vertically at right, including the name of the award won. Backs have season highlights in black-and-white. The unnumbered cards are checklisted here alphabetically.

		NM/M
Complete Set (10):		18.00
Common Player:		2.00
(1)	Bill Castro (Unsung Hero)	2.00
(2)	Cecil Cooper (Walk of Fame)	2.00
(3)	Chad Fox (Most Valuable Pitcher)	2.50
(4)	Ray King (Manager's Award)	2.00
(5)	Ray King (Community Service Award)	2.00
(6)	Mark Loretta (Harvey Kuenn Award)	2.50
(7)	Allan H. (Bud) Selig (Walk of Fame)	2.50
(8)	Richie Sexson (Home Run Champion)	3.00
(9)	Richie Sexson (MVP)	3.00
(10)	Ben Sheets (Newcomer of the Year)	3.00

2002 Milwaukee Brewers Police

Fans at the May 30 Brewers game received this team set of 2-1/2" x 3-1/2" safety cards. Fronts have action photos with a black-and-white photo of an architectural detail of Miller Park in the top-left corner. Backs repeat the Miller Park photo and have a safety message from the player. Cards are checklisted here by uniform number.

		NM/M
Complete Set (30):		3.00
Common Player:		.25
00	Curtis Leskanic	.25
1	Luis Lopez	.25
2	Tyler Houston	.25
5	Geoff Jenkins	.50
7	Eric Young	.25
8	Mark Loretta	.25
9	Paul Bako	.25
10	Ron Belliard	.25
11	Richie Sexson	.50
12	Matt Stairs	.35
15	Ben Sheets	.35
16	Lenny Harris	.25
18	Jose Hernandez	.25
21	Jamey Wright	.25
22	Alex Sanchez	.25
23	Alex Ochoa	.25
25	Raul Casanova	.25
31	Paul Rigdon	.25
32	Nick Neugebauer	.25
37	Ruben Quevedo	.25
29	Glendon Rusch	.25
40	Chad Fox	.25
41	Jeffrey Hammonds	.25
46	Ray King	.25
48	Mike Buddie	.25
48	Mike DeJean	.25
49	Jose Cabrera	.25
51	Luis Vizcaino	.25
52	Nelson Figueroa	.25
95	Takahito Nomura	.25

2003 Milwaukee Brewers Diamond Celebration

Winners of various annual awards by the Milwaukee Brewers are featured in this 3" x 5" card set which was issued at the team's Diamond Celebration dinner, January 31, one cello-wrapped set per place setting. Fronts have a black-and-sepia photo with a black frameline. A dinner logo is at bottom with the honoree's name, award and uniform number (for players) in white. Backs have season highlights in black and red. Production was reported as 1,000 sets. The unnumbered cards are checklisted here alphabetically.

		NM/M
Complete Set (10):		15.00
Common Card:		1.00
(1)	Harry Dalton (Walk of Fame)	1.00
(2)	Mike DeJean (Most Valuable Pitcher)	1.50
(3)	Jeffrey Hammonds (Community Service Award)	2.00
(4)	Ernie Harwell (Bud Selig Award)	1.50
(5)	Alex Sanchez (Harvey Kuenn Award)	1.50
(6)	Richie Sexson (Home Run Champion)	5.00
(7)	Bob Uecker (Walk of Fame)	3.00
(8)	Luis Vizcaino (Newcomer of the Year)	2.00
(9)	Eric Young (Unsung Hero Award)	2.00
(10)	Doug Melvin, Ned Yost, Ulice Payne, Jr. (Dawning of a New Era)	1.00

2003 Milwaukee Brewers Safety

This team set was a stadium giveaway to the first 10,000 youngsters attending the April 19 game. The 2-1/2" x 3-1/2" cards have neck-to-cap color portraits on front, with player name, position and uniform number. Backs are in gold with a health or safety tip.

		NM/M
Complete Set (30):		3.00
Common Player:		.25
3	Ned Yost	.25
5	Geoff Jenkins	.50
6	Keith Ginter	.25
7	Eric Young	.25
9	Enrique Cruz	.25
10	Royce Clayton	.25
11	Richie Sexson	.50
12	Eddie Perez	.25
15	Ben Sheets	.35
18	Wes Helms	.25
20	Scott Podsednik	.50
21	Keith Osik	.25
23	Alex Sanchez	.25
24	John Vander Wal	.25
26	Wayne Franklin	.25
27	Brady Clark	.25
28	Valerio de los Santos	.25
29	Jason Conti	.25
33	Curtis Leskanic	.25
39	Glendon Rusch	.25
40	John Foster	.25
41	Jeffrey Hammonds	.25
46	Todd Ritchie	.25
47	Shane Nance	.25
48	Mike DeJean	.25
50	Matt Kinney	.25
51	Luis Vizcaino	.25
52	Matt Ford	.25
56	Jayson Durocher	.25
---	Brewers Coaches	

2004 Milwaukee Brewers Safety

This team set was a stadium giveaway to youngsters attending the May 1 game. The 2-1/2" x 3-1/2" cards have color portraits on front, with player name, position and uniform number. Backs have a health or safety tip.

		NM/M
Complete Set (30):		5.00
Common Player:		.25
1	Bernie Brewer (Mascot)	.25
2	Bill Hall	.25
3	Ned Yost	.25
4	Paul Molitor	2.00
5	Geoff Jenkins	.45
6	Keith Ginter	.25
11	Lyle Overbay	.50
12	Ben Grieve	.25
15	Ben Sheets	.50
18	Wes Helms	.25
20	Scott Podsednik	.50
21	Chad Moeller	.25
22	Trent Durrington	.25
27	Brady Clark	.25
29	Gary Bennett	.25
30	Craig Counsell	.25
33	Adrian Hernandez	.25
33	Wes Obermueller	.25
37	Junior Spivey	.25
39	Chris Capuano	.25
41	Dan Kolb	.25
43	Dave Burba	.25
48	Ben Ford	.25
49	Doug Davis	.25
50	Matt Kinney	.25
51	Luis Vizcaino	.25
55	Brooks Kieschnick	.25
57	Jeff Bennett	.25
---	Brewers Coaches	.25
---	Klements Sausages	.25

2005 Milwaukee Brewers Safety

This team set was a stadium giveaway to the first 10,000 youngsters attending the May 1 game. The 2-1/2" x 3-1/2" cards have color portraits on front, with player name, position and uniform number. Backs have a health or safety tip.

		NM/M
Complete Set (29):		3.00
Common Player:		.25
3	Ned Yost	.25
5	Geoff Jenkins	.50
6	Keith Ginter	.25
7	Eric Young	.25
9	Enrique Cruz	.25
10	Royce Clayton	.25
11	Richie Sexson	.50
12	Eddie Perez	.25
15	Ben Sheets	.35
18	Wes Helms	.25
20	Scott Podsednik	.50
21	Keith Osik	.25
23	Alex Sanchez	.25
24	John Vander Wal	.25
26	Wayne Franklin	.25
27	Brady Clark	.25
28	Valerio de los Santos	.25
29	Jason Conti	.25
33	Curtis Leskanic	.25
39	Glendon Rusch	.25
40	John Foster	.25
41	Jeffrey Hammonds	.25
46	Todd Ritchie	.25
47	Shane Nance	.25
48	Mike DeJean	.25
50	Matt Kinney	.25
51	Luis Vizcaino	.25
52	Matt Ford	.25
56	Jayson Durocher	.25
---	Brewers Coaches	

		NM/M
Complete Set (30):		6.00
Common Player:		.25
2	Bill Hall	.25
3	Ned Yost	.25
5	Geoff Jenkins	.50
6	Jeff Cirillo	.25
7	J.J. Hardy	.35
10	David Krynzel	.35
11	Lyle Overbay	.50
15	Ben Sheets	.50
18	Wes Helms	.25
24	Chad Moeller	.25
24	Chris Magruder	.25
27	Damian Miller	.25
27	Brady Clark	.25
31	Russell Branyan	.25
33	Wes Obermueller	.25
37	Junior Spivey	.25
38	Matt Wise	.25
39	Chris Capuano	.25
40	Ben Hendrickson	.25
41	Tommy Phelps	.25
45	Carlos Lee	.50
46	Mike Adams	.25
47	Jorge de la Rosa	.25
49	Doug Davis	.25
52	Ricky Bottalico	.25
53	Victor Santos	.25
57	Jeff Bennett	.25
58	Gary Glover	.25
59	Derrick Turnbow	.25
---	Coaches (Ned Yost, Butch Wynegar, Bill Castro, Marcus Hanel, Dave Nelson, Rich Dauer, Mike Maddux, Rich Donnelly)	.25

1983 Minnesota Twins Team Issue

The Minnesota Twins produced a 36-card set in 1983 to be sold at concession stands and through the mail. The full-color borderless cards measure 2-1/2" x 3-1/2" and displayed the player's uniform number on a white Twins jersey at the bottom of the card. The backs contain full career statistics.

		NM/M
Complete Set (36):		7.00
Common Player:		.25
1	John Castino	.25

2	Jim Eisenreich	.50
3	Ray Smith	.25
4	Scott Ullger	.25
5	Gary Gaetti	.75
6	Mickey Hatcher	.25
7	Bobby Mitchell	.25
8	Len Faedo	.25
9	Kent Hrbek	2.00
10	Tim Laudner	.25
11	Frank Viola	1.00
12	Bryan Oelkers	.25
13	Rick Lysander	.25
14	Dave Engle	.25
15	Len Whitehouse	.25
16	Pete Filson	.25
17	Tom Brunansky	.25
18	Randy Bush	.25
19	Brad Havens	.25
20	Al Williams	.25
21	Gary Ward	.25
22	Jack O'Connor	.25
23	Bobby Castillo	.25
24	Ron Washington	.25
25	Ron Davis	.25
26	Tom Kelly	.25
27	Billy Gardner	.25
28	Rick Stelmaszek	.25
29	Jim Lemon	.25
30	Johnny Podres	.25
31	Minnesota's Native Sons (Jim Eisenreich, Kent Hrbek, Tim Laudner)	.75
32	Twins' Catchers (Dave Engle, Tim Laudner)	.25
33	The Lumber Company (Tom Brunansky, Gary Gaetti, Kent Hrbek, Gary Ward)	.75
34	Twins' Coaches (Billy Gardner, Tom Kelly, Jim Lemon, Johnny Podres, Rick Stelmaszek)	.25
35	Team Photo	.40
36	Metrodome/Checklist	.25

1984 Minnesota Twins Team Issue

This team-issued set from the Minnesota Twins consists of 36 full-color, borderless cards, each measuring 2-1/2" x 3-1/2". As in the previous year, the player's uniform number appears on a white Twins jersey at the bottom of the card. The backs are printed in red and blue on white stock and include career stats. The set features several special cards, including one of Harmon Killebrew.

		NM/M
Complete Set (36):		7.50
Common Player:		.25
1	John Castino	.25
2	Jim Eisenreich	.35
3	Al Jimenez	.25
4	Dave Meier	.25
5	Gary Gaetti	.50
6	Mickey Hatcher	.25
7	Jeff Reed	.25
8	Tim Teufel	.25
9	Len Faedo	.25
10	Kent Hrbek	1.00
11	Tim Laudner	.25
12	Frank Viola	.50
13	Ken Schrom	.25
14	Larry Pashnick	.25
15	Dave Engle	.25
16	Keith Comstock	.25
17	Pete Filson	.25
18	Tom Brunansky	.25
19	Randy Bush	.25
20	Darrell Brown	.25
21	Al Williams	.25
22	Mike Walters	.25
23	John Butcher	.25
24	Bobby Castillo	.25
25	Ron Washington	.25
26	Ron Davis	.25
27	Tom Kelly	.25
28	Billy Gardner	.25
29	Rick Stelmaszek	.25
30	Jim Lemon	.25
31	Johnny Podres	.25
32	Mike Smithson	.25
33	Harmon Killebrew	4.00
34	Team Photo	.50
35	Logo Card	.25
36	Metrodome/Checklist	.25

1985 Minnesota Twins Team Issue

Similar in format to the previous two years, this 36-card team-issued set features full-color, borderless cards. The player's uniform number is again displayed on a white Twins jersey in the lower right corner, and the 1985 All-Star Game logo is shown in the lower left. The All-Star Game logo also appears on a special card in the set that lists on the back all Twins who have been selected for previous All-Star Games. The set was sold at ballpark concession stands and through the mail.

		NM/M
Complete Set (36):		15.00
Common Player:		.20
1	Alvaro Espinoza	.25
2	Roy Smalley	.25
3	Pedro Oliva	.75
4	Dave Meier	.25
5	Gary Gaetti	.50
6	Mickey Hatcher	.25
7	Jeff Reed	.25
8	Tim Teufel	.25
9	Mark Salas	.25
10	Kent Hrbek	1.00
11	Tim Laudner	.25
12	Frank Viola	.50
13	Ken Schrom	.25
14	Rick Lysander	.25
15	Dave Engle	.25
16	Andre David	.25
17	Len Whitehouse	.25
18	Pete Filson	.25
19	Tom Brunansky	.25
20	Randy Bush	.25
21	Greg Gagne	.75
22	John Butcher	.25
23	Mike Stenhouse	.25
24	Kirby Puckett	10.00
25	Tom Klawitter	.25
26	Curt Wardle	.25
27	Rich Yett	.25
28	Ron Washington	.25
29	Ron Davis	.25
30	Tom Kelly	.25
31	Billy Gardner	.25
32	Rick Stelmaszek	.25
33	Johnny Podres	.40
34	Mike Smithson	.25
35	1985 All-Star Game Logo Card	.25
36	Twins Logo/Checklist	.25

1986 Minnesota Twins Team Issue

This team-issued set contains 36 2-9/16" x 3-1/2" full-color cards. Fronts feature the Twins 25th anniversary logo and a jersey at the bottom of each card with the player's uniform number. All cards, except an action shot of Bert Blyleven, are posed photos, with a facsimile autograph on each. The set also includes a checklist and a team photo.

		NM/M
Complete Set (36):		6.00
Common Player:		.15

1	Chris Pittaro	.15
2	Steve Lombardozzi	.15
3	Roy Smalley	.15
4	Pedro Oliva	.50
5	Gary Gaetti	.30
6	Mickey Hatcher	.15
7	Jeff Reed	.15
8	Mark Salas	.15
9	Kent Hrbek	.50
10	Tim Laudner	.15
11	Frank Viola	.30
12	Dennis Burtt	.15
13	Alex Sanchez	.15
14	Roy Smith	.15
15	Billy Beane	.15
16	Pete Filson	.15
17	Tom Brunansky	.15
18	Randy Bush	.15
19	Frank Eufemia	.15
20	Mark Davidson	.15
21	Bert Blyleven	.40
22	Greg Gagne	.25
23	John Butcher	.15
24	Kirby Puckett	5.00
25	Bill Latham	.15
26	Ron Washington	.15
27	Ron Davis	.15
28	Tom Kelly	.15
29	Dick Such	.15
30	Rick Stelmaszek	.15
31	Ray Miller	.15
32	Wayne Terwilliger	.15
33	Mike Smithson	.15
34	Alvis Woods	.15
35	Team Photo	.15
36	Twins Logo/Checklist	.15

1987 Minnesota Twins Team Issue

The Minnesota Twins produced a 32-card set of 2-1/2" x 3-1/2" full-color baseball cards to be sold at the ballpark and through their souvenir catalog. The card fronts are borderless, containing only the player photo. The backs are printed in blue and red on white card stock and carry the player's personal data and career record. The Twins also produced a post card set that was similar in design to the standard-size card set, but utilized different photos.

		NM/M
Complete Set (33):		12.50
Common Player:		.25
1	Steve Lombardozzi	.25
2	Roy Smalley	.25
3	Pedro Oliva	.50
4	Greg Gagne	.25
5	Gary Gaetti	.30
6	Tom Kelly	.25
7	Tom Nieto	.25
8	Mark Salas	.25
9	Kent Hrbek	.50
10	Tim Laudner	.25
11	Frank Viola	.35
12	Les Straker	.25
13	George Frazier	.25
14	Keith Atherton	.25
15	Tom Brunansky	.25
16	Randy Bush	.25
17	Al Newman	.25
18	Mark Davidson	.25
19	Bert Blyleven	.35
20	Dan Gladden	.25
21	Kirby Puckett	7.50

22	Mark Portugal	.25
23	Juan Berenguer	.25
24	Jeff Reardon	.25
25	Dick Such	.25
26	Rick Stelmaszek	.25
27	Rick Renick	.25
28	Wayne Terwilliger	.25
29	Joe Klink	.25
30	Mike Smithson	.25
31	Team Photo	.25
32	Twins Champions Logo	.25
33	Twins Logo/Checklist	.25

1988 Minnesota Twins Fire Safety

This 8-1/4" x 3-3/4" booklet contains a dozen postcards called Color-Grams featuring caricatures (suitable for coloring) of star players. Postcards are attached along a perforated edge to a baseball card-size stub with a black-and-white photo of the featured player. Backs include the player name and personal information. The card stubs include the same information, along with a fire prevention tip. Twins Color-Grams were produced as a public service by the U.S. Forest Service and Dept. of Agriculture and were distributed to fans at the Metrodome.

		NM/M
Complete Booklet:		10.00
Complete Set, Singles (12):		7.50
Common Player:		.50
(1)	Bert Blyleven	.75
(2)	Randy Bush	.50
(3)	Gary Gaetti	.60
(4)	Greg Gagne	.50
(5)	Dan Gladden	.50
(6)	Kent Hrbek	1.00
(7)	Gene Larkin	.50
(8)	Tim Laudner	.50
(9)	Al Newman	.50
(10)	Kirby Puckett	4.00
(11)	Jeff Reardon	.50
(12)	Frank Viola	.50

1988 Minnesota Twins Team Issue

The Twins issued this set to commemorate the team's 1987 World Series victory. The slightly oversized cards (2-5/8" x 3-7/16") feature color player photos printed on heavy stock with a gold-embossed "1987 World Champions" logo in the lower-left corner. Numbered card backs are red, white and blue and contain player name, personal info and stats. A limited edition of 5000 sets were printed but only a few hundred were sold before the sets were taken off the market due to Major League Baseball licensing restrictions on the use of the World Series logo.

		NM/M
Complete Set (33):		60.00
Common Player:		1.50
1	Steve Lombardozzi	1.50
2	Roy Smalley	1.50
3	Pedro Oliva	4.00
4	Greg Gagne	3.00
5	Gary Gaetti	4.00
6	Gene Larkin	2.00
7	Tom Kelly	2.00
8	Kent Hrbek	6.00
9	Tim Laudner	2.00
10	Frank Viola	4.00
11	Les Straker	1.50
12	Don Baylor	4.00
13	George Frazier	1.50
14	Keith Atherton	1.50
15	Tom Brunansky	1.50
16	Randy Bush	1.50
17	Al Newman	1.50
18	Mark Davidson	1.50
19	Bert Blyleven	4.00
20	Dan Schatzeder	1.50
21	Dan Gladden	2.00
22	Sal Butera	1.50
23	Kirby Puckett	25.00
24	Joe Niekro	2.00
25	Juan Berenguer	1.50
26	Jeff Reardon	3.00
27	Dick Such	1.50
28	Rick Stelmaszek	1.50
29	Rick Renick	1.50
30	Wayne Terwilliger	1.50
31	Team Photo	1.50
32	World Champions Team Logo Card	1.50
33	Team Logo Card/ Checklist	1.50

1997 Minnesota Twins 10th Anniversary

The 10th anniversary of the team's 1987 World Series victory is recalled with this set given to fans on August 8 during the reunion weekend at the Metrodome. The 2-1/2" x 3-1/2" cards have 10-year-old color action photos on front with the anniversary logo and player identification. On back are a black-and-white portrait photo, uniform number, biographical details, the player's 1987 season and post-season performance and the sponsor's logo. The cards are checklisted here in alphabetical order.

		NM/M
Complete Set (25):		10.00
Common Player:		.25
(1)	Keith Atherton	.25
(2)	Don Baylor	.40
(3)	Juan Berenguer	.25
(4)	Bert Blyleven	.35
(5)	Tom Brunansky	.25
(6)	Randy Bush	.25
(7)	Sal Butera	.25
(8)	Mark Davidson	.25
(9)	George Frazier	.25
(10)	Gary Gaetti	.50
(11)	Greg Gagne	.50
(12)	Dan Gladden	.50
(13)	Kent Hrbek	1.00
(14)	Tom Kelly	.25
(15)	Gene Larkin	.25
(16)	Tim Laudner	.25
(17)	Steve Lombardozzi	.25
(18)	Al Newman	.25
(19)	Joe Niekro	.40
(20)	Kirby Puckett	5.00
(21)	Jeff Reardon	.25
(22)	Dan Schatzeder	.25
(23)	Roy Smalley	.25
(24)	Les Straker	.25
(25)	Frank Viola	.40

2002 Minnesota Twins Police

More than 300 agencies comprising the Minnesota Crime Prevention Association distributed this multi-sport set. Eight players each from the Twins, Vikings and Wild were included, along with McGruff the Crime Dog. Distribution of the baseball players cards was between August 6-19. The baseball cards have game-action photos which are borderless at top and sides. Two team logos are in the top corners and a blue strip at bottom has player name, uniform number and position. Backs have a black-and-white portrait photo, a safety tip and sponsors logos. Only the baseball players from the issue are listed here.

		NM/M
Complete (Baseball) Set (8):		5.00
Common Player:		.50
1	Eddie Guardado	.50
2	Cristian Guzman	1.00
3	Jacque Jones	1.00
4	Corey Koskie	1.00

5	Doug Mientkiewicz	.50
6	A.J. Pierzynski	.50
7	Luis Rivas	.50
8	Torii Hunter	1.50

2003 Minnesota Twins Police

Sponsored by the Minnesota Crime Prevention Association, this set features eight popular players and McGruff the Crime Dog. Standard 2-1/2" x 3-1/2" cards have game-action photos on front, borderless at top and sides. A blue stripe at bottom has uniform number, player name and position. The team's 2002 A.L. Central Division Champions logo and "Gotta See 'Em" 2003 season logo are in the top corners. A facsimile autograph appears on front. Backs are in black, white and blue with a portrait photo, player data and a safety tip, along with the sponsor's and printer's logos.

		NM/M
Complete Set (9):		5.00
Common Player:		.50
1	Torii Hunter	1.00
2	Doug Mientkiewicz	.75
3	Corey Koskie	.75
4	A.J. Pierzynski	.75
5	Brad Radke	.50
6	Jacque Jones	.75
7	Eddie Guardado	.50
8	Eric Milton	.50
9	McGruff the Crime Dog	.50

2004 Minnesota Twins Police

Sponsored by the Minnesota Crime Prevention Association, this set features eight popular players. Standard 2-1/2" x 3-1/2" cards have game-action photos on front, borderless at top and sides. A blue stripe at bottom has uniform number, player name and position. The team's 2003 A.L. Central Division Champions logo is in the top-right corner. A facsimile autograph appears on front. Backs are in black and white with a portrait photo, player data and a safety tip, along with the sponsor's and printer's logos.

		NM/M
Complete Set (8):		5.00
Common Player:		.50
1	Torii Hunter	.75
2	Doug Mientkiewicz	.50
3	Corey Koskie	.50
4	Shannon Stewart	.50
5	Brad Radke	.50
6	Cristian Guzman	.50
7	Johan Santana	2.00
8	Kyle Lohse	.50

2004 Minnesota Twins Team Issue

To build support in its drive to retain Major League Baseball in the Twin Cities and build a new outdoor stadium, the team issued this card set at its winter TwinsFest. Cards are

2003 Minnesota Twins Police

2-1/2" x 3-1/2" printed on thin semi-gloss stock. There are five player cards and seven cards depicting artists' views of the proposed ballpark.

		NM/M
Complete Set (12):		6.00
Common Player:		.50
16	Doug Mientkiewicz	.50
22	Brad Radke	.50
23	Shannon Stewart	.75
27	Corey Koskie	.75
48	Torii Hunter	1.00
---	A Ballpark for Minnesota ("As the new home . . .")	.50
---	A Ballpark for Minnesota ("Got off the bench . . .")	.50
---	A Ballpark for Minnesota ("Minnesota's new ballpark will honor . . .")	.50
---	A Ballpark for Minnesota ("Minnesota's new ballpark will mark . . .")	.50
---	A Ballpark for Minnesota ("Much like those . . .")	.50
---	A Ballpark for Minnesota ("The exterior . . .")	.50
---	A Ballpark for Minnesota ("With total seating . . .")	.50

2005 Star Tribune Minnesota Twins Medallion Collection

A set of 21 commemorative medallions was sponsored by the Star Tribune in this promotion. Coupons found in the newspaper between May 2-25 could be redeemed at newsstands (along with $2.99) for that day's medallion. Larger and thicker than a quarter, the 1-3/16" diameter medals are struck in nickel and have on their fronts an enameled portrait photo. A team logo dominates the back. A colorful, photo-filled 7-3/4" x 13" album was available to house the pieces. The medals are listed here in alphabetical order.

		NM/M
Complete Set (21):		90.00
Common Player:		3.00
Album:		3.00
(1)	Grant Balfour	3.00
(2)	Juan Castro	3.00
(3)	Michael Cuddyer	3.00
(4)	Lew Ford	3.00
(5)	Ron Gardenhire	3.00
(6)	Torii Hunter	4.50
(7)	Jacque Jones	4.50
(8)	Matthew LeCroy	3.00
(9)	Kyle Lohse	3.00
(10)	Joe Mauer	10.00
(11)	Joe Mays	3.00
(12)	Justin Morneau	10.00
(13)	Joe Nathan	3.00
(14)	Brad Radke	4.50
(15)	Juan Rincon	3.00
(16)	Luis Rivas	3.00
(17)	J.C. Romero	3.00
(18)	Johan Santana	12.50
(19)	Carlos Silva	3.00
(20)	Shannon Stewart	3.00
(21)	Twins Back To Back To Back Championships	3.00

2005 Minnesota Twins Police

Sponsored by the Minnesota Crime Prevention Association, this set features seven popular players and McGruff the Crime Dog. Standard 2-1/2" x 3-1/2" cards have game-action photos on front, bordered in dark blue. A strip at bottom has uniform number, player name and position. Team logos are in each upper corner. Backs are in black-and-white with a small portrait photo, player information, safety tip, along with the sponsor's and printer's logos. The set was distributed by area police agencies and at a Twins game in May.

		NM/M
Complete Set (8):		8.00
Common Player:		1.00
7	Joe Mauer	2.00
22	Brad Radke	1.00
23	Shannon Stewart	1.00
36	Joe Nathan	1.50
48	Torii Hunter	1.50
49	Kyle Lohse	1.50
57	Johan Santana	1.50
---	McGruff The Crime Dog	1.00

1992 MJB Holoprisms

The Holoprism set consists of two four-card hologram sets of Rookies of the Year Jeff Bagwell and Chuck Knoblauch. Each player set was packaged in a special plastic case. The production was limited to 250,000 of each set, numbered and with a letter of authenticity. Each player autographed 500 cards, which were randomly inserted.

		NM/M
Complete Bagwell Set (4):		6.00
Common Bagwell Card:		1.50
Complete Knoblauch Set (4):		6.00
Common Knoblauch Card:		1.00
Autographed Bagwell Card:		75.00
Autographed Knoblauch Card:		40.00
R1	Jeff Bagwell/Btg	2.00
R1a	Jeff Bagwell (Overprinted "PROTOTYPE" on back).	2.00
R2	Jeff Bagwell/Fldg	2.00
R3	Jeff Bagwell/Btg	2.00
R4	Jeff Bagwell/Btg	2.00
R1	Chuck Knoblauch/Btg	1.00
R1a	Chuck Knoblauch (Overprinted "PROTOTYPE" on back).	1.00
R2	Chuck Knoblauch/Fldg	1.00
R3	Chuck Knoblauch/Btg	1.00
R4	Chuck Knoblauch/Btg	1.00

2000 MLB Showdown Promos

To introduce its baseball card game, Wizards of the Coast produced a series of promo cards that were locally distributed to hobby stores to encourage people to join gaming leagues. The promos differ from the issued cards in the use of silver-foil highlights and the presence of large "FUTURE STAR" or "DIAMOND STAR" in the background, instead of a team logo, or "HOME RUN HITTER" at top. Because of the manner of distribution, some promos are more difficult to find in the hobby market.

		NM/M
Complete Set (43):		10.00
Common Player:		.40
(1)	Sandy Alomar Jr.	.40
(2)	Craig Biggio	.40
(3)	Carlos Delgado	.60
(4)	Damion Easley	.40
(5)	Mark Grace	.40
(6)	Rusty Greer	.40
(7)	Tony Gwynn	1.00
(8a)	Andruw Jones (8 OB)	.60
(8b)	Andruw Jones (10 OB)	.60
(9)	Chipper Jones	1.00
(10)	Jeff Kent	.40
(11)	Edgar Martinez	.40
(12)	Gary Sheffield	.60
(13)	B.J. Surhoff	.40
(14)	Jason Varitek	.40
(15)	Robin Ventura	.40
(16)	Bernie Williams	.40
(1)	Bob Abreu	.40
(2)	Ron Belliard	.40
(3)	Sean Casey	.40
(4)	Luis Castillo	.40
(5)	J.D. Drew	.60
(6)	Erubiel Durazo	.40
(7)	Carlos Febles	.40
(8)	Troy Glaus	.65
(9)	Ben Grieve	.40
(10)	Todd Helton	.65
(11)	Corey Koskie	.40
(12)	Warren Morris	.40
1	Barry Bonds	2.00
2	Jose Canseco	.60
3	Nomar Garciaparra	1.00
4	Jason Giambi	.60
5	Shawn Green	.50
6	Ken Griffey Jr.	1.25
7	Andruw Jones	.75
8	Chipper Jones	1.00
9	Mark McGwire	1.50
10	Rafael Palmeiro	.65
11	Mike Piazza	1.25
12	Manny Ramirez	.75
13	Alex Rodriguez	1.50
14	Sammy Sosa	1.25

2000 MLB Showdown 1st Edition

Yet another attempt to bridge the gap between baseball cards as player-related collectibles and as interactive game, MLB Showdown from veteran gamers Wizards of the Coast enjoyed significant initial interest. Issued as a starter deck and in nine-card booster packs, the debut set has 462 player cards, including 63 premium holofoil star cards and 75 strategy cards. The holo premium foils were inserted in booster packs at a rate of 1:3. Promo cards were locally distributed. While collectors compete with gamers for these cards in the market, relative values placed on the cards by each group of buyers may differ. Cards without the silver-foil "1st Edition" logo were released in booster packs and are worth about half the values shown here.

		NM/M
Complete Set (517):		200.00
Common Player:		.15
Starter Box:		6.00
Starter Deck:		2.00
Booster Box (36):		25.00
Booster Pack (9):		1.00
1	Garret Anderson	.15
2	Tim Belcher	.15
3	Gary DiSarcina (Photo is Tim Salmon.)	.15
4	Darin Erstad	.30
5	Chuck Finley (Foil)	2.00
6	Troy Glaus	.65
7	Todd Greene	.15
8	Jeff Huson	.15
9	Orlando Palmeiro	.15
10	Troy Percival	.15
11	Mark Petkovsek	.15
12	Tim Salmon	.15
13	Steve Sparks	.15
14	Mo Vaughn	.15
15	Matt Walbeck	.15
16	Jay Bell (Foil)	2.00
17	Andy Benes	.15
18	Omar Daal	.15
19	Steve Finley	.15
20	Andy Fox	.15
21	Hanley Frias	.15
22	Bernard Gilkey	.15
23	Luis Gonzalez (Foil)	2.00
24	Randy Johnson (Foil)	3.00
25	Travis Lee	.15
26	Matt Mantei	.15
27	Dan Plesac	.15
28	Kelly Stinnett	.15
29	Greg Swindell	.15
30	Matt Williams (Foil)	2.00
31	Tony Womack	.15
32	Bret Boone	.15
33	Tom Glavine	.40
34	Jose Hernandez	.15
35	Brian Hunter	.15
36	Andruw Jones	.75
37	Chipper Jones (Foil)	4.00
38	Brian Jordan	.15
39	Ryan Klesko	.15
40	Keith Lockhart	.15
41	Greg Maddux (Foil)	4.00
42	Kevin Millwood (Foil)	2.00
43	Eddie Perez	.15
44	Mike Remlinger	.15
45	John Rocker	.15
46	John Smoltz	.15
47	Walt Weiss	.15
48	Gerald Williams	.15
49	Rich Amaral	.15
50	Brady Anderson	.15
51	Albert Belle	.15
52	Mike Bordick	.15
53	Jeff Conine	.15
54	Delino DeShields	.15
55	Scott Erickson	.15
56	Charles Johnson	.15
57	Mike Mussina	.35
58	Jesse Orosco	.15
59	Sidney Ponson	.15
60	Jeff Reboulet	.15
61	Cal Ripken Jr. (Foil)	7.00
62	B.J. Surhoff	.15
63	Mike Timlin	.15
64	Rod Beck	.15
65	Damon Buford	.15
66	Rheal Cormier	.15
67	Nomar Garciaparra (Foil)	4.00
68	Butch Huskey	.15
69	Darren Lewis	.15
70	Derek Lowe	.15
71	Pedro Martinez (Foil)	3.00
72	Trot Nixon	.15
73	Jose Offerman	.15
74	Troy O'Leary	.15
75	Mark Portugal	.15
76	Pat Rapp	.15
77	Mike Stanley	.15
78	John Valentin	.15
79	Jason Varitek	.25
80	Tim Wakefield	.15
81	Rick Aguilera	.15
82	Jeff Blauser	.15
83	Kyle Farnsworth	.15
84	Gary Gaetti	.15
85	Mark Grace	.15
86	Lance Johnson	.15
87	Jon Lieber	.15
88	Mickey Morandini	.15
89	Jose Nieves	.15
90	Jeff Reed	.15
91	Henry Rodriguez	.15
92	Scott Sanders	.15
93	Benito Santiago	.15
94	Sammy Sosa	4.50
95	Steve Trachsel	.15
96	James Baldwin	.15
97	Mike Caruso	.15
98	Ray Durham	.15
99	Brook Fordyce	.15
100	Bob Howry	.15
101	Paul Konerko	.25
102	Carlos Lee	.35
103	Greg Norton	.15
104	Magglio Ordonez	.15
105	Jim Parque	.15
106	Bill Simas	.15
107	Chris Singleton	.15
108	Mike Sirotka	.15
109	Frank Thomas (Foil)	3.00
110	Craig Wilson	.15
111	Aaron Boone	.15
112	Mike Cameron	.15
113	Sean Casey (Foil)	2.00
114	Danny Graves	.15
115	Pete Harnisch	.15
116	Barry Larkin (Foil)	2.00
117	Pokey Reese	.15
118	Scott Sullivan	.15
119	Eddie Taubensee	.15
120	Brett Tomko	.15
121	Michael Tucker	.15
122	Greg Vaughn	.15
123	Ron Villone	.15
124	Scott Williamson (Foil)	2.00
125	Dmitri Young	.15
126	Roberto Alomar (Foil)	2.00
127	Harold Baines	.15
128	Dave Burba	.15
129	Bartolo Colon	.15
130	Einar Diaz	.15
131	Travis Fryman	.15
132	Mike Jackson	.15
133	David Justice	.15
134	Kenny Lofton (Foil)	2.00
135	Charles Nagy	.15
136	Manny Ramirez (Foil)	3.00
137	Richie Sexson	.15
138	Paul Shuey	.15
139	Jim Thome (Foil)	2.50
140	Omar Vizquel	.15
141	Enrique Wilson	.15
142	Kurt Abbott	.15
143	Pedro Astacio	.15
144	Jeff Barry	.15
145	Dante Bichette	.15
146	Henry Blanco	.15
147	Brian Bohanon	.15
148	Vinny Castilla	.15
149	Jerry Dipoto	.15
150	Todd Helton	.65
151	Darryl Kile	.15
152	Curtis Leskanic	.15
153	Neifi Perez	.15
154	Terry Shumpert	.15
155	Dave Veres	.15
156	Larry Walker (Foil)	2.00
157	Brad Ausmus	.15
158	Frank Catalanotto	.15
159	Tony Clark	.15
160	Deivi Cruz	.15
161	Damion Easley	.15
162	Juan Encarnacion	.15
163	Karim Garcia	.15
164	Bobby Higginson	.15
165	Todd Jones	.15
166	Gabe Kapler	.15
167	Dave Mlicki	.15
168	Brian Moehler	.15
169	C.J. Nitkowski	.15
170	Dean Palmer (Foil)	2.00
171	Jeff Weaver	.15
172	Antonio Alfonseca	.15
173	Bruce Aven	.15
174	Dave Berg	.15
175	Luis Castillo (Foil)	2.00
176	Ryan Dempster	.15
177	Brian Edmondson	.15
178	Alex Gonzalez	.15
179	Mark Kotsay	.15
180	Derrek Lee	.50
181	Braden Looper	.15
182	Mike Lowell	.15
183	Brian Meadows	.15
184	Mike Redmond	.15
185	Dennis Springer	.15
186	Preston Wilson	.15
187	Jeff Bagwell (Foil)	3.00
188	Derek Bell	.15
189	Craig Biggio	.15
190	Tim Bogar	.15
191	Ken Caminiti	.15
192	Scott Elarton	.15
193	Tony Eusebio	.15
194	Carl Everett (Foil)	2.00
195	Mike Hampton (Foil)	2.00
196	Richard Hidalgo	.15
197	Stan Javier	.15
198	Jose Lima	.15
199	Jay Powell	.15
200	Shane Reynolds	.15
201	Bill Spiers	.15
202	Billy Wagner (Foil)	2.00
203	Carlos Beltran (Foil)	2.50
204	Johnny Damon	.35
205	Jermaine Dye	.15
206	Carlos Febles	.15
207	Jeremy Giambi	.15
208	Chad Kreuter	.15
209	Jeff Montgomery	.15
210	Joe Randa	.15
211	Jose Rosado	.15
212	Rey Sanchez	.15
213	Scott Service	.15
214	Tim Spehr	.15
215	Jeff Suppan	.15
216	Mike Sweeney	.15
217	Jay Witasick	.15
218	Adrian Beltre	.50
219	Pedro Borbon	.15
220	Kevin Brown (Foil)	2.00
221	Mark Grudzielanek	.15
222	Dave Hansen	.15
223	Todd Hundley	.15
224	Eric Karros	.15
225	Raul Mondesi	.15
226	Chan Ho Park	.15
227	Jeff Shaw	.15
228	Gary Sheffield (Foil)	2.50
229	Ismael Valdes	.15
230	Jose Vizcaino	.15
231	Devon White	.15
232	Eric Young	.15
233	Ron Belliard	.15
234	Sean Berry	.15
235	Jeromy Burnitz (Foil)	2.00
236	Jeff Cirillo	.15
237	Marquis Grissom	.15
238	Geoff Jenkins	.15
239	Scott Karl	.15
240	Mark Loretta	.15
241	Mike Myers	.15
242	David Nilsson (Foil)	2.00
243	Hideo Nomo	.50
244	Alex Ochoa	.15
245	Jose Valentin	.15
246	Bob Wickman	.15
247	Steve Woodard	.15
248	Chad Allen	.15
249	Ron Coomer	.15
250	Cristian Guzman	.15
251	Denny Hocking	.15
252	Torii Hunter	.15
253	Corey Koskie	.15
254	Matt Lawton	.15
255	Joe Mays	.15
256	Doug Mientkiewicz	.15
257	Eric Milton	.15
258	Brad Radke (Foil)	2.00
259	Terry Steinbach	.15
260	Mike Trombley	.15
261	Todd Walker	.19
262	Bob Wells	.15
263	Shane Andrews	.15
264	Michael Barrett	.15
265	Orlando Cabrera	.15
266	Brad Fullmer	.15
267	Vladimir Guerrero (Foil)	3.00
268	Wilton Guerrero	.15
269	Dustin Hermanson	.15
270	Steve Kline	.15
271	Manny Martinez	.15
272	Mike Thurman	.15
273	Ugueth Urbina	.15
274	Javier Vazquez	.15
275	Jose Vidro	.15
276	Rondell White	.15
277	Chris Widger	.15
278	Edgardo Alfonzo (Foil)	2.00
279	Armando Benitez	.15
280	Roger Cedeno	.15
281	Dennis Cook	.15
282	Shawon Dunston	.15
283	Matt Franco	.15
284	Darryl Hamilton	.15
285	Rickey Henderson (Foil)	3.00
286	Orel Hershiser	.15
287	Al Leiter	.15
288	John Olerud	.15
289	Rey Ordonez	.15
290	Mike Piazza (Foil)	5.00
291	Kenny Rogers	.15
292	Robin Ventura	.15
293	Turk Wendell	.15
294	Masato Yoshii	.15
295	Scott Brosius	.15
296	Roger Clemens (Foil)	4.50
297	David Cone (Foil)	2.00
298	Chad Curtis	.15
299	Chili Davis	.15
300	Orlando Hernandez	.15
301	Derek Jeter (Foil)	7.00
302	Chuck Knoblauch	.15
303	Ricky Ledee	.15
304	Tino Martinez	.15
305	Ramiro Mendoza	.15
306	Paul O'Neill	.15
307	Andy Pettitte	.35
308	Jorge Posada	.15
309	Mariano Rivera (Foil)	2.00
310	Mike Stanton	.15
311	Bernie Williams (Foil)	2.00
312	Kevin Appier	.15
313	Eric Chavez	.25
314	Ryan Christensen	.15
315	Jason Giambi	2.50
316	Ben Grieve	.15
317	Buddy Groom	.15
318	Gil Heredia	.15
319	A.J. Hinch	.15
320	John Jaha	.15
321	Doug Jones	.15
322	Omar Olivares	.15
323	Tony Phillips	.15
324	Matt Stairs	.15
325	Miguel Tejada	.25
326	Randy Velarde (Foil)	2.00
327	Bobby Abreu (Foil)	2.00
328	Marlon Anderson	.15
329	Alex Arias	.15
330	Rico Brogna	.15
331	Paul Byrd	.15
332	Ron Gant	.15
333	Doug Glanville	.15
334	Wayne Gomes	.15
335	Kevin Jordan	.15
336	Mike Lieberthal	.15
337	Steve Montgomery	.15
338	Chad Ogea	.15
339	Scott Rolen	.60
340	Curt Schilling (Foil)	2.50
341	Kevin Sefcik	.15
342	Mike Benjamin	.15
343	Kris Benson	.15
344	Adrian Brown	.15
345	Brant Brown	.15
346	Brad Clontz	.15
347	Brian Giles (Foil)	2.00
348	Jason Kendall (Foil)	2.00
349	Al Martin	.15
350	Warren Morris	.15
351	Todd Ritchie	.15
352	Scott Sauerbeck	.15
353	Jason Schmidt	.15
354	Ed Sprague	.15
355	Mike Williams	.15
356	Kevin Young	.15
357	Andy Ashby	.15
358	Ben Davis	.15
359	Tony Gwynn (Foil)	4.00
360	Sterling Hitchcock	.15
361	Trevor Hoffman (Foil)	2.00
362	Damian Jackson	.15
363	Wally Joyner	.15
364	Phil Nevin	.15
365	Eric Owens	.15
366	Ruben Rivera	.15
367	Reggie Sanders	.15
368	John Vander Wal	.15
369	Quilvio Veras	.15
370	Matt Whisenant	.15
371	Woody Williams	.15
372	Rich Aurilia	.15
373	Marvin Benard	.15
374	Barry Bonds (Foil)	7.00
375	Ellis Burks	.15
376	Alan Embree	.15
377	Shawn Estes	.15
378	John Johnstone	.15
379	Jeff Kent	.15
380	Brent Mayne	.15
381	Bill Mueller	.15
382	Robb Nen	.15
383	Russ Ortiz	.15
384	Kirk Rueter	.15
385	F.P. Santangelo	.15
386	J.T. Snow	.15
387	David Bell	.15
388	Jay Buhner	.15
389	Russ Davis	.15
390	Freddy Garcia	.15
391	Ken Griffey Jr. (Foil)	5.00
392	John Halama	.15
393	Brian L. Hunter	.15
394	Raul Ibanez	.15
395	Tom Lampkin	.15
396	Edgar Martinez (Foil)	2.00
397	Jose Mesa	.15
398	Jamie Moyer	.15
399	Jose Paniagua	.15
400	Alex Rodriguez (Foil)	6.00
401	Dan Wilson	.15
402	Manny Aybar	.15
403	Ricky Bottalico	.15
404	Kent Bottenfield	.15
405	Darren Bragg	.15
406	Alberto Castillo	.15
407	J.D. Drew	.60
408	Jose Jiminez	.15
409	Ray Lankford	.15
410	Joe McEwing	.15
411	Willie McGee	.15
412	Mark McGwire (Foil)	6.00
413	Darren Oliver	.15
414	Lance Painter	.15
415	Edgar Renteria	.15
416	Fernando Tatis (Foil)	2.00
417	Wilson Alvarez	.15
418	Rolando Arrojo	.15
419	Wade Boggs	1.00
420	Miguel Cairo	.15
421	Jose Canseco (Foil)	2.50
422	John Flaherty	.15
423	Roberto Hernandez	.15
424	Dave Martinez	.15
425	Fred McGriff	.15
426	Paul Sorrento	.15
427	Kevin Stocker	.15
428	Bubba Trammell	.15
429	Rick White	.15
430	Randy Winn	.15
431	Bobby Witt	.15
432	Royce Clayton	.15
433	Tim Crabtree	.15
434	Juan Gonzalez	.45
435	Tom Goodwin	.15
436	Rusty Greer	.15
437	Rick Helling	.15
438	Mark McLemore	.15
439	Mike Morgan	.15
440	Rafael Palmeiro (Foil)	3.00
441	Ivan Rodriguez (Foil)	3.00
442	Aaron Sele	.15
443	Lee Stevens	.15
444	Mike Venafro	.15
445	John Wetteland	.15
446	Todd Zeile	.15
447	Jeff Zimmerman (Foil)	2.00
448	Tony Batista	.15
449	Homer Bush	.15
450	Jose Cruz Jr.	.15
451	Carlos Delgado	.40
452	Kelvim Escobar	.15
453	Tony Fernandez (Foil)	2.00
454	Darrin Fletcher	.15
455	Shawn Green (Foil)	2.00
456	Pat Hentgen	.15
457	Billy Koch	.15
458	Graeme Lloyd	.15
459	Brian McRae	.15
460	David Segui	.15
461	Shannon Stewart	.15
462	David Wells	.15
S1	Bad Call (Umpire)	.10
S2	Big Inning (Mike Stanley)	.10
S3	Bobbled in the Outfield (Tony Phillips)	.10
S4	Clutch Hitting (Manny Ramirez)	.10
S5	Do or Die (Chuck Knoblauch)	.10
S6	Down the Middle (?)	.10
S7	Ducks on the Pond (Carl Everett)	.10
S8	Favorable Matchup (Barry Bonds)	.30
S9	Free Steal (Juan Encarnacion)	.10
S10	Get Under It (Jose Offerman)	.10
S11	Great Lead (Rickey Henderson)	.20
S12	Hard Slide (Damian Jackson)	.10
S13	High Fives (Derek Jeter)	.10
S14	Last Chance (Paul O'Neill)	.10
S15	Long Single (Derek Jeter)	.30
S16	Out of Gas (Jeff Zimmerman)	.10
S17	Out of Position (Rickey Henderson, Ryan Klesko)	.15
S18	Play the Percentages (Chipper Jones)	.10
S19	Rally Cap (Omar Vizquel)	.10
S20	Rattled (Mike Hennenan)	.10
S21	Runner Not Held (Miguel Tejada)	.10
S22	Slow Roller (Brian Bohanon)	.10
S23	Stick a Fork in Him (Kevin Millwood)	.10
S24	Swing for the Fences (Sammy Sosa)	.15
S25	To the Warning Track (Ricky Ledee)	.10
S26	Whiplash (Mark McGwire)	.25
S27	Wide Throw (Roberto Alomar)	.10
S28	Wild Pitch (Eddie Taubensee)	.10
S29	By the Book (Walt Weiss)	.10
S30	Dominating (Billy Wagner)	.10
S31	Full Windup (Orlando Hernandez)	.10
S32	Good Fielding (Rey Ordonez, Ryan Klesko)	.10
S33	Gun 'Em Down! (Jason Kendall)	.10
S34	He's Got a Gun (Sammy Sosa)	.10
S35	In the Groove (David Cone)	.10
S36	In the Zone (Pedro Martinez)	.10
S37	Infield In (S.F. Giants)	.10
S38	Intimidation (Randy Johnson)	.15
S39	Just Over the Wall (Ken Griffey, Jr.)	.25
S40	Knock the Ball Down (?)	.10
S41	Lefty Specialist (Jesse Orosco)	.10
S42	Nerves of Steel (Mariano Rivera)	.10
S43	Nothing but Heat (Randy Johnson)	.10
S44	Pitch Out (Bobby Hughes)	.10
S45	Pumped Up (John Rocker)	.10
S46	Quick Pitch (Greg Maddux)	.10
S47	Rally Killer (Carlos Baerga)	.10
S48	Short Fly (Chuck Knoblauch, Bernie Williams)	.10
S49	Three Up, Three Down (Pedro Martinez)	.10
S50	Trick Pitch (Derek Jeter)	.30
S51	Belt-High (Sammy Sosa)	.15
S52	Change In Strategy (Joe Torre)	.10
S53	Grounder to Second (Pokey Reese)	.10
S54	Stealing Signals (Mark Grace)	.10
S55	Swing at Anything (Cal Ripken, Jr.)	.30

2000 MLB Showdown Pennant Run Promos

To promote its forthcoming Pennant Run edition, Wizards of the Coast issued eight specially marked sample cards. The promos have silver-foil player names and a large "W." The promos were issued one per copy of TopDeck magazine (a gamer's publication) which carried a $5.99 cover price.

		NM/M
Complete Set (8):		3.00
Common Player:		.50
1	Peter Bergeron	.50
2	Matt Clement	.50
3	Ramon Hernandez	.50
4	Gabe Kapler	.50
5	Adam Kennedy	.50

6 Sean Lowe .50
7 Joe Nathan .50
8 Daryle Ward .50

2000 MLB Showdown Pennant Run

Issued just after the 2000 season opened, this is essentially an update to the interactive game MLB Showdown from veteran gamers Wizards of the Coast. Players in the set are generally those who changed teams during the off-season, or promising rookies. The Pennant Run edition was issued in a Booster box of 36 nine-card (seven player, two strategy) packs. The set has 130 "regular" player cards, 20 premium holofoil star cards and 25 strategy cards. The holo premium cards were inserted in packs at a rate of 1:3. While collectors compete with gamers for these cards in the market, relative values placed on the cards by each group of buyers may differ.

	NM/M
Complete Set (175):	30.00
Common Player:	.15
Booster Pack (9):	1.00
Booster Box (36):	20.00

1 Kent Bottenfield .15
2 Ken Hill .15
3 Adam Kennedy .15
4 Ben Molina .15
5 Scott Spiezio .15
6 Brian Anderson .15
7 Erubiel Durazo (Foil) 1.00
8 Armando Reynoso .15
9 Russ Springer .15
10 Todd Stottlemyre .15
11 Tony Womack .15
12 Andres Galarraga (Foil) 1.00
13 Javy Lopez (Foil) 1.00
14 Kevin McGlinchy .15
15 Terry Mulholland .15
16 Reggie Sanders .15
17 Harold Baines .15
18 Will Clark .15
19 Mike Trombley .15
20 Manny Alexander .15
21 Carl Everett (Foil) 1.00
22 Ramon Martinez (Foil) 1.00
23 Bret Saberhagen .15
24 John Wasdin .15
25 Joe Girardi .15
26 Ricky Gutierrez .15
27 Glenallen Hill .15
28 Kevin Tapani .15
29 Kerry Wood (Foil) 2.00
30 Eric Young .15
31 Keith Foulke (Foil) 1.00
32 Mark Johnson .15
33 Sean Lowe .15
34 Jose Valentin .15
35 Dante Bichette .15
36 Ken Griffey Jr. (Foil) 6.00
37 Denny Neagle .15
38 Steve Parris .15
39 Dennis Reyes .15
40 Sandy Alomar Jr. .15
41 Chuck Finley (Foil) 1.00
42 Steve Karsay .15
43 Steve Reed .15
44 Jaret Wright .15
45 Jeff Cirillo .15
46 Tom Goodwin .15
47 Jeffrey Hammonds .15
48 Mike Lansing .15
49 Aaron Ledesma .15
50 Brent Mayne .15
51 Doug Brocail .15
52 Robert Fick .15
53 Juan Gonzalez .60
54 Hideo Nomo .60
55 Luis Polonia .15
56 Brant Brown .15
57 Alex Fernandez .15
58 Cliff Floyd .15
59 Dan Miceli .15
60 Vladimir Nunez .15
61 Moises Alou (Foil) 1.00
62 Roger Cedeno (Foil) 1.00
63 Octavio Dotel .15
64 Mitch Meluskey .15

65 Daryle Ward .15
66 Mark Quinn (Foil) 1.00
67 Brad Rigby .15
68 Blake Stein .15
69 Mac Suzuki .15
70 Terry Adams .15
71 Darren Dreifort .15
72 Kevin Elster .15
73 Shawn Green (Foil) 1.50
74 Todd Hollandsworth .15
75 Gregg Olson .15
76 Kevin Barker .15
77 Jose Hernandez .15
78 Dave Weathers .15
79 Hector Carrasco .15
80 Eddie Guardado .15
81 Jacque Jones .15
82 David Ortiz .50
83 Peter Bergeron .15
84 Hideki Irabu .15
85 Lee Stevens .15
86 Anthony Telford .15
87 Derek Bell .15
88 John Franco .15
89 Mike Hampton (Foil) 1.00
90 Bobby J. Jones .15
91 Todd Pratt .15
92 Todd Zeile .15
93 Jason Grimsley .15
94 Roberto Kelly .15
95 Jim Leyritz .15
96 Ramiro Mendoza .15
97 Rich Becker .15
98 Ramon Hernandez .15
99 Tim Hudson (Foil) 2.00
100 Jason Isringhausen .15
101 Mike Magnante .15
102 Olmedo Saenz .15
103 Mickey Morandini .15
104 Robert Person .15
105 Desi Relaford .15
106 Jason Christiansen .15
107 Wil Cordero .15
108 Francisco Cordova .15
109 Chad Hermansen .15
110 Pat Meares .15
111 Aramis Ramirez .15
112 Bret Boone .15
113 Matt Clement .15
114 Carlos Hernandez .15
115 Ryan Klesko .15
116 Dave Magadan .15
117 Al Martin .15
118 Bobby Estalella .15
119 Livan Hernandez .15
120 Doug Mirabelli .15
121 Joe Nathan .15
122 Mike Cameron .15
123 Mark McLemore .15
124 Gil Meche .15
125 John Olerud .15
126 Arthur Rhodes .15
127 Aaron Sele (Foil) 1.00
128 Jim Edmonds (Foil) 1.00
129 Pat Hentgen .15
130 Darryl Kile .15
131 Eli Marrero .15
132 Dave Veres .15
133 Fernando Vina .15
134 Vinny Castilla .15
135 Juan Guzman .15
136 Ryan Rupe .15
137 Greg Vaughn (Foil) 1.00
138 Gerald Williams .15
139 Esteban Yan .15
140 Tom Evans .15
141 Gabe Kapler .15
142 Ruben Mateo (Foil) 1.00
143 Kenny Rogers .15
144 David Segui .15
145 Tony Batista .15
146 Chris Carpenter .15
147 Brad Fullmer .15
148 Alex Gonzalez .15
149 Roy Halladay .15
150 Raul Mondesi (Foil) 1.00
S1 Afterburners (Aaron Boone) .10
S2 Change Sides (Chipper Jones) .15
S3 Patience is a Virtue (Bob Abreu) .10
S4 Payoff Pitch (Fernando Tatis) .10
S5 Pointers (Rod Carew) .15
S6 Professional Baserunner (J.D. Drew) .10
S7 Professional Hitter (John VanderWal) .10
S8 Protect the Runner (Pokey Reese) .10
S9 Rough Outing (Greg Maddux) .10
S10 Shelled (Cincinnati Reds) .10
S11 Take What is Given (Larry Walker) .10
S12 Tricky Hop (Alex Rodriguez) .40
S13 Aggressive Coaching (Alex Rodriguez) .40
S14 Cut Off in the Gap (N.Y. Mets) .10
S15 Great Start (Kevin Brown) .10
S16 Insult to Injury (Paul O'Neill) .10
S17 Job Well Done (Scott Williamson) .10

S18 Low and Away (Jamie Moyer) .10
S19 Outfield In (Bernie Williams) .10
S20 Put Out the Fire (John Franco) .10
S21 Rotation Play (Pittsburgh Pirates) .10
S22 Swiss Army Closer (John Rocker) .10
S23 Whoops (Mike Lansing) .10
S24 Pep Talk (Roger Clemens, Joe Torre) .15
S25 Revenue Sharing (Derek Jeter) .50

2001 MLB Showdown Promos

To introduce its 2001 card game, Wizards of the Coast produced a series of promo cards which were locally distributed to hobby stores to encourage people to join gaming leagues. The promos differ from the issued cards in the use of a designation at top of "ACE PITCHER," "FUTURE STAR" or "DIAMOND STAR" and the absence of the large team logo in the background. Because of the manner of distribution, some promos are more difficult to find in the hobby market.

	NM/M
Complete Set (64):	35.00
Common Player:	.50

(1) Kris Benson .50
(2) Kevin Brown .50
(3) Roger Clemens 1.75
(4) Bartolo Colon .50
(5) Jeff D'Amico .50
(6) Ryan Dempster .50
(7) Adam Eaton .50
(8) Scott Elarton .50
(9) Livan Hernandez .50
(10) Tim Hudson .65
(11) Randy Johnson 1.00
(12) Darryl Kile .50
(13) Al Leiter .50
(14) Jon Lieber .50
(15) Greg Maddux 1.50
(16) Pedro Martinez 1.00
(17) Brad Radke .50
(18) Javier Vazquez .50
(19) Jeff Weaver .50
(20) David Wells .50
(1) Roberto Alomar .50
(2) Carlos Delgado .65
(3) Jason Giambi .75
(4) Troy Glaus .75
(5) Bobby Higginson .50
(6) David Justice .50
(7) Jeff Kent .50
(8) Ivan Rodriguez .65
(9) Gary Sheffield .75
(10) Frank Thomas 1.00
(11) Greg Vaughn .50
(12) Robin Ventura .50
(13) Rondell White .50
(1) Peter Bergeron .50
(2) Pat Burrell .75
(3) Sean Casey .50
(4) J.D. Drew .75
(5) Richard Hidalgo .50
(6) Melvin Mora .50
(7) Eric Owens .50
(8) Aramis Ramirez .50
(9) Preston Wilson .50
(1) Joe Crede .50
(2) Corey Patterson .75
(3) Albert Pujols 15.00
(4) Ben Sheets .50
(5) Alfonso Soriano .75

2001 MLB Showdown 1st Edition

MLB Showdown returned for a second season in 2001. Issued as a 50-card starter set, a 60-card "Draft Pack" and in nine-card booster packs, the set has 416 "regular" player cards, 46 premium holofoil star cards and 75 strategy cards. The holo premium cards were inserted in booster packs at a rate of

1:3. Promo cards were locally distributed. While collectors compete with gamers for these cards in the market, relative values placed on the cards by each group of buyers may differ. Cards without the silver-foil "1st Edition" logo were released in booster packs and are worth about half the prices shown here.

	NM/M
Complete Set (537):	195.00
Common Player:	.15
Starter Box:	12.00
Booster Pack (9):	1.50
Booster Box (36):	25.00

1 Garret Anderson .15
2 Darin Erstad (Foil) 2.00
3 Ron Gant .15
4 Troy Glaus (Foil) 3.00
5 Shigetosi Hasegawa .15
6 Adam Kennedy .15
7 Al Levine .15
8 Ben Molina .15
9 Troy Percival .15
10 Mark Petkovsek .15
11 Tim Salmon .15
12 Scott Schoeneweis .15
13 Scott Spezio .15
14 Mo Vaughn .15
15 Jarrod Washburn .15
16 Brian Anderson .15
17 Danny Bautista .15
18 Jay Bell .15
19 Greg Colbrunn .15
20 Steve Finley .15
21 Luis Gonzalez (Foil) 2.00
22 Randy Johnson (Foil) 3.50
23 Byung-Hyun Kim .15
24 Matt Mantei .15
25 Mike Morgan .15
26 Curt Schilling .30
27 Kelly Stinnett .15
28 Greg Swindell .15
29 Matt Williams .15
30 Tony Womack .15
31 Andy Ashby .15
32 Bobby Bonilla .15
33 Rafael Furcal (Foil) 2.00
34 Andres Galarraga .15
35 Tom Glavine (Foil) 2.50
36 Andruw Jones .50
37 Chipper Jones (Foil) 4.00
38 Brian Jordan .15
39 Wally Joyner .15
40 Keith Lockhart .15
41 Javy Lopez .15
42 Greg Maddux (Foil) 4.00
43 Kevin Millwood .15
44 Mike Remlinger .15
45 John Rocker .15
46 B.J. Surhoff .15
47 Quilvio Veras .15
48 Brady Anderson .15
49 Albert Belle .15
50 Jeff Conine .15
51 Delino DeShields .15
52 Buddy Groom .15
53 Trenidad Hubbard .15
54 Luis Matos .15
55 Jose Mercedes .15
56 Melvin Mora .15
57 Mike Mussina (Foil) 2.50
58 Sidney Ponson .15
59 Pat Rapp .15
60 Chris Richard .15
61 Cal Ripken Jr. (Foil) 7.00
62 Mike Trombley .15
63 Rolando Arrojo .15
64 Dante Bichette .15
65 Rheal Cormier .15
66 Carl Everett .15
67 Rich Garces .15
68 Nomar Garciaparra (Foil) 4.00
69 Mike Lansing .15
70 Darren Lewis .15
71 Derek Lowe .15
72 Pedro Martinez (Foil) 3.50
73 Ramon Martinez .15
74 Trot Nixon .15
75 Jose Offerman .15
76 Troy O'Leary .15
77 Jason Varitek .15
78 Rick Aguilera .15
79 Damon Buford .15
80 Joe Girardi .15
81 Mark Grace .15

82 Willie Greene .15
83 Ricky Gutierrez .15
84 Felix Heredia .15
85 Jon Lieber .15
86 Jeff Reed .15
87 Sammy Sosa (Foil) 4.50
88 Kevin Tapani .15
89 Todd Van Poppel .15
90 Rondell White .15
91 Kerry Wood .35
92 Eric Young .15
93 James Baldwin .15
94 Ray Durham .15
95 Keith Foulke (Foil) 2.00
96 Bob Howry .15
97 Charles Johnson (Foil) 2.00
98 Mark L. Johnson .15
99 Paul Konerko .25
100 Carlos Lee .25
101 Magglio Ordonez .15
102 Jim Parque .15
103 Herbert Perry .15
104 Bill Simas .15
105 Chris Singleton .15
106 Mike Sirotka .15
107 Frank Thomas (Foil) 3.50
108 Jose Valentin .15
109 Kelly Wunsch .15
110 Aaron Boone .15
111 Sean Casey .15
112 Danny Graves .15
113 Ken Griffey Jr. (Foil) 5.00
114 Pete Harnisch .15
115 Barry Larkin (Foil) 2.00
116 Alex Ochoa .15
117 Steve Parris .15
118 Pokey Reese .15
119 Chris Stynes .15
120 Scott Sullivan .15
121 Eddie Taubensee .15
122 Michael Tucker .15
123 Ron Villone .15
124 Dmitri Young .15
125 Roberto Alomar (Foil) 2.00
126 Sandy Alomar Jr. .15
127 Jason Bere .15
128 Dave Burba .15
129 Bartolo Colon .15
130 Wil Cordero .15
131 Chuck Finley .15
132 Travis Fryman .15
133 Steve Karsay .15
134 Kenny Lofton .15
135 Manny Ramirez (Foil) 3.50
136 David Segui .15
137 Jim Thome .45
138 Omar Vizquel .15
139 Bob Wickman .15
140 Pedro Astacio .15
141 Brian Bohannon .15
142 Jeff Cirillo .15
143 Jeff Frye .15
144 Jeffrey Hammonds .15
145 Todd Helton (Foil) 3.00
146 Todd Hollandsworth .15
147 Butch Huskey .15
148 Jose Jimenez .15
149 Brent Mayne .15
150 Neifi Perez .15
151 Terry Shumpert .15
152 Larry Walker .15
153 Gabe White (Foil) 2.00
154 Masato Yoshii .15
155 Matt Anderson .15
156 Brad Ausmus .15
157 Rich Becker .15
158 Tony Clark .15
159 Deivi Cruz .15
160 Damion Easley .15
161 Juan Encarnacion .15
162 Juan Gonzalez .30
163 Shane Halter .15
164 Bobby Higginson .15
165 Todd Jones (Foil) 2.00
166 Brian Moehler .15
167 Hideo Nomo .35
168 Dean Palmer .15
169 Jeff Weaver .15
170 Antonio Alfonseca .15
171 Luis Castillo (Foil) 2.00
172 Ryan Dempster (Foil) 2.00
173 Cliff Floyd .15
174 Alex Gonzalez .15
175 Mark Kotsay .15
176 Derrek Lee .35
177 Braden Looper .15
178 Mike Lowell .15
179 Brad Penny .15
180 Mike Redmond .15
181 Henry Rodriguez .15
182 Jesus Sanchez .15
183 Mark Smith .15
184 Preston Wilson .15
185 Moises Alou .15
186 Jeff Bagwell (Foil) 3.50
187 Lance Berkman .15
188 Craig Biggio .15
189 Tim Bogar .15
190 Jose Cabrera .15
191 Octavio Dotel .15
192 Scott Elarton (Foil) 2.00
193 Richard Hidalgo .15
194 Chris Holt .15
195 Jose Lima .15
196 Julio Lugo .15
197 Mitch Meluskey .15
198 Bill Spiers .15
199 Daryle Ward .15

200 Carlos Beltran .40
201 Ricky Bottalico .15
202 Johnny Damon (Foil) 2.50
203 Jermaine Dye .15
204 Carlos Febles .15
205 Dave McCarty .15
206 Mark Quinn .15
207 Joe Randa .15
208 Dan Reichert .15
209 Rey Sanchez .15
210 Jose Santiago .15
211 Jeff Suppan .15
212 Mac Suzuki .15
213 Mike Sweeney .15
214 Gregg Zaun .15
215 Terry Adams .15
216 Adrian Beltre .15
217 Kevin Brown (Foil) 2.00
218 Alex Cora .15
219 Darren Dreifort .15
220 Tom Goodwin .15
221 Shawn Green .25
222 Mark Grudzielanek .15
223 Dave Hansen .15
224 Todd Hundley .15
225 Eric Karros .15
226 Chad Kreuter .15
227 Chan Ho Park .15
228 Jeff Shaw .15
229 Gary Sheffield (Foil) 2.50
230 Juan Acevedo .15
231 Ron Belliard .15
232 Henry Blanco .15
233 Jeromy Burnitz .15
234 Jeff D'Amico (Foil) 2.00
235 Valerio de los Santos .15
236 Marquis Grissom .15
237 Charlie Hayes .15
238 Jimmy Haynes .15
239 Jose Hernandez .15
240 Geoff Jenkins .15
241 Curtis Leskanic .15
242 Mark Loretta .15
243 Richie Sexson .15
244 Dave Weathers .15
245 Jay Canizaro .15
246 Ron Coomer .15
247 Cristian Guzman .15
248 LaTroy Hawkins .15
249 Denny Hocking .15
250 Torii Hunter .15
251 Jacque Jones .15
252 Corey Koskie .15
253 Matt Lawton .15
254 Matt LeCroy .15
255 Eric Milton .15
256 David Ortiz .40
257 Brad Radke (Foil) 2.00
258 Mark Redman .15
259 Bob Wells .15
260 Michael Barrett .15
261 Peter Bergeron .15
262 Milton Bradley .15
263 Orlando Cabrera .15
264 Vladimir Guerrero (Foil) 3.50
265 Wilton Guerrero .15
266 Dustin Hermanson .15
267 Terry Jones .15
268 Steve Kline .15
269 Felipe Lira .15
270 Mike Mordecai .15
271 Lee Stevens .15
272 Anthony Telford .15
273 Javier Vazquez .15
274 Jose Vidro (Foil) 2.00
275 Edgardo Alfonzo (Foil) 2.00
276 Derek Bell .15
277 Armando Benitez .15
278 Mike Bordick .15
279 Mike Hampton (Foil) 2.00
280 Lenny Harris .15
281 Al Leiter .15
282 Jay Payton .15
283 Mike Piazza (Foil) 5.00
284 Todd Pratt .15
285 Glendon Rusch .15
286 Bubba Trammell .15
287 Robin Ventura .15
288 Turk Wendell .15
289 Rick White .15
290 Todd Zeile .15
291 Scott Brosius .15
292 Roger Clemens (Foil) 4.50
293 Jason Grimsley .15
294 Orlando Hernandez .15
295 Derek Jeter (Foil) 7.00
296 Dave Justice .15
297 Chuck Knoblauch .15
298 Tino Martinez .15
299 Denny Neagle .15
300 Jeff Nelson .15
301 Paul O'Neill .15
302 Andy Pettitte .25
303 Jorge Posada .15
304 Mariano Rivera (Foil) 2.00
305 Jose Vizcaino .15
306 Bernie Williams (Foil) 2.00
307 Kevin Appier .15
308 Eric Chavez .15
309 Ryan Christenson .15
310 Jason Giambi (Foil) 3.00
311 Jeremy Giambi .15
312 Ben Grieve .15
313 Gil Heredia .15
314 Ramon Hernandez .15
315 Tim Hudson (Foil) 2.50
316 Jason Isringhausen .15
317 Terrence Long (Foil) 2.00

318	Jim Mecir	.15
319	Mark Mulder	.15
320	Matt Stairs	.15
321	Miguel Tejada	.25
322	Randy Velarde	.15
323	Bobby Abreu	.15
324	Jeff Brantley	.15
325	Pat Burrell	.45
326	Omar Daal	.15
327	Rob Ducey	.15
328	Doug Glanville	.15
329	Wayne Gomes	.15
330	Kevin Jordan	.15
331	Travis Lee	.15
332	Mike Lieberthal	.15
333	Vicente Padilla	.15
334	Robert Person	.15
335	Scott Rolen (Foil)	2.50
336	Kevin Sefcik	.15
337	Randy Wolf	.15
338	Jimmy Anderson	.15
339	Mike Benjamin	.15
340	Kris Benson	.15
341	Adrian Brown	.15
342	Brian Giles (Foil)	2.00
343	Jason Kendall (Foil)	2.00
344	Pat Meares	.15
345	Wayne Morris	.15
346	Aramis Ramirez	.15
347	Todd Ritchie	.15
348	Scott Sauerbeck	.15
349	Jose Silva	.15
350	John Vander Wal	.15
351	Mike Williams	.15
352	Kevin Young	.15
353	Carlos Almanzar	.15
354	Bret Boone	.15
355	Matt Clement	.15
356	Adam Eaton	.15
357	Wiki Gonzalez	.15
358	Trevor Hoffman (Foil)	2.00
359	Damian Jackson	.15
360	Ryan Klesko	.15
361	Phil Nevin (Foil)	2.00
362	Eric Owens	.15
363	Desi Relaford	.15
364	Ruben Rivera	.15
365	Kevin Walker	.15
366	Woody Williams	.15
367	Jay Witasick	.15
368	Rich Aurilia	.15
369	Marvin Benard	.15
370	Barry Bonds (Foil)	7.00
371	Ellis Burks	.15
372	Bobby Estella	.15
373	Doug Henry	.15
374	Livan Hernandez	.15
375	Jeff Kent (Foil)	2.00
376	Doug Mirabelli	.15
377	Bill Mueller	.15
378	Calvin Murray	.15
379	Robb Nen (Foil)	2.00
380	Russ Ortiz	.15
381	Armando Rios	.15
382	Felix Rodriguez	.15
383	Kirk Rueter	.15
384	J.T. Snow	.15
385	Paul Abbott	.15
386	David Bell	.15
387	Jay Buhner	.15
388	Mike Cameron	.15
389	John Halama	.15
390	Rickey Henderson	.50
391	Al Martin	.15
392	Edgar Martinez (Foil)	2.00
393	Mark McLemore	.15
394	John Olerud	.15
395	Jose Paniagua	.15
396	Arthur Rhodes	.15
397	Alex Rodriguez (Foil)	6.00
398	Kazuhiro Sasaki (Foil)	2.00
399	Aaron Sele	.15
400	Dan Wilson	.15
401	Rick Ankiel (Foil)	2.00
402	Will Clark	.15
403	J.D. Drew	.45
404	Jim Edmonds (Foil)	2.00
405	Pat Hentgen	.15
406	Darryl Kile	.15
407	Ray Lankford	.15
408	Mike Matheny	.15
409	Mark McGwire (Foil)	6.00
410	Craig Paquette	.15
411	Placido Polanco	.15
412	Edgar Renteria	.15
413	Garrett Stephenson	.15
414	Fernando Tatis	.15
415	Mike Timlin	.15
416	Dave Veres	.15
417	Fernando Vina	.15
418	Miguel Cairo	.15
419	Vinny Castilla	.15
420	Steve Cox	.15
421	Doug Creek	.15
422	John Flaherty	.15
423	Jose Guillen	.15
424	Roberto Hernandez (Foil)	2.00
425	Russ Johnson	.15
426	Albie Lopez	.15
427	Felix Martinez	.15
428	Fred McGriff	.15
429	Bryan Rekar	.15
430	Greg Vaughn	.15
431	Gerald Williams	.15
432	Esteban Yan	.15
433	Luis Alicea	.15
434	Frank Catalanotto	.15
435	Royce Clayton	.15

436	Tim Crabtree	.15
437	Chad Curtis	.15
438	Rusty Greer	.15
439	Rick Helling	.15
440	Gabe Kapler	.15
441	Mike Lamb	.15
442	Ricky Ledee	.15
443	Rafael Palmeiro	.45
444	Ivan Rodriguez (Foil)	3.00
445	Kenny Rogers	.15
446	Mike Venafro	.15
447	John Wetteland	.15
448	Tony Batista (Foil)	2.00
449	Jose Cruz, Jr.	.15
450	Carlos Delgado (Foil)	2.50
451	Kelvim Escobar	.15
452	Darrin Fletcher	.15
453	Brad Fullmer	.15
454	Alex S. Gonzalez	.15
455	Mark Guthrie	.15
456	Billy Koch	.15
457	Esteban Loaiza	.15
458	Raul Mondesi	.15
459	Mickey Morandini	.15
460	Paul Quantrill	.15
461	Shannon Stewart	.15
462	David Wells (Foil)	2.00
S1	Change Sides (Jorge Posada)	.05
S2	Clutch Hitter (Nomar Garciaparra)	.15
S3	Clutch Hitting (Manny Ramirez)	.10
S4	Contact Hitter (Bernie Williams)	.05
S5	Deep in the Gap (Sammy Sosa)	.15
S6	Dog Meat (Brian Buchanon)	.05
S7	Double Steal (Jay Canizaro)	.05
S8	Down the Middle (Michael Tucker)	.05
S9	Drag Bunt (Unidentified)	.05
S10	Drained (Luis Castillo)	.05
S11	Ducks on the Pond (Carl Everett)	.05
S12	Favorable Matchup (Carlos Delgado)	.10
S13	Fight It Off (Unidentified)	.05
S14	Free Swinger (Benji Molina)	.05
S15	Fuel on the Fire (Eric Young)	.05
S16	Hiding an Injury (Unidentified)	.05
S17	In Motion (Nomar Garciaparra)	.15
S18	Last Chance (Alex Ochoa)	.05
S19	Lean Into It (Unidentified)	.05
S20	Nuisance (Rickey Henderson)	.10
S21	Off-Balance (Alex Gonzalez)	.05
S22	Out of Gas (Hideo Nomo)	.10
S23	Overthrow (Sean Casey)	.05
S24	Play the Percentages (Unidentified)	.05
S25	Power Hitter (Unidentified)	.05
S26	Protect the Runner (Chuck Knoblauch)	.05
S27	Pull the Ball (Todd Helton)	.10
S28	Rally Cap (Tim Salmon)	.05
S29	Rough Outing (Randy Johnson)	.10
S30	Runner Not Held (Johnny Damon)	.05
S31	Running on Fumes (Unidentified)	.05
S32	Ruptured Disk (Alex Rodriguez)	.25
S33	Sail Into Center (Pokey Reese)	.05
S34	Say the Magic Word (Mark McGwire)	.25
S35	Shell Shocked (Unidentified)	.05
S36	Singles Hitter (Homer Bush)	.05
S37	Smash up the Middle (Unidentified)	.05
S38	Stick a Fork in Him (Unidentified)	.05
S39	Take What's Given (Unidentified)	.05
S40	To the Warning Track (Brian Giles)	.05
S41	Turn On It (Shawon Dunston)	.05
S42	Anointed Closer (Cutis Leskanic)	.05
S43	By the Book (Unidentified)	.05
S44	Cannon (Bobby Higginson)	.05
S45	Choke (Unidentified)	.05
S46	Fast Worker (Greg Maddux)	.15
S47	Flamethrower (unidentified)	.05
S48	Full Windup (Kevin Brown)	.05
S49	Goose Egg (Omar Vizquel)	.05
S50	Great Start (Tom Glavine)	.10
S51	Great Throw (Neifi Perez)	.05
S52	Gutsy Play (Mike Lamb)	.05
S53	Highlight Reel (Pokey Reese)	.05

S54	Insult to Injury (Unidentified)	.05
S55	In the Groove (Randy Johnson)	.10
S56	Job Well Done (Unidentified)	.05
S57	Just Foul (Unidentified)	.05
S58	Just Over the Wall (Bernie Williams)	.05
S59	Leaping Catch (Barry Bonds)	.35
S60	Lefty Specialist (Jason Christensen)	.05
S61	Low and Away (Eddie Taubensee)	.05
S62	Mound Conference (Unidentified)	.05
S63	Nerves of Steel (Todd Jones)	.05
S64	Pitchout (Unidentified)	.05
S65	Scuff the Ball (Brian Moehler)	.05
S66	Sloppy Bunt (Livan Hernandez)	.05
S67	Soft Hands (Omar Vizquel)	.05
S68	Submarine Pitch (Byung-Hyun Kim)	.05
S69	Visibly Upset (Unidentified)	.05
S70	What Were You Thinking??? (Benito Santiago)	.05
S71	Air It Out (Kevin Brown)	.05
S72	Bear Down (Pedro Martinez)	.10
S73	Brainstorm (Bobby Cox)	.05
S74	Game of Inches (Dmitri Young)	.05
S75	Second Look (Moises Alou)	.05

2001 MLB Showdown Pennant Run Promos

To promote its Pennant Run update edition, Wizards of the Coast issued eight specially marked sample cards to persons attending All-Star FanFest, the National Sports Collectors Convention and the Origins Gaming Convention (Gen Con) in the summer of 2001. The promos are virtually identical to the issued versions of the same players' cards except for the presence on front of a large logo indicating the show at which the cards were distributed.

		NM/M
Complete Set (6):		7.50
Common Player:		1.00
008	C.C. Sabathia	1.00
017	Juan Pierre	1.00
084	Wes Helms	1.00
087	Ben Sheets	1.00
127	Luis Rivas	1.00
169	Ichiro (Suzuki)	3.50

2001 MLB Showdown Pennant Run

Issued after the 2002 season opened, this is essentially an update to the interactive MLB Showdown game. Players in the set are generally those who changed teams during the off-season, or promising

rookies. The Pennant Run edition was issued in a Booster box of 36 nine-card (seven player, two strategy) packs. The set has 100 "regular" player cards, 25 SP (1:3) holofoil star cards and 25 strategy cards. Cards #91-125 are a Super Season player subset. While collectors compete with gamers for these cards in the market, relative values placed on the cards by each group of buyers may differ.

		NM/M
Complete Set (200):		75.00
Common Player:		.15
Booster Pack (9):		1.50
Booster Box (36):		25.00
001	Randy Velarde	.15
002	Dustin Hermanson	.15
003	Jamie Moyer	.15
004	Aaron Fultz	.15
005	Barry Zito (Foil)	2.50
006	Adam Piatt	.15
007	Ben Grieve	.15
008	C.C. Sabathia (Foil)	2.00
009	Eddie Guardado	.15
010	Matt Kinney	.15
011	Blake Stein	.15
012	Billy Wagner (Foil)	2.00
013	Chris Holt	.15
014	Homer Bush	.15
015	Vladimir Nunez	.15
016	C.J. Nitkowski	.15
017	Juan Pierre	.25
018	Jose Valentin	.15
019	Juan Gonzalez	.30
020	Derek Bell	.15
021	Wade Miller	.15
022	Shawn Estes	.15
023	Enrique Wilson	.15
024	Dave Magadan	.15
025	Jason Christiansen	.15
026	Paul Shuey	.15
027	Mark Wohlers	.15
028	John Riedling	.15
029	Francisco Cordova	.15
030	Craig House	.15
031	Scott Strickland	.15
032	Octavio Dotel	.15
033	Jimmy Rollins (Foil)	2.00
034	Carl Pavano	.15
035	Sandy Alomar Jr.	.15
036	Hideki Irabu	.15
037	Tom Gordon	.15
038	Roosevelt Brown	.15
039	Alex Rodriguez (Foil)	4.00
040	Andres Galarraga	.15
041	Rob Bell	.15
042	Jason Schmidt	.15
043	Rod Beck	.15
044	Paul Rigdon	.15
045	Dan Miceli	.15
046	Ricky Bones	.15
047	Mike Hampton (Foil)	2.00
048	Cliff Politte	.15
049	Chris Stynes	.15
050	Ramiro Mendoza	.15
051	Todd Walker	.15
052	Fernando Seguignol	.15
053	Mark Guthrie	.15
054	Tony Armas Jr.	.15
055	Billy McMillon	.15
056	Gary Bennett	.15
057	Corey Patterson (Foil)	2.00
058	Juan Guzman	.15
059	Joe Crede	.25
060	A.J. Pierzynski	.15
061	Ben Davis	.15
062	Alan Embree	.15
063	Jon Garland (Foil)	2.00
064	Ryan Kohlmeier	.15
065	Andy Benes	.15
066	Ron Gant	.15
067	Jerry Hairston Jr.	.15
068	Odalis Perez	.15
069	Lance Painter	.15
070	Jose Segui	.15
071	Russ Davis	.15
072	Jeff Zimmerman	.15
073	Dennys Reyes	.15
074	Jamey Wright	.15
075	Rico Brogna	.15
076	Geraldo Guzman	.15
077	Eric Gagne	.15
078	Bruce Chen	.15
079	Justin Speier	.15
080	Randy Keisler	.15
081	Ellis Burks (Foil)	2.00
082	Alfonso Soriano	.50
083	Jeff Nelson	.15
084	Wes Helms	.15
085	Freddy Garcia (Foil)	2.00
086	Erubiel Durazo	.15
087	Ben Sheets (Foil)	2.00
088	Jose Ortiz (Foil)	2.00
089	Paul Wilson	.15
090	Onan Masaoka	.15
091	Jose Rosado	.15
092	A.J. Burnett	.15
093	Bubba Trammell	.15
094	Mike Fetters	.15
095	Jacob Cruz	.15
096	John Franco	.15
097	Armando Reynoso	.15
098	Lou Pote	.15

099	D'Angelo Jiminez (Foil)	2.00
100	Julio Zuleta	.15
101	Charles Johnson (Foil)	2.00
102	Tsuyoshi Shinjo	.15
103	Brett Tomko	.15
104	Marcus Giles	.15
105	Craig Counsell	.15
106	Ruben Mateo	.15
107	Andy Ashby	.15
108	Marlon Anderson	.15
109	Mark Grace	.15
110	Russ Branyan	.15
111	Julian Tavarez	.15
112	Joey Hamilton	.15
113	Jason LaRue	.15
114	Benji Gil	.15
115	Bill Mueller	.15
116	Mike Stanton	.15
117	Ray King	.15
118	Timoniel Perez	.15
119	Johnny Damon (Foil)	2.50
120	Matt Morris	.15
121	Kevin Appier	.15
122	Frank Castillo	.15
123	Mike Darr	.15
124	Felipe Crespo	.15
125	John Smoltz (Foil)	2.00
126	Ben Weber	.15
127	Luis Rivas	.15
128	Travis Harper	.15
129	Aubrey Huff	.15
130	Paul LoDuca	.15
131	Eric Davis	.15
132	Fernando Tatis	.15
133	Ugueth Urbina	.15
134	Steve Kline	.15
135	Tanyon Sturtze	.15
136	Scott Hatteberg	.15
137	Tomokazu Ohka (Foil)	2.00
138	Melvin Mora	.15
139	Kip Wells	.15
140	Ken Caminiti	.15
141	Dave Martinez	.15
142	Robert Fick	.15
143	Mike Bordick	.15
144	Doug Mientkiewicz	.15
145	Darryl Hamilton	.15
146	Shane Reynolds	.15
147	Vernon Wells (Foil)	2.00
148	Rey Ordonez	.15
149	Brad Ausmus	.15
150	Jay Powell	.15
151	Todd Hundley	.15
152	Travis Miller	.15
153	Tyler Houston	.15
154	Nelson Cruz	.15
155	Manny Ramirez (Foil)	3.00
156	Luis Lopez	.15
157	Luis Sojo	.15
158	Tony Gwynn (Foil)	3.50
159	Roger Cedeno	.15
160	Royce Clayton	.15
161	Olmedo Saenz	.15
162	Brook Fordyce	.15
163	Dee Brown	.15
164	David Wells (Foil)	2.00
165	Jack Wilson	.15
166	Pedro Feliz	.15
167	Hideo Nomo	.15
168	Albert Pujols (Foil)	20.00
169	Ichiro (Suzuki) (Foil)	6.00
170	Ramon Ortiz	.15
171	Mike Holtz	.15
172	Chris Woodward	.15
173	Mike Mussina (Foil)	2.50
174	Carlos Guillen	.15
175	Ben Petrick	.15
S1	Advance on Throw (Johnny Damon, Shane Halter)	.05
S2	Ball in the Dirt (Roberto Alomar, Ruben Mateo)	.05
S3	Constant Pressure (Sammy Sosa, Mark McGwire)	.35
S4	Emergency Bunt (Jeff Leifer)	.05
S5	First-Pitch Swinging (Cal Ripken, Jr.)	.50
S6	Go Up Hacking (Mike Piazza)	.35
S7	Speedster (Derek Jeter)	.50
S8	Sprint to Second (Jose Valentin)	.05
S9	Wild Thing (Benito Santiago)	.05
S10	Wipeout (J.D. Drew)	.10
S11	Caught Napping (Tony Gwynn)	.20
S12	Comebacker (Greg Maddux)	.20
S13	Confusion (Julio Zuleta, Dmitri Young)	.05
S14	Double-Play Whiz (Ray Durham)	.05
S15	Fired Up (Abraham Nunez)	.05
S16	Focused (Rey Ordonez)	.05
S17	Going the Distance (Roger Clemens)	.25
S18	Great Pickoff Move (Rick Ankiel)	.05
S19	Groundball Pitcher (Greg Maddux)	.20
S20	Hung It (Danny Graves)	.05
S21	Pitch Around (Mark McGwire)	.40
S22	Pour It On (Al Leiter)	.05
S23	Clutch Performance (Barry Bonds)	.50
S24	Dot Racing (Mascots)	.05

S25	It's Crunch Time (Dennys Reyes)	.05
	Checklist 1 (001-066)	.05
	Checklist 2 (067-132)	.05
	Checklist 3 (133-S25)	.05
	Pitcher Usage Card	.05

2002 MLB Showdown Promos

		NM/M
Complete Set (10):		20.00
Common Player:		2.00
(1)	Shawn Green	2.00
(2)	Ichiro	4.00
(3)	Derek Jeter	5.00
(4)	Andruw Jones	2.50
(5)	Trot Nixon	2.00
(6)	Andy Pettitte	2.00
(7)	Alex Rodriguez	4.00
(8)	Sammy Sosa	3.00
(9)	Kerry Wood	2.00
(10)	Jeff Zimmerman	2.00

2002 MLB Showdown

MLB Showdown's third season issue in 2002 has 300 "regular" player cards, 56 premium holofoil star cards and 50 strategy cards, including short-prints. The holo premium cards were inserted in booster packs at a rate of 1:3. While collectors compete with gamers in the market, relative values placed on the cards by each group of buyers may differ.

		NM/M
Complete Set (406):		175.00
Common Player:		.15
Starter Set:		6.00
Booster Pack:		1.50
Booster Box (36):		20.00
1	Garret Anderson	.15
2	David Eckstein	.15
3	Darin Erstad	.30
4	Troy Glaus (Foil)	2.50
5	Adam Kennedy	.15
6	Ben Molina	.15
7	Ramon Ortiz	.15
8	Troy Percival	.15
9	Tim Salmon	.15
10	Scott Schoeneweis	.15
11	Scott Spiezio	.15
12	Jarrod Washburn	.15
13	Miguel Batista	.15
14	Jay Bell	.15
15	Craig Counsell	.15
16	David Dellucci	.15
17	Erubiel Durazo	.15
18	Steve Finley	.15
19	Luis Gonzalez (Foil)	2.00
20	Mark Grace	.15
21	Randy Johnson (Foil)	3.00
22	Byun-Hun Kim	.15
23	Albie Lopez	.15
24	Curt Schilling (Foil)	2.50
25	Matt Williams	.15
26	Tony Womack	.15
27	Marcus Giles (Foil)	2.00
28	Tom Glavine	.25
29	Andruw Jones	.15
30	Chipper Jones (Foil)	4.00
31	Brian Jordan	.15
32	Steve Karsay	.15
33	Javy Lopez	.15
34	Greg Maddux (Foil)	4.00
35	Jason Marquis	.15
36	Mike Remlinger	.15
37	Rey Sanchez	.15
38	B.J. Surhoff	.15
39	Brady Anderson	.15
40	Tony Batista (Foil)	2.00
41	Mike Bordick	.15
42	Jeff Conine	.15
43	Buddy Groom	.15
44	Jerry Hairston Jr.	.15
45	Jason Johnson	.15
46	Melvin Mora	.15
47	Chris Richard	.15
48	B.J. Ryan	.15
49	Josh Towers	.15
50	Rolando Arrojo	.15
51	Rod Beck	.15
52	Dante Bichette	.15
53	David Cone	.15
54	Carl Everett	.15
55	Rich Garces	.15
56	Derek Lowe	.15

#	Player	Price
57	Trot Nixon	.15
58	Hideo Nomo	.35
59	Jose Offerman	.15
60	Troy O'Leary	.15
61	Manny Ramirez (Foil)	3.00
62	Delino DeShields	.15
63	Kyle Farnsworth	.15
64	Jeff Fassero	.15
65	Ricky Gutierrez	.15
66	Todd Hundley	.15
67	Jon Lieber	.15
68	Fred McGriff	.15
69	Bill Mueller	.15
70	Corey Patterson	.15
71	Sammy Sosa (Foil)	5.00
72	Julian Tavares	.15
73	Kerry Wood	.30
74	Eric Young	.15
75	Mark Buehrle (Foil)	2.00
76	Royce Clayton	.15
77	Joe Crede	.15
78	Ray Durham	.15
79	Keith Foulke	.15
80	Bob Howry	.15
81	Mark L. Johnson	.15
82	Paul Konerko	.25
83	Carlos Lee	.25
84	Sean Lowe	.15
85	Magglio Ordonez	.15
86	Jose Valentin	.15
87	Aaron Boone	.15
88	Jim Brower	.15
89	Sean Casey	.15
90	Brady Clark	.15
91	Adam Dunn (Foil)	2.00
92	Danny Graves	.15
93	Ken Griffey Jr. (Foil)	6.00
94	Pokey Reese	.15
95	Chris Reitsma	.15
96	Kelly Stinnett	.15
97	Dmitri Young	.15
98	Roberto Alomar (Foil)	2.00
99	Danys Baez	.15
100	Russell Branyan	.15
101	Ellis Burks	.15
102	Bartolo Colon	.15
103	Marty Cordova	.15
104	Einar Diaz	.15
105	Juan Gonzalez	.30
106	Ricardo Rincon	.15
107	C.C. Sabathia (Foil)	2.00
108	Paul Shuey	.15
109	Jim Thome (Foil)	2.50
110	Omar Vizquel	.15
111	Bob Wickman	.15
112	Shawn Chacon	.15
113	Jeff Cirillo	.15
114	Mike Hampton	.15
115	Todd Helton (Foil)	2.50
116	Greg Norton	.15
117	Ben Petrick	.15
118	Juan Pierre	.15
119	Terry Shumpert	.15
120	Larry Walker (Foil)	2.00
121	Matt Anderson	.15
122	Roger Cedeno	.15
123	Tony Clark	.15
124	Deivi Cruz	.15
125	Damion Easley	.15
126	Shane Halter	.15
127	Bobby Higginson (Foil)	2.00
128	Jose Macias	.15
129	Steve Sparks	.15
130	Jeff Weaver	.15
131	Antonio Alfonseca	.15
132	Josh Beckett (Foil)	2.50
133	A.J. Burnett	.15
134	Luis Castillo	.15
135	Ryan Dempster	.15
136	Cliff Floyd	.15
137	Alex Gonzalez	.15
138	Braden Looper	.15
139	Mike Lowell	.15
140	Eric Owens	.15
141	Brad Penny	.15
142	Preston Wilson	.15
143	Moises Alou	.15
144	Brad Ausmus	.15
145	Jeff Bagwell (Foil)	3.00
146	Lance Berkman (Foil)	2.00
147	Craig Biggio	.15
148	Octavio Dotel	.15
149	Richard Hidalgo	.15
150	Julio Lugo	.15
151	Wade Miller	.15
152	Roy Oswalt (Foil)	2.00
153	Shane Reynolds	.15
154	Jose Vizcaino	.15
155	Daryle Ward	.15
156	Carlos Beltran (Foil)	2.50
157	Dee Brown	.15
158	Roberto Hernandez	.15
159	Mark Quinn	.15
160	Joe Randa	.15
161	Dan Reichert	.15
162	Jeff Suppan	.15
163	Mike Sweeney	.15
164	Kris Wilson	.15
165	Terry Adams	.15
166	Adrian Beltre	.15
167	Alex Cora	.15
168	Tom Goodwin	.15
169	Shawn Green	.25
170	Marquis Grissom	.15
171	Mark Grudzielanek	.15
172	Eric Karros	.15
173	Paul LoDuca (Foil)	2.00
174	Chan Ho Park	.15
175	Luke Prokopec	.15
176	Gary Sheffield	.30
177	Ronnie Belliard	.15
178	Henry Blanco	.15
179	Jeromy Burnitz	.15
180	Mike DeJean	.15
181	Chad Fox	.15
182	Jose Hernandez	.15
183	Geoff Jenkins	.15
184	Mark Loretta	.15
185	Nick Neugebauer	.15
186	Richie Sexson	.15
187	Ben Sheets (Foil)	2.00
188	Devon White	.15
189	Cristian Guzman (Foil)	2.00
190	Torii Hunter	.15
191	Jacque Jones	.15
192	Corey Koskie	.15
193	Joe Mays	.15
194	Doug Mientkiewicz	.15
195	Eric Milton	.15
196	David Ortiz	.40
197	A.J. Pierzynski	.15
198	Brad Radke	.15
199	Luis Rivas	.15
200	Tony Armas Jr.	.15
201	Michael Barrett	.15
202	Peter Bergeron	.15
203	Orlando Cabrera	.15
204	Vladimir Guerrero (Foil)	3.00
205	Graeme Lloyd	.15
206	Scott Strickland	.15
207	Fernando Tatis	.15
208	Mike Thurman	.15
209	Javier Vazquez	.15
210	Jose Vidro	.15
211	Brad Wilkerson	.15
212	Edgardo Alfonzo	.15
213	Kevin Appier	.15
214	Armando Benitez	.15
215	Alex Escobar	.15
216	John Franco	.15
217	Al Leiter	.15
218	Rey Ordonez	.15
219	Mike Piazza (Foil)	6.00
220	Glendon Rusch	.15
221	Tsuyoshi Shinjo	.15
222	Steve Trachsel	.15
223	Todd Zeile	.15
224	Roger Clemens (Foil)	5.00
225	Derek Jeter (Foil)	9.00
226	Nick Johnson	.15
227	David Justice	.15
228	Tino Martinez	.15
229	Ramiro Mendoza	.15
230	Mike Mussina (Foil)	2.50
231	Andy Pettitte	.25
232	Jorge Posada	.15
233	Mariano Rivera (Foil)	2.00
234	Alfonso Soriano	.40
235	Mike Stanton	.15
236	Bernie Williams (Foil)	2.00
237	Eric Chavez	.15
238	Johnny Damon	.30
239	Jermaine Dye	.15
240	Jason Giambi (Foil)	2.50
241	Jeremy Giambi	.15
242	Ramon Hernandez	.15
243	Tim Hudson (Foil)	2.00
244	Jason Isringhausen	.15
245	Terrence Long	.15
246	Mark Mulder (Foil)	2.00
247	Olmedo Saenz	.15
248	Miguel Tejada	.25
249	Barry Zito	.25
250	Bobby Abreu	.15
251	Marlon Anderson	.15
252	Ricky Bottalico	.15
253	Pat Burrell	.35
254	Omar Daal	.15
255	Johnny Estrada	.15
256	Nelson Figueroa	.15
257	Travis Lee	.15
258	Robert Person	.15
259	Scott Rolen (Foil)	2.50
260	Jimmy Rollins (Foil)	2.00
261	Randy Wolf	.15
262	Brian Giles (Foil)	2.00
263	Jason Kendall	.15
264	Josias Manzanillo	.15
265	Warren Morris	.15
266	Aramis Ramirez	.15
267	Todd Ritchie	.15
268	Craig Wilson	.15
269	Jack Wilson	.15
270	Kevin Young	.15
271	Ben Davis	.15
272	Wiki Gonzalez	.15
273	Rickey Henderson	.45
274	Junior Herndon	.15
275	Trevor Hoffman	.15
276	Damian Jackson	.15
277	D'Angelo Jimenez	.15
278	Mark Kotsay	.15
279	Phil Nevin (Foil)	2.00
280	Bubba Trammell	.15
281	Rich Aurilia (Foil)	2.00
282	Marvin Benard	.15
283	Barry Bonds (Foil)	9.00
284	Shawn Estes	.15
285	Pedro Feliz	.15
286	Jeff Kent (Foil)	2.00
287	Robb Nen	.15
288	Russ Ortiz	.15
289	Felix Rodriguez	.15
290	Kirk Rueter	.15
291	Benito Santiago	.15
292	J.T. Snow	.15
293	John Vander Wal	.15
294	Bret Boone (Foil)	2.00
295	Mike Cameron	.15
296	Freddy Garcia (Foil)	2.00
297	Carlos Guillen	.15
298	Edgar Martinez (Foil)	2.00
299	Mark McLemore	.15
300	Jamie Moyer	.15
301	Jeff Nelson	.15
302	John Olerud	.15
303	Arthur Rhodes	.15
304	Kazuhiro Sasaki (Foil)	2.00
305	Aaron Sele	.15
306	Ichiro (Foil)	9.00
307	Dan Wilson	.15
308	J.D. Drew (Foil)	2.50
309	Jim Edmonds (Foil)	2.00
310	Dustin Hermanson	.15
311	Darryl Kile	.15
312	Steve Kline	.15
313	Mike Matheny	.15
314	Matt Morris	.15
315	Craig Paquette	.15
316	Placido Polanco	.15
317	Albert Pujols (Foil)	8.00
318	Edgar Renteria	.15
319	Bud Smith	.15
320	Dave Veres	.15
321	Fernando Vina	.15
322	Brent Abernathy	.15
323	Steve Cox	.15
324	Ben Grieve	.15
325	Aubrey Huff	.15
326	Joe Kennedy (Foil)	2.00
327	Tanyon Sturtze	.15
328	Jason Tyner	.15
329	Greg Vaughn	.15
330	Paul Wilson	.15
331	Esteban Yan	.15
332	Frank Catalanotto	.15
333	Chad Curtis	.15
334	Doug Davis	.15
335	Gabe Kapler	.15
336	Mike Lamb	.15
337	Darren Oliver	.15
338	Rafael Palmeiro	.40
339	Alex Rodriguez (Foil)	8.00
340	Ivan Rodriguez (Foil)	2.50
341	Mike Venafro	.15
342	Michael Young	.15
343	Jeff Zimmerman	.15
344	Chris Carpenter	.15
345	Jose Cruz	.15
346	Carlos Delgado (Foil)	2.50
347	Kelvim Escobar	.15
348	Darrin Fletcher	.15
349	Brad Fullmer	.15
350	Alex S. Gonzalez	.15
351	Billy Koch	.15
352	Esteban Loaiza	.15
353	Raul Mondesi	.15
354	Paul Quantrill	.15
355	Shannon Stewart	.15
356	Vernon Wells	.15
S01	Bad Call (Bernie Williams)	.05
S02	Clutch Hitting (Mike Piazza)	.25
S03	Crowd the Plate (Troy Glaus)	.10
S04	Down the Middle/SP (Unidentified)	.50
S05	Drag Bunt/SP (Corey Patterson)	.50
S06	Ducks on the Pond (Unidentified)	.05
S07	Fuel on the Fire/SP (Barry Bonds)	1.50
S08	Last Chance (Craig Biggio)	.05
S09	Nuisance/SP (Unidentified)	.05
S10	Out of Gas (Unidentified)	.05
S11	Payoff Pitch/SP (Manny Ramirez)	.75
S12	Professional Baserunner/SP (Unidentified)	.50
S13	Protect the Runner/SP (Unidentified)	.50
S14	Pull the Ball (Rafael Palmeiro)	.10
S15	Rally Cap (Tom Goodwin)	.05
S16	Rough Outing (Unidentified)	.05
S17	Runner Not Held (Unidentified)	.05
S18	Running on Fumes/SP (Unidentified)	.50
S19	Ruptured Duck/SP (Unidentified)	.50
S20	Sit on the Fastball (Jose Cruz)	.05
S21	Stick a Fork in Him (Kevin Appier)	.05
S22	Sweet Swing (Barry Bonds)	.75
S23	Take What's Given/SP (Johnny Damon)	.60
S24	To the Warning Track (Unidentified)	.05
S25	Turn On It (Lance Berkman)	.05
S26	By the Book (Brad Radke)	.05
S27	Cut Off in the Gap/SP (Unidentified)	.50
S28	Full Windup (Andy Pettitte)	.15
S29	Great Start (Barry Zito)	.05
S30	Great Throw (Ichiro)	.30
S31	Highlight Reel/SP (Brent Abernathy)	.50
S32	Insult to Injury (Curt Schilling)	.05
S33	In the Groove (Mark Mulder)	.05
S34	Intimidation (Mariano Rivera)	.05
S35	Job Well Done/SP (Arthur Rhodes)	.50
S36	Just Over the Wall/SP (Unidentified)	.50
S37	Knock the Ball Down (Abraham Nunez)	.05
S38	Lefty Specialist (Billy Wagner)	.05
S39	Low and Away (Randy Johnson)	.10
S40	Nerves of Steel (Trevor Hoffman)	.05
S41	Pitchout/SP (Unidentified)	.50
S42	Pumped Up (Unidentified)	.50
S43	Put Out the Fire (Kazuhiro Sasaki)	.05
S44	Rally Killer/SP (Unidentified)	.50
S45	Sloppy Bunt/SP (Unidentified)	.50
S46	Submarine Pitch/SP (Byung-Hyun Kim)	.50
S47	Change in Strategy (Unidentified)	.05
S48	Grounder to Second/SP (Unidentified)	.50
S49	It's Crunch Time/SP (Unidentified)	.50
S50	Second Look (Sean Casey)	.05

2002 MLB Showdown All-Star Edition

This specially marked edition of the MLB Showdown interactive game cards was produced for distribution at the All-Star FanFest. Cards have an All-Star Game logo on front and most picture the players in All-Star uniforms.

#	Player	NM/M
	Complete Game Set (50):	20.00
	Common Player:	.50
1	Garret Anderson	.50
2	Tony Batista	.50
3	Mark Buehrle	.50
4	Johnny Damon	.65
5	Robert Fick	.50
6	Freddy Garcia	.50
7	Nomar Garciaparra	1.00
8	Jason Giambi	.65
9	Roy Halladay	.50
10	Shea Hillenbrand	.50
11	Torii Hunter	.50
12	Ichiro	1.50
13	Derek Jeter	2.00
14	Paul Konerko	.60
15	Derek Lowe	.50
16	Jorge Posada	.50
17	Manny Ramirez	.75
18	Mariano Rivera	.50
19	Alex Rodriguez	1.50
20	Kazuhiro Sasaki	.50
21	Alfonso Soriano	.60
22	Mike Sweeney	.50
23	Robin Ventura	.50
24	Omar Vizquel	.50
25	Barry Zito	.50
26	Lance Berkman	.50
27	Barry Bonds	2.00
28	Luis Castillo	.50
29	Adam Dunn	.50
30	Eric Gagne	.50
31	Luis Gonzalez	.50
32	Shawn Green	.50
33	Vladimir Guerrero	.75
34	Todd Helton	.60
35	Jose Hernandez	.50
36	Mike Lowell	.50
37	Andruw Jones	.50
38	Robb Nen	.50
39	Vicente Padilla	.50
40	Odalis Perez	.50
41	Mike Piazza	1.25
42	Scott Rolen	.60
43	Jimmy Rollins	.60
44	Benito Santiago	.50
45	Curt Schilling	.60
46	John Smoltz	.50
47	Sammy Sosa	1.25
48	Junior Spivey	.50
49	Jose Vidro	.50
50	Mike Williams	.50

2002 MLB Showdown League Prize Cards

#	Card	NM/M
	Complete Set (15):	15.00
	Common Card:	.25
(1)	Bobby Abreu	2.00
(2)	Miguel Batista	2.00
(3)	Armando Benitez	2.00
(4)	Mike Cameron	2.00
(5)	Magglio Ordonez	2.00
(6)	Rafael Palmeiro	3.00
(7)	Brad Penny	2.00
(8)	Aramis Ramirez	2.00
(9)	Miguel Tejada	2.00
(10)	Bad Call	.25
(11)	By the Book	.25
(12)	Change in Strategy	.25
(13)	Ducks on the Pond	.25
(14)	Lefty Specialist	.25
(15)	Rally Cap	.25

2002 MLB Showdown Pennant Run

Issued after the 2001 season opened, this is essentially an update to the interactive game MLB Showdown from veteran gamers Wizards of the Coast. Many players in the set changed teams over the off-season, or were promising rookies. The Pennant Run edition was issued in a Booster box of 36 nine-card (seven player, two strategy) packs. The set has 130 "regular" player cards, 25 premium holofoil star cards and 25 strategy cards. The holo premium cards were inserted in packs at a rate of 1:3. While collectors compete with gamers for these cards in the market, relative values placed on the cards by each group of buyers may differ.

#	Player	NM/M
	Complete Set (150):	60.00
	Common Player:	.15
	Booster Pack (9):	1.50
	Booster Box (36):	20.00
1	J.C. Romero	.15
2	Robb Nen	.15
3	Raul Mondesi	.15
4	Mike Piazza	.65
5	Scott Rolen	.30
6	Shigetoshi Hasegawa	.15
7	Shannon Stewart	.15
8	David Eckstein (Foil)	2.00
9	Melvin Mora	.15
10	Jose Rijo	.15
11	Einar Diaz	.15
12	A.J. Burnett	.15
13	Mike Sweeney	.15
14	Jorge Posada (Foil)	2.00
15	Mark Kotsay	.15
16	Doug Davis	.15
17	Steve Woodard	.15
18	Sun voo Kim	.15
19	Sean Casey	.15
20	Juan Acevedo	.15
21	Dustan Mohr	.15
22	Mariano Rivera	.15
23	Kip Wells	.15
24	Kenny Lofton (Foil)	2.00
25	Steve Cox	.15
26	Josh Fogg (Foil)	2.00
27	Ruben Sierra	.15
28	Sandy Alomar Jr.	.15
29	Vicente Padilla (Foil)	2.00
30	Carlos Beltran	.30
31	Mike Lowell	.15
32	Omar Vizquel	.15
33	Ricky Stone	.15
34	Geoff Jenkins	.15
35	Eric Karros	.15
36	Ryan Drese	.15
37	Adam Dunn	.25
38	Hank Blalock	.40
39	Marcus Giles	.15
40	Joe Randa	.15
41	Bob Wickman	.15
42	Roy Halladay	.15
43	Craig Counsell	.15
44	Derek Lowe	.15
45	Ray Durham	.15
46	Paul Shuey	.15
47	Cliff Floyd	.15
48	Shawn Green	.25
49	Torii Hunter	.15
50	Edgardo Alfonzo	.15
51	Carlos Pena	.15
52	Sean Burroughs	.15
53	Placido Polanco	.15
54	Rafael Palmeiro	.45
55	Nate Cornejo	.15
56	Tim Salmon	.15
57	Craig Biggio	.15
58	Eric Hinske (Foil)	2.00
59	Rickey Henderson	.45
60	Nick Johnson	.15
61	Rey Ordonez	.15
62	Jose Hernandez	.15
63	Antonio Alfonseca	.15
64	Alfonso Soriano (Foil)	2.50
65	Eric Chavez	.25
66	B.J. Surhoff (Foil)	2.00
67	Austin Kearns (Foil)	2.00
68	Jacob Cruz	.15
69	Armando Benitez	.15
70	Derek Jeter	1.00
71	Ryan Jensen	.15
72	Kevin Mench	.15
73	Mike Remlinger	.15
74	Luis Castillo	.15
75	Kazuhisa Ishii (Foil)	2.00
76	Bobby Abreu	.15
77	Dave Veres	.15
78	Tony Batista	.15
79	Rey Sanchez	.15
80	Jason Grimsley	.15
81	Al Leiter (Foil)	2.00
82	Kerry Wood (Foil)	2.00
83	Ellis Burks	.15
84	Corey Patterson	.15
85	Adrian Beltre	.15
86	Barry Zito	.25
87	Doug Mientkiewicz	.15
88	Jeffrey Hammonds	.15
89	Jeremy Giambi	.15
90	Tsuyoshi Shinjo	.15
91	Roger Clemens (Foil)	3.50
92	John Franco	.15
93	Alex Rodriguez (Foil)	5.00
94	Barry Bonds (Foil)	15.00
95	Fred McGriff	.15
96	Chuck Finley	.15
97	Jose Rijo	.15
98	Jeff Bagwell (Foil)	2.50
99	Ron Gant	.15
100	Tom Glavine	.25
101	Mike Mussina	.25
102	Gary Sheffield	.30
103	Barry Larkin	.15
104	Jim Thome	.45
105	Chipper Jones (Foil)	3.00
106	Rickey Henderson	.50
107	Randy Johnson (Foil)	2.50
108	Mike Piazza (Foil)	4.00
109	John Smoltz	.15
110	Edgar Martinez	.15
111	Larry Walker	.15
112	Pedro Martinez (Foil)	2.50
113	Sammy Sosa (Foil)	3.50
114	Roberto Alomar (Foil)	2.00
115	Curt Schilling (Foil)	2.00
116	Chuck Knoblauch	.15
117	Frank Thomas	6.00
118	Jeff Kent	.15
119	Kenny Lofton	.15
120	Ken Griffey Jr.	7.50
121	Trevor Hoffman (Foil)	2.00
122	Mo Vaughn	.15
123	Robin Ventura	.15
124	Ellis Burks	.15
125	Tim Raines	.15
S1	Bad Call (Bernie Williams)	.05
S2	Clutch Hitting (Mike Piazza)	.10
S3	Crowd the Plate (Troy Glaus)	.05
S4	Down the Middle (Unidentified)	.05
S5	Ducks on the Pond (Unidentified)	.05
S6	Free Steal (Alex Rodriguez)	.10
S7	Overthrow (Unidentified)	.05
S8	Payoff Pitch (Unidentified)	.05
S9	Rally Cap (Tom Goodwin)	.05
S10	Rattled (Nate Cornejo)	.05
S11	Shell Shocked (Rick Ankiel)	.05
S12	Shelled (Scott Sullivan)	.05
S13	Comebacker (Dave Williams)	.05
S14	Fast Worker (Unidentified)	.05
S15	Full Windup (Andy Pettitte)	.05
S16	Great Thrower (Ichiro Suzuki)	.15
S17	Hung It (Unidentified)	.05
S18	In the Groove (Mark Mulder)	.05
S19	In the Zone (Curt Schilling)	.05
S20	Insult to Injury (Trevor Hoffman)	.05
S21	Nerves of Steel (Unidentified)	.05
S22	Pitchout (Unidentified)	.05

S23 Scuff the Ball (Brian Moehler) .05
S24 Bear Down (Brian Giles) .05
S25 Change in Strategy (Unidentified) .05

2002 MLB Showdown Stars Promos

These four cards were made available at MLB Showdown Spring Training events. They are similar in format to other cards in the series.

		NM/M
Complete Set (4):		6.00
Common Player:		2.00
1	Eric Chavez	2.00
2	Nick Johnson	2.00
3	Jason Marquis	2.00
4	Bud Smith	2.00

2002 MLB Showdown Trading Deadline

Issued after the 2002 season opened, this is an update to the interactive game MLB Showdown from Wizards of the Coast. Players in the set are generally those who changed teams during the off-season, or promising rookies. The Trading Deadline edition was issued in a Booster box of 36 nine-card (seven player, two strategy) packs. The set has 125 "regular" player cards, 25 premium holofoil star cards and 25 strategy cards. The holo premium cards were inserted in packs at a rate of 1:3. While collectors compete with gamers for these cards in the market, relative values placed on these cards by each group of buyers may differ.

		NM/M
Complete Set (175):		55.00
Common Player:		.15
Booster Pack (7+2):		1.50
Booster Box (36):		20.00
1	Jason Giambi (Foil)	2.50
2	Chris Singleton	.15
3	Ben Davis	.15
4	Tsuyoshi Shinjo	.15
5	Brian Jordan	.15
6	Tony Clark	.15
7	Moises Alou (Foil)	2.00
8	Todd Walker	.15
9	Ricky Gutierrez	.15
10	Brad Fullmer	.15
11	Jeromy Burnitz	.15
12	Gary Sheffield (Foil)	2.50
13	Marty Cordova (Foil)	2.00
14	Todd Zeile	.15
15	Alex Gonzalez	.15
16	Kenny Lofton	.15
17	Vinny Castilla	.15
18	Craig Paquette	.15
19	Michael Tucker	.15
20	Cesar Izturis	.15
21	Eric Young	.15
22	Chuck Knoblauch	.15
23	Roberto Alomar (Foil)	2.00
24	David Bell	.15
25	Johnny Damon	.35
26	Roger Cedeno	.15
27	Robin Ventura	.15
28	David Justice (Foil)	2.00
29	Brady Anderson	.15
30	Pokey Reese	.15
31	Reggie Sanders (Foil)	2.00
32	Jeff Cirillo (Foil)	2.00
33	Juan Encarnacion	.15
34	Tino Martinez (Foil)	2.00
35	Carl Everett (Foil)	2.00
36	Danny Bautista	.15
37	Rafael Furcal	.15
38	Dmitri Young	.15
39	Jay Gibbons	.15
40	Brian Buchanan	.15
41	David Segui	.15
42	Barry Larkin (Foil)	2.00
43	John Vander Wal	.15
44	Brent Mayne	.15
45	Neifi Perez	.15
46	Lenny Harris	.15
47	Jason LaRue	.15
48	Travis Fryman	.15
49	Juan Uribe	.15
50	Shea Hillenbrand	.15
51	Aaron Rowand	.15
52	Jose Ortiz	.15
53	Robert Fick	.15
54	Doug Glanville	.15
55	Charles Johnson (Foil)	2.00
56	Derrek Lee	.45
57	Carlos Febles	.15
58	Luis Rivas	.15
59	Lee Stevens	.15
60	Mike Lieberthal	.15
61	Ryan Klesko (Foil)	2.00
62	Chris Gomez	.15
63	Randy Winn	.15
64	Rusty Greer	.15
65	Felipe Lopez	.15
66	Carlos Pena	.15
67	Toby Hall	.15
68	Milton Bradley	.15
69	Matt Lawton	.15
70	Gregg Zaun	.15
71	Eric Hinske	.15
72	Alex Ochoa	.15
73	Rondell White	.15
74	Armando Rios	.15
75	Desi Relaford	.15
76	Nomar Garciaparra (Foil)	4.00
77	Frank Thomas (Foil)	3.00
78	Mitch Meluskey	.15
79	Morgan Ensberg	.15
80	Mo Vaughn (Foil)	2.00
81	Adrian Brown	.15
82	Juan Gonzalez (Foil)	2.50
83	Tom Wilson	.15
84	Matt Stairs	.15
85	Andres Galarraga	.15
86	Sidney Ponson	.15
87	Jesus Colome	.15
88	Juan Cruz	.15
89	Eddie Guardado	.15
90	Jon Garland	.15
91	Denny Neagle	.15
92	Chad Durbin	.15
93	Kevin Brown (Foil)	2.00
94	Elmer Dessens	.15
95	Eric Gagne	.15
96	Jamey Wright	.15
97	Pedro Martinez (Foil)	3.00
98	Jason Bere	.15
99	Ugueth Urbina	.15
100	Carl Pavano	.15
101	Kip Wells	.15
102	Paul Abbott	.15
103	Billy Wagner (Foil)	2.00
104	Erik Hiljus	.15
105	Brandon Duckworth	.15
106	Ruben Quevedo	.15
107	Jimmy Anderson	.15
108	Bobby Jones	.15
109	Livan Hernandez	.15
110	Curtis Leskanic	.15
111	Tom Gordon	.15
112	Jeff Austin	.15
113	Joel Pineiro	.15
114	Chad Bradford	.15
115	Woody Williams	.15
116	Victor Zambrano (Foil)	2.00
117	Jose Mesa	.15
118	Roy Halladay	.15
119	Steve Karsay	.15
120	Hideo Nomo	.50
121	Jeff Farnsworth	.15
122	Dave Weathers	.15
123	Sean Lowe	.15
124	Mike Myers	.15
125	Jason Schmidt	.15
126	Mike Williams	.15
127	Terry Adams	.15
128	Chan Ho Park (Foil)	2.00
129	Jeff D'Amico	.15
130	Kevin Appier (Foil)	2.00
131	Glendon Rusch	.15
132	Jason Isringhausen	.15
133	Todd Ritchie	.15
134	Shawn Estes	.15
135	Kevin Millwood	.15
136	Aaron Sele	.15
137	Rick Helling	.15
138	Billy Koch	.15
139	Paul Quantrill	.15
140	Tim Spooneybarger	.15
141	Jorge Julio	.15
142	Carlos Hernandez	.15
143	Rick Ankiel	.15
144	Scott Erickson	.15
145	Denny Hocking	.15
146	Kazuhisa Ishii	.15
147	Pedro Astacio	.15
148	Satoru Komiyama	.15
149	Kurt Ainsworth	.15
150	John Smoltz (Foil)	2.00
S1	Big Inning (Luis Gonzalez)	.05
S2	Do or Die (Jeff Cirillo)	.05
S3	Free Steal (Alex Rodriguez)	.15
S4	Lean into It (Tsuyoshi Shinjo)	.05
S5	Overthrow (Cubs, Mets)	.05
S6	Pointers (Corey Patterson)	.05
S7	Professional Hitter (David Justice)	.05
S8	Rattled (Nate Cornejo)	.05
S9	Shelled (Scott Sullivan)	.05
S10	Shell Shocked (Rick Ankiel)	.05
S11	Swing for the Fences (Unidentified)	.05
S12	Tricky Hop (Marlon Anderson)	.05
S13	Whiplash (Unidentified)	.05
S14	Choke (Aaron Boone)	.05
S15	Comebacker (Dave Williams)	.05
S16	Fast Worker (Takahito Nomura)	.05
S17	Focused (Paul Abbott)	.05
S18	Hung It (Unidentified)	.05
S19	In the Zone (Rick Helling)	.05
S20	Scuff the Ball (Brian Moehler)	.05
S21	Swiss Army Closer (Joel Piniero)	.05
S22	What Were You Thinking??? (Unidentified)	.05
S23	Whoops! (Alex Gonzalez)	.05
S24	Bear Down (Brian Giles)	.05
S25	Game of Inches (Rich Aurilia)	.05

2003 MLB Showdown Promos

		NM/M
Complete Set (50):		35.00
Common Player:		1.00
P01	Aaron Guiel	1.00
P02	Abraham Nunez	1.00
P03	Al Levine	1.00
P04	Armando Rios	1.00
P05	Aubrey Huff	1.00
P06	Brandon Berger	1.00
P07	Carlos Baerga	1.00
P08	Chris Richard	1.00
P09	Corky Miller	1.00
P10	Damaso Marte	1.00
P11	Darren Holmes	1.00
P12	Denny Hocking	1.00
P13	Erubiel Durazo	1.00
P14	Giovanni Carrara	1.00
P15	Joe McEwing	1.00
P16	Kerry Robinson	1.00
P17	Lenny Harris	1.00
P18	Mark Derosa	1.00
P19	Mark Ellis	1.00
P20	Michael Tejera	1.00
P21	Olmedo Saenz	1.00
P22	Pedro Feliz	1.00
P23	Tomas Perez	1.00
P24	Wendell Magee	1.00
P25	Willis Roberts	1.00
P26	Benito Santiago	1.00
P27	Mike Sweeney	1.00
P28	Fernando Vina	1.00
P29	Troy Glaus	1.50
P30	Barry Larkin	1.00
P31	Manny Ramirez	1.50
P32	Steve Finley	1.00
P33	Shannon Stewart	1.00
P34	Frank Thomas	1.50
P35	Jamie Moyer	1.00
P36	Jon Lieber	1.00
P37	Mark Mulder	1.00
P38	Roger Clemens	2.50
P39	Jorge Posada	1.00
P40	Corey Koskie	1.00
P41	Shawn Green	1.00
P42	Phil Nevin	1.00
P43	Gary Sheffield	1.00
P44	Craig Biggio	1.00
P45	Alan Embree	1.00
P46	Jesse Orosco	1.00
P47	Mike Stanton	1.00
P48	Brandon Duckworth	1.00
P49	Troy Percival	1.00
P50	Robb Nen	1.00

2003 MLB Showdown

MLB Showdown's 2003 edition has has 300 "regular" player cards, 56 premium holofoil star cards and 50 strategy cards. The foil premium cards were inserted in booster packs at a rate of 1:3. While collectors compete with gamers for these cards in the market, relative values placed on the cards by each group of buyers may differ.

		NM/M
Complete Set (354):		150.00
Common Player:		.15
Two-Player Starter Set:		9.00
Draft Pack:		7.50
Booster Pack (7+2):		2.00
Booster Box (36):		40.00
1	Garret Anderson (Foil)	2.00
2	David Eckstein (Foil)	2.00
3	Darin Erstad	.30
4	Brad Fullmer	.15
5	Troy Glaus	.35
6	Adam Kennedy	.15
7	Bengie Molina	.15
8	Ramon Ortiz	.15
9	Orlando Palmeiro	.15
10	Troy Percival	.15
11	Tim Salmon	.15
12	Jarrod Washburn (Foil)	2.00
13	Miguel Batista	.15
14	Danny Bautista	.15
15	Craig Counsell	.15
16	Steve Finley	.15
17	Luis Gonzalez (Foil)	2.00
18	Mark Grace	.15
19	Randy Johnson (Foil)	7.50
20	Byung-Hyun Kim	.15
21	Quinton McCracken	.15
22	Curt Schilling (Foil)	4.50
23	Junior Spivey (Foil)	2.00
24	Tony Womack	.15
25	Vinny Castilla	.15
26	Julio Franco	.15
27	Rafael Furcal (Foil)	2.00
28	Marcus Giles	.15
29	Tom Glavine (Foil)	3.50
30	Andruw Jones (Foil)	7.50
31	Keith Lockhart	.15
32	Javy Lopez	.15
33	Greg Maddux (Foil)	8.00
34	Kevin Millwood	.15
35	Gary Sheffield	.30
36	John Smoltz (Foil)	2.00
37	Tony Batista	.15
38	Mike Bordick	.15
39	Jeff Conine	.15
40	Marty Cordova	.15
41	Jay Gibbons	.15
42	Geronimo Gil	.15
43	Jerry Hairston	.15
44	Jorge Julio	.15
45	Rodrigo Lopez	.15
46	Gary Matthews Jr.	.15
47	Melvin Mora	.15
48	Sidney Ponson	.15
49	Chris Singleton	.15
50	John Burkett	.15
51	Tony Clark	.15
52	Johnny Damon	.35
53	Alan Embree	.15
54	Nomar Garciaparra (Foil)	8.00
55	Shea Hillenbrand	.15
56	Derek Lowe (Foil)	2.00
57	Pedro Martinez (Foil)	7.50
58	Trot Nixon	.15
59	Manny Ramirez	.35
60	Rey Sanchez	.15
61	Ugueth Urbina	.15
62	Jason Varitek	.15
63	Moises Alou	.15
64	Mark Bellhorn	.15
65	Roosevelt Brown	.15
66	Matt Clement	.15
67	Joe Girardi	.15
68	Alex Gonzalez	.15
69	Todd Hundley	.15
70	Jon Lieber	.15
71	Fred McGriff	.15
72	Bill Mueller	.15
73	Corey Patterson	.15
74	Mark Prior (Foil)	6.00
75	Sammy Sosa (Foil)	9.00
76	Mark Buehrle (Foil)	2.00
77	Jon Garland	.15
78	Tony Graffanino	.15
79	Paul Konerko (Foil)	3.50
80	Carlos Lee	.25
81	Magglio Ordonez (Foil)	2.00
82	Frank Thomas	.35
83	Dan Wright	.15
84	Aaron Boone	.15
85	Sean Casey	.15
86	Elmer Dessens	.15
87	Adam Dunn	.15
88	Danny Graves	.15
89	Joey Hamilton	.15
90	Jimmy Haynes	.15
91	Austin Kearns (Foil)	2.00
92	Barry Larkin	.15
93	Jason LaRue	.15
94	Reggie Taylor	.15
95	Todd Walker	.15
96	Danys Baez	.15
97	Milton Bradley	.15
98	Ellis Burks	.15
99	Einar Diaz	.15
100	Ricky Gutierrez	.15
101	Matt Lawton	.15
102	Chris Magruder	.15
103	C.C. Sabathia	.15
104	Lee Stevens	.15
105	Jim Thome (Foil)	3.50
106	Omar Vizquel	.15
107	Bob Wickman	.15
108	Gary Bennett	.15
109	Mike Hampton	.15
110	Todd Helton	.35
111	Jose Jimenez	.15
112	Denny Neagle	.15
113	Jose Ortiz	.15
114	Juan Pierre	.15
115	Juan Uribe	.15
116	Larry Walker (Foil)	2.00
117	Todd Zeile	.15
118	Juan Acevedo	.15
119	Robert Fick	.15
120	Bobby Higginson	.15
121	Damian Jackson	.15
122	Craig Paquette	.15
123	Carlos Pena	.15
124	Mark Redman	.15
125	Randall Simon	.15
126	Steve Sparks	.15
127	Dmitri Young	.15
128	A.J. Burnett	.15
129	Luis Castillo	.15
130	Juan Encarnacion	.15
131	Alex Gonzalez	.15
132	Charles Johnson	.15
133	Derrek Lee	.40
134	Mike Lowell	.15
135	Vladimir Nunez	.15
136	Eric Owens	.15
137	Preston Wilson	.15
138	Brad Ausmus	.15
139	Lance Berkman (Foil)	2.00
140	Craig Biggio	.15
141	Geoff Blum	.15
142	Richard Hidalgo	.15
143	Julio Lugo	.15
144	Orlando Merced	.15
145	Billy Wagner	.15
146	Carlos Beltran	.40
147	Paul Byrd	.15
148	Raul Ibanez	.15
149	Chuck Knoblauch	.15
150	Brent Mayne	.15
151	Neifi Perez	.15
152	Joe Randa	.15
153	Mike Sweeney	.15
154	Adrian Beltre	.25
155	Eric Gagne (Foil)	2.00
156	Shawn Green	.25
157	Marquis Grissom	.15
158	Mark Grudzielanek	.15
159	Kazuhisa Ishii (Foil)	2.00
160	Cesar Izturis	.15
161	Brian Jordan	.15
162	Eric Karros	.15
163	Paul LoDuca (Foil)	2.00
164	Hideo Nomo	.30
165	Jesse Orosco	.15
166	Odalis Perez	.15
167	Mike DeJean	.15
168	Jose Hernandez	.15
169	Geoff Jenkins	.15
170	Alex Sanchez	.15
171	Richie Sexson	.15
172	Ben Sheets	.15
173	Eric Young	.15
174	Eddie Guardado	.15
175	Cristian Guzman	.15
176	Torii Hunter (Foil)	2.00
177	Jacque Jones	.15
178	Corey Koskie	.15
179	Doug Mientkiewicz	.15
180	Eric Milton	.15
181	A.J. Pierzynski	.15
182	Michael Barrett	.15
183	Orlando Cabrera	.15
184	Cliff Floyd	.15
185	Vladimir Guerrero (Foil)	7.50
186	Tomo Ohka	.15
187	Fernando Tatis	.15
188	Javier Vazquez	.15
189	Jose Vidro (Foil)	2.00
190	Brad Wilkerson	.15
191	Edgardo Alfonzo	.15
192	Roberto Alomar	.30
193	Pedro Astacio	.15
194	Armando Benitez	.15
195	Jeromy Burnitz	.15
196	Al Leiter	.15
197	Rey Ordonez	.15
198	Timo Perez	.15
199	Mike Piazza (Foil)	10.00
200	Steve Trachsel	.15
201	Mo Vaughn	.15
202	Roger Clemens	.50
203	Jason Giambi (Foil)	4.50
204	Derek Jeter	1.00
205	Nick Johnson	.15
206	Steve Karsay	.15
207	Mike Mussina (Foil)	2.50
208	Jorge Posada	.15
209	Mariano Rivera (Foil)	2.00
210	Alfonso Soriano (Foil)	4.50
211	Mike Stanton	.15
212	Robin Ventura	.15
213	Jeff Weaver	.15
214	Rondell White	.15
215	Bernie Williams (Foil)	2.00
216	Eric Chavez	.15
217	Jermaine Dye	.15
218	Scott Hatteberg	.15
219	Tim Hudson	.15
220	Billy Koch	.15
221	Terrence Long	.15
222	Mark Mulder	.15
223	Miguel Tejada (Foil)	2.00
224	Barry Zito (Foil)	2.50
225	Bobby Abreu	.15
226	Marlon Anderson	.15
227	Pat Burrell	.35
228	Brandon Duckworth	.15
229	Jeremy Giambi	.15
230	Doug Glanville	.15
231	Mike Lieberthal	.15
232	Jose Mesa	.15
233	Vicente Padilla	.15
234	Jimmy Rollins	.25
235	Adrian Brown	.15
236	Josh Fogg	.15
237	Brian Giles	.15
238	Jason Kendall	.15
239	Pokey Reese	.15
240	Kip Wells	.15
241	Mike Williams (Foil)	2.00
242	Craig Wilson	.15
243	Jack Wilson	.15
244	Kevin Young	.15
245	Trevor Hoffman (Foil)	2.00
246	Mark Kotsay	.15
247	Ray Lankford	.15
248	Brian Lawrence	.15
249	Phil Nevin	.15
250	Kurt Ainsworth	.15
251	David Bell	.15
252	Barry Bonds (Foil)	65.00
253	Ryan Jensen	.15
254	Jeff Kent (Foil)	2.00
255	Robb Nen	.15
256	Reggie Sanders	.15
257	Benito Santiago	.15
258	Tsuyoshi Shinjo	.15
259	J.T. Snow	.15
260	Bret Boone	.15
261	Mike Cameron	.15
262	Jeff Cirillo	.15
263	Freddy Garcia	.15
264	Carlos Guillen	.15
265	Mark McLemore	.15
266	Jamie Moyer	.15
267	John Olerud	.15
268	Joel Pineiro (Foil)	2.00
269	Kazuhiro Sasaki (Foil)	2.00
270	Ruben Sierra	.15
271	Dan Wilson	.15
272	Ichiro (Foil)	12.50
273	J.D. Drew	.30
274	Jim Edmonds (Foil)	2.00
275	Jason Isringhausen	.15
276	Matt Morris (Foil)	2.00
277	Albert Pujols (Foil)	12.50
278	Edgar Renteria	.15
279	Scott Rolen (Foil)	2.50
280	Jason Simontacchi	.15
281	Fernando Vina	.15
282	Brent Abernathy	.15
283	Steve Cox	.15
284	Chris Gomez	.15
285	Ben Grieve	.15
286	Joe Kennedy	.15
287	Tanyon Sturtze	.15
288	Paul Wilson	.15
289	Randy Winn (Foil)	2.00
290	Juan Gonzalez	.30
291	Hideki Irabu	.15
292	Rafael Palmeiro (Foil)	6.00
293	Herbert Perry	.15
294	Alex Rodriguez (Foil)	10.00
295	Ivan Rodriguez	.40
296	Kenny Rogers	.15
297	Ismael Valdes	.15
298	Mike Young	.15
299	Dave Berg	.15
300	Carlos Delgado	.30
301	Kelvim Escobar	.15
302	Roy Halladay	.15
303	Eric Hinske (Foil)	2.00
304	Shannon Stewart	.15
S1	Bad Call (Sean Casey)	.10
S2	Clutch Hitting (Ellis Burks)	.10
S3	Down the Middle (Danny Graves)	.10
S4	Drag Bunt (Mark Mulder)	.10
S5	Ducks on the Pond (Unidentified)	.10
S6	Furl on the Fire (Benito Santiago)	.10
S7	Goodbye Baseball! (Ichiro Suzuki)	.40
S8	Great Addition (Ichiro Suzuki)	.40
S9	Last Chance (Ichiro Suzuki)	.40
S10	Nuisance (Barry Larkin)	.10
S11	Protect the Runner (Jacque Jones)	.10
S12	Pull the Ball (Jim Thome)	.10
S13	Rally Cap (Tino Martinez)	.10
S14	Rookie's Big Chance (Eric Hinske)	.10
S15	Runner Not Held (Unidentified)	.10
S16	See It Clearly (Vladimir Guerrero)	.10
S17	Serious Wheels (Deivi Cruz)	.10
S18	Sit on the Fastball (Carlos Guillen)	.10
S19	Take What's Given (David Eckstein)	.10
S20	Turn On It (Derek Jeter)	.50
S21	Valuable Asset (Barry Bonds)	.50
S22	Aces Up (Mark Mulder)	.10
S23	By the Book (Dan Reichert)	.10
S24	Change It Up (Denny Neagle)	.10
S25	Cut Off in the Gap (Juan Encarnacion)	.10
S26	Full Windup (Chris Reitsma)	.10
S27	Good Leather (Juan Encarnacion)	.10
S29	Great Start (Mark Mulder)	.10
S30	Great Throw (Danny Bautista)	
S30	Highlight Reel (Jose Hernandez)	

S31 In the Groove (Unidentified) .10
S32 Insult to Injury (David Eckstein) .10
S33 Job Well Done (Unidentified) .10
S34 Just Over the Wall (David Justice) .10
S35 Knock the Ball Down (Luis Gonzalez) .10
S36 Lefty Specialist (Ricardo Rincon) .10
S37 Nerves of Steel (Eric Gagne) .10
S38 Paint the Corner (Carlos Febles) .10
S39 Pumped Up (Raul Ibanez) .10
S40 Put Out the Fire (Mark Wohlers) .10
S41 Rally Killer (Abraham Nunez) .10
S42 Submarine Pitch (Byung-Hyun Kim) .10
S43 Throwing Heat (Dave Roberts) .10
S44 What a Relief! (Unidentified) .10
S45 Change in Strategy (Unidentified) .10
S46 Feast of Famine (Giovanni Carrara) .10
S47 Grounder to Second (Barry Larkin) .10
S48 It's Crunch Time (Shane Halter) .10
S49 Just Over the Rail (Shane Halter) .10
S50 Outmanaged (Art Howe, Ray Knight) .10

2003 MLB Showdown Trading Deadline

NM/M
Complete Set (170): 75.00
Common Player: .15
Booster Pack (9): 1.50
Booster Box (36): 40.00
1 So Taguchi .15
2 Ryan Drese .15
3 Mike Hampton .15
4 Sandy Alomar Jr. .15
5 Steve Sparks .15
6 Chan Ho Park .15
7 Roger Cedeno .15
8 Antonio Osuna .15
9 Ryan Dempster .15
10 Jesse Orosco .15
11 Angel Berroa .15
12 Sean Burroughs .15
13 Matt Mantei .15
14 Einar Diaz .15
15 Ken Griffey Jr. 1.00
16 Rey Sanchez .15
17 Antonio Alfonseca .15
18 Carl Crawford .15
19 Rey Ordonez .15
20 Brandon Inge .15
21 Hank Blalock .40
22 Albie Lopez .15
23 Aaron Sele .15
24 Willie Bloomquist .15
25 Shigetoshi Hasegawa .15
26 Steve Kline .15
27 Ramiro Mendoza .15
28 Mike Stanton .15
29 Carlos Zambrano .15
30 Dean Palmer .15
31 Mark Grudzielanek .15
32 Matt Williams .15
33 Michael Cuddyer .15
34 Glendon Rusch .15
35 Hee Seop Choi .15
36 Mike Bordick .15
37 Ray King .15
38 Bill Mueller .15
39 John McDonald .15
40 Brent Butler .15
41 Josh Bard .15
42 Xavier Nady .15
43 J.C. Romero .15
44 Paul Shuey .15
45 Eric Karros .15
46 Runelvys Hernandez .15
47 Braden Looper .15
48 Dave Roberts .15
49 Deivi Cruz .15
50 Todd Hollandsworth .15
51 Billy Koch .15
52 Brandon Villafuerte .15
53 Ricardo Rincon .15
54 Joe Crede .15
55 Juan Pierre .15
57 Ugueth Urbina .15
58 Luis Vizcaino (Foil) 2.00
59 Ben Weber .15
60 Kerry Wood .30
61 Tim Worrell .15
62 Royce Clayton .15
63 Chone Figgins .15
64 Ken Huckaby .15
65 Brian Anderson .15
66 Aramis Ramirez .15
67 Edgar Martinez .15
68 Keith Foulke .15
69 LaTroy Hawkins .15
70 Mike Remlinger .15
71 Lyle Overbay .15
72 Buddy Groom .15
73 Orlando Hudson .15
74 Francisco Rodriguez (Foil) 2.00
75 Craig Biggio .15
76 Todd Zeile .15
77 Vernon Wells .15
78 Casey Fossum .15
79 Wes Helms .15
80 Robert Fick .15
81 Scott Spiezio .15
82 Ty Wigginton .15
83 Elmer Dessens .15
84 Arthur Rhodes .15
85 Matt Stairs .15
86 Miguel Olivo .15
87 Tino Martinez .15
88 Travis Hafner .15
89 Octavio Dotel .15
90 Jimmy Rollins .30
91 Placido Polanco .15
92 Kevin Brown .15
93 John Patterson .15
94 Andy Pettitte .15
95 Bobby Kielty .15
96 Jeremy Giambi .15
97 Brandon Phillips .15
98 Fred McGriff .15
99 Damian Moss .15
100 Russ Ortiz .15
101 Mark Teixeira .35
102 Tom Glavine (Foil) 2.50
103 Chris Woodward .15
104 Brad Radke .15
105 Edgardo Alfonzo .15
106 Jose Contreras (Foil) 2.00
107 Josh Beckett .30
108 Johan Santana .30
109 Brandon Larson .15
110 Randall Simon .15
111 Randy Winn (Foil) 2.00
112 Ray Durham .15
113 Omar Daal (Foil) 2.00
114 David Wells (Foil) 2.00
115 Wade Miller .15
116 Bartolo Colon (Foil) 2.00
117 Ryan Klesko (Foil) 2.00
118 Jeff Bagwell .50
119 Roy Oswalt (Foil) 2.00
120 Orlando Hernandez (Foil) 2.00
121 Ivan Rodriguez (Foil) 4.00
122 Tim Wakefield .15
123 Josh Phelps .15
124 Woody Williams .15
125 Chipper Jones (Foil) 5.00
126 Randy Wolf .15
127 Kevin Millwood (Foil) 2.00
128 Rocco Baldelli (Foil) 4.00
129 Jeff Kent (Foil) 2.00
130 Hideki Matsui (Foil) 7.00
131 Jim Thome (Foil) 3.00
132 Kazuhiro Sasaki .15
133 Jason Jennings (Foil) 2.00
134 Rafael Furcal .15
135 Derek Jeter (Foil) 7.50
136 Benito Santiago .15
137 Jeff Bagwell .50
138 Carlos Beltran .25
139 Scott Rolen (Foil) 2.50
140 Kerry Wood (Foil) 2.50
141 Tim Salmon .15
142 Ichiro (Foil) 12.00
143 Mike Piazza (Foil) 6.00
144 Albert Pujols (Foil) 6.00
145 Nomar Garciaparra (Foil) 5.00
S1 Clutch Hitting .10
S2 Clutch Rookie .10
S3 Great Addition .10
S4 Headed Home .10
S5 High Fives .10
S6 Long Gone? .10
S7 On the Move .10
S8 Take What's Given .10
S9 Who is This Guy? .10
S10 Addition by Subtraction .10
S11 De-nied! .10
S12 Digging Deep .10
S13 Lock it Down .10
S14 New Arrival .10
S15 Not So Fast .10
S16 Pitch Around .10
S17 Rookie Fireballer .10
S18 Split-Finger Fastball .10
S19 Still Learning .10
S20 Three Up, Three Down .10
S21 Triple Dip .10
S22 Brainstorm .10
S23 Outmanaged .10
S24 Stealing Signals .10
S25 Swing at Anything .10

2003 MLB Showdown Pennant Run

Ten-player Super Season and Hall of Fame Heroes subsets were added to the 105 regular player cards and 25 strategy cards in this late-season card gaming issue. As with all MLB Showdown issues, baseball card collectors compete with game players for examples in the market, with each group often placing different values on specific cards.

NM/M
Complete Set (150): 100.00
Common Player: .15
Booster Pack (7+2): 2.00
Booster Box (36): 40.00
1 Josh Beckett .40
2 Jeremy Bonderman .15
3 Carlos Febles .15
4 Tom Goodwin .15
5 Luis Rivas .15
6 Scott Sullivan .15
7 John Thomson .15
8 Lance Carter .15
9 Terry Mulholland .15
10 Jake Westbrook .15
11 Chris George .15
12 Jake Peavy .15
13 Felix Rodriguez .15
14 Marlon Byrd .15
15 Toby Hall .15
16 Rocky Biddle .15
17 Brandon Lyon .15
18 Roberto Hernandez .15
19 Carlos Silva .15
20 Chris Hammond .15
21 Eric Munson .15
22 David Dellucci .15
23 R.A. Dickey .15
24 Cliff Politte .15
25 Russ Springer .15
26 Kirk Reuter .15
27 Vance Wilson .15
28 Scott Williamson .15
29 Ryan Franklin .15
30 Juan Castro .15
31 Craig Monroe .15
32 Joe Beimel .15
33 Scott Schoeneweis .15
34 John Halama .15
35 Eli Marrero .15
36 Felipe Lopez .15
37 Casey Blake .15
38 Mike MacDougal .15
39 Kris Benson .15
40 Francisco Cordero .15
41 Tom Gordon .15
42 Neifi Perez .15
43 Chad Bradford .15
44 Miguel Cairo .15
45 Mike Matheny .15
46 Mike Timlin .15
47 D.J. Carrasco .15
48 Eddie Perez .15
49 Gregg Zaun .15
50 Ronnie Belliard .15
51 Ricardo Rodriguez .15
52 B.J. Ryan .15
53 Michael Tucker .15
54 Rheal Cormier .15
55 Felix Heredia .15
56 Alex Cora .15
57 Travis Lee .15
58 Ted Lilly .15
59 Tom Wilson .15
60 Jeff D'Amico .15
61 Adam Eaton .15
62 Travis Harper .15
63 Mark Loretta .15
64 Ricky Stone .15
65 Wil Cordero .15
66 Cliff Floyd .15
67 Livan Hernandez .15
68 Paul Quantrill .15
69 Ben Davis .15
70 Shawn Estes .15
71 Chris Stynes .15
72 Jay Payton .15
73 Ramon Hernandez .15
74 Jason Johnson .15
75 John Vander Wal .15
76 Shawn Chacon (Foil) 2.00
77 D'Angelo Jimenez .15
78 Desi Relaford .15
79 Rich Aurilia .15
80 Rod Barajas .15
81 Jose Cruz (Foil) 2.00
82 Kyle Lohse .15
83 Rondell White .15
84 Gil Meche (Foil) 2.00
85 Jose Guillen .15
86 Kenny Lofton .15
87 Zach Day (Foil) 2.00
88 Mark Redman .15
89 Melvin Mora (Foil) 2.00
90 Todd Walker .15
91 Torii Hunter .15
92 Frank Catalanotto .15
93 Andres Galarraga .15
94 Jason Schmidt .15
95 Eric Byrnes .15
96 Hank Blalock (Foil) 4.00
97 Jacque Jones (Foil) 2.00
98 Michael Young .15
99 Carl Everett .15
100 Preston Wilson .15
101 Esteban Loaiza .15
102 Raul Mondesi (Foil) 2.00
103 Carlos Delgado (Foil) 2.50
104 Gary Sheffield (Foil) 2.50
105 Kevin Appier .15
106 Jesse Orosco .15
107 Pat Hentgen .15
108 Matt Williams .15
109 David Cone (Foil) 2.00
110 Mark Grace (Foil) 2.00
111 Carlos Baerga (Foil) 2.00
112 Greg Maddux (Foil) 5.00
113 Kevin Brown (Foil) 2.00
114 Ivan Rodriguez (Foil) 3.00
115 John Olerud (Foil) 2.00
116 Larry Doby .75
117 Yogi Berra (Foil) 7.50
118 Hoyt Wilhelm (Foil) 6.00
119 Pee Wee Reese .75
120 Brooks Robinson (Foil) 7.50
121 Robin Yount (Foil) 7.50
122 Reggie Jackson (Foil) 7.50
123 Harmon Killebrew (Foil) 7.50
124 Rod Carew (Foil) 6.00
125 Nolan Ryan (Foil) 12.00
S1 Change Sides .10
S2 Emergency Bunt .10
S3 Get Under It .10
S4 In Motion .10
S5 Out of Position .10
S6 Passed Ball .10
S7 Say the Magic Word .10
S8 Suicide Squeeze .10
S9 To the Warning Track .10
S10 Block the Plate .10
S11 Comebacker .10
S12 Good Matchup .10
S13 Ground Rule Double .10
S14 In the Zone .10
S15 Infield In .10
S16 Pickoff Attempt .10
S17 Play the Odds .10
S18 Playing Shallow .10
S19 Quick Pitch .10
S20 Sinker .10
S21 Up and In .10
S22 Good Scouting .10
S23 Looking Ahead .10
S24 Old Tricks .10
S25 Think Twice .10

2004 MLB Showdown Promo

This promo card was inserted into each issue of the September 2004, Beckett Baseball Monthly.

NM/M
P71 Alex Rodriguez .50

2004 MLB Showdown

MLB Showdown's 2004 edition has 298 "regular" player cards, 50 premium holofoil star cards and 50 strategy cards. The foil premium cards were inserted in booster packs at a rate of 1:3. While collectors compete with gamers for these cards in the market, relative values placed on the cards by each group of buyers may differ.

NM/M
Complete Set (398): 200.00
Common Player: .15
Two-Player Starter Set: 17.50
Draft Pack (60): 10.00
Booster Pack (8+3): 2.00
Booster Box: 75.00
1 Garret Anderson (Foil) 2.00
2 David Eckstein .15
3 Darin Erstad .25
4 Troy Glaus .25
5 Bengie Molina .15
6 Ramon Ortiz .15
7 Eric Owens .15
8 Tim Salmon .15
9 Scot Shields .15
10 Scott Spezio .15
11 Jarrod Washburn .15
12 Rod Barajas .15
13 Alex Cintron .15
14 Elmer Dessens .15
15 Steve Finley .15
16 Luis Gonzalez (Foil) 2.00
17 Mark Grace .15
18 Shea Hillenbrand .15
19 Matt Kata .15
20 Quinton McCracken .15
21 Curt Schilling (Foil) 2.50
22 Vinny Castilla .15
23 Robert Fick .15
24 Rafael Furcal .15
25 Marcus Giles .15
26 Andruw Jones .35
27 Chipper Jones (Foil) 7.50
28 Ray King .15
29 Javy Lopez (Foil) 2.00
30 Greg Maddux .50
31 Russ Ortiz .15
32 Gary Sheffield (Foil) 2.50
33 Tony Batista .15
34 Deivi Cruz .15
35 Travis Driskill .15
36 Brook Fordyce .15
37 Jay Gibbons .15
38 Pat Hentgen .15
39 Jorge Julio .15
40 Rodrigo Lopez .15
41 Luis Matos (Foil) 2.00
42 Melvin Mora .15
43 Brian Roberts .15
44 B.J. Surhoff .15
45 Johnny Damon .30
46 Alan Embree .15
47 Nomar Garciaparra (Foil) 7.50
48 Byung-Hyun Kim .15
49 Derek Lowe .15
50 Pedro Martinez (Foil) 6.00
51 Bill Mueller (Foil) 2.00
52 Trot Nixon .15
53 David Ortiz .35
54 Manny Ramirez .15
55 Jason Varitek .15
56 Tim Wakefield .15
57 Todd Walker .15
59 Antonio Alfonseca .15
60 Moises Alou .15
61 Paul Bako .15
62 Alex Gonzalez .15
63 Tom Goodwin .15
64 Mark Grudzielanek .15
65 Eric Karros .15
66 Kenny Lofton .15
67 Ramon Martinez .15
68 Corey Patterson .15
69 Mark Prior (Foil) 7.50
70 Aramis Ramirez .15
71 Mike Remlinger .15
72 Sammy Sosa (Foil) 9.00
73 Kerry Wood (Foil) 4.50
74 Carlos Zambrano .15
75 Mark Buehrle .15
76 Bartolo Colon .15
77 Joe Crede .15
78 Tom Gordon .15
79 Paul Konerko .25
80 Carlos Lee .25
81 Damaso Marte .15
82 Miguel Olivo .15
83 Magglio Ordonez (Foil) 2.00
84 Frank Thomas .35
85 Jose Valentin .15
86 Sean Casey .15
87 Juan Castro .15
88 Adam Dunn .15
89 Denny Graves .15
90 Ken Griffey Jr. 1.00
91 D'Angelo Jimenez .15
92 Austin Kearns .15
93 Barry Larkin .15
94 Jason LaRue .15
95 Chris Reitsma .15
96 Reggie Taylor .15
97 Paul Wilson .15
98 Danys Baez .15
99 Josh Bard .15
100 Casey Blake .15
101 Jason Boyd .15
102 Milton Bradley (Foil) 2.00
103 Ellis Burks .15
104 Coco Crisp .15
105 Jody Gerut .15
106 Travis Hafner .15
107 Matt Lawton .15
108 John McDonald .15
109 Terry Mulholland .15
110 C.C. Sabathia .15
111 Omar Vizquel .15
112 Ronnie Belliard .15
113 Shawn Chacon .15
113 Todd Helton (Foil) 3.00
114 Charles Johnson .15
115 Darren Oliver .15
116 Jay Payton .15
117 Justin Speier .15
118 Chris Stynes .15
119 Larry Walker .15
120 Preston Wilson .15
121 Jeremy Bonderman .15
122 Shane Halter .15
123 Bobby Higginson .15
124 Brandon Inge .15
125 Wilfredo Ledezma .15
126 Chris Mears .15
127 Warren Morris .15
128 Carlos Pena .15
129 Ramon Santiago .15
130 Andres Torres .15
131 Dmitri Young .15
132 Josh Beckett .25
133 Miguel Cabrera .15
134 Luis Castillo .15
135 Juan Encarnacion .15
136 Alex Gonzalez .15
137 Derrek Lee .35
138 Braden Looper .15
139 Mike Lowell .15
140 Juan Pierre .15
141 Mark Redman .15
142 Ivan Rodriguez (Foil) 4.50
143 Tim Spooneybarger .15
144 Dontrelle Willis (Foil) 2.00
145 Brad Ausmus .15
146 Jeff Bagwell .35
147 Lance Berkman .15
148 Craig Biggio .15
149 Geoff Blum .15
150 Octavio Dotel (Foil) 2.00
151 Morgan Ensberg .15
152 Adam Everett .15
153 Richard Hidalgo (Foil) 2.00
154 Jeff Kent .15
155 Brad Lidge .15
156 Roy Oswalt .15
157 Jeriome Robertson .15
158 Billy Wagner (Foil) 2.00
159 Carlos Beltran (Foil) 2.50
160 Angel Berroa .15
161 Jason Grimsley .15
162 Aaron Guiel .15
163 Runelvys Hernandez .15
164 Raul Ibanez .15
165 Curtis Leskanic .15
166 Jose Lima .15
167 Mike MacDougal .15
168 Brent Mayne .15
169 Joe Randa .15
170 Desi Relaford .15
171 Mike Sweeney .15
172 Michael Tucker .15
173 Adrian Beltre .25
174 Kevin Brown (Foil) 2.00
175 Ron Coomer .15
176 Alex Cora .15
177 Eric Gagne (Foil) 2.00
178 Shawn Green .15
179 Cesar Izturis .15
180 Brian Jordan .15
181 Paul LoDuca .15
182 Fred McGriff .15
183 Hideo Nomo .25
184 Paul Quantrill .15
185 Dave Roberts .15
186 Royce Clayton .15
187 Keith Ginter .15
188 Wes Helms .15
189 Geoff Jenkins .15
190 Brooks Kieschnick .15
191 Eddie Perez .15
192 Scott Podsednik (Foil) 2.00
193 Richie Sexson (Foil) 2.00
194 Ben Sheets .15
195 John Vander Wal .15
196 Chris Gomez .15
197 Cristian Guzman .15
198 LaTroy Hawkins .15
199 Torii Hunter .15
200 Jacque Jones .15
201 Corey Koskie .15
202 Doug Mientkiewicz .15
203 A.J. Pierzynski .15
204 Brad Radke .15
205 Shannon Stewart (Foil) 2.00
206 Michael Barrett .15
207 Orlando Cabrera (Foil) 2.00
208 Endy Chavez .15
209 Zach Day .15
210 Vladimir Guerrero (Foil) 6.00
211 Fernando Tatis .15
212 Javier Vazquez .15
213 Jose Vidro .15
214 Brad Wilkerson .15
215 Tony Clark .15
216 Cliff Floyd .15
217 John Franco .15
218 Joe McEwing .15
219 Timo Perez .15
220 Jason Phillips .15
221 Mike Piazza .65
222 Jose Reyes (Foil) 3.00
223 Steve Traschel .15
224 Dave Weathers .15
225 Ty Wigginton .15
226 Roger Clemens (Foil) 9.00
227 Chris Hammond .15
228 Derek Jeter (Foil) 12.00
229 Nick Johnson .15
230 Hideki Matsui .35
231 Mike Mussina (Foil) 4.50

232	Andy Pettitte	.15
233	Jorge Posada	.15
234	Mariano Rivera	.15
235	Alfonso Soriano	.25
236	Jeff Weaver	.15
237	Bernie Williams	.15
238	Enrique Wilson	.15
239	Chad Bradford	.15
240	Eric Byrnes	.15
241	Mark Ellis	.15
242	Keith Foulke	2.00
243	Scott Hatteberg	.15
244	Ramon Hernandez	.15
245	Tim Hudson (Foil)	3.00
246	Terrence Long	.15
247	Mark Mulder (Foil)	2.00
248	Ricardo Rincon	.15
249	Chris Singleton	.15
250	Miguel Tejada	.15
251	Barry Zito	.15
252	Bobby Abreu	.15
253	David Bell	.15
254	Pat Burrell	.30
255	Marlon Byrd	.15
256	Rheal Cormier	.15
257	Vicente Padilla	.15
258	Tomas Perez	.15
259	Placido Polanco	.15
260	Jimmy Rollins	.15
261	Carlos Silva	.15
262	Jim Thome (Foil)	3.00
263	Randy Wolf (Foil)	2.00
264	Kris Benson	.15
265	Jeff D'Amico	.15
266	Adam Hyzdu	.15
267	Jason Kendall (Foil)	2.00
268	Brian Meadows	.15
269	Abraham Nunez	.15
270	Reggie Sanders	.15
271	Matt Stairs	.15
272	Jack Wilson	.15
273	Gary Bennett	.15
274	Sean Burroughs	.15
275	Adam Eaton	.15
276	Luther Hackman	.15
277	Ryan Klesko	.15
278	Brian Lawrence	.15
279	Mark Loretta	.15
280	Phil Nevin	.15
281	Ramon Vazquez	.15
282	Edgardo Alfonzo	.15
283	Rich Aurilia	.15
284	Jim Brower	.15
285	Jose Cruz	.15
286	Ray Durham	.15
287	Andres Galarraga	.15
288	Marquis Grissom	.15
289	Neifi Perez	.15
290	Felix Rodriguez	.15
291	Benito Santiago	.15
292	Jason Schmidt (Foil)	2.00
293	J.T. Snow	.15
294	Tim Worrell	.15
295	Bret Boone (Foil)	2.00
296	Mike Cameron	.15
297	Ryan Franklin	.15
298	Carlos Guillen	.15
299	Shigetoshi Hasegawa	.15
300	Edgar Martinez	.15
301	Mark McLemore	.15
302	Jamie Moyer (Foil)	2.00
303	John Olerud	.15
304	Ichiro (Foil)	10.00
305	Dan Wilson	.15
306	Randy Winn	.15
307	J.D. Drew	.30
308	Jeff Fassero	.15
309	Bo Hart	.15
310	Jason Isringhausen	.15
311	Tino Martinez	.15
312	Mike Matheny	.15
313	Orlando Palmeiro	.15
314	Albert Pujols (Foil)	10.00
315	Edgar Renteria (Foil)	2.00
316	Garrett Stephenson	.15
317	Woody Williams (Foil)	2.00
318	Rocco Baldelli	.35
319	Lance Carter	.15
320	Carl Crawford	.15
321	Toby Hall	.15
322	Travis Harper	.15
323	Aubrey Huff (Foil)	2.00
324	Travis Lee	.15
325	Julio Lugo	.15
326	Damian Rolls	.15
327	Jorge Sosa	.15
328	Hank Blalock	.35
329	Francisco Cordero	.15
330	Aaron Fultz	.15
331	Juan Gonzalez	.25
332	Rafael Palmeiro	.35
333	Alex Rodriguez (Foil)	12.00
334	Mark Teixeira	.35
335	John Thompson	.15
336	Ismael Valdes	.15
337	Michael Young	.15
338	Frank Catalanotto	.15
339	Carlos Delgado	.15
340	Kelvim Escobar	.15
341	Roy Halliday (Foil)	2.00
342	Eric Hinske	.15
343	Orlando Hudson	.15
344	Greg Myers	.15
345	Josh Phelps	.15
346	Cliff Politte	.15
347	Vernon Wells (Foil)	2.00
348	Chris Woodward	.15
S1	Bad Call	.10

S2	Burned	.10
S3	Check Swing	.10
S4	Deep in the Gap	.10
S5	Drained	.10
S6	Ducks on the Pond	.10
S7	Great Addition	.10
S8	Hard Slide	.10
S9	Inside the Park Home Run	.10
S10	Options	.10
S11	Out of the Frying Pan	.10
S12	Play the Percentages	.10
S13	Pointers	.10
S14	Poor Positioning	.10
S15	Pull the Ball	.10
S16	Rough Outing	.10
S17	Slow Roller	.10
S18	Stick a Fork in Him	.10
S19	Sweet Swing	.10
S20	Take What's Given	.10
S21	Think Again	.10
S22	Turn on It	.10
S23	Aces Up	.10
S24	Caught Him Leaning	.10
S25	Caught the Corner	.10
S26	Choke	.10
S27	Cover Second	.10
S28	Dominating	.10
S29	Foul Ball	.10
S30	Good Leather	.10
S31	Hooking Foul	.10
S32	In the Zone	.10
S33	Infield In	.10
S34	Lined out of Play	.10
S35	Locate	.10
S36	Locked In	.10
S37	Nerves of Steel	.10
S38	Paint the Corner	.10
S39	Power Pitching	.10
S40	Short Fly	.10
S41	Sloppy Bunt	.10
S42	Split-Finger Fastball	.10
S43	Top-Level Strategy	.10
S44	Tough As Nails	.10
S45	Change in Strategy	.10
S46	Close Call	.10
S47	New Strategies	.10
S48	Second Look	.10
S49	Swing at Anything	.10
S50	Think Twice	.10

2004 MLB Showdown League Promos

		NM/M
Complete Set (50):		125.00
Common Player:		3.00
P01	Barry Larkin	3.00
P02	Barry Zito	3.00
P03	C.C. Sabathia	3.00
P04	Carlos Delgado	3.00
P05	Derek Lowe	3.00
P06	Fernando Tatis	3.00
P07	Frank Thomas	4.00
P08	Greg Maddux	6.00
P09	Hideki Matsui	6.00
P10	Jason Isringhausen	3.00
P11	Jeff Kent	3.00
P12	Jimmy Rollins	3.00
P13	Mike Piazza	4.50
P14	Josh Beckett	3.00
P15	Juan Pierre	3.00
P16	Ken Griffey Jr.	5.00
P17	Luis Castillo	3.00
P18	Mike Remlinger	3.00
P19	Moises Alou	3.00
P20	Paul LoDuca	3.00
P21	Preston Wilson	3.00
P22	Rafael Furcal	3.00
P23	Reggie Sanders	3.00
P24	Shigetoshi Hasegawa	3.00
P25	Tony Batista	3.00
P26	Brady Clark	3.00
P27	Carlos Febles	3.00
P28	Damian Jackson	3.00
P29	Darren Bragg	3.00
P30	David Segui	3.00
P31	Jesse Foppert	3.00
P32	Greg Norton	3.00
P33	Hee Seop Choi	3.00
P34	Henry Mateo	3.00
P35	Jake Peavy	3.00
P36	Jeff Reboulet	3.00
P37	Kevin Witt	3.00
P38	Luis Hernandez	3.00
P39	Mike Kinkade	3.00
P40	Paul Shuey	3.00
P41	Ricky Ledee	3.00
P42	Ricky Stone	3.00
P43	Roger Cedeno	3.00
P44	Ron Calloway	3.00
P45	Ryan Wagner	3.00
P46	Shawn Estes	3.00
P47	Todd Pratt	3.00
P48	Tom Wilson	3.00
P49	Tony Graffanino	3.00
P50	Troy O'Leary	3.00

2004 MLB Showdown Pennant Run

WILLIE McCOVEY

		NM/M
Complete Set (125):		250.00
Common Player:		.15
Booster Box (36):		75.00
Booster Pack (9+2):		2.00
001	Shawn Chacon	.15
002	Bobby Crosby	.15
003	Russ Ortiz	.15
004	Jason Simontacchi	.15
005	Oscar Villarreal	.15
006	Rocky Biddle	.15
007	Joe Borowski	.15
008	Shawn Estes	.15
009	Adam LaRoche	.15
010	Carl Everett	.15
011	Willie Harris	.15
012	Carlos Silva	.15
013	Aaron Rowand	.15
014	Francisco Cordero	.15
015	Ryan Freel	.15
016	Trevor Hoffman	.15
017	Edgar Renteria	.15
018	Mike Maroth	.15
019	Carlos Pena	.15
020	John Smoltz	.15
021	Carlos Guillen	.15
022	Buddy Groom	.15
023	Aaron Miles	.15
024	Jason Schmidt (Foil)	2.00
025	Danny Kolb	.15
026	Marco Scutaro	.15
027	Gary Sheffield	.35
028	Eric Gagne (Foil)	4.50
029	Kazuhisa Ishii	.15
030	B.J. Ryan	.15
031	Mark Mulder (Foil)	2.00
032	Gerald Laird	.15
033	Joe Mauer	.40
034	Nate Robertson	.15
035	Hideki Matsui	1.50
036	Ray Lankford	.15
037	Jacob Peavy	.15
038	Esteban Loaiza	.15
039	Mike Stanton	.15
040	Kevin Gregg	.15
041	Steve Traschel	.15
042	Albert Pujols (Foil)	12.00
043	Shingo Takatsu	.15
044	Ichiro (Foil)	10.00
045	Milton Bradley	.15
046	Eric Chavez	.25
047	Paul LoDuca	2.00
048	Kip Wells	.15
049	Miguel Cabrera (Foil)	3.00
050	Johnny Estrada	.15
051	Pedro Martinez (Foil)	6.00
052	Jason Giambi	.40
053	Kenny Rogers	.15
054	Alex Rodriguez (Foil)	12.00
055	Chone Figgins	.15
056	Ken Harvey	.15
057	Todd Helton	.35
058	Javy Lopez	.15
059	R.A. Dickey	.15
060	J.D. Drew	.15
061	Melvin Mora	.15
062	Denny Bautista	.15
063	Kerry Wood	.30
064	Randy Johnson	.40
065	Scott Rolen (Foil)	4.50
066	Roger Clemens (Foil)	7.50
067	Brad Penny	.15
068	Matt Clement	.15
069	Ron Belliard (Foil)	2.00
070	Alfonso Soriano (Foil)	4.00
071	Lew Ford	.15
072	Sean Casey	2.00
073	Troy Glaus	.30
074	Mike Lowell	.15
075	Juan Uribe	.15
076	Adrian Beltre	.15
077	Jack Wilson	.15
078	Craig Counsell	.15
079	Lyle Overbay (Foil)	2.00
080	Jose Contreras	.15
081	Jason Jennings	.15
082	Matt Mantei	.15
083	Luis Vizcaino	.15
084	Luis Ayala	.15
085	Danny Patterson	.15
086	C.J. Nitkowski	.15
087	Larry Bigbie	.15
088	Mike Lieberthal	.15
089	Mike Timlin	.15
090	Robert Mackowiak	.15
091	Kevin Cash	.15
092	Danys Baez	.15
093	J.C. Romero	.15
094	Dan Miceli	.15
095	Armando Benitez	.15
096	Hank Blalock	.40
097	Vinny Castilla	.15
098	Danny Graves	.15
099	Derek Jeter	2.50
100	Jim Thome (Foil)	4.50
101	Mark Loretta	.15
102	Victor Martinez	.30
103	Ken Griffey Jr.	2.00
104	Miguel Tejada	.25
105	Mike Piazza	1.50
106	Ivan Rodriguez	.35
107	Tom Glavine	.15
108	Carl Crawford (Foil)	2.00
109	Jeff Kent	.15
110	Ben Sheets	.15
111	Sammy Sosa	1.25
112	Vladimir Guerrero	.40
113	Curt Schilling	.30
114	Carl Pavano	.15
115	Manny Ramirez (Foil)	6.00
116	Billy Williams (Cooperstown)	6.00
117	Ralph Kiner (Cooperstown)	6.00
118	Whitey Ford (Foil)(Cooperstown)	8.00
119	Jim Palmer (Foil)(Cooperstown)	8.00
120	Willie McCovey (Foil)(Cooperstown)	8.00
121	Phil Rizzuto (Cooperstown)	6.00
122	Orlando Cepeda (Cooperstown)	6.00
123	Eddie Mathews (Foil)(Cooperstown)	8.00
124	Tom Seaver (Foil)(Cooperstown)	8.00
125	Bob Feller (Foil)(Cooperstown)	10.00
S1	Down the Middle	.10
S2	Grooved	.10
S3	Lost in the Sun	.10
S4	Protect the Runner	.10
S5	Running on Fumes	.10
S6	Serious Wheels	.10
S7	Smash Up the Middle	.10
S8	Superior Talent	.10
S9	Swat!	.10
S10	Timing	.10
S11	Calculated Risk	.10
S12	Chin Music	.10
S13	Great Start	.10
S14	High and Tight	.10
S15	Intimidation	.10
S16	On Your Toes	.10
S17	Rally Killer	.10
S18	Setup Man	.10
S19	Whiff!	.10
S20	Dugout General	.10
S21	Old Tricks	.10
S22	Out of Sync	.10
S23	Revelation	.10
S24	Stealing Signals	.10
S25	Superstar	.10

2004 MLB Showdown Trading Deadline

MIKE SCHMIDT

		NM/M
Complete Set (150):		200.00
Common Player:		.25
Booster Box (36):		75.00
Booster Pack (9+2):		2.00
1	Jose Mesa	.15
2	Pokey Reese	.15
3	Rey Sanchez	.15
4	Jeff Weaver	.15
5	Todd Zeile	.15
6	Carlos Rivera	.15
7	Orlando Palmeiro	.15
8	Roberto Alomar	.15
9	Doug Glanville	.15
10	Khalil Greene	.30
11	Victor Martinez	.25
12	Jeffrey Hammonds	.15
13	Bobby Kielty	.15
14	Brian Schneider	.15
15	Arthur Rhodes	.15
16	David Dellucci	.15
17	Eric Young Jr.	.15
18	Grant Balfour	.15
19	Javy Lopez	.15
20	Jeff Nelson	.15
21	Kelvim Escobar	.15
22	Braden Looper	.15
23	Tino Martinez	.15
24	Laynce Nix	.15
25	Horacio Ramirez	.15
26	Hideki Matsui	.50
27	Kevin Mench	.15
28	Scott Sullivan	.15
29	Michael Barrett	.15
30	Jose Cruz	.15
31	Robert Fick	.15
32	Brad Fullmer	.15
33	Eric Karros	.15
34	Mark Kotsay	.15
35	Fernando Vina	.15
36	Tim Worrell	.15
37	Mike Cameron	.15
38	Howie Clark	.15
39	Tom Gordon	.15
40	Adam Kennedy	.15
41	Rafael Palmeiro	.35
42	Reed Johnson	.15
43	Aquilino Lopez	.15
44	Julian Tavarez	.15
45	Ben Broussard	.15
46	Miguel Cabrera	.25
47	Raul Ibanez	.15
48	Randall Simon	.15
49	Ronnie Belliard	.15
50	Scott Spiezio	.15
51	Ellis Burks	.15
52	LaTroy Hawkins	.15
53	Pat Hentgen	.15
54	Eddie Guardado	.15
55	Todd Walker	.15
56	Ivan Rodriguez	.35
57	Raul Mondesi	.15
58	Jeromy Burnitz	.15
59	Rich Aurilia	.15
60	Keith Foulke	.15
61	Ramon Hernandez	.15
62	Kenny Lofton	.15
63	Rafael Soriano (Foil)	2.00
64	Jody Gerut	.15
65	Randy Johnson	.40
66	John Burkett	.15
67	Brian Giles (Foil)	2.00
68	Matt Morris	.15
69	Derek Lee	.35
70	Miguel Tejada	.25
71	Ted Lilly	.15
72	David Wells	.15
73	Carl Everett	.15
74	A.J. Pierzynski	.15
75	Gary Sheffield	.25
76	Juan Gonzalez	.20
77	Brandon Webb	.15
78	Joel Pineiro	.15
79	Scott Rolen (Foil)	3.00
80	Jim Edmonds (Foil)	4.00
81	Curt Schilling (Foil)	4.00
82	Kevin Brown (Foil)	3.00
83	Chad Cordero	.15
84	Rich Harden	.15
85	Lyle Overbay	.15
86	Paul Quantrill	.15
87	Rondell White	.15
88	Joe Nathan	.15
89	Jose Valverde	.15
90	Francisco Rodriguez	.15
91	Billy Wagner	.15
92	Jason Giambi	.25
93	Jason Lane	.15
94	Frank Thomas	.45
95	Greg Maddux	.50
96	Andy Pettitte	.20
97	Jay Payton	.15
98	Roger Clemens	.15
99	Bartolo Colon (Foil)	2.00
100	Vladimir Guerrero	.15
101	Kazuo Matsui (Foil)	4.00
102	Javier Vazquez	.15
103	Esteban Loaiza (Foil)	2.00
104	Alex Rodriguez (Foil)	20.00
105	Javy Lopez (Super Season)(Foil)	3.00
106	Tino Martinez (Super Season)	2.00
107	Vladimir Guerrero (Super Season)(Foil)	7.50
108	Derek Jeter (Super Season)(Foil)	12.00
109	Craig Biggio (Super Season)	3.00
110	Tom Glavine (Super Season)	2.00
111	Nomar Garciaparra (Super Season)(Foil)	7.50
112	Mike Mussina (Super Season)(Foil)	4.50
113	Todd Helton (Super Season)(Foil)	4.50
114	Greg Maddux (Super Season)(Foil)	6.00
115	Roger Clemens (Super Season)(Foil)	7.50
116	Rollie Fingers (Cooperstown)(Foil)	9.00
117	Luis Aparicio (Cooperstown)	9.00
118	Lou Brock (Cooperstown)	9.00
119	Joe Morgan (Cooperstown)	9.00
120	Richie Ashburn (Cooperstown)(Foil)	9.00
121	Al Kaline (Cooperstown)(Foil)	9.00
122	Bob Gibson (Cooperstown)(Foil)	9.00
123	Willie Stargell (Cooperstown)	9.00
124	Warren Spahn (Cooperstown)	9.00
125	Mike Schmidt (Cooperstown)(Foil)	75.00
S1	Dialed In	.10
S2	En Fuego!	.10
S3	Last Chance	.10
S4	On the Move	.10
S5	Opposite-Field Power	.10
S6	Out of Gas	.10
S7	Quick Thinking	.10
S8	Swing for the Fences	.10
S9	Wheelhouse	.10
S10	Beaned	.10
S11	Broken Bat	.10
S12	Caught Napping	.10
S13	Chopper	.10
S14	Dying Quail	.10
S15	Great Reactions	.10
S16	Insult to Injury	.10
S17	Lefty Shift	.10
S18	Pumped Up	.10
S19	Punched Out	.10
S20	Robbed!	.10
S21	Feast or Famine	.10
S22	Home-Field Advantage	.10
S23	Just Over the Rail	.10
S24	Late Call	.10
S25	Outmanaged	.10

2005 MLB Showdown League Promos

		NM/M
Complete Set (25):		30.00
Common Player:		3.00
P01	Scot Shields	3.00
P02	Mark Derosa	3.00
P03	Larry Bigbie	3.00
P04	Greg Maddux	6.00
P05	Aaron Rowand	3.50
P06	C.C. Sabathia	3.00
P07	Jason Johnson	3.50
P08	Tim Spooneybarger	3.00
P09	Jeff Kent	4.50
P10	Nate Field	3.00
P11	Jimmy Gobble	3.00
P12	Edwin Jackson	3.50
P13	Jose Lima	3.00
P14	Justin Morneau	3.00
P15	Juan Rincon	3.00
P16	Luis Rivas	3.00
P17	Joe McEwing	3.00
P18	Eric Valent	3.00
P19	Billy Wagner	5.00
P20	Jack Wilson	3.00
P21	Pedro Feliz	4.50
P22	Willie Bloomquist	4.00
P23	Geoff Blum	4.00
P24	Mark Teixeira	3.50
P25	Michael Young	4.50

2005 MLB Showdown

MICHAEL BARRETT

MLB Showdown's 2004 edition has 298 "regular" player cards, 50 premium holofoil star cards and 50 strategy cards. The foil premium cards were inserted in booster packs at a rate of 1:3. While collectors compete with gamers for these cards in the market, relative values placed on the cards by each group of buyers may differ.

	NM/M
Complete Set (398):	300.00
Common Player:	.15
Two-Player Starter:	12.50
Booster Box (36):	65.00
Booster Pack (8+3):	2.50

#	Player	Price
1	Garret Anderson	.15
2	David Eckstein	.15
3	Darin Erstad	.15
4	Chone Figgins	.15
5	Troy Glaus	.15
6	Kevin Gregg	.15
7	Vladimir Guerrero (Foil)	5.00
8	Jose Guillen	.15
9	Adam Kennedy	.15
10	Troy Percival	.15
11	Francisco Rodriguez	.15
12	Tim Salmon	.15
13	Danny Bautista	.15
14	Alex Cintron	.15
15	Luis Gonzalez	.15
16	Scott Hairston	.15
17	Shea Hillenbrand	.15
18	Randy Johnson (Foil)	7.50
19	Mike Koplove	.15
20	Chad Tracy	.15
21	Brandon Webb	.15
22	Antonio Alfonseca	.15
23	J.D. Drew (Foil)	3.00
24	Johnny Estrada (Foil)	3.00
25	Julio Franco	.15
26	Rafael Furcal	.15
27	Marcus Giles	.15
28	Andruw Jones	.35
29	Chipper Jones	.35
30	Eli Marrero	.15
31	John Smoltz	.15
32	John Thomson	.15
33	Jaret Wright	.15
34	Buddy Groom	.15
35	Jerry Hairston	.15
36	Jorge Julio	.15
37	Rodrigo Lopez	.15
38	Melvin Mora	.15
39	Rafael Palmeiro	.30
40	Brian Roberts	.25
41	B.J. Ryan	.15
42	B.J. Surhoff	.15
43	Miguel Tejada (Foil)	3.00
44	Mark Bellhorn	.15
45	Johnny Damon	.30
46	Alan Embree	.15
47	Keith Foulke	.15
48	Gabe Kapler	.15
49	Pedro Martinez	.35
50	Bill Mueller	.15
51	David Ortiz (Foil)	5.00
52	Manny Ramirez (Foil)	5.00
53	Pokey Reese	.15
54	Curt Schilling	.30
55	Mike Timlin	.15
56	Jason Varitek	.15
57	Moises Alou	.15
58	Michael Barrett	.15
59	Matt Clement	.15
60	Kyle Farnsworth	.15
61	Nomar Garciaparra	.35
62	LaTroy Hawkins	.15
63	Todd Hollandsworth	.15
64	Derrek Lee	.30
65	Greg Maddux	.35
66	Kent Mercker	.15
67	Corey Patterson	.15
68	Aramis Ramirez	.15
69	Kerry Wood	.25
70	Mark Buehrle	.15
71	Joe Crede	.15
72	Freddy Garcia	.15
73	Paul Konerko (Foil)	3.00
74	Carlos Lee	.25
75	Damaso Marte	.15
76	Aaron Rowand	.15
77	Shingo Takatsu	.15
78	Juan Uribe	.15
79	Jose Valentin	.15
80	Sean Casey	.15
81	Juan Castro	.15
82	Adam Dunn (Foil)	3.00
83	Ryan Freel	.15
84	Aaron Harang	.15
85	D'Angelo Jimenez	.15
86	Barry Larkin	.15
87	Jason LaRue	.15
88	Wily Mo Pena	.15
89	Phil Norton	.15
90	John Riedling	.15
91	Paul Wilson	.15
92	Ronnie Belliard	.15
93	Casey Blake	.15
94	Ben Broussard	.15
95	Coco Crisp	.30
96	Travis Hafner (Foil)	3.00
97	Matt Lawton	.15
98	Cliff Lee	.15
99	Victor Martinez	.15
100	David Riske	.15
101	C.C. Sabathia	.15
102	Omar Vizquel	.15
103	Jake Westbrook	.15
104	Jeromy Burnitz	.15

#	Player	Price
105	Vinny Castilla	.15
106	Shawn Chacon	.15
107	Royce Clayton	.15
108	Todd Helton (Foil)	3.00
109	Jason Jennings	.15
110	Charles Johnson	.15
111	Aaron Miles	.15
112	Steve Reed	.15
113	Mark Sweeney	.15
114	Carlos Guillen	.15
115	Omar Infante	.15
116	Mike Maroth	.15
117	Craig Monroe	.15
118	Carlos Pena	.15
119	Nate Robertson	.15
120	Ivan Rodriguez (Foil)	3.00
121	Alex Sanchez	.15
122	Ugueth Urbina	.15
123	Rondell White	.15
124	Esteban Yan	.15
125	Dmitri Young	.15
126	Josh Beckett	.25
127	Armando Benitez	.15
128	Miguel Cabrera (Foil)	4.00
129	Luis Castillo	.15
130	Jeff Conine	.15
131	Alex Gonzalez	.15
132	Mike Lowell	.15
133	Carl Pavano	.15
134	Matt Perisho	.15
135	Juan Pierre	.15
136	Tim Spooneybarger	.15
137	Dontrelle Willis	.15
138	Brad Ausmus	.15
139	Jeff Bagwell	.30
140	Carlos Beltran (Foil)	5.00
141	Lance Berkman (Foil)	2.00
142	Craig Biggio	.15
143	Roger Clemens	.40
144	Morgan Ensberg	.15
145	Adam Everett	.15
146	Mike Gallo	.15
147	Jeff Kent	.15
148	Mike Lamb	.15
149	Brad Lidge	.15
150	Dan Miceli	.15
151	Wade Miller	.15
152	Roy Oswalt	.15
153	Angel Berroa	.15
154	Shawn Camp	.15
155	Tony Graffanino	.15
156	Ken Harvey	.15
157	Darrell May	.15
158	Joe Randa	.15
159	Desi Relaford	.15
160	Matt Stairs	.15
161	Scott Sullivan	.15
162	Mike Sweeney	.15
163	Wilson Alvarez	.15
164	Adrian Beltre (Foil)	4.00
165	Milton Bradley	.15
166	Hee Seop Choi	.15
167	Eric Gagne	.15
168	Shawn Green	.15
169	Kazuhisa Ishii	.15
170	Cesar Izturis	.15
171	Jose Lima	.15
172	Jeff Weaver	.15
173	Jeff Bennett	.15
174	Javy Lopez	.15
175	Brady Clark	.15
176	Craig Counsell	.15
177	Doug Davis	.15
178	Bill Hall	.15
179	Geoff Jenkins	.15
180	Brooks Kieschnick	.15
181	Dan Kolb	.15
182	Chad Moeller	.15
183	Lyle Overbay	.15
184	Scott Podsednik	.15
185	Victor Santos	.15
186	Henry Blanco	.15
187	Michael Cuddyer	.15
188	Lew Ford	.15
189	Cristian Guzman	.15
190	Torii Hunter	.15
191	Jacque Jones	.15
192	Corey Koskie	.15
193	Scott Linebrink	.15
194	Brad Radke	.15
195	Johan Santana	20.00
196	Ben Sheets	.15
197	Wes Helms	.15
198	Ken Griffey Jr.	.45
199	Danny Graves	.15
200	Runelvys Hernandez	.15
201	Chris Woodward	.15
202	Paul LoDuca	.15
203	Scot Shields	.15
204	Todd Walker	.15
205	Gregg Zaun	.15
206	Ricky Bottalico	.15
207	Mike Cameron	.15
208	Cliff Floyd	.15
209	Tom Glavine	.15
210	Richard Hidalgo	.15
211	Al Leiter	.15
212	Braden Looper	.15
213	Kazuo Matsui	.15
214	Jason Phillips	.15
215	Mike Piazza (Foil)	5.00
216	Jose Reyes	.15
217	David Wright	.50
218	Kevin Brown	.15
219	Miguel Cairo	.15
220	Tom Gordon	.15
221	Derek Jeter	.50
222	Kenny Lofton	.15

#	Player	Price
223	Jorge Posada (Foil)	2.00
224	Paul Quantrill	.15
225	Mariano Rivera	.15
226	Alex Rodriguez (Foil)	15.00
227	Gary Sheffield (Foil)	3.00
228	Javier Vazquez	.15
229	Enrique Wilson	.15
230	Eric Byrnes	.15
231	Eric Chavez (Foil)	3.00
232	Bobby Crosby	.15
233	Erubiel Durazo (Foil)	2.00
234	Jermaine Dye	.15
235	Scott Hatteberg	.15
236	Bobby Kielty	.15
237	Mark Kotsay	.15
238	Mark Mulder	.15
239	Ricardo Rincon	.15
240	Marco Scutaro	.15
241	Barry Zito	.15
242	Bobby Abreu (Foil)	2.00
243	David Bell	.15
244	Pat Burrell	.30
245	Rheal Cormier	.15
246	Mike Lieberthal	.15
247	Jason Michaels	.15
248	Eric Milton	.15
249	Vicente Padilla	.15
250	Placido Polanco	.15
251	Lance Carter	.15
252	Jimmy Rollins	.15
253	Jim Thome (Foil)	4.00
254	Chase Utley	.15
255	Billy Wagner	.15
256	Randy Wolf	.15
257	Jason Bay	.15
258	Jose Castillo	.15
259	Jason Kendall (Foil)	2.00
260	Robert Mackowiak	.15
261	Jose Mesa	.15
262	Oliver Perez	.15
263	Tike Redman	.15
264	Salomon Torres	.15
265	Daryle Ward	.15
266	Kip Wells	.15
267	Eric Munson	.15
268	Craig Wilson	.15
269	Jack Wilson	.15
270	Sean Burroughs	.15
271	Brian Giles	.15
272	Khalil Greene	.25
273	Ramon Hernandez	.15
274	Trevor Hoffman	.15
275	Ryan Klesko	.15
276	Mark Loretta (Foil)	2.00
277	Phil Nevin	.15
278	Akinori Otsuka	.15
279	Jay Payton	.15
280	Jake Peavey	.15
281	David Wells	.15
282	Edgardo Alfonzo	.15
283	Jim Brower	.15
284	Deivi Cruz	.15
285	Ray Durham	.15
286	Scott Eyre	.15
287	Marquis Grissom	.15
288	Dustan Mohr	.15
289	A.J. Pierzynski	.15
290	Jason Schmidt	.15
291	J.T. Snow (Foil)	2.00
292	Brett Tomko	.15
293	Michael Tucker	.15
294	Bret Boone	.15
295	Ryan Franklin	.15
296	Eddie Guardado	.15
297	Shigetoshi Hasegawa	.15
298	Raul Ibanez	.15
299	Edgar Martinez	.15
300	Joel Pineiro	.15
301	Scott Spezio	.15
302	Ichiro Suzuki (Foil)	10.00
303	Dan Wilson	.15
304	Randy Winn	.15
305	Chris Carpenter	.15
306	Jim Edmonds (Foil)	2.00
307	Jason Isringhausen	.15
308	Ray King	.15
309	Mike Matheny	.15
310	Matt Morris	.15
311	Albert Pujols (Foil)	12.50
312	Edgar Renteria	.15
313	Scott Rolen (Foil)	4.00
314	Reggie Sanders	.15
315	Julian Tavares	.15
316	Larry Walker	.15
317	Woody Williams	.15
318	Tony Womack	.15
319	Danys Baez	.15
320	Rocco Baldelli	.25
321	Dewan Brazleton	.15
322	Carl Crawford	.15
323	Jose Cruz	.15
324	Toby Hall	.15
325	Travis Harper	.15
326	Aubrey Huff	.15
327	Julio Lugo	.15
328	Tino Martinez	.15
329	Rod Barajas	.15
330	Hank Blalock (Foil)	4.00
331	Francisco Cordero	.15
332	Chan Ho Park	.15
333	Kevin Mench	.15
334	Laynce Nix	.15
335	Kenny Rogers	.15
336	Brian Shouse	.15
337	Alfonso Soriano (Foil)	4.00
338	Mark Teixeira	.25
339	Michael Young	.25
340	Miguel Batista	.15

#	Player	Price
341	Frank Catalanotto	.15
342	Carlos Delgado	.15
343	Roy Halliday	.15
344	Eric Hinske	.15
345	Orlando Hudson	.15
346	Reed Johnson	.15
347	Justin Speier	.15
348	Vernon Wells	.15
S01	Goodbye Baseball	.10
S02	Great Addition	.10
S03	Hacker	.10
S04	Helping Himself	.10
S05	High Pitch Count	.10
S06	Hit the Foul Pole	.10
S07	Make Contact	.10
S08	Pull the Ball	.10
S09	Rattled	.10
S10	Role Player	.10
S11	Scuffing	.10
S12	See it Clearly	.10
S13	Serious Wheels	.10
S14	Sprint to Second	.10
S15	Steal the Sign	.10
S16	Turn on It	.10
S17	Upper-Deck Shot	.10
S18	Valuable Asset	.10
S19	Weakest Link	.10
S20	Work the Count	.10
S21	6-4-3	.10
S22	Aces Up	.10
S23	Can of Corn	.10
S24	De-nied!	.10
S25	Fireballer	.10
S26	Full Windup	.10
S27	Good Leather	.10
S28	Hooking Foul	.10
S29	Knuckleball	.10
S30	Lined out of Play	.10
S31	Masterpiece	.10
S32	Out Pitch	.10
S33	Paint the Corner	.10
S34	Playing Shallow	.10
S35	Robbed!	.10
S36	Shut the Door	.10
S37	Up and In	.10
S38	Working the Edge	.10
S39	25th Man	.10
S40	Change in Strategy	.10
S41	Close Call	.10
S42	Fake to Third	.10
S43	Fan Interference	.10
S44	Field General	.10
S45	Intensity	.10
S46	Mind Games	.10
S47	New Strategies	.10
S48	Scouting Report	.10
S49	Second Look	.10
S50	Swing at Anything	.10

2005 MLB Showdown Trading Deadline

	NM/M
Complete Set (200):	90.00
Common Player:	.25
Booster Pack (8+3):	3.00
Booster Box (36):	65.00

#	Player	Price
1	Steve Finley	.25
2	Josh Phelps	.25
3	Magglio Ordonez	.25
4	Nick Johnson	.25
5	Carlos Lee (Foil)	3.00
6	Quinton McCracken	.25
7	Shawn Estes	.25
8	J.J. Putz	.25
9	Mike DeJean	.25
10	Juan Gonzalez	.25
11	Eric Young	.25
12	Matt Mantei	.25
13	Neal Cotts	.25
14	Mike Sweeney	.25
15	Glendon Rusch	.25
16	Termeel Sledge	.25
17	Ron Villone	.25
18	Troy Glaus	.25
19	Wilson Valdez	.25
20	B.J. Surhoff	.25
21	Kazuhisa Ishii	.25
22	Dustin Hermanson	.25
23	Al Leiter	.25
24	Octavio Dotel	.25
25	Henry Blanco	.25
26	J.D. Drew (Foil)	5.00
27	Kevin Millwood	.25
28	Sandy Alomar Jr.	.25
29	John Riedling	.25
30	Rich Harden (Foil)	3.00
31	Aaron Sele	.25
32	Carlos Beltran (Foil)	4.00
33	Jose Lima	.25
34	Richard Hidalgo	.25
35	Placido Polanco	.25
36	Neifi Perez	.25
37	Wilson Alvarez	.25
38	So Taguchi	.25
39	Matt Perisho	.25
40	Roberto Hernandez	.25
41	Todd Walker	.25
42	Jason Kendall	.25
43	Brett Myers	.25
44	Carlos Silva	.25
45	Randy Johnson (Foil)	8.00
46	Jeremy Bonderman	.25
47	Orlando Cabrera	.25
48	Carlos Delgado (Foil)	4.00
49	A.J. Pierzynski	.25
50	Omar Vizquel	.25
51	Lenny Harris	.25

#	Player	Price
52	Chris Carpenter	.25
53	Miguel Cairo	.25
54	Sammy Sosa (Foil)	8.00
55	Royce Clayton	.25
56	Cal Eldred	.25
57	Rich Aurilia	.25
58	Orlando Palmeiro	.25
59	Bengie Molina	.25
60	Ismael Valdez	.25
61	Nate Bump	.25
62	David Wells	.25
63	Jermaine Dye	.25
64	Carlos Zambrano	.25
65	David Newhan	.25
66	Russ Springer	.25
67	Elmer Dessens	.25
68	Kris Benson	.25
69	Al Reyes	.25
70	Tino Martinez	.25
71	Ruben Sierra	.25
72	Antonio Osuna	.25
73	Moises Alou	.25
74	Brad Wilkerson (Foil)	3.00
75	Jason Christiansen	.25
76	Geoff Blum	.25
77	Dennys Reyes	.25
78	Craig Counsell	.25
79	Rey Sanchez	.25
80	Mark Hendrickson	.25
81	Doug Mirabelli	.25
82	Jeromy Burnitz	.25
83	Carl Pavano	.25
84	Richie Sexson	.25
85	Eric Milton	.25
86	Mark DeRosa	.25
87	Bob Wickman	.25
88	Hideo Nomo	.25
89	Tony Armas Jr.	.25
90	Desi Relaford	.25
91	Russ Ortiz	.25
92	Jose Vidro	.25
93	Jeff Kent (Foil)	7.00
94	Esteban Yan	.25
95	Tim Hudson (Foil)	3.00
96	Jay Payton	.25
97	Tony Womack	.25
98	Gregg Zaun	.25
99	David Weathers	.25
100	Scott Podsednik (Foil)	3.00
101	Mark Mulder (Foil)	3.00
102	Jose Guillen	.25
103	Grady Sizemore	.25
104	Paul Bako	.25
105	Jeff DaVanon	.25
106	Jeff Nelson	.25
107	Troy Percival	.25
108	Brian Lawrence	.25
109	Mike Redmond	.25
110	Odalis Perez	.25
111	John Franco	.25
112	Doug Brocail	.25
113	Einar Diaz	.25
114	Mark Grudzielanek	.25
115	Jason Marquis	.25
116	Jayson Werth	.25
117	John Mabry	.25
118	Alexis Rios	.25
119	Livan Hernandez	.25
120	Zack Greinke	.25
121	Chris Hammond	.25
122	Kent Mercker	.25
123	Ryan Drese	.25
124	Pedro Martinez (Foil)	8.00
125	Alex Cora	.25
126	Kenny Lofton	.25
127	Adrian Beltre (Foil)	3.00
128	David Eckstein	.25
129	Derek Lowe	.25
130	Joe Randa	.25
131	Jose Valentin	.25
132	David Bush	.25
133	Brian Schneider	.25
134	Matt Clement	.25
135	Paul Byrd	.25
136	Jose Vizcaino	.25
137	Todd Pratt	.25
138	Jose Offerman	.25
139	Dan Wilson	.25
140	Frank Francisco	.25
141	Woody Williams	.25
142	Juan Castro	.25
143	Jerry Hairston Jr.	.25
144	Jeff Suppan	.25
145	Steve Reed	.25
146	Jon Lieber	.25
147	Cristian Guzman	.25
148	Shawn Green (Foil)	5.00
149	Damion Easley	.25
150	Bronson Arroyo	.25
151	Raul Mondesi	.25
152	Roger Cedeno	.25
153	Carlos Baerga	.25
154	Jose Hernandez	.25
155	Antonio Alfonseca	.25
156	Ricky Ledee	.25
157	Armando Benitez	.25
158	Esteban Loaiza	.25
159	Steve Kline	.25
160	Corey Koskie	.25
161	Vinny Castilla (Foil)	3.00
162	Tony Clark	.25
163	Edgar Renteria (Foil)	3.00
164	Brian Jordan	.25
165	David Dellucci	.25
166	Hoyt Wilhelm (Foil)	5.00
167	Pee Wee Reese	.25
168	Larry Doby	.25
169	Yogi Berra (Foil)	8.00
170	Robin Yount (Foil)	5.00
171	Brooks Robinson (Foil)	5.00

#	Player	Price
172	Reggie Jackson (Foil)	8.00
173	Rod Carew (Foil)	5.00
174	Harmon Killebrew (Foil)	4.00
175	Nolan Ryan (Foil)	15.00
S1	Free Steal	.25
S2	Get Under It	.25
S3	Go Yard!	.25
S4	Just Called Up	.25
S5	Leadoof Man	.25
S6	Lofted	.25
S7	Missed the Cutoff	.25
S8	Momentum Swing	.25
S9	Shaken	.25
S10	Shelled	.25
S11	Texas Leaguer	.25
S12	Caught Looking	.25
S13	Great Range	.25
S14	High Heat	.25
S15	Just Over the Wall	.25
S16	Slider	.25
S17	Stranded	.25
S18	Superior Athlete	.25
S19	Taking a Risk	.25
S20	Team Defense	.25
S21	Brainstorm	.25
S22	Change the Scorecard	.25
S23	Good Coaching	.25
S24	Preparation	.25
S25	Shell Game	.25

1992 Modell's Team Mets

EDDIE MURRAY   #33 Infielder

Team Mets, the junior fan club, included in its 1992 membership benefits a nine-card perforated sheet sponsored by Modell's Sporting Goods. Cards feature color action photos highlighted by team-color stripes of blue and orange, with a white outer border. The 7-1/2" x 10-1/2" sheet can be separated into standard-size 2-1/2" x 3-1/2" cards. Team Mets and Modell's logos are featured on back, along with 1991 stats and highlights, career numbers and personal data. Cards are checklisted here according to the uniform numbers found on the front.

	NM/M
Complete Set (9):	5.00
Common Player:	.50

#	Player	Price
1	Vince Coleman	.50
9	Todd Hundley	.50
12	Willie Randolph	.50
16	Dwight Gooden	.50
17	David Cone	.50
18	Bret Saberhagen	.50
20	Howard Johnson	.50
25	Bobby Bonilla	.50
33	Eddie Murray	2.00

1991 MooTown Snackers

CHRIS SABO   CINCINNATI REDS / THIRD BASE

Produced by the Sargento Cheese Co., cards were available in Mootown Snacker packages or by sending in a special set redemption coupon from a package to obtain the entire set for $5.95 and three UPCs. Fronts feature action photos with uniform logos airbrushed off. Photos are bordered at top and bottom in red. Backs are in red, black and white and feature statistics and a facsimile autograph. Each player card is attached to a perforated panel on its right which has the checklist and a coupon to order the complete set. Cards without the offer coupon still attached are worth 50% of the values quoted here.

		NM/M
Complete Set (24):		10.00
Common Player:		.25
1	Jose Canseco	.50
2	Kirby Puckett	1.00
3	Barry Bonds	2.00
4	Ken Griffey Jr.	1.50
5	Ryne Sandberg	1.00
6	Tony Gwynn	1.00
7	Kal Daniels	.25
8	Ozzie Smith	1.00
9	Dave Justice	.25
10	Sandy Alomar, Jr.	.25
11	Wade Boggs	1.00
12	Ozzie Guillen	.25
13	Dave Magadan	.25
14	Cal Ripken, Jr.	2.00
15	Don Mattingly	1.25
16	Ruben Sierra	.25
17	Robin Yount	.75
18	Len Dykstra	.25
19	George Brett	1.25
20	Lance Parrish	.25
21	Chris Sabo	.25
22	Craig Biggio	.25
23	Kevin Mitchell	.25
24	Cecil Fielder	.25

1992 MooTown Snackers

The unusual venue of cheese snack packs was the source for these cards. Produced as two-piece panels, there is a player card attached by perforations to a card offering a complete set for $7 and proofs of purchase. The player cards have cheese-yellow borders at top and bottom with an action photo at center. Produced by Michael Schecter Assoc., the cards have had uniform and cap logos removed because they are licensed only by the Players Association and not by MLB. Backs are printed in black and yellow on white and include a facsimile autograph. Cards with the complete set offer no longer attached are worth 50 percent of the values shown here.

		NM/M
Complete Set (24):		7.50
Common Player:		.25
1	Albert Belle	.25
2	Jeff Bagwell	.75
3	Jose Rijo	.25
4	Roger Clemens	1.25
5	Kevin Maas	.25
6	Kirby Puckett	1.00
7	Ken Griffey Jr.	1.50
8	Will Clark	.25
9	Felix Jose	.25
10	Cecil Fielder	.25
11	Darryl Strawberry	.25
12	John Smiley	.25
13	Roberto Alomar	.35
14	Paul Molitor	.75
15	Andre Dawson	.25
16	Terry Mulholland	.25
17	Fred McGriff	.25
18	Dwight Gooden	.25
19	Rickey Henderson	.75
20	Nolan Ryan	2.00
21	George Brett	1.25
22	Tom Glavine	.40
23	Cal Ripken Jr.	2.00
24	Frank Thomas	.75

1983 Mother's Cookies Giants

After putting out Pacific Coast League sets in 1952-53, Mother's Cookies distributed this full-color set of 20 San Francisco Giants cards three decades later. The 2-1/2" x 3-1/2" cards were produced by hobbyist Barry Colla and include the Giants logo and player's name on the card fronts.

JACK CLARK

Backs are numbered and contain biographical information, sponsor's logo and a space for the player's autograph. Fifteen cards were given to every fan at the Aug. 7, 1983, Giants game, with each fan also receiving a coupon good for five additional cards.

		NM/M
Complete Set (20):		6.00
Common Player:		.35
1	Frank Robinson	2.00
2	Jack Clark	.50
3	Chili Davis	.45
4	Johnnie LeMaster	.35
5	Greg Minton	.35
6	Bob Brenly	.35
7	Fred Breining	.35
8	Jeff Leonard	.35
9	Darrell Evans	.50
10	Tom O'Malley	.35
11	Duane Kuiper	.35
12	Mike Krukow	.35
13	Atlee Hammaker	.35
14	Gary Lavelle	.35
15	Bill Laskey	.35
16	Max Venable	.35
17	Joel Youngblood	.35
18	Dave Bergman	.35
19	Mike Vail	.35
20	Andy McGaffigan	.35

1984 Mother's Cookies A's

DAVE KINGMAN

Following the success of their one set in 1983, Mother's Cookies issued five more team sets of cards in 1984. Cards measure 2-1/2" x 3-1/2" with rounded corners. Fronts feature unbordered color photos. Horizontal backs have biographical data, card number, Mother's Cookies logo and space for player autograph. There are 28 cards in the A's set, with 20 of the cards distributed during a stadium promotion. Fans also received a coupon redeemable for eight additional cards. Since those cards did not necessarily complete collectors' sets, Mother's Cookies cards become very popular among traders. The A's set includes cards for the manager, coaches and a checklist.

		NM/M
Complete Set (28):		9.00
Common Player:		.25
1	Steve Boros	.25
2	Rickey Henderson	5.00
3	Joe Morgan	2.00
4	Dwayne Murphy	.25
5	Mike Davis	.25
6	Bruce Bochte	.25
7	Carney Lansford	.25
8	Steve McCatty	.25
9	Mike Heath	.25
10	Chris Codiroli	.25
11	Bill Almon	.25
12	Bill Caudill	.25
13	Donnie Hill	.25
14	Lary Sorenson	.25
15	Dave Kingman	.50
16	Garry Hancock	.25
17	Jeff Burroughs	.25

18	Tom Burgmeier	.25
19	Jim Essian	.25
20	Mike Warren	.25
21	Davey Lopes	.25
22	Ray Burris	.25
23	Tony Phillips	.25
24	Tim Conroy	.25
25	Jeff Bettendorf	.25
26	Keith Atherton	.25
27	A's Coaches (Clete Boyer, Bob Didier, Jackie Moore, Ron Schueler, Billy Williams)	.25
28	Oakland Coliseum/Checklist	.25

Astros

JOE NIEKRO
Astros

Mother's Cookies issued a full-color team set for the Astros in 1984. Cards measure 2-1/2" x 3-1/2" with rounded corners. Card fronts feature unbordered color photos. Horizontal backs have biographical data, card number, Mother's Cookies logo and space for player autograph. There are 28 cards in the Astros set, with 20 of the cards distributed during a stadium promotion. Fans also received a coupon redeemable for eight additional cards. Since those cards did not necessarily complete collectors' sets, Mother's Cookies cards became very popular among traders. The Astros set includes one card for the coaches and a checklist.

		NM/M
Complete Set (28):		7.00
Common Player:		.25
1	Nolan Ryan	6.00
2	Joe Niekro	.25
3	Alan Ashby	.25
4	Bill Doran	.25
5	Phil Garner	.25
6	Ray Knight	.25
7	Dickie Thon	.25
8	Jose Cruz	.25
9	Jerry Mumphrey	.25
10	Terry Puhl	.25
11	Enos Cabell	.25
12	Harry Spilman	.25
13	Dave Smith	.25
14	Mike Scott	.25
15	Bob Lillis	.25
16	Bob Knepper	.25
17	Frank DiPino	.25
18	Tom Wieghaus	.25
19	Denny Walling	.25
20	Tony Scott	.25
21	Alan Bannister	.25
22	Bill Dawley	.25
23	Vern Ruhle	.25
24	Mike LaCoss	.25
25	Mike Madden	.25
26	Craig Reynolds	.25
27	Astros Coaches (Cot Deal, Don Leppert, Denis Menke, Les Moss, Jerry Walker)	.25
28	Astros Logo/Checklist	.25

Giants

JUAN MARICHAL
GIANTS ALL-STAR

Mother's Cookies issued a second annual full-color card set for the S.F. Giants in 1984. Cards measure

2-1/2" x 3-1/2" with rounded corners. Fronts feature drawings of former Giant All-Star team selections. Horizontal backs have brief biographical information, card number and Mother's Cookies logo and autograph space. There are 28 cards in the Giants set, with 20 of the cards distributed during a stadium promotion. Fans also received a coupon redeemable for eight additional cards. Since those cards did not necessarily complete collectors' sets, Mother's Cookies cards became very popular among card traders.

		NM/M
Complete Set (28):		7.50
Common Player:		.15
1	Willie Mays	4.50
2	Willie McCovey	1.00
3	Juan Marichal	.50
4	Gaylord Perry	.50
5	Tom Haller	.15
6	Jim Davenport	.15
7	Jack Clark	.25
8	Greg Minton	.15
9	Atlee Hammaker	.15
10	Gary Lavelle	.15
11	Orlando Cepeda	.50
12	Bobby Bonds	.25
13	John Antonelli	.15
14	Bob Schmidt (Photo actually Wes Westrum.)	.15
15	Sam Jones	.15
16	Mike McCormick	.15
17	Ed Bailey	.15
18	Stu Miller	.15
19	Felipe Alou	.25
20	Jim Hart	.15
21	Dick Dietz	.15
22	Chris Speier	.15
23	Bobby Murcer	.25
24	John Montefusco	.15
25	Vida Blue	.25
26	Ed Whitson	.15
27	Darrell Evans	.25
28	All-Star Game Logo/Checklist	.15

Mariners

ALVIN DAVIS
Mariners

Mother's Cookies issued a full-color set for the Mariners in 1984. Cards measure 2-1/2" x 3-1/2" with rounded corners. Fronts feature unbordered color photos. Horizontal backs have brief biographical data, card number and space for player autograph. There are 28 cards in the set with 20 of the cards distributed during a stadium promotion. Fans also received a coupon redeemable for eight additional cards. Since those cards did not necessarily complete collectors' sets, Mother's Cookies cards became very popular among traders. The set includes one card each for the manager, coaches and a checklist.

		NM/M
Complete Set (28):		6.00
Common Player:		.25
1	Del Crandall	.25
2	Barry Bonnell	.25
3	Dave Henderson	.25
4	Bob Kearney	.25
5	Mike Moore	.25
6	Spike Owen	.25
7	Gorman Thomas	.25
8	Ed Vande Berg	.25
9	Matt Young	.25
10	Larry Milbourne	.25
11	Dave Beard	.25
12	Jim Beattie	.25
13	Mark Langston	.25
14	Orlando Mercado	.25
15	Jack Perconte	.25
16	Pat Putnam	.25
17	Paul Mirabella	.25
18	Domingo Ramos	.25
19	Al Cowens	.25
20	Mike Stanton	.25
21	Steve Henderson	.25
22	Bob Stoddard	.25

23	Alvin Davis	.25
24	Phil Bradley	.25
25	Roy Thomas	.25
26	Darnell Coles	.25
27	Mariners Coaches (Chuck Cottier, Frank Funk, Ben Hines, Phil Roof, Rick Sweet)	.25
28	Seattle Kingdome/Checklist	.25

Padres

TERRY KENNEDY
Padres

Mother's Cookies issued a full-color set for the Padres in 1984. Cards measure 2-1/2" x 3-1/2", with rounded corners. Fronts feature unbordered color photos. Horizontal backs have brief biographical data, card number, sponsor's logo and space for player autograph. There are 28 cards in the set, with 20 of the cards distributed during a stadium promotion. Fans also received a coupon redeemable for eight additional cards. Since those cards did not necessarily complete collectors' sets, Mother's Cookies cards became very popular among traders. The Padres set includes one card each for the manager, coaches and a checklist.

		NM/M
Complete Set (28):		9.00
Common Player:		.25
1	Dick Williams	.25
2	Rich Gossage	.50
3	Tim Lollar	.25
4	Eric Show	.25
5	Terry Kennedy	.25
6	Kurt Bevacqua	.25
7	Steve Garvey	1.50
8	Garry Templeton	.25
9	Tony Gwynn	5.00
10	Alan Wiggins	.25
11	Dave Dravecky	.25
12	Tim Flannery	.25
13	Kevin McReynolds	.25
14	Bobby Brown	.25
15	Ed Whitson	.25
16	Doug Gwosdz	.25
17	Luis DeLeon	.25
18	Andy Hawkins	.25
19	Craig Lefferts	.25
20	Carmelo Martinez	.25
21	Sid Monge	.25
22	Graig Nettles	.25
23	Mario Ramirez	.25
24	Luis Salazar	.25
25	Champ Summers	.25
26	Mark Thurmond	.25
27	Padres Coaches (Harry Dunlop, Deacon Jones, Jack Krol, Norm Sherry, Ozzie Virgil)	.25
28	Jack Murphy Stadium/Checklist	.25

1985 Mother's Cookies A's

DAVE KINGMAN
Oakland A's

Mother's Cookies again issued five full-color sets for Major League teams in 1985. Cards measure 2-1/2" x 3-1/2" with rounded corners. Fronts feature unbordered color photos. Horizontal backs have brief biographical data, card

number, Mother's Cookies logo and space for player autograph. The set was distributed in its entirety during a stadium promotion.

		NM/M
Complete Set (28):		7.00
Common Player:		.25
1	Jackie Moore	.25
2	Dave Kingman	.40
3	Don Sutton	1.25
4	Mike Heath	.25
5	Alfredo Griffin	.25
6	Dwayne Murphy	.25
7	Mike Davis	.25
8	Carney Lansford	.25
9	Chris Codiroli	.25
10	Bruce Bochte	.25
11	Mickey Tettleton	.25
12	Donnie Hill	.25
13	Rob Picciolo	.25
14	Dave Collins	.25
15	Dusty Baker	.50
16	Tim Conroy	.25
17	Keith Atherton	.25
18	Jay Howell	.25
19	Mike Warren	.25
20	Steve McCatty	.25
21	Bill Krueger	.25
22	Curt Young	.25
23	Dan Meyer	.25
24	Mike Gallego	.25
25	Jeff Kaiser	.25
26	Steve Henderson	.25
27	A's Coaches (Clete Boyer, Bob Didier, Dave McKay, Wes Stock, Billy Williams)	.25
28	Oakland Coliseum/Checklist	.25

Astros

DICKIE THON
Houston Astros

Mother's Cookies issued a second annual full-color set for the Astros in 1985. Cards measure 2-1/2" x 3-1/2" with rounded corners. Fronts feature unbordered color photos. Horizontal backs have biographical information, card number, Mother's Cookies logo and space for player autograph. The set was distributed in its entirety during a stadium promotion.

		NM/M
Complete Set (28):		8.00
Common Player:		.25
1	Bob Lillis	.25
2	Nolan Ryan	7.50
3	Phil Garner	.25
4	Jose Cruz	.25
5	Denny Walling	.25
6	Joe Niekro	.30
7	Terry Puhl	.25
8	Bill Doran	.25
9	Dickie Thon	.25
10	Enos Cabell	.25
11	Frank Dipino (DiPino)	.25
12	Julio Solano	.25
13	Alan Ashby	.25
14	Craig Reynolds	.25
15	Jerry Mumphrey	.25
16	Bill Dawley	.25
17	Mark Bailey	.25
18	Mike Scott	.25
19	Harry Spilman	.25
20	Bob Knepper	.25
21	Dave Smith	.25
22	Kevin Bass	.25
23	Tim Tolman	.25
24	Jeff Calhoun	.25
25	Jim Pankovits	.25
26	Ron Mathis	.25
27	Astros Coaches (Cot Deal, Matt Galante, Don Leppert, Denis Menke, Jerry Walker)	.25
28	Astros Logo/Checklist	.25

Giants

Mother's Cookies issued a third annual full-color set for the Giants in 1985. Cards measure 2-1/2" x 3-1/2" with rounded corners. Fronts feature unbordered color photos. Horizontal backs have brief biographical information, card number, Mother's Cookies logo and space for player autograph. The set was distributed in its entirety during a stadium promotion.

	NM/M
Complete Set (28):	6.00
Common Player:	.25
1 Jim Davenport	.25
2 Chili Davis	.25
3 Dan Gladden	.25
4 Jeff Leonard	.25
5 Manny Trillo	.25
6 Atlee Hammaker	.25
7 Bob Brenly	.25
8 Greg Minton	.25
9 Bill Laskey	.25
10 Vida Blue	.30
11 Mike Krukow	.25
12 Frank Williams	.25
13 Jose Uribe	.25
14 Johnnie LeMaster	.25
15 Scot Thompson	.25
16 Dave LaPoint	.25
17 David Green	.25
18 Chris Brown	.25
19 Joel Youngblood	.25
20 Mark Davis	.25
21 Jim Gott	.25
22 Doug Gwosdz	.25
23 Scott Garrelts	.25
24 Gary Rajsich	.25
25 Rob Deer	.25
26 Brad Wellman	.25
27 Coaches (Rocky Bridges, Chuck Hiller, Tom McCraw, Bob Miller, Jack Mull)	.25
28 Candlestick Park/Checklist	.25

Mariners

Mother's Cookies issued a second annual full-color set for the Mariners in 1985. Cards measure 2-1/2" x 3-1/2" with rounded corners. Fronts feature unbordered color photos. Horizontal backs have biographical information, card number, Mother's Cookies logo and space for player autograph. The set was distributed in its entirety during a stadium promotion.

	NM/M
Complete Set (28):	6.00
Common Player:	.25
1 Chuck Cottier	.25
2 Alvin Davis	.25
3 Mark Langston	.25
4 Dave Henderson	.25
5 Ed Vande Berg	.25
6 Al Cowens	.25
7 Spike Owen	.25
8 Mike Moore	.25
9 Gorman Thomas	.25
10 Barry Bonnell	.25
11 Jack Perconte	.25
12 Domingo Ramos	.25
13 Bob Kearney	.25
14 Matt Young	.25
15 Jim Beattie	.25
16 Mike Stanton	.25
17 Dave Valle	.25
18 Ken Phelps	.25
19 Salome Barojas	.25
20 Jim Presley	.25
21 Phil Bradley	.25
22 Dave Geisel	.25
23 Harold Reynolds	.50
24 Edwin Nunez	.25
25 Mike Morgan	.25
26 Ivan Calderon	.25
27 Mariners Coaches (Deron Johnson, Jim Mahoney, Marty Martinez, Phil Regan, Phil Roof)	.25
28 Seattle Kingdome/Checklist	.25

Padres

Mother's Cookies issued a second annual full-color Padres team set in 1985. Cards have rounded corners and measure 2-1/2" x 3-1/2". Glossy fronts feature unbordered color photos. Horizontal backs have biographical data, card number, Mother's Cookies logo and space for player autograph. The set was distributed in its entirety during a stadium promotion.

	NM/M
Complete Set (28):	6.00
Common Player:	.25
1 Dick Williams	.25
2 Tony Gwynn	4.50
3 Kevin McReynolds	.25
4 Graig Nettles	.25
5 Rich Gossage	.40
6 Steve Garvey	1.50
7 Garry Templeton	.25
8 Dave Dravecky	.25
9 Eric Show	.25
10 Terry Kennedy	.25
11 Luis DeLeon	.25
12 Bruce Bochy	.25
13 Andy Hawkins	.25
14 Kurt Bevacqua	.25
15 Craig Lefferts	.25
16 Mario Ramirez	.25
17 LaMarr Hoyt	.25
18 Jerry Royster	.25
19 Tim Stoddard	.25
20 Tim Flannery	.25
21 Mark Thurmond	.25
22 Greg Booker	.25
23 Bobby Brown	.25
24 Carmelo Martinez	.25
25 Al Bumbry	.25
26 Jerry Davis	.25
27 Padres Coaches (Galen Cisco, Harry Dunlop, Deacon Jones, Jack Krol, Ozzie Virgil)	.25
28 Jack Murphy Stadium/Checklist	.25

1986 Mother's Cookies A's

Mother's Cookies produced four full-color team sets in 1986, with only the San Diego Padres not repeating from the 1985 group. The third annual set for the Oakland A's measures 2-1/2" x 3-1/2" with rounded corners. Glossy fronts feature unbordered color photos. Horizontal backs have brief biographical information, card number and Mother's Cookies logo. There are 28 cards in the A's set, with 20 of the cards distributed during a stadium promotion. Each fan also received a coupon redeemable for eight additional cards which could be traded to complete a set.

	NM/M
Complete Set (28):	10.00
Common Player:	.25
1 Jackie Moore	.25
2 Dave Kingman	.40
3 Dusty Baker	.40
4 Joaquin Andujar	.25
5 Alfredo Griffin	.25
6 Dwayne Murphy	.25
7 Mike Davis	.25
8 Carney Lansford	.25
9 Jose Canseco	6.00
10 Bruce Bochte	.25
11 Mickey Tettleton	.25
12 Donnie Hill	.25
13 Jose Rijo	.25
14 Rick Langford	.25
15 Chris Codiroli	.25
16 Moose Haas	.25
17 Keith Atherton	.25
18 Jay Howell	.25
19 Tony Phillips	.25
20 Steve Henderson	.25
21 Bill Krueger	.25
22 Steve Ontiveros	.25
23 Bill Bathe	.25
24 Rickey Peters	.25
25 Tim Birtsas	.25
26 Trainers (Frank Ciensczyk, Larry Davis, Steve Vucinich, Barry Weinberg)	.25
27 Coaches (Bob Didier, Dave McKay, Jeff Newman, Ron Plaza, Wes Stock, Bob Watson)	.25
28 Oakland Coliseum/Checklist	.25

Astros

Mother's Cookies produced a third annual Astros team set in 1985. The round-cornered, glossy front 2-1/2" x 3-1/2" cards feature unbordered color paintings of Houston's past All-Star Game performers. Backs have biographical information, card number and Mother's Cookies logo. There are 28 cards in the set, with 20 of the cards distributed during a stadium promotion. Each fan also received a coupon redeemable for eight additional cards that could be traded to complete a set.

	NM/M
Complete Set (28):	9.00
Common Player:	.25
1 Dick Farrell	.25
2 Hal Woodeschick (Woodeshick)	.25
3 Joe Morgan	1.00
4 Claude Raymond	.25
5 Mike Cuellar	.25
6 Rusty Staub	.25
7 Jimmy Wynn	.25
8 Larry Dierker	.25
9 Denis Menke	.25
10 Don Wilson	.25
11 Cesar Cedeno	.25
12 Lee May	.25
13 Bob Watson	.25
14 Ken Forsch	.25
15 Joaquin Andujar	.25
16 Terry Puhl	.25
17 Joe Niekro	.30
18 Craig Reynolds	.25
19 Joe Sambito	.25
20 Jose Cruz	.25
21 J.R. Richard	.30
22 Bob Knepper	.25
23 Nolan Ryan	7.50
24 Ray Knight	.25
25 Bill Dawley	.25
26 Dickie Thon	.25
27 Jerry Mumphrey	.25
28 Astros Logo/Checklist	.25

Giants

Mother's Cookies produced a fourth annual set for the Giants in 1985. Round-cornered, glossy

front cards measure 2-1/2" x 3-1/2" and feature unbordered color photos. Horizontal backs have biographical data, card number, and Mother's Cookies logo. There are 28 cards in the set, with 20 of the cards distributed during a stadium promotion. Each fan also received a coupon redeemable for eight additional cards which could be traded to complete the set.

	NM/M
Complete Set (28):	6.00
Common Player:	.25
1 Roger Craig	.25
2 Chili Davis	.25
3 Dan Gladden	.25
4 Jeff Leonard	.25
5 Bob Brenly	.25
6 Atlee Hammaker	.25
7 Will Clark	5.00
8 Greg Minton	.25
9 Candy Maldonado	.25
10 Vida Blue	.25
11 Mike Krukow	.25
12 Bob Melvin	.25
13 Jose Uribe	.25
14 Dan Driessen	.25
15 Jeff Robinson	.25
16 Rob Thompson	.25
17 Mike LaCoss	.25
18 Chris Brown	.25
19 Scott Garrelts	.25
20 Mark Davis	.25
21 Jim Gott	.25
22 Brad Wellman	.25
23 Roger Mason	.25
24 Bill Laskey	.25
25 Brad Gulden	.25
26 Joel Youngblood	.25
27 Juan Berenguer	.25
28 Coaches/Checklist (Bill Fahey, Bob Lillis, Gordy MacKenzie, Jose Morales, Norm Sherry)	.25

Mariners

Mother's Cookies produced a third annual set for the M's in 1985. Round-cornered, glossy front cards measure 2-1/2" x 3-1/2" and feature unbordered color photos. Horizontal backs have brief biographical information, card number and sponsor's logo. There are 28 cards in the set, with 20 distributed during a stadium promotion. Each fan also received a coupon redeemable for eight additional cards which could be traded to complete the set.

	NM/M
Complete Set (28):	6.00
Common Player:	.25
1 Dick Williams	.25
2 Alvin Davis	.25
3 Mark Langston	.25
4 Dave Henderson	.25
5 Steve Yeager	.25
6 Al Cowens	.25
7 Jim Presley	.25
8 Phil Bradley	.25
9 Gorman Thomas	.25
10 Barry Bonnell	.25
11 Milt Wilcox	.25
12 Domingo Ramos	.25
13 Paul Mirabella	.25
14 Matt Young	.25
15 Ivan Calderon	.25
16 Bill Swift	.25
17 Pete Ladd	.25
18 Ken Phelps	.25
19 Karl Best	.25
20 Spike Owen	.25
21 Mike Moore	.25
22 Danny Tartabull	.25
23 Bob Kearney	.25
24 Edwin Nunez	.25
25 Mike Morgan	.25
26 Roy Thomas	.25
27 Jim Beattie	.25
28 Coaches/Checklist (Deron Johnson, Marty Martinez, Phil Regan, Phil Roof, Ozzie Virgil)	.25

1987 Mother's Cookies A's

Continuing with a tradition of producing beautiful baseball cards, Mother's Cookies of Oakland, Calif. issued a 28-card set featuring every Oakland A's player to have been elected to the All-Star Game since 1968. The full-color photos came from the private collection of nationally known photographer Doug McWilliams. Twenty of the 28 cards were given out to fans attending the A's game on July 5. An additional eight cards were available by redeeming a mail-in certificate. The cards measure 2-1/2" x 3-1/2" and feature rounded corners. Backs carry the player's All-Star Game statistics.

	NM/M
Complete Set (28):	12.00
Common Player:	.25
1 Bert Campaneris	.25
2 Rick Monday	.25
3 John Odom	.25
4 Sal Bando	.25
5 Reggie Jackson	2.50
6 Catfish Hunter	1.00
7 Vida Blue	.25
8 Dave Duncan	.25
9 Joe Rudi	.25
10 Rollie Fingers	.75
11 Ken Holtzman	.25
12 Dick Williams	.25
13 Alvin Dark	.25
14 Gene Tenace	.25
15 Claudell Washington	.25
16 Phil Garner	.25
17 Wayne Gross	.25
18 Matt Keough	.25
19 Jeff Newman	.25
20 Rickey Henderson	1.50
21 Tony Armas	.25
22 Mike Norris	.25
23 Billy Martin	.40
24 Bill Caudill	.25
25 Jay Howell	.25
26 Jose Canseco	2.00
27 Jose and Reggie (Jose Canseco, Reggie Jackson)	2.50
28 A's Logo/Checklist	.25

Astros

Twenty of 28 cards featuring Astros players were given out to the first 25,000 fans attending the July 17 game at the Astrodome. An additional eight cards (though not necessarily the exact eight needed to complete a set) were available from the sponsor by redeeming a mail-in certificate. The cards have rounded corners, glossy fronts and measure 2-1/2" x 3-1/2". Backs are printed in purple and orange and contain personal data, the Mother's Cookies logo, card number and a spot for the player's autograph.

	NM/M
Complete Set (28):	10.00
Common Player:	.25
1 Hal Lanier	.25
2 Mike Scott	.25
3 Jose Cruz	.25
4 Bill Doran	.25
5 Bob Knepper	.25
6 Phil Garner	.25
7 Terry Puhl	.25
8 Nolan Ryan	7.50
9 Kevin Bass	.25
10 Glenn Davis	.25
11 Alan Ashby	.25
12 Charlie Kerfeld	.25
13 Denny Walling	.25
14 Danny Darwin	.25
15 Mark Bailey	.25
16 Davey Lopes	.25
17 Dave Meads	.25
18 Aurelio Lopez	.25
19 Craig Reynolds	.25
20 Dave Smith	.25
21 Larry Anderson (Andersen)	.25
22 Jim Pankovits	.25
23 Jim Deshaies	.25
24 Bert Pena	.25
25 Dickie Thon	.25
26 Billy Hatcher	.25
27 Coaches (Yogi Berra, Matt Galante, Denis Menke, Les Moss, Gene Tenace)	.25
28 Houston Astrodome/Checklist	.25

Dodgers

Mother's Cookies produced for the first time in 1987 a team set featuring the L.A. Dodgers. Twenty of the 28 cards are given to youngsters 14 and under at Dodger Stadium on August 9. An additional eight cards were available from Mother's Cookies via a mail-in coupon. The borderless, full-color cards measure 2-1/2" x 3-1/2" and have rounded corners. A special album designed to house the set was available for $3.95 through a mail-in offer.

	NM/M
Complete Set (28):	10.00
Common Player:	.25
1 Tom Lasorda	.40
2 Pedro Guerrero	.25
3 Steve Sax	.25
4 Fernando Valenzuela	.25
5 Mike Marshall	.25
6 Orel Hershiser	.75
7 Mariano Duncan	.25
8 Bill Madlock	.25
9 Bob Welch	.25
10 Mike Scioscia	.25
11 Mike Ramsey	.25
12 Matt Young	.25
13 Franklin Stubbs	.25
14 Tom Niedenfuer	.25
15 Reggie Williams	.25
16 Rick Honeycutt	.25
17 Dave Anderson	.25
18 Alejandro Pena	.25
19 Ken Howell	.25
20 Len Matuszek	.25
21 Tim Leary	.25
22 Tracy Woodson	.25
23 Alex Trevino	.25
24 Ken Landreaux	.25
25 Mickey Hatcher	.25

26	Brian Holton	.25
27	Coaches (Joey Amalfitano, Mark Cresse, Don McMahon, Manny Mota, Ron Perranoski, Bill Russell)	.25
28	Dodger Stadium/Checklist	.25

Giants

Distribution of the 1987 Mother's Cookies Giants cards took place at Candlestick Park on June 27. Twenty of the 28 cards in the set were given to the first 25,000 fans entering the park. The starter packet of 20 cards contained a mail-in coupon card which was good for an additional eight cards. The glossy-front cards measure 2-1/2" x 3-1/2" with rounded corners. Backs are printed in red and purple and contain personal and statistical information along with the Mother's Cookies logo.

		NM/M
Complete Set (28):		9.00
Common Player:		.25
1	Roger Craig	.25
2	Will Clark	1.00
3	Chili Davis	.25
4	Bob Brenly	.25
5	Chris Brown	.25
6	Mike Krukow	.25
7	Candy Maldonado	.25
8	Jeffrey Leonard	.25
9	Greg Minton	.25
10	Robby Thompson	.25
11	Scott Garrelts	.25
12	Bob Melvin	.25
13	Jose Uribe	.25
14	Mark Davis	.25
15	Eddie Milner	.25
16	Harry Spilman	.25
17	Kelly Downs	.25
18	Chris Speier	.25
19	Jim Gott	.25
20	Joel Youngblood	.25
21	Mike LaCoss	.25
22	Matt Williams	3.00
23	Roger Mason	.25
24	Mike Aldrete	.25
25	Jeff Robinson	.25
26	Mark Grant	.25
27	Coaches (Bill Fahey, Bob Lillis, Gordon MacKenzie, Jose Morales, Norm Sherry, Don Zimmer)	.25
28	Candlestick Park/Checklist	.25

Mariners

For the fourth consecutive year, Mother's Cookies issued a team set featuring the Mariners. Twenty of the 28 cards were distributed to the first 20,000 fans entering the Kingdome on August 9. An additional eight cards (though not necessarily the eight cards needed to complete the set) were available by redeeming a mail-in certificate. Collectors were encouraged to trade to complete a set. The 2-1/2" x 3-1/2" full-color cards feature glossy fronts and rounded corners. A specially designed album to house the set was available.

		NM/M
Complete Set (28):		6.00
Common Player:		.25
1	Dick Williams	.25
2	Alvin Davis	.25
3	Mike Moore	.25
4	Jim Presley	.25
5	Mark Langston	.25
6	Phil Bradley	.25
7	Ken Phelps	.25
8	Mike Morgan	.25
9	David Valle	.25
10	Harold Reynolds	.40
11	Edwin Nunez	.25
12	Bob Kearney	.25
13	Scott Bankhead	.25
14	Scott Bradley	.25
15	Mickey Brantley	.25
16	Mark Huismann	.25
17	Mike Kingery	.25
18	John Moses	.25
19	Donell Nixon	.25
20	Rey Quinones	.25
21	Domingo Ramos	.25
22	Jerry Reed	.25
23	Rich Renteria	.25
24	Rich Monteleone	.25
25	Mike Trujillo	.25
26	Bill Wilkinson	.25
27	John Christensen	.25
28	Coaches/Checklist (Billy Connors, Frank Howard, Phil Roof, Bobby Tolan, Ozzie Virgil)	.25

Rangers

While Mother's Cookies of Oakland had produced high-quality baseball card sets of various teams since 1983, the Rangers participated in the promotion for the first time in 1987. Twenty cards from the 28-card set were handed out to the first 25,000 fans entering Arlington Stadium on July 17. An additional eight cards (though not necessarily the eight needed to complete a set) were available by redeeming a mail-in certificate. The cards measure 2-1/2" x 3-1/2" with rounded corners and glossy finish, like all Mother's Cookies issued in 1987.

		NM/M
Complete Set (28):		9.00
Common Player:		.25
1	Bobby Valentine	.25
2	Pete Incaviglia	.50
3	Charlie Hough	.25
4	Oddibe McDowell	.25
5	Larry Parrish	.25
6	Scott Fletcher	.25
7	Steve Buechele	.25
8	Tom Paciorek	.25
9	Pete O'Brien	.25
10	Darrell Porter	.25
11	Greg Harris	.25
12	Don Slaught	.25
13	Ruben Sierra	.50
14	Curtis Wilkerson	.25
15	Dale Mohorcic	.25
16	Ron Meredith	.25
17	Mitch Williams	.25
18	Bob Brower	.25
19	Edwin Correa	.25
20	Geno Petralli	.25
21	Mike Loynd	.25
22	Jerry Browne	.25
23	Jose Guzman	.25
24	Jeff Kunkel	.25
25	Bobby Witt	.25
26	Jeff Russell	.25
27	Trainers (Danny Wheat, Bill Zeigler)	.25
28	Coaches/Checklist (Joe Ferguson, Tim Foli, Tom House, Art Howe, Dave Oliver, Tom Robson)	.25

Mark McGwire

A four-card set featuring outstanding rookie Mark McGwire of the Oakland A's was produced by Mother's Cookies in 1987. Cards are 2-1/2" x 3-1/2" and have rounded corners

and glossy finish like other Mother's issues. The set was obtainable by sending in eight proof-of-purchase seals or could be secured at the National Sports Collectors Convention held July 9-12 in San Francisco. Convention goers received one card as a bonus for each Mother's Cookies baseball card album purchased.

		NM/M
Complete Set (4):		10.00
Uncut Strip:		10.00
Common Card:		3.00
1	Mark McGwire/Portrait	3.00
2	Mark McGwire (Leaning on bat rack.)	3.00
3	Mark McGwire (Beginning batting swing.)	3.00
4	Mark McGwire (Batting follow-through.)	3.00

1988 Mother's Cookies A's

Complete at 28 cards, the 1988 Mother's Cookies A's set features full-color, borderless cards with rounded corners in the standard 2-1/2" x 3-1/2" format. Backs are printed in red and purple and include biographical information, the Mother's Cookies logo and card number. Starter sets of 20 cards were distributed at the stadium along with a promotional card redeemable for another eights cards (not necessarily those needed to complete the set). An album to house the cards was also available.

		NM/M
Complete Set (28):		16.00
Common Player:		.35
1	Tony LaRussa	.50
2	Mark McGwire	6.00
3	Dave Stewart	.35
4	Mickey Tettleton	.35
5	Dave Parker	.35
6	Carney Lansford	.35
7	Jose Canseco	.75
8	Don Baylor	.50
9	Bob Welch	.35
10	Dennis Eckersley	1.25
11	Walt Weiss	.50
12	Tony Phillips	.35
13	Steve Ontiveros	.35
14	Dave Henderson	.35
15	Stan Javier	.35
16	Ron Hassey	.35
17	Curt Young	.35
18	Glenn Hubbard	.35
19	Storm Davis	.35
20	Eric Plunk	.35
21	Matt Young	.35
22	Mike Gallego	.35
23	Rick Honeycutt	.35
24	Doug Jennings	.35
25	Gene Nelson	.35
26	Greg Cadaret	.35
27	Coaches (Dave Duncan, Rene Lachemann, Jim Lefebvre, Dave McKay, Mike Paul, Bob Watson)	.35
28	Jose Canseco, Mark McGwire	2.50

Astros

One of six team sets issued by Mother's Cookies in 1988, the 28-card Astros set is similar in design to other Mother's Cookies sets. Glossy-front cards are 2-1/2" x 3-1/2" size with rounded corners and feature full-color, borderless photos on the fronts. Backs feature red and purple printing and include brief biographical information, the Mother's logo and card number. Twenty of the cards were distributed in a stadium promotion, along with a redemption card that could be exchanged for an additional eight cards (but not necessarily the eight needed to complete the set). An album was also available to house the set.

		NM/M
Complete Set (28):		12.00
Common Player:		.35
1	Hal Lanier	.35
2	Mike Scott	.35
3	Gerald Young	.35
4	Bill Doran	.35
5	Bob Knepper	.35
6	Billy Hatcher	.35
7	Terry Puhl	.35
8	Nolan Ryan	10.00
9	Kevin Bass	.35
10	Glenn Davis	.35
11	Alan Ashby	.35
12	Steve Henderson	.35
13	Denny Walling	.35
14	Danny Darwin	.35
15	Mark Bailey	.35
16	Ernie Camacho	.35
17	Rafael Ramirez	.35
18	Jeff Heathcock	.35
19	Craig Reynolds	.35
20	Dave Smith	.35
21	Larry Andersen	.35
22	Jim Pankovits	.35
23	Jim Deshaies	.35
24	Juan Agosto	.35
25	Chuck Jackson	.35
26	Joaquin Andujar	.35
27	Coaches (Yogi Berra, Gene Clines, Matt Galante, Marc Hill, Denis Menke, Les Moss)	.35
28	Trainers/Checklist (Doc Ewell, Dave Labossiere, Dennis Liborio)	.35

Dodgers

Similar in design to other Mother's Cookies sets, the 1988 Dodgers issue features full-color, borderless photos with backs printed in red and purple. The 28 cards in the set measure 2-1/2" x 3-1/2" with rounded corners. Starter packs of 20 cards were distributed at a ballpark promotion along with a coupon card that could be exchanged for an additional eight cards at a local card show or through the mail. Backs include brief player information, the Moth-

er's Cookies logo and card number. The promotion also included a special album to house the set.

		NM/M
Complete Set (28):		8.00
Common Player:		.35
1	Tom Lasorda	.45
2	Pedro Guerrero	.35
3	Steve Sax	.35
4	Fernando Valenzuela	.35
5	Mike Marshall	.35
6	Orel Hershiser	.50
7	Alfredo Griffin	.35
8	Kirk Gibson	.35
9	Don Sutton	1.25
10	Mike Scioscia	.35
11	Franklin Stubbs	.35
12	Mike Davis	.35
13	Jesse Orosco	.35
14	John Shelby	.35
15	Rick Dempsey	.35
16	Jay Howell	.35
17	Dave Anderson	.35
18	Alejandro Pena	.35
19	Jeff Hamilton	.35
20	Danny Heep	.35
21	Tim Leary	.35
22	Brad Havens	.35
23	Tim Belcher	.35
24	Ken Howell	.35
25	Mickey Hatcher	.35
26	Brian Holton	.35
27	Mike Devereaux	.35
28	Coaches/Checklist (Joe Amalfitano, Mark Cresse, Joe Ferguson, Ben Hines, Manny Mota, Ron Perranoski, Bill Russell)	.35

Giants

One of six team sets issued in 1988 by Mother's Cookies, this 28-card Giants set featured full-color borderless photos on a standard-size card with rounded corners. Backs, printed in red and purple, include brief player data, the Mother's Cookies logo and card number. Twenty different cards were distributed as a starter set at a stadium promotion along with a coupon card that could be redeemed for an additional eight cards (not necessarily those needed to complete the set). The redemption cards could be exchanged through the mail or redeemed at a local card show.

		NM/M
Complete Set (28):		10.00
Common Player:		.35
1	Roger Craig	.35
2	Will Clark	.75
3	Kevin Mitchell	.35
4	Bob Brenly	.35
5	Mike Aldrete	.35
6	Mike Krukow	.35
7	Candy Maldonado	.35
8	Jeffrey Leonard	.35
9	Dave Dravecky	.35
10	Robby Thompson	.35
11	Scott Garrelts	.35
12	Bob Melvin	.35
13	Jose Uribe	.35
14	Brett Butler	.35
15	Rick Reuschel	.35
16	Harry Spilman	.35
17	Kelly Downs	.35
18	Chris Speier	.35
19	Atlee Hammaker	.35
20	Joel Youngblood	.35
21	Mike LaCoss	.35
22	Don Robinson	.35
23	Mark Wasinger	.35
24	Craig Lefferts	.35
25	Phil Garner	.35
26	Joe Price	.35
27	Coaches (Dusty Baker, Bill Fahey, Bob Lillis, Gordie MacKenzie, Jose Morales, Norm Sherry)	.35
28	Logo Card/Checklist	.35

Mariners

Similar in design to other Mother's Cookies sets, the 28-card Mariners issue features full-color, borderless photos on a 2-1/2" x 3-1/2" card with rounded corners. Backs, printed in red and purple, include brief biographical information, the Mother's Cookies logo and card number. Twenty-card starter packs were distributed at a stadium promotion, where fans received a coupon card that could be exchanged for an additional eight cards (not necessarily those needed to complete the set). The coupon card could be redeemed through the mail or exchanged at a local baseball card show. As with the rest of the 1988 Mother's Cookies sets, an album was also available to house the cards.

		NM/M
Complete Set (28):		6.00
Common Player:		.35
1	Dick Williams	.35
2	Alvin Davis	.35
3	Mike Moore	.35
4	Jim Presley	.35
5	Mark Langston	.35
6	Henry Cotto	.35
7	Ken Phelps	.35
8	Steve Trout	.35
9	David Valle	.35
10	Harold Reynolds	.50
11	Edwin Nunez	.35
12	Glenn Wilson	.35
13	Scott Bankhead	.35
14	Scott Bradley	.35
15	Mickey Brantley	.35
16	Bruce Fields	.35
17	Mike Kingery	.35
18	Mike Campbell	.35
19	Mike Jackson	.35
20	Rey Quinones	.35
21	Mario Diaz	.35
22	Jerry Reed	.35
23	Rich Renteria	.35
24	Julio Solano	.35
25	Bill Swift	.35
26	Bill Wilkinson	.35
27	Coaches (Billy Connors, Frank Howard, Phil Roof, Jim Snyder, Ozzie Virgil)	.35
28	Trainers/Checklist (Henry Genzale, Rick Griffin)	.35

Rangers

This 28-card issue was one of six team sets issued in 1988 by Mother's Cookies. The Rangers issue features full-color, borderless cards printed in standard 2-1/2" x 3-1/2" format with rounded corners. Backs are printed in red and purple and include player information, Mother's Cookies logo and card number. Twenty-card starter packs were distributed as a stadium promotion that included a redemption card good for another eight

cards (not necessarily those needed to complete the set) either through the mail or at a local card show.

		NM/M
Complete Set (28):		7.00
Common Player:		.35
1	Bobby Valentine	.35
2	Pete Incaviglia	.35
3	Charlie Hough	.35
4	Oddibe McDowell	.35
5	Larry Parrish	.35
6	Scott Fletcher	.35
7	Steve Buechele	.35
8	Steve Kemp	.35
9	Pete O'Brien	.35
10	Ruben Sierra	.35
11	Mike Stanley	.35
12	Jose Cecena	.35
13	Cecil Espy	.35
14	Curtis Wilkerson	.35
15	Dale Mohorcic	.35
16	Ray Hayward	.35
17	Mitch Williams	.35
18	Bob Brower	.35
19	Paul Kilgus	.35
20	Geno Petralli	.35
21	James Steels	.35
22	Jerry Browne	.35
23	Jose Guzman	.35
24	DeWayne Vaughn	.35
25	Bobby Witt	.35
26	Jeff Russell	.35
27	Coaches (Richard Egan, Tom House, Art Howe, Davey Lopes, David Oliver, Tom Robson)	.35
28	Trainers/Checklist (Danny Wheat, Bill Zeigler)	.35

Will Clark

In a baseball spring training-related promotion, Mother's Cookies of Oakland, Calif. produced a full-color four-card set featuring San Francisco Giants first baseman Will Clark. The cards, which have glossy finishes and rounded corners, came cellophane-wrapped in specially marked 18-ounce packages of Mother's Cookies products. The cards are identical in style to the other Mother's Cookies issues.

		NM/M
Complete Set (4):		4.00
4-Card Uncut Panel:		4.00
Common Card:		1.00
1	Will Clark (Bat on shoulder.)	1.00
2	Will Clark/Kneeling	1.00
3	Will Clark (Batting follow-through.)	1.00
4	Will Clark (Heading for first base.)	1.00

Mark McGwire

For the second consecutive year, Mother's Cookies devoted a four-card set to Oakland A's slugger Mark McGwire. The full-color cards have rounded corners and measure 2-1/2" x 3-1/2". The cards were issued in specially marked 18-ounce packages of Mother's Cookies products in the northern Cali-

fornia area. The cards are identical in design to the team issues produced by Mother's.

		NM/M
Complete Set (4):		7.00
4-Card Uncut Panel:		9.00
Common Card:		2.00
1	Mark McGwire (Holding oversized bat.)	2.00
2	Mark McGwire/Fldg	2.00
3	Mark McGwire/Kneeling	2.00
4	Mark McGwire (Bat in air.)	2.00

1989 Mother's Cookies A's

The 1989 Mother's Cookies A's set consists of 28 cards designed in the traditional style: a glossy 2-1/2" x 3-1/2" card with a borderless photo and rounded corners. A starter set of the cards was used as a stadium promotion and distributed to fans attending the July 30 Oakland game.

		NM/M
Complete Set (28):		13.50
Common Player:		.35
1	Tony LaRussa	.35
2	Mark McGwire	5.00
3	Terry Steinbach	.35
4	Dave Parker	.35
5	Carney Lansford	.35
6	Dave Stewart	.35
7	Jose Canseco	1.00
8	Walt Weiss	.35
9	Bob Welch	.35
10	Dennis Eckersley	1.25
11	Tony Phillips	.35
12	Mike Moore	.35
13	Dave Henderson	.35
14	Curt Young	.35
15	Ron Hassey	.35
16	Eric Plunk	.35
17	Luis Polonia	.35
18	Storm Davis	.35
19	Glenn Hubbard	.35
20	Greg Cadaret	.35
21	Stan Javier	.35
22	Felix Jose	.35
23	Mike Gallego	.35
24	Todd Burns	.35
25	Rick Honeycutt	.35
26	Gene Nelson	.35
27	A's Coaches (Dave Duncan, Rene Lacheman, Art Kusnyer, Tommie Reynolds, Merv Rettenmund)	.35
28	Walt Weiss, Mark McGwire, Jose Canseco	2.50

Astros

The 1989 Astros team set issued by Mother's Cookies consists of 28 cards in 2-1/2" x 3-1/2" format in the traditional style of glossy borderless photos and rounded corners. Partial sets were distributed to fans attending the July 22 game at the Astrodome. The cards feature the photography of Barry Colla and display the Mother's Cookies logo on the back.

		NM/M
Complete Set (28):		11.00
Common Player:		.35
1	Art Howe	.35
2	Mike Scott	.35
3	Gerald Young	.35
4	Bill Doran	.35
5	Billy Hatcher	.35
6	Terry Puhl	.35
7	Bob Knepper	.35
8	Kevin Bass	.35
9	Glenn Davis	.35
10	Alan Ashby	.35
11	Bob Forsch	.35
12	Greg Gross	.35
13	Danny Darwin	.35
14	Craig Biggio	3.00
15	Jim Clancy	.35
16	Rafael Ramirez	.35
17	Alex Trevino	.35
18	Craig Reynolds	.35

19	Dave Smith	.35
20	Larry Andersen	.35
21	Eric Yelding	.35
22	Jim Deshaies	.35
23	Juan Agosto	.35
24	Rick Rhoden	.35
25	Ken Caminiti	1.00
26	Dave Meads	.35
27	Astros Coaches (Yogi Berra, Matt Galante, Phil Garner, Les Moss, Ed Napoleon, Ed Ott)	.35
28	Trainers/Checklist (Dave Labossiere, Doc Ewell, Dennis Liborio)	.35

Dodgers

This 28-card set features the players and coaches of the L.A. Dodgers. The cards follow the traditional Mother's Cookies style featuring rounded corners, borderless color photos, horizontal backs and 2-1/2" x 3-1/2" size. Initially 20 cards were given away as starter sets at Dodger Stadium.

		NM/M
Complete Set (28):		9.00
Common Player:		.35
1	Tom Lasorda	.40
2	Eddie Murray	2.00
3	Mike Scioscia	.35
4	Fernando Valenzuela	.35
5	Mike Marshall	.35
6	Orel Hershiser	.50
7	Alfredo Griffin	.35
8	Kirk Gibson	.35
9	John Tudor	.35
10	Willie Randolph	.35
11	Franklin Stubbs	.35
12	Mike Davis	.35
13	Mike Morgan	.35
14	John Shelby	.35
15	Rick Dempsey	.35
16	Jay Howell	.35
17	Dave Anderson	.35
18	Alejandro Pena	.35
19	Jeff Hamilton	.35
20	Ricky Horton	.35
21	Tim Leary	.35
22	Ray Searage	.35
23	Tim Belcher	.35
24	Tim Crews	.35
25	Mickey Hatcher	.35
26	Mariano Duncan	.35
27	Coaches (Joe Amalfitano, Mark Cresse, Joe Ferguson, Ben Hines, Manny Mota, Ron Perranoski, Bill Russell)	.35
28	Checklist	.35

Giants

The 1989 Mother's Cookies Giants set consists of 28 cards, all featuring borderless, color photos with rounded corners. Starter sets of the cards were distributed as a stadium promotion to fans attending the August 6 game at Candlestick Park.

		NM/M
Complete Set (28):		9.00
Common Player:		.35
1	Roger Craig	.35
2	Will Clark	1.00
3	Kevin Mitchell	.35
4	Kelly Downs	.35
5	Brett Butler	.35
6	Mike Krukow	.35
7	Candy Maldonado	.35
8	Terry Kennedy	.35
9	Dave Dravecky	.35
10	Robby Thompson	.35
11	Scott Garrelts	.35
12	Matt Williams	1.00
13	Jose Uribe	.35
14	Tracy Jones	.35
15	Rick Reuschel	.35
16	Ernest Riles	.35
17	Jeff Brantley	.35
18	Chris Speier	.35
19	Atlee Hammaker	.35
20	Ed Jurak	.35
21	Mike LaCoss	.35
22	Don Robinson	.35

23	Kirt Manwaring	.35
24	Craig Lefferts	.35
25	Donnell Nixon	.35
26	Joe Price	.35
27	Rich Gossage	.75
28	Coaches/Checklist (Bill Fahey, Dusty Baker, Bob Lillis, Wendell Kim, Norm Sherry)	.35

Mariners

For the sixth straight season, Mother's Cookies released a Mariners team set. The 1989 issue features 28 cards. Starter sets of 20 cards were distributed at a Mariners home game. The cards are 2-1/2" x 3-1/2" and feature borderless, glossy full color photos. Card backs are horizontal. Rookie sensation Ken Griffey Jr. was included in the 1989 issue.

		NM/M
Complete Set (28):		12.50
Common Player:		.35
1	Jim Lefebvre	.35
2	Alvin Davis	.35
3	Ken Griffey Jr.	9.00
4	Jim Presley	.35
5	Mark Langston	.35
6	Henry Cotto	.35
7	Mickey Brantley	.35
8	Jeffrey Leonard	.35
9	Dave Valle	.35
10	Harold Reynolds	.50
11	Edgar Martinez	3.00
12	Tom Niedenfuer	.35
13	Scott Bankhead	.35
14	Scott Bradley	.35
15	Omar Vizquel	.35
16	Erik Hanson	.35
17	Bill Swift	.35
18	Mike Campbell	.35
19	Mike Jackson	.35
20	Rich Renteria	.35
21	Mario Diaz	.35
22	Jerry Reed	.35
23	Darnell Coles	.35
24	Steve Trout	.35
25	Mike Schooler	.35
26	Julio Solano	.35
27	Coaches (Gene Clines, Bob Didier, Rusty Kuntz, Mike Paul, Bill Plummer)	.35
28	Checklist/Trainers (Henry Genzale, Rick Griffin)	.35

Rangers

The 1989 Mother's Cookies Rangers team set features the traditional glossy borderless photos and rounded corners. The 2-1/2" x 3-1/2" set of 28 cards features the photography of Barry Colla. Partial sets were distributed to fans attending the July 30 game at Arlington Stadium.

		NM/M
Complete Set (28):		8.00
Common Player:		.35
1	Bobby Valentine	.35
2	Nolan Ryan	6.00
3	Julio Franco	.35
4	Charlie Hough	.35
5	Rafael Palmeiro	4.00
6	Jeff Russell	.35
7	Ruben Sierra	.35
8	Steve Buechele	.35
9	Buddy Bell	.35
10	Pete Incaviglia	.35
11	Geno Petralli	.35
12	Cecil Espy	.35
13	Scott Fletcher	.35
14	Bobby Witt	.35
15	Brad Arnsberg	.35
16	Rick Leach	.35
17	Jamie Moyer	.35
18	Kevin Brown	.35
19	Jeff Kunkel	.35
20	Cecilio McMurtry	.35
21	Kenny Rogers	.35
22	Mike Stanley	.35
23	Cecilio Guante	.35
24	Jim Sundberg	.35

25	Jose Guzman	.35
26	Jeff Stone	.35
27	Coaches (Dick Egan, Tom Robson, Toby Harrah, Dave Oliver, Tom House, Davey Lopes)	.35
28	Trainers/Checklist (Bill Ziegler, Danny Wheat)	.35

Jose Canseco

This special insert glossy set features Canseco in two posed (one standing, one kneeling) and two action (one batting, one running) shots. Full-color card fronts have rounded corners. Flip sides are numbered, printed in red and purple, and carry 1988 stats and career notes. Cards are individually cellowrapped and inserted in Mother's Fudge 'N Chips, Oatmeal Raisin and Cocadas cookie bags.

		NM/M
Complete Set (4):		5.00
Four-Card Uncut Panel:		6.00
Common Card:		1.50
1	Jose Canseco (Ball in hand.)	1.50
2	Jose Canseco (On one knee grasping bat.)	1.50
3	Jose Canseco (Swinging-in action.)	1.50
4	Jose Canseco (Baserunning)	1.50

Will Clark

Will Clark is featured on a special-edition glossy set inserted in Mother's big bag chocolate chip cookies. The standard-size (2-1/2" x 3-1/2") cards feature Clark in two posed (batting and catching) and two action (batting and running) shots. Purple and red backs list 1986-88 stats.

		NM/M
Complete Set (4):		4.00
Four-Card Uncut Panel:		4.00
Common Card:		1.00
1	Will Clark (Displaying ball in glove.)	1.00
2	Will Clark (Batting stance.)	1.00
3	Will Clark (In action-after swing.)	1.00
4	Will Clark (Heading towards first.)	1.00

Ken Griffey, Jr.

This set featuring Ken Griffey, Jr. was issued by Mother's Cookies and was available only in cookie packages in Washington and Oregon. The cards were also available at a Seattle Mariners Kingdome baseball card show on August 20, where the set was introduced. The cards were then packed inside specially marked bags of cookies, one card per bag.

		NM/M
Complete Set (4):		15.00
Four-Card Uncut Panel:		20.00
Common Card:		5.00
1	Ken Griffey Jr. (Arms folded.)	5.00
2	Ken Griffey Jr. (Ball in hand.)	5.00
3	Ken Griffey Jr. (Bat over left shoulder.)	5.00
4	Ken Griffey Jr. (Back of jersey showing.)	5.00

Mark McGwire

This special edition features full-color glossy player photos by Barry Colla on standard-size (2-1/2" x 3-1/2") cards with rounded corners. Photos feature four different batting poses. Numbered flip sides, printed in purple and red, carry 1987-88 statistics. Cards are indi-

vidually cello-wrapped and were inserted in Mother's Cookie Parade variety cookie bags.

		NM/M
Complete Set (4):		6.00
Common Player:		1.50
1	Mark McGwire (Bat on shoulder.)	1.50
2	Mark McGwire (Batting stance.)	1.50
3	Mark McGwire (Bat in front.)	1.50
4	Mark McGwire (Batting follow through.)	1.50

Rookies of the Year

This four-card set features the American League Rookies of the Year for 1986, 1987 and 1988, all members of the Oakland A's. The 2-1/2" x 3-1/2" cards feature full color photos in the traditional Mother's Cookies format. One card was devoted to each player along with a special card showcasing all three players. The cards were distributed one per box in Mother's Cookies.

		NM/M
Complete Set (4):		15.00
Four-Card Uncut Panel:		15.00
Common Card:		.75
1	Jose Canseco	2.25
2	Mark McGwire	7.50
3	Walt Weiss	.75
4	Walt Weiss, Mark McGwire, Jose Canseco	5.50

1990 Mother's Cookies A's

This 28-card set features cards distributed at an A's home game. Cards measure 2-1/2" x 3-1/2" and feature rounded corners. Backs include biographical information and autograph space.

		NM/M
Complete Set (28):		15.00
Common Player:		.35
1	Tony LaRussa	.35
2	Mark McGwire	4.00
3	Terry Steinbach	.35
4	Rickey Henderson	2.00
5	Dave Stewart	.35
6	Jose Canseco	.75
7	Dennis Eckersley	1.00
8	Carney Lansford	.35
9	Mike Moore	.35
10	Walt Weiss	.35
11	Scott Sanderson	.35
12	Ron Hassey	.35
13	Rick Honeycutt	.35
14	Ken Phelps	.35
15	Jamie Quirk	.35
16	Bob Welch	.35
17	Felix Jose	.35
18	Dave Henderson	.35
19	Mike Norris	.35
20	Todd Burns	.35
21	Lance Blankenship	.35
22	Gene Nelson	.35
23	Stan Javier	.35
24	Curt Young	.35
25	Mike Gallego	.35
26	Joe Klink	.35
27	Coaches (Dave Duncan, Art Kuysner, Rene Lacheman, Dave McKay, Merv Rettenmund, Tommie Reynolds)	.35
28	Checklist/Trainers (Frank Ciensczyk, Larry Davis, Steve Vucinich, Barry Weinberg)	.35

Astros

This 28-card set features cards styled like past Mother's Cookies releases. The cards were distributed in 20-card packs at an Astros home game. The cards were never distributed in complete set form.

KEN OBERKFELL
Astros

		NM/M
Complete Set (28):		10.00
Common Player:		.35
1	Art Howe	.35
2	Glenn Davis	.35
3	Eric Anthony	.35
4	Mike Scott	.35
5	Craig Biggio	2.00
6	Ken Caminiti	.50
7	Bill Doran	.35
8	Gerald Young	.35
9	Terry Puhl	.35
10	Mark Portugal	.35
11	Mark Davidson	.35
12	Jim Deshaies	.35
13	Bill Gullickson	.35
14	Franklin Stubbs	.35
15	Danny Darwin	.35
16	Ken Oberkfell	.35
17	Dave Smith	.35
18	Dan Schatzeder	.35
19	Rafael Ramirez	.35
20	Larry Andersen	.35
21	Alex Trevino	.35
22	Glenn Wilson	.35
23	Jim Clancy	.35
24	Eric Yelding	.35
25	Casey Candaele	.35
26	Juan Agosto	.35
27	Coaches (Bill Bowman, Bob Cluck, Phil Garner, Matt Galante, Rudy Jaramillo, Ed Napoleon)	.35
28	Checklist/Trainers (Doc Ewell, Dave Labossiere, Dennis Liborio)	.35

Dodgers

JOHN WETTELAND
Dodgers

Distributed as a promotional item, these cards are styled like past Mother's Cookies releases. Fans 14 and under received a 20-card pack at a Dodgers home game. Cards were also available at a Labor Day card show in Anaheim. The cards were not distributed in complete set form.

		NM/M
Complete Set (28):		10.00
Common Player:		.35
1	Tom Lasorda	.45
2	Fernando Valenzuela	.35
3	Kal Daniels	.35
4	Mike Scioscia	.35
5	Eddie Murray	3.00
6	Mickey Hatcher	.35
7	Juan Samuel	.35
8	Alfredo Griffin	.35
9	Tim Belcher	.35
10	Hubie Brooks	.35
11	Jose Gonzalez	.35
12	Orel Hershiser	.45
13	Kirk Gibson	.35
14	Chris Gwynn	.35
15	Jay Howell	.35
16	Rick Dempsey	.35
17	Ramon Martinez	.50
18	Lenny Harris	.35
19	John Wetteland	.35
20	Mike Sharperson	.35
21	Mike Morgan	.35
22	Ray Searage	.35
23	Jeff Hamilton	.35
24	Jim Gott	.35
25	John Shelby	.35
26	Tim Crews	.35
27	Don Aase	.35

| 28 | Coaches (Joe Amalfitano, Mark Cresse, Joe Ferguson, Ben Hines, Manny Mota, Ron Perranoski, Bill Russell) | .35 |

Giants

Like the other Mother's Cookies issues of 1990, Giants cards were distributed as a promotional item. Fans 14 and under were given a 20-card starter set at a Giants game. Cards could also be obtained at the Labor Day card show in San Francisco. The cards were not released in complete set form.

		NM/M
Complete Set (28):		10.00
Common Player:		.35
1	Roger Craig	.35
2	Will Clark	1.00
3	Gary Carter	3.00
4	Kelly Downs	.35
5	Kevin Mitchell	.35
6	Steve Bedrosian	.35
7	Brett Butler	.35
8	Rick Reuschel	.35
9	Matt Williams	1.00
10	Robby Thompson	.35
11	Mike LaCoss	.35
12	Terry Kennedy	.35
13	Atlee Hammaker	.35
14	Rick Leach	.35
15	Ernest Riles	.35
16	Scott Garrelts	.35
17	Jose Uribe	.35
18	Greg Litton	.35
19	Dave Anderson	.35
20	Don Robinson	.35
21	Coaches (Dusty Baker, Bill Fahey, Wendell Kim, Bob Lillis, Norm Sherry)	.35
22	Bill Bathe	.35
23	Randy O'Neal	.35
24	Kevin Bass	.35
25	Jeff Brantley	.35
26	John Burkett	.35
27	Ernie Camacho	.35
28	Checklist	.35

Mariners

HENRY COTTO
Mariners

This 28-card set features the traditional Mother's Cookies style with borderless full-color photos with rounded corners. Backs feature biographical information and autograph space. The cards were released as a promotion at a Mariners home game and at a Kingdome card show.

		NM/M
Complete Set (28):		17.50
Common Player:		.35
1	Jim Lefebvre	.35
2	Alvin Davis	.35
3	Ken Griffey Jr.	7.00
4	Jeffrey Leonard	.35
5	David Valle	.35
6	Harold Reynolds	.35
7	Jay Buhner	.75
8	Erik Hanson	.35
9	Henry Cotto	.35
10	Edgar Martinez	.35
11	Bill Swift	.35
12	Omar Vizquel	.75
13	Randy Johnson	5.00
14	Greg Briley	.35
15	Gene Harris	.35
16	Matt Young	.35
17	Pete O'Brien	.35
18	Brent Knackert	.35
19	Mike Jackson	.35
20	Brian Holman	.35
21	Mike Schooler	.35
22	Darnell Coles	.35
23	Keith Comstock	.35
24	Scott Bankhead	.35
25	Scott Bradley	.35
26	Mike Brumley	.35
27	Coaches (Gene Clines, Bob Didier, Rusty Kuntz, Mike Paul, Bill Plummer)	.35
28	Checklist/Trainers (Henry Genzale, Rick Griffin, Tom Newberg)	.35

Rangers

Putting together a complete set of these cards was not an easy task. The cards were distributed in 20-card packs at a Rangers home game and also could be obtained at a Dallas card convention. The cards were not released in complete set form. The cards feature the traditional Mother's Cookies style of glossy photos and rounded corners.

		NM/M
Complete Set (28):		12.50
Common Player:		.35
1	Bobby Valentine	.35
2	Nolan Ryan	6.00
3	Ruben Sierra	.35
4	Pete Incaviglia	.35
5	Charlie Hough	.35
6	Harold Baines	.35
7	Gino Petralli	.35
8	Jeff Russell	.35
9	Rafael Palmeiro	2.00
10	Julio Franco	.35
11	Jack Daugherty	.35
12	Gary Pettis	.35
13	Brian Bohanon	.35
14	Steve Buechele	.35
15	Bobby Witt	.35
16	Thad Bosley	.35
17	Gary Mielke	.35
18	Jeff Kunkel	.35
19	Mike Jeffcoat	.35
20	Mike Stanley	.35
21	Kevin Brown	.35
22	Kenny Rogers	.35
23	Jeff Huson	.35
24	Jamie Moyer	.35
25	Cecil Espy	.35
26	John Russell	.35
27	Coaches (Toby Harrah, Tom House, Davey Lopes, Dave Oliver, Tom Robson)	.35
28	Checklist/Trainers (Joe Macko, Marty Stajduhar, Danny Wheat, Bill Zeigler)	.35

Jose Canseco

JOSE CANSECO
Oakland Athletics

This special insert glossy set features Canseco in four posed shots. Full-color card fronts have rounded corners. Flip sides are numbered, printed in red and purple and feature the Mother's Cookies logo. The cards are individually cello-wrapped and inserted one per Mother's Cookies bag.

		NM/M
Complete Set (4):		4.00
Four-Card Uncut Panel:		5.00
Common Card:		1.50
1	Jose Canseco/Sitting (Bat on shoulder.)	1.50
2	Jose Canseco (Bat behind neck.)	1.50
3	Jose Canseco (Batting stance.)	1.50
4	Jose Canseco (On dugout step.)	1.50

Will Clark

1990 marks the third consecutive year that Mother's Cookies devoted a set to Giants slugger Will Clark. The set features four posed full-color shots. The cards follow the same design as all recent Mother's Cookies cards.

		NM/M
Complete Set (4):		4.00
Four-Card Uncut Panel:		4.00
Common Card:		1.00
1	Will Clark (Bat on shoulder.)	1.00
2	Will Clark (Closeup in stance.)	1.00
3	Will Clark (Open in stance.)	1.00
4	Will Clark (Bat behind neck.)	1.00

Mark McGwire

1990 marks the fourth year that A's slugger Mark McGwire was featured on a special four-card Mother's Cookies set. The photos for the cards were once again by Barry Colla. Four different posed shots of McGwire are showcased.

		NM/M
Complete Set (4):		6.00
Four-Card Uncut Panel:		7.50
Common Card:		2.00
1	Mark McGwire (Bat on shoulder.)	2.00
2	Mark McGwire (Leaning against bat rack.)	2.00
3	Mark McGwire (Glove in hand.)	2.00
4	Mark McGwire (On dugout step.)	2.00

Nolan Ryan

Unlike other special Mother's Cookies player sets, the Nolan Ryan cards feature "5000 K's" along with his name and team on the card fronts. The set honors the strikeout king's monumental feat. The cards follow the classic Mother's Cookies style.

		NM/M
Complete Set (4):		4.00
Four-Card Uncut Panel:		5.00
Common Card:		2.00
1	Nolan Ryan (Facing with ball in hand.)	2.00
2	Nolan Ryan (Standing in dugout.)	2.00
3	Nolan Ryan (Gripping ball behind back.)	2.00
4	Nolan Ryan (Sitting on dugout step.)	2.00

Matt Williams

MATT WILLIAMS
Giants

Matt Williams made his Mother's Cookies single-player card set debut in 1990. Four posed shots of the Giants third baseman are showcased. Williams is featured twice in batting poses and twice as a fielder on the glossy, round-cornered 2-1/2" x 3-1/2" cards.

		NM/M
Complete Set (4):		2.50
Four-Card Uncut Panel:		2.50
Common Card:		.75
1	Matt Williams (Bat on shoulder.)	.75
2	Matt Williams (In batting stance.)	.75
3	Matt Williams (Glove in hand.)	.75
4	Matt Williams/Fldg	.75

1991 Mother's Cookies A's

The incomparable photography of Barry Colla captures the Oakland A's in their home-field environs for the 28 cards in this set. Glossy fronts feature borderless posed photos. The player's name and team appear in white in an upper corner. Backs have minimal

---

biographical data, player position, uniform and card numbers and appropriate logos.

		NM/M
Complete Set (28):		12.00
Common Player:		.25
1	Tony LaRussa	.25
2	Mark McGwire	3.50
3	Terry Steinbach	.25
4	Rickey Henderson	1.50
5	Dave Stewart	.25
6	Jose Canseco	.75
7	Dennis Eckersley	1.00
8	Carney Lansford	.25
9	Bob Welch	.25
10	Walt Weiss	.25
11	Mike Moore	.25
12	Vance Law	.25
13	Rick Honeycutt	.25
14	Harold Baines	.25
15	Jamie Quirk	.25
16	Ernest Riles	.25
17	Willie Wilson	.25
18	Dave Henderson	.25
19	Kirk Dressendorfer	.25
20	Todd Burns	.25
21	Lance Blankenship	.25
22	Gene Nelson	.25
23	Eric Show	.25
24	Curt Young	.25
25	Mike Gallego	.25
26	Joe Klink	.25
27	Steve Chitren	.25
28	Coaches/Checklist (Rene Lachman, Dave Duncan, Dave McKay, Tommie Reynolds, Art Kuysner, Reggie Jackson, Rick Burleson)	.25

Astros

JEFF BAGWELL
Astros

This 28-card set was produced in the now-familiar Mother's Cookies card format. Glossy fronts feature rounded corners and full-bleed posed color photos (apparently taken at San Francisco's Candlestick Park, home base of photographer Barry Colla) with the player's name and team in white in an upper corner. Backs are printed in red and purple and include a few biographical details, along with cookie company and MLB logos, uniform and card numbers and a line for autographing.

		NM/M
Complete Set (28):		10.00
Common Player:		.25
1	Art Howe	.25
2	Steve Finley	.25
3	Pete Harnisch	.25
4	Mike Scott	.25
5	Craig Biggio	.50
6	Ken Caminiti	.25
7	Eric Yelding	.25
8	Jeff Bagwell	6.00
9	Jim Deshaies	.25
10	Mark Portugal	.25
11	Mark Davidson	.25
12	Jimmy Jones	.25
13	Luis Gonzalez	2.00
14	Karl Rhodes	.25
15	Curt Schilling	.25
16	Ken Oberkfell	.25
17	Mark McLemore	.25
18	David Rohde	.25
19	Rafael Ramirez	.25
20	Al Osuna	.25
21	Jim Corsi	.25
22	Carl Nichols	.25
23	Jim Clancy	.25
24	Dwayne Henry	.25
25	Casey Candaele	.25
26	Xavier Hernandez	.25
27	Darryl Kile	.25
28	Coaches/Checklist (Cluck Galante, Rudy Jaramillo, Phil Garner, Bob Cluck, Ed Ott)	.25

Dodgers

LENNY HARRIS
Dodgers

Dodger Stadium is the background for Barry Colla's portraits of the Los Angeles manager, coaches and players appearing in this 28-card set. Standard-size cards with rounded corners feature borderless UV-coated fronts on which the only printing is the player's name and team in white in an upper corner. Backs are in red and purple and include a few biographical details, position, uniform and card numbers, a space for an autograph and the logos of the cookie company and MLB.

		NM/M
Complete Set (28):		7.50
Common Player:		.25
1	Tom Lasorda	.40
2	Darryl Strawberry	.25
3	Kal Daniels	.25
4	Mike Scioscia	.25
5	Eddie Murray	2.00
6	Brett Butler	.25
7	Juan Samuel	.25
8	Alfredo Griffin	.25
9	Tim Belcher	.25
10	Ramon Martinez	.25
11	Jose Gonzalez	.25
12	Orel Hershiser	.40
13	Bob Ojeda	.25
14	Chris Gwynn	.25
15	Jay Howell	.25
16	Gary Carter	2.00
17	Kevin Gross	.25
18	Lenny Harris	.25
19	Mike Hartley	.25
20	Mike Sharperson	.25
21	Mike Morgan	.25
22	John Candelaria	.25
23	Jeff Hamilton	.25
24	Jim Gott	.25
25	Barry Lyons	.25
26	Tim Crews	.25
27	Stan Javier	.25
28	Coaches/Checklist (Ron Perranoski, Bill Russell, Manny Mota, Joe Ferguson, Ben Hines, Joe Amalfitano, Mark Cresse)	.25

Giants

KEVIN BASS
Giants

For the ninth consecutive year Mother's Cookies sponsored a promotional card set for the Giants. As in the beginning, the cards highlight the work of photographer Barry Colla with posed portraits of the personnel in Candlestick Park. Fronts of the round-cornered borderless cards are UV-coated and have the player's name and team printed in white in an upper corner. Backs are in red and purple and include cookie company and Major League Baseball logos along with a few biographical details and both uniform and card numbers.

		NM/M
Complete Set (28):		7.00
Common Player:		.25
1	Roger Craig	.25

2	Will Clark	.50
3	Steve Decker	.25
4	Kelly Downs	.25
5	Kevin Mitchell	.25
6	Willie McGee	.25
7	Buddy Black	.25
8	Dave Righetti	.25
9	Matt Williams	.50
10	Robby Thompson	.25
11	Mike LaCoss	.25
12	Terry Kennedy	.25
13	Mark Leonard	.25
14	Rick Reuschel	.25
15	Mike Felder	.25
16	Scott Garrelts	.25
17	Jose Uribe	.25
18	Greg Litton	.25
19	Dave Anderson	.25
20	Don Robinson	.25
21	Mike Kingery	.25
22	Trevor Wilson	.25
23	Kirt Manwaring	.25
24	Kevin Bass	.25
26	John Burkett	.25
27	Coaches (Norm Sherry, Wendell Kim, Bob Lillis, Dusty Baker, Bill Fahey)	.25
28	Trainers/Checklist (Mark Letendre, Greg Lynn)	.25

Rangers

The unusual venue of the players' locker room provides the backdrop for photos for this 28-card set sponsored by Mother's Cookies. Besides a look at the player's wardrobe, the full-bleed glossy front photos feature the player's name and position vertically along the left side. Backs have uniform and card numbers, some biographical data and logos of the cookie company and Major League Baseball.

		NM/M
Complete Set (28):		12.50
Common Player:		.25
1	Bobby Valentine	.25
2	Nolan Ryan	6.00
3	Ruben Sierra	.25
4	Juan Gonzalez	3.00
5	Steve Buechele	.25
6	Bobby Witt	.25
7	Geno Petralli	.25
8	Jeff Russell	.25
9	Rafael Palmeiro	2.00
10	Julio Franco	.25
11	Jack Daugherty	.25
12	Gary Pettis	.25
13	John Barfield	.25
14	Scott Chiamparino	.25
15	Kevin Reimer	.25
16	Rich Gossage	.25
17	Brian Downing	.25
18	Denny Walling	.25
19	Mike Jeffcoat	.25
20	Mike Stanley	.25
21	Kevin Brown	.25
22	Kenny Rogers	.25
23	Jeff Huson	.25
24	Mario Diaz	.25
25	Brad Arnsberg	.25
26	John Russell	.25
27	Gerald Alexander	.25
28	Coaches/Checklist (Orlando Gomez, Toby Harrah, Tom House, Davey Lopes, Dave Oliver, Tom Robson)	.25

Griffeys

This four-card set was packaged with Mother's Cookies sold in the Pacific Northwest. Each card features a borderless glossy posed photo on front. The traditional rounded corners of Mother's cards are found on the issue. Backs have a few stats and career notes.

	NM/M
Complete Set, Singles (4):	5.00
Complete Set, Uncut Strip:	5.00
Common Card:	1.00

KEN GRIFFEY FATHER & SON

1	Ken Griffey Jr.	3.00
2	Ken Griffey, Sr.	1.00
3	Ken Griffey Jr., Ken Griffey Sr. (Holding gloves.)	1.00
4	Ken Griffey Jr., Ken Griffey Sr. (Holding bats.)	1.50

Nolan Ryan 300 Wins

Mother's Cookies in 1991 created a four-card Nolan Ryan set honoring baseball's most recent 300-game winner. One card was included in specially marked packages of cookies. Card fronts have the traditional Mother's Cookies look: Barry Colla photography on full-bleed cards with rounded corners. Backs have a few statistics and career notes.

		NM/M
Complete Set (4):		2.00
Four-Card Uncut Panel:		2.00
Common Card:		.75
1	Nolan Ryan/Standing (Front view.)	.75
2	Nolan Ryan/Kneeling	.75
3	Nolan Ryan/Standing (Side view.)	.75
4	Nolan Ryan (Gripping "300" ball.)	.75

1992 Mother's Cookies A's

The commemorative patch marking the Oakland A's 25th season on the West Coast is visible on several of Barry Colla's photos in this 28-card issue. The traditional Mother's Cookies card format of 2-1/2" x 3-1/2", round-cornered cards with UV-coated borderless front photos is followed in this set. The player's name and team are in white in an upper corner. Backs have cookie company and Major League Baseball logos, along with the player's position, uniform and card numbers, space for an autograph and minimal biographical data. Back printing is in red and purple on white.

	NM/M
Complete Set (28):	7.50
Common Player:	.25

1	Tony LaRussa	.25
2	Mark McGwire	3.50
3	Terry Steinbach	.25
4	Rickey Henderson	1.50
5	Dave Stewart	.25
6	Jose Canseco	.75
7	Dennis Eckersley	1.00
8	Carney Lansford	.25
9	Bob Welch	.25
10	Walt Weiss	.25
11	Mike Moore	.25
12	Goose Gossage	.25
13	Rick Honeycutt	.25
14	Harold Baines	.25
15	Jamie Quirk	.25
16	Jeff Parrett	.25
17	Willie Wilson	.25
18	Dave Henderson	.25
19	Joe Slusarski	.25
20	Mike Bordick	.25
21	Lance Blankenship	.25
22	Gene Nelson	.25
23	Vince Horsman	.25
24	Ron Darling	.25
25	Randy Ready	.25
26	Scott Hemond	.25
27	Scott Brosius	.25
28	Coaches/Checklist (Tommie Reynolds, Dave Duncan, Doug Rader, Rene Lacheman, Art Kusnyer, Dave McKay)	.25

Astros

ANDUJAR CEDENO Astros

The Astrodome provides the backdrop for Barry Colla's photos of Astros personnel seen on this 28-card set sponsored by Mother's Cookies. Cards are in standard 2-1/2" x 3-1/2" and feature rounded corners. Glossy fronts are borderless and have no graphics except the player's name and team in an upper corner. Backs are printed in red and purple and have a few biographical details along with uniform and card numbers, the player's position, an autograph line and the logos of the cookie company and MLB.

		NM/M
Complete Set (28):		7.50
Common Player:		.25
1	Art Howe	.25
2	Steve Finley	.25
3	Pete Harnisch	.25
4	Pete Incaviglia	.25
5	Craig Biggio	.50
6	Ken Caminiti	.25
7	Eric Anthony	.25
8	Jeff Bagwell	4.00
9	Andujar Cedeno	.25
10	Mark Portugal	.25
11	Eddie Taubensee	.25
12	Jimmy Jones	.25
13	Joe Boever	.25
14	Benny Distefano	.25
15	Juan Guerrero	.25
16	Doug Jones	.25
17	Scott Servais	.25
18	Butch Henry	.25
19	Rafael Ramirez	.25
20	Al Osuna	.25
21	Rob Murphy	.25
22	Chris Jones	.25
23	Rob Mallicoat	.25
24	Darryl Kile	.25
25	Casey Candaele	.25
26	Xavier Hernandez	.25
27	Coaches (Bob Cluck, Matt Galante, Rudy Jaramillo, Ed Ott, Tom Spencer)	.25
28	Trainers / Checklist (Doc Ewell, Dennis Liborio, Dave Labossiere)	.25

Dodgers

A commemorative patch marking Dodger Stadium's 30th anniversary is featured on some of the Barry Colla photos seen on this 28-card set. Cards have the now-traditional round-corner, glossy-front borderless format with player name and team in white in an upper

ERIC KARROS Dodgers

corner. Printed in red and purple, the backs have a few biographical details along with uniform and card numbers and appropriate logos.

		NM/M
Complete Set (28):		6.00
Common Player:		.25
1	Tom Lasorda	.35
2	Brett Butler	.25
3	Tom Candiotti	.25
4	Eric Davis	.25
5	Lenny Harris	.25
6	Orel Hershiser	.35
7	Ramon Martinez	.25
8	Jose Offerman	.25
9	Mike Scioscia	.25
10	Darryl Strawberry	.25
11	Todd Benzinger	.25
12	John Candelaria	.25
13	Tim Crews	.25
14	Kal Daniels	.25
15	Jim Gott	.25
16	Kevin Gross	.25
17	Dave Hansen	.25
18	Carlos Hernandez	.25
19	Jay Howell	.25
20	Stan Javier	.25
21	Eric Karros	.50
22	Roger McDowell	.25
23	Bob Ojeda	.25
24	Juan Samuel	.25
25	Mike Sharperson	.25
26	Mitch Webster	.25
27	Steve Wilson	.25
28	Coaches/Checklist (Joe Amalfitano, Mark Cresse, Joe Ferguson, Ben Hines, Manny Mota, Ron Perranoski, Ron Roenicke)	.25

Giants

JOHN BURKETT Giants

In 1983 Mother's Cookies re-entered the baseball card world with a set of S.F. Giants cards. In 1992, the company sponsored its 10th consecutive Giants team issue. As in the '83 set, the cards feature the photography of Barry Colla. In 2-1/2" x 3-1/2" size with rounded corners and UV-coating on the borderless fronts, the cards continue the format used since 1984. Backs are also in the familiar style, with a bit of biographical data and appropriate logos.

		NM/M
Complete Set (28):		7.50
Common Player:		.25
1	Roger Craig	.25
2	Will Clark	.50
3	Bill Swift	.25
4	Royce Clayton	.25
5	John Burkett	.25
6	Willie McGee	.25
7	Buddy Black	.25
8	Dave Righetti	.25
9	Matt Williams	.50
10	Robby Thompson	.25
11	Darren Lewis	.25
12	Mike Jackson	.25
13	Mark Leonard	.25
14	Rod Beck	.25
15	Mike Felder	.25
16	Bryan Hickerson	.25
17	Jose Uribe	.25
18	Greg Litton	.25

19	Cory Snyder	.25
20	Jim McNamara	.25
21	Kelly Downs	.25
22	Trevor Wilson	.25
23	Kirt Manwaring	.25
24	Kevin Bass	.25
25	Jeff Brantley	.25
26	Dave Burba	.25
27	Chris James	.25
28	Coaches/Checklist (Carlos Alfonso, Dusty Baker, Bob Brenly, Wendell Kim, Bob Lillis)	.25

Mariners

CALVIN JONES Mariners

After a one-year absence from the Mother's Cookies lineup, the M's returned in 1992 with a set. Standard-size cards have rounded corners and UV-coated fronts. The only graphics appearing on the borderless photos are the player and team name in white in an upper corner. Backs are printed in red and purple and have basic biographical data, uniform and card numbers, space for an autograph and appropriate sponsor and licensor logos.

		NM/M
Complete Set (28):		12.50
Common Player:		.25
1	Bill Plummer	.25
2	Ken Griffey Jr.	4.00
3	Harold Reynolds	.25
4	Kevin Mitchell	.25
5	David Valle	.25
6	Jay Buhner	.40
7	Erik Hanson	.25
8	Pete O'Brien	.25
9	Henry Cotto	.25
10	Mike Schooler	.25
11	Tino Martinez	1.00
12	Dennis Powell	.25
13	Randy Johnson	2.00
14	Dave Cochrane	.25
15	Greg Briley	.25
16	Omar Vizquel	.40
17	Dave Fleming	.25
18	Matt Sinatro	.25
19	Jeff Nelson	.25
20	Edgar Martinez	.25
21	Calvin Jones	.25
22	Russ Swan	.25
23	Jim Acker	.25
24	Jeff Schaffer	.25
25	Clay Parker	.25
26	Brian Holman	.25
27	Coaches (Marty Martinez, Gene Clines, Roger Hansen, Dan Warthen, Russ Nixon, Rusty Kuntz)	.25
28	Mascot/Checklist	.25

Padres

OSCAR AZOCAR Padres

The Padres ended a six-year hiatus when they re-appeared in the Mother's Cookies lineup for 1992. The 28-card set follows the traditional Mother's format: 2-1/2" x 3-1/2" cards with rounded corners, glossy borderless front photos and the player and team name in white in an upper corner. Backs have appropriate log-

os, uniform and card numbers, player data and room for an autograph, all printed in red and purple.

		NM/M
Complete Set (28):		10.00
Common Player:		.25
1	Greg Riddoch	.25
2	Greg Harris	.25
3	Gary Sheffield	1.00
4	Fred McGriff	.40
5	Kurt Stillwell	.25
6	Benito Santiago	.25
7	Tony Gwynn	4.00
8	Tony Fernandez	.25
9	Jerald Clark	.25
10	Dave Eiland	.25
11	Randy Myers	.25
12	Oscar Azocar	.25
13	Dann Bilardello	.25
14	Jose Melendez	.25
15	Darrin Jackson	.25
16	Andy Benes	.25
17	Tim Teufel	.25
18	Jeremy Hernandez	.25
19	Kevin Ward	.25
20	Bruce Hurst	.25
21	Larry Andersen	.25
22	Rich Rodriguez	.25
23	Pat Clements	.25
24	Craig Lefferts	.25
25	Craig Shipley	.25
26	Mike Maddux	.25
27	Coaches (Bruce Kimm, Rob Picciolo, Merv Rettenmund, Mike Roarke, Jim Snyder)	.25
28	Team Logo/Checklist	.25

Rangers

JEFF RUSSELL Rangers

The clubhouse wall provides the universal backdrop for the posed photos in this 28-card set. Standard-size cards have a high-gloss borderless front photo with rounded corners and the player and team name in white in an upper corner. Backs are in red and purple and have a few player biographical details along with uniform and card numbers, space for an autograph and the logos of the sponsor and licensor.

		NM/M
Complete Set (28):		15.00
Common Player:		.25
1	Bobby Valentine	.25
2	Nolan Ryan	5.00
3	Ruben Sierra	.25
4	Juan Gonzalez	2.00
5	Ivan Rodriguez	4.00
6	Bobby Witt	.25
7	Geno Petralli	.25
8	Jeff Russell	.25
9	Rafael Palmeiro	1.50
10	Julio Franco	.25
11	Jack Daugherty	.25
12	Dickie Thon	.25
13	Floyd Bannister	.25
14	Scott Chiamparino	.25
15	Kevin Reimer	.25
16	Jeff Robinson	.25
17	Brian Downing	.25
18	Brian Bohanon	.25
19	Jose Guzman	.25
20	Terry Mathews	.25
21	Kevin Brown	.25
22	Kenny Rogers	.25
23	Jeff Huson	.25
24	Monty Fariss	.25
25	Al Newman	.25
26	Dean Palmer	.25
27	John Cangelosi	.25
28	Coaches/Checklist (Ray Burris, Orlando Gomez, Toby Harrah, Tom House, Dave Oliver, Tom Robson)	.25

Jeff Bagwell

The set consists of four standard-size cards with a full-bleed color photo on the fronts of the cards and rounded corners. Bagwell's name appears horizontally in white on the front of the card and the backs are printed in purple and

JEFF BAGWELL

red. Along with the Major League merchandise logo on the bottom of the card there is an area for the player's autograph.

		NM/M
Complete Set (4):		9.00
Four-Card Uncut Panel:		10.00
Common Card:		2.50
1	Jeff Bagwell (Head and shoulders.)	2.50
2	Jeff Bagwell (Bat on shoulder.)	2.50
3	Jeff Bagwell (Waist-up.)	2.50
4	Jeff Bagwell (Ball in glove.)	2.50

Chuck Knoblauch

American League 1991 Rookie of the Year Chuck Knoblauch is featured in this four-card set. Similar in format to other Mother's cards, the glossy fronts have rounded corners and feature full-bleed color photos. The red and purple backs have statistical and biographical data along with appropriate logos.

		NM/M
Complete Set (4):		4.00
Common Card:		1.00
1	Chuck Knoblauch (Bat on shoulder.)	1.00
2	Chuck Knoblauch (Head and shoulders.)	1.00
3	Chuck Knoblauch (Waist-up.)	1.00
4	Chuck Knoblauch/Fldg	1.00

Nolan Ryan 7 No-Hitters

Mother's Cookie Co. produced an eight-card set in 1992 commemorating Nolan Ryan's seven no-hitters. Cards were found in specially marked packages of Mother's Cookies. The company also made available uncut sheets of the eight cards through the mail. Fronts feature photos contemporary with Ryan's no-hitters in a borderless, round-cornered format with glossy surface. "Nolan Ryan/7 No-Hitters" appears in white vertically in the upper-left corner. Backs are printed in red and purple and

include a bit of biographical data along with details of each no-hitter. The eighth card in the set offers room to write in information about a future no-hitter which never materialized prior to Ryan's retirement following the 1993 season.

		NM/M
Complete Set (8):		6.00
Eight-Card Uncut Panel:		6.00
Common Card:		1.00
1	Nolan Ryan/Portrait/ Angels	1.00
2	Nolan Ryan/Ptchg/Angels	1.00
3	Nolan Ryan/ Waving/Angels	1.00
4	Nolan Ryan/Angels (Holding four "0" balls.)	1.00
5	Nolan Ryan/Astros	1.00
6	Nolan Ryan/ Pitching/Rangers	1.00
7	Nolan Ryan/ Pitching/Rangers	1.00
8	Nolan Ryan/Rangers (Palms up.)	1.00

1993 Mother's Cookies Angels

GARY GAETTI
Angels

In its 11th year of renewed baseball card production, Mother's Cookies sponsored trading card promotions with seven major league teams including, for the first time, the California Angels. At special promotional games, youngsters entering the ballpark were given packs of 28 cards. Each of the paper envelopes contained 20 different player cards and eight cards of another player. Instructions on the envelope encouraged trading to complete a set of 28. All of the team sets were identical in format. Cards measure the standard 2-1/2" x 3-1/2" with rounded corners. Fronts feature borderless posed photos, the work of photographer Barry Colla. The only graphic elements on the front are the player's name and team in white, generally in an upper corner. In 1993 the Mother's cards featured a somewhat less glossy front finish than in previous years. Backs are printed in red and purple. Data includes the player's position, uniform and card numbers, a few biographical bits, a "How Obtained" statement and a space for an autograph, along with the logos of the cookie company and Major League Baseball.

		NM/M
Complete Set (28):		9.00
Common Player:		.25
1	Buck Rodgers	.25
2	Gary DiSarcina	.25
3	Chuck Finley	.25
4	J.T. Snow	.50
5	Gary Gaetti	.25
6	Chili Davis	.25
7	Tim Salmon	2.50
8	Mark Langston	.25
9	Scott Sanderson	.25
10	John Orton	.25
11	Julio Valera	.25
12	Chad Curtis	.25
13	Kelly Gruber	.25
14	Rene Gonzalez	.25
15	Luis Polonia	.25
16	Greg Myers	.25
17	Gene Nelson	.25
18	Torey Lovullo	.25
19	Scott Lewis	.25
20	Chuck Crim	.25
21	John Farrell	.25
22	Steve Frey	.25
23	Stan Javier	.25
24	Ken Patterson	.25
25	Ron Tingley	.25
26	Damion Easley	.25
27	Joe Grahe	.25
28	Coaches/Checklist (Jimmie Reese, Rod Carew, Bobby Knoop, Chuck Hernandez, Ken Macha, John Wathan, Rick Turner)	.25

A's

		NM/M
Complete Set (28):		6.00
Common Player:		.25
1	Tony LaRussa	.25
2	Mark McGwire	2.00
3	Terry Steinbach	.25
4	Dennis Eckersley	.75
5	Ruben Sierra	.25
6	Rickey Henderson	1.00
7	Mike Bordick	.25
8	Rick Honeycutt	.25
9	Dave Henderson	.25
10	Bob Welch	.25
11	Dale Sveum	.25
12	Ron Darling	.25
13	Jerry Browne	.25
14	Bobby Witt	.25
15	Troy Neel	.25
16	Goose Gossage	.25
17	Brent Gates	.25
18	Storm Davis	.25
19	Scott Hemond	.25
20	Kelly Downs	.25
21	Kevin Seitzer	.25
22	Lance Blankenship	.25
23	Mike Mohler	.25
24	Edwin Nunez	.25
25	Joe Boever	.25
26	Shawn Hillegas	.25
27	Coaches (Dave Duncan, Art Kusnyer, Greg Luzinski, Dave McKay, Tommie Reynolds)	.25
28	Checklist (Frank Ciensczyk (equipment manager))	.25

Astros

ERIC ANTHONY
Astros

		NM/M
Complete Set (28):		9.00
Common Player:		.25
1	Art Howe	.25
2	Steve Finley	.25
3	Pete Harnisch	.25
4	Craig Biggio	.50
5	Doug Drabek	.25
6	Scott Servais	.25
7	Jeff Bagwell	2.50
8	Eric Anthony	.25
9	Ken Caminiti	.25
10	Andujar Cedeno	.25
11	Mark Portugal	.25
12	Jose Uribe	.25
13	Rick Parker	.25
14	Doug Jones	.25
15	Luis Gonzalez	.50
16	Kevin Bass	.25
17	Greg Swindell	.25
18	Eddie Taubensee	.25
19	Darryl Kile	.25
20	Brian Williams	.25
21	Chris James	.25
22	Chris Donnels	.25
23	Xavier Hernandez	.25
24	Casey Candaele	.25
25	Eric Bell	.25
26	Mark Grant	.25
27	Tom Edens	.25
28	Coaches/Checklist (Bill Bowman, Bob Cluck, Matt Galante, Rudy Jaramillo, Ed Ott, Tom Spencer)	.25

Dodgers

		NM/M
Complete Set (28):		20.00
Common Player:		.25
1	Tommy Lasorda	.35
2	Eric Karros	.25
3	Brett Butler	.25
4	Mike Piazza	9.00
5	Jose Offerman	.25
6	Tim Wallach	.25
7	Eric Davis	.25
8	Darryl Strawberry	.25
9	Jody Reed	.25
10	Orel Hershiser	.35
11	Tom Candiotti	.25
12	Ramon Martinez	.25
13	Lenny Harris	.25
14	Mike Sharperson	.25

TOM CANDIOTTI
Dodgers

15	Omar Daal	.25
16	Pedro Martinez	6.00
17	Jim Gott	.25
18	Carlos Hernandez	.25
19	Kevin Gross	.25
20	Cory Snyder	.25
21	Todd Worrell	.25
22	Mitch Webster	.25
23	Steve Wilson	.25
24	Dave Hansen	.25
25	Roger McDowell	.25
26	Pedro Astacio	.25
27	Rick Trlicek	.25
28	Coaches/Checklist (Joe Amalfitano, Mark Cresse, Joe Ferguson, Ben Hines, Manny Mota, Ron Perranoski, Ron Roenicke)	.25

Giants

WILL CLARK
Giants

		NM/M
Complete Set (28):		8.00
Common Player:		.25
1	Dusty Baker	.40
2	Will Clark	.50
3	Matt Williams	.50
4	Barry Bonds	7.50
5	Bill Swift	.25
6	Royce Clayton	.25
7	John Burkett	.25
8	Willie McGee	.25
9	Kirt Manwaring	.25
10	Dave Righetti	.25
11	Todd Benzinger	.25
12	Rod Beck	.25
13	Darren Lewis	.25
14	Robby Thompson	.25
15	Mark Carreon	.25
16	Dave Martinez	.25
17	Jeff Brantley	.25
18	Dave Burba	.25
19	Mike Benjamin	.25
20	Mike Jackson	.25
21	Craig Colbert	.25
22	Bud Black	.25
23	Trevor Wilson	.25
24	Kevin Rogers	.25
25	Jeff Reed	.25
26	Bryan Hickerson	.25
27	Gino Minutelli	.25
28	Coaches / Checklist (Bobby Bonds, Bob Brenly, Wendell Kim, Bob Lillis, Dick Pole, Denny Sommers)	.25

Mariners

MIKE FELDER
Mariners

		NM/M
Complete Set (28):		10.00

1	Lou Piniella	.25
2	Dave Fleming	.25
3	Pete O'Brien	.25
4	Ken Griffey Jr.	6.00
5	Henry Cotto	.25
6	Jay Buhner	.25
7	David Valle	.25
8	Dwayne Henry	.25
9	Mike Felder	.25
10	Norm Charlton	.25
11	Edgar Martinez	.25
12	Erik Hanson	.25
13	Mike Blowers	.25
14	Omar Vizquel	.25
15	Randy Johnson	2.00
16	Russ Swan	.25
17	Tino Martinez	.25
18	Rich DeLucia	.25
19	Jeff Nelson	.25
20	Chris Bosio	.25
21	Tim Leary	.25
22	Mackey Sasser	.25
23	Dennis Powell	.25
24	Mike Hampton	.25
25	Fernando Vina	.25
26	John Cummings	.25
27	Rich Amaral	.25
28	Coaches/Checklist (Sammy Ellis, John McLaren, Ken Griffey Sr., Sam Perlozzo, Sam Mejias, Lee Elia)	.25

Padres

		NM/M
Complete Set (28):		10.00
Common Player:		.25
1	Jim Riggleman	.25
2	Gary Sheffield	1.00
3	Tony Gwynn	6.00
4	Fred McGriff	.25
5	Greg Harris	.25
6	Tim Teufel	.25
7	Dave Eiland	.25
8	Phil Plantier	.25
9	Bruce Hurst	.25
10	Ricky Gutierrez	.25
11	Rich Rodriguez	.25
12	Derek Bell	.25
13	Bob Geren	.25
14	Andy Benes	.25
15	Darrell Sherman	.25
16	Frank Seminara	.25
17	Guillermo Velasquez	.25
18	Gene Harris	.25
19	Dan Walters	.25
20	Craig Shipley	.25
21	Phil Clark	.25
22	Jeff Gardner	.25
23	Mike Scioscia	.25
24	Wally Whitehurst	.25
25	Roger Mason	.25
26	Kerry Taylor	.25
27	Tim Scott	.25
28	Coaches/Checklist (Dave Bialas, Bruce Bochy, Rob Picciolo, Dan Radison, Merv Rettenmund, Mike Roarke)	.25

Nolan Ryan Farewell

Nolan Ryan's final 10 major league seasons with the Astros and Rangers are captured in this set. Cards are in standard Mother's Cookies format: 2-1/2" x 3-1/2" with rounded corners, borderless front

photos and UV-coated. Each card has a "Nolan Ryan Farewell Set" diamond logo in an upper corner. Backs are printed in red and purple and have a few biographical details along with the year the picture on front was created. Each card has stats for one year from 1984-1992 or cumulative All-Star stats along with Major League totals. Cards were available either cello-wrapped singly in cookie packages or as a complete set via a mail-in offer.

		NM/M
Complete Set (10):		6.00
Uncut Sheet (10):		6.00
Common Card:		.75
1	Nolan Ryan (1984 Astros)	.75
2	Nolan Ryan (1985 Astros)	.75
3	Nolan Ryan (1986 Astros)	.75
4	Nolan Ryan (1987 Astros)	.75
5	Nolan Ryan (1988 Astros)	.75
6	Nolan Ryan (1989 Rangers)	.75
7	Nolan Ryan (1990 Rangers)	.75
8	Nolan Ryan (1991 Rangers)	.75
9	Nolan Ryan (1992 Rangers)	.75
10	Nolan Ryan (All-Star Stats)	.75

1994 Mother's Cookies Angels

Originally scheduled to be given away at a promotional date during the 1994 season, these cards were caught in the strike and not distributed until the March 30-April 1 home-and-home series between the replacement players of the Angels and those of the Oakland A's. The cards were distributed in a paper envelope containing 20 different cards and eight cards of a 21st player. The idea was to trade to complete a set. The 2-1/2" x 3-1/2" cards have rounded corners and feature borderless color photos on front with the player's name and team in one of the corners. Backs are printed in red and purple and include some biographical data, uniform and card numbers, logos of Mother's Cookies and Major League Baseball and a line for an autograph.

		NM/M
Complete Set (28):		12.50
Common Player:		.25
1	Marcel Lacheman	.25
2	Mark Langston	.25
3	J.T. Snow	.25
4	Chad Curtis	.25
5	Tim Salmon	1.00
6	Gary DiSarcina	.25
7	Bo Jackson	2.50
8	Dwight Smith	.25
9	Chuck Finley	.25
10	Rod Correia	.25
11	Spike Owen	.25
12	Harold Reynolds	.25
13	Chris Turner	.25
14	Chili Davis	.25
15	Bob Patterson	.25
16	Jim Edmonds	4.00
17	Joe Magrane	.25
18	Craig Lefferts	.25
19	Scott Lewis	.25
20	Rex Hudler	.25
21	Mike Butcher	.25
22	Brian Anderson	.25
23	Greg Myers	.25
24	Mark Leiter	.25
25	Joe Grahe	.25
26	Jorge Fabregas	.25
27	John Dopson	.25
28	Angels Coaches/Checklist (Chuck Hernandez, Ken Macha, Bobby Knoop, Joe Maddon, Rod Carew, Max Oliveras)	.25

A's

Departing little from previous years, this 28-card set of the players, manager and coaches of the Oakland A's features the inimitable photography of Barry Colla. Cards are 2-1/2" x 3-1/2" with rounded corners and borderless photos. The player's name and team are in white in one of the corners. Backs are printed in red and purple and feature a few biographical bits, a uniform number and card number, a line for an autograph and the logos of Mother's Cookies and Major League Baseball. Originally intended to be given away at a game during the strike-shortened 1994 season, the cards were instead given out at the March 30-April 1 home-and-home exhibition series between the A's and the California Angels. To promote old-fashioned card trading, each package of cards contained 20 cards, plus eight cards of a 21st player. Considerable trading was thus required to complete a set.

		NM/M
Complete Set (28):		12.00
Common Player:		.25
1	Tony LaRussa	.25
2	Mark McGwire	5.00
3	Terry Steinbach	.25
4	Dennis Eckersley	1.50
5	Mike Bordick	.25
6	Rickey Henderson	2.00
7	Ruben Sierra	.25
8	Stan Javier	.25
9	Todd Van Poppel	.25
10	Bob Welch	.25
11	Miguel Jimenez	.25
12	Steve Karsay	.25
13	Geronimo Berroa	.25
14	Bobby Witt	.25
15	Troy Neel	.25
16	Ron Darling	.25
17	Scott Hemond	.25
18	Steve Ontiveros	.25
19	Mike Aldrete	.25
20	Carlos Reyes	.25
21	Brent Gates	.25
22	Mark Acre	.25
23	Eric Helfand	.25
24	Vince Horsman	.25
25	Bill Taylor	.25
26	Scott Brosius	.25
27	John Briscoe	.25
28	Athletics' Coaches/Checklist (Dave Duncan, Jim Lefebvre, Carney Lansford, Tommie Reynolds, Art Kusnyer, Dave McKay)	.25

Astros

Distributed at an early 1995 game because the 1994 strike wiped out the planned promotional date, these cards were handed out in packages that contained 20 different cards and eight cards of a 21st player. The idea was to trade

the duplicates to form a team set. The round-cornered 2-1/2" x 3-1/2" cards have a borderless color photo on front. Backs are printed in red and purple and include a few biographical notes, uniform and card numbers, a line for an autograph and logos of Mother's Cookies and Major League Baseball.

		NM/M
Complete Set (28):		10.00
Common Player:		.25
1	Terry Collins	.25
2	Mitch Williams	.25
3	Jeff Bagwell	2.50
4	Luis Gonzalez	.50
5	Craig Biggio	.50
6	Darryl Kile	.25
7	Ken Caminiti	.25
8	Steve Finley	.25
9	Pete Harnisch	.25
10	Sid Bream	.25
11	Mike Felder	.25
12	Tom Edens	.25
13	James Mouton	.25
14	Doug Drabek	.25
15	Greg Swindell	.25
16	Chris Donnels	.25
17	John Hudek	.25
18	Andujar Cedeno	.25
19	Scott Servais	.25
20	Todd Jones	.25
21	Kevin Bass	.25
22	Shane Reynolds	.25
23	Brian Williams	.25
24	Tony Eusebio	.25
25	Mike Hampton	.25
26	Andy Stankiewicz	.25
27	Astros Coaches (Ben Hines, Julio Linares, Matt Galante, Steve Henderson, Mel Stottlemyre, Sr.)	.25
28	Astros Trainers/Checklist (Dave Labossiere, Dennis Liborio, Rex Jones)	.25

Dodgers

Plans to distribute this set were postponed when the players' strike wiped out the latter part of the 1994 season. Instead, the cards were distributed at an early 1995 promotional contest. Each package of 28 cards contained 20 different cards and eight cards of a 21st player. This required extensive trading to complete a team set. Cards feature borderless color photos on a 2-1/2" x 3-1/2" round-cornered format. Backs are printed in red and purple and include uniform and card numbers, biographical data, an autograph line and the logos of Mother's Cookies and Major League Baseball.

		NM/M
Complete Set (28):		9.00
Common Player:		.25
1	Tommy Lasorda	.25
2	Mike Piazza	5.00
3	Delino DeShields	.25
4	Eric Karros	.25
5	Jose Offerman	.25
6	Brett Butler	.25
7	Orel Hershiser	.35
8	Henry Rodriguez	.25
9	Raul Mondesi	.25
10	Tim Wallach	.25
11	Ramon Martinez	.25
12	Mitch Webster	.25
13	Todd Worrell	.25
14	Jeff Treadway	.25
15	Tom Candiotti	.25
16	Pedro Astacio	.25
17	Chris Gwynn	.25
18	Jim Gott	.25
19	Omar Daal	.25
20	Cory Snyder	.25
21	Kevin Gross	.25
22	Dave Hansen	.25
23	Al Osuna	.25
24	Darren Dreifort	.25
25	Roger McDowell	.25
26	Carlos Hernandez	.25
27	Gary Wayne	.25
28	Dodgers Coaches/Checklist (Ron Perranoski, Joe Amalfitano, Reggie Smith, Joe Ferguson, Bill Russell, Mark Cresse)	.25

Giants

Unable to distribute these cards in 1994 because the strike wiped out a planned promotional date, the Giants gave away the cards at an early 1995 game. Cards were distributed in packages containing 20 different players and eight cards of a 21st player; requiring extensive trading to complete a team set. The 2-1/2" x 3-1/2" round-cornered cards feature borderless color photos on front. Backs have red and purple printing and include a few biographical notes, card and uniform numbers, Mother's Cookies and Major League Baseball logos and a line for an autograph.

		NM/M
Complete Set (28):		15.00
Common Player:		.25
1	Dusty Baker	.40
2	Robby Thompson	.25
3	Barry Bonds	7.50
4	Royce Clayton	.25
5	John Burkett	.25
6	Bill Swift	.25
7	Matt Williams	.50
8	Rod Beck	.25
9	Steve Scarsone	.25
10	Mark Portugal	.25
11	John Patterson	.25
12	Darren Lewis	.25
13	Kirt Manwaring	.25
14	Salomon Torres	.25
15	Willie McGee	.25
16	Dave Martinez	.25
17	Darryl Strawberry	.25
18	Steve Frey	.25
19	Rich Monteleone	.25
20	Todd Benzinger	.25
21	Jeff Reed	.25
22	Mike Benjamin	.25
23	Mike Jackson	.25
24	Pat Gomez	.25
25	Dave Burba	.25
26	Bryan Hickerson	.25
27	Mark Carreon	.25
28	Giants Coaches/Checklist (Bobby Bonds, Bob Lillis, Wendell Kim, Bob Brenly, Dick Pole, Denny Sommers)	

Mariners

When the players struck on Aug. 12, 1994, it killed the Mariners' plans to distribute these cards at a promotional date. Instead, packages of the cards were given away during the winter as players and management toured the Northwest drumming up fan interest. Cards were issued in a group containing 20 different players and eight cards of a 21st player. It was

necessary to trade the duplicates to finish a team set. Cards are 2-1/2" x 3-1/2" with round corners and feature borderless color photos on front. Backs are in red and purple and include biographical bits, uniform and card numbers and the logos of Mother's Cookies and Major League Baseball.

		NM/M
Complete Set (28):		10.00
Common Player:		.25
1	Lou Piniella	.25
2	Randy Johnson	2.00
3	Eric Anthony	.25
4	Ken Griffey Jr.	5.00
5	Felix Fermin	.25
6	Jay Buhner	.25
7	Chris Bosio	.25
8	Reggie Jefferson	.25
9	Greg Hibbard	.25
10	Dave Fleming	.25
11	Rich Amaral	.25
12	Rich Gossage	.25
13	Edgar Martinez	.25
14	Bobby Ayala	.25
15	Darren Bragg	.25
16	Tino Martinez	.25
17	Mike Blowers	.25
18	John Cummings	.25
19	Keith Mitchell	.25
20	Bill Haselman	.25
21	Greg Pirkl	.25
22	Mackey Sasser	.25
23	Tim Davis	.25
24	Dan Wilson	.25
25	Jeff Nelson	.25
26	Kevin King	.25
27	Torey Lovullo	.25
28	Mariners Coaches/Checklist (Sam Perlozzo, Lee Elia, Sammy Ellis, John McLaren, Sam Mejias)	.25

Padres

The cancellation of the latter part of the 1994 season by the players' strike wiped out a planned promotional date on which these cards were to have been given out. Instead, the cards were distributed at an early 1995 game. Packages were given out consisting of 20 different cards plus eight cards of a 21st player, which could be traded to complete a team set. Cards are 2-1/2" x 3-1/2" with round corners and a borderless color photo on front. Backs are printed in red and purple and have a few biographical notes, card and uniform numbers, an autograph line and logos of Mother's Cookies and Major League Baseball.

		NM/M
Complete Set (28):		9.00
Common Player:		.25
1	Jim Riggleman	.25
2	Tony Gwynn	5.00
3	Andy Benes	.25
4	Bip Roberts	.25
5	Phil Clark	.25
6	Wally Whitehurst	.25
7	Archi Cianfrocco	.25
8	Derek Bell	.25
9	Ricky Gutierrez	.25
10	Mark Davis	.25
11	Phil Plantier	.25
12	Brian Johnson	.25
13	Billy Bean	.25
14	Craig Shipley	.25
15	Tim Hyers	.25
16	Gene Harris	.25
17	Scott Sanders	.25
18	A.J. Sager	.25
19	Keith Lockhart	.25
20	Tim Mauser	.25
21	Andy Ashby	.25
22	Brad Ausmus	.25
23	Trevor Hoffman	.25
24	Luis Lopez	.25
25	Doug Brocail	.25
26	Dave Staton	.25
27	Pedro A. Martinez	.25
28	Padres Coaches/Checklist (Sonny Siebert, Rob Picciolo, Dave Bialas, Dan Radison, Merv Rettenmund, Bruce Bochy)	.25

Rookies of the Year

In 1994 Mother's Cookies issued three different four-card sets of the 1993 Rookies of the Year. Cards of Mike Piazza of the Dodgers and Tim Salmon of California were available, one per package, in each of six varieties of Mother's Big Cookies. There was also a four-card set featuring both players on each of the four cards. These cards were packaged one per bag of Mother's Major League Double Headers. The specially marked packages with the trading cards inside also carried details about Mother's Commemorative Uncut Strips of each of the three different sets in a mail-in offer. In addition, the company created two chase cards designed to put the real cookie fans to the test. The "One in a Thousand - Rookies of the Year" - foil trading cards were inserted one in every 1,000 packages, with either blue or red foil, and fewer than 10,000 of the foil cards produced.

		NM/M
Complete Set (12):		8.00
Four-Card Uncut Piazza Panel:		6.00
Four-Card Uncut Salmon Panel:		2.00
Four-Card Uncut Piazza-Salmon Panel:		4.00
Common Card:		.50
1	Tim Salmon (Bat on shoulder.)	.50
2	Tim Salmon (Batting stance.)	.50
3	Tim Salmon (Dugout pose.)	.50
4	Tim Salmon/Fldg	.50
5	Mike Piazza (Bat on shoulder.)	1.50
6	Mike Piazza (Batting stance.)	1.50
7	Mike Piazza (Dugout pose.)	1.50
8	Mike Piazza/Catching	1.50
9	Tim Salmon, Mike Piazza (Bats on shoulders.)	.50
10	Tim Salmon, Mike Piazza (Arm around shoulder.)	.50
11	Tim Salmon, Mike Piazza (Shaking hands.)	.50
12	Tim Salmon, Mike Piazza (Back to back.)	.50
BF	Tim Salmon, Mike Piazza (Shaking hands; 1 in 1,000 blue foil.)	9.00
RF	Tim Salmon, Mike Piazza/Kneeling (1 in 1,000 red foil.)	9.00

Nolan Ryan Final Farewell

A virtual reprint of the 1993 Farewell Set, the 1994 version uses the same photos and, except for

card #10, presents the same information on the card backs. Card #10 in the 1994 set offers 1993 season and final Major League stats instead of the All-Star stats on the 1993 version. Some minor differences in photo cropping between the two sets will be noticed, as well as the fact that many of the back elements which had been printed in red on the 1993 cards are in purple on the 1994 cards, and vice versa. Cards can be distinguished by the presence of a 1993 or 1994 copyright line on the back.

		NM/M
Complete Set (10):		6.00
10-Card Uncut Panel:		10.00
Common Card:		1.00
1	Nolan Ryan (1984 Astros)	1.00
2	Nolan Ryan (1985 Astros)	1.00
3	Nolan Ryan (1986 Astros)	1.00
4	Nolan Ryan (1987 Astros)	1.00
5	Nolan Ryan (1988 Astros)	1.00
6	Nolan Ryan (1989 Rangers)	1.00
7	Nolan Ryan (1990 Rangers)	1.00
8	Nolan Ryan (1991 Rangers)	1.00
9	Nolan Ryan (1992 Rangers)	1.00
10	Nolan Ryan (1993 Rangers)	1.00

1995 Mother's Cookies Angels

Seven teams in the Western U.S. participated in Mother's Cookies 13th season of sponsoring team sets. Virtually identical in format to previous years, the 2-1/2" x 3-1/2" round-cornered cards were given away at promotional dates. To promote old-fashioned card trading, the cards were distributed in a paper envelope containing 20 different cards, plus eight cards of a 21st player. Considerable trading was thus required to complete a team set. As in previous years, Barry Colla's superb photos capture the players, manager and coaches of each team in a 28-card set. Backs are again printed in red and purple with a few bits of biographical data, uniform and card numbers and space for an autograph, along with the sponsor's logo.

		NM/M
Complete Set (28):		9.00
Common Player:		.25
1	Marcel Lachemann	.25
2	Mark Langston	.25
3	J.T. Snow	.25
4	Tim Salmon	1.50
5	Chili Davis	.25
6	Gary DiSarcina	.25
7	Tony Phillips	.25
8	Jim Edmonds	2.50
9	Chuck Finley	.25
10	Mark Dalesandro	.25
11	Greg Myers	.25
12	Spike Owen	.25
13	Lee Smith	.25
14	Eduardo Perez	.25
15	Bob Patterson	.25
16	Mitch Williams	.25
17	Garret Anderson	.50
18	Mike Bielecki	.25
19	Shawn Boskie	.25
20	Damion Easley	.25
21	Mike Butcher	.25
22	Brian Anderson	.25
23	Andy Allanson	.25

24	Scott Sanderson	.25
25	Troy Percival	.25
26	Rex Hudler	.25
27	Mike James	.25
28	Coaches/checklist	
	(Mick Billmyer,	
	Rick Burleson, Rod Carew,	
	Chuck Hernandez,	
	Bobby Knoop,	
	Bill Lachemann,	
	Joe Maddon)	.25

A's

DENNIS ECKERSLEY
Athletics

		NM/M
Complete Set (29):		7.50
Common Player:		.25
1	Tony LaRussa	.25
2	Mark McGwire	2.50
3	Terry Steinbach	.25
4	Dennis Eckersley	.75
5	Rickey Henderson	1.00
6	Ron Darling	.25
7	Ruben Sierra	.25
8	Mike Aldrete	.25
9	Stan Javier	.25
10	Mike Bordick	.25
11	Dave Stewart	.25
12	Geronimo Berroa	.25
13	Todd Van Poppel	.25
14	Todd Stottlemyre	.25
15	Eric Helfand	.25
16	Dave Leiper	.25
17	Rick Honeycutt	.25
18	Steve Ontiveros	.25
19	Mike Gallego	.25
20	Carlos Reyes	.25
21	Brent Gates	.25
22	Craig Paquette	.25
23	Mike Harkey	.25
24	Andy Tomberlin	.25
25	Jim Corsi	.25
26	Mark Acre	.25
27	Scott Brosius	.25
28	Coaches/Checklist	
	(Dave Duncan, Art Kusnyer,	
	Carney Lansford,	
	Jim Lefebvre, Dave McKay,	
	Tommie Reynolds)	.25
29	Ariel Prieto	
	(Late-season update.)	2.50
---	Mother's Coupon	
	(Spanish)	.05

Astros

TONY EUSEBIO
Astros

		NM/M
Complete Set (28):		9.00
Common Player:		.25
1	Terry Collins	.25
2	Jeff Bagwell	2.50
3	Luis Gonzalez	.50
4	Darryl Kile	.25
5	Derek Bell	.25
6	Scott Servais	.25
7	Craig Biggio	.50
8	Dave Magadan	.25
9	Milt Thompson	.25
10	Derrick May	.25
11	Doug Drabek	.25
12	Tony Eusebio	.25
13	Phil Nevin	.25
14	James Mouton	.25
15	Phil Plantier	.25
16	Pedro Martinez	.25
17	Orlando Miller	.25
18	John Hudek	.25
19	Doug Brocail	.25
20	Craig Shipley	.25
21	Shane Reynolds	.25

22	Mike Hampton	.25
23	Todd Jones	.25
24	Greg Swindell	.25
25	Jim Dougherty	.25
26	Brian Hunter	.25
27	Dave Veres	.25
28	Coaches/Checklist	
	(Jesse Barfield, Matt Galante,	
	Steve Henderson,	
	Julio Linares,	
	Mel Stottlemyre)	.25

Dodgers

ISMAEL VALDES
Dodgers

		NM/M
Complete Set (28):		12.00
Common Player:		.25
1	Tommy Lasorda	.25
2	Mike Piazza	4.00
3	Raul Mondesi	.25
4	Ramon Martinez	.25
5	Eric Karros	.25
6	Roberto Kelly	.25
7	Tim Wallach	.25
8	Jose Offerman	.25
9	Delino DeShields	.25
10	Dave Hansen	.25
11	Pedro Astacio	.25
12	Mitch Webster	.25
13	Hideo Nomo	6.00
14	Billy Ashley	.25
15	Chris Gwynn	.25
16	Todd Hollandsworth	.25
17	Omar Daal	.25
18	Todd Worrell	.25
19	Todd Williams	.25
20	Carlos Hernandez	.25
21	Tom Candiotti	.25
22	Antonio Osuna	.25
23	Ismael Valdes	.25
24	Rudy Seanez	.25
25	Joey Eischen	.25
26	Greg Hansell	.25
27	Rick Parker	.25
28	Coaches/Checklist	
	(Joe Amalfitano, Mark Cresse,	
	Manny Mota, Bill Russell,	
	Reggie Smith,	
	Dave Wallace)	.25

Giants

GLENALLEN HILL
Giants

		NM/M
Complete Set (28):		12.00
Common Player:		.25
1	Dusty Baker	.40
2	Robby Thompson	.25
3	Barry Bonds	6.00
4	Royce Clayton	.25
5	Glenallen Hill	.25
6	Terry Mulholland	.25
7	Matt Williams	.50
8	Mark Portugal	.25
9	John Patterson	.25
10	Rod Beck	.25
11	Mark Leiter	.25
12	Kirt Manwaring	.25
13	Steve Scarsone	.25
14	Darren Lewis	.25
15	Tom Lampkin	.25
16	William Van Landingham	.25
17	Joe Rosselli	.25
18	Chris Hook	.25
19	Mark Dewey	.25
20	J.R. Phillips	.25
21	Jeff Reed	.25
22	Pat Gomez	.25
23	Mike Benjamin	.25
24	Trevor Wilson	.25
25	Dave Burba	.25

26	Jose Bautista	.25
27	Mark Carreon	.25
28	Coaches/Checklist	
	(Bobby Bonds, Bob Brenly,	
	Wendell Kim, Bob Lillis,	
	Dick Pole)	.25

Mariners

JOEY CORA
Mariners

		NM/M
Complete Set (28):		12.00
Common Player:		.25
1	Lou Piniella	.25
2	Randy Johnson	2.00
3	Dave Fleming	.25
4	Ken Griffey Jr.	4.00
5	Edgar Martinez	.25
6	Jay Buhner	.25
7	Alex Rodriguez	7.50
8	Joey Cora	.25
9	Tim Davis	.25
10	Mike Blowers	.25
11	Chris Bosio	.25
12	Dan Wilson	.25
13	Rich Amaral	.25
14	Bobby Ayala	.25
15	Darren Bragg	.25
16	Bob Wells	.25
17	Doug Strange	.25
18	Chad Kreuter	.25
19	Rafael Carmona	.25
20	Luis Sojo	.25
21	Tim Belcher	.25
22	Steve Frey	.25
23	Tino Martinez	.25
24	Felix Fermin	.25
25	Jeff Nelson	.25
26	Alex Diaz	.25
27	Bill Risley	.25
28	Coaches/Checklist	
	(Bobby Cuellar, Lee Elia,	
	John McLaren, Sam Mejias,	
	Sam Perlozzo,	
	Matt Sinatro)	.25

Padres

FERNANDO VALENZUELA
Padres

		NM/M
Complete Set (28):		9.00
Common Player:		.25
1	Bruce Bochy	.25
2	Tony Gwynn	4.00
3	Ken Caminiti	.25
4	Bip Roberts	.25
5	Andujar Cedeno	.25
6	Andy Benes	.25
7	Phil Clark	.25
8	Fernando Valenzuela	.25
9	Roberto Petagine	.25
10	Brian Johnson	.25
11	Scott Livingstone	.25
12	Brian Williams	.25
13	Jody Reed	.25
14	Steve Finley	.25
15	Jeff Tabaka	.25
16	Ray Holbert	.25
17	Tim Worrell	.25
18	Eddie Williams	.25
19	Brad Ausmus	.25
20	Willie Blair	.25
21	Trevor Hoffman	.25
22	Scott Sanders	.25
23	Andy Ashby	.25
24	Joey Hamilton	.25
25	Andres Berumen	.25
26	Melvin Nieves	.25
27	Bryce Florie	.25

28	Coaches/Checklist	
	(Davey Lopes, Graig Nettles,	
	Rob Picciolo,	
	Merv Rettenmund,	
	Sonny Siebert)	.25

1996 Mother's Cookies Angels

GARRET ANDERSON
Angels

After a four-year absence, the California Angels returned to participate in Mother's Cookies 14th season of sponsoring team sets. Virtually identical in format to previous years, the 2-1/2" x 3-1/2" round-cornered cards were given away at promotional dates. To promote old-fashioned card trading, the cards were distributed in a paper envelope containing 20 different cards, plus eight cards of a 21st player. Considerable trading was thus required to complete a team set. As in previous years, superb photos capture the players, manager and coaches of each team in a 28-card set. Backs are again printed in red and purple with a few bits of biographical data, uniform and card numbers and space for an autograph, along with the sponsor's logo.

		NM/M
Complete Set (28):		7.50
Common Player:		.25
1	Marcel Lachemann	.25
2	Chili Davis	.25
3	Mark Langston	.25
4	Tim Salmon	.75
5	Jim Abbott	.25
6	Jim Edmonds	1.00
7	Gary DiSarcina	.25
8	J.T. Snow	.25
9	Chuck Finley	.25
10	Tim Wallach	.25
11	Lee Smith	.25
12	George Arias	.25
13	Troy Percival	.25
14	Randy Velarde	.25
15	Garret Anderson	.35
16	Jorge Fabregas	.25
17	Shawn Boskie	.25
18	Mark Eichhorn	.25
19	Jack Howell	.25
20	Jason Grimsley	.25
21	Rex Hudler	.25
22	Mike Aldrete	.25
23	Mike James	.25
24	Scott Sanderson	.25
25	Don Slaught	.25
26	Mark Holzemer	.25
27	Dick Schofield	.25
28	Coaches/Checklist	
	(Mick Billmyer,	
	Rick Burleson, Rod Carew,	
	Chuck Hernandez,	
	Bobby Knoop,	
	Bill Lachemann,	
	Joe Maddon)	.25

A's

JASON GIAMBI
Athletics

		NM/M
Complete Set (28):		7.50
Common Player:		.25
1	Art Howe	.25
2	Mark McGwire	2.00

3	Jason Giambi	2.50
4	Terry Steinbach	.25
5	Mike Bordick	.25
6	Brent Gates	.25
7	Scott Brosius	.25
8	Doug Johns	.25
9	Jose Herrera	.25
10	John Wasdin	.25
11	Ernie Young	.25
12	Pedro Munoz	.25
13	Steve Wojciechowski	.25
14	Geronimo Berroa	.25
15	Phil Plantier	.25
16	Bobby Chouinard	.25
17	George Williams	.25
18	Jim Corsi	.25
19	Mike Mohler	.25
20	Torey Lovullo	.25
21	Carlos Reyes	.25
22	Buddy Groom	.25
23	Don Wengert	.25
24	Bill Taylor	.25
25	Todd Van Poppel	.25
26	Rafael Bournigal	.25
27	Damon Mashore	.25
28	Coaches/Checklist (Bob Alejo,	
	Bob Cluck, Duffy Dyer,	
	Brad Fischer, Denny Walling,	
	Ron Washington)	.25

Astros

DEREK BELL
Astros

		NM/M
Complete Set (28):		7.50
Common Player:		.25
1	Terry Collins	.25
2	Jeff Bagwell	2.50
3	Craig Biggio	.50
4	Derek Bell	.25
5	Darryl Kile	.25
6	Sean Berry	.25
7	Doug Drabek	.25
8	Derrick May	.25
9	Orlando Miller	.25
10	Mike Hampton	.25
11	Rick Wilkins	.25
12	Brian Hunter	.25
13	Shane Reynolds	.25
14	James Mouton	.25
15	Greg Swindell	.25
16	Bill Spiers	.25
17	Alvin Morman	.25
18	Tony Eusebio	.25
19	John Hudek	.25
20	Doug Brocail	.25
21	Anthony Young	.25
22	John Cangelosi	.25
23	Jeff Tabaka	.25
24	Mike Simms	.25
25	Todd Jones	.25
26	Ricky Gutierrez	.25
27	Mark Small	.25
28	Coaches/Checklist	
	(Matt Galante,	
	Steve Henderson,	
	Julio Linares, Brent Strom,	
	Rick Sweet)	.25

Dodgers

		NM/M
Complete Set (28):		10.00
Common Player:		.25
1	Tommy Lasorda	.25
2	Mike Piazza	4.00
3	Hideo Nomo	2.50
4	Raul Mondesi	.25
5	Eric Karros	.25
6	Delino DeShields	.25
7	Greg Gagne	.25

8	Brett Butler	.25
9	Todd Hollandsworth	.25
10	Mike Blowers	.25
11	Ismael Valdes	.25
12	Pedro Astacio	.25
13	Billy Ashley	.25
14	Tom Candiotti	.25
15	Dave Hansen	.25
16	Joey Eischen	.25
17	Milt Thompson	.25
18	Chan Ho Park	1.50
19	Antonio Osuna	.25
20	Carlos Hernandez	.25
21	Ramon Martinez	.25
22	Scott Radinsky	.25
23	Chad Fonville	.25
24	Darren Hall	.25
25	Todd Worrell	.25
26	Mark Guthrie	.25
27	Roger Cedeno	.25
28	Coaches/Checklist	
	(Joe Amalfitano, Mark Cresse,	
	Manny Mota, Bill Russell,	
	Reggie Smith,	
	Dave Wallace)	.25

Giants

ROD BECK

		NM/M
Complete Set (28):		9.00
Common Player:		.25
1	Dusty Baker	.40
2	Barry Bonds	5.00
3	Rod Beck	.25
4	Matt Williams	.50
5	Robby Thompson	.25
6	Glenallen Hill	.25
7	Kirt Manwaring	.25
8	Mark Carreon	.25
9	Osvaldo Fernandez	.25
10	J.R. Phillips	.25
11	Shawon Dunston	.25
12	Mark Leiter	.25
13	William Van Landingham	.25
14	Stan Javier	.25
15	Allen Watson	.25
16	Mel Hall	.25
17	Doug Creek	.25
18	Steve Scarsone	.25
19	Mark Dewey	.25
20	Mark Gardner	.25
21	David McCarty	.25
22	Tom Lampkin	.25
23	Jeff Juden	.25
24	Steve Decker	.25
25	Rich DeLucia	.25
26	Kim Batiste	.25
27	Steve Bourgeois	.25
28	Checklist/Coaches	
	(Carlos Alfonso,	
	Bobby Bonds, Jim Davenport,	
	Wendell Kim, Bob Lillis,	
	Juan Lopez, Dick Pole,	
	Mike Sadek)	.25

Mariners

JAY BUHNER
Mariners

		NM/M
Complete Set (28):		15.00
Common Player:		.25
1	Lou Piniella	.25
2	Randy Johnson	1.00
3	Jay Buhner	.25
4	Ken Griffey Jr.	3.00
5	Ricky Jordan	.25
6	Rich Amaral	.25
7	Edgar Martinez	.25
8	Joey Cora	.25
9	Alex Rodriguez	6.00
10	Sterling Hitchcock	.25

11	Chris Bosio	.25
12	John Marzano	.25
13	Bob Wells	.25
14	Rafael Carmona	.25
15	Dan Wilson	.25
16	Norm Charlton	.25
17	Paul Sorrento	.25
18	Mike Jackson	.25
19	Luis Sojo	.25
20	Bobby Ayala	.25
21	Alex Diaz	.25
22	Doug Strange	.25
23	Bob Wolcott	.25
24	Darren Bragg	.25
25	Paul Menhart	.25
26	Edwin Hurtado	.25
27	Russ Davis	.25
28	Cocahes/Checklist (Bobby Cuellar, Lee Elia, John McLaren, Sam Mejias, Matt Sinatro, Steve Smith)	.25

Padres

FERNANDO VALENZUELA
Padres

		NM/M
Complete Set (28):		9.00
Common Player:		.25
1	Bruce Bochy	.25
2	Tony Gwynn	3.50
3	Wally Joyner	.25
4	Rickey Henderson	1.50
5	Ken Caminiti	.25
6	Scott Sanders	.25
7	Steve Finley	.25
8	Fernando Valenzuela	.25
9	Brian Johnson	.25
10	Jody Reed	.25
11	Bob Tewksbury	.25
12	Andujar Cedeno	.25
13	Sean Bergman	.25
14	Marc Newfield	.25
15	Craig Shipley	.25
16	Scott Livingstone	.25
17	Trevor Hoffman	.25
18	Doug Bochtler	.25
19	Archi Cianfrocco	.25
20	Joey Hamilton	.25
21	Andy Ashby	.25
22	Chris Gwynn	.25
23	Luis Lopez	.25
24	Tim Worrell	.25
25	Brad Ausmus	.25
26	Willie Blair	.25
27	Bryce Florie	.25
28	Coaches/Checklist (Tim Flannery, Grady Little, Davey Lopes, Rob Picciolo, Merv Rettenmund, Dan Warthen)	.25

Rangers

JIM ELSTER

		NM/M
Complete Set (28):		9.00
Common Player:		.25
1	Johnny Oates	.25
2	Will Clark	.50
3	Juan Gonzalez	2.50
4	Ivan Rodriguez	3.50
5	Darryl Hamilton	.25
6	Dean Palmer	.25
7	Mickey Tettleton	.25
8	Craig Worthington	.25
9	Rusty Greer	.25
10	Kevin Gross	.25
11	Rick Helling	.25
12	Kevin Elster	.25
13	Bobby Witt	.25
14	Mark McLemore	.25
15	Warren Newson	.25

16	Mike Henneman	.25
17	Ken Hill	.25
18	Gil Heredia	.25
19	Roger Pavlik	.25
20	Dave Valle	.25
21	Mark Brandenburg	.25
22	Kurt Stillwell	.25
23	Ed Vosberg	.25
24	Dennis Cook	.25
25	Damon Buford	.25
26	Benji Gil	.25
27	Darren Oliver	.25
28	Cocahes/Checklist (Dick Bosman, Bucky Dent, Larry Hardy, Rudy Jaramillo, Ed Napoleon, Jerry Narron)	.25

1997 Mother's Cookies Angels

TIM SALMON

Fans attending the August 3 game at Anaheim Stadium received a starter set of 21 of the 28 cards in this team set, plus seven duplicates. They were encouraged to trade to fill their sets. The 2-1/2" x 3-1/2" round-corner cards have player portrait photos on front. To the left and bottom are red and blue stripes. The player name is at bottom in white, and the team logo is at bottom-right. Backs have minimal player data, a sponsor's logo and space for an autograph.

		NM/M
Complete Set (28):		7.50
Common Player:		.25
1	Terry Collins	.25
2	Tim Salmon	.50
3	Eddie Murray	2.50
4	Mark Langston	.25
5	Jim Edmonds	.75
6	Tony Phillips	.25
7	Gary DiSarcina	.25
8	Garret Anderson	.25
9	Chuck Finley	.25
10	Darin Erstad	2.00
11	Jim Leyritz	.25
12	Shigetoshi Hasegawa	.25
13	Luis Alicea	.25
14	Troy Percival	.25
15	Allen Watson	.25
16	Craig Grebeck	.25
17	Mike Holtz	.25
18	Chad Kreuter	.25
19	Dennis Springer	.25
20	Jason Dickson	.25
21	Mike James	.25
22	Orlando Palmeiro	.25
23	Dave Hollins	.25
24	Mark Gubicza	.25
25	Pep Harris	.25
26	Jack Howell	.25
27	Rich DeLucia	.25
28	Angels Coaches/Checklist (Larry Bowa, Rod Carew, Joe Coleman, Marcel Lachemann, Joe Maddon, Dave Parker)	.25

A's

MARK McGWIRE

Fans attending the August 10 game at the Coliseum received a starter set of 21 of the 28 cards in this team set, plus seven duplicates. They were encouraged to

trade to fill their sets. The 2-1/2" x 3-1/2" round-corner cards have player portrait photos on front. To the left and bottom are green and gold stripes. The player name is at bottom in white, and the team logo is at bottom-right. Backs have minimal player data, a sponsor's logo and space for an autograph.

		NM/M
Complete Set (28):		9.00
Common Player:		.25
1	Art Howe	.25
2	Mark McGwire	2.50
3	Jose Canseco	1.00
4	Jason Giambi	1.50
5	Geronimo Berroa	.25
6	Ernie Young	.25
7	Scott Brosius	.25
8	Dave Magadan	.25
9	Mike Mohler	.25
10	George Williams	.25
11	Tony Batista	.25
12	Steve Karsay	.25
13	Rafael Bournigal	.25
14	Ariel Prieto	.25
15	Buddy Groom	.25
16	Matt Stairs	.25
17	Brent Mayne	.25
18	Bill Taylor	.25
19	Scott Spiezio	.25
20	Richie Lewis	.25
21	Mark Acre	.25
22	Dave Telgheder	.25
23	Willie Adams	.25
24	Izzy Molina	.25
25	Don Wengert	.25
26	Damon Mashore	.25
27	Aaron Small	.25
28	A's Coaches/Checklist (Bob Alejo, Bob Cluck, Duffy Dyer, Brad Fischer, Denny Walling, Ron Washington)	.25

Astros

DARRYL KILE

Children attending a promotional game at the Astrodome received a starter set of 21 of the 28 cards in this team set, plus seven duplicates. They were encouraged to trade to fill their sets. The 2-1/2" x 3-1/2" round-corner cards have portrait photos on front. To the left and bottom are navy and gold stripes. The player name is at bottom in white, and the team logo is at bottom-right. Backs have minimal player data, a sponsor's logo and space for an autograph.

		NM/M
Complete Set (28):		9.00
Common Player:		.25
1	Larry Dierker	.25
2	Jeff Bagwell	2.50
3	Craig Biggio	.50
4	Darryl Kile	.50
5	Luis Gonzalez	.50
6	Shane Reynolds	.25
7	James Mouton	.25
8	Sean Berry	.25
9	Billy Wagner	.75
10	Ricky Gutierrez	.25
11	Mike Hampton	.25
12	Tony Eusebio	.25
13	Derek Bell	.25
14	Ray Montgomery	.25
15	Bill Spiers	.25
16	Sid Fernandez	.25
17	Brad Ausmus	.25
18	John Hudek	.25
19	Bob Abreu	.25
20	Russ Springer	.25
21	Chris Holt	.25
22	Tom Martin	.25
23	Donne Wall	.25
24	Thomas Howard	.25
25	Jose Lima	.25
26	Pat Listach	.25
27	Ramon Garcia	.25

28	Astros Coaches/Checklist (Alan Ashby, Jose Cruz, Mike Cubbage, Tom McCraw, Vern Ruhle, Bill Virdon)	.25

Dodgers

HIDEO NOMO

Children attending the July 13 game at Dodger Stadium received a starter set of 21 of the 28 cards in this team set, plus seven duplicates. They were encouraged to trade to fill their sets. The 2-1/2" x 3-1/2" round-corner cards have player portrait photos on front. To the left and bottom are red and blue stripes. The player name is at bottom in white, and the team logo is at bottom-right. Backs have minimal player data, a sponsor's logo and space for an autograph.

		NM/M
Complete Set (28):		12.00
Common Player:		.25
1	Bill Russell	.25
2	Eric Karros	.25
3	Mike Piazza	4.00
4	Raul Mondesi	.25
5	Hideo Nomo	2.00
6	Todd Hollandsworth	.25
7	Greg Gagne	.25
8	Brett Butler	.25
9	Ramon Martinez	.25
10	Todd Zeile	.25
11	Ismael Valdes	.25
12	Chip Hale	.25
13	Tom Candiotti	.25
14	Billy Ashley	.25
15	Chan Ho Park	.25
16	Wayne Kirby	.25
17	Mark Guthrie	.25
18	Juan Castro	.25
19	Todd Worrell	.25
20	Tom Prince	.25
21	Scott Radinsky	.25
22	Pedro Astacio	.25
23	Wilton Guerrero	.25
24	Darren Hall	.25
25	Darren Dreifort	.25
26	Nelson Liriano	.25
27	Dodgers Coaches (Joe Amalfitano, Mark Cresse, Manny Mota, Mike Scioscia, Reggie Smith, Dave Wallace)	.25
28	Robinson 50th Anniversary Logo/Checklist	.25

Giants

MARVIN BENARD   GIANTS

Twenty thousand fans attending the July 27 game at 3Com Park received a starter set of 21 of the 28 cards in this team set, plus seven duplicates. They were encouraged to trade to fill their sets. The 2-1/2" x 3-1/2" round-corner cards have player portrait photos on front. To the left and bottom are black and orange stripes. The player name is at bottom in white, and the team logo is at bottom-right. Backs have minimal player data, a sponsor's logo and space for an autograph.

		NM/M
Complete Set (28):		10.00
Common Player:		.25
1	Dusty Baker	.25
2	Barry Bonds	5.00
3	J.T. Snow	.25
4	Rod Beck	.25
5	Glenallen Hill	.25
6	Rick Wilkins	.25
7	Jeff Kent	.50
8	Shawn Estes	.25
9	Darryl Hamilton	.25
10	Jose Vizcaino	.25
11	Julian Tavares	.25
12	Mark Gardner	.25
13	Stan Javier	.25
14	Osvaldo Fernandez	.25
15	Jim Poole	.25
16	Marvin Benard	.25
17	William Van Landingham	.25
18	Bill Mueller	.25
19	Mark Lewis	.25
20	Damon Berryhill	.25
21	Doug Henry	.25
22	Rich Rodriguez	.25
23	Kirk Rueter	.25
24	Rich Aurilia	.25
25	Joe Roa	.25
26	Marcus Jensen	.25
27	Miguel Murphy (Equipment Manager)	.25
28	Giants Coaches/Checklist (Carlos Alfonso, Gene Clines, Sonny Jackson, Juan Lopez, Ron Perranoski, Dick Pole)	.25

Padres

TONY GWYNN   PADRES

Partial sets of Mother's Cookies Padres were given to children 14 and under attending the June 22 game at Jack Murphy Stadium. Team colors of royal blue and orange form border strips to the left and bottom of the posed photo. A team logo appears at lower-right.

		NM/M
Complete Set (28):		9.00
Common Player:		.25
1	Bruce Bochy	.25
2	Tony Gwynn	3.00
3	Ken Caminiti	.25
4	Wally Joyner	.25
5	Rickey Henderson	1.50
6	Greg Vaughn	.25
7	Steve Finley	.25
8	Fernando Valenzuela	.25
9	John Flaherty	.25
10	Sterling Hitchcock	.25
11	Quilvio Veras	.25
12	Don Slaught	.25
13	Sean Bergman	.25
14	Chris Gomez	.25
15	Craig Shipley	.25
16	Joey Hamilton	.25
17	Scott Livingstone	.25
18	Trevor Hoffman	.25
19	Doug Bochtler	.25
20	Chris Jones	.25
21	Andy Ashby	.25
22	Archi Cianfrocco	.25
23	Tim Worrell	.25
24	Will Cunnane	.25
25	Carlos Hernandez	.25
26	Tim Scott	.25
27	Dario Veras	.25
28	Coaches/Checklist (Greg Booker, Tim Flannery, Davey Lopes, Rob Picciolo, Merv Rettenmund, Dan Warthen)	.25

Rangers

Fans attending a promotional game at the Ballpark in Arlington received a starter set of 21 of the 28 cards in this team set, plus seven duplicates. They were encouraged to trade to fill their sets. The 2-1/2" x 3-1/2" round-corner cards have player portrait photos on front. To the left and bottom are red and blue stripes. The player name is at bot-

IVAN RODRIGUEZ

tom in white, and the team logo is at bottom-right. Backs have minimal player data, a sponsor's logo and space for an autograph.

		NM/M
Complete Set (28):		8.00
Common Player:		.25
1	Johnny Oates	.25
2	Will Clark	.50
3	Juan Gonzalez	2.50
4	Ivan Rodriguez	3.50
5	John Wetteland	.25
6	Mickey Tettleton	.25
7	Dean Palmer	.25
8	Rusty Greer	.25
9	Ed Vosberg	.25
10	Lee Stevens	.25
11	Benji Gil	.25
12	Mike Devereaux	.25
13	Bobby Witt	.25
14	Mark McLemore	.25
15	Warren Newson	.25
16	Eric Gunderson	.25
17	Ken Hill	.25
18	Damon Buford	.25
19	Roger Pavlik	.25
20	Billy Ripken	.25
21	John Burkett	.25
22	Darren Oliver	.25
23	Mike Simms	.25
24	Julio Santana	.25
25	Henry Mercedes	.25
26	Xavier Hernandez	.25
27	Danny Patterson	.25
28	Rangers Coaches/Checklist (Dick Bosman, Bucky Dent, Larry Hardy, Rudy Jaramillo, Ed Napoleon, Jerry Narron)	.25

1998 Mother's Cookies A's

TOM CANDIOTTI

The first 25,000 fans at the August 2 game in Oakland received a starter set of 21 of the 28 cards in this team set, plus seven duplicates. They were encouraged to trade to fill their sets. The 2-1/2" x 3-1/2" round-corner cards have player portrait photos on front. To the left and bottom are green and gold stripes. The player name is at the bottom in white, and the team logo is at bottom-left. Backs have minimal player data, a sponsor's logo and space for an autograph, all printed in red and purple on a purple background.

		NM/M
Complete Set (28):		8.00
Common Player:		.25
1	Art Howe	.25
2	Rickey Henderson	1.00
3	Jason Giambi	2.00
4	Tom Candiotti	.25
5	Matt Stairs	.25
6	Kenny Rogers	.25
7	Scott Spiezio	.25
8	Ben Grieve	.50
9	Kevin Mitchell	.25
10	A.J. Hinch	.25
11	Bill Taylor	.25
12	Rafael Bournigal	.25
13	Miguel Tejada	3.00
14	Kurt Abbott	.25

15	Buddy Groom	.25
16	Dave Magadan	.25
17	Mike Oquist	.25
18	Mike Macfarlane	.25
19	Mike Fetters	.25
20	Ryan Christenson	.25
21	T.J. Mathews	.25
22	Mike Mohler	.25
23	Jason McDonald	.25
24	Blake Stein	.25
25	Mike Blowers	.25
26	Jimmy Haynes	.25
27	Aaron Small	.25
28	Cocahes/Checklist (Duffy Dyer, Brad Fischer, Gary Jones, Rick Peterson, Denny Walling, Ron Washington)	.25

Astros

The first 25,000 fans at the September 13 game at the Astrodome received a starter set of 21 of the 28 cards in this team set, plus seven duplicates. They were encouraged to trade to fill their sets. The 2-1/2" x 3-1/2" round-corner cards have player portrait photos on front. To the left and bottom are team-color blue and gold stripes. The player name is at the bottom in white, and the team logo is at bottom-left. Backs have minimal player data, a sponsor's logo and space for an autograph, all printed in red and purple on a purple background.

		NM/M
	Complete Set (28):	9.00
	Common Player:	.25
1	Larry Dierker	.25
2	Jeff Bagwell	3.00
3	Craig Biggio	.50
4	Derek Bell	.25
5	Shane Reynolds	.25
6	Sean Berry	.25
7	Moises Alou	.25
8	Carl Everett	.25
9	Billy Wagner	.25
10	Tony Eusebio	.25
11	Mike Hampton	.25
12	Ricky Gutierrez	.25
13	Jose Lima	.25
14	Brad Ausmus	.25
15	Bill Spiers	.25
16	C.J. Nitkowski	.25
17	Randy Johnson	4.00
18	Mike Magnante	.25
19	Dave Clark	.25
20	Sean Bergman	.25
21	Richard Hidalgo	.25
22	Pete Shourek	.25
23	Jay Powell	.25
24	Trever Miller	.25
25	Tim Bogar	.25
26	Doug Henry	.25
27	Scott Elarton	.25
28	Coaches (Jose Cruz, Mike Cubbage, Dave Engle, Matt Galante, Tom McCraw, Vern Ruhle)	.25

Dodgers

CHARLES JOHNSON

The first 25,000 kids at the August 16 game in Los Angeles received a starter set of 21 of the 28 cards in

this team set, plus seven duplicates. They were encouraged to trade to fill their sets. The 2-1/2" x 3-1/2" round-corner cards have player portrait photos on front. To the left and bottom are red and blue stripes. The player name is at the bottom in white, and the team logo is at bottom-left. Backs have minimal player data, a sponsor's logo and space for an autograph, all printed in red and purple on a purple background.

		NM/M
	Complete Set (28):	7.50
	Common Player:	.25
1	Glenn Hoffman	.25
2	Eric Karros	.25
3	Bobby Bonilla	.25
4	Raul Mondesi	.25
5	Gary Sheffield	1.00
6	Ramon Martinez	.25
7	Charles Johnson	.25
8	Jose Vizcaino	.25
9	Scott Radinsky	.25
10	Jim Eisenreich	.25
11	Ismael Valdes	.25
12	Eric Young	.25
13	Chan Ho Park	.25
14	Roger Cedeno	.25
15	Antonio Osuna	.25
16	Dave Mlicki	.25
17	Mark Guthrie	.25
18	Juan Castro	.25
19	Darren Dreifort	.25
20	Tom Prince	.25
21	Jeff Shaw	.25
22	Alex Cora	.25
23	Matt Luke	.25
24	Darren Hall	.25
25	Trenidad Hubbard	.25
26	Jim Bruske	.25
27	Tripp Cromer	.25
28	Dodgers Coaches (Joe Amalfitano, Mickey Hatcher, Charlie Hough, Manny Mota, Mike Scioscia, John Shelby)	.25

Giants

SHAWN ESTES

The first 25,000 fans at the July 26 game at 3Com Park received a starter set of 21 of the 28 cards in this team set, plus seven duplicates. They were encouraged to trade to fill their sets. The 2-1/2" x 3-1/2" round-corner cards have player portrait photos on front. To the left and bottom are black and orange stripes. The player name is at the bottom in white, and the team logo is at bottom-left. Backs have minimal player data, a sponsor's logo and space for an autograph, all printed in red and purple on a purple background.

		NM/M
	Complete Set (28):	9.00
	Common Player:	.25
1	Dusty Baker	.25
2	Barry Bonds	5.00
3	Shawn Estes	.25
4	Jeff Kent	.50
5	Orel Hershiser	.50
6	Brian Johnson	.25
7	J.T. Snow	.25
8	Bill Mueller	.25
9	Kirk Rueter	.25
10	Darryl Hamilton	.25
11	Rich Aurilia	.25
12	Mark Gardner	.25
13	Stan Javier	.25
14	Robb Nen	.25
15	Rich Rodriguez	.25
16	Brent Mayne	.25
17	Julian Tavares	.25
18	Rey Sanchez	.25
19	Chris Jones	.25
20	Charlie Hayes	.25
21	Danny Darwin	.25
22	Jim Poole	.25
23	Marvin Benard	.25
24	Steve Reed	.25

25	Alex Diaz	.25
26	John Johnstone	.25
27	Rene De La Rosa, Mike Krukow, Duane Kuiper, Jon Miller, Amaury Pi-Gonzalez, Ted Robinson (Broadcasters)	.25
28	Giants Coaches/Checklist (Carlos Alfonso, Gene Clines, Sonny Jackson, Juan Lopez, Ron Perranoski, Ron Wotus)	.25

Padres

Fans at a designated Pads' home game received a starter set of 21 of the 28 cards in this team set, plus seven duplicates. They were encouraged to trade to fill their sets. The 2-1/2" x 3-1/2" round-corner cards have player portrait photos on front. To the left and bottom are blue and orange stripes. The player name is at the bottom in white, and the team logo is at bottom-left. Backs have minimal player data, a sponsor's logo and space for an autograph, all printed in red and purple on a purple background.

		NM/M
	Complete Set (28):	9.00
	Common Player:	.25
1	Bruce Bochy	.25
2	Tony Gwynn	4.00
3	Ken Caminiti	.25
4	Kevin Brown	.40
5	Wally Joyner	.25
6	Sterling Hitchcock	.25
7	Greg Vaughn	.25
8	Steve Finley	.25
9	Joey Hamilton	.25
10	Carlos Hernandez	.25
11	Quilvio Veras	.25
12	Trevor Hoffman	.25
13	Chris Gomez	.25
14	Andy Ashby	.25
15	Greg Myers	.25
16	Mark Langston	.25
17	Andy Sheets	.25
18	Dan Miceli	.25
19	James Mouton	.25
20	Brian Boehringer	.25
21	Archi Cianfrocco	.25
22	Mark Sweeney	.25
23	Pete Smith	.25
24	Eddie Williams	.25
25	Ed Giovanola	.25
26	Carlos Reyes	.25
27	Donne Wall	.25
28	Padres Coaches (Greg Booker, Tim Flannery, Davey Lopes, Rob Picciolo, Merv Rettenmund, Dave Stewart)	.25

1998 Mr. Sub Roger Clemens

The date attributed is speculative, since the cards carry no copyright. This set appears to have been issued by a Canadian sub sandwich chain to honor Roger Clemens first four Cy Young Awards. Borderless fronts of the 2-1/2" x 3-1/2" cards have color portrait and action artwork of Clemens in a Blue Jays uniform, with a sepia multi-exposure image of Cy Young in the background, all four cards in the set share the front design, with the only difference being the card number at top-left. Backs are dominated by a large coin-like design with black-and-white artwork of Clemens. The first three cards have back pictures in a Red Sox uniform, the last card shows him with Toronto. The date of his CY Award is shown on each "coin." Beneath the central design

on the graduated blue background are MLB and Mr. Sub logos and "www.RocketRoger.com."

		NM/M
	Complete Set (4):	6.00
	Common Card:	1.50
1	Roger Clemens/1986	1.50
2	Roger Clemens/1987	1.50
3	Roger Clemens/1991	1.50
4	Roger Clemens/1997	1.50

1992 Mr. Turkey

Mr. Turkey, a division of Sara Lee, offered a set of Major League Superstar cards during the 1992 season. A total of 26 cards, one player representing each team, were included in various Mr. Turkey meat packages. The cardboard packaging allows for the printing directly on the carton instead of inserting the cards inside the package. Collectors were able to collect the cards individually or as an uncut sheet, available by sending to the company.

		NM/M
	Complete Set (26):	10.00
	Uncut Sheet:	15.00
	Common Player:	.35
1	Jim Abbott	.40
2	Roberto Alomar	.50
3	Sandy Alomar, Jr.	.40
4	Craig Biggio	.40
5	George Brett	2.00
6	Will Clark	.40
7	Roger Clemens	2.00
8	Cecil Fielder	.40
9	Carlton Fisk	1.00
10	Andres Galarraga	.40
11	Dwight Gooden	.40
12	Ken Griffey Jr.	3.00
13	Tony Gwynn	1.50
14	Rickey Henderson	1.00
15	Dave Justice	.40
16	Don Mattingly	1.00
17	Dale Murphy	.75
18	Kirby Puckett	1.50
19	Cal Ripken, Jr.	3.50
20	Nolan Ryan	3.50
21	Chris Sabo	.40
22	Ryne Sandberg	1.50
23	Ozzie Smith	1.50
24	Darryl Strawberry	.40
25	Andy Van Slyke	.40
26	Robin Yount	1.00

1995 Mr. Turkey

LAY ONE DOWN

Five retired players are featured in this issue. The 2-1/2" x 3-1/2" cards have a sepia or color photo on front, along with a Baseball Greats logo. Uniform logos have been removed from the photos. Backs have personal and career data, and logos of the sponsor and the players' licensing agent. The cards are unnumbered.

		NM/M
	Complete Set (5):	10.00
	Common Player:	2.00
(1)	Bob Feller	2.00
(2)	Al Kaline	2.00
(3)	Tug McGraw	2.00
(4)	Boog Powell	2.00
(5)	Warren Spahn	2.00

1983 Mr. Z's Pizza Milwaukee Brewers

These 5" x 7" color cards were given away (bagged in cellophane) with the purchase of frozen pizzas.

		NM/M
	Complete Set (3):	7.50
	Common Player:	1.00
(1)	Cecil Cooper	1.00
(2)	Paul Molitor	4.00
(3)	Robin Yount	4.00

1984 Mr. Z's Pizza Milwaukee Brewers

These 5" x 7" color cards were given away with the purchase of frozen pizza and other Brewer-logo food products.

		NM/M
	Complete Set (3):	4.00
	Common Player:	1.00
(1)	George Bamberger	1.00
(2)	Rollie Fingers	2.00
(3)	Jim Gantner	1.00

1985 Mr. Z's Pizza Pete Rose

These 5" x 7" cards were issued in Mr. Z's pizzas, each one picturing Pete Rose. Fronts have borderless action photos with a headline in black or white and a facsimile autograph. Backs have a red border with photos of Reds team merchandise which could be obtained by saving pizza labels.

		NM/M
	Complete Set (11):	35.00
	Common Card:	4.00
(1)	Another Hit! (Pete Rose)	4.00
(2)	Classic Rose (Pete Rose)	4.00
(3)	Lay One Down (Pete Rose)	4.00
(4)	Line Up Time (Pete Rose)	4.00
(5)	On Deck (Pete Rose)	4.00
(6)	One Hit Closer! (Pete Rose (No facsimile autograph).)	4.00
(7)	Pete's Back (Pete Rose)	4.00
(8)	Play Ball! (Pete Rose)	4.00
(9)	Player-Manager (Pete Rose)	4.00

(10)	Rounding Third Heading for Home (Pete Rose)	4.00
(11)	Send in the Lefty (Pete Rose)	4.00

2001 Mrs. Baird's Breadwinners Texas Rangers

Every third loaf of Mrs. Baird's bread and buns included one of 10 Texas Rangers cards; other packages had ticket discount coupons, autographed memorabilia or cards, or one of 500 foil parallel sets. The cards feature game-action photos on a red and white background. The player's name is vertically in white on a blue strip at left. A Mrs. Baird's logo and "BREAD WINNERS" appear in the black band at top. A team logo is at lower-left. Horizontal backs have another photo with the Rangers stadium at top, personal data at left and 2000 season notes at right. Series 1 (#1-5) cards were available from April through June, Series 2 (#6-10) cards were in packages during July-August. Headquartered in the Dallas area, the bakery's products were distributed throughout Texas and Oklahoma and in parts of Louisiana and New Mexico.

		NM/M
	Complete Set (11):	7.50
	Common Player:	.50
	Foil Parallel:	3X
1	Pudge Rodriguez	1.50
2	Gabe Kapler	.50
3	Rusty Greer	.50
4	Rafael Palmeiro	1.50
5	Kenny Rogers	.50
6	Alex Rodriguez	2.50
7	Ruben Mateo	.50
8	Rick Helling	.50
9	Ken Caminiti	.50
10	Andres Galarraga	.50
---	Header/Checklist	.05

1981 MSA Discs

Unlike the contemporary Peter Pan/Sunbeam blank-back discs, this set of 2-3/4" diameter discs carry on their backs the advertising of Michael Schechter Associates, their producer.

		NM/M
	Complete Set (32):	135.00
	Common Player:	4.00
(1)	Buddy Bell	4.00
(2)	Johnny Bench	8.00
(3)	Bruce Bochte	4.00
(4)	George Brett	12.50
(5)	Bill Buckner	4.00
(6)	Rod Carew	8.00
(7)	Steve Carlton	8.00
(8)	Cesar Cedeno	4.00
(9)	Jack Clark	4.00
(10)	Cecil Cooper	4.00
(11)	Bucky Dent	4.00
(12)	Carlton Fisk	8.00
(13)	Steve Garvey	6.50
(14)	Goose Gossage	4.00
(15)	Mike Hargrove	4.00
(16)	Keith Hernandez	4.00
(17)	Bob Horner	4.00
(18)	Reggie Jackson	12.50
(19)	Steve Kemp	4.00

		NM/M
(20)	Ron LeFlore	4.00
(21)	Fred Lynn	4.00
(22)	Lee Mazzilli	4.00
(23)	Eddie Murray	8.00
(24)	Mike Norris	4.00
(25)	Dave Parker	4.00
(26)	J.R. Richard	4.00
(27)	Pete Rose	15.00
(28)	Mike Schmidt	12.50
(29)	Tom Seaver	9.00
(30)	Roy Smalley	4.00
(31)	Willie Stargell	8.00
(32)	Garry Templeton	4.00

1981 MSA/Peter Pan-Sunbeam Bakery Discs

Only the MSA copyright is found on these 2-3/4" diameter player discs, the names of Peter Pan or Sunbeam Bakery, the sponsors that packed the discs in loaves of bread, are nowhere to be seen. Like other MSA disc issues, the black-and-white player picture appears on a baseball design with side panels in various colors. Player information appears at each side and in the center panel, along with the Players Association logo. Because the discs are not licensed by the leagues, uniform logos have been removed from the photos. Backs are blank. The unnumbered discs are checklisted here in alphabetical order. A 16-3/4" x 22-5/8" red, white and blue display poster with slots for inserting the discs is known bearing the Peter Pan advertising.

		NM/M
Complete Set (32):		75.00
Common Player:		2.00
Pete Pan Poster:		25.00
(1)	Buddy Bell	2.00
(2)	Johnny Bench	4.50
(3)	Bruce Bochte	2.00
(4)	George Brett	7.50
(5)	Bill Buckner	2.00
(6)	Rod Carew	4.50
(7)	Steve Carlton	4.50
(8)	Cesar Cedeno	2.00
(9)	Jack Clark	2.00
(10)	Cecil Cooper	2.00
(11)	Bucky Dent	2.00
(12)	Carlton Fisk	4.50
(13)	Steve Garvey	3.50
(14)	Goose Gossage	2.00
(15)	Mike Hargrove	2.00
(16)	Keith Hernandez	2.00
(17)	Bob Horner	2.00
(18)	Reggie Jackson	7.50
(19)	Steve Kemp	2.00
(20)	Ron LeFlore	2.00
(21)	Fred Lynn	2.00
(22)	Lee Mazzilli	2.00
(23)	Eddie Murray	4.50
(24)	Mike Norris	2.00
(25)	Dave Parker	2.00
(26)	J.R. Richard	2.00
(27)	Pete Rose	9.00
(28)	Mike Schmidt	7.50
(29)	Tom Seaver	5.00
(30)	Roy Smalley	2.00
(31)	Willie Stargell	4.50
(32)	Garry Templeton	2.00

1985 MSA/Subway Sandwiches Discs

Identical in form and format to other Schechter discs of the era, the Subway giveaways are nowhere marked as such, only the MSA copyright appears. The 2-3/4" diameter discs have black-and-white player portraits in the white center panel of a baseball design. The variously colored end panels contain player information and a 1985 date. The Players Association logo appears beneath the photo. Because the discs are not licensed by Major League Baseball, team logos have been airbrushed off uniforms. The unnumbered, blank-backed discs are checklisted here in alphabetical order.

		NM/M
Complete Set (36):		95.00
Common Player:		3.00
(1)	Buddy Bell	3.00
(2)	Mike Boddicker	3.00
(3)	George Brett	10.00
(4)	Bill Buckner	3.00
(5)	Rod Carew	6.50
(6)	Steve Carlton	6.50
(7)	Cesar Cedeno	3.00
(8)	Dave Concepcion	3.00
(9)	Cecil Cooper	3.00
(10)	Al Cowens	3.00
(11)	Goose Gossage	3.00
(12)	Pedro Guerrero	3.00
(13)	Ron Guidry	3.00
(14)	Tony Gwynn	9.00
(15)	Mike Hargrove	3.00
(16)	Bob Horner	3.00
(17)	Kent Hrbek	3.00
(18)	Rick Langford	3.00
(19)	Dennis Leonard	3.00
(20)	Willie McGee	3.00
(21)	Jack Morris	3.00
(22)	Terry Puhl	3.00
(23)	Dan Quisenberry	3.00
(24)	Johnny Ray	3.00
(25)	Cal Ripken Jr.	15.00
(26)	Ryne Sandberg	9.00
(27)	Mike Schmidt	10.00
(28)	Tom Seaver	6.50
(29)	Rick Sutcliffe	3.00
(30)	Bruce Sutter	4.50
(31)	Alan Trammell	3.00
(32)	Fernando Valenzuela	3.00
(33)	Greg Walker	3.00
(34)	Willie Wilson	3.00
(35)	Dave Winfield	6.50
(36)	Geoff Zahn	3.00

1992 MTV Rock n' Jock

The third annual softball charity game featuring music and sports personalities was the occasion for issue of this three-card set. Fronts have a multi-colored starred border with the player action photo (presumably taken at theprevious year's game). Backs are in black-and-white with the MTV and event logos, the date and place of the game and the notation that the card is from a "Limited Edition of 20,000."

		NM/M
Complete Set (3):		6.00
Common Player:		.50
1	M.C. Hammer	.50
2	Frank Thomas	2.00
3	Ken Griffey Jr.	4.00

N

1989 Nabisco Don Mattingly

Issued as a mail-in premium for Ritz cracker proofs of purchase, this sheet measures 10-5/8" x 13-15/16" and includes eight 2-1/2" x 3-1/2" cards and a 5"x7" card. The individual cards are not perforated and are seldom seen cut from the sheet. For lack of licensing by Major League Baseball, the photos on front have generally had the team logos airbrushed away. Cards are numbered on front and back with a year identifying the

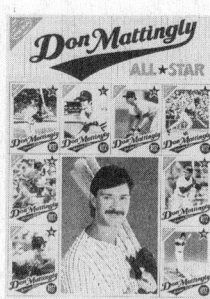

photo. Backs are printed in red, white and blue and contain biographical data and career highlights on the small cards, while the large card offers complete major and minor league stats and major awards won. The sheet was produced for Nabisco by Topps.

		NM/M
Complete Sheet:		7.50
Common Card:		1.00
72	Don Mattingly (Boyhood photo.)	1.00
81	Don Mattingly (Minor league photo.)	1.00
84	Don Mattingly/Fldg	1.00
85-89	Don Mattingly/Btg	1.00
----	Don Mattingly (5" x 7" pose)	1.00

1992 Nabisco Canadian Tradition

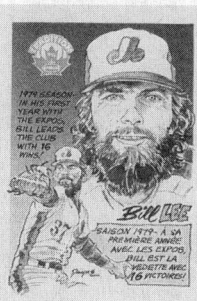

Nabisco released a 36-card set of former Toronto Blue Jays and Montreal Expos inside several of its products in 1992. Three cards were included per box. A colorful 9" x 12" album with plastic sheets was available via a mail-in offer. The cards are artist renderings of the players, similar in style to the famous sports drawings that appeared on the pages of the Sporting News over the years. Text on the drawings is in both English and French. Backs are printed in red, white and blue and include the team and Nabisco logos along with English and French descriptions of the Famous Moment.

		NM/M
Complete Set (36):		25.00
Common Player:		.75
Album:		7.50
1	Bill Lee	.75
2	Cliff Johnson	.75
3	Ken Singleton	.75
4	Al Woods	.75
5	Ron Hunt	.75
6	Barry Bonnell	.75
7	Tony Perez	4.00
8	Willie Upshaw	.75
9	Coco Laboy	.75
10	Famous Moments (Blue Jays Win A.L. East/1985)	.75
11	Bob Bailey	.75
12	Dave McKay	.75
13	Rodney Scott	.75
14	Jerry Garvin	.75
15	Famous Moments (Expos Win N.L. East/1981)	.75
16	Rick Bosetti	.75
17	Larry Parrish	.75
18	Bill Singer	.75
19	Ron Fairly	.75
20	Damaso Garcia	.75
21	Al Oliver	1.50
22	Famous Moments (Blue Jays Win Eastern Division/1989)	.75
23	Claude Raymond	.75
24	Buck Martinez	.75
25	Rusty Staub	1.50
26	Otto Velez	.75
27	Mack Jones	.75
28	Garth Iorg	.75
29	Bill Stoneman	.75
30	Doug Ault	.75
31	Famous Moments (Expos Host All-Star Game/1982)	.75
32	Jesse Jefferson	.75
33	Steve Rogers	.75
34	Ernie Whitt	.75
35	John Boccabella	.75
36	Bob Bailor	.75

1993 Nabisco All-Star Autographs

In a promotion with the Major League Baseball Players Alumni, Nabisco produced this six-card set of former stars. For $5 and proofs of purchase, collectors could receive an authentically autographed card. The 2-1/2" x 3-1/2" cards featured color photos on front on which the team logos have been airbrushed away, since Major League Baseball did not license the issue. Backs gave biographical and career information along with a black-and-white childhood photo of the player. The unnumbered cards are checklisted here in alphabetical order. Don Drysdale's death on July 3, in the midst of the promotion, curtailed availability of cards with his autograph. Each card came cased with a certificate of authenticity. Unautographed cards and 12-card uncut sheets are known.

		NM/M
Complete Set (6):		90.00
Common Player:		6.00
(1)	Ernie Banks	13.50
(2)	Don Drysdale	45.00
(3)	Catfish Hunter	20.00
(4)	Phil Niekro	6.00
(5)	Brooks Robinson	7.50
(6)	Willie Stargell	25.00

1994 Nabisco All-Star Legends Autographs

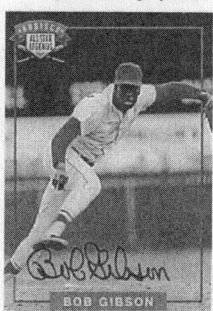

For a second year in 1994, Nabisco continued its program of offering autographed cards of former stars for $5 and proofs of purchase from its snack products. Cards retained the same basic format of using airbrushed color photos on front and black-and-white childhood photos on back. Fronts have a "Nabisco All-Star Legends" logo in the upper-left. Backs have career and biographical data and the logos of the sponsor and the Major League Baseball Players Alumni. The unnumbered cards are checklisted here alphabetically. Each card came with a certificate of authenticity. The Sparky Lyle card was not part of the mail-in promotion but was distributed in person

2001 Nabisco Latino Legends of Baseball

A trio of popular Latino former stars is featured in this in-store giveaway from Nabisco. Fronts have portrait and action photos of the player in an 8" x 10" format. Because the cards are not licensed by MLB, uniform logos have been removed from the photos. Backs have personal information and career data printed in Spanish.

		NM/M
Complete Set (3):		20.00
Common Player:		4.00
(1)	Roberto Clemente	15.00
(2)	Minnie Minoso	4.00
(3)	Tony Perez	6.00

2002 Nabisco Philadelphia Phillies

At the July 7 game at Veterans Stadium, youngsters 14 and under received this set. On thin card stock, the 2-1/2" x 3-1/2" cards have red, white and blue borders around game-action photos. Nabisco and Acme logos are in the upper corners. At bottom is the team logo and player name. Horizontal backs are also in red, white and blue with a large batter silhouette, biographical data and a line each of minor and major league stats. The checklist is arranged by uniform numbers which appear on back.

		NM/M
Complete Set (35):		9.00
Common Player:		.25
3	Todd Pratt	.25
5	Pat Burrell	1.00
6	Doug Glanville	.25
8	Jeremy Giambi	.25
8	Marlon Anderson	.35
9	Tomas Perez	.25
10	Larry Bowa	.25
11	Jimmy Rollins	.75
13	Turk Wendell	.25
15	Dave Hollins	.25
16	Travis Lee	.35
17	Scott Rolen	.75
18	John Vukovich	.25
19	Dan Plesac	.25
21	Greg Gross	.25
22	Jason Michaels	.25
24	Mike Lieberthal	.35
25	Gary Varsho	.25
27	Ricky Bottalico	.25
29	Tony Scott	.25
31	Robert Person	.25
37	Ricky Ledee	.25
37	Rheal Cormier	.25
40	Jose Santiago	.25
43	Randy Wolf	.25
44	Vicente Padilla	.25
46	Vern Ruhle	.25
47	David Coggin	.25
49	Jose Mesa	.25
50	Doug Nickle	.25
51	Terry Adams	.25
52	Carlos Silva	.25
55	Bobby Abreu	.35
56	Brandon Duckworth	.25
59	Ramon Henderson	.25

2000 Team Nabisco All-Stars

This series was issued in Nabisco snack and cookie packages. Fronts have color photos on which team logos have been removed. The player figure is set against a background that has a large purple-blue baseball at bottom and red and white rays at top. The sponsor logo is at top-right. Backs have a smaller version of the photo, career stats and highlights. The unnumbered cards are checklisted here alphabetically.

		NM/M
Complete Set (5):		30.00
Common Player:		6.00
(1)	Bob Gibson	9.00
(2)	Sparky Lyle	12.00
(3)	Jim Palmer	6.00
(4)	Frank Robinson	8.00
(5)	Duke Snider	10.00

		NM/M
Complete Set (11):		9.00
Common Player:		.50
(1)	Lawrence "Yogi" Berra	1.50
(2)	Gary Carter	1.00
(3)	Orlando Cepeda	1.00
(4)	George Foster	.50
(5)	Steve Garvey	.75
(6)	John Kruk	.50
(7)	Joe Morgan	1.00
(8)	Dot Richardson	.50
(9)	Brooks Robinson	1.00
(10)	Mike Schmidt	2.00
(11)	Ozzie Smith	2.00

1983 Nalley Potato Chips Mariners

These large (8-11/16" x 10-11/16") photo cards were issued only in the area of Washington state by Nalley Potato Chips. The six Seattle Mariners are pictured in full color on the entire back panel of each box. On the side panels, detailed player stats and biographies are listed on one side, with a Mariners schedule and ticket discount offer on the other side.

		NM/M
Complete Set (6):		45.00
Common Player:		7.50
8	Rick Sweet	7.50
16	Al Cowens	7.50
21	Todd Cruz	7.50
22	Richie Zisk	7.50
36	Gaylord Perry	20.00
37	Bill Caudill	7.50

1995 National Packtime

An unusual joint venture by the six major baseball card licensees resulted in this 18-card set which was available only via a mail-in offer. The set was obtained by sending in $2 and 28 wrappers from any of the companies' 1995 baseball cards prior to June 30, 1995. Most of the card designs were similar to the respective company's regular issues of the same brand. Each card is gold-foil enhanced and each carries the crossed-bats National Packtime logo on front. Cards are numbered on back from 1-18. A reported 130,000 of the sets were exchanged for wrappers.

		NM/M
Complete Set (18):		3.00
Common Player:		
1	Frank Thomas (Donruss)	.40
2	Matt Williams (Fleer Ultra)	.15
3	Juan Gonzalez (Pacific Crown)	.35
4	Bob Hamelin (Pinnacle)	.15
5	Mike Piazza (Topps)	.50
6	Ken Griffey Jr. (Upper Deck)	.50
7	Barry Bonds (Donruss)	.75
8	Tim Salmon (Fleer Ultra)	.15
9	Jose Canseco (Pacific Crown)	.35
10	Cal Ripken Jr. (Pinnacle)	.75
11	Raul Mondesi (Topps)	.15
12	Alex Rodriguez (Upper Deck)	.60
13	Will Clark (Donruss)	.20
14	Fred McGriff (Fleer Ultra)	.15
15	Tony Gwynn (Pacific Crown)	.45
16	Kenny Lofton (Pinnacle)	.15
17	Deion Sanders (Topps)	.20
18	Jeff Bagwell (Upper Deck)	.40

Welcome to the Show

This special set was another joint venture by the major card manufacturers, Major League Baseball and the Players Association. Sets of six cards were given to attendees at the National Sports Collectors Convention. In designs similar to the companies' regular-issue cards of 1995, these handouts carry a National Packtime logo on front and a red, white and black "WELCOME TO THE SHOW" logo on back. Cards are various numbered "of" 5, 6 or 8, though only six were issued. A paper accompanying the six-card packs assured collectors they were receiving the entire set.

		NM/M
Complete Set (6):		3.00
Common Player:		.50
1 of 6	Greg Maddux (Leaf)	1.00
1/8	Albert Belle (Upper Deck)	.60
2 of 6	Darren Daulton (Ultra)	.50
2 of 6	Don Mattingly (Topps)	1.50
3 of 5	Hideo Nomo (Pinnacle)	.75
3 of 6	Randy Johnson (Pacific)	.75

1986 National Photo Royals

These 2-7/8" x 4-1/4" cards were a team product issued in conjunction with National Photo. The 24-card set includes 21 players, manager Dick Howser, a Royals' 1985 World Championship commemorative card and a discount offer card from National Photo. Card fronts feature full-color action photos with a blue "Kansas City Royals" at the top of each card. Each player's name, number and position are also included. Card

backs list complete professional career statistics, along with the National Photo logo.

[10] DICK HOWSER, Manager

		NM/M
Complete Set (24):		3.50
Common Player:		.15
1	Buddy Biancalana	.15
3	Jorge Orta	.15
4	Greg Pryor	.15
5	George Brett	3.00
6	Willie Wilson	.25
8	Jim Sundberg	.15
10	Dick Howser	.15
11	Hal McRae	.15
20	Frank White	.15
21	Lonnie Smith	.15
22	Dennis Leonard	.15
23	Mark Gubicza	.15
24	Darryl Motley	.15
25	Danny Jackson	.15
26	Steve Farr	.15
29	Dan Quisenberry	.25
31	Bret Saberhagen	.15
35	Lynn Jones	.15
37	Charlie Leibrandt	.15
48	Mark Huismann	.15
40	Buddy Black	.15
45	Steve Balboni	.15
----	Header Card	.15
----	Discount Card	.15

1988 Negro League Stars

Josh Gibson

Players associated with the segregated Negro Leagues around Pittsburgh are featured on this set sponsored by the Duquesne Light Co. and the Pittsburgh Pirates and handed out at the September 10 Pirates game. The 2-1/2" x 3-1/2" cards were issued on a perforated sheet. Fronts have sepia photos. A yellow banner at top reads "NEGRO LEAGUE STARS," a commemorative circle logo appears at lower-right. Backs are in black-and-white with a career summary, biographical data, and the Pirates logo.

		NM/M
Complete Set (20):		12.00
Uncut Sheet:		12.50
Common Player:		.40
1	Rube Foster	.60
2	1913 Homestead Grays	.40
3	Cum Posey	.75
4	1926 Pittsburgh Crawford	.40
5	Gus Greenlee	.40
6	Pop Lloyd	.60
7	Oscar Charleston	.60
8	Smoky Joe Williams	.60
9	Judy Johnson	.40
10	Martin Dihigo	.60
11	Satchel Paige	1.50
12	Josh Gibson	1.50
13	Sam Streeter	.40
14	Cool Papa Bell	.60
15	Ted Page	.40
16	Buck Leonard	1.00
17	Ray Dandridge	.60
18	Lefty Melix, Willis Moody	.40
19	Harold Tinker	.40
20	Monte Irvin	.80

1984 Nestle

STEVE GARVEY 1B

The 792 cards in the 1984 Nestle set are identical to the Topps regular issue except that the candy company's logo replaces the Topps logo in the upper-right corner of the front. The set was offered as a premium in uncut 132-card sheet form (24" x 48"). A few enterprising individuals bought up the majority of the reported 4,000 set production and had the sheets cut into single cards. Due to the ease in handling individual cards, as opposed to large press sheets, sets of single cards sell for more than sheet sets.

	NM/M
Complete Set, Sheets (6)	100.00
Complete Set, Singles (792)	130.00
Common Player:	.25
Sheet A:	60.00
Sheet B:	10.00
Sheet C:	10.00
Sheet D:	10.00
Sheet E:	10.00
Sheet F:	10.00

Don Mattingly "Proof/Test"

DON MATTINGLY OF-1B

This fantasy card has been frequently encountered in the market since the days of Mattingly's dominance in the baseball card world in the late 1980s. The card is seen in several variations, always in black-and-white with a blank-back. Some versions of this unauthorized collectors issues carry notations of proof- or test-card status on front and/or back.

Dream Team

Cal Ripken ORIOLES Shortstop

This set was issued by the Nestle candy company in conjunction with Topps. Cards are in standard 2-1/2" x 3-1/2" size and feature the top 22 players of 1984, 11 from each league. This full-color "Dream Team" includes one player at each position, plus right- and left-handed starting pitchers and one reliev-

er. Card fronts and backs each have a Nestle logo An unnumbered checklist was included with the set.

		NM/M
Complete Set (23):		9.00
Common Player:		.35
Uncut Sheet:		10.00
1	Eddie Murray	.75
2	Lou Whitaker	.35
3	George Brett	2.00
4	Cal Ripken	3.50
5	Jim Rice	.50
6	Dave Winfield	.75
7	Lloyd Moseby	.35
8	Lance Parrish	.35
9	LaMarr Hoyt	.35
10	Ron Guidry	.35
11	Dan Quisenberry	.35
12	Steve Garvey	.50
13	Johnny Ray	.35
14	Mike Schmidt	2.00
15	Ozzie Smith	1.50
16	Andre Dawson	.50
17	Tim Raines	.35
18	Dale Murphy	.50
19	Tony Pena	.35
20	John Denny	.35
21	Steve Carlton	.75
22	Al Holland	.35
----	Checklist	.05

1987 Nestle

Ted Williams OUTFIELD BOSTON RED SOX

Nestle, in conjunction with Topps, issued a 33-card set in 1987. Cards #1-11 feature black-and-white photos of players from the "Golden Era." Cards #12-33 feature full-color photos of American (12-22) and National League (23-33) players from the "Modern Era" of baseball. The cards measure 2-1/2" x 3-1/2" and have all team emblems airbrushed away. Three cards were inserted in specially marked six-packs of various Nestle candy bars. Two complete sets were available through a mail-in offer for $1.50 and three proofs of purchase.

		NM/M
Complete Set (33):		10.00
Common Player:		.30
1	Lou Gehrig	.75
2	Rogers Hornsby	.30
3	Pie Traynor	.30
4	Honus Wagner	.50
5	Babe Ruth	2.00
6	Tris Speaker	.30
7	Ty Cobb	.65
8	Mickey Cochrane	.30
9	Walter Johnson	.30
10	Carl Hubbell	.30
11	Jimmie Foxx	.30
12	Rod Carew	.30
13	Nellie Fox	.30
14	Brooks Robinson	.30
15	Luis Aparicio	.30
16	Frank Robinson	.30
17	Mickey Mantle	3.00
18	Ted Williams	.75
19	Yogi Berra	.30
20	Bob Feller	.30
21	Whitey Ford	.30
22	Harmon Killebrew	.30
23	Stan Musial	.60
24	Jackie Robinson	.75
25	Eddie Mathews	.30
26	Ernie Banks	.30
27	Roberto Clemente	1.50
28	Willie Mays	.75
29	Hank Aaron	.75
30	Johnny Bench	.30
31	Bob Gibson	.30
32	Warren Spahn	.30
33	Duke Snider	.30

1988 Nestle

This 44-card set was produced by Mike Schechter Associates for Nestle. "Dream Team" packets of three player cards and one checklist card were inserted in six-packs of Nestle's candy bars.

Jose Canseco OUTFIELD A's

The issue features current players divided into four Dream Teams (East and West teams for each league). The "1988 Nestle" header appears at the top of the red and yellow-bordered cards. Below the player closeup (in an airbrushed cap) is a blue oval player name banner. Card backs are red, white and blue with personal stats, career highlights and major league totals. The bright red, blue and yellow checklist card outlines two special offers; one for an uncut sheet of all 44 player cards and one for a 1988 replica autographed baseball.

		NM/M
Complete Set, Singles (44):		10.00
Complete Set, Uncut Sheet:		10.00
Common Player:		.25
1	Roger Clemens	2.25
2	Dale Murphy	.50
3	Eric Davis	.25
4	Gary Gaetti	.25
5	Ozzie Smith	2.00
6	Mike Schmidt	2.25
7	Ozzie Guillen	.25
8	John Franco	.25
9	Andre Dawson	.50
10	Mark McGwire	2.50
11	Bret Saberhagen	.25
12	Benny Santiago	.25
13	Jose Uribe	.25
14	Will Clark	.25
15	Don Mattingly	2.25
16	Juan Samuel	.25
17	Jack Clark	.25
18	Darryl Strawberry	.25
19	Bill Doran	.25
20	Pete Incaviglia	.25
21	Dwight Gooden	.25
22	Willie Randolph	.25
23	Tim Wallach	.25
24	Pedro Guerrero	.25
25	Steve Bedrosian	.25
26	Gary Carter	1.00
27	Jeff Reardon	.25
28	Dave Righetti	.25
29	Frank White	.25
30	Buddy Bell	.25
31	Tim Raines	.25
32	Wade Boggs	2.00
33	Dave Winfield	1.00
34	George Bell	.25
35	Alan Trammell	.25
36	Joe Carter	.25
37	Jose Canseco	.75
38	Carlton Fisk	1.00
39	Kirby Puckett	2.00
40	Tony Gwynn	2.00
41	Matt Nokes	.25
42	Keith Hernandez	.25
43	Nolan Ryan	3.00
44	Wally Joyner	.25

2002 Nestle

CHIPPER JONES 3B

Specially marked boxes of Nestle's ice cream novelties contained one of six Topps-produced cards sealed to the cardboard in a protective plastic pouch. The 2-1/2" x 3-1/2" cards have a color action photo and black-and-white portrait photo on front. Both pictures have

had uniform logos removed because the cards are licensed only by the players, and not by MLB. Topps and Nestle's logos appear at top. Backs have another color photo, biographical data, recent stats, career highlights and sponsor/copyright information. Authentically autographed A-Rod and Chipper cards were random inserts.

		NM/M
Complete Set (6):		12.00
Common Player:		2.00
1	Barry Bonds	3.50
2	Chipper Jones	2.00
2	Chipper Jones/Auto.	35.00
3	Mike Piazza	2.50
4	Alex Rodriguez	2.50
4	Alex Rodriguez/Auto.	60.00
5	Sammy Sosa	2.00
6	Ichiro	2.50

1991-1992 NewSport

O. SMITH Shortstop

This set of glossy player cards was issued in France as four-card panels stapled into issues of a monthly magazine devoted to American sports; hence all of the text is in French. The approximately 4" x 6" cards have a month of issue in tiny type on the back. Fronts have large color game-action photos or poses bordered in white. At top is the player's last name and initial, and his position. The NewSport and MLB logos are at bottom. Backs are in black-and-white with biographical details, major league stats and career summary. The unnumbered cards are checklisted here in alphabetical order. In 2001 a hoard of more than 14,000 of the cards, comprising 175 sets and thousands of four-card panels, was offered in a major hobby auction but did not meet a $5,000 minimum bid.

		NM/M
Complete Set (32):		55.00
Common Player:		1.00
(1)	Roberto Alomar	1.50
(2)	Wade Boggs	4.00
(3)	George Brett	4.50
(4)	Will Clark	1.00
(5)	Eric Davis	1.00
(6)	Rob Dibble	1.00
(7)	Doug Drabek	1.00
(8)	Cecil Fielder	1.00
(9)	Julio Franco	1.00
(10)	Ken Griffey Jr.	5.00
(11)	Rickey Henderson	3.00
(12)	Kent Hrbek	1.00
(13)	Bo Jackson	1.50
(14)	Howard Johnson	1.00
(15)	Barry Larkin	1.00
(16)	Don Mattingly	4.50
(17)	Fred McGriff	1.00
(18)	Mark McGwire	6.00
(19)	Jack Morris	1.00
(20)	Lloyd Moseby	1.00
(21)	Terry Pendleton	1.00
(22)	Kirby Puckett	4.00
(23)	Cal Ripken Jr.	7.50
(24)	Nolan Ryan	7.50
(25)	Bret Saberhagen	1.00
(26)	Ryne Sandberg	4.00
(27)	Benito Santiago	1.00
(28)	Mike Scioscia	1.00
(29)	Ozzie Smith	4.00
(30)	Darryl Strawberry	1.00
(31)	Andy Van Slyke	1.00
(32)	Frank Viola	1.00

1989 J.J. Nissen Super Stars

Distributed with bakery products, these standard-size cards feature central color photos on which uniform logos have been airbrushed away due to lack of a Major League Baseball license by Michael

Schechter Associates, the cards' manufacturer. Front graphics are in shades of red, orange and yellow. Backs are printed in black-and-white. The complete set price does not include the Mark Grace card with Vance Law's photo.

		NM/M
Complete Set (20):		7.00
Common Player:		.25
1	Wally Joyner	.25
2	Wade Boggs	1.00
3	Ellis Burks	.25
4	Don Mattingly	1.25
5	Jose Canseco	.75
6	Mike Greenwell	.25
7	Eric Davis	.25
8	Kirby Puckett	1.00
9	Kevin Seitzer	.25
10	Darryl Strawberry	.25
11	Gregg Jefferies	.25
12a	Mark Grace (Photo actually Vance Law.)	3.00
12b	Mark Grace (Correct photo.)	.35
13	Matt Nokes	.25
14	Mark McGwire	1.50
15	Bobby Bonilla	.25
16	Roger Clemens	1.25
17	Frank Viola	.25
18	Orel Hershiser	.25
19	David Cone	.25
20	Ted Williams	2.00

2001 Norstan Milwaukee Brewers Walk of Fame

To commemorate the Walk of Fame in their newly opened ballpark, the Brewers gave this set of inaugural inductees' cards to the first 30,000 fans at the July 12 game. Sponsored by Norstan, whose logo appears in red on front, the 2-1/2" x 3-1/2" cards have sepia toned game-action photos on front with facsimile autograph; at left is a vertical bar with player name and uniform number. Black-and-white backs have another action photo.

		NM/M
Complete Set (4):		8.00
Common Player:		1.00
(1)	Hank Aaron	4.00
(2)	Rollie Fingers	1.00
(3)	Paul Molitor	2.00
(4)	Robin Yount	2.00

1984 N.Y. Mets M.V.P. Club

This nine-card, uncut panel was issued - along with other souvenir items - as a promotion by the New York Mets M.V.P. (Most Valuable Person) Club. Available from the club by mail, the perforated panel features eight full-color player cards, plus a special promotional card in the center. The full panel measures 7-1/2" x 10-1/2", with individual cards measuring the standard 2-1/2" x 3-1/2". Card backs are numbered in the upper right corner and include player stats and career highlights.

KEITH HERNANDEZ   First Base

		NM/M
Complete Singles Set (9):		3.00
Common Player:		.25
Panel:		4.50
1	Dave Johnson	.25
2	Ron Darling	.25
3	George Foster	.25
4	Keith Hernandez	.50
5	Jesse Orosco	.25
6	Rusty Staub	.40
7	Darryl Strawberry	1.50
8	Mookie Wilson	.35
----	Membership Card	.05

1985 N.Y. Mets Super Fan Club

KEITH HERNANDEZ   First Base

This nine-card panel was issued as part of a souvenir package by the New York Mets Super Fan Club. The full-color, perforated panel measures 7-1/2" x 10-1/2" and features eight standard-size player cards, plus a special promotional card in the center. The uncut sheet was available by mail directly from the club. The backs are numbered in the upper right corner and include player statistics and career highlights.

		NM/M
Complete Singles Set (9):		3.50
Common Player:		.25
Panel:		4.50
1	Wally Backman	.25
2	Bruce Berenyi	.25
3	Gary Carter	2.00
4	George Foster	.25
5	Dwight Gooden	1.00
6	Keith Hernandez	.50
7	Doug Sisk	.25
8	Darryl Strawberry	.35
----	Membership Card	.05

1985 N.Y. Mets Police

16
Dwight Gooden
PITCHER

This collectors' issue came out of Florida, where the Mets conducted spring training. The cards were not authorized by the team, the Kiwanis Club or any police agency; they were manufactured strictly for sale to unsuspecting collectors. In format they resemble

contemporary safety issues, measuring 2-5/8" x 4-1/4" with color player photos on front and an anti-drug message on back (ironic, considering the percentage of players in the set who had well-publicized substance abuse problems). Because of their unlicensed nature no collectible value is quoted.

Complete Set (6):

1986 N.Y. Mets Super Fan Club

This special nine-card panel was issued by the fan club of the 1986 World Champion New York Mets, along with other souvenir items gained with membership in the club. Included in the full-color set are eight top Mets players, with a promotional card in the center of the panel. Individual cards measure 2-1/2" x 3-1/2", and are perforated at the edges to facilitate separation. The full panel measures 70-1/2" x 10-1/2". Card fronts feature posed photos of each player, along with name, position and team logo. Backs feature career and personal data, and are printed in the team's blue and orange colors.

		NM/M
Complete Singles Set (9):		2.00
Common Player:		.15
Panel:		2.00
1	Wally Backman	.25
2	Gary Carter	1.00
3	Ron Darling	.25
4	Dwight Gooden	.35
5	Keith Hernandez	.45
6	Howard Johnson	.25
7	Roger McDowell	.25
8	Darryl Strawberry	.35
----	Membership Card	.05

1992 N.Y. Mets Spring Training Superstars

A series of large-format (13-3/4" x 22-3/4") color pictures of Mets players was issued during spring training 1992 by The Port St. Lucie News and The Stuart News in Florida. The pictures are printed on heavy newspaper stock and feature color action photos with a light blue frame and white border. A box at bottom has the player's major league career stats. Various advertisements appear on back. The unnumbered pictures are listed here alphabetically and it is possible this list is not complete.

		NM/M
Complete Set (9):		35.00
Common Player:		4.00
(1)	Bobby Bonilla	4.00

(2)	Kevin Elster	4.00
(3)	John Franco	4.00
(4)	Todd Hundley	4.00
(5)	Howard Johnson	4.00
(6)	Dave Magadan	4.00
(7)	Eddie Murray	8.00
(8)	Willie Randolph	4.00
(9)	Bret Saberhagen	6.00

1997 N.Y. Mets Motion Cards

This issue was handed out to fans as a stadium promotion. The 3-1/2" x 2-1/2" cards have a borderless action scene on front, in which the players move when the card is tilted. Backs are conventionally printed with another player action photo, 1996 stats and biographical details.

		NM/M
Complete Set (4):		9.00
Common Player:		2.00
0	Rey Ordonez	3.00
1	Lance Johnson	2.00
9	Todd Hundley	2.50
31	John Franco	2.00

1982 N.Y. Yankees Yearbook

American League stars of the 1940s-1960s are featured in a two-page cardboard panel stapled into the Yankees yearbook in 1982. The cards were the work of TCMA and done in the style of early-1950s Bowman cards, although the size is the standard 2-1/2" x 3-1/2". Like the '51 Bowmans, the yearbook cards have a color painting of the player on front with his name in a black strip near the bottom. Backs have a career summary and a bit of personal data along with the TCMA copyright notice. The yearbook originally sold for $3.

		NM/M
Complete Yearbook:		18.00
Complete Set, Singles (18):		16.00
Common Player:		1.00
1	Joe DiMaggio	6.00
2	Billy Pierce	1.00
3	Phil Rizzuto	2.00
4	Ted Williams	5.00
5	Billy Martin	1.50
6	Mel Parnell	1.00
7	Harmon Killebrew	1.50
8	Yogi Berra	2.00
9	Roy Sievers	1.00
10	Bill Dickey	1.50
11	Hank Greenberg	2.00
12	Allie Reynolds	1.00
13	Joe Sewell	1.00
14	Virgil Trucks	1.00
15	Mickey Mantle	8.00
16	Boog Powell	1.00
17	Whitey Ford	1.50
18	Lou Boudreau	1.50

1985 N.Y. Yankees Police

This collectors' issue came out of Florida, where the Yankees conducted spring training. The cards were not authorized by the team, the Kiwanis Club or any police agency; they were manufactured strictly for sale to unsuspecting collectors. In format they resemble contemporary safety issues, measuring 2-5/8" x 4-1/4" with color player photos on front and an anti-

30
Willie Randolph
INFIELDER

drug message on back. Because they were unlicensed, no collector value is attributed.

2003 N.Y. Mets Spring Training

Several media outlets at the team's spring training headquarters in Port St. Luice, Fla., sponsored this set of cards as a stadium giveaway on March 12. Several of the cards are the first to show the team's newest stars in their Mets uniforms. Distributed in a paper envelope, the cards are a mix of portrait and action photos in a blank-back 3-1/8" x 4-7/8" format.

		NM/M
Complete Set (7):		15.00
Common Player:		.50
(1)	Roberto Alomar	1.50
(2)	Armando Benitez	.50
(3)	Cliff Floyd	.50
(4)	Tom Glavine	2.50
(5)	Al Leiter	.50
(6)	Mike Piazza	10.00
(7)	Mo Vaughn	1.50

2004 N.Y. Post Yankees Medallion Collection

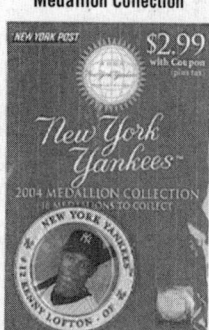

A set of 16 commemorative medallions was issued by the N.Y. Post in this early-season promotion. Coupons found in the newspaper between April 27 and May 16 could be redeemed at newsstands (along with $2.99) for that day's medallion. Larger and thicker than a quarter, the 1-3/16" diameter medals are struck in nickel and have on their fronts an enameled portrait photo. Backs have the team logo. A bronze "Next Century" medallion was available with the complete set and a colorful, photo-filled 9-1/2" x 9" album was available to house the pieces. The medals are listed here by uniform number.

		NM/M
Complete Set (16):		60.00
Common Player:		3.00
Album:		3.00
2	Derek Jeter	7.50
11	Gary Sheffield	4.50
12	Kenny Lofton	3.00
13	Alex Rodriguez	6.00
14	Enrique Wilson	3.00
20	Jorge Posada	3.00
22	Jon Lieber	3.00
25	Jason Giambi	4.50
27	Kevin Brown	3.00
33	Javier Vazquez	3.00
35	Mike Mussina	4.50
42	Mariano Rivera	4.50
51	Bernie Williams	3.00
52	Jose Contreras	3.00
55	Hideki Matsui	7.50
---	Next Century	3.00

2005 N.Y. Post Yankees Immortals Medallion Collection

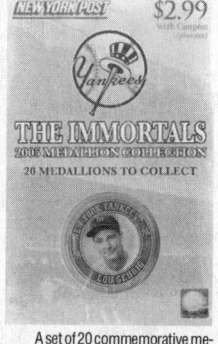

A set of 20 commemorative medallions was issued by the N.Y. Post in this promotion. Coupons found in the newspaper between April 18 and May 13 could be redeemed at newsstands (along with $2.99) for that day's medallion. Larger and thicker than a quarter, the 1-3/16" diameter medals are struck in nickel and have on their fronts an enameled portrait photo. Backs have a pinstriped jersey with the player's number. A triple-fold, colorful, photo-filled 14" x 22" album was available to house the pieces. The medals are listed here in the order of their issue.

		NM/M
Complete Set (20):		75.00
Common Player:		3.00
Album:		3.00
(1)	Lou Gehrig	7.50
(2)	Mickey Mantle	10.00
(3)	Graig Nettles	3.00
(4)	Jim "Catfish" Hunter	3.00
(5)	Reggie Jackson	5.00
(6)	Yogi Berra	5.00
(7)	Ron Guidry	3.00
(8)	Lefty Gomez	3.00
(9)	Tony Lazzeri	3.00
(10)	Phil Rizzuto	4.50
(11)	Roger Maris	4.50
(12)	Don Mattingly	4.50
(13)	Don Larsen	3.00
(14)	Elston Howard	3.00
(15)	Thurman Munson	4.50
(16)	Joe DiMaggio	7.50
(17)	Whitey Ford	4.50
(18)	Billy Martin	3.00
(19)	Casey Stengel	3.00
(20)	Babe Ruth	9.00

2004 N.Y. Yankees Collector's Series

Jorge Posada

Each spring training program sold at 2004 Yankees games at Legends Field in Tampa included one 8" x 10" color card of a current or former Yankees player. Each card was issued only on a single day, making assembly of complete sets difficult. Fronts have a large color game-action photo with the famous Yankee Stadium facade at top. Backs have biographical data, a few stats or, in the case of retired players, a career summary.

		NM/M
Complete Set (13):		75.00
Common Player:		5.00
1	Jorge Posada	6.00
2	Ron Guidry	5.00
3	Mike Mussina	5.00
4	Gary Sheffield	5.00
5	Mariano Rivera	5.00
6	Hideki Matsui	7.50
7	Don Mattingly	10.00
8	Jason Giambi	6.00
9	Reggie Jackson	6.00

10	Yogi Berra	6.00
11	Bucky Dent	5.00
12	Derek Jeter	10.00
13	Alex Rodriguez	10.00

1981 O-Pee-Chee

The Canadian version of the 1981 Topps set consists of 374 cards. This O-Pee-Chee set features many cards which note a player team change on front. These notations could be accomplished as the OPC cards were printed after the Topps. The cards measure 2-1/2" x 3-1/2" and have texts that are written in both English and French. The cards were printed on both white and gray stock. Cards with gray stock are valued 2-3X those with white stock.

NM/M

Complete Set (374): 40.00
Common Player: .10
Wax Pack (8): 2.50
Wax Box (36): 60.00

1	Frank Pastore	.10
2	Phil Huffman	.10
3	Len Barker	.10
4	Robin Yount	2.00
5	Dave Stieb	.15
6	Gary Carter	4.00
7	Butch Hobson	.10
8	Lance Parrish	.10
9	Bruce Sutter	1.50
10	Mike Flanagan	.10
11	Paul Mirabella	.10
12	Craig Reynolds	.10
13	Joe Charboneau	.50
14	Dan Driessen	.10
15	Larry Parrish	.10
16	Ron Davis	.10
17	Cliff Johnson	.10
18	Bruce Bochte	.10
19	Jim Clancy	.10
20	Bill Russell	.10
21	Ron Oester	.10
22	Danny Darwin	.10
23	Willie Aikens	.10
24	Don Stanhouse	.10
25	Sixto Lezcano	.10
26	U.L. Washington	.10
27	Champ Summers	.10
28	Enrique Romo	.10
29	Gene Tenace	.10
30	Jack Clark	.10
31	Checklist 1-125	.10
32	Ken Oberkfell	.10
33	Rick Honeycutt	.10
34	Al Bumbry	.10
35	John Tamargo	.10
36	Ed Farmer	.10
37	Gary Roenicke	.10
38	Tim Foli	.10
39	Eddie Murray	2.00
40	Roy Howell	.10
41	Bill Gullickson	.15
42	Jerry White	.10
43	Tim Blackwell	.10
44	Steve Henderson	.10
45	Enos Cabell	.10
46	Rick Bossetti	.10
47	Bill North	.10
48	Rich Gossage	.15
49	Bob Shirley	.10
50	Dave Lopes	.10
51	Shane Rawley	.10
52	Lloyd Moseby	.75
53	Burt Hooton	.10
54	Ivan DeJesus	.10
55	Mike Norris	.10
56	Del Unser	.10
57	Dave Revering	.10
58	Joel Youngblood	.10
59	Steve McCatty	.10
60	Willie Randolph	.10
61	Butch Wynegar	.10
62	Gary Lavelle	.10
63	Willie Montanez	.10
64	Terry Puhl	.10
65	Scott McGregor	.10
66	Buddy Bell	.10
67	Toby Harrah	.10
68	Jim Rice	.45
69	Darrell Evans	.10
70	Al Oliver	.10
71	Hal Dues	.10
72	Barry Evans	.10
73	Doug Bair	.10
74	Mike Hargrove	.10
75	Reggie Smith	.10
76	Mario Mendoza	.10
77	Mike Barlow	.10
78	Garth Iorg	.10
79	Jeff Reardon	1.00
80	Roger Erickson	.10
81	Dave Stapleton	.10
82	Barry Bonnell	.10
83	Dave Concepcion	.10
84	Johnnie LeMaster	.10
85	Mike Caldwell	.10
86	Wayne Gross	.10
87	Rick Camp	.10
88	Joe Lefebvre	.10
89	Darrell Jackson	.10
90	Bake McBride	.10
91	Tim Stoddard	.10
92	Mike Easler	.10
93	Jim Bibby	.10
94	Kent Tekulve	.10
95	Jim Sundberg	.10
96	Tommy John	.15
97	Chris Speier	.10
98	Clint Hurdle	.10
99	Phil Garner	.10
100	Rod Carew	2.00
101	Steve Stone	.10
102	Joe Niekro	.10
103	Jerry Martin	.10
104	Ron LeFlore	.10
105	Jose Cruz	.10
106	Don Money	.10
107	Bobby Brown	.10
108	Larry Herndon	.10
109	Dennis Eckersley	1.50
110	Carl Yastrzemski	2.50
111	Greg Minton	.10
112	Dan Schatzeder	.10
113	George Brett	4.00
114	Tom Underwood	.10
115	Roy Smalley	.10
116	Carlton Fisk	2.00
117	Pete Falcone	.10
118	Dale Murphy	1.00
119	Tippy Martinez	.10
120	Larry Bowa	.10
121	Julio Cruz	.10
122	Jim Gantner	.10
123	Al Cowens	.10
124	Jerry Garvin	.10
125	Andre Dawson	3.00
126	Charlie Leibrandt	.10
127	Willie Stargell	2.00
128	Andre Thornton	.10
129	Art Howe	.10
130	Larry Gura	.10
131	Jerry Remy	.10
132	Rick Dempsey	.10
133	Alan Trammell	.15
134	Mike LaCoss	.10
135	Gorman Thomas	.10
136	Expos Future Stars (Bobby Pate, Tim Raines, Roberto Ramos)	3.00
137	Bill Madlock	.10
138	Rich Dotson	.10
139	Oscar Gamble	.10
140	Bob Forsch	.10
141	Miguel Dilone	.10
142	Jackson Todd	.10
143	Dan Meyer	.10
144	Garry Templeton	.10
145	Mickey Rivers	.10
146	Alan Ashby	.10
147	Dale Berra	.10
148	Randy Jones	.10
149	Joe Nolan	.10
150	Mark Fidrych	.25
151	Tony Armas	.10
152	Steve Kemp	.10
153	Jerry Reuss	.10
154	Rick Langford	.10
155	Chris Chambliss	.10
156	Bob McClure	.10
157	John Wathan	.10
158	John Curtis	.10
159	Steve Howe	.10
160	Garry Maddox	.10
161	Dan Graham	.10
162	Doug Corbett	.10
163	Rob Dressler	.10
164	Bucky Dent	.10
165	Alvis Woods	.10
166	Floyd Bannister	.10
167	Lee Mazzilli	.10
168	Don Robinson	.10
169	John Mayberry	.10
170	Woodie Fryman	.10
171	Gene Richards	.10
172	Rick Burleson	.10
173	Bump Wills	.10
174	Glenn Abbott	.10
175	Dave Collins	.10
176	Mike Krukow	.10
177	Rick Monday	.10
178	Dave Parker	.10
179	Rudy May	.10
180	Pete Rose	6.00
181	Elias Sosa	.10
182	Bob Grich	.10
183	Fred Norman	.10
184	Jim Dwyer	.10
185	Dennis Leonard	.10
186	Gary Matthews	.10
187	Ron Hassey	.10
188	Doug DeCinces	.10
189	Craig Swan	.10
190	Cesar Cedeno	.10
191	Rick Sutcliffe	.10
192	Kiko Garcia	.10
193	Pete Vuckovich	.10
194	Tony Bernazard	.10
195	Keith Hernandez	.10
196	Jerry Mumphrey	.10
197	Jim Kern	.10
198	Jerry Dybzinski	.10
199	John Lowenstein	.10
200	George Foster	.10
201	Phil Niekro	1.50
202	Bill Buckner	.10
203	Steve Carlton	2.00
204	John D'Acquisto	.10
205	Rick Reuschel	.10
206	Dan Quisenberry	.10
207	Mike Schmidt	4.00
208	Bob Watson	.10
209	Jim Spencer	.10
210	Jim Palmer	1.50
211	Derrel Thomas	.10
212	Steve Nicosia	.10
213	Omar Moreno	.10
214	Richie Zisk	.10
215	Larry Hisle	.10
216	Mike Torrez	.10
217	Rich Hebner	.10
218	Britt Burns	.10
219	Ken Landreaux	.10
220	Tom Seaver	2.00
221	Bob Davis	.10
222	Jorge Orta	.10
223	Bobby Bonds	.10
224	Pat Zachry	.10
225	Ruppert Jones	.10
226	Duane Kuiper	.10
227	Rodney Scott	.10
228	Tom Paciorek	.10
229	Rollie Fingers	1.50
230	George Hendrick	.10
231	Tony Perez	2.50
232	Grant Jackson	.10
233	Damaso Garcia	.10
234	Lou Whitaker	.10
235	Scott Sanderson	.10
236	Mike Ivie	.10
237	Charlie Moore	.10
238	Blue Jays Future Stars (Luis Leal, Brian Milner, Ken Schrom)	.45
239	Rick Miller	.10
240	Nolan Ryan	9.00
241	Checklist 126-250	.10
242	Chet Lemon	.10
243	Dave Palmer	.10
244	Ellis Valentine	.10
245	Carney Lansford	.10
246	Ed Ott	.10
247	Glenn Hubbard	.10
248	Joey McLaughlin	.10
249	Jerry Narron	.10
250	Ron Guidry	.10
251	Steve Garvey	.75
252	Victor Cruz	.10
253	Bobby Murcer	.10
254	Ozzie Smith	3.00
255	John Stearns	.10
256	Bill Campbell	.10
257	Rennie Stennett	.10
258	Rick Waits	.10
259	Gary Lucas	.10
260	Ron Cey	.10
261	Rickey Henderson	8.00
262	Sammy Stewart	.10
263	Brian Downing	.10
264	Mark Bomback	.10
265	John Candelaria	.10
266	Renie Martin	.10
267	Stan Bahnsen	.10
268	Expos Team	.50
269	Ken Forsch	.10
270	Greg Luzinski	.10
271	Ron Jackson	.10
272	Wayne Garland	.10
273	Milt May	.10
274	Rick Wise	.10
275	Dwight Evans	.10
276	Sal Bando	.10
277	Alfredo Griffin	.10
278	Rick Sofield	.10
279	Bob Knepper	.10
280	Ken Griffey	.10
281	Ken Singleton	.10
282	Ernie Whitt	.10
283	Billy Sample	.10
284	Jack Morris	.10
285	Dick Ruthven	.10
286	Johnny Bench	2.00
287	Dave Smith	.10
288	Amos Otis	.10
289	Dave Goltz	.10
290	Bob Boone	.10
291	Aurelio Lopez	.10
292	Tom Hume	.10
293	Charlie Lea	.10
294	Bert Blyleven	.10
295	Hal McRae	.10
296	Bob Stanley	.10
297	Bob Bailor	.10
298	Jerry Koosman	.10
299	Eliott Maddox	.10
300	Paul Molitor	2.50
301	Matt Keough	.10
302	Pat Putnam	.10
303	Dan Ford	.10
304	John Castino	.10
305	Barry Foote	.10
306	Lou Piniella	.15
307	Gene Garber	.10
308	Rick Manning	.10
309	Don Baylor	.10
310	Vida Blue	.10
311	Doug Flynn	.10
312	Rick Rhoden	.10
313	Fred Lynn	.10
314	Rich Dauer	.10
315	Kirk Gibson	2.50
316	Ken Reitz	.10
317	Lonnie Smith	.10
318	Steve Yeager	.10
319	Rowland Office	.10
320	Tom Burgmeier	.10
321	Leon Durham	.10
322	Neil Allen	.10
323	Ray Burris	.10
324	Mike Willis	.10
325	Ray Knight	.10
326	Rafael Landestoy	.10
327	Moose Haas	.10
328	Ross Baumgarten	.10
329	Joaquin Andujar	.10
330	Frank White	.10
331	Blue Jays Team	.50
332	Dick Drago	.10
333	Sid Monge	.10
334	Joe Sambito	.10
335	Rick Cerone	.10
336	Eddie Whitson	.10
337	Sparky Lyle	.10
338	Checklist 251-374	.10
339	Jon Matlack	.10
340	Ben Oglivie	.10
341	Dwayne Murphy	.10
342	Terry Crowley	.10
343	Frank Taveras	.10
344	Steve Rogers	.10
345	Warren Cromartie	.10
346	Bill Caudill	.10
347	Harold Baines	1.50
348	Frank LaCorte	.10
349	Glenn Hoffman	.10
350	J.R. Richard	.10
351	Otto Velez	.10
352	Ted Simmons	.10
353	Terry Kennedy	.10
354	Al Hrabosky	.10
355	Bob Horner	.10
356	Cecil Cooper	.10
357	Bob Welch	.10
358	Paul Moskau	.10
359	Dave Rader	.10
360	Willie Wilson	.10
361	Dave Kingman	.10
362	Joe Rudi	.10
363	Rich Gale	.10
364	Steve Trout	.10
365	Graig Nettles	.10
366	Lamar Johnson	.10
367	Denny Martinez	.10
368	Manny Trillo	.10
369	Frank Tanana	.10
370	Reggie Jackson	2.50
371	Bill Lee	.10
372	Jay Johnstone	.10
373	Jason Thompson	.10
374	Tom Hutton	.10

Posters

Inserted inside the regular 1981 O-Pee-Chee wax packs, these full-color posters measure approximately 4-7/8" x 6-7/8". The set is complete at 24 posters and includes 12 players each from the Blue Jays and Expos. The blank-backed posters are numbered in the border below the photo where the caption is written in both French and English. The photos are surrounded by a blue border for Blue Jays players or a red border for Expos. Because they were inserted in wax packs, the posters are usually found quarter-folded; such folds are not considered in grading.

NM/M

Complete Set (24): 10.00
Common Player: .50

1	Willie Montanez	.50
2	Rodney Scott	.50
3	Chris Speier	.50
4	Larry Parrish	.50
5	Warren Cromartie	.50
6	Andre Dawson	2.00
7	Ellis Valentine	.50
8	Gary Carter	5.00
9	Steve Rogers	.50
10	Woodie Fryman	.50
11	Jerry White	.50
12	Scott Sanderson	.50
13	John Mayberry	.50
14	Damasa Garcia (Damaso)	.50
15	Alfredo Griffin	.50
16	Garth Iorg	.50
17	Alvis Woods	.50
18	Rick Bosetti	.50
19	Barry Bonnell	.50
20	Ernie Whitt	.50
21	Jim Clancy	.50
22	Dave Stieb	1.50
23	Otto Velez	.50
24	Lloyd Moseby	.50

1982 O-Pee-Chee

The 1982 O-Pee-Chee set, complete at 396 cards, is nearly identical in design to the 1982 Topps set, except the Canadian-issued cards display the O-Pee-Chee logo on the front of the card and list the player's position in both French and English. The backs of the cards, which measure the standard 2-1/2" x 3-1/2", are also bilingual. Some of the cards carry an extra line on the front indicating an off-season team change.

NM/M

Complete Set (396): 35.00
Common Player: .10
Wax Pack: 1.50
Wax Box (36): 40.00

1	Dan Spillner	.10
2	Ken Singleton/AS	.10
3	John Candelaria	.10
4	Frank Tanana	.10
5	Reggie Smith	.10
6	Rick Monday	.10
7	Scott Sanderson	.10
8	Rich Dauer	.10
9	Ron Guidry	.15
10	Ron Guidry/IA	.10
11	Tom Brookens	.10
12	Moose Haas	.10
13	Chet Lemon	.10
14	Steve Howe	.10
15	Ellis Valentine	.10
16	Toby Harrah	.10
17	Darrell Evans	.10
18	Johnny Bench	2.00
19	Ernie Whitt	.10
20	Garry Maddox	.10
21	Graig Nettles/IA	.10
22	Al Oliver/IA	.10
23	Bob Boone	.10
24	Pete Rose/IA	2.00
25	Jerry Remy	.10
26	Jorge Orta	.10
27	Bobby Bonds	.10
28	Jim Clancy	.10
29	Dwayne Murphy	.10
30	Tom Seaver	2.00
31	Tom Seaver/IA	1.50
32	Claudell Washington	.10
33	Bob Shirley	.10
34	Bob Forsch	.10
35	Willie Aikens	.10
36	Rod Carew/AS	.60
37	Willie Randolph	.10
38	Charlie Lea	.10
39	Lou Whitaker	.10
40	Dave Parker	.10
41	Dave Parker/IA	.10
42	Mark Belanger	.10
43	Rick Langford	.10
44	Rollie Fingers/IA	.10
45	Rick Cerone	.10
46	Johnny Wockenfuss	.10
47	Jack Morris/AS	.10
48	Cesar Cedeno	.10
49	Alvis Woods	.10
50	Buddy Bell	.10
51	Mickey Rivers/IA	.10
52	Steve Rogers	.10
53	Blue Jays Team	.50
54	Ron Hassey	.10
55	Rick Burleson	.10
56	Harold Baines	.10
57	Craig Reynolds	.10
58	Carlton Fisk/AS	.60
59	Jim Kern	.10
60	Tony Armas	.10
61	Warren Cromartie	.10
62	Graig Nettles	.10
63	Jerry Koosman	.10
64	Pat Zachry	.10
65	Terry Kennedy	.10
66	Richie Zisk	.10
67	Rich Gale	.10
68	Steve Carlton	2.00
69	Greg Luzinski/IA	.10
70	Tim Raines	2.00
71	Roy Lee Jackson	.10
72	Carl Yastrzemski	2.00
73	John Castino	.10
74	Joe Niekro	.10
75	Tommy John	.15
76	Dave Winfield/AS	.75
77	Miguel Dilone	.10
78	Gary Gray	.10
79	Tom Hume	.10
80	Jim Palmer	1.50
81	Jim Palmer/IA	.75
82	Vida Blue/IA	.10
83	Garth Iorg	.10
84	Rennie Stennett	.10
85	Davey Lopes/IA	.10
86	Dave Concepcion	.10
87	Matt Keough	.10
88	Jim Spencer	.10
89	Steve Henderson	.10
90	Nolan Ryan	7.50
91	Carney Lansford	.10
92	Bake McBride	.10
93	Dave Stapleton	.10
94	Expos Team	.50
95	Ozzie Smith	4.00
96	Rich Hebner	.10
97	Tim Foli	.10
98	Darrell Porter	.10
99	Barry Bonnell	.10
100	Mike Schmidt	3.00
101	Mike Schmidt/IA	1.50
102	Dan Briggs	.10
103	Al Cowens	.10
104	Grant Jackson	.10
105	Kirk Gibson	.10
106	Dan Schatzeder	.10
107	Juan Berenguer	.10
108	Jack Morris	.15
109	Dave Revering	.10
110	Carlton Fisk	2.00
111	Carlton Fisk/IA	1.00
112	Billy Sample	.10
113	Steve McCatty	.10
114	Ken Landreaux	.10
115	Gaylord Perry	1.00
116	Elias Sosa	.10
117	Rich Gossage/IA	.10
118	Expos Future Stars (Terry Francona, Brad Mills, Bryn Smith)	.25
119	Billy Almon	.10
120	Gary Lucas	.10
121	Ken Oberkfell	.10
122	Steve Carlton/IA	1.00
123	Jeff Reardon	.50
124	Bill Buckner	.10
125	Danny Ainge	2.50
126	Paul Splittorff	.10
127	Lonnie Smith	.10
128	Rudy May	.10
129	Checklist 1-132	.10
130	Julio Cruz	.10
131	Stan Bahnsen	.10
132	Pete Vuckovich	.10
133	Luis Salazar	.10
134	Dan Ford	.10
135	Denny Martinez	.10
136	Lary Sorensen	.10
137	Fergie Jenkins	1.50
138	Rick Camp	.10
139	Wayne Nordhagen	.10
140	Ron LeFlore	.10
141	Rick Sutcliffe	.10
142	Rick Waits	.10
143	Mookie Wilson	.10
144	Greg Minton	.10
145	Bob Horner	.10
146	Joe Morgan/IA	1.00
147	Larry Gura	.10
148	Alfredo Griffin	.10
149	Pat Putnam	.10
150	Ted Simmons	.10
151	Gary Matthews	.10
152	Greg Luzinski	.10
153	Mike Flanagan	.10
154	Jim Morrison	.10
155	Frank White	.10
156	Otto Velez	.10
157	Doug Corbett	.10
158	Brian Downing	.10
159	Willie Randolph/IA	.10
160	Luis Tiant	.10
161	Andre Thornton	.10
162	Amos Otis	.10

No	Player	Price
163	Paul Mirabella	.10
164	Bert Blyleven	.10
165	Rowland Office	.10
166	Gene Tenace	.10
167	Cecil Cooper	.10
168	Bruce Benedict	.10
169	Mark Clear	.10
170	Jim Bibby	.10
171	Ken Griffey Sr./IA	.10
172	Bill Gullickson	.10
173	Mike Scioscia	.10
174	Doug DeCinces	.10
175	Jerry Mumphrey	.10
176	Rollie Fingers	1.00
177	George Foster/IA	.10
178	Mitchell Page	.10
179	Steve Garvey	.50
180	Steve Garvey/IA	.25
181	Woodie Fryman	.10
182	Larry Herndon	.10
183	Frank White/IA	.10
184	Alan Ashby	.10
185	Phil Niekro	1.00
186	Leon Roberts	.10
187	Rod Carew	2.00
188	Willie Stargell/IA	1.00
189	Joel Youngblood	.10
190	J.R. Richard	.10
191	Tim Wallach	.50
192	Broderick Perkins	.10
193	Johnny Grubb	.10
194	Larry Bowa	.10
195	Paul Molitor	3.00
196	Willie Upshaw	.10
197	Roy Smalley	.10
198	Chris Speier	.10
199	Don Aase	.10
200	George Brett	3.00
201	George Brett/IA	1.50
202	Rick Manning	.10
203	Blue Jays Future Stars (Jesse Barfield, Brian Milner, Boomer Wells)	2.00
204	Rick Reuschel	.10
205	Neil Allen	.10
206	Leon Durham	.10
207	Jim Gantner	.10
208	Joe Morgan	2.00
209	Gary Lavelle	.10
210	Keith Hernandez	.10
211	Joe Charboneau	.10
212	Mario Mendoza	.10
213	Willie Randolph/AS	.10
214	Lance Parrish	.10
215	Mike Krukow	.10
216	Ron Cey	.10
217	Ruppert Jones	.10
218	Dave Lopes	.10
219	Steve Yeager	.10
220	Manny Trillo	.10
221	Dave Concepcion/IA	.10
222	Butch Wynegar	.10
223	Lloyd Moseby	.20
224	Bruce Bochte	.10
225	Ed Ott	.10
226	Checklist 133-264	.10
227	Ray Burris	.10
228	Reggie Smith/IA	.10
229	Oscar Gamble	.10
230	Willie Wilson	.10
231	Brian Kingman	.10
232	John Stearns	.10
233	Duane Kuiper	.10
234	Don Baylor	.10
235	Mike Easler	.10
236	Lou Piniella	.10
237	Robin Yount	2.00
238	Kevin Saucier	.10
239	Jon Matlack	.10
240	Bucky Dent	.10
241	Bucky Dent/IA	.10
242	Milt May	.10
243	Lee Mazzilli	.10
244	Gary Carter	3.00
245	Ken Reitz	.10
246	Scott McGregor/AS	.10
247	Pedro Guerrero	.10
248	Art Howe	.10
249	Dick Tidrow	.10
250	Tug McGraw	.10
251	Fred Lynn	.10
252	Fred Lynn/IA	.10
253	Gene Richards	.10
254	Jorge Bell	4.00
255	Tony Perez	2.50
256	Tony Perez/IA	.10
257	Rich Dotson	.10
258	Bo Diaz	.10
259	Rodney Scott	.10
260	Bruce Sutter	1.50
261	George Brett/AS	1.00
262	Rick Dempsey	.10
263	Mike Phillips	.10
264	Jerry Garvin	.10
265	Al Bumbry	.10
266	Hubie Brooks	.10
267	Vida Blue	.10
268	Rickey Henderson	3.00
269	Rick Peters	.10
270	Rusty Staub	.20
271	Sixto Lezcano	.10
272	Bump Wills	.10
273	Gary Allenson	.10
274	Randy Jones	.10
275	Bob Watson	.10
276	Dave Kingman	.10
277	Terry Puhl	.10
278	Jerry Reuss	.10
279	Sammy Stewart	.10
280	Ben Oglivie	.10
281	Kent Tekulve	.10
282	Ken Macha	.10
283	Ron Davis	.10
284	Bob Grich	.10
285	Sparky Lyle	.10
286	Rich Gossage/AS	.10
287	Dennis Eckersley	1.00
288	Garry Templeton	.10
289	Bob Stanley	.10
290	Ken Singleton	.10
291	Mickey Hatcher	.10
292	Dave Palmer	.10
293	Damaso Garcia	.10
294	Don Money	.10
295	George Hendrick	.10
296	Steve Kemp	.10
297	Dave Smith	.10
298	Bucky Dent/AS	.10
299	Steve Trout	.10
300	Reggie Jackson	2.50
301	Reggie Jackson/IA	1.00
302	Doug Flynn	.10
303	Wayne Gross	.10
304	Johnny Bench/IA	1.00
305	Don Sutton	1.00
306	Don Sutton/IA	.40
307	Mark Bomback	.10
308	Charlie Moore	.10
309	Jeff Burroughs	.10
310	Mike Hargrove	.10
311	Enos Cabell	.10
312	Lenny Randle	.10
313	Ivan DeJesus	.10
314	Bob Martinez	.10
315	Burt Hooton	.10
316	Scott McGregor	.10
317	Dick Ruthven	.10
318	Mike Heath	.10
319	Ray Knight	.10
320	Chris Chambliss	.10
321	Chris Chambliss/IA	.10
322	Ross Baumgarten	.10
323	Bill Lee	.10
324	Gorman Thomas	.10
325	Jose Cruz	.10
326	Al Oliver	.10
327	Jackson Todd	.10
328	Ed Farmer	.10
329	U.L. Washington	.10
330	Ken Griffey	.10
331	John Milner	.10
332	Don Robinson	.10
333	Cliff Johnson	.10
334	Fernando Valenzuela	.15
335	Jim Sundberg	.10
336	George Foster	.10
337	Pete Rose/AS	1.50
338	Davey Lopes/AS	.10
339	Mike Schmidt/AS	1.00
340	Dave Concepcion/AS	.10
341	Andre Dawson/AS	.25
342	George Foster/AS	.10
343	Dave Parker/AS	.10
344	Gary Carter/AS	1.00
345	Fernando Valenzuela/AS	.10
346	Tom Seaver/AS	.60
347	Bruce Sutter/AS	.75
348	Darrell Porter/IA	.10
349	Dave Collins	.10
350	Amos Otis/IA	.10
351	Frank Taveras	.10
352	Dave Winfield	3.00
353	Larry Parrish	.10
354	Roberto Ramos	.10
355	Dwight Evans	.10
356	Mickey Rivers	.10
357	Butch Hobson	.10
358	Carl Yastrzemski/IA	1.00
359	Ron Jackson	.10
360	Len Barker	.10
361	Pete Rose	4.00
362	Kevin Hickey	.10
363	Rod Carew/IA	1.00
364	Hector Cruz	.10
365	Bill Madlock	.10
366	Jim Rice	.40
367	Ron Cey (IA)	.10
368	Luis Leal	.10
369	Dennis Leonard	.10
370	Mike Norris	.10
371	Tom Paciorek	.10
372	Willie Stargell	2.00
373	Dan Driessen	.10
374	Larry Bowa/IA	.10
375	Dusty Baker	.10
376	Joey McLaughlin	.10
377	Reggie Jackson/IA	.60
378	Mike Caldwell	.10
379	Andre Dawson	1.00
380	Dave Stieb	.20
381	Alan Trammell	.10
382	John Mayberry	.10
383	John Wathan	.10
384	Hal McRae	.10
385	Ken Forsch	.10
386	Jerry White	.10
387	Tom Veryzer	.10
388	Joe Rudi	.10
389	Bob Knepper	.10
390	Eddie Murray	2.00
391	Dale Murphy	.50
392	Bob Boone/IA	.10
393	Al Hrabosky	.10
394	Checklist 265-396	.10
395	Omar Moreno	.10
396	Rich Gossage	.15

Posters

MONTREAL EXPOS — GARY CARTER

The 24 posters in this Canadian set, which features 12 players from the Expos and 12 from the Blue Jays, were inserted in regular 1982 O-Pee-Chee wax packs. The posters measure approximately 4-7/8" x 6-7/8" and are usually found quarter-folded for pack insertion. Such fold lines are not considered in grading. The blank-backed posters are numbered in the bottom border where the captions appear in both French and English. Red borders surround the photos of Blue Jays players, while blue borders are used for the Expos.

No	Player	NM/M
	Complete Set (24):	12.00
	Common Player:	.50
1	John Mayberry	.50
2	Damaso Garcia	.50
3	Ernie Whitt	.50
4	Lloyd Moseby	.50
5	Alvis Woods	.50
6	Dave Stieb	.75
7	Roy Lee Jackson	.50
8	Joey McLaughlin	.50
9	Luis Leal	.50
10	Aurelio Rodriguez	.50
11	Otto Velez	.50
12	Juan Berenger (Berenguer)	.50
13	Warren Cromartie	.50
14	Rodney Scott	.50
15	Larry Parrish	.50
16	Gary Carter	5.00
17	Tim Raines	2.00
18	Andre Dawson	2.00
19	Terry Francona	.50
20	Steve Rogers	.50
21	Bill Gullickson	.50
22	Scott Sanderson	.50
23	Jeff Reardon	.50
24	Jerry White	.50

Stickers

The Canadian OPC stickers are identical to the Topps version except for the bi-lingual printing on backs.

1983 O-Pee-Chee

CARL YASTRZEMSKI — RED SOX

Again complete at 396 cards, the 1983 O-Pee-Chee set borrows its design from the 1983 Topps set, except the Canadian-issued cards display the O-Pee-Chee logo on the front of the card and show the player's position in both French and English. The backs of the cards are also printed in both languages. The cards measure the standard 2-1/2" x 3-1/2". Some cards carry the extra line on the front indicating an off-season trade.

No	Player	NM/M
	Complete Set (396):	30.00
	Common Player:	.05
	Wax Pack:	3.00
	Wax Box (36):	60.00
1	Rusty Staub	.15
2	Larry Parrish	.10
3	George Brett	1.75
4	Carl Yastrzemski	1.50
5	Al Oliver (Super Veteran)	.05
6	Bill Virdon	.05
7	Gene Richards	.05
8	Steve Balboni	.05
9	Joey McLaughlin	.05
10	Gorman Thomas	.05
11	Chris Chambliss	.05
12	Ray Burris	.05
13	Larry Herndon	.05
14	Ozzie Smith	1.50
15	Ron Cey	.05
16	Willie Wilson	.05
17	Kent Tekulve	.05
18	Kent Tekulve (Super Veteran)	.05
19	Oscar Gamble	.05
20	Carlton Fisk	1.25
21	Dale Murphy/AS	.05
22	Randy Lerch	.05
23	Dale Murphy	.45
24	Steve Mura	.05
25	Hal McRae	.05
26	Dennis Lamp	.05
27	Ron Washington	.05
28	Bruce Bochte	.05
29	Randy Jones	.05
30	Jim Rice	.15
31	Bill Gullickson	.05
32	Dave Concepcion/AS	.05
33	Ted Simmons (Super Veteran)	.05
34	Bobby Cox	.05
35	Rollie Fingers	.60
36	Rollie Fingers (Super Veteran)	.10
37	Mike Hargrove	.05
38	Roy Smalley	.05
39	Terry Puhl	.05
40	Fernando Valenzuela	.05
41	Garry Maddox	.05
42	Dale Murray	.05
43	Bob Dernier	.05
44	Don Robinson	.05
45	John Mayberry	.05
46	Richard Dotson	.05
47	Wayne Nordhagen	.05
48	Lary Sorenson	.05
49	Willie McGee	.15
50	Bob Horner	.05
51	Rusty Staub (Super Veteran)	.05
52	Tom Seaver	1.25
53	Chet Lemon	.05
54	Scott Sanderson	.05
55	Mookie Wilson	.05
56	Reggie Jackson	1.50
57	Tim Blackwell	.05
58	Keith Moreland	.05
59	Alvis Woods	.05
60	Johnny Bench	1.25
61	Johnny Bench (Super Veteran)	.30
62	Jim Gott	.05
63	Rick Monday	.05
64	Gary Matthews	.05
65	Jack Morris	.15
66	Lou Whitaker	.05
67	U.L. Washington	.05
68	Eric Show	.05
69	Lee Lacy	.05
70	Steve Carlton	1.25
71	Steve Carlton (Super Veteran)	.10
72	Tom Paciorek	.05
73	Manny Trillo	.05
74	Tony Perez	.05
	Tony Perez (Super Veteran)	.05
75	Amos Otis	.05
76	Rick Mahler	.05
77	Hosken Powell	.05
78	Bill Caudill	.05
79	Dan Petry	.05
80	George Foster	.05
81	Joe Morgan	.05
82	Burt Hooton	.05
83	Ryne Sandberg	8.00
84	Alan Ashby	.05
85	Ken Singleton	.05
86	Tom Hume	.05
87	Dennis Leonard	.05
88	Jim Gantner	.05
89	Leon Roberts	.05
90	Jerry Reuss	.05
91	Ben Oglivie	.05
92	Sparky Lyle	.05
	Sparky Lyle (Super Veteran)	.05
93	John Castino	.05
94	Phil Niekro	.60
95	Alan Trammell	.10
96	Gaylord Perry	.05
97	Tom Herr	.05
98	Vance Law	.05
99	Dickie Noles	.05
100	Pete Rose	2.00
101	Pete Rose (Super Veteran)	.50
102	Dave Concepcion	.05
103	Darrell Porter	.05
104	Ron Guidry	.05
105	Steve Rogers/AS	.05
106	Greg Minton	.05
107	Glenn Hoffman	.05
108	Luis Leal	.05
109	Ken Griffey	.05
110	Expos Team	.05
111	Luis Pujols	.05
112	Julio Cruz	.05
113	Jim Slaton	.05
114	Jim Slaton	.05
115	Chili Davis	.05
116	Pedro Guerrero	.05
117	Mike Ivie	.05
118	Chris Welsh	.05
119	Frank Pastore	.05
120	Len Barker	.05
121	Chris Speier	.05
122	Bobby Murcer	.05
123	Bill Russell	.05
124	Lloyd Moseby	.05
125	Leon Durham	.05
126	Carl Yastrzemski (Super Veteran)	.05
127	John Candelaria	.05
128	Phil Garner	.05
129	Checklist 1-132	.05
130	Dave Stieb	.05
131	Geoff Zahn	.05
132	Todd Cruz	.05
133	Tony Pena	.05
134	Hubie Brooks	.05
135	Dwight Evans	.05
136	Willie Aikens	.05
137	Woodie Fryman	.05
138	Rick Dempsey	.05
139	Bruce Berenyi	.05
140	Willie Randolph	.05
141	Eddie Murray	1.25
142	Mike Caldwell	.05
143	Tony Gwynn	8.00
144	Tommy John	.05
	Tommy John (Super Veteran)	.05
145	Don Sutton	.60
146	Don Sutton (Super Veteran)	.10
147	Rick Manning	.05
148	George Hendrick	.05
149	Johnny Ray	.05
150	Bruce Sutter	1.00
151	Bruce Sutter (Super Veteran)	.25
152	Jay Johnstone	.05
153	Jerry Koosman	.05
154	Johnnie LeMaster	.05
155	Dan Quisenberry	.05
156	Luis Salazar	.05
157	Steve Bedrosian	.05
158	Jim Sundberg	.05
159	Gaylord Perry (Super Veteran)	.10
160	Dave Kingman	.05
161	Dave Kingman (Super Veteran)	.05
162	Mark Clear	.05
163	Cal Ripken	8.00
164	Dave Palmer	.05
165	Dan Driessen	.05
166	Tug McGraw	.05
167	Denny Martinez	.10
168	Juan Eichelberger	.05
169	Doug Flynn	.05
170	Steve Howe	.05
171	Frank White	.05
172	Mike Flanagan	.05
173	Andre Dawson/AS	.15
174	Manny Trillo/AS	.05
175	Bo Diaz	.05
176	Dave Righetti	.05
177	Harold Baines	.05
178	Vida Blue	.05
179	Luis Tiant (Super Veteran)	.05
180	Rickey Henderson	1.50
181	Rick Rhoden	.05
182	Fred Lynn	.05
183	Ed Vande Berg	.05
184	Dwayne Murphy	.05
185	Tim Lollar	.05
186	Dave Tobik	.05
187	Tug McGraw (Super Veteran)	.05
188	Rick Miller	.05
189	Dan Schatzeder	.05
190	Cecil Cooper	.05
191	Jim Beattie	.05
192	Rich Dauer	.05
193	Al Cowens	.05
194	Roy Lee Jackson	.05
195	Mike Gates	.05
196	Tommy John	.10
197	Bob Forsch	.05
198	Steve Garvey	.05
199	Brad Mills	.05
200	Rod Carew	1.25
201	Rod Carew	.05
	Rod Carew (Super Veteran)	.05
202	Blue Jays Team	.05
203	Floyd Bannister	.05
204	Bruce Benedict	.05
205	Dave Parker	.05
206	Ken Oberkfell	.05
207	Graig Nettles	.05
	Graig Nettles (Super Veteran)	.05
208	Sparky Lyle	.05
209	Jason Thompson	.05
210	Jack Clark	.05
211	Jim Kaat	.05
212	John Stearns	.05
213	Tom Burgmeier	.05
214	Jerry White	.05
215	Mario Soto	.05
216	Scott McGregor	.05
217	Tim Stoddard	.05
218	Bill Laskey	.05
219	Reggie Jackson (Super Veteran)	.05
220	Dusty Baker	.05
221	Joe Niekro	.05
222	Damaso Garcia	.05
223	John Montefusco	.05
224	Mickey Rivers	.05
225	Enos Cabell	.05
226	LaMarr Hoyt	.05
227	Tim Raines	.20
228	Joaquin Andujar	.05
229	Tim Wallach	.15
230	Fergie Jenkins	.05
231	Fergie Jenkins (Super Veteran)	.05
232	Tom Brunansky	.05
233	Ivan DeJesus	.05
234	Bryn Smith	.05
235	Claudell Washington	.05
236	Steve Renko	.05
237	Dan Norman	.05
238	Cesar Cedeno	.05
239	Dave Stapleton	.05
240	Rich Gossage	.10
241	Rich Gossage (Super Veteran)	.05
242	Bob Stanley	.05
243	Rich Gale	.05
244	Sixto Lezcano	.05
245	Steve Sax	.05
246	Jerry Mumphrey	.05
247	Dave Smith	.05
248	Bake McBride	.05
249	Checklist 133-264	.05
250	Bill Buckner	.05
251	Kent Hrbek	.05
252	Gene Tenace	.05
253	Charlie Lea	.05
254	Rick Cerone	.05
255	Gene Garber	.05
256	Gene Garber (Super Veteran)	.05
257	Jesse Barfield	.30
258	Dave Winfield	1.50
259	Don Money	.05
260	Steve Kemp	.05
261	Steve Yeager	.05
262	Keith Hernandez	.05
263	Tippy Martinez	.05
264	Joe Morgan (Super Veteran)	.05
265	Joel Youngblood	.05
266	Bruce Sutter/AS	.25
267	Terry Francona	.05
268	Neil Allen	.05
269	Ron Oester	.05
270	Dennis Eckersley	.60
271	Dale Berra	.05
272	Al Bumbry	.05
273	Lonnie Smith	.05
274	Terry Kennedy	.05
275	Ray Knight	.05
276	Mike Norris	.05
277	Rance Mulliniks	.05
278	Dan Spillner	.05
279	Bucky Dent	.05
280	Bert Blyleven	.05
281	Barry Bonnell	.05
282	Reggie Smith	.05
283	Reggie Smith (Super Veteran)	.05
284	Ted Simmons	.05
285	Lance Parrish	.05
286	Larry Christenson	.05
287	Ruppert Jones	.05
288	Bob Welch	.05
289	John Wathan	.05
290	Jeff Reardon	.05
291	Dave Revering	.05
292	Craig Swan	.05
293	Graig Nettles	.05
294	Alfredo Griffin	.05
295	Jerry Remy	.05
296	Joe Sambito	.05
297	Ron LeFlore	.05
298	Brian Downing	.05
299	Jim Palmer	1.00
300	Mike Schmidt	1.75
301	Mike Schmidt (Super Veteran)	.35
302	Ernie Whitt	.05
303	Andre Dawson	.75
304	Bobby Murcer (Super Veteran)	.05
305	Larry Bowa	.05
306	Lee Mazzilli	.05
307	Lou Piniella	.05
308	Buck Martinez	.05
309	Jerry Martin	.05
310	Greg Luzinski	.05
311	Al Oliver	.05
312	Mike Torrez	.05
313	Dick Ruthven	.05
314	Gary Carter/AS	.05
315	Rick Burleson	.05
316	Phil Niekro (Super Veteran)	.10
317	Moose Haas	.05
318	Carney Lansford	.05
319	Tim Foli	.05
320	Steve Rogers	.05
321	Kirk Gibson	.05
322	Glenn Hubbard	.05
323	Luis DeLeon	.05
324	Mike Marshall	.05
325	Von Hayes	.05
326	Garth Iorg	.05
327	Jose Cruz	.05
328	Jim Palmer (Super Veteran)	.10
329	Darrell Evans	.05
330	Buddy Bell	.05
331	Mike Krukow	.05

No.	Player	Price
332	Omar Moreno	.05
333	Dave LaRoche	.05
334	Dave LaRoche (Super Veteran)	.05
335	Bill Madlock	.05
336	Garry Templeton	.05
337	John Lowenstein	.05
338	Willie Upshaw	.05
339	Dave Hostetler	.05
340	Larry Gura	.05
341	Doug DeCinces	.05
342	Mike Schmidt/AS	.25
343	Charlie Hough	.05
344	Andre Thornton	.05
345	Jim Clancy	.05
346	Ken Forsch	.05
347	Sammy Stewart	.05
348	Alan Bannister	.05
349	Checklist 265-396	.05
350	Robin Yount	1.25
351	Warren Cromartie	.05
352	Tim Raines/AS	.05
353	Tony Armas	.05
354	Tom Seaver (Super Veteran)	.30
355	Tony Perez	1.00
356	Toby Harrah	.05
357	Dan Ford	.05
358	Charlie Puleo	.05
359	Dave Collins	.05
360	Nolan Ryan	6.00
361	Nolan Ryan (Super Veteran)	2.50
362	Bill Almon	.05
363	Eddie Milner	.05
364	Gary Lucas	.05
365	Dave Lopes	.05
366	Bob Boone	.05
367	Biff Pocoroba	.05
368	Richie Zisk	.05
369	Tony Bernazard	.05
370	Gary Carter	1.50
371	Paul Molitor	1.50
372	Art Howe	.05
373	Pete Rose/AS	.50
374	Glenn Adams	.05
375	Pete Vukovich	.05
376	Gary Lavelle	.05
377	Lee May	.05
378	Lee May (Super Veteran)	.05
379	Butch Wynegar	.05
380	Ron Davis	.05
381	Bob Grich	.05
382	Gary Roenicke	.05
383	Jim Kaat	.10
384	Steve Carlton/AS	.05
385	Mike Easler	.05
386	Rod Carew/AS	.05
387	Bobby Grich/AS	.05
388	George Brett/AS	.25
389	Robin Yount/AS	.05
390	Reggie Jackson/AS	.05
391	Rickey Henderson/AS	.25
392	Fred Lynn/AS	.05
393	Carlton Fisk/AS	.05
394	Pete Vuckovich/AS	.05
395	Larry Gura /AS	.05
396	Dan Quisenberry/AS	.05

1984 O-Pee-Chee

Almost identical in design to the 1984 Topps set, the 1984 O-Pee-Chee set contains 396 cards. The O-Pee-Chee cards display the Canadian company's logo in the upper right corner and the backs of the cards are printed in both English and French. The cards measure 2-1/2" x 3-1/2", and some include the extra line on the front of the card to indicate a trade.

		NM/M
Complete Set (396):		22.50
Common Player:		.05
Wax Pack:		1.00
Wax Box (36):		25.00
1	Pascual Perez	.10
2	Cal Ripken	6.00
3	Lloyd Moseby	.15
4	Mel Hall	.05
5	Willie Wilson	.05
6	Mike Morgan	.05
7	Gary Lucas	.05
8	Don Mattingly	8.00
9	Jim Gott	.05
10	Robin Yount	1.50

No.	Player	Price
11	Joey McLaughlin	.05
12	Billy Sample	.05
13	Oscar Gamble	.05
14	Bill Russell	.05
15	Burt Hooton	.05
16	Omar Moreno	.05
17	Dave Lopes	.05
18	Dale Berra	.05
19	Rance Mulliniks	.05
20	Greg Luzinski	.05
21	Doug Sisk	.05
22	Don Robinson	.05
23	Keith Moreland	.05
24	Richard Dotson	.05
25	Glenn Hubbard	.05
26	Rod Carew	1.50
27	Alan Wiggins	.05
28	Frank Viola	.05
29	Phil Niekro	1.00
30	Wade Boggs	2.50
31	Dave Parker	.05
32	Bobby Ramos	.05
33	Tom Burgmeier	.05
34	Eddie Milner	.05
35	Don Sutton	1.00
36	Glenn Wilson	.05
37	Mike Krukow	.05
38	Dave Collins	.05
39	Garth Iorg	.05
40	Dusty Baker	.05
41	Tony Bernazard	.05
42	Claudell Washington	.05
43	Cecil Cooper	.05
44	Dan Driessen	.05
45	Jerry Mumphrey	.05
46	Rick Rhoden	.05
47	Rudy Law	.05
48	Julio Franco	.05
49	Mike Norris	.05
50	Chris Chambliss	.05
51	Pete Falcone	.05
52	Mike Marshall	.05
53	Amos Otis	.05
54	Jesse Orosco	.05
55	Dave Concepcion	.05
56	Gary Allenson	.05
57	Dan Schatzeder	.05
58	Jerry Remy	.05
59	Carney Lansford	.05
60	Paul Molitor	2.50
61	Chris Codiroli	.05
62	Dave Hostetler	.05
63	Ed Vande Berg	.05
64	Ryne Sandberg	2.50
65	Kirk Gibson	.05
66	Nolan Ryan	6.00
67	Gary Ward	.05
68	Luis Salazar	.05
69	Dan Quisenberry	.05
70	Gary Matthews	.05
71	Pete O'Brien	.05
72	John Wathan	.05
73	Jody Davis	.05
74	Kent Tekulve	.05
75	Bob Forsch	.05
76	Alfredo Griffin	.05
77	Bryn Smith	.05
78	Mike Torrez	.05
79	Mike Hargrove	.05
80	Steve Rogers	.05
81	Bake McBride	.05
82	Doug DeCinces	.05
83	Richie Zisk	.05
84	Randy Bush	.05
85	Atlee Hammaker	.05
86	Chet Lemon	.05
87	Frank Pastore	.05
88	Alan Trammell	.05
89	Terry Francona	.05
90	Pedro Guerrero	.05
91	Dan Spillner	.05
92	Lloyd Moseby	.05
93	Bob Knepper	.05
94	Ted Simmons	.05
95	Aurelio Lopez	.05
96	Bill Buckner	.05
97	LaMarr Hoyt	.05
98	Tom Brunansky	.05
99	Ron Oester	.05
100	Reggie Jackson	1.50
101	Ron Davis	.05
102	Ken Oberkfell	.05
103	Dwayne Murphy	.05
104	Jim Slaton	.05
105	Tony Armas	.05
106	Ernie Whitt	.05
107	Johnnie LeMaster	.05
108	Randy Moffitt	.05
109	Terry Forster	.05
110	Ron Guidry	.05
111	Bill Virdon	.05
112	Doyle Alexander	.05
113	Lonnie Smith	.05
114	Checklist	.05
115	Andre Thornton	.05
116	Jeff Reardon	.15
117	Tom Herr	.05
118	Charlie Hough	.05
119	Phil Garner	.05
120	Keith Hernandez	.05
121	Rich Gossage	.10
122	Ted Simmons	.05
123	Butch Wynegar	.05
124	Damaso Garcia	.05
125	Britt Burns	.05
126	Bert Blyleven	.05
127	Carlton Fisk	1.50
128	Rick Manning	.05
129	Bill Laskey	.05
130	Ozzie Smith	2.50
131	Bo Diaz	.05
132	Tom Paciorek	.05
133	Dave Rozema	.05
134	Dave Stieb	.15
135	Brian Downing	.05
136	Rick Camp	.05
137	Willie Aikens	.05
138	Charlie Moore	.05
139	George Frazier	.05
140	Storm Davis	.05
141	Glenn Hoffman	.05
142	Charlie Lea	.05
143	Mike Vail	.05
144	Steve Sax	.05
145	Gary Lavelle	.05
146	Gorman Thomas	.05
147	Dan Petry	.05
148	Mark Clear	.05
149	Dave Beard	.05
150	Dale Murphy	.75
151	Steve Trout	.05
152	Tony Pena	.05
153	Geoff Zahn	.05
154	Dave Henderson	.05
155	Frank White	.05
156	Dick Ruthven	.05
157	Gary Gaetti	.05
158	Lance Parrish	.05
159	Joe Price	.05
160	Mario Soto	.05
161	Tug McGraw	.05
162	Bob Ojeda	.05
163	George Hendrick	.05
164	Scott Sanderson	.05
165	Ken Singleton	.05
166	Terry Kennedy	.05
167	Gene Garber	.05
168	Juan Bonilla	.05
169	Larry Parrish	.05
170	Jerry Reuss	.05
171	John Tudor	.05
172	Dave Kingman	.05
173	Garry Templeton	.05
174	Bob Boone	.05
175	Graig Nettles	.05
176	Lee Smith	.05
177	LaMarr Hoyt	.05
178	Bill Krueger	.05
179	Buck Martinez	.05
180	Manny Trillo	.05
181	Lou Whitaker	.05
182	Darryl Strawberry	1.00
183	Neil Allen	.05
184	Jim Rice	.25
185	Sixto Lezcano	.05
186	Tom Hume	.05
187	Garry Maddox	.05
188	Bryan Little	.05
189	Jose Cruz	.05
190	Ben Oglivie	.05
191	Cesar Cedeno	.05
192	Nick Esasky	.05
193	Ken Forsch	.05
194	Jim Palmer	1.25
195	Jack Morris	.15
196	Steve Howe	.05
197	Harold Baines	.05
198	Bill Doran	.05
199	Willie Hernandez	.05
200	Andre Dawson	1.25
201	Bruce Kison	.05
202	Bobby Cox	.05
203	Matt Keough	.05
204	Ron Guidry	.05
205	Greg Minton	.05
206	Al Holland	.05
207	Luis Leal	.05
208	Jose Oquendo	.05
209	Leon Durham	.05
210	Joe Morgan	1.50
211	Lou Whitaker/AS	.05
212	George Brett/AS	.75
213	Bruce Hurst	.05
214	Steve Carlton	1.50
215	Tippy Martinez	.05
216	Ken Landreaux	.05
217	Alan Ashby	.05
218	Dennis Eckersley	1.00
219	Craig McMurtry	.05
220	Fernando Valenzuela	.05
221	Cliff Johnson	.05
222	Rick Honeycutt	.05
223	George Brett	3.00
224	Rusty Staub	.20
225	Lee Mazzilli	.05
226	Pat Putnam	.05
227	Bob Welch	.05
228	Rick Cerone	.05
229	Lee Lacy	.05
230	Rickey Henderson	2.50
231	Gary Redus	.05
232	Tim Wallach	.25
233	Checklist	.05
234	Rafael Ramirez	.05
235	Matt Young	.05
236	Ellis Valentine	.05
237	John Castino	.05
238	Eric Show	.05
239	Bob Horner	.05
240	Eddie Murray	1.50
241	Billy Almon	.05
242	Greg Brock	.05
243	Bruce Sutter	1.00
244	Dwight Evans	.05
245	Rick Sutcliffe	.05
246	Terry Crowley	.05
247	Fred Lynn	.05
248	Bill Dawley	.05
249	Dave Stapleton	.05
250	Bill Madlock	.05
251	Jim Sundberg	.05
252	Steve Yeager	.05
253	Jim Wohlford	.05
254	Shane Rawley	.05
255	Bruce Benedict	.05
256	Dave Geisel	.05
257	Julio Cruz	.05
258	Luis Sanchez	.05
259	Von Hayes	.05
260	Scott McGregor	.05
261	Tom Seaver	1.50
262	Doug Flynn	.05
263	Wayne Gross	.05
264	Larry Gura	.05
265	John Montefusco	.05
266	Dave Winfield/AS	1.00
267	Tim Lollar	.05
268	Ron Washington	.05
269	Mickey Rivers	.05
270	Mookie Wilson	.05
271	Moose Haas	.05
272	Rick Dempsey	.05
273	Dan Quisenberry	.05
274	Steve Henderson	.05
275	Len Matuszek	.05
276	Frank Tanana	.05
277	Dave Righetti	.05
278	Jorge Bell	.35
279	Ivan DeJesus	.05
280	Floyd Bannister	.05
281	Dale Murray	.05
282	Andre Robertson	.05
283	Rollie Fingers	1.00
284	Tommy John	.10
285	Darrell Porter	.05
286	Lary Sorensen	.05
287	Warren Cromartie	.05
288	Jim Beattie	.05
289	Blue Jays Team	.25
290	Dave Dravecky	.05
291	Eddie Murray/AS	.50
292	Greg Bargar	.05
293	Tom Underwood	.05
294	U.L. Washington	.05
295	Mike Flanagan	.05
296	Rich Gedman	.05
297	Bruce Berenyi	.05
298	Jim Gantner	.05
299	Bill Caudill	.05
300	Pete Rose	4.00
301	Steve Kemp	.05
302	Barry Bonnell	.05
303	Joel Youngblood	.05
304	Rick Langford	.05
305	Roy Smalley	.05
306	Ken Griffey	.05
307	Al Oliver	.05
308	Ron Hassey	.05
309	Len Barker	.05
310	Willie McGee	.05
311	Jerry Koosman	.05
312	Jorge Orta	.05
313	Pete Vuckovich	.05
314	George Wright	.05
315	Bob Grich	.05
316	Jesse Barfield	.25
317	Willie Upshaw	.05
318	Bill Gullickson	.10
319	Ray Burris	.05
320	Bob Stanley	.05
321	Ray Knight	.05
322	Ken Schrom	.05
323	Johnny Ray	.05
324	Brian Giles	.05
325	Darrell Evans	.05
326	Mike Caldwell	.05
327	Ruppert Jones	.05
328	Chris Speier	.05
329	Bobby Castillo	.05
330	John Candelaria	.05
331	Bucky Dent	.05
332	Expos Team	.25
333	Larry Herndon	.05
334	Chuck Rainey	.05
335	Don Baylor	.05
336	Bob James	.05
337	Jim Clancy	.05
338	Duane Kuiper	.05
339	Roy Lee Jackson	.05
340	Hal McRae	.05
341	Larry McWilliams	.05
342	Tim Foli	.05
343	Fergie Jenkins	2.00
344	Dickie Thon	.05
345	Kent Hrbek	.05
346	Larry Bowa	.05
347	Buddy Bell	.05
348	Toby Harrah	.05
349	Dan Ford	.05
350	George Foster	.05
351	Lou Piniella	.05
352	Dave Stewart	.25
353	Mike Easler	.05
354	Jeff Burroughs	.05
355	Jason Thompson	.05
356	Glenn Abbott	.05
357	Ron Cey	.05
358	Bob Dernier	.05
359	Jim Acker	.05
360	Willie Randolph	.05
361	Mike Schmidt	3.00
362	David Green	.05
363	Cal Ripken Jr./AS	2.00
364	Jim Rice/AS	.05
365	Steve Bedrosian	.05
366	Gary Carter	2.50
367	Chili Davis	.05
368	Hubie Brooks	.05
369	Steve McCatty	.05
370	Tim Raines	.35
371	Joaquin Andujar	.05
372	Gary Roenicke	.05
373	Ron Kittle	.05
374	Rich Dauer	.05
375	Dennis Leonard	.05
376	Rick Burleson	.05
377	Eric Rasmussen	.05
378	Dave Winfield	2.50
379	Checklist	.05
380	Steve Garvey	.50
381	Jack Clark	.05
382	Odell Jones	.05
383	Terry Puhl	.05
384	Joe Niekro	.05
385	Tony Perez	2.00
386	George Hendrick/AS	.05
387	Johnny Ray/AS	.05
388	Mike Schmidt/AS	.75
389	Ozzie Smith/AS	.75
390	Tim Raines/AS	.25
391	Dale Murphy/AS	.25
392	Andre Dawson/AS	.35
393	Gary Carter/AS	1.00
394	Steve Rogers/AS	.15
395	Steve Carlton/AS	.50
396	Jesse Orosco/AS	.05

Stickers

83 RICK MONDAY	357 PETE O'BRIEN

Bi-lingual backs are the only difference between the OPC 1984 sticker set and the Topps issue. The sets share a checklist and, generally, values, although some Blue Jays and Expos stars may command a small premium in the Canadian version.

1985 O-Pee-Chee

This 396-card set is almost identical in design to the 1985 Topps set. Measuring 2-1/2" x 3-1/2", the fronts of the Canadian-issued cards display the O-Pee-Chee logo in the upper left corner, and the backs of the cards are printed in both French and English. A "traded" line appears on the front of some of the cards to indicate a change in teams.

		NM/M
Complete Set (396):		15.00
Common Player:		.05
Wax Pack (15):		1.50
Wax Box (36):		40.00
1	Tom Seaver	1.50
2	Gary Lavelle	.05
3	Tim Wallach	.15
4	Jim Wohlford	.05
5	Jeff Robinson	.05
6	Willie Wilson	.05
7	Cliff Johnson	.05
8	Willie Randolph	.05
9	Larry Herndon	.05
10	Kirby Puckett	4.00
11	Mookie Wilson	.05
12	Dave Lopes	.05
13	Tim Lollar	.05
14	Chris Bando	.05
15	Jerry Koosman	.05
16	Bobby Meacham	.05
17	Mike Scott	.05
18	Rich Gedman	.05
19	George Frazier	.05
20	Chet Lemon	.05
21	Dave Concepcion	.05
22	Jason Thompson	.05
23	Bret Saberhagen	.05
24	Jesse Barfield	.15
25	Steve Bedrosian	.05
26	Roy Smalley	.05
27	Bruce Berenyi	.05
28	Butch Wynegar	.05
29	Alan Ashby	.05
30	Cal Ripken	4.00
31	Luis Leal	.05
32	Dave Dravecky	.05
33	Tito Landrum	.05
34	Pedro Guerrero	.05
35	Graig Nettles	.05
36	Fred Breining	.05
37	Roy Lee Jackson	.05
38	Steve Henderson	.05
39	Gary Pettis	.05
40	Phil Niekro	.75
41	Dwight Gooden	.10
42	Luis Sanchez	.05
43	Lee Smith	.05
44	Dickie Thon	.05
45	Greg Minton	.05
46	Mike Flanagan	.05
47	Bud Black	.05
48	Tony Fernandez	.05
49	Carlton Fisk	1.50
50	John Candelaria	.05
51	Bob Watson	.05
52	Rick Leach	.05
53	Rick Rhoden	.05
54	Cesar Cedeno	.05
55	Frank Tanana	.05
56	Larry Bowa	.05
57	Willie McGee	.05
58	Rich Dauer	.05
59	Jorge Bell	.35
60	George Hendrick	.05
61	Donnie Moore	.05
62	Mike Ramsey	.05
63	Nolan Ryan	4.00
64	Mark Bailey	.05
65	Bill Buckner	.05
66	Jerry Reuss	.05
67	Mike Schmidt	2.50
68	Von Hayes	.05
69	Phil Bradley	.05
70	Don Baylor	.05
71	Julio Cruz	.05
72	Rick Sutcliffe	.05
73	Storm Davis	.05
74	Mike Krukow	.05
75	Willie Upshaw	.05
76	Craig Lefferts	.05
77	Lloyd Moseby	.05
78	Ron Davis	.05
79	Rick Mahler	.05
80	Keith Hernandez	.05
81	Vance Law	.05
82	Joe Price	.05
83	Dennis Lamp	.05
84	Gary Ward	.05
85	Mike Marshall	.05
86	Marvell Wynne	.05
87	David Green	.05
88	Bryn Smith	.05
89	Sixto Lezcano	.05
90	Rich Gossage	.10
91	Jeff Burroughs	.05
92	Bobby Brown	.05
93	Oscar Gamble	.05
94	Rick Dempsey	.05
95	Jose Cruz	.05
96	Johnny Ray	.05
97	Joel Youngblood	.05
98	Eddie Whitson	.05
99	Milt Wilcox	.05
100	George Brett	2.50
101	Jim Acker	.05
102	Jim Sundberg	.05
103	Ozzie Virgil	.05
104	Mike Fitzgerald	.05
105	Ron Kittle	.05
106	Pascual Perez	.05
107	Barry Bonnell	.05
108	Lou Whitaker	.05
109	Gary Roenicke	.05
110	Alejandro Pena	.05
111	Doug DeCinces	.05
112	Doug Flynn	.05
113	Tom Herr	.05
114	Bob James	.05
115	Rickey Henderson	2.00
116	Pete Rose	3.00
117	Greg Gross	.05
118	Eric Show	.05
119	Buck Martinez	.05
120	Steve Kemp	.05
121	Checklist 1-132	.05
122	Tom Brunansky	.05
123	Dave Kingman	.05
124	Garry Templeton	.05
125	Kent Tekulve	.05
126	Darryl Strawberry	.05
127	Mark Gubicza	.05
128	Ernie Whitt	.05
129	Don Robinson	.05
130	Al Oliver	.05
131	Mario Soto	.05
132	Jeff Leonard	.05
133	Andre Dawson	.35
134	Bruce Hurst	.05
135	Bobby Cox	.05
136	Matt Young	.05
137	Bob Forsch	.05
138	Ron Darling	.05
139	Steve Trout	.05
140	Geoff Zahn	.05
141	Ken Forsch	.05
142	Jerry Willard	.05
143	Bill Gullickson	.05
144	Mike Mason	.05

#	Player	Price
145	Alvin Davis	.05
146	Gary Redus	.05
147	Willie Aikens	.05
148	Steve Yeager	.05
149	Dickie Noles	.05
150	Jim Rice	.25
151	Moose Haas	.05
152	Steve Balboni	.05
153	Frank LaCorte	.05
154	Argenis Salazar	.05
155	Bob Grich	.05
156	Craig Reynolds	.05
157	Bill Madlock	.05
158	Pat Tabler	.05
159	Don Slaught	.05
160	Lance Parrish	.05
161	Ken Schrom	.05
162	Wally Backman	.05
163	Dennis Eckersley	.75
164	Dave Collins	.05
165	Dusty Baker	.05
166	Claudell Washington	.05
167	Rick Camp	.05
168	Garth Iorg	.05
169	Shane Rawley	.05
170	George Foster	.05
171	Tony Bernazard	.05
172	Don Sutton	.75
173	Jerry Remy	.05
174	Rick Honeycutt	.05
175	Dave Parker	.05
176	Buddy Bell	.05
177	Steve Garvey	.20
178	Miguel Dilone	.05
179	Tommy John	.10
180	Dave Winfield	2.00
181	Alan Trammell	.05
182	Rollie Fingers	.75
183	Larry McWilliams	.05
184	Carmen Castillo	.05
185	Al Holland	.05
186	Jerry Mumphrey	.05
187	Chris Chambliss	.05
188	Jim Clancy	.05
189	Glenn Wilson	.05
190	Rusty Staub	.05
191	Ozzie Smith	2.00
192	Howard Johnson	.05
193	Jimmy Key	1.00
194	Terry Kennedy	.05
195	Glenn Hubbard	.05
196	Pete O'Brien	.05
197	Keith Moreland	.05
198	Eddie Milner	.05
199	Dave Engle	.05
200	Reggie Jackson	1.50
201	Burt Hooton	.05
202	Gorman Thomas	.05
203	Larry Parrish	.05
204	Bob Stanley	.05
205	Steve Rogers	.05
206	Phil Garner	.05
207	Ed Vande Berg	.05
208	Jack Clark	.05
209	Bill Campbell	.05
210	Gary Matthews	.05
211	Dave Palmer	.05
212	Tony Perez	1.50
213	Sammy Stewart	.05
214	John Tudor	.05
215	Bob Brenly	.05
216	Jim Gantner	.05
217	Bryan Clark	.05
218	Doyle Alexander	.05
219	Bo Diaz	.05
220	Fred Lynn	.05
221	Eddie Murray	1.50
222	Hubie Brooks	.05
223	Tom Hume	.05
224	Al Cowens	.05
225	Mike Boddicker	.05
226	Len Matuszek	.05
227	Danny Darwin	.05
228	Scott McGregor	.05
229	Dave LaPoint	.05
230	Gary Carter	2.00
231	Joaquin Andujar	.05
232	Rafael Ramirez	.05
233	Wayne Gross	.05
234	Neil Allen	.05
235	Gary Maddox	.05
236	Mark Thurmond	.05
237	Julio Franco	.05
238	Ray Burris	.05
239	Tim Teufel	.05
240	Dave Stieb	.15
241	Brett Butler	.05
242	Greg Brock	.05
243	Barbaro Garbey	.05
244	Greg Walker	.05
245	Chili Davis	.05
246	Darrell Porter	.05
247	Tippy Martinez	.05
248	Terry Forster	.05
249	Harold Baines	.05
250	Jesse Orosco	.05
251	Brad Gulden	.05
252	Mike Hargrove	.05
253	Nick Esasky	.05
254	Frank Williams	.05
255	Lonnie Smith	.05
256	Daryl Sconiers	.05
257	Bryan Little	.05
258	Terry Francona	.05
259	Mark Langston	.15
260	Dave Righetti	.05
261	Checklist 133-264	.05
262	Bob Horner	.05

#	Player	Price
263	Mel Hall	.05
264	John Shelby	.05
265	Juan Samuel	.05
266	Frank Viola	.05
267	Jim Fanning	.05
268	Dick Ruthven	.05
269	Bobby Ramos	.05
270	Dan Quisenberry	.05
271	Dwight Evans	.05
272	Andre Thornton	.05
273	Orel Hershiser	.50
274	Ray Knight	.05
275	Bill Caudill	.05
276	Charlie Hough	.05
277	Tim Raines	.25
278	Mike Squires	.05
279	Alex Trevino	.05
280	Ron Romanick	.05
281	Tom Niedenfuer	.05
282	Mike Stenhouse	.05
283	Terry Puhl	.05
284	Hal McRae	.05
285	Dan Driessen	.05
286	Rudy Law	.05
287	Walt Terrell	.05
288	Jeff Kunkel	.05
289	Bob Knepper	.05
290	Cecil Cooper	.05
291	Bob Welch	.05
292	Frank Pastore	.05
293	Dan Schatzeder	.05
294	Tom Nieto	.05
295	Joe Niekro	.05
296	Ryne Sandberg	2.00
297	Gary Lucas	.05
298	John Castino	.05
299	Bill Doran	.05
300	Rod Carew	1.50
301	John Montefusco	.05
302	Johnnie LeMaster	.05
303	Jim Beattie	.05
304	Gary Gaetti	.05
305	Dale Berra	.05
306	Rick Reuschel	.05
307	Ken Oberkfell	.05
308	Kent Hrbek	.05
309	Mike Witt	.05
310	Manny Trillo	.05
311	Jim Gott	.05
312	LaMarr Hoyt	.05
313	Dave Schmidt	.05
314	Ron Oester	.05
315	Doug Sisk	.05
316	John Lowenstein	.05
317	Derrel Thomas	.05
318	Ted Simmons	.05
319	Darrell Evans	.05
320	Dale Murphy	.50
321	Ricky Horton	.05
322	Ken Phelps	.05
323	Lee Mazzilli	.05
324	Don Mattingly	2.50
325	John Denny	.05
326	Ken Singleton	.05
327	Brook Jacoby	.05
328	Greg Luzinski	.05
329	Bob Ojeda	.05
330	Leon Durham	.05
331	Bill Laskey	.05
332	Ben Oglivie	.05
333	Willie Hernandez	.05
334	Bob Dernier	.05
335	Bruce Benedict	.05
336	Rance Mulliniks	.05
337	Rick Cerone	.05
338	Britt Burns	.05
339	Danny Heep	.05
340	Robin Yount	1.50
341	Andy Van Slyke	.05
342	Curt Wilkerson	.05
343	Bill Russell	.05
344	Dave Henderson	.05
345	Charlie Lea	.05
346	Terry Pendleton	.05
347	Carney Lansford	.05
348	Bob Boone	.05
349	Mike Easler	.05
350	Wade Boggs	2.00
351	Atlee Hammaker	.05
352	Joe Morgan	1.50
353	Damaso Garcia	.05
354	Floyd Bannister	.05
355	Bert Blyleven	.05
356	John Butcher	.05
357	Fernando Valenzuela	.05
358	Tony Pena	.05
359	Mike Smithson	.05
360	Steve Carlton	1.50
361	Alfredo Griffin	.05
362	Craig McMurtry	.05
363	Bill Dawley	.05
364	Richard Dotson	.05
365	Carmelo Martinez	.05
366	Ron Cey	.05
367	Tony Scott	.05
368	Dave Bergman	.05
369	Steve Sax	.05
370	Bruce Sutter	1.00
371	Mickey Rivers	.05
372	Kirk Gibson	.05
373	Scott Sanderson	.05
374	Brian Downing	.05
375	Jeff Reardon	.15
376	Frank DiPino	.05
377	Checklist 265-396	.05
378	Alan Wiggins	.05
379	Charles Hudson	.05
380	Ken Griffey	.05

#	Player	Price
381	Tom Paciorek	.05
382	Jack Morris	.15
383	Tony Gwynn	2.00
384	Jody Davis	.05
385	Jose DeLeon	.05
386	Bob Kearney	.05
387	George Wright	.05
388	Ron Guidry	.05
389	Rick Manning	.05
390	Sid Fernandez	.05
391	Bruce Bochte	.05
392	Dan Petry	.05
393	Tim Stoddard	.05
394	Tony Armas	.05
395	Paul Molitor	2.00
396	Mike Heath	.05

Posters

TORONTO BLUE JAYS
Photo: DAMASO GARCIA #7

The 1985 O-Pee-Chee poster set consists of 12 players each from the Expos and Blue Jays. The blank-backed posters measure approximately 4-7/8" x 6-7/8" and generally have fold marks because they were inserted in the OPC wax packs. The card number, written in both French and English, appears in the bottom border. The full-color player photos are surrounded by a red border for Expos and a blue border for Blue Jays.

		NM/M
Complete Set (24):		9.00
Common Player:		.50
1	Mike Fitzgerald	.50
2	Dan Driessen	.50
3	Dave Palmer	.50
4	U.L. Washington	.50
5	Hubie Brooks	.75
6	Tim Wallach	.50
7	Tim Raines	2.50
8	Herm Winningham	.50
9	Andre Dawson	2.50
10	Charlie Lea	.50
11	Steve Rogers	.50
12	Jeff Reardon	.60
13	Buck Martinez	.50
14	Willie Upshaw	.50
15	Damaso Garcia	.50
16	Tony Fernandez	1.00
17	Rance Mulliniks	.50
18	George Bell	1.00
19	Lloyd Moseby	.50
20	Jesse Barfield	.60
21	Doyle Alexander	.50
22	Dave Stieb	.85
23	Bill Caudill	.50
24	Gary Lavelle	.50

Stickers

Bi-lingual backs are the only difference between the OPC 1985 sticker set and the Topps issue. The sets share a checklist and, generally, values, although some Blue Jays and Expos stars may command a small premium in the Canadian version.

1986 O-Pee-Chee

EXPOS
RAZOR SHINES
O-Pee-Chee

As usual, the 1986 O-Pee-Chee set was issued in close simulation of the Topps cards for the same year. The 396 cards in the set are 2-1/2" x 3-1/2" and use almost all of the same

pictures as the Topps set. The O-Pee-Chee cards, being a Canadian issue, list player information in both English and French. There is an abundance of players from the two Canadian teams - Toronto and Montreal. As the O-Pee-Chee set was issued later in the year than the Topps regular issue, players who changed teams after the printing date are noted with a traded line at the bottom of the player photo. O-Pee-Chee's logo appears in the upper right of each card front.

		NM/M
Complete Set (396):		12.00
Common Player:		.05
Wax Box (36):		16.00
1	Pete Rose	1.50
2	Ken Landreaux	.05
3	Rob Picciolo	.05
4	Steve Garvey	.10
5	Andy Hawkins	.05
6	Rudy Law	.05
7	Lonnie Smith	.05
8	Dwayne Murphy	.05
9	Moose Haas	.05
10	Tony Gwynn	1.00
11	Bob Ojeda	.05
12	Jose Uribe	.05
13	Bob Kearney	.05
14	Julio Cruz	.05
15	Eddie Whitson	.05
16	Rick Schu	.05
17	Mike Stenhouse	.05
18	Lou Thornton	.05
19	Ryne Sandberg	1.00
20	Lou Whitaker	.05
21	Mark Brouhard	.05
22	Gary Lavelle	.05
23	Manny Lee	.05
24	Don Slaught	.05
25	Willie Wilson	.05
26	Mike Marshall	.05
27	Ray Knight	.05
28	Mario Soto	.05
29	Dave Anderson	.05
30	Eddie Murray	.75
31	Dusty Baker	.05
32	Steve Yeager	.05
33	Andy Van Slyke	.05
34	Dave Righetti	.05
35	Jeff Reardon	.05
36	Burt Hooton	.05
37	Johnny Ray	.05
38	Glenn Hoffman	.05
39	Rick Mahler	.05
40	Ken Griffey	.05
41	Brad Wellman	.05
42	Joe Hesketh	.05
43	Mark Salas	.05
44	Jorge Orta	.05
45	Damaso Garcia	.05
46	Jim Acker	.05
47	Bill Madlock	.05
48	Bill Almon	.05
49	Rick Manning	.05
50	Dan Quisenberry	.05
51	Jim Gantner	.05
52	Kevin Bass	.05
53	Len Dykstra	.05
54	John Franco	.05
55	Fred Lynn	.05
56	Jim Morrison	.05
57	Bill Doran	.05
58	Leon Durham	.05
59	Andre Thornton	.05
60	Dwight Evans	.05
61	Larry Herndon	.05
62	Bob Boone	.05
63	Kent Hrbek	.05
64	Floyd Bannister	.05
65	Harold Baines	.05
66	Pat Tabler	.05
67	Carmelo Martinez	.05
68	Ed Lynch	.05
69	George Foster	.05
70	Dave Winfield	1.00
71	Ken Schrom	.05
72	Toby Harrah	.05
73	Jackie Gutierrez	.05
74	Rance Mulliniks	.05
75	Jose DeLeon	.05
76	Ron Romanick	.05
77	Charlie Leibrandt	.05
78	Bruce Benedict	.05
79	Dave Schmidt	.05
80	Darryl Strawberry	.05
81	Wayne Krenchicki	.05
82	Tippy Martinez	.05
83	Phil Garner	.05
84	Darrell Porter	.05
85	Tony Perez	1.00
86	Tom Waddell	.05
87	Tim Hulett	.05
88	Barbaro Garbey	.05
89	Randy St. Claire	.05
90	Garry Templeton	.05
91	Tim Teufel	.05
92	Al Cowens	.05
93	Scot Thompson	.05
94	Tom Herr	.05
95	Ozzie Virgil	.05
96	Jose Cruz	.05
97	Gary Gaetti	.05
98	Roger Clemens	2.00

#	Player	Price
99	Vance Law	.05
100	Nolan Ryan	2.50
101	Mike Smithson	.05
102	Rafael Santana	.05
103	Darrell Evans	.05
104	Rich Gossage	.05
105	Gary Ward	.05
106	Jim Gott	.05
107	Rafael Ramirez	.05
108	Ted Power	.05
109	Ron Guidry	.05
110	Scott McGregor	.05
111	Mike Scioscia	.05
112	Glenn Hubbard	.05
113	U.L. Washington	.05
114	Al Oliver	.05
115	Jay Howell	.05
116	Brook Jacoby	.05
117	Willie McGee	.05
118	Jerry Royster	.05
119	Barry Bonnell	.05
120	Steve Carlton	.75
121	Alfredo Griffin	.05
122	David Green	.05
123	Greg Walker	.05
124	Frank Tanana	.05
125	Dave Lopes	.05
126	Mike Krukow	.05
127	Jack Howell	.05
128	Greg Harris	.05
129	Herm Winningham	.05
130	Alan Trammell	.05
131	Checklist 1-132	.05
132	Razor Shines	.05
133	Bruce Sutter	.65
134	Carney Lansford	.05
135	Joe Niekro	.05
136	Ernie Whitt	.05
137	Charlie Moore	.05
138	Mel Hall	.05
139	Roger McDowell	.05
140	John Candelaria	.05
141	Bob Rodgers	.05
142	Manny Trillo	.05
143	Dave Palmer	.05
144	Robin Yount	.75
145	Pedro Guerrero	.05
146	Von Hayes	.05
147	Lance Parrish	.05
148	Mike Heath	.05
149	Brett Butler	.05
150	Joaquin Andujar	.05
151	Graig Nettles	.05
152	Pete Vuckovich	.05
153	Jason Thompson	.05
154	Bert Roberge	.05
155	Bob Grich	.05
156	Roy Smalley	.05
157	Ron Hassey	.05
158	Bob Stanley	.05
159	Orel Hershiser	.05
160	Chet Lemon	.05
161	Terry Puhl	.05
162	Dave LaPoint	.05
163	Onix Concepcion	.05
164	Steve Balboni	.05
165	Mike Davis	.05
166	Dickie Thon	.05
167	Zane Smith	.05
168	Jeff Burroughs	.05
169	Alex Trevino	.05
170	Gary Carter	1.00
171	Tito Landrum	.05
172	Sammy Stewart	.05
173	Wayne Gross	.05
174	Britt Burns	.05
175	Steve Sax	.05
176	Jody Davis	.05
177	Joel Youngblood	.05
178	Fernando Valenzuela	.05
179	Storm Davis	.05
180	Don Mattingly	1.25
181	Steve Bedrosian	.05
182	Jesse Orosco	.05
183	Gary Roenicke	.05
184	Don Baylor	.05
185	Rollie Fingers	.50
186	Ruppert Jones	.05
187	Scott Fletcher	.05
188	Bob Dernier	.05
189	Mike Mason	.05
190	George Hendrick	.05
191	Wally Backman	.05
192	Oddibe McDowell	.05
193	Bruce Hurst	.05
194	Ron Cey	.05
195	Dave Concepcion	.05
196	Doyle Alexander	.05
197	Dale Murray	.05
198	Mark Langston	.05
199	Dennis Eckersley	.50
200	Mike Schmidt	1.50
201	Nick Esasky	.05
202	Ken Dayley	.05
203	Rick Cerone	.05
204	Larry McWilliams	.05
205	Brian Downing	.05
206	Danny Darwin	.05
207	Bill Caudill	.05
208	Dave Rozema	.05
209	Eric Show	.05
210	Brad Komminsk	.05
211	Chris Bando	.05
212	Chris Speier	.05
213	Jim Clancy	.05
214	Randy Bush	.05
215	Frank White	.05
216	Dan Petry	.05

#	Player	Price
217	Tim Wallach	.05
218	Mitch Webster	.05
219	Dennis Lamp	.05
220	Bob Horner	.05
221	Dave Henderson	.05
222	Dave Smith	.05
223	Willie Upshaw	.05
224	Cesar Cedeno	.05
225	Ron Darling	.05
226	Lee Lacy	.05
227	John Tudor	.05
228	Jim Presley	.05
229	Bill Gullickson	.05
230	Terry Kennedy	.05
231	Bob Knepper	.05
232	Rick Rhoden	.05
233	Richard Dotson	.05
234	Jesse Barfield	.10
235	Butch Wynegar	.05
236	Jerry Reuss	.05
237	Juan Samuel	.05
238	Larry Parrish	.05
239	Bill Buckner	.05
240	Pat Sheridan	.05
241	Tony Fernandez	.05
242	Rich Thompson	.05
243	Rickey Henderson	1.00
244	Craig Lefferts	.05
245	Jim Sundberg	.05
246	Phil Niekro	.50
247	Terry Harper	.05
248	Spike Owen	.05
249	Bret Saberhagen	.05
250	Dwight Gooden	.50
251	Rich Dauer	.05
252	Keith Hernandez	.05
253	Bo Diaz	.05
254	Ozzie Guillen	.05
255	Tony Armas	.05
256	Andre Dawson	.25
257	Doug DeCinces	.05
258	Tim Burke	.05
259	Dennis Boyd	.05
260	Tony Pena	.05
261	Sal Butera	.05
262	Wade Boggs	1.00
263	Checklist 133-254	.05
264	Ron Oester	.05
265	Ron Davis	.05
266	Keith Moreland	.05
267	Paul Molitor	1.00
268	John Denny	.05
269	Frank Viola	.05
270	Jack Morris	.10
271	Dave Collins	.05
272	Bert Blyleven	.05
273	Jerry Willard	.05
274	Matt Young	.05
275	Charlie Hough	.05
276	Dave Dravecky	.05
277	Garth Iorg	.05
278	Hal McRae	.05
279	Curt Wilkerson	.05
280	Tim Raines	.20
281	Bill Laskey	.05
282	Jerry Mumphrey	.05
283	Pat Clements	.05
284	Bob James	.05
285	Buddy Bell	.05
286	Tom Brookens	.05
287	Dave Parker	.05
288	Ron Kittle	.05
289	Johnnie LeMaster	.05
290	Carlton Fisk	.75
291	Jimmy Key	.05
292	Gary Matthews	.05
293	Marvell Wynne	.05
294	Danny Cox	.05
295	Kirk Gibson	.05
296	Mariano Duncan	.05
297	Ozzie Smith	1.00
298	Craig Reynolds	.05
299	Bryn Smith	.05
300	George Brett	1.50
301	Walt Terrell	.05
302	Greg Gross	.05
303	Claudell Washington	.05
304	Howard Johnson	.05
305	Phil Bradley	.05
306	R.J. Reynolds	.05
307	Bob Brenly	.05
308	Hubie Brooks	.05
309	Alvin Davis	.05
310	Donnie Hill	.05
311	Dick Schofield	.05
312	Tom Filer	.05
313	Mike Fitzgerald	.05
314	Marty Barrett	.05
315	Mookie Wilson	.05
316	Alan Knicely	.05
317	Ed Romero	.05
318	Glenn Wilson	.05
319	Bud Black	.05
320	Jim Rice	.20
321	Terry Pendleton	.05
322	Dave Kingman	.05
323	Gary Pettis	.05
324	Dan Schatzeder	.05
325	Juan Beniquez	.05
326	Kent Tekulve	.05
327	Mike Pagliarulo	.05
328	Pete O'Brien	.05
329	Kirby Puckett	1.00
330	Rick Sutcliffe	.05
331	Alan Ashby	.05
332	Willie Randolph	.05
333	Tom Henke	.05
334	Ken Oberkfell	.05

No.	Player	Price
335	Don Sutton	.50
336	Dan Gladden	.05
337	George Vuckovich	.05
338	Jorge Bell	.10
339	Jim Dwyer	.05
340	Cal Ripken	2.50
341	Willie Hernandez	.05
342	Gary Redus	.05
343	Jerry Koosman	.05
344	Jim Wohlford	.05
345	Donnie Moore	.05
346	Floyd Youmans	.05
347	Gorman Thomas	.05
348	Cliff Johnson	.05
349	Ken Howell	.05
350	Jack Clark	.05
351	Gary Lucas	.05
352	Bob Clark	.05
353	Dave Stieb	.05
354	Tony Bernazard	.05
355	Lee Smith	.05
356	Mickey Hatcher	.05
357	Ed Vande Berg	.05
358	Rick Dempsey	.05
359	Bobby Cox	.05
360	Lloyd Moseby	.05
361	Shane Rawley	.05
362	Garry Maddox	.05
363	Buck Martinez	.05
364	Ed Nunez	.05
365	Luis Leal	.05
366	Dale Berra	.05
367	Mike Boddicker	.05
368	Greg Brock	.05
369	Al Holland	.05
370	Vince Coleman	.05
371	Rod Carew	.75
372	Ben Oglivie	.05
373	Lee Mazzilli	.05
374	Terry Francona	.05
375	Rich Gedman	.05
376	Charlie Lea	.05
377	Joe Carter	.50
378	Bruce Bochte	.05
379	Bobby Meacham	.05
380	LaMarr Hoyt	.05
381	Jeff Leonard	.05
382	Ivan Calderon	.05
383	Chris Brown	.05
384	Steve Trout	.05
385	Cecil Cooper	.05
386	Cecil Fielder	1.50
387	Tim Flannery	.05
388	Chris Codiroli	.05
389	Glenn Davis	.05
390	Tom Seaver	.75
391	Julio Franco	.05
392	Tom Brunansky	.05
393	Rob Wilfong	.05
394	Reggie Jackson	.75
395	Scott Garrelts	.05
396	Checklist 255-396	.05

E	Carlton Fisk	1.00
F	Dwight Gooden	.20
G	Pedro Guerrero	.20
H	Ron Guidry	.20
Panel		4.00
I	Reggie Jackson	1.50
J	Don Mattingly	2.00
K	Oddibe McDowell	.15
L	Willie McGee	.15
Panel		3.00
M	Dale Murphy	.65
N	Pete Rose	2.50
O	Bret Saberhagen	.15
P	Fernando Valenzuela	.15

Stickers

Bi-lingual backs are the only difference between the OPC 1986 sticker set and the Topps issue. The sets share a checklist and, generally, values, although some Blue Jays and Expos stars may command a small premium in the Canadian version.

	NM/M
Complete Set:	15.00
Common Player:	.05
Album:	2.00

Tattoos

Topps and its Canadian shadow O-Pee-Chee returned to tattoos in 1986, marketing a set of 24 different tattoo sheets. Each sheet of tattoos measures 3-7/16" x 14" and includes both player portrait and smaller generic action tattoos. The player tattoos measure about 1-1/2" x 2-1/2". With 24 sheets, eight players per sheet, there are 192 players represented in the set. The sheets are numbered. The OPC version is distinguished from Topps by copyright notice.

1987 O-Pee-Chee

O-Pee-Chee of London, Ont., under license from the Topps Chewing Gum Co., continued a practice started in 1965 by issuing a baseball card set for 1987. The 396-card set is identical in design to the regular Topps set, save the name "O-Pee-Chee" replacing "Topps" in the lower right corner. Because the set is issued after its American counterpart, several cards appear with trade notations and corrected logos on the fronts. The cards, which are printed on white stock and are the standard 2-1/2" x 3-1/2", feature backs written in both English and French.

	NM/M
Complete Set (396):	15.00
Common Player:	.05
Wax Pack:	1.00
Wax Box (36):	17.50

No.	Player	Price
1	Ken Oberkfell	.05
2	Jack Howell	.05
3	Hubie Brooks	.05
4	Bob Grich	.05
5	Rick Leach	.05
6	Phil Niekro	.50
7	Rickey Henderson	1.00
8	Terry Pendleton	.05
9	Jay Tibbs	.05
10	Cecil Cooper	.05
11	Mario Soto	.05
12	George Bell	.15
13	Nick Esasky	.05
14	Larry McWilliams	.05
15	Dan Quisenberry	.05
16	Ed Lynch	.05
17	Pete O'Brien	.05
18	Luis Aguayo	.05
19	Matt Young	.05
20	Gary Carter	1.00
21	Tom Paciorek	.05
22	Doug DeCinces	.05
23	Lee Smith	.05
24	Jesse Barfield	.05
25	Bert Blyleven	.05
26	Greg Brock	.05
27	Dan Petry	.05
28	Rick Dempsey	.05
29	Jimmy Key	.05
30	Tim Raines	.15
31	Bruce Hurst	.05
32	Manny Trillo	.05
33	Andy Van Slyke	.05
34	Ed Vande Berg	.05
35	Sid Bream	.05
36	Dave Winfield	1.00
37	Scott Garrelts	.05
38	Dennis Leonard	.05
39	Marty Barrett	.05
40	Dave Righetti	.05
41	Bo Diaz	.05
42	Gary Redus	.05
43	Tom Niedenfuer	.05
44	Greg Harris	.05
45	Jim Presley	.05
46	Danny Gladden	.05
47	Roy Smalley	.05
48	Wally Backman	.05
49	Tom Seaver	.75
50	Dave Smith	.05
51	Mel Hall	.05
52	Tim Flannery	.05
53	Julio Cruz	.05
54	Dick Schofield	.05
55	Tim Wallach	.05
56	Glenn Davis	.05
57	Darren Daulton	.05
58	Chico Walker	.05
59	Garth Iorg	.05
60	Tony Pena	.05
61	Ron Hassey	.05
62	Dave Dravecky	.05
63	Jorge Orta	.05
64	Al Nipper	.05
65	Tom Browning	.05
66	Marc Sullivan	.05
67	Todd Worrell	.05
68	Glenn Hubbard	.05
69	Carney Lansford	.05
70	Charlie Hough	.05
71	Lance McCullers	.05
72	Walt Terrell	.05
73	Bob Kearney	.05
74	Dan Pasqua	.05
75	Ron Darling	.05
76	Robin Yount	.75
77	Pat Tabler	.05
78	Tom Foley	.05
79	Juan Nieves	.05
80	Wally Joyner	.05
81	Wayne Krenchicki	.05
82	Kirby Puckett	1.00
83	Bob Ojeda	.05
84	Mookie Wilson	.05
85	Kevin Bass	.05
86	Kent Tekulve	.05
87	Mark Salas	.05
88	Brian Downing	.05
89	Ozzie Guillen	.05
90	Dave Stieb	.05
91	Rance Mulliniks	.05
92	Mike Witt	.05
93	Charlie Moore	.05
94	Jose Uribe	.05
95	Oddibe McDowell	.05
96	Ray Soff	.05
97	Glenn Wilson	.05
98	Brook Jacoby	.05
99	Darryl Motley	.05
100	Steve Garvey	.10
101	Frank White	.05
102	Mike Moore	.05
103	Rick Aguilera	.05
104	Buddy Bell	.05
105	Floyd Youmans	.05
106	Lou Whitaker	.05
107	Ozzie Smith	1.00
108	Jim Gantner	.05
109	R.J. Reynolds	.05
110	John Tudor	.05
111	Alfredo Griffin	.05
112	Mike Flanagan	.05
113	Neil Allen	.05
114	Ken Griffey	.05
115	Donnie Moore	.05
116	Bob Horner	.05
117	Ron Shepherd	.05
118	Cliff Johnson	.05
119	Vince Coleman	.05
120	Eddie Murray	.75
121	Dwayne Murphy	.05
122	Jim Clancy	.05
123	Ken Landreaux	.05
124	Tom Nieto	.05
125	Bob Brenly	.05
126	George Brett	1.25
127	Vance Law	.05
128	Checklist 1-132	.05
129	Bob Knepper	.05
130	Dwight Gooden	.05
131	Juan Bonilla	.05
132	Tim Burke	.05
133	Bob McClure	.05
134	Scott Bailes	.05
135	Mike Easler	.05
136	Ron Romanick	.05
137	Rich Gedman	.05
138	Bob Dernier	.05
139	John Denny	.05
140	Bret Saberhagen	.05
141	Herm Winningham	.05
142	Rick Sutcliffe	.05
143	Ryne Sandberg	1.00
144	Mike Scioscia	.05
145	Charlie Kerfeld	.05
146	Jim Rice	.15
147	Steve Trout	.05
148	Jesse Orosco	.05
149	Mike Boddicker	.05
150	Wade Boggs	1.00
151	Dane Iorg	.05
152	Rick Burleson	.05
153	Duane Ward	.05
154	Rick Reuschel	.05
155	Nolan Ryan	2.00
156	Bill Caudill	.05
157	Danny Darwin	.05
158	Ed Romero	.05
159	Bill Almon	.05
160	Julio Franco	.05
161	Kent Hrbek	.05
162	Chili Davis	.05
163	Kevin Gross	.05
164	Carlton Fisk	.75
165	Jeff Reardon	.05
166	Bob Boone	.05
167	Rick Honeycutt	.05
168	Dan Schatzeder	.05
169	Jim Wohlford	.05
170	Phil Bradley	.05
171	Ken Schrom	.05
172	Ron Oester	.05
173	Juan Beniquez	.05
174	Tony Armas	.05
175	Bob Stanley	.05
176	Steve Buechele	.05
177	Keith Moreland	.05
178	Cecil Fielder	.50
179	Gary Gaetti	.05
180	Chris Brown	.05
181	Tom Herr	.05
182	Lee Lacy	.05
183	Ozzie Virgil	.05
184	Paul Molitor	1.00
185	Roger McDowell	.05
186	Mike Marshall	.05
187	Ken Howell	.05
188	Rob Deer	.05
189	Joe Hesketh	.05
190	Jim Sundberg	.05
191	Kelly Gruber	.10
192	Cory Snyder	.05
193	Dave Concepcion	.05
194	Kirk McCaskill	.05
195	Mike Pagliarulo	.05
196	Rick Manning	.05
197	Brett Butler	.05
198	Tony Gwynn	1.00
199	Mariano Duncan	.05
200	Pete Rose	1.25
201	John Cangelosi	.05
202	Danny Cox	.05
203	Butch Wynegar	.05
204	Chris Chambliss	.05
205	Graig Nettles	.05
206	Chet Lemon	.05
207	Don Aase	.05
208	Mike Mason	.05
209	Alan Trammell	.05
210	Lloyd Moseby	.05
211	Richard Dotson	.05
212	Mike Fitzgerald	.05
213	Darrell Porter	.05
214	Checklist 133-264	.05
215	Mark Langston	.05
216	Steve Farr	.05
217	Dann Bilardello	.05
218	Gary Ward	.05
219	Cecilio Guante	.05
220	Joe Carter	.15
221	Ernie Whitt	.05
222	Denny Walling	.05
223	Charlie Leibrandt	.05
224	Wayne Tolleson	.05
225	Mike Smithson	.05
226	Zane Smith	.05
227	Terry Puhl	.05
228	Eric Davis	.05
229	Don Mattingly	1.25
230	Don Baylor	.05
231	Frank Tanana	.05
232	Tom Brookens	.05
233	Steve Bedrosian	.05
234	Wallace Johnson	.05
235	Alvin Davis	.05
236	Tommy John	.05
237	Jim Morrison	.05
238	Ricky Horton	.05
239	Shane Rawley	.05
240	Steve Balboni	.05
241	Mike Krukow	.05
242	Rick Mahler	.05
243	Bill Doran	.05
244	Mark Clear	.05
245	Willie Upshaw	.05
246	Hal McRae	.05
247	Jose Canseco	.45
248	George Hendrick	.05
249	Doyle Alexander	.05
250	Teddy Higuera	.05
251	Tom Hume	.05
252	Denny Martinez	.05
253	Eddie Milner	.05
254	Steve Sax	.05
255	Juan Samuel	.05
256	Dave Bergman	.05
257	Bob Forsch	.05
258	Steve Yeager	.05
259	Don Sutton	.50
260	Vida Blue	.05
261	Tom Brunansky	.05
262	Joe Sambito	.05
263	Mitch Webster	.05
264	Checklist 265-396	.05
265	Darrell Evans	.05
266	Dave Kingman	.05
267	Howard Johnson	.05
268	Greg Pryor	.05
269	Tippy Martinez	.05
270	Jody Davis	.05
271	Steve Carlton	.75
272	Andres Galarraga	.15
273	Fernando Valenzuela	.05
274	Jeff Hearron	.05
275	Ray Knight	.05
276	Bill Madlock	.05
277	Tom Henke	.05
278	Gary Pettis	.05
279	Jimy Williams	.05
280	Jeffrey Leonard	.05
281	Bryn Smith	.05
282	John Cerutti	.05
283	Gary Roenicke	.05
284	Joaquin Andujar	.05
285	Dennis Boyd	.05
286	Tim Hulett	.05
287	Craig Lefferts	.05
288	Tito Landrum	.05
289	Manny Lee	.05
290	Leon Durham	.05
291	Johnny Ray	.05
292	Franklin Stubbs	.05
293	Bob Rodgers	.05
294	Terry Francona	.05
295	Len Dykstra	.05
296	Tom Candiotti	.05
297	Frank DiPino	.05
298	Craig Reynolds	.05
299	Jerry Hairston Sr.	.05
300	Reggie Jackson	1.00
301	Luis Aquino	.05
302	Greg Walker	.05
303	Terry Kennedy	.05
304	Phil Garner	.05
305	John Franco	.05
306	Bill Buckner	.05
307	Kevin Mitchell	.05
308	Don Slaught	.05
309	Harold Baines	.05
310	Frank Viola	.05
311	Dave Lopes	.05
312	Cal Ripken	2.00
313	John Candelaria	.05
314	Bob Sebra	.05
315	Bud Black	.05
316	Brian Fisher	.05
317	Clint Hurdle	.05
318	Ernie Riles	.05
319	Dave LaPoint	.05
320	Barry Bonds	6.00
321	Tim Stoddard	.05
322	Ron Cey	.05
323	Al Newman	.05
324	Jerry Royster	.05
325	Garry Templeton	.05
326	Mark Gubicza	.05
327	Andre Thornton	.05
328	Bob Welch	.05
329	Tony Fernandez	.05
330	Mike Scott	.05
331	Jack Clark	.05
332	Danny Tartabull	.05
333	Greg Minton	.05
334	Ed Correa	.05
335	Candy Maldonado	.05
336	Dennis Lamp	.05
337	Sid Fernandez	.05
338	Greg Gross	.05
339	Willie Hernandez	.05
340	Roger Clemens	1.50
341	Mickey Hatcher	.05
342	Bob James	.05
343	Jose Cruz	.05
344	Bruce Sutter	.65
345	Andre Dawson	.25
346	Shawon Dunston	.05
347	Scott McGregor	.05
348	Carmelo Martinez	.05
349	Storm Davis	.05
350	Keith Hernandez	.05
351	Andy McGaffigan	.05
352	Dave Parker	.05
353	Ernie Camacho	.05
354	Eric Show	.05
355	Don Carman	.05
356	Floyd Bannister	.05
357	Willie McGee	.05
358	Atlee Hammaker	.05
359	Dale Murphy	.30
360	Pedro Guerrero	.05
361	Will Clark	.10
362	Bill Campbell	.05
363	Alejandro Pena	.05
364	Dennis Rasmussen	.05
365	Rick Rhoden	.05
366	Randy St. Claire	.05
367	Willie Wilson	.05
368	Dwight Evans	.05
369	Moose Haas	.05
370	Fred Lynn	.05
371	Mark Eichhorn	.05
372	Dave Schmidt	.05
373	Jerry Reuss	.05
374	Lance Parrish	.05
375	Ron Guidry	.05
376	Jack Morris	.05
377	Willie Randolph	.05
378	Joel Youngblood	.05
379	Darryl Strawberry	.05
380	Rich Gossage	.50
381	Dennis Eckersley	.50
382	Gary Lucas	.05
383	Ron Davis	.05
384	Pete Incaviglia	.05
385	Orel Hershiser	.10
386	Kirk Gibson	.05
387	Don Robinson	.05
388	Darnell Coles	.05
389	Von Hayes	.05
390	Gary Matthews	.05
391	Jay Howell	.05
392	Tim Laudner	.05
393	Rod Scurry	.05
394	Tony Bernazard	.05
395	Damaso Garcia	.05
396	Mike Schmidt	1.25

Box Panels

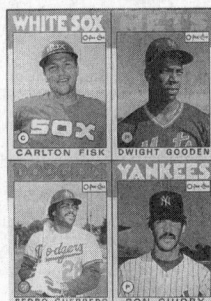

The Canadian card company licensed by Topps to distribute cards in Canada is O-Pee-Chee. In 1986, O-Pee-Chee issued wax pack boxes with baseball cards printed on the box bottoms. Four cards appear on four different boxes making a complete set of 16. The cards are identical to the 1986 Topps wax box issue with the exception of the OPC logo replacing Topps and the addition of French on the card backs. These bilingual cards were issued in Canada but are readily available in the USA. The cards are the standard 2-1/2" x 3-1/2" size, printed in full-color with black and red backs. The panel cards are not numbered but instead are lettered from A through P.

	NM/M
Complete Panel Set (4):	12.00
Complete Singles Set (16):	11.00
Common Panel:	3.50
Common Single Player:	.15
Panel	4.50
A Jorge Bell	.50
B Wade Boggs	1.00
C George Brett	1.50
D Vince Coleman	.20
Panel	3.50

Box Panels

For the second consecutive year, O-Pee-Chee placed baseball cards on the bottoms of its wax pack boxes. The 2-1/8" x 3" cards were issued in panels of four and are slightly smaller in size than the regular issue OPC cards. The card fronts are identical in design to the regular issue, while the backs contain a newspaper-type commentary in both French and English. Collectors may note the 1987 Topps wax box cards were issued on side panels as opposed to box bottoms. Because the OPC wax boxes are smaller in size than their U.S. counterparts, printing cards on side panels was not possible.

	NM/M
Complete Panel Set (2):	5.00
Complete Singles Set (8):	5.00
Common Single Player:	.15
Panel	2.00
A Don Baylor	.15
B Steve Carlton	.50
C Ron Cey	.15
D Cecil Cooper	.15
Panel	4.00
E Rickey Henderson	.15
F Jim Rice	.35
G Don Sutton	.50
H Dave Winfield	.15

Stickers

Bi-lingual backs are the only difference between the OPC 1987 sticker set and the Topps issue. The sets share a checklist and, generally, values, although some Blue Jays and Expos stars may command a small premium in the Canadian version.

1988 O-Pee-Chee

Under license from Topps, O-Pee-Chee uses the same player photos as the Topps issue, but the Canadian edition includes only 396 cards (one-half the number in the Topps set). The OPC set was printed after the U.S. press run, so several cards carry overprints on the fronts, indicating changes in players' teams. New teams are named in the overprints; card headers bear the former team names. This set follows the same basic design as the 1988 Topps cards. The OPC logo appears in place of the Topps logo, both front and back. A four-card subset consists of #1 and #2 draft choices for the Expos (Nathan Minchey and Delino DeShields) and Blue Jays (Alex Sanchez and Derek Bell). These cards are distinguished by a yellow or orange triangle in the lower-right corner bearing the player's name above the words "Choisi au repecharge." Card backs are bilingual (English-French) and printed in black on orange. This series was marketed primarily in Canada in four separate display boxes, with four cards printed one each box bottom. Individual card packs contain seven cards and one stick of gum.

	NM/M
Unopened Fact. Set (396):	9.00
Complete Set (396):	7.50
Common Player:	.05
Wax Pack (7):	.25
Wax Box (48):	7.50

#	Player	Price
1	Chris James	.05
2	Steve Buechele	.05
3	Mike Henneman	.05
4	Eddie Murray	.60
5	Bret Saberhagen	.05
6	Nathan Minchey (Draft Pick)	.05
7	Harold Reynolds	.05
8	Bo Jackson	.10
9	Mike Easler	.05
10	Ryne Sandberg	.75
11	Mike Young	.05
12	Tony Phillips	.05
13	Andres Thomas	.05
14	Tim Burke	.05
15	Chili Davis	.05
16	Jim Lindeman	.05
17	Ron Oester	.05
18	Craig Reynolds	.05
19	Juan Samuel	.05
20	Kevin Gross	.05
21	Cecil Fielder	.05
22	Greg Swindell	.05
23	Jose DeLeon	.05
24	Jim Deshaies	.05
25	Andres Galarraga	.10
26	Mitch Williams	.05
27	R.J. Reynolds	.05
28	Jose Nunez	.05
29	Angel Salazar	.05
30	Sid Fernandez	.05
31	Keith Moreland	.05
32	John Kruk	.05
33	Rob Deer	.05
34	Ricky Horton	.05
35	Harold Baines	.05
36	Jamie Moyer	.05
37	Kevin McReynolds	.05
38	Ozzie Smith	.75
39	Ron Darling	.05
40	Orel Hershiser	.05
41	Bob Melvin	.05
42	Alfredo Griffin	.05
43	Dick Schofield	.05
44	Terry Steinbach	.05
45	Kent Hrbek	.05
46	Darnell Coles	.05
47	Jimmy Key	.05
48	Alan Ashby	.05
49	Julio Franco	.05
50	Hubie Brooks	.05
51	Chris Bando	.05
52	Fernando Valenzuela	.05
53	Kal Daniels	.05
54	Jim Clancy	.05
55	Phil Bradley	.05
56	Andy McGaffigan	.05
57	Mike LaValliere	.05
58	Dave Magadan	.05
59	Danny Cox	.05
60	Rickey Henderson	.75
61	Jim Rice	.20
62	Calvin Schiraldi	.05
63	Jerry Mumphrey	.05
64	Ken Caminiti	.05
65	Leon Durham	.05
66	Shane Rawley	.05
67	Ken Oberkfell	.05
68	Keith Hernandez	.05
69	Bob Brenly	.05
70	Roger Clemens	.90
71	Gary Pettis	.05
72	Dennis Eckersley	.50
73	Dave Smith	.05
74	Cal Ripken	1.00
75	Joe Carter	.15
76	Denny Martinez	.05
77	Juan Beniquez	.05
78	Tim Laudner	.05
79	Ernie Whitt	.05
80	Mark Langston	.05
81	Dale Sveum	.05
82	Dion James	.05
83	Dave Valle	.05
84	Bill Wegman	.05
85	Howard Johnson	.05
86	Benito Santiago	.05
87	Casey Candaele	.05
88	Delino DeShields (Draft Pick)	3.00
89	Dave Winfield	.75
90	Dale Murphy	.20
91	Jay Howell	.05
92	Ken Williams	.05
93	Bob Sebra	.05
94	Tim Wallach	.10
95	Lance Parrish	.05
96	Todd Benzinger	.05
97	Scott Garrelts	.05
98	Jose Guzman	.05
99	Jeff Reardon	.05
100	Jack Clark	.05
101	Tracy Jones	.05
102	Barry Larkin	.05
103	Curt Young	.05
104	Juan Nieves	.05
105	Terry Pendleton	.05
106	Rob Ducey	.05
107	Scott Bailes	.05
108	Eric King	.05
109	Mike Pagliarulo	.05
110	Teddy Higuera	.05
111	Pedro Guerrero	.05
112	Chris Brown	.05
113	Kelly Gruber	.05
114	Jack Howell	.05
115	Johnny Ray	.05
116	Mark Eichhorn	.05
117	Tony Pena	.05
118	Bob Welch	.05
119	Mike Kingery	.05
120	Kirby Puckett	.75
121	Charlie Hough	.05
122	Tony Bernazard	.05
123	Tom Candiotti	.05
124	Ray Knight	.05
125	Bruce Hurst	.05
126	Steve Jeltz	.05
127	Ron Guidry	.05
128	Duane Ward	.05
129	Greg Minton	.05
130	Buddy Bell	.05
131	Denny Walling	.05
132	Donnie Hill	.05
133	Wayne Tolleson	.05
134	Bob Rodgers	.05
135	Todd Worrell	.05
136	Brian Dayett	.05
137	Chris Bosio	.05
138	Mitch Webster	.05
139	Jerry Browne	.05
140	Jesse Barfield	.05
141	Doug DeCinces	.05
142	Andy Van Slyke	.05
143	Doug Drabek	.05
144	Jeff Parrett	.05
145	Bill Madlock	.05
146	Larry Herndon	.05
147	Bill Buckner	.05
148	Carmelo Martinez	.05
149	Ken Howell	.05
150	Eric Davis	.05
151	Randy Ready	.05
152	Jeffrey Leonard	.05
153	Dave Steib	.05
154	Jeff Stone	.05
155	Dave Righetti	.05
156	Gary Matthews	.05
157	Gary Carter	.75
158	Bob Boone	.05
159	Glenn Davis	.05
160	Willie McGee	.05
161	Bryn Smith	.05
162	Mark McLemore	.05
163	Dale Mohorcic	.05
164	Mike Flanagan	.05
165	Robin Yount	.60
166	Bill Doran	.05
167	Rance Mulliniks	.05
168	Wally Joyner	.05
169	Cory Snyder	.05
170	Rich Gossage	.05
171	Rick Mahler	.05
172	Henry Cotto	.05
173	George Bell	.15
174	B.J. Surhoff	.05
175	Kevin Bass	.05
176	Jeff Reed	.05
177	Frank Tanana	.05
178	Darryl Strawberry	.05
179	Lou Whitaker	.05
180	Terry Kennedy	.05
181	Mariano Duncan	.05
182	Ken Phelps	.05
183	Bob Dernier	.05
184	Ivan Calderon	.05
185	Rick Rhoden	.05
186	Rafael Palmeiro	.50
187	Kelly Downs	.05
188	Spike Owen	.05
189	Bobby Bonilla	.05
190	Candy Maldonado	.05
191	John Cerutti	.05
192	Devon White	.25
193	Brian Fisher	.05
194	Alex Sanchez (Draft Pick)	.20
195	Dan Quisenberry	.05
196	Dave Engle	.05
197	Lance McCullers	.05
198	Franklin Stubbs	.05
199	Scott Bradley	.05
200	Wade Boggs	.75
201	Kirk Gibson	.05
202	Brett Butler	.05
203	Dave Anderson	.05
204	Donnie Moore	.05
205	Nelson Liriano	.05
206	Danny Gladden	.05
207	Dan Pasqua	.05
208	Robbie Thompson	.05
209	Richard Dotson	.05
210	Willie Randolph	.05
211	Danny Tartabull	.05
212	Greg Brock	.05
213	Albert Hall	.05
214	Dave Schmidt	.05
215	Von Hayes	.05
216	Herm Winningham	.05
217	Mike Davis	.05
218	Charlie Leibrandt	.05
219	Mike Stanley	.05
220	Tom Henke	.05
221	Dwight Evans	.05
222	Willie Wilson	.05
223	Stan Jefferson	.05
224	Mike Dunne	.05
225	Mike Scioscia	.05
226	Larry Parrish	.05
227	Mike Scott	.05
228	Wallace Johnson	.05
229	Jeff Musselman	.05
230	Pat Tabler	.05
231	Paul Molitor	.75
232	Bob James	.05
233	Joe Niekro	.05
234	Oddibe McDowell	.05
235	Gary Ward	.05
236	Ted Power	.05
237	Pascual Perez	.05
238	Luis Polonia	.05
239	Mike Diaz	.05
240	Lee Smith	.05
241	Willie Upshaw	.05
242	Tom Neidenfuer	.05
243	Tim Raines	.20
244	Jeff Robinson	.05
245	Rich Gedman	.05
246	Scott Bankhead	.05
247	Andre Dawson	.25
248	Brook Jacoby	.05
249	Mike Marshall	.05
250	Nolan Ryan	1.00
251	Tom Foley	.05
252	Bob Brower	.05
253	Checklist 1-132	.05
254	Scott McGregor	.05
255	Ken Griffey	.05
256	Ken Schrom	.05
257	Gary Gaetti	.05
258	Ed Nunez	.05
259	Frank Viola	.05
260	Vince Coleman	.05
261	Reid Nichols	.05
262	Tim Flannery	.05
263	Glenn Braggs	.05
264	Garry Templeton	.05
265	Bo Diaz	.05
266	Matt Nokes	.05
267	Barry Bonds	1.00
268	Bruce Ruffin	.05
269	Ellis Burks	.05
270	Mike Witt	.05
271	Ken Gerhart	.05
272	Lloyd Moseby	.05
273	Garth Iorg	.05
274	Mike Greenwell	.05
275	Kevin Seitzer	.05
276	Luis Salazar	.05
277	Shawon Dunston	.05
278	Rick Reuschel	.05
279	Randy St. Claire	.05
280	Pete Incaviglia	.05
281	Mike Boddicker	.05
282	Jay Tibbs	.05
283	Shane Mack	.05
284	Walt Terrell	.05
285	Jim Presley	.05
286	Greg Walker	.05
287	Dwight Gooden	.05
288	Jim Morrison	.05
289	Gene Garber	.05
290	Tony Fernandez	.05
291	Ozzie Virgil	.05
292	Carney Lansford	.05
293	Jim Acker	.05
294	Tommy Hinzo	.05
295	Bert Blyleven	.05
296	Ozzie Guillen	.05
297	Zane Smith	.05
298	Milt Thompson	.05
299	Len Dykstra	.05
300	Don Mattingly	.85
301	Bud Black	.05
302	Jose Uribe	.05
303	Manny Lee	.05
304	Sid Bream	.05
305	Steve Sax	.05
306	Billy Hatcher	.05
307	John Shelby	.05
308	Lee Mazzilli	.05
309	Bill Long	.05
310	Tom Herr	.05
311	Derek Bell (Draft Pick)	3.00
312	George Brett	.85
313	Bob McClure	.05
314	Jimy Williams	.05
315	Dave Parker	.05
316	Doyle Alexander	.05
317	Dan Plesac	.05
318	Mel Hall	.05
319	Ruben Sierra	.05
320	Alan Trammell	.05
321	Mike Schmidt	.85
322	Wally Ritchie	.05
323	Rick Leach	.05
324	Danny Jackson	.05
325	Glenn Hubbard	.05
326	Frank White	.05
327	Larry Sheets	.05
328	John Cangelosi	.05
329	Bill Gullickson	.05
330	Eddie Whitson	.05
331	Brian Downing	.05
332	Gary Redus	.05
333	Wally Backman	.05
334	Dwayne Murphy	.05
335	Claudell Washington	.05
336	Dave Concepcion	.05
337	Jim Gantner	.05
338	Marty Barrett	.05
339	Mickey Hatcher	.05
340	Jack Morris	.05
341	John Franco	.05
342	Ron Robinson	.05
343	Greg Gagne	.05
344	Steve Bedrosian	.05
345	Scott Fletcher	.05
346	Vance Law	.05
347	Joe Johnson	.05
348	Jim Eisenreich	.05
349	Alvin Davis	.05
350	Will Clark	.10
351	Mike Aldrete	.05
352	Billy Ripken	.05
353	Dave Stewart	.05
354	Neal Heaton	.05
355	Roger McDowell	.05
356	John Tudor	.05
357	Floyd Bannister	.05
358	Rey Quinones	.05
359	Glenn Wilson	.05
360	Tony Gwynn	.75
361	Greg Maddux	.75
362	Juan Castillo	.05
363	Willie Fraser	.05
364	Nick Esasky	.05
365	Floyd Youmans	.05
366	Chet Lemon	.05
367	Matt Young	.05
368	Gerald Young	.05
369	Bob Stanley	.05
370	Jose Canseco	.45
371	Joe Hesketh	.05
372	Rick Sutcliffe	.05
373	Checklist 133-264	.05
374	Checklist 265-396	.05
375	Tom Brunansky	.05
376	Jody Davis	.05
377	Sam Horn	.05
378	Mark Gubicza	.05
379	Rafael Ramirez	.05
380	Joe Magrane	.05
381	Pete O'Brien	.05
382	Lee Guetterman	.05
383	Eric Bell	.05
384	Gene Larkin	.05
385	Carlton Fisk	.60
386	Mike Fitzgerald	.05
387	Kevin Mitchell	.05
388	Jim Winn	.05
389	Mike Smithson	.05
390	Darrell Evans	.05
391	Terry Leach	.05
392	Charlie Kerfeld	.05
393	Mike Krukow	.05
394	Mark McGwire	.90
395	Fred McGriff	.10
396	DeWayne Buice	.05

Box Panels

A Topps licensee, O-Pee-Chee of Canada issued this 16-card set on wax display box bottoms. Cards feature popular current players and are identified by alphabet (A-P) rather than numbers. Player photos are the same ones used on the Topps U.S. issue and cards follow the same design as Topps' regular issue set. The OPC logo replaces the Topps logo on both front and back. Orange and black card backs are bilingual (French/English) and include complete major and minor league career stats.

		NM/M
Complete Panel Set (4):		8.00
Complete Singles Set (16):		8.00
Common Single Player:		.10
Panel		1.00
A	Don Baylor	.10
B	Steve Bedrosian	.10
C	Juan Beniquez	.10
D	Bob Boone	.15
Panel		2.00
E	Darrell Evans	.10
F	Tony Gwynn	1.00
G	John Kruk	.10
H	Marvell Wynne	.05
Panel		1.00
I	Joe Carter	.25
J	Eric Davis	1.00
K	Howard Johnson	.10
L	Darryl Strawberry	.10
Panel		5.00
M	Rickey Henderson	1.00
N	Nolan Ryan	3.00
O	Mike Schmidt	1.50
P	Kent Tekulve	.10

Stickers/Stickercards

This is the Canadian version of Topps' sticker issue for 1988, virtually identical except for the substitution of the OPC logo and copyright notice on the front of the stickercard. The Canadian version shares the Topps' checklists and, essentially, the price structure, although Canadian star players command a small premium in the OPC version.

1989 O-Pee-Chee

At 396 cards, the 1989 O-Pee-Chee issue is half the size of the corresponding Topps set. As in previous years, the design of the OPC cards is virtually identical to the Topps version, though the Topps logo on front has been replaced with an O-Pee-Chee logo in one of the upper corners and the backs are printed in both English and French for the Canadian market. Cards of players who changed teams often contain an overprint indicating the player's new team and date of the transaction.

		NM/M
Complete Set (396):		10.00
Common Player:		.05
Wax Box (48):		12.00
1	Brook Jacoby	.05
2	Atlee Hammaker	.05
3	Jack Clark	.05
4	Dave Steib	.10
5	Bud Black	.05
6	Damon Berryhill	.05
7	Mike Scioscia	.05
8	Jose Uribe	.05
9	Mike Aldrete	.05
10	Andre Dawson	.25
11	Bruce Sutter	.45
12	Dale Sveum	.05
13	Dan Quisenberry	.05
14	Tom Niedenfuer	.05
15	Robby Thompson	.05
16	Ron Robinson	.05
17	Brian Downing	.05
18	Rick Rhoden	.05
19	Greg Gagne	.05
20	Allan Anderson	.05
21	Eddie Whitson	.05
22	Billy Ripken	.05
23	Mike Fitzgerald	.05
24	Shane Rawley	.05
25	Frank White	.05
26	Don Mattingly	.75
27	Fred Lynn	.05
28	Mike Moore	.05
29	Kelly Gruber	.05
30	Dwight Gooden	.05
31	Dan Pasqua	.05
32	Dennis Rasmussen	.05
33	B.J. Surhoff	.05
34	Sid Fernandez	.05
35	John Tudor	.05
36	Mitch Webster	.05
37	Doug Drabek	.05
38	Bobby Witt	.05
39	Mike Maddux	.05
40	Steve Sax	.05
41	Orel Hershiser	.05
42	Pete Incaviglia	.05
43	Guillermo Hernandez	.05
44	Kevin Coffman	.05
45	Kal Daniels	.05
46	Carlton Fisk	.50
47	Carney Lansford	.05
48	Tim Burke	.05
49	Alan Trammell	.05
50	George Bell	.15
51	Tony Gwynn	.60
52	Bob Brenly	.05
53	Ruben Sierra	.05
54	Otis Nixon	.05
55	Julio Franco	.05
56	Pat Tabler	.05
57	Alvin Davis	.05
58	Kevin Seitzer	.05
59	Mark Davis	.05
60	Tom Brunansky	.05
61	Jeff Treadway	.05
62	Alfredo Griffin	.05
63	Keith Hernandez	.05
64	Alex Trevino	.05
65	Rick Reuschel	.05
66	Bob Walk	.05
67	Dave Palmer	.05
68	Pedro Guerrero	.05
69	Jose Oquendo	.05
70	Mark McGwire	.85
71	Mike Boddicker	.05
72	Wally Backman	.05
73	Pascual Perez	.05
74	Joe Hesketh	.05
75	Tom Henke	.05
76	Nelson Liriano	.05
77	Doyle Alexander	.05
78	Tim Wallach	.10
79	Scott Bankhead	.05
80	Cory Snyder	.05
81	Dave Magadan	.05
82	Randy Ready	.05
83	Steve Buechele	.05
84	Bo Jackson	.10
85	Kevin McReynolds	.05
86	Jeff Reardon	.05
87	Tim Raines	.25
88	Melido Perez	.05
89	Dave LaPoint	.05
90	Vince Coleman	.05
91	Floyd Youmans	.05
92	Buddy Bell	.05
93	Andres Galarraga	.15
94	Tony Pena	.05
95	Gerald Young	.05
96	Rick Cerone	.05
97	Ken Oberkfell	.05
98	Larry Sheets	.05
99	Chuck Crim	.05
100	Mike Schmidt	.75
101	Ivan Calderon	.05
102	Kevin Bass	.05
103	Chili Davis	.05
104	Randy Myers	.05
105	Ron Darling	.05
106	Willie Upshaw	.05
107	Jose DeLeon	.05
108	Fred Manrique	.05
109	Johnny Ray	.05
110	Paul Molitor	.60
111	Rance Mulliniks	.05
112	Jim Presley	.05
113	Lloyd Moseby	.05
114	Lance Parrish	.05
115	Jody Davis	.05
116	Matt Nokes	.05
117	Dave Anderson	.05
118	Checklist	.05
119	Rafael Belliard	.05
120	Frank Viola	.05
121	Roger Clemens	.85
122	Luis Salazar	.05
123	Mike Stanley	.05
124	Jim Traber	.05
125	Mike Krukow	.05
126	Sid Bream	.05
127	Joel Skinner	.05

No.	Player	Price
128	Milt Thompson	.05
129	Terry Clark	.05
130	Gerald Perry	.05
131	Bryn Smith	.05
132	Kirby Puckett	.60
133	Bill Long	.05
134	Jim Gantner	.05
135	Jose Rijo	.05
136	Joey Meyer	.05
137	Geno Petralli	.05
138	Wallace Johnson	.05
139	Mike Flanagan	.05
140	Shawon Dunston	.05
141	Eric Plunk	.05
142	Bobby Bonilla	.05
143	Jack McDowell	.05
144	Mookie Wilson	.05
145	Dave Stewart	.10
146	Gary Pettis	.05
147	Eric Show	.05
148	Eddie Murray	.50
149	Lee Smith	.05
150	Fernando Valenzuela	.05
151	Bob Walk	.05
152	Harold Baines	.05
153	Albert Hall	.05
154	Don Carman	.05
155	Marty Barrett	.05
156	Chris Sabo	.05
157	Bret Saberhagen	.05
158	Danny Cox	.05
159	Tom Foley	.05
160	Jeffrey Leonard	.05
161	Brady Anderson	.05
162	Rich Gossage	.05
163	Greg Brock	.05
164	Joe Carter	.10
165	Mike Dunne	.05
166	Jeff Russell	.05
167	Dan Plesac	.05
168	Willie Wilson	.05
169	Mike Jackson	.05
170	Tony Fernandez	.05
171	Jamie Moyer	.05
172	Jim Gott	.05
173	Mel Hall	.05
174	Mark McGwire	.85
175	John Shelby	.05
176	Jeff Parrett	.05
177	Tim Belcher	.05
178	Rich Gedman	.05
179	Ozzie Virgil	.05
180	Mike Scott	.05
181	Dickie Thon	.05
182	Rob Murphy	.05
183	Oddibe McDowell	.05
184	Wade Boggs	.60
185	Claudell Washington	.05
186	Randy Johnson	2.00
187	Paul O'Neill	.05
188	Todd Benzinger	.05
189	Kevin Mitchell	.05
190	Mike Witt	.05
191	Sil Campusano	.05
192	Ken Gerhart	.05
193	Bob Rodgers	.05
194	Floyd Bannister	.05
195	Ozzie Guillen	.05
196	Ron Gant	.05
197	Neal Heaton	.05
198	Bill Swift	.05
199	Dave Parker	.05
200	George Brett	.75
201	Bo Diaz	.05
202	Brad Moore	.05
203	Rob Ducey	.05
204	Bert Blyleven	.05
205	Dwight Evans	.05
206	Roberto Alomar	.60
207	Henry Cotto	.05
208	Harold Reynolds	.05
209	Jose Guzman	.05
210	Dale Murphy	.15
211	Mike Pagliarulo	.05
212	Jay Howell	.05
213	Rene Gonzalez	.05
214	Scott Garrelts	.05
215	Kevin Gross	.05
216	Jack Howell	.05
217	Kurt Stillwell	.05
218	Mike LaValliere	.05
219	Jim Clancy	.05
220	Gary Gaetti	.05
221	Hubie Brooks	.05
222	Bruce Ruffin	.05
223	Jay Buhner	.05
224	Cecil Fielder	.15
225	Willie McGee	.05
226	Bill Doran	.05
227	John Farrell	.05
228	Nelson Santovenia	.05
229	Jimmy Key	.05
230	Ozzie Smith	.60
231	Dave Schmidt	.05
232	Jody Reed	.05
233	Gregg Jefferies	.05
234	Tom Browning	.05
235	John Kruk	.05
236	Charles Hudson	.05
237	Todd Stottlemyre	.10
238	Don Slaught	.05
239	Tim Laudner	.05
240	Greg Maddux	.60
241	Brett Butler	.05
242	Checklist	.05
243	Bob Boone	.05
244	Willie Randolph	.05
245	Jim Rice	.15
246	Rey Quinonez	.05
247	Checklist	.05
248	Stan Javier	.05
249	Tim Leary	.05
250	Cal Ripken, Jr.	1.00
251	John Dopson	.05
252	Billy Hatcher	.05
253	Robin Yount	.50
254	Mickey Hatcher	.05
255	Bob Horner	.05
256	Benito Santiago	.05
257	Luis Rivera	.05
258	Fred McGriff	.10
259	Dave Wells	.10
260	Dave Winfield	.60
261	Rafael Ramirez	.05
262	Nick Esasky	.05
263	Barry Bonds	1.00
264	Joe Magrane	.05
265	Kent Hrbek	.05
266	Jack Morris	.05
267	Jeff Robinson	.05
268	Ron Kittle	.05
269	Candy Maldonado	.05
270	Wally Joyner	.05
271	Glenn Braggs	.05
272	Ron Hassey	.05
273	Jose Lind	.05
274	Mark Eichhorn	.05
275	Danny Tartabull	.05
276	Paul Kilgus	.05
277	Mike Davis	.05
278	Andy McGaffigan	.05
279	Scott Bradley	.05
280	Bob Knepper	.05
281	Gary Redus	.05
282	Rickey Henderson	.60
283	Andy Allanson	.05
284	Rick Leach	.05
285	John Candelaria	.05
286	Dick Schofield	.05
287	Bryan Harvey	.05
288	Randy Bush	.05
289	Ernie Whitt	.05
290	John Franco	.05
291	Todd Worrell	.05
292	Teddy Higuera	.05
293	Keith Moreland	.05
294	Juan Berenguer	.05
295	Scott Fletcher	.05
296	Roger McDowell	.10
297	Mark Grace	.05
298	Chris James	.05
299	Frank Tanana	.05
300	Darryl Strawberry	.05
301	Charlie Leibrandt	.05
302	Gary Ward	.05
303	Brian Fisher	.05
304	Terry Steinbach	.05
305	Dave Smith	.05
306	Greg Minton	.05
307	Lance McCullers	.05
308	Phil Bradley	.05
309	Terry Kennedy	.05
310	Rafael Palmeiro	.45
311	Ellis Burks	.05
312	Doug Jones	.05
313	Dennis Martinez	.10
314	Pete O'Brien	.05
315	Greg Swindell	.05
316	Walt Weiss	.05
317	Pete Stanicek	.05
318	Gene Nelson	.05
319	Danny Jackson	.05
320	Lou Whitaker	.05
321	Will Clark	.10
322	John Smiley	.05
323	Mike Marshall	.05
324	Gary Carter	.60
325	Jesse Barfield	.05
326	Dennis Boyd	.05
327	Dave Henderson	.05
328	Chet Lemon	.05
329	Bob Melvin	.05
330	Eric Davis	.05
331	Ted Power	.05
332	Carmelo Martinez	.05
333	Bob Ojeda	.05
334	Steve Lyons	.05
335	Dave Righetti	.05
336	Steve Balboni	.05
337	Calvin Schiraldi	.05
338	Vance Law	.05
339	Zane Smith	.05
340	Kirk Gibson	.05
341	Jim Deshaies	.05
342	Tom Brookens	.05
343	Pat Borders	.10
344	Devon White	.10
345	Charlie Hough	.05
346	Rex Hudler	.05
347	John Cerutti	.05
348	Kirk McCaskill	.05
349	Len Dykstra	.05
350	Andy Van Slyke	.05
351	Jeff Robinson	.05
352	Rick Schu	.05
353	Bruce Benedict	.05
354	Bill Wegman	.05
355	Mark Langston	.05
356	Steve Farr	.05
357	Richard Dotson	.05
358	Andres Thomas	.05
359	Alan Ashby	.05
360	Ryne Sandberg	.60
361	Kelly Downs	.05
362	Jeff Musselman	.05
363	Barry Larkin	.05
364	Rob Deer	.05
365	Mike Henneman	.05
366	Nolan Ryan	1.00
367	Johnny Paredes	.05
368	Bobby Thigpen	.05
369	Mickey Brantley	.05
370	Dennis Eckersley	.45
371	Manny Lee	.05
372	Juan Samuel	.05
373	Tracy Jones	.05
374	Mike Greenwell	.05
375	Terry Pendleton	.05
376	Steve Lombardozzi	.05
377	Mitch Williams	.05
378	Glenn Davis	.05
379	Mark Gubicza	.05
380	Orel Hershiser	.05
381	Jimmy Williams	.05
382	Kirk Gibson	.05
383	Howard Johnson	.05
384	Dave Cone	.05
385	Von Hayes	.05
386	Luis Polonia	.05
387	Dan Gladden	.05
388	Pete Smith	.05
389	Jose Canseco	.35
390	Mickey Hatcher	.05
391	Wil Tejada	.05
392	Duane Ward	.05
393	Rick Mahler	.05
394	Rick Sutcliffe	.05
395	Dave Martinez	.05
396	Ken Dayley	.05

Box Panels

Continuing its practice of printing baseball cards on the bottom panels of its wax pack boxes, OPC in 1989 issued a special 16-card set, printing four cards on each of four different box-bottom panels. The cards are identical in design to the regular 1989 OPC cards. They are designated by letter (from A through P) rather than by number.

		NM/M
Complete Panel Set (4):		10.00
Complete Singles Set (16):		10.00
Common Panel:		1.50
Common Single Player:		.10
Panel		2.50
A	George Brett	1.50
B	Bill Buckner	.10
C	Darrell Evans	.10
D	Rich Gossage	.10
Panel		1.50
E	Greg Gross	.10
F	Rickey Henderson	1.00
G	Keith Hernandez	.10
H	Tom Lasorda	.25
Panel		7.50
I	Jim Rice	.50
J	Cal Ripken, Jr.	3.00
K	Nolan Ryan	3.00
L	Mike Schmidt	1.50
Panel		1.50
M	Bruce Sutter	.75
N	Don Sutton	.50
O	Kent Tekulve	.05
P	Dave Winfield	1.00

Stickers/Stickercards

Once again sharing a checklist with the 1989 Topps sticker issue, the OPC version differs only in the substitution of the O-Pee-Chee logo and copyright notice on the front of the stickercard. Values are also essentially the same, although Expos and Blue Jays stars carry a small premium in the OPC version.

1990 O-Pee-Chee

Virtually identical to the contemporary 1990 Topps set, the OPC issue features the same 792 cards. On most cards the fronts are indistinguishable, even to the use of a Topps logo on the Canadian product. A number of the OPC cards differ from their Topps counterparts in that there is a notice of team change printed in black on the front. Backs of the OPC cards feature a few lines of French in areas such as the stat headings, the career summary and monthly scoreboard. The OPC cards omit the Topps copyright line and feature an OPC copyright line on back.

	NM/M
Unopened Fact. Set (792):	15.00
Complete Set (792):	12.00
Common Player:	.05
Wax Pack:	.75
Wax Box (36):	20.00

Stickers

Once again sharing a checklist with the 1990 Topps sticker issue, the OPC version differs only in the substitution of the O-Pee-Chee logo and copyright notice on the stickercard. Values are also essentially the same, although Expos and Blue Jays stars carry a small premium in the OPC version.

Sample Sheet

This 7-1/2" x 10-1/2" sample sheet debuts the 1991 OPC set. Fronts reproduce the basic design while the back, printed in blue on white, contains an ad for OPC.

	NM/M
Complete Sheet:	5.00

1991 O-Pee-Chee

Once again for 1991, OPC utilized the contemporary Topps set of 792 cards as the basis for its own issue. The OPC cards are again printed on a lighter, whiter stock and differ from the Topps cards in the addition of French to the card backs, along with the OPC copyright. Many card fronts in OPC carry a small black typographical notice concerning team changes by the players.

	NM/M
Complete Set (792):	10.00
Common Player:	.05
Wax Box (36):	9.00

Premier

The O-Pee-Chee Co. of London, Ontario, Canada produced this 132-card set. The card fronts feature action photos, while the flip sides display a posed photo and career statistics. The cards were packaged seven cards per pack in a tamper-proof foil wrap. Several Expo and Blue Jay players are featured. Two special cards are included in this set. Card #62 honors Rickey Henderson's stolen base record, while card #102 commemorates Nolan Ryan's seventh no-hitter. Traded players and free agents are featured with their new teams.

	NM/M
Unopened Fact. Set (132):	4.00
Complete Set (132):	3.00
Common Player:	.05
Wax Pack (7):	.75
Wax Box (36):	9.00

No.	Player	Price
1	Roberto Alomar	.40
2	Sandy Alomar	.05
3	Moises Alou	.20
4	Brian Barnes	.05
5	Steve Bedrosian	.05
6	George Bell	.10
7	Juan Bell	.05
8	Albert Belle	.20
9	Bud Black	.05
10	Mike Boddicker	.05
11	Wade Boggs	.75
12	Barry Bonds	1.00
13	Denis Boucher	.10
14	George Brett	.85
15	Hubie Brooks	.05
16	Brett Butler	.05
17	Ivan Calderon	.05
18	Jose Canseco	.25
19	Gary Carter	.75
20	Joe Carter	.10
21	Jack Clark	.05
22	Will Clark	.05
23	Roger Clemens	.90
24	Alex Cole	.05
25	Vince Coleman	.05
26	Jeff Conine	.05
27	Milt Cuyler	.05
28	Danny Darwin	.05
29	Eric Davis	.05
30	Glenn Davis	.05
31	Andre Dawson	.25
32	Ken Dayley	.05
33	Steve Decker	.05
34	Delino DeShields	.10
35	Lance Dickson	.05
36	Kirk Dressendorfer	.05
37	Shawon Dunston	.05
38	Dennis Eckersley	.50
39	Dwight Evans	.05
40	Howard Farmer	.05
41	Junior Felix	.05
42	Alex Fernandez	.10
43	Tony Fernandez	.05
44	Cecil Fielder	.15
45	Carlton Fisk	.60
46	Willie Fraser	.05
47	Gary Gaetti	.05
48	Andres Galarraga	.10
49	Ron Gant	.05
50	Kirk Gibson	.05
51	Bernard Gilkey	.05
52	Leo Gomez	.05
53	Rene Gonzalez	.05
54	Juan Gonzalez	.45
55	Doc Gooden	.05
56	Ken Griffey Jr.	.90
57	Kelly Gruber	.05
58	Pedro Guerrero	.05
59	Tony Gwynn	.75
60	Chris Hammond	.05
61	Ron Hassey	.05
62	Rickey Henderson	.75
63	Tom Henke	.05
64	Orel Hershiser	.05
65	Chris Hoiles	.05
66	Todd Hundley	.05
67	Pete Incaviglia	.05
68	Danny Jackson	.05
69	Barry Jones	.05
70	David Justice	.05
71	Jimmy Key	.05
72	Ray Lankford	.05
73	Darren Lewis	.05
74	Kevin Maas	.05
75	Denny Martinez	.10
76	Tino Martinez	.05
77	Don Mattingly	.85
78	Willie McGee	.05
79	Fred McGriff	.15
80	Hensley Meulens	.05
81	Kevin Mitchell	.05
82	Paul Molitor	.75
83	Mickey Morandini	.05
84	Jack Morris	.05
85	Dale Murphy	.15
86	Eddie Murray	.60
87	Chris Nabholz	.05
88	Tim Naehring	.05
89	Otis Nixon	.05
90	Jose Offerman	.05
91	Bob Ojeda	.05
92	John Olerud	.15
93	Gregg Olson	.05
94	Dave Parker	.05
95	Terry Pendleton	.05
96	Kirby Puckett	.75
97	Rock Raines	.10
98	Jeff Reardon	.05
99	Dave Righetti	.05
100	Cal Ripken	1.00
101	Mel Rojas	.05
102	Nolan Ryan	1.00
103	Ryne Sandberg	.75
104	Scott Sanderson	.05
105	Benito Santiago	.05
106	Pete Schourek	.05
107	Gary Scott	.05
108	Terry Shumpert	.05
109	Ruben Sierra	.05
110	Doug Simons	.05
111	Dave Smith	.05
112	Ozzie Smith	.75
113	Cory Snyder	.05
114	Luis Sojo	.05
115	Dave Stewart	.10
116	Dave Stieb	.05
117	Darryl Strawberry	.05
118	Pat Tabler	.05
119	Wade Taylor	.05
120	Bobby Thigpen	.05
121	Frank Thomas	.60
122	Mike Timlin	.05
123	Alan Trammell	.05
124	Mo Vaughn	.05
125	Tim Wallach	.05
126	Devon White	.10
127	Mark Whiten	.05
128	Bernie Williams	.10
129	Willie Wilson	.05
130	Dave Winfield	.75
131	Robin Yount	.60
132	Checklist	.05

1992 O-Pee-Chee

Once again closely following the format of the 1992 Topps set, and for the most part corresponding to its 792-card checklist, the 1992 OPCs differ on the front only in the substitution of an O-Pee-Chee logo for the Topps logo, and in the inclusion of team-change information for many of the players who moved after the Topps cards were printed. On backs, the light blue "Topps" logo printed behind the stats has been removed, and the logo beneath the card number changed from "Topps" to "O-Pee-Chee." The addition of a few lines of French above the stats and in the career summary can be seen on the OPC cards, as well as the substitution of an OPC copyright line for that of Topps. Where the 1992 Topps set features All-Star cards in the number range 386-407, the OPC set has a group of player cards who are not represented in the Topps set, including four "Tribute" cards honoring Gary Carter. Card #45 in the OPC set is also a Carter Tribute card, whereas in the Topps set it is a regular card.

	NM/M
Unopened Fact. Set (792):	15.00
Complete Set (792):	10.00
Common Player:	.05
Wax Box (36):	12.00
45 Gary Carter - Tribute	1.00
386 Lance Blankenship	.10
387 Gary Carter - Tribute	1.00
388 Ron Tingley	.10
389 Gary Carter - Tribute	1.00
390 Gene Harris	.10
391 Jeff Schaefer	.10
392 Mark Grant	.10
393 Carl Willis	.10
394 Al Leiter	.25
395 Ron Robinson	.10
396 Tim Hullett	.10
397 Craig Worthington	.10
398 John Orton	.10
399 Gary Carter - Tribute	1.00
400 John Dopson	.10
401 Moises Alou	.60
402 Gary Carter - Tribute	1.00
403 Matt Young	.10
404 Wayne Edwards	.10
405 Nick Esasky	.10
406 Dave Eiland	.10
407 Mike Brumley	.10

Premier

JOSE MELENDEZ

O-Pee-Chee increased the number of cards in its premier set to 198 for 1992. The cards feature white borders surrounding full-color player photos. The O-Pee-Chee banner appears at the top of the card and the player's name and position appear at the bottom. The backs feature an additional player photo, statistics and player information. Traded players and free agents are featured with their new teams.

	NM/M
Factory Set (198):	5.00
Complete Set (198):	4.00
Common Player:	.10
Wax Box (36):	9.00
1 Wade Boggs	.75
2 John Smiley	.10
3 Checklist	.10
4 Ron Gant	.10
5 Mike Bordick	.10
6 Charlie Hayes	.10
7 Kevin Morton	.10
8 Checklist	.10
9 Chris Gwynn	.10
10 Melido Perez	.10
11 Danny Gladden	.10
12 Brian McRae	.15
13 Denny Martinez	.15
14 Bob Scanlan	.10
15 Julio Franco	.10
16 Ruben Amaro	.10
17 Mo Sanford	.10
18 Scott Bankhead	.10
19 Dickie Thon	.10
20 Chris James	.10
21 Mike Huff	.10
22 Orlando Merced	.10
23 Chris Sabo	.10

24 Jose Canseco	.40
25 Reggie Sanders	.10
26 Chris Nabholz	.10
27 Kevin Seitzer	.10
28 Ryan Bowen	.10
29 Gary Carter	.75
30 Wayne Rosenthal	.10
31 Alan Trammell	.10
32 Doug Drabek	.10
33 Craig Shipley	.10
34 Ryne Sandberg	.75
35 Chuck Knoblauch	.10
36 Bret Barberie	.10
37 Tim Naehring	.10
38 Omar Olivares	.10
39 Royce Clayton	.10
40 Brent Mayne	.10
41 Darrin Fletcher	.10
42 Howard Johnson	.10
43 Steve Sax	.10
44 Greg Swindell	.10
45 Andre Dawson	.25
46 Kent Hrbek	.10
47 Doc Gooden	.10
48 Mark Leiter	.10
49 Tom Glavine	.25
50 Mo Vaughn	.10
51 Doug Jones	.10
52 Brian Barnes	.10
53 Rob Dibble	.10
54 Kevin McReynolds	.10
55 Ivan Rodriguez	.50
56 Scott Livingstone	.10
57 Mike Magnante	.10
58 Pete Schourek	.10
59 Frank Thomas	.60
60 Kirk McCaskill	.10
61 Wally Joyner	.10
62 Rick Aguilera	.10
63 Eric Karros	.10
64 Tino Martinez	.10
65 Bryan Hickerson	.10
66 Ruben Sierra	.10
67 Willie Randolph	.10
68 Bill Landrum	.10
69 Bip Roberts	.10
70 Cecil Fielder	.15
71 Pat Kelly	.10
72 Kenny Lofton	.10
73 John Franco	.10
74 Phil Plantier	.10
75 Dave Martinez	.10
76 Warren Newson	.10
77 Chito Martinez	.10
78 Brian Hunter	.10
79 Jack Morris	.10
80 Eric King	.10
81 Nolan Ryan	1.50
82 Bret Saberhagen	.10
83 Roberto Kelly	.10
84 Ozzie Smith	.75
85 Chuck McElroy	.10
86 Carlton Fisk	.60
87 Mike Mussina	.50
88 Mark Carreon	.10
89 Ken Hill	.10
90 Rick Cerone	.10
91 Deion Sanders	.15
92 Don Mattingly	.85
93 Danny Tartabull	.10
94 Keith Miller	.10
95 Gregg Jefferies	.10
96 Barry Larkin	.10
97 Kevin Mitchell	.10
98 Rick Sutcliffe	.10
99 Mark McGwire	1.25
100 Albert Belle	.10
101 Gregg Olson	.10
102 Kirby Puckett	.75
103 Luis Gonzalez	.10
104 Randy Myers	.10
105 Roger Clemens	.90
106 Tony Gwynn	.75
107 Jeff Bagwell	.60
108 John Wetteland	.10
109 Bernie Williams	.10
110 Scott Kamieniecki	.10
111 Robin Yount	.60
112 Dean Palmer	.10
113 Tim Belcher	.10
114 George Brett	.85
115 Frank Viola	.10
116 Kelly Gruber	.10
117 David Justice	.10
118 Scott Leuis	.10
119 Jeff Fassero	.10
120 Sammy Sosa	.90
121 Al Osuna	.10
122 Wilson Alvarez	.10
123 Jose Offerman	.10
124 Mel Rojas	.10
125 Shawon Dunston	.10
126 Pete Incaviglia	.10
127 Von Hayes	.10
128 Dave Gallagher	.10
129 Eric Davis	.10
130 Roberto Alomar	.35
131 Mike Gallego	.10
132 Robin Ventura	.10
133 Bill Swift	.10
134 John Kruk	.10
135 Craig Biggio	.10
136 Eddie Taubensee	.10
137 Cal Ripken, Jr.	1.50
138 Charles Nagy	.10
139 Jose Melendez	.10
140 Jim Abbott	.10
141 Paul Molitor	.75

142 Tom Candiotti	.10
143 Bobby Bonilla	.10
144 Matt Williams	.10
145 Brett Butler	.10
146 Will Clark	.10
147 Rickey Henderson	.75
148 Ray Lankford	.10
149 Bill Pecota	.10
150 Dave Winfield	.75
151 Darren Lewis	.10
152 Bob MacDonald	.10
153 David Segui	.10
154 Benny Santiago	.10
155 Chuck Finley	.10
156 Andujar Cedeno	.10
157 Barry Bonds	1.50
158 Joe Grahe	.10
159 Frank Castillo	.10
160 Dave Burba	.10
161 Leo Gomez	.10
162 Orel Hershiser	.10
163 Delino DeShields	.15
164 Sandy Alomar	.10
165 Denny Neagle	.10
166 Fred McGriff	.15
167 Ken Griffey Jr.	1.00
168 Juan Guzman	.10
169 Bobby Rose	.10
170 Steve Avery	.10
171 Rich DeLucia	.10
172 Mike Timlin	.10
173 Randy Johnson	.65
174 Paul Gibson	.10
175 David Cone	.10
176 Marquis Grissom	.15
177 Kurt Stillwell	.10
178 Mark Whiten	.10
179 Darryl Strawberry	.10
180 Mike Morgan	.10
181 Scott Scudder	.10
182 George Bell	.15
183 Alvin Davis	.10
184 Len Dykstra	.10
185 Kyle Abbott	.10
186 Chris Haney	.10
187 Junior Noboa	.10
188 Dennis Eckersley	.50
189 Derek Bell	.20
190 Lee Smith	.10
191 Andres Galarraga	.15
192 Jack Armstrong	.10
193 Eddie Murray	.60
194 Joe Carter	.15
195 Terry Pendleton	.10
196 Darryl Kile	.10
197 Rod Beck	.10
198 Hubie Brooks	.10

1993 O-Pee-Chee

Blue Jays

DEVON WHITE OUTFIELDER

For the first time in history, the 1993 O-Pee-Chee set differed significantly from the Topps set; photographs and designs are entirely different. Team names are scripted across the top, but a yellow triangle with a new team name appears on the front for players who have been traded. Two insert sets honoring the 1992 World Champion Toronto Blue Jays were also produced.

	NM/M
Complete Set (396):	15.00
Common Player:	.10
Wax Pack (8):	.75
Wax Box:	15.00
1 Jim Abbott	.10
2 Eric Anthony	.10
3 Harold Baines	.10
4 Roberto Alomar	.45
5 Steve Avery	.10
6 James Austin	.10
7 Mark Wohlers	.10
8 Steve Buechele	.10
9 Pedro Astacio	.10
10 Moises Alou	.20
11 Rod Beck	.10
12 Sandy Alomar	.10
13 Brett Boone	.10
14 Bryan Harvey	.10
15 Bobby Bonilla	.10
16 Brady Anderson	.10
17 Andy Benes	.10
18 Ruben Amaro	.10
19 Jay Bell	.10
20 Kevin Brown	.10
21 Scott Bankhead	.10

22 Denis Boucher	.10
23 Kevin Appier	.10
24 Pat Kelly	.10
25 Rick Aguilera	.10
26 George Bell	.10
27 Steve Farr	.10
28 Chad Curtis	.10
29 Jeff Bagwell	.60
30 Lance Blankenship	.10
31 Derek Bell	.10
32 Damon Berryhill	.10
33 Ricky Bones	.10
34 Rheal Cormier	.10
35 Andre Dawson	.30
36 Brett Butler	.10
37 Sean Berry	.10
38 Bud Black	.10
39 Carlos Baerga	.10
40 Jay Buhner	.10
41 Charlie Hough	.10
42 Sid Fernandez	.10
43 Luis Mercedes	.10
44 Jerald Clark	.10
45 Wes Chamberlain	.10
46 Barry Bonds	1.50
47 Jose Canseco	.30
48 Tim Belcher	.10
49 David Nied	.10
50 George Brett	.85
51 Cecil Fielder	.10
52 Chili Davis	.10
53 Alex Fernandez	.10
54 Charlie Hayes	.10
55 Rob Ducey	.10
56 Craig Biggio	.10
57 Mike Bordick	.10
58 Pat Borders	.10
59 Jeff Blauser	.10
60 Chris Bosio	.10
61 Bernard Gilkey	.10
62 Shawon Dunston	.10
63 Tom Candiotti	.10
64 Darrin Fletcher	.10
65 Jeff Brantley	.10
66 Albert Belle	.10
67 Dave Fleming	.10
68 John Franco	.10
69 Glenn Davis	.10
70 Tony Fernandez	.10
71 Darren Daulton	.10
72 Doug Drabek	.10
73 Julio Franco	.10
74 Tom Browning	.10
75 Tom Gordon	.10
76 Travis Fryman	.10
77 Scott Erickson	.10
78 Carlton Fisk	.60
79 Roberto Kelly	.10
80 Gary DiSarcina	.10
81 Ken Caminiti	.10
82 Ron Darling	.10
83 Joe Carter	.15
84 Sid Bream	.10
85 Cal Eldred	.10
86 Mark Grace	.10
87 Eric Davis	.10
88 Ivan Calderon	.10
89 John Burkett	.10
90 Felix Fermin	.10
91 Ken Griffey Jr.	1.00
92 Doc Gooden	.10
93 Mike Devereaux	.10
94 Tony Gwynn	.75
95 Mariano Duncan	.10
96 Jeff King	.10
97 Juan Gonzalez	.50
98 Norm Charlton	.10
99 Mark Gubicza	.10
100 Danny Gladden	.10
101 Greg Gagne	.10
102 Ozzie Guillen	.10
103 Don Mattingly	.85
104 Damion Easley	.10
105 Casey Candaele	.10
106 Dennis Eckersley	.50
107 David Cone	.10
108 Ron Gant	.10
109 Mike Fetters	.10
110 Mike Harkey	.10
111 Kevin Gross	.10
112 Archi Cianfrocco	.10
113 Will Clark	.10
114 Glenallen Hill	.10
115 Erik Hanson	.10
116 Todd Hundley	.10
117 Leo Gomez	.10
118 Bruce Hurst	.10
119 Len Dykstra	.10
120 Jose Lind	.10
121 Jose Guzman	.10
122 Rob Dibble	.10
123 Gregg Jefferies	.10
124 Bill Gullickson	.10
125 Brian Harper	.10
126 Roberto Hernandez	.10
127 Sam Militello	.10
128 Junior Felix	.10
129 Andujar Cedeno	.10
130 Rickey Henderson	.75
131 Bob MacDonald	.10
132 Tom Glavine	.25
133 Scott Fletcher	.10
134 Brian Jordan	.10
135 Greg Maddux	.75
136 Orel Hershiser	.10
137 Greg Colbrunn	.10
138 Royce Clayton	.10
139 Thomas Howard	.10

140 Randy Johnson	.75
141 Jeff Innis	.10
142 Chris Hoiles	.10
143 Darrin Jackson	.10
144 Tommy Greene	.10
145 Mike LaValliere	.10
146 David Hulse	.10
147 Barry Larkin	.10
148 Wally Joyner	.10
149 Mike Henneman	.10
150 Kent Hrbek	.10
151 Bo Jackson	.15
152 Rich Monteleone	.10
153 Chuck Finley	.10
154 Steve Finley	.10
155 Dave Henderson	.10
156 Kelly Gruber	.10
157 Brian Hunter	.10
158 Darryl Hamilton	.10
159 Derrick May	.10
160 Jay Howell	.10
161 Wil Cordero	.10
162 Bryan Hickerson	.10
163 Reggie Jefferson	.10
164 Edgar Martinez	.10
165 Nigel Wilson	.10
166 Howard Johnson	.10
167 Tim Hulett	.10
168 Mike Maddux	.10
169 Dave Hollins	.10
170 Zane Smith	.10
171 Rafael Palmeiro	.45
172 Dave Martinez	.10
173 Rusty Meacham	.10
174 Mark Leiter	.10
175 Chuck Knoblauch	.10
176 Lance Johnson	.10
177 Matt Nokes	.10
178 Luis Gonzalez	.10
179 Jack Morris	.10
180 David Justice	.10
181 Doug Henry	.10
182 Felix Jose	.10
183 Delino DeShields	.15
184 Rene Gonzales	.10
185 Pete Harnisch	.10
186 Mike Moore	.10
187 Juan Guzman	.10
188 John Olerud	.20
189 Ryan Klesko	.10
190 John Jaha	.10
191 Ray Lankford	.10
192 Jeff Fassero	.10
193 Darren Lewis	.10
194 Mark Lewis	.10
195 Alan Mills	.10
196 Wade Boggs	.75
197 Hal Morris	.10
198 Ron Karkovice	.10
199 John Grahe	.10
200 Butch Henry	.10
201 Mark McGwire	1.25
202 Tom Henke	.10
203 Ed Sprague	.10
204 Charlie Leibrandt	.10
205 Pat Listach	.10
206 Omar Olivares	.10
207 Mike Morgan	.10
208 Eric Karros	.10
209 Marquis Grissom	.15
210 Willie McGee	.10
211 Derek Lilliquist	.10
212 Tino Martinez	.10
213 Jeff Kent	.10
214 Mike Mussina	.35
215 Randy Myers	.10
216 John Kruk	.10
217 Tom Brunansky	.10
218 Paul O'Neill	.10
219 Scott Livingstone	.10
220 John Valentin	.10
221 Eddie Zosky	.10
222 Pete Smith	.10
223 Bill Wegman	.10
224 Todd Zeile	.10
225 Tim Wallach	.10
226 Mitch Williams	.10
227 Tim Wakefield	.10
228 Frank Viola	.10
229 Nolan Ryan	1.50
230 Kirk McCaskill	.10
231 Melido Perez	.10
232 Mark Langston	.10
233 Xavier Hernandez	.10
234 Jerry Browne	.10
235 Dave Stieb	.15
236 Mark Lemke	.10
237 Paul Molitor	.75
238 Geronimo Pena	.10
239 Ken Hill	.10
240 Jack Clark	.10
241 Greg Myers	.10
242 Pete Incaviglia	.10
243 Ruben Sierra	.10
244 Todd Stottlemyre	.10
245 Pat Hentgen	.10
246 Melvin Nieves	.10
247 Jaime Navarro	.10
248 Donovan Osborne	.10
249 Brian Barnes	.10
250 Cory Snyder	.10
251 Kenny Lofton	.10
252 Kevin Mitchell	.10
253 Dave Magadan	.10
254 Ben McDonald	.10
255 Fred McGriff	.20
256 Mickey Morandini	.10
257 Randy Tomlin	.10

258 Dean Palmer	.10
259 Roger Clemens	1.00
260 Joe Oliver	.10
261 Jeff Montgomery	.10
262 Tony Phillips	.10
263 Shane Mack	.10
264 Jack McDowell	.10
265 Mike Macfarlane	.10
266 Luis Polonia	.10
267 Doug Jones	.10
268 Terry Steinbach	.10
269 Jimmy Key	.10
270 Pat Tabler	.10
271 Otis Nixon	.10
272 Dave Nilsson	.10
273 Tom Pagnozzi	.10
274 Ryne Sandberg	.75
275 Ramon Martinez	.10
276 Tim Laker	.10
277 Bill Swift	.10
278 Charles Nagy	.10
279 Harold Reynolds	.10
280 Eddie Murray	.60
281 Gregg Olson	.10
282 Frank Seminara	.10
283 Terry Mulholland	.10
284 Kevin Palmer	.10
285 Mike Greenwell	.10
286 Jose Rijo	.10
287 Brian McRae	.10
288 Frank Tanana	.10
289 Pedro Munoz	.10
290 Tim Raines	.15
291 Andy Stankiewicz	.10
292 Tim Salmon	.10
293 Jimmy Jones	.10
294 Dave Stewart	.15
295 Mike Timlin	.10
296 Greg Olson	.10
297 Dan Plesac	.10
298 Mike Perez	.10
299 Jose Offerman	.10
300 Denny Martinez	.15
301 Robby Thompson	.10
302 Bret Saberhagen	.10
303 Joe Orsulak	.10
304 Tim Naehring	.10
305 Bip Roberts	.10
306 Kirby Puckett	.75
307 Steve Sax	.10
308 Danny Tartabull	.10
309 Jeff Juden	.10
310 Duane Ward	.10
311 Alejandro Pena	.10
312 Kevin Seitzer	.10
313 Ozzie Smith	.75
314 Mike Piazza	1.00
315 Chris Nabholz	.10
316 Tony Pena	.10
317 Gary Sheffield	.25
318 Mark Portugal	.10
319 Walt Weiss	.10
320 Manuel Lee	.10
321 David Wells	.15
322 Terry Pendleton	.10
323 Billy Spiers	.10
324 Lee Smith	.10
325 Bob Scanlan	.10
326 Mike Scioscia	.10
327 Spike Owen	.10
328 Mackey Sasser	.10
329 Arthur Rhodes	.10
330 Ben Rivera	.10
331 Ivan Rodriguez	.50
332 Phil Plantier	.10
333 Chris Sabo	.10
334 Mickey Tettleton	.10
335 John Smiley	.10
336 Bobby Thigpen	.10
337 Randy Velarde	.10
338 Luis Sojo	.10
339 Scott Servais	.10
340 Bob Welch	.10
341 Devon White	.15
342 Jeff Reardon	.10
343 B.J. Surhoff	.10
344 Bob Tewksbury	.10
345 Jose Vizcaino	.10
346 Mike Sharperson	.10
347 Mel Rojas	.10
348 Matt Williams	.10
349 Steve Olin	.10
350 Mike Schooler	.10
351 Ryan Thompson	.10
352 Cal Ripken	1.50
353 Benny Santiago	.10
354 Curt Schilling	.25
355 Andy Van Slyke	.10
356 Kenny Rogers	.10
357 Jody Reed	.10
358 Reggie Sanders	.10
359 Kevin McReynolds	.10
360 Alan Trammell	.10
361 Kevin Tapani	.10
362 Frank Thomas	.60
363 Bernie Williams	.10
364 John Smoltz	.10
365 Robin Yount	.60
366 John Wetteland	.10
367 Bob Zupcic	.10
368 Julio Valera	.10
369 Brian Williams	.10
370 Willie Wilson	.10
371 Dave Winfield	.75
372 Deion Sanders	.10
373 Greg Vaughn	.10
374 Todd Worrell	.10
375 Darryl Strawberry	.10

376	John Vander Wal	.10
377	Mike Benjamin	.10
378	Mark Whiten	.10
379	Omar Vizquel	.10
380	Anthony Young	.10
381	Rick Sutcliffe	.10
382	Candy Maldonado	.10
383	Francisco Cabrera	.10
384	Larry Walker	.20
385	Scott Cooper	.10
386	Gerald Williams	.10
387	Robin Ventura	.10
388	Carl Willis	.10
389	Lou Whitaker	.10
390	Hipolito Pichardo	.10
391	Rudy Seanez	.10
392	Greg Swindell	.10
393	Mo Vaughn	.10
394	Checklist 1 of 3	.10
395	Checklist 2 of 3	.10
396	Checklist 3 of 3	.10

World Champs

This 18-card insert set commemorates the Toronto Blue Jays' 1992 World Series victory; 17 players and Manager Cito Gaston are featured. Cards were randomly inserted, one World Champs or World Series Heroes card per every 69-cent, eight-card pack. Fronts and backs each feature the World's Championship logo. Backs include stats from the 1992 ALCS and World Series.

		NM/M
Complete Set (18):		4.00
Common Player:		.25
1	Roberto Alomar	1.00
2	Pat Borders	.25
3	Joe Carter	.65
4	David Cone	.35
5	Kelly Gruber	.25
6	Juan Guzman	.25
7	Tom Henke	.25
8	Jimmy Key	.35
9	Manuel Lee	.25
10	Candy Maldonado	.25
11	Jack Morris	.35
12	John Olerud	.50
13	Ed Sprague	.25
14	Todd Stottlemyre	.25
15	Duane Ward	.25
16	Devon White	.35
17	Dave Winfield	1.50
18	Cito Gaston	.25

World Series Heroes

This insert set honors four of the Toronto Blue Jays' World Series stars. Cards were randomly inserted in every 69-cent, eight-card pack, one World Champs or World Series Heroes card per pack.

		NM/M
Complete Set (4):		1.50
Common Player:		.25
1	Pat Borders	.25
2	Jimmy Key	.25
3	Ed Sprague	.25
4	Dave Winfield	1.50

Premier

For the third consecutive year, O-Pee-Chee produced a set under

DAVID CONE • P

its Premier brand name. The regular set, issued in three series, has 132 cards and 48 insert cards. The insert sets are titled Star Performers (gold borders), Foil Star Performers (full-bleed photos and gold stamping), and Top Draft Picks (two each featuring the Toronto Blue Jays and Montreal Expos top picks). O-Pee-Chee announced it produced only 4,000 cases for this set.

		NM/M
Complete Set (132):		4.00
Common Player:		.05
Wax Box:		8.00
1	Barry Bonds	1.50
2	Chad Curtis	.05
3	Chris Bosio	.05
4	Cal Eldred	.05
5	Dan Walter	.05
6	Rene Arocha	.05
7	Delino DeShields	.05
8	Spike Owen	.05
9	Jeff Russell	.05
10	Phil Plantier	.05
11	Mike Christopher	.05
12	Darren Daulton	.05
13	Scott Cooper	.05
14	Paul O'Neill	.05
15	Jimmy Key	.05
16	Dickie Thon	.05
17	Greg Gohr	.05
18	Andre Dawson	.25
19	Steve Cooke	.05
20	Tony Fernandez	.05
21	Mark Gardner	.05
22	Dave Martinez	.05
23	Jose Guzman	.05
24	Chili Davis	.05
25	Randy Knorr	.05
26	Mike Piazza	1.00
27	Benji Gil	.05
28	Dave Winfield	.45
29	Wil Cordero	.05
30	Butch Henry	.05
31	Eric Young	.05
32	Orestes Destrade	.05
33	Randy Myers	.05
34	Tom Brunansky	.05
35	Dan Wilson	.05
36	Juan Guzman	.05
37	Tim Salmon	.05
38	Bill Krueger	.05
39	Larry Walker	.25
40	David Hulse	.05
41	Ken Ryan	.05
42	Jose Lind	.05
43	Benny Santiago	.05
44	Ray Lankford	.05
45	Dave Stewart	.05
46	Don Mattingly	.60
47	Fernando Valenzuela	.05
48	Scott Fletcher	.05
49	Wade Boggs	.50
50	Norm Charlton	.05
51	Carlos Baerga	.05
52	John Olerud	.15
53	Willie Wilson	.05
54	Dennis Moeller	.05
55	Joe Orsulak	.05
56	John Smiley	.05
57	Al Martin	.05
58	Andres Galarraga	.15
59	Billy Ripken	.05
60	Dave Stieb	.05
61	Dave Magadan	.05
62	Todd Worrell	.05
63	Sherman Obando	.05
64	Kent Bottenfield	.05
65	Vinny Castilla	.05
66	Charlie Hayes	.05
67	Mike Hartley	.05
68	Harold Baines	.05
69	John Cummings	.05
70	J.T. Snow	.05
71	Graeme Lloyd	.05
72	Frank Bolick	.05
73	Doug Drabek	.05
74	Milt Thompson	.05
75	Tim Pugh	.05
76	John Kruk	.05
77	Tom Henke	.05
78	Kevin Young	.05
79	Ryan Thompson	.05
80	Mike Hampton	.05
81	Jose Canseco	.30

82	Mike Lansing	.15
83	Candy Maldonado	.05
84	Alex Arias	.05
85	Troy Neel	.05
86	Greg Swindell	.05
87	Tim Wallach	.05
88	Andy Van Slyke	.05
89	Harold Baines	.05
90	Bryan Harvey	.05
91	Jerald Clark	.05
92	David Cone	.05
93	Ellis Burks	.05
94	Scott Bankhead	.05
95	Pete Incaviglia	.05
96	Cecil Fielder	.10
97	Sean Berry	.05
98	Gregg Jefferies	.05
99	Billy Brewer	.05
100	Scott Sanderson	.05
101	Walt Weiss	.05
102	Travis Fryman	.05
103	Barry Larkin	.05
104	Darren Holmes	.05
105	Ivan Calderon	.05
106	Terry Jorgensen	.05
107	David Nied	.05
108	Tim Bogar	.05
109	Roberto Kelly	.05
110	Mike Moore	.05
111	Carlos Garcia	.05
112	Mike Bielecki	.05
113	Trevor Hoffman	.05
114	Rich Amaral	.05
115	Jody Reed	.05
116	Charlie Leibrandt	.05
117	Greg Gagne	.05
118	Darrell Sherman	.05
119	Jeff Conine	.05
120	Tim Laker	.05
121	Kevin Seitzer	.05
122	Jeff Mutis	.05
123	Rico Rossy	.05
124	Paul Molitor	.45
125	Cal Ripken	1.50
126	Greg Maddux	.60
127	Greg McMichael	.05
128	Felix Jose	.05
129	Dick Schofield	.05
130	Jim Abbott	.05
131	Kevin Reimer	.05
132	Checklist	.05

Premier Star Performers

STAR PERFORMERS

EDGAR MARTINEZ • THIRD BASE

O-Pee-Chee released a 22-card insert set in two forms: Star Performers (featuring a gold border design) and Foil Star Performers (featuring full-bleed photos and gold stamping). The players are identical in both sets, but foil cards are generally worth more. There are 34 Star Performers per 36-card wax box and one Foil Star Performer card per box.

		NM/M
Complete Set (22):		4.50
Common Player:		.10
Foil:		6X
1	Frank Thomas	.50
2	Fred McGriff	.15
3	Roberto Alomar	.40
4	Ryne Sandberg	.65
5	Gary Sheffield	.25
6	Juan Gonzalez	.40
7	Eric Karros	.10
8	Ken Griffey Jr.	.75
9	Deion Sanders	.10
10	Kirby Puckett	.65
11	Will Clark	.10
12	Joe Carter	.15
13	Barry Bonds	1.50
14	Pat Listach	.10
15	Mark McGwire	1.00
16	Kenny Lofton	.10
17	Roger Clemens	.75
18	Greg Maddux	.65
19	Nolan Ryan	1.50
20	Tom Glavine	.20
21	Dennis Eckersley	.40

Premier Top Draft Picks

These randomly inserted cards feature four prospects; two each for Montreal and Toronto. Card fronts are foil-stamped and have a vertical banner with the player's name. The

B.J. WALLACE • EXPOS' 1ST DRAFT PICK

Expos

OPC Premier logo is in the corner. On back is another player photo, a team logo and a bi-lingual rationale for the player's draft status.

		NM/M
Complete Set (4):		2.50
Common Player:		.50
1	B.J. Wallace	.50
2	Shannon Stewart	2.00
3	Rod Henderson	.50
4	Todd Steverson	.50

1994 O-Pee-Chee Sample Sheet

The basic '94 OPC card set and all of its chase card sets were previewed on this sample sheet sent to dealers. Measuring 8" x 11", the sheet's cards vary slightly from issued cards in terms of foil highlights. Card fronts on the sample sheet are highlighted in red foil while there is no foil on the backs. Each of the card backs (except the jumbo All-Star) includes the notation "Pre-Production Sample."

	NM/M
Complete Sheet:	6.00

1994 O-Pee-Chee

ED SPRAGUE • THIRD BASE • THROWN OUT

Limited to 2,500 cases (about 112,000 of each card in the regular 270-card set) the '94 OPC issue features color photos on front and back along with complete major league stats (and some minor league stats) on back. Team names are in a color-coded strip at left. Career summaries and some other data are printed in both English and French.

		NM/M
Complete Set (270):		15.00
Common Player:		.05
Wax Pack (15):		.75
Wax Box (36):		15.00
1	Paul Molitor	.75
2	Kirt Manwaring	.05
3	Brady Anderson	.05
4	Scott Cooper	.05
5	Kevin Stocker	.05
6	Alex Fernandez	.05
7	Jeff Montgomery	.05
8	Danny Tartabull	.05

9	Damion Easley	.05
10	Andujar Cedeno	.05
11	Steve Karsay	.05
12	Dave Stewart	.05
13	Fred McGriff	.05
14	Jaime Navarro	.05
15	Allen Watson	.05
16	Ryne Sandberg	.75
17	Arthur Rhodes	.05
18	Marquis Grissom	.05
19	John Burkett	.05
20	Robby Thompson	.05
21	Denny Martinez	.05
22	Ken Griffey Jr.	1.00
23	Orestes Destrade	.05
24	Dwight Gooden	.05
25	Rafael Palmeiro	.40
26	Pedro Martinez	.25
27	Wes Chamberlain	.05
28	Juan Gonzalez	.50
29	Kevin Mitchell	.05
30	Dante Bichette	.05
31	Howard Johnson	.05
32	Mickey Tettleton	.05
33	Robin Ventura	.05
34	Terry Mulholland	.05
35	Bernie Williams	.05
36	Eduardo Perez	.05
37	Rickey Henderson	.65
38	Terry Pendleton	.05
39	John Smoltz	.05
40	Derrick May	.05
41	Pedro Martinez	.60
42	Mark Portugal	.05
43	Albert Belle	.05
44	Edgar Martinez	.05
45	Gary Sheffield	.35
46	Bret Saberhagen	.05
47	Ricky Gutierrez	.05
48	Orlando Merced	.05
49	Mike Greenwell	.05
50	Jose Rijo	.05
51	Jeff Granger	.05
52	Mike Henneman	.05
53	Dave Winfield	.05
54	Don Mattingly	.85
55	J.T. Snow	.05
56	Todd Van Poppel	.05
57	Chipper Jones	.75
58	Darryl Hamilton	.05
59	Delino DeShields	.05
60	Rondell White	.05
61	Eric Anthony	.05
62	Charlie Hough	.05
63	Sid Fernandez	.05
64	Derek Bell	.05
65	Phil Plantier	.05
66	Curt Schilling	.20
67	Roger Clemens	1.00
68	Jose Lind	.05
69	Andres Galarraga	.05
70	Tim Belcher	.05
71	Ron Karkovice	.05
72	Alan Trammell	.05
73	Pete Harnisch	.05
74	Mark McGwire	1.50
75	Ryan Klesko	.05
76	Ramon Martinez	.05
77	Gregg Jefferies	.05
78	Steve Buechele	.05
79	Bill Swift	.05
80	Matt Williams	.05
81	Randy Johnson	.60
82	Mike Mussina	.50
83	Andy Benes	.05
84	Dave Staton	.05
85	Steve Cooke	.05
86	Andy Van Slyke	.05
87	Ivan Rodriguez	.50
88	Frank Viola	.05
89	Aaron Sele	.05
90	Ellis Burks	.05
91	Wally Joyner	.05
92	Rick Aguilera	.05
93	Kirby Puckett	.75
94	Roberto Hernandez	.05
95	Mike Stanley	.05
96	Roberto Alomar	.25
97	James Mouton	.05
98	Chad Curtis	.05
99	Mitch Williams	.05
100	Carlos Delgado	.40
101	Greg Maddux	.75
102	Brian Harper	.05
103	Tom Pagnozzi	.05
104	Jose Offerman	.05
105	John Wetteland	.05
106	Carlos Baerga	.05
107	Dave Magadan	.05
108	Bobby Jones	.05
109	Tony Gwynn	.75
110	Jeromy Burnitz	.05
111	Bip Roberts	.05
112	Carlos Garcia	.05
113	Jeff Russell	.05
114	Armando Reynoso	.05
115	Ozzie Guillen	.05
116	Bo Jackson	.10
117	Terry Steinbach	.05
118	Deion Sanders	.05
119	Randy Myers	.05
120	Mark Whiten	.05
121	Manny Ramirez	.60
122	Ben McDonald	.05
123	Darren Daulton	.05
124	Kevin Young	.05
125	Barry Larkin	.05
126	Cecil Fielder	.05

127	Frank Thomas	.60
128	Luis Polonia	.05
129	Steve Finley	.05
130	John Olerud	.05
131	John Jaha	.05
132	Darren Lewis	.05
133	Orel Hershiser	.05
134	Chris Bosio	.05
135	Ryan Thompson	.05
136	Chris Sabo	.05
137	Tommy Greene	.05
138	Andre Dawson	.25
139	Bobby Kelly	.05
140	Ken Hill	.05
141	Greg Gagne	.05
142	Julio Franco	.05
143	Chili Davis	.05
144	Dennis Eckersley	.50
145	Joe Carter	.05
146	Mark Grace	.05
147	Mike Piazza	.90
148	J.R. Phillips	.05
149	Rich Amaral	.05
150	Benny Santiago	.05
151	Jeff King	.05
152	Dean Palmer	.05
153	Hal Morris	.05
154	Mike MacFarlane	.05
155	Chuck Knoblauch	.05
156	Pat Kelly	.05
157	Greg Swindell	.05
158	Chuck Finley	.05
159	Devon White	.05
160	Duane Ward	.05
161	Sammy Sosa	.85
162	Javier Lopez	.05
163	Eric Karros	.05
164	Royce Clayton	.05
165	Salomon Torres	.05
166	Jeff Kent	.05
167	Chris Hoiles	.05
168	Len Dykstra	.05
169	Jose Canseco	.35
170	Bret Boone	.05
171	Charlie Hayes	.05
172	Lou Whitaker	.05
173	Jack McDowell	.05
174	Jimmy Key	.05
175	Mark Langston	.05
176	Darryl Kile	.05
177	Juan Guzman	.05
178	Pat Borders	.05
179	Cal Eldred	.05
180	Jose Guzman	.05
181	Ozzie Smith	.75
182	Rod Beck	.05
183	Dave Fleming	.05
184	Eddie Murray	.60
185	Cal Ripken	2.00
186	Dave Hollins	.05
187	Will Clark	.05
188	Otis Nixon	.05
189	Joe Oliver	.05
190	Roberto Mejia	.05
191	Felix Jose	.05
192	Tony Phillips	.05
193	Wade Boggs	.75
194	Tim Salmon	.05
195	Ruben Sierra	.05
196	Steve Avery	.05
197	B.J. Surhoff	.05
198	Todd Zeile	.05
(199)	Raul Mondesi (No card number on back.)	
200	Barry Bonds	2.00
201	Sandy Alomar	.05
202	Bobby Bonilla	.05
203	Mike Devereaux	.05
204	Rickey Bottalico	.05
205	Kevin Brown	.05
206	Jason Bere	.05
207	Reggie Sanders	.05
208	David Nied	.05
209	Travis Fryman	.05
210	James Baldwin	.05
211	Jim Abbott	.05
212	Jeff Bagwell	.60
213	Bob Welch	.05
214	Jeff Blauser	.05
215	Brett Butler	.05
216	Pat Listach	.05
217	Bob Tewksbury	.05
218	Mike Lansing	.05
219	Wayne Kirby	.05
220	Chuck Carr	.05
221	Harold Baines	.05
222	Jay Bell	.05
223	Cliff Floyd	.05
224	Rob Dibble	.05
225	Kevin Appier	.05
226	Eric Davis	.05
227	Matt Walbeck	.05
228	Tim Raines	.05
229	Paul O'Neill	.05
230	Craig Biggio	.05
231	Brent Gates	.05
232	Rob Butler	.05
233	Dave Justice	.05
234	Rene Arocha	.05
235	Mike Morgan	.05
236	Denis Boucher	.05
237	Kenny Lofton	.05
238	Jeff Conine	.05
239	Bryan Harvey	.05
240	Danny Jackson	.05
241	Al Martin	.05
242	Tom Henke	.05
243	Erik Hanson	.05

244	Walt Weiss	.05
245	Brian McRae	.05
246	Kevin Tapani	.05
247	David McCarty	.05
248	Doug Drabek	.05
249	Troy Neel	.05
250	Tom Glavine	.20
251	Ray Lankford	.05
252	Wil Cordero	.05
253	Larry Walker	.05
254	Charles Nagy	.05
255	Kirk Rueter	.05
256	John Franco	.05
257	John Kruk	.05
258	Alex Gonzalez	.05
259	Mo Vaughn	.05
260	David Cone	.05
261	Kent Hrbek	.05
262	Lance Johnson	.05
263	Luis Gonzalez	.10
264	Mike Bordick	.05
265	Ed Sprague	.05
266	Moises Alou	.05
267	Omar Vizquel	.05
268	Jay Buhner	.05
269	Checklist	.05
270	Checklist	.05

All-Star Redemption Cards

A series of 25 All-Star redemption cards was one of the several inserts which were found at the rate of one per pack in '94 OPC foil. Fronts feature a color photo floating over a white background. The player's name is displayed in gold script at top and the card number is repeated along the top and left or right of the photo. Backs have information on how to redeem the cards for a super-size version of the set. Approximately 78,000 of each of the 25 cards in the insert set were produced.

		NM/M
Complete Set (25):		9.00
Common Player:		.50
1	Frank Thomas	.65
2	Paul Molitor	1.00
3	Barry Bonds	2.50
4	Juan Gonzalez	.60
5	Jeff Bagwell	.75
6	Carlos Baerga	.50
7	Ryne Sandberg	1.00
8	Ken Griffey Jr.	2.00
9	Mike Piazza	1.50
10	Tim Salmon	.50
11	Marquis Grissom	.50
12	Albert Belle	.50
13	Fred McGriff	.50
14	Jack McDowell	.50
14p	Jack McDowell ("Pre-Production Sample")	.50
15	Cal Ripken, Jr.	.50
16	John Olerud	.50
17	Kirby Puckett	1.00
18	Roger Clemens	1.50
19	Larry Walker	.60
20	Cecil Fielder	.50
21	Roberto Alomar	.60
22	Greg Maddux	1.00
23	Joe Carter	.50
24	Dave Justice	.50
25	Kenny Lofton	.50

Jumbo All-Stars

Each of the 60,000 foil-pack boxes of '94 OPC contained one jumbo (5" x 7") All-Star card from a set of 25. Fronts are identical to the All-Star redemption card inserts found in foil packs, with a UV coating. Backs are blank. Each of the jumbo All-Stars was produced in a quantity of 2,400. A factory-set version of the jumbo All-Stars was also available by redeeming five of the AS inserts and $20. The factory-set AS jumbos differ from the box-toppers in that they have gold-foil enhancements and are numbered to 5,000 each.

		NM/M
Complete Set (25):		75.00
Common Player:		2.00
Complete Factory Set:		35.00
Factory Set Singles:		.75X
1	Frank Thomas	4.00
2	Paul Molitor	5.00
3	Barry Bonds	9.00
4	Juan Gonzalez	3.00
5	Jeff Bagwell	4.00
6	Carlos Baerga	2.00
7	Ryne Sandberg	5.00
8	Ken Griffey Jr.	7.50
9	Mike Piazza	6.00
10	Tim Salmon	2.00
11	Marquis Grissom	2.50
12	Albert Belle	2.00
13	Fred McGriff	2.50
14	Jack McDowell	2.00
15	Cal Ripken	9.00
16	John Olerud	2.50
17	Kirby Puckett	5.00
18	Roger Clemens	6.00
19	Larry Walker	2.50
20	Cecil Fielder	2.00
21	Roberto Alomar	3.00
22	Greg Maddux	5.00
23	Joe Carter	2.50
24	Dave Justice	2.00
25	Kenny Lofton	2.00

Diamond Dynamos

"Baseball's brightest new stars" was the stated criteria for inclusion in this chase card set. Fronts feature a full-bleed action photo with the player's name and "Diamond Dynamos" logo at bottom in red foil. Backs have a second player photo, personal data, a bi-lingual career summary and gold-foil presentation of the player's name and "Twenty-first Century Stars." An average of 1-2 of the cards was inserted per foil box, creating a production run of 5,000 of each card.

		NM/M
Complete Set (18):		5.00
Common Player:		.25
1	Mike Piazza	4.00
2	Roberto Mejia	.25
3	Wayne Kirby	.25
4	Kevin Stocker	.25
5	Chris Gomez	.25
6	Bobby Jones	.25
7	David McCarty	.25
8	Kirk Rueter	.25
9	J.T. Snow	.25
10	Wil Cordero	.25
11	Tim Salmon	.25
12	Jeff Conine	.25
13	Jason Bere	.25
14	Greg McMichael	.25
15	Brent Gates	.25
16	Allen Watson	.25
17	Aaron Sele	.25
18	Carlos Garcia	.25

Hot Prospects

Nine of 1994's hottest rookies are featured in this insert set. Fronts feature full-bleed photos with the player's name in gold foil at bottom. An "O-Pee-Chee Hot Prospects" logo appears in an upper corner. Backs are in shades of red, yellow and orange and include another

player photo, biographical data, a career summary and complete minor league stats.

		NM/M
Complete Set (9):		7.50
Common Player:		.50
1	Cliff Floyd	.50
2	James Mouton	.50
3	Salomon Torres	.50
4	Raul Mondesi	.50
5	Carlos Delgado	3.00
6	Manny Ramirez	3.00
7	Javier Lopez	.50
8	Alex Gonzalez	.50
9	Ryan Klesko	.50

Toronto Blue Jays

The Blue Jays' starting line-up for the final game of the 1993 World Series is honored on this insert set. Fronts have a large typographic background of "World Series Champions '92 & '93." There is a color player photo with his name in red foil at bottom. Backs repeat the typographic background in black and include 1992 and 1993 World Series stats along with the player's Series highlights in both English and French. A gold-foil seal marking the back-to-back championships is at top center. Stated odds of finding a Blue Jays insert card are one per foil box, indicating a production of about 6,666 of each card.

		NM/M
Complete Set (9):		6.00
Common Player:		.50
1	Rickey Henderson	2.00
2	Devon White	.75
3	Paul Molitor	2.00
4	Joe Carter	.75
5	John Olerud	1.00
6	Roberto Alomar	1.50
7	Ed Sprague	.50
8	Pat Borders	.50
9	Tony Fernandez	.50

2009 O-Pee-Chee

	NM/M
Complete Set (600):	125.00
Common Player (1-560):	.15
Common RC (561-600):	
RC's inserted 1:3	
Moments (543-560) inserted 1:6	
League Leaders (531-542) 1:8	
Hobby Pack (6):	1.50

Hobby Box (36):		50.00
1	Melvin Mora	.15
2	Jim Thome	.40
3	Jonathan Sanchez	.15
4	Cesar Izturis	.15
5	A.J. Pierzynski	.15
6	Adam LaRoche	.25
7	J.D. Drew	.25
8	Brian Schneider	.15
9	John Grabow	.15
10	Jimmy Rollins	.50
11	Jeff Baker	.15
12	Daniel Cabrera	.15
13	Kyle Lohse	.15
14	Jason Giambi	.40
15	Nate McLouth	.40
16	Gary Matthews	.15
17	Cody Ross	.15
18	Justin Masterson	.25
19	Jose Lopez	.15
20	Brian Roberts	.40
21	Cla Meredith	.15
22	Ben Francisco	.15
23	Brian McCann	.25
24	Carlos Guillen	.15
25	Chien-Ming Wang	.75
26	Brandon Phillips	.40
27	Saul Rivera	.15
28	Torii Hunter	.25
29	Jamie Moyer	.15
30	Kevin Youkilis	.50
31	Martin Prado	.15
32	Magglio Ordonez	.25
33	Nomar Garciaparra	.40
34	Takashi Saito	.15
35	Chase Headley	.15
36	Mike Pelfrey	.15
37	Ronny Cedeno	.15
38	Dallas McPherson	.15
39	Zack Greinke	.75
40	Matt Cain	.15
41	Xavier Nady	.15
42	Willy Aybar	.15
43	Edgar Gonzalez	.15
44	Gabe Gross	.15
45	Joey Votto	.50
46	Jason Michaels	.15
47	Eric Chavez	.15
48	Jason Bartlett	.25
49	Jeremy Guthrie	.15
50	Matt Holliday	.40
51	Ross Ohlendorf	.15
52	Gil Meche	.15
53	B.J. Upton	.40
54	Ryan Doumit	.15
55	Jay Bruce	.75
56	Huston Street	.15
57	Bobby Crosby	.15
58	Jose Valverde	.15
59	Brian Tallet	.15
60	Adam Dunn	.50
61	Victor Martinez	.40
62	Jeff Francoeur	.25
63	Emilio Bonifacio	.15
64	Chone Figgins	.25
65	Alexei Ramirez	.50
66	Brian Giles	.25
67	Khalil Greene	.15
68	Phil Hughes	.25
69	Mike Aviles	.25
70	Ryan Braun	1.00
71	Braden Looper	.15
72	Jhonny Peralta	.15
73	Ian Stewart	.15
74	James Loney	.25
75	Chase Utley	.75
76	Reed Johnson	.15
77	Jorge Cantu	.25
78	Julio Lugo	.15
79	Raul Ibanez	.40
80	Lance Berkman	.40
81	Joel Peralta	.15
82	Mark Hendrickson	.15
83	Jeff Suppan	.15
84	Scott Olsen	.15
85	Joba Chamberlain	.75
86	Fausto Carmona	.15
87	Andy Pettitte	.40
88	Jimmie Johnson	.15
89	Chris Snyder	.15
90	Nick Swisher	.15
91	Edgar Renteria	.25
92	Brandon Inge	.15
93	Aubrey Huff	.25
94	Stephen Drew	.40
95	Denard Span	.25
96	Carl Crawford	.40
97	Felix Pie	.15
98	Jeremy Sowers	.15
99	Trevor Hoffman	.25
100	Albert Pujols	2.00
101	Radhames Liz	.15
102	Doug Davis	.15
103	Joel Hanrahan	.15
104	Seth Smith	.15
105	Francisco Liriano	.40
106	Bobby Abreu	.40
107	Willie Harris	.15
108	Travis Ishikawa	.15
109	Travis Hafner	.15
110	Adrian Gonzalez	.50
111	Shin-Soo Choo	.40
112	Robinson Cano	.40
113	Matt Capps	.15
114	Gerald Laird	.15
115	Max Scherzer	.40
116	Mike Jacobs	.15
117	Asdrubal Cabrera	.15
118	J.J. Hardy	.40
119	Justin Upton	.50
120	Mariano Rivera	.50
121	Jack Cust	.15
122	Orlando Hudson	.25
123	Brian Wilson	.15
124	Heath Bell	.15
125	Chipper Jones	1.00
126	Jason Marquis	.15
127	Rocco Baldelli	.15
128	Rafael Perez	.15
129	Carlos Gomez	.15
130	Kerry Wood	.25
131	Adam Wainwright	.25
132	Michael Bourn	.15
133	Cristian Guzman	.15
134	Dustin McGowan	.15
135	James Shields	.25
136	Matt Lindstrom	.15
137	Rick Ankiel	.40
138	J.P. Howell	.15
139	Ben Zobrist	.15
140	Tim Hudson	.25
141	Clayton Kershaw	.40
142	Edwin Encarnacion	.15
143	Kevin Millwood	.25
144	Jack Hannahan	.15
145	Alex Gordon	.40
146	Chad Durbin	.15
147	Derrek Lee	.50
148	Kevin Gregg	.15
149	Clint Barmes	.15
150	Dustin Pedroia	.75
151	Brad Hawpe	.15
152	Steven Shell	.15
153	Jesse Crain	.15
154	Edwar Ramirez	.15
155	Jair Jurrjens	.25
156	Matt Albers	.15
157	Endy Chavez	.15
158	Steve Pearce	.15
159	John Maine	.25
160	Ryan Theriot	.15
161	Eric Stults	.15
162	Cha Seung Baek	.15
163	Alex Gonzalez	.15
164	Dan Haren	.40
165	Edwin Jackson	.15
166	Felipe Lopez	.15
167	David DeJesus	.15
168	Todd Wellemeyer	.15
169	Joey Gathright	.15
170	Roy Oswalt	.25
171	Carlos Pena	.25
172	Nick Hundley	.15
173	Adrian Beltre	.25
174	Omar Vizquel	.25
175	Cole Hamels	.50
176	Jarrod Saltalamacchia	.15
177	Yuniesky Betancourt	.15
178	Placido Polanco	.25
179	Ryan Spilborghs	.15
180	Josh Beckett	.50
181	Cory Wade	.15
182	Aaron Laffey	.15
183	Kosuke Fukudome	.25
184	Miguel Montero	.15
185	Edinson Volquez	.25
186	Jon Garland	.15
187	Andruw Jones	.25
188	Vernon Wells	.15
189	Zach Duke	.15
190	David Wright	1.00
191	Ryan Madson	.15
192	Hideki Okajima	.15
193	Ryan Church	.15
194	Adam Jones	.40
195	Geovany Soto	.40
196	Jeremy Hermida	.15
197	Juan Rivera	.15
198	David Weathers	.15
199	Jorge Campillo	.15
200	Derek Jeter	2.00
201	Brett Myers	.15
202	Brett Gardner	.15
203	Rafael Furcal	.25
204	Wandy Rodriguez	.15
205	Ricky Nolasco	.25
206	Ryan Freel	.15
207	Jeremy Bonderman	.15
208	Mike Wuertz	.15
209	Hank Blalock	.25
210	Alfonso Soriano	.50
211	Jeff Clement	.15
212	Garrett Atkins	.25
213	Luis Vizcaino	.15
214	Tim Redding	.15
215	Ryan Ludwick	.40
216	Mark Teahen	.15
217	Chris Young	.25
218	David Aardsma	.15
219	Ubaldo Jimenez	.15
220	Ryan Howard	1.00
221	Skip Schumaker	.15
222	Craig Counsell	.15
223	Chris Iannetta	.15
224	Jason Kubel	.25
225	Johan Santana	.75
226	Luke Hochevar	.15
227	Jason Bay	.50
228	Alex Hinshaw	.15
229	Jon Rauch	.15
230	Carlos Quentin	.40
231	Coco Crisp	.15
232	Casey Blake	.15
233	Carlos Marmol	.15
234	Fernando Rodney	.15
235	Jed Lowrie	.15
236	Brad Penny	.15
237	Reggie Willits	.15
238	Mike Hampton	.15
239	Mike Lowell	.25
240	Randy Johnson	.75
241	Jarrod Washburn	.15
242	B.J. Ryan	.15
243	Javier Vazquez	.40
244	Todd Helton	.50
245	Matt Garza	.25
246	Ramon Hernandez	.15
247	Johnny Cueto	.25
248	Willy Taveras	.25
249	Carlos Silva	.15
250	Manny Ramirez	.75
251	A.J. Burnett	.25
252	Aaron Cook	.15
253	Josh Bard	.15
254	Aaron Harang	.25
255	Jeff Samardzija	.15
256	Brad Lidge	.25
257	Pedro Feliz	.15
258	Kazuo Matsui	.15
259	Joe Blanton	.15
260	Ian Kinsler	.50
261	Rich Harden	.15
262	Kelly Johnson	.15
263	Anibal Sanchez	.15
264	Mike Adams	.15
265	Chad Billingsley	.40
266	Chris Davis	.40
267	Brandon Moss	.15
268	Matt Kemp	.50
269	Jose Arredondo	.15
270	Mark Teixeira	.50
271	Glen Perkins	.15
272	Pat Burrell	.25
273	Luke Scott	.15
274	Scott Feldman	.15
275	Ichiro Suzuki	1.00
276	Cliff Floyd	.15
277	Bill Hall	.15
278	Bronson Arroyo	.15
279	Lyle Overbay	.15
280	Aramis Ramirez	.40
281	Jeff Keppinger	.15
282	Brandon Morrow	.15
283	Ryan Shealy	.15
284	Andrew Sonnanstine	.15
285	Josh Johnson	.25
286	Carlos Ruiz	.15
287	Gregg Zaun	.15
288	Kenji Johjima	.15
289	Mike Gonzalez	.15
290	Carlos Delgado	.50
291	Gary Sheffield	.40
292	Brian Anderson	.15
293	Josh Hamilton	.75
294	Tom Gorzelanny	.15
295	Yunel Escobar	.15
296	Scott Hairston	.15
297	Luis Castillo	.15
298	Gabe Kapler	.15
299	Nelson Cruz	.40
300	Tim Lincecum	1.00
301	Brian Bannister	.15
302	Frank Francisco	.15
303	Jose Guillen	.25
304	Erick Aybar	.15
305	Brad Ziegler	.15
306	John Baker	.15
307	Hong-Chih Kuo	.15
308	Jo Jo Reyes	.15
309	Josh Willingham	.15
310	Billy Wagner	.15
311	Nick Blackburn	.15
312	David Purcey	.15
313	Rafael Soriano	.15
314	Zach Miner	.15
315	Andre Ethier	.40
316	Rickie Weeks	.25
317	Akinori Iwamura	.15
318	Hideki Matsui	.50
319	Ryan Rowland-Smith	.15
320	Miguel Cabrera	.75
321	Manny Parra	.15
322	Jack Wilson	.15
323	Jeremy Reed	.15
324	Chris Coste	.15
325	Grady Sizemore	.75
326	Andy LaRoche	.15
327	Joel Pineiro	.15
328	Brian Buscher	.15
329	Randy Wolf	.15
330	Jake Peavy	.50
331	Curtis Granderson	.50
332	Kyle Kendrick	.15
333	Joe Saunders	.15
334	Russell Martin	.25
335	Conor Jackson	.15
336	Paul Konerko	.40
337	Kevin Slowey	.15
338	Mark DeRosa	.25
339	Garret Anderson	.25
340	Michael Young	.25
341	Greg Dobbs	.15
342	Brian Moehler	.15
343	Alex Rios	.40
344	Mike Napoli	.15
345	Bobby Jenks	.15
346	Daric Barton	.15
347	Jason Kendall	.15
348	Chad Qualls	.15
349	Milton Bradley	.25
350	Joe Mauer	.50
351	Livan Hernandez	.15
352	Chris Ray	.15
353	Bob Howry	.15

Base Set (continued)

#	Player		#	Player	
354	Manny Corpas	.15	472	Travis Buck	.15
355	Ervin Santana	.25	473	Dioner Navarro	.15
356	Billy Butler	.25	474	Mark Buehrle	.25
357	Russ Springer	.15	475	Hanley Ramirez	1.00
358	Micah Owings	.15	476	John Lannan	.15
359	Corey Hart	.25	477	Lastings Milledge	.15
360	Francisco Rodriguez	.25	478	Dallas Braden	.15
361	Ted Lilly	.25	479	Orlando Cabrera	.25
362	Adam Everett	.15	480	Jose Reyes	.75
363	Scott Rolen	.25	481	Jorge Posada	.50
364	Troy Tulowitzki	.40	482	Jason Isringhausen	.15
365	Jacoby Ellsbury	.75	483	Rich Aurilia	.15
366	Jayson Werth	.40	484	Hunter Pence	.50
367	Gio Gonzalez	.15	485	Carlos Zambrano	.40
368	Mark Ellis	.15	486	Randy Winn	.15
369	Brendan Harris	.15	487	Carlos Beltran	.50
370	David Ortiz	.75	488	Armando Galarraga	.15
371	Carlos Lee	.40	489	Wilson Betemit	.15
372	Jonathan Broxton	.25	490	Vladimir Guerrero	.75
373	Jesse Litsch	.15	491	Ryan Garko	.15
374	Barry Zito	.15	492	Ian Snell	.15
375	Daisuke Matsuzaka	.75	493	Yadier Molina	.15
376	Kevin Kouzmanoff	.15	494	Tom Glavine	.50
377	Jesse Carlson	.15	495	Cameron Maybin	.25
378	Brian Fuentes	.15	496	Vicente Padilla	.15
379	Mark Reynolds	.25	497	Keiichi Yabu	.15
380	Brandon Webb	.50	498	Oliver Perez	.15
381	Scott Kazmir	.15	499	Carlos Villanueva	.15
382	Blake DeWitt	.15	500	Alex Rodriguez	1.50
383	Kurt Suzuki	.15	501	Baltimore Orioles	.25
384	Chris Volstad	.15	502	Boston Red Sox	.40
385	Gavin Floyd	.15	503	Chicago White Sox	.25
386	Paul Maholm	.15	504	Houston Astros	.25
387	Freddy Sanchez	.25	505	Oakland Athletics	.25
388	Scott Baker	.25	506	Toronto Blue Jays	.25
389	John Danks	.25	507	Atlanta Braves	.25
390	C.C. Sabathia	.75	508	Milwaukee Brewers	.25
391	Ryan Dempster	.25	509	St. Louis Cardinals	.50
392	Tim Wakefield	.25	510	Chicago Cubs	.25
393	Mike Cameron	.25	511	Arizona Diamondbacks	.25
394	Aaron Rowand	.25	512	Los Angeles Dodgers	.50
395	Howie Kendrick	.15	513	San Francisco Giants	.25
396	Marlon Byrd	.15	514	Cleveland Indians	.25
397	David Bush	.15	515	Seattle Mariners	.25
398	George Sherrill	.15	516	Florida Marlins	.25
399	Francisco Cordero	.15	517	New York Mets	.50
400	Evan Longoria	1.00	518	Washington Nationals	.25
401	Hiroki Kuroda	.15	519	San Diego Padres	.25
402	Sean Gallagher	.15	520	Pittsburgh Pirates	.25
403	Yovani Gallardo	.50	521	Tampa Bay Rays	.50
404	Ryan Sweeney	.15	522	Cincinnati Reds	.25
405	Chris Dickerson	.15	523	Colorado Rockies	.25
406	Jason Varitek	.25	524	Kansas City Royals	.25
407	Erik Bedard	.25	525	Detroit Tigers	.25
408	J.J. Putz	.15	526	Minnesota Twins	.25
409	Wily Mo Pena	.15	527	New York Yankees	.50
410	Rich Hill	.15	528	Philadelphia Phillies	.50
411	Delmon Young	.25	529	Los Angeles Dodgers	.50
412	David Eckstein	.15	530	Texas Rangers	.25
413	Marcus Thames	.15	531	Dustin Pedroia, Joe Mauer, Milton Bradley	1.00
414	Dontrelle Willis	.25	532	Albert Pujols, Chipper Jones, Matt Holliday	2.00
415	Joakim Soria	.15	533	Alex Rodriguez, Carlos Quentin, Miguel Cabrera	1.50
416	Chan Ho Park	.15	534	Adam Dunn, Carlos Delgado, Ryan Howard	1.00
417	Jered Weaver	.40	535	Josh Hamilton, Justin Morneau, Miguel Cabrera	1.00
418	Justin Duchscherer	.15	536	Adrian Gonzalez, David Wright, Ryan Howard	1.00
419	Casey Kotchman	.25	537	Cliff Lee, Daisuke Matsuzaka, Roy Halladay	.50
420	John Lackey	.25	538	Jake Peavy, Johan Santana, Tim Lincecum	1.00
421	Peter Moylan	.15	539	Cliff Lee, Daisuke Matsuzaka, Roy Halladay	.50
422	Bengie Molina	.15	540	Brandon Webb, Ryan Dempster, Tim Lincecum	1.00
423	Mark Loretta	.15	541	A.J. Burnett, Ervin Santana, Roy Halladay	.50
424	Dan Wheeler	.15	542	Dan Haren, Johan Santana, Tim Lincecum	1.00
425	Ken Griffey Jr.	1.50	543	Grady Sizemore	1.00
426	Justin Verlander	.50	544	Ichiro Suzuki	1.50
427	Troy Glaus	.25	545	Hanley Ramirez	1.00
428	Daniel Murphy	.15	546	Jose Reyes	1.00
429	Brandon Backe	.15	547	Johan Santana	1.00
430	Nick Markakis	.50	548	Adrian Gonzalez	.50
431	Travis Metcalf	.15	549	Carlos Zambrano	.50
432	Austin Kearns	.15	550	Jonathan Papelbon	.50
433	Adam Lind	.25	551	Josh Hamilton	1.00
434	Jody Gerut	.15	552	Derek Jeter	2.00
435	Jonathan Papelbon	.40	553	Kevin Youkilis	.75
436	Duaner Sanchez	.15	554	Joe Mauer	.75
437	David Murphy	.15	555	Kosuke Fukudome	.50
438	Eddie Guardado	.15	556	Chipper Jones	1.00
439	Johnny Damon	.50	557	Lance Berkman	.75
440	Derek Lowe	.25	558	Michael Young	1.00
441	Miguel Olivo	.15	559	Evan Longoria	2.00
442	Shaun Marcum	.15	560	Alex Rodriguez	1.50
443	Ty Wigginton	.15	561	Travis Snider RC	2.00
444	Elijah Dukes	.15	562	James McDonald RC	1.50
445	Felix Hernandez	.40	563	Brian Duensing RC	1.00
446	Joe Inglett	.15	564	Josh Outman RC	1.00
447	Kelly Shoppach	.15	565	Josh Geer (RC)	1.00
448	Eric Hinske	.15	566	Kevin Jepsen (RC)	1.00
449	Fred Lewis	.15	567	Scott Lewis (RC)	1.00
450	Cliff Lee	.40	568	Jason Motte (RC)	1.00
451	Miguel Tejada	.40	569	Ricky Romero (RC)	1.50
452	Jensen Lewis	.15	570	Landon Powell (RC)	1.00
453	Ryan Zimmerman	.40	571	Scott Elbert (RC)	1.00
454	Jon Lester	.50	572	Bobby Parnell RC	1.00
455	Justin Morneau	.50	573	Ryan Perry RC	1.00
456	John Smoltz	.50	574	Phil Coke RC	1.50
457	Emmanuel Burriss	.15			
458	Joe Nathan	.25			
459	Jeff Niemann	.15			
460	Roy Halladay	.50			
461	Matt Diaz	.15			
462	Oscar Salazar	.15			
463	Chris Perez	.15			
464	Matt Joyce	.15			
465	Dan Uggla	.40			
466	Jermaine Dye	.40			
467	Shane Victorino	.40			
468	Chris Getz	.15			
469	Chris B. Young	.25			
470	Prince Fielder	.75			
471	Juan Pierre	.15			

#	Player	
575	Trevor Cahill RC	2.00
576	Jesse Chavez RC	1.00
577	George Kottaras (RC)	1.00
578	Trevor Crowe RC	1.00
579	David Freese RC	1.00
580	Matt Tuiasosopo (RC)	1.00
581	Brett Anderson RC	1.50
582	Casey McGehee (RC)	1.00
583	Elvis Andrus RC	1.50
584	Shawn Kelley RC	1.50
585	Mike Hinckley (RC)	1.00
586	Donald Veal RC	1.00
587	Colby Rasmus (RC)	1.50
588	Shairon Martis RC	1.00
589	Walter Silva RC	1.00
590	Chris Jakubauskas RC	1.00
591	Brad Nelson (RC)	1.00
592	Alfredo Simon (RC)	1.00
593	Koji Uehara RC	1.50
594	Rick Porcello RC	5.00
595	Kenshin Kawakami RC	2.00
596	Dexter Fowler (RC)	2.00
597	Jordan Schafer (RC)	1.50
598	David Patton RC	1.00
599	Luis Cruz RC	1.00
600	Joe Martinez RC	1.00

Black

Black:	2-3X
Black RC:	1-2X
Inserted 1:6	

Black Blank Back

Blank Back:	10-20X
Blank Back RC:	5-10X

Black Mini

Black:	4-8X
Black RC:	2-4X

Retro

#	Player	NM/M
	Common Player (1-33):	2.00
1	Sidney Crosby	15.00
2	Alexander Ovechkin	8.00
3	Carey Price	5.00
4	Henrik Lundqvist	4.00
5	Jonathan Toews	6.00
6	Martin Brodeur	6.00
7	Evgeni Malkin	8.00
8	Jarome Iginla	5.00
9	Henrik Zetterberg	5.00
10	Roberto Luongo	4.00
11	Travis Snider	3.00
12	Russell Martin	2.00
13	Justin Morneau	2.00
14	Joey Votto	2.00
15	Alex Rios	2.00
16	Jon Lester	2.00
17	Ryan Howard	5.00
18	Johan Santana	4.00
19	C.C. Sabathia	3.00
20	Roy Halladay	2.00
21	Chase Utley	4.00
22	Chipper Jones	4.00
23	Ryan Braun	5.00
24	Ken Griffey Jr.	6.00
25	B.J. Upton	2.00
26	Hanley Ramirez	5.00
27	Alex Rodriguez	6.00
28	Cole Hamels	4.00
29	Albert Pujols	10.00
30	Derek Jeter	10.00
31	Manny Ramirez	4.00
32	David Wright	5.00
33	Evan Longoria	6.00

2008 Highlights & Milestones

#	Player	NM/M
	Common Player:	1.00
1	Brad Lidge	1.00
2	Ken Griffey Jr.	3.00
3	Melvin Mora	1.00
4	Derek Jeter	4.00
5	Josh Hamilton	2.00
6	Alfonso Soriano	1.50
7	Francisco Rodriguez	1.50
8	Jon Lester	1.50
9	Carlos Zambrano	1.00
10	Adrian Beltre	1.00
11	Carlos Gomez	1.00
12	Kelly Shoppach	1.00
13	Manny Ramirez	2.00
14	Carlos Delgado	1.50
15	C.C. Sabathia	2.00

All-Rookie Team

#	Player	NM/M
	Common Player:	1.00
1	Geovany Soto	1.50
2	Joey Votto	1.50
3	Alexei Ramirez	1.50
4	Evan Longoria	5.00
5	Mike Aviles	1.00
6	Jacoby Ellsbury	3.00
7	Jay Bruce	2.50
8	Kosuke Fukudome	1.50
9	Jair Jurrjens	1.00
10	Denard Span	1.00

Face of the Franchise

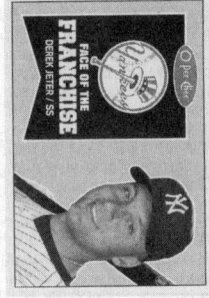

#	Player	NM/M
	Common Player:	1.00
1	Vladimir Guerrero	1.50
2	Roy Oswalt	1.00
3	Eric Chavez	1.00
4	Roy Halladay	1.50
5	Chipper Jones	2.00
6	Ryan Braun	3.00
7	Albert Pujols	5.00
8	Carlos Zambrano	1.00
9	Brandon Webb	1.50
10	Russell Martin	1.00
11	Tim Lincecum	3.00
12	Grady Sizemore	2.00
13	Ichiro Suzuki	4.00
14	Hanley Ramirez	2.50
15	David Wright	3.00
16	Ryan Zimmerman	1.50
17	Brian Roberts	1.00
18	Adrian Gonzalez	1.50
19	Jimmy Rollins	2.00
20	Nate McLouth	1.00
21	Michael Young	1.00
22	Evan Longoria	4.00
23	David Ortiz	2.00
24	Jay Bruce	3.00
25	Troy Tulowitzki	1.50
26	Alex Gordon	1.00
27	Miguel Cabrera	2.00
28	Joe Mauer	1.50
29	Carlos Quentin	1.00
30	Derek Jeter	5.00

Midsummer Memories

#	Player	NM/M
	Common Player:	1.00
1	Ken Griffey Jr.	3.00
2	Hank Blalock	1.00
3	Michael Young	1.00
4	Ichiro Suzuki	3.00
5	Miguel Tejada	1.00
6	Alfonso Soriano	1.50
7	Jimmy Rollins	1.50
8	Derek Jeter	4.00
9	Justin Morneau	1.50
10	J.D. Drew	1.00
11	Carl Crawford	1.00
12	Vladimir Guerrero	1.50
13	Mark Teixeira	1.50
14	David Ortiz	1.50
15	Manny Ramirez	1.50

New York, New York

#	Player	NM/M
	Common Player:	1.50
1	C.C. Sabathia	2.50
2	Jorge Posada	2.50
3	Derek Jeter	12.00
4	Alex Rodriguez	6.00
5	Chien-Ming Wang	3.00
6	Joba Chamberlain	5.00
7	A.J. Burnett	2.00
8	Mariano Rivera	3.00
9	Nick Swisher	1.50
10	Robinson Cano	2.50
11	Mark Teixeira	4.00
12	Johnny Damon	3.00
13	Hideki Matsui	3.00
14	Andy Pettitte	2.50
15	Xavier Nady	1.50
16	Jose Reyes	3.00
17	David Wright	5.00
18	John Maine	1.50
19	Daniel Murphy	1.50
20	Francisco Rodriguez	1.50
21	Carlos Delgado	2.00
22	Luis Castillo	1.50
23	Ryan Church	1.50
24	Brian Schneider	1.50
25	J.J. Putz	1.50
26	Mike Pelfrey	1.50
27	Oliver Perez	1.50
28	Jeremy Reed	1.50
29	Johan Santana	4.00
30	Carlos Beltran	2.00

New York, New York - Multi Sport

#	Player	NM/M
	Common Player:	2.00
1	C.C. Sabathia	3.00
2	Henrik Lundqvist	6.00
3	Jose Reyes	4.00
4	Derek Jeter	12.00
5	David Wright	6.00
6	Rick DiPietro	4.00
7	Joba Chamberlain	5.00
8	Alex Rodriguez	8.00
9	Johan Santana	4.00
10	Carlos Beltran	2.00

OPC 1971 Buybacks

No Pricing

Materials

Inserted 1:108 Hobby
Inserted 1:216 Retail

Code	Players	NM/M
BBP	A.J. Burnett, Brad Penny, Josh Beckett	10.00
BHH	Corey Hart, Jeremy Hermida, Rocco Baldelli	10.00
BMY	Adrian Beltre, Kevin Youkilis, Melvin Mora	15.00
BYP	Jonathan Papelbon, Josh Beckett, Kevin Youkilis	20.00
CBG	Chad Billingsley, Fausto Carmona, Zack Greinke	10.00
CFM	Jeff Francoeur, Michael Cuddyer, Nick Markakis	15.00
CKR	Brian Roberts, Ian Kinsler, Robinson Cano	10.00
CSW	Josh Willingham, Michael Cuddyer, Nick Swisher	10.00
DLO	Carlos Lee, Jermaine Dye, Magglio Ordonez	10.00
EFG	Chone Figgins, Curtis Granderson, Jacoby Ellsbury	15.00
ELK	Andre Ethier, James Loney, Matt Kemp	15.00
FOD	Carlos Delgado, David Ortiz, Prince Fielder	15.00
GDH	J.J. Hardy, Khalil Greene, Stephen Drew	10.00
HAG	Carlos Gonzalez, Garrett Atkins, Todd Helton	10.00
HMC	Justin Morneau, Miguel Cabrera, Travis Hafner	12.00
HML	Evan Longoria, Josh Hamilton, Justin Morneau	20.00
HMW	Jake Westbrook, Travis Hafner, Victor Martinez	10.00
HRR	Alex Rios, Roy Halladay, Scott Rolen	15.00
JCP	Derek Jeter, Jorge Posada, Robinson Cano	25.00
KJN	Howie Kendrick, Jayson Nix, Kelly Johnson	10.00
LRF	Aramis Ramirez, Derrek Lee, Kosuke Fukudome	10.00
LWS	Billy Wagner, Brad Lidge, Takashi Saito	10.00
MFJ	Brian McCann, Jeff Francoeur, Kelly Johnson	10.00
MMM	Joe Mauer, Russell Martin, Victor Martinez	10.00
NMC	Joe Mauer, Joe Nathan, Michael Cuddyer	15.00
OHG	David Ortiz, Jason Giambi, Travis Hafner	10.00
OHP	Brad Penny, Roy Halladay, Roy Oswalt	10.00
PBO	Clay Buchholz, David Ortiz, Jonathan Papelbon	10.00
PCF	Albert Pujols, Miguel Cabrera, Prince Fielder	20.00
PHB	Andy Pettitte, Cole Hamels, Erik Bedard	10.00
RPV	Ivan Rodriguez, Jason Varitek, Jorge Posada	10.00
VWB	Clay Buchholz, Jered Weaver, Justin Verlander	10.00
YDR	Chris B. Young, Mark Reynolds, Stephen Drew	10.00
YKM	Ian Kinsler, Kevin Millwood, Michael Young	10.00

Signatures

Inserted 1:216 Hobby
Inserted 1:1,080 Retail

Code	Player	NM/M
AJ	Joaquin Arias	8.00
AL	Aaron Laffey	8.00
AR	Alexei Ramirez	35.00
BR	Brian Barton	8.00
CD	Chris Duncan	20.00
CH	Corey Hart	20.00
CS	Clint Sammons	8.00
CW	Cory Wade	12.00
DM	David Murphy	8.00
ED	Elijah Dukes	8.00
EV	Edinson Volquez	15.00
FC	Fausto Carmona	8.00
HE	Chase Headley	12.00
HJ	J.A. Happ	20.00
IK	Ian Kennedy	12.00
JA	Jonathan Albaladejo	12.00
JC	Jeff Clement	12.00
JH	Justin Hampson	8.00
JM	John Maine	10.00
KJ	Kelly Johnson	8.00
KK	Kevin Kouzmanoff	8.00
KM	Kyle McClellan	8.00
KS	Kurt Suzuki	12.00
MB	Michael Bourn	12.00
MH	Micah Hoffpauir	20.00
MR	Mike Rabelo	8.00
NB	Nick Blackburn	10.00
RO	Ross Ohlendorf	8.00
SA	Jarrod Saltalamacchia	15.00
SM	Sean Marshall	10.00
SP	Steve Pearce	8.00

The Award Show

#	Player	NM/M
	Common Player:	1.00
1	Yadier Molina	1.50
2	Adrian Gonzalez	1.50
3	Brandon Phillips	1.00
4	David Wright	3.00
5	Jimmy Rollins	1.50
6	Carlos Beltran	1.50
7	Shane Victorino	1.50
8	Geovany Soto	1.50
9	Tim Lincecum	3.00
10	Albert Pujols	5.00
11	Joe Mauer	1.50
12	Carlos Pena	1.50
13	Dustin Pedroia	2.50
14	Adrian Beltre	1.00
15	Torii Hunter	1.50

		NM/M
16	Grady Sizemore	2.00
17	Ichiro Suzuki	3.00
18	Evan Longoria	3.00
19	Cliff Lee	1.00
20	Dustin Pedroia	2.50

1987 Oakland Athletics Fire Safety

The 1987 Smokey Bear A's set is not comparable to earlier Forestry Service issues. The cards are bound together in a book titled "Smokey Bear's Fire Prevention Color-Grams." Each Color-Gram features two cards in one. A near-standard size (2-1/2" x 3-3/4") black-and-white card is attached to a large perforated (3-3/4"x 6") card, also black-and-white. The large card, which has a postcard back, features a caricature of the player and is intended to be colored and mailed. Backs contain personal and statistical information and carry a Smokey Bear cartoon fire sfaety message. The books were distributed at an A's game during the 1987 season.

		NM/M
Complete Book:		4.50
Complete Singles Set (12):		3.00
Common Player:		.25
(1)	Joaquin Andujar	.25
(2)	Jose Canseco	1.50
(3)	Mike Davis	.25
(4)	Alfredo Griffin	.25
(5)	Moose Haas	.25
(6)	Jay Howell	.25
(7)	Reggie Jackson	1.50
(8)	Carney Lansford	.25
(9)	Dwayne Murphy	.25
(10)	Tony Phillips	.25
(11)	Dave Stewart	.25
(12)	Curt Young	.25

1992 Oakland A's Dream Team

Following fan balloting in 1991, the Oakland A's named an all-time Dream Team for their 25th anniversary season in 1992 and issued a card set of those players. Cards were distributed in two versions. Perforated sheets of eight cards each were included in the second and third editions of the team's magazine. Imperforate four-card strips were also handed out to the first 10,000 fans attending each of four selected home games in 1992. Cards measure 2-9/16" x 3-3/4". Fronts have gray borders. At upperleft is a green and yellow Dream Team pennant; a 25th anniversary logo at lower-right is also in team colors. A red box beneath the color player photo has the name and position in red and white. Black-and-white backs have uniform and card numbers, career stats and highlights and a few biographical bits.

		NM/M
Complete Set (16):		20.00
Common Player:		1.00
1	Mark McGwire	5.00
2	Mike Gallego	1.00
3	Bert Campaneris	1.00
4	Carney Lansford	1.00
5	Reggie Jackson	4.00
6	Rickey Henderson	3.00
7	Jose Canseco	3.00
8	Dave Parker	1.00
9	Terry Steinbach	1.00
10	Dave Stewart	1.00
11	Jim "Catfish" Hunter	2.00
12	Vida Blue	1.00
13	Bob Welch	1.00
14	Dennis Eckersley	2.00
15	Rollie Fingers	2.00
16	Tony LaRussa	1.00

1995 Oakland A's CHP

This safety set was sponsored by the California Highway Patrol. Fronts of the 2-1/2" x 3-1/2" cards have borderless game-action photos with a pair of team logos in the upper corner, a CHiPs badge at bottom-left and the player's name at lower-right. Black-and-white backs have player data and a driving safety tip.

		NM/M
Complete Set (8):		15.00
Common Player:		.50
1	Brent Gates	.50
2	Mark McGwire	10.00
3	Geronimo Berroa	.50
4	Jason Giambi	7.00
5	Terry Steinbach	.50
6	Mike Bordick	.50
7	Todd Van Poppel	.50
8	Ariel Prieto	.50

1999 Plumbers Local 342 Oakland A's

Borrowing from the concept used for many years by Mother's Cookies, this team set was de-signed to encourage trading when it was distributed to 15,000 fans on May 2. Cards were given away in shrink-wrapped packs of 28, containing 20 single cards and eight of one of the others. Sponsored by a trade union, the Plumbers Steamfitters Refrigeration Local 342, the set has color photos on front, surrounded by borders which morph from yellow to dark green. A "Generation '99 A's" logo is at lower-left. Backs have minimal player data.

		NM/M
Complete Set (28):		12.50
Common Player:		.25
1	Art Howe	.25
2	Ben Grieve	.50
3	Jason Giambi	3.00
4	Kenny Rogers	.25
5	Matt Stairs	.25
6	Tom Candiotti	.25
7	Tony Phillips	.25
8	Eric Chavez	1.50
9	Tim Raines	.50
10	A.J. Hinch	.25
11	Bill Taylor	.25
12	Miguel Tejada	1.50
13	Tim Worrell	.25
14	Scott Spezio	.25
15	Buddy Groom	.25
16	Olmedo Saenz	.25
17	T.J. Mathews	.25
18	Mike Macfarlane	.25
19	Brad Rigby	.25
20	Ryan Christenson	.25
21	Doug Jones	.25
22	Terry Clark	.25
23	Jorge Velandia	.25
24	Gil Heredia	.25
25	John Jaha	.25
26	Jimmy Haynes	.25
27	Jason McDonald	.25
28	A's Coaches/Checklist (Thad Bosley, Brad Fischer, Dave Hudgens, Ken Macha, Rick Peterson, Ron Washington)	.25

2000 Plumbers Local 342 Oakland A's

This team set was designed to encourage trading when it was distributed to fans at a promotional game. Cards were given away in packs of 28, containing 20 single cards and eight of one of the others. Sponsored by a trade union, the Plumbers Steamfitters Refrigeration Local 342, the set has color photos on front, surrounded by green borders. Backs have minimal player data.

		NM/M
Complete Set (28):		15.00
Common Player:		.50
1	Art Howe	.50
2	Jason Giambi	4.00
3	Tim Hudson	2.00
4	Matt Stairs	.50
5	Kevin Appier	.50
6	Ben Grieve	.50
7	Randy Velarde	.50
8	Eric Chavez	1.50
9	Mark Mulder	.75
10	Sal Fasano	.50
11	Doug Jones	.50
12	Miguel Tejada	1.50
13	Omar Oliveres	.50
14	Jeremy Giambi	.50
15	Gil Heredia	.50
16	Olmedo Saenz	.50
17	T.J. Mathews	.50
18	Ramon Hernandez	.50
19	Jeff Tam	.50
20	Ryan Christenson	.50
21	John Jaha	.50
22	Rich Sauveur	.50
23	Terrence Long	.50
24	Mike Magnante	.50
25	Scott Service	.50
26	Frank Menechino	.50
27	Jason Isringhausen	.50
28	Coaches/Checklist	.50

2001 Oakland A's Cal Ripken Farewell

To mark his final trip to Oakland as a player, the A's issued these cards to the first 20,000 fans at the September 3-5 games. The cards commemorate career highlights. Fronts have action photos from earlier seasons and a smaller second photo of more current vintage. Red-and-black backs have a ghost-image photo details of the highlight and specifics of the giveaway.

		NM/M
Complete Set (3):		9.00
Common Card:		3.00

		NM/M
1	Cal Ripken Jr. (Rookie Season 1982)	3.00
2	Cal Ripken Jr. (All-Star Game 1987)	3.00
3	Cal Ripken Jr. (2,131 - Record Breaker)	3.00

2002 Plumbers Local 342 Oakland A's

This team set was designed to encourage trading when it was distributed to 15,000 fans on August 18. Cards were given away in shrink-wrapped packs of 28, containing 20 single cards and eight of one of the others. Sponsored by a trade union, the Plumbers Steamfitters Refrigeration Local 342, the set has borderless color photos on front. A team-colors green and gold strip at bottom has the the player name and "BASEBALL A's STYLE." Backs are in black, green and gold with player data and a large union logo.

		NM/M
Complete Set (28):		15.00
Common Player:		.50
1	Art Howe	.50
2	Tim Hudson	2.00
3	David Justice	.50
4	Mark Mulder	.75
5	Jermaine Dye	.50
6	Barry Zito	2.00
7	Miguel Tejada	1.50
8	Eric Chavez	1.50
9	Terrence Long	.50
10	John Mabry	.50
11	Billy Koch	.50
12	Adam Piatt	.50
13	Ramon Hernandez	.50
14	Randy Velarde	.50
15	Scott Hatteberg	.50
16	Mike Magnante	.50
17	Greg Myers	.50
18	Cory Lidle	.50
19	Olmedo Saenz	.50
20	Jim Mecir	.50
21	Eric Byrnes	.50
22	Mark Ellis	.50
23	Mike Venafro	.50
24	Carlos Pena	.50
25	Mike Fyhrie	.50
26	Aaron Harang	.50
27	Chad Bradford	.50
28	A's Coaches (Thad Bosley, Brad Fischer, Ken Macha, Rick Peterson, Mike Quade, Ron Washington)	.50

2003 Plumbers Local 342 Oakland A's

This team set was designed to encourage trading when it was distributed to fans at a promotional game. Twenty-eight cards were given away in paper envelopes, containing 20 single cards and eight of one of the others. Sponsored by the Plumbers Steamfitters Refrigeration Local 342, the set has borderless color photos on front. A team-colors green and gold strip at bottom has the player name, posi-tion and team logo. Backs are in white, green and gold with player data and a large union logo.

		NM/M
Complete Set (28):		15.00
Common Player:		.50
1	Ken Macha	.50
2	Tim Hudson	2.00
3	Miguel Tejada	1.50
4	Mark Mulder	.75
5	Ramon Hernandez	.50
6	Barry Zito	2.00
7	Jose Guillen	.50
8	Eric Chavez	1.50
9	Terrence Long	.50
10	Ricardo Rincon	.50
11	Erubiel Durazo	.50
12	Mark Ellis	.50
13	Keith Foulke	.50
14	Eric Byrnes	.50
15	Ted Lilly	.50
16	Scott Hatteberg	.50
17	Rich Harden	1.00
18	Chris Singleton	.50
19	Chad Bradford	.50
20	Jermaine Dye	.50
21	Chad Harville	.50
22	Adam Melhuse	.50
23	Jim Mecir	.50
24	John Halama	.50
25	Mike Neu	.50
26	Billy McMillon	.50
27	Frank Menechino	.50
28	A's Coaches (Brad Fischer, Terry Francona, Bob Geren, Dave Hudgens, Rick Peterson, Ron Washington)	.50

1983 O'Connell & Son Ink Baseball Greats

This set of 4-1/2" x 6-1/2" blank-back cards features the artwork of T.S. O'Connell done in the style of 1959 Topps cards. Player portraits are in black-and-white, while backgrounds and team logos are in color. Production was limited to 2,000 sets.

		NM/M
Complete Set (20):		65.00
Common Player:		2.50
(1)	Hank Aaron	6.50
(2)	Johnny Bench	2.50
(3)	Yogi Berra	3.50
(4)	George Brett	4.50
(5)	Roy Campanella	3.50
(6)	Rod Carew	2.50
(7)	Roberto Clemente	10.00
(8)	Bob Gibson	2.50
(9)	Al Kaline	3.00
(10)	Mickey Mantle	12.50
(11)	Joe Morgan	2.50
(12)	Stan Musial	3.50
(13)	Jim Rice	2.50
(14)	Frank Robinson	2.50
(15)	Pete Rose	6.50
(16)	Tom Seaver	2.50
(17)	Duke Snider	3.50
(18)	Honus Wagner	4.50
(19)	Carl Yastrzemski	2.50
(20)	Robin Yount	2.50

1984-91 O'Connell & Son Ink Mini Prints

This series of 2-1/2" x 3-1/2" blank-backed cards was issued over the period of 1984-91. Cards #1-180 were sold in annual series of 36 each from 1984-88; the 21-card Sixth Series was issued in 1990. The final 43 cards, plus unnumbered checklists for the first six series were distributed in issues of the company's newsletter, "The Infield Dirt." All cards feature black-and-white pen-and-ink player portraits by T.S. O'Connell and have only the player name and card number on front. Several styles of background, some in color, are found among the various series. Production was limited to 2,000 of each card.

		NM/M
Complete Set (250):		450.00
Common Player:		1.50
	First Series	45.00
1	Ted Williams	7.50
2	Minnie Minoso	1.50
3	Sandy Koufax	4.50
4	Al Kaline	4.50
5	Whitey Ford	3.00
6	Wade Boggs	3.00
7	Nolan Ryan	12.00
8	Greg Luzinski	1.50
9	Cal Ripken	12.00
10	Carl Yastrzemski	4.50
11	Dale Murphy	2.00
12	Rocky Colavito	7.50
13	George Brett	7.50
14	Willie McCovey	3.00
15	Rod Carew	2.50
16	Bob Gibson	2.50
17	Robin Yount	3.00
18	Steve Carlton	2.50
19	Harmon Killebrew	2.50
20	Willie Mays	7.50
21	Reggie Jackson	5.00
22	Eddie Mathews	2.50
23	Eddie Murray	2.50
24	Johnny Bench	2.50
25	Mickey Mantle	18.00
26	Willie Stargell	2.50
27	Rickey Henderson	2.50
28	Roger Maris	6.00
29	Darryl Strawberry	1.50
30	Pete Rose	9.00
31	Jim Rice	1.50
32	Thurman Munson	3.00
33	Brooks Robinson	2.50
34	Fernando Valenzuela	1.50
35	Tony Oliva	1.50
36	Hank Aaron	7.50
	Second Series	45.00
37	Joe Morgan	2.50
38	Kent Hrbek	1.50
39	Yogi Berra	3.00
40	Stan Musial	7.50
41	Gary Matthews	1.50
42	Larry Doby	1.50
43	Steve Garvey	2.50
44	Bob Horner	1.50
45	Ron Guidry	1.50
46	Ernie Banks	3.00
47	Carlton Fisk	2.50
48	"Pee Wee" Reese	2.50
49	Bobby Shantz	1.50
50	Joe DiMaggio	12.00
51	Enos Slaughter	1.50
52	Gary Carter	2.50
53	Bob Feller	2.50
54	Phil Rizzuto	2.50
55	Dave Concepcion	1.50
56	Ron Kittle	1.50
57	Dwight Evans	1.50
58	Johnny Mize	1.50
59	Richie Ashburn	2.50
60	Roberto Clemente	12.00
61	Fred Lynn	1.50
62	Billy Williams	1.50
63	Dave Winfield	2.50
64	Robin Roberts	2.50
65	Billy Martin	1.50
66	Duke Snider	3.00
67	Luis Aparicio	2.50
68	Mickey Vernon	1.50
69	Mike Schmidt	6.00
70	Frank Robinson	2.50
71	Bill Madlock	1.50
72	Rollie Fingers	2.50
	Third Series	45.00
73	Rod Carew	2.50

#	Player	Price
74	Carl Erskine	1.50
75	Lou Brock	2.50
76	Brooks Robinson	2.50
77	Roberto Clemente	12.00
78	Nellie Fox	2.50
79	Bud Harrelson	1.50
80	Ted Williams	7.50
81	Walter Johnson	2.50
82	Cal Ripken	12.00
83	Lefty Grove	2.00
84	Lou Whitaker	1.50
85	Johnny Bench	2.50
86	Ty Cobb	6.00
87	Mike Schmidt	6.00
88	George Brett	7.50
89	Jim Bunning	1.50
90	Babe Ruth	12.00
91	Satchel Paige	5.00
92	Warren Spahn	1.50
93	Dale Murphy	2.50
94	Early Wynn	1.50
95	Reggie Jackson	2.50
96	Charlie Gehringer	1.50
97	Jackie Robinson	9.00
98	Lou Gehrig	10.00
99	Hank Aaron	7.50
100	Mickey Mantle	18.00
101	Sandy Koufax	9.00
102	Ryne Sandberg	4.00
103	Don Mattingly	6.00
104	Darryl Strawberry	1.50
105	Tom Seaver	2.50
106	Bill Klem	1.50
107	Dwight Gooden	1.50
108	Pete Rose	9.00
	Fourth Series	45.00
109	Elston Howard	2.50
110	Honus Wagner	3.00
111	Waite Hoyt	1.50
112	Bill Bruton	1.50
113	Gil Hodges	2.50
114	Vic Power	1.50
115	Al Kaline	4.50
116	Al Lopez	1.50
117	Rocky Bridges	1.50
118	Jim Gilliam	1.50
119	Christy Mathewson	1.50
120	Hank Greenberg	3.00
121	Eddie Mathews	1.50
122	Van Mungo	1.50
123	Harry Simpson	1.50
124	Carl Yastrzemski	2.50
125	Pete Rose	9.00
126	Dizzy Dean	1.50
127	Chi Chi Olivo	1.50
128	Johnny Vander Meer	1.50
129	Roberto Clemente	12.00
130	Carl Hubbell	1.50
131	Willie Mays	7.50
132	Willie Stargell	2.50
133	Sam Jethroe	1.50
134	Pete Rose	9.00
135	Jackie Robinson	9.00
136	Yogi Berra	3.00
137	Grover Alexander	2.00
138	Joe Morgan	2.50
139	Rube Foster	1.50
140	Mickey Mantle	18.00
141	Ted Williams	7.50
142	Jimmie Foxx	2.50
143	Pepper Martin	1.50
144	Hank Aaron	7.50
	Fifth Series	45.00
145	Vida Blue	1.50
146	Carl Furillo	2.00
147	Lloyd Waner	1.50
148	Eddie Dyer	1.50
149	Casey Stengel	2.50
150	Mickey Mantle	18.00
151	Gil Hodges	2.50
152	Don Mossi	1.50
153	Ron Swoboda	1.50
154	Hoyt Wilhelm	1.50
155	Ed Roush (Edd)	1.50
156	Mickey Lolich	2.00
157	Jim Palmer	2.50
158	Thurman Munson	3.00
159	Don Zimmer	1.50
160	Hank Aaron	7.50
161	Johnny Bench	2.50
162	Orlando Cepeda	1.50
163	Honus Wagner	3.00
164	Tom Seaver	2.50
165	Willie Mays	7.50
166	Elmer Riddle	1.50
167	Tony Oliva	1.50
168	Elmer Flick	1.50
169	Curt Flood	1.50
170	Carl Yastrzemski	2.50
171	Charlie Keller	1.50
172	Christy Mathewson	2.50
173	Eddie Plank	1.50
174	Lou Gehrig	10.00
175	John McGraw	1.50
176	Mule Haas	1.50
177	Paul Waner	1.50
178	Steve Blass	1.50
179	Honus Wagner	3.00
180	Jack Barry	1.50
	Sixth Series	45.00
181	Rocky Colavito	4.50
182	Danny Murtaugh	1.50
183	John Edwards	1.50
184	Pete Rose	9.00
185	Roy Campanella	3.00
186	Jerry Grote	1.50
187	Leo Durocher	1.50
188	Rollie Fingers	2.50

#	Player	Price
189	Wes Parker	1.50
190	Joe Rudi	1.50
191	Bill Veeck	2.50
192	Mark Fidrych	2.50
193	George Foster	1.50
194	Early Wynn	1.50
195	Frank Howard	1.50
196	Graig Nettles	2.50
197	Juan Pizzaro	1.50
198	Jose Cruz	1.50
199	Joe Jackson	12.00
200	Stan Musial	7.50
201	Chuck Klein	1.50
	Seventh Series	45.00
202	Ryne Sandberg	6.00
203	Richie Allen	2.50
204	Bo Jackson	2.50
205	Kevin Mitchell	1.50
206	Al Smith, Early Wynn, Larry Doby	2.50
207	Mickey Mantle	18.00
208	Will Clark	2.50
209	Cecil Fielder	1.50
210	Bobby Richardson	2.50
211	Nolan Ryan	12.00
212	Casey Stengel	2.50
213	Ted Kluszewski	3.00
214	Gaylord Perry	1.50
215	Johnny Vander Meer	1.50
216	Willie Mays	7.50
217	Goose Goslin	1.50
218	Bobby Shantz	1.50
219	Terry Pendleton	1.50
220	Richie Ashburn	2.50
221	Robin Yount	3.00
222	Cal Ripken	12.00
223	Danny Ainge	1.50
224	Bob Friend	1.50
225	Orel Hershiser	2.50
226	Wade Boggs	3.00
227	Bill Mazeroski (1960 World Series home run.)	3.00
228	Stan Musial	7.50
229	Chris Short	1.50
230	Johnny Bench	2.50
231	Nellie Fox	2.50
232	Ron Santo	2.50
233	Tony Gwynn	6.00
234	Phil Niekro	2.50
235	Frank Thomas	4.50
236	Greg Gross	1.50
237	Ken Griffey Jr.	9.00
238	Benito Santiago	1.50
239	Dwight Gooden	1.50
240	Darryl Strawberry	1.50
241	Roy Campanella	3.00
242	Roger Clemens	6.00
243	Kirby Puckett	7.50
244	Nolan Ryan	12.00
---	First Series Checklist	.25
---	Second Series Checklist	.25
---	Third Series Checklist	.25
---	Fourth Series Checklist	.25
---	Fifth Series Checklist	.25
---	Sixth Series Checklist	.25

1986 Oh Henry! Cleveland Indians

This 30-card set of Cleveland Indians players was distributed by the team at a special Photo/Baseball Card Day at Municipal Stadium. The cards were printed on an 11" x 29" three-panel, perforated foldout piece which featured four action shots of the Indians on the cover. Unfolded, there are two panels containing the baseball cards and a third which contains a team photo. Cards measure 2-1/4" x 3-1/8". The players' studio portraits are framed in blue with a white border and list player name, number and position. Card fronts also include a picture of the sponsoring candy bar. Card backs include facsimile autograph and professional records. Each card is perforated for separation.

		NM/M
	Complete Set, Foldout:	9.00
	Common Player:	.40
2	Brett Butler	.40
4	Tony Bernazard	.40
6	Andy Allanson	.40
7	Pat Corrales	.40
8	Carmen Castillo	.40
10	Pat Tabler	.40
13	Ernie Camacho	.40
14	Julio Franco	.50
15	Dan Rohn	.40
18	Ken Schrom	.40
20	Otis Nixon	.40
22	Fran Mullins	.40
23	Chris Bando	.40
24	Ed Williams	.40
26	Brook Jacoby	.40
27	Mel Hall	.40
29	Andre Thornton	.50
30	Joe Carter	.75
35	Phil Niekro	2.00
36	Jamie Easterly	.40
37	Don Schulze	.40
42	Rich Yett	.40
43	Scott Bailes	.40
44	Neal Heaton	.40
46	Jim Kern	.40
48	Dickie Noles	.40
49	Tom Candiotti	.40
53	Reggie Ritter	.40
54	Tom Waddell	.40
---	Coaching Staff (Jack Aker, Bobby Bonds, Doc Edwards, John Goryl)	.40
---	Team Photo	.40

1995 Oh Henry! Toronto Blue Jays

The candy bar company, Oh Henry!, sponsored this card set giveaway. The 2-1/2" x 3-1/2" cards have an action photo on a green background with the team name repeated in white diagonally. A large colorful "LET'S PLAY BALL" team logo is at top-left. The player name and uniform number are overprinted at bottom. Backs are printed in black-and-white with personal data, career highlights, stats, and sponsor's logo. Cards are listed here alphabetically.

		NM/M
	Complete Set (36):	12.00
	Common Player:	.25
(1)	Roberto Alomar	.75
(2)	Bob Bailor	.25
(3)	Howard Battle	.25
(4)	Joe Carter	.45
(5)	Tony Castillo	.25
(6)	Domingo Cedeno	.25
(7)	Galen Cisco	.25
(8)	David Cone	.35
(9)	Brad Cornett	.25
(10)	Danny Cox	.25
(11)	Tim Crabtree	.25
(12)	Carlos Delgado	1.00
(13)	Cito Gaston	.25
(14)	Alex Gonzalez	.50
(15)	Shawn Green	2.00
(16)	Juan Guzman	.25
(17)	Darren Hall	.25
(18)	Pat Hentgen	.25
(19)	Larry Hisle	.25
(20)	Dennis Holmberg	.25
(21)	Michael Huff	.25
(22)	Randy Knorr	.25
(23)	Al Leiter	.25
(24)	Nick Leyva	.25
(25)	Angel Martinez	.25
(26)	Paul Molitor	2.50
(27)	John Olerud	.50
(28)	Tomas Perez	.25
(29)	Aaron Small	.25
(30)	Paul Spoljaric	.25
(31)	Ed Sprague	.25
(32)	Gene Tenace	.25
(33)	Mike Timlin	.25
(34)	Duane Ward	.25
(35)	Devon White	.40
(36)	Woody Williams	.25

1996 Oh Henry! Toronto Blue Jays

In celebration of the team's 20th anniversary, Oh Henry! sponsored a card set giveaway at SkyDome on June 11. The first 25,000 fans received a boxed set of current and former players. The 2-1/2" x 3-1/2" cards have a borderless photo on front. The central portion of the picture is in color, the edges are in black-and-white. The player name and uniform number are overprinted at bottom. The team's anniversary logo is in the upper-left corner. On former players' cards there is a gold "ALUMNI" banner under the logo ball. Backs are printed in blue and white with career summary and stats, a few bits of personal data and logos of the team and sponsor. Cards are listed here alphabetically.

		NM/M
	Complete Set (36):	8.00
	Common Player:	.25
(1)	George Bell	.35
(2)	Brian Bohanon	.25
(3)	Joe Carter	.40
(4)	Tony Castillo	.25
(5)	Domingo Cedeno	.25
(6)	Tim Crabtree	.25
(7)	Felipe Crespo	.25
(8)	Carlos Delgado	1.50
(9)	Cito Gaston	.25
(10)	Alex Gonzalez	.50
(11)	Shawn Green	1.00
(12)	Alfredo Griffin	.25
(13)	Kelly Gruber	.25
(14)	Juan Guzman	.25
(15)	Erik Hanson	.25
(16)	Pat Hentgen	.25
(17)	Marty Janzen	.25
(18)	Nick Leyva	.25
(19)	Sandy Martinez	.25
(20)	Lloyd Moseby	.35
(21)	Otis Nixon	.25
(22)	Charlie O'Brien	.25
(23)	John Olerud	.75
(24)	Robert Perez	.25
(25)	Paul Quantrill	.25
(26)	Mel Queen	.25
(27)	Bill Risley	.25
(28)	Juan Samuel	.25
(29)	Ed Sprague	.25
(30)	Dave Steib	.35
(31)	Gene Tenace	.25
(32)	Mike Timlin	.25
(33)	Willie Upshaw	.25
(34)	Jeffrey Ware	.25
(35)	Ernie Whitt	.25
(36)	Woody Williams	.25

1997 Oh Henry! Toronto Blue Jays

The first 25,000 fans entering SkyDome for the Blue Jays' May 6 game received a team card set sponsored by the candy bar company. In 2-1/2" x 3-1/2" size, fronts feature color action photos with a splash of "infield dirt" vertically at left. The player's name and uniform number appear at top-left. "Oh!" and the team logo are printed in bottom corners. Backs are printed in blue and white with a few personal data, stats and career highlights.

		NM/M
	Complete Set (36):	7.50
	Common Player:	.25
2	Otis Nixon	.25
3	Felipe Crespo	.25
4	Alfredo Griffin	.25
5	Jacob Brumfield	.25
6	Orlando Merced	.25
7	Shannon Stewart	.50
8	Alex Gonzalez	.40
11	Jim Lett	.25
12	Juan Samuel	.25
13	Carlos Garcia	.25
15	Shawn Green	1.00
17	Nick Leyva	.25
18	Robert Perez	.25
19	Benito Santiago	.25
21	Roger Clemens	2.50
22	Charlie O'Brien	.25
24	Paul Spoljaric	.25
25	Carlos Delgado	1.50
26	Willie Upshaw	.25
29	Joe Carter	.30
31	Robert Person	.25
33	Ed Sprague	.25
34	Mel Queen	.25
37	Tim Crabtree	.25
39	Erik Hanson	.25
40	Mike Timlin	.25
41	Pat Hentgen	.25
43	Cito Gaston	.25
44	Gene Tenace	.25
48	Paul Quantrill	.25
49	Luis Andujar	.25
54	Woody Williams	.25
55	Bill Risley	.25
57	Juan Guzman	.25

1998 Oh Henry! Toronto Blue Jays

This stadium giveaway card set was issued in a flip-top cardboard box decorated with the team logo and checklist. The 2-1/2" x 3-1/2" cards have (mostly) game action photos on their borderless fronts. Sponsor logo at player name and uniform number are at top, team logo and motto "BRING IT ON." at bottom. Backs are blue-and-white with player data, stats and career highlights. The checklist is arranged by uniform number.

		NM/M
	Complete Set (36):	7.50
	Common Player:	.25
1	Tony Fernandez	.25
3	Felipe Crespo	.25
4	Craig Grebeck	.25
5	Mark Dalesandro	.25
7	Eddie Rodriguez	.25
8	Alex Gonzalez	.45
9	Darren Fletcher	.25
10	Jim Lett	.25
11	Juan Samuel	.25
14	Kevin Brown	.25
15	Shawn Green	1.00
16	Jack Hubbard	.25
17	Tim Johnson	.25
19	Benito Santiago	.25
19	Dan Plesac	.25
20	Mike Stanley	.25
21	Roger Clemens	3.00
22	Sal Butera	.25
23	Jose Cruz Jr.	.25
24	Shannon Stewart	.35
25	Carlos Delgado	1.50

1999 Oh Henry! Toronto Blue Jays

This boxed set was a stadium give-away. Fronts of the 2-1/2" x 3-1/2" cards have game-action photos on a wood-look background. Backs have personal data, career highlights and stats printed in blue. The checklist is arranged by uniform number.

		NM/M
	Complete Set (36):	7.50
	Common Player:	.25
1	Tony Fernandez	.25
3	Norberto Martin	.25
4	Craig Grebeck	.25
5	Mark Dalesandro	.25
7	Pat Kelly	.25
8	Alex Gonzalez	.25
9	Darrin Fletcher	.25
10	Jim Lett	.25
11	Jim Fregosi	.25
12	Willie Greene	.25
13	Pete Munro	.25
15	Shawn Green	.75
16	Lloyd Moseby	.25
17	Dave Hollins	.25
18	Homer Bush	.25
19	Dan Plesac	.25
22	Mike Matheny	.25
23	Jose Cruz	.25
24a	Paul Spoljaric	.25
24b	Shannon Stewart	.35
25	Carlos Delgado	1.50
26	Chris Carpenter	.25
29	Geronimo Berroa	.25
32	Marty Pevey	.25
32	Roy Halladay	.75
33	David Wells	.25
34	Mel Queen	.25
35	Terry Bevington	.25
39	Gary Matthews	.25
40	Graeme Lloyd	.25
41	Pat Hentgen	.25
42	Tom Davey	.25
47	Kelvim Escobar	.25
48	Paul Quantrill	.25
50	Joey Hamilton	.25
77	Bill Risley	.25

#	Player	Price
26	Chris Carpenter	.25
28	Randy Myers	.25
30	Woody Williams	.25
31	Robert Person	.25
37	Ed Sprague	.25
34	Mel Queen	.25
38	Gary Matthews	.25
39	Erik Hanson	.25
40	Carlos Almanzar	.25
41	Pat Hentgen	.25
44	Jose Canseco	1.00
45	Kelvim Escobar	.25
48	Paul Quantrill	.25
55	Bill Risley	.25
57	Juan Guzman	.25

2000 Oh Henry! Toronto Blue Jays

This boxed set was a stadium give-away. Fronts of the 2-1/2" x 3-1/2" cards have game-action photos on a dark blue background. Backs have personal data, career highlights and stats printed in blue.

	NM/M
Complete Set (36):	10.00
Common Player:	.25
3 Lee Elia	.25
4 Craig Grebeck	.25
7 Tony Batista	.25
8 Alex Gonzalez	.25
9 Darrin Fletcher	.25
10 Vernon Wells	.50
11 Jim Fregosi	.25
13 Peter Munro	.25
15 Marty Cordova	.25
18 Homer Bush	.25
20 Brad Fullmer	.25
22 Rick Langford	.25
23 Jose Cruz	.25
24 Shannon Stewart	.25
25 Carlos Delgado	1.50
26 Chris Carpenter	.25
28 Lance Painter	.25
29 Bobby Knoop	.25
30 Alberto Castillo	.25
32 Roy Halladay	.75
33 David Wells	.50
34 Clayton Andrews	.25
35 Terry Bevington	.25
37 Frank Castillo	.25
41 Cito Gaston	.25
43 Raul Mondesi	.25
44 Billy Koch	.25
47 Kelvim Escobar	.25
48 Paul Quantrill	.25
49 John Bale	.25
50 Joey Hamilton	.25
51 Pedro Borbon	.25
52 John Frascatore	.25
55 DeWayne Wise	.25
56 Roly de Armas	.25
77/00 Diamond / Ace (Mascots)	.25

2001 Oh Henry! Toronto Blue Jays

The team's 25th season is commemorated with this stadium give-away boxed set. Fronts have action photos on a blue background with team and sponsor logos. Backs have a large 25th anniversary logo, complete stats, personal data and career highlights.

	NM/M
Complete Set (36):	8.00
Common Player:	.25
1 Cookie Rojas	.25
2 Jeff Frye	.25
5 Chris Woodward	.25
7 Tony Batista	.25
8 Alex Gonzalez	.35
9 Darrin Fletcher	.25
13 Buck Martinez	.25
14 Ryan Freel	.25
16 Garth Iorg	.25
17 Chris Michalak	.25
18 Homer Bush	.25
19 Dan Plesac	.25
20 Brad Fullmer	.25
21 Esteban Loaiza	.25
22 Brian Simmons	.25
23 Jose Cruz Jr.	.25
24 Shannon Stewart	.50
25 Carlos Delgado	1.00
26 Chris Carpenter	.25
28 Lance Painter	.25
30 Alberto Castillo	.25
33 Mike Sirotka	.25
35 Terry Bevington	.25
39 Steve Parris	.25
41 Cito Gaston	.25
43 Raul Mondesi	.25
44 Billy Koch	.25
45 Kelvim Escobar	.25
47 Gil Patterson	.25
48 Paul Quantrill	.25
50 Joey Hamilton	.25
51 Pedro Borbon	.25
52 John Frascatore	.25
53 Mark Connor	.25
--- First Pitch (Bill Singer)	.25
--- Home Run Record (Raul Mondesi, Tony Batista, Jose Cruz Jr., Carlos Delgado)	.25

1982-1988 Ohio Baseball Hall of Fame

Ohio natives and players who made their mark playing in the

Frank Robinson 1978

Buckeye State are featured in this collectors' issue, along with executives and a few other figures. Fronts of the 3-3/8" x 5-5/8" cards have black-and-white player photos surrounded by red borders. The player's name and year of induction are at bottom. Black-and-white backs have lengthy career summaries. Original production was 2,500 sets which were sold into the hobby at $7 apiece. Later inductees were added to the set through at least 1988, but the checklist after #65 is incomplete and may represent skip-numbering.

	NM/M
Complete Set (93):	100.00
Common Player:	2.00
1 Ohio Baseball Hall of Fame	2.00
2 Checklist	.50
3 Nick Cullop	2.00
4 Dean Chance	2.00
5 Bob Feller	3.00
6 Jesse Haines	2.00
7 Waite Hoyt	2.00
8 Ernie Lombardi	2.00
9 Mike Powers	2.00
10 Edd Roush	2.00
11 Red Ruffing	2.00
12 Luke Sewell	2.00
13 Tris Speaker	3.00
14 Cy Young	3.00
15 Walter Alston	2.00
16 Lou Boudreau	2.00
17 Warren Giles	2.00
18 Ted Kluszewski	3.00
19 William McKinley	2.00
20 Roger Peckinpaugh	2.00
21 Johnny Vander Meer	2.00
22 Early Wynn	2.00
23 Earl Averill	2.00
24 Stan Coveleski	2.00
25 Lefty Grove	2.00
26 Nap Lajoie	2.00
27 Al Lopez	2.00
28 Eddie Onslow	2.00
29 Branch Rickey	2.00
30 Frank Robinson	3.00
31 George Sisler	2.00
32 Bob Lemon	2.00
33 Satchel Paige	2.00
34 Bucky Walters	2.00
35 Gus Bell	2.00
36 Rocky Colavito	3.00
37 Mel Harder	2.00
38 Tommy Henrich	2.00
39 Miller Huggins	2.00
40 Fred Hutchinson	2.00
41 Eppa Rixey	2.00
42 Joe Sewell	2.00
43 George Uhle	2.00
44 Bill Veeck	2.00
45 Estel Crabtree	2.00
46 Harvey Haddix	2.00
47 Noodles Hahn	2.00
48 Joe Jackson	4.00
49 Kenesaw Landis	2.00
50 Thurman Munson	3.00
51 Gabe Paul	2.00
52 Vada Pinson	2.00
53 Wally Post	2.00
54 Vic Wertz	2.00
55 Paul Derringer	2.00
56 John Galbreath	2.00
57 Richard Marquard	2.00
58 Bill McKechnie	2.00
59 Rocky Nelson	2.00
60 Al Rosen	2.00
61 Lew Fonseca	2.00
62 Larry MacPhail	2.00
63 Joe Nuxhall	2.00
64 Birdie Tebbetts	2.00
65 Gene Woodling	2.00
66 Ethan Allen	2.00
67 Mike Garcia	2.00
68 Bob Howsam	2.00
69 Addie Joss	2.00
70 Ken Keltner	2.00
71 "Tot" Pressnell	2.00
72 Roger Bresnahan	2.00

	NM/M
73 Bill Mazeroski	3.00
75a Frank McCormick	2.00
75b George H. Sisler	2.00
76 Bill Wambsganss	2.00
79 Woody English	2.00
80 Roy McMillan	3.00
81 Frank Baumholtz	2.00
83 Sam McDowell	2.50
84 James Campbell	2.00
86 Ned Garver	2.00
87 Bob Purkey	2.00
90 Harold Cooper	2.00
91 Dennis Galehouse	2.00
92 Brooks Lawrence	2.50
93 Tony Lucadello	2.00

1992 Old Style Chicago Cubs

1966 - 1973, 1976 - 1977

RANDY HUNDLEY

More than two dozens Cubs stars are featured in this set of 2-1/2" x 3-1/2" cards. Front have sepia player photos with their years at Chicago indicated on top. Backs are printed in black, red and blue on white with a few stats and career highlights, sponsor and team logos and a picture of the Cubs uniform in the player's debut year. The unnumbered cards are checklisted here in alphabetical order.

	NM/M
Complete Set (28):	15.00
Common Player:	.50
(1) Grover Alexander	.50
(2) Cap Anson	.50
(3) Ernie Banks	3.00
(4) Mordecai Brown	.50
(5) Phil Cavarretta	.50
(6) Frank Chance	.50
(7) Kiki Cuyler	.50
(8) Johnny Evers	.50
(9) Charlie Grimm	.50
(10) Stan Hack	.50
(11) Gabby Hartnett	.50
(12) Billy Herman	.50
(13) Rogers Hornsby	.50
(14) Ken Hubbs	1.00
(15) Randy Hundley	.50
(16) Fergie Jenkins	.75
(17) Bill Lee	.50
(18) Andy Pafko	.50
(19) Rick Reuschel	.50
(20) Charlie Root	.50
(21) Ron Santo	.75
(22) Hank Sauer	.50
(23) Riggs Stephenson	.50
(24) Bruce Sutter	.75
(25) Joe Tinker	.50
(26) Hippo Vaughn	.50
(27) Billy Williams	1.00
(28) Hack Wilson	.50

1993 Old Style Billy Williams

BILLY WILLIAMS

The career of long-time Cubs star, batting coach and Hall of Famer Billy Williams is traced in this four-card set given to fans attending the Aug. 17, 1993, game at Wrigley Field between the Cubs and Expos. Fronts of the first three cards have black-and-white photos, the last card is in color. Backs have biographical and career information along with the sponsor's logo.

	NM/M
Complete Set (4):	8.00
Common Card:	2.00
(1) Billy Williams/ Btg/Personal	2.00
(2) Billy Williams/ Fldg/Playing Career)	2.00
(3) Billy Williams/ Btg/Playing Career	2.00
(4) Billy Williams/Portrait/ Coaching Career)	2.00

1999 Old Style Chicago Cubs All-Century Team

MARK GRACE

Cubs greats of the 20th Century are featured in this stadium give-away set. The set was distributed over the course of three games at Wrigley Field in seven-card cello-wrapped packs. With the exception of all-time manager Frank Chance, the cards were packaged alphabetically; Chance was included in the third "series" pack. Fronts of the 2-1/2" x 3-1/2" cards have black-and-white or color photos in a fancy white frame on a tan background. Color team and sponsor logos appear in the left-hand corners. Black-and-white backs have player data, career highlights and lifetime Cubs stats. The player's uniform number, if any, appears on both front and back. Cards have a glossy surface on both front and back.

	NM/M
Complete Set (21):	20.00
Common Player:	.50
(1) Grover Alexander	.50
(2) Ernie Banks	2.50
(3) Mordecai Brown	.50
(4) Phil Cavarretta	.50
(5) Frank Chance	.50
(6) Andre Dawson	1.00
(7) Mark Grace	2.00
(8) Charlie Grimm	.50
(9) Stan Hack	.50
(10) Gabby Hartnett	.50
(11) Billy Herman	.50
(12) Fergie Jenkins	.75
(13) Andy Pafko	.50
(14) Ryne Sandberg	2.50
(15) Ron Santo	1.50
(16) Lee Smith	.50
(17) Sammy Sosa	3.00
(18) Bruce Sutter	.75
(19) Joe Tinker	.50
(20) Billy Williams	.75
(21) Hack Wilson	.50

1982 On Deck Cookies Discs

CECIL COOPER

These 2-3/4" discs were packaged with a large cookie and sold for 25-29 cents in areas including Florida and New Jersey. The fronts have a 1981 copyright date, but the backs indicate "1982 Collectors Series." Fronts have black-and-white player portraits in the center panel of a baseball design. The end panels can be any one of several pastel colors. Backs are in red and black and repeat the baseball motif and include a copyright for "All sports baking Co., Inc." Each side carries the Players Union logo through

which the discs were licensed by Michael Schechter Associates. Because they are not licensed through Major League Baseball, player pictures have no uniform logos.

	NM/M
Complete Set (32):	60.00
Common Player:	1.50
(1) Buddy Bell	1.50
(2) Johnny Bench	4.00
(3) Bruce Bochte	1.50
(4) George Brett	7.50
(5) Bill Buckner	1.50
(6) Rod Carew	4.00
(7) Steve Carlton	4.00
(8) Cesar Cedeno	1.50
(9) Jack Clark	1.50
(10) Cecil Cooper	1.50
(11) Bucky Dent	1.50
(12) Carlton Fisk	4.00
(13) Steve Garvey	2.50
(14) Goose Gossage	1.50
(15) Mike Hargrove	1.50
(16) Keith Hernandez	1.50
(17) Bob Horner	1.50
(18) Reggie Jackson	7.50
(19) Steve Kemp	1.50
(20) Ron LeFlore	1.50
(21) Fred Lynn	1.50
(22) Lee Mazilli	1.50
(23) Eddie Murray	4.00
(24) Mike Norris	1.50
(25) Dave Parker	1.50
(26) J.R. Richard	1.50
(27) Pete Rose	9.00
(28) Mike Schmidt	7.50
(29) Tom Seaver	4.00
(30) Willie Stargell	4.00
(31) Roy Smalley	1.50
(32) Garry Templeton	1.50

1994 Oscar Mayer Superstar Pop-Ups

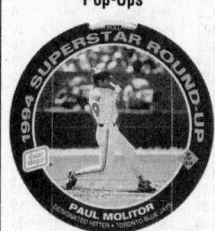

PAUL MOLITOR

Oscar Mayer Bologna packages in 1994 included one pop-up card in each, but unlike the similar Kraft cards, in this case it was 30 round cards (2-1/2 inches in diameter), with the Oscar Mayer logo on the front and trivia questions on the backs. The promotion ran from April through May, or as long as the supplies lasted. The cards were licensed by the Major League Baseball Players Association, but not by Major League Baseball, so the team logos were airbrushed from player's caps and uniforms. Through an on-pack and in-store mail-in offer, collectors could order complete sets of cards for $1.95 per league (15 cards), plus the appropriate proofs of purchase. Officials of Kraft USA, parent company of Oscar Mayer, announced that they printed 266,000 sets.

	NM/M
Complete Set (30):	10.00
Common Player:	.50
1 Jim Abbott	.50
2 Kevin Appier	.50
3 Roger Clemens	1.25
4 Cecil Fielder	.50
5 Juan Gonzalez	.60
6 Ken Griffey Jr.	1.50
7 Kenny Lofton	.50
8 Jack McDowell	.50
9 Paul Molitor	.75
10 Kirby Puckett	1.00
11 Cal Ripken Jr.	2.00
12 Tim Salmon	.50
13 Ruben Sierra	.50
14 Frank Thomas	.75
15 Greg Vaughn	.50
16 Jeff Bagwell	.75
17 Barry Bonds	2.00
18 Bobby Bonilla	.50
19 Jeff Conine	.50
20 Lenny Dykstra	.50
21 Andres Galarraga	.50
22 Marquis Grissom	.50
23 Tony Gwynn	.50
24 Gregg Jefferies	.50
25 John Kruk	.50
26 Greg Maddux	1.00
27 Mike Piazza	1.25
28 Jose Rijo	.50

	NM/M
29 Ryne Sandberg	1.00
30 Andy Van Slyke	.50

1987-89 Our Own Tea Discs

DARRYL STRAWBERRY NEW YORK METS OUTFIELD

Our Own Tea was one of the regional brands which appears on the series of player disc folders which were packaged with various iced tea mixes and other products between 1987-89.

(See 1987-89 Super Star Discs for checklists and values.)

P

1988 Pacific Baseball Legends

ROGER MARIS OUTFIELDER

Pacific Trading Cards rounded up 110 photos of the greatest baseball players from the past 40 years for its 1988 "Baseball Legends" set. All players featured in the set are (or were) members of the Major League Baseball Alumni Association. Card fronts feature silver outer borders and large, clear full-color player photos outlined in black against colorful banner-style inner borders of red, blue, green, orange or gold. The player's name and position are printed in white letters on the lower portion of the banner. Card backs are numbered and carry the Baseball Legends logo, player biography, major league career stats, and personal information. The cards were sold in boxed sets via candy wholesalers, with emphasis on Midwest and New England states. Complete collector sets in clear plastic boxes were made available via dealers or directly from Pacific Trading Cards. Four cards were issued in both error and corrected versions.

	NM/M
Complete Set (110) (No checklist.):	15.00
Common Player:	.10
Wax Pack (10):	.75
Wax Box (36):	15.00
1 Hank Aaron	2.00
2 Red Shoendienst (Schoendienst)	.30
3 Brooks Robinson	.30
4 Luke Appling	.30
5 Gene Woodling	.10
6 Stan Musial	1.00
7 Mickey Mantle	6.00
8 Richie Ashburn	.40
9 Ralph Kiner	.40
10 Phil Rizzuto	.50
11 Harvey Haddix	.10
12 Ken Boyer	.20
13 Clete Boyer	.10
14 Ken Harrelson	.10
15 Robin Roberts	.40
16 Catfish Hunter	.40
17 Frank Howard	.20
18 Jim Perry	.10
19a Elston Howard (Reversed photo.)	.20

#	Player	Price
19b	Elston Howard (Correct photo.)	.20
20	Jim Bouton	.20
21	Pee Wee Reese	.50
22a	Mel Stottlemyer	.20
22b	Mel Stottlemyre	.20
23	Hank Sauer	.10
24	Willie Mays	1.00
25	Tom Tresh	.20
26	Roy Sievers	.10
27	Leo Durocher	.30
28	Al Dark	.20
29	Tony Kubek	.30
30	Johnny Vander Meer	.20
31	Joe Adcock	.20
32	Bob Lemon	.40
33	Don Newcombe	.40
34	Thurman Munson	.50
35	Earl Battey	.10
36	Ernie Banks	.60
37	Matty Alou	.10
38	Dave McNally	.10
39	Mickey Lolich	.20
40	Jackie Robinson	1.00
41	Allie Reynolds	.30
42a	Don Larson	.20
42b	Don Larsen	.20
43	Fergie Jenkins	.30
44	Jim Gilliam	.20
45	Bobby Thomson	.20
46	Sparky Anderson	.20
47	Roy Campanella	.60
48	Marv Throneberry	.20
49	Bill Virdon	.10
50	Ted Williams	1.00
51	Minnie Minoso	.20
52	Bob Turley	.20
53	Yogi Berra	.60
54	Juan Marichal	.40
55	Duke Snider	.60
56	Harvey Kuenn	.40
57	Nellie Fox	.40
58	Felipe Alou	.10
59	Tony Oliva	.20
60	Bill Mazeroski	.40
61	Bobby Shantz	.20
62	Mark Fidrych	.20
63	Johnny Mize	.40
64	Ralph Terry	.10
65	Gus Bell	.10
66	Jerry Koosman	.20
67	Mike McCormick	.10
68	Lou Burdette	.20
69	George Kell	.40
70	Vic Raschi	.20
71	Chuck Connors	.40
72	Ted Kluszewski	.50
73	Bobby Doerr	.30
74	Bobby Richardson	.30
75	Carl Erskine	.40
76	Hoyt Wilhelm	.40
77	Bob Purkey	.10
78	Bob Friend	.10
79	Monte Irvin	.30
80a	Jim Longborg	.20
80b	Jim Lonborg	.20
81	Wally Moon	.10
82	Moose Skowron	.20
83	Tommy Davis	.20
84	Enos Slaughter	.40
85	Sal Maglie	.20
86	Harmon Killebrew	.50
87	Gil Hodges	.50
88	Jim Kaat	.20
89	Roger Maris	.60
90	Billy Williams	.40
91	Luis Aparicio	.40
92	Jim Bunning	.40
93	Bill Freehan	.10
94	Orlando Cepeda	.30
95	Early Wynn	.40
96	Tug McGraw	.30
97	Ron Santo	.30
98	Del Crandall	.10
99	Sal Bando	.10
100	Joe DiMaggio	2.00
101	Bob Feller	.50
102	Larry Doby	.40
103	Rollie Fingers	.30
104	Al Kaline	.60
105	Johnny Podres	.20
106	Lou Boudreau	.30
107	Zoilo Versalles	.10
108	Dick Groat	.10
109	Warren Spahn	.50
110	Johnny Bench	.60
----	Checklist	2.00

1989 Pacific Legends II

Pacific Trading Cards issued its Baseball Legends II set as a carry over of its initial set. The photos are printed on silver background and have colorful inner borders of red, blue, orange or gold. Players' names and positions are printed in white letters below the photos. The card backs once again present the "Baseball Legends" logo, player biography, major league career statistics, and personal information. The Baseball Legends II are numbered 110-220 and were available in wax packs at a limited number of retail chains. The

complete set was also made available via dealers or could be ordered directly from Pacific Trading Cards.

		NM/M
Complete Set (110) (No checklist.):		12.50
Common Player:		.10
Wax Pack (10):		.75
Wax Box (36):		15.00
111	Reggie Jackson	.50
112	Rich Reese	.10
113	Frankie Frisch	.10
114	Ed Kranepool	.10
115	Al Hrabosky	.10
116	Eddie Mathews	.20
117	Ty Cobb	1.00
118	Jim Davenport	.10
119	Buddy Lewis	.10
120	Virgil Trucks	.10
121	Del Ennis	.10
122	Dick Radatz	.10
123	Andy Pafko	.10
124	Wilbur Wood	.10
125	Joe Sewell	.10
126	Herb Score	.10
127	Paul Waner	.10
128	Lloyd Waner	.10
129	Brooks Robinson	.20
130	Bo Belinsky	.10
131	Phil Cavaretta	.10
132	Claude Osteen	.10
133	Tito Francona	.10
134	Billy Pierce	.10
135	Roberto Clemente	3.00
136	Spud Chandler	.10
137	Enos Slaughter	.10
138	Ken Holtzman	.10
139	John Hopp	.10
140	Tony LaRussa	.20
141	Ryne Duren	.10
142	Glenn Beckert	.10
143	Ken Keltner	.10
144	Hank Bauer	.10
145	Roger Craig	.10
146	Frank Baker	.10
147	Jim O'Toole	.10
148	Rogers Hornsby	.20
149	Jose Cardenal	.10
150	Bobby Doerr	.10
151	Mickey Cochrane	.10
152	Gaylord Perry	.10
153	Frank Thomas	.10
154	Ted Williams	1.00
155	Sam McDowell	.10
156	Bob Feller	.20
157	Bert Campaneris	.10
158	Thornton Lee	.10
159	Gary Peters	.10
160	Joe Medwick	.10
161	Joe Nuxhall	.10
162	Joe Schultz	.10
163	Harmon Killebrew	.20
164	Bucky Walters	.10
165	Bobby Allison	.10
166	Lou Boudreau	.10
167	Joe Cronin	.10
168	Mike Torrez	.10
169	Rich Rollins	.10
170	Tony Cuccinello	.10
171	Hoyt Wilhelm	.10
172	Ernie Harwell	.10
173	George Foster	.10
174	Lou Gehrig	1.50
175	Dave Kingman	.10
176	Babe Ruth	2.00
177	Joe Black	.10
178	Roy Face	.10
179	Earl Weaver	.10
180	Johnny Mize	.10
181	Roger Cramer	.10
182	Jim Piersall	.10
183	Ned Garver	.10
184	Billy Williams	.10
185	Lefty Grove	.10
186	Jim Grant	.10
187	Elmer Valo	.10
188	Ewell Blackwell	.10
189	Mel Ott	.20
190	Harry Walker	.10
191	Bill Campbell	.10
192	Walter Johnson	.40
193	Jim "Catfish" Hunter	.10
194	Charlie Keller	.10
195	Hank Greenberg	.40
196	Bobby Murcer	.10
197	Al Lopez	.10
198	Vida Blue	.10
199	Shag Crawford	.10
200	Arky Vaughan	.10
201	Smoky Burgess	.10
202	Rip Sewell	.10
203	Earl Averill	.10
204	Milt Pappas	.10
205	Mel Harder	.10
206	Sam Jethroe	.10
207	Randy Hundley	.10
208	Jessie Haines	.10
209	Jack Brickhouse	.10
210	Whitey Ford	.20
211	Honus Wagner	1.25
212	Phil Niekro	.10
213	Gary Bell	.10
214	Jon Matlack	.10
215	Moe Drabowsky	.10
216	Edd Roush	.10
217	Joel Horlen	.10
218	Casey Stengel	.20
219	Burt Hooton	.10
220	Joe Jackson	3.00
----	Checklist	2.00

1990 Pacific Legends

The cards in this 110-card set feature the same style as the previous Pacific Legends releases. The cards are available in wax packs as well as in complete set form. Several players found in the first two legends releases are also found in this issue along with new players.

		NM/M
Complete Set (110):		10.00
Common Player:		.10
Wax Pack (10):		.50
Wax Box (36):		12.50
1	Hank Aaron	2.00
2	Tommie Agee	.10
3	Luke Appling	.20
4	Sal Bando	.10
5	Ernie Banks	1.00
6	Don Baylor	.20
7	Yogi Berra	.75
8	Vida Blue	.10
9	Lou Boudreau	.10
10	Clete Boyer	.10
11	George Bamberger	.10
12	Lou Brock	.30
13	Ralph Branca	.10
14	Carl Erskine	.10
15	Bert Campaneris	.10
16	Steve Carlton	.50
17	Rod Carew	.50
18	Rocky Colovito	.40
19	Frank Crosetti	.10
20	Larry Doby	.20
21	Bobby Doerr	.10
22	Walt Dropo	.10
23	Rick Ferrell	.10
24	Joe Garagiola	.50
25	Ralph Garr	.10
26	Dick Groat	.10
27	Steve Garvey	.40
28	Bob Gibson	.50
29	Don Drysdale	.40
30	Billy Herman	.10
31	Bobby Grich	.10
32	Monte Irvin	.20
33	Dave Johnson	.10
34	Don Kessinger	.10
35	Harmon Killebrew	.50
36	Ralph Kiner	.20
37	Vern Law	.20
38	Ed Lopat	.10
39	Bill Mazeroski	.40
40	Rick Monday	.10
41	Manny Mota	.10
42	Don Newcombe	.20
43	Gaylord Perry	.20
44	Jim Piersall	.10
45	Johnny Podres	.20
46	Boog Powell	.20
47	Robin Roberts	.20
48	Ron Santo	.30
49	Herb Score	.20
50	Enos Slaughter	.50
51	Warren Spahn	.50
52	Rusty Staub	.20
53	Frank Torre	.10
54	Bob Horner	.10
55	Lee May	.10
56	Bill White	.20
57	Hoyt Wilhelm	.10
58	Billy Williams	.20
59	Ted Williams	1.50
60	Tom Seaver	.50
61	Carl Yaztrzemski	.75
62	Marv Throneberry	.10
63	Steve Stone	.10
64	Rico Petrocelli	.10
65	Orlando Cepeda	.30
66	Eddie Mathews	.50
67	Joe Sewell	.10
68	Jim "Catfish" Hunter	.20
69	Alvin Dark	.10
70	Richie Ashburn	.30
71	Dusty Baker	.10
72	George Foster	.10
73	Eddie Yost	.10
74	Buddy Bell	.10
75	Manny Sanguillen	.10
76	Jim Bunning	.20
77	Smoky Burgess	.10
78	Al Rosen	.20
79	Gene Conley	.10
80	Dave Dravecky	.10
81	Charlie Gehringer	.20
82	Billy Pierce	.10
83	Willie Horton	.10
84	Ron Hunt	.10
85	Bob Feller	.40
86	George Kell	.20
87	Dave Kingman	.20
88	Jerry Koosman	.10
89	Clem Labine	.10
90	Tony LaRussa	.20
91	Dennis Leonard	.10
92	Dale Long	.10
93	Sparky Lyle	.10
94	Gil McDougald	.10
95	Don Mossi	.10
96	Phil Niekro	.10
97	Tom Paciorek	.10
98	Mel Parnell	.10
99	Lou Pinella	.20
100	Bobby Richardson	.20
101	Phil Rizzuto	.60
102	Brooks Robinson	.40
103	Pete Runnels	.10
104	Diego Segui	.10
105	Bobby Shantz	.10
106	Bobby Thomson	.20
107	Joe Torre	.30
108	Earl Weaver	.30
109	Willie Wilson	.10
110	Jesse Barfield	.10

Senior League

An early supporter of the short-lived "old-timers" league, Pacific issued a card set depicting the players of the Senior Professional Baseball Association. Sold in wax packs as well as complete boxed sets, the cards have silver borders on front with yellow stars above and to the right of the player photo. Color team logos are at bottom-left. Red, white and blue backs have appropriate logos, card number, a few biographical details and a short career summary in a horizontal format. The cards were issued with a set of 15 team logo stickers with a puzzle back. Shades of the 1989 Fleer Billy Ripken card, the card of Jim Nettles contains a photo which shows a vulgarity written on the knob of his bat. A cleaned-up version was issued later, and is much scarcer. Many other errors from the regular-edition set were corrected in a glossy edition of 20,000 complete sets, while several new errors were created.

		NM/M
Complete Set (220):		4.00
Common Player:		.05
Glossy:		2X
1	Bobby Tolan	.05
2	Sergio Ferrer	.05
3	David Rajsich	.05
4	Ron LeFlore	.10
5	Steve Henderson	.05
6	Jerry Martin	.05
7	Gary Rajsich	.05
8	Elias Sosa	.05
9	Jon Matlack	.05
10	Steve Kemp	.05
11	Lenny Randle	.05
12	Roy Howell	.05
13	Milt Wilcox	.05
14	Alan Bannister	.05
15	Dock Ellis	.05
16	Mike Williams	.05
17	Luis Gomez	.05
18	Joe Sambito	.05
19	Bake McBride	.05
20a	Pat Zachry (Photo actually Dick Bosman.)	
20b	Dick Bosman	.10
21	Dwight Lowry	.05
22	Ozzie Virgil Sr.	.05
23	Randy Lerch	.05
24	Butch Benton	.05
25	Tom Zimmer	.05
26a	Al Holland (Photo actually Nardi Contreras.)	.05
26b	Nardi Contreras	.10
27	Sammy Stewart	.05
28	Bill Lee	.05
29	Ferguson Jenkins	.50
30	Leon Roberts	.05
31	Rick Wise	.05
32	Butch Hobson	.05
33	Pete LaCock	.05
34	Bill Campbell	.05
35	Doug Simunic	.05
36	Mario Guerrero	.05
37	Jim Willoughby	.05
38	Joe Pittman	.05
39	Mark Bomback	.05
40	Tommy McMillian	.05
41	Gary Allanson	.05
42	Cecil Cooper	.10
43	John LaRosa	.05
44	Darrell Brandon	.05
45	Bernie Carbo	.05
46	Mike Cuellar	.10
47	Al Bumbry	.05
48a	Gene Richards (Photo actually Tony Scott.)	.05
49a	Tony Scott	.10
49b	Pedro Borbon	.05
50	Julio Solo	.05
51a	Ed Nottle (Back reads Sun Sox.)	.05
51b	Ed Nottle (Back reads Super Sox.)	.10
52	Jim Bibby	.05
53	Doug Griffin	.05
54	Ed Clements	.05
55	Dalton Jones	.05
56	Earl Weaver	.25
57	Jesus DeLaRosa	.05
58	Paul Casanova	.05
59	Frank Riccelli	.05
60	Rafael Landestoy	.05
61	George Hendrick	.05
62	Cesar Cedeno	.10
63	Bert Campaneris	.10
64	Derrel Thomas	.05
65	Bobby Ramos	.05
66	Grant Jackson	.05
67	Steve Whitaker	.05
68	Pedro Ramos	.05
69	Joe Hicks	.05
70	Taylor Duncan	.05
71	Tom Shopay	.05
72	Ken Clay	.05
73	Mike Kekich	.05
74	Ed Halicki	.05
75	Ed Figueroa	.05
76	Paul Blair	.05
77	Luis Tiant	.10
78	Stan Bahnsen	.05
79	Rennie Stennett	.05
80	Bobby Molinaro	.05
81	Jim Gideon	.05
82	Orlando Gonzalez	.05
83	Amos Otis	.05
84	Dennis Leonard	.05
85	Pat Putman	.05
86	Rick Manning	.05
87	Pat Dobson	.05
88	Marty Castillo	.05
89	Steve McCatty	.05
90	Doug Bird	.05
91	Rick Waits	.05
92	Ron Jackson	.05
93	Tim Hosley	.05
94	Steve Luebber	.05
95	Rich Gale	.05
96	Champ Summers	.05
97	Dave LaRoche	.05
98	Bobby Jones	.05
99	Kim Allen	.05
100	Wayne Garland	.05
101	Tom Spencer	.05
102	Dan Driessen	.05
103	Ron Pruitt	.05
104	Tim Ireland	.05
105	Dan Driessen	.05
106	Pepe Frias	.05
107	Eric Rasmussen	.05
108	Don Hood	.05
109a	Joe Coleman (Photo actually Tony Torchia.)	.05
109b	Tony Torchia	.05
110	Jim Slaton	.05
111	Clint Hurdle	.05
112	Larry Milbourne	.05
113	Al Holland	.05
114	George Foster	.10
115	Graig Nettles	.10
116	Oscar Gamble	.05
117	Ross Grimsley	.05
118	Bill Travers	.05
119	Jose Beniquez	.05
120a	Jerry Grote (In Action)	.05
120b	Jerry Grote (Catcher)	.10
121	John D'Acquisto	.05
122	Tom Murphy	.05
123	Walt Williams	.05
124	Roy Thomas	.05
125a	Jerry Grote (Photo actually Fred Stanley.)	.05
125b	Fred Stanley (Jerry Grote back.)	.10
126a	Jim Nettles (Vulgarity on bat knob.)	.50
126b	Jim Nettles (No vulgarity.)	3.00
127	Randy Niemann	.05
128a	Bobby Bonds	.10
128b	Bobby Bonds (No name/position on front.)	.50
129	Ed Glynn	.05
130	Ed Hicks	.05
131	Ivan Murrell	.05
132	Graig Nettles	.05
133	Hal McRae	.20
134	Pat Kelly	.05
135	Sammy Stewart	.05
136	Bruce Kison	.05
137	Jim Morrison	.05
138	Omar Moreno	.05
139	Tom Brown	.05
140	Steve Dillard	.05
141	Gary Alexander	.05
142	Al Oliver	.10
143	Rick Lysander	.05
144	Tippy Martinez	.05
145	Al Cowens	.05
146	Gene Clines	.05
147	Willie Aikens	.05
148	Tommy Moore	.05
149	Clete Boyer	.05
150	Stan Cliburn	.05
151	Ken Kravec	.05
152	Garth Iorg	.05
153	Rick Peterson	.05
154	Wayne Nordhagen	.05
155	Danny Meyer	.05
156	Wayne Garrett	.05
157	Wayne Krenchicki	.05
158	Graig Nettles	.10
159	Earl Stephenson	.05
160	Carl Taylor	.05
161	Rollie Fingers	.50
162	Toby Harrah	.05
163	Mickey Rivers	.05
164	Dave Kingman	.05
165	Paul Mirabella	.05
166	Dick Williams	.05
167	Luis Pujols	.05
168	Tito Landrum	.05
169	Tom Underwood	.05
170	Mark Wagner	.05
171	Odell Jones	.05
172	Doug Capilla	.05
173	Alfie Rondon	.05
174	Lowell Palmer	.05
175	Juan Eichelberger	.05
176	Wes Clements	.05
177	Rodney Scott	.05
178	Ron Washington	.05
179	Al Hrabosky	.05
180	Sid Monge	.05
181	Randy Johnson	.05
182	Tim Stoddard	.05
183	Dick Williams	.05
184	Lee Lacy	.05
185	Jerry White	.05
186	Dave Kingman	.10
187	Checklist 1-110	.05
188	Jose Cruz	.10
189	Jamie Easterly	.05
190	Ike Blessit	.05
191	Johnny Grubb	.05
192	Dave Cash	.05
193	Doug Corbett	.05
194	Bruce Bochy	.05
195	Mark Corey	.05
196	Gil Rondon	.05
197	Jerry Martin	.05
198	Gerry Pirtle	.05
199	Gates Brown	.05
200	Bob Galasso	.05
201	Bake McBride	.05
202	Wayne Granger	.05
203	Larry Milbourne	.05
204	Tom Paciorek	.05
205	U.L. Washington	.05
206	Larvell Blanks	.05
207	Bob Shirley	.05
208	Pete Falcone	.05
209	Sal Butera	.05
210	Roy Branch	.05
211	Dyar Miller	.05
212	Paul Siebert	.05
213	Ken Reitz	.05
214	Bill Madlock	.10
215	Vida Blue	.15
216	Dave Hilton	.05
217	Pedro Ramos, Charlie Bree	.05
218	Checklist 111-220	.05
219	Pat Dobson, Earl Weaver	.05
220	Curt Flood	.15

1991 Pacific Senior League

In 1991 Pacific Trading Cards produced its second set of cards of Senior Professional Baseball Association players. The cards feature color photos on the front, with the player's name and position along the bottom and team nickname and logo on a banner vertically on the left side. There are 160 cards in the glossy set, with some multi-player and in-action cards included. For reasons unknown, some of the cards (including those of Rice, Fingers, Blue, Dave Cash, Dan Norman, Ron LeFlore, Cesar Cedeno, Rafael Landestoy and Dan Driessen) were apparently printed in two versions.

		NM/M
	Complete Set (160):	3.00
	Common Player:	.05
1	Dan Driessen	.05
2	Marty Castillo	.05
3	Jerry White	.05
4	Bud Anderson	.05
5	Ron Jackson	.05
6	Fred Stanley	.05
7	Steve Luebber	.05
8	Jery Terrell	.05
9	Pat Dobson	.05
10	Ken Kravec	.05
11	Gil Rondon	.05
12	Dyar Miller	.05
13	Bobby Molinaro	.05
14	Jerry Martin	.05
15	Rick Waits	.05
16	Steve McCatty	.05
17	Roger Slagle	.05
18	Mike Ramsey	.05
19	Rich Gale	.05
20	Larry Harlow	.05
21	Dan Rohn	.05
22	Don Cooper	.05
23	Marv Foley	.05
24	Rafael Landestoy	.05
25	Eddie Milner	.05
26a	Amos Otis (Green jersey pose.)	.05
26b	Amos Otis (White jersey action.)	.05
27	Odell Jones	.05
28	Tippy Martinez	.05
29	Stu Cliburn	.05
30	Stan Cliburn	.05
31	Tony Cloninger	.05
32	Jeff Jones	.05
33	Ken Reitz	.05
34	Dave Sax	.05
35	Orlando Gonzalez	.05
36	Jose Cruz	.10
37	Mickey Mahler	.05
38	Derek Botelho	.05
39	Rick Lysander	.05
40	Cesar Cedeno	.10
41	Garth Iorg	.05
42	Wayne Krenchicki	.05
43	Clete Boyer	.05
44	Dan Boone	.05
45	George Vukovich	.05
46	Omar Moreno	.05
47	Ron Washington	.05
48	Ron Washington (MVP)	.05
49	Rick Peterson	.05
50	Tack Wilson	.05
51	Stan Cliburn, Stu Cliburn	.05
52	Rick Lysander (POY)	.05
53	Cesar Cedeno, Pete LaCock	.05
54	Jim Marshall, Clete Boyer	.05
55	Doug Simunic	.05
56	Pat Kelly	.05
57	Roy Branch	.05
58	Dave Cash	.05
59	Bobby Jones	.05
60	Hector Cruz	.05
61	Reggie Cleveland	.05
62	Gary Lance	.05
63	Ron LeFlore	.05
64	Dan Norman	.05
65	Renie Martin	.05
66	Pete Mackanin	.05
67	Frank Riccelli	.05
68	Alfie Rondon	.05
69	Rodney Scott	.05
70	Jim Tracy	.05
71	Ed Dennis	.05
72	Rick Lindell	.05
73	Jeff Youngbauer	.05
74	Jeff Youngbauer	.05
75	Russ Foster	.05

76	Jeff Capriati	.05
77	Art DeFreites	.05
78	Alfie Rondon/Action	.05
79	Reggie Cleveland/Action	.05
80	Dave Cash/Action	.05
81	Vida Blue	.15
82	Ed Glynn	.05
83	Bob Owchinko	.05
84	Bill Fleming	.05
85	Ron Roenicke, Gary Roenicke	.05
86	Tom Thompson	.05
87	Derrell Thomas	.05
88	Jim Willoughby	.05
89	Jim Pankovits	.05
90	Jack Cooley	.05
91	Lenn Sakata	.05
92	Mike Brocki	.05
93	Chuck Fick	.05
94	Tom Benedict	.05
95	Anthony Davis	.05
96	Cardell Camper	.05
97	Leon Roberts	.05
98	Roger Erickson	.05
99	Kim Allen	.05
100	Dave Skaggs	.05
101	Joe Decker	.05
102	U.L. Washington	.05
103	Don Fletcher	.05
104	Gary Roenicke	.05
105	Rich Dauer	.05
106	Ron Roenicke	.05
107	Mike Norris	.05
108	Ferguson Jenkins	.50
109	Ronn Reynolds	.05
110	Pete Falcone	.05
111	Gary Allenson	.05
112	Mark Wagner	.05
113	Jack Lazorko	.05
114	Bob Galasso	.05
115	Ron Davis	.05
116	Lenny Randle	.05
117	Ricky Peters	.05
118	Jim Dwyer	.05
119	Juan Eichelberger	.05
120	Pete LaCock	.05
121	Tony Scott	.05
122	Rick Lancellotti	.05
123	Barry Bonnell	.05
124	Dave Hilton	.05
125	Bill Campbell	.05
126	Rollie Fingers	.05
127	Jim Marshall	.05
128	Razor Shines	.05
129	Guy Sularz	.05
130	Roy Thomas	.05
131	Joel Youngblood	.05
132	Ernie Camacho	.05
133	Dave Hilton, Jim Marshall, Fred Stanley	.05
134	Ken Landreaux	.05
135	Dave Rozema	.05
136	Tom Zimmer	.05
137	Elias Sosa	.05
138	Ozzie Virgil Sr.	.05
139	Al Holland	.05
140	Milt Wilcox	.05
141	Jerry Reed	.05
142	Chris Welch	.05
143	Luis Gomez	.05
144	Steve Henderson	.05
145	Butch Benton	.05
146	Bill Lee	.05
147	Todd Cruz	.05
148	Jim Rice	.45
149	Tito Landrum	.05
150	Ozzie Virgil Jr.	.05
151	Joe Pittman	.05
152	Bobby Tolan	.05
153	Len Barker	.05
154	Dave Rajsich	.05
155	Glenn Gulliver	.05
156	Gary Rajsich	.05
157	Joe Sambito	.05
158	Frank Vito	.05
159	Ozzie Virgil Sr., Ozzie Virgil Jr.	.05
160	Dave Rajsich, Gary Rajsich	.05

Nolan Ryan

The career and family life of Nolan Ryan (to 1991) were the subject matter of this 110-card set by Pacific Trading Card Co. Sold in both foil packs and factory sets, the cards have a UV-coated front featuring a photo flanked on the left by "Nolan

Ryan" printed vertically in a color accent stripe. At lower left is a flaming baseball "Texas Express" logo. A photo caption appears beneath the photo. On back the blazing ball motif is repeated, with a photo or career highlights in its center.

		NM/M
	Factory Set (110):	8.00
	Complete Set (110):	5.00
	Common Card:	.10
	Wax Pack (12):	.50
	Wax Box (36):	12.00
1	Future Hall of Famer	.10
2	From Little League to the Major Leagues	.10
3	A Dream Come True	.10
4	Signed by the Mets	.10
5	Fireball Pitcher	.10
6	Mets Rookie Pitcher	.10
7	First Major League Win	.10
8	Early in 1969	.10
9	Tensions of a Pennant Race	.10
10	Mets Clinch NL East	.10
11	Keep the Ball Down	.10
12	Playoff Victory	.10
13	World Series Victory	.10
14	The Amazin' Mets	.10
15	Met Strikeout Record	.10
16	One of the Worst Trades in Baseball	.10
17	Slow Start with Mets	.10
18	Pitcher New York Mets	.10
19	Traded to the Angels	.10
20	Meeting New Friends	.10
21	Throwing Fast Balls	.10
22	Move the Ball Around	.10
23	Nolan Heat	.10
24	No-Hitter Number 1	.10
25	Looking Back on Number 1	.10
26	No-Hitter Number 2	.10
27	Single Season Strikeout Record	.10
28	21 Wins in 1973	.10
29	Fastest Pitch Ever Thrown at 100.9 MPH	.10
30	No-Hitter Number 3	.10
31	No-Hitter Number 4	.10
32	Ryan and Tanana	.10
33	Learning Change-Up	.10
34	Pitcher California Angels	.10
35	Nolan Joins Astros	.10
36	Starting Pitcher Nolan Ryan	.10
37	Taking Batting Practice	.10
38	The Game's Greatest Power Pitcher	.10
39	3000 Career Strikeouts	.10
40	A Ryan Home Run	.10
41	The Fast Ball Grip	.10
42	Record 5th No-Hitter	.10
43	No-Hitter Number 5	.10
44	A Dream Fulfilled	.10
45	Nolan Passes Walter Johnson	.10
46	Strikeout 4000	.10
47	Astros Win Western Division Title	.10
48	Pitcher Houston Astros	.10
49	Milestone Strikeouts	.10
50	Post Season Participant	.10
51	Hurling for Houston	.10
52	135 N.L. Wins	.10
53	Through with Chew	.10
54	Signed by Rangers 1989	.10
55	Pleasant Change for Nolan	.10
56	Real Special Moment	.10
57	1989 All-Star Game	.10
58	Pitching in 1989 All-Star Game	.10
59	5000 Strikeouts; A Standing Ovation	.10
60	Great Moments in 1989	.10
61	Nolan with Dan Smith, Rangers First Pic	.10
62	Ranger Club Record 16 Strikeouts	.10
63	Last Pitch No-Hitter Number 6	.10
64	Sweet Number 6	.10
65	Oldest to Throw No-Hitter	.10
66	Another Ryan Win	.10
67	20th Pitcher to Win 300	.10
68	300 Win Battery	.10
69	300 Game Winner	.10
70	Perfect Mechanics	.10
71	22 Seasons with 100 or more Strikeouts	.10
72	11th Strikeout Title	.10
73	232 Strikeouts, 1990	.10
74	The 1990 Season	.10
75	Pitcher Texas Rangers	.10
76	1991, Nolan's 25th Season	.10
77	Throwing Spirals	.10
78	Running the Steps	.10
79	Hard Work and Conditioning	.10
80	The Rigid Workout	.10
81	Ryan's Routine	.10
82	Ryan's Routine Between Starts	.10
83	Running in Outfield	.10
84	B.P. in Texas	.10

85	18 Career Low-Hitters	.10
86	My Job is to Give My Team/Chance to Win	.10
87	The Spring Workout	.10
88	Power versus Power	.10
89	Awesome Power	.10
90	Blazing Speed	.10
91	The Pick Off	.10
92	Real Gamer	.10
93	Ranger Battery Mates	.10
94	The Glare	.10
95	The High Leg Kick	.10
96	Day Off	.10
97	A New Ball	.10
98	Going to Rosin Bag	.10
99	Time for Relief	.10
100	Lone Star Legend	.10
101	Fans' Favorite	.10
102	Watching Nolan Pitch	.10
103	Our Family of Five	.10
104	Texas Beefmaster	.10
105	Gentleman Rancher	.10
106	Texas Cowboy Life	.10
107	The Ryan Family	.10
108	Participating in Cutting Horse Contest	.10
109	Nolan Interviews	.10
110	Lynn Nolan Ryan	.10

Nolan Ryan Milestones

No-Hitter #1

Issued as inserts in the 1991 Nolan Ryan foil packs was this set of eight career highlight cards. The format is basically the same as the regular-issue cards, except that the inserts are bordered in either silver (edition of 10,000) or gold (edition of 1,000). The unnumbered cards are checklisted here in chronological order. The inserts were found only in foil and wax packs.

		NM/M
	Complete Set, Silver (8):	50.00
	Complete Set, Gold (8):	65.00
	Common Card, Silver:	7.50
	Common Card, Gold:	12.00
(1a)	Rookie Pitcher/Silver	7.50
(1b)	Rookie Pitcher/Gold	12.00
(2a)	No-Hitter 1/Silver	7.50
(2b)	No-Hitter 1/Gold	12.00
(3a)	No-Hitter 2/Silver	7.50
(3b)	No-Hitter 2/Gold	12.00
(4a)	No-Hitter 3/Silver	7.50
(4b)	No-Hitter 3/Gold	12.00
(5a)	No-Hitter 4/Silver	7.50
(5b)	No-Hitter 4/Gold	12.00
(6a)	No-Hitter 5/Silver	7.50
(6b)	No-Hitter 5/Gold	12.00
(7a)	Sweet 6/Silver	7.50
(7b)	Sweet 6/Gold	12.00
(8a)	25th Season/Silver	7.50
(8b)	25th Season/Gold	12.00

Nolan Ryan 7th No-Hitter

Number Seven

On May 1, 1991, before the home crowd at Arlington, Nolan Ryan posted his seventh career no-hitter, blanking the Blue Jays. In commemoration of the event, Pacific produced a seven-card insert set for random inclusion in its Nolan Ryan "Texas Express" foil packs. Each card was produced in an edition of 10,000 silver-foil bor-

dered cards and 1,000 with gold-foil borders. The design follows the basic format of the regular Ryan issue, with the flaming baseball series logo at lower-left on the front, the card's title in a colored stripe beneath the photo, and Ryan's name printed vertically in a colored stripe at left. Backs repeat the flaming ball design at center, containing information about the no-hitter.

		NM/M
	Complete Set, Silver (7):	50.00
	Complete Set, Gold (7):	125.00
	Common Card, Silver:	12.00
	Common Card, Gold:	25.00
1a	Last Pitch/Silver	12.00
1b	Last Pitch/Gold	25.00
2a	No-Hitter #7/Silver	12.00
2b	No-Hitter #7/Gold	25.00
3a	The Best/Silver	12.00
3b	The Best/Gold	25.00
4a	Time to Celebrate/Silver	12.00
4b	Time to Celebrate/Gold	25.00
5a	Congratulations from Rangers Fans/Silver	12.00
5b	Congratulations from Rangers Fans/Gold	25.00
6a	Catcher Mike Stanley/Silver	12.00
6b	Catcher Mike Stanley/Gold	25.00
7a	All in a Day's Work/Silver	12.00
7b	All in a Day's Work/Gold	25.00

Nolan Ryan 7th No-Hitter Hologram

No-Hitter #7

Even more elusive and exclusive than the gold- and silver-foil bordered "7th No-Hitter" inserts found in wax and foil packs was this edition produced with gold and silver holographic borders (1,000 each in gold and silver. The hologram 7th No-Hitter inserts were found only in 99-cent cello packs.

		NM/M
	Complete Set, Silver (7):	300.00
	Complete Set, Gold (7):	300.00
	Common Card, Silver:	50.00
	Common Card, Gold:	50.00
1a	Last Pitch/Silver	50.00
1b	Last Pitch/Gold	50.00
2a	No-Hitter #7/Silver	50.00
2b	No-Hitter #7/Gold	50.00
3a	The Best/Silver	50.00
3b	The Best/Gold	50.00
4a	Time to Celebrate/Silver	50.00
4b	Time to Celebrate/Gold	50.00
5a	Congratulations from Rangers Fans/Silver	50.00
5b	Congratulations from Rangers Fans/Gold	50.00
6a	Catcher Mike Stanley/Silver	50.00
6b	Catcher Mike Stanley/Gold	50.00
7a	All in a Day's Work/Silver	50.00
7b	All in a Day's Work/Gold	50.00

1992 Pacific Nolan Ryan

The 1992 Nolan Ryan "Texas Express" Series 2 is numbered 111 to 220, featuring the same design as the original 110-card issue of 1991. The set includes photos of Ryan from boyhood to his seventh no-hitter, and two bonus subsets were also randomly inserted in the foil packs.

		NM/M
	Complete Set (110):	6.00
	Common Player:	.10
111	The Golden Arm	.10
112	Little League All-Star	.10
113	All-State Pitcher	.10
114	Nolan Ryan Field	.10
115	Nolan at Age 20	.10
116	Nolan Ryan Jacksonville Suns	.10

117	Surrounded By Friends	.10
118	Nolan the Cowboy	.10
119	The Simple Life	.10
120	Nolan Loves Animals	.10
121	Growing Up in New York	.10
122	New York Strikeout Record	.10
123	Traded	.10
124	Hall of Fame Victims	.10
125	Number 500	.10
126	California Victory	.10
127	20 Win Season	.10
128	Throwing Heat	.10
129	Strikeout Record	.10
130	Number One	.10
131	1,000th Strikeout	.10
132	Number Two	.10
133	2,000th Strikeout	.10
134	Number Three	.10
135	Pure Speed	.10
136	Independence Day Fireworks	.10
137	Fast Ball Pitcher	.10
138	Number Four	.10
139	Free Agent	.10
140	Houston Bound	.10
141	Big Dollars	.10
142	Strong Houston Staff	.10
143	Number Five	.10
144	Astro MVp	.10
145	Western Divison Game	.10
146	National League All-Star	.10
147	Major League Record	.10
148	Nolan Breaks Johnson's Record	.10
149	Reese and Nolan	.10
150	100th National League Win	.10
151	4,000th Strikeout	.10
152	League Leader	.10
153	250th Career Win	.10
154	The Seldom of Swat	.10
155	4,500th Strikeout	.10
156	Like Father Like Son	.10
157	Spoiled in the Ninth	.10
158	Leaving Houston	.10
159	Houston Star	.10
160	Ryan Test Free Agency	.10
161	Awesome Heat	.10
162	Brotherly Love	.10
163	Astros Return	.10
164	Texas Size Decision	.10
165	Texas Legend	.10
166	Drawing a Crowd	.10
167	Great Start	.10
168	5,000th Strikeout	.10
169	Texas All-Star	.10
170	Number Six	.10
171	300th Win	.10
172	1990 League Leader	.10
173	Man of the Year	.10
174	Spring Training 1991	.10
175	Fast Ball Grip	.10
176	Strong Arm	.10
177	Stanley's Delight	.10
178	After Nolan's 7th No-Hitter	.10
179	Stretching Before the Game	.10
180	The Rangers Sign Nolan for 1992 and 199	.10
181	Heading to the Bullpen	.10
182	Nolan Ryan - Banker	.10
183	Time with Fans	.10
184	Solid 1992 Season	.10
185	Ranger Team Leader	.10
186	More Records	.10
187	Number Seven	.10
188	Nolan Passes Niekro	.10
189	Ryan Trails Sutton	.10
190	Ranger Strikeout Mark	.10
191	Consectutive K's	.10
192	5,500th Strikeout	.10
193	Twenty-Five First Timers	.10
194	No-Hitters Ended in the Ninth	.10
195	Constant Work-Outs	.10
196	Nolan in Motion	.10
197	Pitching in Fenway Park	.10
198	Goose and Nolan	.10
199	Talking Over Strategy	.10
200	Don't Mess With Texas	.10
201	314-278 Thru 1991	.10
202	All-Time Leader	.10
203	High Praise	.10
204	Manager's Delight	.10
205	733 Major League Starts	.10
206	Ryan the Quarterback	.10
207	Hard Work Pays Off	.10
208	Passing Along Wisdom	.10
209	Still Dominant	.10
210	Nolan's Fast Ball	.10
211	Seven No-Hitters	.10
212	Training for Perfection	.10
213	Nolan's Edge - Speed	.10
214	This One was for Them	.10
215	Another Day's Work	.10
216	Pick Off at Third	.10
217	Ready to Pitch	.10
218	Spring Training 1992	.10
219	Nolan Receives The Victor Award	.10
220	Nolan's 26th Season	.10

Nolan Ryan Gold Inserts

Pacific produced this insert set for the 1992 Nolan Ryan "Texas Express" sequel. There are eight differ-

Number Two

13 WINS IN 1968

Rangers' Opening Night Pitcher

No-Hitter #1

ent gold-foil bordered cards, one for each of Ryan's no-hitters, plus an additional card combining all seven. Design is similar to the 1991-92 Ryan cards from Pacific. Backs feature box scores of the no-hitters. The cards are unnumbered. According to the manufacturer, 10,000 of each insert were produced.

	NM/M
Complete Set (8):	65.00
Common Ryan:	10.00
(1) Number One	10.00
(2) Number Two	10.00
(3) Number Three	10.00
(4) Number Four	10.00
(5) Number Five	10.00
(6) Number Six	10.00
(7) Number Seven	10.00
(8) Seven No-Hitters	10.00

Nolan Ryan Limited

One of two insert sets included in both regular and jumbo foil packs of 1992 Pacific Nolan Ryan cards was this six-card presentation. Cards have the basic format of the regular issue except the "Texas Express" logo on front has been replaced by a Rangers team logo. Vertically formatted backs have a color photo at left and a few paragraphs of career summary at center. Each card was printed in an edition of 3,000, and Ryan personally autographed 1,000 of card #1. A second version of these cards, without the words "Limited Edition" on back beneath the Rangers and MLB logos, was produced for inclusion in the July 1992 issue of "Trading Cards" magazine. The magazine versions of these cards are worth about 10 percent of the inserts.

	NM/M
Complete Set (6):	30.00
Common Card:	7.50
1 Nolan Ryan	7.50
1a Nolan Ryan/Auto.	90.00
2 Nolan Ryan	7.50
3 The Texas Express	7.50
4 Seventh No-Hitter	7.50
5 Texas Legacy	7.50
6 Quarter Century	7.50

1992 Pacific Tom Seaver

In a style similar to its popular Nolan Ryan sets, Pacific produced a Tom Seaver set of 110 cards in 1992. The company also produced two limited edition subsets as part of the "Tom Terrific" card series. Cards were sold in both foil packs and factory sets. UV-coated fronts have white borders with silver, violet or magenta highlight stripes. A baseball symbol at lower-left has "Tom" above and "Terrific" be-

neath. This image is duplicated on back, with the ball containing either a photo or career highlights.

	NM/M
Complete Set (110):	4.00
Common Player:	.05
1 Stand-out High School Basketball Player	.05
2 Pro Ball Player	.05
3 Destined to be a Met	.05
4 Brave or Met	.05
5 Mets Luck of the Draw	.05
6 Sent to Jacksonville	.05
7 First Major League Win	.05
8 1967 Rookie of the Year	.05
9 Humble Beginnings	.05
10 Predicting the Future	.05
11 Rookie All-Star	.05
12 16 Wins in 1968	.05
13 1968 N.L. All-Star	.05
14 The Amazing Mets	.05
15 1969 Cy Young Winner	.05
16 Pitcher of the Year	.05
17 Strikeout Leader	.05
18 Ties Major League Record	.05
19 Mr. Consistency	.05
20 Finishing in Style	.05
21 Twenty-Game Winner	.05
22 Second Cy Young Award	.05
23 Batting Star	.05
24 At Bat in the World Series	.05
25 Championship Series Record	.05
26 Injury Plagued Season	.05
27 Comeback	.05
28 Super September	.05
29 Sporting News All-Star	.05
30 Strikeout Record	.05
31 USC Alumni Star	.05
32 Winning Smile	.05
33 One-Hitter	.05
34 Traded to the Reds	.05
35 New York Mets Pitcher	.05
36 Winning with the Reds	.05
37 No-Hitter	.05
38 N.L. Leader	.05
39 Smooth Swing	.05
40 No Decision in the Championship Series	.05
41 Injury Shortened Season	.05
42 Bouncing Back	.05
43 Eighth All-Star Appearance	.05
44 Spring Training 1982	.05
45 Back to New York	.05
46 Cincinnati Reds Pitcher	.05
47 Back in the Big Apple	.05
48 Opening Day Star	.05
49 Not Much Run Support	.05
50 Pair of Shutouts	.05
51 4,000 Inning Mark	.05
52 One Season in New York	.05
53 Chicago Bound	.05
54 Chicago White Sox Pitcher	.05
55 Win 300	.05
56 16 Wins in 1985	.05
57 Blast From the Past	.05
58 Moving Up in the Record Book	.05
59 Cy Young Winners	.05
60 Two Legends of the Game	.05
61 Singing Praise	.05
62 300th Win Tribute	.05
63 The Seaver Family	.05
64 20th Major League Season	.05
65 Traded to the Red Sox	.05
66 Chicago White Sox Career Record	.05
67 Red Sox Man	.05
68 Boston Red Sox Pitcher	.05
69 One Last Try	.05
70 Major League Records	.05
71 Lowest N.L. Career ERA	.05
72 Pitching in Comiskey Park	.05
73 273 N.L. Wins	.05
74 300 Win Honors	.05
75 311 Major League Wins	.05
76 41 Retired	.05
77 Championship Series 2.84 ERA	.05
78 June 1976 Age 32	.05
79 8-Time N.L. All-Star	.05
80 Broadcasting Career	.05
81 300th Win Celebration	.05
82 Tom and Nolan	.05
83 4th Best ERA All-Time	.05
84 15th All-Time in Victories	.05
85 300 Win Club	.05
86 Hall of Fame	.05
87 Pitching in Wrigley Field	.05
88 Power Pitching	.05
89 Spring Training 1980	.05
90 Pitching in Riverfront Stadium 1980	.05
91 Tom Terrific	.05
92 Super Seaver	.05
93 Top 10 All-Time	.05
94 16 Opening Day Starts	.05
95 3,272 Strikeouts	.05
96 Six Opening Day Wins	.05
97 239 Innings Pitched in 1985	.05
98 A Day Off	.05
99 Concentration (You Can't Let Up)	.05
100 Velocity, Movement, and Location	.05
101 Strikeout King	.05
102 The Most Important Pitch	.05
103 Cincinnati Reds Number 41	.05
104 George Thomas Seaver	.05
105 Dazzling Dean of the Reds' Staff	.05
106 Tom Receives the Judge Emil Fuchs Award	.05
107 Boston Mound Ace	.05
108 Fly Ball to Center	.05
109 August 4, 1985 Yankee Stadium	.05
110 Breaking Walter Johnson's Record	.05

Tom Seaver Milestones

Inserted into foil packs of its 1992 Seaver set, Pacific produced a gold-foil bordered set limited to 10,000 each of six different cards featuring career milestones. A white-bordered version of 3,000 cards each was also produced. One thousand of the "Rookie Phenomenon" cards were personally autographed by Seaver among the inserts. On each card, an action photo of Seaver is flanked at left with his name vertically printed in a fading color stripe. The "Tom Terrific" baseball logo carried is carried over from the regular set at lower-left. Backs have a second photo at left, and a summary of the career highlight.

	NM/M
Complete Set (6):	12.50
Complete Set, Gold (6):	15.00
Common Card:	2.50
Common Card, Gold:	3.50
1a Rookie Phenomenon	2.50
1b Rookie Phenomenon/ Gold	3.50
1c Rookie Phenomenon (Auto. edition of 1,000.)	25.00
2a Miracle Mets	2.50
2b Miracle Mets/Gold	3.50
3a Strikeout Record	2.50
3b Strikeout Record/Gold	3.50
4a No-Hitter	2.50
4b No-Hitter/Gold	3.50
5a 300th Win	2.50
5b 300th Win/Gold	3.50
6a Hall of Fame	2.50
6b Hall of Fame/Gold	3.50

1993 Pacific Nolan Ryan 27th Season

Pacific marked the record-breaking 27th season of Nolan Ryan's career by re-issuing all 220 cards in its popular Nolan Ryan set with a special logo. The first series of the set (110 cards) had been issued in 1991 and the second series was issued in 1992 and numbered 111-220. In 1993 the company released a 30-card update for the pitcher's final season, complete with the special logo. Later the company decided to reissue cards 1-220 with the same

logo because of the demand for the cards. Refer to 1991 and 1992 sets for card 1-220 checklists.

	NM/M
Complete Set (250):	10.00
Common Player:	.10
221 Rangers' Opening Night	.10
222 Slow Start in 1992	.10
223 Still Productive	.10
224 Getting Hot	.10
225 Closing Strong	.10
226 No Decision	.10
227 No Run Support	.10
228 Two Complete Games	.10
229 8-2/3 Inning Shutout	.10
230 Multiple Stikeout Games	.10
231 Ejected|	.10
232 319 and Counting	.10
233 Strikeout	.10
234 24 of 26 Seasons	.10
235 Smile, Nolan|	.10
236 Texas Ranger Marks	.10
237 Ranger Ace	.10
238 Another Record	.10
239 6th Place All-Time Innings Pitched	.10
240 27 Games Started in 1992	.10
241 Seaver & Ryan	.10
242 Angels' Number 30 Retired	.10
243 Angels' Nolan Ryan Night	.10
244 Angels' Hall of Fame	.10
245 Great Friends	.10
246 Cowboys	.10
247 Spring Training	.10
248 Smokin' Fastball	.10
249 The Texas Express	.10
250 Pacific Pride	.10

Limited

Continuing with its "Limited Edition" insert set from the 1992 Nolan Ryan issue, this insert set picks up with numbers 7-12, featuring 1992 highlights in Ryan's career.

	NM/M
Complete Set (6):	20.00
Common Player:	5.00
7-12 Nolan Ryan	5.00

Limited Gold

A gold-foil bordered version of the six 1993 Nolan Ryan "Limited Edition" insert cards was created as a card show give-away and random

pack insert. Gold versions of cards #7-9 were given out at a Bellevue, Wash., show, while gold cards of #10-12 were found in foil packs. Just 3,000 of each foil-pack insert was produced.

	NM/M
Complete Set (6):	35.00
Common Player:	7.50
7-12 Nolan Ryan	7.50

Prism

An insert set unique to the 1993 Pacific Nolan Ryan 27th Season set was this issue of 20 prism cards. Fronts feature an action photo of Ryan against a prismatic background. Backs have another photo and a few brief biographical notes on a marbled background. Each prism card was produced in a silver edition of 10,000, a gold edition of 1,500 and a gold-edition uncut sheet of 20 cards serially numbered to 1,000. The prism cards were inserted into 25-cent foil packs of Pacific's 1993 Nolan Ryan issue.

	NM/M
Complete Set (Silver)(20):	55.00
Common Card (Silver):	3.50
1 Nolan Ryan/Silver	3.50
1a Nolan Ryan/Gold	6.00
2 Nolan Ryan/Silver	3.50
2a Nolan Ryan/Gold	6.00
3 Nolan Ryan/Silver	3.50
3a Nolan Ryan/Gold	6.00
4 Nolan Ryan/Silver	3.50
4a Nolan Ryan/Gold	6.00
5 Nolan Ryan/Silver	3.50
5a Nolan Ryan/Gold	6.00
6 Nolan Ryan/Silver	3.50
6a Nolan Ryan/Gold	6.00
7 Nolan Ryan/Silver	3.50
7a Nolan Ryan/Gold	6.00
8 Nolan Ryan/Silver	3.50
8a Nolan Ryan/Gold	6.00
9 Nolan Ryan/Silver	3.50
9a Nolan Ryan/Gold	6.00
10 Nolan Ryan/Silver	3.50
10a Nolan Ryan/Gold	6.00
11 Nolan Ryan/Silver	3.50
11a Nolan Ryan/Gold	6.00
12 Nolan Ryan/Silver	3.50
12a Nolan Ryan/Gold	6.00
13 Nolan Ryan/Silver	3.50
13a Nolan Ryan/Gold	6.00
14 Nolan Ryan/Silver	3.50
14a Nolan Ryan/Gold	6.00
15 Nolan Ryan/Silver	3.50
15a Nolan Ryan/Gold	6.00
16 Nolan Ryan/Silver	3.50
16a Nolan Ryan/Gold	6.00
17 Nolan Ryan/Silver	3.50
17a Nolan Ryan/Gold	6.00
18 Nolan Ryan/Silver	3.50
18a Nolan Ryan/Gold	6.00
19 Nolan Ryan/Silver	3.50
19a Nolan Ryan/Gold	6.00
20 Nolan Ryan/Silver	3.50
20a Nolan Ryan/Gold	6.00
Complete Set (Gold)(20):	85.00
Common Card (Gold):	6.00
Uncut Sheet (Gold):	110.00

1993 Pacific/McCormick Nolan Ryan Milestones

Great moments in Nolan Ryan's career are featured in this set produced by Pacific for McCormick & Co., a food products company. Fronts are similar to several of Pacific's other Ryan issues and include a "Farewell to a Legend" logo in the lower-left corner. The career highlight represented by the photo is named in a red strip at bottom. Backs share an action photo of Ryan over which are printed stats, information about the highlight or other data. Sponsors' logos are in the corners. Cards are UV coated on both sides.

	NM/M
Complete Set (21):	7.50
Common Player:	.50
1 No-Hitter #1 (Nolan Ryan)	.50
2 No-Hitter #2 (Nolan Ryan)	.50
3 No-Hitter #3 (Nolan Ryan)	.50
4 No-Hitter #4 (Nolan Ryan)	.50
5 No-Hitter #5 (Nolan Ryan)	.50
6 Last Pitch No-Hitter #6 (Nolan Ryan)	.50
7 No-Hitter #7 (Nolan Ryan)	.50
8 1st Strikeout (Nolan Ryan)	.50
9 1,000 Strikeout (Nolan Ryan)	.50
10 2,000 Strikeout (Nolan Ryan)	.50
11 3,000 Strikeout (Nolan Ryan)	.50
12 Nolan Breaks Johnson's Record (Nolan Ryan)	.50
13 4,000 Strikeout (Nolan Ryan)	.50
14 5,000 Strikeout (Nolan Ryan)	.50
15 5,500th Strikeout (Nolan Ryan)	.50
16 First Major League Win (Nolan Ryan)	.50
17 250th Career Win (Nolan Ryan)	.50
18 300th Win (Nolan Ryan)	.50
19 100.9 MPH Pitch (Nolan Ryan)	.50
20 Lone Star Legend (Nolan Ryan)	.50
--- Header Card	.10

1993 Pacific

MATT WILLIAMS

This set marks the first time a major league set was designed entirely for the Spanish-speaking market. Distribution areas included retail markets in the United States, Mexico, South America and the Caribbean. The cards are glossy and feature Spanish text on both sides. Cards are numbered in alphabetical order by team, beginning with Atlanta. Insert sets are: Prism (20 cards featuring Spanish players and their accomplishments), Beisbol De Estralla (Stars of Baseball), Hot Players and Amigos (a 30-card set which features two or more players per card).

	NM/M
Complete Set (660):	20.00
Common Player:	.05
1 Rafael Belliard	.05
2 Sid Bream	.05
3 Francisco Cabrera	.05
4 Marvin Freeman	.05
5 Ron Gant	.05
6 Tom Glavine	.05
7 Brian Hunter	.05
8 Dave Justice	.05
9 Ryan Klesko	.05
10 Melvin Nieves	.05
11 Deion Sanders	.05
12 John Smoltz	.05
13 Mark Wohlers	.05
14 Brady Anderson	.05
15 Glenn Davis	.05
16 Mike Devereaux	.05
17 Leo Gomez	.05

No.	Player	Price
18	Chris Hoiles	.05
19	Chito Martinez	.05
20	Ben McDonald	.05
21	Mike Mussina	.40
22	Gregg Olson	.05
23	Joe Orsulak	.05
24	Cal Ripken, Jr.	1.50
25	David Segui	.05
26	Rick Sutcliffe	.05
27	Wade Boggs	.65
28	Tom Brunansky	.05
29	Ellis Burks	.05
30	Roger Clemens	.75
31	John Dopson	.05
32	John Flaherty	.05
33	Mike Greenwell	.05
34	Tony Pena	.05
35	Carlos Quintana	.05
36	Luis Rivera	.05
37	Mo Vaughn	.55
38	Frank Viola	.05
39	Matt Young	.05
40	Scott Bailes	.05
41	Bert Blyleven	.05
42	Chad Curtis	.05
43	Gary DiSarcina	.05
44	Chuck Finley	.05
45	Mike Fitzgerald	.05
46	Gary Gaetti	.05
47	Rene Gonzales	.05
48	Mark Langston	.05
49	Scott Lewis	.05
50	Luis Polonia	.05
51	Tim Salmon	.05
52	Lee Stevens	.05
53	Steve Buechele	.05
54	Frank Castillo	.05
55	Doug Dascenzo	.05
56	Andre Dawson	.25
57	Shawon Dunston	.05
58	Mark Grace	.05
59	Mike Morgan	.05
60	Luis Salazar	.05
61	Rey Sanchez	.05
62	Ryne Sandberg	.65
63	Dwight Smith	.05
64	Jerome Walton	.05
65	Rick Wilkins	.05
66	Wilson Alvarez	.05
67	George Bell	.05
68	Joey Cora	.05
69	Alex Fernandez	.05
70	Carlton Fisk	.50
71	Craig Grebeck	.05
72	Ozzie Guillen	.05
73	Jack McDowell	.05
74	Scott Radinsky	.05
75	Tim Raines	.05
76	Bobby Thigpen	.05
77	Frank Thomas	.50
78	Robin Ventura	.05
79	Tom Browning	.05
80	Jacob Brumfield	.05
81	Rob Dibble	.05
82	Bill Doran	.05
83	Billy Hatcher	.05
84	Barry Larkin	.05
85	Hal Morris	.05
86	Joe Oliver	.05
87	Jeff Reed	.05
88	Jose Rijo	.05
89	Bip Roberts	.05
90	Chris Sabo	.05
91	Sandy Alomar, Jr.	.05
92	Brad Arnsberg	.05
93	Carlos Baerga	.05
94	Albert Belle	.05
95	Felix Fermin	.05
96	Mark Lewis	.05
97	Kenny Lofton	.05
98	Carlos Martinez	.05
99	Rod Nicholas	.05
100	Dave Rohde	.05
101	Scott Scudder	.05
102	Paul Sorrento	.05
103	Mark Whiten	.05
104	Mark Carreon	.05
105	Milt Cuyler	.05
106	Rob Deer	.05
107	Cecil Fielder	.05
108	Travis Fryman	.05
109	Dan Gladden	.05
110	Bill Gullickson	.05
111	Les Lancaster	.05
112	Mark Leiter	.05
113	Tony Phillips	.05
114	Mickey Tettleton	.05
115	Alan Trammell	.05
116	Lou Whitaker	.05
117	Jeff Bagwell	.50
118	Craig Biggio	.05
119	Joe Boever	.05
120	Casey Candaele	.05
121	Andujar Cedeno	.05
122	Steve Finley	.05
123	Luis Gonzalez	.05
124	Pete Harnisch	.05
125	Jimmy Jones	.05
126	Mark Portugal	.05
127	Rafael Ramirez	.05
128	Mike Simms	.05
129	Eric Yelding	.05
130	Luis Aquino	.05
131	Kevin Appier	.05
132	Mike Boddicker	.05
133	George Brett	.75
134	Tom Gordon	.05
135	Mark Gubicza	.05
136	David Howard	.05
137	Gregg Jefferies	.05
138	Wally Joyner	.05
139	Brian McRae	.05
140	Jeff Montgomery	.05
141	Terry Shumpert	.05
142	Curtis Wilkerson	.05
143	Brett Butler	.05
144	Eric Davis	.05
145	Kevin Gross	.05
146	Dave Hansen	.05
147	Lenny Harris	.05
148	Carlos Hernandez	.05
149	Orel Hershiser	.05
150	Jay Howell	.05
151	Eric Karros	.05
152	Ramon Martinez	.05
153	Jose Offerman	.05
154	Mike Sharperson	.05
155	Darryl Strawberry	.05
156	Jim Gantner	.05
157	Darryl Hamilton	.05
158	Doug Henry	.05
159	John Jaha	.05
160	Pat Listach	.05
161	Jaime Navarro	.05
162	Dave Nilsson	.05
163	Jesse Orosco	.05
164	Kevin Seitzer	.05
165	B.J. Surhoff	.05
166	Greg Vaughn	.05
167	Robin Yount	.50
168	Rick Aguilera	.05
169	Scott Erickson	.05
170	Mark Guthrie	.05
171	Kent Hrbek	.05
172	Chuck Knoblauch	.05
173	Gene Larkin	.05
174	Shane Mack	.05
175	Pedro Munoz	.05
176	Mike Pagliarulo	.05
177	Kirby Puckett	.65
178	Kevin Tapani	.05
179	Gary Wayne	.05
180	Moises Alou	.05
181	Brian Barnes	.05
182	Archie Cianfrocco	.05
183	Delino DeShields	.05
184	Darrin Fletcher	.05
185	Marquis Grissom	.05
186	Ken Hill	.05
187	Dennis Martinez	.05
188	Bill Sampen	.05
189	John VanderWal	.05
190	Larry Walker	.05
191	Tim Wallach	.05
192	Bobby Bonilla	.05
193	Daryl Boston	.05
194	Vince Coleman	.05
195	Kevin Elster	.05
196	Sid Fernandez	.05
197	John Franco	.05
198	Dwight Gooden	.05
199	Howard Johnson	.05
200	Willie Randolph	.05
201	Bret Saberhagen	.05
202	Dick Schofield	.05
203	Pete Schourek	.05
204	Greg Cadaret	.05
205	John Habyan	.05
206	Pat Kelly	.05
207	Kevin Maas	.05
208	Don Mattingly	.75
209	Matt Nokes	.05
210	Melido Perez	.05
211	Scott Sanderson	.05
212	Andy Stankiewicz	.05
213	Danny Tartabull	.05
214	Randy Velarde	.05
215	Bernie Williams	.05
216	Harold Baines	.05
217	Mike Bordick	.05
218	Scott Brosius	.05
219	Jerry Browne	.05
220	Ron Darling	.05
221	Dennis Eckersley	.40
222	Rickey Henderson	.50
223	Rick Honeycutt	.05
224	Mark McGwire	1.25
225	Ruben Sierra	.05
226	Terry Steinbach	.05
227	Bob Welch	.05
228	Willie Wilson	.05
229	Ruben Amaro	.05
230	Kim Batiste	.05
231	Juan Bell	.05
232	Wes Chamberlain	.05
233	Darren Daulton	.05
234	Mariano Duncan	.05
235	Len Dykstra	.05
236	Dave Hollins	.05
237	Stan Javier	.05
238	John Kruk	.05
239	Mickey Morandini	.05
240	Terry Mulholland	.05
241	Mitch Williams	.05
242	Stan Belinda	.05
243	Jay Bell	.05
244	Carlos Garcia	.05
245	Jeff King	.05
246	Mike LaValliere	.05
247	Lloyd McClendon	.05
248	Orlando Merced	.05
249	Paul Miller	.05
250	Gary Redus	.05
251	Don Slaught	.05
252	Zane Smith	.05
253	Andy Van Slyke	.05
254	Tim Wakefield	.05
255	Andy Benes	.05
256	Dann Bilardello	.05
257	Tony Gwynn	.65
258	Greg Harris	.05
259	Darrin Jackson	.05
260	Mike Maddux	.05
261	Fred McGriff	.05
262	Rich Rodriguez	.05
263	Benito Santiago	.05
264	Gary Sheffield	.35
265	Kurt Stillwell	.05
266	Tim Teufel	.05
267	Bud Black	.05
268	John Burkett	.05
269	Will Clark	.05
270	Royce Clayton	.05
271	Bryan Hickerson	.05
272	Chris James	.05
273	Darren Lewis	.05
274	Willie McGee	.05
275	Jim McNamara	.05
276	Francisco Oliveras	.05
277	Robby Thompson	.05
278	Matt Williams	.05
279	Trevor Wilson	.05
280	Bret Boone	.05
281	Greg Briley	.05
282	Jay Buhner	.05
283	Henry Cotto	.05
284	Rich DeLucia	.05
285	Dave Fleming	.05
286	Ken Griffey Jr.	1.00
287	Erik Hanson	.05
288	Randy Johnson	.50
289	Tino Martinez	.05
290	Edgar Martinez	.05
291	Dave Valle	.05
292	Omar Vizquel	.05
293	Luis Alicea	.05
294	Bernard Gilkey	.05
295	Felix Jose	.05
296	Ray Lankford	.05
297	Omar Olivares	.05
298	Jose Oquendo	.05
299	Tom Pagnozzi	.05
300	Geronimo Pena	.05
301	Gerald Perry	.05
302	Ozzie Smith	.65
303	Lee Smith	.05
304	Bob Tewksbury	.05
305	Todd Zeile	.05
306	Kevin Brown	.05
307	Todd Burns	.05
308	Jose Canseco	.35
309	Hector Fajardo	.05
310	Julio Franco	.05
311	Juan Gonzalez	.25
312	Jeff Huson	.05
313	Rob Maurer	.05
314	Rafael Palmeiro	.45
315	Dean Palmer	.05
316	Ivan Rodriguez	.45
317	Nolan Ryan	1.50
318	Dickie Thon	.05
319	Roberto Alomar	.20
320	Derek Bell	.05
321	Pat Borders	.05
322	Joe Carter	.05
323	Kelly Gruber	.05
324	Juan Guzman	.05
325	Manny Lee	.05
326	Jack Morris	.05
327	John Olerud	.05
328	Ed Sprague	.05
329	Todd Stottlemyre	.05
330	Duane Ward	.05
331	Steve Avery	.05
332	Damon Berryhill	.05
333	Jeff Blauser	.05
334	Mark Lemke	.05
335	Greg Maddux	.65
336	Kent Mercker	.05
337	Otis Nixon	.05
338	Greg Olson	.05
339	Bill Pecota	.05
340	Terry Pendleton	.05
341	Mike Stanton	.05
342	Todd Frohwirth	.05
343	Tim Hulett	.05
344	Mark McLemore	.05
345	Luis Mercedes	.05
346	Alan Mills	.05
347	Sherman Obando	.05
348	Jim Poole	.05
349	Harold Reynolds	.05
350	Arthur Rhodes	.05
351	Jeff Tackett	.05
352	Fernando Valenzuela	.05
353	Scott Bankhead	.05
354	Ivan Calderon	.05
355	Scott Cooper	.05
356	Danny Darwin	.05
357	Scott Fletcher	.05
358	Tony Fossas	.05
359	Greg Harris	.05
360	Joe Hesketh	.05
361	Jose Melendez	.05
362	Paul Quantrill	.05
363	John Valentin	.05
364	Mike Butcher	.05
365	Chuck Crim	.05
366	Chili Davis	.05
367	Damion Easley	.05
368	Steve Frey	.05
369	Joe Grahe	.05
370	Greg Myers	.05
371	John Orton	.05
372	J.T. Snow	.05
373	Ron Tingley	.05
374	Julio Valera	.05
375	Paul Assenmacher	.05
376	Jose Bautista	.05
377	Jose Guzman	.05
378	Greg Hibbard	.05
379	Candy Maldonado	.05
380	Derrick May	.05
381	Dan Plesac	.05
382	Tommy Shields	.05
383	Sammy Sosa	.75
384	Jose Vizcaino	.05
385	Greg Walbeck	.05
386	Ellis Burks	.05
387	Roberto Hernandez	.05
388	Mike Huff	.05
389	Bo Jackson	.10
390	Lance Johnson	.05
391	Ron Karkovice	.05
392	Kirk McCaskill	.05
393	Donn Pall	.05
394	Dan Pasqua	.05
395	Steve Sax	.05
396	Dave Stieb	.05
397	Bobby Ayala	.05
398	Tim Belcher	.05
399	Jeff Branson	.05
400	Cesar Hernandez	.05
401	Roberto Kelly	.05
402	Randy Milligan	.05
403	Kevin Mitchell	.05
404	Juan Samuel	.05
405	Reggie Sanders	.05
406	John Smiley	.05
407	Dan Wilson	.05
408	Mike Christopher	.05
409	Dennis Cook	.05
410	Alvaro Espinoza	.05
411	Glenallen Hill	.05
412	Reggie Jefferson	.05
413	Derek Lilliquist	.05
414	Jose Mesa	.05
415	Charles Nagy	.05
416	Junior Ortiz	.05
417	Eric Plunk	.05
418	Ted Power	.05
419	Scott Aldred	.05
420	Andy Ashby	.05
421	Freddie Benavides	.05
422	Dante Bichette	.05
423	Willie Blair	.05
424	Vinny Castilla	.05
425	Jerald Clark	.05
426	Alex Cole	.05
427	Andres Galarraga	.05
428	Joe Girardi	.05
429	Charlie Hayes	.05
430	Butch Henry	.05
431	Darren Holmes	.05
432	Dale Murphy	.20
433	David Nied	.05
434	Jeff Parrett	.05
435	Steve Reed RC	.05
436	Armando Reynoso	.05
437	Bruce Ruffin	.05
438	Bryn Smith	.05
439	Jim Tatum	.05
440	Eric Young	.05
441	Skeeter Barnes	.05
442	Tom Bolton	.05
443	Kirk Gibson	.05
444	Chad Krueter	.05
445	Bill Krueger	.05
446	Scott Livingstone	.05
447	Bob MacDonald	.05
448	Mike Moore	.05
449	Mike Munoz	.05
450	Gary Thurman	.05
451	David Wells	.05
452	Alex Arias	.05
453	Jack Armstrong	.05
454	Bret Barberie	.05
455	Ryan Bowen	.05
456	Cris Carpenter	.05
457	Chuck Carr	.05
458	Jeff Conine	.05
459	Steve Decker	.05
460	Orestes Destrade	.05
461	Monty Fariss	.05
462	Junior Felix	.05
463	Bryan Harvey	.05
464	Trevor Hoffman	.05
465	Charlie Hough	.05
466	Dave Magadan	.05
467	Bob McClure	.05
468	Rob Natal	.05
469	Scott Pose	.05
470	Rich Renteria	.05
471	Benito Santiago	.05
472	Matt Turner	.05
473	Walt Weiss	.05
474	Eric Anthony	.05
475	Chris Donnels	.05
476	Doug Drabek	.05
477	Xavier Hernandez	.05
478	Doug Jones	.05
479	Darryl Kile	.05
480	Scott Servais	.05
481	Greg Swindell	.05
482	Eddie Taubensee	.05
483	Jose Uribe	.05
484	Brian Williams	.05
485	Billy Brewer	.05
486	David Cone	.05
487	Greg Gagne	.05
488	Phil Hiatt	.05
489	Jose Lind	.05
490	Brent Mayne	.05
491	Kevin McReynolds	.05
492	Keith Miller	.05
493	Hipolito Pichardo	.05
494	Harvey Pulliam	.05
495	Rico Rossay	.05
496	Pedro Astacio	.05
497	Tom Candiotti	.05
498	Tom Goodwin	.05
499	Jim Gott	.05
500	Pedro Martinez	.50
501	Roger McDowell	.05
502	Mike Piazza	.75
503	Jody Reed	.05
504	Rick Trlicek	.05
505	Mitch Weber	.05
506	Steve Wilson	.05
507	James Austin	.05
508	Ricky Bones	.05
509	Alex Diaz	.05
510	Mike Fetters	.05
511	Teddy Higuera	.05
512	Graeme Lloyd	.05
513	Carlos Maldonado	.05
514	Josias Manzanillo	.05
515	Kevin Reimer	.05
516	Bill Spiers	.05
517	Bill Wegman	.05
518	Willie Banks	.05
519	J.T. Bruett	.05
520	Brian Harper	.05
521	Terry Jorgensen	.05
522	Scott Leius	.05
523	Pat Mahomes	.05
524	Dave McCarty	.05
525	Jeff Reboulet	.05
526	Mike Trombley	.05
527	Carl Willis	.05
528	Dave Winfield	.50
529	Sean Berry	.05
530	Frank Bolick	.05
531	Kent Bottenfield	.05
532	Wil Cordero	.05
533	Jeff Fassero	.05
534	Tim Laker	.05
535	Mike Lansing	.05
536	Chris Nabholz	.05
537	Mel Rojas	.05
538	John Wetteland	.05
539	Ted Wood (Front photo actually Frank Bollick.)	.05
540	Mike Draper	.05
541	Tony Fernandez	.05
542	Todd Hundley	.05
543	Jeff Innis	.05
544	Jeff McKnight	.05
545	Eddie Murray	.50
546	Charlie O'Brien	.05
547	Frank Tanana	.05
548	Ryan Thompson	.05
549	Chico Walker	.05
550	Anthony Young	.05
551	Jim Abbott	.05
552	Wade Boggs	.75
553	Steve Farr	.05
554	Neal Heaton	.05
555	Steve Howe	.05
556	Dion James	.05
557	Scott Kamieniecki	.05
558	Jimmy Key	.05
559	Jim Leyritz	.05
560	Paul O'Neill	.05
561	Spike Owen	.05
562	Lance Blankenship	.05
563	Joe Boever	.05
564	Storm Davis	.05
565	Kelly Downs	.05
566	Eric Fox	.05
567	Rich Gossage	.05
568	Dave Henderson	.05
569	Shawn Hillegas	.05
570	Mike Mohler RC	.05
571	Troy Neel	.05
572	Dale Sveum	.05
573	Larry Anderson	.05
574	Bob Ayrault	.05
575	Jose DeLeon	.05
576	Jim Eisenreich	.05
577	Pete Incaviglia	.05
578	Danny Jackson	.05
579	Ricky Jordan	.05
580	Ben Rivera	.05
581	Curt Schilling	.25
582	Milt Thompson	.05
583	David West	.05
584	John Candelaria	.05
585	Steve Cooke	.05
586	Tom Foley	.05
587	Al Martin	.05
588	Blas Minor	.05
589	Dennis Moeller	.05
590	Denny Neagle	.05
591	Tom Prince	.05
592	Randy Tomlin	.05
593	Bob Walk	.05
594	Kevin Young	.05
595	Pat Gomez	.05
596	Ricky Gutierrez	.05
597	Gene Harris	.05
598	Jeremy Hernandez	.05
599	Phil Plantier	.05
600	Tim Scott	.05
601	Frank Seminara	.05
602	Darrell Sherman	.05
603	Craig Shipley	.05
604	Guillermo Velasquez	.05
605	Dan Walters	.05
606	Mike Benjamin	.05
607	Barry Bonds	1.50
608	Jeff Brantley	.05
609	Dave Burba	.05
610	Craig Colbert	.05
611	Mike Jackson	.05
612	Kirt Manwaring	.05
613	Dave Martinez	.05
614	Dave Righetti	.05
615	Kevin Rogers	.05
616	Bill Swift	.05
617	Rich Amaral	.05
618	Mike Blowers	.05
619	Chris Bosio	.05
620	Norm Charlton	.05
621	John Cummings	.05
622	Mike Felder	.05
623	Bill Haselman	.05
624	Tim Leary	.05
625	Pete O'Brien	.05
626	Russ Swan	.05
627	Fernando Vina	.05
628	Rene Arocha	.05
629	Rod Brewer	.05
630	Ozzie Canseco	.05
631	Rheal Cormier	.05
632	Brian Jordan	.05
633	Joe Magrane	.05
634	Donovan Osborne	.05
635	Mike Perez	.05
636	Stan Royer	.05
637	Hector Villanueva	.05
638	Tracy Woodson	.05
639	Benji Gil	.05
640	Tom Henke	.05
641	David Hulse	.05
642	Charlie Leibrandt	.05
643	Robb Nen	.05
644	Dan Peltier	.05
645	Billy Ripken	.05
646	Kenny Rogers	.05
647	John Russell	.05
648	Dan Smith	.05
649	Matt Whiteside	.05
650	William Canate	.05
651	Darnell Coles	.05
652	Al Leiter	.05
653	Domingo Martinez	.05
654	Paul Molitor	.50
655	Luis Sojo	.05
656	Dave Stewart	.05
657	Mike Timlin	.05
658	Turner Ward	.05
659	Devon White	.05
660	Eddie Zosky	.05

Beisbol Amigos

In groups of two, three or more, and generally from the same team, Latin players are paired in this second series insert set. The cards feature player photos (sometimes posed, sometimes superimposed) on a background of red, white and black baseballs. The players' last names and a card title are printed in Spanish on front and repeated on back. Also on back a few career highlights and stats are printed in red on a marbled background - again all in Spanish.

		NM/M
Complete Set (30):		7.50
Common Player:		.50
1	Edgar Martinez	.50
2	Luis Polonia, Stan Javier	.50
3	George Bell, Julio Franco	.50
4	Ozzie Guillen, Ivan Rodriguez	.60
5	Carlos Baerga, Sandy Alomar Jr.	.50
6	Sandy Alomar Jr., Alvaro Espinoza, Paul Sorrento, Carlos Baerga, Felix Fermin, Junior Ortiz, Jose Mesa, Carlos Martinez	.50
7	Sandy Alomar Jr., Roberto Alomar	1.00
8	Jose Lind, Felix Jose	.50
9	Ricky Bones, Jaime Navarro	.50
10	Jaime Navarro, Jesse Orosco	.50
11	Tino Martinez, Edgar Martinez	.50
12	Juan Gonzalez, Ivan Rodriguez	.75
13	Juan Gonzalez, Julio Franco	.60
14	Julio Franco, Jose Canseco, Rafael Palmeiro	.60
15	Juan Gonzalez, Jose Canseco	.65
16	Ivan Rodriguez, Benji Gil	.60

17 Jose Guzman, Frank Castillo .50
18 Rey Sanchez, Jose Vizcaino .50
19 Derrick May, Sammy Sosa 2.00
20 Sammy Sosa, Candy Maldonado 2.00
21 Jose Rijo, Juan Samuel .50
22 Freddie Benavides, Andres Galarraga .50
23 Guillermo Velasquez, Benito Santiago .50
24 Luis Gonzalez, Andujar Cedeno .50
25 Wil Cordero, Dennis Martinez .50
26 Moises Alou, Wil Cordero .50
27 Ozzie Canseco, Jose Canseco .75
28 Jose Oquendo, Luis Alicea .50
29 Luis Alicea, Rene Arocha .50
30 Geronimo Pena, Luis Alicea .50

Estrellas de Beisbol

Pacific produced a gold-foil "Stars of Baseball" set of 20 that was randomly inserted as part of the company's first series Spanish language major league set in 1993. Each card features a color action photo on the front surrounded by a gold-foil border. Production was limited to 10,000 of each card.

NM/M
Complete Set (20): 6.00
Common Player: .50
1 Moises Alou .50
2 Bobby Bonilla .50
3 Tony Fernandez .50
4 Felix Jose .50
5 Dennis Martinez .50
6 Orlando Merced .50
7 Jose Oquendo .50
8 Geronimo Pena .50
9 Jose Rijo .50
10 Benito Santiago .50
11 Sandy Alomar Jr. .50
12 Carlos Baerga .50
13 Jose Canseco 1.50
14 Juan "Igor" Gonzalez 2.00
15 Juan Guzman .50
16 Edgar Martinez .50
17 Rafael Palmeiro 2.00
18 Ruben Sierra .50
19 Danny Tartabull .50
20 Omar Vizquel .50

Jugadores Calientes

Three dozen "hot players" with a decidedly Hispanic predominance are featured in this glittery Series 2 insert set. Player action photos appear in front of a silver prismatic foil background. Names appear at bottom in boldly styled, but hard to read, letters in bright colors. Horizontal backs have a pair of player photos and a large team logo, along with a few stats, all printed in Spanish.

NM/M
Complete Set (36): 20.00

Common Player: .50
1 Rich Amaral .50
2 George Brett 1.75
3 Jay Buhner .50
4 Roger Clemens 2.00
5 Kirk Gibson .50
6 Juan Gonzalez 1.00
7 Ken Griffey Jr. 2.00
8 Bo Jackson .75
9 Kenny Lofton .50
10 Mark McGwire 2.25
11 Sherman Obando .50
12 John Olerud .50
13 Carlos Quintana .50
14 Ivan Rodriguez 1.00
15 Nolan Ryan 2.50
16 J.T. Snow .50
17 Fernando Valenzuela .50
18 Dave Winfield 1.25
19 Moises Alou .50
20 Jeff Bagwell 1.25
21 Barry Bonds 2.50
22 Bobby Bonilla .50
23 Vinny Castilla .50
24 Andujar Cedeno .50
25 Orestes Destrade .50
26 Andres Galarraga .50
27 Mark Grace .50
28 Tony Gwynn 1.50
29 Roberto Kelly .50
30 John Kruk .50
31 Dave Magadan .50
32 Derrick May .50
33 Orlando Merced .50
34 Mike Piazza 2.00
35 Armando Reynoso .50
36 Jose Vizcaino .50

Prism Insert

Pacific produced a prism card that was randomly inserted in its Series 1 Spanish-language set in 1993. Each of the 20 cards has a color photo of a star Latino player on the front superimposed over a prismatic silver-foil background. Card backs contain an action photo and a brief player biography on a marbled background. Production was limited to 10,000 of each card.

NM/M
Complete Set (20): 60.00
Common Player: 3.00
1 Francisco Cabrera 3.00
2 Jose Lind 3.00
3 Dennis Martinez 3.00
4 Ramon Martinez 3.00
5 Jose Rijo 3.00
6 Benito Santiago 3.00
7 Roberto Alomar 9.00
8 Sandy Alomar Jr. 3.00
9 Carlos Baerga 3.00
10 George Bell 3.00
11 Jose Canseco 6.00
12 Alex Fernandez 3.00
13 Julio Franco 3.00
14 Igor (Juan) Gonzalez 12.00
15 Ozzie Guillen 3.00
16 Teddy Higuera 3.00
17 Edgar Martinez 3.00
18 Hipolito Pichardo 3.00
19 Luis Polonia 3.00
20 Ivan Rodriguez 7.50

1994 Pacific Crown Promos

Virtually identical in format to the regular 1994 Pacific Crown issue, the eight cards in the promo set have a "P-" prefix to the card number. Each side has a large "For Promotional Use Only" printed diagonally in black. The cards were sent to dealers as a preview to Pacific's 1994 bilingual issue.

NM/M
Complete Set (8): 6.00
Common Player: .75
1 Carlos Baerga .75
2 Joe Carter .75
3 Juan Gonzalez .75
4 Ken Griffey Jr. 2.00
5 Greg Maddux 1.50
6 Mike Piazza 1.75
7 Tim Salmon .75
8 Frank Thomas 1.25

1994 Pacific Crown

Following its 1993 Spanish-language set, Pacific's 1994 "Crown Collection" offering is bilingual, featuring both English and Spanish for most of the back printing. Fronts have an action photo which is borderless at the top and sides. A gold-foil line separates the bottom of the photo from a marbled strip that is color-coded by team. The player's name appears in two lines at the left of the strip, a gold-foil crown logo is at left. A Pacific logo appears in one of the upper corners of the photo. Backs have a photo, again borderless at top and sides, with a Pacific logo in one upper corner and the card number and MLB logos in the lower corners. At bottom is a gray marble strip with a few biographical details, 1993 and career stats and a ghost-image color team logo. The 660 cards in the set were issued in a single series.

NM/M
Complete Set (660): 20.00
Common Player: .05
Pack (12): 1.00
Wax Box (36): 20.00
1 Steve Avery .05
2 Steve Bedrosian .05
3 Damon Beryhill .05
4 Jeff Blauser .05
5 Sid Bream .05
6 Francisco Cabrera .05
7 Ramon Caraballo .05
8 Ron Gant .05
9 Tom Glavine .25
10 Chipper Jones .75
11 Dave Justice .05
12 Ryan Klesko .05
13 Mark Lemke .05
14 Javier Lopez .05
15 Greg Maddux .75
16 Fred McGriff .05
17 Greg McMichael .05
18 Kent Mercker .05
19 Otis Nixon .05
20 Terry Pendleton .05
21 Deion Sanders .05
22 John Smoltz .05
23 Tony Tarasco .05
24 Manny Alexander .05
25 Brady Anderson .05
26 Harold Baines .05
27 Damion Buford (Damon) .05
28 Paul Carey .05
29 Mike Devereaux .05
30 Todd Frohwirth .05
31 Leo Gomez .05
32 Jeffrey Hammonds .05
33 Chris Hoiles .05
34 Tim Hullett .05
35 Ben McDonald .05
36 Mark McLemore .05
37 Alan Mills .05
38 Mike Mussina .35
39 Sherman Obando .05
40 Gregg Olson .05
41 Mike Pagliarulo .05
42 Jim Poole .05
43 Harold Reynolds .05
44 Cal Ripken, Jr. 2.00
45 David Segui .05
46 Fernando Valenzuela .05
47 Jack Voight .05
48 Scott Bankhead .05
49 Roger Clemens 1.00
50 Scott Cooper .05
51 Danny Darwin .05
52 Andre Dawson .20
53 John Dopson .05
54 Scott Fletcher .05
55 Tony Fossas .05
56 Mike Greenwell .05
57 Billy Hatcher .05
58 Jeff McNeely .05
59 Jose Melendez .05
60 Tim Naehring .05
61 Tony Pena .05
62 Carlos Quintana .05
63 Paul Quantrill .05
64 Luis Rivera .05
65 Jeff Russell .05
66 Aaron Sele .05
67 John Valentin .05
68 Mo Vaughn .05
69 Frank Viola .05
70 Bob Zupcic .05
71 Mike Butcher .05
72 Ron Correia .05
73 Chad Curtis .05
74 Chili Davis .05
75 Gary DiSarcina .05
76 Damion Easley .05
77 John Farrell .05
78 Chuck Finley .05
79 Joe Grahe .05
80 Stan Javier .05
81 Mark Langston .05
82 Phil Leftwich .05
83 Torey Lovullo .05
84 Joe Magrane .05
85 Greg Myers .05
86 Eduardo Perez .05
87 Luis Polonia .05
88 Tim Salmon .05
89 J.T. Snow .05
90 Kurt Stillwell .05
91 Ron Tingley .05
92 Chris Turner .05
93 Julio Valera .05
94 Jose Bautista .05
95 Shawn Boskie .05
96 Steve Buechele .05
97 Frank Castillo .05
98 Mark Grace .05
99 Jose Guzman .05
100 Mike Harkey .05
101 Greg Hibbard .05
102 Doug Jennings .05
103 Derrick May .05
104 Mike Morgan .05
105 Randy Myers .05
106 Karl Rhodes .05
107 Kevin Robinson .05
108 Rey Sanchez .05
109 Ryne Sandberg .75
110 Tommy Shields .05
111 Dwight Smith .05
112 Sammy Sosa .75
113 Jose Vizcaino .05
114 Turk Wendell .05
115 Rick Wilkins .05
116 Willie Wilson .05
117 Eddie Zambrano .05
118 Wilson Alvarez .05
119 Tim Belcher .05
120 Jason Bere .05
121 Rodney Bolton .05
122 Ellis Burks .05
123 Joey Cora .05
124 Alex Fernandez .05
125 Ozzie Guillen .05
126 Craig Grebeck .05
127 Roberto Hernandez .05
128 Bo Jackson .10
129 Lance Johnson .05
130 Ron Karkovice .05
131 Mike Lavalliere .05
132 Norberto Martin .05
133 Kirk McCaskill .05
134 Jack McDowell .05
135 Scott Radinsky .05
136 Tim Raines .05
137 Steve Sax .05
138 Frank Thomas .60
139 Dan Pasqua .05
140 Robin Ventura .05
141 Jeff Branson .05
142 Tom Browning .05
143 Jacob Brumfield .05
144 Tim Costo .05
145 Rob Dibble .05
146 Brian Dorsett .05
147 Steve Foster .05
148 Cesar Hernandez .05
149 Roberto Kelly .05
150 Barry Larkin .05
151 Larry Luebbers .05
152 Kevin Mitchell .05
153 Joe Oliver .05
154 Tim Pugh .05
155 Jeff Reardon .05
156 Jose Rijo .05
157 Bip Roberts .05
158 Chris Sabo .05
159 Juan Samuel .05
160 Reggie Sanders .05
161 John Smiley .05
162 Jerry Spradlin .05
163 Gary Varsho .05
164 Sandy Alomar Jr. .05
165 Carlos Baerga .25
166 Albert Belle .05
167 Mark Clark .05
168 Alvaro Espinoza .05
169 Felix Fermin .05
170 Reggie Jefferson .05
171 Wayne Kirby .05
172 Tom Kramer .05
173 Jesse Levis .05
174 Kenny Lofton .05
175 Candy Maldonado .05
176 Carlos Martinez .05
177 Jose Mesa .05
178 Jeff Mutis .05
179 Charles Nagy .05
180 Bob Ojeda .05
181 Junior Ortiz .05
182 Eric Plunk .05
183 Manny Ramirez .60
184 Paul Sorrento .05
185 Jeff Treadway .05
186 Bill Wertz .05
187 Freddie Benavides .05
188 Dante Bichette .05
189 Willie Blair .05
190 Daryl Boston .05
191 Pedro Castellano .05
192 Vinny Castilla .05
193 Jerald Clark .05
194 Alex Cole .05
195 Andres Galarraga .05
196 Joe Girardi .05
197 Charlie Hayes .05
198 Darren Holmes .05
199 Chris Jones .05
200 Curt Leskanic .05
201 Roberto Mejia .05
202 David Nied .05
203 J. Owens .05
204 Steve Reed .05
205 Armando Reynoso .05
206 Bruce Ruffin .05
207 Keith Shepherd .05
208 Jim Tatum .05
209 Eric Young .05
210 Skeeter Barnes .05
211 Danny Bautista .05
212 Tom Bolton .05
213 Eric Davis .05
214 Storm Davis .05
215 Cecil Fielder .05
216 Travis Fryman .05
217 Kirk Gibson .05
218 Dan Gladden .05
219 John Doherty .05
220 Chris Gomez .05
221 David Haas .05
222 Bill Krueger .05
223 Chad Kreuter .05
224 Mark Leiter .05
225 Bob MacDonald .05
226 Mike Moore .05
227 Tony Phillips .05
228 Rich Rowland .05
229 Mickey Tettleton .05
230 Alan Trammell .05
231 David Wells .05
232 Lou Whitaker .05
233 Luis Aquino .05
234 Alex Arias .05
235 Jack Armstrong .05
236 Ryan Bowen .05
237 Chuck Carr .05
238 Matias Carrillo .05
239 Jeff Conine .05
240 Henry Cotto .05
241 Orestes Destrade .05
242 Chris Hammond .05
243 Bryan Harvey .05
244 Charlie Hough .05
245 Richie Lewis .05
246 Mitch Lyden .05
247 Dave Magadan .05
248 Bob Natal .05
249 Benito Santiago .05
250 Gary Sheffield .30
251 Matt Turner .05
252 David Weathers .05
253 Walt Weiss .05
254 Darrell Whitmore .05
255 Nigel Wilson .05
256 Eric Anthony .05
257 Jeff Bagwell .60
258 Kevin Bass .05
259 Craig Biggio .05
260 Ken Caminiti .05
261 Andujar Cedeno .05
262 Chris Donnels .05
263 Doug Drabek .05
264 Tom Edens .05
265 Steve Finley .05
266 Luis Gonzalez .05
267 Pete Harnisch .05
268 Xavier Hernandez .05
269 Todd Jones .05
270 Darryl Kile .05
271 Al Osuna .05
272 Rick Parker .05
273 Mark Portugal .05
274 Scott Servais .05
275 Greg Swindell .05
276 Eddie Taubensee .05
277 Jose Uribe .05
278 Brian Williams .05
279 Kevin Appier .05
280 Billy Brewer .05
281 David Cone .05
282 Greg Gagne .05
283 Tom Gordon .05
284 Chris Gwynn .05
285 John Habyan .05
286 Chris Haney .05
287 Phil Hiatt .05
288 David Howard .05
289 Felix Jose .05
290 Wally Joyner .05
291 Jose Koslofski .05
292 Jose Lind .05
293 Brent Mayne .05
294 Mike Mcfarlane .05
295 Brian McRae .05
296 Kevin McReynolds .05
297 Keith Miller .05
298 Jeff Montgomery .05
299 Hipolito Pichardo .05
300 Rico Rossy .05
301 Curtis Wilkerson .05
302 Pedro Astacio .05
303 Rafael Bournigal .05
304 Brett Butler .05
305 Tom Candiotti .05
306 Omar Daal .05
307 Jim Gott .05
308 Kevin Gross .05
309 Dave Hansen .05
310 Carlos Hernandez .05
311 Orel Hershiser .05
312 Eric Karros .05
313 Pedro Martinez .60
314 Ramon Martinez .05
315 Roger McDowell .05
316 Raul Mondesi .05
317 Jose Offerman .05
318 Mike Piazza 1.00
319 Jody Reed .05
320 Henry Rodriguez .05
321 Cory Snyder .05
322 Darryl Strawberry .05
323 Tim Wallach .05
324 Steve Wilson .05
325 Juan Bell .05
326 Ricky Bones .05
327 Alex Diaz .05
328 Cal Eldred .05
329 Darryl Hamilton .05
330 Doug Henry .05
331 John Jaha .05
332 Pat Listach .05
333 Graeme Lloyd .05
334 Carlos Maldonado .05
335 Angel Miranda .05
336 Jaime Navarro .05
337 Dave Nilsson .05
338 Rafael Novoa .05
339 Troy O'Leary .05
340 Jesse Orosco .05
341 Kevin Seitzer .05
342 Bill Spiers .05
343 William Suero .05
344 B.J. Surhoff .05
345 Dickie Thon .05
346 Jose Valentin .05
347 Greg Vaughn .05
348 Robin Yount .60
349 Willie Banks .05
350 Bernardo Brito .05
351 Scott Erickson .05
352 Mark Guthrie .05
353 Chip Hale .05
354 Brian Harper .05
355 Kent Hrbek .05
356 Terry Jorgenson .05
357 Chuck Knoblauch .05
358 Gene Larkin .05
359 Scott Leius .05
360 Shane Mack .05
361 David McCarty .05
362 Pat Meares .05
363 Pedro Munoz .05
364 Derek Parks .05
365 Kirby Puckett .75
366 Jeff Reboulet .05
367 Kevin Tapani .05
368 Mike Trombley .05
369 George Tsamis .05
370 Carl Willis .05
371 Dave Winfield .60
372 Moises Alou .05
373 Brian Barnes .05
374 Sean Berry .05
375 Frank Bolick .05
376 Wil Cordero .05
377 Delino DeShields .05
378 Jeff Fassero .05
379 Darren Fletcher .05
380 Cliff Floyd .05
381 Lou Frazier .05
382 Marquis Grissom .05
383 Gil Heredia .05
384 Mike Lansing .05
385 Oreste Marrero .05
386 Dennis Martinez .05
387 Curtis Pride .05
388 Mel Rojas .05
389 Kirk Rueter .05
390 Joe Siddall .05
391 John Vander Wal .05
392 Larry Walker .05
393 John Wetteland .05
394 Rondell White .05
395 Tom Bogar .05
396 Bobby Bonilla .05

#	Player	Price
397	Jeromy Burnitz	.05
398	Mike Draper	.05
399	Sid Fernandez	.05
400	John Franco	.05
401	Dave Gallagher	.05
402	Dwight Gooden	.05
403	Eric Hillman	.05
404	Todd Hundley	.05
405	Butch Huskey	.05
406	Jeff Innis	.05
407	Howard Johnson	.05
408	Jeff Kent	.05
409	Ced Landrum	.05
410	Mike Maddux	.05
411	Josias Manzanillo	.05
412	Jeff McKnight	.05
413	Eddie Murray	.60
414	Tito Navarro	.05
415	Joe Orsulak	.05
416	Bret Saberhagen	.05
417	Dave Telgheder	.05
418	Ryan Thompson	.05
419	Chico Walker	.05
420	Jim Abbott	.05
421	Wade Boggs	.75
422	Mike Gallego	.05
423	Mark Hutton	.05
424	Dion James	.05
425	Domingo Jean	.05
426	Pat Kelly	.05
427	Jimmy Key	.05
428	Jim Leyritz	.05
429	Kevin Maas	.05
430	Don Mattingly	1.00
431	Bobby Munoz	.05
432	Matt Nokes	.05
433	Paul O'Neill	.05
434	Spike Owen	.05
435	Melido Perez	.05
436	Lee Smith	.05
437	Andy Stankiewicz	.05
438	Mike Stanley	.05
439	Danny Tartabull	.05
440	Randy Velarde	.05
441	Bernie Williams	.05
442	Gerald Williams	.05
443	Mike Witt	.05
444	Marcos Armas	.05
445	Lance Blankenship	.05
446	Mike Bordick	.05
447	Ron Darling	.05
448	Dennis Eckersley	.45
449	Brent Gates	.05
450	Goose Gossage	.05
451	Scott Hemond	.05
452	Dave Henderson	.05
453	Shawn Hillegas	.05
454	Rick Honeycutt	.05
455	Scott Lydy	.05
456	Mark McGwire	1.50
457	Henry Mercedes	.05
458	Mike Mohler	.05
459	Troy Neel	.05
460	Edwin Nunez	.05
461	Craig Paquette	.05
462	Ruben Sierra	.05
463	Terry Steinbach	.05
464	Todd Van Poppel	.05
465	Bob Welch	.05
466	Bobby Witt	.05
467	Ruben Amaro	.05
468	Larry Anderson	.05
469	Kim Batiste	.05
470	Wes Chamberlain	.05
471	Darren Daulton	.05
472	Mariano Duncan	.05
473	Len Dykstra	.05
474	Jim Eisenreich	.05
475	Tommy Greene	.05
476	Dave Hollins	.05
477	Pete Incaviglia	.05
478	Danny Jackson	.05
479	John Kruk	.05
480	Tony Longmire	.05
481	Jeff Manto	.05
482	Mike Morandini	.05
483	Terry Mulholland	.05
484	Todd Pratt	.05
485	Ben Rivera	.05
486	Curt Schilling	.25
487	Kevin Stocker	.05
488	Milt Thompson	.05
489	David West	.05
490	Mitch Williams	.05
491	Jeff Ballard	.05
492	Jay Bell	.05
493	Scott Bullett	.05
494	Dave Clark	.05
495	Steve Cooke	.05
496	Midre Cummings	.05
497	Mark Dewey	.05
498	Carlos Garcia	.05
499	Jeff King	.05
500	Al Martin	.05
501	Lloyd McClendon	.05
502	Orlando Merced	.05
503	Blas Minor	.05
504	Denny Neagle	.05
505	Tom Prince	.05
506	Don Slaught	.05
507	Zane Smith	.05
508	Randy Tomlin	.05
509	Andy Van Slyke	.05
510	Paul Wagner	.05
511	Tim Wakefield	.05
512	Bob Walk	.05
513	John Wehner	.05
514	Kevin Young	.05
515	Billy Bean	.05
516	Andy Benes	.05
517	Derek Bell	.05
518	Doug Brocail	.05
519	Jarvis Brown	.05
520	Phil Clark	.05
521	Mark Davis	.05
522	Jeff Gardner	.05
523	Pat Gomez	.05
524	Ricky Gutierrez	.05
525	Tony Gwynn	.75
526	Gene Harris	.05
527	Kevin Higgins	.05
528	Trevor Hoffman	.05
529	Luis Lopez	.05
530	Pedro A. Martinez	.05
531	Melvin Nieves	.05
532	Phil Plantier	.05
533	Frank Seminara	.05
534	Craig Shipley	.05
535	Tim Tuefel	.05
536	Guillermo Velasquez	.05
537	Wally Whitehurst	.05
538	Rod Beck	.05
539	Todd Benzinger	.05
540	Barry Bonds	2.00
541	Jeff Brantley	.05
542	Dave Burba	.05
543	John Burkett	.05
544	Will Clark	.05
545	Royce Clayton	.05
546	Brian Hickerson (Bryan)	.05
547	Mike Jackson	.05
548	Darren Lewis	.05
549	Kirt Manwaring	.05
550	Dave Martinez	.05
551	Willie McGee	.05
552	Jeff Reed	.05
553	Dave Righetti	.05
554	Kevin Rogers	.05
555	Steve Scarsone	.05
556	Bill Swift	.05
557	Robby Thompson	.05
558	Salomon Torres	.05
559	Matt Williams	.05
560	Trevor Wilson	.05
561	Rich Amaral	.05
562	Mike Blowers	.05
563	Chris Bosio	.05
564	Jay Buhner	.05
565	Norm Charlton	.05
566	Jim Converse	.05
567	Rich DeLucia	.05
568	Mike Felder	.05
569	Dave Fleming	.05
570	Ken Griffey Jr.	1.00
571	Bill Haselman	.05
572	Dwayne Henry	.05
573	Brad Holman	.05
574	Randy Johnson	.60
575	Greg Litton	.05
576	Edgar Martinez	.05
577	Tino Martinez	.05
578	Jeff Nelson	.05
579	Mark Newfield	.05
580	Roger Salkeld	.05
581	Mackey Sasser	.05
582	Brian Turang	.05
583	Omar Vizquel	.05
584	Dave Valle	.05
585	Luis Alicea	.05
586	Rene Arocha	.05
587	Rheal Cormier	.05
588	Tripp Cromer	.05
589	Bernard Gilkey	.05
590	Lee Guetterman	.05
591	Gregg Jefferies	.05
592	Tim Jones	.05
593	Paul Kilgus	.05
594	Les Lancaster	.05
595	Omar Olivares	.05
596	Jose Oquendo	.05
597	Donovan Osborne	.05
598	Tom Pagnozzi	.05
599	Erik Pappas	.05
600	Geronimo Pena	.05
601	Mike Perez	.05
602	Gerald Perry	.05
603	Stan Royer	.05
604	Ozzie Smith	.75
605	Bob Tewksbury	.05
606	Allen Watson	.05
607	Mark Whiten	.05
608	Todd Zeile	.05
609	Jeff Bronkey	.05
610	Kevin Brown	.05
611	Jose Canseco	.35
612	Doug Dascenzo	.05
613	Butch Davis	.05
614	Mario Diaz	.05
615	Julio Franco	.05
616	Benji Gil	.05
617	Juan Gonzalez	.30
618	Tom Henke	.05
619	Jeff Huson	.05
620	David Hulse	.05
621	Craig Lefferts	.05
622	Rafael Palmeiro	.50
623	Dean Palmer	.05
624	Bob Patterson	.05
625	Roger Pavlik	.05
626	Gary Redus	.05
627	Ivan Rodriguez	.50
628	Kenny Rogers	.05
629	Jon Shave	.05
630	Doug Strange	.05
631	Matt Whiteside	.05
632	Roberto Alomar	.15
633	Pat Borders	.05
634	Scott Brow	.05
635	Rob Butler	.05
636	Joe Carter	.05
637	Tony Castillo	.05
638	Mark Eichhorn	.05
639	Tony Fernandez	.05
640	Huck Flener RC	.05
641	Alfredo Griffin	.05
642	Juan Guzman	.05
643	Rickey Henderson	.60
644	Pat Hentgen	.05
645	Randy Knorr	.05
646	Al Leiter	.05
647	Dominigo Martinez	.05
648	Paul Molitor	.60
649	Jack Morris	.05
650	John Olerud	.05
651	Ed Sprague	.05
652	Dave Stewart	.05
653	Devon White	.05
654	Woody Williams	.05
655	Barry Bonds (MVP)	1.00
656	Greg Maddux (CY)	.40
657	Jack McDowell (CY)	.05
658	Mike Piazza (ROY)	.65
659	Tim Salmon (ROY)	.05
660	Frank Thomas (MVP)	.25

All Latino All-Star Team

Latino All-Stars is the theme of the third insert set found randomly packed in Pacific Spanish for 1994. Cards feature a player action photo on front, with a gold foil pinstripe around the sides and top. The player's name appears in gold script at bottom and there is a baseball logo in the corner. On backs a portrait photo of the player is set against a background of his native flag. Season highlights of 1993 are presented in English and Spanish. Eight thousand sets were produced.

		NM/M
Complete Set (20):		4.00
Common Player:		.25
1	Benito Santiago	.25
2	Dave Magadan	.25
3	Andres Galarraga	.25
4	Luis Gonzalez	.25
5	Jose Offerman	.25
6	Bobby Bonilla	.25
7	Dennis Martinez	.25
8	Mariano Duncan	.25
9	Orlando Merced	.25
10	Jose Rijo	.25
11	Danny Tartabull	.25
12	Ruben Sierra	.25
13	Ivan Rodriguez	1.00
14	Juan Gonzalez	1.00
15	Jose Canseco	.50
16	Rafael Palmeiro	1.00
17	Roberto Alomar	.50
18	Eduardo Perez	.25
19	Alex Fernandez	.25
20	Omar Vizquel	.25

Homerun Leaders

A gold prismatic background behind a color action player photo is the featured design on this Pacific insert set. Backs have another player photo against a ballfield backdrop. A huge baseball is overprinted with the player's name and number of 1993 homers. A league designation is among the logos featured on back. A total of 8,000 of these inserts sets was the announced production.

		NM/M
Complete Set (20):		25.00
Common Player:		1.00
1	Juan Gonzalez	1.50
2	Ken Griffey Jr.	3.00
3	Frank Thomas	2.50
4	Albert Belle	1.00
5	Rafael Palmeiro	1.50
6	Joe Carter	1.00
7	Dean Palmer	1.00
8	Mickey Tettleton	1.00
9	Tim Salmon	1.00
10	Danny Tartabull	1.00
11	Barry Bonds	5.00
12	Dave Justice	1.00
13	Matt Williams	1.00
14	Fred McGriff	1.00
15	Ron Gant	1.00
16	Mike Piazza	3.00
17	Bobby Bonilla	1.00
18	Phil Plantier	1.00
19	Sammy Sosa	3.00
20	Rick Wilkins	1.00

Jewels of the Crown

One of three inserts into 1994 Pacific Spanish foil packs. The design features a player action photo set against a silver prismatic background. On back is another color player photo against a background of colored silk and a large jewel. Season highlight stats and awards won are presented in both English and Spanish. The announced production run of these inserts was 8,000 sets.

		NM/M
Complete Set (36):		40.00
Common Player:		1.00
1	Robin Yount	2.50
2	Juan Gonzalez	1.25
3	Rafael Palmeiro	2.00
4	Paul Molitor	2.50
5	Roberto Alomar	1.25
6	John Olerud	1.00
7	Randy Johnson	2.50
8	Ken Griffey Jr.	4.00
9	Wade Boggs	3.00
10	Don Mattingly	3.50
11	Kirby Puckett	3.00
12	Tim Salmon	1.00
13	Frank Thomas	2.50
14	Fernando Valenzuela (Comeback Player)	1.00
15	Cal Ripken, Jr.	6.00
16	Carlos Baerga	1.00
17	Kenny Lofton	1.00
18	Cecil Fielder	1.00
19	John Burkett	1.00
20	Andres Galarraga (Comeback Player)	1.00
21	Charlie Hayes	1.00
22	Orestes Destrade	1.00
23	Jeff Conine	1.00
24	Jeff Bagwell	2.50
25	Mark Grace	1.00
26	Ryne Sandberg	3.00
27	Gregg Jefferies	1.00
28	Barry Bonds	6.00
29	Mike Piazza	3.50
30	Greg Maddux	3.00
31	Darren Daulton	1.00
32	John Kruk	1.00
33	Len Dykstra	1.00
34	Orlando Merced	1.00
35	Tony Gwynn	3.00
36	Robby Thompson	1.00

Jewels of the Crown - Retail

Using the same design, photos, graphics and card numbers, the retail version of the Jewels of the Crown insert set varies only in the silver prismatic foil background on front. While the scarcer hobby version has a diamond-shaped pattern to the foil, the retail version has numerous circles as a background pattern. The retail cards were inserted one per pack of retail product and are thus much more common than the hobby version.

		NM/M
Complete Set (36):		40.00
Common Player:		.75
1	Robin Yount	2.50
2	Juan Gonzalez	1.25
3	Rafael Palmeiro	1.25
4	Paul Molitor	2.50
5	Roberto Alomar	1.00
6	John Olerud	.75
7	Randy Johnson	2.50
8	Ken Griffey Jr.	4.00
9	Wade Boggs	3.00
10	Don Mattingly	3.50
11	Kirby Puckett	3.00
12	Tim Salmon	.75
13	Frank Thomas	2.50
14	Fernando Valenzuela (Comeback Player)	.75
15	Cal Ripken, Jr.	5.00
16	Carlos Baerga	.75
17	Kenny Lofton	.75
18	Cecil Fielder	.75
19	John Burkett	.75
20	Andres Galarraga (Comeback Player)	.75
21	Charlie Hayes	.75
22	Orestes Destrade	.75
23	Jeff Conine	.75
24	Jeff Bagwell	2.50
25	Mark Grace	.75
26	Ryne Sandberg	3.00
27	Gregg Jefferies	.75
28	Barry Bonds	5.00
29	Mike Piazza	3.50
30	Greg Maddux	3.00
31	Darren Daulton	.75
32	John Kruk	.75
33	Len Dykstra	.75
34	Orlando Merced	.75
35	Tony Gwynn	3.00
36	Robby Thompson	.75

1995 Pacific

The base cards in Pacific's Crown Collection baseball issue for 1995 feature borderless color action photos on front, graphically highlighted by the player at bottom in gold foil and a color team logo on a baseball at lower-left. Backs have a playing field design in the background with a portrait photo at left. At right are 1994 stats, career highlights and a ghosted image of the team logo. Most back printing is in both English and Spanish. The 450 cards in the series are arranged alphabetically within team, with the teams arranged in city-alpha order. Several chase cards series are found in the 12-card foil packs.

		NM/M
Complete Set (450):		20.00
Common Player:		.05
Pack (12):		1.00
Wax Box (36):		20.00
1	Steve Avery	.05
2	Rafael Belliard	.05
3	Jeff Blauser	.05
4	Tom Glavine	.25
5	Dave Justice	.05
6	Mike Kelly	.05
7	Roberto Kelly	.05
8	Ryan Klesko	.05
9	Mark Lemke	.05
10	Javier Lopez	.05
11	Greg Maddux	.75
12	Fred McGriff	.05
13	Greg McMichael	.05
14	Jose Oliva	.05
15	John Smoltz	.05
16	Tony Tarasco	.05
17	Brady Anderson	.05
18	Harold Baines	.05
19	Armando Benitez	.05
20	Mike Devereaux	.05
21	Leo Gomez	.05
22	Jeffrey Hammonds	.05
23	Chris Hoiles	.05
24	Ben McDonald	.05
25	Mark McLemore	.05
26	Jamie Moyer	.05
27	Mike Mussina	.40
28	Rafael Palmeiro	.50
29	Jim Poole	.05
30	Cal Ripken Jr.	2.00
31	Lee Smith	.05
32	Mark Smith	.05
33	Jose Canseco	.35
34	Roger Clemens	1.00
35	Scott Cooper	.05
36	Andre Dawson	.25
37	Tony Fossas	.05
38	Mike Greenwell	.05
39	Chris Howard	.05
40	Jose Melendez	.05
41	Nate Minchey	.05
42	Tim Naehring	.05
43	Otis Nixon	.05
44	Carlos Rodriguez	.05
45	Aaron Sele	.05
46	Lee Tinsley	.05
47	Sergio Valdez	.05
48	John Valentin	.05
49	Mo Vaughn	.05
50	Brian Anderson	.05
51	Garret Anderson	.05
52	Rod Correia	.05
53	Chad Curtis	.05
54	Mark Dalesandro	.05
55	Chili Davis	.05
56	Gary DiSarcina	.05
57	Damion Easley	.05
58	Jim Edmonds	.05
59	Jorge Fabregas	.05
60	Chuck Finley	.05
61	Bo Jackson	.10
62	Mark Langston	.05
63	Eduardo Perez	.05
64	Tim Salmon	.05
65	J.T. Snow	.05
66	Willie Banks	.05
67	Jose Bautista	.05
68	Shawon Dunston	.05
69	Kevin Foster	.05
70	Mark Grace	.05
71	Jose Guzman	.05
72	Jose Hernandez	.05
73	Blaise Illsey	.05
74	Derrick May	.05
75	Randy Myers	.05
76	Karl Rhodes	.05
77	Kevin Roberson	.05
78	Rey Sanchez	.05
79	Sammy Sosa	.75
80	Steve Trachsel	.05
81	Eddie Zambrano	.05
82	Wilson Alvarez	.05
83	Jason Bere	.05
84	Joey Cora	.05
85	Jose DeLeon	.05
86	Alex Fernandez	.05
87	Julio Franco	.05
88	Ozzie Guillen	.05
89	Joe Hall	.05
90	Roberto Hernandez	.05
91	Darrin Jackson	.05
92	Lance Johnson	.05
93	Norberto Martin	.05
94	Jack McDowell	.05
95	Tim Raines	.05
96	Olmedo Saenz	.05
97	Frank Thomas	.60
98	Robin Ventura	.05
99	Bret Boone	.05
100	Jeff Brantley	.05
101	Jacob Brumfield	.05
102	Hector Carrasco	.05
103	Brian Dorsett	.05
104	Tony Fernandez	.05
105	Willie Greene	.05
106	Erik Hanson	.05
107	Kevin Jarvis	.05
108	Barry Larkin	.05
109	Kevin Mitchell	.05
110	Hal Morris	.05
111	Jose Rijo	.05
112	Johnny Ruffin	.05
113	Deion Sanders	.05
114	Reggie Sanders	.05
115	Sandy Alomar Jr.	.05
116	Ruben Amaro	.05
117	Carlos Baerga	.05
118	Albert Belle	.05
119	Alvaro Espinoza	.05
120	Rene Gonzales	.05

#	Player	Price		#	Player	Price		#	Player	Price
121	Wayne Kirby	.05		239	Jesse Orosco	.05		357	Derek Bell	.05
122	Kenny Lofton	.05		240	Jody Reed	.05		358	Andy Benes	.05
123	Candy Maldonado	.05		241	Jose Valentin	.05		359	Phil Clark	.05
124	Dennis Martinez	.05		242	Greg Vaughn	.05		360	Donnie Elliott	.05
125	Eddie Murray	.60		243	Turner Ward	.05		361	Ricky Gutierrez	.05
126	Charles Nagy	.05		244	Rick Aguilera	.05		362	Tony Gwynn	.75
127	Tony Pena	.05		245	Rich Becker	.05		363	Trevor Hoffman	.05
128	Manny Ramirez	.60		246	Jim Deshaies	.05		364	Tim Hyers	.05
129	Paul Sorrento	.05		247	Steve Dunn	.05		365	Luis Lopez	.05
130	Jim Thome	.40		248	Scott Erickson	.05		366	Jose Martinez	.05
131	Omar Vizquel	.05		249	Kent Hrbek	.05		367	Pedro A. Martinez	.05
132	Dante Bichette	.05		250	Chuck Knoblauch	.05		368	Phil Plantier	.05
133	Ellis Burks	.05		251	Scott Leius	.05		369	Bip Roberts	.05
134	Vinny Castilla	.05		252	David McCarty	.05		370	A.J. Sager	.05
135	Marvin Freeman	.05		253	Pat Meares	.05		371	Jeff Tabaka	.05
136	Andres Galarraga	.05		254	Pedro Munoz	.05		372	Todd Benzinger	.05
137	Joe Girardi	.05		255	Kirby Puckett	.75		373	Barry Bonds	2.00
138	Charlie Hayes	.05		256	Carlos Pulido	.05		374	John Burkett	.05
139	Mike Kingery	.05		257	Kevin Tapani	.05		375	Mark Carreon	.05
140	Nelson Liriano	.05		258	Matt Walbeck	.05		376	Royce Clayton	.05
141	Roberto Mejia	.05		259	Dave Winfield	.60		377	Pat Gomez	.05
142	David Nied	.05		260	Moises Alou	.05		378	Erik Johnson	.05
143	Steve Reed	.05		261	Juan Bell	.05		379	Darren Lewis	.05
144	Armando Reynoso	.05		262	Freddie Benavides	.05		380	Kirt Manwaring	.05
145	Bruce Ruffin	.05		263	Sean Berry	.05		381	Dave Martinez	.05
146	John Vander Wal	.05		264	Wil Cordero	.05		382	John Patterson	.05
147	Walt Weiss	.05		265	Jeff Fassero	.05		383	Mark Portugal	.05
148	Skeeter Barnes	.05		266	Darrin Fletcher	.05		384	Darryl Strawberry	.05
149	Tim Belcher	.05		267	Cliff Floyd	.05		385	Salomon Torres	.05
150	Junior Felix	.05		268	Marquis Grissom	.05		386	Bill Van Landingham	.05
151	Cecil Fielder	.05		269	Gil Heredia	.05		387	Matt Williams	.05
152	Travis Fryman	.05		270	Ken Hill	.05		388	Rich Amaral	.05
153	Kirk Gibson	.05		271	Pedro Martinez	.60		389	Bobby Ayala	.05
154	Chris Gomez	.05		272	Mel Rojas	.05		390	Mike Blowers	.05
155	Buddy Groom	.05		273	Larry Walker	.05		391	Chris Bosio	.05
156	Chad Kreuter	.05		274	John Wetteland	.05		392	Jay Buhner	.05
157	Mike Moore	.05		275	Rondell White	.05		393	Jim Converse	.05
158	Tony Phillips	.05		276	Tim Bogar	.05		394	Tim Davis	.05
159	Juan Samuel	.05		277	Bobby Bonilla	.05		395	Felix Fermin	.05
160	Mickey Tettleton	.05		278	Rico Brogna	.05		396	Dave Fleming	.05
161	Alan Trammell	.05		279	Jeromy Burnitz	.05		397	Goose Gossage	.05
162	David Wells	.05		280	John Franco	.05		398	Ken Griffey Jr.	1.00
163	Lou Whitaker	.05		281	Eric Hillman	.05		399	Randy Johnson	.60
164	Kurt Abbott	.05		282	Todd Hundley	.05		400	Edgar Martinez	.05
165	Luis Aquino	.05		283	Jeff Kent	.05		401	Tino Martinez	.05
166	Alex Arias	.05		284	Mike Maddux	.05		402	Alex Rodriguez	1.50
167	Bret Barberie	.05		285	Joe Orsulak	.05		403	Dan Wilson	.05
168	Jerry Browne	.05		286	Luis Rivera	.05		404	Luis Alicea	.05
169	Chuck Carr	.05		287	Bret Saberhagen	.05		405	Rene Arocha	.05
170	Matias Carrillo	.05		288	David Segui	.05		406	Bernard Gilkey	.05
171	Greg Colbrunn	.05		289	Ryan Thompson	.05		407	Gregg Jefferies	.05
172	Jeff Conine	.05		290	Fernando Vina	.05		408	Ray Lankford	.05
173	Carl Everett	.05		291	Jose Vizcaino	.05		409	Terry McGriff	.05
174	Robb Nen	.05		292	Jim Abbott	.05		410	Omar Olivares	.05
175	Yorkis Perez	.05		293	Wade Boggs	.75		411	Jose Oquendo	.05
176	Pat Rapp	.05		294	Russ Davis	.05		412	Vicente Palacios	.05
177	Benito Santiago	.05		295	Mike Gallego	.05		413	Geronimo Pena	.05
178	Gary Sheffield	.35		296	Xavier Hernandez	.05		414	Mike Perez	.05
179	Darrell Whitmore	.05		297	Steve Howe	.05		415	Gerald Perry	.05
180	Jeff Bagwell	.60		298	Jimmy Key	.05		416	Ozzie Smith	.75
181	Kevin Bass	.05		299	Don Mattingly	1.00		417	Bob Tewksbury	.05
182	Craig Biggio	.05		300	Terry Mulholland	.05		418	Mark Whiten	.05
183	Andujar Cedeno	.05		301	Paul O'Neill	.05		419	Todd Zeile	.05
184	Doug Drabek	.05		302	Luis Polonia	.05		420	Esteban Beltre	.05
185	Tony Eusebio	.05		303	Mike Stanley	.05		421	Kevin Brown	.05
186	Steve Finley	.05		304	Danny Tartabull	.05		422	Cris Carpenter	.05
187	Luis Gonzalez	.05		305	Randy Velarde	.05		423	Will Clark	.05
188	Pete Harnisch	.05		306	Bob Wickman	.05		424	Hector Fajardo	.05
189	John Hudek	.05		307	Bernie Williams	.05		425	Jeff Frye	.05
190	Orlando Miller	.05		308	Mark Acre	.05		426	Juan Gonzalez	.30
191	James Mouton	.05		309	Geronimo Berroa	.05		427	Rusty Greer	.05
192	Roberto Petagine	.05		310	Mike Bordick	.05		428	Rick Honeycutt	.05
193	Shane Reynolds	.05		311	Dennis Eckersley	.50		429	David Hulse	.05
194	Greg Swindell	.05		312	Rickey Henderson	.60		430	Manny Lee	.05
195	Dave Veres	.05		313	Stan Javier	.05		431	Junior Ortiz	.05
196	Kevin Appier	.05		314	Miguel Jimenez	.05		432	Dean Palmer	.05
197	Stan Belinda	.05		315	Francisco Matos	.05		433	Ivan Rodriguez	.50
198	Vince Coleman	.05		316	Mark McGwire	1.50		434	Dan Smith	.05
199	David Cone	.05		317	Troy Neel	.05		435	Roberto Alomar	.15
200	Gary Gaetti	.05		318	Steve Ontiveros	.05		436	Pat Borders	.05
201	Greg Gagne	.05		319	Carlos Reyes	.05		437	Scott Brow	.05
202	Mark Gubicza	.05		320	Ruben Sierra	.05		438	Rob Butler	.05
203	Bob Hamelin	.05		321	Terry Steinbach	.05		439	Joe Carter	.05
204	Dave Henderson	.05		322	Bob Welch	.05		440	Tony Castillo	.05
205	Felix Jose	.05		323	Bobby Witt	.05		441	Domingo Cedeno	.05
206	Wally Joyner	.05		324	Larry Andersen	.05		442	Brad Cornett	.05
207	Jose Lind	.05		325	Kim Batiste	.05		443	Carlos Delgado	.35
208	Mike Macfarlane	.05		326	Darren Daulton	.05		444	Alex Gonzalez	.05
209	Brian McRae	.05		327	Mariano Duncan	.05		445	Juan Guzman	.05
210	Jeff Montgomery	.05		328	Lenny Dykstra	.05		446	Darren Hall	.05
211	Hipolito Pichardo	.05		329	Jim Eisenreich	.05		447	Paul Molitor	.60
212	Pedro Astacio	.05		330	Danny Jackson	.05		448	John Olerud	.05
213	Brett Butler	.05		331	John Kruk	.05		449	Robert Perez	.05
214	Omar Daal	.05		332	Tony Longmire	.05		450	Devon White	.05
215	Delino DeShields	.05		333	Tom Marsh	.05				
216	Darren Dreifort	.05		334	Mickey Morandini	.05				
217	Carlos Hernandez	.05		335	Bobby Munoz	.05				
218	Orel Hershiser	.05		336	Todd Pratt	.05				
219	Garey Ingram	.05		337	Tom Quinlan	.05				
220	Eric Karros	.05		338	Kevin Stocker	.05				
221	Ramon Martinez	.05		339	Fernando Valenzuela	.05				
222	Raul Mondesi	.05		340	Jay Bell	.05				
223	Jose Offerman	.05		341	Dave Clark	.05				
224	Mike Piazza	1.00		342	Steve Cooke	.05				
225	Henry Rodriguez	.05		343	Carlos Garcia	.05				
226	Ismael Valdes	.05		344	Jeff King	.05				
227	Tim Wallach	.05		345	Jon Lieber	.05				
228	Jeff Cirillo	.05		346	Ravelo Manzanillo	.05				
229	Alex Diaz	.05		347	Al Martin	.05				
230	Cal Eldred	.05		348	Orlando Merced	.05				
231	Mike Fetters	.05		349	Denny Neagle	.05				
232	Brian Harper	.05		350	Alejandro Pena	.05				
233	Ted Higuera	.05		351	Don Slaught	.05				
234	John Jaha	.05		352	Zane Smith	.05				
235	Graeme Lloyd	.05		353	Andy Van Slyke	.05				
236	Jose Mercedes	.05		354	Rick White	.05				
237	Jaime Navarro	.05		355	Kevin Young	.05				
238	Dave Nilsson	.05		356	Andy Ashby	.05				

A die-cut gold holographic foil crown is featured in this chase set. The player's name at bottom is rendered in the same foil. Backs have a dark blue background, a portrait photo and a 1994 season recap.

		NM/M
Complete Set (20):		30.00
Common Player:		.45
1	Greg Maddux	2.50
2	Fred McGriff	.45
3	Rafael Palmeiro	1.50
4	Cal Ripken Jr.	4.50
5	Jose Canseco	1.00
6	Frank Thomas	2.00
7	Albert Belle	.45
8	Manny Ramirez	2.00
9	Andres Galarraga	.45
10	Jeff Bagwell	2.00
11	Chan Ho Park	.45
12	Raul Mondesi	.45
13	Mike Piazza	3.00
14	Kirby Puckett	2.50
15	Barry Bonds	4.50
16	Ken Griffey Jr.	3.00
17	Alex Rodriguez	3.50
18	Juan Gonzalez	1.00
19	Roberto Alomar	1.00
20	Carlos Delgado	1.25

Hot Hispanics

Acknowledging its bilingual card license and market niche, this insert set of Latinos Destacados (Hot Hispanics) features top Latin players in the majors. The series logo and a gold-foil holographic player name rise from a row of flames at bottom-front. On the reverse is another player photo, on an inferno background, along with 1994 season highlights and a large team logo.

		NM/M
Complete Set (36):		20.00
Common Player:		.25
1	Roberto Alomar	1.25
2	Moises Alou	.25
3	Wilson Alvarez	.25
4	Carlos Baerga	.25
5	Geronimo Berroa	.25
6	Jose Canseco	1.00
7	Hector Carrasco	.25
8	Wil Cordero	.25
9	Carlos Delgado	1.50
10	Damion Easley	.25
11	Tony Eusebio	.25
12	Hector Fajardo	.25
13	Andres Galarraga	.25
14	Carlos Garcia	.25
15	Chris Gomez	.25
16	Alex Gonzalez	.25
17	Juan Gonzalez	1.25
18	Luis Gonzalez	.25
19	Felix Jose	.25
20	Javier Lopez	.25
21	Luis Lopez	.25
22	Dennis Martinez	.25
23	Orlando Miller	.25
24	Raul Mondesi	.25
25	Jose Oliva	.25
26	Rafael Palmeiro	2.00
27	Yorkis Perez	.25
28	Manny Ramirez	2.50
29	Jose Rijo	.25
30	Alex Rodriguez	4.00
31	Ivan Rodriguez	2.00
32	Carlos Rodriguez	.25
33	Sammy Sosa	3.00
34	Tony Tarasco	.25
35	Ismael Valdes	.25
36	Bernie Williams	.25

Marquee Prism

Etched gold holographic foil is the background to the action photos in this insert set. Player names at bottom-front are shadowed in team colors. Backs repeat the front photo in miniature version in a box at one side that offers career stats and a highlight. On the other end is a portrait photo on a background of baseballs.

Gold Crown Die-Cut

		NM/M
Complete Set (36):		22.50
Common Player:		.35
1	Jose Canseco	.65
2	Gregg Jefferies	.35
3	Fred McGriff	.35
4	Joe Carter	.35
5	Tim Salmon	.35
6	Wade Boggs	1.25
7	Dave Winfield	1.00
8	Bob Hamelin	.35
9	Cal Ripken Jr.	3.00
10	Don Mattingly	1.50
11	Juan Gonzalez	.50
12	Carlos Delgado	.65
13	Barry Bonds	3.00
14	Albert Belle	.35
15	Raul Mondesi	.35
16	Jeff Bagwell	1.00
17	Mike Piazza	1.50
18	Rafael Palmeiro	.75
19	Frank Thomas	1.00
20	Matt Williams	.35
21	Ken Griffey Jr.	2.00
22	Will Clark	.35
23	Bobby Bonilla	.35
24	Kenny Lofton	.35
25	Paul Molitor	1.00
26	Kirby Puckett	1.25
27	Dave Justice	.35
28	Jeff Conine	.35
29	Bret Boone	.35
30	Larry Walker	.35
31	Cecil Fielder	.35
32	Manny Ramirez	1.00
33	Javier Lopez	.35
34	Jimmy Key	.35
35	Andres Galarraga	.35
36	Tony Gwynn	1.25

1995 Pacific Prism

The rainbow prismatic foil background on the card fronts provides the visual punch to Pacific's premium brand cards. In a throwback to the 1950s, the cards were sold in single-card packs for $1.75. Production was limited to 2,999 cases of 36-pack boxes. Backs have a large portrait photo on a conventionally printed rainbow background. In keeping with the company's license, the 1994 season summary printed at bottom on back is in both English and Spanish. One checklist, team or Pacific logo was inserted into each pack to protect the Prism card.

		NM/M
Complete Set (143):		65.00
Common Player:		.25
Pack (2):		.60
Wax Box (36):		12.50
1	Dave Justice	.25
2	Ryan Klesko	.25
3	Javier Lopez	.25
4	Greg Maddux	2.00
5	Fred McGriff	.25
6	Tony Tarasco	.25
7	Jeffrey Hammonds	.25
8	Mike Mussina	.75
9	Rafael Palmeiro	1.25
10	Cal Ripken Jr.	5.00
11	Lee Smith	.25
12	Roger Clemens	2.50

#	Player	Price
13	Scott Cooper	.25
14	Mike Greenwell	.25
15	Carlos Rodriguez	.25
16	Mo Vaughn	.25
17	Chili Davis	.25
18	Jorge Fabregas	.25
20	Bo Jackson	.35
21a	Tim Salmon	.25
21b	Jim Edmonds (should be #18)	
22	Mark Grace	.25
23	Jose Guzman	.25
24	Randy Myers	.25
25	Rey Sanchez	.25
26	Sammy Sosa	2.50
27	Wilson Alvarez	.25
28	Julio Franco	.25
29	Ozzie Guillen	.25
30	Jack McDowell	.25
31	Frank Thomas	1.50
32	Bret Boone	.25
33	Barry Larkin	.25
34	Hal Morris	.25
35	Jose Rijo	.25
36	Deion Sanders	.25
37	Carlos Baerga	.25
38	Albert Belle	.25
39	Kenny Lofton	.25
40	Dennis Martinez	.25
41	Manny Ramirez	1.50
42	Omar Vizquel	.25
43	Dante Bichette	.25
44	Marvin Freeman	.25
45	Andres Galarraga	.25
46	Mike Kingery	.25
47	Danny Bautista	.25
48	Cecil Fielder	.25
49	Travis Fryman	.25
50	Tony Phillips	.25
51	Alan Trammell	.25
52	Lou Whitaker	.25
53	Alex Arias	.25
54	Bret Barberie	.25
55	Jeff Conine	.25
56	Charles Johnson	.25
57	Gary Sheffield	.65
58	Jeff Bagwell	1.50
59	Craig Biggio	.25
60	Doug Drabek	.25
61	Tony Eusebio	.25
62	Luis Gonzalez	.25
63	David Cone	.25
64	Bob Hamelin	.25
65	Felix Jose	.25
66	Wally Joyner	.25
67	Brian McRae	.25
68	Brett Butler	.25
69	Garey Ingram	.25
70	Ramon Martinez	.25
71	Raul Mondesi	.25
72	Mike Piazza	2.50
73	Henry Rodriguez	.25
74	Ricky Bones	.25
75	Pat Listach	.25
76	Dave Nilsson	.25
77	Jose Valentin	.25
78	Rick Aguilera	.25
79	Denny Hocking	.25
80	Shane Mack	.25
81	Pedro Munoz	.25
82	Kirby Puckett	2.00
83	Dave Winfield	1.50
84	Moises Alou	.25
85	Wil Cordero	.25
86	Cliff Floyd	.25
87	Marquis Grissom	.25
88	Pedro Martinez	1.50
89	Larry Walker	.25
90	Bobby Bonilla	.25
91	Jeromy Burnitz	.25
92	John Franco	.25
93	Jeff Kent	.25
94	Jose Vizcaino	.25
95	Wade Boggs	2.00
96	Jimmy Key	.25
97	Don Mattingly	2.50
98	Paul O'Neill	.25
99	Luis Polonia	.25
100	Danny Tartabull	.25
101	Geronimo Berroa	.25
102	Rickey Henderson	1.50
103	Ruben Sierra	.25
104	Terry Steinbach	.25
105	Darren Daulton	.25
106	Mariano Duncan	.25
107	Lenny Dykstra	.25
108	Mike Lieberthal	.25
109	Tony Longmire	.25
110	Tom Marsh	.25
111	Jay Bell	.25
112	Carlos Garcia	.25
113	Orlando Merced	.25
114	Andy Van Slyke	.25
115	Derek Bell	.25
116	Tony Gwynn	2.00
117	Luis Lopez	.25
118	Bip Roberts	.25
119	Rod Beck	.25
120	Barry Bonds	5.00
121	Darryl Strawberry	.25
122	Bill Van Landingham	.25
123	Matt Williams	.25
124	Jay Buhner	.25
125	Felix Fermin	.25
126	Ken Griffey Jr.	3.00
127	Randy Johnson	1.50
128	Edgar Martinez	.25
129	Alex Rodriguez	4.00
130	Rene Arocha	.25
131	Gregg Jefferies	.25
132	Mike Perez	.25

133	Ozzie Smith	2.00
134	Jose Canseco	.65
135	Will Clark	.25
136	Juan Gonzalez	1.00
137	Ivan Rodriguez	1.25
138	Roberto Alomar	.50
139	Joe Carter	.25
140	Carlos Delgado	.75
141	Alex Gonzalez	.25
142	Juan Guzman	.25
143	Paul Molitor	1.50
144	John Olerud	.25

Team Logos

Inserted one card per pack to provide some protection to the Prism card was a checklist, team or Pacific logo card. The large color logos are on a background of a playing field. Backs have a short English/Spanish history of the team.

		NM/M
Complete Set (31):		2.00
Common Player:		.10
1	Baltimore Orioles	.10
2	Boston Red Sox	.10
3	California Angels	.10
4	Chicago White Sox	.10
5	Cleveland Indians	.10
6	Detroit Tigers	.10
7	Kansas City Royals	.10
8	Milwaukee Brewers	.10
9	Minnesota Twins	.10
10	New York Yankees	.10
11	Oakland Athletics	.10
12	Seattle Mariners	.10
13	Texas Rangers	.10
14	Toronto Blue Jays	.10
15	Atlanta Braves	.10
16	Chicago Cubs	.10
17	Cincinnati Reds	.10
18	Colorado Rockies	.10
19	Florida Marlins	.10
20	Houston Astros	.10
21	Los Angeles Dodgers	.10
22	Montreal Expos	.10
23	New York Mets	.10
24	Philadelphia Phillies	.10
25	Pittsburgh Pirates	.10
26	St. Louis Cardinals	.10
27	San Diego Padres	.10
28	San Francisco Giants	.10
1	Checklist 1-72	.05
2	Checklist 73-144	.05
---	Pacific Logo Card	.05

Mariners Memories

To commemorate the M's magical 1995 season leading up to the A.L. Western Division pennant and the American League championship series, Pacific issued this boxed set. The first 17 cards in the set depict post-season action, with backs done in newspaper style. The rest of the set features the individual players in borderless action photos on front and smaller color portraits on the back. All cards feature silver-foil highlights on front. The set was sold in a team-colors cardboard box. The set was released in late December and includes full 1995 stats for the players.

		NM/M
Complete Set (50):		10.00
Common Player:		.10
1	Griffey slams M's to brink (Ken Griffey Jr.)	.50
2	Mariners clinch tie in Texas (Vince Coleman)	.10
3	Mariners win the West (Luis Sojo)	.10
4	At last, something to celebrate (Randy Johnson)	.25
5	Johnson stands tall (Randy Johnson)	.25
6	Griffey has big debut (Ken Griffey Jr.)	.50
7	Tino ignites Mariners (Edgar Martinez, Tino Martinez)	.10
8	Mariners tie Yankee series (Edgar Martinez)	.10
9	Griffey scores winning run (Ken Griffey Jr.)	.50
10	Thunder in the Kingdome	.10
11	Series win ends years of futility	.10
12	Bob who? beats Cleveland (Bob Wolcott)	.10
13	Buhner rocks Cleveland (Jay Buhner)	.10
14	Johnson salutes Kingdome crowd (Randy Johnson)	.25
15	Fans give their all (Lou Piniella)	.10
16	Cora eludes tag (Joey Cora)	.10
17	Voice of M's calls winner (Dave Niehaus)	.10
18	Rich Amaral	.10
19	Bobby Ayala	.10
20	Tim Belcher	.10
21	Andy Benes	.10
22	Mike Blowers	.10
23	Chris Bosio	.10
24	Darren Bragg	.10
25	Jay Buhner	.25
26	Rafael Carmona	.10
27	Norm Charlton	.10
28	Vince Coleman	.10
29	Joey Cora	.10
30	Alex Diaz	.10
31	Felix Fermin	.10
32	Ken Griffey Jr.	3.00
33	Lee Guetterman	.10
34	Randy Johnson	3.00
35	Edgar Martinez	.25
36	Tino Martinez	.25
37	Jeff Nelson	.10
38	Warren Newson	.10
39	Greg Pirkl	.10
40	Arquimedez Pozo	.10
41	Bill Risley	.10
42	Alex Rodriquez (Rodriguez)	5.00
43	Luis Sojo	.10
44	Doug Strange	.10
45	Salomon Torres	.10
46	Bob Wells	.10
47	Chris Widger	.10
48	Dan Wilson	.10
49	Bob Wolcott	.10
50	Lou Piniella	.25

1996 Pacific Crown Collection

Pacific's base set for 1996 features 450 gold-foil enhanced cards. Fronts have borderless game-action photos with the issuer's logo in an upper corner and the player's name at bottom center in gold. Horizontal backs have a portrait photo at right, career highlights in both English and Spanish at left, and 1995 stats at top. Cards were sold in 12-card foil packs which could include one of six types of insert cards.

		NM/M
Complete Set (450):		17.50
Common Player:		.05
Pack (12):		1.00
Wax Box (36):		25.00
1	Steve Avery	.05
2	Ryan Klesko	.05
3	Pedro Borbon	.05
4	Chipper Jones	1.00
5	Kent Mercker	.05
6	Greg Maddux	1.00
7	Greg McMichael	.05
8	Mark Wohlers	.05
9	Fred McGriff	.10
10	John Smoltz	.15
11	Rafael Belliard	.05
12	Mark Lemke	.05
13	Tom Glavine	.30
14	Javier Lopez	.05
15	Jeff Blauser	.05
16	Dave Justice	.05
17	Marquis Grissom	.05
18	Greg Maddux (NL Cy Young)	.50
19	Randy Myers	.05
20	Scott Servais	.05
21	Sammy Sosa	1.00
22	Kevin Foster	.05
23	Jose Hernandez	.05
24	Jim Bullinger	.05
25	Mike Perez	.05
26	Shawon Dunston	.05
27	Rey Sanchez	.05
28	Frank Castillo	.05
29	Jaime Navarro	.05
30	Brian McRae	.05
31	Mark Grace	.25
32	Roberto Rivera	.05
33	Luis Gonzalez	.05
34	Hector Carrasco	.05
35	Bret Boone	.05
36	Thomas Howard	.05
37	Hal Morris	.05
38	John Smiley	.05
39	Jeff Brantley	.05
40	Barry Larkin	.05
41	Mariano Duncan	.05
42	Xavier Hernandez	.05
43	Pete Schourek	.05
44	Reggie Sanders	.05
45	Dave Burba	.05
46	Jeff Branson	.05
47	Mark Portugal	.05
48	Ron Gant	.05
49	Benito Santiago	.05
50	Barry Larkin (NL MVP)	.05
51	Steve Reed	.05
52	Kevin Ritz	.05
53	Dante Bichette	.05
54	Darren Holmes	.05
55	Ellis Burks	.05
56	Walt Weiss	.05
57	Armando Reynoso	.05
58	Vinny Castilla	.05
59	Jason Bates	.05
60	Mike Kingery	.05
61	Bryan Rekar	.05
62	Curtis Leskanic	.05
63	Bret Saberhagen	.05
64	Andres Galarraga	.05
65	Larry Walker	.05
66	Joe Girardi	.05
67	Quilvio Veras	.05
68	Robb Nen	.05
69	Mario Diaz	.05
70	Chuck Carr	.05
71	Alex Arias	.05
72	Pat Rapp	.05
73	Rich Garces	.05
74	Kurt Abbott	.05
75	Andre Dawson	.25
76	Greg Colbrunn	.05
77	John Burkett	.05
78	Terry Pendleton	.05
79	Jesus Tavarez	.05
80	Charles Johnson	.05
81	Yorkis Perez	.05
82	Jeff Conine	.05
83	Gary Sheffield	.45
84	Brian Hunter	.05
85	Derrick May	.05
86	Greg Swindell	.05
87	Derek Bell	.05
88	Dave Veres	.05
89	Jeff Bagwell	.75
90	Todd Jones	.05
91	Orlando Miller	.05
92	Pedro A. Martinez	.05
93	Tony Eusebio	.05
94	Craig Biggio	.05
95	Shane Reynolds	.05
96	James Mouton	.05
97	Doug Drabek	.05
98	Dave Magadan	.05
99	Ricky Gutierrez	.05
100	Hideo Nomo	.50
101	Delino DeShields	.05
102	Tom Candiotti	.05
103	Mike Piazza	1.50
104	Ramon Martinez	.05
105	Pedro Astacio	.05
106	Chad Fonville	.05
107	Raul Mondesi	.05
108	Ismael Valdes	.05
109	Jose Offerman	.05
110	Todd Worrell	.05
111	Eric Karros	.05
112	Brett Butler	.05
113	Juan Castro	.05
114	Roberto Kelly	.05
115	Omar Daal	.05
116	Antonio Osuna	.05
117	Hideo Nomo (NL Rookie of Year)	.50
118	Mike Lansing	.05
119	Mel Rojas	.05
120	Sean Berry	.05
121	David Segui	.05
122	Tavo Alvarez	.05
123	Pedro Martinez	.75
124	F.P. Santangelo RC	.05
125	Rondell White	.05
126	Cliff Floyd	.05
127	Henry Rodriguez	.05
128	Tony Tarasco	.05
129	Yamil Benitez	.05
130	Carlos Perez	.05
131	Wil Cordero	.05
132	Jeff Fassero	.05
133	Moises Alou	.05
134	John Franco	.05
135	Rico Brogna	.05
136	Dave Mlicki	.05
137	Bill Pulsipher	.05
138	Jose Vizcaino	.05
139	Carl Everett	.05
140	Edgardo Alfonzo	.05
141	Bobby Jones	.05
142	Alberto Castillo	.05
143	Joe Orsulak	.05
144	Jeff Kent	.05
145	Ryan Thompson	.05
146	Jason Isringhausen	.05
147	Todd Hundley	.05
148	Alex Ochoa	.05
149	Charlie Hayes	.05
150	Michael Mimbs	.05
151	Darren Daulton	.05
152	Toby Borland	.05
153	Andy Van Slyke	.05
154	Mickey Morandini	.05
155	Sid Fernandez	.05
156	Tom Marsh	.05
157	Kevin Stocker	.05
158	Paul Quantrill	.05
159	Gregg Jefferies	.05
160	Ricky Bottalico	.05
161	Lenny Dykstra	.05
162	Mark Whiten	.05
163	Tyler Green	.05
164	Jim Eisenreich	.05
165	Heathcliff Slocumb	.05
166	Esteban Loaiza	.05
167	Rich Aude	.05
168	Jason Christiansen	.05
169	Ramon Morel	.05
170	Orlando Merced	.05
171	Paul Wagner	.05
172	Jeff King	.05
173	Jay Bell	.05
174	Jacob Brumfield	.05
175	Nelson Liriano	.05
176	Dan Miceli	.05
177	Carlos Garcia	.05
178	Denny Neagle	.05
179	Angelo Encarnacion	.05
180	Al Martin	.05
181	Midre Cummings	.05
182	Eddie Williams	.05
183	Roberto Petagine	.05
184	Tony Gwynn	1.00
185	Andy Ashby	.05
186	Melvin Nieves	.05
187	Phil Clark	.05
188	Brad Ausmus	.05
189	Bip Roberts	.05
190	Fernando Valenzuela	.05
191	Marc Newfield	.05
192	Steve Finley	.05
193	Trevor Hoffman	.05
194	Andujar Cedeno	.05
195	Jody Reed	.05
196	Ken Caminiti	.05
197	Joey Hamilton	.05
198	Tony Gwynn (NL Batting Champ)	.50
199	Shawn Barton	.05
200	Deion Sanders	.05
201	Rikkert Faneyte	.05
202	Barry Bonds	2.50
203	Matt Williams	.05
204	Jose Bautista	.05
205	Mark Leiter	.05
206	Mark Carreon	.05
207	Robby Thompson	.05
208	Terry Mulholland	.05
209	Rod Beck	.05
210	Royce Clayton	.05
211	J.R. Phillips	.05
212	Kirt Manwaring	.05
213	Glenallen Hill	.05
214	William Van Landingham	.05
215	Scott Cooper	.05
216	Bernard Gilkey	.05
217	Allen Watson	.05
218	Donovan Osborne	.05
219	Ray Lankford	.05
220	Tony Fossas	.05
221	Tom Pagnozzi	.05
222	John Mabry	.05
223	Tripp Cromer	.05
224	Mark Petkovsek	.05
225	Mike Morgan	.05
226	Ozzie Smith	1.00
227	Tom Henke	.05
228	Jose Oquendo	.05
229	Brian Jordan	.05
230	Cal Ripken Jr.	2.50
231	Scott Erickson	.05
232	Harold Baines	.05
233	Jeff Manto	.05
234	Jesse Orosco	.05
235	Jeffrey Hammonds	.05
236	Brady Anderson	.05
237	Manny Alexander	.05
238	Chris Hoiles	.05
239	Rafael Palmeiro	.60
240	Ben McDonald	.05
241	Curtis Goodwin	.05
242	Bobby Bonilla	.05
243	Mike Mussina	.60
244	Kevin Brown	.05
245	Armando Benitez	.05
246	Jose Canseco	.50
247	Erik Hanson	.05
248	Mo Vaughn	.05
249	Tim Naehring	.05
250	Vaughn Eshelman	.05
251	Mike Greenwell	.05
252	Troy O'Leary	.05
253	Tim Wakefield	.05
254	Dwayne Hosey	.05
255	John Valentin	.05
256	Rick Aguilera	.05
257	Mike MacFarlane	.05
258	Roger Clemens	1.50
259	Luis Alicea	.05
260	Mo Vaughn (AL MVP)	.05
261	Mark Langston	.05
262	Jim Edmonds	.05
263	Rod Correla	.05
264	Tim Salmon	.05
265	J.T. Snow	.05
266	Orlando Palmeiro	.05
267	Jorge Fabregas	.05
268	Jim Abbott	.05
269	Eduardo Perez	.05
270	Lee Smith	.05
271	Gary DiSarcina	.05
272	Damion Easley	.05
273	Tony Phillips	.05
274	Garret Anderson	.05
275	Chuck Finley	.05
276	Chili Davis	.05
277	Lance Johnson	.05
278	Alex Fernandez	.05
279	Robin Ventura	.05
280	Chris Snopek	.05
281	Brian Keyser	.05
282	Lyle Mouton	.05
283	Luis Andujar RC	.05
284	Tim Raines	.05
285	Larry Thomas	.05
286	Ozzie Guillen	.05
287	Frank Thomas	.75
288	Roberto Hernandez	.05
289	Dave Martinez	.05
290	Ray Durham	.05
291	Ron Karkovice	.05
292	Wilson Alvarez	.05
293	Omar Vizquel	.05
294	Eddie Murray	.75
295	Sandy Alomar	.05
296	Orel Hershiser	.05
297	Jose Mesa	.05
298	Julian Tavarez	.05
299	Dennis Martinez	.05
300	Carlos Baerga	.05
301	Manny Ramirez	.75
302	Jim Thome	.60
303	Kenny Lofton	.50
304	Tony Pena	.05
305	Alvaro Espinoza	.05
306	Paul Sorrento	.05
307	Albert Belle	.05
308	Danny Bautista	.05
309	Chris Gomez	.05
310	Jose Lima	.05
311	Phil Nevin	.05
312	Alan Trammell	.05
313	Chad Curtis	.05
314	John Flaherty	.05
315	Travis Fryman	.05
316	Todd Steverson	.05
317	Brian Bohanon	.05
318	Lou Whitaker	.05
319	Bobby Higginson	.05
320	Steve Rodriguez	.05
321	Cecil Fielder	.05
322	Felipe Lira	.05
323	Juan Samuel	.05
324	Bob Hamelin	.05
325	Tom Goodwin	.05
326	Johnny Damon	.25
327	Hipolito Pichardo	.05
328	Dilson Torres	.05
329	Kevin Appier	.05
330	Mark Gubicza	.05
331	Jon Nunnally	.05
332	Gary Gaetti	.05
333	Brent Mayne	.05
334	Brent Cookson	.05
335	Tom Gordon	.05
336	Wally Joyner	.05
337	Greg Gagne	.05
338	Fernando Vina	.05
339	Joe Oliver	.05
340	John Jaha	.05
341	Jeff Cirillo	.05
342	Pat Listach	.05
343	Dave Nilsson	.05
344	Steve Sparks	.05
345	Ricky Bones	.05
346	David Hulse	.05
347	Scott Karl	.05
348	Darryl Hamilton	.05
349	B.J. Surhoff	.05
350	Angel Miranda	.05
351	Sid Roberson	.05
352	Matt Mieske	.05
353	Jose Valentin RC	.05
354	Matt Lawton RC	.25
355	Eddie Guardado	.05
356	Brad Radke	.05
357	Pedro Munoz	.05
358	Scott Stahoviak	.05
359	Erik Schullstrom	.05
360	Pat Meares	.05
361	Marty Cordova	.05
362	Scott Leius	.05
363	Matt Walbeck	.05
364	Rich Becker	.05
365	Kirby Puckett	1.00
366	Oscar Munoz	.05
367	Chuck Knoblauch	.05
368	Marty Cordova (AL Rookie of Year)	.05
369	Bernie Williams	.05
370	Mike Stanley	.05
371	Andy Pettitte	.25
372	Jack McDowell	.05
373	Sterling Hitchcock	.05
374	David Cone	.05
375	Randy Velarde	.05
376	Don Mattingly	1.50
377	Melido Perez	.05
378	Wade Boggs	1.00
379	Ruben Sierra	.05
380	Tony Fernandez	.05
381	John Wetteland	.05
382	Mariano Rivera	.15
383	Derek Jeter	2.50
384	Paul O'Neill	.05
385	Mark McGwire	2.00
386	Scott Brosius	.05
387	Don Wengert	.05
388	Terry Steinbach	.05
389	Brent Gates	.05
390	Craig Paquette	.05
391	Mike Bordick	.05
392	Ariel Prieto	.05
393	Dennis Eckersley	.65
394	Carlos Reyes	.05
395	Todd Stottlemyre	.05
396	Rickey Henderson	.75
397	Geronimo Berroa	.05
398	Steve Ontiveros	.05
399	Mike Gallego	.05
400	Stan Javier	.05
401	Randy Johnson	.75
402	Norm Charlton	.05
403	Mike Blowers	.05
404	Tino Martinez	.05
405	Dan Wilson	.05
406	Andy Benes	.05
407	Alex Diaz	.05
408	Edgar Martinez	.05
409	Chris Bosio	.05
410	Ken Griffey Jr.	1.50
411	Luis Sojo	.05
412	Bob Wolcott	.05
413	Vince Coleman	.05
414	Rich Amaral	.05
415	Jay Buhner	.05
416	Alex Rodriguez	2.00
417	Joey Cora	.05
418	Randy Johnson (AL Cy Young)	.25
419	Edgar Martinez (AL Batting Champ)	.05
420	Ivan Rodriguez	.65
421	Mark McLemore	.05
422	Mickey Tettleton	.05
423	Juan Gonzalez	.40
424	Will Clark	.05
425	Kevin Gross	.05
426	Dean Palmer	.05
427	Kenny Rogers	.05
428	Bob Tewksbury	.05
429	Benji Gil	.05
430	Jeff Russell	.05
431	Rusty Greer	.05
432	Roger Pavlik	.05
433	Esteban Beltre	.05
434	Otis Nixon	.05
435	Paul Molitor	.75
436	Carlos Delgado	.50
437	Ed Sprague	.05
438	Juan Guzman	.05
439	Domingo Cedeno	.05
440	Pat Hentgen	.05
441	Tomas Perez	.05
442	John Olerud	.25
443	Shawn Green	.25
444	Al Leiter	.05
445	Joe Carter	.05
446	Robert Perez	.05
447	Devon White	.05
448	Tony Castillo	.05
449	Alex Gonzalez	.05
450	Roberto Alomar	.20
450p	Roberto Alomar (Unmarked promo card, "Games: 128" on back.)	1.50

Cramer's Choice

One of the most unusually shaped baseball cards of all time is the Cramer's Choice insert set from the 1996 Pacific Crown Collection. The set features the 10 best players as chosen by Pacific founder and president, Mike Cramer. Cards are in a die-cut pyramidal design 3-1/2" tall and 2-1/2" at the base. They player picture on front is set against a silver-foil background, while the player name and other information is in gold foil on a faux marble base at bottom; the effect is a simulation of a trophy. Backs repeat the marbled background and have a bilingual justification from Cramer concerning his choice of the player as one of the 10 best. Average insertion rate is one card per case (720 packs). Cards are numbered with a "CC" prefix.

		NM/M
Complete Set (10):		150.00
Common Player:		6.00
1	Roberto Alomar	7.50
2	Wade Boggs	15.00
3	Cal Ripken Jr.	30.00
4	Greg Maddux	15.00
5	Frank Thomas	12.50
6	Tony Gwynn	15.00
7	Mike Piazza	20.00
8	Ken Griffey Jr.	25.00
9	Manny Ramirez	12.50
10	Edgar Martinez	6.00

Estrellas Latinas

Three dozen of the best contemporary Latino ballplayers are honored in this chase set. Cards feature action photos silhouetted on a black background shot through with gold-foil streaks and stars. The player name, set and insert set logos are in gold at left. Backs have a portrait photo and English/Spanish career summary. The Latino Stars insert cards are inserted at an average rate of one per nine packs; about four per foil box. Cards are numbered with an "EL" prefix.

		NM/M
Complete Set (36):		16.00
Common Player:		.25
1	Roberto Alomar	.50
2	Moises Alou	.25
3	Carlos Baerga	.25
4	Geronimo Berroa	.25
5	Ricky Bones	.25
6	Bobby Bonilla	.25
7	Jose Canseco	.65
8	Vinny Castilla	.25
9	Pedro Martinez	1.50
10	John Valentin	.25
11	Andres Galarraga	.25
12	Juan Gonzalez	.75
13	Ozzie Guillen	.25
14	Esteban Loaiza	.25
15	Javier Lopez	.25
16	Dennis Martinez	.25
17	Edgar Martinez	.25
18	Tino Martinez	.25
19	Orlando Merced	.25
20	Jose Mesa	.25
21	Raul Mondesi	.25
22	Jaime Navarro	.25
23	Rafael Palmeiro	.75
24	Carlos Perez	.25
25	Manny Ramirez	1.50
26	Alex Rodriguez	3.50
27	Ivan Rodriguez	1.25
28	David Segui	.25
29	Ruben Sierra	.25
30	Sammy Sosa	2.00
31	Julian Tavarez	.25
32	Ismael Valdes	.25
33	Fernando Valenzuela	.25
34	Quilvio Veras	.25
35	Omar Vizquel	.25
36	Bernie Williams	.25

Gold Crown Die-Cuts

One of Pacific's most popular inserts of the previous year returns in 1996. The Gold Crown die-cuts have the top of the card cut away to

form a gold-foil crown design with an action photo below. The player's name is also in gold foil. Backs repeat the gold crown design at top, have a portrait photo at lower-right and a few words about the player, in both English and Spanish. Insertion rate was advertised as one per 37 packs, on average. Cards are numbered with a "DC" prefix.

		NM/M
Complete Set (36):		45.00
Common Player:		.75
1	Roberto Alomar	1.00
2	Will Clark	.75
3	Johnny Damon	1.00
4	Don Mattingly	2.50
5	Edgar Martinez	.75
6	Manny Ramirez	1.50
7	Mike Piazza	2.50
8	Quilvio Veras	.75
9	Rickey Henderson	1.50
10	Jeff Bagwell	1.50
11	Andres Galarraga	.75
12	Tim Salmon	.75
13	Ken Griffey Jr.	2.50
14	Sammy Sosa	2.00
15	Cal Ripken Jr.	4.50
16	Raul Mondesi	.75
17	Jose Canseco	1.00
18	Frank Thomas	1.50
19	Hideo Nomo	1.00
20	Wade Boggs	2.00
21	Reggie Sanders	.75
22	Carlos Baerga	.75
23	Mo Vaughn	.75
24	Ivan Rodriguez	1.25
25	Kirby Puckett	2.00
26	Albert Belle	.75
27	Vinny Castilla	.75
28	Greg Maddux	2.00
29	Dante Bichette	.75
30	Deion Sanders	.75
31	Chipper Jones	2.00
32	Cecil Fielder	.75
33	Randy Johnson	1.50
34	Mark McGwire	3.50
35	Tony Gwynn	2.00
36	Barry Bonds	4.50

Hometown of the Players

The hometown roots of 20 top players are examined in this chase set. Fronts have action photos with large areas of the background replaced with textured gold foil, including solid and outline versions of the player's name. Backs have a portrait photo, a representation of the player's native flag and a few words about his hometown. Card numbers have an "HP" prefix and are inserted at an average rate of one per 18 packs; about two per box.

		NM/M
Complete Set (20):		15.00
Common Player:		.50
1	Mike Piazza	1.50
2	Greg Maddux	1.00
3	Tony Gwynn	1.00
4	Carlos Baerga	.50
5	Don Mattingly	1.50
6	Cal Ripken Jr.	2.50
7	Chipper Jones	1.00

8	Andres Galarraga	.50
9	Manny Ramirez	.75
10	Roberto Alomar	.60
11	Ken Griffey Jr.	1.50
12	Jose Canseco	.60
13	Frank Thomas	.75
14	Vinny Castilla	.50
15	Roberto Kelly	.50
16	Dennis Martinez	.50
17	Kirby Puckett	1.00
18	Raul Mondesi	.50
19	Hideo Nomo	.60
20	Edgar Martinez	.50

Milestones

A textured metallic blue-foil background is featured on this insert set. Behind the player action photo is a spider's web design with flying baseballs, team logo and a number representing the milestone. The player's name is in purple foil, outlined in white, vertically at right. Backs have a portrait photo and bi-lingual description of the milestone. Average insertion rate for this insert series is one per 37 packs. Cards are numbered with a "M" prefix.

		NM/M
Complete Set (10):		12.50
Common Player:		.50
1	Albert Belle	.50
2	Don Mattingly	2.25
3	Tony Gwynn	2.00
4	Jose Canseco	.50
5	Marty Cordova	.50
6	Wade Boggs	2.00
7	Greg Maddux	2.00
8	Eddie Murray	1.50
9	Ken Griffey Jr.	2.50
10	Cal Ripken Jr.	3.00

October Moments

Post-season baseball has never been better represented on a card than in Pacific's "October Moments" chase set. Action photos are set against a background of a stadium decked in the traditional Fall Classic bunting, all rendered in metallic copper foil. At bottom is a textured silver strip with the player name in copper and a swirl of fallen leaves. Backs have a repeat of the leaves and bunting themes with a player portrait at center and English/Spanish description of his October heroics. These cards are found at an average rate of once per 37 packs. Cards are numbered with an "OM" prefix.

		NM/M
Complete Set (20):		30.00
Common Player:		.60
1	Carlos Baerga	.60
2	Albert Belle	.75
3	Dante Bichette	.60
4	Jose Canseco	1.25
5	Tom Glavine	1.00
6	Ken Griffey Jr.	5.00
7	Randy Johnson	2.50
8	Chipper Jones	3.50

9	Dave Justice	.60
10	Ryan Klesko	.60
11	Kenny Lofton	.60
12	Javier Lopez	.60
13	Greg Maddux	3.50
14	Edgar Martinez	.60
15	Don Mattingly	4.00
16	Hideo Nomo	1.25
17	Mike Piazza	4.00
18	Manny Ramirez	2.50
19	Reggie Sanders	.60
20	Jim Thome	1.50

1996 Pacific Prism

Only the best in baseball make the cut for the Prism checklist. Sold in one-card foil packs the cards feature action photos set against an etched silver-foil background highlighted by slashes approximating team colors. Backs are conventionally printed in a horizontal format with a player portrait photo at left center on a purple background. A short 1995 season recap is feature in both English and Spanish. Card numbers are prefixed with a "P."

		NM/M
Complete Set (144):		50.00
Common Player:		.35
Golds:		1.5X
Pack (2):		.65
Wax Box (36):		20.00
1	Tom Glavine	.75
2	Chipper Jones	2.00
3	David Justice	.35
4	Ryan Klesko	.35
5	Javier Lopez	.35
6	Greg Maddux	2.00
7	Fred McGriff	.35
8	Frank Castillo	.35
9	Luis Gonzalez	.35
10	Mark Grace	.35
11	Brian McRae	.35
12	Jaime Navarro	.35
13	Sammy Sosa	2.00
14	Bret Boone	.35
15	Ron Gant	.35
16	Barry Larkin	.35
17	Reggie Sanders	.35
18	Benito Santiago	.35
19	Dante Bichette	.35
20	Vinny Castilla	.35
21	Andres Galarraga	.35
22	Bryan Rekar	.35
23	Roberto Alomar	1.00
23p	Roberto Alomar ("Azulejos" rather than "Los Azulajos" on back, unmarked promo card.)	1.00
24	Jeff Conine	.35
25	Andre Dawson	.50
26	Charles Johnson	.35
27	Gary Sheffield	1.00
28	Quilvio Veras	.35
29	Jeff Bagwell	1.50
30	Derek Bell	.35
31	Craig Biggio	.35
32	Tony Eusebio	.35
33	Karim Garcia	.35
34	Eric Karros	.35
35	Ramon Martinez	.35
36	Raul Mondesi	.35
37	Hideo Nomo	1.00
38	Mike Piazza	3.00
39	Ismael Valdes	.35
40	Moises Alou	.35
41	Wil Cordero	.35
42	Pedro Martinez	1.50
43	Mel Rojas	.35
44	David Segui	.35
45	Edgardo Alfonzo	.35
46	Rico Brogna	.35
47	John Franco	.35
48	Jason Isringhausen	.35
49	Jose Vizcaino	.35
50	Ricky Bottalico	.35
51	Darren Daulton	.35
52	Lenny Dykstra	.35
53	Tyler Green	.35
54	Gregg Jefferies	.35
55	Jay Bell	.35
56	Jason Christiansen	.35
57	Carlos Garcia	.35
58	Esteban Loaiza	.35

59	Orlando Merced	.35
60	Andujar Cedeno	.35
61	Tony Gwynn	2.00
62	Melvin Nieves	.35
63	Phil Plantier	.35
64	Fernando Valenzuela	.35
65	Barry Bonds	4.50
66	J.R. Phillips	.35
67	Deion Sanders	.35
68	Matt Williams	.35
69	Bernard Gilkey	.35
70	Tom Henke	.35
71	Brian Jordan	.35
72	Ozzie Smith	2.00
73	Manny Alexander	.35
74	Bobby Bonilla	.35
75	Mike Mussina	1.00
76	Rafael Palmeiro	1.00
77	Cal Ripken Jr.	4.50
78	Jose Canseco	1.00
79	Roger Clemens	2.50
80	John Valentin	.35
81	Mo Vaughn	.35
82	Tim Wakefield	.35
83	Garret Anderson	.35
84	Damion Easley	.35
85	Jim Edmonds	.35
86	Tim Salmon	.35
87	Wilson Alvarez	.35
88	Alex Fernandez	.35
89	Ozzie Guillen	.35
90	Roberto Hernandez	.35
91	Frank Thomas	1.50
92	Robin Ventura	.35
93	Carlos Baerga	.35
94	Albert Belle	.35
95	Kenny Lofton	.35
96	Dennis Martinez	.35
97	Eddie Murray	1.50
98	Manny Ramirez	1.50
99	Omar Vizquel	.35
100	Chad Curtis	.35
101	Cecil Fielder	.35
102	Felipe Lira	.35
103	Alan Trammell	.35
104	Kevin Appier	.35
105	Johnny Damon	.35
106	Gary Gaetti	.35
107	Wally Joyner	.35
108	Ricky Bones	.35
109	John Jaha	.35
110	B.J. Surhoff	.35
111	Jose Valentin	.35
112	Fernando Vina	.35
113	Marty Cordova	.35
114	Chuck Knoblauch	.35
115	Scott Leius	.35
116	Pedro Munoz	.35
117	Kirby Puckett	2.00
118	Wade Boggs	2.00
119	Don Mattingly	2.50
120	Jack McDowell	.35
121	Paul O'Neill	.35
122	Ruben Rivera	.35
123	Bernie Williams	.35
124	Geronimo Berroa	.35
125	Rickey Henderson	1.50
126	Mark McGwire	3.50
127	Terry Steinbach	.35
128	Danny Tartabull	.35
129	Jay Buhner	.35
130	Joey Cora	.35
131	Ken Griffey Jr.	3.00
132	Randy Johnson	1.50
133	Edgar Martinez	.35
134	Tino Martinez	.35
135	Will Clark	.35
136	Juan Gonzalez	.75
137	Dean Palmer	.35
138	Ivan Rodriguez	1.25
139	Mickey Tettleton	.35
140	Larry Walker	.35
141	Joe Carter	.35
142	Carlos Delgado	1.00
143	Alex Gonzalez	.35
144	Paul Molitor	1.50

Gold

Exactly paralleling the cards in the regular Prism set, this chase card insert replaces the silver foil on front with gold foil. All else remains the same. Stated odds of picking a Gold Prism parallel card are about one per 18 packs, on average (two per box).

Red Hot Stars

Bright red metallic foil provides the background for these inserts. Color action photos are in the foreground, while player name and multiple team logos are worked into the background. Backs are conventionally printed with another player photo and a few words - in both English and Spanish - about the player's 1995 season. Card numbers have an RH prefix. Stated odds of finding a Red Hot Stars insert are one per 37 packs.

		NM/M
Complete Set (144):		100.00
Common Player:		.50
Stars:		1.5X

Fence Busters

Home run heroes are featured in this insert set. The player's big swing is photographed in the foreground while a baseball flies out of the etched metallic foil stadium background. The player's name is in blue foil. Backs have another player photo and details of his 1995 season home run output, in both English and Spanish. Cards are numbered with an FB prefix. Stated odds of finding a Fence Busters insert are one per 37 packs, on average.

		NM/M
Complete Set (19):		50.00
Common Player:		1.50
1	Albert Belle	1.50
2	Dante Bichette	1.50
3	Barry Bonds	7.50
4	Jay Buhner	1.50
5	Jose Canseco	2.25
6	Ken Griffey Jr.	5.00
7	Chipper Jones	4.00
8	David Justice	1.50
9	Eric Karros	1.50
10	Edgar Martinez	1.50
11	Mark McGwire	6.00
12	Eddie Murray	3.00
13	Mike Piazza	5.00
14	Kirby Puckett	4.00
15	Cal Ripken Jr.	7.50
16	Tim Salmon	1.50
17	Sammy Sosa	4.00
18	Frank Thomas	3.00
19	Mo Vaughn	1.50

Flame Throwers

Burning baseballs are the background for the game's best pitchers in this die-cut insert set. The gold-foil highlighted flames have their tails die-cut at the card's left end. The featured pitcher is shown in action in the foreground. The name at bottom and company logo are in gold foil. Backs are conventionally printed with another action photo and 1995 highlight printed in both English and Spanish. Card numbers carry an FT prefix. Stated odds of finding a Flame Throwers card are one in 73 packs, about every two boxes.

		NM/M
Complete Set (10):		25.00
Common Player:		1.50
1	Roger Clemens	6.50
2	David Cone	1.50
3	Tom Glavine	2.50
4	Randy Johnson	4.50
5	Greg Maddux	6.00
6	Ramon Martinez	1.50
7	Jose Mesa	1.50
8	Mike Mussina	2.50
9	Hideo Nomo	3.00
10	Jose Rijo	1.50

NM/M

		NM/M
Complete Set (20):		25.00
Common Player:		.50
1	Roberto Alomar	.75
2	Jeff Bagwell	1.50
3	Albert Belle	.50
4	Wade Boggs	2.00
5	Barry Bonds	4.00
6	Jose Canseco	1.00
7	Ken Griffey Jr.	2.50
8	Tony Gwynn	2.00
9	Randy Johnson	1.50
10	Chipper Jones	2.00
11	Greg Maddux	2.00
12	Edgar Martinez	.50
13	Don Mattingly	2.50
14	Mike Piazza	2.50
15	Kirby Puckett	2.00
16	Manny Ramirez	1.50
17	Cal Ripken Jr.	4.00
18	Tim Salmon	.50
19	Frank Thomas	1.50
20	Mo Vaughn	.50

Carlos Baerga Celebrities Softball

This set was produced for distribution to fans attending the second annual Carlos Baerga Celebrities Softball Game in Puerto Rico. Packs were handed out containing two of the cards from this set, a regular Pacific Crown Collection card, a Pacific logo card and an information card about card shops on the island. The softball celebrities cards have a blue and red marbled border with player names at bottom in gold foil. Players are shown in action during the '95 game. Backs feature a portrait photo of the player and English/Spanish description of his participation in the event.

		NM/M
Complete Set (8):		12.00
Common Player:		1.00
1	Carlos Baerga	1.00
2	Mike Piazza	4.00
3	Bernie Williams	1.00
4	Frank Thomas	2.50
5	Roberto Alomar	1.25
6	Edgar Martinez	1.00
7	Kenny Lofton	1.00
8	Sammy Sosa	4.00

Nolan Ryan Career Highlights

Highlights of Ryan's career with the Texas Rangers are featured in this 11-card set given to fans attending the September 13 game at Arlington during Nolan Ryan Appreciation Week, when the team retired his jersey. Ten cards feature action photos on front with gold-foil graphics. Backs share a background photo of Ryan's classic windup and describe the action pictured on front. Sponsors' and licensors' logos are at top and bottom. An 11th unnumbered card is a checklist.

		NM/M
Complete Set (11):		9.00
Common Player:		1.00
---	Header Card/Checklist	.25
1	King of K's (Nolan Ryan)	1.00
2	324 Career Wins (Nolan Ryan)	1.00
3	Miracle Man (Nolan Ryan)	1.00
4	Low-Hit Nolan (Nolan Ryan)	1.00
5	Milestone K's (Nolan Ryan)	1.00
6	Pure Heat (Nolan Ryan)	1.00
7	No-Hit Nolan (Nolan Ryan)	1.00
8	Ryan's Farewell (Nolan Ryan)	1.00
9	Legendary Career (Nolan Ryan)	1.00
10	Retiring #34 (Nolan Ryan)	1.00

Advil Nolan Ryan

Nolan Ryan, who starred in TV commericals for Advil pain reliever at the end of his career continued his association with the product via a baseball card set in 1996. A pair of cards marking the all-time strikeout leader's first and last Ks were available in-store with the purchase of a bottle of Advil. A 27-card set of career highlight cards was available by mail for $5.50 and proof of purchase. All of the Ryan cards have full-bleed front photos with gold-foil highlights and the Advil and Pacific logos. Backs have a background photo of Ryan pitching, with a description of the highlight. Cards are UV coated on each side. The mail-in set was issued in a collectors' box.

		NM/M
Complete Set (29):		6.00
Common Card:		.25
IN-STORE CARDS		
1a	First Strikeout (Nolan Ryan)	.50
2a	Last strikeout (Nolan Ryan)	.50
MAIL-IN SET		
1	New York Mets Rookie Pitcher (Nolan Ryan)	.25
2	California Angels (Nolan Ryan)	.25
3	Houston Astros (Nolan Ryan)	.25
4	Texas Rangers (Nolan Ryan)	.25
5	No-Hitter #1 (Nolan Ryan)	.25
6	No-Hitter #2 (Nolan Ryan)	.25
7	No-Hitter #3 (Nolan Ryan)	.25
8	No-Hitter #4 (Nolan Ryan)	.25
9	No-Hitter #5 (Nolan Ryan)	.25
10	No-Hitter #6 (Nolan Ryan)	.25
11	No-Hitter #7 (Nolan Ryan)	.25
12	First Major League Win (Nolan Ryan)	.25
13	250th Win (Nolan Ryan)	.25
14	300th Win (Nolan Ryan)	.25
15	324th Win (Nolan Ryan)	.25
16	1,000th Strikeout (Nolan Ryan)	.25
17	2,000th Strikeout (Nolan Ryan)	.25
18	3,000th Strikeout (Nolan Ryan)	.25
19	Nolan Breaks Johnson Record (Nolan Ryan)	.25
20	4,000th Strikeout (Nolan Ryan)	.25
21	5,000th Strikeout (Nolan Ryan)	.25
22	World Series Victory (Nolan Ryan)	.25
23	Fastest Pitch Ever Thrown (Nolan Ryan)	.25
24	Ryan Home Run (Nolan Ryan)	.25
25	The Greatest Power Pitcher (Nolan Ryan)	.25
26	1989 All-Star Game (Nolan Ryan)	.25
27	Last Appearance (Nolan Ryan)	.25

1997 Pacific Crown

The 450-card, regular-sized set was available in 12-card packs. The card fronts feature the player's name in gold foil along the left border with the team logo in the bottom right corner. The card backs feature a head shot of the player in the lower left quadrant with a short highlight in both Spanish and English. Inserted in packs were: Card-Supials, Cramer's Choice, Latinos Of The Major Leagues, Fireworks Die-Cuts, Gold Crown Die-Cuts and Triple Crown Die-Cuts. A parallel silver version (67 sets) was available.

		NM/M
Complete Set (450):		30.00
Common Player:		.05
Silver Stars/RC's:		15X
Light Blue:		1X
Pack (12):		1.25
Wax Box (36):		32.50
1	Garret Anderson	.05
2	George Arias	.05
3	Chili Davis	.05
4	Gary DiSarcina	.05
5	Jim Edmonds	.05
6	Darin Erstad	.15
7	Jorge Fabregas	.05
8	Chuck Finley	.05
9	Rex Hudler	.05
10	Mark Langston	.05
11	Orlando Palmeiro	.05
12	Troy Percival	.05
13	Tim Salmon	.05
14	J.T. Snow	.05
15	Randy Velarde	.05
16	Manny Alexander	.05
17	Roberto Alomar	.25
18	Brady Anderson	.05
19	Armando Benitez	.05
20	Bobby Bonilla	.05
21	Rocky Coppinger	.05
22	Scott Erickson	.05
23	Jeffrey Hammonds	.05
24	Chris Hoiles	.05
25	Eddie Murray	.75
26	Mike Mussina	.60
27	Randy Myers	.05
28	Rafael Palmeiro	.65
29	Cal Ripken Jr.	2.50
30	B.J. Surhoff	.05
31	Tony Tarasco	.05
32	Esteban Beltre	.05
33	Darren Bragg	.05
34	Jose Canseco	.60
35	Roger Clemens	1.50
36	Wil Cordero	.05
37	Alex Delgado	.05
38	Jeff Frye	.05
39	Nomar Garciaparra	1.00
40	Tom Gordon	.05
41	Mike Greenwell	.05
42	Reggie Jefferson	.05
43	Tim Naehring	.05
44	Troy O'Leary	.05
45	Heathcliff Slocumb	.05
46	Lee Tinsley	.05
47	John Valentin	.05
48	Mo Vaughn	.05
49	Wilson Alvarez	.05
50	Harold Baines	.05
51	Ray Durham	.05
52	Alex Fernandez	.05
53	Ozzie Guillen	.05
54	Roberto Hernandez	.05
55	Ron Karkovice	.05
56	Darren Lewis	.05
57	Norberto Martin	.05
58	Dave Martinez	.05
59	Lyle Mouton	.05
60	Jose Munoz	.05
61	Tony Phillips	.05
62	Rich Sauveur	.05
63	Danny Tartabull	.05
64	Frank Thomas	.75
65	Robin Ventura	.05
66	Sandy Alomar Jr.	.05
67	Albert Belle	.05
68	Julio Franco	.05
69	Brian Giles RC	.50
70	Danny Graves	.05
71	Orel Hershiser	.05
72	Jeff Kent	.05
73	Kenny Lofton	.05
74	Dennis Martinez	.05
75	Jack McDowell	.05
76	Jose Mesa	.05
77	Charles Nagy	.05
78	Manny Ramirez	.75
79	Julian Tavarez	.05
80	Jim Thome	.60
81	Jose Vizcaino	.05
82	Omar Vizquel	.05
83	Brad Ausmus	.05
84	Kimera Bartee	.05
85	Raul Casanova	.05
86	Tony Clark	.05
87	Travis Fryman	.05
88	Bobby Higginson	.05
89	Mark Lewis	.05
90	Jose Lima	.05
91	Felipe Lira	.05
92	Phil Nevin	.05
93	Melvin Nieves	.05
94	Curtis Pride	.05
95	Ruben Sierra	.05
96	Alan Trammell	.05
97	Kevin Appier	.05
98	Tim Belcher	.05
99	Johnny Damon	.35
100	Tom Goodwin	.05
101	Bob Hamelin	.05
102	David Howard	.05
103	Jason Jacome	.05
104	Keith Lockhart	.05
105	Mike Macfarlane	.05
106	Jeff Montgomery	.05
107	Jose Offerman	.05
108	Hipolito Pichardo	.05
109	Joe Randa	.05
110	Bip Roberts	.05
111	Chris Stynes	.05
112	Mike Sweeney	.05
113	Joe Vitiello	.05
114	Jeromy Burnitz	.05
115	Chuck Carr	.05
116	Jeff Cirillo	.05
117	Mike Fetters	.05
118	David Hulse	.05
119	John Jaha	.05
120	Scott Karl	.05
121	Jesse Levis	.05
122	Mark Loretta	.05
123	Mike Matheny	.05
124	Ben McDonald	.05
125	Matt Mieske	.05
126	Angel Miranda	.05
127	Dave Nilsson	.05
128	Jose Valentin	.05
129	Fernando Vina	.05
130	Ron Villone	.05
131	Gerald Williams	.05
132	Rick Aguilera	.05
133	Rich Becker	.05
134	Ron Coomer	.05
135	Marty Cordova	.05
136	Eddie Guardado	.05
137	Denny Hocking	.05
138	Roberto Kelly	.05
139	Chuck Knoblauch	.05
140	Matt Lawton	.05
141	Pat Meares	.05
142	Paul Molitor	.75
143	Greg Myers	.05
144	Jeff Reboulet	.05
145	Scott Stahoviak	.05
146	Todd Walker	.05
147	Wade Boggs	1.00
148	David Cone	.05
149	Mariano Duncan	.05
150	Cecil Fielder	.05
151	Dwight Gooden	.05
152	Derek Jeter	2.50
153	Jim Leyritz	.05
154	Tino Martinez	.05
155	Paul O'Neill	.05
156	Andy Pettitte	.05
157	Tim Raines	.15
158	Mariano Rivera	.05
159	Ruben Rivera	.05
160	Kenny Rogers	.05
161	Darryl Strawberry	.05
162	John Wetteland	.05
163	Bernie Williams	.05
164	Tony Batista	.05
165	Geronimo Berroa	.05
166	Mike Bordick	.05
167	Scott Brosius	.05
168	Brent Gates	.05
169	Jason Giambi	.65
170	Jose Herrera	.05
171	Brian Lesher	.05
172	Damon Mashore RC	.05
173	Mark McGwire	2.00
174	Ariel Prieto	.05
175	Carlos Reyes	.05
176	Matt Stairs	.05
177	Terry Steinbach	.05
178	John Wasdin	.05
179	Ernie Young	.05
180	Rich Amaral	.05
181	Bobby Ayala	.05
182	Jay Buhner	.05
183	Rafael Carmona	.05
184	Norm Charlton	.05
185	Joey Cora	.05
186	Ken Griffey Jr.	1.50
187	Sterling Hitchcock	.05
188	Dave Hollins	.05
189	Randy Johnson	.75
190	Edgar Martinez	.05
191	Jamie Moyer	.05
192	Alex Rodriguez	2.00
193	Paul Sorrento	.05
194	Salomon Torres	.05
195	Bob Wells	.05
196	Dan Wilson	.05
197	Will Clark	.05
198	Kevin Elster	.05
199	Rene Gonzales	.05
200	Juan Gonzalez	.40
201	Rusty Greer	.05
202	Darryl Hamilton	.05
203	Mike Henneman	.05
204	Ken Hill	.05
205	Mark McLemore	.05
206	Darren Oliver	.05
207	Dean Palmer	.05
208	Roger Pavlik	.05
209	Ivan Rodriguez	.65
210	Kurt Stillwell	.05
211	Mickey Tettleton	.05
212	Bobby Witt	.05
213	Tilson Brito	.05
214	Jacob Brumfield	.05
215	Miguel Cairo	.05
216	Joe Carter	.05
217	Felipe Crespo	.05
218	Carlos Delgado	.60
219	Alex Gonzalez	.05
220	Shawn Green	.15
221	Juan Guzman	.05
222	Pat Hentgen	.05
223	Charlie O'Brien	.05
224	John Olerud	.05
225	Robert Perez	.05
226	Tomas Perez	.05
227	Juan Samuel	.05
228	Ed Sprague	.05
229	Mike Timlin	.05
230	Rafael Belliard	.05
231	Jermaine Dye	.05
232	Tom Glavine	.25
233	Marquis Grissom	.05
234	Andruw Jones	.75
235	Chipper Jones	1.00
236	David Justice	.05
237	Ryan Klesko	.05
238	Mark Lemke	.05
239	Javier Lopez	.05
240	Greg Maddux	1.00
241	Fred McGriff	.05
242	Denny Neagle	.05
243	Eddie Perez	.05
244	John Smoltz	.05
245	Mark Wohlers	.05
246	Brant Brown	.05
247	Scott Bullett	.05
248	Leo Gomez	.05
249	Luis Gonzalez	.05
250	Mark Grace	.05
251	Jose Hernandez	.05
252	Brooks Kieschnick	.05
253	Brian McRae	.05
254	Jaime Navarro	.05
255	Mike Perez	.05
256	Rey Sanchez	.05
257	Ryne Sandberg	1.00
258	Scott Servais	.05
259	Sammy Sosa	1.00
260	Pedro Valdes RC	.05
261	Turk Wendell	.05
262	Bret Boone	.05
263	Jeff Branson	.05
264	Jeff Brantley	.05
265	Dave Burba	.05
266	Hector Carrasco	.05
267	Eric Davis	.05
268	Willie Greene	.05
269	Lenny Harris	.05
270	Thomas Howard	.05
271	Barry Larkin	.05
272	Hal Morris	.05
273	Joe Oliver	.05
274	Eric Owens	.05
275	Jose Rijo	.05
276	Reggie Sanders	.05
277	Eddie Taubensee	.05
278	Jason Bates	.05
279	Dante Bichette	.05
280	Ellis Burks	.05
281	Vinny Castilla	.05
282	Andres Galarraga	.05
283	Quinton McCracken	.05
284	Jayhawk Owens	.05
285	Jeff Reed	.05
286	Bryan Rekar	.05
287	Armando Reynoso	.05
288	Kevin Ritz	.05
289	Bruce Ruffin	.05
290	John Vander Wal	.05
291	Larry Walker	.05
292	Walt Weiss	.05
293	Eric Young	.05
294	Kurt Abbott	.05
295	Alex Arias	.05
296	Miguel Batista	.05
297	Kevin Brown	.05
298	Luis Castillo	.05
299	Greg Colbrunn	.05
300	Jeff Conine	.05
301	Charles Johnson	.05
302	Al Leiter	.05
303	Robb Nen	.05
304	Joe Orsulak	.05
305	Yorkis Perez	.05
306	Edgar Renteria	.05
307	Gary Sheffield	.30
308	Jesus Tavarez	.05
309	Quilvio Veras	.05
310	Devon White	.05
311	Jeff Bagwell	.75
312	Derek Bell	.05
313	Sean Berry	.05
314	Craig Biggio	.05
315	Doug Drabek	.05
316	Tony Eusebio	.05
317	Ricky Gutierrez	.05
318	Xavier Hernandez	.05
319	Brian L. Hunter	.05
320	Darryl Kile	.05
321	Derrick May	.05
322	Orlando Miller	.05
323	James Mouton	.05
324	Bill Spiers	.05
325	Pedro Astacio	.05
326	Brett Butler	.05
327	Juan Castro	.05
328	Roger Cedeno	.05
329	Delino DeShields	.05
330	Karim Garcia	.10
331	Todd Hollandsworth	.05
332	Eric Karros	.05
333	Oreste Marrero	.05
334	Ramon Martinez	.05
335	Raul Mondesi	.05
336	Hideo Nomo	.50
337	Antonio Osuna	.05
338	Chan Ho Park	.05
339	Mike Piazza	1.50
340	Ismael Valdes	.05
341	Moises Alou	.05
342	Omar Daal	.05
343	Jeff Fassero	.05
344	Cliff Floyd	.05
345	Mark Grudzielanek	.05
346	Mike Lansing	.05
347	Pedro Martinez	.75
348	Sherman Obando	.05
349	Jose Paniagua	.05
350	Henry Rodriguez	.05
351	Mel Rojas	.05
352	F.P. Santangelo	.05
353	Dave Segui	.05
354	Dave Silvestri	.05
355	Ugueth Urbina	.05
356	Rondell White	.05
357	Edgardo Alfonzo	.05
358	Carlos Baerga	.05
359	Tim Bogar	.05
360	Rico Brogna	.05
361	Alvaro Espinoza	.05
362	Carl Everett	.05
363	John Franco	.05
364	Bernard Gilkey	.05
365	Todd Hundley	.05
366	Butch Huskey	.05
367	Jason Isringhausen	.05
368	Bobby Jones	.05
369	Lance Johnson	.05
370	Brent Mayne	.05
371	Alex Ochoa	.05
372	Rey Ordonez	.05
373	Ron Blazier	.05
374	Ricky Bottalico	.05
375	David Doster	.05
376	Lenny Dykstra	.05
377	Jim Eisenreich	.05
378	Bobby Estalella	.05
379	Gregg Jefferies	.05
380	Kevin Jordan	.05
381	Ricardo Jordan	.05
382	Mickey Morandini	.05
383	Ricky Otero	.05
384	Benito Santiago	.05
385	Gene Schall	.05
386	Curt Schilling	.25
387	Kevin Sefcik	.05
388	Kevin Stocker	.05
389	Jermaine Allensworth	.05
390	Jay Bell	.05
391	Jason Christiansen	.05
392	Francisco Cordova	.05
393	Mark Johnson	.05
394	Jason Kendall	.05
395	Jeff King	.05
396	Jon Lieber	.05
397	Nelson Liriano	.05
398	Esteban Loaiza	.05
399	Al Martin	.05
400	Orlando Merced	.05
401	Ramon Morel	.05
402	Luis Alicea	.05
403	Alan Benes	.05

404	Andy Benes	.05
405	Terry Bradshaw	.05
406	Royce Clayton	.05
407	Dennis Eckersley	.65
408	Gary Gaetti	.05
409	Mike Gallego	.05
410	Ron Gant	.05
411	Brian Jordan	.05
412	Ray Lankford	.05
413	John Mabry	.05
414	Willie McGee	.05
415	Tom Pagnozzi	.05
416	Ozzie Smith	1.00
417	Todd Stottlemyre	.05
418	Mark Sweeney	.05
419	Andy Ashby	.05
420	Ken Caminiti	.05
421	Archi Cianfrocco	.05
422	Steve Finley	.05
423	Chris Gomez	.05
424	Tony Gwynn	1.00
425	Joey Hamilton	.05
426	Rickey Henderson	.75
427	Trevor Hoffman	.05
428	Brian Johnson	.05
429	Wally Joyner	.05
430	Scott Livingstone	.05
431	Jody Reed	.05
432	Craig Shipley	.05
433	Fernando Valenzuela	.05
434	Greg Vaughn	.05
435	Rich Aurilia	.05
436	Kim Batiste	.05
437	Jose Bautista	.05
438	Rod Beck	.05
439	Marvin Benard	.05
440	Barry Bonds	2.50
441	Shawon Dunston	.05
442	Shawn Estes	.05
443	Osvaldo Fernandez	.05
444	Stan Javier	.05
445	David McCarty	.05
446	Bill Mueller RC	.15
447	Steve Scarsone	.05
448	Robby Thompson	.05
449	Rick Wilkins	.05
450	Matt Williams	.05

Light Blue

This parallel insert was produced exclusively for insertion in Wal-Mart/Sam's jumbo packs at the rate of one per pack. Following the format of the regular-issue, they use light blue foil, rather than the standard gold. Light blue inserts should not be confused with the much scarcer silver inserts which are visually similar.

	NM/M
Complete Set (450):	60.00
Common Player:	.25
Stars:	1X

Silver

This parallel insert was produced in an edition of only 67 cards per player. Following the format of the regular-issue, they use silver foil, rather than the standard gold. Silver parallels were inserted at an advertised rate of one per 73 packs. Silver inserts should not be confused with the much more common light blue inserts which are visually similar.

	NM/M
Common Player:	1.00
Stars/Rookies:	12X

Card-Supials

The 36-card, regular-sized set was inserted every 37 packs of 1997 Pacific Crown baseball. The

---

card fronts feature a gold-foil spiral with the player's name printed along a curve on the bottom edge. The team logo appears in the lower right corner. The card backs feature an action shot and are numbered "x of 36." The cards come with a mini (1-1/4" x 1-3/4") card that slides into a pocket on the back. The mini cards depict the same action shot as the larger card backs.

	NM/M
Complete Set (72):	80.00
Complete Large Set (36):	60.00
Complete Small Set (36):	45.00
Common Large:	.75

Small Cards: 75 Percent

1	Roberto Alomar	1.00
2	Brady Anderson	.75
3	Eddie Murray	2.00
4	Cal Ripken Jr.	5.00
5	Jose Canseco	1.00
6	Mo Vaughn	.75
7	Frank Thomas	2.00
8	Albert Belle	.75
9	Omar Vizquel	.75
10	Chuck Knoblauch	.75
11	Paul Molitor	2.00
12	Wade Boggs	2.50
13	Derek Jeter	5.00
14	Andy Pettitte	1.00
15	Mark McGwire	3.50
16	Jay Buhner	.75
17	Ken Griffey Jr.	5.00
18	Alex Rodriguez	3.50
19	Juan Gonzalez	1.00
20	Ivan Rodriguez	1.50
21	Andruw Jones	2.00
22	Chipper Jones	2.50
23	Ryan Klesko	.75
24	Greg Maddux	2.50
25	Ryne Sandberg	2.50
26	Andres Galarraga	.75
27	Gary Sheffield	1.00
28	Jeff Bagwell	2.00
29	Todd Hollandsworth	.75
30	Hideo Nomo	1.00
31	Mike Piazza	3.00
32	Todd Hundley	.75
33	Dennis Eckersley	1.50
34	Ken Caminiti	.75
35	Tony Gwynn	2.50
36	Barry Bonds	5.00

Cramer's Choice Awards

The 10-card, regular-sized set was inserted every 721 packs and features a die-cut pyramid design. A color player photo is imaged over silver foil with the player's name and position in gold foil over a green marble background along the bottom. The card backs feature a headshot with a brief career highlight in both Spanish and English. The cards are numbered with a "CC" prefix.

	NM/M
Complete Set (10):	75.00
Common Player:	4.50
1 Roberto Alomar	5.00
2 Frank Thomas	9.00
3 Albert Belle	4.50
4 Andy Pettitte	4.50

5	Ken Griffey Jr.	17.50
6	Alex Rodriguez	25.00
7	Chipper Jones	12.00
8	John Smoltz	4.50
9	Mike Piazza	15.00
10	Tony Gwynn	12.00

Fireworks Die-Cuts

The 20-card, regular-sized, die-cut set was inserted every 73 packs of 1997 Crown. The card fronts feature a color action shot with generic fireworks over a stadium on the upper half. The horizontal card backs contain close-up shots with highlights in Spanish and English. The cards are numbered with the "FW" prefix.

	NM/M
Complete Set (20):	40.00
Common Player:	.75
1 Roberto Alomar	1.00
2 Brady Anderson	.75
3 Eddie Murray	2.50
4 Cal Ripken Jr.	2.50
5 Frank Thomas	2.50
6 Albert Belle	.75
7 Derek Jeter	7.50
8 Andy Pettitte	1.00
9 Bernie Williams	.75
10 Mark McGwire	6.50
11 Ken Griffey Jr.	5.00
12 Alex Rodriguez	6.50
13 Juan Gonzalez	1.25
14 Andruw Jones	2.50
15 Chipper Jones	3.50
16 Hideo Nomo	1.25
17 Mike Piazza	5.00
18 Henry Rodriguez	.75
19 Tony Gwynn	3.50
20 Barry Bonds	7.50

Gold Crown Die-Cuts

The 36-card, regular-sized, die-cut set was inserted every 37 packs. The card fronts feature a die-cut, gold-foil crown on the top border and the player's name appears in gold along the bottom edge. The card backs contain a headshot and a Spanish/English highlight and are numbered with the "GC" prefix.

	NM/M
Complete Set (36):	65.00
Common Player:	1.00
1 Roberto Alomar	1.25
2 Brady Anderson	1.00
3 Mike Mussina	1.50
4 Eddie Murray	2.75
5 Cal Ripken Jr.	8.50
6 Jose Canseco	2.00
7 Frank Thomas	2.75
8 Albert Belle	1.50
9 Omar Vizquel	1.00
10 Wade Boggs	3.50
11 Derek Jeter	8.50
12 Andy Pettitte	1.25
13 Mariano Rivera	1.25
14 Bernie Williams	1.00
15 Mark McGwire	6.50
16 Ken Griffey Jr.	5.00
17 Edgar Martinez	1.00
18 Alex Rodriguez	6.50
19 Juan Gonzalez	1.50
20 Ivan Rodriguez	2.50

21	Andruw Jones	2.75
22	Chipper Jones	3.50
23	Ryan Klesko	1.00
24	John Smoltz	1.00
25	Ryne Sandberg	3.50
26	Andres Galarraga	1.00
27	Edgar Renteria	1.00
28	Jeff Bagwell	2.75
29	Todd Hollandsworth	1.00
30	Hideo Nomo	1.50
31	Mike Piazza	5.00
32	Todd Hundley	1.00
33	Brian Jordan	1.00
34	Ken Caminiti	1.00
35	Tony Gwynn	3.50
36	Barry Bonds	8.50

Latinos of the Major Leagues

The 36-card, regular-sized set was inserted twice every 37 packs. The card fronts feature a color action shot over the player's name in gold foil. The card backs have another action shot and a Spanish/English highlight.

	NM/M
Complete Set (36):	45.00
Common Player:	1.00
1 George Arias	1.00
2 Roberto Alomar	1.50
3 Rafael Palmeiro	2.50
4 Bobby Bonilla	1.00
5 Jose Canseco	1.00
6 Wilson Alvarez	1.00
7 Dave Martinez	1.00
8 Julio Franco	1.00
9 Manny Ramirez	3.00
10 Omar Vizquel	1.00
11 Marty Cordova	1.00
12 Roberto Kelly	1.00
13 Tino Martinez	1.00
14 Mariano Rivera	1.50
15 Ruben Rivera	1.00
16 Bernie Williams	1.00
17 Geronimo Berroa	1.00
18 Joey Cora	1.00
19 Edgar Martinez	1.00
20 Alex Rodriguez	6.00
21 Juan Gonzalez	2.00
22 Ivan Rodriguez	2.50
23 Andruw Jones	3.00
24 Javier Lopez	1.00
25 Sammy Sosa	4.50
26 Vinny Castilla	1.00
27 Andres Galarraga	1.00
28 Ramon Martinez	1.00
29 Raul Mondesi	1.00
30 Ismael Valdes	1.00
31 Pedro Martinez	3.00
32 Henry Rodriguez	1.00
33 Carlos Baerga	1.00
34 Rey Ordonez	1.00
35 Fernando Valenzuela	1.00
36 Osvaldo Fernandez	1.00

Triple Crown Die-Cuts

The 20-card, regular-sized, die-cut set was inserted every 145 packs of Crown baseball. The horizontal card fronts feature the same gold-foil, die-cut crown as on the Gold Crown Die-Cut inserts. The card backs feature a headshot, Spanish/English text and are numbered with the "TC" prefix.

	NM/M
Complete Set (20):	75.00
Common Player:	2.00
1 Brady Anderson	2.00
2 Rafael Palmeiro	4.00
3 Mo Vaughn	2.00
4 Frank Thomas	5.00
5 Albert Belle	2.00

6	Jim Thome	4.00
7	Cecil Fielder	2.00
8	Mark McGwire	10.00
9	Ken Griffey Jr.	7.50
10	Alex Rodriguez	10.00
11	Juan Gonzalez	3.00
12	Andruw Jones	5.00
13	Chipper Jones	6.00
14	Dante Bichette	2.00
15	Ellis Burks	2.00
16	Andres Galarraga	2.00
17	Jeff Bagwell	5.00
18	Mike Piazza	7.50
19	Ken Caminiti	2.00
20	Barry Bonds	12.50

1997 Pacific Invincible

The 1997 Pacific Invincible 150-card set was sold in three-card packs. The card fronts feature gold foil parallel lines with a color action shot. The bottom right quadrant contains a transparent cel headshot. The card backs have Spanish/English text and another color action shot. The reverse cel has the player's hat team logo air-brushed off to prevent reverse print. Insert sets are: Sluggers & Hurlers, Sizzling Lumber, Gate Attractions, Gems of the Diamond (2:1), and Light Blue (retail only) and Platinum (hobby) parallel sets of the 150 base cards.

	NM/M
Complete Set (150):	30.00
Common Player:	.25
Light Blues:	1X
Platinums:	2X
Pack (3):	1.00
Wax Box (36):	25.00
1 Chili Davis	.25
2 Jim Edmonds	.25
3 Darin Erstad	.50
4 Orlando Palmeiro	.25
5 Tim Salmon	.25
6 J.T. Snow	.25
7 Roberto Alomar	.50
8 Brady Anderson	.25
9 Eddie Murray	1.50
10 Mike Mussina	1.00
11 Rafael Palmeiro	1.25
12 Cal Ripken Jr.	4.00
13 Jose Canseco	1.00
14 Roger Clemens	2.50
15 Nomar Garciaparra	2.00
16 Reggie Jefferson	.25
17 Mo Vaughn	.25
18 Wilson Alvarez	.25
19 Harold Baines	.25
20 Alex Fernandez	.25
21 Danny Tartabull	.25
22 Frank Thomas	1.50
23 Robin Ventura	.25
24 Sandy Alomar Jr.	.25
25 Albert Belle	.25
26 Kenny Lofton	.25
27 Jim Thome	.75
28 Omar Vizquel	.25
29 Raul Casanova	.25
30 Tony Clark	.25
31 Travis Fryman	.25
32 Bobby Higginson	.25
33 Melvin Nieves	.25
34 Justin Thompson	.25
35 Johnny Damon	.50
36 Tom Goodwin	.25
37 Jeff Montgomery	.25
38 Jose Offerman	.25
39 John Jaha	.25
40 Jeff Cirillo	.25
41 Dave Nilsson	.25
42 Jose Valentin	.25
43 Fernando Vina	.25
44 Marty Cordova	.25
45 Roberto Kelly	.25
46 Chuck Knoblauch	.25
47 Paul Molitor	1.50
48 Todd Walker	.25
49 Wade Boggs	2.00
50 Cecil Fielder	.25
51 Derek Jeter	4.00
52 Tino Martinez	.25
53 Andy Pettitte	.40
54 Mariano Rivera	.40
55 Bernie Williams	.25

56	Tony Batista	.25
57	Geronimo Berroa	.25
58	Jason Giambi	.75
59	Mark McGwire	3.00
60	Terry Steinbach	.25
61	Jay Buhner	.25
62	Joey Cora	.25
63	Ken Griffey Jr.	2.50
64	Edgar Martinez	.25
65	Alex Rodriguez	3.00
66	Paul Sorrento	.25
67	Will Clark	.25
68	Juan Gonzalez	.75
69	Rusty Greer	.25
70	Dean Palmer	.25
71	Ivan Rodriguez	1.25
72	Joe Carter	.25
73	Carlos Delgado	.75
74	Juan Guzman	.25
75	Pat Hentgen	.25
76	Ed Sprague	.25
77	Jermaine Dye	.25
78	Andruw Jones	1.50
79	Chipper Jones	2.00
80	Ryan Klesko	.25
81	Javier Lopez	.25
82	Greg Maddux	2.00
83	John Smoltz	.25
84	Mark Grace	.25
85	Luis Gonzalez	.25
86	Brooks Kieschnick	.25
87	Jaime Navarro	.25
88	Ryne Sandberg	2.00
89	Sammy Sosa	2.00
90	Bret Boone	.25
91	Jeff Brantley	.25
92	Eric Davis	.25
93	Barry Larkin	.25
94	Reggie Sanders	.25
95	Ellis Burks	.25
96	Dante Bichette	.25
97	Vinny Castilla	.25
98	Andres Galarraga	.25
99	Eric Young	.25
100	Kevin Brown	.25
101	Jeff Conine	.25
102	Charles Johnson	.25
103	Edgar Renteria	.25
104	Gary Sheffield	.75
105	Jeff Bagwell	1.50
106	Derek Bell	.25
107	Sean Berry	.25
108	Craig Biggio	.25
109	Shane Reynolds	.25
110	Karim Garcia	.25
111	Todd Hollandsworth	.25
112	Ramon Martinez	.25
113	Raul Mondesi	.25
114	Hideo Nomo	.75
115	Mike Piazza	2.50
116	Ismael Valdes	.25
117	Moises Alou	.25
118	Mark Grudzielanek	.25
119	Pedro Martinez	1.50
120	Henry Rodriguez	.25
121	F.P. Santangelo	.25
122	Carlos Baerga	.25
123	Bernard Gilkey	.25
124	Todd Hundley	.25
125	Lance Johnson	.25
126	Alex Ochoa	.25
127	Rey Ordonez	.25
128	Lenny Dykstra	.25
129	Gregg Jefferies	.25
130	Ricky Otero	.25
131	Benito Santiago	.25
132	Jermaine Allensworth	.25
133	Francisco Cordova	.25
134	Carlos Garcia	.25
135	Jason Kendall	.25
136	Al Martin	.25
137	Dennis Eckersley	1.25
138	Ron Gant	.25
139	Brian Jordan	.25
140	John Mabry	.25
141	Ozzie Smith	2.00
142	Ken Caminiti	.25
143	Steve Finley	.25
144	Tony Gwynn	2.00
145	Wally Joyner	.25
146	Fernando Valenzuela	.25
147	Barry Bonds	4.00
148	Jacob Cruz	.25
149	Osvaldo Fernandez	.25
150	Matt Williams	.25

Gate Attractions

The 32-card, regular-sized set was inserted every 73 packs of Pacific Invincible baseball. The card fronts feature a generic baseball glove background with the player's name and position in a gold-foil circle. The center of the card is a cel action shot within a common baseball image. The player's team logo appears in the upper right corner. The card backs contain a headshot in the upper left corner with highlights in Spanish and English. The player's image in the cel is etched in gray in reverse. The cards are numbered with the "GA" prefix.

		NM/M
Complete Set (32):		80.00
Common Player:		1.00
1	Roberto Alomar	1.00
2	Brady Anderson	1.00
3	Cal Ripken Jr.	8.00
4	Frank Thomas	2.50
5	Kenny Lofton	1.00
6	Omar Vizquel	1.00
7	Paul Molitor	2.50
8	Wade Boggs	3.00
9	Derek Jeter	8.00
10	Andy Pettitte	1.50
11	Bernie Williams	1.00
12	Geronimo Berroa	1.00
13	Mark McGwire	6.00
14	Ken Griffey Jr.	4.50
15	Alex Rodriguez	6.00
16	Juan Gonzalez	1.50
17	Andruw Jones	2.50
18	Chipper Jones	3.00
19	Greg Maddux	3.00
20	Ryne Sandberg	3.00
21	Sammy Sosa	3.00
22	Andres Galarraga	1.00
23	Jeff Bagwell	2.50
24	Todd Hollandsworth	1.00
25	Hideo Nomo	1.50
26	Mike Piazza	4.50
27	Todd Hundley	1.00
28	Lance Johnson	1.00
29	Ozzie Smith	3.00
30	Ken Caminiti	1.00
31	Tony Gwynn	3.00
32	Barry Bonds	8.00

Gems of the Diamond

Essentially the base set for 1997 Pacific Prism Invincible, these cards are found two per three-card pack. Fronts of the 2-1/2" x 3-1/2" cards have action photos with earth-tone borders and a color team logo at bottom. Backs have a large player portrait photos in a diamond at right-center and are numbered with a "GD-" prefix.

		NM/M
Complete Set (220):		20.00
Common Player:		.10
1	Jim Abbott	.10
2	Shawn Boskie	.10
3	Gary DiSarcina	.10
4	Jim Edmonds	.10
5	Todd Greene	.10
6	Jack Howell	.10
7	Jeff Schmidt	.10
8	Shad Williams	.10
9	Roberto Alomar	.35
10	Cesar Devarez	.10
11	Alan Mills	.10
12	Eddie Murray	.75
13	Jesse Orosco	.10
14	Arthur Rhodes	.10
15	Bill Ripken	.10
16	Cal Ripken Jr.	2.50
17	Mark Smith	.10
18	Roger Clemens	1.50
19	Vaughn Eshelman	.10
20	Rich Garces	.10
21	Bill Haselman	.10
22	Dwayne Hosey	.10
23	Mike Maddux	.10
24	Jose Malave	.10
25	Aaron Sele	.10
26	James Baldwin	.10
27	Pat Borders	.10
28	Mike Cameron	.10

29	Tony Castillo	.10
30	Domingo Cedeno	.10
31	Greg Norton	.10
32	Frank Thomas	.75
33	Albert Belle	.10
34	Einar Diaz	.10
35	Alan Embree	.10
36	Albie Lopez	.10
37	Chad Ogea	.10
38	Tony Pena	.10
39	Joe Roa	.10
40	Fausto Cruz	.10
41	Joey Eischen	.10
42	Travis Fryman	.10
43	Mike Myers	.10
44	A.J. Sager	.10
45	Duane Singleton	.10
46	Justin Thompson	.10
47	Jeff Granger	.10
48	Les Norman	.10
49	Jon Nunnally	.10
50	Craig Paquette	.10
51	Michael Tucker	.10
52	Julio Valera	.10
53	Kevin Young	.10
54	Cal Eldred	.10
55	Ramon Garcia	.10
56	Marc Newfield	.10
57	Al Reyes	.10
58	Tim Unroe	.10
59	Tim Vanegmond	.10
60	Turner Ward	.10
61	Bob Wickman	.10
62	Chuck Knoblauch	.10
63	Paul Molitor	.75
64	Kirby Puckett	1.00
65	Tom Quinlan	.10
66	Rich Robertson	.10
67	Dave Stevens	.10
68	Matt Walbeck	.10
69	Wade Boggs	1.00
70	Tony Fernandez	.10
71	Andy Fox	.10
72	Joe Girardi	.10
73	Charlie Hayes	.10
74	Pat Kelly	.10
75	Jeff Nelson	.10
76	Melido Perez	.10
77	Mark Acre	.10
78	Allen Battle	.10
79	Rafael Bournigal	.10
80	Mark McGwire	2.00
81	Pedro Munoz	.10
82	Scott Spiezio	.10
83	Don Wengert	.10
84	Steve Wojciechowski	.10
85	Alex Diaz	.10
86	Ken Griffey Jr.	1.50
87	Raul Ibanez	.10
88	Mike Jackson	.10
89	John Marzano	.10
90	Greg McCarthy	.10
91	Alex Rodriguez	2.00
92	Andy Sheets	.10
93	Makoto Suzuki	.10
94	Benji Gil	.10
95	Juan Gonzalez	.40
96	Kevin Gross	.10
97	Gil Heredia	.10
98	Luis Ortiz	.10
99	Jeff Russell	.10
100	Dave Valle	.10
101	Marty Janzen	.10
102	Sandy Martinez	.10
103	Julio Mosquera	.10
104	Otis Nixon	.10
105	Paul Spoljaric	.10
106	Shannon Stewart	.10
107	Woody Williams	.10
108	Steve Avery	.10
109	Mike Bielecki	.10
110	Pedro Borbon	.10
111	Ed Giovanola	.10
112	Chipper Jones	1.00
113	Greg Maddux	1.00
114	Mike Mordecai	.10
115	Terrell Wade	.10
116	Terry Adams	.10
117	Brian Dorsett	.10
118	Doug Glanville	.10
119	Tyler Houston	.10
120	Robin Jennings	.10
121	Ryne Sandberg	1.00
122	Terry Shumpert	.10
123	Amaury Telemaco	.10
124	Steve Trachsel	.10
125	Curtis Goodwin	.10
126	Mike Kelly	.10
127	Chad Mottola	.10
128	Mark Portugal	.10
129	Roger Salkeld	.10
130	John Smiley	.10
131	Lee Smith	.10
132	Roger Bailey	.10
133	Andres Galarraga	.25
134	Darren Holmes	.10
135	Curtis Leskanic	.10
136	Mike Munoz	.10
137	Jeff Reed	.10
138	Mark Thompson	.10
139	Jamey Wright	.10
140	Andre Dawson	.25
141	Craig Grebeck	.10
142	Matt Mantei	.10
143	Billy McMillon	.10
144	Kurt Miller	.10
145	Ralph Milliard	.10
146	Bob Natal	.10

147	Joe Siddall	.10
148	Bob Abreu	.25
149	Doug Brocail	.10
150	Danny Darwin	.10
151	Mike Hampton	.10
152	Todd Jones	.10
153	Kirt Manwaring	.10
154	Alvin Morman	.10
155	Billy Ashley	.10
156	Tom Candiotti	.10
157	Darren Dreifort	.10
158	Greg Gagne	.10
159	Wilton Guerrero	.10
160	Hideo Nomo	.40
161	Mike Piazza	1.50
162	Tom Prince	.10
163	Todd Worrell	.10
164	Moises Alou	.10
165	Shane Andrews	.10
166	Derek Aucoin	.10
167	Raul Chavez	.10
168	Darrin Fletcher	.10
169	Mark Leiter	.10
170	Henry Rodriguez	.10
171	Dave Veres	.10
172	Paul Byrd	.10
173	Alberto Castillo	.10
174	Mark Clark	.10
175	Rey Ordonez	.10
176	Roberto Petagine	.10
177	Andy Tomberlin	.10
178	Derek Wallace	.10
179	Paul Wilson	.10
180	Ruben Amaro Jr.	.10
181	Toby Borland	.10
182	Rich Hunter	.10
183	Tony Longmire	.10
184	Wendell Magee Jr.	.10
185	Bobby Munoz	.10
186	Scott Rolen	.60
187	Mike Williams	.10
188	Trey Beamon	.10
189	Jason Christiansen	.10
190	Elmer Dessens	.10
191	Angelo Encarnacion	.10
192	Carlos Garcia	.10
193	Mike Kingery	.10
194	Chris Peters	.10
195	Tony Womack	.10
196	Brian Barber	.10
197	David Bell	.10
198	Tony Fossas	.10
199	Rick Honeycutt	.10
200	T.J. Mathews	.10
201	Miguel Mejia	.10
202	Donovan Osborne	.10
203	Ozzie Smith	1.00
204	Andres Berumen	.10
205	Ken Caminiti	.10
206	Chris Gwynn	.10
207	Tony Gwynn	1.00
208	Rickey Henderson	.75
209	Scott Sanders	.10
210	Jason Thompson	.10
211	Fernando Valenzuela	.10
212	Tim Worrell	.10
213	Barry Bonds	2.50
214	Jay Canizaro	.10
215	Doug Creek	.10
216	Jacob Cruz	.10
217	Glenallen Hill	.10
218	Tom Lampkin	.10
219	Jim Poole	.10
220	Desi Wilson	.10

Sizzling Lumber

The 36-card, regular-sized, die-cut set was inserted every 37 packs of Invincible. The cards have die-cut flames along the right border with a bat running parallel. The player's name appears in gold foil along the top border with his position in English and Spanish in gold foil along the bottom. The card backs feature a headshot in the upper half and contain Spanish and English text. The cards are numbered with the "SL" prefix.

		NM/M
Complete Set (36):		50.00
Common Player:		.50
1A	Cal Ripken Jr.	6.50
1B	Rafael Palmeiro	2.50
1C	Roberto Alomar	1.00
2A	Frank Thomas	3.00

2B	Robin Ventura	.50
2C	Harold Baines	.50
3A	Albert Belle	.50
3B	Manny Ramirez	3.00
3C	Kenny Lofton	.50
4A	Derek Jeter	6.50
4B	Bernie Williams	.50
4C	Wade Boggs	3.50
5A	Mark McGwire	5.00
5B	Jason Giambi	2.00
5C	Geronimo Berroa	.50
6A	Ken Griffey Jr.	4.00
6B	Alex Rodriguez	5.00
6C	Jay Buhner	.50
7A	Juan Gonzalez	1.50
7B	Dean Palmer	.50
7C	Ivan Rodriguez	2.50
8A	Ryan Klesko	.50
8B	Chipper Jones	3.50
8C	Andruw Jones	3.00
9A	Dante Bichette	.50
9B	Andres Galarraga	.50
10A	Vinny Castilla	.50
10B	Jeff Bagwell	3.00
10C	Craig Biggio	.50
10C	Derek Bell	.50
11A	Mike Piazza	4.00
11B	Raul Mondesi	.50
11C	Karim Garcia	.50
12A	Tony Gwynn	3.50
12B	Ken Caminiti	.50
12C	Greg Vaughn	.50

Sluggers & Hurlers

The 24-card, regular-sized set was inserted every 145 packs of Pacific Invincible baseball. The cards are numbered with an "SH-xA" or "SH-xaB". Each "A" card is the left half of a two-card set with the two players from the same team having their logo in the fit-together center. Each card has the player's name printed in gold foil along the bottom border with gold-foil swirls around the team logo. The card backs have a circular headshot with text in English and Spanish.

		NM/M
Complete Set (24):		80.00
Common Player:		2.00
SH-1a	Cal Ripken Jr.	10.00
SH-1b	Mike Mussina	2.50
SH-2a	Jose Canseco	2.50
SH-2b	Roger Clemens	6.00
SH-3a	Frank Thomas	3.50
SH-3b	Wilson Alvarez	2.00
SH-4a	Kenny Lofton	2.00
SH-4b	Orel Hershiser	2.00
SH-5a	Derek Jeter	10.00
SH-5b	Andy Pettitte	2.00
SH-6a	Ken Griffey Jr.	6.00
SH-6b	Randy Johnson	3.50
SH-7a	Alex Rodriguez	7.50
SH-7b	Jamie Moyer	2.00
SH-8a	Andruw Jones	3.50
SH-8b	Greg Maddux	4.50
SH-9a	Chipper Jones	4.50
SH-9b	John Smoltz	2.00
SH-10a	Jeff Bagwell	3.50
SH-10b	Shane Reynolds	2.00
SH-11a	Mike Piazza	6.00
SH-11b	Hideo Nomo	2.50
SH-12a	Tony Gwynn	4.50
SH-12b	Fernando Valenzuela	2.00

Carlos Baerga Celebrities Softball

This set was produced for distribution to fans attending the third annual Carlos Baerga Celebrities Softball Game in Puerto Rico on December 14. Packs were handed out containing two cards from this set, a 1997 Pacific Crown Collection card, a '97 Pacific Invincible card, a Pacific logo card and an information card about card shops on the island. The softball celebrities cards have gold-foil highlighted borderless action photos from the 1996 game. Pacific and the charity game's logos are in upper-

right and lower left. Horizontal backs have a player portrait photo at left and English/Spanish description of his participation in the event.

		NM/M
Complete Set (10):		16.00
Common Player:		1.00
1	Carlos Baerga	1.00
2	Bernie Williams	1.00
3	Ivan Rodriguez	5.00
4	Sandy Alomar Jr.	2.00
5	Joey Cora	1.00
6	Roberto Alomar	1.50
7	Moises Alou	1.00
8	Rey Ordonez	1.00
9	Derek Jeter	10.00
10	David Justice	1.00

NationsBank Florida Marlins

Certainly one of the nicest team card sets ever given away at a promotional game was this Marlins set produced by Pacific and sponsored by NationsBank. The cello-wrapped set was given out to the first 16,000 children attending the June 27 Marlins game. The 2-1/2" x 3-1/2" cards are UV-coated on both sides with a gold-foil "wave" containing the player names on front. The producer, sponsor and team logos also appear on front. Backs have a swirling teal background with a player color portrait in the upper-right. Personal data, 1996 and career stats and a short career summary - in both English and Spanish - are also found on back.

		NM/M
Complete Set (33):		6.00
Common Player:		.25
1	Kurt Abbott	.25
2	Moises Alou	.25
3	Alex Arias	.25
4	Bobby Bonilla	.25
5	Kevin Brown	.25
6	John Cangelosi	.25
7	Luis Castillo	.25
8	Jeff Conine	.25
9	Jim Eisenreich	.25
10	Alex Fernandez	.25
11	Cliff Floyd	.25
12	Rick Helling	.25
13	Felix Heredia	.25
14	Mark Hutton	.25
15	Charles Johnson	.25
16	Al Leiter	.25
17	Robb Nen	.25
18	Jay Powell	.25
19	Pat Rapp	.25
20	Edgar Renteria	.25
21	Tony Saunders	.25
22	Gary Sheffield	.75
23	Devon White	.25
24	Gregg Zaun	.25
25	Jim Leyland	.25
26	Rich Donnelly	.25
27	Bruce Kimm	.25
28	Jerry Manuel	.25
29	Milt May	.25
30	Larry Rothschild	.25
31	Tommy Sandt	.25
32	Billy the Marlin (Mascot)	.25
(33)	Header Card/Checklist	.10

1998 Pacific

Pacific Baseball for 1998 is a 450-card, bilingual set. The base set features full-bleed photos with the Pacific Crown Collection logo in the upper-left and the player's name, position and team at the bottom. Inserts include Cramer's Choice Awards, In The Cage Laser-Cuts, Home Run Hitters, Team Checklist Laser-Cuts, Gold Crown Die-Cuts and Latinos of the Major Leagues. Three foil-color parallels were issued: Reds were found one per Wal-Mart exclusive retail pack; Silvers were found one per Hobby pack. Platinum Blues, numbered to 67 each, were found one per 73 packs.

		NM/M
Complete Set (450):		40.00
Common Player:		.05
Silvers:		3X
Inserted 1:1 H		
Reds:		6X
Inserted 1:1 R		
Platinum Blues:		15X
Inserted 1:73		
Pack (12):		1.00
Wax Box (36):		20.00
1	Luis Alicea	.05
2	Garret Anderson	.05
3	Jason Dickson	.05
4	Gary DiSarcina	.05
5	Jim Edmonds	.15
6	Darin Erstad	.05
7	Chuck Finley	.05
8	Shigetosi Hasegawa	.05
9	Rickey Henderson	.75
10	Dave Hollins	.05
11	Mark Langston	.05
12	Orlando Palmeiro	.05
13	Troy Percival	.05
14	Tony Phillips	.05
15	Tim Salmon	.05
16	Allen Watson	.05
17	Roberto Alomar	.25
18	Brady Anderson	.05
19	Harold Baines	.05
20	Armando Benitez	.05
21	Geronimo Berroa	.05
22	Mike Bordick	.05
23	Eric Davis	.05
24	Scott Erickson	.05
25	Chris Hoiles	.05
26	Jimmy Key	.05
27	Aaron Ledesma	.05
28	Mike Mussina	.50
29	Randy Myers	.05
30	Jesse Orosco	.05
31	Rafael Palmeiro	.65
32	Jeff Reboulet	.05
33	Cal Ripken Jr.	2.00
34	B.J. Surhoff	.05
35	Steve Avery	.05
36	Darren Bragg	.05
37	Wil Cordero	.05
38	Jeff Frye	.05
39	Nomar Garciaparra	1.00
40	Tom Gordon	.05
41	Bill Haselman	.05
42	Scott Hatteberg	.05
43	Butch Henry	.05
44	Reggie Jefferson	.05
45	Tim Naehring	.05
46	Troy O'Leary	.05
47	Jeff Suppan	.05
48	John Valentin	.05
49	Mo Vaughn	.25
50	Tim Wakefield	.05
51	James Baldwin	.05
52	Albert Belle	.25
53	Tony Castillo	.05
54	Doug Drabek	.05
55	Ray Durham	.05
56	Jorge Fabregas	.05
57	Ozzie Guillen	.05
58	Matt Karchner	.05
59	Norberto Martin	.05
60	Dave Martinez	.05
61	Lyle Mouton	.05
62	Jaime Navarro	.05
63	Frank Thomas	.75
64	Mario Valdez	.05

No.	Player	Price
65	Robin Ventura	.05
66	Sandy Alomar Jr.	.05
67	Paul Assenmacher	.05
68	Tony Fernandez	.05
69	Brian Giles	.05
70	Marquis Grissom	.05
71	Orel Hershiser	.05
72	Mike Jackson	.05
73	David Justice	.05
74	Albie Lopez	.05
75	Jose Mesa	.05
76	Charles Nagy	.05
77	Chad Ogea	.05
78	Manny Ramirez	.75
79	Jim Thome	.60
80	Omar Vizquel	.05
81	Matt Williams	.05
82	Jaret Wright	.05
83	Willie Blair	.05
84	Raul Casanova	.05
85	Tony Clark	.05
86	Deivi Cruz	.05
87	Damion Easley	.05
88	Travis Fryman	.05
89	Bobby Higginson	.05
90	Brian Hunter	.05
91	Todd Jones	.05
92	Dan Miceli	.05
93	Brian Moehler	.05
94	Melvin Nieves	.05
95	Jody Reed	.05
96	Justin Thompson	.05
97	Bubba Trammell	.05
98	Kevin Appier	.05
99	Jay Bell	.05
100	Yamil Benitez	.05
101	Johnny Damon	.35
102	Chili Davis	.05
103	Jermaine Dye	.05
104	Jed Hansen	.05
105	Jeff King	.05
106	Mike Macfarlane	.05
107	Felix Martinez	.05
108	Jeff Montgomery	.05
109	Jose Offerman	.05
110	Dean Palmer	.05
111	Hipolito Pichardo	.05
112	Jose Rosado	.05
113	Jeromy Burnitz	.05
114	Jeff Cirillo	.05
115	Cal Eldred	.05
116	John Jaha	.05
117	Doug Jones	.05
118	Scott Karl	.05
119	Jesse Levis	.05
120	Mark Loretta	.05
121	Ben McDonald	.05
122	Jose Mercedes	.05
123	Matt Mieske	.05
124	Dave Nilsson	.05
125	Jose Valentin	.05
126	Fernando Vina	.05
127	Gerald Williams	.05
128	Rick Aguilera	.05
129	Rich Becker	.05
130	Ron Coomer	.05
131	Marty Cordova	.05
132	Eddie Guardado	.05
133	LaTroy Hawkins	.05
134	Denny Hocking	.05
135	Chuck Knoblauch	.05
136	Matt Lawton	.05
137	Pat Meares	.05
138	Paul Molitor	.75
139	David Ortiz	.50
140	Brad Radke	.05
141	Terry Steinbach	.05
142	Bob Tewksbury	.05
143	Javier Valentin	.05
144	Wade Boggs	1.00
145	David Cone	.05
146	Chad Curtis	.05
147	Cecil Fielder	.05
148	Joe Girardi	.05
149	Dwight Gooden	.05
150	Hideki Irabu	.05
151	Derek Jeter	2.00
152	Tino Martinez	.05
153	Ramiro Mendoza	.05
154	Paul O'Neill	.05
155	Andy Pettitte	.20
156	Jorge Posada	.05
157	Mariano Rivera	.15
158	Rey Sanchez	.05
159	Luis Sojo	.05
160	David Wells	.05
161	Bernie Williams	.05
162	Rafael Bournigal	.05
163	Scott Brosius	.05
164	Jose Canseco	.50
165	Jason Giambi	.60
166	Ben Grieve	.05
167	Dave Magadan	.05
168	Brent Mayne	.05
169	Jason McDonald	.05
170	Izzy Molina	.05
171	Ariel Prieto	.05
172	Carlos Reyes	.05
173	Scott Spiezio	.05
174	Matt Stairs	.05
175	Bill Taylor	.05
176	Dave Telgheder	.05
177	Steve Wojciechowski	.05
178	Rich Amaral	.05
179	Bobby Ayala	.05
180	Jay Buhner	.05
181	Rafael Carmona	.05
182	Ken Cloude	.05
183	Joey Cora	.05
184	Russ Davis	.05
185	Jeff Fassero	.05
186	Ken Griffey Jr.	1.25
187	Raul Ibanez	.05
188	Randy Johnson	.75
189	Roberto Kelly	.05
190	Edgar Martinez	.05
191	Jamie Moyer	.05
192	Omar Olivares	.05
193	Alex Rodriguez	1.50
194	Heathcliff Slocumb	.05
195	Paul Sorrento	.05
196	Dan Wilson	.05
197	Scott Bailes	.05
198	John Burkett	.05
199	Domingo Cedeno	.05
200	Will Clark	.05
201	Hanley Frias RC	.05
202	Juan Gonzalez	.40
203	Tom Goodwin	.05
204	Rusty Greer	.05
205	Wilson Heredia	.05
206	Darren Oliver	.05
207	Billy Ripken	.05
208	Ivan Rodriguez	.65
209	Lee Stevens	.05
210	Fernando Tatis	.05
211	John Wetteland	.05
212	Bobby Witt	.05
213	Jacob Brumfield	.05
214	Joe Carter	.05
215	Roger Clemens	1.25
216	Felipe Crespo	.05
217	Jose Cruz Jr.	.50
218	Carlos Delgado	.50
219	Mariano Duncan	.05
220	Carlos Garcia	.05
221	Alex Gonzalez	.05
222	Juan Guzman	.05
223	Pat Hentgen	.05
224	Orlando Merced	.05
225	Tomas Perez	.05
226	Paul Quantrill	.05
227	Benito Santiago	.05
228	Woody Williams	.05
229	Rafael Belliard	.05
230	Jeff Blauser	.05
231	Pedro Borbon	.05
232	Tom Glavine	.25
233	Tony Graffanino	.05
234	Andruw Jones	.75
235	Chipper Jones	1.00
236	Ryan Klesko	.05
237	Mark Lemke	.05
238	Kenny Lofton	.05
239	Javier Lopez	.05
240	Fred McGriff	.05
241	Greg Maddux	1.00
242	Denny Neagle	.05
243	John Smoltz	.05
244	Michael Tucker	.05
245	Mark Wohlers	.05
246	Manny Alexander	.05
247	Miguel Batista	.05
248	Mark Clark	.05
249	Doug Glanville	.05
250	Jeremi Gonzalez	.05
251	Mark Grace	.05
252	Jose Hernandez	.05
253	Lance Johnson	.05
254	Brooks Kieschnick	.05
255	Kevin Orie	.05
256	Ryne Sandberg	1.00
257	Scott Servais	.05
258	Sammy Sosa	1.00
259	Kevin Tapani	.05
260	Ramon Tatis	.05
261	Bret Boone	.05
262	Dave Burba	.05
263	Brook Fordyce	.05
264	Willie Greene	.05
265	Barry Larkin	.05
266	Pedro A. Martinez	.05
267	Hal Morris	.05
268	Joe Oliver	.05
269	Eduardo Perez	.05
270	Pokey Reese	.05
271	Felix Rodriguez	.05
272	Deion Sanders	.25
273	Reggie Sanders	.05
274	Jeff Shaw	.05
275	Scott Sullivan	.05
276	Brett Tomko	.05
277	Roger Bailey	.05
278	Dante Bichette	.05
279	Ellis Burks	.05
280	Vinny Castilla	.05
281	Frank Castillo	.05
282	Mike DeJean RC	.05
283	Andres Galarraga	.05
284	Darren Holmes	.05
285	Kirt Manwaring	.05
286	Quinton McCracken	.05
287	Neifi Perez	.05
288	Steve Reed	.05
289	John Thomson	.05
290	Larry Walker	.05
291	Walt Weiss	.05
292	Kurt Abbott	.05
293	Antonio Alfonseca	.05
294	Moises Alou	.05
295	Alex Arias	.05
296	Bobby Bonilla	.05
297	Kevin Brown	.05
298	Craig Counsell	.05
299	Darren Daulton	.05
300	Jim Eisenreich	.05
301	Alex Fernandez	.05
302	Felix Heredia	.05
303	Livan Hernandez	.05
304	Charles Johnson	.05
305	Al Leiter	.05
306	Robb Nen	.05
307	Edgar Renteria	.05
308	Gary Sheffield	.45
309	Devon White	.05
310	Bob Abreu	.10
311	Brad Ausmus	.05
312	Jeff Bagwell	.75
313	Derek Bell	.05
314	Sean Berry	.05
315	Craig Biggio	.05
316	Ramon Garcia	.05
317	Luis Gonzalez	.05
318	Ricky Gutierrez	.05
319	Mike Hampton	.05
320	Richard Hidalgo	.05
321	Thomas Howard	.05
322	Darryl Kile	.05
323	Jose Lima	.05
324	Shane Reynolds	.05
325	Bill Spiers	.05
326	Tom Candiotti	.05
327	Roger Cedeno	.05
328	Greg Gagne	.05
329	Karim Garcia	.05
330	Wilton Guerrero	.05
331	Todd Hollandsworth	.05
332	Eric Karros	.05
333	Ramon Martinez	.05
334	Raul Mondesi	.05
335	Otis Nixon	.05
336	Hideo Nomo	.40
337	Antonio Osuna	.05
338	Chan Ho Park	.05
339	Mike Piazza	1.25
340	Dennis Reyes	.05
341	Ismael Valdes	.05
342	Todd Worrell	.05
343	Todd Zeile	.05
344	Darrin Fletcher	.05
345	Mark Grudzielanek	.05
346	Vladimir Guerrero	.75
347	Dustin Hermanson	.05
348	Mike Lansing	.05
349	Pedro Martinez	.75
350	Ryan McGuire	.05
351	Jose Paniagua	.05
352	Carlos Perez	.05
353	Henry Rodriguez	.05
354	F.P. Santangelo	.05
355	David Segui	.05
356	Ugueth Urbina	.05
357	Marc Valdes	.05
358	Jose Vidro	.05
359	Rondell White	.05
360	Juan Acevedo	.05
361	Edgardo Alfonzo	.05
362	Carlos Baerga	.05
363	Carl Everett	.05
364	John Franco	.05
365	Bernard Gilkey	.05
366	Todd Hundley	.05
367	Butch Huskey	.05
368	Bobby Jones	.05
369	Takashi Kashiwada	.05
370	Greg McMichael	.05
371	Brian McRae	.05
372	Alex Ochoa	.05
373	John Olerud	.05
374	Rey Ordonez	.05
375	Turk Wendell	.05
376	Ricky Bottalico	.05
377	Rico Brogna	.05
378	Lenny Dykstra	.05
379	Bobby Estalella	.05
380	Wayne Gomes	.05
381	Tyler Green	.05
382	Gregg Jefferies	.05
383	Mark Leiter	.05
384	Mike Lieberthal	.05
385	Mickey Morandini	.05
386	Scott Rolen	.60
387	Curt Schilling	.25
388	Kevin Stocker	.05
389	Danny Tartabull	.05
390	Jermaine Allensworth	.05
391	Adrian Brown	.05
392	Jason Christiansen	.05
393	Steve Cooke	.05
394	Francisco Cordova	.05
395	Jose Guillen	.05
396	Jason Kendall	.05
397	Jon Lieber	.05
398	Esteban Loaiza	.05
399	Al Martin	.05
400	Kevin Polcovich RC	.05
401	Joe Randa	.05
402	Ricardo Rincon	.05
403	Tony Womack	.05
404	Kevin Young	.05
405	Andy Benes	.05
406	Royce Clayton	.05
407	Delino DeShields	.05
408	Mike Difelice	.05
409	Dennis Eckersley	.60
410	John Frascatore	.05
411	Gary Gaetti	.05
412	Ron Gant	.05
413	Brian Jordan	.05
414	Ray Lankford	.05
415	Willie McGee	.05
416	Mark McGwire	1.50
417	Matt Morris	.05
418	Luis Ordaz	.05
419	Todd Stottlemyre	.05
420	Andy Ashby	.05
421	Jim Bruske	.05
422	Ken Caminiti	.05
423	Will Cunnane	.05
424	Steve Finley	.05
425	John Flaherty	.05
426	Chris Gomez	.05
427	Tony Gwynn	1.00
428	Joey Hamilton	.05
429	Carlos Hernandez	.05
430	Sterling Hitchcock	.05
431	Trevor Hoffman	.05
432	Wally Joyner	.05
433	Greg Vaughn	.05
434	Quilvio Veras	.05
435	Wilson Alvarez	.05
436	Rod Beck	.05
437	Barry Bonds	2.00
438	Jacob Cruz	.05
439	Shawn Estes	.05
440	Darryl Hamilton	.05
441	Roberto Hernandez	.05
442	Glenallen Hill	.05
443	Stan Javier	.05
444	Brian Johnson	.05
445	Jeff Kent	.05
446	Bill Mueller	.05
447	Kirk Rueter	.05
448	J.T. Snow	.05
449	Julian Tavarez	.05
450	Jose Vizcaino	.05

Red/Silver/Blue

Red, Silver and Platinum Blue parallels were printed for all 450 cards in Pacific, with the gold foil found on base cards being replaced by one of those foils. Red foil versions were inserted one per Wal-Mart pack (retail). Silver versions were inserted one per hobby pack. Platinum Blues, limited to 67 sets, were a one per 73 pack insert.

	NM/M
Common Red:	1.50
Red Stars:	6X
Common Silver:	.75
Silver Stars:	3X
Common Platinum Blue:	3.00
Platinum Blue Stars:	15X

Cramer's Choice

Cramer's Choice Awards is a 10-card die-cut insert. The cards feature the top player at each position as selected by Pacific CEO Mike Cramer. Each card is shaped like a trophy.

		NM/M
Complete Set (10):		150.00
Common Player:		7.50
Inserted 1:721		
1	Greg Maddux	15.00
2	Roberto Alomar	7.50
3	Cal Ripken Jr.	30.00
4	Nomar Garciaparra	15.00
5	Larry Walker	7.50
6	Mike Piazza	17.50
7	Mark McGwire	25.00
8	Tony Gwynn	15.00
9	Ken Griffey Jr.	20.00
10	Roger Clemens	17.50

Gold Crown Die-Cuts

Gold Crown Die-Cuts is a 36-card insert seeded one per 37 packs. Each card has a holographic silver foil background and gold etching. The cards are die-cut around a crown design at the top.

		NM/M
Complete Set (36):		85.00
Common Player:		1.50
1	Chipper Jones	4.00
2	Greg Maddux	4.00
3	Denny Neagle	1.50
4	Roberto Alomar	2.00
5	Rafael Palmeiro	2.50
6	Cal Ripken Jr.	8.00
7	Nomar Garciaparra	4.00
8	Mo Vaughn	1.50
9	Frank Thomas	3.00
10	Sandy Alomar Jr.	1.50
11	David Justice	1.50
12	Manny Ramirez	3.00
13	Andres Galarraga	1.50
14	Larry Walker	1.50
15	Moises Alou	1.50
16	Livan Hernandez	1.50
17	Gary Sheffield	2.00
18	Jeff Bagwell	3.00
19	Raul Mondesi	1.50
20	Hideo Nomo	2.00
21	Mike Piazza	4.50
22	Derek Jeter	8.00
23	Tino Martinez	1.50
24	Bernie Williams	1.50
25	Ben Grieve	1.50
26	Mark McGwire	6.50
27	Tony Gwynn	4.00
28	Barry Bonds	8.00
29	Ken Griffey Jr.	5.00
30	Randy Johnson	3.00
31	Edgar Martinez	1.50
32	Alex Rodriguez	6.50
33	Juan Gonzalez	2.00
34	Ivan Rodriguez	2.50
35	Roger Clemens	4.50
36	Jose Cruz Jr.	1.50

Home Run Hitters

This 20-card set was inserted one per 73 packs. The full-foil cards feature a color player photo with their home run total from 1997 embossed in the background.

		NM/M
Complete Set (20):		50.00
Common Player:		1.00
1	Rafael Palmeiro	3.00
2	Mo Vaughn	1.00
3	Sammy Sosa	4.00
4	Albert Belle	1.00
5	Frank Thomas	3.50
6	David Justice	1.00
7	Jim Thome	3.00
8	Matt Williams	1.00
9	Vinny Castilla	1.00
10	Andres Galarraga	1.00
11	Larry Walker	1.00
12	Jeff Bagwell	3.50
13	Mike Piazza	4.50
14	Tino Martinez	1.00
15	Mark McGwire	6.00
16	Barry Bonds	7.50
17	Jay Buhner	1.00
18	Ken Griffey Jr.	5.00
19	Alex Rodriguez	6.00
20	Juan Gonzalez	6.00

In the Cage

This insert set features top players in a die-cut batting cage. The netting on the cage is laser-cut. In The Cage laser-cuts were inserted one per 145 packs.

		NM/M
Complete Set (20):		175.00
Common Player:		4.00
1	Chipper Jones	12.00
2	Roberto Alomar	4.00
3	Cal Ripken Jr.	25.00
4	Nomar Garciaparra	12.00
5	Frank Thomas	10.00
6	Sandy Alomar Jr.	4.00
7	David Justice	4.00
8	Larry Walker	4.00
9	Bobby Bonilla	4.00
10	Mike Piazza	16.00
11	Tino Martinez	4.00
12	Bernie Williams	4.00
13	Mark McGwire	20.00
14	Tony Gwynn	12.00
15	Barry Bonds	25.00
16	Ken Griffey Jr.	16.00
17	Edgar Martinez	4.00
18	Alex Rodriguez	20.00
19	Juan Gonzalez	6.00
20	Ivan Rodriguez	7.50

Latinos of the Major Leagues

This 36-card set features Major League players of Hispanic descent. The background has a world map on the left, the player's team logo in the center and an American flag on the right.

		NM/M
Complete Set (36):		30.00
Common Player:		.50
Inserted 2:37		
1	Andruw Jones	2.50
2	Javier Lopez	.50
3	Roberto Alomar	1.25
4	Geronimo Berroa	.50
5	Rafael Palmeiro	2.00
6	Nomar Garciaparra	3.00
7	Sammy Sosa	3.00
8	Ozzie Guillen	.50
9	Sandy Alomar Jr.	.50
10	Manny Ramirez	2.50
11	Omar Vizquel	.50
12	Vinny Castilla	.50
13	Andres Galarraga	.50
14	Moises Alou	.50
15	Bobby Bonilla	.50
16	Livan Hernandez	.50
17	Edgar Renteria	.50
18	Wilton Guerrero	.50
19	Raul Mondesi	.50
20	Ismael Valdes	.50
21	Fernando Vina	.50
22	Pedro Martinez	2.50
23	Edgardo Alfonzo	.50
24	Carlos Baerga	.50
25	Rey Ordonez	.50
26	Tino Martinez	.50
27	Mariano Rivera	1.00
28	Bernie Williams	.50
29	Jose Canseco	1.50
30	Joey Cora	.50
31	Roberto Kelly	.50
32	Edgar Martinez	.50
33	Alex Rodriguez	3.50
34	Juan Gonzalez	1.50
35	Ivan Rodriguez	2.00
36	Jose Cruz Jr.	.50

Team Checklists

Team Checklists is a 30-card insert in the bilingual Pacific Baseball set. One card was created for each team. A player photo is featured on the right with the team logo laser-cut into a bat barrel design on the left.

		NM/M
Complete Set (30):		60.00
Common Player:		.50
1	Tim Salmon, Jim Edmonds	.50
2	Cal Ripken Jr., Roberto Alomar	6.00
3	Nomar Garciaparra, Mo Vaughn	3.50
4	Frank Thomas, Albert Belle	2.50
5	Sandy Alomar Jr., Manny Ramirez	2.50

6	Justin Thompson, Tony Clark	.50
7	Johnny Damon, Jermaine Dye	.75
8	Dave Nilsson, Jeff Cirillo	.50
9	Paul Molitor, Chuck Knoblauch	2.50
10	Tino Martinez, Derek Jeter	6.00
11	Ben Grieve, Jose Canseco	1.00
12	Ken Griffey Jr., Alex Rodriguez	5.00
13	Juan Gonzalez, Ivan Rodriguez	2.00
14	Jose Cruz Jr., Roger Clemens	4.00
15	Greg Maddux, Chipper Jones	3.50
16	Sammy Sosa, Mark Grace	3.50
17	Barry Larkin, Deion Sanders	.50
18	Larry Walker, Andres Galarraga	.50
19	Moises Alou, Bobby Bonilla	2.50
20	Jeff Bagwell, Craig Biggio	2.50
21	Mike Piazza, Hideo Nomo	4.00
22	Pedro Martinez, Henry Rodriguez	2.50
23	Rey Ordonez, Carlos Baerga	.50
24	Curt Schilling, Scott Rolen	1.50
25	Al Martin, Tony Womack	.50
26	Mark McGwire, Dennis Eckersley	5.00
27	Tony Gwynn, Wally Joyner	3.50
28	Barry Bonds, J.T. Snow	6.00
29	Matt Williams, Jay Bell	.50
30	Fred McGriff, Roberto Hernandez	.50

1998 Pacific Aurora

The Aurora base set consists of 200 cards printed on 24-point board. The cards have a color photo bordered on two sides by a thick green (National League) or red (A.L.) border. A portrait photo appears in the upper-right corner. Back has another portrait photo, 1997 and career stats, career highlights and personal data. Aurora was sold in six-card foil packs. Inserts include Pennant Fever (with three parallels), Hardball Cel-Fusions, Kings of the Major Leagues, On Deck Laser-Cuts and Pacific Cubes.

		NM/M
	Complete Set (200):	20.00
	Common Player:	.05
	Pack (6):	1.00
	Wax Box (36):	20.00
1	Garret Anderson	.05
2	Jim Edmonds	.05
3	Darin Erstad	.15
4	Cecil Fielder	.05
5	Chuck Finley	.05
6	Todd Greene	.05
7	Ken Hill	.05
8	Tim Salmon	.05
9	Roberto Alomar	.20
10	Brady Anderson	.05
11	Joe Carter	.05
12	Mike Mussina	.35
13	Rafael Palmeiro	.65
14	Cal Ripken Jr.	2.50
15	B.J. Surhoff	.05
16	Steve Avery	.05
17	Nomar Garciaparra	1.00
18	Pedro Martinez	.75
19	John Valentin	.05
20	Jason Varitek	.05
21	Mo Vaughn	.05
22	Albert Belle	.05
23	Ray Durham	.05
24	Magglio Ordonez RC	1.50
25	Frank Thomas	.75
26	Robin Ventura	.05
27	Sandy Alomar Jr.	.05
28	Travis Fryman	.05
29	Dwight Gooden	.05
30	David Justice	.05
31	Kenny Lofton	.05
32	Manny Ramirez	.75
33	Jim Thome	.60
34	Omar Vizquel	.05
35	Enrique Wilson	.05
36	Jaret Wright	.05
37	Tony Clark	.05
38	Bobby Higginson	.05
39	Brian Hunter	.05
40	Bip Roberts	.05
41	Justin Thompson	.05
42	Jeff Conine	.05
43	Johnny Damon	.35
44	Jermaine Dye	.05
45	Jeff King	.05
46	Jeff Montgomery	.05
47	Hal Morris	.05
48	Dean Palmer	.05
49	Terry Pendleton	.05
50	Rick Aguilera	.05
51	Marty Cordova	.05
52	Paul Molitor	.75
53	Otis Nixon	.05
54	Brad Radke	.05
55	Terry Steinbach	.05
56	Todd Walker	.05
57	Chili Davis	.05
58	Derek Jeter	2.50
59	Chuck Knoblauch	.05
60	Tino Martinez	.05
61	Paul O'Neill	.05
62	Andy Pettitte	.20
63	Mariano Rivera	.15
64	Bernie Williams	.05
65	Jason Giambi	.50
66	Ben Grieve	.05
67	Rickey Henderson	.75
68	A.J. Hinch	.05
69	Kenny Rogers	.05
70	Jay Buhner	.05
71	Joey Cora	.05
72	Ken Griffey Jr.	1.50
73	Randy Johnson	.75
74	Edgar Martinez	.05
75	Jamie Moyer	.05
76	Alex Rodriguez	2.00
77	David Segui	.05
78	Rolando Arrojo RC	.35
79	Wade Boggs	1.00
80	Roberto Hernandez	.05
81	Dave Martinez	.05
82	Fred McGriff	.05
83	Paul Sorrento	.05
84	Kevin Stocker	.05
85	Will Clark	.05
86	Juan Gonzalez	.40
87	Tom Goodwin	.05
88	Rusty Greer	.05
89	Ivan Rodriguez	.65
90	John Wetteland	.05
91	Jose Canseco	.40
92	Roger Clemens	1.25
93	Jose Cruz Jr.	.05
94	Carlos Delgado	.50
95	Pat Hentgen	.05
96	Jay Bell	.05
97	Andy Benes	.05
98	Karim Garcia	.05
99	Travis Lee	.05
100	Devon White	.05
101	Matt Williams	.05
102	Andres Galarraga	.05
103	Tom Glavine	.30
104	Andruw Jones	.75
105	Chipper Jones	1.00
106	Ryan Klesko	.05
107	Javy Lopez	.05
108	Greg Maddux	1.00
109	Walt Weiss	.05
110	Rod Beck	.05
111	Jeff Blauser	.05
112	Mark Grace	.05
113	Lance Johnson	.05
114	Mickey Morandini	.05
115	Henry Rodriguez	.05
116	Sammy Sosa	1.00
117	Kerry Wood	.35
118	Lenny Harris	.05
119	Damian Jackson	.05
120	Barry Larkin	.05
121	Reggie Sanders	.05
122	Brett Tomko	.05
123	Dante Bichette	.05
124	Ellis Burks	.05
125	Vinny Castilla	.05
126	Todd Helton	.75
127	Darryl Kile	.05
128	Larry Walker	.05
129	Bobby Bonilla	.05
130	Livan Hernandez	.05
131	Charles Johnson	.05
132	Derek Lee	.50
133	Edgar Renteria	.05
134	Gary Sheffield	.35
135	Moises Alou	.05
136	Jeff Bagwell	.75
137	Derek Bell	.05
138	Craig Biggio	.05
139	John Halama RC	.15
140	Mike Hampton	.05
141	Richard Hidalgo	.05
142	Wilton Guerrero	.05
143	Todd Hollandsworth	.05
144	Eric Karros	.05
145	Paul Konerko	.05
146	Raul Mondesi	.05
147	Hideo Nomo	.40
148	Chan Ho Park	.05
149	Mike Piazza	1.25
150	Jeromy Burnitz	.05
151	Todd Dunn	.05
152	Marquis Grissom	.05
153	John Jaha	.05
154	Dave Nilsson	.05
155	Fernando Vina	.05
156	Mark Grudzielanek	.05
157	Vladimir Guerrero	.75
158	F.P. Santangelo	.05
159	Jose Vidro	.05
160	Rondell White	.05
161	Edgardo Alfonzo	.05
162	Carlos Baerga	.05
163	John Franco	.05
164	Todd Hundley	.05
165	Brian McRae	.05
166	John Olerud	.05
167	Rey Ordonez	.05
168	Masato Yoshii RC	.25
169	Ricky Bottalico	.05
170	Doug Glanville	.05
171	Gregg Jefferies	.05
172	Desi Relaford	.05
173	Scott Rolen	.60
174	Curt Schilling	.30
175	Jose Guillen	.05
176	Jason Kendall	.05
177	Al Martin	.05
178	Abraham Nunez	.05
179	Kevin Young	.05
180	Royce Clayton	.05
181	Delino DeShields	.05
182	Gary Gaetti	.05
183	Ron Gant	.05
184	Brian Jordan	.05
185	Ray Lankford	.05
186	Willie McGee	.05
187	Mark McGwire	2.00
188	Kevin Brown	.05
189	Ken Caminiti	.05
190	Steve Finley	.05
191	Tony Gwynn	1.00
192	Wally Joyner	.05
193	Ruben Rivera	.05
194	Quilvio Veras	.05
195	Barry Bonds	2.50
196	Shawn Estes	.05
197	Orel Hershiser	.05
198	Jeff Kent	.05
199	Robb Nen	.05
200	J.T. Snow	.05

Cubes

A cardboard cube presenting player photos on top and three sides, plus a side of stats was created as a hobby-only insert for Pacific Aurora. The assembled, shrink-wrapped cubes were packed one per box.

		NM/M
	Complete Set (20):	75.00
	Common Player:	1.50
	Inserted 1:Box	
1	Travis Lee	1.50
2	Chipper Jones	4.00
3	Greg Maddux	4.00
4	Cal Ripken Jr.	10.00
5	Nomar Garciaparra	4.00
6	Frank Thomas	3.00
7	Manny Ramirez	3.00
8	Larry Walker	1.50
9	Hideo Nomo	2.00
10	Mike Piazza	5.00
11	Derek Jeter	10.00
12	Ben Grieve	1.50
13	Mark McGwire	7.50
14	Tony Gwynn	4.00
15	Barry Bonds	10.00
16	Ken Griffey Jr.	6.00
17	Alex Rodriguez	7.50
18	Wade Boggs	4.00
19	Juan Gonzalez	2.00
20	Jose Cruz Jr.	1.50

Hardball Cel-Fusion

Hardball Cel-Fusion features a die-cut celluloid baseball fused to a foiled and etched card.

		NM/M
	Complete Set (20):	60.00
	Common Player:	2.00
	Inserted 1:73	
1	Travis Lee	2.00
2	Chipper Jones	6.00

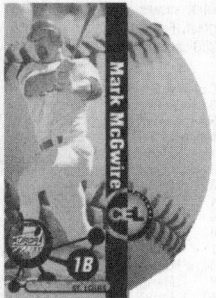

3	Greg Maddux	6.00
4	Cal Ripken Jr.	15.00
5	Nomar Garciaparra	6.00
6	Frank Thomas	4.50
7	David Justice	2.00
8	Jeff Bagwell	4.50
9	Hideo Nomo	3.00
10	Mike Piazza	7.50
11	Derek Jeter	15.00
12	Ben Grieve	2.00
13	Scott Rolen	3.00
14	Mark McGwire	12.00
15	Tony Gwynn	6.00
16	Ken Griffey Jr.	9.00
17	Alex Rodriguez	12.00
18	Ivan Rodriguez	3.50
19	Roger Clemens	7.50
20	Jose Cruz Jr.	2.00

Kings of the Major Leagues

This 10-card insert features star players on fully-foiled cards. A marble-look semi-circular panel at bottom has the player identification. The action photo at center is set against a bronze orb and concentric circles of gold-foil repeat the "Kings of the Major Leagues" title. Backs have a color portrait on a red and black background along with a few sentences about the player.

		NM/M
	Complete Set (10):	75.00
	Common Player:	7.50
	Inserted 1:361	
1	Chipper Jones	9.00
2	Greg Maddux	9.00
3	Cal Ripken Jr.	20.00
4	Nomar Garciaparra	9.00
5	Frank Thomas	7.50
6	Mike Piazza	10.00
7	Mark McGwire	15.00
8	Tony Gwynn	9.00
9	Ken Griffey Jr.	12.00
10	Alex Rodriguez	15.00

On Deck Laser-Cut

On Deck Laser-Cut is a 20-card insert in packs of 1998 Pacific Aurora. Fronts have an action photo at top, with an intricately die-cut pattern in gold foil below. Backs feature a portrait photo.

		NM/M
	Complete Set (20):	30.00
	Common Player:	.60
	Inserted 1:9	
1	Travis Lee	.60
2	Chipper Jones	2.25
3	Greg Maddux	2.25
4	Cal Ripken Jr.	6.00
5	Nomar Garciaparra	.60
6	Frank Thomas	1.50
7	Manny Ramirez	1.50
8	Larry Walker	.60
9	Hideo Nomo	1.00
10	Mike Piazza	2.50
11	Derek Jeter	6.00
12	Ben Grieve	.60
13	Mark McGwire	4.50
14	Tony Gwynn	2.25
15	Barry Bonds	6.00
16	Ken Griffey Jr.	3.00
17	Alex Rodriguez	4.50
18	Wade Boggs	2.25
19	Juan Gonzalez	1.00
20	Jose Cruz Jr.	.60

Pennant Fever

Pennant Fever is a 50-card insert seeded one per pack. Each card is fully foiled and etched. The color player image is duplicated in the upper-left corner with an image stamped in gold foil. Pennant Fever has four parallels. Red cards are a 1:4 retail insert. The Silver retail parallel is numbered to 250, Platinum Blue is numbered to 100 and the Copper hobby parallel is numbered to 20. Tony Gwynn signed his card serially numbered one in each insert.

		NM/M
	Complete Set (50):	25.00
	Common Player:	.20
	Inserted 1:1	
	Reds (1:4 Retail):	2X
	Silvers (250 Sets):	4X
	Platinum Blues (100 Sets):	12X
	Coppers (20 Sets):	40X
1	Tony Gwynn	1.00
2	Derek Jeter	2.00
3	Alex Rodriguez	1.50
4	Paul Molitor	.75
5	Nomar Garciaparra	1.00
6	Jeff Bagwell	.75
7	Ivan Rodriguez	.65
8	Cal Ripken Jr.	2.00
9	Matt Williams	.20
10	Chipper Jones	1.00
11	Edgar Martinez	.20
12	Wade Boggs	1.00
13	Paul Konerko	.30
14	Ben Grieve	.20
15	Sandy Alomar Jr.	.20
16	Travis Lee	.20
17	Scott Rolen	.65
18	Ryan Klesko	.20
19	Juan Gonzalez	.40
20	Albert Belle	.20
21	Roger Clemens	1.25
22	Javy Lopez	.20
23	Jose Cruz Jr.	.20
24	Ken Griffey Jr.	1.25
25	Mark McGwire	1.50
26	Brady Anderson	.20
27	Jaret Wright	.20
28	Roberto Alomar	.30
29	Joe Carter	.20
30	Hideo Nomo	.40
31	Mike Piazza	1.25
32	Andres Galarraga	.20
33	Larry Walker	.20
34	Tim Salmon	.20
35	Frank Thomas	.75
36	Moises Alou	.20
37	David Justice	.20
38	Manny Ramirez	.75
39	Jim Edmonds	.20
40	Barry Bonds	2.00
41	Jim Thome	.65
42	Mo Vaughn	.20
43	Rafael Palmeiro	.65
44	Darin Erstad	.30
45	Pedro Martinez	.75
46	Greg Maddux	1.00
47	Jose Canseco	.45
48	Vladimir Guerrero	.75
49	Bernie Williams	.75
50	Randy Johnson	.75

1998 Pacific Crown Royale

The Crown Royale base set consists of 144 die-cut cards. The cards have a horizontal layout and are die-cut around a crown design at the top. The cards are double-foiled and etched. Inserts include Diamond Knights, Pillars of the

Game, Race to the Record, All-Star Die-Cuts, Firestone on Baseball and Cramer's Choice Awards.

		NM/M
	Complete Set (144):	60.00
	Common Player:	.20
	Pack (6):	1.00
	Wax Box (24):	20.00
1	Garret Anderson	.20
2	Jim Edmonds	.20
3	Darin Erstad	.50
4	Tim Salmon	.20
5	Jarrod Washburn	.20
6	David Dellucci	.20
7	Travis Lee	.20
8	Devon White	.20
9	Matt Williams	.20
10	Andres Galarraga	.20
11	Tom Glavine	.35
12	Andruw Jones	2.00
13	Chipper Jones	3.00
14	Ryan Klesko	.20
15	Javy Lopez	.20
16	Greg Maddux	3.00
17	Walt Weiss	.20
18	Roberto Alomar	.75
19	Harold Baines	.20
20	Eric Davis	.20
21	Mike Mussina	1.00
22	Rafael Palmeiro	1.50
23	Cal Ripken Jr.	5.00
24	Nomar Garciaparra	3.00
25	Pedro Martinez	2.00
26	Troy O'Leary	.20
27	Mo Vaughn	.20
28	Tim Wakefield	.20
29	Mark Grace	.20
30	Mickey Morandini	.20
31	Sammy Sosa	3.00
32	Kerry Wood	.50
33	Albert Belle	.20
34	Mike Caruso	.20
35	Ray Durham	.20
36	Frank Thomas	2.00
37	Robin Ventura	.20
38	Bret Boone	.20
39	Sean Casey	.25
40	Barry Larkin	.20
41	Reggie Sanders	.20
42	Sandy Alomar Jr.	.20
43	David Justice	.20
44	Kenny Lofton	.20
45	Manny Ramirez	2.00
46	Jim Thome	1.00
47	Omar Vizquel	.20
48	Jaret Wright	.20
49	Dante Bichette	.20
50	Ellis Burks	.20
51	Vinny Castilla	.20
52	Todd Helton	2.00
53	Larry Walker	.20
54	Tony Clark	.20
55	Damion Easley	.20
56	Bobby Higginson	.20
57	Cliff Floyd	.20
58	Livan Hernandez	.20
59	Derrek Lee	.75
60	Edgar Renteria	.20
61	Moises Alou	.20
62	Jeff Bagwell	2.00
63	Derek Bell	.20
64	Craig Biggio	.20
65	Johnny Damon	.35
66	Jeff King	.20
67	Hal Morris	.20
68	Dean Palmer	.20
69	Bobby Bonilla	.20
70	Eric Karros	.20
71	Raul Mondesi	.20
72	Gary Sheffield	.75
73	Jeromy Burnitz	.20
74	Jeff Cirillo	.20
75	Marquis Grissom	.20
76	Fernando Vina	.20
77	Marty Cordova	.20
78	Pat Meares	.20
79	Paul Molitor	2.00
80	Terry Steinbach	.20
81	Todd Walker	.20
82	Brad Fullmer	.20
83	Vladimir Guerrero	2.00
84	Carl Pavano	.20
85	Rondell White	.20
86	Carlos Baerga	.20
87	Hideo Nomo	1.00
88	John Olerud	.20
89	Rey Ordonez	.20
90	Mike Piazza	3.00
91	Masato Yoshii RC	.75
92	Orlando Hernandez RC	.75
93	Hideki Irabu	.20
94	Derek Jeter	5.00
95	Chuck Knoblauch	.20
96	Ricky Ledee	.20
97	Tino Martinez	.20
98	Paul O'Neill	.20

99	Bernie Williams	.20
100	Jason Giambi	1.25
101	Ben Grieve	.20
102	Rickey Henderson	2.00
103	Matt Stairs	.20
104	Bob Abreu	.25
105	Doug Glanville	.20
106	Scott Rolen	1.50
107	Curt Schilling	.35
108	Jose Guillen	.20
109	Jason Kendall	.20
110	Jason Schmidt	.20
111	Kevin Young	.20
112	Delino DeShields	.20
113	Brian Jordan	.20
114	Ray Lankford	.20
115	Mark McGwire	4.00
116	Tony Gwynn	3.00
117	Wally Joyner	.20
118	Ruben Rivera	.20
119	Greg Vaughn	.20
120	Rich Aurilia	.20
121	Barry Bonds	5.00
122	Bill Mueller	.20
123	Robb Nen	.20
124	Jay Buhner	.20
125	Ken Griffey Jr.	3.50
126	Edgar Martinez	.20
127	Shane Monahan	.20
128	Alex Rodriguez	4.00
129	David Segui	.20
130	Rolando Arrojo **RC**	.75
131	Wade Boggs	1.00
132	Quinton McCracken	.20
133	Fred McGriff	.20
134	Bobby Smith	.20
135	Will Clark	.20
136	Juan Gonzalez	1.00
137	Rusty Greer	.20
138	Ivan Rodriguez	1.50
139	Aaron Sele	.20
140	John Wetteland	.20
141	Jose Canseco	1.00
142	Roger Clemens	3.50
143	Carlos Delgado	1.25
144	Shawn Green	.50

All-Stars

This 20-card insert was seeded one per 25 packs. The featured players all participated in the 1998 All-Star Game. The background features the sun rising over a mountain with a die-cut at the top of the card.

		NM/M
Complete Set (20):		110.00
Common Player:		1.50
Inserted 1:25		
1	Roberto Alomar	2.00
2	Cal Ripken Jr.	15.00
3	Kenny Lofton	1.50
4	Jim Thome	5.00
5	Derek Jeter	15.00
6	David Wells	1.50
7	Ken Griffey Jr.	10.00
8	Alex Rodriguez	12.00
9	Juan Gonzalez	4.00
10	Ivan Rodriguez	4.00
11	Gary Sheffield	2.50
12	Chipper Jones	7.50
13	Greg Maddux	7.50
14	Walt Weiss	1.50
15	Larry Walker	1.50
16	Craig Biggio	1.50
17	Mike Piazza	10.00
18	Mark McGwire	12.00
19	Tony Gwynn	7.50
20	Barry Bonds	15.00

Cramer's Choice Awards

Premium-sized Cramer's Choice Awards were inserted one per box. The 10 players in the set are featured on a die-cut card designed to resemble a trophy. Pacific CEO Mike Cramer signed and hand-numbered ten sets of Cramer's Choice Awards.

		NM/M
Complete Set (10):		65.00
Common Player:		4.00
Inserted 1:box		
1	Cal Ripken Jr.	15.00
2	Ken Griffey Jr.	9.00

3	Alex Rodriguez	12.00
4	Juan Gonzalez	5.00
5	Travis Lee	4.00
6	Chipper Jones	7.50
7	Greg Maddux	7.50
8	Kerry Wood	5.00
9	Mark McGwire	12.00
10	Tony Gwynn	7.50

Diamond Knights

Diamond Knights is a 25-card, one per pack insert. Each card features a color action photo and the player's name, team and position listed on a Medieval-type border at the bottom.

		NM/M
Complete Set (25):		20.00
Common Player:		.35
Inserted 1:1		
1	Andres Galarraga	.35
2	Chipper Jones	1.00
3	Greg Maddux	1.00
4	Cal Ripken Jr.	2.50
5	Nomar Garciaparra	1.50
6	Mo Vaughn	.35
7	Kerry Wood	.45
8	Frank Thomas	.75
9	Vinny Castilla	.35
10	Jeff Bagwell	.75
11	Craig Biggio	.35
12	Paul Molitor	.75
13	Mike Piazza	1.50
14	Orlando Hernandez	.35
15	Derek Jeter	2.50
16	Ricky Ledee	.35
17	Mark McGwire	2.00
18	Tony Gwynn	1.00
19	Barry Bonds	2.50
20	Ken Griffey Jr.	1.75
21	Alex Rodriguez	2.00
22	Wade Boggs	1.00
23	Juan Gonzalez	.45
24	Ivan Rodriguez	.65
25	Jose Canseco	.50

Firestone on Baseball

This 26-card insert features star players with commentary by sports personality Roy Firestone. The fronts have a color photo of the player and a portrait of Firestone in the lower-right corner. The card backs have text by Firestone on

what makes the featured player great. Firestone signed a total of 300 cards in this insert.

		NM/M
Complete Set (26):		50.00
Common Player:		.35
Firestone Auto. Card:		18.00
Inserted 1:12		
1	Travis Lee	.35
2	Chipper Jones	3.00
3	Greg Maddux	3.00
4	Cal Ripken Jr.	6.00
5	Nomar Garciaparra	3.00
6	Mo Vaughn	.35
7	Kerry Wood	1.00
8	Frank Thomas	2.25
9	Manny Ramirez	2.25
10	Larry Walker	.35
11	Gary Sheffield	1.00
12	Paul Molitor	1.50
13	Hideo Nomo	1.50
14	Mike Piazza	3.50
15	Ben Grieve	.35
16	Mark McGwire	5.00
17	Tony Gwynn	3.00
18	Barry Bonds	6.00
19	Ken Griffey Jr.	4.00
20	Randy Johnson	2.25
21	Alex Rodriguez	5.00
22	Wade Boggs	3.00
23	Juan Gonzalez	1.50
24	Ivan Rodriguez	1.75
25	Roger Clemens	3.50
26	Roy Firestone	.35

Home Run Fever

Home Run Fever features players who had a shot at breaking Roger Maris' home run record in 1998. Fronts have a player photo on the left and a blackboard with numbers from 1 to 60 on the right. Ten circles featuring disappearing ink contained numbers 61 through 70. Collectors could rub the circles to reveal the player's potential record home run total.

		NM/M
Complete Set (10):		30.00
Common Player:		1.50
Inserted 1:73		
1	Andres Galarraga	1.50
2	Sammy Sosa	4.50
3	Albert Belle	1.50
4	Jim Thome	3.00
5	Mark McGwire	7.50
6	Greg Vaughn	1.50
7	Ken Griffey Jr.	6.00
8	Alex Rodriguez	7.50
9	Juan Gonzalez	2.50
10	Jose Canseco	2.50

Pillars of the Game

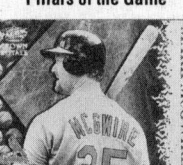

This 25-card insert was seeded one per pack. Each card features a star player with a background of holographic silver foil.

		NM/M
Complete Set (25):		20.00
Common Player:		.35
Inserted 1:1		
1	Jim Edmonds	.35
2	Travis Lee	.35
3	Chipper Jones	1.00
4	Tom Glavine, John Smoltz, Greg Maddux	1.00
5	Cal Ripken Jr.	2.50
6	Nomar Garciaparra	1.00
7	Mo Vaughn	.35
8	Sammy Sosa	1.00
9	Kerry Wood	.40
10	Frank Thomas	.75
11	Jim Thome	.65
12	Larry Walker	.35
13	Moises Alou	.35
14	Raul Mondesi	.35
15	Mike Piazza	1.25
16	Hideki Irabu	.35
17	Bernie Williams	.35
18	Ben Grieve	.35
19	Scott Rolen	.65
20	Mark McGwire	2.00
21	Tony Gwynn	1.00
22	Ken Griffey Jr.	1.50

23	Alex Rodriguez	2.00
24	Juan Gonzalez	.40
25	Roger Clemens	1.25

1998 Pacific Invincible

Invincible consists of a 150-card base set with a horizontal format featuring a player photo on the left and a portrait in a cel window on the right. The regular cards were inserted one per five-card pack. Silver (2:37) and Platinum Blue (1:73) parallels were also created. Inserts include Moments in Time, Team Checklists, Photoengravings, Interleague Players, Gems of the Diamond and Cramer's Choice Awards.

		NM/M
Complete Set (150):		60.00
Common Player:		.20
Silvers:		4X
Inserted 2:37		
Platinum Blues:		6X
Inserted 1:73		
Pack (5):		1.25
Wax Box (36):		32.50
1	Garret Anderson	.20
2	Jim Edmonds	.20
3	Darin Erstad	.35
4	Chuck Finley	.20
5	Tim Salmon	.20
6	Roberto Alomar	.35
7	Brady Anderson	.20
8	Geronimo Berroa	.20
9	Eric Davis	.20
10	Mike Mussina	.50
11	Rafael Palmeiro	1.00
12	Cal Ripken Jr.	6.00
13	Steve Avery	.20
14	Nomar Garciaparra	2.50
15	John Valentin	.20
16	Mo Vaughn	.20
17	Albert Belle	.20
18	Ozzie Guillen	.20
19	Norberto Martin	.20
20	Frank Thomas	1.50
21	Robin Ventura	.20
22	Sandy Alomar Jr.	.20
23	David Justice	.20
24	Kenny Lofton	.20
25	Manny Ramirez	1.50
26	Jim Thome	1.00
27	Omar Vizquel	.20
28	Matt Williams	.20
29	Jaret Wright	.20
30	Raul Casanova	.20
31	Tony Clark	.20
32	Deivi Cruz	.20
33	Bobby Higginson	.20
34	Justin Thompson	.20
35	Yamil Benitez	.20
36	Johnny Damon	.35
37	Jermaine Dye	.20
38	Jed Hansen	.20
39	Larry Sutton	.20
40	Jeromy Burnitz	.20
41	Jeff Cirillo	.20
42	Dave Nilsson	.20
43	Jose Valentin	.20
44	Fernando Vina	.20
45	Marty Cordova	.20
46	Chuck Knoblauch	.20
47	Paul Molitor	1.50
48	Brad Radke	.20
49	Terry Steinbach	.20
50	Wade Boggs	2.50
51	Hideki Irabu	.20
52	Derek Jeter	6.00
53	Tino Martinez	.20
54	Andy Pettitte	.30
55	Mariano Rivera	.30
56	Bernie Williams	.20
57	Jose Canseco	.75
58	Jason Giambi	.75
59	Ben Grieve	.20
60	Aaron Small	.20
61	Jay Buhner	.20
62	Ken Cloude	.20
63	Joey Cora	.20
64	Ken Griffey Jr.	3.50
65	Randy Johnson	1.50
66	Edgar Martinez	.20
67	Alex Rodriguez	5.00
68	Will Clark	.20
69	Juan Gonzalez	.75
70	Rusty Greer	.20
71	Ivan Rodriguez	1.00
72	Joe Carter	.20
73	Roger Clemens	3.00
74	Jose Cruz Jr.	.20
75	Carlos Delgado	.75
76	Andruw Jones	1.50
77	Chipper Jones	2.50
78	Ryan Klesko	.20
79	Javier Lopez	.20

80	Greg Maddux	2.50
81	Miguel Batista	.20
82	Jeremi Gonzalez	.20
83	Mark Grace	.20
84	Kevin Orie	.20
85	Sammy Sosa	2.50
86	Barry Larkin	.20
87	Deion Sanders	.20
88	Reggie Sanders	.20
89	Chris Stynes	.20
90	Dante Bichette	.20
91	Vinny Castilla	.20
92	Andres Galarraga	.20
93	Neifi Perez	.20
94	Larry Walker	.20
95	Moises Alou	.20
96	Bobby Bonilla	.20
97	Kevin Brown	.20
98	Craig Counsell	.20
99	Livan Hernandez	.20
100	Edgar Renteria	.20
101	Gary Sheffield	.60
102	Jeff Bagwell	1.50
103	Craig Biggio	.20
104	Luis Gonzalez	.20
105	Darryl Kile	.20
106	Wilton Guerrero	.20
107	Eric Karros	.20
108	Ramon Martinez	.20
109	Raul Mondesi	.20
110	Hideo Nomo	.75
111	Chan Ho Park	.20
112	Mike Piazza	3.00
113	Mark Grudzielanek	.20
114	Vladimir Guerrero	1.50
115	Pedro Martinez	1.50
116	Henry Rodriguez	.20
117	David Segui	.20
118	Edgardo Alfonzo	.20
119	Carlos Baerga	.20
120	John Franco	.20
121	John Olerud	.20
122	Rey Ordonez	.20
123	Ricky Bottalico	.20
124	Gregg Jefferies	.20
125	Mickey Morandini	.20
126	Scott Rolen	1.00
127	Curt Schilling	.45
128	Jose Guillen	.20
129	Esteban Loaiza	.20
130	Al Martin	.20
131	Tony Womack	.20
132	Dennis Eckersley	1.00
133	Gary Gaetti	.20
134	Curtis King	.20
135	Ray Lankford	.20
136	Mark McGwire	5.00
137	Ken Caminiti	.20
138	Steve Finley	.20
139	Tony Gwynn	2.50
140	Carlos Hernandez	.20
141	Wally Joyner	.20
142	Barry Bonds	6.00
143	Jacob Cruz	.20
144	Shawn Estes	.20
145	Stan Javier	.20
146	J.T. Snow	.20
147	Nomar Garciaparra (ROY)	1.00
148	Scott Rolen (ROY)	.60
149	Ken Griffey Jr. (MVP)	1.75
150	Larry Walker (MVP)	.20

Cramer's Choice

The 10-card Cramer's Choice Awards insert features top players on cards with a die-cut trophy design. This set has six different foil variations, each with a different production number. Green (99 hand-numbered sets), Dark Blue (80), Light Blue (50), Red (25), Gold (15) and Purple (10) versions were included in Invincible.

		NM/M
Complete Green Set (10):		200.00
Common Green (99 Sets):		10.00
Dark Blues (80 Sets):		1X
Light Blues (50 Sets):		1.5X
Reds (25 Sets):		2X
Golds (15 Sets):		3X
Purples (10 Sets):		5X
1	Greg Maddux	20.00
2	Roberto Alomar	10.00
3	Cal Ripken Jr.	40.00

4	Nomar Garciaparra	20.00
5	Larry Walker	10.00
6	Mike Piazza	22.50
7	Mark McGwire	30.00
8	Tony Gwynn	20.00
9	Ken Griffey Jr.	25.00
10	Roger Clemens	22.50

Gems of the Diamond

Gems of the Diamond is a 220-card insert seeded four per pack. The cards feature a color photo inside a white border.

		NM/M
Complete Set (220):		20.00
Common Player:		.10
1	Jim Edmonds	.10
2	Todd Greene	.10
3	Ken Hill	.10
4	Mike Holtz	.10
5	Mike James	.10
6	Chad Kreuter	.10
7	Tim Salmon	.10
8	Roberto Alomar	.20
9	Brady Anderson	.10
10	David Dellucci	.10
11	Jeffrey Hammonds	.10
12	Mike Mussina	.40
13	Rafael Palmeiro	.65
14	Arthur Rhodes	.10
15	Cal Ripken Jr.	2.50
16	Nerio Rodriguez	.10
17	Tony Tarasco	.10
18	Lenny Webster	.10
19	Mike Benjamin	.10
20	Rich Garces	.10
21	Nomar Garciaparra	1.00
22	Shane Mack	.10
23	Jose Malave	.10
24	Jesus Tavarez	.10
25	Mo Vaughn	.20
26	John Wasdin	.10
27	Jeff Abbott	.10
28	Albert Belle	.10
29	Mike Cameron	.10
30	Al Levine	.10
31	Robert Machado	.10
32	Greg Norton	.10
33	Magglio Ordonez	.20
34	Mike Sirotka	.10
35	Frank Thomas	.75
36	Mario Valdez	.10
37	Sandy Alomar Jr.	.20
38	David Justice	.20
39	Jack McDowell	.10
40	Eric Plunk	.10
41	Manny Ramirez	.75
42	Kevin Seitzer	.10
43	Paul Shuey	.10
44	Omar Vizquel	.10
45	Kimera Bartee	.10
46	Glenn Dishman	.10
47	Orlando Miller	.10
48	Mike Myers	.10
49	Phil Nevin	.10
50	A.J. Sager	.10
51	Ricky Bones	.10
52	Scott Cooper	.10
53	Shane Halter	.10
54	David Howard	.10
55	Glendon Rusch	.10
56	Joe Vitiello	.10
57	Jeff D'Amico	.10
58	Mike Fetters	.10
59	Mike Matheny	.10
60	Jose Mercedes	.10
61	Ron Villone	.10
62	Jack Voigt	.10
63	Brent Brede	.10
64	Chuck Knoblauch	.10
65	Paul Molitor	.75
66	Todd Ritchie	.10
67	Frankie Rodriguez	.10
68	Scott Stahoviak	.10
69	Greg Swindell	.10
70	Todd Walker	.10
71	Wade Boggs	1.00
72	Hideki Irabu	.10
73	Derek Jeter	2.50
74	Pat Kelly	.10
75	Graeme Lloyd	.10
76	Tino Martinez	.10
77	Jeff Nelson	.10
78	Scott Pose	.10
79	Mike Stanton	.10
80	Darryl Strawberry	.10
81	Bernie Williams	.10

82	Tony Batista	.10
83	Mark Bellhorn	.10
84	Ben Grieve	.10
85	Pat Lennon	.10
86	Brian Lesher	.10
87	Miguel Tejada	.20
88	George Williams	.10
89	Joey Cora	.10
90	Rob Ducey	.10
91	Ken Griffey Jr.	1.50
92	Randy Johnson	.75
93	Edgar Martinez	.10
94	John Marzano	.10
95	Greg McCarthy	.10
96	Alex Rodriguez	2.00
97	Andy Sheets	.10
98	Mike Timlin	.10
99	Lee Tinsley	.10
100	Damon Buford	.10
101	Alex Diaz	.10
102	Benji Gil	.10
103	Juan Gonzalez	.40
104	Eric Gunderson	.10
105	Danny Patterson	.10
106	Ivan Rodriguez	.65
107	Mike Simms	.10
108	Luis Andujar	.10
109	Joe Carter	.10
110	Roger Clemens	1.25
111	Jose Cruz Jr.	.10
112	Shawn Green	.30
113	Robert Perez	.10
114	Juan Samuel	.10
115	Ed Sprague	.10
116	Shannon Stewart	.10
117	Danny Bautista	.10
118	Chipper Jones	1.00
119	Ryan Klesko	.10
120	Keith Lockhart	.10
121	Javier Lopez	.10
122	Greg Maddux	1.00
123	Kevin Millwood	.10
124	Mike Mordecai	.10
125	Eddie Perez	.10
126	Randall Simon	.10
127	Miguel Cairo	.10
128	Dave Clark	.10
129	Kevin Foster	.10
130	Mark Grace	.10
131	Tyler Houston	.10
132	Mike Hubbard	.10
133	Kevin Orie	.10
134	Ryne Sandberg	1.00
135	Sammy Sosa	1.00
136	Lenny Harris	.10
137	Kent Mercker	.10
138	Mike Morgan	.10
139	Deion Sanders	.10
140	Chris Stynes	.10
141	Gabe White	.10
142	Jason Bates	.10
143	Vinny Castilla	.10
144	Andres Galarraga	.10
145	Curtis Leskanic	.10
146	Jeff McCurry	.10
147	Mike Munoz	.10
148	Larry Walker	.10
149	Jamey Wright	.10
150	Moises Alou	.10
151	Bobby Bonilla	.10
152	Kevin Brown	.10
153	John Cangelosi	.10
154	Jeff Conine	.10
155	Cliff Floyd	.10
156	Jay Powell	.10
157	Edgar Renteria	.10
158	Tony Saunders	.10
159	Gary Sheffield	.40
160	Jeff Bagwell	.75
161	Tim Bogar	.10
162	Tony Eusebio	.10
163	Chris Holt	.10
164	Ray Montgomery	.10
165	Luis Rivera	.10
166	Eric Anthony	.10
167	Brett Butler	.10
168	Juan Castro	.10
169	Tripp Cromer	.10
170	Raul Mondesi	.40
171	Hideo Nomo	.40
172	Mike Piazza	1.25
173	Tom Prince	.10
174	Adam Riggs	.10
175	Shane Andrews	.10
176	Shayne Bennett	.10
177	Raul Chavez	.10
178	Pedro Martinez	.75
179	Sherman Obando	.10
180	Andy Stankiewicz	.10
181	Alberto Castillo	.10
182	Shawn Gilbert	.10
183	Luis Lopez	.10
184	Roberto Petagine	.10
185	Armando Reynoso	.10
186	Midre Cummings	.10
187	Kevin Jordan	.10
188	Desi Relaford	.10
189	Scott Rolen	.65
190	Ken Ryan	.10
191	Kevin Sefcik	.10
192	Emil Brown	.10
193	Lou Collier	.10
194	Francisco Cordova	.10
195	Kevin Elster	.10
196	Mark Smith	.10
197	Marc Wilkins	.10
198	Manny Aybar	.10
199	Jose Bautista	.10

200	David Bell	.10
201	Rigo Beltran	.10
202	Delino DeShields	.10
203	Dennis Eckersley	.65
204	John Mabry	.10
205	Eli Marrero	.10
206	Willie McGee	.10
207	Mark McGwire	2.00
208	Ken Caminiti	.10
209	Tony Gwynn	1.00
210	Chris Jones	.10
211	Craig Shipley	.10
212	Pete Smith	.10
213	Jorge Velandia	.10
214	Dario Veras	.10
215	Rich Aurilia	.10
216	Damon Berryhill	.10
217	Barry Bonds	2.50
218	Osvaldo Fernandez	.10
219	Dante Powell	.10
220	Rich Rodriguez	.10

Interleague Players

Interleague Players is a 30-card insert featuring 15 sets of players - one National League and one American League player. The dark blue backgrounds have red lightning bolts and the white borders are made of a leather-like material. When a set of players is placed next to each other, they form the MLB Interleague logo in the center. Interleague Players cards were inserted one per 73 packs.

		NM/M
Complete Set (30):		120.00
Common Player:		1.50
Inserted 1:73		
1A	Roberto Alomar	2.50
1N	Craig Biggio	1.50
2A	Cal Ripken Jr.	12.00
2N	Chipper Jones	6.00
3A	Nomar Garciaparra	6.00
3N	Scott Rolen	3.50
4A	Mo Vaughn	1.50
4N	Andres Galarraga	1.50
5A	Frank Thomas	4.50
5N	Tony Gwynn	6.00
6A	Albert Belle	1.50
6N	Barry Bonds	12.00
7A	Hideki Irabu	1.50
7N	Hideo Nomo	2.50
8A	Derek Jeter	12.00
8N	Rey Ordonez	1.50
9A	Tino Martinez	1.50
9N	Mark McGwire	10.00
10A	Alex Rodriguez	10.00
10N	Edgar Renteria	1.50
11A	Ken Griffey Jr.	7.50
11N	Larry Walker	1.50
12A	Randy Johnson	4.50
12N	Greg Maddux	6.00
13A	Ivan Rodriguez	3.50
13N	Mike Piazza	6.50
14A	Roger Clemens	6.50
14N	Pedro Martinez	4.50
15A	Jose Cruz Jr.	1.50
15N	Wilton Guerrero	1.50

Moments in Time

Moments in Time (20 cards, 1:145) is designed as a baseball scoreboard. The cards have a horizontal layout with the date of an important game in the player's career at the top. The player's stats from the game are featured and a picture is located on the scoreboard screen.

	NM/M
Complete Set (20):	100.00
Common Player:	3.00
Inserted 1:145	

1	Chipper Jones	10.00
2	Cal Ripken Jr.	17.50
3	Frank Thomas	7.50
4	David Justice	3.00
5	Andres Galarraga	3.00
6	Larry Walker	3.00
7	Livan Hernandez	3.00
8	Wilton Guerrero	3.00
9	Hideo Nomo	4.50
10	Mike Piazza	12.00
11	Pedro Martinez	7.50
12	Bernie Williams	3.00
13	Ben Grieve	3.00
14	Scott Rolen	6.00
15	Mark McGwire	15.00
16	Tony Gwynn	10.00
17	Ken Griffey Jr.	13.50
18	Alex Rodriguez	15.00
19	Juan Gonzalez	4.50
20	Jose Cruz Jr.	3.00

Photoengravings

Photoengravings is an 18-card insert seeded one per 37 packs. Each card has a unique "old-style" design with a player photo in a frame in the center.

		NM/M
Complete Set (18):		50.00
Common Player:		1.00
Inserted 1:37		
1	Greg Maddux	3.50
2	Cal Ripken Jr.	7.50
3	Nomar Garciaparra	3.50
4	Frank Thomas	2.50
5	Larry Walker	1.00
6	Mike Piazza	4.00
7	Hideo Nomo	2.00
8	Pedro Martinez	2.50
9	Derek Jeter	7.50
10	Tino Martinez	1.00
11	Mark McGwire	6.00
12	Tony Gwynn	3.50
13	Barry Bonds	7.50
14	Ken Griffey Jr.	5.00
15	Alex Rodriguez	6.00
16	Ivan Rodriguez	2.25
17	Roger Clemens	4.00
18	Jose Cruz Jr.	1.00

Team Checklists

Team Checklists is a 30-card insert seeded 2:37. The fronts feature a player collage with the team logo in the background. The back has a complete checklist for that team in Invincible and more player photos.

	NM/M
Complete Set (30):	60.00
Common Player:	1.00
Inserted 2:37	

1	Anaheim Angels (Jim Edmonds, Tim Salmon, Darin Erstad, Garret Anderson, Rickey Henderson)	2.50
2	Atlanta Braves (Greg Maddux, Chipper Jones, Javy Lopez, Ryan Klesko, Andruw Jones)	3.00
3	Baltimore Orioles (Cal Ripken Jr., Roberto Alomar, Brady Anderson, Mike Mussina, Rafael Palmeiro)	6.00
4	Boston Red Sox (Nomar Garciaparra, Mo Vaughn, Steve Avery, John Valentin)	3.00
5	Chicago Cubs (Sammy Sosa, Mark Grace, Ryne Sandberg, Jeremi Gonzalez)	
6	Chicago White Sox (Frank Thomas, Albert Belle, Robin Ventura, Ozzie Guillen)	2.50
7	Cincinnati Reds (Barry Larkin, Deion Sanders, Reggie Sanders, Brett Tomko)	1.00
8	Cleveland Indians (Sandy Alomar Jr., Manny Ramirez, David Justice, Jim Thome, Omar Vizquel)	2.50
9	Colorado Rockies (Andres Galarraga, Larry Walker, Vinny Castilla, Dante Bichette, Ellis Burks)	1.00
10	Detroit Tigers (Jason Thompson, Tony Clark, Deivi Cruz, Bobby Higginson)	1.00
11	Florida Marlins (Gary Sheffield, Edgar Renteria, Livan Hernandez, Charles Johnson, Bobby Bonilla)	1.00
12	Houston Astros (Jeff Bagwell, Craig Biggio, Richard Hidalgo, Darryl Kile)	2.50
13	Kansas City Royals (Johnny Damon, Jermaine Dye, Chili Davis, Jose Rosado)	1.00
14	Los Angeles Dodgers (Mike Piazza, Wilton Guerrero, Raul Mondesi, Hideo Nomo, Ramon Martinez)	4.00
15	Milwaukee Brewers (David Nilsson, Fernando Vina, Jeromy Burnitz, Julio Franco, Jeff Cirillo)	1.00
16	Minnesota Twins (Paul Molitor, Chuck Knoblauch, Brad Radke, Terry Steinbach, Marty Cordova)	2.50
17	Montreal Expos (Henry Rodriguez, Vladimir Guerrero, Pedro Martinez, David Segui, Mark Grudzielanek)	2.50
18	New York Mets (Carlos Baerga, Todd Hundley, Rey Ordonez, John Olerud, Edgardo Alfonzo)	1.00
19	New York Yankees (Derek Jeter, Tino Martinez, Bernie Williams, Andy Pettitte, Mariano Rivera)	6.00
20	Oakland Athletics (Jose Canseco, Ben Grieve, Jason Giambi, Matt Stairs)	1.75
21	Philadelphia Phillies (Curt Schilling, Scott Rolen, Gregg Jefferies, Lenny Dykstra, Ricky Bottalico)	1.75
22	Pittsburgh Pirates (Al Martin, Tony Womack, Jose Guillen, Esteban Loaiza)	1.00
23	St. Louis Cardinals (Mark McGwire, Dennis Eckersley, Delino DeShields, Willie McGee, Ray Lankford)	4.50
24	San Diego Padres (Tony Gwynn, Ken Caminiti, Wally Joyner, Steve Finley)	3.00
25	San Francisco Giants (Barry Bonds, J.T. Snow, Stan Javier, Rod Beck, Jose Vizcaino)	6.00
26	Seattle Mariners (Ken Griffey Jr., Alex Rodriguez, Edgar Martinez, Randy Johnson, Jay Buhner)	4.50
27	Texas Rangers (Juan Gonzalez, Ivan Rodriguez, Will Clark, John Wetteland, Rusty Greer)	2.00
28	Toronto Blue Jays (Jose Cruz Jr., Roger Clemens, Pat Hentgen, Joe Carter)	4.00
29	Arizona Diamondbacks (Yamil Benitez, Devon White, Matt Williams, Jay Bell)	1.00
30	Tampa Bay Devil Rays (Wade Boggs, Paul Sorrento, Fred McGriff, Roberto Hernandez)	3.00

1998 Pacific Omega

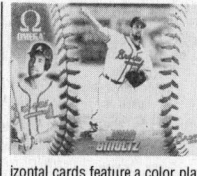

The Omega base set consists of 250 three-image cards. The horizontal cards feature a color player photo in the center with the image duplicated in foil on the right. Another color photo is on the left. The photos are divided by a baseball seam design. Red-foil parallels were a 1:4 pack insert in Wal-Mart exclusive packaging.

	NM/M
Complete Set (250):	25.00
Common Player:	.10
Reds:	4X
Pack (6):	1.00
Wax Box (36):	15.00

1	Garret Anderson	.10
2	Gary DiSarcina	.10
3	Jim Edmonds	.10
4	Darin Erstad	.20
5	Cecil Fielder	.10
6	Chuck Finley	.10
7	Shigetosi Hasegawa	.10
8	Tim Salmon	.10
9	Brian Anderson	.10
10	Jay Bell	.10
11	Andy Benes	.10
12	Yamil Benitez	.10
13	Jorge Fabregas	.10
14	Travis Lee	.10
15	Devon White	.10
16	Matt Williams	.10
17	Andres Galarraga	.10
18	Tom Glavine	.35
19	Andruw Jones	.75
20	Chipper Jones	1.00
21	Ryan Klesko	.10
22	Javy Lopez	.10
23	Greg Maddux	1.00
24	Kevin Millwood RC	.50
25	Denny Neagle	.10
26	John Smoltz	.10
27	Roberto Alomar	.20
28	Brady Anderson	.10
29	Joe Carter	.10
30	Eric Davis	.10
31	Jimmy Key	.10
32	Mike Mussina	.40
33	Rafael Palmeiro	.65
34	Cal Ripken Jr.	2.50
35	B.J. Surhoff	.10
36	Dennis Eckersley	.65
37	Nomar Garciaparra	1.00
38	Reggie Jefferson	.10
39	Derek Lowe	.10
40	Pedro Martinez	.75
41	Brian Rose	.10
42	John Valentin	.10
43	Jason Varitek	.10
44	Mo Vaughn	.10
45	Jeff Blauser	.10
46	Jeremi Gonzalez	.10
47	Mark Grace	.10
48	Lance Johnson	.10
49	Kevin Orie	.10
50	Henry Rodriguez	.10
51	Sammy Sosa	1.00
52	Kerry Wood	.35
53	Albert Belle	.10
54	Mike Cameron	.10
55	Mike Caruso	.10
56	Ray Durham	.10
57	Jaime Navarro	.10
58	Greg Norton	.10
59	Magglio Ordonez RC	1.50
60	Frank Thomas	.75
61	Robin Ventura	.10
62	Bret Boone	.10
63	Willie Greene	.10
64	Barry Larkin	.10
65	Jon Nunnally	.10
66	Eduardo Perez	.10
67	Reggie Sanders	.10
68	Brett Tomko	.10
69	Sandy Alomar Jr.	.10
70	Travis Fryman	.10
71	David Justice	.10
72	Kenny Lofton	.10
73	Charles Nagy	.10
74	Manny Ramirez	.75
75	Jim Thome	.65
76	Omar Vizquel	.10
77	Enrique Wilson	.10
78	Jaret Wright	.10
79	Dante Bichette	.10
80	Ellis Burks	.10
81	Vinny Castilla	.10
82	Todd Helton	.75
83	Darryl Kile	.10
84	Mike Lansing	.10
85	Neifi Perez	.10
86	Larry Walker	.10
87	Raul Casanova	.10
88	Tony Clark	.10
89	Luis Gonzalez	.10
90	Bobby Higginson	.10
91	Brian Hunter	.10

92	Bip Roberts	.10
93	Justin Thompson	.10
94	Josh Booty	.10
95	Craig Counsell	.10
96	Livan Hernandez	.10
97	Ryan Jackson RC	.10
98	Mark Kotsay	.10
99	Derrek Lee	.50
100	Mike Piazza	1.25
101	Edgar Renteria	.10
102	Cliff Floyd	.10
103	Moises Alou	.10
104	Jeff Bagwell	.75
105	Derrick Bell	.10
106	Sean Berry	.10
107	Craig Biggio	.10
108	John Halama RC	.15
109	Richard Hidalgo	.10
110	Shane Reynolds	.10
111	Tim Belcher	.10
112	Brian Bevil	.10
113	Jeff Conine	.10
114	Johnny Damon	.25
115	Jeff King	.10
116	Jeff Montgomery	.10
117	Dean Palmer	.10
118	Terry Pendleton	.10
119	Bobby Bonilla	.10
120	Wilton Guerrero	.10
121	Todd Hollandsworth	.10
122	Charles Johnson	.10
123	Eric Karros	.10
124	Paul Konerko	.20
125	Ramon Martinez	.10
126	Raul Mondesi	.10
127	Hideo Nomo	.40
128	Gary Sheffield	.45
129	Ismael Valdes	.10
130	Jeromy Burnitz	.10
131	Jeff Cirillo	.10
132	Todd Dunn	.10
133	Marquis Grissom	.10
134	John Jaha	.10
135	Scott Karl	.10
136	Dave Nilsson	.10
137	Jose Valentin	.10
138	Fernando Vina	.10
139	Rick Aguilera	.10
140	Marty Cordova	.10
141	Pat Meares	.10
142	Paul Molitor	.75
143	David Ortiz	.50
144	Brad Radke	.10
145	Terry Steinbach	.10
146	Todd Walker	.10
147	Shane Andrews	.10
148	Brad Fullmer	.10
149	Mark Grudzielanek	.10
150	Vladimir Guerrero	.75
151	F.P. Santangelo	.10
152	Jose Vidro	.10
153	Rondell White	.10
154	Carlos Baerga	.10
155	Bernard Gilkey	.10
156	Todd Hundley	.10
157	Butch Huskey	.10
158	Bobby Jones	.10
159	Brian McRae	.10
160	John Olerud	.10
161	Rey Ordonez	.10
162	Masato Yoshii RC	.25
163	David Cone	.10
164	Hideki Irabu	.10
165	Derek Jeter	2.50
166	Chuck Knoblauch	.10
167	Tino Martinez	.10
168	Paul O'Neill	.10
169	Andy Pettitte	.30
170	Mariano Rivera	.15
171	Darryl Strawberry	.10
172	David Wells	.10
173	Bernie Williams	.10
174	Ryan Christenson RC	.15
175	Jason Giambi	.60
176	Ben Grieve	.10
177	Rickey Henderson	.75
178	A.J. Hinch	.10
179	Kenny Rogers	.10
180	Ricky Bottalico	.10
181	Rico Brogna	.10
182	Doug Glanville	.10
183	Gregg Jefferies	.10
184	Mike Lieberthal	.10
185	Scott Rolen	.65
186	Curt Schilling	.35
187	Jermaine Allensworth	.10
188	Lou Collier	.10
189	Jose Guillen	.10
190	Jason Kendall	.10
191	Al Martin	.10
192	Tony Womack	.10
193	Kevin Young	.10
194	Royce Clayton	.10
195	Delino DeShields	.10
196	Gary Gaetti	.10
197	Ron Gant	.10
198	Brian Jordan	.10
199	Ray Lankford	.10
200	Mark McGwire	2.00
201	Todd Stottlemyre	.10
202	Kevin Brown	.10
203	Ken Caminiti	.10
204	Steve Finley	.10
205	Tony Gwynn	1.00
206	Carlos Hernandez	.10
207	Wally Joyner	.10
208	Greg Vaughn	.10
209	Barry Bonds	2.50

#	Player	
210	Shawn Estes	.10
211	Orel Hershiser	.10
212	Stan Javier	.10
213	Jeff Kent	.10
214	Bill Mueller	.10
215	Robb Nen	.10
216	J.T. Snow	.10
217	Jay Buhner	.10
218	Ken Cloude	.10
219	Joey Cora	.10
220	Ken Griffey Jr.	1.50
221	Glenallen Hill	.10
222	Randy Johnson	.75
223	Edgar Martinez	.10
224	Jamie Moyer	.10
225	Alex Rodriguez	2.00
226	David Segui	.10
227	Dan Wilson	.10
228	Rolando Arrojo RC	.25
229	Wade Boggs	1.00
230	Miguel Cairo	.10
231	Roberto Hernandez	.10
232	Quinton McCracken	.10
233	Fred McGriff	.10
234	Paul Sorrento	.10
235	Kevin Stocker	.10
236	Will Clark	.10
237	Juan Gonzalez	.40
238	Rusty Greer	.10
239	Rick Helling	.10
240	Roberto Kelly	.10
241	Ivan Rodriguez	.65
242	Aaron Sele	.10
243	John Wetteland	.10
244	Jose Canseco	.50
245	Roger Clemens	1.25
246	Jose Cruz Jr.	.10
247	Carlos Delgado	.50
248	Alex Gonzalez	.10
249	Ed Sprague	.10
250	Shannon Stewart	.10

EO Portraits

MARK McGWIRE St. Louis

EO Portraits is a 20-card insert seeded 1:73. Each card has a color action photo with a player portrait laser-cut into the card. A "1-of-1" parallel features a laser-cut number on the card as well. The "EO" stands for "Electro Optical" technology.

NM/M
Complete Set (20): 70.00
Common Player: 1.25
Inserted 1:73

#	Player	
1	Cal Ripken Jr.	10.00
2	Nomar Garciaparra	5.00
3	Mo Vaughn	1.25
4	Frank Thomas	4.00
5	Manny Ramirez	4.00
6	Ben Grieve	1.25
7	Ken Griffey Jr.	6.50
8	Alex Rodriguez	7.50
9	Juan Gonzalez	2.00
10	Ivan Rodriguez	3.50
11	Travis Lee	1.25
12	Greg Maddux	5.00
13	Chipper Jones	5.00
14	Kerry Wood	2.00
15	Larry Walker	1.25
16	Jeff Bagwell	4.00
17	Mike Piazza	6.00
18	Mark McGwire	7.50
19	Tony Gwynn	5.00
20	Barry Bonds	10.00

Face to Face

Face to Face features two star players on each card. It is a 10-card insert seeded one per 145 packs.

NM/M
Complete Set (10): 50.00
Common Player: 2.00
Inserted 1:145

#	Players	
1	Alex Rodriguez, Nomar Garciaparra	9.00
2	Mark McGwire, Ken Griffey Jr.	9.00
3	Mike Piazza, Sandy Alomar Jr.	6.00
4	Kerry Wood, Roger Clemens	6.00
5	Cal Ripken Jr., Paul Molitor	10.00
6	Tony Gwynn, Wade Boggs	5.00
7	Frank Thomas, Chipper Jones	5.00
8	Travis Lee, Ben Grieve	2.00
9	Hideo Nomo, Hideki Irabu	3.50
10	Juan Gonzalez, Manny Ramirez	3.50

Online

Online is a 36-card insert seeded about one per nine packs. The foiled and etched cards feature a color player photo in front of a hi-tech designed background. The card fronts also include the internet address for the player's web site on bigleaguers.com.

NM/M
Complete Set (36): 35.00
Common Player: .45
Inserted 1:9

#	Player	
1	Cal Ripken Jr.	5.00
2	Nomar Garciaparra	2.00
3	Pedro Martinez	1.50
4	Mo Vaughn	.45
5	Frank Thomas	1.50
6	Sandy Alomar Jr.	.45
7	Manny Ramirez	1.50
8	Jaret Wright	.45
9	Paul Molitor	1.50
10	Derek Jeter	5.00
11	Bernie Williams	.45
12	Ben Grieve	.45
13	Ken Griffey Jr.	3.00
14	Edgar Martinez	.45
15	Alex Rodriguez	4.00
16	Wade Boggs	2.00
17	Juan Gonzalez	.75
18	Ivan Rodriguez	1.00
19	Roger Clemens	2.50
20	Travis Lee	.45
21	Matt Williams	.45
22	Andres Galarraga	.45
23	Chipper Jones	2.00
24	Greg Maddux	2.00
25	Sammy Sosa	2.00
26	Kerry Wood	.75
27	Barry Larkin	.45
28	Larry Walker	.45
29	Derrek Lee	1.00
30	Jeff Bagwell	1.50
31	Hideo Nomo	.75
32	Mike Piazza	2.50
33	Scott Rolen	1.00
34	Mark McGwire	4.00
35	Tony Gwynn	2.00
36	Barry Bonds	5.00

Prism

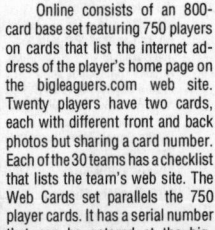

MIKE PIAZZA

This 20-card insert was seeded one per 37 packs. Horizontal card fronts feature prismatic foil technology.

NM/M
Complete Set (20): 30.00
Common Player: .75
Inserted 1:37

#	Player	
1	Cal Ripken Jr.	4.50
2	Nomar Garciaparra	2.50
3	Pedro Martinez	1.50
4	Frank Thomas	1.50
5	Manny Ramirez	1.50
6	Brian Giles	.75
7	Derek Jeter	4.50
8	Ben Grieve	.75
9	Ken Griffey Jr.	3.00
10	Alex Rodriguez	3.50
11	Juan Gonzalez	1.00
12	Travis Lee	.75
13	Chipper Jones	2.50
14	Greg Maddux	2.50
15	Kerry Wood	1.00
16	Larry Walker	.75
17	Hideo Nomo	1.00
18	Mike Piazza	3.00
19	Mark McGwire	3.50
20	Tony Gwynn	2.50

Rising Stars

Rising Stars is a multi-tiered hobby-only insert. The 20 base cards are found about 1:9 packs. Each card has two or three prospects from the same team. Five tiers of partial parallels of the insert are sequentially numbered.

NM/M
Complete Set (30): 15.00
Common Player: .50
Inserted 1:9
Tier 1 (# to 100): 3X
Tier 2 (# to 75): 4X
Tier 3 (# to 50): 5X
Tier 4 (# to 25): 10X
Tier 5 (1 of 1): Value Undetermined

#	Players	
1	Nerio Rodriguez, Sidney Ponson	.50
2	Frank Catalanotto, Roberto Duran, Sean Runyan	.50
3	Kevin L. Brown, Carlos Almanzar	.50
4	Aaron Boone, Pat Watkins, Scott Winchester	.50
5	Brian Meadows, Andy Larkin, Antonio Alfonseca	.50
6	DaRond Stovall, Trey Moore, Shayne Bennett	.50
7	Felix Martinez, Larry Sutton, Brian Bevil	.50
8	Homer Bush, Mike Buddie	.50
9	Rich Butler, Esteban Yan	.50
10	Damon Hollins, Brian Edmondson	.50
11	Lou Collier, Jose Silva, Javier Martinez	.50
12	Steve Sinclair, Mark Dalesandro	.50
13	Jason Varitek, Brian Rose, Brian Shouse	.50
14	Mike Caruso, Jeff Abbott, Tom Fordham	.50
15	Jason Johnson, Bobby Smith	.50
16	Dave Berg, Mark Kotsay, Jesus Sanchez	.50
17	Richard Hidalgo, John Halama, Trever Miller	.50
18	Geoff Jenkins, Bobby Hughes, Steve Woodard	.50
19	Eli Marrero, Cliff Politte, Mike Busby	.50
20	Desi Relaford, Darrin Winston	.50
21	Todd Helton, Bobby Jones	1.50
22	Rolando Arrojo, Miguel Cairo, Dan Carlson	.50
23	David Ortiz, Javier Valentin, Eric Milton	1.25
24	Magglio Ordonez, Greg Norton	1.00
25	Brad Fullmer, Javier Vazquez, Rick DeHart	.50
26	Paul Konerko, Matt Luke	1.00
27	Derrek Lee, Ryan Jackson, John Roskos	1.25
28	Ben Grieve, A.J. Hinch, Ryan Christenson	.50
29	Travis Lee, Karim Garcia, David Dellucci	.65
30	Kerry Wood, Marc Pisciotta	1.00

1998 Pacific Online

Online consists of an 800-card base set featuring 750 players on cards that list the internet address of the player's home page on the bigleaguers.com web site. Twenty players have two cards, each with different front and back photos but sharing a card number. Each of the 30 teams has a checklist that lists the team's web site. The Web Cards set parallels the 750 player cards. It has a serial number that can be entered at the big-

leaguers.com Web site to determine if a prize has been won. Red-foil versions of each card were produced for retail-only jumbo packs; they may carry a modest premium.

NM/M
Complete Set (800): 60.00
Common Player: .05
Web Stars/RC's: 2X
Inserted 1:1
Pack (9): .75
Wax Box (36): 20.00

#	Player	
1	Garret Anderson	.05
2	Rich DeLucia RC	.05
3	Jason Dickson	.05
4	Gary DiSarcina	.05
5	Jim Edmonds	.15
6	Darin Erstad	.05
7	Cecil Fielder	.05
8	Chuck Finley	.05
9	Carlos Garcia	.05
10	Shigetosi Hasegawa	.05
11	Ken Hill	.05
12	Dave Hollins	.05
13	Mike Holtz	.05
14	Mike James	.05
15	Norberto Martin	.05
16	Damon Mashore	.05
17	Jack McDowell	.05
18	Phil Nevin	.05
19	Omar Olivares	.05
20	Troy Percival	.05
21	Rich Robertson	.05
22	Tim Salmon	.05
23	Craig Shipley	.05
24	Matt Walbeck	.05
25	Allen Watson	.05
26	Jim Edmonds (Angels Checklist)	.05
27	Brian Anderson	.05
28	Tony Batista	.05
29	Jay Bell	.05
30	Andy Benes	.05
31	Yamil Benitez	.05
32	Willie Blair	.05
33	Brent Brede	.05
34	Scott Brow	.05
35	Omar Daal	.05
36	David Dellucci	.05
37	Edwin Diaz	.05
38	Jorge Fabregas	.05
39	Andy Fox	.05
40	Karim Garcia	.05
41a	Travis Lee/Btg	.05
41b	Travis Lee/Fldg	.05
42	Barry Manuel	.05
43	Gregg Olson	.05
44	Felix Rodriguez	.05
45	Clint Sodowsky	.05
46	Russ Springer	.05
47	Andy Stankiewicz	.05
48	Kelly Stinnett	.05
49	Jeff Suppan	.05
50	Devon White	.05
51	Matt Williams	.05
52	Travis Lee (Diamondbacks Checklist)	.05
53	Danny Bautista	.05
54	Rafael Belliard	.05
55	Adam Butler RC	.10
56	Mike Cather	.05
57	Brian Edmondson	.05
58	Alan Embree	.05
59	Andres Galarraga	.05
60	Tom Glavine	.35
61	Tony Graffanino	.05
62	Andruw Jones	.65
63a	Chipper Jones/Btg	.75
63b	Chipper Jones/Fldg	.75
64	Ryan Klesko	.05
65	Keith Lockhart	.05
66	Javy Lopez	.05
67a	Greg Maddux/Btg	.05
67b	Greg Maddux/Pitching	.75
68	Dennis Martinez	.05
69	Kevin Millwood RC	.50
70	Denny Neagle	.05
71	Eddie Perez	.05
72	Curtis Pride	.05
73	John Smoltz	.05
74	Michael Tucker	.05
75	Walt Weiss	.05
76	Gerald Williams	.05
77	Mark Wohlers	.05
78	Chipper Jones (Braves Checklist)	.40
79	Roberto Alomar	.15
80	Brady Anderson	.05
81	Harold Baines	.05
82	Armando Benitez	.05
83	Mike Bordick	.05
84	Joe Carter	.05
85	Norm Charlton	.05
86	Eric Davis	.05
87	Doug Drabek	.05
88	Scott Erickson	.05
89	Jeffrey Hammonds	.05
90	Chris Hoiles	.05
91	Scott Kamieniecki	.05
92	Jimmy Key	.05
93	Terry Mathews	.05
94	Alan Mills	.05
95	Mike Mussina	.25
96	Jesse Orosco	.05
97	Rafael Palmeiro	.60
98	Sidney Ponson	.05
99	Jeff Reboulet	.05
100	Arthur Rhodes	.05
101a	Cal Ripken Jr./Btg	2.00
101b	Cal Ripken Jr./Btg (Close-up.)	2.00
102	Nerio Rodriguez	.05
103	B.J. Surhoff	.05
104	Lenny Webster	.05
105	Cal Ripken Jr. (Orioles Checklist)	1.00
106	Steve Avery	.05
107	Mike Benjamin	.05
108	Darren Bragg	.05
109	Damon Buford	.05
110	Jim Corsi	.05
111	Dennis Eckersley	.60
112	Rich Garces	.05
113a	Nomar Garciaparra/Btg	.75
113b	Nomar Garciaparra/Fldg	.75
114	Tom Gordon	.05
115	Scott Hatteberg	.05
116	Butch Henry	.05
117	Reggie Jefferson	.05
118	Mark Lemke	.05
119	Darren Lewis	.05
120	Jim Leyritz	.05
121	Derek Lowe	.05
122	Pedro Martinez	.65
123	Troy O'Leary	.05
124	Brian Rose	.05
125	Bret Saberhagen	.05
126	Donnie Sadler	.05
127	Brian Shouse	.05
128	John Valentin	.05
129	Jason Varitek	.05
130	Mo Vaughn	.05
131	Tim Wakefield	.05
132	John Wasdin	.05
133	Nomar Garciaparra (Red Sox Checklist)	.45
134	Terry Adams	.05
135	Manny Alexander	.05
136	Rod Beck	.05
137	Jeff Blauser	.05
138	Brant Brown	.05
139	Mark Clark	.05
140	Jeremi Gonzalez	.05
141	Mark Grace	.05
142	Jose Hernandez	.05
143	Tyler Houston	.05
144	Lance Johnson	.05
145	Sandy Martinez	.05
146	Matt Mieske	.05
147	Mickey Morandini	.05
148	Terry Mulholland	.05
149	Kevin Orie	.05
150	Bob Patterson	.05
151	Marc Pisciotta	.05
152	Henry Rodriguez	.05
153	Scott Servais	.05
154	Sammy Sosa	.05
155	Kevin Tapani	.05
156	Steve Trachsel	.05
157a	Kerry Wood/Pitching	.30
157b	Kerry Wood/Pitching (Close-up.)	.30
158	Kerry Wood (Cubs Checklist)	.20
159	Jeff Abbott	.05
160	James Baldwin	.05
161	Albert Belle	.05
162	Jason Bere	.05
163	Mike Cameron	.05
164	Mike Caruso	.05
165	Carlos Castillo	.05
166	Tony Castillo	.05
167	Ray Durham	.05
168	Scott Eyre	.05
169	Tom Fordham	.05
170	Keith Foulke	.05
171	Lou Frazier	.05
172	Matt Karchner	.05
173	Chad Kreuter	.05
174	Jaime Navarro	.05
175	Greg Norton	.05
176	Charlie O'Brien	.05
177	Magglio Ordonez	.15
178	Ruben Sierra	.05
179	Bill Simas	.05
180	Mike Sirotka	.05
181	Chris Snopek	.05
182a	Frank Thomas (In batter's box.)	.65
182b	Frank Thomas/Swinging	.65
183	Robin Ventura	.05
184	Frank Thomas (White Sox Checklist)	.40
185	Stan Belinda	.05
186	Aaron Boone	.15
187	Bret Boone	.05
188	Brook Fordyce	.05
189	Willie Greene	.05
190	Pete Harnisch	.05
191	Lenny Harris	.05
192	Mark Hutton	.05
193	Damian Jackson	.05
194	Ricardo Jordan	.05
195	Barry Larkin	.05
196	Eduardo Perez	.05
197	Pokey Reese	.05
198	Mike Remlinger	.05
199	Reggie Sanders	.05
200	Jeff Shaw	.05
201	Chris Stynes	.05
202	Scott Sullivan	.05
203	Eddie Taubensee	.05
204	Brett Tomko	.05
205	Pat Watkins	.05
206	David Weathers	.05
207	Gabe White	.05
208	Scott Winchester	.05
209	Barry Larkin (Reds Checklist)	.05
210	Sandy Alomar Jr.	.05
211	Paul Assenmacher	.05
212	Geronimo Berroa	.05
213	Pat Borders	.05
214	Jeff Branson	.05
215	Dave Burba	.05
216	Bartolo Colon	.05
217	Shawon Dunston	.05
218	Travis Fryman	.05
219	Brian Giles	.05
220	Dwight Gooden	.05
221	Mike Jackson	.05
222	David Justice	.05
223	Kenny Lofton	.05
224	Jose Mesa	.05
225	Alvin Morman	.05
226	Charles Nagy	.05
227	Chad Ogea	.05
228	Eric Plunk	.05
229	Manny Ramirez	.65
230	Paul Shuey	.05
231	Jim Thome	.65
232	Ron Villone	.05
233	Omar Vizquel	.05
234	Enrique Wilson	.05
235	Jaret Wright	.05
236	Manny Ramirez (Indians Checklist)	.40
237	Pedro Astacio	.05
238	Jason Bates	.05
239	Dante Bichette	.05
240	Ellis Burks	.05
241	Vinny Castilla	.05
242	Greg Colbrunn	.05
243	Mike DeJean	.05
244	Jerry Dipoto	.05
245	Curtis Goodwin	.05
246	Todd Helton	.65
247	Bobby Jones	.05
248	Darryl Kile	.05
249	Mike Lansing	.05
250	Curtis Leskanic	.05
251	Nelson Liriano	.05
252	Kirt Manwaring	.05
253	Chuck McElroy	.05
254	Mike Munoz	.05
255	Neifi Perez	.05
256	Jeff Reed	.05
257	Mark Thompson	.05
258	John Vander Wal	.05
259	Dave Veres	.05
260a	Larry Walker/Btg	.05
260b	Larry Walker/Btg (Close-up.)	.05
261	Jamey Wright	.05
262	Larry Walker (Rockies Checklist)	.05
263	Kimera Bartee	.05
264	Doug Brocail	.05
265	Raul Casanova	.05
266	Frank Castillo	.05
267	Frank Catalanotto	.05
268	Tony Clark	.05
269	Deivi Cruz	.05
270	Roberto Duran	.05
271	Damion Easley	.05
272	Bryce Florie	.05
273	Luis Gonzalez	.05
274	Bob Higginson	.05
275	Brian Hunter	.05
276	Todd Jones	.05
277	Greg Keagle	.05
278	Jeff Manto	.05
279	Brian Moehler	.05
280	Joe Oliver	.05
281	Joe Randa	.05
282	Billy Ripken	.05
283	Bip Roberts	.05
284	Sean Runyan	.05
285	A.J. Sager	.05
286	Justin Thompson	.05
287	Tony Clark (Tigers Checklist)	.05
288	Antonio Alfonseca	.05
289	Dave Berg	.05
290	Josh Booty	.05
291	John Cangelosi	.05
292	Craig Counsell	.05
293	Vic Darensbourg	.05
294	Cliff Floyd	.05
295	Oscar Henriquez	.05
296	Felix Heredia	.05
297	Ryan Jackson RC	.05
298	Mark Kotsay	.05

No	Player	Price
299	Andy Larkin	.05
300	Derrek Lee	.60
301	Brian Meadows	.05
302	Rafael Medina	.05
303	Jay Powell	.05
304	Edgar Renteria	.05
305	Jesus Sanchez RC	.05
306	Rob Stanifer	.05
307	Gregg Zaun	.05
308	Derrek Lee (Marlins Checklist)	.30
309	Moises Alou	.05
310	Brad Ausmus	.05
311a	Jeff Bagwell/Btg	.65
311b	Jeff Bagwell/Fldg	.65
312	Derek Bell	.05
313	Sean Bergman	.05
314	Sean Berry	.05
315	Craig Biggio	.05
316	Tim Bogar	.05
317	Jose Cabrera	.05
318	Dave Clark	.05
319	Tony Eusebio	.05
320	Carl Everett	.05
321	Ricky Gutierrez	.05
322	John Halama	.05
323	Mike Hampton	.05
324	Doug Henry	.05
325	Richard Hidalgo	.05
326	Jack Howell	.05
327	Jose Lima	.05
328	Mike Magnante	.05
329	Trever Miller	.05
330	C.J. Nitkowski	.05
331	Shane Reynolds	.05
332	Bill Spiers	.05
333	Billy Wagner	.05
334	Jeff Bagwell (Astros Checklist)	.40
335	Tim Belcher	.05
336	Brian Bevil	.05
337	Johnny Damon	.35
338	Jermaine Dye	.05
339	Sal Fasano	.05
340	Shane Halter	.05
341	Chris Haney	.05
342	Jed Hansen	.05
343	Jeff King	.05
344	Jeff Montgomery	.05
345	Hal Morris	.05
346	Jose Offerman	.05
347	Dean Palmer	.05
348	Terry Pendleton	.05
349	Hipolito Pichardo	.05
350	Jim Pittsley	.05
351	Pat Rapp	.05
352	Jose Rosado	.05
353	Glendon Rusch	.05
354	Scott Service	.05
355	Larry Sutton	.05
356	Mike Sweeney	.05
357	Joe Vitiello	.05
358	Matt Whisenant	.05
359	Ernie Young	.05
360	Jeff King (Royals Checklist)	.05
361	Bobby Bonilla	.05
362	Jim Bruske	.05
363	Juan Castro	.05
364	Roger Cedeno	.05
365	Mike Devereaux	.05
366	Darren Dreifort	.05
367	Jim Eisenreich	.05
368	Wilton Guerrero	.05
369	Mark Guthrie	.05
370	Darren Hall	.05
371	Todd Hollandsworth	.05
372	Thomas Howard	.05
373	Trenidad Hubbard	.05
374	Charles Johnson	.05
375	Eric Karros	.05
376	Paul Konerko	.20
377	Matt Luke	.05
378	Ramon Martinez	.05
379	Raul Mondesi	.05
380	Hideo Nomo	.35
381	Antonio Osuna	.05
382	Chan Ho Park	.05
383	Tom Prince	.05
384	Scott Radinsky	.05
385	Gary Sheffield	.40
386	Ismael Valdes	.05
387	Jose Vizcaino	.05
388	Eric Young	.05
389	Gary Sheffield (Dodgers Checklist)	.10
390	Jeromy Burnitz	.05
391	Jeff Cirillo	.05
392	Cal Eldred	.05
393	Chad Fox	.05
394	Marquis Grissom	.05
395	Bob Hamelin	.05
396	Bobby Hughes	.05
397	Darrin Jackson	.05
398	John Jaha	.05
399	Geoff Jenkins	.05
400	Doug Jones	.05
401	Jeff Juden	.05
402	Scott Karl	.05
403	Jesse Levis	.05
404	Mark Loretta	.05
405	Mike Matheny	.05
406	Jose Mercedes	.05
407	Mike Myers	.05
408	Marc Newfield	.05
409	Dave Nilsson	.05
410	Al Reyes	.05
411	Jose Valentin	.05
412	Fernando Vina	.05
413	Paul Wagner	.05
414	Bob Wickman	.05
415	Steve Woodard	.05
416	Marquis Grissom (Brewers Checklist)	.05
417	Rick Aguilera	.05
418	Ron Coomer	.05
419	Marty Cordova	.05
420	Brent Gates	.05
421	Eddie Guardado	.05
422	Denny Hocking	.05
423	Matt Lawton	.05
424	Pat Meares	.05
425	Orlando Merced	.05
426	Eric Milton	.05
427	Paul Molitor	.65
428	Mike Morgan	.05
429	Dan Naulty	.05
430	Otis Nixon	.05
431	Alex Ochoa	.05
432	David Ortiz	.40
433	Brad Radke	.05
434	Todd Ritchie	.05
435	Frank Rodriguez	.05
436	Terry Steinbach	.05
437	Greg Swindell	.05
438	Bob Tewksbury	.05
439	Mike Trombley	.05
440	Javier Valentin	.05
441	Todd Walker	.05
442	Paul Molitor (Twins Checklist)	.40
443	Shane Andrews	.05
444	Miguel Batista	.05
445	Shayne Bennett	.05
446	Rick DeHart	.05
447	Brad Fullmer	.05
448	Mark Grudzielanek	.05
449	Vladimir Guerrero	.65
450	Dustin Hermanson	.05
451	Steve Kline	.05
452	Scott Livingstone	.05
453	Mike Maddux	.05
454	Derrick May	.05
455	Ryan McGuire	.05
456	Trey Moore	.05
457	Mike Mordecai	.05
458	Carl Pavano	.05
459	Carlos Perez	.05
460	F.P. Santangelo	.05
461	DaRond Stovall	.05
462	Anthony Telford	.05
463	Ugueth Urbina	.05
464	Marc Valdes	.05
465	Jose Vidro	.05
466	Rondell White	.05
467	Chris Widger	.05
468	Vladimir Guerrero (Expos Checklist)	.40
469	Edgardo Alfonzo	.05
470	Carlos Baerga	.05
471	Rich Becker	.05
472	Brian Bohanon	.05
473	Alberto Castillo	.05
474	Dennis Cook	.05
475	John Franco	.05
476	Matt Franco	.05
477	Bernard Gilkey	.05
478	John Hudek	.05
479	Butch Huskey	.05
480	Bobby Jones	.05
481	Al Leiter	.05
482	Luis Lopez	.05
483	Brian McRae	.05
484	Dave Mlicki	.05
485	John Olerud	.05
486	Rey Ordonez	.05
487	Craig Paquette	.05
488a	Mike Piazza/Btg	1.00
488b	Mike Piazza/Btg (Close-up.)	1.00
489	Todd Pratt	.05
490	Mel Rojas	.05
491	Tim Spehr	.05
492	Turk Wendell	.05
493	Masato Yoshii RC	.25
494	Mike Piazza (Mets Checklist)	.45
495	Willie Banks	.05
496	Scott Brosius	.05
497	Mike Buddie	.05
498	Homer Bush	.05
499	David Cone	.05
500	Chad Curtis	.05
501	Chili Davis	.05
502	Joe Girardi	.05
503	Darren Holmes	.05
504	Hideki Irabu	.05
505a	Derek Jeter/Btg	2.00
505b	Derek Jeter/Btg	2.00
506	Chuck Knoblauch	.05
507	Graeme Lloyd	.05
508	Tino Martinez	.05
509	Ramiro Mendoza	.05
510	Jeff Nelson	.05
511	Paul O'Neill	.20
512	Andy Pettitte	.20
513	Jorge Posada	.05
514	Tim Raines	.05
515	Mariano Rivera	.15
516	Luis Sojo	.05
517	Mike Stanton	.05
518	Darryl Strawberry	.05
519	Dale Sveum	.05
520	David Wells	.05
521	Bernie Williams	.05
522	Bernie Williams (Yankees Checklist)	.05
523	Kurt Abbott	.05
524	Mike Blowers	.05
525	Rafael Bournigal	.05
526	Tom Candiotti	.05
527	Ryan Christenson	.05
528	Mike Fetters	.05
529	Jason Giambi	.50
530a	Ben Grieve/Btg	.05
530b	Ben Grieve/Running	.05
531	Buddy Groom	.05
532	Jimmy Haynes	.05
533	Rickey Henderson	.65
534	A.J. Hinch	.05
535	Mike Macfarlane	.05
536	Dave Magadan	.05
537	T.J. Mathews	.05
538	Jason McDonald	.05
539	Kevin Mitchell	.05
540	Mike Mohler	.05
541	Mike Oquist	.05
542	Ariel Prieto	.05
543	Kenny Rogers	.05
544	Aaron Small	.05
545	Scott Spiezio	.05
546	Matt Stairs	.05
547	Bill Taylor	.05
548	Dave Telgheder	.05
549	Jack Voigt	.05
550	Ben Grieve (A's Checklist)	.05
551	Bob Abreu	.10
552	Ruben Amaro	.05
553	Alex Arias	.05
554	Matt Beech	.05
555	Ricky Bottalico	.05
556	Billy Brewer	.05
557	Rico Brogna	.05
558	Doug Glanville	.05
559	Wayne Gomes	.05
560	Mike Grace	.05
561	Tyler Green	.05
562	Rex Hudler	.05
563	Gregg Jefferies	.05
564	Kevin Jordan	.05
565	Mark Leiter	.05
566	Mark Lewis	.05
567	Mike Lieberthal	.05
568	Mark Parent	.05
569	Yorkis Perez	.05
570	Desi Relaford	.05
571	Scott Rolen	.50
572	Curt Schilling	.35
573	Kevin Sefcik	.05
574	Jerry Spradlin	.05
575	Garrett Stephenson	.05
576	Darrin Winston	.05
577	Scott Rolen (Phillies Checklist)	.20
578	Jermaine Allensworth	.05
579	Jason Christiansen	.05
580	Lou Collier	.05
581	Francisco Cordova	.05
582	Elmer Dessens	.05
583	Freddy Garcia	.05
584	Jose Guillen	.05
585	Jason Kendall	.05
586	Jon Lieber	.05
587	Esteban Loaiza	.05
588	Al Martin	.05
589	Javier Martinez	.05
590	Kevin Polcovich	.05
591	Ricardo Rincon	.05
592	Jason Schmidt	.05
593	Jose Silva	.05
595	Mark Smith	.05
596	Doug Strange	.05
597	Turner Ward	.05
598	Mark Wilkins	.05
599	Mike Williams	.05
600	Tony Womack	.05
601	Kevin Young	.05
602	Tony Womack (Pirates Checklist)	.05
603	Manny Aybar	.05
604	Kent Bottenfield	.05
605	Jeff Brantley	.05
606	Mike Busby	.05
607	Royce Clayton	.05
608	Delino DeShields	.05
609	John Frascatore	.05
610	Gary Gaetti	.05
611	Ron Gant	.05
612	David Howard	.05
613	Brian Hunter	.05
614	Brian Jordan	.05
615	Tom Lampkin	.05
616	Ray Lankford	.05
617	Braden Looper	.05
618	John Mabry	.05
619	Eli Marrero	.05
620	Willie McGee	.05
621a	Mark McGwire/Btg	1.50
621b	Mark McGwire/Fldg	1.50
622	Kent Mercker	.05
623	Matt Morris	.05
624	Donovan Osborne	.05
625	Tom Pagnozzi	.05
626	Lance Painter	.05
627	Mark Petkovsek	.05
628	Todd Stottlemyre	.05
629	Mark McGwire (Cardinals Checklist)	.75
630	Andy Ashby	.05
631	Brian Boehringer	.05
632	Kevin Brown	.05
633	Ken Caminiti	.10
634	Steve Finley	.05
635	Ed Giovanola	.05
636	Chris Gomez	.05
637a	Tony Gwynn (Blue jersey.)	.75
637b	Tony Gwynn (White jersey.)	.75
SAMPLE	Tony Gwynn (SAMPLE overprint on back.)	1.00
638	Joey Hamilton	.05
639	Carlos Hernandez	.05
640	Sterling Hitchcock	.05
641	Trevor Hoffman	.05
642	Wally Joyner	.05
643	Dan Miceli	.05
644	James Mouton	.05
645	Greg Myers	.05
646	Carlos Reyes	.05
647	Andy Sheets	.05
648	Pete Smith	.05
649	Mark Sweeney	.05
650	Greg Vaughn	.05
651	Quilvio Veras	.05
652	Tony Gwynn (Padres Checklist)	.40
653	Rich Aurilia	.05
654	Marvin Benard	.05
655a	Barry Bonds/Btg	2.00
655b	Barry Bonds/Btg (Close-up.)	2.00
656	Danny Darwin	.05
657	Shawn Estes	.05
658	Mark Gardner	.05
659	Darryl Hamilton	.05
660	Charlie Hayes	.05
661	Orel Hershiser	.05
662	Stan Javier	.05
663	Brian Johnson	.05
664	John Johnstone	.05
665	Jeff Kent	.05
666	Brent Mayne	.05
667	Bill Mueller	.05
668	Robb Nen	.05
669	Jim Poole	.05
670	Steve Reed	.05
671	Rich Rodriguez	.05
672	Kirk Rueter	.05
673	Rey Sanchez	.05
674	J.T. Snow	.05
675	Julian Tavarez	.05
676	Barry Bonds (Giants Checklist)	1.00
677	Rich Amaral	.05
678	Bobby Ayala	.05
679	Jay Buhner	.05
680	Ken Cloude	.05
681	Joey Cora	.05
682	Russ Davis	.05
683	Rob Ducey	.05
684	Jeff Fassero	.05
685	Tony Fossas	.05
686a	Ken Griffey Jr./Btg	1.25
686b	Ken Griffey Jr./Fldg	1.25
687	Glenallen Hill	.05
688	Jeff Huson	.05
689	Randy Johnson	.65
690	Edgar Martinez	.05
691	John Marzano	.05
692	Jamie Moyer	.05
693a	Alex Rodriguez/Btg	1.50
693b	Alex Rodriguez/Fldg	1.50
694	David Segui	.05
695	Heathcliff Slocumb	.05
696	Paul Spoljaric	.05
697	Bill Swift	.05
698	Mike Timlin	.05
699	Bob Wells	.05
700	Dan Wilson	.05
701	Ken Griffey Jr. (Mariners Checklist)	.50
702	Wilson Alvarez	.05
703	Rolando Arrojo RC	.30
704a	Wade Boggs/Btg	.75
704b	Wade Boggs/Fldg	.75
705	Rich Butler	.05
706	Miguel Cairo	.05
707	Mike Difelice	.05
708	John Flaherty	.05
709	Roberto Hernandez	.05
710	Mike Kelly	.05
711	Aaron Ledesma	.05
712	Albie Lopez	.05
713	Dave Martinez	.05
714	Quinton McCracken	.05
715	Fred McGriff	.05
716	Jim Mecir	.05
717	Tony Saunders	.05
718	Bobby Smith	.05
719	Paul Sorrento	.05
720	Dennis Springer	.05
721	Kevin Stocker	.05
722	Ramon Tatis	.05
723	Bubba Trammell	.05
724	Esteban Yan	.05
725	Wade Boggs (Devil Rays Checklist)	.40
726	Luis Alicea	.05
727	Scott Bailes	.05
728	John Burkett	.05
729	Domingo Cedeno	.05
730	Will Clark	.05
731	Kevin Elster	.05
732a	Juan Gonzalez (Bat)	.35
732b	Juan Gonzalez (No bat.)	.35
733	Tom Goodwin	.05
734	Rusty Greer	.05
735	Eric Gunderson	.05
736	Bill Haselman	.05
737	Rick Helling	.10
738	Roberto Kelly	.05
739	Mark McLemore	.05
740	Darren Oliver	.05
741	Danny Patterson	.05
742	Roger Pavlik	.05
743a	Ivan Rodriguez/Btg	.60
743b	Ivan Rodriguez/Fldg	.60
744	Aaron Sele	.05
745	Mike Simms	.05
746	Lee Stevens	.05
747	Fernando Tatis	.05
748	John Wetteland	.05
749	Bobby Witt	.05
750	Juan Gonzalez (Rangers Checklist)	.20
751	Carlos Almanzar	.05
752	Kevin Brown	.05
753	Jose Canseco	.40
754	Chris Carpenter	.05
755	Roger Clemens	1.00
756	Felipe Crespo	.05
757	Jose Cruz Jr.	.05
758	Mark Dalesandro	.05
759	Carlos Delgado	.50
760	Kelvim Escobar	.05
761	Tony Fernandez	.05
762	Darrin Fletcher	.05
763	Alex Gonzalez	.05
764	Craig Grebeck	.05
765	Shawn Green	.35
766	Juan Guzman	.05
767	Erik Hanson	.05
768	Pat Hentgen	.05
769	Randy Myers	.05
770	Robert Person	.05
771	Dan Plesac	.05
772	Paul Quantrill	.05
773	Bill Risley	.05
774	Juan Samuel	.05
775	Steve Sinclair	.05
776	Ed Sprague	.05
777	Mike Stanley	.05
778	Shannon Stewart	.05
779	Woody Williams	.05
780	Roger Clemens (Blue Jays Checklist)	.45

Web Cards

This 800-card parallel set allowed collectors to use Pacific's web site to find out the prize they had won. The cards used gold foil on the front instead of the silver foil used on base cards, and contained an eight-digit code on the back that was the claim number.

Web Stars/RC's:	2X
Inserted 1:1	

1998 Pacific Paramount

Paramount was Pacific's first fully-licensed baseball card product. The 250 base cards feature full-bleed photos with the player's name and team listed at the bottom. The base set is paralleled three times. Gold retail (1:1), Copper hobby (1:1) and Platinum Blue (1:73) versions were included. Inserts in the product are Special Delivery Die-Cuts, Team Checklist Die-Cuts, Cooperstown Bound, Fielder's Choice Laser-Cuts and Inaugural Issue.

	NM/M
Complete Set (250):	20.00
Common Player:	.05

Gold (1:1R):	1X
Copper (1:1H):	1X
Red (1:1 ANCO):	2X
Platinum Blue (1:73):	4X
Holographic Silver:	20X
Production 99 Sets	
Pack (6):	1.00
Wax Box (36):	15.00

No	Player	Price
1	Garret Anderson	.10
2	Gary DiSarcina	.10
3	Jim Edmonds	.10
4	Darin Erstad	.20
5	Cecil Fielder	.10
6	Chuck Finley	.10
7	Todd Greene	.10
8	Shigetosi Hasegawa	.10
9	Tim Salmon	.10
10	Roberto Alomar	.20
11	Brady Anderson	.10
12	Joe Carter	.10
13	Eric Davis	.10
14	Ozzie Guillen	.10
15	Mike Mussina	.40
16	Rafael Palmeiro	.65
17	Cal Ripken Jr.	2.50
18	B.J. Surhoff	.10
19	Steve Avery	.10
20	Nomar Garciaparra	1.00
21	Reggie Jefferson	.10
22	Pedro Martinez	.75
23	Tim Naehring	.10
24	John Valentin	.10
25	Mo Vaughn	.10
26	James Baldwin	.10
27	Albert Belle	.10
28	Ray Durham	.10
29	Benji Gil	.10
30	Jaime Navarro	.10
31	Magglio Ordonez RC	1.50
32	Frank Thomas	.75
33	Robin Ventura	.10
34	Sandy Alomar Jr.	.10
35	Geronimo Berroa	.10
36	Travis Fryman	.10
37	David Justice	.10
38	Kenny Lofton	.10
39	Charles Nagy	.10
40	Manny Ramirez	.75
41	Jim Thome	.65
42	Omar Vizquel	.10
43	Jaret Wright	.10
44	Raul Casanova	.10
45	Frank Catalanotto RC	.20
46	Tony Clark	.10
47	Bobby Higginson	.10
48	Brian Hunter	.10
49	Todd Jones	.10
50	Bip Roberts	.10
51	Justin Thompson	.10
52	Kevin Appier	.10
53	Johnny Damon	.35
54	Jermaine Dye	.10
55	Jeff King	.10
56	Jeff Montgomery	.10
57	Dean Palmer	.10
58	Jose Rosado	.10
59	Larry Sutton	.10
60	Rick Aguilera	.10
61	Marty Cordova	.10
62	Pat Meares	.10
63	Paul Molitor	.75
64	Otis Nixon	.10
65	Brad Radke	.10
66	Terry Steinbach	.10
67	Todd Walker	.10
68	Hideki Irabu	.10
69	Derek Jeter	2.50
70	Chuck Knoblauch	.10
71	Tino Martinez	.10
72	Paul O'Neill	.10
73	Andy Pettitte	.20
74	Mariano Rivera	.15
75	Bernie Williams	.10
76	Mark Bellhorn	.10
77	Tom Candiotti	.10
78	Jason Giambi	.50
79	Ben Grieve	.10
80	Rickey Henderson	.75
81	Jason McDonald	.10
82	Aaron Small	.10
83	Miguel Tejada	.20
84	Jay Buhner	.10
85	Joey Cora	.10
86	Jeff Fassero	.10
87	Ken Griffey Jr.	1.50
88	Randy Johnson	.75
89	Edgar Martinez	.10
90	Alex Rodriguez	2.00
91	David Segui	.10
92	Dan Wilson	.10
93	Wilson Alvarez	.10
94	Wade Boggs	1.00
95	Miguel Cairo	.10
96	John Flaherty	.10
97	Dave Martinez	.10
98	Quinton McCracken	.10
99	Fred McGriff	.10
100	Paul Sorrento	.10
101	Kevin Stocker	.10
102	John Burkett	.10
103	Will Clark	.10
104	Juan Gonzalez	.40
105	Rusty Greer	.10
106	Roberto Kelly	.10
107	Ivan Rodriguez	.65
108	Fernando Tatis	.10
109	John Wetteland	.10
110	Jose Canseco	.40

111	Roger Clemens	1.25
112	Jose Cruz Jr.	.10
113	Carlos Delgado	.50
114	Alex Gonzalez	.10
115	Pat Hentgen	.10
116	Ed Sprague	.10
117	Shannon Stewart	.10
118	Brian Anderson	.10
119	Jay Bell	.10
120	Andy Benes	.10
121	Yamil Benitez	.10
122	Jorge Fabregas	.10
123	Travis Lee	.10
124	Devon White	.10
125	Matt Williams	.10
126	Bob Wolcott	.10
127	Andres Galarraga	.10
128	Tom Glavine	.35
129	Andruw Jones	.75
130	Chipper Jones	1.00
131	Ryan Klesko	.10
132	Javy Lopez	.10
133	Greg Maddux	1.00
134	Denny Neagle	.10
135	John Smoltz	.10
136	Rod Beck	.10
137	Jeff Blauser	.10
138	Mark Grace	.10
139	Lance Johnson	.10
140	Mickey Morandini	.10
141	Kevin Orie	.10
142	Sammy Sosa	1.00
143	Aaron Boone	.10
144	Bret Boone	.10
145	Dave Burba	.10
146	Lenny Harris	.10
147	Barry Larkin	.10
148	Reggie Sanders	.10
149	Brett Tomko	.10
150	Pedro Astacio	.10
151	Dante Bichette	.10
152	Ellis Burks	.10
153	Vinny Castilla	.10
154	Todd Helton	.75
155	Darryl Kile	.10
156	Jeff Reed	.10
157	Larry Walker	.10
158	Bobby Bonilla	.10
159	Todd Dunwoody	.10
160	Livan Hernandez	.10
161	Charles Johnson	.10
162	Mark Kotsay	.10
163	Derek Lee	.60
164	Edgar Renteria	.10
165	Gary Sheffield	.50
166	Moises Alou	.10
167	Jeff Bagwell	.75
168	Derek Bell	.10
169	Craig Biggio	.10
170	Mike Hampton	.10
171	Richard Hidalgo	.10
172	Chris Holt	.10
173	Shane Reynolds	.10
174	Wilton Guerrero	.10
175	Eric Karros	.10
176	Paul Konerko	.20
177	Ramon Martinez	.10
178	Raul Mondesi	.10
179	Hideo Nomo	.40
180	Chan Ho Park	.10
181	Mike Piazza	1.25
182	Ismael Valdes	.10
183	Jeromy Burnitz	.10
184	Jeff Cirillo	.10
185	Todd Dunn	.10
186	Marquis Grissom	.10
187	John Jaha	.10
188	Doug Jones	.10
189	Dave Nilsson	.10
190	Jose Valentin	.10
191	Fernando Vina	.10
192	Orlando Cabrera	.10
193	Steve Falteisek	.10
194	Mark Grudzielanek	.10
195	Vladimir Guerrero	.75
196	Carlos Perez	.10
197	F.P. Santangelo	.10
198	Jose Vidro	.10
199	Rondell White	.10
200	Edgardo Alfonzo	.10
201	Carlos Baerga	.10
202	John Franco	.10
203	Bernard Gilkey	.10
204	Todd Hundley	.10
205	Butch Huskey	.10
206	Bobby Jones	.10
207	Brian McRae	.10
208	John Olerud	.10
209	Rey Ordonez	.10
210	Ricky Bottalico	.10
211	Bobby Estalella	.10
212	Doug Glanville	.10
213	Gregg Jefferies	.10
214	Mike Lieberthal	.10
215	Desi Relaford	.10
216	Scott Rolen	.65
217	Curt Schilling	.35
218	Adrian Brown	.10
219	Emil Brown	.10
220	Francisco Cordova	.10
221	Jose Guillen	.10
222	Al Martin	.10
223	Abraham Nunez	.10
224	Tony Womack	.10
225	Kevin Young	.10
226	Alan Benes	.10
227	Royce Clayton	.10
228	Gary Gaetti	.10

229	Ron Gant	.10
230	Brian Jordan	.10
231	Ray Lankford	.10
232	Mark McGwire	2.00
233	Todd Stottlemyre	.10
234	Kevin Brown	.10
235	Ken Caminiti	.10
236	Steve Finley	.10
237	Tony Gwynn	1.00
238	Wally Joyner	.10
239	Ruben Rivera	.10
240	Greg Vaughn	.10
241	Quilvio Veras	.10
242	Barry Bonds	2.50
243	Jacob Cruz	.10
244	Shawn Estes	.10
245	Orel Hershiser	.10
246	Stan Javier	.10
247	Brian Johnson	.10
248	Jeff Kent	.10
249	Robb Nen	.10
250	J.T. Snow	.10

Gold/Copper/Red

Gold, Copper and Red foil versions of all 250 cards in Paramount were inserted at a rate of one per pack. Gold versions were retail exclusive, Copper versions were hobby exclusive and Red versions were ANCO pack exclusive. The only difference is these parallels use a different color foil than the base cards.

	NM/M
Common Gold/Copper Player:	.25
Gold/Copper Stars:	1X
Inserted 1:1	
Common Red Player:	.30
Red Stars:	2X

Holographic Silver

Holographics Silver parallel cards were issued for all 250 cards in the Paramount set. These were inserted into hobby packs, with only 99 sets produced.

	NM/M
Common Player:	1.00
Holographic Silver Stars:	20X
Production 99 Sets	

Platinum Blue

This parallel set reprinted all 250 cards in Paramount using blue foil stamping on the card front. These were inserted one per 73 packs.

	NM/M
Common Platinum Blue Player:	1.00
Platinum Blue Stars:	4X
Inserted 1:73	

Cooperstown Bound

Cooperstown Bound is a 10-card insert seeded one per 361 packs. Each card features a color player photo with a silver foil column on the left. The cards are fully foiled and etched.

	NM/M
Complete Set (10):	60.00
Common Player:	8.00
Inserted 1:361	
Pacific Proofs:	6X

Production 20 Sets

1	Greg Maddux	10.00
2	Cal Ripken Jr.	15.00
3	Frank Thomas	8.00
4	Mike Piazza	8.00
5	Paul Molitor	8.00
6	Mark McGwire	12.00
7	Tony Gwynn	8.00
8	Barry Bonds	15.00
9	Ken Griffey Jr.	10.00
10	Wade Boggs	8.00

Fielder's Choice

Fielder's Choice Laser-Cuts is a 20-card insert seeded one per 73 packs. Each card is die-cut around a baseball glove that appears in the background. The webbing of the glove is laser-cut.

		NM/M
Complete Set (20):		45.00
Common Player:		.75
Inserted 1:73		
1	Chipper Jones	3.00
2	Greg Maddux	3.00
3	Cal Ripken Jr.	6.00
4	Nomar Garciaparra	3.00
5	Frank Thomas	2.50
6	David Justice	.75
7	Larry Walker	.75
8	Jeff Bagwell	2.50
9	Hideo Nomo	1.25
10	Mike Piazza	3.50
11	Derek Jeter	6.00
12	Ben Grieve	.75
13	Mark McGwire	4.50
14	Tony Gwynn	3.00
15	Barry Bonds	6.00
16	Ken Griffey Jr.	4.00
17	Alex Rodriguez	4.50
18	Wade Boggs	3.00
19	Ivan Rodriguez	2.00
20	Jose Cruz Jr.	.75

Special Delivery

Special Delivery cards are die-cut to resemble a postage stamp. Each card front is foiled and etched and features three photos of the player. Special Delivery is a 20-card insert seeded one per 37 packs.

		NM/M
Complete Set (20):		30.00
Common Player:		.50
Inserted 1:37		
1	Chipper Jones	2.50
2	Greg Maddux	2.50
3	Cal Ripken Jr.	5.00
4	Nomar Garciaparra	2.50
5	Pedro Martinez	2.00
6	Frank Thomas	2.00
7	David Justice	.50
8	Larry Walker	.50
9	Jeff Bagwell	2.00

10	Hideo Nomo	1.00
11	Mike Piazza	3.00
12	Vladimir Guerrero	2.00
13	Derek Jeter	5.00
14	Ben Grieve	.50
15	Mark McGwire	4.00
16	Tony Gwynn	2.50
17	Barry Bonds	5.00
18	Ken Griffey Jr.	3.50
19	Alex Rodriguez	4.00
20	Jose Cruz Jr.	.50

Team Checklists

Team Checklists (30 cards, 2:37) feature a player photo surrounded by two bats. The card is die-cut around the photo and the bats at the top. The bottom has the player's name, position and team.

		NM/M
Complete Set (30):		25.00
Common Player:		.25
Inserted 1:18		
1	Tim Salmon	.25
2	Cal Ripken Jr.	4.00
3	Nomar Garciaparra	1.50
4	Frank Thomas	1.00
5	Manny Ramirez	1.00
6	Tony Clark	.25
7	Dean Palmer	.25
8	Paul Molitor	1.00
9	Derek Jeter	4.00
10	Ben Grieve	.25
11	Ken Griffey Jr.	2.50
12	Wade Boggs	1.50
13	Ivan Rodriguez	.75
14	Roger Clemens	2.00
15	Matt Williams	.25
16	Chipper Jones	1.50
17	Sammy Sosa	1.50
18	Barry Larkin	.25
19	Larry Walker	.25
20	Livan Hernandez	.25
21	Jeff Bagwell	1.00
22	Mike Piazza	2.00
23	John Jaha	.25
24	Vladimir Guerrero	1.00
25	Todd Hundley	.25
26	Scott Rolen	.75
27	Kevin Young	.25
28	Mark McGwire	3.00
29	Tony Gwynn	1.50
30	Barry Bonds	4.00

1998 Pacific Revolution

Pacific Revolution consists of a 150-card base set. The base cards are dual-foiled, etched and embossed. Inserts include Showstoppers, Prime Time Performers Laser-Cuts, Foul Pole Laser-Cuts, Major League Icons and Shadow Series.

		NM/M
Complete Set (150):		65.00
Common Player:		.25
Pack (3):		1.00
Wax Box (24):		20.00
1	Garret Anderson	.25
2	Jim Edmonds	.25
3	Darin Erstad	.40
4	Chuck Finley	.25
5	Tim Salmon	.25
6	Jay Bell	.25
7	Travis Lee	.25

8	Devon White	.25
9	Matt Williams	.25
10	Andres Galarraga	.25
11	Tom Glavine	.45
12	Andruw Jones	2.50
13	Chipper Jones	3.50
14	Ryan Klesko	.25
15	Javy Lopez	.25
16	Greg Maddux	3.50
17	Walt Weiss	.25
18	Roberto Alomar	.40
19	Joe Carter	.25
20	Mike Mussina	1.25
21	Rafael Palmeiro	2.00
22	Cal Ripken Jr.	6.00
23	B.J. Surhoff	.25
24	Nomar Garciaparra	3.00
25	Reggie Jefferson	.25
26	Pedro Martinez	2.50
27	Troy O'Leary	.25
28	Mo Vaughn	.25
29	Mark Grace	.25
30	Mickey Morandini	.25
31	Henry Rodriguez	.25
32	Sammy Sosa	3.00
33	Kerry Wood	1.25
34	Albert Belle	.25
35	Ray Durham	.25
36	Magglio Ordonez **RC**	2.00
37	Frank Thomas	2.50
38	Robin Ventura	.25
39	Bret Boone	.25
40	Barry Larkin	.25
41	Reggie Sanders	.25
42	Brett Tomko	.25
43	Sandy Alomar	.25
44	David Justice	.25
45	Kenny Lofton	.25
46	Manny Ramirez	2.50
47	Jim Thome	2.00
48	Omar Vizquel	.25
49	Jaret Wright	.25
50	Dante Bichette	.25
51	Ellis Burks	.25
52	Vinny Castilla	.25
53	Todd Helton	2.50
54	Larry Walker	.25
55	Tony Clark	.25
56	Deivi Cruz	.25
57	Damion Easley	.25
58	Bobby Higginson	.25
59	Brian Hunter	.25
60	Cliff Floyd	.25
61	Livan Hernandez	.25
62	Derek Lee	1.50
63	Edgar Renteria	.25
64	Moises Alou	.25
65	Jeff Bagwell	2.50
66	Derek Bell	.25
67	Craig Biggio	.25
68	Richard Hidalgo	.25
69	Johnny Damon	.40
70	Jeff King	.25
71	Hal Morris	.25
72	Dean Palmer	.25
73	Bobby Bonilla	.25
74	Charles Johnson	.25
75	Paul Konerko	.35
76	Raul Mondesi	.25
77	Gary Sheffield	.75
78	Jeromy Burnitz	.25
79	Marquis Grissom	.25
80	Dave Nilsson	.25
81	Fernando Vina	.25
82	Marty Cordova	.25
83	Pat Meares	.25
84	Paul Molitor	2.50
85	Brad Radke	.25
86	Terry Steinbach	.25
87	Todd Walker	.25
88	Brad Fullmer	.25
89	Vladimir Guerrero	2.50
90	Carl Pavano	.25
91	Rondell White	.25
92	Bernard Gilkey	.25
93	Hideo Nomo	1.25
94	John Olerud	.25
95	Rey Ordonez	.25
96	Mike Piazza	4.00
97	Masato Yoshii **RC**	.65
98	Hideki Irabu	.25
99	Derek Jeter	6.00
100	Chuck Knoblauch	.25
101	Tino Martinez	.25
102	Paul O'Neill	.25
103	Darryl Strawberry	.25
104	Bernie Williams	.25
105	Jason Giambi	1.50
106	Ben Grieve	.25
107	Rickey Henderson	2.50
108	Matt Stairs	.25
109	Doug Glanville	.25
110	Desi Relaford	.25
111	Scott Rolen	1.50
112	Curt Schilling	.45
113	Jason Kendall	.25
114	Al Martin	.25
115	Jason Schmidt	.25
116	Kevin Young	.25
117	Delino DeShields	.25
118	Gary Gaetti	.25
119	Brian Jordan	.25
120	Ray Lankford	.25
121	Mark McGwire	5.00
122	Kevin Brown	.25
123	Steve Finley	.25
124	Tony Gwynn	3.50
125	Wally Joyner	.25

126	Greg Vaughn	.25
127	Barry Bonds	6.00
128	Orel Hershiser	.25
129	Jeff Kent	.25
130	Bill Mueller	.25
131	Jay Buhner	.25
132	Ken Griffey Jr.	4.50
133	Randy Johnson	2.50
134	Edgar Martinez	.25
135	Alex Rodriguez	5.00
136	David Segui	.25
137	Rolando Arrojo **RC**	.75
138	Wade Boggs	3.50
139	Quinton McCracken	.25
140	Fred McGriff	.25
141	Will Clark	.25
142	Juan Gonzalez	1.25
143	Tom Goodwin	.25
144	Ivan Rodriguez	2.00
145	Aaron Sele	.25
146	John Wetteland	.25
147	Jose Canseco	.50
148	Roger Clemens	4.00
149	Jose Cruz Jr.	.25
150	Carlos Delgado	.65

Shadows

Shadows is a full parallel of the Revolution base set. Limited to 99 sequentially numbered sets, each card is embossed with a special "Shadow Series" stamp.

	NM/M
Common Player:	2.00
Stars/Rookies:	6X

Foul Pole

Foul Pole Laser-Cuts is a 20-card insert seeded one per 49 packs. Each card features a color player photo on the left and a foul pole on the right. The foul pole design includes netting that is laser cut.

		NM/M
Complete Set (20):		100.00
Common Player:		2.00
Inserted 1:49		
1	Cal Ripken Jr.	15.00
2	Nomar Garciaparra	7.50
3	Mo Vaughn	2.00
4	Frank Thomas	6.00
5	Manny Ramirez	6.00
6	Bernie Williams	2.00
7	Ben Grieve	2.00
8	Ken Griffey Jr.	10.00
9	Alex Rodriguez	12.00
10	Juan Gonzalez	3.00
11	Ivan Rodriguez	5.00
12	Travis Lee	2.00
13	Chipper Jones	7.50
14	Sammy Sosa	7.50
15	Vinny Castilla	2.00
16	Moises Alou	2.00
17	Gary Sheffield	3.00
18	Mike Piazza	12.00
19	Mark McGwire	12.00
20	Barry Bonds	15.00

Major League Icons

Major League Icons is a 10-card insert seeded one per 121 packs. Each card features a player photo on a die-cut shield, with the shield on a flaming stand.

		NM/M
Complete Set (10):		50.00
Common Player:		4.50
Inserted 1:121		
1	Cal Ripken Jr.	15.00
2	Nomar Garciaparra	7.50
3	Frank Thomas	6.00
4	Ken Griffey Jr.	10.00
5	Alex Rodriguez	12.50
6	Chipper Jones	7.50
7	Kerry Wood	4.50
8	Mike Piazza	9.00
9	Mark McGwire	12.50
10	Tony Gwynn	7.50

Prime Time Performers

Prime Time Performers is a 20-card insert seeded one per 25 packs. The cards are designed like a TV program guide with the team logo laser-cut on the TV screen. The color player photo is located on the left.

		NM/M
Complete Set (20):		25.00
Common Player:		.50
Inserted 1:25		
1	Cal Ripken Jr.	4.50
2	Nomar Garciaparra	2.00
3	Frank Thomas	1.50
4	Jim Thome	1.25
5	Hideki Irabu	.50
6	Derek Jeter	4.50
7	Ben Grieve	.50
8	Ken Griffey Jr.	3.00
9	Alex Rodriguez	3.50
10	Juan Gonzalez	.75
11	Ivan Rodriguez	1.25
12	Travis Lee	.50
13	Chipper Jones	2.00
14	Greg Maddux	2.00
15	Kerry Wood	.75
16	Larry Walker	.50
17	Jeff Bagwell	1.50
18	Mike Piazza	2.50
19	Mark McGwire	3.50
20	Tony Gwynn	2.00

Rookies and Hardball Heroes

This hobby-only insert combines 20 hot prospects with 10 veteran stars. Horizontal cards have action photos on a flashy metallic-foil background. A portrait photo is on back. The first 20 cards in the set, the youngsters, are paralleled in a gold edition which was limited to just 50 cards of each.

		NM/M
Complete Set (30):		20.00
Common Player:		.25
Inserted 1:6		
Gold (1-20):		10X
Production 50 Sets		
1	Justin Baughman	.25
2	Jarrod Washburn	.25
3	Travis Lee	.25
4	Kerry Wood	.25
5	Magglio Ordonez	.50
6	Todd Helton	1.00
7	Derrek Lee	.25
8	Richard Hidalgo	.25
9	Mike Caruso	.25

10	David Ortiz	.75
11	Brad Fullmer	.25
12	Masato Yoshii	.25
13	Orlando Hernandez	.25
14	Ricky Ledee	.25
15	Ben Grieve	.25
16	Carlton Loewer	.25
17	Desi Relaford	.25
18	Ruben Rivera	.25
19	Rolando Arrojo	.25
20	Matt Perisho	.25
21	Chipper Jones	2.00
22	Greg Maddux	2.00
23	Cal Ripken Jr.	5.00
24	Nomar Garciaparra	2.00
25	Frank Thomas	1.00
26	Mark McGwire	4.00
27	Tony Gwynn	2.00
28	Ken Griffey Jr.	3.00
29	Alex Rodriguez	4.00
30	Juan Gonzalez	.50

Showstoppers

This 36-card insert was seeded two per 25 packs. The cards feature holographic foil. The color photo is centered above the team logo and the Showstoppers logo.

		NM/M
Complete Set (36):		30.00
Common Player:		.45
Inserted 1:12		
1	Cal Ripken Jr.	5.00
2	Nomar Garciaparra	2.50
3	Pedro Martinez	2.00
4	Mo Vaughn	.45
5	Frank Thomas	2.00
6	Manny Ramirez	2.00
7	Jim Thome	1.75
8	Jaret Wright	.45
9	Paul Molitor	2.00
10	Orlando Hernandez	.60
11	Derek Jeter	5.00
12	Bernie Williams	.45
13	Ben Grieve	.45
14	Ken Griffey Jr.	3.50
15	Alex Rodriguez	4.00
16	Wade Boggs	2.50
17	Juan Gonzalez	1.00
18	Ivan Rodriguez	1.75
19	Jose Canseco	.75
20	Roger Clemens	3.00
21	Travis Lee	.45
22	Andres Galarraga	.45
23	Chipper Jones	2.50
24	Greg Maddux	2.50
25	Sammy Sosa	2.50
26	Kerry Wood	.75
27	Vinny Castilla	.45
28	Larry Walker	.45
29	Moises Alou	.45
30	Raul Mondesi	.45
31	Gary Sheffield	.75
32	Hideo Nomo	1.00
33	Mike Piazza	3.00
34	Mark McGwire	4.00
35	Tony Gwynn	2.50
36	Barry Bonds	5.00

Nestle's Latinos

Produced by Pacific this set of Latino ballplayers' cards was issued in three-card packs with the purchase of certain Nestle's food products in Los Angeles, Miami, Houston and San Antonio. Cards

are found in two styles. Five of the cards have gold-foil graphic highlights on both top and bottom on front. On back the card number is in a white circle. The second style has foil only at bottom front and on back the card number is in a black circle. Both types have Pacific and Nestle logos on front and back.

		NM/M
Complete Set (20):		8.00
Common Player:		.25
1	Ismael Valdes	.25
2	Juan Gonzalez	.50
3	Ivan Rodriguez	.65
4	Joey Cora	.25
5	Livan Hernandez	.25
1	Bernie Williams	.25
2	Tino Martinez	.25
3	Alex Rodriguez	1.50
4	Edgar Martinez	.25
5	Andres Galarraga	.25
6	Manny Ramirez	.75
7	Carlos Baerga	.25
8	Pedro Martinez	.75
9	Vinny Castilla	.25
10	Sammy Sosa	1.00
11	Nomar Garciaparra	1.00
12	Javy Lopez	.25
13	Sandy Alomar	.25
14	Roberto Alomar	.40
15	Jose Canseco	.50

Home Run Heroes

This retail exclusive product was sold as a complete set sealed in a tin lithographed can. The 2-1/2" x 3-1/2" cards have color action photos on front of the players in the followthrough of their home run swing. The figures are set on an artificial background which includes a sign giving the date and distance of their final home run of the 1998 season. Their team logo is in the "turf" at their feet. Fronts are highlighted with gold foil. On back are a portrait photo, a season summary and 1998 stats, along with appropriate licensor and manufacturer logos.

		NM/M
Complete Set (6):		2.50
Common Player:		.25
1	Mark McGwire	1.00
2	Sammy Sosa	.65
3	Ken Griffey Jr.	.75
4	Greg Vaughn	.25
5	Albert Belle	.25
6	Jose Canseco	.50

Home Run History

This boxed set commemorating the great home run chase of 1998 was an exclusive to one of the television home-shopping shows. Each player is featured on 35 cards, with several depicting both players. Fronts have portraits or action shots which are borderless at the top and sides. At bottom is a gold-foil highlighted panel with the player's name,

card title and date. Backs have another photo and details of the highlight. A pair of die-cut bonus cards were included in the boxed set.

		NM/M
Complete Set (70+2):		10.00
Common Card:		.50
1	Mark McGwire (Portrait of a Hero)	.50
2	Sammy Sosa (Portrait of a Hero)	.50
3	Mark McGwire (Fan Favorite)	.50
4	Sammy Sosa (Fan Favorite)	.50
5	Mark McGwire (Well-Rounded Superstar)	.50
6	Sammy Sosa (Well-Rounded Superstar)	.50
7	Mark McGwire (Cardinals Slugger)	.50
8	Sammy Sosa (Cubs Slugger)	.50
9	Mark McGwire (Home Run #48)	.50
10	Sammy Sosa (20 HRs in June)	.50
11	Mark McGwire (Home Run #50)	.50
12	Sammy Sosa (Home Run #50)	.50
13	Mark McGwire (Home Run #57)	.50
14	Sammy Sosa (Home Run #51)	.50
15	Mark McGwire (Home Run #58)	.50
16	Sammy Sosa (Home Run #56)	.50
17	Mark McGwire (Home Run #59)	.50
18	Sammy Sosa (Home Run #59)	.50
19	Mark McGwire (Home Run #60)	.50
20	Sammy Sosa (Home Run #60)	.50
21	Mark McGwire (Home Run #61)	.50
22	Sammy Sosa (Home Run #61)	.50
23	Mark McGwire (Home Run #62)	.50
24	Sammy Sosa (Home Run #62)	.50
25	Mark McGwire (The Record Falls)	.50
26	Sammy Sosa (Tied at 62!)	.50
27	Mark McGwire (The Home Run Ball)	.50
28	Sammy Sosa (Sammy Sosa Day)	.50
29	Mark McGwire (Achievement Award)	.50
30	Sammy Sosa (Achievement Award)	.50
31	Mark McGwire (What a Ride!)	.50
32	Sammy Sosa (A Season of Accolades)	.50
33	Mark McGwire (Home Run #63)	.50
34	Sammy Sosa (Sammy, You're the Man)	.50
35	Mark McGwire (Home Run #64)	.50
36	Sammy Sosa (Home Run #63)	.50
37	Mark McGwire (Home Run #65)	.50
38	Sammy Sosa (Home Run #64)	.50
39	Mark McGwire (Home Run #67)	.50
40	Sammy Sosa (Home Run #65)	.50
41	Mark McGwire (Home Run #68)	.50
42	Sammy Sosa (Home Run #66)	.50
43	Mark McGwire (70!!!)	.50
44	Sammy Sosa (Cubs Win Wild Card)	.50
45	Mark McGwire (Last Swing of the Bat)	.50
46	Sammy Sosa (18 Stolen Bases)	.50
47	Mark McGwire (Power at the Plate)	.50
48	Sammy Sosa (Grand Sam)	.50
49	Mark McGwire (130 Runs Scored)	.50
50	Sammy Sosa (134 Runs Scored)	.50
51	Mark McGwire (32 HRs on the Road)	.50
52	Sammy Sosa (31 HRs on the Road)	.50
53	Mark McGwire (38 HRs at Home)	.50
54	Sammy Sosa (35 HRs at Home)	.50
55	Mark McGwire (11 First-Inning Home Runs)	.50
56	Sammy Sosa (12 First-Inning Home Runs)	.50

57	Mark McGwire (10 Multiple-HR Games)	.50
58	Sammy Sosa (11 Multiple-HR Games)	.50
59	Mark McGwire (545-Foot Blast)	.50
60	Sammy Sosa (500-Foot Blast)	.50
61	Mark McGwire (St. Louis' Favorite Son)	.50
62	Sammy Sosa (Chicago's Favorite Son)	.50
63	Mark McGwire (A Season of Celebration)	.50
64	Sammy Sosa (A Season of Celebration)	.50
65	Mark McGwire (Curtain Call)	.50
66	Sammy Sosa (Curtain Call)	.50
67	Mark McGwire, Sammy Sosa (Awesome Power)	.50
68	Mark McGwire, Sammy Sosa (Ambassadors of the Game)	.50
69	Mark McGwire, Sammy Sosa (Transcending Sports)	.50
70	Mark McGwire, Sammy Sosa (Friends to the End/Checklist)	.50

Home Run History Bonus Cards

Though they are not identified as such, this pair of Gold Crown-style die-cut cards were bonus inserts in the Home Run History boxed set. Fronts have gold-foil highlights with the pivotal number in blue-sky tones. Backs have portrait photos and a few words about the remarkable record.

		NM/M
1	Mark McGwire (Home Run Champ)	1.50
1	Cal Ripken Jr. (Consecutive Games)	2.00

National Convention Redemption

This card of Pacific spokesman Tony Gwynn was given away at the card company's booth in a redemption program during the 1998 National Sports Collectors Convention in August 1998. The card front has a color photo of Gwynn on red and yellow rayed background. At lower-right is a gold-foil convention logo. Back has an action photo, copyright information and logos.

		NM/M
1998	Tony Gwynn	3.00

1999 Pacific Sample

This card of Pacific spokesman Tony Gwynn introduces the 1999 series. The sample card follows the format of the issued version but is overprinted "SAMPLE" on back and lacks Gwynn's 1998 season and career stats.

		NM/M
	Tony Gwynn	2.00

1999 Pacific

The 450-card base set features full bleed fronts enhanced with silver foil stamping. Card backs have year-by-year statistics, a small photo and a brief career highlight caption. There are two parallels, Platinum Blues and Reds. Platinum Blues have blue foil stamping and are seeded 1:73 packs. Reds are retail exclusive with red foil stamping and are seeded one per retail pack.

		NM/M
Complete Set (500):		30.00
Common Player:		.10
Platinum Blues (1:73):		15X
Reds (1:1R):		2.5X
Pack (10):		1.00
Wax Box (36):		35.00
1	Garret Anderson	.10
2	Jason Dickson	.10
3	Gary DiSarcina	.10
4	Jim Edmonds	.25
5	Darin Erstad	.25
6	Chuck Finley	.10
7	Shigetosi Hasegawa	.10
8	Ken Hill	.10
9	Dave Hollins	.10
10	Phil Nevin	.10
11	Troy Percival	.10
12a	Tim Salmon/Action	.10
12b	Tim Salmon/Portrait	.10
13	Brian Anderson	.10
14	Tony Batista	.10
15	Jay Bell	.10
16	Andy Benes	.10
17	Yamil Benitez	.10
18	Omar Daal	.10
19	David Dellucci	.10
20	Karim Garcia	.10
21	Bernard Gilkey	.10
22a	Travis Lee/Action	.10
22b	Travis Lee/Portrait	.10
23	Aaron Small	.10
24	Kelly Stinnett	.10
25	Devon White	.10
26	Matt Williams	.10
27a	Bruce Chen/Action	.10
27b	Bruce Chen/Portrait	.10
28a	Andres Galarraga/Action	.10
28b	Andres Galarraga/Portrait	.10
29	Tom Glavine	.35
30	Ozzie Guillen	.10
31	Andruw Jones	1.00
32a	Chipper Jones/Action	1.50
32b	Chipper Jones/Portrait	1.50
33	Ryan Klesko	.10
34	George Lombard	.10
35	Javy Lopez	.10
36a	Greg Maddux/Action	1.50
36b	Greg Maddux/Portrait	1.50
37a	Marty Malloy/Action	.10
37b	Marty Malloy/Portrait	.10
38	Dennis Martinez	.10
39	Kevin Millwood	.10
40a	Alex Rodriguez/Action	2.50
40b	Alex Rodriguez/Portrait	2.50
41	Denny Neagle	.10
42	John Smoltz	.10
43	Michael Tucker	.10
44	Walt Weiss	.10
45a	Roberto Alomar/Action	.10

No.	Player	Price
45b	Roberto Alomar/Portrait	.25
46	Brady Anderson	.10
47	Harold Baines	.10
48	Mike Bordick	.10
49a	Danny Clyburn/Action	.10
49b	Danny Clyburn/Portrait	.10
50	Eric Davis	.10
51	Scott Erickson	.10
52	Chris Hoiles	.10
53	Jimmy Key	.10
54a	Ryan Minor/Action	.10
54b	Ryan Minor/Portrait	.10
55	Mike Mussina	.40
56	Jesse Orosco	.10
57a	Rafael Palmeiro/Action	.75
57b	Rafael Palmeiro/Portrait	.75
58	Sidney Ponson	.10
59	Arthur Rhodes	.10
60a	Cal Ripken Jr./Action	3.00
60b	Cal Ripken Jr./Portrait	3.00
61	B.J. Surhoff	.10
62	Steve Avery	.10
63	Darren Bragg	.10
64	Dennis Eckersley	.75
65a	Nomar Garciaparra/Action	1.50
65b	Nomar Garciaparra/Portrait	1.50
66a	Sammy Sosa/Action	1.50
66b	Sammy Sosa/Portrait	1.50
67	Tom Gordon	.10
68	Reggie Jefferson	.10
69	Darren Lewis	.10
70a	Mark McGwire/Action	2.50
70b	Mark McGwire/Portrait	2.50
71	Pedro Martinez	1.00
72	Troy O'Leary	.10
73	Bret Saberhagen	.10
74	Mike Stanley	.10
75	John Valentin	.10
76	Jason Varitek	.10
77	Mo Vaughn	.10
78	Tim Wakefield	.10
79	Manny Alexander	.10
80	Rod Beck	.10
81	Brant Brown	.10
82	Mark Clark	.10
83	Gary Gaetti	.10
84	Mark Grace	.10
85	Jose Hernandez	.10
86	Lance Johnson	.10
87a	Jason Maxwell/Action	.10
87b	Jason Maxwell/Portrait	.10
88	Mickey Morandini	.10
89	Terry Mulholland	.10
90	Henry Rodriguez	.10
91	Scott Servais	.10
92	Kevin Tapani	.10
93	Pedro Valdes	.10
94	Kerry Wood	.40
95	Jeff Abbott	.10
96	James Baldwin	.10
97	Albert Belle	.10
98	Mike Cameron	.10
99	Mike Caruso	.10
100	Wil Cordero	.10
101	Ray Durham	.10
102	Jaime Navarro	.10
103	Greg Norton	.10
104	Magglio Ordonez	.25
105	Mike Sirotka	.10
106a	Frank Thomas/Action	1.00
106b	Frank Thomas/Portrait	1.00
107	Robin Ventura	.10
108	Craig Wilson	.10
109	Aaron Boone	.10
110	Bret Boone	.10
111	Sean Casey	.15
112	Pete Harnisch	.10
113	John Hudek	.10
114	Barry Larkin	.10
115	Eduardo Perez	.10
116	Mike Remlinger	.10
117	Reggie Sanders	.10
118	Chris Stynes	.10
119	Eddie Taubensee	.10
120	Brett Tomko	.10
121	Pat Watkins	.10
122	Dmitri Young	.10
123	Sandy Alomar Jr.	.10
124	Dave Burba	.10
125	Bartolo Colon	.10
126	Joey Cora	.10
127	Brian Giles	.10
128	Dwight Gooden	.10
129	Mike Jackson	.10
130	David Justice	.10
131	Kenny Lofton	.10
132	Charles Nagy	.10
133	Chad Ogea	.10
134a	Manny Ramirez/Action	1.00
134b	Manny Ramirez/Portrait	1.00
135	Richie Sexson	.10
136a	Jim Thome/Action	.75
136b	Jim Thome/Portrait	.75
137	Omar Vizquel	.10
138	Jaret Wright	.10
139	Pedro Astacio	.10
140	Jason Bates	.10
141a	Dante Bichette/Action	.10
141b	Dante Bichette/Portrait	.10
142a	Vinny Castilla/Action	.10
142b	Vinny Castilla/Portrait	.10
143a	Edgar Clemente/Action	.10
143b	Edgar Clemente/Portrait	.10
144a	Derrick Gibson/Action	.10
144b	Derrick Gibson/Portrait	.10
145	Curtis Goodwin	.10

No.	Player	Price
146a	Todd Helton/Action	1.00
146b	Todd Helton/Portrait	1.00
147	Todd Jones	.10
148	Darryl Kile	.10
149	Mike Lansing	.10
150	Chuck McElroy	.10
151	Neifi Perez	.10
152	Jeff Reed	.10
153	John Thomson	.10
154a	Larry Walker/Action	.10
154b	Larry Walker/Portrait	.10
155	Jamey Wright	.10
156	Kimera Bartee	.10
157	Geronimo Berroa	.10
158	Raul Casanova	.10
159	Frank Catalanotto	.10
160	Tony Clark	.10
161	Deivi Cruz	.10
162	Damion Easley	.10
163	Juan Encarnacion	.10
164	Luis Gonzalez	.10
165	Seth Greisinger	.10
166	Bob Higginson	.10
167	Brian Hunter	.10
168	Todd Jones	.10
169	Justin Thompson	.10
170	Antonio Alfonseca	.10
171	Dave Berg	.10
172	John Cangelosi	.10
173	Craig Counsell	.10
174	Todd Dunwoody	.10
175	Cliff Floyd	.10
176	Alex Gonzalez	.10
177	Livan Hernandez	.10
178	Ryan Jackson	.10
179	Mark Kotsay	.10
180	Derrek Lee	.65
181	Matt Mantei	.10
182	Brian Meadows	.10
183	Edgar Renteria	.10
184a	Moises Alou/Action	.10
184b	Moises Alou/Portrait	.10
185	Brad Ausmus	.10
186a	Jeff Bagwell/Action	1.00
186b	Jeff Bagwell/Portrait	1.00
187	Derek Bell	.10
188	Sean Berry	.10
189	Craig Biggio	.10
190	Carl Everett	.10
191	Ricky Gutierrez	.10
192	Mike Hampton	.10
193	Doug Henry	.10
194	Richard Hidalgo	.10
195	Randy Johnson	1.00
196a	Russ Johnson/Action	.10
196b	Russ Johnson/Portrait	.10
197	Shane Reynolds	.10
198	Bill Spiers	.10
199	Kevin Appier	.10
200	Tim Belcher	.10
201	Jeff Conine	.10
202	Johnny Damon	.35
203	Jermaine Dye	.10
204a	Jeremy Giambi (Batting stance.)	.10
204b	Jeremy Giambi (Follow-through.)	.10
205	Jeff King	.10
206	Shane Mack	.10
207	Jeff Montgomery	.10
208	Hal Morris	.10
209	Jose Offerman	.10
210	Dean Palmer	.10
211	Jose Rosado	.10
212	Glendon Rusch	.10
213	Larry Sutton	.10
214	Mike Sweeney	.10
215	Bobby Bonilla	.10
216	Alex Cora	.10
217	Darren Dreifort	.10
218	Mark Grudzielanek	.10
219	Todd Hollandsworth	.10
220	Trenidad Hubbard	.10
221	Charles Johnson	.10
222	Eric Karros	.10
223	Matt Luke	.10
224	Ramon Martinez	.10
225	Raul Mondesi	.10
226	Chan Ho Park	.10
227	Jeff Shaw	.10
228	Gary Sheffield	.40
229	Eric Young	.10
230	Jeromy Burnitz	.10
231	Jeff Cirillo	.10
232	Marquis Grissom	.10
233	Bobby Hughes	.10
234	John Jaha	.10
235	Geoff Jenkins	.10
236	Scott Karl	.10
237	Mark Loretta	.10
238	Mike Matheny	.10
239	Mike Myers	.10
240	Dave Nilsson	.10
241	Bob Wickman	.10
242	Jose Valentin	.10
243	Fernando Vina	.10
244	Rick Aguilera	.10
245	Ron Coomer	.10
246	Marty Cordova	.10
247	Denny Hocking	.10
248	Matt Lawton	.10
249	Pat Meares	.10
250a	Paul Molitor/Action	1.00
250b	Paul Molitor/Portrait	1.00
251	Otis Nixon	.10
252	Alex Ochoa	.10
253	David Ortiz	.65
254	A.J. Pierzynski	.10

No.	Player	Price
255	Brad Radke	.10
256	Terry Steinbach	.10
257	Bob Tewksbury	.10
258	Todd Walker	.10
259	Shane Andrews	.10
260	Shayne Bennett	.10
261	Orlando Cabrera	.10
262	Brad Fullmer	.10
263	Vladimir Guerrero	1.00
264	Wilton Guerrero	.10
265	Dustin Hermanson	.10
266	Terry Jones	.10
267	Steve Kline	.10
268	Carl Pavano	.10
269	F.P. Santangelo	.10
270a	Fernando Seguignol/Action	.10
270b	Fernando Seguignol/Portrait	.10
271	Ugueth Urbina	.10
272	Jose Vidro	.10
273	Chris Widger	.10
274	Edgardo Alfonzo	.10
275	Carlos Baerga	.10
276	John Franco	.10
277	Todd Hundley	.10
278	Butch Huskey	.10
279	Bobby Jones	.10
280	Al Leiter	.10
281	Greg McMichael	.10
282	Brian McRae	.10
283	Hideo Nomo	.50
284	John Olerud	.10
285	Rey Ordonez	.10
286a	Mike Piazza/Action	1.75
286b	Mike Piazza/Portrait	1.75
287	Turk Wendell	.10
288	Masato Yoshii	.10
289	David Cone	.10
290	Chad Curtis	.10
291	Joe Girardi	.10
292	Orlando Hernandez	.10
293a	Hideki Irabu/Action	.10
293b	Hideki Irabu/Portrait	.10
294a	Derek Jeter/Action	3.00
294b	Derek Jeter/Portrait	3.00
295	Chuck Knoblauch	.10
296a	Mike Lowell/Action	.10
296b	Mike Lowell/Portrait	.10
297	Tino Martinez	.10
298	Ramiro Mendoza	.10
299	Paul O'Neill	.10
300	Andy Pettitte	.25
301	Jorge Posada	.10
302	Tim Raines	.10
303	Mariano Rivera	.15
304	David Wells	.10
305a	Bernie Williams/Action	.10
305b	Bernie Williams/Portrait	.10
306	Mike Blowers	.10
307	Tom Candiotti	.10
308a	Eric Chavez/Action	.15
308b	Eric Chavez/Portrait	.15
309	Ryan Christenson	.10
310	Jason Giambi	.65
311a	Ben Grieve/Action	.10
311b	Ben Grieve/Portrait	.10
312	Rickey Henderson	1.00
313	A.J. Hinch	.10
314	Jason McDonald	.10
315	Bip Roberts	.10
316	Kenny Rogers	.10
317	Scott Spiezio	.10
318	Matt Stairs	.10
319	Miguel Tejada	.20
320	Bob Abreu	.20
321	Alex Arias	.10
322a	Gary Bennett RC/Action	.10
322b	Gary Bennett RC/Portrait	.10
323	Ricky Bottalico	.10
324	Rico Brogna	.10
325	Bobby Estalella	.10
326	Doug Glanville	.10
327	Kevin Jordan	.10
328	Mark Leiter	.10
329	Wendell Magee	.10
330	Mark Portugal	.10
331	Desi Relaford	.10
332	Scott Rolen	.65
333	Curt Schilling	.35
334	Kevin Sefcik	.10
335	Adrian Brown	.10
336	Emil Brown	.10
337	Lou Collier	.10
338	Francisco Cordova	.10
339	Freddy Garcia	.10
340	Jose Guillen	.10
341	Jason Kendall	.10
342	Al Martin	.10
343	Abraham Nunez	.10
344	Aramis Ramirez	.10
345	Ricardo Rincon	.10
346	Jason Schmidt	.10
347	Turner Ward	.10
348	Tony Womack	.10
349	Kevin Young	.10
350	Juan Acevedo	.10
351	Delino DeShields	.10
352a	J.D. Drew/Action	.40
352b	J.D. Drew/Portrait	.40
353	Ron Gant	.10
354	Brian Jordan	.10
355	Ray Lankford	.10
356	Eli Marrero	.10
357	Kent Mercker	.10
358	Matt Morris	.10
359	Luis Ordaz	.10
360	Donovan Osborne	.10

No.	Player	Price
361	Placido Polanco	.10
362	Fernando Tatis	.10
363	Andy Ashby	.10
364	Kevin Brown	.10
365	Ken Caminiti	.10
366	Steve Finley	.10
367	Chris Gomez	.10
368a	Tony Gwynn/Action	1.50
368b	Tony Gwynn/Portrait	1.50
369	Joey Hamilton	.10
370	Carlos Hernandez	.10
371	Trevor Hoffman	.10
372	Wally Joyner	.10
373	Jim Leyritz	.10
374	Ruben Rivera	.10
375	Greg Vaughn	.10
376	Quilvio Veras	.10
377	Rich Aurilia	.10
378a	Barry Bonds/Action	3.00
378b	Barry Bonds/Portrait	3.00
379	Ellis Burks	.10
380	Joe Carter	.10
381	Stan Javier	.10
382	Brian Johnson	.10
383	Jeff Kent	.10
384	Jose Mesa	.10
385	Bill Mueller	.10
386	Robb Nen	.10
387a	Armando Rios/Action	.10
387b	Armando Rios/Portrait	.10
388	Kirk Rueter	.10
389	Rey Sanchez	.10
390	J.T. Snow	.10
391	David Bell	.10
392	Jay Buhner	.10
393	Ken Cloude	.10
394	Russ Davis	.10
395	Jeff Fassero	.10
396a	Ken Griffey Jr./Action	2.00
396b	Ken Griffey Jr./Portrait	2.00
397	Giomar Guevara RC	.10
398	Carlos Guillen	.10
399	Edgar Martinez	.10
400	Shane Monahan	.10
401	Jamie Moyer	.10
402	David Segui	.10
403	Makoto Suzuki	.10
404	Mike Timlin	.10
405	Dan Wilson	.10
406	Wilson Alvarez	.10
407	Rolando Arrojo	.10
408	Wade Boggs	1.50
409	Miguel Cairo	.10
410	Roberto Hernandez	.10
411	Mike Kelly	.10
412	Aaron Ledesma	.10
413	Albie Lopez	.10
414	Dave Martinez	.10
415	Quinton McCracken	.10
416	Fred McGriff	.10
417	Bryan Rekar	.10
418	Paul Sorrento	.10
419	Randy Winn	.10
420	John Burkett	.10
421	Will Clark	.10
422	Royce Clayton	.10
423a	Juan Gonzalez/Action	.50
423b	Juan Gonzalez/Portrait	.50
424	Tom Goodwin	.10
425	Rusty Greer	.10
426	Rick Helling	.10
427	Roberto Kelly	.10
428	Mark McLemore	.10
429a	Ivan Rodriguez/Action	.75
429b	Ivan Rodriguez/Portrait	.75
430	Aaron Sele	.10
431	Lee Stevens	.10
432	Todd Stottlemyre	.10
433	John Wetteland	.10
434	Todd Zeile	.10
435	Jose Canseco	.50
436a	Roger Clemens/Action	1.75
436b	Roger Clemens/Portrait	1.75
437	Felipe Crespo	.10
438a	Jose Cruz Jr./Action	.10
438b	Jose Cruz Jr./Portrait	.10
439	Carlos Delgado	.50
440a	Tom Evans/Action	.10
440b	Tom Evans/Portrait	.10
441	Tony Fernandez	.10
442	Darrin Fletcher	.10
443	Alex Gonzalez	.10
444	Shawn Green	.30
445	Roy Halladay	.10
446	Pat Hentgen	.10
447	Juan Samuel	.10
448	Benito Santiago	.10
449	Shannon Stewart	.10
450	Woody Williams	.10

Cramer's Choice

Pacific CEO Michael Cramer personally chose this 10-card set. Die-cut in a trophy shape, the cards are enhanced with silver holographic etching and gold foil stamping across the card bottom. Cards are serially numbered to 299.

		NM/M
Complete Set (10):		65.00
Common Player:		7.50
Inserted 1:721		
1	Cal Ripken Jr.	20.00
2	Nomar Garciaparra	12.50
3	Frank Thomas	10.00
4	Ken Griffey Jr.	15.00

5	Alex Rodriguez	17.50
6	Greg Maddux	12.50
7	Sammy Sosa	12.50
8	Kerry Wood	7.50
9	Mark McGwire	17.50
10	Tony Gwynn	12.50

Dynagon Diamond

Dynagon Diamond captures 20 of baseball's biggest stars in action against a mirror-patterned full-foil background. These are seeded about 1:9. A Titanium parallel with each card numbered to 99 was exclusive to hobby packs.

		NM/M
Complete Set (20):		20.00
Common Player:		.40
Inserted 1:9		
Titanium (99 Sets):		8X
1	Cal Ripken Jr.	2.50
2	Nomar Garciaparra	1.00
3	Frank Thomas	.75
4	Derek Jeter	2.50
5	Ben Grieve	.40
6	Ken Griffey Jr.	1.50
7	Alex Rodriguez	2.00
8	Juan Gonzalez	.50
9	Travis Lee	.40
10	Chipper Jones	1.00
11	Greg Maddux	1.00
12	Sammy Sosa	1.00
13	Kerry Wood	.50
14	Jeff Bagwell	.75
15	Hideo Nomo	.50
16	Mike Piazza	12.50
17	J.D. Drew	.50
18	Mark McGwire	2.00
19	Tony Gwynn	1.00
20	Barry Bonds	2.50

Gold Crown Die-Cuts

This 36-card die-cut set is shaped like a crown at the top and features dual foiling, 24-pt. stock and gold foil stamping. These are seeded 1:37 packs.

		NM/M
Complete Set (36):		75.00
Common Player:		.75
Inserted 1:37		
1	Darin Erstad	1.00
2	Cal Ripken Jr.	7.50
3	Nomar Garciaparra	4.00
4	Pedro Martinez	3.00
5	Mo Vaughn	.75
6	Frank Thomas	3.00
7	Kenny Lofton	.75
8	Manny Ramirez	3.00
9	Paul Molitor	3.00
10	Derek Jeter	7.50
11	Bernie Williams	.75
12	Ben Grieve	.75
13	Ken Griffey Jr.	5.00
14	Alex Rodriguez	6.00
15	Wade Boggs	4.00
16	Juan Gonzalez	1.50
17	Ivan Rodriguez	2.50
18	Jose Canseco	1.50
19	Roger Clemens	4.50
20	Travis Lee	.75
21	Chipper Jones	4.00
22	Greg Maddux	4.00
23	Sammy Sosa	4.00
24	Kerry Wood	1.50
25	Todd Helton	3.00
26	Larry Walker	.75
27	Jeff Bagwell	3.00
28	Craig Biggio	.75
29	Raul Mondesi	.75
30	Vladimir Guerrero	3.00
31	Mike Piazza	4.50
32	Scott Rolen	2.00
33	J.D. Drew	1.50
34	Mark McGwire	6.00
35	Tony Gwynn	4.00
36	Barry Bonds	7.50

Hot Cards

This dealer-only 10-card set was awarded to any dealer that had sold any packs/boxes that produced a card for the Pacific Hot Cards Registry Program. Fronts have a metallic foil background. Backs have a portrait photo and are serial numbered within an edition of 500 each.

		NM/M
Complete Set (10):		75.00
Common Player:		3.00
1	Alex Rodriguez	12.50
2	Tony Gwynn	7.50
3	Ken Griffey Jr.	10.00
4	Sammy Sosa	7.50
5	Ivan Rodriguez	6.00
6	Derek Jeter	15.00
7	Cal Ripken Jr.	15.00
8	Mark McGwire	12.50
9	J.D. Drew	4.50
10	Bernie Williams	3.00

Team Checklists

This 30-card horizontal insert set features a star player from each team on the card front, with each team's complete checklist on the card back. Fronts feature a holographic silver-foiled and embossed logo of the player's respective team. These are seeded 2:37 packs.

		NM/M
Complete Set (30):		30.00
Common Player:		.30
Inserted 1:18		
1	Darin Erstad	.50
2	Cal Ripken Jr.	3.00
3	Nomar Garciaparra	1.50
4	Frank Thomas	1.00
5	Manny Ramirez	1.00
6	Damion Easley	.30
7	Jeff King	.30
8	Paul Molitor	1.00
9	Derek Jeter	3.00
10	Ben Grieve	.30
11	Ken Griffey Jr.	2.00
12	Wade Boggs	1.50
13	Juan Gonzalez	.60
14	Roger Clemens	1.75
15	Travis Lee	.30
16	Chipper Jones	1.50
17	Sammy Sosa	1.50
18	Barry Larkin	.30
19	Todd Helton	1.00
20	Mark Kotsay	.30
21	Jeff Bagwell	1.00
22	Raul Mondesi	.30
23	Jeff Cirillo	.30
24	Vladimir Guerrero	.30

25	Mike Piazza	1.75
26	Scott Rolen	.75
27	Jason Kendall	.30
28	Mark McGwire	2.50
29	Tony Gwynn	1.50
30	Barry Bonds	3.00

Timelines

Timelines features 20 superstars, giving a chronological history of each player complete with photos from early in their careers. Three photos of the player are on the card front. Inserted exclusively in hobby packs these are limited to 199 serially numbered sets.

		NM/M
Complete Set (20):		200.00
Common Player:		6.00
Inserted 1:181 H		
1	Cal Ripken Jr.	30.00
2	Frank Thomas	12.00
3	Jim Thome	10.00
4	Paul Molitor	12.00
5	Bernie Williams	6.00
6	Derek Jeter	30.00
7	Ken Griffey Jr.	20.00
8	Alex Rodriguez	25.00
9	Wade Boggs	15.00
10	Jose Canseco	9.00
11	Roger Clemens	17.50
12	Andres Galarraga	6.00
13	Chipper Jones	15.00
14	Greg Maddux	15.00
15	Sammy Sosa	15.00
16	Larry Walker	6.00
17	Randy Johnson	12.00
18	Mike Piazza	17.50
19	Mark McGwire	25.00
20	Tony Gwynn	15.00

1999 Pacific Aurora

The 200-card set features two photos on the card front and one on the back. Card backs also have '98 and career stats along with personal information. The player's name and Aurora logo is stamped with gold foil. A parallel "Opening Day" issued is stamped with a gold foil seal and numbered within an edition of 31 each.

		NM/M
Complete Set (200):		20.00
Common Player:		.10
Opening Days:		20X
Production 31 Sets		
Reds:		2X
Retail Only (1:6)		
Pack (6):		1.50
Wax Box (36):		22.50
1	Garret Anderson	.10
2	Jim Edmonds	.10
3	Darin Erstad	.30
4	Matt Luke	.10
5	Tim Salmon	.10
6	Mo Vaughn	.10
7	Jay Bell	.10
8	David Dellucci	.10
9	Steve Finley	.10
10	Bernard Gilkey	.10
11	Randy Johnson	1.00
12	Travis Lee	.10
13	Matt Williams	.10
14	Andres Galarraga	.10
15	Tom Glavine	.35
16	Andruw Jones	1.00
17	Chipper Jones	1.50
18	Brian Jordan	.10
19	Javy Lopez	.10
20	Greg Maddux	1.50
21	Albert Belle	.10
22	Will Clark	.10
23	Scott Erickson	.10
24	Mike Mussina	.40
25	Cal Ripken Jr.	3.00
26	B.J. Surhoff	.10
27	Nomar Garciaparra	1.50
28	Reggie Jefferson	.10
29	Darren Lewis	.10
30	Pedro Martinez	1.00
31	John Valentin	.10
32	Rod Beck	.10
33	Mark Grace	.10
34	Lance Johnson	.10
35	Mickey Morandini	.10
36	Sammy Sosa	1.50
37	Kerry Wood	.40
38	James Baldwin	.10
39	Mike Caruso	.10
40	Ray Durham	.10
41	Magglio Ordonez	.25
42	Frank Thomas	1.00
43	Aaron Boone	.10
44	Sean Casey	.20
45	Barry Larkin	.10
46	Hal Morris	.10
47	Denny Neagle	.10
48	Greg Vaughn	.10
49	Pat Watkins	.10
50	Roberto Alomar	.25
51	Sandy Alomar Jr.	.10
52	David Justice	.10
53	Kenny Lofton	.10
54	Manny Ramirez	1.00
55	Richie Sexson	.10
56	Jim Thome	.75
57	Omar Vizquel	.10
58	Dante Bichette	.10
59	Vinny Castilla	.10
60	Edgard Clemente RC	.10
61	Derrick Gibson	.10
62	Todd Helton	1.00
63	Darryl Kile	.10
64	Larry Walker	.10
65	Tony Clark	.10
66	Damion Easley	.10
67	Bob Higginson	.10
68	Brian Hunter	.10
69	Dean Palmer	.10
70	Justin Thompson	.10
71	Craig Counsell	.10
72	Todd Dunwoody	.10
73	Cliff Floyd	.10
74	Alex Gonzalez	.10
75	Livan Hernandez	.10
76	Mark Kotsay	.10
77	Derrek Lee	.65
78	Moises Alou	.10
79	Jeff Bagwell	1.00
80	Derek Bell	.10
81	Craig Biggio	.10
82	Ken Caminiti	.10
83	Richard Hidalgo	.10
84	Shane Reynolds	.10
85	Jeff Conine	.10
86	Johnny Damon	.35
87	Jermaine Dye	.10
88	Jeff King	.10
89	Jeff Montgomery	.10
90	Mike Sweeney	.10
91	Kevin Brown	.10
92	Mark Grudzielanek	.10
93	Eric Karros	.10
94	Raul Mondesi	.10
95	Chan Ho Park	.10
96	Gary Sheffield	.40
97	Jeromy Burnitz	.10
98	Jeff Cirillo	.10
99	Marquis Grissom	.10
100	Geoff Jenkins	.10
101	Dave Nilsson	.10
102	Jose Valentin	.10
103	Fernando Vina	.10
104	Marty Cordova	.10
105	Matt Lawton	.10
106	David Ortiz	.60
107	Brad Radke	.10
108	Todd Walker	.10
109	Shane Andrews	.10
110	Orlando Cabrera	.10
111	Brad Fullmer	.10
112	Vladimir Guerrero	1.00
113	Wilton Guerrero	.10
114	Carl Pavano	.10
115	Fernando Seguignol	.10
116	Ugueth Urbina	.10
117	Edgardo Alfonzo	.10
118	Bobby Bonilla	.10
119	Rickey Henderson	1.00
120	Hideo Nomo	.60
121	John Olerud	.10
122	Rey Ordonez	.10
123	Mike Piazza	2.00
124	Masato Yoshii	.10
125	Scott Brosius	.10
126	Orlando Hernandez	.10
127	Hideki Irabu	.10
128	Derek Jeter	3.00
129	Chuck Knoblauch	.10
130	Tino Martinez	.10
131	Jorge Posada	.10
132	Bernie Williams	.10
133	Eric Chavez	.20
134	Ryan Christenson	.10
135	Jason Giambi	.65
136	Ben Grieve	.10
137	A.J. Hinch	.10
138	Matt Stairs	.10
139	Miguel Tejada	.20
140	Bob Abreu	.20
141	Gary Bennett RC	.10
142	Desi Relaford	.10
143	Scott Rolen	.75
144	Curt Schilling	.35
145	Kevin Sefcik	.10
146	Brian Giles	.10
147	Jose Guillen	.10
148	Jason Kendall	.10
149	Aramis Ramirez	.10
150	Tony Womack	.10
151	Kevin Young	.10
152	Eric Davis	.10
153	J.D. Drew	.50
154	Ray Lankford	.10
155	Eli Marrero	.10
156	Mark McGwire	2.50
157	Luis Ordaz	.10
158	Edgar Renteria	.10
159	Andy Ashby	.10
160	Tony Gwynn	1.50
161	Trevor Hoffman	.10
162	Wally Joyner	.10
163	Jim Leyritz	.10
164	Ruben Rivera	.10
165	Reggie Sanders	.10
166	Quilvio Veras	.10
167	Rich Aurilia	.10
168	Marvin Benard	.10
169	Barry Bonds	3.00
170	Ellis Burks	.10
171	Jeff Kent	.10
172	Bill Mueller	.10
173	J.T. Snow	.10
174	Jay Buhner	.10
175	Jeff Fassero	.10
176	Ken Griffey Jr.	2.25
177	Carlos Guillen	.10
178	Edgar Martinez	.10
179	Alex Rodriguez	2.50
180	David Segui	.10
181	Dan Wilson	.10
182	Rolando Arrojo	.10
183	Wade Boggs	1.50
184	Jose Canseco	.40
185	Aaron Ledesma	.10
186	Dave Martinez	.10
187	Quinton McCracken	.10
188	Fred McGriff	.10
189	Juan Gonzalez	.60
190	Tom Goodwin	.10
191	Rusty Greer	.10
192	Roberto Kelly	.10
193	Rafael Palmeiro	.75
194	Ivan Rodriguez	.75
195	Roger Clemens	2.00
196	Jose Cruz Jr.	.10
197	Carlos Delgado	.60
198	Alex Gonzalez	.10
199	Roy Halladay	.10
200	Pat Hentgen	.10

Complete Players

The 10 players featured in this serial numbered 20-card set each have two cards, designed to fit together. Card fronts feature a red border on the top and bottom with the rest of the card done in gold foil etching. Each card is serially numbered to 299.

		NM/M
Complete Set (10):		40.00
Common Player:		3.00
Production 299 Sets		
1	Cal Ripken Jr.	9.00
2	Nomar Garciaparra	4.50
3	Sammy Sosa	4.50
4	Kerry Wood	3.00
5	Frank Thomas	4.50
6	Mike Piazza	5.00
7	Mark McGwire	7.50
8	Tony Gwynn	4.50
9	Ken Griffey Jr.	6.00
10	Alex Rodriguez	7.50

Kings of the Major Leagues

The full foiled card fronts also utilize gold foil stamping. Pacific's crown as well as the featured player's team are shadow boxed in the background with the player's image in the foreground. These are seeded 1:361.

		NM/M
Complete Set (10):		80.00
Common Player:		5.00
Inserted 1:361		
1	Cal Ripken Jr.	17.50
2	Nomar Garciaparra	9.00
3	Sammy Sosa	9.00
4	Kerry Wood	5.00
5	Frank Thomas	7.50
6	Mike Piazza	10.00
7	Mark McGwire	15.00
8	Tony Gwynn	9.00
9	Ken Griffey Jr.	12.50
10	Alex Rodriguez	15.00

On Deck

Twenty of the game's hottest players are featured in this laser-cut and silver foil stamped set. The player's team logo is laser cut into the bottom half of the card beneath the player photo.

		NM/M
Complete Set (20):		17.50
Common Player:		.50
Inserted 1:9		
1	Chipper Jones	1.00
2	Cal Ripken Jr.	3.00
3	Nomar Garciaparra	1.00
4	Sammy Sosa	1.00
5	Frank Thomas	.75
6	Manny Ramirez	.75
7	Todd Helton	.75
8	Larry Walker	.50
9	Jeff Bagwell	.75
10	Vladimir Guerrero	.75
11	Mike Piazza	1.50
12	Derek Jeter	3.00
13	Bernie Williams	.50
14	J.D. Drew	.50
15	Mark McGwire	2.50
16	Tony Gwynn	1.00
17	Ken Griffey Jr.	2.00
18	Alex Rodriguez	2.50
19	Juan Gonzalez	.50
20	Ivan Rodriguez	.65

Pennant Fever

Regular Pennant Fever inserts feature gold foil stamping of 20 of the hottest players in the hobby. These are seeded 4:37 packs. There are also three parallel versions: Platinum Blue, Silver and Copper. Platinum Blues are limited to 100 serial numbered sets. Silvers are retail exclusive and limited to 250 numbered sets and Coppers are hobby exclusive and limited to 20 numbered sets. Pacific spokesman Tony Gwynn autographed 97 regular Pennant Fever cards and one each of the Silver, Blue and Copper.

		NM/M
Complete Set (20):		30.00
Common Player:		.75
Silver (250 Sets):		2X
Platinum Blue (100):		6X
Copper (20):		20X
Tony Gwynn Autograph:		25.00
1	Chipper Jones	2.00
2	Greg Maddux	2.00
3	Cal Ripken Jr.	5.00
4	Nomar Garciaparra	2.00
5	Sammy Sosa	2.00
6	Kerry Wood	.75
7	Frank Thomas	1.50
8	Manny Ramirez	1.50
9	Todd Helton	1.50
10	Jeff Bagwell	1.50
11	Mike Piazza	2.50
12	Derek Jeter	5.00
13	Bernie Williams	.75
14	J.D. Drew	.75
15	Mark McGwire	4.00
16	Tony Gwynn	2.00
17	Ken Griffey Jr.	3.00
18	Alex Rodriguez	4.00
19	Juan Gonzalez	.75
20	Ivan Rodriguez	1.25

Styrotechs

This 20-card set features styrene stock, making the cards more resilient. Fronts have a black border highlighted with gold foil. Backs have a photo and brief career highlights. These are seeded 1:37 packs.

		NM/M
Complete Set (20):		35.00
Common Player:		1.00
Inserted 1:37		
1	Chipper Jones	3.00
2	Greg Maddux	3.00
3	Cal Ripken Jr.	6.00
4	Nomar Garciaparra	3.00
5	Sammy Sosa	3.00
6	Kerry Wood	1.25
7	Frank Thomas	2.00
8	Manny Ramirez	2.00
9	Larry Walker	1.00
10	Jeff Bagwell	2.00
11	Mike Piazza	4.00
12	Derek Jeter	6.00
13	Bernie Williams	1.00
14	J.D. Drew	1.25
15	Mark McGwire	5.00
16	Tony Gwynn	3.00
17	Ken Griffey Jr.	4.50
18	Alex Rodriguez	5.00
19	Juan Gonzalez	1.25
20	Ivan Rodriguez	1.50

1999 Pacific Crown Collection Sample

This card of Pacific spokesman Tony Gwynn introduces the 1999 Crown series. The sample card follows the format of the issued version but is overprinted "SAMPLE" on back.

		NM/M
	Tony Gwynn	2.00

1999 Pacific Crown Collection

TOM GLAVINE

Released in one series the 300-card set has white borders and gold-foil highlights on front. Backs have a small photo along with English and Spanish narrative. A Platinum Blue parallel to the base set utilizes platinum blue holographic foil and is seeded 1:73 packs. A WalMart-exclusive red-foiled parallel is seeded 1:9 packs. Twelve-card packs had an S.R.P. of $2.49.

		NM/M
Complete Set (300):		20.00
Common Player:		.10
Red Stars:		6X
Inserted 1:9		
Platinum Blue Stars:		30X
Inserted 1:73		
Pack (12):		1.00
Wax Box (36):		22.50
1	Garret Anderson	.10
2	Gary DiSarcina	.10
3	Jim Edmonds	.10
4	Darin Erstad	.25
5	Shigetosi Hasegawa	.10
6	Norberto Martin	.10
7	Omar Olivares	.10
8	Orlando Palmeiro	.10
9	Tim Salmon	.10
10	Randy Velarde	.10
11	Tony Batista	.10
12	Jay Bell	.10
13	Yamil Benitez	.10
14	Omar Daal	.10
15	David Dellucci	.10
16	Karim Garcia	.10
17	Travis Lee	.10
18	Felix Rodriguez	.10
19	Devon White	.10
20	Matt Williams	.10
21	Andres Galarraga	.10
22	Tom Glavine	.35
23	Ozzie Guillen	.10
24	Andruw Jones	1.00
25	Chipper Jones	1.50
26	Ryan Klesko	.10
27	Javy Lopez	.10
28	Greg Maddux	1.50
29	Dennis Martinez	.10
30	Odaliz Perez	.10
31	Rudy Seanez	.10
32	John Smoltz	.10
33	Roberto Alomar	.25
34	Armando Benitez	.10
35	Scott Erickson	.10
36	Juan Guzman	.10
37	Mike Mussina	.35
38	Jesse Orosco	.10
39	Rafael Palmeiro	.75
40	Sidney Ponson	.10
41	Cal Ripken Jr.	3.00
42	B.J. Surhoff	.10
43	Lenny Webster	.10
44	Dennis Eckersley	.75
45	Nomar Garciaparra	1.50
46	Darren Lewis	.10
47	Pedro Martinez	1.00
48	Troy O'Leary	.10
49	Bret Saberhagen	.10
50	John Valentin	.10
51	Mo Vaughn	.10
52	Tim Wakefield	.10
53	Manny Alexander	.10
54	Rod Beck	.10
55	Gary Gaetti	.10
56	Mark Grace	.10
57	Felix Heredia	.10
58	Jose Hernandez	.10
59	Henry Rodriguez	.10
60	Sammy Sosa	1.50
61	Kevin Tapani	.10
62	Kerry Wood	.45
63	James Baldwin	.10
64	Albert Belle	.10
65	Mike Caruso	.10
66	Carlos Castillo	.10
67	Wil Cordero	.10
68	Jaime Navarro	.10
69	Magglio Ordonez	.25
70	Frank Thomas	1.00
71	Robin Ventura	.10
72	Bret Boone	.10
73	Sean Casey	.10
74	Guillermo Garcia RC	.10

#	Player	
75	Barry Larkin	.10
76	Melvin Nieves	.10
77	Eduardo Perez	.10
78	Roberto Petagine	.10
79	Reggie Sanders	.10
80	Eddie Taubensee	.10
81	Brett Tomko	.10
82	Sandy Alomar Jr.	.10
83	Bartolo Colon	.10
84	Joey Cora	.10
85	Einar Diaz	.10
86	David Justice	.10
87	Kenny Lofton	.10
88	Manny Ramirez	1.00
89	Jim Thome	.75
90	Omar Vizquel	.10
91	Enrique Wilson	.10
92	Pedro Astacio	.10
93	Dante Bichette	.10
94	Vinny Castilla	.10
95	Edgard Clemente RC	.10
96	Todd Helton	1.00
97	Darryl Kile	.10
98	Mike Munoz	.10
99	Neifi Perez	.10
100	Jeff Reed	.10
101	Larry Walker	.10
102	Gabe Alvarez	.10
103	Kimera Bartee	.10
104	Frank Castillo	.10
105	Tony Clark	.10
106	Deivi Cruz	.10
107	Damion Easley	.10
108	Luis Gonzalez	.10
109	Marino Santana	.10
110	Justin Thompson	.10
111	Antonio Alfonseca	.10
112	Alex Fernandez	.10
113	Cliff Floyd	.10
114	Alex Gonzalez	.10
115	Livan Hernandez	.10
116	Mark Kotsay	.10
117	Derrek Lee	.65
118	Edgar Renteria	.10
119	Jesus Sanchez	.10
120	Moises Alou	.10
121	Jeff Bagwell	1.00
122	Derek Bell	.10
123	Craig Biggio	.10
124	Tony Eusebio	.10
125	Ricky Gutierrez	.10
126	Richard Hidalgo	.10
127	Randy Johnson	1.00
128	Jose Lima	.10
129	Shane Reynolds	.10
130	Johnny Damon	.40
131	Carlos Febles	.10
132	Jeff King	.10
133	Mendy Lopez	.10
134	Hal Morris	.10
135	Jose Offerman	.10
136	Jose Rosado	.10
137	Jose Santiago	.10
138	Bobby Bonilla	.10
139	Roger Cedeno	.10
140	Alex Cora	.10
141	Eric Karros	.10
142	Raul Mondesi	.10
143	Antonio Osuna	.10
144	Chan Ho Park	.10
145	Gary Sheffield	.30
146	Ismael Valdes	.10
147	Jeromy Burnitz	.10
148	Jeff Cirillo	.10
149	Valerio de los Santos	.10
150	Marquis Grissom	.10
151	Scott Karl	.10
152	Dave Nilsson	.10
153	Al Reyes	.10
154	Rafael Roque	.10
155	Jose Valentin	.10
156	Fernando Vina	.10
157	Rick Aguilera	.10
158	Hector Carrasco	.10
159	Marty Cordova	.10
160	Eddie Guardado	.10
161	Paul Molitor	1.00
162	Otis Nixon	.10
163	Alex Ochoa	.10
164	David Ortiz	.45
165	Frank Rodriguez	.10
166	Todd Walker	.10
167	Miguel Batista	.10
168	Orlando Cabrera	.10
169	Vladimir Guerrero	1.00
170	Wilton Guerrero	.10
171	Carl Pavano	.10
172	Robert Perez	.10
173	F.P. Santangelo	.10
174	Fernando Seguignol	.10
175	Ugueth Urbina	.10
176	Javier Vazquez	.10
177	Edgardo Alfonzo	.10
178	Carlos Baerga	.10
179	John Franco	.10
180	Luis Lopez	.10
181	Hideo Nomo	.50
182	John Olerud	.10
183	Rey Ordonez	.10
184	Mike Piazza	1.75
185	Armando Reynoso	.10
186	Masato Yoshii	.10
187	David Cone	.10
188	Orlando Hernandez	.10
189	Hideki Irabu	.10
190	Derek Jeter	3.00
191	Ricky Ledee	.10
192	Tino Martinez	.10

#	Player	
193	Ramiro Mendoza	.10
194	Paul O'Neill	.10
195	Jorge Posada	.10
196	Mariano Rivera	.15
197	Luis Sojo	.10
198	Bernie Williams	.10
199	Rafael Bournigal	.10
200	Eric Chavez	.20
201	Ryan Christenson	.10
202	Jason Giambi	.60
203	Ben Grieve	.10
204	Rickey Henderson	1.00
205	A.J. Hinch	.10
206	Kenny Rogers	.10
207	Miguel Tejada	.20
208	Jorge Velandia	.10
209	Bobby Abreu	.20
210	Marlon Anderson	.10
211	Alex Arias	.10
212	Bobby Estalella	.10
213	Doug Glanville	.10
214	Scott Rolen	.65
215	Curt Schilling	.35
216	Kevin Sefcik	.10
217	Adrian Brown	.10
218	Francisco Cordova	.10
219	Freddy Garcia	.10
220	Jose Guillen	.10
221	Jason Kendall	.10
222	Al Martin	.10
223	Abraham Nunez	.10
224	Aramis Ramirez	.10
225	Ricardo Rincon	.10
226	Kevin Young	.10
227	J.D. Drew	.40
228	Ron Gant	.10
229	Jose Jimenez	.10
230	Brian Jordan	.10
231	Ray Lankford	.10
232	Eli Marrero	.10
233	Mark McGwire	2.50
234	Luis Ordaz	.10
235	Placido Polanco	.10
236	Fernando Tatis	.10
237	Andy Ashby	.10
238	Kevin Brown	.10
239	Ken Caminiti	.10
240	Steve Finley	.10
241	Chris Gomez	.10
242	Tony Gwynn	1.50
243	Carlos Hernandez	.10
244	Trevor Hoffman	.10
245	Wally Joyner	.10
246	Ruben Rivera	.10
247	Greg Vaughn	.10
248	Quilvio Veras	.10
249	Rich Aurilia	.10
250	Barry Bonds	3.00
251	Stan Javier	.10
252	Jeff Kent	.10
253	Ramon Martinez	.10
254	Jose Mesa	.10
255	Armando Rios	.10
256	Rich Rodriguez	.10
257	Rey Sanchez	.10
258	J.T. Snow	.10
259	Julian Tavarez	.10
260	Jeff Fassero	.10
261	Ken Griffey Jr.	2.00
262	Giomar Guevara RC	.10
263	Carlos Guillen	.10
264	Raul Ibanez	.10
265	Edgar Martinez	.10
266	Jamie Moyer	.10
267	Alex Rodriguez	2.50
268	David Segui	.10
269	Makoto Suzuki	.10
270	Wilson Alvarez	.10
271	Rolando Arrojo	.10
272	Wade Boggs	1.50
273	Miguel Cairo	.10
274	Roberto Hernandez	.10
275	Aaron Ledesma	.10
276	Albie Lopez	.10
277	Quinton McCracken	.10
278	Fred McGriff	.10
279	Esteban Yan	.10
280	Luis Alicea	.10
281	Will Clark	.10
282	Juan Gonzalez	.50
283	Rusty Greer	.10
284	Rick Helling	.10
285	Xavier Hernandez	.10
286	Roberto Kelly	.10
287	Esteban Loaiza	.10
288	Ivan Rodriguez	.75
289	Aaron Sele	.10
290	John Wetteland	.10
291	Jose Canseco	.40
292	Roger Clemens	1.75
293	Felipe Crespo	.10
294	Jose Cruz Jr.	.10
295	Carlos Delgado	.60
296	Kelvim Escobar	.10
297	Tony Fernandez	.10
298	Alex Gonzalez	.10
299	Tomas Perez	.10
300	Juan Samuel	.10

In The Cage

These die-cut inserts have a netting like background with laser cutting, giving the look that the player is hitting in a batting cage. These are seeded 1:145 packs.

	NM/M
Complete Set (20):	80.00
Common Player:	2.00

	Inserted 1:145	
1	Chipper Jones	7.50
2	Cal Ripken Jr.	15.00
3	Nomar Garciaparra	7.50
4	Sammy Sosa	7.50
5	Frank Thomas	5.00
6	Manny Ramirez	5.00
7	Todd Helton	5.00
8	Moises Alou	2.00
9	Vladimir Guerrero	5.00
10	Mike Piazza	9.00
11	Derek Jeter	15.00
12	Ben Grieve	2.00
13	J.D. Drew	3.00
14	Mark McGwire	12.00
15	Tony Gwynn	7.50
16	Ken Griffey Jr.	10.00
17	Edgar Martinez	2.00
18	Alex Rodriguez	12.00
19	Juan Gonzalez	2.50
20	Ivan Rodriguez	4.00

Latinos/Major Leagues

This 36-card set salutes the many Latino players in the major leagues.

	NM/M
Complete Set (36):	25.00
Common Player:	.30

	Inserted 1:18	
1	Roberto Alomar	.60
2	Rafael Palmeiro	2.00
3	Nomar Garciaparra	3.50
4	Pedro Martinez	2.50
5	Magglio Ordonez	1.50
6	Sandy Alomar Jr.	.30
7	Bartolo Colon	.30
8	Manny Ramirez	2.50
9	Omar Vizquel	.30
10	Enrique Wilson	.30
11	David Ortiz	1.50
12	Orlando Hernandez	.30
13	Tino Martinez	.30
14	Mariano Rivera	.45
15	Bernie Williams	.30
16	Edgar Martinez	.30
17	Alex Rodriguez	5.00
18	David Segui	.30
19	Rolando Arrojo	.30
20	Juan Gonzalez	1.25
21	Ivan Rodriguez	2.00
22	Jose Canseco	1.00
23	Jose Cruz Jr.	.30
24	Andres Galarraga	.30
25	Andruw Jones	2.50
26	Javy Lopez	.30
27	Sammy Sosa	3.50
28	Vinny Castilla	.30
29	Alex Gonzalez	.30
30	Moises Alou	.30
31	Bobby Bonilla	.30
32	Raul Mondesi	.30
33	Fernando Vina	.30
34	Vladimir Guerrero	2.50
35	Carlos Baerga	.30
36	Rey Ordonez	.30

Pacific Cup

These die-cut inserts are shaped like a trophy with the featured player's photo in the foreground. These are seeded 1:721 packs.

	NM/M
Complete Set (10):	80.00
Common Player:	5.00

	Inserted 1:721	
1	Cal Ripken Jr.	20.00

2	Nomar Garciaparra	8.00
3	Frank Thomas	6.00
4	Ken Griffey Jr.	12.00
5	Alex Rodriguez	16.00
6	Greg Maddux	8.00
7	Sammy Sosa	8.00
8	Kerry Wood	5.00
9	Mark McGwire	16.00
10	Tony Gwynn	8.00

Players Choice

In conjunction with the annual Players Choice Awards ceremonies, Pacific produced a special edition of the cards of some of the players involved. Cards have a "Players Choice" foil stamp on front. Quantities produced were in the range of 25-40 of each.

	NM/M
Complete Set (6):	55.00
Common Player:	5.00
10 Randy Velarde	5.00
41 Cal Ripken Jr.	30.00
47 Pedro Martinez	12.00
88 Manny Ramirez	12.00
112 Alex Fernandez	5.00
128 Jose Lima	5.00

Tape Measure

This 20-card insert set is fully foiled in platinum blue with rainbow highlights in the background of the player photo.

	NM/M
Complete Set (20):	20.00
Common Player:	.60

	Inserted 1:73	
1	Andres Galarraga	.60
2	Chipper Jones	2.50
3	Nomar Garciaparra	2.50
4	Sammy Sosa	2.50
5	Frank Thomas	1.50
6	Manny Ramirez	1.50
7	Vinny Castilla	.60
8	Moises Alou	.60
9	Jeff Bagwell	1.50
10	Raul Mondesi	.60
11	Vladimir Guerrero	1.50
12	Mike Piazza	2.75
13	J.D. Drew	1.00
14	Mark McGwire	3.50
15	Greg Vaughn	.60
16	Ken Griffey Jr.	3.00
17	Alex Rodriguez	3.50
18	Juan Gonzalez	1.00
19	Ivan Rodriguez	1.25
20	Jose Canseco	1.00

Team Checklists

This features holographic silver-foil stamping and a horizontal format. The backs have a complete team checklist for the featured player's team.

	NM/M
Complete Set (30):	25.00
Common Player:	.50

	Inserted 1:37	
1	Darin Erstad	.60
2	Travis Lee	.50
3	Chipper Jones	2.00
4	Cal Ripken Jr.	4.00

5	Nomar Garciaparra	1.75
6	Sammy Sosa	1.75
7	Frank Thomas	1.25
8	Barry Larkin	.50
9	Manny Ramirez	1.25
10	Larry Walker	.50
11	Bob Higginson	.50
12	Livan Hernandez	.50
13	Moises Alou	.50
14	Jeff King	.50
15	Raul Mondesi	.50
16	Marquis Grissom	.50
17	David Ortiz	1.00
18	Vladimir Guerrero	1.25
19	Mike Piazza	2.00
20	Derek Jeter	4.00
21	Ben Grieve	.50
22	Scott Rolen	.75
23	Jason Kendall	.50
24	Mark McGwire	3.00
25	Tony Gwynn	1.75
26	Barry Bonds	4.00
27	Ken Griffey Jr.	2.50
28	Wade Boggs	1.75
29	Juan Gonzalez	.75
30	Jose Canseco	.60

1999 Pacific Crown Royale

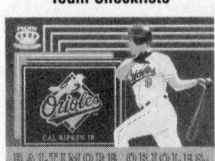

The Crown Royale 144-card base set has a horizontal format die-cut around a crown design at the top. The cards are double foiled and etched. There are 18 short-printed rookies and prospects cards, which were inserted at a rate of about one per eight packs. There are two parallels: Limited Series and Opening Day. Limited Series is produced on 24-point stock with silver foil and limited to 99 numbered sets. Opening Day is limited to 72 numbered sets.

	NM/M
Complete Set (144):	75.00
Common Player:	.25
Common SP:	.50
Limited Series (99 Sets):	6X
SP's:	2X
Opening Day (72 Sets):	12X
SP's:	2X
Pack (6):	2.00
Wax Box (24):	35.00
1	Jim Edmonds	.25
2	Darin Erstad	.50
3	Troy Glaus	2.00
4	Tim Salmon	.25
5	Mo Vaughn	.25
6	Jay Bell	.25
7	Steve Finley	.25
8	Randy Johnson	2.00
9	Travis Lee	.25
10	Matt Williams	.25
11	Andruw Jones	.25
12	Chipper Jones	3.00
13	Brian Jordan	.25
14	Ryan Klesko	.25
15	Javy Lopez	.25
16	Greg Maddux	3.00
17	Randall Simon/SP	.50
18	Albert Belle	.25
19	Will Clark	.25
20	Delino DeShields	.25
21	Mike Mussina	.25
22	Cal Ripken Jr.	6.00
23	Nomar Garciaparra	2.00
24	Pedro Martinez	2.00
25	Jose Offerman	.25
26	John Valentin	.25
27	Mark Grace	.25
28	Lance Johnson	.25
29	Henry Rodriguez	.25
30	Sammy Sosa	3.00
31	Kerry Wood	1.00
32	Mike Caruso	.25
33	Ray Durham	.25
34	Magglio Ordonez	.40
35	Brian Simmons/SP	.50
36	Frank Thomas	2.00
37	Mike Cameron	.25
38	Barry Larkin	.25
39	Greg Vaughn	.25
40	Dmitri Young	.25
41	Roberto Alomar	.40
42	Sandy Alomar Jr.	.25
43	David Justice	.25
44	Kenny Lofton	.25
45	Manny Ramirez	2.00
46	Jim Thome	1.50
47	Dante Bichette	.25
48	Vinny Castilla	.25
49	Todd Helton	2.00
50	Larry Walker	.25
51	Tony Clark	.25
52	Damion Easley	.25
53	Bob Higginson	.25
54	Brian Hunter	.25

55	Gabe Kapler/SP	.50
56	Jeff Weaver/SP RC	2.50
57	Cliff Floyd	.25
58	Alex Gonzalez/SP	.50
59	Mark Kotsay	.25
60	Derrek Lee	1.00
61	Preston Wilson/SP	.75
62	Moises Alou	.25
63	Jeff Bagwell	2.00
64	Derek Bell	.25
65	Craig Biggio	.25
66	Ken Caminiti	.25
67	Carlos Beltran/SP	2.00
68	Johnny Damon	.45
69	Carlos Febles/SP	.65
70	Jeff King	.25
71	Kevin Brown	.25
72	Todd Hundley	.25
73	Eric Karros	.25
74	Raul Mondesi	.25
75	Gary Sheffield	.75
76	Jeromy Burnitz	.25
77	Jeff Cirillo	.25
78	Marquis Grissom	.25
79	Fernando Vina	.25
80	Chad Allen/SP RC	.50
81	Matt Lawton	.25
82	Doug Mientkiewicz/SP	.75
83	Brad Radke	.25
84	Todd Walker	.25
85	Michael Barrett/SP	.50
86	Brad Fullmer	.25
87	Vladimir Guerrero	2.00
88	Wilton Guerrero	.25
89	Ugueth Urbina	.25
90	Bobby Bonilla	.25
91	Rickey Henderson	2.00
92	Rey Ordonez	.25
93	Mike Piazza	3.50
94	Robin Ventura	.25
95	Roger Clemens	3.50
96	Orlando Hernandez	.25
97	Derek Jeter	6.00
98	Chuck Knoblauch	.25
99	Tino Martinez	.25
100	Bernie Williams	.25
101	Eric Chavez/SP	1.50
102	Jason Giambi	.25
103	Ben Grieve	.25
104	Tim Raines	.25
105	Marlon Anderson/SP	.65
106	Doug Glanville	.25
107	Scott Rolen	1.25
108	Curt Schilling	.40
109	Brian Giles	.25
110	Jose Guillen	.25
111	Jason Kendall	.25
112	Kevin Young	.25
113	J.D. Drew/SP	2.00
114	Jose Jimenez/SP	.50
115	Ray Lankford	.25
116	Mark McGwire	5.00
117	Fernando Tatis	.25
118	Matt Clement/SP	.75
119	Tony Gwynn	3.00
120	Trevor Hoffman	.25
121	Wally Joyner	.25
122	Reggie Sanders	.25
123	Barry Bonds	6.00
124	Ellis Burks	.25
125	Jeff Kent	.25
126	J.T. Snow	.25
127	Freddy Garcia/SP RC	1.00
128	Ken Griffey Jr.	4.00
129	Edgar Martinez	.25
130	Alex Rodriguez	5.00
131	David Segui	.25
132	Rolando Arrojo	.25
133	Wade Boggs	3.00
134	Jose Canseco	.65
135	Quinton McCracken	.25
136	Fred McGriff	.25
137	Juan Gonzalez	1.00
138	Rusty Greer	.25
139	Rafael Palmeiro	1.50
140	Ivan Rodriguez	1.50
141	Jose Cruz Jr.	.25
142	Carlos Delgado	.75
143	Shawn Green	.75
144	Roy Halladay/SP	1.00

Century 21

This 10-card set features some of baseball's most dominating players, on a full silver foil front. These are seeded 1:25 packs.

		NM/M
Complete Set (10):		30.00
Common Player:		2.00
Inserted 1:25		
1	Cal Ripken Jr.	7.50
2	Nomar Garciaparra	4.00
3	Sammy Sosa	4.00
4	Frank Thomas	3.00
5	Mike Piazza	4.50
6	J.D. Drew	2.00
7	Mark McGwire	6.00
8	Tony Gwynn	4.00
9	Ken Griffey Jr.	5.00
10	Alex Rodriguez	6.00

Cramer's Choice Premiums

This enlarged (about 5" x 7") 10-card set is die-cut into a trophy shape. Cards are enhanced with silver holographic fronts with silver holographic etching and gold-foil stamping across the bottom. They are found one per box. Six serially numbered parallels were randomly seeded: Dark Blue (35 each), Green (30), Red (25), Light Blue (20), Gold (10) and Purple (1).

		NM/M
Complete Set (10):		20.00
Common Player:		2.00
Inserted 1:Box		
Dark Blue (35 Sets):		5X
Green (30):		6X
Red (25):		8X
Light Blue (20):		10X
Gold (10):		15X
Purple (1): Value Undetermined		
1	Cal Ripken Jr.	6.50
2	Nomar Garciaparra	3.00
3	Sammy Sosa	3.00
4	Frank Thomas	2.50
5	Mike Piazza	3.50
6	Derek Jeter	6.50
7	J.D. Drew	2.00
8	Mark McGwire	5.00
9	Tony Gwynn	3.00
10	Ken Griffey Jr.	4.00

Gold Crown Die-Cut Premiums

This enlarged six-card set was an unannounced premium box-topper. They were limited to 1,036 numbered sets, found less than once every other box.

		NM/M
Complete Set (6):		15.00
Common Player:		2.50
Inserted 6:10 boxes		
1	Cal Ripken Jr.	7.00
2	Mike Piazza	4.50
3	Ken Griffey Jr.	5.00
4	Tony Gwynn	3.00
5	Mark McGwire	6.00
6	J.D. Drew	2.50

Living Legends

This 10-card set spotlights baseball's top stars on a fully foiled card front. These are serial numbered to 375 sets.

	NM/M
Complete Set (10):	100.00

Common Player:		7.50
Production 375 Sets		
1	Greg Maddux	10.00
2	Cal Ripken Jr.	20.00
3	Nomar Garciaparra	10.00
4	Sammy Sosa	10.00
5	Frank Thomas	7.50
6	Mike Piazza	12.00
7	Mark McGwire	15.00
8	Tony Gwynn	10.00
9	Ken Griffey Jr.	13.50
10	Alex Rodriguez	15.00

Master Performers

This 20-card set features a full foiled front with the player photo in a frame like border. Master Performers are seeded 2:25 packs.

		NM/M
Complete Set (20):		40.00
Common Player:		1.00
Inserted 2:25		
1	Chipper Jones	2.50
2	Greg Maddux	2.50
3	Cal Ripken Jr.	5.00
4	Nomar Garciaparra	2.50
5	Sammy Sosa	2.50
6	Frank Thomas	2.00
7	Raul Mondesi	1.00
8	Vladimir Guerrero	2.00
9	Mike Piazza	3.00
10	Roger Clemens	3.00
11	Derek Jeter	5.00
12	Scott Rolen	1.75
13	J.D. Drew	1.50
14	Mark McGwire	4.00
15	Tony Gwynn	2.50
16	Barry Bonds	5.00
17	Ken Griffey Jr.	3.50
18	Alex Rodriguez	4.00
19	Juan Gonzalez	1.50
20	Ivan Rodriguez	1.75

Pillars of the Game

This 25-card set features holographic silver foil fronts on a horizontal format.

		NM/M
Complete Set (25):		30.00
Common Player:		.50
Inserted 1:1		
1	Mo Vaughn	.50
2	Chipper Jones	2.00
3	Greg Maddux	2.00
4	Albert Belle	.50
5	Cal Ripken Jr.	4.00
6	Nomar Garciaparra	2.00
7	Sammy Sosa	2.00
8	Frank Thomas	1.50
9	Manny Ramirez	1.50
10	Jeff Bagwell	1.50
11	Raul Mondesi	.50
12	Vladimir Guerrero	1.50
13	Mike Piazza	2.25
14	Roger Clemens	2.25
15	Derek Jeter	4.00

16	Bernie Williams	.50
17	Ben Grieve	.50
18	J.D. Drew	1.00
19	Mark McGwire	3.00
20	Tony Gwynn	2.00
21	Barry Bonds	4.00
22	Ken Griffey Jr.	2.50
23	Alex Rodriguez	3.00
24	Juan Gonzalez	2.50
25	Ivan Rodriguez	1.25

Pivotal Players

This 25-card set features holographic silver foil fronts with a flame in the background of the player photo.

		NM/M
Complete Set (25):		20.00
Common Player:		.50
Inserted 1:1		
1	Mo Vaughn	.50
2	Chipper Jones	2.00
3	Greg Maddux	2.00
4	Albert Belle	.50
5	Cal Ripken Jr.	4.00
6	Nomar Garciaparra	2.00
7	Sammy Sosa	2.00
8	Frank Thomas	1.50
9	Manny Ramirez	1.50
10	Craig Biggio	.50
11	Raul Mondesi	.50
12	Vladimir Guerrero	1.50
13	Mike Piazza	2.25
14	Roger Clemens	2.50
15	Derek Jeter	4.00
16	Bernie Williams	.50
17	Ben Grieve	.50
18	Scott Rolen	.60
19	J.D. Drew	.75
20	Mark McGwire	3.00
21	Tony Gwynn	2.00
22	Ken Griffey Jr.	2.50
23	Alex Rodriguez	3.00
24	Juan Gonzalez	.75
25	Ivan Rodriguez	1.00

Home Run Heroes

These cards were part of an unannounced multi-manufacturer (Fleer, Upper Deck, Topps, Pacific) insert program which was exclusive to Wal-Mart. Each company produced cards of Mark McGwire and Sammy Sosa, along with two other premier sluggers. Each company's cards share a "Power Elite" logo at top and "Home Run Heroes" logo vertically at right.

		NM/M
Complete Set (4):		3.50
Common Player:		.50
13	Mark McGwire	1.50
14	Sammy Sosa	1.25
15	Juan Gonzalez	.50
16	Manny Ramirez	.50

1999 Pacific Invincible

The base set consists of 150 cards. Each features an action photo with a portrait in a cel window at bottom. There are two parallels to the base set: Opening Day and Platinum Blue. Both parallels are limited to 67 serial numbered sets.

		NM/M
Complete Set (150):		60.00
Common Player:		.25
Opening Day (69 Sets):		6X
Platinum Blues (67):		6X
Pack (3):		1.50
Wax Box (24):		35.00
1	Jim Edmonds	.25
2	Darin Erstad	.50
3	Troy Glaus	2.50
4	Tim Salmon	.25
5	Mo Vaughn	.25
6	Steve Finley	.25
7	Randy Johnson	2.50
8	Travis Lee	.25
9	Dante Powell	.25
10	Matt Williams	.25
11	Bret Boone	.25
12	Andruw Jones	2.50
13	Chipper Jones	3.00
14	Brian Jordan	.25
15	Ryan Klesko	.25
16	Javy Lopez	.25
17	Greg Maddux	3.00
18	Brady Anderson	.25
19	Albert Belle	.25
20	Will Clark	.25
21	Mike Mussina	.75
22	Cal Ripken Jr.	6.00
23	Nomar Garciaparra	3.00
24	Pedro Martinez	2.50
25	Trot Nixon	.25
26	Jose Offerman	.25
27	Donnie Sadler	.25
28	John Valentin	.25
29	Mark Grace	.25
30	Lance Johnson	.25
31	Henry Rodriguez	.25
32	Sammy Sosa	3.00
33	Kerry Wood	1.25
34	McKay Christensen	.25
35	Ray Durham	.25
36	Jeff Liefer	.25
37	Frank Thomas	2.50
38	Mike Cameron	.25
39	Barry Larkin	.25
40	Greg Vaughn	.25
41	Dmitri Young	.25
42	Roberto Alomar	.50
43	Sandy Alomar Jr.	.25
44	David Justice	.25
45	Kenny Lofton	.25
46	Manny Ramirez	2.50
47	Jim Thome	2.25
48	Dante Bichette	.25
49	Vinny Castilla	.25
50	Darryl Hamilton	.25
51	Todd Helton	2.50
52	Neifi Perez	.25
53	Larry Walker	.25
54	Tony Clark	.25
55	Damion Easley	.25
56	Bob Higginson	.25
57	Brian Hunter	.25
58	Gabe Kapler	.25
59	Cliff Floyd	.25
60	Alex Gonzalez	.25
61	Mark Kotsay	.25
62	Derek Lee	2.00
63	Braden Looper	.25
64	Moises Alou	.25
65	Jeff Bagwell	2.50
66	Craig Biggio	.25
67	Ken Caminiti	.25
68	Scott Elarton	.25
69	Mitch Meluskey	.25
70	Carlos Beltran	.65
71	Johnny Damon	.50
72	Carlos Febles	.25
73	Jeremy Giambi	.25
74	Kevin Brown	.25
75	Todd Hundley	.25
76	Paul LoDuca	.25
77	Raul Mondesi	.25
78	Gary Sheffield	1.00
79	Geoff Jenkins	.25
80	Jeromy Burnitz	.25
81	Marquis Grissom	.25
82	Jose Valentin	.25
83	Fernando Vina	.25
84	Corey Koskie	.25
85	Matt Lawton	.25
86	Christian Guzman	.25
87	Torii Hunter	.25
88	Doug Mientkiewicz	.25
89	Michael Barrett	.25
90	Brad Fullmer	.25
91	Vladimir Guerrero	2.50

92	Fernando Seguignol	.25
93	Ugueth Urbina	.25
94	Bobby Bonilla	.25
95	Rickey Henderson	2.50
96	Rey Ordonez	.25
97	Mike Piazza	3.50
98	Robin Ventura	.25
99	Roger Clemens	3.50
100	Derek Jeter	6.00
101	Chuck Knoblauch	.25
102	Tino Martinez	.25
103	Paul O'Neill	.25
104	Bernie Williams	.25
105	Eric Chavez	.50
106	Ryan Christenson	.25
107	Jason Giambi	1.25
108	Ben Grieve	.25
109	Miguel Tejada	.50
110	Marlon Anderson	.25
111	Doug Glanville	.25
112	Scott Rolen	2.25
113	Curt Schilling	.50
114	Brian Giles	.25
115	Warren Morris	.25
116	Jason Kendall	.25
117	Kris Benson	.25
118	J.D. Drew	1.25
119	Ray Lankford	.25
120	Mark McGwire	5.00
121	Matt Clement	.25
122	Tony Gwynn	3.00
123	Trevor Hoffman	.25
124	Wally Joyner	.25
125	Reggie Sanders	.25
126	Barry Bonds	6.00
127	Ellis Burks	.25
128	Jeff Kent	.25
129	Stan Javier	.25
130	J.T. Snow	.25
131	Jay Buhner	.25
132	Freddy Garcia RC	.25
133	Ken Griffey Jr.	4.00
134	Russ Davis	.25
135	Edgar Martinez	.25
136	Alex Rodriguez	5.00
137	David Segui	.25
138	Rolando Arrojo	.25
139	Wade Boggs	1.00
140	Jose Canseco	.25
141	Quinton McCracken	.25
142	Fred McGriff	.25
143	Juan Gonzalez	1.25
144	Tom Goodwin	.25
145	Rusty Greer	.25
146	Ivan Rodriguez	2.25
147	Jose Cruz Jr.	.25
148	Carlos Delgado	1.00
149	Shawn Green	.75
150	Roy Halladay	.25

Diamond Magic

This 10-card set features a horizontal format with silver foil stamping on the front. Diamond Magic's are seeded 1:49 packs.

		NM/M
Complete Set (10):		35.00
Common Player:		3.00
Inserted 1:49		
1	Cal Ripken Jr.	7.50
2	Nomar Garciaparra	4.00
3	Sammy Sosa	4.00
4	Frank Thomas	3.50
5	Mike Piazza	4.50
6	J.D. Drew	3.00
7	Mark McGwire	6.00
8	Tony Gwynn	4.00
9	Ken Griffey Jr.	5.00
10	Alex Rodriguez	6.00

Flash Point

This 20-card set features gold etching and gold foil stamping on the card front. These were seeded 1:25 packs.

		NM/M
Complete Set (20):		50.00
Common Player:		1.25
Inserted 1:25		
1	Mo Vaughn	1.25
2	Chipper Jones	4.00
3	Greg Maddux	3.50
4	Cal Ripken Jr.	9.00
5	Nomar Garciaparra	3.50
6	Sammy Sosa	3.50
7	Frank Thomas	2.50
8	Manny Ramirez	2.50
9	Vladimir Guerrero	2.50
10	Mike Piazza	4.00
11	Roger Clemens	4.00
12	Derek Jeter	9.00
13	Ben Grieve	1.25
14	Scott Rolen	2.00
15	J.D. Drew	1.50
16	Mark McGwire	7.50
17	Tony Gwynn	3.50
18	Ken Griffey Jr.	5.00
19	Alex Rodriguez	7.50
20	Juan Gonzalez	1.50

Giants of the Game

This jumbo mail-in redemption set of baseball's top stars is limited to 10 serially numbered specimens of each card.

		NM/M
Complete Set (10):		300.00
Common Player:		25.00
Production 10 Sets		
1	Cal Ripken Jr.	75.00
2	Nomar Garciaparra	35.00
3	Sammy Sosa	35.00
4	Frank Thomas	30.00
5	Mike Piazza	40.00
6	J.D. Drew	25.00
7	Mark McGwire	60.00
8	Tony Gwynn	35.00
9	Ken Griffey Jr.	50.00
10	Alex Rodriguez	60.00

Sandlot Heroes

Sandlot Heroes salutes baseball's top players on a horizontal format with holographic silver foil stamping on front. These were inserted one per pack. Each player can be found in two versions. A special edition, serially numbered to 10 of each and overprinted with a SportsFest logo, was created for use as a redemption prize at Pacific's booth at the show.

		NM/M
Complete Set (20):		15.00
Common Player:		.50
Inserted 1:1		
SportsFest (10 Sets):		25X
1	Mo Vaughn	.50
2	Chipper Jones	1.00
3	Greg Maddux	1.00
4	Cal Ripken Jr.	3.00
5	Nomar Garciaparra	1.00
6	Sammy Sosa	1.00
7	Frank Thomas	.75
8	Manny Ramirez	.75
9	Vladimir Guerrero	.75
10	Mike Piazza	1.25
11	Roger Clemens	1.25
12	Derek Jeter	3.00
13	Eric Chavez	.50
14	Ben Grieve	.50
15	J.D. Drew	.60
16	Mark McGwire	2.00
17	Tony Gwynn	1.00
18	Ken Griffey Jr.	1.50
19	Alex Rodriguez	2.00
20	Juan Gonzalez	.60

Seismic Force

This 20-card set has a dot pattern behind the featured player with the left side and bottom of the card in a gold border. These were seeded one per pack. A specially marked SportsFest version was created for use as a redemption prize at Pacific's booth at the show. These are serially numbered to just 20 apiece.

		NM/M
Complete Set (20):		15.00
Common Player:		.50
Inserted 1:1		
SportsFest (20 Sets):		15X
1	Mo Vaughn	.50
2	Chipper Jones	1.00
3	Greg Maddux	1.00
4	Cal Ripken Jr.	3.00
5	Nomar Garciaparra	1.00
6	Sammy Sosa	1.00
7	Frank Thomas	.75
8	Manny Ramirez	.75
9	Vladimir Guerrero	.75
10	Mike Piazza	1.25
11	Bernie Williams	.50
12	Derek Jeter	3.00
13	Ben Grieve	.50
14	J.D. Drew	.60
15	Mark McGwire	2.00
16	Tony Gwynn	1.00
17	Ken Griffey Jr.	1.50
18	Alex Rodriguez	2.00
19	Juan Gonzalez	.50
20	Ivan Rodriguez	.65

Thunder Alley

Thunder Alley focuses on baseball's top power hitters. These were inserted 1:121 packs.

		NM/M
Complete Set (20):		75.00
Common Player:		2.50
Inserted 1:121		
1	Mo Vaughn	2.50
2	Chipper Jones	6.00
3	Cal Ripken Jr.	12.00
4	Nomar Garciaparra	6.00
5	Sammy Sosa	6.00
6	Frank Thomas	5.00
7	Manny Ramirez	5.00
8	Todd Helton	5.00
9	Vladimir Guerrero	5.00
10	Mike Piazza	7.50
11	Derek Jeter	12.00
12	Ben Grieve	2.50
13	Scott Rolen	4.50
14	J.D. Drew	3.00
15	Mark McGwire	10.00
16	Tony Gwynn	6.00
17	Ken Griffey Jr.	9.00
18	Alex Rodriguez	10.00
19	Juan Gonzalez	3.00
20	Ivan Rodriguez	4.50

1999 Pacific Omega Sample

The Omega brand for '99 was launched with this sample card of spokesman Tony Gwynn. The card is in the same format as the regular-issue cards, except for the "SAMPLE" overprint on back and in the card-number circle at bottom-right.

	NM/M
SAMPLE Tony Gwynn	2.00

1999 Pacific Omega

This single-series product features both portrait and action photos on front in a horizontal format. Four parallel versions distinguished by the color of foil highlights were random inserts in the

six-card packs. Gold parallels are serially numbered to 299 each; Copper to 99; Platinum Blue to 75 and Premiere Date to 50.

		NM/M
Complete Set (250):		20.00
Common Player:		.10
Gold (299 Sets):		4X
Copper (99):		10X
Platinum Blue (75):		15X
Premiere Date (50):		20X
Wax Pack (6):		1.50
Wax Box (36):		35.00
1	Garret Anderson	.10
2	Jim Edmonds	.10
3	Darin Erstad	.10
4	Chuck Finley	.10
5	Troy Glaus	.75
6	Troy Percival	.10
7	Chris Pritchett	.10
8	Tim Salmon	.10
9	Mo Vaughn	.10
10	Jay Bell	.10
11	Steve Finley	.10
12	Luis Gonzalez	.10
13	Randy Johnson	.75
14	Byung-Hyun Kim RC	.75
15	Travis Lee	.10
16	Matt Williams	.10
17	Tony Womack	.10
18	Bret Boone	.10
19	Mark DeRosa	.10
20	Tom Glavine	.35
21	Andruw Jones	.75
22	Chipper Jones	1.00
23	Brian Jordan	.10
24	Ryan Klesko	.10
25	Javy Lopez	.10
26	Greg Maddux	1.00
27	John Smoltz	.10
28	Bruce Chen, Odalis Perez	.10
29	Brady Anderson	.10
30	Harold Baines	.10
31	Albert Belle	.10
32	Will Clark	.10
33	Delino DeShields	.10
34	Jerry Hairston Jr.	.10
35	Charles Johnson	.10
36	Mike Mussina	.40
37	Cal Ripken Jr.	2.50
38	B.J. Surhoff	.10
39	Jin Ho Cho	.10
40	Nomar Garciaparra	1.00
41	Pedro Martinez	.75
42	Jose Offerman	.10
43	Troy O'Leary	.10
44	John Valentin	.10
45	Jason Varitek	.10
46	Juan Pena RC, Brian Rose	.10
47	Mark Grace	.10
48	Glenallen Hill	.10
49	Tyler Houston	.10
50	Mickey Morandini	.10
51	Henry Rodriguez	.10
52	Sammy Sosa	1.00
53	Kevin Tapani	.10
54	Mike Caruso	.10
55	Ray Durham	.10
56	Paul Konerko	.20
57	Carlos Lee	.10
58	Magglio Ordonez	.20
59	Mike Sirotka	.10
60	Frank Thomas	.75
61	Mark L. Johnson, Chris Singleton	.10
62	Mike Cameron	.10
63	Sean Casey	.20
64	Pete Harnisch	.10
65	Barry Larkin	.10
66	Pokey Reese	.10
67	Greg Vaughn	.10
68	Scott Williamson	.10
69	Dmitri Young	.10
70	Roberto Alomar	.25
71	Sandy Alomar Jr.	.10
72	Travis Fryman	.10
73	David Justice	.10
74	Kenny Lofton	.10
75	Manny Ramirez	.75
76	Richie Sexson	.10
77	Jim Thome	.65
78	Omar Vizquel	.10
79	Jaret Wright	.10
80	Dante Bichette	.10
81	Vinny Castilla	.10
82	Todd Helton	.75
83	Darryl Hamilton	.10
84	Darryl Kile	.10
85	Neifi Perez	.10
86	Larry Walker	.25
87	Tony Clark	.10
88	Damion Easley	.10
89	Juan Encarnacion	.10
90	Bobby Higginson	.10
91	Gabe Kapler	.10
92	Dean Palmer	.10
93	Justin Thompson	.10
94	Masao Kida RC, Jeff Weaver RC	1.00
95	Bruce Aven	.10
96	Luis Castillo	.10
97	Alex Fernandez	.10
98	Cliff Floyd	.10
99	Alex Gonzalez	.10
100	Mark Kotsay	.10
101	Preston Wilson	.10
102	Moises Alou	.10
103	Jeff Bagwell	.75
104	Derek Bell	.10
105	Craig Biggio	.10
106	Mike Hampton	.10
107	Richard Hidalgo	.10
108	Jose Lima	.10
109	Billy Wagner	.10
110	Russ Johnson, Daryle Ward	.10
111	Carlos Beltran	.50
112	Johnny Damon	.35
113	Jermaine Dye	.10
114	Carlos Febles	.10
115	Jeremy Giambi	.10
116	Joe Randa	.10
117	Mike Sweeney	.10
118	Orber Moreno RC, Jose Santiago	.10
119	Kevin Brown	.10
120	Todd Hundley	.10
121	Eric Karros	.10
122	Raul Mondesi	.10
123	Chan Ho Park	.10
124	Angel Pena	.10
125	Gary Sheffield	.45
126	Devon White	.10
127	Eric Young	.10
128	Ron Belliard	.10
129	Jeromy Burnitz	.10
130	Jeff Cirillo	.10
131	Marquis Grissom	.10
132	Geoff Jenkins	.10
133	David Nilsson	.10
134	Hideo Nomo	.40
135	Fernando Vina	.10
136	Ron Coomer	.10
137	Marty Cordova	.10
138	Corey Koskie	.10
139	Brad Radke	.10
140	Todd Walker	.10
141	Chad Allen RC, Torii Hunter	.10
142	Cristian Guzman, Jacque Jones	.10
143	Michael Barrett	.10
144	Orlando Cabrera	.10
145	Vladimir Guerrero	.75
146	Wilton Guerrero	.10
147	Ugueth Urbina	.10
148	Rondell White	.10
149	Chris Widger	.10
150	Edgardo Alfonzo	.10
151	Roger Cedeno	.10
152	Octavio Dotel	.10
153	Rickey Henderson	.75
154	John Olerud	.10
155	Rey Ordonez	.10
156	Mike Piazza	1.25
157	Robin Ventura	.10
158	Scott Brosius	.10
159	Roger Clemens	1.25
160	David Cone	.10
161	Chili Davis	.10
162	Orlando Hernandez	.10
163	Derek Jeter	2.50
164	Chuck Knoblauch	.10
165	Tino Martinez	.10
166	Paul O'Neill	.10
167	Bernie Williams	.10
168	Jason Giambi	.60
169	Ben Grieve	.10
170	Chad Harville RC	.10
171	Tim Hudson RC	2.00
172	Tony Phillips	.10
173	Kenny Rogers	.10
174	Matt Stairs	.10
175	Miguel Tejada	.25
176	Eric Chavez	.25
177	Bobby Abreu	.20
178	Ron Gant	.10
179	Doug Glanville	.10
180	Mike Lieberthal	.10
181	Desi Relaford	.10
182	Scott Rolen	.65
183	Curt Schilling	.35
184	Marlon Anderson, Randy Wolf	.10
185	Brant Brown	.10
186	Brian Giles	.10
187	Jason Kendall	.10
188	Al Martin	.10
189	Ed Sprague	.10
190	Kevin Young	.10
191	Kris Benson, Warren Morris	.10
192	Kent Bottenfield	.10
193	Eric Davis	.10
194	J.D. Drew	.45
195	Ray Lankford	.10
196	Joe McEwing RC	.25
197	Mark McGwire	2.00
198	Edgar Renteria	.10
199	Fernando Tatis	.10
200	Andy Ashby	.10
201	Ben Davis	.10
202	Tony Gwynn	1.00
203	Trevor Hoffman	.10
204	Wally Joyner	.10
205	Gary Matthews Jr.	.10
206	Ruben Rivera	.10
207	Reggie Sanders	.10
208	Rich Aurilia	.10
209	Marvin Benard	.10
210	Barry Bonds	2.50
211	Ellis Burks	.10
212	Stan Javier	.10
213	Jeff Kent	.10
214	Robb Nen	.10
215	J.T. Snow	.10
216	David Bell	.10
217	Jay Buhner	.10
218	Freddy Garcia RC	.50
219	Ken Griffey Jr.	1.50
220	Brian Hunter	.10
221	Butch Huskey	.10
222	Edgar Martinez	.10
223	Jamie Moyer	.10
224	Alex Rodriguez	2.00
225	David Segui	.10
226	Rolando Arrojo	.10
227	Wade Boggs	1.00
228	Miguel Cairo	.10
229	Jose Canseco	.60
230	Dave Martinez	.10
231	Fred McGriff	.10
232	Kevin Stocker	.10
233	Mike Duvall RC, David Lamb	.10
234	Royce Clayton	.10
235	Juan Gonzalez	.40
236	Rusty Greer	.10
237	Ruben Mateo	.10
238	Rafael Palmeiro	.65
239	Ivan Rodriguez	.65
240	John Wetteland	.10
241	Todd Zeile	.10
242	Jeff Zimmerman	.10
243	Homer Bush	.10
244	Jose Cruz Jr.	.10
245	Carlos Delgado	.60
246	Tony Fernandez	.10
247	Shawn Green	.35
248	Shannon Stewart	.10
249	David Wells	.10
250	Roy Halladay, Billy Koch	.10

Debut Duos

The careers of two players who made their major league debuts the same season are compared in this scarce (1:145) insert series. Fronts feature action photos of the pair, backs have portraits.

		NM/M
Complete Set (10):		45.00
Common Player:		2.50
Inserted 1:145		
1	Nomar Garciaparra, Vladimir Guerrero	6.00
2	Derek Jeter, Andy Pettitte	12.00
3	Garret Anderson, Alex Rodriguez	9.00
4	Chipper Jones, Raul Mondesi	6.00
5	Pedro Martinez, Mike Piazza	6.50
6	Mo Vaughn, Bernie Williams	2.50
7	Juan Gonzalez, Ken Griffey Jr.	7.50
8	Sammy Sosa, Larry Walker	6.00
9	Barry Bonds, Mark McGwire	12.00
10	Wade Boggs, Tony Gwynn	6.00

Diamond Masters

		NM/M
Complete Set (36):		27.50
Common Player:		.25
Inserted 1:9		
1	Darin Erstad	.35
2	Mo Vaughn	.25
3	Matt Williams	.25
4	Andruw Jones	.75
5	Chipper Jones	1.00
6	Greg Maddux	1.00
7	Nomar Garciaparra	1.00
8	Nomar Garciaparra	1.00
9	Pedro Martinez	.75
10	Sammy Sosa	1.00
11	Frank Thomas	.75
12	Kenny Lofton	.25
13	Manny Ramirez	.75
14	Larry Walker	.25
15	Gabe Kapler	.25
16	Jeff Bagwell	.75
17	Craig Biggio	.25
18	Raul Mondesi	.25
19	Vladimir Guerrero	.75
20	Mike Piazza	1.25
21	Roger Clemens	1.25
22	Derek Jeter	3.00
23	Bernie Williams	.25
24	Scott Rolen	.65
25	J.D. Drew	.60
26	Mark McGwire	2.00
27	Fernando Tatis	.25
28	Tony Gwynn	1.00
29	Barry Bonds	3.00
30	Ken Griffey Jr.	1.50
31	Alex Rodriguez	2.00
32	Jose Canseco	.60
33	Juan Gonzalez	.40
34	Ruben Mateo	.25
35	Ivan Rodriguez	.65
36	Rusty Greer	.25

EO Portraits

		NM/M
Complete Set (20):		60.00
Common Player:		1.00
Inserted 1:73		
1-of-1 numbered parallels exist.		
1	Mo Vaughn	1.00
2	Chipper Jones	5.00
3	Greg Maddux	5.00
4	Cal Ripken Jr.	10.00
5	Nomar Garciaparra	5.00
6	Sammy Sosa	5.00
7	Frank Thomas	4.00
8	Manny Ramirez	4.00
9	Jeff Bagwell	4.00
10	Mike Piazza	5.50
11	Roger Clemens	5.50
12	Derek Jeter	10.00
13	Scott Rolen	3.00
14	Mark McGwire	8.00
15	Tony Gwynn	5.00
16	Barry Bonds	10.00
17	Ken Griffey Jr.	6.00
18	Alex Rodriguez	8.00
19	Jose Canseco	2.50
20	Juan Gonzalez	2.00

Hit Machine 3000

Within days of Tony Gwynn's 3,000 hit on August 6, Pacific had rushed into production a special insert honoring the achievement of its long-time spokesman. A total of 3,000 serially numbered sets of 20 cards were issued as random pack inserts in Omega. Fronts feature various game-action and studio photos of Gwynn, and are highlighted in silver foil. Backs have two more color photos of Gwynn and a few sentences about the player. A serial number in printed on front.

		NM/M
Complete Set (20):		24.00
Common Player:		1.50
1	The Hitting Machine	1.50
2	The Eyes Have It	1.50
3	The Art of Hitting	1.50
4	Solid as a Rock	1.50
5	Seeing Doubles	1.50
6	Pitcher's Worst Nightmare	1.50
7	Portrait of an All-Star	1.50
8	An American Hero	1.50
9	Fan Favorite	1.50
10	Mr. Batting Title	1.50
11	4-for-5!	1.50
12	Mission Accomplished	1.50
13	One Hit Away	1.50
14	A Tip of the Hat	1.50
15	It's a Base Hit!	1.50
16	2997th - Grand Slam!	1.50
17	2998th Hit	1.50
18	2999th Hit - 2-Run Double	1.50
19	3000th Hit!	1.50
20	3000 Hits, 8874 At-Bats, 18 Years	1.50

HR '99

		NM/M
Complete Set (20):		20.00
Common Player:		.25
Inserted 1:37		
1	Mo Vaughn	.25
2	Matt Williams	.25
3	Chipper Jones	2.00
4	Albert Belle	.25
5	Nomar Garciaparra	2.00
6	Sammy Sosa	2.00
7	Frank Thomas	1.25
8	Manny Ramirez	1.25
9	Jeff Bagwell	1.25
10	Raul Mondesi	.25
11	Vladimir Guerrero	1.25
12	Mike Piazza	2.25
13	Derek Jeter	4.00
14	Mark McGwire	3.00
15	Fernando Tatis	.25
16	Barry Bonds	4.00
17	Ken Griffey Jr.	2.50
18	Alex Rodriguez	3.00
19	Jose Canseco	.75
20	Juan Gonzalez	.65

5-Tool Talents

		NM/M
Complete Set (30):		40.00
Common Player:		.40
Inserted 4:37		
1	Randy Johnson	1.50
2	Greg Maddux	2.00
3	Pedro Martinez	1.50
4	Kevin Brown	.40
5	Roger Clemens	2.50
6	Carlos Lee	.40
7	Gabe Kapler	.40
8	Carlos Beltran	.75
9	J.D. Drew	.75
10	Ruben Mateo	.40
11	Chipper Jones	2.00
12	Sammy Sosa	2.00
13	Manny Ramirez	1.50
14	Vladimir Guerrero	1.50
15	Mark McGwire	4.00
16	Ken Griffey Jr.	3.00
17	Jose Canseco	.75
18	Nomar Garciaparra	2.00
19	Frank Thomas	1.50
20	Larry Walker	.40
21	Jeff Bagwell	1.50
22	Mike Piazza	2.50
23	Tony Gwynn	2.00
24	Juan Gonzalez	.75
25	Cal Ripken Jr.	5.00
26	Derek Jeter	5.00
27	Scott Rolen	1.25
28	Barry Bonds	5.00
29	Alex Rodriguez	4.00
30	Ivan Rodriguez	1.25

5-Tool Talents Tiered

A parallel of the 5-Tool Talents inserts is fractured into five tiers of increasing scarcity, differentiated by the color of foil highlights and the serially numbered limited edition. The breakdown is: Tier 1, blue, 100 sets; Tier 2, red, 75 sets; Tier 3, green, 50 sets; Tier 4, purple, 25 sets; Tier 5, gold, one set. The unique gold cards are not priced due to their rarity.

		NM/M
1	Randy Johnson	4.00
6	Carlos Lee	2.00
11	Chipper Jones	5.00
18	Nomar Garciaparra	5.00
21	Jeff Bagwell	4.00
28	Barry Bonds	7.50
2	Greg Maddux	7.50
7	Gabe Kapler	2.00
16	Manny Ramirez	6.00
14	Ken Griffey Jr.	10.00
19	Frank Thomas	6.00
8	Ivan Rodriguez	5.00
3	Pedro Martinez	12.50
4	Carlos Beltran	6.00
15	Mark McGwire	20.00
20	Larry Walker	2.00
25	Cal Ripken Jr.	30.00
26	Derek Jeter	30.00
9	Kevin Brown	7.50
4	J.D. Drew	15.00
12	Sammy Sosa	25.00
5	Jose Canseco	20.00
23	Tony Gwynn	25.00
29	Alex Rodriguez	35.00

Paramount Sample

Pacific spokesman Tony Gwynn is featured on the sample card issued to introduce the brand for 1999. The card carries a large "SAMPLE" overprint diagonally on back.

	NM/M
Tony Gwynn	2.00

1999 Pacific Paramount

The 250-card base set is highlighted by silver foil stamping and a white border. Card backs have a small photo along with 1998 statistics and career totals and a brief career note. There are six parallels to the base set: Copper, Platinum Blue, Holographic Silver, Opening Day Issue, Gold and Holographic Gold. Each parallel is enhanced with the appropriate foil color. Coppers are found exclusively in hobby packs at a rate of one per pack. Platinum Blues are seeded one per 73 packs, Holographic Silvers are hobby only and limited to 99 serial numbered sets. Opening Day Issue is limited to 74 numbered sets. Golds are found one per retail pack. Holographic Golds are limited to 199 numbered sets.

	NM/M
Complete Set (250):	25.00
Common Player:	.10
Copper (1:1H):	2X
Red (1:1R):	2X
Gold (1:1R):	2X
Platinum Blue (1:73):	4X
Holographic Gold (199):	10X
Holographic Silver (99 Sets):	15X
Opening Day (74):	15X
Pack (6):	1.00
Wax Box (36):	25.00

1	Garret Anderson	.10
2	Gary DiSarcina	.10
3	Jim Edmonds	.10
4	Darin Erstad	.25
5	Chuck Finley	.10
6	Troy Glaus	.75
7	Troy Percival	.10
8	Tim Salmon	.10
9	Mo Vaughn	.10
10	Tony Batista	.10
11	Jay Bell	.10
12	Andy Benes	.10
13	Steve Finley	.10
14	Luis Gonzalez	.10
15	Randy Johnson	.75
16	Travis Lee	.10
17	Todd Stottlemyre	.10
18	Matt Williams	.10
19	David Dellucci	.10
20	Bret Boone	.10
21	Andres Galarraga	.20
22	Tom Glavine	.35
23	Andruw Jones	.75
24	Chipper Jones	1.50
25	Brian Jordan	.10
26	Ryan Klesko	.10
27	Javy Lopez	.10
28	Greg Maddux	1.50
29	John Smoltz	.10
30	Brady Anderson	.10
31	Albert Belle	.10
32	Will Clark	.10
33	Delino DeShields	.10
34	Charles Johnson	.10
35	Mike Mussina	.40
36	Cal Ripken Jr.	3.00
37	B.J. Surhoff	.10
38	Nomar Garciaparra	1.50
39	Reggie Jefferson	.10
40	Darren Lewis	.10
41	Pedro Martinez	.75
42	Troy O'Leary	.10
43	Jose Offerman	.10
44	Donnie Sadler	.10
45	John Valentin	.10
46	Rod Beck	.10
47	Gary Gaetti	.10
48	Mark Grace	.10
49	Lance Johnson	.10
50	Mickey Morandini	.10
51	Henry Rodriguez	.10
52	Sammy Sosa	1.50
53	Kerry Wood	.40
54	Mike Caruso	.10
55	Ray Durham	.10
56	Paul Konerko	.20
57	Jaime Navarro	.10
58	Greg Norton	.10
59	Magglio Ordonez	.30
60	Frank Thomas	.75
61	Aaron Boone	.10
62	Mike Cameron	.10
63	Barry Larkin	.10
64	Hal Morris	.10
65	Pokey Reese	.10
66	Brett Tomko	.10
67	Greg Vaughn	.10
68	Dmitri Young	.10
69	Roberto Alomar	.25
70	Sandy Alomar Jr.	.10
71	Bartolo Colon	.10
72	Travis Fryman	.10
73	David Justice	.10
74	Kenny Lofton	.10
75	Manny Ramirez	.75
76	Richie Sexson	.10
77	Jim Thome	.65
78	Omar Vizquel	.10
79	Dante Bichette	.10
80	Vinny Castilla	.10
81	Darryl Hamilton	.10
82	Todd Helton	.75
83	Darryl Kile	.10
84	Mike Lansing	.10
85	Neifi Perez	.10
86	Larry Walker	.20
87	Tony Clark	.10
88	Damion Easley	.10
89	Bob Higginson	.10
90	Brian Hunter	.10
91	Dean Palmer	.10
92	Justin Thompson	.10
93	Todd Dunwoody	.10
94	Cliff Floyd	.10
95	Alex Gonzalez	.10
96	Livan Hernandez	.10
97	Mark Kotsay	.10
98	Derrek Lee	.60
99	Kevin Orie	.10
100	Moises Alou	.10
101	Jeff Bagwell	.75
102	Derek Bell	.10
103	Craig Biggio	.10
104	Ken Caminiti	.10
105	Ricky Gutierrez	.10
106	Richard Hidalgo	.10
107	Billy Wagner	.10
108	Jeff Conine	.10
109	Johnny Damon	.35
110	Carlos Febles	.10
111	Jeremy Giambi	.10
112	Jeff King	.10
113	Jeff Montgomery	.10
114	Joe Randa	.10
115	Kevin Brown	.10
116	Mark Grudzielanek	.10
117	Todd Hundley	.10
118	Eric Karros	.10
119	Raul Mondesi	.10
120	Chan Ho Park	.10
121	Gary Sheffield	.40
122	Devon White	.10
123	Eric Young	.10
124	Jeromy Burnitz	.10
125	Jeff Cirillo	.10
126	Marquis Grissom	.10
127	Geoff Jenkins	.10
128	Dave Nilsson	.10
129	Jose Valentin	.10
130	Fernando Vina	.10
131	Rick Aguilera	.10
132	Ron Coomer	.10
133	Marty Cordova	.10
134	Matt Lawton	.10
135	David Ortiz	.50
136	Brad Radke	.10
137	Terry Steinbach	.10
138	Javier Valentin	.10
139	Todd Walker	.10
140	Orlando Cabrera	.10
141	Brad Fullmer	.10
142	Vladimir Guerrero	.75
143	Wilton Guerrero	.10
144	Carl Pavano	.10
145	Ugueth Urbina	.10
146	Rondell White	.10
147	Chris Widger	.10
148	Edgardo Alfonzo	.10
149	Bobby Bonilla	.10
150	Rickey Henderson	.75
151	Brian McRae	.10
152	Hideo Nomo	.40
153	John Olerud	.10
154	Rey Ordonez	.10
155	Mike Piazza	1.75
156	Robin Ventura	.10
157	Masato Yoshii	.10
158	Roger Clemens	1.75
159	David Cone	.10
160	Orlando Hernandez	.10
161	Hideki Irabu	.10
162	Derek Jeter	3.00
163	Chuck Knoblauch	.10
164	Tino Martinez	.10
165	Paul O'Neill	.10
166	Darryl Strawberry	.10
167	Bernie Williams	.10
168	Eric Chavez	.20
169	Ryan Christenson	.10
170	Jason Giambi	.50
171	Ben Grieve	.10
172	Tony Phillips	.10
173	Tim Raines	.10
174	Scott Spiezio	.10
175	Miguel Tejada	.20
176	Bobby Abreu	.20
177	Rico Brogna	.10
178	Ron Gant	.10
179	Doug Glanville	.10
180	Desi Relaford	.10
181	Scott Rolen	.65
182	Curt Schilling	.35
183	Brant Brown	.10
184	Brian Giles	.10
185	Jose Guillen	.10
186	Jason Kendall	.10
187	Al Martin	.10
188	Ed Sprague	.10
189	Kevin Young	.10
190	Eric Davis	.10
191	J.D. Drew	.40
192	Ray Lankford	.10
193	Eli Marrero	.10
194	Mark McGwire	2.50
195	Edgar Renteria	.10
196	Fernando Tatis	.10
197	Andy Ashby	.10
198	Tony Gwynn	1.50
199	Carlos Hernandez	.10
200	Trevor Hoffman	.10
201	Wally Joyner	.10
202	Jim Leyritz	.10
203	Ruben Rivera	.10
204	Matt Clement	.10
205	Quilvio Veras	.10
206	Rich Aurilia	.10
207	Marvin Benard	.10
208	Barry Bonds	3.00
209	Ellis Burks	.10
210	Jeff Kent	.10
211	Bill Mueller	.10
212	Robb Nen	.10
213	J.T. Snow	.10
214	Jay Buhner	.10
215	Jeff Fassero	.10
216	Ken Griffey Jr.	2.00
217	Carlos Guillen	.10
218	Butch Huskey	.10
219	Edgar Martinez	.10
220	Alex Rodriguez	2.50
221	David Segui	.10
222	Dan Wilson	.10
223	Rolando Arrojo	.10
224	Wade Boggs	1.50
225	Jose Canseco	.50
226	Roberto Hernandez	.10
227	Dave Martinez	.10
228	Quinton McCracken	.10
229	Fred McGriff	.10
230	Kevin Stocker	.10
231	Randy Winn	.10
232	Royce Clayton	.10
233	Juan Gonzalez	.40
234	Tom Goodwin	.10
235	Rusty Greer	.10
236	Rick Helling	.10
237	Rafael Palmeiro	.65
238	Ivan Rodriguez	.65
239	Aaron Sele	.10
240	John Wetteland	.10
241	Todd Zeile	.10
242	Jose Cruz Jr.	.10
243	Carlos Delgado	.50
244	Tony Fernandez	.10
245	Cecil Fielder	.10
246	Alex Gonzalez	.10
247	Shawn Green	.35
248	Roy Halladay	.10
249	Shannon Stewart	.10
250	David Wells	.10

Cooperstown Bound

This 10-card set focuses on players who seem destined for the Hall of Fame. These inserts feature silver foil stamping and are seeded 1:361 packs.

		NM/M
Complete Set (10):		35.00
Common Player:		3.00
Inserted 1:361		
1	Greg Maddux	4.00
2	Cal Ripken Jr.	10.00
3	Nomar Garciaparra	4.00
4	Sammy Sosa	4.00
5	Frank Thomas	3.00
6	Mike Piazza	5.00
7	Mark McGwire	10.00
8	Tony Gwynn	4.00
9	Ken Griffey Jr.	6.00
10	Alex Rodriguez	8.00

Fielder's Choice

This 20-card set is die-cut into a glove shape and enhanced with gold foil stamping. These are seeded 1:73 packs.

		NM/M
Complete Set (20):		60.00
Common Player:		2.50
Inserted 1:73		
1	Chipper Jones	5.00
2	Greg Maddux	5.00
3	Cal Ripken Jr.	10.00
4	Nomar Garciaparra	5.00
5	Sammy Sosa	5.00
6	Kerry Wood	3.00
7	Frank Thomas	4.00
8	Manny Ramirez	4.00
9	Todd Helton	4.00
10	Jeff Bagwell	4.00
11	Mike Piazza	5.50
12	Derek Jeter	10.00
13	Bernie Williams	2.50
14	J.D. Drew	3.00
15	Mark McGwire	7.50
16	Tony Gwynn	5.00
17	Ken Griffey Jr.	6.00
18	Alex Rodriguez	7.50
19	Juan Gonzalez	2.00
20	Ivan Rodriguez	3.50

Personal Bests

This 36-card set features holographic silver foil stamping on the card front. Card backs include a close-up photo of the featured player and a career note. These are seeded 1:37 packs.

		NM/M
Complete Set (36):		45.00
Common Player:		.50
Inserted 1:37		
1	Darin Erstad	.65
2	Mo Vaughn	.50
3	Travis Lee	.50

4	Chipper Jones	3.00
5	Greg Maddux	3.00
6	Albert Belle	.50
7	Cal Ripken Jr.	6.00
8	Nomar Garciaparra	3.00
9	Sammy Sosa	3.00
10	Kerry Wood	1.00
11	Frank Thomas	2.00
12	Greg Vaughn	.50
13	Manny Ramirez	2.00
14	Todd Helton	2.00
15	Larry Walker	.50
16	Jeff Bagwell	2.00
17	Craig Biggio	.50
18	Raul Mondesi	.50
19	Vladimir Guerrero	2.00
20	Hideo Nomo	1.00
21	Mike Piazza	3.50
22	Roger Clemens	3.50
23	Derek Jeter	6.00
24	Bernie Williams	.50
25	Eric Chavez	.75
26	Ben Grieve	.50
27	Scott Rolen	1.50
28	J.D. Drew	1.25
29	Mark McGwire	4.50
30	Tony Gwynn	3.00
31	Barry Bonds	6.00
32	Ken Griffey Jr.	4.00
33	Alex Rodriguez	4.50
34	Jose Canseco	1.25
35	Juan Gonzalez	1.00
36	Ivan Rodriguez	1.50

Team Checklists

This 30-card set features gold foil etching and stamping on the card front. Card backs show the featured player's team checklist for the base set. These were seeded 2:37 packs.

		NM/M
Complete Set (30):		40.00
Common Player:		.50
Inserted 2:37		
1	Mo Vaughn	.50
2	Travis Lee	.50
3	Chipper Jones	3.00
4	Cal Ripken Jr.	6.00
5	Nomar Garciaparra	3.00
6	Sammy Sosa	3.00
7	Frank Thomas	2.50
8	Greg Vaughn	.50
9	Manny Ramirez	2.50
10	Larry Walker	.50
11	Damion Easley	.50
12	Mark Kotsay	.50
13	Jeff Bagwell	2.50
14	Jeremy Giambi	.50
15	Raul Mondesi	.50
16	Marquis Grissom	.50
17	Brad Radke	.50
18	Vladimir Guerrero	2.50
19	Mike Piazza	3.50
20	Roger Clemens	3.50
21	Ben Grieve	.50
22	Scott Rolen	.50
23	Brian Giles	.50
24	Mark McGwire	5.00
25	Tony Gwynn	5.00
26	Barry Bonds	6.00
27	Ken Griffey Jr.	4.00
28	Jose Canseco	1.25
29	Juan Gonzalez	1.25
30	Jose Cruz Jr.	.50

1999 Pacific Prism Sample

This card of Pacific spokesman Tony Gwynn introduces the 1999 Prism series. The sample card follows the format of the issued version but is overprinted "SAMPLE" on back.

	NM/M
Tony Gwynn	2.00

1999 Pacific Prism

This 150-card base set has a full, holographic silver card front. Card backs feature two more player photos along with 1998 and career statistics. Hobby packs consist of five cards. There are also four parallels including Holographic Gold, Holographic Mirror, Holographic Blue, Holographic Purple and Red. Golds are limited to 480 serial numbered sets, Mirrors 160 sets, Blues 80 numbered sets, and, Purples 320 sets. Red parallels are a retail-only insert and are seeded at a rate of one per 12.5 packs.

	NM/M
Complete Set (150):	50.00
Common Player:	.15
Red (2:25R):	3X
HoloGold (480 Sets):	3X
HoloPurple (320):	4X
HoloMirror (160):	8X
HoloBlue (80):	15X
Retail Pack (3):	1.00
Hobby Pack (5):	1.50

1	Garret Anderson	.15
2	Jim Edmonds	.15
3	Darin Erstad	.30
4	Chuck Finley	.15
5	Tim Salmon	.15
6	Jay Bell	.15
7	David Dellucci	.15
8	Travis Lee	.15
9	Matt Williams	.15
10	Andres Galarraga	.15
11	Tom Glavine	.40
12	Andruw Jones	1.50
13	Chipper Jones	2.00
14	Ryan Klesko	.15
15	Javy Lopez	.15
16	Greg Maddux	2.00
17	Roberto Alomar	.50
18	Ryan Minor	.15
19	Mike Mussina	.40
20	Rafael Palmeiro	1.25
21	Cal Ripken Jr.	4.00
22	Nomar Garciaparra	2.00
23	Pedro Martinez	1.50
24	John Valentin	.15
25	Mo Vaughn	.15
26	Tim Wakefield	.15
27	Rod Beck	.15
28	Mark Grace	.15
29	Lance Johnson	.15
30	Sammy Sosa	2.00
31	Kerry Wood	.50
32	Albert Belle	.15
33	Mike Caruso	.15
34	Magglio Ordonez	.30
35	Frank Thomas	1.50
36	Robin Ventura	.15
37	Aaron Boone	.15

#	Player	
38	Barry Larkin	.15
39	Reggie Sanders	.15
40	Brett Tomko	.15
41	Sandy Alomar Jr.	.15
42	Bartolo Colon	.15
43	David Justice	.15
44	Kenny Lofton	.15
45	Manny Ramirez	1.50
46	Richie Sexson	1.00
47	Jim Thome	1.00
48	Omar Vizquel	.15
49	Dante Bichette	.15
50	Vinny Castilla	.15
51	Edgard Clemente RC	.15
52	Todd Helton	1.50
53	Quinton McCracken	.15
54	Larry Walker	.15
55	Tony Clark	.15
56	Damion Easley	.15
57	Luis Gonzalez	.15
58	Bob Higginson	.15
59	Brian Hunter	.15
60	Cliff Floyd	.15
61	Alex Gonzalez	.15
62	Livan Hernandez	.15
63	Derrek Lee	.65
64	Edgar Renteria	.15
65	Moises Alou	.15
66	Jeff Bagwell	1.50
67	Derek Bell	.15
68	Craig Biggio	.15
69	Randy Johnson	1.50
70	Johnny Damon	.35
71	Jeff King	.15
72	Hal Morris	.15
73	Dean Palmer	.15
74	Eric Karros	.15
75	Raul Mondesi	.15
76	Chan Ho Park	.15
77	Gary Sheffield	.50
78	Jeromy Burnitz	.15
79	Jeff Cirillo	.15
80	Marquis Grissom	.15
81	Jose Valentin	.15
82	Fernando Vina	.15
83	Paul Molitor	1.50
84	Otis Nixon	.15
85	David Ortiz	.65
86	Todd Walker	.15
87	Vladimir Guerrero	1.50
88	Carl Pavano	.15
89	Fernando Seguignol	.15
90	Ugueth Urbina	.15
91	Carlos Baerga	.15
92	Bobby Bonilla	.15
93	Hideo Nomo	.75
94	John Olerud	.15
95	Rey Ordonez	.15
96	Mike Piazza	2.25
97	David Cone	.15
98	Orlando Hernandez	.15
99	Hideki Irabu	.15
100	Derek Jeter	4.00
101	Tino Martinez	.15
102	Bernie Williams	.15
103	Eric Chavez	.25
104	Jason Giambi	1.00
105	Ben Grieve	.15
106	Rickey Henderson	1.50
107	Bob Abreu	.25
108	Doug Glanville	.15
109	Scott Rolen	1.00
110	Curt Schilling	.40
111	Emil Brown	.15
112	Jose Guillen	.15
113	Jason Kendall	.15
114	Al Martin	.15
115	Aramis Ramirez	.15
116	Kevin Young	.15
117	J.D. Drew	.75
118	Ron Gant	.15
119	Brian Jordan	.15
120	Eli Marrero	.15
121	Mark McGwire	3.00
122	Kevin Brown	.15
123	Tony Gwynn	2.00
124	Trevor Hoffman	.15
125	Wally Joyner	.15
126	Greg Vaughn	.15
127	Barry Bonds	4.00
128	Ellis Burks	.15
129	Jeff Kent	.15
130	Robb Nen	.15
131	J.T. Snow	.15
132	Jay Buhner	.15
133	Ken Griffey Jr.	2.50
134	Edgar Martinez	.15
135	Alex Rodriguez	3.00
136	David Segui	.15
137	Rolando Arrojo	.15
138	Wade Boggs	2.00
139	Aaron Ledesma	.15
140	Fred McGriff	.15
141	Will Clark	.15
142	Juan Gonzalez	.15
143	Rusty Greer	.15
144	Ivan Rodriguez	1.25
145	Aaron Sele	.40
146	Jose Canseco	.40
147	Roger Clemens	2.25
148	Jose Cruz Jr.	.15
149	Carlos Delgado	.50
150	Alex Gonzalez	.15

Ahead of the Game

Each card features full gold foil and etching with a close-up

photo of baseball's top 20 stars. These are seeded 1:49 packs.

		NM/M
Complete Set (20):		40.00
Common Player:		1.00
Inserted 1:49		
1	Darin Erstad	1.25
2	Travis Lee	1.00
3	Chipper Jones	3.00
4	Cal Ripken Jr.	6.00
5	Nomar Garciaparra	3.00
6	Sammy Sosa	3.00
7	Kerry Wood	1.25
8	Frank Thomas	2.00
9	Manny Ramirez	2.00
10	Todd Helton	2.00
11	Jeff Bagwell	2.00
12	Mike Piazza	3.50
13	Derek Jeter	6.00
14	Bernie Williams	1.00
15	J.D. Drew	1.25
16	Mark McGwire	5.00
17	Tony Gwynn	3.00
18	Ken Griffey Jr.	4.00
19	Alex Rodriguez	5.00
20	Ivan Rodriguez	1.50

Ballpark Legends

This 10 card set salutes baseball's biggest stars. These inserts feature silver foil stamping and etching with an image of a ballpark in the background of the player photo. These are seeded 1:193 packs.

		NM/M
Complete Set (10):		40.00
Common Player:		2.50
Inserted 1:193		
1	Cal Ripken Jr.	10.00
2	Nomar Garciaparra	5.00
3	Frank Thomas	4.00
4	Ken Griffey Jr.	6.00
5	Alex Rodriguez	7.50
6	Greg Maddux	5.00
7	Sammy Sosa	5.00
8	Kerry Wood	2.50
9	Mark McGwire	7.50
10	Tony Gwynn	5.00

Diamond Glory

Card fronts feature full copper foil stamping with a star in the background of the player's photo. The 20-card set features 20 of baseball's most exciting players including several top 1999 rookies. These are seeded 2:25 packs.

		NM/M
Complete Set (20):		25.00
Common Player:		.60
Inserted 2:25		
1	Darin Erstad	.60
2	Travis Lee	.60
3	Chipper Jones	2.00
4	Greg Maddux	2.00
5	Cal Ripken Jr.	3.50
6	Nomar Garciaparra	2.00
7	Sammy Sosa	2.00
8	Kerry Wood	.75
9	Frank Thomas	1.50
10	Todd Helton	1.50
11	Jeff Bagwell	1.50
12	Mike Piazza	2.25
13	Derek Jeter	3.50
14	Bernie Williams	.60
15	J.D. Drew	.75
16	Mark McGwire	3.00
17	Tony Gwynn	2.00
18	Ken Griffey Jr.	2.50
19	Alex Rodriguez	3.00
20	Juan Gonzalez	.75

Epic Performers

This hobby-only set features top hobby favorites and is seeded at 1:97 packs.

		NM/M
Complete Set (10):		60.00
Common Player:		4.00
Inserted 1:97 H		
1	Cal Ripken Jr.	15.00
2	Nomar Garciaparra	7.50
3	Frank Thomas	6.00
4	Ken Griffey Jr.	10.00
5	Alex Rodriguez	12.50
6	Greg Maddux	7.50
7	Sammy Sosa	7.50
8	Kerry Wood	4.00
9	Mark McGwire	12.50
10	Tony Gwynn	7.50

1999 Pacific Private Stock

The premiere issue of Private Stock base cards features holographic silver foil on 30-pt. cardboard. Card backs have selected box scores from the '98 season, with a brief commentary on the player. Packs consist of six cards.

		NM/M
Complete Set (150):		25.00
Common Player:		.10
Pack (6):		1.50
Wax Box (24):		20.00
Wax Box (36):		25.00
1	Jeff Bagwell	1.00
2	Roger Clemens	1.75
3	J.D. Drew	.60
4	Nomar Garciaparra	.75
5	Juan Gonzalez	.50
6	Ken Griffey Jr.	2.00
7	Tony Gwynn	1.50
8	Derek Jeter	3.00
9	Chipper Jones	1.50
10	Travis Lee	.10
11	Greg Maddux	1.50
12	Mark McGwire	2.50
13	Mike Piazza	1.75
14	Manny Ramirez	.50
15	Cal Ripken Jr.	3.00
16	Alex Rodriguez	2.50
17	Ivan Rodriguez	.75
18	Sammy Sosa	1.50
19	Frank Thomas	1.00
20	Kerry Wood	.40
21	Roberto Alomar	.25
22	Moises Alou	.10
23	Albert Belle	.10
24	Craig Biggio	.10
25	Wade Boggs	1.50
26	Barry Bonds	3.00
27	Jose Canseco	.50
28	Jim Edmonds	.10
29	Darin Erstad	.25
30	Andres Galarraga	.10
31	Tom Glavine	.35
32	Ben Grieve	.10
33	Vladimir Guerrero	1.00
34	Wilton Guerrero	.10
35	Todd Helton	1.00
36	Andruw Jones	1.00
37	Ryan Klesko	.10
38	Kenny Lofton	.10
39	Javy Lopez	.10
40	Pedro Martinez	1.00
41	Paul Molitor	1.00
42	Raul Mondesi	.10
43	Rafael Palmeiro	.75
44	Tim Salmon	.10
45	Jim Thome	.75
46	Mo Vaughn	.75
47	Larry Walker	.10
48	David Wells	.10
49	Bernie Williams	.75
50	Jaret Wright	.10
51	Bobby Abreu	.15
52	Garret Anderson	.10
53	Rolando Arrojo	.10
54	Tony Batista	.10
55	Rod Beck	.10
56	Derek Bell	.10
57	Marvin Benard	.10
58	Dave Berg	.10
59	Dante Bichette	.10
60	Aaron Boone	.10
61	Bret Boone	.10
62	Scott Brosius	.10
63	Brant Brown	.10
64	Kevin Brown	.10
65	Jeromy Burnitz	.10
66	Ken Caminiti	.10
67	Mike Caruso	.10
68	Sean Casey	.20
69	Vinny Castilla	.10
70	Eric Chavez	.20
71	Ryan Christenson	.10
72	Jeff Cirillo	.10
73	Tony Clark	.10
74	Will Clark	.10
75	Edgard Clemente RC	.10
76	David Cone	.10
77	Marty Cordova	.10
78	Jose Cruz Jr.	.10
79	Eric Davis	.10
80	Carlos Delgado	.50
81	David Dellucci	.10
82	Delino DeShields	.10
83	Gary DiSarcina	.10
84	Damion Easley	.10
85	Dennis Eckersley	.65
86	Cliff Floyd	.10
87	Jason Giambi	.65
88	Doug Glanville	.10
89	Alex Gonzalez	.10
90	Mark Grace	.10
91	Rusty Greer	.10
92	Jose Guillen	.10
93	Carlos Guillen	.10
94	Jeffrey Hammonds	.10
95	Rick Helling	.10
96	Bob Henley	.10
97	Livan Hernandez	.10
98	Orlando Hernandez	.10
99	Bob Higginson	.10
100	Trevor Hoffman	.10
101	Randy Johnson	1.00
102	Brian Jordan	.10
103	Wally Joyner	.10
104	Eric Karros	.10
105	Jason Kendall	.10
106	Jeff Kent	.10
107	Jeff King	.10
108	Mark Kotsay	.10
109	Ray Lankford	.10
110	Barry Larkin	.10
111	Mark Loretta	.10
112	Edgar Martinez	.10
113	Tino Martinez	.10
114	Quinton McCracken	.10
115	Fred McGriff	.10
116	Ryan Minor	.10
117	Hal Morris	.10
118	Bill Mueller	.10
119	Mike Mussina	.40
120	Dave Nilsson	.10
121	Otis Nixon	.10
122	Hideo Nomo	.50
123	Paul O'Neill	.10
124	Jose Offerman	.10
125	John Olerud	.10
126	Rey Ordonez	.10
127	David Ortiz	.50
128	Dean Palmer	.10
129	Chan Ho Park	.10
130	Aramis Ramirez	.10
131	Edgar Renteria	.10
132	Armando Rios	.10
133	Henry Rodriguez	.10
134	Scott Rolen	.75
135	David Segui	.10
136	Richie Sexson	.10
137	Gary Sheffield	.45
138	John Smoltz	.10
139	Matt Stairs	.10
140	Justin Thompson	.10
141	Greg Vaughn	.10
142	Omar Vizquel	.10
143	Tim Wakefield	.10
144	Tim Wakefield	.10
145	Todd Walker	.10
146	Devon White	.10
147	Rondell White	.10
148	Matt Williams	.10
149	Enrique Wilson RC	.25
150	Kevin Young	.10

Exclusive Series

This 20-card set is a partial parallel to the base set. Taking the first 20 cards from the set and serially numbering them to 299 sets. These are inserted exclusively in hobby packs.

		NM/M
Complete Set (20):		50.00
Common Player:		1.00
Production: 299 Sets H		
1	Jeff Bagwell	2.00
2	Roger Clemens	3.50
3	J.D. Drew	1.25
4	Nomar Garciaparra	3.00
5	Juan Gonzalez	1.25
6	Ken Griffey Jr.	4.00
7	Tony Gwynn	3.00
8	Derek Jeter	6.00
9	Chipper Jones	3.00
10	Travis Lee	1.00
11	Greg Maddux	3.00
12	Mark McGwire	5.00
13	Mike Piazza	3.50
14	Manny Ramirez	2.00
15	Cal Ripken Jr.	6.00
16	Alex Rodriguez	5.00
17	Ivan Rodriguez	1.50
18	Sammy Sosa	3.00
19	Frank Thomas	2.00
20	Kerry Wood	1.25

Platinum Series

Another partial parallel of the first 50 cards in the base set. Cards have a platinum holographic sheen to them with a Platinum stamp on the front. These are limited to 199 numbered sets.

		NM/M
Complete Set (50):		160.00
Common Player:		.75
Production 199 Sets		
1	Jeff Bagwell	5.00
2	Roger Clemens	6.50
3	J.D. Drew	3.00
4	Nomar Garciaparra	6.00
5	Juan Gonzalez	2.50
6	Ken Griffey Jr.	8.00
7	Tony Gwynn	6.00
8	Derek Jeter	12.00
9	Chipper Jones	6.00
10	Travis Lee	.75
11	Greg Maddux	6.00
12	Mark McGwire	10.00
13	Mike Piazza	6.50
14	Manny Ramirez	5.00
15	Cal Ripken Jr.	12.00
16	Alex Rodriguez	10.00
17	Ivan Rodriguez	4.00
18	Sammy Sosa	6.00
19	Frank Thomas	5.00
20	Kerry Wood	2.00
21	Roberto Alomar	1.50
22	Moises Alou	.75
23	Albert Belle	.75
24	Craig Biggio	.75
25	Wade Boggs	6.00
26	Barry Bonds	12.00
27	Jose Canseco	3.00
28	Jim Edmonds	.75
29	Darin Erstad	1.50
30	Andres Galarraga	.75
31	Tom Glavine	2.00
32	Ben Grieve	.75
33	Vladimir Guerrero	5.00
34	Wilton Guerrero	.75
35	Todd Helton	5.00
36	Andruw Jones	5.00
37	Ryan Klesko	.75
38	Kenny Lofton	.75
39	Javy Lopez	.75
40	Pedro Martinez	5.00
41	Paul Molitor	5.00
42	Raul Mondesi	.75
43	Rafael Palmeiro	4.00
44	Tim Salmon	.75
45	Jim Thome	3.50
46	Mo Vaughn	.75
47	Larry Walker	.75
48	David Wells	.75
49	Bernie Williams	.75
50	Jaret Wright	.75

Preferred Series

Another partial parallel of the first 20 base cards. Each card is stamped with a holographic Preferred logo and are numbered to 399 sets.

		NM/M
Complete Set (20):		37.50
Common Player:		.60
Production: 399 Sets		
1	Jeff Bagwell	1.50
2	Roger Clemens	2.25
3	J.D. Drew	.75
4	Nomar Garciaparra	2.00
5	Juan Gonzalez	.75
6	Ken Griffey Jr.	2.50
7	Tony Gwynn	2.00
8	Derek Jeter	5.00
9	Chipper Jones	2.00
10	Travis Lee	.60
11	Greg Maddux	2.00
12	Mark McGwire	3.50
13	Mike Piazza	2.25
14	Manny Ramirez	1.50
15	Cal Ripken Jr.	5.00
16	Alex Rodriguez	3.50
17	Ivan Rodriguez	1.25
18	Sammy Sosa	2.00
19	Frank Thomas	1.50
20	Kerry Wood	.75

Vintage Series

This insert set is a partial parallel of the first 50 cards in the base set and has a Vintage holographic stamp on the card fronts. These are limited to 99 numbered sets.

		NM/M
Complete Set (50):		375.00
Common Player:		2.50
Production: 99 Sets		
1	Jeff Bagwell	12.50
2	Roger Clemens	17.50
3	J.D. Drew	7.50
4	Nomar Garciaparra	15.00
5	Juan Gonzalez	6.00
6	Ken Griffey Jr.	20.00
7	Tony Gwynn	15.00
8	Derek Jeter	30.00
9	Chipper Jones	15.00
10	Travis Lee	2.50
11	Greg Maddux	15.00
12	Mark McGwire	25.00
13	Mike Piazza	17.50
14	Manny Ramirez	12.50
15	Cal Ripken Jr.	30.00
16	Alex Rodriguez	25.00
17	Ivan Rodriguez	10.00
18	Sammy Sosa	15.00
19	Frank Thomas	12.50
20	Kerry Wood	6.00
21	Roberto Alomar	3.50
22	Moises Alou	2.50
23	Albert Belle	2.50
24	Craig Biggio	2.50
25	Wade Boggs	15.00
26	Barry Bonds	30.00
27	Jose Canseco	2.50
28	Jim Edmonds	

29	Darin Erstad	3.50
30	Andres Galarraga	2.50
31	Tom Glavine	5.00
32	Ben Grieve	2.50
33	Vladimir Guerrero	12.50
34	Wilton Guerrero	2.50
35	Todd Helton	12.50
36	Andruw Jones	12.50
37	Ryan Klesko	2.50
38	Kenny Lofton	2.50
39	Javy Lopez	2.50
40	Pedro Martinez	12.50
41	Paul Molitor	12.50
42	Raul Mondesi	2.50
43	Rafael Palmeiro	10.00
44	Tim Salmon	2.50
45	Jim Thome	10.00
46	Mo Vaughn	2.50
47	Larry Walker	2.50
48	David Wells	2.50
49	Bernie Williams	2.50
50	Jaret Wright	2.50

PS-206

This 150-card set takes reverent reach back into collecting history with its smaller format (1.5" x 2.5"). Card fronts have a white border with silver foil stamping and a blue back, these are found one per pack. A parallel also exists with a red back, which are seeded 1:25 packs.

NM/M
Complete Set (150): 20.00
Common Player: .15
Inserted 1:1
Red Parallels: 4X
Inserted 1:25

1	Jeff Bagwell	.75
2	Roger Clemens	1.25
3	J.D. Drew	.50
4	Nomar Garciaparra	1.00
5	Juan Gonzalez	.40
6	Ken Griffey Jr.	1.50
7	Tony Gwynn	1.00
8	Derek Jeter	3.00
9	Chipper Jones	1.00
10	Travis Lee	.15
11	Greg Maddux	1.00
12	Mark McGwire	2.00
13	Mike Piazza	1.25
14	Manny Ramirez	.75
15	Cal Ripken Jr.	3.00
16	Alex Rodriguez	2.00
17	Ivan Rodriguez	.65
18	Sammy Sosa	1.00
19	Frank Thomas	.75
20	Kerry Wood	.40
21	Roberto Alomar	.30
22	Moises Alou	.15
23	Albert Belle	.15
24	Craig Biggio	.15
25	Wade Boggs	1.00
26	Barry Bonds	3.00
27	Jose Canseco	.50
28	Jim Edmonds	.15
29	Darin Erstad	.30
30	Andres Galarraga	.15
31	Tom Glavine	.35
32	Ben Grieve	.15
33	Vladimir Guerrero	.75
34	Wilton Guerrero	.15
35	Todd Helton	.75
36	Andruw Jones	.75
37	Ryan Klesko	.15
38	Kenny Lofton	.15
39	Javy Lopez	.15
40	Pedro Martinez	.75
41	Paul Molitor	.75
42	Raul Mondesi	.15
43	Rafael Palmeiro	.65
44	Tim Salmon	.15
45	Jim Thome	.65
46	Mo Vaughn	.15
47	Larry Walker	.15
48	David Wells	.15
49	Bernie Williams	.15
50	Jaret Wright	.15
51	Bobby Abreu	.15
52	Garret Anderson	.15
53	Rolando Arrojo	.15
54	Tony Batista	.15
55	Rod Beck	.15
56	Derek Bell	.15
57	Marvin Benard	.15
58	Dave Berg	.15
59	Dante Bichette	.15
60	Aaron Boone	.15
61	Bret Boone	.15
62	Scott Brosius	.15
63	Brant Brown	.15
64	Kevin Brown	.15
65	Jeromy Burnitz	.15
66	Ken Caminiti	.15
67	Mike Caruso	.15
68	Sean Casey	.25
69	Vinny Castilla	.15
70	Eric Chavez	.25
71	Ryan Christenson	.15
72	Jeff Cirillo	.15
73	Tony Clark	.15
74	Will Clark	.15
75	Edgard Clemente	.15
76	David Cone	.15
77	Marty Cordova	.15
78	Jose Cruz Jr.	.15
79	Eric Davis	.15
80	Carlos Delgado	.60
81	David Dellucci	.15
82	Delino DeShields	.15
83	Gary DiSarcina	.15
84	Damion Easley	.15
85	Dennis Eckersley	.65
86	Cliff Floyd	.15
87	Jason Giambi	.60
88	Doug Glanville	.15
89	Alex Gonzalez	.15
90	Mark Grace	.15
91	Rusty Greer	.15
92	Jose Guillen	.15
93	Carlos Guillen	.15
94	Jeffrey Hammonds	.15
95	Rick Helling	.15
96	Bob Henley	.15
97	Livan Hernandez	.15
98	Orlando Hernandez	.15
99	Bob Higginson	.15
100	Trevor Hoffman	.15
101	Randy Johnson	.75
102	Brian Jordan	.15
103	Wally Joyner	.15
104	Eric Karros	.15
105	Jason Kendall	.15
106	Jeff Kent	.15
107	Jeff King	.15
108	Mark Kotsay	.15
109	Ray Lankford	.15
110	Barry Larkin	.15
111	Mark Loretta	.15
112	Edgar Martinez	.15
113	Tino Martinez	.15
114	Quinton McCracken	.15
115	Fred McGriff	.15
116	Ryan Minor	.15
117	Hal Morris	.15
118	Bill Mueller	.15
119	Mike Mussina	.40
120	Dave Nilsson	.15
121	Otis Nixon	.15
122	Hideo Nomo	.40
123	Paul O'Neill	.15
124	Jose Offerman	.15
125	John Olerud	.15
126	Rey Ordonez	.15
127	David Ortiz	.50
128	Dean Palmer	.15
129	Chan Ho Park	.15
130	Aramis Ramirez	.15
131	Edgar Renteria	.15
132	Armando Rios	.15
133	Henry Rodriguez	.15
134	Scott Rolen	.60
135	Curt Schilling	.35
136	David Segui	.15
137	Richie Sexson	.15
138	Gary Sheffield	.50
139	John Smoltz	.15
140	Matt Stairs	.15
141	Justin Thompson	.15
142	Greg Vaughn	.15
143	Omar Vizquel	.15
144	Tim Wakefield	.15
145	Todd Walker	.15
146	Devon White	.15
147	Rondell White	.15
148	Matt Williams	.15
149	Enrique Wilson	.15
150	Kevin Young	.15

Homerun History

This holographic silver foiled commemorative set honors Mark McGwire and Sammy Sosa's historic '98 seasons. Two cards were added to the end of the set, which are Silver Crown Die-Cuts honoring Ripken Jr.'s consecutive games streak and McGwire's 70 home runs. These are inserted 2:25 packs.

NM/M
Complete Set (22): 25.00
Common McGwire: 1.50
Common Sosa: 1.00
Inserted 1:12

1	Home Run #61 (Mark McGwire)	3.00
2	Home Run #59 (Sammy Sosa)	1.00
3	Home Run #62 (Mark McGwire)	1.50
4	Home Run #60 (Sammy Sosa)	1.00
5	Home Run #63 (Mark McGwire)	1.50
6	Home Run #61 (Sammy Sosa)	3.00
7	Home Run #64 (Mark McGwire)	1.50
8	Home Run #62 (Sammy Sosa)	1.00
9	Home Run #65 (Mark McGwire)	1.50
10	Home Run #63 (Sammy Sosa)	1.00
11	Home Run #67 (Mark McGwire)	1.50
12	Home Run #64 (Sammy Sosa)	1.00
13	Home Run #68 (Mark McGwire)	1.50
14	Home Run #65 (Sammy Sosa)	1.00
15	Home Run #70 (Mark McGwire)	5.00
16	Home Run #66 (Sammy Sosa)	3.00
17	A Season of Celebration (Mark McGwire)	1.50
18	A Season of Celebration (Sammy Sosa)	1.00
19	Awesome Power (Sammy Sosa, Mark McGwire)	1.50
20	Transcending Sports (Mark McGwire, Sammy Sosa)	1.50
21	Crown Die-Cut (Mark McGwire)	1.50
22	Crown Die-Cut (Cal Ripken Jr.)	1.00

1999 Pacific Revolution

The 150-card set features dual foiled etching and embossing enhanced by gold-foil stamping. Card backs have year-by-year statistics along with a close-up photo. There are 25 short-printed rookie and prospect cards, which were inserted at a rate of about one per four packs. There are three parallels to the base set: Premiere Date, Red and Shadow. Reds are retail exclusive and are limited to 299 numbered sets. Shadows have light blue foil stamping and are limited to 99 numbered sets. Premiere Date are seeded exclusively in hobby packs at a rate of 1:25 packs.

NM/M
Complete Set (150): 60.00
Common Player: .15
Shadow (99 Sets H): 6X
SP: 3X
Red (299 R): 2X
SP: 1.5X
Premiere Date (49 H): 12X
SP: 6X
Wax Pack (3): 2.00
Wax Box (24): 35.00

1	Jim Edmonds	.15
2	Darin Erstad	.30
3	Troy Glaus	.15
4	Tim Salmon	.15
5	Mo Vaughn	.15
6	Steve Finley	.15
7	Luis Gonzalez	.15
8	Randy Johnson	1.00
9	Travis Lee	.15
10	Matt Williams	.15
11	Andruw Jones	1.00
12	Chipper Jones	1.50
13	Brian Jordan	.15
14	Javy Lopez	.15
15	Greg Maddux	1.50
16	Kevin McGlinchy/SP RC	1.00
17	John Smoltz	.15
18	Brady Anderson	.15
19	Albert Belle	.15
20	Will Clark	.15
21	Willis Otanez/SP RC	.25
22	Calvin Pickering/SP RC	.25
23	Cal Ripken Jr.	4.00
24	Nomar Garciaparra	1.50
25	Pedro Martinez	1.00
26	Troy O'Leary	.15
27	Jose Offerman	.15
28	Mark Grace	.15
29	Mickey Morandini	.15
30	Henry Rodriguez	.15
31	Sammy Sosa	1.50
32	Ray Durham	.15
33	Carlos Lee/SP	.50
34	Jeff Liefer/SP RC	.35
35	Magglio Ordonez	.30
36	Frank Thomas	1.00
37	Mike Cameron	.15
38	Sean Casey	.35
39	Barry Larkin	.15
40	Greg Vaughn	.15
41	Roberto Alomar	.35
42	Sandy Alomar Jr.	.15
43	David Justice	.15
44	Kenny Lofton	.15
45	Manny Ramirez	1.00
46	Richie Sexson	.15
47	Jim Thome	.65
48	Dante Bichette	.15
49	Vinny Castilla	.15
50	Darryl Hamilton	.15
51	Todd Helton	1.00
52	Larry Walker	.15
53	Tony Clark	.15
54	Damion Easley	.15
55	Bob Higginson	.15
56	Gabe Kapler/SP	.25
57	Alex Gonzalez/SP RC	.35
58	Mark Kotsay	.15
59	Kevin Orie	.15
60	Preston Wilson/SP	1.00
61	Jeff Bagwell	1.00
62	Derek Bell	.15
63	Craig Biggio	.15
64	Ken Caminiti	.15
65	Carlos Beltran/SP	.65
66	Johnny Damon	.35
67	Jermaine Dye	.15
68	Carlos Febles/SP	.35
69	Kevin Brown	.15
70	Todd Hundley	.15
71	Eric Karros	.15
72	Raul Mondesi	.15
73	Gary Sheffield	.45
74	Jeromy Burnitz	.15
75	Jeff Cirillo	.15
76	Marquis Grissom	.15
77	Fernando Vina	.15
78	Chad Allen/SP RC	.25
79	Corey Koskie/SP RC	1.50
80	Doug Mientkiewicz/SP RC	1.00
81	Brad Radke	.15
82	Todd Walker	.15
83	Michael Barrett/SP RC	.35
84	Vladimir Guerrero	1.00
85	Wilton Guerrero	.15
86	Guillermo Mota/SP RC	.35
87	Rondell White	.15
88	Edgardo Alfonzo	.15
89	Rickey Henderson	1.00
90	John Olerud	.15
91	Mike Piazza	2.00
92	Robin Ventura	.15
93	Roger Clemens	2.00
94	Chili Davis	.15
95	Derek Jeter	4.00
96	Chuck Knoblauch	.15
97	Tino Martinez	.15
98	Paul O'Neill	.15
99	Bernie Williams	.15
100	Eric Chavez/SP	.35
101	Jason Giambi	.65
102	Ben Grieve	.15
103	John Jaha	.15
104	Olmedo Saenz/SP RC	.25
105	Bobby Abreu	.25
106	Doug Glanville	.15
107	Desi Relaford	.15
108	Scott Rolen	.75
109	Curt Schilling	.35
110	Brian Giles	.15
111	Jason Kendall	.15
112	Pat Meares	.15
113	Kevin Young	.15
114	J.D. Drew/SP	1.00
115	Ray Lankford	.15
116	Eli Marrero	.15
117	Joe McEwing/SP RC	.35
118	Mark McGwire	3.00
119	Fernando Tatis	.15
120	Tony Gwynn	1.50
121	Trevor Hoffman	.15
122	Wally Joyner	.15
123	Reggie Sanders	.15
124	Barry Bonds	4.00
125	Ellis Burks	.15
126	Jeff Kent	.15
127	Ramon Martinez/SP RC	.25
128	Joe Nathan/SP RC	.25
129	Freddy Garcia/SP RC	1.00
130	Ken Griffey Jr.	2.50
131	Brian Hunter	.15
132	Edgar Martinez	.15
133	Alex Rodriguez	3.00
134	David Segui	.15
135	Wade Boggs	1.50
136	Jose Canseco	.45
137	Quinton McCracken	.15
138	Fred McGriff	.15
139	Kelly Dransfeldt/SP RC	.25
140	Juan Gonzalez	.50
141	Rusty Greer	.15
142	Rafael Palmeiro	.75
143	Ivan Rodriguez	.75
144	Lee Stevens	.15
145	Jose Cruz Jr.	.15
146	Carlos Delgado	.60
147	Shawn Green	.50
148	Roy Halladay/SP RC	1.50
149	Shannon Stewart	.15
150	Kevin Witt/SP RC	.35

Shadow

This hobby-only parallel insert features blue metallic-foil background and graphics on front. Backs are identical to the base version except they include a dot-matrix applied serial number at left within an edition of 99.

NM/M
Common Player: 4.00
Stars: 6X
SP's: 3X

Diamond Legacy

This 36-card set features a holographic patterned foil card front. Card backs have a small close-up photo along with a career note. These were seeded 2:25 packs.

NM/M
Complete Set (36): 60.00
Common Player: .50
Inserted 2:25

1	Troy Glaus	2.00
2	Mo Vaughn	.50
3	Matt Williams	.50
4	Chipper Jones	3.00
5	Andruw Jones	2.00
6	Greg Maddux	3.00
7	Albert Belle	.50
8	Cal Ripken Jr.	3.00
9	Nomar Garciaparra	3.00
10	Sammy Sosa	3.00
11	Frank Thomas	2.00
12	Manny Ramirez	2.00
13	Todd Helton	2.00
14	Larry Walker	.50
15	Gabe Kapler	.50
16	Jeff Bagwell	2.00
17	Craig Biggio	.50
18	Raul Mondesi	.50
19	Vladimir Guerrero	2.00
20	Mike Piazza	3.50
21	Roger Clemens	3.50
22	Derek Jeter	6.00
23	Bernie Williams	.50
24	Ben Grieve	.50
25	Scott Rolen	1.75
26	J.D. Drew	1.50
27	Mark McGwire	5.00
28	Fernando Tatis	.50
29	Tony Gwynn	3.00
30	Barry Bonds	6.00
31	Ken Griffey Jr.	4.00
32	Alex Rodriguez	5.00
33	Jose Canseco	1.25
34	Juan Gonzalez	1.00
35	Ivan Rodriguez	1.75
36	Shawn Green	1.50

Foul Pole

This 20-card set features netting down the right side of each card, with the player photo on the left side. The player name, position and logo are stamped with gold foil. These were seeded 1:49 packs.

NM/M
Complete Set (20): 100.00
Common Player: 1.50
Inserted 1:49

1	Chipper Jones	8.00
2	Andruw Jones	6.00
3	Cal Ripken Jr.	16.00
4	Nomar Garciaparra	8.00
5	Sammy Sosa	8.00
6	Frank Thomas	6.00
7	Manny Ramirez	6.00
8	Jeff Bagwell	6.00
9	Raul Mondesi	1.50
10	Vladimir Guerrero	6.00
11	Mike Piazza	9.00
12	Derek Jeter	16.00
13	Bernie Williams	1.50
14	Scott Rolen	5.00
15	J.D. Drew	3.00
16	Mark McGwire	12.00
17	Tony Gwynn	8.00
18	Ken Griffey Jr.	10.00
19	Alex Rodriguez	12.00
20	Juan Gonzalez	3.00

Icons

This 10-card set spotlights the top players, each card is die-cut in the shape of a shield with silver foil etching and stamping. These were seeded 1:121 packs.

NM/M
Complete Set (10): 50.00
Common Player: 4.00
Inserted 1:121

1	Cal Ripken Jr.	10.00
2	Nomar Garciaparra	5.00
3	Sammy Sosa	5.00
4	Frank Thomas	4.00
5	Mike Piazza	6.50
6	Derek Jeter	10.00
7	Mark McGwire	8.00
8	Tony Gwynn	5.00
9	Ken Griffey Jr.	7.50
10	Alex Rodriguez	8.00

Thorn in the Side

This 20-card set features full holographic silver foil and is die-cut in the upper right portion. Card backs analyzes the featured player's success against a certain opponent over the years. These were seeded 1:25 packs.

		NM/M
Complete Set (20):		35.00
Common Player:		1.00
Inserted 1:25		
1	Mo Vaughn	1.00
2	Chipper Jones	3.00
3	Greg Maddux	3.00
4	Cal Ripken Jr.	6.00
5	Nomar Garciaparra	3.00
6	Sammy Sosa	3.00
7	Frank Thomas	2.25
8	Manny Ramirez	2.25
9	Jeff Bagwell	2.25
10	Mike Piazza	3.50
11	Derek Jeter	6.00
12	Bernie Williams	1.00
13	J.D. Drew	1.50
14	Mark McGwire	4.50
15	Tony Gwynn	3.00
16	Barry Bonds	6.00
17	Ken Griffey Jr.	4.00
18	Alex Rodriguez	4.50
19	Juan Gonzalez	1.50
20	Ivan Rodriguez	2.00

Tripleheader

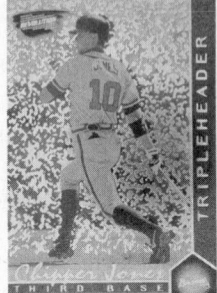

This 30-card set features spotted gold foil blotching around the player image with the name, postion, team and logo stamped in gold foil. These were seeded 4:25 hobby packs. The set is also broken down into three separate tiers of 10 cards. Tier 1 (cards 1-10) are limited to 99 numbered sets. Tier 2 (11-20) 199 numbered sets and Tier 3 (21-30) 299 numbered sets.

		NM/M
Complete Set (30):		30.00
Common Player:		.25
Inserted 4:25 H		
Tier 1 (1-10)		
Production 99 Sets H		
Tier 2 (11-20)		
Production 199 Sets H		
Tier 3 (21-30)		
Production 299 Sets H		
1	Greg Maddux	1.50
2	Cal Ripken Jr.	3.00
3	Nomar Garciaparra	1.50
4	Sammy Sosa	1.50
5	Frank Thomas	1.00
6	Mike Piazza	1.75
7	Mark McGwire	2.50
8	Tony Gwynn	1.50
9	Ken Griffey Jr.	2.00
10	Alex Rodriguez	2.50
11	Mo Vaughn	.25
12	Chipper Jones	1.50
13	Manny Ramirez	1.00
14	Larry Walker	.25
15	Jeff Bagwell	1.00
16	Vladimir Guerrero	.25
17	Derek Jeter	3.00
18	J.D. Drew	.60
19	Barry Bonds	3.00
20	Juan Gonzalez	.50
21	Troy Glaus	1.00
22	Andruw Jones	1.00
23	Matt Williams	.25
24	Craig Biggio	.25
25	Raul Mondesi	.25

26	Roger Clemens	1.75
27	Bernie Williams	.25
28	Scott Rolen	.75
29	Jose Canseco	.50
30	Ivan Rodriguez	.75

2000 Pacific Sample

Tony Gwynn was once again the spokesman for Pacific's 2000 line-up of baseball cards products. To showcase its base brand for the year, Pacific produced this sample card, so overprinted and "numbered" on back, but otherwise virtually identical to the issued version.

		NM/M
SAMPLE Tony Gwynn		3.00

2000 Pacific

The base set consists of 500-cards with the Pacific logo and player name stamped in silver foil on the card front. Card backs have a small photo along with complete career statistics and a brief career highlight. 50 players in the base set also have another version and are priced equally.

		NM/M
Complete Set (500):		60.00
Common Player:		.10
Pack (12):		1.50
Wax Box (24):		25.00
1	Garret Anderson	.15
2	Tim Belcher	.10
3	Gary DiSarcina	.10
4	Trent Durrington	.10
5	Jim Edmonds	.15
6a	Darin Erstad/Action	.35
6b	Darin Erstad/Portrait	.35
7	Chuck Finley	.10
8	Troy Glaus	.75
9	Todd Greene	.10
10	Bret Hemphill	.10
11	Ken Hill	.10
12	Ramon Ortiz	.10
13	Troy Percival	.10
14	Mark Petkovsek	.10
15	Tim Salmon	.20
16a	Mo Vaughn	.15
16b	Mo Vaughn/Portrait	.15
17	Jay Bell	.10
18	Omar Daal	.10
19	Erubiel Durazo	.10
20	Steve Finley	.10
21	Bernard Gilkey	.10
22	Luis Gonzalez	.20
23	Randy Johnson	.75
24	Byung-Hyun Kim	.10
25	Travis Lee	.10
26	Matt Mantei	.10
27	Armando Reynoso	.10
28	Rob Ryan	.10
29	Kelly Stinnett	.10
30	Todd Stottlemyre	.10
31a	Matt Williams/Action	.15
31b	Matt Williams/Portrait	.15
32	Tony Womack	.10
33	Bret Boone	.10
34	Andres Galarraga	.15
35	Tom Glavine	.35
36	Ozzie Guillen	.10
37a	Andruw Jones/Action	.75
37b	Andruw Jones/Portrait	.75
38a	Chipper Jones/Action	1.00
38b	Chipper Jones/Portrait	1.00
39	Brian Jordan	.15
40	Ryan Klesko	.15
41	Javy Lopez	.15
42a	Greg Maddux/Action	1.00
42b	Greg Maddux/Portrait	1.00
43	Kevin Millwood	.15
44	John Rocker	.15
45	Randall Simon	.10
46	John Smoltz	.15
47	Gerald Williams	.10
48	Brady Anderson	.15
49a	Albert Belle/Action	.15
49b	Albert Belle/Portrait	.15
50	Mike Bordick	.10
51	Will Clark	.25
52	Jeff Conine	.10
53	Delino DeShields	.10
54	Jerry Hairston Jr.	.10

55	Charles Johnson	.10
56	Eugene Kingsale	.10
57	Ryan Minor	.10
58	Mike Mussina	.35
59	Sidney Ponson	.10
60a	Cal Ripken Jr./Action	2.50
60b	Cal Ripken Jr./Portrait	2.50
61	B.J. Surhoff	.10
62	Mike Timlin	.10
63	Rod Beck	.10
64a	Nomar Garciaparra/Action	1.50
64b	Nomar Garciaparra/Portrait	1.50
65	Tom Gordon	.10
66	Butch Huskey	.10
67	Derek Lowe	.10
68a	Pedro Martinez/Action	.75
68b	Pedro Martinez/Portrait	.75
69	Trot Nixon	.10
70	Jose Offerman	.10
71	Troy O'Leary	.10
72	Pat Rapp	.10
73	Donnie Sadler	.10
74	Mike Stanley	.10
75	John Valentin	.10
76	Jason Varitek	.10
77	Wilton Veras	.15
78	Tim Wakefield	.10
79	Rick Aguilera	.10
80	Manny Alexander	.10
81	Roosevelt Brown	.10
82	Mark Grace	.20
83	Glenallen Hill	.10
84	Lance Johnson	.10
85	Jon Lieber	.10
86	Cole Liniak	.10
87	Chad Meyers	.10
88	Mickey Morandini	.10
89	Jose Nieves	.10
90	Henry Rodriguez	.10
91a	Sammy Sosa/Action	1.50
91b	Sammy Sosa/Portrait	1.50
92	Kevin Tapani	.10
93	Kerry Wood	.50
94	Mike Caruso	.10
95	Ray Durham	.10
96	Brook Fordyce	.10
97	Bobby Howry	.10
98	Paul Konerko	.25
99	Carlos Lee	.10
100	Aaron Myette	.10
101	Greg Norton	.10
102	Magglio Ordonez	.25
103	Jim Parque	.10
104	Liu Rodriguez	.10
105	Chris Singleton	.10
106	Mike Sirotka	.10
107a	Frank Thomas/Action	.75
107b	Frank Thomas/Portrait	.75
108	Kip Wells	.10
109	Aaron Boone	.10
110	Mike Cameron	.10
111a	Sean Casey/Action	.20
111b	Sean Casey/Portrait	.20
112	Jeffrey Hammonds	.10
113	Pete Harnisch	.10
114a	Barry Larkin/Action	.15
114b	Barry Larkin/Portrait	.15
115	Jason LaRue	.10
116	Denny Neagle	.10
117	Pokey Reese	.10
118	Scott Sullivan	.10
119	Eddie Taubensee	.10
120	Greg Vaughn	.10
121	Scott Williamson	.10
122	Dmitri Young	.10
123a	Roberto Alomar/Action	.35
123b	Roberto Alomar/Portrait	.35
124	Sandy Alomar Jr.	.10
125	Harold Baines	.10
126	Russell Branyan	.10
127	Dave Burba	.10
128	Bartolo Colon	.10
129	Travis Fryman	.15
130	Mike Jackson	.10
131	David Justice	.15
132a	Kenny Lofton/Action	.15
132b	Kenny Lofton/Portrait	.15
133	Charles Nagy	.10
134a	Manny Ramirez/Action	.75
134b	Manny Ramirez/Portrait	.75
135	Dave Roberts	.10
136	Richie Sexson	.15
137	Jim Thome	.60
138	Omar Vizquel	.15
139	Jaret Wright	.15
140	Pedro Astacio	.10
141	Dante Bichette	.10
142	Brian Bohanon	.10
143a	Vinny Castilla/Action	.15
143b	Vinny Castilla/Portrait	.15
144	Edgard Clemente	.10
145	Derrick Gibson	.10
146	Todd Helton	.75
147	Darryl Kile	.10
148	Mike Lansing	.10
149	Kirt Manwaring	.10
150	Neifi Perez	.10
151	Ben Petrick	.10
152	Juan Sosa RC	.20
153	Dave Veres	.10
154a	Larry Walker/Action	.15
154b	Larry Walker/Portrait	.15
155	Brad Ausmus	.10
156	Dave Borkowski	.10
157	Tony Clark	.15
158	Francisco Cordero	.10

159	Deivi Cruz	.10
160	Damion Easley	.10
161	Juan Encarnacion	.10
162	Robert Fick	.10
163	Bobby Higginson	.10
164	Gabe Kapler	.15
165	Brian Moehler	.10
166	Dean Palmer	.10
167	Luis Polonia	.10
168	Justin Thompson	.10
169	Jeff Weaver	.10
170	Antonio Alfonseca	.10
171	Bruce Aven	.10
172	A.J. Burnett	.15
173	Luis Castillo	.10
174	Ramon Castro	.10
175	Ryan Dempster	.10
176	Alex Fernandez	.10
177	Cliff Floyd	.10
178	Amaury Garcia	.10
179	Alex Gonzalez	.10
180	Mark Kotsay	.10
181	Mike Lowell	.15
182	Brian Meadows	.10
183	Kevin Orie	.10
184	Julio Ramirez	.10
185	Preston Wilson	.15
186	Moises Alou	.10
187a	Jeff Bagwell/Action	.75
187b	Jeff Bagwell/Portrait	.75
188	Glen Barker	.10
189	Derek Bell	.10
190a	Craig Biggio/Action	.15
190b	Craig Biggio/Portrait	.15
191	Ken Caminiti	.10
192	Scott Elarton	.10
193	Carl Everett	.10
194	Mike Hampton	.10
195	Carlos Hernandez	.10
196	Richard Hidalgo	.10
197	Jose Lima	.10
198	Shane Reynolds	.15
199	Bill Spiers	.10
200	Billy Wagner	.15
201a	Carlos Beltran/Action	.50
201b	Carlos Beltran/Portrait	.50
202	Dermal Brown	.10
203	Johnny Damon	.25
204	Jermaine Dye	.10
205	Carlos Febles	.10
206	Jeremy Giambi	.10
207	Mark Quinn	.10
208	Joe Randa	.10
209	Dan Reichert	.10
210	Jose Rosado	.10
211	Rey Sanchez	.10
212	Jeff Suppan	.10
213	Mike Sweeney	.10
214a	Kevin Brown/Action	.15
214b	Kevin Brown/Portrait	.15
215	Darren Dreifort	.10
216	Eric Gagne	.10
217	Mark Grudzielanek	.10
218	Todd Hollandsworth	.10
219	Todd Hundley	.10
220	Eric Karros	.10
221	Raul Mondesi	.15
222	Chan Ho Park	.10
223	Jeff Shaw	.10
224a	Gary Sheffield/Action	.30
224b	Gary Sheffield/Portrait	.30
225	Ismael Valdes	.10
226	Devon White	.10
227	Eric Young	.10
228	Kevin Barker	.10
229	Ron Belliard	.10
230a	Jeromy Burnitz/Action	.10
230b	Jeromy Burnitz/Portrait	.10
231	Jeff Cirillo	.10
232	Marquis Grissom	.10
233	Geoff Jenkins	.10
234	Mark Loretta	.10
235	David Nilsson	.10
236	Hideo Nomo	.75
237	Alex Ochoa	.10
238	Kyle Peterson	.10
239	Fernando Vina	.10
240	Bob Wickman	.10
241	Steve Woodard	.10
242	Chad Allen	.10
243	Ron Coomer	.10
244	Marty Cordova	.10
245	Cristian Guzman	.10
246	Denny Hocking	.10
247	Jacque Jones	.10
248	Corey Koskie	.10
249	Matt Lawton	.10
250	Joe Mays	.10
251	Eric Milton	.10
252	Brad Radke	.10
253	Mark Redman	.10
254	Terry Steinbach	.10
255	Todd Walker	.10
256	Tony Armas Jr.	.10
257	Michael Barrett	.10
258	Peter Bergeron	.10
259	Geoff Blum	.10
260	Orlando Cabrera	.10
261	Trace Coquillette RC	.15
262	Brad Fullmer	.10
263a	Vladimir Guerrero/Action	.75
263b	Vladimir Guerrero/Portrait	.75
264	Wilton Guerrero	.10
265	Dustin Hermanson	.10
266	Manny Martinez	.10
267	Ryan McGuire	.10
268	Ugueth Urbina	.10
269	Jose Vidro	.10
270	Rondell White	.10
271	Chris Widger	.10
272	Edgardo Alfonzo	.15
273	Armando Benitez	.10

274	Roger Cedeno	.10
275	Dennis Cook	.10
276	Octavio Dotel	.10
277	John Franco	.10
278	Darryl Hamilton	.10
279	Rickey Henderson	.75
280	Orel Hershiser	.10
281	Al Leiter	.10
282a	John Olerud/Action	.15
282b	John Olerud/Portrait	.15
283	Rey Ordonez	.10
284a	Mike Piazza/Action	1.50
284b	Mike Piazza/Portrait	1.50
285	Kenny Rogers	.10
286	Jorge Toca	.10
287	Robin Ventura	.15
288	Scott Brosius	.10
289a	Roger Clemens/Action	1.25
289b	Roger Clemens/Portrait	1.25
290	David Cone	.15
291	Chili Davis	.10
292	Orlando Hernandez	.15
293	Hideki Irabu	.10
294a	Derek Jeter/Action	2.50
294b	Derek Jeter/Portrait	2.50
295	Chuck Knoblauch	.10
296	Ricky Ledee	.10
297	Jim Leyritz	.10
298	Tino Martinez	.15
299	Paul O'Neill	.15
300	Andy Pettitte	.25
301	Jorge Posada	.15
302	Mariano Rivera	.25
303	Alfonso Soriano	.75
304a	Bernie Williams/Action	.20
304b	Bernie Williams/Portrait	.20
305	Ed Yarnall	.10
306	Kevin Appier	.10
307	Rich Becker	.10
308	Eric Chavez	.25
309	Jason Giambi	.60
310	Ben Grieve	.10
311	Ramon Hernandez	.10
312	Tim Hudson	.25
313	John Jaha	.10
314	Doug Jones	.10
315	Omar Olivares	.10
316	Mike Oquist	.10
317	Matt Stairs	.10
318	Miguel Tejada	.25
319	Randy Velarde	.10
320	Bobby Abreu	.15
321	Marlon Anderson	.10
322	Alex Arias	.10
323	Rico Brogna	.10
324	Paul Byrd	.10
325	Ron Gant	.10
326	Doug Glanville	.10
327	Wayne Gomes	.10
328	Mike Lieberthal	.10
329	Robert Person	.10
330	Desi Relaford	.10
331a	Scott Rolen/Action	.60
331b	Scott Rolen/Portrait	.60
332a	Curt Schilling/Action	.35
332b	Curt Schilling/Portrait	.35
333	Kris Benson	.10
334	Adrian Brown	.10
335	Brant Brown	.10
336	Brian Giles	.15
337	Chad Hermansen	.10
338	Jason Kendall	.15
339	Al Martin	.10
340	Pat Meares	.10
341a	Warren Morris/Action	.10
341b	Warren Morris/Portrait	.10
342	Todd Ritchie	.10
343	Jason Schmidt	.10
344	Ed Sprague	.10
345	Mike Williams	.10
346	Kevin Young	.10
347	Rick Ankiel	.25
348	Ricky Bottalico	.10
349	Kent Bottenfield	.10
350	Darren Bragg	.10
351	Eric Davis	.15
352a	J.D. Drew/Action	.35
352b	J.D. Drew/Portrait	.35
353	Adam Kennedy	.10
354	Ray Lankford	.10
355	Joe McEwing	.10
356a	Mark McGwire/Action	2.00
356b	Mark McGwire/Portrait	2.00
357	Matt Morris	.10
358	Darren Oliver	.10
359	Edgar Renteria	.10
360	Fernando Tatis	.10
361	Andy Ashby	.10
362	Ben Davis	.10
363a	Tony Gwynn/Action	1.00
363b	Tony Gwynn/Portrait	1.00
364	Sterling Hitchcock	.10
365	Trevor Hoffman	.15
366	Damian Jackson	.10
367	Wally Joyner	.10
368	Dave Magadan	.10
369	Gary Matthews Jr.	.10
370	Phil Nevin	.10
371	Eric Owens	.10
372	Ruben Rivera	.10
373a	Reggie Sanders/Action	.10
373b	Reggie Sanders/Portrait	.10
374	Quilvio Veras	.10
375	Rich Aurilia	.10
376	Marvin Benard	.10
377a	Barry Bonds/Action	2.50
377b	Barry Bonds/Portrait	2.50
378	Ellis Burks	.10
379	Shawn Estes	.10
380	Livan Hernandez	.10
381a	Jeff Kent/Action	.15

381b	Jeff Kent/Portrait	.15
382	Brent Mayne	.10
383	Bill Mueller	.10
384	Calvin Murray	.10
385	Robb Nen	.10
386	Russ Ortiz	.10
387	Kirk Rueter	.10
388	J.T. Snow	.10
389	David Bell	.10
390	Jay Buhner	.15
391	Russ Davis	.10
392a	Freddy Garcia/Action	.10
392b	Freddy Garcia/Portrait	.10
393a	Ken Griffey Jr./Action	1.50
393b	Ken Griffey Jr./Portrait	1.50
394	Carlos Guillen	.10
395	John Halama	.10
396	Brian Hunter	.10
397	Ryan Jackson	.10
398	Edgar Martinez	.10
399	Gil Meche	.10
400	Jose Mesa	.10
401	Jamie Moyer	.10
402a	Alex Rodriguez/Action	2.00
402b	Alex Rodriguez/Portrait	2.00
403	Dan Wilson	.10
404	Wilson Alvarez	.10
405	Rolando Arrojo	.10
406a	Wade Boggs/Action	1.00
406b	Wade Boggs/Portrait	1.00
407	Miguel Cairo	.10
408a	Jose Canseco/Action	.40
408b	Jose Canseco/Portrait	.40
409	John Flaherty	.10
410	Jose Guillen	.10
411	Roberto Hernandez	.10
412	Terrell Lowery	.10
413	Dave Martinez	.10
414	Quinton McCracken	.10
415a	Fred McGriff/Action	.15
415b	Fred McGriff/Portrait	.15
416	Ryan Rupe	.10
417	Kevin Stocker	.10
418	Bubba Trammell	.10
419	Royce Clayton	.10
420a	Juan Gonzalez/Action	.75
420b	Juan Gonzalez/Portrait	.75
421	Tom Goodwin	.10
422	Rusty Greer	.10
423	Rick Helling	.10
424	Roberto Kelly	.10
425	Ruben Mateo	.10
426	Mark McLemore	.10
427	Mike Morgan	.10
428	Rafael Palmeiro	.65
429a	Ivan Rodriguez/Action	.65
429b	Ivan Rodriguez/Portrait	.65
430	Aaron Sele	.10
431	Lee Stevens	.10
432	John Wetteland	.10
433	Todd Zeile	.10
434	Jeff Zimmerman	.10
435	Tony Batista	.10
436	Casey Blake	.10
437	Homer Bush	.10
438	Chris Carpenter	.10
439	Jose Cruz Jr.	.10
440a	Carlos Delgado/Action	.50
440b	Carlos Delgado/Portrait	.50
441	Tony Fernandez	.10
442	Darrin Fletcher	.10
443	Alex Gonzalez	.10
444a	Shawn Green/Action	.35
444b	Shawn Green/Portrait	.35
445	Roy Halladay	.10
446	Billy Koch	.10
447	David Segui	.10
448	Shannon Stewart	.10
449	David Wells	.10
450	Vernon Wells	.15

Copper

Coppers are a parallel set to the 500-card base set and are identical to the base cards besides the copper foil stamping. Inserted exclusively in hobby packs Coppers are limited to 99 serial numbered sets.

		NM/M
Common Copper:		5.00
Stars:		4-8X
Production 99 Sets		

Platinum Blue

A parallel to the 500-card base set these have identical photos as the regular cards besides platinum blue foil stamping. A total of 75 serial numbered sets were produced.

	NM/M
Common Player:	8.00
Stars:	6-10X
Production 75 Sets	

Premiere Date

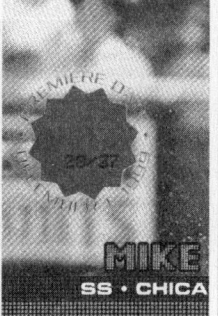

A parallel to the 500-card base set these are sequentially numbered to 37 sets.

	NM/M
Common Player:	15.00
Stars:	8X to15X
Production 37 Sets	

Ruby Red (Seven-11)

This parallel to the base set of 2000 Pacific was available only in 10-card retail "Jewel Collection" packs at Seven-11 convenience stores. Other than the use of red metallic foil for the player name and Pacific logo, the cards are identical to the regular-issue version.

	NM/M
Complete Set (500):	65.00
Common Player:	.15
Stars/Rookies	1.5X

Command Performers

	NM/M
Complete Set (20):	45.00
Common Player:	1.00
Inserted 1:24 Retail	

1	Chipper Jones	3.00
2	Greg Maddux	3.00
3	Cal Ripken Jr.	6.00
4	Nomar Garciaparra	4.00
5	Sammy Sosa	4.00
6	Sean Casey	1.00
7	Manny Ramirez	2.00
8	Larry Walker	1.00
9	Jeff Bagwell	2.00
10	Vladimir Guerrero	2.00
11	Mike Piazza	4.00
12	Roger Clemens	3.50
13	Derek Jeter	6.00
14	Mark McGwire	5.00
15	Tony Gwynn	3.00
16	Barry Bonds	6.00
17	Ken Griffey Jr.	4.00
18	Alex Rodriguez	5.00
19	Ivan Rodriguez	1.50
20	Shawn Green	1.25

Cramer's Choice Awards

This die-cut set is shaped in a trophy-like design on a holographic silver foil design. Cramer's Choice are seeded 1:721 packs.

	NM/M
Complete Set (10):	300.00
Common Player:	25.00
Inserted 1:721	

1	Chipper Jones	25.00
2	Cal Ripken Jr.	50.00
3	Nomar Garciaparra	30.00
4	Sammy Sosa	30.00
5	Mike Piazza	30.00
6	Derek Jeter	50.00
7	Mark McGwire	40.00
8	Tony Gwynn	25.00
9	Ken Griffey Jr.	30.00
10	Alex Rodriguez	40.00

Diamond Leaders

Designed on a horizontal format each card features three statistical leaders from the 1999 season for each respective team. Card fronts have gold holofoil stamping while card backs give statistical leaders for eight categories for the featured team. These were seeded 2:25 packs.

	NM/M
Complete Set (30):	25.00
Common Card:	.50
Inserted 2:25	

1	Anaheim Angels (Garret Anderson, Chuck Finley, Troy Percival, Mo Vaughn)	.50
2	Baltimore Orioles (Albert Belle, Mike Mussina, B.J. Surhoff)	.50
3	Boston Red Sox (Nomar Garciaparra, Pedro J. Martinez, Troy O'Leary)	3.00
4	Chicago White Sox (Ray Durham, Magglio Ordonez, Frank Thomas)	1.50
5	Cleveland Indians (Bartolo Colon, Manny Ramirez, Omar Vizquel)	1.50
6	Detroit Tigers (Deivi Cruz, Dave Mlicki, David Palmer)	.50
7	Kansas City Royals (Johnny Damon, Jermaine Dye, Jose Rosado, Mike Sweeney)	.50
8	Minnesota Twins (Corey Koskie, Eric Milton, Brad Radke)	.50
9	New York Yankees (Orlando Hernandez, Derek Jeter, Mariano Rivera, Bernie Williams)	4.00
10	Oakland Athletics (Jeremy Giambi, Tim Hudson, Matt Stairs)	1.00
11	Seattle Mariners (Freddy Garcia, Ken Griffey Jr., Edgar Martinez)	3.00
12	Tampa Bay Devil Rays (Jose Canseco, Roberto Hernandez, Fred McGriff)	.75
13	Texas Rangers (Rafael Palmeiro, Ivan Rodriguez, John Wetteland)	1.00
14	Toronto Blue Jays (Carlos Delgado, Shannon Stewart, David Wells)	1.00
15	Arizona Diamondbacks (Luis Gonzalez, Randy Johnson, Matt Williams)	1.50
16	Atlanta Braves (Chipper Jones, Brian Jordan, Greg Maddux)	2.00
17	Chicago Cubs (Mark Grace, Jon Lieber, Sammy Sosa)	3.00
18	Cincinnati Reds (Sean Casey, Pete Harnisch, Greg Vaughn)	.50
19	Colorado Rockies (Pedro Astacio, Dante Bichette, Larry Walker)	.50
20	Florida Marlins (Luis Castillo, Alex Fernandez, Preston Wilson)	.50
21	Houston Astros (Jeff Bagwell, Mike Hampton, Billy Wagner)	1.50
22	Los Angeles Dodgers (Kevin Brown, Mark Grudzielanek, Eric Karros)	.50
23	Milwaukee Brewers (Jeromy Burnitz, Jeff Cirillo, Marquis Grissom, Hideo Nomo)	1.00
24	Montreal Expos (Vladimir Guerrero, Dustin Hermanson, Ugueth Urbina)	1.50
25	New York Mets (Roger Cedeno, Rickey Henderson, Mike Piazza)	3.00
26	Philadelphia Phillies (Bobby Abreu, Mike Lieberthal, Curt Schilling)	.75
27	Pittsburgh Pirates (Brian Giles, Jason Kendall, Kevin Young)	.50
28	St. Louis Cardinals (Kent Bottenfield, Ray Lankford, Mark McGwire)	3.50
29	San Diego Padres (Tony Gwynn, Trevor Hoffman, Reggie Sanders)	2.00
30	San Francisco Giants (Barry Bonds, Jeff Kent, Russ Ortiz)	4.00

Gold Crown Die-Cuts

Printed on a 24-point stock this set features Pacific's classic crown shaped design on a dual foiled holographic gold and silver stock. These were seeded 1:25 packs.

	NM/M
Complete Set (36):	150.00
Common Player:	1.50
Inserted 1:25	

1	Mo Vaughn	1.50
2	Matt Williams	1.50
3	Andruw Jones	6.00
4	Chipper Jones	8.00
5	Greg Maddux	8.00
6	Cal Ripken Jr.	15.00
7	Nomar Garciaparra	10.00
8	Pedro Martinez	6.00
9	Sammy Sosa	10.00
10	Magglio Ordonez	2.50
11	Frank Thomas	6.00
12	Sean Casey	1.50
13	Roberto Alomar	2.50
14	Manny Ramirez	6.00
15	Larry Walker	1.50
16	Jeff Bagwell	6.00
17	Craig Biggio	1.50
18	Carlos Beltran	4.00
19	Vladimir Guerrero	6.00
20	Mike Piazza	10.00
21	Roger Clemens	9.00
22	Derek Jeter	15.00
23	Bernie Williams	2.00
24	Scott Rolen	5.00
25	Warren Morris	1.50
26	J.D. Drew	2.00
27	Mark McGwire	12.00
28	Tony Gwynn	8.00
29	Barry Bonds	15.00
30	Ken Griffey Jr.	10.00
31	Alex Rodriguez	12.00
32	Jose Canseco	2.00
33	Juan Gonzalez	6.00
34	Rafael Palmeiro	5.00
35	Ivan Rodriguez	5.00
36	Shawn Green	3.00

Reflections

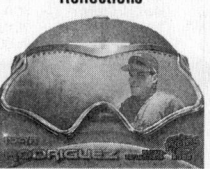

This 20-card die-cut set features a unique sunglasses-on-cap design utilizing cel technology for added effect on the sunglasses portion of the insert. The backs have a small photo of the featured player. These were seeded 1:97 packs.

	NM/M
Common Player:	3.00
Inserted 1:97	

1	Andruw Jones	6.00
2	Chipper Jones	8.00
3	Cal Ripken Jr.	20.00
4	Nomar Garciaparra	12.00
5	Sammy Sosa	12.00
6	Frank Thomas	6.00
7	Manny Ramirez	6.00
8	Jeff Bagwell	6.00
9	Vladimir Guerrero	6.00
10	Mike Piazza	12.00
11	Derek Jeter	20.00
12	Bernie Williams	3.00
13	Scott Rolen	3.00
14	J.D. Drew	3.00
15	Mark McGwire	15.00
16	Tony Gwynn	8.00
17	Ken Griffey Jr.	12.00
18	Alex Rodriguez	15.00
19	Juan Gonzalez	6.00
20	Ivan Rodriguez	3.00

Past & Present

Inserted exclusively in hobby packs at a rate of 1:49, these inserts have a silver prism front and a cardboard textured back. The fronts have a current photo of the player while the backs have a photo taken years before.

	NM/M
Complete Set (20):	80.00
Common Player:	1.50
Inserted 1:49 H	

1	Chipper Jones	5.00
2	Greg Maddux	5.00
3	Cal Ripken Jr.	10.00
4	Nomar Garciaparra	6.00
5	Pedro Martinez	4.00
6	Sammy Sosa	6.00
7	Frank Thomas	4.00
8	Manny Ramirez	4.00
9	Larry Walker	1.50
10	Jeff Bagwell	4.00
11	Mike Piazza	6.00
12	Roger Clemens	5.50
13	Derek Jeter	10.00
14	Mark McGwire	8.00
15	Tony Gwynn	5.00
16	Barry Bonds	10.00
17	Ken Griffey Jr.	6.00
18	Alex Rodriguez	8.00
19	Wade Boggs	5.00
20	Ivan Rodriguez	3.00

Ornaments

This 20-card set features a number of different Christmas patterned die-cut shapes, including ornaments, wreaths and Christmas trees. Each card comes with a string intended to hang from a tree on a holographic foil design. These were seeded 2:25 packs.

	NM/M
Complete Set (20):	40.00
Common Player:	1.00
Inserted 2:25	

1	Mo Vaughn	1.00
2	Chipper Jones	3.00
3	Greg Maddux	3.00
4	Cal Ripken Jr.	4.00
5	Nomar Garciaparra	4.00
6	Sammy Sosa	4.00
7	Frank Thomas	2.00
8	Manny Ramirez	2.00
9	Larry Walker	1.00
10	Jeff Bagwell	2.00
11	Mike Piazza	4.00
12	Roger Clemens	3.50
13	Scott Rolen	1.50
14	J.D. Drew	1.25
15	Mark McGwire	5.00
16	Tony Gwynn	3.00
17	Ken Griffey Jr.	4.00
18	Alex Rodriguez	5.00
19	Ivan Rodriguez	1.50

2000 Pacific Aurora Sample

Nearly identical to the issued version of spokesman Tony Gwynn's card, this features a large white diagonal "SAMPLE" overprint on back and in the space where a card number usually appears.

	NM/M
Tony Gwynn	3.00

2000 Pacific Aurora

	NM/M
Complete Set (151):	25.00
Common Player:	.15
Pack (10):	2.00
Wax Box (24):	30.00

1	Darin Erstad	.25
2	Troy Glaus	.75
3	Tim Salmon	.25
4	Mo Vaughn	.15
5	Jay Bell	.15
6	Erubiel Durazo	.15
7	Luis Gonzalez	.25
8	Randy Johnson	.75
9	Matt Williams	.15
10	Tom Glavine	.35
11	Andruw Jones	.75
12	Chipper Jones	1.00
13	Brian Jordan	.15
14	Greg Maddux	1.00
15	Kevin Millwood	.15
16	Albert Belle	.15
17	Will Clark	.25
18	Mike Mussina	.35
19	Cal Ripken Jr.	2.50
20	B.J. Surhoff	.15
21	Nomar Garciaparra	1.50
22	Pedro Martinez	.75
23	Troy O'Leary	.15
24	Wilton Veras	.15
25	Mark Grace	.25
26	Henry Rodriguez	.15
27	Sammy Sosa	1.50
28	Kerry Wood	.50
29	Ray Durham	.15
30	Paul Konerko	.25
31	Carlos Lee	.15
32	Magglio Ordonez	.25
33	Chris Singleton	.15
34	Frank Thomas	.75
35	Mike Cameron	.15
36	Sean Casey	.25
37	Barry Larkin	.25
38	Pokey Reese	.15
39	Eddie Taubensee	.15
40	Roberto Alomar	.40
41	David Justice	.15
42	Kenny Lofton	.25
43	Manny Ramirez	.75
44	Richie Sexson	.15
45	Jim Thome	.60
46	Omar Vizquel	.15
47	Todd Helton	.75
48	Mike Lansing	.15
49	Neifi Perez	.15
50	Ben Petrick	.15
51	Larry Walker	.25
52	Tony Clark	.15
53	Damion Easley	.15
54	Juan Encarnacion	.15
55	Juan Gonzalez	.75
56	Dean Palmer	.15
57	Luis Castillo	.15
58	Cliff Floyd	.15
59	Alex Gonzalez	.15
60	Mike Lowell	.15
61	Preston Wilson	.15
62	Jeff Bagwell	.75
63	Craig Biggio	.15
64	Ken Caminiti	.15
65	Jose Lima	.15
66	Billy Wagner	.15
67	Carlos Beltran	.50
68	Johnny Damon	.25
69	Jermaine Dye	.15
70	Mark Quinn	.15
71	Mike Sweeney	.15
72	Kevin Brown	.15
73	Shawn Green	.35
74	Eric Karros	.15
75	Chan Ho Park	.15
76	Gary Sheffield	.40
77	Ron Belliard	.15
78	Jeromy Burnitz	.15
79	Marquis Grissom	.15
80	Geoff Jenkins	.15
81	David Nilsson	.15
82	Ron Coomer	.15
83	Jacque Jones	.15
84	Brad Radke	.15
85	Todd Walker	.15
86	Michael Barrett	.15
87	Peter Bergeron	.15
88	Vladimir Guerrero	.75
89	Jose Vidro	.15
90	Rondell White	.15
91	Edgardo Alfonzo	.15
92	Darryl Hamilton	.15
93	Rey Ordonez	.15
94	Mike Piazza	1.50
95	Robin Ventura	.15
96	Roger Clemens	1.25
97	Orlando Hernandez	.15
98	Derek Jeter	2.50
99	Tino Martinez	.15
100	Mariano Rivera	.25
101	Bernie Williams	.25
102	Eric Chavez	.25
103	Jason Giambi	.60
104	Ben Grieve	.15
105	Tim Hudson	.25
106	John Jaha	.15
107	Matt Stairs	.15
108	Bobby Abreu	.15
109	Doug Glanville	.15
110	Mike Lieberthal	.15
111	Scott Rolen	.60
112	Curt Schilling	.40
113	Brian Giles	.15
114	Chad Hermansen	.15
115	Jason Kendall	.15
116	Warren Morris	.15
117	Kevin Young	.15
118	Rick Ankiel	.15
119	J.D. Drew	.25
120	Ray Lankford	.15
121	Mark McGwire	2.00
122	Edgar Renteria	.15
123	Fernando Tatis	.15
124	Ben Davis	.15
125	Tony Gwynn	1.00
126	Trevor Hoffman	.15

127	Phil Nevin	.15
128	Barry Bonds	2.50
129	Ellis Burks	.15
130	Jeff Kent	.15
131	J.T. Snow	.15
132	Freddy Garcia	.15
133	Ken Griffey Jr.	1.50
133a	Ken Griffey Jr. Reds	2.00
134	Edgar Martinez	.15
135	Alex Rodriguez	2.00
136	Dan Wilson	.15
137	Jose Canseco	.40
138	Roberto Hernandez	.15
139	Dave Martinez	.15
140	Fred McGriff	.15
141	Rusty Greer	.15
142	Ruben Mateo	.65
143	Rafael Palmeiro	.65
144	Ivan Rodriguez	.65
145	Jeff Zimmerman	.15
146	Homer Bush	.15
147	Carlos Delgado	.50
148	Raul Mondesi	.15
149	Shannon Stewart	.15
150	Vernon Wells	.15

Copper

Stars: 2-4X
Production 399 Sets

Platinum Blue

Stars: 5-10X
Production 67 Sets

Silver

Stars: 3-6X
Production 199 Sets

At-Bat Styrotechs

		NM/M
Complete Set (20):		125.00
Common Player:		2.00
Production 299 Sets		
1	Chipper Jones	7.50
2	Cal Ripken Jr.	15.00
3	Nomar Garciaparra	10.00
4	Sammy Sosa	10.00
5	Frank Thomas	6.00
6	Manny Ramirez	6.00
7	Larry Walker	2.00
8	Jeff Bagwell	6.00
9	Carlos Beltran	2.00
10	Vladimir Guerrero	6.00
11	Mike Piazza	10.00
12	Derek Jeter	15.00
13	Bernie Williams	2.00
14	Mark McGwire	12.00
15	Tony Gwynn	7.50
16	Barry Bonds	15.00
17	Ken Griffey Jr.	10.00
18	Alex Rodriguez	12.00
19	Jose Canseco	3.00
20	Ivan Rodriguez	5.00

Dugout View Net-Fusions

		NM/M
Complete Set (20):		110.00
Common Player:		2.50
Inserted 1:37		
1	Mo Vaughn	2.50
2	Chipper Jones	8.00
3	Cal Ripken Jr.	15.00
4	Nomar Garciaparra	10.00
5	Sammy Sosa	10.00
6	Manny Ramirez	6.00
7	Larry Walker	2.00
8	Juan Gonzalez	6.00
9	Jeff Bagwell	6.00
10	Craig Biggio	2.50
11	Shawn Green	3.00
12	Vladimir Guerrero	6.00
13	Mike Piazza	10.00
14	Derek Jeter	15.00
15	Scott Rolen	5.00
16	Mark McGwire	12.00
17	Tony Gwynn	8.00
18	Ken Griffey Jr.	10.00
19	Alex Rodriguez	12.00
20	Rafael Palmeiro	4.00

Pennant Fever

		NM/M
Complete Set (20):		25.00
Common Player:		1.00
T. Gwynn Auto./147		75.00
Inserted 4:37		
1	Andruw Jones	1.50
2	Chipper Jones	2.00
3	Greg Maddux	2.00
4	Cal Ripken Jr.	4.00
5	Nomar Garciaparra	2.50
6	Pedro Martinez	1.50
7	Sammy Sosa	2.50
8	Manny Ramirez	1.50
9	Jim Thome	1.00
10	Jeff Bagwell	1.50
11	Mike Piazza	2.50
12	Roger Clemens	2.25
13	Derek Jeter	4.00
14	Bernie Williams	1.00
15	Mark McGwire	3.00
16	Tony Gwynn	2.00
17	Ken Griffey Jr.	2.50
18	Alex Rodriguez	3.00
19	Rafael Palmeiro	1.00
20	Ivan Rodriguez	1.00

Pinstripes

		NM/M
Complete Set (50):		30.00
Common Player:		.25
Premiere Date:		3-6X
Production 51 Sets		
4	Mo Vaughn	1.00
7	Randy Johnson	1.50
9	Matt Williams	.25
11	Andruw Jones	1.50
12	Chipper Jones	2.00
14	Greg Maddux	2.00
19	Cal Ripken Jr.	4.00
21	Nomar Garciaparra	2.50
22	Pedro Martinez	1.50
27	Sammy Sosa	2.50
32	Magglio Ordonez	.35
34	Frank Thomas	1.50
36	Sean Casey	.35
37	Barry Larkin	.35
42	Kenny Lofton	.25
43	Manny Ramirez	1.50
45	Jim Thome	1.50
47	Todd Helton	1.50
51	Larry Walker	.25
55	Juan Gonzalez	1.50
62	Jeff Bagwell	1.50
63	Craig Biggio	.25
67	Carlos Beltran	.50
73	Shawn Green	.40
76	Gary Sheffield	.40
88	Jeromy Burnitz	.25
88	Vladimir Guerrero	1.50
91	Edgardo Alfonzo	.25
94	Mike Piazza	2.50
96	Roger Clemens	2.25
97	Orlando Hernandez	.25
98	Derek Jeter	4.00
101	Bernie Williams	.35
102	Eric Chavez	.35
105	Tim Hudson	.35
111	Scott Rolen	1.25
112	Curt Schilling	.50
113	Brian Giles	.25
114	Rick Ankiel	.25
121	Mark McGwire	3.00
125	Tony Gwynn	2.00
128	Barry Bonds	4.00
130	Jeff Kent	.25
133	Ken Griffey Jr.	2.50
135	Alex Rodriguez	3.00
137	Jose Canseco	.50
140	Fred McGriff	.25
143	Rafael Palmeiro	.75
144	Ivan Rodriguez	.75
147	Carlos Delgado	1.00

Star Factor

		NM/M
Complete Set (10):		200.00

Common Player:		20.00
Inserted 1:361		
1	Chipper Jones	20.00
2	Cal Ripken Jr.	40.00
3	Nomar Garciaparra	25.00
4	Sammy Sosa	25.00
5	Mike Piazza	25.00
6	Derek Jeter	40.00
7	Mark McGwire	30.00
8	Tony Gwynn	20.00
9	Ken Griffey Jr.	25.00
10	Alex Rodriguez	30.00

2000 Pacific Crown Collection Sample

Nearly identical to the issued version of spokesman Tony Gwynn's card, this features a large white diagonal "SAMPLE" overprint on back and in the space where a card number usually appears.

		NM/M
Tony Gwynn		3.00

2000 Pacific Crown Collection

This 300-card base set has a white bordered design with the logo, player name and team stamped in gold foil. Card backs have a small close-up photo, a brief career highlight and 1999 statistics along with career totals.

		NM/M
Complete Set (300):		25.00
Common Player:		.10
Pack (10):		1.50
Wax Box (36):		30.00
1	Garret Anderson	.10
2	Darin Erstad	.25
3	Ben Molina	.10
4	Ramon Ortiz	.10
5	Orlando Palmeiro	.10
6	Troy Percival	.15
7	Tim Salmon	.25
8	Mo Vaughn	.25
9	Checklist (Mo Vaughn)	.10
10	Jay Bell	.10
11	Omar Daal	.10
12	Erubiel Durazo	.25
13	Steve Finley	.10
14	Hanley Frias	.10
15	Luis Gonzalez	.25
16	Randy Johnson	.75
17	Matt Williams	.10
18	Checklist (Matt Williams)	.10
19	Andres Galarraga	.10
20	Tom Glavine	.35
21	Andruw Jones	.75
22	Chipper Jones	1.00
23	Brian Jordan	.10
24	Javy Lopez	.10
25	Greg Maddux	1.00
26	Kevin Millwood	.10
27	Eddie Perez	.10
28	John Smoltz	.10
29	Checklist (Chipper Jones)	.50
30	Albert Belle	.15
31	Jesse Garcia	.10
32	Jerry Hairston Jr.	.10
33	Charles Johnson	.10
34	Mike Mussina	.30
35	Sidney Ponson	.10
36	Cal Ripken Jr.	2.50
37	B.J. Surhoff	.10
38	Checklist (Cal Ripken Jr.)	1.00
39	Nomar Garciaparra	1.50
40	Pedro Martinez	.75
41	Ramon Martinez	.10
42	Trot Nixon	.10
43	Jose Offerman	.10
44	Troy O'Leary	.10
45	John Valentin	.10
46	Wilton Veras	.10
47	Checklist (Nomar Garciaparra)	.75
48	Mark Grace	.15
49	Felix Heredia	.10
50	Jose Molina	.10
51	Jose Nieves	.10
52	Henry Rodriguez	.10
53	Sammy Sosa	1.50
54	Kerry Wood	.65
55	Checklist (Sammy Sosa)	.60
56	Mike Caruso	.10
57	Carlos Castillo	.10
58	Jason Dellaero	.10
59	Carlos Lee	.10
60	Magglio Ordonez	.25
61	Jesus Pena	.10
62	Liu Rodriguez	.10
63	Frank Thomas	.75
64	Checklist (Magglio Ordonez)	.15
65	Aaron Boone	.10
66	Mike Cameron	.10
67	Sean Casey	.20
68	Juan Guzman	.10
69	Barry Larkin	.10
70	Pokey Reese	.10
71	Eddie Taubensee	.10
72	Greg Vaughn	.10
73	Checklist (Sean Casey)	.15
74	Roberto Alomar	.25
75	Sandy Alomar Jr.	.10
76	Bartolo Colon	.10
77	Jacob Cruz	.10
78	Einar Diaz	.10
79	David Justice	.10
80	Kenny Lofton	.10
81	Manny Ramirez	.75
82	Richie Sexson	.10
83	Jim Thome	.75
84	Omar Vizquel	.10
85	Enrique Wilson	.10
86	Checklist (Manny Ramirez)	.40
87	Pedro Astacio	.10
88	Henry Blanco	.10
89	Vinny Castilla	.10
90	Edgard Clemente	.10
91	Todd Helton	.75
92	Neifi Perez	.10
93	Terry Shumpert	.10
94	Juan Sosa RC	.20
95	Larry Walker	.10
96	Checklist (Vinny Castilla)	.10
97	Tony Clark	.10
98	Deivi Cruz	.10
99	Damion Easley	.10
100	Juan Encarnacion	.10
101	Karim Garcia	.10
102	Luis Garcia	.10
103	Juan Gonzalez	.75
104	Jose Macias	.10
105	Dean Palmer	.10
106	Checklist (Juan Encarnacion)	.10
107	Antonio Alfonseca	.10
108	Armando Almanza	.10
109	Bruce Aven	.10
110	Luis Castillo	.10
111	Ramon Castro	.10
112	Alex Fernandez	.10
113	Cliff Floyd	.10
114	Alex Gonzalez	.10
115	Michael Tejera RC	.10
116	Preston Wilson	.10
117	Checklist (Luis Castillo)	.10
118	Jeff Bagwell	.75
119	Craig Biggio	.10
120	Jose Cabrera	.10
121	Tony Eusebio	.10
122	Carl Everett	.10
123	Ricky Gutierrez	.10
124	Mike Hampton	.10
125	Richard Hidalgo	.10
126	Jose Lima	.10
127	Billy Wagner	.10
128	Checklist (Jeff Bagwell)	.40
129	Carlos Beltran	.50
130	Johnny Damon	.25
131	Jermaine Dye	.10
132	Carlos Febles	.10
133	Jeremy Giambi	.10
134	Jose Rosado	.10
135	Rey Sanchez	.10
136	Jose Santiago	.10
137	Checklist (Carlos Beltran)	.10
138	Kevin Brown	.10
139	Craig Counsell	.10
140	Shawn Green	.40
141	Eric Karros	.10
142	Angel Pena	.10
143	Gary Sheffield	.25
144	Ismael Valdes	.10
145	Jose Vizcaino	.10
146	Devon White	.10
147	Checklist (Eric Karros)	.10
148	Ron Belliard	.10
149	Jeromy Burnitz	.10
150	Jeff Cirillo	.10
151	Marquis Grissom	.10
152	Geoff Jenkins	.10
153	Dave Nilsson	.10
154	Rafael Roque	.10
155	Jose Valentin	.10
156	Fernando Vina	.10
157	Jeromy Burnitz	.10
158	Chad Allen	.10
159	Ron Coomer	.10
160	Eddie Guardado	.10
161	Cristian Guzman	.10
162	Jacque Jones	.10
163	Javier Valentin	.10
164	Todd Walker	.10
165	Checklist (Ron Coomer)	.10
166	Michael Barrett	.10
167	Miguel Batista	.10
168	Vladimir Guerrero	.75
169	Wilton Guerrero	.10
170	Fernando Seguignol	.10
171	Ugueth Urbina	.10
172	Javier Vazquez	.10
173	Jose Vidro	.10
174	Rondell White	.10
175	Checklist (Vladimir Guerrero)	.25
176	Edgardo Alfonzo	.10
177	Armando Benitez	.10
178	Roger Cedeno	.10
179	Octavio Dotel	.10
180	Melvin Mora	.10
181	Rey Ordonez	.10
182	Mike Piazza	1.50
183	Jorge Toca	.10
184	Robin Ventura	.10
185	Checklist (Edgardo Alfonzo)	.10
186	Roger Clemens	1.25
187	David Cone	.10
188	Orlando Hernandez	.10
189	Derek Jeter	2.50
190	Ricky Ledee	.10
191	Tino Martinez	.10
192	Ramiro Mendoza	.10
193	Jorge Posada	.10
194	Mariano Rivera	.15
195	Alfonso Soriano	.75
196	Bernie Williams	.30
197	Checklist (Derek Jeter)	1.00
198	Eric Chavez	.15
199	Jason Giambi	.60
200	Ben Grieve	.10
201	Ramon Hernandez	.10
202	Tim Hudson	.25
203	John Jaha	.10
204	Omar Olivares	.10
205	Olmedo Saenz	.10
206	Matt Stairs	.10
207	Miguel Tejada	.20
208	Checklist (Tim Hudson)	.10
209	Rico Brogna	.10
210	Bobby Abreu	.10
211	Marlon Anderson	.10
212	Alex Arias	.10
213	Doug Glanville	.10
214	Robert Person	.10
215	Scott Rolen	.35
216	Curt Schilling	.10
217	Checklist (Scott Rolen)	.25
218	Francisco Cordova	.10
219	Brian Giles	.10
220	Jason Kendall	.10
221	Warren Morris	.10
222	Abraham Nunez	.10
223	Aramis Ramirez	.10
224	Jose Silva	.10
225	Kevin Young	.10
226	Checklist (Brian Giles)	.10
227	Rick Ankiel	.25
228	Ricky Bottalico	.10
229	J.D. Drew	.25
230	Ray Lankford	.10
231	Mark McGwire	2.00
232	Eduardo Perez	.10
233	Placido Polanco	.10
234	Edgar Renteria	.10
235	Fernando Tatis	.10
236	Checklist (Mark McGwire)	.85
237	Carlos Almanzar	.10
238	Wiki Gonzalez	.10
239	Tony Gwynn	1.00
240	Trevor Hoffman	.10
241	Damian Jackson	.10
242	Wally Joyner	.10
243	Ruben Rivera	.10
244	Reggie Sanders	.10
245	Quivlio Veras	.10
246	Checklist (Tony Gwynn)	.50
247	Rich Aurilia	.10
248	Marvin Benard	.10
249	Barry Bonds	2.50
250	Ellis Burks	.10
251	Miguel Del Toro	.10
252	Edwards Guzman	.10
253	Livan Hernandez	.10
254	Jeff Kent	.10
255	Russ Ortiz	.10
256	Armando Rios	.10
257	Checklist (Barry Bonds)	1.00
258	Rafael Bournigal	.10
259	Freddy Garcia	.10
260	Ken Griffey Jr.	15.00
261	Carlos Guillen	.10
262	Raul Ibanez	.10
263	Edgar Martinez	.10
264	Jose Mesa	.10
265	Jamie Moyer	.10
266	John Olerud	.10
267	Jose Paniagua	.10
268	Alex Rodriguez	2.00
269	Checklist (Alex Rodriguez)	1.00
270	Wilson Alvarez	.10
271	Rolando Arrojo	.10
272	Wade Boggs	1.00
273	Miguel Cairo	.10
274	Jose Canseco	.40
275	Jose Guillen	.10
276	Roberto Hernandez	.10
277	Albie Lopez	.10
278	Fred McGriff	.10
279	Esteban Yan	.10
280	Checklist (Jose Canseco)	.20
281	Rusty Greer	.10
282	Roberto Kelly	.10
283	Esteban Loaiza	.10
284	Ruben Mateo	.10
285	Rafael Palmeiro	.65
286	Ivan Rodriguez	.65
287	Aaron Sele	.10
288	John Wetteland	.10
289	Checklist (Ivan Rodriguez)	.25
290	Tony Batista	.10
291	Jose Cruz Jr.	.10
292	Carlos Delgado	.50
293	Kelvim Escobar	.10
294	Tony Fernandez	.10
295	Billy Koch	.10
296	Raul Mondesi	.10
297	Willis Otanez	.10
298	David Segui	.10
299	David Wells	.10
300	Checklist (Carlos Delgado)	.20

Holographic Purple

A parallel to the 300-card base set, holographic purple stamping replaces the gold foil to differentiate these from the base cards. These are limited to 199 numbered sets.

Stars: 4-8X
Production 199 Sets

Platinum Blue

A parallel to the 300-card base set, these have blue foil stamping in place of gold foil and are limited to 67 serial numbered sets.

Stars: 8-15X
Production 67 Sets

In The Cage

These inserts have a die-cut design around an image of a batting cage, with net-fusion technology used to mimic the netting in a batting cage. These were inserted 1:145 packs.

		NM/M
Complete Set (20):		250.00
Common Player:		5.00
Inserted 1:145		
1	Mo Vaughn	5.00
2	Chipper Jones	15.00
3	Cal Ripken Jr.	30.00
4	Nomar Garciaparra	20.00
5	Sammy Sosa	20.00
6	Frank Thomas	10.00
7	Roberto Alomar	6.00
8	Manny Ramirez	10.00
9	Larry Walker	5.00
10	Jeff Bagwell	10.00
11	Vladimir Guerrero	10.00
12	Mike Piazza	20.00

13	Derek Jeter	30.00
14	Bernie Williams	5.00
15	Mark McGwire	25.00
16	Tony Gwynn	15.00
16	Ken Griffey Jr.	20.00
18	Alex Rodriguez	25.00
19	Rafael Palmeiro	8.00
20	Ivan Rodriguez	8.00

Latinos of the Major Leagues

ORLANDO HERNANDEZ

This set salutes major league's who have a latino heritage. These were seeded 2:37 packs and have a horizontal format with two images of the featured player on the card front.

		NM/M
Complete Set (36):		20.00
Common Player:		.25
Inserted 2:37		
Parallel:		2-4X
Production 99 Sets		
1	Erubiel Durazo	.25
2	Luis Gonzalez	.25
3	Andruw Jones	1.00
4	Nomar Garciaparra	2.00
5	Pedro Martinez	1.00
6	Sammy Sosa	2.00
7	Carlos Lee	.25
8	Magglio Ordonez	.65
9	Roberto Alomar	.65
10	Manny Ramirez	1.00
11	Omar Vizquel	.25
12	Vinny Castilla	.25
13	Juan Gonzalez	1.00
14	Luis Castillo	.25
15	Jose Lima	.25
16	Carlos Beltran	.75
17	Vladimir Guerrero	1.00
18	Edgardo Alfonzo	.25
19	Roger Cedeno	.25
20	Rey Ordonez	.25
21	Orlando Hernandez	.25
22	Tino Martinez	.25
23	Mariano Rivera	.35
24	Bernie Williams	.50
25	Miguel Tejada	.50
26	Bobby Abreu	.25
27	Fernando Tatis	.25
28	Freddy Garcia	.25
29	Edgar Martinez	.25
30	Alex Rodriguez	3.00
31	Jose Canseco	.65
32	Ruben Mateo	.25
33	Rafael Palmeiro	.75
34	Ivan Rodriguez	.75
35	Carlos Delgado	.65
36	Raul Mondesi	.25

Moment of Truth

ALEX RODRIGUEZ

These inserts feature gold foil stamping and a shadow image of the player in the background of the player photo. These were inserted 1:37 packs.

		NM/M
Complete Set (30):		50.00
Common Player:		.50
Inserted 1:37		
1	Mo Vaughn	.50
2	Chipper Jones	3.00
3	Greg Maddux	3.00
4	Albert Belle	.50
5	Cal Ripken Jr.	6.00
6	Nomar Garciaparra	4.00
7	Pedro Martinez	2.00
8	Sammy Sosa	4.00
9	Frank Thomas	2.00
10	Barry Larkin	.50
11	Kenny Lofton	1.00
12	Manny Ramirez	2.00
13	Larry Walker	.50
14	Juan Gonzalez	2.00
15	Jeff Bagwell	2.00
16	Craig Biggio	.50
17	Carlos Beltran	1.00
18	Vladimir Guerrero	2.00
19	Mike Piazza	4.00
20	Roger Clemens	3.50
21	Derek Jeter	6.00
22	Bernie Williams	.75
23	Mark McGwire	5.00
24	Tony Gwynn	3.00
25	Barry Bonds	6.00
26	Ken Griffey Jr.	4.00
27	Alex Rodriguez	5.00
28	Rafael Palmeiro	1.50
29	Ivan Rodriguez	1.50
30	Carlos Delgado	1.00

Pacific Cup

Pacific Cup's have a horizontal format with gold foil stamping and an image of a trophy cup beside the player photo. These were inserted 1:721 packs.

		NM/M
Complete Set (10):		220.00
Inserted 1:721		
1	Cal Ripken Jr.	40.00
2	Nomar Garciaparra	25.00
3	Pedro Martinez	15.00
4	Sammy Sosa	25.00
5	Vladimir Guerrero	15.00
6	Derek Jeter	40.00
7	Mark McGwire	35.00
8	Tony Gwynn	20.00
9	Ken Griffey Jr.	25.00
10	Alex Rodriguez	35.00

Timber 2000

SAMMY SOSA

These 1:73 pack inserts have a horizontal format highlighted by gold foil stamping. A black bat is in the background of the player image with 2000 written in the bat head.

		NM/M
Complete Set (20):		100.00
Common Player:		2.00
Inserted 1:73		
1	Chipper Jones	8.00
2	Nomar Garciaparra	10.00
3	Sammy Sosa	10.00
4	Magglio Ordonez	2.00
5	Manny Ramirez	6.00
6	Vinny Castilla	2.00
7	Juan Gonzalez	6.00
8	Jeff Bagwell	6.00
9	Shawn Green	3.00
10	Vladimir Guerrero	6.00
11	Mike Piazza	10.00
12	Derek Jeter	15.00
13	Bernie Williams	2.00
14	Mark McGwire	12.00
15	Ken Griffey Jr.	10.00
16	Alex Rodriguez	12.00
17	Jose Canseco	3.00
18	Rafael Palmeiro	5.00
19	Ivan Rodriguez	5.00
20	Carlos Delgado	4.00

2000 Pacific Crown Royale

CHIPPER JONES

The Crown Royale 144-card base set has a horizontal format die-cut around a crown design at the top. The cards are double foiled with gold and silver foil etching.

		NM/M
Complete Set (144):		40.00
Common Player:		.25
Common SP:		1.00
Pack (6):		2.50
Box (24):		45.00
1	Darin Erstad	.40
2	Troy Glaus	1.00
3	Adam Kennedy/SP	1.00
4	Derrick Turnbow/SP RC	1.00
5	Mo Vaughn	.25
6	Erubiel Durazo	.25
7	Steve Finley	.25
8	Randy Johnson	1.00
9	Travis Lee	.25
10	Matt Williams	.25
11	Rafael Furcal/SP	1.00
12	Andres Galarraga	.25
13	Andruw Jones	1.00
14	Chipper Jones	1.50
15	Javy Lopez	.25
16	Greg Maddux	1.50
17	Albert Belle	.35
18	Will Clark	.35
19	Mike Mussina	.40
20	Cal Ripken Jr.	3.00
21	Carl Everett	.25
22	Nomar Garciaparra	2.00
23	Pedro Martinez	1.00
24	Jason Varitek	.25
25	Scott Downs/SP RC	1.00
26	Mark Grace	.35
27	Sammy Sosa	2.00
28	Kerry Wood	.65
29	Ray Durham	.25
30	Paul Konerko	.25
31	Carlos Lee	.25
32	Magglio Ordonez	.40
33	Frank Thomas	1.00
34	Rob Bell SP	1.00
35	Sean Casey	.25
36	Ken Griffey Jr.	2.00
37	Barry Larkin	.25
38	Pokey Reese	.25
39	Roberto Alomar	.40
40	David Justice	.25
41	Kenny Lofton	.25
42	Manny Ramirez	1.00
43	Richie Sexson	.25
44	Jim Thome	.75
45	Rolando Arrojo	.25
46	Jeff Cirillo	.25
47	Tom Goodwin	.25
48	Todd Helton	1.00
49	Larry Walker	.25
50	Tony Clark	.25
51	Juan Encarnacion	.25
52	Juan Gonzalez	1.00
53	Hideo Nomo	1.00
54	Dean Palmer	.25
55	Cliff Floyd	.25
56	Alex Gonzalez	.25
57	Mike Lowell	.25
58	Brad Penny/SP	1.00
59	Preston Wilson	.25
60	Moises Alou	.25
61	Jeff Bagwell	1.00
62	Craig Biggio	.25
63	Roger Cedeno	.25
64	Julio Lugo/SP	.25
65	Carlos Beltran	.60
66	Johnny Damon	.40
67	Jermaine Dye	.25
68	Carlos Febles	.25
69	Mark Quinn/SP	1.00
70	Kevin Brown	.25
71	Shawn Green	.50
72	Eric Karros	.25
73	Gary Sheffield	.50
74	Kevin Barker/SP	1.00
75	Ron Belliard	.25
76	Jeromy Burnitz	.25
77	Geoff Jenkins	.25
78	Jacque Jones	.25
79	Corey Koskie	.25
80	Matt LeCroy/SP	.25
81	Brad Radke	.25
82	Peter Bergeron/SP	1.00
83	Matt Blank/SP	1.00
84	Vladimir Guerrero	.25
85	Hideki Irabu	.25
86	Rondell White	.25
87	Edgardo Alfonzo	.25
88	Mike Hampton	.25
89	Rickey Henderson	1.00
90	Rey Ordonez	.25
91	Jay Payton/SP	1.00
92	Mike Piazza	2.00
93	Roger Clemens	1.75
94	Orlando Hernandez	.25
95	Derek Jeter	3.00
96	Tino Martinez	.25
97	Alfonso Soriano/SP	2.50
98	Bernie Williams	.40
99	Eric Chavez	.40
100	Jason Giambi	.75
101	Ben Grieve	.50
102	Tim Hudson	.50
103	Terrence Long/SP	1.00
104	Mark Mulder/SP	1.00
105	Adam Piatt/SP	1.00
106	Bobby Abreu	.25
107	Doug Glanville	.25
108	Mike Lieberthal	.25
109	Scott Rolen	.75
110	Brian Giles	.25
111	Chad Hermansen/SP	1.00
112	Jason Kendall	.25
113	Warren Morris	.25
114	Rick Ankiel/SP	1.00
115	Justin Brunette/SP RC	1.00
116	J.D. Drew	.40
117	Mark McGwire	2.50
118	Fernando Tatis	.25
119	Wiki Gonzalez/SP	1.00
120	Tony Gwynn	1.50
121	Trevor Hoffman	.25
122	Ryan Klesko	1.00
123	Barry Bonds	3.00
124	Ellis Burks	.25
125	Jeff Kent	.25
126	Calvin Murray/SP	1.00
127	J.T. Snow	.25
128	Freddy Garcia	.25
129	John Olerud	.25
130	Alex Rodriguez	2.50
131	Kazuhiro Sasaki/SP RC	3.00
132	Jose Canseco	.50
133	Vinny Castilla	.25
134	Fred McGriff	.25
135	Greg Vaughn	.25
136	Gabe Kapler	.25
137	Mike Lamb/SP RC	1.00
138	Ruben Mateo/SP	1.00
139	Rafael Palmeiro	.75
140	Ivan Rodriguez	.75
141	Tony Batista	.25
142	Carlos Delgado	.75
143	Raul Mondesi	.25
144	Shannon Stewart	.25

Limited Series

A parallel to the 144-card base set, silver foil replaces gold foil to differentiate these from regular cards. They are also limited to 144 serial numbered sets.

Stars:	2-4X
Production 144 Sets	

Red

Identical in design to the base set, these have red foil instead of gold and are the base cards in retail packaging.

All singles:	1X
Base cards in retail packs.	

Platinum Blue

A parallel to the 144-card base set these have blue foil in place of gold foil to differentiate them from regular cards. They are limited to 75 serial numbered sets.

Stars:	3-6X
Production 75 Sets	

Premiere Date

A parallel to the 144-card base set these are found exclusively in hobby packs and are limited to 121 serial numbered sets.

Stars:	2-4X
Production 121 Sets	

Card-Supials

CAL RIPKEN JR.

These inserts feature a superstar's regular sized card paired with a top prospect teammate's smaller card. The standard sized card has a horizontal format with gold foil stamping, the small prospect card has gold foil stamping on a vertical format. These were seeded 2:25 packs.

		NM/M
Complete Set (20):		40.00
Common Card:		1.00
Inserted 2:25		
1	Randy Johnson, Erubiel Durazo	2.00
2	Chipper Jones, Andruw Jones	3.00
3	Cal Ripken Jr., Matt Riley	6.00
4	Nomar Garciaparra, Jason Varitek	4.00
5	Sammy Sosa, Kerry Wood	4.00
6	Frank Thomas, Magglio Ordonez	2.00
7	Ken Griffey Jr., Sean Casey	4.00
8	Manny Ramirez, Richie Sexson	2.00
9	Larry Walker, Ben Petrick	1.00
10	Juan Gonzalez, Juan Encarnacion	2.00
11	Jeff Bagwell, Lance Berkman	2.00
12	Shawn Green, Eric Gagne	1.00
13	Vladimir Guerrero, Peter Bergeron	2.00
14	Mike Piazza, Edgardo Alfonzo	4.00
15	Derek Jeter, Alfonso Soriano	5.00
16	Scott Rolen, Bobby Abreu	1.50
17	Mark McGwire, Rick Ankiel	5.00
18	Tony Gwynn, Ben Davis	3.00
19	Alex Rodriguez, Freddy Garcia	5.00
20	Ivan Rodriguez, Ruben Mateo	1.50

Cramer's Choice Jumbo

This enlarged 10-card set is die-cut into a trophy shape. The jumbo cards are enhanced with a silver holo-foiled front with gold foil stamping and etching across the bottom portion. These were found one per box exclusively in hobby boxes. Six parallels also were randomly inserted with each individual color replacing the gold foil stamping. Aqua's are limited to 20 numbered sets, Blue's 35 sets, Gold's 10 sets, Green's 30 sets, Purple's one set and Red's 25 sets.

		NM/M
Complete Set (10):		35.00
Common Player:		1.00
Inserted 1:Box H		
Aqua:		5-10X
Production 20 Sets		
Blue:		2-5X
Production 35 Sets		
Gold:		10-20X
Production 10 Sets		
Green:		3-6X
Production 30 Sets		
Red:		4-8X
Production 25 Sets		
1	Cal Ripken Jr.	6.00
2	Nomar Garciaparra	4.00
3	Ken Griffey Jr.	4.00
4	Sammy Sosa	4.00
5	Mike Piazza	4.00
6	Derek Jeter	6.00
7	Rick Ankiel	1.00
8	Mark McGwire	4.00
9	Tony Gwynn	2.00
10	Alex Rodriguez	5.00

Feature Attractions

CAL RIPKEN JR.

This 25-card set has a horizontal format with the featured player's achievements on a billboard in the background. These were seeded one per hobby pack and one per two retail packs. An Exclusive Showing parallel is also randomly inserted and is limited to 20 serial numbered sets.

		NM/M
Complete Set (25):		10.00
Common Player:		.25
Inserted 1:1		
Exclusive Showing:		30-50X
Production 20 Sets		
1	Erubiel Durazo	.25
2	Chipper Jones	1.00
3	Greg Maddux	1.00
4	Cal Ripken Jr.	2.50
5	Nomar Garciaparra	1.50
6	Pedro Martinez	.75
7	Sammy Sosa	1.50
8	Frank Thomas	.75
9	Ken Griffey Jr.	1.50
10	Manny Ramirez	.75
11	Larry Walker	.25
12	Juan Gonzalez	.75
13	Jeff Bagwell	.75
14	Carlos Beltran	.50
15	Shawn Green	.50
16	Vladimir Guerrero	.75
17	Mike Piazza	1.50
18	Roger Clemens	1.25
19	Derek Jeter	2.50
20	Ben Grieve	.25
21	Rick Ankiel	.35
22	Mark McGwire	1.50
23	Tony Gwynn	1.00
24	Alex Rodriguez	2.00
25	Ivan Rodriguez	.65

Final Numbers

These inserts are found one per hobby pack and one per two retail packs. The logo, player name and team are stamped in silver foil and has "Final Numbers" written down the right hand portion of the front. A holographic parallel limited to 10 serial numbered sets is also randomly inserted.

		NM/M
Complete Set (25):		10.00
Common Player:		.25
Inserted 1:1		
1	Randy Johnson	.75
2	Andruw Jones	.75
3	Chipper Jones	1.00
4	Cal Ripken Jr.	2.50
5	Nomar Garciaparra	1.50
6	Pedro Martinez	.75
7	Sammy Sosa	1.50
8	Ken Griffey Jr.	1.50
9	Sean Casey	.35
10	Manny Ramirez	.75
11	Larry Walker	.25
12	Jeff Bagwell	.75
13	Craig Biggio	.25
14	Shawn Green	.50
15	Vladimir Guerrero	.75
16	Mike Piazza	1.50
17	Derek Jeter	2.50
18	Bernie Williams	.35
19	Scott Rolen	.65
20	Mark McGwire	2.00
21	Tony Gwynn	1.00
22	Barry Bonds	2.50
23	Alex Rodriguez	2.00
24	Jose Canseco	.40
25	Ivan Rodriguez	.65

Jumbo

These jumbo cards are identical in design to the base cards besides their enlarged size. These were found exclusively in hobby boxes and were found as a box topper in 6:10 boxes.

		NM/M
Complete Set (6):		25.00
Inserted 6:10 boxes H		
1	Cal Ripken Jr.	6.00
2	Nomar Garciaparra	4.00
3	Ken Griffey Jr.	4.00
4	Derek Jeter	6.00
5	Mark McGwire	5.00
6	Alex Rodriguez	5.00

Proofs

Proofs are the actual printer's proofs used to produce this set. The inserts are transparent and have a coal black tint. These were inserted 1:25 packs. A parallel is also randomly inserted and is limited to 50 serial numbered sets.

		NM/M
Complete Set (36):		90.00
Common Player:		1.00
Inserted 1:25		
Proofs:		2-3X
1	Erubiel Durazo	1.50
2	Randy Johnson	3.00
3	Chipper Jones	5.00
4	Greg Maddux	5.00
5	Cal Ripken Jr.	10.00
6	Nomar Garciaparra	8.00
7	Pedro Martinez	3.00
8	Sammy Sosa	5.00

9	Frank Thomas	2.50
10	Sean Casey	1.50
11	Ken Griffey Jr.	5.00
12	Manny Ramirez	2.50
13	Jim Thome	2.50
14	Larry Walker	1.50
15	Juan Gonzalez	2.50
16	Jeff Bagwell	2.50
17	Craig Biggio	1.50
18	Carlos Beltran	2.00
19	Shawn Green	2.00
20	Vladimir Guerrero	2.50
21	Edgardo Alfonzo	1.00
22	Mike Piazza	5.00
23	Roger Clemens	6.00
24	Derek Jeter	10.00
25	Alfonso Soriano	4.00
26	Bernie Williams	2.00
27	Ben Grieve	1.00
28	Rick Ankiel	1.00
29	Mark McGwire	8.00
30	Tony Gwynn	3.00
31	Barry Bonds	8.00
32	Alex Rodriguez	8.00
33	Jose Canseco	2.00
34	Vinny Castilla	1.00
35	Ivan Rodriguez	2.00
36	Rafael Palmeiro	2.00

Sweet Spot Signatures

These die-cut autographed cards are done on a horizontal format with an image of a baseball beside the player photo. The signature is on the "sweet spot" of the baseball image. Red foil stamping is used on the seams of the baseball and the player name. No insertion ratio was announced.

		NM/M
	Common Player:	5.00
1	Adam Kennedy	5.00
2	Trot Nixon	8.00
3	Magglio Ordonez	10.00
4	Sean Casey	8.00
5	Travis Dawkins	5.00
6	Todd Helton	25.00
7	Ben Petrick	5.00
8	Jeff Weaver	6.00
9	Preston Wilson	5.00
10	Lance Berkman	10.00
11	Roger Cedeno	5.00
12	Eric Gagne	10.00
13	Kevin Barker	5.00
14	Kyle Peterson	5.00
15	Tony Armas Jr.	5.00
16	Peter Bergeron	5.00
17	Alfonso Soriano	40.00
18	Ben Grieve	5.00
19	Ramon Hernandez	5.00
20	Brian Giles	8.00
21	Chad Hermansen	5.00
22	Warren Morris	5.00
23	Ben Davis	5.00
24	Rick Ankiel	15.00
25	Chad Hutchinson	5.00
26	Freddy Garcia	10.00
27	Gabe Kapler	5.00
28	Ruben Mateo	5.00
29	Billy Koch	5.00
30	Vernon Wells	5.00

2000 Pacific Invincible

The base set consists of 150 cards. The player image is on an acetate stock with a blue sky background. The rest of the card is on standard UV coated stock and has the player name stamped in gold foil.

	NM/M
Complete Set (150):	75.00
Common Player:	.25
Pack (3):	
Box (36):	50.00

1	Darin Erstad	.50
2	Troy Glaus	1.50
3	Ramon Ortiz	.25
4	Tim Salmon	.35
5	Mo Vaughn	.25
6	Erubiel Durazo	.25
7	Luis Gonzalez	.35
8	Randy Johnson	1.50
9	Matt Williams	.25
10	Rafael Furcal	.25
11	Andres Galarraga	.25
12	Tom Glavine	.40
13	Andruw Jones	1.50
14	Chipper Jones	2.00
15	Greg Maddux	2.00
16	Kevin Millwood	.25
17	Albert Belle	.35
18	Will Clark	.35
19	Mike Mussina	.40
20	Matt Riley	.25
21	Cal Ripken Jr.	4.00
22	Carl Everett	.25
23	Nomar Garciaparra	2.50
24	Steve Lomasney	.25
25	Pedro Martinez	1.50
26	Tomo Ohka RC	.75
27	Wilton Veras	.25
28	Mark Grace	.25
29	Sammy Sosa	2.50
30	Kerry Wood	.75
31	Eric Young	.25
32	Julio Zuleta RC	.25
33	Paul Konerko	.35
34	Carlos Lee	.25
35	Magglio Ordonez	.35
36	Josh Paul	.25
37	Frank Thomas	1.50
38	Rob Bell	.25
39	Dante Bichette	.25
40	Sean Casey	.35
41	Ken Griffey Jr.	2.50
42	Barry Larkin	.25
43	Pokey Reese	.25
44	Roberto Alomar	.40
45	Manny Ramirez	1.50
46	Richie Sexson	.25
47	Jim Thome	1.50
48	Omar Vizquel	.25
49	Jeff Cirillo	.25
50	Todd Helton	1.50
51	Neifi Perez	.25
52	Larry Walker	.25
53	Tony Clark	.25
54	Juan Encarnacion	.25
55	Juan Gonzalez	1.50
56	Hideo Nomo	1.00
57	Luis Castillo	.25
58	Alex Gonzalez	.25
59	Brad Penny	.25
60	Preston Wilson	.25
61	Moises Alou	.25
62	Jeff Bagwell	1.50
63	Lance Berkman	.25
64	Craig Biggio	.25
65	Roger Cedeno	.25
66	Jose Lima	.25
67	Carlos Beltran	.50
68	Johnny Damon	.35
69	Chad Durbin RC	.25
70	Jermaine Dye	.25
71	Carlos Febles	.25
72	Mark Quinn	.25
73	Kevin Brown	.25
74	Eric Gagne	.25
75	Shawn Green	.50
76	Eric Karros	.25
77	Gary Sheffield	.40
78	Kevin Barker	.25
79	Ron Belliard	.25
80	Jeromy Burnitz	.25
81	Geoff Jenkins	.25
82	Jacque Jones	.25
83	Corey Koskie	.25
84	Matt LeCroy	.25
85	David Ortiz	.35
86	Johan Santana RC	20.00
87	Todd Walker	.25
88	Peter Bergeron	.25
89	Vladimir Guerrero	1.50
90	Jose Vidro	.25
91	Rondell White	.25
92	Edgardo Alfonzo	.25
93	Derek Bell	.25
94	Mike Hampton	.25
95	Rey Ordonez	.25
96	Mike Piazza	2.50
97	Robin Ventura	.25
98	Roger Clemens	2.25
99	Orlando Hernandez	.25
100	Derek Jeter	4.00
101	Alfonso Soriano	.75
102	Bernie Williams	.35
103	Eric Chavez	.40
104	Jason Giambi	.75
105	Ben Grieve	.25
106	Tim Hudson	.40
107	Miguel Tejada	.40
108	Bobby Abreu	.25
109	Doug Glanville	.25
110	Mike Lieberthal	.25
111	Scott Rolen	.40
112	Brian Giles	.25
113	Chad Hermansen	.25
114	Jason Kendall	.25
115	Warren Morris	.25
116	Aramis Ramirez	.25
117	Rick Ankiel	.40
118	J.D. Drew	.40

119	Mark McGwire	3.00
120	Fernando Tatis	.25
121	Fernando Vina	.25
122	Bret Boone	.25
123	Ben Davis	.25
124	Tony Gwynn	2.00
125	Trevor Hoffman	.25
126	Ryan Klesko	.25
127	Rich Aurilia	.25
128	Barry Bonds	4.00
129	Ellis Burks	.25
130	Jeff Kent	.25
131	Freddy Garcia	.25
132	Carlos Guillen	.25
133	Edgar Martinez	.25
134	John Olerud	.25
135	Robert Ramsay	.25
136	Alex Rodriguez	3.00
137	Kazuhiro Sasaki RC	3.00
138	Jose Canseco	.50
139	Vinny Castilla	.25
140	Fred McGriff	.25
141	Greg Vaughn (Front photo is Mo Vaughn.)	.25
142	Dan Wheeler	.25
143	Gabe Kapler	.25
144	Ruben Mateo	.25
145	Rafael Palmeiro	.75
146	Ivan Rodriguez	.75
147	Tony Batista	.25
148	Carlos Delgado	.65
149	Raul Mondesi	.25
150	Vernon Wells	.25

Holographic Purple

A parallel to the 150-card set, holographic purple stamping replaces the gold foil from the base cards. These are limited to 299 serial numbered sets.

Stars:	2-3X
Production 299 Sets	

Platinum Blue

A parallel to the 150-card base set these differ only from the regular cards in that blue foil stamping replaces gold. Each card is also serially numbered on the card front in an edition of 67 sets.

Stars:	4-8X
Production 67 Sets	

Diamond Aces

This insert set highlights the top pitchers in the game. Silver-foil stamping is used on the card fronts, which are designed to duplicate the look of an Ace in a deck of playing cards. These were seeded 1 per pack. A parallel limited to 399 serial numbered sets is also randomly seeded.

		NM/M
Complete Set (20):		5.00
Common Player:		.25
Inserted 1:1		
Edition of 399 Parallel:		2-3X
1	Randy Johnson	.75
2	Greg Maddux	1.00
3	Tom Glavine	.40
4	John Smoltz	.25
5	Mike Mussina	.50
6	Pedro Martinez	.75
7	Kerry Wood	.60

8	Bartolo Colon	.25
9	Brad Penny	.25
10	Billy Wagner	.25
11	Kevin Brown	.25
12	Mike Hampton	.25
13	Roger Clemens	1.50
14	David Cone	.25
15	Orlando Hernandez	.25
16	Mariano Rivera	.40
17	Tim Hudson	.40
18	Trevor Hoffman	.25
19	Rick Ankiel	.25
20	Freddy Garcia	.25

Eyes of the World

This 20-card set has a horizontal format with gold foil stamping. The background of the player photo has a partial globe with a star and the country the featured player is from stamped in gold foil. These were inserted 1:25 packs.

		NM/M
Complete Set (20):		30.00
Common Player:		.75
Inserted 1:25		
1	Erubiel Durazo	.75
2	Andruw Jones	2.00
3	Cal Ripken Jr.	6.00
4	Nomar Garciaparra	4.00
5	Pedro Martinez	2.00
6	Sammy Sosa	4.00
7	Ken Griffey Jr.	4.00
8	Manny Ramirez	2.00
9	Larry Walker	.75
10	Juan Gonzalez	2.00
11	Carlos Beltran	1.25
12	Vladimir Guerrero	2.00
13	Orlando Hernandez	.75
14	Derek Jeter	6.00
15	Mark McGwire	5.00
16	Tony Gwynn	3.00
17	Freddy Garcia	.75
18	Alex Rodriguez	5.00
19	Jose Canseco	1.25
20	Ivan Rodriguez	1.50

Game Gear

		NM/M
Common Card:		4.00
1	Jeff Bagwell/Jsy/1,000	8.00
2	Tom Glavine/Jsy/1,000	6.00
3	Mark Grace/Jsy/1,000	8.00
4	Eric Karros/Jsy/1,000	4.00
5	Edgar Martinez/Jsy/800	6.00
6	Manny Ramirez/Jsy/975	8.00
7	Cal Ripken Jr./ Jsy/1,000	25.00
8	Alex Rodriguez/Jsy/900	15.00
9	Ivan Rodriguez/Jsy/675	6.00
10	Mo Vaughn Jsy/1,000	4.00
11	Edgar Martinez/ Bat-Jsy/200	8.00
12	Manny Ramirez/Jsy/145	15.00
13	Alex Rodriguez/ Bat-Jsy/200	25.00
14	Ivan Rodriguez/ Bat-Jsy/200	10.00
15	Edgar Martinez/Bat/200	6.00
16	Manny Ramirez/Bat/200	15.00
17	Ivan Rodriguez/Bat/200	8.00
18	Alex Rodriguez/Bat/200	20.00
19	Jeff Bagwell/Patch/125	30.00
20	Tom Glavine/Patch/110	25.00
21	Mark Grace/Patch/125	25.00
22	Tony Gwynn/Patch/65	40.00
23	Chipper Jones/Patch/80	40.00
24	Eric Karros/Patch/125	15.00
25	Greg Maddux/Patch/80	50.00
26	Edgar Martinez/ Patch/125	20.00
27	Manny Ramirez/ Patch/125	30.00
28	Cal Ripken Jr./ Patch/125	65.00
29	Alex Rodriguez/ Patch/125	50.00
30	Ivan Rodriguez/ Patch/125	25.00
31	Frank Thomas/ Patch/125	25.00
32	Mo Vaughn/Patch/125	15.00

Kings of the Diamond

Twenty of the top hitters in the game are featured on a design in-

tended to duplicate the look of a King card in a playing deck of cards. These were seeded one per pack. A parallel version limited to 299 serial numbered sets is also randomly seeded.

		NM/M
Complete Set (30):		10.00
Common Player:		.20
Inserted 1:1		
1	Mo Vaughn	.20
2	Erubiel Durazo	.20
3	Andruw Jones	.65
4	Chipper Jones	.75
5	Cal Ripken Jr.	1.50
6	Nomar Garciaparra	1.00
7	Sammy Sosa	1.00
8	Frank Thomas	.65
9	Sean Casey	.25
10	Ken Griffey Jr.	1.00
11	Manny Ramirez	.65
12	Larry Walker	.20
13	Juan Gonzalez	.65
14	Jeff Bagwell	.65
15	Craig Biggio	.20
16	Carlos Beltran	.50
17	Shawn Green	.35
18	Vladimir Guerrero	.65
19	Mike Piazza	1.00
20	Derek Jeter	1.50
21	Bernie Williams	.40
22	Ben Grieve	.20
23	Scott Rolen	.40
24	Mark McGwire	1.25
25	Tony Gwynn	.75
26	Barry Bonds	1.50
27	Alex Rodriguez	1.25
28	Jose Canseco	.25
29	Rafael Palmeiro	.50
30	Ivan Rodriguez	.50

Lighting The Fire

These full foiled inserts are die-cut in the shape of a flame, with an image of a baseball at the core of the fiery image. These were inserted 1:49 packs.

		NM/M
Complete Set (20):		120.00
Common Player:		3.00
Inserted 1:49		
1	Chipper Jones	8.00
2	Greg Maddux	8.00
3	Cal Ripken Jr.	15.00
4	Nomar Garciaparra	10.00
5	Pedro Martinez	6.00
6	Ken Griffey Jr.	10.00
7	Sammy Sosa	10.00
8	Manny Ramirez	6.00
9	Juan Gonzalez	6.00
10	Jeff Bagwell	6.00
11	Shawn Green	3.00
12	Vladimir Guerrero	6.00
13	Mike Piazza	10.00
14	Roger Clemens	9.00
15	Derek Jeter	15.00
16	Mark McGwire	12.00
17	Tony Gwynn	8.00
18	Alex Rodriguez	12.00
19	Jose Canseco	3.00
20	Ivan Rodriguez	5.00

Ticket To Stardom

These unique cards have a design intended to replicate a ticket stub. Two images of the featured player are on the front, the bigger

primary photo is vertical, while the smaller photo is horizontal. Silver foil stamping is used throughout. These are found 1:121 packs.

		NM/M
Complete Set (20):		250.00
Common Player:		5.00
Inserted 1:121		
1	Andruw Jones	10.00
2	Chipper Jones	15.00
3	Cal Ripken Jr.	30.00
4	Nomar Garciaparra	20.00
5	Pedro Martinez	10.00
6	Ken Griffey Jr.	20.00
7	Sammy Sosa	20.00
8	Manny Ramirez	10.00
9	Jeff Bagwell	10.00
10	Shawn Green	5.00
11	Vladimir Guerrero	10.00
12	Mike Piazza	20.00
13	Derek Jeter	30.00
14	Alfonso Soriano	8.00
15	Scott Rolen	6.00
16	Rick Ankiel	5.00
17	Mark McGwire	25.00
18	Tony Gwynn	15.00
19	Alex Rodriguez	25.00
20	Ivan Rodriguez	8.00

Wild Vinyl

This scarce 10-card insert set is serial numbered on the card front, limited to only 10 sets.

Complete Set (10):	
Common Player:	
Production 10 Sets	

2000 Pacific Omega

	NM/M
Complete Set (255):	300.00
Common Player:	.10
Common (151-255):	4.00
Production 999 Sets	

1	Garret Anderson	.10
2	Darin Erstad	.25
3	Troy Glaus	.75
4	Tim Salmon	.20
5	Mo Vaughn	.10
6	Jay Bell	.10
7	Steve Finley	.10
8	Luis Gonzalez	.10
9	Randy Johnson	.75
10	Matt Williams	.10
11	Andres Galarraga	.10
12	Andruw Jones	.75
13	Chipper Jones	1.00
14	Brian Jordan	.10

#	Player	Price
15	Greg Maddux	1.00
16	B.J. Surhoff	.10
17	Brady Anderson	.10
18	Albert Belle	.10
19	Mike Mussina	.40
20	Cal Ripken Jr.	2.50
21	Carl Everett	.10
22	Nomar Garciaparra	1.50
23	Pedro Martinez	.75
24	Jason Varitek	.10
25	Mark Grace	.20
26	Sammy Sosa	1.50
27	Rondell White	.10
28	Kerry Wood	.35
29	Eric Young	.10
30	Ray Durham	.10
31	Carlos Lee	.10
32	Magglio Ordonez	.25
33	Frank Thomas	.75
34	Sean Casey	.20
35	Ken Griffey Jr.	1.50
36	Barry Larkin	.10
37	Pokey Reese	.10
38	Roberto Alomar	.40
39	Kenny Lofton	.10
40	Manny Ramirez	.75
41	David Segui	.10
42	Jim Thome	.60
43	Omar Vizquel	.10
44	Jeff Cirillo	.10
45	Jeffrey Hammonds	.10
46	Todd Helton	.75
47	Todd Hollandsworth	.10
48	Larry Walker	.10
49	Tony Clark	.10
50	Juan Encarnacion	.10
51	Juan Gonzalez	.75
52	Bobby Higginson	.10
53	Hideo Nomo	.75
54	Dean Palmer	.10
55	Luis Castillo	.10
56	Cliff Floyd	.10
57	Derek Lee	.10
58	Mike Lowell	.10
59	Henry Rodriguez	.10
60	Preston Wilson	.10
61	Moises Alou	.10
62	Jeff Bagwell	.75
63	Craig Biggio	.10
64	Ken Caminiti	.10
65	Richard Hidalgo	.10
66	Carlos Beltran	.40
67	Johnny Damon	.25
68	Jermaine Dye	.10
69	Joe Randa	.10
70	Mike Sweeney	.10
71	Adrian Beltre	.20
72	Kevin Brown	.10
73	Shawn Green	.35
74	Eric Karros	.10
75	Chan Ho Park	.10
76	Gary Sheffield	.30
77	Ron Belliard	.10
78	Jeromy Burnitz	.10
79	Geoff Jenkins	.10
80	Richie Sexson	.10
81	Ron Coomer	.10
82	Jacque Jones	.10
83	Corey Koskie	.10
84	Matt Lawton	.10
85	Vladimir Guerrero	.75
86	Lee Stevens	.10
87	Jose Vidro	.10
88	Edgardo Alfonzo	.10
89	Derek Bell	.10
90	Mike Bordick	.10
91	Mike Piazza	1.50
92	Robin Ventura	.10
93	Jose Canseco	.40
94	Roger Clemens	1.25
95	Orlando Hernandez	.10
96	Derek Jeter	2.50
97	David Justice	.10
98	Tino Martinez	.10
99	Jorge Posada	.10
100	Bernie Williams	.40
101	Eric Chavez	.20
102	Jason Giambi	.50
103	Ben Grieve	.10
104	Miguel Tejada	.25
105	Bobby Abreu	.10
106	Doug Glanville	.10
107	Travis Lee	.10
108	Mike Lieberthal	.10
109	Scott Rolen	.65
110	Brian S. Giles	.10
111	Jason Kendall	.10
112	Warren Morris	.10
113	Kevin Young	.10
114	Will Clark	.20
115	J.D. Drew	.20
116	Jim Edmonds	.10
117	Mark McGwire	2.00
118	Edgar Renteria	.10
119	Fernando Tatis	.10
120	Fernando Vina	.10
121	Bret Boone	.10
122	Tony Gwynn	1.00
123	Trevor Hoffman	.10
124	Phil Nevin	.10
125	Eric Owens	.10
126	Barry Bonds	2.50
127	Ellis Burks	.10
128	Jeff Kent	.10
129	J.T. Snow	.10
130	Jay Buhner	.10
131	Mike Cameron	.10
132	Rickey Henderson	.75
133	Edgar Martinez	.10
134	John Olerud	.10
135	Alex Rodriguez	2.00
136	Kazuhiro Sasaki RC	1.00

#	Player	Price
137	Fred McGriff	.10
138	Greg Vaughn	.10
139	Gerald Williams	.10
140	Rusty Greer	.10
141	Gabe Kapler	.10
142	Ricky Ledee	.10
143	Rafael Palmeiro	.65
144	Ivan Rodriguez	.65
145	Tony Batista	.10
146	Jose Cruz Jr.	.10
147	Carlos Delgado	.50
148	Brad Fullmer	.10
149	Shannon Stewart	.10
150	David Wells	.10
151	Juan Alvarez, Jeff DaVanon	6.00
152	Seth Etherton, Adam Kennedy	4.00
153	Ramon Ortiz, Lou Pote	4.00
154	Derrick Turnbow RC, Eric Weaver	4.00
155	Rod Barajas, Jason Conti	4.00
156	Byung-Hyun Kim, Rob Ryan	4.00
157	David Cortes, George Lombard	4.00
158	Ivanon Coffie, Melvin Mora	4.00
159	Ryan Kohlmeier RC, Luis Matos RC	6.00
160	Willie Morales, John Parrish RC	4.00
161	Chris Richard RC, Jay Spurgeon RC	5.00
162	Israel Alcantara, Tomokazu Ohka RC	5.00
163	Paxton Crawford RC, Sang-Hoon Lee RC	4.00
164	Mike Mahoney RC, Wilton Veras	4.00
165	Daniel Garibay RC, Ross Gload RC	4.00
166	Gary Matthews Jr., Phil Norton	4.00
167	Roosevelt Brown, Ruben Quevedo	4.00
168	Lorenzo Barcelo RC, Rocky Biddle RC	4.00
169	Mark Buehrle RC, John Garland	8.00
170	Aaron Myette, Josh Paul	4.00
171	Kip Wells, Kelly Wunsch	4.00
172	Rob Bell, Travis Dawkins	4.00
173	Hector Mercado RC, John Riedling RC	4.00
174	Russell Branyan, Sean DePaula	4.00
175	Tim Drew, Mark Watson	4.00
176	Craig House RC, Ben Petrick	5.00
177	Robert Fick, Jose Macias	4.00
178	Javier Cardona RC, Brandon Villafuerte	4.00
179	Armando Almanza, A.J. Burnett	4.00
180	Ramon Castro, Pablo Ozuna	4.00
181	Lance Berkman, Jason Green	4.00
182	Julio Lugo, Tony McKnight	4.00
183	Mitch Meluskey, Wade Miller	4.00
184	Chad Durbin RC, Hector Ortiz RC	5.00
185	Dermal Brown, Mark Quinn	4.00
186	Eric Gagne, Mike Judd	4.00
187	Kane Davis RC, Valerio de los Santos	4.00
188	Santiago Perez, Paul Rigdon RC	4.00
189	Matt Kinney, Matt LeCroy	4.00
190	Jason Maxwell, A.J. Pierzynski	4.00
191	J.C. Romero RC, Johan Santana RC	50.00
192	Tony Armas Jr., Peter Bergeron	4.00
193	Matt Blank, Milton Bradley	4.00
194	Tomas De la Rossa, Scott Forster	4.00
195	Yovanny Lara RC, Talmadge Nunnari RC	4.00
196	Brian Schneider, Andy Tracy	4.00
197	Scott Strickland, T.J. Tucker	4.00
198	Eric Cammack, Jim Mann RC	4.00
199	Grant Roberts, Jorge Toca	4.00
200	Alfonso Soriano, Jay Tessmer	8.00
201	Terrence Long, Mark Mulder	4.00
202	Pat Burrell, Cliff Politte	4.00
203	Jimmy Anderson, Bronson Arroyo	4.00
204	Mike Darr, Kory DeHaan	4.00
205	Adam Eaton, Wiki Gonzalez	4.00
206	Brandon Kolb RC, Kevin Walker	4.00
207	Damon Minor, Calvin Murray	4.00
208	Kevin Hodges, Joel Pineiro RC	40.00
209	Rob Ramsay RC, Kazuhiro Sasaki RC	8.00

#	Player	Price
210	Rick Ankiel, Mike Matthews	4.00
211	Steve Cox, Travis Harper	4.00
212	Kenny Kelly RC, Damian Rolls RC	4.00
213	Doug Davis, Scott Sheldon	4.00
214	Brian Sikorski, Pedro Valdes	4.00
215	Francisco Cordero, B.J. Waszgis	4.00
216	Matt DeWitt, Josh Phelps RC	8.00
217	Vernon Wells, Dewayne Wise	4.00
218	Geraldo Guzman RC, Jason Marquis	4.00
219	Rafael Furcal, Steve Sisco RC	4.00
220	B.J. Ryan, Kevin Beirne	4.00
221	Matt Ginter RC, Brad Penny	4.00
222	Julio Zuleta RC, Eric Munson	5.00
223	Dan Reichert, Jeff Williams	4.00
224	Jason LaRue, Danny Ardoin	4.00
225	Ray King, Mark Redman	4.00
226	Joe Crede, Mike Bell	4.00
227	Juan Pierre RC, Jay Payton	6.00
228	Wayne Franklin, Randy Choate RC	4.00
229	Chris Truby, Adam Piatt	4.00
230	Kevin Nicholson, Chris Woodward	4.00
231	Barry Zito RC, Jason Boyd	15.00
232	Brian O'Connor RC, Miguel Del Toro	4.00
233	Carlos Guillen, Aubrey Huff	4.00
234	Chad Hermansen, Jason Tyner	4.00
235	Aaron Fultz, Ryan Vogelsong	4.00
236	Shawn Wooten, Vance Wilson	4.00
237	Danny Klassen, Mike Lamb	4.00
238	Chad Bradford, Gene Stechschulte RC	4.00
239	Ismael Villegas, Hector Ramirez	4.00
240	Matt T. Williams, Luis Vizcaino, Mike Garcia, Domingo Guzman, Justin Brunette RC, Pasqual Coco RC	4.00
241	Frank Charles, Keith McDonald RC	4.00
242	Carlos Casimiro RC, Morgan Burkhart RC	4.00
243	Raul Gonzalez RC, Shawn Gilbert	4.00
244	Darrell Einertson, Jeff Sparks RC	4.00
245	Augie Ojeda RC, Brady Clark, Todd Belitz, Eric Byrnes RC	6.00
246	Leo Estrella RC, Charlie Greene	4.00
247	Trace Coquillette, Pedro Feliz RC	6.00
248	Tike Redman RC, David Newhan	4.00
249	Rodrigo Lopez RC, John Bales	6.00
250	Corey Patterson, Jose Ortiz RC	6.00
251	Britt Reames RC, Oswaldo Mairena RC	4.00
252	Xavier Nady RC, Timoniel Perez RC	6.00
253	Tom Jacquez, Vicente Padilla	4.00
254	Elvis Pena RC, Adam Melhuse RC	4.00
255	Ben Weber, Alex Cabrera RC	6.00

Gold

Stars (1-150):   4-8X
Production 120 Sets

Platinum Blue

Stars (1-150):   6-10X
Production 55 Sets

Premiere Date

Stars (1-150):   4-8X
Production 77 Sets

AL Contenders

		NM/M
Complete Set (18):		20.00
Common Player:		.50
Inserted 2:37		
1	Darin Erstad	.75
2	Troy Glaus	1.50
3	Mo Vaughn	.50
4	Albert Belle	.50
5	Cal Ripken Jr.	4.00
6	Nomar Garciaparra	3.00
7	Pedro Martinez	1.50
8	Frank Thomas	1.50
9	Manny Ramirez	1.50
10	Jim Thome	1.25
11	Juan Gonzalez	1.50
12	Roger Clemens	2.50
13	Derek Jeter	4.00
14	Bernie Williams	.75
15	Jason Giambi	1.00
16	Alex Rodriguez	3.50
17	Edgar Martinez	.50
18	Carlos Delgado	1.00

EO Portraits

		NM/M
Complete Set (20):		125.00
Common Player:		3.00
Inserted 1:73		
1-of-1 die-cut parallels exist.		
1	Chipper Jones	8.00
2	Greg Maddux	8.00
3	Cal Ripken Jr.	15.00
4	Pedro Martinez	6.00
5	Nomar Garciaparra	10.00
6	Sammy Sosa	10.00
7	Frank Thomas	6.00
8	Ken Griffey Jr.	10.00
9	Gary Sheffield	4.00
10	Vladimir Guerrero	6.00
11	Mike Piazza	6.00
12	Roger Clemens	9.00
13	Derek Jeter	15.00
14	Pat Burrell	3.00
15	Tony Gwynn	8.00
16	Barry Bonds	15.00
17	Alex Rodriguez	12.00
18	Rick Ankiel	3.00
19	Mark McGwire	12.00
20	Ivan Rodriguez	6.00

Full Court

	NM/M
Complete Set (36):	30.00
Common Player:	.50
Inserted 4:37 H	

Copper

Stars (1-150):   8-15X
Production 45 Sets

#	Player	Price
1	Magglio Ordonez	.50
2	Manny Ramirez	1.50
3	Todd Helton	1.50
4	David Justice	.50
5	Bernie Williams	.50
6	Jason Giambi	1.00
7	Scott Rolen	1.00
8	Jeff Kent	.50
9	Edgar Martinez	.50
10	Randy Johnson	1.50
11	Greg Maddux	2.00
12	Mike Mussina	.60
13	Pedro Martinez	1.50
14	Chuck Finley	.50
15	Kevin Brown	.50
16	Roger Clemens	2.25
17	Tim Hudson	.50
18	Rick Ankiel	.50
19	Troy Glaus	1.50
20	Chipper Jones	2.00
21	Nomar Garciaparra	2.50
22	Jeff Bagwell	1.50
23	Shawn Green	.60
24	Vladimir Guerrero	1.50
25	Mike Piazza	2.50
26	Jim Edmonds	.50
27	Rafael Palmeiro	.75
28	Cal Ripken Jr.	4.00
29	Sammy Sosa	2.50
30	Frank Thomas	1.50
31	Ken Griffey Jr.	2.50
32	Gary Sheffield	.50
33	Barry Bonds	4.00
34	Alex Rodriguez	3.00
35	Mark McGwire	3.00
36	Carlos Delgado	1.00

MLB Generations

		NM/M
Complete Set (20):		100.00
Common Card:		3.00
Inserted 1:145		
1	Mark McGwire, Pat Burrell	12.00
2	Cal Ripken Jr., Alex Rodriguez	15.00
3	Randy Johnson, Rick Ankiel	6.00
4	Tony Gwynn, Darin Erstad	8.00
5	Barry Bonds, Magglio Ordonez	15.00
6	Frank Thomas, Jason Giambi	6.00
7	Roger Clemens, Kerry Wood	10.00
8	Mike Piazza, Mitch Meluskey	10.00
9	Ken Griffey Jr., Andruw Jones	10.00
10	Bernie Williams, J.D. Drew	4.00
11	Chipper Jones, Troy Glaus	8.00
12	Andres Galarraga, Todd Helton	6.00
13	Juan Gonzalez, Vladimir Guerrero	6.00
14	Craig Biggio, Rafael Furcal	3.00
15	Sammy Sosa, Jermaine Dye	10.00
16	Larry Walker, Richard Hidalgo	3.00
17	Greg Maddux, Adam Eaton	8.00
18	Barry Larkin, Derek Jeter	15.00
19	Roberto Alomar, Jose Vidro	4.00
20	Jeff Kent, Edgardo Alfonzo	3.00

NL Contenders

		NM/M
Complete Set (18):		20.00
Common Player:		.50
Inserted 2:37		

#	Player	Price
1	Randy Johnson	1.50
2	Chipper Jones	2.00
3	Greg Maddux	2.00
4	Sammy Sosa	2.50
5	Sean Casey	.50
6	Ken Griffey Jr.	2.50
7	Todd Helton	1.50
8	Jeff Bagwell	1.50
9	Shawn Green	.50
10	Gary Sheffield	.75
11	Vladimir Guerrero	1.50
12	Mike Piazza	2.50
13	Scott Rolen	1.00
14	Barry Bonds	4.00
15	Rick Ankiel	.50
16	J.D. Drew	.50
17	Jim Edmonds	.50
18	Mark McGwire	3.00

Signatures

		NM/M
Common Player:		5.00
1	Darin Erstad	10.00
2	Nomar Garciaparra	125.00
3	Cal Eldred	5.00
4	Magglio Ordonez	10.00
5	Frank Thomas	30.00
6	Brady Clark	5.00
7	Richard Hidalgo	5.00
8	Gary Sheffield	10.00
9	Pat Burrell	15.00
10	Jim Edmonds	10.00

Stellar Performers

		NM/M
Complete Set (20):		50.00
Common Player:		1.00
Inserted 1:37		
1	Darin Erstad	1.00
2	Chipper Jones	3.00
3	Greg Maddux	3.00
4	Cal Ripken Jr.	6.00
5	Pedro Martinez	2.00
6	Nomar Garciaparra	4.00
7	Sammy Sosa	4.00
8	Frank Thomas	3.00
9	Ken Griffey Jr.	4.00
10	Todd Helton	2.00
11	Jeff Bagwell	2.00
12	Vladimir Guerrero	3.00
13	Mike Piazza	4.00
14	Derek Jeter	6.00
15	Roger Clemens	3.50
16	Tony Gwynn	3.00
17	Barry Bonds	6.00
18	Alex Rodriguez	5.00
19	Mark McGwire	5.00
20	Ivan Rodriguez	1.50

Opening Day 2K

As part of a multi-manufacturer promotion, Pacific issued eight cards of an "Opening Day 2K" set. Packages containing some of the 32 cards in the issue were distributed by MLB teams early in the season. The cards were also available exclusively as inserts in Pacific Crown Collection and Pacific Aurora packs sold at K-Mart stores early in the season. The Pacific OD2K cards have gold-foil graphic highlights on front. Backs have a portrait photo and are numbered with an "OD" prefix.

		NM/M
Complete Set (8):		4.00
Common Player:		.50
25	Mo Vaughn	.50
26	Chipper Jones	1.00
27	Nomar Garciaparra	1.00
28	Larry Walker	.65
29	Corey Koskie	.50
30	Scott Rolen	.75
31	Tony Gwynn	1.00
32	Jose Canseco	.65

2000 Pacific Paramount Sample

Nearly identical to the issued version of spokesman Tony Gwynn's card, this features a large white diagonal "SAMPLE" overprint on back and in the space where a card number usually appears.

	NM/M
Tony Gwynn	3.00

2000 Pacific Paramount

		NM/M
Complete Set (250):		25.00
Common Player:		.10
Pack (6):		1.50
Wax Box (36):		40.00
1	Garret Anderson	.10
2	Jim Edmonds	.10
3	Darin Erstad	.25
4	Chuck Finley	.10
5	Troy Glaus	.75
6	Troy Percival	.10
7	Tim Salmon	.20
8	Mo Vaughn	.10
9	Jay Bell	.10
10	Erubiel Durazo	.10
11	Steve Finley	.10
12	Luis Gonzalez	.20
13	Randy Johnson	.75
14	Travis Lee	.10
15	Matt Mantei	.10
16	Matt Williams	.10
17	Tony Womack	.10
18	Bret Boone	.10
19	Tom Glavine	.35
20	Andruw Jones	.75
21	Chipper Jones	1.00
22	Brian Jordan	.10
23	Javy Lopez	.10
24	Greg Maddux	1.00
25	Kevin Millwood	.10
26	John Rocker	.10
27	John Smoltz	.10
28	Brady Anderson	.10
29	Albert Belle	.10
30	Will Clark	.20
31	Charles Johnson	.10
32	Mike Mussina	.35
33	Cal Ripken Jr.	2.00
34	B.J. Surhoff	.10
35	Nomar Garciaparra	1.25
36	Derek Lowe	.10
37	Pedro Martinez	.75
38	Trot Nixon	.10
39	Troy O'Leary	.10
40	Jose Offerman	.10
41	John Valentin	.10
42	Jason Varitek	.10
43	Mark Grace	.20
44	Glenallen Hill	.10
45	Jon Lieber	.10
46	Cole Liniak	.10
47	Jose Nieves	.10
48	Henry Rodriguez	.10
49	Sammy Sosa	1.25
50	Kerry Wood	.65
51	Jason Dellaero	.10
52	Ray Durham	.10
53	Paul Konerko	.10
54	Carlos Lee	.10
55	Greg Norton	.10
56	Magglio Ordonez	.10
57	Chris Singleton	.10
58	Frank Thomas	.75
59	Aaron Boone	.10
60	Mike Cameron	.10
61	Sean Casey	.20
62	Pete Harnisch	.10
63	Barry Larkin	.10
64	Pokey Reese	.10
65	Greg Vaughn	.10
66	Scott Williamson	.10
67	Roberto Alomar	.35
68	Sean DePaula RC	.20
69	Travis Fryman	.10
70	David Justice	.10
71	Kenny Lofton	.10
72	Manny Ramirez	.75
73	Richie Sexson	.10
74	Jim Thome	.65
75	Omar Vizquel	.10
76	Pedro Astacio	.10
77	Vinny Castilla	.10
78	Derrick Gibson	.10
79	Todd Helton	.75
80	Neifi Perez	.10
81	Ben Petrick	.10
82	Larry Walker	.10
83	Brad Ausmus	.10
84	Tony Clark	.10
85	Deivi Cruz	.10
86	Damion Easley	.10
87	Juan Encarnacion	.10
88	Juan Gonzalez	.75
89	Bobby Higginson	.10
90	Dave Mlicki	.10
91	Dean Palmer	.10
92	Bruce Aven	.10
93	Luis Castillo	.10
94	Ramon Castro	.10
95	Cliff Floyd	.10
96	Alex Gonzalez	.10
97	Mike Lowell	.10
98	Preston Wilson	.10
99	Jeff Bagwell	.75
100	Derek Bell	.10
101	Craig Biggio	.35
102	Ken Caminiti	.10
103	Carl Everett	.10
104	Mike Hampton	.10
105	Jose Lima	.10
106	Billy Wagner	.10
107	Daryle Ward	.10
108	Carlos Beltran	.40
109	Johnny Damon	.25
110	Jermaine Dye	.10
111	Carlos Febles	.10
112	Mark Quinn	.10
113	Joe Randa	.10
114	Jose Rosado	.10
115	Mike Sweeney	.10
116	Kevin Brown	.10
117	Shawn Green	.35
118	Mark Grudzielanek	.10
119	Todd Hollandsworth	.10
120	Eric Karros	.10
121	Chan Ho Park	.10
122	Gary Sheffield	.35
123	Devon White	.10
124	Eric Young	.10
125	Kevin Barker	.10
126	Ron Belliard	.10
127	Jeromy Burnitz	.10
128	Jeff Cirillo	.10
129	Marquis Grissom	.10
130	Geoff Jenkins	.10
131	David Nilsson	.10
132	Chad Allen	.10
133	Ron Coomer	.10
134	Jacque Jones	.10
135	Corey Koskie	.10
136	Matt Lawton	.10
137	Brad Radke	.10
138	Todd Walker	.10
139	Michael Barrett	.10
140	Peter Bergeron	.10
141	Brad Fullmer	.10
142	Vladimir Guerrero	.75
143	Ugueth Urbina	.10
144	Jose Vidro	.10
145	Rondell White	.10
146	Edgardo Alfonzo	.10
147	Armando Benitez	.10
148	Roger Cedeno	.10
149	Rickey Henderson	.75
150	Melvin Mora	.10
151	John Olerud	.10
152	Rey Ordonez	.10
153	Mike Piazza	1.25
154	Jorge Toca	.10
155	Robin Ventura	.10
156	Roger Clemens	1.00
157	David Cone	.10
158	Orlando Hernandez	.10
159	Derek Jeter	2.00
160	Chuck Knoblauch	.10
161	Ricky Ledee	.10
162	Tino Martinez	.10
163	Paul O'Neill	.10
164	Mariano Rivera	.20
165	Alfonso Soriano	.75
166	Bernie Williams	.25
167	Eric Chavez	.25
168	Jason Giambi	.50
169	Ben Grieve	.10
170	Tim Hudson	.25
171	John Jaha	.10
172	Matt Stairs	.10
173	Miguel Tejada	.25
174	Randy Velarde	.10
175	Bobby Abreu	.10
176	Marlon Anderson	.10
177	Rico Brogna	.10
178	Ron Gant	.10
179	Doug Glanville	.10
180	Mike Lieberthal	.10
181	Scott Rolen	.65
182	Curt Schilling	.35
183	Brian Giles	.10
184	Chad Hermansen	.10
185	Jason Kendall	.10
186	Al Martin	.10
187	Pat Meares	.10
188	Warren Morris	.10
189	Ed Sprague	.10
190	Kevin Young	.10
191	Rick Ankiel	.25
192	Kent Bottenfield	.10
193	Eric Davis	.10
194	J.D. Drew	.25
195	Adam Kennedy	.10
196	Ray Lankford	.10
197	Joe McEwing	.10
198	Mark McGwire	1.50
199	Edgar Renteria	.10
200	Fernando Tatis	.10
201	Mike Darr	.10
202	Ben Davis	.10
203	Tony Gwynn	1.00
204	Trevor Hoffman	.10
205	Damian Jackson	.10
206	Phil Nevin	.10
207	Reggie Sanders	.10
208	Quilvio Veras	.10
209	Rich Aurilia	.10
210	Marvin Benard	.10
211	Barry Bonds	2.00
212	Ellis Burks	.10
213	Livan Hernandez	.10
214	Jeff Kent	.10
215	Russ Ortiz	.10
216	J.T. Snow	.10
217	Paul Abbott	.10
218	David Bell	.10
219	Freddy Garcia	.10
220	Ken Griffey Jr.	1.50
221	Carlos Guillen	.10
222	Brian Hunter	.10
223	Edgar Martinez	.10
224	Jamie Moyer	.10
225	Alex Rodriguez	1.50
226	Wade Boggs	1.00
227	Miguel Cairo	.10
228	Jose Canseco	.40
229	Roberto Hernandez	.10
230	Dave Martinez	.10
231	Quinton McCracken	.10
232	Fred McGriff	.10
233	Kevin Stocker	.10
234	Royce Clayton	.10
235	Rusty Greer	.10
236	Ruben Mateo	.10
237	Rafael Palmeiro	.65
238	Ivan Rodriguez	.65
239	Aaron Sele	.10
240	John Wetteland	.10
241	Todd Zeile	.10
242	Tony Batista	.10
243	Homer Bush	.10
244	Carlos Delgado	.50
245	Tony Fernandez	.10
246	Billy Koch	.10
247	Raul Mondesi	.10
248	Shannon Stewart	.10
249	David Wells	.10
250	Vernon Wells	.10

Copper
Stars: 2X
Inserted 1:1 H

Emerald
Stars: 1-2X
Yng Stars & RC's: 1X
Inserted 1:1 7-11 pack.

Gold
Inserted 1:1 R
Stars: 1-2X
Yng Stars & RC's: 1X

Holographic Gold
Stars: 3-6X
Production 199 Sets

Holographic Green
Stars: 6-10X
Production 99 Sets, 7-11 insert.

Holographic Silver

Stars: 5-10X
Production 99 Sets

Platinum Blue
Stars: 6-12X
Production 67 Sets

Premiere Date
Stars: 8-15X
Production 50 Sets

Ruby Red
Stars: 1-2X
RC's: 1X
Inserted 9 per 7-11 pack.

Cooperstown Bound

		NM/M
Complete Set (10):		220.00
Common Player:		20.00
Inserted 1:361		
Proofs:		2X
Production 20 Sets, hobby only.		
Canvas Proofs: Values Undetermined		
Production One Set		
1	Greg Maddux	20.00
2	Cal Ripken Jr.	40.00
3	Nomar Garciaparra	25.00
4	Sammy Sosa	25.00
5	Roger Clemens	30.00
6	Derek Jeter	40.00
7	Mark McGwire	30.00
8	Tony Gwynn	30.00
9	Ken Griffey Jr.	25.00
10	Alex Rodriguez	30.00

Double Vision

		NM/M
Complete Set (36):		220.00
Common Player:		3.00
Inserted 1:37		
1	Chipper Jones	8.00
2	Cal Ripken Jr.	15.00
3	Nomar Garciaparra	10.00
4	Pedro Martinez	6.00
5	Sammy Sosa	10.00
6	Manny Ramirez	6.00
7	Jeff Bagwell	6.00
8	Craig Biggio	3.00
9	Vladimir Guerrero	6.00
10	Mike Piazza	10.00
11	Roger Clemens	9.00
12	Derek Jeter	15.00
13	Mark McGwire	12.00
14	Tony Gwynn	8.00
15	Ken Griffey Jr.	10.00
16	Alex Rodriguez	12.00
17	Rafael Palmeiro	5.00
18	Ivan Rodriguez	5.00
19	Chipper Jones	8.00
20	Cal Ripken Jr.	15.00
21	Nomar Garciaparra	10.00
22	Pedro Martinez	6.00
23	Sammy Sosa	10.00
24	Manny Ramirez	6.00
25	Jeff Bagwell	6.00
26	Craig Biggio	3.00
27	Vladimir Guerrero	6.00
28	Mike Piazza	10.00
29	Roger Clemens	9.00
30	Derek Jeter	15.00
31	Mark McGwire	12.00
32	Tony Gwynn	8.00
33	Ken Griffey Jr.	10.00
34	Alex Rodriguez	12.00
35	Rafael Palmeiro	5.00
36	Ivan Rodriguez	5.00

Fielder's Choice

		NM/M
Complete Set (20):		150.00
Common Player:		3.00
Inserted 1:73		
Gold Parallel (10 Sets issued):		6-8X
1	Andruw Jones	5.00
2	Chipper Jones	8.00
3	Greg Maddux	8.00
4	Cal Ripken Jr.	20.00
5	Nomar Garciaparra	10.00
6	Sammy Sosa	10.00
7	Sean Casey	3.00
8	Manny Ramirez	5.00
9	Larry Walker	3.00
10	Jeff Bagwell	5.00
11	Mike Piazza	10.00
12	Derek Jeter	20.00
13	Bernie Williams	3.00
14	Scott Rolen	4.00
15	Mark McGwire	15.00
16	Tony Gwynn	8.00
17	Barry Bonds	20.00
18	Ken Griffey Jr.	10.00
19	Alex Rodriguez	15.00
20	Ivan Rodriguez	4.00

Maximum Impact

		NM/M
Complete Set (20):		25.00
Common Player:		.50
Inserted 2:25 7-11 packs.		
1	Chipper Jones	2.00
2	Cal Ripken Jr.	4.00
3	Nomar Garciaparra	2.50
4	Pedro Martinez	1.50
5	Sammy Sosa	2.50
6	Manny Ramirez	1.50
7	Larry Walker	.50
8	Jeff Bagwell	1.50
9	Carlos Beltran	.75
10	Vladimir Guerrero	1.50
11	Mike Piazza	2.50
12	Derek Jeter	4.00
13	Roger Clemens	2.25
14	Mark McGwire	3.00
15	Tony Gwynn	2.00
16	Barry Bonds	4.00
17	Ken Griffey Jr.	2.50
18	Alex Rodriguez	3.00
19	Ivan Rodriguez	1.00
20	Carlos Delgado	.75

Season in Review

		NM/M
Complete Set (30):		25.00
Common Player:		.50
Inserted 2:37		
1	Randy Johnson	1.50
2	Matt Williams	.50
3	Chipper Jones	2.00
4	Greg Maddux	2.00
5	Cal Ripken Jr.	4.00
6	Nomar Garciaparra	2.50
7	Pedro Martinez	1.50
8	Sammy Sosa	2.50
9	Manny Ramirez	1.50
10	Larry Walker	.50
11	Jeff Bagwell	1.50
12	Craig Biggio	.50
13	Carlos Beltran	.75
14	Mark Quinn	.50
15	Vladimir Guerrero	1.50
16	Mike Piazza	2.50
17	Robin Ventura	.50
18	Roger Clemens	2.25
19	David Cone	.50
20	Derek Jeter	4.00
21	Mark McGwire	3.00
22	Fernando Tatis	.50
23	Tony Gwynn	2.00
24	Barry Bonds	4.00
25	Ken Griffey Jr.	2.50
26	Alex Rodriguez	3.00
27	Wade Boggs	2.00
28	Jose Canseco	.65
29	Rafael Palmeiro	1.00
30	Ivan Rodriguez	1.00

Update

		NM/M
Complete Set (100):		10.00
Common Player:		.10
Production 12,500 Sets; retail exclusive		
1-U	Adam Kennedy	.10
2-U	Bengie Molina	.10
3-U	Derrick Turnbow	.10
4-U	Randy Johnson	.75
5-U	Danny Klassen	.10
6-U	Vicente Padilla	.10
7-U	Rafael Furcal	.10
8-U	Andres Galarraga	.10
9-U	Chipper Jones	1.00
10-U	Fernando Lunar	.10
11-U	Willie Morales	.10
12-U	Cal Ripken Jr.	2.00
13-U	B.J. Ryan	.10
14-U	Carl Everett	.10
15-U	Nomar Garciaparra	1.25
16-U	Pedro Martinez	.75
17-U	Wilton Veras	.10
18-U	Scott Downs	.10
19-U	Daniel Garibay	.10
20-U	Sammy Sosa	1.25
21-U	Julio Zuleta	.10
22-U	Josh Paul	.10
23-U	Frank Thomas	.75
24-U	Rob Bell	.10
25-U	Dante Bichette	.10
26-U	Travis Dawkins	.10
27-U	Ken Griffey Jr.	1.25
28-U	Chuck Finley	.10
29-U	Manny Ramirez	.75
30-U	Paul Rigdon	.10
31-U	Jeff Cirillo	.10
32-U	Larry Walker	.75
33-U	Masato Yoshii	.10
34-U	Robert Fick	.10
35-U	Jose Macias	.10
36-U	Juan Gonzalez	.75
37-U	Hideo Nomo	.10
38-U	Jason Grilli	.10
39-U	Pablo Ozuna	.10
40-U	Brad Penny	.75
41-U	Jeff Bagwell	.75
42-U	Lance Berkman	.75

43-U	Roger Cedeno	.10
44-U	Octavio Dotel	.10
45-U	Chad Durbin	.10
46-U	Eric Gagne	.10
47-U	Shawn Green	.35
48-U	Jose Hernandez	.10
49-U	Matt LeCroy	.10
50-U	Johan Santana	.10
51-U	Vladimir Guerrero	.75
52-U	Hideki Irabu	.10
53-U	Andrew Tracy	.10
54-U	Derek Bell	.10
55-U	Eric Cammack	.10
56-U	Mike Hampton	.10
57-U	Jay Payton	.10
58-U	Mike Piazza	1.25
59-U	Todd Zeile	.10
60-U	Roger Clemens	1.00
61-U	Darrell Einertson	.10
62-U	Derek Jeter	2.00
63-U	Jason Giambi	.60
64-U	Terrence Long	.10
65-U	Mark Mulder	.10
66-U	Adam Piatt	.10
67-U	Luis Vizcaino	.10
68-U	Pat Burrell	.35
69-U	Scott Rolen	.65
70-U	Chad Hermansen	.10
71-U	Rick Ankiel	.25
72-U	Jim Edmonds	.10
73-U	Mark McGwire	1.50
74-U	Gene Stechschulte	.10
75-U	Fernando Vina	.10
76-U	Bret Boone	.10
77-U	Tony Gwynn	1.00
78-U	Ryan Klesko	.10
79-U	David Newhan	.10
80-U	Kevin Walker	.10
81-U	Barry Bonds	2.00
82-U	Aaron Fultz	.10
83-U	Ben Weber	.10
84-U	Rickey Henderson	.75
85-U	Kevin Hodges	.10
86-U	John Olerud	.10
87-U	Robert Ramsay	.10
88-U	Alex Rodriguez	1.50
89-U	Kazuhiro Sasaki	.15
90-U	Vinny Castilla	.10
91-U	Jeff Sparks	.10
92-U	Greg Vaughn	.10
93-U	Francisco Cordero	.10
94-U	Gabe Kapler	.10
95-U	Mike Lamb	.10
96-U	Ivan Rodriguez	.65
97-U	Clayton Andrews	.10
98-U	Brad Fullmer	.10
99-U	Raul Mondesi	.10
100-U	Dewayne Wise	.10

2000 Pacific Prism

	NM/M
Complete Set (150):	10.00
Common Player:	.10
Pack (5):	1.50
Wax Box (24):	15.00

1	Jeff DaVanon RC	.10
2	Troy Glaus	.50
3	Tim Salmon	.15
4	Mo Vaughn	.10
5	Jay Bell	.10
6	Erubiel Durazo	.10
7	Luis Gonzalez	.20
8	Randy Johnson	.50
9	Matt Williams	.10
10	Andres Galarraga	.10
11	Andruw Jones	.50
12	Chipper Jones	.75
13	Brian Jordan	.10
14	Greg Maddux	.65
15	Kevin Millwood	.10
16	John Smoltz	.10
17	Albert Belle	.15
18	Mike Mussina	.25
19	Calvin Pickering	.10
20	Cal Ripken Jr.	1.50
21	B.J. Surhoff	.10
22	Nomar Garciaparra	1.00
23	Pedro Martinez	.50
24	Troy O'Leary	.10
25	John Valentin	.10
26	Jason Varitek	.10
27	Mark Grace	.15
28	Henry Rodriguez	.10
29	Sammy Sosa	1.00
30	Kerry Wood	.25
31	Ray Durham	.10
32	Carlos Lee	.10
33	Magglio Ordonez	.10
34	Chris Singleton	.10
35	Frank Thomas	1.00
36	Sean Casey	.15
37	Travis Dawkins	.10
38	Barry Larkin	.10
39	Pokey Reese	.10
40	Scott Williamson	.10
41	Roberto Alomar	.20
42	Bartolo Colon	.10
43	David Justice	.10
44	Manny Ramirez	.50
45	Richie Sexson	.10
46	Jim Thome	.50
47	Omar Vizquel	.10
48	Pedro Astacio	.10
49	Todd Helton	.50
50	Neifi Perez	.10
51	Ben Petrick	.10
52	Larry Walker	.10
53	Tony Clark	.10
54	Damion Easley	.10
55	Juan Gonzalez	.50
56	Dean Palmer	.10
57	A.J. Burnett	.10
58	Luis Castillo	.10
59	Cliff Floyd	.10
60	Alex Gonzalez	.10
61	Preston Wilson	.10
62	Jeff Bagwell	.50
63	Craig Biggio	.50
64	Ken Caminiti	.10
65	Jose Lima	.10
66	Billy Wagner	.10
67	Carlos Beltran	.30
68	Johnny Damon	.25
69	Jermaine Dye	.10
70	Carlos Febles	.10
71	Mike Sweeney	.10
72	Kevin Brown	.10
73	Shawn Green	.25
74	Eric Karros	.10
75	Chan Ho Park	.10
76	Gary Sheffield	.30
77	Ron Belliard	.10
78	Jeromy Burnitz	.10
79	Marquis Grissom	.10
80	Geoff Jenkins	.10
81	Mark Loretta	.10
82	Ron Coomer	.10
83	Jacque Jones	.10
84	Corey Koskie	.10
85	Brad Radke	.10
86	Todd Walker	.10
87	Michael Barrett	.10
88	Peter Bergeron	.10
89	Vladimir Guerrero	.50
90	Jose Vidro	.10
91	Rondell White	.10
92	Edgardo Alfonzo	.10
93	Rickey Henderson	.50
94	Rey Ordonez	.10
95	Mike Piazza	1.00
96	Robin Ventura	.10
97	Roger Clemens	.75
98	Orlando Hernandez	.10
99	Derek Jeter	1.50
100	Tino Martinez	.10
101	Mariano Rivera	.15
102	Alfonso Soriano	.50
103	Bernie Williams	.20
104	Eric Chavez	.15
105	Jason Giambi	.30
106	Ben Grieve	.10
107	Tim Hudson	.20
108	John Jaha	.10
109	Bobby Abreu	.10
110	Doug Glanville	.10
111	Mike Lieberthal	.10
112	Scott Rolen	.40
113	Curt Schilling	.25
114	Brian Giles	.10
115	Jason Kendall	.10
116	Warren Morris	.10
117	Kevin Young	.10
118	Rick Ankiel	.10
119	J.D. Drew	.15
120	Chad Hutchinson	.10
121	Ray Lankford	.10
122	Mark McGwire	1.25
123	Fernando Tatis	.10
124	Bret Boone	.10
125	Ben Davis	.10
126	Tony Gwynn	.65
127	Trevor Hoffman	.10
128	Barry Bonds	1.50
129	Ellis Burks	.10
130	Jeff Kent	.10
131	J.T. Snow	.10
132	Freddy Garcia	.10
133	Ken Griffey Jr.	1.00
134	Edgar Martinez	.10
135	John Olerud	.10
136	Alex Rodriguez	1.25
137	Jose Canseco	.20
138	Vinny Castilla	.10
139	Roberto Hernandez	.10
140	Fred McGriff	.10
141	Rusty Greer	.10
142	Ruben Mateo	.10
143	Rafael Palmeiro	.40
144	Ivan Rodriguez	.40
145	Lee Stevens	.10
146	Tony Batista	.10
147	Carlos Delgado	.35
148	Shannon Stewart	.10
149	David Wells	.10
150	Vernon Wells	.10

Drops Silver

One of eight silver-foil parallels to Prism, this version features a raindrop-like patterned background. Inserted into both hobby and retail packaging, production was reported as 799 of 100 of the cards, and 916 of the other 50 cards (indicated with a (*) in the checklist. The cards are not serially numbered.

		NM/M
Common Player:		.50
Stars:		2-4X
1	Jeff DaVanon RC	.50
2	Troy Glaus	1.00
3	Tim Salmon	.60
4	Mo Vaughn (*)	.50
5	Jay Bell	.50
6	Erubiel Durazo	.50
7	Luis Gonzalez	.50
8	Randy Johnson (*)	1.00
9	Matt Williams (*)	.50
10	Andres Galarraga	.50
11	Andruw Jones (*)	1.00
12	Chipper Jones (*)	1.50
13	Brian Jordan	.50
14	Greg Maddux (*)	1.50
15	Kevin Millwood	.50
16	John Smoltz	.50
17	Albert Belle	.50
18	Mike Mussina (*)	.60
19	Calvin Pickering	.50
20	Cal Ripken Jr. (*)	3.00
21	B.J. Surhoff	.50
22	Nomar Garciaparra (*)	2.00
23	Pedro Martinez (*)	1.00
24	Troy O'Leary	.50
25	John Valentin	.50
26	Jason Varitek	.50
27	Mark Grace	.60
28	Henry Rodriguez	.50
29	Sammy Sosa (*)	2.00
30	Kerry Wood (*)	.65
31	Ray Durham	.50
32	Carlos Lee	.50
33	Magglio Ordonez (*)	.50
34	Chris Singleton	.50
35	Frank Thomas (*)	1.00
36	Sean Casey (*)	.50
37	Travis Dawkins	.50
38	Barry Larkin	.50
39	Pokey Reese	.50
40	Scott Williamson	.50
41	Roberto Alomar (*)	.60
42	Bartolo Colon	.50
43	David Justice	.50
44	Manny Ramirez (*)	1.00
45	Richie Sexson	.50
46	Jim Thome (*)	1.00
47	Omar Vizquel	.50
48	Pedro Astacio	.50
49	Todd Helton (*)	1.00
50	Neifi Perez	.50
51	Ben Petrick	.50
52	Larry Walker (*)	.50
53	Tony Clark	.50
54	Damion Easley	.50
55	Juan Gonzalez (*)	1.00
56	Dean Palmer	.50
57	A.J. Burnett	.50
58	Luis Castillo	.50
59	Cliff Floyd	.50
60	Alex Gonzalez	.50
61	Preston Wilson (*)	.50
62	Jeff Bagwell (*)	1.00
63	Craig Biggio (*)	.50
64	Ken Caminiti	.50
65	Jose Lima	.50
66	Billy Wagner	.50
67	Carlos Beltran (*)	.65
68	Johnny Damon	.65
69	Jermaine Dye	.50
70	Carlos Febles	.50
71	Mike Sweeney	.50
72	Kevin Brown (*)	.50
73	Shawn Green (*)	.75
74	Eric Karros	.50
75	Chan Ho Park	.50
76	Gary Sheffield (*)	.60
77	Ron Belliard	.50
x8	Jeromy Burnitz (*)	.50
79	Marquis Grissom	.50
80	Geoff Jenkins	.50
81	Mark Loretta	.50
82	Ron Coomer	.50
83	Jacque Jones	.50
84	Corey Koskie	.50
85	Brad Radke	.50
86	Todd Walker	.50
87	Michael Barrett	.50
88	Peter Bergeron	.50
89	Vladimir Guerrero (*)	1.00
90	Jose Vidro	.50
91	Rondell White	.50
92	Edgardo Alfonzo (*)	.50
93	Rickey Henderson	1.00
94	Rey Ordonez	.50
95	Mike Piazza (*)	2.00
96	Robin Ventura	.50
97	Roger Clemens (*)	1.75
98	Orlando Hernandez	.50
99	Derek Jeter (*)	3.00
100	Tino Martinez	.50
101	Mariano Rivera	.50
102	Alfonso Soriano	.75
103	Bernie Williams (*)	.60
104	Eric Chavez	.50
105	Jason Giambi	.75
106	Ben Grieve	.50
107	Tim Hudson	.75
108	John Jaha	.50
109	Bobby Abreu	.50
110	Doug Glanville	.50
111	Mike Lieberthal	.50
112	Scott Rolen (*)	.75
113	Curt Schilling	.50
114	Brian Giles (*)	.50
115	Jason Kendall	.50
116	Warren Morris	.50
117	Kevin Young	.50
118	Rick Ankiel (*)	.50
119	J.D. Drew (*)	.60
120	Chad Hutchinson	.50
121	Ray Lankford	.50
122	Mark McGwire (*)	2.50
123	Fernando Tatis	.50
124	Bret Boone	.60
125	Ben Davis	.50
126	Tony Gwynn (*)	1.50
127	Trevor Hoffman	.50
128	Barry Bonds (*)	3.00
129	Ellis Burks	.50
130	Jeff Kent	.50
131	J.T. Snow	.50
132	Freddy Garcia	.50
133	Ken Griffey Jr. (*)	2.00
134	Edgar Martinez	.50
135	John Olerud	.50
136	Alex Rodriguez (*)	2.50
137	Jose Canseco (*)	.60
138	Vinny Castilla	.50
139	Roberto Hernandez	.50
140	Fred McGriff	.50
141	Rusty Greer	.50
142	Ruben Mateo (*)	.50
143	Rafael Palmeiro (*)	.75
144	Ivan Rodriguez (*)	.75
145	Lee Stevens	.50
146	Tony Batista	.50
147	Carlos Delgado (*)	.60
148	Shannon Stewart	.50
149	David Wells	.50
150	Vernon Wells	.50

Holographic Blue

	NM/M
Common Player:	1.00
Stars:	4-6X
Production 80 Sets	

Holographic Gold

	NM/M
Common Player:	.50
Stars:	2-4X
Production 480 Sets	

Holographic Mirror

	NM/M
Common Player:	1.50
Stars:	4-6X
Production 160 Sets	

Holographic Purple

	NM/M
Common Player:	1.00
Stars:	6-8X
Production 99 Sets	

Pebbly Dots

One of eight silver-foil versions of Prism, there is virtually no way to describe the silver metallic

foil background of this parallel set dubbed "Pebbly Dots" by the maker to allow its differentiation from the set labeled "Texture Silver," other than perhaps the vaguely vertical orientation of the texture. Production of 100 of the cards was 691 apiece, with the other 50 cards produced in an edition of 448 each indicated with an (*) in the checklist. They were inserted into both hobby and retail packaging. The cards are not serially numbered.

		NM/M
Complete Set (150):		50.00
Common Player:		.50
1	Jeff DaVanon RC	.50
2	Troy Glaus	.75
3	Tim Salmon	.60
4	Mo Vaughn (*)	.50
5	Jay Bell	.50
6	Erubiel Durazo	.50
7	Luis Gonzalez	.60
8	Randy Johnson (*)	.75
9	Matt Williams (*)	.50
10	Andres Galarraga	.50
11	Andruw Jones (*)	.75
12	Chipper Jones (*)	1.00
13	Brian Jordan	.50
14	Greg Maddux (*)	1.00
15	Kevin Millwood	.50
16	John Smoltz	.50
17	Albert Belle	.50
18	Mike Mussina (*)	.60
19	Calvin Pickering	.50
20	Cal Ripken Jr. (*)	3.00
21	B.J. Surhoff	.50
22	Nomar Garciaparra (*)	2.00
23	Pedro Martinez (*)	.75
24	Troy O'Leary	.50
25	John Valentin	.50
26	Jason Varitek	.60
27	Mark Grace	.50
28	Henry Rodriguez	.50
29	Sammy Sosa (*)	2.00
30	Kerry Wood (*)	.65
31	Ray Durham	.50
32	Carlos Lee	.50
33	Magglio Ordonez (*)	.50
34	Chris Singleton	.50
35	Frank Thomas (*)	.75
36	Sean Casey (*)	.60
37	Travis Dawkins	.50
38	Barry Larkin	.50
39	Pokey Reese	.50
40	Scott Williamson	.50
41	Roberto Alomar (*)	.60
42	Bartolo Colon	.50
43	David Justice	.50
44	Manny Ramirez (*)	.75
45	Richie Sexson	.50
46	Jim Thome (*)	.75
47	Omar Vizquel	.50
48	Pedro Astacio	.50
49	Todd Helton (*)	.75
50	Neifi Perez	.50
51	Ben Petrick	.50
52	Larry Walker (*)	.50
53	Tony Clark	.50
54	Damion Easley	.50
55	Juan Gonzalez (*)	.75
56	Dean Palmer	.50
57	A.J. Burnett	.50
58	Luis Castillo	.50
59	Cliff Floyd	.50
60	Alex Gonzalez	.50
61	Preston Wilson (*)	.50
62	Jeff Bagwell (*)	.75
63	Craig Biggio (*)	.50
64	Ken Caminiti	.50
65	Jose Lima	.50
66	Billy Wagner	.50
67	Carlos Beltran (*)	.65
68	Johnny Damon	.50
69	Jermaine Dye	.50
70	Carlos Febles	.50
71	Mike Sweeney	.50
72	Kevin Brown (*)	.50
73	Shawn Green (*)	.65
74	Eric Karros	.50
75	Chan Ho Park	.50
76	Gary Sheffield (*)	.60
77	Ron Belliard	.50
78	Jeromy Burnitz (*)	.50
79	Marquis Grissom	.50
80	Geoff Jenkins	.50
81	Mark Loretta	.50
82	Ron Coomer	.50
83	Jacque Jones	.50
84	Corey Koskie	.50
85	Brad Radke	.50
86	Todd Walker	.50
87	Michael Barrett	.50
88	Peter Bergeron	.50
89	Vladimir Guerrero (*)	.75
90	Jose Vidro	.50
91	Rondell White	.50
92	Edgardo Alfonzo (*)	.50
93	Rickey Henderson	.75
94	Rey Ordonez	.50
95	Mike Piazza (*)	2.00
96	Robin Ventura	.50
97	Roger Clemens (*)	1.50
98	Orlando Hernandez	.50
99	Derek Jeter (*)	3.00
100	Tino Martinez	.50
101	Mariano Rivera	.50
102	Alfonso Soriano	.65
103	Bernie Williams (*)	.60
104	Eric Chavez	.50
105	Jason Giambi	.50
106	Ben Grieve	.50
107	Tim Hudson	.60
108	John Jaha	.50
109	Bobby Abreu	.50
110	Doug Glanville	.50
111	Mike Lieberthal	.50
112	Scott Rolen (*)	.60
113	Curt Schilling	.50
114	Brian Giles (*)	.50
115	Jason Kendall	.50
116	Warren Morris	.50
117	Kevin Young	.50
118	Rick Ankiel (*)	.50
119	J.D. Drew (*)	.60
120	Chad Hutchinson	.50
121	Ray Lankford	.50
122	Mark McGwire (*)	2.50
123	Fernando Tatis	.50
124	Bret Boone	.50
125	Ben Davis	.50
126	Tony Gwynn (*)	1.00
127	Trevor Hoffman	.50
128	Barry Bonds (*)	3.00
129	Ellis Burks	.50
130	Jeff Kent	.50
131	J.T. Snow	.50
132	Freddy Garcia	.50
133	Ken Griffey Jr. (*)	2.00
134	Edgar Martinez	.50
135	John Olerud	.50
136	Alex Rodriguez (*)	2.50
137	Jose Canseco (*)	.60
138	Vinny Castilla	.50
139	Roberto Hernandez	.50
140	Fred McGriff	.50
141	Rusty Greer	.50
142	Ruben Mateo (*)	.50
143	Rafael Palmeiro (*)	.65
144	Ivan Rodriguez (*)	.65
145	Lee Stevens	.50
146	Tony Batista	.50
147	Carlos Delgado (*)	.60
148	Shannon Stewart	.50
149	David Wells	.50
150	Vernon Wells	.50

Premiere Date

Sixty-one of each card in '00 Prism were embossed with a round seal at center: "PREMIERE DATE / PRISM / 2000 / APR. 12, 2000" and have a dot-matrix serial number at bottom-right on front.

	NM/M
Common Player:	1.50
Stars:	8-10X
Production 61 Sets	

Rapture Gold

This complete-set parallel to Prism, features a diagonally striped metallic gold-foil background. A retail-only insert, 565 sets were produced. The cards are not serially numbered.

Complete Set (150): 50.00
Common Player: .50
Stars: 2-3X

Rapture Silver

One of eight silver-foil parallels to Prism, this version features a diagonally striped background. A hobby-only insert, 916 sets were produced. The cards are not serially numbered.

NM/M
Complete Set (150): 50.00
Common Player: .50
Stars: 2-3X

Sheen Silver

One of eight silver-foil versions of Prism, there is virtually no way to describe the silver metallic foil background of this partial-parallel set dubbed "Sheen Silver" by the maker, other than perhaps the diagonal orientation of the jagged-edged forms. Production was reported as 565 each for cards in the numerical range of #1-40 and #80-110, and 448 each for cards skip-numbered between #42-79 and #111-150. They were inserted into both hobby and retail packaging. The cards are not serially numbered. The 100-card partial-parallel does not include most of the top stars.

NM/M
Complete Set (100): 40.00
Common Player: .50

1	Jeff DaVanon **RC**	.50
3	Troy Glaus	1.50
5	Tim Salmon	.50
6	Jay Bell	.50
7	Erubiel Durazo	.50
10	Luis Gonzalez	.50
13	Andres Galarraga	.50
15	Brian Jordan	.50
16	Kevin Millwood	.50
17	John Smoltz	.50
19	Albert Belle	.50
21	Calvin Pickering	.50
24	B.J. Surhoff	.50
25	Troy O'Leary	.50
26	John Valentin	.50
27	Jason Varitek	.50
	Mark Grace	.50

28	Henry Rodriguez	.50
31	Ray Durham	.50
32	Carlos Lee	.50
34	Chris Singleton	.50
37	Travis Dawkins	.50
38	Barry Larkin	.50
39	Pokey Reese	.50
40	Scott Williamson	.50
42	Bartolo Colon	.50
43	David Justice	.50
45	Richie Sexson	.50
47	Omar Vizquel	.50
48	Pedro Astacio	.50
50	Neifi Perez	.50
51	Ben Petrick	.50
53	Tony Clark	.50
56	Damion Easley	.50
	Dean Palmer	.50
57	A.J. Burnett	.50
58	Luis Castillo	.50
59	Cliff Floyd	.50
60	Alex Gonzalez	.50
64	Ken Caminiti	.50
65	Jose Lima	.50
66	Billy Wagner	.50
68	Johnny Damon	.50
69	Jermaine Dye	.50
70	Carlos Febles	.50
73	Mike Sweeney	.50
74	Eric Karros	.50
74	Chan Ho Park	.50
77	Ron Belliard	.50
79	Marquis Grissom	.50
80	Geoff Jenkins	.50
81	Mark Loretta	.50
82	Ron Coomer	.50
83	Jacque Jones	.50
84	Corey Koskie	.50
85	Brad Radke	.50
86	Todd Walker	.50
87	Michael Barrett	.50
88	Peter Bergeron	.50
90	Jose Vidro	.50
91	Rondell White	.50
93	Rickey Henderson	1.50
94	Rey Ordonez	.50
96	Robin Ventura	.50
98	Orlando Hernandez	.50
100	Tino Martinez	.50
101	Mariano Rivera	.50
102	Alfonso Soriano	1.00
104	Eric Chavez	.50
105	Jason Giambi	1.00
106	Ben Grieve	.50
107	Tim Hudson	.50
108	John Jaha	.50
109	Bobby Abreu	.50
110	Doug Glanville	.50
111	Mike Lieberthal	.50
113	Curt Schilling	.50
115	Jason Kendall	.50
116	Warren Morris	.50
117	Kevin Young	.50
120	Chad Hutchinson	.50
121	Ray Lankford	.50
123	Fernando Tatis	.50
124	Bret Boone	.50
125	Ben Davis	.50
127	Trevor Hoffman	.50
129	Ellis Burks	.50
130	Jeff Kent	.50
131	J.T. Snow	.50
134	Edgar Martinez	.50
135	John Olerud	.50
138	Vinny Castilla	.50
139	Roberto Hernandez	.50
140	Fred McGriff	.50
141	Rusty Greer	.50
145	Lee Stevens	.50
146	Tony Batista	.50
148	Shannon Stewart	.50
149	David Wells	.50
150	Vernon Wells	.50

Slider Silver

One of eight silver-foil versions of Prism, there is virtually no way to describe the silver metallic foil background of this parallel set dubbed "Slider Silver" by the maker, other than perhaps noting the horizontally oriented arrowhead-shaped forms in the background. Production was reported as either 334 each, 448, or 565, depending on press sheet. The number of each card produced is noted parenthetically in this checklist. They were inserted into both hobby and retail packaging. The cards are not serially numbered.

NM/M
Complete Set (150): 50.00
Common Player: .50

1	Jeff DaVanon/334 **RC**	.50
2	Troy Glaus/334	.75
3	Tim Salmon/334	.60
4	Mo Vaughn/565	.50
5	Jay Bell/334	.50
6	Erubiel Durazo/334	.50
7	Luis Gonzalez /334	.60
8	Randy Johnson/565	.75
9	Matt Williams/565	.50
10	Andres Galarraga/334	.50
11	Andruw Jones/565	.75
12	Chipper Jones/565	1.00
13	Brian Jordan/334	.50
14	Greg Maddux/565	1.00
15	Kevin Millwood/334	.50
16	John Smoltz/334	.50
17	Albert Belle/334	.50
18	Mike Mussina/565	.45
19	Calvin Pickering/334	.50
20	Cal Ripken Jr./565	3.00
21	B.J. Surhoff/334	.50
22	Nomar Garciaparra/565	2.00
23	Pedro Martinez/565	.75
24	Troy O'Leary/334	.50
25	John Valentin/334	.50
26	Jason Varitek/334	.50
27	Mark Grace/334	.50
28	Henry Rodriguez/334	.50
29	Sammy Sosa/565	2.00
30	Kerry Wood/565	.60
31	Ray Durham/334	.50
32	Carlos Lee/334	.50
33	Magglio Ordonez/565	.60
34	Chris Singleton/334	.50
35	Frank Thomas/565	.75
36	Sean Casey/565	.60
37	Travis Dawkins/334	.50
38	Barry Larkin/334	.50
39	Pokey Reese/334	.50
40	Scott Williamson/334	.50
41	Roberto Alomar/565	.60
42	Bartolo Colon/448	.50
43	David Justice/448	.50
44	Manny Ramirez /565	.75
45	Richie Sexson/448	.50
46	Jim Thome/565	.65
47	Omar Vizquel/448	.50
48	Pedro Astacio/448	.50
49	Todd Helton/565	.75
50	Neifi Perez/448	.50
51	Ben Petrick/448	.50
52	Larry Walker/565	.50
53	Tony Clark/448	.50
54	Damion Easley/448	.50
55	Juan Gonzalez/565	.75
56	Dean Palmer/448	.50
57	A.J. Burnett/448	.50
58	Luis Castillo/448	.50
59	Cliff Floyd/448	.50
60	Alex Gonzalez/448	.50
61	Preston Wilson/565	.50
62	Jeff Bagwell/565	.75
63	Craig Biggio/565	.50
64	Ken Caminiti/448	.50
65	Jose Lima/448	.50
66	Billy Wagner/448	.50
67	Carlos Beltran/565	.65
68	Johnny Damon/448	.50
69	Jermaine Dye/448	.50
70	Carlos Febles/448	.50
71	Mike Sweeney/448	.50
72	Kevin Brown/565	.50
73	Shawn Green/565	.60
74	Eric Karros/448	.50
75	Chan Ho Park/448	.50
76	Gary Sheffield/565	.50
77	Ron Belliard/334	.50
78	Jeromy Burnitz/565	.50
79	Marquis Grissom/448	.50
80	Geoff Jenkins/334	.50
81	Mark Loretta/334	.50
82	Ron Coomer/334	.50
83	Jacque Jones/334	.50
84	Corey Koskie/334	.50
85	Brad Radke/334	.50
86	Todd Walker/334	.50
87	Michael Barrett/334	.50
88	Peter Bergeron/334	.50
89	Vladimir Guerrero/565	.75
90	Jose Vidro/334	.50
91	Rondell White/334	.50
92	Edgardo Alfonzo/565	.50
93	Rickey Henderson/334	.75
94	Rey Ordonez/334	.50
95	Mike Piazza/565	2.00
96	Robin Ventura/334	.50
97	Roger Clemens/565	1.50
98	Orlando Hernandez/334	.50
99	Derek Jeter/565	3.00
100	Tino Martinez/334	.50
101	Mariano Rivera/334	.50
102	Alfonso Soriano/334	2.00
103	Bernie Williams/334	.60
104	Eric Chavez/334	.50
105	Jason Giambi/334	.75
106	Ben Grieve/334	.50
107	Tim Hudson/334	.60
108	John Jaha/334	.50
109	Bobby Abreu/334	.50
110	Doug Glanville/334	.50
111	Mike Lieberthal/448	.50
112	Scott Rolen/565	.65
113	Curt Schilling/448	.60
114	Brian Giles/565	.50
115	Jason Kendall/448	.50
116	Warren Morris/448	.50
117	Kevin Young/448	.50
118	Rick Ankiel/565	.60
119	J.D. Drew/565	.60
120	Chad Hutchinson/448	.50
121	Ray Lankford/448	.50
122	Mark McGwire/448	2.50
123	Fernando Tatis/448	.50
124	Bret Boone/448	.50
125	Ben Davis/448	.50
126	Tony Gwynn/565	1.00
127	Trevor Hoffman/448	.50
128	Barry Bonds/565	3.00
129	Ellis Burks/448	.50
130	Jeff Kent/448	.50
131	J.T. Snow/448	.50
132	Freddy Garcia/565	.50
133	Ken Griffey Jr./565	2.00
134	Edgar Martinez/448	.50
135	John Olerud/448	.50
136	Alex Rodriguez/565	2.50
137	Jose Canseco/565	.60
138	Vinny Castilla/448	.50
139	Roberto Hernandez/448	.50
140	Fred McGriff/448	.50
141	Rusty Greer/448	.50
142	Ruben Mateo/565	.50
143	Rafael Palmeiro/565	.65
144	Ivan Rodriguez/565	.65
145	Lee Stevens/448	.50
146	Tony Batista/448	.50
147	Carlos Delgado/565	.60
148	Shannon Stewart/448	.50
149	David Wells/448	.50
150	Vernon Wells/448	.50

Texture Silver

One of eight silver-foil versions of Prism, there is virtually no way to describe the silver metallic foil background of this parallel set dubbed "Texture Silver" by the maker to allow its differentiation from the set labeled "Silver Pebbly Drops," other than perhaps the vaguely diagonal orientation of the texture. Production was reported as 448 sets inserted only into retail packaging. The cards are not serially numbered.

NM/M
Complete Set (150): 50.00
Common Player: .50
Stars: 2-3X

Tinsel Silver

One of eight silver-foil parallels to Prism, this version features a horizontally striped background that the makers labeled "Tinsel Silver." Inserted only into hobby packaging, production was reported as 331 sets. The cards are not serially numbered.

NM/M
Complete Set (150): 50.00
Common Player: .50
Stars: 2-3X

Woodgrain Silver

One of eight silver-foil parallels to Prism, this version features

a mottled patterned background which the makers insist resembles woodgrain. Inserted only into retail packaging, production was reported as 331 sets. The cards are not serially numbered.

NM/M
Complete Set (150): 50.00
Common Player: .50
Stars: 2-3X

A.L. Legends

NM/M
Complete Set (10): 15.00
Common Player: .50
Inserted 1:25

1	Mo Vaughn	.50
2	Cal Ripken Jr.	4.00
3	Nomar Garciaparra	2.50
4	Manny Ramirez	1.50
5	Roger Clemens	2.00
6	Derek Jeter	4.00
7	Ken Griffey Jr.	2.50
8	Alex Rodriguez	3.00
9	Jose Canseco	.75
10	Rafael Palmeiro	1.00

Center Stage

NM/M
Complete Set (20): 40.00
Common Player: 1.00
Inserted 1:25

1	Chipper Jones	3.00
2	Cal Ripken Jr.	6.00
3	Nomar Garciaparra	4.00
4	Pedro Martinez	2.00
5	Sammy Sosa	4.00
6	Sean Casey	1.00
7	Manny Ramirez	2.00
8	Jim Thome	1.50
9	Jeff Bagwell	2.00
10	Carlos Beltran	1.50
11	Vladimir Guerrero	2.00
12	Mike Piazza	4.00
13	Derek Jeter	6.00
14	Bernie Williams	1.00
15	Scott Rolen	1.50
16	Mark McGwire	5.00
17	Tony Gwynn	3.00
18	Ken Griffey Jr.	4.00
19	Alex Rodriguez	5.00
20	Ivan Rodriguez	1.50

Diamond Dial-A-Stats

NM/M
Complete Set (10): 90.00
Common Player: 8.00

Inserted 1:193

1	Chipper Jones	8.00
2	Greg Maddux	8.00
3	Cal Ripken Jr.	20.00
4	Sammy Sosa	10.00
5	Mike Piazza	10.00
6	Roger Clemens	9.00
7	Mark McGwire	15.00
8	Tony Gwynn	8.00
9	Ken Griffey Jr.	10.00
10	Alex Rodriguez	15.00

N.L. Legends

NM/M
Complete Set (10): 15.00
Common Player: .50
Inserted 1:25

1	Chipper Jones	2.00
2	Greg Maddux	2.00
3	Sammy Sosa	2.50
4	Larry Walker	.50
5	Jeff Bagwell	1.00
6	Vladimir Guerrero	1.00
7	Mike Piazza	2.50
8	Mark McGwire	3.00
9	Tony Gwynn	2.00
10	Barry Bonds	4.00

Prospects

NM/M
Complete Set (10): 12.00
Common Player: 1.00
Inserted 1:97

1	Erubiel Durazo	1.00
2	Wilton Veras	1.00
3	Ben Petrick	1.00
4	Mark Quinn	1.00
5	Peter Bergeron	1.00
6	Alfonso Soriano	5.00
7	Tim Hudson	2.00
8	Chad Hermansen	1.00
9	Rick Ankiel	1.50
10	Ruben Mateo	1.00

2000 Pacific Private Stock

This base set consists of 150-cards, each card image uses an artist's computer generated brush strokes. Short-printed prospects are seeded 1:4 packs. The logo, player name and team are stamped in gold foil.

NM/M
Complete Set (150): 50.00
Common Player: .15
Common SP Prospect: 1.00
Inserted 1:4
Pack (7): 2.00
Wax Box (24): 35.00

1	Darin Erstad	.25
2	Troy Glaus	.75
3	Tim Salmon	.15
4	Mo Vaughn	.15
5	Jay Bell	.15
6	Luis Gonzalez	.25
7	Randy Johnson	.75

#	Player	Price
8	Matt Williams	.15
9	Andruw Jones	.75
10	Chipper Jones	1.00
11	Brian Jordan	.15
12	Greg Maddux	1.00
13	Kevin Millwood	.15
14	Albert Belle	.20
15	Mike Mussina	.35
16	Cal Ripken Jr.	2.00
17	B.J. Surhoff	.15
18	Nomar Garciaparra	1.25
19	Butch Huskey	.15
20	Pedro Martinez	.75
21	Troy O'Leary	.15
22	Mark Grace	.25
23	Bo Porter/SP	1.00
24	Henry Rodriguez	.15
25	Sammy Sosa	1.25
26	Kerry Wood	.40
27	Jason Dellaero/SP	1.00
28	Ray Durham	.15
29	Paul Konerko	.20
30	Carlos Lee	.15
31	Magglio Ordonez	.25
32	Frank Thomas	.75
33	Mike Cameron	.15
34	Sean Casey	.25
35	Barry Larkin	.15
36	Greg Vaughn	.15
37	Roberto Alomar	.40
38	Russell Branyan/SP	1.00
39	Kenny Lofton	.15
40	Manny Ramirez	.75
41	Richie Sexson	.15
42	Jim Thome	.75
43	Omar Vizquel	.15
44	Dante Bichette	.15
45	Vinny Castilla	.15
46	Todd Helton	.75
47	Ben Petrick/SP	1.00
48	Juan Sosa/SP	1.00
49	Larry Walker	.15
50	Tony Clark	.15
51	Damion Easley	.15
52	Juan Encarnacion	.15
53	Robert Fick/SP	1.00
54	Dean Palmer	.15
55	A.J. Burnett/SP	1.00
56	Luis Castillo	.15
57	Alex Gonzalez	.15
58	Julio Ramirez/SP	1.00
59	Preston Wilson	.15
60	Jeff Bagwell	.75
61	Craig Biggio	.15
62	Ken Caminiti	.15
63	Carl Everett	.15
64	Mike Hampton	.15
65	Billy Wagner	.15
66	Carlos Beltran	.50
67	Dermal Brown/SP	1.00
68	Jermaine Dye	.15
69	Carlos Febles	.15
70	Mark Quinn/SP	1.00
71	Mike Sweeney	.15
72	Kevin Brown	.15
73	Eric Gagne/SP	1.50
74	Eric Karros	.15
75	Raul Mondesi	.15
76	Gary Sheffield	.40
77	Jeromy Burnitz	.15
78	Jeff Cirillo	.15
79	Geoff Jenkins	.15
80	David Nilsson	.15
81	Ron Coomer	.15
82	Jacque Jones	.15
83	Corey Koskie	.15
84	Brad Radke	.15
85	Tony Armas Jr./SP	1.50
86	Peter Bergeron/SP	1.00
87	Vladimir Guerrero	.75
88	Jose Vidro	.15
89	Rondell White	.15
90	Edgardo Alfonzo	.15
91	Roger Cedeno	.15
92	Rickey Henderson	.75
93	Jay Payton/SP	1.00
94	Mike Piazza	1.25
95	Jorge Toca/SP	1.00
96	Robin Ventura	.15
97	Roger Clemens	1.00
98	David Cone	.15
99	Derek Jeter	2.00
100	D'Angelo Jimenez/SP	1.00
101	Tino Martinez	.15
102	Alfonso Soriano/SP	3.00
103	Bernie Williams	.25
104	Jason Giambi	.50
105	Ben Grieve	.15
106	Tim Hudson	.25
107	Matt Stairs	.15
108	Bobby Abreu	.15
109	Doug Glanville	.15
110	Scott Rolen	.65
111	Curt Schilling	.40
112	Brian Giles	.15
113	Chad Hermansen/SP	1.00
114	Jason Kendall	.15
115	Warren Morris	.15
116	Rick Ankiel/SP	1.00
117	J.D. Drew	.25
118	Adam Kennedy/SP	1.00
119	Ray Lankford	.15
120	Mark McGwire	1.50
121	Fernando Tatis	.15
122	Mike Darr/SP	1.00
123	Ben Davis	.15
124	Tony Gwynn	1.00
125	Trevor Hoffman	.15
126	Reggie Sanders	.15
127	Barry Bonds	2.00
128	Ellis Burks	.15
129	Jeff Kent	.15

#	Player	Price
130	J.T. Snow	.15
131	Freddy Garcia	.15
132	Ken Griffey Jr.	1.25
133	Carlos Guillen/SP	1.00
134	Edgar Martinez	.15
135	Alex Rodriguez	1.50
136	Miguel Cairo	.15
137	Jose Canseco	.40
138	Steve Cox/SP	1.00
139	Roberto Hernandez	.15
140	Fred McGriff	.15
141	Juan Gonzalez	.75
142	Rusty Greer	.15
143	Ruben Mateo/SP	1.00
144	Rafael Palmeiro	.65
145	Ivan Rodriguez	.65
146	Carlos Delgado	.50
147	Tony Fernandez	.15
148	Shawn Green	.35
149	Shannon Stewart	.15
150	Vernon Wells/SP	1.00

Gold Portraits

A parallel to the 150-card base set that have a gold foiled border. These are found exclusively in hobby packs and are limited to 99 serial numbered sets.

Stars:	5-10X
Prospects:	1-2X
Production 99 Sets	

Silver Portraits

A parallel to the 150-card base set. These have a silver foiled border. Found exclusively in retail packs, these are limited to 199 serial numbered sets.

Stars:	3-6X
Prospects:	1-2X
Production 199 Sets	

Premiere Date

A parallel to the 150-card base set these are limited to 34 serial numbered sets.

Stars:	5-10X
Prospects:	1-2X
Inserted 1:24	

Canvas

This 20-card set is printed on real artist's canvas and has the look of a miniature piece of art.

		NM/M
Complete Set (20):		120.00
Common Player:		2.00
Inserted 1:49		
1	Chipper Jones	8.00
2	Greg Maddux	8.00
3	Cal Ripken Jr.	15.00
4	Nomar Garciaparra	10.00
5	Sammy Sosa	10.00
6	Frank Thomas	6.00
7	Manny Ramirez	6.00
8	Larry Walker	2.00
9	Jeff Bagwell	6.00
10	Vladimir Guerrero	6.00
11	Mike Piazza	10.00
12	Roger Clemens	9.00
13	Derek Jeter	15.00
14	Mark McGwire	12.00
15	Tony Gwynn	8.00
16	Barry Bonds	15.00
17	Ken Griffey Jr.	10.00
18	Alex Rodriguez	12.00
19	Juan Gonzalez	6.00
20	Ivan Rodriguez	5.00

Extreme Action

The focus of this 20-card set is the action photography, hence the name Extreme Action. They are seeded 2:25 packs.

		NM/M
Complete Set (20):		25.00
Common Player:		.50
Inserted 2:25		
1	Andruw Jones	1.50
2	Chipper Jones	2.00
3	Cal Ripken Jr.	4.00
4	Nomar Garciaparra	2.50
5	Sammy Sosa	2.50
6	Frank Thomas	1.50
7	Roberto Alomar	.60
8	Manny Ramirez	1.50
9	Larry Walker	.50
10	Jeff Bagwell	1.50
11	Vladimir Guerrero	1.50
12	Mike Piazza	2.50
13	Derek Jeter	4.00
14	Bernie Williams	.50
15	Scott Rolen	1.00
16	Mark McGwire	3.00
17	Tony Gwynn	2.00
18	Ken Griffey Jr.	2.50
19	Alex Rodriguez	3.00
20	Ivan Rodriguez	1.00

Reserve

Found exclusively in hobby packs these have a paper thin stock, enhanced with gold foil stamping. These are seeded 1:25 packs.

		NM/M
Complete Set (20):		50.00
Common Player:		1.00
Inserted 1:25		
1	Chipper Jones	3.00
2	Greg Maddux	3.00
3	Cal Ripken Jr.	6.00
4	Nomar Garciaparra	4.00
5	Sammy Sosa	4.00
6	Frank Thomas	2.00
7	Manny Ramirez	2.00
8	Larry Walker	1.00
9	Jeff Bagwell	2.00
10	Vladimir Guerrero	2.00
11	Mike Piazza	4.00
12	Roger Clemens	3.50
13	Derek Jeter	6.00
14	Mark McGwire	5.00
15	Tony Gwynn	3.00
16	Barry Bonds	6.00
17	Ken Griffey Jr.	4.00
18	Alex Rodriguez	5.00
19	Ivan Rodriguez	1.50
20	Shawn Green	1.25

PS-2000

This miniature 60-card set has a white border with gold foil stamping and are seeded two per pack.

		NM/M
Complete Set (60):		15.00
Common Player:		.15
Inserted 2:Pack		
1	Mo Vaughn	.15
2	Greg Maddux	1.00
3	Andruw Jones	.75
4	Chipper Jones	1.00
5	Cal Ripken Jr.	2.50
6	Nomar Garciaparra	1.50
7	Pedro Martinez	.75
8	Sammy Sosa	1.50
9	Jason Dellaero	.15
10	Magglio Ordonez	.15
11	Frank Thomas	.75
12	Sean Casey	.25
13	Russell Branyan	.15
14	Manny Ramirez	.75
15	Richie Sexson	.15
16	Ben Petrick	.15
17	Juan Sosa	.15
18	Larry Walker	.15
19	Robert Fick	.15
20	Craig Biggio	.15
21	Jeff Bagwell	.75
22	Carlos Beltran	.50
23	Dermal Brown	.15
24	Mark Quinn	.15
25	Eric Gagne	.15
26	Jeromy Burnitz	.15
27	Tony Armas Jr.	.15
28	Peter Bergeron	.15
29	Vladimir Guerrero	.75
30	Edgardo Alfonzo	.15
31	Mike Piazza	1.50
32	Jorge Toca	.15
33	Roger Clemens	1.25
34	Alfonso Soriano	.65
35	Bernie Williams	.25
36	Derek Jeter	2.50
37	Tim Hudson	.25
38	Bobby Abreu	.15
39	Scott Rolen	.65
40	Brian Giles	.15
41	Chad Hermansen	.15
42	Warren Morris	.15
43	Rick Ankiel	.25
44	J.D. Drew	.25
45	Adam Kennedy	.15
46	Mark McGwire	2.00
47	Mike Darr	.15
48	Tony Gwynn	1.00
49	Barry Bonds	2.50
50	Ken Griffey Jr.	1.50
51	Carlos Guillen	.15
52	Alex Rodriguez	1.50
53	Juan Gonzalez	.75
54	Ruben Mateo	.15
55	Ivan Rodriguez	.65
56	Rafael Palmeiro	.65
57	Jose Canseco	.40
58	Steve Cox	.15
59	Shawn Green	.30
60	Vernon Wells	.15

PS-2000 New Wave

This miniature 20-card set has copper foil stamping and is limited to 199 serial numbered sets.

		NM/M
Complete Set (20):		40.00
Common Player:		1.00
Production 199 Sets		
1	Andruw Jones	3.50
2	Chipper Jones	5.00
3	Nomar Garciaparra	6.00
4	Magglio Ordonez	1.00
5	Sean Casey	1.00
6	Manny Ramirez	3.50
7	Richie Sexson	1.00

#	Player	Price
15	Tony Gwynn	3.00
16	Barry Bonds	6.00
17	Ken Griffey Jr.	4.00
18	Alex Rodriguez	5.00
19	Ivan Rodriguez	1.50
20	Shawn Green	1.25

8	Carlos Beltran	2.00
9	Jeromy Burnitz	1.00
10	Vladimir Guerrero	3.50
11	Edgardo Alfonzo	1.00
12	Derek Jeter	10.00
13	Tim Hudson	1.00
14	Bobby Abreu	1.00
15	Scott Rolen	2.50
16	Brian Giles	1.00
17	Warren Morris	1.00
18	J.D. Drew	1.25
19	Alex Rodriguez	8.00
20	Shawn Green	1.25

PS-2000 Rookies

This miniature 20-card set has holographic silver foil stamping and is limited to 99 serial numbered sets.

		NM/M
Complete Set (20):		20.00
Common Player:		1.00
Inserted 99 Sets		
1	Jason Dellaero	1.00
2	Russell Branyan	1.00
3	Ben Petrick	1.00
4	Juan Sosa	1.00
5	Robert Fick	1.00
6	Dermal Brown	1.00
7	Mark Quinn	1.00
8	Eric Gagne	1.50
9	Tony Armas Jr.	1.00
10	Peter Bergeron	1.00
11	Jorge Toca	1.00
12	Alfonso Soriano	6.00
13	Chad Hermansen	1.00
14	Rick Ankiel	1.00
15	Adam Kennedy	1.50
16	Mike Darr	1.00
17	Carlos Guillen	1.00
18	Steve Cox	1.00
19	Ruben Mateo	1.00
20	Vernon Wells	1.50

PS-2000 Stars

This miniature 20-card set is limited to 299 serial numbered sets.

		NM/M
Complete Set (20):		40.00
Common Player:		1.00
Production 299 Sets		
1	Mo Vaughn	1.00
2	Greg Maddux	4.00
3	Cal Ripken Jr.	8.00
4	Pedro Martinez	3.00
5	Sammy Sosa	5.00
6	Frank Thomas	3.00
7	Larry Walker	1.00
8	Craig Biggio	1.00
9	Jeff Bagwell	3.00
10	Mike Piazza	5.00
11	Roger Clemens	4.50
12	Bernie Williams	1.00
13	Mark McGwire	6.00
14	Tony Gwynn	3.00
15	Barry Bonds	8.00
16	Ken Griffey Jr.	5.00
17	Juan Gonzalez	3.00
18	Ivan Rodriguez	2.00
19	Rafael Palmeiro	2.00
20	Jose Canseco	1.50

2000 Pacific Revolution

The base set consists of 150 cards with silver holofoil throughout the card front. "Revolution" is embossed on the left portion and the logo is stamped in gold foil. Twenty-five short-printed prospects are seeded 1:4 packs.

		NM/M
Complete Set (150):		60.00
Common Player:		.25
Common SP:		1.00
Pack (3):		2.00
Box:		35.00
1	Darin Erstad	.50
2	Troy Glaus	1.00
3	Adam Kennedy/SP	1.50
4	Mo Vaughn	.25
5	Erubiel Durazo	.25
6	Steve Finley	.25

7	Luis Gonzalez	.35
8	Randy Johnson	1.00
9	Travis Lee	.25
10	Vicente Padilla/SP	1.00
11	Matt Williams	.25
12	Rafael Furcal/SP	1.00
13	Andres Galarraga	.25
14	Andruw Jones	.75
15	Chipper Jones	1.50
16	Greg Maddux	1.50
17	Luis Rivera/SP	1.00
18	Albert Belle	.25
19	Mike Bordick	.35
20	Will Clark	.35
21	Mike Mussina	.40
22	Cal Ripken Jr.	3.00
23	B.J. Surhoff	.25
24	Carl Everett	.25
25	Nomar Garciaparra	2.00
26	Pedro Martinez	1.00
27	Jason Varitek	.25
28	Wilton Veras/SP	1.00
29	Shane Andrews	.25
30	Scott Downs/SP **RC**	1.00
31	Mark Grace	.35
32	Sammy Sosa	2.00
33	Kerry Wood	.50
34	Ray Durham	.25
35	Paul Konerko	.35
36	Carlos Lee	.25
37	Magglio Ordonez	.25
38	Frank Thomas	1.00
39	Rob Bell/SP	1.00
40	Sean Casey	.40
41	Ken Griffey Jr.	2.00
42	Barry Larkin	.25
43	Pokey Reese	.25
44	Roberto Alomar	.40
45	David Justice	.25
46	Kenny Lofton	.25
47	Manny Ramirez	1.00
48	Richie Sexson	.25
49	Jim Thome	1.00
50	Jeff Cirillo	.25
51	Jeffrey Hammonds	.25
52	Todd Helton	1.00
53	Larry Walker	.25
54	Tony Clark	.25
55	Juan Gonzalez	1.00
56	Hideo Nomo	1.00
57	Dean Palmer	.25
58	Alex Gonzalez	.25
59	Mike Lowell	.25
60	Pablo Ozuna/SP	1.00
61	Brad Penny/SP	1.00
62	Preston Wilson	.25
63	Moises Alou	.25
64	Jeff Bagwell	1.00
65	Craig Biggio	.25
66	Ken Caminiti	.25
67	Julio Lugo/SP	1.00
68	Carlos Beltran	.60
69	Johnny Damon	.40
70	Jermaine Dye	.25
71	Carlos Febles	.25
72	Mark Quinn/SP	1.00
73	Kevin Brown	.25
74	Shawn Green	.65
75	Chan Ho Park	.25
76	Gary Sheffield	.50
77	Kevin Barker/SP	1.00
78	Ron Belliard	.25
79	Jeromy Burnitz	.25
80	Geoff Jenkins	.25
81	Cristian Guzman	.25
82	Jacque Jones	.25
83	Corey Koskie	.25
84	Matt Lawton	.25
85	Peter Bergeron/SP	1.00
86	Vladimir Guerrero	1.00
87	Andy Tracy/SP	1.00
88	Jose Vidro	.25
89	Rondell White	.25
90	Edgardo Alfonzo	.25
91	Derek Bell	.25
92	Eric Cammack/SP	1.00
93	Mike Piazza	2.00
94	Robin Ventura	.25
95	Roger Clemens	1.75
96	Orlando Hernandez	.25
97	Derek Jeter	3.00
98	Tino Martinez	.25
99	Alfonso Soriano/SP	3.00
100	Bernie Williams	.35
101	Eric Chavez	.25
102	Jason Giambi	.75
103	Ben Grieve	.25
104	Terrence Long/SP	1.00

105	Mark Mulder/SP	1.00
106	Adam Piatt/SP	1.00
107	Bobby Abreu	.25
108	Rico Brogna	.25
109	Doug Glanville	.25
110	Mike Lieberthal	.25
111	Scott Rolen	.75
112	Brian Giles	.25
113	Chad Hermansen/SP	1.00
114	Jason Kendall	.25
115	Warren Morris	.25
116	Rick Ankiel/SP	1.00
117	J.D. Drew	.40
118	Jim Edmonds	.25
119	Mark McGwire	2.50
120	Fernando Tatis	.25
121	Fernando Vina	.25
122	Tony Gwynn	1.50
123	Trevor Hoffman	.25
124	Ryan Klesko	.25
125	Eric Owens	.25
126	Barry Bonds	3.00
127	Ellis Burks	.25
128	Bobby Estalella	.25
129	Jeff Kent	.25
130	Scott Linebrink/SP **RC**	1.00
131	Jay Buhner	.25
132	Stan Javier	.25
133	Edgar Martinez	.25
134	John Olerud	.25
135	Alex Rodriguez	2.50
136	Kazuhiro Sasaki/SP **RC**	2.00
137	Jose Canseco	.40
138	Vinny Castilla	.25
139	Fred McGriff	.25
140	Greg Vaughn	.25
141	Gabe Kapler	.25
142	Mike Lamb/SP **RC**	1.00
143	Ruben Mateo	.25
144	Rafael Palmeiro	.75
145	Ivan Rodriguez	.75
146	Tony Batista	.25
147	Jose Cruz Jr.	.75
148	Carlos Delgado	.75
149	Brad Fullmer	.25
150	Raul Mondesi	.25

Red

A parallel to the 150-card base set these insert have red foil in place of the gold from the base version. These are also serial numbered on the card front, limited to 299 sets.

Stars:	1-2X
SP's:	1X
Production 299 Sets	

Shadow

This parallel to the 150-card base set replaces the gold foil highlights with blue foil on front and has an embossed box at center which reads "SHADOW SERIES." Backs have a serial number ink-jetted from within an edition of 99 each.

Stars:	3-6X
SP's:	1-2X
Production 99 Sets	

Foul Pole Net-Fusions

These inserts utilize net-fusion technology, with netting infused in the left and right portion. The player name and logo are stamped in gold foil. These are found on the average of 1:49 packs.

		NM/M
Complete Set (20):		110.00
Common Player:		2.00
Inserted 1:49		
1	Chipper Jones	8.00
2	Cal Ripken Jr.	15.00
3	Nomar Garciaparra	10.00
4	Pedro Martinez	6.00

5	Sammy Sosa	10.00
6	Frank Thomas	6.00
7	Ken Griffey Jr.	10.00
8	Manny Ramirez	6.00
9	Jeff Bagwell	6.00
10	Shawn Green	3.00
11	Vladimir Guerrero	6.00
12	Mike Piazza	10.00
13	Derek Jeter	15.00
14	Bernie Williams	2.00
15	Rick Ankiel	4.00
16	Mark McGwire	12.00
17	Tony Gwynn	8.00
18	Barry Bonds	15.00
19	Alex Rodriguez	12.00
20	Ivan Rodriguez	5.00

Game-Ball Signatures

This 25-card autographed set has a piece of baseball leather embedded into the front on which the player penned his signature.

		NM/M
Common Player:		5.00
1	Randy Johnson	40.00
2	Greg Maddux	90.00
3	Rafael Furcal	7.50
4	Shane Andrews	5.00
5	Sean Casey	10.00
6	Travis Dawkins	5.00
7	Alex Gonzalez	5.00
8	Shane Reynolds	5.00
9	Eric Gagne	10.00
10	Kevin Barker	5.00
11	Eric Milton	5.00
12	Mark Quinn	5.00
13	Alfonso Soriano	40.00
14	Brian Giles	6.00
15	Mark Mulder	10.00
16	Adam Piatt	5.00
17	Warren Morris	5.00
18	Rick Ankiel	15.00
19	Adam Kennedy	6.00
20	Fernando Tatis	5.00
21	Barry Bonds	100.00
22	Alex Rodriguez	75.00
23	Ruben Mateo	5.00
24	Billy Koch	5.00
25	Brad Penny	5.00

Icons

These die-cut cards feature silver foil stamping and the player's team logo in the background. These are found on the average of 1:121 packs.

		NM/M
Complete Set (20):		250.00
Common Player:		8.00
Inserted 1:121		
1	Randy Johnson	10.00
2	Chipper Jones	15.00
3	Greg Maddux	15.00
4	Cal Ripken Jr.	30.00
5	Nomar Garciaparra	20.00
6	Pedro Martinez	10.00
7	Sammy Sosa	20.00
8	Frank Thomas	15.00
9	Ken Griffey Jr.	20.00
10	Juan Gonzalez	10.00
11	Jeff Bagwell	10.00
12	Vladimir Guerrero	10.00
13	Mike Piazza	20.00
14	Roger Clemens	17.50
15	Derek Jeter	30.00
16	Mark McGwire	25.00

17	Tony Gwynn	15.00
18	Barry Bonds	30.00
19	Alex Rodriguez	25.00
20	Ivan Rodriguez	8.00

On Deck

These inserts have a die-cut rounded bottom and feature the player in a simulated on-deck circle enhanced by green foil stamping. These are seeded 1:25 packs.

		NM/M
Complete Set (20):		40.00
Common Player:		1.00
Inserted 1:25		
1	Chipper Jones	3.00
2	Cal Ripken Jr.	6.00
3	Nomar Garciaparra	4.00
4	Sammy Sosa	4.00
5	Frank Thomas	4.00
6	Ken Griffey Jr.	4.00
7	Manny Ramirez	2.00
8	Larry Walker	1.00
9	Juan Gonzalez	2.00
10	Jeff Bagwell	2.00
11	Shawn Green	1.50
12	Vladimir Guerrero	2.00
13	Mike Piazza	4.00
14	Derek Jeter	6.00
15	Scott Rolen	1.50
16	Mark McGwire	5.00
17	Tony Gwynn	3.00
18	Alex Rodriguez	5.00
19	Jose Canseco	1.50
20	Ivan Rodriguez	1.75

Season Opener

This 36-card set has a horizontal format with the set name, team logo, player name and Revolution logo stamped in gold foil. These are seeded 2:25 packs.

		NM/M
Complete Set (36):		35.00
Common Player:		.50
Inserted 2:25		
1	Erubiel Durazo	.50
2	Randy Johnson	1.50
3	Andruw Jones	1.50
4	Chipper Jones	2.00
5	Greg Maddux	2.00
6	Cal Ripken Jr.	4.00
7	Nomar Garciaparra	3.00
8	Pedro Martinez	1.50
9	Sammy Sosa	2.50
10	Frank Thomas	1.50
11	Magglio Ordonez	.50
12	Ken Griffey Jr.	2.50
13	Barry Larkin	.50
14	Kenny Lofton	.50
15	Manny Ramirez	1.50
16	Jim Thome	1.50
17	Larry Walker	.50
18	Juan Gonzalez	1.50
19	Jeff Bagwell	1.50
20	Craig Biggio	.50
21	Carlos Beltran	.75
22	Shawn Green	.75
23	Vladimir Guerrero	1.50
24	Mike Piazza	2.50
25	Orlando Hernandez	.50
26	Derek Jeter	4.00
27	Bernie Williams	.50
28	Eric Chavez	.50
29	Scott Rolen	1.00
30	Jim Edmonds	.50
31	Tony Gwynn	2.00
32	Barry Bonds	3.00
33	Alex Rodriguez	3.00
34	Jose Canseco	.65
35	Ivan Rodriguez	1.00
36	Rafael Palmeiro	1.00

17	Tony Gwynn	15.00
18	Barry Bonds	30.00
19	Alex Rodriguez	25.00
20	Ivan Rodriguez	8.00

Triple Header

This 30-card set is broken down into three tiers with cards 1-10 spotlighting batting average leaders, 11-20 home run leaders and 21-30 strikeout leaders. The base versions are seeded 4:25 packs. A parallel version for each of the three groups is also inserted. Cards 1-20 are limited to 99 serial numbered sets while cards 21-30 are limited to 599 serial numbered sets.

		NM/M
Complete Set (30):		25.00
Common Player:		.25
Inserted 4:25		
Parallel (1-10):		3-6X
99 Sets Produced		
Parallel (11-20):		3-6X
99 Sets Produced		
Parallel (21-30):		1-2X
599 Sets Produced		
1	Chipper Jones	1.50
2	Cal Ripken Jr.	3.00
3	Nomar Garciaparra	2.00
4	Frank Thomas	1.00
5	Larry Walker	.25
6	Vladimir Guerrero	1.00
7	Mike Piazza	2.00
8	Derek Jeter	3.00
9	Tony Gwynn	1.50
10	Ivan Rodriguez	.75
11	Sammy Sosa	2.00
12	Ken Griffey Jr.	2.00
13	Manny Ramirez	1.00
14	Jeff Bagwell	1.00
15	Shawn Green	.40
16	Mark McGwire	2.50
17	Barry Bonds	3.00
18	Alex Rodriguez	2.50
19	Jose Canseco	.50
20	Rafael Palmeiro	.75
21	Randy Johnson	1.00
22	Tom Glavine	.40
23	Greg Maddux	1.50
24	Mike Mussina	.40
25	Pedro Martinez	1.00
26	Kerry Wood	.60
27	Chuck Finley	.25
28	Kevin Brown	.25
29	Roger Clemens	1.75
30	Rick Ankiel	.25

2000 Pacific Vanguard Sample

To introduce the hobby to its new Vanguard brand, Pacific issued this card of principal spokesman Tony Gwynn. Using the same "Vision-Glow" technology as the regular-issue cards, the sample has a large white diagonal overprint on back and "SAMPLE" instead of a card number.

	NM/M
Tony Gwynn	3.00

2000 Pacific Vanguard

		NM/M
Complete Set (100):		30.00
Common Player:		.15
Pack (4):		2.00
Wax Box (24):		35.00
1	Troy Glaus	1.00

	RAFAEL PALMEIRO	

2	Tim Salmon	.25
3	Mo Vaughn	.15
4	Albert Belle	.15
5	Mike Mussina	.35
6	Cal Ripken Jr.	3.00
7	Nomar Garciaparra	2.00
8	Pedro Martinez	1.00
9	Troy O'Leary	.15
10	Wilton Veras	.15
11	Magglio Ordonez	.15
12	Chris Singleton	.15
13	Frank Thomas	1.00
14	Roberto Alomar	.40
15	Russell Branyan	.15
16	Manny Ramirez	1.00
17	Jim Thome	.75
18	Omar Vizquel	.15
19	Tony Clark	.15
20	Juan Gonzalez	1.00
21	Dean Palmer	.15
22	Carlos Beltran	.50
23	Johnny Damon	.30
24	Jermaine Dye	.15
25	Mark Quinn	.15
26	Jacque Jones	.15
27	Corey Koskie	.15
28	Brad Radke	.15
29	Roger Clemens	1.75
30	Derek Jeter	3.00
31	Alfonso Soriano	.75
32	Bernie Williams	.30
33	Eric Chavez	.30
34	Jason Giambi	.75
35	Ben Grieve	.15
36	Tim Hudson	.30
37	Mike Cameron	.15
38	Freddy Garcia	.15
39	Edgar Martinez	.15
40	Alex Rodriguez	2.50
41	Jose Canseco	.50
42	Vinny Castilla	.15
43	Fred McGriff	.15
44	Rusty Greer	.15
45	Ruben Mateo	.15
46	Rafael Palmeiro	.75
47	Ivan Rodriguez	.65
48	Carlos Delgado	.75
49	Shannon Stewart	.15
50	Vernon Wells	.15
51	Erubiel Durazo	.15
52	Randy Johnson	1.00
53	Matt Williams	.15
54	Andruw Jones	1.00
55	Chipper Jones	1.50
56	Greg Maddux	1.50
57	Mark Grace	.25
58	Sammy Sosa	2.00
59	Kerry Wood	.50
60	Sean Casey	.25
61	Ken Griffey Jr.	2.00
62	Barry Larkin	.15
63	Todd Helton	1.00
64	Ben Petrick	.15
65	Larry Walker	.15
66	Luis Castillo	.15
67	Alex Gonzalez	.15
68	Preston Wilson	.15
69	Jeff Bagwell	1.00
70	Craig Biggio	.15
71	Billy Wagner	.15
72	Kevin Brown	.15
73	Shawn Green	.40
74	Gary Sheffield	.40
75	Kevin Barker	.15
76	Ron Belliard	.15
77	Jeromy Burnitz	.15
78	Michael Barrett	.15
79	Peter Bergeron	.15
80	Vladimir Guerrero	1.00
81	Edgardo Alfonzo	.15
82	Rey Ordonez	.15
83	Mike Piazza	2.00
84	Robin Ventura	.15
85	Bobby Abreu	.15
86	Mike Lieberthal	.15
87	Scott Rolen	.75
88	Brian Giles	.15
89	Chad Hermansen	.15
90	Jason Kendall	.15
91	Rick Ankiel	.25
92	J.D. Drew	.25
93	Mark McGwire	2.50
94	Fernando Tatis	.15
95	Ben Davis	.15
96	Tony Gwynn	1.50
97	Trevor Hoffman	.15
98	Barry Bonds	3.00
99	Ellis Burks	.15
100	Jeff Kent	.15

Gold

A.L. (1-50):	2-4X
Production 199 Sets R	
N.L. (51-100):	3-6X
Production 99 Sets R	

Green

A.L. (1-50):	3-6X
Production 99 Sets	
N.L. (51-100):	2-4X
Production 199 Sets	

Purple

Production 10 Sets	
(Values Undetermined)	

Premiere Date

Stars:	3-5X
Production 135 Sets H	

A.L. Vanguard Press

		NM/M
Complete Set (10):		10.00
Common Player:		.65
Inserted 2:25		
1	Cal Ripken Jr.	3.00
2	Nomar Garciaparra	2.00
3	Pedro Martinez	1.00
4	Manny Ramirez	1.00
5	Carlos Beltran	.65
6	Roger Clemens	1.50
7	Derek Jeter	3.00
8	Alex Rodriguez	2.50
9	Rafael Palmeiro	.75
10	Ivan Rodriguez	.75

Cosmic Force

		NM/M
Complete Set (10):		30.00
Common Player:		3.00
Inserted 1:73		
1	Chipper Jones	3.00
2	Cal Ripken Jr.	6.00
3	Nomar Garciaparra	4.00
4	Sammy Sosa	4.00
5	Ken Griffey Jr.	4.00
6	Mike Piazza	4.00
7	Derek Jeter	6.00
8	Mark McGwire	5.00
9	Tony Gwynn	3.00
10	Alex Rodriguez	5.00

Diamond Architects

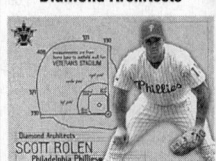

		NM/M
Complete Set (20):		25.00
Common Player:		.50
Inserted 1:25		
1	Chipper Jones	2.00
2	Greg Maddux	2.00
3	Cal Ripken Jr.	4.00
4	Nomar Garciaparra	2.50
5	Sammy Sosa	2.50
6	Ken Griffey Jr.	2.50
7	Manny Ramirez	.50
8	Larry Walker	.50
9	Jeff Bagwell	.50
10	Vladimir Guerrero	1.50
11	Mike Piazza	2.50
12	Roger Clemens	2.25
13	Derek Jeter	4.00
14	Bernie Williams	.50
15	Scott Rolen	1.00
16	Mark McGwire	2.00
17	Tony Gwynn	2.00
18	Alex Rodriguez	3.00
19	Rafael Palmeiro	.50
20	Ivan Rodriguez	.75

Game Worn Jersey

		NM/M
Inserted 1:120		
1	Greg Maddux	10.00
2	Tony Gwynn	10.00
3	Alex Rodriguez	20.00
4	Frank Thomas	8.00
5	Chipper Jones	10.00

High Voltage

		NM/M
Complete Set (36):		10.00
Common Player:		.15
Inserted 1:1		
1	Mo Vaughn	.15
2	Erubiel Durazo	.15
3	Randy Johnson	.60
4	Andruw Jones	.60
5	Chipper Jones	.75
6	Greg Maddux	.75
7	Cal Ripken Jr.	2.00
8	Nomar Garciaparra	1.25
9	Pedro Martinez	.60
10	Sammy Sosa	1.25
11	Frank Thomas	.60
12	Sean Casey	.25
13	Ken Griffey Jr.	1.25
14	Barry Larkin	.15
15	Manny Ramirez	.60
16	Jim Thome	.50
17	Larry Walker	.15
18	Jeff Bagwell	.60
19	Craig Biggio	.15
20	Carlos Beltran	.40
21	Shawn Green	.25
22	Vladimir Guerrero	.60
23	Edgardo Alfonzo	.15
24	Mike Piazza	1.50
25	Roger Clemens	1.00
26	Derek Jeter	2.00
27	Bernie Williams	.25
28	Scott Rolen	.60
29	Brian Giles	.15
30	Rick Ankiel	.15
31	Mark McGwire	1.50
32	Tony Gwynn	.75
33	Barry Bonds	2.00
34	Alex Rodriguez	1.50
35	Rafael Palmeiro	.60
36	Ivan Rodriguez	.60

N.L. Vanguard Press

Guerrero sets Expos' homer record

Above: The Expos count on Vladimir to drive the Montreal offense.

		NM/M
Complete Set (10):		10.00
Common Player:		.50
Inserted 2:37		
1	Chipper Jones	1.50
2	Greg Maddux	1.50
3	Sammy Sosa	2.00
4	Ken Griffey Jr.	2.00
5	Larry Walker	.50
6	Jeff Bagwell	1.00
7	Vladimir Guerrero	1.00
8	Mike Piazza	2.00
9	Mark McGwire	2.50
10	Tony Gwynn	1.50

1991 Pacific Gas & Electric S.F. Giants

Perforated panels of six 2-3/4" x 3-3/4" Giants cards were included in each of five editions of Giants Magazine, the team's official program, for 1991. The set was sponsored by PG&E. Cards have color action photos on front with a graduated gray frame and white borders. At bottom is a team typographical logo, crossed bats and a red ribbon with player identification. A pentagon at top has the date "91." Backs are in black-and-white with a large sponsor's ad, the player's career stats, a few biographical details and uniform and card numbers.

		NM/M
Complete Set (30):		15.00
Common Player:		.50
1	Kevin Mitchell	.50
2	Robby Thompson	.50
3	John Burkett	.50
4	Kelly Downs	.50
5	Terry Kennedy	.50
6	Roger Craig	.50
7	Jeff Brantley	.50
8	Greg Litton	.50
9	Trevor Wilson	.50
10	Kevin Bass	.50
11	Matt Williams	1.00
12	Jose Uribe	.50
13	Steve Decker	.50
14	Will Clark	1.00
15	Dave Righetti	.50
16	Mike Kingery	.50
17	Mike LaCoss	.50
18	Dave Anderson	.50
19	Bud Black	.50
20	Mike Benjamin	.50
21	Don Robinson	.50
22	Mark Leonard	.50
23	Willie McGee	.50
24	Francisco Oliveras	.50
25	Kirt Manwaring	.50
26	Rick Parker	.50
27	Mike Remlinger	.50
28	Mike Felder	.50
29	Scott Garrelts	.50
30	Tony Perezchica	.50

1992 Pacific Gas & Electric S.F. Giants

Perforated panels of six 2-3/4" x 3-3/4" Giants cards were included in each of six editions of Giants Magazine, the team's official program, for 1992. The set was sponsored by PG&E. Cards have color action photos on front with a wood-look frame and white borders. At top is a gold ribbon with player name and position. At bottom is the team logo, crossed bats, uniform number and the year of issue. Horizontal backs are in black-and-white with a large sponsor's ad, the player's career stats, a few biographical details, uniform number and energy conservation tip. Cards are unnumbered and are listed here by panel.

		NM/M
Complete Set, Panels (6):		25.00
Complete Set, Singles (36):		20.00
Common Player:		.50
PANEL 1		5.00
(1)	Rod Beck	.50
(2)	Wendell Kim	.50
(3)	Gil Heredia	.50
(4)	Mike Benjamin	.50
(5)	Matt Williams	1.00
(6)	Robby Thompson	.50
PANEL 2		5.00
(7)	Will Clark/AS	1.00
(8)	Bob Brenly	.50
(9)	Bryan Hickerson	.50
(10)	Bob Lillis	.50
(11)	Royce Clayton	.50
(12)	Mark Leonard (Dropping bat.)	.50
PANEL 3		5.00
(13)	Roger Craig	.50
(14)	Jeff Brantley	.50
(15)	Darren Lewis	.50
(16)	Mark Leonard/Btg	.50
(17)	John Burkett	.50
(18)	Mike Felder	.50
PANEL 4		5.00
(19)	Kelly Downs	.50
(20)	Jose Uribe	.50
(21)	Bud Black	.50
(22)	Kirt Manwaring	.50
(23)	Trevor Wilson	.50
(24)	Kevin Bass	.50
PANEL 5		5.00
(25)	Mike Jackson	.50
(26)	Will Clark	1.00
(27)	Jim McNamara	.50
(28)	Dusty Baker	.50
(29)	Scott Garrelts	.50
(30)	Chris James	.50
PANEL 6		5.00
(31)	Dave Righetti	.50
(32)	Cory Snyder	.50
(33)	Dave Burba	.50
(34)	Carlos Alfonso	.50
(35)	Bill Swift	.50
(36)	Willie McGee	.50

2001 Pacific

		NM/M
Complete Set (500):		40.00
Common Player:		.10
Pack (12):		1.00
Box (36):		25.00
1	Garret Anderson	.10
2	Gary DiSarcina	.10
3	Darin Erstad	.25
4	Seth Etherton	.10
5	Ron Gant	.10
6	Troy Glaus	.75
7	Shigetosi Hasegawa	.10
8	Adam Kennedy	.10
9	Ben Molina	.10
10	Ramon Ortiz	.10
11	Troy Percival	.10
12	Tim Salmon	.20
13	Scott Schoeneweis	.10
14	Mo Vaughn	.10
15	Jarrod Washburn	.10
16	Brian Anderson	.10
17	Danny Bautista	.10
18	Jay Bell	.10
19	Greg Colbrunn	.10
20	Erubiel Durazo	.10
21	Steve Finley	.10
22	Luis Gonzalez	.20
23	Randy Johnson	.75
24	Byung-Hyun Kim	.10
25	Matt Mantei	.10
26	Armando Reynoso	.10
27	Todd Stottlemyre	.10
28	Matt Williams	.10
29	Tony Womack	.10
30	Andy Ashby	.10
31	Bobby Bonilla	.10
32	Rafael Furcal	.10
33	Andres Galarraga	.10
34	Tom Glavine	.35
35	Andruw Jones	.75
36	Chipper Jones	1.00
37	Brian Jordan	.10
38	Wally Joyner	.10
39	Keith Lockhart	.10
40	Javy Lopez	.10
41	Greg Maddux	1.00
42	Kevin Millwood	.10
43	John Rocker	.10
44	Reggie Sanders	.10
45	John Smoltz	.10
46	B.J. Surhoff	.10
47	Quilvio Veras	.10
48	Walt Weiss	.10
49	Brady Anderson	.10
50	Albert Belle	.15
51	Jeff Conine	.10
52	Delino DeShields	.10
53	Brook Fordyce	.10
54	Jerry Hairston Jr.	.10
55	Mark Lewis	.10
56	Luis Matos	.10
57	Melvin Mora	.10
58	Mike Mussina	.35
59	Chris Richard	.10
60	Cal Ripken Jr.	2.00
61	Manny Alexander	.10
62	Rolando Arrojo	.10
63	Midre Cummings	.10
64	Carl Everett	.10
65	Nomar Garciaparra	1.25
66	Mike Lansing	.10
67	Darren Lewis	.10
68	Derek Lowe	.10
69	Pedro Martinez	.75
70	Ramon Martinez	.10
71	Trot Nixon	.10
72	Troy O'Leary	.10
73	Jose Offerman	.10
74	Tomo Ohka	.10
75	Jason Varitek	.10
76	Rick Aguilera	.10
77	Shane Andrews	.10
78	Brant Brown	.10
79	Damon Buford	.10
80	Joe Girardi	.10
81	Mark Grace	.20
82	Willie Greene	.10
83	Ricky Gutierrez	.10
84	Jon Lieber	.10
85	Sammy Sosa	1.25
86	Kevin Tapani	.10
87	Rondell White	.10
88	Kerry Wood	.50
89	Eric Young	.10
90	Harold Baines	.10
91	James Baldwin	.10
92	Ray Durham	.10
93	Cal Eldred	.10
94	Keith Foulke	.10
95	Charles Johnson	.10
96	Paul Konerko	.20
97	Carlos Lee	.10
98	Magglio Ordonez	.10
99	Jim Parque	.10
100	Herbert Perry	.10
101	Chris Singleton	.10
102	Mike Sirotka	.10
103	Frank Thomas	.75
104	Jose Valentin	.10
105	Rob Bell	.10
106	Aaron Boone	.10
107	Sean Casey	.20
108	Danny Graves	.10
109	Ken Griffey Jr.	1.25
110	Pete Harnisch	.10
111	Brian L. Hunter	.10
112	Barry Larkin	.10
113	Pokey Reese	.10
114	Benito Santiago	.10
115	Chris Stynes	.10
116	Michael Tucker	.10
117	Ron Villone	.10
118	Scott Williamson	.10
119	Dmitri Young	.10
120	Roberto Alomar	.35
121	Sandy Alomar Jr.	.10
122	Russell Branyan	.10
123	Dave Burba	.10
124	Bartolo Colon	.10
125	Wil Cordero	.10
126	Einar Diaz	.10
127	Chuck Finley	.10
128	Travis Fryman	.10
129	Kenny Lofton	.10
130	Charles Nagy	.10
131	Manny Ramirez	.75
132	David Segui	.10
133	Jim Thome	.65
134	Omar Vizquel	.10
135	Brian Bohanon	.10
136	Jeff Cirillo	.10
137	Jeff Frye	.10
138	Jeffrey Hammonds	.10
139	Todd Helton	.75
140	Todd Hollandsworth	.10
141	Jose Jimenez	.10
142	Brent Mayne	.10
143	Neifi Perez	.10
144	Ben Petrick	.10
145	Juan Pierre	.10
146	Larry Walker	.10
147	Todd Walker	.10
148	Masato Yoshii	.10
149	Brad Ausmus	.10
150	Rich Becker	.10
151	Tony Clark	.10
152	Deivi Cruz	.10
153	Damion Easley	.10
154	Juan Encarnacion	.10
155	Robert Fick	.10
156	Juan Gonzalez	.75
157	Bobby Higginson	.10
158	Todd Jones	.10
159	Wendell Magee Jr.	.10
160	Brian Moehler	.10
161	Hideo Nomo	.75
162	Dean Palmer	.10
163	Jeff Weaver	.10
164	Antonio Alfonseca	.10
165	David Berg	.10
166	A.J. Burnett	.10
167	Luis Castillo	.10
168	Ryan Dempster	.10
169	Cliff Floyd	.10
170	Alex Gonzalez	.10
171	Mark Kotsay	.10
172	Derrek Lee	.10
173	Mike Lowell	.10
174	Mike Redmond	.10
175	Henry Rodriguez	.10
176	Jesus Sanchez	.10
177	Preston Wilson	.10
178	Moises Alou	.10
179	Jeff Bagwell	.75
180	Glen Barker	.10
181	Lance Berkman	.10
182	Craig Biggio	.10
183	Tim Bogar	.10
184	Ken Caminiti	.10
185	Roger Cedeno	.10
186	Scott Elarton	.10
187	Tony Eusebio	.10
188	Richard Hidalgo	.10
189	Jose Lima	.10
190	Mitch Meluskey	.10
191	Shane Reynolds	.10
192	Bill Spiers	.10
193	Billy Wagner	.10
194	Daryle Ward	.10
195	Carlos Beltran	.40
196	Ricky Bottalico	.10
197	Johnny Damon	.25
198	Jermaine Dye	.10
199	Jorge Fabregas	.10
200	David McCarty	.10
201	Mark Quinn	.10
202	Joe Randa	.10
203	Jeff Reboulet	.10
204	Rey Sanchez	.10
205	Blake Stein	.10
206	Jeff Suppan	.10
207	Mac Suzuki	.10
208	Mike Sweeney	.10
209	Gregg Zaun	.10
210	Adrian Beltre	.25
211	Kevin Brown	.10
212	Alex Cora	.10
213	Darren Dreifort	.10
214	Tom Goodwin	.10
215	Shawn Green	.30
216	Mark Grudzielanek	.10
217	Todd Hundley	.10
218	Eric Karros	.10
219	Chad Kreuter	.10
220	Jim Leyritz	.10
221	Chan Ho Park	.10
222	Jeff Shaw	.10
223	Gary Sheffield	.25
224	Devon White	.10
225	Ron Belliard	.10
226	Henry Blanco	.10
227	Jeromy Burnitz	.10
228	Jeff D'Amico	.10
229	Marquis Grissom	.10
230	Charlie Hayes	.10
231	Jimmy Haynes	.10
232	Tyler Houston	.10
233	Geoff Jenkins	.10
234	Mark Loretta	.10
235	James Mouton	.10
236	Richie Sexson	.10
237	Jamey Wright	.10
238	Jay Canizaro	.10
239	Ron Coomer	.10
240	Cristian Guzman	.10
241	Denny Hocking	.10
242	Torii Hunter	.10
243	Jacque Jones	.10
244	Corey Koskie	.10
245	Matt Lawton	.10
246	Matt LeCroy	.10
247	Eric Milton	.10
248	David Ortiz	.25
249	Brad Radke	.10
250	Mark Redman	.10
251	Michael Barrett	.10
252	Peter Bergeron	.10
253	Milton Bradley	.10
254	Orlando Cabrera	.10
255	Vladimir Guerrero	.75
256	Wilton Guerrero	.10
257	Dustin Hermanson	.10
258	Hideki Irabu	.10
259	Fernando Seguignol	.10
260	Lee Stevens	.10
261	Andy Tracy	.10
262	Javier Vazquez	.10
263	Jose Vidro	.10
264	Edgardo Alfonzo	.10
265	Derek Bell	.10
266	Armando Benitez	.10
267	Mike Bordick	.10
268	John Franco	.10
269	Darryl Hamilton	.10
270	Mike Hampton	.10
271	Lenny Harris	.10
272	Al Leiter	.10
273	Joe McEwing	.10
274	Rey Ordonez	.10
275	Jay Payton	.10
276	Mike Piazza	1.25
277	Glendon Rusch	.10
278	Bubba Trammell	.10
279	Robin Ventura	.10
280	Todd Zeile	.10
281	Scott Brosius	.10
282	Jose Canseco	.25
283	Roger Clemens	1.00
284	David Cone	.10
285	Dwight Gooden	.10
286	Orlando Hernandez	.10
287	Glenallen Hill	.10
288	Derek Jeter	2.00
289	David Justice	.10
290	Chuck Knoblauch	.10
291	Tino Martinez	.10
292	Denny Neagle	.10
293	Paul O'Neill	.10
294	Andy Pettitte	.20
295	Jorge Posada	.10
296	Mariano Rivera	.20
297	Luis Sojo	.10
298	Jose Vizcaino	.10
299	Bernie Williams	.25
300	Kevin Appier	.10
301	Eric Chavez	.20
302	Ryan Christenson	.10
303	Jason Giambi	.50
304	Jeremy Giambi	.10
305	Ben Grieve	.10
306	Gil Heredia	.10
307	Ramon Hernandez	.10
308	Tim Hudson	.20
309	Jason Isringhausen	.10
310	Terrence Long	.10
311	Mark Mulder	.10
312	Adam Piatt	.10
313	Matt Stairs	.10
314	Miguel Tejada	.25
315	Randy Velarde	.10
316	Alex Arias	.10
317	Pat Burrell	.25
318	Omar Daal	.10
319	Travis Lee	.10
320	Mike Lieberthal	.10
321	Randy Wolf	.10
322	Bobby Abreu	.10
323	Jeff Brantley	.10
324	Bruce Chen	.10
325	Doug Glanville	.10
326	Kevin Jordan	.10
327	Robert Person	.10
328	Scott Rolen	.65
329	Jimmy Anderson	.10
330	Mike Benjamin	.10
331	Kris Benson	.10
332	Adam Brown	.10
333	Brian Giles	.10
334	Jason Kendall	.10
335	Pat Meares	.10
336	Warren Morris	.10
337	Aramis Ramirez	.10
338	Todd Ritchie	.10
339	Jason Schmidt	.10
340	John Vander Wal	.10
341	Mike Williams	.10
342	Enrique Wilson	.10
343	Kevin Young	.10
344	Rick Ankiel	.20
345	Andy Benes	.10
346	Will Clark	.15
347	Eric Davis	.10
348	J.D. Drew	.20
349	Shawon Dunston	.10
350	Jim Edmonds	.10
351	Pat Hentgen	.10
352	Darryl Kile	.10
353	Ray Lankford	.10
354	Mike Matheny	.10
355	Mark McGwire	1.50
356	Craig Paquette	.10
357	Edgar Renteria	.10
358	Garrett Stephenson	.10
359	Fernando Tatis	.10
360	Dave Veres	.10
361	Fernando Vina	.10
362	Bret Boone	.10
363	Matt Clement	.10
364	Ben Davis	.10
365	Adam Eaton	.10
366	Wiki Gonzalez	.10
367	Tony Gwynn	1.00
368	Damian Jackson	.10
369	Ryan Klesko	.10
370	John Mabry	.10
371	Dave Magadan	.10
372	Phil Nevin	.10
373	Eric Owens	.10
374	Desi Relaford	.10
375	Ruben Rivera	.10
376	Woody Williams	.10
377	Rich Aurilia	.10
378	Marvin Benard	.10
379	Barry Bonds	2.00
380	Ellis Burks	.10
381	Bobby Estalella	.10
382	Shawn Estes	.10
383	Mark Gardner	.10
384	Livan Hernandez	.10
385	Jeff Kent	.10
386	Bill Mueller	.10
387	Robb Nen	.10
388	Russ Ortiz	.10
389	Armando Rios	.10
390	Kirk Rueter	.10
391	J.T. Snow	.10
392	David Bell	.10
393	Jay Buhner	.10
394	Mike Cameron	.10
395	Freddy Garcia	.10
396	Carlos Guillen	.10
397	John Halama	.10
398	Rickey Henderson	.75
399	Al Martin	.10
400	Edgar Martinez	.10
401	Mark McLemore	.10
402	Jamie Moyer	.10
403	John Olerud	.10
404	Joe Oliver	.10
405	Alex Rodriguez	1.50
406	Kazuhiro Sasaki	.15
407	Aaron Sele	.10
408	Dan Wilson	.10
409	Miguel Cairo	.10
410	Vinny Castilla	.10
411	Steve Cox	.10
412	John Flaherty	.10
413	Jose Guillen	.10
414	Roberto Hernandez	.10
415	Russ Johnson	.10
416	Felix Martinez	.10

417	Fred McGriff	.10
418	Greg Vaughn	.10
419	Gerald Williams	.10
420	Luis Alicea	.10
421	Frank Catalanotto	.10
422	Royce Clayton	.10
423	Chad Curtis	.10
424	Rusty Greer	.10
425	Bill Haselman	.10
426	Rick Helling	.10
427	Gabe Kapler	.10
428	Mike Lamb	.10
429	Ricky Ledee	.10
430	Ruben Mateo	.10
431	Rafael Palmeiro	.65
432	Ivan Rodriguez	.65
433	Kenny Rogers	.10
434	John Wetteland	.10
435	Jeff Zimmerman	.10
436	Tony Batista	.10
437	Homer Bush	.10
438	Chris Carpenter	.10
439	Marty Cordova	.10
440	Jose Cruz Jr.	.10
441	Carlos Delgado	.40
442	Darrin Fletcher	.10
443	Brad Fullmer	.10
444	Alex S. Gonzalez	.10
445	Billy Koch	.10
446	Raul Mondesi	.10
447	Mickey Morandini	.10
448	Shannon Stewart	.10
449	Steve Trachsel	.10
450	David Wells	.10
451	Juan Alvarez	.10
452	Shawn Wooten	.10
453	Ismael Villegas	.10
454	Carlos Casimiro	.10
455	Morgan Burkhart	.10
456	Paxton Crawford	.10
457	Dernell Stenson	.10
458	Ross Gload	.10
459	Raul Gonzalez	.10
460	Corey Patterson	.10
461	Julio Zuleta	.10
462	Rocky Biddle	.10
463	Joe Crede	.10
464	Matt Ginter	.10
465	Aaron Myette	.10
466	Mike Bell	.10
467	Travis Dawkins	.10
468	Mark Watson	.10
469	Elvis Pena	.10
470	Eric Munson	.10
471	Pablo Ozuna	.10
472	Frank Charles	.10
473	Mike Judd	.10
474	Hector Ramirez	.10
475	Jack Cressend	.10
476	Talmadge Nunnari	.10
477	Jorge Toca	.10
478	Alfonso Soriano	.65
479	Jay Tessmer	.10
480	Jake Westbrook	.10
481	Todd Belitz	.10
482	Eric Byrnes	.10
483	Jose Ortiz	.10
484	Tike Redman	.10
485	Domingo Guzman	.10
486	Rodrigo Lopez	.10
487	Pedro Feliz	.10
488	Damon Minor	.10
489	Ryan Vogelsong	.10
490	Joel Pineiro	.10
491	Justin Brunette	.10
492	Keith McDonald	.10
493	Aubrey Huff	.10
494	Kenny Kelly	.10
495	Damian Rolls	.10
496	John Bale	.10
497	Pasqual Coco	.10
498	Matt DeWitt	.10
499	Leo Estrella	.10
500	Josh Phelps	.10

Hobby Limited
Stars: 8-15X
Production 70 Sets

Retail Limited
Stars: 4-8X
Production 85 Sets

Premiere Date

Stars: 20-30X
Production 35 Sets

Extreme

Stars: 15-25X
Production 45 Sets

AL Decade's Best

		NM/M
Complete Set (18):		20.00
Common Player:		.50
Inserted 2:721		
1	Rickey Henderson	1.50
2	Rafael Palmeiro	1.00
3	Cal Ripken Jr.	4.00
4	Jose Canseco	.75
5	Juan Gonzalez	1.50
6	Frank Thomas	1.50
7	Albert Belle	.50
8	Edgar Martinez	.50
9	Mo Vaughn	.50
10	Derek Jeter	4.00
11	Mark McGwire	3.00
12	Alex Rodriguez	3.00
13	Ken Griffey Jr.	2.50
14	Nomar Garciaparra	2.50
15	Roger Clemens	2.00
16	Bernie Williams	.50
17	Ivan Rodriguez	1.00
18	Pedro Martinez	1.50

Cramer's Choice Awards

		NM/M
Complete Set (10):		275.00
Common Player:		15.00
Inserted 1:721		

Styrene & Canvas pricing unavailable.

1	Cal Ripken Jr.	50.00
2	Nomar Garciaparra	30.00
3	Sammy Sosa	30.00
4	Frank Thomas	15.00
5	Ken Griffey Jr.	30.00
6	Mike Piazza	30.00
7	Derek Jeter	50.00
8	Mark McGwire	40.00
9	Barry Bonds	50.00
10	Alex Rodriguez	40.00

Gold Crown Die-Cuts

		NM/M
Complete Set (36):		100.00
Common Player:		1.50
Inserted 1:73		
1	Darin Erstad	1.50
2	Troy Glaus	4.00
3	Randy Johnson	4.00
4	Rafael Furcal	1.50
5	Andruw Jones	4.00
6	Chipper Jones	5.00
7	Greg Maddux	5.00
8	Cal Ripken Jr.	10.00
9	Nomar Garciaparra	8.00
10	Pedro Martinez	4.00
11	Sammy Sosa	8.00
12	Kerry Wood	2.50
13	Frank Thomas	4.00
14	Ken Griffey Jr.	8.00
15	Manny Ramirez	4.00
16	Todd Helton	4.00
17	Jeff Bagwell	4.00
18	Shawn Green	1.50
19	Gary Sheffield	1.50
20	Vladimir Guerrero	4.00
21	Mike Piazza	8.00
22	Jose Canseco	2.00
23	Roger Clemens	6.00
24	Derek Jeter	10.00
25	Jason Giambi	2.50
26	Pat Burrell	2.00
26	Rick Ankiel (Should be #27.)	1.50
28	Jim Edmonds	1.50
29	Mark McGwire	9.00
30	Tony Gwynn	5.00
31	Barry Bonds	10.00
32	Rickey Henderson	4.00
33	Edgar Martinez	1.50
34	Alex Rodriguez	9.00
35	Ivan Rodriguez	3.00
36	Carlos Delgado	1.50

Pacific NL Decade's Best

		NM/M
Complete Set (18):		15.00
Common Player:		.50
Inserted 2:37		
1	Barry Bonds	4.00
2	Jeff Bagwell	1.00
3	Tom Glavine	.65
4	Gary Sheffield	.65
5	Fred McGriff	.50
6	Greg Maddux	1.50
7	Mike Piazza	2.00
8	Tony Gwynn	1.50
9	Hideo Nomo	1.00
10	Andres Galarraga	.50
11	Larry Walker	.50
12	Scott Rolen	.75
13	Pedro Martinez	1.50
14	Sammy Sosa	2.00
15	Mark McGwire	3.00
16	Kerry Wood	.75
17	Chipper Jones	1.50
18	Mark Grace	.75

Pacific On The Horizon

		NM/M
Complete Set (10):		20.00
Common Player:		2.00
Inserted 1:145		
1	Rafael Furcal	2.00
2	Corey Patterson	2.50
3	Russell Branyan	2.00
4	Juan Pierre	2.50
5	Mark Quinn	2.00
6	Alfonso Soriano	6.00
7	Adam Piatt	2.00
8	Pat Burrell	4.50
9	Kazuhiro Sasaki	2.50
10	Aubrey Huff	2.00

Pacific Ornaments

		NM/M
Complete Set (24):		25.00
Common Player:		.50
Inserted 2:37		
1	Rafael Furcal	.50
2	Chipper Jones	2.00
3	Greg Maddux	2.00
4	Cal Ripken Jr.	4.00
5	Nomar Garciaparra	2.50
6	Pedro Martinez	1.50
7	Sammy Sosa	2.50
8	Frank Thomas	1.50
9	Ken Griffey Jr.	2.50
10	Manny Ramirez	1.50
11	Todd Helton	1.50
12	Vladimir Guerrero	1.50
13	Mike Piazza	2.50
14	Roger Clemens	2.25
15	Derek Jeter	4.00
16	Pat Burrell	1.00
17	Rick Ankiel	.50
18	Mark McGwire	3.00
19	Barry Bonds	4.00
20	Alex Rodriguez	3.00
21	Troy Glaus	1.50
22	Tom Glavine	.50
23	Jim Edmonds	.50
24	Ivan Rodriguez	1.00

2001 Pacific Paramount Samples

While the Paramount brand was never produced due to Pacific's loss of its licensing early in 2001, a trio of base-set sample cards were created and distributed to media and dealers. Fronts have vignetted photos and silver-foil highlights. Backs have portrait photos and the usual data and stats. Cards have "SAMPLE" in place of the card number on back.

		NM/M
Complete Set (3):		7.50
Common Player:		3.00
(1)	Barry Bonds	3.00
(2)	Vladimir Guerrero	3.00
(3)	Greg Maddux	3.00

2001 Pacific Private Stock

		NM/M
Complete Set (150):		50.00
Common Player:		.25
Common (126-150):		1.00
Inserted 1:4		
Hobby Pack (7):		10.00
Hobby Box (10):		75.00
1	Darin Erstad	.50
2	Troy Glaus	1.00
3	Tim Salmon	.35
4	Mo Vaughn	.25
5	Steve Finley	.25
6	Luis Gonzalez	.35
7	Randy Johnson	1.00
8	Matt Williams	.25
9	Rafael Furcal	.25
10	Andres Galarraga	.25
11	Tom Glavine	.45
12	Andruw Jones	1.00
13	Chipper Jones	1.50
14	Greg Maddux	1.50
15	B.J. Surhoff	.25
16	Brady Anderson	.25
17	Albert Belle	.25
18	Mike Mussina	.45
19	Cal Ripken Jr.	3.00
20	Carl Everett	.25
21	Nomar Garciaparra	2.00
22	Pedro Martinez	1.00
23	Mark Grace	.35
24	Sammy Sosa	2.00
25	Kerry Wood	.50
26	Carlos Lee	.25
27	Magglio Ordonez	.25
28	Frank Thomas	1.00
29	Sean Casey	.35
30	Ken Griffey Jr.	2.00
31	Barry Larkin	.25
32	Pokey Reese	.25
33	Roberto Alomar	.40
34	Kenny Lofton	.25
35	Manny Ramirez	1.00
36	Jim Thome	.75
37	Omar Vizquel	.25
38	Jeff Cirillo	.25
39	Jeffrey Hammonds	.25
40	Todd Helton	1.00
41	Larry Walker	.25
42	Tony Clark	.25
43	Juan Encarnacion	.25
44	Juan Gonzalez	1.00
45	Hideo Nomo	1.00
46	Cliff Floyd	.25
47	Derrek Lee	.25
48	Henry Rodriguez	.25
49	Preston Wilson	.25
50	Jeff Bagwell	1.00
51	Craig Biggio	.25
52	Richard Hidalgo	.25
53	Moises Alou	.25
54	Carlos Beltran	.50
55	Johnny Damon	.40
56	Jermaine Dye	.25
57	Mac Suzuki	.25
58	Mike Sweeney	.25
59	Adrian Beltre	.40
60	Kevin Brown	.25
61	Shawn Green	.50
62	Eric Karros	.25
63	Chan Ho Park	.25
64	Gary Sheffield	.40
65	Jeromy Burnitz	.25
66	Geoff Jenkins	.25
67	Richie Sexson	.25
68	Jacque Jones	.25
69	Matt Lawton	.25
70	Eric Milton	.25
71	Vladimir Guerrero	1.00
72	Jose Vidro	.25
73	Edgardo Alfonzo	.25
74	Mike Hampton	.25
75	Mike Piazza	2.00
76	Robin Ventura	.25
77	Jose Canseco	.50
78	Roger Clemens	1.75
79	Derek Jeter	3.00
80	David Justice	.25
81	Jorge Posada	.25
82	Bernie Williams	.35
83	Jason Giambi	.65
84	Ben Grieve	.25
85	Tim Hudson	.25
86	Terrence Long	.25
87	Miguel Tejada	.35
88	Bobby Abreu	.25
89	Pat Burrell	.50
90	Mike Lieberthal	.25
91	Scott Rolen	.75
92	Kris Benson	.25
93	Brian Giles	.25
94	Jason Kendall	.25
95	Aramis Ramirez	.25
96	Rick Ankiel	.25
97	Will Clark	.35
98	J.D. Drew	.25
99	Jim Edmonds	.25
100	Mark McGwire	2.50
101	Fernando Tatis	.25
102	Adam Eaton	.25
103	Tony Gwynn	1.50
104	Phil Nevin	.25
105	Eric Owens	.25
106	Barry Bonds	3.00
107	Jeff Kent	.25
108	J.T. Snow	.25
109	Rickey Henderson	1.00
110	Edgar Martinez	.25
111	John Olerud	.25
112	Alex Rodriguez	2.50
113	Kazuhiro Sasaki	.25
114	Vinny Castilla	.25
115	Fred McGriff	.25
116	Greg Vaughn	.25
117	Gabe Kapler	.25
118	Ruben Mateo	.25
119	Rafael Palmeiro	.75
120	Ivan Rodriguez	.75
121	Tony Batista	.25
122	Jose Cruz Jr.	.25
123	Carlos Delgado	.75
124	Shannon Stewart	.25
125	David Wells	.25
126	Shawn Wooten	1.00
127	George Lombard	1.00
128	Morgan Burkhart	1.00
129	Ross Gload	1.00
130	Corey Patterson	1.00
131	Julio Zuleta	1.00
132	Joe Crede	1.00
133	Matt Ginter	1.00
134	Travis Dawkins	1.00
135	Eric Munson	1.00
136	Dee Brown	1.00
137	Luke Prokopec	1.00
138	Timoniel Perez	1.00
139	Alfonso Soriano	2.00
140	Jake Westbrook	1.00
141	Eric Byrnes	1.00
142	Adam Hyzdu	1.00
143	Jimmy Rollins	1.50
144	Xavier Nady	1.00
145	Ryan Vogelsong	1.00
146	Joel Pineiro	2.00
147	Aubrey Huff	1.00
148	Kenny Kelly	1.00
149	Josh Phelps	1.00
150	Vernon Wells	1.00

Silver
Stars: .5-1.5X
SP's: .5-1X
Base cards in retail.

Gold Portraits
Stars: 6-10X
SP's (126-150): 1-2X
Production 75 Sets H

Silver Portraits

Stars: 2-5X
SP's: 1X
Production 290 Sets R

Premiere Date
Stars: 4-8X
SP's: 1-2X
Production 90 Sets

Artist's Canvas

		NM/M
Complete Set (20):		50.00
Common Player:		1.00
Inserted 1:21		
1	Randy Johnson	2.50
2	Chipper Jones	4.00
3	Greg Maddux	4.00
4	Cal Ripken Jr.	8.00
5	Nomar Garciaparra	5.00
6	Pedro Martinez	2.50
7	Sammy Sosa	5.00
8	Frank Thomas	2.50
9	Ken Griffey Jr.	5.00
10	Manny Ramirez	2.50
11	Vladimir Guerrero	2.50
12	Mike Piazza	5.00
13	Roger Clemens	4.50
14	Derek Jeter	6.00
15	Jason Giambi	2.50
16	Rick Ankiel	1.00
17	Mark McGwire	6.00
18	Barry Bonds	8.00
19	Alex Rodriguez	6.00
20	Ivan Rodriguez	2.00

Extreme Action

		NM/M
Complete Set (20):		20.00
Common Player:		.50
Inserted 1:11		
1	Troy Glaus	1.00
2	Rafael Furcal	.50
3	Chipper Jones	1.50
4	Cal Ripken Jr.	3.00
5	Nomar Garciaparra	2.00
6	Sammy Sosa	2.00
7	Ken Griffey Jr.	2.00
8	Manny Ramirez	1.00
9	Todd Helton	1.00
10	Jeff Bagwell	1.00
11	Vladimir Guerrero	1.00
12	Derek Jeter	3.00
13	Mike Piazza	2.00
14	Pat Burrell	.75
15	Jim Edmonds	.50
16	Mark McGwire	2.50
17	Barry Bonds	3.00
18	Alex Rodriguez	2.50
19	Ivan Rodriguez	2.00
20	Carlos Delgado	.75

Game Gear

		NM/M
Common Player:		4.00
Inserted 1:1 H		
1	Garret Anderson/Bat	6.00
2	Darin Erstad/Jsy	5.00
3	Ron Gant/Bat	4.00
4	Troy Glaus/Jsy	8.00
5	Tim Salmon/Bat	5.00
6	Mo Vaughn/Jsy/Gray	4.00
7	Mo Vaughn/Jsy/White	4.00
8	Mo Vaughn/Bat	4.00
9	Jay Bell/Jsy	4.00
10	Jay Bell/Bat	4.00
11	Erubiel Durazo/Jsy/Black	4.00
12	Erubiel Durazo/Jsy/White	4.00
13	Erubiel Durazo/Bat	4.00
14	Steve Finley/Bat	4.00
15	Randy Johnson	10.00
16	Byung-Hyun Kim/Jsy/White	4.00
17	Byung-Hyun Kim/Jsy/Gray	
18	Matt Williams/Jsy/Gray	4.00
19	Matt Williams/Jsy/White	4.00
20	Matt Williams/Jsy/Purple	4.00
21	Bobby Bonilla/Jsy	4.00
22	Rafael Furcal/Bat	5.00
23	Andruw Jones/Bat	8.00
24	Chipper Jones/Jsy	10.00
25	Chipper Jones/Bat	10.00
26	Brian Jordan/Jsy	4.00
27	Javier Lopez/Bat	4.00
28	Greg Maddux/Jsy	15.00
29	Greg Maddux/Bat	15.00
30	Brady Anderson/Bat	4.00
31	Albert Belle/Bat	4.00
32	Nomar Garciaparra/Bat	15.00
33	Pedro Martinez/Bat	10.00
34	Jose Offerman/Bat	4.00
35	Damon Buford/Jsy	4.00
36	Jose Nieves/Bat	4.00
38	Kerry Wood/Bat	8.00
39	James Baldwin/Jsy	4.00
40	Ray Durham/Jsy	4.00
41	Ray Durham/Bat	4.00
42	Carlos Lee/Bat	4.00
43	Magglio Ordonez/Jsy	6.00
44	Magglio Ordonez/Bat	6.00
45	Chris Singleton/Jsy	4.00
46	Aaron Boone/Jsy	4.00
47	Sean Casey/Bat	4.00
48	Barry Larkin/Jsy	4.00
49	Pokey Reese/Jsy	4.00
50	Pokey Reese/Bat	4.00
51	Dmitri Young/Bat	4.00
52	Roberto Alomar/Bat	8.00
53	Einar Diaz/Bat	4.00
54	Kenny Lofton/Bat	4.00
55	David Segui/Bat	4.00
56	Omar Vizquel/Jsy	5.00
57	Luis Castillo/Jsy	4.00
58	Jeff Cirillo/Jsy	4.00
59	Jeff Frye/Bat	4.00
60	Todd Helton/Jsy	8.00
61	Todd Helton/Jsy	8.00
62	Neifi Perez/Bat	4.00
63	Larry Walker/Jsy	4.00
64	Larry Walker/Bat	4.00
65	Masato Yoshii/Jsy	4.00
66	Brad Ausmus/Jsy	4.00
67	Rich Becker/Bat	4.00
68	Tony Clark/Bat	4.00
69	Deivi Cruz/Bat	4.00
70	Juan Gonzalez/Bat	6.00
71	Dean Palmer/Bat	4.00
72	Cliff Floyd/Jsy/White	4.00
73	Cliff Floyd/Jsy/Teal	4.00
74	Cliff Floyd/Bat	4.00
75	Alex Gonzalez/Jsy	4.00
76	Alex Gonzalez/Marlins Bat	4.00
77	Mark Kotsay/Bat	4.00
78	Derrek Lee/Bat	4.00
79	Pablo Ozuna/Bat	4.00
80	Craig Biggio/Bat	4.00
81	Ken Caminiti/Bat	4.00
82	Roger Cedeno/Bat	4.00
83	Ricky Bottalico/Bat	4.00
84	Dee Brown/Bat	4.00
85	Jermaine Dye/Bat	4.00
86	David McCarty/Bat	4.00
87	Hector Ortiz/Bat	4.00
88	Joe Randa/Bat	4.00
89	Adrian Beltre/Jsy	4.00
90	Kevin Brown/Jsy	6.00
91	Alex Cora/Bat	4.00
92	Darren Dreifort/Bat	4.00
93	Shawn Green/Jsy/White	6.00
94	Shawn Green/Jsy/Gray	6.00
95	Todd Hundley/Bat	4.00
96	Eric Karros/Bat	4.00
97	Chan Ho Park/Jsy	4.00
98	Chan Ho Park/Bat	4.00
101	Gary Sheffield/Bat	6.00
102	Ismael Valdes/Bat	4.00
103	Jeromy Burnitz/Bat	4.00
104	Marquis Grissom/Bat	4.00
105	Matt Lawton/Bat	4.00
106	Fernando Seguignol/Bat	4.00
107	Edgardo Alfonzo/White Swing	4.00
108	Edgardo Alfonzo/Jsy/White Drop	4.00
109	Edgardo Alfonzo/Jsy/Black	4.00
110	Derek Bell/Jsy/White	4.00
111	Derek Bell/Jsy/Black	4.00
112	Armando Benitez/Bat	4.00
113	Al Leiter/Bat	4.00
114	Rey Ordonez/Jsy/Gray Field	4.00
115	Rey Ordonez/Jsy/White	4.00
116	Rey Ordonez/Jsy/Gray Bunt	4.00
117	Rey Ordonez/Bat	4.00
118	Jay Payton/Bat	4.00
119	Mike Piazza/Jsy	10.00
120	Robin Ventura/Jsy/Black Hit	4.00
121	Robin Ventura/Jsy/Black Field	4.00
122	Robin Ventura/Jsy White	4.00
123	Luis Polonia/Bat	4.00
124	Bernie Williams/Bat	6.00
125	Eric Chavez/Jsy	4.00
126	Jason Giambi/Jsy	8.00
127	Jason Giambi/Bat	8.00
128	Ben Grieve/Jsy	4.00
129	Ben Grieve/Bat	4.00
130	Ramon Hernandez/Bat	4.00
131	Tim Hudson/Jsy	6.00
132	Terrence Long/Bat	4.00
133	Mark Mulder/Bat	6.00
134	Adam Piatt/Jsy	4.00
135	Olmedo Saenz/Bat	4.00
136	Matt Stairs/Bat	4.00
137	Mike Stanley/Bat	4.00
138	Miguel Tejada/Bat	6.00
139	Travis Lee/Bat	4.00
140	Brian Giles/Bat	5.00
141	Jason Kendall/Jsy	4.00
142	Will Clark/Bat	6.00
143	J.D. Drew/Bat	4.00
144	Jim Edmonds/Bat	10.00
145	Mark McGwire/Bat	50.00
146	Edgar Renteria/Bat	4.00
147	Garrett Stephenson/Jsy	4.00
148	Tony Gwynn/Jsy	10.00
149	Ruben Rivera/Bat	4.00
150	Barry Bonds/Jsy	40.00
151	Barry Bonds/Bat	40.00
152	Ellis Burks/Jsy	4.00
153	J.T. Snow/Bat	4.00
154	Jay Buhner/Jsy	4.00
155	Jay Buhner/Bat	4.00
156	Carlos Guillen/Jsy	4.00
157	Carlos Guillen/Bat	4.00
158	Rickey Henderson/Bat	15.00
159	Edgar Martinez/Bat	6.00
160	Gil Meche/Bat	4.00
161	John Olerud/Bat	5.00
162	Joe Oliver/Bat	4.00
163	Alex Rodriguez/Jsy	30.00
164	Kazuhiro Sasaki/Jsy	4.00
165	Dan Wilson/Jsy	4.00
166	Dan Wilson/Bat	4.00
167	Vinny Castilla/Bat	4.00
168	Jose Guillen/Bat	4.00
169	Fred McGriff/Jsy	5.00
170	Rusty Greer/Bat	4.00
171	Mike Lamb/Bat	4.00
172	Ruben Mateo/Jsy	4.00
173	Ruben Mateo/Bat	4.00
174	Rafael Palmeiro/Jsy	8.00
178	Rafael Palmeiro/Bat	4.00
179	Tony Batista/Bat	4.00
180	Marty Cordova/Bat	4.00
181	Jose Cruz Jr./Bat	4.00
181	Alex Gonzalez/Blue Jays Bat	4.00
182	Raul Mondesi/Bat	4.00

Game Jersey Patch

		NM/M
Common Player:		8.00
2	Darin Erstad	8.00
4	Troy Glaus	15.00
6	Mo Vaughn/Gray	8.00
7	Mo Vaughn/White	8.00
9	Jay Bell	8.00
11	Erubiel Durazo/Black	8.00
12	Erubiel Durazo/White	8.00
15	Randy Johnson	40.00
16	Byung-Hyun Kim/White	8.00
17	Byung-Hyun Kim/Gray	8.00
18	Matt Williams/White	8.00
19	Matt Williams/White	8.00
20	Matt Williams/Purple	8.00
21	Bobby Bonilla	8.00
24	Chipper Jones	25.00
26	Brian Jordan	8.00
28	Greg Maddux	80.00
35	Damon Buford	8.00
39	James Baldwin	8.00
40	Ray Durham	8.00
43	Magglio Ordonez	20.00
45	Chris Singleton	8.00
48	Barry Larkin	15.00
54	Pokey Reese	8.00
54	Kenny Lofton	10.00
56	Omar Vizquel	10.00
57	Luis Castillo	8.00
58	Jeff Cirillo	8.00
60	Todd Helton	20.00
63	Larry Walker	10.00
65	Masato Yoshii	8.00
66	Brad Ausmus	8.00
72	Cliff Floyd/White	8.00
73	Cliff Floyd Teal	8.00
75	Alex Gonzalez	8.00
79	Pablo Ozuna	8.00
89	Adrian Beltre	8.00
90	Kevin Brown	15.00
93	Shawn Green/White	15.00
94	Shawn Green/Gray	15.00
95	Todd Hundley	8.00
98	Chan Ho Park	8.00
107	Edgardo Alfonzo/White Swing	8.00
108	Edgardo Alfonzo/White Drop	8.00
109	Edgardo Alfonzo/Black	8.00
110	Derek Bell/White	8.00
111	Derek Bell/Black	8.00
114	Rey Ordonez/Gray Field	8.00
115	Rey Ordonez/White	8.00
116	Rey Ordonez/Gray Bunt	8.00
119	Mike Piazza	75.00
120	Robin Ventura/Black Hit	10.00
121	Robin Ventura/Black Field	10.00
122	Robin Ventura/White	10.00
125	Eric Chavez	15.00
126	Jason Giambi	15.00
128	Ben Grieve	8.00
131	Tim Hudson	15.00
133	Mark Mulder	15.00
134	Adam Piatt	8.00
141	Jason Kendall	10.00
147	Garrett Stephenson	8.00
148	Tony Gwynn	40.00
150	Barry Bonds	90.00
152	Ellis Burks	8.00
154	Jay Buhner	8.00
156	Carlos Guillen	8.00
164	Kazuhiro Sasaki	15.00
165	Dan Wilson	8.00
169	Fred McGriff	10.00
172	Ruben Mateo	8.00
174	Rafael Palmeiro	25.00

Reserve

		NM/M
Complete Set (20):		25.00
Common Player:		.50
Inserted 1:21 H		
1	Randy Johnson	1.50
2	Chipper Jones	2.00
3	Greg Maddux	2.00
4	Cal Ripken Jr.	4.00
5	Nomar Garciaparra	2.50
6	Pedro Martinez	1.50
7	Sammy Sosa	2.50
8	Frank Thomas	1.50
9	Ken Griffey Jr.	4.00
10	Todd Helton	1.50
11	Vladimir Guerrero	1.50
12	Mike Piazza	2.50
13	Roger Clemens	2.25
14	Derek Jeter	4.00
15	Rick Ankiel	.50
16	Mark McGwire	3.00
17	Tony Gwynn	2.00
18	Barry Bonds	4.00
19	Alex Rodriguez	3.00
20	Ivan Rodriguez	1.00

PS-206 Action

		NM/M
Complete Set (60):		20.00
Common Player:		.15
Inserted 2:Pack		
1	Darin Erstad	.25
2	Troy Glaus	.65
3	Randy Johnson	.65
4	Rafael Furcal	.15
5	Tom Glavine	.40
6	Andruw Jones	.65
7	Chipper Jones	.75
8	Greg Maddux	.75
9	Albert Belle	.15
10	Mike Mussina	.40
11	Cal Ripken Jr.	1.50
12	Nomar Garciaparra	1.00
13	Pedro Martinez	.65
14	Mark Grace	.25
15	Sammy Sosa	1.00
16	Kerry Wood	.35
17	Magglio Ordonez	.15
18	Frank Thomas	.65
19	Ken Griffey Jr.	1.00
20	Barry Larkin	.15
21	Roberto Alomar	.35
22	Manny Ramirez	.65
23	Jim Thome	.60
24	Jeff Cirillo	.15
25	Todd Helton	.65
26	Larry Walker	.15
27	Juan Gonzalez	.65
28	Hideo Nomo	.65
29	Preston Wilson	.65
30	Jeff Bagwell	.65
31	Craig Biggio	.15
32	Johnny Damon	.25
33	Jermaine Dye	.15
34	Shawn Green	.30
35	Gary Sheffield	.25
36	Vladimir Guerrero	.65
37	Mike Piazza	1.00
38	Jose Canseco	.40
39	Roger Clemens	.85
40	Derek Jeter	1.50
41	Bernie Williams	.30
42	Jason Giambi	.50
43	Ben Grieve	.15
44	Pat Burrell	.40
45	Scott Rolen	.50
46	Rick Ankiel	.25
47	J.D. Drew	.15
48	Jim Edmonds	.15
49	Mark McGwire	1.25
50	Tony Gwynn	.75
51	Barry Bonds	1.50
52	Jeff Kent	.15
53	Edgar Martinez	.15
54	Alex Rodriguez	1.25
55	Kazuhiro Sasaki	.15
56	Fred McGriff	.15
57	Rafael Palmeiro	.50
58	Ivan Rodriguez	.50
59	Tony Batista	.15
60	Carlos Delgado	.25

PS-206 New Wave

		NM/M
Complete Set (20):		30.00
Common Player:		1.00
Inserted 2:Hobby Case		
1	Darin Erstad	1.50
2	Troy Glaus	5.00
3	Rafael Furcal	1.00
4	Andruw Jones	5.00
5	Magglio Ordonez	1.00
6	Carlos Lee	1.00
7	Todd Helton	5.00
8	Johnny Damon	1.50
9	Jermaine Dye	1.00
10	Vladimir Guerrero	5.00
11	Jason Giambi	4.00
12	Ben Grieve	1.00
13	Pat Burrell	3.00
14	Rick Ankiel	1.00
15	J.D. Drew	1.50
16	Adam Eaton	1.00
17	Kazuhiro Sasaki	1.00
18	Ruben Mateo	1.00
19	Tony Batista	1.00
20	Carlos Delgado	3.00

PS-206 Rookies

		NM/M
Complete Set (20):		50.00
Common Player:		3.00
Inserted 1:Case		
1	George Lombard	3.00
2	Morgan Burkhart	3.00
3	Corey Patterson	5.00
4	Julio Zuleta	3.00
5	Joe Crede	3.00
6	Matt Ginter	3.00
7	Aaron Myette	3.00
8	Travis Dawkins	3.00
9	Eric Munson	3.00
10	Dee Brown	3.00
11	Luke Prokopec	3.00
12	Jorge Toca	3.00
13	Alfonso Soriano	7.50
14	Eric Byrnes	3.00
15	Adam Hyzdu	3.00
16	Jimmy Rollins	4.00
17	Joel Pineiro	4.00
18	Aubrey Huff	4.00
19	Kenny Kelly	3.00
20	Vernon Wells	3.00

PS-206 Stars

		NM/M
Complete Set (20):		50.00
Common Player:		1.00
Inserted 3:Hobby Case		
1	Chipper Jones	3.00
2	Greg Maddux	3.00
3	Cal Ripken Jr.	6.00
4	Nomar Garciaparra	4.00
5	Pedro Martinez	2.00
6	Sammy Sosa	4.00
7	Frank Thomas	2.00
8	Ken Griffey Jr.	4.00
9	Manny Ramirez	2.00
10	Jeff Bagwell	2.00
11	Gary Sheffield	1.00
12	Mike Piazza	4.00
13	Roger Clemens	3.50
14	Derek Jeter	6.00
15	Rick Ankiel	1.00
16	Mark McGwire	5.00
17	Tony Gwynn	3.00
18	Barry Bonds	6.00
19	Alex Rodriguez	5.00
20	Ivan Rodriguez	1.50

2000 Palm Beach Post Montreal Expos

At each of the spring training games between March 3-April 1 each copy of the newspaper sold at the ballpark contained a random insert of two Expos and two Cardinals cards. The 3-1/8" x 4-3/4" blank-back cards have action color photos on front.

		NM/M
Complete Set (20):		15.00
Common Player:		.50
(1)	Felipe Alou	.65
(2)	Michael Barrett	.50
(3)	Geoff Blum	.50
(4)	Orlando Cabrera	.75
(5)	Brad Fullmer	.65
(6)	Vladimir Guerrero	5.00
(7)	Dustin Hermanson	.75
(8)	Hideki Irabu	.50
(9)	Steve Kline	.50
(10)	Graeme Lloyd	.50
(11)	Trey Moore	.50
(12)	Mickey Morandini	.50
(13)	Mike Mordecai	.50
(14)	Carl Pavano	.75
(15)	Anthony Telford	.50
(16)	Ugueth Urbina	.75
(17)	Jose Vidro	.75
(18)	Rondell White/Btg	1.00
(19)	Rondell White/Standing	1.00
(20)	Chris Widger	.50

2000 Palm Beach Post St. Louis Cardinals

During spring training each copy of the newspaper sold at the ballpark contained a random insert of two Expos and two Cardinals cards. The 3-1/8" x 4-3/4" blank-back cards have action color photos on front.

		NM/M
Complete Set (20):		20.00
Common Player:		.50
(1)	Rick Ankiel	.50
(2)	Andy Benes	.50
(3)	Kent Bottenfield	.50
(4)	Eric Davis	.50
(5)	J.D. Drew	2.00
(6)	Pat Hentgen	.50
(7)	Chad Hutchinson	.50
(8)	Darryl Kile	.50
(9)	Ray Lankford	.50
(10)	Tony LaRussa	.50
(11)	Eli Marrero	.50
(12)	Joe McEwing	.50
(13)	Mark McGwire/Btg	5.00
(14)	Mark McGwire/Standing	5.00
(15)	Matt Morris	.50
(16)	Edgar Renteria	.50
(17)	Heathcliff Slocumb	.50
(18)	Fernando Tatis	.50
(19)	Dave Veres	.50
(20)	Fernando Vina	.50

2001 Palm Beach Post N.Y. Mets

During spring training the local newspaper distributed (in unknown manner) this set of 2-1/2" x 3-1/2" cards printed on thin stock. Fronts have purplish-gray gray borders and game-action photos. Backs are in black-and-white with a portrait photo, career notes, stats and player personal data. The set is checklisted here by uniform number, as printed on front and back.

		NM/M
Complete Set (10):		10.00
Common Player:		.50
4	Robin Ventura	.50
10	Todd Zeile	.50
22	Al Leiter	.50
31	Mike Piazza	6.00
45	Rick Reed	.50
49	John Franco	.50
?	Armando Benitez	.50
50	Benny Agbayani	.50

2002 Palm Beach Post N.Y. Mets

During spring training the local newspaper distributed (in unknown manner) this set of 2-1/2" x 3-1/2" cards printed on thin stock. Fronts have purple borders and posed or game-action photos. Backs are in black-and-white and have a large team logo and minimal player personal data. The set is checklisted here by uniform number, as printed on front and back.

		NM/M
Complete Set (10):		8.00
Common Player:		.50
2	Bobby Valentine	.50
6	Timo Perez	.50
10	Rey Ordonez	.50
13	Edgardo Alfonzo	.50
22	Al Leiter	.50
31	Mike Piazza	5.00
44	Jay Payton	.50
45	John Franco	.50
47	Joe McEwing	.50
49	Armando Benitez	.50

1988 Panini Stickers

BOSTON RED SOX
ROGER CLEMENS

This set of 480 stickers features 312 major league players, both rookies and superstar veterans. The full-color stickers measure 2-11/16" x 1-7/8" (team emblem and uniform stickers are slightly larger). Individual players, duos and group action shots are included in the set which also contains 14 stickers that depict 1987 season highlights. Panini also produced a 64-page album with Don Mattingly on the cover and two pages devoted to each team with a space marked for each sticker in the set. Individual sticker packets contained a total of six stickers; four players, one team logo and one uniform sticker. Panini offered a collectors' sticker exchange service in which up to 30 stickers could be traded or specific stickers purchased for 10 cents each. The 26 team logo/pennant stickers (numbered A-1 through Z-1) are listed as #455-480 in the following checklist.

		NM/M
Complete Set (480):		15.00
Common Player:		.05
Sticker Album:		1.00
Wax Pack (6):		.25
Wax Box (100):		7.50
1	World Series Trophy	.05
2	Orioles Logo	.05
3	Orioles Uniform	.05
4	Eric Bell	.05
5	Mike Boddicker	.05
6	Dave Schmidt	.05
7	Terry Kennedy	.05
8	Eddie Murray	.45
9	Bill Ripken	.05
10	Orioles Action (Tony Armas, Cal Ripken Jr.)	.05
11	Orioles Action (Tony Armas, Cal Ripken Jr.)	.25
12	Ray Knight	.05
13	Cal Ripken, Jr.	1.00
14	Ken Gerhart	.05
15	Fred Lynn	.05

#	Player	Price
16	Larry Sheets	.05
17	Mike Young	.05
18	Red Sox Logo	.05
19	Red Sox Uniform	.05
20	Oil Can Boyd	.05
21	Roger Clemens	.65
22	Bruce Hurst	.05
23	Bob Stanley	.05
24	Rich Gedman	.05
25	Dwight Evans	.05
26	Red Sox Action (Marty Barrett, Tim Laudner)	.05
27	Red Sox Action (Marty Barrett, Tim Laudner)	.05
28	Marty Barrett	.05
29	Wade Boggs	.50
30	Spike Owen	.05
31	Ellis Burks	.05
32	Mike Greenwell	.05
33	Jim Rice	.10
34	Angels Logo	.05
35	Angels Uniform	.05
36	Kirk McCaskill	.05
37	Don Sutton	.40
38	Mike Witt	.05
39	Bob Boone	.05
40	Wally Joyner	.05
41	Mark McLemore	.05
42	Angels Action (Juan Bonilla, Devon White)	.05
43	Angels Action (Juan Bonilla, Devon White)	.05
44	Jack Howell	.05
45	Dick Schofield	.05
46	Brian Downing	.05
47	Ruppert Jones	.05
48	Gary Pettis	.05
49	Devon White	.05
50	White Sox Logo	.05
51	White Sox Uniform	.05
52	Floyd Bannister	.05
53	Richard Dotson	.05
54	Bob James	.05
55	Carlton Fisk	.45
56	Greg Walker	.05
57	Fred Manrique	.05
58	White Sox Action (Ozzie Guillen, Donnie Hill, Pat Sheridan)	.05
59	White Sox Action (Ozzie Guillen, Donnie Hill, Pat Sheridan)	.05
60	Steve Lyons	.05
61	Ozzie Guillen	.05
62	Harold Baines	.05
63	Ivan Calderon	.05
64	Gary Redus	.05
65	Ken Williams	.05
66	Indians Logo	.05
67	Indians Uniform	.05
68	Scott Bailes	.05
69	Tom Candiotti	.05
70	Greg Swindell	.05
71	Chris Bando	.05
72	Joe Carter	.05
73	Tommy Hinzo	.05
74	Indians Action (Juan Bonilla, Joe Carter)	.05
75	Indians Action (Juan Bonilla, Joe Carter)	.05
76	Brook Jacoby	.05
77	Julio Franco	.05
78	Brett Butler	.05
79	Mel Hall	.05
80	Cory Snyder	.05
81	Pat Tabler	.05
82	Tigers Logo	.05
83	Tigers Uniform	.05
84	Willie Hernandez	.05
85	Jack Morris	.05
86	Frank Tanana	.05
87	Walt Terrell	.05
88	Matt Nokes	.05
89	Darrell Evans	.05
90	Tigers Action (Darrell Evans, Carlton Fisk)	.05
91	Tigers Action (Darrell Evans, Carlton Fisk)	.05
92	Lou Whitaker	.05
93	Tom Brookens	.05
94	Alan Trammell	.05
95	Kirk Gibson	.05
96	Chet Lemon	.05
97	Pat Sheridan	.05
98	Royals Logo	.05
99	Royals Uniform	.05
100	Charlie Leibrandt	.05
101	Dan Quisenberry	.05
102	Bret Saberhagen	.05
103	Jamie Quirk	.05
104	George Brett	.60
105	Frank White	.05
106	Royals Action (Bret Saberhagen)	.05
107	Royals Action (Bret Saberhagen)	.05
108	Kevin Seitzer	.05
109	Angel Salazar	.05
110	Bo Jackson	.10
111	Lonnie Smith	.05
112	Danny Tartabull	.05
113	Willie Wilson	.05
114	Brewers Logo	.05
115	Brewers Uniform	.05
116	Ted Higuera	.05
117	Juan Nieves	.05
118	Dan Plesac	.05
119	Bill Wegman	.05
120	B.J. Surhoff	.05
121	Greg Brock	.05
122	Brewers Action (Jim Gantner, Lou Whitaker)	.05
123	Brewers Action (Jim Gantner, Lou Whitaker)	.05
124	Jim Gantner	.05
125	Paul Molitor	.45
126	Dale Sveum	.05
127	Glenn Braggs	.05
128	Rob Deer	.05
129	Robin Yount	.45
130	Twins Logo	.05
131	Twins Uniform	.05
132	Bert Blyleven	.05
133	Jeff Reardon	.05
134	Frank Viola	.05
135	Tim Laudner	.05
136	Kent Hrbek	.05
137	Steve Lombardozzi	.05
138	Twins Action (Steve Lombardozzi, Frank White)	.05
139	Twins Action (Steve Lombardozzi, Frank White)	.05
140	Gary Gaetti	.05
141	Greg Gagne	.05
142	Tom Brunansky	.05
143	Dan Gladden	.05
144	Kirby Puckett	.50
145	Gene Larkin	.05
146	Yankees Logo	.05
147	Yankees Uniform	.05
148	Tommy John	.05
149	Rick Rhoden	.05
150	Dave Righetti	.05
151	Rick Cerone	.05
152	Don Mattingly	.60
153	Willie Randolph	.05
154	Yankees Action (Scott Fletcher, Don Mattingly)	.25
155	Yankees Action (Scott Fletcher, Don Mattingly)	.20
156	Mike Pagliarulo	.05
157	Wayne Tolleson	.05
158	Rickey Henderson	.45
159	Dan Pasqua	.05
160	Gary Ward	.05
161	Dave Winfield	.45
162	Athletics Logo	.05
163	Athletics Uniform	.05
164	Dave Stewart	.05
165	Curt Young	.05
166	Terry Steinbach	.05
167	Mark McGwire	.75
168	Tony Phillips	.05
169	Carney Lansford	.05
170	Athletics Action (Mike Gallego, Tony Phillips)	.05
171	Athletics Action (Mike Gallego, Tony Phillips)	.05
172	Alfredo Griffin	.05
173	Jose Canseco	.30
174	Mike Davis	.05
175	Reggie Jackson	.60
176	Dwayne Murphy	.05
177	Luis Polonia	.05
178	Mariners Logo	.05
179	Mariners Uniform	.05
180	Scott Bankhead	.05
181	Mark Langston	.05
182	Edwin Nunez	.05
183	Scott Bradley	.05
184	Dave Valle	.05
185	Alvin Davis	.05
186	Mariners Action (Jack Howell, Rey Quinones)	.05
187	Mariners Action (Jack Howell, Rey Quinones)	.05
188	Harold Reynolds	.05
189	Jim Presley	.05
190	Rey Quinones	.05
191	Phil Bradley	.05
192	Mickey Brantley	.05
193	Mike Kingery	.05
194	Rangers Logo	.05
195	Rangers Uniform	.05
196	Edwin Correa	.05
197	Charlie Hough	.05
198	Bobby Witt	.05
199	Mike Stanley	.05
200	Pete O'Brien	.05
201	Jerry Browne	.05
202	Rangers Action (Steve Buechele, Eddie Murray)	.05
203	Rangers Action (Steve Buechele, Eddie Murray)	.05
204	Steve Buechele	.05
205	Larry Parrish	.05
206	Scott Fletcher	.05
207	Pete Incaviglia	.05
208	Oddibe McDowell	.05
209	Ruben Sierra	.05
210	Blue Jays Logo	.05
211	Blue Jays Uniform	.05
212	Mark Eichhorn	.05
213	Tom Henke	.05
214	Jimmy Key	.05
215	Dave Stieb	.05
216	Ernie Whitt	.05
217	Willie Upshaw	.05
218	Blue Jays Action (Harold Reynolds, Willie Upshaw)	.05
219	Blue Jays Action (Harold Reynolds, Willie Upshaw)	.05
220	Garth Iorg	.05
221	Kelly Gruber	.05
222	Tony Fernandez	.05
223	Jesse Barfield	.05
224	George Bell	.05
225	Lloyd Moseby	.05
226	National League Logo	.05
227	Terry Kennedy	.05
	Don Mattingly	.20
228	Wade Boggs, Willie Randolph	.05
229	Bret Saberhagen	.05
230	George Bell, Cal Ripken Jr.	.45
231	Rickey Henderson, Dave Winfield	.10
232	Gary Carter, Jack Clark	.05
233	Mike Scott	.05
234	Ryne Sandberg, Mike Schmidt	.25
235	Ozzie Smith, Eric Davis	.10
236	Andre Dawson, Darryl Strawberry	.05
237	Braves Logo	.05
238	Braves Uniform	.05
239	Rick Mahler	.05
240	Zane Smith	.05
241	Ozzie Virgil	.05
242	Gerald Perry	.05
243	Glenn Hubbard	.05
244	Ken Oberkfell	.05
245	Braves Action (Glenn Hubbard, Jeffrey Leonard)	.05
246	Braves Action (Glenn Hubbard, Jeffrey Leonard)	.05
247	Rafael Ramirez	.05
248	Ken Griffey	.05
249	Albert Hall	.05
250	Dion James	.05
251	Dale Murphy	.20
252	Gary Roenicke	.05
253	Cubs Logo	.05
254	Cubs Uniform	.05
255	Jamie Moyer	.05
256	Lee Smith	.05
257	Rick Sutcliffe	.05
258	Jody Davis	.05
259	Leon Durham	.05
260	Ryne Sandberg	.50
261	Cubs Action (Jody Davis)	.05
262	Cubs Action (Jody Davis)	.05
263	Keith Moreland	.05
264	Shawon Dunston	.05
265	Andre Dawson	.25
266	Dave Martinez	.05
267	Jerry Mumphrey	.05
268	Rafael Palmeiro	.45
269	Reds Logo	.05
270	Reds Uniform	.05
271	John Franco	.05
272	Ted Power	.05
273	Bo Diaz	.05
274	Nick Esasky	.05
275	Dave Concepcion	.05
276	Kurt Stillwell	.05
277	Reds Action (Bob Melvin, Dave Parker)	.05
278	Reds Action (Bob Melvin, Dave Parker)	.05
279	Buddy Bell	.05
280	Barry Larkin	.05
281	Kal Daniels	.05
282	Eric Davis	.05
283	Tracy Jones	.05
284	Dave Parker	.05
285	Astros Logo	.05
286	Astros Uniform	.05
287	Jim Deshaies	.05
288	Nolan Ryan	1.00
289	Mike Scott	.05
290	Dave Smith	.05
291	Alan Ashby	.05
292	Glenn Davis	.05
293	Astros Action (Alan Ashby, Gary Carter)	.05
294	Astros Action (Alan Ashby, Gary Carter)	.05
295	Bill Doran	.05
296	Denny Walling	.05
297	Craig Reynolds	.05
298	Kevin Bass	.05
299	Jose Cruz	.05
300	Billy Hatcher	.05
301	Dodgers Logo	.05
302	Dodgers Uniform	.05
303	Orel Hershiser	.05
304	Fernando Valenzuela	.05
305	Bob Welch	.05
306	Matt Young	.05
307	Mike Scioscia	.05
308	Franklin Stubbs	.05
309	Dodgers Action (Mariano Duncan, Junior Ortiz)	.05
310	Dodgers Action (Mariano Duncan, Junior Ortiz)	.05
311	Steve Sax	.05
312	Jeff Hamilton	.05
313	Dave Anderson	.05
314	Pedro Guerrero	.05
315	Mike Marshall	.05
316	John Shelby	.05
317	Expos Logo	.05
318	Expos Uniform	.05
319	Neal Heaton	.05
320	Bryn Smith	.05
321	Floyd Youmans	.05
322	Mike Fitzgerald	.05
323	Andres Galarraga	.05
324	Vance Law	.05
325	Expos Action (John Kruk, Tim Raines)	.05
326	Expos Action (John Kruk, Tim Raines)	.05
327	Tim Wallach	.05
328	Hubie Brooks	.05
329	Casey Candaele	.05
330	Tim Raines	.05
331	Mitch Webster	.05
332	Herm Winningham	.05
333	Mets Logo	.05
334	Mets Uniform	.05
335	Ron Darling	.05
336	Sid Fernandez	.05
337	Dwight Gooden	.05
338	Gary Carter	.45
339	Keith Hernandez	.05
340	Wally Backman	.05
341	Mets Action (Mike Diaz, Darryl Strawberry, Tim Teufel, Mookie Wilson)	.05
342	Mets Action (Mike Diaz, Darryl Strawberry, Tim Teufel, Mookie Wilson)	.05
343	Howard Johnson	.05
344	Rafael Santana	.05
345	Lenny Dykstra	.05
346	Kevin McReynolds	.05
347	Darryl Strawberry	.05
348	Mookie Wilson	.05
349	Phillies Logo	.05
350	Phillies Uniform	.05
351	Steve Bedrosian	.05
352	Shane Rawley	.05
353	Bruce Ruffin	.05
354	Kent Tekulve	.05
355	Lance Parrish	.05
356	Von Hayes	.05
357	Phillies Action (Tony Pena, Glenn Wilson)	.05
358	Phillies Action (Tony Pena, Glenn Wilson)	.05
359	Juan Samuel	.05
360	Mike Schmidt	.60
361	Steve Jeltz	.05
362	Chris James	.05
363	Milt Thompson	.05
364	Glenn Wilson	.05
365	Pirates Logo	.05
366	Pirates Uniform	.05
367	Mike Dunne	.05
368	Brian Fisher	.05
369	Mike LaValliere	.05
370	Sid Bream	.05
371	Jose Lind	.05
372	Bobby Bonilla	.05
373	Pirates Action (Bobby Bonilla)	.05
374	Pirates Action (Bobby Bonilla)	.05
375	Al Pedrique	.05
376	Barry Bonds	1.00
377	John Cangelosi	.05
378	Mike Diaz	.05
379	R.J. Reynolds	.05
380	Andy Van Slyke	.05
381	Cardinals Logo	.05
382	Cardinals Uniform	.05
383	Danny Cox	.05
384	Bob Forsch	.05
385	Joe Magrane	.05
386	Todd Worrell	.05
387	Tony Pena	.05
388	Jack Clark	.05
389	Cardinals Action (Jody Davis, Tom Herr)	.05
390	Cardinals Action (Jody Davis, Tom Herr)	.05
391	Tom Herr	.05
392	Terry Pendleton	.05
393	Ozzie Smith	.50
394	Vince Coleman	.05
395	Curt Ford	.05
396	Willie McGee	.05
397	Padres Logo	.05
398	Padres Uniform	.05
399	Lance McCullers	.05
400	Eric Show	.05
401	Ed Whitson	.05
402	Benito Santiago	.05
403	John Kruk	.05
404	Tim Flannery	.05
405	Padres Action (Randy Ready, Benito Santiago)	.05
406	Padres Action (Randy Ready, Benito Santiago)	.05
407	Randy Ready	.05
408	Chris Brown	.05
409	Garry Templeton	.05
410	Tony Gwynn	.50
411	Stan Jefferson	.05
412	Carmelo Martinez	.05
413	Giants Logo	.05
414	Giants Uniform	.05
415	Kelly Downs	.05
416	Scott Garrelts	.05
417	Mike Krukow	.05
418	Mike LaCoss	.05
419	Bob Brenly	.05
420	Will Clark	.05
421	Giants Action (Will Clark, Mike Fitzgerald)	.05
422	Giants Action (Will Clark, Mike Fitzgerald)	.05
423	Robby Thompson	.05
424	Kevin Mitchell	.05
425	Jose Uribe	.05
426	Mike Aldrete	.05
427	Jeffrey Leonard	.05
428	Candy Maldonado	.05
429	Mike Schmidt	.40
430	Don Mattingly	.40
431	Juan Nieves	.05
432	Paul Molitor	.25
433	Benito Santiago	.05
434	Rickey Henderson	.25
435	Nolan Ryan	.65
436	Kevin Seitzer	.05
437	Tony Gwynn	.35
438	Mark McGwire	.55
439	Howard Johnson	.05
440	Steve Bedrosian	.05
441	Darrell Evans	.05
442	Eddie Murray	.25
443	1987 A.L. Championship Series (Kirby Puckett, Alan Trammell, Lou Whitaker)	.05
444	1987 A.L. Championship Series (Kirby Puckett, Alan Trammell, Lou Whitaker)	.05
445	American League Championship Series MVP (Gary Gaetti)	.05
446	National League Championship Series MVP (Jeffrey Leonard)	.05
447	1987 N.L. Championship Series (Kevin Mitchell, Tony Pena)	.05
448	1987 N.L. Championship Series (Kevin Mitchell, Tony Pena)	.05
449	1987 World Series (Tom Brunansky, Tony Pena)	.05
450	1987 World Series (Tom Brunansky, Tony Pena)	.05
451	World Series Celebration	.05
452	World Series Celebration	.05
453	World Series Celebration	.05
454	World Series Celebration	.05
(455)	Orioles Logo/Pennant	.05
(456)	Red Sox Logo/Pennant	.05
(457)	Angels Logo/Pennant	.05
(458)	White Sox Logo/Pennant	.05
(459)	Indians Logo/Pennant	.05
(460)	Tigers Logo/Pennant	.05
(461)	Royals Logo/Pennant	.05
(462)	Brewers Logo/Pennant	.05
(463)	Twins Logo/Pennant	.05
(464)	Yankees Logo/Pennant	.05
(465)	Athletics Logo/Pennant	.05
(466)	Mariners Logo/Pennant	.05
(467)	Rangers Logo/Pennant	.05
(468)	Blue Jays Logo/Pennant	.05
(469)	Braves Logo/Pennant	.05
(470)	Cubs Logo/Pennant	.05
(471)	Reds Logo/Pennant	.05
(472)	Astros Logo/Pennant	.05
(473)	Dodgers Logo/Pennant	.05
(474)	Expos Logo/Pennant	.05
(475)	Mets Logo/Pennant	.05
(476)	Phillies Logo/Pennant	.05
(477)	Pirates Logo/Pennant	.05
(478)	Cardinals Logo/Pennant	.05
(479)	Padres Logo/Pennant	.05
(480)	Giants Logo/Pennant	.05

1989 Panini Stickers

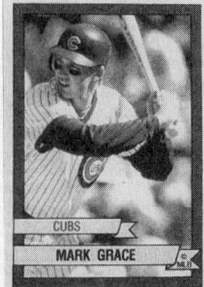

MARK GRACE — CUBS

For a second straight year, the Italian sticker manufacturer produced a 480-piece set for the American market. The 1-7/8" x 2-11/16" stickers were sold in packs of six for 30 cents. Packs contain five player stickers and a foil depicting team logos, lettering or ballparks. A 64-page album depicting Jose Canseco on the cover was offered for 69 cents. The 1989 Panini stickers used more action photos than the previous year. Color photos had banners at the bottom with team and player name. Backs had appropriate logos, sticker number and ads for Panini's sticker book.

	NM/M
Complete Set (480):	12.50
Common Player:	.05
Sticker Album:	1.00
Wax Pack (6):	.25
Wax Box (100):	7.50

#	Player	Price
1	World Series Trophy	.05
2	World Series Trophy	.05
3	Mike Schmidt	.40
4	Tom Browning	.05
5	Doug Jones	.05
6	Wrigley Field	.05
7	Wade Boggs	.30
8	Jose Canseco	.20
9	Orel Hershiser	.05
10	Oakland A's Win ALCS	.05
11	Oakland A's Win ALCS	.05
12	Dennis Eckersley (ALCS MVP)	.20
13	Orel Hershiser (NLCS MVP)	.05
14	Dodgers Win NLCS	.05
15	Dodgers Win NLCS	.05
16	Kirk Gibson	.05
17	Kirk Gibson	.05
18	Orel Hershiser	.05
19	Orel Hershiser	.05
20	Mark McGwire	.50
21	Tim Belcher	.05
22	Jay Howell	.05
23	Mickey Hatcher	.05
24	Mike Davis	.05
25	Orel Hershiser (World Series MVP)	.05
26	Dodgers Win World Series	.05
27	Dodgers Win World Series	.05
28	Dodgers Win World Series	.05
29	Dodgers Win World Series	.05
30	Braves Logo	.05
31	Jose Alvarez	.05
32	Tommy Gregg	.05
33	Paul Assenmacher	.05
34	Tom Glavine	.25
35	Rick Mahler	.05
36	Pete Smith	.05
37	Atlanta Stadium	.05
38	Braves Script	.05
39	Bruce Sutter	.20
40	Gerald Perry	.05
41	Jeff Blauser	.05
42	Ron Gant	.05
43	Andres Thomas	.05
44	Dion James	.05
45	Dale Murphy	.20
46	Cubs Logo	.05
47	Doug Dascenzo	.05
48	Mike Harkey	.05
49	Greg Maddux	.50
50	Jeff Pico	.05
51	Rick Sutcliffe	.05
52	Damon Berryhill	.05
53	Wrigley Field	.05
54	Cubs Script	.05
55	Mark Grace	.15
56	Ryne Sandberg	.50
57	Vance Law	.05
58	Shawon Dunston	.05
59	Andre Dawson	.25
60	Rafael Palmeiro	.40
61	Mitch Webster	.05
62	Reds Logo	.05
63	Jack Armstrong	.05
64	Chris Sabo	.05
65	Tom Browning	.05
66	John Franco	.05
67	Danny Jackson	.05
68	Jose Rijo	.05
69	Riverfront Stadium	.05
70	Reds Script	.05
71	Bo Diaz	.05
72	Nick Esasky	.05
73	Jeff Treadway	.05
74	Barry Larkin	.05
75	Kal Daniels	.05
76	Eric Davis	.05
77	Paul O'Neill	.05
78	Astros Logo	.05
79	Craig Biggio	.05
80	John Fishel	.05
81	Juan Agosto	.05
82	Bob Knepper	.05
83	Nolan Ryan	1.00
84	Mike Scott	.05
85	The Astrodome	.05
86	Astros Script	.05
87	Dave Smith	.05
88	Glenn Davis	.05
89	Bill Doran	.05
90	Rafael Ramirez	.05
91	Kevin Bass	.05
92	Billy Hatcher	.05
93	Gerald Young	.05
94	Dodgers Logo	.05
95	Tim Belcher	.05
96	Tim Crews	.05
97	Orel Hershiser	.05
98	Jay Howell	.05
99	Tim Leary	.05
100	John Tudor	.05

No.	Player	Price
101	Dodgers Stadium	.05
102	Dodgers Script	.05
103	Fernando Valenzuela	.05
104	Mike Scioscia	.05
105	Mickey Hatcher	.05
106	Steve Sax	.05
107	Kirk Gibson	.05
108	Mike Marshall	.05
109	John Shelby	.05
110	Expos Logo	.05
111	Randy Johnson	.40
112	Nelson Santovenia	.05
113	Tim Burke	.05
114	Dennis Martinez	.05
115	Pascual Perez	.05
116	Bryn Smith	.05
117	Olympic Stadium	.05
118	Expos Script	.05
119	Andres Galarraga	.05
120	Wallace Johnson	.05
121	Tom Foley	.05
122	Tim Wallach	.05
123	Hubie Brooks	.05
124	Tracy Jones	.05
125	Tim Raines	.05
126	Mets Logo	.05
127	Kevin Elster	.05
128	Gregg Jefferies	.05
129	David Cone	.05
130	Ron Darling	.05
131	Dwight Gooden	.05
132	Roger McDowell	.05
133	Shea Stadium	.05
134	Mets Script	.05
135	Randy Myers	.05
136	Gary Carter	.40
137	Keith Hernandez	.05
138	Lenny Dykstra	.05
139	Kevin McReynolds	.05
140	Darryl Strawberry	.05
141	Mookie Wilson	.05
142	Phillies Logo	.05
143	Ron Jones	.05
144	Ricky Jordan	.05
145	Steve Bedrosian	.05
146	Don Carman	.05
147	Kevin Gross	.05
148	Bruce Ruffin	.05
149	Veterans Stadium	.05
150	Phillies Script	.05
151	Von Hayes	.05
152	Juan Samuel	.05
153	Mike Schmidt	.55
154	Phil Bradley	.05
155	Bob Dernier	.05
156	Chris James	.05
157	Milt Thompson	.05
158	Pirates Logo	.05
159	Randy Kramer	.05
160	Scott Medvin	.05
161	Doug Drabek	.05
162	Mike Dunne	.05
163	Jim Gott	.05
164	Jeff Robinson	.05
165	Three Rivers Stadium	.05
166	Pirates Script	.05
167	John Smiley	.05
168	Mike LaValliere	.05
169	Sid Bream	.05
170	Jose Lind	.05
171	Bobby Bonilla	.05
172	Barry Bonds	1.00
173	Andy Van Slyke	.05
174	Cardinals Logo	.05
175	Luis Alicea	.05
176	John Costello	.05
177	Jose DeLeon	.05
178	Joe Magrane	.05
179	Todd Worrell	.05
180	Tony Pena	.05
181	Busch Stadium	.05
182	Cardinals Script	.05
183	Pedro Guerrero	.05
184	Jose Oquendo	.05
185	Terry Pendleton	.50
186	Ozzie Smith	.50
187	Tom Brunansky	.05
188	Vince Coleman	.05
189	Willie McGee	.05
190	Padres Logo	.05
191	Roberto Alomar	.15
192	Sandy Alomar, Jr.	.05
193	Mark Davis	.05
194	Andy Hawkins	.05
195	Dennis Rasmussen	.05
196	Eric Show	.05
197	Jack Murphy Stadium	.05
198	Padres Script	.05
199	Benito Santiago	.05
200	John Kruk	.05
201	Randy Ready	.05
202	Garry Templeton	.05
203	Tony Gwynn	.50
204	Carmelo Martinez	.05
205	Marvell Wynne	.05
206	Giants Logo	.05
207	Dennis Cook	.05
208	Kirt Manwaring	.05
209	Kelly Downs	.05
210	Rick Reuschel	.05
211	Don Robinson	.05
212	Will Clark	.05
213	Candlestick Park	.05
214	Giants Script	.05
215	Robby Thompson	.05
216	Kevin Mitchell	.05
217	Jose Uribe	.05
218	Matt Williams	.05
219	Mike Aldrete	.05
220	Brett Butler	.05
221	Candy Maldonado	.05
222	Tony Gwynn	.30
223	Darryl Strawberry	.05
224	Andres Galarraga	.05
225	Orel Hershiser	.05
	Danny Jackson	.05
226	Nolan Ryan	.50
227	Dwight Gooden/AS	.05
228	Gary Carter/AS	.05
229	Vince Coleman/AS	.05
230	Andre Dawson/AS	.05
231	Darryl Strawberry/AS	.05
232	Will Clark/AS	.05
233	Ryne Sandberg/AS	.25
234	Bobby Bonilla/AS	.05
235	Ozzie Smith/AS	.30
236	Terry Steinbach/AS	.05
237	Frank Viola/AS	.05
238	Jose Canseco/AS	.10
239	Rickey Henderson/AS	.20
240	Dave Winfield/AS	.20
241	Cal Ripken, Jr./AS	.50
242	Wade Boggs/AS	.25
243	Paul Molitor/AS	.20
244	Mark McGwire/AS	.40
245	Wade Boggs	.30
246	Jose Canseco	.10
247	Kirby Puckett	.30
248	Frank Viola	.05
249	Roger Clemens	.35
250	Orioles Logo	.05
251	Bob Milacki	.05
252	Craig Worthington	.05
253	Jeff Ballard	.05
254	Tom Niedenfuer	.05
255	Dave Schmidt	.05
256	Terry Kennedy	.05
257	Memorial Stadium	.05
258	Orioles Script	.05
259	Mickey Tettleton	.05
260	Eddie Murray	.40
261	Billy Ripken	.05
262	Cal Ripken, Jr.	1.00
263	Joe Orsulak	.05
264	Larry Sheets	.05
265	Pete Stanicek	.05
266	Red Sox Logo	.05
267	Steve Curry	.05
268	Jody Reed	.05
269	"Oil Can" Boyd	.05
270	Roger Clemens	.55
271	Bruce Hurst	.05
272	Lee Smith	.05
273	Fenway Park	.05
274	Red Sox Script	.05
275	Todd Benzinger	.05
276	Marty Barrett	.05
277	Wade Boggs	.50
278	Ellis Burks	.05
279	Dwight Evans	.05
280	Mike Greenwell	.05
281	Jim Rice	.10
282	Angels Logo	.05
283	Dante Bichette	.05
284	Bryan Harvey	.05
285	Kirk McCaskill	.05
286	Mike Witt	.05
287	Bob Boone	.05
288	Brian Downing	.05
289	Anaheim Stadium	.05
290	Angels Script	.05
291	Wally Joyner	.05
292	Johnny Ray	.05
293	Jack Howell	.05
294	Dick Schofield	.05
295	Tony Armas	.05
296	Chili Davis	.05
297	Devon White	.05
298	White Sox Logo	.05
299	Dave Gallagher	.05
300	Melido Perez	.05
301	Shawn Hillegas	.05
302	Jack McDowell	.05
303	Bobby Thigpen	.05
304	Carlton Fisk	.40
305	Comiskey Park	.05
306	White Sox Script	.05
307	Greg Walker	.05
308	Steve Lyons	.05
309	Ozzie Guillen	.05
310	Harold Baines	.05
311	Daryl Boston	.05
312	Lance Johnson	.05
313	Dan Pasqua	.05
314	Indians Logo	.05
315	Luis Medina	.05
316	Ron Tingley	.05
317	Tom Candiotti	.05
318	John Farrell	.05
319	Doug Jones	.05
320	Greg Swindell	.05
321	Cleveland Stadium	.05
322	Indians Script	.05
323	Andy Allanson	.05
324	Willie Upshaw	.05
325	Julio Franco	.05
326	Brook Jacoby	.05
327	Joe Carter	.05
328	Mel Hall	.05
329	Cory Snyder	.05
330	Tigers Logo	.05
331	Paul Gibson	.05
332	Torey Luvullo	.05
333	Mike Henneman	.05
334	Jack Morris	.05
335	Jeff Robinson	.05
336	Frank Tanana	.05
337	Tiger Stadium	.05
338	Tigers Script	.05
339	Matt Nokes	.05
340	Tom Brookens	.05
341	Lou Whitaker	.05
342	Luis Salazar	.05
343	Alan Trammell	.05
344	Chet Lemon	.05
345	Gary Pettis	.05
346	Royals Logo	.05
347	Luis de los Santos	.05
348	Gary Thurman	.05
349	Steve Farr	.05
350	Mark Gubicza	.05
351	Charlie Leibrandt	.05
352	Bret Saberhagen	.05
353	Royals Stadium	.05
354	Royals Script	.05
355	George Brett	.55
356	Frank White	.05
357	Kevin Seitzer	.05
358	Bo Jackson	.10
359	Pat Tabler	.05
360	Danny Tartabull	.05
361	Willie Wilson	.05
362	Brewers Logo	.05
363	Joey Meyer	.05
364	Gary Sheffield	.25
365	Don August	.05
366	Ted Higuera	.05
367	Dan Plesac	.05
368	B.J. Surhoff	.05
369	County Stadium	.05
370	Brewers Script	.05
371	Greg Brock	.05
372	Jim Gantner	.05
373	Paul Molitor	.40
374	Dale Sveum	.05
375	Glenn Braggs	.05
376	Rob Deer	.05
377	Robin Yount	.40
378	Twins Logo	.05
379	German Gonzalez	.05
380	Kelvin Torve	.05
381	Allan Anderson	.05
382	Jeff Reardon	.05
383	Frank Viola	.05
384	Tim Laudner	.05
385	HHH Metrodome	.05
386	Twins Script	.05
387	Kent Hrbek	.05
388	Gene Larkin	.05
389	Gary Gaetti	.05
390	Greg Gagne	.05
391	Randy Bush	.05
392	Dan Gladden	.05
393	Kirby Puckett	.50
394	Yankees Logo	.05
395	Roberto Kelly	.05
396	Al Leiter	.05
397	John Candelaria	.05
398	Rich Dotson	.05
399	Rick Rhoden	.05
400	Dave Righetti	.05
401	Yankee Stadium	.05
402	Yankees Script	.05
403	Don Slaught	.05
404	Don Mattingly	.55
405	Willie Randolph	.05
406	Mike Pagliarulo	.05
407	Rafael Santana	.05
408	Rickey Henderson	.40
409	Dave Winfield	.40
410	A's Logo	.05
411	Todd Burns	.05
412	Walt Weiss	.05
413	Storm Davis	.05
414	Dennis Eckersley	.35
415	Dave Stewart	.05
416	Bob Welch	.05
417	Oakland Coliseum	.05
418	A's Script	.05
419	Terry Steinbach	.05
420	Mark McGwire	.75
421	Carney Lansford	.05
422	Jose Canseco	.35
423	Dave Henderson	.05
424	Dave Parker	.05
425	Luis Polonia	.05
426	Mariners Logo	.05
427	Mario Diaz	.05
428	Edgar Martinez	.05
429	Scott Bankhead	.05
430	Mark Langston	.05
431	Mike Moore	.05
432	Scott Bradley	.05
433	The Kingdome	.05
434	Mariners Script	.05
435	Alvin Davis	.05
436	Harold Reynolds	.05
437	Jim Presley	.05
438	Rey Quinonez	.05
439	Mickey Brantley	.05
440	Jay Buhner	.05
441	Henry Cotto	.05
442	Rangers Logo	.05
443	Cecil Espy	.05
444	Chad Kreuter	.05
445	Jose Guzman	.05
446	Charlie Hough	.05
447	Jeff Russell	.05
448	Bobby Witt	.05
449	Arlington Stadium	.05
450	Rangers Script	.05
451	Geno Petralli	.05
452	Pete O'Brien	.05
453	Steve Buechele	.05
454	Scott Fletcher	.05
455	Pete Incaviglia	.05
456	Oddibe McDowell	.05
457	Ruben Sierra	.05
458	Blue Jays Logo	.05
459	Rob Ducey	.05
460	Todd Stottlemyre	.05
461	Tom Henke	.05
462	Jimmy Key	.05
463	Dave Steib	.05
464	Pat Borders	.05
465	Exhibition Stadium	.05
466	Blue Jays Script	.05
467	Fred McGriff	.05
468	Manny Lee	.05
469	Kelly Gruber	.05
470	Tony Fernandez	.05
471	Jesse Barfield	.05
472	George Bell	.05
473	Lloyd Moseby	.05
474	Orel Hershiser	.05
475	Frank Viola	.05
476	Chris Sabo	.05
477	Jose Canseco	.10
478	Walt Weiss	.05
479	Kirk Gibson	.05
480	Jose Canseco	.10

1990 Panini Stickers

BRAVES

JOHN SMOLTZ

Nearly 400 individual player and specialty stickers comprise the 1990 issue from this Italian company. Sold in packs of five regular and one foil sticker, the set includes 388 2-1/8" x 3" stickers. Fronts feature color action photos. Backs are printed in black-and-white and include a sticker number and appropriate logos. A 68-page album with Nolan Ryan on the cover was sold as an adjunct to the stickers. Among the foil stickers in the set are those featuring the team logo and batting helmet of each team.

	NM/M
Complete Set (388):	9.00
Common Player:	.05
English Album:	1.00
French Album:	3.00
Wax Pack (5+1):	.25
Wax Box (100):	7.50

No.	Player	Price
1	Randy Milligan	.05
2	Gregg Olson	.05
3	Bill Ripken	.05
4	Phil Bradley	.05
5	Joe Orsulak	.05
6	Bob Milacki	.05
7	Cal Ripken, Jr.	1.00
8	Mickey Tettleton	.05
9	Orioles Logo (Foil)	.05
10	Orioles Helmet (Foil)	.05
11	Craig Worthington	.05
12	Mike Devereaux	.05
13	Jeff Ballard	.05
14	Lee Smith	.05
15	Marty Barrett	.05
16	Mike Greenwell	.05
17	Dwight Evans	.05
18	John Dopson	.05
19	Wade Boggs	.50
20	Mike Boddicker	.05
21	Ellis Burks	.05
22	Red Sox Logo (Foil)	.05
23	Red Sox Helmet (Foil)	.05
24	Roger Clemens	.55
25	Jody Reed	.05
26	Nick Esasky	.05
27	Brian Downing	.05
28	Bert Blyleven	.05
29	Devon White	.05
30	Claudell Washington	.05
31	Wally Joyner	.05
32	Chuck Finley	.05
33	Johnny Ray	.05
34	Jim Abbott	.05
35	Angels Logo (Foil)	.05
36	Angels Helmet (Foil)	.05
37	Kirk McCaskill	.05
38	Lance Parrish	.05
39	Chili Davis	.05
40	Steve Lyons	.05
41	Ozzie Guillen	.05
42	Melido Perez	.05
43	Scott Fletcher	.05
44	Carlton Fisk	.40
45	Greg Walker	.05
46	Dave Gallagher	.05
47	Ivan Calderon	.05
48	White Sox Logo (Foil)	.05
49	White Sox Helmet (Foil)	.05
50	Bobby Thigpen	.05
51	Ron Kittle	.05
52	Daryl Boston	.05
53	John Farrell	.05
54	Jerry Browne	.05
55	Pete O'Brien	.05
56	Cory Snyder	.05
57	Tom Candiotti	.05
58	Brook Jacoby	.05
59	Greg Swindell	.05
60	Felix Fermin	.05
61	Indians Logo (Foil)	.05
62	Indians Helmet (Foil)	.05
63	Doug Jones	.05
64	Dion James	.05
65	Joe Carter	.05
66	Mike Heath	.05
67	Dave Bergman	.05
68	Gary Ward	.05
69	Mike Henneman	.05
70	Alan Trammell	.05
71	Lou Whitaker	.05
72	Frank Tanana	.05
73	Fred Lynn	.05
74	Tigers Logo (Foil)	.05
75	Tigers Helmet (Foil)	.05
76	Jack Morris	.05
77	Chet Lemon	.05
78	Gary Pettis	.05
79	Kurt Stillwell	.05
80	Jim Eisenreich	.05
81	Bret Saberhagen	.05
82	Mark Gubicza	.05
83	Frank White	.05
84	Bo Jackson	.10
85	Jeff Montgomery	.05
86	Kevin Seitzer	.05
87	Royals Logo (Foil)	.05
88	Royals Helmet (Foil)	.05
89	Tom Gordon	.05
90	Danny Tartabull	.05
91	George Brett	.55
92	Robin Yount	.40
93	B.J. Surhoff	.05
94	Jim Gantner	.05
95	Dan Plesac	.05
96	Ted Higuera	.05
97	Glenn Braggs	.05
98	Paul Molitor	.40
99	Chris Bosio	.05
100	Brewers Logo (Foil)	.05
101	Brewers Helmet (Foil)	.05
102	Rob Deer	.05
103	Chuck Crim	.05
104	Greg Brock	.05
105	Kirby Puckett	.50
106	Gary Gaetti	.05
107	Roy Smith	.05
108	Jeff Reardon	.05
109	Randy Bush	.05
110	Al Newman	.05
111	Dan Gladden	.05
112	Kent Hrbek	.05
113	Twins Logo (Foil)	.05
114	Twins Helmet (Foil)	.05
115	Greg Gagne	.05
116	Brian Harper	.05
117	Allan Anderson	.05
118	Lee Guetterman	.05
119	Roberto Kelly	.05
120	Jesse Barfield	.05
121	Alvaro Espinoza	.05
122	Mel Hall	.05
123	Chuck Cary	.05
124	Dave Righetti	.05
125	Don Mattingly	.55
126	Yankees Logo (Foil)	.05
127	Yankees Helmet (Foil)	.05
128	Bob Geren	.05
129	Steve Sax	.05
130	Andy Hawkins	.05
131	Bob Welch	.05
132	Mark McGwire	.75
133	Dave Henderson	.05
134	Carney Lansford	.05
135	Walt Weiss	.05
136	Mike Moore	.05
137	Dennis Eckersley	.35
138	Rickey Henderson	.40
139	A's Logo (Foil)	.05
140	A's Helmet (Foil)	.05
141	Dave Stewart	.05
142	Jose Canseco	.30
143	Terry Steinbach	.05
144	Harold Reynolds	.05
145	Darnell Coles	.05
146	Brian Holman	.05
147	Scott Bankhead	.05
148	Greg Briley	.05
149	Alvin Davis	.05
150	Jeffrey Leonard	.05
151	Mike Schooler	.05
152	Mariners Logo (Foil)	.05
153	Mariners Helmet (Foil)	.05
154	Randy Johnson	.40
155	Ken Griffey Jr.	.65
156	Dave Valle	.05
157	Pete Incaviglia	.05
158	Fred Manrique	.05
159	Jeff Russell	.05
160	Nolan Ryan	1.00
161	Geno Petralli	.05
162	Ruben Sierra	.05
163	Julio Franco	.05
164	Rafael Palmeiro	.35
165	Rangers Logo (Foil)	.05
166	Rangers Helmet (Foil)	.05
167	Harold Baines	.05
168	Kevin Brown	.05
169	Steve Buechele	.05
170	Fred McGriff	.05
171	Kelly Gruber	.05
172	Todd Stottlemyre	.05
173	Dave Steib	.05
174	Mookie Wilson	.05
175	Pat Borders	.05
176	Tony Fernandez	.05
177	John Cerutti	.05
178	Blue Jays Logo (Foil)	.05
179	Blue Jays Helmet (Foil)	.05
180	George Bell	.05
181	Jimmy Key	.05
182	Nelson Liriano	.05
183	Kirby Puckett (BA leader)	.30
184	Carney Lansford (Stats leader)	.05
185	Nolan Ryan (K Leader)	.50
186	American League Logo (Foil)	.05
187	National League Logo (Foil)	.05
188	World's Championship Trophy (Foil)	.05
189	1988 L.A. Dodgers World Series Ring (Foil)	.05
190	1987 Minnesota Twins World Series Ring (Foil)	.05
191	1986 N.Y. Mets World Series Ring (Foil)	.05
192	1985 K.C. Royals World Series Ring (Foil)	.05
193	1984 Detroit Tigers World Series Ring (Foil)	.05
194	1983 Baltimore Orioles World Series Ring (Foil)	.05
195	1982 Cardinals World Series Ring (Foil)	.05
196	1981 L.A. Dodgers World Series Ring (Foil)	.05
197	1980 Phillies World Series Ring (Foil)	.05
198	Dave Stewart, Bo Jackson/AS	.05
199	Wade Boggs, Kirby Puckett/AS	.15
200	Harold Baines/AS	.05
201	Julio Franco/AS	.05
202	Cal Ripken, Jr./AS	.50
203	Ruben Sierra/AS	.05
204	Mark McGwire/AS	.40
205	Terry Steinbach/AS	.05
206	Rick Reuschel/AS	.05
	Ozzie Smith/AS	.05
207	Tony Gwynn, Will Clark/AS	.05
208	Kevin Mitchell/AS	.05
209	Eric Davis/AS	.05
210	Howard Johnson/AS	.05
211	Pedro Guerrero/AS	.05
212	Ryne Sandberg/AS	.25
213	Benito Santiago/AS	.05
214	Kevin Mitchell (HR Leaders)	.05
215	Mark Davis (Saves leader.)	.05
	Vince Coleman (SB Leader)	.05
216	Jeff Blauser	.05
217	Jeff Treadway	.05
218	Tom Glavine	.20
219	Joe Boever	.05
220	Oddibe McDowell	.05
221	Dale Murphy	.20
222	Derek Lilliquist	.05
223	Tommy Gregg	.05
224	Braves Logo (Foil)	.05
225	Braves Helmet (Foil)	.05
226	Lonnie Smith	.05
227	John Smoltz	.05
228	Andres Thomas	.05
229	Jerome Walton	.05
230	Ryne Sandberg	.50
231	Mitch Williams	.05
232	Rick Sutcliffe	.05
233	Damon Berryhill	.05
234	Dwight Smith	.05
235	Shawon Dunston	.05
236	Greg Maddux	.05
237	Cubs Logo (Foil)	.05
238	Cubs Helmet (Foil)	.05
239	Andre Dawson	.25
240	Mark Grace	.05
241	Mike Bielecki	.05
242	Jose Rijo	.05
243	John Franco	.05
244	Paul O'Neill	.05
245	Eric Davis	.05
246	Tom Browning	.05
247	Chris Sabo	.05
248	Rob Dibble	.05
249	Todd Benzinger	.05
250	Reds Logo (Foil)	.05
251	Reds Helmet (Foil)	.05
252	Barry Larkin	.05
253	Rolando Roomes	.05
254	Danny Jackson	.05
255	Terry Puhl	.05
256	Dave Smith	.05
257	Glenn Davis	.05
258	Craig Biggio	.05
259	Ken Caminiti	.05
260	Kevin Bass	.05
261	Mike Scott	.05

263 Gerald Young .05
264 Astros Logo (Foil) .05
265 Astros Helmet (Foil) .05
266 Rafael Ramirez .05
267 Jim Deshaies .05
268 Bill Doran .05
269 Fernando Valenzuela .05
270 Alfredo Griffin .05
271 Kirk Gibson .05
272 Mike Marshall .05
273 Eddie Murray .40
274 Jay Howell .05
275 Orel Hershiser .05
276 Mike Scioscia .05
277 Dodgers Logo (Foil) .05
278 Dodgers Helmet (Foil) .05
279 Willie Randolph .05
280 Kal Daniels .05
281 Tim Belcher .05
282 Pascual Perez .05
283 Tim Raines .05
284 Andres Galarraga .05
285 Spike Owen .05
286 Tim Wallach .05
287 Mark Langston .05
288 Dennis Martinez .05
289 Nelson Santovenia .05
290 Expos Logo (Foil) .05
291 Expos Helmet (Foil) .05
292 Tom Foley .05
293 Dave Martinez .05
294 Tim Burke .05
295 Ron Darling .05
296 Kevin Elster .05
297 Dwight Gooden .05
298 Gregg Jefferies .05
299 Sid Fernandez .05
300 Dave Magadan .05
301 David Cone .05
302 Darryl Strawberry .05
303 Mets Logo (Foil) .05
304 Mets Helmet (Foil) .05
305 Kevin McReynolds .05
306 Howard Johnson .05
307 Randy Myers .05
308 Roger McDowell .05
309 Tom Herr .05
310 John Kruk .05
311 Randy Ready .05
312 Jeff Parrett .05
313 Lenny Dykstra .05
314 Ken Howell .05
315 Ricky Jordan .05
316 Phillies Logo (Foil) .05
317 Phillies Helmet (Foil) .05
318 Dickie Thon .05
319 Von Hayes .05
320 Dennis Cook .05
321 Jay Bell .05
322 Barry Bonds 1.00
323 John Smiley .05
324 Andy Van Slyke .05
325 Bobby Bonilla .05
326 Bill Landrum .05
327 Randy Kramer .05
328 Jose Lind .05
329 Pirates Logo (Foil) .05
330 Pirates Helmet (Foil) .05
331 Gary Redus .05
332 Doug Drabek .05
333 Mike LaValliere .05
334 Jose DeLeon .05
335 Pedro Guerrero .05
336 Vince Coleman .05
337 Terry Pendleton .05
338 Ozzie Smith .50
339 Willie McGee .05
340 Todd Worrell .05
341 Jose Oquendo .05
342 Cardinals Logo (Foil) .05
343 Cardinals Helmet (Foil) .05
344 Tom Brunansky .05
345 Milt Thompson .05
346 Joe Magrane .05
347 Ed Whitson .05
348 Jack Clark .05
349 Roberto Alomar .10
350 Chris James .05
351 Tony Gwynn .50
352 Mark Davis .05
353 Greg W. Harris .05
354 Garry Templeton .05
355 Padres Logo (Foil) .05
356 Padres Helmet (Foil) .05
357 Bruce Hurst .05
358 Benito Santiago .05
359 Bip Roberts .05
360 Dave Dravecky .05
361 Kevin Mitchell .05
362 Craig Lefferts .05
363 Will Clark .05
364 Steve Bedrosian .05
365 Brett Butler .05
366 Matt Williams .05
367 Scott Garrelts .05
368 Giants Logo (Foil) .05
369 Giants Helmet (Foil) .05
370 Rick Reuschel .05
371 Robby Thompson .05
372 Jose Uribe .05
373 Ben McDonald (Headliner) .05
374 Carlos Martinez (Headliner) .05
375 Steve Olin (Headliner) .05
376 Bill Spiers (Headliner) .05
377 Junior Felix (Headliner) .05
378 Joe Oliver (Headliner) .05
379 Eric Anthony (Headliner) .05

380 Ramon Martinez (Headliner) .05
381 Todd Zeile (Headliner) .05
382 Andy Benes (Headliner) .05
383 Vince Coleman (Highlight) .05
384 Bo Jackson (Highlight) .05
385 Howard Johnson (Highlight) .05
386 Dave Dravecky (Highlight) .05
387 Nolan Ryan (Highlight) .50
388 Cal Ripken, Jr. (Highlight) .50

1991 Panini Stickers

For 1991 the Panini stickers were considerably downsized in both the number of pieces in the set (271) and in the size of each sticker (1-1/2" x 2-9-16"). Player stickers have a color action photo at center with a few stats at bottom. There are foil pennant and team logo stickers for each team as well as 1990 season highlights kicking off the set. Backs are printed in black-and-white and have MLB and Players Association logos, along with Panini advertising. A colorful album was available to house the stickers, featuring on its cover Ken Griffey, Jr., Ryne Sandberg and Rickey Henderson.

NM/M
Complete Set (271): 12.50
Common Player: .05
Album: 1.00
Wax Pack (5+1): .25
Wax Box (100): 9.00
1 Mark Langston, Mike Witt (No-hitter.) .05
2 Randy Johnson (No-hitter.) .20
3 Nolan Ryan (No-hitter.) .50
4 Dave Stewart (No-hitter.) .05
5 Fernando Valenzuela (No-hitter.) .05
6 Andy Hawkins (No-hitter.) .05
7 Melido Perez (No-hitter.) .05
8 Terry Mullholland (No-hitter.) .05
9 Dave Steib (No-hitter.) .05
10 Craig Biggio .05
11 Jim Deshaies .05
12 Dave Smith .05
13 Eric Yelding .05
14 Astros Pennant .05
15 Astros Logo .05
16 Mike Scott .05
17 Ken Caminiti .05
18 Danny Darwin .05
19 Glenn Davis .05
20 Braves Pennant .05
21 Braves Logo .05
22 Lonnie Smith .05
23 Charlie Leibrandt .05
24 Jim Presley .05
25 Greg Olson .05
26 John Smoltz .05
27 Ron Gant .05
28 Jeff Treadway .05
29 Dave Justice .05
30 Jose Oquendo .05
31 Joe Magrane .05
32 Cardinals Pennant .05
33 Cardinals Logo .05
34 Todd Zeile .05
35 Vince Coleman .05
36 Bob Tewksbury .05
37 Pedro Guerrero .05
38 Lee Smith .05
39 Ozzie Smith .50
40 Ryne Sandberg .50
41 Andre Dawson .05
42 Cubs Pennant .05
43 Greg Maddux .50
44 Jerome Walton .05
45 Cubs Logo .05
46 Mike Harkey .05
47 Shawon Dunston .05
48 Mark Grace .05
49 Joe Girardi .05
50 Ramon Martinez .05
51 Lenny Harris .05
52 Mike Morgan .05

53 Eddie Murray .40
54 Dodgers Pennant .05
55 Dodgers Logo .05
56 Hubie Brooks .05
57 Mike Scioscia .05
58 Kal Daniels .05
59 Fernando Valenzuela .05
60 Expos Pennant .05
61 Expos Logo .05
62 Spike Owen .05
63 Tim Raines .05
64 Tim Wallach .05
65 Larry Walker .05
66 Dave Martinez .05
67 Mark Gardner .05
68 Dennis Martinez .05
69 Delino DeShields .05
70 Jeff Brantley .05
71 Kevin Mitchell .05
72 Giants Pennant .05
73 Giants Logo .05
74 Don Robinson .05
75 Brett Butler .05
76 Matt Williams .05
77 Robby Thompson .05
78 John Burkett .05
79 Will Clark .05
80 David Cone .05
81 Dave Magadan .05
82 Mets Pennant .05
83 Gregg Jefferies .05
84 Frank Viola .05
85 Mets Logo .05
86 Howard Johnson .05
87 John Franco .05
88 Darryl Strawberry .05
89 Dwight Gooden .05
90 Joe Carter .05
91 Ed Whitson .05
92 Andy Benes .05
93 Benito Santiago .05
94 Padres Pennant .05
95 Padres Logo .05
96 Roberto Alomar .10
97 Bip Roberts .05
98 Jack Clark .05
99 Tony Gwynn .50
100 Phillies Pennant .05
101 Phillies Logo .05
102 Charlie Hayes .05
103 Lenny Dykstra .05
104 Dale Murphy .20
105 Von Hayes .05
106 Dickie Thon .05
107 John Kruk .05
108 Ken Howell .05
109 Darren Daulton .05
110 Jay Bell .05
111 Bobby Bonilla .05
112 Pirates Pennant .05
113 Pirates Logo .05
114 Barry Bonds 1.00
115 Neal Heaton .05
116 Doug Drabek .05
117 Jose Lind .05
118 Andy Van Slyke .05
119 Sid Bream .05
120 Paul O'Neill .05
121 Randy Myers .05
122 Reds Pennant .05
123 Mariano Duncan .05
124 Eric Davis .05
125 Red Logo .05
126 Jack Armstrong .05
127 Chris Sabo .05
128 Rob Dibble .05
129 Barry Larkin .05
130 National League Logo .05
131 American League Logo .05
132 Dave Winfield .40
133 Lance Parrish .05
134 Chili Davis .05
135 Chuck Finley .05
136 Angels Pennant .05
137 Angels Logo .05
138 Johnny Ray .05
139 Dante Bichette .05
140 Jim Abbott .05
141 Wally Joyner .05
142 A's Pennant .05
143 A's Logo .05
144 Dave Stewart .05
145 Mark McGwire .75
146 Rickey Henderson .40
147 Walt Weiss .05
148 Dennis Eckersley .35
149 Jose Canseco .30
150 Dave Henderson .05
151 Bob Welch .05
152 Tony Fernandez .05
153 David Wells .05
154 Blue Jays Pennant .05
155 Blue Jays Logo .05
156 Pat Borders .05
157 Fred McGriff .05
158 George Bell .05
159 John Olerud .05
160 Dave Steib .05
161 Kelly Gruber .05
162 Billy Spiers .05
163 Dan Plesac .05
164 Brewers Pennant .05
165 Mark Knudson .05
166 Robin Yount .40
167 Brewers Logo .05
168 Paul Molitor .05
169 B.J. Surhoff .05
170 Gary Sheffield .30

171 Dave Parker .05
172 Sandy Alomar .05
173 Doug Jones .05
174 Tom Candiotti .05
175 Mitch Webster .05
176 Indians Pennant .05
177 Indians Logo .05
178 Brook Jacoby .05
179 Candy Maldonado .05
180 Carlos Baerga .05
181 Chris James .05
182 Mariners Pennant .05
183 Mariners Logo .05
184 Mike Schooler .05
185 Alvin Davis .05
186 Erik Hanson .05
187 Edgar Martinez .05
188 Randy Johnson .40
189 Ken Griffey Jr. .60
190 Jay Buhner .05
191 Harold Reynolds .05
192 Cal Ripken Jr. 1.00
193 Gregg Olson .05
194 Orioles Pennant .05
195 Orioles Logo .05
196 Mike Devereaux .05
197 Ben McDonald .05
198 Craig Worthington .05
199 Dave Johnson .05
200 Joe Orsulak .05
201 Randy Milligan .05
202 Ruben Sierra .05
203 Bobby Witt .05
204 Rangers Pennant .05
205 Nolan Ryan 1.00
206 Jeff Huson .05
207 Rangers Logo .05
208 Kevin Brown .05
209 Steve Buechele .05
210 Julio Franco .05
211 Rafael Palmeiro .05
212 Ellis Burks .05
213 Dwight Evans .05
214 Wade Boggs .50
215 Roger Clemens .55
216 Red Sox Pennant .05
217 Red Sox Logo .05
218 Jeff Reardon .05
219 Tony Pena .05
220 Jody Reed .05
221 Carlos Quintana .05
222 Royals Pennant .05
223 Royals Logo .05
224 George Brett .55
225 Bret Saberhagen .05
226 Bo Jackson .10
227 Kevin Seitzer .05
228 Mark Gubicza .05
229 Jim Eisenreich .05
230 Gerald Perry .05
231 Tom Gordon .05
232 Cecil Fielder .05
233 Lou Whitaker .05
234 Tigers Pennant .05
235 Tigers Logo .05
236 Mike Henneman .05
237 Mike Heath .05
238 Alan Trammell .05
239 Lloyd Moseby .05
240 Dan Petry .05
241 Dave Bergman .05
242 Brian Harper .05
243 Rick Aguilera .05
244 Twins Pennant .05
245 Greg Gagne .05
246 Gene Larkin .05
247 Twins Logo .05
248 Kirby Puckett .50
249 Kevin Tapani .05
250 Gary Gaetti .05
251 Kent Hrbek .05
252 Bobby Thigpen .05
253 Lance Johnson .05
254 Greg Hibbard .05
255 Carlton Fisk .40
256 White Sox Pennant .05
257 White Sox Logo .05
258 Ivan Calderon .05
259 Barry Jones .05
260 Robin Ventura .05
261 Ozzie Guillen .05
262 Yankees Pennant .05
263 Yankees Logo .05
264 Kevin Maas .05
265 Bob Geren .05
266 Dave Righetti .05
267 Don Mattingly .55
268 Roberto Kelly .05
269 Alvaro Espinoza .05
270 Oscar Azocar .05
271 Steve Sax .05

Canadian

While the U.S. sticker set from Panini was downsized both in physical format and number of stickers in the set, a special issue for the Canadian market was produced in the 2-1/8" x 3" size to a total of 360 pieces. The relatively simple design has a color game-action photo with a wide white border. The black player name and team at bottom are highlighted by a red (American League) or blue (National League) splash of color at lower-left. Black-and-white

CHET LEMON
DETROIT TIGERS

backs have a sticker number and a few words about the collection in English and French. Besides player stickers there are foil specialty stickers for the teams and a subset of All-Star stickers.

NM/M
Complete Set (360): 20.00
Common Player: .05
Album: 3.00
1 Major League Baseball Logo (foil) .05
2 MLB Players Association Logo (foil) .05
3 Panini Logo (foil) .05
4 Houston Astros Pennant (Foil) .05
5 Houston Astros Logo (Foil) .05
6 Craig Biggio .05
7 Glenn Davis .05
8 Casey Candaele .05
9 Ken Caminiti .05
10 Rafael Ramirez .05
11 Glenn Wilson .05
12 Eric Yelding .05
13 Franklin Stubbs .05
14 Mike Scott .05
15 Danny Darwin .05
16 Atlanta Braves Pennant (Foil) .05
17 Atlanta Braves Logo (Foil) .05
18 Greg Olson .05
19 Tommy Gregg .05
20 Jeff Treadway .05
21 Jim Presley .05
22 Jeff Blauser .05
23 Ron Gant .05
24 Lonnie Smith .05
25 Dave Justice .05
26 John Smoltz .05
27 Charlie Leibrandt .05
28 St. Louis Cardinals Pennant (Foil) .05
29 St. Louis Cardinals Logo (Foil) .05
30 Tom Pagnozzi .05
31 Pedro Guerrero .05
32 Jose Oquendo .05
33 Todd Zeile .05
34 Ozzie Smith .50
35 Vince Coleman .05
36 Milt Thompson .05
37 Rex Hudler .05
38 Joe Magrane .05
39 Lee Smith .05
40 Chicago Cubs Pennant (Foil) .05
41 Chicago Cubs Logo (Foil) .05
42 Joe Girardi .05
43 Mark Grace .05
44 Ryne Sandberg .50
45 Luis Salazar .05
46 Shawon Dunston .05
47 Dwight Smith .05
48 Jerome Walton .05
49 Andre Dawson .05
50 Greg Maddux .50
51 Mike Harkey .05
52 Los Angeles Dodgers Pennant (Foil) .05
53 Los Angeles Dodgers Logo (Foil) .05
54 Mike Scioscia .05
55 Eddie Murray .40
56 Juan Samuel .05
57 Lenny Harris .05
58 Alfredo Griffin .05
59 Hubie Brooks .05
60 Kal Daniels .05
61 Stan Javier .05
62 Ramon Martinez .05
63 Mike Morgan .05
64 San Francisco Giants Pennant (Foil) .05
65 San Francisco Giants Logo (Foil) .05
66 Terry Kennedy .05
67 Will Clark .05
68 Robby Thompson .05
69 Matt Williams .05
70 Jose Uribe .05
71 Kevin Mitchell .05
72 Brett Butler .05
73 Don Robinson .05
74 John Burkett .05
75 Jeff Brantley .05

76 New York Mets Pennant (Foil) .05
77 New York Mets Logo (Foil) .05
78 Mackey Sasser .05
79 Dave Magadan .05
80 Gregg Jefferies .05
81 Howard Johnson .05
82 Kevin Elster .05
83 Kevin McReynolds .05
84 Daryl Boston .05
85 Darryl Strawberry .05
86 Dwight Gooden .05
87 Frank Viola .05
88 San Diego Padres Pennant (Foil) .05
89 San Diego Padres Logo (Foil) .05
90 Benito Santiago .05
91 Jack Clark .05
92 Roberto Alomar .10
93 Mike Pagliarulo .05
94 Garry Templeton .05
95 Joe Carter .05
96 Bip Roberts .05
97 Tony Gwynn .50
98 Ed Whitson .05
99 Andy Benes .05
100 Philadelphia Phillies Pennant (Foil) .05
101 Philadelphia Phillies Logo (Foil) .05
102 Darren Daulton .05
103 Ricky Jordan .05
104 Randy Ready .05
105 Charlie Hayes .05
106 Dickie Thon .05
107 Von Hayes .05
108 Lenny Dykstra .05
109 Dale Murphy .20
110 Ken Howell .05
111 Roger McDowell .05
112 Pittsburgh Pirates Pennant (Foil) .05
113 Pittsburgh Pirates Logo (Foil) .05
114 Mike LaValliere .05
115 Sid Bream .05
116 Jose Lind .05
117 Jeff King .05
118 Jay Bell .05
119 Barry Bonds 1.00
120 Bobby Bonilla .05
121 Andy Van Slyke .05
122 Doug Drabek .05
123 Neal Heaton .05
124 Cincinnati Reds Pennant (Foil) .05
125 Cincinnati Reds Logo (Foil) .05
126 Joe Oliver .05
127 Todd Benzinger .05
128 Mariano Duncan .05
129 Chris Sabo .05
130 Barry Larkin .05
131 Eric Davis .05
132 Billy Hatcher .05
133 Paul O'Neill .05
134 Jose Rijo .05
135 Randy Myers .05
136 Montreal Expos Pennant (Foil) .05
137 Montreal Expos Logo (Foil) .05
138 Mike Fitzgerald .05
139 Andres Galarraga .05
140 Delino DeShields .05
141 Tim Wallach .05
142 Spike Owen .05
143 Tim Raines .05
144 Dave Martinez .05
145 Larry Walker .05
146 Expos batting Helmet (Foil) .05
147 Dennis Boyd .05
148 Tim Burke .05
149 Bill Sampen .05
150 Dennis Martinez .05
151 Marquis Grissom .05
152 Otis Nixon .05
153 Jerry Goff .05
154 Steve Frey .05
155 National League Logo (Foil) .05
156 American League Logo (Foil) .05
157 Benito Santiago/AS .05
158 Will Clark/AS .05
159 Ryne Sandberg/AS .25
160 Chris Sabo/AS .05
161 Ozzie Smith/AS .25
162 Kevin Mitchell/AS .05
163 Lenny Dykstra/AS .05
164 Darryl Strawberry/AS .05
165 Jack Armstrong/AS .05
166 Sandy Alomar, Jr./AS .05
167 Mark McGwire/AS .45
168 Steve Sax/AS .05
169 Wade Boggs/AS .25
170 Cal Ripken, Jr./AS .50
171 Rickey Henderson/AS .20
172 Ken Griffey Jr./AS .40
173 Jose Canseco/AS .15
174 Bob Welch/AS .05
175 All-Star Game - Wrigley Field .05
176 World's Championship Trophy (Foil) .05

177 California Angels Pennant (Foil) .05
178 California Angels Logo (Foil) .05
179 Lance Parrish .05
180 Wally Joyner .05
181 Johnny Ray .05
182 Jack Howell .05
183 Dick Schofield .05
184 Dave Winfield .40
185 Devon White .05
186 Dante Bichette .05
187 Chuck Finley .05
188 Jim Abbott .05
189 Oakland A's Pennant (Foil) .05
190 Oakland A's Logo (Foil) .05
191 Terry Steinbach .05
192 Mark McGwire .85
193 Willie Randolph .05
194 Carney Lansford .05
195 Walt Weiss .05
196 Rickey Henderson .40
197 Dave Henderson .05
198 Jose Canseco .30
199 Dave Stewart .05
200 Dennis Eckersley .35
201 Milwaukee Brewers Pennant (Foil) .05
202 Milwaukee Brewers Logo (Foil) .05
203 B.J. Surhoff .05
204 Greg Brock .05
205 Paul Molitor .40
206 Gary Sheffield .20
207 Billy Spiers .05
208 Robin Yount .40
209 Rob Deer .05
210 Dave Parker .05
211 Mark Knudson .05
212 Dan Plesac .05
213 Cleveland Indians Pennant (Foil) .05
214 Cleveland Indians Logo (Foil) .05
215 Sandy Alomar, Jr. .05
216 Brook Jacoby .05
217 Jerry Browne .05
218 Carlos Baerga .05
219 Felix Fermin .05
220 Candy Maldonado .05
221 Cory Snyder .05
222 Alex Cole, Jr. .05
223 Tom Candiotti .05
224 Doug Jones .05
225 Seattle Mariners Pennant (Foil) .05
226 Seattle Mariners Logo (Foil) .05
227 Dave Valle .05
228 Pete O'Brien .05
229 Harold Reynolds .05
230 Edgar Martinez .05
231 Omar Vizquel .05
232 Henry Cotto .05
233 Ken Griffey Jr. .75
234 Jay Buhner .05
235 Eric Hanson (Erik) .05
236 Mike Schooler .05
237 Baltimore Orioles Pennant (Foil) .05
238 Baltimore Orioles Logo (Foil) .05
239 Mickey Tettleton .05
240 Randy Milligan .05
241 Billy Ripken .05
242 Craig Worthington .05
243 Cal Ripken, Jr. 1.00
244 Steve Finley .05
245 Mike Devereaux .05
246 Joe Orsulak .05
247 Ben McDonald .05
248 Gregg Olson .05
249 Texas Rangers Pennant (Foil) .05
250 Texas Rangers Logo (Foil) .05
251 Geno Petralli .05
252 Rafael Palmeiro .40
253 Julio Franco .05
254 Steve Buechele .05
255 Jeff Huson .05
256 Gary Pettis .05
257 Ruben Sierra .05
258 Pete Incaviglia .05
259 Nolan Ryan 1.00
260 Bobby Witt .05
261 Boston Red Sox Pennant (Foil) .05
262 Boston Red Sox Logo (Foil) .05
263 Tony Pena .05
264 Carlos Quintana .05
265 Jody Reed .05
266 Wade Boggs .50
267 Luis Rivera .05
268 Mike Greenwell .05
269 Ellis Burks .05
270 Tom Brunansky .05
271 Roger Clemens .60
272 Jeff Reardon .05
273 Kansas City Royals Pennant (Foil) .05
274 Kansas City Royals Logo (Foil) .05
275 Mike Macfarlane .05
276 George Brett .60
277 Bill Pecota .05
278 Kevin Seitzer .05
279 Kurt Stillwell .05

280 Jim Eisenreich .05
281 Bo Jackson .10
282 Danny Tartabull .05
283 Bret Saberhagen .05
284 Tom Gordon .05
285 Detroit Tigers Pennant (Foil) .05
286 Detroit Tigers Logo (Foil) .05
287 Mike Heath .05
288 Cecil Fielder .05
289 Lou Whitaker .05
290 Tony Phillips .05
291 Alan Trammell .05
292 Chet Lemon .05
293 Lloyd Moseby .05
294 Gary Ward .05
295 Dan Petry .05
296 Jack Morris .05
297 Minnesota Twins Pennant (Foil) .05
298 Minnesota Twins Logo (Foil) .05
299 Brian Harper .05
300 Kent Hrbek .05
301 Al Newman .05
302 Gary Gaetti .05
303 Greg Gagne .05
304 Dan Gladden .05
305 Kirby Puckett .50
306 Gene Larkin .05
307 Kevin Tapani .05
308 Rick Aguilera .05
309 Chicago White Sox Pennant (Foil) .05
310 Chicago White Sox Logo (Foil) .05
311 Carlton Fisk .40
312 Carlos Martinez .05
313 Scott Fletcher .05
314 Robin Ventura .05
315 Ozzie Guillen .05
316 Sammy Sosa .65
317 Lance Johnson .05
318 Ivan Calderon .05
319 Greg Hibbard .05
320 Bobby Thigpen .05
321 New York Yankees Pennant (Foil) .05
322 New York Yankees Logo (Foil) .05
323 Bob Geren .05
324 Don Mattingly .60
325 Steve Sax .05
326 Jim Leyritz .05
327 Alvaro Espinoza .05
328 Roberto Kelly .05
329 Oscar Azocar .05
330 Jesse Barfield .05
331 Chuck Cary .05
332 Dave Righetti .05
333 Toronto Blue Jays Pennant (Foil) .05
334 Toronto Blue Jays Logo (Foil) .05
335 Pat Borders .05
336 Fred McGriff .05
337 Manny Lee .05
338 Kelly Gruber .05
339 Tony Fernandez .05
340 George Bell .05
341 Mookie Wilson .05
342 Junior Felix .05
343 Blue Jays Batting Helmet (Foil) .05
344 Dave Steib .05
345 Tom Henke .05
346 Greg Myers .05
347 Glenallen Hill .05
348 John Olerud .05
349 Todd Stottlemyre .05
350 David Wells .05
351 Jimmy Key .05
352 Mark Langston (No-hitter.) .05
353 Randy Johnson (No-hitter.) .20
354 Nolan Ryan (No-hitter.) .50
355 Dave Stewart (No-hitter.) .05
356 Fernando Valenzuela (No-hitter.) .05
357 Andy Hawkins (No-hitter.) .05
358 Melido Perez (No-hitter.) .05
359 Terry Mulholland (No-hitter.) .05
360 Dave Stieb (No-hitter.) .05

Top 15 Stickers (Canadian)

WILLIE McGEE
ST. LOUIS CARDINALS
BATTING AVERAGE
MOYENNE AU BÂTON .335

The four leaders from each league in major statistical categories from the 1990 season are featured in this set of stickers marketed in Canada. The 2-1/2" x 3-1/2" stickers feature a large color photo at top. In the white border at bottom is the player's name and team, the stat in which he excelled (printed in both English and French), the number achieved, and, at lower-left, his rank among the top four. A series of team logo metallic stickers honors the teams which led in various stats. Backs are printed in black with appropriate logos and sticker number. A colorful album could be purchased to the house the sticker collection.

	NM/M
Complete Set (136):	10.00
Common Player:	.10

1 Willie McGee .10
2 Eddie Murray .30
3 Dave Magadan .10
4 Lenny Dykstra .10
5 George Brett .45
6 Rickey Henderson .30
7 Rafael Palmeiro .30
8 Alan Trammell .10
9 Ryne Sandberg .40
10 Darryl Strawberry .10
11 Kevin Mitchell .10
12 Barry Bonds .75
13 Cecil Fielder .10
14 Mark McGwire .65
15 Jose Canseco .15
16 Fred McGriff .10
17 Matt Williams .10
18 Bobby Bonilla .10
19 Joe Carter .10
20 Barry Bonds .75
21 Cecil Fielder .10
22 Kelly Gruber .10
23 Mark McGwire .65
24 Jose Canseco .15
25 Brett Butler .10
26 Lenny Dykstra .10
27 Ryne Sandberg .40
28 Barry Larkin .10
29 Rafael Palmeiro .30
30 Wade Boggs .40
31 Roberto Kelly .10
32 Mike Greenwell .10
33 Barry Bonds .75
34 Ryne Sandberg .40
35 Kevin Mitchell .10
36 Ron Gant .10
37 Cecil Fielder .10
38 Rickey Henderson .30
39 Jose Canseco .10
40 Fred McGriff .10
41 Vince Coleman .10
42 Eric Yelding .10
43 Barry Bonds .75
44 Brett Butler .10
45 Rickey Henderson .30
46 Steve Sax .10
47 Roberto Kelly .10
48 Alex Cole, Jr. .10
49 Ryne Sandberg .40
50 Bobby Bonilla .10
51 Brett Butler .10
52 Ron Gant .10
53 Rickey Henderson .30
54 Cecil Fielder .10
55 Harold Reynolds .10
56 Robin Yount .30
57 Doug Drabek .10
58 Ramon Martinez .10
59 Frank Viola .10
60 Dwight Gooden .10
61 Bob Welch .10
62 Dave Stewart .10
63 Roger Clemens .45
64 Dave Stieb .10
65 Danny Darwin .10
66 Zane Smith .10
67 Ed Whitson .10
68 Frank Viola .10
69 Roger Clemens .45
70 Chuck Finley .10
71 Dave Stewart .10
72 Kevin Appier .10
73 David Cone .10
74 Dwight Gooden .10
75 Ramon Martinez .10
76 Frank Viola .10
77 Nolan Ryan .75
78 Bobby Witt .10
79 Erik Hanson .10
80 Roger Clemens .45
81 John Franco .10
82 Randy Myers .10
83 Lee Smith .10
84 Craig Lefferts .10
85 Bobby Thigpen .10
86 Dennis Eckersley .25
87 Doug Jones .10
88 Gregg Olson .10
89 Mike Morgan .10
90 Bruce Hurst .10
91 Mark Gardner .10
92 Doug Drabek .10
93 Dave Stewart .10
94 Roger Clemens .45
95 Kevin Appier .10
96 Melido Perez .10
97 National League Logo .10
98 Greg Maddux .40
99 Benito Santiago .10
100 Andres Galarraga .10
101 Ryne Sandberg .40
102 Tim Wallach .10
103 Ozzie Smith .40
104 Tony Gwynn .40
105 Barry Bonds .75
106 Andy Van Slyke .10
107 American League Logo .10
108 Mike Boddicker .10
109 Sandy Alomar Jr. .10
110 Mark McGwire .65
111 Harold Reynolds .10
112 Kelly Gruber .10
113 Ozzie Guillen .10
114 Ellis Burks .10
115 Gary Pettis .10
116 Ken Griffey Jr. .50
117 Cincinnati Reds Logo .10
118 New York Mets Logo .10
119 New York Mets Script .10
120 Chicago Cubs Logo .10
121 Montreal Expos Logo .10
122 Boston Red Sox Logo .10
123 Detroit Tigers Logo .10
124 Toronto Blue Jays Logo .10
125 Boston Red Sox Script .10
126 Milwaukee Brewers Logo .10
127 Philadelphia Phillies Logo .10
128 Cincinnati Reds Logo .10
129 Montreal Expos Logo .10
130 New York Mets Logo .10
131 Cincinnati Reds Logo .10
132 California Angels Logo .10
133 Toronto Blue Jays Logo .10
134 Oakland A's Logo .10
135 Oakland A's Script .10
136 Chicago White Sox Logo .10

1992 Panini Stickers

TIM WALLACH THIRD BASE 204

A 288-piece set comprised Panini's annual baseball issue in 1992. Stickers were sold in packs of six for 39 cents. A colorful album for housing the stickers was also available, picturing members of the World Champion Twins. Individual stickers measured 2-1/8" x 3". Player stickers feature a color action photo at center, with a shark's tooth border at right. A colored diamond is overprinted on the first letters of the name, while a rule of the same color is printed around the photo. On American League stickers the color highlights are in magenta; teal for N.L. Stickers are numbered by position within team, and each team set includes a foil-glitter team logo sticker. Similar special stickers honor the 1991 All-Star Game starters and a few other special themes. Backs of the foils are printed in blue and promote sticker collecting. Backs of the player stickers are special themes. Backs of the foils are printed in blue and in full color and include trivia questions, "Play Ball" game situations and score cards for the game.

	NM/M
Complete Set (288):	10.00
Common Player:	.05
Album:	1.00
Wax Pack (5+1):	.25
Wax Box (50):	5.00

1 Panini Logo (Foil) .05
2 Major League Baseball Logo (Foil) .05
3 Players Association Logo (Foil) .05
4 Lance Parrish .05
5 Wally Joyner .05
6 Luis Sojo .05
7 Gary Gaetti .05
8 Dick Schofield .05
9 Junior Felix .05
10 Luis Polonia .05
11 Mark Langston .05
12 Jim Abbott .05
13 California Angels Logo (Foil) .05
14 Terry Steinbach .05
15 Mark McGwire .75
16 Mike Gallego .05
17 Carney Lansford .05
18 Walt Weiss .05
19 Jose Canseco .30
20 Dave Henderson .05
21 Rickey Henderson .40
22 Dennis Eckersley .35
23 Oakland A's Logo (Foil) .05
24 Pat Borders .05
25 John Olerud .05
26 Roberto Alomar .20
27 Kelly Gruber .05
28 Manuel Lee .05
29 Joe Carter .05
30 Devon White .05
31 Candy Maldonado .05
32 Jimmy Key .05
33 Toronto Blue Jays Logo (Foil) .05
34 B.J. Surhoff .05
35 Franklin Stubbs .05
36 Willie Randolph .05
37 Jim Gantner .05
38 Bill Spiers .05
39 Dante Bichette .05
40 Robin Yount .40
41 Greg Vaughn .05
42 Jaime Navarro .05
43 Milwaukee Brewers Logo (Foil) .05
44 Sandy Alomar Jr. .05
45 Mike Aldrete .05
46 Mark Lewis .05
47 Carlos Baerga .05
48 Felix Fermin .05
49 Mark Whiten .05
50 Alex Cole .05
51 Albert Belle .10
52 Greg Swindell .05
53 Cleveland Indians Logo (Foil) .05
54 Dave Valle .05
55 Pete O'Brien .05
56 Harold Reynolds .05
57 Edgar Martinez .05
58 Omar Vizquel .05
59 Jay Buhner .05
60 Ken Griffey Jr. .60
61 Greg Briley .05
62 Randy Johnson .40
63 Seattle Mariners Logo (Foil) .05
64 Chris Hoiles .05
65 Randy Milligan .05
66 Billy Ripken .05
67 Leo Gomez .05
68 Cal Ripken Jr. 1.00
69 Dwight Evans .05
70 Mike Devereaux .05
71 Joe Orsulak .05
72 Gregg Olson .05
73 Baltimore Orioles Logo (Foil) .05
74 Ivan Rodriguez .40
75 Rafael Palmeiro .05
76 Julio Franco .05
77 Dean Palmer .05
78 Jeff Huson .05
79 Ruben Sierra .05
80 Gary Pettis .05
81 Juan Gonzalez .40
82 Nolan Ryan 1.00
83 Texas Rangers Logo (Foil) .05
84 Tony Pena .05
85 Carlos Quintana .05
86 Jody Reed .05
87 Wade Boggs .50
88 Luis Rivera .05
89 Tom Brunansky .05
90 Ellis Burks .05
91 Mike Greenwell .05
92 Roger Clemens .55
93 Boston Red Sox Logo (Foil) .05
94 Todd Benzinger .05
95 Terry Shumpert .05
96 Bill Pecota .05
97 Kurt Stillwell .05
98 Danny Tartabull .05
99 Brian McRae .05
100 Kirk Gibson .05
101 Bret Saberhagen .05
102 George Brett .55
103 Kansas City Royals Logo (Foil) .05
104 Mickey Tettleton .05
105 Cecil Fielder .05
106 Lou Whitaker .05
107 Travis Fryman .05
108 Alan Trammell .05
109 Rob Deer .05
110 Milt Cuyler .05
111 Lloyd Moseby .05
112 Bill Gullickson .05
113 Detroit Tigers Logo (Foil) .05
114 Brian Harper .05
115 Kent Hrbek .05
116 Chuck Knoblauch .05
117 Mike Pagliarulo .05
118 Greg Gagne .05
119 Shane Mack .05
120 Kirby Puckett .50
121 Dan Gladden .05
122 Jack Morris .05
123 Minnesota Twins Logo (Foil) .05
124 Carlton Fisk .40
125 Frank Thomas .40
126 Joey Cora .05
127 Robin Ventura .05
128 Ozzie Guillen .05
129 Sammy Sosa .60
130 Lance Johnson .05
131 Tim Raines .05
132 Bobby Thigpen .05
133 Chicago White Sox Logo (Foil) .05
134 Matt Nokes .05
135 Don Mattingly .55
136 Steve Sax .05
137 Pat Kelly .05
138 Alvaro Espinoza .05
139 Jesse Barfield .05
140 Roberto Kelly .05
141 Mel Hall .05
142 Scott Sanderson .05
143 New York Yankees Logo (Foil) .05
144 A.L. HR Leaders (Cecil Fielder, Jose Canseco) .05
145 A.L. BA Leader (Julio Franco) .05
146 A.L. ERA Leader (Roger Clemens) .25
147 N.L. HR Leader (Howard Johnson) .05
148 N.L. BA Leader (Terry Pendleton) .05
149 N.L. ERA Leader (Dennis Martinez) .05
150 Houston Astros Logo (Foil) .05
151 Craig Biggio .05
152 Jeff Bagwell .40
153 Casey Candaele .05
154 Ken Caminiti .05
155 Andujar Cedeno .05
156 Mike Simms .05
157 Steve Finley .05
158 Luis Gonzalez .05
159 Pete Harnisch .05
160 Atlanta Braves Logo (Foil) .05
161 Greg Olson .05
162 Sid Bream .05
163 Mark Lemke .05
164 Terry Pendleton .05
165 Rafael Belliard .05
166 Dave Justice .05
167 Ron Gant .05
168 Lonnie Smith .05
169 Steve Avery .05
170 St. Louis Cardinals Logo (Foil) .05
171 Tom Pagnozzi .05
172 Pedro Guerrero .05
173 Jose Oquendo .05
174 Todd Zeile .05
175 Ozzie Smith .50
176 Felix Jose .05
177 Ray Lankford .05
178 Jose DeLeon .05
179 Lee Smith .05
180 Chicago Cubs Logo (Foil) .05
181 Hector Villanueva .05
182 Mark Grace .10
183 Ryne Sandberg .50
184 Luis Salazar .05
185 Shawon Dunston .05
186 Andre Dawson .20
187 Jerome Walton .05
188 George Bell .05
189 Greg Maddux .50
190 Los Angeles Dodgers Logo (Foil) .05
191 Mike Scioscia .05
192 Eddie Murray .40
193 Juan Samuel .05
194 Lenny Harris .05
195 Alfredo Griffin .05
196 Darryl Strawberry .05
197 Brett Butler .05
198 Kal Daniels .05
199 Orel Hershiser .05
200 Montreal Expos Logo (Foil) .05
201 Gilberto Reyes .05
202 Andres Galarraga .05
203 Delino DeShields .05
204 Tim Wallach .05
205 Spike Owen .05
206 Larry Walker .05
207 Marquis Grissom .05
208 Ivan Calderon .05
209 Dennis Martinez .05
210 San Francisco Giants Logo (Foil) .05
211 Steve Decker .05
212 Will Clark .05
213 Robby Thompson .05
214 Matt Williams .05
215 Jose Uribe .05
216 Kevin Bass .05
217 Willie McGee .05
218 Kevin Mitchell .05
219 Dave Righetti .05
220 New York Mets Logo (Foil) .05
221 Rick Cerone .05
222 Dave Magadan .05
223 Gregg Jefferies .05
224 Howard Johnson .05

225	Kevin Elster	.05
226	Hubie Brooks	.05
227	Vince Coleman	.05
228	Kevin McReynolds	.05
229	Frank Viola	.05
230	San Diego Padres Logo (Foil)	.05
231	Benito Santiago	.05
232	Fred McGriff	.05
233	Bip Roberts	.05
234	Jack Howell	.05
235	Tony Fernandez	.05
236	Tony Gwynn	.50
237	Darrin Jackson	.05
238	Bruce Hurst	.05
239	Craig Lefferts	.05
240	Philadelphia Phillies Logo (Foil)	.05
241	Darren Daulton	.05
242	John Kruk	.05
243	Mickey Morandini	.05
244	Charlie Hayes	.05
245	Dickie Thon	.05
246	Dale Murphy	.25
247	Lenny Dykstra	.05
248	Von Hayes	.05
249	Terry Mulholland	.05
250	Pittsburgh Pirates Logo (Foil)	.05
251	Mike LaValliere	.05
252	Orlando Merced	.05
253	Jose Lind	.05
254	Steve Buechele	.05
255	Jay Bell	.05
256	Bobby Bonilla	.05
257	Andy Van Slyke	.05
258	Barry Bonds	1.00
259	Doug Drabek	.05
260	Cincinnati Reds Logo (Foil)	.05
261	Joe Oliver	.05
262	Hal Morris	.05
263	Bill Doran	.05
264	Chris Sabo	.05
265	Barry Larkin	.05
266	Paul O'Neill	.05
267	Eric Davis	.05
268	Glenn Braggs	.05
269	Jose Rijo	.05
270	Toronto Sky Dome (Foil)	.05
271	Sandy Alomar Jr. (All-Star Foil)	
272	Cecil Fielder (All-Star Foil)	.05
273	Roberto Alomar (All-Star Foil)	.10
274	Wade Boggs (All-Star Foil)	.25
275	Cal Ripken Jr. (All-Star Foil)	.50
276	Dave Henderson (All-Star Foil)	.05
277	Ken Griffey Jr. (All-Star Foil)	.40
278	Rickey Henderson (All-Star Foil)	.20
279	Jack Morris (All-Star Foil)	.05
280	Benito Santiago (All-Star Foil)	.05
281	Will Clark (All-Star Foil)	.05
282	Ryne Sandberg (All-Star Foil)	.25
283	Chris Sabo (All-Star Foil)	.05
284	Ozzie Smith (All-Star Foil)	.25
285	Andre Dawson (All-Star Foil)	.05
286	Tony Gwynn (All-Star Foil)	.25
287	Ivan Calderon (All-Star Foil)	.05
288	Tom Glavine (All-Star Foil)	.05

Canadian

ROBIN VENTURA
THIRD BASE/TROISIÈME BUT

The Canadian version of the 1992 Panini stickers mirrors the U.S. set's checklist (and price guide). In the same size (2-1/8" x 3") and format, the Canadian stickers differ from the U.S. version in the addition of French position on front and bilingual back.

	NM/M
Complete Set (288):	10.00
Common Player:	.05
Album:	1.00

1993 Panini Stickers

The 1993 issue is complete at 300 stickers. Besides 10 player stickers for each major league

AATLANTA BRAVES
DAVE JUSTICE

team, there are stickers for league leaders and major 1992-season award winners. There is a gold-foil team logo sticker for each team and one of the player stickers on each team is produced in a glitter technology. Stickers measure 2-3/8" x 3-3/8". Fronts have an action photo at center with team logo in the lower-left corner. Backs are printed in green and include the sticker number and appropriate Panini and baseball logos. A 58-page album was available to house the stickers.

	NM/M
Complete Set (300):	10.00
Common Player:	.05
Sticker Album:	1.00
1	California Angels Logo	.05
2	Mark Langston	.05
3	Ron Tingley	.05
4	Gary Gaetti	.05
5	Kelly Gruber	.05
6	Gary Disarcina	.05
7	Damion Easley (Glitter)	.05
8	Luis Polonia	.05
9	Lee Stevens	.05
10	Chad Curtis	.05
11	Rene Gonzales	.05
12	Oakland A's Logo	.05
13	Dennis Eckersley	.35
14	Terry Steinbach	.05
15	Mark McGwire	.75
16	Mike Bordick (Glitter)	.05
17	Carney Lansford	.05
18	Jerry Browne	.05
19	Rickey Henderson	.40
20	Dave Henderson	.05
21	Ruben Sierra	.05
22	Ron Darling	.05
23	Toronto Blue Jays Logo	.05
24	Jack Morris	.05
25	Pat Borders	.05
26	John Olerud	.05
27	Roberto Alomar	.10
28	Luis Sojo	.05
29	Dave Stewart	.05
30	Devon White	.05
31	Joe Carter	.05
32	Derek Bell	.05
33	Juan Guzman (Glitter)	.05
34	Milwaukee Brewers Logo	.05
35	Jaime Navarro	.05
36	B.J. Surhoff	.05
37	Franklin Stubbs	.05
38	Billy Spiers	.05
39	Pat Listach (Glitter)	.05
40	Kevin Seitzer	.05
41	Darryl Hamilton	.05
42	Robin Yount	.40
43	Kevin Reimer	.05
44	Greg Vaughn	.05
45	Cleveland Indians Logo	.05
46	Charles Nagy	.05
47	Sandy Alomar Jr.	.05
48	Reggie Jefferson	.05
49	Mark Lewis	.05
50	Felix Fermin	.05
51	Carlos Baerga	.05
52	Albert Belle	.05
53	Kenny Lofton (Glitter)	.05
54	Mark Whiten	.05
55	Paul Sorrento	.05
56	Seattle Mariners Logo	.05
57	Dave Fleming	.05
58	Dave Valle	.05
59	Pete O'Brien	.05
60	Randy Johnson	.40
61	Omar Vizquel	.05
62	Edgar Martinez	.05
63	Ken Griffey Jr. (Glitter)	.75
64	Henry Cotto	.05
65	Jay Buhner	.05
66	Tino Martinez	.05
67	Baltimore Orioles Logo	.05
68	Ben McDonald	.05
69	Mike Mussina (Glitter)	.35
70	Chris Hoiles	.05
71	Randy Milligan	.05
72	Billy Ripken	.05
73	Cal Ripken Jr.	1.00
74	Leo Gomez	.05
75	Mike Devereaux	.05
76	Brady Anderson	.05
77	Joe Orsulak	.05

78	Texas Rangers Logo	.05
79	Kevin Brown	.05
80	Ivan Rodriguez (Glitter)	.40
81	Rafael Palmeiro	.05
82	Julio Franco	.05
83	Jeff Huson	.05
84	Dean Palmer	.05
85	Jose Canseco	.30
86	Juan Gonzalez	.40
87	Nolan Ryan	1.00
88	Brian Downing	.05
89	Boston Red Sox Logo	.05
90	Roger Clemens	.55
91	Tony Pena	.05
92	Mo Vaughn	.05
93	Scott Cooper	.05
94	Luis Rivera	.05
95	Ellis Burks	.05
96	Mike Greenwell	.05
97	Andre Dawson	.20
98	Ivan Calderon	.05
99	Phil Plantier (Glitter)	.05
100	Kansas City Royals Logo	.05
101	Kevin Appier	.05
102	Mike MacFarlane	.05
103	Wally Joyner	.05
104	Jim Eisenreich	.05
105	Greg Gagne	.05
106	Gregg Jefferies	.05
107	Kevin McReynolds	.05
108	Brian McRae (Glitter)	.05
109	Keith Miller	.05
110	George Brett	.55
111	Detroit Tigers Logo	.05
112	Bill Gullickson	.05
113	Mickey Tettleton	.05
114	Cecil Fielder	.05
115	Tony Phillips	.05
116	Scott Livingstone	.05
117	Travis Fryman (Glitter)	.05
118	Dan Gladden	.05
119	Rob Deer	.05
120	Frank Tanana	.05
121	Skeeter Barnes	.05
122	Minnesota Twins Logo	.05
123	Scott Erickson	.05
124	Brian Harper	.05
125	Kent Hrbek	.05
126	Chuck Knoblauch (Glitter)	.05
127	Willie Banks	.05
128	Scott Leius	.05
129	Shane Mack	.05
130	Kirby Puckett	.50
131	Chili Davis	.05
132	Pedro Munoz	.05
133	Chicago White Sox Logo	.05
134	Jack McDowell	.05
135	Carlton Fisk	.40
136	Frank Thomas (Glitter)	.45
137	Steve Sax	.05
138	Ozzie Guillen	.05
139	Robin Ventura	.05
140	Tim Raines	.05
141	Lance Johnson	.05
142	Ron Karkovice	.05
143	George Bell	.05
144	New York Yankees Logo	.05
145	Scott Sanderson	.05
146	Matt Nokes	.05
147	Kevin Maas (Glitter)	.05
148	Randy Velarde	.05
149	Andy Stankiewicz	.05
150	Pat Kelly	.05
151	Paul O'Neill	.05
152	Wade Boggs	.50
153	Danny Tartabull	.05
154	Don Mattingly	.50
155	Edgar Martinez (B.A. Leader)	.05
156	Kevin Brown (W-L Record)	.05
157	Dennis Eckersley (Saves leader.)	.15
158	Gary Sheffield (B.A. leader.)	.05
159	Tom Glavine, Greg Maddux (W-L Leaders)	.05
160	Lee Smith (Saves leader.)	.05
161	Dennis Eckersley (Cy Young)	.15
162	Dennis Eckersley (MVP)	.15
163	Pat Listach (Rookie/Year)	.05
164	Greg Maddux (Cy Young)	.50
165	Barry Bonds (MVP)	.50
166	Eric Karros (Rookie/Year)	.05
167	Houston Astros Logo	.05
168	Pete Harnisch	.05
169	Eddie Taubensee	.05
170	Jeff Bagwell (Glitter)	.45
171	Craig Biggio	.05
172	Andujar Cedeno	.05
173	Ken Caminiti	.05
174	Steve Finley	.05
175	Luis Gonzalez	.05
176	Eric Anthony	.05
177	Casey Candaele	.05
178	Atlanta Braves Logo	.05
179	Tom Glavine	.25
180	Greg Olson	.05
181	Sid Bream	.05
182	Mark Lemke	.05
183	Jeff Blauser	.05
184	Terry Pendleton	.05
185	Ron Gant	.05
186	Otis Nixon	.05
187	Dave Justice	.05
188	Deion Sanders (Glitter)	.20
189	St. Louis Cardinals Logo	.05

190	Bob Tewksbury	.05
191	Tom Pagnozzi	.05
192	Lee Smith	.05
193	Geronimo Pena	.05
194	Ozzie Smith	.50
195	Todd Zeile	.05
196	Ray Lankford	.05
197	Bernard Gilkey	.05
198	Felix Jose	.05
199	Donovan Osborne (Glitter)	.05
200	Chicago Cubs Logo	.05
201	Mike Morgan	.05
202	Rick Wilkins	.05
203	Mark Grace (Glitter)	.05
204	Ryne Sandberg	.50
205	Shawon Dunston	.05
206	Steve Buechele	.05
207	Kal Daniels	.05
208	Sammy Sosa	.50
209	Derrick May	.05
210	Doug Dascenzo	.05
211	Los Angeles Dodgers Logo	.05
212	Ramon Martinez	.05
213	Mike Scioscia	.05
214	Eric Karros (Glitter)	.05
215	Tim Wallach	.05
216	Jose Offerman	.05
217	Mike Sharperson	.05
218	Brett Butler	.05
219	Darryl Strawberry	.05
220	Lenny Harris	.05
221	Eric Davis	.05
222	Montreal Expos Logo	.05
223	Ken Hill	.05
224	Darrin Fletcher	.05
225	Greg Colbrunn (Glitter)	.05
226	Delino DeShields	.05
227	Wil Cordero	.05
228	Dennis Martinez	.05
229	John Vander Wal	.05
230	Marquis Grissom	.05
231	Larry Walker	.05
232	Moises Alou	.05
233	San Francisco Giants Logo	.05
234	Billy Swift	.05
235	Kirt Manwaring	.05
236	Will Clark	.05
237	Robby Thompson	.05
238	Royce Clayton (Glitter)	.05
239	Matt Williams	.05
240	Willie McGee	.05
241	Mark Leonard	.05
242	Cory Snyder	.05
243	Barry Bonds	1.00
244	New York Mets Logo	.05
245	Dwight Gooden	.05
246	Todd Hundley (Glitter)	.05
247	Eddie Murray	.40
248	Sid Fernandez	.05
249	Tony Fernandez	.05
250	Dave Magadan	.05
251	Howard Johnson	.05
252	Vince Coleman	.05
253	Bobby Bonilla	.05
254	Daryl Boston	.05
255	San Diego Padres Logo	.05
256	Bruce Hurst	.05
257	Dan Walters	.05
258	Fred McGriff	.05
259	Kurt Stillwell	.05
260	Craig Shipley	.05
261	Gary Sheffield (Glitter)	.35
262	Tony Gwynn	.50
263	Oscar Azocar	.05
264	Darrin Jackson	.05
265	Andy Benes	.05
266	Philadelphia Phillies Logo	.05
267	Terry Mulholland	.05
268	Curt Schilling	.25
269	Darren Daulton	.05
270	John Kruk	.05
271	Mickey Morandini (Glitter)	.05
272	Mariano Duncan	.05
273	Dave Hollins	.05
274	Lenny Dykstra	.05
275	Wes Chamberlain	.05
276	Stan Javier	.05
277	Pittsburgh Pirates Logo	.05
278	Zane Smith	.05
279	Tim Wakefield (Glitter)	.05
280	Mike LaValliere	.05
281	Orlando Merced	.05
282	Stan Belinda	.05
283	Jay Bell	.05
284	Jeff King	.05
285	Andy Van Slyke	.05
286	Bob Walk	.05
287	Gary Varsho	.05
288	Cincinnati Reds Logo	.05
289	Jose Rijo	.05
290	Joe Oliver	.05
291	Hal Morris	.05
292	Bip Roberts	.05
293	Barry Larkin	.05
294	Chris Sabo	.05
295	Roberto Kelly	.05
296	Kevin Mitchell	.05
297	Rob Dibble	.05
298	Reggie Sanders (Glitter)	.05
299	Florida Marlins Logo	.05
300	Colorado Rockies Logo	.05

1994 Panini Stickers

With set size at the reduced count of 268, Panini retained the larger format 2-3/8" x 3-3/8" sticker

Walt Weiss

size. Stickers featured green borders surrounding a color action photo on front. Below the player photo is a pennant with the team logo and player name. Backs have a sticker number at center, with appropriate licensor logos and Panini advertising in black-and-white. The set includes 16 foil stickers honoring major 1993 season award winners in the A.L. and N.L. and four World Series action stickers. The set is arranged alphabetically within team and league. Stickers were sold in packs of six for 49 cents. A colorful album to house the stickers was also available.

	NM/M
Complete Set (268):	5.00
Common Player:	.05
1	World Series Action (Foil)	.05
2	World Series Action (Foil)	.05
3	World Series Action (Foil)	.05
4	World Series Action (Foil)	.05
5	BA Leader (John Olerud (Foil))	.05
6	HR Leader (Juan Gonzalez (Foil))	.20
7	RBI Leader (Albert Belle (Foil))	.05
8	Wins Leader (Jack McDowell (Foil))	.05
9	K Leader (Randy Johnson (Foil))	.20
10	Saves Leader (Jeff Montgomery (Foil))	.05
11	BA Leader (Andres Galarraga (Foil))	.05
12	HR Leader (Barry Bonds (Foil))	.50
13	RBI Leader (Barry Bonds (Foil))	.50
14	Wins Leaders (Tom Glavine, John Burkett (Foil))	.05
15	K Leader (Jose Rijo (Foil))	.05
16	Saves Leader (Randy Myers (Foil))	.05
17	Brady Anderson	.05
18	Harold Baines	.05
19	Mike Devereaux	.05
20	Chris Hoiles	.05
21	Mike Mussina	.30
22	Harold Reynolds	.05
23	Cal Ripken Jr.	1.00
24	David Segui	.05
25	Fernando Valenzuela	.05
26	Roger Clemens	.60
27	Scott Cooper	.05
28	Andre Dawson	.20
29	Scott Fletcher	.05
30	Mike Greenwell	.05
31	Billy Hatcher	.05
32	Tony Pena	.05
33	John Valentin	.05
34	Mo Vaughn	.05
35	Chad Curtis	.05
36	Gary DiSarcina	.05
37	Damion Easley	.05
38	Mark Langston	.05
39	Torey Lovullo	.05
40	Greg Myers	.05
41	Luis Polonia	.05
42	Tim Salmon	.05
43	J.T. Snow	.05
44	George Bell	.05
45	Ellis Burks	.05
46	Joey Cora	.05
47	Ozzie Guillen	.05
48	Roberto Hernandez	.05
49	Bo Jackson	.10
50	Jack McDowell	.05
51	Frank Thomas	.40
52	Robin Ventura	.05
53	Sandy Alomar Jr.	.05
54	Carlos Baerga	.05
55	Albert Belle	.05
56	Felix Fermin	.05
57	Wayne Kirby	.05
58	Kenny Lofton	.05
59	Charles Nagy	.05
60	Paul Sorrento	.05
61	Jeff Treadway	.05
62	Eric Davis	.05
63	Cecil Fielder	.05
64	Travis Fryman	.05

65	Bill Gullickson	.05
66	Mike Moore	.05
67	Tony Phillips	.05
68	Mickey Tettleton	.05
69	Alan Trammell	.05
70	Lou Whitaker	.05
71	Kevin Appier	.05
72	Greg Gagne	.05
73	Tom Gordon	.05
74	Felix Jose	.05
75	Wally Joyner	.05
76	Jose Lind	.05
77	Mike Macfarlane	.05
78	Brian McRae	.05
79	Kevin McReynolds	.05
80	Darryl Hamilton	.05
81	Teddy Higuera	.05
82	John Jaha	.05
83	Pat Listach	.05
84	Dave Nilsson	.05
85	Kevin Reimer	.05
86	Kevin Seitzer	.05
87	B. J. Surhoff	.05
88	Greg Vaughn	.05
89	Willie Banks	.05
90	Brian Harper	.05
91	Kent Hrbek	.05
92	Chuck Knoblauch	.05
93	Shane Mack	.05
94	Pat Meares	.05
95	Pedro Munoz	.05
.5	Kirby Puckett	.50
97	Dave Winfield	.40
98	Jim Abbott	.05
99	Wade Boggs	.50
100	Mike Gallego	.05
101	Pat Kelly	.05
102	Don Mattingly	.60
103	Paul O'Neill	.05
104	Mike Stanley	.05
105	Danny Tartabull	.05
106	Bernie Williams	.05
107	Mike Bordick	.05
108	Dennis Eckersley	.35
109	Dave Henderson	.05
110	Mark McGwire	.75
111	Troy Neel	.05
112	Ruben Sierra	.05
113	Terry Steinbach	.05
114	Todd Van Poppel	.05
115	Bob Welch	.05
116	Bret Boone	.05
117	Jay Buhner	.05
118	Ken Griffey Jr.	.65
119	Randy Johnson	.40
120	Rich Amaral	.05
121	Edgar Martinez	.05
122	Tino Martinez	.05
123	Dave Valle	.05
124	Omar Vizquel	.05
125	Jose Canseco	.25
126	Julio Gonzalez	.05
127	Juan Gonzalez	.20
128	Tom Henke	.05
129	Manuel Lee	.05
130	Rafael Palmeiro	.35
131	Dean Palmer	.05
132	Ivan Rodriguez	.35
133	Doug Strange	.05
134	Roberto Alomar	.10
135	Pat Borders	.05
136	Joe Carter	.05
137	Tony Fernandez	.05
138	Juan Guzman	.05
139	Rickey Henderson	.40
140	Paul Molitor	.40
141	John Olerud	.05
142	Devon White	.05
143	Jeff Blauser	.05
144	Ron Gant	.05
145	Tom Glavine	.20
146	Dave Justice	.05
147	Greg Maddux	.50
148	Fred McGriff	.05
149	Terry Pendleton	.05
150	Deion Sanders	.05
151	John Smoltz	.05
152	Shawon Dunston	.05
153	Mark Grace	.05
154	Derrick May	.05
155	Randy Myers	.05
156	Ryne Sandberg	.50
157	Dwight Smith	.05
158	Sammy Sosa	.50
159	Jose Vizcaino	.05
160	Rick Wilkins	.05
161	Tom Browning	.05
162	Roberto Kelly	.05
163	Barry Larkin	.05
164	Kevin Mitchell	.05
165	Hal Morris	.05
166	Joe Oliver	.05
167	Jose Rijo	.05
168	Chris Sabo	.05
169	Reggie Sanders	.05
170	Freddie Benavides	.05
171	Dante Bichette	.05
172	Vinny Castilla	.05
173	Jerald Clark	.05
174	Andres Galarraga	.05
175	Charlie Hayes	.05
176	Chris Jones	.05
177	Roberto Mejia	.05
178	Eric Young	.05
179	Bret Barberie	.05
180	Chuck Carr	.05
181	Jeff Conine	.05
182	Orestes Destrade	.05

183	Bryan Harvey	.05
184	Rich Renteria	.05
185	Benito Santiago	.05
186	Gary Sheffield	.20
187	Walt Weiss	.05
188	Eric Anthony	.05
189	Jeff Bagwell	.40
190	Craig Biggio	.05
191	Ken Caminiti	.05
192	Andujar Cedeno	.05
193	Doug Drabek	.05
194	Steve Finley	.05
195	Doug Jones	.05
196	Darryl Kile	.05
197	Brett Butler	.05
198	Tom Candiotti	.05
199	Dave Hansen	.05
200	Orel Hershiser	.05
201	Eric Karros	.05
202	Jose Offerman	.05
203	Mike Piazza	.60
204	Cory Snyder	.05
205	Darryl Strawberry	.05
206	Moises Alou	.05
207	Sean Berry	.05
208	Wil Cordero	.05
209	Delino DeShields	.05
210	Marquis Grissom	.05
211	Ken Hill	.05
212	Mike Lansing	.05
213	Larry Walker	.05
214	John Wetteland	.05
215	Bobby Bonilla	.05
216	Jeromy Burnitz	.05
217	Dwight Gooden	.05
218	Todd Hundley	.05
219	Howard Johnson	.05
220	Jeff Kent	.05
221	Eddie Murray	.40
222	Bret Saberhagen	.05
223	Ryan Thompson	.05
224	Darren Daulton	.05
225	Mariano Duncan	.05
226	Lenny Dykstra	.05
227	Jim Eisenreich	.05
228	Dave Hollins	.05
229	John Kruk	.05
230	Curt Schilling	.20
231	Kevin Stocker	.05
232	Mitch Williams	.05
233	Jay Bell	.05
234	Steve Cooke	.05
235	Carlos Garcia	.05
236	Jeff King	.05
237	Orlando Merced	.05
238	Don Slaught	.05
239	Zane Smith	.05
240	Andy Van Slyke	.05
241	Kevin Young	.05
242	Bernard Gilkey	.05
243	Gregg Jefferies	.05
244	Brian Jordan	.05
245	Ray Lankford	.05
246	Tom Pagnozzi	.05
247	Geronimo Pena	.05
248	Ozzie Smith	.50
249	Bob Tewksbury	.05
250	Mark Whiten	.05
251	Brad Ausmus	.05
252	Derek Bell	.05
253	Andy Benes	.05
254	Phil Clark	.05
255	Jeff Gardner	.05
256	Tony Gwynn	.50
257	Trevor Hoffman	.05
258	Phil Plantier	.05
259	Craig Shipley	.05
260	Rod Beck	.05
261	Barry Bonds	1.00
262	John Burkett	.05
263	Will Clark	.05
264	Royce Clayton	.05
265	Willie McGee	.05
266	Bill Swift	.05
267	Robby Thompson	.05
268	Matt Williams	.05
Album:		1.00
Wax Pack (5+1):		.25
Wax Box (50):		5.00

2005 Parody Productions Boston Baseball Heroes

This deck of poker-format (2-1/2" x 3-1/2", round-cornered, linen finish) playing cards features color caricatures of past and contemporary Red Sox stars.

Player name, sometimes a nickname, and his dates of service with the team are included. Backs have a baseball on a red background with white borders. The issue is apparently not licensed by MLB or the players.

		NM/M
Complete Set (55):		10.00
Common Player:		.25
AS	Curt Schilling	.35
2S	Jason Varitek	.25
3S	Mo Vaughn	.25
4S	Bill Mueller	.25
5S	Wade Boggs	1.00
6S	Nomar Garciaparra	1.00
7S	Manny Ramirez	1.00
8S	Johnny Damon	.40
9S	Trot Nixon	.25
10S	Tim Wakefield	.25
JS	Pedro Martinez	.35
QS	Roger Clemens	1.50
KS	David Ortiz	.50
AD	Mel Parnell	.25
2D	Sammy White	.25
3D	Billy Goodman	.25
4D	Bobby Doerr	.25
5D	Frank Malzone	.25
6D	Johnny Pesky	.25
7D	Jimmy Piersall	.35
8D	Dominic DiMaggio	.35
9D	Jackie Jensen	.35
10D	Vern Stephens	.25
JD	Dave Ferriss	.25
QD	Tex Hughson	.25
KD	Ted Williams	2.00
AC	Cy Young	.50
2C	Wally Schang	.25
3C	Jimmy Foxx	.50
4C	Jack Berry (Barry)	.25
5C	Jimmy Collins	.25
6C	Joe Cronin	.25
7C	Duffy Lewis	.25
8C	Doc Cramer	.25
9C	Harry Hooper	.25
10C	Bill Carrigan	.25
JC	Lefty Grove	.35
QC	Joe Wood	.25
KC	Tris Speaker	.40
AH	Luis Tiant	.35
2H	Carlton Fisk	.40
3H	George Scott	.25
4H	Tony Conigliaro	.35
5H	Rico Petrocelli	.25
6H	Rick Burleson	.25
7H	Reggie Smith	.25
8H	Fred Lynn	.35
9H	Dwight Evans	.35
10H	Jim Rice	.35
JH	Dick Radatz	.25
QH	Bill Lee	.25
KH	Carl Yastrzemski	1.50
---	Ken Coleman (Broadcaster)	.25
---	Ned Martin (Broadcaster)	.25
---	Tom Yawkey (Owner)	.25

2005 Parody Productions Chicago (Cubs) Baseball Heroes

This deck of poker-format (2-1/2" x 3-1/2", round-cornered, linen finish) playing cards features color caricatures of past and contemporary Cubs stars. Player name, sometimes a nickname, and his dates of service with the team are included. Backs have a baseball on a blue background with white borders. The issue is apparently not licensed by MLB or the players.

		NM/M
Complete Set (55):		10.00
Common Player:		.25
AS	Mark Prior	1.00
2S	Joe Girardi	.25
3S	Mark Grace	.35
4S	Ryne Sandberg	2.00
5S	Aramis Ramirez	.25
7S	Moises Alou	.25
8S	Corey Patterson	.25

9S	Andre Dawson	.50
10S	Carlos Zambrano	.25
JS	Kerry Wood	.35
QS	Lee Smith	.25
KS	Sammy Sosa	1.50
AD	Fergie Jenkins	.50
2D	Randy Hundley	.25
3D	Phil Cavarretta	.25
4D	Glenn Beckert	.25
5D	Ron Santo	.50
6D	Don Kessinger	.25
7D	Billy Williams	.75
8D	Hank Sauer	.25
9D	Jose Cardenal	.25
10D	Billy Herman	.25
JD	Bill Hands	.25
QD	Ken Holtzman	.25
KD	Ernie Banks	2.00
AC	Mordecai Brown	.25
2C	Gabby Hartnett	.25
3C	Frank Chance	.35
4C	Johnny Evers	.35
5C	Stan Hack	.25
6C	Joe Tinker	.35
7C	Bill Nicholson	.25
8C	Andy Pafko	.25
9C	Lewis Wilson	.35
10C	Kiki Cuyler	.25
JC	Charley Root	.25
QC	Grover Cleveland Alexander	.35
KC	Cap Anson	.35
AH	Greg Maddux	1.50
2H	Jody Davis	.25
3H	Bill Buckner	.25
4H	Manny Trillo	.25
5H	Bill Madlock	.25
6H	Ivan DeJesus	.25
7H	Gary Matthews	.25
8H	Leon Durham	.25
9H	Keith Moreland	.25
10H	Rick Reuschel	.25
JH	Rick Sutcliffe	.25
QH	Bruce Sutter	.50
KH	Dave Kingman	.25
---	Jack Brickhouse (Broadcaster)	.25
---	Harry Carey (Caray) (Broadcaster)	.50
---	Charlie Grimm	.25

2005 Parody Productions Cincinnati Baseball Heroes

This deck of poker-format (2-1/2" x 3-1/2", round-cornered, linen finish) playing cards features color caricatures of past and contemporary Reds stars. Player name, sometimes a nickname, and his dates of service with the team are included. Backs have a baseball on a red background with white borders. The issue is apparently not licensed by MLB or the players.

		NM/M
Complete Set (55):		10.00
Common Player:		.25
AS	Don Gullett	.25
2S	Johnny Bench	1.50
3S	Tony Perez	1.50
4S	Joe Morgan	1.50
5S	Pete Rose	2.00
6S	Dave Concepcion	.50
7S	George Foster	.25
8S	Cesar Geronimo	.25
9S	Ken Griffey	.50
10S	Sparky Anderson	1.00
JS	Rawly Eastwick	.25
QS	Pedro Borbon	.25
KS	Fred Norman	.25
AD	Johnny Vander Meer	.25
2D	Ernie Lombardi	.25
3D	Ted Kluszewski	1.00
4D	Johnny Temple	.25
5D	Ray Knight	.25
6D	Roy McMillan	.25
7D	Gus Bell	.25
8D	Eric Davis	.25
9D	Vada Pinson	.50
10D	Fred Hutchinson	.25
JD	Joe Nuxhall	.35
QD	Bucky Walters	.25
KD	Frank Robinson	1.50
AC	Eppa Rixey	.25

2C	Bubbles Hargrave	.25
3C	Frank McCormick	.25
4C	Hughie Critz	.25
5C	Heinie Groh	.25
6C	Billy Myers	.25
7C	Wally Post	.25
8C	Edd Roush	.25
9C	Red Lucas	.25
10C	Bill McKechnie	.25
JC	Dolf Luque	.25
QC	Paul Derringer	.25
KC	Noodles Hahn	.25
AH	Jose Rijo	.25
2H	Jason LaRue	.35
3H	Sean Casey	.50
4H	Tommy Helms	.25
5H	Chris Sabo	.25
6H	Barry Larkin	.25
7H	Adam Dunn	.50
8H	Ken Griffey Jr.	2.00
9H	Paul O'Neill	.25
10H	Lou Piniella	.25
JH	Mario Soto	.25
QH	Rob Dibble	.25
KH	Tom Browning	.25
---	Marty Brennaman (Announcer)	.25
---	Powel Crosley (Owner)	.25
---	Marge Schott (Owner)	.25

2005 Parody Productions L.A. & Brooklyn Baseball Heroes

This deck of poker-format (2-1/2" x 3-1/2", round-cornered, linen finish) playing cards features color caricatures of past and contemporary Dodgers stars. Player name, sometimes a nickname, and his dates of service with the team are included. Backs have a baseball on a blue background with white borders. The issue is apparently not licensed by MLB or the players.

		NM/M
Complete Set (55):		10.00
Common Player:		.25
AS	Eric Gagne	.25
2S	Mike Scioscia	.25
3S	Eric Karros	.25
4S	Steve Sax	.25
5S	Adrian Beltre	.25
6S	Cesar Izturis	.25
7S	Gary Sheffield	.25
8S	Milton Bradley	.25
9S	Shawn Green	.35
10S	Ramon Martinez	.25
JS	Hideo Nomo	.50
QS	Kevin Brown	.25
KS	Mike Piazza	1.00
AD	Sandy Koufax	2.00
2D	John Roseboro	.25
3D	Wes Parker	.25
4D	Jim Gilliam	.25
5D	Bill Buckner	.25
6D	Maury Wills	.35
7D	Tommy Davis	.25
8D	Willie Davis	.25
9D	Ron Fairly	.25
10D	Ron Perranoski	.25
JD	Johnny Podres	.25
QD	Don Drysdale	.50
KD	Frank Howard	.40
AC	Don Newcombe	.50
2C	Roy Campanella	.50
3C	Gil Hodges	.50
4C	Jackie Robinson	1.50
5C	Billy Cox	.25
6C	Pee Wee Reese	.50
7C	Zach Wheat	.25
8C	Duke Snider	.50
9C	Carl Furillo	.25
10C	Dazzy Vance	.25
JC	Clem Labine	.25
QC	Carl Erskine	.25
KC	Jake Daubert	.25
AH	Orel Hershiser	.25
2H	Steve Yeager	.25
3H	Steve Garvey	.35
4H	Davey Lopes	.25
5H	Ron Cey	.25
6H	Bill Russell	.25
7H	Dusty Baker	.25
8H	Claude Osteen	.25

9H	Reggie Smith	.25
10H	Burt Hooten (Hooton)	.25
JH	Fernando Valenzuela	.35
QH	Don Sutton	.25
KH	Kirk Gibson	.25
---	Walter Alston	.25
---	Tommy Lasorda	.25
---	Vin Scully (Announcer)	.25

2005 Parody Productions N.Y. (Yankees) Baseball Heroes

This deck of poker-format (2-1/2" x 3-1/2", round-cornered, linen finish) playing cards features color caricatures of past and contemporary Yankees stars. Player name, sometimes a nickname, and his dates of service with the team are included. Backs have a baseball on a white pinstriped background. The issue is apparently not licensed by MLB or the players.

		NM/M
Complete Set (55):		10.00
Common Player:		.25
AS	Roger Clemens	1.50
2S	Jorge Posada	.25
3S	Tino Martinez	.25
4S	Alfonso Soriano	.25
5S	Alex Rodriguez	1.50
6S	Derek Jeter	1.50
7S	Hideki Matsui	.50
8S	Bernie Williams	.25
9S	Paul O'Neill	.25
10S	Mike Mussina	.25
JS	Andy Petitte	.25
QS	Mariano Rivera	.25
KS	Don Mattingly	1.00
AD	Whitey Ford	.50
2D	Yogi Berra	.50
3D	Joe Pepitone	.35
4D	Bobby Richardson	.25
5D	Clete Boyer	.25
6D	Phil Rizzuto	.35
7D	Roy White	.25
8D	Roger Maris	.50
9D	Hank Bauer	.25
10D	Allie Reynolds	.25
JD	Ed Lopat	.25
QD	Mel Stottlemyre	.25
KD	Mickey Mantle	2.00
AC	Charles Ruffing	.25
2C	Bill Dickey	.25
3C	Lou Gehrig	2.00
4C	Tony Lazzeri	.25
5C	Red Rolfe	.25
6C	Frank Crosetti	.25
7C	Earle Combs	.25
8C	Joe DiMaggio	2.00
9C	Charlie Keller	.25
10C	Waite Hoyt	.25
JC	Herb Pennock	.25
QC	Lefty Gomez	.25
KC	George Herman Ruth	2.00
AH	Ron Guidry	.25
2H	Thurman Munson	.50
3H	Chris Chambliss	.25
4H	Willie Randolph	.25
5H	Graig Nettles	.25
6H	Bucky Dent	.25
7H	Dave Winfield	.50
8H	Mickey Rivers	.25
9H	Bobby Murcer	.25
10H	Jim Hunter	.35
JH	Dave Righetti	.25
QH	Rich Gossage	.25
KH	Reggie Jackson	.50
---	Billy Martin	.40
---	Casey Stengel	.40
---	Joe Torre	.40

1988 Pepsi-Cola/ Kroger Tigers

Approximately 38,000 sets of cards were given to fans at Tiger Stadium on July 30th, 1988. The set, sponsored by Pepsi-Cola and Kroger, includes 25 oversized (2-7/8" x 4-1/4") cards printed on glossy white stock with blue and orange borders. The card backs include small black and white close-up photos, the players'

---

(41) DARRELL EVANS, IF

professional records and sponsor logos. The numbers in the following checklist refer to the players' uniform.

		NM/M
Complete Set (25):		4.00
Common Player:		.25
1	Lou Whitaker	.50
2	Alan Trammell	1.00
8	Mike Heath	.25
11	Sparky Anderson	.50
12	Luis Salazar	.25
14	Dave Bergman	.25
15	Pat Sheridan	.25
16	Tom Brookens	.25
19	Doyle Alexander	.25
21	Guillermo Hernandez	.25
22	Ray Knight	.25
24	Gary Pettis	.25
25	Eric King	.25
26	Frank Tanana	.25
31	Larry Herndon	.25
32	Jim Walewander	.25
33	Matt Nokes	.25
34	Chet Lemon	.25
35	Walt Terrell	.25
39	Mike Henneman	.25
41	Darrell Evans	.50
44	Jeff Robinson	.25
47	Jack Morris	.25
48	Paul Gibson	.25
---	Coaches (Billy Consolo, Alex Grammas, Billy Muffett, Vada Pinson, Dick Tracewski)	.25

1989 Pepsi-Cola Mark McGwire

During the summer of 1989, selected Pepsi products in the Northern California area carried these special McGwire cards. Photos were posed with McGwire wearing a generic white uniform trimmed in A's colors and bearing his number 25 and a Pepsi logo patch. Backs have the same biographical details, recent stats and career highlights. A card number is printed at lower-right.

		NM/M
Complete Set (12):		10.00
Common Card:		1.50
1	Mark McGwire/Btg (Left foot raised.)	1.50
2	Mark McGwire/Fldg	1.50
3	Mark McGwire (Reaching for ball with glove.)	1.50
4	Mark McGwire/Btg (Foot down.)	1.50
5	Mark McGwire (Kneeling with bat.)	1.50
6	Mark McGwire (Stretching for throw at first.)	1.50
7	Mark McGwire (Bat on shoulder.)	1.50
8	Mark McGwire (Holding bat.)	1.50
9	Mark McGwire (Bat on shoulder.)	1.50
10	Mark McGwire (Holding bat.)	1.50
11	Mark McGwire (Holding bat.)	1.50
12	Mark McGwire (Batting follow-through.)	1.50

1990 Pepsi-Cola Boston Red Sox

Pepsi combined with Score to produce this special 20-card Boston Red Sox team set. Cards were inserted regionally in 12-packs of Pepsi and Diet Pepsi. The card fronts feature full-color action photos with the team name across the top border and the player's name along the bottom border. The Pepsi and Diet Pepsi logos also appear on the bottom border. The card backs represent standard Score card backs, but are not numbered and also once again feature the Pepsi and Diet Pepsi logos.

		NM/M
Complete Set (20):		5.00
Common Player:		.25
(1)	Marty Barrett	.25
(2)	Mike Boddicker	.25
(3)	Wade Boggs	1.50
(4)	Bill Buckner	.35
(5)	Ellis Burks	.25
(6)	Roger Clemens	3.00
(7)	John Dopson	.25
(8)	Dwight Evans	.35
(9)	Wes Gardner	.25
(10)	Rich Gedman	.25
(11)	Mike Greenwell	.25
(12)	Dennis Lamp	.25
(13)	Rob Murphy	.25
(14)	Tony Pena	.25
(15)	Carlos Quintana	.25
(16)	Jeff Reardon	.25
(17)	Jody Reed	.25
(18)	Luis Rivera	.25
(19)	Kevin Romine	.25
(20)	Lee Smith	.25

Jose Canseco

Single cards from this issue were distributed in packs of Pepsi products in the San Francisco Bay area. Each card has a photo of Canseco in a generic red, white and blue uniform. Fronts have a blue border with a Pepsi logo. Backs have biographical data, recent stats and career highlights. The cards are numbered in the lower-right corner.

		NM/M
Complete Set (10):		5.00
Common Card:		.75
1	Jose Canseco (Batting follow-through.)	.75
2	Jose Canseco (Batting follow-through.)	.75
3	Jose Canseco/Fldg	.75
4	Jose Canseco/Btg	.75
5	Jose Canseco (Holding glove.)	.75
6	Jose Canseco (Batting follow-through.)	.75
7	Jose Canseco (On dugout steps.)	.75
8	Jose Canseco/Btg	.75
9	Jose Canseco/Portrait	.75
10	Jose Canseco/Portrait	.75

1991 Pepsi-Cola Superstars

This Florida regional issue was distributed by gluing cards in-

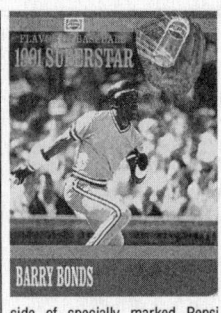

side of specially marked Pepsi products. Both front and back feature a "Flavor of Baseball" headline and logo of a glove catching a flying Pepsi can. Fronts have an action photo with colored strips at top and bottom. Player photos have uniform logos deleted. Backs have career stats, a few biographical details and a card number. The cards are slightly larger than current standards, measuring 2-5/8" x 3-1/2".

		NM/M
Complete Set (17):		18.50
Common Player:		.35
1	Dwight Gooden	.35
2	Andre Dawson	.65
3	Ryne Sandberg	2.00
4	Dave Steib	.35
5	Jose Rijo	.35
6	Roger Clemens	2.50
7	Barry Bonds	4.00
8	Cal Ripken, Jr.	4.00
9	Dave Justice	.35
10	Cecil Fielder	.35
11	Don Mattingly	2.50
12	Ozzie Smith	2.00
13	Kirby Puckett	2.00
14	Rafael Palmeiro	1.50
15	Bobby Bonilla	.35
16	Len Dykstra	.35
17	Jose Canseco	1.00

Cincinnati Reds

This team set was produced for inclusion in packages of Pepsi products in the Ohio area by Michael Schechter Assoc. Like most MSA issues, the cards have had cap and uniform logos airbrushed away because they are licensed only by the Players Union, and not MLB. Fronts have red borders with Pepsi, Diet Pepsi and MLBPA logos. Backs are in red, white and blue with the soda logos at top a few biographical notes, complete major and minor league stats and a facsimile autograph. The unnumbered cards are checklisted here alphabetically.

		NM/M
Complete Set (20):		8.00
Common Player:		.50
(1)	Jack Armstrong	.50
(2)	Todd Benzinger	.50
(3)	Glenn Braggs	.50
(4)	Tom Browning	.50
(5)	Norm Charlton	.50
(6)	Eric Davis	.75
(7)	Rob Dibble	.50
(8)	Bill Doran	.50
(9)	Mariano Duncan	.50
(10)	Billy Hatcher	.50
(11)	Barry Larkin	.75
(12)	Hal Morris	.50
(13)	Randy Myers	.50
(14)	Joe Oliver	.50
(15)	Paul O'Neill	.75
(16)	Lou Piniella	.75
(17)	Jeff Reed	.50
(18)	Jose Rijo	.50
(19)	Chris Sabo	.75
(20)	Herm Winningham	.50

Red Sox

For the second consecutive year, Pepsi/Diet Pepsi sponsored Boston Red Sox trading cards. The cards were inserted in specially marked packs of Pepsi and Diet Pepsi and were made available from July 1 through August 10. A consumer sweepstakes was also included with this promotion. Player jersey numbers are featured on the backs of the cards. Danny Darwin's jersey is incorrectly listed as #46. He actually wears #44 for the BoSox. Wade Boggs is not featured on a 1991 Pepsi-Cola Red Sox card.

		NM/M
Complete Set (20):		6.00
Common Player:		.25
2	Luis Rivera	.25
5	Jody Reed	.25
6	Tony Pena	.25
11	Tim Naehring	.25
12	Ellis Burks	.25
15	Dennis Lamp	.25
18	Carlos Quintana	.25
19	Dana Kiecker	.25
20	John Marzano	.25
21	Roger Clemens	5.00
23	Tom Brunansky	.25
25	Jack Clark	.25
27	Greg Harris	.25
29	Phil Plantier	.25
30	Matt Young	.25
38	Jeff Gray	.25
39	Mike Greenwell	.25
41	Jeff Reardon	.25
46	Danny Darwin	.25
50	Tom Bolton	.25

Griffeys

This regionally released set features Ken Griffey, Sr. and Jr. and was distributed in Pepsi products. In the photos the players are shown in generic white uniforms with Pepsi logo patches. Backs are printed in black-and-white and include biographical data, recent stats and career highlights. Card numbers are in the lower-right.

		NM/M
Complete Set (8):		7.50
Common Card:		.25
1	Ken Griffey Jr. (Swinging bat.)	2.00
2	Ken Griffey Jr./Throwing	2.00
3	Ken Griffey Jr./Catching	2.00
4	Ken Griffey Jr. (Bat on shoulder.)	2.00
5	Ken Griffey Jr. (Leaning on father.)	.75
6	Ken Griffey Jr. (Standing with father.)	.75
7	Ken Griffey Sr./Btg	.25
8	Ken Griffey Sr./Fldg	.25

Rickey Henderson

A third annual issue distributed with Pepsi products in the San Francisco Bay area this set features photos of the all-time base stealing king in airbrushed uniforms. Bor-

ders are red, white and blue pinstripes. A line-art figure of a base runner appears in the lower-right. Backs have a few bits of biographical data, career stats and a career highlight. Card numbers are printed in the lower-right.

		NM/M
Complete Set (10):		9.00
Common Card:		1.00
Uncut Prize Sheet:		25.00
1	Rickey Henderson (Batting follow-through.)	1.00
2	Rickey Henderson (Base running.)	1.00
3	Rickey Henderson (Warm-up stretches.)	1.00
4	Rickey Henderson (Taking lead-off.)	1.00
5	Rickey Henderson (Bat on shoulder.)	1.00
6	Rickey Henderson (Batting follow-through.)	1.00
7	Rickey Henderson (Squatting with bat.)	1.00
8	Rickey Henderson (Throwing follow-through.)	1.00
9	Rickey Henderson (Leading off.)	1.00
10	Rickey Henderson (Warm-up swings.)	1.00

Rickey Henderson Discs

Intended as a giveaway with Pepsi fountain drinks, this four-piece set of "3-D" discs pictures Rickey Henderson in a generic Pepsi-logo uniform. Each 2-1/4" diameter disc has two pictures of Henderson which change when the disc is moved. There is a purple border around the color photos, with "Pepsi," decorative stars and Henderson's name in white. Backs are printed in red and blue on white and are identical and unnumbered. The date and Pepsi logo are at top with 1990 season and career stats beneath.

		NM/M
Complete Set (4):		2.50
Common Disc:		1.00
(1)	Rickey Henderson (Bat on shoulder/ follow-through.)	1.00
(2)	Rickey Henderson (Warm-up swing/batting follow-through.)	1.00
(3)	Rickey Henderson (Lead-off/running for 2nd.)	1.00
(4)	Rickey Henderson (Lead-off/headfirst slide.)	1.00

1996 Pepsi-Cola Cubs Convention

In conjunction with the Chicago Cubs 11th annual winter fan convention, Pepsi issued this boxed set featuring past and current Cubs with an emphasis on those appearing as convention guests. Individual cards are 4" x 5-1/2" and feature black-and-white or color photos inside a black border with white piping. The team and convention logos are printed in red, white and blue. Backs are printed in black on white and feature stats and biographical data plus the team

and sponsor logos. The unnumbered cards are checklisted here in alphabetical order.

		NM/M
Complete Set (24):		8.00
Common Player:		.25
(1)	Ernie Banks	3.00
(2)	Glenn Beckert	.25
(3)	Larry Bowa	.25
(4)	Harry Caray	.25
(5)	Frank Castillo	.25
(6)	Jody Davis	.25
(7)	Dynamic Duo (Scott Bullett, Ozzie Timmons)	.25
(8)	Flashback Favorites (Milt Pappas, Tim Stoddard)	.25
(9)	Golden Voices (Jack Brickhouse, Vince Lloyd)	.25
(10)	Randy Hundley	.25
(11)	Fergie Jenkins	.50
(12)	Don Kessinger	.35
(13)	Gary Matthews	.25
(14)	Brian McRae	.25
(15)	Jim Riggleman	.25
(16)	Ron Santo	.50
(17)	Sensational 70's (Jose Cardenal, Rick Monday)	.25
(18)	Scott Servais	.25
(19)	Rick Sutcliffe	.25
(20)	Steve Trachsel	.25
(21)	Billy Williams	.75
(22)	Wrigleyville Sluggers (Keith Moreland, Richie Hebner)	.25
(23)	Young Guns (Turk Wendell, Terry Adams)	.25
(24)	Vine Line subscription offer (Ernie Banks)	.25

1998 Pepsi-Cola Arizona Diamondbacks

Pepsi-Cola and Circle K stores ran a baseball-season promotion to distribute 15 cards of Arizona Diamondback players on a regional basis. By use of a punchcard to record the purchase of five 20-oz. or one-liter Pepsi products a customer could receive a series of three players cards each month. Produced by Pinnacle, the D'back cards have action photos on front against a stylized semi-circular background. Team, Pinnacle and Pepsi logos are in three of the corners with the player name at lower-right. Backs have a red, white and blue Pepsi-style whirlpool background, another player photo, major league stats, a career highlight and licensor logos. Final production of the cards differs considerably from the player checklist provided on the punchcard and ads.

		NM/M
Complete Set (15):		6.00
Common Card:		.50
1	Andy Benes	.50
2	Willie Blair	.50
3	Jorge Fabregas	.50
4	Jay Bell	.50
5	Travis Lee	1.00
6	Matt Williams	.50
7	Devon White	.50
8	Karim Garcia	.65
9	Yamil Benitez	.50
10	Brian Anderson	.50
11	Scott Brow	.50
12	Felix Rodriguez	.50
13	Jeff Suppan	.50
14	Andy Fox	.50
15	Andy Stankiewicz	.50

Cubs Convention

In conjunction with the Chicago Cubs 13th annual winter fan convention, Pepsi issued this boxed set featuring past and current Cubs with an emphasis on those appearing as convention guests. Individual cards are 3-1/2" x 4" and feature black-and-white or color photos bordered in blue and sand. The team and convention logos are printed in red, white and blue. Backs are printed in black on white and feature stats and biographical data plus the team and sponsor logos. The unnumbered cards are checklisted here in alphabetical order.

		NM/M
Complete Set (30):		7.00
Common Card:		.25
(1)	Terry Adams	.25
(2)	Alumni Club (Carmen Fanzone, Paul Reuschel)	.25
(3)	Alumni Club (Oscar Gamble, Larry Bowa)	.25
(4)	Ernie Banks	2.00
(5)	Behind the Plate (Randy Hundley, Jody Davis)	.25
(6)	Booth Banter (Pat Hughes, Josh Lewin)	.25
(7)	Jack Brickhouse	.25
(8)	Harry Caray	.25
(9)	Catching Corps (Mike Hubbard, Tyler Houston)	.25
(10)	Andre Dawson	.50
(11)	Flame-Throwers (Kevin Foster, Marc Pisciotta)	.25
(12)	Future Stars (Kerry Wood, Pat Cline)	.50
(13)	Mark Grace	.50
(14)	Hot Prospects (Robin Jennings, Rodney Myers)	.25
(15)	Mound Mates (Mark Clark, Jeremi Gonzalez)	.25
(16)	New Cubs (Jeff Blauser, Mickey Morandini)	.25
(17)	No-Hit Hurlers (Milt Pappas, Don Cardwell)	.25
(18)	Kevin Orie	.25
(19)	Outfield Greats (Andy Pafko, Gary Matthews)	.35
(20)	Jim Riggleman	.25
(21)	Ron Santo	1.00
(22)	Scott Servais	.25
(23)	Sammy Sosa	2.00
(24)	Rick Sutcliffe	.25
(25)	Steve Trachsel	.25
(26)	Veteran Hurlers (Bob Patterson, Kevin Tapani)	.25
(27)	Billy Williams	1.00
(28)	1969 Cubs (Dick Selma, Willie Smith)	.25
(29)	1969 Infield (Glenn Beckert, Don Kessinger)	.25
(30)	89er's (Mike Bielecki, Vance Law)	.25

1999 Pepsi-Cola Arizona Diamondbacks

Sponsored by Pepsi and produced by Fleer, this team-set promotion features action photos on front on a metallic-foil background which approximates the colors and design of the soft drink logo, which also appears at lower-left. The player's uniform is at top-left. On back is a portrait photo on a repeat of the red, white and blue background.

Full Major League stats are provided, along with career highlights and biographical data. At bottom is a row of licensor and sponsor logos.

		NM/M
Complete Set (15):		9.00
Common Player:		.50
1	Jay Bell	.50
2	Andy Benes	.50
3	Randy Johnson	3.00
4	Matt Williams	.50
5	Steve Finley	.50
6	Todd Stottlemyre	.50
7	Omar Daal	.50
8	Travis Lee	.50
9	Armando Reynoso	.50
10	Gregg Olson	.50
11	Tony Batista	.50
12	Greg Swindell	.50
13	Greg Colbrunn	.50
14	Damian Miller	.50
15	Kelly Stinnett	.50
---	Checklist 1	.10
---	Checklist 2	.10
---	Checklist 3	.10
---	Checklist 4	.10

2000 Pepsi-Cola Arizona Diamondbacks

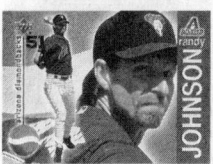

Pepsi-Cola and Circle K stores ran a baseball-season promotion to distribute 15 cards of Arizona Diamondback players on a regional basis. Produced by Upper Deck, the D'back cards have large portrait and smaller action photos in a horizontal format on a red, white and blue wave background. Team, UD and Pepsi logos appear in the corners with the player name at right. Backs have the same background, another player photo, major league stats, a career highlight and licensor logos. Cards were distributed in three five-card series, with a checklist card in each pack.

		NM/M
Complete Set (18):		9.00
Common Player:		.50
1	Jay Bell	.50
2	Matt Williams	.50
3	Greg Swindell	.50
4	Matt Williams	.50
5	Erubiel Durazo	.50
6	Todd Stottlemyre	.50
7	Randy Johnson	3.00
8	Tony Womack	.50
9	Greg Colbrunn	.50
10	Brian Anderson	.50
11	Omar Daal	.50
12	Travis Lee	.50
13	Steve Finley	.50
14	Luis Gonzalez	.50
15	Kelly Stinnett	.50
	Checklist 1	.10
	Checklist 2	.10
	Checklist 3	.10

Detroit Tigers

Pepsi-Cola ran a late-season promotion to distribute 15 cards of Detroit Tigers players on a regional

basis. Produced by Upper Deck, the cards have large portrait and smaller action photos in a horizontal format on a red, white and blue wave background. Team, UD and Pepsi logos appear in the corners with the player name at right. Backs have the same background, another action photo, major league stats, a careeer highlight and licensor logos. Cards were distributed in one per 12-pack of Pepsi products.

		NM/M
Complete Set (15):		5.00
Common Player:		.50
1	Damion Easley	.50
2	Dave Mlicki	.50
3	Jeff Weaver	.50
4	Deivi Cruz	.50
5	Juan Encarnacion	.50
6	Brian Moehler	.50
7	Robert Fick	.50
8	Juan Gonzalez	1.50
9	Phil Garner	.50
10	Brad Ausmus	.50
11	Todd Jones	.50
12	Bobby Higginson	.50
13	Tony Clark	.50
14	Dean Palmer	.50
15	Doug Brocail	.50

2001 Pepsi-Cola Arizona Diamondbacks

Pepsi-Cola ran a baseball-season promotion to distribute 15 cards of Arizona Diamondback players on a regional basis. Produced by Upper Deck, the D'back cards have a circular action photo in a horizontal format on a red, white and blue wave background at left. At right is a rattlesnake skin design. Team, UD and Pepsi logos appear at right, with the player name at left. Backs have the same background, another player photo, recent major league stats, a career highlight and licensor logos. Cards were distributed in five three-card series. They are checklisted here by uniform number which appears on front.

		NM/M
Complete Set (15):		10.00
Common Player:		.25
5	Tony Womack	.25
9	Matt Williams	.25
12	Steve Finley	.25
16	Reggie Sanders	.25
17	Mark Grace	.50
20	Luis Gonzalez	.25
22	Greg Swindell	.25
27	Armando Reynoso	.25
28	Greg Colbrunn	.25
30	Todd Stottlemyre	.25
31	Matt Mantei	.25
33	Jay Bell	.25
34	Brian Anderson	.25
38	Curt Schilling	2.00
51	Randy Johnson	3.00

2002 Pepsi-Cola Seattle Mariners

Pepsi-Cola and the Mariners teamed up for this 25th Anniversary promotion distributing eight cards on a regional basis. Produced by Upper Deck, the M's cards have a game-action photo at left. At right is the team name along with Pepsi and anniversary logos. Backs have

player stats and career highlights, a few sentences of team history and licensor logos. Cards were distributed in two-card cello packs.

		NM/M
Complete Set (8):		10.00
Common Player:		.50
1	John Olerud	.50
2	Mike Cameron	.50
3	Edgar Martinez	.75
4	Ichiro	6.00
5	Bret Boone	.75
6	Jeff Nelson	.50
7	Freddy Garcia	.50
8	Jamie Moyer	.50

2003 Pepsi-Cola

Unusual for modern promotional cards, Pepsi chose a smaller, 2" x 2-3/4" format for its Fleer-produced issue. Specially marked 24-can "Value Cubes" of Pepsi products included one of the cards. A total of 9.75 million (about 325,000 sets) were reportedly produced. Fronts have action photos in a format similar to the soda logo, with red border at top and blue at bottom. Fleer, Pepsi and MLB logos appear. Backs have a team logo, player data, recent stats and career highlights, along with appropriate logos and copyright information. There is one player from each team in the issue.

		NM/M
Complete Set (30):		6.00
Common Player:		.15
1	Troy Glaus	.30
2	Chipper Jones	.35
3	Randy Johnson	.30
4	Tony Batista	.15
5	Magglio Ordonez	.30
6	Ken Griffey Jr.	.40
7	Omar Vizquel	.15
8	Todd Helton	.30
9	Bobby Higginson	.15
10	Luis Castillo	.15
11	Jeff Bagwell	.30
12	Mike Sweeney	.15
13	Shawn Green	.25
14	Richie Sexson	.15
15	Torii Hunter	.15
16	Vladimir Guerrero	.30
17	Mike Piazza	.35
18	Jason Giambi	.25
19	Barry Zito	.15
20	Pat Burrell	.25
21	Brian Giles	.15
22	Trevor Hoffman	.15
23	Barry Bonds	.75
24	Ichiro	.50
25	Albert Pujols	.60
26	Ben Grieve	.15
27	Alex Rodriguez	.60
28	Carlos Delgado	.25
29	Kerry Wood	.20
30	Pedro Martinez	.30

2004 Pepsi-Cola Arizona Diamondbacks

Pepsi-Cola offered this team set of Arizona Diamondback players as a stadium giveaway. Pro-

duced by Upper Deck, the cards have a game-action photo on a blue background. Backs have the same background, two more player photos, recent major league stats, a career highlight and licensor logos.

		NM/M
Complete Set (15):		7.00
Common Player:		.25
1	Randy Johnson	5.00
2	Richie Sexson	.35
3	Roberto Alomar	.35
4	Shea Hillenbrand	.35
5	Alex Cintron	.25
6	Matt Kata	.25
7	Robby Hammock	.25
8	Luis Gonzalez	.25
9	Steve Finley	.25
10	Danny Bautista	.25
11	Matt Mantei	.25
12	Brandon Webb	.35
13	Elmer Dessens	.25
14	Oscar Villarreal	.25
15	Jose Valverde	.25

1980-2001 Perez-Steele Hall of Fame Postcards

In 1980, Perez-Steele Galleries of Ft. Washington, Pa., produced the first in an ongoing series of limited-edition (10,000 each) postcards devoted to members of the Hall of Fame. The company updated its series regularly through 2001 to add new inductees. The 3-1/2" x 5-1/2" cards feature color portrait and smaller sepia action watercolor paintings by Dick Perez. Decorative postcard backs have a few words about the player, card and series number and individual set number from within the edition of 10,000. Cards were sold by series only, in a color-coded box which includes a checklist. To a great degree, value of unsigned Perez-Steele cards depends on whether the player is still alive to autograph them.

		NM/M
Complete Set (270):		750.00
Common Player:		2.00
First Series, 1980		75.00
1	Ty Cobb	20.00
2	Walter Johnson	6.00
3	Christy Mathewson	7.50
4	Babe Ruth	25.00
5	Honus Wagner	7.50
6	Morgan Bulkeley	2.00
7	Ban Johnson	2.00
8	Nap Lajoie	4.00
9	Connie Mack	4.00
10	John McGraw	2.00
11	Tris Speaker	4.00
12	George Wright	2.00
13	Cy Young	7.50
14	Grover Alexander	4.00
15	Alexander Cartwright	2.00
16	Henry Chadwick	2.00
17	Cap Anson	2.00
18	Eddie Collins	2.00
19	Candy Cummings	2.00
20	Charles Comiskey	2.00
21	Buck Ewing	2.00
22	Lou Gehrig	20.00
23	Willie Keeler	2.00
24	Hoss Radbourne	2.00
25	George Sisler	2.00
26	A.G. Spalding	2.00
27	Rogers Hornsby	4.00
28	Kenesaw Landis	2.00
29	Roger Breshnahan	2.00
30	Dan Brouthers	2.00
---	First Series Checklist	1.00
Second Series, 1980		50.00
31	Fred Clarke	2.00
32	Jimmy Collins	2.00
33	Ed Delahanty	2.00
34	Hugh Duffy	2.00
35	Hughie Jennings	2.00
36	King Kelly	2.00

37	Jim O'Rourke	2.00
38	Wilbert Robinson	2.00
39	Jesse Burkett	2.00
40	Frank Chance	2.00
41	Jack Chesbro	2.00
42	Johnny Evers	2.00
43	Clark Griffith	2.00
44	Thomas McCarthy	2.00
45	Joe McGinnity	2.00
46	Eddie Plank	2.00
47	Joe Tinker	2.00
48	Rube Waddell	2.00
49	Ed Walsh	2.00
50	Mickey Cochrane	2.00
51	Frankie Frisch	2.00
52	Lefty Grove	2.00
53	Carl Hubbell	2.00
54	Herb Pennock	2.00
55	Pie Traynor	2.00
56	Mordecai Brown	2.00
57	Charlie Gehringer	2.00
58	Kid Nichols	2.00
59	Jimmie Foxx	4.00
60	Mel Ott	2.00
---	Second Series Checklist	1.00
Third Series, 1980		75.00
61	Harry Heilmann	2.00
62	Paul Waner	2.00
63	Ed Barrow	2.00
64	Chief Bender	2.00
65	Tom Connolly	2.00
66	Dizzy Dean	7.50
67	Bill Klem	2.00
68	Al Simmons	2.00
69	Bobby Wallace	2.00
70	Harry Wright	2.00
71	Bill Dickey	2.00
72	Rabbit Maranville	2.00
73	Bill Terry	2.00
74	Frank Baker	2.00
75	Joe DiMaggio	20.00
76	Gabby Hartnett	2.00
77	Ted Lyons	2.00
78	Ray Schalk	2.00
79	Dazzy Vance	2.00
80	Joe Cronin	2.00
81	Hank Greenberg	7.50
82	Sam Crawford	2.00
83	Joe McCarthy	2.00
84	Zack Wheat	2.00
85	Max Carey	2.00
86	Billy Hamilton	2.00
87	Bob Feller	6.00
88	Bill McKechnie	2.00
89	Jackie Robinson	10.00
90	Edd Roush	2.00
---	Third Series Checklist	1.00
Fourth Series, 1981		65.00
91	John Clarkson	2.00
92	Elmer Flick	2.00
93	Sam Rice	2.00
94	Eppa Rixey	2.00
95	Luke Appling	2.00
96	Red Faber	2.00
97	Burleigh Grimes	2.00
98	Miller Huggins	2.00
99	Tim Keefe	2.00
100	Heinie Manush	2.00
101	John Ward	2.00
102	Pud Galvin	2.00
103	Casey Stengel	3.00
104	Ted Williams	20.00
105	Branch Rickey	2.00
106	Red Ruffing	2.00
107	Lloyd Waner	2.00
108	Kiki Cuyler	2.00
109	Goose Goslin	2.00
110	Joe Medwick	2.00
111	Roy Campanella	7.50
112	Stan Coveleski	2.00
113	Waite Hoyt	2.00
114	Stan Musial	10.00
115	Lou Boudreau	2.00
116	Earle Combs	2.00
117	Ford Frick	2.00
118	Jesse Haines	2.00
119	David Bancroft	2.00
120	Jake Beckley	2.00
---	Fourth Series Checklist	1.00
Fifth Series, 1981		85.00
121	Chick Hafey	2.00
122	Harry Hooper	2.00
123	Joe Kelley	2.00
124	Rube Marquard	2.00
125	Satchel Paige	10.00
126	George Weiss	2.00
127	Yogi Berra	6.00
128	Josh Gibson	4.00
129	Lefty Gomez	2.00
130	William Harridge	2.00
131	Sandy Koufax	15.00
132	Buck Leonard	2.00
133	Early Wynn	2.00
134	Ross Youngs	2.00
135	Roberto Clemente	20.00
136	Billy Evans	2.00
137	Monte Irvin	4.00
138	George Kelly	2.00
139	Warren Spahn	4.00
140	Mickey Welch	2.00
141	Cool Papa Bell	2.00
142	Jim Bottomley	2.00
143	Jocko Conlan	2.00
144	Whitey Ford	5.00
145	Mickey Mantle	25.00
146	Sam Thompson	2.00
147	Earl Averill	2.00
148	Bucky Harris	2.00

149	Billy Herman	2.00
150	Judy Johnson	2.00
---	Fifth Series Checklist	1.00
Sixth Series, 1981		85.00
151	Ralph Kiner	2.00
152	Oscar Charleston	2.00
153	Roger Connor	2.00
154	Cal Hubbard	2.00
155	Bob Lemon	2.00
156	Freddie Lindstrom	2.00
157	Robin Roberts	4.00
158	Ernie Banks	6.00
159	Martin DiHigo	2.00
160	John Lloyd	2.00
161	Al Lopez	2.00
162	Amos Rusie	2.00
163	Joe Sewell	2.00
164	Addie Joss	2.00
165	Larry MacPhail	2.00
166	Eddie Mathews	2.00
167	Warren Giles	2.00
168	Willie Mays	15.00
169	Hack Wilson	2.00
170	Al Kaline	5.00
171	Chuck Klein	2.00
172	Duke Snider	5.00
173	Tom Yawkey	2.00
174	Rube Foster	2.00
175	Bob Gibson	4.00
176	Johnny Mize	2.00
A	Abner Doubleday	2.00
B	Stephen Clark	2.00
C	Paul Kerr	2.00
D	Edward W. Stack	2.00
---	Sixth Series Checklist	1.00
Seventh Series, 1983		55.00
177	Hank Aaron	20.00
178	Happy Chandler	3.00
179	Travis Jackson	3.00
180	Frank Robinson	10.00
181	Walter Alston	3.00
182	George Kell	6.00
183	Juan Marichal	7.50
184	Brooks Robinson	10.00
Eighth Series, 1985		55.00
185	Luis Aparicio	7.50
186	Don Drysdale	3.00
187	Rick Ferrell	3.00
188	Harmon Killebrew	6.00
189	Pee Wee Reese	3.00
190	Lou Brock	6.00
191	Enos Slaughter	3.00
192	Arky Vaughn	3.00
193	Hoyt Wilhelm	3.00
Ninth Series, 1987		15.00
194	Bobby Doerr	2.00
195	Ernie Lombardi	2.00
196	Willie McCovey	2.00
197	Ray Dandridge	2.00
198	Catfish Hunter	2.00
199	Billy Williams	4.00
E	Frank Steele, Peggy Steele, Dick Perez	2.00
Tenth Series, 1989		20.00
200	Willie Stargell	2.00
201	Al Barlick	2.00
202	Johnny Bench	4.00
203	Red Schoendienst	4.00
204	Carl Yastrzemski	4.00
F	George Bush, Edward Stack	4.00
Eleventh Series, 1991		30.00
205	Joe Morgan	4.00
206	Jim Palmer	4.00
207	Rod Carew	4.00
208	Ferguson Jenkins	4.00
209	Tony Lazzeri	2.00
210	Gaylord Perry	4.00
211	Bill Veeck	2.00
Twelfth Series, 1993		35.00
212	Rollie Fingers	4.00
213	Bill McGowan	3.00
214	Hal Newhouser	3.00
215	Tom Seaver	6.00
216	Reggie Jackson	7.50
217	Steve Carlton	6.00
218	Leo Durocher	3.00
219	Phil Rizzuto	6.00
Thirteenth Series, 1995		40.00
220	Richie Ashburn	4.00
221	Leon Day	3.00
222	William Hulbert	3.00
223	Mike Schmidt	10.00
224	Vic Willis	3.00
225	Jim Bunning	6.00
226	Andrew "Rube" Foster	3.00
227	Ned Hanlon	3.00
228	Earl Weaver	6.00
Fourteenth Series, 1997		85.00
229	Nellie Fox	6.00
230	Tommy Lasorda	6.00
231	Phil Niekro	4.00
232	Willie Wells	3.00
233	George Davis	3.00
234	Larry Doby	4.00
235	Lee MacPhail	4.00
236	Joe Rogan	3.00
237	Don Sutton	4.00
238	George Brett	15.00
239	Orlando Cepeda	6.00
240	Nestor Chylak	3.00
241	Nolan Ryan	20.00
242	Frank Selee	3.00
243	Joe Williams	3.00
244	Robin Yount	7.50
Fifteenth Series, 2001		50.00
245	Sparky Anderson	6.00
246	Carlton Fisk	7.50

247	Bid McPhee	3.00
248	Tony Perez	6.00
249	Turkey Stearnes	3.00
250	Bill Mazeroski	7.50
251	Kirby Puckett	7.50
252	Hilton Smith	3.00
253	Dave Winfield	7.50
G	Franklin A. Steele	5.00

Autographed

Because the cards are so popular with autograph collectors, a listing of Perez-Steele Hall of Fame postcards which are possible to acquire in authentically autographed form is provided here, along with current retail values. Only those players who were alive at the time of their cards' issue are included in this listing; no cards from Series 1 and very few from Series 2 are available in autographed form.

		NM/M
Common Player:		15.00
53	Carl Hubbell	80.00
57	Charlie Gehringer	80.00
71	Bill Dickey	65.00
73	Bill Terry	90.00
75	Joe DiMaggio	325.00
77	Ted Lyons	235.00
80	Joe Cronin	750.00
81	Hank Greenberg	300.00
87	Bob Feller	25.00
90	Edd Roush	75.00
95	Luke Appling	50.00
97	Burleigh Grimes	190.00
104	Ted Williams	300.00
106	Red Ruffing	450.00
107	Lloyd Waner	2,250
111	Roy Campanella	300.00
112	Stan Coveleski	300.00
113	Waite Hoyt	495.00
114	Stan Musial	75.00
115	Lou Boudreau	25.00
125	Satchel Paige	2,500
127	Yogi Berra	40.00
129	Lefty Gomez	60.00
131	Sandy Koufax	90.00
132a	Buck Leonard (Pre-stroke.)	45.00
132b	Buck Leonard (Post-stroke.)	25.00
133	Early Wynn	40.00
137	Monte Irvin	20.00
138	George Kelly	350.00
139	Warren Spahn	30.00
141	Cool Papa Bell	75.00
143	Jocko Conlan	60.00
144	Whitey Ford	40.00
145	Mickey Mantle	300.00
147	Earl Averill	450.00
149	Billy Herman	35.00
150	Judy Johnson	60.00
151	Ralph Kiner	30.00
155	Bob Lemon	30.00
157	Robin Roberts	25.00
158	Ernie Banks	30.00
161	Al Lopez	75.00
163	Joe Sewell	45.00
166	Eddie Mathews	40.00
168	Willie Mays	75.00
170	Al Kaline	25.00
172	Duke Snider	30.00
175	Bob Gibson	25.00
176	Johnny Mize	35.00
D	Edward W. Stack	15.00
177	Hank Aaron	45.00
178	Happy Chandler	50.00
179	Travis Jackson	80.00
180	Frank Robinson	35.00
181	Walter Alston	675.00
182	George Kell	20.00
183	Juan Marichal	20.00
184	Brooks Robinson	22.50
185	Luis Aparicio	22.50
186	Don Drysdale	40.00
187	Rick Ferrell	25.00
188	Harmon Killebrew	30.00
189	Pee Wee Reese	55.00
190	Lou Brock	25.00
191	Enos Slaughter	20.00
192	Hoyt Wilhelm	30.00
193	Bobby Doerr	17.50

196	Willie McCovey	35.00
197	Ray Dandridge	30.00
198	Catfish Hunter	40.00
199	Billy Williams	22.50
E	Frank Steele, Peggy Steele, Dick Perez	15.00
200	Willie Stargell	35.00
201	Al Barlick	20.00
202	Johnny Bench	45.00
203	Red Schoendienst	25.00
204	Carl Yastrzemski	65.00
F	George Bush, Edward Stack	60.00
205	Joe Morgan	35.00
206	Jim Palmer	25.00
207	Rod Carew	45.00
208	Ferguson Jenkins	30.00
210	Gaylord Perry	17.50
212	Rollie Fingers	35.00
214	Hal Newhouser	60.00
215	Tom Seaver	60.00
216	Reggie Jackson	75.00
217	Steve Carlton	45.00
219	Phil Rizzuto	40.00
220	Richie Ashburn	30.00
223	Mike Schmidt	75.00
225	Jim Bunning	35.00
228	Earl Weaver	35.00
230	Tommy Lasorda	35.00
231	Phil Niekro	35.00
234	Larry Doby	90.00
235	Lee MacPhail	35.00
237	Don Sutton	35.00
238	George Brett	100.00
239	Orlando Cepeda	40.00
241	Nolan Ryan	100.00
244	Robin Yount	100.00
245	Sparky Anderson	45.00
246	Carlton Fisk	60.00
247	Tony Perez	45.00
250	Bill Mazeroski	45.00
251	Kirby Puckett	85.00
253	Dave Winfield	85.00

1981 Perez-Steele Yankee Greats Promotional Postcard

To advertise the availability of a "Yankee Greats" lithograph by Dick Perez, the Perez-Steele Galleries issued this promotional postcard. The 3-1/2" x 5-1/2" card is printed on thin cardboard with a reproduction of the lithograph on front. Printed in blue, the postcard-style back has information on the lithograph, which was issued in a size of 19" x 24-1/2" in an edition of 1,000 signed pieces.

	NM/M
Yankee Greats (Babe Ruth, Lou Gehrig, Earle Combs)	4.00

1985-95 Perez-Steele Great Moments Postcards

Yet another collectors issue devoted solely to Hall of Fame players, the Great Moments series borrows the format of the 1911 Turkey Red cabinet cards. The 5-3/4" x 8" cards are printed on textured card-

board (which was noticeably downgraded beginning with the 1993 series). Fronts have Dick Perez paintings surrounded by a greenish-brown border; backs are in black-and-white. Each card carries a series checklist on back and an individual set serial number from within an edition of 5,000. Cards were issued in series of 12.

		NM/M
Complete Set (108):		400.00
Common Player:		3.00
1	Babe Ruth	20.00
2	Al Kaline	6.00
3	Jackie Robinson	10.00
4	Lou Gehrig	15.00
5	Whitey Ford	6.00
6	Christy Mathewson	5.00
7	Roy Campanella	7.50
8	Walter Johnson	5.00
9	Hank Aaron	12.50
10	Cy Young	5.00
11	Stan Musial	12.50
12	Ty Cobb	15.00
13	Ted Williams	15.00
14	Warren Spahn	3.00
15	Lloyd Waner, Paul Waner	3.00
16	Sandy Koufax	12.50
17	Robin Roberts	3.00
18	Dizzy Dean	4.00
19	Mickey Mantle	25.00
20	Satchel Paige	10.00
21	Ernie Banks	3.00
22	Willie McCovey	3.00
23	Johnny Mize	3.00
24	Honus Wagner	7.50
25	Willie Keeler	3.00
26	Pee Wee Reese	3.00
27	Monte Irvin	3.00
28	Eddie Mathews	3.00
29	Enos Slaughter	3.00
30	Rube Marquard	3.00
31	Charlie Gehringer	3.00
32	Roberto Clemente	15.00
33	Duke Snider	4.50
34	Ray Dandridge	3.00
35	Carl Hubbell	3.00
36	Bobby Doerr	3.00
37	Bill Dickey	3.00
38	Willie Stargell	3.00
39	Brooks Robinson	3.00
40	Joe Tinker, Johnny Evers, Frank Chance	5.00
41	Billy Herman	3.00
42	Grover Alexander	4.00
43	Luis Aparicio	3.00
44	Lefty Gomez	3.00
45	Eddie Collins	3.00
46	Judy Johnson	3.00
47	Harry Heilmann	3.00
48	Harmon Killebrew	3.00
49	Johnny Bench	4.50
50	Max Carey	3.00
51	Cool Papa Bell	3.00
52	Rube Waddell	3.00
53	Yogi Berra	6.00
54	Herb Pennock	3.00
55	Red Schoendienst	3.00
56	Juan Marichal	3.00
57	Frankie Frisch	3.00
58	Buck Leonard	3.00
59	George Kell	3.00
60	Chuck Klein	3.00
61	King Kelly	3.00
62	Jim Hunter	3.00
63	Lou Boudreau	3.00
64	Al Lopez	3.00
65	Willie Mays	12.50
66	Lou Brock	3.00
67	Bob Lemon	3.00
68	Joe Sewell	3.00
69	Billy Williams	3.00
70	Rick Ferrell	3.00
71	Arky Vaughn	3.00
72	Carl Yastrzemski	4.50
73	Tom Seaver	6.00
74	Rollie Fingers	3.00
75	Ralph Kiner	3.00
76	Frank Baker	3.00
77	Rod Carew	3.00
78	Goose Goslin	3.00
79	Gaylord Perry	3.00
80	Hack Wilson	3.00
81	Hal Newhouser	3.00
82	Early Wynn	3.00
83	Bob Feller	4.00
84	Branch Rickey (W/Jackie Robinson.)	3.00
85	Jim Palmer	3.00
86	Al Barlick	3.00
87	Willie Mays, Mickey Mantle, Duke Snider	20.00
88	Hank Greenberg	6.00
89	Joe Morgan	3.00
90	Chief Bender	3.00
91	Pee Wee Reese, Jackie Robinson	5.00
92	Jim Bottomley	3.00
93	Ferguson Jenkins	3.00
94	Frank Robinson	4.00
95	Hoyt Wilhelm	3.00
96	Cap Anson	3.00
97	Jim Bunning	3.00
98	Richie Ashburn	4.00

99	Steve Carlton	3.00
100	Mike Schmidt	6.00
101	Nellie Fox	3.00
102	Tommy Lasorda	3.00
103	Leo Durocher	3.00
104	Reggie Jackson	6.00
105	Phil Rizzuto	4.50
106	Phil Niekro	3.00
107	Willie Wells	3.00
108	Earl Weaver	3.00

Autographed

Because the Perez-Steele postcards are so popular with autograph collectors, separate listings for authentically autographed examples of the cards are provided here. Those cards not listed cannot possibly have been signed because the player was deceased prior to issue.

		NM/M
Complete Set (70):		1,800
Common Player:		17.50
2	Al Kaline	30.00
5	Whitey Ford	35.00
7	Roy Campanella	400.00
9	Hank Aaron	60.00
11	Stan Musial	60.00
13	Ted Williams	300.00
14	Warren Spahn	30.00
16	Sandy Koufax	95.00
17	Robin Roberts	25.00
19	Mickey Mantle	300.00
21	Ernie Banks	55.00
22	Willie McCovey	40.00
23	Johnny Mize	40.00
26	Pee Wee Reese	60.00
27	Monte Irvin	20.00
28	Eddie Mathews	50.00
29	Enos Slaughter	27.50
31	Charlie Gehringer	65.00
33	Duke Snider	40.00
34	Ray Dandridge	45.00
35	Carl Hubbell	65.00
36	Bobby Doerr	17.50
37	Bill Dickey	65.00
38	Willie Stargell	35.00
39	Brooks Robinson	30.00
41	Billy Herman	40.00
43	Luis Aparicio	25.00
44	Lefty Gomez	55.00
48	Harmon Killebrew	35.00
49	Johnny Bench	40.00
51	Cool Papa Bell	90.00
53	Yogi Berra	35.00
55	Red Schoendienst	25.00
56	Juan Marichal	25.00
58	Buck Leonard	40.00
59	George Kell	20.00
62	Jim Hunter	55.00
63	Lou Boudreau	30.00
64	Al Lopez	60.00
65	Willie Mays	80.00
66	Lou Brock	30.00
67	Bob Lemon	35.00
68	Joe Sewell	50.00
69	Billy Williams	25.00
70	Rick Ferrell	35.00
72	Carl Yastrzemski	60.00
73	Tom Seaver	50.00
74	Rollie Fingers	32.50
75	Ralph Kiner	27.50
77	Rod Carew	35.00
79	Gaylord Perry	25.00
81	Hal Newhouser	30.00
82	Early Wynn	40.00
83	Bob Feller	30.00
85	Jim Palmer	32.50
86	Al Barlick	25.00
87	Willie Mays, Mickey Mantle, Duke Snider	325.00
89	Joe Morgan	30.00
93	Ferguson Jenkins	20.00
94	Frank Robinson	40.00
95	Hoyt Wilhelm	30.00
97	Jim Bunning	30.00
98	Richie Ashburn	25.00
99	Steve Carlton	45.00
100	Mike Schmidt	75.00
102	Tommy Lasorda	50.00
104	Reggie Jackson	50.00
105	Phil Rizzuto	35.00
106	Phil Niekro	25.00
108	Earl Weaver	30.00

1989 Perez-Steele Celebration Postcards

The Celebrations postcard issue from Perez-Steele was an attempt to offer collectors an original medium on which to obtain autographs of Hall of Famers. All 44 of the players included in the issue were alive when the set was conceived and most were still around when it was actually issued. The 3-1/2" x 5-1/2" cards have color portrait and action paintings by Dick Perez on front, which features a linen texture. Backs have postcard indicia, Perez-Steele and Hall of Fame logos, card number and individual serial number from within the edition limit of 10,000. Cards were originally sold only as complete sets.

		NM/M
Complete Set (45):		100.00
Common Player:		2.50
1	Hank Aaron	10.00
2	Luis Aparicio	2.50
3	Ernie Banks	6.00
4	Cool Papa Bell	2.50
5	Johnny Bench	6.00
6	Yogi Berra	6.00
7	Lou Boudreau	2.50
8	Roy Campanella	7.50
9	Happy Chandler	2.50
10	Jocko Conlan	2.50
11	Ray Dandridge	2.50
12	Bill Dickey	3.00
13	Bobby Doerr	2.50
14	Rick Ferrell	2.50
15	Charlie Gehringer	3.00
16	Lefty Gomez	3.00
17	Billy Herman	2.50
18	Catfish Hunter	2.50
19	Monte Irvin	2.50
20	Judy Johnson	2.50
21	Al Kaline	6.00
22	George Kell	2.50
23	Harmon Killebrew	2.50
24	Ralph Kiner	2.50
25	Bob Lemon	2.50
26	Buck Leonard	2.50
27	Al Lopez	2.50
28	Mickey Mantle	20.00
29	Juan Marichal	2.50
30	Eddie Mathews	2.50
31	Willie McCovey	2.50
32	Johnny Mize	2.50
33	Stan Musial	7.50
34	Pee Wee Reese	2.50
35	Brooks Robinson	2.50
36	Joe Sewell	2.50
37	Enos Slaughter	2.50
38	Duke Snider	6.00
39	Warren Spahn	2.50
40	Willie Stargell	2.50
41	Bill Terry	2.50
42	Billy Williams	2.50
43	Ted Williams	15.00
44	Carl Yastrzemski	2.50
---	Checklist	1.00

Autographed

Because of their popularity as an autograph vehicle, values for authentically signed examples of the Perez-Steele Celebrations postcards are presented here. Cards of Lefty Gomez (#16), Judy Johnson (#20) and Bill Terry (#41) cannot exist with genuine autographs because those players were deceased by the time the cards were issued.

		NM/M
Common Player:		15.00
1	Hank Aaron	40.00
2	Luis Aparicio	15.00
3	Ernie Banks	30.00
4	Cool Papa Bell	60.00
5	Johnny Bench	35.00
6	Yogi Berra	35.00
7	Lou Boudreau	20.00
8	Roy Campanella	400.00

9	Happy Chandler	35.00
10	Jocko Conlan	450.00
11	Ray Dandridge	30.00
12	Bill Dickey	65.00
13	Bobby Doerr	15.00
14	Rick Ferrell	20.00
15	Charlie Gehringer	45.00
17	Billy Herman	30.00
18	Catfish Hunter	30.00
19	Monte Irvin	22.50
21	Al Kaline	25.00
22	George Kell	20.00
23	Harmon Killebrew	30.00
24	Ralph Kiner	25.00
25	Bob Lemon	30.00
26	Buck Leonard	30.00
27	Al Lopez	75.00
28	Mickey Mantle	300.00
29	Juan Marichal	30.00
30	Eddie Mathews	40.00
31	Willie McCovey	30.00
32	Johnny Mize	30.00
33	Stan Musial	50.00
34	Pee Wee Reese	55.00
35	Brooks Robinson	25.00
36	Joe Sewell	40.00
37	Enos Slaughter	25.00
38	Duke Snider	30.00
39	Warren Spahn	25.00
40	Willie Stargell	30.00
42	Billy Williams	20.00
43	Ted Williams	250.00
44	Carl Yastrzemski	60.00

1990-92 Perez-Steele Master Works Postcards

A blending of the designs of classic early baseball cards with the artwork of one of today's most recognized baseball artists produced the Perez-Steele Master Works postcard series. Each of the players in the collection (living players selected for inclusion on the basis of autograph possibilities) is shown on five different cards, one of original design and four adapting the formats of the 1909 Ramly (T204), 1911 "Gold Borders" (T205) and 1908 Rose Co. postcards (PC760) and 1888 Goodwin Champions (N162). The Ramly and Rose takeoffs feature gold-foil embossing. Postcard backs are printed in brown (#1-25) or dark green (#26-50). Information on back includes a description of the card set on which the design is based, card and series number and the individual set serial number from within the edition of 10,000. Series 1 (#1-25) was issued in 1990; Series 2 (#26-50) in 1992. Each was available only as a complete boxed set.

		NM/M
Complete Set (52):		150.00
Common Player:		3.00
1	Charlie Gehringer (Ramly)	3.00
2	Charlie Gehringer (Goodwin)	3.00
3	Charlie Gehringer (Rose)	3.00
4	Charlie Gehringer (Gold Border)	3.00
5	Charlie Gehringer (Perez-Steele)	3.00
6	Mickey Mantle (Ramly)	15.00
7	Mickey Mantle (Goodwin)	15.00
8	Mickey Mantle (Rose)	15.00
9	Mickey Mantle (Gold Border)	15.00
10	Mickey Mantle (Perez-Steele)	15.00
11	Willie Mays (Ramly)	9.00
12	Willie Mays (Goodwin)	9.00
13	Willie Mays (Rose)	9.00
14	Willie Mays (Gold Border)	9.00

15	Willie Mays (Perez-Steele)	9.00
16	Duke Snider (Ramly)	6.00
17	Duke Snider (Goodwin)	6.00
18	Duke Snider (Rose)	6.00
19	Duke Snider (Gold Border)	6.00
20	Duke Snider (Perez-Steele)	6.00
21	Warren Spahn (Ramly)	3.00
22	Warren Spahn (Goodwin)	3.00
23	Warren Spahn (Rose)	3.00
24	Warren Spahn (Gold Border)	3.00
25	Warren Spahn (Perez-Steele)	3.00
---	Checklist 1-25	1.00
26	Yogi Berra (Ramly)	5.00
27	Yogi Berra (Goodwin)	5.00
28	Yogi Berra (Rose)	5.00
29	Yogi Berra (Gold Border)	5.00
30	Yogi Berra (Perez-Steele)	5.00
31	Johnny Mize (Ramly)	3.00
32	Johnny Mize (Goodwin)	3.00
33	Johnny Mize (Rose)	3.00
34	Johnny Mize (Gold Border)	3.00
35	Johnny Mize (Perez-Steele)	3.00
36	Willie Stargell (Ramly)	3.00
37	Willie Stargell (Goodwin)	3.00
38	Willie Stargell (Rose)	3.00
39	Willie Stargell (Gold Border)	3.00
40	Willie Stargell (Perez-Steele)	3.00
41	Ted Williams (Ramly)	12.00
42	Ted Williams (Goodwin)	12.00
43	Ted Williams (Rose)	12.00
44	Ted Williams (Gold Border)	12.00
45	Ted Williams (Perez-Steele)	12.00
46	Carl Yastrzemski (Ramly)	4.00
47	Carl Yastrzemski (Goodwin)	4.00
48	Carl Yastrzemski (Rose)	4.00
49	Carl Yastrzemski (Gold Border)	4.00
50	Carl Yastrzemski (Perez-Steele)	4.00
---	Checklist 26-50	1.00

1985 Performance Printing Texas Rangers

A local printing company sponsored this 28-card set of the Texas Rangers. The 2-3/8" x 3-1/2" cards are in full color and are numbered on the back by uniform number. Card fronts feature full-color, game-action photos. The 25 players on the Rangers' active roster at press time are included, along with manager Bobby Valentine and unnumbered coaches and trainer cards. The black and white card backs have a smaller portrait photo of each player, as well as biographical information and career statistics.

		NM/M
Complete Set (28):		9.00
Common Player:		.50
0	Oddibe McDowell	.50
1	Bill Stein	.50
2	Bobby Valentine	.50
3	Wayne Tolleson	.50
4	Don Slaught	.50
5	Alan Bannister	.50
6	Bobby Jones	.50
7	Glenn Brummer	.50
8	Luis Pujols	.50
9	Pete O'Brien	.50
11	Toby Harrah	.50
13	Tommy Dunbar	.50
14	Larry Parrish	.50
16	Mike Mason	.50
19	Curtis Wilkerson	.50
24	Dave Schmidt	.50
25	Buddy Bell	.50
30	Greg Harris	.50
32	Dave Rozema	.50
33	Gary Ward	.50
35	Dickie Noles	.50
41	Chris Welsh	.50
44	Cliff Johnson	.50
46	Burt Hooton	.50
48	Dave Stewart	.50
49	Charlie Hough	.50
----	Trainers (Danny Wheat, Bill Ziegler)	.50
----	Rangers Coaches (Rich Donnelly, Glenn Ezell, Tom House, Art Howe, Wayne Terwilliger)	.50

1986 Performance Printing Texas Rangers

For the second time, the Texas Rangers issued a full-color card set in conjunction with this local printing company. Fronts of the 28-card set include player name, position and team logo beneath the color photo. Backs of the 2-3/8" x 3-1/2" cards are in black and white, with a small portrait photo of each player along with personal and professional statistics. Cards were distributed at the August 23 Rangers home game, and the set includes all of the Rangers' fine rookies such as Bobby Witt, Pete Incaviglia, Edwin Correa and Ruben Sierra.

		NM/M
Complete Set (28):		5.00
Common Player:		.25
0	Oddibe McDowell	.25
1	Scott Fletcher	.25
2	Bobby Valentine	.25
3	Ruben Sierra	.35
4	Don Slaught	.25
9	Pete O'Brien	.25
11	Toby Harrah	.25
12	Geno Petralli	.25
15	Larry Parrish	.25
16	Mike Mason	.25
17	Darrell Porter	.25
18	Edwin Correa	.25
19	Curtis Wilkerson	.25
22	Steve Buechele	.25
23	Jose Guzman	.25
24	Ricky Wright	.25
27	Greg Harris	.25
28	Mitch Williams	.25
29	Pete Incaviglia	.50
32	Gary Ward	.25
34	Dale Mohorcic	.25
42	Jeff Russell	.25
44	Tom Paciorek	.25
46	Mike Loynd	.25
48	Bobby Witt	.25
49	Charlie Hough	.25
----	Coaching Staff (Joe Ferguson, Tim Foli, Tom House, Art Howe, Tom Robson)	.25
----	Trainers (Danny Wheat, Bill Zeigler)	.25

1981 Perma-Graphics All-Star Credit Cards

Using the same "credit card" style of its previous 1981 issue, Perma-Graphics issued an 18-card set in the fall of 1981 featuring starting players from the 1981 All-Star Game. The front of the card contains a full-color photo, plus the player's name, position and team. The back includes personal data, career records, highlights and an "autograph panel."

		NM/M
Complete Set (18):		15.00
Common Player:		1.00
1	Gary Carter	1.50
2	Dave Concepcion	1.00
3	Andre Dawson	1.25
4	George Foster	1.00
5	Davey Lopes	1.00
6	Dave Parker	1.00
7	Pete Rose	5.00
8	Mike Schmidt	4.00
9	Fernando Valenzuela	1.00
10	George Brett	4.00
11a	Rod Carew (Outfield)	2.50
11b	Rod Carew (First base.)	2.50
11c	Rod Carew (First base, #20 on back.)	2.50
11d	Rod Carew (First base, #29 on back.)	2.50
12	Bucky Dent	1.00
13	Carlton Fisk	1.50
14	Reggie Jackson	3.00
15	Jack Morris	1.00
16	Willie Randolph	1.00
17	Ken Singleton	1.00
18	Dave Winfield	1.50

Super Star Credit Cards

Issued in 1981 by Perma-Graphics of Maryland Heights, Mo., this innovative 32-card set was printed on high-impact, permanently laminated vinyl to give the appearance of a real credit card. The front of the wallet-sized cards includes career statistics and highlights, along with an "autograph panel" for obtaining the player's signature.

		NM/M
Complete Set (32):		25.00
Common Player:		1.00
1	Johnny Bench	2.00
2	Mike Schmidt	4.00
3	George Brett	4.00
4	Carl Yastrzemski	2.00
5	Pete Rose	5.00
6	Bob Horner	1.00
7	Reggie Jackson	3.00
8	Keith Hernandez	1.00
9	George Foster	1.00
10	Garry Templeton	1.00
11	Tom Seaver	2.00
12	Steve Garvey	1.25
13	Dave Parker	1.00
14	Willie Stargell	1.50
15	Cecil Cooper	1.00
16	Steve Carlton	1.50
17	Ted Simmons	1.00
18	Dave Kingman	1.00
19	Rickey Henderson	1.50
20	Fred Lynn	1.00
21	Dave Winfield	1.50
22a	Rod Carew (Uniform #20 on back.)	2.00
22b	Rod Carew (Uniform #29 on back.)	2.00
23	Jim Rice	1.25
24	Bruce Sutter	1.50
25	Cesar Cedeno	1.00
26	Nolan Ryan	6.00
27	Dusty Baker	1.00
28	Jim Palmer	1.50
29	Gorman Thomas	1.00
30	Ben Oglivie	1.00
31	Willie Wilson	1.00
32	Gary Carter	1.50

1982 Perma-Graphics All-Star Credit Cards

Perma-Graphics issued its second "All-Star Credit Card" set in the fall of 1982. Consisting of 18 cards, the set pictured the starters from both leagues in the 1982 All-Star Game. The set was also available in a more limited "gold" version.

		NM/M
Complete Set (18):		15.00
Common Player:		1.00
Gold:		3X
1	Dennis Eckersley	1.50
2	Cecil Cooper	1.00
3	Carlton Fisk	1.00
4	Robin Yount	2.00
5	Bobby Grich	1.00
6	Rickey Henderson	2.00

7	Reggie Jackson	3.00
8	Fred Lynn	1.00
9	George Brett	4.00
10	Gary Carter	2.00
11	Dave Concepcion	1.00
12	Andre Dawson	1.25
13	Tim Raines	1.00
14	Dale Murphy	1.25
15	Steve Rogers	1.00
16	Pete Rose	5.00
17	Mike Schmidt	4.00
18	Manny Trillo	1.00

Super Star Credit Cards

Perma-Graphics reduced its "Superstar Credit Card Set" to 24 players in 1982, maintaining the same basic credit card appearance. The player photos on the front of the cards are surrounded by a wood-tone border and the backs include the usual personal data, career statistics, highlights and autograph panel. The set was also issued in a limited-edition "gold" version.

		NM/M
Complete Set (24):		25.00
Common Player:		1.00
Gold:		3X
1	Johnny Bench	2.00
2	Tom Seaver	2.00
3	Mike Schmidt	4.00
4	Gary Carter	1.50
5	Willie Stargell	1.50
6	Tim Raines	1.00
7	Bill Madlock	1.00
8	Keith Hernandez	1.00
9	Pete Rose	5.00
10	Steve Carlton	1.50
11	Steve Garvey	1.25
12	Fernando Valenzuela	1.00
13	Carl Yastrzemski	1.00
14	Dave Winfield	1.50
15	Carney Lansford	1.00
16	Rollie Fingers	1.00
17	Tony Armas	1.00
18	Cecil Cooper	1.00
19	George Brett	4.00
20	Reggie Jackson	3.00
21	Rod Carew	1.50
22	Eddie Murray	1.50
23	Rickey Henderson	1.50
24	Kirk Gibson	1.00

1983 Perma-Graphics All-Star Credit Cards

The final issue from Perma-Graphics, this 18-card set was produced in the fall of 1983 and features the 18 starting players from the 1983 All-Star Game. Similar to other Perma-Graphics sets, the cards were printed on wallet-size vinyl to give the appearance of a real credit card. The set was also available in a limited-edition "gold" version.

		NM/M
Complete Set (18):		17.50
Common Player:		1.00

Gold:		3X
1	George Brett	4.00
2	Rod Carew	2.00
3	Fred Lynn	1.00
4	Jim Rice	1.50
5	Ted Simmons	1.00
6	Dave Stieb	1.00
7	Manny Trillo	1.00
8	Dave Winfield	2.00
9	Robin Yount	2.00
10	Gary Carter	1.00
11	Andre Dawson	1.50
12	Dale Murphy	1.50
13	Al Oliver	1.00
14	Tim Raines	1.00
15	Steve Sax	1.00
16	Mike Schmidt	4.00
17	Ozzie Smith	3.00
18	Mario Soto	1.00

Super Star Credit Cards

Similar in design to its previous sets, Perma-Graphics increased the number of cards in its 1983 "Superstar" set to 36, including 18 players from each league. The front of the vinyl card has a full-color photo with the player's name, team, league and position below. The backs contain career records, highlights and autograph panel. The cards were also issued in a special "gold" version, more limited than the regular edition.

		NM/M
Complete Set (36):		25.00
Common Player:		1.00
Gold:		3X
1	Bill Buckner	1.00
2	Steve Carlton	2.00
3	Gary Carter	2.00
4	Andre Dawson	1.25
5	Pedro Guerrero	1.00
6	George Hendrick	1.00
7	Keith Hernandez	1.00
8	Bill Madlock	1.00
9	Dale Murphy	1.25
10	Al Oliver	1.00
11	Dave Parker	1.00
12	Darrell Porter	1.00
13	Pete Rose	5.00
14	Mike Schmidt	4.00
15	Lonnie Smith	1.00
16	Ozzie Smith	1.50
17	Bruce Sutter	1.50
18	Fernando Valenzuela	1.00
19	George Brett	4.00
20	Rod Carew	2.00
21	Cecil Cooper	1.00
22	Doug DeCinces	1.00
23	Rollie Fingers	1.50
24	Damaso Garcia	1.00
25	Toby Harrah	1.00
26	Rickey Henderson	2.00
27	Reggie Jackson	3.00
28	Hal McRae	1.00
29	Eddie Murray	2.00
30	Lance Parrish	1.00
31	Jim Rice	1.25
32	Gorman Thomas	1.00
33	Willie Wilson	1.00
34	Dave Winfield	2.00
35	Carl Yastrzemski	2.50
36	Robin Yount	2.00

1983 Gaylord Perry Career Highlights

Although their name does not appear anywhere on the six cards in this set, Topps was the manufacturer of this career highlights issue which was distributed by Perry's own memorabilia company. In standard 2-1/2" x 3-1/2" format, card fronts feature a color photo with various colored borders and name plates. The year of the career highlight printed on back is presented in the lower-right. Backs have a card number in a peanut and a write-up of the career accomplishment, printed in brown and orange.

		NM/M
Complete Set (6):		8.00
Common Card:		1.50
1	Gaylord Perry (First win.)	1.50
2	Gaylord Perry (No-hitter.)	1.50
3	Gaylord Perry (Cy Young Award)	1.50
4	Gaylord Perry (2,500th K)	1.50
5	Gaylord Perry (Cy Young/3,000th K)	1.50
6	Gaylord Perry (300th win)	1.50

1981 Peter Pan Bakery Discs

(See 1981 MSA/Peter Pan - Sunbeam Bakery Discs.)

1991 Petro Canada All-Star FanFest Standups

Petro-Canada Standups are vaguely reminiscent of the 1964 Topps Standups. The set was distributed at Fanfest in Toronto in conjunction with the All-Star Game. The folded card as issued measures 2-7/8" x 3-9/16". The card can be unfolded to reveal a die-cut action figure of the player superimposed in front of a photo of stadium surroundings. The base which the player stands on has major league and All-Star Game statistics, with career highlights on the back and a player quiz.

	NM/M
Complete Set (26):	12.50

Common Player:		.25
1	Cal Ripken, Jr.	3.00
2	Greg Olson	.25
3	Roger Clemens	2.00
4	Ryne Sandberg	1.50
5	Dave Winfield	1.00
6	Eric Davis	.25
7	Carlton Fisk	1.00
8	Mike Scott	.25
9	Sandy Alomar, Jr.	.25
10	Tim Wallach	.25
11	Cecil Fielder	.25
12	Dwight Gooden	.25
13	George Brett	2.00
14	Dale Murphy	.50
15	Paul Molitor	1.00
16	Barry Bonds	3.00
17	Kirby Puckett	1.50
18	Ozzie Smith	1.50
19	Don Mattingly	2.00
20	Will Clark	.25
21	Rickey Henderson	1.00
22	Orel Hershiser	.25
23	Ken Griffey Jr.	2.50
24	Tony Gwynn	1.50
25	Nolan Ryan	3.00
26	Kelly Gruber	.25

1998-99 Philadelphia A's Historical Society

A major undertaking by the Philadelphia A's Historical Society was the creation of this collectors card set in conjunction with the group's fourth reunion in 1998. Card designs are strongly reminiscent of the classic Topps and Bowman cards of the early 1950s. Fronts have a painting of each player by Ron Joyner, noted sports artist. Backs have a cartoon, career stats with the A's and lifetime, biographical data and career highlights. Backs are printed in blue and black on white. A card of 1908-09 A's Joe Jackson has been printed in a limited edition of 500 numbered cards and is available only in those sets sold directly through the Society at its original $18.50 price. Seventy-five sets of the cards, which included a sample Joe Jackson card and a pair of large-format cards of Jimmie Foxx and Roger Cramer, were sold as uncut sheets.

		NM/M
Complete Set, W/Jackson (42):		24.00
Complete Set, No/Jackson (41):		18.50
Complete Set, uncut sheet:		60.00
Common Player:		.50
1	Connie Mack	.75
2	Sam Chapman	.60
3	Bobby Shantz	.60
4	Al Brancato	.50
5	Bob Dillinger	.50
6	Irv Hall	.50
7	Joe Hauser	.50
8	Taffy Wright	.50
9	Gus Zernial	.60
10	Ray Murray	.50
11	Skeeter Kell	.50
12	Morrie Martin	.50
13	Pete Suder	.50
14	Pinky Higgins	.50
15	Allie Clark	.50
16	Hank Wyse	.50
17	George Kell	.75
18	Hank Majeski	.50
19	Jimmie Foxx	1.00
20	Crash Davis	.50
21	Elmer Valo	.50
22	Ray Coleman	.50
23	Carl Scheib	.50
24	Billy Hitchcock	.50
25	Earle Brucker Jr.	.50
26	Dave Philley	.50
27	Joe DeMaestri	.50
28	Eddie Collins Jr.	.50
29	Eddie Joost	.50
30	Spook Jacobs	.50
31	Ferris Fain	.60
32	Eddie Robinson	.50
33	Vic Power	.60
34	Lou Brissie	.50
35	Bill Renna	.50
36	Nellie Fox	1.00
37	Lou Limmer	.50
38	Eddie Collins Sr.	1.00
39	Roger Cramer	.50
40	Joe Astroth	.50
---	Joe Jackson (# of 500)	8.00
---	Joe Jackson (Sample overprint.)	4.00
---	Roger Cramer (3-1/2" x 6")	2.00
---	Jimmie Foxx (3-1/2" x 8-1/2")	4.00
41	Bill Werber (Issued 1999)	.50

Philadelphia A's Historical Society Update

Selected by the Society's members as "Fan Favorites" of each decade from the 1900s through the 1930s, this collectors' issue updates the group's original 1998-99 card issue. Cards are in 2-5/8" x 3-3/4" format with painted portraits on front. Black, blue and white backs have a cartoon highlight, personal data, career summary and lifetime A's and major league stats. The cards were also pictured on a 10-3/4" x 12-3/4" "Decades of Greatness" uncut sheet.

		NM/M
Complete Set (4):		6.00
Common Player:		2.00
Uncut Sheet:		10.00
42	Rube Oldring	2.00
43	Stuffy McInnis	2.00
44	Bing Miller	2.00
45	Bob Johnson	2.00

1985 Philadelphia Phillies Police

This is a brilliantly colored 2-5/8" x 4-1/8" set, co-sponsored by the Phillies and Cigna Corp. Card fronts include the player name, number, position and team logo. The 16 cards are numbered on the back and include biographical information and a safety tip. The cards were distributed by several Philadelphia area police departments.

		NM/M
Complete Set (16):		4.00
Common Player:		.15
1	Juan Samuel	.15
2	Von Hayes	.15
3	Ozzie Virgil	.15
4	Mike Schmidt	3.50
5	Greg Gross	.15
6	Tim Corcoran	.15
7	Jerry Koosman	.15
8	Jeff Stone	.15
9	Glenn Wilson	.15
10	Steve Jeltz	.15
11	Garry Maddox	.15
12	Steve Carlton	1.50
13	John Denny	.15
14	Kevin Gross	.15
15	Shane Rawley	.15
16	Charlie Hudson	.15

1986 Philadelphia Phillies Fire Safety

For the second straight year, the Philadelphia Phillies issued a 16-card safety set. However, in 1986 the set was issued in conjunction with the Philadelphia Fire Department rather than the police. Cigna Corp. remained a sponsor. The cards, which measure 2-5/8" x 4-1/8" in size, feature full color photos. Along with other pertinent information, the card backs contain a short player biography and a "Tips From The Dugout" fire safety hint.

		NM/M
Complete Set (16):		3.00
Common Player:		.15
1	Juan Samuel	.15
2	Don Carman	.15
3	Von Hayes	.15
4	Kent Tekulve	.15
5	Greg Gross	.15
6	Shane Rawley	.15
7	Darren Daulton	.25
8	Kevin Gross	.15
9	Steve Jeltz	.15
10	Mike Schmidt	3.00
11	Steve Bedrosian	.15
12	Gary Redus	.15
13	Charles Hudson	.15
14	John Russell	.15
15	Fred Toliver	.15
16	Glenn Wilson	.15

2005 Philadelphia Phillies Medallion Collection

A set of 21 commemorative medallions was sponsored by the Philadelphia Daily News and The Inquirer in this early-season promotion. Coupons found in the newspapers between April 18 and May 18 could be redeemed at newsstands (along with $2.99) for that day's medallion. Larger and thicker than a quarter, the 1-3/16" diameter medals are struck in nickel and have on their fronts an enameled portrait photo. A team logo dominates the back. A colorful, photo-filled 7-3/4" x 13" album was available to house the pieces. The medals are listed here in order of their issue.

		NM/M
Complete Set (21):		65.00
Common Player:		3.00
Album:		3.00
(1)	Jim Thome	5.00
(2)	Placido Polanco	3.00
(3)	Randy Wolf	3.00
(4)	Mike Lieberthal	3.00
(5)	Jon Lieber	3.00
(6)	Jimmy Rollins	4.50
(7)	Kenny Lofton	3.00
(8)	Brett Myers	3.00
(9)	Tomas Perez	3.00
(10)	Rheal Cormier	3.00
(11)	Vicente Padilla	3.00
(12)	David Bell	3.00
(13)	Bobby Abreu	4.50
(14)	Tim Worrell	3.00
(15)	Ryan Madson	3.00
(16)	Chase Utley	4.50
(17)	Charlie Manuel	3.00
(18)	Jason Michaels	3.00
(19)	Pat Burrell	5.00
(20)	Billy Wagner	3.00
(21)	Phillie Phanatic (Mascot)	3.00

1989 Phoenix Holsum Super Stars Discs

(See 1989 Holsum for checklist and price guide. Distributed in Arizona.)

1992 Pinnacle

Score entered the high-end card market with the release of this 620-card set. The cards feature black borders surrounding a white frame with a full-color action photo inside. The player extends beyond the natural background. The backs are horizontal and feature a closeup photo, statistics, team logo, biographical information and career notes. Several subsets can be found within the set including "Idols, Sidelines, Grips, Shades" and "Technicians." The set was released in two 310-card series.

		NM/M
Complete Set (620):		15.00
Common Player:		.05
Foil Pack (16):		.75
Foil Box (36):		17.50
Jumbo Pack (24+3):		1.50
Jumbo Box (12):		22.50
1	Frank Thomas	.75
2	Benito Santiago	.05
3	Carlos Baerga	.05
4	Cecil Fielder	.05
5	Barry Larkin	.05
6	Ozzie Smith	1.00
7	Willie McGee	.05
8	Paul Molitor	.75
9	Andy Van Slyke	.05
10	Ryne Sandberg	1.00
11	Kevin Seitzer	.05
12	Len Dykstra	.05
13	Edgar Martinez	.05
14	Ruben Sierra	.05
15	Howard Johnson	.05
16	Dave Henderson	.05
17	Devon White	.05
18	Terry Pendleton	.05
19	Steve Finley	.05
20	Kirby Puckett	1.00
21	Orel Hershiser	.05
22	Hal Morris	.05
23	Don Mattingly	1.25
24	Delino DeShields	.05
25	Dennis Eckersley	.60
26	Ellis Burks	.05
27	Jay Buhner	.05
28	Matt Williams	.05
29	Lou Whitaker	.05
30	Alex Fernandez	.05
31	Albert Belle	.05
32	Todd Zeile	.05
33	Tony Pena	.05
34	Jay Bell	.05
35	Rafael Palmeiro	.65
36	Wes Chamberlain	.05
37	George Bell	.05
38	Robin Yount	.75
39	Vince Coleman	.05
40	Bruce Hurst	.05
41	Harold Baines	.05
42	Chuck Finley	.05
43	Ken Caminiti	.05
44	Ben McDonald	.05
45	Roberto Alomar	.15
46	Chili Davis	.05
47	Bill Doran	.05
48	Jerald Clark	.05
49	Jose Lind	.05
50	Nolan Ryan	2.00
51	Phil Plantier	.05
52	Gary DiSarcina	.05
53	Kevin Bass	.05
54	Pat Kelly	.05
55	Mark Wohlers	.05
56	Walt Weiss	.05
57	Lenny Harris	.05
58	Ivan Calderon	.05
59	Harold Reynolds	.05
60	George Brett	1.25
61	Gregg Olson	.05
62	Orlando Merced	.05
63	Steve Decker	.05
64	John Franco	.05
65	Greg Maddux	1.00
66	Alex Cole	.05
67	Dave Hollins	.05
68	Kent Hrbek	.05
69	Tom Pagnozzi	.05
70	Jeff Bagwell	.75
71	Jim Gantner	.05
72	Matt Nokes	.05
73	Brian Harper	.05
74	Andy Benes	.05
75	Tom Glavine	.35
76	Terry Steinbach	.05
77	Dennis Martinez	.05
78	John Olerud	.05
79	Ozzie Guillen	.05
80	Darryl Strawberry	.05
81	Gary Gaetti	.05
82	Dave Righetti	.05
83	Chris Hoiles	.05
84	Andujar Cedeno	.05
85	Jack Clark	.05
86	David Howard	.05
87	Bill Gullickson	.05
88	Bernard Gilkey	.05
89	Kevin Elster	.05
90	Kevin Maas	.05
91	Mark Lewis	.05
92	Greg Vaughn	.05
93	Bret Barberie	.05
94	Dave Smith	.05
95	Roger Clemens	1.25
96	Doug Drabek	.05
97	Omar Vizquel	.05
98	Jose Guzman	.05
99	Juan Samuel	.05
100	Dave Justice	.05
101	Tom Browning	.05
102	Mark Gubicza	.05
103	Mickey Morandini	.05
104	Ed Whitson	.05
105	Lance Parrish	.05
106	Scott Erickson	.05
107	Jack McDowell	.05
108	Dave Stieb	.05
109	Mike Moore	.05
110	Travis Fryman	.05
111	Dwight Gooden	.05
112	Fred McGriff	.05
113	Alan Trammell	.05
114	Roberto Kelly	.05
115	Andre Dawson	.25
116	Bill Landrum	.05
117	Brian McRae	.05
118	B.J. Surhoff	.05
119	Chuck Knoblauch	.05
120	Steve Olin	.05
121	Robin Ventura	.05
122	Will Clark	.05
123	Tino Martinez	.05
124	Dale Murphy	.25
125	Pete O'Brien	.05
126	Ray Lankford	.05
127	Juan Gonzalez	.40
128	Ron Gant	.05
129	Marquis Grissom	.05
130	Jose Canseco	.50
131	Mike Greenwell	.05
132	Mark Langston	.05
133	Brett Butler	.05
134	Kelly Gruber	.05
135	Chris Sabo	.05
136	Mark Grace	.05
137	Tony Fernandez	.05
138	Glenn Davis	.05
139	Pedro Munoz	.05
140	Craig Biggio	.05
141	Pete Schourek	.05
142	Mike Boddicker	.05
143	Robby Thompson	.05
144	Mel Hall	.05
145	Bryan Harvey	.05
146	Mike LaValliere	.05
147	John Kruk	.05
148	Joe Carter	.05
149	Greg Olson	.05
150	Julio Franco	.05
151	Darryl Hamilton	.05
152	Felix Fermin	.05
153	Jose Offerman	.05
154	Paul O'Neill	.05
155	Tommy Greene	.05
156	Ivan Rodriguez	.65
157	Dave Stewart	.05
158	Jeff Reardon	.05
159	Felix Jose	.05
160	Doug Dascenzo	.05
161	Tim Wallach	.05
162	Dan Plesac	.05
163	Luis Gonzalez	.05
164	Mike Henneman	.05
165	Mike Devereaux	.05
166	Luis Polonia	.05
167	Mike Sharperson	.05
168	Chris Donnels	.05
169	Greg Harris	.05
170	Deion Sanders	.05
171	Mike Schooler	.05
172	Jose DeJesus	.05
173	Jeff Montgomery	.05
174	Milt Cuyler	.05
175	Wade Boggs	1.00
176	Kevin Tapani	.05
177	Bill Spiers	.05
178	Tim Raines	.05
179	Randy Milligan	.05
180	Rob Dibble	.05
181	Kirt Manwaring	.05
182	Pascual Perez	.05
183	Juan Guzman	.05
184	John Smiley	.05
185	David Segui	.05
186	Omar Olivares	.05
187	Joe Slusarski	.05
188	Erik Hanson	.05
189	Mark Portugal	.05
190	Walt Terrell	.05
191	John Smoltz	.05
192	Wilson Alvarez	.05
193	Jimmy Key	.05
194	Larry Walker	.05
195	Lee Smith	.05
196	Pete Harnisch	.05
197	Mike Harkey	.05
198	Frank Tanana	.05
199	Terry Mulholland	.05
200	Cal Ripken, Jr.	2.00
201	Dave Magadan	.05
202	Bud Black	.05
203	Terry Shumpert	.05
204	Mike Mussina	.40
205	Mo Vaughn	.05
206	Steve Farr	.05
207	Darrin Jackson	.05
208	Jerry Browne	.05
209	Jeff Russell	.05
210	Mike Scioscia	.05
211	Rick Aguilera	.05
212	Jaime Navarro	.05
213	Randy Tomlin	.05
214	Bobby Thigpen	.05
215	Mark Gardner	.05
216	Norm Charlton	.05
217	Mark McGwire	1.75
218	Skeeter Barnes	.05
219	Bob Tewksbury	.05
220	Junior Felix	.05
221	Sam Horn	.05
222	Jody Reed	.05
223	Luis Sojo	.05
224	Jerome Walton	.05
225	Darryl Kile	.05
226	Mickey Tettleton	.05
227	Dan Pasqua	.05
228	Jim Gott	.05
229	Bernie Williams	.05
230	Shane Mack	.05
231	Steve Avery	.05
232	Dave Valle	.05
233	Mark Leonard	.05
234	Spike Owen	.05
235	Gary Sheffield	.20
236	Steve Chitren	.05
237	Zane Smith	.05
238	Tom Gordon	.05
239	Jose Oquendo	.05
240	Todd Stottlemyre	.05
241	Darren Daulton	.05
242	Tim Naehring	.05
243	Tony Phillips	.05
244	Shawon Dunston	.05
245	Manuel Lee	.05
246	Mike Pagliarulo	.05
247	Jim Thome (Rookie Prospect)	.65
248	Luis Mercedes (Rookie Prospect)	.05
249	Cal Eldred (Rookie Prospect)	.05
250	Derek Bell (Rookie Prospect)	.05
251	Arthur Rhodes (Rookie Prospect)	.05
252	Scott Cooper (Rookie Prospect)	.05
253	Roberto Hernandez (Rookie Prospect)	.05
254	Mo Sanford (Rookie Prospect)	.05
255	Scott Servais (Rookie Prospect)	.05
256	Eric Karros (Rookie Prospect)	.05
257	Andy Mota	.05
258	Keith Mitchell	.05
259	Joel Johnston	.05
260	John Wehner (Rookie Prospect)	.05
261	Gino Minutelli (Rookie Prospect)	.05
262	Greg Gagne	.05
263	Stan Royer (Rookie Prospect)	.05
264	Carlos Garcia (Rookie Prospect)	.05
265	Andy Ashby (Rookie Prospect)	.05
266	Kim Batiste (Rookie Prospect)	.05
267	Julio Valera (Rookie Prospect)	.05
268	Royce Clayton (Rookie Prospect)	.05
269	Gary Scott (Rookie Prospect)	.05
270	Kirk Dressendorfer (Rookie Prospect)	.05

271	Sean Berry (Rookie Prospect)	.05
272	Lance Dickson (Rookie Prospect)	.05
273	Rob Maurer (Rookie Prospect)	.05
274	Scott Brosius (Rookie Prospect)	.05
275	Dave Fleming (Rookie Prospect)	.05
276	Lenny Webster (Rookie Prospect)	.05
277	Mike Humphreys (Rookie Prospect)	.05
278	Freddie Benavides (Rookie Prospect)	.05
279	Harvey Pulliam (Rookie Prospect)	.05
280	Jeff Carter (Rookie Prospect)	.05
281	Jim Abbott, Nolan Ryan (Idols)	.25
282	Wade Boggs, George Brett (Idols)	.25
283	Ken Griffey Jr., Rickey Henderson (Idols)	.50
284	Dale Murphy, Wally Joyner (Idols)	.10
285	Chuck Knoblauch, Ozzie Smith (Idols)	.20
286	Robin Ventura, Lou Gehrig (Idols)	.20
287	Robin Yount (Sidelines - Motocross)	.30
288	Bob Tewksbury (Sidelines - Cartoonist)	.05
289	Kirby Puckett (Sidelines - Pool Player)	.50
290	Kenny Lofton (Sidelines - Basketball Player)	.05
291	Jack McDowell (Sidelines - Guitarist)	.05
292	John Burkett (Sidelines - Bowler)	.05
293	Dwight Smith (Sidelines - Singer)	.05
294	Nolan Ryan (Sidelines - Cattle Rancher)	1.00
295	Manny Ramirez RC (1st Round Draft Pick)	2.50
296	Cliff Floyd RC (1st Round Draft Pick)	.50
297	Al Shirley RC (1st Round Draft Pick)	.05
298	Brian Barber RC (1st Round Draft Pick)	.05
299	Jon Farrell RC (1st Round Draft Pick)	.05
300	Scott Ruffcorn RC (1st Round Draft Pick)	.05
301	Tyrone Hill RC (1st Round Draft Pick)	.05
302	Benji Gil RC (1st Round Draft Pick)	.05
303	Tyler Green RC (1st Round Draft Pick)	.05
304	Allen Watson (Shades)	.05
305	Jay Buhner (Shades)	.05
306	Roberto Alomar (Shades)	.05
307	Chuck Knoblauch (Shades)	.05
308	Darryl Strawberry (Shades)	.05
309	Danny Tartabull (Shades)	.05
310	Bobby Bonilla (Shades)	.05
311	Mike Felder	.05
312	Storm Davis	.05
313	Tim Teufel	.05
314	Tom Brunansky	.05
315	Rex Hudler	.05
316	Dave Otto	.05
317	Jeff King	.05
318	Dan Gladden	.05
319	Bill Pecota	.05
320	Franklin Stubbs	.05
321	Gary Carter	.75
322	Melido Perez	.05
323	Eric Davis	.05
324	Greg Myers	.05
325	Pete Incaviglia	.05
326	Von Hayes	.05
327	Greg Swindell	.05
328	Steve Sax	.05
329	Chuck McElroy	.05
330	Gregg Jefferies	.05
331	Joe Oliver	.05
332	Paul Faries	.05
333	David West	.05
334	Craig Grebeck	.05
335	Chris Hammond	.05
336	Billy Ripken	.05
337	Scott Sanderson	.05
338	Dick Schofield	.05
339	Bob Milacki	.05
340	Kevin Reimer	.05
341	Jose DeLeon	.05
342	Henry Cotto	.05
343	Daryl Boston	.05
344	Kevin Gross	.05
345	Milt Thompson	.05
346	Luis Rivera	.05
347	Al Osuna	.05
348	Rob Deer	.05
349	Tim Leary	.05
350	Mike Stanton	.05
351	Dean Palmer	.05
352	Trevor Wilson	.05
353	Mark Eichhorn	.05
354	Scott Aldred	.05
355	Mark Whiten	.05
356	Leo Gomez	.05
357	Rafael Belliard	.05
358	Carlos Quintana	.05
359	Mark Davis	.05
360	Chris Nabholz	.05
361	Carlton Fisk	.75
362	Joe Orsulak	.05
363	Eric Anthony	.05
364	Greg Hibbard	.05
365	Scott Leius	.05
366	Hensley Meulens	.05
367	Chris Bosio	.05
368	Brian Downing	.05
369	Sammy Sosa	1.00
370	Stan Belinda	.05
371	Joe Grahe	.05
372	Luis Salazar	.05
373	Lance Johnson	.05
374	Kal Daniels	.05
375	Dave Winfield	.75
376	Brook Jacoby	.05
377	Mariano Duncan	.05
378	Ron Darling	.05
379	Randy Johnson	.75
380	Chito Martinez	.05
381	Andres Galarraga	.05
382	Willie Randolph	.05
383	Charles Nagy	.05
384	Tim Belcher	.05
385	Duane Ward	.05
386	Vicente Palacios	.05
387	Mike Gallego	.05
388	Rich DeLucia	.05
389	Scott Radinsky	.05
390	Damon Berryhill	.05
391	Kirk McCaskill	.05
392	Pedro Guerrero	.05
393	Kevin Mitchell	.05
394	Dickie Thon	.05
395	Bobby Bonilla	.05
396	Bill Wegman	.05
397	Dave Martinez	.05
398	Rick Sutcliffe	.05
399	Larry Andersen	.05
400	Tony Gwynn	1.00
401	Rickey Henderson	.75
402	Greg Cadaret	.05
403	Keith Miller	.05
404	Bip Roberts	.05
405	Kevin Brown	.05
406	Mitch Williams	.05
407	Frank Viola	.05
408	Darren Lewis	.05
409	Bob Walk	.05
410	Bob Walk	.05
411	Todd Frohwirth	.05
412	Brian Hunter	.05
413	Ron Karkovice	.05
414	Mike Morgan	.05
415	Joe Hesketh	.05
416	Don Slaught	.05
417	Tom Henke	.05
418	Kurt Stillwell	.05
419	Hector Villanueva	.05
420	Glenallen Hill	.05
421	Pat Borders	.05
422	Charlie Hough	.05
423	Charlie Leibrandt	.05
424	Eddie Murray	.75
425	Jesse Barfield	.05
426	Mark Lemke	.05
427	Kevin McReynolds	.05
428	Gilberto Reyes	.05
429	Ramon Martinez	.05
430	Steve Buechele	.05
431	David Wells	.05
432	Kyle Abbott (Rookie Prospect)	.05
433	John Habyan	.05
434	Kevin Appier	.05
435	Gene Larkin	.05
436	Sandy Alomar, Jr.	.05
437	Mike Jackson	.05
438	Todd Benzinger	.05
439	Teddy Higuera	.05
440	Reggie Sanders (Rookie Prospect)	.05
441	Mark Carreon	.05
442	Bret Saberhagen	.05
443	Gene Nelson	.05
444	Jay Howell	.05
445	Roger McDowell	.05
446	Sid Bream	.05
447	Mackey Sasser	.05
448	Bill Swift	.05
449	Hubie Brooks	.05
450	David Cone	.05
451	Bobby Witt	.05
452	Brady Anderson	.05
453	Lee Stevens	.05
454	Luis Aquino	.05
455	Carney Lansford	.05
456	Carlos Hernandez (Rookie Prospect)	.05
457	Danny Jackson	.05
458	Gerald Young	.05
459	Tom Candiotti	.05
460	Billy Hatcher	.05
461	John Wetteland	.05
462	Mike Bordick	.05
463	Don Robinson	.05
464	Jeff Johnson	.05
465	Lonnie Smith	.05
466	Paul Assenmacher	.05
467	Alvin Davis	.05
468	Jim Eisenreich	.05
469	Brent Mayne	.05
470	Jeff Brantley	.05
471	Tim Burke	.05
472	Pat Mahomes RC (Rookie Prospect)	.05
473	Ryan Bowen	.05
474	Bryn Smith	.05
475	Mike Flanagan	.05
476	Reggie Jefferson (Rookie Prospect)	.05
477	Jeff Blauser	.05
478	Craig Lefferts	.05
479	Todd Worrell	.05
480	Scott Scudder	.05
481	Kirk Gibson	.05
482	Kenny Rogers	.05
483	Jack Morris	.05
484	Russ Swan	.05
485	Mike Huff	.05
486	Ken Hill	.05
487	Geronimo Pena	.05
488	Charlie O'Brien	.05
489	Mike Maddux	.05
490	Scott Livingstone (Rookie Prospect)	.05
491	Carl Willis	.05
492	Kelly Downs	.05
493	Dennis Cook	.05
494	Joe Magrane	.05
495	Bob Kipper	.05
496	Jose Mesa	.05
497	Charlie Hayes	.05
498	Joe Girardi	.05
499	Doug Jones	.05
500	Barry Bonds	2.00
501	Bill Krueger	.05
502	Glenn Braggs	.05
503	Eric King	.05
504	Frank Castillo	.05
505	Mike Gardiner	.05
506	Cory Snyder	.05
507	Steve Howe	.05
508	Jose Rijo	.05
509	Sid Fernandez	.05
510	Archi Cianfrocco RC (Rookie Prospect)	.05
511	Mark Guthrie	.05
512	Bob Ojeda	.05
513	John Doherty (Rookie Prospect)	.05
514	Dante Bichette	.05
515	Juan Berenguer	.05
516	Jeff Robinson	.05
517	Mike MacFarlane	.05
518	Matt Young	.05
519	Otis Nixon	.05
520	Brian Holman	.05
521	Chris Haney	.05
522	Jeff Kent RC (Rookie Prospect)	.75
523	Chad Curtis RC (Rookie Prospect)	.25
524	Vince Horsman	.05
525	Rod Nichols	.05
526	Peter Hoy RC (Rookie Prospect)	.05
527	Shawn Boskie	.05
528	Alejandro Pena	.05
529	Dave Burba (Rookie Prospect)	.05
530	Ricky Jordan	.05
531	David Silvestri (Rookie Prospect)	.05
532	John Patterson (Rookie Prospect)	.05
533	Jeff Branson (Rookie Prospect)	.05
534	Derrick May	.05
535	Esteban Beltre (Rookie Prospect)	.05
536	Jose Melendez	.05
537	Wally Joyner	.05
538	Eddie Taubensee (Rookie Prospect)	.05
539	Jim Abbott	.05
540	Brian Williams RC (Rookie Prospect)	.05
541	Donovan Osborne (Rookie Prospect)	.05
542	Patrick Lennon (Rookie Prospect)	.05
543	Mike Groppuso RC (Rookie Prospect)	.05
544	Jarvis Brown RC (Rookie Prospect)	.05
545	Shawn Livesy RC (1st Round Draft Pick)	.05
546	Jeff Ware (1st Round Draft Pick)	.05
547	Danny Tartabull	.05
548	Bobby Jones RC (1st Round Draft Pick)	.05
549	Ken Griffey Jr.	1.50
550	Rey Sanchez RC	.05
551	Pedro Astacio RC (Rookie Prospect)	.10
552	Juan Guerrero RC (Rookie Prospect)	.05
553	Jacob Brumfield RC (Rookie Prospect)	.05
554	Ben Rivera RC (Rookie Prospect)	.05
555	Brian Jordan RC (Rookie Prospect)	.40
556	Denny Neagle (Rookie Prospect)	.05
557	Cliff Brantley	.05
558	Anthony Young (Rookie Prospect)	.05
559	John VanderWal RC (Rookie Prospect)	.05
560	Monty Fariss RC (Rookie Prospect)	.05
561	Russ Springer RC (Rookie Prospect)	.05
562	Pat Listach RC	.05
563	Pat Hentgen (Rookie Prospect)	.05
564	Andy Stankiewicz (Rookie Prospect)	.05
565	Mike Perez (Rookie Prospect)	.05
566	Mike Bielecki	.05
567	Butch Henry (Rookie Prospect)	.05
568	Dave Nilsson RC (Rookie Prospect)	.05
569	Scott Hatteberg RC (Rookie Prospect)	.05
570	Ruben Amaro Jr. (Rookie Prospect)	.05
571	Todd Hundley (Rookie Prospect)	.05
572	Moises Alou (Rookie Prospect)	.05
573	Hector Fajardo (Rookie Prospect)	.05
574	Todd Van Poppel (Rookie Prospect)	.05
575	Willie Banks (Rookie Prospect)	.05
576	Bob Zupcic (Rookie Prospect)	.05
577	J.J. Johnson RC (1st Round Draft Pick)	.05
578	John Burkett	.05
579	Trever Miller (1st Round Draft Pick)	.05
580	Scott Bankhead	.05
581	Rich Amaral (Rookie Prospect)	.05
582	Kenny Lofton (Rookie Prospect)	.05
583	Matt Stairs (Rookie Prospect)	.05
584	Don Mattingly, Rod Carew (Idols)	.25
585	Jack Morris, Steve Avery (Idols)	.05
586	Roberto Alomar, Sandy Alomar (Idols)	.10
587	Scott Sanderson, Catfish Hunter (Idols)	.05
588	Dave Justice, Willie Stargell (Idols)	.05
589	Rex Hudler, Roger Staubach (Idols)	.05
590	David Cone, Jackie Gleason (Idols)	.05
591	Willie Davis, Tony Gwynn (Idols)	.15
592	Orel Hershiser (Sidelines)	.05
593	John Wetteland (Sidelines)	.05
594	Tom Glavine (Sidelines)	.05
595	Randy Johnson (Sidelines)	.25
596	Jim Gott (Sidelines)	.05
597	Donald Harris	.05
598	Shawn Hare RC	.05
599	Chris Gardner	.05
600	Rusty Meacham	.05
601	Benito Santiago (Shades)	.05
602	Eric Davis (Shades)	.05
603	Jose Lind (Shades)	.05
604	Dave Justice (Shades)	.05
605	Tim Raines (Shades)	.05
606	Randy Tomlin (Grips)	.05
607	Jack McDowell (Grips)	.05
608	Greg Maddux (Grips)	.30
609	Charles Nagy (Grips)	.05
610	Tom Candiotti (Grips)	.05
611	David Cone (Grips)	.05
612	Steve Avery (Grips)	.10
613	Rod Beck RC	.05
614	Rickey Henderson (Technician)	.25
615	Benito Santiago (Technician)	.05
616	Ruben Sierra (Technician)	.05
617	Ryne Sandberg (Technician)	.05
618	Nolan Ryan (Technician)	1.00
619	Brett Butler (Technician)	.05
620	Dave Justice (Technician)	.05

cards with their baseball heroes. Both front and back are horizontal in format and include photos of both the rookie and his idol.

	NM/M
Complete Set (18):	20.00
Common Player:	.50
1 Reggie Sanders, Eric Davis	.50
2 Hector Fajardo, Jim Abbott	.50
3 Gary Cooper, George Brett	3.50
4 Mark Wohlers, Roger Clemens	3.50
5 Luis Mercedes, Julio Franco	.50
6 Willie Banks, Dwight Gooden	.50
7 Kenny Lofton, Rickey Henderson	1.50
8 Keith Mitchell, Dave Henderson	.50
10 Kim Batiste, Barry Larkin	.50
11 Thurman Munson, Todd Hundley	1.00
12 Eddie Zosky, Cal Ripken Jr.	4.50
13 Todd Van Poppel, Nolan Ryan	4.50
14 Ryne Sandberg, Jim Thome	2.50
15 Dave Fleming, Bobby Murcer	.50
16 Royce Clayton, Ozzie Smith	2.50
17 Don Harris, Darryl Strawberry	.50
18 Alan Trammell, Chad Curtis	.50
Derek Bell, Dave Winfield	1.50

contained one of these horizontal-format cards of the game's top hitters. The player's name is printed in gold foil at the bottom of the card, along with a red and white Slugfest logo. Backs, which are vertical, have a color player photo, a career summary and a few lifetime stats.

	NM/M
Complete Set (15):	15.00
Common Player:	.30
1 Cecil Fielder	.30
2 Mark McGwire	2.50
3 Jose Canseco	.65
4 Barry Bonds	3.00
5 Dave Justice	.30
6 Bobby Bonilla	.30
7 Ken Griffey Jr.	2.00
8 Ron Gant	.30
9 Ryne Sandberg	1.50
10 Ruben Sierra	.30
11 Frank Thomas	1.00
12 Will Clark	.30
13 Kirby Puckett	1.50
14 Cal Ripken, Jr.	3.00
15 Jeff Bagwell	1.00

Team Pinnacle

The most sought-after of the 1992 Pinnacle inserts is this 12-piece set of "two-headed" cards. An American and a National League superstar at each position are featured on each card, with two cards each for starting and relief pitchers. The ultra-realistic artwork of Chris Greco is featured on the cards, which were inserted into Series 1 foil packs.

	NM/M
Complete Set (12):	40.00
Common Player:	1.50
1 Roger Clemens, Ramon Martinez	8.00
2 Jim Abbott, Steve Avery	1.50
3 Benito Santiago, Ivan Rodriguez	3.00
4 Frank Thomas, Will Clark	3.00
5 Roberto Alomar, Ryne Sandberg	6.00
6 Robin Ventura, Matt Williams	1.50
7 Cal Ripken, Jr., Barry Larkin	10.00
8 Danny Tartabull, Barry Bonds	8.00
9 Brett Butler, Ken Griffey Jr.	8.00
10 Ruben Sierra, Dave Justice	1.50
11 Dennis Eckersley, Rob Dibble	1.50
12 Scott Radinsky, John Franco	1.50

Team 2000

Rookies

Styled after the regular 1992 Pinnacle cards, this 30-card boxed set features the year's top rookies. The cards have a game-action photo which is borderless on the top and sides. Beneath the photo a team color-coded strip carries the player's name in gold foil, with a gold-bordered team logo at left. A black strip at bottom has the notation "1992 Rookie." Horizontal backs follow a similar design and include a bit of player information, Pinnacle's anti-counterfeiting strip and some gold-foil enhancements.

	NM/M
Complete Set (30):	2.00
Common Player:	.05
1 Luis Mercedes	.05
2 Scott Cooper	.05
3 Kenny Lofton	.25
4 John Doherty	.05
5 Pat Listach	.05
6 Andy Stankiewicz	.05
7 Derek Bell	.25
8 Gary DiSarcina	.05
9 Roberto Hernandez	.15
10 Joel Johnston	.05
11 Pat Mahomes	.05
12 Todd Van Poppel	.05
13 Dave Fleming	.05
14 Monty Fariss	.05
15 Gary Scott	.05
16 Moises Alou	.25
17 Todd Hundley	.25
18 Kim Batiste	.05
19 Denny Neagle	.05
20 Donovan Osborne	.05
21 Mark Wohlers	.05
22 Reggie Sanders	.10
23 Brian Williams	.05
24 Eric Karros	.25
25 Frank Seminara	.05
26 Royce Clayton	.25
27 Dave Nilsson	.05
28 Matt Stairs	.05
29 Chad Curtis	.25
30 Carlos Hernandez	.25

Rookie Idols

Carrying on with the Idols subset theme in the regular issue, these Series 2 foil-pack inserts feature 18 young prospects sharing

Slugfest

Each specially marked Slugfest jumbo pack of '92 Pinnacle

Young stars projected to be the superstars of the 2000 season were chosen for this insert set found three at a time in jumbo packs. Cards #1-40 were included in Series 1 packaging, while cards #41-80 were inserted with Series 2 Pinnacle. Cards feature gold foil highlights on both front and back.

This boxed set highlighting the career of Mickey Mantle was issued in a reported edition of 180,000 sets. Fronts and backs feature an assortment of black-and-white, color and colorized photos. Fronts have gold-foil stamped highlights. Card backs have a few sentences about Mantle's life or career.

This set offers many of the same features which made the debut Pinnacle set so popular in 1992. Subsets are titled Rookies, Now & Then (which shows the player as he looked as a rookie and in 1993), Idols (active players and their heroes on the same card), Hometown Heroes (players who are playing with their hometown team), Draft Picks and Rookies. More than 100 rookies and 10 draft picks are featured. All regular cards have an action photo, a black border and the Pinnacle name in gold foil. Series 1 cards feature portraits of players on the two new expansion teams; Series 2 cards feature action shots of them. Team Pinnacle insert cards returned, while Rookie Team Pinnacle cards made their debut. Other insert sets are titled Team 2001, Slugfest and Tribute, which features five cards each of Nolan Ryan and George Brett.

		NM/M
Complete Set (80):		3.00
Common Player:		.05
1	Mike Mussina	.30
2	Phil Plantier	.05
3	Frank Thomas	.50
4	Travis Fryman	.05
5	Kevin Appier	.05
6	Chuck Knoblauch	.05
7	Pat Kelly	.05
8	Ivan Rodriguez	.40
9	Dave Justice	.05
10	Jeff Bagwell	.50
11	Marquis Grissom	.05
12	Andy Benes	.05
13	Gregg Olson	.05
14	Kevin Morton	.05
15	Tim Naehring	.05
16	Dave Hollins	.05
17	Sandy Alomar Jr.	.05
18	Albert Belle	.05
19	Charles Nagy	.05
20	Brian McRae	.05
21	Larry Walker	.05
22	Delino DeShields	.05
23	Jeff Johnson	.05
24	Bernie Williams	.05
25	Jose Offerman	.05
26	Juan Gonzalez	.25
27	Juan Guzman	.05
28	Eric Anthony	.05
29	Brian Hunter	.05
30	John Smoltz	.05
31	Deion Sanders	.05
32	Greg Maddux	.75
33	Andujar Cedeno	.05
34	Royce Clayton	.05
35	Kenny Lofton	.05
36	Cal Eldred	.05
37	Jim Thome	.50
38	Gary DiSarcina	.05
39	Brian Jordan	.05
40	Chad Curtis	.05
41	Ben McDonald	.05
42	Jim Abbott	.05
43	Robin Ventura	.05
44	Milt Cuyler	.05
45	Gregg Jefferies	.05
46	Scott Radinsky	.05
47	Ken Griffey Jr.	1.00
48	Roberto Alomar	.15
49	Ramon Martinez	.05
50	Bret Barberie	.05
51	Ray Lankford	.05
52	Leo Gomez	.05
53	Tommy Greene	.05
54	Mo Vaughn	.05
55	Sammy Sosa	.75
56	Carlos Baerga	.05
57	Mark Lewis	.05
58	Tom Gordon	.05
59	Gary Sheffield	.25
60	Scott Erickson	.05
61	Pedro Munoz	.05
62	Tino Martinez	.05
63	Darren Lewis	.05
64	Dean Palmer	.05
65	John Olerud	.05
66	Steve Avery	.05
67	Pete Harnisch	.05
68	Luis Gonzalez	.05
69	Kim Batiste	.05
70	Reggie Sanders	.05
71	Luis Mercedes	.05
72	Todd Van Poppel	.05
73	Gary Scott	.05
74	Monty Fariss	.05
75	Kyle Abbott	.05
76	Eric Karros	.05
77	Mo Sanford	.05
78	Todd Hundley	.05
79	Reggie Jefferson	.05
80	Pat Mahomes	.05

Mickey Mantle

		NM/M
Complete Set (30):		20.00
Common Card:		1.00
1	Father and Son	1.00
2	High School	1.00
3	Commerce Comet	1.00
4	Spring Training	1.00
5	The Beginning	1.00
6	No. 6	1.00
7	The Rookie	1.00
8	Tape-Measure Shots	1.00
9	Shortstop	1.00
10	Outfield	1.00
11	Speed, Speed, Speed	1.00
12	Contracts	1.00
13	Three-time MVP	1.00
14	Triple Crown	1.00
15	Series Slam	1.00
16	Series Star	1.00
17	Switch Hitter	1.00
18	Fan Favorite	1.00
19	Milestones	1.00
20	Enthusiasm	1.00
21	Hitting	1.00
22	First Base	1.00
23	Courage	1.00
24	Mick & Stan (Musial)	1.00
25	Whitey & Yogi (Ford, Berra)	1.00
26	Mick & Billy (Martin)	1.00
27	Mick & Casey (Stengel)	1.00
28	Awards	1.00
29	Retirement	1.00
30	Cooperstown	1.00

1993 Pinnacle Promos

Dave Fleming

On six of the eight cards issued to premiere Pinnacle's '93 set, the difference between the promo version and the issued version is so slight it can easily go unnoticed — the "TM" in the upper-right corner on front is larger on the promo than on the regular card. Promo cards #3 and 5 are easier to spot because the team logos on back of the promos are the old Expos and Mariners logos, rather than the new versions found on issued cards.

		NM/M
Complete Set (8):		10.00
Common Player:		1.25
1	Gary Sheffield	3.00
2	Cal Eldred	1.25
3	Larry Walker	1.25
4	Deion Sanders	1.50
5	Dave Fleming	1.25
6	Carlos Baerga	1.25
7	Bernie Williams	1.25
8	John Kruk	1.25

1993 Pinnacle

		NM/M
Complete Set (620):		17.50
Common Player:		.05
Series 1 Pack (15):		.35
Series 1 Box (36):		8.00
Series 2 Pack (15):		.75
Series 2 Box (36):		20.00
1	Gary Sheffield	.30
2	Cal Eldred	.05
3	Larry Walker	.05
4	Deion Sanders	.05
5	Dave Fleming	.05
6	Carlos Baerga	.05
7	Bernie Williams	.05
8	John Kruk	.05
9	Jimmy Key	.05
10	Jeff Bagwell	.60
11	Jim Abbott	.05
12	Terry Steinbach	.05
13	Bob Tewksbury	.05
14	Eric Karros	.05
15	Ryne Sandberg	.75
16	Will Clark	.05
17	Edgar Martinez	.05
18	Eddie Murray	.60
19	Andy Van Slyke	.05
20	Cal Ripken, Jr.	2.00
21	Ivan Rodriguez	.50
22	Barry Larkin	.05
23	Don Mattingly	.85
24	Gregg Jefferies	.05
25	Roger Clemens	.85
26	Cecil Fielder	.05
27	Kent Hrbek	.05
28	Robin Ventura	.05
29	Rickey Henderson	.60
30	Roberto Alomar	.15
31	Luis Polonia	.05
32	Andujar Cedeno	.05
33	Pat Listach	.05
34	Mark Grace	.05
35	Otis Nixon	.05
36	Felix Jose	.05
37	Mike Sharperson	.05
38	Dennis Martinez	.05
39	Willie McGee	.05
40	Kenny Lofton	.05
41	Randy Johnson	.60
42	Andy Benes	.05
43	Bobby Bonilla	.05
44	Mike Mussina	.50
45	Len Dykstra	.05
46	Ellis Burks	.05
47	Chris Sabo	.05
48	Jay Bell	.05
49	Jose Canseco	.40
50	Craig Biggio	.05
51	Wally Joyner	.05
52	Mickey Tettleton	.05
53	Tim Raines	.05
54	Brian Harper	.05
55	Rene Gonzales	.05
56	Mark Langston	.05
57	Jack Morris	.05
58	Mark McGwire	1.50
59	Ken Caminiti	.05
60	Terry Pendleton	.05
61	Dave Nilsson	.05
62	Tom Pagnozzi	.05
63	Mike Morgan	.05
64	Darryl Strawberry	.05
65	Charles Nagy	.05
66	Ken Hill	.05
67	Matt Williams	.05
68	Jay Buhner	.05
69	Vince Coleman	.05
70	Brady Anderson	.05
71	Fred McGriff	.05
72	Ben McDonald	.05
73	Terry Mulholland	.05
74	Randy Tomlin	.05
75	Nolan Ryan	2.00
76	Frank Viola	.05
77	Jose Rijo	.05
78	Shane Mack	.05
79	Travis Fryman	.05
80	Jack McDowell	.05
81	Mark Gubicza	.05
82	Matt Nokes	.05
83	Bert Blyleven	.05
84	Eric Anthony	.05
85	Mike Bordick	.05
86	John Olerud	.05
87	B.J. Surhoff	.05
88	Bernard Gilkey	.05
89	Shawon Dunston	.05
90	Tom Glavine	.30
91	Brett Butler	.05
92	Moises Alou	.05
93	Albert Belle	.05
94	Darren Lewis	.05
95	Omar Vizquel	.05
96	Dwight Gooden	.05
97	Gregg Olson	.05
98	Tony Gwynn	.75
99	Darren Daulton	.05
100	Dennis Eckersley	.50
101	Rob Dibble	.05
102	Mike Greenwell	.05
103	Jose Lind	.05
104	Julio Franco	.05
105	Tom Gordon	.05
106	Scott Livingstone	.05
107	Chuck Knoblauch	.05
108	Frank Thomas	.60
109	Melido Perez	.05
110	Ken Griffey Jr.	1.00
111	Harold Baines	.05
112	Gary Gaetti	.05
113	Pete Harnisch	.05
114	David Wells	.05
115	Charlie Leibrandt	.05
116	Ray Lankford	.05
117	Kevin Seitzer	.05
118	Robin Yount	.60
119	Lenny Harris	.05
120	Chris James	.05
121	Delino DeShields	.05
122	Kirt Manwaring	.05
123	Glenallen Hill	.05
124	Hensley Meulens	.05
125	Darrin Jackson	.05
126	Todd Hundley	.05
127	Dave Hollins	.05
128	Sam Horn	.05
129	Roberto Hernandez	.05
130	Vicente Palacios	.05
131	George Brett	.85
132	Dave Martinez	.05
133	Kevin Appier	.05
134	Pat Kelly	.05
135	Pedro Munoz	.05
136	Mark Carreon	.05
137	Lance Johnson	.05
138	Devon White	.05
139	Julio Valera	.05
140	Eddie Taubensee	.05
141	Willie Wilson	.05
142	Stan Belinda	.05
143	John Smoltz	.05
144	Darryl Hamilton	.05
145	Sammy Sosa	.75
146	Carlos Hernandez	.05
147	Tom Candiotti	.05
148	Mike Felder	.05
149	Rusty Meacham	.05
150	Ivan Calderon	.05
151	Pete O'Brien	.05
152	Erik Hanson	.05
153	Billy Ripken	.05
154	Kurt Stillwell	.05
155	Jeff Kent	.05
156	Mickey Morandini	.05
157	Randy Milligan	.05
158	Reggie Sanders	.05
159	Luis Rivera	.05
160	Orlando Merced	.05
161	Dean Palmer	.05
162	Mike Perez	.05
163	Scott Erikson	.05
164	Kevin McReynolds	.05
165	Kevin Maas	.05
166	Ozzie Guillen	.05
167	Rob Deer	.05
168	Danny Tartabull	.05
169	Lee Stevens	.05
170	Dave Henderson	.05
171	Derek Bell	.05
172	Steve Finley	.05
173	Greg Olson	.05
174	Geronimo Pena	.05
175	Paul Quantrill	.05
176	Steve Buechele	.05
177	Kevin Gross	.05
178	Tim Wallach	.05
179	Dave Valle	.05
180	Dave Silvestri	.05
181	Bud Black	.05
182	Henry Rodriguez	.05
183	Tim Teufel	.05
184	Mark McLemore	.05
185	Bret Saberhagen	.05
186	Chris Hoiles	.05
187	Ricky Jordan	.05
188	Don Slaught	.05
189	Mo Vaughn	.05
190	Joe Oliver	.05
191	Juan Gonzalez	.30
192	Scott Leius	.05
193	Milt Cuyler	.05
194	Chris Haney	.05
195	Ron Karkovice	.05
196	Steve Farr	.05
197	John Orton	.05
198	Kelly Gruber	.05
199	Ron Darling	.05
200	Ruben Sierra	.05
201	Chuck Finley	.05
202	Mike Moore	.05
203	Pat Borders	.05
204	Sid Bream	.05
205	Todd Zeile	.05
206	Rick Wilkins	.05
207	Jim Gantner	.05
208	Frank Castillo	.05
209	Dave Hansen	.05
210	Trevor Wilson	.05
211	Sandy Alomar, Jr.	.05
212	Sean Berry	.05
213	Tino Martinez	.05
214	Chito Martinez	.05
215	Dan Walters	.05
216	John Franco	.05
217	Glenn Davis	.05
218	Mariano Duncan	.05
219	Mike LaValliere	.05
220	Rafael Palmeiro	.50
221	Jack Clark	.05
222	Hal Morris	.05
223	Ed Sprague	.05
224	John Valentin	.05
225	Sam Militello	.05
226	Bob Wickman	.05
227	Damion Easley	.05
228	John Jaha	.05
229	Bob Ayrault	.05
230	Mo Sanford/ED	.05
231	Walt Weiss/ED	.05
232	Dante Bichette/ED	.05
233	Steve Decker/ED	.05
234	Jerald Clark/ED	.05
235	Bryan Harvey/ED	.05
236	Joe Girardi/ED	.05
237	Dave Magadan/ED	.05
238	David Nied (Rookie Prospect)	.05
239	Eric Wedge **RC** (Rookie Prospect)	.05
240	Rico Brogna (Rookie Prospect)	.05
241	J.T. Bruett (Rookie Prospect)	.05
242	Jonathan Hurst (Rookie Prospect)	.05
243	Bret Boone (Rookie Prospect)	.05
244	Manny Alexander (Rookie Prospect)	.05
245	Scooter Tucker (Rookie Prospect)	.05
246	Troy Neel (Rookie Prospect)	.05
247	Eddie Zosky (Rookie Prospect)	.05
248	Melvin Nieves (Rookie Prospect)	.05
249	Ryan Thompson (Rookie Prospect)	.05
250	Shawn Barton (Rookie Prospect)	.05
251	Ryan Klesko (Rookie Prospect)	.05
252	Mike Piazza (Rookie Prospect)	1.00
253	Steve Hosey (Rookie Prospect)	.05
254	Shane Reynolds (Rookie Prospect)	.05
255	Dan Wilson (Rookie Prospect)	.05
256	Tom Marsh (Rookie Prospect)	.05
257	Barry Manuel (Rookie Prospect)	.05
258	Paul Miller (Rookie Prospect)	.05
259	Pedro Martinez (Rookie Prospect)	.60
260	Steve Cooke (Rookie Prospect)	.05
261	Johnny Guzman (Rookie Prospect)	.05
262	Mike Butcher (Rookie Prospect)	.05
263	Bien Figueroa (Rookie Prospect)	.05
264	Rich Rowland (Rookie Prospect)	.05
265	Shawn Jeter (Rookie Prospect)	.05
266	Gerald Williams (Rookie Prospect)	.05
267	Derek Parks (Rookie Prospect)	.05
268	Henry Mercedes (Rookie Prospect)	.05
269	David Hulse **RC** (Rookie Prospect)	.05
270	Tim Pugh **RC** (Rookie Prospect)	.05
271	William Suero (Rookie Prospect)	.05
272	Ozzie Canseco (Rookie Prospect)	.05
273	Fernando Ramsey (Rookie Prospect)	.05
274	Bernardo Brito (Rookie Prospect)	.05
275	Dave Mlicki (Rookie Prospect)	.05
276	Tim Salmon (Rookie Prospect)	.05
277	Mike Raczka (Rookie Prospect)	.05
278	Ken Ryan **RC** (Rookie Prospect)	.05
279	Rafael Bournigal (Rookie Prospect)	.05
280	Wil Cordero (Rookie Prospect)	.05
281	Billy Ashley (Rookie Prospect)	.05
282	Paul Wagner (Rookie Prospect)	.05
283	Blas Minor (Rookie Prospect)	.05
284	Rick Trlicek (Rookie Prospect)	.05
285	Willie Greene (Rookie Prospect)	.05
286	Ted Wood (Rookie Prospect)	.05
287	Phil Clark (Rookie Prospect)	.05
288	Jesse Levis (Rookie Prospect)	.05
289	Tony Gwynn (Now & The n)	.40
290	Nolan Ryan (Now & Then)	1.00
291	Dennis Martinez (Now & Then)	.05
292	Eddie Murray (Now & Then)	.30
293	Robin Yount (Now & Then)	.30
294	George Brett (Now & Then)	.45
295	Dave Winfield (Now & Then)	.30
296	Bert Blyleven (Now & Then)	.05
297	Jeff Bagwell (Idols – Carl Yastrzemski)	.30
298	John Smoltz (Idols – Jack Morris)	.05
299	Larry Walker (Idols – Mike Bossy)	.05
300	Gary Sheffield (Idols – Barry Larkin)	.15
301	Ivan Rodriguez (Idols – Carlton Fisk)	.30
302	Delino DeShields (Idols – Malcolm X)	.05
303	Tim Salmon (Idols – Dwight Evans)	.05
304	Bernard Gilkey (Hometown Heroes)	.05
305	Cal Ripken, Jr. (Hometown Heroes)	1.00
306	Barry Larkin (Hometown Heroes)	.05
307	Kent Hrbek (Hometown Heroes)	.05
308	Rickey Henderson (Hometown Heroes)	.30
309	Darryl Strawberry (Hometown Heroes)	.05
310	John Franco (Hometown Heroes)	.05
311	Todd Stottlemyre	.05
312	Luis Gonzalez	.05
313	Tommy Greene	.05
314	Randy Velarde	.05
315	Steve Avery	.05
316	Jose Oquendo	.05
317	Rey Sanchez	.05
318	Greg Vaughn	.05
319	Orel Hershiser	.05
320	Paul Sorrento	.05
321	Royce Clayton	.05
322	John Vander Wal	.05
323	Henry Cotto	.05
324	Pete Schourek	.05
325	David Segui	.05
326	Arthur Rhodes	.05
327	Bruce Hurst	.05
328	Wes Chamberlain	.05
329	Ozzie Smith	.75
330	Scott Cooper	.05
331	Felix Fermin	.05
332	Mike Macfarlane	.05
333	Dan Gladden	.05
334	Kevin Tapani	.05
335	Steve Sax	.05
336	Jeff Montgomery	.05
337	Gary DiSarcina	.05
338	Lance Blankenship	.05
339	Brian Williams	.05
340	Duane Ward	.05
341	Chuck McElroy	.05
342	Joe Magrane	.05
343	Jaime Navarro	.05
344	Dave Justice	.05
345	Jose Offerman	.05
346	Marquis Grissom	.05
347	Bill Swift	.05
348	Jim Thome	.50
349	Archi Cianfrocco	.05
350	Anthony Young	.05
351	Leo Gomez	.05
352	Bill Gullickson	.05
353	Alan Trammell	.05
354	Dan Pasqua	.05
355	Jeff King	.05
356	Kevin Brown	.05
357	Tim Belcher	.05
358	Bip Roberts	.05
359	Brent Mayne	.05
360	Rheal Cormier	.05
361	Mark Guthrie	.05
362	Craig Grebeck	.05

Mickey Mantle

MICKEY MANTLE

363 Andy Stankiewicz .05
364 Juan Guzman .05
365 Bobby Witt .05
366 Mark Portugal .05
367 Brian McRae .05
368 Mark Lemke .05
369 Bill Wegman .05
370 Donovan Osborne .05
371 Derrick May .05
372 Carl Willis .05
373 Chris Nabholz .05
374 Mark Lewis .05
375 John Burkett .05
376 Luis Mercedes .05
377 Ramon Martinez .05
378 Kyle Abbott .05
379 Mark Wohlers .05
380 Bob Walk .05
381 Kenny Rogers .05
382 Tim Naehring .05
383 Alex Fernandez .05
384 Keith Miller .05
385 Mike Henneman .05
386 Rick Aguilera .05
387 George Bell .05
388 Mike Gallego .05
389 Howard Johnson .05
390 Kim Batiste .05
391 Jerry Browne .05
392 Damon Berryhill .05
393 Ricky Bones .05
394 Omar Olivares .05
395 Mike Harkey .05
396 Pedro Astacio .05
397 John Wetteland .05
398 Rod Beck .05
399 Thomas Howard .05
400 Mike Devereaux .05
401 Tim Wakefield .05
402 Curt Schilling .30
403 Zane Smith .05
404 Bob Zupcic .05
405 Tom Browning .05
406 Tony Phillips .05
407 John Doherty .05
408 Pat Mahomes .05
409 John Habyan .05
410 Steve Olin .05
411 Chad Curtis .05
412 Joe Grahe .05
413 John Patterson .05
414 Brian Hunter .05
415 Doug Henry .05
416 Lee Smith .05
417 Bob Scanlan .05
418 Kent Mercker .05
419 Mel Rojas .05
420 Mark Whiten .05
421 Carlton Fisk .60
422 Candy Maldonado .05
423 Doug Drabek .05
424 Wade Boggs .75
425 Mark Davis .05
426 Kirby Puckett .75
427 Joe Carter .05
428 Paul Molitor .60
429 Eric Davis .05
430 Darryl Kile .05
431 Jeff Parrett/ED .05
432 Jeff Blauser .05
433 Dan Plesac .05
434 Andres Galarraga/ED .05
435 Jim Gott .05
436 Jose Mesa .05
437 Ben Rivera .05
438 Dave Winfield .60
439 Norm Charlton .05
440 Chris Bosio .05
441 Wilson Alvarez .05
442 Dave Stewart .05
443 Doug Jones .05
444 Jeff Russell .05
445 Ron Gant .05
446 Paul O'Neill .05
447 Charlie Hayes/ED .05
448 Joe Hesketh .05
449 Chris Hammond .05
450 Hipolito Pichardo .05
451 Scott Radinsky .05
452 Bobby Thigpen .05
453 Xavier Hernandez .05
454 Lonnie Smith .05
455 Jamie Arnold RC (1st Draft Pick) .05
456 B.J. Wallace RC (1st Draft Pick) .05
457 Derek Jeter RC (Rookie Prospect) 10.00
458 Jason Kendall RC (Rookie Prospect) .75
459 Rick Helling RC (Rookie Prospect) .05
460 Derek Wallace RC (Rookie Prospect) .05
461 Sean Lowe RC (Rookie Prospect) .05
462 Shannon Stewart RC (Rookie Prospect) .60
463 Benji Grigsby RC (Rookie Prospect) .05
464 Todd Steverson RC (Rookie Prospect) .05
465 Dan Serafini RC (Rookie Prospect) .05
466 Michael Tucker (Rookie Prospect) .05
467 Chris Roberts (Rookie Prospect) .05
468 Pete Janicki RC (1st Draft Pick) .05
469 Jeff Schmidt RC (1st Draft Pick) .05
470 Don Mattingly (Now & Then) .45
471 Cal Ripken, Jr. (Now & Then) 1.00
472 Jack Morris (Now & Then) .05
473 Terry Pendleton (Now & Then) .05
474 Dennis Eckersley (Now & Then) .25
475 Carlton Fisk (Now & Then) .30
476 Wade Boggs (Now & Then) .35
477 Len Dykstra (Idols - Ken Stabler) .05
478 Danny Tartabull (Idols - Jose Tartabull) .05
479 Jeff Conine (Idols - Dale Murphy) .10
480 Gregg Jefferies (Idols - Ron Cey) .05
481 Paul Molitor (Idols - Harmon Killebrew) .30
482 John Valentin (Idols - Dave Concepcion) .05
483 Alex Arias (Idols - Dave Winfield) .10
484 Barry Bonds (Hometown Heroes) 1.00
485 Doug Drabek (Hometown Heroes) .05
486 Dave Winfield (Hometown Heroes) .30
487 Brett Butler (Hometown Heroes) .05
488 Harold Baines (Hometown Heroes) .05
489 David Cone (Hometown Heroes) .05
490 Willie McGee (Hometown Heroes) .05
491 Robby Thompson .05
492 Pete Incaviglia .05
493 Manuel Lee .05
494 Rafael Belliard .05
495 Scott Fletcher .05
496 Jeff Frye .05
497 Andre Dawson .25
498 Mike Scioscia .05
499 Spike Owen .05
500 Sid Fernandez .05
501 Joe Orsulak .05
502 Benito Santiago/ED .05
503 Dale Murphy .25
504 Barry Bonds 2.00
505 Jose Guzman .05
506 Tony Pena .05
507 Greg Swindell .05
508 Mike Pagliarulo .05
509 Lou Whitaker .05
510 Greg Gagne .05
511 Butch Henry/ED .05
512 Jeff Brantley .05
513 Jack Armstrong/ED .05
514 Danny Jackson .05
515 Junior Felix/ED .05
516 Milt Thompson .05
517 Greg Maddux .75
518 Eric Young/ED .05
519 Jody Reed .05
520 Roberto Kelly .05
521 Darren Holmes/ED .05
522 Craig Lefferts .05
523 Charlie Hough/ED .05
524 Bo Jackson .10
525 Bill Spiers .05
526 Orestes Destrade/ED .05
527 Greg Hibbard .05
528 Roger McDowell .05
529 Cory Snyder .05
530 Harold Reynolds .05
531 Kevin Reimer .05
532 Rick Sutcliffe .05
533 Tony Fernandez .05
534 Tom Brunansky .05
535 Jeff Reardon .05
536 Chili Davis .05
537 Bob Ojeda .05
538 Greg Colbrunn .05
539 Phil Plantier .05
540 Brian Jordan .05
541 Pete Smith .05
542 Frank Tanana .05
543 John Smiley .05
544 David Cone .05
545 Daryl Boston/ED .05
546 Tom Henke .05
547 Bill Krueger .05
548 Freddie Benavides/ED .05
549 Randy Myers .05
550 Reggie Jefferson .05
551 Kevin Mitchell .05
552 Dave Stieb .05
553 Bret Barberie/ED .05
554 Tim Crews .05
555 Doug Dascenzo .05
556 Alex Cole/ED .05
557 Jeff Innis .05
558 Carlos Garcia .05
559 Steve Howe .05
560 Kirk McCaskill .05
561 Frank Seminara .05
562 Cris Carpenter/ED .05
563 Mike Stanley .05
564 Carlos Quintana .05
565 Mitch Williams .05
566 Juan Bell .05
567 Eric Fox .05
568 Al Leiter .05
569 Mike Stanton .05
570 Scott Kamienicki .05
571 Ryan Bowen/ED .05
572 Andy Ashby/ED .05
573 Bob Welch .05
574 Scott Sanderson .05
575 Joe Kmak (Rookie Prospect) .05
576 Scott Pose/ED (Rookie Prospect) .05
577 Ricky Gutierrez (Rookie Prospect) .05
578 Mike Trombley (Rookie Prospect) .05
579 Sterling Hitchcock RC (Rookie Prospect) .10
580 Rodney Bolton (Rookie Prospect) .05
581 Tyler Green (Rookie Prospect) .05
582 Tim Costo (Rookie Prospect) .05
583 Tim Laker RC (Rookie Prospect) .05
584 Steve Reed/ED RC (Rookie Prospect) .05
585 Tom Kramer RC (Rookie Prospect) .05
586 Robb Nen (Rookie Prospect) .05
587 Jim Tatum RC (Rookie Prospect) .05
588 Frank Bolick (Rookie Prospect) .05
589 Kevin Young (Rookie Prospect) .05
590 Matt Whiteside RC (Rookie Prospect) .05
591 Cesar Hernandez (Rookie Prospect) .05
592 Mike Mohler RC (Rookie Prospect) .05
593 Alan Embree (Rookie Prospect) .05
594 Terry Jorgensen (Rookie Prospect) .05
595 John Cummings RC (Rookie Prospect) .05
596 Domingo Martinez (Rookie Prospect) .05
597 Benji Gil (Rookie Prospect) .05
598 Todd Pratt RC (Rookie Prospect) .05
599 Rene Arocha RC (Rookie Prospect) .05
600 Dennis Moeller (Rookie Prospect) .05
601 Jeff Conine/ED (Rookie Prospect) .05
602 Trevor Hoffman/ED (Rookie Prospect) .05
603 Daniel Smith (Rookie Prospect) .05
604 Lee Tinsley (Rookie Prospect) .05
605 Dan Peltier (Rookie Prospect) .05
606 Billy Brewer (Rookie Prospect) .05
607 Matt Walbeck RC (Rookie Prospect) .05
608 Richie Lewis/ED (Rookie Prospect) .05
609 J.T. Snow RC (Rookie Prospect) .40
610 Pat Gomez RC (Rookie Prospect) .05
611 Phil Hiatt (Rookie Prospect) .05
612 Alex Arias/ED (Rookie Prospect) .05
613 Kevin Rogers (Rookie Prospect) .05
614 Al Martin (Rookie Prospect) .05
615 Greg Gohr (Rookie Prospect) .05
616 Grame Lloyd RC (Rookie Prospect) .05
617 Kent Bottenfield (Rookie Prospect) .05
618 Chuck Carr/ED (Rookie Prospect) .05
619 Darrell Sherman RC (Rookie Prospect) .05
620 Mike Lansing RC (Rookie Prospect) .15

Expansion Opening Day

This nine-card set features 18 players for the two N.L. expansion teams: Florida Marlins and Colorado Rockies. Each "two-headed" card shows a projected Opening Day starter for each team. Cards were available one per Series 2 hobby box. Complete sets were available through a special mail-in offer.

	NM/M
Complete Set (9):	2.50
Common Player:	.25

1 Charlie Hough, David Nied .25
2 Benito Santiago, Joe Girardi .40
3 Orestes Destrade, Andres Galarraga .75
4 Bret Barberie, Eric Young .25
5 Dave Magadan, Charlie Hayes .25
6 Walt Weiss, Freddie Benavides .25
7 Jeff Conine, Jerald Clark .50
8 Scott Pose, Alex Cole .25
9 Junior Felix, Dante Bichette .40

Rookie Team Pinnacle

These 10 cards were randomly inserted into Series 2 packs. Rookie Team Pinnacle is printed in gold foil on both sides of the card. Cards are numbered 1 of 10, etc., and use the special Dufex process. Each card shows two players painted by artist Christopher Greco. Stated odds of finding a Rookie Team Pinnacle insert were one in 90 packs.

	NM/M
Complete Set (10):	20.00
Common Player:	1.50

1 Pedro Martinez, Mike Trombley 6.00
2 Kevin Rogers, Sterling Hitchcock 1.50
3 Mike Piazza, Jesse Levis 10.00
4 Ryan Klesko, J.T. Snow 1.50
5 John Patterson, Bret Boone 1.50
6 Domingo Martinez, Kevin Young 1.50
7 Wil Cordero, Manny Alexander 1.50
8 Steve Hosey, Tim Salmon 1.50
9 Ryan Thompson, Gerald Williams 1.50
10 Melvin Nieves, David Hulse 1.50

Slugfest

Baseball's top sluggers are featured in this 30-card insert set. Slugfest is printed in gold foil on the card front.

	NM/M
Complete Set (30):	12.50
Common Player:	.25

1 Juan Gonzalez .50
2 Mark McGwire 2.00
3 Cecil Fielder .25
4 Joe Carter .25
5 Fred McGriff .25
6 Barry Bonds 2.50
7 Gary Sheffield .50
8 Dave Hollins .25
9 Frank Thomas 1.00
10 Danny Tartabull .25
11 Albert Belle .25
12 Ruben Sierra .25
13 Larry Walker .25
14 Jeff Bagwell 1.00
15 Dave Justice .25
16 Kirby Puckett 1.25
17 John Kruk .25
18 Howard Johnson .25
19 Darryl Strawberry .25
20 Will Clark .25
21 Kevin Mitchell .25
22 Mickey Tettleton .25
23 Don Mattingly 1.50
24 Jose Canseco .75
25 Sam Militello .25
26 Andre Dawson .50
27 Ryne Sandberg 1.25
28 Ken Griffey Jr. 1.75
29 Carlos Baerga .25
30 Travis Fryman .25

Team Pinnacle

These cards were randomly inserted in Series 1 at a rate of about one in every 24 packs. Each card features two players painted by artist Christopher Greco. An eleventh card, featuring relief pitchers, was available only via a mail-in offer.

	NM/M
Complete Set (11):	40.00
Common Player:	1.50

1 Greg Maddux, Mike Mussina 10.00
2 Tom Glavine, John Smiley 2.00
3 Darren Daulton, Ivan Rodriguez 3.00
4 Fred McGriff, Frank Thomas 4.00
5 Delino DeShields, Carlos Baerga 1.50
6 Gary Sheffield, Edgar Martinez 1.50
7 Ozzie Smith, Pat Listach 8.00
8 Barry Bonds, Juan Gonzalez 15.00
9 Kirby Puckett, Andy Van Slyke 8.00
10 Larry Walker, Joe Carter 1.50
11 Rick Aguilera, Rob Dibble 1.50

Team 2001

This insert set features 30 players who are expected to be stars in the year 2001. Cards were randomly inserted into 27-card jumbo packs from Series 1.

	NM/M
Complete Set (30):	5.00
Common Player:	.05

1 Wil Cordero .05
2 Cal Eldred .05
3 Mike Mussina .60
4 Chuck Knoblauch .05
5 Melvin Nieves .05
6 Tim Wakefield .05
7 Carlos Baerga .05
8 Bret Boone .05
9 Jeff Bagwell 1.00
10 Travis Fryman .05
11 Royce Clayton .05
12 Delino DeShields .05
13 Juan Gonzalez .50
14 Pedro Martinez 1.00
15 Bernie Williams .05
16 Billy Ashley .05
17 Marquis Grissom .05
18 Kenny Lofton .05
19 Ray Lankford .05
20 Tim Salmon .05
21 Steve Hosey .05
22 Charles Nagy .05
23 Dave Fleming .05
24 Reggie Sanders .05
25 Sam Militello .05
26 Eric Karros .05
27 Ryan Klesko .05
28 Dean Palmer .05
29 Ivan Rodriguez .75
30 Sterling Hitchcock .05

Tribute

George Brett

These Hall of Famers each have five-card sets devoted to their career achievements. Each card commemorates a career milestone. Cards are random inserts in Series 2, about one every 24 packs. Fronts have a gold-foil stamped "Tribute" vertically at right.

	NM/M
Complete Set (10):	10.00
George Brett Card (1-5):	1.00
Nolan Ryan Card (6-10):	1.50

1 Kansas City Royalty (George Brett) 1.00
2 The Chase for .400 (George Brett) 1.00
3 Pine Tar Pandemonium - "The Bat" (George Brett) 1.00
4 MVP and a World Series, Too (George Brett) 1.00
5 3,000 or Bust (George Brett) 1.00
6 The Rookie (Nolan Ryan) 1.50
7 Angel of No Mercy (Nolan Ryan) 1.50
8 Astronomical Success (Nolan Ryan) 1.50
9 5,000 Ks (Nolan Ryan) 1.50
10 No-Hitter No. 7 (Nolan Ryan) 1.50

Cooperstown

NOLAN RYAN

This boxed set features "today's superstar players bound to become Cooperstown inductees." In standard 2-1/2" x 3-1/2" format, the cards feature on both front and back an action photo which is borderless at the top and sides. At bottom-center of each photo is a half-moon green and gold-foil "Cooperstown Card" logo. On front, the player's name is gold-foil stamped in a black bar at bottom. On back is a black box, again with the player's name in gold-foil, plus a few stats justifying the player's Hall of Fame potential. Pinnacle's trademark optical-variable anti-counterfeiting device is at the bottom. Cards are UV coated on both sides. A special edition of 1,000 of the Cooperstown sets was produced in Pinnacle's "Dufex" technology and distributed at the 1993 SCAI trade show. Other than being printed on foil, the cards are identical to the regular-issue Cooperstown cards. Each of the Pinnacle Cooperstown cards can also be found in a sample version which differs from the issued cards principally in the appearance on back of a large "PROMO" overprint.

		NM/M
Complete Set (30):		7.50
Common Player:		.25
Dufex:		25X
Promo:		30X
1	Nolan Ryan	2.00
2	George Brett	.85
3	Robin Yount	.65
4	Carlton Fisk	.65
5	Dale Murphy	.35
6	Dennis Eckersley	.50
7	Rickey Henderson	.65
8	Ryne Sandberg	.75
9	Ozzie Smith	.75
10	Dave Winfield	.65
11	Andre Dawson	.35
12	Kirby Puckett	.75
13	Wade Boggs	.75
14	Don Mattingly	.85
15	Barry Bonds	2.00
16	Will Clark	.25
17	Cal Ripken, Jr.	2.00
18	Roger Clemens	.85
19	Dwight Gooden	.25
20	Tony Gwynn	.75
21	Joe Carter	.25
22	Ken Griffey Jr.	1.00
23	Paul Molitor	.60
24	Frank Thomas	.60
25	Juan Gonzalez	.35
26	Barry Larkin	.25
27	Eddie Murray	.60
28	Cecil Fielder	.25
29	Roberto Alomar	.35
30	Mark McGwire	1.50

Joe DiMaggio

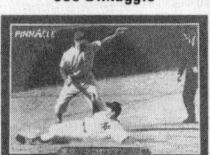

Sold in a special tin box in a limited edition of 200,000 sets, this set highlights the career of "The Yankee Clipper." Fronts feature black-and-white or colorized photos with a black border and gold-foil highlights. Backs feature a woodgrain center panel with a portion of DiMaggio's career recounted. The boxed set includes an "Authenticator" lens through which the name "DiMaggio" can be seen when placed over the optical-variable printing on back. Genuine DiMaggio autographed cards were randomly inserted into 9,000 sets.

		NM/M
Complete Set (30):		7.50
Common Card:		.35
1	An American Hero	.50
2	San Francisco Seals	.35
3	Seals Farewell	.35
4	First Game	.35
5	The Rookie	.35
6	Rookie All-Star (With Dizzy Dean.)	.45
7	Fan Favorite	.35
8	Teammates' Awe	.35
9	Classic Swing	.35
10	Joltin' Power	.35
11	Rapid Robert vs. Joltin' Joe (With Bob Feller.)	.45
12	The Complete Hitter	.35
13	Makin' It Look Easy	.35
14	Extra Swings	.35
15	The Run Producer	.35
16	Quiet Confidence	.35
17	Sticks 'N' Bones	.35
18	A Link to the Past (With Lou Gehrig.)	.50
19	The Center of Attention	.35
20	The DiMaggio Mystique	.35
21	Joe McCarthy (With Joe McCarthy.)	.35
22	World War II	.35
23	Fearless Baserunner	.35
24	The Summer of '41	.35
25	Career Statistics	.50
26	No. 45	.35
27	Chasing Ruth	.35
28	The Final Season	.35
29	Retirement	.35
30	Baseball's Greatest Living Player	.50

Joe DiMaggio Autographs

Eighteen hundred of each of five different insert cards were personally autographed by the Yankee Clipper and randomly inserted into the Joe DiMaggio box set tins at a rate of about one autograph per 22 sets. Fronts of the 2-1/8" x 3-1/2" cards have sepia artwork of DiMaggio at a particular stage of his career. In the wide white border at bottom is the autograph. Backs have a photo, part of a narrative about DiMaggio's career, and a serial number. A certificate of authenticity accompanies each signed card.

		NM/M
Complete Set (5):		850.00
1-5	Joe DiMaggio	175.00

Home Run Club

Pinnacle released this boxed set produced in a special metallic-foil printing process called "Dufex." Limited to 200,000 numbered sets, the cards are UV-coated and gold-foil stamped. The checklist includes 28 American League and 20 National League sluggers.

		NM/M
Complete Set (48):		6.00
Common Player:		.10
1	Juan Gonzalez	.40
2	Fred McGriff	.10
3	Cecil Fielder	.10
4	Barry Bonds	1.50
5	Albert Belle	.10
6	Gary Sheffield	.25
7	Joe Carter	.10
8	Mark McGwire	1.25
9	Darren Daulton	.10
10	Jose Canseco	.50
11	Dave Hollins	.10
12	Ryne Sandberg	.85
13	Ken Griffey Jr.	1.00
14	Larry Walker	.10
15	Rob Deer	.10
16	Andre Dawson	.25
17	Frank Thomas	.75
18	Mickey Tettleton	.10
19	Charlie Hayes	.10
20	Ron Gant	.10
21	Rickey Henderson	.75
22	Matt Williams	.10
23	Kevin Mitchell	.10
24	Robin Ventura	.10
25	Dean Palmer	.10
26	Mike Piazza	1.00
27	J.T. Snow	.75
28	Jeff Bagwell	.75

29	John Olerud	.10
30	Greg Vaughn	.10
31	Dave Justice	.10
32	Dave Winfield	.75
33	Danny Tartabull	.10
34	Eric Anthony	.10
35	Eddie Murray	.75
36	Jay Buhner	.10
37	Derek Bell	.10
38	Will Clark	.10
39	Carlos Baerga	.10
40	Mo Vaughn	.10
41	Bobby Bonilla	.10
42	Tim Salmon	.10
43	Bo Jackson	.10
44	Howard Johnson	.10
45	Kent Hrbek	.10
46	Ruben Sierra	.10
47	Cal Ripken, Jr.	1.50
48	Travis Fryman	.10

1994 Pinnacle Samples

Basically the same as the issued versions, these promo cards differ in the presence of a diagonal "SAMPLE" overprint on front and back. Cello-wrapped packs of hobby and retail versions were produced, with appropriate header cards.

		NM/M
Complete Set (12):		10.00
Common Player:		.50
2	Carlos Baerga	.50
3	Sammy Sosa	2.00
5	John Olerud	.75
7	Moises Alou	.50
8	Steve Avery	.50
10	Cecil Fielder	.50
11	Greg Maddux	2.00
269	Jeff Granger	.50
---	Jeff Granger (Museum) (Blank-back.)	1.00
---	Jeff Granger (Museum) (Black print on back.)	1.00
TR1	Paul Molitor (Tribute)	1.50
---	Hobby Version Header Card	.05
---	Retail Version Header Card	.05

1994 Pinnacle

Pinnacle's 1994 mid-priced brand features full bleed photos, gold-foil graphics and UV coating. On front, player and team names appear in a shield-and-bar motif in the lower-left corner. On horizontal backs, the front photo is reproduced as a subdued background photo, over which are printed recent stats and a few biographical details. A different player photo is featured at left, while the brand's optical-variable anti-counterfeiting device is at bottom center. Subsets include major award winners, Rookie Prospects and Draft Picks which are appropriately noted with gold-foil lettering on front. The issue was produced in two series of 270 cards each.

		NM/M
Complete Set (540):		15.00
Common Player:		.05

		NM/M
Artist's Proofs:		20X
Museums:		6X
Series 1 or 2 Pack (14):		.75
Series 1 or 2 Box (24):		12.50
1	Frank Thomas	.65
2	Carlos Baerga	.05
3	Sammy Sosa	.75
4	Tony Gwynn	.75
5	John Olerud	.05
6	Ryne Sandberg	.75
7	Moises Alou	.05
8	Steve Avery	.05
9	Tim Salmon	.05
10	Cecil Fielder	.05
11	Greg Maddux	.75
12	Barry Larkin	.05
13	Mike Devereaux	.05
14	Charlie Hayes	.05
15	Albert Belle	.05
16	Andy Van Slyke	.05
17	Mo Vaughn	.05
18	Brian McRae	.05
19	Cal Eldred	.05
20	Craig Biggio	.05
21	Kirby Puckett	.75
22	Derek Bell	.05
23	Don Mattingly	.85
24	John Burkett	.05
25	Roger Clemens	.85
26	Barry Bonds	2.00
27	Paul Molitor	.65
28	Mike Piazza	1.00
29	Robin Ventura	.05
30	Jeff Conine	.05
31	Wade Boggs	.75
32	Dennis Eckersley	.50
33	Bobby Bonilla	.05
34	Len Dykstra	.05
35	Manny Alexander	.05
36	Ray Lankford	.05
37	Greg Vaughn	.05
38	Chuck Finley	.05
39	Todd Benzinger	.05
40	Dave Justice	.05
41	Rob Dibble	.05
42	Tom Henke	.05
43	David Nied	.05
44	Sandy Alomar Jr.	.05
45	Pete Harnisch	.05
46	Jeff Russell	.05
47	Terry Mulholland	.05
48	Kevin Appier	.05
49	Randy Tomlin	.05
50	Cal Ripken, Jr.	2.00
51	Andy Benes	.05
52	Jimmy Key	.05
53	Kirt Manwaring	.05
54	Kevin Tapani	.05
55	Jose Guzman	.05
56	Todd Stottlemyre	.05
57	Jack McDowell	.05
58	Orel Hershiser	.05
59	Chris Hammond	.05
60	Chris Nabholz	.05
61	Ruben Sierra	.05
62	Dwight Gooden	.05
63	John Kruk	.05
64	Omar Vizquel	.05
65	Tim Naehring	.05
66	Dwight Smith	.05
67	Mickey Tettleton	.05
68	J.T. Snow	.05
69	Greg McMichael	.05
70	Kevin Mitchell	.05
71	Kevin Brown	.05
72	Scott Cooper	.05
73	Jim Thome	.60
74	Joe Girardi	.05
75	Eric Anthony	.05
76	Orlando Merced	.05
77	Felix Jose	.05
78	Tommy Greene	.05
79	Bernard Gilkey	.05
80	Phil Plantier	.05
81	Danny Tartabull	.05
82	Trevor Wilson	.05
83	Chuck Knoblauch	.05
84	Rick Wilkins	.05
85	Devon White	.05
86	Lance Johnson	.05
87	Eric Karros	.05
88	Gary Sheffield	.35
89	Wil Cordero	.05
90	Ron Darling	.05
91	Darren Daulton	.05
92	Joe Orsulak	.05
93	Steve Cooke	.05
94	Darryl Hamilton	.05
95	Aaron Sele	.05
96	John Doherty	.05
97	Gary DiSarcina	.05
98	Jeff Blauser	.05
99	John Smiley	.05
100	Ken Griffey Jr.	1.00
101	Dean Palmer	.05
102	Felix Fermin	.05
103	Jerald Clark	.05
104	Doug Drabek	.05
105	Curt Schilling	.30
106	Jeff Montgomery	.05
107	Rene Arocha	.05
108	Carlos Garcia	.05
109	Wally Whitehurst	.05
110	Jim Abbott	.05
111	Royce Clayton	.05
112	Chris Hoiles	.05
113	Mike Morgan	.05
114	Joe Magrane	.05

115	Tom Candiotti	.05
116	Ron Karkovice	.05
117	Ryan Bowen	.05
118	Rod Beck	.05
119	John Wetteland	.05
120	Terry Steinbach	.05
121	Dave Hollins	.05
122	Jeff Kent	.05
123	Ricky Bones	.05
124	Brian Jordan	.05
125	Chad Kreuter	.05
126	John Valentin	.05
127	Billy Hathaway	.05
128	Wilson Alvarez	.05
129	Tino Martinez	.05
130	Rodney Bolton	.05
131	David Segui	.05
132	Wayne Kirby	.05
133	Eric Young	.05
134	Scott Servais	.05
135	Scott Radinsky	.05
136	Bret Barberie	.05
137	John Roper	.05
138	Ricky Gutierrez	.05
139	Bernie Williams	.05
140	Bud Black	.05
141	Jose Vizcaino	.05
142	Gerald Williams	.05
143	Duane Ward	.05
144	Danny Jackson	.05
145	Allen Watson	.05
146	Scott Fletcher	.05
147	Delino DeShields	.05
148	Shane Mack	.05
149	Jim Eisenreich	.05
150	Troy Neel	.05
151	Jay Bell	.05
152	B.J. Surhoff	.05
153	Mark Whiten	.05
154	Mike Henneman	.05
155	Todd Hundley	.05
156	Greg Myers	.05
157	Ryan Klesko	.05
158	Dave Fleming	.05
159	Mickey Morandini	.05
160	Blas Minor	.05
161	Reggie Jefferson	.05
162	David Hulse	.05
163	Greg Swindell	.05
164	Roberto Hernandez	.05
165	Brady Anderson	.05
166	Jack Armstrong	.05
167	Phil Clark	.05
168	Melido Perez	.05
169	Darren Lewis	.05
170	Sam Horn	.05
171	Mike Harkey	.05
172	Juan Guzman	.05
173	Bob Natal	.05
174	Deion Sanders	.05
175	Carlos Quintana	.05
176	Mel Rojas	.05
177	Willie Banks	.05
178	Ben Rivera	.05
179	Kenny Lofton	.05
180	Leo Gomez	.05
181	Roberto Mejia	.05
182	Mike Perez	.05
183	Travis Fryman	.05
184	Ben McDonald	.05
185	Steve Frey	.05
186	Kevin Young	.05
187	Dave Magadan	.05
188	Bobby Munoz	.05
189	Pat Rapp	.05
190	Jose Offerman	.05
191	Vinny Castilla	.05
192	Ivan Calderon	.05
193	Ken Caminiti	.05
194	Benji Gil	.05
195	Chuck Carr	.05
196	Derrick May	.05
197	Pat Kelly	.05
198	Jeff Brantley	.05
199	Jose Lind	.05
200	Steve Buechele	.05
201	Wes Chamberlain	.05
202	Eduardo Perez	.05
203	Bret Saberhagen	.05
204	Gregg Jefferies	.05
205	Darrin Fletcher	.05
206	Kent Hrbek	.05
207	Kim Batiste	.05
208	Jeff King	.05
209	Donovan Osborne	.05
210	Dave Nilsson	.05
211	Al Martin	.05
212	Mike Moore	.05
213	Sterling Hitchcock	.05
214	Geronimo Pena	.05
215	Kevin Higgins	.05
216	Norm Charlton	.05
217	Don Slaught	.05
218	Mitch Williams	.05
219	Derek Lilliquist	.05
220	Armando Reynoso	.05
221	Kenny Rogers	.05
222	Doug Jones	.05
223	Luis Aquino	.05
224	Mike Oquist	.05
225	Darryl Scott	.05
226	Kurt Abbott	.05
227	Andy Tomberlin	.05
228	Norberto Martin	.05
229	Pedro Castellano	.05
230	Curtis Pride RC	.05
231	Jeff McNeely	.05
232	Scott Lydy	.05

233	Darren Oliver	.05
234	Danny Bautista	.05
235	Butch Huskey	.05
236	Chipper Jones	.75
237	Eddie Zambrano	.05
238	Jean Domingo	.05
239	Javier Lopez	.05
240	Nigel Wilson	.05
241	Drew Denson RC	.05
242	Raul Mondesi	.05
243	Luis Ortiz	.05
244	Manny Ramirez	.65
245	Greg Blosser	.05
246	Rondell White	.05
247	Steve Karsay	.05
248	Scott Stahoviak	.05
249	Jose Valentin	.05
250	Marc Newfield	.05
251	Keith Kessinger	.05
252	Carl Everett	.05
253	John O'Donoghue	.05
254	Turk Wendell	.05
255	Scott Ruffcorn	.05
256	Tony Tarasco	.05
257	Andy Cook	.05
258	Matt Mieske	.05
259	Luis Lopez	.05
260	Ramon Caraballo	.05
261	Salomon Torres	.05
262	Brooks Kieschnick RC	.05
263	Daron Kirkreit RC	.05
264	Bill Wagner RC	.10
265	Matt Drews RC	.05
266	Scott Christman	.05
267	Torii Hunter RC	1.00
268	Jamey Wright RC	.05
269	Jeff Granger	.05
270	Trot Nixon RC	1.00
271	Randy Myers	.05
272	Trevor Hoffman	.05
273	Bob Wickman	.05
274	Willie McGee	.05
275	Hipolito Pichardo	.05
276	Bobby Witt	.05
277	Gregg Olson	.05
278	Randy Johnson	.65
279	Robb Nen	.05
280	Paul O'Neill	.05
281	Lou Whitaker	.05
282	Chad Curtis	.05
283	Doug Henry	.05
284	Tom Glavine	.30
285	Mike Greenwell	.05
286	Roberto Kelly	.05
287	Roberto Alomar	.15
288	Charlie Hough	.05
289	Alex Fernandez	.05
290	Jeff Bagwell	.65
291	Wally Joyner	.05
292	Andujar Cedeno	.05
293	Rick Aguilera	.05
294	Darryl Strawberry	.05
295	Mike Mussina	.35
296	Jeff Gardner	.05
297	Chris Gwynn	.05
298	Matt Williams	.05
299	Brent Gates	.05
300	Mark McGwire	1.50
301	Jim Deshaies	.05
302	Edgar Martinez	.05
303	Danny Darwin	.05
304	Pat Meares	.05
305	Benito Santiago	.05
306	Jose Canseco	.40
307	Jim Gott	.05
308	Paul Sorrento	.05
309	Scott Kamieniecki	.05
310	Larry Walker	.05
311	Mark Langston	.05
312	John Jaha	.05
313	Stan Javier	.05
314	Hal Morris	.05
315	Robby Thompson	.05
316	Pat Hentgen	.05
317	Tom Gordon	.05
318	Joey Cora	.05
319	Luis Alicea	.05
320	Andre Dawson	.25
321	Darryl Kile	.05
322	Jose Rijo	.05
323	Luis Gonzalez	.05
324	Billy Ashley	.05
325	David Cone	.05
326	Bill Swift	.05
327	Phil Hiatt	.05
328	Craig Paquette	.05
329	Bob Welch	.05
330	Tony Phillips	.05
331	Archi Cianfrocco	.05
332	Dave Winfield	.65
333	David McCarty	.05
334	Al Leiter	.05
335	Tom Browning	.05
336	Mark Grace	.05
337	Jose Mesa	.05
338	Mike Stanley	.05
339	Roger McDowell	.05
340	Damion Easley	.05
341	Angel Miranda	.05
342	John Smoltz	.05
343	Jay Buhner	.05
344	Bryan Harvey	.05
345	Joe Carter	.05
346	Dante Bichette	.05
347	Jason Bere	.05
348	Frank Viola	.05
349	Ivan Rodriguez	.60
350	Juan Gonzalez	.05

No.	Player	Price		No.	Player	Price
351	Steve Finley	.05		469	Roger Pavlik	.05
352	Mike Felder	.05		470	Greg W. Harris	.05
353	Ramon Martinez	.05		471	Xavier Hernandez	.05
354	Greg Gagne	.05		472	Erik Hanson	.05
355	Ken Hill	.05		473	Jesse Orosco	.05
356	Pedro Munoz	.05		474	Greg Colbrunn	.05
357	Todd Van Poppel	.05		475	Harold Reynolds	.05
358	Marquis Grissom	.05		476	Greg Harris	.05
359	Milt Cuyler	.05		477	Pat Borders	.05
360	Reggie Sanders	.05		478	Melvin Nieves	.05
361	Scott Erickson	.05		479	Mariano Duncan	.05
362	Billy Hatcher	.05		480	Greg Hibbard	.05
363	Gene Harris	.05		481	Tim Pugh	.05
364	Rene Gonzales	.05		482	Bobby Ayala	.05
365	Kevin Rogers	.05		483	Sid Fernandez	.05
366	Eric Plunk	.05		484	Tim Wallach	.05
367	Todd Zeile	.05		485	Randy Milligan	.05
368	John Franco	.05		486	Walt Weiss	.05
369	Brett Butler	.05		487	Matt Walbeck	.05
370	Bill Spiers	.05		488	Mike Macfarlane	.05
371	Terry Pendleton	.05		489	Jerry Browne	.05
372	Chris Bosio	.05		490	Chris Sabo	.05
373	Orestes Destrade	.05		491	Tim Belcher	.05
374	Dave Stewart	.05		492	Spike Owen	.05
375	Darren Holmes	.05		493	Rafael Palmeiro	.60
376	Doug Strange	.05		494	Brian Harper	.05
377	Brian Turang	.05		495	Eddie Murray	.65
378	Carl Willis	.05		496	Ellis Burks	.05
379	Mark McLemore	.05		497	Karl Rhodes	.05
380	Bobby Jones	.05		498	Otis Nixon	.05
381	Scott Sanders	.05		499	Lee Smith	.05
382	Kirk Rueter	.05		500	Bip Roberts	.05
383	Randy Velarde	.05		501	Pedro Martinez	.65
384	Fred McGriff	.05		502	Brian L. Hunter	.05
385	Charles Nagy	.05		503	Tyler Green	.05
386	Rich Amaral	.05		504	Bruce Hurst	.05
387	Geronimo Berroa	.05		505	Alex Gonzalez	.05
388	Eric Davis	.05		506	Mark Portugal	.05
389	Ozzie Smith	.75		507	Bob Ojeda	.05
390	Alex Arias	.05		508	Dave Henderson	.05
391	Brad Ausmus	.05		509	Bo Jackson	.10
392	Cliff Floyd	.05		510	Bret Boone	.05
393	Roger Salkeld	.05		511	Mark Eichhorn	.05
394	Jim Edmonds	.05		512	Luis Polonia	.05
395	Jeromy Burnitz	.05		513	Will Clark	.05
396	Dave Staton	.05		514	Dave Valle	.05
397	Rob Butler	.05		515	Dan Wilson	.05
398	Marcos Armas	.05		516	Dennis Martinez	.05
399	Darrell Whitmore	.05		517	Jim Leyritz	.05
400	Ryan Thompson	.05		518	Howard Johnson	.05
401	Ross Powell RC	.05		519	Jody Reed	.05
402	Joe Oliver	.05		520	Julio Franco	.05
403	Paul Carey	.05		521	Jeff Reardon	.05
404	Bob Hamelin	.05		522	Willie Greene	.05
405	Chris Turner	.05		523	Shawon Dunston	.05
406	Nate Minchey	.05		524	Keith Mitchell	.05
407	Lonnie Maclin RC	.05		525	Rick Helling	.05
408	Harold Baines	.05		526	Mark Kiefer	.05
409	Brian Williams	.05		527	Chan Ho Park RC	.75
410	Johnny Ruffin	.05		528	Tony Longmire	.05
411	Julian Tavarez RC	.05		529	Rich Becker	.05
412	Mark Hutton	.05		530	Tim Hyers	.05
413	Carlos Delgado	.50		531	Darrin Jackson	.05
414	Chris Gomez	.05		532	Jack Morris	.05
415	Mike Hampton	.05		533	Rick White	.05
416	Alex Diaz	.05		534	Mike Kelly	.05
417	Jeffrey Hammonds	.05		535	James Mouton	.05
418	Jayhawk Owens	.05		536	Steve Trachsel	.05
419	J.R. Phillips	.05		537	Tony Eusebio	.05
420	Cory Bailey RC	.05		538	Kelly Stinnett	.05
421	Denny Hocking	.05		539	Paul Spoljaric	.05
422	Jon Shave	.05		540	Darren Dreifort	.05
423	Damon Buford	.05				
424	Troy O'Leary	.05				
425	Tripp Cromer	.05				
426	Albie Lopez	.05				
427	Tony Fernandez	.05				
428	Ozzie Guillen	.05				
429	Alan Trammell	.05				
430	John Wasdin RC	.05				
431	Marc Valdes	.05				
432	Brian Anderson RC	.20				
433	Matt Brunson RC	.05				
434	Wayne Gomes RC	.05				
435	Jay Powell RC	.05				
436	Kirk Presley RC	.05				
437	Jon Ratliff RC	.05				
438	Derrek Lee RC	2.00				
439	Tom Pagnozzi	.05				
440	Kent Mercker	.05				
441	Phil Leftwich RC	.05				
442	Jamie Moyer	.05				
443	John Flaherty	.05				
444	Mark Wohlers	.05				
445	Jose Bautista	.05				
446	Andres Galarraga	.05				
447	Mark Lemke	.05				
448	Tim Wakefield	.05				
449	Pat Listach	.05				
450	Rickey Henderson	.65				
451	Mike Gallego	.05				
452	Bob Tewksbury	.05				
453	Kirk Gibson	.05				
454	Pedro Astacio	.05				
455	Mike Lansing	.05				
456	Sean Berry	.05				
457	Bob Walk	.05				
458	Chili Davis	.05				
459	Ed Sprague	.05				
460	Kevin Stocker	.05				
461	Mike Stanton	.05				
462	Tim Raines	.05				
463	Mike Bordick	.05				
464	David Wells	.05				
465	Tim Laker	.05				
466	Cory Snyder	.05				
467	Alex Cole	.05				
468	Pete Incaviglia	.05				

Artist's Proof

A specially designated version of the regular Pinnacle set, described as the first day's production of the first 1,000 of each card, was issued as a random pack insert. Cards feature a small gold-foil "Artist's Proof" rectangle embossed above the player/team name shield on front. In all other respects the cards are identical to the regular-issue versions.

	NM/M
Complete Set (540):	250.00
Common Player:	1.50
Stars/Rookies:	20X

Museum Collection

Each card in the 1994 Pinnacle set was produced in a parallel "Museum Collection" version. The inserts were produced utilizing the company's Dufex foil-printing technology on front, with rays emanating from the Pinnacle logo. Backs are identical to the regular-issue version except for the substitution of a "1994 Museum Collection" logo for the optical-variable anti-counterfeiting bar at bottom-center. Museums were random package inserts, appearing at the rate of about once per four packs.

	NM/M
Complete Set (540):	225.00
Common Player:	1.00
Stars/Rookies:	6X

Rookie Team Pinnacle

The popular Rookie Team Pinnacle insert card tradition continued in 1994 with a series of nine "two-headed" cards featuring the top prospect from each league at each position. The cards again feature the ultra-realistic artwork of Chris Greco. Each side is enhanced with gold-foil presentations of the player's name, the Pinnacle logo and the Rookie Team Pinnacle logo. The inserts were packaged, on average, one per 90 packs of hobby foil only.

		NM/M
Complete Set (9):		12.00
Common Player:		.75
1	Carlos Delgado, Javier Lopez	2.50
2	Bob Hamelin, J.R. Phillips	.75
3	Jon Shave, Keith Kessinger	.75
4	Butch Huskey, Luis Ortiz	.75
5	Chipper Jones, Kurt Abbott	5.00
6	Rondell White, Manny Ramirez	3.00
7	Cliff Floyd, Jeffrey Hammonds	.75
8	Marc Newfield, Nigel Wilson	.75
9	Salomon Torres, Mark Hutton	.75

Team Pinnacle

The double-sided Team Pinnacle insert set features 18 of the top players in the game. They were inserted into Series 2 at a rate of one every 90 packs.

		NM/M
Complete Set (9):		35.00
Common Player:		1.50
1	Jeff Bagwell, Frank Thomas	4.00
2	Carlos Baerga, Robby Thompson	1.50
3	Matt Williams, Dean Palmer	1.50
4	Cal Ripken, Jr., Jay Bell	12.00
5	Ivan Rodriguez, Mike Piazza	6.00
6	Len Dykstra, Ken Griffey Jr.	8.00
7	Juan Gonzalez, Barry Bonds	10.00
8	Tim Salmon, Dave Justice	1.50
9	Greg Maddux, Jack McDowell	8.00

Run Creators

This insert set, exclusive to Pinnacle jumbo packaging, features the top 44 performers of the previous season in the arcane statistic of "runs created." Fronts have an action photo on which the stadium background has been muted in soft-focus red or blue. The player's last name appears at right in gold foil; the logo, "The Run Creators" is in one of the lower corners. Backs are printed in teal with a color team logo at center, beneath the stats that earned the player's inclusion in the series. The player's runs created are in gold foil above the write-up. Cards are numbered with an "RC" prefix.

		NM/M
Complete Set (44):		17.50
Common Player:		.25
1	John Olerud	.25
2	Frank Thomas	1.00
3	Ken Griffey Jr.	3.00
4	Paul Molitor	1.00
5	Rafael Palmeiro	.75
6	Roberto Alomar	.35
7	Juan Gonzalez	.50
8	Albert Belle	.25
9	Travis Fryman	.25
10	Rickey Henderson	1.00
11	Tony Phillips	.25
12	Mo Vaughn	.25
13	Tim Salmon	.25
14	Kenny Lofton	.25
15	Carlos Baerga	.25
16	Greg Vaughn	.25
17	Jay Buhner	.25
18	Chris Hoiles	.25
19	Mickey Tettleton	.25
20	Kirby Puckett	1.50
21	Danny Tartabull	.25
22	Devon White	.25
23	Barry Bonds	4.00
24	Lenny Dykstra	.25
25	John Kruk	.25
26	Fred McGriff	.25
27	Gregg Jefferies	.25
28	Mike Piazza	3.00
29	Jeff Blauser	.25
30	Andres Galarraga	.25
31	Darren Daulton	.25
32	Dave Justice	.25
33	Craig Biggio	.25
34	Mark Grace	.25
35	Tony Gwynn	1.50
36	Jeff Bagwell	1.00
37	Jay Bell	.25
38	Marquis Grissom	.25
39	Matt Williams	.25
40	Charlie Hayes	.25
41	Dante Bichette	.25
42	Bernard Gilkey	.25
43	Brett Butler	.25
44	Rick Wilkins	.25

Tribute

A hobby-only insert set, found approximately one per 18 foil packs, this nine-card series honors players who reached significant season or career milestones or otherwise had special achievements in 1993. Fronts feature full-bleed action photos. At left is a black strip with "TRIBUTE" in gold foil. A colored strip at bottom has the player name in gold foil and a short description of why he is being feted beneath. The Pinnacle logo is in gold foil at top. The same gold-foil enhancements are found on back, along with a portrait photo. In a black box at bottom are details of the tribute. The Pinnacle optical-variable anti-counterfeiting device is at bottom center. Card numbers are prefixed with "TR."

		NM/M
Complete Set (18):		15.00
Common Player:		.25
1	Paul Molitor	1.00
2	Jim Abbott	.25
3	Dave Winfield	1.00
4	Bo Jackson	.35
5	Dave Justice	.25
6	Len Dykstra	.25
7	Mike Piazza	2.50
8	Barry Bonds	4.50
9	Randy Johnson	1.00
10	Ozzie Smith	1.50
11	Mark Whiten	.25
12	Greg Maddux	1.50
13	Cal Ripken, Jr.	4.50
14	Frank Thomas	1.00
15	Juan Gonzalez	.45
16	Roberto Alomar	.25
17	Ken Griffey Jr.	3.00
18	Lee Smith	.25

New Generation

Baseball's hottest rookies and second-year players were featured in this boxed set. Cards are typical Pinnacle quality with full-bleed action photos, UV coating and gold-foil stamping on front and back. A total of 100,000 sets was produced, with a suggested retail price of $9.95.

		NM/M
Complete Set (25):		5.00
Common Player:		.25
1	Tim Salmon	.25
2	Mike Piazza	2.00
3	Jason Bere	.25
4	Jeffrey Hammonds	.25
5	Aaron Sele	.25
6	Salomon Torres	.25
7	Wil Cordero	.25
8	Allen Watson	.25
9	J.T. Snow	.25
10	Cliff Floyd	.25
10a	Cliff Floyd (Overprinted "SAMPLE" card.)	.50
11	Jeff McNeely	.25
12	Butch Huskey	.25
13	J.R. Phillips	.25
14	Bobby Jones	.25
15	Javier Lopez	.25
16	Scott Ruffcorn	.25
17	Manny Ramirez	1.25
18	Carlos Delgado	1.00
19	Rondell White	.25
20	Chipper Jones	1.50
21	Billy Ashley	.25
22	Nigel Wilson	.25
23	Jeromy Burnitz	.25
24	Danny Bautista	.25
25	Darrell Whitmore	.25

Power Surge

The major leagues' heaviest hitters are featured in this boxed set. Cards are typical Pinnacle quality with gold-foil stamping on front, UV coating on both sides and high-tech graphics. Fronts feature game-action photos while backs have smaller portrait and action photos on a marbled background, along with 1993 and career stats and a description of the player's power potential. Cards are numbered with a "PS" prefix. A total of 100,000 sets was produced.

		NM/M
Complete Set (25):		4.00
Common Player:		.25
1	Dave Justice	.25
2	Chris Hoiles	.25
3	Mo Vaughn	.25
4	Tim Salmon	.25
5	J.T. Snow	.25
6	Frank Thomas	.65
7	Sammy Sosa	.75
8	Rick Wilkins	.25
9	Robin Ventura	.25
10	Reggie Sanders	.25
11	Albert Belle	.25
12	Carlos Baerga	.25
12a	Carlos Baerga (Overprinted "SAMPLE" card.)	.50
13	Manny Ramirez	.65
14	Travis Fryman	.25
15	Gary Sheffield	.35
16	Jeff Bagwell	.65
17	Mike Piazza	1.00
18	Eric Karros	.25
19	Cliff Floyd	.25
20	Mark Whiten	.25
21	Phil Plantier	.25
22	Derek Bell	.25
23	Ken Griffey Jr.	1.00
24	Juan Gonzalez	.35
25	Dean Palmer	.25

The Naturals

The Naturals boxed set puts a game-action photo against a textured-foil background. Backs picture the player on a background of nature photography, including lightning, blue skies and clouds. Pinnacle produced 100,000 sets, which come in a numbered, sealed box with a certificate of authenticity.

		NM/M
Complete Set (25):		6.00
Common Player:		.15
1	Frank Thomas	.50
2	Barry Bonds	1.50
3	Ken Griffey Jr.	1.00
4	Juan Gonzalez	.25
5	Dave Justice	.15
6	Albert Belle	.15
7	Kenny Lofton	.15
8	Roberto Alomar	.15

9 Tim Salmon .15
10 Randy Johnson .50
11 Kirby Puckett .65
12 Tony Gwynn .65
13 Fred McGriff .15
14 Ryne Sandberg .65
15 Greg Maddux .65
16 Matt Williams .15
17 Lenny Dykstra .15
18 Gary Sheffield .35
18a Gary Sheffield (Overprinted "SAMPLE" card.) .50
19 Mike Piazza 1.00
20 Dean Palmer .15
21 Travis Fryman .15
22 Carlos Baerga .15
23 Cal Ripken, Jr. 1.50
24 John Olerud .15
25 Roger Clemens .75

1995 Pinnacle Series 1 Samples

This eight-card cello-wrapped sample set was sent to dealers to preview the 1995 Pinnacle Series 1 cards. The cards are identical to regular-issue Pinnacle cards except they carry a white diagonal "SAMPLE" notation on front and back.

NM/M
Complete Set (9): 6.00
Common Player: .50
16 Mickey Morandini .50
22US Wil Cordero (Upstart) (Card not included in most packs.) 2.00
119 Gary Sheffield 1.00
122 Ivan Rodriguez 1.50
132 Alex Rodriguez (Rookie) 3.00
208 Bo Jackson .75
223 Jose Rijo .50
224 Ryan Klesko .50
---- Header card .05

1995 Pinnacle

THOME

The 1995 Pinnacle set was produced in two series of 225 base cards each, plus inserts. Fronts have borderless photos with a large embossed gold foil "wave" at bottom containing the player's last name and team logo. Horizontal backs have a portrait photo at left, an action photo at right and a few sentences about the player at center. Stats at the bottom offer previous year, career and career-best numbers. Subsets with the base cards include rookie specials in both Series 1 and 2 have a design featuring a green stripe at one side or bottom with the player's name in gold and a special round gold-foil logo. A similar design, with red stripes, is used for Series 1 cards featuring Draft Picks. In Series 2, a 30-card Swing Men subset has a blue vortex background design and special gold-foil identifier. Basic pack configurations offered 12-card ($2.49) and 15-card

($2.99) counts in both retail and hobby versions, each with some unique inserts.

NM/M
Complete Set (450): 15.00
Common Player: .10
Artist's Proofs: 10X
Museum Collection: 4X
Hobby Pack (12): 1.00
Hobby Wax Box (24): 15.00
Retail Pack (12): 1.00
Retail Wax Box (36): 20.00
1 Jeff Bagwell .75
2 Roger Clemens 1.25
3 Mark Whiten .10
4 Shawon Dunston .10
5 Bobby Bonilla .10
6 Kevin Tapani .10
7 Eric Karros .10
8 Cliff Floyd .10
9 Pat Kelly .10
10 Jeffrey Hammonds .10
11 Jeff Conine .10
12 Fred McGriff .10
13 Chris Bosio .10
14 Mike Mussina .40
15 Danny Bautista .10
16 Mickey Morandini .10
17 Chuck Finley .10
18 Jim Thome .65
19 Luis Ortiz .10
20 Walt Weiss .10
21 Don Mattingly 1.25
22 Bob Hamelin .10
23 Melido Perez .10
24 Kevin Mitchell .10
25 John Smoltz .10
26 Hector Carrasco .10
27 Pat Hentgen .10
28 Derrick May .10
29 Mike Kingery .10
30 Chuck Carr .10
31 Billy Ashley .10
32 Todd Hundley .10
33 Luis Gonzalez .10
34 Marquis Grissom .10
35 Jeff King .10
36 Eddie Williams .10
37 Tom Pagnozzi .10
38 Chris Hoiles .10
39 Sandy Alomar .10
40 Mike Greenwell .10
41 Lance Johnson .10
42 Junior Felix .10
43 Felix Jose .10
44 Scott Leius .10
45 Ruben Sierra .10
46 Kevin Seitzer .10
47 Wade Boggs 1.00
48 Reggie Jefferson .10
49 Jose Canseco .40
50 Dave Justice .10
51 John Smiley .10
52 Joe Carter .10
53 Rick Wilkins .10
54 Ellis Burks .10
55 Dave Weathers .10
56 Pedro Astacio .10
57 Ryan Thompson .10
58 James Mouton .10
59 Mel Rojas .10
60 Orlando Merced .10
61 Matt Williams .10
62 Bernard Gilkey .10
63 J.R. Phillips .10
64 Lee Smith .10
65 Jim Edmonds .10
66 Darrin Jackson .10
67 Scott Cooper .10
68 Ron Karkovice .10
69 Chris Gomez .10
70 Kevin Appier .10
71 Bobby Jones .10
72 Doug Drabek .10
73 Matt Mieske .10
74 Sterling Hitchcock .10
75 John Valentin .10
76 Reggie Sanders .10
77 Wally Joyner .10
78 Turk Wendell .10
79 Wendell Hayes .10
80 Bret Barberie .10
81 Troy Neel .10
82 Ken Caminiti .10
83 Milt Thompson .10
84 Paul Sorrento .10'
85 Trevor Hoffman .10
86 Jay Bell .10
87 Mark Portugal .10
88 Sid Fernandez .10
89 Charles Nagy .10
90 Jeff Montgomery .10
91 Chuck Knoblauch .10
92 Jeff Frye .10
93 Tony Gwynn 1.00
94 John Olerud .10
95 David Nied .10
96 Chris Hammond .10
97 Edgar Martinez .10
98 Kevin Stocker .10
99 Jeff Fassero .10
100 Curt Schilling .30
101 Dave Clark .10
102 Delino DeShields .10
103 Leo Gomez .10
104 Dave Hollins .15
105 Tim Naehring .10

106 Otis Nixon .10
107 Ozzie Guillen .10
108 Jose Lind .10
109 Stan Javier .10
110 Greg Vaughn .10
111 Chipper Jones 1.00
112 Ed Sprague .10
113 Mike Macfarlane .10
114 Steve Finley .10
115 Ken Hill .10
116 Carlos Garcia .10
117 Lou Whitaker .10
118 Todd Zeile .10
119 Gary Sheffield .40
120 Ben McDonald .10
121 Pete Harnisch .10
122 Ivan Rodriguez .65
123 Wilson Alvarez .10
124 Travis Fryman .10
125 Pedro Munoz .10
126 Mark Lemke .10
127 Jose Valentin .10
128 Ken Griffey Jr. 1.50
129 Omar Vizquel .10
130 Milt Cuyler .10
131 Steve Traschel .10
132 Alex Rodriguez 2.00
133 Garret Anderson .10
134 Armando Benitez .10
135 Shawn Green .35
136 Jorge Fabregas .10
137 Orlando Miller .10
138 Rikkert Faneyte .10
139 Ismael Valdes .10
140 Jose Oliva .10
141 Aaron Small .10
142 Tim Davis .10
143 Ricky Bottalacio .10
144 Mike Matheny .10
145 Roberto Petagine .10
146 Fausto Cruz .10
147 Bryce Florie .10
148 Jose Lima .10
149 John Hudek .10
150 Duane Singleton .10
151 John Mabry .10
152 Robert Eenhoorn .10
153 Jon Lieber .10
154 Garey Ingram .10
155 Paul Shuey .10
156 Mike Lieberthal .10
157 Steve Dunn .10
158 Charles Johnson .10
159 Ernie Young .10
160 Jose Martinez .10
161 Kurt Miller .10
162 Joey Eischen .10
163 Dave Stevens .10
164 Brian Hunter .10
165 Jeff Cirillo .10
166 Mark Smith .10
167 McKay Christensen RC .10
168 C.J. Nitkowski RC .10
169 Antone Williamson RC .10
170 Paul Konerko RC .10
171 Scott Elarton RC .15
172 Jacob Shumate .10
173 Terrence Long .10
174 Mark Johnson RC .10
175 Ben Grieve .10
176 Jayson Peterson RC .10
177 Checklist .10
178 Checklist .10
179 Checklist .10
180 Checklist .10
181 Brian Anderson .10
182 Steve Buechele .10
183 Mark Clark .10
184 Cecil Fielder .10
185 Steve Avery .10
186 Devon White .10
187 Craig Shipley .10
188 Brady Anderson .10
189 Kenny Lofton .10
190 Alex Cole .10
191 Brent Gates .10
192 Dean Palmer .10
193 Alex Gonzalez .10
194 Steve Cooke .10
195 Ray Lankford .10
196 Mark McGwire 2.00
197 Marc Newfield .10
198 Pat Rapp .10
199 Darren Lewis .10
200 Carlos Baerga .10
201 Rickey Henderson .75
202 Kurt Abbott .10
203 Kirt Manwaring .10
204 Cal Ripken Jr. 2.50
205 Darren Daulton .10
206 Greg Colbrunn .10
207 Darryl Hamilton .10
208 Bo Jackson .10
209 Tony Phillips .10
210 Geronimo Berroa .10
211 Rich Becker .10
212 Tony Tarasco .10
213 Karl Rhodes .10
214 Phil Plantier .10
215 J.T. Snow .10
216 Mo Vaughn .10
217 Greg Gagne .10
218 Rickey Bones .10
219 Mike Bordick .10
220 Chad Curtis .10
221 Royce Clayton .10
222 Roberto Alomar .15
223 Jose Rijo .10

224 Ryan Klesko .10
225 Mark Langston .10
226 Frank Thomas .75
227 Juan Gonzalez .40
228 Ron Gant .10
229 Javier Lopez .10
230 Sammy Sosa 1.00
231 Kevin Brown .10
232 Gary DiSarcina .10
233 Albert Belle .10
234 Jay Buhner .10
235 Pedro Martinez .75
236 Bob Tewksbury .10
237 Mike Piazza 1.50
238 Darryl Kile .10
239 Bryan Harvey .10
240 Andres Galarraga .10
241 Jeff Blauser .10
242 Jeff Kent .10
243 Bobby Munoz .10
244 Greg Maddux 1.00
245 Paul O'Neill .10
246 Lenny Dykstra .10
247 Todd Van Poppel .10
248 Bernie Williams .05
249 Glenallen Hill .10
250 Duane Ward .10
251 Dennis Eckersley .60
252 Pat Mahomes .10
253 Rusty Greer (Photo actually Jeff Frye.) .10
254 Roberto Kelly .10
255 Randy Myers .10
256 Scott Ruffcorn .10
257 Robin Ventura .10
258 Eduardo Perez .10
259 Aaron Sele .10
260 Paul Molitor .75
261 Juan Guzman .10
262 Darren Oliver .10
263 Mike Stanley .10
264 Tom Glavine .30
265 Rico Brogna .10
266 Craig Biggio .10
267 Darrell Whitmore .10
268 Jimmy Key .10
269 Will Clark .10
270 David Cone .10
271 Brian Jordan .10
272 Barry Bonds 2.50
273 Danny Tartabull .10
274 Ramon Martinez .10
275 Al Martin .10
276 Fred McGriff (Swing Men) .10
277 Carlos Delgado (Swing Men) .25
278 Juan Gonzalez (Swing Men) .20
279 Shawn Green (Swing Men) .20
280 Carlos Baerga (Swing Men) .10
281 Cliff Floyd (Swing Men) .10
282 Ozzie Smith (Swing Men) .50
283 Alex Rodriguez (Swing Men) 1.00
284 Kenny Lofton (Swing Men) .10
285 Dave Justice (Swing Men) .10
286 Tim Salmon (Swing Men) .10
287 Manny Ramirez (Swing Men) .40
288 Will Clark (Swing Men) .10
289 Garret Anderson (Swing Men) .10
290 Billy Ashley (Swing Men) .10
291 Tony Gwynn (Swing Men) .50
292 Raul Mondesi (Swing Men) .10
293 Rafael Palmeiro (Swing Men) .30
294 Matt Williams (Swing Men) .10
295 Don Mattingly (Swing Men) .60
296 Kirby Puckett (Swing Men) .50
297 Paul Molitor (Swing Men) .40
298 Albert Belle (Swing Men) .10
299 Barry Bonds (Swing Men) 1.25
300 Mike Piazza (Swing Men) .85
301 Jeff Bagwell (Swing Men) .40
302 Frank Thomas (Swing Men) .40
303 Chipper Jones (Swing Men) .50
304 Ken Griffey Jr. (Swing Men) .75
305 Cal Ripken Jr. (Swing Men) 1.25
306 Eric Anthony .10
307 Todd Benzinger .10
308 Jacob Brumfield .10
309 Wes Chamberlain .10
310 Tino Martinez .10
311 Roberto Mejia .10
312 Jose Offerman .10
313 David Segui .10
314 Eric Young .10
315 Rey Sanchez .10
316 Raul Mondesi .10
317 Bret Boone .10
318 Andre Dawson .30
319 Brian McRae .10
320 Dave Nilsson .10
321 Moises Alou .10
322 Don Slaught .10

323 Dave McCarty .10
324 Mike Huff .10
325 Rick Aguilera .10
326 Rod Beck .10
327 Kenny Rogers .10
328 Andy Benes .10
329 Allen Watson .10
330 Randy Johnson .75
331 Willie Greene .10
332 Hal Morris .10
333 Ozzie Smith 1.00
334 Jason Bere .10
335 Scott Erickson .10
336 Dante Bichette .10
337 Willie Banks .10
338 Eric Davis .10
339 Rondell White .10
340 Kirby Puckett 1.00
341 Deion Sanders .10
342 Eddie Murray .75
343 Mike Harkey .10
344 Joey Hamilton .10
345 Roger Salkeld .10
346 Wil Cordero .10
347 John Wetteland .10
348 Geronimo Pena .10
349 Kirk Gibson .10
350 Manny Ramirez .75
351 William Van Landingham .10
352 B.J. Surhoff .10
353 Ken Ryan .10
354 Terry Steinbach .10
355 Bret Saberhagen .10
356 John Jaha .10
357 Joe Girardi .10
358 Steve Karsay .10
359 Alex Fernandez .10
360 Salomon Torres .10
361 John Burkett .10
362 Derek Bell .10
363 Tom Henke .10
364 Gregg Jefferies .10
365 Jack McDowell .10
366 Andujar Cedeno .10
367 Dave Winfield .75
368 Carl Everett .10
369 Danny Jackson .10
370 Jeromy Burnitz .10
371 Mark Grace .10
372 Larry Walker .10
373 Bill Swift .10
374 Dennis Martinez .10
375 Mickey Tettleton .10
376 Mel Nieves .10
377 Cal Eldred .10
378 Orel Hershiser .10
379 David Wells .10
380 Gary Gaetti .10
381 Tim Raines .10
382 Barry Larkin .10
383 Jason Jacome .10
384 Tim Wallach .10
385 Robby Thompson .10
386 Frank Viola .10
387 Dave Stewart .10
388 Bip Roberts .10
389 Ron Darling .10
390 Carlos Delgado .45
391 Tim Salmon .10
392 Alan Trammell .10
393 Kevin Foster .10
394 Jim Abbott .10
395 John Kruk .10
396 Andy Van Slyke .10
397 Dave Magadan .10
398 Rafael Palmeiro .65
399 Mike Devereaux .10
400 Benito Santiago .10
401 Brett Butler .10
402 John Franco .10
403 Matt Walbeck .10
404 Terry Pendleton .10
405 Chris Sabo .10
406 Andrew Lorraine .10
407 Dan Wilson .10
408 Mike Lansing .10
409 Ray McDavid .10
410 Shane Andrews .10
411 Tom Gordon .10
412 Chad Ogea .10
413 James Baldwin .10
414 Russ Davis .10
415 Ray Holbert .10
416 Ray Durham .10
417 Matt Nokes .10
418 Rodney Henderson .10
419 Gabe White .10
420 Todd Hollandsworth .10
421 Midre Cummings .10
422 Harold Baines .10
423 Troy Percival .10
424 Joe Vitiello .10
425 Andy Ashby .10
426 Michael Tucker .10
427 Mark Gubicza .10
428 Jim Bullinger .10
429 Jose Malave .10
430 Pete Schourek .10
431 Bobby Ayala .10
432 Marvin Freeman .10
433 Pat Listach .10
434 Eddie Taubensee .10
435 Steve Howe .10
436 Kent Mercker .10
437 Hector Fajardo .10
438 Scott Kamieniecki .10
439 Robb Nen .10
440 Mike Kelly .10

441 Tom Candiotti .10
442 Albie Lopez .10
443 Jeff Granger .10
444 Rich Aude .10
445 Luis Polonia .10
446 A.L. Checklist (Frank Thomas) .40
447 A.L. Checklist (Ken Griffey Jr.) .65
448 N.L. Checklist (Mike Piazza) .75
449 N.L. Checklist (Jeff Bagwell) .40
450 Insert Checklist (Frank Thomas, Ken Griffey Jr., Mike Piazza, Jeff Bagwell) .40

Artist's Proof

ASTACIO

Said to represent the first 1,000 of each card printed, the Artist's Proof chase set is a parallel issue with a counterpart for each of the regular-issue cards. The proofs differ in the use of silver, rather than gold foil for front graphic highlights, and the inclusion of a rectangular silver-foil "ARTIST'S PROOF" logo on front. The AP inserts were reported seeded at an average rate of one per 26 packs.

NM/M
Complete Set (450): 300.00
Common Player: 1.00
Stars/Rookies: 10X

Museum Collection

HAMILTON

Pinnacle's Dufex foil-printing technology on the card fronts differentiates this parallel insert from the corresponding cards in the regular issue. Backs have a rectangular "1995 Museum Collection" logo at lower-left. Museum inserts are found at an average rate of one per four packs. Because of production difficulties, trade cards had to be issued in place of seven of the rookie cards in Series 2. Those redemption cards were valid only through Dec. 31, 1995.

NM/M
Complete Set (450): 200.00
Common Player: .50
Stars/Rookies: 4X
Redemption Card .25

E.T.A. '95

JOE VITIELLO
ETA95

This hobby-only chase set identifies six players picked to arrive in the major leagues for a 1995 debut. Both sides have borderless action photos on which the background has been subdued and posterized. Gold-foil headlines on each side of the card give the player's credentials. These inserts are found on average of once per 24 packs.

		NM/M
Complete Set (6):		5.00
Common Player:		.70
1	Ben Grieve	.75
2	Alex Ochoa	.75
3	Joe Vitiello	.75
4	Johnny Damon	3.00
5	Trey Beamon	.75
6	Brooks Kieschnick	.75

Gate Attraction

Series 2 jumbo packs are the exclusive source for this chase set. Printed on metallic foil, the cards have a color photo at top and a second photo at bottom that is shown in gold tones only. A "Gate Attraction" seal is in the lower-left corner. Backs have a large portrait photo on a color-streaked background, plus a few words about the player.

		NM/M
Complete Set (18):		25.00
Common Player:		.50
1	Ken Griffey Jr.	3.50
2	Frank Thomas	1.50
3	Cal Ripken Jr.	5.00
4	Jeff Bagwell	1.50
5	Mike Piazza	3.50
6	Barry Bonds	5.00
7	Kirby Puckett	2.00
8	Albert Belle	.50
9	Tony Gwynn	2.00
10	Raul Mondesi	.50
11	Will Clark	.50
12	Don Mattingly	2.75
13	Roger Clemens	2.75
14	Paul Molitor	1.50
15	Matt Williams	.50
16	Greg Maddux	2.00
17	Kenny Lofton	.50
18	Cliff Floyd	.50

New Blood

Both hobby and retail packs of Series 2 hide this insert set of young stars, at an average rate of one card per 90 packs. A player photo appears in the red and silver foil-printed background, and there is a color action photo in the foreground. Conventionally printed backs feature the same photos, but with their prominence reversed. A few words of text describe the player's star potential.

		NM/M
Complete Set (9):		10.00
Common Player:		.75
1	Alex Rodriguez	5.00
2	Shawn Green	1.50
3	Brian Hunter	.75
4	Garret Anderson	.75
5	Charles Johnson	.75
6	Chipper Jones	3.00
7	Carlos Delgado	1.50

8	Billy Ashley	.75
9	J.R. Phillips	.75

Performers

Series 1 jumbos were the only place to find this chase set. Fronts have a deep red background with a golden pyramid at center and a silver apex, all in foil printing. A color player action photo is in the center foreground. The reverse repeats the front photo in the background, in one color, and has a second color photo, along with a few words about the player.

		NM/M
Complete Set (18):		15.00
Common Player:		.35
1	Frank Thomas	2.00
2	Albert Belle	.35
3	Barry Bonds	3.50
4	Juan Gonzalez	1.00
5	Andres Galarraga	.35
6	Raul Mondesi	.35
7	Paul Molitor	2.00
8	Tim Salmon	.35
9	Mike Piazza	2.50
10	Gregg Jefferies	.35
11	Will Clark	.35
12	Greg Maddux	2.25
13	Manny Ramirez	2.00
14	Kirby Puckett	2.25
15	Shawn Green	1.25
16	Rafael Palmeiro	1.75
17	Paul O'Neill	.35
18	Jason Bere	.35

Red Hot

These Series 2 inserts are found at an average rate of one per 16 packs and feature top veteran stars. Fronts have a large action photo on right, over a background of foil-printed red and yellow flames. A vertical strip at left of graduated red tones has a player portrait photo and the "RED HOT" flame logo, again printed in foil. Backs are conventionally printed and have a black background with large flaming "RED HOT" letters and a color player photo.

		NM/M
Complete Set (25):		35.00
Common Player:		.75
1	Cal Ripken Jr.	5.50
2	Ken Griffey Jr.	4.00
3	Frank Thomas	1.50
4	Jeff Bagwell	1.50
5	Mike Piazza	4.00
6	Barry Bonds	5.50
7	Albert Belle	.75
8	Tony Gwynn	2.00
9	Kirby Puckett	2.00
10	Don Mattingly	2.50
11	Matt Williams	.75
12	Greg Maddux	2.50
13	Raul Mondesi	.75
14	Paul Molitor	1.50
15	Manny Ramirez	1.50
16	Joe Carter	.75
17	Will Clark	.75
18	Roger Clemens	2.50
19	Tim Salmon	.75
20	Dave Justice	.75

21	Kenny Lofton	.75
22	Deion Sanders	.75
23	Roberto Alomar	1.00
24	Cliff Floyd	.75
25	Carlos Baerga	.75

White Hot

Similar in format to the Red Hot inserts, and featuring the same players, the hobby-only White Hot cards are a chase set of a chase set. Seeded once per 36 packs on average (more than twice as scarce as the Red Hots), the White Hot cards have fronts totally printed in the Dufex process, with predominantly blue and white background colors, while the backs are highlighted by blue foil printing in the "WHITE HOT" background lettering on black background.

		NM/M
Complete Set (25):		140.00
Common Player:		2.50
1	Cal Ripken Jr.	16.00
2	Ken Griffey Jr.	13.50
3	Frank Thomas	8.00
4	Jeff Bagwell	8.00
5	Mike Piazza	13.50
6	Barry Bonds	16.00
7	Albert Belle	2.50
8	Tony Gwynn	10.00
9	Kirby Puckett	10.00
10	Don Mattingly	12.00
11	Matt Williams	2.50
12	Greg Maddux	10.00
13	Raul Mondesi	2.50
14	Paul Molitor	8.00
15	Manny Ramirez	8.00
16	Joe Carter	2.50
17	Will Clark	2.50
18	Roger Clemens	12.00
19	Tim Salmon	2.50
20	Dave Justice	2.50
21	Kenny Lofton	2.50
22	Deion Sanders	2.50
23	Roberto Alomar	3.50
24	Cliff Floyd	2.50
25	Carlos Baerga	2.50

Team Pinnacle

This nine-card Series 1 insert set becomes an 18-card challenge if the collector decides to hunt for both versions of each card. As in the past the Team Pinnacle cards picture National and American League counterparts at each position on different sides of the same card. In 1995 each card is printed with one side in Pinnacle's Dufex foil technology, and the other side conventionally printed. Thus card #1 can be found with Mike Mussina in Dufex and Greg Maddux conventionally printed, or with Maddux in Dufex and Mussina conventional. Team Pinnacle cards are found inserted at an average rate of only one per 90 packs. Card numbers have a "TP" prefix.

		NM/M
Complete Set (9):		35.00

Common Player:		1.50
1	Mike Mussina,	
	Greg Maddux	8.00
2	Carlos Delgado,	
	Mike Piazza	6.00
3	Frank Thomas,	
	Jeff Bagwell	4.00
4	Roberto Alomar,	
	Craig Biggio	3.00
5	Cal Ripken Jr.,	
	Ozzie Smith	12.00
6	Travis Fryman,	
	Matt Williams	1.50
7	Ken Griffey Jr.,	
	Barry Bonds	10.00
8	Albert Belle, Dave Justice	1.50
9	Kirby Puckett,	
	Tony Gwynn	8.00

Team Pinnacle Pin Trade Cards

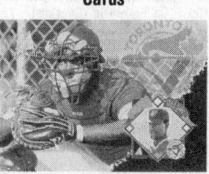

In one of the hobby's first major attempts to cross-promote pin- and card-collecting, Series 2 Pinnacle packs offered a special insert set of cards which could be redeemed for a collector's pin of the same player. Seeded at the rate of one per 48 regular packs and one per 36 jumbo packs, the pin redemption cards were valid until Nov. 15, 1995. Payment of $2 handling fee was required for redemption.

		NM/M
Complete Set (18):		40.00
Common Player:		.75
1	Greg Maddux	4.00
2	Mike Mussina	1.50
3	Mike Piazza	5.00
4	Carlos Delgado	1.50
5	Jeff Bagwell	3.00
6	Frank Thomas	3.00
7	Craig Biggio	.75
8	Roberto Alomar	1.00
9	Ozzie Smith	4.00
10	Cal Ripken Jr.	6.00
11	Matt Williams	.75
12	Travis Fryman	.75
13	Barry Bonds	6.00
14	Ken Griffey Jr.	6.00
15	Dave Justice	.75
16	Albert Belle	.75
17	Tony Gwynn	4.00
18	Kirby Puckett	4.00

Team Pinnacle Collector Pins

Redemption cards in Series 2 packs could be traded in (until Nov. 15, 1995) for an enameled pin of the player pictured on the trade card. Pins are about 1-3/8" x 1-1/4". A raised relief portrait of the player is at center with his name in pennants above and his team logo at bottom, along with the Pinnacle logo. Backs are gold-tone with a post-and-button style of pinback. The unnumbered pins are listed here in the same sequence as the redemption cards.

		NM/M
Complete Set (18):		135.00
Common Player:		5.00
(1)	Greg Maddux	10.00
(2)	Mike Mussina	6.00
(3)	Mike Piazza	8.00
(4)	Carlos Delgado	6.00
(5)	Jeff Bagwell	8.00
(6)	Frank Thomas	5.00
(7)	Craig Biggio	5.00
(8)	Roberto Alomar	6.00
(9)	Ozzie Smith	10.00
(10)	Cal Ripken Jr.	20.00
(11)	Matt Williams	5.00
(12)	Travis Fryman	5.00
(13)	Barry Bonds	20.00
(14)	Ken Griffey Jr.	15.00
(15)	Dave Justice	5.00
(16)	Albert Belle	5.00
(17)	Tony Gwynn	10.00
(18)	Kirby Puckett	10.00

Pin-Cards

Virtually nothing is known of this issue except that it is connected in some way to the Series 2 Pinnacle player pin issue. The front features portrait and action photos on a red background with gold-foil graphics. Backs have career highlights, a large color photo and a card number with "PPC" prefix. To date only a single card is known.

Upstarts

The most dominant young players in the game were featured in this insert series. Cards are printed with most of the photo's background covered by the legs of a large blue-and-gold star device, which includes the team logo at its red center. A blue circular "'95 UPSTARTS" logo at bottom-left has the player name in gold. These cards are exclusive to Series 1, found at an average rate of one per eight packs.

		NM/M
Complete Set (30):		10.00
Common Player:		.15
1	Frank Thomas	1.50
2	Roberto Alomar	.30
3	Mike Piazza	2.50
4	Javier Lopez	.15
5	Albert Belle	.15
6	Carlos Delgado	.75
7	Rusty Greer	.15
8	Tim Salmon	.15
9	Raul Mondesi	.15
10	Juan Gonzalez	.75
11	Manny Ramirez	1.50
12	Sammy Sosa	2.00
13	Jeff Kent	.15
14	Melvin Nieves	.15
15	Rondell White	.75
16	Shawn Green	.75
17	Bernie Williams	.15
18	Aaron Sele	.15
19	Jason Bere	.15
20	Joey Hamilton	.15
21	Mike Kelly	.15
22	Wil Cordero	.15
23	Moises Alou	.15
24	Roberto Kelly	.15
25	Deion Sanders	.15
26	Steve Karsay	.15
27	Bret Boone	.15
28	Willie Greene	.15
29	Billy Ashley	.15
30	Brian Anderson	.15

FanFest

Pinnacle's sponsorship of the July 7-11 All-Star FanFest was marked with the issue of this set. Cards were distributed in two-card packs at various venues around the All-Star celebration in Arlington, Texas. Each card features the FanFest logo at lower-left on front, with the player's name and team logo in a stylized gold-foil baseball diamond at lower-right. A

full-bleed action photo comprises the rest of the front. Horizontal backs show a portrait photo of the player before a photo of The Ballpark at Arlington. The FanFast logo is repeated at bottom-center.

		NM/M
Complete Set (30):		7.50
Common Player:		.15
1	Cal Ripken Jr.	1.50
2	Roger Clemens	.75
3	Don Mattingly	.75
4	Albert Belle	.15
5	Kirby Puckett	.65
6	Cecil Fielder	.15
7	Kevin Appier	.15
8	Will Clark	.15
9	Juan Gonzalez	.25
10	Ivan Rodriguez	.45
11	Ken Griffey Jr.	1.00
12	Tim Salmon	.15
13	Frank Thomas	.50
14	Roberto Alomar	.20
15	Rickey Henderson	.50
16	Raul Mondesi	.15
17	Matt Williams	.15
18	Ozzie Smith	.65
19	Deion Sanders	.15
20	Tony Gwynn	.65
21	Greg Maddux	.65
22	Sammy Sosa	.65
23	Mike Piazza	1.00
24	Barry Bonds	1.50
25	Jeff Bagwell	.50
26	Len Dykstra	.15
27	Rico Brogna	.15
28	Larry Walker	.15
29	Gary Sheffield	.35
30	Wil Cordero	.15

1996 Pinnacle Samples

Pinnacle's 1996 issue was premiered with this nine-card sample set. The cards are virtually identical in format to the regular-issue cards, but feature a large white "SAMPLE" printed diagonally on front and back. The cards were sent to dealers and hobby media in a cello pack.

		NM/M
Complete Set (9):		5.00
Common Player:		.75
1	Greg Maddux	1.50
2	Bill Pulsipher	.75
3	Dante Bichette	.75
4*	Mike Piazza	2.00
5	Garret Anderson	.75
165	Ruben Rivera	.75
168	Tony Clark	.75
2	Mo Vaughn	
	(Pinnacle Power)	1.00
---	Header Card	.10

1996 Pinnacle

Pinnacle's 400-card regular-issue set has borderless front photos highlighted by prismatic gold-foil graphics in a triangle at bottom. Backs have another photo along with stats and data. Parallel Starburst and Starburst Artist's Proof sets contain only 200 of the cards in the base issue. Series 1 inserts include a Cal Ripken Jr. "Tribute" card,

RUBEN RIVERA

numbered "1 of 1," along with Team Pinnacle, Pinnacle Power, Team Tomorrow, Essence of the Game and First Rate. Series 2 inserts are Christie Brinkley Collection, Project Stardom, Skylines, Slugfest and Team Spirit. Pinnacle was sold in 10-card hobby and retail foil packs, and 18-card jumbo packs.

	NM/M
Complete Set (400):	15.00
Common Player:	.10
Series 1 or 2 Pack (10):	.75
Series 1 or 2 Box (24):	15.00

#	Player	Price
1	Greg Maddux	1.00
2	Bill Pulsipher	.10
3	Dante Bichette	.10
4	Mike Piazza	1.50
5	Garret Anderson	.10
6	Steve Finley	.10
7	Andy Benes	.10
8	Chuck Knoblauch	.10
9	Tom Gordon	.10
10	Jeff Bagwell	.75
11	Wil Cordero	.10
12	John Mabry	.10
13	Jeff Frye	.10
14	Travis Fryman	.10
15	John Wetteland	.10
16	Jason Bates	.10
17	Danny Tartabull	.10
18	Charles Nagy	.10
19	Robin Ventura	.10
20	Reggie Sanders	.10
21	Dave Clark	.10
22	Jaime Navarro	.10
23	Joey Hamilton	.10
24	Al Leiter	.10
25	Deion Sanders	.10
26	Tim Salmon	.10
27	Tino Martinez	.10
28	Mike Greenwell	.10
29	Phil Plantier	.10
30	Bobby Bonilla	.10
31	Kenny Rogers	.10
32	Chili Davis	.10
33	Joe Carter	.10
34	Mike Mussina	.40
35	Matt Mieske	.10
36	Jose Canseco	.40
37	Brad Radke	.10
38	Juan Gonzalez	.40
39	David Segui	.10
40	Alex Fernandez	.10
41	Jeff Kent	.10
42	Todd Zeile	.10
43	Darryl Strawberry	.10
44	Jose Rijo	.10
45	Ramon Martinez	.10
46	Manny Ramirez	.75
47	Gregg Jefferies	.10
48	Bryan Rekar	.10
49	Jeff King	.10
50	John Olerud	.10
51	Marc Newfield	.10
52	Charles Johnson	.10
53	Robby Thompson	.10
54	Brian Hunter	.10
55	Mike Blowers	.10
56	Keith Lockhart	.10
57	Ray Lankford	.10
58	Tim Wallach	.10
59	Ivan Rodriguez	.65
60	Ed Sprague	.10
61	Paul Molitor	.75
62	Eric Karros	.10
63	Glenallen Hill	.10
64	Jay Bell	.10
65	Tom Pagnozzi	.10
66	Greg Colbrunn	.10
67	Edgar Martinez	.10
68	Paul Sorrento	.10
69	Kirt Manwaring	.10
70	Pete Schourek	.10
71	Orlando Merced	.10
72	Shawon Dunston	.10
73	Ricky Bottalico	.10
74	Brady Anderson	.10
75	Steve Ontiveros	.10
76	Jim Abbott	.10
77	Carl Everett	.10
78	Mo Vaughn	.10
79	Pedro Martinez	.75
80	Harold Baines	.10
81	Alan Trammell	.10
82	Steve Avery	.10
83	Jeff Cirillo	.10
84	John Valentin	.10
85	Bernie Williams	.10
86	Andre Dawson	.30
87	Dave Winfield	.75
88	B.J. Surhoff	.10
89	Jeff Blauser	.10
90	Barry Larkin	.10
91	Cliff Floyd	.10
92	Sammy Sosa	1.00
93	Andres Galarraga	.10
94	Dave Nilsson	.10
95	James Mouton	.10
96	Marquis Grissom	.10
97	Matt Williams	.10
98	John Jaha	.10
99	Don Mattingly	1.25
100	Tim Naehring	.10
101	Kevin Appier	.10
102	Bobby Higginson	.10
103	Andy Pettitte	.25
104	Ozzie Smith	.10
105	Kenny Lofton	.10
106	Ken Caminiti	.10
107	Walt Weiss	.10
108	Jack McDowell	.10
109	Brian McRae	.10
110	Gary Gaetti	.10
111	Curtis Goodwin	.10
112	Dennis Martinez	.10
113	Omar Vizquel	.10
114	Chipper Jones	1.00
115	Mark Gubicza	.10
116	Ruben Sierra	.10
117	Eddie Murray	.75
118	Chad Curtis	.10
119	Hal Morris	.10
120	Ben McDonald	.10
121	Marty Cordova	.10
122	Ken Griffey Jr.	1.50
123	Gary Sheffield	.40
124	Charlie Hayes	.10
125	Shawn Green	.40
126	Jason Giambi	.50
127	Mark Langston	.10
128	Mark Whiten	.10
129	Greg Vaughn	.10
130	Mark McGwire	1.75
131	Hideo Nomo	.40
132	Eric Karros, Raul Mondesi, Hideo Nomo, Mike Piazza	.10
133	Jason Bere	.10
134	Ken Griffey Jr. (The Naturals)	.65
135	Frank Thomas (The Naturals)	.40
136	Cal Ripken Jr. (The Naturals)	1.00
137	Albert Belle (The Naturals)	.10
138	Mike Piazza (The Naturals)	.65
139	Dante Bichette (The Naturals)	.10
140	Sammy Sosa (The Naturals)	.50
141	Mo Vaughn (The Naturals)	.10
142	Tim Salmon (The Naturals)	.10
143	Reggie Sanders (The Naturals)	.10
144	Cecil Fielder (The Naturals)	.10
145	Jim Edmonds (The Naturals)	.10
146	Rafael Palmeiro (The Naturals)	.10
147	Edgar Martinez (The Naturals)	.10
148	Barry Bonds (The Naturals)	1.00
149	Manny Ramirez (The Naturals)	.35
150	Larry Walker (The Naturals)	.10
151	Jeff Bagwell (The Naturals)	.35
152	Ron Gant (The Naturals)	.10
153	Andres Galarraga (The Naturals)	.10
154	Eddie Murray (The Naturals)	.35
155	Kirby Puckett (The Naturals)	.50
156	Will Clark (The Naturals)	.10
157	Don Mattingly (The Naturals)	.60
158	Mark McGwire (The Naturals)	.75
159	Dean Palmer (The Naturals)	.10
160	Matt Williams (The Naturals)	.10
161	Fred McGriff (The Naturals)	.10
162	Joe Carter (The Naturals)	.10
163	Juan Gonzalez (The Naturals)	.15
164	Alex Ochoa	.10
165	Ruben Rivera	.10
166	Tony Clark	.10
167	Brian Barber	.10
168	Matt Lawton	.10
169	Terrell Wade	.10
170	Johnny Damon	.30
171	Derek Jeter	2.00
172	Phil Nevin	.10
173	Robert Perez	.10
174	C.J. Nitkowski	.10
175	Joe Vitiello	.10
176	Roger Cedeno	.10
177	Ron Coomer	.10
178	Chris Widger	.10
179	Jimmy Haynes	.10
180	Mike Sweeney RC	.50
181	Howard Battle	.10
182	John Wasdin	.10
183	Jim Pittsley	.10
184	Bob Wolcott	.10
185	LaTroy Hawkins	.10
186	Nigel Wilson	.10
187	Dustin Hermanson	.10
188	Chris Snopek	.10
189	Mariano Rivera	.15
190	Jose Herrera	.10
191	Chris Stynes	.10
192	Larry Thomas	.10
193	David Bell	.10
194	Frank Thomas (Checklist)	.40
195	Ken Griffey Jr. (Checklist)	.65
196	Cal Ripken Jr. (Checklist)	.75
197	Jeff Bagwell (Checklist)	.35
198	Mike Piazza (Checklist)	.60
199	Barry Bonds (Checklist)	.75
200	Garret Anderson, Chipper Jones (Checklist)	.25
201	Frank Thomas	.75
202	Michael Tucker	.10
203	Kirby Puckett	1.00
204	Alex Gonzalez	.10
205	Tony Gwynn	1.00
206	Moises Alou	.10
207	Albert Belle	.10
208	Barry Bonds	2.00
209	Fred McGriff	.10
210	Dennis Eckersley	.65
211	Craig Biggio	.10
212	David Cone	.10
213	Will Clark	.10
214	Cal Ripken Jr.	2.00
215	Wade Boggs	1.00
216	Pete Schourek	.10
217	Darren Daulton	.10
218	Carlos Baerga	.10
219	Larry Walker	.10
220	Denny Neagle	.10
221	Jim Edmonds	.10
222	Lee Smith	.10
223	Jason Isringhausen	.10
224	Jay Buhner	.10
225	John Olerud	.10
226	Jeff Conine	.10
227	Dean Palmer	.10
228	Jim Abbott	.10
229	Raul Mondesi	.10
230	Tom Glavine	.35
231	Kevin Seitzer	.10
232	Lenny Dykstra	.10
233	Brian Jordan	.10
234	Rondell White	.10
235	Bret Boone	.10
236	Randy Johnson	.75
237	Paul O'Neill	.10
238	Jim Thome	.65
239	Edgardo Alfonzo	.10
240	Terry Pendleton	.10
241	Harold Baines	.10
242	Roberto Alomar	.20
243	Mark Grace	.10
244	Derek Bell	.10
245	Vinny Castilla	.10
246	Cecil Fielder	.10
247	Roger Clemens	1.25
248	Orel Hershiser	.10
249	J.T. Snow	.10
250	Rafael Palmeiro	.65
251	Bret Saberhagen	.10
252	Todd Hollandsworth	.10
253	Ryan Klesko	.10
254	Greg Maddux (Hardball Heroes)	.50
255	Ken Griffey Jr. (Hardball Heroes)	.65
256	Hideo Nomo (Hardball Heroes)	.15
257	Frank Thomas (Hardball Heroes)	.40
258	Cal Ripken Jr. (Hardball Heroes)	1.00
259	Jeff Bagwell (Hardball Heroes)	.35
260	Barry Bonds (Hardball Heroes)	1.00
261	Mo Vaughn (Hardball Heroes)	.10
262	Albert Belle (Hardball Heroes)	.10
263	Sammy Sosa (Hardball Heroes)	.50
264	Reggie Sanders (Hardball Heroes)	.10
265	Mike Piazza (Hardball Heroes)	.65
266	Chipper Jones (Hardball Heroes)	.50
267	Tony Gwynn (Hardball Heroes)	.50
268	Kirby Puckett (Hardball Heroes)	.50
269	Wade Boggs (Hardball Heroes)	.45
270	Will Clark (Hardball Heroes)	.10
271	Gary Sheffield (Hardball Heroes)	.10
272	Dante Bichette (Hardball Heroes)	.10
273	Randy Johnson (Hardball Heroes)	.35
274	Matt Williams (Hardball Heroes)	.10
275	Alex Rodriguez (Hardball Heroes)	.75
276	Tim Salmon (Hardball Heroes)	.10
277	Johnny Damon (Hardball Heroes)	.10
278	Manny Ramirez (Hardball Heroes)	.35
279	Derek Jeter (Hardball Heroes)	1.00
280	Eddie Murray (Hardball Heroes)	.35
281	Ozzie Smith (Hardball Heroes)	.35
282	Garret Anderson (Hardball Heroes)	.10
283	Raul Mondesi (Hardball Heroes)	.10
284	Terry Steinbach	.10
285	Carlos Garcia	.10
286	Dave Justice	.10
287	Eric Anthony	.10
288	Benji Gil	.10
289	Bob Hamelin	.10
290	Dwayne Hosey	.10
291	Andy Pettitte	.25
292	Rod Beck	.10
293	Shane Andrews	.10
294	Julian Tavarez	.10
295	Willie Greene	.10
296	Ismael Valdes	.10
297	Glenallen Hill	.10
298	Troy Percival	.10
299	Ray Durham	.10
300	Jeff Conine (.300 Series)	.10
301.8	Ken Griffey Jr. (.300 Series)	.75
302	Will Clark (.300 Series)	.10
303	Mike Greenwell (.300 Series)	.10
304.9	Carlos Baerga (.300 Series)	.10
305.3	Paul Molitor (.300 Series)	.35
305.6	Jeff Bagwell (.300 Series)	.35
306	Mark Grace (.300 Series)	.10
307	Don Mattingly (.300 Series)	.60
308	Hal Morris (.300 Series)	.10
309	Butch Huskey	.10
310	Ozzie Guillen	.10
311	Erik Hanson	.10
312	Kenny Lofton (.300 Series)	.10
313	Edgar Martinez (.300 Series)	.10
314	Kurt Abbott	.10
315	John Smoltz	.10
316	Ariel Prieto	.10
317	Mark Carreon	.10
318	Kirby Puckett (.300 Series)	.50
319	Carlos Perez	.10
320	Gary DiSarcina	.10
321	Trevor Hoffman	.10
322	Mike Piazza (.300 Series)	.65
323	Frank Thomas (.300 Series)	.40
324	Juan Acevedo	.10
325	Bip Roberts	.10
326	Javier Lopez	.10
327	Benito Santiago	.10
328	Mark Lewis	.10
329	Royce Clayton	.10
330	Tom Gordon	.10
331	Ben McDonald	.10
332	Dan Wilson	.10
333	Ron Gant	.10
334	Wade Boggs (.300 Series)	.45
335	Paul Molitor	.75
336	Tony Gwynn (.300 Series)	.50
337	Sean Berry	.10
338	Rickey Henderson	.35
339	Wil Cordero	.10
340	Kent Mercker	.10
341	Kenny Rogers	.10
342	Ryne Sandberg	1.00
343	Charlie Hayes	.10
344	Andy Benes	.10
345	Sterling Hitchcock	.10
346	Bernard Gilkey	.10
347	Julio Franco	.10
348	Ken Hill	.10
349	Russ Davis	.10
350	Mike Blowers	.10
351	B.J. Surhoff	.10
352	Lance Johnson	.10
353	Darryl Hamilton	.10
354	Shawon Dunston	.10
355	Rick Aguilera	.10
356	Danny Tartabull	.10
357	Todd Stottlemyre	.10
358	Mike Bordick	.10
359	Jack McDowell	.10
360	Todd Zeile	.10
361	Tino Martinez	.10
362	Greg Gagne	.10
363	Mike Kelly	.10
364	Tim Raines	.10
365	Ernie Young	.10
366	Mike Stanley	.10
367	Wally Joyner	.10
368	Karim Garcia	.10
369	Paul Wilson	.10
370	Sal Fasano	.10
371	Jason Schmidt	.10
372	Livan Hernandez RC	.25
373	George Arias	.10
374	Steve Gibralter	.10
375	Jermaine Dye	.10
376	Jason Kendall	.10
377	Brooks Kieschnick	.10
378	Jeff Ware	.10
379	Alan Benes	.10
380	Rey Ordonez	.10
381	Jay Powell	.10
382	Osvaldo Fernandez RC	.15
383	Wilton Guerrero RC	.10
384	Eric Owens	.10
385	George Williams	.10
386	Chan Ho Park	.10
387	Jeff Suppan	.10
388	F.P. Santangelo RC	.10
389	Terry Adams	.10
390	Bob Abreu	.10
391	Quinton McCracken RC	.10
392	Mike Busby RC	.10
393	Cal Ripken Jr. (Checklist)	.75
394	Ken Griffey Jr. (Checklist)	.60
395	Frank Thomas (Checklist)	.40
396	Chipper Jones (Checklist)	.50
397	Greg Maddux (Checklist)	.50
398	Mike Piazza (Checklist)	.65
399	Ken Griffey Jr., Frank Thomas, Cal Ripken Jr., Greg Maddux, Chipper Jones, Mike Piazza (Checklist)	.50

Artist's Proof

AP is a parallel to the Starburst partial parallel of '96 Pinnacle. Like Starburst, the Artist's Proof cards are printed in Dufex technology on front, with the AP cards having the words "ARTIST'S PROOF" repeated throughout the background. AP backs are identical to Starburst. Stated insertion rate for the Artist's Proofs was one per 47 packs in hobby and one per 67 retail packs.

	NM/M
Common Artist's Proof:	2.00
Stars:	3X

Starburst

PETE SCHOUREK

For 1996 Pinnacle abbreviated its parallel insert set to just half of the cards from the base issue. Only 200 select players are included in the Starburst Dufex-printed parallel set found on average of once per seven hobby packs and once per 10 retail packs.

	NM/M
Complete Set (200):	150.00
Common Player:	.40
Common Artist's Proof:	.75
Artist's Proofs:	2X

#	Player	Price
1	Greg Maddux	3.00
2	Bill Pulsipher	.40
3	Dante Bichette	.40
4	Mike Piazza	4.00
5	Garret Anderson	.40
6	Chuck Knoblauch	.40
7	Jeff Bagwell	2.25
8	Wil Cordero	.40
9	Travis Fryman	.40
10	Reggie Sanders	.40
11	Deion Sanders	.40
12	Tim Salmon	.40
13	Tino Martinez	.40
14	Bobby Bonilla	.40
15	Joe Carter	.40
16	Mike Mussina	1.25
17	Jose Canseco	1.25
18	Manny Ramirez	2.25
19	Gregg Jefferies	.40
20	Charles Johnson	.40
21	Brian Hunter	.40
22	Ray Lankford	.40
23	Ivan Rodriguez	2.00
24	Paul Molitor	2.25
25	Eric Karros	.40
26	Edgar Martinez	.40
27	Shawon Dunston	.40
28	Mo Vaughn	.40
29	Pedro Martinez	2.25
30	Marty Cordova	.40
31	Ken Caminiti	.40
32	Gary Sheffield	.75
33	Shawn Green	.75
34	Cliff Floyd	.40
35	Andres Galarraga	.40
36	Matt Williams	.40
37	Don Mattingly	3.50
38	Kevin Appier	.40
39	Ozzie Smith	3.00
40	Kenny Lofton	.40
41	Ken Griffey Jr.	4.00
42	Jack McDowell	.40
43	Gary Gaetti	.40
44	Dennis Martinez	.40
45	Chipper Jones	3.00
46	Eddie Murray	2.25
47	Bernie Williams	.40
48	Andre Dawson	.60
49	Dave Winfield	2.25
50	B.J. Surhoff	.40
51	Barry Larkin	.40
52	Alan Trammell	.40
53	Sammy Sosa	3.00
54	Hideo Nomo	1.00
55	Mark McGwire	4.50
56	Jay Bell	.40
57	Juan Gonzalez	1.00
58	Chili Davis	.40
59	Robin Ventura	.40
60	John Mabry	.40
61	Ken Griffey Jr. (Naturals)	2.00
62	Frank Thomas (Naturals)	1.25
63	Cal Ripken Jr. (Naturals)	3.00
64	Albert Belle (Naturals)	.40
65	Mike Piazza (Naturals)	2.00
66	Dante Bichette (Naturals)	.40
67	Sammy Sosa (Naturals)	1.50
68	Mo Vaughn (Naturals)	.40
69	Tim Salmon (Naturals)	.40
70	Reggie Sanders (Naturals)	.40
71	Cecil Fielder (Naturals)	.40
72	Jim Edmonds (Naturals)	.40
73	Rafael Palmeiro (Naturals)	.75
74	Edgar Martinez (Naturals)	.40
75	Barry Bonds (Naturals)	3.00
76	Manny Ramirez (Naturals)	1.25
77	Larry Walker (Naturals)	.40
78	Jeff Bagwell (Naturals)	1.25
79	Ron Gant (Naturals)	.40
80	Andres Galarraga (Naturals)	.40
81	Eddie Murray (Naturals)	1.25
82	Kirby Puckett (Naturals)	1.50
83	Will Clark (Naturals)	.40
84	Don Mattingly (Naturals)	1.75
85	Mark McGwire (Naturals)	2.25
86	Dean Palmer (Naturals)	.40
87	Matt Williams (Naturals)	.40
88	Fred McGriff (Naturals)	.40
89	Joe Carter (Naturals)	.40
90	Juan Gonzalez (Naturals)	.65
91	Alex Ochoa	.40
92	Ruben Rivera	.40
93	Tony Clark	.40
94	Pete Schourek	.40
95	Terrell Wade	.40
96	Johnny Damon	.65
97	Derek Jeter	6.00
98	Phil Nevin	.40
99	Robert Perez	.40
100	Dustin Hermanson	.40
101	Frank Thomas	2.25
102	Michael Tucker	.40
103	Kirby Puckett	3.00
104	Alex Gonzalez	.40
105	Tony Gwynn	3.00
106	Moises Alou	.40
107	Albert Belle	.40
108	Barry Bonds	6.00
109	Fred McGriff	.40
110	Dennis Eckersley	1.50
111	Craig Biggio	.40
112	David Cone	.40
113	Will Clark	.40
114	Cal Ripken Jr.	6.00
115	Wade Boggs	3.00
116	Pete Schourek	.40
117	Darren Daulton	.40
118	Carlos Baerga	.40
119	Larry Walker	.40
120	Denny Neagle	.40
121	Jim Edmonds	.40
122	Lee Smith	.40
123	Jason Isringhausen	.40
124	Jay Buhner	.40
125	John Olerud	.40
126	Jeff Conine	.40
127	Dean Palmer	.40
128	Jim Abbott	.40

129	Raul Mondesi	.40
130	Tom Glavine	.60
131	Kevin Seitzer	.40
132	Lenny Dykstra	.40
133	Brian Jordan	.40
134	Rondell White	.40
135	Bret Boone	.40
136	Randy Johnson	2.25
137	Paul O'Neill	.40
138	Jim Thome	.75
139	Edgardo Alfonzo	.40
140	Terry Pendleton	.40
141	Harold Baines	.40
142	Roberto Alomar	.45
143	Mark Grace	.40
144	Derek Bell	.40
145	Vinny Castilla	.40
146	Cecil Fielder	.40
147	Roger Clemens	3.50
148	Orel Hershiser	.40
149	J.T. Snow	.40
150	Rafael Palmeiro	1.75
151	Bret Saberhagen	.40
152	Todd Hollandsworth	.40
153	Ryan Klesko	.40
154	Greg Maddux (Hardball Heroes)	1.50
155	Ken Griffey Jr. (Hardball Heroes)	2.00
156	Hideo Nomo (Hardball Heroes)	.65
157	Frank Thomas (Hardball Heroes)	1.25
158	Cal Ripken Jr. (Hardball Heroes)	3.00
159	Jeff Bagwell (Hardball Heroes)	1.25
160	Barry Bonds (Hardball Heroes)	3.00
161	Mo Vaughn (Hardball Heroes)	.40
162	Albert Belle (Hardball Heroes)	.40
163	Sammy Sosa (Hardball Heroes)	1.50
164	Reggie Sanders (Hardball Heroes)	.40
165	Mike Piazza (Hardball Heroes)	2.00
166	Chipper Jones (Hardball Heroes)	1.50
167	Tony Gwynn (Hardball Heroes)	1.50
168	Kirby Puckett (Hardball Heroes)	1.50
169	Wade Boggs (Hardball Heroes)	1.25
170	Will Clark (Hardball Heroes)	.40
171	Gary Sheffield (Hardball Heroes)	.45
172	Dante Bichette (Hardball Heroes)	.40
173	Randy Johnson (Hardball Heroes)	1.25
174	Matt Williams (Hardball Heroes)	.40
175	Alex Rodriguez (Hardball Heroes)	4.50
176	Tim Salmon (Hardball Heroes)	.40
177	Johnny Damon (Hardball Heroes)	.40
178	Manny Ramirez (Hardball Heroes)	1.25
179	Derek Jeter (Hardball Heroes)	3.00
180	Eddie Murray (Hardball Heroes)	1.25
181	Ozzie Smith (Hardball Heroes)	1.50
182	Garret Anderson (Hardball Heroes)	.40
183	Raul Mondesi (Hardball Heroes)	.40
184	Jeff Conine (.300 Series)	.40
185	Ken Griffey Jr. (.300 Series)	2.00
186	Will Clark (.300 Series)	.40
187	Mike Greenwell (.300 Series)	.40
188	Carlos Baerga (.300 Series)	.40
189	Paul Molitor (.300 Series)	1.25
190	Jeff Bagwell (.300 Series)	1.25
191	Mark Grace (.300 Series)	.40
192	Don Mattingly (.300 Series)	1.75
193	Hal Morris (.300 Series)	.40
194	Kenny Lofton (.300 Series)	.40
195	Edgar Martinez (.300 Series)	.40
196	Kirby Puckett (.300 Series)	1.50
197	Mike Piazza (.300 Series)	2.00
198	Frank Thomas (.300 Series)	1.25
199	Wade Boggs (.300 Series)	1.25
200	Tony Gwynn (.300 Series)	1.50

Foil Series 2

The 200 cards from Series 2 were paralleled in a special foil edition which was sold at retail outlets only in five-card $2.99 packs. Fronts have a metallic foil background to differentiate them from the regular-issue Series 2 version.

	NM/M
Complete Set (200):	15.00
Common Player:	.20
Stars:	1.5X

Christie Brinkley Collection Promo

To promote its Brinkley-photographed insert cards in Series 2 Pinnacle, the company issued a card of the celebrity photographer. In the same format as the player inserts, the promo card has a gold-foil enhanced borderless glamor photo on front. The back repeats a detail of the front photo and has details of the insert series.

	NM/M
Christie Brinkley	5.00

Christie Brinkley Collection

Supermodel Christie Brinkley took the photos for these 1996 Pinnacle Series 2 inserts. The cards capture players from the 1995 World Series participants during a spring training photo session. Cards were seeded one per every 23 hobby packs or 32 retail packs.

		NM/M
Complete Set (16):		15.00
Common Player:		.75
1	Greg Maddux	3.50
2	Ryan Klesko	.75
3	Dave Justice	.75
4	Tom Glavine	1.50
5	Chipper Jones	4.00
6	Fred McGriff	.75
7	Javier Lopez	.75
8	Marquis Grissom	.75
9	Jason Schmidt	.75
10	Albert Belle	.75
11	Manny Ramirez	2.25
12	Carlos Baerga	.75
13	Sandy Alomar	.75
14	Jim Thome	2.25
15	Julio Franco	.75
16	Kenny Lofton	.75

Essence of the Game

Essence of the Game is an 18-card insert set found only in hobby packs at a one per 23 packs rate in Series 1. Cards are printed on clear plastic with the front photo also appearing in an inverted fashion on back. Micro-etched Dufex printing technology is utilized on the front.

		NM/M
Complete Set (18):		35.00
Common Player:		.75
1	Cal Ripken Jr.	6.00
2	Greg Maddux	3.00
3	Frank Thomas	2.50
4	Matt Williams	.75
5	Chipper Jones	3.00
6	Reggie Sanders	.75
7	Ken Griffey Jr.	4.00
8	Kirby Puckett	3.00
9	Hideo Nomo	1.50
10	Mike Piazza	4.00
11	Jeff Bagwell	2.50
12	Mo Vaughn	.75
13	Albert Belle	.75
14	Tim Salmon	.75
15	Don Mattingly	3.50
16	Will Clark	.75
17	Eddie Murray	2.50
18	Barry Bonds	6.00

First Rate

Retail-exclusive First Rate showcases former first round draft picks playing in the majors. Printed in Dufex foil throughout, a red swirl pattern covers the left 2/3 of the front. Backs show the player again, within a large numeral "1." These inserts are found at an average rate of one per 23 packs in Series 1.

		NM/M
Complete Set (18):		40.00
Common Player:		1.25
1	Ken Griffey Jr.	5.00
2	Frank Thomas	2.50
3	Mo Vaughn	1.25
4	Chipper Jones	4.00
5	Alex Rodriguez	6.50
6	Kirby Puckett	3.50
7	Gary Sheffield	1.75
8	Matt Williams	1.25
9	Barry Bonds	7.50
10	Craig Biggio	1.25
11	Robin Ventura	1.25
12	Michael Tucker	1.25
13	Derek Jeter	7.50
14	Manny Ramirez	2.50
15	Barry Larkin	1.25
16	Shawn Green	1.75
17	Will Clark	1.25
18	Mark McGwire	6.50

Pinnacle Power

Pinnacle Power inserts are seeded at the rate of one per 47 packs in both hobby and retail Series 1. The sluggers are featured on a two-layered front. The bottom layer is silver Dufex foil with solid black on top; a color action photo of the player is at center, giving the card a die-cut appearance.

		NM/M
Complete Set (20):		40.00
Common Player:		1.25
1	Frank Thomas	2.50
2	Mo Vaughn	1.25
2p	Mo Vaughn (Promo)	1.50
3	Ken Griffey Jr.	4.50
4	Matt Williams	1.25
5	Barry Bonds	6.00
6	Reggie Sanders	1.25
7	Mike Piazza	4.50
8	Jim Edmonds	1.25
9	Dante Bichette	1.25
10	Sammy Sosa	3.50
11	Jeff Bagwell	2.50
12	Fred McGriff	1.25
13	Albert Belle	1.25
14	Tim Salmon	1.25
15	Joe Carter	1.25
16	Manny Ramirez	2.50
17	Eddie Murray	2.50
18	Cecil Fielder	1.25
19	Larry Walker	1.25
20	Juan Gonzalez	1.75

Project Stardom

These inserts feature young players on their way to stardom. The cards, which use Dufex technology, are seeded one per every 35 packs of Series 2 hobby packs.

		NM/M
Complete Set (18):		35.00
Common Player:		1.00
1	Paul Wilson	1.00
2	Derek Jeter	8.50
3	Karim Garcia	1.00
4	Johnny Damon	2.75
5	Alex Rodriguez	7.50
6	Chipper Jones	8.00
7	Charles Johnson	1.00
8	Bob Abreu	1.25
9	Alan Benes	1.00
10	Richard Hidalgo	1.00
11	Brooks Kieschnick	1.00
12	Garret Anderson	1.00
13	Livan Hernandez	1.00
14	Manny Ramirez	5.00
15	Jermaine Dye	1.00
16	Todd Hollandsworth	1.00
17	Raul Mondesi	1.00
18	Ryan Klesko	1.00

Cal Ripken Tribute

A special Cal Ripken Tribute card was issued in Series 1 Pinnacle packs at a rate of 1:150. Front features an etched metallic foil background, a gold-foil facsimile autograph and a "2,131+ Consecutive Games Played" starburst. Back has a photo of the scoreboard on that historic occasion, and a photo of Ripken being driven around Camden Yards in a red Corvette. The card is numbered "1 of 1," but it is not unique.

		NM/M
1 of 1	Cal Ripken Jr.	5.00

Skylines

These inserts feature player portraits looming over the city skyline where they play their home games. Printed on a clear plastic stock, the cards were seeded one per every 29 Series 2 magazine packs, and one per 50 retail packs.

		NM/M
Complete Set (18):		375.00
Common Player:		10.00
1	Ken Griffey Jr.	50.00
2	Frank Thomas	30.00
3	Greg Maddux	40.00
4	Cal Ripken Jr.	65.00
5	Albert Belle	10.00
6	Mo Vaughn	10.00
7	Mike Piazza	50.00
8	Wade Boggs	40.00
9	Will Clark	10.00
10	Barry Bonds	65.00
11	Gary Sheffield	10.00
12	Hideo Nomo	25.00
13	Tony Gwynn	40.00
14	Kirby Puckett	40.00
15	Chipper Jones	40.00
16	Jeff Bagwell	30.00
17	Manny Ramirez	30.00
18	Raul Mondesi	10.00

Slugfest

These Series 2 inserts feature the game's heaviest hitters on all-foil Dufex cards. The cards were seeded one per every 35 retail packs.

		NM/M
Complete Set (18):		40.00
Common Player:		1.25
1	Frank Thomas	2.75
2	Ken Griffey Jr.	4.00
3	Jeff Bagwell	2.75
4	Barry Bonds	5.00
5	Mo Vaughn	1.25
6	Albert Belle	1.25
7	Mike Piazza	4.00
8	Matt Williams	1.25
9	Dante Bichette	1.25
10	Sammy Sosa	3.00
11	Gary Sheffield	2.00
12	Reggie Sanders	1.25
13	Manny Ramirez	2.75
14	Eddie Murray	2.75
15	Juan Gonzalez	2.25
16	Dean Palmer	1.25
17	Rafael Palmeiro	2.75
18	Cecil Fielder	1.25

Team Pinnacle

Team Pinnacle inserts offer 18 players in a double-sided nine-card set. Each card can be found with Dufex printing on one side and regular gold-foil printing on the other. Inserted one per 72 packs of Series 1, Team Pinnacle pairs up an American League player and a National Leaguer at the same position on each card.

		NM/M
Complete Set (9):		35.00
Common Player:		1.50
1	Frank Thomas, Jeff Bagwell	4.00
2	Chuck Knoblauch, Craig Biggio	1.50
3	Jim Thome, Matt Williams	3.00
4	Barry Larkin, Cal Ripken Jr.	12.00
5	Barry Bonds, Tim Salmon	10.00
6	Ken Griffey Jr., Reggie Sanders	8.00
7	Albert Belle, Sammy Sosa	6.00
8	Ivan Rodriguez, Mike Piazza	6.00
9	Greg Maddux, Randy Johnson	8.00

Team Spirit

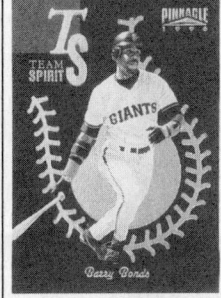

One in every 72 Series 2 hobby packs or every 103 retail packs has one of these die-cut insert cards. Each card has a holographic baseball design behind an embossed glossy action photo of the player on a flat black background. Backs are conventionally printed.

		NM/M
Complete Set (12):		45.00
Common Player:		1.25
1	Greg Maddux	4.00
2	Ken Griffey Jr.	5.00
3	Derek Jeter	8.00
4	Mike Piazza	5.00
5	Cal Ripken Jr.	8.00
6	Frank Thomas	2.75
7	Jeff Bagwell	2.75
8	Mo Vaughn	1.25
9	Albert Belle	1.25
10	Chipper Jones	4.00
11	Johnny Damon	1.50
12	Barry Bonds	8.00

Team Tomorrow

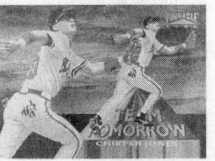

Team Tomorrow showcases young superstars on a horizontal Dufex design. While the player appears twice on the card front, the left side is merely a close-up of the same shot appearing on the right. These inserts are exclusive to Series 1 jumbo packs, found on average at the rate of one per 19 packs.

		NM/M
Complete Set (10):		20.00
Common Player:		.50
1	Ruben Rivera	.50
2	Johnny Damon	1.00
3	Raul Mondesi	.50
4	Manny Ramirez	3.00
5	Hideo Nomo	1.50
6	Chipper Jones	4.00
7	Garret Anderson	.50
8	Alex Rodriguez	5.00
9	Derek Jeter	6.00
10	Karim Garcia	.50

1996 Pinnacle/Aficionado

Pinnacle's 1996 Aficionado set gives every card the look of maple woodgrain. The 200 regular issue cards include 160 cards in an antique-look sepia-tone finish. The horizontal front also has a rainbow holographic foil image of the player. The back has comparison statistics that show how the player compares with the league average at that position and the league average at that position in different eras. There are also 60 four-color cards, which include 25 rookie cards, and a 10-card Global Reach subset. This subset, which honors baseball's international flavor, features Aficionado's new heligram printing process. Artist's Proof parallel cards, seeded about one per 35 packs, were also created. These cards mirror the regular issue and use a unique gold foil stamp. There were three insert sets: Slick Picks, Rivals and Magic Numbers.

		NM/M
Complete Set (200):		20.00
Common Player:		.10
Common Artist's Proof:		.50
Artist's Proof Stars:		8X
Pack (5):		1.50
Wax Box (16):		30.00
1	Jack McDowell	.10
2	Jay Bell	.10
3	Rafael Palmeiro	1.25
4	Wally Joyner	.10
5	Ozzie Smith	2.00
6	Mark McGwire	3.00
7	Kevin Seitzer	.10
8	Fred McGriff	.10
9	Roger Clemens	2.25
9s	Roger Clemens (Marked "SAMPLE.")	4.00
10	Randy Johnson	1.50
11	Cecil Fielder	.10
12	David Cone	.10
13	Chili Davis	.10
14	Andres Galarraga	.10
15	Joe Carter	.10
16	Ryne Sandberg	2.00
17	Paul O'Neill	.10
18	Cal Ripken Jr.	4.00
19	Wade Boggs	2.00
20	Greg Gagne	.10
21	Edgar Martinez	.10
22	Greg Maddux	2.00
23	Ken Caminiti	.10
24	Kirby Puckett	2.00
25	Craig Biggio	.10
26	Will Clark	.10
27	Ron Gant	.10
28	Eddie Murray	1.50
29	Lance Johnson	.10
30	Tony Gwynn	2.00
31	Dante Bichette	.10
32	Darren Daulton	.10
33	Danny Tartabull	.10
34	Jeff King	.10
35	Tom Glavine	.40
36	Rickey Henderson	1.50
37	Jose Canseco	1.00
38	Barry Larkin	.10
39	Dennis Martinez	.10
40	Ruben Sierra	.10
41	Bobby Bonilla	.10
42	Jeff Conine	.10
43	Lee Smith	.10
44	Charlie Hayes	.10
45	Walt Weiss	.10
46	Jay Buhner	.10
47	Kenny Rogers	.10
48	Paul Molitor	1.50
49	Hal Morris	.10
50	Todd Stottlemyre	.10
51	Mike Stanley	.10
52	Mark Grace	.10
53	Lenny Dykstra	.10
54	Andre Dawson	.25
55	Dennis Eckersley	1.25
56	Ben McDonald	.10
57	Ray Lankford	.10
58	Mo Vaughn	.10
59	Frank Thomas	1.50
60	Julio Franco	.10
61	Jim Abbott	.10
62	Greg Vaughn	.10
63	Marquis Grissom	.10
64	Tino Martinez	.10
65	Kevin Appier	.10
66	Matt Williams	.10
67	Sammy Sosa	2.00
68	Larry Walker	.10
69	Ivan Rodriguez	1.25
70	Eric Karros	.10
71	Bernie Williams	.10
72	Carlos Baerga	.10
73	Jeff Bagwell	1.50
74	Pete Schourek	.10
75	Ken Griffey Jr.	2.50
76	Bernard Gilkey	.10
77	Albert Belle	.10
78	Chuck Knoblauch	.10
79	John Smoltz	.10
80	Barry Bonds	4.00
81	Vinny Castilla	.10
82	John Olerud	.10
83	Mike Mussina	1.00
84	Alex Fernandez	.10
85	Shawon Dunston	.10
86	Travis Fryman	.10
87	Moises Alou	.10
88	Dean Palmer	.10

89	Gregg Jefferies	.10
90	Jim Thome	1.25
91	Dave Justice	.10
92	B.J. Surhoff	.10
93	Ramon Martinez	.10
94	Gary Sheffield	.40
95	Andy Benes	.10
96	Reggie Sanders	.10
97	Roberto Alomar	.35
98	Omar Vizquel	.10
99	Juan Gonzalez	.75
100	Robin Ventura	.10
101	Jason Isringhausen	.10
102	Greg Colbrunn	.10
103	Brian Jordan	.10
104	Shawn Green	.40
105	Brian Hunter	.10
106	Rondell White	.10
107	Ryan Klesko	.10
107s	Ryan Klesko (Marked "SAMPLE.")	1.00
108	Sterling Hitchcock	.10
109	Manny Ramirez	1.50
110	Bret Boone	.10
111	Michael Tucker	.10
112	Julian Tavarez	.10
113	Benji Gil	.10
114	Kenny Lofton	.10
115	Mike Kelly	.10
116	Ray Durham	.10
117	Trevor Hoffman	.10
118	Butch Huskey	.10
119	Phil Nevin	.10
120	Pedro Martinez	1.50
121	Wil Cordero	.10
122	Tim Salmon	.10
123	Jim Edmonds	.10
124	Mike Piazza	2.50
125	Rico Brogna	.10
126	John Mabry	.10
127	Chipper Jones	2.00
128	Johnny Damon	.35
129	Raul Mondesi	.10
130	Denny Neagle	.10
131	Marc Newfield	.10
132	Hideo Nomo	.75
133	Joe Vitiello	.10
134	Garret Anderson	.10
135	Dave Nilsson	.10
136	Alex Rodriguez	3.00
137	Russ Davis	.10
138	Frank Rodriguez	.10
139	Royce Clayton	.10
140	John Valentin	.10
141	Marty Cordova	.10
142	Alex Gonzalez	.10
143	Carlos Delgado	.75
144	Willie Greene	.10
145	Cliff Floyd	.10
146	Bobby Higginson	.10
147	J.T. Snow	.10
148	Derek Bell	.10
149	Edgardo Alfonzo	.10
150	Charles Johnson	.10
151	Hideo Nomo (Global Reach)	.60
152	Larry Walker (Global Reach)	
153	Bob Abreu (Global Reach)	.10
154	Karim Garcia (Global Reach)	.10
155	Dave Nilsson (Global Reach)	.10
156	Chan Ho Park (Global Reach)	.10
157	Dennis Martinez (Global Reach)	.10
158	Sammy Sosa (Global Reach)	1.25
159	Rey Ordonez (Global Reach)	.10
160	Roberto Alomar (Global Reach)	.10
161	George Arias	.10
162	Jason Schmidt	.10
163	Derek Jeter	4.00
164	Chris Snopek	.10
165	Todd Hollandsworth	.10
166	Sal Fasano	.10
167	Jay Powell	.10
168	Paul Wilson	.10
169	Jim Pittsley	.10
170	LaTroy Hawkins	.10
171	Bob Abreu	.10
172	Mike Grace RC	.10
173	Karim Garcia	.10
174	Richard Hidalgo	.10
175	Felipe Crespo	.10
176	Terrell Wade	.10
177	Steve Gibralter	.10
178	Jermaine Dye	.10
179	Alan Benes	.10
180	Wilton Guerrero RC	.10
181	Brooks Kieschnick	.10
182	Roger Cedeno	.10
183	Osvaldo Fernandez RC	.10
184	Matt Lawton RC	.50
185	George Williams	.10
186	Jimmy Haynes	.10
187	Mike Busby RC	.10
188	Chan Ho Park	.10
189	Marc Barcelo	.10
190	Jason Kendall	.10
191	Rey Ordonez	.10
192	Tyler Houston	.10
193	John Wasdin	.10
194	Jeff Suppan	.10
195	Jeff Ware	.10

196	Checklist	.10
197	Checklist	.10
198	Checklist	.10
199	Checklist	.10
200	Checklist	.10

First Pitch Previews

This parallel set differs from the regularly issued version in that there is a "FIRST PITCH / PREVIEW" label printed on the front on the end opposite the heligram player portrait. Also, whereas on the regular cards, the player portrait is in silver metallic composition, the First Pitch Preview cards have the portrait in gold. These cards were most often obtained by visiting Pinnacle's site on the Internet and answering a trivia question.

	NM/M
Complete Set (200):	250.00
Common Player:	2.00

Magic Numbers

This insert set focuses on 10 of the game's best players, printing them on a wooden stock which carries the distinct grain and color of natural wood. The cards, seeded one every 72 packs, compares players with others who have worn the same uniform number. Each card can also be found with a large black "SAMPLE" printed on back.

		NM/M
Complete Set (10):		15.50
Common Player:		.75
Samples:		1X
1	Ken Griffey Jr.	3.25
2	Greg Maddux	2.50
3	Frank Thomas	1.50
4	Mo Vaughn	.75
5	Jeff Bagwell	1.50
6	Chipper Jones	2.50
7	Albert Belle	.75
8	Cal Ripken Jr.	4.50
9	Matt Williams	.75
10	Sammy Sosa	2.50

Rivals

These inserts concentrate on the many matchups and rivalries that make baseball fun. Each card uses spot embossing. The cards are seeded one per every 24 packs.

		NM/M
Complete Set (24):		65.00
Common Player:		2.00
1	Ken Griffey Jr.,	
	Frank Thomas	4.00

2	Frank Thomas, Cal Ripken Jr.	4.50
3	Cal Ripken Jr., Mo Vaughn	4.00
4	Mo Vaughn, Ken Griffey Jr.	2.50
5	Ken Griffey Jr., Cal Ripken Jr.	5.00
6	Frank Thomas, Mo Vaughn	2.00
7	Cal Ripken Jr., Ken Griffey Jr.	5.00
8	Mo Vaughn, Frank Thomas	2.00
9	Ken Griffey Jr., Mo Vaughn	2.50
10	Frank Thomas, Ken Griffey Jr.	4.00
11	Cal Ripken Jr., Frank Thomas	4.50
12	Mo Vaughn, Cal Ripken Jr.	4.00
13	Mike Piazza, Jeff Bagwell	2.50
14	Jeff Bagwell, Barry Bonds	4.50
15	Jeff Bagwell, Mike Piazza	2.50
16	Tony Gwynn, Mike Piazza	3.00
17	Mike Piazza, Barry Bonds	5.00
18	Jeff Bagwell, Tony Gwynn	2.00
19	Barry Bonds, Mike Piazza	5.00
20	Tony Gwynn, Jeff Bagwell	2.00
21	Mike Piazza, Tony Gwynn	3.00
22	Barry Bonds, Jeff Bagwell	4.50
23	Tony Gwynn, Barry Bonds	4.50
24	Barry Bonds, Tony Gwynn	4.50

Slick Picks

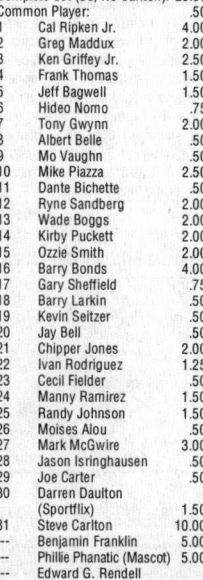

This insert set pictures 32 of the best players in baseball on cards which use Spectroetch printing. Each card notes where that player was selected in the annual draft, emphasizing that there are numerous bargains available throughout the amateur draft. The cards were seeded one per 10 packs, making them the easiest to obtain of the set's insert cards.

		NM/M
Complete Set (32):		40.00
Common Player:		.50
1	Mike Piazza	2.50
2	Cal Ripken Jr.	4.00
3	Ken Griffey Jr.	2.50
4	Paul Wilson	.50
5	Frank Thomas	1.50
6	Mo Vaughn	.50
7	Barry Bonds	4.00
8	Albert Belle	.50
9	Jeff Bagwell	1.50
10	Dante Bichette	.50
11	Hideo Nomo	.75
12	Raul Mondesi	.50
13	Manny Ramirez	1.50
14	Greg Maddux	2.00
15	Tony Gwynn	2.00
16	Ryne Sandberg	2.00
17	Reggie Sanders	.50
18	Derek Jeter	4.00
19	Johnny Damon	.75
20	Alex Rodriguez	3.00
21	Ryan Klesko	.50
22	Jim Thome	1.50
23	Kenny Lofton	.50
24	Tino Martinez	.50
25	Randy Johnson	1.50
26	Wade Boggs	2.00
27	Juan Gonzalez	.75
28	Kirby Puckett	2.00
29	Tim Salmon	.50
30	Chipper Jones	2.00
31	Garret Anderson	.50
32	Eddie Murray	1.50

FanFest

In conjunction with its title sponsorship of baseball's All-Star FanFest, July 5-9 in Philadelphia, the company distributed two-card foil packs prior to and at the show. Fronts have a negative posterized image of Independence Hall as a backdrop for a player action photo. Textured gold-foil bottom corners hold a team logo and a Liberty Bell silhouette with the player's position. The player name appears in gold foil above the FanFest logo at bottom center. Backs repeat the

negative background and have another player photo, a few words about him and all the appropriate logos. The Darren Daulton card is in Sportflix technology as a tribute to the recently retired Phillies fan favorite. Card #31, Steve Carlton, was not distributed in packs. Cards of the Phillie Phanatic team mascot, the city's mayor and several other local dignitaries were produced and given to those persons.

		NM/M
Complete Set (30, No Carlton):		25.00
Common Player:		.50
1	Cal Ripken Jr.	4.00
2	Greg Maddux	2.00
3	Ken Griffey Jr.	2.50
4	Frank Thomas	1.50
5	Jeff Bagwell	1.50
6	Hideo Nomo	.75
7	Tony Gwynn	.50
8	Albert Belle	.50
9	Mo Vaughn	.50
10	Mike Piazza	2.50
11	Dante Bichette	.50
12	Ryne Sandberg	2.00
13	Wade Boggs	2.00
14	Kirby Puckett	2.00
15	Ozzie Smith	2.00
16	Barry Bonds	4.00
17	Gary Sheffield	.75
18	Barry Larkin	.50
19	Kevin Seitzer	.50
20	Jay Bell	.50
21	Chipper Jones	2.00
22	Ivan Rodriguez	1.25
23	Cecil Fielder	.50
24	Manny Ramirez	1.50
25	Randy Johnson	1.50
26	Moises Alou	.50
27	Mark McGwire	3.00
28	Jason Isringhausen	.50
29	Joe Carter	.50
30	Darren Daulton (Sportflix)	1.50
31	Steve Carlton	10.00
---	Benjamin Franklin	5.00
---	Phillie Phanatic (Mascot)	5.00
---	Edward G. Rendell (Mayor)	3.00

FanFest Playing Cards

A special version of Pinnacle's FanFest cards was produced for construction of a large "house of cards" at the FanFest site. Following the event, some of the cards made their way into the hobby. Similar in format to the regular cards, the special issue was produced on textured playing-card stock in a 2-1/4" x 3-1/2" format with rounded corners. The playing cards lack the gold-foil found on regular cards and thus the player's name is nowhere to be found. Backs have a large gold-and-white Pinnacle logo on a black background. Cards are listed here using the numbering found on the regular version; the playing cards are unnumbered.

		NM/M
Complete Set (29):		300.00
Common Player:		10.00
(1)	Cal Ripken Jr.	30.00
(2)	Greg Maddux	17.50
(3)	Ken Griffey Jr.	20.00
(4)	Frank Thomas	15.00
(5)	Jeff Bagwell	15.00
(6)	Hideo Nomo	12.50
(7)	Tony Gwynn	17.50
(8)	Albert Belle	10.00
(9)	Mo Vaughn	10.00
(10)	Mike Piazza	20.00
(11)	Dante Bichette	10.00
(12)	Ryne Sandberg	17.50
(13)	Wade Boggs	17.50
(14)	Kirby Puckett	17.50
(15)	Ozzie Smith	17.50
(16)	Barry Bonds	30.00
(17)	Gary Sheffield	12.50
(18)	Barry Larkin	10.00
(19)	Kevin Seitzer	10.00
(20)	Jay Bell	10.00
(21)	Chipper Jones	17.50
(22)	Ivan Rodriguez	12.50
(23)	Cecil Fielder	10.00
(24)	Manny Ramirez	15.00
(25)	Randy Johnson	15.00
(26)	Moises Alou	10.00
(27)	Mark McGwire	25.00
(28)	Jason Isringhausen	10.00
(29)	Joe Carter	10.00

1997 Pinnacle

Pinnacle baseball consists of 200 base cards. Fronts have the player's name stamped within a foil baseball-diamond shape at the bottom of each card. Backs contain summaries of the players' 1996 and lifetime statistics. Included within the base set is a 30-card Rookies subset, a 12-card Clout subset and three checklists. Inserts include two parallel sets (Artist's Proof and Museum Collection), Passport to the Majors, Shades, Team Pinnacle, Cardfrontations, and Home/Away. Cards were sold in 10-card packs for $2.49 each.

		NM/M
Complete Set (200):		10.00
Common Player:		.05
Pack (10):		1.00
Wax Box (24):		12.50
Wax Retail Box (16):		10.00
1	Cecil Fielder	.05
2	Garret Anderson	.05
3	Charles Nagy	.05
4	Darryl Hamilton	.05
5	Greg Myers	.05
6	Eric Davis	.05
7	Jeff Frye	.05
8	Marquis Grissom	.05
9	Curt Schilling	.35
10	Jeff Fassero	.05
11	Alan Benes	.05
12	Orlando Miller	.05
13	Alex Fernandez	.05
14	Andy Pettitte	.25
15	Andre Dawson	.25
16	Mark Grudzielanek	.05
17	Joe Vitiello	.05
18	Juan Gonzalez	.40
19	Mark Whiten	.05
20	Lance Johnson	.05
21	Trevor Hoffman	.05
22	Marc Newfield	.05
23	Jim Eisenreich	.05
24	Joe Carter	.05
25	Jose Canseco	.30
26	Bill Swift	.05
27	Ellis Burks	.05
28	Ben McDonald	.05
29	Edgar Martinez	.05
30	Jamie Moyer	.05
31	Chan Ho Park	.05
32	Carlos Delgado	.50
33	Kevin Mitchell	.05
34	Carlos Garcia	.05
35	Darryl Strawberry	.05
36	Jim Thome	.60
37	Jose Offerman	.05
38	Ryan Klesko	.05
39	Ruben Sierra	.05

40	Devon White	.05
41	Brian Jordan	.05
42	Tony Gwynn	.75
43	Rafael Palmeiro	.50
44	Dante Bichette	.05
45	Scott Stahoviak	.05
46	Roger Cedeno	.05
47	Ivan Rodriguez	.50
48	Bob Abreu	.05
49	Darryl Kile	.05
50	Darren Dreifort	.05
51	Shawon Dunston	.05
52	Mark McGwire	1.50
53	Tim Salmon	.05
54	Gene Schall	.05
55	Roger Clemens	.85
56	Rondell White	.05
57	Ed Sprague	.05
58	Craig Paquette	.05
59	David Segui	.05
60	Jaime Navarro	.05
61	Tom Glavine	.35
62	Jeff Brantley	.05
63	Kimera Bartee	.05
64	Fernando Vina	.05
65	Eddie Murray	.65
66	Lenny Dykstra	.05
67	Kevin Elster	.05
68	Vinny Castilla	.05
69	Todd Greene	.05
70	Brett Butler	.05
71	Robby Thompson	.05
72	Reggie Jefferson	.05
73	Todd Hundley	.05
74	Jeff King	.05
75	Ernie Young	.05
76	Jeff Bagwell	.65
77	Dan Wilson	.05
78	Paul Molitor	.65
79	Kevin Seitzer	.05
80	Kevin Brown	.05
81	Ron Gant	.05
82	Dwight Gooden	.05
83	Todd Stottlemyre	.05
84	Ken Caminiti	.05
85	James Baldwin	.05
86	Jermaine Dye	.05
87	Harold Baines	.05
88	Pat Hentgen	.05
89	Frank Rodriguez	.05
90	Mark Johnson	.05
91	Jason Kendall	.05
92	Alex Rodriguez	1.50
93	Alan Trammell	.05
94	Scott Brosius	.05
95	Delino DeShields	.05
96	Chipper Jones	.75
97	Barry Bonds	2.00
98	Brady Anderson	.05
99	Ryne Sandberg	.75
100	Albert Belle	.05
101	Jeff Cirillo	.05
102	Frank Thomas	.65
103	Mike Piazza	1.00
104	Rickey Henderson	.65
105	Rey Ordonez	.05
106	Mark Grace	.05
107	Terry Steinbach	.05
108	Ray Durham	.05
109	Barry Larkin	.05
110	Tony Clark	.05
111	Bernie Williams	.05
112	John Smoltz	.05
113	Moises Alou	.05
114	Alex Gonzalez	.05
115	Rico Brogna	.05
116	Eric Karros	.05
117	Jeff Conine	.05
118	Todd Hollandsworth	.05
119	Troy Percival	.05
120	Paul Wilson	.05
121	Orel Hershiser	.05
122	Ozzie Smith	.75
123	Dave Hollins	.05
124	Ken Hill	.05
125	Rick Wilkins	.05
126	Scott Servais	.05
127	Fernando Valenzuela	.05
128	Mariano Rivera	.15
129	Mark Loretta	.05
130	Shane Reynolds	.05
131	Darren Oliver	.05
132	Steve Trachsel	.05
133	Darren Bragg	.05
134	Jason Dickson	.05
135	Darren Fletcher	.05
136	Gary Gaetti	.05
137	Joey Cora	.05
138	Terry Pendleton	.05
139	Derek Jeter	2.00
140	Danny Tartabull	.05
141	John Flaherty	.05
142	B.J. Surhoff	.05
143	Mark Sweeney	.05
144	Chad Mottola	.05
145	Andujar Cedeno	.05
146	Tim Belcher	.05
147	Mark Thompson	.05
148	Rafael Bournigal	.05
149	Marty Cordova	.05
150	Osvaldo Fernandez	.05
151	Mike Stanley	.05
152	Ricky Bottalico	.05
153	Donnie Wall	.05
154	Omar Vizquel	.05
155	Mike Mussina	.30
156	Brant Brown	.05
157	F.P. Santangelo	.05

158	Ryan Hancock	.05
159	Jeff D'Amico	.05
160	Luis Castillo	.05
161	Darin Erstad	.10
162	Ugueth Urbina	.05
163	Andruw Jones	.65
164	Steve Gibralter	.05
165	Robin Jennings	.05
166	Mike Cameron	.05
167	George Arias	.05
168	Chris Stynes	.05
169	Justin Thompson	.05
170	Jamey Wright	.05
171	Todd Walker	.05
172	Nomar Garciaparra	.75
173	Jose Paniagua	.05
174	Marvin Benard	.05
175	Rocky Coppinger	.05
176	Quinton McCracken	.05
177	Amaury Telemaco	.05
178	Neifi Perez	.05
179	Todd Greene	.05
180	Jason Thompson	.05
181	Wilton Guerrero	.05
182	Edgar Renteria	.05
183	Billy Wagner	.05
184	Alex Ochoa	.05
185	Billy McMillon	.05
186	Kenny Lofton	.05
187	Andres Galarraga (Clout)	.05
188	Chuck Knoblauch (Clout)	.05
189	Greg Maddux (Clout)	.75
190	Mo Vaughn (Clout)	.40
191	Cal Ripken Jr. (Clout)	2.00
192	Hideo Nomo (Clout)	.05
193	Ken Griffey Jr. (Clout)	1.00
194	Sammy Sosa (Clout)	.75
195	Jay Buhner (Clout)	.05
196	Manny Ramirez (Clout)	.65
197	Matt Williams (Clout)	.05
198	Andruw Jones (Checklist)	.30
199	Darin Erstad (Checklist)	.05
200	Trey Beamon (Checklist)	.05

Artist's Proofs

Artist's Proofs parallels for 1997 Pinnacle were issued in a "fractured" set form. That is, three levels of scarcity were created, with each card available in only one of those levels. For 125 of the players, bronze is the scarcity level; 50 of the players have a silver-level scarcity and 25 players are found in the top-shelf gold level, with a reported production of 300 each. Stated odds of finding an AP parallel were 1:47 in hobby and retail packs, and 1:55 in magazine packs.

	NM/M
Common Bronze (125):	1.00
Bronze Stars:	30X
Common Silver (50):	2.50
Silver Stars:	12X
Common Gold (25):	4.00
Gold Stars:	10X

Museum Collection

Each of the 200 cards in 1997 Pinnacle Series 1 was also issued in a graphically enhanced Museum Collection parallel set. The Museum cards utilize basically the same design as the regular-issue Pinnacle cards, but the front is printed in the

company's Dufex gold-foil technology. On back, a small rectangular logo verifies the card's special status.

	NM/M
Complete Set (200):	100.00
Common Player:	1.00
Stars/Rookies:	6X

Cardfrontations

This hobby-only set was inserted every 23 packs of 1997 Pinnacle baseball. Fronts depict a player portrait imaged over a foil rainbow background. The same player is then pictured in action shots with the "Cardfrontation" logo in gold foil in the lower right half. The player's name appears in gold foil below the gold-foil team logo. Backs depict another player's portrait with text describing interaction between the two players. The cards are numbered as "x of 20."

	NM/M
Complete Set (20):	35.00
Common Player:	.50
1	Greg Maddux, Mike Piazza	3.00
2	Tom Glavine, Ken Caminiti	.75
3	Randy Johnson, Cal Ripken Jr.	5.00
4	Kevin Appier, Mark McGwire	4.00
5	Andy Pettitte, Juan Gonzalez	1.00
6	Pat Hentgen, Albert Belle	.50
7	Hideo Nomo, Chipper Jones	2.00
8	Ismael Valdes, Sammy Sosa	2.50
9	Mike Mussina, Manny Ramirez	1.50
10	David Cone, Jay Buhner	.50
11	Mark Wohlers, Gary Sheffield	.75
12	Alan Benes, Barry Bonds	5.00
13	Roger Clemens, Ivan Rodriguez	2.50
14	Mariano Rivera, Ken Griffey Jr.	3.00
15	Dwight Gooden, Frank Thomas	1.50
16	John Wetteland, Darin Erstad	
17	John Smoltz, Brian Jordan	.50
18	Kevin Brown, Jeff Bagwell	1.50
19	Jack McDowell, Alex Rodriguez	4.00
20	Charles Nagy, Bernie Williams	.50

Home/Away

The 24-card, shirt-shaped, die-cut set was inserted every 33 retail packs. The background on front and back is a facsimile of the player's home or road jersey. A color action photo is on front with gold-foil graphics. Backs have a few words about the player.

	NM/M
Complete Set (12):	65.00

Common Player:		2.00
1	Chipper Jones	5.00
2	Ken Griffey Jr.	6.00
3	Mike Piazza	6.00
4	Frank Thomas	4.00
5	Jeff Bagwell	4.00
6	Alex Rodriguez	8.00
7	Barry Bonds	10.00
8	Mo Vaughn	2.00
9	Derek Jeter	10.00
10	Mark McGwire	8.00
11	Cal Ripken Jr.	10.00
12	Albert Belle	2.00

Passport to the Majors

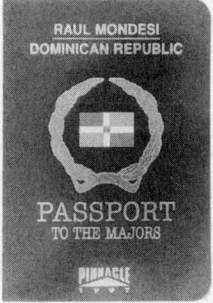

The 25-card, regular-sized set was inserted every 36 packs of 1997 Pinnacle baseball. The cards fold out and resemble a mini passport.

	NM/M
Complete Set (25):	55.00
Common Player:	1.00
1	Greg Maddux	4.00
2	Ken Griffey Jr.	6.00
3	Frank Thomas	3.00
4	Cal Ripken Jr.	10.00
5	Mike Piazza	6.00
6	Alex Rodriguez	7.50
7	Mo Vaughn	1.00
8	Chipper Jones	4.00
9	Roberto Alomar	1.00
10	Edgar Martinez	1.00
11	Javier Lopez	1.00
12	Ivan Rodriguez	2.50
13	Juan Gonzalez	1.50
14	Carlos Baerga	1.00
15	Sammy Sosa	4.00
16	Manny Ramirez	3.00
17	Raul Mondesi	1.00
18	Henry Rodriguez	1.00
19	Rafael Palmeiro	2.50
20	Rey Ordonez	1.00
21	Hideo Nomo	1.50
22	Makoto Suzuki	1.00
23	Chan Ho Park	1.00
24	Larry Walker	1.00
25	Ruben Rivera	1.00

Shades

This set was inserted every 23 retail packs of Pinnacle baseball. The horizontal cards are die-cut at the top of a pair of sunglasses whose lenses contain color portrait and action pictures of the player. The player face beneath the shades is printed on silver foil stock. Backs have a mirror-image of the front photos in the lenses and a baseball diamond in the background.

	NM/M
Complete Set (10):	15.00
Common Player:	.75
1	Ken Griffey Jr.	3.00
2	Juan Gonzalez	1.50
3	John Smoltz	.75
4	Gary Sheffield	1.00
5	Cal Ripken Jr.	5.00
6	Mo Vaughn	.75
7	Brian Jordan	.75
8	Mike Piazza	3.00
9	Frank Thomas	2.25
10	Alex Rodriguez	4.00

Team Pinnacle

This insert features top National League players from a position on one side with the best American League players on the other. One side of the card is in Dufex printing and there is actually two

versions of each card, as either side can feature the Dufex foil. Team Pinnacle is inserted every 90 packs.

	NM/M
Complete Set (10):	30.00
Common Player:	1.50
1	Frank Thomas, Jeff Bagwell	4.00
2	Chuck Knoblauch, Eric Young	1.50
3	Ken Caminiti, Jim Thome	3.00
4	Alex Rodriguez, Chipper Jones	6.00
5	Mike Piazza, Ivan Rodriguez	5.00
6	Albert Belle, Barry Bonds	8.00
7	Ken Griffey Jr., Ellis Burks	6.00
8	Juan Gonzalez, Gary Sheffield	3.00
9	John Smoltz, Andy Pettitte	2.00
10	All Players	2.00

1997 New Pinnacle Samples

This group of sample cards was sent to dealers to introduce the New Pinnacle brand which took the place of a second series of Pinnacle in 1997. Cards are virtually identical to the issued versions except for the large diagonal black-and-white "SAMPLE" overprint on front and back.

	NM/M
Complete Set (6):	7.50
Common Player:	.50
2	Sammy Sosa	3.00
45	Mike Piazza	3.00
57	Jeff Bagwell	1.50
81	Alex Rodriguez	5.00
127	Ryan Klesko	.50
175	Andruw Jones	2.00

1997 New Pinnacle

In lieu of a second series of Pinnacle Baseball, the company offered collectors New Pinnacle, a 200-card set sold in 10-card packs for $2.99. Two parallel versions of the 200-card set exist in Museum Collection and Artist's Proofs. Other inserts include Press Plates, Spellbound, Keeping the Pace and Interleague Encounter. Collectors who obtained four Press Plates of the same player's card back or front were eligible to win cash prizes.

	NM/M
Complete Set (200):	12.50
Common Player:	.05
Common Museum:	1.00
Museum Stars:	8X
Common Red Artist's Proof:	1.00

Red AP Stars:	10X
Common Blue Artist's Proof:	3.00
Blue AP Stars:	25X
Common Green Artist's Proof:	6.00
Green AP Stars:	35X
Pack (10):	1.50
Wax Box (18):	15.00

1	Ken Griffey Jr.	1.00
2	Sammy Sosa	.75
3	Greg Maddux	.75
4	Matt Williams	.05
5	Jason Isringhausen	.05
6	Gregg Jefferies	.05
7	Chili Davis	.05
8	Paul O'Neill	.05
9	Larry Walker	.05
10	Ellis Burks	.05
11	Cliff Floyd	.05
12	Albert Belle	.05
13	Javier Lopez	.05
14	David Cone	.05
15	Jose Canseco	.40
16	Todd Zeile	.05
17	Bernard Gilkey	.05
18	Andres Galarraga	.05
19	Chris Snopek	.05
20	Tim Salmon	.05
21	Roger Clemens	.85
22	Reggie Sanders	.05
23	John Jaha	.05
24	Andy Pettitte	.25
25	Kenny Lofton	.05
26	Robb Nen	.05
27	John Wetteland	.05
28	Bobby Bonilla	.05
29	Hideo Nomo	.40
30	Cecil Fielder	.05
31	Garret Anderson	.05
32	Pat Hentgen	.05
33	David Justice	.05
34	Billy Wagner	.05
35	Al Leiter	.05
36	Mark Wohlers	.05
37	Rondell White	.05
38	Charles Johnson	.05
39	Mark Grace	.05
40	Pedro Martinez	.65
41	Tom Goodwin	.05
42	Manny Ramirez	.65
43	Greg Vaughn	.05
44	Brian Jordan	.05
45	Mike Piazza	1.00
46	Roberto Hernandez	.05
47	Wade Boggs	.75
48	Scott Sanders	.05
49	Alex Gonzalez	.05
50	Kevin Brown	.05
51	Bob Higginson	.05
52	Ken Caminiti	.05
53	Derek Jeter	2.00
54	Carlos Baerga	.05
55	Jay Buhner	.05
56	Tim Naehring	.05
57	Jeff Bagwell	.65
58	Steve Finley	.05
59	Kevin Appier	.05
60	Jay Bell	.05
61	Ivan Rodriguez	.60
62	Terrell Wade	.05
63	Rusty Greer	.05
64	Juan Guzman	.05
65	Fred McGriff	.05
66	Tino Martinez	.05
67	Ray Lankford	.05
68	Juan Gonzalez	.40
69	Ron Gant	.05
70	Jack McDowell	.05
71	Tony Gwynn	.75
72	Joe Carter	.05
73	Wilson Alvarez	.05
74	Jason Giambi	.60
75	Brian Hunter	.05
76	Michael Tucker	.05
77	Andy Benes	.05
78	Brady Anderson	.05
79	Ramon Martinez	.05
80	Troy Percival	.05
81	Alex Rodriguez	1.50
82	Jim Thome	.60
83	Denny Neagle	.05
84	Rafael Palmeiro	.60
85	Jose Valentin	.05
86	Marc Newfield	.05
87	Mariano Rivera	.15
88	Alan Benes	.05
89	Jimmy Key	.05
90	Joe Randa	.05
91	Cal Ripken Jr.	2.00
92	Craig Biggio	.05
93	Dean Palmer	.05
94	Gary Sheffield	.45
95	Ismael Valdez	.05
96	John Valentin	.05
97	Johnny Damon	.35
98	Mo Vaughn	.05
99	Paul Sorrento	.05
100	Randy Johnson	.05
101	Raul Mondesi	.05
102	Roberto Alomar	.20
103	Royce Clayton	.05
104	Mark Grudzielanek	.05
105	Wally Joyner	.05
106	Wil Cordero	.05
107	Will Clark	.05
108	Chuck Knoblauch	.05
109	Derek Bell	.05
110	Henry Rodriguez	.05
111	Edgar Renteria	.05

112	Travis Fryman	.05
113	Eric Young	.05
114	Sandy Alomar Jr.	.05
115	Darin Erstad	.25
116	Barry Larkin	.05
117	Barry Bonds	2.00
118	Frank Thomas	.65
119	Carlos Delgado	.50
120	Jason Kendall	.05
121	Todd Hollandsworth	.05
122	Jim Edmonds	.05
123	Chipper Jones	.75
124	Jeff Fassero	.05
125	Deion Sanders	.05
126	Matt Lawton	.05
127	Ryan Klesko	.05
128	Mike Mussina	.40
129	Paul Molitor	.65
130	Dante Bichette	.05
131	Bill Pulsipher	.05
132	Todd Hundley	.05
133	J.T. Snow	.05
134	Chuck Finley	.05
135	Shawn Green	.30
136	Charles Nagy	.05
137	Willie Greene	.05
138	Marty Cordova	.05
139	Eddie Murray	.65
140	Ryne Sandberg	.75
141	Alex Fernandez	.05
142	Mark McGwire	1.50
143	Eric Davis	.05
144	Jermaine Dye	.05
145	Ruben Sierra	.05
146	Damon Buford	.05
147	John Smoltz	.05
148	Alex Ochoa	.05
149	Moises Alou	.05
150	Rico Brogna	.05
151	Terry Steinbach	.05
152	Jeff King	.05
153	Carlos Garcia	.05
154	Tom Glavine	.35
155	Edgar Martinez	.05
156	Kevin Elster	.05
157	Darryl Hamilton	.05
158	Jason Dickson	.05
159	Kevin Orie	.05
160	Bubba Trammell RC	.25
161	Jose Guillen	.05
162	Brant Brown	.05
163	Wendell Magee	.05
164	Scott Spiezio	.05
165	Todd Walker	.05
166	Rod Myers RC	.05
167	Damon Mashore	.05
168	Wilton Guerrero	.05
169	Vladimir Guerrero	.65
170	Nomar Garciaparra	.75
171	Shannon Stewart	.05
172	Scott Rolen	.60
173	Bob Abreu	.05
174	Danny Patterson RC	.05
175	Andruw Jones	.65
176	Brian Giles RC	.50
177	Dmitri Young	.05
178	Cal Ripken Jr. (East Meets West)	1.00
179	Chuck Knoblauch (East Meets West)	.05
180	Alex Rodriguez (East Meets West)	.75
181	Andres Galarraga (East Meets West)	.05
182	Pedro Martinez (East Meets West)	.35
183	Brady Anderson (East Meets West)	.05
184	Barry Bonds (East Meets West)	1.00
185	Ivan Rodriguez (East Meets West)	.30
186	Gary Sheffield (East Meets West)	.05
187	Denny Neagle (East Meets West)	.05
188	Mark McGwire (Aura)	.75
189	Ellis Burks (Aura)	.05
190	Alex Rodriguez (Aura)	.75
191	Mike Piazza (Aura)	.65
192	Barry Bonds (Aura)	1.00
193	Albert Belle (Aura)	.05
194	Chipper Jones (Aura)	.40
195	Juan Gonzalez (Aura)	.20
196	Brady Anderson (Aura)	.05
197	Frank Thomas (Aura)	.35
198	Checklist (Vladimir Guerrero)	.35
199	Checklist (Todd Walker)	.05
200	Checklist (Scott Rolen)	.05

Artist's Proof

This 200-card parallel set features a special AP seal and foil treatment and is fractured into three levels of scarcity - Red (125 cards), Blue (50 cards) and Green (25 cards). Cards were inserted at a rate of 1:39 packs. "Artist's Proof" is stamped along the lower edge.

	NM/M
Common Red Artist's Proof:	1.00
Red Artist's Proofs:	10X
Common Blue Artist's Proof:	2.00
Blue Artist's Proofs:	25X

	NM/M
Common Green Artist's Proof:	6.00
Green Artist's Proofs:	35X

Museum Collection

Dufex printing on gold-foil backgrounds differentiates the Musuem Collection parallel of New Pinnacle from the regular-issue cards. Museums were inserted at an average rate of one per nine packs.

	NM/M
Complete Set (200):	200.00
Common Player:	1.00
Stars/Rookies:	8X

Interleague Encounter

Inserted 1:240 packs, this 10-card set showcases 20 American League and National League rivals with the date of their first interleague match-up on double-sided mirror mylar cards.

		NM/M
Complete Set (10):		60.00
Common Player:		2.50
1	Albert Belle, Brian Jordan	2.50
2	Andruw Jones, Brady Anderson	4.50
3	Ken Griffey Jr., Tony Gwynn	7.50
4	Cal Ripken Jr., Chipper Jones	12.00
5	Mike Piazza, Ivan Rodriguez	7.50
6	Derek Jeter, Vladimir Guerrero	12.00
7	Greg Maddux, Mo Vaughn	6.00
8	Alex Rodriguez, Hideo Nomo	10.00
9	Juan Gonzalez, Barry Bonds	12.00
10	Frank Thomas, Jeff Bagwell	4.50

Keeping the Pace

Top sluggers who were considered candidates to break Roger Maris' single-season record of 61 home runs were featured in this insert set. Cards feature Dot Matrix holographic borders and backgrounds on front. Backs present career stats

of an all-time great and project future numbers for the current player. The cards were inserted 1:89 packs.

		NM/M
Complete Set (18):		100.00
Common Player:		1.00
1	Juan Gonzalez	3.00
2	Greg Maddux	7.50
3	Ivan Rodriguez	4.50
4	Ken Griffey Jr.	12.00
5	Alex Rodriguez	13.50
6	Barry Bonds	15.00
7	Frank Thomas	6.00
8	Chuck Knoblauch	1.00
9	Derek Jeter	15.00
10	Roger Clemens	9.00
11	Kenny Lofton	1.00
12	Tony Gwynn	7.50
13	Troy Percival	1.00
14	Cal Ripken Jr.	15.00
15	Andy Pettitte	1.50
16	Hideo Nomo	3.00
17	Randy Johnson	2.50
18	Mike Piazza	12.00

Press Plates

Just when collectors thought they had seen every type of insert card imaginable, New Pinnacle proved them wrong by cutting up and inserting into packs (about one per 1,250) the metal plates used to print the set. There are black, blue, red and yellow plates for the front and back of each card. Rather than touting the collector value of the plates, Pinnacle created a treasure hunt by offering $20,000-35,000 to anybody assembling a complete set of four plates for either the front or back of any card. The $35,000, which would have been awarded for completion prior to August 22, was unclaimed. The amount decreased to $20,000 for any set redeemed by the end of 1997.

Spellbound

Each of the 50 cards in this insert features a letter of the alphabet as the basic card design. The letters can be used to spell out the names of nine players featured in the set.

Cards feature micro-etched foil and are inserted 1:19 packs. Cards of Griffey, Ripken and the Jones were inserted only in hobby packs; retail packs have cards of Belle, Thomas, Piazza and the Rodriguezes. Values shown are per card; multiply by number of cards to determine a player's set value.

		NM/M
Complete Set (50):		110.00
1-5AB	Albert Belle	1.00
1-6AJ	Andruw Jones	2.00
1-4AR	Alex Rodriguez	4.50
1-7CJ	Chipper Jones	2.50
1-6CR	Cal Ripken Jr.	6.00
1-5FT	Frank Thomas	2.00
1-5IR	Ivan Rodriguez	1.50
1-6KG	Ken Griffey Jr.	3.50
1-6MP	Mike Piazza	3.50

1997 Pinnacle Certified

This 150-card base features a mirror-like mylar finish and a peel-off protector on each card front. Backs feature the player's 1996 statistics against each opponent. There are four different parallel sets, each with varying degrees of scarcity: Certified Red (1:5), Mirror Red (1:99), Mirror Blue (1:199) and Mirror Gold (1:299). Other inserts include Lasting Impressions, Certified Team, and Certified Gold Team. Cards were sold in six-card packs for a suggested price of $4.99.

	NM/M
Complete Set (150):	30.00
Common Player:	.15
Common Certified Red:	1.00
Certified Red Stars:	5X
Common Mirror Red:	3.00
Mirror Red Stars:	12X
Common Mirror Blue:	4.00
Mirror Blue Stars:	15X
Common Mirror Gold:	7.50
Mirror Gold Stars:	35X
Jose Cruz Jr. Redemption:	2.00
Pack (6):	2.00
Wax Box (20):	35.00

1	Barry Bonds	3.00
2	Mo Vaughn	.15
3	Matt Williams	.15
4	Ryne Sandberg	1.25
5	Jeff Bagwell	1.00
6	Alan Benes	.15
7	John Wetteland	.15
8	Fred McGriff	.15
9	Craig Biggio	.15
10	Bernie Williams	.15
11	Brian L. Hunter	.15
12	Sandy Alomar Jr.	.15
13	Ray Lankford	.15
14	Ryan Klesko	.15
15	Jermaine Dye	.15
16	Andy Benes	.15
17	Albert Belle	.15
18	Tony Clark	.15
19	Dean Palmer	.15
20	Bernard Gilkey	.15
21	Ken Caminiti	.15
22	Alex Rodriguez	2.25
23	Tim Salmon	.15
24	Larry Walker	.15
25	Barry Larkin	.15
26	Mike Piazza	1.50
27	Brady Anderson	.15
28	Cal Ripken Jr.	3.00
29	Charles Nagy	.15
30	Paul Molitor	1.00
31	Darin Erstad	.25
32	Rey Ordonez	.15
33	Wally Joyner	.15
34	David Cone	.15
35	Sammy Sosa	1.25
36	Dante Bichette	.15
37	Eric Karros	.15
38	Omar Vizquel	.15
39	Roger Clemens	1.25
40	Joe Carter	.15
41	Frank Thomas	3.00
42	Javier Lopez	.15
43	Mike Mussina	.45
44	Gary Sheffield	.60
45	Tony Gwynn	1.25
46	Jason Kendall	.15
47	Jim Thome	.75
48	Andres Galarraga	.15
49	Mark McGwire	2.25
50	Troy Percival	.15
51	Derek Jeter	3.00
52	Todd Hollandsworth	.15
53	Ken Griffey Jr.	1.50
54	Randy Johnson	1.00
55	Pat Hentgen	.15
56	Rusty Greer	.15
57	John Jaha	.15
58	Kenny Lofton	.15
59	Chipper Jones	1.25
60	Robb Nen	.15
61	Rafael Palmeiro	.30
62	Mariano Rivera	.15
63	Hideo Nomo	.50
64	Greg Vaughn	.15
65	Ron Gant	.15
66	Eddie Murray	.15
67	John Smoltz	.15
68	Manny Ramirez	.50
69	Juan Gonzalez	.50
70	F.P. Santangelo	.15
71	Moises Alou	.15
72	Alex Ochoa	.15
73	Chuck Knoblauch	.15
74	Raul Mondesi	.15
75	J.T. Snow	.15
76	Rickey Henderson	1.00
77	Bobby Bonilla	.15
78	Wade Boggs	1.25
79	Ivan Rodriguez	.75
80	Brian Jordan	.15
81	Al Leiter	.15
82	Jay Buhner	.15
83	Greg Maddux	1.25
84	Edgar Martinez	.15
85	Kevin Brown	.15
86	Eric Young	.15
87	Todd Hundley	.15
88	Ellis Burks	.15
89	Marquis Grissom	.15
90	Jose Canseco	.60
91	Henry Rodriguez	.15
92	Andy Pettitte	.45
93	Mark Grudzielanek	.15
94	Dwight Gooden	.15
95	Roberto Alomar	.50
96	Paul Wilson	.15
97	Will Clark	.15
98	Rondell White	.15
99	Charles Johnson	.15
100	Jim Edmonds	.15
101	Jason Giambi	.60
102	Billy Wagner	.15
103	Edgar Renteria	.15
104	Johnny Damon	.45
105	Jason Isringhausen	.15
106	Andruw Jones	1.00
107	Jose Guillen	.15
108	Kevin Orie	.15
109	Brian Giles RC	1.25
110	Danny Patterson	.15
111	Vladimir Guerrero	1.00
112	Scott Rolen	.75
113	Damon Mashore	.15
114	Nomar Garciaparra	1.25
115	Todd Walker	.15
116	Wilton Guerrero	.15
117	Bob Abreu	.25
118	Brooks Kieschnick	.15
119	Pokey Reese	.15
120	Todd Greene	.15
121	Dmitri Young	.15
122	Raul Casanova	.15
123	Glendon Rusch	.15
124	Jason Dickson	.15
125	Jorge Posada	.15
126	Rod Myers RC	.15
127	Bubba Trammell RC	.40
128	Scott Spiezio	.15
129	Hideki Irabu RC	.40
130	Wendell Magee	.15
131	Bartolo Colon	.15
132	Chris Holt	.15
133	Calvin Maduro	.15
134	Ray Montgomery	.15
135	Shannon Stewart	.15
136	Ken Griffey Jr. (Certified Stars)	1.00
137	Vladimir Guerrero (Certified Stars)	.50
138	Roger Clemens (Certified Stars)	.75
139	Mark McGwire (Certified Stars)	1.25
140	Albert Belle (Certified Stars)	.15
141	Derek Jeter (Certified Stars)	1.50
142	Juan Gonzalez (Certified Stars)	.25
143	Greg Maddux (Certified Stars)	.60
144	Alex Rodriguez (Certified Stars)	1.25
145	Jeff Bagwell (Certified Stars)	.50
146	Cal Ripken Jr. (Certified Stars)	1.50
147	Tony Gwynn (Certified Stars)	.60
148	Frank Thomas (Certified Stars)	.50
149	Hideo Nomo (Certified Stars)	.25
150	Andruw Jones (Certified Stars)	.50

Red

This parallel set features a red tint to the triangular mylar background left and right of the photo on front. "CERTIFIED RED" is printed vertically on both edges. Backs are identical to regular Certified cards. A peel-off protection coating is on the front of the card. Cards were inserted 1:5 packs.

	NM/M
Common Certified Red:	1.00
Certified Red Stars:	5X

Mirror Red

This parallel set features a red design element on the front of each card. Cards were inserted 1:99 packs.

	NM/M
Common Mirror Red:	3.00
Mirror Red Stars:	12X

Mirror Blue

This parallel set features a blue design element on the front of each card. Cards were inserted 1:199 packs.

	NM/M
Common Mirror Blue:	4.00
Mirror Blue Stars:	15X

Mirror Gold

This parallel set features a holographic gold design on the front of each card. Cards were inserted 1:299 packs.

	NM/M
Common Mirror Gold:	7.50
Mirror Gold Stars:	35X

Mirror Black

The exact nature of these cards is undetermined. They may have been intentionally created and "secretly" seeded in packs as an insert or they may have been test cards which were mistakenly inserted. They are not marked in any fashion.

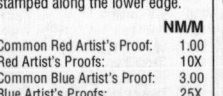

The cards are said to reflect in bright green under direct light. It is commonly believed that each "Mirror Black" card exists in only a single piece, but that has not been verified. Neither is it confirmed that a Mirror Black parallel exists for each of the 151 cards in the base set. Even the most undistinguished player's card can sell for $100 or more due to the scarcity of the type.

	NM/M
Common Player:	100.00

Lasting Impression

This insert features an hourglass die-cut design and a mirror mylar finish and pictures some of baseball's top veteran stars. Backs are conventionally printed and include a color portrait photo and a few words about the player. Cards were inserted 1:19 packs.

		NM/M
Complete Set (20):		40.00
Common Player:		1.00
1	Cal Ripken Jr.	7.50
2	Ken Griffey Jr.	5.00
3	Mo Vaughn	1.00
4	Brian Jordan	1.00
5	Mark McGwire	6.00
6	Chuck Knoblauch	1.00
7	Sammy Sosa	3.00
8	Brady Anderson	1.00
9	Frank Thomas	2.00
10	Tony Gwynn	3.00
11	Roger Clemens	4.00
12	Alex Rodriguez	6.00
13	Paul Molitor	2.00
14	Kenny Lofton	1.00
15	John Smoltz	1.00
16	Roberto Alomar	1.50
17	Randy Johnson	2.00
18	Ryne Sandberg	3.00
19	Manny Ramirez	2.00
20	Mike Mussina	1.50

Team

The top 20 players in the game are honored on cards with frosted silver mylar printing. Cards were inserted 1:19 packs. A parallel version of this set, Certified Gold Team, has a gold mylar design with each card numbered to 500; while a super-premium parallel, Mirror Gold, is numbered to 25. Each card can also be found in a promo version overprinted "SAMPLE."

		NM/M
Complete Set (20):		30.00
Common Player:		.50
Gold:		3X
Mirror Gold:		15X
Sample:		1X
1	Frank Thomas	1.50
2	Jeff Bagwell	1.50
3	Derek Jeter	4.00
4	Chipper Jones	2.00
5	Alex Rodriguez	3.00
6	Ken Caminiti	.50
7	Cal Ripken Jr.	4.00

8	Mo Vaughn	.50
9	Ivan Rodriguez	1.00
10	Mike Piazza	2.50
11	Juan Gonzalez	.75
12	Barry Bonds	4.00
13	Ken Griffey Jr.	2.50
14	Andruw Jones	1.50
15	Albert Belle	.50
16	Gary Sheffield	.75
17	Andy Pettitte	.65
18	Hideo Nomo	.75
19	Greg Maddux	2.00
20	John Smoltz	.50

1997 Totally Certified Samples

This trio of promo cards previews the high-tech, all-numbered Totally Certified issue. The samples are similar in format to the issued versions except they carry a large, black "SAMPLE" overprint diagonally on front and back. Also, backs have a gold-foil "PROMO" instead of the individual serial number.

		NM/M
Complete Set (3):		5.00
Common Player:		1.00
18	Tony Clark (Platinum Red)	1.00
39	Roger Clemens (Platinum Blue)	3.00
41	Frank Thomas (Platinum Gold)	2.00

1997 Totally Certified Platinum Red

Totally Certified doesn't have a true base set. Instead, the product consists of three different 150-card parallel sets. Packs consisted of three cards for $6.99 each. The first of three parallels is the Platinum Red set, inserted two per pack, and featuring micro-etched holographic mylar stock with red accents and foil stamping. Each card in the Red set is sequentially-numbered to 3,999.

		NM/M
Complete Set (150):		75.00
Common Player:		.25
Pack (3):		3.00
Wax Box (20):		45.00
1	Barry Bonds	4.00
2	Mo Vaughn	.25
3	Matt Williams	.25
4	Ryne Sandberg	2.00
5	Jeff Bagwell	1.25
6	Alan Benes	.25
7	John Wetteland	.25
8	Fred McGriff	.25
9	Craig Biggio	.25
10	Bernie Williams	.25
11	Brian Hunter	.25
12	Sandy Alomar Jr.	.25
13	Ray Lankford	.25
14	Ryan Klesko	.25
15	Jermaine Dye	.25
16	Andy Benes	.25
17	Albert Belle	.25
18	Tony Clark	.25
19	Dean Palmer	.25
20	Bernard Gilkey	.25

21	Ken Caminiti	.25
22	Alex Rodriguez	3.00
23	Tim Salmon	.25
24	Larry Walker	.25
25	Barry Larkin	.25
26	Mike Piazza	2.50
27	Brady Anderson	.25
28	Cal Ripken Jr.	4.00
29	Charles Nagy	.25
30	Paul Molitor	1.25
31	Darin Erstad	.35
32	Rey Ordonez	.25
33	Wally Joyner	.25
34	David Cone	.25
35	Sammy Sosa	2.00
36	Dante Bichette	.25
37	Eric Karros	.25
38	Omar Vizquel	.25
39	Roger Clemens	2.25
40	Joe Carter	.25
41	Frank Thomas	1.25
42	Javier Lopez	.25
43	Mike Mussina	.75
44	Gary Sheffield	.60
45	Tony Gwynn	2.00
46	Jason Kendall	.25
47	Jim Thome	1.00
48	Andres Galarraga	.25
49	Mark McGwire	3.00
50	Troy Percival	.25
51	Derek Jeter	4.00
52	Todd Hollandsworth	.25
53	Ken Griffey Jr.	2.50
54	Randy Johnson	1.25
55	Pat Hentgen	.25
56	Rusty Greer	.25
57	John Jaha	.25
58	Kenny Lofton	.25
59	Chipper Jones	2.00
60	Robb Nen	.25
61	Rafael Palmeiro	1.00
62	Mariano Rivera	.35
63	Hideo Nomo	.65
64	Greg Vaughn	.25
65	Ron Gant	.25
66	Eddie Murray	1.25
67	John Smoltz	.25
68	Manny Ramirez	1.25
69	Juan Gonzalez	.65
70	F.P. Santangelo	.25
71	Moises Alou	.25
72	Alex Ochoa	.25
73	Chuck Knoblauch	.25
74	Raul Mondesi	.25
75	J.T. Snow	.25
76	Rickey Henderson	1.25
77	Bobby Bonilla	.25
78	Wade Boggs	2.00
79	Ivan Rodriguez	1.00
80	Brian Jordan	.25
81	Al Leiter	.25
82	Jay Buhner	.25
83	Greg Maddux	2.00
84	Edgar Martinez	.25
85	Kevin Brown	.25
86	Eric Young	.25
87	Todd Hundley	.25
88	Ellis Burks	.25
89	Marquis Grissom	.25
90	Jose Canseco	.60
91	Henry Rodriguez	.25
92	Andy Pettitte	.50
93	Mark Grudzielanek	.25
94	Dwight Gooden	.25
95	Roberto Alomar	.35
96	Paul Wilson	.25
97	Will Clark	.25
98	Rondell White	.25
99	Charles Johnson	.25
100	Jim Edmonds	.25
101	Jason Giambi	.75
102	Billy Wagner	.25
103	Edgar Renteria	.25
104	Johnny Damon	.45
105	Jason Isringhausen	.25
106	Andruw Jones	1.25
107	Jose Guillen	.25
108	Kevin Orie	.25
109	Brian Giles **RC**	2.00
110	Danny Patterson	.25
111	Vladimir Guerrero	1.25
112	Scott Rolen	1.00
113	Damon Mashore	.25
114	Nomar Garciaparra	2.00
115	Todd Walker	.25
116	Wilton Guerrero	.25
117	Bob Abreu	.35
118	Brooks Kieschnick	.25
119	Pokey Reese	.25
120	Todd Greene	.25
121	Dmitri Young	.25
122	Raul Casanova	.25
123	Glendon Rusch	.25
124	Jason Dickson	.25
125	Jorge Posada	.25
126	Rod Myers	.25
127	Bubba Trammell	.25
128	Scott Spiezio	.25
129	Hideki Irabu	.25
130	Wendell Magee	.25
131	Bartolo Colon	.25
132	Chris Holt	.25
133	Calvin Maduro	.25
134	Ray Montgomery	.25
135	Shannon Stewart	.25
136	Ken Griffey Jr. (Certified Stars)	1.50
137	Vladimir Guerrero (Certified Stars)	.60
138	Roger Clemens (Certified Stars)	1.25
139	Mark McGwire (Certified Stars)	1.50
140	Albert Belle (Certified Stars)	.25
141	Derek Jeter (Certified Stars)	2.00
142	Juan Gonzalez (Certified Stars)	.30
143	Greg Maddux (Certified Stars)	1.00
144	Alex Rodriguez (Certified Stars)	1.50
145	Jeff Bagwell (Certified Stars)	.60
146	Cal Ripken Jr. (Certified Stars)	2.00
147	Tony Gwynn (Certified Stars)	1.00
148	Frank Thomas (Certified Stars)	.60
149	Hideo Nomo (Certified Stars)	.30
150	Andruw Jones (Certified Stars)	.60

Platinum Blue

Featuring blue accents and foil stamping, the Platinum Blue cards are sequentially numbered on back in gold foil to 1,999 and inserted per pack.

	NM/M
Complete Set (150):	200.00
Common Player:	1.00
Platinum Blue Stars:	1.5X

Platinum Gold

The most difficult to find of the Totally Certified cards, the Platinum Gold versions are sequentially-numbered to 30 per card and inserted 1:79 packs.

	NM/M
Common Player:	25.00
Platinum Gold Stars:	30X

1997 Pinnacle FanFest

As title sponsor for baseball's All-Star FanFest in Cleveland, July 4-8, Pinnacle issued a number of special cards including this set which was distributed in three-card cello packs both prior to and during

the event. To help promote the event, six of the cards were issued with a schedule back, as well as the regular back design. Fronts have action photos highlighted at bottom by a stadium facade in gold foil. The FanFest logo is at bottom center. Backs feature a player portrait photo within a large star. Also on back are a few stats and personal data, a few words about the player and appropriate logos. Cards are numbered with an "FF" prefix and "of 21" following the number. Card #21 of the host team's Sandy Alomar, Jr., was not issued in packs. A redemption card, which could be traded in at area card shops for the Alomar card, was substituted.

		NM/M
Complete Set (21):		12.50
Common Player:		.25
FF1	Frank Thomas	.65
FF2	Jeff Bagwell	.65
FF3	Chuck Knoblauch	.25
FF4	Craig Biggio	.25
FF5	Alex Rodriguez	1.50
FF6	Chipper Jones	.75
FF7	Cal Ripken Jr.	1.50
FF8	Ken Caminiti	.25
FF9	Juan Gonzalez	.45
FF10	Barry Bonds	2.00
FF11	Ken Griffey Jr.	1.00
FF12	Andruw Jones	.65
FF13	Manny Ramirez	.65
FF14	Tony Gwynn	.75
FF15a	Ivan Rodriguez (Schedule back.)	2.50
FF15b	Ivan Rodriguez (Regular back.)	.50
FF16a	Mike Piazza (Schedule back.)	4.50
FF16b	Mike Piazza (Regular back.)	1.00
FF17a	Andy Pettitte (Schedule back.)	2.00
FF17b	Andy Pettitte (Regular back.)	.40
FF18a	Hideo Nomo (Schedule back.)	1.50
FF18b	Hideo Nomo (Regular back.)	.45
FF19a	Roger Clemens (Schedule back.)	4.00
FF19b	Roger Clemens (Regular back.)	.85
FF20a	Greg Maddux (Schedule back.)	3.50
FF20b	Greg Maddux (Regular back.)	.75
FF21	Sandy Alomar Jr.	2.50
----	Sandy Alomar Jr. (Trade-in card.)	.25

Larry Doby

Marking the 50th anniversary of the American League's integration, Pinnacle, title sponsor of baseball's All-Star FanFest, issued a special card of black A.L. pioneer Larry Doby, who debuted in 1947 with the Indians. FanFest and the All-Star Game were held in Cleveland in 1997, with Doby attending many of the functions. In the same format as its FanFest set of current players, the special Doby card has a black-and-white action photo on front, with gold-foil highlights at bottom. Back repeats the front photo within a star and offers some career notes and stats. The Doby card was given away to FanFest volunteer workers and laminated into identification badges for FanFest dealers.

	NM/M
Larry Doby	4.00

Personal Cards

Continuing a tradition begun a year earlier, Pinnacle, the title

sponsor for baseball's FanFest, produced a series of cards for various local and media celebrities. The cards are in the same format as the FanFest player cards, with color photos on front and gold-foil highlights. Backs have a photo detail within a star design and a few words about the personality, along with stats such as Indians' games attended, popcorn consumed, etc. Cards are numbered with a PC prefix and are difficult to find because their distribution was controlled by the person pictured. Rick Manning was an Indians outfielder from 1975-83. Mike Hegan played in the American League from 1964-77; his father, Jim, was a staple behind the plate for the Indians between 1941-57. Six of the cards feature members of the Fox network which televised the 1997 All-Star Game.

		NM/M
Complete Set (12):		30.00
Common Player:		2.00
PC1	Macie McInnis (Fox)	2.00
PC2	Bill Martin (Fox)	2.00
PC3	Dick Gaddard (Fox)	2.00
PC4	Jack Corrigan (WUAB-TV)	2.00
PC5	Mike Hegan (WUAB-TV)	6.00
PC6	Rick Manning (Sports Channel)	5.00
PC7	John Sanders (Sports Channel)	2.00
PC8	Mayor Michael R. White	4.50
PC9	Wilma Smith (Fox)	2.00
PC10	Tim Taylor (Fox)	2.00
PC11	Robin Swoboda (Fox)	2.00
PC12	Slider (Mascot)	3.00

1997 Pinnacle Inside

The first baseball card set to be sold within a sealed tin can, Inside Baseball consists of a 150-card base set featuring both a color and black-and-white photo of the player on front. Included in the base set are 20 Rookies cards and three checklists. Inserts include the Club Edition and Diamond Edition parallel sets, Dueling Dugouts and Fortysomething. In addition, 24 different cans, each featuring a different player, were available. Cans containing one pack of 10 cards were sold for $2.99 each.

		NM/M
Complete Set (150):		15.00
Common Player:		.05
Common Club Edition:		.75
Club Edition Stars:		5X
Common Diamond Edition:		5.00
Diamond Edition Stars:		25X
Unopened Can (10):		2.00
Case Cans (48):		60.00
1	David Cone	.05
2	Sammy Sosa	1.00
3	Joe Carter	.05
4	Juan Gonzalez	.40

5	Hideo Nomo	.40
6	Moises Alou	.05
7	Marc Newfield	.05
8	Alex Rodriguez	2.00
9	Kimera Bartee	.05
10	Chuck Knoblauch	.05
11	Jason Isringhausen	.05
12	Jermaine Allensworth	.05
13	Frank Thomas	.75
14	Paul Molitor	.75
15	John Mabry	.05
16	Greg Maddux	1.00
17	Rafael Palmeiro	.65
18	Brian Jordan	.05
19	Ken Griffey Jr.	1.50
20	Brady Anderson	.05
21	Ruben Sierra	.05
22	Travis Fryman	.05
23	Cal Ripken Jr.	2.50
24	Will Clark	.05
25	Todd Hollandsworth	.05
26	Kevin Brown	.05
27	Mike Piazza	1.50
28	Craig Biggio	.05
29	Paul Wilson	.05
30	Andres Galarraga	.05
31	Chipper Jones	1.00
32	Jason Giambi	.65
33	Ernie Young	.05
34	Marty Cordova	.05
35	Albert Belle	.05
36	Roger Clemens	1.25
37	Ryne Sandberg	1.00
38	Henry Rodriguez	.05
39	Jay Buhner	.05
40	Raul Mondesi	.05
41	Jeff Fassero	.05
42	Edgar Martinez	.05
43	Trey Beamon	.05
44	Mo Vaughn	.40
45	Gary Sheffield	.40
46	Ray Durham	.05
47	Brett Butler	.05
48	Ivan Rodriguez	.65
49	Fred McGriff	.05
50	Dean Palmer	.05
51	Rickey Henderson	.75
52	Andy Pettitte	.30
53	Bobby Bonilla	.05
54	Shawn Green	.50
55	Tino Martinez	.05
56	Tony Gwynn	1.00
57	Tom Glavine	.35
58	Eric Young	.05
59	Kevin Appier	.05
60	Barry Bonds	2.50
61	Wade Boggs	1.00
62	Jason Kendall	.05
63	Jeff Bagwell	.75
64	Jeff Conine	.05
65	Greg Vaughn	.05
66	Eric Karros	.05
67	Manny Ramirez	.75
68	John Smoltz	.05
69	Terrell Wade	.05
70	John Wetteland	.05
71	Kenny Lofton	.05
72	Jim Thome	.65
73	Bill Pulsipher	.05
74	Darryl Strawberry	.05
75	Roberto Alomar	.25
76	Bobby Higginson	.05
77	James Baldwin	.05
78	Mark McGwire	2.00
79	Jose Canseco	.40
80	Mark Grudzielanek	.05
81	Ryan Klesko	.05
82	Javier Lopez	.05
83	Ken Caminiti	.05
84	Dave Nilsson	.05
85	Tim Salmon	.05
86	Cecil Fielder	.05
87	Derek Jeter	2.50
88	Garret Anderson	.05
89	Dwight Gooden	.05
90	Carlos Delgado	.50
91	Ugueth Urbina	.05
92	Chan Ho Park	.05
93	Eddie Murray	.75
94	Alex Ochoa	.05
95	Rusty Greer	.05
96	Mark Grace	.05
97	Pat Hentgen	.05
98	John Jaha	.05
99	Charles Johnson	.05
100	Jermaine Dye	.05
101	Quinton McCracken	.05
102	Troy Percival	.05
103	Shane Reynolds	.05
104	Rondell White	.05
105	Charles Nagy	.05
106	Alan Benes	.05
107	Tom Goodwin	.05
108	Ron Gant	.05
109	Dan Wilson	.05
110	Darin Erstad	.10
111	Matt Williams	.05
112	Barry Larkin	.05
113	Mariano Rivera	.15
114	Larry Walker	.05
115	Jim Edmonds	.05
116	Michael Tucker	.05
117	Todd Hundley	.05
118	Alex Fernandez	.05
119	J.T. Snow	.05
120	Ellis Burks	.05
121	Steve Finley	.05
122	Mike Mussina	.40

123	Curtis Pride	.05
124	Derek Bell	.05
125	Dante Bichette	.05
126	Terry Steinbach	.05
127	Randy Johnson	.75
128	Andruw Jones	.75
129	Vladimir Guerrero	.75
130	Ruben Rivera	.05
131	Billy Wagner	.05
132	Scott Rolen	.65
133	Rey Ordonez	.05
134	Karim Garcia	.05
135	George Arias	.05
136	Todd Greene	.05
137	Robin Jennings	.05
138	Raul Casanova	.05
139	Josh Booty	.05
140	Edgar Renteria	.05
141	Chad Mottola	.05
142	Dmitri Young	.05
143	Tony Clark	.05
144	Todd Walker	.05
145	Kevin Brown	.05
146	Nomar Garciaparra	1.00
147	Neifi Perez	.05
148	Derek Jeter, Todd Hollandsworth	.50
149	Pat Hentgen, John Smoltz	.05
150	Juan Gonzalez, Ken Caminiti	.05

Club Edition

A 150-card parallel set featuring a special silver foil design and "CLUB EDITION" notation on back, these cards were inserted 1:7 can of Inside.

	NM/M
Complete Club Edition Set (150):	300.00
Common Club Edition:	.75
Stars:	5X

Diamond Edition

A second parallel set, this time featuring a special die-cut design and gold holographic stamping. Cards were inserted 1:63 packs.

	NM/M
Common Diamond Edition:	5.00
Stars:	25X

Cans

In addition to the cards, collectors had the option of collecting the 24 different player cans which are the "packs" in which the cards were sold. About the size of a can of peas (3" diameter, 4-1/2" tall), the cans feature several color and black-and-white reproductions of the player's Inside card. The package had to be opened with a can opener to access the cards. Values shown are for empty cans which have been opened from the bottom; top-opened cans have little collectible value.

	NM/M
Complete Set (24):	10.00
Common Can:	.25
Sealed Cans:	2X
1	Ken Griffey Jr.	.75
2	Juan Gonzalez	.30
3	Frank Thomas	.40
4	Cal Ripken Jr.	1.50
5	Derek Jeter	1.50
6	Andruw Jones	.40
7	Alex Rodriguez	1.00
8	Mike Piazza	.75
9	Mo Vaughn	.25
10	Jeff Bagwell	.40
11	Ken Caminiti	.25
12	Andy Pettitte	.30
13	Barry Bonds	1.50
14	Mark McGwire	1.00
15	Ryan Klesko	.25
16	Manny Ramirez	.50
17	Ivan Rodriguez	.35
18	Chipper Jones	.50
19	Albert Belle	.25
20	Tony Gwynn	.50
21	Kenny Lofton	.25
22	Greg Maddux	.50
23	Hideo Nomo	.40
24	John Smoltz	.25

Dueling Dugouts

This 20-card insert set features a veteran player on one side, a rising star on the other, and a spinning wheel that reveals their respective achievements in various statistical categories. Cards were inserted 1:23 packs.

		NM/M
Complete Set (20):		65.00
Common Player:		1.25
1	Alex Rodriguez, Cal Ripken Jr.	10.00
2	Jeff Bagwell, Ken Caminiti	3.00
3	Barry Bonds, Albert Belle	10.00
4	Mike Piazza, Ivan Rodriguez	6.00
5	Chuck Knoblauch, Roberto Alomar	1.25
6	Ken Griffey Jr., Andruw Jones	6.00
7	Chipper Jones, Jim Thome	4.00
8	Frank Thomas, Mo Vaughn	3.00
9	Fred McGriff, Mark McGwire	7.50
10	Brian Jordan, Tony Gwynn	4.00
11	Barry Larkin, Derek Jeter	10.00
12	Kenny Lofton, Bernie Williams	1.25
13	Juan Gonzalez, Manny Ramirez	3.00
14	Will Clark, Rafael Palmeiro	2.50
15	Greg Maddux, Roger Clemens	4.50
16	John Smoltz, Andy Pettitte	1.25
17	Mariano Rivera, John Wetteland	1.25
18	Hideo Nomo, Mike Mussina	2.00
19	Todd Hollandsworth, Darin Erstad	1.25
20	Vladimir Guerrero, Karim Garcia	3.00

Fortysomething

The top home run hitters in the game are pictured in this 16-card set. Cards were inserted 1:47 packs.

		NM/M
Complete Set (16):		50.00
Common Player:		1.00
1	Juan Gonzalez	3.00
2	Barry Bonds	12.00
3	Ken Caminiti	1.00
4	Mark McGwire	10.00
5	Todd Hundley	1.00
6	Albert Belle	1.00
7	Ellis Burks	1.00
8	Jay Buhner	1.00
9	Brady Anderson	1.00
10	Vinny Castilla	1.00
11	Mo Vaughn	1.00
12	Ken Griffey Jr.	7.50
13	Sammy Sosa	6.50
14	Andres Galarraga	1.00
15	Gary Sheffield	2.00
16	Frank Thomas	5.00

Mint Collection

The 30-card Mint Collection set came in three-card packs that also contained two coins. Cards come in two versions: die-cut and foil. Three foil versions appear with Bronze as the "common." Silver (1:15) and Gold (1:48) parallels also appear. The coins that come with each pack arrive in brass, silver and gold and can be matched up with the corresponding player's die-cut card. Fronts feature a player action shot on the left side with a shadowed portrait at right. On the die-cut versions, the coin-size hole is in the lower-right; the foil team stamp for the common cards is in the same location. Backs are numbered as "x of 30" and deliver a short text.

		NM/M
Complete Set (30):		25.00
Common Player:		.25
Silver Cards:		4X
Gold Cards:		6X
Die-Cuts: 50 Percent		
Wax Box (24):		25.00
1	Ken Griffey Jr.	2.00
2	Frank Thomas	1.25
3	Alex Rodriguez	2.50
4	Cal Ripken Jr.	3.00
5	Mo Vaughn	.25
6	Juan Gonzalez	.60
7	Mike Piazza	2.00
8	Albert Belle	.25
9	Chipper Jones	1.50
10	Andruw Jones	1.25
11	Greg Maddux	1.50
12	Hideo Nomo	.50
13	Jeff Bagwell	1.25
14	Manny Ramirez	.25
15	Mark McGwire	2.50
16	Derek Jeter	3.00
17	Sammy Sosa	1.50
18	Barry Bonds	3.00
19	Chuck Knoblauch	.25
20	Dante Bichette	.25
21	Tony Gwynn	1.50
22	Ken Caminiti	.25
23	Gary Sheffield	.60

24	Tim Salmon	.25
25	Ivan Rodriguez	1.00
26	Henry Rodriguez	.25
27	Barry Larkin	.25
28	Ryan Klesko	.25
29	Brian Jordan	.25
30	Jay Buhner	.25

Mint Collection Coins

Two coins from the 30-coin set were included in each three-card pack of 1997 Pinnacle Mint Collection. Brass coins are common while nickel-silver coins were inserted every 20 packs and gold-plated coins were inserted every 48 packs. Redemption cards for solid silver coins were found every 2,300 packs and a redemption card for a solid gold coin was inserted one per 47,200 packs. Only one of each 24K gold coin was produced. The front of the coins feature the player's portrait while the backs have a baseball diamond with "Limited Edition, Pinnacle Mint Collection 1997" printed.

		NM/M
Complete Set (30):		35.00
Common Brass Coin:		.25
Nickel Coins:		2X
Gold Plated Coins:		6X
Silver Coins:		20X
24K Gold Coins: Value Undetermined		
1	Ken Griffey Jr.	2.50
2	Frank Thomas	1.50
3	Alex Rodriguez	3.00
4	Cal Ripken Jr.	4.00
5	Mo Vaughn	.25
6	Juan Gonzalez	.75
7	Mike Piazza	2.50
8	Albert Belle	.25
9	Chipper Jones	2.00
10	Andruw Jones	1.50
11	Greg Maddux	2.00
12	Hideo Nomo	.75
13	Jeff Bagwell	1.50
14	Manny Ramirez	1.50
15	Mark McGwire	3.00
16	Derek Jeter	4.00
17	Sammy Sosa	1.50
18	Barry Bonds	4.00
19	Chuck Knoblauch	.25
20	Dante Bichette	.25
21	Tony Gwynn	2.00
22	Ken Caminiti	.25
23	Gary Sheffield	.65
24	Tim Salmon	.25
25	Ivan Rodriguez	1.00
26	Henry Rodriguez	.25
27	Barry Larkin	.25
28	Ryan Klesko	.25
29	Brian Jordan	.25
30	Jay Buhner	.25

1997 Pinnacle X-Press

The 150-card set features 115 base cards, a 22-card Rookies subset, 10 Peak Performers and three checklist cards. Each of the regular cards features a horizontal design with two photos of each player on front. Inserts include Swing for the Fences (regular player cards as well as base and booster cards that can be used to accumulate points for a sweepstakes), Men of Summer, Far & Away, Melting Pot, and Metal Works Silver and Gold redemptions. Cards were sold in eight-card packs for $1.99. X-Press Metal Works boxes were also available for $14.99 and contained a regular pack, one metal card and a master deck used to play the Swing for the Fences game.

		NM/M
Complete Set (150):		7.50
Common Player:		.05
Men of Summer:		4X
Pack (8):		.75
Wax Box (24):		10.00
1	Larry Walker	.05
2	Andy Pettitte	.30
3	Matt Williams	.05
4	Juan Gonzalez	.40
5	Frank Thomas	.75
6	Kenny Lofton	.05
7	Ken Griffey Jr.	1.25
8	Andres Galarraga	.05
9	Greg Maddux	1.00
10	Hideo Nomo	.40
11	Cecil Fielder	.05
12	Jose Canseco	.40
13	Tony Gwynn	1.00
14	Eddie Murray	.75
15	Alex Rodriguez	1.50
16	Mike Piazza	1.25
17	Ken Hill	.05
18	Chuck Knoblauch	.05
19	Ellis Burks	.05
20	Rafael Palmeiro	.65
21	Vinny Castilla	.05
22	Rusty Greer	.05
23	Chipper Jones	1.00
24	Rey Ordonez	.05
25	Mariano Rivera	.15
26	Garret Anderson	.05
27	Edgar Martinez	.05
28	Dante Bichette	.05
29	Todd Hundley	.05
30	Barry Bonds	2.00
31	Barry Larkin	.05
32	Derek Jeter	2.00
33	Marquis Grissom	.05
34	David Justice	.05
35	Ivan Rodriguez	.65
36	Jay Buhner	.05
37	Fred McGriff	.05
38	Brady Anderson	.05
39	Tony Clark	.05
40	Eric Young	.05
41	Charles Nagy	.05
42	Mark McGwire	1.50
43	Paul O'Neill	.05
44	Tino Martinez	.05
45	Ryne Sandberg	1.00
46	Bernie Williams	.05
47	Albert Belle	.05
48	Jeff Cirillo	.05
49	Tim Salmon	.05
50	Steve Finley	.05
51	Lance Johnson	.05
52	John Smoltz	.05
53	Javier Lopez	.05
54	Roger Clemens	1.00
55	Kevin Appier	.05
56	Ken Caminiti	.05
57	Cal Ripken Jr.	2.00
58	Moises Alou	.05
59	Marty Cordova	.05
60	David Cone	.05
61	Manny Ramirez	.75
62	Ray Durham	.05
63	Jermaine Dye	.05
64	Craig Biggio	.05
65	Will Clark	.05
66	Omar Vizquel	.05
67	Bernard Gilkey	.05
68	Greg Vaughn	.05
69	Wade Boggs	1.00
70	Dave Nilsson	.05
71	Mark Grace	.05
72	Dean Palmer	.05
73	Sammy Sosa	1.00
74	Mike Mussina	.30
75	Alex Fernandez	.05
76	Henry Rodriguez	.05
77	Travis Fryman	.05
78	Jeff Bagwell	.75
79	Pat Hentgen	.05
80	Gary Sheffield	.40
81	Jim Edmonds	.05
82	Darin Erstad	.10
83	Mark Grudzielanek	.05
84	Jim Thome	.65
85	Bobby Higginson	.05
86	Al Martin	.05
87	Jason Giambi	.50
88	Mo Vaughn	.05
89	Jeff Conine	.05
90	Edgar Renteria	.05
91	Andy Ashby	.05
92	Ryan Klesko	.05
93	John Jaha	.05
94	Paul Molitor	.75
95	Brian Hunter	.05
96	Randy Johnson	.75
97	Joey Hamilton	.05
98	Billy Wagner	.05
99	John Wetteland	.05
100	Jeff Fassero	.05
101	Rondell White	.05
102	Kevin Brown	.05
103	Andy Benes	.05
104	Raul Mondesi	.05
105	Todd Hollandsworth	.05
106	Alex Ochoa	.05
107	Bobby Bonilla	.05
108	Brian Jordan	.05
109	Tom Glavine	.35
110	Ron Gant	.05
111	Jason Kendall	

#	Player	Price
112	Roberto Alomar	.30
113	Troy Percival	.05
114	Michael Tucker	.05
115	Joe Carter	.05
116	Andruw Jones	.75
117	Nomar Garciaparra	1.00
118	Todd Walker	.05
119	Jose Guillen	.05
120	Bubba Trammell RC	.20
121	Wilton Guerrero	.05
122	Bob Abreu	.15
123	Vladimir Guerrero	.75
124	Dmitri Young	.05
125	Kevin Orie	.05
126	Glendon Rusch	.05
127	Brooks Kieschnick	.05
128	Scott Spiezio	.05
129	Brian Giles RC	.75
130	Jason Dickson	.05
131	Damon Mashore	.05
132	Wendell Magee	.05
133	Matt Morris	.05
134	Scott Rolen	.65
135	Shannon Stewart	.05
136	Deivi Cruz RC	.15
137	Hideki Irabu RC	.15
138	Larry Walker (Peak Performers)	.05
139	Ken Griffey Jr. (Peak Performers)	.65
140	Frank Thomas (Peak Performers)	.40
141	Ivan Rodriguez (Peak Performers)	.30
142	Randy Johnson (Peak Performers)	.40
143	Mark McGwire (Peak Performers)	.75
144	Tino Martinez (Peak Performers)	.05
145	Tony Clark (Peak Performers)	.05
146	Mike Piazza (Peak Performers)	.50
147	Alex Rodriguez (Peak Performers)	.75
148	Checklist (Roger Clemens)	.50
149	Checklist (Greg Maddux)	.45
150	Checklist (Hideo Nomo)	.20

Men of Summer

This parallel set of the 150 cards in the base X-Press issue differs in that the fronts are printed on foil backgrounds and the backs have a notation "MEN OF SUMMER" printed in gold vertically at top.

	NM/M
Complete Set (150):	50.00
Common Player:	.25
Stars:	3X

Far & Away

DARIN ERSTAD

This 18-card insert highlights the top home run hitters in baseball and is printed with Dufex technology. Cards were inserted 1:19 packs.

		NM/M
Complete Set (18):		25.00
Common Player:		.50
1	Albert Belle	.50
2	Mark McGwire	4.50
3	Frank Thomas	1.75
4	Mo Vaughn	.50
5	Jeff Bagwell	1.75
6	Juan Gonzalez	1.00
7	Mike Piazza	3.50
8	Andruw Jones	1.75
9	Chipper Jones	2.50
10	Gary Sheffield	1.00
11	Sammy Sosa	2.50
12	Darin Erstad	.75
13	Jay Buhner	.50
14	Ken Griffey Jr.	3.50
15	Ken Caminiti	.50
16	Brady Anderson	.50
17	Manny Ramirez	1.75
18	Alex Rodriguez	4.50

Melting Pot

This insert showcases the talents of major leaguers from various countries. Fronts have color player photos on a background which combines shiny silver foil and textured foil in the design of the player's native flag. Backs have another photo and are ink-jet numbered in a white stripe at bottom in an edition of 500 each. Stated insertion rate was one per 288 packs. Each card can also be found in a promo card version overprinted "SAMPLE."

		NM/M
Complete Set (20):		110.00
Common Player:		1.50
Samples:		1X
1	Jose Guillen	1.50
2	Vladimir Guerrero	8.00
3	Andruw Jones	8.00
4	Larry Walker	1.50
5	Manny Ramirez	8.00
6	Ken Griffey Jr.	10.00
7	Alex Rodriguez	12.00
8	Frank Thomas	8.00
9	Juan Gonzalez	4.00
10	Ivan Rodriguez	6.00
11	Hideo Nomo	4.00
12	Rafael Palmeiro	6.00
13	Dave Nilsson	1.50
14	Nomar Garciaparra	9.00
15	Wilton Guerrero	1.50
16	Sammy Sosa	9.00
17	Edgar Renteria	1.50
18	Cal Ripken Jr.	16.00
19	Derek Jeter	16.00
20	Rey Ordonez	1.50

Metal Works

KEN GRIFFEY JR.

Each Home Plate Box of X-Press contains one heavy bronze Metal Works "card." The 2-3/8" x 3-1/2" slabs have a player portrait on front. Backs have a few words about the player. Redemption cards for silver-plated parallels were inserted 1:470 packs, while a silver slab was found 1:54 Home Plate Boxes. Silver Metal Works are serially numbered to 400 each. Gold-plated Metal Works were produced in an edition of 200 each, with redemption cards inserted 1:950 packs or one per 108 Home Plate Boxes.

		NM/M
Complete Set (20):		25.00
Common Player:		.50
Silver:		3X
Gold:		6X
1	Ken Griffey Jr.	2.00
2	Frank Thomas	1.00
3	Andruw Jones	1.00
4	Alex Rodriguez	2.50
5	Derek Jeter	3.00
6	Cal Ripken Jr.	3.00
7	Mike Piazza	2.00
8	Chipper Jones	1.50
9	Juan Gonzalez	.65
10	Greg Maddux	1.50
11	Tony Gwynn	1.50
12	Jeff Bagwell	1.00
13	Albert Belle	.50
14	Mark McGwire	2.50
15	Nomar Garciaparra	1.50
16	Mo Vaughn	.50
17	Andy Pettitte	.65
18	Manny Ramirez	1.00
19	Kenny Lofton	.50
20	Roger Clemens	1.75

Swing for the Fences

These inserts allowed collectors to play an interactive game based on the number of home runs hit by the home run champion of each league. Cards feature 60 different players and were inserted 1:2 packs. Base cards feature a number between 20-42 printed on them and are found one in every master deck. Booster cards feature a plus-or-minus point total (i.e. +7, -2) that can be used to add or subtract points to get to the winning home run total. Booster cards are found 1:2 packs. Collectors who accumulated the winning home run totals were eligible to win prizes ranging from autographs to a trip to the 1998 All-Star Game. The unnumbered cards are checklisted here in alphabetical order.

		NM/M
Complete Set (60):		20.00
Common Player:		.15
(1)	Sandy Alomar Jr.	.15
(2)	Moises Alou	.15
(3)	Brady Anderson	.15
(4)	Jeff Bagwell	1.00
(5)	Derek Bell	.15
(6)	Jay Bell	.15
(7)	Albert Belle	.15
(8)	Geronimo Berroa	.15
(9)	Dante Bichette	.15
(10)	Barry Bonds	2.50
(11)	Bobby Bonilla	.15
(12)	Jay Buhner	.15
(13)	Ellis Burks	.15
(14)	Ken Caminiti	.15
(15)	Jose Canseco	.40
(16)	Joe Carter	.15
(17)	Vinny Castilla	.15
(18)	Tony Clark	.15
(19)	Carlos Delgado	.50
(20)	Jim Edmonds	.15
(21)	Cecil Fielder	.15
(22)	Andres Galarraga	.15
(23)	Ron Gant	.15
(24)	Bernard Gilkey	.15
(25)	Juan Gonzalez	.50
(26)	Ken Griffey Jr. (AL WINNER)	4.00
(27)	Vladimir Guerrero	1.00
(28)	Todd Hundley	.15
(29)	John Jaha	.15
(30)	Andruw Jones	1.00
(31)	Chipper Jones	1.25
(32)	David Justice	.15
(33)	Jeff Kent	.15
(34)	Ryan Klesko	.15
(35)	Barry Larkin	.15
(36)	Mike Lieberthal	.15
(37)	Javy Lopez	.15
(38)	Edgar Martinez	.15
(39)	Tino Martinez	.15
(40)	Fred McGriff	.15
(41)	Mark McGwire (AL/NL WINNER)	4.00
(42)	Raul Mondesi	.15
(43)	Tim Naehring	.15
(44)	Dave Nillson	.15
(45)	Rafael Palmeiro	.75
(46)	Dean Palmer	.15
(47)	Mike Piazza	1.50
(48)	Cal Ripken Jr.	2.50
(49)	Henry Rodriguez	.15
(50)	Tim Salmon	.15
(51)	Gary Sheffield	.40
(52)	Sammy Sosa	1.25
(53)	Terry Steinbach	.15
(54)	Frank Thomas	1.00
(55)	Jim Thome	.75
(56)	Mo Vaughn	.15
(57)	Larry Walker (NL Winner)	1.25
(58)	Rondell White	.15
(59)	Matt Williams	.15
(60)	Todd Zeile	.15

Swing/Fences Gold

BELLE

Collectors who correctly matched Swing for the Fences insert game cards of the final 1997 season American and National home run champions with proper point cards equal to the number of home runs each hit could exchange them for a random assortment of 10 upgraded cards featuring gold-foil highlights and a premium card stock. The first 1,000 redemptions received an autographed Andruw Jones gold card. The redemption period ended March 1, 1998.

	NM/M
Complete Set (60):	125.00
Common Player:	1.00
Stars:	4X
Andruw Jones Autograph:	25.00

1998 Pinnacle Samples

PIAZZA

Six stars from its 1998 issue were issued in a promo card version with "SAMPLE" printed in large black letters diagonally on back. They were distributed in two-card cello packs.

		NM/M
Complete Set (6):		6.00
Common Player:		1.00
8	Nomar Garciaparra	2.00
9	Ken Griffey Jr.	2.00
24	Frank Thomas	1.25
33	Mike Piazza	2.00
56	Chipper Jones	1.50
72	Larry Walker	1.00

1998 Pinnacle

BAGWELL

Pinnacle's 200-card base set features full-bleed photos on front. Three different backs are produced for each card #1-157: home stats, away stats and seasonal stats. The set also includes cards, 24 Rookies, six Field of Vision, 10 Goin' Jake cards and three checklists. Parallel sets include Artist's Proofs, Press Plates and Museum Collection. Inserts include Epix, Hit it Here, Spellbound and Uncut.

		NM/M
Complete Set (200):		12.50
Common Player:		.05
Pack (10):		1.00
Wax Box (18):		12.00
1	Tony Gwynn/AS	1.00
2	Pedro Martinez/AS	.75
3	Kenny Lofton/AS	.05
4	Curt Schilling/AS	.35
5	Shawn Estes/AS	.05
6	Tom Glavine/AS	.35
7	Mike Piazza/AS	1.50
8	Ray Lankford/AS	.05
9	Barry Larkin/AS	.05
10	Tony Womack/AS	.05
11	Jeff Blauser/AS	.05
12	Rod Beck/AS	.05
13	Larry Walker/AS	.05
14	Greg Maddux/AS	1.00
15	Mark Grace/AS	.05
16	Ken Caminiti/AS	.05
17	Bobby Jones/AS	.05
18	Chipper Jones/AS	1.00
19	Javier Lopez/AS	.05
20	Moises Alou/AS	.05
21	Royce Clayton/AS	.05
22	Darryl Kile/AS	.05
23	Barry Bonds/AS	2.50
24	Steve Finley/AS	.05
25	Andres Galarraga/AS	.05
26	Denny Neagle/AS	.05
27	Todd Hundley/AS	.05
28	Jeff Bagwell	.75
29	Andy Pettitte	.25
30	Darin Erstad	.15
31	Carlos Delgado	.50
32	Matt Williams	.05
33	Will Clark	.05
34	Vinny Castilla	.05
35	Brad Radke	.05
36	John Olerud	.05
37	Andruw Jones	.75
38	Jason Giambi	.50
39	Scott Rolen	.65
40	Gary Sheffield	.40
41	Jimmy Key	.05
42	Kevin Appier	.05
43	Wade Boggs	1.00
44	Hideo Nomo	.40
45	Manny Ramirez	.75
46	Wilton Guerrero	.05
47	Travis Fryman	.05
48	Chili Davis	.05
49	Jeromy Burnitz	.05
50	Craig Biggio	.05
51	Tim Salmon	.05
52	Jose Cruz Jr.	.05
53	Sammy Sosa	1.00
54	Hideki Irabu	.05
55	Chan Ho Park	.05
56	Robin Ventura	.05
57	Jose Guillen	.05
58	Deion Sanders	.05
59	Jose Canseco	.40
60	Jay Buhner	.05
61	Rafael Palmeiro	.65
62	Vladimir Guerrero	.75
63	Mark McGwire	2.00
64	Derek Jeter	2.50
65	Bobby Bonilla	.05
66	Raul Mondesi	.05
67	Paul Molitor	.75
68	Joe Carter	.05
69	Marquis Grissom	.05
70	Juan Gonzalez	.40
71	Kevin Orie	.05
72	Rusty Greer	.05
73	Henry Rodriguez	.05
74	Fernando Tatis	.05
75	John Valentin	.05
76	Matt Morris	.05
77	Ray Durham	.05
78	Geronimo Berroa	.05
79	Scott Brosius	.05
80	Willie Greene	.05
81	Rondell White	.05
82	Doug Drabek	.05
83	Derek Bell	.05
84	Butch Huskey	.05
85	Doug Jones	.05
86	Jeff Kent	.05
87	Jim Edmonds	.05
88	Mark McLemore	.05
89	Todd Zeile	.05
90	Edgardo Alfonzo	.05
91	Carlos Baerga	.05
92	Jorge Fabregas	.05
93	Alan Benes	.05
94	Troy Percival	.05
95	Edgar Renteria	.05
96	Jeff Fassero	.05
97	Reggie Sanders	.05
98	Dean Palmer	.05
99	J.T. Snow	.05
100	Dave Nilsson	.05
101	Dan Wilson	.05
102	Robb Nen	.05
103	Damion Easley	.05
104	Kevin Foster	.05
105	Jose Offerman	.05
106	Steve Cooke	.05
107	Matt Stairs	.05
108	Darryl Hamilton	.05
109	Steve Karsay	.05
110	Gary DiSarcina	.05
111	Dante Bichette	.05
112	Billy Wagner	.05
113	David Segui	.05
114	Bobby Higginson	.05
115	Jeffrey Hammonds	.05
116	Kevin Brown	.05
117	Paul Sorrento	.05
118	Mark Leiter	.05
119	Charles Nagy	.05
120	Danny Patterson	.05
121	Brian McRae	.05
122	Jay Bell	.05
123	Jamie Moyer	.05
124	Carl Everett	.05
125	Greg Colbrunn	.05
126	Jason Kendall	.05
127	Luis Sojo	.05
128	Mike Lieberthal	.05
129	Reggie Jefferson	.05
130	Cal Eldred	.05
131	Orel Hershiser	.05
132	Doug Glanville	.05
133	Willie Blair	.05
134	Neifi Perez	.05
135	Sean Berry	.05
136	Chuck Finley	.05
137	Alex Gonzalez	.05
138	Dennis Eckersley	.65
139	Kenny Rogers	.05
140	Troy O'Leary	.05
141	Roger Bailey	.05
142	Yamil Benitez	.05
143	Wally Joyner	.05
144	Bobby Witt	.05
145	Pete Schourek	.05
146	Terry Steinbach	.05
147	B.J. Surhoff	.05
148	Esteban Loaiza	.05
149	Heathcliff Slocumb	.05
150	Ed Sprague	.05
151	Gregg Jefferies	.05
152	Scott Erickson	.05
153	Jaime Navarro	.05
154	David Wells	.05
155	Alex Fernandez	.05
156	Tim Belcher	.05
157	Mark Grudzielanek	.05
158	Scott Hatteberg	.05
159	Paul Konerko	.15
160	Ben Grieve	.05
161	Abraham Nunez	.05
162	Shannon Stewart	.05
163	Jaret Wright	.05
164	Derrek Lee	.50
165	Todd Dunwoody	.05
166	Steve Woodard RC	.10
167	Ryan McGuire	.05
168	Jeremi Gonzalez	.05
169	Mark Kotsay	.05
170	Brett Tomko	.05
171	Bobby Estalella	.05
172	Livan Hernandez	.05
173	Todd Helton	.75
174	Garrett Stephenson	.05
175	Pokey Reese	.05
176	Tony Saunders	.05
177	Antone Williamson	.05
178	Bartolo Colon	.05
179	Karim Garcia	.05
180	Juan Encarnacion	.05
181	Jacob Cruz	.05
182	Alex Rodriguez (Field of Vision)	2.00
183	Cal Ripken Jr., Roberto Alomar (Field of Vision)	1.00
184	Roger Clemens (Field of Vision)	1.25
185	Derek Jeter (Field of Vision)	2.00
186	Frank Thomas (Field of Vision)	.75
187	Ken Griffey Jr. (Field of Vision)	1.50
188	Mark McGwire (Goin' Jake)	1.00
189	Tino Martinez (Goin' Jake)	.05
190	Larry Walker (Goin' Jake)	.05
191	Brady Anderson (Goin' Jake)	.05
192	Jeff Bagwell (Goin' Jake)	.75
193	Ken Griffey Jr. (Goin' Jake)	1.50
194	Chipper Jones (Goin' Jake)	1.00
195	Ray Lankford (Goin' Jake)	.05
196	Jim Thome (Goin' Jake)	.65
197	Nomar Garciaparra (Goin' Jake)	1.00
198	Checklist (1997 HR Contest)	.05
199	Checklist (1997 HR Contest Winner)	.05
200	Checklist (Overall View of the Park)	.05
9	Ken Griffey Jr./AS (Overprinted "SAMPLE" on back.)	2.00
24	Frank Thomas/AS (Overprinted "SAMPLE" on back.)	1.50

Artist's Proofs

Artist's Proofs is a 100-card partial parallel of the Pinnacle base set. The gold-foil Dufex cards were renumbered with a "PP" prefix and inserted one per 39 packs. A red AP seal appears on front.

		NM/M
Complete Set (100):		375.00
Common Artist's Proof:		1.50
1	Tony Gwynn/AS	12.50
2	Pedro Martinez/AS	10.00
3	Kenny Lofton/AS	1.50
4	Curt Schilling/AS	3.00
5	Shawn Estes/AS	1.50
6	Tom Glavine/AS	3.00
7	Mike Piazza/AS	16.00
8	Ray Lankford/AS	1.50
9	Barry Larkin/AS	1.50
10	Tony Womack/AS	1.50
11	Jeff Blauser/AS	1.50
12	Rod Beck/AS	1.50
13	Larry Walker/AS	1.50
14	Greg Maddux/AS	12.50
15	Mark Grace/AS	1.50
16	Ken Caminiti/AS	1.50
17	Bobby Jones/AS	1.50
18	Chipper Jones/AS	12.50
19	Javier Lopez/AS	1.50
20	Moises Alou/AS	1.50
21	Royce Clayton/AS	1.50
22	Darryl Kile/AS	1.50
23	Barry Bonds/AS	25.00
24	Steve Finley/AS	1.50
25	Andres Galarraga/AS	1.50
26	Denny Neagle/AS	1.50
27	Todd Hundley/AS	1.50
28	Jeff Bagwell	10.00
29	Andy Pettitte	2.50
30	Darin Erstad	2.00
31	Carlos Delgado	4.00
32	Matt Williams	1.50
33	Will Clark	1.50
34	Brad Radke	1.50
35	John Olerud	1.50
36	Andruw Jones	10.00
37	Scott Rolen	7.50
38	Gary Sheffield	3.00
39	Jimmy Key	1.50
40	Wade Boggs	12.50
41	Hideo Nomo	5.00
42	Manny Ramirez	10.00
43	Wilton Guerrero	1.50
44	Travis Fryman	1.50
45	Craig Biggio	1.50
46	Tim Salmon	1.50
47	Jose Cruz Jr.	1.50
48	Sammy Sosa	12.50
49	Hideki Irabu	1.50
50	Jose Guillen	1.50
51	Deion Sanders	1.50
52	Jose Canseco	4.00
53	Jay Buhner	1.50
54	Rafael Palmeiro	7.50
55	Vladimir Guerrero	10.00
56	Mark McGwire	20.00
57	Derek Jeter	25.00
58	Bobby Bonilla	1.50
59	Raul Mondesi	1.50
60	Paul Molitor	10.00
61	Joe Carter	1.50
62	Marquis Grissom	1.50
63	Juan Gonzalez	5.00
64	Dante Bichette	1.50
65	Shannon Stewart (Rookie)	1.50
66	Jaret Wright (Rookie)	1.50
67	Derrek Lee (Rookie)	6.00
68	Todd Dunwoody (Rookie)	1.50
69	Steve Woodard (Rookie)	1.50
70	Ryan McGuire (Rookie)	1.50
71	Jeremi Gonzalez (Rookie)	1.50
72	Mark Kotsay (Rookie)	1.50
73	Brett Tomko (Rookie)	1.50
74	Bobby Estalella (Rookie)	1.50
75	Livan Hernandez (Rookie)	1.50
76	Todd Helton (Rookie)	10.00
77	Garrett Stephenson (Rookie)	1.50
78	Pokey Reese (Rookie)	1.50
79	Tony Saunders (Rookie)	1.50
80	Antone Williamson (Rookie)	1.50
81	Bartolo Colon (Rookie)	1.50
82	Karim Garcia (Rookie)	1.50
83	Juan Encarnacion (Rookie)	1.50
84	Jacob Cruz (Rookie)	1.50
85	Alex Rodriguez (Field of Vision)	20.00
86	Cal Ripken Jr., Roberto Alomar (Field of Vision)	15.00
87	Roger Clemens (Field of Vision)	13.50
88	Derek Jeter (Field of Vision)	25.00
89	Frank Thomas (Field of Vision)	10.00
90	Ken Griffey Jr. (Field of Vision)	16.00
91	Mark McGwire (Goin' Jake)	20.00
92	Tino Martinez (Goin' Jake)	1.50
93	Larry Walker (Goin' Jake)	1.50
94	Brady Anderson (Goin' Jake)	1.50
95	Jeff Bagwell (Goin' Jake)	10.00
96	Ken Griffey Jr. (Goin' Jake)	16.00
97	Chipper Jones (Goin' Jake)	12.50
98	Ray Lankford (Goin' Jake)	1.50
99	Jim Thome (Goin' Jake)	7.50
100	Nomar Garciaparra (Goin' Jake)	12.50

Museum Collection

Museum Collection is a 100-card partial parallel of the Pinnacle base set. The silver-foil Dufex cards were renumbered with a "PP" prefix. Backs have a small "Museum Collection" logo at bottom-center. The cards were inserted one per nine packs.

		NM/M
Complete Museum Set (100):		110.00
Common Museum:		.50
1	Tony Gwynn/AS	2.50
2	Pedro Martinez/AS	2.50
3	Kenny Lofton/AS	.50
4	Curt Schilling/AS	1.50
5	Shawn Estes/AS	.50
6	Tom Glavine/AS	1.50
7	Mike Piazza/AS	4.00
8	Ray Lankford/AS	.50
9	Barry Larkin/AS	.50
10	Tony Womack/AS	.50
11	Jeff Blauser/AS	.50
12	Rod Beck/AS	.50
13	Larry Walker/AS	.50
14	Greg Maddux/AS	3.00
15	Mark Grace/AS	.50
16	Ken Caminiti/AS	.50
17	Bobby Jones/AS	.50
18	Chipper Jones/AS	3.00
19	Javier Lopez/AS	.50
20	Moises Alou/AS	.50
21	Royce Clayton/AS	.50
22	Darryl Kile/AS	.50
23	Barry Bonds/AS	6.00
24	Steve Finley/AS	.50
25	Andres Galarraga/AS	.50
26	Denny Neagle/AS	.50
27	Todd Hundley/AS	.50
28	Jeff Bagwell	2.50
29	Andy Pettitte	1.00
30	Darin Erstad	1.00
31	Carlos Delgado	.50
32	Matt Williams	.50
33	Will Clark	.50
34	Brad Radke	.50
35	John Olerud	.50
36	Andruw Jones	2.50
37	Scott Rolen	2.00
38	Gary Sheffield	1.50
39	Jimmy Key	.50
40	Wade Boggs	3.00
41	Hideo Nomo	1.25
42	Manny Ramirez	2.50
43	Wilton Guerrero	.50
44	Travis Fryman	.50
45	Craig Biggio	.50
46	Tim Salmon	.50
47	Jose Cruz Jr.	.50
48	Sammy Sosa	3.00
49	Hideki Irabu	.50
50	Jose Guillen	.50
51	Deion Sanders	.50
52	Jose Canseco	1.50
53	Jay Buhner	.50
54	Rafael Palmeiro	2.00
55	Vladimir Guerrero	2.50
56	Mark McGwire	5.00

Power Packs Supers

Two dozen regular and subset (Goin' Jake, Field of Vision) cards from Pinnacle are paralleled in this super-size (3-1/2" x 5") version which was included along with 21 regular cards in a $5.99 "Power Pack." Other than being four times the size of the regular card, these supers differ only in their numbering which specifies "x of 24" on back. Each card can also be found in a promo version with a large black "SAMPLE" overprinted on back.

		NM/M
Complete Set (24):		30.00
Common Player:		.50
Samples:		1.5X
1	Alex Rodriguez (Field of Vision)	3.00
2	Cal Ripken Jr., Roberto Alomar (Field of Vision)	2.00
3	Roger Clemens (Field of Vision)	2.25
4	Derek Jeter (Field of Vision)	3.50
5	Frank Thomas (Field of Vision)	1.50
6	Ken Griffey Jr. Field of Vision)	2.50
7	Mark McGwire (Goin' Jake)	3.00
8	Tino Martinez (Goin' Jake)	.50
9	Larry Walker (Goin' Jake)	.50

10	Brady Anderson (Goin' Jake)	.50
11	Jeff Bagwell (Goin' Jake)	1.50
12	Ken Griffey Jr. (Goin' Jake)	2.50
13	Chipper Jones (Goin' Jake)	2.00
14	Ray Lankford (Goin' Jake)	.50
15	Jim Thome (Goin' Jake)	1.00
16	Nomar Garciaparra (Goin' Jake)	2.00
17	Mike Piazza	2.50
18	Andruw Jones	1.50
19	Greg Maddux	2.00
20	Tony Gwynn	2.00
21	Larry Walker	.50
22	Jeff Bagwell	2.00
23	Chipper Jones	2.00
24	Scott Rolen	1.00

Epix

This cross-brand insert was included in Pinnacle, Score, Pinnacle Certified and Zenith. Twenty-four cards were seeded in Pinnacle packs (1:21). The four-tiered set highlights a memorable Game, Season, Moment and Play in a player's career. The holographic foil cards came in three colors: orange, purple and emerald.

		NM/M
Complete Set (24):		45.00
Common Player:		1.00
Purples:		2X
Emeralds:		4X
1	Ken Griffey Jr./G	3.00
2	Juan Gonzalez/G	1.25
3	Jeff Bagwell/G	2.00
4	Ivan Rodriguez/G	1.50
5	Nomar Garciaparra/G	2.50
6	Ryne Sandberg/G	2.50
7	Frank Thomas/S	4.00
8	Derek Jeter/S	5.00
9	Tony Gwynn/S	3.00
10	Albert Belle/S	1.00
11	Scott Rolen/S	1.50
12	Barry Larkin/S	1.00
13	Alex Rodriguez/M	4.00
14	Cal Ripken Jr./M	5.00
15	Chipper Jones/M	2.50
16	Roger Clemens/M	2.75
17	Mo Vaughn/M	1.00
18	Mark McGwire/M	4.00
19	Mike Piazza/M	3.00
20	Andruw Jones/P	.50
21	Greg Maddux/P	2.50
22	Barry Bonds/P	5.00
23	Paul Molitor/P	2.00
24	Eddie Murray/P	2.00

Hit It Here

Hit it Here is seeded one per 17 packs. The micro-etched silver foil cards feature a color player photo with a red "Hit it Here" target at left. Each card has a serial number. If the pictured player hit for the cycle on Opening Day 1998, the collector with the correct serially numbered card would have won $1 million. Each card was also produced in a promo version without serial number and with a large black "SAMPLE" overprint on back.

Press Plates

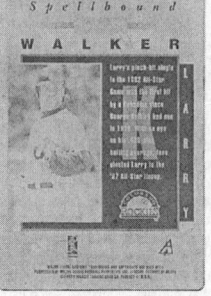

Pinnacle cut up and inserted into packs (about one per 1,250) the metal plates used to print the regular and insert cards in the set. There are black, blue, magenta and yellow plates for the front and back of each card. Because of their unique nature, establishment of catalog values isn't feasible.

	NM/M
Common Player:	50.00

Spellbound

Spellbound is a 50-card insert seeded one per 17 packs. Nine players are featured in the set. The cards feature a photo of the player with a letter from his first or last name in the background. Each player has enough cards to spell his first or last name or a nickname. Values shown are per card and should be multiplied by the number of cards in a player's name to arrive at a value for a complete-player card.

		NM/M
Complete Set (50):		90.00
Common Card:		.75
Inserted 1:17		
1	Mark McGwire (M)	3.50
2	Mark McGwire (C)	3.50
3	Mark McGwire (G)	3.50
4	Mark McGwire (W)	3.50
5	Mark McGwire (I)	3.50
6	Mark McGwire (R)	3.50
7	Mark McGwire (E)	3.50
8	Roger Clemens (R)	2.50
9	Roger Clemens (O)	2.50
10	Roger Clemens (C)	2.50
11	Roger Clemens (K)	2.50
12	Roger Clemens (E)	2.50
13	Roger Clemens (T)	2.50
14	Frank Thomas (B)	1.50
15	Frank Thomas (I)	1.50
16	Frank Thomas (G)	1.50
17	Frank Thomas (H)	1.50
18	Frank Thomas (U)	1.50
19	Frank Thomas (R)	1.50
20	Frank Thomas (T)	1.50
21	Scott Rolen (R)	1.25
22	Scott Rolen (O)	1.25
23	Scott Rolen (L)	1.25
24	Scott Rolen (E)	1.25
25	Scott Rolen (N)	1.25
26	Ken Griffey Jr. (G)	3.00
27	Ken Griffey Jr. (R)	3.00
28	Ken Griffey Jr. (I)	3.00
29	Ken Griffey Jr. (F)	3.00
30	Ken Griffey Jr. (F)	3.00
31	Ken Griffey Jr. (E)	3.00
32	Ken Griffey Jr. (Y)	3.00
33	Larry Walker (W)	.75
34	Larry Walker (A)	.75
35	Larry Walker (L)	.75
36	Larry Walker (K)	.75
37	Larry Walker (E)	.75
38	Larry Walker (R)	.75
39	Nomar Garciaparra (N)	2.25
40	Nomar Garciaparra (O)	2.25
41	Nomar Garciaparra (M)	2.25
42	Nomar Garciaparra (A)	2.25
43	Nomar Garciaparra (R)	2.25
44	Cal Ripken Jr. (C)	4.50
45	Cal Ripken Jr. (A)	4.50
46	Cal Ripken Jr. (L)	4.50
47	Tony Gwynn (T)	2.25
48	Tony Gwynn (O)	2.25
49	Tony Gwynn (N)	2.25
50	Tony Gwynn (Y)	2.25

All-Star FanFest John Elway

The quarterback of the World's Champion Denver Broncos was featured on a card harkening back to his minor league baseball playing days. During the July 1998 All-Star FanFest in Denver, Pinnacle sold a special card of Elway, with proceeds benefiting the city's schools. Initial cost was $2 per card. Front has a black-and-white posed action photo with blue and white pinstriped backgrounds. Back has a ghosted photo of Elway in his Broncos uniform and provides details of his baseball career.

	NM/M
John Elway	3.00

Certified Mirrors

Among several card issues that were aborted by Pinnacle's bankruptcy in mid-1998, but that have leaked into the hobby market in dribs and drabs, are specimens of some of the intended mirror parallels for a Pinnacle Certified set. The majority of cards seen have been Mirror Reds, with a few Mirror Gold issues and even fewer Mirror Blues. Many cards are known in only a single example, and some commons have not yet been verified, though it is presumed that all cards among the first 99 numbers on the unissued Certified base set checklist will be found eventually.

		NM/M
Common Player:		15.00
1	Vladimir Guerrero	25.00
2	Andruw Jones	25.00
3	Paul Molitor	25.00
4	Jose Cruz Jr.	25.00
5	Edgar Martinez	15.00
6	Andy Pettitte	15.00
7	Darin Erstad	15.00
8	Barry Larkin	15.00
9	Derek Jeter	60.00
10	Rusty Greer	15.00

11	Brady Anderson	15.00
12	Tony Clark	15.00
13	Manny Ramirez	25.00
14	Jim Thome	20.00
15	Matt Williams	15.00
16	Ivan Rodriguez	20.00
17	Scott Rolen	20.00
18	Gary Sheffield	15.00
19	David Justice	15.00
20	Roberto Alomar	15.00
21	Ken Caminiti	15.00
22	Sammy Sosa	40.00
23	Albert Belle	15.00
24	Chuck Knoblauch	15.00
25	Mo Vaughn	15.00
26	Raul Mondesi	15.00
27	Tim Salmon	15.00
28	Bernie Williams	15.00
29	Tony Gwynn	25.00
30	Pedro Martinez	25.00
31	Roger Clemens	40.00
32	Craig Biggio	15.00
33	Randy Johnson	25.00
34	Tino Martinez	15.00
35	Chipper Jones	25.00
36	Kenny Lofton	15.00
37	Greg Maddux	25.00
38	Hideo Nomo	20.00
39	Andres Galarraga	15.00
40	Nomar Garciaparra	30.00
41	Juan Gonzalez	20.00
42	Mark McGwire	50.00
43	Mike Piazza	30.00
44	Jeff Bagwell	25.00
45	Barry Bonds	60.00
46	Larry Walker	15.00
47	Alex Rodriguez	60.00
48	Frank Thomas	30.00
49	Cal Ripken Jr.	75.00
50	Ken Griffey Jr.	50.00
51	Todd Walker	15.00
52	Jose Guillen	15.00
53	Vinny Castilla	15.00
54	Shannon Stewart	15.00
55	Jim Edmonds	15.00
56	Bobby Higginson	15.00
57	Jay Buhner	15.00
58	Mike Mussina	15.00
59	Todd Greene	15.00
60	Chan Ho Park	15.00
61	Livan Hernandez	15.00
62	Sandy Alomar Jr.	15.00
63	Fred McGriff	15.00
64	Travis Fryman	15.00
65	Jaret Wright	15.00
66	Bobby Bonilla	15.00
67	Moises Alou	15.00
68	Rafael Palmeiro	25.00
69	Charles Johnson	15.00
70	Ray Lankford	15.00
71	Kevin Brown	15.00
72	Neifi Perez	15.00
73	Rondell White	15.00
74	Bartolo Colon	15.00
75	Bob Abreu	15.00
76	Eric Young	15.00
77	Jason Giambi	20.00
78	Edgardo Alfonzo	15.00
79	Dante Bichette	15.00
80	Eric Karros	15.00
81	Matt Morris	15.00
82	Tom Glavine	15.00
83	Randy Hundley	15.00
84	Jason Dickson	15.00
85	Ryan Klesko	15.00
86	Mark Grace	15.00
87	Brett Tomko	15.00
88	Kevin Orie	15.00
89	Robin Ventura	15.00
90	Jose Canseco	15.00
91	Brian Jordan	15.00
92	Jason Kendall	15.00
93	Mike Cameron	15.00
94	Curt Schilling	20.00
95	Carlos Delgado	15.00
96	Garret Anderson	15.00
97	John Smoltz	15.00
98	Wade Boggs	25.00
99	Javy Lopez	15.00

1998 Pinnacle Inside

Pinnacle Inside features cards in a can. The 150 base cards have full-bleed photos on front with stats on the right and the player's name and position at bottom. The Club Edition parallel (1:7) is printed on silver foil board and the Diamond Edition parallel (1:67) is printed on prismatic foil board. Each pack of cards was packaged inside a collectible can. Inserts include Behind the Numbers and Stand Up Guys.

	NM/M
Complete Set (150):	12.00
Common Player:	.05
Club Edition (1:7):	4X
Diamond Edition (1:67):	10X
Can (10):	1.00
Box (48):	45.00

1	Darin Erstad	.15
2	Derek Jeter	2.50
3	Alex Rodriguez	2.00
4	Bobby Higginson	.05
5	Nomar Garciaparra	1.00
6	Kenny Lofton	.05
7	Ivan Rodriguez	.65
8	Cal Ripken Jr.	2.50
9	Todd Hundley	.05
10	Chipper Jones	1.00
11	Barry Larkin	.05
12	Roberto Alomar	.15
13	Mo Vaughn	.05
14	Sammy Sosa	1.00
15	Sandy Alomar Jr.	.05
16	Albert Belle	.05
17	Scott Rolen	.65
18	Pokey Reese	.05
19	Ryan Klesko	.05
20	Andres Galarraga	.05
21	Justin Thompson	.05
22	Gary Sheffield	.40
23	David Justice	.05
24	Ken Griffey Jr.	1.50
25	Andruw Jones	.75
26	Jeff Bagwell	.75
27	Vladimir Guerrero	.75
28	Mike Piazza	1.50
29	Chuck Knoblauch	.05
30	Rondell White	.05
31	Greg Maddux	1.00
32	Andy Pettitte	.20
33	Larry Walker	.05
34	Bobby Estalella	.05
35	Frank Thomas	.75
36	Tony Womack	.05
37	Tony Gwynn	1.00
38	Barry Bonds	2.50
39	Randy Johnson	.75
40	Mark McGwire	2.00
41	Juan Gonzalez	.40
42	Tim Salmon	.05
43	John Smoltz	.05
44	Rafael Palmeiro	.65
45	Mark Grace	.05
46	Mike Cameron	.05
47	Jim Thome	.65
48	Neifi Perez	.05
49	Kevin Brown	.05
50	Craig Biggio	.05
51	Bernie Williams	.05
52	Hideo Nomo	.40
53	Bob Abreu	.15
54	Edgardo Alfonzo	.05
55	Wade Boggs	1.00
56	Jose Guillen	.05
57	Ken Caminiti	.05
58	Paul Molitor	.75
59	Shawn Estes	.05
60	Edgar Martinez	.05
61	Livan Hernandez	.05
62	Ray Lankford	.05
63	Rusty Greer	.05
64	Jim Edmonds	.35
65	Tom Glavine	.05
66	Alan Benes	.05
67	Will Clark	.05
68	Garret Anderson	.05
69	Javier Lopez	.05
70	Mike Mussina	.35
71	Kevin Orie	.05
72	Matt Williams	.05
73	Bobby Bonilla	.05
74	Ruben Rivera	.05
75	Jason Giambi	.60
76	Todd Walker	.05
77	Tino Martinez	.05
78	Matt Morris	.05
79	Fernando Tatis	.05
80	Todd Greene	.05
81	Fred McGriff	.05
82	Brady Anderson	.05
83	Mark Kotsay	.05
84	Raul Mondesi	.05
85	Moises Alou	.05
86	Roger Clemens	1.25
87	Wilton Guerrero	.05
88	Shannon Stewart	.05
89	Chan Ho Park	.05
90	Carlos Delgado	.60
91	Jose Cruz Jr.	.60
92	Shawn Green	.35
93	Robin Ventura	.05
94	Reggie Sanders	.05
95	Orel Hershiser	.05
96	Dante Bichette	.05
97	Charles Johnson	.05
98	Pedro Martinez	.75
99	Mariano Rivera	.15
100	Joe Randa	.05
101	Jeff Kent	.05
102	Jay Buhner	.05
103	Brian Jordan	.05
104	Jason Kendall	.05
105	Scott Spiezio	.05
106	Desi Relaford	.05
107	Bernard Gilkey	.05
108	Manny Ramirez	.75
109	Tony Clark	.05
110	Eric Young	.05
111	Johnny Damon	.30
112	Glendon Rusch	.05
113	Ben Grieve	.05
114	Homer Bush	.05
115	Miguel Tejada	.25
116	Lou Collier	.05
117	Derrek Lee	.60
118	Jacob Cruz	.05
119	Raul Ibanez	.05
120	Ryan Mclaren	.05
121	Antone Williamson	.05
122	Abraham Nunez	.05
123	Jeff Abbott	.05
124	Brett Tomko	.05
125	Richie Sexson	.05
126	Todd Helton	.75
127	Juan Encarnacion	.05
128	Richard Hidalgo	.05
129	Paul Konerko	.10
130	Brad Fullmer	.05
131	Jeremi Gonzalez	.05
132	Jaret Wright	.05
133	Derek Jeter (Inside Tips)	1.25
134	Frank Thomas (Inside Tips)	.40
135	Nomar Garciaparra (Inside Tips)	.50
136	Kenny Lofton (Inside Tips)	.05
137	Jeff Bagwell (Inside Tips)	.40
138	Todd Hundley (Inside Tips)	.05
139	Alex Rodriguez (Inside Tips)	1.00
140	Ken Griffey Jr. (Inside Tips)	.75
141	Sammy Sosa (Inside Tips)	.50
142	Greg Maddux (Inside Tips)	.50
143	Albert Belle (Inside Tips)	.05
144	Cal Ripken Jr. (Inside Tips)	1.25
145	Mark McGwire (Inside Tips)	1.00
146	Chipper Jones (Inside Tips)	.50
147	Charles Johnson (Inside Tips)	.05
148	Checklist (Ken Griffey Jr.)	.75
149	Checklist (Jose Cruz Jr.)	.05
150	Checklist (Larry Walker)	.05

Club Edition

This parallel set is virtually identical to the regular Inside cards, except for the addition of a "CLUB EDITION" notice to the right of the player's first name, and the use of gold foil highlights instead of silver on front.

	NM/M
Complete Set (150):	50.00
Common Player:	2.00
Stars:	4X
Inserted 1:7	

Diamond Edition

Diamond Edition cards parallel all 150 cards in Pinnacle Inside. The fronts have the insert name. These are printed on prismatic foil board and inserted one per 67 cans.

	NM/M
Common Card:	6.00
Stars:	10X
Inserted 1:67	

Behind the Numbers

Behind the Numbers is seeded one per 23 cans. Fronts feature an action photo printed in front of the player's number. The card is die-cut around the large metallic foil numerals. The back has a portrait photo and text explaining why the player wears that number.

	NM/M
Complete Set (20):	85.00
Common Player:	1.50
Inserted 1:23	
1	Ken Griffey Jr.	7.50
2	Cal Ripken Jr.	12.00
3	Alex Rodriguez	10.00
4	Jose Cruz Jr.	1.50
5	Mike Piazza	7.50
6	Nomar Garciaparra	5.50
7	Scott Rolen	2.50
8	Andruw Jones	4.00
9	Frank Thomas	4.00
10	Mark McGwire	10.00
11	Ivan Rodriguez	3.00
12	Greg Maddux	5.50
13	Roger Clemens	6.50
14	Derek Jeter	12.00
15	Tony Gwynn	5.50
16	Ben Grieve	1.50
17	Jeff Bagwell	4.00
18	Chipper Jones	6.00
19	Hideo Nomo	2.00
20	Sandy Alomar Jr.	1.50

Stand Up Guys

This 50-card insert was seeded one per can. Each card has a match; the two cards join together in the center to form a stand-up collectible featuring four Major League players. Each card can also be found in a promo edition with a large "SAMPLE" overprint.

	NM/M
Complete Set (50):	35.00
Common Card:	.25
Sample:	3X
1-A/B	Ken Griffey Jr., Cal Ripken Jr.	2.00
1-C/D	Tony Gwynn, Mike Piazza	1.25
2-A/B	Andruw Jones, Alex Rodriguez	1.50
2-C/D	Scott Rolen, Nomar Garciaparra	1.50
3-A/B	Andruw Jones, Greg Maddux	1.00
3-C/D	Javy Lopez, Chipper Jones	1.00
4-A/B	Jay Buhner, Randy Johnson	.75
4-C/D	Ken Griffey Jr., Alex Rodriguez	1.50
5-A/B	Frank Thomas, Jeff Bagwell	.75
5-C/D	Mark McGwire, Mo Vaughn	1.50
6-A/B	Nomar Garciaparra, Derek Jeter	2.00
6-C/D	Alex Rodriguez, Barry Larkin	1.50
7-A/B	Mike Piazza, Ivan Rodriguez	1.25
7-C/D	Charles Johnson, Javy Lopez	.25
8-A/B	Cal Ripken Jr., Chipper Jones	2.00
8-C/D	Ken Caminiti, Scott Rolen	.65
9-A/B	Jose Cruz Jr., Vladimir Guerrero	.75
9-C/D	Andruw Jones, Jose Guillen	.75
10-A/B	Larry Walker, Dante Bichette	.25
10-C/D	Ellis Burks, Neifi Perez	.25
11-A/B	Sammy Sosa, Sammy Sosa	1.00
11-C/D	Vladimir Guerrero, Manny Ramirez	.75
12-A/B	Greg Maddux, Roger Clemens	1.00
12-C/D	Hideo Nomo, Randy Johnson	.75
13-A/B	Ben Grieve, Paul Konerko	.40
13-C/D	Jose Cruz Jr., Fernando Tatis	.25
14-A/B	Ryne Sandberg, Chuck Knoblauch	1.00
14-C/D	Roberto Alomar, Craig Biggio	.35
15-A/B	Cal Ripken Jr., Brady Anderson	2.00
15-C/D	Rafael Palmeiro, Roberto Alomar	.65
16-A/B	Darin Erstad, Jim Edmonds	.35
16-C/D	Tim Salmon, Garret Anderson	.25
17-A/B	Mike Piazza, Hideo Nomo	1.25
17-C/D	Raul Mondesi, Eric Karros	.25
18-A/B	Ivan Rodriguez, Juan Gonzalez	.65
18-C/D	Will Clark, Rusty Greer	.25
19-A/B	Derek Jeter, Bernie Williams	2.00
19-C/D	Tino Martinez, Andy Pettitte	.25
20-A/B	Kenny Lofton, Ken Griffey Jr.	1.25
20-C/D	Brady Anderson, Bernie Williams	.25
21-A/B	Paul Molitor, Eddie Murray	.75
21-C/D	Ryne Sandberg, Rickey Henderson	1.00
22-A/B	Tony Clark, Frank Thomas	.75
22-C/D	Jeff Bagwell, Mark McGwire	1.50
23-A/B	Manny Ramirez, Jim Thome	.75
23-C/D	David Justice, Sandy Alomar Jr.	.25
24-A/B	Barry Bonds, Albert Belle	2.00
24-C/D	Larry Walker, Dante Bichette	.60
25-A/B	Ken Griffey Jr., Frank Thomas	1.25
25-C/D	Alex Rodriguez, Andruw Jones	1.50

Cans

Ten-card packs of Pinnacle Inside were packaged in collectible cans. The 24 cans featured a player photo or team logo. Cans were created to honor the Florida Marlins' world championship and the expansion Arizona and Tampa Bay teams. Gold parallel versions of the cans were found one every 47 cans. Values shown are for bottom-opened cans; cans opened from the top have little collectible value.

	NM/M
Complete Set (23):	15.00
Common Can:	.40
Gold Cans:	2X
1	Ken Griffey Jr.	1.25
2	Frank Thomas	.65
3	Alex Rodriguez	1.50
4	Andruw Jones	.65
5	Mike Piazza	1.25
6	Ben Grieve	.40

7	Hideo Nomo	.50
8	Vladimir Guerrero	.65
9	Roger Clemens	1.00
10	Tony Gwynn	.75
11	Mark McGwire	1.50
12	Cal Ripken Jr.	2.00
13	Jose Cruz Jr.	.40
14	Greg Maddux	.75
15	Chipper Jones	.75
16	Derek Jeter	2.00
17	Juan Gonzalez	.50
18	Nomar Garciaparra (AL ROY)	1.00
19	Scott Rolen (NL ROY)	.65
20	Florida Marlins World Series Winner	.40
21	Larry Walker (NL MVP)	.40
22	Tampa Bay Devil Rays	.40
23	Arizona Diamondbacks	.40

1998 Pinnacle Mint Collection

Mint Collection consists of 30 cards and 30 matching coins with numerous parallels of each. The cards come in four different versions. The base card features a player photo at left with a circular bronze foil team logo at right. The base cards were inserted one per hobby pack and two per retail pack. Die-cut versions removed the team logo and were inserted two per hobby and one per retail packs. Silver Mint Team (1:15 hobby, 1:23 retail) and Gold Mint Team (1:47 hobby, 1:71 retail) parallels were printed on silver foil and gold foil board, respectively.

	NM/M
Complete Set (30):	10.00
Common Die-Cut:	.25
Bronze (1:1H):	2X
Silver (1:15H):	5X
Gold (1:47):	12X
Pack (3+2):	1.00
Wax Box (24):	12.00
1	Jeff Bagwell	.65
2	Albert Belle	.25
3	Barry Bonds	2.00
4	Tony Clark	.25
5	Roger Clemens	1.00
6	Juan Gonzalez	.35
7	Ken Griffey Jr.	1.25
8	Tony Gwynn	.75
9	Derek Jeter	2.00
10	Randy Johnson	.65
11	Chipper Jones	.75
12	Greg Maddux	.75
13	Tino Martinez	.25
14	Mark McGwire	1.50
15	Hideo Nomo	.35
16	Andy Pettitte	.25
17	Mike Piazza	1.25
18	Cal Ripken Jr.	2.00
19	Alex Rodriguez	1.50
20	Ivan Rodriguez	.50
21	Sammy Sosa	.50
22	Frank Thomas	.65
23	Mo Vaughn	.25
24	Larry Walker	.25
25	Jose Cruz Jr.	.25
26	Nomar Garciaparra	.75
27	Vladimir Guerrero	.65
28	Livan Hernandez	.25
29	Andruw Jones	.65
30	Scott Rolen	.50

Coins

Two base coins were included in each pack of Mint Collection. The coins feature the player's image, name and number on the front along with his team's name and logo. The back has the Mint Collection logo. Seven parallels were included: Nickel-Silver (1:41), Brass Proof (numbered to 500), Nickel

Proof (numbered to 250), Gold Proof (numbered to 100), Gold-Plated (1:199), Solid Silver (1:288 hobby, 1:960 retail) and Solid Gold by redemption (1-of-1).

	NM/M
Complete Set (30):	20.00
Common Brass Coin:	.50
Brass Proof (500):	5X
Nickel (1:41):	3X
Nickel Proof (250):	12X
Silver:	12X
Inserted 1:288 H, 1:960 R	
Gold Plated (1:199):	15X
Gold Proof (100):	20X
1 Jeff Bagwell	.75
2 Albert Belle	.50
3 Barry Bonds	2.00
4 Tony Clark	.50
5 Roger Clemens	1.50
6 Juan Gonzalez	.50
7 Ken Griffey Jr.	1.50
8 Tony Gwynn	1.00
9 Derek Jeter	2.00
10 Randy Johnson	1.00
11 Chipper Jones	1.00
12 Greg Maddux	1.50
13 Tino Martinez	.50
14 Mark McGwire	1.50
15 Hideo Nomo	.50
16 Andy Pettitte	.75
17 Mike Piazza	1.00
18 Cal Ripken Jr.	2.00
19 Alex Rodriguez	2.00
20 Ivan Rodriguez	.75
21 Sammy Sosa	.75
22 Frank Thomas	.75
23 Mo Vaughn	.50
24 Larry Walker	.50
25 Jose Cruz Jr.	.50
26 Nomar Garciaparra	.75
27 Vladimir Guerrero	.75
28 Livan Hernandez	.50
29 Andruw Jones	.75
30 Scott Rolen	.75

Mint Gems

Scott Rolen

Mint Gems is a six-card insert printed on silver foil board. The cards were inserted 1:31 hobby packs and 1:47 retail. The oversized Mint Gems coins are twice the size of the regular coins. The six coins were inserted 1:31 hobby packs.

	NM/M
Complete Set (6)	20.00
Common Player:	2.00
Coins:	1X
1 Ken Griffey Jr.	6.00
2 Larry Walker	2.00
3 Roger Clemens	5.00
4 Pedro Martinez	4.00
5 Nomar Garciaparra	4.50
6 Scott Rolen	3.00

1998 Pinnacle Performers

Pinnacle Performers consists of a 150-card base set. The Peak Performers parallel adds silver foil to the base cards and was inserted 1:7. Inserts in the home run-themed product include Big Bang, Launching Pad, Player's Card and Power Trip.

	NM/M
Complete Set (150):	12.00
Common Player:	.05
Peak Performers (1:7):	2X
Pack (10):	1.00
Wax Box (24):	15.00
1 Ken Griffey Jr.	1.00
2 Frank Thomas	.65
3 Cal Ripken Jr.	1.50
4 Alex Rodriguez	1.25
5 Greg Maddux	.75
6 Mike Piazza	1.00
7 Chipper Jones	.75
8 Tony Gwynn	.75
9 Derek Jeter	1.50
10 Jeff Bagwell	.65
11 Juan Gonzalez	.35
12 Nomar Garciaparra	.75
13 Andruw Jones	.65
14 Hideo Nomo	.35
15 Roger Clemens	.85
16 Mark McGwire	1.25
17 Scott Rolen	.60
18 Vladimir Guerrero	.65
19 Barry Bonds	1.50
20 Darin Erstad	.15
21 Albert Belle	.05
22 Kenny Lofton	.05
23 Mo Vaughn	.05
24 Tony Clark	.05
25 Ivan Rodriguez	.60
26 Jose Cruz Jr.	.05
27 Larry Walker	.05
28 Jaret Wright	.05
29 Andy Pettitte	.05
30 Roberto Alomar	.20
31 Randy Johnson	.65
32 Manny Ramirez	.65
33 Paul Molitor	.65
34 Mike Mussina	.35
35 Jim Thome	.60
36 Tino Martinez	.05
37 Gary Sheffield	.45
38 Chuck Knoblauch	.05
39 Bernie Williams	.05
40 Tim Salmon	.05
41 Sammy Sosa	.75
42 Wade Boggs	.75
43 Will Clark	.05
44 Andres Galarraga	.05
45 Raul Mondesi	.05
46 Rickey Henderson	.65
47 Jose Canseco	.45
48 Pedro Martinez	.65
49 Jay Buhner	.05
50 Ryan Klesko	.05
51 Barry Larkin	.05
52 Charles Johnson	.05
53 Tom Glavine	.35
54 Edgar Martinez	.05
55 Fred McGriff	.05
56 Moises Alou	.05
57 Dante Bichette	.05
58 Jim Edmonds	.05
59 Mark Grace	.05
60 Chan Ho Park	.05
61 Justin Thompson	.05
62 John Smoltz	.05
63 Craig Biggio	.05
64 Ken Caminiti	.05
65 Richard Hidalgo	.05
66 Carlos Delgado	.50
67 David Justice	.05
68 J.T. Snow	.05
69 Jason Giambi	.50
70 Garret Anderson	.05
71 Rondell White	.05
72 Matt Williams	.05
73 Brady Anderson	.05
74 Eric Karros	.05
75 Javier Lopez	.05
76 Pat Hentgen	.05
77 Todd Hundley	.05
78 Ray Lankford	.05
79 Denny Neagle	.05
80 Sandy Alomar Jr.	.05
81 Jason Kendall	.05
82 Omar Vizquel	.05
83 Kevin Brown	.05
84 Kevin Appier	.05
85 Al Martin	.05
86 Rusty Greer	.05
87 Bobby Bonilla	.05
88 Shawn Estes	.05
89 Rafael Palmeiro	.60
90 Edgar Renteria	.05
91 Alan Benes	.05
92 Bobby Higginson	.05
93 Mark Grudzielanek	.05
94 Jose Guillen	.05
95 Neifi Perez	.05
96 Jeff Abbott	.05
97 Todd Walker	.05
98 Eric Young	.05
99 Brett Tomko	.05
100 Mike Cameron	.05
101 Karim Garcia	.05
102 Brian Jordan	.05
103 Jeff Suppan	.05
104 Robin Ventura	.05
105 Henry Rodriguez	.05
106 Shannon Stewart	.05
107 Kevin Orie	.05
108 Bartolo Colon	.05
109 Bob Abreu	.15
110 Vinny Castilla	.05
111 Livan Hernandez	.05

112 Derrek Lee	.50
113 Mark Kotsay	.05
114 Todd Greene	.05
115 Edgardo Alfonzo	.05
116 A.J. Hinch	.05
117 Paul Konerko	.15
118 Todd Helton	.65
119 Miguel Tejada	.20
120 Fernando Tatis	.05
121 Ben Grieve	.05
122 Travis Lee	.05
123 Kerry Wood	.25
124 Eli Marrero	.05
125 David Ortiz	.50
126 Juan Encarnacion	.05
127 Brad Fullmer	.05
128 Richie Sexson	.05
129 Aaron Boone	.05
130 Enrique Wilson	.05
131 Javier Valentin	.05
132 Abraham Nunez	.05
133 Ricky Ledee	.05
134 Carl Pavano	.05
135 Bobby Estalella	.05
136 Homer Bush	.05
137 Brian Rose	.05
138 Ken Griffey Jr. (Far and Away)	.50
139 Frank Thomas (Far and Away)	.35
140 Cal Ripken Jr. (Far and Away)	.75
141 Alex Rodriguez (Far and Away)	.65
142 Greg Maddux (Far and Away)	.40
143 Chipper Jones (Far and Away)	.40
144 Mike Piazza (Far and Away)	.50
145 Tony Gwynn (Far and Away)	.40
146 Derek Jeter (Far and Away)	.75
147 Jeff Bagwell (Far and Away)	.35
148 Checklist (Hideo Nomo)	.20
149 Checklist (Roger Clemens)	.45
150 Checklist (Greg Maddux)	.35

Peak Performers

This 150-card parallel set is printed on silver foil vs. the white cardboard stock used on regular-issue cards. The parallel set name is printed down the right side in gold letters. They were seeded one per seven packs.

	NM/M
Complete Set (150):	100.00
Common Player:	2.00
Stars:	6X
Inserted 1:7	

Big Bang

This 20-card insert features top power hitters. The micro-etched cards are sequentially numbered to 2,500. Each player has a Seasonal Outburst parallel, with a red overlay and numbered to that player's best seasonal home run total. Each card is also found in a promo edition with a large black "SAMPLE" overprinted on back.

	NM/M
Complete Set (20):	27.50
Common Player:	.50
Production 2,500 Sets	
Sample:	1X
1 Ken Griffey Jr.	2.50
2 Frank Thomas	1.50
3 Mike Piazza	2.50
4 Chipper Jones	2.00
5 Alex Rodriguez	3.00
6 Nomar Garciaparra	2.00
7 Jeff Bagwell	1.50
8 Cal Ripken Jr.	3.50
9 Albert Belle	.50
10 Mark McGwire	3.00
11 Juan Gonzalez	.75
12 Larry Walker	.50
13 Tino Martinez	.50
14 Jim Thome	1.00
15 Manny Ramirez	1.50
16 Barry Bonds	3.50
17 Mo Vaughn	.50
18 Jose Cruz Jr.	.50
19 Tony Clark	.50
20 Andruw Jones	1.50

Big Bang Seasonal Outburst

Season Outburst parallels the Big Bang insert. The cards have a red overlay and are sequentially numbered to each player's season-high home run total. Unnumbered versions of the cards, likely leaked into the market after Pinnacle went bankrupt in mid-1998, have been seen; their value is much lower than the issued version.

	NM/M
Complete Set (20):	500.00
Common Player:	10.00
#'d to player's 1997 HR total	
Unnumbered: 25 Percent	
1 Ken Griffey Jr./56	40.00
2 Frank Thomas/35	20.00
3 Mike Piazza/40	40.00
4 Chipper Jones/21	65.00
5 Alex Rodriguez/23	75.00
6 Nomar Garciaparra/30	40.00
7 Jeff Bagwell/43	20.00
8 Cal Ripken Jr./17	80.00
9 Albert Belle/30	65.00
10 Mark McGwire/58	65.00
11 Juan Gonzalez/42	12.50
12 Larry Walker/49	10.00
13 Tino Martinez/44	10.00
14 Jim Thome/40	15.00
15 Manny Ramirez/26	25.00
16 Barry Bonds/40	75.00
17 Mo Vaughn/35	10.00
18 Jose Cruz Jr./26	10.00
19 Tony Clark/32	10.00
20 Andruw Jones/18	25.00

Launching Pad

Launching PAD

Launching Pad is a 20-card insert seeded one per nine packs. It features top sluggers on foil-on-foil cards with an outer space background.

	NM/M
Complete Set (20):	25.00
Common Player:	.50
Inserted 1:9	
1 Ben Grieve	.50
2 Ken Griffey Jr.	2.50
3 Derek Jeter	3.50
4 Frank Thomas	1.00
5 Travis Lee	.50
6 Vladimir Guerrero	1.00
7 Tony Gwynn	2.00
8 Jose Cruz Jr.	.50
9 Cal Ripken Jr.	3.50
10 Chipper Jones	2.00
11 Scott Rolen	.75
12 Andruw Jones	1.00
13 Ivan Rodriguez	.75
14 Todd Helton	1.00
15 Nomar Garciaparra	2.00
16 Mark McGwire	3.00
17 Gary Sheffield	.60
18 Bernie Williams	.50
19 Alex Rodriguez	3.00
20 Mike Piazza	2.50

Power Trip

This 10-card insert was seeded 1:21. Printed on silver foil, each card is sequentially-numbered to 10,000. Cards backs have details about one of the player's power-hitting highlights of the previous season.

	NM/M
Complete Set (10):	16.00
Common Player:	1.00
Production 10,000 Sets	
1 Frank Thomas	1.00
2 Alex Rodriguez	3.00
3 Nomar Garciaparra	1.50
4 Jeff Bagwell	1.00
5 Cal Ripken Jr.	4.00
6 Mike Piazza	2.00
7 Chipper Jones	1.50
8 Ken Griffey Jr.	2.00
9 Mark McGwire	3.00
10 Juan Gonzalez	1.00

Swing for the Fences

Pinnacle Performers included the "Swing for the Fences" sweepstakes. Fifty players were featured on cards with numbers on an all-red background. Fifty Home Run Points cards were also inserted, with each card featuring a point total on the front. Collectors who found the player cards of the AL and NL home run leaders, as well as enough point cards to match each of their season totals, were eligible to win prizes. A player or point card was inserted in each pack.

	NM/M
Complete Set (50):	24.00
Common Player:	.25
Inserted 1:1	
1 Brady Anderson	.25
2 Albert Belle	.25
3 Jay Buhner	.25
4 Jose Canseco	.50
5 Tony Clark	.25
6 Jose Cruz Jr.	.25
7 Jim Edmonds	.25
8 Cecil Fielder	.25
9 Travis Fryman	.25
10 Nomar Garciaparra	1.00
11 Juan Gonzalez	.40
12 Ken Griffey Jr.	1.50
13 David Justice	.25
14 Travis Lee	.25
15 Edgar Martinez	.25
16 Tino Martinez	.25
17 Rafael Palmeiro	.65
18 Manny Ramirez	.75
19 Cal Ripken Jr.	2.50
20 Alex Rodriguez	.25
21 Tim Salmon	.25
22 Frank Thomas	.75
23 Jim Thome	.65
24 Mo Vaughn	.25
25 Bernie Williams	.25
26 Fred McGriff	.25
27 Jeff Bagwell	.75
28 Dante Bichette	.25
29 Barry Bonds	2.50
30 Ellis Burks	.25
31 Ken Caminiti	.25
32 Vinny Castilla	.25
33 Andres Galarraga	.25

34 Vladimir Guerrero	.75
35 Todd Helton	.75
36 Todd Hundley	.25
37 Andruw Jones	.75
38 Chipper Jones	1.00
39 Eric Karros	.25
40 Ryan Klesko	.25
41 Ray Lankford	.25
42 Mark McGwire	2.00
43 Raul Mondesi	.25
44 Mike Piazza	1.50
45 Scott Rolen	.65
46 Gary Sheffield	.50
47 Sammy Sosa	1.00
48 Larry Walker	.25
49 Matt Williams	.25
50 WILDCARD	.25

Swing/Fences Prize Cards

This set was evidently intended to be one of the prizes in Pinnacle's Swing for the Fences sweepstakes, but the cards were never officially distributed due to the company's midyear bankruptcy. Making their way out the back into hobby channels in later years, the cards feature action photos on a silver prismatic foil background. Unnumbered backs have the player's career home run totals versus each team.

	NM/M
Complete Set (10):	10.00
Common Player:	.50
(1) Jeff Bagwell	1.00
(2) Barry Bonds	3.00
(3) Nomar Garciaparra	1.50
(4) Juan Gonzalez	.50
(5) Ken Griffey Jr.	2.00
(6) Chipper Jones	1.50
(7) Mark McGwire	2.50
(8) Mike Piazza	1.50
(9) Alex Rodriguez	2.50
(10) Frank Thomas	1.00

1998 Pinnacle Plus

Pinnacle Plus consists of a 200-card base set. Five subsets are included: Field of Vision, Naturals, All-Stars, Devil Rays and Diamondbacks. Artist's Proof is a 60-card partial parallel of the base set, inserted 1:35 packs. Gold Artist's Proof cards are numbered to 100 and Mirror Artist's Proofs are 1-of-1 inserts. Inserts include Lasting Memories, Yardwork, A Piece of the Game, All-Star Epix, Team Pinnacle, Gold Team Pinnacle, Pinnabilia and Certified Souvenir.

	NM/M
Complete Set (200):	12.00
Common Player:	.05
Pack (10):	1.00
Wax Box (20):	12.00
1 Roberto Alomar/AS	.20
2 Sandy Alomar Jr./AS	.05
3 Brady Anderson/AS	.05
4 Albert Belle/AS	.05
5 Jeff Cirillo/AS	.05
6 Roger Clemens/AS	1.25
7 David Cone/AS	.05
8 Nomar Garciaparra/AS	1.00
9 Ken Griffey Jr./AS	.50
10 Jason Dickson/AS	.05

11	Edgar Martinez/AS	.05
12	Tino Martinez/AS	.05
13	Randy Johnson/AS	.75
14	Mark McGwire/AS	2.00
15	David Justice/AS	.05
16	Mike Mussina/AS	.40
17	Chuck Knoblauch/AS	.05
18	Joey Cora/AS	.05
19	Pat Hentgen/AS	.05
20	Randy Myers/AS	.05
21	Cal Ripken Jr./AS	2.50
22	Mariano Rivera/AS	.15
23	Jose Rosado/AS	.05
24	Frank Thomas/AS	.75
25	Alex Rodriguez/AS	2.00
26	Justin Thompson/AS	.05
27	Ivan Rodriguez/AS	.65
28	Bernie Williams/AS	.05
29	Pedro Martinez/AS	.75
30	Tony Clark	.05
31	Garret Anderson	.05
32	Travis Fryman	.05
33	Mike Piazza	1.50
34	Carl Pavano	.05
35	Kevin Millwood RC	1.00
36	Miguel Tejada	.20
37	Willie Blair	.05
38	Devon White	.05
39	Andres Galarraga	.05
40	Barry Larkin	.05
41	Al Leiter	.05
42	Moises Alou	.05
43	Eric Young	.05
44	John Jaha	.05
45	Bernard Gilkey	.05
46	Freddy Garcia	.05
47	Ruben Rivera	.05
48	Robb Nen	.05
49	Ray Lankford	.05
50	Kenny Lofton	.05
51	Joe Carter	.05
52	Jason McDonald	.05
53	Quinton McCracken	.05
54	Kerry Wood	.50
55	Mike Lansing	.05
56	Chipper Jones	1.00
57	Barry Bonds	2.50
58	Brad Fullmer	.05
59	Jeff Bagwell	.75
60	Rondell White	.05
61	Geronimo Berroa	.05
62	Magglio Ordonez RC	1.50
63	Dwight Gooden	.05
64	Brian Hunter	.05
65	Todd Walker	.05
66	Frank Catalanotto RC	.05
67	Tony Saunders	.05
68	Travis Lee	.05
69	Michael Tucker	.05
70	Reggie Sanders	.05
71	Derrek Lee	.50
72	Larry Walker	.05
73	Marquis Grissom	.05
74	Craig Biggio	.05
75	Kevin Brown	.05
76	J.T. Snow	.05
77	Eric Davis	.05
78	Jeff Abbott	.05
79	Jermaine Dye	.05
80	Otis Nixon	.05
81	Curt Schilling	.35
82	Enrique Wilson	.05
83	Tony Gwynn	1.00
84	Orlando Cabrera	.05
85	Ramon Martinez	.05
86	Greg Vaughn	.05
87	Alan Benes	.05
88	Dennis Eckersley	.65
89	Jim Thome	.65
90	Juan Encarnacion	.05
91	Jeff King	.05
92	Shannon Stewart	.05
93	Roberto Hernandez	.15
94	Raul Ibanez	.05
95	Darryl Kile	.05
96	Charles Johnson	.05
97	Rich Becker	.05
98	Hal Morris	.05
99	Ismael Valdes	.05
100	Orel Hershiser	.05
101	Mo Vaughn	.05
102	Aaron Boone	.05
103	Jeff Conine	.05
104	Paul O'Neill	.05
105	Tom Candiotti	.05
106	Wilson Alvarez	.05
107	Mike Stanley	.05
108	Carlos Delgado	.50
109	Tony Batista	.05
110	Dante Bichette	.05
111	Henry Rodriguez	.05
112	Karim Garcia	.05
113	Shane Reynolds	.05
114	Ken Caminiti	.05
115	Jose Silva	.05
116	Juan Gonzalez	.40
117	Brian Jordan	.05
118	Jim Leyritz	.05
119	Manny Ramirez	.75
120	Fred McGriff	.05
121	Brooks Kieschnick	.05
122	Sean Casey	.15
123	John Smoltz	.05
124	Rusty Greer	.05
125	Cecil Fielder	.05
126	Mike Cameron	.05
127	Reggie Jefferson	.05
128	Bobby Higginson	.05
129	Kevin Appier	.05
130	Robin Ventura	.05
131	Ben Grieve	.05
132	Wade Boggs	1.00
133	Jose Cruz Jr.	.05
134	Jeff Suppan	.05
135	Vinny Castilla	.05
136	Sammy Sosa	1.00
137	Mark Wohlers	.05
138	Jay Bell	.05
139	Brett Tomko	.05
140	Gary Sheffield	.40
141	Tim Salmon	.05
142	Jaret Wright	.05
143	Kenny Rogers	.05
144	Brian Anderson	.05
145	Darrin Fletcher	.05
146	John Flaherty	.05
147	Dmitri Young	.05
148	Andruw Jones	.75
149	Matt Williams	.05
150	Bobby Bonilla	.05
151	Mike Hampton	.05
152	Al Martin	.05
153	Mark Grudzielanek	.05
154	Dave Nilsson	.05
155	Roger Cedeno	.05
156	Greg Maddux	1.00
157	Mark Kotsay	.05
158	Steve Finley	.05
159	Wilson Delgado	.05
160	Ron Gant	.05
161	Jim Edmonds	.05
162	Jeff Blauser	.05
163	Dave Burba	.05
164	Pedro Astacio	.05
165	Livan Hernandez	.05
166	Neifi Perez	.05
167	Ryan Klesko	.05
168	Fernando Tatis	.05
169	Richard Hidalgo	.05
170	Carlos Perez	.05
171	Bob Abreu	.15
172	Francisco Cordova	.05
173	Todd Helton	.75
174	Doug Glanville	.05
175	Brian Rose	.05
176	Yamil Benitez	.05
177	Darin Erstad	.15
178	Scott Rolen	.60
179	John Wetteland	.05
180	Paul Sorrento	.05
181	Walt Weiss	.05
182	Vladimir Guerrero	.75
183	Ken Griffey Jr. (The Naturals)	.75
184	Alex Rodriguez (The Naturals)	1.00
185	Cal Ripken Jr. (The Naturals)	1.25
186	Frank Thomas (The Naturals)	.40
187	Chipper Jones (The Naturals)	.50
188	Hideo Nomo (The Naturals)	.20
189	Nomar Garciaparra (The Naturals)	.60
190	Mike Piazza (The Naturals)	1.00
191	Greg Maddux (The Naturals)	.50
192	Tony Gwynn (The Naturals)	.50
193	Mark McGwire (The Naturals)	1.00
194	Roger Clemens (The Naturals)	.65
195	Mike Piazza (Field of Vision)	.75
196	Mark McGwire (Field of Vision)	1.00
197	Chipper Jones (Field of Vision)	.50
198	Larry Walker (Field of Vision)	.05
199	Hideo Nomo (Field of Vision)	.20
200	Barry Bonds (Field of Vision)	1.25

Artist's Proofs

Artist's Proofs is a 60-card partial parallel of the Pinnacle Plus base set. The dot matrix hologram cards were inserted 1:35. Gold Artist's Proofs added a gold finish and are sequentially numbered to 100. Mirror Artist's Proofs are a "1-of-1" insert. Card numbers have an "AP" prefix.

		NM/M
Complete Set (60):		150.00
Common Player:		.75
Inserted 1:35		
Golds:		10X
Production 100 Sets		
1	Roberto Alomar/AS	1.50
2	Albert Belle/AS	.75
3	Roger Clemens/AS	8.00
4	Nomar Garciaparra/AS	7.50
5	Ken Griffey Jr./AS	10.00
6	Tino Martinez/AS	.75
7	Randy Johnson/AS	.75
8	Mark McGwire/AS	12.50
9	David Justice/AS	.75
10	Chuck Knoblauch/AS	.75
11	Cal Ripken Jr./AS	15.00
12	Frank Thomas/AS	6.00
13	Alex Rodriguez/AS	12.50
14	Ivan Rodriguez/AS	5.00
15	Bernie Williams/AS	.75
16	Pedro Martinez	6.00
17	Tony Clark	.75
18	Mike Piazza	10.00
19	Miguel Tejada	1.00
20	Andres Galarraga	.75
21	Barry Larkin	.75
22	Kenny Lofton	.75
23	Chipper Jones	7.50
24	Barry Bonds	15.00
25	Brad Fullmer	.75
26	Jeff Bagwell	6.00
27	Todd Walker	.75
28	Travis Lee	.75
29	Larry Walker	.75
30	Craig Biggio	.75
31	Tony Gwynn	7.50
32	Jim Thome	5.00
33	Juan Encarnacion	.75
34	Mo Vaughn	.75
35	Karim Garcia	.75
36	Ken Caminiti	.75
37	Juan Gonzalez	3.00
38	Manny Ramirez	6.00
39	Fred McGriff	.75
40	Rusty Greer	.75
41	Bobby Higginson	.75
42	Ben Grieve	.75
43	Wade Boggs	7.50
44	Jose Cruz Jr.	.75
45	Sammy Sosa	7.50
46	Gary Sheffield	2.00
47	Tim Salmon	.75
48	Jaret Wright	.75
49	Andruw Jones	6.00
50	Matt Williams	.75
51	Greg Maddux	7.50
52	Jim Edmonds	.75
53	Livan Hernandez	.75
54	Neifi Perez	.75
55	Fernando Tatis	.75
56	Richard Hidalgo	.75
57	Todd Helton	6.00
58	Darin Erstad	1.50
59	Scott Rolen	5.00
60	Vladimir Guerrero	6.00

A Piece of the Game

Inserted 1:17 hobby packs (1:19 retail), this 10-card insert features baseball's top players on micro-etched foil cards.

		NM/M
Complete Set (10):		8.00
Common Player:		.50
Inserted 1:19		
1	Ken Griffey Jr.	1.00
2	Frank Thomas	.75
3	Alex Rodriguez	1.50
4	Chipper Jones	.75
5	Cal Ripken Jr.	2.00
6	Mike Piazza	1.00
7	Greg Maddux	.75
8	Juan Gonzalez	.50
9	Nomar Garciaparra	.75
10	Larry Walker	.50

Epix All-Star Moment

The All-Star Epix insert is part of the cross-brand Epix set. The cards honor the All-Star Game achievements of baseball's stars on

cards with dot matrix holograms. All-Star Epix was seeded 1:21. Cards #1-12 were distributed in Score Rookie/Traded.

		NM/M
Complete Set (12):		25.00
Common Player:		1.00
Purples:		1.5X
Emeralds:		2.5X
Inserted 1:21		
13	Alex Rodriguez	3.50
14	Cal Ripken Jr.	5.00
15	Chipper Jones	2.50
16	Roger Clemens	2.75
17	Mo Vaughn	1.00
18	Mark McGwire	3.50
19	Mike Piazza	3.00
20	Andruw Jones	2.00
21	Greg Maddux	2.50
22	Barry Bonds	5.00
23	Paul Molitor	2.00
24	Hideo Nomo	1.50

Lasting Memories

Lasting Memories is a 30-card insert seeded 1:5. Printed on foil board, the cards feature a player photo with a sky background.

		NM/M
Complete Set (30):		16.00
Common Player:		.25
Inserted 1:5		
1	Nomar Garciaparra	.75
2	Ken Griffey Jr.	1.00
3	Livan Hernandez	.25
4	Hideo Nomo	.40
5	Ben Grieve	.25
6	Scott Rolen	.50
7	Roger Clemens	.85
8	Cal Ripken Jr.	2.00
9	Mo Vaughn	.25
10	Frank Thomas	.65
11	Mark McGwire	1.50
12	Barry Larkin	.25
13	Matt Williams	.25
14	Jose Cruz Jr.	.25
15	Andruw Jones	.65
16	Mike Piazza	1.00
17	Jeff Bagwell	.65
18	Chipper Jones	.75
19	Juan Gonzalez	.40
20	Kenny Lofton	.25
21	Greg Maddux	.75
22	Ivan Rodriguez	.50
23	Alex Rodriguez	1.50
24	Derek Jeter	2.00
25	Albert Belle	.25
26	Barry Bonds	2.00
27	Larry Walker	.25
28	Sammy Sosa	.75
29	Tony Gwynn	.75
30	Randy Johnson	.65

Team Pinnacle

Team Pinnacle is a 15-card, double-sided insert. Printed on mirror-mylar, the cards were inserted 1:71. The hobby-only Gold Team Pinnacle parallel was inserted 1:199 packs.

		NM/M
Complete Set (15):		50.00
Common Player:		1.50
Inserted 1:71		
Golds:		2X

		NM/M
Inserted 1:199		
1	Mike Piazza, Ivan Rodriguez	6.00
2	Mark McGwire, Mo Vaughn	5.00
3	Roberto Alomar, Craig Biggio	2.00
4	Alex Rodriguez, Barry Larkin	8.00
5	Cal Ripken Jr., Chipper Jones	10.00
6	Ken Griffey Jr., Larry Walker	6.00
7	Juan Gonzalez, Tony Gwynn	4.00
8	Albert Belle, Barry Bonds	8.00
9	Kenny Lofton, Andruw Jones	3.00
10	Tino Martinez, Jeff Bagwell	3.00
11	Frank Thomas, Andres Galarraga	3.00
12	Roger Clemens, Greg Maddux	8.00
13	Pedro Martinez, Hideo Nomo	4.00
14	Nomar Garciaparra, Scott Rolen	5.00
15	Ben Grieve, Paul Konerko	1.50

Yardwork

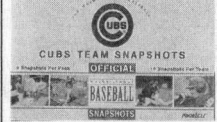

Yardwork is a 15-card insert seeded one per 19 packs. It features the top home run hitters in Major League Baseball.

		NM/M
Complete Set (15):		12.50
Common Player:		.35
Inserted 1:9		
1	Mo Vaughn	.35
2	Frank Thomas	.75
3	Albert Belle	.35
4	Nomar Garciaparra	1.00
5	Tony Clark	.35
6	Ken Griffey Jr.	1.50
7	Juan Gonzalez	.60
8	Sammy Sosa	1.00
9	Jose Cruz Jr.	.35
10	Jeff Bagwell	.75
11	Mike Piazza	1.50
12	Larry Walker	.35
13	Mark McGwire	2.00
14	Barry Bonds	2.50

1998 Pinnacle Snapshots

CUBS TEAM SNAPSHOTS

One of Pinnacle's last issues was a team-oriented presentation of large-format (4"x6") cards called Snapshots. Like their namesake, the focus on this issue is on candid photos rather than posed portraits or game-action pictures. The cards are printed on thin high-gloss cardboard stock resembling photo paper. Fronts, many of them horizontally formatted, are borderless and have no graphic enhancement. Backs are lightly printed with Pinnacle and licensor logos and a card number expressed "x of 18." The player's name is nowhere to be found. Snapshots were sold regionally in single-team boxes of 25 packs with eight cards each.

Angels

		NM/M
Complete Set (18):		7.50
Common Player:		.50
1	Jason Dickson	.50
2	Gary DiSarcina	.50
3	Garret Anderson	.50
4	Shigetosi Hasegawa	.50
5	Ken Hill	.50
6	Todd Greene	.50
7	Tim Salmon	.75
8	Jim Edmonds	.60
9	Garret Anderson	.50
10	Dave Hollins	.50
11	Todd Greene	.50
12	Troy Percival	.50
13	Gary DiSarcina	.50
14	Cecil Fielder	.50
15	Darin Erstad	.75
16	Chuck Finley	.50
17	Jim Edmonds	.50
18	Jason Dickson	.50

Braves

		NM/M
Complete Set (18):		11.00
Common Player:		.50
1	Ryan Klesko	.50
2	Walt Weiss	.50
3	Tom Glavine	.75
4	Randall Simon	.50
5	John Smoltz	.50
6	Chipper Jones	1.50
7	Javier Lopez	.50
8	Greg Maddux	1.50
9	Andruw Jones	1.00
10	Michael Tucker	.50
11	Andres Galarraga	.50
12	Andres Galarraga	.50
13	Greg Maddux	1.50
14	Wes Helms	.50
15	Bruce Chen	.50
16	Denny Neagle	.50
17	Mark Wohlers	.50
18	Kevin Millwood	.60

Cardinals

		NM/M
Complete Set (18):		10.00
Common Player:		.50
1	Alan Benes	.50
2	Ron Gant	.50
3	Donovan Osborne	.50
4	Eli Marrero	.50
5	Mark McGwire	2.50
6	Delino DeShields	.50
7	Tom Pagnozzi	.50
8	Delino DeShields	.50
9	Mark McGwire	2.50
10	Royce Clayton	.50
11	Brian Jordan	.50
12	Ray Lankford	.50
13	Brian Jordan	.50
14	Matt Morris	.50
15	John Mabry	.50

		NM/M
16	Luis Ordaz	.50
17	Ron Gant	.50
18	Todd Stottlemyre	.50

Cubs

		NM/M
Complete Set (18):		9.00
Common Player:		.50
1	Mark Grace	.60
2	Manny Alexander	.50
3	Jeremi Gonzalez	.50
4	Brant Brown	.50
5	Mark Grace	.60
6	Lance Johnson	.50
7	Mark Clark	.50
8	Kevin Foster	.50
9	Brant Brown	.50
10	Kevin Foster	.50
11	Kevin Tapani	.50
12	Sammy Sosa	1.50
13	Sammy Sosa	1.50
14	Pat Cline	.50
15	Kevin Orie	.50
16	Steve Trachsel	.50
17	Lance Johnson	.50
18	Robin Jennings	.50

Devil Rays

		NM/M
Complete Set (18):		7.50
Common Player:		.50
1	Kevin Stocker	.50
2	Paul Sorrento	.50
3	John Flaherty	.50
4	Wade Boggs	1.50
5	Rich Butler	.50
6	Wilson Alvarez	.50
7	Bubba Trammell	.50
8	David Martinez	.50
9	Brooks Kieschnick	.50
10	Tony Saunders	.50
11	Esteban Yan	.50
12	Quinton McCracken	.50
13	Albie Lopez	.50
14	Roberto Hernandez	.50
15	Fred McGriff	.50
16	Bubba Trammell	.50
17	Brooks Kieschnick	.50
18	Fred McGriff	.50

Diamondbacks

		NM/M
Complete Set (18):		7.50
Common Player:		.50
1	Travis Lee	1.00
2	Matt Williams	.50
3	Jay Bell	.50
4	Devon White	.50
5	Andy Benes	.50
6	Tony Batista	.50
7	Jay Bell	.50
8	Edwin Diaz	.50
9	Devon White	.50
10	Bob Wolcott	.50
11	Karim Garcia	1.00
12	Yamil Benitez	.50
13	Jorge Fabregas	.50
14	Jeff Suppan	.50
15	Ben Ford	.50
16	Brian Anderson	.50
17	Travis Lee	1.00
18	Matt Williams	.50

Dodgers

		NM/M
Complete Set (18):		12.00
Common Player:		.50

1	Mike Piazza	2.50
2	Eric Karros	.50
3	Raul Mondesi	.50
4	Wilton Guerrero	.50
5	Darren Dreifort	.50
6	Roger Cedeno	.50
7	Todd Zeile	.50
8	Paul Konerko	.75
9	Todd Hollandsworth	.50
10	Ismael Valdes	.50
11	Hideo Nomo	1.00
12	Ramon Martinez	.50
13	Chan Ho Park	.75
14	Eric Young	.50
15	Dennis Reyes	.50
16	Eric Karros	.50
17	Mike Piazza	2.50
18	Raul Mondesi	.50

Indians

		NM/M
Complete Set (18):		7.50
Common Player:		.50
1	Manny Ramirez	1.50
2	Travis Fryman	.50
3	Jaret Wright	.50
4	Brian Giles	.50
5	Bartolo Colon	.50
6	Kenny Lofton	.50
7	David Justice	.50
8	Brian Giles	.50
9	Sandy Alomar Jr.	.50
10	Jose Mesa	.50
11	Jim Thome	1.00
12	Sandy Alomar Jr.	.50
13	Omar Vizquel	.50
14	Geronimo Berroa	.50
15	John Smiley	.50
16	Chad Ogea	.50
17	Charles Nagy	.50
18	Enrique Wilson	.50

Mariners

		NM/M
Complete Set (18):		12.00
Common Player:		.50
1	Alex Rodriguez	2.50
2	Jay Buhner	.50
3	Russ Davis	.50
4	Joey Cora	.50
5	Joey Cora	.50
6	Jay Buhner	.50
7	Ken Griffey Jr.	2.00
8	Raul Ibanez	.50
9	Rich Amaral	.50
10	Shane Monahan	.50
11	Alex Rodriguez	2.50
12	Dan Wilson	.50
13	Bob Wells	.50
14	Randy Johnson	1.00
15	Randy Johnson	1.00
16	Jeff Fassero	.50
17	Ken Cloude	.50
18	Edgar Martinez	.50

Mets

		NM/M
Complete Set (18):		7.50
Common Player:		.50
1	Rey Ordonez	.50
2	Todd Hundley	.50
3	Preston Wilson	.50
4	Rich Becker	.50
5	Bernard Gilkey	.50
6	Rey Ordonez	.50
7	Butch Huskey	.50
8	Carlos Baerga	.50
9	Edgardo Alfonzo	.50
10	Bill Pulsipher	.50
11	John Franco	.50
12	Todd Pratt	.50
13	Brian McRae	.50
14	Bobby Jones	.50
15	John Olerud	.50
16	Todd Hundley	.50
17	Jay Payton	.50
18	Paul Wilson	.50

Orioles

		NM/M
Complete Set (18):		12.50
Common Player:		.50
1	Cal Ripken Jr.	3.00
2	Rocky Coppinger	.50
3	Eric Davis	.50
4	Chris Hoiles	.50
5	Mike Mussina	.75
6	Joe Carter	.50
7	Rafael Palmeiro	1.00
8	B.J. Surhoff	.50

9	Jimmy Key	.50
10	Scott Erickson	.50
11	Armando Benitez	.50
12	Roberto Alomar	.65
13	Cal Ripken Jr.	3.00
14	Mike Bordick	.50
15	Roberto Alomar	.65
16	Jeffrey Hammonds	.50
17	Rafael Palmeiro	1.00
18	Brady Anderson	.50

Rangers

		NM/M
Complete Set (18):		9.00
Common Player:		.50
1	Ivan Rodriguez	1.00
2	Fernando Tatis	.50
3	Danny Patterson	.50
4	Will Clark	.66
5	Kevin Elster	.50
6	Rusty Greer	.50
7	Darren Oliver	.50
8	John Burkett	.50
9	Tom Goodwin	.50
10	Roberto Kelly	.50
11	Aaron Sele	.50
12	Rick Helling	.50
13	Mark McLemore	.50
14	Lee Stevens	.50
15	John Wetteland	.50
16	Will Clark	.65
17	Juan Gonzalez	.75
18	Roger Pavlik	.50

Red Sox

		NM/M
Complete Set (18):		9.00
Common Player:		.50
1	Tim Naehring	.50
2	Brian Rose	.50
3	Darren Bragg	.50
4	Pedro Martinez	1.00
5	Mo Vaughn	.50
6	Jim Leyritz	.50
7	Troy O'Leary	.50
8	Mo Vaughn	.50
9	Nomar Garciaparra	1.50
10	Michael Coleman	.50
11	Tom Gordon	.50
12	Tim Naehring	.50
13	Nomar Garciaparra	1.50
14	John Valentin	.50
15	Steve Avery	.50
16	Damon Buford	.50
17	Troy O'Leary	.50
18	Bret Saberhagen	.50

Rockies

		NM/M
Complete Set (18):		7.50
Common Player:		.50
1	Larry Walker	.50
2	Pedro Astacio	.50
3	Jamey Wright	.50
4	Darryl Kile	.50
5	Kirt Manwaring	.50
6	Todd Helton	1.50
7	Mike Lansing	.50
8	Neifi Perez	.50
9	Dante Bichette	.50
10	Derrick Gibson	.50
11	Neifi Perez	.50
12	Darryl Kile	.50
13	Larry Walker	.50
14	Roger Bailey	.50
15	Ellis Burks	.50

16	Dante Bichette	.50
17	Derrick Gibson	.50
18	Ellis Burks	.50

Yankees

		NM/M
Complete Set (18):		12.50
Common Player:		.75
1	Andy Pettitte	.75
2	Darryl Strawberry	.50
3	Joe Girardi	.50
4	Derek Jeter	3.00
5	Andy Pettitte	.75
6	Tim Raines	.50
7	Mariano Rivera	.75
8	Tino Martinez	.50
9	Derek Jeter	3.00
10	Hideki Irabu	.50
11	Tino Martinez	.50
12	David Cone	.50
13	Bernie Williams	.65
14	David Cone	.50
15	Bernie Williams	.65
16	Chuck Knoblauch	.50
17	Paul O'Neill	.50
18	David Wells	.50

Sport Block

By manipulating the eight cubes of which this novelty is comprised, pictures of eight popular players and the team logo can be displayed. The cube measures 2-3/4" x 2-3/4" x 2-3/4".

		NM/M
Complete Set (10):		20.00
Common Team:		3.00
(1)	Anaheim Angels (Garret Anderson, Jason Dickson, Jim Edmonds, Darin Erstad, Chuck Finley, Todd Greene, Troy Percival, Tim Salmon, Angels Logo)	3.00
(2)	Arizona Diamondbacks	3.00
(3)	Atlanta Braves (Andres Galarraga, Tom Glavine, Andruw Jones, Chipper Jones, Ryan Klesko, Javier Lopez, Greg Maddux, John Smoltz, Braves Logo)	3.00
(4)	Baltimore Orioles	3.00
(5)	Boston Red Sox (Darren Bragg, Nomar Garciaparra, Reggie Jefferson, Jim Leyritz, Pedro Martinez, Troy O'Leary, John Valentin, Mo Vaughn, Red Sox Logo)	3.00
(6)	Cleveland Indians	3.00
(7)	Los Angeles Dodgers (Eric Karros, Paul Konerko, Ramon Martinez, Raul Mondesi, Hideo Nomo, Chan Ho Park, Mike Piazza, Ismael Valdes, Dodgers Logo)	3.00
(8)	New York Yankees	3.00
(9)	Seattle Mariners (Jay Buhner, Russ Davis, Jeff Fassero, Ken Griffey Jr., Randy Johnson, Edgar Martinez, Alex Rodriguez, Dan Wilson, Mariners Logo)	3.00
(10)	Tampa Bay Devil Rays (Wilson Alvarez, Wade Boggs, Dave Martinez, Quinton McCracken, Fred McGriff, Tony Saunders, Paul Sorrento, Bubba Trammell, Devil Rays Logo)	3.00

Totally Certified Platinum Gold

Among several card issues that were aborted by Pinnacle's bankruptcy in mid-1998, but which have leaked into the hobby market in dribs and drabs, are 10 Totally Certified Platinum Gold cards that were intended to be random pack inserts in 1998 Certified. Each of the cards was produced in an edition of 30 serially numbered pieces. To date, confirma-

---

tion of back-door release of the Platinum Red and Platinum Blue versions has not been made.

		NM/M
Complete Set (10):		125.00
Common Player:		7.50
1	Vladimir Guerrero	15.00
2	Andruw Jones	12.00
3	Paul Molitor	15.00
4	Jose Cruz Jr.	7.50
5	Edgar Martinez	7.50
6	Andy Pettitte	9.00
7	Darin Erstad	9.00
8	Barry Larkin	7.50
9	Derek Jeter	40.00
10	Rusty Greer	7.50

1998 Team Pinnacle Baseball

With each $30 membership in Pinnacle's collectors' club, "Team Pinnacle," the member received a litho tin box with 10 each special baseball, football and hockey cards, and a pack of unnumbered promo cards. In standard 2-1/2" x 3-1/2", cards have game-action photos on front, bordered in a dominant team color and enhanced with a gold-foil Team Pinnacle logo at bottom. Backs have portrait photos, a few personal details, career highlights and the player's uniform number ghosted in the background.

		NM/M
Complete Set (10):		16.00
Common Player:		1.00
B1	Ken Griffey Jr.	2.00
B2	Frank Thomas	1.25
B3	Cal Ripken Jr.	3.00
B4	Alex Rodriguez	2.50
B5	Mike Piazza	2.00
B6	Derek Jeter	3.00
B7	Greg Maddux	1.50
B8	Chipper Jones	1.50
B9	Mark McGwire	2.50
B10	Juan Gonzalez	1.00
---	Cal Ripken Jr. (Unmarked sample.)	2.50

Team Pinnacle (Unissued)

This four-card set was reportedly created for distribution to members of the card company's "Team Pinnacle" but was

---

never officially issued due to the manufacturer's bankruptcy. The 2-1/2" x 3-1/2" cards have game-action photos on front with a wide diagonal color stripe at top and a gold-foil "98 TEAM PINNACLE" logo at bottom. Backs have a color portrait photo along with some stats and highlights. The cards are unnumbered.

		NM/M
Complete Set (4):		7.50
Common Player:		3.00
(1)	John Elway/Football	2.00
(2)	Ken Griffey Jr.	2.00
(3)	Derek Jeter	3.00
(4)	Eric Lindros/Hockey	2.00

Uncut

Advertised as the "BIGGEST CARD EVER!" these 13-3/8 x 18-5/8 cards are approximately 30 times larger than standard cards. Sold in individual cello bags with a suggested retail price of around $10, the cards are super-size replicas of the same players' cards found in the Field of Vision subset in regular 1998 Pinnacle. The giant cards have an etched metallic foil front not found on the regular cards. They are packaged with a die-cut cardboard backing which tends to bruise the edges or chip off small patches of ink.

		NM/M
Complete Set (6):		20.00
Common Card:		3.00
182	Alex Rodriguez	6.00
183	Cal Ripken Jr., Roberto Alomar	4.50
184	Roger Clemens	3.50
185	Derek Jeter	7.50
186	Frank Thomas	3.00
186p	Frank Thomas ("SAMPLE" on back.)	4.50
187	Ken Griffey Jr.	4.50

2004 Pitt Ohio Express 1979 Pirates

The purpose for which the Pennsylvania trucking company produced this card set, and the manner of their distribution, is unclear. The set commemorates the World Champion Pittsburgh Pirates of 1979. Fronts of the approximately 4-3/4" x 3-5/8" cards have large black-and-white portrait photos. Highlighted by gold graphics, the fronts also include a team logo, player name, position and uniform number. Backs have an ad for the trucking company.

		NM/M
Complete Set (18):		20.00
Common Player:		2.00
(1)	Matt Alexander	2.00
(2)	Tony Bartirome	2.00
(3)	Jim Bibby	2.00
(4)	Mike Easler	2.00
(5)	Grant Jackson	2.00
(6)	Bruce Kison	2.00
(7)	Lee Lacy	2.00

(8)	Bill Madlock	3.00
(9)	Omar Moreno	2.00
(10)	Steve Nicosia	2.00
(11)	Ed Ott	2.00
(12)	Dave Parker	4.00
(13)	Dave Roberts	2.00
(14)	Don Robinson	2.00
(15)	Jim Rooker	2.00
(16)	Manny Sanguillen	3.00
(17)	Chuck Tanner	2.00
(18)	Kent Tekulve	2.00

1992 Pittsburgh Brewing Co. Roberto Clemente Tribute

The first 15,000 fans at Three Rivers Stadium on September 6 at a special promotional Clemente tribute night received this perforated pair of cards honoring the Pirates superstar. The 7" square panel has a pair of two-part cards. Each side has a 3-1/2" x 5-1/2" picture portion at top and a 1-1/2" tab at bottom, perforated for easy separation. The left side has a portrait of the Pirate great with his first name; at right is his last name and an action picture. Back of the portrait card has career stats; back of the action card has career highlights. Artwork on each card is by Tom Mosser. The sponsor logo is on back of each tab along with a quotation and copyright information.

	NM/M
Complete Panel:	18.00
Complete Set (2):	15.00
#21 Roberto/Portrait	7.50
#21 Clemente/Action	7.50

1985 Pittsburgh Pirates Yearbook Cards

This 18-card set was issued on two nine-card perforated panels inserted into the Bucs' 1985 yearbook. Individual cards measure 2-1/2" x 3-1/2" and feature color photos surrounded by black and gold borders. The player's name, position and uniform number are printed in a white panel at bottom. Backs are in black-and-white and offer complete major and minor league stats, along with the logos of sponsor Cameron/Coca-Cola.

		NM/M
Complete Set (18):		7.50
Common Player:		.50
2	Jim Morrison	.50
3	Johnny Ray	.50
5	Bill Madlock	.60
6	Tony Pena	.50
7	Chuck Tanner	.50
10	Tim Foli	.50
13	Steve Kemp	.50
15	George Hendrick	.50
23	Jose DeLeon	.50
27	Kent Tekulve	.50
28	Sixto Lezcano	.50
29	Rick Rhoden	.50
30	Jason Thompson	.50
34	Marvell Wynne	.50
45	Don Robinson	.50
48	John Candelaria	.50
49	Larry McWilliams	.50
51	Doug Frobel	.50

1996 Pizza Hut

In conjunction with a foam bat/ball promotion, Pizza Hut issued a small set of small cards (2-1/2" x 2-1/4") featuring players involved in the endorsement. The player portrait photos on the cards are devoid of cap logos and surrounded by a rainbow border. Player names are in yellow with a nickname in red. A choking hazard warning is in black-and-white on bottom. Backs are printed in red and black and have career summaries, logos and copyright notice. The unnumbered cards are checklisted here alphabetically.

	NM/M
Complete Set (4):	8.00
Common Card:	1.50
(1) Jeff Bagwell (Thumper), Orel Hershiser (Bulldawg)	1.50
(2) David Cone (Controller), Mike Piazza (Crusher)	3.00
(3) Ken Griffey Jr. (Junior), Greg Maddux (Surgeon)	3.00
(4) Randy Johnson (Big Unit), Mo Vaughn (Hit Dog)	1.50

2001 Playoff Absolute Memorabilia

	NM/M
Complete Set (200):	
Common Player:	.25
Common SP (151-200):	5.00
Production 700	
Pack (6):	8.00
Box (18) w/baseball:	150.00
1	Alex Rodriguez	2.50
2	Barry Bonds	3.00
3	Cal Ripken Jr.	3.00
4	Chipper Jones	1.50
5	Derek Jeter	3.00
6	Troy Glaus	1.00
7	Frank Thomas	1.00
8	Greg Maddux	1.50
9	Ivan Rodriguez	.75
10	Jeff Bagwell	1.00
11	Ryan Dempster	.25
12	Todd Helton	1.00
13	Ken Griffey Jr.	2.00
14	Manny Ramirez	1.00
15	Mark McGwire	2.50
16	Mike Piazza	2.00
17	Nomar Garciaparra	2.00
18	Pedro Martinez	1.00
19	Randy Johnson	1.00
20	Rick Ankiel	.50
21	Rickey Henderson	1.00
22	Roger Clemens	1.75
23	Sammy Sosa	2.00
24	Tony Gwynn	2.00
25	Vladimir Guerrero	1.00
26	Kazuhiro Sasaki	.50
27	Roberto Alomar	.50
28	Barry Zito	.35
29	Pat Burrell	.50
30	Harold Baines	.25
31	Carlos Delgado	.65
32	J.D. Drew	.50
33	Jim Edmonds	.25
34	Darin Erstad	.50
35	Jason Giambi	.75
36	Tom Glavine	.50
37	Juan Gonzalez	1.00
38	Mark Grace	.35
39	Shawn Green	.25
40	Tim Hudson	.50
41	Andruw Jones	.25
42	David Justice	.25

43	Jeff Kent	.25
44	Barry Larkin	.25
45	Rafael Furcal	.50
46	Mike Mussina	.50
47	Hideo Nomo	1.00
48	Rafael Palmeiro	.75
49	Adam Piatt	.25
50	Scott Rolen	.75
51	Gary Sheffield	.50
52	Bernie Williams	.35
53	Bob Abreu	.25
54	Edgardo Alfonzo	.25
55	Edgar Renteria	.25
56	Phil Nevin	.25
57	Craig Biggio	.25
58	Andres Galarraga	.25
59	Edgar Martinez	.25
60	Fred McGriff	.25
61	Magglio Ordonez	.25
62	Jim Thome	.25
63	Matt Williams	.25
64	Kerry Wood	.65
65	Moises Alou	.25
66	Brady Anderson	.25
67	Garret Anderson	.25
68	Russell Branyan	.25
69	Tony Batista	.25
70	Vernon Wells	.25
71	Carlos Beltran	.60
72	Adrian Beltre	.25
73	Kris Benson	.25
74	Lance Berkman	.25
75	Kevin Brown	.25
76	Dee Brown	.25
77	Jeromy Burnitz	.25
78	Timoniel Perez	.25
79	Sean Casey	.40
80	Luis Castillo	.25
81	Eric Chavez	.35
82	Jeff Cirillo	.25
83	Bartolo Colon	.25
84	David Cone	.25
85	Freddy Garcia	.25
86	Johnny Damon	.40
87	Ray Durham	.25
88	Jermaine Dye	.25
89	Juan Encarnacion	.25
90	Terrence Long	.25
91	Carl Everett	.25
92	Steve Finley	.25
93	Cliff Floyd	.25
94	Brad Fullmer	.25
95	Brian Giles	.25
96	Luis Gonzalez	.35
97	Rusty Greer	.25
98	Jeffrey Hammonds	.25
99	Mike Hampton	.25
100	Orlando Hernandez	.25
101	Richard Hidalgo	.25
102	Geoff Jenkins	.25
103	Jacque Jones	.25
104	Brian Jordan	.25
105	Gabe Kapler	.25
106	Eric Karros	.25
107	Jason Kendall	.25
108	Adam Kennedy	.25
109	Deion Sanders	.25
110	Ryan Klesko	.25
111	Chuck Knoblauch	.25
112	Paul Konerko	.25
113	Carlos Lee	.25
114	Kenny Lofton	.25
115	Javy Lopez	.25
116	Tino Martinez	.25
117	Ruben Mateo	.25
118	Kevin Millwood	.25
119	Jimmy Rollins	.25
120	Raul Mondesi	.25
121	Trot Nixon	.25
122	John Olerud	.25
123	Paul O'Neill	.35
124	Chan Ho Park	.25
125	Andy Pettitte	.35
126	Jorge Posada	.25
127	Mark Quinn	.25
128	Aramis Ramirez	.25
129	Mariano Rivera	.25
130	Tim Salmon	.35
131	Curt Schilling	.50
132	Richie Sexson	.25
133	John Smoltz	.25
134	J.T. Snow	.25
135	Jay Payton	.25
136	Shannon Stewart	.25
137	B.J. Surhoff	.25
138	Mike Sweeney	.25
139	Fernando Tatis	.25
140	Miguel Tejada	.35
141	Jason Varitek	.25
142	Greg Vaughn	.25
143	Mo Vaughn	.25
144	Robin Ventura	.25
145	Jose Vidro	.25
146	Omar Vizquel	.25
147	Larry Walker	.25
148	David Wells	.25
149	Rondell White	.25
150	Preston Wilson	.25
151	Bud Smith RC	5.00
152	Cory Aldridge RC	5.00
153	Wilmy Caceres RC	5.00
154	Josh Beckett RC	5.00
155	Wilson Betemit RC	10.00
156	Jason Michaels RC	5.00
157	Albert Pujols RC	100.00
158	Andres Torres RC	5.00
159	Jack Wilson RC	8.00
160	Alex Escobar RC	5.00
161	Ben Sheets RC	5.00
162	Rafael Soriano RC	10.00

163	Nate Frese RC	5.00
164	Carlos Garcia RC	5.00
165	Brandon Larson RC	5.00
166	Alexis Gomez RC	5.00
167	Jason Hart RC	5.00
168	Nick Johnson RC	5.00
169	Donaldo Mendez RC	5.00
170	Christian Parker RC	5.00
171	Jackson Melian RC	5.00
172	Jack Cust RC	5.00
173	Adrian Hernandez RC	5.00
174	Joe Crede RC	8.00
175	Jose Mieses RC	5.00
176	Roy Oswalt RC	5.00
177	Eric Munson RC	5.00
178	Xavier Nady RC	5.00
179	Horacio Ramirez RC	5.00
180	Abraham Nunez RC	5.00
181	Jose Ortiz RC	5.00
182	Jeremy Owens RC	5.00
183	Claudio Vargas RC	5.00
184	Marcus Giles	5.00
185	Aubrey Huff	5.00
186	C.C. Sabathia	8.00
187	Adam Dunn	5.00
188	Adam Pettyjohn RC	5.00
189	Elpidio Guzman RC	5.00
190	Jay Gibbons RC	5.00
191	Wilkin Ruan RC	5.00
192	Tsuyoshi Shinjo RC	8.00
193	Alfonso Soriano	8.00
194	Corey Patterson	5.00
195	Ichiro Suzuki RC	60.00
196	Billy Sylvester RC	5.00
197	Juan Uribe RC	5.00
198	Johnny Estrada RC	5.00
199	Carlos Valderrama RC	5.00
200	Matt White RC	5.00

Ball Hoggs

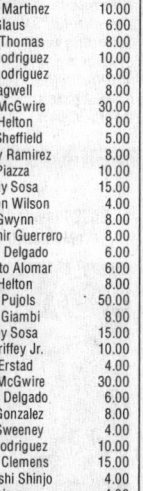

	NM/M
Common Player:	8.00
Production 75 unless noted.	
1	Vladimir Guerrero	15.00
2	Troy Glaus	10.00
3	Tony Gwynn	20.00
4	Cal Ripken/125	50.00
5	Todd Helton	15.00
6	Jacque Jones/125	8.00
7	Shawn Green/100	8.00
8	Ichiro Suzuki	85.00
9	Scott Rolen	15.00
10	Roger Clemens	30.00
11	Ken Griffey/25	50.00
14	Sammy Sosa	25.00
15	J.D. Drew	10.00
16	Barry Bonds/100	40.00
17	Pat Burrell	15.00
18	Mark McGwire/100	65.00
19	Mike Piazza	20.00
20	Magglio Ordonez/150	10.00
21	Miguel Tejada	10.00
22	Albert Pujols/100	150.00
23	Derek Jeter	40.00
24	Johnny Damon	15.00
25	Mike Sweeney	8.00
26	Ben Grieve	8.00
27	Jeff Kent	8.00
28	Andres Galarraga	8.00
29	Richie Sexson	10.00
30	Juan Encarnacion	8.00
31	Ruben Mateo	8.00
33	Manny Ramirez	15.00
35	Ivan Rodriguez	15.00
36	Darin Erstad	8.00
37	Carlos Delgado	10.00
38	Jeff Bagwell	8.00
39	Jermaine Dye	8.00
40	Jose Ortiz	8.00
41	Gary Sheffield	10.00
42	Eric Chavez	8.00
43	Mark Grace	15.00
44	Rafael Palmeiro	15.00
45	Tsuyoshi Shinjo/100	8.00
46	Terrence Long	8.00
47	Carlos Delgado/25	20.00
48	Frank Thomas	15.00
49	Chipper Jones/25	40.00
50	Jason Giambi	15.00

Ballpark Souvenirs

	NM/M
Common Player:	4.00
Production 400 Sets	
Doubles:	1-1.5X
Production 200 Sets	
Triples:	1.5-2X
Production 75 Sets	
Home Runs:	2-4X

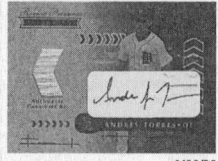

33	Manny Ramirez	20.00
35	Ivan Rodriguez	20.00
36	Darin Erstad	15.00
37	Carlos Delgado	20.00
38	Jeff Bagwell	20.00
39	Jermaine Dye	15.00
40	Jose Ortiz	15.00
42	Eric Chavez	15.00
43	Mark Grace	30.00
44	Rafael Palmeiro	30.00
45	Tsuyoshi Shinjo	20.00
46	Terrence Long	15.00
47	Carlos Delgado	20.00
48	Frank Thomas	25.00
50	Jason Giambi	25.00

Rookie Premiere Autographs

	NM/M
Production 25 Sets	
1	Barry Bonds	20.00
2	Cal Ripken Jr.	25.00
3	Pedro Martinez	10.00
4	Troy Glaus	6.00
5	Frank Thomas	8.00
6	Alex Rodriguez	10.00
7	Ivan Rodriguez	8.00
8	Jeff Bagwell	8.00
9	Mark McGwire	30.00
10	Todd Helton	8.00
11	Gary Sheffield	5.00
12	Manny Ramirez	8.00
13	Mike Piazza	10.00
14	Sammy Sosa	15.00
15	Preston Wilson	4.00
16	Tony Gwynn	8.00
17	Vladimir Guerrero	8.00
18	Carlos Delgado	6.00
19	Roberto Alomar	5.00
20	Todd Helton	8.00
21	Albert Pujols	50.00
22	Jason Giambi	8.00
23	Sammy Sosa	15.00
24	Ken Griffey Jr.	8.00
25	Darin Erstad	4.00
26	Mark McGwire	30.00
27	Carlos Delgado	6.00
28	Juan Gonzalez	8.00
29	Mike Sweeney	4.00
30	Alex Rodriguez	10.00
31	Roger Clemens	15.00
32	Tsuyoshi Shinjo	4.00
33	Ben Grieve	4.00
34	Jeff Kent	4.00
35	Vladimir Guerrero	8.00
36	Shawn Green	6.00
37	Rafael Palmeiro	8.00
38	Tony Gwynn	8.00
39	Scott Rolen	8.00
40	Ken Griffey Jr.	10.00
41	Albert Pujols	50.00
42	Barry Bonds	20.00
43	Mark Grace	8.00
44	Bernie Williams	6.00
45	Frank Thomas	8.00
46	Jermaine Dye	4.00
47	Mike Piazza	10.00
48	Chipper Jones	10.00
49	Richie Sexson	6.00
50	Magglio Ordonez	6.00

Production 25 Sets		
151	Bud Smith	15.00
152	Cory Aldridge	15.00
154	Josh Beckett	40.00
155	Wilson Betemit	15.00
157	Albert Pujols	500.00
158	Andres Torres	15.00
160	Alex Escobar	15.00
161	Ben Sheets	30.00
162	Rafael Soriano	25.00
164	Carlos Garcia	15.00
165	Brandon Larson	20.00
167	Jason Hart	15.00
168	Nick Johnson	25.00
169	Donaldo Mendez	15.00
170	Christian Parker	15.00
171	Jackson Melian	15.00
173	Adrian Hernandez	15.00
174	Joe Crede	15.00
175	Jose Mieses	15.00
176	Roy Oswalt	30.00
178	Xavier Nady	20.00
179	Horacio Ramirez	15.00
180	Abraham Nunez	15.00
181	Jose Ortiz	15.00
182	Jeremy Owens	15.00
183	Claudio Vargas	15.00
184	Marcus Giles	20.00
186	C.C. Sabathia	40.00
187	Adam Dunn	50.00
188	Adam Pettyjohn	.15.00
190	Jay Gibbons	15.00
191	Wilkin Ruan	15.00
193	Alfonso Soriano	60.00
194	Corey Patterson	20.00
196	Billy Sylvester	15.00
197	Juan Uribe	15.00
198	Johnny Estrada	15.00
199	Carlos Valderrama	15.00
200	Matt White	15.00

Signing Bonus Baseballs

	NM/M
Common Auto. Baseball:	15.00
Inserted 1:Box	
Al Oliver/500	15.00
Andre Dawson/550	25.00
Barry Bonds/25	250.00
Bill Madlock/525	15.00
Bill Mazeroski/25	75.00
Billy Williams/325	20.00
Bob Feller/550	20.00
Bob Gibson/25	100.00
Bobby Doerr/300	25.00
Bobby Richardson/500	20.00
Boog Powell/500	15.00
Brian Jordan/25	40.00
Bucky Dent/500	15.00
Charles Johnson/25	40.00
Chipper Jones/25	100.00
Clete Boyer/500	20.00
Dale Murphy/25	80.00
Dave Concepcion/500	15.00
Dave Kingman/500	15.00
Don Larsen/200	40.00
Don Newcombe/500	15.00
Don Zimmer/25	40.00
Duke Snider/25	100.00
Earl Weaver/300	20.00
Enos Slaughter/525	20.00
Fergie Jenkins/1000	20.00
Frank Howard/500	20.00
Frank Robinson/25	100.00
Frank Thomas/25	85.00
Gary Carter/200	30.00
Gaylord Perry/1000	15.00
George Foster/500	15.00
George Kell/300	20.00
Goose Gossage/500	15.00
Greg Maddux/25	100.00
Hank Aaron/25	300.00
Hank Bauer/500	15.00
Harmon Killebrew/200	60.00
Henry Rodriguez/400	15.00
Herb Score/500	15.00
Hoyt Wilhelm/500	20.00
J.D. Drew/75	20.00
Javy Lopez/25	40.00
Jim Edmonds/25	40.00

Boss Hoggs

	NM/M
Production 25 Sets	
4	Cal Ripken	80.00
6	Jacque Jones	15.00
7	Shawn Green	15.00
8	Ichiro Suzuki	100.00
9	Scott Rolen	20.00
11	Ken Griffey	50.00
14	Sammy Sosa	50.00
15	J.D. Drew	15.00
16	Barry Bonds	80.00
17	Pat Burrell	20.00
18	Mark McGwire	100.00
19	Mike Piazza	75.00
20	Magglio Ordonez	20.00
21	Miguel Tejada	20.00
23	Derek Jeter	85.00
24	Johnny Damon	15.00
25	Mike Sweeney	15.00
26	Ben Grieve	15.00
27	Jeff Kent	15.00
28	Andres Galarraga	15.00
29	Richie Sexson	20.00
30	Juan Encarnacion	15.00
31	Ruben Mateo	15.00

Jim Palmer/500	20.00
Joe Pepitone/500	20.00
Johnny Bench/25	120.00
Johnny Podres/500	25.00
Juan Marichal/485	20.00
Kirby Puckett/25	100.00
Larry Doby/300	30.00
Lou Brock/25	75.00
Luis Tiant/500	15.00
Magglio Ordonez/200	25.00
Manny Ramirez/25	60.00
Maury Wills/500	20.00
Mike Schmidt/25	150.00
Minnie Minoso/100	15.00
Monte Irvin/500	25.00
Moose Skowron/25	20.00
Nolan Ryan/25	200.00
Ozzie Smith/25	100.00
Phil Rizzuto/25	75.00
Ralph Kiner/100	40.00
Randy Johnson/25	100.00
Red Schoendienst/500	20.00
Reggie Jackson/25	80.00
Rickey Henderson/25	100.00
Robin Roberts/500	25.00
Roger Clemens/25	125.00
Rollie Fingers/575	20.00
Ryne Sandberg/25	100.00
Sean Casey/25	30.00
Stan Musial/25	100.00
Steve Carlton/25	75.00
Steve Garvey/1000	15.00
Todd Helton/25	50.00
Tom Glavine/25	50.00
Tom Seaver/25	75.00
Tommy John/1000	15.00
Tony Gwynn/25	75.00
Tony Perez/400	15.00
Wade Boggs/25	75.00
Warren Spahn/500	60.00
Whitey Ford/25	75.00
Willie Mays/25	150.00
Willie McCovey/25	60.00
Willie Stargell/25	75.00
Yogi Berra/25	75.00

Spectrum

Stars (1-150):	No Pricing
Production 10	
RK's (151-200):	2-4X
Production 25	

Tools Of The Trade

NM/M

Common Player:	5.00
Jerseys (1-20):	
Production 300	
Bats (21-40):	
Production 125	
Batting Glove (41-45):	
Production 50	
Hat (46-50):	
Production 100	
Autographs:	No Pricing
Production 25 Sets	
1 Vladimir Guerrero	10.00
2 Troy Glaus	6.00
3 Tony Gwynn	10.00
4 Todd Helton	8.00
5 Scott Rolen	8.00
6 Roger Clemens	20.00
7 Pedro Martinez	10.00
8 Richie Sexson	6.00
9 Magglio Ordonez	5.00
10 Ben Grieve	5.00
11 Jeff Bagwell	8.00
12 Edgar Martinez	5.00
13 Greg Maddux	25.00
15 Frank Thomas	10.00
16 Edgardo Alfonzo	5.00
17 Cal Ripken Jr.	40.00
18 Jose Vidro	5.00
19 Andruw Jones	8.00
20 Barry Bonds	50.00
21 Juan Gonzalez	8.00
22 Andruw Jones	8.00
23 Cal Ripken Jr.	60.00
24 Greg Maddux	30.00
25 Manny Ramirez	20.00
26 Roberto Alomar	8.00
27 Shawn Green	6.00
28 Edgardo Alfonzo	5.00
29 Rafael Palmeiro	10.00
30 Hideo Nomo	100.00
31 Andres Galarraga	6.00
32 Todd Helton	15.00
33 Darin Erstad	5.00
34 Ivan Rodriguez	15.00

36	Sean Casey	6.00
37	Vladimir Guerrero	20.00
39	Troy Glaus	8.00
40	Jeff Bagwell	10.00
41	Barry Bonds	100.00
42	Cal Ripken Jr.	125.00
43	Roberto Alomar	30.00
44	Sean Casey	20.00
45	Tony Gwynn	40.00
46	Bernie Williams	25.00
47	Barry Zito	25.00
49	Tom Glavine	25.00

2002 Playoff Absolute Memorabilia Samples

Selected issues of the September 2002 Beckett Baseball Card Monthly included a sample 2002 Playoff Absolute Memorabilia card rubber-cemented inside. The cards differ from the issued version only in the appearance on back of a (usually) silver-foil "SAMPLE" notation. Some cards were produced with the overprint in gold-foil, in much more limited quantities. The number of different players' cards involved in the promotion is unknown.

NM/M

Common Player:	.10
Stars:	1.5-2X
Gold:	20X

2002 Playoff Absolute Memorabilia

NM/M

Complete Set (200):	
Common Player:	.50
Common RK/Prospect (151-200):	3.00
Production 1,000	
Pack (6):	
Box + 8 x 10:	140.00
1 David Eckstein	.50
2 Darin Erstad	.75
3 Troy Glaus	1.50
4 Garret Anderson	.50
5 Tim Salmon	.50
6 Curt Schilling	1.00
7 Randy Johnson	1.50
8 Luis Gonzalez	.50
9 Mark Grace	.60
10 Tom Glavine	.75
11 Greg Maddux	2.00
12 Chipper Jones	2.00
13 Gary Sheffield	.75
14 John Smoltz	.50
15 Andruw Jones	1.50
16 Wilson Betemit	.50
17 Tony Batista	.50
18 Javier Vazquez	.50
19 Scott Erickson	.50
20 Josh Towers	.50
21 Pedro J. Martinez	1.50
22 Johnny Damon	.60
23 Manny Ramirez	1.50
24 Rickey Henderson	1.50
25 Trot Nixon	.50
26 Nomar Garciaparra	2.50
27 Juan Cruz	.50
28 Kerry Wood	1.25
29 Fred McGriff	.50
30 Moises Alou	.50
31 Sammy Sosa	2.50
32 Corey Patterson	.50
33 Mark Buehrle	.50
34 Keith Foulke	.50
35 Frank Thomas	1.50
36 Kenny Lofton	.50
37 Magglio Ordonez	.50
38 Barry Larkin	.50
39 Ken Griffey Jr.	2.50
40 Adam Dunn	.75
41 Juan Encarnacion	.50
42 Sean Casey	.60
43 Bartolo Colon	.50
44 C.C. Sabathia	.50
45 Travis Fryman	.50
46 Jim Thome	1.50
47 Omar Vizquel	.50
48 Ellis Burks	.50
49 Russell Branyan	.50
50 Mike Hampton	.50
51 Todd Helton	.50
52 Jose Ortiz	.50

53	Juan Uribe	.50
54	Juan Pierre	.50
55	Larry Walker	.50
56	Mike Rivera	.50
57	Robert Fick	.50
58	Bobby Higginson	.50
59	Josh Beckett	.50
60	Richard Hidalgo	.50
61	Cliff Floyd	.50
62	Mike Lowell	.50
63	Roy Oswalt	.50
64	Morgan Ensberg	.50
65	Jeff Bagwell	1.50
66	Craig Biggio	.50
67	Lance Berkman	.50
68	Carlos Beltran	.75
69	Mike Sweeney	.50
70	Neifi Perez	.50
71	Kevin Brown	.50
72	Hideo Nomo	1.50
73	Paul LoDuca	.60
74	Adrian Beltre	.60
75	Shawn Green	.75
76	Eric Karros	.50
77	Brad Radke	.50
78	Corey Koskie	.50
79	Doug Mientkiewicz	.50
80	Torii Hunter	.50
81	Jacque Jones	.50
82	Ben Sheets	.50
83	Richie Sexson	.50
84	Geoff Jenkins	.50
85	Tony Armas	.50
86	Michael Barrett	.50
87	Jose Vidro	.50
88	Vladimir Guerrero	1.50
89	Roger Clemens	2.25
90	Derek Jeter	4.00
91	Bernie Williams	.60
92	Jason Giambi	1.25
93	Jorge Posada	.50
94	Mike Mussina	.65
95	Andy Pettitte	.65
96	Nick Johnson	.50
97	Alfonso Soriano	1.25
98	Shawn Estes	.50
99	Al Leiter	.50
100	Mike Piazza	2.50
101	Roberto Alomar	.75
102	Mo Vaughn	.50
103	Jeromy Burnitz	.50
104	Tim Hudson	.65
105	Barry Zito	.50
106	Mark Mulder	.50
107	Eric Chavez	.65
108	Miguel Tejada	.65
109	Jeremy Giambi	.50
110	Jermaine Dye	.50
111	Mike Lieberthal	.50
112	Scott Rolen	1.25
113	Pat Burrell	.75
114	Brandon Duckworth	.50
115	Bobby Abreu	.50
116	Jason Kendall	.50
117	Aramis Ramirez	.50
118	Brian Giles	.50
119	Pokey Reese	.50
120	Phil Nevin	.50
121	Ryan Klesko	.50
122	Carlos Pena	.50
123	Trevor Hoffman	.50
124	Barry Bonds	4.00
125	Rich Aurilia	.50
126	Jeff Kent	.50
127	Tsuyoshi Shinjo	.50
128	Ichiro Suzuki	2.00
129	Edgar Martinez	.50
130	Freddy Garcia	.50
131	Bret Boone	.50
132	Matt Morris	.50
133	Tino Martinez	.50
134	Albert Pujols	3.00
135	J.D. Drew	.75
136	Jim Edmonds	.50
137	Gabe Kapler	.50
138	Paul Wilson	.50
139	Ben Grieve	.50
140	Wade Miller	.50
141	Chan Ho Park	.50
142	Alex Rodriguez	3.00
143	Rafael Palmeiro	1.25
144	Juan Gonzalez	1.50
145	Ivan Rodriguez	1.25
146	Carlos Delgado	.75
147	Jose Cruz Jr.	.50
148	Shannon Stewart	.50
149	Raul Mondesi	.50
150	Vernon Wells	.50
151	So Taguchi RC	8.00
152	Kazuhisa Ishii RC	8.00
153	Hank Blalock	3.00
154	Sean Burroughs	3.00
155	Geronimo Gil	3.00
156	Jon Rauch	3.00
157	Fernando Rodney	3.00
158	Miguel Asencio RC	3.00
159	Franklyn German RC	3.00
160	Luis Ugueto RC	3.00
161	Jorge Sosa RC	3.00
162	Felix Escalona RC	3.00
163	Colby Lewis	3.00
164	Mark Teixeira	6.00
165	Mark Prior	6.00
166	Francis Beltran RC	3.00
167	Joe Thurston	3.00
168	Earl Snyder RC	3.00
169	Takahito Nomura RC	3.00
170	Bill Hall	3.00

171	Marlon Byrd	3.00
172	Dave Williams	3.00
173	Yorvit Torrealba	3.00
174	Brandon Backe RC	3.00
175	Jorge de la Rosa RC	3.00
176	Brian Mallette RC	3.00
177	Rodrigo Rosario RC	3.00
178	Anderson Machado RC	3.00
179	Jorge Padilla RC	3.00
180	Allan Simpson RC	3.00
181	Doug DeVore RC	3.00
182	Steve Bechler RC	3.00
183	Raul Chavez	3.00
184	Tom Shearn RC	3.00
185	Ben Howard RC	3.00
186	Chris Baker RC	3.00
187	Travis Hughes RC	3.00
188	Kevin Mench	3.00
189	Drew Henson	3.00
190	Mike Moriarty RC	3.00
191	Corey Thurman RC	3.00
192	Bobby Hill	3.00
193	Steve Kent RC	3.00
194	Satoru Komiyama RC	3.00
195	Jason Lane	3.00
196	Angel Berroa	3.00
197	Brandon Puffer RC	3.00
198	Brian Fitzgerald RC	3.00
199	Rene Reyes RC	3.00
200	Hee Seop Choi	5.00

Spectrum

Stars (1-150):	3-5X
Production 100	
SP's:	1-1.5X
Production 50	

Absolutely Ink

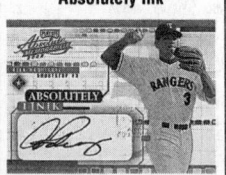

NM/M

Common Autograph:	5.00
Inserted 1:27	
Gold Parallel #'d to 25 not priced.	
Jsy Parallel #'d to Jsy # not priced.	
Adrian Beltre	20.00
Alex Rodriguez/50	100.00
Ben Sheets	20.00
Bobby Doerr	15.00
Blaine Neal	5.00
Carlos Beltran	25.00
Carlos Pena	5.00
Corey Patterson/150	15.00
Dave Parker	10.00
David Justice/65	25.00
Don Mattingly/75	65.00
Duaner Sanchez	5.00
Eric Chavez/150	15.00
Freddy Garcia	10.00
Gary Carter	25.00
Ivan Rodriguez/50	40.00
J.D. Drew/100	20.00
Jack Cust	5.00
Jason Michaels	5.00
Jermaine Dye/125	10.00
Jose Vidro	8.00
Josh Towers	6.00
Kerry Wood/50	40.00
Kirby Puckett/50	75.00
Luis Gonzalez/75	25.00
Luis Rivera	5.00
Manny Ramirez/40	40.00
Marcus Giles	10.00
Mark Prior/100	30.00
Mark Teixeira/100	25.00
Marlon Byrd/250	15.00
Matt Ginter	5.00
Moises Alou/150	15.00
Nate Frese	5.00
Nick Johnson	5.00
Pablo Ozuna	5.00
Paul LoDuca/200	20.00
Richie Sexson	15.00
Roberto Alomar/100	40.00
Roy Oswalt/300	15.00
Ryan Klesko/75	15.00
Sean Casey/125	10.00
Shannon Stewart	8.00
So Taguchi	8.00
Terrence Long	5.00
Timoniel Perez	5.00
Tony Gwynn/50	60.00
Troy Glaus/300	15.00
Vladimir Guerrero/225	40.00
Wade Miller	15.00
Wilson Betemit	5.00

Signing Bonus

Common Player:	NM/M
Bobby Abreu/53	40.00
Roberto Alomar/100	50.00
Moises Alou/250	50.00
Carlos Beltran/50	50.00
Adrian Beltre/29	40.00
Adrian Beltre/150	30.00
Angel Berroa/50	20.00
Angel Berroa/100	25.00
Wilson Betemit/250	25.00
Hank Blalock/50	50.00
Hank Blalock/100	40.00
Lou Brock/100	60.00
Lou Brock/200	50.00
Kevin Brown/27	50.00
Kevin Brown/100	25.00
Kevin Brown/150	25.00
Mark Buehrle/56	60.00
Mark Buehrle/200	40.00
Marlon Byrd/61	25.00
Steve Carlton/100	50.00
Steve Carlton/150	40.00
Sean Casey/100	30.00
Eric Chavez/28	50.00
Juan Cruz/51	25.00
J.D. Drew/100	30.00
Brandon Duckworth/56	25.00
Brandon Duckworth/150	15.00
Adam Dunn/44	60.00
Jermaine Dye/100	50.00
Jermaine Dye/250	30.00
Morgan Ensberg/100	30.00
Cliff Floyd/200	15.00
Freddy Garcia/34	50.00
Freddy Garcia/125	25.00
Troy Glaus/50	65.00
Troy Glaus/100	40.00
Tom Glavine/200	60.00
Luis Gonzalez/125	30.00
Vladimir Guerrero/27	120.00
Vladimir Guerrero/150	80.00
Richard Hidalgo/100	20.00
Richard Hidalgo/135	20.00
Richard Hidalgo/150	20.00
Tim Hudson/50	60.00
Tim Hudson/100	40.00
Reggie Jackson/44	75.00
Nick Johnson/200	30.00
Andruw Jones/75	75.00
Al Kaline/250	60.00
Gabe Kapler/125	25.00
Gabe Kapler/175	25.00
Ryan Klesko/30	40.00
Jason Lane/100	30.00
Barry Larkin/50	60.00
Barry Larkin/100	50.00
Paul LoDuca/50	40.00
Fred Lynn/150	30.00
Fred Lynn/250	30.00
Greg Maddux/31	200.00
Edgar Martinez/150	50.00
Pedro J. Martinez/45	125.00
Don Mattingly/100	140.00
Willie McCovey/190	40.00
Willie McCovey/250	40.00
Wade Miller/52	25.00
Wade Miller/150	25.00
Wade Miller/250	25.00
Paul Molitor/75	50.00
Paul Molitor/100	40.00
Paul Molitor/125	40.00
Mark Mulder/40	35.00
Jose Ortiz/125	15.00
Roy Oswalt/44	40.00
Roy Oswalt/100	40.00
Jim Palmer/150	30.00
Jim Palmer/250	25.00
Dave Parker/150	25.00
Corey Patterson/250	25.00
Carlos Pena/125	15.00
Carlos Pena/250	15.00
Tony Perez/24	40.00
Tony Perez/50	40.00
Juan Pierre/75	25.00
Mark Prior/50	50.00
Mark Prior/75	40.00
Mark Prior/125	40.00
Kirby Puckett/34	125.00
Albert Pujols/100	250.00
Aramis Ramirez/50	25.00
Aramis Ramirez/125	40.00
Phil Rizzuto/10	265.00
Phil Rizzuto/250	70.00
Brooks Robinson/150	70.00
Brooks Robinson/250	60.00
Nolan Ryan/200	200.00
Nolan Ryan/34	200.00
Ryne Sandberg/50	150.00
Mike Schmidt/100	100.00
Richie Sexson/100	30.00
Ben Sheets/100	30.00
Ben Sheets/150	30.00
Alfonso Soriano/100	50.00
Shannon Stewart/100	25.00
Shannon Stewart/150	25.00
Mike Sweeney/100	30.00
So Taguchi/99	40.00
Mark Teixeira/23	65.00
Mark Teixeira/100	60.00
Miguel Tejada/40	60.00
Miguel Tejada/50	60.00
Frank Thomas/35	120.00
Javier Vazquez/125	25.00
Jose Vidro/150	20.00
Kerry Wood/34	75.00
Barry Zito/50	60.00

Team Tandems

NM/M

Complete Set (40):		80.00
Common Card:		1.00
Inserted 1:12		
Golds:		2-3X
Inserted 1:72		
1	Troy Glaus, Darin Erstad	1.50
2	Curt Schilling, Randy Johnson	3.00
3	Chipper Jones, Andruw Jones	3.00
4	Greg Maddux, Tom Glavine	4.00
5	Nomar Garciaparra, Manny Ramirez	6.00
6	Pedro J. Martinez, Trot Nixon	3.00
7	Kerry Wood, Sammy Sosa	5.00
8	Frank Thomas, Magglio Ordonez	2.00
9	Ken Griffey Jr., Barry Larkin	5.00
10	C.C. Sabathia, Jim Thome	2.50
11	Todd Helton, Larry Walker	2.00
12	Bobby Higginson, Shane Halter	1.00
13	Cliff Floyd, Brad Penny	1.00
14	Jeff Bagwell, Craig Biggio	2.00
15	Shawn Green, Adrian Beltre	1.50
16	Ben Sheets, Richie Sexson	1.50
17	Vladimir Guerrero, Jose Vidro	3.00
18	Mike Piazza, Roberto Alomar	5.00
19	Roger Clemens, Mike Mussina	6.00
20	Derek Jeter, Jason Giambi	8.00
21	Barry Zito, Tim Hudson	1.50
22	Eric Chavez, Miguel Tejada	1.50
23	Pat Burrell, Scott Rolen	3.00
24	Brian Giles, Aramis Ramirez	1.50
25	Ryan Klesko, Phil Nevin	1.50
26	Barry Bonds, Rich Aurilia	8.00
27	Ichiro Suzuki, Kazuhisa Sasaki	1.50
28	Albert Pujols, J.D. Drew	6.00
29	Alex Rodriguez, Ivan Rodriguez	6.00
30	Carlos Delgado, Shannon Stewart	1.50
31	Mo Vaughn, Roger Cedeno	1.50
32	Carlos Beltran, Mike Sweeney	1.50
33	Edgar Martinez, Bret Boone	1.50
34	Juan Gonzalez, Rafael Palmeiro	2.00
35	Johnny Damon, Rickey Henderson	1.50
36	Sean Casey, Adam Dunn	2.00
37	Jeff Kent, Tsuyoshi Shinjo	1.50
38	Lance Berkman, Richard Hidalgo	1.50
39	So Taguchi, Tino Martinez	1.50
40	Hideo Nomo, Kazuhisa Ishii	1.50

Team Tandems G-U

NM/M

Common Card:		5.00
Inserted 1:33		
Golds:		2-3X
Production 50		
1	Troy Glaus, Darin Erstad	8.00
2	Curt Schilling, Randy Johnson	10.00
3	Chipper Jones, Andruw Jones	10.00
4	Greg Maddux, Tom Glavine	20.00
5	Nomar Garciaparra, Manny Ramirez	25.00
6	Pedro J. Martinez, Trot Nixon	15.00

#	Player	Price
7	Kerry Wood, Sammy Sosa	15.00
8	Frank Thomas, Magglio Ordonez	10.00
9	Ken Griffey Jr., Barry Larkin	15.00
10	C.C. Sabathia, Jim Thome	15.00
11	Todd Helton, Larry Walker	8.00
12	Bobby Higginson, Shane Halter	8.00
13	Cliff Floyd, Brad Penny	5.00
14	Jeff Bagwell, Craig Biggio	15.00
15	Shawn Green, Adrian Beltre	8.00
16	Ben Sheets, Richie Sexson	8.00
17	Vladimir Guerrero, Jose Vidro	12.00
18	Mike Piazza, Roberto Alomar	15.00
19	Roger Clemens, Mike Mussina	50.00
20	Derek Jeter, Jason Giambi	30.00
21	Barry Zito, Tim Hudson	15.00
22	Eric Chavez, Miguel Tejada	10.00
23	Pat Burrell, Scott Rolen	15.00
24	Brian Giles, Aramis Ramirez	10.00
25	Ryan Klesko, Phil Nevin	8.00
26	Barry Bonds, Rich Aurilia	15.00
28	Albert Pujols, J.D. Drew	15.00
29	Alex Rodriguez, Ivan Rodriguez	15.00
30	Carlos Delgado, Shannon Stewart	8.00
31	Mo Vaughn, Roger Cedeno	5.00
32	Carlos Beltran, Mike Sweeney	8.00
33	Edgar Martinez, Bret Boone	8.00
34	Juan Gonzalez, Rafael Palmeiro	12.00
35	Johnny Damon, Rickey Henderson	10.00
36	Sean Casey, Adam Dunn	15.00
37	Jeff Kent, Tsuyoshi Shinjo	10.00
38	Lance Berkman, Richard Hidalgo	8.00
39	So Taguchi, Tino Martinez	15.00
40	Hideo Nomo, Kazuhisa Ishii	35.00

Team Quads

NM/M
Complete Set (20): 75.00
Common Card: 2.00
Inserted 1:18
Golds: 2X
Inserted 1:72

#	Players	Price
1	Troy Glaus, Darin Erstad, Garret Anderson, Troy Percival	2.00
2	Curt Schilling, Randy Johnson, Luis Gonzalez, Mark Grace	4.00
3	Chipper Jones, Andruw Jones, Greg Maddux, Tom Glavine	5.00
4	Nomar Garciaparra, Manny Ramirez, Trot Nixon, Pedro J. Martinez	6.00
5	Kerry Wood, Sammy Sosa, Fred McGriff, Moises Alou	6.00
6	Frank Thomas, Magglio Ordonez, Mark Buehrle, Kenny Lofton	3.00
7	Ken Griffey Jr., Barry Larkin, Juan Encarnacion, Sean Casey	6.00
8	C.C. Sabathia, Jim Thome, Bartolo Colon, Russell Branyan	4.00
9	Todd Helton, Larry Walker, Juan Pierre, Mike Hampton	2.50
10	Jeff Bagwell, Craig Biggio, Lance Berkman, Richard Hidalgo	2.00
11	Shawn Green, Adrian Beltre, Hideo Nomo, Paul LoDuca	2.00
12	Mike Piazza, Roberto Alomar, Mo Vaughn, Roger Cedeno	6.00
13	Roger Clemens, Derek Jeter, Jason Giambi, Mike Mussina	10.00
14	Barry Zito, Tim Hudson, Eric Chavez, Miguel Tejada	2.50
15	Pat Burrell, Scott Rolen, Bobby Abreu, Marlon Byrd	4.00
16	Bernie Williams, Jorge Posada, Alfonso Soriano, Andy Pettitte	3.00
17	Barry Bonds, Rich Aurilia, Tsuyoshi Shinjo, Jeff Kent	8.00
18	Ichiro Suzuki, Kazuhiro Sasaki, Bret Boone, Edgar Martinez	6.00
19	Albert Pujols, J.D. Drew, Jim Edmonds, Tino Martinez	8.00
20	Alex Rodriguez, Ivan Rodriguez, Juan Gonzalez, Rafael Palmeiro	8.00

Team Quads Game-Used

NM/M
Numbered to 100
Prime: No Pricing
Production 25

#	Players	Price
1	Troy Glaus, Darin Erstad, Garret Anderson, Troy Percival	25.00
2	Curt Schilling, Randy Johnson, Luis Gonzalez, Mark Grace	30.00
3	Chipper Jones, Andruw Jones, Greg Maddux, Tom Glavine	40.00
4	Nomar Garciaparra, Manny Ramirez, Trot Nixon, Pedro J. Martinez	50.00
5	Kerry Wood, Sammy Sosa, Fred McGriff, Moises Alou	35.00
6	Frank Thomas, Magglio Ordonez, Mark Buehrle, Kenny Lofton	25.00
8	C.C. Sabathia, Jim Thome, Bartolo Colon, Russell Branyan	40.00
9	Todd Helton, Larry Walker, Juan Pierre, Mike Hampton	30.00
10	Jeff Bagwell, Craig Biggio, Lance Berkman, Richard Hidalgo	30.00
11	Shawn Green, Adrian Beltre, Hideo Nomo, Paul LoDuca	40.00
12	Mike Piazza, Roberto Alomar, Mo Vaughn, Roger Cedeno	40.00
13	Roger Clemens, Derek Jeter, Jason Giambi, Mike Mussina	75.00
14	Barry Zito, Tim Hudson, Eric Chavez, Miguel Tejada	20.00
15	Pat Burrell, Scott Rolen, Bobby Abreu, Marlon Byrd	35.00
16	Bernie Williams, Jorge Posada, Alfonso Soriano, Andy Pettitte	30.00
17	Barry Bonds, Rich Aurilia, Tsuyoshi Shinjo, Jeff Kent	40.00
18	Ichiro Suzuki, Kazuhiro Sasaki, Bret Boone, Edgar Martinez	50.00
19	Albert Pujols, J.D. Drew, Jim Edmonds, Tino Martinez	40.00
20	Alex Rodriguez, Ivan Rodriguez, Juan Gonzalez, Rafael Palmeiro	40.00

Tools of the Trade

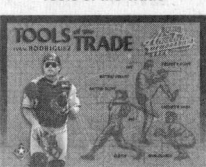

NM/M
Complete Set (95): 120.00
Common Player: 1.00
Inserted 1:9
Golds: 2-3X
Inserted 1:45

#	Player	Price
1	Mike Mussina	2.00
2	Rickey Henderson	2.00
3	Raul Mondesi	1.00
4	Nomar Garciaparra	6.00
5	Randy Johnson	3.00
6	Roger Clemens	6.00
7	Shawn Green	1.00
8	Todd Helton	2.00
9	Aramis Ramirez	1.50
10	Barry Larkin	1.50
11	Byung-Hyun Kim	1.00
12	C.C. Sabathia	1.00
13	Curt Schilling	2.50
14	Darin Erstad	1.50
15	Eric Karros	1.00
16	Freddy Garcia	1.00
17	Greg Maddux	4.00
18	Jason Kendall	1.00
19	Jim Thome	3.00
20	Juan Gonzalez	1.00
21	Kazuhiro Sasaki	1.00
22	Kerry Wood	3.00
23	Luis Gonzalez	1.50
24	Mark Mulder	1.00
25	Rich Aurilia	1.00
26	Ray Durham	1.00
27	Ben Grieve	1.00
28	Bret Boone	1.00
29	Edgar Martinez	1.00
30	Ivan Rodriguez	1.00
31	Jorge Posada	1.00
32	Mike Piazza	6.00
33	Pat Burrell	1.50
34	Robin Ventura	1.00
35	Trot Nixon	1.00
36	Adrian Beltre	1.00
37	Bernie Williams	1.50
38	Bobby Abreu	1.50
39	Carlos Delgado	1.50
40	Craig Biggio	1.50
41	Garret Anderson	1.50
42	Jermaine Dye	1.00
43	Johnny Damon	1.00
44	Tim Salmon	1.00
45	Tino Martinez	1.00
46	Fred McGriff	1.00
47	Gary Sheffield	1.00
48	Adam Dunn	2.00
49	Joe Mays	1.00
50	Kenny Lofton	1.00
51	Josh Beckett	1.00
52	Bud Smith	1.00
53	Johnny Estrada	1.00
54	Charles Johnson	1.00
55	Craig Wilson	1.00
56	Terrence Long	1.00
57	Andy Pettitte	1.50
58	Brian Giles	1.00
59	Juan Pierre	1.00
60	Cliff Floyd	1.00
61	Ivan Rodriguez	2.00
62	Andruw Jones	2.00
63	Lance Berkman	1.00
64	Mark Buehrle	1.00
65	Miguel Tejada	1.00
66	Wade Miller	1.00
67	Johnny Estrada	1.00
68	Tsuyoshi Shinjo	1.00
69	Scott Rolen	2.50
70	Roberto Alomar	2.00
71	Mark Grace	2.00
72	Larry Walker	1.50
73	Jim Edmonds	1.50
74	Jeff Kent	1.00
75	Frank Thomas	2.50
76	Carlos Beltran	1.50
77	Barry Zito	1.00
78	Alex Rodriguez	8.00
79	Troy Glaus	1.00
80	Ryan Klesko	1.00
81	Tom Glavine	1.00
82	Ben Sheets	1.00
83	Manny Ramirez	2.50
84	Shannon Stewart	1.00
85	Vladimir Guerrero	4.00
86	Chipper Jones	3.00
87	Jeff Bagwell	2.50
88	Richie Sexson	1.50
89	Sean Casey	1.50
90	Tim Hudson	1.50
91	J.D. Drew	1.50
92	Ivan Rodriguez	2.00
93	Magglio Ordonez	1.50
94	John Buck	1.00
95	Paul LoDuca	1.00

Tools of Trade G-U

NM/M
Common Player: 5.00
Jerseys #'d to 300.
Bats #'d to 250.
Shoes #'d to 150.
Shin Guard #'d to 150.
Glove #'d to 125.
Mask #'d to 100.
Hat #'d to 50.
Doubles #'d to 200.
Triples #'d to 75.
Quads #'d to 50.

#	Player/Item	Price
1	Mike Mussina/Jsy	10.00
2	Rickey Henderson/Jsy	10.00
3	Raul Mondesi/Jsy	5.00
4	Nomar Garciaparra/Jsy	15.00
5	Randy Johnson/Jsy	10.00
6	Roger Clemens/Jsy	15.00
7	Shawn Green/Jsy	5.00
8	Todd Helton/Jsy	8.00
9	Aramis Ramirez/Jsy	8.00
10	Barry Larkin/Jsy	5.00
11	Byung-Hyun Kim/Jsy	5.00
12	C.C. Sabathia/Jsy	5.00
13	Curt Schilling/Jsy	10.00
14	Darin Erstad/Jsy	5.00
15	Eric Karros/Jsy	5.00
16	Freddy Garcia/Jsy	5.00
17	Greg Maddux/Jsy	15.00
18	Jason Kendall/Jsy	5.00
19	Jim Thome/Jsy	10.00
20	Juan Gonzalez/Jsy	8.00
21	Kazuhiro Sasaki/Jsy	5.00
22	Kerry Wood/Jsy	10.00
23	Luis Gonzalez/Jsy	8.00
24	Mark Mulder/Jsy	8.00
25	Rich Aurilia/Jsy	5.00
26	Ray Durham/Jsy	5.00
27	Ben Grieve/Jsy	5.00
28	Bret Boone/Jsy	5.00
29	Edgar Martinez/Jsy	8.00
30	Ivan Rodriguez/Jsy	8.00
31	Jorge Posada/Jsy	10.00
32	Mike Piazza/Jsy	15.00
33	Pat Burrell/Bat	8.00
34	Robin Ventura/Bat	5.00
35	Trot Nixon/Bat	5.00
36	Adrian Beltre/Bat	5.00
37	Bernie Williams/Bat	8.00
38	Bobby Abreu/Bat	8.00
39	Carlos Delgado/Bat	8.00
40	Craig Biggio/Bat	8.00
41	Garret Anderson/Bat	8.00
42	Jermaine Dye/Bat	8.00
43	Johnny Damon/Bat	8.00
44	Tim Salmon/Bat	8.00
45	Tino Martinez/Bat	10.00
46	Fred McGriff/Bat	8.00
47	Gary Sheffield/Bat	8.00
48	Adam Dunn/Shoe	15.00
49	Joe Mays/Shoe	8.00
50	Kenny Lofton/Shoe	10.00
51	Josh Beckett/Shoe	10.00
52	Bud Smith/Shoe	5.00
53	Johnny Estrada/Shin	10.00
54	Charles Johnson/Shin	8.00
55	Craig Wilson/Shin	15.00
56	Terrence Long/Glove	8.00
57	Andy Pettitte/Glove	15.00
58	Brian Giles/Glove	10.00
59	Juan Pierre/Glove	10.00
60	Cliff Floyd/Glove	10.00
61	Ivan Rodriguez/Glove	15.00
62	Andruw Jones/Hat	15.00
63	Lance Berkman/Hat	15.00
64	Mark Buehrle/Hat	10.00
65	Miguel Tejada/Hat	15.00
66	Wade Miller/Hat	10.00
67	Johnny Estrada/Shin	10.00
68	T. Shinjo/Bat/Shoe	15.00
69	S. Rolen/Bat/Shoe	20.00
70	R. Alomar/Bat/Shoe	20.00
71	M. Grace/Glv/Jsy	15.00
72	L. Walker/Bat/Jsy	15.00
73	J. Edmonds/Jsy/Bat	15.00
74	J. Kent/Jsy/Bat	10.00
75	F. Thomas/Jsy/Bat	15.00
76	C. Beltran/Jsy/Bat	10.00
77	B. Zito/Shoe/Jsy	15.00
78	A. Rodriguez/Jsy/Bat	25.00
79	T. Glaus/Dualjsy	15.00
80	R. Klesko/Bat/Glv	8.00
81	T. Glavine/Jsy/Bat	10.00
82	B. Sheets/Bat/Jsy	20.00
83	M. Ramirez/Shoe/Glv/Jsy	25.00
84	S. Stewart/Hat/Jsy/Bat	15.00
85	V. Guerrero/Jsy/Bat	45.00
86	C. Jones/Glv/Jsy/Bat	40.00
87	J. Bagwell/Jsy/Hat/Bat	40.00
88	R. Sexson/Bat/Jsy/Glv/Shoe	40.00
89	S. Casey/Jsy/Hat/Shoe/Bat	30.00
90	T Hudson/Shoe/Hat/Glv/Jsy	30.00
91	JD Drew/Shoe/Jsy/Hat/Bat	40.00
92	I Rodriguez/Jsy/Mask/Chst/Glv	60.00
93	M Ordonez/Hat/Glv/Jsy/Shoe	40.00
94	J Buck/Glv/Chst/Shin/Msk	20.00
95	P LoDuca/Jsy/Chst/Shin/Msk	30.00

2002 Playoff Piece of the Game

NM/M
Complete Set (100):
Common Player: .50
Common SP (51-100): 5.00
Pack (5): 15.00
Box (6): 75.00

#	Player	Price
1	Vladimir Guerrero	1.50
2	Troy Glaus	1.50
3	Ichiro Suzuki	2.50
4	Chipper Jones	2.00
5	Roberto Alomar	.75
6	Scott Rolen	1.25
7	Randy Johnson	1.50
8	Roger Clemens	2.25
9	Nomar Garciaparra	2.50
10	Greg Maddux	2.00
11	Barry Bonds	4.00
12	Derek Jeter	4.00
13	Albert Pujols	3.00
14	Kerry Wood	1.25
15	Jim Thome	1.50
16	Manny Ramirez	1.50
17	Carlos Delgado	.75
18	Magglio Ordonez	.50
19	Torii Hunter	.50
20	Garret Anderson	.50
21	Eric Chavez	.60
22	Rafael Palmeiro	1.25
23	Andruw Jones	1.50
24	Cliff Floyd	.50
25	Sammy Sosa	2.50
26	Mike Mussina	.60
27	Jeff Bagwell	1.50
28	Miguel Tejada	.60
29	Curt Schilling	1.00
30	Tom Glavine	.75
31	Frank Thomas	1.50
32	Jim Edmonds	.50
33	Juan Gonzalez	1.50
34	Todd Helton	1.50
35	Shawn Green	.75
36	Alfonso Soriano	1.25
37	Lance Berkman	.50
38	Barry Zito	.60
39	Ryan Klesko	.50
40	Larry Walker	.50
41	Craig Biggio	.50
42	Luis Gonzalez	.50
43	Ivan Rodriguez	1.25
44	J.D. Drew	.75
45	Roy Oswalt	.50
46	Jason Giambi	1.25
47	Brian Giles	.50
48	Richie Sexson	.50
49	Pat Burrell	.75
50	Alex Rodriguez	3.00
51	So Taguchi RC	8.00
52	Allan Simpson RC	5.00
53	Oliver Perez RC	10.00
54	Ben Howard RC	5.00
55	Kirk Saarloos RC	5.00
56	Francis Beltran RC	5.00
57	Jorge Padilla RC	5.00
58	Brandon Puffer RC	5.00
59	Brian Mallette RC	5.00
60	Kyle Kane RC	5.00
61	Travis Driskill RC	5.00
62	Jeremy Lambert RC	5.00
63	Steve Kent RC	5.00
64	Julius Matos RC	5.00
65	Julio Mateo RC	5.00
66	Kazuhisa Ishii RC	8.00
67	Franklyn German RC	5.00
68	John Foster RC	5.00
69	Luis Ugueto RC	5.00
70	Shawn Sedlacek RC	5.00
71	Earl Snyder RC	5.00
72	Alex Pelaez RC	5.00
73	Victor Alvarez RC	5.00
74	Tom Shearn RC	5.00
75	Corey Thurman RC	5.00
76	Eric Junge RC	5.00
77	Hansel Izquierdo RC	5.00
78	Elio Serrano RC	5.00
79	J.J. Trujillo RC	5.00
80	Chris Snelling RC	6.00
81	Satoru Komiyama RC	8.00
82	Brandon Backe RC	5.00
83	Anderson Machado RC	5.00
84	Doug DeVore RC	5.00
85	Steve Bechler RC	5.00
86	John Ennis RC	5.00
87	Rodrigo Rosario RC	5.00
88	Jorge Sosa RC	5.00
89	Ken Huckaby RC	5.00
90	Mike Moriarty RC	5.00
91	Michael Crudale RC	5.00
92	Kevin Frederick RC	5.00
93	Aaron Guiel RC	5.00
94	Jose Rodriguez RC	5.00
95	Andy Shibilo RC	5.00
96	Deivis Santos RC	5.00
97	Felix Escalona RC	5.00
98	Miguel Asencio RC	5.00
99	Takahito Nomura RC	5.00
100	Cam Esslinger RC	5.00

Materials

NM/M
Common Materials (1-90): 4.00
Team Connections (91-95): Production 500
Superstar Combos (96-100): Production 250
Bronze Materials (1-90): 1-2X — Production 250
Bronze Team Connect. (91-95): 1.5-2X — Production 100
Bronze Combos (96-100): 2-3X — Production 50
Silver Materials (1-90): 1.5-2.5X — Production 150
Silver Tm. Connect. (91-95): 1.5-3X — Production 50
Silver Combos (96-100): No Pricing — Production 25
Gold Materials (1-90): 2-5X — Production 25
Gold Tm. Connect. (91-95): No Pricing — Production 10
Gold Combos (96-100): No Pricing — Production 10
Platinum Materials (1-90): No Pricing — Production 25
Platinum Tm Connect. (91-95): No Pricing — Production 10
Platinum Combos (96-100): No Pricing — Production 5

#	Player/Item	Price
1	Adam Dunn/Bat	8.00
2	Adrian Beltre/Bat	4.00
3	Albert Pujols/Base	10.00
4	Alex Rodriguez/Jsy	12.00
5	Alex Rodriguez/Bat	12.00
6	Andruw Jones/Jsy	5.00
7	Andruw Jones/Bat	5.00
8	Barry Bonds/Base	15.00
9	Barry Larkin/Jsy	5.00
10	Juan Gonzalez/Jsy	5.00
11	Bernie Williams/Jsy	6.00
12	Carlos Delgado/Jsy	5.00
13	Chipper Jones/Jsy	10.00
14	Chipper Jones/Bat	8.00
15	Craig Biggio/Jsy	5.00
16	Craig Biggio/Bat	5.00
17	Cristian Guzman/Jsy	5.00
18	Curt Schilling/Jsy	6.00
19	Derek Jeter/Base	15.00
20	Edgar Martinez/Jsy	5.00
21	Edgardo Alfonzo/Jsy	4.00
22	Ellis Burks/Jsy	4.00
23	Frank Thomas/Bat	6.00
24	Freddy Garcia/Jsy	4.00
25	Greg Maddux/Jsy	10.00
26	Harmon Killebrew/Pants	15.00
27	Hideo Nomo/Jsy	12.00
28	Ichiro Suzuki/Base	15.00
29	Ivan Rodriguez/Jsy	8.00
30	Ivan Rodriguez/Bat	8.00
31	J.D. Drew/Bat	6.00
32	J.D. Drew/Jsy	6.00
33	Javy Lopez/Jsy	6.00
34	Jeff Bagwell/Jsy	6.00
35	Jim Edmonds/Jsy	6.00
36	Jim Edmonds/Bat	6.00
37	John Olerud/Bat	4.00
38	John Smoltz/Jsy	6.00
39	Jose Cruz Jr./Jsy	4.00
40	Jose Vidro/Jsy	4.00
41	Juan Gonzalez/Bat	6.00
42	Juan Pierre/Jsy	4.00
43	Ken Griffey Jr./Base	10.00
44	Kenny Lofton/Jsy	4.00
45	Kerry Wood/Jsy	6.00
46	Kevin Brown/Jsy	4.00
47	Lance Berkman/Jsy	6.00
48	Lance Berkman/Bat	6.00
49	Larry Walker/Jsy	5.00
50	Luis Gonzalez/Jsy	5.00
51	Magglio Ordonez/Jsy	5.00
52	Magglio Ordonez/Bat	5.00
53	Manny Ramirez/Jsy	8.00
54	Manny Ramirez/Bat	8.00
55	Vladimir Guerrero/Jsy	8.00
56	Mark Grace/Bat	8.00
57	Michael Barrett/Jsy	

2002 Playoff Piece of the Game (continued)

#	Player	Price
58	Miguel Tejada/Jsy	8.00
59	Mike Piazza/Jsy	12.00
60	Mike Piazza/Bat	12.00
61	Mike Schmidt/Bat	15.00
62	Mike Sweeney/Jsy	4.00
63	Nolan Ryan/Jsy	30.00
64	Nomar Garciaparra/Jsy	15.00
65	Paul LoDuca/Jsy	4.00
66	Rafael Palmeiro/Jsy	8.00
67	Rafael Palmeiro/Bat	8.00
68	Jose Canseco/Bat	8.00
69	Raul Mondesi/Jsy	4.00
70	Reggie Jackson/Bat	8.00
71	Rickey Henderson/Bat	8.00
72	Roberto Alomar/Bat	6.00
73	Robin Ventura/Jsy	4.00
74	Rod Carew/Bat	10.00
75	Roger Clemens/Jsy	15.00
76	Sammy Sosa/Base	10.00
77	Sean Casey/Jsy	5.00
78	Shannon Stewart/Jsy	4.00
79	Shawn Green/Jsy	6.00
80	Shawn Green/Bat	6.00
81	Tim Hudson/Jsy	6.00
82	Todd Helton/Bat	8.00
83	Tom Glavine/Jsy	6.00
84	Tony Gwynn/Jsy	10.00
85	Tony Gwynn/Jsy	10.00
86	Tony Gwynn/Bat	10.00
87	Troy Glaus/Jsy	6.00
88	Tsuyoshi Shinjo/Bat	4.00
89	Vladimir Guerrero/Jsy	8.00
90	Vladimir Guerrero/Bat	8.00
91	Nomar Garciaparra, Pedro J. Martinez	30.00
92	Randy Johnson, Curt Schilling	15.00
93	Andruw Jones, Chipper Jones	15.00
94	Todd Helton, Larry Walker	15.00
95	Jeff Bagwell, Craig Biggio	15.00
96	Alex Rodriguez	25.00
97	Greg Maddux	25.00
98	Mike Piazza	25.00
99	Lance Berkman	15.00
100	Vladimir Guerrero	20.00

2002 Playoff Piece of the Game - LCS Programs

A perforated sheet of Piece of the Game cards was inserted into some of the programs sold for the American and National League Championship Series. The 8-1/2" x 11" sheet features eight player cards and a header card advertising the brand. Each 3-1/2" x 2-1/2" card is perforated on all sides and differs from the regularly issued version only in the card number on back. Sheet cards have either an "ALCS-" or "NLCS-" prefix to the number. Other programs could be found with similar sheets of Donruss Originals, Donruss Studio or Donruss Diamond Kings cards.

	NM/M
Complete Sheet Set (2):	14.00
Common Player:	.50
ALCS SHEET	7.00
17 Jim Thome	1.00
18 Garret Anderson	.50
19 Alfonso Soriano	1.00
20 Nomar Garciaparra	2.50
21 Eric Chavez	.60
22 Magglio Ordonez	1.00
23 Roger Clemens	2.25
24 Torii Hunter	.50
--- Header Card	.10
NLCS SHEET	7.00
9 Jeff Bagwell	1.50
10 Shawn Green	.75
11 Vladimir Guerrero	1.50
12 Greg Maddux	2.00
13 Luis Gonzalez	.50
14 Todd Helton	1.50
15 Richie Sexson	.50
16 Chipper Jones	2.00
--- Header Card	.10

2003 Playoff Absolute Memorabilia

	NM/M
Complete Set (200):	
Common Player:	.50
Common SP (151-200):	3.00
Production 1,500	
Pack (6):	
Box (18 + Glass Plaque):	85.00

#	Player	Price
1	Nomar Garciaparra	2.50
2	Barry Bonds	4.00
3	Greg Maddux	2.00
4	Roger Clemens	3.00
5	Derek Jeter	4.00
6	Alex Rodriguez	3.00
7	Chipper Jones	2.00
8	Sammy Sosa	2.50
9	Alfonso Soriano	1.00
10	Albert Pujols	3.00
11	Adam Dunn	1.00
12	Tom Glavine	.75
13	Pedro J. Martinez	1.50
14	Jim Thome	1.00
15	Hideo Nomo	1.50
16	Roberto Alomar	.75
17	Barry Zito	.65
18	Troy Glaus	1.50
19	Kerry Wood	1.00
20	Magglio Ordonez	.50
21	Todd Helton	1.50
22	Craig Biggio	.50
23	Roy Oswalt	.50
24	Torii Hunter	.50
25	Miguel Tejada	.65
26	Tsuyoshi Shinjo	.50
27	Scott Rolen	1.00
28	Rafael Palmeiro	1.00
29	Victor Martinez	.75
30	Hank Blalock	.75
31	Jason Lane	.50
32	Junior Spivey	.50
33	Gary Sheffield	.75
34	Corey Patterson	.50
35	Corky Miller	.50
36	Brian Tallet	.50
37	Cliff Lee	1.00
38	Jason Jennings	.50
39	Kirk Saarloos	.50
40	Wade Miller	.50
41	Angel Berroa	.50
42	Mike Sweeney	.50
43	Paul LoDuca	.50
44	A.J. Pierzynski	.50
45	Drew Henson	.50
46	Eric Chavez	.65
47	Tim Hudson	.75
48	Aramis Ramirez	.50
49	Jack Wilson	.50
50	Ryan Klesko	.50
51	Antonio Perez	.50
52	Dewon Brazelton	.50
53	Mark Teixeira	.75
54	Eric Hinske	.50
55	Freddy Sanchez	.50
56	Mike Rivera	.50
57	Alfredo Amezaga	.50
58	Cliff Floyd	.50
59	Brandon Larson	.50
60	Richard Hidalgo	.50
61	Cesar Izturis	.50
62	Richie Sexson	.50
63	Michael Cuddyer	.50
64	Javier Vazquez	.50
65	Brandon Claussen	.50
66	Carlos Rivera	.50
67	Vernon Wells	.50
68	Kenny Lofton	.50
69	Aubrey Huff	.50
70	Adam LaRoche	.50
71	Jeff Baker	.50
72	Jose Castillo	.50
73	Joe Borchard	.50
74	Walter Young	.50
75	Jose Morban	.50
76	Vinnie Chulk	.50
77	Christian Parker	.50
78	Mike Piazza	2.50
79	Ichiro Suzuki	2.50
80	Kazuhisa Ishii	.50
81	Rickey Henderson	1.50
82	Ken Griffey Jr.	2.50
83	Jason Giambi	.75
84	Randy Johnson	1.50
85	Curt Schilling	.75
86	Manny Ramirez	1.50
87	Barry Larkin	.50
88	Jeff Bagwell	1.50
89	Vladimir Guerrero	1.50
90	Mike Mussina	.65
91	Juan Gonzalez	1.50
92	Andruw Jones	1.50
93	Frank Thomas	1.50
94	Sean Casey	.50
95	Josh Beckett	.50
96	Lance Berkman	.50
97	Shawn Green	.75
98	Bernie Williams	.65
99	Pat Burrell	.75
100	Edgar Martinez	.50
101	Ivan Rodriguez	1.00
102	Jeremy Guthrie	.50
103	Alexis Rios	.50
104	Nic Jackson	.50
105	Jason Anderson	.50
106	Travis Chapman	.50
107	Mac Suzuki	.50
108	Toby Hall	.50
109	Mark Prior	1.50
110	So Taguchi	.50
111	Marlon Byrd	.50
112	Garret Anderson	.50
113	Luis Gonzalez	.50
114	Jay Gibbons	.50
115	Mark Buehrle	.50
116	Wily Mo Pena	.50
117	C.C. Sabathia	.50
118	Ricardo Rodriguez	.50
119	Robert Fick	.50
120	Rodrigo Rosario	.50
121	Alexis Gomez	.50
122	Carlos Beltran	1.00
123	Joe Thurston	.50
124	Ben Sheets	.50
125	Jose Vidro	.50
126	Nick Johnson	.50
127	Mark Mulder	.50
128	Bobby Abreu	.50
129	Brian Giles	.50
130	Brian Lawrence	.50
131	Jeff Kent	.50
132	Chris Snelling	.50
133	Kevin Mench	.50
134	Carlos Delgado	.75
135	Orlando Hudson	.50
136	Juan Cruz	.50
137	Jim Edmonds	.50
138	Geronimo Gil	.50
139	Joe Crede	.50
140	Wilson Valdez	.50
141	Runelvys Hernandez	.50
142	Nick Neugebauer	.50
143	Takahito Nomura	.50
144	Andres Galarraga	.50
145	Mark Grace	.65
146	Brandon Duckworth	.50
147	Oliver Perez	.50
148	Xavier Nady	.50
149	Rafael Soriano	.50
150	Ben Kozlowski	.50
151	Prentice Redman RC	3.00
152	Craig Brazell RC	3.00
153	Nook Logan RC	3.00
154	Greg Aquino RC	3.00
155	Matt Kata RC	3.00
156	Ian Ferguson RC	3.00
157	Chien-Ming Wang RC	30.00
158	Beau Kemp RC	3.00
159	Alejandro Machado RC	3.00
160	Michael Hessman RC	3.00
161	Francisco Rosario RC	3.00
162	Pedro Liriano	3.00
163	Richard Fischer RC	3.00
164	Franklin Perez	3.00
165	Oscar Villarreal RC	3.00
166	Arnie Munoz RC	3.00
167	Tim Olson RC	3.00
168	Jose Contreras RC	5.00
169	Francisco Cruceta RC	3.00
170	Jeremy Bonderman	8.00
171	Jeremy Griffiths	3.00
172	John Webb	3.00
173	Phil Seibel RC	3.00
174	Aaron Looper RC	3.00
175	Brian Stokes RC	3.00
176	Guillermo Quiroz RC	3.00
177	Fernando Cabrera RC	3.00
178	Josh Hall RC	3.00
179	Diegomar Markwell RC	3.00
180	Andrew Brown RC	3.00
181	Doug Waechter RC	3.00
182	Felix Sanchez RC	3.00
183	Gerardo Garcia	3.00
184	Matt Bruback RC	3.00
185	Michel Hernandez RC	3.00
186	Rett Johnson RC	3.00
187	Ryan Cameron RC	3.00
188	Rob Hammock RC	3.00
189	Clint Barmes RC	8.00
190	Brandon Webb RC	15.00
191	Shane Bazzell RC	3.00
192	Joe Valentine RC	3.00
193	Josh Stewart RC	3.00
194	Pete LaForest RC	3.00
195	Shane Victorino RC	8.00
196	Terrmel Sledge RC	3.00
197	Lew Ford RC	3.00
198	Todd Wellemeyer RC	6.00
200	Hideki Matsui RC	10.00

Spectrum

Stars (1-150):	3-5X
Rookies (151-200):	.75-2X
Production 100 Sets	

Absolutely Ink

	NM/M
Inserted 1:552	
Blues:	No Pricing
Production 10-25	

Golds

No Pricing
Production 5-10

#	Player	Price
1	Vladimir Guerrero	50.00
8	Eric Hinske	15.00
9	Jose Vidro	8.00
16	Rodrigo Rosario	8.00
17	Brandon Claussen	20.00
18	Jermaine Dye	8.00
22	Jeremy Guthrie	50.00
24	Brian Lawrence	8.00
29	Barry Larkin	50.00
30	Drew Henson	40.00
36	Mark Teixeira	30.00
38	Roberto Alomar	30.00
39	Barry Zito	35.00

Glass Plaques

NM/M

One Per Box:

Player / Variation	Price
Roberto Alomar/Bat/Jsy/	40.00
Roberto Alomar/Jsy/100	30.00
Jeff Bagwell/Bat/Jsy/150	30.00
Ernie Banks/Jsy/150	40.00
Lance Berkman/Bat/Jsy/	40.00
Lance Berkman/Jsy/150	30.00
Barry Bonds/Ball/Base/50	85.00
Barry Bonds/Ball/Base/100	75.00
Barry Bonds/Base/200	60.00
George Brett/Bat/Jsy/50	125.00
George Brett/Jsy/200	50.00
Pat Burrell/Bat/Jsy/100	50.00
Pat Burrell/Jsy/150	30.00
Steve Carlton/Auto./50	60.00
Steve Carlton/Bat/Jsy/100	40.00
Steve Carlton/Jsy/100	30.00
Roger Clemens/Glv/Jsy/50	150.00
Roger Clemens/Jsy/100	60.00
Roger Clemens/Glv/Jsy/150	150.00
Roger Clemens/Jsy/200	60.00
Roberto Clemente/Bat/Jsy/150	80.00
Roberto Clemente/Jsy/200	60.00
Jose Contreras/Jsy/100	30.00
Jose Contreras/Jsy/150	25.00
Adam Dunn/Bat/Jsy/100	40.00
Adam Dunn/Jsy/150	30.00
Bob Feller/Auto./50	65.00
Bob Feller/Jsy/Bat/50	50.00
Bob Feller/Jsy/100	30.00
Nomar Garciaparra/Bat/Jsy/100	65.00
Nomar Garciaparra/Jsy/200	55.00
Jason Giambi/Bat/Jsy/100	50.00
Jason Giambi/Jsy/150	40.00
Troy Glaus/Bat/Jsy/100	40.00
Troy Glaus/Jsy/150	35.00
Juan Gonzalez/Bat/Jsy/100	40.00
Juan Gonzalez/Jsy/150	30.00
Luis Gonzalez/Bat/Jsy/100	30.00
Luis Gonzalez/Jsy/150	25.00
Mark Grace/Auto./50	100.00
Mark Grace/Bat/Jsy/100	45.00
Mark Grace/Jsy/150	35.00
Shawn Green/Bat/Jsy/100	40.00
Shawn Green/Jsy/150	25.00
Ken Griffey Jr./Ball/Base/100	50.00
Ken Griffey Jr./Base/200	40.00
Vladimir Guerrero/Bat/Jsy/100	40.00
Vladimir Guerrero/Jsy/150	35.00
Tony Gwynn/Bat/Jsy/150	50.00
Tony Gwynn/Jsy/200	40.00
Todd Helton/Bat/Jsy/100	40.00
Todd Helton/Jsy/150	30.00
Rickey Henderson/Bat/Jsy/100	40.00
Rickey Henderson/Jsy/200	30.00
Tim Hudson/Auto./50	65.00
Tim Hudson/Hat/Jsy/100	30.00
Tim Hudson/Jsy/150	25.00
Torii Hunter/Auto./50	65.00
Torii Hunter/Hat/Jsy/100	40.00
Torii Hunter/Jsy/150	30.00
Kazuhisa Ishii/Bat/Jsy/100	30.00
Kazuhisa Ishii/Jsy/200	25.00
Derek Jeter/Ball/Base/150	60.00
Derek Jeter/Base/200	50.00
Randy Johnson/Bat/Jsy/100	50.00
Randy Johnson/Jsy/150	40.00
Andruw Jones/Bat/Jsy/100	35.00
Andruw Jones/Jsy/150	30.00
Chipper Jones/Bat/Jsy/100	40.00
Chipper Jones/Jsy/150	30.00
Al Kaline/Bat/Jsy/100	40.00
Al Kaline/Jsy/150	35.00
Barry Larkin/Auto./50	60.00
Barry Larkin/Bat/Jsy/100	40.00
Barry Larkin/Jsy/150	30.00
Greg Maddux/Bat/Jsy/100	50.00
Greg Maddux/Jsy/200	40.00
Pedro Martinez/Bat/Jsy/100	40.00
Pedro Martinez/Jsy/150	35.00
Hideki Matsui/Ball/Base/50	110.00
Hideki Matsui/Ball/Base/150	75.00
Hideki Matsui/Base/200	55.00
Don Mattingly/Bat/Jsy/100	65.00
Don Mattingly/Jsy/200	50.00
Mark Mulder/Auto./150	50.00
Mark Mulder/Jsy/150	25.00
Mark Mulder/Jsy/100	30.00
Stan Musial/Bat/Jsy/100	65.00
Stan Musial/Jsy/200	60.00
Hideo Nomo/Bat/Jsy/50	60.00
Hideo Nomo/Bat/Jsy/100	40.00
Hideo Nomo/Jsy/200	30.00
Magglio Ordonez/Auto./50	50.00
Magglio Ordonez/Bat/Jsy/100	40.00
Magglio Ordonez/Jsy/150	25.00
Roy Oswalt/Auto./50	50.00
Roy Oswalt/Bat/Jsy/100	30.00
Roy Oswalt/Jsy/150	25.00
Rafael Palmeiro/Bat/Jsy/100	40.00
Rafael Palmeiro/Jsy/150	30.00
Mike Piazza/Bat/Jsy/50	75.00
Mike Piazza/Bat/Jsy/100	40.00
Mike Piazza/Jsy/200	40.00
Mark Prior/Bat/Jsy/100	60.00
Mark Prior/Jsy/150	40.00
Albert Pujols/Bat/Jsy/100	75.00
Albert Pujols/Jsy/150	60.00
Manny Ramirez/Bat/Jsy/100	40.00
Manny Ramirez/Jsy/150	30.00
Cal Ripken Jr./Bat/Jsy/100	90.00
Cal Ripken Jr./Jsy/200	70.00
Frank Robinson/Auto./50	65.00
Frank Robinson/Bat/Jsy/100	40.00
Frank Robinson/Jsy/150	30.00
Alex Rodriguez/Bat/Jsy/100	50.00
Alex Rodriguez/Jsy/200	40.00
Nolan Ryan/Jkt/150	90.00
Nolan Ryan/Jsy/200	75.00
Nolan Ryan/Jsy/	100.00
Ryne Sandberg/Bat/Jsy/100	100.00
Ryne Sandberg/Jsy/200	65.00
Curt Schilling/Glv/Jsy/50	50.00
Curt Schilling/Jsy/150	30.00
Mike Schmidt/Bat/Jsy/100	70.00
Mike Schmidt/Jsy/200	50.00
Ozzie Smith/Bat/Jsy/100	65.00
Ozzie Smith/Jsy/150	50.00
Alfonso Soriano/Bat/Jsy/150	50.00
Alfonso Soriano/Jsy/150	50.00
Sammy Sosa/Bat/Jsy/150	50.00
Sammy Sosa/Jsy/200	40.00
Junior Spivey/Auto./50	50.00
Junior Spivey/Bat/Jsy/100	30.00
Junior Spivey/Jsy/150	25.00
Ichiro Suzuki/Ball/Base/50	80.00
Ichiro Suzuki/Ball/Base/150	60.00
Ichiro Suzuki/Base/200	40.00
Mark Teixeira/Bat/Jsy/100	
Mark Teixeira/Jsy/150	30.00
Miguel Tejada/Auto./50	60.00
Miguel Tejada/Bat/Jsy/100	40.00
Miguel Tejada/Jsy/150	30.00
Frank Thomas/Bat/Jsy/100	40.00
Frank Thomas/Jsy/150	30.00
Bernie Williams/Bat/Jsy/100	40.00
Bernie Williams/Jsy/150	35.00
Kerry Wood/Auto./50	80.00
Kerry Wood/Bat/Jsy/100	45.00
Kerry Wood/Jsy/150	35.00
Barry Zito/Auto./50	75.00
Barry Zito/Hat/Jsy/100	40.00
Barry Zito/Jsy/150	35.00

Player's Collection - Bat

	NM/M
Common Player:	4.00
Production 75 Sets	

#	Player	Price
81	Alex Rodriguez	15.00
82	Alfonso Soriano	12.00
83	Barry Larkin	8.00
84	Roberto Alomar	8.00
85	Ivan Rodriguez	8.00
86	Jason Giambi	8.00
87	Jeff Bagwell	8.00
88	Juan Gonzalez	8.00
89	Larry Walker	4.00
90	Luis Gonzalez	4.00
91	Magglio Ordonez	6.00
92	Manny Ramirez	8.00
93	Marlon Byrd	4.00
94	Mike Piazza	12.00
95	Pat Burrell	8.00
96	Todd Helton	8.00
97	Rickey Henderson	8.00
98	Andruw Jones	8.00
99	Craig Biggio	4.00
100	Mark Prior	10.00

Player's Collection - Jersey

	NM/M
Common Player:	4.00
Production 75 Sets	

#	Player	Price
1	Adam Dunn	6.00
2	Adrian Beltre	4.00
3	Alex Rodriguez	15.00
4	Alfonso Soriano	12.00
5	Andruw Jones	8.00
6	Andy Pettitte	6.00
7	Barry Larkin	6.00
8	Barry Zito	6.00
9	Ben Grieve	4.00
10	Bernie Williams	8.00
11	Cal Ripken Jr.	40.00
12	Carlos Delgado	6.00
13	C.C. Sabathia	4.00
14	Chipper Jones	10.00
15	Craig Biggio	6.00
16	Curt Schilling	6.00
17	Alex Rodriguez	15.00
18	Frank Thomas	8.00
19	Freddy Garcia	4.00
20	Jay Bell	4.00
21	Roger Clemens	15.00
22	Tony Gwynn	10.00
23	Ivan Rodriguez	8.00
24	Jason Giambi	8.00
25	Jason Jennings	4.00
26	Jay Payton	4.00
27	J.D. Drew	5.00
28	Jeff Bagwell	8.00
29	Jeromy Burnitz	4.00
30	Jim Edmonds	6.00
31	Jim Thome	8.00
32	Joe Borchard	4.00
33	Joe Mays	4.00
34	John Olerud	5.00
35	David Wells	4.00
36	Juan Gonzalez	8.00
37	Kazuhiro Sasaki	4.00
38	Chan Ho Park	4.00
39	Kerry Wood	10.00
40	Kevin Brown	4.00
41	Lance Berkman	6.00
42	Larry Walker	6.00
43	Bret Boone	4.00
44	Magglio Ordonez	8.00
45	Manny Ramirez	8.00
46	Mark Mulder	6.00
47	Mark Prior	10.00
48	Matt Williams	4.00
49	Miguel Tejada	5.00
50	Mike Piazza	12.00
51	Nomar Garciaparra	15.00
52	Doug Davis	4.00
53	Paul Konerko	4.00
54	Paul LoDuca	4.00
55	Pedro J. Martinez	10.00
56	Preston Wilson	4.00
57		

58	Marlon Byrd	4.00
59	Reggie Sanders	4.00
60	Richie Sexson	6.00
61		4.00
62	Rickey Henderson	8.00
63	Robert Person	4.00
64		4.00
65	Roger Clemens	15.00
66	Roy Oswalt	6.00
67	Ryan Klesko	4.00
68	Sammy Sosa	15.00
69	Shawn Green	6.00
70	Steve Finley	4.00
71	Terrence Long	4.00
72	Tim Hudson	6.00
73	Toby Hall	4.00
74	Todd Helton	8.00
75	Travis Lee	4.00
76	Troy Glaus	8.00
77	Tsuyoshi Shinjo	4.00
78	Vernon Wells	6.00
79	Vladimir Guerrero	8.00
80	Wes Helms	4.00

Rookie Materials Jersey Number

NM/M

Many not priced due to scarcity.

2	Yogi Berra/35	40.00
3	Vladimir Guerrero/27	35.00
4	Randy Johnson/51	25.00
5	Andruw Jones/25	25.00
10	Alfonso Soriano/33	35.00
13	Rafael Palmeiro/25	20.00

Rookie Materials Season

NM/M

Common Player: 5.00
Quantity produced listed.

1	Stan Musial/42	75.00
2	Yogi Berra/47	40.00
3	Vladimir Guerrero/97	15.00
4	Randy Johnson/89	20.00
5	Andruw Jones/96	10.00
6	Jeff Kent/92	5.00
8	Hideo Nomo/95	20.00
9	Ivan Rodriguez/91	10.00
10	Alfonso Soriano/101	20.00
11	Scott Rolen/96	15.00
12	Juan Gonzalez/89	15.00
13	Rafael Palmeiro/86	15.00
14	Mike Schmidt/73	60.00
15	Cal Ripken Jr./82	75.00

Signing Bonus

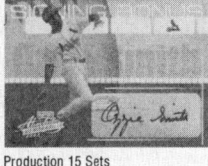

Production 15 Sets
No Pricing

Spectrum Signatures

NM/M

Common Autograph: 6.00
Varying quantities produced.

10	Albert Pujols/10	325.00
16	Roberto Alomar/15	100.00
17	Barry Zito/25	50.00
20	Magglio Ordonez/25	50.00
23	Roy Oswalt/25	30.00
24	Torii Hunter/25	40.00
29	Victor Martinez/100	30.00
30	Hank Blalock/50	30.00
32	Junior Spivey/50	15.00
34	Corey Patterson/50	20.00
35	Corky Miller/100	6.00
36	Brian Tallet/100	6.00
37	Cliff Lee/100	20.00
38	Jason Jennings/100	8.00
39	Kirk Saarloos/100	6.00
40	Wade Miller/50	15.00
41	Angel Berroa/100	10.00
42	Mike Sweeney/50	15.00
43	Paul LoDuca/50	20.00
44	A.J. Pierzynski/100	15.00
45	Drew Henson/50	25.00
46	Tim Hudson/50	40.00
47	Antonio Perez/25	3.00
48	Dewon Brazelton/50	15.00
49	Mark Teixeira/50	40.00

54	Eric Hinske/100	15.00
55	Freddy Sanchez/100	15.00
57	Alfredo Amezaga/100	10.00
59	Brandon Larson/100	8.00
60	Richard Hidalgo/100	10.00
62	Richie Sexson/25	30.00
63	Michael Cuddyer/100	8.00
68	Kenny Lofton/50	30.00
69	Aubrey Huff/100	15.00
70	Adam LaRoche/100	15.00
71	Jeff Baker/100	10.00
72	Jose Castillo/100	10.00
73	Joe Borchard/100	10.00
74	Walter Young/100	8.00
76	Vinnie Chulk/100	8.00
80	Kazuhisa Ishii/25	60.00
87	Barry Larkin/50	50.00
89	Vladimir Guerrero/50	60.00
92	Andruw Jones/25	60.00
95	Josh Beckett/100	25.00
100	Edgar Martinez/50	25.00
102	Jeremy Guthrie/100	15.00
103	Alexis Rios/100	20.00
104	Nic Jackson/100	8.00
105	Jason Anderson/100	8.00
106	Travis Chapman/100	8.00
107	Mac Suzuki/304	15.00
109	Mark Prior/50	30.00
111	Marlon Byrd/100	10.00
114	Jay Gibbons/100	10.00
118	Ricardo Rodriguez/100	10.00
119	Robert Fick/100	10.00
120	Rodrigo Rosario/250	8.00
121	Alexis Gomez/100	10.00
124	Ben Sheets/50	20.00
126	Nick Johnson/50	10.00
127	Mark Mulder/50	40.00
132	Chris Snelling/100	8.00
133	Kevin Mench/100	10.00
135	Orlando Hudson/50	15.00
139	Joe Crede/100	10.00
140	Wilson Valdez/25	10.00
141	Runelvys Hernandez/100	10.00
143	Takahito Nomura/47	15.00
147	Oliver Perez/50	15.00
148	Xavier Nady/100	12.00
150	Ben Kozlowski/100	8.00
151	Prentice Redman/250	10.00
152	Craig Brazell/250	10.00
153	Nook Logan/250	6.00
154	Greg Aquino/250	8.00
155	Matt Kata/250	15.00
156	Ian Ferguson/250	6.00
157	Chien-Ming Wang/250	200.00
158	Beau Kemp/250	6.00
159	Alejandro Machado/250	6.00
160	Michael Hessman/160	6.00
161	Francisco Rosario/250	6.00
162	Pedro Liriano/250	6.00
163	Richard Fischer/250	6.00
164	Franklin Perez/250	6.00
165	Oscar Villarreal/250	10.00
166	Arnie Munoz/250	6.00
167	Tim Olson/250	8.00
168	Jose Contreras/250	25.00
169	Francisco Cruceta/250	8.00
170	Jeremy Bonderman/250	40.00
171	Jeremy Griffiths/250	6.00
172	John Webb/250	6.00
173	Phil Seibel/250	6.00
174	Aaron Looper/250	6.00
175	Brian Stokes/250	6.00
176	Guillermo Quiroz/250	8.00
177	Fernando Cabrera/250	8.00
178	Josh Hall/250	10.00
179	Diegomar Markwell/250	6.00
180	Andrew Brown/250	8.00
181	Doug Waechter/250	8.00
182	Felix Sanchez/250	6.00
183	Gerardo Garcia/250	8.00
184	Matt Bruback/250	6.00
185	Michel Hernandez/250	6.00
186	Rett Johnson/250	6.00
187	Ryan Cameron/250	6.00
188	Rob Hammock/250	15.00
189	Clint Barmes/250	15.00
190	Brandon Webb/250	50.00
191	Jon Leicester/250	6.00
192	Shane Bazzell/250	10.00
193	Joe Valentine/250	8.00
194	Josh Stewart/250	15.00
195	Pete LaForest/250	8.00
196	Shane Victorino/250	6.00
197	Terrmel Sledge/250	6.00
198	Lew Ford/250	8.00
199	Todd Wellemeyer/250	10.00

Team Tandems

NM/M

Common Duo: 2.00
Inserted 1:48
Spectrums: 1-2X
Production 100 Sets

1	Mark Prior, Sammy Sosa	5.00
2	Vladimir Guerrero, Jose Vidro	3.00
3	Bernie Williams, Alfonso Soriano	6.00
4	Mike Sweeney, Carlos Beltran	2.00
5	Magglio Ordonez, Paul Konerko	2.00
6	Adam Dunn, Austin Kearns	3.00
7	Randy Johnson, Curt Schilling	4.00

8	Hideo Nomo, Kazuhisa Ishii	2.00
9	Pat Burrell, Bobby Abreu	3.00
10	Todd Helton, Larry Walker	2.00

Team Tandems Material

NM/M

Common Duo: No Pricing
Quantity produced listed.
Spectrums:
Production 25 or 10

1	Mark Prior, Sammy Sosa/100	30.00
2	Vladimir Guerrero, Jose Vidro/100	10.00
3	Bernie Williams, Alfonso Soriano/100	20.00
4	Mike Sweeney, Carlos Beltran/100	6.00
5	Magglio Ordonez, Paul Konerko/100	6.00
6	Adam Dunn, Austin Kearns/100	15.00
7	Randy Johnson, Curt Schilling/100	15.00
8	Hideo Nomo, Kazuhisa Ishii/40	50.00
9	Pat Burrell, Bobby Abreu/40	20.00
10	Todd Helton, Larry Walker/100	8.00

Team Trios

NM/M

Common Trio: 5.00
Inserted 1:88
Spectrums: 1-2X
Production 50 Sets

1	Greg Maddux, Chipper Jones, Andruw Jones	8.00
2	Sammy Sosa, Mark Prior, Kerry Wood	8.00
3	Pedro Martinez, Nomar Garciaparra, Manny Ramirez	8.00
4	Jason Giambi, Roger Clemens, Alfonso Soriano	8.00
5	Alex Rodriguez, Rafael Palmeiro, Mark Teixeira	8.00
6	Mike Piazza, Roberto Alomar, Tsuyoshi Shinjo	6.00
7	Jeff Bagwell, Craig Biggio, Lance Berkman	5.00
8	Troy Glaus, Garret Anderson, Troy Percival	5.00
9	Miguel Tejada, Eric Chavez, Barry Zito	5.00
10	Luis Gonzalez, Randy Johnson, Curt Schilling	6.00

Team Trios Materials

NM/M

Quantity produced listed 5.00
Spectrums: No Pricing
Production 10 or 25

1	Greg Maddux, Chipper Jones, Andruw Jones/100	30.00
2	Sammy Sosa, Mark Prior, Kerry Wood/30	30.00
3	Pedro Martinez, Nomar Garciaparra, Manny Ramirez/50	50.00
4	Jason Giambi, Roger Clemens, Alfonso Soriano/100	40.00
5	Alex Rodriguez, Rafael Palmeiro, Mark Teixeira/100	25.00
6	Mike Piazza, Roberto Alomar, Tsuyoshi Shinjo/40	40.00
7	Jeff Bagwell, Craig Biggio, Lance Berkman/100	25.00
8	Troy Glaus, Garret Anderson, Troy Percival/40	25.00
9	Miguel Tejada, Eric Chavez, Barry Zito/100	20.00
10	Luis Gonzalez, Randy Johnson, Curt Schilling/100	25.00

Tools of the Trade

NM/M

Complete Set (110): 125.00
Common Player: 1.00

Inserted 1:5

1	Sammy Sosa	4.00
2	Nomar Garciaparra	5.00
3	Andruw Jones	1.50
4	Troy Glaus	1.00
5	Greg Maddux	4.00
6	Rickey Henderson	1.00
7	Alex Rodriguez	6.00
8	Manny Ramirez	1.50
9	Lance Berkman	1.00
10	Roger Clemens	5.00
11	Ivan Rodriguez	1.00
12	Kazuhisa Ishii	1.00
13	Alfonso Soriano	3.00
14	Austin Kearns	1.00
15	Mike Piazza	3.00
16	Curt Schilling	1.00
17	Jeff Bagwell	1.50
18	Todd Helton	1.50
19	Randy Johnson	2.00
20	Vladimir Guerrero	1.50
21	Kerry Wood	1.00
22	Rafael Palmeiro	1.00
23	Roy Oswalt	1.00
24	Chipper Jones	3.00
25	Pat Burrell	1.00
26	Jason Giambi	2.00
27	Pedro J. Martinez	1.00
28	Roberto Alomar	1.00
29	Shawn Green	1.00
30	Adam Dunn	1.00
31	Juan Gonzalez	1.50
32	Mark Prior	1.00
33	Hideo Nomo	1.00
34	Torii Hunter	1.00
35	Mark Teixeira	1.00
36	Craig Biggio	1.00
37	Rafael Palmeiro	1.00
38	Jeff Bagwell	1.50
39	Albert Pujols	1.00
40	Richie Sexson	1.00
41	Alex Rodriguez	6.00
42	Carlos Delgado	1.50
43	Frank Thomas	1.50
44	Sammy Sosa	1.00
45	Marlon Byrd	1.00
46	Mark Prior	1.00
47	Adrian Beltre	1.00
48	Tom Glavine	1.00
49	So Taguchi	1.00
50	Jeff Bagwell	1.50
51	Mike Sweeney	1.00
52	Luis Gonzalez	1.00
53	Chipper Jones	3.00
54	Jason Giambi	2.00
55	Miguel Tejada	1.00
56	Todd Helton	1.50
57	Andruw Jones	1.50
58	Mike Piazza	3.00
59	Manny Ramirez	1.50
60	Randy Johnson	1.00
61	Carlos Beltran	1.00
62	Victor Martinez	1.00
63	Orlando Hudson	1.00
64	Jeff Kent	1.00
65	Greg Maddux	4.00
66	Garret Anderson	1.00
67	Joe Thurston	1.00
68	Mark Teixeira	1.00
69	Kazuhisa Ishii	1.00
70	Austin Kearns	1.00
71	Pat Burrell	1.00
72	Joe Borchard	1.00
73	Josh Phelps	1.00
74	Travis Hafner	1.00
75	So Taguchi	1.00
76	Victor Martinez	1.00
77	Paul LoDuca	1.00
78	Bernie Williams	1.00
79	Josh Phelps	1.00
80	Marlon Byrd	1.00
81	Manny Ramirez	1.00
82	Jason Giambi	2.00
83	Jeff Bagwell	1.50
84	Sammy Sosa	1.00
85	Josh Phelps	1.00
86	Tim Hudson	1.00
87	Randy Johnson	2.00
88	Troy Glaus	1.00
89	Joe Thurston	1.00
90	Miguel Tejada	1.00
91	Adam Dunn	1.00
92	Magglio Ordonez	1.00
93	Mike Sweeney	1.00
94	Andruw Jones	1.50
95	Carlos Beltran	1.00
96	Joe Borchard	1.00
97	Austin Kearns	1.00
98	Richie Sexson	1.00
99	Mark Prior	5.00
100	Mark Teixeira	1.00
101	Ryan Klesko	1.00
102	Jason Jennings	1.00
103	Travis Hafner	1.00
104	Mark Buehrle	1.00
105	Eric Hinske	1.00
106	Rafael Palmeiro	1.00
107	Roy Oswalt	1.00
108	Kerry Wood	1.00
109	Brian Giles	1.00
110	Ivan Rodriguez	1.00

Tools of the Trade Materials

NM/M

Common Player: 3.00
Quantity produced listed
Spectrums: 1-2.5X
Production 10 to 50

1	Sammy Sosa/250	10.00
2	Nomar Garciaparra/250	10.00
3	Andruw Jones/250	5.00
4	Troy Glaus/250	5.00
5	Greg Maddux/250	10.00
6	Rickey Henderson/40	25.00
7	Alex Rodriguez/250	10.00
8	Manny Ramirez/250	5.00
9	Lance Berkman/250	4.00
10	Roger Clemens/250	15.00
11	Ivan Rodriguez/	·6.00
12	Kazuhisa Ishii/40	15.00
13	Alfonso Soriano/250	10.00
14	Austin Kearns/250	5.00
15	Mike Piazza/250	8.00
16	Curt Schilling/250	5.00
17	Jeff Bagwell/250	5.00
18	Todd Helton/250	6.00
19	Randy Johnson/250	6.00
20	Vladimir Guerrero/250	6.00
21	Kerry Wood/250	6.00
22	Rafael Palmeiro/250	5.00
23	Roy Oswalt/250	3.00
24	Chipper Jones/250	8.00
25	Pat Burrell/40	15.00
26	Jason Giambi/250	8.00
27	Pedro J. Martinez/250	5.00
28	Roberto Alomar/40	15.00
29	Shawn Green/250	5.00
30	Adam Dunn/250	5.00
31	Juan Gonzalez/40	15.00
32	Mark Prior/250	8.00
33	Hideo Nomo/250	8.00
34	Torii Hunter/250	5.00
35	Mark Teixeira/250	5.00
36	Craig Biggio/250	4.00
37	Rafael Palmeiro/250	5.00
38	Jeff Bagwell/250	5.00
39	Albert Pujols/200	12.00
40	Richie Sexson/250	4.00
41	Alex Rodriguez/250	10.00
42	Carlos Delgado/250	3.00
43	Frank Thomas/75	8.00
44	Sammy Sosa/250	10.00
45	Marlon Byrd/250	3.00
46	Mark Prior/250	8.00
47	Adrian Beltre/250	3.00
48	Tom Glavine/250	5.00
49	So Taguchi/250	3.00
50	Jeff Bagwell/250	5.00
51	Mike Sweeney/250	3.00
52	Luis Gonzalez/250	3.00
53	Chipper Jones/100	8.00
54	Jason Giambi/250	6.00
55	Miguel Tejada/250	5.00
56	Todd Helton/250	5.00
57	Andruw Jones/250	5.00
58	Mike Piazza/250	8.00
59	Manny Ramirez/250	6.00
60	Randy Johnson/250	6.00
61	Carlos Beltran/250	3.00
62	Victor Martinez/250	3.00
63	Orlando Hudson/250	3.00
64	Jeff Kent/250	5.00
65	Greg Maddux/250	8.00
66	Garret Anderson/150	4.00
67	Joe Thurston/250	3.00
68	Mark Teixeira/250	3.00
69	Kazuhisa Ishii/250	3.00
70	Austin Kearns/250	4.00
71	Pat Burrell/100	5.00
72	Joe Borchard/250	3.00
73	Josh Phelps/250	3.00
74	Travis Hafner/250	3.00
75	So Taguchi/125	3.00
76	Victor Martinez/125	3.00
77	Paul LoDuca/125	3.00
78	Bernie Williams/125	8.00
79	Josh Phelps/125	5.00
80	Marlon Byrd/125	5.00
81	Manny Ramirez/100	10.00
82	Jason Giambi/125	10.00
83	Jeff Bagwell/50	15.00
84	Sammy Sosa/125	20.00
85	Josh Phelps/125	5.00
86	Tim Hudson/125	5.00
87	Randy Johnson/125	10.00
88	Troy Glaus/125	5.00
89	Joe Thurston/125	4.00
90	Miguel Tejada/125	5.00
91	Adam Dunn/100	15.00
92	Magglio Ordonez/100	10.00
93	Mike Sweeney/100	10.00
94	Andruw Jones/100	15.00
95	Carlos Beltran/100	8.00
96	Joe Borchard/100	8.00
97	Austin Kearns/100	15.00
98	Richie Sexson/50	15.00
99	Mark Prior/50	50.00
100	Mark Teixeira/50	20.00
101	Ryan Klesko/50	10.00
102	Jason Jennings/50	10.00
103	Travis Hafner/50	15.00
104	Mark Buehrle/50	15.00
105	Eric Hinske/50	20.00
106	Rafael Palmeiro/50	40.00
107	Roy Oswalt/50	20.00
108	Kerry Wood/50	25.00
109	Brian Giles/50	15.00
110	Ivan Rodriguez/50	25.00

Total Bases

NM/M

Complete Set (30): 60.00
Common Player: 1.00
Inserted 1:16

1	Albert Pujols	6.00
2	Nomar Garciaparra	6.00
3	Jason Giambi	3.00
4	Miguel Tejada	1.00
5	Rafael Palmeiro	1.50
6	Sammy Sosa	5.00
7	Pat Burrell	1.50
8	Lance Berkman	1.00
9	Bernie Williams	1.50
10	Jim Thome	2.00
11	Carlos Beltran	1.00
12	Eric Chavez	1.00
13	Alex Rodriguez	6.00
14	Magglio Ordonez	1.00
15	Brian Giles	3.00
16	Alfonso Soriano	3.00
17	Shawn Green	1.00
18	Vladimir Guerrero	2.00
19	Garret Anderson	1.00
20	Todd Helton	2.00
21	Barry Bonds	8.00
22	Jeff Kent	1.00
23	Torii Hunter	1.00
24	Ichiro Suzuki	4.00
25	Derek Jeter	8.00
26	Chipper Jones	4.00
27	Jeff Bagwell	2.00
28	Mike Piazza	4.00
29	Rickey Henderson	1.50
30	Ken Griffey Jr.	4.00

Total Bases Materials 1B

NM/M

Common Player: 4.00
Quantity produced listed

1	Albert Pujols/109	12.00
2	Nomar Garciaparra/112	12.00
3	Jason Giambi/100	8.00
4	Miguel Tejada/140	4.00
5	Rafael Palmeiro/58	5.00
6	Sammy Sosa/98	15.00
7	Pat Burrell/87	8.00
8	Lance Berkman/90	4.00
9	Bernie Williams/146	6.00
10	Jim Thome/73	8.00
11	Carlos Beltran/94	4.00
12	Eric Chavez/93	4.00
13	Alex Rodriguez/101	15.00
14	Magglio Ordonez/103	4.00
15	Brian Giles/68	4.00
16	Alfonso Soriano/117	10.00
17	Shawn Green/92	4.00
18	Vladimir Guerrero/128	6.00
19	Garret Anderson/107	4.00
20	Todd Helton/109	8.00
21	Barry Bonds/70	20.00
22	Jeff Kent/114	4.00
23	Torii Hunter/92	4.00
24	Ichiro Suzuki/165	25.00
25	Derek Jeter/147	25.00
26	Chipper Jones/117	8.00
27	Jeff Bagwell/100	8.00
28	Mike Piazza/76	10.00
29	Rickey Henderson/28	40.00
30	Ken Griffey Jr./36	40.00

Total Bases Materials 2B

NM/M

Quantity produced listed

1	Albert Pujols/40	40.00
2	Nomar Garciaparra/25	25.00
3	Jason Giambi/34	15.00
4	Miguel Tejada/30	15.00
5	Rafael Palmeiro/34	15.00
7	Pat Burrell/39	10.00
8	Lance Berkman/35	8.00
9	Bernie Williams/37	15.00
11	Carlos Beltran/44	8.00
12	Eric Chavez/31	8.00
13	Alex Rodriguez/32	50.00
14	Magglio Ordonez/47	8.00
15	Brian Giles/37	8.00
16	Alfonso Soriano/51	10.00
17	Shawn Green/31	10.00
18	Vladimir Guerrero/37	15.00
19	Garret Anderson/56	8.00
20	Todd Helton/39	15.00

21	Barry Bonds/31	50.00
22	Jeff Kent/42	8.00
23	Torii Hunter/37	15.00
24	Derek Jeter/26	50.00
26	Chipper Jones/35	25.00
27	Jeff Bagwell/33	25.00
28	Mike Piazza/23	35.00

Total Bases Materials 3B
No pricing due to scarcity.

Total Bases Materials HR

		NM/M
Quantity produced listed		
1	Albert Pujols/34	40.00
3	Jason Giambi/41	20.00
4	Miguel Tejada/41	10.00
5	Rafael Palmeiro/43	15.00
6	Sammy Sosa/49	30.00
7	Pat Burrell/37	15.00
8	Lance Berkman/42	10.00
10	Jim Thome/52	15.00
11	Carlos Beltran/29	10.00
12	Eric Chavez/34	12.00
13	Alex Rodriguez/57	25.00
14	Magglio Ordonez/58	8.00
15	Brian Giles/38	8.00
16	Alfonso Soriano/39	30.00
17	Shawn Green/42	8.00
18	Vladimir Guerrero/39	15.00
19	Garret Anderson/29	15.00
20	Todd Helton/30	15.00
21	Barry Bonds/46	40.00
22	Jeff Kent/37	8.00
23	Torii Hunter/29	25.00
26	Chipper Jones/26	35.00
27	Jeff Bagwell/31	20.00
28	Mike Piazza/33	30.00

2003 Playoff Piece of the Game

		NM/M
Common Player:		4.00
Pack (1):		12.00
Box (6):		60.00
1	Adam Dunn/Bat	8.00
2	Adam Dunn/Jsy	8.00
3	Adrian Beltre/Bat	6.00
4	Albert Pujols/Bat	15.00
5	Albert Pujols/Bat	15.00
6	Alex Rodriguez/Bat	15.00
7	Alex Rodriguez/Blue Jsy	10.00
8	Alex Rodriguez/White Jsy	10.00
9	Alfonso Soriano/Bat	8.00
10	Alfonso Soriano/Gray Jsy	8.00
11	Alfonso Soriano/White Jsy	8.00
12	Brett Myers/Jsy	4.00
13	Andruw Jones/Jsy	6.00
14	Austin Kearns/Jsy	6.00
15	Barry Larkin/Jsy	6.00
16	Barry Zito/Jsy	6.00
17	Bernie Williams/Jsy	6.00
18	Brian Giles/Bat	4.00
19	Zach Day/Jsy	4.00
20	Carlos Beltran/Bat	4.00
21	Brandon Phillips/Bat	4.00
22	Carlos Lee/Bat	4.00
23	Casey Fossum/Jsy	4.00
24	Chipper Jones/Jsy	8.00
25	Marcus Giles/Jsy	4.00
26	Craig Biggio/Jsy	6.00
27	Curt Schilling/Jsy	6.00
28	Derek Jeter/Base	15.00
29	Edgar Martinez/Jsy	6.00
30	Eric Chavez/Jsy	6.00
31	Eric Hinske/Bat	4.00
32	Frank Thomas/190/Bat	4.00
33	Aubrey Huff/Jsy	4.00
34	Gary Carter/Jacket	8.00
35	Greg Maddux/Gray Jsy	8.00
36	Greg Maddux/White Jsy	8.00
37	Hideki Matsui/Base RC	15.00
38	Hideo Nomo/White Jsy	4.00
39	Rod Carew/Jacket	8.00
40	Ichiro Suzuki/Base	10.00
41	Ivan Rodriguez/Bat	8.00
42	Jason Giambi/Bat	6.00
43	Jason Giambi/Jsy	6.00
44	J.C. Romero/Jsy	4.00
45	Jason Giambi/White Jsy	6.00
46	Jeff Bagwell/Jsy	6.00
47	Josh Bard/Jsy	4.00
48	Jim Thome/Jsy	8.00
49	Jay Gibbons/Jsy	4.00
50	Jorge Posada/Jsy	6.00
51	Juan Gonzalez/Bat	4.00
52	Kazuhisa Ishii/Bat	4.00
53	George Brett/Bat	15.00
54	Kenny Lofton/Bat	4.00
55	Kerry Wood/Jsy	8.00
56	Kevin Brown/Jsy	4.00
57	Kirk Saarloos/Jsy	4.00
58	Lance Berkman/Jsy	5.00
59	Larry Walker/Jsy	4.00
60	Magglio Ordonez/Jsy	4.00
61	Manny Ramirez/Jsy	8.00
62	Mark Mulder/Jsy	4.00
63	Mark Prior/Jsy	8.00
64	Matt Williams/Jsy	4.00
65	Miguel Tejada/Jsy	6.00
66	Mike Mussina/Jsy	6.00
67	Mike Piazza/Bat	10.00
68	Mike Piazza/Black Jsy	10.00
69	Mike Piazza/White Jsy	10.00
70	Nomar Garciaparra/Bat	10.00
71	Nomar Garciaparra/Gray Jsy	10.00
72	Nomar Garciaparra/White Jsy	10.00
73	Paul LoDuca/Jsy	4.00
74	Pedro Martinez/Jsy	8.00
75	Rafael Palmeiro/Jsy	8.00
76	Randy Johnson/Gray Jsy	8.00
77	Randy Johnson/White Jsy	8.00
78	Rickey Henderson/Jsy	8.00
79	Roberto Alomar/Jsy	8.00
80	Rod Carew/Jkt	8.00
81	Roger Clemens/Gray Jsy	15.00
82	Roger Clemens/White Jsy	15.00
83	Cal Ripken Jr./Jsy	25.00
84	Roy Oswalt/Jsy	4.00
85	Jeremy Bonderman/Jsy	8.00
86	Ryne Sandberg/Bat	10.00
87	Sammy Sosa/Bat	12.00
88	Sammy Sosa/Grey Jsy	15.00
89	Sammy Sosa/White Jsy	15.00
90	Scott Rolen/Jsy	8.00
91	Frank Catalanotto/Jsy	4.00
92	Shawn Green/Jsy	4.00
93	Tim Hudson/Jsy	5.00
94	Todd Helton/Jsy	8.00
95	Tony Gwynn/Jsy	8.00
96	Torii Hunter/Jsy	6.00
97	Troy Glaus/Jsy	6.00
98	Runelvys Hernandez/Jsy	4.00
99	Vernon Wells/Jsy	4.00
100	Vladimir Guerrero/Jsy	8.00

Autographs

		NM/M
Common Player:		
Varying quantities produced.		
Prime Autos:		No Pricing
Production 4-20		
12	Brett Myers	10.00
18	Brian Giles/30	30.00
19	Zach Day	8.00
21	Brandon Phillips	10.00
22	Carlos Lee	12.00
24	Casey Fossum	10.00
25	Marcus Giles	10.00
29	Edgar Martinez/100	40.00
30	Eric Chavez/75	25.00
31	Eric Hinske	10.00
33	Aubrey Huff	10.00
41	Ivan Rodriguez/50	75.00
42	Ivan Rodriguez/75	40.00
44	J.C. Romero	8.00
47	Josh Bard	8.00
49	Jay Gibbons	10.00
51	Juan Gonzalez/50	50.00
57	Kirk Saarloos	8.00
62	Mark Mulder/100	25.00
63	Mark Prior/25	75.00
64	Matt Williams	15.00
74	Paul LoDuca	15.00
84	Roy Oswalt/50	25.00
85	Jeremy Bonderman	50.00
86	Ryne Sandberg/40	100.00
90	Scott Rolen/50	40.00
95	Frank Catalanotto	8.00
96	Torii Hunter/140	20.00
98	Runelvys Hernandez	10.00
100	Vladimir Guerrero/150	40.00

Prime Materials

No Pricing
Production 25 Sets

Bronze Materials

Cards (1-100):	1-1.5X
Production 150 Sets	

Silver Materials
Cards (1-100):	1-2X
Production 75 Sets	

Gold Materials
Cards (1-100):	1.5-2.5X
Production 50 Sets	

Platinum Materials
No pricing due to scarcity.
Production 25 Sets

2003 Playoff Portraits Promos

To introduce its textured artwork issue, Playoff produced several types of promo cards. Two styles of white-bordered samples were issued; one has a blank-back and was distributed to dealers with ordering information, the other has a sample-marked back and was found one per box of Playoff Absolute. Otherwise unmarked promos with green top and bottom borders were distributed at All-Star FanFest, while similar promos with red top and bottom borders were handed out the Atlantic City National convention. Checklists for each of these styles are undetermined.

Common Player:

2003 Playoff Portraits Samples

Each issue of the October 2003 Beckett Baseball Card Monthly included a sample 2003 Playoff Portraits card rubber-cemented inside. The cards differ from the issued version only in the appearance on back of a (usually) black dot-matrix printed "SAMPLE" notation. Some cards were produced with the overprint in silver, in much more limited quantities. The number of different players' cards involved in the promotion is unknown.

	NM/M
Common Player:	.10
Stars:	1.5-2X
Silvers:	10X

2003 Playoff Portraits

		NM/M
Complete Set (144):		40.00
Common Player:		.25
Pack (7):		4.00
Box (20):		60.00
1	Vladimir Guerrero	1.50
2	Luis Gonzalez	.35
3	Andruw Jones	1.50
4	Manny Ramirez	1.50
5	Derek Jeter	4.00
6	Eric Hinske	.25
7	Curt Schilling	.45
8	Adam Dunn	1.00
9	Jason Jennings	.25
10	Mike Piazza	2.50
11	Jason Giambi	.75
12	Jeff Bagwell	1.00

Greg Maddux • Atlanta Braves

13	Rickey Henderson	1.50
14	Randy Johnson	1.50
15	Roger Clemens	3.00
16	Troy Glaus	1.00
17	Hideo Nomo	.50
18	Joe Borchard	.25
19	Torii Hunter	.25
20	Lance Berkman	.25
21	Todd Helton	1.50
22	Mike Mussina	.40
23	Vernon Wells	.25
24	Pat Burrell	.25
25	Ichiro Suzuki	2.50
26	Shawn Green	.50
27	Frank Thomas	1.50
28	Barry Zito	.40
29	Barry Bonds	4.00
30	Ken Griffey Jr.	2.50
31	Albert Pujols	3.00
32	Roberto Alomar	.25
33	Barry Larkin	.25
34	Tony Gwynn	2.00
35	Chipper Jones	2.00
36	Pedro J. Martinez	1.50
37	Juan Gonzalez	.75
38	Greg Maddux	2.00
39	Tim Hudson	.35
40	Sammy Sosa	1.50
41	Victor Martinez	.50
42	Mark Buehrle	.25
43	Austin Kearns	.25
44	Kerry Wood	1.00
45	Nomar Garciaparra	1.00
46	Alfonso Soriano	1.00
47	Mark Prior	.75
48	Richie Sexson	.25
49	Mark Teixeira	.75
50	Craig Biggio	.25
51	Rafael Palmeiro	1.00
52	Carlos Beltran	.75
53	Bernie Williams	.35
54	Eric Chavez	.35
55	Paul Konerko	.35
56	Nolan Ryan	4.00
57	Mark Mulder	.25
58	Miguel Tejada	.35
59	Roy Oswalt	.25
60	Jim Edmonds	.25
61	Ryan Klesko	.25
62	Cal Ripken Jr.	4.00
63	Josh Beckett	.25
64	Kazuhisa Ishii	.25
65	Alex Rodriguez	3.00
66	Mike Sweeney	.25
67	C.C. Sabathia	.25
68	Jose Vidro	.25
69	Magglio Ordonez	.75
70	Carlos Delgado	.25
71	Jorge Posada	.25
72	Bobby Abreu	.25
73	Brian Giles	.25
74	Kirby Puckett	2.00
75	Yogi Berra	1.00
76	Ryne Sandberg	2.00
77	Tom Glavine	.45
78	Jim Thome	1.00
79	Chris Snelling	.25
80	Drew Henson	.25
81	Junior Spivey	.25
82	Mike Schmidt	3.00
83	Jeff Kent	.25
84	Stan Musial	2.00
85	Garret Anderson	.25
86	Jose Contreras RC	3.00
87	Ivan Rodriguez	1.00
88	Hideki Matsui RC	6.00
89	Don Mattingly	3.00
90	Angel Berroa	.25
91	George Brett	3.00
92	Jermaine Dye	.25
93	John Olerud	.25
94	Josh Phelps	.25
95	Sean Casey	.35
96	Larry Walker	.25
97	Jason Lane	.25
98	Travis Hafner	.25
99	Terrence Long	.25
100	Shannon Stewart	.25
101	Richard Hidalgo	.25
102	Joe Thurston	.25
103	Ben Sheets	.25
104	Orlando Cabrera	.25
105	Aramis Ramirez	.25
106	So Taguchi	.25
107	Frank Robinson	.75
108	Phil Nevin	.25
109	Dennis Tankersley	.25
110	J.D. Drew	.50
111	Paul LoDuca	.25
112	Ozzie Smith	2.00
113	Carlos Lee	.25
114	Nick Johnson	.25
115	Edgar Martinez	.75
116	Hank Blalock	.75
117	Orlando Hudson	.25
118	Corey Patterson	.25
119	Steve Carlton	.50
120	Wade Miller	.25
121	Adrian Beltre	.75
122	Scott Rolen	1.00
123	Brian Lawrence	.25
124	Rich Aurilia	.25
125	Tsuyoshi Shinjo	.25
126	John Buck	.25
127	Marlon Byrd	.25
128	Michael Cuddyer	.25
129	Marshall McDougall	.25
130	Travis Chapman	.25
131	Jose Morban	.25
132	Adam LaRoche	.25
133	Jose Castillo	.25
134	Walter Young	.25
135	Jeff Baker	.25
136	Jeremy Guthrie	.25
137	Pedro J. Martinez	.75
138	Randy Johnson	.75
139	Alex Rodriguez	1.50
140	Hideo Nomo	.50
141	Roger Clemens	.50
142	Rickey Henderson	.50
143	Jason Giambi	.40
144	Mike Piazza	1.00

Artifacts Bronze

		NM/M
Common Player:		4.00
Production 100 or less.		
Silvers:		1-1.5X
Production 50 or less.		
Golds:		No Pricing
Production 25 or less.		
Bronze Combos:		1-1.5X
Production 100 or less.		
Silver Combos:		No Pricing
Production 25 or less.		
Gold Combos:		No Pricing
Production 10 or less.		
1	Vladimir Guerrero/100	8.00
2	Luis Gonzalez/100	5.00
3	Andruw Jones/100	8.00
4	Manny Ramirez/50	10.00
5	Derek Jeter/100	20.00
6	Eric Hinske/100	4.00
7	Curt Schilling/100	4.00
8	Adam Dunn/50	10.00
9	Jason Jennings/100	4.00
10	Mike Piazza/100	12.00
11	Jason Giambi/100	6.00
12	Jeff Bagwell/100	15.00
13	Rickey Henderson/100	20.00
14	Randy Johnson/100	8.00
15	Roger Clemens/100	20.00
16	Troy Glaus/100	6.00
17	Hideo Nomo/100	6.00
19	Torii Hunter/100	6.00
20	Lance Berkman/100	6.00
21	Todd Helton/100	15.00
22	Mike Mussina/100	8.00
23	Vernon Wells/100	4.00
24	Pat Burrell/100	4.00
25	Ichiro Suzuki/100	25.00
26	Shawn Green/100	6.00
27	Frank Thomas/100	10.00
28	Barry Zito/100	6.00
29	Barry Bonds/100	20.00
30	Ken Griffey Jr./100	15.00
31	Albert Pujols/100	20.00
32	Roberto Alomar/50	6.00
33	Barry Larkin/100	6.00
34	Tony Gwynn/100	15.00
35	Chipper Jones/100	10.00
36	Pedro Martinez/100	10.00
37	Juan Gonzalez/50	10.00
38	Greg Maddux/100	15.00
39	Tim Hudson/100	6.00
40	Sammy Sosa/100	20.00
41	Victor Martinez/100	6.00
42	Mark Buehrle/100	6.00
43	Austin Kearns/100	4.00
44	Kerry Wood/50	15.00
45	Nomar Garciaparra/100	15.00
46	Alfonso Soriano/100	10.00
47	Mark Prior/50	10.00
48	Richie Sexson/100	4.00
49	Mark Teixeira/50	8.00
50	Craig Biggio/50	8.00
51	Rafael Palmeiro/50	10.00
52	Carlos Beltran/50	10.00
53	Bernie Williams/50	10.00
54	Eric Chavez/100	6.00
55	Paul Konerko/50	6.00
56	Nolan Ryan/50	35.00
57	Mark Mulder/50	6.00
58	Miguel Tejada/50	6.00
59	Roy Oswalt/50	8.00
60	Jim Edmonds/50	8.00
61	Ryan Klesko/50	6.00
62	Cal Ripken Jr/100	40.00
63	Josh Beckett/100	6.00
64	Kazuhisa Ishii/50	6.00
65	Alex Rodriguez/100	15.00
66	Mike Sweeney/50	4.00
67	C.C. Sabathia/50	6.00
68	Jose Vidro/50	4.00
69	Magglio Ordonez/50	6.00
70	Carlos Delgado/50	8.00
71	Jorge Posada/100	8.00
72	Bobby Abreu/100	6.00
73	Brian Giles/50	4.00
74	Kirby Puckett/50	30.00
75	Yogi Berra/50	25.00
76	Ryne Sandberg/50	40.00
77	Tom Glavine/50	8.00
78	Jim Thome/50	10.00
79	Chris Snelling/50	5.00
80	Drew Henson/50	10.00
81	Junior Spivey/50	8.00
82	Mike Schmidt/50	50.00
83	Jeff Kent/50	6.00
84	Stan Musial/100	30.00
85	Garret Anderson/50	8.00
87	Ivan Rodriguez/50	12.00
89	Hideki Matsui/100	25.00
89	Don Mattingly/100	30.00
90	Angel Berroa/100	4.00
91	George Brett/50	50.00
92	Jermaine Dye/50	4.00
93	John Olerud/50	4.00
94	Josh Phelps/50	4.00
95	Sean Casey/50	4.00
96	Larry Walker/50	8.00
97	Jason Lane/50	4.00
98	Travis Hafner/100	6.00
99	Terrence Long/50	4.00
100	Shannon Stewart/50	4.00
101	Richard Hidalgo/50	4.00
102	Joe Thurston/50	4.00
103	Ben Sheets/100	6.00
104	Orlando Cabrera/50	6.00
105	Aramis Ramirez/50	6.00
106	So Taguchi/50	5.00
107	Frank Robinson/50	12.00
109	Dennis Tankersley/100	4.00
110	J.D. Drew/100	6.00
111	Paul LoDuca/50	6.00
112	Ozzie Smith/50	40.00
113	Carlos Lee/50	4.00
114	Nick Johnson/100	4.00
115	Edgar Martinez/50	8.00
116	Hank Blalock/50	15.00
117	Orlando Hudson/100	4.00
118	Corey Patterson/100	4.00
119	Steve Carlton/50	10.00
120	Wade Miller/50	4.00
121	Adrian Beltre/50	8.00
122	Scott Rolen/50	20.00
123	Brian Lawrence/50	4.00
124	Rich Aurilia/50	4.00
125	Tsuyoshi Shinjo/50	8.00
126	John Buck/50	4.00
127	Marlon Byrd/100	4.00
128	Michael Cuddyer/50	4.00
130	Travis Chapman/100	4.00
131	Jose Morban/100	4.00
132	Adam LaRoche/100	4.00
133	Jose Castillo/100	4.00
134	Walter Young/100	4.00

Beige
	1-30X
Production 250 Sets	

Bronze
Bronze:	2-4X
Production 100 Sets	

Bronze Autographs

		NM/M
Common Bronze Auto.:		
Production 100 or less.		
Silvers:		1-1.5X
Production 50 or less.		
No Pricing for production 25 or less.		
Golds:		No Pricing
Production 25 or less.		
1	Vladimir Guerrero/100	35.00
3	Andruw Jones/25	50.00
6	Eric Hinske/100	6.00
8	Adam Dunn/50	35.00
9	Jason Jennings/60	8.00
16	Troy Glaus/60	25.00
18	Joe Borchard/100	6.00
19	Torii Hunter/25	40.00
31	Albert Pujols/25	150.00
32	Roberto Alomar/100	35.00
33	Barry Larkin/95	25.00
34	Tony Gwynn/60	75.00
35	Chipper Jones/25	75.00
37	Juan Gonzalez/25	50.00
41	Victor Martinez/100	20.00
42	Mark Buehrle/100	10.00
44	Kerry Wood/40	60.00
47	Mark Prior/25	60.00
48	Richie Sexson/100	6.00
49	Mark Teixeira/25	50.00

#	Player	Price
50	Craig Biggio/25	40.00
56	Nolan Ryan/25	150.00
57	Mark Mulder/100	20.00
59	Roy Oswalt/40	25.00
61	Ryan Klesko/40	20.00
62	Cal Ripken Jr./25	150.00
67	C.C. Sabathia/50	15.00
72	Bobby Abreu/100	15.00
73	Brian Giles/50	15.00
74	Kirby Puckett/50	60.00
77	Tom Glavine/100	35.00
79	Chris Snelling/100	10.00
80	Drew Henson/25	40.00
81	Junior Spivey/100	10.00
82	Mike Schmidt/50	75.00
83	Jeff Kent/25	40.00
84	Stan Musial/50	65.00
85	Garret Anderson/25	30.00
86	Jose Contreras/50	40.00
89	Don Mattingly/50	90.00
90	Angel Berroa/100	10.00
92	Jermaine Dye/100	10.00
94	Josh Phelps/100	10.00
96	Jason Lane/100	8.00
98	Travis Hafner/100	12.00
99	Terrence Long/100	10.00
100	Shannon Stewart/100	8.00
101	Richard Hidalgo/25	20.00
102	Joe Thurston/100	10.00
103	Ben Sheets/100	15.00
105	Aramis Ramirez/40	15.00
106	So Taguchi/29	30.00
108	Phil Nevin/100	12.00
109	Dennis Tankersley/100	8.00
110	J.D. Drew/25	30.00
111	Paul LoDuca/100	15.00
113	Carlos Lee/100	10.00
114	Nick Johnson/100	10.00
115	Edgar Martinez/100	35.00
117	Orlando Hudson/100	8.00
118	Corey Patterson/100	15.00
119	Steve Carlton/25	40.00
120	Wade Miller/100	6.00
121	Adrian Beltre/25	30.00
122	Scott Rolen/100	30.00
123	Brian Lawrence/100	6.00
126	John Buck/100	6.00
127	Marlon Byrd/100	10.00
128	Michael Cuddyer/100	8.00
129	Marshall McDougall/100	6.00
130	Travis Chapman/100	6.00
131	Jose Morban/100	6.00
132	Adam LaRoche/100	12.00
133	Jose Castillo/100	6.00
134	Walter Young/100	6.00
135	Jeff Baker/100	6.00
136	Jeremy Guthrie/100	10.00

Silver

Larry Walker • Colorado Rockies®

Production 50 or less.

Silver Autographs

Production 50 or less.

2003 Playoff Prestige Samples

Each issue of the July 2003 Beckett Baseball Card Monthly included a sample 2003 Playoff Prestige card rubber-cemented inside. The cards differ from the issued version only in the appearance on back of a (usually) silver-foil "SAMPLE" notation. Some cards were produced with the overprint in gold-foil, in much more limited quantities. The number of different players' cards involved in the promotion is unknown.

	NM/M
Common Player:	.10
Stars:	1.5-2X
Gold:	10X

2003 Playoff Prestige

	NM/M
Complete Set (200):	35.00
Common Player:	.15
Pack (6):	2.00
Box (24):	45.00

#	Player	Price
1	Darin Erstad	.25
2	David Eckstein	.15
3	Garret Anderson	.15
4	Jarrod Washburn	.15
5	Tim Salmon	.15
6	Troy Glaus	.50
7	Jay Gibbons	.15
8	Marty Cordova	.15
9	Melvin Mora	.15
10	Rodrigo Lopez	.15
11	Tony Batista	.15
12	Cliff Floyd	.15
13	Derek Lowe	.15
14	Johnny Damon	.50
15	Manny Ramirez	.75
16	Nomar Garciaparra	.75
17	Pedro J. Martinez	.75
18	Rickey Henderson	.75
19	Shea Hillenbrand	.15
20	Carlos Lee	.15
21	Frank Thomas	.75
22	Magglio Ordonez	.15
23	Mark Buehrle	.15
24	Paul Konerko	.15
25	C.C. Sabathia	.15
26	Danys Baez	.15
27	Ellis Burks	.15
28	Travis Hafner	.15
29	Omar Vizquel	.15
30	Bobby Higginson	.15
31	Carlos Pena	.15
32	Mark Redman	.15
33	Robert Fick	.15
34	Steve Sparks	.15
35	Carlos Beltran	.50
36	Joe Randa	.15
37	Mike Sweeney	.15
38	Paul Byrd	.15
39	Raul Ibanez	.15
40	Runelvys Hernandez	.15
41	Brad Radke	.15
42	Corey Koskie	.15
43	Cristian Guzman	.15
44	David Ortiz	1.00
45	Doug Mientkiewicz	.15
46	Dustan Mohr	.15
47	Jacque Jones	.15
48	Torii Hunter	.15
49	Alfonso Soriano	.75
50	Andy Pettitte	.50
51	Bernie Williams	.40
52	David Wells	.15
53	Derek Jeter	2.00
54	Jason Giambi	.50
55	Jeff Weaver	.15
56	Jorge Posada	.50
57	Mike Mussina	.50
58	Roger Clemens	1.25
59	Barry Zito	.25
60	David Justice	.25
61	Eric Chavez	.25
62	Jermaine Dye	.15
63	Mark Mulder	.15
64	Miguel Tejada	.40
65	Ray Durham	.15
66	Tim Hudson	.40
67	Bret Boone	.15
68	Chris Snelling	.15
69	Edgar Martinez	.15
70	Freddy Garcia	.15
71	Ichiro Suzuki	1.50
72	Jamie Moyer	.15
73	John Olerud	.15
74	Kazuhiro Sasaki	.15
75	Aubrey Huff	.15
76	Joe Kennedy	.15
77	Paul Wilson	.15
78	Alex Rodriguez	1.75
79	Chan Ho Park	.15
80	Hank Blalock	.50
81	Ivan Rodriguez	.50
82	Juan Gonzalez	.50
83	Kevin Mench	.15
84	Rafael Palmeiro	.50
85	Carlos Delgado	.40
86	Eric Hinske	.15
87	Jose Cruz	.15
88	Josh Phelps	.15
89	Roy Halladay	.15
90	Shannon Stewart	.15
91	Vernon Wells	.15
92	Curt Schilling	.40
93	Junior Spivey	.15
94	Luis Gonzalez	.25
95	Mark Grace	.25
96	Randy Johnson	.75
97	Andruw Jones	.40
98	Chipper Jones	1.00
99	Gary Sheffield	.40
100	Greg Maddux	1.00
101	John Smoltz	.15
102	Kevin Millwood	.15
103	Mike Hampton	.15
104	Corey Patterson	.15
105	Fred McGriff	.15
106	Kerry Wood	.50
107	Mark Prior	.40
108	Moises Alou	.15
109	Sammy Sosa	1.00
110	Adam Dunn	.50
111	Austin Kearns	.15
112	Barry Larkin	.15
113	Ken Griffey Jr.	1.50
114	Sean Casey	.15
115	Jason Jennings	.15
116	Jay Payton	.15
117	Larry Walker	.15
118	Todd Helton	.50
119	A.J. Burnett	.15
120	Josh Beckett	.15
121	Juan Encarnacion	.15
122	Mike Lowell	.15
123	Craig Biggio	.15
124	Daryle Ward	.15
125	Jeff Bagwell	.50
126	Lance Berkman	.15
127	Roy Oswalt	.15
128	Adrian Beltre	.40
129	Hideo Nomo	.40
130	Kazuhisa Ishii	.15
131	Kevin Brown	.15
132	Odalis Perez	.15
133	Paul LoDuca	.15
134	Shawn Green	.40
135	Jeff Kent	.15
136	Ben Sheets	.15
137	Jeffrey Hammonds	.15
138	Jose Hernandez	.15
139	Richie Sexson	.15
140	Bartolo Colon	.15
141	Brad Wilkerson	.15
142	Javier Vazquez	.15
143	Jose Vidro	.15
144	Michael Barrett	.15
145	Vladimir Guerrero	.75
146	Al Leiter	.15
147	Mike Piazza	1.50
148	Mo Vaughn	.15
149	Pedro Astacio	.15
150	Roberto Alomar	.40
151	Roger Cedeno	.15
152	Tom Glavine	.40
153	Bobby Abreu	.15
154	Jimmy Rollins	.25
155	Mike Lieberthal	.15
156	Pat Burrell	.40
157	Vicente Padilla	.15
158	Jim Thome	.50
159	Aramis Ramirez	.15
160	Brian Giles	.15
161	Jason Kendall	.15
162	Josh Fogg	.15
163	Kip Wells	.15
164	Mark Kotsay	.15
165	Oliver Perez	.15
166	Phil Nevin	.15
167	Ryan Klesko	.15
168	Sean Burroughs	.15
169	Trevor Hoffman	.15
170	Barry Bonds	2.00
171	Benito Santiago	.15
172	Reggie Sanders	.15
173	Rich Aurilia	.15
174	Russ Ortiz	.15
175	Albert Pujols	1.75
176	J.D. Drew	.25
177	Jim Edmonds	.15
178	Matt Morris	.15
179	Tino Martinez	.15
180	Scott Rolen	.50
181	Joe Borchard	.15
182	Freddy Sanchez	.15
183	Jose Contreras RC	3.00
184	Jeff Baker	.15
185	Ryan Church	.15
186	Mario Ramos	.15
187	Corwin Malone	.15
188	Jimmy Gobble	.15
189	Jon Adkins	.15
190	Tim Kalita	.15
191	Nelson Castro	.15
192	Colin Young	.15
193	Luis Martinez	.15
194	Todd Donovan	.15
195	Jeremy Ward	.15
196	Wilson Valdez	.15
197	Hideki Matsui RC	6.00
198	Mitch Wylie	.15
199	Adam Walker	.15
200	Clifford Bartosh	.15

X-tra Points

Stars (1-180):	4-8X
Production 150	
Prospects (181-200):	4-8X
Production 50	

Award Winners

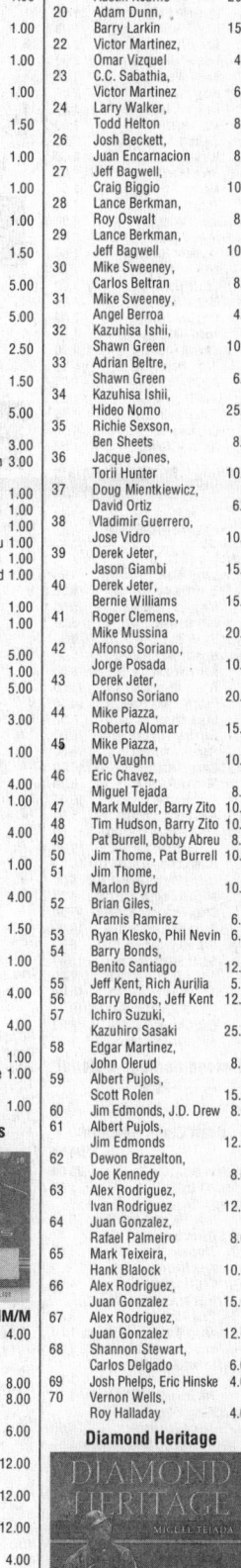

	NM/M
Complete Set (15):	25.00
Common Player:	1.00
#'d to year of award	

#	Player	Price
1	Barry Zito	1.00
2	Barry Bonds	5.00
3	Randy Johnson	1.50
4	Roger Clemens	2.50
5	Ichiro Suzuki	3.00
6	Chipper Jones	2.00
7	Ken Griffey Jr.	3.00
8	Miguel Tejada	1.00
9	Greg Maddux	2.00
10	Jeff Bagwell	1.50
11	Rickey Henderson	1.50
12	Tom Glavine	1.00
13	Albert Pujols	4.00
14	Nomar Garciaparra	3.00
15	Derek Jeter	5.00

Connections

	NM/M
Complete Set (70):	90.00
Common Duo:	1.00
Inserted 1:8	
Century Connections:	3-6X
Production 100 Sets	

#	Players	Price
1	Troy Glaus, Garret Anderson	1.50
2	Troy Glaus, Tim Salmon	1.50
3	Randy Johnson, Curt Schilling	1.50
4	Matt Williams, Luis Gonzalez	1.00
5	Greg Maddux, John Smoltz	2.00
6	Andruw Jones, Chipper Jones	2.00
7	Greg Maddux, Kevin Millwood	2.00
8	Tony Batista, Geronimo Gil	1.00
9	Pedro J. Martinez, Nomar Garciaparra	3.00
10	Manny Ramirez, Nomar Garciaparra	3.00
11	Nomar Garciaparra, Rickey Henderson	3.00
12	Trot Nixon, Manny Ramirez	1.50
13	Kerry Wood, Mark Prior	1.00
14	Sammy Sosa, Fred McGriff	3.00
15	Sammy Sosa, Corey Patterson	3.00
16	Frank Thomas, Magglio Ordonez	1.50
17	Joe Borchard, Magglio Ordonez	1.00
18	Adam Dunn, Austin Kearns	1.00
19	Barry Larkin, Ken Griffey Jr.	3.00
20	Adam Dunn, Barry Larkin	1.00
21	Adam Dunn, Ken Griffey Jr.	3.00
22	Victor Martinez, Omar Vizquel	1.00
23	C.C. Sabathia, Victor Martinez	1.00
24	Larry Walker, Todd Helton	1.00
25	Carlos Pena, Robert Fick	1.00
26	Josh Beckett, Juan Encarnacion	1.00
27	Jeff Bagwell, Craig Biggio	1.50
28	Lance Berkman, Roy Oswalt	1.00
29	Lance Berkman, Jeff Bagwell	1.50
30	Mike Sweeney, Carlos Beltran	1.00
31	Mike Sweeney, Angel Berroa	1.00
32	Kazuhisa Ishii, Shawn Green	1.00
33	Adrian Beltre, Shawn Green	1.00
34	Kazuhisa Ishii, Hideo Nomo	1.50
35	Richie Sexson, Ben Sheets	1.00
36	Jacque Jones, Torii Hunter	1.00
37	Doug Mientkiewicz, David Ortiz	1.00
38	Vladimir Guerrero, Jose Vidro	1.50
39	Derek Jeter, Jason Giambi	5.00
40	Derek Jeter, Bernie Williams	5.00
41	Roger Clemens, Mike Mussina	2.50
42	Alfonso Soriano, Jorge Posada	1.50
43	Derek Jeter, Alfonso Soriano	5.00
44	Mike Piazza, Roberto Alomar	3.00
45	Mike Piazza, Mo Vaughn	3.00
46	Eric Chavez, Miguel Tejada	1.00
47	Mark Mulder, Barry Zito	1.00
48	Tim Hudson, Barry Zito	1.00
49	Pat Burrell, Bobby Abreu	1.00
50	Jim Thome, Pat Burrell	1.00
51	Jim Thome, Marlon Byrd	1.00
52	Brian Giles, Aramis Ramirez	1.00
53	Ryan Klesko, Phil Nevin	1.00
54	Barry Bonds, Benito Santiago	5.00
55	Jeff Kent, Rich Aurilia	1.00
56	Barry Bonds, Jeff Kent	5.00
57	Ichiro Suzuki, Kazuhiro Sasaki	3.00
58	Edgar Martinez, John Olerud	1.00
59	Albert Pujols, Scott Rolen	4.00
60	Jim Edmonds, J.D. Drew	1.00
61	Albert Pujols, Jim Edmonds	4.00
62	Dewon Brazelton, Joe Kennedy	1.00
63	Alex Rodriguez, Ivan Rodriguez	4.00
64	Juan Gonzalez, Rafael Palmeiro	1.50
65	Mark Teixeira, Hank Blalock	1.00
66	Alex Rodriguez, Juan Gonzalez	4.00
67	Alex Rodriguez, Juan Gonzalez	4.00
68	Shannon Stewart, Carlos Delgado	1.00
69	Josh Phelps, Eric Hinske	1.00
70	Vernon Wells, Roy Halladay	1.00

Material Connections

	NM/M
Common Duo:	4.00
Production 400 Sets	

#	Players	Price
1	Troy Glaus, Garret Anderson	8.00
2	Troy Glaus, Tim Salmon	8.00
4	Matt Williams, Luis Gonzalez	6.00
5	Greg Maddux, John Smoltz	12.00
6	Andruw Jones, Chipper Jones	12.00
7	Greg Maddux, Kevin Millwood	12.00
8	Tony Batista, Geronimo Gil	4.00
9	Pedro J. Martinez, Nomar Garciaparra	15.00
10	Manny Ramirez, Nomar Garciaparra	15.00
11	Nomar Garciaparra, Rickey Henderson	15.00
12	Trot Nixon, Manny Ramirez	10.00
13	Kerry Wood, Mark Prior	10.00
14	Sammy Sosa, Fred McGriff	10.00
15	Sammy Sosa, Corey Patterson	10.00
16	Frank Thomas, Magglio Ordonez	8.00
17	Joe Borchard, Magglio Ordonez	6.00
18	Adam Dunn, Austin Kearns	20.00
20	Adam Dunn, Barry Larkin	15.00
22	Victor Martinez, Omar Vizquel	4.00
23	C.C. Sabathia, Victor Martinez	6.00
24	Larry Walker, Todd Helton	8.00
26	Josh Beckett, Juan Encarnacion	8.00
27	Jeff Bagwell, Craig Biggio	10.00
28	Lance Berkman, Roy Oswalt	8.00
29	Lance Berkman, Jeff Bagwell	10.00
30	Mike Sweeney, Carlos Beltran	8.00
31	Mike Sweeney, Angel Berroa	4.00
32	Kazuhisa Ishii, Shawn Green	10.00
33	Adrian Beltre, Shawn Green	6.00
34	Kazuhisa Ishii, Hideo Nomo	25.00
35	Richie Sexson, Ben Sheets	8.00
36	Jacque Jones, Torii Hunter	10.00
37	Doug Mientkiewicz, David Ortiz	6.00
38	Vladimir Guerrero, Jose Vidro	10.00
39	Derek Jeter, Jason Giambi	15.00
40	Derek Jeter, Bernie Williams	15.00
41	Roger Clemens, Mike Mussina	20.00
42	Alfonso Soriano, Jorge Posada	10.00
43	Derek Jeter, Alfonso Soriano	20.00
44	Mike Piazza, Roberto Alomar	15.00
45	Mike Piazza, Mo Vaughn	10.00
46	Eric Chavez, Miguel Tejada	8.00
47	Mark Mulder, Barry Zito	10.00
48	Tim Hudson, Barry Zito	10.00
49	Pat Burrell, Bobby Abreu	8.00
50	Jim Thome, Pat Burrell	10.00
51	Jim Thome, Marlon Byrd	10.00
52	Brian Giles, Aramis Ramirez	6.00
53	Ryan Klesko, Phil Nevin	6.00
54	Barry Bonds, Benito Santiago	12.00
55	Jeff Kent, Rich Aurilia	5.00
56	Barry Bonds, Jeff Kent	12.00
57	Ichiro Suzuki, Kazuhiro Sasaki	25.00
58	Edgar Martinez, John Olerud	8.00
59	Albert Pujols, Scott Rolen	15.00
60	Jim Edmonds, J.D. Drew	8.00
61	Albert Pujols, Jim Edmonds	12.00
62	Dewon Brazelton, Joe Kennedy	8.00
63	Alex Rodriguez, Ivan Rodriguez	12.00
64	Juan Gonzalez, Rafael Palmeiro	8.00
65	Mark Teixeira, Hank Blalock	10.00
66	Alex Rodriguez, Juan Gonzalez	15.00
67	Alex Rodriguez, Juan Gonzalez	12.00
68	Shannon Stewart, Carlos Delgado	6.00
69	Josh Phelps, Eric Hinske	4.00
70	Vernon Wells, Roy Halladay	4.00

Diamond Heritage

	NM/M
Complete Set (30):	35.00
Common Player:	1.00
Inserted 1:21	
Golds:	5-10X
Production 50 Sets	

#	Player	Price
1	Larry Walker	1.00
2	Troy Glaus	1.50
3	Magglio Ordonez	1.00
4	Roy Oswalt	1.00
5	Barry Zito	1.00
6	Nomar Garciaparra	3.00
7	Kerry Wood	1.25
8	Roger Clemens	2.50
9	Pedro J. Martinez	1.50
10	Mark Prior	1.00
11	Sammy Sosa	3.00
12	Randy Johnson	1.50
13	Greg Maddux	2.00
14	Manny Ramirez	1.50
15	Torii Hunter	1.00
16	Alex Rodriguez	4.00
17	Mike Piazza	3.00
18	Vladimir Guerrero	1.50
19	Ivan Rodriguez	1.25
20	Lance Berkman	1.00
21	Miguel Tejada	1.00
22	Chipper Jones	2.00
23	Todd Helton	1.50
24	Shawn Green	1.00
25	Scott Rolen	1.25
26	Adam Dunn	1.25
27	Jim Thome	1.25
28	Rafael Palmeiro	1.25
29	Eric Chavez	1.00
30	Andruw Jones	1.50

Diamond Heritage Materials

NM/M
Common Player: 5.00
Production 200 unless noted.
Autographs: No Pricing
Production 15 to 25

#	Player	Price
1	Larry Walker	6.00
2	Troy Glaus	6.00
3	Magglio Ordonez	5.00
4	Roy Oswalt	5.00
5	Barry Zito	8.00
6	Nomar Garciaparra	15.00
7	Kerry Wood	8.00
8	Roger Clemens	15.00
9	Pedro J. Martinez	10.00
10	Mark Prior	6.00
11	Sammy Sosa	15.00
12	Randy Johnson	10.00
13	Greg Maddux	10.00
14	Manny Ramirez	8.00
15	Torii Hunter	10.00
16	Alex Rodriguez/Bat/100	15.00
17	Mike Piazza/Bat/100	15.00
18	V. Guerrero/Bat/100	10.00
19	Ivan Rodriguez/Bat/100	10.00
20	Lance Berkman/Bat/100	8.00
21	Miguel Tejada/Bat/100	8.00
22	Chipper Jones/Bat/100	15.00
23	Todd Helton/Bat/100	8.00
24	Shawn Green/Bat/100	8.00
25	Scott Rolen/Bat/100	15.00
26	Adam Dunn/Bat/100	12.00
27	Jim Thome/Bat/100	8.00
28	Rafael Palmeiro/Bat/100	10.00
29	Eric Chavez/Bat/100	8.00
30	Andruw Jones/Bat/100	8.00

Diamond Heritage Material Auto

Quantity produced listed.

Draft Class Reunion

NM/M
Complete Set (10): 20.00
Common Player: 1.00
Inserted 1:24

#	Players	Price
1	Mike Piazza, John Olerud	3.00
2	Derek Jeter, Shannon Stewart	5.00
3	Alex Rodriguez, Torii Hunter	4.00
4	Nomar Garciaparra, Paul Konerko	3.00
5	Kerry Wood, Todd Helton	1.50
6	Eric Chavez, Billy Koch	1.50
7	Lance Berkman, Troy Glaus	1.50
8	Pat Burrell, Mark Mulder	1.50
9	Barry Zito, Jason Jennings	1.00
10	Mark Prior, Mark Teixeira	1.50

Infield/Outfield Tandems Material

NM/M
Common Duo: 8.00
Production 100 Sets

#	Players	Price
1	Troy Glaus, Garret Anderson	10.00
2	Mark Grace, Luis Gonzalez	10.00
3	Nomar Garciaparra, Manny Ramirez	20.00
4	Alfonso Soriano, Bernie Williams	15.00
5	Jeff Bagwell, Lance Berkman	15.00
6	Alex Rodriguez, Juan Gonzalez	15.00
7	Barry Larkin, Adam Dunn	15.00
8	Scott Rolen, Jim Edmonds	20.00
9	Todd Helton, Larry Walker	10.00
10	Adrian Beltre, Shawn Green	10.00
11	Jose Vidro, Vladimir Guerrero	12.00
12	Mike Sweeney, Carlos Beltran	10.00
13	Josh Phelps, Vernon Wells	8.00
14	Paul Konerko, Magglio Ordonez	10.00
15	Phil Nevin, Ryan Klesko	10.00

Inside The Numbers

NM/M
Complete Set (25): 35.00
Common Player: 1.00
Production 2,002 Sets
Die-Cuts: 10-25X
#'d to jersey number

#	Player	Price
1	Roger Clemens	2.50
2	Greg Maddux	2.00
3	Miguel Tejada	1.00
4	Alex Rodriguez	4.00
5	Ichiro Suzuki	2.50
6	Sammy Sosa	3.00
7	Jim Thome	1.50
8	Derek Jeter	5.00
9	Randy Johnson	1.50
10	Barry Zito	1.00
11	Jason Giambi	1.50
12	Shawn Green	1.00
13	Curt Schilling	1.00
14	Albert Pujols	4.00
15	Vladimir Guerrero	1.50
16	Pedro J. Martinez	1.50
17	Alfonso Soriano	1.50
18	Barry Bonds	5.00
19	Magglio Ordonez	1.00
20	Chipper Jones	2.00
21	Pat Burrell	1.00
22	Luis Gonzalez	1.00
23	Jeff Bagwell	1.00
24	Garret Anderson	1.00
25	Larry Walker	1.00

League Leaders

NM/M
Complete Set (15): 25.00
Common Player: 1.00
Production 2,002 Sets

#	Player	Price
1	Manny Ramirez	2.00
2	Sammy Sosa	3.00
3	Alex Rodriguez	4.00
4	Alfonso Soriano	2.00
5	Vladimir Guerrero	2.00
6	Nomar Garciaparra	3.00
7	Johnny Damon	2.00
8	Alfonso Soriano	2.00
9	Barry Bonds	5.00
10	Barry Zito	1.00
11	Pedro J. Martinez	2.00
12	John Smoltz	1.00
13	Randy Johnson	2.00
14	Lance Berkman	1.00
15	Randy Johnson	2.00

League Leaders Materials

NM/M
Common Player: 4.00
Production 250 Sets

#	Player	Price
1	Manny Ramirez/Jsy	8.00
2	Sammy Sosa/Base	8.00
3	Alex Rodriguez/Jsy	10.00
4	Alfonso Soriano/Jsy	10.00
5	Vladimir Guerrero/Jsy	8.00
6	Nomar Garciaparra/Jsy	10.00
7	Johnny Damon/Bat	4.00
8	Alfonso Soriano/Jsy	8.00
9	Barry Bonds/Base	12.00
10	Barry Zito/Jsy	6.00
11	Pedro J. Martinez/Jsy	6.00
12	John Smoltz	6.00
13	Randy Johnson/Jsy	6.00
14	Lance Berkman/Jsy	6.00
15	Randy Johnson/Jsy	6.00

Player Collection

NM/M
Common Player: 4.00
Production 325 Sets

#	Player	Price
1	Adam Dunn	8.00
2	Adrian Beltre	6.00
3	Alex Rodriguez	20.00
4	Alfonso Soriano	10.00
5	Andruw Jones	8.00
6	Andy Pettitte	6.00
7	Barry Larkin	4.00
8	Barry Zito	4.00
9	Ben Grieve	4.00
10	Bernie Williams	4.00
11	Cal Ripken Jr.	25.00
12	Carlos Delgado	5.00
13	C.C. Sabathia	4.00
14	Chipper Jones	12.00
15	Craig Biggio	4.00
16	Curt Schilling	5.00
17	Alex Rodriguez	20.00
18	Frank Thomas	8.00
19	Freddy Garcia	4.00
20	Jay Bell	4.00
21	Roger Clemens	15.00
22	Tony Gwynn	12.00
23	Ivan Rodriguez	8.00
24	Jason Giambi	8.00
25	Jason Jennings	4.00
26	Jay Payton	4.00
27	J.D. Drew	6.00
28	Jeff Bagwell	8.00
29	Jeromy Burnitz	4.00
30	Jim Edmonds	4.00
31	Jim Thome	8.00
32	Joe Borchard	4.00
33	Joe Mays	4.00
34	John Olerud	4.00
35	David Wells	4.00
36	Juan Gonzalez	8.00
37	Kazuhiro Sasaki	4.00
38	Chan Ho Park	4.00
39	Kerry Wood	8.00
40	Kevin Brown	4.00
41	Lance Berkman	4.00
42	Larry Walker	4.00
43	Bret Boone	4.00
44	Magglio Ordonez	4.00
45	Manny Ramirez	8.00
46	Mark Mulder	4.00
47	Mark Prior	6.00
48	Matt Williams	4.00
49	Miguel Tejada	4.00
50	Mike Piazza	15.00
51	Nomar Garciaparra	15.00
52	Doug Davis	4.00
53	Paul Konerko	4.00
54	Paul LoDuca	4.00
55	Pedro J. Martinez	8.00
56	Preston Wilson	4.00
57	Rafael Palmeiro	8.00
58	Marlon Byrd	4.00
59	Reggie Sanders	4.00
60	Richie Sexson	4.00
61	Rickey Henderson	10.00
62	Rickey Henderson	10.00
63	Robert Person	4.00
64	Jeff Bagwell	8.00
65	Roger Clemens	15.00
66	Roy Oswalt	4.00
67	Ryan Klesko	4.00
68	Sammy Sosa	15.00
69	Shawn Green	5.00
70	Steve Finley	4.00
71	Terrence Long	4.00
72	Tim Hudson	4.00
73	Toby Hall	4.00
74	Todd Helton	8.00
75	Travis Lee	4.00
76	Troy Glaus	8.00
77	Tsuyoshi Shinjo	4.00
78	Vernon Wells	8.00
79	Vladimir Guerrero	8.00
80	Wes Helms	4.00
81	Alex Rodriguez	20.00
82	Alfonso Soriano	10.00
83	Barry Larkin	4.00
84	Roberto Alomar	5.00
85	Ivan Rodriguez	8.00
86	Jason Giambi	6.00
87	Jeff Bagwell	8.00
88	Juan Gonzalez	8.00
89	Larry Walker	4.00
90	Luis Gonzalez	4.00
91	Magglio Ordonez	4.00
92	Manny Ramirez	8.00
93	Marlon Byrd	4.00
94	Mike Piazza	15.00
95	Pat Burrell	8.00
96	Todd Helton	8.00
97	Rickey Henderson	10.00
98	Andruw Jones	8.00
99	Craig Biggio	8.00
100	Mark Prior	6.00

Signature Impressions

NM/M
Varying quantities produced.

#	Player	Price
1	A.J. Pierzynski/50	20.00
2	Adam Dunn/25	60.00
3	Barry Zito/25	50.00
5	Bobby Abreu/20	30.00
6	Brandon Phillips/25	25.00
7	Don Mattingly/15	250.00
9	Eric Hinske/25	25.00
12	John Candelaria/30	15.00
16	Lance Berkman/25	30.00
18	Miguel Tejada/25	40.00
22	Roy Oswalt/25	30.00
27	Yogi Berra/15	100.00
28	Joe Kennedy/50	5.00
30	Lenny Dykstra/50	25.00
39	Toby Hall/50	10.00
46	Victor Martinez/25	45.00
47	Brian Giles/15	40.00
50	Jeremy Bonderman/100	35.00

Stars of MLB

NM/M
Common Player: 5.00
Production 150 Sets
Patches: 4-8X
Production 25 Sets
Autographs: No Pricing
Production 25
Patch Autographs: No Pricing
Production 5 to 10

#	Player	Price
1	Roger Clemens	12.00
2	Randy Johnson	8.00
3	Sammy Sosa	12.00
4	Vladimir Guerrero	8.00
5	Lance Berkman	5.00
6	Alfonso Soriano	5.00
7	Alex Rodriguez	15.00
8	Roberto Alomar	6.00
9	Miguel Tejada	5.00
10	Pedro J. Martinez	5.00
11	Greg Maddux	10.00
12	Barry Zito	5.00
13	Magglio Ordonez	5.00
14	Chipper Jones	10.00
15	Manny Ramirez	8.00
16	Troy Glaus	5.00
17	Pat Burrell	6.00
18	Roy Oswalt	5.00
19	Mike Piazza	12.00
20	Nomar Garciaparra	12.00

2004 Playoff Absolute Memorabilia

NM/M
Complete Set (250):
Common Player (1-200): 1.50
Production 1,349
Common Non-Auto. (201-250): 2.00
Production 1,000
Common Auto. (201-250): 8.00
Production 500-700
Pack (4): 40.00
Box (6): 185.00

#	Player	Price
1	Troy Glaus	2.00
2	Garret Anderson	2.00
3	Tim Salmon	2.00
4	Bartolo Colon	1.50
5	Troy Percival	1.50
6	Nolan Ryan Angels	10.00
7	Vladimir Guerrero	4.00
8	Richie Sexson	1.50
9	Shea Hillenbrand	1.50
10	Luis Gonzalez	1.50
11	Brandon Webb	1.50
12	Randy Johnson	4.00
13	Robby Hammock	1.50
14	Edgar Gonzalez	1.50
15	Roberto Alomar	1.50
16	Andruw Jones	3.00
17	Chipper Jones	4.00
18	Dale Murphy	2.00
19	Rafael Furcal	1.50
20	J.D. Drew	1.50
21	Bubba Nelson	1.50
22	Julio Franco	1.50
23	Adam LaRoche	1.50
24	Michael Hessman	1.50
25	Warren Spahn	3.00
26	Jay Gibbons	1.50
27	Cal Ripken Jr.	10.00
28	Miguel Tejada	2.50
29	Adam Loewen	2.00
30	Rafael Palmeiro	3.00
31	Javy Lopez	1.50
32	Luis Matos	1.50
33	Jason Varitek	2.00
34	Carl Yastrzemski	5.00
35	Manny Ramirez	3.00
36	Trot Nixon	1.50
37	Curt Schilling	3.00
38	Pedro J. Martinez	4.00
39	Nomar Garciaparra	5.00
40	Luis Tiant	1.50
41	Kevin Youkilis	1.50
42	Michel Hernandez	1.50
43	Sammy Sosa	5.00
44	Greg Maddux	4.00
45	Kerry Wood	4.00
46	Mark Prior	4.00
47	Ernie Banks	4.00
48	Aramis Ramirez	2.00
49	Brendan Harris	1.50
50	Todd Wellemeyer	1.50
51	Frank Thomas	3.00
52	Magglio Ordonez	2.00
53	Carlos Lee	1.50
54	Joe Crede	1.50
55	Joe Borchard	1.50
56	Mark Buehrle	1.50
57	Sean Casey	2.00
58	Adam Dunn	2.50
59	Austin Kearns	2.00
60	Ken Griffey Jr.	5.00
61	Barry Larkin	2.00
62	Ryan Wagner	1.50
63	Jody Gerut	1.50
64	Jeremy Guthrie	1.50
65	Travis Hafner	1.50
66	Brian Tallet	1.50
67	Todd Helton	3.00
68	Preston Wilson	1.50
69	Jeff Baker	1.50
70	Clint Barmes	1.50
71	Joe Kennedy	1.50
72	Jack Morris	1.50
73	George Kell	1.50
74	Preston Larrison	1.50
75	Dmitri Young	1.50
76	Ivan Rodriguez	3.00
77	Dontrelle Willis	2.00
78	Josh Beckett	2.50
79	Miguel Cabrera	4.00
80	Mike Lowell	2.00
81	Luis Castillo	1.50
82	Juan Pierre	1.50
83	Jeff Bagwell	3.00
84	Jeff Kent	2.00
85	Craig Biggio	2.00
86	Lance Berkman	2.00
87	Andy Pettitte	2.00
88	Roy Oswalt	2.00
89	Chris Burke	1.50
90	Jason Lane	1.50
91	Roger Clemens	6.00
92	Mike Sweeney	1.50
93	Carlos Beltran	2.00
94	Angel Berroa	1.50
95	Juan Gonzalez	2.50
96	Ken Harvey	1.50
97	Byron Gettis	1.50
98	Alexis Gomez	1.50
99	Ian Ferguson	1.50
100	Duke Snider	3.00
101	Shawn Green	2.00
102	Hideo Nomo	2.00
103	Kazuhisa Ishii	1.50
104	Edwin Jackson	1.50
105	Fred McGriff	2.00
106	Hong-Chih Kou	1.50
107	Don Sutton RC	1.50
108	Rickey Henderson	2.00
109	Cesar Izturis	1.50
110	Robin Ventura	1.50
111	Paul LoDuca	1.50
112	Rickie Weeks	2.00
113	Scott Podsednik	2.00
114	Junior Spivey	1.50
115	Lyle Overbay	2.00
116	Tony Oliva	1.50
117	Jacque Jones	1.50
118	Shannon Stewart	1.50
119	Torii Hunter	2.00
120	Johan Santana	2.00
121	J.D. Durbin	1.50
122	Jason Kubel	2.00
123	Michael Cuddyer	1.50
124	Nick Johnson	1.50
125	Jose Vidro	1.50
126	Orlando Cabrera	1.50
127	Zach Day	1.50
128	Mike Piazza	5.00
129	Tom Glavine	2.00
130	Jae Weong Seo	1.50
131	Gary Carter	2.00
132	Phil Seibel	1.50
133	Edwin Almonte	1.50
134	Aaron Boone	1.50
135	Kenny Lofton	2.00
136	Don Mattingly	6.00
137	Jason Giambi	3.00
138	Alex Rodriguez Yanks	8.00
139	Jorge Posada	2.00
140	Bernie Williams	2.00
141	Hideki Matsui	5.00
142	Mike Mussina	2.00
143	Mariano Rivera	2.00
144	Gary Sheffield	2.00
145	Derek Jeter	8.00
146	Chien-Ming Wang	1.50
147	Javier Vazquez	1.50
148	Jose Contreras	1.50
149	Whitey Ford	2.00
150	Kevin Brown	2.00
151	Eric Chavez	2.00
152	Barry Zito	2.00
153	Mark Mulder	2.00
154	Tim Hudson	2.00
155	Rich Harden	1.50
156	Eric Byrnes	1.50
157	Jim Thome	4.00
158	Bobby Abreu	2.00
159	Marlon Byrd	1.50
160	Lenny Dykstra	2.00
161	Steve Carlton	2.00
162	Ryan Howard	2.00
163	Bobby Hill	1.50
164	Jose Castillo	1.50
165	Jay Payton	1.50
166	Ryan Klesko	1.50
167	Brian Giles	1.50
168	Henri Stanley	1.50
169	Jason Schmidt	2.00
170	Jerome Williams	1.50
171	J.T. Snow	1.50
172	Bret Boone	2.00
173	Edgar Martinez	2.00
174	Ichiro Suzuki	5.00
175	Jamie Moyer	1.50
176	Rich Aurilia	1.50
177	Chris Snelling	1.50
178	Scott Rolen	4.00
179	Albert Pujols	6.00
180	Jim Edmonds	2.00
181	Stan Musial	4.00
182	Dan Haren	1.50
183	Red Schoendienst	1.50
184	Aubrey Huff	1.50
185	Delmon Young	1.50
186	Rocco Baldelli	2.00
187	Dewon Brazelton	1.50
188	Mark Teixeira	2.50
189	Hank Blalock	3.00
190	Nolan Ryan Ranger	10.00
191	Alfonso Soriano	4.00
192	Michael Young	1.50
193	Vernon Wells	1.50
194	Roy Halladay	2.00
195	Carlos Delgado	2.50
196	Dustin McGowan	1.50
197	Josh Phelps	1.50
198	Alexis Rios	1.50
199	Eric Hinske	1.50
200	Josh Towers	1.50
201	Kazuo Matsui/1,000 RC	5.00
202	Fernando Nieve AU/500 RC	8.00
203	Mike Rouse/1,000	3.00
204	Dennis Sarfate AU/500 RC	8.00
205	Josh Labandeira AU/500 RC	8.00
206	Chris Oxspring AU/500 RC	8.00
207	Alfredo Simon/1,000 RC	2.00
208	Cory Sullivan AU/500 RC	8.00
209	Ruddy Yan AU/500 RC	8.00
210	Jason Bartlett AU/500 RC	8.00
211	Akinori Otsuka/1,000 RC	5.00
212	Lincoln Holdzkom/1,000 RC	2.00
213	Justin Leone/1,000 RC	4.00
214	Jorge Sequea AU/500 RC	8.00
215	John Gall/1,000 RC	3.00
216	Jerome Gamble/1,000 RC	2.00
217	Tim Bittner AU/500 RC	8.00
218	Ronny Cedeno AU/500 RC	12.00
219	Justin Hampson/1,000 RC	2.00
220	Ryan Wing AU/500	8.00
221	Mariano Gomez AU/500 RC	8.00
222	Carlos Vasquez/1,000 RC	8.00
223	Casey Daigle AU/500 RC	8.00
224	Renyel Pinto AU/500 RC	8.00
225	Chris Shelton AU/500 RC	15.00
226	Mike Gosling AU/700	8.00
227	Aarom Baldiris AU/700 RC	8.00
228	Ramon Ramirez AU/700 RC	8.00
229	Roberto Novoa AU/500 RC	8.00
230	Sean Henn AU/500	10.00
231	Jamie Brown AU/500 RC	8.00
232	Nick Regilio AU/500 RC	8.00
233	David Crouthers AU/700	8.00
234	Greg Dobbs AU/500 RC	8.00
235	Angel Chavez AU/500 RC	8.00
236	Willy Taveras AU/500 RC	20.00
237	Justin Knoedler AU/500 RC	8.00
238	Ian Snell AU/700 RC	10.00
239	Jason Frasor AU/500 RC	8.00
240	Jerry Gil AU/500 RC	8.00
241	Carlos Hines AU/500 RC	8.00
242	Ivan Ochoa AU/500 RC	8.00
243	Jose Capellan AU/700 RC	10.00
244	Onil Joseph AU/700 RC	8.00
245	Hector Gimenez AU/700 RC	8.00
246	Shawn Hill AU/700 RC	8.00
247	Freddy Guzman AU/700 RC	8.00
248	Graham Koonce AU/500 RC	8.00
249	Ronald Belisario AU/500 RC	8.00
250	Merkin Valdez AU/700 RC	8.00

Retail

Cards (1-200): .15X
1-200 are not serial numbered.

Spectrum Silver

Stars (1-200): 1-2X
Gold Auto. (201-250): .25-.4X
Non-Auto. (201-250): 1X
Production 100 Sets

Spectrum Gold

Stars (1-200): 2-4X
Gold Auto. (201-250): .5X
Non-Auto. (201-250): 1-2X
Production 50 Sets

Spectrum Platinum

No Pricing
Production One Set

Absolutely Ink

NM/M

Quantity produced listed.
Spectrum: .75-1.5X
Production 1-25
No pricing 15 or less.

1	Adam Dunn/100	25.00
2	Al Kaline/100	25.00
3	Alan Trammell/100	15.00
6	Andre Dawson/Cubs/100	15.00
7	Andre Dawson/Expos/100	15.00
8	Andruw Jones/100	25.00
9	Angel Berroa/50	10.00
10	Aramis Ramirez/50	25.00
11	Aubrey Huff/100	12.00
12	Austin Kearns/100	15.00
13	Barry Larkin/50	30.00
16	Bert Blyleven/100	15.00
17	Billy Williams/100	15.00
19	Bob Feller/100	20.00
20	Bob Gibson/25	35.00
21	Bobby Doerr/100	15.00
22	Brandon Webb/100	10.00
23	Brett Myers/50	15.00
24	Brooks Robinson/100	40.00
27	Carlos Beltran/100	15.00
28	Carlos Lee/100	10.00
31	Craig Biggio/50	25.00
33	Dale Murphy/100	15.00
34	Darryl Strawberry/100	15.00
35	Dave Concepcion/50	20.00
36	Dave Parker/100	15.00
38	Don Mattingly/100	60.00
39	Dontrelle Willis/100	20.00
40	Duke Snider/100	30.00
41	Dwight Gooden/100	15.00
42	Edgar Martinez/50	30.00
43	Eric Chavez/50	25.00
44	Ernie Banks/100	50.00
45	Fergie Jenkins/100	15.00
46	Frank Robinson/100	20.00
47	Frank Thomas/25	50.00
48	Fred Lynn/100	15.00
49	Fred McGriff/25	50.00
50	Garret Anderson/100	15.00
51	Gary Carter/Expos/100	15.00
52	Gary Carter/Mets/100	15.00
53	Gary Sheffield/50	25.00
57	Gaylord Perry/100	15.00
57	Hank Blalock/100	25.00
57	Harold Baines/50	25.00
62	Jacque Jones/100	15.00
62	Jae Weong Seo/100	15.00
64	Jamie Moyer/25	25.00
65	Jason Varitek/50	35.00
65	Jay Gibbons/50	15.00
67	Jim Edmonds/25	35.00
67	Jim Palmer/100	20.00
69	Jim Rice/50	15.00
71	Johan Santana/100	40.00
72	Jorge Posada/50	40.00
73	Josh Beckett/75	40.00
74	Juan Gonzalez/25	40.00
75	Keith Hernandez/100	15.00
76	Kirby Puckett/25	60.00
77	Luis Tiant/100	15.00
78	Magglio Ordonez/100	15.00
81	Mark Grace/25	50.00
82	Mark Mulder/100	20.00
83	Mark Prior/100	40.00
84	Mark Teixeira/100	25.00
85	Marty Marion/100	15.00
86	Mike Lowell/25	25.00
90	Nolan Ryan/25	125.00
91	Orel Hershiser/100	30.00
92	Orlando Cepeda/100	15.00

97	Phil Niekro/100	15.00
99	Ralph Kiner/100	20.00
101	Red Schoendienst/100	15.00
103	Robin Roberts/50	15.00
104	Robin Ventura/100	15.00
106	Rocco Baldelli/25	30.00
109	Sammy Sosa/21	150.00
110	Sean Casey/23	25.00
111	Shannon Stewart/50	15.00
113	Stan Musial/100	60.00
114	Steve Carlton/50	40.00
115	Steve Garvey/100	15.00
117	Tommy John/100	15.00
118	Tony Gwynn/25	60.00
119	Tony Oliva/100	15.00
120	Torii Hunter/100	15.00
121	Trot Nixon/50	30.00
122	Troy Glaus/50	20.00
123	Vernon Wells/25	20.00
124	Vladimir Guerrero/100	35.00
125	Will Clark/100	35.00

Absolutely Ink Material

NM/M

Quantity produced listed
Prime: .5-1X
Production 1-25
No pricing 15 or less.

1	Adam Dunn/Jsy/100	30.00
2	Al Kaline/Pants/50	50.00
3	Alan Trammell/Jsy/100	20.00
6	Andre Dawson/Cubs Jsy/100	20.00
7	Andre Dawson/Expos Jsy/100	15.00
9	Angel Berroa/Jsy/100	10.00
11	Aubrey Huff/Jsy/100	15.00
12	Austin Kearns/Jsy/100	15.00
16	Bert Blyleven/Jsy/100	15.00
17	Billy Williams/Jsy/100	15.00
19	Bob Feller/Jsy/100	25.00
21	Bobby Doerr/Jsy/100	25.00
22	Brandon Webb/Jsy/100	15.00
23	Brett Myers/Jsy/100	15.00
24	Brooks Robinson/Jsy/100	40.00
27	Carlos Beltran/Jsy/100	40.00
28	Carlos Lee/Jsy/100	15.00
33	Dale Murphy/Jsy/100	30.00
34	Darryl Strawberry/Jsy/100	20.00
35	Dave Concepcion/Jsy/50	20.00
36	Dave Parker/Jsy/100	15.00
38	Don Mattingly/Jsy/50	75.00
39	Dontrelle Willis/Jsy/20	25.00
41	Dwight Gooden/Jsy/60	20.00
42	Edgar Martinez/Jsy/100	30.00
44	Ernie Banks/Jsy/50	50.00
45	Fergie Jenkins/Pants/100	20.00
46	Frank Robinson/Jsy/50	40.00
48	Fred Lynn/Jsy/100	15.00
49	Fred McGriff/Jsy/20	60.00
51	Garret Anderson/Jsy/100	15.00
51	Gary Carter/Expos Jsy/100	20.00
52	Gary Carter/Mets Jkt/100	20.00
53	Gary Sheffield/Jsy/100	20.00
57	Gaylord Perry/Jsy/100	15.00
57	Hank Blalock/Jsy/100	30.00
57	Harold Baines/Jsy/100	20.00
63	Jae Weong Seo/Jsy/100	15.00
64	Jamie Moyer/Jsy/100	15.00
65	Jason Varitek/Jsy/100	30.00
66	Jay Gibbons/Jsy/100	15.00
67	Jim Palmer/Jsy/100	25.00
69	Jim Rice/Jsy/100	20.00
70	Joe Carter/Jsy/50	20.00
71	Johan Santana/Jsy/100	40.00
72	Jorge Posada/Jsy/15	75.00
75	Keith Hernandez/Jsy/100	20.00
77	Luis Tiant /Jsy/100	20.00
82	Mark Mulder/Jsy/20	40.00
85	Marty Marion/Jsy/100	20.00
86	Mike Lowell/Jsy/60	20.00
92	Orlando Cepeda/Bat/65	20.00
97	Phil Niekro/Jsy/100	25.00
99	Ralph Kiner/Jsy/100	25.00
101	Red Schoendienst/Jsy/60	20.00
103	Robin Roberts/Hat/50	25.00
104	Robin Ventura/Jsy/65	25.00
110	Sean Casey/Jsy/75	20.00

111	Shannon Stewart/Jsy/100	15.00
114	Steve Carlton/Jsy/50	40.00
115	Steve Garvey/Bat/100	20.00
117	Tommy John/Jsy/100	15.00
119	Tony Oliva/Jsy/100	20.00
120	Torii Hunter/Jsy/50	20.00
121	Trot Nixon/Jsy/100	30.00
124	Vladimir Guerrero/Jsy/55	50.00
125	Will Clark/Jsy/100	40.00

Absolutely Ink Triple

No Pricing
Production 1-10
Prime: No Pricing
Production 1-5

Marks of Fame

NM/M

Production 100 Sets
Spectrum: 1-2X
Production 25 Sets

1	Nolan Ryan	15.00
2	Ernie Banks	6.00
3	Bob Feller	4.00
4	Duke Snider	5.00
5	Sammy Sosa	8.00
6	Whitey Ford	6.00
7	Steve Carlton	4.00
8	Tony Gwynn	4.00
9	Jim Bunning	4.00
10	Stan Musial	8.00
11	Cal Ripken Jr.	20.00
12	George Brett	4.00
13	Gary Carter	4.00
14	Jim Palmer	4.00
15	Gaylord Perry	4.00

Marks of Fame Signature

NM/M

Quantity produced listed
Spectrum: .75-1.5X
Production 1-25
No pricing 15 or less.

1	Nolan Ryan/50	120.00
2	Ernie Banks/50	50.00
3	Bob Feller/100	25.00
4	Duke Snider/100	25.00
5	Sammy Sosa/21	125.00
6	Whitey Ford/50	50.00
7	Steve Carlton/100	25.00
8	Tony Gwynn/25	75.00
9	Jim Bunning/100	20.00
10	Stan Musial/60	60.00
11	George Brett/25	100.00
12	Gary Carter/100	15.00
14	Jim Palmer/50	25.00
15	Gaylord Perry/100	15.00

Signature Club

NM/M

Quantity produced listed
2	Gary Sheffield/Bat/50	20.00
4	Will Clark/Bat/50	25.00
5	Ernie Banks/Bat/50	50.00

Signature Material

NM/M

Quantity produced listed
Prime: No Pricing
Production Five Sets
Combo: 1X
Production 25-50
Combo Prime: No Pricing
Production Five Sets

| 2 | Gary Carter/Jsy/50 | 25.00 |
| 3 | Dale Murphy/Jsy/50 | 35.00 |

| 4 | Don Mattingly/Jsy/25 | 100.00 |
| 5 | Stan Musial/Jsy/25 | 100.00 |

Signature Spectrum Silver

NM/M

Quantity produced listed.
1	Troy Glaus/34	25.00
2	Garret Anderson/100	15.00
6	Nolan Ryan Angels/25	150.00
7	Vladimir Guerrero/100	40.00
8	Richie Sexson/34	20.00
9	Shea Hillenbrand/100	10.00
11	Brandon Webb/100	10.00
13	Robby Hammock/250	10.00
14	Edgar Gonzalez/100	10.00
15	Roberto Alomar/32	50.00
16	Andruw Jones/50	20.00
18	Dale Murphy/100	15.00
19	Rafael Furcal/100	12.00
21	Bubba Nelson/250	10.00
22	Julio Franco/100	15.00
23	Adam LaRoche/100	10.00
24	Michael Hessman/250	10.00
26	Jay Gibbons/100	10.00
29	Adam Loewen/100	10.00
32	Luis Matos/100	10.00
33	Jason Varitek/50	35.00
36	Trot Nixon/100	15.00
40	Luis Tiant/100	15.00
41	Kevin Youkilis/25	15.00
42	Michel Hernandez/190	10.00
43	Sammy Sosa/21	150.00
45	Kerry Wood/50	40.00
46	Mark Prior/100	40.00
47	Ernie Banks/100	40.00
48	Aramis Ramirez/30	20.00
49	Brendan Harris/250	10.00
50	Todd Wellemeyer/250	10.00
51	Frank Thomas/50	40.00
52	Magglio Ordonez/100	10.00
53	Carlos Lee/100	15.00
54	Joe Crede/100	10.00
55	Joe Borchard/250	10.00
57	Sean Casey/50	10.00
58	Adam Dunn/100	25.00
59	Austin Kearns/100	10.00
61	Barry Larkin/50	30.00
62	Ryan Wagner/100	10.00
63	Jody Gerut/100	10.00
64	Jeremy Guthrie/50	10.00
65	Travis Hafner/100	10.00
66	Brian Tallet/250	10.00
68	Preston Wilson/100	10.00
69	Jeff Baker/50	10.00
70	Clint Barmes/250	10.00
71	Joe Kennedy/250	10.00
73	George Kell/100	15.00
74	Preston Larrison/250	10.00
77	Dontrelle Willis/100	20.00
78	Josh Beckett/25	35.00
79	Miguel Cabrera/100	30.00
80	Mike Lowell/25	25.00
81	Luis Castillo/100	10.00
83	Jeff Bagwell/50	40.00
85	Craig Biggio/50	30.00
86	Lance Berkman/25	40.00
87	Andy Pettitte/25	50.00
88	Roy Oswalt/25	25.00
89	Chris Burke/250	10.00
90	Jason Lane/231	10.00
93	Carlos Beltran/100	25.00
94	Angel Berroa/100	15.00
95	Juan Gonzalez/25	40.00
96	Ken Harvey/200	15.00
97	Byron Gettis/250	10.00
98	Alexis Gomez/250	10.00
99	Ian Ferguson/104	10.00
100	Duke Snider/100	25.00
103	Kazuhisa Ishii/25	10.00
104	Edwin Jackson/100	10.00
105	Fred McGriff/50	15.00
106	Hong-Chih Kuo/50	50.00
107	Don Sutton/100	15.00
109	Cesar Izturis/101	10.00
110	Robin Ventura/25	20.00
111	Paul LoDuca/50	10.00
112	Rickie Weeks/21	40.00
113	Scott Podsednik/100	15.00
114	Junior Spivey/89	10.00
115	Lyle Overbay/89	15.00
116	Tony Oliva/72	15.00
117	Jacque Jones/100	15.00
118	Shannon Stewart/100	15.00
119	Torii Hunter/100	15.00
120	Johan Santana/100	30.00
121	J.D. Durbin/89	10.00
122	Jason Kubel/250	10.00
123	Michael Cuddyer/225	10.00
124	Nick Punto/200	10.00
125	Jose Vidro/25	10.00
126	Orlando Cabrera/25	20.00
127	Zach Day/100	10.00
130	Jae Weong Seo/100	10.00
131	Gary Carter/100	15.00
132	Phil Seibel/177	10.00
133	Edwin Almonte/250	10.00
136	Don Mattingly/50	50.00
139	Jorge Posada/50	40.00
144	Gary Sheffield/100	15.00
146	Chien-Ming Wang/50	150.00
147	Javier Vazquez/25	15.00
148	Jose Contreras/25	35.00
149	Whitey Ford/100	40.00
151	Eric Chavez/50	25.00
153	Mark Mulder/100	25.00
154	Tim Hudson/50	30.00
155	Rich Harden/100	15.00
156	Eric Byrnes/250	10.00

159	Marlon Byrd/100	10.00
160	Lenny Dykstra/100	15.00
161	Steve Carlton/100	25.00
162	Ryan Howard/250	75.00
163	Bobby Hill/250	10.00
164	Jose Castillo/100	10.00
165	Jay Payton/100	10.00
168	Henri Stanley/112	10.00
170	Jerome Williams/100	15.00
171	J.T. Snow/89	15.00
173	Edgar Martinez/50	30.00
175	Jamie Moyer/19	15.00
176	Rich Aurilia/25	15.00
177	Chris Snelling/177	10.00
180	Scott Rolen/100	30.00
181	Jim Edmonds/50	10.00
182	Stan Musial/100	60.00
183	Red Schoendienst/100	15.00
184	Aubrey Huff/100	10.00
185	Delmon Young/100	10.00
186	Rocco Baldelli/50	20.00
187	Dewon Brazelton/50	10.00
188	Mark Teixeira/100	20.00
189	Hank Blalock/30	30.00
190	Nolan Ryan Rgr/25	125.00
192	Michael Young/100	25.00
194	Roy Halladay/50	10.00
196	Dustin McGowan/250	10.00
197	Josh Phelps/75	10.00
198	Alexis Rios/100	15.00
200	Josh Towers/158	10.00
202	Fernando Nieve/250	10.00
204	Dennis Sarfate/100	10.00
205	Josh Labandeira/250	10.00
206	Chris Oxspring/250	10.00
207	Alfredo Simon/100	10.00
208	Cory Sullivan/100	10.00
209	Ruddy Yan/250	10.00
210	Jason Bartlett/250	10.00
211	Akinori Otsuka/50	10.00
212	Lincoln Holdzkom/250	10.00
213	Justin Leone/250	10.00
214	Jorge Sequea/250	10.00
215	John Gall/50	25.00
217	Tim Bittner/250	10.00
219	Justin Hampson/250	10.00
220	Ryan Wing/100	10.00
221	Mariano Gomez/250	10.00
222	Carlos Vasquez/250	10.00
223	Casey Daigle/150	10.00
224	Renyel Pinto/250	10.00
225	Chris Shelton/250	35.00
229	Roberto Novoa/250	10.00
230	Sean Henn/250	10.00
231	Jamie Brown/200	10.00
232	Nick Regilio/250	10.00
234	Greg Dobbs/250	10.00
235	Angel Chavez/250	10.00
236	Willy Taveras/225	10.00
237	Justin Knoedler/225	10.00
239	Jason Frasor/225	10.00
240	Jerry Gil/225	10.00
241	Carlos Hines/225	10.00
242	Ivan Ochoa/250	10.00
248	Graham Koonce/250	10.00
249	Ronald Belisario/225	10.00

Signature Spectrum Gold

NM/M

Quantity produced listed
1	Troy Glaus/15	35.00
2	Garret Anderson/100	15.00
7	Vladimir Guerrero/25	60.00
8	Richie Sexson/25	25.00
9	Shea Hillenbrand/100	10.00
11	Brandon Webb/100	10.00
15	Roberto Alomar/50	50.00
18	Dale Murphy/100	25.00
19	Rafael Furcal/100	12.00
22	Julio Franco/100	10.00
23	Adam LaRoche/100	10.00
26	Jay Gibbons/100	10.00
29	Adam Loewen/100	10.00
32	Luis Matos/100	15.00
33	Jason Varitek/100	40.00
36	Trot Nixon/100	20.00
40	Luis Tiant/50	15.00
41	Kevin Youkilis/25	20.00
45	Kerry Wood/50	40.00
46	Mark Prior/100	40.00
47	Ernie Banks/100	40.00
52	Magglio Ordonez/100	15.00
53	Carlos Lee/100	15.00
54	Joe Crede/50	15.00
59	Austin Kearns/100	10.00
61	Barry Larkin/25	40.00
62	Ryan Wagner/100	10.00
63	Jody Gerut/100	15.00
64	Jeremy Guthrie/25	15.00
65	Travis Hafner/25	25.00
68	Preston Wilson/100	10.00
69	Jeff Baker/25	15.00
73	George Kell/100	15.00
79	Miguel Cabrera/35	35.00
81	Luis Castillo/50	10.00
83	Jeff Bagwell/25	50.00
87	Andy Pettitte/25	50.00
93	Carlos Beltran/25	40.00
94	Angel Berroa/100	10.00
100	Duke Snider/25	25.00
103	Edwin Jackson/50	10.00
106	Hong-Chih Kuo/50	75.00
107	Don Sutton/25	25.00
112	Rickie Weeks/24	40.00
113	Scott Podsednik/100	10.00
116	Tony Oliva/50	25.00

117	Jacque Jones/100	15.00
119	Torii Hunter/100	15.00
130	Jae Weong Seo/100	10.00
131	Gary Carter/100	15.00
136	Don Mattingly/100	50.00
139	Jorge Posada/50	50.00
144	Gary Sheffield/25	25.00
146	Chien-Ming Wang/25	180.00
153	Mark Mulder/50	15.00
155	Rich Harden/50	15.00
159	Marlon Byrd/100	10.00
160	Lenny Dykstra/100	15.00
161	Steve Carlton/50	40.00
164	Jose Castillo/50	15.00
165	Jay Payton/100	10.00
170	Jerome Williams/50	25.00
178	Scott Rolen/50	40.00
181	Stan Musial/100	60.00
182	Dan Haren/25	15.00
183	Red Schoendienst/100	15.00
184	Aubrey Huff/100	10.00
185	Delmon Young/100	20.00
187	Dewon Brazelton/25	15.00
188	Mark Teixeira/50	30.00
189	Hank Blalock/25	40.00
192	Michael Young/25	25.00
194	Roy Halladay/25	25.00
198	Alexis Rios/50	25.00
202	Fernando Nieve/100	10.00
205	Josh Labandeira/100	10.00
206	Chris Oxspring/100	15.00
207	Cory Sullivan/100	10.00
209	Ruddy Yan/100	10.00
210	Jason Bartlett/100	15.00
212	Lincoln Holdzkom/100	10.00
213	Justin Leone/100	10.00
214	Jorge Sequea/100	10.00
217	Tim Bittner/100	10.00
219	Justin Hampson/100	10.00
220	Ryan Wing/100	10.00
221	Mariano Gomez/100	10.00
222	Carlos Vasquez/100	10.00
224	Renyel Pinto/100	10.00
230	Sean Henn/100	10.00
232	Nick Regilio/100	10.00
234	Greg Dobbs/100	15.00
235	Angel Chavez/100	10.00
242	Ivan Ochoa/100	10.00
248	Graham Koonce/100	10.00

Team Tandem

NM/M

Production 250 Sets
Spectrum: 2-4X
Production 25 Sets
1	Vladimir Guerrero, Reggie Jackson	3.00
2	Dale Murphy, Chipper Jones	3.00
3	Gary Carter, Mike Piazza	4.00
4	Miguel Tejada, Cal Ripken Jr.	8.00
5	Gary Sheffield, Derek Jeter	6.00
6	Curt Schilling, Pedro J. Martinez	3.00
7	Roger Clemens, Andy Pettitte	5.00
8	Mike Sweeney, George Brett	6.00
9	Kazuhisa Ishii, Hideo Nomo	3.00
10	Austin Kearns, Adam Dunn	
11	Miguel Cabrera, Dontrelle Willis	
12	Don Mattingly, Derek Jeter	8.00
13	Barry Zito, Eric Chavez	2.00
14	Jim Thome, Mike Schmidt	4.00
15	Albert Pujols, Stan Musial	8.00
16	Nolan Ryan, Alex Rodriguez	8.00
17	Kerry Wood, Mark Prior	4.00
18	Rafael Palmeiro, Jay Gibbons	3.00
19	Nomar Garciaparra, Manny Ramirez	4.00
20	Ivan Rodriguez, Mike Piazza	4.00

Team Tandem Material

NM/M

Production 250 Sets
Prime: No Pricing
Production Five Sets
1	Reggie Jackson/Bat, Vladimir Guerrero/Bat	10.00
2	Chipper Jones/Jsy, Dale Murphy/Jsy	10.00
3	Gary Carter/Jsy, Mike Piazza/Jsy	10.00
4	Miguel Tejada/Bat, Cal Ripken Jr./Bat	25.00
5	Derek Jeter/Bat, Gary Sheffield/Bat	25.00
6	Curt Schilling/Bat, Pedro J. Martinez/Bat	10.00
7	Roger Clemens/Bat, Andy Pettitte/Bat	15.00
8	Mike Sweeney/Jsy, George Brett/Jsy	10.00
9	Kazuhisa Ishii/Jsy, Hideo Nomo/Jsy	10.00

10	Austin Kearns/Jsy, Adam Dunn/Jsy 10.00
11	Dontrelle Willis/Jsy, Miguel Cabrera/Jsy 10.00
12	Don Mattingly/Jsy, Derek Jeter/Jsy 35.00
13	Barry Zito/Jsy, Eric Chavez/Jsy 8.00
14	Jim Thome/Jsy, Mike Schmidt/Jsy 20.00
15	Albert Pujols/Jsy, Stan Musial/Jsy 40.00
16	Nolan Ryan/Jsy, Alex Rodriguez/Jsy 25.00
17	Mark Prior/Jsy, Kerry Wood/Jsy 15.00
18	Rafael Palmeiro/Jsy, Jay Gibbons/Jsy 10.00
19	Nomar Garciaparra/Jsy, Manny Ramirez/Jsy 15.00
20	Ivan Rodriguez/Jsy, Mike Piazza/Jsy 10.00

Team Trio
NM/M
Production 100 Sets
Spectrum: 1.5-2X
Production 25 Sets
1 Sammy Sosa, Kerry Wood, Mark Prior
2 Hank Blalock, Mark Teixeira, Alex Rodriguez
3 Vernon Wells, Roy Halladay, Carlos Delgado 4.00
4 Mike Mussina, Jorge Posada, Mariano Rivera 6.00
5 Shannon Stewart, Torii Hunter, Jacque Jones 4.00
6 Carlos Beltran, Mike Sweeney, Angel Berroa 4.00
7 Dontrelle Willis, Miguel Cabrera, Josh Beckett 6.00
8 Jeff Bagwell, Craig Biggio, Lance Berkman 6.00
9 Nomar Garciaparra, Pedro J. Martinez, Manny Ramirez 10.00
10 Shawn Green, Kazuhisa Ishii, Hideo Nomo
11 Mark Mulder, Barry Zito, Tim Hudson 4.00
12 Jim Edmonds, Scott Rolen, Albert Pujols 15.00
13 Cal Ripken Jr., Jay Gibbons, Rafael Palmeiro 20.00
14 Sammy Sosa, Mark Grace, Ryne Sandberg
15 Nolan Ryan, Roger Clemens, Randy Johnson 20.00

Team Trio Material
NM/M
Production 100 Sets
Prime: No Pricing
Production Five Sets
1 Sammy Sosa, Kerry Wood, Mark Prior 25.00
2 Hank Blalock, Mark Teixeira, Alex Rodriguez 15.00
3 Vernon Wells, Roy Halladay, Carlos Delgado 8.00
4 Mike Mussina, Jorge Posada, Mariano Rivera 25.00
5 Shannon Stewart, Torii Hunter, Jacque Jones 8.00
6 Carlos Beltran, Mike Sweeney, Angel Berroa 8.00
7 Dontrelle Willis, Miguel Cabrera, Josh Beckett 15.00
8 Jeff Bagwell, Craig Biggio, Lance Berkman 10.00
9 Nomar Garciaparra, Pedro J. Martinez, Manny Ramirez 20.00
10 Shawn Green, Kazuhisa Ishii, Hideo Nomo
11 Mark Mulder, Barry Zito, Tim Hudson 8.00
12 Jim Edmonds, Scott Rolen, Albert Pujols 25.00
13 Cal Ripken Jr., Jay Gibbons, Rafael Palmeiro 40.00
14 Sammy Sosa, Mark Grace, Ryne Sandberg 35.00
15 Nolan Ryan, Roger Clemens, Randy Johnson/25 80.00

Team Quad
NM/M
Production 100 Sets
Spectrum: 1.5-2X
Production 25 Sets
1 Jeff Kent, Lance Berkman, Craig Biggio, Jeff Bagwell 6.00
2 Nomar Garciaparra, Manny Ramirez, Pedro Martinez, Trot Nixon 10.00
3 Paul Konerko, Carlos Lee, Magglio Ordonez, Frank Thomas 6.00

4 John Smoltz, Chipper Jones, Andruw Jones, Rafael Furcal 6.00
5 Garret Anderson, Troy Percival, Troy Glaus, Darin Erstad
6 Steve Finley, Brandon Webb, Randy Johnson, Luis Gonzalez 6.00
7 Paul LoDuca, Hideo Nomo, Shawn Green, Kazuhisa Ishii 6.00
8 Larry Walker, Todd Helton, Jason Jennings, Preston Wilson 10.00
9 Dontrelle Willis, Brad Penny, Josh Beckett 4.00
10 Jose Reyes, Jae Weong Seo, Tom Glavine, Mike Piazza 10.00
11 Bernie Williams, Derek Jeter, Jason Giambi, Alfonso Soriano 15.00
12 Rich Harden, Tim Hudson, Barry Zito, Mark Mulder 4.00
13 Kevin Millwood, Marlon Byrd, Jim Thome, Bobby Abreu 8.00
14 Edgar Renteria, Jim Edmonds, Albert Pujols, Scott Rolen 10.00
15 Roger Clemens, Andy Pettitte, Wade Miller, Roy Oswalt 10.00

Team Quad Material
NM/M
Production 100 Sets
Prime: No Pricing
Production Five Sets
1 Jeff Kent, Lance Berkman, Craig Biggio, Jeff Bagwell 20.00
2 Nomar Garciaparra, Manny Ramirez, Pedro Martinez, Trot Nixon 35.00
3 Paul Konerko, Carlos Lee, Magglio Ordonez, Frank Thomas 20.00
4 John Smoltz, Chipper Jones, Andruw Jones, Rafael Furcal 20.00
5 Garret Anderson, Troy Percival, Troy Glaus, Darin Erstad 10.00
6 Steve Finley, Brandon Webb, Randy Johnson, Luis Gonzalez 20.00
7 Paul LoDuca, Hideo Nomo, Shawn Green, Kazuhisa Ishii 20.00
8 Larry Walker, Todd Helton, Jason Jennings, Preston Wilson 20.00
9 Dontrelle Willis, Brad Penny, Josh Beckett 20.00
10 Jose Reyes, Jae Weong Seo, Tom Glavine, Mike Piazza
11 Bernie Williams, Derek Jeter, Jason Giambi, Alfonso Soriano 40.00
12 Rich Harden, Tim Hudson, Barry Zito, Mark Mulder 10.00
13 Kevin Millwood, Marlon Byrd, Jim Thome, Bobby Abreu 20.00
14 Edgar Renteria, Jim Edmonds, Albert Pujols, Scott Rolen 40.00
15 Roger Clemens, Andy Pettitte, Wade Miller, Roy Oswalt 30.00

Tools of Trade Blue
NM/M
Common Player: 1.50
Production 250 Sets
Black: No Pricing
Production One Set
Blue Spectrum: 1-1.5X
Production 125 Sets
Green: 1-1.5X
Production 150 Sets
Green Spectrum: 2-3X
Production 50 Sets
Red: 1X
Production 200 Sets
Red Spectrum: 1-2X
Production 100 Sets
1 Adam Dunn/H 2.50
2 Adam Dunn/A 2.50
3 Alan Trammell 2.00
4 Albert Pujols/H 6.00
5 Albert Pujols/A 6.00
6 Alex Rodriguez 6.00
7 Alex Rodriguez 6.00
8 Alfonso Soriano 4.00
9 Andre Dawson 2.00
10 Andruw Jones/H 2.00
11 Andruw Jones/A 2.00
12 Andy Pettitte/H 2.00
13 Andy Pettitte/A 2.00
14 Angel Berroa 1.50
15 Aubrey Huff 1.50
16 Austin Kearns 2.00
17 Barry Zito 2.00
18 Barry Zito 2.00
19 Barry Zito/A 2.00
20 Bernie Williams 2.00
21 Bobby Abreu 2.00
22 Brandon Webb 1.50
23 Cal Ripken Jr./H 8.00
24 Cal Ripken Jr./A 8.00
25 Cal Ripken Jr. 8.00
26 Carlos Beltran 2.00
27 Carlos Delgado/H 2.00
28 Carlos Delgado/A 2.00
29 Carlos Lee 1.50
30 Chipper Jones/H 3.00
31 Chipper Jones/A 3.00
32 Craig Biggio/H 2.00
33 Craig Biggio/A 2.00
34 Curt Schilling 2.00
35 Curt Schilling 2.00
36 Dale Murphy/H 2.00
37 Dale Murphy/A 2.00
38 Darryl Strawberry 1.50
39 Derek Jeter/H 8.00
40 Derek Jeter/A 8.00
41 Don Mattingly/H 8.00
42 Don Mattingly/A 8.00
43 Dontrelle Willis/H 2.00
44 Dontrelle Willis/A 2.00
45 Dwight Gooden 1.50
46 Edgar Martinez 1.50
47 Eric Chavez 2.00
48 Frank Thomas/A 2.00
49 Frank Thomas 2.00
50 Garret Anderson 2.00
51 Gary Carter 2.00
52 Gary Sheffield 2.00
53 George Brett/H 6.00
54 George Brett/A 6.00
55 Greg Maddux 4.00
56 Hank Blalock 2.00
57 Hideo Nomo 2.00
58 Ivan Rodriguez 2.00
59 Ivan Rodriguez 2.00
60 Jacque Jones 1.50
61 Jae Weong Seo 1.50
62 Jason Giambi 2.00
63 Jason Giambi 2.00
64 Javy Lopez 2.00
65 Jay Gibbons 1.50
66 Jeff Bagwell 2.00
67 Jeff Bagwell 2.00
68 Jeff Kent 1.50
69 Jim Edmonds 2.00
70 Jim Thome 3.00
71 Jorge Posada 2.00
72 Jose Canseco 2.00
73 Jose Reyes 2.00
74 Josh Beckett 2.00
75 Juan Gonzalez 2.00
76 Kazuhisa Ishii 1.50
77 Kerry Wood 3.00
78 Kerry Wood 3.00
79 Kirby Puckett 3.00
80 Lance Berkman 2.00
81 Lou Brock 2.00
82 Luis Castillo 1.50
83 Luis Gonzalez 1.50
84 Magglio Ordonez 1.50
85 Manny Ramirez 2.00
86 Manny Ramirez 2.00
87 Marcus Giles 1.50
88 Mark Grace 2.00
89 Mark Mulder 2.00
90 Mark Prior 4.00
91 Mark Prior 4.00
92 Mark Teixeira 2.00
93 Marlon Byrd 1.50
94 Miguel Cabrera 3.00
95 Miguel Tejada 2.00
96 Mike Lowell 2.00
97 Mike Mussina 2.00
98 Mike Mussina 2.00
99 Mike Piazza 4.00
100 Mike Piazza 4.00
101 Mike Piazza 4.00
102 Mike Schmidt 5.00
103 Mike Schmidt 5.00
104 Mike Sweeney 1.50
105 Nick Johnson 1.50
106 Nolan Ryan 8.00
107 Nolan Ryan 8.00
108 Nolan Ryan 8.00
109 Nomar Garciaparra 5.00
110 Nomar Garciaparra 5.00
111 Pat Burrell 2.00
112 Paul LoDuca 1.50
113 Pedro Martinez 3.00
114 Pedro Martinez 3.00
115 Preston Wilson 1.50
116 Rafael Palmeiro 2.00
117 Rafael Palmeiro 2.00
118 Randy Johnson 4.00
119 Randy Johnson 4.00
120 Richie Sexson 2.00
121 Rickey Henderson 2.00
122 Rickey Henderson 2.00
123 Rickey Henderson 2.00
124 Roberto Alomar 2.00
125 Rocco Baldelli 2.00
126 Rod Carew 2.00
127 Roger Clemens 6.00
128 Roger Clemens 6.00
129 Roy Halladay 2.00
130 Roy Oswalt 1.50
131 Ryne Sandberg 5.00
132 Sammy Sosa 5.00
133 Sammy Sosa 5.00
134 Sammy Sosa 5.00
135 Scott Rolen 4.00
136 Shawn Green 2.00
137 Steve Carlton 2.00
138 Tim Hudson 2.00
139 Todd Helton 2.00
140 Todd Helton 2.00
141 Tom Glavine 2.00
142 Tom Glavine 2.00
143 Tony Gwynn 4.00
144 Tony Gwynn 4.00
145 Torii Hunter 2.00
146 Trot Nixon 2.00
147 Troy Glaus 2.00
148 Vernon Wells 2.00
149 Vladimir Guerrero 4.00
150 Will Clark 3.00

Tools of Trade Sig Blue Spectrum
NM/M
Quantity produced listed
Black: No Pricing
Production One Set
Green: No Pricing
Production 1-10
Red: .75-1.5X
Production 1-50
No pricing 15 or less.
3 Alan Trammell/100 15.00
10 Andre Dawson/100 15.00
16 Angel Berroa/100 8.00
16 Aubrey Huff/100 10.00
17 Austin Kearns/100 15.00
22 Brandon Webb/100 8.00
26 Carlos Beltran/100 20.00
29 Carlos Lee/100 15.00
36 Dale Murphy H/50 30.00
37 Dale Murphy A/50 30.00
38 Darryl Strawberry/50 30.00
41 Don Mattingly H/50 75.00
42 Don Mattingly A/50 75.00
43 Dontrelle Willis H/25 30.00
44 Dontrelle Willis A/25 30.00
45 Dwight Gooden/50 25.00
46 Edgar Martinez/25 50.00
48 Frank Thomas A/25 50.00
49 Frank Thomas/50 50.00
50 Garret Anderson/100 15.00
51 Gary Carter/100 15.00
60 Jacque Jones/50 20.00
61 Jae Weong Seo/25 25.00
65 Jay Gibbons/50 15.00
69 Jim Edmonds/25 35.00
71 Jorge Posada/25 40.00
73 Jose Reyes/25 25.00
75 Juan Gonzalez/20 41.00
77 Kerry Wood H/25 50.00
78 Kerry Wood/25 50.00
81 Lou Brock/100 25.00
84 Magglio Ordonez/50 20.00
87 Marcus Giles/50 40.00
88 Mark Grace/25 40.00
89 Mark Mulder/100 25.00
90 Mark Prior H/50 60.00
91 Mark Prior A/50 60.00
92 Mark Teixeira/50 30.00
93 Marlon Byrd/50 15.00
94 Miguel Cabrera/100 35.00
102 Mike Schmidt H/25 75.00
103 Mike Schmidt A/25 75.00
106 Nolan Ryan/25 125.00
107 Nolan Ryan/25 125.00
108 Nolan Ryan/25 125.00
112 Paul LoDuca/50 25.00
115 Preston Wilson/100 15.00
129 Roy Halladay/25 30.00
130 Roy Oswalt/25 25.00
135 Scott Rolen/50 40.00
137 Steve Carlton/30 30.00
143 Tony Gwynn A/25 60.00
144 Tony Gwynn/25 60.00
145 Torii Hunter/50 25.00
146 Trot Nixon/25 30.00
149 Vladimir Guerrero/65 65.00
150 Will Clark/50 50.00

Tools of Trade Mater. Sig. Sing
NM/M
Quantity produced listed.
Combo: 1-2X
Production 1-25
Combo Prime: No Pricing
Production 1-5
Trio: No Pricing
Production 1-10
Quad: No Pricing
Production 1-10
1 Adam Dunn/H/Jsy/25 50.00
2 Adam Dunn/A/Jsy/25 50.00
3 Alan Trammell/Jsy/25 50.00
10 Andre Dawson/Jsy/25 25.00
15 Angel Berroa/Jsy/50 15.00
17 Austin Kearns/28 25.00
21 Bobby Abreu/Jsy/25 25.00
22 Brandon Webb/Jsy/25 25.00
26 Carlos Beltran/Jsy/15 25.00
29 Carlos Lee/Jsy/25 25.00
36 Dale Murphy/Jsy/25 40.00
37 Dale Murphy/Jsy/25 40.00
38 Darryl Strawberry/ Jsy/39
43 Dontrelle Willis/Jsy/25 30.00
44 Dontrelle Willis/Jsy/25 30.00
45 Dwight Gooden/Jsy/16 35.00
50 Garret Anderson/Jsy/16 30.00
61 Jae Weong Seo/Jsy/25
71 Jorge Posada/Jsy/20 60.00
74 Josh Beckett/Jsy/21 40.00

82 Luis Castillo/Jsy/25 20.00
89 Mark Mulder/Jsy/20 40.00
93 Marlon Byrd/Jsy/29 20.00
94 Miguel Cabrera/Jsy/20 50.00
96 Mike Lowell/Jsy/19 30.00
112 Paul LoDuca/Jsy/25 25.00
115 Preston Wilson/Jsy/44 20.00
125 Rocco Baldelli/Jsy/25 30.00
129 Roy Halladay/Jsy/32 25.00
137 Steve Carlton/Jsy/25 50.00
145 Torii Hunter/Jsy/25 25.00
146 Trot Nixon/Jsy/25 50.00

Tools of Trade Mater. Combo
NM/M
Production 25-250
Single: No Pricing
Production 1-5
Combo Price Single: 2-4X
Production 1-25
Trio: 1-30X
Production 5-100
No pricing 15 or less.
Quad: 2-4X
Production 1-50
No pricing 15 or less.
Five: 3-5X
Production 10-25
Six: 3-6X
Production 5-25
1 Adam Dunn/Bat-Jsy/250 6.00
2 Adam Dunn/Bat-Jsy/250 6.00
3 Alan Trammell/ Bat-Jsy/250 4.00
4 Albert Pujols/ Bat-Jsy/250 20.00
5 Albert Pujols/ Bat-Jsy/250 20.00
6 Alex Rodriguez/ Bat-Jsy/250 10.00
7 Alex Rodriguez/ Bat-Jsy/250 10.00
7 Alex Rodriguez/ Bat-Jsy/250 10.00
8 Alex Rodriguez/ Bat-Jsy/100 10.00
9 Alfonso Soriano/ Bat-Jsy/100 10.00
10 Andre Dawson/ Bat-Jsy 5.00
11 Andruw Jones/ Bat-Jsy/100 8.00
12 Andruw Jones/ Bat-Jsy/250 8.00
13 Andy Pettitte/ Bat-Jsy/100 10.00
14 Andy Pettitte/ Bat-Jsy/100 10.00
15 Angel Berroa/ Bat-Jsy 4.00
16 Aubrey Huff/Bat-Jsy/250 4.00
17 Austin Kearns/ Bat-Jsy/250 6.00
18 Barry Zito/Bat-Jsy/250 6.00
19 Barry Zito/Bat-Jsy/250 6.00
20 Bernie Williams/ Bat-Jsy/250 8.00
21 Bobby Abreu/ Bat-Jsy/250 6.00
22 Brandon Webb/ Bat-Jsy/250 4.00
23 Cal Ripken Jr./ Bat-Jsy/250 30.00
24 Cal Ripken Jr./ Bat-Jsy/250 30.00
25 Cal Ripken Jr./ Bat-Jsy/250 30.00
26 Carlos Beltran/ Bat-Jsy/250 6.00
27 Carlos Delgado/ Bat-Jsy/250 6.00
28 Carlos Delgado/ Bat-Jsy/250 6.00
29 Carlos Lee/Bat-Jsy/250 4.00
30 Chipper Jones/ Bat-Jsy/250 10.00
31 Chipper Jones/ Bat-Jsy/250 10.00
32 Craig Biggio/Bat-Jsy/250 6.00
33 Craig Biggio/Bat-Jsy/100 6.00
34 Curt Schilling/ Bat-Jsy/250 6.00
35 Curt Schilling/ Bat-Jsy/250 8.00
36 Dale Murphy/Bat-Jsy/250 8.00
37 Dale Murphy/Bat-Jsy/100 8.00
38 Darryl Strawberry/ Bat-Jsy/250 4.00
39 Derek Jeter/Bat-Jsy/250 30.00
40 Derek Jeter/Bat-Jsy/100 30.00
41 Don Mattingly/ Bat-Jsy/250 15.00
42 Don Mattingly/ Bat-Jsy/250 15.00
43 Dontrelle Willis/ Bat-Jsy/250 6.00
44 Dontrelle Willis/ Bat-Jsy/250 6.00
45 Dwight Gooden/ Bat-Jsy/250 6.00
46 Edgar Martinez/ Bat-Jsy/250 6.00
47 Eric Chavez/Bat-Jsy/250 6.00
48 Frank Thomas/ Bat-Jsy/250 10.00
49 Frank Thomas/ Bat-Jsy/250 10.00
50 Garret Anderson/ Bat-Jsy/250 10.00
51 Gary Carter/Bat-Jsy/250 6.00
52 Gary Sheffield/ Bat-Jsy/250 6.00
53 George Brett/ Bat-Jsy/250 20.00
54 George Brett/ Bat-Jsy/250 20.00
55 Greg Maddux/ Bat-Jsy/250 10.00
56 Hank Blalock/ Bat-Jsy/250 8.00
57 Hideo Nomo/ Bat-Jsy/250 10.00
58 Ivan Rodriguez/ Bat-Jsy/250 8.00
59 Ivan Rodriguez/ Bat-Jsy/250 8.00
60 Jacque Jones/ Bat-Jsy/250 4.00
62 Jason Giambi/ Bat-Jsy/250 8.00
63 Jason Giambi/ Bat-Jsy/250 8.00
64 Javy Lopez/Bat-Jsy/250 6.00
65 Jay Gibbons/Bat-Jsy/250 4.00
66 Jeff Bagwell/Bat-Jsy/250 8.00
67 Jeff Bagwell/Bat-Jsy/250 8.00
68 Jeff Kent/Bat-Jsy/250 8.00
69 Jim Edmonds/ Bat-Jsy/250 8.00
70 Jim Thome/Bat-Jsy/250 12.00
71 Jorge Posada/ Bat-Jsy/250 8.00
72 Jose Canseco/ Bat-Jsy/250 8.00
73 Jose Reyes/Bat-Jsy/250 8.00
74 Josh Beckett/Bat-Jsy/250 8.00
75 Juan Gonzalez/ Bat-Jsy/250 8.00
76 Kazuhisa Ishii/ Bat-Jsy/250 4.00
77 Kerry Wood/ Bat-Jsy/250 10.00
78 Kerry Wood/ Bat-Jsy/250 10.00
79 Kirby Puckett/ Bat-Jsy/250 10.00
80 Lance Berkman/ Bat-Jsy/250 8.00
81 Lou Brock/Bat-Jsy/250 8.00
82 Luis Castillo/Bat-Jsy/250 4.00
83 Luis Gonzalez/ Bat-Jsy/250 4.00
84 Magglio Ordonez/ Bat-Jsy/250 6.00
85 Manny Ramirez/ Bat-Jsy/250 8.00
86 Manny Ramirez/ Bat-Jsy/250 8.00
87 Marcus Giles/ Bat-Jsy/250 10.00
88 Mark Grace/Bat-Jsy/250 8.00
89 Mark Mulder/Bat-Jsy/250 6.00
90 Mark Prior/Bat-Jsy/250 10.00
91 Mark Prior/Bat-Jsy/250 10.00
92 Mark Teixeira/ Bat-Jsy/250 6.00
93 Marlon Byrd/Bat-Jsy/250 4.00
94 Miguel Cabrera/ Bat-Jsy/250 10.00
95 Miguel Tejada/ Bat-Jsy/250 6.00
96 Mike Lowell/Bat-Jsy/250 6.00
97 Mike Mussina/ Jsy-Pants/250 8.00
98 Mike Mussina/ Jsy/250 8.00
99 Mike Piazza/ Bat-Jsy/250 12.00
100 Mike Piazza/ Bat-Jsy/250 12.00
101 Mike Piazza/ Bat-Jsy/250 12.00
102 Mike Schmidt/ Bat-Jsy/250 20.00
103 Mike Schmidt/ Bat-Jsy/250 20.00
104 Mike Sweeney/ Bat-Jsy/250 4.00
105 Nick Johnson/ Bat-Jsy/250 4.00
106 Nolan Ryan/Jkt-Jsy/250 30.00
107 Nolan Ryan/Jkt-Jsy/250 30.00
108 Nolan Ryan/ Jsy-Pants/250 30.00
109 Nomar Garciaparra/ Bat-Jsy/250 15.00
110 Nomar Garciaparra/ Bat-Jsy/250 15.00
111 Pat Burrell/Bat-Jsy/250 6.00
112 Paul LoDuca/Bat-Jsy/250 4.00
113 Pedro J. Martinez/ Bat-Jsy/250
114 Pedro Martinez/ Bat-Jsy/250 10.00
115 Preston Wilson/ Bat-Jsy/250 4.00
116 Rafael Palmeiro/ Bat-Jsy/250 8.00
117 Rafael Palmeiro/ Bat-Jsy/250 8.00
118 Randy Johnson/ Bat-Jsy/250 10.00
119 Randy Johnson/ Bat-Jsy/250 10.00
120 Richie Sexson/ Bat-Jsy/250 6.00
121 Rickey Henderson/ Bat-Jsy/250

#	Card	Price
122	Rickey Henderson/Bat-Jsy/250	8.00
123	Rickey Henderson/Bat-Jsy/250	8.00
124	Roberto Alomar/Bat-Jsy/250	8.00
125	Rocco Baldelli/Bat-Jsy/250	6.00
126	Rod Carew/Bat-Jsy/250	8.00
127	Roger Clemens/Bat-Jsy/250	15.00
128	Roger Clemens/Bat-Jsy/250	15.00
129	Roy Halladay/Jsy/250	4.00
130	Roy Oswalt/Bat-Jsy/250	6.00
131	Ryne Sandberg/Bat-Jsy/250	15.00
132	Sammy Sosa/Bat-Jsy/250	15.00
133	Sammy Sosa/Bat-Jsy/250	15.00
134	Sammy Sosa/Bat-Jsy/250	15.00
135	Scott Rolen/Bat-Jsy/250	10.00
136	Shawn Green/Bat-Jsy/250	6.00
137	Steve Carlton/Bat-Jsy/250	6.00
138	Tim Hudson/Bat-Jsy/250	6.00
139	Todd Helton/Bat-Jsy/250	8.00
140	Todd Helton/Bat-Jsy/250	8.00
141	Tom Glavine/Bat-Jsy/250	8.00
142	Tom Glavine/Bat-Jsy/250	8.00
143	Tony Gwynn/Bat-Jsy/250	12.00
144	Tony Gwynn/Bat-Jsy/250	12.00
145	Torii Hunter/Bat-Jsy/250	6.00
146	Trot Nixon/Bat-Jsy/250	6.00
147	Troy Glaus/Bat-Jsy/250	6.00
148	Vernon Wells/Bat-Jsy/250	4.00
149	Vladimir Guerrero/Bat-Jsy/250	10.00
150	Will Clark/Bat-Jsy/250	10.00

2004 Playoff Honors

NM/M
Complete Set (250):
Common Player (1-200): .15
Common SP (201-250): 3.00
Production 1,999
Common SP Auto. (226-250): 8.00
Pack (6): 5.00
Box (12): 55.00

#	Player	Price
1	Bartolo Colon	.15
2	Garret Anderson	.40
3	Tim Salmon	.25
4	Troy Glaus	.25
5	Vladimir Guerrero	.75
6	Brandon Webb	.15
7	Brian Bruney	.15
8	Luis Gonzalez	.25
9	Randy Johnson	.75
10	Richie Sexson	.40
11	Robby Hammock	.15
12	Roberto Alomar	.40
13	Shea Hillenbrand	.15
14	Steve Finley	.15
15	Adam LaRoche	.15
16	Andruw Jones	.50
17	Bubba Nelson	.15
18	Chipper Jones	.75
19	Dale Murphy	.50
20	J.D. Drew	.25
21	John Smoltz	.25
22	Marcus Giles	.15
23	Rafael Furcal	.25
24	Warren Spahn	.75
25	Greg Maddux	1.00
26	Adam Loewen	.15
27	Cal Ripken Jr.	3.00
28	Javy Lopez	.25
29	Jay Gibbons	.15
30	Luis Matos	.15
31	Miguel Tejada	.40
32	Rafael Palmeiro	.50
33	Bobby Doerr	.15
34	Curt Schilling	.50
35	Edwin Almonte	.15
36	Jason Varitek	.25
37	Kevin Youkilis	.15
38	Manny Ramirez	.50
39	Nomar Garciaparra	1.00
40	Pedro J. Martinez	.75
41	Trot Nixon	.25
42	Andre Dawson	.25
43	Aramis Ramirez	.40
44	Brendan Harris	.15
45	Derrek Lee	.25
46	Ernie Banks	.75
47	Kerry Wood	.75
48	Mark Prior	1.00
49	Ryne Sandberg	1.00
50	Sammy Sosa	1.50
51	Carlos Lee	.15
52	Frank Thomas	.50
53	Joe Borchard	.15
54	Joe Crede	.15
55	Magglio Ordonez	.25
56	Adam Dunn	.50
57	Austin Kearns	.25
58	Barry Larkin	.40
59	Brandon Larson	.15
60	Ken Griffey Jr.	1.00
61	Ryan Wagner	.15
62	Sean Casey	.25
63	Bob Feller	.25
64	Brian Tallet	.15
65	C.C. Sabathia	.25
66	Jeremy Guthrie	.15
67	Jody Gerut	.15
68	Clint Barmes	.15
69	Jeff Baker	.15
70	Joe Kennedy	.15
71	Larry Walker	.25
72	Preston Wilson	.15
73	Todd Helton	.50
74	Alan Trammell	.25
75	Dmitri Young	.15
76	Ivan Rodriguez	.50
77	Jeremy Bonderman	.15
78	Preston Larrison	.15
79	Dontrelle Willis	.25
80	Josh Beckett	.50
81	Juan Pierre	.15
82	Luis Castillo	.15
83	Miguel Cabrera	.75
84	Mike Lowell	.25
85	Andy Pettitte	.25
86	Chris Burke	.25
87	Craig Biggio	.25
88	Jeff Bagwell	.50
89	Jeff Kent	.25
90	Lance Berkman	.25
91	Morgan Ensberg	.15
92	Richard Hidalgo	.15
93	Roger Clemens	1.50
94	Roy Oswalt	.25
95	Angel Berroa	.15
96	Byron Gettis	.15
97	Carlos Beltran	.40
98	George Brett	2.00
99	Juan Gonzalez	.50
100	Mike Sweeney	.15
101	Duke Snider	.50
102	Edwin Jackson	.15
103	Eric Gagne	.50
104	Hideo Nomo	.40
105	Hong-Chih Kuo	.15
106	Kazuhisa Ishii	.15
107	Paul LoDuca	.15
108	Robin Ventura	.15
109	Shawn Green	.25
110	Junior Spivey	.15
111	Rickie Weeks	.25
112	Scott Podsednik	.15
113	J.D. Durbin	.15
114	Jacque Jones	.15
115	Jason Kubel	.25
116	Johan Santana	.25
117	Shannon Stewart	.15
118	Torii Hunter	.25
119	Brad Wilkerson	.15
120	Jose Vidro	.15
121	Nick Johnson	.15
122	Orlando Cabrera	.15
123	Gary Carter	.25
124	Jae Weong Seo	.15
125	Lenny Dykstra	.25
126	Mike Piazza	1.00
127	Tom Glavine	.25
128	Alex Rodriguez	1.50
129	Bernie Williams	.40
130	Chien-Ming Wang	1.00
131	Derek Jeter	2.00
132	Don Mattingly	1.50
133	Gary Sheffield	.25
134	Hideki Matsui	1.50
135	Jason Giambi	.25
136	Javier Vazquez	.25
137	Jorge Posada	.40
138	Jose Contreras	.25
139	Kevin Brown	.25
140	Mariano Rivera	.40
141	Mike Mussina	.40
142	Whitey Ford	.50
143	Barry Zito	.40
144	Eric Chavez	.25
145	Mark Mulder	.40
146	Rich Harden	.25
147	Tim Hudson	.25
148	Reggie Jackson	.50
149	Rickey Henderson	.50
150	Brett Myers	.15
151	Bobby Abreu	.25
152	Jim Thome	.75
153	Kevin Millwood	.15
154	Marlon Byrd	.15
155	Mike Schmidt	1.50
156	Ryan Howard	3.00
157	Jack Wilson	.15
158	Jason Kendall	.25
159	Brian Giles	.25
160	David Wells	.15
161	Jay Payton	.15
162	Phil Nevin	.15
163	Ryan Klesko	.15
164	Sean Burroughs	.15
165	A.J. Pierzynski	.15
166	J.T. Snow	.15
167	Jason Schmidt	.50
168	Jerome Williams	.15
169	Will Clark	.50
170	Bret Boone	.15
171	Chris Snelling	.15
172	Edgar Martinez	.25
173	Ichiro Suzuki	1.50
174	Randy Winn	.15
175	Rich Aurilia	.15
176	Shigetoshi Hasegawa	.15
177	Albert Pujols	.75
178	Dan Haren	.15
179	Edgar Renteria	.25
180	Jim Edmonds	.40
181	Matt Morris	.15
182	Scott Rolen	.75
183	Stan Musial	1.00
184	Aubrey Huff	.15
185	Chad Gaudin	.15
186	Delmon Young	.25
187	Fred McGriff	.25
188	Rocco Baldelli	.75
189	Alfonso Soriano	.75
190	Hank Blalock	.50
191	Mark Teixeira	.40
192	Nolan Ryan	2.00
193	Alexis Rios	.15
194	Carlos Delgado	.40
195	Dustin McGowan	.15
196	Guillermo Quiroz	.15
197	Josh Phelps	.15
198	Roy Halladay	.25
199	Vernon Wells	.15
200	Vinnie Chulk	.15
201	Jose Capellan/1,999 RC	5.00
202	Kazuo Matsui/1,999 RC	5.00
203	David Crouthers/1,999	3.00
204	Akinori Otsuka/1,999 RC	5.00
205	Nick Regilio/1,999 RC	3.00
206	Justin Hampson/1,999	3.00
207	Lincoln Holdzkom/1,999 RC	3.00
208	Jorge Sequea/1,999 RC	3.00
209	Justin Leone/1,999 RC	5.00
210	Renyel Pinto/1,999 RC	5.00
211	Mariano Gomez/1,999 RC	3.00
212	Onil Joseph Auto./1,000 RC	5.00
213	Josh Labandeira AU/1,000 RC	10.00
214	Cory Sullivan/1,999 RC	5.00
215	Carlos Vasquez/Auto./675 RC	8.00
216	Chris Shelton/1,999 RC	8.00
217	Willy Taveras/1,999 RC	8.00
218	John Gall/1,999 RC	5.00
219	Jerry Gil/1,999 RC	3.00
220	Jason Frasor/1,999 RC	3.00
221	Justin Knoedler/1,999 RC	3.00
222	Ronald Belisario/1,999 RC	3.00
223	Mike Rouse/1,999	3.00
224	Dennis Sarfate/1,999 RC	3.00
225	Casey Daigle/1,999 RC	3.00
226	Shingo Takatsu/Auto./800 RC	10.00
227	Jason Bartlett/Auto./800 RC	8.00
228	Alfredo Simon/Auto./1,000 RC	8.00
229	Chris Oxspring/1,999 RC	3.00
230	Fernando Nieve/Auto./1,000 RC	8.00
231	Ruddy Yan/Auto./800 RC	8.00
232	Ryan Wing/1,999	3.00
233	Tim Bittner/Auto./1,000 RC	8.00
234	Ramon Ramirez/Auto./1,000 RC	8.00
235	Sean Henn/Auto./1,000	8.00
236	Roberto Novoa RC	4.00
237	Jerome Gamble/Auto./800 RC	8.00
238	Jamie Brown/Auto./800 RC	8.00
239	Ian Snell/Auto./800 RC	30.00
240	Freddy Guzman/Auto./800 RC	8.00
241	Aarom Baldiris/Auto./1,000 RC	8.00
242	Greg Dobbs/1,999 RC	3.00
243	Ivan Ochoa/1,999 RC	3.00
244	Angel Chavez/Auto./800 RC	8.00
245	Merkin Valdez/Auto./800 RC	10.00
246	Mike Gosling/Auto./800 RC	8.00
247	Carlos Hines/Auto./800 RC	8.00
248	Graham Koonce/Auto./1,000	10.00
249	William Bergolla/Auto./1,000 RC	8.00
250	Hector Gimenez/Auto./1,000 RC	8.00

Credits Bronze
Bronze (1-200): 3-6X
Bronze (201-250): .5-1X
Production 100 Sets

Credits Silver
Silver (1-200): 4-8X
Silver (201-250): No Pricing
Production 50 Sets

Credits Gold
Gold (1-200): 8-15X
Gold (201-250): No Pricing
Production 25 Sets

Credits Platinum
No Pricing
Production One Set

Awards
NM/M
Common Player: 2.00
Quantity produced listed.

#	Player	Price
1	Phil Rizzuto/1,950	3.00
2	Fred Lynn/1,975	2.00
3	George Brett/1,980	8.00
4	Cal Ripken Jr./1,983	10.00
5	Don Mattingly/1,985	8.00
6	Rickey Henderson/1,990	3.00
7	Stan Musial/1,943	5.00
8	Marty Marion/1,944	5.00
9	Ernie Banks/1,958	5.00
10	Sammy Sosa/1,998	6.00
11	Terry Pendleton/1,991	3.00
12	Ryne Sandberg/1,984	6.00
13	Andre Dawson/1,987	3.00
14	George Foster/1,977	2.00
15	Dave Parker/1,978	2.00
16	Keith Hernandez/1,979	3.00
17	Mike Schmidt/1,980	5.00
18	Dale Murphy/1,982	3.00
19	Whitey Ford/1,961	3.00
20	Roy Halladay/2,003	3.00
21	Orel Hershiser/1,988	3.00
22	Bob Feller/1,940	3.00
23	Dwight Gooden/1,985	2.00
24	Steve Carlton/1,972	3.00
25	Randy Johnson/2,002	4.00

Awards Signature
NM/M
Quantity produced listed

#	Player	Price
1	Phil Rizzuto/50	25.00
4	Fred Lynn/100	15.00
5	Stan Musial/50	50.00
9	Marty Marion/50	10.00
10	Sammy Sosa/21	125.00
11	Terry Pendleton/100	10.00
13	Andre Dawson/100	15.00
14	George Foster/100	10.00
15	Dave Parker/88	15.00
16	Keith Hernandez/100	20.00
17	Whitey Ford/50	25.00
20	Roy Halladay/25	25.00
21	Orel Hershiser/45	40.00
22	Bob Feller/100	15.00
23	Dwight Gooden/100	10.00

Champions
NM/M
Common Player: 2.00
Quantity produced listed.

#	Player	Price
1	Stan Musial/1,951	5.00
2	Warren Spahn/1,958	5.00
3	Bob Gibson/1,968	3.00
4	Mike Schmidt/1,980	6.00
5	Dale Murphy/1,982	4.00
6	Steve Carlton/1,983	4.00
7	Will Clark/1,988	4.00
8	Nolan Ryan/1,990	10.00
9	Ryne Sandberg/1,990	6.00
10	Roger Clemens/1,990	8.00
11	George Brett/1,990	8.00
12	Tony Gwynn/1,997	5.00
13	Todd Helton/2,000	3.00
14	Troy Glaus/2,000	2.00
15	Sammy Sosa/2,000	6.00
16	Pedro J. Martinez/2,000	4.00
17	Mark Mulder/2,001	2.00
18	Manny Ramirez/2,002	3.00
19	Lance Berkman/2,002	2.00
20	Alex Rodriguez/Rgr/2,002	6.00

Champions Jersey
NM/M
Common Jersey: 5.00
Quantity produced listed.

#	Player	Price
1	Stan Musial/100	30.00
2	Warren Spahn/100	10.00
3	Bob Gibson/100	10.00
4	Mike Schmidt/100	20.00
5	Dale Murphy/82	10.00
6	Steve Carlton/100	8.00
7	Will Clark/100	10.00
8	Nolan Ryan/100	25.00
9	Ryne Sandberg/100	8.00
10	Roger Clemens/100	15.00
11	George Brett/100	25.00
12	Tony Gwynn/250	10.00
13	Todd Helton/250	8.00
14	Troy Glaus/250	5.00
15	Sammy Sosa/250	8.00
16	Pedro J. Martinez/250	8.00
17	Mark Mulder/250	5.00
18	Manny Ramirez/250	6.00
19	Lance Berkman/250	5.00
20	Alex Rodriguez/250	8.00

Champions Signature
NM/M
Quantity produced listed.

#	Player	Price
1	Stan Musial/50	50.00
3	Bob Gibson/50	25.00
7	Will Clark/50	40.00
8	Nolan Ryan/34	100.00

Champions Jersey Signature
No Pricing
Production Five Sets

Class Reunion
NM/M
Quantity produced listed.

#	Player	Price
1	Eddie Murray, Gary Carter/2,003	3.00
2	Carlton Fisk, Tony Perez/2,000	3.00
3	Nolan Ryan, George Brett/1,999	10.00
4	Rod Carew, Fergie Jenkins/1,991	3.00
5	Joe Morgan, Jim Palmer/1,990	3.00
6	Carl Yastrzemski, Johnny Bench/1,989	5.00
7	Harmon Killebrew, Luis Aparicio/1,984	3.00
8	Brooks Robinson, Juan Marichal/1,983	3.00
9	Al Kaline, Duke Snider/1,980	3.00
10	Roberto Clemente, Warren Spahn/1,973	8.00
11	Mark Prior, Mark Teixeira/2,001	3.00
12	Josh Beckett, Barry Zito/1,999	3.00
13	Mark Mulder, Adam Dunn/1,998	3.00
14	Vernon Wells, Lance Berkman/1,997	3.00
15	Eric Chavez, Nick Johnson/1,996	3.00
16	Kerry Wood, Roy Halladay/1,995	4.00
17	Todd Helton, Carlos Beltran/1,995	4.00
18	Derek Jeter, Jason Giambi/1,992	8.00
20	Chipper Jones, Mike Mussina/1,990	4.00

Class Reunion Material

NM/M
Quantity produced listed.

#	Players	Price
1	Eddie Murray/Jsy, Gary Carter/Jsy	15.00
2	Carlton Fisk/Jsy, Tony Perez/Bat/250	20.00
3	Nolan Ryan/Jsy, George Brett/Jsy/100	50.00
4	Rod Carew/Jsy, Fergie Jenkins/Pants/250	15.00
5	Joe Morgan/Jsy, Jim Palmer/Jsy/100	15.00
6	Carl Yastrzemski/Jsy, Johnny Bench/Jsy/250	30.00
7	Harmon Killebrew/Jsy, Luis Aparicio/Jsy/250	15.00
8	Brooks Robinson/Jsy, Juan Marichal/Jsy/100	15.00
9	Al Kaline/Jsy, Duke Snider/Jsy/25	35.00
10	Roger Clemens/Jsy, Warren Spahn/Jsy/100	80.00
11	Mark Prior/Jsy, Mark Teixeira/Jsy/250	10.00
12	Josh Beckett/Jsy, Barry Zito/Jsy/1,999	8.00
13	Mark Mulder/Jsy, Adam Dunn/Jsy/250	10.00
14	Vernon Wells/Jsy, Lance Berkman/Jsy/250	8.00
15	Eric Chavez/Jsy, Nick Johnson/Jsy/250	8.00
16	Kerry Wood/Jsy, Roy Halladay/Jsy/250	12.00
17	Todd Helton/Jsy, Carlos Beltran/Jsy/250	10.00
18	Derek Jeter/Jsy, Jason Giambi/Jsy/250	20.00
19	Manny Ramirez/Jsy, Shawn Green/Jsy/250	10.00
20	Chipper Jones/Jsy, Mike Mussina/Jsy/250	10.00

Game Day Souvenir

NM/M

#	Player	Price
2	Bob Gibson/Jsy/75	6.00
3	Frank Robinson/Bat/61	10.00
4	Tony Gwynn/Pants/99	20.00
5	Warren Spahn/Jsy/53	20.00
6	George Brett/Bat/77	25.00
7	Cal Ripken Jr./Hat/19	100.00
8	Frank Thomas/Bat/93	15.00
9	Sammy Sosa/Jsy/100	15.00
10	Harmon Killebrew/Bat/75	15.00

Game Day Souvenir Signature
No Pricing
Production Five Sets

Piece of the Game Bat
NM/M

#	Player	Price
1	Albert Pujols/250	15.00
2	Angel Berroa/250	4.00
3	Aubrey Huff/250	4.00
4	Barry Zito/250	6.00
5	Bobby Abreu/250	4.00
6	Carlos Beltran/250	4.00
7	Chipper Jones/250	8.00
8	Derek Jeter/50	20.00
9	Eric Chavez/150	6.00
10	Eric Hinske/50	6.00
11	Gary Sheffield/250	4.00
12	George Brett/250	15.00
13	Jay Gibbons/250	4.00
14	Jim Edmonds/250	4.00
15	Josh Beckett/250	6.00
16	Manny Ramirez/250	6.00
17	Mark Mulder/250	6.00
18	Marlon Byrd/250	4.00
19	Mike Lowell/250	4.00
20	Mike Schmidt/250	20.00
21	Nolan Ryan/250	20.00
22	Rafael Furcal/250	4.00
23	Randy Johnson/100	10.00
24	Rod Carew/250	8.00
25	Torii Hunter/250	4.00

Piece of the Game Bat Signature
No Pricing
Production 1-10

Piece of the Game Jersey
NM/M
Quantity produced listed.

#	Player	Price
1	Albert Pujols/250	15.00
2	Angel Berroa/250	4.00
3	Aubrey Huff/250	4.00
4	Barry Zito/250	6.00
5	Bobby Abreu/250	4.00
6	Carlos Beltran/250	4.00
7	Chipper Jones/250	8.00
8	Derek Jeter/50	40.00
9	Eric Chavez/250	5.00
10	Eric Hinske/100	4.00
12	George Brett/250	15.00
13	Jay Gibbons/250	4.00
14	Jim Edmonds/250	4.00
15	Josh Beckett/250	6.00
16	Manny Ramirez/250	6.00
17	Mark Mulder/100	6.00
18	Marlon Byrd/250	4.00
19	Mike Lowell/250	4.00
20	Mike Schmidt/100	35.00
21	Nolan Ryan/100	25.00
22	Rafael Furcal/250	4.00
23	Randy Johnson/250	8.00
24	Rod Carew/100	8.00
25	Torii Hunter/250	4.00

Piece of the Game Jersey Signature
Quantity produced listed.

Piece of the Game Combo
NM/M

#	Player	Price
1	Albert Pujols/Bat-Jsy/100	25.00
2	Angel Berroa/Bat-Pants/100	6.00
3	Aubrey Huff/Bat-Jsy/100	6.00
4	Barry Zito/Bat-Jsy/100	8.00
5	Bobby Abreu/Bat-Jsy/100	6.00
6	Carlos Beltran/Bat-Jsy/100	6.00
7	Chipper Jones/Bat-Jsy/100	10.00
8	Derek Jeter/Bat-Jsy/100	40.00
9	Eric Chavez/Bat-Jsy/50	8.00
10	Eric Hinske/Bat-Jsy/25	
11	George Brett/Bat-Jsy/100	25.00
12	Jay Gibbons/Bat-Jsy/100	6.00
13	Jim Edmonds/Bat-Jsy/100	8.00
15	Josh Beckett/Bat-Jsy/100	10.00
16	Manny Ramirez/Bat-Jsy/100	10.00
17	Mark Mulder/Bat-Jsy/25	15.00
18	Marlon Byrd/Bat-Jsy/25	6.00
19	Mike Lowell/Bat-Jsy/100	6.00
20	Mike Schmidt/Bat-Jsy/50	35.00
21	Nolan Ryan/Bat-Jsy/100	35.00
22	Rafael Furcal/Bat-Jsy/100	
23	Randy Johnson/Bat-Jsy/100	
24	Rod Carew/Bat-Jsy/100	15.00
25	Torii Hunter/Bat-Jsy/100	6.00

Piece of the Game Combo Signature
No Pricing
Production 1-10

Prime Signature Autograph

		NM/M
1	Garret Anderson/50	15.00
2	Rafael Palmeiro/50	40.00
3	Vladimir Guerrero/50	50.00
5	Dontrelle Willis/50	30.00
6	Miguel Cabrera/100	35.00
7	Shannon Stewart/100	10.00
9	Gary Sheffield/100	25.00
12	Tom Glavine/25	40.00
13	Brandon Webb/100	10.00
14	Carlos Lee/100	10.00
17	Magglio Ordonez/100	15.00
19	Andruw Jones/100	20.00
21	Sammy Sosa/50	100.00
22	Juan Gonzalez/50	25.00
23	Jeff Bagwell/25	50.00
24	Rickey Henderson/25	75.00
25	Mike Schmidt/50	60.00
26	Jim Rice/100	15.00
27	Billy Williams/100	15.00
28	Lou Brock/100	20.00
29	Robin Yount/75	75.00
30	Nolan Ryan/50	85.00
31	Darryl Strawberry/100	15.00
32	Cal Ripken Jr./25	200.00
33	Andre Dawson/50	15.00
34	Don Mattingly/50	75.00
35	Paul Molitor/25	50.00
36	Bo Jackson/50	75.00
37	Ernie Banks/50	50.00
38	Orel Hershiser/100	20.00
39	Mark Grace/50	40.00
40	Carlton Fisk/50	25.00

Prime Signature Autograph Bat

Quantity produced listed.

Prime Signature Autograph Jersey

		NM/M
2	Rafael Palmeiro/25	75.00
6	Miguel Cabrera/20	75.00
7	Shannon Stewart/23	15.00
29	Robin Yount/19	75.00
31	Darryl Strawberry/25	25.00
34	Don Mattingly/23	100.00
39	Mark Grace/17	65.00

Prime Signature Insert

		NM/M
Production 2,500 Sets		
1	Garret Anderson	2.00
2	Rafael Palmeiro	3.00
3	Vladimir Guerrero	3.00
4	Alex Rodriguez	5.00
5	Dontrelle Willis	2.00
6	Miguel Cabrera	3.00
7	Shannon Stewart	2.00
8	Mike Piazza	4.00
9	Gary Sheffield	2.00
10	Ivan Rodriguez	3.00
11	Randy Johnson	3.00
12	Tom Glavine	2.00
13	Brandon Webb	2.00
14	Carlos Lee	2.00
15	Hideo Nomo	2.00
16	Mike Mussina	3.00
17	Magglio Ordonez	2.00
18	Austin Kearns	2.00
19	Andruw Jones	3.00
20	Mariano Rivera	3.00
21	Sammy Sosa	4.00
22	Juan Gonzalez	3.00
23	Jeff Bagwell	3.00
24	Rickey Henderson	3.00
25	Mike Schmidt	3.00
26	Jim Rice	2.00
27	Billy Williams	2.00
28	Lou Brock	2.00
29	Robin Yount	4.00
30	Nolan Ryan	8.00
31	Darryl Strawberry	2.00
32	Cal Ripken Jr.	10.00
33	Andre Dawson	2.00
34	Don Mattingly	5.00
35	Paul Molitor	3.00
36	Bo Jackson	3.00
37	Ernie Banks	4.00
38	Orel Hershiser	2.00
39	Mark Grace	3.00
40	Carlton Fisk	3.00

Quad Material

		NM/M
Quantity produced listed.		
1	Matt Williams, Mark Grace, Will Clark, Keith Hernandez/100	60.00
2	Jason Giambi, Jim Thome, Carlos Delgado, Rafael Palmeiro/100	
3	Albert Pujols, Ernie Banks, Jeff Bagwell, Jim Thome/100	50.00
4	Paul Molitor, Joe Morgan, Ryne Sandberg, Alfonso Soriano/50	50.00
5	Cal Ripken Jr., Derek Jeter, Alex Rodriguez, Nomar Garciaparra/100	75.00
6	Ozzie Smith, Robin Yount, Alan Trammell, Dave Concepcion/50	50.00

8	Johnny Bench, Carlton Fisk, Gary Carter, Mike Piazza/100	40.00
9	Todd Helton, Brian Giles, Edgar Renteria, Scott Rolen/25	40.00
10	Carlos Delgado, Alfonso Soriano, Alex Rodriguez, Troy Glaus/100	20.00
11	Harmon Killebrew, Reggie Jackson, Mike Schmidt, Sammy Sosa/100	65.00
12	Stan Musial, Rickey Henderson, Tony Gwynn, Lou Brock/25	80.00
13	Cal Ripken Jr., George Brett, Paul Molitor, Rod Carew/100	75.00
14	Sammy Sosa, Vladimir Guerrero, Manny Ramirez, Magglio Ordonez/100	40.00
15	Andruw Jones, Jim Edmonds, Torii Hunter, Vernon Wells/100	20.00
16	Chipper Jones, Shawn Green, Andruw Jones, Lance Berkman/100	20.00
17	Tony Gwynn, Dale Murphy, Kirby Puckett, Andre Dawson/100	75.00
19	Nolan Ryan, Roger Clemens, Kerry Wood, Josh Beckett/100	75.00
21	Dennis Eckersley, John Smoltz, Mariano Rivera, Lee Smith/100	40.00
22	Mike Mussina, Greg Maddux, Jack Morris, Bert Blyleven/100	40.00
23	Steve Carlton, Tom Glavine, Barry Zito, Andy Pettitte/100	20.00
24	Whitey Ford, Warren Spahn, Bob Feller, Juan Marichal/25	80.00
25	Nolan Ryan, Roger Clemens, Steve Carlton, Randy Johnson/100	80.00

Rookie Year Jersey Number

		NM/M
1	Gary Carter/50	10.00
2	Robin Yount/50	30.00
3	Roger Clemens/25	40.00
4	Gary Sheffield/50	8.00
5	Mike Piazza/25	30.00
6	Hideo Nomo/25	30.00
7	Alex Rodriguez/50	20.00
8	Mark Prior/25	15.00
9	Dontrelle Willis/100	10.00
10	Angel Berroa/100	8.00

Rookie Year Jersey Signature

No Pricing
Production 1-10

Signature Bronze

		NM/M
Quantity produced listed.		
2	Garret Anderson/100	15.00
5	Vladimir Guerrero/50	50.00
6	Brandon Webb/100	8.00
7	Brian Bruney/96	8.00
11	Robby Hammock/100	8.00
13	Shea Hillenbrand/100	8.00
14	Adam LaRoche/100	10.00
16	Andruw Jones/100	25.00
17	Bubba Nelson/100	8.00
22	Marcus Giles/100	15.00
23	Rafael Furcal/50	15.00
26	Adam Loewen/100	8.00
27	Cal Ripken Jr./25	150.00
29	Jay Gibbons/100	8.00
30	Luis Matos/100	8.00
33	Bobby Doerr/100	15.00
35	Edwin Almonte/99	8.00
36	Jason Varitek/50	30.00
37	Kevin Youkilis/100	15.00
42	Andre Dawson/100	15.00
43	Aramis Ramirez/25	25.00
44	Brendan Harris/100	8.00
45	Derrek Lee/100	20.00
46	Ernie Banks/25	60.00
47	Kerry Wood/25	50.00
48	Mark Prior/50	40.00
50	Sammy Sosa/50	125.00
51	Carlos Lee/100	10.00
52	Frank Thomas/25	50.00
53	Joe Borchard/100	8.00
54	Joe Crede/50	10.00
55	Magglio Ordonez/50	15.00
58	Barry Larkin/25	40.00
59	Brandon Larson/100	8.00
61	Ryan Wagner/25	8.00
63	Bob Feller/100	20.00
64	Brian Tallet/100	8.00
66	Jeremy Guthrie/100	8.00
67	Jody Gerut/100	8.00
68	Clint Barmes/100	8.00
69	Jeff Baker/25	8.00
72	Preston Wilson/100	15.00
74	Alan Trammell/100	15.00

78	Preston Larrison/100	8.00
79	Dontrelle Willis/25	30.00
83	Miguel Cabrera/100	40.00
85	Andy Pettitte/25	50.00
86	Chris Burke/100	8.00
88	Jeff Bagwell/25	50.00
91	Morgan Ensberg/100	10.00
96	Byron Gettis/100	8.00
97	Carlos Beltran/100	30.00
98	George Brett/25	100.00
101	Duke Snider/100	20.00
102	Edwin Jackson/100	10.00
105	Hong-Chih Kuo/100	15.00
106	Kazuhisa Ishii/25	40.00
107	Paul LoDuca/100	15.00
108	Robin Ventura/100	15.00
110	Junior Spivey/50	10.00
112	Scott Podsednik/100	15.00
113	J.D. Durbin/100	8.00
114	Jacque Jones/100	15.00
116	Johan Santana/100	15.00
117	Shannon Stewart/50	10.00
123	Gary Carter/100	15.00
125	Lenny Dykstra/100	15.00
130	Chien-Ming Wang/100	100.00
132	Don Mattingly/100	80.00
133	Gary Sheffield/50	25.00
137	Jorge Posada/50	25.00
142	Whitey Ford/50	25.00
145	Mark Mulder/100	15.00
146	Rich Harden/100	15.00
147	Tim Hudson/25	15.00
148	Reggie Jackson/25	50.00
149	Rickey Henderson/25	80.00
150	Brett Myers/100	8.00
154	Marlon Byrd/100	8.00
155	Mike Schmidt/50	60.00
156	Ryan Howard/50	80.00
161	Jay Payton/100	10.00
168	Jerome Williams/50	10.00
169	Will Clark/50	50.00
171	Chris Snelling/100	8.00
176	Shigetoshi Hasegawa/100	8.00
178	Dan Haren/100	10.00
180	Jim Edmonds/25	30.00
182	Scott Rolen/50	30.00
183	Stan Musial/50	60.00
184	Aubrey Huff/100	15.00
185	Chad Gaudin/100	8.00
186	Delmon Young/50	30.00
191	Mark Teixeira/25	25.00
192	Nolan Ryan/50	100.00
193	Alexis Rios/100	15.00
195	Dustin McGowan/100	10.00
196	Guillermo Quiroz/50	10.00
197	Josh Phelps/25	15.00
198	Roy Halladay/25	25.00
200	Vinnie Chulk/25	15.00
201	Jose Capellan/100	35.00
203	David Crouthers/100	8.00
204	Akinori Otsuka/100	35.00
205	Nick Regilio/100	8.00
206	Justin Hampson/100	8.00
207	Lincoln Holdzkom/100	8.00
208	Jorge Sequea/100	8.00
209	Justin Leone/100	15.00
210	Renyel Pinto/100	10.00
211	Mariano Gomez/100	8.00
214	Cory Sullivan/100	8.00
216	Chris Shelton/100	40.00
217	Willy Taveras/25	8.00
218	John Gall/100	15.00
222	Ronald Belisario/100	8.00
223	Mike Rouse/100	8.00
224	Dennis Sarfate/100	8.00

Signature Silver

Silver: .75-1.5X Bronze
Production 1-100
No pricing 25 or less.

Signature Gold

Gold: .75-1.5X Bronze
Production 1-50
No pricing 25 or less.

Signature Platinum

No Pricing
Production One Set

Signs of Greatness

		NM/M
Quantity produced listed.		
1	Mark Prior/25	50.00
2	Scott Podsednik/25	25.00
4	Dontrelle Willis/25	30.00
5	Rocco Baldelli/25	40.00
6	Brandon Webb/25	15.00
7	Rich Harden/25	40.00
8	Miguel Cabrera/25	50.00
9	Josh Beckett/25	40.00
10	Mark Teixeira/25	40.00

Tandem Material

		NM/M
Common Duo:		10.00
Quantity produced listed.		

1	Bo Jackson, Deion Sanders/100	30.00
2	Eddie Murray, Rafael Palmeiro/250	15.00
3	Alex Rodriguez, Dale Murphy/250	15.00
4	Carlton Fisk, Ivan Rodriguez/250	15.00
5	Rickey Henderson, Lou Brock/50	30.00
6	Sammy Sosa, Ernie Banks/250	25.00
7	Warren Spahn, Steve Carlton/150	15.00
8	Carl Yastrzemski, Darrell Evans/250	25.00
9	Keith Hernandez, Lenny Dykstra/250	10.00
10	Pee Wee Reese, Marty Marion/150	15.00
11	Hideo Nomo, Chipper Jones/250	15.00
12	Willie McCovey, Reggie Jackson/100	20.00
13	Mark Prior, Barry Zito/250	10.00
14	Cal Ripken Jr., Miguel Tejada/Bat/100	50.00
15	Roberto Clemente, Vladimir Guerrero/Bat/100	75.00
16	Gary Carter, Mike Piazza/250	15.00
17	Jim Rice, Fred Lynn/50	20.00
18	Willie Stargell, Keith Hernandez/250	15.00
19	Nomar Garciaparra, Mark Teixeira/100	20.00
20	Derek Jeter, Phil Rizzuto/50	50.00
21	Eric Chavez, Hank Blalock/100	10.00
22	Eric Davis, Darryl Strawberry/150	15.00
23	Rickey Henderson, Deion Sanders/100	15.00
24	Dave Parker, Austin Kearns/250	10.00
25	Luis Aparicio, Dave Concepcion/100	15.00
26	Rafael Palmeiro, Will Clark/100	25.00
27	Ryne Sandberg, Ozzie Smith/250	50.00
28	Alex Rodriguez M's, Jose Canseco/250	15.00
29	Sammy Sosa, Juan Gonzalez/250	15.00
30	Pedro J. Martinez, Juan Marichal/50	20.00
32	Dwight Gooden, Gary Sheffield/250	10.00
33	Lou Boudreau, Omar Vizquel/100	15.00
34	Mark Prior, Ron Santo Bat/100	30.00
35	Albert Pujols, Ken Boyer/250	25.00
36	Tom Seaver, Curt Schilling/250	15.00
37	Joe Morgan, Jeff Kent/250	10.00
38	Steve Garvey, Ozzie Smith/250	25.00
39	Mike Piazza, Ivan Rodriguez/250	15.00
	Mike Schmidt, Jim Thome/100	25.00

2004 Playoff Prestige

		NM/M
Complete Set (200):		35.00
Common Player:		.15
Pack (6):		3.50
Box (24):		75.00
1	Bengie Molina	.15
2	Garret Anderson	.25
3	Jarrod Washburn	.15
4	Scott Spiezio	.15
5	Tim Salmon	.25
6	Troy Glaus	.40
7	Alex Cintron	.15
8	Brandon Webb	.25
9	Curt Schilling	.50
10	Edgar Gonzalez	.50
11	Luis Gonzalez	.25
12	Randy Johnson	.75
13	Steve Finley	.15

14	Andruw Jones	.50
15	Bubba Nelson	.50
16	Chipper Jones	1.00
17	Gary Sheffield	.40
18	Greg Maddux	1.00
19	Javy Lopez	.40
20	John Smoltz	.25
21	Marcus Giles	.25
22	Rafael Furcal	.25
23	Brian Roberts	.15
24	Jason Johnson	.15
25	Jay Gibbons	.25
26	Luis Matos	.15
27	Melvin Mora	.15
28	Tony Batista	.15
29	Bill Mueller	.25
30	David Ortiz	.40
31	Johnny Damon	.25
32	Kevin Youkilis	1.00
33	Manny Ramirez	.50
34	Nomar Garciaparra	1.50
35	Pedro Martinez	.75
36	Trot Nixon	.25
37	Aramis Ramirez	.25
38	Brendan Harris	.50
39	Carlos Zambrano	.15
40	Corey Patterson	.25
41	Kenny Lofton	.25
42	Kerry Wood	.75
43	Mark Prior	1.50
44	Sammy Sosa	1.50
45	Bartolo Colon	.25
46	Carlos Lee	.25
47	Esteban Loaiza	.15
48	Frank Thomas	.50
49	Joe Crede	.15
50	Magglio Ordonez	.40
51	Roberto Alomar	.40
52	Adam Dunn	.40
53	Austin Kearns	.40
54	Josh Hall	.15
55	Ken Griffey Jr.	1.00
56	Sean Casey	.25
57	Micheal Nakamura	.15
58	C.C. Sabathia	.15
59	Casey Blake	.15
60	Jody Gerut	.15
61	Matt Lawton	.15
62	Milton Bradley	.15
63	Omar Vizquel	.25
64	Jason Jennings	.15
65	Jay Payton	.25
66	Larry Walker	.25
67	Preston Wilson	.25
68	Todd Helton	.50
69	Bobby Higginson	.15
70	Carlos Pena	.15
71	Dmitri Young	.15
72	Jeremy Bonderman	.15
73	Preston Larrison	.50
74	Derrek Lee	.25
75	Dontrelle Willis	.40
76	Ivan Rodriguez	.50
77	Josh Beckett	.50
78	Juan Pierre	.15
79	Miguel Cabrera	.75
80	Mike Lowell	.25
81	Chris Burke	.15
82	Craig Biggio	.25
83	Jeff Bagwell	.50
84	Jeff Kent	.25
85	Lance Berkman	.40
86	Richard Hidalgo	.25
87	Roy Oswalt	.25
88	Aaron Guiel	.15
89	Angel Berroa	.25
90	Carlos Beltran	.40
91	Jeremy Affeldt	.15
92	Michael Sweeney	.25
93	Runelvys Hernandez	.15
94	Dave Roberts	.15
95	Eric Gagne	.40
96	Hideo Nomo	.40
97	Kevin Brown	.25
98	Paul Lo Duca	.15
99	Shawn Green	.40
100	Ben Sheets	.25
101	Geoff Jenkins	.40
102	Richie Sexson	.40
103	Rickie Weeks	1.00
104	Scott Podsednik	.50
105	J.D. Durbin	.50
106	Jacque Jones	.15
107	Jason Kubel	.50
108	Shannon Stewart	.25
109	Torii Hunter	.40
110	Chad Cordero	.25
111	Javier Vazquez	.25
112	Jose Vidro	.15
113	Livan Hernandez	.15
114	Orlando Cabrera	.25
115	Tony Armas Jr.	.15
116	Vladimir Guerrero	.75
117	Al Leiter	.25
118	Cliff Floyd	.15
119	Jae Weong So	.15
120	Jose Reyes	.50
121	Mike Piazza	1.00
122	Tom Glavine	.25
123	Aaron Boone	.15
124	Alfonso Soriano	.75
125	Andy Pettitte	.25
126	Derek Jeter	.15
127	Hideki Matsui	.75
128	Jason Giambi	.15
129	Jorge Posada	.50
130	Jose Contreras	.25
131	Mike Mussina	.50

132	Barry Zito	.40
133	Eric Byrnes	.15
134	Eric Chavez	.40
135	Jose Guillen	.15
136	Mark Mulder	.40
137	Miguel Tejada	.40
138	Ramon Hernandez	.15
139	Rich Harden	.15
140	Tim Hudson	.40
141	Bobby Abreu	.25
142	Brett Myers	.15
143	Jim Thome	.75
144	Kevin Millwood	.15
145	Mike Lieberthal	.15
146	Ryan Howard	1.50
147	Craig Wilson	.15
148	Jack Wilson	.15
149	Jason Kendall	.15
150	Kip Wells	.15
151	Reggie Sanders	.15
152	Albert Pujols	1.50
153	Edgar Renteria	.25
154	Jim Edmonds	.40
155	Matt Morris	.25
156	Scott Rolen	.75
157	Tino Martinez	.15
158	Woody Williams	.15
159	Brian Giles	.25
160	Freddy Guzman RC	.50
161	Jake Peavy	.15
162	Khalil Greene	.50
163	Phil Nevin	.15
164	Ryan Klesko	.25
165	Ray Durham	.15
166	Jason Schmidt	.25
167	Jerome Williams	.50
168	Jesse Foppert	.15
169	Jose Cruz	.15
170	Marquis Grissom	.15
171	Merkin Valdez RC	1.50
172	Rich Aurilia	.15
173	Bret Boone	.25
174	Freddy Garcia	.15
175	Ichiro Suzuki	1.50
176	Jamie Moyer	.15
177	John Olerud	.25
178	Mike Cameron	.15
179	Randy Winn	.15
180	Aubrey Huff	.25
181	Carl Crawford	.25
182	Chad Gaudin	.50
183	Rocco Baldelli	.50
184	Toby Hall	.15
185	Travis Lee	.15
186	Alex Rodriguez	1.50
187	Hank Blalock	.40
188	John Thomson	.15
189	Juan Gonzalez	.25
190	Mark Teixeira	.40
191	Michael Young	.15
192	Rafael Palmeiro	.50
193	Ramon Nivar	.50
194	Carlos Delgado	.50
195	Dustin McGowan	.50
196	Frank Catalanotto	.15
197	Vinnie Chulk	.15
198	Orlando Hudson	.15
199	Roy Halladay	.40
200	Vernon Wells	.25

Xtra Bases Black

Black (1-200):	4-8X
Production 75 Sets	

Xtra Bases Black Autographs

No Pricing
Production 25 Sets

PXtra Bases Green Autographs

No Pricing

Xtra Bases Purple

Purple (1-200):	2-5X
Production 150 Sets	

Xtra Bases Purple Autographs

		NM/M
Production 100 Sets		
10	Edgar Gonzalez	6.00
15	Bubba Nelson	8.00
32	Kevin Youkilis	15.00
38	Brendan Harris	8.00
57	Micheal Nakamura	6.00
73	Preston Larrison	6.00

79	Miguel Cabrera	35.00
81	Chris Burke	15.00
105	J.D. Durbin	10.00
107	Jason Kubel	8.00
146	Ryan Howard	75.00
193	Ramon Nivar	8.00
195	Dustin McGowan	10.00
198	Orlando Hudson	8.00

Xtra Bases Red Autographs
Complete Set:
Common Player:

Achievements

		NM/M
1	Hideo Nomo/95 ROY	1.50
2	Don Mattingly/85 MVP	6.00
3	Roger Clemens/86 CY/MVP	6.00
4	Greg Maddux/95 CY	4.00
5	Stan Musial/43 MVP	4.00
6	Roberto Clemente/66 MVP	
7	Derek Jeter/96 ROY	6.00
8	Albert Pujols/01 ROY	6.00
9	Cal Ripken Jr./91 MVP	8.00
10	George Brett/80 MVP	8.00
11	Carl Yastrzemski/67 MVP	4.00
12	Rickey Henderson/90 MVP	
13	Sammy Sosa/98 MVP	5.00
14	Randy Johnson/02 CY	3.00
15	Bob Gibson/68 CY/MVP	3.00

Autographs
Quantity produced listed

		NM/M
8	Brandon Webb/100	20.00
10	Edgar Gonzalez PROS/150	8.00
15	Bubba Nelson PROS/250	10.00
25	Jay Gibbons/50	20.00
32	Kevin Youkilis PROS/100	20.00
36	Trot Nixon/25	40.00
37	Aramis Ramirez/25	25.00
38	Brendan Harris PROS/400	8.00
49	Joe Crede/25	15.00
54	Josh Hall/25	15.00
57	Mike Nakamura/250	8.00
60	Jody Gerut/50	15.00
73	Preston Larrison PROS/250	8.00
75	Dontrelle Willis/25	40.00
79	Miguel Cabrera/100	30.00
81	Chris Burke PROS/250	10.00
93	Runelvys Hernandez/50	10.00
98	Paul Lo Duca/25	15.00
102	Richie Sexson/25	25.00
105	J.D. Durbin PROS/500	10.00
106	Jacque Jones/50	12.00
107	Jason Kubel PROS/400	8.00
112	Shannon Stewart/50	15.00
102	Jose Vidro/25	15.00
114	Orlando Cabrera/25	20.00
119	Jae Weong Seo/25	20.00
133	Eric Byrnes/50	15.00
136	Mark Mulder/25	20.00
139	Rich Harden/50	25.00
146	Ryan Howard PROS/400	75.00
193	Ramon Nivar PROS/100	8.00
195	Dustin McGowan PROS/100	10.00
197	Vinnie Chulk/112	8.00
198	Orlando Hudson/100	10.00

Changing Stripes

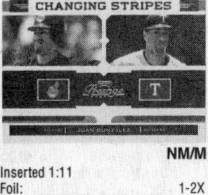

		NM/M
Inserted 1:11		
Foil:		1-2X
Holofoil:		2-3X
Production 150 Sets		
1	Rickey Henderson/ A-s-Yanks	4.00

2	Mike Mussina/O's-Yanks	2.00
3	Jim Thome/Indians-Phils	3.00
4	Hideo Nomo/Sox-Dodgers	1.50
5	Scott Rolen/Phils-Cards	3.00
6	Jason Giambi/A's-Yanks	3.00
7	Randy Johnson/Astros-D'backs	3.00
8	Shawn Green/Jays-Dodgers	1.50
9	Curt Schilling/Phils-D'backs	2.00
10	Alex Rodriguez/M's-Rangers	5.00
11	Greg Maddux/Cubs-Braves	4.00
12	Randy Johnson/M's-Astros	3.00
13	Hideo Nomo/Dodgers-Mets	1.50
14	Juan Rodriguez/Rgr-Marlins	2.00
15	Juan Gonzalez/Indians-Rangers	2.00
16	Manny Ramirez/Indians-Sox	2.00
17	Mike Piazza/Dodgers-Mets	4.00
18	Nolan Ryan/Angels-Astros	8.00
19	Nolan Ryan/Astros-Rangers	8.00
20	Pedro Martinez/Expos-Sox	3.00
21	Reggie Jackson/Yanks-Angels	2.00
22	Roberto Alomar/Mets-Sox	1.50
23	Rod Carew/Twins-Angels	2.00
24	Roger Clemens/Sox-Yanks	6.00
25	Sammy Sosa/Sox-Cubs	5.00

Changing Stripes Dual Jersey

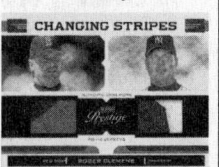

		NM/M
Prodcution 150 Sets		
Primes:		No Pricing
Production 25 Sets		
1	Rickey Henderson/ A's-Yanks	10.00
2	Mike Mussina/O's-Yanks	8.00
3	Jim Thome/Indians-Phils	10.00
4	Hideo Nomo/Sox-Dodgers	15.00
5	Scott Rolen/Phils-Cards	10.00
6	Jason Giambi/A's-Yanks	12.00
7	Randy Johnson/Astros-D'backs	10.00
8	Shawn Green/Jays-Dodgers	6.00
9	Curt Schilling/Phils-D'backs	8.00
10	Alex Rodriguez/M's-Rangers	15.00
12	Randy Johnson/M's-Astros	10.00
13	Hideo Nomo/Dodgers-Mets	15.00
14	Ivan Rodriguez/Rgr-Marlins	10.00
15	Juan Gonzalez/Indians-Rangers	8.00
16	Manny Ramirez/Indians-Sox	8.00
17	Mike Piazza/Dodgers-Mets	10.00
18	Nolan Ryan/Angels-Astros	30.00
19	Nolan Ryan/Astrs-Rangers	30.00
20	Pedro Martinez/Expos-Sox	10.00
22	Roberto Alomar/Mets-Sox	8.00
23	Rod Carew/Twins-Angels	12.00
24	Roger Clemens/Sox-Yankss	15.00
25	Sammy Sosa/Sox-Cubs	15.00

Connections

		NM/M
Inserted 1:9		
Foil:		1.5-2X
Holofoil:		No Pricing
Production 21 Sets		
1	Derek Jeter, Alfonso Soriano	4.00
2	Greg Maddux, Chipper Jones	2.00
3	Albert Pujols, Scott Rolen	3.00

4	Randy Johnson, Curt Schilling	1.50
5	Nomar Garciaparra, Manny Ramirez	3.00
6	Alex Rodriguez, Mark Teixeira	3.00
7	Barry Zito, Tim Hudson	.75
8	Sammy Sosa, Mark Prior	2.00
9	Derek Jeter, Jason Giambi	4.00
10	Roger Clemens, Mike Mussina	3.00
11	Mark Prior, Kerry Wood	2.00
12	Alex Rodriguez, Hank Blalock	3.00
13	Frank Thomas, Magglio Ordonez	1.00
14	Nomar Garciaparra, Pedro Martinez	3.00
15	Carlos Delgado, Vernon Wells	1.00
16	Miguel Tejada, Eric Chavez	.75
17	Jeff Bagwell, Lance Berkman	1.00
18	Jim Thome, Bobby Abreu	1.50
19	Todd Helton, Preston Wilson	1.00
20	Vladimir Guerrero, Javier Vazquez	1.50

Connections Material

		NM/M
Production 250 Sets		
1	Derek Jeter/Bat, Alfonso Soriano/Bat	20.00
2	Greg Maddux/Bat, Chipper Jones/Jsy	12.00
3	Albert Pujols/Bat, Scott Rolen/Bat	15.00
4	Randy Johnson/Bat, Curt Schilling/Bat	10.00
5	Nomar Garciaparra/Bat, Manny Ramirez/Bat	10.00
6	Alex Rodriguez/Bat, Mark Teixeira/Bat	10.00
7	Barry Zito/Bat, Tim Hudson/Bat	10.00
8	Sammy Sosa/Bat, Mark Prior/Bat	15.00
9	Derek Jeter/Bat, Jason Giambi/Bat	20.00
10	Roger Clemens/Jsy, Mike Mussina/Bat	15.00
11	Mark Prior/Bat, Kerry Wood/Bat	10.00
12	Alex Rodriguez/Bat, Hank Blalock/Bat	10.00
13	Frank Thomas/Bat, Magglio Ordonez/Bat	8.00
14	Nomar Garciaparra/Bat, Pedro Martinez/Bat	15.00
15	Carlos Delgado/Bat, Vernon Wells/Bat	8.00
16	Miguel Tejada/Bat, Eric Chavez/Bat	8.00
17	Jeff Bagwell/Bat, Lance Berkman/Bat	10.00
18	Jim Thome/Jsy, Bobby Abreu/Bat	10.00
19	Todd Helton/Bat, Preston Wilson	8.00
20	Vladimir Guerrero/Bat, Javier Vazquez/Jsy	10.00

Diamond Heritage

		NM/M
Inserted 1:13		
1	Mike Piazza	3.00
2	Greg Maddux	2.50

3	Nomar Garciaparra	3.00
4	Chipper Jones	2.00
5	Albert Pujols	4.00
6	Derek Jeter	5.00
7	Shawn Green	.75
8	Alex Rodriguez	4.00
9	Jim Thome	2.00
10	Jason Giambi	1.50
11	Sammy Sosa	3.00
12	Hank Blalock	1.00
13	Garret Anderson	.75
14	Manny Ramirez	1.50
15	Scott Rolen	1.50
16	Jeff Bagwell	1.50
17	Randy Johnson	2.00
18	Ichiro Suzuki	3.00
19	Ivan Rodriguez	1.50
20	Alfonso Soriano	1.50

Diamond Heritage Material

		NM/M
Inserted 1:92		
1	Mike Piazza/Bat	10.00
2	Greg Maddux/Bat	8.00
3	Nomar Garciaparra/Bat	10.00
4	Chipper Jones/Jsy	8.00
5	Albert Pujols/Bat	15.00
6	Derek Jeter/Jsy	15.00
7	Shawn Green/Bat	5.00
8	Alex Rodriguez/Bat	10.00
9	Jim Thome/Jsy	8.00
10	Jason Giambi/Bat	8.00
11	Sammy Sosa/Bat	12.00
12	Hank Blalock/Bat	6.00
13	Garret Anderson/Bat	6.00
14	Manny Ramirez/Bat	6.00
15	Scott Rolen/Bat	6.00
16	Jeff Bagwell/Bat	6.00
17	Randy Johnson/Bat	8.00
18	Ivan Rodriguez/Bat	6.00
19	Ivan Rodriguez/Bat	6.00
20	Alfonso Soriano/Bat	6.00

League Leaders Single

		NM/M
Foil		2-3X
Production 100 Sets		
Holofoil:		No Pricing
Production 25 Sets		
1	Alex Rodriguez/AL HR	3.00
2	Albert Pujols/NL Hit	3.00
3	Albert Pujols/NL Avg	3.00
4	Nomar Garciaparra/AL Hit	2.00
5	Mark Prior/NL ERA	2.00
6	Pedro Martinez/NL ERA	1.00
7	Kerry Wood/NL SO	1.00
8	Derek Jeter/AL Avg	3.00
9	Jason Giambi/AL BB	1.00
10	Roger Clemens/AL SO	2.00

League Leaders Single Material

		NM/M
Production 250 Sets		
1	Alex Rodriguez/Bat	10.00
2	Albert Pujols/Bat	15.00
3	Albert Pujols/Bat	15.00
4	Nomar Garciaparra/Bat	10.00
5	Mark Prior/Jsy	10.00
6	Pedro Martinez/Jsy	8.00
7	Kerry Wood/Jsy	8.00
8	Derek Jeter/Jsy	15.00
9	Jason Giambi/Jsy	6.00
10	Roger Clemens/Jsy	12.00

League Leaders Double

		NM/M
Production 500 Sets		
Foil:		1-2X
Production 75 Sets		
Holofoil:		No Pricing
Production 10 Sets		
1	Alex Rodriguez, Jim Thome/HR	5.00
2	Mark Prior, Pedro Martinez/ERA	4.00
3	Roger Clemens, Kerry Wood/SO	5.00
4	Nomar Garciaparra, Albert Pujols/Hit	5.00
5	Derek Jeter, Albert Pujols/Avg	5.00

League Leaders Double Material

		NM/M
Production 100 Sets		
1	Alex Rodriguez/Bat, Jim Thome/Bat	20.00
2	Mark Prior/Jsy, Pedro Martinez/Jsy	15.00
3	Roger Clemens/Jsy, Kerry Wood/Jsy	20.00
4	Nomar Garciaparra/Bat, Albert Pujols/Bat	25.00
5	Derek Jeter/Jsy, Albert Pujols/Bat	25.00

League Leaders Quad

		NM/M
Production 250 Sets		
Foil:		1-2X
Production 50 Sets		
Holofoil:		No Pricing
Production Five Sets		
1	Albert Pujols, Todd Helton, Edgar Renteria, Gary Sheffield	10.00
2	Derek Jeter, Manny Ramirez, Nomar Garciaparra, Ichiro Suzuki	10.00
3	Mark Prior, Curt Schilling, Nomar Garciaparra, Kevin Brown	8.00
4	Richie Sexson, Sammy Sosa, Albert Pujols, Jim Thome	10.00
5	Alex Rodriguez, Frank Thomas, Jason Giambi, Carlos Delgado	8.00

League Leaders Quad Material

		NM/M
Production 50 Sets		
1	Albert Pujols, Todd Helton, Edgar Renteria, Gary Sheffield	30.00
3	Mark Prior, Curt Schilling, Hideo Nomo, Kevin Brown	30.00
4	Richie Sexson, Sammy Sosa, Albert Pujols, Jim Thome	40.00
5	Alex Rodriguez, Frank Thomas, Jason Giambi, Carlos Delgado	35.00

Players Collection Jersey

		NM/M
Inserted 1:79		
Platinum:		1-2X
Production 50		
1-3	Adam Dunn	5.00
4-7	Alex Rodriguez	10.00
8-9	Andruw Jones	6.00
10	Austin Kearns	6.00
11	Brandon Webb	4.00
12	C.C. Sabathia	4.00
13	Cal Ripken Jr.	25.00
14	Carlos Beltran	5.00
15	Carlos Delgado	6.00
16	Carlos Lee	4.00
17-18	Chipper Jones	8.00
19	Craig Biggio	4.00
20	Curt Schilling	6.00
21	David Wells	4.00
22	Don Mattingly	15.00
23	Dontrelle Willis	6.00
24-25	Frank Thomas	8.00
26	Fred McGriff	6.00
27	Garret Anderson	6.00
28-29	Gary Sheffield	6.00
30	Greg Maddux	10.00
31-32	Hank Blalock	6.00
33	Hee Seop Choi	4.00
34-36	Hideo Nomo	6.00
37-38	Ivan Rodriguez	6.00
39	Jason Giambi	6.00
40	Jim Edmonds	6.00
41	Jim Thome	8.00
42	John Olerud	4.00
43	John Smoltz	6.00
44	Josh Beckett	4.00
45	Josh Phelps	4.00
46-47	Juan Gonzalez	6.00
48	Kazuhisa Ishii	4.00
49	Lance Berkman	5.00
50-51	Larry Walker	5.00
52	Luis Gonzalez	5.00
53-54	Magglio Ordonez	6.00
55-56	Manny Ramirez	6.00
57-58	Mark Teixeira	8.00
59	Mark Teixeira	6.00
60	Mike Mussina	6.00
61-63	Mike Piazza	8.00
64-65	Nomar Garciaparra	8.00
66	Pat Burrell	4.00
67	Paul Konerko	5.00
68	Paul Lo Duca	5.00
69	Pedro Martinez	8.00
70	Rafael Furcal	5.00
71-72	Rafael Palmeiro	6.00
73	Ramon Hernandez	4.00
74-76	Rickey Henderson	8.00

77-78	Roberto Alomar	6.00
79	Robin Ventura	5.00
80-81	Roger Clemens	10.00
82	Roy Halladay	6.00
83-85	Sammy Sosa	12.00
86	Scott Rolen	8.00
87	Shannon Stewart	6.00
88-90	Shawn Green	5.00
91	Terrence Long	4.00
92	Tim Hudson	6.00
93-94	Todd Helton	8.00
95-96	Tom Glavine	6.00
97	Torii Hunter	6.00
98	Vernon Wells	4.00
99-100	Vladimir Guerrero	8.00

Prestigious Pros

		NM/M
Inserted 1:23		
1	Mark Prior	3.00
2	Derek Jeter	5.00
3	Mike Mussina	1.50
4	Nomar Garciaparra	3.00
5	Roger Clemens	4.00
6	Jason Giambi	1.50
7	Randy Johnson	2.00
8	Rafael Palmeiro	1.50
9	Barry Zito	1.00
10	Pat Burrell	1.00

Stars of MLB

		NM/M
Foil:		1-2X
Production 100 Sets		
Holofoil:		No Pricing
Prod. 25 Sets		
1	Albert Pujols	6.00
2	Derek Jeter	8.00
3	Mike Piazza	4.00
4	Greg Maddux	4.00
5	Ichiro Suzuki	5.00
6	Nomar Garciaparra	5.00
7	Ivan Rodriguez	2.00
8	Randy Johnson	3.00
9	Alex Rodriguez	6.00
10	Sammy Sosa	3.00
11	Alfonso Soriano	3.00
12	Vladimir Guerrero	3.00
13	Jason Giambi	3.00
14	Mark Prior	4.00
15	Chipper Jones	3.00

Stars of MLB Jersey

		NM/M
Production 250 Sets		
Prime:		1-2X
Production 50		
1	Albert Pujols	15.00
2	Derek Jeter	15.00
3	Mike Piazza	8.00
4	Greg Maddux	10.00
5	Nomar Garciaparra	8.00
6	Ivan Rodriguez	6.00
7	Randy Johnson	8.00
9	Alex Rodriguez	10.00
10	Sammy Sosa	12.00
11	Alfonso Soriano	8.00
12	Vladimir Guerrero	8.00

13	Jason Giambi	6.00
14	Mark Prior	10.00
15	Chipper Jones	8.00

Stars of MLB Jersey Autographs

		NM/M
Quantity produced listed.
14	Mark Prior/50	75.00

2004 Playoff Prime Cuts

		NM/M
Complete Set (50):		150.00
Common Player:		1.50
Production 949 Sets		
Box (1):		185.00
1	Roger Clemens	6.00
2	Nomar Garciaparra	6.00
3	Albert Pujols	6.00
4	Sammy Sosa	6.00
5	Greg Maddux	4.00
6	Jason Giambi	3.00
7	Hideo Nomo	1.50
8	Mike Piazza	4.00
9	Ichiro Suzuki	5.00
10	Jeff Bagwell	2.00
11	Derek Jeter	8.00
12	Manny Ramirez	2.00
13	Rickey Henderson	1.50
14	Alex Rodriguez	6.00
15	Troy Glaus	1.50
16	Mike Mussina	1.50
17	Kerry Wood	1.00
18	Kazuhisa Ishii	1.00
19	Hideki Matsui	8.00
20	Frank Thomas	2.00
21	Barry Bonds	8.00
22	Adam Dunn	1.50
23	Randy Johnson	3.00
24	Alfonso Soriano	3.00
25	Pedro J. Martinez	3.00
26	Andruw Jones	2.00
27	Mark Prior	4.00
28	Vladimir Guerrero	3.00
29	Chipper Jones	4.00
30	Todd Helton	2.00
31	Rafael Palmeiro	2.00
32	Mark Grace	2.00
33	Pedro J. Martinez	3.00
34	Randy Johnson	3.00
35	Randy Johnson	3.00
36	Roger Clemens	6.00
37	Roger Clemens	6.00
38	Alex Rodriguez	4.00
39	Greg Maddux	4.00
40	Mike Piazza	4.00
41	Mike Piazza	4.00
42	Hideo Nomo	1.50
43	Rickey Henderson	1.50
44	Rickey Henderson	1.50
45	Barry Bonds	8.00
46	Ivan Rodriguez	2.00
47	George Brett	8.00
48	Cal Ripken Jr.	8.00
49	Nolan Ryan	10.00
50	Don Mattingly	6.00

Century

		NM/M
Cards (1-50):		1-2X
Production 100 Sets		
Century Gold:		No Pricing
Production 10 Sets		
Century Proof:		No Pricing
Production One Set		

Icons Material

		NM/M
Varying quantities produced.
4	Johnny Bench/50	35.00
5	Lefty Grove/25	75.00
6	Carlton Fisk/50	25.00
7	Mel Ott/25	75.00
8	Bob Feller/25	75.00
9	Jackie Robinson/25	30.00
10	Ted Williams/50	135.00
11	Roy Campanella/50	40.00
12	Stan Musial/50	40.00
13	Yogi Berra/50	40.00
14	Babe Ruth/25	750.00
15	Roberto Clemente/50	100.00
16	Warren Spahn/50	40.00
17	Ernie Banks/50	40.00
18	Eddie Mathews/50	35.00
19	Ryne Sandberg/50	40.00
20	Rod Carew/50	25.00
21	Duke Snider/50	25.00
22	Jim Palmer/50	20.00

24	Frank Robinson/50	20.00
25	Brooks Robinson/50	25.00
26	Harmon Killebrew/50	40.00
27	Carl Yastrzemski/50	40.00
28	Reggie Jackson/50	25.00
29	Mike Schmidt/50	40.00
30	Robin Yount/50	30.00
31	George Brett/50	40.00
32	Nolan Ryan/50	40.00
33	Kirby Puckett/50	40.00
34	Cal Ripken Jr./50	40.00
35	Don Mattingly/50	35.00
36	Tony Gwynn/50	65.00
37	Deion Sanders/19	45.00
38	Dave Winfield/19	40.00
39	Eddie Murray/19	60.00
40	Tom Seaver/19	50.00
41	Willie Stargell/19	50.00
42	Wade Boggs/19	50.00
43	Ozzie Smith/19	60.00
44	Willie McCovey/19	40.00
45	Reggie Jackson/19	40.00
46	Whitey Ford/19	40.00
47	Lou Brock/19	40.00
48	Lou Boudreau/19	30.00
49	Steve Carlton/19	45.00
50	Rod Carew/19	40.00
51	Bob Gibson/19	35.00
52	Thurman Munson/19	60.00
53	Roger Maris/19	80.00
54	Nolan Ryan/50	40.00
55	Nolan Ryan/50	40.00
56	Bo Jackson/19	50.00
57	Joe Morgan/19	30.00
58	Phil Rizzuto/19	35.00
59	Gary Carter/19	40.00
60	Paul Molitor/19	50.00
61	Don Drysdale/19	50.00
62	Jim "Catfish" Hunter/19	30.00
63	Fergie Jenkins/19	30.00
64	Pee Wee Reese/19	40.00
65	Dave Winfield/19	40.00
66	Wade Boggs/19	40.00
67	Lefty Grove/19	60.00
68	Rickey Henderson/19	45.00
69	Roger Clemens/19	50.00
70	Roger Clemens/19	50.00

Icons Material Signature

		NM/M
Varying quantities produced.
4	Johnny Bench/18	75.00
8	Bob Feller/45	50.00
12	Stan Musial/30	100.00
13	Yogi Berra/42	65.00
21	Duke Snider/35	50.00
26	Harmon Killebrew/30	100.00
33	Kirby Puckett/16	80.00
69	Roger Clemens/19	150.00

Icons Material Signature Prime

		NM/M
Many not priced due to scarcity.
6	Carlton Fisk/50	60.00
11	Roy Campanella/1 (8/05 auction)	2,020
12	Stan Musial/20	120.00
16	Warren Spahn/25	90.00
17	Ernie Banks/50	70.00
19	Ryne Sandberg/50	100.00
20	Rod Carew/50	50.00
22	Jim Palmer/50	40.00
24	Frank Robinson/50	40.00
25	Brooks Robinson/50	50.00
26	Harmon Killebrew/20	100.00
27	Carl Yastrzemski/50	90.00
28	Reggie Jackson/50	60.00
29	Mike Schmidt/20	125.00
30	Robin Yount/50	75.00
31	George Brett/50	100.00
32	Nolan Ryan/50	120.00
33	Kirby Puckett/34	70.00
34	Cal Ripken Jr./50	150.00
35	Don Mattingly/50	100.00
36	Tony Gwynn/50	70.00
37	Deion Sanders/50	50.00
38	Dave Winfield/50	50.00
39	Eddie Murray/25	75.00
42	Wade Boggs/50	60.00
43	Ozzie Smith/50	75.00
44	Willie McCovey/50	50.00
45	Reggie Jackson/50	60.00
46	Whitey Ford/50	50.00
47	Lou Brock/25	50.00
48	Lou Boudreau/50	50.00
49	Steve Carlton/50	50.00
50	Rod Carew/50	50.00
51	Bob Gibson/50	70.00
54	Nolan Ryan/50	125.00
55	Nolan Ryan/50	125.00
56	Bo Jackson/50	60.00
57	Joe Morgan/50	45.00
58	Phil Rizzuto/50	45.00
59	Gary Carter/50	50.00
60	Paul Molitor/50	55.00
63	Fergie Jenkins/50	45.00
65	Dave Winfield/50	45.00
66	Wade Boggs/50	50.00
68	Rickey Henderson/50	85.00
69	Roger Clemens/25	150.00
70	Roger Clemens/50	120.00

Icons Material Combo Prime

		NM/M
Varying quantities produced.
6	Carlton Fisk/25	50.00
7	Mel Ott/25	85.00

11	Roy Campanella/25	70.00
15	Roberto Clemente/25	200.00
17	Ernie Banks/25	85.00
18	Eddie Mathews/25	50.00
19	Ryne Sandberg/25	80.00
20	Rod Carew/25	50.00
24	Frank Robinson/25	40.00
25	Brooks Robinson/25	50.00
27	Carl Yastrzemski/25	80.00
28	Reggie Jackson/25	50.00
29	Mike Schmidt/25	75.00
30	Robin Yount/25	50.00
31	George Brett/25	75.00
32	Nolan Ryan/25	75.00
33	Kirby Puckett/25	60.00
34	Cal Ripken Jr./25	120.00
35	Don Mattingly/25	50.00
36	Tony Gwynn/25	80.00
37	Deion Sanders/19	50.00
38	Dave Winfield/19	50.00
39	Eddie Murray/19	70.00
41	Willie Stargell/19	60.00
42	Wade Boggs/19	60.00
43	Ozzie Smith/19	70.00
44	Willie McCovey/19	50.00
45	Reggie Jackson/19	50.00
46	Whitey Ford/19	50.00
47	Lou Brock/19	50.00
48	Lou Boudreau/19	50.00
49	Steve Carlton/19	60.00
50	Rod Carew/19	50.00
52	Thurman Munson/19	70.00
53	Roger Maris/19	110.00
54	Nolan Ryan/19	75.00
55	Nolan Ryan/19	75.00
56	Bo Jackson/19	50.00
57	Joe Morgan/19	40.00
58	Phil Rizzuto/19	45.00
59	Gary Carter/19	50.00
60	Paul Molitor/19	60.00
63	Fergie Jenkins/19	40.00
64	Pee Wee Reese/19	50.00
65	Dave Winfield/19	40.00
66	Wade Boggs/19	50.00
69	Roger Clemens/19	50.00
70	Roger Clemens/19	60.00

Icons Signature

		NM/M
Varying quantities produced.
4	Johnny Bench/50	60.00
6	Carlton Fisk/50	40.00
8	Bob Feller/50	40.00
12	Stan Musial/50	65.00
13	Yogi Berra/50	50.00
16	Warren Spahn/25	100.00
17	Ernie Banks/50	50.00
19	Ryne Sandberg/50	70.00
21	Duke Snider/25	50.00
22	Jim Palmer/25	40.00
24	Frank Robinson/50	40.00
25	Brooks Robinson/50	50.00
26	Harmon Killebrew/25	75.00
27	Carl Yastrzemski/50	60.00
28	Reggie Jackson/25	50.00
29	Mike Schmidt/20	75.00
30	Robin Yount/25	65.00
31	George Brett/25	120.00
32	Nolan Ryan/50	110.00
33	Kirby Puckett/34	60.00
34	Cal Ripken Jr./25	200.00
35	Don Mattingly/50	85.00
36	Tony Gwynn/25	70.00
38	Dave Winfield/50	50.00
39	Eddie Murray/25	70.00
42	Wade Boggs/25	60.00
43	Ozzie Smith/25	75.00
44	Willie McCovey/25	50.00
45	Reggie Jackson/25	50.00
47	Lou Brock/25	50.00
48	Lou Boudreau/25	90.00
51	Bob Gibson/25	40.00
56	Bo Jackson/25	65.00
57	Joe Morgan/25	35.00
59	Gary Carter/25	40.00
60	Paul Molitor/25	55.00
65	Dave Winfield/25	40.00
66	Wade Boggs/25	60.00

Prime Cut Materials

		NM/M
Varying quantities produced.
1	Roger Clemens/150	40.00
2	Nomar Garciaparra/150	45.00
3	Albert Pujols/150	40.00
4	Sammy Sosa/150	40.00
5	Greg Maddux/150	40.00
6	Jason Giambi/125	40.00
7	Hideo Nomo/150	30.00
8	Mike Piazza/150	30.00
9	Ichiro Suzuki/25	50.00
10	Jeff Bagwell/150	35.00
11	Derek Jeter/25	50.00
12	Manny Ramirez/25	25.00
13	Rickey Henderson/50	30.00
14	Alex Rodriguez/25	60.00
15	Troy Glaus/25	40.00
17	Kerry Wood/25	40.00

18	Kazuhisa Ishii/25	30.00
19	Hideki Matsui/25	65.00
20	Frank Thomas/25	50.00
21	Barry Bonds/25	50.00
22	Adam Dunn/25	40.00
23	Randy Johnson/25	40.00
24	Alfonso Soriano/35	40.00
25	Pedro J. Martinez/25	40.00
26	Andruw Jones/25	30.00
27	Mark Prior/50	40.00
28	Vladimir Guerrero/25	40.00
29	Chipper Jones/25	40.00
30	Todd Helton/25	35.00
31	Rafael Palmeiro/25	30.00
32	Mark Grace/25	35.00
33	Pedro J. Martinez/25	40.00
34	Randy Johnson/25	40.00
35	Randy Johnson/25	40.00
36	Roger Clemens/50	45.00
38	Alex Rodriguez/25	60.00
40	Mike Piazza/25	30.00
42	Hideo Nomo/50	25.00
43	Rickey Henderson/50	30.00
44	Rickey Henderson/50	30.00
46	Ivan Rodriguez/25	30.00
47	George Brett/50	50.00
48	Cal Ripken Jr./50	65.00
49	Nolan Ryan/50	50.00
50	Don Mattingly/50	40.00

Prime Cut Material Signature

		NM/M
Varying quantities produced.
1	Roger Clemens/25	185.00
3	Albert Pujols/25	180.00
5	Greg Maddux/25	175.00
10	Jeff Bagwell/25	70.00
12	Manny Ramirez/25	60.00
13	Rickey Henderson/25	100.00
14	Alex Rodriguez/25	180.00
15	Troy Glaus/50	40.00
16	Mike Mussina/25	70.00
17	Kerry Wood/25	90.00
18	Kazuhisa Ishii/50	50.00
20	Frank Thomas/25	80.00
22	Adam Dunn/50	60.00
24	Alfonso Soriano/25	85.00
26	Andruw Jones/25	60.00
27	Mark Prior/25	75.00
28	Vladimir Guerrero/50	75.00
29	Chipper Jones/50	85.00
30	Todd Helton/50	60.00
31	Rafael Palmeiro/25	75.00
32	Mark Grace/50	70.00
36	Roger Clemens/25	185.00
38	Alex Rodriguez/25	180.00
44	Rickey Henderson/25	100.00
46	Ivan Rodriguez/25	50.00
47	George Brett/25	120.00
48	Cal Ripken Jr./50	200.00
49	Nolan Ryan/50	140.00
50	Don Mattingly/50	120.00

Material Combos

		NM/M
Production 25 Sets
1	Roger Clemens	60.00
2	Nomar Garciaparra	50.00
3	Albert Pujols	80.00
4	Sammy Sosa	50.00
5	Greg Maddux	50.00
6	Jason Giambi	40.00
7	Hideo Nomo	30.00
8	Mike Piazza	50.00
9	Ichiro Suzuki	70.00
10	Jeff Bagwell	40.00
11	Derek Jeter	60.00
12	Manny Ramirez	30.00
13	Rickey Henderson	40.00
14	Alex Rodriguez	70.00
15	Troy Glaus	35.00
16	Mike Mussina	40.00
17	Kerry Wood	50.00
18	Kazuhisa Ishii	75.00
19	Hideki Matsui	75.00
20	Frank Thomas	45.00
21	Barry Bonds	60.00
22	Adam Dunn	35.00
23	Randy Johnson	50.00
24	Alfonso Soriano	40.00
25	Pedro J. Martinez	45.00
26	Andruw Jones	35.00
27	Mark Prior	50.00
28	Vladimir Guerrero	45.00
29	Chipper Jones	45.00
30	Todd Helton	45.00
31	Rafael Palmeiro	40.00
32	Mark Grace	45.00
33	Pedro J. Martinez	45.00
34	Randy Johnson	50.00
35	Randy Johnson	50.00
36	Roger Clemens	60.00
38	Alex Rodriguez	70.00
40	Mike Piazza	40.00
42	Hideo Nomo	40.00
43	Rickey Henderson	40.00

44	Rickey Henderson	40.00
46	Ivan Rodriguez	35.00
47	George Brett	85.00
48	Cal Ripken Jr.	140.00
49	Nolan Ryan	75.00
50	Don Mattingly	75.00

Signature

		NM/M
Varying quantities produced.
1	Roger Clemens/25	150.00
3	Albert Pujols/25	150.00
10	Jeff Bagwell/25	60.00
13	Rickey Henderson/25	80.00
14	Alex Rodriguez/25	150.00
15	Troy Glaus/25	35.00
16	Mike Mussina/25	60.00
17	Kerry Wood/25	80.00
18	Kazuhisa Ishii/25	40.00
20	Frank Thomas/25	70.00
22	Adam Dunn/25	50.00
24	Alfonso Soriano/25	75.00
26	Andruw Jones/25	50.00
27	Mark Prior/25	60.00
28	Vladimir Guerrero/25	60.00
29	Chipper Jones/25	75.00
31	Rafael Palmeiro/25	65.00
32	Mark Grace/25	60.00
36	Roger Clemens/25	150.00
37	Roger Clemens/25	150.00
38	Alex Rodriguez/25	150.00
43	Rickey Henderson/25	80.00
44	Rickey Henderson/25	80.00
46	Ivan Rodriguez/25	50.00
47	George Brett/25	120.00
48	Cal Ripken Jr./25	200.00
49	Nolan Ryan/25	125.00
50	Don Mattingly/25	100.00

Timeline Dual Achievement Material

		NM/M
Varying quantities produced.
3	Stan Musial, Ted Williams/25	185.00
4	George Brett, Mike Schmidt/25	75.00
5	Cal Ripken Jr., Dale Murphy/19	90.00
6	Mike Schmidt, Roger Clemens/19	65.00
10	George Brett, Nolan Ryan/19	100.00
12	Al Kaline, Duke Snider/19	50.00

Timeline Dual Achieve. Material Sig.

		NM/M
Varying quantities produced.
4	George Brett, Mike Schmidt/24	150.00
5	Cal Ripken Jr., Dale Murphy/25	200.00
6	Mike Schmidt, Roger Clemens/24	220.00
7	Babe Ruth, Ty Cobb/1 (4/04 Auction)	18,000
10	George Brett, Nolan Ryan/25	220.00

Timeline Dual Achieve. Material Prime

		NM/M
Varying quantities produced.
4	George Brett, Mike Schmidt/19	120.00
5	Cal Ripken Jr., Dale Murphy/19	120.00
6	Mike Schmidt, Roger Clemens/19	90.00
10	George Brett, Nolan Ryan/19	140.00

Timeline Dual Achieve Material Combo

No Pricing

Timeline Dual Achievement Signature

		NM/M
Production 24 or 25
4	George Brett, Mike Schmidt/24	160.00
5	Cal Ripken Jr., Dale Murphy/25	180.00
6	Mike Schmidt, Roger Clemens/24	220.00
10	George Brett, Nolan Ryan/25	220.00
12	Al Kaline, Duke Snider/25	100.00

Timeline Dual League Leader Material

		NM/M
Production 9 or 19
4	Jim Palmer, Steve Carlton/19	40.00
7	Nolan Ryan, Steve Carlton/19	70.00
8	Don Mattingly, Tony Gwynn/19	70.00
9	Nolan Ryan, Roger Clemens/19	80.00

Timeline Dual League Leader Mat Prime

Production 9 or 19
7	Nolan Ryan, Steve Carlton/19	80.00
8	Don Mattingly, Tony Gwynn/19	80.00
9	Nolan Ryan, Roger Clemens/19	100.00

Timeline Dual League Leader Mat. Sig.

		NM/M
Varying quantities produced.
4	Jim Palmer, Steve Carlton/19	60.00
7	Nolan Ryan, Steve Carlton/19	200.00
8	Don Mattingly, Tony Gwynn/19	150.00
9	Nolan Ryan, Roger Clemens/19	350.00

Timeline Dual League Leader Signature

		NM/M
Production 25 or 50
4	Jim Palmer, Steve Carlton/50	60.00
7	Nolan Ryan, Steve Carlton/50	180.00
8	Don Mattingly, Tony Gwynn/50	140.00
9	Nolan Ryan, Roger Clemens/25	300.00

Timeline Dual League Leader Mat Combo

		NM/M
Production 9 or 19
7	Nolan Ryan, Steve Carlton/19	80.00
8	Don Mattingly, Tony Gwynn/19	80.00
9	Nolan Ryan, Roger Clemens/19	100.00

Timeline - Material

		NM/M
Varying quantities produced.
4	Ted Williams/50	140.00
5	Roy Campanella/50	30.00
6	Stan Musial/50	35.00
7	Yogi Berra/50	25.00
9	Roberto Clemente/50	85.00
12	Carl Yastrzemski/50	35.00
13	Mike Schmidt/50	30.00
14	George Brett/50	35.00
15	Nolan Ryan/50	35.00
16	Stan Musial/50	35.00
17	Ted Williams/50	140.00
18	Roberto Clemente/50	90.00
19	Greg Maddux/50	25.00
21	Robin Yount/50	20.00
22	Nolan Ryan/50	35.00
23	Ted Williams/50	140.00
24	George Brett/50	30.00
25	Yogi Berra/50	25.00
26	Rod Carew/50	20.00
27	Dale Murphy/25	40.00

Timeline Material Signature

		NM/M
Varying quantities produced.
6	Stan Musial/33	100.00
7	Yogi Berra/42	75.00
16	Stan Musial/38	100.00
25	Yogi Berra/42	75.00

Timeline Material Prime

		NM/M
Varying quantities produced.
5	Roy Campanella/25	40.00
10	Will Clark/19	50.00
12	Carl Yastrzemski/25	75.00
13	Mike Schmidt/25	50.00
14	George Brett/25	50.00
15	Nolan Ryan/25	50.00
19	Greg Maddux/25	40.00
21	Robin Yount/25	40.00
22	Nolan Ryan/25	50.00
24	George Brett/25	50.00
26	Rod Carew/25	40.00
27	Dale Murphy/25	40.00

Timeline Material Combo

		NM/M
Varying quantities produced.
10	Will Clark/19	60.00
12	Carl Yastrzemski/19	80.00
13	Mike Schmidt/19	60.00
14	George Brett/19	65.00
15	Nolan Ryan/19	100.00
19	Greg Maddux/19	50.00
21	Robin Yount/19	50.00
22	Nolan Ryan/19	100.00
24	George Brett/19	65.00
26	Rod Carew/19	40.00
27	Dale Murphy/19	40.00

Timeline Signature

		NM/M
Varying quantities produced.
6	Stan Musial/50	70.00
7	Yogi Berra/50	50.00

#	Player	Price
10	Will Clark/25	100.00
12	Carl Yastrzemski/50	80.00
13	Mike Schmidt/20	85.00
14	George Brett/25	90.00
15	Nolan Ryan/50	110.00
16	Stan Musial/50	70.00
19	Greg Maddux/31	120.00
21	Robin Yount/25	75.00
22	Nolan Ryan/50	110.00
24	George Brett/25	90.00
25	Yogi Berra/50	50.00
27	Dale Murphy/25	50.00

Timeline Material Signature Prime

NM/M
Varying quantities produced.

#	Player	Price
10	Will Clark/50	75.00
12	Carl Yastrzemski/50	80.00
13	Mike Schmidt/20	120.00
14	George Brett/25	100.00
15	Nolan Ryan/50	125.00
19	Greg Maddux/50	125.00
21	Robin Yount/50	75.00
22	Nolan Ryan/50	125.00
24	George Brett/25	100.00

2004 Playoff Prime Cuts II

NM/M

		Price
Complete Set (100):		
Common (1-91):		1.50
Common (92-100):		3.00
Production 699		
Wood Box (One Pack):		150.00
1	Mark Prior	2.00
2	Derek Jeter	8.00
3	Eric Chavez	1.50
4	Carlos Delgado	1.50
5	Albert Pujols	8.00
6	Miguel Cabrera	2.00
7	Ivan Rodriguez	2.00
8	Javy Lopez	1.50
9	Hank Blalock	2.00
10	Chipper Jones	3.00
11	Gary Sheffield	3.00
12	Alfonso Soriano	3.00
13	Alex Rodriguez/Yanks	6.00
14	Edgar Renteria	1.50
15	Jim Edmonds	1.50
16	Garret Anderson	1.50
17	Lance Berkman	1.50
18	Brandon Webb	1.50
19	Mike Lowell	1.50
20	Mark Mulder	1.50
21	Sammy Sosa	5.00
22	Roger Clemens/Astros	8.00
23	Mark Teixeira	1.50
24	Manny Ramirez	3.00
25	Rafael Palmeiro	2.00
26	Ichiro Suzuki	6.00
27	Vladimir Guerrero	3.00
28	Austin Kearns	1.50
29	Troy Glaus	1.50
30	Ken Griffey Jr.	4.00
31	Greg Maddux	4.00
32	Roy Halladay	1.50
33	Roy Oswalt	1.50
34	Kerry Wood	3.00
35	Mike Mussina/Yanks	2.00
36	Michael Young	1.50
37	Juan Gonzalez	1.50
38	Curt Schilling	2.00
39	Shannon Stewart	1.50
40	Todd Helton	2.00
41	Larry Walker/Cards	1.50
42	Mariano Rivera	2.00
43	Nomar Garciaparra	4.00
44	Adam Dunn	2.00
45	Pedro J. Martinez/Sox	3.00
46	Bernie Williams	1.50
47	Tom Glavine	2.00
48	Torii Hunter	1.50
49	David Ortiz	3.00
50	Frank Thomas	4.00
51	Randy Johnson/D'backs	3.00
52	Jason Giambi	1.50
53	Carlos Lee	1.50
54	Mike Sweeney	1.50
55	Hideki Matsui	6.00
56	Dontrelle Willis	1.50
57	Tim Hudson	1.50
58	Jose Vidro	1.50
59	Jeff Bagwell	2.00
60	Rocco Baldelli	1.50
61	Craig Biggio	1.50
62	Mike Piazza/Mets	4.00
63	Magglio Ordonez	1.50
64	Hideo Nomo	1.50
65	Miguel Tejada	1.50
66	Vernon Wells	1.50
67	Barry Larkin	1.50
68	Jacque Jones	1.50
69	Scott Rolen	3.00
70	Jeff Kent	1.50
71	Steve Finley	1.50
72	Kazuo Matsui	6.00
73	Carlos Beltran	2.00
74	Shawn Green	1.50
75	Barry Zito	1.50
76	Aramis Ramirez	1.50
77	Paul LoDuca	1.50
78	Kazuhisa Ishii	1.50
79	Aubrey Huff	1.50
80	Jim Thome	3.00
81	Andy Pettitte/Astros	1.50
82	Andruw Jones	1.50
83	Josh Beckett	1.50
84	Sean Casey	1.50
85	Alex Rodriguez/M's	6.00
86	Roger Clemens/Yanks	6.00
87	Mike Mussina/O's	2.00
88	Pedro Martinez/Dgr	3.00
89	Randy Johnson/Astros	3.00
90	Mike Piazza/Dgr	4.00
91	Andy Pettitte/Yanks	1.50
92	Cal Ripken Jr.	15.00
93	Dale Murphy	3.00
94	Don Mattingly	8.00
95	Gary Carter	3.00
96	George Brett	8.00
97	Nolan Ryan	10.00
98	Ozzie Smith	8.00
99	Steve Carlton	3.00
100	Tony Gwynn	6.00

Silver

Silver (1-91):	1-2X
Silver (92-100):	1-1.5X
Production 50 Sets	

Gold

Gold (1-91):	2-4X
Gold (92-100):	1.5-2X
Production 25 Sets	

Platinum

No Pricing
Production One Set

Icons

NM/M

Common Player:		4.00
Production 50 Sets		
Gold:		No Pricing
Production 10 Sets		
Platinum:		No Pricing
Production One Set		
Silver:		1-1.5X
Production 25 Sets		
1	Dale Murphy	6.00
2	Eddie Mathews	8.00
3	Brooks Robinson	8.00
4	Cal Ripken Jr.	25.00
5	Cal Ripken Jr.	25.00
6	Eddie Murray	8.00
7	Frank Robinson	4.00
8	Jim Palmer	4.00
9	Bobby Doerr	4.00
10	Carl Yastrzemski	10.00
11	Carlton Fisk	6.00
12	Dennis Eckersley	6.00
13	Luis Aparicio	4.00
14	Luis Tiant	4.00
15	Ted Williams	12.00
16	Wade Boggs	4.00
17	Duke Snider	6.00
18	Jackie Robinson	8.00
19	Pee Wee Reese	6.00
20	Burleigh Grimes	4.00
21	Nolan Ryan	20.00
22	Reggie Jackson	6.00
23	Rod Carew	6.00
24	Rod Carew	6.00
25	Billy Williams	4.00
26	Ernie Banks	8.00
27	Mark Grace	6.00
28	Ron Santo	4.00
29	Paul Molitor	6.00
30	Bo Jackson	6.00
31	Carlton Fisk	6.00
32	Johnny Bench	8.00
33	Tom Seaver	6.00
34	Tony Perez	4.00
35	Bob Feller	4.00
36	Lou Boudreau	4.00
37	Al Kaline	8.00
38	Alan Trammell	4.00
39	Ty Cobb	8.00
40	Don Sutton	4.00
41	Nolan Ryan	20.00
42	Roger Maris	8.00
43	Bo Jackson	6.00
44	George Brett	12.00
45	George Brett	12.00
46	Maury Wills	4.00
47	Warren Spahn	6.00
48	Robin Yount	10.00
49	Harmon Killebrew	6.00
50	Kirby Puckett	8.00
51	Paul Molitor	6.00
52	Andre Dawson	4.00
53	Mel Ott	6.00
54	Mel Ott	6.00
55	Duke Snider	6.00
56	Rickey Henderson	8.00
57	Tom Seaver	6.00
58	Babe Ruth	15.00
59	Babe Ruth	15.00
60	Jim "Catfish" Hunter	4.00
61	Dave Righetti	4.00
62	Dave Winfield	6.00
63	Don Mattingly	15.00
64	Don Mattingly	15.00
65	Lou Gehrig	10.00
66	Lou Gehrig	10.00
67	Phil Niekro	4.00
68	Phil Rizzuto	6.00
69	Reggie Jackson	6.00
70	Rickey Henderson	6.00
71	Roger Maris	8.00
72	Thurman Munson	8.00
73	Thurman Munson	8.00
74	Wade Boggs	6.00
75	Whitey Ford	6.00
76	Yogi Berra	8.00
77	Lefty Grove	4.00
78	Mike Schmidt	10.00
79	Mike Schmidt	10.00
80	Steve Carlton	4.00
81	Ralph Kiner	4.00
82	Roberto Clemente	15.00
83	Roberto Clemente	15.00
84	Dave Winfield	4.00
85	Rickey Henderson	6.00
86	Steve Garvey	4.00
87	Tony Gwynn	8.00
88	Tony Gwynn	8.00
89	Gaylord Perry	4.00
90	Joe Morgan	6.00
91	Juan Marichal	4.00
92	Steve Carlton	4.00
93	Will Clark	4.00
94	Willie McCovey	4.00
95	Bob Gibson	6.00
96	Lou Brock	6.00
97	Stan Musial	10.00
98	Fergie Jenkins	4.00
99	Nolan Ryan	20.00
100	Harmon Killebrew	8.00

Icons Material Combo

NM/M
Many not priced.
Prime: No Pricing
Production 1-10

#	Player	Price
4	Cal Ripken Jr./Bat-Jsy/25	75.00
5	Cal Ripken Jr./Jkt-Pants/25	75.00
6	Eddie Murray/Bat-Jsy/25	30.00
7	Frank Robinson/Bat-Jsy/20	20.00
10	Carl Yastrzemski/Bat-Jsy/25	40.00
15	Carlton Fisk/Bat-Jsy/25	25.00
16	Ted Williams/Bat-Jsy/25	100.00
17	Duke Snider/Jsy-Pants/25	25.00
18	Jackie Robinson/Jkt-Jsy/25	80.00
21	Nolan Ryan/Jkt-Jsy/25	50.00
22	Reggie Jackson/Hat-Jsy/25	25.00
23	Rod Carew/Bat-Jsy/25	25.00
24	Rod Carew/Jkt-Jsy/25	25.00
29	Paul Molitor/Jsy-Pants/25	25.00
31	Carlton Fisk/Bat-Jsy/25	25.00
33	Tom Seaver/Bat-Jsy/25	25.00
39	Ty Cobb/Bat-Pants/25	150.00
41	Nolan Ryan/Bat-Jsy/25	50.00
42	Roger Maris/Jsy-Pants/25	75.00
44	George Brett/Bat-Jsy/25	50.00
45	George Brett/Hat-Jsy/25	50.00
47	Warren Spahn/Jsy-Jsy/25	30.00
49	Robin Yount/Bat-Jsy/19	50.00
49	Harmon Killebrew/Jsy-Jsy/25	40.00
53	Mel Ott/Bat-Jsy/25	50.00
54	Mel Ott/Bat-Pants/25	50.00
55	Duke Snider/Jsy-Pants/25	25.00
58	Babe Ruth/Bat-Jsy/25	300.00
59	Babe Ruth/Bat-Pants/25	300.00
65	Lou Gehrig/Bat-Jsy/25	200.00
66	Lou Gehrig/Bat-Pants/25	200.00
69	Reggie Jackson/Bat-Jsy/25	25.00
71	Roger Maris/Bat-Pants/25	60.00
72	Thurman Munson/Bat-Jsy/25	50.00
73	Thurman Munson/Bat-Pants/25	50.00
75	Whitey Ford/Jsy-Jsy/16	40.00
78	Mike Schmidt/Bat-Jsy/25	50.00
79	Mike Schmidt/Hat-Jsy/25	50.00
82	Roberto Clemente/Bat-Jsy/21	150.00
83	Roberto Clemente/Bat-Hat/21	150.00
93	Will Clark/Bat-Jsy/22	30.00
94	Willie McCovey/Jsy-Jsy/25	25.00
99	Nolan Ryan/Jsy-Pants/25	50.00
100	Harmon Killebrew/Bat-Jsy/25	40.00

Icons Material Number

NM/M
Many not priced.

#	Player	Price
1	Dale Murphy/Jsy/25	20.00
3	Brooks Robinson/Jsy/25	20.00
4	Cal Ripken Jr./Jsy/25	60.00
5	Cal Ripken Jr./Jkt/25	60.00
6	Eddie Murray/Jsy/25	30.00
7	Frank Robinson/Jsy/25	15.00
8	Jim Palmer/Jsy/25	15.00
9	Bobby Doerr/Jsy/25	10.00
10	Carl Yastrzemski/Jsy/25	40.00
11	Carlton Fisk/Jsy/25	20.00
15	Ted Williams/Jsy/100	100.00
18	Duke Snider/Jsy/25	20.00
19	Jackie Robinson/Jkt/50	65.00
19	Pee Wee Reese/Jsy/25	15.00
20	Burleigh Grimes/Pants/25	50.00
21	Nolan Ryan/Jsy/25	40.00
22	Reggie Jackson/Jsy/25	20.00
23	Rod Carew/Jsy/25	20.00
24	Rod Carew/Jkt/25	20.00
25	Billy Williams/Jsy/25	10.00
26	Ernie Banks/Jsy/25	25.00
29	Paul Molitor/Pants/25	20.00
31	Carlton Fisk/Jsy/25	20.00
32	Johnny Bench/Jsy/25	30.00
33	Tom Seaver/Jsy/25	20.00
35	Bob Feller/Jsy/15	15.00
36	Lou Boudreau/Jsy/25	25.00
39	Ty Cobb/Pants/50	100.00
41	Nolan Ryan/Jsy/25	40.00
42	Roger Maris/Jsy/25	50.00
43	George Brett/Jsy/25	40.00
44	George Brett/Jsy/25	40.00
46	Warren Spahn/Jsy/25	40.00
47	Robin Yount/Jsy/25	30.00
48	Harmon Killebrew/Jsy/25	30.00
50	Kirby Puckett/Jsy/25	25.00
51	Paul Molitor/Jsy/25	20.00
52	Mel Ott/Jsy/25	40.00
54	Mel Ott/Jsy/25	20.00
58	Duke Snider/Jsy/25	20.00
58	Babe Ruth/Jsy/25	300.00
60	Babe Ruth/Jsy/25	180.00
60	Jim "Catfish" Hunter/Jsy/25	20.00
63	Don Mattingly/Jsy/25	40.00
64	Don Mattingly/Jsy/25	40.00
65	Lou Gehrig/Jsy/25	150.00
66	Lou Gehrig/Pants/50	100.00
68	Phil Rizzuto/Pants/25	20.00
69	Reggie Jackson/Jsy/25	20.00
71	Roger Maris/Jsy/25	40.00
72	Thurman Munson/Jsy/50	35.00
73	Thurman Munson/Pants/50	35.00
77	Lefty Grove/Hat/25	120.00
78	Mike Schmidt/Jsy/20	40.00
79	Mike Schmidt/Jkt/20	40.00
82	Roberto Clemente/Jsy/21	100.00
83	Roberto Clemente/Hat/21	100.00
91	Juan Marichal/Jsy/25	15.00
93	Will Clark/Jsy/22	25.00
94	Willie McCovey/Jsy/25	25.00
96	Bob Gibson/Jsy/25	25.00
96	Lou Brock/Jkt/20	20.00
99	Nolan Ryan/Jsy/25	40.00
100	Harmon Killebrew/Jsy/25	35.00

Icons Material Prime

No Pricing
Production 1-10

Icons Sign. Century Silver

NM/M

#	Player	Price
1	Dale Murphy/25	40.00
3	Brooks Robinson/50	30.00
4	Cal Ripken Jr./25	180.00
5	Cal Ripken Jr./25	180.00
6	Eddie Murray/50	50.00
7	Frank Robinson/50	30.00
8	Jim Palmer/50	30.00
9	Bobby Doerr/50	30.00
10	Carl Yastrzemski/50	75.00
11	Carlton Fisk/27	40.00
12	Dennis Eckersley/43	30.00
13	Luis Aparicio/25	25.00
16	Wade Boggs/26	40.00
17	Duke Snider/50	30.00
21	Nolan Ryan/30	100.00
22	Reggie Jackson/50	50.00
23	Rod Carew/29	35.00
24	Rod Carew/29	35.00
25	Billy Williams/26	20.00
29	Paul Molitor/25	35.00
30	Bo Jackson/25	50.00
31	Carlton Fisk/25	40.00
32	Johnny Bench/50	40.00
33	Tom Seaver/50	40.00
34	Tony Perez/25	40.00
35	Bob Feller/30	30.00
37	Al Kaline/50	40.00
40	Don Sutton/20	30.00
41	Nolan Ryan/34	100.00
43	Bo Jackson/25	50.00
44	George Brett/25	100.00
45	George Brett/25	100.00
48	Robin Yount/19	65.00
49	Harmon Killebrew/50	40.00
51	Paul Molitor/30	30.00
54	Duke Snider/50	40.00
56	Rickey Henderson/24	60.00
57	Tom Seaver/25	40.00
62	Dave Winfield/31	35.00
63	Don Mattingly/50	60.00
64	Don Mattingly/50	60.00
67	Phil Niekro/35	20.00
68	Phil Rizzuto/35	20.00
69	Reggie Jackson/50	50.00
70	Rickey Henderson/24	60.00
75	Whitey Ford/25	50.00
76	Yogi Berra/25	50.00
78	Mike Schmidt/20	80.00
79	Mike Schmidt/20	80.00
80	Steve Carlton/30	30.00
81	Ralph Kiner/25	45.00
84	Dave Winfield/31	35.00
85	Rickey Henderson/50	60.00
87	Tony Gwynn/50	40.00
88	Tony Gwynn/50	40.00
89	Gaylord Perry/36	20.00
90	Joe Morgan/24	25.00
91	Juan Marichal/27	25.00
92	Steve Carlton/30	30.00
93	Will Clark/22	50.00
94	Willie McCovey/25	30.00
95	Bob Gibson/45	30.00
97	Stan Musial/65	65.00
98	Lou Brock/30	30.00
99	Nolan Ryan/34	100.00
100	Harmon Killebrew/50	40.00

Icons Signature Century Gold

NM/M
Many not priced.

#	Player	Price
1	Dale Murphy/25	40.00
3	Brooks Robinson/25	40.00
7	Frank Robinson/25	35.00
8	Jim Palmer/25	35.00
9	Bobby Doerr/25	30.00
17	Duke Snider/25	40.00
32	Johnny Bench/25	50.00
34	Tony Perez/24	40.00
35	Bob Feller/19	40.00
37	Al Kaline/25	50.00
43	Bo Jackson/16	75.00
49	Harmon Killebrew/25	50.00
51	Paul Molitor/25	35.00
55	Duke Snider/25	40.00
64	Don Mattingly/23	75.00
64	Don Mattingly/23	75.00
80	Steve Carlton/25	35.00
81	Ralph Kiner/25	45.00
87	Tony Gwynn/19	50.00
88	Tony Gwynn/19	50.00
92	Steve Carlton/25	50.00
95	Bob Gibson/25	40.00
96	Lou Brock/20	40.00
97	Stan Musial/25	90.00
100	Harmon Killebrew/50	50.00

Icons Sign. Century Platinum

No Pricing
Production One Set

Icons Sign. Material Combo

NM/M
Many not priced.
Prime: No Pricing
Production 1-10

#	Player	Price
1	Dale Murphy/Bat-Jsy/25	45.00
7	Frank Robinson/Bat-Jsy/20	45.00
8	Jim Palmer/Hat-Jsy/22	50.00
9	Bobby Doerr/Bat-Jsy/25	40.00
17	Duke Snider/Jsy-Pants/25	50.00
25	Billy Williams/Bat-Jsy/26	30.00
29	Paul Molitor/Jsy-Pants/25	50.00
34	Tony Perez/Bat-Fld Glv/24	50.00
48	Robin Yount/Bat-Jsy/19	100.00
49	Harmon Killebrew/Jsy-Jsy/25	80.00
51	Paul Molitor/Bat-Jsy/25	50.00
63	Don Mattingly/Bat-Jsy/23	100.00
64	Don Mattingly/Hat-Jsy/23	100.00
78	Mike Schmidt/Bat-Jsy/20	100.00
79	Mike Schmidt/Hat-Jkt/20	100.00
80	Steve Carlton/Fld Glv-Pants/32	50.00
87	Tony Gwynn/Fld Glv-Jsy/19	80.00
88	Tony Gwynn/Jsy-Pants/19	80.00
92	Steve Carlton/Bat-Jsy/32	50.00
93	Will Clark/Bat-Jsy/22	75.00
98	Fergie Jenkins/Fld Glv-Hat/31	40.00

Icons Sign. Material Number

NM/M
Many not priced.
Prime: No Pricing
Production 1-10

#	Player	Price
7	Frank Robinson/Jsy/20	40.00
8	Jim Palmer/Jsy/20	40.00
9	Bobby Doerr/Jsy/25	30.00
11	Carlton Fisk/Jsy/27	40.00
12	Dennis Eckersley/Jsy/43	30.00
16	Wade Boggs/Jsy/26	40.00
21	Nolan Ryan/Jsy/30	50.00
22	Reggie Jackson/Jsy/44	50.00
25	Billy Williams/Jsy/25	25.00
27	Mark Grace/Jsy/17	45.00
35	Bob Feller/Jsy/19	30.00
40	Don Sutton/Jsy/20	30.00
41	Nolan Ryan/Jsy/34	100.00
43	Bo Jackson/Jsy/16	75.00
48	Robin Yount/Jsy/19	65.00
62	Dave Winfield/Pants/31	40.00
63	Dave Winfield/Jsy/23	40.00
64	Don Mattingly/Jkt/23	80.00
69	Reggie Jackson/Jsy/44	50.00
78	Mike Schmidt/Jsy/20	80.00
79	Mike Schmidt/Jsy/20	80.00
80	Steve Carlton/Pants/32	40.00
84	Dave Winfield/Jsy/31	40.00
87	Tony Gwynn/Jsy/19	75.00
88	Tony Gwynn/Jsy/19	75.00
89	Gaylord Perry/Jsy/36	20.00
91	Juan Marichal/Jsy/27	25.00
92	Steve Carlton/Jsy/32	40.00
93	Will Clark/Jsy/22	65.00
95	Bob Gibson/Jsy/45	35.00
96	Lou Brock/Jkt/20	40.00
98	Fergie Jenkins/Hat/31	25.00
99	Nolan Ryan/Jsy/34	100.00

Material Combo

NM/M
Many not priced due to scarcity.
Prime: No Pricing
Production 1-9

#	Player	Price
1	Mark Prior/Hat-Jsy/22	20.00
2	Alfonso Soriano/Bat-Jsy/25	25.00
15	Jim Edmonds/Bat-Jsy/15	20.00
16	Garret Anderson/Bat-Jsy/16	15.00
21	Sammy Sosa/Bat-Jsy/21	40.00
22	Roger Clemens/Bat-Jsy/22	50.00
24	Manny Ramirez/Bat-Jsy/24	25.00
25	Rafael Palmeiro/Bat-Jsy/25	20.00
27	Vladimir Guerrero/Bat-Jsy/27	25.00
31	Greg Maddux/Bat-Jsy/31	40.00
35	Mike Mussina/Bat-Jsy/35	25.00
40	Todd Helton/Bat-Jsy/17	25.00
86	Roger Clemens/Fld Glv-Jsy/22	50.00
92	Cal Ripken Jr./Bat-Jsy/25	75.00
93	Dale Murphy/Bat-Jsy/25	20.00
94	Don Mattingly/Bat-Jsy/25	50.00
96	George Brett/Bat-Jsy/25	50.00
97	Nolan Ryan/Bat-Jkt/25	60.00
98	Ozzie Smith/Bat-Jsy/45	50.00

Material Number

NM/M
Most not priced.
Prime: No Pricing
Production 1-10

#	Player	Price
86	Roger Clemens/Jsy/25	40.00
92	Cal Ripken Jr./Jsy/25	60.00
93	Dale Murphy/Jsy/25	40.00
94	Don Mattingly/Jsy/25	40.00
96	George Brett/Jsy/25	50.00
97	Nolan Ryan/Jkt/25	50.00
98	Ozzie Smith/Jsy/25	30.00

Signature Century Silver

NM/M
Many not priced.

#	Player	Price
1	Mark Prior/22	30.00
2	Miguel Cabrera/24	40.00
9	Hank Blalock/25	40.00
11	Gary Sheffield/25	40.00
15	Jim Edmonds/25	25.00
16	Garret Anderson/25	25.00
17	Lance Berkman/25	30.00
20	Mark Mulder/25	30.00
21	Sammy Sosa/21	125.00
23	Mark Teixeira/40	40.00
24	Manny Ramirez/24	75.00
25	Rafael Palmeiro/25	40.00
31	Greg Maddux/31	100.00
34	Kerry Wood/34	50.00
35	Mike Mussina/35	40.00
44	Juan Gonzalez/22	40.00
44	Adam Dunn/44	40.00
49	David Ortiz/34	50.00
50	Frank Thomas/35	50.00
63	Craig Biggio/25	35.00
63	Magglio Ordonez/30	25.00
66	Vernon Wells/25	25.00
69	Scott Rolen/27	50.00
82	Andruw Jones/35	35.00
83	Josh Beckett/21	25.00
87	Mike Mussina/35	40.00
92	Cal Ripken Jr./35	175.00
93	Dale Murphy/25	40.00
94	Don Mattingly/25	75.00
95	Gary Carter/25	40.00
97	Nolan Ryan/34	100.00
99	Steve Carlton/32	40.00
100	Tony Gwynn/25	50.00

Signature Century Gold

No Pricing
Production 1-17

Signature Century Platinum

No Pricing
Production One Set

Signature Material Combo

		NM/M
Most not priced.
Prime: No Pricing
Production 1-9

1	Mark Prior/Hat-Jsy/22	50.00
20	Mark Mulder/Jsy-Jsy/20	35.00
40	Todd Helton/Bat-Jsy/17	75.00
83	Josh Beckett/Bat-Jsy/21	35.00
93	Dale Murphy/Bat-Jsy/94	
94	Don Mattingly/Bat-Jsy/25	100.00

Signature Material Number

		NM/M
Most not priced.
Prime: No Pricing
Production 1-9

1	Mark Prior/Jsy/22	40.00
17	Lance Berkman/Jsy/17	50.00
20	Mark Mulder/Jsy/20	60.00
40	Todd Helton/Jsy/17	60.00
57	Tim Hudson/Jsy/15	35.00
83	Josh Beckett/Jsy/21	
94	Don Mattingly/Jsy/23	100.00
97	Nolan Ryan/Jkt/34	125.00
99	Steve Carlton/Jsy/32	40.00
100	Tony Gwynn/Jsy/19	80.00

Timeline

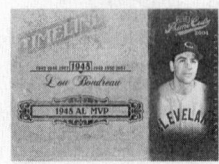

		NM/M
Common Player: 4.00
Production 50 Sets
Century Gold: No Pricing
Production 10 Sets
Century Platinum: No Pricing
Production One Set
Century Silver: 1-1.5X
Production 25 Sets

1	Al Kaline	8.00
2	Alex Rodriguez	10.00
3	Andre Dawson	4.00
4	Babe Ruth	15.00
5	Barry Zito	4.00
6	Bob Feller	6.00
7	Bob Gibson	6.00
8	Bobby Doerr	6.00
9	Brooks Robinson	6.00
10	Cal Ripken Jr.	25.00
11	Carl Hubbell	4.00
12	Carl Yastrzemski	10.00
13	Carlton Fisk	6.00
14	Jim "Catfish" Hunter	6.00
15	Chipper Jones	8.00
16	Cy Young	6.00
17	Dale Murphy	6.00
18	Dave Parker	4.00
19	Dennis Eckersley	4.00
20	Don Drysdale	6.00
21	Don Mattingly	15.00
22	Duke Snider	6.00
23	Dwight Gooden	4.00
24	Early Wynn	4.00
25	Eddie Mathews	8.00
26	Eddie Murray	6.00
27	Enos Slaughter	4.00
28	Ernie Banks	8.00
29	Fergie Jenkins	4.00
30	Frank Robinson	6.00
31	Frank Thomas	8.00
32	Frankie Frisch	4.00
33	Fred Lynn	4.00
34	Gary Carter	4.00
35	Gaylord Perry	4.00
36	George Brett	15.00
37	Greg Maddux	10.00
38	Hal Newhouser	4.00
39	Harmon Killebrew	8.00
40	Honus Wagner	6.00
41	Hoyt Wilhelm	4.00
42	Ivan Rodriguez	8.00
43	Jackie Robinson	6.00
44	Jason Giambi	4.00
45	Jeff Bagwell	6.00
46	Jim Palmer	4.00
47	Jimmie Foxx	8.00
48	Joe Morgan	4.00
49	Johnny Bench	8.00
50	Johnny Mize	4.00
51	Jose Canseco	6.00
52	Juan Gonzalez	6.00
53	Juan Marichal	4.00
54	Keith Hernandez	4.00
55	Kirby Puckett	8.00
56	Lefty Grove	4.00
57	Lou Boudreau	4.00
58	Lou Brock	6.00
59	Lou Gehrig	10.00
60	Luis Aparicio	4.00
61	Marty Marion	4.00
62	Mel Ott	6.00
63	Miguel Tejada	6.00
64	Mike Schmidt	10.00
65	Nellie Fox	6.00
66	Nolan Ryan	15.00
67	Orel Hershiser	4.00
68	Orlando Cepeda	4.00
69	Paul Molitor	6.00
70	Pedro Martinez	8.00
71	Pee Wee Reese	4.00
72	Phil Niekro	4.00
73	Phil Rizzuto	6.00
74	Ralph Kiner	4.00
75	Randy Johnson	8.00
76	Red Schoendienst	4.00
77	Reggie Jackson	6.00
78	Rickey Henderson	4.00
79	Roberto Clemente	15.00
80	Robin Yount	8.00
81	Rod Carew	6.00
82	Roger Clemens	10.00
83	Roger Maris	10.00
84	Rogers Hornsby	8.00
85	Roy Campanella	8.00
86	Ozzie Smith	10.00
87	Sammy Sosa	6.00
88	Satchel Paige	6.00
89	Stan Musial	10.00
90	Steve Carlton	8.00
91	Ted Williams	10.00
92	Thurman Munson	4.00
93	Tom Seaver	4.00
94	Ty Cobb	10.00
95	Walter Johnson	6.00
96	Warren Spahn	8.00
97	Whitey Ford	6.00
98	Willie McCovey	6.00
99	Willie Stargell	6.00
100	Yogi Berra	8.00

Timeline Material Combo

		NM/M
Quantity produced listed.

4	Babe Ruth/Jsy-Jsy/25	350.00
7	Bob Gibson/Hat-Jsy/25	35.00
10	Cal Ripken Jr./Jkt-Jsy/25	75.00
13	Carlton Fisk/Bat-Jsy/27	25.00
14	Jim "Catfish" Hunter/Jsy/27	25.00
17	Dale Murphy/Bat-Jsy/25	25.00
21	Don Mattingly/Btg Glv-Pants/25	50.00
25	Eddie Mathews/Bat-Jsy/41	40.00
26	Eddie Murray/Bat-Jsy/33	40.00
36	George Brett/Hat-Jsy/25	60.00
39	Harmon Killebrew/Bat-Jsy/25	50.00
43	Jackie Robinson/Jkt-Jsy/42	100.00
46	Jim Palmer/Hat-Jsy/22	20.00
47	Jimmie Foxx/Bat-Fld Glv/25	125.00
49	Johnny Bench/Bat-Jsy/25	40.00
58	Lou Brock/Bat-Jsy/20	25.00
59	Lou Gehrig/Jsy-Pants/25	250.00
62	Mel Ott/Jsy-Pants/25	50.00
64	Mike Schmidt/Bat-Jsy/20	60.00
66	Nolan Ryan/Jsy-Pants/25	60.00
68	Orlando Cepeda/Bat-Pants/25	20.00
71	Pee Wee Reese/Bat-Jsy/25	30.00
77	Reggie Jackson/Bat-Jsy/25	30.00
79	Roberto Clemente/Hat-Jsy/21	150.00
80	Robin Yount/Bat-Jsy/19	50.00
81	Rod Carew/Bat-Jsy/29	30.00
82	Roger Clemens/Jsy/21	40.00
83	Roger Maris/Jsy-Pants/25	75.00
85	Roy Campanella/Bat-Jsy/39	35.00
86	Ozzie Smith/Bat-Jsy/21	40.00
87	Sammy Sosa/Bat-Jsy/21	40.00
90	Steve Carlton/Hat-Jsy/32	20.00
91	Ted Williams/Jsy-Jsy/25	140.00
92	Thurman Munson/Jsy-Pants/10	50.00
94	Ty Cobb/Bat-Pants/25	160.00
96	Warren Spahn/Jsy-Jsy/21	40.00
98	Willie McCovey/Bat-Jsy/25	25.00

Timeline Material Combo CY

Quantity produced listed.

Timeline Material Number

		NM/M
Quantity produced listed.

4	Babe Ruth/Jsy/25	350.00
6	Bob Feller/Pants/19	25.00
7	Bob Gibson/Jsy/25	30.00
10	Cal Ripken Jr./Jsy/25	60.00
12	Carl Yastrzemski/Jsy/25	40.00
13	Carlton Fisk/Jsy/27	25.00
14	Jim "Catfish" Hunter/Jsy/27	20.00
20	Don Drysdale/Jsy/25	40.00
22	Duke Snider/Pants/25	25.00
24	Early Wynn/Jsy/24	15.00
25	Eddie Mathews/Jsy/25	30.00
26	Eddie Murray/Jsy/25	25.00
28	Ernie Banks/Jsy/25	35.00
32	Frankie Frisch/Jkt/25	40.00
36	George Brett/Jsy/25	40.00
39	Harmon Killebrew/Jsy/25	35.00
43	Jackie Robinson/Jkt/42	60.00
46	Jim Palmer/Jsy/22	15.00
47	Jimmie Foxx/Fld Glv/25	85.00
49	Johnny Bench/Jsy/25	25.00
53	Juan Marichal/Jsy/27	15.00
55	Kirby Puckett/Jsy/25	30.00
58	Lou Brock/Jsy/20	25.00
59	Lou Gehrig/Jsy/25	180.00
62	Mel Ott/Jsy/25	40.00
64	Mike Schmidt/Jsy/20	50.00
66	Nolan Ryan/Jsy/25	50.00
68	Orlando Cepeda/Pants/25	15.00
71	Pee Wee Reese/Jsy/25	25.00
74	Ralph Kiner/Bat/25	25.00
77	Reggie Jackson/Jsy/25	25.00
80	Robin Yount/Jsy/19	40.00
81	Rod Carew/Jsy/25	25.00
82	Roger Clemens/Jsy/21	30.00
83	Roger Maris/Jsy/25	60.00
84	Rogers Hornsby/Bat/25	75.00
85	Roy Campanella/Pants/25	30.00
86	Ozzie Smith/Jsy/25	35.00
87	Sammy Sosa/Jsy/21	30.00
88	Satchel Paige/Jsy/25	75.00
90	Steve Carlton/Jsy/25	15.00
91	Ted Williams/Jsy/25	100.00
92	Thurman Munson/Jsy/25	40.00
93	Tom Seaver/Pants/25	25.00
94	Ty Cobb/Pants/25	140.00
96	Warren Spahn/Jsy/25	35.00
98	Willie McCovey/Jsy/8	25.00

Timeline Material Position

		NM/M
Quantity produced listed.

4	Babe Ruth/Jsy/25	350.00
6	Bob Feller/Pants/19	25.00
7	Bob Gibson/Jsy/25	30.00
10	Cal Ripken Jr./Jsy/25	60.00
12	Carl Yastrzemski/Jsy/25	40.00
13	Carlton Fisk/Jsy/27	25.00
14	Jim "Catfish" Hunter/Jsy/27	20.00
20	Don Drysdale/Jsy/25	40.00
22	Duke Snider/Pants/25	25.00
24	Early Wynn/Jsy/24	15.00
25	Eddie Mathews/Jsy/25	30.00
26	Eddie Murray/Jsy/25	25.00
28	Ernie Banks/Jsy/25	35.00
32	Frankie Frisch/Jkt/25	40.00
36	George Brett/Jsy/25	40.00
39	Harmon Killebrew/Jsy/25	35.00
43	Jackie Robinson/Jkt/42	60.00
47	Jimmie Foxx/Fld Glv/25	85.00
49	Johnny Bench/Jsy/25	25.00
53	Juan Marichal/Jsy/27	15.00
55	Kirby Puckett/Jsy/25	30.00
58	Lou Brock/Jsy/25	25.00
59	Lou Gehrig/Jsy/25	180.00
62	Mel Ott/Jsy/25	40.00
64	Mike Schmidt/Jsy/20	50.00
66	Nolan Ryan/Jsy/25	50.00
68	Orlando Cepeda/Pants/25	15.00
71	Pee Wee Reese/Bat/25	25.00
74	Ralph Kiner/Bat/25	25.00
77	Reggie Jackson/Jsy/25	25.00
80	Robin Yount/Jsy/19	40.00
81	Rod Carew/Jsy/25	25.00
82	Roger Clemens/Jsy/21	30.00
83	Roger Maris/Jsy/25	60.00
84	Rogers Hornsby/Bat/25	75.00
86	Ozzie Smith/Jsy/25	35.00
87	Sammy Sosa/Jsy/21	30.00
88	Satchel Paige/CO Jsy/25	75.00
90	Steve Carlton/Jsy/25	15.00
92	Thurman Munson/Jsy/15	50.00
93	Tom Seaver/Pants/25	25.00
96	Warren Spahn/Jsy/21	35.00
98	Willie McCovey/Jsy/25	25.00

Timeline Material Prime

No Pricing
Production 1-10

Timeline Material Quad

No Pricing
Production 1-25

Timeline Material Trio

		NM/M
Most not priced.
Trio HOF: No Pricing
Production 1-9
Trio MVP: No Pricing
Production 1-10
Trio Stats: No Pricing
Production 1-15

10	Cal Ripken Jr./Jkt-Jsy-Pants/25	100.00
17	Dale Murphy/Bat-Jsy/25	40.00
21	Don Mattingly/Bat-Jkt-Pants/25	75.00
26	Eddie Murray/Bat-Jsy-Shoe/25	85.00
80	Robin Yount/Bat-Jsy/19	70.00
82	Roger Clemens/Bat-Jsy/21	50.00

Timeline Sig. Material Combo

		NM/M
Most not priced.

7	Bob Gibson/Hat-Jsy/25	50.00
8	Bobby Doerr/Bat-Jsy/25	50.00
58	Lou Brock/Bat-Jsy/20	50.00

Timeline Sign. Mat. Combo CY

		NM/M
Most not priced.

7	Bob Gibson/Hat-Jsy/25	50.00
46	Jim Palmer/Hat-Jsy/22	50.00
90	Steve Carlton/Hat-Jsy/32	50.00

Timeline Sign. Mat. Number

		NM/M
Most not priced.

6	Bob Feller/Pants/19	40.00
7	Bob Gibson/Jsy/25	50.00
8	Bobby Doerr/Jsy/25	40.00
21	Don Mattingly/Pants/23	80.00
46	Jim Palmer/Jsy/22	40.00
53	Juan Marichal/Jsy/27	40.00
58	Lou Brock/Jsy/20	50.00
66	Nolan Ryan/Jsy/34	150.00
90	Steve Carlton/Jsy/32	40.00

Timeline Sign. Mat. Position

		NM/M
Most not priced.

6	Bob Feller/Pants/19	40.00
8	Bobby Doerr/Jsy/25	40.00
21	Don Mattingly/Pants/23	80.00
46	Jim Palmer/Jsy/22	40.00
53	Juan Marichal/Jsy/27	40.00
58	Lou Brock/Jsy/20	50.00
66	Nolan Ryan/Jsy/34	150.00
67	Orel Hershiser/Jsy/25	30.00

Timeline Sign. Mat. Prime

No Pricing
Production 1-9

Timeline Sign. Material Quad

		NM/M
Most not priced.

21	Don Mattingly/25	180.00

Timeline Sign. Material Trio

		NM/M
No Pricing
Production 1-9
Trio HOF: No Pricing
Production 1-9
Trio MVP: No Pricing
Production 1-8
Trio Stats: No Pricing
Production 1-9

91	Ted Williams/Bat-Jkt-Jsy/1 (2/06 Auction)	1,483

2005 Playoff Absolute Memorabilia

		NM/M
Complete Set (100):		
Common Player:		.50
Retail:		.3X
Retail doesn't have foil front.

Pack (4):		40.00
Box (4):		150.00
1	Andruw Jones	.75
2	B.J. Upton	.75
3	Jim Edmonds	.75
4	Johan Santana	1.00
5	Jeff Bagwell	.75
6	Derek Jeter	3.00
7	Eric Chavez	.75
8	Albert Pujols	3.00
9	Craig Biggio	.75
10	Hank Blalock	.75
11	Chipper Jones	1.00
12	Jacque Jones	.50
13	Alfonso Soriano	1.00
14	Carl Crawford	.50
15	Ben Sheets	.50
16	Garret Anderson	.75
17	Luis Gonzalez	.50
18	Andy Pettitte	.75
19	Miguel Tejada	.75
20	Carlos Delgado	.50
21	Austin Kearns	.50
22	Adrian Beltre	.50
23	Rafael Palmeiro	.75
24	Greg Maddux	2.00
25	Jason Bay	.50
26	Jason Varitek	.75
27	David Ortiz	1.00
28	Dontrelle Willis	.75
29	Adam Dunn	1.00
30	Carlos Lee	.50
31	Manny Ramirez	1.00
32	Rocco Baldelli	.50
33	Jeff Kent	.50
34	Jake Peavy	.75
35	Vernon Wells	.50
36	Ichiro Suzuki	2.00
37	C.C. Sabathia	.50
38	Hideki Matsui	2.00
39	Gary Sheffield	.75
40	Paul LoDuca	.50
41	Vladimir Guerrero	1.00
42	Omar Vizquel	.50
43	Lance Berkman	.50
44	Shawn Green	.50
45	Josh Beckett	.50
46	Barry Zito	.50
47	Roger Clemens	3.00
48	Sean Casey	.50
49	Edgar Renteria	.50
50	Mark Teixeira	.75
51	Frank Thomas	.75
52	Khalil Greene	.50
53	Bobby Abreu	.75
54	Rafael Furcal	.50
55	Jose Vidro	.50
56	Nomar Garciaparra	1.00
57	Melvin Mora	.50
58	Trot Nixon	.50
59	Magglio Ordonez	.50
60	Michael Young	.50
61	Richie Sexson	.50
62	Alex Rodriguez	3.00
63	Tim Hudson	.50
64	Todd Helton	.75
65	Mike Lowell	.50
66	Mark Mulder	.50
67	Sammy Sosa	1.50
68	Mark Prior	1.00
69	Shannon Stewart	.50
70	Miguel Cabrera	1.00
71	Troy Glaus	.50
72	Scott Rolen	.50
73	Ken Griffey Jr.	2.00
74	Mike Piazza	1.00
75	Roy Halladay	.50
76	Larry Walker	.75
77	Kerry Wood	.50
78	Mike Mussina	.75
79	Curt Schilling	1.00
80	Rich Harden	.50
81†	Victor Martinez	.50
82	Roy Oswalt	.50
83	Pedro Martinez	1.00
84	Tom Glavine	.50
85	Randy Johnson	1.00
86	Ivan Rodriguez	.50
87	Carlos Beltran	.75
88	Torii Hunter	.50
89	Hideo Nomo	.50
90	Jim Thome	1.00
91	Aramis Ramirez	.50
92	J.D. Drew	.50
93	Javy Lopez	.50
94	David Wright	2.00
95	Bobby Crosby	.75
96	Jeff Niemann RC	3.00
97	Yuniesky Betancourt RC	3.00
98	Tadahito Iguchi RC	1.00
99	Philip Humber RC	3.00
100	Justin Verlander RC	5.00

Black

Black:		2-4X
Inserted 1:18 Retail

Blue

Blue:		1-2X
Inserted 1:3 Retail

Red

Red:		2-3X
Inserted 1:8 Retail

Spectrum Gold

No Pricing
Production 10 Sets

Spectrum Platinum

No Pricing
Production One Set

Spectrum Silver

Silver:		2-3X
Production 100 Sets

Absolutely Ink Swatch Single

		NM/M
Production 5-50

1	Rafael Furcal/Jsy/50	15.00

Ab. Ink Swatch Single Spectrum

		NM/M
Production 1-25
Prime: No Pricing
Production One Set

1	Rafael Furcal/Jsy/25	20.00
3	Dale Murphy/Jsy/25	35.00
5	Bill Madlock/Bat/25	20.00
7	Bobby Crosby/Jsy/25	20.00
11	Lyle Overbay/Jsy/25	15.00
13	Omar Vizquel/Jsy/25	25.00
18	Travis Hafner/Jsy/25	15.00
23	Mark Teixeira/Jsy/25	50.00
27	Darryl Strawberry/Jsy/25	20.00
28	Alexis Rios/Bat/25	15.00
30	Magglio Ordonez/Jsy/25	15.00
31	Jay Gibbons/Jsy/25	20.00
35	Keith Hernandez/Jsy/25	20.00
38	Carlos Zambrano/Jsy/25	30.00
39	Brett Myers/Jsy/25	15.00
40	Rich Harden/Jsy/25	15.00
41	Danny Kolb/Jsy/25	15.00
47	Carlos Lee/Jsy/25	20.00
51	Dave Parker/Bat/25	20.00
53	C.C. Sabathia/Jsy/25	20.00
55	Brandon Webb/Pants/25	25.00
56	Sean Casey/Jsy/25	20.00
57	Johan Santana/Jsy/25	50.00
58	Miguel Cabrera/Jsy/25	50.00
59	Bert Blyleven/Jsy/25	20.00

Ab. Ink Swatch Single Spectrum (right column continued)

(This is a continuation of the main 2005 Absolute listings on the far right)

3	Dale Murphy/Jsy/50	25.00
4	Duke Snider/Pants/50	25.00
5	Bill Madlock/Bat/50	20.00
7	Bobby Crosby/Jsy/50	15.00
8	Cal Ripken Jr./50	140.00
9	Hank Blalock/Jsy/50	25.00
10	Vernon Wells/Jsy/50	20.00
11	Lyle Overbay/Jsy/50	15.00
13	Omar Vizquel/Jsy/50	20.00
15	Ben Sheets/Jsy/50	20.00
16	Aramis Ramirez/Jsy/50	30.00
18	Travis Hafner/Jsy/50	15.00
19	Mike Lowell/Jsy/50	15.00
20	Frank Robinson/Bat/50	30.00
22	Juan Gonzalez/Jsy/50	25.00
27	Darryl Strawberry/Jsy/50	20.00
28	Alexis Rios/Bat/50	15.00
30	Magglio Ordonez/Jsy/50	15.00
31	Jay Gibbons/Jsy/50	15.00
32	Steve Carlton/Jsy/50	35.00
34	Kerry Wood/Jsy/50	25.00
36	Eric Chavez/Jsy/50	25.00
37	Keith Hernandez/Jsy/50	15.00
38	Carlos Zambrano/Jsy/50	25.00
39	Brett Myers/Jsy/50	15.00
40	Rich Harden/Jsy/50	20.00
41	Danny Kolb/Jsy/50	15.00
42	Mark Prior/Jsy/50	40.00
43	Joey Gathright/Jsy/50	15.00
44	David Cone/Jsy/50	15.00
45	Carlos Lee/Jsy/50	20.00
47	Jack Morris/Jsy/50	20.00
48	Torii Hunter/Jsy/50	20.00
49	Garret Anderson/Jsy/50	25.00
51	Dave Parker/Bat/50	20.00
52	C.C. Sabathia/Jsy/50	15.00
53	Dennis Eckersley/Jsy/50	20.00
54	Barry Larkin/Jsy/50	40.00
55	Brandon Webb/Pants/50	15.00
56	Sean Casey/Jsy/50	20.00
57	Johan Santana/Jsy/50	40.00
58	Miguel Cabrera/Jsy/50	50.00
59	Bert Blyleven/Jsy/50	15.00
60	Casey Kotchman/Jsy/50	15.00
61	Dwight Gooden/Jsy/50	15.00
62	Milton Bradley/Jsy/50	15.00
63	John Kruk/Jsy/50	25.00
64	Michael Young/Jsy/50	20.00
66	Robin Ventura/Jsy/50	15.00
67	Tim Hudson/Jsy/25	30.00
68	Will Clark/Bat/50	40.00
69	Lew Ford/Jsy/50	15.00
70	Jody Gerut/Jsy/50	15.00
72	Don Sutton/Jsy/50	15.00
73	B.J. Upton/Bat/50	20.00
74	Austin Kearns/Jsy/50	15.00
77	Ryan Wagner/Jsy/50	15.00
78	Jermaine Dye/Jsy/50	15.00
80	Al Oliver/Jsy/50	15.00
81	Angel Berroa/Pants/50	15.00
82	Edgar Renteria/Jsy/50	20.00
83	Dennis Eckersley/Jsy/25	25.00
84	Roy Oswalt/Jsy/50	20.00
86	Dave Righetti/Jsy/50	20.00
87	Aubrey Huff/Jsy/50	20.00
89	Jose Vidro/Jsy/50	15.00
90	Harold Baines/Jsy/50	15.00
93	Ken Harvey/Jsy/50	15.00
95	Jason Bay/Jsy/50	20.00
96	Dwight Evans/Jsy/50	30.00
97	Luis Tiant/Jsy/50	15.00
98	Ron Santo/Bat/50	30.00
99	Brian Roberts/Jsy/50	15.00
100	Marty Marion/Jsy/50	15.00

60 Casey Kotchman/Jsy/25 25.00
61 Dwight Gooden/Jsy/25 25.00
62 Milton Bradley/Jsy/25 25.00
63 John Kruk/Jsy/25 25.00
64 Michael Young/Jsy/25 25.00
69 Lew Ford/Jsy/25 15.00
70 Jody Gerut/Jsy/25 15.00
71 Don Sutton/Jsy/25 20.00
73 Austin Kearns/Jsy/25 15.00
77 Ryan Wagner/Jsy/25 15.00
78 Jermaine Dye/Jsy/25 15.00
80 Al Oliver/Jsy/25 15.00
81 Angel Berroa/Pants/25 15.00
89 Jose Vidro/Jsy/25 15.00
90 Harold Baines/Jsy/25 20.00
92 Mark Mulder/Jsy/25 20.00
93 Ken Harvey/Jsy/25 15.00
95 Jason Bay/Jsy/25 25.00
96 Dwight Evans/Jsy/25 25.00
97 Luis Tiant/Pants/25 15.00
98 Ron Santo/Bat/25 30.00
99 Brian Roberts/Jsy/25 40.00
100 Marty Marion/Jsy/25 15.00

Absolutely Ink Swatch Double
NM/M
Production 1-50
1 Rafael Furcal B-J/50 20.00
3 Dale Murphy B-J/50 30.00
7 Bobby Crosby J-J/50 20.00
8 Cal Ripken Jr. J-P/25 150.00
10 Vernon Wells J-J/50 20.00
11 Lyle Overbay J-J/50 15.00
13 Omar Vizquel J-J/25 20.00
16 Aramis Ramirez J-J/25 30.00
18 Travis Hafner BG-J/50 15.00
22 Juan Gonzalez J-J/25 25.00
23 Mark Teixeira J-J/25 35.00
27 Darryl Strawberry J-J/50 20.00
30 Magglio Ordonez B-J/50 20.00
31 Jay Gibbons B-J/50 15.00
32 Steve Carlton FG-J/50 40.00
37 Keith Hernandez B-J/50 15.00
38 Carlos Zambrano J-J/25 25.00
39 Brett Myers J-J/50 15.00
41 Danny Kolb J-J/50 15.00
42 Mark Prior FG-J/50 40.00
43 Joey Gathright B-J/50 15.00
44 David Cone J-J/50 15.00
45 Carlos Lee FG-J/50 15.00
49 Garret Anderson J-J/25 20.00
51 Dave Parker J-J/25 15.00
52 C.C. Sabathia J-J/50 20.00
53 Dennis Eckersley A's J-P/50 20.00
55 Brandon Webb B-P/50 15.00
56 Sean Casey B-J/50 15.00
57 Johan Santana J-J/25 60.00
58 Miguel Cabrera J-J/50 15.00
59 Bert Blyleven J-J/50 15.00
60 Casey Kotchman B-J/50 20.00
62 Milton Bradley J-J/50 15.00
63 John Kruk J-J/50 25.00
64 Michael Young B-J/50 15.00
69 Lew Ford J-J/50 15.00
70 Jody Gerut B-J/50 15.00
71 Don Sutton J-J/50 15.00
73 Austin Kearns J-J/50 15.00
77 Ryan Wagner J-J/50 15.00
78 Jermaine Dye J-J/50 15.00
80 Al Oliver B-J/50 15.00
81 Angel Berroa B-P/50 15.00
82 Edgar Renteria J-J/50 20.00
84 Roy Oswalt FG-J/25 25.00
86 Dave Righetti J-J/50 20.00
87 Aubrey Huff H-J/25 15.00
89 Jose Vidro B-J/50 15.00
90 Harold Baines B-J/50 15.00
94 Ken Harvey J-J/50 15.00
95 Jason Bay B-J/50 40.00
96 Dwight Evans B-J/50 40.00
99 Brian Roberts B-J/50 40.00

Absolutely Ink Swatch Double Spectrum
NM/M
Production 1-25
Prime: No Pricing
Production One Set
1 Rafael Furcal B-J/25 20.00
3 Dale Murphy B-J/25 40.00
7 Bobby Crosby J-J/25 25.00
10 Vernon Wells J-J/25 20.00
11 Lyle Overbay J-J/25 15.00
18 Travis Hafner BG-J/25 30.00
27 Darryl Strawberry J-J/25 25.00
31 Jay Gibbons B-J/25 20.00
37 Keith Hernandez B-J/25 20.00
38 Carlos Zambrano J-J/25 30.00
39 Brett Myers J-J/25 15.00
41 Danny Kolb J-J/25 15.00
43 Carlos Lee FG-J/25 20.00
55 Brandon Webb B-P/25 15.00
59 Bert Blyleven J-J/25 15.00
60 Casey Kotchman B-J/25 20.00
62 Milton Bradley B-J/25 15.00
63 John Kruk J-J/25 25.00
64 Michael Young B-J/25 15.00
69 Lew Ford B-J/25 15.00
70 Jody Gerut B-J/25 15.00
71 Don Sutton J-J/25 15.00
73 Austin Kearns J-J/25 20.00
77 Ryan Wagner J-J/25 15.00
78 Jermaine Dye J-J/25 15.00

81 Angel Berroa B-P/25 15.00
89 Jose Vidro B-J/25 15.00
90 Harold Baines J-J/25 20.00
93 Ken Harvey J-J/25 15.00
95 Jason Bay B-J/25 25.00
96 Dwight Evans B-J/25 40.00
99 Brian Roberts J-J/25 40.00

Absolutely Ink Swatch Triple
NM/M
Production 1-75
1 Rafael Furcal/50 20.00
3 Dale Murphy/50 30.00
8 Cal Ripken Jr./25 160.00
9 Hank Blalock/25 30.00
13 Omar Vizquel/25 30.00
16 Aramis Ramirez/25 35.00
18 Travis Hafner/25 25.00
22 Juan Gonzalez/25 30.00
23 Mark Teixeira/75 40.00
27 Darryl Strawberry/50 20.00
31 Jay Gibbons/25 20.00
37 Keith Hernandez/25 25.00
45 Carlos Lee/50 20.00
49 Garret Anderson/25 30.00
52 C.C. Sabathia/25 20.00
53 Dennis Eckersley/25 25.00
55 Brandon Webb/50 20.00
56 Sean Casey/25 25.00
58 Miguel Cabrera/25 50.00
60 Casey Kotchman/50 25.00
64 Michael Young/25 25.00
69 Lew Ford/25 15.00
70 Jody Gerut/25 15.00
73 Austin Kearns/50 15.00
77 Ryan Wagner/25 15.00
78 Jermaine Dye/25 15.00
81 Angel Berroa/50 15.00
86 Dave Righetti/25 20.00
89 Jose Vidro/25 15.00
90 Harold Baines/50 20.00
95 Jason Bay/25 25.00
96 Dwight Evans/25 40.00

Ab. Ink Swatch Triple Spectrum
NM/M
Production 1-25
Prime: No Pricing
Production One Set
1 Rafael Furcal/25 20.00
3 Dale Murphy/25 40.00
18 Travis Hafner/25 25.00
23 Mark Teixeira/25 50.00
27 Darryl Strawberry/25 20.00
45 Carlos Lee/25 20.00
60 Casey Kotchman/25 25.00
64 Michael Young/25 30.00
69 Lew Ford/25 15.00
70 Jody Gerut/25 15.00
73 Austin Kearns/25 20.00
77 Ryan Wagner/25 15.00
78 Jermaine Dye/25 15.00
81 Angel Berroa/25 15.00
89 Jose Vidro/25 20.00
90 Harold Baines/25 20.00

Absolute Memorabilia Heroes
NM/M
Common Player: 1.50
Production 250 Sets
Spectrum: 1-2X
Production 50 Sets
Reverse Spectrum: 2-4X
Production 25 Sets
1 Billy Martin 3.00
2 Rickey Henderson 2.00
3 Alan Trammell 2.00
5 Lenny Dykstra 1.50
6 Jeff Bagwell 2.00
7 Steve Garvey 1.50
8 Jim "Catfish" Hunter 2.00
9 Cal Ripken Jr. 10.00
10 Gary Sheffield 3.00
11 Edgar Martinez 1.50
12 Roberto Alomar 2.00
13 Luis Tiant 1.50
14 Jim Rice 2.00
15 Carlos Beltran 2.00
16 Hideo Nomo 2.00
17 Mark Grace 2.00
18 Joe Cronin 2.00
19 Tony Gwynn 3.00
20 Bo Jackson 3.00
21 Roger Clemens 5.00
22 Roger Clemens 5.00
23 Don Mattingly 5.00
24 Willie Mays 5.00
25 Andruw Jones 2.00
26 Andre Dawson 2.00
27 Carlton Fisk 2.00
28 Robin Yount 3.00
29 Joe Carter 1.50
30 Dale Murphy 2.00
31 Greg Maddux 3.00
32 Ichiro Suzuki 4.00

33 Jose Canseco 2.00
34 Nolan Ryan 8.00
35 Frank Thomas 2.00
36 Fred Lynn 1.50
37 Curt Schilling 2.00
37 Curt Schilling 2.00
38 Dave Parker 1.50
40 Randy Johnson 2.50
41 Randy Johnson 2.50
42 Vladimir Guerrero 2.50
43 Bernie Williams 1.50
44 Wade Boggs 2.00
45 Pedro Martinez 2.50
46 Andy Pettitte 1.50
47 Fergie Jenkins 2.00
48 Darryl Strawberry 1.50
49 Rafael Palmeiro 2.00
50 Albert Pujols 5.00

Heroes Swatch Double
NM/M
Production 25-50
Spectrum Prime: No Pricing
Production 1-25
1 Billy Martin J-P/50 25.00
2 Rickey Henderson B-J/50 10.00
3 Alan Trammell B-J/50 10.00
4 Lenny Dykstra B-J/50 8.00
5 Jeff Bagwell B-J/50 8.00
6 Steve Garvey B-J/50 8.00
7 Jim "Catfish" Hunter J-J/50 10.00
8 Cal Ripken Jr. J-P/50 40.00
9 Reggie Jackson JK-J/50 10.00
10 Gary Sheffield FG-J/50 8.00
11 Edgar Martinez J-J/50 8.00
12 Roberto Alomar J-J/50 8.00
13 Luis Tiant H-J/50 8.00
14 Jim Rice J-P/50 8.00
15 Carlos Beltran B-J/50 8.00
16 Hideo Nomo B-J/50 10.00
17 Mark Grace FG-J/50 10.00
18 Joe Cronin J-P/50 30.00
19 Tony Gwynn B-J/50 15.00
20 Bo Jackson B-J/50 10.00
21 Roger Clemens J-J/50 25.00
22 Roger Clemens J-J/50 25.00
23 Don Mattingly B-J/50 20.00
24 Willie Mays B-J/50 50.00
25 Andruw Jones B-J/50 8.00
26 Andre Dawson J-P/50 8.00
28 Robin Yount H-J/50 15.00
29 Joe Carter B-J/50 8.00
30 Dale Murphy B-J/50 8.00
31 Greg Maddux J-J/50 15.00
32 Jose Canseco H-J/50 10.00
34 Nolan Ryan B-J/50 30.00
35 Frank Thomas J-P/50 10.00
36 Fred Lynn B-J/50 8.00
37 Curt Schilling J-J/50 10.00
38 Curt Schilling J-J/50 10.00
39 Dave Parker B-J/50 8.00
40 Randy Johnson J-J/50 10.00
41 Randy Johnson J-J/25 10.00
42 Vladimir Guerrero J-J/50 10.00
43 Bernie Williams J-J/50 8.00
44 Wade Boggs B-J/50 10.00
45 Pedro Martinez J-J/50 8.00
46 Andy Pettitte J-J/50 8.00
47 Fergie Jenkins H-J/50 8.00
48 Darryl Strawberry J-P/50 8.00
49 Rafael Palmeiro J-J/50 10.00
50 Albert Pujols J-J/50 30.00

Heroes Auto. Swatch Double Spec Prime
NM/M
No Pricing
Production 1-15
Triple: No Pricing
Production One Set

Heroes Swatch Triple
NM/M
Production 1-50
Spectrum Prime: No Pricing
Production 1-15
1 Billy Martin/25 35.00
2 Rickey Henderson/25 15.00
3 Alan Trammell/25 10.00
4 Lenny Dykstra/25 10.00
5 Jeff Bagwell/50 10.00
6 Steve Garvey/50 10.00
8 Cal Ripken Jr./25 50.00
9 Reggie Jackson/50 15.00
10 Gary Sheffield/50 10.00
11 Edgar Martinez/50 10.00
12 Roberto Alomar/50 10.00
14 Jim Rice/50 10.00
15 Carlos Beltran/50 15.00
16 Hideo Nomo/25 20.00
17 Mark Grace/50 15.00
18 Joe Cronin/50 40.00
19 Tony Gwynn/25 25.00
20 Bo Jackson/50 20.00
21 Roger Clemens/50 25.00
22 Roger Clemens/50 25.00
23 Don Mattingly/25 30.00
25 Andruw Jones/50 10.00
26 Andre Dawson/25 15.00
28 Robin Yount/25 60.00
31 Greg Maddux/50 15.00
34 Nolan Ryan/25 40.00
36 Frank Thomas/25 15.00
36 Fred Lynn/50 10.00
37 Curt Schilling/50 15.00

38 Curt Schilling/50 15.00
39 Dave Parker/50 10.00
42 Vladimir Guerrero/50 15.00
43 Bernie Williams/25 10.00
45 Pedro Martinez/50 15.00
47 Andy Pettitte/50 10.00
49 Fergie Jenkins/25 10.00
50 Rafael Palmeiro/50 15.00
50 Albert Pujols/50 40.00

Marks of Fame
NM/M
Common Player: 2.00
Production 150 Sets
Spectrum: 2-3X
Production 25 Sets
1 Bobby Doerr 2.00
2 Reggie Jackson 3.00
3 Harmon Killebrew 4.00
4 Duke Snider 3.00
5 Brooks Robinson 3.00
6 Al Kaline 4.00
7 Carlton Fisk 3.00
8 Willie Stargell 3.00
9 Enos Slaughter 2.00
10 Nolan Ryan 10.00
11 Luis Aparicio 2.00
12 Hoyt Wilhelm 2.00
13 Orlando Cepeda 2.00
14 Mike Schmidt 6.00
15 Frank Robinson 3.00
16 Whitey Ford 3.00
17 Don Sutton 2.00
18 Joe Morgan 2.00
19 Bob Feller 3.00
21 Lou Brock 3.00
22 Warren Spahn 4.00
23 Jim Palmer 2.00
24 Reggie Jackson 3.00
25 Willie Mays 8.00
26 George Brett 8.00
27 Billy Williams 2.00
28 Juan Marichal 2.00
29 Early Wynn 2.00
31 Rod Carew 3.00
32 Maury Wills 2.00
32 Fergie Jenkins 2.00
33 Steve Carlton 3.00
34 Eddie Murray 3.00
35 Kirby Puckett 3.00
36 Johnny Bench 4.00
37 Gaylord Perry 2.00
38 Gary Carter 2.00
39 Tony Perez 2.00
40 Tony Oliva 2.00
41 Luis Aparicio 2.00
42 Tom Seaver 3.00
43 Paul Molitor 2.00
44 Dennis Eckersley 2.00
45 Willie McCovey 3.00
46 Bob Gibson 3.00
47 Robin Roberts 2.00
48 Carl Yastrzemski 4.00
49 Ozzie Smith 4.00
49 Nolan Ryan 10.00
50 Stan Musial 6.00

Marks of Fame Auto. Swatch Single
NM/M
Production 5-125
1 Bobby Doerr/Pants/125 20.00
3 Harmon Killebrew/Jsy/50 40.00
4 Duke Snider/Jsy/50 40.00
5 Brooks Robinson/Jsy/125 30.00
6 Al Kaline/Bat/125 35.00
7 Carlton Fisk/Jkt/50 40.00
10 Nolan Ryan/Pants/50 80.00
11 Luis Aparicio/Jsy/125 20.00
13 Orlando Cepeda/Pants/50 25.00
14 Mike Schmidt/Jsy/50 60.00
15 Frank Robinson/Bat/125 30.00
16 Whitey Ford/Jsy/50 50.00
17 Don Sutton/Jsy/125 20.00
19 Bob Feller/Pants/125 30.00
20 Lou Brock/Jkt/125 30.00
22 Jim Palmer/Pants/50 25.00
26 Billy Williams/Jsy/50 25.00
27 Juan Marichal/Pants/125 25.00
31 Rod Carew/Jsy/50 35.00
31 Fergie Jenkins/Pants/125 25.00
32 Steve Carlton/Pants/125 25.00
35 Johnny Bench/Pants/50 50.00
37 Gaylord Perry/Pants/125 15.00
37 Gary Carter/Pants/50 25.00
38 Tony Perez FG-J/25 25.00
39 Tony Oliva/Jsy/125 25.00
40 Luis Aparicio/Bat/100 25.00
42 Tom Seaver/Pants/50 35.00
42 Paul Molitor/Pants/50 35.00
44 Dennis Eckersley/Jsy/125 35.00
44 Willie McCovey/Pants/50 35.00
46 Robin Roberts/Hat/50 50.00
48 Ozzie Smith/Pants/50 50.00
49 Nolan Ryan/Jkt/50 80.00
50 Stan Musial/Pants/50 60.00

Marks of Fame Swatch Double
NM/M
Production 1-50
Spectrum Prime: No Pricing
Production 1-25
1 Bobby Doerr/50 10.00
2 Reggie Jackson B-P/50 10.00
3 Harmon Killebrew B-J/50 15.00
4 Duke Snider J-P/25 15.00
5 Brooks Robinson B-J/50 15.00
7 Carlton Fisk B-JK/50 10.00
8 Willie Stargell B-J/50 10.00
9 Enos Slaughter J-J/50 10.00
10 Nolan Ryan J-P/50 25.00
11 Luis Aparicio B-J/50 8.00
12 Hoyt Wilhelm B-J/50 8.00
13 Orlando Cepeda B-P/50 10.00
14 Mike Schmidt B-J/50 20.00
16 Frank Robinson B-S/50 15.00
16 Whitey Ford B-J/50 15.00
17 Don Sutton B-J/50 8.00
18 Joe Morgan B-J/50 8.00
20 Lou Brock B-JK/50 10.00
22 Warren Spahn J-P/50 12.00
23 Jim Palmer H-P/50 10.00
24 Reggie Jackson J-J/50 10.00
26 Willie Mays B-J/50 50.00
26 Billy Williams J-J/50 8.00
28 Juan Marichal J-P/50 8.00
28 Early Wynn J-J/50 8.00
31 Rod Carew J-J/50 10.00
31 Fergie Jenkins FG-P/50 8.00
32 Steve Carlton B-J/50 8.00
33 Eddie Murray B-J/50 15.00
34 Kirby Puckett B-J/50 15.00
36 Johnny Bench B-J/50 15.00
36 Gaylord Perry J-J/50 8.00
38 Gary Carter B-J/50 8.00
39 Tony Oliva B-J/50 8.00
41 Tom Seaver J-P/50 15.00
42 Paul Molitor B-J/50 15.00
43 Dennis Eckersley J-J/50 10.00
45 Willie McCovey J-P/50 10.00
47 Carl Yastrzemski B-J/50 20.00
48 Ozzie Smith H-P/50 20.00
49 Nolan Ryan JK-J/50 25.00
50 Stan Musial B-P/50 50.00

Marks of Fame Auto. Swatch Double
NM/M
Production 1-75
Prime: No Pricing
Production 1-10
1 Bobby Doerr B-P/50 25.00
3 Harmon Killebrew B-J/50 40.00
4 Duke Snider J-P/50 40.00
5 Brooks Robinson B-J/25 40.00
7 Carlton Fisk B-JK/25 40.00
9 Nolan Ryan B-P/25 100.00
11 Luis Aparicio B-J/25 20.00
12 Hoyt Wilhelm J-J/25 25.00
13 Orlando Cepeda B-P/25 25.00
14 Mike Schmidt B-J/25 75.00
16 Frank Robinson B-S/25 50.00
16 Whitey Ford J-J/25 50.00
17 Don Sutton J-J/25 20.00
20 Lou Brock B-JK/25 50.00
22 Jim Palmer H-P/25 30.00
27 Juan Marichal J-P/25 25.00
29 Rod Carew B-J/25 40.00
32 Steve Carlton B-J/25 50.00
35 Johnny Bench B-J/25 50.00
36 Gaylord Perry J-J/25 20.00
37 Gary Carter B-J/25 25.00
38 Tony Perez FG-J/25 25.00
39 Tony Oliva B-J/75 20.00
41 Tom Seaver J-P/25 40.00
42 Paul Molitor B-J/25 35.00
43 Dennis Eckersley J-J/25 35.00
44 Willie McCovey J-P/25 40.00
48 Ozzie Smith H-P/25 50.00
49 Nolan Ryan JK-J/25 100.00
50 Stan Musial B-P/25 80.00

Marks of Fame Swatch Triple
NM/M
Production 1-25
Spectrum Prime: No Pricing
Production 1-15
1 Bobby Doerr/25 15.00
7 Carlton Fisk/25 15.00
8 Willie Stargell/25 15.00
9 Nolan Ryan/25 40.00
11 Luis Aparicio/25 12.00
12 Hoyt Wilhelm/25 10.00
14 Mike Schmidt/25 30.00
18 Joe Morgan/25 15.00
20 Lou Brock/25 15.00
21 Warren Spahn/25 50.00
23 Reggie Jackson/25 15.00
24 Willie Mays/25 60.00
29 Juan Marichal/25 15.00
29 Rod Carew/25 15.00
32 Steve Carlton/25 15.00
33 Eddie Murray/25 20.00
34 Kirby Puckett/25 20.00
35 Johnny Bench/25 20.00
35 Gary Carter/25 12.00
39 Tony Oliva/25 12.00

41 Tom Seaver/25 15.00
42 Paul Molitor/25 15.00
43 Dennis Eckersley/25 12.00
44 Willie McCovey/25 15.00
47 Carl Yastrzemski/25 35.00
48 Ozzie Smith/25 25.00
49 Nolan Ryan/25 40.00
50 Stan Musial/25 40.00

Marks of Fame Auto. Swatch Triple
No Pricing
Production 1-10
Prime: No Pricing
Production One Set

Team Tandems
NM/M
Common Card: 1.50
Production 250 Sets
Spectrum: .75-1.5X
Production 150 Sets
1 Mark Prior, Kerry Wood 2.00
2 Barry Zito, Tim Hudson 1.50
3 Curt Schilling, Pedro Martinez 2.50
4 Will Clark, Matt Williams 2.00
5 Bernie Williams, Jason Giambi 2.00
6 Vernon Wells, Roy Halladay 1.50
7 Josh Beckett, A.J. Burnett 1.50
8 Dale Murphy, Phil Niekro 2.00
9 Mike Schmidt, Steve Carlton 5.00
10 Tony Oliva, Harmon Killebrew 2.00
11 Robin Yount, Paul Molitor 2.50
12 Francisco Rodriguez, Troy Percival 1.50
13 Ben Sheets, Danny Kolb 1.50
14 Andruw Jones, Rafael Furcal 1.50
15 Todd Helton, Preston Wilson 1.50
16 Wade Boggs, Fred McGriff 2.00
17 Manny Ramirez, David Ortiz 2.50
18 Miguel Cabrera, Dontrelle Willis 2.00
19 Edgar Renteria, Scott Rolen 2.00
20 Carlos Beltran, Jeff Kent 2.00
21 Eric Davis, Deion Sanders 2.00
22 Frank Thomas, Paul Konerko 2.00
23 Mike Piazza, Al Leiter 3.00
24 Sean Burroughs, Ryan Klesko 1.50
25 Ken Harvey, Mike Sweeney 1.50
26 David Sanders, Hideki Matsui 4.00
27 Steve Carlton, Mark Buehrle 2.00
28 Gaylord Perry, Randy Johnson 2.00
29 Joe Morgan, Steve Carlton 2.00
30 Vladimir Guerrero, Orlando Cabrera 2.00
31 Scott Rolen, John Kruk 2.00
32 Aaron Boone, Dmitri Young 1.50
33 Rickey Henderson, Vladimir Guerrero 2.00
34 Charles Johnson, Cliff Floyd 1.50
35 Cal Ripken Jr., Rafael Palmeiro 8.00

Team Tandems Swatch Single
NM/M
Production 10-125
1 Mark Prior, Kerry Wood/125 6.00
2 Barry Zito, Tim Hudson/125 5.00
3 Curt Schilling, Pedro Martinez/125 8.00
4 Will Clark, Matt Williams/125 8.00
5 Bernie Williams, Jason Giambi/125 8.00
6 Vernon Wells, Roy Halladay/125
7 Josh Beckett, A.J. Burnett/125 5.00
8 Dale Murphy, Phil Niekro/125 15.00
9 Mike Schmidt, Steve Carlton/125 15.00
10 Tony Oliva, Harmon Killebrew/50 15.00
11 Robin Yount, Paul Molitor/125 15.00
12 Felix Rodriguez, Troy Percival/25 10.00
13 Ben Sheets, Danny Kolb/125 5.00
14 Andruw Jones, Rafael Furcal/125 5.00

15	Todd Helton, Preston Wilson/125	5.00
16	Wade Boggs, Fred McGriff/50	10.00
17	Manny Ramirez, David Ortiz/125	12.00
18	Miguel Cabrera, Dontrelle Willis/125	10.00
19	Edgar Renteria, Scott Rolen/125	10.00
20	Carlos Beltran, Jeff Kent Bat/125	8.00
21	Eric Davis Bat, Deion Sanders/125	8.00
22	Frank Thomas, Paul Konerko/50	10.00
23	Mike Piazza, Al Leiter/125	12.00
24	Sean Burroughs, Ryan Klesko/125	5.00
25	Ken Harvey, Mike Sweeney/125	5.00
26	Deion Sanders, Hideki Matsui/125	25.00
27	Steve Carlton, Mark Buehrle/50	8.00
28	Gaylord Perry, Randy Johnson/125	10.00
29	Joe Morgan, Steve Carlton/125	10.00
31	Scott Rolen, John Kruk/125	10.00
32	Aaron Boone, Dmitri Young/125	5.00
33	Rickey Henderson Hat, Vladimir Guerrero/25	15.00
34	Charles Johnson, Cliff Floyd/125	5.00
35	Cal Ripken Jr., Rafael Palmeiro/125	25.00

Team Tandems Swatch Single Spectrum
NM/M

Production 1-75
1	Mark Prior, Kerry Wood/75	6.00
2	Barry Zito, Tim Hudson/75	5.00
3	Curt Schilling, Pedro Martinez/75	10.00
4	Will Clark, M. Williams/75	8.00
5	Bernie Williams, Jason Giambi/75	5.00
6	Vernon Wells, Roy Halladay/75	5.00
7	Josh Beckett, A.J. Burnett/75	5.00
8	Dale Murphy, Phil Niekro/75	10.00
11	Robin Yount, Paul Molitor/75	15.00
13	Ben Sheets, Danny Kolb/75	5.00
14	Andruw Jones, Rafael Furcal/75	5.00
15	Todd Helton, Preston Wilson/75	5.00
17	Manny Ramirez, David Ortiz/75	10.00
18	Miguel Cabrera, Dontrelle Willis/75	8.00
19	Edgar Renteria, Scott Rolen/75	8.00
20	Carlos Beltran, Jeff Kent Bat/75	8.00
21	Eric Davis Bat, Deion Sanders/75	8.00
23	Mike Piazza, Al Leiter/75	10.00
24	Sean Burroughs, Ryan Klesko/75	5.00
25	Ken Harvey, Mike Sweeney/75	5.00
26	Deion Sanders, Hideki Matsui/75	25.00
28	Gaylord Perry, Randy Johnson/75	8.00
31	Scott Rolen, John Kruk/75	8.00
32	Aaron Boone, D. Young/75	5.00
34	Charles Johnson, Cliff Floyd/75	5.00
35	Cal Ripken Jr., Rafael Palmeiro/75	25.00

Team Tandems Swatch Double
NM/M

Production 1-125
Spectrum: 1-2X
Production 1-50
No pricing 20 or less.
1	Mark Prior, Kerry Wood/125	8.00
2	Barry Zito, Tim Hudson/125	8.00
3	Curt Schilling, Pedro Martinez/125	15.00
5	Bernie Williams, Jason Giambi/125	10.00
7	Josh Beckett, A.J. Burnett/125	8.00
8	Dale Murphy, Phil Niekro/125	20.00

10	Tony Oliva, Harmon Killebrew/50	30.00
11	Robin Yount, Paul Molitor/125	20.00
14	Andruw Jones, Rafael Furcal/125	8.00
15	Todd Helton, Preston Wilson/125	10.00
16	Wade Boggs, Fred McGriff/125	15.00
17	Manny Ramirez, David Ortiz/125	15.00
18	Miguel Cabrera, Dontrelle Willis/125	12.00
20	Carlos Beltran, Jeff Kent/50	12.00
21	Eric Davis, Deion Sanders/25	15.00
22	Frank Thomas, Paul Konerko/50	15.00
23	Mike Piazza, Al Leiter/125	20.00
24	Sean Burroughs, Ryan Klesko/50	10.00
26	Deion Sanders, Hideki Matsui/125	35.00
27	Steve Carlton, Mark Buehrle/50	12.00
29	Joe Morgan, Steve Carlton/25	15.00
33	Rickey Henderson, Vladimir Guerrero/50	15.00
34	Charles Johnson, Cliff Floyd/125	8.00
35	Cal Ripken Jr., Rafael Palmeiro/125	40.00

Team Trios
NM/M

Common Card:
Production 200 Sets
Spectrum: 1X
Production 125 Sets
1	Cal Ripken Jr., Jim Palmer, Eddie Murray	10.00
2	Roger Clemens, Wade Boggs, Evans	5.00
3	Rafael Palmeiro, Miguel Tejada, Javy Lopez	2.00
4	Carl Crawford, Rocco Baldelli, B.J. Upton	1.50
5	Mark Buehrle, Magglio Ordonez, Carlos Lee	1.50
6	Victor Martinez, Travis Hafner, Jody Gerut	1.50
7	Bobby Abreu, Brett Myers, Kevin Millwood	1.50
8	Sammy Sosa, Aramis Ramirez, Carlos Zambrano	3.00
9	Bo, George Brett, Carlos Beltran	5.00
10	Hideo Nomo, Adrian Beltre, Shawn Green	2.00
11	Wilson, Wilson, Jason Bay	1.50
12	Tom Seaver, Nolan Ryan, Dwight Gooden	8.00
13	David Dellucci, Laynce Nix, Kevin Mench	1.50
14	Alan Trammell, Morris, Gibson	2.00
15	M. Will, Grace, Randy Johnson	2.00
16	Dawson, Gary Carter, Tony Perez	2.00
17	Dale Murphy, John Kruk, Lenny Dykstra	2.00
18	B. Roberts, Ian Gibb, Larry Bigbie	1.50
19	Mike Lowell, Ivan Rodriguez, Brad Penny	2.00
20	Murray, Darryl Strawberry, Oliver	2.00
21	Darryl Strawberry, Rickey Henderson, Gary Sheffield	2.00
22	Roberto Alomar, Joe Crede, Durham	2.00
23	Jason Kendall, Giles, Aramis Ramirez	1.50
24	Delmon, Aubrey Huff, Tino	2.00
25	Jeff Bagwell, Cruz, Joe Morgan	2.00
26	Snow, Rich Aurilia, Jeff Kent	2.00
27	Jenkins, Nolan Ryan, Cordero	8.00
28	Lofton, Jim Thome, Roberto Alomar	3.00
29	Atkins, Todd Helton, Jennings	2.00
30	Gary Carter, Pedro, Randy Johnson	2.50

Team Trios Swatch Single
NM/M

Production 50 unless noted.
1	Cal Ripken Jr., Jim Palmer, Murray	40.00
2	Roger Clemens, Wade Boggs, Evans	25.00
3	Rafael Palmeiro, Miguel Tejada, Javy Lopez	12.00

4	Carl Crawford, Rocco Baldelli, B.J. Upton	
5	Mark Buehrle, Magglio Ordonez, Carlos Lee	10.00
6	Victor Martinez, Travis Hafner, Jody Gerut	10.00
7	Bobby Abreu, Brett Myers, Kevin Millwood	10.00
8	Sammy Sosa, Aramis Ramirez, Carlos Zambrano	15.00
9	Bo, George Brett, Carlos Beltran	30.00
10	Hideo Nomo, Adrian Beltre, Shawn Green	15.00
11	Wilson, Wilson, Jason Bay	10.00
12	Tom Seaver, Nolan Ryan, Dwight Gooden	35.00
13	David Dellucci, Laynce Nix, Kevin Mench	8.00
14	Alan Trammell, Morris, Gibson	15.00
15	M. Will, Grace, Randy Johnson	15.00
16	Dawson, Gary Carter, Tony Perez	15.00
17	Dale Murphy, Tomas Kurka, Lenny Dykstra	20.00
18	Roberts, Ian Gibb, Larry Bigbie	15.00
19	Mike Lowell, Ivan Rodriguez, Brad Penny	15.00
20	Murray, Darryl Strawberry, Oliver	20.00
21	Darryl Strawberry, Rickey Henderson, Gary Sheffield	15.00
22	Roberto Alomar, Joe Crede, Durham	10.00
23	Jason Kendall, Giles, Aramis Ramirez	10.00
24	Delmon, Aubrey Huff, Tino	10.00
25	Jeff Bagwell, Cruz, Joe Morgan	12.00
26	Snow, Rich Aurilia, Jeff Kent	8.00
27	Jenkins, Nolan Ryan, Cordero	25.00
28	Lofton, Jim Thome, Roberto Alomar	20.00
29	Atkins, Todd Helton, Jennings	15.00
30	Gary Carter, Pedro, Randy Johnson	15.00

Team Trios Swatch Double
NM/M

Production 25-100
Spectrum: .75-1.5X
Production 5-35
No pricing production 20 or less.
Prime Black: No Pricing
Production 5-10
1	Cal Ripken Jr., Jim Palmer, Murray/100	75.00
2	Roger Clemens, Wade Boggs, Evans/100	50.00
3	Rafael Palmeiro, Miguel Tejada, Javy Lopez/50	25.00
5	Mark Buehrle, Magglio Ordonez, Carlos Lee/100	15.00
6	Victor Martinez, Travis Hafner, Jody Gerut/50	20.00
9	Bo, George Brett, Carlos Beltran/100	40.00
10	Hideo Nomo, Adrian Beltre, Shawn Green/100	25.00
11	Wilson, Wilson, Jason Bay/100	15.00
12	Tom Seaver, Nolan Ryan, Dwight Gooden/100	50.00
14	Alan Trammell, Morris, Gibson/50	30.00
15	M. Will, Mark Grace, Randy Johnson/50	30.00
16	Dawson, Gary Carter, Tony Perez/100	20.00
19	Mike Lowell, Ivan Rodriguez, Brad Penny/50	25.00
20	Murray, Darryl Strawberry, Oliver/100	30.00
21	Darryl Strawberry, Rickey Henderson, Gary Sheffield/100	25.00
22	Roberto Alomar, Joe Crede, Durham/100	20.00
28	Lofton, Jim Thome, Roberto Alomar/25	40.00
29	Atkins, Todd Helton, Jennings/100	20.00
30	Gary Carter, Pedro, Randy Johnson/50	30.00

Team Quads
NM/M

Common Quad:
Production 150 Sets
Spectrum: 1X
Production 100 Sets
1	St. Louis Card/Active	6.00
2	Cleveland Indians	2.00
3	California Angels	2.00
4	Boston Red Sox	5.00
5	New York Yanks/Active	6.00
6	Atlanta Braves	3.00
7	Oakland A's	3.00
9	Anaheim Angels	2.00
10	Minnesota Twins/Active	3.00
11	New York Mets	4.00
12	Houston Astros	3.00
13	San Diego Padres	4.00
14	Cincinnati Reds	2.00
15	Texas Rangers/Retro	6.00
16	New York Yanks/Retro	8.00
17	St. Louis Cards/Retro	6.00
18	Pittsburgh Pirates	2.00
19	Chicago Cubs	4.00
20	Minnesota Twins/Retro	3.00

Team Quads Swatch Single
NM/M

Production 25-100
1	St. Louis Card/Active/100	25.00
2	Cleveland Indians/100	30.00
3	California Angels/100	15.00
4	Boston Red Sox/100	20.00
5	New York Yanks/Active/100	30.00
6	Atlanta Braves/100	25.00
7	Oakland A's/100	10.00
8	Anaheim Angels/100	15.00
9	Texas Rangers/Active/100	10.00
10	Minnesota Twins/Active/25	25.00
11	New York Mets/100	20.00
12	Houston Astros/100	30.00
13	San Diego Padres/100	25.00
14	Cincinnati Reds/100	10.00
15	Texas Rangers/Retro/100	30.00
16	New York Yanks/Retro/100	50.00
17	St. Louis Cards/Retro/50	50.00
18	Pittsburgh Pirates/100	15.00
19	Chicago Cubs/100	25.00
20	Minnesota Twins/Retro/100	20.00

Team Quads Swatch Single Spectrum
NM/M

Production 10-35
Prime Black: No Pricing
Production 10 Sets
1	St. Louis Card/Active/35	40.00
2	Cleveland Indians/35	50.00
3	California Angels/35	50.00
4	Boston Red Sox/35	30.00
5	New York Yanks/Active/35	40.00
6	Atlanta Braves/35	40.00
7	Oakland A's/35	20.00
8	Anaheim Angels/35	25.00
9	Texas Rangers/Active/35	20.00
11	New York Mets/35	30.00
12	Houston Astros/35	50.00
14	San Diego Padres/35	50.00
14	Cincinnati Reds/35	20.00
15	Texas Rangers/Retro/35	40.00
16	New York Yanks/Retro/35	75.00
18	Pittsburgh Pirates/35	20.00
19	Chicago Cubs/35	40.00
20	Minnesota Twins/Retro/35	30.00

Team Quads Swatch Double
NM/M

Production 25-75
1	St. Louis Card/Active/75	25.00
3	California Angels/75	30.00
4	Boston Red Sox/75	30.00
5	New York Yanks/Active/25	75.00
6	Atlanta Braves/75	60.00
7	Oakland A's/75	20.00
8	Anaheim Angels/75	40.00
9	Texas Rangers/Active/75	20.00
10	Minnesota Twins/Active/75	40.00
11	New York Mets/75	30.00
12	Houston Astros/25	75.00
13	San Diego Padres/75	40.00
14	Cincinnati Reds/75	20.00
15	Texas Rangers/Retro/75	50.00
18	Pittsburgh Pirates/75	20.00
20	Minnesota Twins/Retro/75	30.00

Team Quads Swatch Double Spectrum
NM/M

Production 1-25
Prime Black: No Pricing
Production 1-5
1	St. Louis Card/Active/25	40.00
3	California Angels/25	50.00
4	Boston Red Sox/25	60.00
5	Texas Rangers/Active/25	30.00
11	New York Mets/25	50.00
13	San Diego Padres/25	60.00
14	Cincinnati Reds/25	40.00
15	Texas Rangers/Retro/2570	40.00

Team Six
NM/M

Common Card: 1.50
Production 100 Sets
Spectrum: 1-1.5X
Production 50 Sets
1	San Francisco Giants	8.00
2	Houston Astros	6.00
3	Cincinnati Reds	5.00
4	St. Louis Cardinals	8.00
5	New York Yankees	10.00
6	Chicago Cubs	6.00
7	Arizona Diamondbacks	1.50
8	Los Angeles Dodgers	6.00
9	Anaheim Angels	4.00
10	Boston Red Sox	8.00
11	Seattle Mariners	8.00
12	Chicago White Sox	4.00
13	Philadelphia Phillies	10.00
14	New York Mets	10.00
15	Atlanta Braves	4.00

Team Six Swatch Single
NM/M

Production 15-50
1	San Francisco Giants/50	80.00
2	Houston Astros/50	40.00
5	New York Yankees/50	60.00
6	Chicago Cubs/50	40.00
7	Arizona Diamondbacks/50	20.00
8	Los Angeles Dodgers/50	40.00
9	Anaheim Angels/50	30.00
10	Boston Red Sox/50	50.00
12	Chicago White Sox/50	40.00
13	Philadelphia Phillies/50	40.00
14	New York Mets/50	40.00
15	Atlanta Braves/50	40.00

Team Six Swatch Single Spectrum
NM/M

Production 5-25
Prime Black: No Pricing
Production Five Sets

1	San Francisco Giants/25	100.00
3	Houston Astros/25	50.00
5	New York Yankees/25	75.00
6	Chicago Cubs/25	50.00
7	Arizona Diamondbacks/25	25.00
8	Los Angeles Dodgers/25	50.00
10	Boston Red Sox/25	65.00
12	Chicago White Sox/25	40.00
13	Philadelphia Phillies/25	50.00
14	New York Mets/25	50.00
15	Atlanta Braves/25	50.00

Tools of the Trade Red
NM/M

Common Player:
Production 250 Sets
Black: 1-1.5X
Production 100 Sets
Blue: 1-1.5X
Production 150 Sets
Rev. Spectrum Red: 1-2X
Production 50 Sets
Rev. Spectrum Blue: No Pricing
Production 10 Sets
1	Ozzie Smith	5.00
2	Carlos Beltran	2.00
3	Dale Murphy	2.00
4	Paul Molitor	2.00
5	George Brett	6.00
6	Stan Musial	5.00
7	Ivan Rodriguez	2.00
8	Carl Yastrzemski	4.00
9	Reggie Jackson	2.00
10	Hideo Nomo	2.00
11	Gary Sheffield	2.00
12	Roberto Alomar	2.00
13	Pedro Martinez	3.00
14	Ernie Banks	3.00
15	Tim Hudson	1.50
16	Dwight Gooden	1.50
17	Lance Berkman	1.50
18	Darryl Strawberry	1.50
19	Larry Walker	2.00
20	Lou Brock	2.00
21	Roger Clemens	2.00
22	Paul LoDuca	1.50
23	Don Mattingly	2.00
24	Willie Mays	6.00
25	Rafael Palmeiro	2.00
26	Roy Oswalt	1.50
27	Vladimir Guerrero	3.00
28	Austin Kearns	1.50
29	Rod Carew	2.00
30	Nolan Ryan	8.00
31	Richie Sexson	2.00
32	Steve Carlton	2.00
33	Eddie Murray	2.00
34	Nolan Ryan	8.00
35	Mike Mussina	2.00
36	Sean Casey	1.50
37	Juan Gonzalez	1.50
38	Curt Schilling	2.00
39	Darryl Strawberry	1.50
40	Alfonso Soriano	3.00
41	Tom Seaver	3.00
42	Mike Schmidt	5.00
43	Todd Helton	2.00
44	Reggie Jackson	2.00
45	Shawn Green	1.50
46	Mike Mussina	2.00
47	Tom Glavine	1.50
48	Torii Hunter	1.50
49	Kerry Wood	2.00
50	Carlos Delgado	2.00
51	Randy Johnson	2.00
52	David Ortiz	3.00
53	Troy Glaus	2.00
54	Rickey Henderson	2.00
55	Craig Biggio	2.00
56	Brad Penny	1.50
57	Gary Carter	2.00
58	Andy Pettitte	2.00
59	Mark Prior	2.00
60	Kirby Puckett	3.00
61	Willie McCovey	3.00
62	Andre Dawson	2.00
63	Greg Maddux	4.00
64	Adrian Beltre	1.50
65	Andruw Jones	2.00
66	Juan Gonzalez	1.50
67	Frank Thomas	2.00
68	Victor Martinez	1.50
69	Randy Johnson	3.00
70	Andre Dawson	2.00
71	Adam Dunn	2.00
72	Carlton Fisk	3.00
73	Cal Ripken Jr.	8.00
74	Kenny Lofton	1.50
75	Barry Zito	1.50
76	Sammy Sosa	4.00
77	Deion Sanders	2.00
78	Tony Gwynn	3.00
79	Mike Piazza	3.00
80	Jeff Bagwell	2.00
81	Manny Ramirez	3.00
82	Carlos Beltran	2.00
83	Mark Grace	2.00
84	Robin Yount	4.00
85	Albert Pujols	6.00
86	Dontrelle Willis	2.00
87	Jim Thome	2.00
88	Magglio Ordonez	1.50
89	Miguel Tejada	2.00
90	Mark Teixeira	2.00
91	Gary Carter	2.00

#	Player	Price
92	Ivan Rodriguez	2.00
93	Jason Giambi	1.50
94	Rickey Henderson	2.00
95	Curt Schilling	2.00
96	Bobby Doerr	2.00
97	Chipper Jones	3.00
98	Eric Chavez	1.50
99	Johnny Bench	4.00
100	Harmon Killebrew	3.00

Tools of Trade Laundry Tag Prime Red
No Pricing
Production One Set

Tools of Trade Swatch Single Jumbo
NM/M

Production 1-100
Prime Red: No Pricing
Production 1-25
Reverse: 1-2X
Production 1-50
Prime Black: No Pricing
Production One Set

#	Player	Price
1	Ozzie Smith/25	30.00
2	Carlos Beltran/Jsy/50	10.00
3	Dale Murphy/Jsy/50	20.00
4	Paul Molitor/Jsy/25	25.00
6	Stan Musial/Pants/50	50.00
9	Ivan Rodriguez/Jsy/100	10.00
10	Hideo Nomo/Jsy/50	15.00
11	Gary Sheffield/Jsy/25	15.00
12	Roberto Alomar/Jsy/100	10.00
13	Pedro Martinez/Jsy/50	12.00
15	Tim Hudson/Jsy/100	8.00
17	Lance Berkman/Jsy/75	8.00
19	Larry Walker/Jsy/150	5.00
20	Lou Brock/Jkt/50	20.00
21	Roger Clemens/Jsy/50	30.00
23	Don Mattingly/Jsy/25	40.00
25	Rafael Palmeiro/Jsy/100	10.00
27	Vladimir Guerrero/Jsy/50	15.00
29	Rod Carew/Jsy/50	15.00
30	Nolan Ryan/Jsy/50	50.00
31	Richie Sexson/Jsy/100	10.00
33	Eddie Murray/Jsy/50	20.00
35	Mike Mussina/Jsy/50	12.00
36	Sean Casey/Jsy/100	8.00
37	Juan Gonzalez/Jsy/25	15.00
38	Curt Schilling/Jsy/100	10.00
39	Darryl Strawberry/Jsy/50	10.00
41	Tom Seaver/Jsy/50	15.00
42	Mike Schmidt/Jsy/25	40.00
43	Todd Helton/Jsy/50	10.00
45	Shawn Green/Jsy/100	8.00
47	Tom Glavine/Jsy/100	10.00
49	Kerry Wood/Jsy/50	10.00
51	R. John/Jsy/50	20.00
52	David Ortiz/Jsy/75	15.00
53	Troy Glaus/Jsy/50	10.00
54	Rickey Henderson/Jsy/25	15.00
55	Craig Biggio/Jsy/75	8.00
56	Brad Penny/Jsy/100	8.00
57	Gary Carter/Jsy/50	10.00
59	Andy Pettitte/Jsy/50	10.00
59	Mark Prior/Jsy/50	10.00
60	Kirby Puckett/Jsy/50	20.00
61	Willie McCovey/Jsy/50	15.00
63	Greg Maddux/Jsy/100	10.00
65	Andruw Jones/Jsy/100	10.00
68	Victor Martinez/Jsy/50	8.00
72	Andre Dawson/Jsy/50	10.00
72	Carlton Fisk/Jsy/100	10.00
73	Cal Ripken Jr./Jsy/100	35.00
74	Kenny Lofton/Hat/25	10.00
75	Barry Zito/Jsy/100	10.00
76	Sammy Sosa/Jsy/100	15.00
77	Deion Sanders/Jsy/100	20.00
78	Tony Gwynn/Jsy/100	20.00
79	Mike Piazza/Jsy/100	10.00
80	Jeff Bagwell/Jsy/100	10.00
84	Mark Grace/Jsy/50	15.00
84	Robin Yount/Jsy/50	20.00
85	Albert Pujols/Jsy/100	30.00
86	Dontrelle Willis/Jsy/100	10.00
89	Miguel Tejada/Jsy/100	12.00
90	Mark Teixeira/Jsy/50	10.00
92	Ivan Rodriguez/Jsy/100	10.00
93	Jason Giambi/Jsy/25	10.00
94	Rickey Henderson/Jsy/25	15.00
95	Curt Schilling/Jsy/50	10.00
96	Bobby Doerr/Pants/25	20.00
97	Chipper Jones/Jsy/25	20.00
98	Eric Chavez/Jsy/100	10.00
99	Johnny Bench/Jsy/25	25.00
100	Harmon Killebrew/Jsy/25	40.00

Tools of the Trade Swatch Double
NM/M

Production 1-150
Prime Red: No Pricing
Production 1-25
Prime Black: No Pricing
Production 1-25

#	Player	Price
1	Ozzie Smith B-P/25	15.00
2	Carlos Beltran J-S/50	8.00
3	Dale Murphy J-J/50	8.00
4	Paul Molitor J-P/150	8.00

#	Player	Price
5	George Brett B-H/25	25.00
6	Stan Musial B-P/25	30.00
7	Ivan Rodriguez J-J/150	8.00
8	Carl Yastrzemski B-J/25	30.00
9	Reggie Jackson J-J/50	10.00
10	Hideo Nomo J-P/150	10.00
11	Gary Sheffield H-J/25	8.00
12	Roberto Alomar B-J/150	8.00
13	Pedro Martinez J-P/150	8.00
15	Tim Hudson H-J/100	5.00
17	Lance Berkman B-J/150	5.00
19	Larry Walker J-J/150	5.00
20	Lou Brock B-JK/150	10.00
21	Roger Clemens B-J/25	30.00
22	Paul LoDuca B-J/50	5.00
23	Don Mattingly BG-P/50	20.00
24	Willie Mays B-P/25	50.00
25	Rafael Palmeiro B-J/150	8.00
27	Vladimir Guerrero B-J/150	8.00
29	Rod Carew JK-JK/150	8.00
30	Nolan Ryan B-JK/25	25.00
31	Richie Sexson H-J/150	8.00
32	Steve Carlton B-H/150	8.00
33	Eddie Murray B-J/150	8.00
34	Nolan Ryan B-J/150	25.00
35	Mike Mussina J-P/125	8.00
36	Sean Casey J-P/150	5.00
38	Curt Schilling J-J/150	8.00
39	Darryl Strawberry B-J/150	5.00
41	Tom Seaver J-P/150	10.00
42	Mike Schmidt B-J/150	15.00
43	Todd Helton B-J/150	8.00
45	Shawn Green B-J/150	5.00
47	Tom Glavine B-J/150	8.00
49	Kerry Wood G-J/100	8.00
50	Carlos Delgado B-J/100	5.00
51	R. John J-P/150	8.00
52	David Ortiz B-J/150	8.00
53	Troy Glaus J-J/150	5.00
54	Rickey Henderson B-J/150	8.00
55	Craig Biggio B-J/150	5.00
56	Brad Penny FG-J/150	5.00
57	Gary Carter J-P/150	8.00
58	Andy Pettitte J-J/150	5.00
59	Mark Prior FG-J/150	10.00
60	Kirby Puckett B-FG/100	10.00
61	Willie McCovey J-P/100	10.00
63	Greg Maddux B-J/50	15.00
64	Adrian Beltre B-J/150	5.00
65	Andruw Jones B-J/150	8.00
67	Frank Thomas J-J/150	8.00
68	Victor Martinez CP-J/150	5.00
69	R. John J-P/150	8.00
71	Adam Dunn B-J/95	8.00
72	Carlton Fisk B-J/150	8.00
73	Cal Ripken Jr. J-P/150	25.00
74	Kenny Lofton B-H/150	5.00
75	Barry Zito J-J/150	5.00
76	Sammy Sosa B-J/150	10.00
77	Deion Sanders J-P/150	10.00
78	Tony Gwynn J-P/150	10.00
79	Mike Piazza J-P/150	10.00
80	Jeff Bagwell J-P/150	8.00
81	Manny Ramirez B-J/150	8.00
83	Mark Grace B-J/50	8.00
84	Robin Yount B-J/150	12.00
85	Albert Pujols B-J/150	20.00
86	Dontrelle Willis B-J/150	8.00
88	Magglio Ordonez B-S/150	5.00
89	Miguel Tejada H-J/150	8.00
90	Mark Teixeira FG-J/150	8.00
91	Gary Carter B-J/25	15.00
92	Ivan Rodriguez CP-J/150	8.00
93	Jason Giambi H-J/50	5.00
94	Rickey Henderson B-P/150	8.00
95	Curt Schilling J-J/150	8.00
96	Bobby Doerr B-P/150	8.00
97	Chipper Jones B-J/150	10.00
99	Johnny Bench B-P/150	10.00
100	Harmon Killebrew H-J/50	10.00

Tools of Trade Auto. Swatch Double
NM/M

Production 1-75
Prime Red: .75-1.5X
Production 1-50
No pricing production 20 or less.
Prime Black: No Pricing
Production One Set

#	Player	Price
1	Ozzie Smith B-P/25	50.00
3	Dale Murphy J-J/50	30.00
4	Paul Molitor J-P/25	40.00
20	Lou Brock B-JK/50	40.00
22	Paul LoDuca B-J/25	25.00
36	Sean Casey J-P/50	25.00
37	Juan Gonzalez J-P/50	30.00
39	Darryl Strawberry B-J/50	25.00
41	Tom Seaver J-P/25	40.00
48	Torii Hunter B-J/40	25.00
56	Brad Penny FG-J/75	10.00
57	Gary Carter J-P/25	30.00
62	Andre Dawson B-J/50	25.00
64	Adrian Beltre B-J/50	25.00
66	Juan Gonzalez B-J/50	30.00
70	Andre Dawson B-J/50	25.00
73	Cal Ripken Jr. J-P/25	160.00
88	Magglio Ordonez B-S/25	20.00
91	Gary Carter B-J/25	30.00
96	Bobby Doerr B-P/50	25.00

#	Player	Price
98	Eric Chavez B-J/25	25.00
100	Harmon Killebrew H-J/25	50.00

Tools/Trade Auto. Swatch Double Reverse
NM/M

Production 1-75

#	Player	Price
20	Lou Brock B-JK/25	40.00
36	Sean Casey J-P/50	25.00
39	Darryl Strawberry B-J/75	20.00
48	Torii Hunter B-J/50	25.00
56	Brad Penny FG-J/50	12.00
62	Andre Dawson B-J/25	30.00
64	Adrian Beltre B-J/25	20.00
66	Juan Gonzalez B-J/25	30.00
70	Andre Dawson B-J/25	30.00

Tools of Trade Swatch Triple
NM/M

Production 1-25
Prime Red: No Pricing
Production 1-25
Prime Black: No Pricing
Production 1-15

#	Player	Price
2	Carlos Beltran/25	15.00
3	Dale Murphy/25	15.00
4	Paul Molitor/25	15.00
5	George Brett/25	35.00
6	Stan Musial/25	40.00
7	Ivan Rodriguez/25	10.00
9	Reggie Jackson/25	15.00
10	Hideo Nomo/25	20.00
12	Roberto Alomar/25	15.00
13	Pedro Martinez/25	15.00
15	Tim Hudson/25	10.00
17	Lance Berkman/25	10.00
19	Larry Walker/25	10.00
21	Roger Clemens/25	30.00
22	Paul LoDuca/25	10.00
23	Don Mattingly/25	15.00
25	Rafael Palmeiro/25	15.00
27	Vladimir Guerrero/25	15.00
29	Rod Carew/25	15.00
30	Nolan Ryan/25	40.00
31	Richie Sexson/25	10.00
33	Eddie Murray/25	20.00
34	Nolan Ryan/25	40.00
36	Sean Casey/25	10.00
37	Juan Gonzalez/25	10.00
42	Mike Schmidt/25	30.00
43	Todd Helton/25	12.00
45	Shawn Green/25	10.00
47	Tom Glavine/25	15.00
49	Kerry Wood/25	15.00
50	Carlos Delgado/25	10.00
51	R. John/25	15.00
52	David Ortiz/25	15.00
53	Troy Glaus/25	10.00
54	Rickey Henderson/25	15.00
55	Craig Biggio/25	10.00
56	Brad Penny/25	10.00
57	Gary Carter/25	15.00
58	Andy Pettitte/25	10.00
59	Mark Prior/25	10.00
60	Kirby Puckett/25	20.00
63	Greg Maddux/25	25.00
64	Adrian Beltre/25	15.00
65	Andruw Jones/25	12.00
67	Frank Thomas/25	10.00
68	Victor Martinez/25	10.00
70	Andre Dawson/25	12.00
72	Carlton Fisk/25	15.00
73	Cal Ripken Jr./25	40.00
74	Kenny Lofton/25	10.00
75	Barry Zito/25	10.00
76	Sammy Sosa/25	20.00
77	Deion Sanders/25	20.00
78	Tony Gwynn/25	20.00
79	Mike Piazza/25	20.00
80	Jeff Bagwell/25	15.00
81	Manny Ramirez/25	15.00
84	Mark Grace/25	15.00
84	Robin Yount/25	20.00
85	Albert Pujols/25	40.00
86	Dontrelle Willis/25	15.00
88	Magglio Ordonez/25	10.00
89	Miguel Tejada/25	15.00
90	Mark Teixeira/25	15.00
91	Gary Carter/25	15.00
92	Ivan Rodriguez/25	15.00
93	Jason Giambi/25	15.00
94	Rickey Henderson/25	15.00
95	Curt Schilling/25	15.00
96	Bobby Doerr/25	15.00
97	Chipper Jones/25	20.00
98	Eric Chavez/25	10.00
99	Johnny Bench/25	20.00
100	Harmon Killebrew/25	30.00

Tools of Trade Auto. Swatch Triple
NM/M

Production 1-75
Prime Red: No Pricing
Production 1-25
Prime Black: No Pricing
Production One Set

#	Player	Price
2	Carlos Beltran/25	40.00
3	Dale Murphy/25	50.00
18	Darryl Strawberry/75	25.00
20	Lou Brock/25	40.00
36	Sean Casey/75	25.00
37	Juan Gonzalez/25	25.00

#	Player	Price
39	Darryl Strawberry/75	20.00
56	Brad Penny/25	20.00
57	Gary Carter/25	30.00
64	Adrian Beltre/25	25.00
66	Juan Gonzalez/50	25.00
70	Andre Dawson/75	25.00
73	Cal Ripken Jr./25	200.00
82	Carlos Beltran/25	40.00
91	Gary Carter/25	30.00
96	Bobby Doerr/25	30.00
100	Harmon Killebrew/25	60.00

Tools/Trade Auto. Swatch Triple Revers
NM/M

Production 1-50

#	Player	Price
18	Darryl Strawberry/50	25.00
20	Lou Brock/50	50.00
36	Sean Casey/25	25.00
37	Juan Gonzalez/30	25.00
39	Darryl Strawberry/50	20.00
70	Andre Dawson/50	25.00

Tools of the Trade Swatch Quad
NM/M

Production 1-100
Prime Red: No Pricing
Production 1-10
Prime Black: No Pricing
Production One Set

#	Player	Price
3	Dale Murphy/25	20.00
4	Paul Molitor/25	30.00
7	Ivan Rodriguez/50	15.00
8	Carl Yastrzemski/50	40.00
9	Reggie Jackson/100	20.00
10	Hideo Nomo/75	15.00
11	Gary Sheffield/30	15.00
12	Roberto Alomar/25	15.00
13	Pedro Martinez/25	15.00
14	Ernie Banks/25	40.00
15	Tim Hudson/50	10.00
17	Lance Berkman/65	10.00
19	Larry Walker/100	10.00
20	Lou Brock/50	25.00
21	Roger Clemens/25	40.00
22	Paul LoDuca/100	10.00
23	Don Mattingly/50	25.00
24	Willie Mays/25	80.00
25	Rafael Palmeiro/100	10.00
26	Roy Oswalt/30	15.00
31	Richie Sexson/100	10.00
33	Eddie Murray/100	15.00
36	Sean Casey/75	10.00
39	Darryl Strawberry/50	15.00
41	Tom Seaver/35	25.00
42	Mike Schmidt/50	40.00
43	Todd Helton/100	12.00
45	Shawn Green/100	10.00
46	Mike Mussina/25	20.00
50	Carlos Delgado/100	10.00
52	David Ortiz/90	30.00
53	Troy Glaus/50	12.00
54	Rickey Henderson/100	25.00
55	Craig Biggio/100	10.00
56	Brad Penny/25	15.00
57	Gary Carter/50	15.00
58	Andy Pettitte/50	15.00
59	Mark Prior/50	15.00
64	Adrian Beltre/50	15.00
65	Andruw Jones/100	10.00
66	Juan Gonzalez/30	15.00
67	Frank Thomas/50	25.00
68	Victor Martinez/50	10.00
70	Andre Dawson/50	15.00
72	Carlton Fisk/25	25.00
73	Cal Ripken Jr./100	50.00
74	Kenny Lofton/100	10.00
75	Barry Zito/100	10.00
76	Sammy Sosa/100	25.00
76	Sammy Sosa/100	25.00
78	Tony Gwynn/100	20.00
79	Mike Piazza/100	25.00
80	Jeff Bagwell/100	15.00
83	Mark Grace/50	20.00
85	Albert Pujols/50	60.00
88	Dontrelle Willis/50	15.00
88	Magglio Ordonez/50	10.00
89	Miguel Tejada/100	15.00
90	Mark Teixeira/100	15.00
92	Ivan Rodriguez/50	15.00
93	Jason Giambi/25	15.00
94	Rickey Henderson/100	15.00
95	Curt Schilling/100	15.00
100	Harmon Killebrew/50	30.00

Tools of Trade Auto. Swatch Quad
NM/M

Production 1-5
Prime Red: No Pricing
Production 1-5

#	Player	Price
3	Dale Murphy/25	60.00
20	Lou Brock/25	80.00
23	Don Mattingly/25	120.00
36	Sean Casey/75	40.00
39	Darryl Strawberry/50	40.00
41	Tom Seaver/25	75.00
42	Mike Schmidt/100	100.00
56	Brad Penny/25	30.00
57	Gary Carter/25	40.00
73	Cal Ripken Jr./25	200.00
78	Tony Gwynn/25	75.00
88	Magglio Ordonez/25	30.00

#	Player	Price
91	Gary Carter/25	40.00
100	Harmon Killebrew/25	80.00

Tools/Trade Auto. Swatch Quad Reverse
No Pricing
Production 1-15

Tools of the Trade Swatch Five
NM/M

Production 1-50
Prime Red: No Pricing
Production 1-10
Prime Black: No Pricing
Production One Set
Reverse: No Pricing
Production 1-15

#	Player	Price
4	Paul Molitor/25	35.00
7	Ivan Rodriguez/25	25.00
13	Roberto Alomar/25	20.00
13	Pedro Martinez/30	30.00
15	Tim Hudson/25	25.00
17	Lance Berkman/25	20.00
22	Paul LoDuca/25	15.00
23	Don Mattingly/25	65.00
25	Rafael Palmeiro/25	25.00
26	Roy Oswalt/25	20.00
28	Austin Kearns/25	20.00
29	Rod Carew/25	40.00
31	Richie Sexson/50	15.00
33	Eddie Murray/25	50.00
36	Sean Casey/25	20.00
42	Mike Schmidt/25	70.00
43	Todd Helton/25	25.00
52	David Ortiz/50	35.00
53	Troy Glaus/25	20.00
54	Rickey Henderson/50	25.00
55	Craig Biggio/50	25.00
56	Brad Penny/45	15.00
57	Gary Carter/40	25.00
58	Andy Pettitte/25	25.00
59	Mark Prior/25	25.00
64	Adrian Beltre/50	20.00
65	Andruw Jones/25	20.00
67	Frank Thomas/25	25.00
68	Victor Martinez/25	20.00
73	Cal Ripken Jr./50	75.00
76	Sammy Sosa/25	35.00
78	Tony Gwynn/50	40.00
79	Mike Piazza/50	50.00
80	Jeff Bagwell/50	25.00
82	Carlos Beltran/20	25.00
84	Robin Yount/25	40.00
88	Magglio Ordonez/50	20.00
89	Miguel Tejada/50	25.00
90	Mark Teixeira/50	20.00
91	Gary Carter/25	25.00
92	Ivan Rodriguez/25	25.00
94	Rickey Henderson/50	25.00
95	Curt Schilling/50	25.00

Tools of the Trade Swatch Six
NM/M

Production 1-50
Reverse: No Pricing
Production 1-10
Prime Red: No Pricing
Production 1-5
Prime Black: No Pricing
Production One Set

#	Player	Price
22	Paul LoDuca/50	20.00
31	Richie Sexson/50	20.00
52	David Ortiz/50	40.00
53	Troy Glaus/50	25.00
57	Gary Carter/50	35.00
59	Mark Prior/50	25.00
73	Cal Ripken Jr./50	85.00
76	Sammy Sosa/25	40.00
78	Tony Gwynn/50	40.00
79	Mike Piazza/50	25.00
80	Jeff Bagwell/25	25.00
90	Mark Teixeira/50	25.00
92	Ivan Rodriguez/25	25.00
94	Rickey Henderson/50	30.00

2005 Playoff Prestige
NM/M

Complete Set (200):		35.00
Common Player:		.25
Hobby Pack (8):		3.00
Hobby Box (24):		65.00

#	Player	Price
1	Rafael Furcal	.25
2	Derek Jeter	2.00
3	Edgar Renteria	.40
4	Jeff Bagwell	.50
5	Nomar Garciaparra	1.25
6	Melvin Mora	.25
7	Craig Biggio	.40
8	Brad Penny	.25
9	Hank Blalock	.50
10	Vernon Wells	.25
11	Gary Sheffield	.50
12	Jeff Kent	.25
13	Carl Crawford	.25
14	Paul Konerko	.25
15	Carlos Beltran	.50
16	Garret Anderson	.25
17	Todd Helton	.50
18	Javy Lopez	.25
19	Mike Lowell	.25
20	Robb Quinlan	.25
21	Andy Pettitte	.40
22	Roger Clemens	2.00
23	Mark Teixeira	.50

#	Player	Price
24	Miguel Cabrera	.75
25	Andruw Jones	.40
26	Josh Beckett	.40
27	Scott Rolen	.25
28	J.J. Putz	.25
29	Adrian Beltre	.50
30	Magglio Ordonez	.25
31	Mike Piazza	1.00
32	Danny Graves	.25
33	Larry Walker	.40
34	Kerry Wood	.75
35	Mike Mussina	.50
36	Joe Nathan	.25
37	Chone Figgins	.25
38	Curt Schilling	.75
39	Brett Myers	.25
40	Jae Weong Seo	.25
41	Danny Kolb	.25
42	Mariano Rivera	.50
43	Francisco Cordero	.25
44	Adam Dunn	.50
45	Pedro Martinez	.75
46	Frank Thomas	.50
47	Tom Glavine	.40
48	Torii Hunter	.40
49	Ben Sheets	.40
50	Shawn Green	.25
51	Randy Johnson	.75
52	C.C. Sabathia	.25
53	Bobby Abreu	.40
54	Octavio Dotel	.25
55	Hideki Matsui	1.50
56	Mark Buehrle	.25
57	Johan Santana	.50
58	Brandon Inge	.25
59	Dewon Brazelton	.25
60	Ryan Wagner	.25
61	Kevin Brown	.25
62	Laynce Nix	.25
63	Jason Bay	.40
64	J.D. Drew	.25
65	Jacque Jones	.25
66	Jason Schmidt	.40
67	Joe Kennedy	.25
68	Miguel Tejada	.50
69	Hideo Nomo	.25
70	Michael Young	.25
71	Lyle Overbay	.25
72	Omar Vizquel	.25
73	Johnny Estrada	.25
74	Khalil Greene	.40
75	Barry Zito	.25
76	Wilson Valdez	.25
77	Nick Green	.25
78	Bucky Jacobsen	.25
79	Keith Foulke	.25
80	Sean Burroughs	.25
81	Carlos Zambrano	.40
82	Orlando Cabrera	.25
83	Shigetoshi Hasegawa	.25
84	Troy Glaus	.40
85	Mike Sweeney	.25
86	Jason Giambi	.25
87	Derek Lee	.25
88	Carlos Delgado	.40
89	Kazuo Matsui	.25
90	Lew Ford	.25
91	Akinori Otsuka	.25
92	Bobby Crosby	.25
93	Jose Reyes	.40
94	Jose Vidro	.25
95	Shingo Takatsu	.25
96	Sean Casey	.25
97	Tim Olson	.25
98	Jeff Suppan	.25
99	Rafael Palmeiro	.25
100	Esteban Loaiza	.25
101	Brian Roberts	.25
102	Jack Wilson	.25
103	Eric Chavez	.40
104	Eric Milton	.25
105	Albert Pujols	2.00
106	Jake Peavy	.25
107	Ivan Rodriguez	.50
108	Chad Cordero	.25
109	Jody Gerut	.25
110	Chipper Jones	.75
111	Barry Larkin	.25
112	Alfonso Soriano	.75
113	Alex Rodriguez	1.50
114	Paul LoDuca	.25
115	Jim Edmonds	.40
116	Aramis Ramirez	.40
117	Lance Berkman	.25
118	Johnny Damon	.75
119	Aubrey Huff	.25
120	Mark Mulder	.25
121	Sammy Sosa	1.50
122	Mark Prior	.75
123	Shannon Stewart	.25
124	Manny Ramirez	.75
125	Jim Thome	.75
126	Doug DeVore	.25
127	Vladimir Guerrero	.75
128	Ken Harvey	.25
129	Jacob Cruz	.25
130	Ken Griffey Jr.	1.00
131	Greg Maddux	1.00
132	Derek Lowe	.25
133	Craig Monroe	.25
134	David Ortiz	.75
135	Dontrelle Willis	.40
136	Tom Gordon	.25
137	David Dellucci	.25
138	Vance Wilson	.25
139	Milton Bradley	.25
140	Ichiro Suzuki	1.50
141	Victor Martinez	.25

142	Wade Miller	.25
143	Francisco Rodriguez	.25
144	Roy Oswalt	.40
145	Carlos Lee	.25
146	Kazuhisa Ishii	.25
147	Tim Hudson	.40
148	Travis Hafner	.25
149	Jermaine Dye	.25
150	Steve Finley	.25
151	Justin Verlander RC	1.50
152	Yadier Molina	.25
153	Andy Green	.25
154	Nick Swisher	.25
155	Clint Nageotte	.25
156	Grady Sizemore	.50
157	Gavin Floyd	.25
158	Josh Kroeger	.25
159	Russ Adams	.25
160	Jeff Baker	.25
161	Dioner Navarro	.25
162	Shawn Hill	.25
163	Ryan Howard	1.00
164	Scott Proctor	.25
165	Jason Kubel	.25
166	Jose Lopez	.25
167	Ryan Church	.25
168	Yhency Brazoban	.25
169	Jeff Francis	.25
170	Angel Guzman	.25
171	John Van Benschoten	.25
172	Adrian Gonzalez	.25
173	Casey Kotchman	.25
174	David Wright	.75
175	B.J. Upton	.50
176	Dallas McPherson	.50
177	Rene Rivera	.25
178	Denny Bautista	.25
179	Logan Kensing	.25
180	Matt Peterson	.25
181	Jeremy Reed	.25
182	Jairo Garcia	.25
183	Val Majewski	.25
184	Victor Diaz	.25
185	David Krynzel	.25
186	Ron Cey	.25
187	Bill Madlock	.25
188	Dave Stewart	.25
189	Billy Ripken	.25
190	Gary Carter	.50
191	Darryl Strawberry	.25
192	Dave Parker	.25
193	Ron Guidry	.25
194	Gaylord Perry	.25
195	Fred Lynn	.25
196	Jack Morris	.25
197	Steve Garvey	.25
198	Andre Dawson	.50
199	Nolan Ryan	2.50
200	Paul Molitor	.75

Red Foil

Red Foil:	8-15X
Production 25 Sets	

Xtra Bases Black

Black:	8-15X
Production 25 Sets	

Xtra Bases Green

Green:	5-10X
Production 50 Sets	

Xtra Bases Purple

Purple:	4-8X
Production 100 Sets	

Xtra Bases Red

Red:	3-6X
Production 150 Sets	

Autographs

		NM/M
Common Autograph:		8.00
20	Robb Quinlan	8.00
28	J.J. Putz	8.00
58	Brandon Inge/SP	15.00
67	Joe Kennedy	8.00
76	Wilson Valdez	8.00
77	Nick Green	8.00
78	Bucky Jacobsen	10.00
97	Tim Olson	10.00
98	Jeff Suppan/SP	15.00
126	Doug DeVore	8.00
129	Jacob Cruz	8.00
133	Craig Monroe	10.00
138	Vance Wilson	8.00
153	Andy Green	8.00
164	Scott Proctor	8.00

Changing Stripes

		NM/M
Complete Set (25):		25.00
Common Player:		.75
Inserted 1:8		
Foil:		2-3X
Production 100 Sets		
Holo-Foil:		3-6X
Production 25 Sets		
1	Ivan Rodriguez	1.00
2	Roger Clemens	4.00
3	Curt Schilling	1.50
4	Alex Rodriguez	4.00
5	Greg Maddux	2.00
6	Juan Gonzalez	.75
7	Pedro Martinez	1.50
8	Roberto Alomar	.75
9	Randy Johnson	1.50
10	Ken Griffey Jr.	2.00
11	Carlos Beltran	1.00
12	Andy Pettitte	1.00
13	Tom Glavine	.75
14	Miguel Tejada	1.50
15	Alfonso Soriano	1.50
16	Shannon Stewart	.75
17	Nomar Garciaparra	2.00
18	Jeff Kent	.75
19	David Ortiz	1.50
20	Sean Casey	.75
21	Rickey Henderson	1.00
22	Carlton Fisk	1.00
23	Phil Niekro	.75
24	Dale Murphy	1.00
25	Reggie Jackson	1.50

Changing Stripes Mat. Dual Jersey

		NM/M
Production 12-250		
1	Ivan Rodriguez/250	10.00
2	Roger Clemens/50	20.00
3	Curt Schilling/250	12.00
6	Juan Gonzalez/250	8.00
7	Pedro Martinez/100	15.00
8	Roberto Alomar/250	10.00
9	Randy Johnson/100	15.00
11	Carlos Beltran/100	15.00
12	Andy Pettitte/250	10.00
13	Tom Glavine/50	15.00
14	Miguel Tejada/250	10.00
15	Alfonso Soriano/100	10.00
16	Shannon Stewart/100	8.00
19	David Ortiz/100	15.00
20	Sean Casey/50	10.00
21	Rickey Henderson/250	10.00
22	Carlton Fisk/250	15.00
23	Phil Niekro/250	8.00
24	Dale Murphy/250	15.00
25	Reggie Jackson/100	15.00

Connections

		NM/M
Complete Set (25):		40.00
Common Duo:		1.50
Inserted 1:8		
Foil:		2-3X
Production 100 Sets		
Holo-Foil:		3-6X
Production 25 Sets		
1	Josh Beckett, Dontrelle Willis	1.50
2	Andruw Jones, Chipper Jones	2.00
3	Kazuo Matsui, Jose Reyes	1.50
4	Bobby Abreu, Jim Thome	2.00
5	Jeff Bagwell, Lance Berkman	2.00
6	Roger Clemens, Roy Oswalt	4.00
7	Scott Rolen, Larry Walker	2.00
8	Albert Pujols, Jim Edmonds	4.00
9	Greg Maddux, Sammy Sosa	2.50
10	Mark Prior, Nomar Garciaparra	2.00
11	Barry Larkin, Sean Casey	1.50
12	Adrian Beltre, Shawn Green	1.50
13	Alex Rodriguez, Derek Jeter	6.00
14	Manny Ramirez, Jason Varitek	3.00
15	Miguel Tejada, Javy Lopez	2.00

Diamond Heritage

		NM/M
Complete Set (15):		20.00
Common Player:		.75
Inserted 1:12		
1	Pedro Martinez	1.50
2	Mark Teixeira	1.00

16	B.J. Upton, Carl Crawford	1.50
17	Frank Thomas, Paul Konerko	2.00
18	Joe Mauer, Justin Morneau	2.00
19	Victor Martinez, Jody Gerut	1.50
20	Bobby Crosby, Barry Zito	1.50
21	Mark Teixeira, Hank Blalock	2.00
22	Reggie Jackson, Rod Carew	2.00
23	Rickey Henderson, Tony Gwynn	2.50
24	Tom Seaver, Johnny Bench	3.00
25	Don Mattingly, Dave Righetti	4.00

Connections Material Dual Bat

		NM/M
Production 25-250		
2	Andruw Jones, Chipper Jones/250	10.00
3	Kazuo Matsui, Jose Reyes/100	10.00
4	Bobby Abreu, Jim Thome/100	12.00
5	Jeff Bagwell, Lance Berkman/250	10.00
6	Roger Clemens, Roy Oswalt/250	15.00
10	Mark Prior, Nomar Garciaparra/100	10.00
11	Barry Larkin, Sean Casey/100	10.00
12	Shawn Green, Adrian Beltre/250	5.00
14	Jason Varitek, Manny Ramirez/100	15.00
15	Miguel Tejada, Javy Lopez/100	10.00
17	Frank Thomas, Paul Konerko/100	10.00
19	Victor Martinez, Jody Gerut/25	12.00
21	Mark Teixeira, Hank Blalock/100	10.00
22	Reggie Jackson, Rod Carew/250	10.00
23	Tony Gwynn, Rickey Henderson/250	15.00
24	Tom Seaver, Johnny Bench/250	15.00

Connections Material Dual Jersey

		NM/M
Production 10-250		
Prime:		1-2X
Production 10-25		
No pricing 20 or less.		
1	Josh Beckett, Dontrelle Willis/250	8.00
2	Andruw Jones, Chipper Jones/250	10.00
3	Kazuo Matsui, Jose Reyes/100	10.00
4	Bobby Abreu, Jim Thome/250	10.00
5	Jeff Bagwell, Lance Berkman/250	10.00
6	Roger Clemens, Roy Oswalt/250	15.00
8	Albert Pujols, Jim Edmonds/250	25.00
11	Barry Larkin, Sean Casey/50	15.00
12	Shawn Green, Adrian Beltre/250	8.00
14	Jason Varitek, Manny Ramirez/50	20.00
15	Miguel Tejada, Javy Lopez/50	12.00
17	Frank Thomas Pants, Paul Konerko/250	10.00
20	Bobby Crosby, Barry Zito/250	8.00
21	Mark Teixeira, Hank Blalock/100	10.00
22	Reggie Jackson, Rod Carew/Jkt/250	12.00
23	Rickey Henderson, Tony Gwynn/250	15.00
24	Tom Seaver, Johnny Bench/Pants/100	15.00
25	Don Mattingly, Dave Righetti/250	20.00

3	Lance Berkman	.75
4	Vladimir Guerrero	1.50
5	Albert Pujols	4.00
6	Roger Clemens	4.00
7	Manny Ramirez	1.50
8	Mike Piazza	2.00
9	Jim Thome	1.50
10	Mark Prior	1.00
11	Gary Sheffield	.75
12	Sammy Sosa	2.50
13	Tim Hudson	.75
14	Hideki Matsui	3.00
15	Jim Edmonds	.75

Diamond Heritage Matieral Bat

		NM/M
Production 100 Sets		
1	Pedro Martinez	10.00
2	Mark Teixeira	10.00
3	Lance Berkman	5.00
4	Vladimir Guerrero	10.00
6	Roger Clemens	15.00
7	Manny Ramirez	10.00
8	Mike Piazza	10.00
9	Jim Thome	10.00
10	Mark Prior	8.00
11	Gary Sheffield	8.00
12	Sammy Sosa	10.00
13	Tim Hudson	5.00
14	Hideki Matsui	25.00
15	Jim Edmonds	8.00

Diamond Heritage Material Jersey

		NM/M
Production 100 Sets		
1	Pedro Martinez	10.00
2	Mark Teixeira	10.00
3	Lance Berkman	5.00
4	Vladimir Guerrero	10.00
5	Albert Pujols	25.00
6	Roger Clemens	15.00
7	Manny Ramirez	10.00
8	Mike Piazza	10.00
9	Jim Thome	10.00
10	Mark Prior	8.00
11	Gary Sheffield	8.00
12	Sammy Sosa	10.00
13	Tim Hudson	5.00
14	Hideki Matsui Pants	25.00
15	Jim Edmonds	8.00

League Leaders Single

		NM/M
Complete Set (10):		25.00
Inserted 1:21		
Foil:		2-4X
Production 100 Sets		
Holo-Foil:		4-8X
Production 25 Sets		
1	Gary Sheffield	2.00
2	Ben Sheets	2.00
3	Adrian Beltre	2.00
4	Scott Rolen	3.00
5	George Brett	4.00
6	Johan Santana	3.00
7	Manny Ramirez	3.00
8	Cal Ripken Jr.	8.00
9	Carlos Zambrano	2.00
10	Tony Gwynn	4.00

League Leader Single Material Bat

		NM/M
Production 250 Sets		
1	Gary Sheffield	8.00
2	Ben Sheets	5.00
3	Adrian Beltre	5.00
5	George Brett	12.00
7	Manny Ramirez	10.00
8	Cal Ripken Jr.	25.00
10	Tony Gwynn	8.00

League Leaders Single Mat. Jersey

		NM/M
Production 25-250		
1	Gary Sheffield/250	8.00
2	Ben Sheets/250	5.00
3	Adrian Beltre/50	8.00
4	Scott Rolen/250	8.00
5	George Brett/250	15.00
6	Johan Santana/25	20.00
7	Manny Ramirez/250	10.00
8	Cal Ripken Jr./250	25.00
9	Carlos Zambrano/250	5.00
10	Tony Gwynn/250	8.00

League Leaders Double

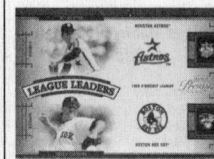

		NM/M
Complete Set (5):		15.00
Inserted 1:39		
Foil:		2-3X
Production 100 Sets		
Holo-Foil:		3-6X

1	Tim Hudson, Roy Oswalt	2.00
2	Ivan Rodriguez, Todd Helton	3.00
3	Mark Teixeira, Jim Edmonds	2.00
4	Nolan Ryan, Roger Clemens	8.00
5	Sammy Sosa, Troy Glaus	3.00

League Leader Double Material Bat

		NM/M
Production 250 Sets		
1	Tim Hudson, Roy Oswalt	8.00
2	Ivan Rodriguez, Todd Helton	15.00
3	Mark Teixeira, Jim Edmonds	10.00
4	Nolan Ryan, Roger Clemens	25.00
5	Sammy Sosa, Troy Glaus	15.00

League Leaders Double Mat. Jersey

		NM/M
Production 50-250		
1	Tim Hudson, Roy Oswalt/100	10.00
2	Ivan Rodriguez, Todd Helton/50	15.00
3	Mark Teixeira, Jim Edmonds/250	15.00
4	Nolan Ryan, Roger Clemens/250	25.00
5	Sammy Sosa, Troy Glaus/250	15.00

League Leaders Quad

		NM/M
Inserted 1:39		
Foil:		1-2X
Production 100 Sets		
Holo-Foil:		3-5X
Production 25 Sets		
1	Wade Boggs, Paul Molitor, Alan Trammell, Kirby Puckett	4.00
2	Dale Murphy, Mike Schmidt, Gary Carter, Darryl Strawberry	6.00
3	Jose Canseco, Kirby Puckett, Will Clark, Darryl Strawberry	6.00
4	Pedro Martinez, Kevin Brown, Randy Johnson, Roger Clemens	6.00
5	Don Mattingly, Dave Parker, Eddie Murray, Dale Murphy	4.00

League Leaders Quad Material Bat

		NM/M
Production 100 Sets		
2	Dale Murphy, Mike Schmidt, Gary Carter, Darryl Strawberry	40.00
4	Pedro Martinez, Kevin Brown, Randy Johnson, Roger Clemens	40.00
5	Don Mattingly, Dave Parker, Eddie Murray, Dale Murphy	50.00

League Leaders Quad Mat. Jersey

		NM/M
Production 100 Sets		
1	Wade Boggs, Paul Molitor, Alan Trammell, Kirby Puckett	40.00
2	Dale Murphy, Mike Schmidt, Gary Carter, Darryl Strawberry	40.00
3	Jose Canseco, Kirby Puckett, Will Clark, Darryl Strawberry	40.00
4	Pedro Martinez, Kevin Brown, Randy Johnson, Roger Clemens	50.00
5	Don Mattingly, Dave Parker, Eddie Murray, Dale Murphy	50.00

Playoff Champions Combo Wild Card

		NM/M
Inserted 1:391		
Division Combo:		.75-1X
League Combo:		.75-1X
World Series Combo:		.75-1X
Redemption Deadline 4-15-06.		

Production 25 Sets

1	Tim Hudson, Roy Oswalt	2.00
2	Ivan Rodriguez, Todd Helton	3.00
3	Mark Teixeira, Jim Edmonds	2.00
4	Nolan Ryan, Roger Clemens	8.00
5	Sammy Sosa, Troy Glaus	3.00

1	Andruw Jones, Johnny Estrada, Chipper Jones	10.00
2	Miguel Cabrera, Josh Beckett, Dontrelle Willis	10.00
3	Chad Cordero, Nick Johnson, Brad Wilkerson	5.00
4	Jim Thome, Bobby Abreu, Chase Utley	10.00
5	Mike Piazza, Kazuo Matsui, David Wright	10.00
6	Albert Pujols, Scott Rolen, Jim Edmonds	10.00
7	Kerry Wood, Mark Prior, Carlos Zambrano	10.00
8	Ben Sheets, Geoff Jenkins, Lyle Overbay	5.00
9	Kip Wells, Jack Wilson, Jason Bay	5.00
10	Austin Kearns, Adam Dunn, Ken Griffey Jr.	10.00
11	Roy Oswalt, Lance Berkman, Jeff Bagwell	10.00
12	Jason Jennings, Matt Holliday, Todd Helton	10.00
13	Eric Gagne, Jayson Werth, Milton Bradley	10.00
14	Alex Cintron, Brandon Webb, Luis Gonzalez	5.00
15	Jason Schmidt, Edgardo Alfonzo, Kirk Rueter	5.00
16	Khalil Greene, Jake Peavy, Trevor Hoffman	5.00
17	Manny Ramirez, Curt Schilling, David Ortiz	15.00
18	Miguel Tejada, Melvin Mora, Javy Lopez	8.00
19	Roy Halladay, Alexis Rios, Gabe Gross	5.00
20	Alex Rodriguez, Derek Jeter, Hideki Matsui	20.00
21	B.J. Upton, Scott Kazmir, Carl Crawford	10.00
22	Frank Thomas, Shingo Takatsu, Aaron Rowand	8.00
23	Victor Martinez, C.C. Sabathia, Travis Hafner	5.00
24	Torii Hunter, Johan Santana, Justin Morneau	10.00
25	Zack Greinke, Mike Sweeney, Ken Harvey	5.00
26	Ivan Rodriguez, Jeremy Bonderman, Carlos Guillen	8.00
27	Rich Harden, Bobby Crosby, Barry Zito	5.00
28	Bret Boone, Ichiro Suzuki, Jeremy Reed	12.00
29	Michael Young, Mark Teixeira, Hank Blalock	10.00
30	Vladimir Guerrero, Darin Erstad, Garret Anderson	10.00

Playoff Game Jersey Collection

Inserted 1:8 Retail

Prestigious Pros Blue

		NM/M
Common Player:		1.00
Production 900 Sets		
Black:		No Pricing
Production 10 Sets		
Bronze:		2-3X
Production 100 Sets		
Gold:		2-4X
Production 50 Sets		
Green:		1-2X
Production 350 Sets		
Orange:		1-1.5X
Production 500 Sets		
Platinum:		3-5X
Production 25 Sets		
Purple:		1-2X
Production 200 Sets		
Red:		1X
Production 70 Sets		
Silver:		2-3X
Production 75 Sets		
1	Ozzie Smith	3.00
2	Derek Jeter	4.00
3	Eric Chavez	1.00
4	Paul Molitor	2.00
5	Jeff Bagwell	1.50
6	Melvin Mora	1.00
7	Craig Biggio	1.50
8	Cal Ripken Jr.	8.00
9	Hank Blalock	1.50
10	Miguel Tejada	2.00
11	Jacque Jones	1.00

12 Alfonso Soriano 2.00
13 Omar Vizquel 1.00
14 Paul Konerko 1.00
15 Tim Hudson 1.00
16 Garret Anderson 1.00
17 Lance Berkman 1.00
18 Randy Johnson 1.00
19 Robin Yount 3.00
20 Mark Mulder 1.00
21 Sean Casey 1.00
22 Jim Palmer 1.50
23 Don Mattingly 5.00
24 Manny Ramirez 2.00
25 Rafael Palmeiro 1.50
26 Vernon Wells 1.00
27 Vladimir Guerrero 2.00
28 Ken Harvey 1.00
29 Rod Carew 1.50
30 Nolan Ryan 8.00
31 Mike Piazza 3.00
32 Steve Carlton 1.50
33 Miguel Cabrera 2.00
34 Kerry Wood 2.00
35 Mike Mussina 1.00
36 Gaylord Perry 1.00
37 Gary Sheffield 1.50
38 Curt Schilling 2.00
39 Don Sutton 1.00
40 Roger Clemens 6.00
41 Victor Martinez 1.00
42 Jason Giambi 1.00
43 Dennis Eckersley 1.00
44 Adam Dunn 1.50
45 Pedro Martinez 2.00
46 Tony Perez 1.00
47 Tom Glavine 1.00
48 Torii Hunter 1.00
49 Hideo Nomo 1.00
50 Scott Rolen 2.00
51 Ichiro Suzuki 1.00
52 C.C. Sabathia 1.00
53 George Brett 5.00
54 David Ortiz 1.00
55 Hideki Matsui 4.00
56 Nomar Garciaparra 1.00
57 Johan Santana 2.00
58 Phil Niekro 1.00
59 Dontrelle Willis 1.00
60 Magglio Ordonez 1.00
61 Livan Hernandez 1.00
62 Edgar Renteria 1.00
63 Todd Helton 1.50
64 Carlos Beltran 1.50
65 Sammy Sosa 4.00
66 Albert Pujols 6.00
67 Mike Lowell 1.00
68 Mark Prior 1.00
69 Ivan Rodriguez 1.50
70 Jake Peavy 1.00
71 Jim Thome 2.00
72 Mark Teixeira 1.50
73 Shawn Green 1.00
74 Rollie Fingers 1.00
75 Barry Zito 1.00
76 Jose Vidro 1.00
77 Ben Sheets 1.00
78 Roy Halladay 1.00
79 Frank Thomas 1.50
80 Chipper Jones 2.00
81 Jason Bay 1.00
82 Tony Gwynn 5.00
83 Shannon Stewart 1.00
84 Carl Crawford 1.00
85 Andruw Jones 1.00
86 Greg Maddux 3.00
87 Barry Larkin 1.00
88 Alex Rodriguez 5.00
89 Rickey Henderson 1.50
90 Troy Glaus 1.00
91 Roy Oswalt 1.00
92 Michael Young 1.00
93 Carlos Lee 1.00
94 Jim Edmonds 1.00
95 Fergie Jenkins 1.00
96 Paul LoDuca 1.00
97 Aubrey Huff 1.00
98 Ken Griffey Jr. 3.00
99 Carlos Delgado 1.50
100 Mike Schmidt

Prestigious Pros Mat. Bat Silver

NM/M
Production 5-50
No pricing 20 or less.
1 Ozzie Smith/50 25.00
3 Eric Chavez/25 10.00
4 Paul Molitor/50 12.00
5 Jeff Bagwell/50 10.00
7 Craig Biggio/25 15.00
8 Cal Ripken Jr./25 40.00
9 Hank Blalock/25 10.00
10 Miguel Tejada/25 12.00
14 Paul Konerko/25 10.00
15 Tim Hudson/25 10.00
17 Garret Anderson/50 10.00
18 Lance Berkman/50 10.00
19 Randy Johnson/25 20.00
21 Robin Yount/50 10.00
23 Sean Casey/25 10.00
24 Don Mattingly/50 25.00
25 Rafael Palmeiro/25 15.00
27 Vladimir Guerrero/25 20.00
28 Ken Harvey/25 8.00
29 Rod Carew/50 8.00
30 Nolan Ryan/50 35.00
31 Mike Piazza/25 20.00

32 Steve Carlton/50 8.00
34 Kerry Wood/25 15.00
35 Mike Mussina/25 10.00
37 Gary Sheffield/25 10.00
38 Curt Schilling/25 15.00
40 Roger Clemens/25 25.00
41 Victor Martinez/25 10.00
42 Jason Giambi/25 10.00
44 Adam Dunn/25 12.00
45 Pedro Martinez/25 15.00
46 Tony Perez/25 8.00
47 Tom Glavine/25 12.00
48 Torii Hunter/50 8.00
49 Hideo Nomo/25 25.00
50 Scott Rolen/25 20.00
53 George Brett/25 25.00
54 David Ortiz/50 12.00
55 Hideki Matsui/25 40.00
56 Nomar Garciaparra/25 20.00
58 Phil Niekro/50 8.00
60 Magglio Ordonez/25 8.00
62 Edgar Renteria/25 10.00
63 Todd Helton/25 15.00
64 Carlos Beltran/25 10.00
65 Sammy Sosa/25 15.00
67 Mike Lowell/25 10.00
68 Mark Prior/25 15.00
69 Ivan Rodriguez/50 10.00
71 Jim Thome/50 10.00
72 Mark Teixeira/25 10.00
73 Shawn Green/25 10.00
77 Ben Sheets/25 10.00
79 Frank Thomas/25 15.00
81 Jason Bay/25 10.00
82 Tony Gwynn/50 15.00
83 Shannon Stewart/25 8.00
85 Andruw Jones/50 10.00
87 Barry Larkin/50 8.00
89 Rickey Henderson/50 15.00
90 Troy Glaus/25 10.00
91 Roy Oswalt/25 10.00
92 Michael Young/25 10.00
93 Carlos Lee/25 10.00
94 Jim Edmonds/50 10.00
96 Paul LoDuca/25 10.00
99 Carlos Delgado/25 10.00
100 Mike Schmidt/50 25.00

Prestigious Pros Mat. Jersey Gold

NM/M
Production 5-50
No pricing 20 or less.
Platinum Patch: No Pricing
Production 5-10
1 Ozzie Smith/50 25.00
3 Eric Chavez/25 10.00
4 Paul Molitor/50 12.00
5 Jeff Bagwell/50 10.00
6 Melvin Mora/25 10.00
7 Craig Biggio/25 15.00
8 Cal Ripken Jr./50 40.00
10 Miguel Tejada/25 12.00
13 Omar Vizquel/25 15.00
14 Paul Konerko/25 8.00
15 Tim Hudson/25 10.00
17 Lance Berkman/25 8.00
18 Randy Johnson/25 20.00
19 Robin Yount/50 15.00
20 Mark Mulder/20 10.00
21 Sean Casey/25 10.00
22 Jim Palmer/50 8.00
23 Don Mattingly/50 25.00
26 Vernon Wells/25 8.00
27 Vladimir Guerrero/25 20.00
28 Ken Harvey/25 8.00
29 Rod Carew/50 8.00
30 Nolan Ryan/50 35.00
31 Mike Piazza/25 20.00
32 Steve Carlton/50 8.00
34 Kerry Wood/25 15.00
35 Mike Mussina/25 10.00
36 Gaylord Perry/50 8.00
37 Gary Sheffield/25 10.00
38 Curt Schilling/25 15.00
39 Don Sutton/50 8.00
40 Roger Clemens/25 25.00
41 Victor Martinez/25 10.00
42 Jason Giambi/25 10.00
43 Dennis Eckersley/50 10.00
45 Pedro Martinez/25 10.00
46 Tony Perez/50 8.00
49 Hideo Nomo/25 25.00
50 Scott Rolen/25 20.00
52 C.C. Sabathia/25 10.00
53 George Brett/50 25.00
55 Hideki Matsui/25 40.00
58 Phil Niekro/50 8.00
59 Dontrelle Willis/25 10.00
60 Magglio Ordonez/25 8.00
61 Livan Hernandez/25 8.00
62 Edgar Renteria/25 10.00
63 Todd Helton/25 15.00
65 Sammy Sosa/25 20.00
66 Albert Pujols/25 35.00
68 Mark Prior/25 15.00
71 Jim Thome/25 15.00
72 Mark Teixeira/25 12.00
73 Shawn Green/25 10.00
74 Rollie Fingers/50 8.00
77 Ben Sheets/25 10.00
79 Roy Halladay/25 10.00
80 Chipper Jones/25 15.00
81 Jason Bay/25 10.00
82 Tony Gwynn/50 15.00

84 Carl Crawford/25 10.00
85 Andruw Jones/25 10.00
86 Greg Maddux/25 20.00
87 Barry Larkin/25 12.00
89 Rickey Henderson/50 15.00
90 Troy Glaus/25 10.00
92 Michael Young/25 10.00
93 Carlos Lee/25 10.00
94 Jim Edmonds/25 12.00
95 Fergie Jenkins/50 10.00
97 Aubrey Huff/25 10.00
99 Carlos Delgado/25 8.00
100 Mike Schmidt/50 25.00

Prestigious Pros Signature Black

No Pricing
Production Five Sets

Signature Xtra Bases Black

No Pricing
Production 3-10

Signature Xtra Bases Purple

NM/M
Production 5-50
6 Melvin Mora/25 25.00
8 Brad Penny/25 10.00
13 Carl Crawford/25 25.00
20 Robb Quinlan/50 8.00
28 J.J. Putz/25 8.00
32 Danny Graves/50 10.00
36 Joe Nathan/50 25.00
37 Chone Figgins/50 10.00
39 Brett Myers/50 10.00
41 Danny Kolb/50 15.00
43 Francisco Cordero/50 10.00
52 C.C. Sabathia/25 25.00
54 Octavio Dotel/50 15.00
56 Mark Buehrle/25 15.00
58 Brandon Inge/50 15.00
59 Dewon Brazelton/50 10.00
60 Ryan Wagner/50 8.00
62 Laynce Nix/50 15.00
63 Jason Bay/25 20.00
65 Jacque Jones/25 20.00
67 Joe Kennedy/50 8.00
71 Lyle Overbay/25 20.00
76 Johnny Estrada/50 15.00
76 Wilson Valdez/50 8.00
77 Nick Green/50 8.00
78 Bucky Jacobsen/50 10.00
79 Keith Foulke/50 35.00
81 Carlos Zambrano/50 35.00
82 Orlando Cabrera/25 20.00
90 Lew Ford/50 15.00
92 Bobby Crosby/50 20.00
97 Tim Olson/50 8.00
98 Jeff Suppan/50 10.00
100 Esteban Loaiza/50 10.00
101 Brian Roberts/50 35.00
102 Jack Wilson/50 15.00
106 Jake Peavy/25 30.00
108 Chad Cordero/50 10.00
109 Jody Gerut/25 10.00
126 Doug DeVore/50 8.00
128 Ken Harvey/50 10.00
129 Jacob Cruz/50 8.00
133 Craig Monroe/50 10.00
136 Tom Gordon/50 15.00
137 David Dellucci/50 20.00
138 Vance Wilson/50 8.00
139 Milton Bradley/50 15.00
141 Victor Martinez/25 30.00
142 Wade Miller/50 15.00
145 Carlos Lee/25 15.00
148 Travis Hafner/50 15.00
149 Jermaine Dye/50 15.00
152 Yadier Molina/50 20.00
153 Andy Green/50 8.00
161 Dioner Navarro/50 12.00
162 Shawn Hill/50 8.00
164 Scott Proctor/50 15.00
165 Jason Kubel/50 15.00
168 Yhency Brazoban/50 10.00
170 Angel Guzman/50 15.00
172 Adrian Gonzalez/50 12.00
173 Casey Kotchman 15.00
187 Bill Madlock/25 20.00
189 Billy Ripken/25 10.00
190 Gary Carter/25 25.00
191 Darryl Strawberry/25 25.00
192 Dave Parker/25 25.00
195 Fred Lynn/25 25.00
196 Jack Morris/25 25.00
198 Andre Dawson/25 25.00

Stars of MLB

NM/M
Complete Set (15): 20.00
Common Player: 1.00
Inserted 1:12
Foil: 2-4X
Production 100 Sets
Holo-Foil: 4-8X
Production 25 Sets
1 Randy Johnson 3.00
2 Adrian Beltre 1.00
4 Eric Chavez 1.00
4 Mike Mussina 1.50
5 Todd Helton 2.00
6 Curt Schilling 2.00
7 Miguel Cabrera 3.00
8 Kerry Wood 2.50
9 David Ortiz 3.00
10 Michael Young 1.00
11 Mark Mulder 1.00
12 Victor Martinez 1.00
13 Johan Santana 2.00
14 Scott Rolen 3.00
15 Carlos Beltran 2.00

Stars of MLB Material Bat

NM/M
No Pricing
Production 50-100
1 Randy Johnson/100 10.00
2 Adrian Beltre/100 5.00
3 Eric Chavez/100 5.00
4 Mike Mussina/100 8.00
5 Todd Helton/100 8.00
6 Curt Schilling/100 10.00
7 Miguel Cabrera/100 8.00
8 Kerry Wood/100 5.00
9 David Ortiz/100 10.00
10 Michael Young/100 5.00
11 Mark Mulder/50 5.00
14 Scott Rolen/100 10.00
15 Carlos Beltran/100 8.00

Stars of MLB Sign. Material Bat

NM/M
Production 10-50
2 Adrian Beltre/50 25.00
3 Eric Chavez/50 20.00
8 Kerry Wood/25 50.00
9 David Ortiz/25 40.00
10 Michael Young/50 25.00
15 Carlos Beltran/50 50.00

Stars of MLB Material Jersey

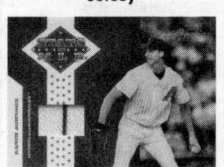

NM/M
Production 100 Sets
Prime: 1-2X
Production 25 Sets
1 Randy Johnson/Pants 10.00
2 Adrian Beltre 5.00
3 Eric Chavez 5.00
4 Mike Mussina 8.00
5 Todd Helton 8.00
6 Curt Schilling 10.00
7 Miguel Cabrera 10.00
8 Kerry Wood 10.00
9 David Ortiz 12.00
10 Michael Young 5.00
11 Mark Mulder 5.00
12 Victor Martinez 5.00
13 Johan Santana 10.00
14 Scott Rolen 10.00
15 Carlos Beltran 8.00

Stars of MLB Sig. Material Jersey

NM/M
Production 10-50
Prime: No Pricing
Production Five Sets
2 Adrian Beltre/50 25.00
3 Eric Chavez/50 20.00
8 Kerry Wood/50 50.00
9 David Ortiz/50 40.00
10 Michael Young/50 25.00
12 Victor Martinez/50 50.00
13 Johan Santana/50 50.00
15 Carlos Beltran/25 50.00

2008 Playoff Contenders

NM/M
Complete Set (1-50):
Common Player (1-50): .50
Common Auto. (51-130): 8.00
SP Autos. are noted.
Pack (5): 5.00

Box (24): 110.00
1 Aaron Shafer .50
2 Adrian Nieto 1.00
3 Andrew Liebel .50
4 Blake Tekotte .50
5 Brad Mills 1.00
6 Brandon Waring 1.00
7 Brett Hunter .50
8 Byron Wiley .75
9 Caleb Gindl .75
10 Carlos Peguero 1.00
11 Carson Blair 1.00
12 Charlie Blackmon 1.00
13 Chris Johnson 1.50
14 Cody Adams 1.00
15 Cody Satterwhite 1.00
16 Cole Rohrbough 1.00
17 Cole St. Clair 1.00
18 Daniel Thomas .50
19 Dennis Raben 1.00
20 Derek Norris 1.00
21 Dominic Brown 4.00
22 Dusty Coleman .50
23 Gerardo Parra .50
24 Greg Halman 1.50
25 J.P. Ramirez 2.00
26 James Darnell 1.00
27 Jason Knapp 2.50
28 Jay Austin .50
29 Jesus Montero 2.00
30 Jharmidy DeJesus .50
31 Jose Duran 1.00
32 Josh Vitters 1.50
33 Kenn Kasparek .50
34 L.J. Hoes 1.50
35 Logan Schafer .50
36 Matt Harrison .50
37 Matt Mitchell .50
38 Max Ramirez 1.00
39 Mike Cisco 1.00
40 Niko Vasquez 1.00
41 Rolando Gomez .50
42 Ryan Kalish .50
43 Stolmy Pimentel .50
44 T.J. Steele .50
45 Tim Murphy .50
46 Tony Delmonico .50
47 Tyler Ladendorf .50
48 Tyler Sample 1.50
49 Vance Worley 1.50
50 Xavier Avery 1.50
51 Aaron Cunningham/283 20.00
52 Alex Buchholz 20.00
53 Allan Dykstra 10.00
54 Andrew Cashner/216 20.00
55 Andrew Walker/288 15.00
56 Angel Morales 25.00
57 Angel Villalona 60.00
58 Anthony Hewitt 10.00
59 Brad Hand/274 20.00
60 Brad Holt/236 20.00
61 Brandon Crawford/339 15.00
62 Bryan Price/165 15.00
63 Buster Posey 50.00
64 Carlos Gutierrez/87 15.00
65 Chase D'Arnaud/304 20.00
66 Chris Davis 15.00
67 Chris Hicks/230 15.00
68 Christian Friedrich 10.00
69 Clark Murphy 15.00
70 Cord Phelps/244 15.00
71 Curtis Petersen/244 15.00
72 Daniel Cortes/292 15.00
73 Dan Schlereth/317 10.00
74 Danny Carroll 10.00
75 Danny Espinosa/395 15.00
76 Dayn Viciedo/395 40.00
77 Derek Holland 25.00
78 Derrick Rose/88 90.00
79 Devaris Gordon 25.00
80 Engel Beltre 15.00
81 Evan Frederickson/177 20.00
82 Gordon Beckham 40.00
83 Greg Veloz/339 20.00
84 Ike Davis 15.00
85 Isaac Galloway 15.00
86 Jared Bolden 15.00
87 Jarek Cunningham/229 20.00
88 Jhoulys Chacin 25.00
89 Jon Jay 15.00
90 Jordan Danks/354 15.00
91 Josh Lindblom/288 15.00
92 Juan Carlos Sulbaran 15.00
93 Juan Ramirez/267 20.00
94 Justin Parker/225 25.00
95 Kirk Nieuwenhuis 8.00
96 Pat Venditte 25.00
97 Lance Lynn 15.00
98 Logan Forsythe/262 20.00
99 Logan Morrison/314 40.00
100 Marcus Lemon 15.00
101 Mark Sobolewski/277 20.00
102 Mat Gamel 30.00
103 Michael Beasley/88 75.00
104 Michael Kohn 10.00
105 Michael Taylor/362 15.00
106 Michel Inoa 25.00
107 Mike Jones 15.00
108 Mike Montgomery 15.00
109 Mike Stanton/149 275.00
110 Neftali Feliz/246 40.00
111 Neftali Soto/249 30.00
112 O.J. Mayo/88 100.00
113 Pedro Baez 20.00
114 Petey Paramore 10.00
115 Rafael Rodriguez 50.00
116 Rashun Dixon 15.00
117 Rick Porcello 40.00

118 Robbie Grossman/227 25.00
119 Roger Kieschnick/289 50.00
120 Ryan Perry 10.00
121 Shane Peterson/399 15.00
122 Shooter Hunt/52 25.00
123 Trey Haley/309 20.00
124 Tyler Chatwood 10.00
125 Tyson Ross 10.00
126 Wilin Rosario 10.00
127 Wilmer Flores/75 150.00
128 Yamaico Navarro 20.00
129 Zach Collier/200 30.00
130 Zach Putnam 15.00

Holo Silver

Holo Silver (1-50): 2-3X
Holo Silver (51-130): .1-.15X
Production 199 Sets

Championship Ticket Autos

Production One Set

Draft Class

NM/M
Common Duo: 2.50
Production 1,500 Sets
Gold: 1-1.5X
Production 250 Sets
Black: 1-2X
Production 100 Sets
1 Ike Davis,
Kirk Nieuwenhuis 4.00
2 Curtis Petersen,
Isaac Galloway 2.50
3 Jon Jay, Lance Lynn 2.50
4 Chris Davis,
Clark Murphy 2.50
5 Trey Haley, Zach Putnam 2.50

Draft Class Black Autos.

NM/M
Production 25 Sets
1 Ike Davis,
Kirk Nieuwenhuis 50.00
3 Jon Jay, Lance Lynn 30.00
4 Chris Davis,
Clark Murphy 20.00
5 Trey Haley,
Zach Putnam 20.00

Legendary Rookies

NM/M
Production 1,500 Sets
Gold: 1-1.5X
Production 250 Sets
Black: 1-2X
Production 100 Sets
1 Willie Mays 8.00
2 Pete Rose 8.00
3 Cal Ripken Jr. 8.00
4 Mike Schmidt 4.00
5 Robin Yount 8.00

Legendary Rookies Black Autos.

NM/M
Production 25 Sets
Most not priced.
2 Pete Rose 90.00

Rookie Roll Call

		NM/M
Common Player:		1.50
Production 1,500 Sets		
Gold:		1-1.5X
Production 250 Sets		
Black:		1-2X
Production 100 Sets		
1	Mat Gamel	3.00
2	Michel Inoa	3.00
3	Rafael Rodriguez	4.00
4	Isaac Galloway	1.50
5	Angel Villalona	5.00

Rookie Roll Call Black Autos.

		NM/M
Common Player:		
Most not priced.		
3	Rafael Rodriguez	100.00
4	Isaac Galloway	20.00

Round Numbers

		NM/M
Common Duo:		2.50
Gold:		1-1.5X
Production 250 Sets		
Black:		1-2X
Production 100 Sets		
1	Buster Posey, Gordon Beckham	5.00
2	Dan Schlereth, Ryan Perry	2.50
3	Allan Dykstra, Anthony Hewitt	2.50
4	Tyler Chatwood, Tyson Ross	2.50
5	Brandon Crawford, Chase D'Arnaud	4.00

Round Numbers Black Autos

		NM/M
Production 25 Sets		
Most not priced		
2	Dan Schlereth, Ryan Perry	20.00

Season Tickets Autographs

		NM/M
Common Auto.:		8.00
1	Aaron Shafer	10.00
2	Adrian Nieto	10.00
3	Andrew Liebel	10.00
4	Blake Tekotte	10.00
5	Brad Mills	15.00
6	Brandon Waring	25.00
7	Brett Hunter	15.00
8	Byron Wiley	15.00
9	Caleb Gindl	25.00
10	Carlos Peguero	8.00
11	Carson Blair	15.00
12	Charlie Blackmon	15.00
14	Cody Adams	8.00
15	Cody Satterwhite	10.00
16	Cole Rohrbough	15.00
17	Cole St. Clair	15.00
18	Daniel Thomas	10.00
19	Dennis Raben	15.00
20	Derek Norris	15.00
21	Dominic Brown	40.00
22	Dusty Coleman	15.00
23	Gerardo Parra	30.00
24	Greg Halman	8.00
25	J.P. Ramirez	20.00
26	James Darnell	15.00
27	Jason Knapp	10.00
28	Jay Austin	10.00
29	Jesus Montero	60.00
30	Jharmidy DeJesus	25.00
31	Jose Duran	15.00
32	Josh Vitters	25.00
33	Kenn Kasparek	8.00
34	L.J. Hoes	30.00
35	Logan Schafer	8.00
36	Matt Harrison	15.00
37	Matt Mitchell	10.00
38	Max Ramirez	10.00
39	Mike Cisco	10.00
40	Niko Vasquez	20.00
41	Rolando Gomez	15.00
42	Ryan Kalish	25.00
43	T.J. Steele	8.00
44	Tim Murphy	8.00
45	Tony Delmonico	15.00
46	Tyler Ladendorf	8.00
47	Tyler Sample	15.00
48	Vance Worley	15.00
49	Xavier Avery	20.00
50	Xavier Avery	20.00

2008 Playoff Prime Cuts

		NM/M
Common Player (1-100):		1.00
Production 249		
Common Auto. (101-150):		8.00
Production 249		
Box:		220.00
1	Al Kaline	2.50
2	Alan Trammell	1.00
3	Andre Dawson	1.50
4	Barry Larkin	1.00
5	Billy Williams	1.00
6	Bo Jackson	2.50
7	Bob Feller	2.00
8	Bob Gibson	2.50
9	Bobby Doerr	1.50
10	Brooks Robinson	2.00
11	Bruce Sutter	1.00
12	Cal Ripken Jr.	8.00
13	Carl Erskine	1.00
14	Carl Yastrzemski	4.00
15	Carlton Fisk	1.50
16	Dale Murphy	1.50
17	Dave Winfield	2.00
18	Deion Sanders	1.50
19	Dennis Eckersley	1.50
20	Denny McLain	1.00
21	Dwight Gooden	1.00
22	Don Drysdale	2.00
23	Don Larsen	2.00
24	Don Mattingly	4.00
25	Don Sutton	2.00
26	Duke Snider	2.00
27	Eddie Mathews	3.00
28	Eddie Murray	2.00
29	Ernie Banks	3.00
30	Fergie Jenkins	1.00
31	Frank Howard	1.00
32	Frank Robinson	2.50
33	Fred Lynn	1.00
34	Gary Carter	1.00
35	Gaylord Perry	1.00
36	George Brett	4.00
37	George Kell	1.00
38	Gil Hodges	1.00
39	Hank Aaron	5.00
40	Harmon Killebrew	2.00
41	Jackie Robinson	3.00
42	Jim Palmer	1.50
43	Jim Rice	1.00
44	Jim Thorpe	2.50
45	Joe Cronin	1.00
46	Joe Jackson	4.00
47	Joe Medwick	1.00
48	Joe Morgan	2.00
49	Johnny Bench	3.00
50	Johnny Pesky	1.00
51	Juan Marichal	2.00
52	Arky Vaughan	1.00
53	Kirk Gibson	1.00
54	Larry Walker	1.00
55	Lou Boudreau	1.00
56	Lou Brock	1.50
57	Lou Gehrig	5.00
58	Luis Aparicio	1.00
59	Mark Fidrych	1.00
60	Marty Marion	1.00
61	Maury Wills	1.00
62	Mike Schmidt	3.00
63	Monte Irvin	1.50
64	Nellie Fox	1.00
65	Nolan Ryan	6.00
66	Orlando Cepeda	1.50
67	Ozzie Smith	3.00
68	Paul Molitor	2.00
69	Pete Rose	5.00
70	Phil Niekro	1.00
71	Randy Jones	1.00
73	Red Schoendienst	1.00
74	Reggie Jackson	2.00
75	Richie Ashburn	1.00
76	Roberto Clemente	5.00
77	Robin Roberts	1.00
78	Robin Yount	2.50
79	Rod Carew	1.50
81	Roger Maris	3.00
82	Ryne Sandberg	3.00
83	Satchel Paige	3.00
84	Sparky Anderson	1.00
85	Stan Musial	2.50
86	Steve Carlton	1.00
87	Steve Garvey	1.00
88	Ted Williams	4.00
89	Tim Raines	1.00
90	Tom Seaver	2.00
91	Tony Gwynn	2.00
92	Tony Perez	1.00
93	Wade Boggs	1.50
94	Warren Spahn	2.00
95	Whitey Ford	2.00
96	Will Clark	1.50
97	Willie Mays	5.00
98	Willie McCovey	1.50
99	Willie Stargell	2.00
100	Yogi Berra	2.50
101	Mike Stanton/Auto./249	125.00
102	Logan Morrison/Auto./249	25.00
103	Daniel Cortes/Auto./249	15.00
104	Jhoulys Chacin/Auto./249	25.00
105	Brandon Crawford/Auto./249	8.00
106	Rick Porcello/Auto./249	30.00
106	Rick Porcello/Jsy/Auto./249	30.00
107	Neftali Feliz/Auto./249	25.00
108	Buster Posey/Auto./249	50.00
108	Buster Posey/Jsy/Auto./249	50.00
109	Gordon Beckham/Auto./249	30.00
109	Gordon Beckham/Jsy/Auto./249	30.00
110	Ike Davis/Auto./249	40.00
110	Ike Davis/Bat/Auto./249	40.00
111	Andrew Cashner/Auto./249	10.00
111	Andrew Cashner/Jsy/Auto./249	10.00
112	Ryan Perry/Auto./249	15.00
113	Anthony Hewitt/Auto./249	8.00
114	Dan Schlereth/Auto./249	8.00
115	Carlos Gutierrez/Auto./249	15.00
116	Shooter Hunt/Auto./249	15.00
117	Brad Holt/Auto./249	15.00
118	Zach Collier/Auto./249	-10.00
119	Evan Frederickson/Auto./249	8.00
120	Christian Friedrich/Auto./249	10.00
121	Cord Phelps/Auto./249	8.00
122	Danny Espinosa/Auto./249	8.00
124	Bryan Price/Auto./249	8.00
125	Juan Ramirez/Auto./249	8.00
126	Xavier Avery/Auto./249	10.00
127	Brad Hand/Auto./249	8.00
128	Jay Austin/Auto./249	8.00
129	Tyson Ross/Auto./249	8.00
130	Michael Taylor/Auto./249	15.00
131	Tyler Ladendorf/Auto./249	8.00
132	Rashun Dixon/Auto./249	15.00
133	Cody Adams/Auto./249	8.00
134	Michel Inoa/Auto./249	25.00
135	Wilin Rosario/Auto./249	12.00
136	Dennis Raben/Auto./249	10.00
137	Cody Satterwhite/Jsy/Auto./249	10.00
138	Wilmer Flores/Auto./249	60.00
139	Zeke Spruill/Auto./249	15.00
140	Jason Knapp/Auto./249	8.00
141	Charlie Blackmon/Auto./249	8.00
142	Tyler Chatwood/Auto./249	8.00
143	Logan Schafer/Auto./249	10.00
144	Isaac Galloway/Auto./249	15.00
145	T.J. Steele/Auto./249	8.00
146	Chase D'Arnaud/Auto./249	8.00
147	Rolando Gomez/Auto./249	8.00
148	Anthony Gose/Auto./249	8.00
149	Adrian Nieto/Auto./249	8.00
150	Allan Dykstra/Auto./249	10.00

Century Gold

No Pricing
Production Five Sets

Century Platinum

Production One Set

Century Silver

No Pricing
Production 25 Sets

Century Signatures

		NM/M
Production 1-99		
Platinum:		No Pricing
Production One Set		
1	Al Kaline/28	35.00
2	Brooks Robinson/74	30.00
12	Cal Ripken Jr./31	120.00
25	Don Sutton/53	15.00
37	George Kell/99	20.00
51	Juan Marichal/43	20.00
60	Marty Marion/94	15.00
65	Nolan Ryan/32	70.00
85	Stan Musial/99	50.00
95	Whitey Ford/26	40.00

Bats

		NM/M
Production 1-99		
2	Alan Trammell/99	8.00
3	Andre Dawson/99	8.00
6	Barry Larkin/99	8.00
6	Bo Jackson/99	12.00
9	Brooks Robinson/99	10.00
12	Cal Ripken Jr./30	10.00
13	Carlton Fisk/27	10.00
16	Dale Murphy/99	10.00
18	Deion Sanders/49	12.00
21	Dwight Gooden/99	6.00
24	Don Mattingly/99	8.00
27	Eddie Mathews/99	15.00
28	Eddie Murray/99	10.00
34	Gary Carter/30	10.00
36	George Brett/30	20.00
40	Harmon Killebrew/31	12.00
46	Joe Morgan/99	8.00
49	Johnny Bench/35	25.00
52	Arky Vaughan/99	25.00
64	Nellie Fox/49	25.00
66	Orlando Cepeda/99	8.00
68	Paul Molitor/49	8.00
77	Roberto Clemente/50	50.00
79	Robin Yount/49	12.00
81	Roger Maris/99	30.00
86	Steve Carlton/29	8.00
91	Tony Gwynn/49	10.00
96	Will Clark/99	8.00
99	Willie Stargell/99	10.00

Biography

		NM/M
Common Player:		1.50
1	Lou Gehrig	6.00
2	Jackie Robinson	3.00
3	Ted Williams	8.00
4	Pete Rose	8.00
5	Jim Thorpe	4.00
6	Joe Jackson	8.00
7	Joe Medwick	2.00
8	Eddie Mathews	4.00
9	Willie Mays	6.00
10	Hank Aaron	8.00
11	Pete Rose	8.00
12	Gil Hodges	1.50
13	Roberto Clemente	6.00
14	Cal Ripken Jr.	10.00
15	Nolan Ryan	8.00
16	Satchel Paige	3.00
17	Roger Maris	4.00
18	Mike Schmidt	5.00
19	Reggie Jackson	2.50
20	George Brett	6.00
21	Pete Rose	6.00
22	Lou Gehrig	6.00
23	Jackie Robinson	3.00
24	Ted Williams	8.00
25	Jim Thorpe	4.00
26	Joe Jackson	8.00
27	Joe Medwick	2.00
28	Eddie Mathews	4.00
29	Willie Mays	6.00
30	Arky Vaughan	1.50
31	Gil Hodges	1.50
32	Roberto Clemente	6.00
33	Satchel Paige	3.00
34	Roger Maris	4.00
35	Cal Ripken Jr.	10.00

Auto. Biography

		NM/M
Production 1-50		
9	Willie Mays/25	180.00
14	Cal Ripken Jr./25	125.00
15	Nolan Ryan/50	100.00
18	Mike Schmidt/50	40.00
19	Reggie Jackson/50	40.00
29	Willie Mays/25	180.00
35	Cal Ripken Jr./24	150.00

Biography Materials

		NM/M
Production 5-50		
Prime:		No Pricing
Production 1-25		
3	Ted Williams/25	50.00
6	Joe Jackson/25	180.00
7	Joe Medwick/50	30.00
8	Eddie Mathews/50	30.00
12	Gil Hodges/25	30.00
13	Roberto Clemente/50	50.00
14	Cal Ripken Jr./40	35.00
16	Satchel Paige/25	60.00
17	Roger Maris/50	40.00
20	George Brett/25	25.00
24	Ted Williams/25	50.00
26	Joe Jackson/25	180.00
27	Joe Medwick/50	30.00
28	Eddie Mathews/50	30.00
31	Gil Hodges/25	30.00
32	Roberto Clemente/50	50.00
33	Satchel Paige/20	60.00
34	Roger Maris/50	40.00
35	Cal Ripken Jr./20	40.00

Colossal

		NM/M
Production 1-50		
Prime:		No Pricing
Production 1-25		
7	Nolan Ryan/30	40.00
12	Roger Maris/25	40.00
21	Gil Hodges/50	30.00
23	Joe Medwick/49	30.00

Colossal Signatures

No Pricing
Production 1-19

Colossal Jersey

		NM/M
Production 1-50		
Prime:		No Pricing
Production 1-19		
12	Roger Maris/25	50.00
21	Gil Hodges/50	30.00
23	Joe Medwick/49	25.00

Colossal Jersey # Signatures

Production 1-19
Prime: No Pricing

Colossal Location

		NM/M
Production 1-99		
Autographs:		No Pricing
Production 1-25		
Prime:		No Pricing
12	Roger Maris/25	50.00
16	Tony Gwynn/99	20.00
21	Gil Hodges/50	25.00
23	Joe Medwick/49	30.00

Colossal Location Signatures

Production 1-19

Colossal Prime Signatures

Production 1-25

Colossal Position

		NM/M
Production 1-99		
Prime:		No Pricing
Production 1-25		
Autographs:		No Pricing
Production 1-19		
12	Roger Maris/25	50.00
16	Tony Gwynn/99	20.00
21	Gil Hodges/50	30.00
23	Joe Medwick/49	25.00

Dual Materials

		NM/M
Production 1-99		
2	Alan Trammell/60	20.00
16	Dale Murphy/50	20.00
21	Dwight Gooden/99	5.00
34	Don Sutton/99	8.00
34	Gary Carter/30	10.00
45	Joe Cronin/49	15.00
46	Joe Jackson/25	150.00
48	Joe Morgan/99	8.00
52	Arky Vaughan/99	25.00
68	Paul Molitor/49	12.00
73	Red Schoendienst/29	8.00
81	Roger Maris/49	35.00
86	Steve Carlton/29	8.00
91	Tony Gwynn/49	8.00
92	Tony Perez/49	8.00
93	Wade Boggs/26	15.00
99	Willie Stargell/99	10.00

Icons

No pricing yet.		
Production 25 Sets		
Gold:		No Pricing
Production 5 Sets		
Platinum:		No Pricing
Production One Set		
Silver:		No Pricing
Production 10 Sets		

Icons Bats

		NM/M
Production 1-99		
7	Brooks Robinson/60	12.00
17	Joe Morgan/99	10.00
21	Dale Murphy/99	10.00
22	Robin Yount/39	15.00
29	Barry Larkin/75	8.00
31	Roberto Clemente/50	40.00
32	Eddie Mathews/99	12.00
41	Roger Maris/99	25.00
45	Tony Gwynn/99	10.00
50	Will Clark/49	12.00

Icons Jersey Number

		NM/M
Production 1-50		
Prime:		No Pricing
Production 1-40		
17	Joe Morgan/50	10.00
28	Dennis Eckersley/43	8.00
45	Tony Gwynn/99	12.00
49	Ozzie Smith/99	15.00

Icons Jersey Position

		NM/M
Production 1-99		
17	Joe Morgan/50	10.00
45	Tony Gwynn/99	12.00
49	Ozzie Smith/90	15.00

Icons Jersey Number Signatures

		NM/M
Production 1-50		
Prime:		No Pricing
Production 1-25		
Autographs:		No Pricing
Production 1-15		

Icons Materials Combos

		NM/M
Production 1-49		
Prime Autos.:		No Pricing
Production 1-8		
17	Joe Morgan/49	10.00
21	Dale Murphy/49	15.00
30	Larry Walker/49	8.00
36	Joe Jackson/25	150.00
41	Roger Maris/49	35.00
45	Tony Gwynn/49	15.00

Icons Materials Signatures MVP

		NM/M
Production 1-49		
7	Joe Morgan/49	30.00

Icons Materials HOF

		NM/M
Production 1-99		
Autographs:		No Pricing
Production 1-25		
Prime:		No Pricing
Production 1-25		
Prime Autos.:		No Pricing
Production 1-6		
17	Joe Morgan/30	10.00
28	Dennis Eckersley/35	8.00
45	Tony Gwynn/99	10.00

Icons Materials Icons

		NM/M
Production 1-99		
Autographs:		No Pricing
Production 1-20		
17	Joe Morgan/25	20.00
28	Dennis Eckersley/35	8.00
29	Barry Larkin/30	15.00
36	Joe Jackson/25	250.00
37	Joe Medwick/25	35.00
43	Ted Williams/25	60.00
45	Tony Gwynn/99	15.00

Jersey Number

		NM/M
Production 1-99		
2	Alan Trammell/75	8.00
3	Andre Dawson/75	10.00
5	Billy Williams/75	8.00
7	Bob Feller/49	10.00
9	Bobby Doerr/49	10.00
10	Brooks Robinson/30	12.00
12	Cal Ripken Jr./30	35.00
16	Dale Murphy/75	15.00
17	Dave Winfield/31	10.00
18	Deion Sanders/75	10.00
21	Dwight Gooden/99	8.00
25	Don Sutton/99	8.00
28	Eddie Murray/33	10.00
35	Gaylord Perry/36	9.00
45	Joe Cronin/49	12.00
48	Joe Morgan/50	8.00
49	Ozzie Smith/75	15.00
68	Paul Molitor/49	10.00
70	Phil Niekro/49	8.00
86	Steve Carlton/49	8.00
91	Tony Gwynn/99	10.00
94	Warren Spahn/99	15.00
99	Willie Stargell/99	12.00

Jersey Position

		NM/M
Production 1-99		
2	Alan Trammell/75	8.00
3	Andre Dawson/99	10.00
5	Billy Williams/75	10.00
7	Bob Feller/49	10.00
9	Bobby Doerr/49	10.00
12	Cal Ripken Jr./30	35.00
16	Dale Murphy/49	15.00
18	Deion Sanders/99	10.00
21	Dwight Gooden/99	10.00
24	Don Mattingly/99	15.00
25	Don Sutton/99	10.00
45	Joe Cronin/49	15.00
48	Joe Morgan/49	15.00
67	Ozzie Smith/75	15.00
68	Paul Molitor/49	10.00
70	Phil Niekro/49	8.00
86	Steve Carlton/49	8.00
91	Tony Gwynn/49	10.00
92	Tony Perez/49	15.00
94	Warren Spahn/99	15.00
99	Willie Stargell/99	10.00

Leaf Limited Phenoms

		NM/M
Common Auto.:		8.00
1	Rick Porcello	25.00
2	Buster Posey	60.00
3	Gordon Beckham	40.00
4	Ike Davis	40.00
5	Andrew Cashner	12.00
6	Jhoulys Chacin	25.00
7	Neftali Feliz	30.00
8	Ryan Perry	15.00
9	Anthony Hewitt	8.00
10	Dan Schlereth	8.00
11	Michel Inoa	20.00
12	Logan Schafer	10.00
13	Rafael Rodriguez	30.00
14	Allan Dykstra	8.00
15	Neftali Soto	20.00
16	Wilson Ramos	8.00
17	Anthony Gose	8.00
18	Tyler Sample	10.00
19	Danny Espinosa	10.00
20	Rashun Dixon	20.00
21	Kyle Hudson	12.00
22	Tim Murphy	8.00
23	Jharmidy DeJesus	8.00
24	Will Smith	12.00
25	Derek Norris	8.00

Material Combos

		NM/M
Production 25-99		
Prime:		No Pricing
Production 1-5		
1	Lou Gehrig, Ted Williams/25	150.00
4	Lou Gehrig, Cal Ripken Jr./25	150.00
5	Ted Williams, Lou Boudreau/99	60.00
6	Joe Jackson, Jim Thorpe/25	250.00
7	Roberto Clemente, Lou Gehrig/25	150.00
9	Ted Williams, Tony Gwynn/99	40.00

| 10 | Joe Medwick, Carl Yastrzemski/99 | 35.00 |

Material Triples

NM/M

Production 5-50
Prime: No Pricing
Production 1-5

| 1 | Pete Rose/50 | 75.00 |

Material Quads

NM/M

Production 5-99
Prime: No Pricing
Production 1-5

| 3 | Johnny Bench, Mike Schmidt, Willie Mays, Paul Molitor | 50.00 |

Playoff Contenders Rookies

NM/M

Common Auto.:		8.00
1	Rick Porcello	30.00
2	Buster Posey	60.00
3	Gordon Beckham	40.00
4	Ike Davis	40.00
5	Andrew Cashner	12.00
6	Jhoulys Chacin	25.00
7	Neftali Feliz	30.00
8	Ryan Perry	15.00
9	Anthony Hewitt	8.00
10	Dan Schlereth	10.00
11	Michel Inoa	20.00
12	Logan Schafer	10.00
13	Rafael Rodriguez	30.00
14	Allan Dykstra	8.00
15	T.J. Steele	8.00
16	Aaron Shafer	10.00
17	Dennis Raben	8.00
18	Cody Satterwhite	15.00
19	James Darnell	8.00
20	Zeke Spruill	20.00
21	Jason Knapp	8.00
22	Charlie Blackmon	10.00
23	O.J. Mayo	75.00
24	Michael Beasley	60.00
25	Derrick Rose	100.00

Signature Combos

Production 10 Sets
Trios: No Pricing
Production 10 Sets
Quads: No Pricing

Souvenir Cuts

NM/M

Production 1-250

| 98 | Joe DiMaggio/250 | 250.00 |

Souvenir Stadium Cuts

NM/M

Production 1-250

| 2 | Joe DiMaggio/250 | 250.00 |

Timeline

NM/M

Common Player:		2.00

Production 50 Sets
Gold: No Pricing
Production Five Sets
Silver: No Pricing
Production 10 Sets

1	Stan Musial	8.00
2	Yogi Berra	8.00
3	Willie Mays	10.00
4	Hank Aaron	12.00
5	Ernie Banks	6.00
6	Frank Robinson	3.00
7	Brooks Robinson	4.00
8	Frank Robinson	3.00
9	Orlando Cepeda	2.00
10	Carl Yastrzemski	8.00
11	Bob Gibson	4.00
12	Willie McCovey	4.00
13	Harmon Killebrew	5.00
14	Johnny Bench	6.00
15	Pete Rose	15.00
16	Reggie Jackson	4.00
17	Joe Morgan	3.00
18	Rod Carew	4.00
19	Mike Schmidt	8.00
20	George Brett	10.00
21	Robin Yount	6.00
22	Cal Ripken Jr.	20.00
23	Ryne Sandberg	10.00
24	Don Mattingly	10.00
25	Roberto Clemente	12.00
26	Eddie Mathews	6.00
27	Gil Hodges	3.00
28	Jackie Robinson	12.00
29	Jim Thorpe	6.00
30	Joe Jackson	15.00
31	Joe Medwick	5.00
32	Lou Gehrig	10.00
33	Nellie Fox	4.00
34	Nolan Ryan	15.00
35	Roger Maris	8.00
36	Satchel Paige	8.00
37	Ted Williams	12.00
38	Tom Seaver	4.00
39	Tony Gwynn	6.00
40	Whitey Ford	4.00
41	Reggie Jackson	4.00
42	Casey Stengel	2.00
43	Early Wynn	2.00
44	Billy Martin	2.00
45	Don Drysdale	3.00

46	Lefty Grove	4.00
47	Enos Slaughter	2.00
48	Jim "Catfish" Hunter	2.00
49	Carlton Fisk	3.00
50	Eddie Murray	4.00

Timeline Bats

NM/M

Production 3-99

7	Brooks Robinson/60	10.00
9	Orlando Cepeda/29	8.00
10	Carl Yastrzemski/67	10.00
17	Joe Morgan/50	8.00
24	Don Mattingly/60	15.00
25	Roberto Clemente/50	40.00
26	Eddie Mathews/99	12.00
35	Roger Maris/99	30.00
39	Tony Gwynn/49	10.00
50	Eddie Murray/99	10.00

Timeline Jersey Location

NM/M

Production 1-99

17	Joe Morgan/50	8.00
39	Tony Gwynn/99	10.00
49	Carlton Fisk/35	8.00

Timeline Jersey Number

NM/M

Production 1-99
Prime: No Pricing
Production 1-25

17	Joe Morgan/50	8.00
22	Cal Ripken Jr./35	25.00
39	Tony Gwynn/99	10.00
49	Carlton Fisk/27	10.00

Timeline Materials Combos Auto.

Production 1-25
Prime: No Pricing
Production 1-10

Timeline Trios Materials

NM/M

Production 1-99
Prime: No Pricing
Production 1-12
Trios MVP: No Pricing
Production 1-25
Trios HOF: No Pricing
Production 1-20

17	Joe Morgan/40	10.00
39	Tony Gwynn/99	12.00
42	Casey Stengel/30	25.00

Timeline Trios Materials Sign.

Production 1-25

Timeline Trios Mat. Sign. HOF

Production 1-20
Prime: No Pricing
Production 1-5

Timeline Trios Mat. Sign. Stats

Production 1-20
Prime: No Pricing
Production 1-10

Timeline Quads Materials

NM/M

Production 1-25

| 39 | Tony Gwynn/99 | 15.00 |

Timeline Quads Materials Sign.

No Pricing
Production 1-20
Prime: No Pricing
Production 1-8

Timeline Mat. Custom Nicknames

NM/M

Production 1-99
Prime: No Pricing
Production 1-25
Custom Numbers: No Pricing
Production 1-25

9	Orlando Cepeda/99	10.00
27	Gil Hodges/50	20.00
30	Joe Jackson/50	200.00
33	Nellie Fox/50	50.00
39	Tony Gwynn/99	10.00

1985 Polaroid/J.C. Penney Indians

While the Cleveland Indians continued its four-year tradition of baseball card promotional game issues in 1985, the sponsor changed from Wheaties to Polaroid/J.C. Penney. The set features 30 player cards, a manager card and a group card of the coaching staff. Though produced in the "safety set" format - slightly oversize (2-13/16" by 4-1/8") with wide white borders - the Indians cards carry no safety message.

Polaroid JCPenney — JOE CARTER Outfielder

Backs, once again numbered by uniform number, contain major and minor league stats.

NM/M

Complete Set (32):		9.00
Common Player:		.50
2	Brett Butler	.50
4	Tony Bernazard	.50
8	Carmen Castillo	.50
10	Pat Tabler	.50
12	Benny Ayala	.50
14	Ernie Camacho	.50
16	Julio Franco	.50
18	Jerry Willard	.50
18	Pat Corrales	.50
20	Otis Nixon	.35
21	Mike Hargrove	.50
22	Mike Fischlin	.50
23	Chris Bando	.50
24	George Vukovich	.50
25	Brook Jacoby	.50
27	Mel Hall	.50
28	Bert Blyleven	1.00
29	Andre Thornton	.30
30	Joe Carter	.50
32	Rick Behenna	.50
33	Roy Smith	.50
35	Jerry Reed	.50
36	Jamie Easterly	.50
38	Dave Von Ohlen	.50
41	Rich Thompson	.50
43	Bryan Clark	.50
44	Neal Heaton	.50
48	Vern Ruhle	.50
49	Jeff Barkley	.50
50	Ramon Romero	.50
54	Tom Waddell	.50
---	Coaches (Bobby Bonds, Johnny Goryl, Don McMahon, Ed Napolean, Dennis Sommers)	.50

2002 Poland Spring Boston Red Sox

BOSTON RED SOX — trot NIXON

This cello-wrapped stadium give-away set was sponsored by the team's bottled water concession. Fronts have poses or action photos with team and sponsor logos in opposite corners. Backs have a U.S. flag ghost image in the background with a close-up repeat of the front photo. Personal data, '01 stats and career highlights appear along with the logos. The set is listed here by uniform number.

NM/M

Complete Set (24):		7.50
Common Player:		.25
3	Grady Little	.25
5	Nomar Garciaparra	2.00
7	Trot Nixon	.50
18	Carlos Baerga	.25
18	Johnny Damon	.75
20	John Burkett	.25
22	Tony Clark	.25
23	Brian Daubach	.25
24	Manny Ramirez	1.50
26	Lou Merloni	.25
28	Doug Mirabelli	.25
29	Shea Hillenbrand	.25
30	Jose Offerman	.25
32	Derek Lowe	.25
33	Jason Varitek	.25

34	Rich Garces	.25
35	Rickey Henderson	1.50
37	Frank Castillo	.25
41	Ugueth Urbina	.25
44	Rolando Arrojo	.25
45	Pedro Martinez	1.50
49	Tim Wakefield	.25
---	Wally the Green Monster	.25
---	Sponsor's Card	.05

1999 Pop Secret Detroit Tigers

This team set was sponsored by the snack food company and distributed at a promotional game at Tiger Stadium. The 2-1/2" x 3-1/2" cards have color photos which are borderless at top, bottom and right. At left are black and blue vertical stripes with player identification. Backs have a color portrait photo, career stats and team and sponsor logos. The unnumbered cards are checklisted here alphabetically.

NM/M

Complete Set (26):		9.00
Common Player:		.50
(1)	Matt Anderson	.50
(2)	Brad Ausmus	.50
(3)	Willie Blair	.50
(4)	Doug Brocail	.50
(5)	Frank Catalanotto	.50
(6)	Tony Clark	.50
(7)	Deivi Cruz	.50
(8)	Damion Easley	.50
(9)	Juan Encarnacion	.50
(10)	Karim Garcia	.50
(11)	Seth Greisinger	.50
(12)	Bill Haselman	.50
(13)	Bobby Higginson	.50
(14)	Gregg Jefferies	.50
(15)	Todd Jones	.50
(16)	Gabe Kapler	1.00
(17)	Masao Kida	.50
(18)	Dave Mlicki	.50
(19)	Brian Moehler	.50
(20)	C.J. Nitkowski	.50
(21)	Dean Palmer	.50
(22)	Larry Parrish	.50
(23)	Luis Polonia	.50
(24)	Justin Thompson	.50
(25)	Jeff Weaver	.50
(26)	The Corner (Tiger Stadium)	.50

1990 Post Cereal

Post — First Collector Series — WILL CLARK — SAN FRANCISCO GIANTS — FIRST BASE

Post Cereal returned in 1990 with a 30-card set. Card fronts feature border terms in white, red and blue, with the Post logo at top-left and the Major League Baseball logo at top-right. Backs show complete major league statistics; underneath is a facsimile autograph. The player photos do not display team logos. Cards were included three per box, inside Alpha-Bits cereal. An uncut sheet version of the set was also offered in a run of 5,000 serially numbered pieces.

NM/M

Complete Set (30):		4.00
Common Player:		.10

Uncut Sheet:		15.00
1	Don Mattingly	.75
2	Roger Clemens	.75
3	Kirby Puckett	.60
4	George Brett	.75
5	Tony Gwynn	.60
6	Ozzie Smith	.60
7	Will Clark	.10
8	Orel Hershiser	.10
9	Ryne Sandberg	.60
10	Darryl Strawberry	.10
11	Nolan Ryan	1.50
12	Mark McGwire	1.00
13	Jim Abbott	.10
14	Bo Jackson	.20
15	Kevin Mitchell	.10
16	Jose Canseco	.35
17	Wade Boggs	.20
18	Dale Murphy	.20
19	Mark Grace	.10
20	Mike Scott	.10
21	Cal Ripken, Jr.	1.50
22	Pedro Guerrero	.10
23	Ken Griffey Jr.	.85
24	Eric Davis	.10
25	Rickey Henderson	.45
26	Robin Yount	.45
27	Von Hayes	.10
28	Alan Trammell	.10
29	Dwight Gooden	.10
30	Joe Carter	.10

1991 Post Cereal

Post — 1991 Collector Series — MARK McGWIRE — OAKLAND A's

These superstar trading cards were inserted in several brands of Post's children's cereals. The cards were produced by Mike Schechter Associates, Inc. and are authorized by the Players Association, but not MLB, so team logos have been removed from the photos. Card backs feature statistics and a facsimile autograph.

NM/M

Complete Set (30):		4.00
Common Player:		.10
1	Dave Justice	.10
2	Mark McGwire	.75
3	Will Clark	.10
4	Jose Canseco	.30
5	Vince Coleman	.10
6	Sandy Alomar, Jr.	.10
7	Darryl Strawberry	.10
8	Len Dykstra	.10
9	Gregg Jefferies	.10
10	Tony Gwynn	.50
11	Ken Griffey Jr.	.75
12	Roger Clemens	.65
13	Chris Sabo	.10
14	Bobby Bonilla	.10
15	Gary Sheffield	.30
16	Ryne Sandberg	.50
17	Nolan Ryan	1.00
18	Barry Larkin	.10
19	Cal Ripken, Jr.	1.00
20	Jim Abbott	.10
21	Barry Bonds	1.00
22	Mark Grace	.10
23	Cecil Fielder	.10
24	Kevin Mitchell	.10
25	Todd Zeile	.10
26	George Brett	.65
27	Rickey Henderson	.45
28	Kirby Puckett	.50
29	Don Mattingly	.65
30	Kevin Maas	.10

Canadian

SÉRIE DES ÉTOILES — 1991 — SUPER STAR SERIES — Post — BENITO SANTIAGO — SAN DIEGO PADRES OF SAN DIEGO

Specially-marked Post cereal boxes sold in Canada included one of 30 cards from a 1991 Super Star series. Cards are bilingual, and include player statistics and biographical information on the backs. The major league logos are airbrushed from the players' caps and uniforms. American Leaguers' cards have blue stripes above and below the photo on front and as a back border color; National Leaguers are in red.

NM/M

Complete Set (30):		10.00
Set in Album:		12.50
Common Player:		.25
1	Delino DeShields	.25
2	Tim Wallach	.25
3	Andres Galarraga	.25
4	Dave Magadan	.25
5	Barry Bonds	2.00
6	Len Dykstra	.25
7	Andre Dawson	.35
8	Ozzie Smith	.65
9	Will Clark	.65
10	Chris Sabo	.25
11	Eddie Murray	.60
12	Dave Justice	.25
13	Benito Santiago	.25
14	Glenn Davis	.25
15	Kelly Gruber	.25
16	Dave Stieb	.25
17	John Olerud	.25
18	Roger Clemens	.85
19	Cecil Fielder	.25
20	Kevin Maas	.25
21	Robin Yount	.60
22	Cal Ripken, Jr.	2.00
23	Sandy Alomar	.25
24	Rickey Henderson	.60
25	Bobby Thigpen	.25
26	Ken Griffey Jr.	1.00
27	Nolan Ryan	2.00
28	Dave Winfield	.60
29	George Brett	.75
30	Kirby Puckett	.65

1992 Post Cereal

Post — 1992 COLLECTOR SERIES — Joe Carter — TORONTO BLUE JAYS

The addition of a back photo is notable on Post's 1992 set. Again packaged at the rate of three cards in specially marked boxes, a complete set was available via a mail-in offer. Front photos have a blue strip at top with the Post logo at upper-left. A red stripe at bottom has the player's name and the logo of the Major League Baseball Player's Association. The absence of a Major League Baseball logo, and the air-brushing of uniform logos on all photos identifies this set as the work of Mike Schechter Associates. Backs have a small photo at left, bordered in red. At right are biographical details, career stats and a facsimile autograph. The cards of 1991 Rookies of the Year Jeff Bagwell and Chuck Knoblauch are designated with a "Rookie Star" banner over the front photo.

NM/M

Complete Set (30):		3.00
Common Player:		.10
1	Jeff Bagwell	.35
2	Ryne Sandberg	.45
3	Don Mattingly	.50
4	Wally Joyner	.10
5	Dwight Gooden	.10
6	Chuck Knoblauch	.10
7	Kirby Puckett	.45
8	Ozzie Smith	.45
9	Cal Ripken, Jr.	.75
10	Darryl Strawberry	.10
11	George Brett	.50
12	Joe Carter	.10
13	Cecil Fielder	.10
14	Will Clark	.10
15	Barry Bonds	.75
16	Roger Clemens	.50
17	Paul Molitor	.35

18	Scott Erickson	.10
19	Wade Boggs	.45
20	Ken Griffey Jr.	.60
21	Bobby Bonilla	.10
22	Terry Pendleton	.10
23	Barry Larkin	.10
24	Frank Thomas	.35
25	Jose Canseco	.25
26	Tony Gwynn	.45
27	Nolan Ryan	.75
28	Howard Johnson	.10
29	Dave Justice	.10
30	Danny Tartabull	.10

Canadian

For the second year in a row Post Cereal of Canada issued a set of cards inserted in cereal boxes. The 1992 cards have a player photo on front (with airbrushed cap) and information on the reverse in both English and French. The back of the card also contains an action photo, which has a pop-up tab which when opened stands up, revealing a statistical base.

		NM/M
Complete Set (18):		9.00
Common Player:		.25
1	Dennis Martinez	.25
2	Benito Santiago	.25
3	Will Clark	.25
4	Ryne Sandberg	1.00
5	Tim Wallach	.25
6	Ozzie Smith	1.00
7	Darryl Strawberry	.25
8	Brett Butler	.25
9	Barry Bonds	2.00
10	Roger Clemens	1.25
11	Sandy Alomar	.25
12	Cecil Fielder	.25
13	Roberto Alomar	.35
14	Kelly Gruber	.25
15	Cal Ripken, Jr.	2.00
16	Jose Canseco	.50
17	Kirby Puckett	1.00
18	Rickey Henderson	.75

1993 Post Cereal

Post Cereal's 1993 Collectors Series cards feature a black border on the bottom and the right side, with the Post logo located at top right and the player's name, team and position along the bottom. Team logos have been air-brushed from the uniforms. Backs have a black background, a color player portrait photo, personal data, a career summary, 1992 and career stats, and a red strip with a white facsimile autograph. A special edition of 5,000 numbered uncut sheets was also produced.

		NM/M
Complete Set (30):		3.00
Common Player:		.10
Uncut Sheet:		10.00
1	Dave Fleming	.10
2	Will Clark	.10
3	Kirby Puckett	.60
4	Roger Clemens	.65
5	Fred McGriff	.10

6	Eric Karros	.10
7	Ken Griffey Jr.	.75
8	Tony Gwynn	.60
9	Cal Ripken, Jr.	1.25
10	Cecil Fielder	.10
11	Gary Sheffield	.25
12	Don Mattingly	.65
13	Ryne Sandberg	.60
14	Frank Thomas	.50
15	Barry Bonds	1.25
16	Paul Molitor	.50
17	Terry Pendleton	.10
18	Darren Daulton	.10
19	Mark McGwire	1.00
20	Nolan Ryan	1.25
21	Tom Glavine	.30
22	Roberto Alomar	.20
23	Juan Gonzalez	.20
24	Bobby Bonilla	.10
25	George Brett	.60
26	Ozzie Smith	.60
27	Andy Van Slyke	.10
28	Barry Larkin	.10
29	John Kruk	.10
30	Robin Yount	.50

Canadian

For the third consecutive year, Post Canada produced a set of cards. The 1993 set features a two-sided card with one side containing a special pop-up feature, much the same as their 1992 offering. There are 18 black-bordered and gold-lettered cards in the set. The cards were available in specially-marked boxes of cereal.

		NM/M
Complete Set (18):		10.00
Common Player:		.25
1	Pat Borders	.25
2	Juan Guzman	.25
3	Roger Clemens	1.25
4	Joe Carter	.25
5	Roberto Alomar	.35
6	Robin Yount	.75
7	Cal Ripken, Jr.	3.00
8	Kirby Puckett	1.00
9	Ken Griffey Jr.	2.00
10	Darren Daulton	.25
11	Andy Van Slyke	.25
12	Bobby Bonilla	.25
13	Larry Walker	.25
14	Ryne Sandberg	1.00
15	Barry Larkin	.25
16	Gary Sheffield	.40
17	Ozzie Smith	1.00
18	Terry Pendleton	.25

1994 Post Cereal

Post cereals' 1994 set was issued three cards at a time in cellophane packages in cereal boxes. A special edition of 5,000 numbered 15-1/2" x 20-1/2" uncut sheets was also produced.

		NM/M
Complete Set (30):		3.00
Common Player:		.10
Uncut Sheet:		15.00
1	Mike Piazza	.75
2	Don Mattingly	.65
3	Juan Gonzalez	.35
4	Kirby Puckett	.60

5	Gary Sheffield	.25
6	David Justice	.10
7	Jack McDowell	.10
8	Mo Vaughn	.25
9	Darren Daulton	.10
10	Bobby Bonilla	.10
11	Barry Bonds	1.00
12	Barry Larkin	.10
13	Tony Gwynn	.60
14	Mark Grace	.10
15	Ken Griffey Jr.	.75
16	Tom Glavine	.35
17	Cecil Fielder	.10
18	Roberto Alomar	.25
19	Mark Whiten	.10
20	Lenny Dykstra	.10
21	Frank Thomas	.45
22	Will Clark	.10
23	Andres Galarraga	.10
24	John Olerud	.10
25	Cal Ripken, Jr.	1.00
26	Tim Salmon	.10
27	Albert Belle	.10
28	Gregg Jefferies	.10
29	Jeff Bagwell	.45
30	Orlando Merced	.10

Canadian

The emphasis was on Expos and Blue Jays players in the 1994 Post cereal cards issued in Canada. Several of the cards featured gold-foil stamping on the fronts. Like all contemporary Post cards, the uniform logos were airbrushed from the photos due to lack of licensing from Major League Baseball.

		NM/M
Complete Set (18):		12.00
Common Player:		.25
1	Joe Carter	1.00
2	Paul Molitor	.75
3	Roberto Alomar	.40
4	John Olerud	.25
5	Dave Stewart	.25
6	Juan Guzman	.25
7	Pat Borders	.25
8	Larry Walker	.25
9	Moises Alou	.25
10	Ken Griffey Jr.	1.50
11	Barry Bonds	2.50
12	Frank Thomas	.75
13	Cal Ripken, Jr.	2.50
14	Mike Piazza	1.50
15	Juan Gonzalez	.40
16	Lenny Dykstra	.25
17	David Justice	.25
18	Kirby Puckett	1.25

1995 Post Cereal

The 1995 Post Collector Series differs dramatically in format from the company's recent cereal-box insert issues. Each card measures 5" x 3-1/2" and is vertically scored at center to allow it to be folded. When folded, the front has a player action photo against a blue marbled background. On back is another photo, with career stats and highlights and a yellow facsimile autograph. In the center of the folded piece is a large game-action photo. All pictures have had the team logos removed for lack of a license by MLB. The cards are licensed by the Players Association. Complete sets of the '95 Post cards were available in a special cardboard display folder. Large quantities of the set made their way into dealer hands by 1998, and the value plummeted.

	NM/M
Complete Set (16):	2.50
Common Player:	.10
1 Wade Boggs	.60
2 Jeff Bagwell	.45
3 Greg Maddux	.60
4 Ken Griffey Jr.	.65
5 Roberto Alomar	.20
6 Kirby Puckett	.60
7 Tony Gwynn	.60
8 Cal Ripken Jr.	1.00
9 Matt Williams	.10
10 Dave Justice	.10
11 Barry Bonds	1.00
12 Mike Piazza	.65
13 Albert Belle	.10
14 Frank Thomas	.45
15 Len Dykstra	.10
16 Will Clark	.10

Canadian

Post cereals celebrated its fifth anniversary of baseball card production for the Canadian market by switching providers to Upper Deck, and issuing a high-quality album to house the 18-card set. Cards feature color action photos that are borderless at top, bottom and right. At left is a vertical black marbled panel with the player's name, team and position. An Upper Deck logo is at top-right; a Post anniversary logo at lower-left. Because the cards are licensed by the Major League Players Association, but not Major League Baseball, team logos have been airbrushed from photos. Backs have another player photo plus bilingual biographical data, career highlights and stats for the previous five seasons and lifetime. A ghost image of the front photo appears under the typography. As might be expected, the set's roster is especially rich in Expos and Blue Jays players.

		NM/M
Complete Set (18):		12.00
Common Player:		.50
Album:		6.00
1	Ken Griffey Jr.	2.00
2	Roberto Alomar	.35
3	Paul Molitor	.75
4	Devon White	.25
5	Moises Alou	.25
6	Ken Hill	.25
7	Paul O'Neill	.25
8	Joe Carter	.25
9	Kirby Puckett	1.50
10	Jimmy Key	.25
11	Frank Thomas	.75
12	David Cone	.25
13	Tony Gwynn	1.50
14	Matt Williams	.25
15	Jeff Bagwell	.75
16	Greg Maddux	1.50
17	Barry Bonds	3.00
18	Cal Ripken Jr.	3.00

2001 Post Collector's Series

(See 2001 Topps/Post Collector's Series.)

2001 Post 500 Home Run Club

(See 2001 Topps/Post 500 Home Run Club for checklist and values.)

2002 Post Collector's Series

(See 2002 Topps/Post Collector's Series.)

2003 Post MVP Action

(See 2003 Upper Deck/Post MVP Action.)

1985 P.R.E. Pete Rose Set

This 120-card set traces the career of Pete Rose through the 1985 season. Many cards feature photos used on earlier Topps cards. Each card, and the box in which they were sold, says the set was "Designed by Topps Chewing Gum Inc." The set was distributed within the hobby by Renata Galasso and the copyright-holder is identified as "P.R.E." (Pete Rose Enterprises?). Besides the Topps photos, the cards include a number of original paintings by Ron Lewis, a few family-album type photos and some game-action shots of career highlights. Backs of the first three cards offer complete minor and major league stats through 1985. Cards #4-90 have a question and answer format on back and the final 30 cards in the set have a puzzle-back depicting many of Rose's Topps cards in full color. Single cards from the set are seldom offered in the market. A borderless version of card #1 was issued in an edition of 1,000, all cards being autographed.

	NM/M
Complete Set (120):	15.00
Single Card:	.25
Autographed #1:	35.00
1-120 Pete Rose	.25

1986 Provigo Expos

This 28-card set was issued in three-card panels of 7-1/2" x 3-3/8". Each card measures 2-1/2" x 3-3/8", and each panel includes two players

and an advertising card. Panels are perforated to allow for separation, if desired. Card fronts have high quality game-action color photos with the player's name, uniform number and Expos and Provigo logos. Card backs include biographical information in both French and English and list the card's number within the set. There are 24 player, one manager and two coaches cards, along with a card of the Expos mascot, Youppi.

		NM/M
Complete Panel Set:		3.00
Complete Singles Set:		2.50
Common Panel:		.15
Common Single Player:		.10
Album:		5.00
Panel 1		.15
1	Hubie Brooks	.15
2	Dann Bilardello	.10
----	Checklist	.02
Panel 2		.15
3	Buck Rodgers	.10
4	Andy McGaffigan	.10
----	Album Offer	.02
Panel 3		.15
5	Mitch Webster	.10
6	Jim Wohlford	.10
----	Album Offer	.02
Panel 4		1.00
7	Tim Raines	.35
8	Jay Tibbs	.10
----	Album Offer	.02
Panel 5		.15
9	Andre Dawson	.50
10	Andres Galarraga	.35
----	Album Offer	.02
Panel 6		.30
11	Tim Wallach	.10
12	Dan Schatzeder	.10
----	Checklist	.02
Panel 7		.15
13	Jeff Reardon	.10
14	Expos' Coaching Staff (Larry Bearnarth, Joe Kerrigan, Bobby Winkles)	.10
----	Album Offer	.02
Panel 8		.15
15	Jason Thompson	.10
16	Bert Roberge	.10
----	$1 Expos Ticket Coupon	.02
Panel 9		.15
17	Al Newman	.10
18	Tim Burke	.10
----	Album Offer	.02
Panel 10		.15
19	Bryn Smith	.10
20	Wayne Krenchicki	.10
----	Album Offer	.02
Panel 11		.15
21	Joe Hesketh	.10
22	Herman Winningham	.10
----	Album Offer	.02
Panel 12		.15
23	Vance Law	.10
24	Floyd Youmans	.10
----	Album Offer	.02
Panel 13		.15
25	Jeff Parrett	.10
26	Mike Fitzgerald	.10
----	Album Offer	.02
Panel 14		.15
27	Youppi (Mascot).	.15
28	Expos' Coaching Staff (Ron Hansen, Ken Macha, Rick Renick)	.10
----	Album Offer	.02

Posters

This Provigo issue is much scarcer than the smaller card panels issued the same year. These posters measure about 9" x 14-7/8". A large (9" x 12-1/2") player portrait is separated from a bottom coupon panel. Backs are blank and can be found in red, white or blue. The player pictures have facsimile autographs and a white strip at bottom with identification, uniform number, team and sponsor logos and card number. Values shown are for complete poster/coupon combinations.

	NM/M
Complete Set (12):	20.00
Common Player:	2.00
1 Tim Raines	4.00
2 Bryn Smith	2.00
3 Hubie Brooks	2.00
4 Buck Rodgers	2.00
5 Mitch Webster	2.00
6 Joe Hesketh	2.00
7 Mike Fitzgerald	2.00
8 Andy McGaffigan	2.00
9 Andre Dawson	7.50
10 Tim Wallach	2.00
11 Jeff Reardon	2.00
12 Vance Law	2.00

1994 PruCare N.Y. Mets

Top names on the 1994 Mets are featured in this issue sponsored by PruCare, a division of Prudential Insurance, whose logo appears on front and back. Cards were issued in a nine-card panel, perforated for easy separation. Individual cards are 2-1/2" x 3-1/2". Fronts have color action photos surrounded by team-color frames and white borders. Backs are printed in orange and blue with personal data, 1993 stats and highlights and career major league stats. The unnumbered cards are checklisted here in alphabetical order.

	NM/M
Complete Sheet:	3.50
Complete Set (9):	3.00
Common Player:	.50
(1) Bobby Bonilla	.50
(2) Jeromy Burnitz	.50
(3) John Franco	.50
(4) Dwight Gooden	.50
(5) Bud Harrelson	.50
(6) Jeff Kent	.50
(7) Kevin McReynolds	.50
(8) Ryan Thompson	.50
(9) Mookie Wilson	.50

1990 Publications International Stickers

Nolan Ryan

This large set was issued in the form of an album with pages of bound-in stickers which were to be removed and placed in the appropriately numbered spots. Arranged by team, the album's spaces have a trivia question about the player whose sticker belongs there. The 1-3/8" x 1-3/4" stickers are unnumbered and are listed here according to the number of their album space.

	NM/M
Complete Album:	20.00
Complete Sticker Set (648):	15.00
Common Player:	.05
(1) Dave Anderson	.05
(2) Tim Belcher	.05
(3) Mike Davis	.05
(4) Rick Dempsey	.05
(5) Kirk Gibson	.05
(6) Alfredo Griffin	.05
(7) Jeff Hamilton	.05
(8) Mickey Hatcher	.05
(9) Orel Hershiser	.05
(10) Ricky Horton	.05
(11) Jay Howell	.05
(12) Tim Leary	.05
(13) Mike Marshall	.05
(14) Eddie Murray	.60
(15) Alejandro Pena	.05
(16) Willie Randolph	.05
(17) Mike Scoscia	.05
(18) John Shelby	.05
(19) Franklin Stubbs	.05
(20) John Tudor	.05
(21) Fernando Valenzuela	.05
(22) Todd Benzinger	.05
(23) Tom Browning	.05
(24) Norm Charlton	.05
(25) Kal Daniels	.05
(26) Eric Davis	.05
(27) Bo Diaz	.05
(28) Rob Dibble	.05
(29) John Franco	.05
(30) Ken Griffey Sr.	.05
(31) Lenny Harris	.05
(32) Danny Jackson	.05
(33) Barry Larkin	.05
(34) Rick Mahler	.05
(35) Ron Oester	.05
(36) Paul O'Neill	.05
(37) Jeff Reed	.05
(38) Jose Rijo	.05
(39) Chris Sabo	.05
(40) Kent Tekulve	.05
(41) Manny Trillo	.05
(42) Joel Youngblood	.05
(43) Roberto Alomar	.15
(44) Greg Booker	.05
(45) Jack Clark	.05
(46) Jerald Clark	.05
(47) Mark Davis	.05
(48) Tim Flannery	.05
(49) Mark Grant	.05
(50) Tony Gwynn	.75
(51) Bruce Hurst	.05
(52) John Kruk	.05
(53) Dave Leiper	.05
(54) Carmelo Martinez	.05
(55) Mark Parent	.05
(56) Dennis Rasmussen	.05
(57) Randy Ready	.05
(58) Benito Santiago	.05
(59) Eric Show	.05
(60) Garry Templeton	.05
(61) Walt Terrell	.05
(62) Ed Whitson	.05
(63) Marvell Wynne	.05
(64) Brett Butler	.05
(65) Will Clark	.05
(66) Kelly Downs	.05
(67) Scott Garrelts	.05
(68) Rich "Goose" Gossage	.05
(69) Atlee Hammaker	.05
(70) Tracy Jones	.05
(71) Terry Kennedy	.05
(72) Mike Krukow	.05
(73) Mike LaCoss	.05
(74) Craig Lefferts	.05
(75) Candy Maldonado	.05
(76) Kirt Manwaring	.05
(77) Kevin Mitchell	.05
(78) Donell Nixon	.05
(79) Rick Reuschel	.05
(80) Ernest Riles	.05
(81) Don Robinson	.05
(82) Chris Speier	.05
(83) Robby Thompson	.05
(84) Jose Uribe	.05
(85) Juan Agosto	.05
(86) Larry Andersen	.05
(87) Kevin Bass	.05
(88) Craig Biggio	.05
(89) Ken Caminiti	.05
(90) Jim Clancy	.05
(91) Danny Darwin	.05
(92) Glenn Davis	.05
(93) Jim Deshaies	.05
(94) Bill Doran	.05
(95) Bob Forsch	.05
(96) Billy Hatcher	.05
(97) Bob Knepper	.05
(98) Terry Puhl	.05
(99) Rafael Ramirez	.05
(100) Craig Reynolds	.05
(101) Rick Rhoden	.05
(102) Mike Scott	.05
(103) Dave Smith	.05
(104) Alex Trevino	.05
(105) Gerald Young	.05
(106) Jose Alvarez	.05
(107) Paul Assenmacher	.05
(108) Bruce Benedict	.05
(109) Jeff Blauser	.05
(110) Joe Boever	.05
(111) Jody Davis	.05
(112) Darrell Evans	.05
(113) Ron Gant	.05
(114) Tommy Gregg	.05
(115) Dion James	.05
(116) Derek Lilliquist	.05
(117) Dale Murphy	.20
(118) Gerald Perry	.05
(119) Charlie Puleo	.05
(120) John Russell	.05
(121) Lonnie Smith	.05
(122) Pete Smith	.05
(123) Zane Smith	.05
(124) John Smoltz	.05
(125) Bruce Sutter	.20
(126) Andres Thomas	.05
(127) Rick Aguilera	.05
(128) Gary Carter	.60
(129) David Cone	.05
(130) Ron Darling	.05
(131) Lenny Dykstra	.05
(132) Kevin Elster	.05
(133) Sid Fernandez	.05
(134) Dwight Gooden	.05
(135) Keith Hernandez	.05
(136) Gregg Jeffries	.05
(137) Howard Johnson	.05
(138) Dave Magadan	.05
(139) Lee Mazzilli	.05
(140) Roger McDowell	.05
(141) Kevin McReynolds	.05
(142) Randy Myers	.05
(143) Bob Ojeda	.05
(144) Mackey Sasser	.05
(145) Darryl Strawberry	.05
(146) Tim Teufel	.05
(147) Mookie Wilson	.05
(148) Rafael Belliard	.05
(149) Barry Bonds	1.50
(150) Bobby Bonilla	.05
(151) Sid Bream	.05
(152) Benny Distefano	.05
(153) Doug Drabek	.05
(154) Brian Fisher	.05
(155) Jim Gott	.05
(156) Neal Heaton	.05
(157) Bill Landrum	.05
(158) Mike LaValliere	.05
(159) Jose Lind	.05
(160) Junior Ortiz	.05
(161) Tom Prince	.05
(162) Gary Redus	.05
(163) R.J. Reynolds	.05
(164) Jeff Robinson	.05
(165) John Smiley	.05
(166) Andy Van Slyke	.05
(167) Bob Walk	.05
(168) Glenn Wilson	.05
(169) Hubie Brooks	.05
(170) Tim Burke	.05
(171) Mike Fitzgerald	.05
(172) Tom Foley	.05
(173) Andres Galarraga	.05
(174) Kevin Gross	.05
(175) Joe Hesketh	.05
(176) Brian Holman	.05
(177) Rex Hudler	.05
(178) Wallace Johnson	.05
(179) Mark Langston	.05
(180) Dave Martinez	.05
(181) Dennis Martinez	.05
(182) Andy McGaffigan	.05
(183) Otis Nixon	.05
(184) Spike Owen	.05
(185) Pascual Perez	.05
(186) Tim Raines	.05
(187) Nelson Santovenia	.05
(188) Bryn Smith	.05
(189) Tim Wallach	.05
(190) Damon Berryhill	.05
(191) Mike Bielecki	.05
(192) Andre Dawson	.20
(193) Shawon Dunston	.05
(194) Mark Grace	.05
(195) Darrin Jackson	.05
(196) Paul Kilgus	.05
(197) Vance Law	.05
(198) Greg Maddux	.75
(199) Pat Perry	.05
(200) Jeff Pico	.05
(201) Ryne Sandberg	.75
(202) Scott Sanderson	.05
(203) Calvin Schiraldi	.05
(204) Dwight Smith	.05
(205) Rick Sutcliffe	.05
(206) Gary Varsho	.05
(207) Jerome Walton	.05
(208) Mitch Webster	.05
(209) Curtis Wilkerson	.05
(210) Mitch Williams	.05
(211) Tom Browning	.05
(212) Cris Carpenter	.05
(213) Vince Coleman	.05
(214) John Costello	.05
(215) Danny Cox	.05
(216) Ken Dayley	.05
(217) Jose DeLeon	.05
(218) Frank DiPino	.05
(219) Pedro Guerrero	.05
(220) Joe Magrane	.05
(221) Greg Mathews	.05
(222) Willie McGee	.05
(223) Jose Oquendo	.05
(224) Tom Pagnozzi	.05
(225) Tony Pena	.05
(226) Terry Pendleton	.05
(227) Dan Quisenberry	.05
(228) Ozzie Smith	.75
(229) Scott Terry	.05
(230) Milt Thompson	.05
(231) Todd Worrell	.05
(232) Steve Bedrosian	.05
(233) Don Carman	.05
(234) Darren Daulton	.05
(235) Bob Dernier	.05
(236) Marvin Freeman	.05
(237) Greg Harris	.05
(238) Von Hayes	.05
(239) Tommy Herr	.05
(240) Ken Howell	.05
(241) Chris James	.05
(242) Steve Jeltz	.05
(243) Ron Jones	.05
(244) Ricky Jordan	.05
(245) Steve Lake	.05
(246) Mike Maddux	.05
(247) Larry McWilliams	.05
(248) Jeff Parrett	.05
(249) Juan Samuel	.05
(250) Mike Schmidt	.85
(251) Dickie Thon	.05
(252) Floyd Youmans	.05
(253) Bobby Bonilla/AS	.05
(254) Will Clark/AS	.05
(255) Eric Davis/AS	.05
(256) Andre Dawson/AS	.05
(257) Bill Doran/AS	.05
(258) John Franco/AS	.05
(259) Kirk Gibson/AS	.05
(260) Dwight Gooden/AS	.05
(261) Tony Gwynn/AS	.35
(262) Keith Hernandez/AS	.05
(263) Orel Hershiser/AS	.05
(264) Danny Jackson/AS	.05
(265) Howard Johnson/AS	.05
(266) Barry Larkin/AS	.05
(267) Joe Magrane/AS	.05
(268) Kevin McReynolds/AS	.05
(269) Tony Pena/AS	.05
(270) Ryne Sandberg/AS	.35
(271) Benito Santiago/AS	.05
(272) Ozzie Smith/AS	.35
(273) Darryl Strawberry/AS	.05
(274) Todd Worrell/AS	.05
(275) Harold Baines/AS	.05
(276) George Bell/AS	.05
(277) Wade Boggs/AS	.35
(278) Bob Boone/AS	.05
(279) Jose Canseco/AS	.20
(280) Joe Carter/AS	.05
(281) Roger Clemens/AS	.40
(282) Dennis Eckersley/AS	.25
(283) Tony Fernandez/AS	.05
(284) Carlton Fisk/AS	.30
(285) Julio Franco/AS	.05
(286) Gary Gaetti/AS	.05
(287) Mike Greenwell/AS	.05
(288) Rickey Henderson/AS	.30
(289) Teddy Higuera/AS	.05
(290) Kent Hrbek/AS	.05
(290) Don Mattingly/AS	.40
(291) Kirby Puckett/AS	.35
(292) Jeff Reardon/AS	.05
(293) Harold Reynolds/AS	.05
(294) Dave Stewart/AS	.05
(295) Alan Trammell/AS	.05
(297) Frank Viola/AS	.05
(298) Dave Winfield/AS	.30
(299) Todd Burns	.05
(300) Greg Cadaret	.05
(301) Jose Canseco	.30
(302) Storm Davis	.05
(303) Dennis Eckersley	.45
(304) Mike Gallego	.05
(305) Ron Hassey	.05
(306) Dave Henderson	.05
(307) Rick Honeycutt	.05
(308) Stan Javier	.05
(309) Carney Lansford	.05
(310) Mark McGwire	1.25
(311) Mike Moore	.05
(312) Dave Parker	.05
(313) Eric Plunk	.05
(314) Luis Polonia	.05
(315) Terry Steinbach	.05
(316) Dave Stewart	.05
(317) Walt Weiss	.05
(318) Bob Welch	.05
(319) Curt Young	.05
(320) Allan Anderson	.05
(321) Wally Backman	.05
(322) Doug Baker	.05
(323) Juan Berenguer	.05
(324) Randy Bush	.05
(325) Jim Dwyer	.05
(326) Gary Gaetti	.05
(327) Greg Gagne	.05
(328) Dan Gladden	.05
(329) Brian Harper	.05
(330) Kent Hrbek	.05
(331) Gene Larkin	.05
(332) Tim Laudner	.05
(333) John Moses	.05
(334) Al Newman	.05
(335) Kirby Puckett	.75
(336) Shane Rawley	.05
(337) Jeff Reardon	.05
(338) Steve Shields	.05
(339) Frank Viola	.05
(340) Gary Wayne	.05
(341) Luis Aquino	.05
(342) Floyd Bannister	.05
(343) Bob Boone	.05
(344) George Brett	.85
(345) Bill Buckner	.05
(346) Jim Eisenreich	.05
(347) Steve Farr	.05
(348) Tom Gordon	.05
(349) Mark Gubicza	.05
(350) Bo Jackson	.10
(351) Charlie Leibrandt	.05
(352) Mike Macfarlane	.05
(353) Jeff Montgomery	.05
(354) Bret Saberhagen	.05
(355) Kevin Seitzer	.05
(356) Kurt Stillwell	.05
(357) Pat Tabler	.05
(358) Danny Tartabull	.05
(359) Gary Thurman	.05
(361) Frank White	.05
(361) Willie Wilson	.05
(362) Jim Abbott	.05
(363) Kent Anderson	.05
(364) Tony Armas	.05
(365) Dante Bichette	.05
(366) Bert Blyleven	.05
(367) Chili Davis	.05
(368) Brian Downing	.05
(369) Chuck Finley	.05
(370) Willie Fraser	.05
(371) Jack Howell	.05
(372) Wally Joyner	.05
(373) Kirk McCaskill	.05
(374) Bob McClure	.05
(375) Greg Minton	.05
(376) Lance Parrish	.05
(377) Dan Petry	.05
(378) Johnny Ray	.05
(379) Dick Schofield	.05
(380) Claudell Washington	.05
(381) Devon White	.05
(382) Mike Witt	.05
(383) Harold Baines	.05
(384) Daryl Boston	.05
(385) Ivan Calderon	.05
(386) Carlton Fisk	.60
(387) Dave Gallagher	.05
(388) Ozzie Guillen	.05
(389) Shawn Hillegas	.05
(390) Barry Jones	.05
(391) Ron Karkovice	.05
(392) Eric King	.05
(393) Ron Kittle	.05
(394) Bill Long	.05
(395) Steve Lyons	.05
(396) Fred Manrique	.05
(397) Donn Pall	.05
(398) Dan Pasqua	.05
(399) Melido Perez	.05
(400) Jerry Reuss	.05
(401) Bobby Thigpen	.05
(402) Greg Walker	.05
(403) Eddie Williams	.05
(404) Buddy Bell	.05
(405) Kevin Brown	.05
(406) Steve Buechele	.05
(407) Cecil Espy	.05
(408) Scott Fletcher	.05
(409) Julio Franco	.05
(410) Cecilio Guante	.05
(411) Jose Guzman	.05
(412) Charlie Hough	.05
(413) Pete Incaviglia	.05
(414) Chad Kreuter	.05
(415) Jeff Kunkel	.05
(416) Rick Leach	.05
(417) Jamie Moyer	.05
(418) Rafael Palmeiro	.50
(419) Geno Petralli	.05
(420) Jeff Russell	.05
(421) Nolan Ryan	1.50
(422) Ruben Sierra	.05
(423) Jim Sundberg	.05
(424) Bobby Witt	.05
(425) Steve Balboni	.05
(426) Scott Bankhead	.05
(427) Scott Bradley	.05
(428) Mickey Brantley	.05
(429) Darnell Coles	.05
(430) Henry Cotto	.05
(431) Alvin Davis	.05
(432) Mario Diaz	.05
(433) Ken Griffey Jr.	1.00
(434) Erik Hanson	.05
(435) Mike Jackson	.05
(436) Jeffrey Leonard	.05
(437) Edgar Martinez	.05
(438) Tom Niedenfuer	.05
(439) Jim Presley	.05
(440) Jerry Reed	.05
(441) Harold Reynolds	.05
(442) Bill Swift	.05
(443) Steve Trout	.05
(444) Dave Valle	.05
(445) Omar Vizquel	.05
(446) Marty Barrett	.05
(447) Mike Boddicker	.05
(448) Wade Boggs	.75
(449) Dennis "Oil Can" Boyd	.05
(450) Ellis Burks	.05
(451) Rick Cerone	.05
(452) Roger Clemens	.85
(453) Nick Esasky	.05
(454) Dwight Evans	.05
(455) Wes Gardner	.05
(456) Rich Gedman	.05
(457) Mike Greenwell	.05
(458) Sam Horn	.05
(459) Randy Kutcher	.05
(460) Dennis Lamp	.05
(461) Rob Murphy	.05
(462) Jody Reed	.05
(463) Jim Rice	.10
(464) Lee Smith	.05
(465) Mike Smithson	.05
(466) Bob Stanley	.05
(467) Doyle Alexander	.05
(468) Dave Bergman	.05
(469) Chris Brown	.05
(470) Paul Gibson	.05
(471) Mike Heath	.05
(472) Mike Henneman	.05
(473) Guillermo Hernandez	.05
(474) Charles Hudson	.05
(475) Chet Lemon	.05
(476) Fred Lynn	.05
(477) Keith Moreland	.05
(478) Jack Morris	.05
(479) Matt Nokes	.05
(480) Gary Pettis	.05
(481) Jeff Robinson	.05
(482) Pat Sheridan	.05
(483) Frank Tanana	.05
(484) Alan Trammell	.05
(485) Lou Whitaker	.05
(486) Frank Williams	.05
(487) Kenny Williams	.05
(488) Don August	.05
(489) Mike Birkbeck	.05
(490) Chris Bosio	.05
(491) Glenn Braggs	.05
(492) Greg Brock	.05
(493) Chuck Crim	.05
(494) Rob Deer	.05
(495) Mike Felder	.05
(496) Jim Gantner	.05
(497) Ted Higuera	.05
(498) Joey Meyer	.05
(499) Paul Mirabella	.05
(500) Paul Molitor	.60
(501) Juan Nieves	.05
(502) Charlie O'Brien	.05
(503) Dan Plesac	.05
(504) Gary Sheffield	.30
(505) B.J. Surhoff	.05
(506) Dale Sveum	.05
(507) Bill Wegman	.05
(508) Robin Yount	.60
(509) George Bell	.05
(510) Pat Borders	.05
(511) John Cerutti	.05
(512) Rob Ducey	.05
(513) Tony Fernandez	.05
(514) Mike Flanagan	.05
(515) Kelly Gruber	.05
(516) Tom Henke	.05
(517) Alexis Infante	.05
(518) Jimmy Key	.05
(519) Tom Lawless	.05
(520) Manny Lee	.05
(521) Al Leiter	.05
(522) Nelson Liriano	.05
(523) Fred McGriff	.05
(524) Lloyd Moseby	.05
(525) Rance Mulliniks	.05
(526) Dave Steib	.05
(527) Todd Stottlemyre	.05
(528) Duane Ward	.05
(529) Ernie Whitt	.05
(530) Jesse Barfield	.05
(531) Bob Brower	.05
(532) John Candelaria	.05
(533) Richard Dotson	.05
(534) Lee Guetterman	.05
(535) Mel Hall	.05
(536) Andy Hawkins	.05
(537) Rickey Henderson	.60
(538) Roberto Kelly	.05
(539) Dave LaPoint	.05
(540) Don Mattingly	.85
(541) Lance McCullers	.05
(542) Mike Pagliarulo	.05
(543) Clay Parker	.05
(544) Ken Phelps	.05
(545) Dave Righetti	.05
(546) Rafael Santana	.05
(547) Steve Sax	.05
(548) Don Slaught	.05
(549) Wayne Tolleson	.05
(550) Dave Winfield	.60
(551) Andy Allanson	.05
(552) Keith Atherton	.05
(553) Scott Bailes	.05
(554) Bud Black	.05
(555) Jerry Browne	.05
(556) Tom Candiotti	.05
(557) Joe Carter	.05
(558) David Clark	.05
(559) John Farrell	.05
(560) Felix Fermin	.05
(561) Brook Jacoby	.05
(562) Doug Jones	.05
(563) Oddibe McDowell	.05
(564) Luis Medina	.05
(565) Pete O'Brien	.05
(566) Jesse Orosco	.05
(567) Joel Skinner	.05
(568) Cory Snyder	.05
(569) Greg Swindell	.05
(570) Rich Yett	.05
(571) Mike Young	.05
(572) Brady Anderson	.05

(573)	Jeff Ballard	.05
(574)	Jose Bautista	.05
(575)	Phil Bradley	.05
(576)	Mike Devereaux	.05
(577)	Kevin Hickey	.05
(578)	Brian Holton	.05
(579)	Bob Melvin	.05
(580)	Bob Milacki	.05
(581)	Gregg Olson	.05
(582)	Joe Orsulak	.05
(583)	Bill Ripken	.05
(584)	Cal Ripken Jr.	1.50
(585)	Dave Schmidt	.05
(586)	Larry Sheets	.05
(587)	Mickey Tettleton	.05
(588)	Mark Thurmond	.05
(589)	Jay Tibbs	.05
(590)	Jim Traber	.05
(591)	Mark Williamson	.05
(592)	Craig Worthington	.05
(593)	Allan Anderson	.05
(594)	Ellis Burks	.05
(595)	Ken Griffey Jr.	1.00
(596)	Bo Jackson	.05
(597)	Roberto Kelly	.05
(598)	Kirk McCaskill	.05
(599)	Fred McGriff	.05
(600)	Mark McGwire	1.25
(601)	Bob Milacki	.05
(602)	Melido Perez	.05
(603)	Jeff Robinson	.05
(604)	Gary Sheffield	.05
(605)	Ruben Sierra	.05
(606)	Greg Swindell	.05
(607)	Roberto Alomar	.15
(608)	Tim Belcher	.05
(609)	Vince Coleman	.05
(610)	Kal Daniels	.05
(611)	Andres Galarraga	.05
(612)	Ron Gant	.05
(613)	Mark Grace	.05
(614)	Gregg Jefferies	.05
(615)	Ricky Jordan	.05
(616)	Jose Lind	.05
(617)	Kevin Mitchell	.05
(618)	Gerald Young	.05
(619)	Base	.05
(620)	Batting Helmets	.05
(621)	Bats	.05
(622)	Batting Gloves	.05
(623)	Los Angeles Dodgers	.05
(624)	Cincinnati Reds	.05
(625)	San Diego Padres	.05
(626)	San Francisco Giants	.05
(627)	Houston Astros	.05
(628)	Atlanta Braves	.05
(629)	New York Mets	.05
(630)	Pittsburgh Pirates	.05
(631)	Montreal Expos	.05
(632)	Chicago Cubs	.05
(633)	St. Louis Cardinals	.05
(634)	Philadelphia Phillies	.05
(635)	Oakland A's	.05
(636)	Minnesota Twins	.05
(637)	Kansas City Royals	.05
(638)	California Angels	.05
(639)	Chicago White Sox	.05
(640)	Texas Rangers	.05
(641)	Seattle Mariners	.05
(642)	Boston Red Sox	.05
(643)	Detroit Tigers	.05
(644)	Milwaukee Brewers	.05
(645)	Toronto Blue Jays	.05
(646)	New York Yankees	.05
(647)	Cleveland Indians	.05
(648)	Baltimore Orioles	.05

Hottest Players Stickers

Established major league stars are featured in this set of large-format (4-1/8" x 5-7/16") blank-back stickers. The stickers are printed four per sheet and were sold with a 36-page album for mounting. The album has player data, stats and highlights for each of the stars. Stickers have color action photos with a white frame at center. There is a red stripe at top of the frame and a blue stripe at bottom, which contains the player name. The unnumbered stickers are checklisted here in alphabetical order.

	NM/M
Complete Set, W/Album (56):	4.00
Common Player:	.05

---

(1)	George Bell	.05
(2)	Wade Boggs	.50
(3)	Bobby Bonilla	.05
(4)	Jose Canseco	.25
(5)	Joe Carter	.05
(6)	Will Clark	.05
(7)	Roger Clemens	.60
(8)	Alvin Davis	.05
(9)	Eric Davis	.05
(10)	Glenn Davis	.05
(11)	Mark Davis	.05
(12)	Carlton Fisk	.35
(13)	John Franco	.05
(14)	Gary Gaetti	.05
(15)	Andres Galarraga	.05
(16)	Dwight Gooden	.05
(17)	Mark Grace	.05
(18)	Pedro Guerrero	.05
(19)	Tony Gwynn	.50
(20)	Rickey Henderson	.35
(21)	Orel Hershiser	.05
(22)	Bo Jackson	.05
(23)	Ricky Jordan	.05
(24)	Wally Joyner	.05
(25)	Don Mattingly	.60
(26)	Fred McGriff	.05
(27)	Kevin Mitchell	.05
(28)	Paul Molitor	.35
(29)	Dale Murphy	.25
(30)	Eddie Murray	.35
(31)	Kirby Puckett	.50
(32)	Tim Raines	.05
(33)	Harold Reynolds	.05
(34)	Cal Ripken Jr.	1.00
(35)	Nolan Ryan	1.00
(36)	Bret Saberhagen	.05
(37)	Ryne Sandberg	.50
(38)	Steve Sax	.05
(39)	Mike Scott	.05
(40)	Ruben Sierra	.50
(41)	Ozzie Smith	.50
(42)	John Smoltz	.05
(43)	Darryl Strawberry	.05
(44)	Greg Swindell	.05
(45)	Mickey Tettleton	.05
(46)	Alan Trammell	.05
(47)	Andy Van Slyke	.05
(48)	Lou Whitaker	.05
(49)	Devon White	.05
(50)	Robin Yount	.35
(51)	Dodger Stadium	.05
(52)	Jack Murphy Stadium	.05
(53)	Shea Stadium	.05
(54)	Three Rivers Stadium	.05
(55)	Tiger Stadium	.05
(56)	Yankee Stadium	.05

Hottest Rookies Stickers

This set of large-format (4-1/8" x 5-7/16") stickers features the rookie crop of 1990 along with other young players who were not technically rookies in 1990. The stickers were sold four per sheet in complete sets which included a 36-page color album to mount the stamps. The album pages have personal data, career stats and highlights about each player. On the stickers, each action photo has a central frame in white with a blue stripe at top and a red stripe at bottom bearing the player name. Backs are, of course, blank. The set is checklisted here alphabetically.

	NM/M
Complete Set, W/Album (56):	4.00
Common Player:	.05

---

(1)	Jim Abbott	.05
(2)	Sandy Alomar	.05
(3)	Kent Anderson	.05
(4)	Eric Anthony	.05
(5)	Jeff Ballard	.05
(6)	Joey Belle	.15
(7)	Andy Benes	.05
(8)	Lance Blankenship	.05
(9)	Jeff Brantley	.05
(10)	Cris Carpenter	.05
(11)	Mark Carreon	.05
(12)	Dennis Cook	.05
(13)	Scott Coolbaugh	.05
(14)	Luis de los Santos	.05
(15)	Junior Felix	.05
(16)	Mark Gardner	.05
(17)	German Gonzalez	.05
(18)	Tom Gordon	.05
(19)	Ken Griffey Jr.	2.00
(20)	Marquis Grissom	.05
(21)	Charlie Hayes	.05
(22)	Gregg Jefferies	.05
(23)	Randy Johnson	1.00
(24)	Felix Jose	.05
(25)	Jeff King	.05
(26)	Randy Kramer	.05
(27)	Derek Lilliquist	.05
(28)	Greg Litton	.05
(29)	Kelly Mann	.05
(30)	Ramon Martinez	.05
(31)	Luis Medina	.05
(32)	Hal Morris	.05
(33)	Joe Oliver	.05
(34)	Gregg Olson	.05
(35)	Dean Palmer	.05
(36)	Carlos Quintana	.05
(37)	Kevin Ritz	.05
(38)	Deion Sanders	.05
(39)	Scott Scudder	.05
(40)	Steve Searcy	.05
(41)	Gary Sheffield	.25
(42)	Dwight Smith	.05
(43)	Sam Sosa	1.50
(44)	Greg Vaughn	.05
(45)	Robin Ventura	.05
(46)	Jerome Walton	.05
(47)	Dave West	.05
(48)	John Wetteland	.05
(49)	Eric Yelding	.05
(50)	Todd Zeile	.05
(51)	Dodger Stadium	.05
(52)	Jack Murphy Stadium	.05
(53)	Shea Stadium	.05
(54)	Three Rivers Stadium	.05
(55)	Tiger Stadium	.05
(56)	Yankee Stadium	.05

1993 Publix Florida Marlins

	NM/M
Complete Set (29):	10.00
Common Player:	.50

6	Rich Renteria	.50
8	Bret Barbarie	.50
09	Benito Santiago	.50
10	Gary Sheffield	1.50
11	Chris Hammond	.50
13	Bob Natal	.50
15	Rene Lachemann	.50
17	Darrell Whitmore	.50
19	Jeff Conine	.50
20	Greg Briley	.50
21	Chuck Carr	.50
22	Walt Weiss	.50
26	Richie Lewis	.50
26	Alex Arias	.50
27	Luis Aquino	.50
29	Henry Cotto	.50
30	Nigel Wilson	.50
31	Robb Nen	.50
34	Bryan Harvey	.50
39	Orestes Destrade	.50
42	Rich Rodriguez	.50
46	Ryan Bowen	.50
48	Pat Rapp	.50
49	Charlie Hough	.50
54	Matt Turner	.50
58	Joe Klink	.50
77	Jack Armstrong	.50
---	Marlins Coaches (Marcel Lachemann, Doug Rader, Vada Pinson, Frank Reberger, Cookie Rojas)	.50
---	Billy (Mascot)	.50
---	$1 Coke-Publix Coupon	.50

Q

1986 Quaker Oats

The Quaker Co., in conjunction with Topps, produced this 33-card set of current basebAll-Stars for packaging in groups of three in Chewy Granola Bars packages. The cards are noted as the "1st Annual Collectors Edition." They are numbered and measure 2-1/2" x 3-1/2." Card fronts feature full-color player photos with the product name at the top and the player name, team

and position below the photo. The complete set was offered via mail order by the Quaker Company.

	NM/M
Complete Set (33):	4.00
Common Player:	.05

1	Willie McGee	.05
2	Dwight Gooden	.05
3	Vince Coleman	.05
4	Gary Carter	.50
5	Jack Clark	.05
6	Steve Garvey	.15
7	Tony Gwynn	.65
8	Dale Murphy	.25
9	Dave Parker	.05
10	Tim Raines	.05
11	Pete Rose	1.00
12	Nolan Ryan	1.50
13	Ryne Sandberg	.65
14	Mike Schmidt	.75
15	Ozzie Smith	.05
16	Darryl Strawberry	.05
17	Fernando Valenzuela	.05
18	Don Mattingly	.75
19	Bret Saberhagen	.05
20	Ozzie Guillen	.05
21	Bert Blyleven	.50
22	Wade Boggs	.65
23	George Brett	.75
24	Darrell Evans	.05
25	Rickey Henderson	.50
26	Reggie Jackson	.75
27	Eddie Murray	.50
28	Phil Niekro	.25
29	Dan Quisenberry	.05
30	Jim Rice	.15
31	Cal Ripken, Jr.	1.50
32	Tom Seaver	.65
33	Dave Winfield	.50
----	Offer Card	.03

R

1993 Rainbow Foods Dave Winfield

Dave Winfield's return to Minnesota where he excelled in college sports was marked by the "Homecoming Collection," tracing the future Hall of Famer's career. The 2-1/2" x 3-1/2" cards have black-and-white or color photos on front and back. Each side also sports a special logo identifying the issue. Rainbow's logo appears on front, while that of a major food brand such as Kraft or Oscar Mayer appear on back, along with information about Winfield's career. Cards were sold in five-card packs with four blue-bordered cards and one gold-bordered parallel card.

	NM/M
Complete Set, Blue (10):	7.50
Common Player, Blue:	1.00
Gold:	2-3X

1	Dave Winfield (University of Minnesota Outfielder)	1.00
2	Dave Winfield (University of Minnesota Pitcher)	1.00

3	Dave Winfield (University of Minnesota BasketbAll-Star)	1.00
4	Dave Winfield (San Diego Padres 1973-1980)	1.00
5	Dave Winfield (N.Y. Yankees 1981-1990)	1.00
6	Dave Winfield (California Angels 1990-1991)	1.00
7	Dave Winfield (Toronto Blue Jays 1992)	1.00
8	Dave Winfield (Minnesota Twins 1993-)	1.00
9	Dave Winfield (7-time Gold Glove Winner)	1.00
10	Dave Winfield (Pride of Minnesota)	1.00

2001 Rainbow Foods Minnesota Twins 10th Anniversary

As part of a three-game celebration of the 10th annivsary of the Twins 1991 World's Championship, Rainbow Foods sponsored a team-set card giveaway on June 29, distributing 10,000 sets. Fronts of the 2-1/2" x 3-1/2" cards have borderless game-action photos with an anniversary logo. Backs have team and sponsor logos and player career highlights on a baseball diamond design in color. The unnumbered cards are checklisted here in alphabetical order.

	NM/M
Complete Set (26):	9.00
Common Player:	.25

(1)	Rick Aguilera	.25
(2)	Steve Bedrosian	.25
(3)	Jarvis Brown	.25
(4)	Randy Bush	.25
(5)	Chili Davis	.25
(6)	Scott Erickson	.25
(7)	Greg Gagne	.25
(8)	Dan Gladden	.25
(9)	Mark Guthrie	.25
(10)	Brian Harper	.25
(11)	Kent Hrbek	.50
(12)	Tom Kelly	.25
(13)	Chuck Knoblauch	.25
(14)	Gene Larkin	.25
(15)	Terry Leach	.25
(16)	Scott Leius	.25
(17)	Shane Mack	.25
(18)	Jack Morris	.25
(19)	Al Newman	.25
(20)	Junior Ortiz	.25
(21)	Mike Pagliarulo	.25
(22)	Kirby Puckett	5.00
(23)	Paul Sorrento	.25
(24)	Kevin Tapani	.25
(25)	David West	.25
(26)	Carl Willis	.25

1989 Rainier Farms Super Stars Discs

This set is one of the scarcer late-1980s disc issues produced by Michael Schechter Associates for various local businesses. The bakery began distribution of the discs by placing them directly in the cello wrapper with a loaf of bread. This resulted in those cards being severely grease stained and often creased. It also resulted in problems with public health officials

who halted the distribution. Since the bakery could not economically and sanitarily package the cards they dropped the promotion and sold the remainder cards into the hobby. Discs measure 2-3/4" in diameter and have a color player photo (with team logos airbrushed away) at center with a white border. A Rainier Farms Homestyle logo is at top in red and black. Backs are printed in dark blue and feature a few stats, biographical details and a card number.

	NM/M
Complete Set (20):	15.00
Common Player:	.60

1	Wally Joyner	.60
2	Wade Boggs	2.25
3	Ozzie Smith	2.25
4	Don Mattingly	2.50
5	Jose Canseco	1.25
6	Tony Gwynn	2.25
7	Eric Davis	.60
8	Kirby Puckett	2.25
9	Kevin Seitzer	.60
10	Darryl Strawberry	.60
11	Gregg Jefferies	.60
12	Mark Grace	.60
13	Matt Nokes	.60
14	Mark McGwire	3.50
15	Bobby Bonilla	.60
16	Roger Clemens	2.50
17	Frank Viola	.60
18	Orel Hershiser	.60
19	Dave Cone	.60
20	Kirk Gibson	.60

1984 Ralston Purina

This set, produced by Topps, features the game's top players. Photos on the 2-1/2" x 3-1/2" cards are all close-up poses. Topps' logo appears only on the card fronts, and the backs are completely different from Topps' regular issue of 1984, featuring a checkerboard look, coinciding with the well-known Ralston Purina logo. Cards are numbered with odd numbers for American Leaguers and even numbered cards for National Leaguers. Four cards were packed in boxes of Cookie Crisp and Donkey Kong Junior brand cereals, and the complete set was available via a mail-in offer in panel form.

	NM/M
Complete Set, Singles (33):	4.00
Complete Set, Panel	4.00
Common Player:	.05

1	Eddie Murray	.25
2	Ozzie Smith	.35
3	Ted Simmons	.05
4	Pete Rose	.75
5	Greg Luzinski	.05
6	Andre Dawson	.15
7	Dave Winfield	.25
8	Tom Seaver	.25
9	Jim Rice	.15
10	Fernando Valenzuela	.05
11	Wade Boggs	.35
12	Dale Murphy	.15
13	George Brett	.50
14	Nolan Ryan	1.00
15	Rickey Henderson	.25
16	Steve Carlton	.25
17	Rod Carew	.25
18	Steve Garvey	.25
19	Reggie Jackson	.50
20	Dave Concepcion	.05
21	Robin Yount	.25
22	Mike Schmidt	.50
23	Jim Palmer	.25
24	Bruce Sutter	.20
25	Dan Quisenberry	.05
26	Bill Madlock	.05
27	Cecil Cooper	.05
28	Gary Carter	.25
29	Fred Lynn	.05
30	Pedro Guerrero	.05
31	Ron Guidry	.05
32	Keith Hernandez	.05
33	Carlton Fisk	.25

1987 Ralston Purina

Ralston Purina, in conjunction with Mike Schechter Associates, issued this set in specially marked boxes of Cookie Crisp and Honey Graham Chex. Three cards, wrapped in cellophane, were inserted in each box. Fronts contain a full-color photo with the team insignia airbrushed away. Above the photo are two yellow crossed bats and a star, with the player's uniform number inside the star. Backs are gray with red printing and contain personal information and career major league statistics. As part of the promotion, the company advertised an uncut sheet of cards which was available by finding an "instant-winner" game card or sending $1 plus two non-winning cards. Cards on the uncut sheet are identical in design to the single cards, save the omission of the words "1987 Collectors Edition" in the upper-right corner.

		NM/M
Complete Set (15):		7.50
Common Player:		.25
1	Nolan Ryan	1.50
2	Steve Garvey	.35
3	Wade Boggs	.65
4	Dave Winfield	.50
5	Don Mattingly	.75
6	Don Sutton	.35
7	Dave Parker	.25
8	Eddie Murray	.50
9	Gary Carter	.50
10	Roger Clemens	.75
11	Fernando Valenzuela	.25
12	Cal Ripken Jr.	1.50
13	Ozzie Smith	.65
14	Mike Schmidt	.75
15	Ryne Sandberg	.65

Collectors' Sheet

Cards obtained from the mail-in redemption uncut sheet offer are identical to the cereal-box insert versions except that they lack the "1987 / COLLECTORS' / EDITION" legend at top-right.

		NM/M
Complete Panel:		8.00
Complete Singles Set (15):		5.00
Common Single Player:		.15
1	Nolan Ryan	1.00
2	Steve Garvey	.25
3	Wade Boggs	.50
4	Dave Winfield	.40
5	Don Mattingly	.65
6	Don Sutton	.30
7	Dave Parker	.15
8	Eddie Murray	.40
9	Gary Carter	.40
10	Roger Clemens	.65
11	Fernando Valenzuela	.15
12	Cal Ripken Jr.	1.00
13	Ozzie Smith	.50
14	Mike Schmidt	.65
15	Ryne Sandberg	.50

1989 Ralston Purina

Ralston Purina, in conjunction with Mike Schechter Associates, issued this "Superstars" set in 1989. As part of a late-spring and early-summer promotion, the standard-size cards were inserted, two per box, in specially-marked boxes of Crisp Crunch, Honey Nut O's, Fruit Rings and Frosted Flakes in most parts of the country. Ads on cereal boxes also offered complete sets through a mail-in offer. Fronts feature player portraits flanked by stars in all four corners. Backs include stats and player data. Team logos have been removed from the photos.

		NM/M
Complete Set (12):		3.00
Common Player:		.10
1	Ozzie Smith	.75
2	Andre Dawson	.20
3	Darryl Strawberry	.10
4	Mike Schmidt	1.00
5	Orel Hershiser	.10
6	Tim Raines	.10
7	Roger Clemens	1.00
8	Kirby Puckett	.75
9	George Brett	1.00
10	Alan Trammell	.10
11	Don Mattingly	1.00
12	Jose Canseco	.35

1990 Real Milk Mike Henneman

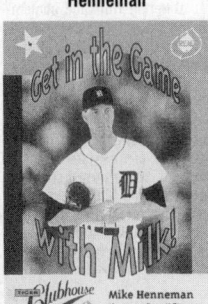

"Get in the Game" urges the headline on each of the cards in this collection featuring then-star Tiger relief pitcher Mike Henneman. The 2-1/2" x 3-1/2" cards have red, white and blue borders with a color photo at center. Backs are in red, black and white with Henneman's stats or career highlights. The set was available as a mail-in premium.

		NM/M
Complete Set (8):		6.00
Common Card:		.25
1	Mike Henneman (Drinking milk.)	2.00
2	Mike Henneman/Pitching	2.00
3	Mike Henneman (In jacket.)	2.00
4	Mike Henneman (Rubbing up ball.)	2.00
5	Milk Carton	.25
6	Hand Holding Carton	.25
--	Title Card	.25
--	Tiger Clubhouse Membership Card	.25

1990 Red Apple Mariners Pin/Cards

It is unknown whether the checklist presented here is complete. This combination promotional issue features a 2-1/2" x 3-13/16" baseball card separated by perforations from a 2-1/2" x 1-7/16" tab. The card portion has a color player photo with a large M's logo. The front of the tab is

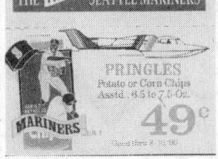

a coupon for a food product. On back the card has a black-and-white portrait photo along with player data and career highlights. The back of the tab has a Red Apple Markets logo. Attached to the tab is a color enameled pin of the player in action.

		NM/M
Common Player:		5.00
(1)	Alvin Davis	6.00
(2)	Ken Griffey Jr.	12.00
(3)	Harold Reynolds	6.00
(4)	David Valle	5.00

1982 Red Lobster Cubs

This 28-card set was co-sponsored by the team and a seafood restaurant chain for distribution at a 1982 Cubs promotional game. Card fronts are unbordered color photos, with player name, number, position and a superimposed facsimile autograph. The set includes 25 players on the 2-1/4" x 3-1/2" cards, along with a card for manager Lee Elia, an unnumbered card for the coaching staff and a team picture. Card backs have complete player statistics and a Red Lobster ad. Production was reported to be 15,000 sets.

		NM/M
Complete Set (28):		60.00
Common Player:		.50
1	Larry Bowa	.50
4	Lee Elia	.50
6	Keith Moreland	.50
7	Jody Davis	.50
10	Leon Durham	.50
15	Junior Kennedy	.50
17	Bump Wills	.50
18	Scot Thompson	.50
21	Jay Johnstone	.50
22	Bill Buckner	.50
23	Ryne Sandberg	50.00
24	Jerry Morales	.50
27	Gary Woods	.50
28	Steve Henderson	.50
29	Bob Molinaro	.50
31	Fergie Jenkins	2.00
33	Al Ripley	.50
34	Randy Martz	.50
36	Mike Proly	.50
37	Ken Kravec	.50
38	Willie Hernandez	.50
39	Bill Campbell	.50
41	Dick Tidrow	.50
46	Lee Smith	1.00
47	Doug Bird	.50
48	Dickie Noles	.50
--	Team Photo	.50

		NM/M
---	Coaching Staff (Billy Connors, Tom Harmon, Gordy MacKenzie, John Vukovich, Billy Williams)	.50

1991 Retort Negro League Legends, Series 1

One of the most extensive collectors' issues featuring former Negro League players was issued over a two-year period by Robert Retort Enterprises. Sold only in a boxed set with accompanying history book, the premiere issue featured 65 individual players, plus game-action and team photos. Fronts of the 3-1/2" x 5-1/2" cards feature sepia photos with a sepia border. Player identification is in the bottom portion. Postcard style backs specify the teams on which the player appeared, have a card number and a serial number from within the edition of 10,000 sets.

		NM/M
Complete Set (100):		35.00
Common Player:		.50
1	Otha Bailey	.50
2	Harry Barnes	.50
3	Gene Benson	.50
4	Bill Beverly	.50
5	Charlie Biot	.50
6	Bob Boyd	.65
7	Allen Bryant	.50
8	Marlin Carter	.50
9	Bill Cash	.50
10	Jim Cohen	.50
11	Elliott Coleman	.50
12	Johnnie Cowan	.50
13	Jimmie Crutchfield	.65
14	Saul Davis	.50
15	Piper Davis	.65
16	Leon Day	2.00
17	Lou Dials	.75
18	Mahlon Duckett	.50
19	Felix Evans	.50
20	Rudy Fernandez	.50
21	Joe Fillmore	.50
22	George Giles	.50
23	Louis Gillis	.50
24	Stanley Glenn	.50
25	Willie Grace	.50
26	Wiley Griggs	.50
27	Albert Haywood	.50
28	Jimmy Hill	.50
29	Cowan Hyde	.50
30	Monte Irvin	1.50
31	Sam Jethroe	1.00
32	Connie Johnson	.65
33	Josh Johnson	.50
34	Clinton Jones	.50
35	Larry Kimbrough	.50
36	Clarence King	.50
37	Jim LaMarque	.50
38	Buck Leonard	2.00
39	Max Manning	.50
40	Verdell Mathis	.50
41	Nath McClinic	.50
42	Clinton McCord	.50
43	Clyde McNeal	.50
44	John Miles	.50
45	Buck O'Neil	2.00
46	Frank Pearson	.50
47	Art Pennington	.75
48	Nathan Peoples	.50
49	Andy Porter	.50
50	Ted Radcliffe	.50
51	Chico Renfroe	.50
52	Bobby Robinson	.50
53	Tommy Sampson	.50
54	Joe Scott	.50
55	Joe Burt Scott	.50
56	Herb Simpson	.50
57	Lonnie Summers	.50
58	Alfred Surratt	.50
59	Bob Thurman	.50
60	Harold Tinker	.50
61	Quincy Trouppe	.75
62	Edsall Walker	.50
63	Al Wilmore	.50
64	Artie Wilson	.75

65	Jim Zapp	.50
66	Grays vs. Stars/1937	.50
67	Grays vs. Eagles/1943	.50
68	Homestead Grays/1944	.50
69	Grays vs. Cuban Stars/1944	.50
70	Grays vs. Cubans/1944	.50
71	Grays vs. Eagles/1945	.50
72	Eagles Pitching Staff/1941	.50
73	Buckeyes Infield/1945	.50
74	Homestead Grays/1948	.50
75	Chicago Murderers Row/1943	.50
76	Indianapolis Clowns/1945	.50
77	East All-Stars/1937	.50
78	East All-Stars/1938	.50
79	East All-Stars/1939	.50
80	East All-Stars/1948	.50
81	West All-Stars/1948	.50
82	Homestead Grays/1931	.50
83	Homestead Grays/1938	.50
84	Pittsburgh Crawfords/1936	.50
85	Kansas City Monarchs/1934	.50
86	Kansas City Monarchs/1949	.50
87	Chicago American Giants/1941	.50
88	Chicago American Giants/1947	.50
89	Memphis Red Sox/1940	.50
90	Memphis Red Sox/1946	.50
91	Birmingham Black Barons/1946	.50
92	Birmingham Black Barons/1948	.50
93	Birmingham Black Barons/1950	.50
94	Harlem Globetrotters/1948	.50
95	Cleveland Buckeyes/1947	.50
96	Philadelphia Stars/1944	.50
97	Newark Eagles/1939	.50
98	Baltimore Elite Giants/1949	.50
99	Indianapolis Clowns/1943	.50
100	Cincinnati Tigers/1937	.50

1993 Retort Negro League Legends, Series 2

One of the most extensive collectors' issues featuring former Negro League players was issued over a two-year period by Robert Retort Enterprises. Sold only in a boxed set, the Series 2 issue features 41 individual players, plus game-action and team photos. Fronts of the 3-1/2" x 5-1/2" cards feature sepia photos with a white border. Player identification is in the bottom border, which also has space for autographing. Postcard style backs specify the teams on which the player appeared, have a card number and a serial number from within the edition of 10,000 sets.

		NM/M
Complete Set (100):		30.00
Common Player:		.50
1	Frank Barnes	.50
2	John Bissant	.50
3	Garnett Blair	.50
4	Jim "Fireball" Bolden	.50
5	Luther Branham	.50
6	Sherwood Brewer	.50
7	Jimmy Dean	.50
8	Frank Duncan, Jr.	.50
9	Wilmer Fields	.50
10	Harold Gordon	.50
11	Bill Greason	.50
12	Acie Griggs	.50
13	Napoleon Gulley	.75
14	Ray Haggins	.50
15	Wilmer Harris	.50
16	Bob Harvey	.50
17	Jehosie Heard	.65
18	Gordon Hopkins	.50
19	Herman Horn	.50
20	James Ivory	.50
21	Henry Kimbro	.75
22	Milford Laurent	.50
23	Ernest Long	.50
24	Frank Marsh	.50
25	Francis Matthews	.50
26	Jim McCurine	.50
27	John Mitchell	.50
28	Lee Moody	.50
29	Rogers Pierre	.50
30	Nathaniel Pollard	.50
31	Merle Porter	.50
32	William Powell	.50
33	Ulysses Redd	.50
34	Harry Rhodes	.50
35	DeWitt Smallwood	.50
36	Joseph Spencer	.50
37	Riley Stewart	.50
38	Earl Taborn	.50
39	Ron Teasley	.50
40	Joe Wiley	.50
41	Buck Leonard	2.00
42	Grays vs. Giants/1945	.50
43	Grays vs. Monarchs/1945	.50
44	Homestead Grays/1948	.50

45	Pittsburgh Crawfords/1928	.50
46	Pittsburgh Crawfords/1935	.50
47	Kansas City Monarchs/1942	.50
48	Buck O'Neil, William Dismukes	.50
49	Chicago American Giants/1942	.50
50	Nashville Elite Giants/1935	.50
51	Baltimore Elite Giants/1941	.50
52	Birmingham Black Barons/1948	.50
53	Birmingham Black Barons/1959	.50
54	Memphis Red Sox/1954	.50
55	Indianapolis ABCs/1923	.50
56	Harlem Globetrotters/1948	.50
57	Harlem Globetrotters/1948	.50
58	Bismarck Barons/1955	.50
59	Culican/1952	.50
60	Santurce/1947	.50
61	Pittsburgh Crawfords/1928	.50
62	Pittsburgh Crawfords/1932	.50
63	Pittsburgh Crawfords/1935	.50
64	Homestead Grays/1937	.50
65	Homestead Grays/1938	.50
66	Homestead Grays/1940	.50
67	Homestead Grays/1945	.50
68	Homestead Grays/1948	.50
69	Kansas City Monarchs/1932	.50
70	Kansas City Monarchs/1934	.50
71	Kansas City Monarchs/1941	.50
72	Kansas City Monarchs/1946	.50
73	Chicago American Giants/1950	.50
74	Memphis Red Sox/1949	.50
75	Birmingham Black Barons/1946	.50
76	Birmingham Black Barons/1948	.50
77	Birmingham Black Barons/1951	.50
78	Birmingham Black Barons/1954	.50
79	St. Louis Stars/1931	.50
80	Newark Dodgers/1935	.50
81	Brooklyn Eagles/1935	.50
82	Newark Eagles/1946	.50
83	Philadelphia Stars/1939	.50
84	Philadelphia Stars/1946	.50
85	Philadelphia Stars/1949	.50
86	Nashville Elite Giants/1935	.50
87	Baltimore Elite Giants/1939	.50
88	Baltimore Elite Giants/1949	.50
89	Cleveland Buckeyes/1947	.50
90	Cincinnati Tigers/1936	.50
91	Miami Ethiopian Clowns/1940	.50
92	Indianapolis Clowns/1944	.50
93	Indianapolis Clowns/1948	.50
94	New York Cubans/1943	.50
95	Harlem Globetrotters/1948	.50
96	House of David/1938	.50
97	E.T. Community/1926	.50
98	Bismarck Giants/1935	.50
99	American All-Stars/1945	.50
100	New York Stars/1949	.50

1988 Revco

This super-glossy boxed set of 33 standard-size cards was produced by Topps for exclusive distribution by Revco stores east of the Mississippi River. Card fronts feature a large blue Revco logo in the upper-left corner opposite a yellow and black boxed "Topps League Leader" label. Player photos are framed in black and orange with a diagonal player identification banner in the lower-right corner. Backs are horizontal, printed in red and black on white stock and include the player name, biographical data, batting/pitching stats and a brief career summary.

		NM/M
Complete Set (33):		4.00
Common Player:		.05
1	Tony Gwynn	.65
2	Andre Dawson	.25
3	Vince Coleman	.05
4	Jack Clark	.05
5	Tim Raines	.05
6	Tim Wallach	.05
7	Juan Samuel	.05
8	Nolan Ryan	1.50
9	Rick Sutcliffe	.05
10	Kent Tekulve	.05
11	Steve Bedrosian	.05
12	Orel Hershiser	.05
13	Rick Rueschel	.05
14	Fernando Valenzuela	.05
15	Bob Welch	.05
16	Wade Boggs	.50
17	Mark McGwire	1.00
18	George Bell	.05
19	Harold Reynolds	.05
20	Paul Molitor	.50
21	Kirby Puckett	.65
22	Kevin Seitzer	.05
23	Brian Downing	.05
24	Dwight Evans	.05
25	Willie Wilson	.05
26	Danny Tartabull	.05
27	Jimmy Key	.05
28	Roger Clemens	.75
29	Dave Stewart	.05
30	Mark Eichhorn	.05
31	Tom Henke	.05
32	Charlie Hough	.05
33	Mark Langston	.05

1996 Revco Cleveland Indians

This set is identified by a logo on front as the "1995 Award Winner Series," but its manner of distribution is unknown. Fronts of the 2-1/2" x 3-1/2" cards have action photos with mottled border. Backs have logos of the 1995 Indians A.L. Championship and of the sponsor, Revco drug stores. Listed on back are the awards earned by the player for the 1995 season. A uniform number also appears, where applicable.

		NM/M
Complete Set (12):		12.00
Common Player:		.50
(1)	Carlos Baerga	.50
(2)	Albert Belle	1.25
(3)	Mike Hargrove	.50
(4)	John Hart (GM)	.50
(5)	Orel Hershiser	1.00
(6)	Kenny Lofton	1.00
(7)	Jose Mesa	.50
(8)	Manny Ramirez	5.00
(9)	Julian Tavares	.50
(10)	Jim Thome	2.50
(11)	Omar Vizquel	1.00
(12)	Cleveland Indians (On-field celebration.)	

1985-86 RGI

(See listings under Renata Galasso.)

Renata Galasso Inc.

1988 Rite Aid

This premiere edition was produced by Topps for distribution by Rite Aid discount drug stores in the Eastern U.S. The boxed set includes 33 standard-size full-color cards with at least one card for each major league team. Four cards in the set highlight MVPs from the 1987 season. Card fronts have white borders and carry a yellow "Team MVP's" header above the player photo which is bordered in red and blue. A large Rite Aid logo appears upper-left; the player's name appears bottom center. The numbered card backs are black on

blue and white card stock in a horizontal layout containing the player name, biography and statistics.

		NM/M
Complete Set (33):		4.00
Common Player:		.05
1	Dale Murphy	.15
2	Andre Dawson	.15
3	Eric Davis	.05
4	Mike Scott	.05
5	Pedro Guerrero	.05
6	Tim Raines	.05
7	Darryl Strawberry	.05
8	Mike Schmidt	.65
9	Mike Dunne	.05
10	Jack Clark	.05
11	Tony Gwynn	.60
12	Will Clark	.05
13	Cal Ripken, Jr.	1.00
14	Wade Boggs	.60
15	Wally Joyner	.05
16	Harold Baines	.05
17	Joe Carter	.05
18	Alan Trammell	.05
19	Kevin Seitzer	.05
20	Paul Molitor	.50
21	Kirby Puckett	.60
22	Don Mattingly	.65
23	Mark McGwire	.75
24	Alvin Davis	.05
25	Ruben Sierra	.05
26	George Bell	.05
27	Jack Morris	.05
28	Jeff Reardon	.05
29	John Tudor	.05
30	Rick Rueschel	.05
31	Gary Gaetti	.05
32	Jeffrey Leonard	.05
33	Frank Viola	.05

1982 Roy Rogers N.Y. Yankees Lids

Members of the N.Y. Yankees (although in uniform which have the logos removed) are featured on these soft drink lids given away at Roy Rogers restaurants in the metropolitan area. Lids are 3-9/16" in diameter with a red plastic ring around a cardboard disc. At the center of the disc is a black-and-white player portrait photo. Player data appears in colored panels at the sides and in the white center section at bottom. The unnumbered lids are checklisted here in alphabetical order.

		NM/M
Complete Set (12):		35.00
Common Player:		2.50
(1)	Rick Cerone	2.50
(2)	Goose Gossage	3.50
(3)	Ken Griffey	2.50
(4)	Ron Guidry	3.00
(5)	Steve Kemp	2.50
(6)	Jerry Mumphrey	2.50
(7)	Graig Nettles	3.00
(8)	Lou Piniella	3.00
(9)	Willie Randolph	3.00
(10)	Andre Robertson	2.50
(11)	Roy Smalley	2.50
(12)	Dave Winfield	7.50

1993 Rolaids Cubs Relief Pitchers

The Chicago Cubs issued a four-card All-Time Cubs Relief Pitchers set as a giveaway at the Sept. 4, 1993 game at Wrigley Field

The four were selected by Cubs fans in a ballot conducted by Rolaids. The standard-sized cards have white borders with a color photo at center. Backs include the player's name, years he pitched for the Cubs, the Rolaids logo and an explanation of the card set's purpose.

		NM/M
Complete Set (4):		4.50
Common Player:		1.00
(1)	Randy Myers	1.00
(2)	Lee Smith	1.50
(3)	Bruce Sutter	2.50
(4)	Mitch Williams	1.00

1993 Nolan Ryan Topps Stickers

Week #8

1981

1975

1990

Twenty-seven of Nolan Ryan's Topps cards from 1968 through 1992 were reproduced, probably without authorization from Topps or Ryan, in a sticker format for regional distribution in Texas area grocery stores. Printed just slightly smaller than the 2-1/2" x 3-1/2" cards, the stickers were issued in strips of three. When the front picture was peeled away, the back of the sticker could be used as a coupon for specific purchases. Stores known to have participated in the program include: Brookshire Bros., Budget Chopper, Minyards and Super S. Strips of three were generally offered on a weekly basis.

	NM/M
Complete Set, Strips (9):	30.00
Common Sticker:	2.00

S

1986 Safeway Houston Astros

Though not marked, these 6" x 9" color player photo were given away over the course of several weeks by area Safeway food stores. The pictures are player portraits in uniform, but without caps because they were licensed by the Players Union, but not MLB. The white-bordered pictures have a facsimile autograph and are blank-backed. Unnumbered, the pictures are checklisted here in alphabetical order.

		NM/M
Complete Set (16):		25.00
Common Player:		1.00
(1)	Alan Ashby	1.00
(2)	Kevin Bass	1.00
(3)	Jose Cruz	1.00
(4)	Glenn Davis	1.00
(5)	Bill Doran	1.00
(6)	Phil Garner	1.00
(7)	Billy Hatcher	1.00
(8)	Charlie Kerfeld	1.00
(9)	Bob Knepper	1.00
(10)	Aurelio Lopez	1.00
(11)	Terry Puhl	1.00
(12)	Craig Reynolds	1.00
(13)	Nolan Ryan	15.00
(14)	Mike Scott	1.00
(15)	Dickie Thon	1.00
(16)	Denny Walling	1.00

2005 Ryne Sandberg Jersey Retirement Day

Stadium giveaway August 28.

	NM/M
Ryne Sandberg	6.00

1984 San Diego Padres Fire Safety

This set of 28 full-color 2-1/2" x 3-1/2" cards pictures Padres players, coaches, broadcasters and the Famous Chicken each posing with

Smokey the Bear. Smokey's portrait and logo of the California and U.S. Forest Services are printed in the bottom border. Backs offer brief player information and a fire prevention tip. The cards were given away at a home game.

		NM/M
Complete Set (28):		7.00
Common Player:		.25
1	Garry Templeton	.25
2	Alan Wiggins	.25
4	Luis Salazar	.25
6	Steve Garvey	1.00
7	Kurt Bevacqua	.25
10	Doug Gwosdz	.25
11	Tim Flannery	.25
16	Terry Kennedy	.25
18	Kevin McReynolds	.25
19	Tony Gwynn	5.00
20	Bobby Brown	.25
30	Eric Show	.25
31	Ed Whitson	.25
35	Luis DeLeon	.25
38	Mark Thurmond	.25
42	Sid Monge	.25
43	Dave Dravecky	.25
48	Tim Lollar	.25
---	Smokey Logo Card	.25
---	The Chicken (Mascot)	.25
---	Dave Campbell (Broadcaster)	.25
---	Jerry Coleman (Broadcaster)	.25
---	Harry Dunlop	.25
---	Harold (Doug) Harvey (Umpire)	.25
---	Jack Krol (Coach)	.25
---	Jack McKeon (Vice President)	.25
---	Norm Sherry (Coach)	.25
---	Ozzie Virgil (Coach)	.25
---	Dick Williams (Manager)	.25

1986-87 San Diego Padres Fire Safety Flip Books

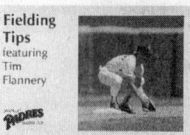

Differing from the contemporary fire safety issues of its time, the 1986-87 Padres promotional effort took the form of 24-page flip books, rather than cards. About 3-1/2" x 2-1/2", the multipage black-and-white books offered photographic playing tips when the pictures were rapidly thumbed. When turned over, the books showed Smokey in action preventing forest fires. The 1987 books, McCullers and Santiago, are slightly larger, at about 4-1/2" x 2-3/4".

		NM/M
Complete Set (5):		25.00
Common Player:		4.00
(1)	Dave Dravecky	4.00
(2)	Tim Flannery	4.00
(3)	Tony Gwynn	15.00
(4)	Lance McCullers	4.00
(5)	Benito Santiago	4.00

1988 San Diego Padres Fire Safety

This oversized (3" x 5") set was produced in conjunction with the U.S. Forest Service as a fire prevention campaign promotion. A full-color player photo, framed by a thin white line, fills the card face. The player number, position and Smokey Bear logo appear at lower-right.

Backs are printed in horizontal postcard format, with player info and a Smokey Bear cartoon on the left half of the card back. The set was available for purchase at the Padres Gift Shop. Cards of Candy Sierra and Larry Bowa were not officially released and are quite rare.

		NM/M
Complete Set (33):		45.00
Common Player:		.50
(1)	Shawn Abner	.50
(2)	Roberto Alomar	8.00
(3)	Sandy Alomar	3.00
(4)	Greg Booker	.50
(5)	Larry Bowa	15.00
(6)	Chris Brown	.50
(7)	Mark Davis	.50
(8)	Pat Dobson	.50
(9)	Tim Flannery	.50
(10)	Mark Grant	.50
(11)	Tony Gwynn	15.00
(12)	Andy Hawkins	.50
(13)	Stan Jefferson	.50
(14)	Jimmy Jones	.50
(15)	John Kruk	.50
(16)	Dave Leiper	.50
(17)	Shane Mack	.50
(18)	Carmelo Martinez	.50
(19)	Lance McCullers	.50
(20)	Keith Moreland	.50
(21)	Eric Nolte	.50
(22)	Amos Otis	.50
(23)	Mark Parent	.50
(24)	Randy Ready	.50
(25)	Greg Riddoch	.50
(26)	Benito Santiago	1.00
(27)	Eric Show	.50
(28)	Candy Sierra	10.00
(29)	Denny Sommers	.50
(30)	Garry Templeton	.50
(31)	Dickie Thon	.50
(32)	Ed Whitson	.50
(33)	Marvell Wynne	.50

1989 San Diego Padres Magazine/S.D. Sports Inserts

During the course of the 1989 season, a 24-card set sponsored by a local baseball card dealer was offered to collectors as an insert to the team's official game program, "Padres Magazine." The cards were offered in six panels of four cards. Each panel included a former Padres star and a career highlight. To complete the set, at least six copies of the $1.50 program had to be purchased. The 2-1/2" x 3-1/2" cards have color portrait photos on front. Backs have player identification and a career stats line, along with trivia about the player.

		NM/M
Complete Set (24):		15.00
Common Player:		.50
1	Jack McKeon	.50
2	Sandy Alomar Jr.	.50
3	Tony Gwynn	6.00
4	Willie McCovey	2.00
5	John Kruk	.50
6	Jack Clark	.50
7	Eric Show	.50
8	Rollie Fingers	1.50
9	The Alomars (Sandy Alomar, Roberto Alomar, Sandy Alomar Jr.)	.65
10	Carmelo Martinez	.50
11	Benito Santiago	.50
12	Nate Colbert	.50
13	Mark Davis	.50
14	Roberto Alomar	1.50
15	Tim Flannery	.50
16	Randy Jones	.50
17	Dennis Rasmussen	.50
18	Greg Harris	.50
19	Garry Templeton	.50
20	Steve Garvey	1.50
21	Bruce Hurst	.50
22	Ed Whitson	.50
23	Chris James	.50
24	Gaylord Perry	1.50

1990 San Diego Padres Magazine/Unocal inserts

The first 24 cards in this set, sponsored by area Unocal service stations, were bound in four-card panels into various issues of Padres Magazine, the team's official program. Sheets measure about 5" x 9" and the individual perforated cards are about 2-1/2" x 3-1/2". A coupon attached to the sheets could be redeemed at participating gas stations for cards #25-27. Fronts have color action photos with team logo at top and sponsor logo at lower-right. Black-and-white backs

Ed Whitson
Pitcher 76

have player data, a line of career stats and highlights of his time with the Padres.

		NM/M
Complete Set (27):		15.00
Common Player:		.50
1	Tony Gwynn	5.00
2	Benito Santiago	.50
3	Mike Pagliarulo	.50
4	Dennis Rasmussen	.50
5	Eric Show	.50
6	Darrin Jackson	.50
7	Mark Parent	.50
8	Jerry Coleman, Rick Monday (Announcers)	.50
9	Andy Benes	.50
10	Roberto Alomar	2.50
11	Craig Lefferts	.50
12	Ed Whitson	.50
13	Calvin Schiraldi	.50
14	Garry Templeton	.50
15	Tony Gwynn	5.00
16	Bob Chandler, Ted Leitner (Announcers)	.50
17	Fred Lynn	.50
18	Jack Clark	.50
19	Mike Dunne	.50
20	Mark Grant	.50
21	Benito Santiago	.50
22	Sandy Alomar Sr., Pat Dobson, Amos Otis, Greg Riddoch, Denny Sommers	.50
23	Bruce Hurst	.50
24	Greg Harris	.50
25	Jack McKeon	1.00
26	Bip Roberts	1.00
27	Joe Carter	4.00

1991 San Diego Padres Magazine/Rally's inserts

The first 24 cards of this set were issued as 5" x 8" perforated panels stapled into issues of "Padres Magazine." Due to substitutions dictated by player moves during the season (which also created Short-Printed cards) it would have been necessary to purchase six of the $2 programs to get the 27-card basic set. Cards #25-27 were only available at Rally's restaurants with a coupon attached to the magazine panels. Single cards measure about 2-1/2" x 3-1/2". Fronts have color portrait photos on a diamond background. Player name and position are in an orange banner at bottom. Team and sponsor logos appear in the upper corners on a dark blue background. Backs are in black-and-white with player identification, a line of career stats and highlights of his tenure in San Diego.

		NM/M
Complete Set (30):		27.50
Common Player:		.50
1	Greg Riddoch	.50
2	Dennis Rasmussen	.50
3	Thomas Howard	.50
4	Tom Lampkin	.50
5	Bruce Hurst	.50
6	Darrin Jackson	.50

7	Jerald Clark	.50
8	Shawn Abner	.50
9	Bip Roberts	.50
10	Marty Barrett	.50
11	Jim Vatcher	.50
12	Greg Gross	.50
13	Greg Harris	.50
14	Ed Whitson	.50
15a	Calvin Schiraldi/SP	1.50
15b	Jerald Clark	.50
16	Rich Rodriguez	.50
17	Larry Andersen	.50
18	Andy Benes	.50
19a	Wes Gardner/SP	1.50
19b	Bruce Hurst	.50
20	Paul Faries	.50
21	Craig Lefferts	.50
22	Tony Gwynn	8.00
23a	Jim Presley/SP	1.50
23b	Bip Roberts	.50
24	Fred McGriff	1.00
25	Gaylord Perry	2.00
26	Benito Santiago	1.50
27	Tony Fernandez	1.50

1992 San Diego Padres Fire Safety

The Padres issued a Smokey the Bear postcard set, sponsored by the U.S. Forest Service. Backs contain the usual fire safety messages, but they are also translated into Spanish. Fronts have full-bleed color photos with the player's name and position in orange in a dark blue box at bottom-center. A color Smokey logo appears in one of the upper corners. The unnumbered cards are checklisted here alphabetically.

		NM/M
Complete Set (36):		15.00
Common Player:		.25
(1)	Larry Andersen	.25
(2)	Oscar Azocar	.25
(3)	Andy Benes	.25
(4)	Dan Bilardello	.25
(5)	Jerald Clark	.25
(6)	Pat Clements	.25
(7)	Dave Eiland	.25
(8)	Tony Fernandez	.25
(9)	Tony Gwynn	6.00
(10)	Gene Harris	.25
(11)	Greg Harris	.25
(12)	Jeremy Hernandez	.25
(13)	Bruce Hurst	.25
(14)	Darrin Jackson	.25
(15)	Tom Lampkin	.25
(16)	Bruce Kimm	.25
(17)	Craig Lefferts	.25
(18)	Mike Maddux	.25
(19)	Fred McGriff	.25
(20)	Jose Melendez	.25
(21)	Randy Myers, Craig Shipley	.25
(22)	Gary Pettis	.25
(23)	Rob Picciolo	.25
(24)	Merv Rettenmund	.25
(25)	Greg Riddoch	.25
(26)	Mike Roarke	.25
(27)	Rich Rodriguez	.25
(28)	Benito Santiago	.25
(29)	Frank Seminara	.25
(30)	Gary Sheffield	2.00
(32)	Jim Snyder	.25
(33)	Dave Staton	.25
(34)	Kurt Stillwell	.25
(35)	Tim Teufel	.25
(36)	Kevin Ward	.25

Police

TONY FERNANDEZ INF

Anti-drug messages are featured on this safety set. The 2-1/2" x 3-1/2" cards have color action photos on front with wide blue borders. Backs are horizontally formatted and feature a few player biographical notes, the D.A.R.E. logo and safety message. Unnumbered cards are checklisted here in alphabetical order. Cards #28-30 in this checklist were not distributed with the rest of the set and are scarcer.

		NM/M
Complete Set (30):		12.00
Common Player:		.25
(1)	Oscar Azocar	.25
(2)	Andy Benes	.25
(3)	Jerald Clark	.25
(4)	Jim Deshaies	.25
(5)	Dave Eiland	.25
(6)	Tony Fernandez	.25
(7)	Tony Gwynn	6.00
(8)	Greg W. Harris	.25
(9)	Bruce Hurst	.25
(10)	Darrin Jackson	.25
(11)	Tom Lampkin	.25
(12)	Fred McGriff	.25
(13)	Merv Rettenmund	.25
(14)	Greg Riddoch	.25
(15)	Benito Santiago	.25
(16)	Frank Seminara	.25
(17)	Gary Sheffield	1.00
(18)	Craig Shipley	.25
(19)	Phil Stephenson	.25
(20)	Kurt Stillwell	.25
(21)	Tim Teufel	.25
(22)	Dan Walters	.25
(23)	Kevin Ward	.25
(24)	Padres relievers (Larry Andersen, Mike Maddux, Jose Melendez, Rich Rodriguez, Tim Scott)	.25
(25)	Coaches (Bruce Kimm, Rob Picciolo, Merv Rettenmund, Mike Roarke, Jim Snyder)	.25
(26)	Bluepper (Mascot)	.25
(27)	Jack Murphy Stadium	.25
(28)	Craig Lefferts	1.00
(29)	Rob Picciolo	1.00
(30)	Fred McGriff, Tony Fernandez, Gary Sheffield, Tony Gwynn	2.00

1991 San Francisco Examiner A's

DAVE HENDERSON
EXAMINER'S FINEST

Evidently issued over the course of the season by the Bay Area daily newspaper, these large-format (8-3/8" x 10-7/8") cards are printed on light cardboard pre-punched for a three-ring binder. Color photos on the fronts are surrounded by team colors of green and yellow. The newspaper's logo appears in black at the top. Backs are in black-and-white with a portrait photo of the player, biographical data, major league stats and career highlights. The unnumbered cards are checklisted here alphabetically.

		NM/M
Complete Set (15):		45.00
Common Player:		2.00
(1)	Harold Baines	2.00
(2)	Jose Canseco	5.00
(3)	Dennis Eckersley	5.00
(4)	Mike Gallego	2.00
(5)	Dave Henderson	2.00
(6)	Rickey Henderson	6.00
(7)	Rick Honeycutt	2.00
(8)	Mark McGwire	10.00
(9)	Mike Moore	2.00
(10)	Gene Nelson	2.00
(11)	Eric Show	2.00
(12)	Terry Steinbach	2.00
(13)	Dave Stewart	2.00
(14)	Walt Weiss	2.00
(15)	Bob Welch	2.00

Giants

Evidently issued over the course of the season by the Bay Area daily newspaper, these large-format (8-3/8" x 10-7/8") cards are printed on light cardboard pre-punched for a three-ring binder. Color photos on the fronts are surrounded by team-color borders of orange and black on a gray background. The newspaper's logo appears in black at the top. Backs are in black-and-white with a portrait photo of the player, biographical

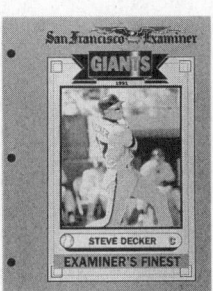

GIANTS
STEVE DECKER
EXAMINER'S FINEST

data, major league stats and career highlights. The unnumbered cards are checklisted here alphabetically.

		NM/M
Complete Set (16):		35.00
Common Player:		2.00
(1)	Kevin Bass	2.00
(2)	Mike Benjamin	2.00
(3)	Bud Black	2.00
(4)	Jeff Brantley	2.00
(5)	John Burkett	2.00
(6)	Will Clark	4.00
(7)	Steve Decker	2.00
(8)	Scott Garrelts	2.00
(9)	Mike LaCoss	2.00
(10)	Willie McGee	2.00
(11)	Kevin Mitchell	2.00
(12)	Dave Righetti	2.00
(13)	Don Robinson	2.00
(14)	Robby Thompson	2.00
(15)	Jose Uribe	2.00
(16)	Matt Williams	4.00

2003 Ron Santo Jersey Retirement Card

SEPTEMBER 23, 2003
Ron Santo
#10
CUBS

This high-gloss, 2-1/2" x 3-1/2" card was a Wrigley Field giveaway on Sept. 23, 2003, on the occasion of the Cubs' retirement of the star third baseman's uniform number. The back has Santo's complete Major League stats.

	NM/M
Ron Santo	6.00

1989 SCD Baseball Card Price Guide Pocket Price Guides

ROYALS

BO JACKSON outfield

Between its premiere issue of April 1988 and the September 1989 issue, SCD's monthly price guide magazine issued a gatefold player poster in each issue. Beginning with the October 1989 issue, panels of five (later six) repli-cards were stapled into the magazine in place of the posters. The 1989 repli-card series depicts contemporary players in the design of the 1964 Topps. Backs are in black-and-white with a photo of the player's rookie card and market advice pertaining to the player.

	NM/M
Complete Set (15):	6.00

Common Player:		.25
1	Mark McGwire	1.50
2	Bo Jackson	.35
3	Ken Griffey	1.50
4	Kevin Mitchell	.25
5	Ryne Sandberg	1.00
6	Will Clark	.25
7	Gregg Jefferies	.25
8	Gary Sheffield	.50
9	Fred McGriff	.25
10	Don Mattingly	1.00
11	Jim Abbott	.25
12	Mitch Williams	.25
13	Glenn Davis	.25
14	Ruben Sierra	.25
15	Robin Yount	.75

1990 SCD Baseball Card Price Guide Pocket Price Guides

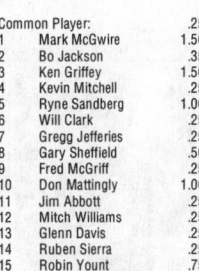

For its first full year of inserting repli-cards in each issue, SCD Baseball Card Price Guide Monthly magazine rendered the game's stars and hot rookies in the style of 1957 Topps cards. Black, white and red backs have a photo of one of the player's other cards, personal data, current values of selected cards and market advice. Cards were printed on panels of five stapled into each month's issue.

		NM/M
Complete Set (60):		20.00
Common Player:		.25
1	Darryl Strawberry	.25
2	Wade Boggs	.75
3	Roger Clemens	1.00
4	Paul Molitor	.60
5	Craig Biggio	.25
6	Ruben Sierra	.25
7	Sandy Alomar Jr.	.25
8	Rickey Henderson	.60
9	Mark Langston	.25
10	Dwight Evans	.25
11	Ben McDonald	.25
12	Bo Jackson	.35
13	Don Mattingly	1.00
14	Todd Zeile	.25
15	Mike Greenwell	.25
16	Eric Anthony	.25
17	Dennis Eckersley	.50
18	Greg Vaughn	.25
19	Kevin Mitchell	.25
20	Ryne Sandberg	.75
21	Will Clark	.25
22	Robin Yount	.60
23	Kirby Puckett	.75
24	Andy Benes	.25
25	Wally Joyner	.25
26	Ozzie Smith	.75
27	John Olerud	.25
28	Devon White	.25
29	Alan Trammell	.25
30	Bobby Bonilla	.25
31	Jose Canseco	.40
32	Fred McGriff	.25
33	Mark Grace	.25
34	Ricky Jordan	.25
35	George Brett	1.00
36	Eric Davis	.25
37	Tony Gwynn	.75
38	Cal Ripken Jr.	2.00
39	Bret Saberhagen	.25
40	Howard Johnson	.25
41	Jerome Walton	.25
42	Mark McGwire	1.50
43	A.L. East Power Hitters (Mike Greenwell, Don Mattingly)	.50
44	Ken Griffey Jr.	1.25
45	Texas' Top Twirlers (Nolan Ryan, Mike Scott)	1.00
46	Barry Larkin	.25
47	Delino DeShields	.25
48	Roberto Alomar	.35
49	Frank Viola	.25
50	Kelly Gruber	.25
51	Michael Jordan	7.50
52	Glenn Davis	.25
53	Marquis Grissom	.25
54	Joe Carter	.25
55	Gregg Jefferies	.25
56	Gary Sheffield	.25
57	Cecil Fielder	.25
58	Matt Williams	.25
59	Ramon Martinez	.25
60	Len Dykstra	.25

1991 SCD Baseball Card Price Guide Pocket Price Guides

MARINERS
ken griffey jr. • outfield

In its third year of including insert cards with each issue, the Price Guide chose the classic 1971 Topps design to showcase the game's top stars and hot rookies. The first five cards have red backgrounds on their backs, the rest are deep green. Backs have a black-and-white photo of one of the player's other cards, along with selected card value data. Also presented are some personal data and the editors' thoughts on each player's future market value.

		NM/M
Complete Set (60):		15.00
Common Player:		.25
1	Ryne Sandberg	.75
2	Bobby Thigpen	.25
3	Rickey Henderson	.65
4	Dwight Gooden	.25
5	Kevin Maas	.25
6	Ron Gant	.25
7	Frank Thomas	.65
8	Doug Drabek	.25
9	Bobby Bonilla	.25
10	Sandy Alomar Jr.	.25
11	Bob Welch	.25
12	Joe Carter	.25
13	Cecil Fielder	.25
14	Dave Justice	.25
15	Barry Bonds	2.00
16	Barry Larkin	.25
17	Ramon Martinez	.25
18	Ben McDonald	.25
19	Roger Clemens	1.00
20	Jose Canseco	.40
21	Will Clark	.25
22	Jeff Conine	.25
23	Chris Sabo	.25
24	Alan Trammell	.25
25	Howard Johnson	.25
26	Dale Murphy	.30
27	Gregg Jefferies	.25
28	Bo Jackson	.30
29	Craig Biggio	.25
30	Delino DeShields	.25
31	Rafael Palmeiro	.50
32	Robin Yount	.65
33	Mark McGwire	1.50
34	Kevin Mitchell	.25
35	George Brett	1.00
36	Tim Wallach	.25
37	Andre Dawson	.30
38	Kirby Puckett	.75
39	Matt Williams	.25
40	Wade Boggs	.75
41	Dave Winfield	.65
42	Don Mattingly	1.00
43	Carlton Fisk	.65
44	Dave Stewart	.25
45	Ken Griffey Jr.	1.25
46	Ruben Sierra	.25
47	George Bell	.25
48	Cal Ripken	2.00
49	Ellis Burks	.25
50	Roberto Alomar	.30
51	Tim Raines	.25
52	Mike Greenwell	.25
53	Benito Santiago	.25
54	Tom Glavine	.35
55	Scott Erickson	.25
56	Chuck Finley	.25
57	Julio Franco	.25
58	Paul Molitor	.65
59	Todd Van Poppel	.25
60	Mo Vaughn	.25

1992 SCD BB Card Price Guide/ Sports Card PG

New collector focus on other team sports resulted in SCD's Baseball Card Price Guide Monthly changing its name to Sports Card Price Guide Monthly with its May 1992 issue. The title change was also reflected in the annual series of repli-cards stapled into each issue. For the first time football, basketball and hockey players joined the base-bAll-Stars. That change was effective with card #19. The '92 series utilized the design of Topps' 1974 baseball cards. Backs are printed in black, white and green and, as in previous years, include a photo of one of the player's cards along with selective current values and a market forecast. Only the set's baseball players are listed here.

		NM/M
Complete (Baseball) Set (56):		20.00
Common Player:		.25
1	Will Clark	.25
2	Albert Belle	.25
3	Luis Gonzalez	.25
4	Ramon Martinez	.25
5	Frank Thomas	.65
6	Travis Fryman	.25
7	Carlton Fisk	.65
8	Bo Jackson	.35
9	Chuck Knoblauch	.25
10	Ron Gant	.25
11	Jose Canseco	.45
12	Roger Clemens	1.00
13	Darren Lewis	.25
14	Kirby Puckett	.75
15	Tom Glavine	.35
16	Royce Clayton	.25
18	Ozzie Smith	.75
20	Robin Ventura	.25
21	Derek Bell	.25
23	Ryne Sandberg	.75
25	Andy Van Slyke	.25
26	Jim Abbott	.25
27	Ken Griffey Jr.	1.25
30	Jeff Bagwell	.65
32	Dwight Gooden	.25
33	Ruben Sierra	.25
35	David Justice	.25
36	Wade Boggs	.75
38	Barry Larkin	.25
39	Felix Jose	.25
40	Howard Johnson	.25
42	Fred McGriff	.25
44	Todd Van Poppel	.25
46	Brien Taylor	.25
48	Cal Ripken Jr.	2.00
50	Dave Winfield	.65
52	Juan Gonzalez	.40
53	Reggie Sanders	.25
57	Gary Sheffield	.45
58	Roberto Alomar	.40
59	Barry Bonds	2.00
60	Tom Glavine	.35
62	Kenny Lofton	.25
63	Joe Carter	.25
66	Paul Molitor	.65
67	Phil Plantier	.25
69	Mark McGwire	1.50
70	Nolan Ryan	2.00
72	Darryl Strawberry	.25
73	Pat Listach	.25
74	Dennis Eckersley	.50
75	Bobby Bonilla	.25
78	Delino DeShields	.25
80	Doug Drabek	.25
81	Deion Sanders	.25
84	Darren Daulton	.25

1993 Sports Card Pocket Price Guide

The final year of production of an annual repli-card insert set for the SCD price guide magazine combined stars and hot rookies from all four major team sports. Cards were produced in the style of Topps' 1973 football issue, with varying colored striped pennants down the left side of the front. Backs are printed in black, white and green (#1-8) and black, white and red (#9-104), and include a cartoon trivia question along with price guide and player data. The repli-cards were printed on sheets of eight stapled

into the magazine's monthly issues. Only the baseball players are listed here.

		NM/M
Complete (Baseball) Set (54):		20.00
Common Player:		.25
1	Tyler Green	.25
3	Ozzie Smith	.75
5	Fred McGriff	.25
7	Marquis Grissom	.25
13	John Smoltz	.25
16	Ruben Sierra	.25
19	Roberto Alomar	.40
20	Gary Sheffield	.40
23	Carlos Baerga	.25
24	Robin Ventura	.25
25	Nigel Wilson	.25
26	David Nied	.25
27	Cal Ripken Jr.	2.00
28	Albert Belle	.25
34	Larry Walker	.25
37	Eric Karros	.25
38	Dwight Gooden	.25
39	Nolan Ryan	2.00
40	Juan Gonzalez	.45
41	Robin Yount	.65
44	Darryl Strawberry	.25
45	George Brett	1.00
46	Ray Lankford	.25
47	Kirby Puckett	.75
48	David Justice	.25
49	Travis Fryman	.25
50	Eddie Murray	.65
51	Tony Gwynn	.75
52	Jack McDowell	.25
57	Ryne Sandberg	.75
58	Deion Sanders	.25
61	Frank Thomas	.65
62	Carlton Fisk	.65
65	Tim Salmon	.25
66	Jeff Conine	.25
67	Benito Santiago	.25
68	Mike Piazza	1.50
70	Andres Galarraga	.25
71	Gregg Jefferies	.25
72	Joe Carter	.25
77	Rickey Henderson	.65
80	Barry Larkin	.25
82	Juan Gonzalez	.45
83	Gary Sheffield	.40
84	Will Clark	.25
89	Mark Grace	.25
90	Cliff Floyd	.25
91	Bobby Bonds Jr.	.25
92	Barry Bonds	2.00
94	Matt Williams	.25
97	Paul Molitor	.65
98	Ken Griffey Jr.	1.50
99	Steve Avery	.25
100	Kirby Puckett	.65

1989 Schafer's Bakery Super Stars Discs

(See 1989 Holsum for checklist and value information. Distributed in Michigan.)

1987 Schnucks St. Louis Cardinals

Sponsored by Schnucks food stores, and distributed at more than 50 locations around St. Louis, the company is not mentioned anywhere on these photos. The set of 6" x 9" photocards depicts the players without caps or other visible uniform logos in color photos against a plain blue backdrop. A facsimile autograph appears in the lower-left corner, with a Players Association logo at upper-

left. Backs are blank. The unnumbered cards are checklisted here alphabetically. A Schnucks spokesman said about 50,000 of each picture were produced.

		NM/M
Complete Set (16):		14.00
Common Player:		.50
(1)	Jack Clark	.50
(2)	Vince Coleman	.75
(3)	Danny Cox	.50
(4)	Curt Ford	.50
(5)	Bob Forsch	.50
(6)	Tom Herr	.50
(7)	Whitey Herzog	.50
(8)	Ricky Horton	.50
(9)	Greg Mathews	.50
(10)	Willie McGee	.75
(11)	Jose Oquendo	.50
(12)	Tony Pena	.50
(13)	Terry Pendleton	.75
(14)	Ozzie Smith	6.00
(15)	John Tudor	.50
(16)	Todd Worrell	.50

1996 Schwebel's Stars Discs

Distributed in loaves of bread in the Youngstown, Ohio, area, the players in this disc set lean heavily towards Cleveland Indians. The 2-3/4" diameter discs were inserted into a special pocket in the bread wrapper to keep them from contact with the bread. Fronts have a purple-to-red graduated color scheme around the border, with a player photo at center. Uniform logos have been removed from the photos because the discs are licensed only by the Players Union; they are a product of Mike Schechter Assoc. Backs are printed in purple with 1995 and career stats along with appropriate logos. A die-cut poster into which the discs could be inserted for display was also available.

		NM/M
Complete Set (20):		20.00
Common Player:		1.00
1	Jim Thome	1.50
2	Orel Hershiser	1.00
3	Greg Maddux	2.50
4	Charles Nagy	1.00
5	Omar Vizquel	1.00
6	Manny Ramirez	2.00
7	Dennis Martinez	1.00
8	Eddie Murray	2.00
9	Albert Belle	1.00
10	Fred McGriff	1.00
11	Jack McDowell	1.00
12	Kenny Lofton	1.00
13	Cal Ripken Jr.	4.00
14	Jose Mesa	1.00
15	Randy Johnson	2.00
16	Ken Griffey Jr.	3.00
17	Carlos Baerga	1.00
18	Frank Thomas	2.00
19	Sandy Alomar Jr.	1.00
20	Barry Bonds	4.00

1988 Score Promo Cards

While these Score promotional sample cards carry a 1988 copyright date on back, they were actually released to hobby dealers late in 1987. They can be easily differentiated from regular-issue 1988 cards by the use of zeros in the stats lines on

back for 1987 and career figures. Most of the promos are otherwise identical to the issued versions of the same players. These were among the first promo cards to be widely distributed within the hobby.

		NM/M
Complete Set (6):		20.00
Common Player:		4.00
30	Mark Langston	4.00
48	Tony Pena	4.00
71	Keith Moreland	4.00
72	Barry Larkin	4.00
121	Dennis Boyd	4.00
149	Denny Walling	4.00

1988 Score Proofs

The first six cards in the eventual 1988 Score debut issue can also be found in proof versions intended to test various inks, finishes, etc. These cards are differentiated from regular issues (and promo cards) by the use of zeros in place of actual stats for 1987 and career on the backs.

		NM/M
Complete Set (6):		150.00
Common Player:		15.00
1	Don Mattingly	45.00
2	Wade Boggs	35.00
3	Tim Raines	15.00
4	Andre Dawson	25.00
5	Mark McGwire	60.00
6	Kevin Seitzer	15.00

1988 Score

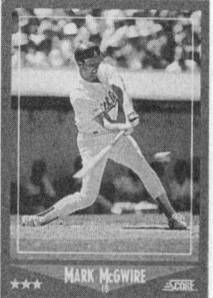

A fifth member joined the group of nationally distributed baseball cards in 1988. Titled "Score," the cards are characterized by extremely sharp color photography and printing. Card backs are full-color also and carry a player portrait along with a brief biography, player data and statistics. The 660 cards in the set are standard 2-1/2" x 3-1/2" format. The fronts come with one of six different border colors which are equally divided at 110 cards per color. The Score set was produced by

Major League Marketing, the same company that marketed the "triple-action" Sportflics card sets.

		NM/M
Unopened Fact. Set (660):		9.00
Complete Set (660):		6.00
Common Player:		.05
Pack:		.35
Wax Box:		9.00
Rack Pack (54):		.75
Rack Box (24):		12.00
1	Don Mattingly	.65
2	Wade Boggs	.50
3	Tim Raines	.20
4	Andre Dawson	.25
5	Mark McGwire	.75
6	Kevin Seitzer	.05
7	Wally Joyner	.05
8	Jesse Barfield	.05
9	Pedro Guerrero	.05
10	Eric Davis	.05
11	George Brett	.65
12	Ozzie Smith	.50
13	Rickey Henderson	.25
14	Jim Rice	.15
15	Matt Nokes RC	.05
16	Mike Schmidt	.65
17	Dave Parker	.05
18	Eddie Murray	.40
19	Andres Galarraga	.05
20	Tony Fernandez	.05
21	Kevin McReynolds	.05
22	B.J. Surhoff	.05
23	Pat Tabler	.05
24	Kirby Puckett	.50
25	Benny Santiago	.05
26	Ryne Sandberg	.50
27	Kelly Downs	.05
28	Jose Cruz	.05
29	Pete O'Brien	.05
30	Mark Langston	.05
31	Lee Smith	.05
32	Juan Samuel	.05
33	Kevin Bass	.05
34	R.J. Reynolds	.05
35	Steve Sax	.05
36	John Kruk	.05
37	Alan Trammell	.05
38	Chris Bosio	.05
39	Brook Jacoby	.05
40	Willie McGee	.05
41	Dave Magadan	.05
42	Fred Lynn	.05
43	Kent Hrbek	.05
44	Brian Downing	.05
45	Jose Canseco	.30
46	Jim Presley	.05
47	Mike Stanley	.05
48	Tony Pena	.05
49	David Cone	.05
50	Rick Sutcliffe	.05
51	Doug Drabek	.05
52	Bill Doran	.05
53	Mike Scioscia	.05
54	Candy Maldonado	.05
55	Dave Winfield	.40
56	Lou Whitaker	.05
57	Tom Henke	.05
58	Ken Gerhart	.05
59	Glenn Braggs	.05
60	Julio Franco	.05
61	Charlie Leibrandt	.05
62	Gary Gaetti	.05
63	Bob Boone	.05
64	Luis Polonia RC	.05
65	Dwight Evans	.05
66	Phil Bradley	.05
67	Mike Boddicker	.05
68	Vince Coleman	.05
69	Howard Johnson	.05
70	Tim Wallach	.05
71	Keith Moreland	.05
72	Barry Larkin	.05
73	Alan Ashby	.05
74	Rick Rhoden	.05
75	Darrell Evans	.05
76	Dave Stieb	.05
77	Dan Plesac	.05
78	Will Clark	.05
79	Frank White	.05
80	Joe Carter	.05
81	Mike Witt	.05
82	Terry Steinbach	.05
83	Alvin Davis	.05
84	Tom Herr	.05
85	Vance Law	.05
86	Kal Daniels	.05
87	Rick Honeycutt	.05
88	Alfredo Griffin	.05
89	Bret Saberhagen	.05
90	Bert Blyleven	.05
91	Jeff Reardon	.05
92	Cory Snyder	.05
93	Greg Walker	.05
94	Joe Magrane RC	.10
95	Rob Deer	.05
96	Ray Knight	.05
97	Casey Candaele	.05
98	John Cerutti	.05
99	Buddy Bell	.05
100	Jack Clark	.05
101	Eric Bell	.05
102	Willie Wilson	.05
103	Dave Schmidt	.05
104	Dennis Eckersley	.35
105	Don Sutton	.35
106	Danny Tartabull	.05
107	Fred McGriff	.05
108	Les Straker RC	.05
109	Lloyd Moseby	.05
110	Roger Clemens	.65
111	Glenn Hubbard	.05
112	Ken Williams RC	.05
113	Ruben Sierra	.05
114	Stan Jefferson	.05
115	Milt Thompson	.05
116	Bobby Bonilla	.05
117	Wayne Tolleson	.05
118	Matt Williams	.05
119	Chet Lemon	.05
120	Dale Sveum	.05
121	Dennis Boyd	.05
122	Brett Butler	.05
123	Terry Kennedy	.05
124	Jack Howell	.05
125	Curt Young	.05
126a	Dale Valle (First name incorrect.)	.25
126b	Dave Valle (Correct spelling.)	.05
127	Curt Wilkerson	.05
128	Tim Teufel	.05
129	Ozzie Virgil	.05
130	Brian Fisher	.05
131	Lance Parrish	.05
132	Tom Browning	.05
133a	Larry Anderson (Incorrect spelling.)	.25
133b	Larry Andersen (Correct spelling.)	.05
134a	Bob Brenley (Incorrect spelling.)	.25
134b	Bob Brenly (Correct spelling.)	.05
135	Mike Marshall	.05
136	Gerald Perry	.05
137	Bobby Meacham	.05
138	Larry Herndon	.05
139	Fred Manrique RC	.05
140	Charlie Hough	.05
141	Ron Darling	.05
142	Herm Winningham	.05
143	Mike Diaz	.05
144	Mike Jackson RC	.05
145	Denny Walling	.05
146	Rob Thompson	.05
147	Franklin Stubbs	.05
148	Albert Hall	.05
149	Bobby Witt	.05
150	Lance McCullers	.05
151	Scott Bradley	.05
152	Mark McLemore	.05
153	Tim Laudner	.05
154	Greg Swindell	.05
155	Marty Barrett	.05
156	Mike Heath	.05
157	Gary Ward	.05
158a	Lee Mazilli (Incorrect spelling.)	.25
158b	Lee Mazzilli (Correct spelling.)	.05
159	Tom Foley	.05
160	Robin Yount	.40
161	Steve Bedrosian	.05
162	Bob Walk	.05
163	Nick Esasky	.05
164	Ken Caminiti RC	.15
165	Jose Uribe	.05
166	Dave Anderson	.05
167	Ed Whitson	.05
168	Ernie Whitt	.05
169	Cecil Cooper	.05
170	Mike Pagliarulo	.05
171	Pat Sheridan	.05
172	Chris Bando	.05
173	Lee Lacy	.05
174	Steve Lombardozzi	.05
175	Mike Greenwell	.05
176	Greg Minton	.05
177	Moose Haas	.05
178	Mike Kingery	.05
179	Greg Harris	.05
180	Bo Jackson	.10
181	Carmelo Martinez	.05
182	Alex Trevino	.05
183	Ron Oester	.05
184	Danny Darwin	.05
185	Mike Krukow	.05
186	Rafael Palmeiro	.40
187	Tim Burke	.05
188	Roger McDowell	.05
189	Garry Templeton	.05
190	Terry Pendleton	.05
191	Larry Parrish	.05
192	Rey Quinones	.05
193	Joaquin Andujar	.05
194	Tom Brunansky	.05
195	Donnie Moore	.05
196	Dan Pasqua	.05
197	Jim Gantner	.05
198	Mark Eichhorn	.05
199	John Grubb	.05
200	Bill Ripken RC	.05
201	Sam Horn RC	.05
202	Todd Worrell	.05
203	Terry Leach	.05
204	Garth Iorg	.05
205	Brian Dayett	.05
206	Bo Diaz	.05
207	Craig Reynolds	.05
208	Brian Holton	.05
209	Marvelle Wynne (Marvell)	.05
210	Dave Concepcion	.05
211	Mike Davis	.05
212	Devon White	.05

No.	Player	Price
213	Mickey Brantley	.05
214	Greg Gagne	.05
215	Oddibe McDowell	.05
216	Jimmy Key	.05
217	Dave Bergman	.05
218	Calvin Schiraldi	.05
219	Larry Sheets	.05
220	Mike Easler	.05
221	Kurt Stillwell	.05
222	Chuck Jackson RC	.05
223	Dave Martinez	.05
224	Tim Leary	.05
225	Steve Garvey	.20
226	Greg Mathews	.05
227	Doug Sisk	.05
228	Dave Henderson	.05
229	Jimmy Dwyer	.05
230	Larry Owen	.05
231	Andre Thornton	.05
232	Mark Salas	.05
233	Tom Brookens	.05
234	Greg Brock	.05
235	Rance Mulliniks	.05
236	Bob Brower	.05
237	Joe Niekro	.05
238	Scott Bankhead	.05
239	Doug DeCinces	.05
240	Tommy John	.05
241	Rich Gedman	.05
242	Ted Power	.05
243	Dave Meads RC	.05
244	Jim Sundberg	.05
245	Ken Oberkfell	.05
246	Jimmy Jones	.05
247	Ken Landreaux	.05
248	Jose Oquendo	.05
249	John Mitchell RC	.05
250	Don Baylor	.05
251	Scott Fletcher	.05
252	Al Newman	.05
253	Carney Lansford	.05
254	Johnny Ray	.05
255	Gary Pettis	.05
256	Ken Phelps	.05
257	Rick Leach	.05
258	Tim Stoddard	.05
259	Ed Romero	.05
260	Sid Bream	.05
261a	Tom Neidenfuer (Incorrect spelling.)	.25
261b	Tom Neidenfuer (Correct spelling.)	.05
262	Rick Dempsey	.05
263	Lonnie Smith	.05
264	Bob Forsch	.05
265	Barry Bonds	1.00
266	Willie Randolph	.05
267	Mike Ramsey	.05
268	Don Slaught	.05
269	Mickey Tettleton	.05
270	Jerry Reuss	.05
271	Marc Sullivan	.05
272	Jim Morrison	.05
273	Steve Balboni	.05
274	Dick Schofield	.05
275	John Tudor	.05
276	Gene Larkin RC	.05
277	Harold Reynolds	.05
278	Jerry Browne	.05
279	Willie Upshaw	.05
280	Ted Higuera	.05
281	Terry McGriff	.05
282	Terry Puhl	.05
283	Mark Wasinger RC	.05
284	Luis Salazar	.05
285	Ted Simmons	.05
286	John Shelby	.05
287	John Smiley RC	.05
288	Curt Ford	.05
289	Steve Crawford	.05
290	Dan Quisenberry	.05
291	Alan Wiggins	.05
292	Randy Bush	.05
293	John Candelaria	.05
294	Tony Phillips	.05
295	Mike Morgan	.05
296	Bill Wegman	.05
297a	Terry Franconia (Incorrect spelling.)	.25
297b	Terry Francona (Correct spelling.)	.05
298	Mickey Hatcher	.05
299	Andres Thomas	.05
300	Bob Stanley	.05
301	Alfredo Pedrique RC	.05
302	Jim Lindeman	.05
303	Wally Backman	.05
304	Paul O'Neill	.05
305	Hubie Brooks	.05
306	Steve Buechele	.05
307	Bobby Thigpen	.05
308	George Hendrick	.05
309	John Moses	.05
310	Ron Guidry	.05
311	Bill Schroeder	.05
312	Jose Nunez RC	.05
313	Bud Black	.05
314	Joe Sambito	.05
315	Scott McGregor	.05
316	Rafael Santana	.05
317	Frank Williams	.05
318	Mike Fitzgerald	.05
319	Rick Mahler	.05
320	Jim Gott	.05
321	Mariano Duncan	.05
322	Jose Guzman	.05
323	Lee Guetterman	.05
324	Dan Gladden	.05

No.	Player	Price
325	Gary Carter	.40
326	Tracy Jones	.05
327	Floyd Youmans	.05
328	Bill Dawley	.05
329	Paul Noce RC	.05
330	Angel Salazar	.05
331	Goose Gossage	.10
332	George Frazier	.05
333	Ruppert Jones	.05
334	Billy Jo Robidoux	.05
335	Mike Scott	.05
336	Randy Myers	.05
337	Bob Sebra	.05
338	Eric Show	.05
339	Mitch Williams	.05
340	Paul Molitor	.40
341	Gus Polidor	.05
342	Steve Trout	.05
343	Jerry Don Gleaton	.05
344	Bob Knepper	.05
345	Mitch Webster	.05
346	John Morris	.05
347	Andy Hawkins	.05
348	Dave Leiper	.05
349	Ernest Riles	.05
350	Dwight Gooden	.05
351	Dave Righetti	.05
352	Pat Dodson	.05
353	John Habyan	.05
354	Jim Deshaies	.05
355	Butch Wynegar	.05
356	Bryn Smith	.05
357	Matt Young	.05
358	Tom Pagnozzi RC	.05
359	Floyd Rayford	.05
360	Darryl Strawberry	.05
361	Sal Butera	.05
362	Domingo Ramos	.05
363	Chris Brown	.05
364	Jose Gonzalez	.05
365	Dave Smith	.05
366	Andy McGaffigan	.05
367	Stan Javier	.05
368	Henry Cotto	.05
369	Mike Birkbeck	.05
370	Len Dykstra	.05
371	Dave Collins	.05
372	Spike Owen	.05
373	Geno Petralli	.05
374	Ron Karkovice	.05
375	Shane Rawley	.05
376	DeWayne Buice RC	.05
377	Bill Pecota RC	.05
378	Leon Durham	.05
379	Ed Olwine	.05
380	Bruce Hurst	.05
381	Bob McClure	.05
382	Mark Thurmond	.05
383	Buddy Biancalana	.05
384	Tim Conroy	.05
385	Tony Gwynn	.50
386	Greg Gross	.05
387	Barry Lyons RC	.05
388	Mike Felder	.05
389	Pat Clements	.05
390	Ken Griffey	.05
391	Mark Davis	.05
392	Jose Rijo	.05
393	Mike Young	.05
394	Willie Fraser	.05
395	Dion James	.05
396	Steve Shields RC	.05
397	Randy St. Claire	.05
398	Danny Jackson	.05
399	Cecil Fielder	.05
400	Keith Hernandez	.05
401	Don Carman	.05
402	Chuck Crim RC	.05
403	Rob Woodward	.05
404	Junior Ortiz	.05
405	Glenn Wilson	.05
406	Ken Howell	.05
407	Jeff Kunkel	.05
408	Jeff Reed	.05
409	Chris James	.05
410	Zane Smith	.05
411	Ken Dixon	.05
412	Ricky Horton	.05
413	Frank DiPino	.05
414	Shane Mack RC	.05
415	Danny Cox	.05
416	Andy Van Slyke	.05
417	Danny Heep	.05
418	John Cangelosi	.05
419a	John Christiansen (Incorrect spelling.)	.25
419b	John Christensen (Correct spelling.)	.05
420	Joey Cora RC	.05
421	Mike LaValliere	.05
422	Kelly Gruber	.05
423	Bruce Benedict	.05
424	Len Matuszek	.05
425	Kent Tekulve	.05
426	Rafael Ramirez	.05
427	Mike Flanagan	.05
428	Mike Gallego	.05
429	Juan Castillo	.05
430	Neal Heaton	.05
431	Phil Garner	.05
432	Mike Dunne RC	.05
433	Wallace Johnson	.05
434	Jack O'Connor	.05
435	Steve Jeltz	.05
436	Donnell Nixon RC	.05
437	Jack Lazorko	.05
438	Keith Comstock RC	.05
439	Jeff Robinson	.05

No.	Player	Price
440	Graig Nettles	.05
441	Mel Hall	.05
442	Gerald Young RC	.05
443	Gary Redus	.05
444	Charlie Moore	.05
445	Bill Madlock	.05
446	Mark Clear	.05
447	Greg Booker	.05
448	Rich Schu	.05
449	Ron Kittle	.05
450	Dale Murphy	.25
451	Bob Dernier	.05
452	Dale Mohorcic	.05
453	Rafael Belliard	.05
454	Charlie Puleo	.05
455	Dwayne Murphy	.05
456	Jim Eisenreich	.05
457	David Palmer	.05
458	Dave Stewart	.05
459	Pascual Perez	.05
460	Glenn Davis	.05
461	Dan Petry	.05
462	Jim Winn	.05
463	Darrell Miller	.05
464	Mike Moore	.05
465	Mike LaCoss	.05
466	Steve Farr	.05
467	Jerry Mumphrey	.05
468	Kevin Gross	.05
469	Bruce Bochy	.05
470	Orel Hershiser	.05
471	Eric King	.05
472	Ellis Burks RC	.25
473	Darren Daulton	.05
474	Mookie Wilson	.05
475	Frank Viola	.05
476	Ron Robinson	.05
477	Bob Melvin	.05
478	Jeff Musselman	.05
479	Charlie Kerfeld	.05
480	Richard Dotson	.05
481	Kevin Mitchell	.05
482	Gary Roenicke	.05
483	Tim Flannery	.05
484	Rich Yett	.05
485	Pete Incaviglia	.05
486	Rick Cerone	.05
487	Tony Armas	.05
488	Jerry Reed	.05
489	Davey Lopes	.05
490	Frank Tanana	.05
491	Mike Loynd	.05
492	Bruce Ruffin	.05
493	Chris Speier	.05
494	Tom Hume	.05
495	Jesse Orosco	.05
496	Robby Wine, Jr. RC	.05
497	Jeff Montgomery RC	.15
498	Jeff Dedmon	.05
499	Luis Aguayo	.05
500	Reggie Jackson (1968-75)	.15
501	Reggie Jackson (1976)	.15
502	Reggie Jackson (1977-81)	.15
503	Reggie Jackson (1982-86)	.15
504	Reggie Jackson (1987)	.15
505	Billy Hatcher	.05
506	Ed Lynch	.05
507	Willie Hernandez	.05
508	Jose DeLeon	.05
509	Joel Youngblood	.05
510	Bob Welch	.05
511	Steve Ontiveros	.05
512	Randy Ready	.05
513	Juan Nieves	.05
514	Jeff Russell	.05
515	Von Hayes	.05
516	Mark Gubicza	.05
517	Ken Dayley	.05
518	Don Aase	.05
519	Rick Reuschel	.05
520	Mike Henneman RC	.10
521	Rick Aguilera	.05
522	Jay Howell	.05
523	Ed Correa	.05
524	Manny Trillo	.05
525	Kirk Gibson	.05
526	Wally Ritchie RC	.05
527	Al Nipper	.05
528	Atlee Hammaker	.05
529	Shawon Dunston	.05
530	Jim Clancy	.05
531	Tom Paciorek	.05
532	Joel Skinner	.05
533	Scott Garrelts	.05
534	Tom O'Malley	.05
535	John Franco	.05
536	Paul Kilgus RC	.05
537	Darrell Porter	.05
538	Walt Terrell	.05
539	Bill Long RC	.05
540	George Bell	.05
541	Jeff Sellers	.05
542	Joe Boever RC	.05
543	Steve Howe	.05
544	Scott Sanderson	.05
545	Jack Morris	.05
546	Todd Benzinger RC	.05
547	Steve Henderson	.05
548	Eddie Milner	.05
549	Jeff Robinson RC	.05
550	Cal Ripken, Jr.	1.00
551	Jody Davis	.05
552	Kirk McCaskill	.05
553	Craig Lefferts	.05
554	Darnell Coles	.05
555	Phil Niekro	.35
556	Mike Aldrete	.05
557	Pat Perry	.05

No.	Player	Price
558	Juan Agosto	.05
559	Rob Murphy	.05
560	Dennis Rasmussen	.05
561	Manny Lee	.05
562	Jeff Blauser RC	.10
563	Bob Ojeda	.05
564	Dave Dravecky	.05
565	Gene Garber	.05
566	Ron Roenicke	.05
567	Tommy Hinzo RC	.05
568	Eric Nolte RC	.05
569	Ed Hearn	.05
570	Mark Davidson RC	.05
571	Jim Walewander RC	.05
572	Donnie Hill	.05
573	Jamie Moyer	.05
574	Ken Schrom	.05
575	Nolan Ryan	1.00
576	Jim Acker	.05
577	Jamie Quirk	.05
578	Jay Aldrich RC	.05
579	Claudell Washington	.05
580	Jeff Leonard	.05
581	Carmen Castillo	.05
582	Daryl Boston	.05
583	Jeff DeWillis RC	.05
584	John Marzano RC	.05
585	Bill Gullickson	.05
586	Andy Allanson	.05
587	Lee Tunnell	.05
588	Gene Nelson	.05
589	Dave LaPoint	.05
590	Harold Baines	.05
591	Bill Buckner	.05
592	Carlton Fisk	.40
593	Rick Manning	.05
594	Doug Jones RC	.10
595	Tom Candiotti	.05
596	Steve Lake	.05
597	Jose Lind RC	.05
598	Ross Jones RC	.05
599	Gary Matthews	.05
600	Fernando Valenzuela	.05
601	Dennis Martinez	.05
602	Les Lancaster RC	.05
603	Ozzie Guillen	.05
604	Tony Bernazard	.05
605	Chili Davis	.05
606	Roy Smalley	.05
607	Ivan Calderon	.05
608	Jay Tibbs	.05
609	Guy Hoffman	.05
610	Doyle Alexander	.05
611	Mike Bielecki	.05
612	Shawn Hillegas RC	.05
613	Keith Atherton	.05
614	Eric Plunk	.05
615	Sid Fernandez	.05
616	Dennis Lamp	.05
617	Dave Engle	.05
618	Harry Spilman	.05
619	Don Robinson	.05
620	John Farrell RC	.05
621	Nelson Liriano RC	.05
622	Floyd Bannister	.05
623	Randy Milligan RC	.05
624	Kevin Elster RC	.10
625	Jody Reed RC	.05
626	Shawn Abner RC	.05
627	Kirt Manwaring RC	.10
628	Pete Stanicek RC	.05
629	Rob Ducey RC	.05
630	Steve Kiefer	.05
631	Gary Thurman RC	.05
632	Darrel Akerfelds RC	.05
633	Dave Clark	.05
634	Roberto Kelly RC	.05
635	Keith Hughes RC	.05
636	John Davis RC	.05
637	Mike Devereaux RC	.10
638	Tom Glavine RC	1.00
639	Keith Miller RC	.05
640	Chris Gwynn RC	.05
641	Tim Crews RC	.05
642	Mackey Sasser RC	.05
643	Vicente Palacios RC	.05
644	Kevin Romine	.05
645	Gregg Jefferies RC	.25
646	Jeff Treadway RC	.05
647	Ron Gant RC	.25
648	Rookie Sluggers (Mark McGwire, Matt Nokes)	.35
649	Speed and Power (Tim Raines, Eric Davis)	.05
650	Game Breakers (Jack Clark, Don Mattingly)	.25
651	Super Shortstops (Tony Fernandez, Cal Ripken, Jr., Alan Trammell)	.05
652	Vince Coleman (Highlight)	.05
653	Kirby Puckett (Highlight)	.25
654	Benito Santiago (Highlight)	.05
655	Juan Nieves (Highlight)	.05
656	Steve Bedrosian (Highlight)	.05
657	Mike Schmidt (Highlight)	.30
658	Don Mattingly (Highlight)	.30
659	Mark McGwire (Highlight)	.35
660	Paul Molitor (Highlight)	.20

Glossy

With production of a reported 5,000 sets, there is a significant premium attached to the glossy version of Score's debut baseball card issue. The specially packaged collector's edition features cards with a high-gloss front finish and was sold only as a complete set.

	NM/M
Complete Set (660):	65.00
Common Player:	.25
Stars:	15X

Box Panels

This 18-card set, produced by Major League Marketing and manufactured by Optigraphics, is the premiere box-bottom set issued under the Score trademark. The set features 18 major league All-star players in full-color action poses, framed by a white border. A "1987 All-Star" banner (red or purple) curves above an orange player name block beneath the player photo. Card backs are printed in red, blue, gold and black and carry the card number, player name and position and league logo. Six colorful "Great Moments in Baseball" trivia cards are also included in this set.

	NM/M
Complete Panel Set:	7.50
Complete Singles Set (18):	7.50
Common Panel:	.50
Common Single Player:	.15
Panel 1	1.00
1 Terry Kennedy	.15
3 Willie Randolph	.15
15 Eric Davis	.15
Panel 2	4.50
3 Don Mattingly	1.00
5 Cal Ripken, Jr.	2.00
11 Jack Clark	.15
Panel 3	3.00
4 Wade Boggs	.75
9 Bret Saberhagen	.25
12 Ryne Sandberg	.75
Panel 4	2.50
6 George Bell	.15
13 Mike Schmidt	1.00
18 Mike Scott	.15
Panel 5	2.00
7 Rickey Henderson	.65
16 Andre Dawson	.25
17 Darryl Strawberry	.25
Panel 6	3.50
8 Dave Winfield	.65
10 Gary Carter	.65
14 Ozzie Smith	.75

Traded/Rookie

This 110-card set featuring rookies and traded veterans is similar in design to the 1988 Score set, except for a change in border color. Individual standard-size player cards (2-1/2" x 3-1/2") feature a bright orange border framing action photos highlighted by a thin white outline. The player name (in white) is centered in the bottom margin, flanked by three yellow stars lower left and a yellow Score logo lower right. The backs carry full-color player portraits on a cream-colored background, plus team name and logo, personal information and a purple stats chart that lists year-by-year and major league totals. A brief player profile follows the stats chart and, on some cards, information is included about the player's trade or acquisition. The boxed update set also includes 10 Magic Motion 3-D trivia cards. The cards are numbered with a "T" suffix.

	NM/M
Complete Set (110):	12.00
Common Player:	.05
1 Jack Clark	.05
2 Danny Jackson	.05
3 Brett Butler	.05
4 Kurt Stillwell	.05
5 Tom Brunansky	.05
6 Dennis Lamp	.05
7 Jose DeLeon	.05
8 Tom Herr	.05
9 Keith Moreland	.05
10 Kirk Gibson	.05
11 Bud Black	.05
12 Rafael Ramirez	.05
13 Luis Salazar	.05
14 Goose Gossage	.05
15 Bob Welch	.05
16 Vance Law	.05
17 Ray Knight	.05
18 Dan Quisenberry	.05
19 Don Slaught	.05
20 Lee Smith	.25
21 Rick Cerone	.05
22 Pat Tabler	.05
23 Larry McWilliams	.05
24 Rick Horton	.05
25 Graig Nettles	.05
26 Dan Petry	.05
27 Jose Rijo	.05
28 Chili Davis	.05
29 Dickie Thon	.05
30 Mackey Sasser	.05
31 Mickey Tettleton	.05
32 Rick Dempsey	.05
33 Ron Hassey	.05
34 Phil Bradley	.05
35 Jay Howell	.05
36 Bill Buckner	.05
37 Alfredo Griffin	.05
38 Gary Pettis	.05
39 Calvin Schiraldi	.05
40 John Candelaria	.05
41 Joe Orsulak	.05
42 Willie Upshaw	.05
43 Herm Winningham	.05
44 Ron Kittle	.05
45 Bob Dernier	.05
46 Steve Balboni	.05
47 Steve Shields	.05
48 Henry Cotto	.05
49 Dave Henderson	.05
50 Dave Parker	.05
51 Mike Young	.05
52 Mark Salas	.05
53 Mike Davis	.05
54 Rafael Santana	.05
55 Don Baylor	.05
56 Dan Pasqua	.05
57 Ernest Riles	.05
58 Glenn Hubbard	.05
59 Mike Smithson	.05
60 Richard Dotson	.05
61 Jerry Reuss	.05
62 Mike Jackson	.05
63 Floyd Bannister	.05
64 Jesse Orosco	.05
65 Larry Parrish	.05
66 Jeff Bittiger RC	.05
67 Ray Hayward RC	.05
68 Ricky Jordan RC	.05
69 Tommy Gregg RC	.05
70 Brady Anderson RC	.50
71 Jeff Montgomery	.05
72 Darryl Hamilton RC	.05
73 Cecil Espy RC	.05
74 Greg Briley RC	.05
75 Joey Meyer RC	.05
76 Mike Macfarlane RC	.05
77 Oswald Peraza RC	.05
78 Jack Armstrong RC	.05
79 Don Heinkel RC	.05
80 Mark Grace RC	1.50
81 Steve Curry RC	.05
82 Damon Berryhill RC	.05
83 Steve Ellsworth RC	.05
84 Pete Smith RC	.05
85 Jack McDowell RC	.05
86 Rob Dibble RC	.05
87 Bryan Harvey RC	.05
88 John Dopson RC	.05
89 Dave Gallagher RC	.05
90 Todd Stottlemyre RC	.05
91 Mike Schooler RC	.05
92 Don Gordon RC	.05
93 Sil Campusano RC	.05
94 Jeff Pico RC	.05
95 Jay Buhner RC	.75
96 Nelson Santovenia RC	.05
97 Al Leiter RC	.05
98 Luis Alicea RC	.05
99 Pat Borders RC	.05

100	Chris Sabo RC	.25
101	Tim Belcher RC	.05
102	Walt Weiss RC	.05
103	Craig Biggio RC	6.00
104	Don August RC	.05
105	Roberto Alomar RC	5.00
106	Todd Burns RC	.05
107	John Costello RC	.05
108	Melido Perez RC	.05
109	Darrin Jackson RC	.05
110	Orestes Destrade RC	.05

Traded/Rookie Glossy

Among the scarcest of the major card companies' high-gloss collector's editions of the late 1980s is the 1988 Score Rookie/Traded issue. Production of the regular-finish set was limited in itself and the glossy version is more so, adding a significant premium value.

	NM/M
Complete Set (110):	60.00
Common Player:	.25
Stars:	3X

Young Superstar Series 1

This 40-card set of 2-1/2" x 3-1/2" cards is divided into five separate eight-card subsets. Similar to the company's regular issue, these cards are distinguished by excellent full-color photography on both front and back. The glossy player photos are centered on a white background and framed by a vivid blue and green border. A player name banner beneath the photo includes the name, position and uniform number. The card backs feature color player portraits beneath a hot pink player name/Score logo banner. Hot pink also frames the personal stats (in green), career stats (in black) and career biography (in blue). The backs also include quotes from well-known baseball authorities discussing player performance. This set was distributed via a write-in offer printed on 1988 Score 17-card package wrappers.

	NM/M
Complete Set (40):	3.00
Common Player:	.10

1	Mark McGwire	2.50
2	Benito Santiago	.10
3	Sam Horn	.10
4	Chris Bosio	.10
5	Matt Nokes	.10
6	Ken Williams	.10
7	Dion James	.10
8	B.J. Surhoff	.10
9	Joe Margrane	.10
10	Kevin Seitzer	.10
11	Stanley Jefferson	.10
12	Devon White	.10
13	Nelson Liriano	.10
14	Chris James	.10
15	Mike Henneman	.10
16	Terry Steinbach	.10
17	John Kruk	.10
18	Matt Williams	.10
19	Kelly Downs	.10
20	Bill Ripken	.10
21	Ozzie Guillen	.10
22	Luis Polonia	.10
23	Dave Magadan	.10
24	Mike Greenwell	.10
25	Will Clark	.10
26	Mike Dunne	.10
27	Wally Joyner	.10
28	Robby Thompson	.10
29	Ken Caminiti	.10
30	Jose Canseco	.50
31	Todd Benzinger	.10
32	Pete Incaviglia	.10
33	John Farrell	.10
34	Casey Candaele	.10
35	Mike Aldrete	.10
36	Ruben Sierra	.10
37	Ellis Burks	.10
38	Tracy Jones	.10
39	Kal Daniels	.10
40	Cory Snyder	.10

Young Superstar Series 2

DON MATTINGLY FIRST BASE 23

This set of 40 standard-size cards and five Magic trivia cards is part of a double series issued by Score. Each series is divided into five smaller sets of eight baseball cards and one trivia card. The design on both series is similar, except for border color. Series I has blue and green borders. Series II has red and blue borders framing full-color player photos. Backs carry color portrait photos and stats in a variety of colors. Young Superstar series were offered via a write-in offer on '88 Score wrappers. For each eight-card subset, collectors were instructed to send two Score wrappers and $1. Complete sets were offered by a number of hobby dealers nationwide.

	NM/M
Complete Set (40):	4.00
Common Player:	.10

1	Don Mattingly	1.00
2	Glenn Braggs	.10
3	Dwight Gooden	.10
4	Jose Lind	.10
5	Danny Tartabull	.10
6	Tony Fernandez	.10
7	Julio Franco	.10
8	Andres Galarraga	.10
9	Bobby Bonilla	.10
10	Eric Davis	.40
11	Gerald Young	.10
12	Barry Bonds	2.00
13	Jerry Browne	.10
14	Jeff Blauser	.10
15	Mickey Brantley	.10
16	Floyd Youmans	.10
17	Bret Saberhagen	.10
18	Shawon Dunston	.10
19	Len Dykstra	.10
20	Darryl Strawberry	.10
21	Rick Aguilera	.10
22	Ivan Calderon	.10
23	Roger Clemens	1.00
24	Vince Coleman	.10
25	Gary Thurman	.10
26	Jeff Treadway	.10
27	Oddibe McDowell	.10
28	Fred McGriff	.10
29	Mark McLemore	.10
30	Jeff Musselman	.10
31	Mitch Williams	.10
32	Dan Plesac	.10
33	Juan Nieves	.10
34	Barry Larkin	.10
35	Greg Mathews	.10
36	Shane Mack	.10
37	Scott Bankhead	.10
38	Eric Bell	.10
39	Greg Swindell	.10
40	Kevin Elster	.10

1989 Score

LANSFORD 4 ATHLETICS CARNEY LANSFORD

This set of 660 cards plus 56 Magic Motion trivia cards is the second annual basic issue from Score. Full-color player photos highlight 651 individual players and nine season highlights, including the first Wrigley Field night game. Action photos are framed by thin brightly colored borders (green, cyan blue, purple, orange, red, royal blue) with a baseball diamond logo/player name beneath the photo. Full-color player close-ups (1-5/16" x 1-5/8") are printed on the pastel-colored backs, along with personal information, stats and career highlights. The cards measure 2-1/2" x 3-1/2".

	NM/M
Unopened Fact. Set (660):	12.00
Complete Set (660):	9.00
Common Player:	.05
Pack (16):	.50
Wax Box (36):	10.00

1	Jose Canseco	.25
2	Andre Dawson	.25
3	Mark McGwire	.65
4	Benny Santiago	.05
5	Rick Reuschel	.05
6	Fred McGriff	.05
7	Kal Daniels	.05
8	Gary Gaetti	.05
9	Ellis Burks	.05
10	Darryl Strawberry	.05
11	Julio Franco	.05
12	Lloyd Moseby	.05
13	Jeff Pico RC	.05
14	Johnny Ray	.05
15	Cal Ripken, Jr.	.75
16	Dick Schofield	.05
17	Mel Hall	.05
18	Bill Ripken	.05
19	Brook Jacoby	.05
20	Kirby Puckett	.50
21	Bill Doran	.05
22	Pete O'Brien	.05
23	Matt Nokes	.05
24	Brian Fisher	.05
25	Jack Clark	.05
26	Gary Pettis	.05
27	Dave Valle	.05
28	Willie Wilson	.05
29	Curt Young	.05
30	Dale Murphy	.20
31	Barry Larkin	.05
32	Dave Stewart	.05
33	Mike LaValliere	.05
34	Glenn Hubbard	.05
35	Ryne Sandberg	.50
36	Tony Pena	.05
37	Greg Walker	.05
38	Von Hayes	.05
39	Kevin Mitchell	.05
40	Tim Raines	.05
41	Keith Hernandez	.05
42	Keith Moreland	.05
43	Ruben Sierra	.05
44	Chet Lemon	.05
45	Willie Randolph	.05
46	Andy Allanson	.05
47	Candy Maldonado	.05
48	Sid Bream	.05
49	Denny Walling	.05
50	Dave Winfield	.40
51	Alvin Davis	.05
52	Cory Snyder	.05
53	Hubie Brooks	.05
54	Chili Davis	.05
55	Kevin Seitzer	.05
56	Jose Uribe	.05
57	Tony Fernandez	.05
58	Tim Teufel	.05
59	Oddibe McDowell	.05
60	Les Lancaster	.05
61	Billy Hatcher	.05
62	Dan Gladden	.05
63	Marty Barrett	.05
64	Nick Esasky	.05
65	Wally Joyner	.05
66	Mike Greenwell	.05
67	Ken Williams	.05
68	Bob Horner	.05
69	Steve Sax	.05
70	Rickey Henderson	.40
71	Mitch Webster	.05
72	Rob Deer	.05
73	Jim Presley	.05
74	Albert Hall	.05
75a	George Brett ("At age 33 ...")	1.00
75b	George Brett ("At age 35 ...")	.50
76	Brian Downing	.05
77	Dave Martinez	.05
78	Scott Fletcher	.05
79	Phil Bradley	.05
80	Ozzie Smith	.50
81	Larry Sheets	.05
82	Mike Aldrete	.05
83	Darnell Coles	.05
84	Len Dykstra	.05
85	Jim Rice	.15
86	Jeff Treadway	.05
87	Jose Lind	.05
88	Willie McGee	.05
89	Mickey Brantley	.05
90	Tony Gwynn	.50
91	R.J. Reynolds	.05
92	Milt Thompson	.05
93	Kevin McReynolds	.05
94	Eddie Murray	.40
95	Lance Parrish	.05
96	Ron Kittle	.05
97	Gerald Young	.05
98	Ernie Whitt	.05
99	Jeff Reed	.05
100	Don Mattingly	.60
101	Gerald Perry	.05
102	Vance Law	.05
103	John Shelby	.05
104	Chris Sabo	.05
105	Danny Tartabull	.05
106	Glenn Wilson	.05
107	Mark Davidson	.05
108	Dave Parker	.05
109	Eric Davis	.05
110	Alan Trammell	.05
111	Ozzie Virgil	.05
112	Frank Tanana	.05
113	Rafael Ramirez	.05
114	Dennis Martinez	.05
115	Jose DeLeon	.05
116	Bob Ojeda	.05
117	Doug Drabek	.05
118	Andy Hawkins	.05
119	Greg Maddux	.50
120	Cecil Fielder (Reversed negative.)	
121	Mike Scioscia	.05
122	Dan Petry	.05
123	Terry Kennedy	.05
124	Kelly Downs	.05
125	Greg Gross	.05
126	Fred Lynn	.05
127	Barry Bonds	.75
128	Harold Baines	.05
129	Doyle Alexander	.05
130	Kevin Elster	.05
131	Mike Heath	.05
132	Teddy Higuera	.05
133	Charlie Leibrandt	.05
134	Tim Laudner	.05
135a	Ray Knight (Photo reversed.)	.40
135b	Ray Knight (Correct photo.)	.05
136	Howard Johnson	.05
137	Terry Pendleton	.05
138	Andy McGaffigan	.05
139	Ken Oberkfell	.05
140	Butch Wynegar	.05
141	Rob Murphy	.05
142	Rich Renteria RC	.05
143	Jose Guzman	.05
144	Andres Galarraga	.05
145	Rick Horton	.05
146	Frank DiPino	.05
147	Glenn Braggs	.05
148	John Kruk	.05
149	Mike Schmidt	.60
150	Lee Smith	.05
151	Robin Yount	.40
152	Mark Eichhorn	.05
153	DeWayne Buice	.05
154	B.J. Surhoff	.05
155	Vince Coleman	.05
156	Tony Phillips	.05
157	Willie Fraser	.05
158	Lance McCullers	.05
159	Greg Gagne	.05
160	Jesse Barfield	.05
161	Mark Langston	.05
162	Kurt Stillwell	.05
163	Dion James	.05
164	Glenn Davis	.05
165	Walt Weiss	.05
166	Dave Concepcion	.05
167	Alfredo Griffin	.05
168	Don Heinkel RC	.05
169	Luis Rivera RC	.05
170	Shane Rawley	.05
171	Darrell Evans	.05
172	Robby Thompson	.05
173	Jody Davis	.05
174	Andy Van Slyke	.05
175	Wade Boggs	.50
176	Garry Templeton	.05
177	Gary Redus	.05
178	Craig Lefferts	.05
179	Carney Lansford	.05
180	Ron Darling	.05
181	Kirk McCaskill	.05
182	Tony Armas	.05
183	Steve Farr	.05
184	Tom Brunansky	.05
185	Bryan Harvey RC	.05
186	Mike Marshall	.05
187	Bo Diaz	.05
188	Willie Upshaw	.05
189	Mike Pagliarulo	.05
190	Mike Krukow	.05
191	Tommy Herr	.05
192	Jim Pankovits	.05
193	Dwight Evans	.05
194	Kelly Gruber	.05
195	Bobby Bonilla	.05
196	Wallace Johnson	.05
197	Dave Stieb	.05
198	Pat Borders RC	.05
199	Rafael Palmeiro	.35
200	Dwight Gooden	.05
201	Pete Incaviglia	.05
202	Chris James	.05
203	Marvell Wynne	.05
204	Pat Sheridan	.05
205	Don Baylor	.05
206	Paul O'Neill	.05
207	Pete Smith	.05
208	Mark McLemore	.05
209	Henry Cotto	.05
210	Kirk Gibson	.05
211	Claudell Washington	.05
212	Randy Bush	.05
213	Joe Carter	.05
214	Bill Buckner	.05
215	Bert Blyleven	.05
216	Brett Butler	.05
217	Lee Mazzilli	.05
218	Spike Owen	.05
219	Bill Swift	.05
220	Tim Wallach	.05
221	David Cone	.05
222	Don Carman	.05
223	Rich Gossage	.05
224	Bob Walk	.05
225	Dave Righetti	.05
226	Kevin Bass	.05
227	Kevin Gross	.05
228	Tim Burke	.05
229	Rick Mahler	.05
230	Lou Whitaker	.05
231	Luis Alicea RC	.05
232	Roberto Alomar	.25
233	Bob Boone	.05
234	Dickie Thon	.05
235	Shawon Dunston	.05
236	Pete Stanicek	.05
237	Craig Biggio	.05
238	Dennis Boyd	.05
239	Tom Candiotti	.05
240	Gary Carter	.40
241	Mike Stanley	.05
242	Ken Phelps	.05
243	Chris Bosio	.05
244	Les Straker	.05
245	Dave Smith	.05
246	John Candelaria	.05
247	Joe Orsulak	.05
248	Storm Davis	.05
249	Floyd Bannister	.05
250	Jack Morris	.05
251	Bret Saberhagen	.05
252	Tom Niedenfuer	.05
253	Neal Heaton	.05
254	Eric Show	.05
255	Juan Samuel	.05
256	Dale Sveum	.05
257	Jim Gott	.05
258	Scott Garrelts	.05
259	Larry McWilliams	.05
260	Steve Bedrosian	.05
261	Jack Howell	.05
262	Jay Tibbs	.05
263	Jamie Moyer	.05
264	Doug Sisk	.05
265	Todd Worrell	.05
266	John Farrell	.05
267	Dave Collins	.05
268	Sid Fernandez	.05
269	Tom Brookens	.05
270	Shane Mack	.05
271	Paul Kilgus	.05
272	Chuck Crim	.05
273	Bob Knepper	.05
274	Mike Moore	.05
275	Guillermo Hernandez	.05
276	Dennis Eckersley	.35
277	Graig Nettles	.05
278	Rich Dotson	.05
279	Larry Herndon	.05
280	Gene Larkin	.05
281	Roger McDowell	.05
282	Greg Swindell	.05
283	Juan Agosto	.05
284	Jeff Robinson	.05
285	Mike Dunne	.05
286	Greg Mathews	.05
287	Kent Tekulve	.05
288	Jerry Mumphrey	.05
289	Jack McDowell	.05
290	Frank Viola	.05
291	Mark Gubicza	.05
292	Dave Schmidt	.05
293	Mike Henneman	.05
294	Jimmy Jones	.05
295	Charlie Hough	.05
296	Rafael Santana	.05
297	Chris Speier	.05
298	Mike Witt	.05
299	Pascual Perez	.05
300	Nolan Ryan	.75
301	Mitch Williams	.05
302	Mookie Wilson	.05
303	Mackey Sasser	.05
304	John Cerutti	.05
305	Jeff Reardon	.05
306	Randy Myers	.05
307	Greg Brock	.05
308	Bob Welch	.05
309	Jeff Robinson	.05
310	Harold Reynolds	.05
311	Jim Walewander	.05
312	Dave Magadan	.05
313	Jim Gantner	.05
314	Walt Terrell	.05
315	Wally Backman	.05
316	Luis Salazar	.05
317	Rick Rhoden	.05
318	Tom Henke	.05
319	Mike Macfarlane	.05
320	Dan Plesac	.05
321	Calvin Schiraldi	.05
322	Stan Javier	.05
323	Devon White	.05
324	Scott Bradley	.05
325	Bruce Hurst	.05
326	Manny Lee	.05
327	Rick Aguilera	.05
328	Bruce Ruffin	.05
329	Ed Whitson	.05
330	Bo Jackson	.10
331	Ivan Calderon	.05
332	Mickey Hatcher	.05
333	Barry Jones RC	.05
334	Ron Hassey	.05
335	Bill Wegman	.05
336	Damon Berryhill	.05
337	Steve Ontiveros	.05
338	Dan Pasqua	.05
339	Bill Pecota	.05
340	Greg Cadaret	.05
341	Scott Bankhead	.05
342	Ron Guidry	.10
343	Danny Heep	.05
344	Bob Brower	.05
345	Rich Gedman	.05
346	Nelson Santovenia RC	.05
347	George Bell	.05
348	Ted Power	.05
349	Mark Grant	.05
350a	Roger Clemens (778 Wins)	2.00
350b	Roger Clemens (78 Wins)	.60
351	Bill Long	.05
352	Jay Bell RC	.05
353	Steve Balboni	.05
354	Bob Kipper	.05
355	Steve Jeltz	.05
356	Jesse Orosco	.05
357	Bob Dernier	.05
358	Mickey Tettleton	.05
359	Duane Ward RC	.05
360	Darrin Jackson RC	.05
361	Rey Quinones	.05
362	Mark Grace	.05
363	Steve Lake	.05
364	Pat Perry	.05
365	Terry Steinbach	.05
366	Alan Ashby	.05
367	Jeff Montgomery	.05
368	Steve Buechele	.05
369	Chris Brown	.05
370	Orel Hershiser	.05
371	Todd Benzinger	.05
372	Ron Gant	.05
373	Paul Assenmacher RC	.05
374	Joey Meyer	.05
375	Neil Allen	.05
376	Mike Davis	.05
377	Jeff Parrett RC	.05
378	Jay Howell	.05
379	Rafael Belliard	.05
380	Luis Polonia	.05
381	Keith Atherton	.05
382	Kent Hrbek	.05
383	Bob Stanley	.05
384	Dave LaPoint	.05
385	Rance Mulliniks	.05
386	Melido Perez	.05
387	Doug Jones	.05
388	Steve Lyons	.05
389	Alejandro Pena	.05
390	Frank White	.05
391	Pat Tabler	.05
392	Eric Plunk RC	.05
393	Mike Maddux RC	.05
394	Allan Anderson RC	.05
395	Bob Brenly	.05
396	Rick Cerone	.05
397	Scott Terry RC	.05
398	Mike Jackson	.05
399	Bobby Thigpen	.05
400	Don Sutton	.35
401	Cecil Espy	.05
402	Junior Ortiz	.05
403	Mike Smithson	.05
404	Bud Black	.05
405	Tom Foley	.05
406	Andres Thomas	.05
407	Rick Sutcliffe	.05
408	Brian Harper	.05
409	John Smiley	.05
410	Juan Nieves	.05
411	Shawn Abner	.05
412	Wes Gardner RC	.05
413	Darren Daulton	.05
414	Juan Berenguer	.05
415	Charles Hudson	.05
416	Rick Honeycutt	.05
417	Greg Booker	.05
418	Tim Belcher	.05
419	Don August	.05
420	Dale Mohorcic	.05
421	Steve Lombardozzi	.05
422	Atlee Hammaker	.05
423	Jerry Don Gleaton	.05
424	Scott Bailes RC	.05
425	Bruce Sutter	.40
426	Randy Ready	.05
427	Jerry Reed	.05
428	Bryn Smith	.05
429	Tim Leary	.05
430	Mark Clear	.05
431	Terry Leach	.05
432	John Moses	.05
433	Ozzie Guillen	.05
434	Gene Nelson	.05
435	Gary Ward	.05
436	Luis Aguayo	.05
437	Fernando Valenzuela	.05
438	Jeff Russell	.05
439	Cecilio Guante	.05
440	Don Robinson	.05
441	Rick Anderson RC	.05

No.	Player	Price
442	Tom Glavine	.35
443	Daryl Boston	.05
444	Joe Price	.05
445	Stewart Cliburn	.05
446	Manny Trillo	.05
447	Joel Skinner	.05
448	Charlie Puleo	.05
449	Carlton Fisk	.40
450	Will Clark	.05
451	Otis Nixon	.05
452	Rick Schu	.05
453	Todd Stottlemyre	.05
454	Tim Birtsas	.05
455	Dave Gallagher RC	.05
456	Barry Lyons	.05
457	Fred Manrique	.05
458	Ernest Riles	.05
459	Doug Jennings RC	.05
460	Joe Magrane	.05
461	Jamie Quirk	.05
462	Jack Armstrong RC	.05
463	Bobby Witt	.05
464	Keith Miller	.05
465	Todd Burns RC	.05
466	John Dopson RC	.05
467	Rich Yett	.05
468	Craig Reynolds	.05
469	Dave Bergman	.05
470	Rex Hudler	.05
471	Eric King	.05
472	Joaquin Andujar	.05
473	Sil Campusano RC	.05
474	Terry Mulholland RC	.05
475	Mike Flanagan	.05
476	Greg Harris	.05
477	Tommy John	.10
478	Dave Anderson	.05
479	Fred Toliver	.05
480	Jimmy Key	.05
481	Donell Nixon	.05
482	Mark Portugal RC	.05
483	Tom Pagnozzi	.05
484	Jeff Kunkel	.05
485	Frank Williams	.05
486	Jody Reed	.05
487	Roberto Kelly	.05
488	Shawn Hillegas	.05
489	Jerry Reuss	.05
490	Mark Davis	.05
491	Jeff Sellers	.05
492	Zane Smith	.05
493	Al Newman RC	.05
494	Mike Young	.05
495	Larry Parrish	.05
496	Herm Winningham	.05
497	Carmen Castillo	.05
498	Joe Hesketh	.05
499	Darrell Miller	.05
500	Mike LaCoss	.05
501	Charlie Lea	.05
502	Bruce Benedict	.05
503	Chuck Finley RC	.05
504	Brad Wellman RC	.05
505	Tim Crews	.05
506	Ken Gerhart	.05
507a	Brian Holton (Born: 1/25/65, Denver.)	.15
507b	Brian Holton (Born: 11/29/59, McKeesport.)	.05
508	Dennis Lamp	.05
509	Bobby Meacham	.05
510	Tracy Jones	.05
511	Mike Fitzgerald	.05
512	Jeff Bittiger RC	.05
513	Tim Flannery	.05
514	Ray Hayward RC	.05
515	Dave Leiper	.05
516	Rod Scurry	.05
517	Carmelo Martinez	.05
518	Curtis Wilkerson	.05
519	Stan Jefferson	.05
520	Dan Quisenberry	.05
521	Lloyd McClendon RC	.05
522	Steve Trout	.05
523	Larry Andersen	.05
524	Don Aase	.05
525	Bob Forsch	.05
526	Geno Petralli	.05
527	Angel Salazar	.05
528	Mike Schooler RC	.05
529	Jose Oquendo	.05
530	Jay Buhner	.05
531	Tom Bolton RC	.05
532	Al Nipper	.05
533	Dave Henderson	.05
534	John Costello RC	.05
535	Donnie Moore	.05
536	Mike Laga	.05
537	Mike Gallego	.05
538	Jim Clancy	.05
539	Joel Youngblood	.05
540	Rick Leach	.05
541	Kevin Romine	.05
542	Mark Salas	.05
543	Greg Minton	.05
544	Dave Palmer	.05
545	Dwayne Murphy	.05
546	Jim Deshaies	.05
547	Don Gordon RC	.05
548	Ricky Jordan	.05
549	Mike Boddicker	.05
550	Mike Scott	.05
551	Jeff Ballard RC	.05
552a	Jose Rijo (Uniform number #24 on card back.)	.15
552b	Jose Rijo (Uniform number #27 on card back.)	.10
553	Danny Darwin	.05
554	Tom Browning	.05
555	Danny Jackson	.05
556	Rick Dempsey	.05
557	Jeffrey Leonard	.05
558	Jeff Musselman	.05
559	Ron Robinson	.05
560	John Tudor	.05
561	Don Slaught	.05
562	Dennis Rasmussen	.05
563	Brady Anderson	.05
564	Pedro Guerrero	.05
565	Paul Molitor	.40
566	Terry Clark RC	.05
567	Terry Puhl	.05
568	Mike Campbell RC	.05
569	Paul Mirabella	.05
570	Jeff Hamilton	.05
571	Oswald Peraza RC	.05
572	Bob McClure	.05
573	Jose Bautista RC	.05
574	Alex Trevino	.05
575	John Franco	.05
576	Mark Parent RC	.05
577	Nelson Liriano	.05
578	Steve Shields	.05
579	Odell Jones	.05
580	Al Leiter	.05
581	Dave Stapleton RC	.05
582	1988 World Series (Jose Canseco, Kirk Gibson, Orel Hershiser, Dave Stewart.)	.10
583	Donnie Hill	.05
584	Chuck Jackson	.05
585	Rene Gonzales RC	.05
586	Tracy Woodson RC	.05
587	Jim Adduci RC	.05
588	Mario Soto	.05
589	Jeff Blauser	.05
590	Jim Traber	.05
591	Jon Perlman RC	.05
592	Mark Williamson RC	.05
593	Dave Meads	.05
594	Jim Eisenreich	.05
595a	Paul Gibson RC (Player in background adjusting cup.)	.25
595b	Paul Gibson RC (Hand airbrushed away.)	.05
596	Mike Birkbeck	.05
597	Terry Francona	.05
598	Paul Zuvella	.05
599	Franklin Stubbs	.05
600	Gregg Jefferies	.05
601	John Cangelosi	.05
602	Mike Sharperson RC	.05
603	Mike Diaz	.05
604	Gary Varsho RC	.05
605	Terry Blocker RC	.05
606	Charlie O'Brien RC	.05
607	Jim Eppard RC	.05
608	John Davis	.05
609	Ken Griffey Sr.	.05
610	Buddy Bell	.05
611	Ted Simmons	.05
612	Matt Williams	.05
613	Danny Cox	.05
614	Al Pedrique	.05
615	Ron Oester	.05
616	John Smoltz	.05
617	Bob Melvin	.05
618	Rob Dibble RC	.10
619	Kirt Manwaring	.05
620	Felix Fermin RC	.05
621	Doug Dascenzo RC	.05
622	Bill Brennan RC	.05
623	Carlos Quintana RC	.05
624	Mike Harkey RC	.05
625	Gary Sheffield RC	1.25
626	Tom Prince RC	.05
627	Steve Searcy RC	.05
628	Charlie Hayes RC	.05
629	Felix Jose RC	.05
630	Sandy Alomar RC	.50
631	Derek Lilliquist RC	.05
632	Geronimo Berroa RC	.05
633	Luis Medina RC	.05
634	Tom Gordon RC	.10
635	Ramon Martinez RC	.25
636	Craig Worthington RC	.05
637	Edgar Martinez RC	.05
638	Chad Krueter RC	.05
639	Ron Jones RC	.05
640	Van Snider RC	.05
641	Lance Blankenship RC	.05
642	Dwight Smith RC	.05
643	Cameron Drew RC	.05
644	Jerald Clark RC	.05
645	Randy Johnson RC	2.00
646	Norm Charlton RC	.05
647	Todd Frohwirth RC	.05
648	Luis de los Santos RC	.05
649	Tim Jones RC	.05
650	Dave West RC	.05
651	Bob Milacki RC	.05
652	1988 Highlight (Wrigley Field)	.05
653	1988 Highlight (Orel Hershiser)	.05
654a	1988 Highlight (Wade Boggs) ("...sixth consecutive seaason..." on back)	2.00
654b	1988 Highlight (Wade Boggs) ("Season" corrected.)	.10
655	1988 Highlight (Jose Canseco)	.15
656	1988 Highlight (Doug Jones)	
657	1988 Highlight (Rickey Henderson)	.10
658	1988 Highlight (Tom Browning)	.05
659	1988 Highlight (Mike Greenwell)	.05
660	1988 Highlight (Joe Morgan) (A.L. Win Streak)	.05

Rookie/Traded

Score issued its second consecutive traded set in 1989 to supplement and update its regular set. The 110-card traded set features the same basic card design as the regular 1989 Score set. The set consists of rookies and traded players pictured with correct teams. The set was sold by hobby dealers in a special box that included an assortment of "Magic Motion" trivia cards. Cards are numbered with a "T" suffix.

		NM/M
Complete Set (110):		10.00
Common Player:		.05
1	Rafael Palmeiro	.35
2	Nolan Ryan	1.00
3	Jack Clark	.05
4	Dave LaPoint	.05
5	Mike Moore	.05
6	Pete O'Brien	.05
7	Jeffrey Leonard	.05
8	Rob Murphy	.05
9	Tom Herr	.05
10	Claudell Washington	.05
11	Mike Pagliarulo	.05
12	Steve Lake	.05
13	Spike Owen	.05
14	Andy Hawkins	.05
15	Todd Benzinger	.05
16	Mookie Wilson	.05
17	Bert Blyleven	.05
18	Jeff Treadway	.05
19	Bruce Hurst	.05
20	Steve Sax	.05
21	Juan Samuel	.05
22	Jesse Barfield	.05
23	Carmelo Castillo	.05
24	Terry Leach	.05
25	Mark Langston	.05
26	Eric King	.05
27	Steve Balboni	.05
28	Len Dykstra	.05
29	Keith Moreland	.05
30	Terry Kennedy	.05
31	Eddie Murray	.45
32	Mitch Williams	.05
33	Jeff Parrett	.05
34	Wally Backman	.05
35	Julio Franco	.05
36	Lance Parrish	.05
37	Nick Esasky	.05
38	Luis Polonia	.05
39	Kevin Gross	.05
40	John Dopson	.05
41	Willie Randolph	.05
42	Jim Clancy	.05
43	Tracy Jones	.05
44	Phil Bradley	.05
45	Milt Thompson	.05
46	Chris James	.05
47	Scott Fletcher	.05
48	Kal Daniels	.05
49	Steve Bedrosian	.05
50	Rickey Henderson	.45
51	Dion James	.05
52	Tim Leary	.05
53	Roger McDowell	.05
54	Mel Hall	.05
55	Dickie Thon	.05
56	Zane Smith	.05
57	Danny Heep	.05
58	Bob McClure	.05
59	Brian Holton	.05
60	Randy Ready	.05
61	Bob Melvin	.05
62	Harold Baines	.05
63	Lance McCullers	.05
64	Jody Davis	.05
65	Darrell Evans	.05
66	Joel Youngblood	.05
67	Frank Viola	.05
68	Mike Aldrete	.05
69	Greg Cadaret	.05
70	John Kruk	.05
71	Pat Sheridan	.05
72	Oddibe McDowell	.05
73	Tom Brookens	.05
74	Bob Boone	.05
75	Walt Terrell	.05
76	Joel Skinner	.05
77	Randy Johnson	1.50
78	Felix Fermin	.05
79	Rick Mahler	.05
80	Rich Dotson	.05
81	Cris Carpenter RC	.05
82	Bill Spiers RC	.05
83	Junior Felix RC	.05
84	Joe Girardi RC	.05
85	Jerome Walton RC	.05
86	Greg Litton RC	.05
87	Greg Harris RC	.05
88	Jim Abbott RC	.05
89	Kevin Brown RC	.05
90	John Wetteland RC	.10
91	Gary Wayne RC	.05
92	Rich Monteleone RC	.05
93	Bob Geren RC	.05
94	Clay Parker RC	.05
95	Steve Finley RC	.05
96	Gregg Olson RC	.05
97	Ken Patterson RC	.05
98	Ken Hill RC	.05
99	Scott Scudder RC	.05
100	Ken Griffey Jr. RC	6.00
101	Jeff Brantley RC	.05
102	Donn Pall RC	.05
103	Carlos Martinez RC	.05
104	Joe Oliver RC	.05
105	Omar Vizquel RC	.25
106	Albert Belle RC	1.00
107	Kenny Rogers RC	.10
108	Mark Carreon RC	.05
109	Rolando Roomes RC	.05
110	Pete Harnisch RC	.05

Rising Stars

CHRIS SABO 3B REDS

Similar in design to the Score Superstar set, this 100-card set showcased a host of rookies. Full-color action photos are surrounded by a bright blue border with a green inner highlight line. Backs display a full-color player portrait above his name and career highlights. The card number and player's rookie year are featured to the right. A "Rising Star" headline highlights the top border. The Score "Rising Star" set was marketed as a combination with a related magazine: "1988-89 Baseball's 100 Hottest Rookies." The set also includes six Magic Motion baseball trivia cards featuring "Rookies to Remember." The magazine/card sets were available at a select group of retailers.

		NM/M
Complete Set (100):		5.00
Common Player:		.10
1	Gregg Jefferies	.10
2	Vicente Palacios	.10
3	Cameron Drew	.10
4	Doug Dascenzo	.10
5	Luis Medina	.10
6	Craig Worthington	.10
7	Rob Ducey	.10
8	Hal Morris	.10
9	Bill Brennan	.10
10	Gary Sheffield	.25
11	Mike Devereaux	.10
12	Hensley Meulens	.10
13	Carlos Quintana	.10
14	Todd Frohwirth	.10
15	Scott Lusader	.10
16	Mark Carreon	.10
17	Torey Lovullo	.10
18	Randy Velarde	.10
19	Billy Bean	.10
20	Lance Blankenship	.10
21	Chris Gwynn	.10
22	Felix Jose	.10
23	Derek Lilliquist	.10
24	Gary Thurman	.10
25	Ron Jones	.10
26	Dave Justice	.10
27	Johnny Paredes	.10
28	Tim Jones	.10
29	Jose Gonzalez	.10
30	Geronimo Berroa	.10
31	Trevor Wilson	.10
32	Morris Madden	.10
33	Lance Johnson	.10
34	Marvin Freeman	.10
35	Jose Cecena	.10
36	Jim Corsi	.10
37	Rolando Roomes	.10
38	Scott Medvin	.10
39	Charlie Hayes	.10
40	Edgar Martinez	.10
41	Van Snider	.10
42	John Fishel	.10
43	Bruce Fields	.10
44	Darryl Hamilton	.10
45	Tom Prince	.10
46	Kirt Manwaring	.10
47	Steve Searcy	.10
48	Mike Harkey	.10
49	German Gonzalez	.10
50	Tony Perezchica	.10
51	Chad Kreuter	.10
52	Luis de los Santos	.10
53	Steve Curry	.10
54	Greg Bailey	.10
55	Ramon Martinez	.10
56	Ron Tingley	.10
57	Randy Kramer	.10
58	Alex Madrid	.10
59	Kevin Reimer	.10
60	Dave Otto	.10
61	Ken Patterson	.10
62	Keith Miller	.10
63	Randy Johnson	2.50
64	Dwight Smith	.10
65	Eric Yelding	.10
66	Bob Geren	.10
67	Shane Turner	.10
68	Tom Gordon	.10
69	Jeff Huson	.10
70	Marty Brown	.10
71	Nelson Santovenia	.10
72	Roberto Alomar	1.00
73	Mike Schooler	.10
74	Pete Smith	.10
75	John Costello	.10
76	Chris Sabo	.10
77	Damon Berryhill	.10
78	Mark Grace	.20
79	Melido Perez	.10
80	Al Leiter	.10
81	Todd Stottlemyre	.10
82	Mackey Sasser	.10
83	Don August	.10
84	Jeff Treadway	.10
85	Jody Reed	.10
86	Mike Campbell	.10
87	Ron Gant	.10
88	Ricky Jordan	.10
89	Terry Clark	.10
90	Roberto Kelly	.10
91	Pat Borders	.10
92	Bryan Harvey	.10
93	Joey Meyer	.10
94	Tim Belcher	.10
95	Walt Weiss	.10
96	Dave Gallagher	.10
97	Mike Macfarlane	.10
98	Craig Biggio	.10
99	Jack Armstrong	.10
100	Todd Burns	.10

Superstars

FRANK VIOLA P Twins

This 100-card set features full-color action photos of baseball's superstars, and six Magic Motion "Rookies to Remember" baseball trivia cards. Card fronts have a bright red border with a blue line inside highlighting the photo. The player ID is displayed in overlapping triangles of white, green, and yellow. The flip side features a full-color player close-up directly beneath a bright red "Superstar" headline. The set was marketed along with the magazine "1989 Baseball's 100 Hottest Players," at select retailers.

		NM/M
Complete Set (100):		6.00
Common Player:		.05
1	Jose Canseco	.35
2	David Cone	.05
3	Dave Winfield	.50
4	George Brett	.75
5	Frank Viola	.05
6	Cory Snyder	.05
7	Alan Trammell	.05
8	Dwight Evans	.05
9	Tim Leary	.05
10	Don Mattingly	.75
11	Kirby Puckett	.65
12	Carney Lansford	.05
13	Dennis Martinez	.05
14	Kent Hrbek	.05
15	Doc Gooden	.05
16	Dennis Eckersley	.40
17	Kevin Seitzer	.05
18	Lee Smith	.05
19	Danny Tartabull	.05
20	Gerald Perry	.05
21	Gary Gaetti	.05
22	Rick Reuschel	.05
23	Keith Hernandez	.05
24	Jeff Reardon	.05
25	Mark McGwire	.85
26	Juan Samuel	.05
27	Jack Clark	.05
28	Robin Yount	.50
29	Steve Bedrosian	.05
30	Kirk Gibson	.05
31	Barry Bonds	1.00
32	Dan Plesac	.05
33	Steve Sax	.05
34	Jeff Robinson	.05
35	Orel Hershiser	.05
36	Julio Franco	.05
37	Dave Righetti	.05
38	Bob Knepper	.05
39	Carlton Fisk	.50
40	Tony Gwynn	.65
41	Doug Jones	.05
42	Bobby Bonilla	.05
43	Ellis Burks	.05
44	Pedro Guerrero	.05
45	Rickey Henderson	.50
46	Glenn Davis	.05
47	Benny Santiago	.05
48	Greg Maddux	.65
49	Teddy Higuera	.05
50	Darryl Strawberry	.05
51	Ozzie Guillen	.05
52	Barry Larkin	.05
53	Tony Fernandez	.05
54	Ryne Sandberg	.65
55	Joe Carter	.05
56	Rafael Palmeiro	.40
57	Paul Molitor	.50
58	Eric Davis	.05
59	Mike Henneman	.05
60	Mike Scott	.05
61	Tom Browning	.05
62	Mark Davis	.05
63	Tom Henke	.05
64	Nolan Ryan	1.00
65	Fred McGriff	.05
66	Dale Murphy	.20
67	Mark Langston	.05
68	Bobby Thigpen	.05
69	Mark Gubicza	.05
70	Mike Greenwell	.05
71	Ron Darling	.05
72	Gerald Young	.05
73	Wally Joyner	.05
74	Andres Galarraga	.05
75	Danny Jackson	.05
76	Mike Schmidt	.75
77	Cal Ripken, Jr.	1.00
78	Alvin Davis	.05
79	Bruce Hurst	.05
80	Andre Dawson	.25
81	Bob Boone	.05
82	Harold Reynolds	.05
83	Eddie Murray	.50
84	Robby Thompson	.05
85	Will Clark	.05
86	Vince Coleman	.05
87	Doug Drabek	.05
88	Ozzie Smith	.65
89	Bob Welch	.05
90	Roger Clemens	.75
91	George Bell	.05
92	Andy Van Slyke	.05
93	Willie McGee	.05
94	Todd Worrell	.05
95	Tim Raines	.05
96	Kevin McReynolds	.05
97	John Franco	.05
98	Jim Gott	.05
99	Johnny Ray	.05
100	Wade Boggs	.65

Yankees

This team set was sponsored by National Westminster Bank and produced by Score as an in-stadium promotion in 1989; distributed to fans attending the July 29 game at Yankee Stadium. The standard-size cards include a full-color player photo with a line drawing of the famous Yankee Stadium facade running along the top of the card. The player's name, "New York Yankees" and position appear below the photo. A second full-color photo is included on the back of the card, along with stats, data and a brief player profile. The set includes a special Thurman Munson commemorative card.

		NM/M
Complete Set (33):		4.00
Common Player:		.15
1	Don Mattingly	2.00
2	Steve Sax	.15
3	Alvaro Espinoza	.15
4	Luis Polonia	.15
5	Jesse Barfield	.15
6	Dave Righetti	.15
7	Dave Winfield	1.00
8	John Candelaria	.15
9	Wayne Tolleson	.15
10	Ken Phelps	.15
11	Rafael Santana	.15
12	Don Slaught	.15
13	Mike Pagliarulo	.15
14	Lance McCullers	.15
15	Dave LaPoint	.15
16	Dale Mohorcic	.15
17	Steve Balboni	.15
18	Roberto Kelly	.15
19	Andy Hawkins	.15
20	Mel Hall	.15
21	Tom Brookens	.15
22	Deion Sanders	.50
23	Richard Dotson	.15
24	Lee Guetterman	.15
25	Bob Geren	.15
26	Jimmy Jones	.15
27	Chuck Cary	.15
28	Ron Guidry	.25
29	Hal Morris	.15
30	Clay Parker	.15
31	Dallas Green	.15
32	Thurman Munson	1.00
33	Sponsor Card	.05

Young Superstars Series 1

These standard-size cards (2-1/2" x 3-1/2") display color action photos with a high-gloss finish. Fronts feature a red and blue border surrounding the photo with the team logo in the lower right. A red band beneath the photo provides the setting for the player ID including name, position, and uniform number. Backs feature a red "Young Superstar" headline above a portrait photo. Above the headline appears the player's personal information and statistics in orange and black. To the right photo a condensed scouting report and career hightlights are revealed. The card number and related logos appear on the bottom portion. Five trivia cards featuring "A Year to Remember" accompanied the series. Each trivia card relates to a highlight from the past 56 years. This set was distributed via a write-in offer with Score card wrappers.

		NM/M
Complete Set (42):		3.00
Common Player:		.10
1	Gregg Jefferies	.10
2	Jody Reed	.10
3	Mark Grace	.10
4	Dave Gallagher	.10

5	Bo Jackson	.15
6	Jay Buhner	.10
7	Melido Perez	.10
8	Bobby Witt	.10
9	David Cone	.10
10	Chris Sabo	.10
11	Pat Borders	.10
12	Mark Grant	.10
13	Mike Macfarlane	.10
14	Mike Jackson	.10
15	Ricky Jordan	.10
16	Ron Gant	.10
17	Al Leiter	.10
18	Jeff Parrett	.10
19	Pete Smith	.10
20	Walt Weiss	.10
21	Doug Drabek	.10
22	Kirt Manwaring	.10
23	Keith Miller	.10
24	Damon Berryhill	.10
25	Gary Sheffield	.25
26	Brady Anderson	.10
27	Mitch Williams	.10
28	Roberto Alomar	.25
29	Bobby Thigpen	.10
30	Bryan Harvey	.10
31	Jose Rijo	.10
32	Dave West	.10
33	Joey Meyer	.10
34	Allan Anderson	.10
35	Rafael Palmeiro	.75
36	Tim Belcher	.10
37	John Smiley	.10
38	Mackey Sasser	.10
39	Greg Maddux	1.00
40	Ramon Martinez	.10
41	Randy Myers	.10
42	Scott Bankhead	.10

Young Superstars Series 2

Score followed up with a second series of Young Superstars in 1989. The second series also included 42 cards and featured the same design as the first series. The set was also distributed via a write-in offer with Score card wrappers.

		NM/M
Complete Set (42):		10.00
Common Player:		.10
1	Sandy Alomar	.10
2	Tom Gordon	.10
3	Ron Jones	.10
4	Todd Burns	.10
5	Paul O'Neill	.10
6	Gene Larkin	.10
7	Eric King	.10
8	Jeff Robinson	.10
9	Bill Wegman	.10
10	Cecil Espy	.10
11	Jose Guzman	.10
12	Kelly Gruber	.10
13	Duane Ward	.10
14	Mark Gubicza	.10
15	Norm Charlton	.10
16	Jose Oquendo	.10
17	Geronimo Berroa	.10
18	Ken Griffey Jr.	9.00
19	Lance McCullers	.10
20	Todd Stottlemyre	.10
21	Craig Worthington	.10
22	Mike Devereaux	.10
23	Tom Glavine	.50
24	Dale Sveum	.10
25	Roberto Kelly	.10
26	Luis Medina	.10
27	Steve Searcy	.10
28	Don August	.10
29	Shawn Hillegas	.10
30	Mike Campbell	.10
31	Mike Harkey	.10
32	Randy Johnson	1.00
33	Craig Biggio	.10
34	Mike Schooler	.10
35	Andres Thomas	.10
36	Jerome Walton	.10
37	Cris Carpenter	.10
38	Kevin Mitchell	.10
39	Eddie Williams	.10
40	Chad Kreuter	.10
41	Danny Jackson	.10
42	Kurt Stillwell	.10

Scoremasters

This unique 42-card boxed set from Score was reproduced from original artwork done by New York artist Jeffrey Rubin. The paintings are reproduced on a standard-size, white, glossy stock, and the set includes the top stars of the game, plus selected rookies.

		NM/M
Complete Set (42):		8.00
Common Player:		.10
1	Bo Jackson	.20
2	Jerome Walton	.10
3	Cal Ripken, Jr.	2.00
4	Mike Scott	.10
5	Nolan Ryan	2.00
6	Don Mattingly	1.00
7	Tom Gordon	.10
8	Jack Morris	.10
9	Carlton Fisk	.75
10	Will Clark	.10
11	George Brett	1.00
12	Kevin Mitchell	.10
13	Mark Langston	.10
14	Dave Stewart	.10
15	Dale Murphy	.30
16	Gary Gaetti	.10
17	Wade Boggs	.85
18	Eric Davis	.10
19	Kirby Puckett	.85
20	Roger Clemens	1.00
21	Orel Hershiser	.10
22	Mark Grace	.10
23	Ryne Sandberg	.85
24	Barry Larkin	.10
25	Ellis Burks	.10
26	Dwight Gooden	.10
27	Ozzie Smith	.85
28	Andre Dawson	.30
29	Julio Franco	.10
30	Ken Griffey Jr.	1.25
31	Ruben Sierra	.10
32	Mark McGwire	1.50
33	Andres Galarraga	.10
34	Joe Carter	.10
35	Vince Coleman	.10
36	Mike Greenwell	.10
37	Tony Gwynn	.85
38	Andy Van Slyke	.10
39	Gregg Jefferies	.10
40	Jose Canseco	.50
41	Dave Winfield	.75
42	Darryl Strawberry	.10

1990 Score Promos

To preview its 1990 baseball cards, Score pre-released the first 110 cards (#221-330) from its unbordered cards as samples. Subtle differences exist on most cards between the samples and the issued version; most easily spotted is that the samples have no statistics on the 1989 season or career lines. Many cards have different versions of the career highlight write-ups on the back, as well. A handful of the sample cards were widely distributed to dealers and the hobby press, while others from the sheet were released more sparingly, creating inequities in the number of

each card available. As few as two examples are known of some of the superstar cards, making them extremely expensive among the single-player specialists.

		NM/M
Common Player:		5.00
221	Steve Buechele	5.00
222	Jesse Barfield	5.00
223	Juan Berenguer	5.00
224	Andy McGaffigan	5.00
225	Pete Smith	5.00
226	Mike Witt	5.00
227	Jay Howell	5.00
228	Scott Bradley	5.00
229	Jerome Walton	5.00
230	Greg Swindell	5.00
231	Atlee Hammaker	5.00
232	Mike Devereaux	5.00
233	Ken Hill	5.00
234	Craig Worthington	5.00
235	Scott Terry	5.00
236	Brett Butler	5.00
237	Doyle Alexander	5.00
238	Dave Anderson	5.00
239	Bob Milacki	5.00
240	Dwight Smith	5.00
241	Otis Nixon	5.00
242	Pat Tabler	5.00
243	Derek Lilliquist	5.00
244	Danny Tartabull	5.00
245	Wade Boggs	65.00
246	Scott Garrelts	5.00
247	Spike Owen	5.00
248	Norm Charlton	5.00
249	Gerald Perry	5.00
250	Nolan Ryan	150.00
251	Kevin Gross	5.00
252	Randy Milligan	5.00
253	Mike LaCoss	5.00
254	Dave Bergman	5.00
255	Tony Gwynn	65.00
256	Felix Fermin	5.00
257	Greg W. Harris	5.00
258	Junior Felix	5.00
259	Mark Davis	5.00
260	Vince Coleman	5.00
261	Paul Gibson	5.00
262	Mitch Williams	5.00
263	Jeff Russell	5.00
264	Omar Vizquel	5.00
265	Andre Dawson	20.00
266	Storm Davis	5.00
267	Guillermo Hernandez	5.00
268	Mike Felder	5.00
269	Tom Candiotti	5.00
270	Bruce Hurst	5.00
271	Fred McGriff	5.00
272	Glenn Davis	5.00
273	John Franco	5.00
274	Rich Yett	5.00
275	Craig Biggio	5.00
276	Gene Larkin	5.00
277	Rob Dibble	5.00
278	Randy Bush	5.00
279	Kevin Bass	5.00
280	Bo Jackson	12.50
281	Wally Backman	5.00
282	Larry Andersen	5.00
283	Chris Bosio	5.00
284	Juan Agosto	5.00
285	Ozzie Smith	65.00
286	George Bell	5.00
287	Rex Hudler	5.00
288	Pat Borders	5.00
289	Danny Jackson	5.00
290	Carlton Fisk	30.00
291	Tracy Jones	5.00
292	Allan Anderson	5.00
293	Johnny Ray	5.00
294	Lee Guetterman	5.00
295	Paul O'Neill	5.00
296	Carney Lansford	5.00
297	Tom Brookens	5.00
298	Claudell Washington	5.00
299	Hubie Brooks	5.00
300	Will Clark	5.00
301	Kenny Rogers	5.00
302	Darrell Evans	5.00
303	Greg Briley	5.00
304	Donn Pall	5.00
305	Teddy Higuera	5.00
306	Dan Pasqua	5.00
307	Dave Winfield	30.00
308	Dennis Powell	5.00
309	Jose DeLeon	5.00
310	Roger Clemens	90.00
311	Melido Perez	5.00
312	Devon White	5.00
313	Dwight Gooden	5.00
314	Carlos Martinez	5.00
315	Dennis Eckersley	25.00
316	Clay Parker	5.00
317	Rick Honeycutt	5.00
318	Tim Laudner	5.00
319	Joe Carter	5.00
320	Robin Yount	30.00
321	Felix Jose	5.00
322	Mickey Tettleton	5.00
323	Mike Gallego	5.00
324	Edgar Martinez	5.00
325	Dave Henderson	5.00
326	Chili Davis	5.00
327	Steve Balboni	5.00
328	Jody Davis	5.00
329	Shawn Hillegas	5.00
330	Jim Abbott	5.00

1990 Score

The regular Score set increased to 704 cards in 1990. Included were a series of cards picturing first-round draft picks, an expanded subset of rookie cards, four World Series specials, five Highlight cards, and a 13-card "Dream Team" series featuring the game's top players pictured on old tobacco-style cards. For the first time in a Score set, team logos are displayed on the card fronts Card backs include a full-color portrait photo with player data. A one-paragraph write-up of each player was again provided by former Sports Illustrated editor Les Woodcock. The Score set was again distributed with "Magic Motion" trivia cards, this year using "Baseball's Most Valuable Players" as its theme.

		NM/M
Hobby Factory Set (714):		8.00
Retail Factory Set (704):		7.00
Complete Set (704):		6.00
Common Player:		.05
Plastic Pack (16):		.40
Plastic Wax Box (36):		9.00
1	Don Mattingly	.50
2	Cal Ripken, Jr.	1.00
3	Dwight Evans	.05
4	Barry Bonds	1.00
5	Kevin McReynolds	.05
6	Ozzie Guillen	.05
7	Terry Kennedy	.05
8	Bryan Harvey	.05
9	Alan Trammell	.05
10	Cory Snyder	.05
11	Jody Reed	.05
12	Roberto Alomar	.20
13	Pedro Guerrero	.05
14	Gary Redus	.05
15	Marty Barrett	.05
16	Ricky Jordan	.05
17	Joe Magrane	.05
18	Sid Fernandez	.05
19	Rich Dotson	.05
20	Jack Clark	.05
21	Bob Walk	.05
22	Ron Karkovice	.05
23	Lenny Harris RC	.05
24	Phil Bradley	.05
25	Andres Galarraga	.05
26	Brian Downing	.05
27	Dave Martinez	.05
28	Eric King	.05
29	Barry Lyons	.05
30	Dave Schmidt	.05
31	Mike Boddicker	.05
32	Tom Foley	.05
33	Brady Anderson	.05
34	Jim Presley	.05
35	Lance Parrish	.05
36	Von Hayes	.05
37	Lee Smith	.05
38	Herm Winningham	.05
39	Alejandro Pena	.05
40	Mike Scott	.05
41	Joe Orsulak	.05
42	Rafael Ramirez	.05
43	Gerald Young	.05
44	Dick Schofield	.05
45	Dave Smith	.05
46	Dave Magadan	.05
47	Dennis Martinez	.05
48	Greg Minton	.05
49	Milt Thompson	.05
50	Orel Hershiser	.05
51	Bip Roberts	.05
52	Jerry Browne	.05
53	Bob Ojeda	.05
54	Fernando Valenzuela	.05
55	Matt Nokes	.05
56	Brook Jacoby	.05
57	Frank Tanana	.05
58	Scott Fletcher	.05
59	Ron Oester	.05
60	Bob Boone	.05
61	Dan Gladden	.05
62	Darnell Coles	.05
63	Gregg Olson	.05
64	Todd Burns	.05
65	Todd Benzinger	.05

66	Dale Murphy	.25
67	Mike Flanagan	.05
68	Jose Oquendo	.05
69	Cecil Espy	.05
70	Chris Sabo	.05
71	Shane Rawley	.05
72	Tom Brunansky	.05
73	Vance Law	.05
74	B.J. Surhoff	.05
75	Lou Whitaker	.05
76	Ken Caminiti	.05
77	Nelson Liriano	.05
78	Tommy Gregg	.05
79	Don Slaught	.05
80	Eddie Murray	.40
81	Joe Boever	.05
82	Charlie Leibrandt	.05
83	Jose Lind	.05
84	Tony Phillips	.05
85	Mitch Webster	.05
86	Dan Plesac	.05
87	Rick Mahler	.05
88	Steve Lyons	.05
89	Tony Fernandez	.05
90	Ryne Sandberg	.45
91	Nick Esasky	.05
92	Luis Salazar	.05
93	Pete Incaviglia	.05
94	Ivan Calderon	.05
95	Jeff Treadway	.05
96	Kurt Stillwell	.05
97	Gary Sheffield	.30
98	Jeffrey Leonard	.05
99	Andres Thomas	.05
100	Roberto Kelly	.05
101	Alvaro Espinoza RC	.05
102	Greg Gagne	.05
103	John Farrell	.05
104	Willie Wilson	.05
105	Glenn Braggs	.05
106	Chet Lemon	.05
107	Jamie Moyer	.05
108	Chuck Crim	.05
109	Dave Valle	.05
110	Walt Weiss	.05
111	Larry Sheets	.05
112	Don Robinson	.05
113	Danny Heep	.05
114	Carmelo Martinez	.05
115	Dave Gallagher	.05
116	Mike LaValliere	.05
117	Bob McClure	.05
118	Rene Gonzales	.05
119	Mark Parent	.05
120	Wally Joyner	.05
121	Mark Gubicza	.05
122	Tony Pena	.05
123	Carmen Castillo	.05
124	Howard Johnson	.05
125	Steve Sax	.05
126	Tim Belcher	.05
127	Tim Burke	.05
128	Al Newman	.05
129	Dennis Rasmussen	.05
130	Doug Jones	.05
131	Fred Lynn	.05
132	Jeff Hamilton	.05
133	German Gonzalez	.05
134	John Morris	.05
135	Dave Parker	.05
136	Gary Pettis	.05
137	Dennis Boyd	.05
138	Candy Maldonado	.05
139	Rick Cerone	.05
140	George Brett	.50
141	Dave Clark	.05
142	Dickie Thon	.05
143	Junior Ortiz	.05
144	Don August	.05
145	Gary Gaetti	.05
146	Kirt Manwaring	.05
147	Jeff Reed	.05
148	Jose Alvarez RC	.05
149	Mike Schooler	.05
150	Mark Grace	.05
151	Geronimo Berroa	.05
152	Barry Jones	.05
153	Geno Petralli	.05
154	Jim Deshaies	.05
155	Barry Larkin	.05
156	Alfredo Griffin	.05
157	Tom Henke	.05
158	Mike Jeffcoat RC	.05
159	Bob Welch	.05
160	Julio Franco	.05
161	Henry Cotto	.05
162	Terry Steinbach	.05
163	Damon Berryhill	.05
164	Tim Crews	.05
165	Tom Browning	.05
166	Frd Manrique	.05
167	Harold Reynolds	.05
168a	Ron Hassey (Uniform #27 on back.)	.05
168b	Ron Hassey (Uniform #24 on back.)	.50
169	Shawon Dunston	.05
170	Bobby Bonilla	.05
171	Tom Herr	.05
172	Mike Heath	.05
173	Rich Gedman	.05
174	Bill Ripken	.05
175	Pete O'Brien	.05
176a	Lloyd McClendon (Uniform number 1 on back.)	.50
176b	Lloyd McClendon (Uniform number 10 on back.)	.05
177	Brian Holton	.05

#	Player	Price
178	Jeff Blauser	.05
179	Jim Eisenreich	.05
180	Bert Blyleven	.05
181	Rob Murphy	.05
182	Bill Doran	.05
183	Curt Ford	.05
184	Mike Henneman	.05
185	Eric Davis	.05
186	Lance McCullers	.05
187	Steve Davis RC	.05
188	Bill Wegman	.05
189	Brian Harper	.05
190	Mike Moore	.05
191	Dale Mohorcic	.05
192	Tim Wallach	.05
193	Keith Hernandez	.05
194	Dave Righetti	.05
195a	Bret Saberhagen ("Joke" on card back.)	.10
195b	Bret Saberhagen ("Joker" on card back.)	.30
196	Paul Kilgus	.05
197	Bud Black	.05
198	Juan Samuel	.05
199	Kevin Seitzer	.05
200	Darryl Strawberry	.05
201	Dave Steib	.05
202	Charlie Hough	.05
203	Jack Morris	.05
204	Rance Mulliniks	.05
205	Alvin Davis	.05
206	Jack Howell	.05
207	Ken Patterson RC	.05
208	Terry Pendleton	.05
209	Craig Lefferts	.05
210	Kevin Brown RC	.05
211	Dan Petry	.05
212	Dave Leiper	.05
213	Daryl Boston	.05
214	Kevin Hickey RC	.05
215	Mike Krukow	.05
216	Terry Francona	.05
217	Kirk McCaskill	.05
218	Scott Bailes	.05
219	Bob Forsch	.05
220	Mike Aldrete	.05
221	Steve Buechele	.05
222	Jesse Barfield	.05
223	Juan Berenguer	.05
224	Andy McGaffigan	.05
225	Pete Smith	.05
226	Mike Witt	.05
227	Jay Howell	.05
228	Scott Bradley	.05
229	Jerome Walton RC	.05
230	Greg Swindell	.05
231	Atlee Hammaker	.05
232a	Mike Devereaux (RF)	.05
232b	Mike Devereaux (CF)	2.00
233	Ken Hill	.05
234	Craig Worthington	.05
235	Scott Terry	.05
236	Brett Butler	.05
237	Doyle Alexander	.05
238	Dave Anderson	.05
239	Bob Milacki	.05
240	Dwight Smith	.05
241	Otis Nixon	.05
242	Pat Tabler	.05
243	Derek Lilliquist	.05
244	Danny Tartabull	.05
245	Wade Boggs	.45
246	Scott Garrelts	.05
247	Spike Owen	.05
248	Norm Charlton	.05
249	Gerald Perry	.05
250	Nolan Ryan	1.00
251	Kevin Gross	.05
252	Randy Milligan	.05
253	Mike LaCoss	.05
254	Dave Bergman	.05
255	Tony Gwynn	.45
256	Felix Fermin	.05
257	Greg Harris	.05
258	Junior Felix RC	.05
259	Mark Davis	.05
260	Vince Coleman	.05
261	Paul Gibson	.05
262	Mitch Williams	.05
263	Jeff Russell	.05
264	Omar Vizquel	.05
265	Andre Dawson	.25
266	Storm Davis	.05
267	Guillermo Hernandez	.05
268	Mike Felder	.05
269	Tom Candiotti	.05
270	Bruce Hurst	.05
271	Fred McGriff	.25
272	Glenn Davis	.05
273	John Franco	.05
274	Rich Yett	.05
275	Craig Biggio	.45
276	Gene Larkin	.05
277	Rob Dibble	.05
278	Randy Bush	.05
279	Kevin Bass	.05
280a	Bo Jackson ("Watham" on back.)	.15
280b	Bo Jackson ("Wathan" on back.)	.50
281	Wally Backman	.05
282	Larry Andersen	.05
283	Chris Bosio	.05
284	Juan Agosto	.05
285	Ozzie Smith	.45
286	George Bell	.05
287	Rex Hudler	.05
288	Pat Borders	.05
289	Danny Jackson	.05
290	Carlton Fisk	.40
291	Tracy Jones	.05
292	Allan Anderson	.05
293	Johnny Ray	.05
294	Lee Guetterman	.05
295	Paul O'Neill	.05
296	Carney Lansford	.05
297	Tom Brookens	.05
298	Claudell Washington	.05
299	Hubie Brooks	.05
300	Will Clark	.05
301	Kenny Rogers	.05
302	Darrell Evans	.05
303	Greg Briley	.05
304	Donn Pall	.05
305	Teddy Higuera	.05
306	Dan Pasqua	.05
307	Dave Winfield	.40
308	Dennis Powell	.05
309	Jose DeLeon	.05
310	Roger Clemens	.50
311	Melido Perez	.05
312	Devon White	.05
313	Dwight Gooden	.05
314	Carlos Martinez RC	.05
315	Dennis Eckersley	.35
316	Clay Parker	.05
317	Rick Honeycutt	.05
318	Tim Laudner	.05
319	Joe Carter	.05
320	Robin Yount	.40
321	Felix Jose	.05
322	Mickey Tettleton	.05
323	Mike Gallego	.05
324	Edgar Martinez	.05
325	Dave Henderson	.05
326	Chili Davis	.05
327	Steve Balboni	.05
328	Jody Davis	.05
329	Shawn Hillegas	.05
330	Jim Abbott	.05
331	John Dopson	.05
332	Mark Williamson	.05
333	Jeff Robinson	.05
334	John Smiley	.05
335	Bobby Thigpen	.05
336	Garry Templeton	.05
337	Marvell Wynne	.05
338a	Ken Griffey Sr. (Uniform #25 on card back.)	.05
338b	Ken Griffey Sr. (Uniform #30 on card back.)	1.00
339	Steve Finley	.05
340	Ellis Burks	.05
341	Frank Williams	.05
342	Mike Morgan	.05
343	Kevin Mitchell	.05
344	Joel Youngblood	.05
345	Mike Greenwell	.05
346	Glenn Wilson	.05
347	John Costello	.05
348	Wes Gardner	.05
349	Jeff Ballard	.05
350	Mark Thurmond	.05
351	Randy Myers	.05
352	Shawn Abner	.05
353	Jesse Orosco	.05
354	Greg Walker	.05
355	Pete Harnisch	.05
356	Steve Farr	.05
357	Dave LaPoint	.05
358	Willie Fraser	.05
359	Mickey Hatcher	.05
360	Rickey Henderson	.40
361	Mike Fitzgerald	.05
362	Bill Schroeder	.05
363	Mark Carreon	.05
364	Ron Jones	.05
365	Jeff Montgomery	.05
366	Bill Krueger RC	.05
367	John Cangelosi	.05
368	Jose Gonzalez	.05
369	Greg Hibbard RC	.05
370	John Smoltz	.05
371	Jeff Brantley RC	.05
372	Frank White	.05
373	Ed Whitson	.05
374	Willie McGee	.05
375	Jose Canseco	.30
376	Randy Ready	.05
377	Don Aase	.05
378	Tony Armas	.05
379	Steve Bedrosian	.05
380	Chuck Finley	.05
381	Kent Hrbek	.05
382	Jim Gantner	.05
383	Mel Hall	.05
384	Mike Marshall	.05
385	Mark McGwire	.75
386	Wayne Tolleson	.05
387	Brian Holton	.05
388	John Wetteland	.05
389	Darren Daulton	.05
390	Rob Deer	.05
391	John Moses	.05
392	Todd Worrell	.05
393	Chuck Cary RC	.05
394	Stan Javier	.05
395	Willie Randolph	.05
396	Bill Buckner	.05
397	Robby Thompson	.05
398	Mike Scioscia	.05
399	Lonnie Smith	.05
400	Kirby Puckett	.45
401	Mark Langston	.05
402	Danny Darwin	.05
403	Greg Maddux	.45
404	Lloyd Moseby	.05
405	Rafael Palmeiro	.35
406	Chad Kreuter	.05
407	Jimmy Key	.05
408	Tim Birtsas	.05
409	Tim Raines	.05
410	Dave Stewart	.05
411	Eric Yelding RC	.05
412	Kent Anderson RC	.05
413	Les Lancaster	.05
414	Rick Dempsey	.05
415	Randy Johnson	.40
416	Gary Carter	.40
417	Rolando Roomes	.05
418	Dan Schatzeder	.05
419	Bryn Smith	.05
420	Ruben Sierra	.05
421	Steve Jeltz	.05
422	Ken Oberkfell	.05
423	Sid Bream	.05
424	Jim Clancy	.05
425	Kelly Gruber	.05
426	Rick Leach	.05
427	Len Dykstra	.05
428	Jeff Pico	.05
429	John Cerutti	.05
430	David Cone	.05
431	Jeff Kunkel	.05
432	Luis Aquino	.05
433	Ernie Whitt	.05
434	Bo Diaz	.05
435	Steve Lake	.05
436	Pat Perry	.05
437	Mike Davis	.05
438	Cecilio Guante	.05
439	Duane Ward	.05
440	Andy Van Slyke	.05
441	Gene Nelson	.05
442	Luis Polonia	.05
443	Kevin Elster	.05
444	Keith Moreland	.05
445	Roger McDowell	.05
446	Ron Darling	.05
447	Ernest Riles	.05
448	Mookie Wilson	.05
449a	Bill Spiers RC (66 missing for year of birth)	.50
449b	Bill Spiers RC (1966 for birth year)	.05
450	Rick Sutcliffe	.05
451	Nelson Santovenia	.05
452	Andy Allanson	.05
453	Bob Melvin	.05
454	Benny Santiago	.05
455	Jose Uribe	.05
456	Bill Landrum RC	.05
457	Bobby Witt	.05
458	Kevin Romine	.05
459	Lee Mazzilli	.05
460	Paul Molitor	.40
461	Ramon Martinez	.05
462	Frank DiPino	.05
463	Walt Terrell	.05
464	Bob Geren RC	.05
465	Rick Reuchel	.05
466	Mark Grant	.05
467	John Kruk	.05
468	Gregg Jefferies	.05
469	R.J. Reynolds	.05
470	Harold Baines	.05
471	Dennis Lamp	.05
472	Tom Gordon	.05
473	Terry Puhl	.05
474	Curtis Wilkerson	.05
475	Dan Quisenberry	.05
476	Oddibe McDowell	.05
477a	Zane Smith (Career ERA 3.93.)	.50
477b	Zane Smith	.05
478	Franklin Stubbs	.05
479	Wallace Johnson	.05
480	Jay Tibbs	.05
481	Tom Glavine	.35
482	Manny Lee	.05
483	Joe Hesketh	.05
484	Mike Bielecki	.05
485	Greg Brock	.05
486	Pascual Perez	.05
487	Kirk Gibson	.05
488	Scott Sanderson	.05
489	Domingo Ramos	.05
490	Kal Daniels	.05
491a	David Wells (Reversed negative on back photo.)	1.50
491b	David Wells (Corrected)	.05
492	Jerry Reed	.05
493	Eric Show	.05
494	Mike Pagliarulo	.05
495	Ron Robinson	.05
496	Brad Komminsk	.05
497	Greg Litton RC	.05
498	Chris James	.05
499	Luis Quinones RC	.05
500	Frank Viola	.05
501	Tim Teufel	.05
502	Terry Leach	.05
503	Matt Williams	.05
504	Tim Leary	.05
505	Doug Drabek	.05
506	Mariano Duncan	.05
507	Charlie Hayes	.05
508	Albert Belle	.05
509	Pat Sheridan	.05
510	Mackey Sasser	.05
511	Jose Rijo	.05
512	Mike Smithson	.05
513	Gary Ward	.05
514	Dion James	.05
515	Jim Gott	.05
516	Drew Hall RC	.05
517	Doug Bair	.05
518	Scott Scudder RC	.05
519	Rick Aguilera	.05
520	Rafael Belliard	.05
521	Jay Buhner	.05
522	Jeff Reardon	.05
523	Steve Rosenberg RC	.05
524	Randy Velarde RC	.05
525	Jeff Musselman	.05
526	Bill Long	.05
527	Gary Wayne RC	.05
528	Dave Johnson RC	.05
529	Ron Kittle	.05
530	Erik Hanson RC	.05
531	Steve Wilson RC	.05
532	Joey Meyer	.05
533	Curt Young	.05
534	Kelly Downs	.05
535	Joe Girardi	.05
536	Lance Blankenship	.05
537	Greg Mathews	.05
538	Donell Nixon	.05
539	Mark Knudson RC	.05
540	Jeff Wetherby RC	.05
541	Darrin Jackson	.05
542	Terry Mulholland	.05
543	Eric Hetzel RC	.05
544	Rick Reed RC	.05
545	Dennis Cook RC	.05
546	Mike Jackson	.05
547	Brian Fisher	.05
548	Gene Harris RC	.05
549	Jeff King RC	.05
550	Dave Dravecky (Salute)	.05
551	Randy Kutcher RC	.05
552	Mark Portugal	.05
553	Jim Corsi RC	.05
554	Todd Stottlemyre	.05
555	Scott Bankhead	.05
556	Ken Dayley	.05
557	Rick Wrona RC	.10
558	Sammy Sosa RC	3.00
559	Keith Miller	.05
560	Ken Griffey Jr.	.65
561a	Ryne Sandberg (Highlight, 3B on front.)	2.00
561b	Ryne Sandberg (Highlight, no position.)	.25
562	Billy Hatcher	.05
563	Jay Bell	.05
564	Jack Daugherty RC	.05
565	Rich Monteleone RC	.05
566	Bo Jackson (All-Star MVP)	.10
567	Tony Fossas RC	.05
568	Roy Smith RC	.05
569	Jaime Navarro RC	.05
570	Lance Johnson	.05
571	Mike Dyer RC	.05
572	Kevin Ritz RC	.05
573	Dave West	.05
574	Gary Mielke RC	.05
575	Scott Lusader RC	.05
576	Joe Oliver	.05
577	Sandy Alomar, Jr.	.05
578	Andy Benes	.05
579	Tim Jones	.05
580	Randy McCament RC	.05
581	Curt Schilling RC	.35
582	John Orton RC	.05
583a	Milt Cuyler RC (998 games)	1.00
583b	Milt Cuyler RC (98 games)	.05
584	Eric Anthony RC	.05
585	Greg Vaughn RC	.15
586	Deion Sanders	.05
587	Jose DeJesus RC	.05
588	Chip Hale RC	.05
589	John Olerud RC	.50
590	Steve Olin RC	.05
591	Marquis Grissom RC	.40
592	Moises Alou RC	.40
593	Mark Lemke RC	.05
594	Dean Palmer RC	.15
595	Robin Ventura	.05
596	Tino Martinez	.05
597	Mike Huff RC	.05
598	Scott Hemond RC	.05
599	Wally Whitehurst RC	.05
600	Todd Zeile RC	.05
601	Glenallen Hill RC	.05
602	Hal Morris RC	.05
603	Juan Bell RC	.05
604	Bobby Rose RC	.05
605	Matt Merullo RC	.05
606	Kevin Maas RC	.05
607	Randy Nosek RC	.05
608a	Billy Bates RC ("12 triples" mentioned in second-last line)	.05
608b	Billy Bates (Triples not mentioned.)	.75
609	Mike Stanton RC	.05
610	Goose Gozzo RC	.05
611	Charles Nagy RC	.40
612	Scott Coolbaugh RC	.05
613	Jose Vizcaino RC	.10
614	Greg Smith RC	.05
615	Jeff Huson RC	.05
616	Mickey Weston RC	.05
617	John Pawlowski RC	.05
618a	Joe Skalski RC (Uniform #27 on card back.)	.05
618b	Joe Skalski RC (Uniform #67 on card back.)	1.00
619	Bernie Williams RC	1.00
620	Shawn Holman RC	.05
621	Gary Eave RC	.05
622	Darrin Fletcher RC	.10
623	Pat Combs RC	.05
624	Mike Blowers RC	.05
625	Kevin Appier RC	.05
626	Pat Austin RC	.05
627	Kelly Mann RC	.05
628	Matt Kinzer RC	.05
629	Chris Hammond RC	.10
630	Dean Wilkins RC	.05
631	Larry Walker RC	.50
632	Blaine Beatty RC	.05
633a	Tom Barrett RC (Uniform #29 on card back.)	.05
633b	Tom Barrett RC (Uniform #14 on card back.)	1.00
634	Stan Belinda RC	.05
635	Tex Smith RC	.05
636	Hensley Meulens RC	.10
637	Juan Gonzalez RC	1.50
638	Lenny Webster RC	.10
639	Mark Gardner RC	.05
640	Tommy Greene RC	.05
641	Mike Hartley RC	.05
642	Phil Stephenson RC	.05
643	Kevin Mmahat RC	.05
644	Ed Whited RC	.05
645	Delino DeShields RC	.15
646	Kevin Blankenship RC	.05
647	Paul Sorrento RC	.05
648	Mike Roesler RC	.05
649	Jason Grimsley RC	.05
650	Dave Justice RC	1.00
651	Scott Cooper RC	.05
652	Dave Eiland RC	.05
653	Mike Munoz RC	.05
654	Jeff Fischer RC	.05
655	Terry Jorgenson RC	.05
656	George Canale RC	.05
657	Brian DuBois RC	.05
658	Carlos Quintana	.05
659	Luis de los Santos RC	.05
660	Jerald Clark	.05
661	Donald Harris RC (1st Round Pick)	.05
662	Paul Coleman RC (1st Round Pick)	.05
663	Frank Thomas RC (1st Round Pick)	2.00
664	Brent Mayne RC (1st Round Pick)	.10
665	Eddie Zosky RC (1st Round Pick)	.05
666	Steve Hosey RC (1st Round Pick)	.05
667	Scott Bryant RC (1st Round Pick)	.05
668	Tom Goodwin RC (1st Round Pick)	.10
669	Cal Eldred RC (1st Round Pick)	.10
670	Earl Cunningham RC (1st Round Pick)	.05
671	Alan Zinter RC (1st Round Pick)	.05
672	Chuck Knoblauch RC (1st Round Pick)	.40
672(a)	Chuck Knoblauch (3,000 autographed cards with a special hologram on back were inserted into 1992 rack packs)	10.00
673	Kyle Abbott RC (1st Round Pick)	.10
674	Roger Salkeld RC (1st Round Pick)	.05
675	Mo Vaughn RC (1st Round Pick)	.50
676	Kiki Jones RC (1st Round Pick)	.05
677	Tyler Houston RC (1st Round Pick)	.10
678	Jeff Jackson RC (1st Round Pick)	.05
679	Greg Gohr RC (1st Round Pick)	.05
680	Ben McDonald RC (1st Round Pick)	.15
681	Greg Blosser RC (1st Round Pick)	.05
682	Willie Green RC (Greene) (1st Round Pick)	.05
683	Wade Boggs (Dream Team)	.25
684	Will Clark (Dream Team)	.05
685	Tony Gwynn (Dream Team)	.25
686	Rickey Henderson (Dream Team)	.20
687	Bo Jackson (Dream Team)	.15
688	Mark Langston (Dream Team)	.05
689	Barry Larkin (Dream Team)	.05
690	Kirby Puckett (Dream Team)	.25
691	Ryne Sandberg (Dream Team)	.25
692	Mike Scott (Dream Team)	.05
693	Terry Steinbach (Dream Team)	.05
694	Bobby Thigpen (Dream Team)	.05
695	Mitch Williams (Dream Team)	.05
696	Nolan Ryan (Highlight)	.40
697	Bo Jackson (FB/BB)	.25
698	Rickey Henderson (ALCS MVP)	.20
699	Will Clark (NLCS MVP)	.05
700	World Series Games 1-2	.05
701	Lights Out: Candlestick	.15
702	World Series Game 3	.05
703	World Series Wrap-up	.05
704	Wade Boggs (Highlight)	.25

Rookie Dream Team

MARK LEMKE   BRAVES•2B

This 10-card "Rookie Dream Team" set, in the same format as those found in the regular-issue 1990 Score, was available only in factory sets for the hobby trade. Factory sets for general retail outlets did not include these cards, nor were they available in Score packs. Cards carry a "B" prefix to their numbers.

		NM/M
Complete Set (10):		1.00
Common Player:		.10
1	A. Bartlett Giamatti	.10
2	Pat Combs	.10
3	Todd Zeile	.10
4	Luis de los Santos	.10
5	Mark Lemke	.10
6	Robin Ventura	.10
7	Jeff Huson	.10
8	Greg Vaughn	.10
9	Marquis Grissom	.10
10	Eric Anthony	.10

Traded

ERIC LINDROS 3B

This 110-card set features players with new teams as well as 1990 Major League rookies. The cards feature full-color action photos framed in yellow with an orange border. The player's ID appears in green below the photo. The team logo is displayed next to the player's name. The card backs feature posed player photos and follow the style of the regular 1990 Score issue. The cards are numbered 1T-110T. Young hockey phenom Eric Lindros is featured trying out for the Toronto Blue Jays.

		NM/M
Complete Set (110):		4.00
Common Player:		.05
1	Dave Winfield	.75
2	Kevin Bass	.05
3	Nick Esasky	.05
4	Mitch Webster	.05
5	Pascual Perez	.05
6	Gary Pettis	.05
7	Tony Pena	.05
8	Candy Maldonado	.05
9	Cecil Fielder	.05
10	Carmelo Martinez	.05
11	Mark Langston	.05
12	Dave Parker	.05
13	Don Slaught	.05
14	Tony Phillips	.05
15	John Franco	.05
16	Randy Myers	.05
17	Jeff Reardon	.05
18	Sandy Alomar, Jr.	.05
19	Joe Carter	.05
20	Fred Lynn	.05
21	Storm Davis	.05
22	Craig Lefferts	.05

23 Pete O'Brien .05
24 Dennis Boyd .05
25 Lloyd Moseby .05
26 Mark Davis .05
27 Tim Leary .05
28 Gerald Perry .05
29 Don Aase .05
30 Ernie Whitt .05
31 Dale Murphy .35
32 Alejandro Pena .05
33 Juan Samuel .05
34 Hubie Brooks .05
35 Gary Carter .75
36 Jim Presley .05
37 Wally Backman .05
38 Matt Nokes .05
39 Dan Petry .05
40 Franklin Stubbs .05
41 Jeff Huson .05
42 Billy Hatcher .05
43 Terry Leach .05
44 Phil Bradley .05
45 Claudell Washington .05
46 Luis Polonia .05
47 Daryl Boston .05
48 Lee Smith .05
49 Tom Brunansky .05
50 Mike Witt .05
51 Willie Randolph .05
52 Stan Javier .05
53 Brad Komminsk .05
54 John Candelaria .05
55 Bryn Smith .05
56 Glenn Braggs .05
57 Keith Hernandez .05
58 Ken Oberkfell .05
59 Steve Jeltz .05
60 Chris James .05
61 Scott Sanderson .05
62 Bill Long .05
63 Rick Cerone .05
64 Scott Bailes .05
65 Larry Sheets .05
66 Junior Ortiz .05
67 Francisco Cabrera RC .05
68 Gary DiSarcina RC .05
69 Greg Olson RC .05
70 Beau Allred RC .05
71 Oscar Azocar RC .05
72 Kent Mercker RC .05
73 John Burkett RC .05
74 Carlos Baerga RC .05
75 Dave Hollins RC .25
76 Todd Hundley RC .25
77 Rick Parker RC .05
78 Steve Cummings RC .05
79 Bill Sampen RC .05
80 Jerry Kutzler RC .05
81 Derek Bell RC .05
82 Kevin Tapani RC .75
83 Jim Leyritz RC .05
84 Ray Lankford RC .25
85 Wayne Edwards RC .05
86 Frank Thomas 2.00
87 Tim Naehring RC .05
88 Willie Blair RC .05
89 Alan Mills RC .05
90 Scott Radinsky RC .05
91 Howard Farmer RC .05
92 Julio Machado RC .05
93 Rafael Valdez RC .05
94 Shawn Boskie RC .05
95 David Segui RC .05
96 Chris Hoiles RC .05
97 D.J. Dozier RC .05
98 Hector Villanueva RC .05
99 Eric Gunderson RC .05
100 Eric Lindros RC 1.00
101 Dave Otto RC .05
102 Dana Kiecker RC .05
103 Tim Drummond RC .05
104 Mickey Pina RC .05
105 Craig Grebeck RC .05
106 Bernard Gilkey RC .25
107 Tim Layana RC .05
108 Scott Chiamparino RC .05
109 Steve Avery RC .05
110 Terry Shumpert RC .05

Rising Stars

TODD ZEILE Cardinals

For the second consecutive year Score produced a 100-card "Rising Stars" set. The 1990 issue was made available as a boxed set and also marketed with a related magazine like the 1989 issue. Magic Motion trivia cards featuring past MVP's accompany the card set. The cards feature full-color action photos on the front and portrait photos on the back.

NM/M
Complete Set (100): 5.00
Common Player: .05
1 Tom Gordon .05
2 Jerome Walton .05
3 Ken Griffey Jr. 1.25
4 Dwight Smith .05
5 Jim Abbott .05
6 Todd Zeile .05
7 Donn Pall .05
8 Rick Reed .05
9 Joey Belle .25
10 Gregg Jefferies .05
11 Kevin Ritz .05
12 Charlie Hayes .05
13 Kevin Appier .05
14 Jeff Huson .05
15 Gary Wayne .05
16 Eric Yelding .05
17 Clay Parker .05
18 Junior Felix .05
19 Derek Lilliquist .05
20 Gary Sheffield .25
21 Craig Worthington .05
22 Jeff Brantley .05
23 Eric Hetzel .05
24 Greg Harris .05
25 John Wetteland .05
26 Joe Oliver .05
27 Kevin Maas .05
28 Kevin Brown .05
29 Mike Stanton .05
30 Greg Vaughn .05
31 Ron Jones .05
32 Gregg Olson .05
33 Joe Girardi .05
34 Ken Hill .05
35 Sammy Sosa 3.00
36 Geronimo Berroa .05
37 Omar Vizquel .05
38 Dean Palmer .05
39 John Olerud .05
40 Deion Sanders .05
41 Randy Kramer .05
42 Scott Lusader .05
43 Dave Johnson .05
44 Jeff Wetherby .05
45 Eric Anthony .05
46 Kenny Rogers .05
47 Matt Winters .05
48 Goose Gozzo .05
49 Carlos Quintana .05
50 Bob Geren .05
51 Chad Kreuter .05
52 Randy Johnson .75
53 Hensley Meulens .05
54 Gene Harris .05
55 Bill Spiers .05
56 Kelly Mann .05
57 Tom McCarthy .05
58 Steve Finley .05
59 Ramon Martinez .05
60 Greg Briley .05
61 Jack Daugherty .05
62 Tim Jones .05
63 Doug Strange .05
64 John Orton .05
65 Scott Scudder .05
66 Mark Gardner (Photo on back actually Steve Frey.) .05
67 Mark Carreon .05
68 Bob Milacki .05
69 Andy Benes .05
70 Carlos Martinez .05
71 Jeff King .05
72 Brad Arnsberg .05
73 Rick Wrona .05
74 Cris Carpenter .05
75 Dennis Cook .05
76 Pete Harnisch .05
77 Greg Hibbard .05
78 Ed Whited .05
79 Scott Coolbaugh .05
80 Billy Bates .05
81 German Gonzalez .05
82 Lance Blankenship .05
83 Lenny Harris .05
84 Milt Cuyler .05
85 Erik Hanson .05
86 Kent Anderson .05
87 Hal Morris .05
88 Mike Brumley .05
89 Ken Patterson .05
90 Mike Devereaux .05
91 Greg Litton .05
92 Rolando Roomes .05
93 Ben McDonald .05
94 Curt Schilling .35
95 Jose DeJesus .05
96 Robin Ventura .05
97 Steve Searcy .05
98 Chip Hale .05
99 Marquis Grissom .05
100 Luis de los Santos .05

Superstars

BO JACKSON Royals

The game's top 100 players are featured in this set. The card fronts feature full-color action photos and are similar in style to the past Score Superstar set. The set was marketed as a boxed set and with a special magazine devoted to baseball's 100 hottest players. Each set includes a series of Magic Motion cards honoring past MVP winners. The player cards measure 2-1/2" x 3-1/2".

NM/M
Complete Set (100): 3.00
Common Player: .05
1 Kirby Puckett .50
2 Steve Sax .05
3 Tony Gwynn .50
4 Willie Randolph .05
5 Jose Canseco .25
6 Ozzie Smith .50
7 Rick Reuschel .05
8 Bill Doran .05
9 Mickey Tettleton .05
10 Don Mattingly .60
11 Greg Swindell .05
12 Bert Blyleven .05
13 Dave Stewart .05
14 Andres Galarraga .05
15 Darryl Strawberry .05
16 Ellis Burks .05
17 Paul O'Neill .05
18 Bruce Hurst .05
19 Dave Smith .05
20 Carney Lansford .05
21 Robby Thompson .05
22 Gary Gaetti .05
23 Jeff Russell .05
24 Chuck Finley .05
25 Mark McGwire .65
26 Alvin Davis .05
27 George Bell .05
28 Cory Snyder .05
29 Keith Hernandez .05
30 Will Clark .75
31 Steve Bedrosian .05
32 Ryne Sandberg .50
33 Tom Browning .05
34 Tim Burke .05
35 John Smoltz .05
36 Phil Bradley .05
37 Bobby Bonilla .05
38 Kirk McCaskill .05
39 Dave Righetti .05
40 Alan Trammell .10
41 Mike Moore .05
42 Harold Reynolds .05
43 Nolan Ryan .75
44 Fred McGriff .05
45 Brian Downing .05
46 Brett Butler .05
47 Mike Scioscia .05
48 John Franco .05
49 Kevin Mitchell .05
50 Mark Davis .05
51 Glenn Davis .05
52 Barry Bonds .75
53 Dwight Evans .05
54 Terry Steinbach .05
55 Dave Gallagher .05
56 Roberto Kelly .05
57 Rafael Palmeiro .35
58 Joe Carter .05
59 Mark Grace .05
60 Pedro Guerrero .05
61 Von Hayes .05
62 Benny Santiago .05
63 Dale Murphy .25
64 John Smiley .05
65 Cal Ripken, Jr. .75
66 Mike Greenwell .05
67 Devon White .05
68 Ed Whitson .05
69 Carlton Fisk .40
70 Lou Whitaker .05
71 Danny Tartabull .05
72 Vince Coleman .05
73 Andre Dawson .25
74 Tim Raines .05
75 George Brett .60
76 Tom Herr .05
77 Andy Van Slyke .05
78 Roger Clemens .60
79 Wade Boggs .05
80 Wally Joyner .05
81 Lonnie Smith .05
82 Howard Johnson .05
83 Julio Franco .05
84 Ruben Sierra .05
85 Dan Plesac .05
86 Bobby Thigpen .05
87 Kevin Seitzer .05
88 Kevin Seitzer .05
89 Dave Steib .05
90 Rickey Henderson .40
91 Jeffrey Leonard .05
92 Robin Yount .40
93 Mitch Williams .05
94 Orel Hershiser .05
95 Eric Davis .05
96 Mark Langston .05
97 Mike Scott .05
98 Paul Molitor .40
99 Dwight Gooden .05
100 Kevin Bass .05

Yankees

New York Yankees
MEL HALL OF

For a second year, National Westminster Bank sponsored a Score-produced team set as a stadium promotion. The set features color player photos on front and back and is graphically enhanced by the team's traditional pinstripe motif. A tribute card to former Yankees infielder and manager Billy Martin, who was killed the previous Christmas, is included in the set. The set was given to fans attending the August 18 game.

NM/M
Complete Set (32): 4.00
Common Player: .15
1 Stump Merrill .15
2 Don Mattingly 2.50
3 Steve Sax .15
4 Alvaro Espinoza .15
5 Jesse Barfield .15
6 Roberto Kelly .15
7 Mel Hall .15
8 Claudell Washington .15
9 Bob Geren .15
10 Jim Leyritz .15
11 Pascual Perez .15
12 Dave LaPoint .15
13 Tim Leary .15
14 Mike Witt .15
15 Chuck Cary .15
16 Dave Righetti .15
17 Lee Guetterman .15
18 Andy Hawkins .15
19 Greg Cadaret .15
20 Eric Plunk .15
21 Jimmy Jones .15
22 Deion Sanders .75
23 Jeff Robinson .15
24 Matt Nokes .15
25 Steve Balboni .15
26 Wayne Tolleson .15
27 Randy Velarde .15
28 Rick Cerone .15
29 Alan Mills .15
30 Billy Martin .30
31 Yankee Stadium .15
32 All-Time Yankee Records .15

Young Superstars Set 1

JOEY BELLE OUTFIELD 36

For the third consecutive year, Score produced Young Superstars boxed sets. The 1990 versions contain 42 player cards plus five Magic-Motion trivia cards. The cards are similar to previous Young Superstar sets, with action photography on the front and a glossy finish. Card backs have a color portrait, major league statistics and scouting reports. Besides the boxed set, cards from Set I were inserted into rack packs.

NM/M
Complete Set (42): 2.00
Common Player: .10
1 Bo Jackson .25
2 Dwight Smith .10
3 Joey Belle .25
4 Gregg Olson .10
5 Jim Abbott .10
6 Felix Fermin .10
7 Brian Holman .10
8 Clay Parker .10
9 Junior Felix .10
10 Joe Oliver .10
11 Steve Finley .10
12 Greg Briley .10
13 Greg Vaughn .10
14 Bill Spiers .10
15 Eric Yelding .10
16 Jose Gonzalez .10
17 Mark Carreon .10
18 Greg Harris .10
19 Felix Jose .10
20 Bob Milacki .10
21 Kenny Rogers .10
22 Rolando Roomes .10
23 Bip Roberts .10
24 Jeff Brantley .10
25 Jeff Ballard .10
26 John Dopson .10
27 Ken Patterson .10
28 Omar Vizquel .10
29 Kevin Brown .10
30 Derek Lilliquist .10
31 David Wells .10
32 Ken Hill .10
33 Greg Litton .10
34 Rob Ducey .10
35 Carlos Martinez .10
36 John Smoltz .10
37 Lenny Harris .10
38 Charlie Hayes .10
39 Tommy Gregg .10
40 John Wetteland .10
41 Jeff Huson .10
42 Eric Anthony .10

Young Superstars Set 2

ROBIN VENTURA THIRD BASE 21

Available only as a boxed set via a mail-order offer, Set II of 1990 Score Young Superstars is identical in format to Set I, with the exception that the graphic elements on the front of Set II cards are in red and green, while in Set I they are in blue and magenta.

NM/M
Complete Set (42): 5.00
Common Player: .10
1 Todd Zeile .10
2 Ben McDonald .10
3 Delino DeShields .10
4 Pat Combs .10
5 John Olerud .10
6 Marquis Grissom .10
7 Mike Stanton .10
8 Robin Ventura .10
9 Larry Walker .10
10 Dante Bichette .10
11 Jack Armstrong .10
12 Jay Bell .10
13 Andy Benes .10
14 Joey Cora .10
15 Rob Dibble .10
16 Jeff King .10
17 Jeff Hamilton .10
18 Erik Hanson .10
19 Pete Harnisch .10
20 Greg Hibbard .10
21 Stan Javier .10
22 Mark Lemke .10
23 Steve Olin .10
24 Tommy Greene .10
25 Sammy Sosa 4.00
26 Gary Wayne .10
27 Deion Sanders .10
28 Steve Wilson .10
29 Joe Girardi .10
30 John Orton .10
31 Kevin Tapani .10
32 Carlos Baerga .10
33 Glenallen Hill .10
34 Mike Blowers .10
35 Dave Hollins .10
36 Lance Blankenship .10
37 Hal Morris .10
38 Lance Johnson .10
39 Chris Gwynn .10
40 Doug Dascenzo .10
41 Jerald Clark .10
42 Carlos Quintana .10

Sportflics 11th National Nolan Ryan

NOLAN RYAN
1990 NATIONAL SPORTS COLLECTORS CONVENTION

This two-fronted card is a unique souvenir given to those who participated in a special 1990 convention tour of the Optigraphics card manufacturing plant in Dallas. The card features Nolan Ryan on two of the company's best-known products, Score on one side, Sportflics on the other. Each side is similar to Ryan's regularly issued card in those sets, but carries logos or typography related to the 11th Annual National Sports Collectors Convention, held in nearby Arlington. Only 600 of the cards were reported produced.

NM/M
Nolan Ryan 100.00

1991 Score Promos

MARK PARENT PADRES C

To preview its 1991 baseball cards Score pre-released the 110 cards from its teal-bordered series (cards #111-220) as samples. The main difference on most cards between the samples and the issued version is that the samples have no statistics on the 1990 season or career lines. Many cards have different career highlight write-ups on back, as well. A handful of the sample cards were widely distributed to dealers and the hobby press, while others from the sheet were released more sparingly. As few as two specimens are known of some superstar cards, driving up their prices among single-player specialty collectors.

NM/M
Common Player: 5.00
111 Juan Berenguer 5.00
112 Mike Heath 5.00
113 Scott Bradley 5.00
114 Jack Morris 5.00
115 Barry Jones 5.00
116 Kevin Romine 5.00
117 Garry Templeton 5.00
118 Scott Sanderson 5.00
119 Roberto Kelly 5.00
120 George Brett 60.00
121 Oddibe McDowell 5.00
122 Jim Acker 5.00
123 Bill Swift 5.00
124 Eric King 5.00
125 Jay Buhner 5.00
126 Matt Young 5.00
127 Alvaro Espinoza 5.00
128 Greg Hibbard 5.00
129 Jeff M. Robinson 5.00

No.	Player	Price
130	Mike Greenwell	5.00
131	Dion James	5.00
132	Donn Pall	5.00
133	Lloyd Moseby	5.00
134	Randy Velarde	5.00
135	Allan Anderson	5.00
136	Mark Davis	5.00
137	Eric Davis	5.00
138	Phil Stephenson	5.00
139	Felix Fermin	5.00
140	Pedro Guerrero	5.00
141	Charlie Hough	5.00
142	Mike Henneman	5.00
143	Jeff Montgomery	5.00
144	Lenny Harris	5.00
145	Bruce Hurst	5.00
146	Eric Anthony	5.00
147	Paul Assenmacher	5.00
148	Jesse Barfield	5.00
149	Carlos Quintana	5.00
150	Dave Stewart	5.00
151	Roy Smith	5.00
152	Paul Gibson	5.00
153	Mickey Hatcher	5.00
154	Jim Eisenreich	5.00
155	Kenny Rogers	5.00
156	Dave Schmidt	5.00
157	Lance Johnson	5.00
158	Dave West	5.00
159	Steve Balboni	5.00
160	Jeff Brantley	5.00
161	Craig Biggio	5.00
162	Brook Jacoby	5.00
163	Dan Gladden	5.00
164	Jeff Reardon	5.00
165	Mark Carreon	5.00
166	Mel Hall	5.00
167	Gary Mielke	5.00
168	Cecil Fielder	5.00
169	Darrin Jackson	5.00
170	Rick Aguilera	5.00
171	Walt Weiss	5.00
172	Steve Farr	5.00
173	Jody Reed	5.00
174	Mike Jeffcoat	5.00
175	Mark Grace	5.00
176	Larry Sheets	5.00
177	Bill Gullickson	5.00
178	Chris Gwynn	5.00
179	Melido Perez	5.00
180	Sid Fernandez	5.00
181	Tim Burke	5.00
182	Gary Pettis	5.00
183	Rob Murphy	5.00
184	Craig Lefferts	5.00
185	Howard Johnson	5.00
186	Ken Caminiti	5.00
187	Tim Belcher	5.00
188	Greg Cadaret	5.00
189	Matt Williams	5.00
190	Dave Magadan	5.00
191	Geno Petralli	5.00
192	Jeff D. Robinson	5.00
193	Jim Deshaies	5.00
194	Willie Randolph	5.00
195	George Bell	5.00
196	Hubie Brooks	5.00
197	Tom Gordon	5.00
198	Mike Fitzgerald	5.00
199	Mike Pagliarulo	5.00
200	Kirby Puckett	40.00
201	Shawon Dunston	5.00
202	Dennis Boyd	5.00
203	Junior Felix	5.00
204	Alejandro Pena	5.00
205	Pete Smith	5.00
206	Tom Glavine	20.00
207	Luis Salazar	5.00
208	John Smoltz	5.00
209	Doug Dascenzo	5.00
210	Tim Wallach	5.00
211	Greg Gagne	5.00
212	Mark Gubicza	5.00
213	Mark Parent	5.00
214	Ken Oberkfell	5.00
215	Gary Carter	30.00
216	Rafael Palmeiro	25.00
217	Tom Niedenfuer	5.00
218	Dave LaPoint	5.00
219	Jeff Treadway	5.00
220	Mitch Williams	5.00

1991 Score

Score introduced a two-series format in 1991. The first series includes cards 1-441. Score cards once again feature multiple border colors within the set, several sub- sets (Master Blaster, K-Man, Highlights and Riflemen), full-color action photos on the front and portraits on the flip side. Score eliminated display of the player's uniform number on the 1991 cards. Black-and-white Dream Team cards, plus Prospects and #1 Draft Picks highlight the 1991 set. The second series was released in February of 1991.

	NM/M
Unopened Fact. Set (900):	10.00
Complete Set (893):	6.00
Common Player:	.05
Series 1 or 2 Pack (16):	.25
Series 1 or 2 Box (36):	6.00

No.	Player	Price
1	Jose Canseco	.25
2	Ken Griffey Jr.	.60
3	Ryne Sandberg	.50
4	Nolan Ryan	.75
5	Bo Jackson	.10
6	Bret Saberhagen	.05
7	Will Clark	.05
8	Ellis Burks	.05
9	Joe Carter	.05
10	Rickey Henderson	.40
11	Ozzie Guillen	.05
12	Wade Boggs	.50
13	Jerome Walton	.05
14	John Franco	.05
15	Ricky Jordan	.05
16	Wally Backman	.05
17	Rob Dibble	.05
18	Glenn Braggs	.05
19	Cory Snyder	.05
20	Kal Daniels	.05
21	Mark Langston	.05
22	Kevin Gross	.05
23	Don Mattingly	.55
24	Dave Righetti	.05
25	Roberto Alomar	.15
26	Robby Thompson	.05
27	Jack McDowell	.05
28	Bip Roberts	.05
29	Jay Howell	.05
30	Dave Steib	.05
31	Johnny Ray	.05
32	Steve Sax	.05
33	Terry Mulholland	.05
34	Lee Guetterman	.05
35	Tim Raines	.05
36	Scott Fletcher	.05
37	Lance Parrish	.05
38	Tony Phillips	.05
39	Todd Stottlemyre	.05
40	Alan Trammell	.05
41	Todd Burns	.05
42	Mookie Wilson	.05
43	Chris Bosio	.05
44	Jeffrey Leonard	.05
45	Doug Jones	.05
46	Mike Scott	.05
47	Andy Hawkins	.05
48	Harold Reynolds	.05
49	Paul Molitor	.40
50	John Farrell	.05
51	Danny Darwin	.05
52	Jeff Blauser	.05
53	John Tudor	.05
54	Milt Thompson	.05
55	Dave Justice	.75
56	Greg Olson RC	.05
57	Willie Blair RC	.05
58	Rick Parker RC	.05
59	Shawn Boskie	.05
60	Kevin Tapani	.05
61	Dave Hollins	.05
62	Scott Radinsky RC	.05
63	Francisco Cabrera	.05
64	Tim Layana RC	.05
65	Jim Leyritz	.05
66	Wayne Edwards	.05
67	Lee Stevens RC	.05
68	Bill Sampen RC	.05
69	Craig Grebeck RC	.05
70	John Burkett	.05
71	Hector Villanueva RC	.05
72	Oscar Azocar RC	.05
73	Alan Mills	.05
74	Carlos Baerga	.60
75	Charles Nagy	.05
76	Tim Drummond	.05
77	Dana Kiecker RC	.05
78	Tom Edens RC	.05
79	Kent Mercker	.05
80	Steve Avery	.05
81	Lee Smith	.05
82	Dave Martinez	.05
83	Dave Winfield	.40
84	Bill Spiers	.05
85	Dan Pasqua	.05
86	Randy Milligan	.05
87	Tracy Jones	.05
88	Greg Myers RC	.05
89	Keith Hernandez	.05
90	Todd Benzinger	.05
91	Mike Jackson	.05
92	Mike Stanley	.05
93	Candy Maldonado	.05
94	John Kruk	.05
95	Cal Ripken, Jr.	.75
96	Willie Fraser	.05
97	Mike Felder	.05
98	Bill Landrum	.05
99	Chuck Crim	.05
100	Chuck Finley	.05
101	Kirt Manwaring	.05
102	Jaime Navarro	.05
103	Dickie Thon	.05
104	Brian Downing	.05
105	Jim Abbott	.05
106	Tom Brookens	.05
107	Darryl Hamilton	.05
108	Bryan Harvey	.05
109	Greg Harris	.05
110	Greg Swindell	.05
111	Juan Berenguer	.05
112	Mike Heath	.05
113	Scott Bradley	.05
114	Jack Morris	.05
115	Barry Jones	.05
116	Kevin Romine	.05
117	Garry Templeton	.05
118	Scott Sanderson	.05
119	Roberto Kelly	.05
120	George Brett	.50
121	Oddibe McDowell	.05
122	Jim Acker	.05
123	Bill Swift	.05
124	Eric King	.05
125	Jay Buhner	.05
126	Matt Young	.05
127	Alvaro Espinoza	.05
128	Greg Hibbard	.05
129	Jeff Robinson	.05
130	Mike Greenwell	.05
131	Dion James	.05
132	Donn Pall	.05
133	Lloyd Moseby	.05
134	Randy Velarde	.05
135	Allan Anderson	.05
136	Mark Davis	.05
137	Eric Davis	.05
138	Phil Stephenson	.05
139	Felix Fermin	.05
140	Pedro Guerrero	.05
141	Charlie Hough	.05
142	Mike Henneman	.05
143	Jeff Montgomery	.05
144	Lenny Harris	.05
145	Bruce Hurst	.05
146	Eric Anthony	.05
147	Paul Assenmacher	.05
148	Jesse Barfield	.05
149	Carlos Quintana	.05
150	Dave Stewart	.05
151	Roy Smith	.05
152	Paul Gibson	.05
153	Mickey Hatcher	.05
154	Jim Eisenreich	.05
155	Kenny Rogers	.05
156	Dave Schmidt	.05
157	Lance Johnson	.05
158	Dave West	.05
159	Steve Balboni	.05
160	Jeff Brantley	.05
161	Craig Biggio	.05
162	Brook Jacoby	.05
163	Dan Gladden	.05
164	Jeff Reardon	.05
165	Mark Carreon	.05
166	Mel Hall	.05
167	Gary Mielke	.05
168	Cecil Fielder	.05
169	Darrin Jackson	.05
170	Rick Aguilera	.05
171	Walt Weiss	.05
172	Steve Farr	.05
173	Jody Reed	.05
174	Mike Jeffcoat	.05
175	Mark Grace	.05
176	Larry Sheets	.05
177	Bill Gullickson	.05
178	Chris Gwynn	.05
179	Melido Perez	.05
180	Sid Fernandez	.05
181	Tim Burke	.05
182	Gary Pettis	.05
183	Rob Murphy	.05
184	Craig Lefferts	.05
185	Howard Johnson	.05
186	Ken Caminiti	.05
187	Tim Belcher	.05
188	Greg Cadaret	.05
189	Matt Williams	.05
190	Dave Magadan	.05
191	Geno Petralli	.05
192	Jeff Robinson	.05
193	Jim Deshaies	.05
194	Willie Randolph	.05
195	George Bell	.05
196	Hubie Brooks	.05
197	Tom Gordon	.05
198	Mike Fitzgerald	.05
199	Mike Pagliarulo	.05
200	Kirby Puckett	.50
201	Shawon Dunston	.05
202	Dennis Boyd	.05
203	Junior Felix	.05
204	Alejandro Pena	.05
205	Pete Smith	.05
206	Tom Glavine	.35
207	Luis Salazar	.05
208	John Smoltz	.05
209	Doug Dascenzo	.05
210	Tim Wallach	.05
211	Greg Gagne	.05
212	Mark Gubicza	.05
213	Mark Parent	.05
214	Ken Oberkfell	.05
215	Gary Carter	.40
216	Rafael Palmeiro	.35
217	Tom Niedenfuer	.05
218	Dave LaPoint	.05
219	Jeff Treadway	.05
220	Mitch Williams	.05
221	Jose DeLeon	.05
222	Mike LaValliere	.05
223	Darrel Akerfelds	.05
224a	Kent Anderson ("Flachy" in first line.)	.05
224b	Kent Anderson ("Flashy" in first line.)	.05
225	Dwight Evans	.05
226	Gary Redus	.05
227	Paul O'Neill	.05
228	Marty Barrett	.05
229	Tom Browning	.05
230	Terry Pendleton	.05
231	Jack Armstrong	.05
232	Mike Boddicker	.05
233	Neal Heaton	.05
234	Marquis Grissom	.05
235	Bert Blyleven	.05
236	Curt Young	.05
237	Don Carman	.05
238	Charlie Hayes	.05
239	Mark Knudson	.05
240	Todd Zeile	.05
241	Larry Walker	.05
242	Jerald Clark	.05
243	Jeff Ballard	.05
244	Jeff King	.05
245	Tom Brunansky	.05
246	Darren Daulton	.05
247	Scott Terry	.05
248	Rob Deer	.05
249	Brady Anderson	.05
250	Len Dykstra	.05
251	Greg Harris	.05
252	Mike Hartley	.05
253	Joey Cora	.05
254	Ivan Calderon	.05
255	Ted Power	.05
256	Sammy Sosa	.50
257	Steve Buechele	.05
258	Mike Devereaux	.05
259	Brad Komminsk	.05
260	Teddy Higuera	.05
261	Shawn Abner	.05
262	Dave Valle	.05
263	Jeff Huson	.05
264	Edgar Martinez	.05
265	Carlton Fisk	.40
266	Steve Finley	.05
267	John Wetteland	.05
268	Kevin Appier	.05
269	Steve Lyons	.05
270	Mickey Tettleton	.05
271	Luis Rivera	.05
272	Steve Jeltz	.05
273	R.J. Reynolds	.05
274	Carlos Martinez	.05
275	Dan Plesac	.05
276	Mike Morgan	.05
277	Jeff Russell	.05
278	Pete Incaviglia	.05
279	Kevin Seitzer	.05
280	Bobby Thigpen	.05
281	Stan Javier	.05
282	Henry Cotto	.05
283	Gary Wayne	.05
284	Shane Mack	.05
285	Brian Holman	.05
286	Gerald Perry	.05
287	Steve Crawford	.05
288	Nelson Liriano	.05
289	Don Aase	.05
290	Randy Johnson	.40
291	Harold Baines	.05
292	Kent Hrbek	.05
293a	Les Lancaster ("Dallas, Texas")	.05
293b	Les Lancaster ("Dallas, Texas")	.05
294	Jeff Musselman	.05
295	Kurt Stillwell	.05
296	Stan Belinda	.05
297	Lou Whitaker	.05
298	Glenn Wilson	.05
299	Omar Vizquel	.05
300	Ramon Martinez	.05
301	Dwight Smith	.05
302	Tim Crews	.05
303	Lance Blankenship	.05
304	Sid Bream	.05
305	Rafael Ramirez	.05
306	Steve Wilson	.05
307	Mackey Sasser	.05
308	Franklin Stubbs	.05
309	Jack Daugherty	.05
310	Eddie Murray	.40
311	Bob Welch	.05
312	Brian Harper	.05
313	Lance McCullers	.05
314	Dave Smith	.05
315	Bobby Bonilla	.05
316	Jerry Don Gleaton	.05
317	Greg Maddux	.50
318	Keith Miller	.05
319	Mark Portugal	.05
320	Robin Ventura	.05
321	Bob Ojeda	.05
322	Mike Harkey	.05
323	Jay Bell	.05
324	Mark McGwire	.65
325	Gary Gaetti	.05
326	Jeff Pico	.05
327	Kevin McReynolds	.05
328	Frank Tanana	.05
329	Eric Yelding	.05
330	Barry Bonds	.75
331	Brian McRae RC	.05
332	Pedro Munoz RC	.05
333	Daryl Irvine RC	.05
334	Chris Hoiles RC	.05
335	Thomas Howard RC	.05
336	Jeff Schulz RC	.05
337	Jeff Manto RC	.05
338	Beau Allred	.05
339	Mike Bordick RC	.10
340	Todd Hundley	.05
341	Jim Vatcher RC	.05
342	Luis Sojo RC	.05
343	Jose Offerman RC	.05
344	Pete Coachman RC	.05
345	Mike Benjamin RC	.05
346	Ozzie Canseco RC	.05
347	Tim McIntosh RC	.05
348	Phil Plantier RC	.05
349	Terry Shumpert RC	.05
350	Darren Lewis RC	.05
351	David Walsh RC	.05
352a	Scott Chiamparino RC (Bats: Left)	.05
352b	Scott Chiamparino RC (Bats: Right)	.05
353	Julio Valera RC	.05
354	Anthony Telford RC	.05
355	Kevin Wickander RC	.05
356	Tim Naehring RC	.05
357	Jim Poole RC	.05
358	Mark Whiten RC	.05
359	Terry Wells RC	.05
360	Rafael Valdez RC	.05
361	Mel Stottlemyre RC	.05
362	David Segui RC	.10
363	Paul Abbott RC	.05
364	Steve Howard RC	.05
365	Karl Rhodes RC	.10
366	Rafael Novoa RC	.05
367	Joe Grahe RC	.05
368	Darren Reed RC	.05
369	Jeff McKnight RC	.05
370	Scott Leius RC	.05
371	Mark Dewey RC	.05
372	Mark Lee RC	.05
373	Rosario McElroy RC	.05
374	Chuck McElroy RC	.05
375	Mike Bell RC	.05
376	Mickey Morandini RC	.05
377	Bill Haselman RC	.05
378	Dave Pavlas RC	.05
379	Derrick May	.05
380	Jeromy Burnitz RC (1st Draft Pick)	.25
381	Donald Peters RC (1st Draft Pick)	.05
382	Alex Fernandez RC (1st Draft Pick)	.05
383	Mike Mussina RC (1st Draft Pick)	1.00
384	Daniel Smith RC (1st Draft Pick)	.05
385	Lance Dickson RC (1st Draft Pick)	.10
386	Carl Everett RC (1st Draft Pick)	.40
387	Thomas Nevers RC (1st Draft Pick)	.05
388	Adam Hyzdu RC (1st Draft Pick)	.05
389	Todd Van Poppel RC (1st Draft Pick)	.10
390	Rondell White RC (1st Draft Pick)	.30
391	Marc Newfield RC (1st Draft Pick)	.05
392	Julio Franco/AS	.05
393	Wade Boggs/AS	.25
394	Ozzie Guillen/AS	.05
395	Cecil Fielder /AS	.05
396	Ken Griffey Jr./AS	.30
397	Rickey Henderson/AS	.20
398	Jose Canseco/AS	.15
399	Roger Clemens/AS	.30
400	Sandy Alomar,Jr./AS	.05
401	Bobby Thigpen/AS	.05
402	Bobby Bonilla (Master Blaster)	.05
403	Eric Davis (Master Blaster)	.05
404	Fred McGriff (Master Blaster)	.05
405	Glenn Davis (Master Blaster)	.05
406	Kevin Mitchell (Master Blaster)	.05
407	Rob Dibble (K-Man)	.05
408	Ramon Martinez (K-Man)	.05
409	David Cone (K-Man)	.05
410	Bobby Witt (K-Man)	.05
411	Mark Langston (K-Man)	.05
412	Bo Jackson (Rifleman)	.10
413	Shawon Dunston (Rifleman)	.05
414	Jesse Barfield (Rifleman)	.05
415	Ken Caminiti (Rifleman)	.05
416	Benito Santiago (Rifleman)	.05
417	Nolan Ryan (Highlight)	.40
418	Bobby Thigpen (HL)	.05
419	Ramon Martinez (HL)	.05
420	Bo Jackson (HL)	.10
421	Carlton Fisk (HL)	.20
422	Jimmy Key	.05
423	Junior Noboa RC	.05
424	Al Newman	.05
425	Pat Borders	.05
426	Von Hayes	.05
427	Tim Teufel	.05
428	Eric Plunk	.05
429	John Moses	.05
430	Mike Witt	.05
431	Otis Nixon	.05
432	Tony Fernandez	.05
433	Rance Mulliniks	.05
434	Dan Petry	.05
435	Bob Geren	.05
436	Steve Frey RC	.05
437	Jamie Moyer	.05
438	Junior Ortiz	.05
439	Tom O'Malley	.05
440	Pat Combs	.05
441	Jose Canseco (Dream Team)	.15
442	Alfredo Griffin	.05
443	Andres Galarraga	.05
444	Bryn Smith	.05
445	Andre Dawson	.25
446	Juan Samuel	.05
447	Mike Aldrete	.05
448	Ron Gant	.05
449	Fernando Valenzuela	.05
450	Vince Coleman	.05
451	Kevin Mitchell	.05
452	Spike Owen	.05
453	Mike Bielecki	.05
454	Dennis Martinez	.05
455	Brett Butler	.05
456	Ron Darling	.05
457	Dennis Rasmussen	.05
458	Ken Howell	.05
459	Steve Bedrosian	.05
460	Frank Viola	.05
461	Jose Lind	.05
462	Chris Sabo	.05
463	Dante Bichette	.05
464	Rick Mahler	.05
465	John Smiley	.05
466	Devon White	.05
467	John Orton	.05
468	Mike Stanton	.05
469	Billy Hatcher	.05
470	Wally Joyner	.05
471	Gene Larkin	.05
472	Doug Drabek	.05
473	Gary Sheffield	.30
474	David Wells	.05
475	Andy Van Slyke	.05
476	Mike Gallego	.05
477	B.J. Surhoff	.05
478	Gene Nelson	.05
479	Mariano Duncan	.05
480	Fred McGriff	.05
481	Jerry Browne	.05
482	Alvin Davis	.05
483	Bill Wegman	.05
484	Dave Parker	.05
485	Dennis Eckersley	.35
486	Erik Hanson	.05
487	Bill Ripken	.05
488	Tom Candiotti	.05
489	Mike Schooler	.05
490	Gregg Olson	.05
491	Chris James	.05
492	Pete Harnisch	.05
493	Julio Franco	.05
494	Greg Briley	.05
495	Ruben Sierra	.05
496	Steve Olin	.05
497	Mike Fetters	.05
498	Mark Williamson	.05
499	Bob Tewksbury	.05
500	Tony Gwynn	.50
501	Randy Myers	.05
502	Keith Comstock	.05
503	Craig Worthington	.05
504	Mark Eichhorn	.05
505	Barry Larkin	.05
506	Dave Johnson	.05
507	Bobby Witt	.05
508	Joe Orsulak	.05
509	Pete O'Brien	.05
510	Brad Arnsberg	.05
511	Storm Davis	.05
512	Bob Milacki	.05
513	Bill Pecota	.05
514	Glenallen Hill	.05
515	Danny Tartabull	.05
516	Mike Moore	.05
517	Ron Robinson	.05
518	Mark Gardner	.05
519	Rick Wrona	.05
520	Mike Scioscia	.05
521	Frank Wills	.05
522	Greg Brock	.05
523	Jack Clark	.05
524	Bruce Ruffin	.05
525	Robin Yount	.40
526	Tom Foley	.05
527	Pat Perry	.05
528	Greg Vaughn	.05
529	Wally Whitehurst	.05
530	Norm Charlton	.05
531	Marvell Wynne	.05
532	Jim Gantner	.05
533	Greg Litton	.05
534	Manny Lee	.05
535	Scott Bailes	.05
536	Charlie Leibrandt	.05
537	Roger McDowell	.05
538	Andy Benes	.05
539	Rick Honeycutt	.05
540	Dwight Gooden	.05
541	Scott Garrelts	.05
542	Dave Clark	.05

#	Player	Price
543	Lonnie Smith	.05
544	Rick Rueschel	.05
545	Delino DeShields	.05
546	Mike Sharperson	.05
547	Mike Kingery	.05
548	Terry Kennedy	.05
549	David Cone	.05
550	Orel Hershiser	.05
551	Matt Nokes	.05
552	Eddie Williams	.05
553	Frank DiPino	.05
554	Fred Lynn	.05
555	Alex Cole RC	.05
556	Terry Leach	.05
557	Chet Lemon	.05
558	Paul Mirabella	.05
559	Bill Long	.05
560	Phil Bradley	.05
561	Duane Ward	.05
562	Dave Bergman	.05
563	Eric Show	.05
564	Xavier Hernandez RC	.05
565	Jeff Parrett	.05
566	Chuck Cary	.05
567	Ken Hill	.05
568	Bob Welch	.05
569	John Mitchell	.05
570	Travis Fryman	.05
571	Derek Lilliquist	.05
572	Steve Lake	.05
573	John Barfield RC	.05
574	Randy Bush	.05
575	Joe Magrane	.05
576	Edgar Diaz	.05
577	Casy Candaele	.05
578	Jesse Orosco	.05
579	Tom Henke	.05
580	Rick Cerone	.05
581	Drew Hall	.05
582	Tony Castillo	.05
583	Jimmy Jones	.05
584	Rick Reed	.05
585	Joe Girardi	.05
586	Jeff Gray RC	.05
587	Luis Polonia	.05
588	Joe Klink RC	.05
589	Rex Hudler	.05
590	Kirk McCaskill	.05
591	Juan Agosto	.05
592	Wes Gardner	.05
593	Rich Rodriguez RC	.05
594	Mitch Webster	.05
595	Kelly Gruber	.05
596	Dale Mohorcic	.05
597	Willie McGee	.05
598	Bill Krueger	.05
599	Bob Walk	.05
600	Kevin Maas	.05
601	Danny Jackson	.05
602	Craig McMurtry	.05
603	Curtis Wilkerson	.05
604	Adam Peterson	.05
605	Sam Horn	.05
606	Tommy Gregg	.05
607	Ken Dayley	.05
608	Carmelo Castillo	.05
609	John Shelby	.05
610	Don Slaught	.05
611	Calvin Schiraldi	.05
612	Dennis Lamp	.05
613	Andres Thomas	.05
614	Jose Gonzales	.05
615	Randy Ready	.05
616	Kevin Bass	.05
617	Mike Marshall	.05
618	Daryl Boston	.05
619	Andy McGaffigan	.05
620	Joe Oliver	.05
621	Jim Gott	.05
622	Jose Oquendo	.05
623	Jose DeJesus	.05
624	Mike Brumley	.05
625	John Olerud	.05
626	Ernest Riles	.05
627	Gene Harris	.05
628	Jose Uribe	.05
629	Darnell Coles	.05
630	Carney Lansford	.05
631	Tim Leary	.05
632	Tim Hulett	.05
633	Kevin Elster	.05
634	Tony Fossas	.05
635	Francisco Oliveras	.05
636	Bob Patterson	.05
637	Gary Ward	.05
638	Rene Gonzales	.05
639	Don Robinson	.05
640	Darryl Strawberry	.05
641	Dave Anderson	.05
642	Scott Scudder	.05
643	Reggie Harris RC	.05
644	Dave Henderson	.05
645	Ben McDonald	.05
646	Bob Kipper	.05
647	Hal Morris	.05
648	Tim Birtsas	.05
649	Steve Searcy	.05
650	Dale Murphy	.20
651	Ron Oester	.05
652	Mike LaCoss	.05
653	Ron Jones	.05
654	Kelly Downs	.05
655	Roger Clemens	.55
656	Herm Winningham	.05
657	Trevor Wilson	.05
658	Jose Rijo	.05
659	Dann Bilardello	.05
660	Gregg Jefferies	.05

#	Player	Price
661	Doug Drabek/AS	.05
662	Randy Myers/AS	.05
663	Benito Santiago/AS	.05
664	Will Clark/AS	.05
665	Ryne Sandberg/AS	.25
666	Barry Larkin/AS	.05
667	Matt Williams/AS	.05
668	Barry Bonds/AS	.35
669	Eric Davis	.05
670	Bobby Bonilla/AS	.05
671	Chipper Jones RC (1st Draft Pick)	3.00
672	Eric Christopherson RC (1st Draft Pick)	.05
673	Robbie Beckett RC (1st Draft Pick)	.05
674	Shane Andrews RC (1st Draft Pick)	.15
675	Steve Karsay RC (1st Draft Pick)	.10
676	Aaron Holbert RC (1st Draft Pick)	.05
677	Donovan Osborne RC (1st Draft Pick)	.05
678	Todd Ritchie RC (1st Draft Pick)	.05
679	Ron Walden RC (1st Draft Pick)	.05
680	Tim Costo RC (1st Draft Pick)	.05
681	Dan Wilson RC (1st Draft Pick)	.10
682	Kurt Miller RC (1st Draft Pick)	.05
683	Mike Lieberthal RC (1st Draft Pick)	.25
684	Roger Clemens (K-Man)	.25
685	Dwight Gooden (K-Man)	.05
686	Nolan Ryan (K-Man)	.35
687	Frank Viola (K-Man)	.05
688	Erik Hanson (K-Man)	.05
689	Matt Williams (Master Blaster)	.05
690	Jose Canseco (Master Blaster)	.10
691	Darryl Strawberry (Master Blaster)	.05
692	Bo Jackson (Master Blaster)	.10
693	Cecil Fielder (Master Blaster)	.05
694	Sandy Alomar, Jr. (Rifleman)	.05
695	Cory Snyder (Rifleman)	.05
696	Eric Davis (Rifleman)	.05
697	Ken Griffey Jr. (Rifleman)	.30
698	Andy Van Slyke (Rifleman)	.05
699	Mark Langston, Mike Witt (No-hitter)	.05
700	Randy Johnson (No-hitter)	.20
701a	Nolan Ryan (No-hitter)(White background on stat box.)	2.00
701b	Nolan Ryan (No-hitter)(Blue background on stat box.)	.35
702	Dave Stewart (No-hitter)	.05
703	Fernando Valenzuela (No-hitter)	.05
704	Andy Hawkins (No-hitter)	.05
705	Melido Perez (No-hitter)	.05
706	Terry Mulholland (No-hitter)	.05
707	Dave Stieb (No-hitter)	.05
708	Brian Barnes RC	.05
709	Bernard Gilkey	.05
710	Steve Decker RC	.05
711	Paul Faries RC	.05
712	Paul Marak RC	.05
713	Wes Chamberlain RC	.05
714	Kevin Belcher RC	.05
715	Dan Boone RC	.05
716	Steve Adkins RC	.05
717	Geronimo Pena RC	.05
718	Howard Farmer RC	.05
719	Mark Leonard RC	.05
720	Tom Lampkin RC	.05
721	Mike Gardiner RC	.05
722	Jeff Conine RC	.25
723	Efrain Valdez RC	.05
724	Chuck Malone RC	.05
725	Leo Gomez RC	.05
726	Paul McClellan RC	.05
727	Mark Leiter RC	.05
728	Rich DeLucia RC	.05
729	Mel Rojas RC	.05
730	Hector Wagner RC	.05
731	Ray Lankford RC	.05
732	Turner Ward RC	.05
733	Gerald Alexander RC	.05
734	Scott Anderson RC	.05
735	Tony Perezchica RC	.05
736	Jimmy Kremers RC	.05
737a	American Flag (SCORE 1991 copyright, unmarked promo.)	.25
737b	American Flag (1991 SCORE in copyright)	.25
738	Mike York RC	.05
739	Mike Rochford RC	.05
740	Scott Aldred RC	.05
741	Rico Brogna RC	.05
742	Dave Burba RC	.05
743	Ray Stephens RC	.05
744	Eric Gunderson RC	.05
745	Troy Afenir RC	.05
746	Jeff Shaw RC	.05
747	Orlando Merced RC	.10
748	Omar Oliveras RC	.05
749	Jerry Kutzler RC	.05
750	Mo Vaughn RC	.05
751	Matt Stark RC	.05
752	Randy Hennis RC	.05

#	Player	Price
753	Andujar Cedeno RC	.05
754	Kelvin Torve RC	.05
755	Joe Kraemer RC	.05
756	Phil Clark RC	.05
757	Ed Vosberg RC	.05
758	Mike Perez RC	.05
759	Scott Lewis RC	.05
760	Steve Chitren RC	.05
761	Ray Young RC	.05
762	Andres Santana RC	.05
763	Rodney McCray RC	.05
764	Sean Berry RC	.05
765	Brent Mayne	.05
766	Mike Simms RC	.05
767	Glenn Sutko RC	.05
768	Gary Disarcina	.05
769	George Brett (HL)	.25
770	Cecil Fielder (HL)	.05
771	Jim Presley	.05
772	John Dopson	.05
773	Bo Jackson (Breaker)	.10
774	Brent Knackert RC	.05
775	Bill Doran	.05
776	Dick Schofield	.05
777	Nelson Santovenia	.05
778	Mark Guthrie RC	.05
779	Mark Lemke	.05
780	Terry Steinbach	.05
781	Tom Bolton	.05
782	Randy Tomlin RC	.05
783	Jeff Kunkel	.05
784	Felix Jose	.05
785	Rick Sutcliffe	.05
786	John Cerutti	.05
787	Jose Vizcaino	.05
788	Curt Schilling	.35
789	Ed Whitson	.05
790	Tony Pena	.05
791	John Candelaria	.05
792	Carmelo Martinez	.05
793	Sandy Alomar, Jr.	.05
794	Jim Neidlinger RC	.05
795	Red's October (Barry Larkin, Chris Sabo)	.10
796	Paul Sorrento	.05
797	Tom Pagnozzi	.05
798	Tino Martinez	.05
799	Scott Ruskin RC	.05
800	Kirk Gibson	.05
801	Walt Terrell	.05
802	John Russell	.05
803	Chili Davis	.05
804	Chris Nabholz RC	.05
805	Juan Gonzalez	.20
806	Ron Hassey	.05
807	Todd Worrell	.05
808	Tommy Greene	.05
809	Joel Skinner	.05
810	Benito Santiago	.05
811	Pat Tabler	.05
812	Scott Erickson RC	.05
813	Moises Alou	.05
814	Dale Sveum	.05
815	Ryne Sandberg (Man of the Year)	.25
816	Rick Dempsey	.05
817	Scott Bankhead	.05
818	Jason Grimsley	.05
819	Doug Jennings	.05
820	Tom Herr	.05
821	Rob Ducey	.05
822	Luis Quinones	.05
823	Greg Minton	.05
824	Mark Grant	.05
825	Ozzie Smith	.50
826	Dave Eiland	.05
827	Danny Heep	.05
828	Hensley Meulens	.05
829	Charlie O'Brien	.05
830	Glenn Davis	.05
831	John Marzano	.05
832	Steve Ontiveros	.05
833	Ron Karkovice	.05
834	Jerry Goff RC	.05
835	Ken Griffey Sr.	.05
836	Kevin Reimer RC	.05
837	Randy Kutcher	.05
838	Mike Blowers	.05
839	Mike Macfarlane	.05
840	Frank Thomas	.40
841	Ken Griffey Sr., Ken Griffey Jr.	.20
842	Jack Howell	.05
843	Mauro Gozzo RC	.05
844	Gerald Young	.05
845	Zane Smith	.05
846	Kevin Brown	.05
847	Sil Campusano	.05
848	Larry Andersen	.05
849	Cal Ripken, Jr. (Franchise)	.35
850	Roger Clemens (Franchise)	.30
851	Sandy Alomar, Jr. (Franchise)	.05
852	Alan Trammell (Franchise)	.05
853	George Brett (Franchise)	.25
854	Robin Yount (Franchise)	.25
855	Kirby Puckett (Franchise)	.25
856	Don Mattingly (Franchise)	.30
857	Rickey Henderson (Franchise)	.20
858	Ken Griffey Jr. (Franchise)	.30
859	Ruben Sierra (Franchise)	.05
860	John Olerud (Franchise)	.05
861	Dave Justice (Franchise)	.05
862	Ryne Sandberg (Franchise)	.25
863	Eric Davis (Franchise)	.05
864	Darryl Strawberry (Franchise)	.05
865	Tim Wallach (Franchise)	.05

#	Player	Price
866	Dwight Gooden (Franchise)	.05
867	Len Dykstra (Franchise)	.05
868	Barry Bonds (Franchise)	.35
869	Todd Zeile (Franchise)	.05
870	Benito Santiago (Franchise)	.05
871	Will Clark (Franchise)	.05
872	Craig Biggio (Franchise)	.05
873	Wally Joyner (Franchise)	.05
874	Frank Thomas (Franchise)	.20
875	Rickey Henderson (MVP)	.20
876	Barry Bonds (MVP)	.35
877	Bob Welch (Cy Young)	.05
878	Doug Drabek (Cy Young)	.05
879	Sandy Alomar, Jr. (ROY)	.05
880	Dave Justice (ROY)	.05
881	Damon Berryhill	.05
882	Frank Viola (Dream Team)	.05
883	Dave Stewart (Dream Team)	.05
884	Doug Jones (Dream Team)	.05
885	Randy Myers (Dream Team)	.05
886	Will Clark (Dream Team)	.05
887	Roberto Alomar (Dream Team)	.10
888	Barry Larkin (Dream Team)	.05
889	Wade Boggs (Dream Team)	.25
890	Rickey Henderson (Dream Team)	.20
891	Kirby Puckett (Dream Team)	.25
892	Ken Griffey Jr. (Dream Team)	.30
893	Benito Santiago (Dream Team)	.05

Mickey Mantle

This special set recalls Mickey Mantle's career as a Yankee. Card fronts are glossy and have red and white borders. The card's caption appears at the bottom in a blue stripe. The backs have a photo and a summary of the caption, plus the card number and serial number. Dealers and media members received the sets, which were limited to 5,000, in a fin-fold plastic wrapper. A total of 2,500 of the cards were numbered and autographed.

		NM/M
Complete Set (7):		35.00
Common Card:		7.50
Autographed Card:		575.00
1	The Rookie	9.00
2	Triple Crown	7.50
3	World Series	7.50
4	Going, Going, Gone	7.50
5	Speed and Grace	7.50
6	A True Yankee	7.50
7	Twilight	7.50

Cooperstown

This seven-card set was included as an insert in every factory set. The card fronts are white, with an oval-vignetted player portrait. The backs have green borders surrounding a yellow background which contains a summary of the player's career.

		NM/M
Complete Set (7):		3.50
Common Player:		.25
B1	Wade Boggs	.50
B2	Barry Larkin	.25
B3	Ken Griffey Jr.	1.00
B4	Rickey Henderson	.35
B5	George Brett	.75
B6	Will Clark	.25
B7	Nolan Ryan	1.50

Hot Rookies

These standard-size cards were inserted one per every 100-card 1991 Score blister pack. Action photos with white borders are featured on the front, and "Hot Rookie" is written in yellow at the top. The background is shaded from yellow to orange. The cards are numbered and each has a color mug shot and a career summary.

		NM/M
Complete Set (10):		2.50
Common Player:		.10

#	Player	Price
1	Dave Justice	.25
2	Kevin Maas	.10
3	Hal Morris	.10
4	Frank Thomas	1.50
5	Jeff Conine	.10
6	Sandy Alomar Jr.	.10
7	Ray Lankford	.10
8	Steve Decker	.10
9	Juan Gonzalez	.50
10	Jose Offerman	.10

Traded

This 110-card set features players with new teams as well as 1991 Major League rookies. The cards are designed in the same style as the regular 1991 Score issue. The cards once again feature a "T" designation along with the card number. The complete set was sold at hobby shops in a special box.

		NM/M
Complete Set (110):		4.00
Common Player:		.05
1	Bo Jackson	.10
2	Mike Flanagan	.05
3	Pete Incaviglia	.05
4	Jack Clark	.05
5	Hubie Brooks	.05
6	Ivan Calderon	.05
7	Glenn Davis	.05
8	Wally Backman	.05
9	Dave Smith	.05
10	Tim Raines	.05
11	Joe Carter	.05
12	Sid Bream	.05
13	George Bell	.05
14	Steve Bedrosian	.05
15	Willie Wilson	.05
16	Darryl Strawberry	.05
17	Danny Jackson	.05
18	Kirk Gibson	.05
19	Willie McGee	.05
20	Junior Felix	.05
21	Steve Farr	.05
22	Pat Tabler	.05
23	Brett Butler	.05
24	Danny Darwin	.05
25	Mickey Tettleton	.05
26	Gary Carter	.50
27	Mitch Williams	.05
28	Candy Maldonado	.05
29	Otis Nixon	.05
30	Brian Downing	.05
31	Tom Candiotti	.05
32	John Candelaria	.05
33	Rob Murphy	.05
34	Deion Sanders	.05
35	Willie Randolph	.05
36	Pete Harnisch	.05
37	Dante Bichette	.05
38	Garry Templeton	.05
39	Gary Gaetti	.05
40	John Cerutti	.05
41	Rick Cerone	.05
42	Mike Pagliarulo	.05
43	Ron Hassey	.05
44	Roberto Alomar	.20
45	Mike Boddicker	.05
46	Bud Black	.05
47	Rob Deer	.05
48	Devon White	.05
49	Luis Sojo	.05
50	Terry Pendleton	.05
51	Kevin Gross	.05
52	Mike Huff	.05
53	Dave Righetti	.05
54	Matt Young	.05
55	Ernest Riles	.05
56	Bill Gullickson	.05
57	Vince Coleman	.05
58	Fred McGriff	.05
59	Franklin Stubbs	.05
60	Eric King	.05
61	Cory Snyder	.05
62	Dwight Evans	.05
63	Gerald Perry	.05
64	Eric Show	.05
65	Shawn Hillegas	.05
66	Tony Fernandez	.05
67	Tim Teufel	.05
68	Mitch Webster	.05
69	Mike Heath	.05
70	Chili Davis	.05
71	Larry Andersen	.05
72	Gary Varsho	.05
73	Juan Berenguer	.05
74	Jack Morris	.05
75	Barry Jones	.05
76	Rafael Belliard	.05
77	Steve Buechele	.05
78	Scott Sanderson	.05
79	Bob Ojeda	.05
80	Curt Schilling	.35
81	Brian Drahman RC	.05
82	Ivan Rodriguez RC	1.00
83	David Howard RC	.05
84	Heath Slocumb RC	.05
85	Mike Timlin RC	.05
86	Darryl Kile RC	.05
87	Pete Schourek RC	.05
88	Bruce Walton RC	.05
89	Al Osuna RC	.05
90	Gary Scott RC	.05
91	Doug Simons RC	.05
92	Chris Jones RC	.05
93	Chuck Knoblauch	.05
94	Dana Allison RC	.05
95	Erik Pappas RC	.05
96	Jeff Bagwell RC	2.50
97	Kirk Dressendorfer RC	.05
98	Freddie Benavides RC	.05
99	Luis Gonzalez RC	.50
100	Wade Taylor RC	.05
101	Ed Sprague RC	.05
102	Bob Scanlan RC	.05
103	Rick Wilkins RC	.05
104	Chris Donnels RC	.05
105	Joe Slusarski RC	.05
106	Mark Lewis RC	.05
107	Pat Kelly RC	.05
108	John Briscoe RC	.05
109	Luis Lopez RC	.05
110	Jeff Johnson RC	.05

Blue Jays

Sold as a special boxed issue including 40 player cards and five trivia cards, this set features the 1991 Blue Jays and their hosting of the 1991 All-Star Game. Cards carry a super-glossy front finish that features a player action photo in a home plate-shaped frame at center. Around the photo are blue and white border designs with the player's name and position at top, and Score and Blue Jays logos at bottom. Backs repeat the blue and white motif with a color player portrait, biographical notes, stats and career summary.

		NM/M
Complete Set (40):		7.00
Common Player:		.25
1	Joe Carter	.35
2	Tom Henke	.25
3	Jimmy Key	.25
4	Al Leiter	.25
5	Dave Steib	.25
6	Todd Stottlemyre	.35
7	Mike Timlin	.25
8	Duane Ward	.25
9	David Wells	.50
10	Frank Wills	.25
11	Pat Borders	.25
12	Greg Myers	.25
13	Roberto Alomar	2.50
14	Rene Gonzalez	.25
15	Kelly Gruber	.25
16	Manny Lee	.25
17	Rance Mulliniks	.25
18	John Olerud	1.00
19	Pat Tabler	.25
20	Derek Bell	.25
21	Jim Acker	.25
22	Rob Ducey	.25
23	Devon White	.35
24	Mookie Wilson	.25
25	Juan Guzman	.25
26	Ed Sprague	.25
27	Ken Dayley	.25
28	Tom Candiotti	.25
29	Candy Maldonado	.25
30	Eddie Zosky	.25
31	Steve Karsay	.25
32	Bob MacDonald	.25
33	Ray Giannelli	.25
34	Jerry Schunk	.25
35	Dave Weathers	.25
36	Cito Gaston	.25
37	Joe Carter/AS	.25
38	Jimmy Key/AS	.25
39	Roberto Alomar/AS	1.50
40	1991 All-Star Game	.25

FanFest/National

Three versions of this set were produced. Two were for distribution at the All-Star FanFest and the National Sports Collectors Convention. These have the name of the appropriate venue printed in a red stripe on back under the player career summary. The third version has a blank red stripe. Fronts have a color action photo against a background of pale green and blue ballplayer silhouettes and yellow baseballs. Backs repeat that motif on a white background. A trapezoid at center has a player portrait photo, color team logo, biological data and career highlights. None of the three versions carries a premium over the others.

		NM/M
Complete Set (10):		2.00
Common Player:		.25
1	Ray Lankford	.25
2	Steve Decker	.25
3	Gary Scott	.25
4	Hensley Meulens	.25
5	Tim Naehring	.25
6	Mark Whiten	.25
7	Ed Sprague	.25
8	Charles Nagy	.25
9	Terry Shumpert	.25
10	Chuck Knoblauch	.25

"Life and Times of Nolan Ryan"

This four-card career highlights set was distributed with a series of four collector magazines. Cards feature color photos with Score and Texas Rangers logos in

---

separate corners. A red stripe above the photo, or to its left, names the highlight; a blue stripe above or to the left of that has his name and position. Horizontally formatted backs have another color photo and a paragraph about the milestone.

		NM/M
Complete Set (4):		6.00
Common Player:		1.50
1	5,000th Career Strikeout (Nolan Ryan)	1.50
2	6th Career No-Hitter (Nolan Ryan)	1.50
3	300th Career Victory (Nolan Ryan)	1.50
4	7th Career No-Hitter (Nolan Ryan)	1.50

Rising Stars

Marketed along with 1990-91 "Baseball's Hottest Rookies" magazine, this 100-card set features top rookies and young players. The cards are similar in design to the Score Superstar set. The magazine/card sets were available to a select group of retailers.

		NM/M
Complete Set (100):		2.50
Common Player:		.05
1	Sandy Alomar, Jr.	.05
2	Tom Edens	.05
3	Terry Shumpert	.05
4	Shawn Boskie	.05
5	Steve Avery	.05
6	Deion Sanders	.05
7	John Burkett	.05
8	Stan Belinda	.05
9	Thomas Howard	.05
10	Wayne Edwards	.05
11	Rick Parker	.05
12	Randy Veres	.05
13	Alex Cole	.05
14	Scott Chaimparino	.05
15	Greg Olson	.05
16	Jose DeJesus	.05
17	Mike Blowers	.05
18	Jeff Huson	.05
19	Willie Blair	.05
20	Howard Farmer	.05
21	Larry Walker	.05
22	Scott Hemond	.05
23	Mel Stottlemyre	.05
24	Mark Whiten	.05
25	Jeff Schulz	.05
26	Gary Disarcina	.05
27	George Canale	.05
28	Dean Palmer	.05
29	Jim Leyritz	.05
30	Carlos Baerga	.05
31	Rafael Valdez	.05
32	Derek Bell	.05
33	Francisco Cabrera	.05
34	Chris Hoiles	.05
35	Craig Grebeck	.05
36	Scott Coolbaugh	.05
37	Kevin Wickander	.05
38	Marquis Grissom	.05
39	Chip Hale	.05
40	Kevin Maas	.05
41	Juan Gonzalez	.50
42	Eric Anthony	.05
43	Luis Sojo	.05
44	Paul Sorrento	.05
45	Dave Justice	.05
46	Oscar Azocar	.05
47	Charles Nagy	.05
48	Robin Ventura	.05
49	Reggie Harris	.05
50	Ben McDonald	.05
51	Hector Villanueva	.05
52	Kevin Tapani	.05
53	Brian Bohanon	.05
54	Tim Layana	.05

55	Delino DeShields	.05
56	Beau Allred	.05
57	Eric Gunderson	.05
58	Kent Mercker	.05
59	Juan Bell	.05
60	Glenallen Hill	.05
61	David Segui	.05
62	Alan Mills	.05
63	Mike Harkey	.05
64	Bill Sampen	.05
65	Greg Vaughn	.05
66	Alex Fernandez	.05
67	Mike Hartley	.05
68	Travis Fryman	.05
69	Dave Rohde	.05
70	Tom Lampkin	.05
71	Mark Gardner	.05
72	Pat Combs	.05
73	Kevin Appier	.05
74	Mike Fetters	.05
75	Greg Myers	.05
76	Steve Searcy	.05
77	Tim Naehring	.05
78	Frank Thomas	1.50
79	Todd Hundley	.05
80	Ed Vosburg	.05
81	Todd Zeile	.05
82	Lee Stevens	.05
83	Scott Radinsky	.05
84	Hensley Meulens	.05
85	Brian DuBois	.05
86	Steve Olin	.05
87	Julio Machado	.05
88	Jose Vizcaino	.05
89	Mark Lemke	.05
90	Felix Jose	.05
91	Wally Whitehurst	.05
92	Dana Kiecker	.05
93	Mike Munoz	.05
94	Adam Peterson	.05
95	Tim Drummond	.05
96	Dave Hollins	.05
97	Craig Wilson	.05
98	Hal Morris	.05
99	Jose Offerman	.05
100	John Olerud	.05

Rookies

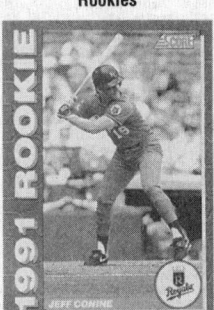

This 40-card boxed set did not receive much attention in the hobby world, but features some of the top young players of 1991. The card fronts feature full-color action photos with a "Rookies" banner along the side border. The backs feature statistics and a player profile. This set was available through hobby dealers and is Score's first release of its kind.

		NM/M
Complete Set (40):		1.00
Common Player:		.05
1	Mel Rojas	.05
2	Ray Lankford	.05
3	Scott Aldred	.05
4	Turner Ward	.05
5	Omar Olivares	.05
6	Mo Vaughn	.05
7	Phil Clark	.05
8	Brent Mayne	.05
9	Scott Lewis	.05
10	Brian Barnes	.05
11	Bernard Gilkey	.05
12	Steve Decker	.05
13	Paul Marak	.05
14	Wes Chamberlain	.05
15	Kevin Belcher	.05
16	Steve Adkins	.05
17	Geronimo Pena	.05
18	Mark Leonard	.05
19	Jeff Conine	.05
20	Leo Gomez	.05
21	Chuck Malone	.05
22	Beau Allred	.05
23	Todd Hundley	.05
24	Lance Dickson	.05
25	Mike Benjamin	.05
26	Jose Offerman	.05
27	Terry Shumpert	.05
28	Darren Lewis	.05
29	Scott Chiamparino	.05
30	Tim Naehring	.05
31	David Segui	.05
32	Karl Rhodes	.05
33	Mickey Morandini	.05
34	Chuck McElroy	.05
35	Tim McIntosh	.05

36	Derrick May	.05
37	Rich DeLucia	.05
38	Tino Martinez	.05
39	Hensley Meulens	.05
40	Andujar Cedeno	.05

Superstars

This 100-card set features full-color action photos on the card fronts and posed shots on the flip sides. The set was marketed along with the magazine "1991 Baseball's Hottest Players." The cards feature red, white, and blue borders. The backs contain brief career highlights. The magazine/card set combo was available to select retailers.

		NM/M
Complete Set (100):		5.00
Common Player:		.05
1	Jose Canseco	.25
2	Bo Jackson	.10
3	Wade Boggs	.50
4	Will Clark	.05
5	Ken Griffey Jr.	.65
6	Doug Drabek	.05
7	Kirby Puckett	.50
8	Joe Orsulak	.05
9	Eric Davis	.05
10	Rickey Henderson	.40
11	Lenny Dykstra	.05
12	Ruben Sierra	.05
13	Paul Molitor	.40
14	Ron Gant	.05
15	Ozzie Guillen	.05
16	Ramon Martinez	.05
17	Edgar Martinez	.05
18	Ozzie Smith	.50
19	Charlie Hayes	.05
20	Barry Larkin	.05
21	Cal Ripken, Jr.	1.00
22	Andy Van Slyke	.05
23	Don Mattingly	.60
24	Dave Stewart	.05
25	Nolan Ryan	1.00
26	Barry Bonds	1.00
27	Gregg Olson	.05
28	Chris Sabo	.05
29	John Franco	.05
30	Gary Sheffield	.25
31	Jeff Treadway	.05
32	Tom Browning	.05
33	Jose Lind	.05
34	Dave Magadan	.05
35	Dale Murphy	.20
36	Tom Candiotti	.05
37	Willie McGee	.05
38	Robin Yount	.40
39	Mark McGwire	.75
40	George Bell	.05
41	Carlton Fisk	.40
42	Bobby Bonilla	.05
43	Randy Milligan	.05
44	Dave Parker	.05
45	Shawon Dunston	.05
46	Brian Harper	.05
47	John Tudor	.05
48	Ellis Burks	.05
49	Bob Welch	.05
50	Roger Clemens	.60
51	Mike Henneman	.05
52	Eddie Murray	.40
53	Kal Daniels	.05
54	Doug Jones	.05
55	Craig Biggio	.05
56	Rafael Palmeiro	.35
57	Wally Joyner	.05
58	Tim Wallach	.05
59	Bret Saberhagen	.05
60	Ryne Sandberg	.50
61	Benito Santiago	.05
62	Darryl Strawberry	.05
63	Alan Trammell	.05
64	Kelly Gruber	.05
65	Dwight Gooden	.05
66	Dave Winfield	.40
67	Rick Aguilera	.05
68	Dave Righetti	.05
69	Jim Abbott	.05
70	Frank Viola	.05
71	Fred McGriff	.05
72	Steve Sax	.05
73	Dennis Eckersley	.35
74	Cory Snyder	.05
75	Mackey Sasser	.05
76	Candy Maldonado	.05

77	Matt Williams	.05
78	Kent Hrbek	.05
79	Randy Myers	.05
80	Gregg Jefferies	.05
81	Joe Carter	.05
82	Mike Greenwell	.05
83	Jack Armstrong	.05
84	Julio Franco	.05
85	George Brett	.60
86	Howard Johnson	.05
87	Andre Dawson	.25
88	Cecil Fielder	.05
89	Tim Raines	.05
90	Chuck Finley	.05
91	Mark Grace	.05
92	Brook Jacoby	.05
93	Dave Steib	.05
94	Tony Gwynn	.50
95	Bobby Thigpen	.05
96	Roberto Kelly	.05
97	Kevin Seitzer	.05
98	Kevin Mitchell	.05
99	Dwight Evans	.05
100	Roberto Alomar	.20

1992 Score Promos

The six known Score promo cards differ from the issued versions in 1992 only in the lack of 1991 and career stats on the back and changes in the career summaries on some of the cards. The promos of Sandberg and Mack were distributed at a St. Louis baseball card show in November 1991, and are somewhat scarcer than the others.

		NM/M
Complete Set (6):		15.00
Common Player:		2.00
1	Ken Griffey Jr.	6.00
4	Dave Justice	2.00
122	Robin Ventura	2.00
200	Ryne Sandberg	5.00
241	Steve Avery	2.00
284	Shane Mack	2.00

1992 Score/Pinnacle Promo Panels

Score debuted both its base-brand (Score) and premium-brand (Pinnacle) sets at one time in 1992 with this issue of four-card panels. Each panel measures 1/16" short each way of 5" x 7" and features Score cards in the upper-left and lower-right, with Pinnacle samples at upper-right and lower-left. Backs have a very light gray overprint, "FOR PROMOTIONAL PURPOSES ONLY NOT FOR RESALE." Cards cut from the panels would be otherwise indistinguishable from the issued versions. Panels are checklisted here alphabetically according to the lowest-numbered Score player. S prefix to the card number indicates Score, P is for Pinnacle. The prefixes do not appear on the cards.

		NM/M
Complete Set (25):		100.00
Common Panel:		

---

(1)	S2 Nolan Ryan, S13 Lonnie Smith, P7 Willie McGee, P18 Terry Pendleton	15.00
(2)	S3 Will Clark, S12 Mark Langston, P8 Paul Molitor, P17 Devon White	4.50
(3)	S4 Dave Justice, S19 Mark Carreon, P1 Frank Thomas, P16 Dave Henderson	4.50
(4)	S5 Dave Henderson, S15 Roberto Alomar, P10 Ryne Sandberg, P20 Kirby Puckett	7.50
(5)	S9 Darryl Strawberry, S14 Jeff Montgomery, P6 Ozzie Smith, P11 Kevin Seitzer	5.00
(6)	S22 Chuck Crim, S33 Jimmy Jones, P27 Jay Buhner, P38 Robin Yount	4.50
(7)	S23 Don Mattingly, S32 Dave Winfield, P28 Matt Williams, P37 George Bell	10.00
(8)	S24 Dickie Thon, S39 Gary Gaetti, P21 Orel Hershiser, P36 Wes Chamberlain	3.00
(9)	S25 Ron Gant, S35 Andres Galarraga, P30 Alex Fernandez, P40 Bruce Hurst	3.00
(10)	S29 Melido Perez, S34 Kevin Gross, P26 Ellis Burks, P31 Albert Belle	3.00
(11)	S42 Rick Aguilera, S53 Doug Jones, P47 Bill Doran, P58 Ivan Calderon	3.00
(12)	S43 Mike Gallego, S52 Todd Zeile, P48 Jerald Clark, P57 Lenny Harris	3.00
(13)	S44 Eric Davis, S59 Randy Ready, P41 Harold Baines, P56 Walt Weiss	3.00
(14)	S45 George Bell, S55 Rafael Palmeiro, P50 Nolan Ryan, P60 George Brett	20.00
(15)	S49 David Wells, S54 Bob Walk, P46 Chili Davis, P51 Phil Plantier	3.00
(16)	S62 Jack McDowell, S73 Juan Samuel, P67 Dave Hollins, P78 John Olerud	3.00
(17)	S63 Jim Acker, S72 Carlton Fisk, P68 Kent Hrbek, P77 Dennis Martinez	3.00
(18)	S64 Jay Buhner, S79 Kirk McCaskill, P61 Gregg Olson, P76 Terry Steinbach	3.00
(19)	S65 Travis Fryman, S75 Andre Dawson, P70 Jeff Bagwell, P80 Darryl Strawberry	4.50
(20)	S69 Ken Caminiti, S74 Todd Stottlemyre, P66 Alex Cole, P71 Jim Gantner	3.00
(21)	S82 Alex Fernandez, S93 Shawn Hillegas, P87 Bill Gullickson, P98 Jose Guzman	3.00
(22)	S83 Ivan Calderon, S92 Ozzie Guillen, P88 Bernard Gilkey, P97 Omar Vizquel	3.00
(23)	S84 Brent Mayne, S99 Tom Bolton, P81 Gary Gaetti, P96 Doug Drabek	
(24)	S85 Jody Reed, S95 Vince Coleman, P90 Kevin Maas, P100 Dave Justice	
(25)	S89 Hensley Meulens, S94 Chili Davis, P86 David Howard, P91 Mark Lewis	3.00

1992 Score

Score used a two series format for the second consecutive year in 1992. Cards 1-442 are featured in the first series. Fronts feature full-color game action photos. Backs feature color head shots of the players, team logo and career stats. Several subsets are included in 1992, including a five-card Joe DiMaggio set. DiMaggio autographed cards were also inserted into random packs. Cards 736-772 can be found with or without a "Rookie Prospects" banner on the

NOLAN RYAN
SCORE 92 PITCHER

card front. Rack packs could be found with random inserts of 1991 Rookie of the Year Chuck Knoblauch's 1990 Score #1 Draft Pick card in a special autographed edition of 3,000. Factory sets contain 17 bonus cards not found in any other packaging.

	NM/M
Unopened Fact. Set (910):	7.50
Complete Set (893):	5.00
Common Player:	.05
Wax Pack (16):	.40
Wax Box (36):	7.50

#	Name	Price
1	Ken Griffey Jr.	.65
2	Nolan Ryan	1.00
3	Will Clark	.05
4	Dave Justice	.05
5	Dave Henderson	.05
6	Bret Saberhagen	.05
7	Fred McGriff	.05
8	Erik Hanson	.05
9	Darryl Strawberry	.05
10	Dwight Gooden	.05
11	Juan Gonzalez	.20
12	Mark Langston	.05
13	Lonnie Smith	.05
14	Jeff Montgomery	.05
15	Roberto Alomar	.20
16	Delino DeShields	.05
17	Steve Bedrosian	.05
18	Terry Pendleton	.05
19	Mark Carreon	.05
20	Mark McGwire	.75
21	Roger Clemens	.60
22	Chuck Crim	.05
23	Don Mattingly	.60
24	Dickie Thon	.05
25	Ron Gant	.05
26	Milt Cuyler	.05
27	Mike Macfarlane	.05
28	Dan Gladden	.05
29	Melido Perez	.05
30	Willie Randolph	.05
31	Albert Belle	.05
32	Dave Winfield	.40
33	Jimmy Jones	.05
34	Kevin Gross	.05
35	Andres Galarraga	.05
36	Mike Devereaux	.05
37	Chris Bosio	.05
38	Mike LaValliere	.05
39	Gary Gaetti	.05
40	Felix Jose	.05
41	Alvaro Espinoza	.05
42	Rick Aguilera	.05
43	Mike Gallego	.05
44	Eric Davis	.05
45	George Bell	.05
46	Tom Brunansky	.05
47	Steve Farr	.05
48	Duane Ward	.05
49	David Wells	.05
50	Cecil Fielder	.05
51	Walt Weiss	.05
52	Todd Zeile	.05
53	Doug Jones	.05
54	Bob Walk	.05
55	Rafael Palmeiro	.35
56	Rob Deer	.05
57	Paul O'Neill	.05
58	Jeff Reardon	.05
59	Randy Ready	.05
60	Scott Erickson	.05
61	Paul Molitor	.40
62	Jack McDowell	.05
63	Jim Acker	.05
64	Jay Buhner	.05
65	Travis Fryman	.05
66	Marquis Grissom	.05
67	Mike Harkey	.05
68	Luis Polonia	.05
69	Ken Caminiti	.05
70	Chris Sabo	.05
71	Gregg Olson	.05
72	Carlton Fisk	.40
73	Juan Samuel	.05
74	Todd Stottlemyre	.05
75	Andre Dawson	.25
76	Alvin Davis	.05
77	Bill Doran	.05
78	B.J. Surhoff	.05
79	Kirk McCaskill	.05
80	Dale Murphy	.25
81	Jose DeLeon	.05
82	Alex Fernandez	.05
83	Ivan Calderon	.05
84	Brent Mayne	.05
85	Jody Reed	.05
86	Randy Tomlin	.05
87	Randy Milligan	.05
88	Pascual Perez	.05
89	Hensley Meulens	.05
90	Joe Carter	.05
91	Mike Moore	.05
92	Ozzie Guillen	.05
93	Shawn Hillegas	.05
94	Chili Davis	.05
95	Vince Coleman	.05
96	Jimmy Key	.05
97	Billy Ripken	.05
98	Dave Smith	.05
99	Tom Bolton	.05
100	Barry Larkin	.05
101	Kenny Rogers	.05
102	Mike Boddicker	.05
103	Kevin Elster	.05
104	Ken Hill	.05
105	Charlie Leibrandt	.05
106	Pat Combs	.05
107	Hubie Brooks	.05
108	Julio Franco	.05
109	Vicente Palacios	.05
110	Kal Daniels	.05
111	Bruce Hurst	.05
112	Willie McGee	.05
113	Ted Power	.05
114	Milt Thompson	.05
115	Doug Drabek	.05
116	Rafael Belliard	.05
117	Scott Garrelts	.05
118	Terry Mulholland	.05
119	Jay Howell	.05
120	Danny Jackson	.05
121	Scott Ruskin	.05
122	Robin Ventura	.05
123	Bip Roberts	.05
124	Jeff Russell	.05
125	Hal Morris	.05
126	Teddy Higuera	.05
127	Luis Sojo	.05
128	Carlos Baerga	.05
129	Jeff Ballard	.05
130	Tom Gordon	.05
131	Sid Bream	.05
132	Rance Mulliniks	.05
133	Andy Benes	.05
134	Mickey Tettleton	.05
135	Rich DeLucia	.05
136	Tom Pagnozzi	.05
137	Harold Baines	.05
138	Danny Darwin	.05
139	Kevin Bass	.05
140	Chris Nabholz	.05
141	Pete O'Brien	.05
142	Jeff Treadway	.05
143	Mickey Morandini	.05
144	Eric King	.05
145	Danny Tartabull	.05
146	Lance Johnson	.05
147	Casey Candaele	.05
148	Felix Fermin	.05
149	Rich Rodriguez	.05
150	Dwight Evans	.05
151	Joe Klink	.05
152	Kevin Reimer	.05
153	Orlando Merced	.05
154	Mel Hall	.05
155	Randy Myers	.05
156	Greg Harris	.05
157	Jeff Brantley	.05
158	Jim Eisenreich	.05
159	Luis Rivera	.05
160	Cris Carpenter	.05
161	Bruce Ruffin	.05
162	Omar Vizquel	.05
163	Gerald Alexander	.05
164	Mark Guthrie	.05
165	Scott Lewis	.05
166	Bill Sampen	.05
167	Dave Anderson	.05
168	Kevin McReynolds	.05
169	Jose Vizcaino	.05
170	Bob Geren	.05
171	Mike Morgan	.05
172	Jim Gott	.05
173	Mike Pagliarulo	.05
174	Mike Jeffcoat	.05
175	Craig Lefferts	.05
176	Steve Finley	.05
177	Wally Backman	.05
178	Kent Mercker	.05
179	John Cerutti	.05
180	Jay Bell	.05
181	Dale Sveum	.05
182	Greg Gagne	.05
183	Donnie Hill	.05
184	Rex Hudler	.05
185	Pat Kelly	.05
186	Jeff Robinson	.05
187	Jeff Gray	.05
188	Jerry Willard	.05
189	Carlos Quintana	.05
190	Dennis Eckersley	.05
191	Kelly Downs	.05
192	Gregg Jefferies	.05
193	Darrin Fletcher	.05
194	Mike Jackson	.05
195	Eddie Murray	.40
196	Billy Landrum	.05
197	Eric Yelding	.05
198	Devon White	.05
199	Larry Walker	.05
200	Ryne Sandberg	.50
201	Dave Magadan	.05
202	Steve Chitren	.05
203	Scott Fletcher	.05
204	Dwayne Henry	.05
205	Scott Coolbaugh	.05
206	Tracy Jones	.05
207	Von Hayes	.05
208	Bob Melvin	.05
209	Scott Scudder	.05
210	Luis Gonzalez	.25
211	Scott Sanderson	.05
212	Chris Donnels	.05
213	Heath Slocumb	.05
214	Mike Timlin	.05
215	Brian Harper	.05
216	Juan Berenguer	.05
217	Mike Henneman	.05
218	Bill Spiers	.05
219	Scott Terry	.05
220	Frank Viola	.05
221	Mark Eichhorn	.05
222	Ernest Riles	.05
223	Ray Lankford	.05
224	Pete Harnisch	.05
225	Bobby Bonilla	.05
226	Mike Scioscia	.05
227	Joel Skinner	.05
228	Brian Holman	.05
229	Gilberto Reyes RC	.05
230	Matt Williams	.05
231	Jaime Navarro	.05
232	Jose Rijo	.05
233	Atlee Hammaker	.05
234	Tim Teufel	.05
235	John Kruk	.05
236	Kurt Stillwell	.05
237	Dan Pasqua	.05
238	Tim Crews	.05
239	Dave Gallagher	.05
240	Leo Gomez	.05
241	Steve Avery	.05
242	Bill Gullickson	.05
243	Mark Portugal	.05
244	Lee Guetterman	.05
245	Benny Santiago	.05
246	Jim Gantner	.05
247	Robby Thompson	.05
248	Terry Shumpert	.05
249	Mike Bell RC	.05
250	Harold Reynolds	.05
251	Mike Felder	.05
252	Bill Pecota	.05
253	Bill Krueger	.05
254	Alfredo Griffin	.05
255	Lou Whitaker	.05
256	Roy Smith	.05
257	Jerald Clark	.05
258	Sammy Sosa	.50
259	Tim Naehring	.05
260	Dave Righetti	.05
261	Paul Gibson	.05
262	Chris James	.05
263	Larry Andersen	.05
264	Storm Davis	.05
265	Jose Lind	.05
266	Greg Hibbard	.05
267	Norm Charlton	.05
268	Paul Kilgus	.05
269	Greg Maddux	.50
270	Ellis Burks	.05
271	Frank Tanana	.05
272	Gene Larkin	.05
273	Ron Hassey	.05
274	Jeff Robinson	.05
275	Steve Howe	.05
276	Daryl Boston	.05
277	Mark Lee	.05
278	Jose Segura RC	.05
279	Lance Blankenship	.05
280	Don Slaught	.05
281	Russ Swan	.05
282	Bob Tewksbury	.05
283	Geno Petralli	.05
284	Shane Mack	.05
285	Bob Scanlan	.05
286	Tim Leary	.05
287	John Smoltz	.05
288	Pat Borders	.05
289	Mark Davidson	.05
290	Sam Horn	.05
291	Lenny Harris	.05
292	Franklin Stubbs	.05
293	Thomas Howard	.05
294	Steve Lyons	.05
295	Francisco Oliveras	.05
296	Terry Leach	.05
297	Barry Jones	.05
298	Lance Parrish	.05
299	Wally Whitehurst	.05
300	Bob Welch	.05
301	Charlie Hayes	.05
302	Charlie Hough	.05
303	Gary Redus	.05
304	Scott Bradley	.05
305	Jose Oquendo	.05
306	Pete Incaviglia	.05
307	Marvin Freeman	.05
308	Gary Pettis	.05
309	Joe Slusarski	.05
310	Kevin Seitzer	.05
311	Jeff Reed	.05
312	Pat Tabler	.05
313	Mike Maddux	.05
314	Bob Milacki	.05
315	Eric Anthony	.05
316	Dante Bichette	.05
317	Steve Decker	.05
318	Jack Clark	.05
319	Doug Dascenzo	.05
320	Scott Leius	.05
321	Jim Lindeman	.05
322	Bryan Harvey	.05
323	Spike Owen	.05
324	Roberto Kelly	.05
325	Stan Belinda	.05
326	Joey Cora	.05
327	Jeff Innis	.05
328	Willie Wilson	.05
329	Juan Agosto	.05
330	Charles Nagy	.05
331	Scott Bailes	.05
332	Pete Schourek	.05
333	Mike Flanagan	.05
334	Omar Olivares	.05
335	Dennis Lamp	.05
336	Tommy Greene	.05
337	Randy Velarde	.05
338	Tom Lampkin	.05
339	John Russell	.05
340	Bob Kipper	.05
341	Todd Burns	.05
342	Ron Jones	.05
343	Dave Valle	.05
344	Mike Heath	.05
345	John Olerud	.05
346	Gerald Young	.05
347	Ken Patterson	.05
348	Les Lancaster	.05
349	Steve Crawford	.05
350	John Candelaria	.05
351	Mike Aldrete	.05
352	Mariano Duncan	.05
353	Julio Machado	.05
354	Ken Williams	.05
355	Walt Terrell	.05
356	Mitch Williams	.05
357	Al Newman	.05
358	Bud Black	.05
359	Joe Hesketh	.05
360	Paul Assenmacher	.05
361	Bo Jackson	.05
362	Jeff Blauser	.05
363	Mike Brumley	.05
364	Jim Deshaies	.05
365	Brady Anderson	.05
366	Chuck McElroy	.05
367	Matt Merullo	.05
368	Tim Belcher	.05
369	Luis Aquino	.05
370	Joe Oliver	.05
371	Greg Swindell	.05
372	Lee Stevens	.05
373	Mark Knudson	.05
374	Bill Wegman	.05
375	Jerry Don Gleaton	.05
376	Pedro Guerrero	.05
377	Randy Bush	.05
378	Greg Harris	.05
379	Eric Plunk	.05
380	Jose DeJesus	.05
381	Bobby Witt	.05
382	Curtis Wilkerson	.05
383	Gene Nelson	.05
384	Wes Chamberlain	.05
385	Tom Henke	.05
386	Mark Lemke	.05
387	Greg Briley	.05
388	Rafael Ramirez	.05
389	Tony Fossas	.05
390	Henry Cotto	.05
391	Tim Hulett	.05
392	Dean Palmer	.05
393	Glenn Braggs	.05
394	Mark Salas	.05
395	Rusty Meacham RC	.05
396	Andy Ashby RC	.10
397	Jose Melendez RC	.05
398	Warren Newson RC	.05
399	Frank Castillo RC	.05
400	Chito Martinez RC	.05
401	Bernie Williams	.05
402	Derek Bell	.05
403	Javier Ortiz RC	.05
404	Tim Sherrill RC	.05
405	Rob MacDonald RC	.05
406	Phil Plantier	.05
407	Troy Afenir	.05
408	Gino Minutelli RC	.05
409	Reggie Jefferson RC	.05
410	Mike Remlinger RC	.05
411	Carlos Rodriguez RC	.05
412	Joe Redfield RC	.05
413	Alonzo Powell RC	.05
414	Scott Livingstone RC	.05
415	Scott Kamieniecki RC	.05
416	Tim Spehr RC	.05
417	Brian Hunter RC	.05
418	Ced Landrum RC	.05
419	Bret Barberie RC	.05
420	Kevin Morton RC	.05
421	Doug Henry RC	.05
422	Doug Piatt RC	.05
423	Pat Rice RC	.05
424	Juan Guzman	.05
425	Nolan Ryan (No-Hit)	.50
426	Tommy Greene (No-Hit)	.05
427	Bob Milacki, Mike Flanagan, Mark Williamson, Gregg Olson (No-Hit)	.05
428	Wilson Alvarez (No-Hit)	.05
429	Otis Nixon (Highlight)	.05
430	Rickey Henderson (Highlight)	.20
431	Cecil Fielder/AS	.05
432	Julio Franco/AS	.05
433	Cal Ripken, Jr./AS	.50
434	Wade Boggs/AS	.25
435	Joe Carter/AS	.05
436	Ken Griffey Jr./AS	.35
437	Ruben Sierra/AS	.05
438	Scott Erickson/AS	.05
439	Tom Henke/AS	.05
440	Terry Steinbach/AS	.05
441	Rickey Henderson (Dream Team)	.20
442	Ryne Sandberg (Dream Team)	.30
443	Otis Nixon	.05
444	Scott Radinsky	.05
445	Mark Grace	.05
446	Tony Pena	.05
447	Billy Hatcher	.05
448	Glenallen Hill	.05
449	Chris Gwynn	.05
450	Tom Glavine	.35
451	John Habyan	.05
452	Al Osuna	.05
453	Tony Phillips	.05
454	Greg Cadaret	.05
455	Rob Dibble	.05
456	Rick Honeycutt	.05
457	Jerome Walton	.05
458	Mookie Wilson	.05
459	Mark Gubicza	.05
460	Craig Biggio	.05
461	Dave Cochrane	.05
462	Keith Miller	.05
463	Alex Cole	.05
464	Pete Smith	.05
465	Brett Butler	.05
466	Jeff Huson	.05
467	Steve Lake	.05
468	Lloyd Moseby	.05
469	Tim McIntosh	.05
470	Dennis Martinez	.05
471	Greg Myers	.05
472	Mackey Sasser	.05
473	Junior Ortiz	.05
474	Greg Olson	.05
475	Steve Sax	.05
476	Ricky Jordan	.05
477	Max Venable	.05
478	Brian McRae	.05
479	Doug Simons	.05
480	Rickey Henderson	.40
481	Gary Varsho	.05
482	Carl Willis	.05
483	Rick Wilkins	.05
484	Donn Pall	.05
485	Edgar Martinez	.05
486	Tom Foley	.05
487	Mark Williamson	.05
488	Jack Armstrong	.05
489	Gary Carter	.40
490	Ruben Sierra	.05
491	Gerald Perry	.05
492	Rob Murphy	.05
493	Zane Smith	.05
494	Darryl Kile	.05
495	Kelly Gruber	.05
496	Jerry Browne	.05
497	Darryl Hamilton	.05
498	Mike Stanton	.05
499	Mark Leonard	.05
500	Jose Canseco	.30
501	Dave Martinez	.05
502	Jose Guzman	.05
503	Terry Kennedy	.05
504	Ed Sprague	.05
505	Frank Thomas	.40
506	Darren Daulton	.05
507	Kevin Tapani	.05
508	Luis Salazar	.05
509	Paul Faries	.05
510	Sandy Alomar, Jr.	.05
511	Jeff King	.05
512	Gary Thurman	.05
513	Chris Hammond	.05
514	Pedro Munoz RC	.05
515	Alan Trammell	.05
516	Geronimo Pena	.05
517	Rodney McCray	.05
518	Manny Lee	.05
519	Junior Felix	.05
520	Kirk Gibson	.05
521	Darrin Jackson	.05
522	John Burkett	.05
523	Jeff Johnson	.05
524	Jim Corsi	.05
525	Robin Yount	.40
526	Jamie Quirk	.05
527	Bob Ojeda	.05
528	Mark Lewis	.05
529	Bryn Smith	.05
530	Kent Hrbek	.05
531	Dennis Boyd	.05
532	Ron Karkovice	.05
533	Don August	.05
534	Todd Frohwirth	.05
535	Wally Joyner	.05
536	Dennis Rasmussen	.05
537	Andy Allanson	.05
538	Rich Gossage	.05
539	John Marzano	.05
540	Cal Ripken, Jr.	1.00
541	Bill Swift	.05
542	Kevin Appier	.05
543	Dave Bergman	.05
544	Bernard Gilkey	.05
545	Mike Greenwell	.05
546	Jose Uribe	.05
547	Jesse Orosco	.05
548	Bob Patterson	.05
549	Mike Stanley	.05
550	Howard Johnson	.05
551	Joe Orsulak	.05
552	Dick Schofield	.05
553	Dave Hollins	.05
554	David Segui	.05
555	Barry Bonds	1.00
556	Mo Vaughn	.05
557	Craig Wilson	.05
558	Bobby Rose	.05
559	Rod Nichols	.05
560	Len Dykstra	.05
561	Craig Grebeck	.05
562	Darren Lewis	.05
563	Todd Benzinger	.05
564	Ed Whitson	.05
565	Jesse Barfield	.05
566	Lloyd McClendon	.05
567	Dan Plesac	.05
568	Danny Cox	.05
569	Skeeter Barnes	.05
570	Bobby Thigpen	.05
571	Deion Sanders	.05
572	Chuck Knoblauch	.05
573	Matt Nokes	.05
574	Herm Winningham	.05
575	Tom Candiotti	.05
576	Jeff Bagwell	.40
577	Brook Jacoby	.05
578	Chico Walker	.05
579	Brian Downing	.05
580	Dave Stewart	.05
581	Francisco Cabrera	.05
582	Rene Gonzales	.05
583	Stan Javier	.05
584	Randy Johnson	.40
585	Chuck Finley	.05
586	Mark Gardner	.05
587	Mark Whiten	.05
588	Garry Templeton	.05
589	Gary Sheffield	.30
590	Ozzie Smith	.50
591	Candy Maldonado	.05
592	Mike Sharperson	.05
593	Carlos Martinez	.05
594	Scott Bankhead	.05
595	Tim Wallach	.05
596	Tino Martinez	.05
597	Roger McDowell	.05
598	Cory Snyder	.05
599	Andujar Cedeno	.05
600	Kirby Puckett	.50
601	Rick Parker	.05
602	Todd Hundley	.05
603	Greg Litton	.05
604	Dave Johnson	.05
605	John Franco	.05
606	Mike Fetters	.05
607	Luis Alicea	.05
608	Trevor Wilson	.05
609	Rob Ducey	.05
610	Ramon Martinez	.05
611	Dave Burba	.05
612	Dwight Smith	.05
613	Kevin Maas	.05
614	John Costello	.05
615	Glenn Davis	.05
616	Shawn Abner	.05
617	Scott Hemond	.05
618	Tom Prince	.05
619	Wally Ritchie	.05
620	Jim Abbott	.05
621	Charlie O'Brien	.05
622	Jack Daugherty	.05
623	Tommy Greene	.05
624	Jeff Shaw	.05
625	Tony Gwynn	.50
626	Mark Leiter	.05
627	Jim Clancy	.05
628	Tim Layana	.05
629	Jeff Schaefer	.05
630	Lee Smith	.05
631	Wade Taylor	.05
632	Mike Simms	.05
633	Terry Steinbach	.05
634	Shawon Dunston	.05
635	Tim Raines	.05
636	Kirt Manwaring	.05
637	Warren Cromartie	.05
638	Luis Quinones	.05
639	Greg Vaughn	.05
640	Kevin Mitchell	.05
641	Chris Hoiles	.05
642	Tom Browning	.05
643	Mitch Webster	.05
644	Steve Olin	.05
645	Tony Fernandez	.05
646	Juan Bell	.05
647	Joe Boever	.05
648	Carney Lansford	.05
649	Mike Benjamin	.05
650	George Brett	.60
651	Tim Burke	.05
652	Jack Morris	.05
653	Orel Hershiser	.05
654	Mike Schooler	.05
655	Andy Van Slyke	.05
656	Dave Stieb	.05
657	Dave Clark	.05
658	Ben McDonald	.05
659	John Smiley	.05
660	Wade Boggs	.50
661	Eric Bullock	.05
662	Eric Show	.05
663	Lenny Webster	.05
664	Mike Huff	.05
665	Rick Sutcliffe	.05
666	Jeff Manto	.05
667	Mike Fitzgerald	.05

668	Matt Young	.05
669	Dave West	.05
670	Mike Hartley	.05
671	Curt Schilling	.35
672	Brian Bohanon	.05
673	Cecil Espy	.05
674	Joe Grahe	.05
675	Sid Fernandez	.05
676	Edwin Nunez	.05
677	Hector Villanueva	.05
678	Sean Berry	.05
679	Dave Eiland	.05
680	David Cone	.05
681	Mike Bordick	.05
682	Tony Castillo	.05
683	John Barfield	.05
684	Jeff Hamilton	.05
685	Ken Dayley	.05
686	Carmelo Martinez	.05
687	Mike Capel	.05
688	Scott Chiamparino	.05
689	Rich Gedman	.05
690	Rich Monteleone	.05
691	Alejandro Pena	.05
692	Oscar Azocar	.05
693	Jim Poole	.05
694	Mike Gardiner	.05
695	Steve Buechele	.05
696	Rudy Seanez	.05
697	Paul Abbott	.05
698	Steve Searcy	.05
699	Jose Offerman	.05
700	Ivan Rodriguez	.35
701	Joe Girardi	.05
702	Tony Perezchica	.05
703	Paul McClellan	.05
704	David Howard RC	.05
705	Dan Petry	.05
706	Jack Howell	.05
707	Jose Mesa	.05
708	Randy St. Claire	.05
709	Kevin Brown	.05
710	Ron Darling	.05
711	Jason Grimsley	.05
712	John Orton	.05
713	Shawn Boskie	.05
714	Pat Clements	.05
715	Brian Barnes	.05
716	Luis Lopez RC	.05
717	Bob McClure	.05
718	Mark Davis	.05
719	Dann Bilardello	.05
720	Tom Edens	.05
721	Willie Fraser	.05
722	Curt Young	.05
723	Neal Heaton	.05
724	Craig Worthington	.05
725	Mel Rojas	.05
726	Daryl Irvine	.05
727	Roger Mason	.05
728	Kirk Dressendorfer	.05
729	Scott Aldred	.05
730	Willie Blair	.05
731	Allan Anderson	.05
732	Dana Kiecker	.05
733	Jose Gonzalez	.05
734	Brian Drahman	.05
735	Brad Komminsk	.05
736	Arthur Rhodes RC	.10
737	Terry Mathews RC	.05
738	Jeff Fassero RC	.05
739	Mike Magnante RC	.05
740	Kip Gross RC	.05
741	Jim Hunter RC	.05
742	Jose Mota RC	.05
743	Joe Bitker	.05
744	Tim Mauser RC	.05
745	Ramon Garcia RC	.05
746	Rod Beck RC	.10
747	Jim Austin RC	.05
748	Keith Mitchell RC	.05
749	Wayne Rosenthal RC	.05
750	Bryan Hickerson RC	.05
751	Bruce Egloff RC	.05
752	John Wehner RC	.05
753	Darren Holmes RC	.05
754	Dave Hansen	.05
755	Mike Mussina	.30
756	Anthony Young RC	.05
757	Ron Tingley	.05
758	Ricky Bones RC	.05
759	Mark Wohlers RC	.05
760	Wilson Alvarez RC	.05
761	Harvey Pulliam RC	.05
762	Ryan Bowen RC	.05
763	Terry Bross RC	.05
764	Joel Johnston RC	.05
765	Terry McDaniel RC	.05
766	Esteban Beltre RC	.05
767	Rob Maurer RC	.05
768	Ted Wood RC	.05
769	Mo Sanford RC	.05
770	Jeff Carter RC	.05
771	Gil Heredia RC	.05
772	Monty Fariss RC	.05
773	Will Clark/AS	.05
774	Ryne Sandberg/AS	.25
775	Barry Larkin/AS	.05
776	Howard Johnson/AS	.05
777	Barry Bonds/AS	.50
778	Brett Butler /AS	.05
779	Tony Gwynn/AS	.25
780	Ramon Martinez/AS	.05
781	Lee Smith/AS	.05
782	Mike Scioscia/AS	.05
783	Dennis Martinez (Highlight)	.05
784	Dennis Martinez (No-Hit)	.05
785	Mark Gardner (No-Hit)	.05
786	Bret Saberhagen (No-Hit)	.05
787	Kent Mercker, Mark Wohlers, Alejandro Pena (No-Hit)	.05
788	Cal Ripken (MVP)	.50
789	Terry Pendleton (MVP)	.35
790	Roger Clemens (CY)	.35
791	Tom Glavine (CY)	.05
792	Chuck Knoblauch (ROY)	.05
793	Jeff Bagwell (ROY)	.20
794	Cal Ripken, Jr. (Man of the Year)	.50
795	David Cone (Highlight)	.05
796	Kirby Puckett (Highlight)	.25
797	Steve Avery (Highlight)	.05
798	Jack Morris (Highlight)	.05
799	Allen Watson RC	.05
800	Manny Ramirez RC	2.00
801	Cliff Floyd RC	.50
802	Al Shirley RC	.05
803	Brian Barber RC	.05
804	Jon Farrell RC	.05
805	Brent Gates RC	.05
806	Scott Ruffcorn RC	.05
807	Tyrone Hill RC	.05
808	Benji Gil RC	.05
809	Aaron Sele RC	.25
810	Tyler Green RC	.05
811	Chris Jones	.05
812	Steve Wilson	.05
813	Cliff Young RC	.05
814	Don Wakamatsu RC	.05
815	Mike Humphreys RC	.05
816	Scott Servais RC	.05
817	Rico Rossy RC	.05
818	John Ramos RC	.05
819	Rob Mallicoat RC	.05
820	Milt Hill RC	.05
821	Carlos Carcia	.05
822	Stan Royer	.05
823	Jeff Plympton RC	.05
824	Braulio Castillo RC	.05
825	David Haas RC	.05
826	Luis Mercedes RC	.05
827	Eric Karros	.05
828	Shawn Hare RC	.05
829	Reggie Sanders	.05
830	Tom Goodwin	.05
831	Dan Gakeler RC	.05
832	Stacy Jones RC	.05
833	Kim Batiste RC	.05
834	Cal Eldred	.05
835	Chris George RC	.05
836	Wayne Housie RC	.05
837	Mike Ignasiak RC	.05
838	Josias Manzanillo RC	.05
839	Jim Olander RC	.05
840	Gary Cooper RC	.05
841	Royce Clayton	.05
842	Hector Fajardo	.05
843	Blaine Beatty	.05
844	Jorge Pedre RC	.05
845	Kenny Lofton	.05
846	Scott Brosius	.05
847	Chris Cron RC	.05
848	Denis Boucher	.05
849	Kyle Abbott	.05
850	Bob Zupcic	.05
851	Rheal Cormier RC	.05
852	Jim Lewis RC	.05
853	Anthony Telford	.05
854	Cliff Brantley RC	.05
855	Kevin Campbell RC	.05
856	Craig Shipley RC	.05
857	Chuck Carr	.05
858	Tony Eusebio RC	.10
859	Jim Thome	.35
860	Vinny Castilla RC	.30
861	Dann Howitt	.05
862	Kevin Ward RC	.05
863	Steve Wapnick RC	.05
864	Rod Brewer	.05
865	Todd Van Poppel	.05
866	Jose Hernandez RC	.05
867	Amalio Carreno RC	.05
868	Calvin Jones RC	.05
869	Jeff Gardner RC	.05
870	Jarvis Brown RC	.05
871	Eddie Taubensee RC	.10
872	Andy Mota RC	.05
873	Chris Haney (Front photo actually Scott Ruskin.)	.05
874	Roberto Hernandez	.05
875	Laddie Renfroe RC	.05
876	Scott Cooper	.05
877	Armando Reynoso RC	.05
878	Ty Cobb (Memorabilia)	.30
879	Babe Ruth (Memorabilia)	.40
880	Honus Wagner (Memorabilia)	.30
881	Lou Gehrig (Memorabilia)	.30
882	Satchel Paige (Memorabilia)	.30
883	Will Clark (Dream Team)	.05
884	Cal Ripken, Jr. (Dream Team)	.50
885	Wade Boggs (Dream Team)	.25
886	Kirby Puckett (Dream Team)	.30
887	Tony Gwynn (Dream Team)	.30
888	Craig Biggio (Dream Team)	.05
889	Scott Erickson (Dream Team)	.05
890	Tom Glavine (Dream Team)	.10
891	Rob Dibble (Dream Team)	.05
892	Mitch Williams (Dream Team)	.05
893	Frank Thomas (Dream Team)	.25

Joe DiMaggio

Colorized vintage photos are featured on the front and back of each of five Joe DiMaggio tribute cards which were issued as random inserts in 1992 Score Series 1 packs. It was reported at the time that 30,000 of each card were produced. A limited number (from an edition of 2,500) of each card were autographed.

		NM/M
Complete Set (5):		25.00
Common Card:		8.00
Autographed Card:		365.00
1	Joe DiMaggio (The Minors)	8.00
2	Joe DiMaggio (The Rookie)	8.00
3	Joe DiMaggio (The MVP)	8.00
4	Joe DiMaggio (The Streak)	8.00
5	Joe DiMaggio (The Legend)	8.00

Factory Set Inserts - Cooperstown

COOPERSTOWN CARD
CARLTON FISK

Available exclusively in factory sets, these bonus cards have posterized color portraits vignetted on a white background. Blue-bordered backs have a yellow "tombstone" at center with career highlights and a quote or two about the player.

		NM/M
Complete Set (4):		1.50
Common Player:		.50
B8	Carlton Fisk	.50
B9	Ozzie Smith	.75
B10	Dave Winfield	.50
B11	Robin Yount	.50

Factory Set Inserts - DiMaggio

Available exclusively in factory sets, these bonus cards honor Joe DiMaggio's career. Fronts have black-and-white photos with silver borders. Color backs have quotes from the Clipper or other ballplayers, plus detailed career highlights.

		NM/M
Complete Set (3):		4.00
Common Card:		1.25
B12	Joe DiMaggio (The Hard Hitter)	1.50
B13	Joe DiMaggio (The Stylish Fielder)	1.50
B14	Joe DiMaggio (The Championship Player)	1.50

Factory Set Inserts - World Series

Available exclusively in factory sets 17 bonus cards are divided into four subsets commemorating the 1991 World Series, potential Hall of Famers, the career of Joe DiMaggio and Carl Yastrzemski's 1967 Triple Crown season. Cards carry a "B" prefix to the card number.

		NM/M
Complete Set (7):		1.00
Common Card:		.15
1	World Series Game 1 (Greg Gagne)	.15
2	World Series Game 2 (Scott Leius)	.15
3	World Series Game 3 (David Justice, Brian Harper)	.15
4	World Series Game 4 (Lonnie Smith, Brian Harper)	.15
5	World Series Game 5 (David Justice)	.15
6	World Series Game 6 (Kirby Puckett)	1.00
7	World Series Game 7 (Gene Larkin)	.15

Factory Set Inserts - Yastrzemski

Available exclusively in factory sets, these bonus cards honor Carl Yastrzemski's 1967 Triple Crown season. Fronts have game-action photos with silver borders and a silver 25 Years logo. Color backs have quotes from Yaz or teammates, plus details of the season's highlights.

		NM/M
Complete Set (3):		2.00
Common Card:		1.00
B15	Carl Yastrzemski (The Impossible Dream)	1.00
B16	Carl Yastrzemski (The Triple Crown)	1.00
B17	Carl Yastrzemski (The World Series)	1.00

Hot Rookies

This 10-card rookie issue was produced as an insert in special blister packs of 1992 Score cards sold at retail outlets. Action photos on front and portraits on back are

TINO MARTINEZ

set against white backgrounds with orange highlights. Cards are standard 2-1/2" x 3-1/2".

		NM/M
Complete Set (10):		4.00
Common Player:		.50
1	Cal Eldred	.50
2	Royce Clayton	.50
3	Kenny Lofton	.75
4	Todd Van Poppel	.50
5	Scott Cooper	.50
6	Todd Hundley	.50
7	Tino Martinez	.75
8	Anthony Telford	.50
9	Derek Bell	.50
10	Reggie Jefferson	.50

Impact Players

Scott Cooper - 3B

Jumbo packs of 1992 Score Series 1 and 2 contained five of these special inserts labeled "90's Impact Players." Front action photos contrast with portrait photos on the backs, which are color-coded by team. Cards #1-45 were packaged with Series 1, cards #46-90 were included in Series 2 packs.

		NM/M
Complete Set (90):		3.00
Common Player:		.05
1	Chuck Knoblauch	.05
2	Jeff Bagwell	.50
3	Juan Guzman	.05
4	Milt Cuyler	.05
5	Ivan Rodriguez	.45
6	Rich DeLucia	.05
7	Orlando Merced	.05
8	Ray Lankford	.05
9	Brian Hunter	.05
10	Roberto Alomar	.25
11	Wes Chamberlain	.05
12	Steve Avery	.05
13	Scott Erickson	.05
14	Jim Abbott	.05
15	Mark Whiten	.05
16	Leo Gomez	.05
17	Doug Henry	.05
18	Brent Mayne	.05
19	Charles Nagy	.05
20	Phil Plantier	.05
21	Mo Vaughn	.05
22	Craig Biggio	.05
23	Derek Bell	.05
24	Royce Clayton	.05
25	Gary Cooper	.05
26	Scott Cooper	.05
27	Juan Gonzalez	.25
28	Ken Griffey Jr.	.75
29	Larry Walker	.05
30	John Smoltz	.05
31	Todd Hundley	.05
32	Kenny Lofton	.05
33	Andy Mota	.05
34	Todd Zeile	.05
35	Arthur Rhodes	.05
36	Jim Thome	.45
37	Todd Van Poppel	.05
38	Mark Wohlers	.05
39	Anthony Young	.05
40	Sandy Alomar Jr.	.05
41	John Olerud	.05
42	Robin Ventura	.05
43	Frank Thomas	.05
44	Dave Justice	.05
45	Hal Morris	.05
46	Ruben Sierra	.05
47	Travis Fryman	.05
48	Mike Mussina	.25
49	Tom Glavine	.35
50	Barry Larkin	.05
51	Will Clark	.05
52	Jose Canseco	.30
53	Bo Jackson	.10
54	Dwight Gooden	.05
55	Barry Bonds	1.00
56	Fred McGriff	.05
57	Roger Clemens	.65
58	Benito Santiago	.05
59	Darryl Strawberry	.05
60	Cecil Fielder	.05
61	John Franco	.05
62	Matt Williams	.05
63	Marquis Grissom	.05
64	Danny Tartabull	.05
65	Ron Gant	.05
66	Paul O'Neill	.05
67	Devon White	.05
68	Rafael Palmeiro	.45
69	Tom Gordon	.05
70	Shawon Dunston	.05
71	Rob Dibble	.05
72	Eddie Zosky	.05
73	Jack McDowell	.05
74	Len Dykstra	.05
75	Ramon Martinez	.05
76	Reggie Sanders	.05
77	Greg Maddux	.60
78	Ellis Burks	.05
79	John Smiley	.05
80	Roberto Kelly	.05
81	Ben McDonald	.05
82	Mark Lewis	.05
83	Jose Rijo	.05
84	Ozzie Guillen	.05
85	Lance Dickson	.05
86	Kim Batiste	.05
87	Gregg Olson	.05
88	Andy Benes	.05
89	Cal Eldred	.05
90	David Cone	.05

The Franchise

CARL YASTRZEMSKI

This four-card set, in both autographed and unautographed form, was a random insert in various premium packaging of Score's 1992 Series II cards. Each of the four cards was produced in an edition of 150,000, with 2,000 of each player's card being autographed and 500 of the triple-player card carrying the autographs of all three superstars.

		NM/M
Complete Set (4):		5.00
Common Player:		1.25
Musial Autograph:		80.00
Mantle Autograph:		450.00
Yastrzemski Autograph:		80.00
Triple Autograph:		1,100
1	Stan Musial	1.50
2	Mickey Mantle	2.50
3	Carl Yastrzemski	1.25
4	Stan Musial, Mickey Mantle, Carl Yastrzemski	1.50

Rookie & Traded

SAMMY SOSA

This 110-card set features traded players, free agents and top rookies from 1992. The cards are styled after the regular 1992 Score cards. Cards 80-110 feature the rookies. The set was released as a boxed set and was available only through hobby dealers.

		NM/M
Complete Set (110):		5.00
Common Player:		.05
1	Gary Sheffield	.20
2	Kevin Seitzer	.05
3	Danny Tartabull	.05
4	Steve Sax	.05
5	Bobby Bonilla	.05
6	Frank Viola	.05
7	Dave Winfield	.60
8	Rick Sutcliffe	.05
9	Jose Canseco	.45
10	Greg Swindell	.05
11	Eddie Murray	.60
12	Randy Myers	.05
13	Wally Joyner	.05
14	Kenny Lofton	.05
15	Jack Morris	.05
16	Charlie Hayes	.05
17	Pete Incaviglia	.05
18	Kevin Mitchell	.05
19	Kurt Stillwell	.05
20	Bret Saberhagen	.05
21	Steve Buechele	.05
22	John Smiley	.05
23	Sammy Sosa	3.00
24	George Bell	.05
25	Curt Schilling	.30
26	Dick Schofield	.05
27	David Cone	.05
28	Dan Gladden	.05
29	Kirk McCaskill	.05
30	Mike Gallego	.05
31	Kevin McReynolds	.05
32	Bill Swift	.05
33	Dave Martinez	.05
34	Storm Davis	.05
35	Willie Randolph	.05
36	Melido Perez	.05
37	Mark Carreon	.05
38	Doug Jones	.05
39	Gregg Jefferies	.05
40	Mike Jackson	.05
41	Dickie Thon	.05
42	Eric King	.05
43	Herm Winningham	.05
44	Derek Lilliquist	.05
45	Dave Anderson	.05
46	Jeff Reardon	.05
47	Scott Bankhead	.05
48	Cory Snyder	.05
49	Al Newman	.05
50	Keith Miller	.05
51	Dave Burba	.05
52	Bill Pecota	.05
53	Chuck Crim	.05
54	Mariano Duncan	.05
55	Dave Gallagher	.05
56	Chris Gwynn	.05
57	Scott Ruskin	.05
58	Jack Armstrong	.05
59	Gary Carter	.60
60	Andres Galarraga	.05
61	Ken Hill	.05
62	Eric Davis	.05
63	Ruben Sierra	.05
64	Darrin Fletcher	.05
65	Tim Belcher	.05
66	Mike Morgan	.05
67	Scott Scudder	.05
68	Tom Candiotti	.05
69	Hubie Brooks	.05
70	Kal Daniels	.05
71	Bruce Ruffin	.05
72	Billy Hatcher	.05
73	Bob Melvin	.05
74	Lee Guetterman	.05
75	Rene Gonzales	.05
76	Kevin Bass	.05
77	Tom Bolton	.05
78	John Wetteland	.05
79	Bip Roberts	.05
80	Pat Listach RC	.05
81	John Doherty RC	.05
82	Sam Militello RC	.05
83	Brian Jordan RC	.05
84	Jeff Kent RC	.10
85	Dave Fleming RC	.05
86	Jeff Tackett RC	.05
87	Chad Curtis RC	.05
88	Eric Fox	.05
89	Denny Neagle RC	.05
90	Donovan Osborne RC	.05
91	Carlos Hernandez RC	.05
92	Tim Wakefield RC	.05
93	Tim Salmon RC	.05
94	Dave Nilsson RC	.05
95	Mike Perez RC	.05
96	Pat Hentgen RC	.05
97	Frank Seminara RC	.05
98	Ruben Amaro Jr. RC	.05
99	Archi Cianfrocco RC	.05
100	Andy Stankiewicz RC	.05
101	Jim Bullinger RC	.05
102	Pat Mahomes RC	.05
103	Hipolito Pichardo RC	.05
104	Bret Boone RC	.05
105	John Vander Wal RC	.05
106	Vince Horsman RC	.05
107	James Austin RC	.05
108	Brian Williams RC	.05
109	Dan Walters RC	.05
110	Wil Cordero RC	.05

Procter & Gamble

In 1992 Score and Procter and Gamble combined to produce an 18-card All-Star set, reportedly two million cards making 101,000 sets offered to collectors originally for $1.49 along with proof of purchase from P & G products. Card fronts feature a color player action photo set against a background of blue star and pink-to-purple diagonal stripes (American Leaguers) or red star and green stripes (National Leaguers). Back designs include a color player portrait photo at upper-right, with personal data, career stats and highlights. Appropriate logos and card number complete the design, which is bordered in color striping similar to the front background.

		NM/M
Complete Set (18):		3.00
Common Player:		.10
1	Sandy Alomar Jr.	.10
2	Mark McGwire	.75
3	Roberto Alomar	.20
4	Wade Boggs	.50
5	Cal Ripken, Jr.	1.00
6	Kirby Puckett	.50
7	Ken Griffey Jr	.65
8	Jose Canseco	.25
9	Kevin Brown	.10
10	Benito Santiago	.10
11	Fred McGriff	.10
12	Ryne Sandberg	.50
13	Terry Pendleton	.10
14	Ozzie Smith	.50
15	Barry Bonds	1.00
16	Tony Gwynn	.50
17	Andy Van Slyke	.10
18	Tom Glavine	.35

Rising Stars

Sold in a blister pack with a book and a handful of "Magic Motion" trivia cards this 100-card set features baseball's top young players. Backs have a player portrait, a career summary and team, league and card company logos.

		NM/M
Complete Set (100):		3.00
Common Player:		.10
1	Milt Cuyler	.10
2	David Howard	.10
3	Brian Hunter	.10
4	Darryl Kile	.10
5	Pat Kelly	.10
6	Luis Gonzalez	.10
7	Mike Benjamin	.10
8	Eric Anthony	.10
9	Moises Alou	.10
10	Darren Lewis	.10
11	Chuck Knoblauch	.10
12	Geronimo Pena	.10
13	Jeff Plympton	.10
14	Bret Barberie	.10
15	Chris Haney	.10
16	Rick Wilkins	.10
17	Julio Valera	.10
18	Joe Slusarski	.10
19	Jose Melendez	.10
20	Pete Schourek	.10
21	Jeff Conine	.10
22	Paul Faries	.10
23	Scott Kamieniecki	.10
24	Bernard Gilkey	.10
25	Wes Chamberlain	.10
26	Charles Nagy	.10
27	Juan Guzman	.10
28	Heath Slocumb	.10
29	Eddie Taubensee	.10
30	Cedric Landrum	.10
31	Jose Offerman	.10
32	Andres Santana	.10
33	David Segui	.10
34	Bernie Williams	.10
35	Jeff Bagwell	1.50
36	Kevin Morton	.10
37	Kirk Dressendorfer	.10
38	Mike Fetters	.10
39	Darren Holmes	.10
40	Jeff Johnson	.10
41	Scott Aldred	.10
42	Kevin Ward	.10
43	Ray Lankford	.10
44	Terry Shumpert	.10
45	Wade Taylor	.10
46	Rob MacDonald	.10
47	Jose Mota	.10
48	Reggie Harris	.10
49	Mike Remlinger	.10
50	Mark Lewis	.10
51	Tino Martinez	.10
52	Ed Sprague	.10
53	Freddie Benavides	.10
54	Rich DeLucia	.10
55	Brian Drahman	.10
56	Steve Decker	.10
57	Scott Livingstone	.10
58	Mike Timlin	.10
59	Bob Scanlan	.10
60	Dean Palmer	.10
61	Frank Castillo	.10
62	Mark Leonard	.10
63	Chuck McElroy	.10
64	Derek Bell	.10
65	Andujar Cedeno	.10
66	Leo Gomez	.10
67	Rusty Meacham	.10
68	Dann Howitt	.10
69	Chris Jones	.10
70	Dave Cochrane	.10
71	Carlos Martinez	.10
72	Hensley Meulens	.10
73	Rich Reed	.10
74	Pedro Munoz	.10
75	Orlando Merced	.10
76	Chito Martinez	.10
77	Ivan Rodriguez	.75
78	Brian Barnes	.10
79	Chris Donnels	.10
80	Todd Hundley	.10
81	Gary Scott	.10
82	John Wehner	.10
83	Al Osuna	.10
84	Luis Lopez	.10
85	Brent Mayne	.10
86	Phil Plantier	.10
87	Joe Bitker	.10
88	Scott Cooper	.10
89	Chris Hammond	.10
90	Tim Sherrill	.10
91	Doug Simons	.10
92	Kip Gross	.10
93	Tim McIntosh	.10
94	Larry Casian	.10
95	Mike Dalton	.10
96	Lance Dickson	.10
97	Joe Grahe	.10
98	Glenn Sutko	.10
99	Gerald Alexander	.10
100	Mo Vaughn	.10

Rookies

A selection of 40 1992 rookie players is featured in this boxed set. Fronts have green borders with a red and white "1992 ROOKIE" notation printed vertically to the left of a game-action photo. Backs repeat the notation on a graduated blue background with a player portrait photo at top, biographical details and a career summary at center and appropriate logos at bottom.

	NM/M
Complete Set (40):	1.50

Superstars

		NM/M
Common Player:		.05
1	Todd Van Poppel	.05
2	Kyle Abbott	.05
3	Derek Bell	.05
4	Jim Thome	.50
5	Mark Wohlers	.05
6	Todd Hundley	.05
7	Arthur Rhodes	.05
8	John Ramos	.05
9	Chris George	.05
10	Kenny Lofton	.05
11	Ted Wood	.05
12	Royce Clayton	.05
13	Scott Cooper	.05
14	Anthony Young	.05
15	Joel Johnston	.05
16	Andy Mota	.05
17	Lenny Webster	.05
18	Andy Ashby	.05
19	Jose Mota	.05
20	Tim McIntosh	.05
21	Terry Bross	.05
22	Harvey Pulliam	.05
23	Hector Fajardo	.05
24	Esteban Beltre	.05
25	Gary DiSarcina	.05
26	Mike Humphreys	.05
27	Jarvis Brown	.05
28	Gary Cooper	.05
29	Chris Donnels	.05
30	Monty Fariss	.05
31	Eric Karros	.05
32	Braulio Castillo	.05
33	Cal Eldred	.05
34	Tom Goodwin	.05
35	Reggie Sanders	.05
36	Scott Servais	.05
37	Kim Batiste	.05
38	Eric Wedge	.05
39	Willie Banks	.05
40	Mo Sanford	.05

Superstars

Available in a blister pack with a book and six "Magic Motion" trivia cards, this 100-card set spotlights the games top veteran stars.

		NM/M
Complete Set (100):		4.00
Common Player:		.05
1	Ken Griffey Jr.	.75
2	Scott Erickson	.05
3	John Smiley	.05
4	Rick Aguilera	.05
5	Jeff Reardon	.05
6	Chuck Finley	.05
7	Kirby Puckett	.50
8	Paul Molitor	.40
9	Dave Winfield	.40
10	Mike Greenwell	.05
11	Bret Saberhagen	.05
12	Pete Harnisch	.05
13	Ozzie Guillen	.05
14	Hal Morris	.05
15	Tom Glavine	.30
16	David Cone	.05
17	Edgar Martinez	.05
18	Willie McGee	.05
19	Jim Abbott	.05
20	Mark Grace	.05
21	George Brett	.65
22	Jack McDowell	.05
23	Don Mattingly	.65
24	Will Clark	.05
25	Dwight Gooden	.05
26	Barry Bonds	1.00
27	Rafael Palmeiro	.35
28	Lee Smith	.05
29	Wally Joyner	.05
30	Wade Boggs	.50
31	Tom Henke	.05
32	Mark Langston	.05
33	Robin Ventura	.05
34	Steve Avery	.05
35	Joe Carter	.05
36	Benito Santiago	.05
37	Dave Stieb	.05
38	Julio Franco	.05
39	Albert Belle	.05
40	Dale Murphy	.25
41	Rob Dibble	.05
42	Dave Justice	.05
43	Jose Rijo	.05
44	Eric Davis	.05
45	Terry Pendleton	.05
46	Kevin Maas	.05
47	Ozzie Smith	.50
48	Andre Dawson	.25
49	Sandy Alomar, Jr.	.05
50	Nolan Ryan	1.00
51	Frank Thomas	.40
52	Craig Biggio	.05
53	Doug Drabek	.05
54	Bobby Thigpen	.05
55	Darryl Strawberry	.05
56	Dennis Eckersley	.35
57	John Franco	.05
58	Paul O'Neill	.05
59	Scott Sanderson	.05
60	Dave Stewart	.05
61	Ivan Calderon	.05
62	Frank Viola	.05
63	Mark McGwire	.75
64	Kelly Gruber	.05
65	Fred McGriff	.05
66	Cecil Fielder	.05
67	Jose Canseco	.30
68	Howard Johnson	.05
69	Juan Gonzalez	.20
70	Tim Wallach	.05
71	John Olerud	.05
72	Carlton Fisk	.40
73	Otis Nixon	.05
74	Roger Clemens	.65
75	Ramon Martinez	.05
76	Ron Gant	.05
77	Barry Larkin	.05
78	Eddie Murray	.40
79	Vince Coleman	.05
80	Bobby Bonilla	.05
81	Tony Gwynn	.50
82	Roberto Alomar	.20
83	Ellis Burks	.05
84	Robin Yount	.40
85	Ryne Sandberg	.50
86	Len Dykstra	.05
87	Ruben Sierra	.05
88	George Bell	.05
89	Cal Ripken, Jr.	1.00
90	Danny Tartabull	.05
91	Gregg Olson	.05
92	Dave Henderson	.05
93	Kevin Mitchell	.05
94	Ben McDonald	.05
95	Matt Williams	.05
96	Roberto Kelly	.05
97	Dennis Martinez	.05
98	Kent Hrbek	.05
99	Felix Jose	.05
100	Rickey Henderson	.40

1993 Score Promos

Only close comparison with regularly issued versions can detect these unmarked promos. The promos feature slightly different croppings of the pictures, situated higher than the normal version.

		NM/M
Complete Set (8):		15.00
Common Player:		1.00
1	Ken Griffey Jr.	4.00
3	Frank Thomas	2.00
4	Ryne Sandberg	3.00
6	Cal Ripken, Jr.	5.00
7	Roger Clemens	2.50
9	Bobby Bonilla	1.00
10	Darren Daulton	1.00
11	Travis Fryman	1.00

1993 Score

Score's 1993 cards have white borders surrounding color action photographs. The player's name is at the bottom of the card, while his team's name and position appears on the left side in a color band. Backs have color portraits, statistics and text. Subsets feature rookies, award winners, draft picks, highlights, World Series highlights, all-star caricatures, dream team players, and the Man of the Year (Kirby Puckett). Insert sets include: Boys of Summer, the Franchise and Stat Leaders, which feature Select's card design.

		NM/M
Complete Set (660):		15.00
Common Player:		.05
Pack (16):		.75
Wax Box (36):		17.50
1	Ken Griffey Jr.	.65
2	Gary Sheffield	.30
3	Frank Thomas	.40
4	Ryne Sandberg	.45
5	Larry Walker	.05
6	Cal Ripken, Jr.	1.00
7	Roger Clemens	.50
8	Bobby Bonilla	.05
9	Carlos Baerga	.05
10	Darren Daulton	.05
11	Travis Fryman	.05
12	Andy Van Slyke	.05
13	Jose Canseco	.30
14	Roberto Alomar	.15
15	Tom Glavine	.30
16	Barry Larkin	.05
17	Gregg Jefferies	.05
18	Craig Biggio	.05
19	Shane Mack	.05
20	Brett Butler	.05
21	Dennis Eckersley	.35
22	Will Clark	.05
23	Don Mattingly	.45
24	Tony Gwynn	.45
25	Ivan Rodriguez	.35
26	Shawon Dunston	.05
27	Mike Mussina	.30
28	Marquis Grissom	.05
29	Charles Nagy	.05
30	Len Dykstra	.05
31	Cecil Fielder	.05
32	Jay Bell	.05
33	B.J. Surhoff	.05
34	Bob Tewksbury	.05
35	Danny Tartabull	.05
36	Terry Pendleton	.05
37	Jack Morris	.05
38	Hal Morris	.05
39	Luis Polonia	.05
40	Ken Caminiti	.05
41	Robin Ventura	.05
42	Darryl Strawberry	.05
43	Wally Joyner	.05
44	Fred McGriff	.05
45	Kevin Tapani	.05
46	Matt Williams	.05
47	Robin Yount	.40
48	Ken Hill	.05
49	Edgar Martinez	.05
50	Mark Grace	.05
51	Juan Gonzalez	.20
52	Curt Schilling	.05
53	Dwight Gooden	.05
54	Chris Hoiles	.05
55	Frank Viola	.05
56	Ray Lankford	.05
57	George Brett	.50
58	Kenny Lofton	.05
59	Nolan Ryan	1.00
60	Mickey Tettleton	.05
61	John Smoltz	.05
62	Howard Johnson	.05
63	Eric Karros	.05
64	Rick Aguilera	.05
65	Steve Finley	.05
66	Mark Langston	.05
67	Bill Swift	.05
68	John Olerud	.05
69	Kevin McReynolds	.05
70	Jack McDowell	.05
71	Rickey Henderson	.40
72	Brian Harper	.05
73	Mike Morgan	.05
74	Rafael Palmeiro	.40
75	Dennis Martinez	.05
76	Tino Martinez	.05
77	Eddie Murray	.40
78	Ellis Burks	.05
79	John Kruk	.05
80	Gregg Olson	.05
81	Bernard Gilkey	.05
82	Milt Cuyler	.05
83	Mike LaValliere	.05
84	Albert Belle	.05
85	Bip Roberts	.05
86	Melido Perez	.05
87	Otis Nixon	.05
88	Bill Spiers	.05
89	Jeff Bagwell	.40
90	Orel Hershiser	.05
91	Andy Benes	.05
92	Devon White	.05
93	Willie McGee	.05
94	Ozzie Guillen	.05
95	Ivan Calderon	.05
96	Keith Miller	.05
97	Steve Buechele	.05

#	Player	Price
98	Kent Hrbek	.05
99	Dave Hollins	.05
100	Mike Bordick	.05
101	Randy Tomlin	.05
102	Omar Vizquel	.05
103	Lee Smith	.05
104	Leo Gomez	.05
105	Jose Rijo	.05
106	Mark Whiten	.05
107	Dave Justice	.05
108	Eddie Taubensee	.05
109	Lance Johnson	.05
110	Felix Jose	.05
111	Mike Harkey	.05
112	Randy Milligan	.05
113	Anthony Young	.05
114	Rico Brogna	.05
115	Bret Saberhagen	.05
116	Sandy Alomar, Jr.	.05
117	Terry Mulholland	.05
118	Darryl Hamilton	.05
119	Todd Zeile	.05
120	Bernie Williams	.05
121	Zane Smith	.05
122	Derek Bell	.05
123	Deion Sanders	.05
124	Luis Sojo	.05
125	Joe Oliver	.05
126	Craig Grebeck	.05
127	Andujar Cedeno	.05
128	Brian McRae	.10
129	Jose Offerman	.05
130	Pedro Munoz	.05
131	Bud Black	.05
132	Mo Vaughn	.05
133	Bruce Hurst	.05
134	Dave Henderson	.05
135	Tom Pagnozzi	.05
136	Erik Hanson	.05
137	Orlando Merced	.05
138	Dean Palmer	.05
139	John Franco	.05
140	Brady Anderson	.05
141	Ricky Jordan	.05
142	Jeff Blauser	.05
143	Sammy Sosa	.45
144	Bob Walk	.05
145	Delino DeShields	.05
146	Kevin Brown	.05
147	Mark Lemke	.05
148	Chuck Knoblauch	.05
149	Chris Sabo	.05
150	Bobby Witt	.05
151	Luis Gonzalez	.05
152	Ron Karkovice	.05
153	Jeff Brantley	.05
154	Kevin Appier	.05
155	Darrin Jackson	.05
156	Kelly Gruber	.05
157	Royce Clayton	.05
158	Chuck Finley	.05
159	Jeff King	.05
160	Greg Vaughn	.05
161	Geronimo Pena	.05
162	Steve Farr	.05
163	Jose Oquendo	.05
164	Mark Lewis	.05
165	John Wetteland	.05
166	Mike Henneman	.05
167	Todd Hundley	.05
168	Wes Chamberlain	.05
169	Steve Avery	.05
170	Mike Devereaux	.05
171	Reggie Sanders	.05
172	Jay Buhner	.05
173	Eric Anthony	.05
174	John Burkett	.05
175	Tom Candiotti	.05
176	Phil Plantier	.05
177	Doug Henry	.05
178	Scott Leius	.05
179	Kirt Manwaring	.05
180	Jeff Parrett	.05
181	Don Slaught	.05
182	Scott Radinsky	.05
183	Luis Alicea	.05
184	Tom Gordon	.05
185	Rick Wilkins	.05
186	Todd Stottlemyre	.05
187	Moises Alou	.05
188	Joe Grahe	.05
189	Jeff Kent	.05
190	Bill Wegman	.05
191	Kim Batiste	.05
192	Matt Nokes	.05
193	Mark Wohlers	.05
194	Paul Sorrento	.05
195	Chris Hammond	.05
196	Scott Livingstone	.05
197	Doug Jones	.05
198	Scott Cooper	.05
199	Ramon Martinez	.05
200	Dave Valle	.05
201	Mariano Duncan	.05
202	Ben McDonald	.05
203	Darren Lewis	.05
204	Kenny Rogers	.05
205	Manuel Lee	.05
206	Scott Erickson	.05
207	Dan Gladden	.05
208	Bob Welch	.05
209	Greg Olson	.05
210	Dan Pasqua	.05
211	Tim Wallach	.05
212	Jeff Montgomery	.05
213	Derrick May	.05
214	Ed Sprague	.05
215	David Haas	.05
216	Darrin Fletcher	.05
217	Brian Jordan	.05
218	Jaime Navarro	.05
219	Randy Velarde	.05
220	Ron Gant	.05
221	Paul Quantrill	.05
222	Damion Easley	.05
223	Charlie Hough	.05
224	Brad Brink RC	.05
225	Barry Manual RC	.05
226	Kevin Koslofski RC	.05
227	Ryan Thompson RC	.05
228	Mike Munoz	.05
229	Dan Wilson RC	.10
230	Peter Hoy RC	.05
231	Pedro Astacio RC	.10
232	Matt Stairs RC	.10
233	Jeff Reboulet RC	.05
234	Manny Alexander RC	.05
235	Willie Banks RC	.05
236	John Jaha RC	.05
237	Scooter Tucker RC	.05
238	Russ Springer RC	.05
239	Paul Miller RC	.05
240	Dan Peltier RC	.05
241	Ozzie Canseco RC	.05
242	Ben Rivera RC	.05
243	John Valentin RC	.05
244	Henry Rodriguez RC	.05
245	Derek Parks RC	.05
246	Carlos Garcia RC	.10
247	Tim Pugh RC	.05
248	Melvin Nieves RC	.05
249	Rich Amaral RC	.05
250	Willie Greene RC	.05
251	Tim Scott RC	.05
252	Dave Silvestri RC	.05
253	Rob Mallicoat RC	.05
254	Donald Harris RC	.05
255	Craig Colbert RC	.05
256	Jose Guzman	.05
257	Domingo Martinez RC	.05
258	William Suero RC	.05
259	Juan Guerrero RC	.05
260	J.T. Snow RC	.45
261	Tony Pena	.05
262	Tim Fortugno RC	.05
263	Tom Marsh RC	.05
264	Kurt Knudsen RC	.05
265	Tim Costo RC	.05
266	Steve Shifflett RC	.05
267	Billy Ashley RC	.05
268	Jerry Nielsen	.05
269	Pete Young RC	.05
270	Johnny Guzman RC	.05
271	Greg Colbrunn RC	.05
272	Jeff Nelson RC	.05
273	Kevin Young RC	.05
274	Jeff Frye RC	.05
275	J.T. Bruett RC	.05
276	Todd Pratt RC	.05
277	Mike Butcher RC	.05
278	John Flaherty RC	.05
279	John Patterson RC	.05
280	Eric Hillman RC	.05
281	Bien Figueros RC	.05
282	Shane Reynolds RC	.05
283	Rich Rowland RC	.05
284	Steve Foster RC	.05
285	Dave Mlicki RC	.05
286	Mike Piazza	.65
287	Mike Trombley RC	.05
288	Jim Pena RC	.05
289	Bob Ayrault RC	.05
290	Henry Mercedes RC	.05
291	Bob Wickman	.05
292	Jacob Brumfield RC	.05
293	David Hulse RC	.05
294	Ryan Klesko RC	.05
295	Doug Linton	.05
296	Steve Cooke RC	.05
297	Eddie Zosky	.05
298	Gerald Williams RC	.05
299	Jonathan Hurst RC	.05
300	Larry Carter RC	.05
301	William Pennyfeather RC	.05
302	Cesar Hernandez RC	.05
303	Steve Hosey RC	.05
304	Blas Minor RC	.05
305	Jeff Grotewold RC	.05
306	Bernardo Brito RC	.05
307	Rafael Bournigal RC	.05
308	Jeff Branson RC	.05
309	Tom Quinlan RC	.05
310	Pat Gomez RC	.05
311	Sterling Hitchcock RC	.10
312	Kent Bottenfield RC	.05
313	Alan Trammell	.05
314	Cris Colon RC	.05
315	Paul Wagner RC	.05
316	Matt Maysey RC	.05
317	Mike Stanton	.05
318	Rick Trlicek RC	.05
319	Kevin Rogers RC	.05
320	Mark Clark RC	.05
321	Pedro Martinez RC	.40
322	Al Martin RC	.05
323	Mike Macfarlane	.05
324	Rey Sanchez RC	.05
325	Roger Pavlik RC	.05
326	Troy Neel RC	.05
327	Kerry Woodson RC	.05
328	Wayne Kirby RC	.05
329	Ken Ryan RC	.05
330	Jesse Levis RC	.05
331	James Austin RC	.05
332	Dan Walters RC	.05
333	Brian Williams	.05
334	Wil Cordero	.05
335	Bret Boone	.05
336	Hipolito Pichardo	.05
337	Pat Mahomes	.05
338	Andy Stankiewicz	.05
339	Jim Bullinger	.05
340	Archi Cianfrocco	.05
341	Ruben Amaro Jr.	.05
342	Frank Seminara	.05
343	Pat Hentgen	.05
344	Dave Nilsson	.05
345	Mike Perez	.05
346	Tim Salmon	.05
347	Tim Wakefield RC	.10
348	Carlos Hernandez	.05
349	Donovan Osborne	.05
350	Denny Naegle	.05
351	Sam Militello	.05
352	Eric Fox	.05
353	John Doherty	.05
354	Chad Curtis	.05
355	Jeff Tackett	.05
356	Dave Fleming	.05
357	Pat Listach	.05
358	Kevin Wickander	.05
359	John VanderWal	.05
360	Arthur Rhodes	.05
361	Bob Scanlan	.05
362	Bob Zupcic	.05
363	Mel Rojas	.05
364	Jim Thome	.35
365	Bill Pecota	.05
366	Mark Carreon	.05
367	Mitch Williams	.05
368	Cal Eldred	.05
369	Stan Belinda	.05
370	Pat Kelly	.05
371	Pheal Cormier	.05
372	Juan Guzman	.05
373	Damon Berryhill	.05
374	Gary DiSarcina	.05
375	Norm Charlton	.05
376	Roberto Hernandez	.05
377	Scott Kamienicki	.05
378	Rusty Meacham	.05
379	Kurt Stillwell	.05
380	Lloyd McClendon	.05
381	Mark Leonard	.05
382	Jerry Browne	.05
383	Glenn Davis	.05
384	Randy Johnson	.40
385	Mike Greenwell	.05
386	Scott Chiamparino	.05
387	George Bell	.05
388	Steve Olin	.05
389	Chuck McElroy	.05
390	Mark Gardner	.05
391	Rod Beck	.05
392	Dennis Rasmussen	.05
393	Charlie Leibrandt	.05
394	Julio Franco	.05
395	Pete Harnisch	.05
396	Sid Bream	.05
397	Milt Thompson	.05
398	Glenallen Hill	.05
399	Chico Walker	.05
400	Alex Cole	.05
401	Trevor Wilson	.05
402	Jeff Conine	.05
403	Kyle Abbott	.05
404	Tom Browning	.05
405	Jerald Clark	.05
406	Vince Horsman	.05
407	Kevin Mitchell	.05
408	Pete Smith	.05
409	Jeff Innis	.05
410	Mike Timlin	.05
411	Charlie Hayes	.05
412	Alex Fernandez	.05
413	Jeff Russell	.05
414	Jody Reed	.05
415	Mickey Morandini	.05
416	Darnell Coles	.05
417	Xavier Hernandez	.05
418	Steve Sax	.05
419	Joe Girardi	.05
420	Mike Fetters	.05
421	Danny Jackson	.05
422	Jim Gott	.05
423	Tim Belcher	.05
424	Jose Mesa	.05
425	Junior Felix	.05
426	Thomas Howard	.05
427	Julio Valera	.05
428	Dante Bichette	.05
429	Mike Sharperson	.05
430	Darryl Kile	.05
431	Lonnie Smith	.05
432	Monty Fariss	.05
433	Reggie Jefferson	.05
434	Bob McClure	.05
435	Craig Lefferts	.05
436	Duane Ward	.05
437	Shawn Abner	.05
438	Roberto Kelly	.05
439	Paul O'Neill	.05
440	Alan Mills	.05
441	Roger Mason	.05
442	Gary Pettis	.05
443	Steve Lake	.05
444	Gene Larkin	.05
445	Larry Anderson	.05
446	Doug Dascenzo	.05
447	Daryl Boston	.05
448	John Candelaria	.05
449	Storm Davis	.05
450	Tom Edens	.05
451	Mike Maddux	.05
452	Tim Naehring	.05
453	John Orton	.05
454	Joey Cora	.05
455	Chuck Crim	.05
456	Dan Plesac	.05
457	Mike Bielecki	.05
458	Terry Jorgensen RC	.05
459	John Habyan	.05
460	Pete O'Brien	.05
461	Jeff Treadway	.05
462	Frank Castillo	.05
463	Jimmy Jones	.05
464	Tommy Greene	.05
465	Tracy Woodson	.05
466	Rich Rodriguez	.05
467	Joe Hesketh	.05
468	Greg Myers	.05
469	Kirk McCaskill	.05
470	Ricky Bones	.05
471	Lenny Webster	.05
472	Francisco Cabrera	.05
473	Turner Ward	.05
474	Dwayne Henry	.05
475	Al Osuna	.05
476	Craig Wilson	.05
477	Chris Nabholz	.05
478	Rafael Belliard	.05
479	Terry Leach	.05
480	Tim Teufel	.05
481	Dennis Eckersley (Award Winner)	.15
482	Barry Bonds (Award Winner)	.50
483	Dennis Eckersley (Award Winner)	.15
484	Greg Maddux (Award Winner)	.25
485	Pat Listach (ROY)	.05
486	Eric Karros (ROY)	.05
487	Jamie Arnold RC	.05
488	B.J. Wallace	.05
489	Derek Jeter RC	8.00
490	Jason Kendall RC	.45
491	Rick Helling	.05
492	Derek Wallace RC	.05
493	Sean Lowe RC	.05
494	Shannon Stewart RC	.65
495	Benji Grigsby RC	.05
496	Todd Steverson RC	.05
497	Dan Serafini RC	.05
498	Michael Tucker	.05
499	Chris Roberts (Draft Pick)	.05
500	Pete Janicki RC (Draft Pick)	.05
501	Jeff Schmidt RC	.05
502	Edgar Martinez/AS	.05
503	Omar Vizquel/AS	.05
504	Ken Griffey Jr./AS	.35
505	Kirby Puckett/AS	.25
506	Joe Carter/AS	.05
507	Ivan Rodriguez/AS	.15
508	Jack Morris/AS	.05
509	Dennis Eckersley/AS	.15
510	Frank Thomas/AS	.45
511	Roberto Alomar/AS	.10
512	Mickey Morandini (Highlight)	.05
513	Dennis Eckersley (Highlight)	.15
514	Jeff Reardon (Highlight)	.05
515	Danny Tartabull (Highlight)	.05
516	Bip Roberts (Highlight)	.05
517	George Brett (Highlight)	.30
518	Robin Yount (Highlight)	.20
519	Kevin Gross (Highlight)	.05
520	Ed Sprague (World Series Highlight)	.05
521	Dave Winfield (World Series Highlight)	.20
522	Ozzie Smith/AS	.05
523	Barry Bonds/AS	.50
524	Andy Van Slyke/AS	.05
525	Tony Gwynn/AS	.25
526	Darren Daulton/AS	.05
527	Greg Maddux/AS	.25
528	Fred McGriff/AS	.05
529	Lee Smith/AS	.05
530	Ryne Sandberg/AS	.25
531	Gary Sheffield/AS	.10
532	Ozzie Smith (Dream Team)	.25
533	Kirby Puckett (Dream Team)	.25
534	Gary Sheffield (Dream Team)	.10
535	Andy Van Slyke (Dream Team)	.05
536	Ken Griffey Jr. (Dream Team)	.35
537	Ivan Rodriguez (Dream Team)	.15
538	Charles Nagy (Dream Team)	.05
539	Tom Glavine (Dream Team)	.10
540	Dennis Eckersley (Dream Team)	.15
541	Frank Thomas (Dream Team)	.20
542	Roberto Alomar (Dream Team)	.10
543	Sean Barry	.05
544	Mike Schooler	.05
545	Chuck Carr	.05
546	Lenny Harris	.05
547	Gary Scott	.05
548	Derek Lilliquist	.05
549	Brian Hunter	.05
550	Kirby Puckett (MOY)	.25
551	Jim Eisenreich	.05
552	Andre Dawson	.25
553	David Nied	.05
554	Spike Owen	.05
555	Greg Gagne	.05
556	Sid Fernandez	.05
557	Mark McGwire	.75
558	Bryan Harvey	.05
559	Harold Reynolds	.05
560	Barry Bonds	1.00
561	Eric Wedge RC	.05
562	Ozzie Smith	.45
563	Rick Sutcliffe	.05
564	Jeff Reardon	.05
565	Alex Arias RC	.05
566	Greg Swindell	.05
567	Brook Jacoby	.05
568	Pete Incaviglia	.05
569	Butch Henry RC	.05
570	Eric Davis	.05
571	Kevin Seitzer	.05
572	Tony Fernandez	.05
573	Steve Reed RC	.05
574	Cory Snyder	.05
575	Joe Carter	.05
576	Greg Maddux	.45
577	Bert Blyleven	.05
578	Kevin Bass	.05
579	Carlton Fisk	.40
580	Doug Drabek	.05
581	Mark Gubicza	.05
582	Bobby Thigpen	.05
583	Chili Davis	.05
584	Scott Bankhead	.05
585	Harold Baines	.05
586	Eric Young RC	.15
587	Lance Parrish	.05
588	Juan Bell	.05
589	Bob Ojeda	.05
590	Joe Orsulak	.05
591	Benito Santiago	.05
592	Wade Boggs	.45
593	Robby Thompson	.05
594	Erik Plunk	.05
595	Hensley Meulens	.05
596	Lou Whitaker	.05
597	Dale Murphy	.25
598	Paul Molitor	.40
599	Greg W. Harris	.05
600	Darren Holmes	.05
601	Dave Martinez	.05
602	Tom Henke	.05
603	Mike Benjamin	.05
604	Rene Gonzales	.05
605	Roger McDowell	.05
606	Kirby Puckett	.45
607	Randy Myers	.05
608	Ruben Sierra	.05
609	Wilson Alvarez	.05
610	Dave Segui	.05
611	Juan Samuel	.05
612	Tom Brunansky	.05
613	Willie Randolph	.05
614	Tony Phillips	.05
615	Candy Maldonado	.05
616	Chris Bosio	.05
617	Bret Barberie	.05
618	Scott Sanderson	.05
619	Ron Darling	.05
620	Dave Winfield	.40
621	Mike Felder	.05
622	Greg Hibbard	.05
623	Mike Scioscia	.05
624	John Smiley	.05
625	Alejandro Pena	.05
626	Terry Steinbach	.05
627	Freddie Benavides	.05
628	Kevin Reimer	.05
629	Braulio Castillo	.05
630	Dave Stieb	.05
631	Dave Magadan	.05
632	Scott Fletcher	.05
633	Cris Carpenter	.05
634	Kevin Maas	.05
635	Todd Worrell	.05
636	Rob Deer	.05
637	Dwight Smith	.05
638	Chito Martinez	.05
639	Jimmy Key	.05
640	Greg Harris	.05
641	Mike Moore	.05
642	Pat Borders	.05
643	Bill Gullickson	.05
644	Greg Gaetti	.05
645	David Howard	.05
646	Jim Abbott	.05
647	Willie Wilson	.05
648	David Wells	.05
649	Andres Galarraga	.05
650	Vince Coleman	.05
651	Rob Dibble	.05
652	Frank Tanana	.05
653	Steve Decker	.05
654	David Cone	.05
655	Jack Armstrong	.05
656	Dave Stewart	.05
657	Billy Hatcher	.05
658	Tim Raines	.05
659	Walt Weiss	.05
660	Jose Lind	.05

Boys of Summer

These cards were available as inserts only in Score 35-card Super Packs, about one in every four packs. Borderless fronts have a color action photo of the player superimposed over the sun. The player's name is in black script in a green strip at bottom, along with a subset logo. On back is a player portrait, again with the sun as a background. Subset, company, team and major league logos are in color on the right, and there is a short career summary on the green background at bottom.

		NM/M
Complete Set (30):		12.50
Common Player:		.25
1	Billy Ashley	.25
2	Tim Salmon	.50
3	Pedro Martinez	4.00
4	Luis Mercedes	.25
5	Mike Piazza	8.00
6	Troy Neel	.25
7	Melvin Nieves	.25
8	Ryan Klesko	.25
9	Ryan Thompson	.25
10	Kevin Young	.25
11	Gerald Williams	.25
12	Willie Greene	.25
13	John Patterson	.25
14	Carlos Garcia	.25
15	Eddie Zosky	.25
16	Sean Berry	.25
17	Rico Brogna	.25
18	Larry Carter	.25
19	Bobby Ayala	.25
20	Alan Embree	.25
21	Donald Harris	.25
22	Sterling Hitchcock	.25
23	David Nied	.25
24	Henry Mercedes	.25
25	Ozzie Canseco	.25
26	David Hulse	.25
27	Al Martin	.25
28	Dan Wilson	.25
29	Paul Miller	.25
30	Rich Rowland	.25

Dream Team

This set which features most of the players in street clothes in sepia-toned photos on a white background, has gold-foil graphics and was available only via a mail-in offer.

		NM/M
Complete Set (12):		5.00
Common Player:		.25
1	Ozzie Smith	1.00
2	Kirby Puckett	1.00
3	Gary Sheffield	.35
4	Andy Van Slyke	.25
5	Ken Griffey Jr.	2.00
6	Ivan Rodriguez	.60
7	Charles Nagy	.25
8	Tom Glavine	.35
9	Dennis Eckersley	.60
10	Frank Thomas	.75
11	Roberto Alomar	.30
--	Header Card	--

The Franchise

These glossy inserts have full-bleed color action photos against a darkened background so that the player stands out. Cards could be found in 16-card packs only; odds of finding one are 1 in every 24 packs. The fronts have gold-foil highlights.

		NM/M
Complete Set (28):		50.00
Common Player:		.60
1	Cal Ripken, Jr.	12.00
2	Roger Clemens	6.00
3	Mark Langston	.60
4	Frank Thomas	3.50
5	Carlos Baerga	.60
6	Cecil Fielder	.60
7	Gregg Jefferies	.60
8	Robin Yount	3.50
9	Kirby Puckett	5.00
10	Don Mattingly	6.00
11	Dennis Eckersley	3.00
12	Ken Griffey Jr.	9.00
13	Juan Gonzalez	3.50
14	Roberto Alomar	1.50
15	Terry Pendleton	.60
16	Ryne Sandberg	5.00
17	Barry Larkin	.60
18	Jeff Bagwell	3.50
19	Brett Butler	.60
20	Larry Walker	.60
21	Bobby Bonilla	.60
22	Darren Daulton	.60
23	Andy Van Slyke	.60
24	Ray Lankford	.60
25	Gary Sheffield	1.50
26	Will Clark	.60
27	Bryan Harvey	.60
28	David Nied	.60

Procter & Gamble Rookies

This set was available via a mail-in offer in the summer of 1993. Ten proofs of purchase were required along with a small amount of cash for postage. Fronts feature a player action photo in a diamond at center with the name, position and team logo in a home plate device at the bottom of the photo. At bottom center is a color photo of the player's home stadium, flanked by silver-foil stripes on a dark green background. Above the player photo are gold-foil Score and P&G logos on a dark green background. A center bar in gold foil has the word "ROOKIE" in green. Backs have a small player portrait photo at top against a dark green background. His name and position are in white at left and personal data at right. At center is a large color photo of the player's hometeam skyline, with the city name in gold type in a green stripe below. At bottom are complete major and minor league stats, MLB and MLBPA logos and the card number.

	NM/M
Complete Set (10):	3.00

Common Player:		.25
1	Wil Cordero	.25
2	Pedro Martinez	2.00
3	Bret Boone	.25
4	Melvin Nieves	.25
5	Ryan Klesko	.25
6	Ryan Thompson	.25
7	Kevin Young	.25
8	Willie Greene	.25
9	Eric Wedge	.25
10	David Nied	.25

1994 Score Samples

Regular and Gold Rush versions of the first eight cards in the 1994 Score set were produced in a special promo version to familiarize buyers with the new issue. Cards have all zeroes in place of the 1993 stats and are overprinted on front and back with a diagonal black "SAMPLE." The samples were distributed in 11-card cello packs containing eight regular sample cards, one of the Gold Rush samples, a Barry Larkin Dream Team promo card and a header.

		NM/M
Complete Set (18):		20.00
Common Player:		.40
1	Barry Bonds	2.00
1	Barry Bonds (Gold Rush)	6.00
2	John Olerud	.40
2	John Olerud (Gold Rush)	1.00
3	Ken Griffey Jr.	1.50
3	Ken Griffey Jr. (Gold Rush)	4.50
4	Jeff Bagwell	1.00
4	Jeff Bagwell (Gold Rush)	3.00
5	John Burkett	.40
5	John Burkett (Gold Rush)	1.00
6	Jack McDowell	.40
6	Jack McDowell (Gold Rush)	1.00
7	Albert Belle	.50
7	Albert Belle (Gold Rush)	1.50
8	Andres Galarraga	.40
8	Andres Galarraga (Gold Rush)	1.00
5	Barry Larkin (Dream Team)	.50
--	Hobby Header Card	.05
--	Retail Header Card	.05

1994 Score

Score's 1994 set, with a new design and UV coating, was issued in two series of 330 cards each. The cards, which use more action photos than before, have dark blue borders with the player's name in a team color-coded strip at the bottom. A special Gold Rush card, done for each card in the set, is included in every pack. Series 1 includes American League checklists, which are printed on the backs of cards depicting panoramic views of each team's ballpark. Series 2 has the National League team checklists. Insert sets include Dream Team players, and National League Gold Stars (Series 2 packs), which use the Gold Rush process and appear once every 18 packs.

		NM/M
Complete Set (660):		15.00
Common Player:		.05
Gold Rush:		2X
Pack (14):		.75
Wax Box (36):		15.00
1	Barry Bonds	1.00
2	John Olerud	.40
3	Ken Griffey Jr.	.65
4	Jeff Bagwell	.40
5	John Burkett	.05
6	Jack McDowell	.05
7	Albert Belle	.05
8	Andres Galarraga	.05
9	Mike Mussina	.30
10	Will Clark	.05
11	Travis Fryman	.05
12	Tony Gwynn	.50
13	Robin Yount	.40
14	Dave Magadan	.05
15	Paul O'Neill	.05
16	Ray Lankford	.05
17	Damion Easley	.05
18	Andy Van Slyke	.05
19	Brian McRae	.05
20	Ryne Sandberg	.50
21	Kirby Puckett	.50
22	Dwight Gooden	.05
23	Don Mattingly	.60
24	Kevin Mitchell	.05
25	Roger Clemens	.60
26	Eric Karros	.05
27	Juan Gonzalez	.20
28	John Kruk	.05
29	Gregg Jefferies	.05
30	Tom Glavine	.05
31	Ivan Rodriguez	.35
32	Jay Bell	.05
33	Randy Johnson	.40
34	Darren Daulton	.05
35	Rickey Henderson	.40
36	Eddie Murray	.40
37	Brian Harper	.05
38	Delino DeShields	.05
39	Jose Lind	.05
40	Benito Santiago	.05
41	Frank Thomas	.40
42	Mark Grace	.05
43	Roberto Alomar	.20
44	Andy Benes	.05
45	Luis Polonia	.05
46	Brett Butler	.05
47	Terry Steinbach	.05
48	Craig Biggio	.05
49	Greg Vaughn	.05
50	Charlie Hayes	.05
51	Mickey Tettleton	.05
52	Jose Rijo	.05
53	Carlos Baerga	.05
54	Jeff Blauser	.05
55	Leo Gomez	.05
56	Bob Tewksbury	.05
57	Mo Vaughn	.05
58	Orlando Merced	.05
59	Tino Martinez	.05
60	Len Dykstra	.05
61	Jose Canseco	.25
62	Tony Fernandez	.05
63	Donovan Osborne	.05
64	Ken Hill	.05
65	Kent Hrbek	.05
66	Bryan Harvey	.05
67	Wally Joyner	.05
68	Derrick May	.05
69	Lance Johnson	.05
70	Willie McGee	.05
71	Mark Langston	.05
72	Terry Pendleton	.05
73	Joe Carter	.05
74	Barry Larkin	.05
75	Jimmy Key	.05
76	Joe Girardi	.05
77	B.J. Surhoff	.05
78	Pete Harnisch	.05
79	Lou Whitaker	.05
80	Cory Snyder	.05
81	Kenny Lofton	.05
82	Fred McGriff	.05
83	Mike Greenwell	.05
84	Mike Perez	.05
85	Cal Ripken, Jr.	1.00
86	Don Slaught	.05
87	Omar Vizquel	.05
88	Curt Schilling	.30
89	Chuck Knoblauch	.05
90	Moises Alou	.05
91	Greg Gagne	.05
92	Bret Saberhagen	.05
93	Ozzie Guillen	.05
94	Matt Williams	.05
95	Chad Curtis	.05
96	Mike Harkey	.05
97	Devon White	.05
98	Walt Weiss	.05
99	Kevin Brown	.05
100	Gary Sheffield	.25
101	Wade Boggs	.50
102	Orel Hershiser	.05
103	Tony Phillips	.05
104	Andujar Cedeno	.05
105	Bill Spiers	.05
106	Otis Nixon	.05
107	Felix Fermin	.05
108	Blp Roberts	.05
109	Dennis Eckersley	.35
110	Dante Bichette	.05
111	Ben McDonald	.05
112	Jim Poole	.05
113	John Dopson	.05
114	Rob Dibble	.05
115	Jeff Treadway	.05
116	Ricky Jordan	.05
117	Mike Henneman	.05
118	Willie Blair	.05
119	Doug Henry	.05
120	Gerald Perry	.05
121	Greg Myers	.05
122	John Franco	.05
123	Roger Mason	.05
124	Chris Hammond	.05
125	Hubie Brooks	.05
126	Kent Mercker	.05
127	Jim Abbott	.05
128	Kevin Bass	.05
129	Rick Aguilera	.05
130	Mitch Webster	.05
131	Eric Plunk	.05
132	Mark Carreon	.05
133	Dave Stewart	.05
134	Willie Wilson	.05
135	Dave Fleming	.05
136	Jeff Tackett	.05
137	Geno Petralli	.05
138	Gene Harris	.05
139	Scott Bankhead	.05
140	Trevor Wilson	.05
141	Alvaro Espinoza	.05
142	Ryan Bowen	.05
143	Mike Moore	.05
144	Bill Pecota	.05
145	Jaime Navarro	.05
146	Jack Daugherty	.05
147	Bob Wickman	.05
148	Chris Jones	.05
149	Todd Stottlemyre	.05
150	Brian Williams	.05
151	Chuck Finley	.05
152	Lenny Harris	.05
153	Alex Fernandez	.05
154	Candy Maldonado	.05
155	Jeff Montgomery	.05
156	David West	.05
157	Mark Williamson	.05
158	Milt Thompson	.05
159	Ron Darling	.05
160	Stan Belinda	.05
161	Henry Cotto	.05
162	Mel Rojas	.05
163	Doug Strange	.05
164	Rene Arocha (1993 Rookie)	.05
165	Tim Hulett	.05
166	Steve Avery	.05
167	Jim Thome	.35
168	Tom Browning	.05
169	Mario Diaz	.05
170	Steve Reed (1993 Rookie)	.05
171	Scott Livingstone	.05
172	Chris Donnels	.05
173	John Jaha	.05
174	Carlos Hernandez	.05
175	Dion James	.05
176	Bud Black	.05
177	Tony Castillo	.05
178	Jose Guzman	.05
179	Torey Lovullo	.05
180	John Vander Wal	.05
181	Mike LaValliere	.05
182	Sid Fernandez	.05
183	Brent Mayne	.05
184	Terry Mulholland	.05
185	Willie Banks	.05
186	Steve Cooke (1993 Rookie)	.05
187	Brent Gates (1993 Rookie)	.05
188	Erik Pappas (1993 Rookie)	.05
189	Bill Haselman (1993 Rookie)	.05
190	Fernando Valenzuela	.05
191	Gary Redus	.05
192	Danny Darwin	.05
193	Mark Portugal	.05
194	Derek Lilliquist	.05
195	Charlie O'Brien	.05
196	Matt Nokes	.05
197	Danny Sheaffer	.05
198	Bill Gullickson	.05
199	Alex Arias (1993 Rookie)	.05
200	Mike Fetters	.05
201	Brian Jordan	.05
202	Joe Grahe	.05
203	Tom Candiotti	.05
204	Jeremy Stanton	.05
205	Mike Stanton	.05
206	David Howard	.05
207	Darren Holmes	.05
208	Rick Honeycutt	.05
209	Danny Jackson	.05
210	Rich Amaral (1993 Rookie)	.05
211	Blas Minor (1993 Rookie)	.05
212	Kenny Rogers	.05
213	Jim Leyritz	.05
214	Mike Morgan	.05
215	Dan Gladden	.05
216	Randy Velarde	.05
217	Mitch Williams	.05
218	Hipolito Pichardo	.05
219	Dave Burba	.05
220	Wilson Alvarez	.05
221	Bob Zupcic	.05
222	Francisco Cabrera	.05
223	Julio Valera	.05
224	Paul Assenmacher	.05
225	Jeff Branson	.05
226	Todd Frohwirth	.05
227	Armando Reynoso	.05
228	Rich Rowland (1993 Rookie)	.05
229	Freddie Benavides (1993 Rookie)	.05
230	Wayne Kirby (1993 Rookie)	.05
231	Darryl Kile	.05
232	Skeeter Barnes	.05
233	Ramon Martinez	.05
234	Tom Gordon	.05
235	Dave Gallagher	.05
236	Ricky Bones	.05
237	Larry Andersen	.05
238	Pat Meares (1993 Rookie)	.05
239	Zane Smith	.05
240	Tim Leary	.05
241	Phil Clark	.05
242	Danny Cox	.05
243	Mike Jackson	.05
244	Mike Gallego	.05
245	Lee Smith	.05
246	Todd Jones (1993 Rookie)	.05
247	Steve Bedrosian	.05
248	Troy Neel	.05
249	Jose Bautista	.05
250	Steve Frey	.05
251	Jeff Reardon	.05
252	Stan Javier	.05
253	Mo Sanford (1993 Rookie)	.05
254	Steve Sax	.05
255	Luis Aquino	.05
256	Domingo Jean (1993 Rookie)	.05
257	Scott Servais	.05
258	Brad Pennington (1993 Rookie)	.05
259	Dave Hansen	.05
260	Goose Gossage	.05
261	Jeff Fassero	.05
262	Junior Ortiz	.05
263	Anthony Young	.05
264	Chris Bosio	.05
265	Ruben Amaro Jr.	.05
266	Mark Eichhorn	.05
267	Dave Clark	.05
268	Gary Thurman	.05
269	Les Lancaster	.05
270	Jamie Moyer	.05
271	Ricky Gutierrez (1993 Rookie)	.05
272	Greg Harris	.05
273	Mike Benjamin	.05
274	Gene Nelson	.05
275	Damon Berryhill	.05
276	Scott Radinsky	.05
277	Mike Aldrete	.05
278	Jerry DiPoto	.05
279	Chris Haney	.05
280	Richie Lewis (1993 Rookie)	.05
281	Jarvis Brown	.05
282	Juan Bell	.05
283	Joe Klink	.05
284	Graeme Lloyd (1993 Rookie)	.05
285	Casey Candaele	.05
286	Bob MacDonald	.05
287	Mike Sharperson	.05
288	Gene Larkin	.05
289	Brian Barnes	.05
290	David McCarty (1993 Rookie)	.05
291	Jeff Innis	.05
292	Bob Patterson	.05
293	Ben Rivera	.05
294	John Habyan	.05
295	Rich Rodriguez	.05
296	Edwin Nunez	.05
297	Rod Brewer	.05
298	Mike Timlin	.05
299	Jesse Orosco	.05
300	Gary Gaetti	.05
301	Todd Benzinger	.05
302	Jeff Nelson	.05
303	Rafael Belliard	.05
304	Matt Whiteside	.05
305	Vinny Castilla	.05
306	Matt Turner	.05
307	Eduardo Perez	.05
308	Joel Johnston	.05
309	Chris Gomez	.05
310	Pat Rapp	.05
311	Jim Tatum	.05
312	Kirk Rueter	.05
313	John Flaherty	.05
314	Tom Kramer	.05
315	Mark Whiten (Highlights)	.05
316	Chris Bosio (Highlights)	.05
317	Orioles Checklist	.05
318	Red Sox Checklist	.05
319	Angels Checklist	.05
320	White Sox Checklist	.05
321	Indians Checklist	.05
322	Tigers Checklist	.05
323	Royals Checklist	.05
324	Brewers Checklist	.05
325	Twins Checklist	.05
326	Yankees Checklist	.05
327	Athletics Checklist	.05
328	Mariners Checklist	.05
329	Rangers Checklist	.05
330	Blue Jays Checklist	.05
331	Frank Viola	.05
332	Ron Gant	.05
333	Charles Nagy	.05
334	Roberto Kelly	.05
335	Brady Anderson	.05
336	Alex Cole	.05
337	Alan Trammell	.05
338	Derek Bell	.05
339	Bernie Williams	.05
340	Jose Offerman	.05
341	Bill Wegman	.05
342	Ken Caminiti	.05
343	Pat Borders	.05
344	Kirt Manwaring	.05
345	Chili Davis	.05
346	Steve Buechele	.05
347	Robin Ventura	.05
348	Teddy Higuera	.05
349	Jerry Browne	.05
350	Scott Kamieniecki	.05
351	Kevin Tapani	.05
352	Marquis Grissom	.05
353	Jay Buhner	.05
354	Dave Hollins	.05
355	Dan Wilson	.05
356	Bob Walk	.05
357	Chris Hoiles	.05
358	Todd Zeile	.05
359	Kevin Appier	.05
360	Chris Sabo	.05
361	David Segui	.05
362	Jerald Clark	.05
363	Tony Pena	.05
364	Steve Finley	.05
365	Roger Pavlik	.05
366	John Smoltz	.05
367	Scott Fletcher	.05
368	Jody Reed	.05
369	David Wells	.05
370	Jose Vizcaino	.05
371	Pat Listach	.05
372	Orestes Destrade	.05
373	Danny Tartabull	.05
374	Greg W. Harris	.05
375	Juan Guzman	.05
376	Larry Walker	.05
377	Gary DiSarcina	.05
378	Bobby Bonilla	.05
379	Tim Raines	.05
380	Tommy Greene	.05
381	Chris Gwynn	.05
382	Jeff King	.05
383	Shane Mack	.05
384	Ozzie Smith	.50
385	Eddie Zambrano **RC**	.05
386	Mike Devereaux	.05
387	Erik Hanson	.05
388	Scott Cooper	.05
389	Dean Palmer	.05
390	John Wetteland	.05
391	Reggie Jefferson	.05
392	Mark Lemke	.05
393	Cecil Fielder	.05
394	Reggie Sanders	.05
395	Darryl Hamilton	.05
396	Daryl Boston	.05
397	Pat Kelly	.05
398	Joe Orsulak	.05
399	Ed Sprague	.05
400	Eric Anthony	.05
401	Scott Sanderson	.05
402	Jim Gott	.05
403	Ron Karkovice	.05
404	Phil Plantier	.05
405	David Cone	.05
406	Robby Thompson	.05
407	Dave Winfield	.40
408	Dwight Smith	.05
409	Ruben Sierra	.05
410	Jack Armstrong	.05
411	Mike Felder	.05
412	Wil Cordero	.05
413	Julio Franco	.05
414	Howard Johnson	.05
415	Mark McLemore	.05
416	Pete Incaviglia	.05
417	John Valentin	.05
418	Tim Wakefield	.05
419	Jose Mesa	.05
420	Bernard Gilkey	.05
421	Kirk Gibson	.05
422	Dave Justice	.05
423	Tom Brunansky	.05
424	John Smiley	.05
425	Kevin Maas	.05
426	Doug Drabek	.05
427	Paul Molitor	.40
428	Darryl Strawberry	.05
429	Tim Naehring	.05
430	Bill Swift	.05
431	Ellis Burks	.05
432	Greg Hibbard	.05
433	Felix Jose	.05
434	Bret Barberie	.05
435	Pedro Munoz	.05
436	Darrin Fletcher	.05
437	Bobby Witt	.05
438	Wes Chamberlain	.05
439	Mackey Sasser	.05
440	Mark Whiten	.05
441	Harold Reynolds	.05
442	Greg Olson	.05
443	Billy Hatcher	.05
444	Joe Oliver	.05
445	Sandy Alomar Jr.	.05
446	Tim Wallach	.05
447	Karl Rhodes	.05

448	Royce Clayton	.05
449	Cal Eldred	.05
450	Rick Wilkins	.05
451	Mike Stanley	.05
452	Charlie Hough	.05
453	Jack Morris	.05
454	Jon Ratliff RC	.05
455	Rene Gonzales	.05
456	Eddie Taubensee	.05
457	Roberto Hernandez	.05
458	Todd Hundley	.05
459	Mike MacFarlane	.05
460	Mickey Morandini	.05
461	Scott Erickson	.05
462	Lonnie Smith	.05
463	Dave Henderson	.05
464	Ryan Klesko	.05
465	Edgar Martinez	.05
466	Tom Pagnozzi	.05
467	Charlie Leibrandt	.05
468	Brian Anderson RC	.10
469	Harold Baines	.05
470	Tim Belcher	.05
471	Andre Dawson	.25
472	Eric Young	.05
473	Paul Sorrento	.05
474	Luis Gonzalez	.05
475	Rob Deer	.05
476	Mike Piazza	.65
477	Kevin Reimer	.05
478	Jeff Gardner	.05
479	Melido Perez	.05
480	Darren Lewis	.05
481	Duane Ward	.05
482	Rey Sanchez	.05
483	Mark Lewis	.05
484	Jeff Conine	.05
485	Joey Cora	.05
486	Trot Nixon RC	.50
487	Kevin McReynolds	.05
488	Mike Lansing	.05
489	Mike Pagliarulo	.05
490	Mariano Duncan	.05
491	Mike Bordick	.05
492	Kevin Young	.05
493	Dave Valle	.05
494	Wayne Gomes RC	.05
495	Rafael Palmeiro	.35
496	Deion Sanders	.05
497	Rick Sutcliffe	.05
498	Randy Milligan	.05
499	Carlos Quintana	.05
500	Chris Turner	.05
501	Thomas Howard	.05
502	Greg Swindell	.05
503	Chad Kreuter	.05
504	Eric Davis	.05
505	Dickie Thon	.05
506	Matt Barnes RC	.05
507	Spike Owen	.05
508	Rod Beck	.05
509	Pat Hentgen	.05
510	Sammy Sosa	.50
511	J.T. Snow	.05
512	Chuck Carr	.05
513	Bo Jackson	.10
514	Dennis Martinez	.05
515	Phil Hiatt	.05
516	Jeff Kent	.05
517	Brooks Kieschnick RC	.05
518	Kirk Presley RC	.05
519	Kevin Seitzer	.05
520	Carlos Garcia	.05
521	Mike Blowers	.05
522	Luis Alicea	.05
523	David Hulse	.05
524	Greg Maddux	.50
525	Gregg Olson	.05
526	Hal Morris	.05
527	Daron Kirkreit	.05
528	David Nied	.05
529	Jeff Russell	.05
530	Kevin Gross	.05
531	John Doherty	.05
532	Matt Brunson RC	.05
533	Dave Nilsson	.05
534	Randy Myers	.05
535	Steve Farr	.05
536	Billy Wagner RC	.10
537	Darnell Coles	.05
538	Frank Tanana	.05
539	Tim Salmon	.05
540	Kim Batiste	.05
541	George Bell	.05
542	Tom Henke	.05
543	Sam Horn	.05
544	Doug Jones	.05
545	Scott Leius	.05
546	Al Martin	.05
547	Bob Welch	.05
548	Scott Christman RC	.05
549	Norm Charlton	.05
550	Mark McGwire	.75
551	Greg McMichael	.05
552	Tim Costo	.05
553	Rodney Bolton	.05
554	Pedro Martinez	.40
555	Marc Valdes	.05
556	Darrell Whitmore	.05
557	Tim Bogar	.05
558	Steve Karsay	.05
559	Danny Bautista	.05
560	Jeffrey Hammonds	.05
561	Aaron Sele	.05
562	Russ Springer	.05
563	Jason Bere	.05
564	Billy Brewer	.05
565	Sterling Hitchcock	.05

566	Bobby Munoz	.05
567	Craig Paquette	.05
568	Bret Boone	.05
569	Dan Peltier	.05
570	Jeromy Burnitz	.05
571	John Wasdin RC	.05
572	Chipper Jones	.50
573	Jamey Wright RC	.05
574	Jeff Granger	.05
575	Jay Powell RC	.05
576	Ryan Thompson	.05
577	Lou Frazier	.05
578	Paul Wagner	.05
579	Brad Ausmus	.05
580	Jack Voigt	.05
581	Kevin Rogers	.05
582	Damon Buford	.05
583	Paul Quantrill	.05
584	Marc Newfield	.05
585	Derrek Lee RC	1.00
586	Shane Reynolds	.05
587	Cliff Floyd	.05
588	Jeff Schwarz	.05
589	Ross Powell RC	.05
590	Gerald Williams	.05
591	Mike Trombley	.05
592	Ken Ryan	.05
593	John O'Donoghue	.05
594	Rod Correia	.05
595	Darrell Sherman	.05
596	Steve Scarsone	.05
597	Sherman Obando	.05
598	Kurt Abbott	.05
599	Dave Telgheder	.05
600	Rick Trlicek	.05
601	Carl Everett	.05
602	Luis Ortiz	.05
603	Larry Luebbers RC	.05
604	Kevin Roberson	.05
605	Butch Huskey	.05
606	Benji Gil	.05
607	Todd Van Poppel	.05
608	Mark Hutton	.05
609	Chip Hale	.05
610	Matt Maysey	.05
611	Scott Ruffcorn	.05
612	Hilly Hathaway	.05
613	Allen Watson	.05
614	Carlos Delgado	.30
615	Roberto Mejia	.05
616	Turk Wendell	.05
617	Tony Tarasco	.05
618	Raul Mondesi	.05
619	Kevin Stocker	.05
620	Javier Lopez	.05
621	Keith Kessinger RC	.05
622	Bob Hamelin	.05
623	John Roper	.05
624	Len Dykstra	
	(World Series)	.05
625	Joe Carter (World Series)	.05
626	Jim Abbott (Highlight)	.05
627	Lee Smith (Highlight)	.05
628	Ken Griffey Jr. (HL)	.35
629	Dave Winfield (Highlight)	.05
630	Darryl Kile (Highlight)	.05
631	Frank Thomas (MVP)	.25
632	Barry Bonds (MVP)	.50
633	Jack McDowell (Cy Young)	.05
634	Greg Maddux (Cy Young)	.25
635	Tim Salmon (ROY)	.05
636	Mike Piazza (ROY)	.40
637	Brian Turang RC	.05
638	Rondell White	.05
639	Nigel Wilson	.05
640	Torii Hunter RC	.75
641	Salomon Torres	.05
642	Kevin Higgins	.05
643	Eric Wedge	.05
644	Roger Salkeld	.05
645	Manny Ramirez	.40
646	Jeff McNeely	.05
647	Braves Checklist	.05
648	Cubs Checklist	.05
649	Reds Checklist	.05
650	Rockies Checklist	.05
651	Marlins Checklist	.05
652	Astros Checklist	.05
653	Dodgers Checklist	.05
654	Expos Checklist	.05
655	Mets Checklist	.05
656	Phillies Checklist	.05
657	Pirates Checklist	.05
658	Cardinals Checklist	.05
659	Padres Checklist	.05
660	Giants Checklist	.05

Gold Rush

Opting to include one insert card in each pack of its 1994 product, Score created a "Gold Rush" version of each card in its regular set. Gold Rush cards are basically the same as their counterparts with a few enhancements. Card fronts are printed on foil with a gold border and a Score Gold Rush logo in one of the upper corners. The background of the photo has been metalized, allowing the color player portion to stand out in sharp contrast. Backs are identical to the regular cards except for the appearance of a large Gold Rush logo under the typography.

	NM/M
Complete Set (660):	40.00
Common Player:	.15
Stars:	2X

Boys of Summer

A heavy emphasis on. rookies and recent rookies is noted in this insert set. Released in two series, cards #1-30 are found in Series 1, with #31-60 packaged with Series 2. Fronts feature a color action photo on which the background has been rendered in a blurred watercolor effect. A hot-color aura separates the player from the background. The player's name appears vertically in gold foil. Backs have the background in reds and orange with a portrait-style player photo on one side and a large "Boys of Summer" logo on the other. A short description of the player's talents appears at center.

		NM/M
Complete Set (60):		25.00
Common Player:		.25
1	Jeff Conine	.25
2	Aaron Sele	.25
3	Kevin Stocker	.25
4	Pat Meares	.25
5	Jeromy Burnitz	.25
6	Mike Piazza	6.00
7	Allen Watson	.25
8	Jeffrey Hammonds	.25
9	Kevin Roberson	.25
10	Hilly Hathaway	.25
11	Kirk Reuter	.25
12	Eduardo Perez	.25
13	Ricky Gutierrez	.25
14	Domingo Jean	.25
15	David Nied	.25
16	Wayne Kirby	.25
17	Mike Lansing	.25
18	Jason Bere	.25
19	Brent Gates	.25
20	Javier Lopez	.25
21	Greg McMichael	.25
22	David Hulse	.25
23	Roberto Mejia	.25
24	Tim Salmon	.50
25	Rene Arocha	.25
26	Bret Boone	.25
27	David McCarty	.25
28	Todd Van Poppel	.25
29	Lance Painter	.25
30	Erik Pappas	.25
31	Chuck Carr	.25
32	Mark Hutton	.25
33	Jeff McNeely	.25
34	Willie Greene	.25
35	Nigel Wilson	.25
36	Rondell White	.25
37	Brian Turang	.25
38	Manny Ramirez	3.00
39	Salomon Torres	.25
40	Melvin Nieves	.25
41	Ryan Klesko	.25
42	Keith Kessinger	.25
43	Eric Wedge	.25
44	Bob Hamelin	.25
45	Carlos Delgado	2.50
46	Marc Newfield	.25
47	Raul Mondesi	.25
48	Tim Costo	.25
49	Pedro Martinez	3.00
50	Steve Karsay	.25
51	Danny Bautista	.25
52	Butch Huskey	.25
53	Kurt Abbott	.25
54	Darrell Sherman	.25
55	Damon Buford	.25
56	Ross Powell	.25
57	Darrell Whitmore	.25
58	Chipper Jones	5.00
59	Jeff Granger	.25
60	Cliff Floyd	.25

Dream Team

Score's 1994 "Dream Team," one top player at each position, was featured in a 10-card insert set. The stars were decked out in vintage uniforms and equipment for the photos. Green and black bars at top and bottom frame the photo, and all printing on the front is in gold foil. Backs have a white background with green highlights. A color player portrait photo is featured, along with a brief justification for the player's selection to the squad. Cards are UV coated on both sides. Stated odds of finding a Dream Team insert were given as one per 72 packs.

		NM/M
Complete Set (10):		15.00
Common Player:		1.00
1	Mike Mussina	2.00
2	Tom Glavine	2.00
3	Don Mattingly	10.00
4	Carlos Baerga	1.00
5	Barry Larkin	1.00
6	Matt Williams	1.00
7	Juan Gonzalez	4.00
8	Andy Van Slyke	1.00
9	Larry Walker	1.00
10	Mike Stanley	1.00

Gold Stars

Limited to inclusion in hobby packs, Score's 60-card "Gold Stars" insert set features 30 National League players, found in Series I packs, and 30 American Leaguers inserted with Series II. Stated odds of finding a Gold Stars card were listed on the wrapper as one in 18 packs. A notation on the cards' back indicates that no more than 6,500 sets of Gold Stars were produced. The high-tech cards feature a color player action photo, the full-bleed background of which has been converted to metallic tones. Backs have a graduated gold background with a portrait-style color player photo.

		NM/M
Complete Set (60):		40.00
Common Player:		.25
1	Barry Bonds	6.00
2	Orlando Merced	.25
3	Mark Grace	.25
4	Darren Daulton	.25
5	Jeff Blauser	.25
6	Deion Sanders	.25
7	John Kruk	.25
8	Jeff Bagwell	2.50
9	Gregg Jefferies	.25
10	Matt Williams	.25
11	Andres Galarraga	.25
12	Jay Bell	.25
13	Mike Piazza	4.50
14	Ron Gant	.25
15	Barry Larkin	.25
16	Tom Glavine	.50
17	Len Dykstra	.25
18	Fred McGriff	.25
19	Andy Van Slyke	.25
20	Gary Sheffield	.75
21	John Burkett	.25
22	Dante Bichette	.25
23	Tony Gwynn	3.50
24	Dave Justice	.25
25	Marquis Grissom	.25
26	Bobby Bonilla	.25
27	Larry Walker	.25
28	Brett Butler	.25
29	Robby Thompson	.25
30	Jeff Conine	.25
31	Joe Carter	.25
32	Ken Griffey Jr.	4.50
33	Juan Gonzalez	1.25
34	Rickey Henderson	2.50
35	Bo Jackson	.35
36	Cal Ripken, Jr.	6.00
37	John Olerud	.25
38	Carlos Baerga	.25
39	Jack McDowell	.25
40	Cecil Fielder	.25
41	Kenny Lofton	.25
42	Roberto Alomar	1.00
43	Randy Johnson	2.50
44	Tim Salmon	.25
45	Frank Thomas	2.50
46	Albert Belle	.25
47	Greg Vaughn	.25
48	Travis Fryman	.25
49	Don Mattingly	4.00
50	Wade Boggs	3.50
51	Mo Vaughn	.25
52	Kirby Puckett	3.50
53	Devon White	.25
54	Tony Phillips	.25
55	Brian Harper	.25
56	Chad Curtis	.25
57	Paul Molitor	2.50
58	Ivan Rodriguez	2.00
59	Rafael Palmeiro	2.00
60	Brian McRae	.25

The Cycle

Leaders in the previous season's production of singles, doubles, triples and home runs are featured in this insert set which was packaged with Series II Score. Player action photos pop out of a circle at center and are surrounded by dark blue borders. "The Cycle" in printed in green at top. The player's name is in gold foil at bottom, printed over an infield diagram in a green strip. The stat which earned the player inclusion in the set is in gold foil at bottom right. On back are the rankings for the statistical category. Cards are numbered with a "TC" prefix.

		NM/M
Complete Set (20):		12.00
Common Player:		.50
1	Brett Butler	.50
2	Kenny Lofton	.50
3	Paul Molitor	2.00
4	Carlos Baerga	.50
5	Gregg Jefferies, Tony Phillips	.50
6	John Olerud	.50
7	Charlie Hayes	.50
8	Len Dykstra	.50
9	Dante Bichette	.50
10	Devon White	.50
11	Lance Johnson	.50
12	Joey Cora, Steve Finley	.50
13	Tony Fernandez	.50
14	David Hulse, Brett Butler	.50
15	Jay Bell, Brian McRae, Mickey Morandini	.50
16	Juan Gonzalez, Barry Bonds	4.00
17	Ken Griffey Jr.	4.00
18	Frank Thomas	2.50
19	Dave Justice	.50
20	Matt Williams, Albert Belle	.50

Cal Ripken, Jr.

Although the cards themselves do not indicate it, this issue was co-sponsored by Burger King and Coke, and distributed in BK restaurants in the Baltimore-Washington area. Cards were available in three-card packs for 25 cents with the purchase of a Coke product. Each pack contains two regular cards and a gold card. Each of the nine cards could be found in a regular and gold version. Cards feature color photos with a semi-circular black border at top or left. "Score '94" appears in orange in one of the upper corners, along with an Orioles logo. Cal Ripken, Jr.'s name appears at the bottom. On the gold premium version, there is a gold-foil circle around the Orioles logo and Ripken's name appears in gold, rather than white. Backs have a smaller color photo, again meeting at a semi-circular edge with the black border at left and bottom. In the black are another Score logo, a card number, an Orioles logo, a headline and a few career details and/or stats. Cards are UV coated on each side. Several hundred of the cards were personally autographed by Ripken and distributed in a drawing.

	NM/M
Complete Set (9):	3.00
Complete Set, Gold (9):	6.00
Common Player:	.50
Common Card, Gold:	1.00
Autographed Card:	200.00
1 Double Honors	.50
1a Double Honors/Gold	1.00
2 Perennial All-Star	.50
2a Perennial All-Star/Gold	1.00
3 Peerless Power	.50
3a Peerless Power/Gold	1.00
4 Fitness Fan	.50
4a Fitness Fan/Gold	1.00
5 Prime Concerns	.50
5a Prime Concerns/Gold	1.00
6 Home Run Club	.50
6a Home Run Club/Gold	1.00
7 The Iron Man	.50
7a The Iron Man/Gold	.50
8 Heavy Hitter	.50
8a Heavy Hitter/Gold	1.00
9 Gold Glover	.50
9a Gold Glover/Gold	1.00

1994 Score Rookie/Traded Samples

To introduce the various types of card which would be included in the 1994 Score Rookie/Traded set, the company produced this sample set. Cards are virtually identical to the issued versions except for the overprint "SAMPLE" running diagonally on front and back. The Rafael Palmeiro "Changing Places" sample card does not feature the red foil logo found on issued cards.

	NM/M
Complete Set (11):	7.50
Common Player:	.50
1RT Lee Smith	.50
2CP Rafael Palmeiro (Changing Places)	2.00
2RT Will Clark	.50
2SU Manny Ramirez (Super Rookie)	2.50
3RT Bo Jackson (Gold Rush)	1.00
4RT Ellis Burks	.50
5RT Eddie Murray	2.00
6RT Delino DeShields	.50
102RT Carlos Delgado	1.50
--- September Call-Up Winner Card	.10
--- Hobby Header Card	.10
--- Retail Header Card	.10

1994 Score Rookie/Traded

Score Rookie & Traded completed the 1994 baseball season with a 165-card update set. These were available in both retail and hobby packs. Score issued Super Rookies and Changing Places insert sets, as well as a Traded Redemption card and a parallel Gold Rush set. Basic cards features red front borders. Team logos are in a bottom corner in a gold polygon. One of the upper corners contains a green polygon with a gold Score logo. Most cards #71-163 feature a square multi-colored "Rookie '94" logo in a lower corner. Backs of all cards have a purple background. Traded players' card backs are vertical and contain two additional photos. Backs of the rookie cards are horizontal and feature a portrait photo at left. The "Rookie '94" logo is repeated in the upper-right corner. This is in reverse of the fronts, on which traded players have a single photo and rookie cards have both portrait and action photos. Card numbers have an "RT" prefix.

	NM/M
Complete Set (165):	5.00
Common Player:	.05
Gold Rush:	2X
Pack (10):	.40
Wax Box (36):	9.00
1 Will Clark	.05
2 Lee Smith	.05
3 Bo Jackson	.10
4 Ellis Burks	.05
5 Eddie Murray	1.00
6 Delino DeShields	.05
7 Erik Hanson	.05
8 Rafael Palmeiro	.75
9 Luis Polonia	.05
10 Omar Vizquel	.05
11 Kurt Abbott	.05
12 Vince Coleman	.05
13 Rickey Henderson	1.00
14 Terry Mulholland	.05
15 Greg Hibbard	.05
16 Walt Weiss	.05
17 Chris Sabo	.05
18 Dave Henderson	.05
19 Rick Sutcliffe	.05
20 Harold Reynolds	.05
21 Jack Morris	.05
22 Dan Wilson	.05
23 Dave Magadan	.05
24 Dennis Martinez	.05
25 Wes Chamberlain	.05
26 Otis Nixon	.05
27 Eric Anthony	.05
28 Randy Milligan	.05
29 Julio Franco	.05
30 Kevin McReynolds	.05
31 Anthony Young	.05
32 Brian Harper	.05
33 Lenny Harris	.05
34 Eddie Taubensee	.05
35 David Segui	.05
36 Stan Javier	.05
37 Felix Fermin	.05
38 Darrin Jackson	.05
39 Tony Fernandez	.05
40 Jose Vizcaino	.05
41 Willie Banks	.05
42 Brian Hunter	.05
43 Reggie Jefferson	.05
44 Junior Felix	.05
45 Jack Armstrong	.05
46 Bip Roberts	.05
47 Jerry Browne	.05
48 Marvin Freeman	.05
49 Jody Reed	.05
50 Alex Cole	.05
51 Sid Fernandez	.05
52 Pete Smith	.05
53 Xavier Hernandez	.05
54 Scott Sanderson	.05
55 Turner Ward	.05
56 Rex Hudler	.05
57 Deion Sanders	.05
58 Sid Bream	.05
59 Tony Pena	.05
60 Bret Boone	.05
61 Bobby Ayala	.05
62 Pedro Martinez	1.00
63 Howard Johnson	.05
64 Mark Portugal	.05
65 Roberto Kelly	.05
66 Spike Owen	.05
67 Jeff Treadway	.05
68 Mike Harkey	.05
69 Doug Jones	.05
70 Steve Farr	.05
71 Billy Taylor	.05
72 Manny Ramirez	1.00
73 Bob Hamelin	.05
74 Steve Karsay	.05
75 Ryan Klesko	.05
76 Cliff Floyd	.05
77 Jeffrey Hammonds	.05
78 Javier Lopez	.05
79 Roger Salkeld	.05
80 Hector Carrasco	.05
81 Gerald Williams	.05
82 Raul Mondesi	.05
83 Sterling Hitchcock	.05
84 Danny Bautista	.05
85 Chris Turner	.05
86 Shane Reynolds	.05
87 Rondell White	.05
88 Salomon Torres	.05
89 Turk Wendell	.05
90 Tony Tarasco	.05
91 Shawn Green	.65
92 Greg Colbrunn	.05
93 Eddie Zambrano	.05
94 Rich Becker	.05
95 Chris Gomez	.05
96 John Patterson	.05
97 Derek Parks	.05
98 Rich Rowland	.05
99 James Mouton	.05
100 Tim Hyers	.05
101 Jose Valentin	.05
102 Carlos Delgado	.65
103 Robert Esenhoorn	.05
104 John Hudek	.05
105 Domingo Cedeno	.05
106 Denny Hocking	.05
107 Greg Pirkl	.05
108 Mark Smith	.05
109 Paul Shuey	.05
110 Jorge Fabregas	.05
111 Rikkert Faneyte	.05
112 Rob Butler	.05
113 Darren Oliver	.05
114 Troy O'Leary	.05
115 Scott Brow	.05
116 Tony Eusebio	.05
117 Carlos Reyes	.05
118 J.R. Phillips	.05
119 Alex Diaz	.05
120 Charles Johnson	.05
121 Nate Minchey	.05
122 Scott Sanders	.05
123 Daryl Boston	.05
124 Joey Hamilton	.05
125 Brian Anderson	.05
126 Dan Miceli	.05
127 Tom Brunansky	.05
128 Dave Staton	.05
129 Mike Oquist	.05
130 John Mabry	.05
131 Norberto Martin	.05
132 Hector Fajardo	.05
133 Mark Hutton	.05
134 Fernando Vina	.05
135 Lee Tinsley	.05
136 Chan Ho Park RC	1.50
137 Paul Spoljaric	.05
138 Matias Carrillo	.05
139 Mark Kiefer	.05
140 Stan Royer	.05
141 Bryan Eversgerd	.05
142 Joe Hall	.05
143 Johnny Ruffin	.05
144 Alex Gonzalez	.05
145 Keith Lockhart	.05
146 Tom Marsh	.05
147 Tony Longmire	.05
148 Keith Mitchell	.05
149 Melvin Nieves	.05
150 Kelly Stinnett	.05
151 Miguel Jimenez	.05
152 Jeff Juden	.05
154 Matt Walbeck	.05
155 Marc Newfield	.05
156 Matt Mieske	.05
157 Marcus Moore	.05
158 Jose Lima RC	.25
159 Mike Kelly	.05
160 Jim Edmonds	.05
161 Steve Trachsel	.05
162 Greg Blosser	.05
163 Mark Acre	.05
164 AL Checklist	.05
165 NL Checklist	.05

Gold Rush

Each pack of Score Rookie and Traded cards included one Gold Rush parallel version of one of the set's cards. The insert cards feature fronts that are printed directly on gold foil and include a Gold Rush logo in an upper corner.

	NM/M
Complete Set (165):	15.00
Common Player:	.15
Stars:	2X

Changing Places

Changing Places documents the relocation of 10 veteran stars. Cards were inserted into one of every 36 retail or hobby packs. Fronts have a color photo of the player in his new uniform and are enhanced with red foil. Backs have a montage of color and black-and-white photos and a few words about the trade. Card numbers have a "CP" prefix.

	NM/M
Complete Set (10):	15.00
Common Player:	1.00
1 Will Clark	1.00
2 Rafael Palmeiro	4.00
3 Roberto Kelly	1.00
4 Bo Jackson	1.25
5 Otis Nixon	1.00
6 Rickey Henderson	5.00
7 Ellis Burks	1.00
8 Lee Smith	1.00
9 Delino DeShields	1.00
10 Deion Sanders	1.00

Super Rookies

Super Rookies is an 18-card set honoring baseball's brightest young stars. They appear only in hobby packs at a rate of one every 36 packs. Fronts are printed on foil, with a multi-colored border. Backs feature another photo, most of which is rendered in single-color blocks, along with a few words about the player and a large Super Rookie logo. Cards are numbered with an "SU" prefix.

	NM/M
Complete Set (18):	15.00
Common Player:	1.00
1 Carlos Delgado	5.00
2 Manny Ramirez	5.00
3 Ryan Klesko	1.00
4 Raul Mondesi	1.00
5 Bob Hamelin	1.00
6 Steve Karsay	1.00
7 Jeffrey Hammonds	1.00
8 Cliff Floyd	1.00
9 Kurt Abbott	1.00
10 Marc Newfield	1.00
11 Javier Lopez	1.00
12 Rich Becker	1.00
13 Greg Pirkl	1.00
14 Rondell White	1.00
15 James Mouton	1.00
16 Tony Tarasco	1.00
17 Brian Anderson	1.00
18 Jim Edmonds	1.00

Redemption Card

The Score Rookie and Traded Redemption card was inserted at a rate of one every 240 packs. It gave collectors a chance to mail in for the best rookie in the annual September call-up: Alex Rodriguez.

	NM/M
September Call-Up Redemption Card (Expired)	2.00
Alex Rodriguez	400.00

1995 Score Samples

This cello-wrapped 10-card sample set of 1995 Score cards was sent to dealers to preview the issue. Cards are identical to the regular-issue versions except they have a diagonal white "SAMPLE" printed on front and back. The SAMPLE notice can be found on each card in either black or white, with the black version appearing to be somewhat less common.

	NM/M
Complete Set (10):	6.00
Common Player:	.50
2 Roberto Alomar	.75
4 Jose Canseco	1.00
5 Matt Williams	.50
5HG Cal Ripken, Jr. (Hall of Gold)	2.50
8DP McKay Christensen ('94 Draft Pick)	.50
221 Jeff Bagwell	1.25
223 Albert Belle	.50
224 Chuck Carr	.05
288 Jorge Fabreges (Rookie)	.50
Header Card	.05

1995 Score

Score 1995 Baseball is composed of 605 cards, issued in two series; the first comprising 330 cards, the second, 275. Cards are identical to the regular-issue versions except they have a diagonal white "SAMPLE" printed on the front and back. The SAMPLE notice can be found on each card in either black or white, with the black version appearing to be somewhat less common. The player's name, position, and team logo is given in white letters on a blue strip across the bottom. Backs resemble the fronts, except with a smaller, portrait photo of the player, which leaves room for statistics and biographical information. Score had a parallel set of Gold Rush cards, along with several other series of inserts. Eleven players in Series 2 can be found in two team variations as a result of a redemption program for updated cards.

	NM/M
Complete Set (605):	13.50
Common Player:	.05
Gold Rush:	2X
Platinums:	3X
Series 1 or 2 Pack (12):	.75
Series 1 or 2 Box (36):	12.50
1 Frank Thomas	.50
2 Roberto Alomar	.15
3 Cal Ripken, Jr.	1.50
4 Jose Canseco	.30
5 Matt Williams	.05
6 Esteban Beltre	.05
7 Domingo Cedeno	.05
8 John Valentin	.05
9 Glenallen Hill	.05
10 Rafael Belliard	.05
11 Randy Myers	.05
12 Mo Vaughn	.05
13 Hector Carrasco	.05
14 Chili Davis	.05
15 Dante Bichette	.05
16 Darren Jackson	.05
17 Mike Piazza	.75
18 Junior Felix	.05
19 Moises Alou	.05
20 Mark Gubicza	.05
21 Bret Saberhagen	.05
22 Len Dykstra	.05
23 Steve Howe	.05
24 Mark Dewey	.05
25 Brian Harper	.05
26 Ozzie Smith	.60
27 Scott Erickson	.05
28 Tony Gwynn	.60
29 Bob Welch	.05
30 Barry Bonds	1.50
31 Leo Gomez	.05
32 Greg Maddux	.60
33 Mike Greenwell	.05
34 Sammy Sosa	.60
35 Darnell Coles	.05
36 Tommy Greene	.05
37 Will Clark	.05
38 Steve Ontiveros	.05
39 Stan Javier	.05
40 Bip Roberts	.05
41 Paul O'Neill	.05
42 Bill Haselman	.05
43 Shane Mack	.05
44 Orlando Merced	.05
45 Kevin Seitzer	.05
46 Trevor Hoffman	.05
47 Greg Gagne	.05
48 Jeff Kent	.05
49 Tony Phillips	.05
50 Ken Hill	.05
51 Carlos Baerga	.05
52 Henry Rodriguez	.05
53 Scott Sanderson	.05
54 Jeff Conine	.05
55 Chris Turner	.05
56 Ken Caminiti	.05
57 Harold Baines	.05
58 Charlie Hayes	.05
59 Roberto Kelly	.05
60 John Olerud	.05
61 Tim Davis	.05
62 Rich Rowland	.05
63 Rey Sanchez	.05
64 Junior Ortiz	.05
65 Ricky Gutierrez	.05
66 Rex Hudler	.05
67 Johnny Ruffin	.05
68 Jay Buhner	.05
69 Tom Pagnozzi	.05
70 Julio Franco	.05
71 Eric Young	.05
72 Mike Bordick	.05
73 Don Slaught	.05
74 Goose Gossage	.05
75 Lonnie Smith	.05
76 Jimmy Key	.05
77 Dave Hollins	.05
78 Mickey Tettleton	.05
79 Luis Gonzalez	.05
80 Dave Winfield	.50
81 Ryan Thompson	.05
82 Felix Jose	.05
83 Rusty Meacham	.05
84 Darryl Hamilton	.05
85 John Wetteland	.05
86 Tom Brunansky	.05
87 Mark Lemke	.05
88 Spike Owen	.05
89 Shawon Dunston	.05
90 Wilson Alvarez	.05
91 Lee Smith	.05
92 Scott Kamieniecki	.05
93 Jacob Brumfield	.05
94 Kirk Gibson	.05
95 Joe Girardi	.05
96 Mike Macfarlane	.05
97 Greg Colbrunn	.05
98 Ricky Bones	.05
99 Delino DeShields	.05
100 Pat Meares	.05
101 Jeff Fassero	.05
102 Jim Leyritz	.05
103 Gary Redus	.05
104 Terry Steinbach	.05
105 Kevin McReynolds	.05
106 Felix Fermin	.05
107 Danny Jackson	.05
108 Chris James	.05
109 Jeff King	.05
110 Pat Hentgen	.05
111 Gerald Perry	.05
112 Tim Raines	.05
113 Eddie Williams	.05
114 Jamie Moyer	.05
115 Bud Black	.05
116 Chris Gomez	.05
117 Luis Lopez	.05
118 Roger Clemens	.65
119 Javier Lopez	.05
120 Dave Nilsson	.05
121 Karl Rhodes	.05
122 Rick Aguilera	.05
123 Tony Fernandez	.05
124 Bernie Williams	.05
125 James Mouton	.05
126 Mark Langston	.05
127 Mike Lansing	.05
128 Joe Orsulak	.05
129 David Hulse	.05
130 Pete Incaviglia	.05
131 Mark Clark	.05
132 Tony Eusebio	.05
133 Chuck Finley	.05
134 Lou Frazier	.05
135 Craig Grebeck	.05
136 Kelly Stinnett	.05
137 Paul Shuey	.05
138 David Nied	.05
139 Billy Brewer	.05
140 Dave Weathers	.05
141 Scott Leius	.05
142 Brian Jordan	.05
143 Melido Perez	.05
144 Tony Tarasco	.05
145 Dan Wilson	.05
146 Rondell White	.05
147 Mike Henneman	.05
148 Brian Johnson	.05
149 Tom Henke	.05
150 John Patterson	.05
151 Bobby Witt	.05
152 Eddie Taubensee	.05
153 Pat Borders	.05
154 Ramon Martinez	.05
155 Mike Kingery	.05
156 Zane Smith	.05
157 Benito Santiago	.05
158 Matias Carrillo	.05
159 Scott Brosius	.05
160 Dave Clark	.05
161 Mark McLemore	.05
162 Curt Schilling	.30
163 J.T. Snow	.05
164 Rod Beck	.05
165 Scott Fletcher	.05
166 Bob Tewksbury	.05
167 Mike LaValliere	.05
168 Dave Hansen	.05
169 Pedro Martinez	.50
170 Kirk Rueter	.05
171 Jose Lind	.05
172 Luis Alicea	.05
173 Mike Moore	.05
174 Andy Ashby	.05

176	Jody Reed	.05	293	Greg O'Halloran	.05	392a	Chad Curtis (Angels)	.05	505	Howard Johnson	.05
177	Darryl Kile	.05	294	Mark Kiefer	.05	392b	Chad Curtis (Tigers)	.10	506	Eric Anthony	.05
178	Carl Willis	.05	295	Jose Oliva	.05	393	Cal Eldred	.05	507	Mark Wohlers	.05
179	Jeromy Burnitz	.05	296	Rich Becker	.05	394	Jason Bere	.05	508	Scott Sanders	.05
180	Mike Gallego	.05	297	Brian Hunter	.05	395	Bret Barberie	.05	509	Pete Harnisch	.05
181	W. Van Landingham **RC**	.05	298	Dave Silvestri	.05	396	Paul Sorrento	.05	510	Wes Chamberlain	.05
182	Sid Fernandez	.05	299	Armando Benitez **RC**	.10	397	Steve Finley	.05	511	Tom Candiotti	.05
183	Kim Batiste	.05	300	Darren Dreifort	.05	398	Cecil Fielder	.05	512	Albie Lopez	.05
184	Greg Myers	.05	301	John Mabry	.05	399	Eric Karros	.05	513	Denny Neagle	.05
185	Steve Avery	.05	302	Greg Pirkl	.05	400	Jeff Montgomery	.05	514	Sean Berry	.05
186	Steve Farr	.05	303	J.R. Phillips	.05	401	Cliff Floyd	.05	515	Billy Hatcher	.05
187	Robb Nen	.05	304	Shawn Green	.30	402	Matt Mieske	.05	516	Todd Jones	.05
188	Dan Pasqua	.05	305	Roberto Petagine	.05	403	Brian Hunter	.05	517	Wayne Kirby	.05
189	Bruce Ruffin	.05	306	Keith Lockhart	.05	404	Alex Cole	.05	518	Butch Henry	.05
190	Jose Valentin	.05	307	Jonathon Hurst	.05	405	Kevin Stocker	.05	519	Sandy Alomar Jr.	.05
191	Willie Banks	.05	308	Paul Spoljaric	.05	406	Eric Davis	.05	520	Kevin Appier	.05
192	Mike Aldrete	.05	309	Mike Lieberthal	.05	407	Marvin Freeman	.05	521	Robert Mejia	.05
193	Randy Milligan	.05	310	Garret Anderson	.05	408	Dennis Eckersley	.40	522	Steve Cooke	.05
194	Steve Karsay	.05	311	John Johnston	.05	409	Todd Zeile	.05	523	Terry Shumpert	.05
195	Mike Stanley	.05	312	Alex Rodriguez	1.50	410	Keith Mitchell	.05	524	Mike Jackson	.05
196	Jose Mesa	.05	313	Kent Mercker	.05	411	Andy Benes	.05	525	Kent Mercker	.05
197	Tom Browning	.05	314	John Valentin	.05	412	Juan Bell	.05	526	David Wells	.05
198	John Vander Wal	.05	315	Kenny Rogers	.05	413	Royce Clayton	.05	527	Juan Samuel	.05
199	Kevin Brown	.05	316	Fred McGriff	.05	414	Ed Sprague	.05	528	Salomon Torres	.05
200	Mike Oquist	.05	317	Atlanta Braves, Baltimore Orioles		415	Mike Mussina	.30	529	Duane Ward	.05
201	Greg Swindell	.05	318	Chicago Cubs, Boston Red Sox	.05	416	Todd Hundley	.05	530a	Rob Dibble (Reds)	.05
202	Eddie Zambrano	.05	319	Cincinnati Reds, California Angels	.05	417	Pat Listach	.05	530b	Rob Dibble (White Sox)	.10
203	Joe Boever	.05	320	Colorado Rockies, Chicago White Sox		418	Joe Oliver	.05	531	Mike Blowers	.05
204	Gary Varsho	.05	321	Cleveland Indians, Florida Marlins	.05	419	Rafael Palmeiro	.40	532	Mark Eichhorn	.05
205	Chris Gwynn	.05	322	Houston Astros, Detroit Tigers		420	Tim Salmon	.05	533	Alex Diaz	.05
206	David Howard	.05	323	Los Angels Dodgers, Kansas City Royals	.05	421	Brady Anderson	.05	534	Dan Miceli	.05
207	Jerome Walton	.05	324	Montreal Expos, Milwaukee Brewers	.05	422	Kenny Lofton	.05	535	Jeff Branson	.05
208	Danny Darwin	.05	325	New York Mets, Minnesota Twins		423	Craig Biggio	.05	536	Dave Stevens	.05
209	Darryl Strawberry	.05	326	Philadelphia Phillies, New York Yankees	.05	424	Bobby Bonilla	.05	537	Charlie O'Brien	.05
210	Todd Van Poppel	.05	327	Pittsburgh Pirates, Oakland Athletics	.05	425	Kenny Rogers	.05	538	Shane Reynolds	.05
211	Scott Livingstone	.05	328	San Diego Padres, Seattle Mariners	.05	426	Derek Bell	.05	539	Rich Amaral	.05
212	Dave Fleming	.05	329	San Francisco Giants, Texas Rangers	.05	427a	Scott Cooper (Red Sox)	.05	540	Rusty Greer	.05
213	Todd Worrell	.05	330	St. Louis Cardinals, Toronto Blue Jays	.05	427b	Scott Cooper (Cardinals)	.10	541	Alex Arias	.05
214	Carlos Delgado	.40	331	Pedro Munoz	.05	428	Ozzie Guillen	.05	542	Eric Plunk	.05
215	Bill Pecota	.05	332	Ryan Klesko	.05	429	Omar Vizquel	.05	543	John Hudek	.05
216	Jim Lindeman	.05	333a	Andre Dawson (Red Sox)	.25	430	Phil Plantier	.05	544	Kirk McCaskill	.05
217	Rick White	.05	333b	Andre Dawson (Marlins)	.35	431	Chuck Knoblauch	.05	545	Jeff Reboulet	.05
218	Jose Oquendo	.05	334	Derrick May	.05	432	Darren Daulton	.05	546	Sterling Hitchcock	.05
219	Tony Castillo	.05	335	Aaron Sele	.05	433	Bob Hamelin	.05	547	Warren Newson	.05
220	Fernando Vina	.05	336	Kevin Mitchell	.05	434	Tom Glavine	.30	548	Bryan Harvey	.05
221	Jeff Bagwell	.50	337	Steve Traschel	.05	435	Walt Weiss	.05	549	Mike Huff	.05
222	Randy Johnson	.50	338	Andres Galarraga	.05	436	Jose Vizcaino	.05	550	Lance Parrish	.05
223	Albert Belle	.05	339a	Terry Pendleton (Braves)	.05	437	Ken Griffey Jr.	.75	551	Ken Griffey Jr. (Hitters Inc.)	.65
224	Chuck Carr	.05	339b	Terry Pendleton (Marlins)	.10	438	Jay Bell	.05	552	Matt Williams (Hitters Inc.)	.05
225	Mark Leiter	.05	340	Gary Sheffield	.30	439	Juan Gonzalez	.25	553	Roberto Alomar (Hitters Inc.)	.10
226	Hal Morris	.05	341	Travis Fryman	.05	440	Jeff Blauser	.05	554	Jeff Bagwell (Hitters Inc.)	.25
227	Robin Ventura	.05	342	Bo Jackson	.10	441	Rickey Henderson	.50	555	Dave Justice (Hitters Inc.)	.05
228	Mike Munoz	.05	343	Gary Gaetti	.05	442	Bobby Ayala	.05	556	Cal Ripken Jr. (Hitters Inc.)	.75
229	Jim Thome	.40	344a	Brett Butler (Dodgers)	.05	443a	David Cone (Royals)	.05	557	Albert Belle (Hitters Inc.)	.25
230	Mario Diaz	.05	344b	Brett Butler (Mets)	.10	443b	David Cone (Blue Jays)	.10	558	Mike Piazza (Hitters Inc.)	.45
231	John Doherty	.05	345	B.J. Surhoff	.05	444	Pedro Martinez	.05	559	Kirby Puckett (Hitters Inc.)	.35
232	Bobby Jones	.05	346a	Larry Walker (Expos)	.25	445	Manny Ramirez	.50	560	Wade Boggs (Hitters Inc.)	.35
233	Raul Mondesi	.05	346b	Larry Walker (Rockies)	.10	446	Mark Portugal	.05	561	Tony Gwynn (Hitters Inc.)	.35
234	Ricky Jordan	.05	347	Kevin Tapani	.05	447	Damion Easley	.05	562	Barry Bonds (Hitters Inc.)	.05
235	John Jaha	.05	348	Rick Wilkins	.05	448	Gary DiSarcina	.05	563	Mo Vaughn (Hitters Inc.)	.05
236	Carlos Garcia	.05	349	Wade Boggs	.60	449	Roberto Hernandez	.05	564	Don Mattingly (Hitters Inc.)	.40
237	Kirby Puckett	.60	350	Mariano Duncan	.05	450	Jeffrey Hammonds	.05	565	Carlos Baerga (Hitters Inc.)	.05
238	Orel Hershiser	.05	351	Ruben Sierra	.05	451	Jeff Treadway	.05	566	Paul Molitor (Hitters Inc.)	.25
239	Don Mattingly	.65	352a	Andy Van Slyke (Pirates)	.05	452a	Jim Abbott (Yankees)	.05	567	Raul Mondesi (Hitters Inc.)	.05
240	Sid Bream	.05	352b	Andy Van Slyke (Orioles)	.10	452b	Jim Abbott (White Sox)	.10	568	Manny Ramirez (Hitters Inc.)	.25
241	Brent Gates	.05	353	Reggie Jefferson	.05	453	Carlos Rodriguez	.05	569	Alex Rodriguez (Hitters Inc.)	.75
242	Tony Longmire	.05	354	Gregg Jefferies	.05	454	Joey Cora	.05	570	Will Clark (Hitters Inc.)	.05
243	Robby Thompson	.05	355	Tim Naehring	.05	455	Bret Boone	.05	571	Frank Thomas (Hitters Inc.)	.30
244	Rick Sutcliffe	.05	356	John Roper	.05	456	Danny Tartabull	.05	572	Moises Alou (Hitters Inc.)	.05
245	Dean Palmer	.05	357	Joe Carter	.05	457	John Franco	.05	573	Jeff Conine (Hitters Inc.)	.05
246	Marquis Grissom	.05	358	Kurt Abbott	.05	458	Roger Salkeld	.05	574	Joe Ausanio	.05
247	Paul Molitor	.50	359	Lenny Harris	.05	459	Fred McGriff	.05	575	Charles Johnson	.05
248	Mark Carreon	.05	360	Lance Johnson	.05	460	Pedro Astacio	.05	576	Ernie Young	.05
249	Jack Voight	.05	361	Brian Anderson	.05	461	Jon Lieber	.05	577	Jeff Granger	.05
250	Greg McMichael (Photo on front is Mike Stanton.)	.05	362	Jim Eisenreich	.05	462	Luis Polonia	.05	578	Robert Perez	.05
			363	Jerry Browne	.05	463	Geronimo Pena	.05	579	Melvin Nieves	.05
251	Damon Berryhill	.05	364	Mark Grace	.05	464	Tom Gordon	.05	580	Gar Finnvold	.05
252	Brian Dorsett	.05	365	Devon White	.05	465	Brad Ausmus	.05	581	Duane Singleton	.05
253	Jim Edmonds	.05	366	Reggie Sanders	.05	466	Willie McGee	.05	582	Chan Ho Park	.05
254	Barry Larkin	.05	367	Ivan Rodriguez	.40	467	Doug Jones	.05	583	Fausto Cruz	.05
255	Jack McDowell	.05	368	Kirt Manwaring	.05	468	John Smoltz	.05	584	Dave Staton	.05
256	Wally Joyner	.05	369	Pat Kelly	.05	469	Troy Neel	.05	585	Denny Hocking	.05
257	Eddie Murray	.50	370	Ellis Burks	.05	470	Luis Sojo	.05	586	Nate Minchey	.05
258	Lenny Webster	.05	371	Charles Nagy	.05	471	John Smiley	.05	587	Marc Newfield	.05
259	Milt Cuyler	.05	372	Kevin Bass	.05	472	Rafael Bournigal	.05	588	Jayhawk Owens	.05
260	Todd Benzinger	.05	373	Lou Whitaker	.05	473	Billy Taylor	.05	589	Darren Bragg	.05
261	Vince Coleman	.05	374	Rene Arocha	.05	474	Juan Guzman	.05	590	Kevin King	.05
262	Todd Stottlemyre	.05	375	Derrick Parks	.05	475	Dave Magadan	.05	591	Kurt Miller	.05
263	Turner Ward	.05	376	Mark Whiten	.05	476	Mike Devereaux	.05	592	Aaron Small	.05
264	Ray Lankford	.05	377	Mark McGwire	1.00	477	Andujar Cedeno	.05	593	Troy O'Leary	.05
265	Matt Walbeck	.05	378	Doug Drabek	.05	478	Edgar Martinez	.05	594	Phil Stidham	.05
266	Deion Sanders	.05	379	Greg Vaughn	.05	479	Troy Neel	.05	595	Steve Dunn	.05
267	Gerald Williams	.05	380	Al Martin	.05	480	Allen Watson	.05	596	Cory Bailey	.05
268	Jim Gott	.05	381	Ron Darling	.05	481	Ron Karkovice	.05	597	Alex Gonzalez	.05
269	Jeff Frye	.05	382	Tim Wallach	.05	482	Joey Hamilton	.05	598	Jim Bowie	.05
270	Jose Rijo	.05	383	Alan Trammell	.05	483	Vinny Castilla	.05	599	Jeff Cirillo	.05
271	Dave Justice	.05	384	Randy Velarde	.05	484	Kevin Gross	.05	600	Mark Hutton	.05
272	Ismael Valdes	.05	385	Chris Sabo	.05	485	Bernard Gilkey	.05	601	Russ Davis	.05
273	Ben McDonald	.05	386	Wil Cordero	.05	486	John Burkett	.05	602	Checklist #331-400	.05
274	Darren Lewis	.05	387	Darrin Fletcher	.05	487	Matt Nokes	.05	603	Checklist #401-469	.05
275	Graeme Lloyd	.05	388	David Segui	.05	488	Mel Rojas	.05	604	Checklist #470-537	.05
276	Luis Ortiz	.05	389	Steve Buechele	.05	489	Craig Shipley	.05	605	Checklist #538-605	.05
277	Julian Tavarez	.05	390	Otis Nixon	.05	490	Chip Hale	.05	----	"You Trade 'em" Redemption Card (Expired Dec. 31, 1995.)	.10
278	Mark Dalesandro	.05	391	Jeff Brantley	.05	491	Bill Swift	.05			
279	Brett Merriman	.05				492	Pat Rapp	.05			
280	Ricky Bottalico	.05				493a	Brian McRae (Royals)	.05			
281	Robert Eenhoorn	.05				493b	Brian McRae (Cubs)	.10			
282	Rikkert Faneyte	.05				494	Mickey Morandini	.05			
283	Mike Kelly	.05				495	Tony Pena	.05			
284	Mark Smith	.05				496	Danny Bautista	.05			
285	Turk Wendell	.05				497	Armando Reynoso	.05			
286	Greg Blosser	.05				498	Ken Ryan	.05			
287	Garey Ingram	.05				499	Billy Ripken	.05			
288	Jorge Fabregas	.05				500	Pat Mahomes	.05			
289	Blaise Ilsley	.05				501	Mark Acre	.05			
290	Joe Hall	.05				502	Geronimo Berroa	.05			
291	Orlando Miller	.05				503	Norberto Martin	.05			
292	Jose Lima	.05				504	Chad Kreuter	.05			

Gold Rush

Besides being collectible in their own right, the gold-foil printed parallel versions of the Score regular-issue cards could be collected into team sets and exchanged with a trade card for platinum versions. The deadline for redemption of Series I was July 1, 1995; Oct. 1, 1995, for Series II. Gold Rush cards were found either one or two per pack, depending on pack card count. Gold Rush versions exist for each card in the Score set and have fronts that are identical to the regular cards except they are printed on foil and have gold borders. Backs of the Gold Rush cards have a small rectangular "GOLD RUSH" logo overprinted.

	NM/M
Complete Set (605):	35.00
Common Player:	.10
Gold Rush Stars:	2X

Platinum Redemption Team Sets

This top of the line parallel set was only available by exchanging a complete Series 1 or Series 2 Gold Rush team set, along with a redemption card. Production of the Platinum sets was limited to 4,950 of each team in each series. Using the same photos and format as the regular issue and Gold Rush cards, the Platinum parallels have card fronts printed on silver prismatic foil. Backs are identical to the regular versions. Platinum series team sets were sent to collectors in specially printed plastic cases with a certificate of authenticity.

	NM/M
Complete Set (587):	250.00
Complete Series 1 (316):	150.00
Complete Series 2 (271)	100.00
Common Player:	.50
Platinum Stars:	4X

Airmail

Young ballplayers with a propensity for hitting the long ball are featured in this insert set found only in Series II jumbo packs. Cards have a player batting action photo set in sky-and-clouds background. A gold-foil stamp in the upper-left corner identifies the series. Backs have a background photo of sunset and dark clouds, with a player portrait photo in the foreground. A few stats and sentences describe the player's power hitting potential. Cards have an AM prefix to the number. Stated odds for insertion rate are an average of one Airmail chase card per 24 packs.

		NM/M
Complete Set (18):		8.00
Common Player:		.25
1	Bob Hamelin	.25
2	John Mabry	.25
3	Marc Newfield	.25
4	Jose Oliva	.25
5	Charles Johnson	.25
6	Russ Davis	.25
7	Ernie Young	.25
8	Billy Ashley	.25
9	Ryan Klesko	.25
10	J.R. Phillips	.25
11	Cliff Floyd	.25
12	Carlos Delgado	1.50
13	Melvin Nieves	.25
14	Raul Mondesi	2.00
15	Manny Ramirez	2.00
16	Mike Kelly	.25
17	Alex Rodriguez	5.00
18	Rusty Greer	.25

Double Gold Champions

A dozen veteran players, who have won at least two of the game's top awards are designated as "Double Gold Champs," in this Series II hobby insert set. Fronts have horizontal action photos at top, with a speckled red border at bottom. Vertical backs have a portrait photo and a list of the major awards won by the player. Cards have a GC prefix to the number. These chase cards were reportedly inserted at an average rate of one per 36.

		NM/M
Complete Set (12):		25.00
Common Player:		.40
1	Frank Thomas	2.00
2	Ken Griffey Jr.	3.50
3	Barry Bonds	5.00
4	Tony Gwynn	2.50
5	Don Mattingly	3.00
6	Greg Maddux	2.50
7	Roger Clemens	3.00
8	Kenny Lofton	.40
9	Jeff Bagwell	2.00
10	Matt Williams	.40
11	Kirby Puckett	2.50
12	Cal Ripken Jr.	5.00

Draft Picks

These cards were randomly included in 1995 Score hobby packs at a rate of one per every 36 packs. The cards showcase 18 of baseball's potential superstars and document their professional beginnings. The card front has the player's team logo and name in the lower-right corner. "'94 Draft Pick" appears in the upper-right corner. The front also has a mug shot and an action shot of the player. The card back has a portrait and career summary and is numbered with a DP prefix.

	NM/M
Complete Set (18):	4.00
Common Player:	.50

1	McKay Christensen	.50
2	Brett Wagner	.50
3	Paul Wilson	.50
4	C.J. Nitkowski	.50
5	Josh Booty	.50
6	Antone Williamson	.50
7	Paul Konerko	1.50
8	Scott Elarton	.50
9	Jacob Shumate	.50
10	Terrence Long	.50
11	Mark Johnson	.50
12	Ben Grieve	.50
13	Doug Million	.50
14	Jayson Peterson	.50
15	Dustin Hermanson	.50
16	Matt Smith	.50
17	Kevin Witt	.50
18	Brian Buchanan	.50

Dream Team Gold

The Major Leagues' top players at each position are featured in this Series I insert set. Fronts are printed entirely on rainbow holographic foil and feature a large and a small player action photo. Backs have a single-color version of one of the front photos as well as a color portrait photo in a circle at center, all in conventional printing technology. Card numbers have a DG prefix.

		NM/M
Complete Set (12):		12.00
Common Player:		.30
1	Frank Thomas	1.25
2	Roberto Alomar	.50
3	Cal Ripken Jr.	4.00
4	Matt Williams	.30
5	Mike Piazza	2.50
6	Albert Belle	.30
7	Ken Griffey Jr.	2.50
8	Tony Gwynn	1.50
9	Paul Molitor	1.25
10	Jimmy Key	.30
11	Greg Maddux	1.50
12	Lee Smith	.30

Hall of Gold

Hall of Gold inserts picture 110 of the top players on gold foil cards. Each card front has the Hall of Gold logo in an upper corner, plus a color action photo of the player, and his name and team logo at the bottom. The card back is numbered using an "HG" prefix and includes another color photo of the player, his team's name, his position, and a career summary. Cards were inserted one per every six regular 1995 Score packs and one per every two jumbo packs. Updated versions of five traded players were issued in Series II, available only via mail-in offer with a trade card found randomly inserted in packs.

		NM/M
Complete Set (110):		25.00
Common Player:		.10
1	Ken Griffey Jr.	1.25
2	Matt Williams	.10
3	Roberto Alomar	.25
4	Jeff Bagwell	.75

5	Dave Justice	.10
6	Cal Ripken Jr.	2.00
7	Randy Johnson	.75
8	Barry Larkin	.10
9	Albert Belle	.10
10	Mike Piazza	1.25
11	Kirby Puckett	1.00
12	Moises Alou	.10
13	Jose Canseco	.45
14	Tony Gwynn	1.00
15	Roger Clemens	1.00
16	Barry Bonds	2.00
17	Mo Vaughn	.10
18	Greg Maddux	1.00
19	Dante Bichette	.10
20	Will Clark	.10
21	Len Dykstra	.10
22	Don Mattingly	1.00
23	Carlos Baerga	.10
24	Ozzie Smith	1.00
25	Paul Molitor	.75
26	Paul O'Neill	.10
27	Deion Sanders	.10
28	Jeff Conine	.10
29	John Olerud	.10
30	Jose Rijo	.10
31	Sammy Sosa	1.00
32	Robin Ventura	.10
33	Raul Mondesi	.10
34	Eddie Murray	.75
35	Marquis Grissom	.10
36	Darryl Strawberry	.10
37	Dave Nilsson	.10
38	Manny Ramirez	.75
39	Delino DeShields	.10
40	Lee Smith	.10
41	Alex Rodriguez	1.50
42	Julio Franco	.10
43	Bret Saberhagen	.10
44	Ken Hill	.10
45	Roberto Kelly	.10
46	Hal Morris	.10
47	Jimmy Key	.10
48	Terry Steinbach	.10
49	Mickey Tettleton	.10
50	Tony Phillips	.10
51	Carlos Garcia	.10
52	Jim Edmonds	.10
53	Rod Beck	.10
54	Shane Mack	.10
55	Ken Caminiti	.10
56	Frank Thomas	.75
57	Kenny Lofton	.10
58	Jack McDowell	.10
59	Jason Bere	.10
60	Joe Carter	.10
61	Gary Sheffield	.45
62	Andres Galarraga	.10
63	Gregg Jefferies	.10
64	Bobby Bonilla	.10
65	Tom Glavine	.35
66	John Smoltz	.10
67	Fred McGriff	.10
68	Craig Biggio	.10
69	Reggie Sanders	.10
70	Kevin Mitchell	.10
71a	Larry Walker (Expos)	.10
71b	Larry Walker (Rockies)	.10
72	Carlos Delgado	.50
73	Andujar Cedeno	.10
74	Ivan Rodriguez	.65
75	Ryan Klesko	.10
76a	John Kruk (Phillies)	.10
76b	John Kruk (White Sox)	.10
77a	Brian McRae (Royals)	.10
77b	Brian McRae (Cubs)	.10
78	Tim Salmon	.10
79	Travis Fryman	.10
80	Chuck Knoblauch	.10
81	Jay Bell	.10
82	Cecil Fielder	.10
83	Cliff Floyd	.10
84	Ruben Sierra	.10
85	Mike Mussina	.45
86	Mark Grace	.10
87	Dennis Eckersley	.65
88	Dennis Martinez	.10
89	Rafael Palmeiro	.65
90	Ben McDonald	.10
91	Dave Hollins	.10
92	Steve Avery	.10
93a	David Cone (Royals)	.10
93b	David Cone (Blue Jays)	.10
94	Darren Daulton	.10
95	Bret Boone	.10
96	Wade Boggs	1.00
97	Doug Drabek	.10
98	Derek Bell	.10
99	Jim Thome	.65
100	Chili Davis	.10
101	Jeffrey Hammonds	.10
102	Rickey Henderson	.75
103	Brett Butler	.10
•104	Tim Wallach	.10
105	Wil Cordero	.10
106	Mark Whiten	.10
107	Bob Hamelin	.10
108	Rondell White	.10
109	Devon White	.10
110a	Tony Tarasco (Braves)	.10
110b	Tony Tarasco (Expos)	.10
----	Redemption Trade Card (Expired Dec. 31, 1995.)	.10

Rookie Dream Team

These Series 2 inserts feature a dozen of 1995's best rookie prospects. Fronts are printed on a silver-foil background. The words "ROOKIE DREAM TEAM" are formed of sky-and-cloud images within the letters. Horizontal backs repeat the motif and include another player photo in a vignette at center. Card numbers have an RDT prefix.

		NM/M
Complete Set (12):		9.00
Common Player:		.50
1	J.R. Phillips	.50
2	Alex Gonzalez	.50
3	Alex Rodriguez	6.00
4	Jose Oliva	.50
5	Charles Johnson	.50
6	Shawn Green	1.50
7	Brian Hunter	.50
8	Garret Anderson	.50
9	Julian Tavarez	.50
10	Jose Lima	.50
11	Armando Benitez	.50
12	Ricky Bottalico	.50

Rookie Greatness

This single-card insert set is the toughest pull among the 1995 Score chase cards. Honoring slugging Braves star Ryan Klesko, the card is inserted at the rate of one per 720 retail packs. An even scarcer autographed version of the card in an edition of just over 6,000 was also created for insertion into hobby packs.

		NM/M
RG1	Ryan Klesko	1.00
SG1	Ryan Klesko/Auto.	7.50

Score Rules

Series I jumbo packs were the only sources for "Score Rules" insert set of rookie and veteran stars. A color player photo at left has a team logo toward the bottom, beneath which is a gold-foil "tie tack" device with the league initials and position. At top-right is a baseball which appears to be dripping orange and green goop down the card. The player's last name is presented vertically with a sepia photo of the player within the letters. Backs repeat the green baseball and ooze motif, with three progressive color proof versions of the sepia front photo and a few sentences about the star. Cards are numbered with an "SR" prefix.

		NM/M
Complete Set (30):		30.00
Common Player:		.30
1	Ken Griffey Jr.	3.50
2	Frank Thomas	1.50
3	Mike Piazza	3.50
4	Jeff Bagwell	1.50
5	Alex Rodriguez	4.50
6	Albert Belle	.30
7	Matt Williams	.30
8	Roberto Alomar	.45
9	Barry Bonds	5.00
10	Raul Mondesi	.30
11	Jose Canseco	.60
12	Kirby Puckett	2.50
13	Fred McGriff	.30
14	Kenny Lofton	.30
15	Greg Maddux	2.50
16	Juan Gonzalez	.75
17	Cliff Floyd	.30
18	Cal Ripken, Jr.	5.00
19	Will Clark	.30
20	Tim Salmon	.30
21	Paul O'Neill	.30
22	Jason Bere	.30
23	Tony Gwynn	2.50
24	Manny Ramirez	1.50
25	Don Mattingly	3.00
26	Dave Justice	.30
27	Javier Lopez	.30
28	Ryan Klesko	.90
29	Carlos Delgado	.90
30	Mike Mussina	.60

Score Rules Supers

While colorful in the standard size, the Score Rules super-size cards found in special collectors kits are positively garish. The 7-1/2" x 10-1/2" cards are virtually identical to the Series 1 inserts, except that on back is a box with a serial number identifying the card from among an edition of 3,000. The Score Rules supers were available only in a collectors kit sold at large retail chains and came packaged with 26 Series 1 and 2 foil packs, a three-ring binder and 10 plastic sheets with a suggested retail price of around $25.

		NM/M
Complete Set (30):		60.00
Common Player:		.90
1	Ken Griffey Jr.	5.00
2	Frank Thomas	3.50
3	Mike Piazza	5.00
4	Jeff Bagwell	3.50
5	Alex Rodriguez	6.00
6	Albert Belle	.90
7	Matt Williams	.90
8	Roberto Alomar	1.25
9	Barry Bonds	7.50
10	Raul Mondesi	.90
11	Jose Canseco	2.50
12	Kirby Puckett	4.50
13	Fred McGriff	.90
14	Kenny Lofton	.90
15	Greg Maddux	4.50
16	Juan Gonzalez	2.00
17	Cliff Floyd	.90
18	Cal Ripken, Jr.	7.50
19	Will Clark	.90
20	Tim Salmon	.90
21	Paul O'Neill	.90
22	Jason Bere	.90
23	Tony Gwynn	4.50
24	Manny Ramirez	3.75
25	Don Mattingly	4.50
26	Dave Justice	.90
27	Javier Lopez	.90
28	Ryan Klesko	.90
29	Carlos Delgado	2.00
30	Mike Mussina	1.50

Ad Prize Cards

In a series of ads in hobby and public media, Score offered a pair of special cards as prizes in a mail-in offer. Cards feature the same basic design as 1995 Score, but are printed on platinum foil on front. Backs are conventionally printed with a portrait photo and a few words about the player.

		NM/M
Complete Set (2):		10.00
AD1	Alex Rodriguez	6.50
AD2	Ivan Rodriguez	3.50

1996 Score Samples

Score premiered its 1996 base brand offering with a cello pack of nine cards, including one of its new Dugout Collection inserts. The samples are virtually identical to the issued versions except that all 1995 and career stats are stated as zeros and the word "SAMPLE" is printed in white letters diagonally across front and back. Each of the cards can be found as a Dugout Collection version, making them eight times scarcer than the other samples.

		NM/M
Complete Set (16):		12.00
Common Player:		.50
3	Ryan Klesko	.50
3	Ryan Klesko (Dugout Collection)	1.00
4	Jim Edmonds	.50
4	Jim Edmonds (Dugout Collection)	1.00
5	Barry Larkin	.50
5	Barry Larkin (Dugout Collection)	1.00
6	Jim Thome	1.00
6	Jim Thome (Dugout Collection)	1.50
7	Raul Mondesi	.50
7	Raul Mondesi (Dugout Collection)	1.00
110	Derek Bell	.50
110	Derek Bell (Dugout Collection)	1.00
240	Derek Jeter	2.00
240	Derek Jeter (Dugout Collection)	4.50
241	Michael Tucker	.50
241	Michael Tucker (Dugout Collection)	1.00

1996 Score

Large, irregularly shaped action photos are featured on the fronts of the basic cards in the 1996 Score issue. Backs feature a portrait photo (in most cases) at left and a full slate of major and minor league stats at right, along with a few words about the player. Slightly different design details and a "ROOKIE" headline identify that subset within the issue.

wide variety of insert cards was produced, most of them exclusive to one type of packaging.

		NM/M
Complete Set (510):		15.00
Common Player:		.05
Wax Pack (10):		.45
Wax Box (36):		10.00
1	Will Clark	.05
2	Rich Becker	.05
3	Ryan Klesko	.05
4	Jim Edmonds	.05
5	Barry Larkin	.05
6	Jim Thome	.40
7	Raul Mondesi	.65
8	Don Mattingly	.65
9	Jeff Conine	.05
10	Rickey Henderson	.50
11	Chad Curtis	.05
12	Darren Daulton	.05
13	Larry Walker	.05
14	Carlos Garcia	.05
15	Carlos Baerga	.05
16	Tony Gwynn	.60
17	Jon Nunally	.05
18	Deion Sanders	.05
19	Mark Grace	.05
20	Alex Rodriguez	1.00
21	Frank Thomas	.50
22	Brian Jordan	.05
23	J.T. Snow	.05
24	Shawn Green	.30
25	Tim Wakefield	.05
26	Curtis Goodwin	.05
27	John Smoltz	.05
28	Devon White	.05
29	Brian Hunter	.05
30	Rusty Greer	.05
31	Rafael Palmeiro	.40
32	Bernard Gilkey	.05
33	John Valentin	.05
34	Randy Johnson	.50
35	Garret Anderson	.05
36	Rikkert Faneyte	.05
37	Ray Durham	.05
38	Bip Roberts	.05
39	Jaime Navarro	.05
40	Mark Johnson	.05
41	Darren Lewis	.05
42	Tyler Green	.05
43	Bill Pulsipher	.05
44	Jason Giambi	.40
45	Kevin Ritz	.05
46	Jack McDowell	.05
47	Felipe Lira	.05
48	Rico Brogna	.05
49	Terry Pendleton	.05
50	Rondell White	.05
51	Andre Dawson	.25
52	Kirby Puckett	.60
53	Wally Joyner	.05
54	B.J. Surhoff	.05
55	Chan Ho Park	.05
56	Greg Vaughn	.05
57	Roberto Alomar	.20
58	Dave Justice	.05
59	Kevin Seitzer	.05
60	Cal Ripken Jr.	1.50
61	Ozzie Smith	.60
62	Mo Vaughn	.05
63	Ricky Bones	.05
64	Gary DiSarcina	.05
65	Matt Williams	.05
66	Wilson Alvarez	.05
67	Lenny Dykstra	.05
68	Brian McRae	.05
69	Todd Stottlemyre	.05
70	Bret Boone	.05
71	Sterling Hitchcock	.05
72	Albert Belle	.50
73	Todd Hundley	.05
74	Vinny Castilla	.05
75	Moises Alou	.05
76	Cecil Fielder	.05
77	Brad Radke	.05
78	Quilvio Veras	.05
79	Eddie Murray	.50
80	James Mouton	.05
81	Pat Listach	.05
82	Mark Gubicza	.05
83	Dave Winfield	.50
84	Fred McGriff	.05
85	Darryl Hamilton	.05
86	Jeffrey Hammonds	.05
87	Pedro Munoz	.05
88	Craig Biggio	.05
89	Cliff Floyd	.05

#	Player	Price
90	Tim Naehring	.05
91	Brett Butler	.05
92	Kevin Foster	.05
93	Patrick Kelly	.05
94	John Smiley	.05
95	Terry Steinbach	.05
96	Orel Hershiser	.05
97	Darrin Fletcher	.05
98	Walt Weiss	.05
99	John Wetteland	.05
100	Alan Trammell	.05
101	Steve Avery	.05
102	Tony Eusebio	.05
103	Sandy Alomar	.05
104	Joe Girardi	.05
105	Rick Aguilera	.05
106	Tony Tarasco	.05
107	Chris Hammond	.05
108	Mike McFarlane	.05
109	Doug Drabek	.05
110	Derek Bell	.05
111	Ed Sprague	.05
112	Todd Hollandsworth	.05
113	Otis Nixon	.05
114	Keith Lockhart	.05
115	Donovan Osborne	.05
116	Dave Magadan	.05
117	Edgar Martinez	.05
118	Chuck Carr	.05
119	J.R. Phillips	.05
120	Sean Bergman	.05
121	Andujar Cedeno	.05
122	Eric Young	.05
123	Al Martin	.05
124	Ken Hill	.05
125	Jim Eisenreich	.05
126	Benito Santiago	.05
127	Ariel Prieto	.05
128	Jim Bullinger	.05
129	Russ Davis	.05
130	Jim Abbott	.05
131	Jason Isringhausen	.05
132	Carlos Perez	.05
133	David Segui	.05
134	Troy O'Leary	.05
135	Pat Meares	.05
136	Chris Hoiles	.05
137	Ismael Valdes	.05
138	Jose Oliva	.05
139	Carlos Delgado	.35
140	Tom Goodwin	.05
141	Bob Tewksbury	.05
142	Chris Gomez	.05
143	Jose Oquendo	.05
144	Mark Lewis	.05
145	Salomon Torres	.05
146	Luis Gonzalez	.05
147	Mark Carreon	.05
148	Lance Johnson	.05
149	Melvin Nieves	.05
150	Lee Smith	.05
151	Jacob Brumfield	.05
152	Armando Benitez	.05
153	Curt Schilling	.30
154	Javier Lopez	.05
155	Frank Rodriguez	.05
156	Alex Gonzalez	.05
157	Todd Worrell	.05
158	Benji Gil	.05
159	Greg Gagne	.05
160	Tom Henke	.05
161	Randy Myers	.05
162	Joey Cora	.05
163	Scott Ruffcorn	.05
164	William Van Landingham	.05
165	Tony Phillips	.05
166	Eddie Williams	.05
167	Bobby Bonilla	.05
168	Denny Neagle	.05
169	Troy Percival	.05
170	Billy Ashley	.05
171	Andy Van Slyke	.05
172	Jose Offerman	.05
173	Mark Parent	.05
174	Edgardo Alfonzo	.05
175	Trevor Hoffman	.05
176	David Cone	.05
177	Dan Wilson	.05
178	Steve Ontiveros	.05
179	Dean Palmer	.05
180	Mike Kelly	.05
181	Jim Leyritz	.05
182	Ron Karkovice	.05
183	Kevin Brown	.05
184	Jose Valentin RC	.05
185	Jorge Fabregas	.05
186	Jose Mesa	.05
187	Brent Mayne	.05
188	Carl Everett	.05
189	Paul Sorrento	.05
190	Pete Shourek	.05
191	Scott Kamieniecki	.05
192	Roberto Hernandez	.05
193	Randy Johnson (Radar Rating)	.25
194	Greg Maddux (Radar Rating)	.35
195	Hideo Nomo (Radar Rating)	.15
196	David Cone (Radar Rating)	.05
197	Mike Mussina (Radar Rating)	.15
198	Andy Benes (Radar Rating)	
199	Kevin Appier (Radar Rating)	

#	Player	Price
200	John Smoltz (Radar Rating)	.05
201	John Wetteland (Radar Rating)	.05
202	Mark Wohlers (Radar Rating)	.05
203	Stan Belinda	.05
204	Brian Anderson	.05
205	Mike Devereaux	.05
206	Mark Wohlers	.05
207	Omar Vizquel	.05
208	Jose Rijo	.05
209	Willie Blair	.05
210	Jamie Moyer	.05
211	Craig Shipley	.05
212	Shane Reynolds	.05
213	Chad Fonville	.05
214	Jose Vizcaino	.05
215	Sid Fernandez	.05
216	Andy Ashby	.05
217	Frank Castillo	.05
218	Kevin Tapani	.05
219	Kent Mercker	.05
220	Karim Garcia	.05
221	Chris Snopek	.05
222	Tim Unroe	.05
223	Johnny Damon	.25
224	LaTroy Hawkins	.05
225	Mariano Rivera	.10
226	Jose Alberro	.05
227	Angel Martinez	.05
228	Jason Schmidt	.05
229	Tony Clark	.05
230	Kevin Jordan	.05
231	Mark Thompson	.05
232	Jim Dougherty	.05
333	Roger Cedeno	.05
234	Ugueth Urbina	.05
235	Ricky Otero	.05
236	Mark Smith	.05
237	Brian Barber	.05
238	Marc Kroon	.05
239	Joe Rosselli	.05
240	Derek Jeter	1.50
241	Michael Tucker	.05
242	Joe Borowski RC	.05
243	Joe Vitiello	.05
244	Orlando Palmeiro	.05
245	James Baldwin	.05
246	Alan Embree	.05
247	Shannon Penn	.05
248	Chris Stynes	.05
249	Oscar Munoz	.05
250	Jose Herrera	.05
251	Scott Sullivan	.05
252	Reggie Williams	.05
253	Mark Grudzielanek	.05
254	Kevin Jordan	.05
255	Terry Bradshaw	.05
256	F.P. Santangelo RC	.05
257	Doug Johns	.05
258	George Williams	.05
259	Larry Thomas	.05
260	Rudy Pemberton	.05
261	Jim Pittsley	.05
262	Les Norman	.05
263	Ruben Rivera	.05
264	Cesar Devarez RC	.05
265	Gregg Zaun	.05
266	Eric Owens	.05
267	John Frascatore	.05
268	Shannon Stewart	.05
269	Checklist	.05
270	Checklist	.05
271	Checklist	.05
272	Checklist	.05
273	Checklist	.05
274	Checklist	.05
275	Checklist	.05
276	Greg Maddux	.60
277	Pedro Martinez	.50
278	Bobby Higginson	.05
279	Ray Lankford	.05
280	Shawon Dunston	.05
281	Gary Sheffield	.35
282	Ken Griffey Jr.	.75
283	Paul Molitor	.50
284	Kevin Appier	.05
285	Chuck Knoblauch	.05
286	Alex Fernandez	.05
287	Steve Finley	.05
288	Jeff Blauser	.05
289	Charles Johnson	.05
290	John Franco	.05
291	Mark Langston	.05
292	Bret Saberhagen	.05
293	John Mabry	.05
294	Ramon Martinez	.05
295	Mike Blowers	.05
296	Paul O'Neill	.05
297	Dave Nilsson	.05
298	Dante Bichette	.05
299	Marty Cordova	.05
300	Jay Bell	.05
301	Mike Mussina	.30
302	Ivan Rodriguez	.40
303	Jose Canseco	.30
304	Jeff Bagwell	.50
305	Manny Ramirez	.50
306	Dennis Martinez	.05
307	Charlie Hayes	.05
308	Joe Carter	.05
309	Travis Fryman	.05
310	Mark McGwire	1.00
311	Reggie Sanders	.05
312	Julian Tavarez	.05
313	Jeff Montgomery	.05
314	Andy Benes	.05
315	John Jaha	.05

#	Player	Price
316	Jeff Kent	.05
317	Mike Piazza	.75
318	Erik Hanson	.05
319	Kenny Rogers	.05
320	Hideo Nomo	.25
321	Gregg Jefferies	.05
322	Chipper Jones	.75
323	Jay Buhner	.05
324	Dennis Eckersley	.40
325	Kenny Lofton	.25
326	Robin Ventura	.05
327	Tom Glavine	.35
328	Tim Salmon	.05
329	Andres Galarraga	.05
330	Hal Morris	.05
331	Brady Anderson	.05
332	Chili Davis	.05
333	Roger Clemens	.65
334	Marquis Grissom	.05
335	Jeff (Mike) Greenwell	.05
336	Sammy Sosa	.60
337	Ron Gant	.05
338	Ken Caminiti	.05
339	Danny Tartabull	.05
340	Barry Bonds	1.50
341	Ben McDonald	.05
342	Ruben Sierra	.05
343	Bernie Williams	.05
344	Wil Cordero	.05
345	Wade Boggs	.60
346	Gary Gaetti	.05
347	Greg Colbrunn	.05
348	Juan Gonzalez	.25
349	Marc Newfield	.05
350	Charles Nagy	.05
351	Robby Thompson	.05
352	Roberto Petagine	.05
353	Darryl Strawberry	.05
354	Tino Martinez	.05
355	Eric Karros	.05
356	Cal Ripken Jr. (Star Struck)	.75
357	Cecil Fielder (Star Struck)	.05
358	Kirby Puckett (Star Struck)	.35
359	Jim Edmonds (Star Struck)	.05
360	Matt Williams (Star Struck)	.05
361	Alex Rodriguez (Star Struck)	.50
362	Barry Larkin (Star Struck)	.05
363	Rafael Palmeiro (Star Struck)	.05
364	David Cone (Star Struck)	.05
365	Roberto Alomar (Star Struck)	.10
366	Eddie Murray (Star Struck)	.25
367	Randy Johnson (Star Struck)	.20
368	Ryan Klesko (Star Struck)	.05
369	Raul Mondesi (Star Struck)	.05
370	Mo Vaughn (Star Struck)	.05
371	Will Clark (Star Struck)	.05
372	Carlos Baerga (Star Struck)	.05
373	Frank Thomas (Star Struck)	.30
374	Larry Walker (Star Struck)	.05
375	Garret Anderson (Star Struck)	.05
376	Edgar Martinez (Star Struck)	.05
377	Don Mattingly (Star Struck)	.40
378	Tony Gwynn (Star Struck)	.35
379	Albert Belle (Star Struck)	.05
380	Jason Isringhausen (Star Struck)	.05
381	Ruben Rivera (Star Struck)	.05
382	Johnny Damon (Star Struck)	.05
383	Karim Garcia (Star Struck)	.05
384	Derek Jeter (Star Struck)	.75
385	David Justice (Star Struck)	.05
386	Royce Clayton	.05
387	Mark Whiten	.05
388	Mickey Tettleton	.05
389	Steve Trachsel	.05
390	Danny Bautista	.05
391	Midre Cummings	.05
392	Scott Leius	.05
393	Manny Alexander	.05
394	Brent Gates	.05
395	Rey Sanchez	.05
396	Andy Pettitte	.20
397	Jeff Cirillo	.05
398	Kurt Abbott	.05
399	Lee Tinsley	.05
400	Paul Assenmacher	.05
401	Scott Erickson	.05
402	Todd Zeile	.05
403	Tom Pagnozzi	.05
404	Ozzie Guillen	.05
405	Jeff Frye	.05
406	Kirt Manwaring	.05
407	Chad Ogea	.05
408	Harold Baines	.05
409	Jason Bere	.05
410	Chuck Finley	.05
411	Jeff Fassero	.05
412	Joey Hamilton	.05
413	John Olerud	.05
414	Kevin Stocker	.05
415	Eric Anthony	.05
416	Aaron Sele	.05
417	Chris Bosio	.05

#	Player	Price
418	Michael Mimbs	.05
419	Orlando Miller	.05
420	Stan Javier	.05
421	Matt Mieske	.05
422	Jason Bates	.05
423	Orlando Merced	.05
424	John Flaherty	.05
425	Reggie Jefferson	.05
426	Scott Stahoviak	.05
427	John Burkett	.05
428	Rod Beck	.05
429	Bill Swift	.05
430	Scott Cooper	.05
431	Mel Rojas	.05
432	Todd Van Poppel	.05
433	Bobby Jones	.05
434	Mike Harkey	.05
435	Sean Berry	.05
436	Glenallen Hill	.05
437	Ryan Thompson	.05
438	Luis Alicea	.05
439	Esteban Loaiza	.05
440	Jeff Reboulet	.05
441	Vince Coleman	.05
442	Ellis Burks	.05
443	Allen Battle	.05
444	Jimmy Key	.05
445	Ricky Bottalico	.05
446	Delino DeShields	.05
447	Albie Lopez	.05
448	Mark Petkovsek	.05
449	Tim Raines	.05
450	Bryan Harvey	.05
451	Pat Hentgen	.05
452	Tim Laker	.05
453	Tom Gordon	.05
454	Phil Plantier	.05
455	Ernie Young	.05
456	Pete Harnisch	.05
457	Roberto Kelly	.05
458	Mark Portugal	.05
459	Mark Leiter	.05
460	Tony Pena	.05
461	Roger Pavlik	.05
462	Jeff King	.05
463	Bryan Rekar	.05
464	Al Leiter	.05
465	Phil Nevin	.05
466	Jose Lima	.05
467	Mike Stanley	.05
468	David McCarty	.05
469	Herb Perry	.05
470	Geronimo Berroa	.05
471	David Wells	.05
472	Vaughn Eshelman	.05
473	Greg Swindell	.05
474	Steve Sparks	.05
475	Luis Sojo	.05
476	Derrick May	.05
477	Joe Oliver	.05
478	Alex Arias	.05
479	Brad Ausmus	.05
480	Gabe White	.05
481	Pat Rapp	.05
482	Damon Buford	.05
483	Turk Wendell	.05
484	Jeff Brantley	.05
485	Curtis Leskanic	.05
486	Robb Nen	.05
487	Lou Whitaker	.05
488	Melido Perez	.05
489	Luis Polonia	.05
490	Scott Brosius	.05
491	Robert Perez	.05
492	Mike Sweeney RC	.50
493	Mark Loretta	.05
494	Alex Ochoa	.05
495	Matt Lawton RC	.10
496	Shawn Estes	.05
497	John Wasdin	.05
498	Marc Kroon	.05
499	Chris Snopek	.05
500	Jeff Suppan	.05
501	Terrell Wade	.05
502	Marvin Benard RC	.10
503	Chris Widger	.05
504	Quinton McCracken	.05
505	Bob Wolcott	.05
506	C.J. Nitkowski	.05
507	Aaron Ledesma	.05
508	Scott Hatteberg	.05
509	Jimmy Haynes	.05
510	Howard Battle	.05

the regular series chosen for inclusion. The white borders of the regular cards are replaced with copper-foil and background printing is also done on foil in this special version. On back is a special "Dugout Collection '96" logo. Advertised insertion rate of the copper-version cards is one per three packs.

	NM/M
Complete Set (220):	60.00
Complete Series 1 (1-110):	30.00
Complete Series 2 (1-110):	30.00
Common Player:	.20
Artist's Proofs:	4X

#	Player	Price
1	Will Clark	.20
2	Rich Becker	.20
3	Ryan Klesko	.20
4	Jim Edmonds	.20
5	Barry Larkin	.20
6	Jim Thome	.65
7	Raul Mondesi	.20
8	Don Mattingly	1.25
9	Jeff Conine	.20
10	Rickey Henderson	.75
11	Chad Curtis	.20
12	Darren Daulton	.20
13	Larry Walker	.20
14	Carlos Baerga	.20
15	Tony Gwynn	1.00
16	Jon Nunnally	.20
17	Deion Sanders	.20
18	Mark Grace	.20
19	Alex Rodriguez	2.00
20	Frank Thomas	.75
21	Brian Jordan	.20
22	J.T. Snow	.20
23	Shawn Green	.50
24	Tim Wakefield	.20
25	Curtis Goodwin	.20
26	John Smoltz	.20
27	Devon White	.20
28	Brian Hunter	.20
29	Rusty Greer	.20
30	Rafael Palmeiro	.65
31	Bernard Gilkey	.20
32	John Valentin	.20
33	Randy Johnson	.75
34	Garret Anderson	.20
35	Ray Durham	.20
36	Bip Roberts	.20
37	Tyler Green	.20
38	Bill Pulsipher	.20
39	Jason Giambi	.50
40	Jack McDowell	.20
41	Rico Brogna	.20
42	Terry Pendleton	.20
43	Rondell White	.20
44	Andre Dawson	.35
45	Kirby Puckett	1.00
46	Wally Joyner	.20
47	B.J. Surhoff	.20
48	Randy Velarde	.20
49	Greg Vaughn	.20
50	Roberto Alomar	.30
51	David Justice	.20
52	Cal Ripken Jr.	3.00
53	Ozzie Smith	1.00
54	Mo Vaughn	.20
55	Gary DiSarcina	.20
56	Matt Williams	.20
57	Lenny Dykstra	.20
58	Bret Boone	.20
59	Albert Belle	.20
60	Vinny Castilla	.20
61	Moises Alou	.20
62	Cecil Fielder	.20
63	Brad Radke	.20
64	Quilvio Veras	.20
65	Eddie Murray	.75
66	Dave Winfield	.75
67	Fred McGriff	.20
68	Craig Biggio	.20
69	Cliff Floyd	.20
70	Tim Naehring	.20
71	John Wetteland	.20
72	Alan Trammell	.20
73	Steve Avery	.20
74	Rick Aguilera	.20
75	Derek Bell	.20
76	Todd Hollandsworth	.20
77	Edgar Martinez	.20
78	Mark Lemke	.20
79	Ariel Prieto	.20
80	Russ Davis	.20
81	Jim Abbott	.20
82	Jason Isringhausen	.20
83	Carlos Perez	.20
84	David Segui	.20
85	Troy O'Leary	.20
86	Ismael Valdes	.20
87	Carlos Delgado	.50
88	Lee Smith	.20
89	Javy Lopez	.20
90	Frank Rodriguez	.20
91	Alex Gonzalez	.20
92	Benji Gil	.20
93	Greg Gagne	.20
94	Randy Myers	.20
95	Bobby Bonilla	.20
96	Billy Ashley	.20
97	Andy Van Slyke	.20
98	Edgardo Alfonzo	.20
99	David Cone	.20
100	Dean Palmer	.20
101	Jose Mesa	.20

#	Player	Price
102	Karim Garcia	.20
103	Johnny Damon	.40
104	LaTroy Hawkins	.15
105	Mark Smith	.20
106	Derek Jeter	3.00
107	Michael Tucker	.20
108	Joe Vitiello	.20
109	Ruben Rivera	.20
110	Gregg Zaun	.20
1	Greg Maddux	1.00
2	Pedro Martinez	.75
3	Bobby Higginson	.20
4	Ray Lankford	.20
5	Shawon Dunston	.20
6	Gary Sheffield	.45
7	Ken Griffey Jr.	1.50
8	Paul Molitor	.75
9	Kevin Appier	.20
10	Chuck Knoblauch	.20
11	Alex Fernandez	.20
12	Steve Finley	.20
13	Jeff Blauser	.20
14	Charles Johnson	.20
15	John Franco	.20
16	Mark Langston	.20
17	Bret Saberhagen	.20
18	John Mabry	.20
19	Ramon Martinez	.20
20	Mike Blowers	.20
21	Paul O'Neill	.20
22	Dave Nilsson	.20
23	Dante Bichette	.20
24	Marty Cordova	.20
25	Jay Bell	.20
26	Mike Mussina	.40
27	Ivan Rodriguez	.65
28	Jose Canseco	.50
29	Jeff Bagwell	.75
30	Manny Ramirez	.75
31	Dennis Martinez	.20
32	Charlie Hayes	.20
33	Joe Carter	.20
34	Travis Fryman	.20
35	Mark McGwire	2.00
36	Reggie Sanders	.20
37	Julian Tavarez	.20
38	Jeff Montgomery	.20
39	Andy Benes	.20
40	John Jaha	.20
41	Jeff Kent	.20
42	Mike Piazza	1.50
43	Erik Hanson	.20
44	Kenny Rogers	.20
45	Hideo Nomo	.50
46	Gregg Jefferies	.20
47	Chipper Jones	1.00
48	Jay Buhner	.20
49	Dennis Eckersley	.65
50	Kenny Lofton	.20
51	Robin Ventura	.20
52	Tom Glavine	.30
53	Tim Salmon	.20
54	Andres Galarraga	.20
55	Hal Morris	.20
56	Brady Anderson	.20
57	Chili Davis	.20
58	Roger Clemens	1.25
59	Marquis Grissom	.20
60	Mike Greenwell	.20
61	Sammy Sosa	1.00
62	Ron Gant	.20
63	Ken Caminiti	.20
64	Danny Tartabull	.20
65	Barry Bonds	3.00
66	Ben McDonald	.20
67	Ruben Sierra	.20
68	Bernie Williams	.20
69	Wil Cordero	.20
70	Wade Boggs	1.00
71	Gary Gaetti	.20
72	Greg Colbrunn	.20
73	Juan Gonzalez	.50
74	Marc Newfield	.20
75	Charles Nagy	.20
76	Robby Thompson	.20
77	Roberto Petagine	.20
78	Darryl Strawberry	.20
79	Tino Martinez	.20
80	Eric Karros	.20
81	Cal Ripken Jr. (Star Struck)	1.50
82	Cecil Fielder (Star Struck)	.20
83	Kirby Puckett (Star Struck)	.50
84	Jim Edmonds (Star Struck)	.20
85	Matt Williams (Star Struck)	.20
86	Alex Rodriguez (Star Struck)	1.00
87	Barry Larkin (Star Struck)	.20
88	Rafael Palmeiro (Star Struck)	.40
89	David Cone (Star Struck)	.20
90	Roberto Alomar (Star Struck)	.25
91	Eddie Murray (Star Struck)	.40
92	Randy Johnson (Star Struck)	.40
93	Ryan Klesko (Star Struck)	.20
94	Raul Mondesi (Star Struck)	.20
95	Mo Vaughn (Star Struck)	.20
96	Will Clark (Star Struck)	.20
97	Carlos Baerga (Star Struck)	.20

Dugout Collection

The concept of a partial parallel set, including the stars and rookies, but not the journeymen and bench warmers, was initiated with Score's "Dugout Collection," with fewer than half of the cards from

98	Frank Thomas (Star Struck)	.45
99	Larry Walker (Star Struck)	.20
100	Garret Anderson (Star Struck)	.20
101	Edgar Martinez (Star Struck)	.20
102	Don Mattingly (Star Struck)	.60
103	Tony Gwynn (Star Struck)	.50
104	Albert Belle (Star Struck)	.20
105	Jason Isringhausen (Star Struck)	.20
106	Ruben Rivera (Star Struck)	.20
107	Johnny Damon (Star Struck)	.35
108	Karim Garcia (Star Struck)	.20
109	Derek Jeter (Star Struck)	1.50
110	David Justice (Star Struck)	.20

Dugout Collection Artist's Proofs

A parallel set within a parallel set, the Artist's Proof logo added to the copper-foil design of the Dugout Collection cards raises the odds of finding one to just once in 36 packs.

	NM/M
Complete Set (220):	300.00
Common Player:	1.00
Artist's Proof Stars:	4X

All-Stars

An exclusive insert found only in 20-card Series 2 jumbo packs at an average rate of one per nine packs, these inserts feature the game's top stars printed in a rainbow holographic-foil technology.

		NM/M
Complete Set (20):		13.50
Common Player:		.25
1	Frank Thomas	1.25
2	Albert Belle	.25
3	Ken Griffey Jr.	2.00
4	Cal Ripken Jr.	3.00
5	Mo Vaughn	.25
6	Matt Williams	.25
7	Barry Bonds	3.00
8	Dante Bichette	.25
9	Tony Gwynn	1.50
10	Greg Maddux	1.50
11	Randy Johnson	1.25
12	Hideo Nomo	.75
13	Tim Salmon	.25
14	Jeff Bagwell	1.25
15	Edgar Martinez	.25
16	Reggie Sanders	.25
17	Larry Walker	.25
18	Chipper Jones	1.50
19	Manny Ramirez	1.25
20	Eddie Murray	1.25

Big Bats

Gold-foil printing highlights cards of 20 of the game's top hitters found in this retail-packaging exclusive insert set. Stated odds of picking a Big Bats card are one in 31 packs.

	NM/M
Complete Set (20):	12.50
Common Player:	.45

BIG Bats Tony GWYNN PADRES

1	Cal Ripken Jr.	3.00
2	Ken Griffey Jr.	2.00
3	Frank Thomas	.75
4	Jeff Bagwell	.75
5	Mike Piazza	2.00
6	Barry Bonds	3.00
7	Matt Williams	.45
8	Raul Mondesi	.45
9	Tony Gwynn	1.25
10	Albert Belle	.45
11	Manny Ramirez	.75
12	Carlos Baerga	.45
13	Mo Vaughn	.45
14	Derek Bell	.45
15	Larry Walker	.45
16	Kenny Lofton	.45
17	Edgar Martinez	.45
18	Reggie Sanders	.45
19	Eddie Murray	.75
20	Chipper Jones	1.25

Diamond Aces

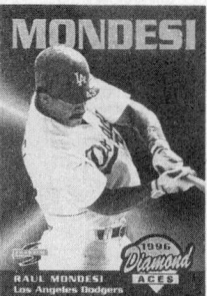

MONDESI
1996 DIAMOND ACES
RAUL MONDESI Los Angeles Dodgers

Thirty of the top veterans and young stars are included in this jumbo-only insert set, seeded at a rate of one per eight packs.

		NM/M
Complete Set (30):		25.00
Common Player:		.35
1	Hideo Nomo	.60
2	Brian Hunter	.35
3	Ray Durham	.35
4	Frank Thomas	1.00
5	Cal Ripken Jr.	3.50
6	Barry Bonds	3.50
7	Greg Maddux	1.25
8	Chipper Jones	1.25
9	Raul Mondesi	.35
10	Mike Piazza	2.00
11	Derek Jeter	3.50
12	Bill Pulsipher	.35
13	Larry Walker	.35
14	Ken Griffey Jr.	2.00
15	Alex Rodriguez	3.00
16	Manny Ramirez	1.00
17	Mo Vaughn	.35
18	Reggie Sanders	.35
19	Derek Bell	.35
20	Jim Edmonds	.35
21	Albert Belle	.35
22	Eddie Murray	1.00
23	Tony Gwynn	1.25
24	Jeff Bagwell	1.00
25	Carlos Baerga	.35
26	Matt Williams	.35
27	Garret Anderson	.35
28	Todd Hollandsworth	.35
29	Johnny Damon	.75
30	Tim Salmon	.35

Dream Team

The hottest player at each position is honored in the Dream Team insert set. Once again featured on holographic foil printing technology, the cards are found in all types of Score packaging at a rate of once per 72 packs.

		NM/M
Complete Set (9):		15.00
Common Player:		.75
1	Cal Ripken Jr.	4.00
2	Frank Thomas	1.50
3	Carlos Baerga	.75
4	Matt Williams	.75
5	Mike Piazza	3.00

Future Franchise

Marc Newfield
FUTURE FRANCHISE

Future Franchise is the most difficult insert to pull from packs of Series 2, at the rate of once per 72 packs, on average. Sixteen young stars are showcased on holographic gold-foil printing in the set.

		NM/M
Complete Set (16):		20.00
Common Player:		.75
1	Jason Isringhausen	.75
2	Chipper Jones	2.50
3	Derek Jeter	5.00
4	Alex Rodriguez	4.00
5	Alex Ochoa	.75
6	Manny Ramirez	1.50
7	Johnny Damon	1.00
8	Ruben Rivera	.75
9	Karim Garcia	.75
10	Garret Anderson	.75
11	Marty Cordova	.75
12	Bill Pulsipher	.75
13	Hideo Nomo	1.00
14	Marc Newfield	.75
15	Charles Johnson	.75
16	Raul Mondesi	.75

Gold Stars

BARRY LARKIN

Appearing once in every 15 packs of Series 2, Gold Stars are labeled with a stamp in the upper-left corner. The set contains 30 top current stars printed on gold-foil and seeded at the average rate of one per 15 packs.

		NM/M
Complete Set (30):		20.00
Common Player:		.20
1	Ken Griffey Jr.	2.00
2	Frank Thomas	1.00
3	Reggie Sanders	.20
4	Tim Salmon	.20
5	Mike Piazza	2.00
6	Tony Gwynn	1.50
7	Gary Sheffield	.45
8	Matt Williams	.20
9	Bernie Williams	.20
10	Jason Isringhausen	.20
11	Albert Belle	.20
12	Chipper Jones	1.50
13	Edgar Martinez	.20
14	Barry Larkin	.20
15	Barry Bonds	3.00
16	Jeff Bagwell	1.00
17	Greg Maddux	1.50
18	Mo Vaughn	.20
19	Ryan Klesko	.20
20	Sammy Sosa	1.50
21	Darren Daulton	.20
22	Ivan Rodriguez	.75
23	Dante Bichette	.20
24	Hideo Nomo	.50
25	Cal Ripken Jr.	3.00
26	Rafael Palmeiro	.75
27	Larry Walker	.20
28	Carlos Baerga	.20
29	Randy Johnson	1.00
30	Manny Ramirez	1.00

Numbers Game

Some of the 1995 season's most impressive statistical accomplishments are featured in this chase set. Cards are enhanced with gold foil and found in all types of Score packs at an average rate of one per 15 packs.

		NM/M
Complete Set (30):		17.50
Common Player:		.15
1	Cal Ripken Jr.	2.50
2	Frank Thomas	.75
3	Ken Griffey Jr.	1.50
4	Mike Piazza	1.50
5	Barry Bonds	2.50
6	Greg Maddux	1.00
7	Jeff Bagwell	.75
8	Derek Bell	.15
9	Tony Gwynn	1.00
10	Hideo Nomo	.50
11	Raul Mondesi	.15
12	Manny Ramirez	.15
13	Albert Belle	.15
14	Matt Williams	.15
15	Jim Edmonds	.15
16	Edgar Martinez	.15
17	Mo Vaughn	.15
18	Reggie Sanders	.15
19	Chipper Jones	1.00
20	Larry Walker	.15
21	Juan Gonzalez	.15
22	Kenny Lofton	.15
23	Don Mattingly	1.25
24	Ivan Rodriguez	.65
25	Randy Johnson	.15
26	Derek Jeter	2.50
27	J.T. Snow	.15
28	Will Clark	.15
29	Rafael Palmeiro	.65
30	Alex Rodriguez	2.00

Power Pace

eric KARROS

Power Pace is exclusive to retail packs in Series 2, where they are found on average every 31 packs. Eighteen top power hitters are featured in this issue in a gold-foil design.

		NM/M
Complete Set (18):		24.00
Common Player:		.50
1	Mark McGwire	4.00
2	Albert Belle	.50
3	Jay Buhner	.50
4	Frank Thomas	1.50
5	Matt Williams	.50
6	Gary Sheffield	.75
7	Mike Piazza	3.00
8	Larry Walker	.50
9	Mo Vaughn	.50
10	Rafael Palmeiro	1.25
11	Dante Bichette	.50
12	Ken Griffey Jr.	3.00
13	Barry Bonds	5.00
14	Manny Ramirez	1.50
15	Sammy Sosa	1.50
16	Tim Salmon	.50
17	Dave Justice	.50
18	Eric Karros	.50

Reflexions

HIDEO NOMO-P

Appearing only in hobby packs this insert set pairs 20 veteran stars with 20 up-and-coming players in a foil-printed format. Odds of finding a Reflexions insert are stated as one per 31 packs.

		NM/M
Complete Set (20):		35.00
Common Player:		.45
1	Cal Ripken Jr., Chipper Jones	5.00
2	Ken Griffey Jr., Alex Rodriguez	4.50
3	Frank Thomas, Mo Vaughn	2.50
4	Kenny Lofton, Brian Hunter	.45
5	Don Mattingly, J.T. Snow	3.75
6	Manny Ramirez, Raul Mondesi	2.50
7	Tony Gwynn, Garret Anderson	3.75
8	Roberto Alomar, Carlos Baerga	.50
9	Andre Dawson, Larry Walker	.50
10	Barry Larkin, Derek Jeter	5.00
11	Barry Bonds, Reggie Sanders	5.00
12	Mike Piazza, Albert Belle	4.00
13	Wade Boggs, Edgar Martinez	3.75
14	David Cone, John Smoltz	.45
15	Will Clark, Jeff Bagwell	2.50
16	Mark McGwire, Cecil Fielder	4.50
17	Greg Maddux, Mike Mussina	3.75
18	Randy Johnson, Hideo Nomo	2.50
19	Jim Thome, Dean Palmer	2.00
20	Chuck Knoblauch, Craig Biggio	.45

Cal Ripken Tribute

The toughest pick among the 1996 Score inserts is this special card marking Cal Ripken's 2,131st consecutive game. The insertion rate is one per 300 packs hobby and retail, one per 150 jumbo packs.

		NM/M
2131	Cal Ripken Jr. (Tribute)	4.00

Titantic Taters

MO VAUGHN
TITANIC TATERS

One of the more creative names in the 1996 insert lineup, Titanic Taters are found one in every 31 packs of Series 2. Gold-foil fronts feature 18 of the game's heaviest hitters.

		NM/M
Complete Set (18):		25.00
Common Player:		.60
1	Albert Belle	.60
2	Frank Thomas	2.00
3	Mo Vaughn	.60
4	Ken Griffey Jr.	3.00
5	Matt Williams	.60
6	Mark McGwire	3.50
7	Dante Bichette	.60
8	Tim Salmon	.60
9	Jeff Bagwell	2.00
10	Rafael Palmeiro	1.50
11	Mike Piazza	3.00
12	Cecil Fielder	.60
13	Larry Walker	.60
14	Sammy Sosa	2.50
15	Manny Ramirez	2.00
16	Gary Sheffield	.90
17	Barry Bonds	5.00
18	Jay Buhner	.60

1997 Score

tom gordon
boston red sox

A total of 551 cards make up the base set, with 330 cards sold in Series I and 221 making up Series II. The basic card design features a color action photo surrounded by a white border. The player's name is above the photo, with the team name underneath. Backs feature text and statistics against a white background with the image of the team logo ghosted into the background. Two parallel insert sets - Artist's Proof and Showcase Series - were part of each series. Other inserts in Series I were Pitcher Perfect, The Franchise, The Glowing Franchise, Titanic Taters (retail exclusive), Stellar Season (magazine packs only), and The Highlight Zone (hobby exclusive). Series II inserts were Blastmasters, Heart of the Order and Stand and Deliver. Cards were sold in 10-card packs for 99 cents each.

	NM/M
Complete Set (551):	16.00
Factory Tin-Box Set (551):	17.50
Common Player:	.05
Showcase:	3X
Artist's Proofs:	10X
Premium Stocks:	3X
Wax Pack (10):	
Wax Box (36):	12.00
1	Jeff Bagwell	.50
2	Mickey Tettleton	.05
3	Johnny Damon	.25
4	Jeff Conine	.05
5	Bernie Williams	.25
6	Will Clark	.05
7	Ryan Klesko	.05
8	Cecil Fielder	.05
9	Paul Wilson	.05
10	Gregg Jefferies	.05
11	Chili Davis	.05
12	Albert Belle	.05
13	Ken Hill	.05
14	Cliff Floyd	.05
15	Jaime Navarro	.05
16	Ismael Valdes	.05
17	Jeff King	.05
18	Chris Bosio	.05
19	Reggie Sanders	.05
20	Darren Daulton	.05
21	Ken Caminiti	.05
22	Mike Piazza	.75
23	Chad Mottola	.05
24	Darin Erstad	.15
25	Dante Bichette	.05
26	Frank Thomas	.50
27	Ben McDonald	.05
28	Raul Casanova	.05
29	Kevin Ritz	.05
30	Garret Anderson	.05
31	Jason Kendall	.05
32	Billy Wagner	.05
33	David Justice	.05
34	Marty Cordova	.05
35	Derek Jeter	1.50
36	Trevor Hoffman	.05
37	Geronimo Berroa	.05
38	Walt Weiss	.05
39	Kirt Manwaring	.05
40	Alex Gonzalez	.05
41	Sean Berry	.05
42	Kevin Appier	.05
43	Rusty Greer	.05
44	Pete Incaviglia	.05

#	Player	Price	#	Player	Price	#	Player	Price	#	Player	Price
45	Rafael Palmeiro	.45	167	Wade Boggs	.65	289	Mike Lansing	.05	411	Mike Timlin	.05
46	Eddie Murray	.50	168	Jay Buhner	.05	290	Scott Servais	.05	412	Joe Vitiello	.05
47	Moises Alou	.05	169	Eric Young	.05	291	Royce Clayton	.05	413	Rondell White	.05
48	Mark Lewis	.05	170	Jose Canseco	.30	292	Mike Grace	.05	414	Jeff Fassero	.05
49	Hal Morris	.05	171	Dwight Gooden	.05	293	James Mouton	.05	415	Rex Hudler	.05
50	Edgar Renteria	.05	172	Fred McGriff	.05	294	Charles Johnson	.05	416	Curt Schilling	.35
51	Rickey Henderson	.50	173	Sandy Alomar Jr.	.05	295	Gary Gaetti	.05	417	Rich Becker	.05
52	Pat Listach	.05	174	Andy Benes	.05	296	Kevin Mitchell	.05	418	William Van Landingham	.05
53	John Wasdin	.05	175	Dean Palmer	.05	297	Carlos Garcia	.05	419	Chris Snopek	.05
54	James Baldwin	.05	176	Larry Walker	.05	298	Desi Relaford	.05	420	David Segui	.05
55	Brian Jordan	.05	177	Charles Nagy	.05	299	Jason Thompson	.05	421	Eddie Murray	.50
56	Edgar Martinez	.05	178	David Cone	.05	300	Osvaldo Fernandez	.05	422	Shane Andrews	.05
57	Wil Cordero	.05	179	Mark Grace	.05	301	Fernando Vina	.05	423	Gary DiSarcina	.05
58	Danny Tartabull	.05	180	Robin Ventura	.05	302	Jose Offerman	.05	424	Brian Hunter	.05
59	Keith Lockhart	.05	181	Roger Clemens	.70	303	Yamil Benitez	.05	425	Willie Greene	.05
60	Rico Brogna	.05	182	Bobby Witt	.05	304	J.T. Snow	.05	426	Felipe Crespo	.05
61	Ricky Bottalico	.05	183	Vinny Castilla	.05	305	Rafael Bournigal	.05	427	Jason Bates	.05
62	Terry Pendleton	.05	184	Gary Sheffield	.35	306	Jason Isringhausen	.05	428	Albert Belle	.05
63	Bret Boone	.05	185	Dan Wilson	.05	307	Bob Higginson	.05	429	Rey Sanchez	.05
64	Charlie Hayes	.05	186	Roger Cedeno	.05	308	Nerio Rodriguez RC	.05	430	Roger Clemens	.70
65	Marc Newfield	.05	187	Mark McGwire	1.00	309	Brian Giles RC	.50	431	Deion Sanders	.05
66	Sterling Hitchcock	.05	188	Darren Bragg	.05	310	Andruw Jones	.50	432	Ernie Young	.05
67	Roberto Alomar	.15	189	Quinton McCracken	.05	311	Billy McMillon	.05	433	Jay Bell	.05
68	John Jaha	.05	190	Randy Myers	.05	312	Arquimedez Pozo	.05	434	Jeff Blauser	.05
69	Greg Colbrunn	.05	191	Jeromy Burnitz	.05	313	Jermaine Allensworth	.05	435	Lenny Dykstra	.05
70	Sal Fasano	.05	192	Randy Johnson	.50	314	Luis Andujar	.05	436	Chuck Carr	.05
71	Brooks Kieschnick	.05	193	Chipper Jones	.75	315	Angel Echevarria	.05	437	Russ Davis	.05
72	Pedro Martinez	.50	194	Greg Vaughn	.05	316	Karim Garcia	.05	438	Carl Everett	.05
73	Kevin Elster	.05	195	Travis Fryman	.05	317	Trey Beamon	.05	439	Damion Easley	.05
74	Ellis Burks	.05	196	Tim Naehring	.05	318	Makoto Suzuki	.05	440	Pat Kelly	.05
75	Chuck Finley	.05	197	B.J. Surhoff	.05	319	Robin Jennings	.05	441	Pat Rapp	.05
76	John Olerud	.05	198	Juan Gonzalez	.25	320	Dmitri Young	.05	442	David Justice	.05
77	Jay Bell	.05	199	Terrell Wade	.05	321	Damon Mashore RC	.05	443	Graeme Lloyd	.05
78	Allen Watson	.05	200	Jeff Frye	.05	322	Wendell Magee	.05	444	Damon Buford	.05
79	Darryl Strawberry	.05	201	Joey Cora	.05	323	Dax Jones RC	.05	445	Jose Valentin	.05
80	Orlando Miller	.05	202	Raul Mondesi	.05	324	Todd Walker	.05	446	Jason Schmidt	.05
81	Jose Herrera	.05	203	Ivan Rodriguez	.45	325	Marvin Benard	.05	447	Dave Martinez	.05
82	Andy Pettitte	.20	204	Armando Reynoso	.05	326	Brian Raabe RC	.05	448	Danny Tartabull	.05
83	Juan Guzman	.05	205	Jeffrey Hammonds	.05	327	Marcus Jensen	.05	449	Jose Vizcaino	.05
84	Alan Benes	.05	206	Darren Dreifort	.05	328	Checklist	.05	450	Steve Avery	.05
85	Jack McDowell	.05	207	Kevin Seitzer	.05	329	Checklist	.05	451	Mike Devereaux	.05
86	Ugueth Urbina	.05	208	Tino Martinez	.05	330	Checklist	.05	452	Jim Eisenreich	.05
87	Rocky Coppinger	.05	209	Jim Bruske	.05	331	Norm Charlton	.05	453	Mark Leiter	.05
88	Jeff Cirillo	.05	210	Jeff Suppan	.05	332	Bruce Ruffin	.05	454	Roberto Kelly	.05
89	Tom Glavine	.35	211	Mark Carreon	.05	333	John Wetteland	.05	455	Benito Santiago	.05
90	Robby Thompson	.05	212	Wilson Alvarez	.05	334	Marquis Grissom	.05	456	Steve Trachsel	.05
91	Barry Bonds	1.50	213	John Burkett	.05	335	Sterling Hitchcock	.05	457	Gerald Williams	.05
92	Carlos Delgado	.40	214	Tony Phillips	.05	336	John Olerud	.05	458	Pete Schourek	.05
93	Mo Vaughn	.05	215	Greg Maddux	.65	337	David Wells	.05	459	Esteban Loaiza	.05
94	Ryne Sandberg	.65	216	Mark Whiten	.05	338	Chili Davis	.05	460	Mel Rojas	.05
95	Alex Rodriguez	1.00	217	Curtis Pride	.05	339	Mark Lewis	.05	461	Tim Wakefield	.05
96	Brady Anderson	.05	218	Lyle Mouton	.05	340	Kenny Lofton	.05	462	Tony Fernandez	.05
97	Scott Brosius	.05	219	Todd Hundley	.05	341	Alex Fernandez	.05	463	Doug Drabek	.05
98	Dennis Eckersley	.45	220	Greg Gagne	.05	342	Ruben Sierra	.05	464	Joe Girardi	.05
99	Brian McRae	.05	221	Rich Amaral	.05	343	Delino DeShields	.05	465	Mike Bordick	.05
100	Rey Ordonez	.05	222	Tom Goodwin	.05	344	John Wasdin	.05	466	Jim Leyritz	.05
101	John Valentin	.05	223	Chris Hoiles	.05	345	Dennis Martinez	.05	467	Erik Hanson	.05
102	Brett Butler	.05	224	Jayhawk Owens	.05	346	Kevin Elster	.05	468	Michael Tucker	.05
103	Eric Karros	.05	225	Kenny Rogers	.05	347	Bobby Bonilla	.05	469	Tony Womack RC	.10
104	Harold Baines	.05	226	Mike Greenwell	.05	348	Jaime Navarro	.05	470	Doug Glanville	.05
105	Javier Lopez	.05	227	Mark Wohlers	.05	349	Chad Curtis	.05	471	Rudy Pemberton	.05
106	Alan Trammell	.05	228	Henry Rodriguez	.05	350	Terry Steinbach	.05	472	Keith Lockhart	.05
107	Jim Thome	.45	229	Robert Perez	.05	351	Ariel Prieto	.05	473	Nomar Garciaparra	.05
108	Frank Rodriguez	.05	230	Jeff Kent	.05	352	Jeff Kent	.05	474	Scott Rolen	.40
109	Bernard Gilkey	.05	231	Darryl Hamilton	.05	353	Carlos Garcia	.05	475	Jason Dickson	.05
110	Reggie Jefferson	.05	232	Alex Fernandez	.05	354	Mark Whiten	.05	476	Glendon Rusch	.05
111	Scott Stahoviak	.05	233	Ron Karkovice	.05	355	Todd Zelle	.05	477	Todd Walker	.05
112	Steve Gibralter	.05	234	Jimmy Haynes	.05	356	Eric Davis	.05	478	Dmitri Young	.05
113	Todd Hollandsworth	.05	235	Craig Biggio	.05	357	Greg Colbrunn	.05	479	Rod Myers RC	.05
114	Ruben Rivera	.05	236	Ray Lankford	.05	358	Moises Alou	.05	480	Wilton Guerrero	.05
115	Dennis Martinez	.05	237	Lance Johnson	.05	359	Allen Watson	.05	481	Jorge Posada	.05
116	Mariano Rivera	.10	238	Matt Williams	.05	360	Jose Canseco	.30	482	Brant Brown	.05
117	John Smoltz	.05	239	Chad Curtis	.05	361	Matt Williams	.05	483	Bubba Trammell RC	.10
118	John Mabry	.05	240	Mark Thompson	.05	362	Jeff King	.05	484	Jose Guillen	.05
119	Tom Gordon	.05	241	Jason Giambi	.40	363	Darryl Hamilton	.05	485	Scott Spiezio	.05
120	Alex Ochoa	.05	242	Barry Larkin	.05	364	Mark Clark	.05	486	Bob Abreu	.10
121	Jamey Wright	.05	243	Paul Molitor	.50	365	J.T. Snow	.05	487	Chris Holt	.05
122	Dave Nilsson	.05	244	Sammy Sosa	.65	366	Kevin Mitchell	.05	488	Deivi Cruz RC	.15
123	Bobby Bonilla	.05	245	Kevin Tapani	.05	367	Orlando Miller	.05	489	Vladimir Guerrero	.50
124	Al Leiter	.05	246	Marquis Grissom	.05	368	Rico Brogna	.05	490	Julio Santana	.05
125	Rick Aguilera	.05	247	Joe Carter	.05	369	Mike James	.05	491	Ray Montgomery	.05
126	Jeff Brantley	.05	248	Ramon Martinez	.05	370	Brad Ausmus	.05	492	Kevin Orie	.05
127	Kevin Brown	.05	249	Tony Gwynn	.65	371	Darryl Kile	.05	493	Todd Hundley (Goin' Yard)	.05
128	George Arias	.05	250	Andy Fox	.05	372	Edgardo Alfonzo	.05	494	Tim Salmon (Goin' Yard)	.05
129	Darren Oliver	.05	251	Troy O'Leary	.05	373	Julian Tavarez	.05	495	Albert Belle (Goin' Yard)	.05
130	Bill Pulsipher	.05	252	Warren Newson	.05	374	Darren Lewis	.05	496	Manny Ramirez (Goin' Yard)	.25
131	Roberto Hernandez	.05	253	Troy Percival	.05	375	Steve Karsay	.05	497	Rafael Palmeiro (Goin' Yard)	.20
132	Delino DeShields	.05	254	Jamie Moyer	.05	376	Lee Stevens	.05	498	Juan Gonzalez (Goin' Yard)	.15
133	Mark Grudzielanek	.05	255	Danny Graves	.05	377	Albie Lopez	.05	499	Ken Griffey Jr. (Goin' Yard)	.40
134	John Wetteland	.05	256	David Wells	.05	378	Orel Hershiser	.05	500	Andruw Jones (Goin' Yard)	.25
135	Carlos Baerga	.05	257	Todd Zeile	.05	379	Lee Smith	.05	501	Mike Piazza (Goin' Yard)	.40
136	Paul Sorrento	.05	258	Raul Ibanez	.05	380	Rick Helling	.05	502	Jeff Bagwell (Goin' Yard)	.25
137	Leo Gomez	.05	259	Tyler Houston	.05	381	Carlos Perez	.05	503	Bernie Williams (Goin' Yard)	.05
138	Andy Ashby	.05	260	LaTroy Hawkins	.05	382	Tony Tarasco	.05	504	Barry Bonds (Goin' Yard)	.65
139	Julio Franco	.05	261	Joey Hamilton	.05	383	Melvin Nieves	.05	505	Ken Caminiti (Goin' Yard)	.05
140	Brian Hunter	.05	262	Mike Sweeney	.05	384	Benji Gil	.05	506	Darin Erstad (Goin' Yard)	.10
141	Jermaine Dye	.05	263	Brant Brown	.05	385	Devon White	.05	507	Alex Rodriguez (Goin' Yard)	.50
142	Tony Clark	.05	264	Pat Hentgen	.05	386	Armando Benitez	.05	508	Frank Thomas (Goin' Yard)	.50
143	Ruben Sierra	.05	265	Mark Johnson	.05	387	Bill Swift	.05	509	Chipper Jones (Goin' Yard)	.40
144	Donovan Osborne	.05	266	Robb Nen	.05	388	John Smiley	.05	510	Mo Vaughn (Goin' Yard)	.05
145	Mark McLemore	.05	267	Justin Thompson	.05	389	Midre Cummings	.05	511	Mark McGwire (Goin' Yard)	.50
146	Terry Steinbach	.05	268	Ron Gant	.05	390	Tim Belcher	.05	512	Fred McGriff (Goin' Yard)	.05
147	Bob Wells	.05	269	Jeff D'Amico	.05	391	Tim Raines	.05	513	Jay Buhner (Goin' Yard)	.05
148	Chan Ho Park	.05	270	Shawn Estes	.05	392	Todd Worrell	.05	514	Jim Thome (Goin' Yard)	.20
149	Tim Salmon	.05	271	Derek Bell	.05	393	Quilvio Veras	.05	515	Gary Sheffield (Goin' Yard)	.20
150	Paul O'Neill	.05	272	Fernando Valenzuela	.05	394	Matt Lawton	.05	516	Dean Palmer (Goin' Yard)	.05
151	Cal Ripken Jr.	1.50	273	Luis Castillo	.05	395	Aaron Sele	.05	517	Henry Rodriguez (Goin' Yard)	.05
152	Wally Joyner	.05	274	Ray Montgomery	.05	396	Bip Roberts	.05	518	Andy Pettitte (Rock & Fire)	.10
153	Omar Vizquel	.05	275	Ed Sprague	.05	397	Denny Neagle	.05	519	Mike Mussina (Rock & Fire)	.10
154	Mike Mussina	.30	276	F.P. Santangelo	.05	398	Tyler Green	.05			
155	Andres Galarraga	.05	277	Todd Greene	.05	399	Hipolito Pichardo	.05			
156	Ken Griffey Jr.	.75	278	Butch Huskey	.05	400	Scott Erickson	.05			
157	Kenny Lofton	.05	279	Steve Finley	.05	401	Bobby Jones	.05			
158	Ray Durham	.05	280	Eric Davis	.05	402	Jim Edmonds	.05			
159	Hideo Nomo	.25	281	Shawn Green	.30	403	Chad Ogea	.05			
160	Ozzie Guillen	.05	282	Al Martin	.05	404	Cal Eldred	.05			
161	Roger Pavlik	.05	283	Michael Tucker	.05	405	Pat Listach	.05			
162	Manny Ramirez	.50	284	Shane Reynolds	.05	406	Todd Stottlemyre	.05			
163	Mark Lemke	.05	285	Matt Mieske	.05	407	Phil Nevin	.05			
164	Mike Stanley	.05	286	Jose Rosado	.05	408	Otis Nixon	.05			
165	Chuck Knoblauch	.05	287	Mark Langston	.05	409	Billy Ashley	.05			
166	Kimera Bartee	.05	288	Ralph Milliard	.05	410	Jimmy Key	.05			

#	Player	Price
520	Greg Maddux (Rock & Fire)	.35
521	John Smoltz (Rock & Fire)	.05
522	Hideo Nomo (Rock & Fire)	.15
523	Troy Percival (Rock & Fire)	.05
524	John Wetteland (Rock & Fire)	.05
525	Roger Clemens (Rock & Fire)	.40
526	Charles Nagy (Rock & Fire)	.05
527	Mariano Rivera (Rock & Fire)	.10
528	Tom Glavine (Rock & Fire)	.15
529	Randy Johnson (Rock & Fire)	.25
530	Jason Isringhausen (Rock & Fire)	.05
531	Alex Fernandez (Rock & Fire)	.05
532	Kevin Brown (Rock & Fire)	.05
533	Chuck Knoblauch (True Grit)	.05
534	Rusty Greer (True Grit)	.05
535	Tony Gwynn (True Grit)	.35
536	Ryan Klesko (True Grit)	.05
537	Ryne Sandberg (True Grit)	.35
538	Barry Larkin (True Grit)	.05
539	Will Clark (True Grit)	.05
540	Kenny Lofton (True Grit)	.05
541	Paul Molitor (True Grit)	.30
542	Roberto Alomar (True Grit)	.10
543	Rey Ordonez (True Grit)	.05
544	Jason Giambi (True Grit)	.05
545	Derek Jeter (True Grit)	.75
546	Cal Ripken Jr. (True Grit)	.75
547	Ivan Rodriguez (True Grit)	.25
548	Checklist (Ken Griffey Jr.)	.35
549	Checklist (Frank Thomas)	.25
550	Checklist (Mike Piazza)	.40
551a	Hideki Irabu/SP RC (English on back; factory sets/retailpacks.)	.25
551b	Hideki Irabu/SP RC (Japanese back; Hobby Reserve packs.)	.35

Premium Stock

This is an upscale version of Score's regular Series 1 1997 issue, designated for hobby sales only. The cards are basically the same as the regular issue, except for the use of gray borders on front and an embossed gold-foil "Premium Stock" logo.

	NM/M
Complete Set (330):	17.50
Common Player:	.10
Premium Stock Stars:	3X

Reserve Collection

This was a hobby-only parallel version of Score Series 2, Cards are similar to regular Series 2 Score except for the use of a textured ray-like silver-foil background on front and a Reserve Collection underprint on back. Cards are numbered with an "HR" prefix. Average insertion rate was one per 11 packs.

	NM/M
Complete Set (221):	250.00
Common Player:	1.00
Reserve Collection Stars:	8X

White Border Artist's Proofs

Specially marked Artist's Proof cards were random inserts in Series 1 retail packs. Like the regular-issue cards, they have white borders, so the gold-foil "ARTIST'S PROOF" logo on front may be overlooked. Only Series 1 (#1-330) are found in this style.

	NM/M
Complete Set (330):	150.00
Common Player:	.50
Artist's Proof Stars:	10X

Showcase

A silver metallic-foil background distinguishes the cards in this parallel set, inserted at a rate of about one per seven packs of both hobby and retail.

	NM/M
Complete Set (551):	200.00
Common Player:	.50
Showcase Stars:	3X

Hobby Reserve

This is a hobby-only parallel version of Score Series 2, similar in concept to the Series 1 Premium Stock. Cards are identical to the regular Series 2 cards except for the addition of a gold Hobby Reserve foil seal on front.

	NM/M
Complete Set (221):	35.00
Common Player:	.10
Hobby Reserve Stars:	3X

Showcase Artist's Proofs

This is a parallel of the Showcase parallel set covering all 551 cards of the base '97 Score set. The Artist's Proofs cards carry over the silver foil background of the Showcase cards on front with a rainbow-wave effect, and are marked with a round red "ARTIST'S PROOF" logo.

NM/M
Common Player: 1.00
Showcase AP Stars: 10X

All-Star Fanfest

Highlighted with red foil and featuring participants in the 1996 All-Star Game, these inserts were a 1:29 seed in special retail boxes of Series 1 Score.

NM/M
Complete Set (20): 15.00
Common Player: .30
1 Frank Thomas 1.00
2 Jeff Bagwell 1.00
3 Chuck Knoblauch .30
4 Ryne Sandberg 1.50
5 Alex Rodriguez 3.00
6 Chipper Jones 1.50
7 Jim Thome .75
8 Ken Caminiti .30
9 Albert Belle .30
10 Tony Gwynn 1.00
11 Ken Griffey Jr. 2.00
12 Andruw Jones 1.00
13 Juan Gonzalez .50
14 Brian Jordan .30
15 Ivan Rodriguez .75
16 Mike Piazza 2.00
17 Andy Pettitte .30
18 John Smoltz .30
19 John Wetteland .30
20 Mark Wohlers .30

Blast Masters

This set was inserted one per 35 Series 2 retail packs and every 23 hobby packs. The set displays the top power hitters in the game over a prismatic gold foil background. The word "Blast" is printed across the top, while "Master" is printed across the bottom, both in red. Backs are predominantly black with a color player photo at center.

NM/M
Complete Set (18): 17.50
Common Player: .25
1 Mo Vaughn .25
2 Mark McGwire 2.25
3 Juan Gonzalez .75
4 Albert Belle .25
5 Barry Bonds 3.00
6 Ken Griffey Jr. 2.00
7 Andruw Jones 1.25
8 Chipper Jones 1.50
9 Mike Piazza 2.00
10 Jeff Bagwell 1.25
11 Dante Bichette .25
12 Alex Rodriguez 2.25
13 Gary Sheffield .60
14 Ken Caminiti .25
15 Sammy Sosa 1.50
16 Vladimir Guerrero 1.25
17 Brian Jordan .25
18 Tim Salmon .25

Heart of the Order

This 36-card set was distributed in Series 2 retail and hobby packs, with cards 1-18 in retail (one per 23 packs) and cards 19-36 in hobby (one per 15). The cards are printed in a horizontal format, with some of the top hitters in the game included in the insert. Fronts are highlighted in red metallic foil. Backs have a color portrait photo and a few words about the player.

NM/M
Complete Set (36): 35.00
Complete Retail Set (1-18): 20.00
Complete Hobby Set (19-36): 15.00
Common Player: .50
1 Ivan Rodriguez 1.00
2 Will Clark .50
3 Juan Gonzalez .75
4 Frank Thomas 1.25
5 Albert Belle .50
6 Robin Ventura .50
7 Alex Rodriguez 3.00
8 Ken Griffey Jr. 2.50
9 Jay Buhner .50
10 Roberto Alomar .65
11 Rafael Palmeiro 1.00
12 Cal Ripken Jr. 4.00
13 Manny Ramirez 1.25
14 Matt Williams .50
15 Jim Thome .50
16 Derek Jeter 4.00
17 Wade Boggs 2.00
18 Bernie Williams .50
19 Chipper Jones 2.00
20 Andruw Jones 1.25
21 Ryan Klesko .50
22 Wilton Guerrero .50
23 Mike Piazza 2.50
24 Raul Mondesi .50
25 Tony Gwynn 2.00
26 Ken Caminiti .50
27 Greg Vaughn .50
28 Brian Jordan .50
29 Ron Gant .50
30 Dmitri Young .50
31 Darin Erstad .50
32 Jim Edmonds .50
33 Tim Salmon .50
34 Chuck Knoblauch .50
35 Paul Molitor 1.25
36 Todd Walker .50

Highlight Zone

Exclusive to 1997 Score Series 1 hobby packs are these Highlight Zone inserts, seeded one per every 35 packs. Within the 18-card set, card numbers 1-9 are in regular hobby packs, while numbers 10-18 are found only in premium stock packs.

NM/M
Complete Set (18): 30.00
Common Player: .60
1 Frank Thomas 1.50
2 Ken Griffey Jr. 3.00
3 Mo Vaughn .60
4 Albert Belle .60
5 Mike Piazza 3.00
6 Barry Bonds 4.50
7 Greg Maddux 2.25
8 Sammy Sosa 2.25
9 Jeff Bagwell 1.50
10 Alex Rodriguez 3.50
11 Chipper Jones 2.50
12 Brady Anderson .60
13 Ozzie Smith 2.25
14 Edgar Martinez .60
15 Cal Ripken Jr. 4.50
16 Ryan Klesko .60
17 Randy Johnson 1.50
18 Eddie Murray 1.50

Andruw Jones Goin' Yard

This special card was a blister-pack topper on Series 2 jumbo retail packs. Jones' home run swing is featured on front with a background of the distances of his blasts. Back has details on Series 2 inserts and the Stand and Deliver promotion.

NM/M
Andruw Jones 2.50

Pitcher Perfect

Seattle Mariners' star pitcher and accomplished photographer Randy Johnson makes his picks for the top talent in this 1997 Score Series 1 insert set. Fronts have player photos with a gold-foil filmstrip graphic at bottom featuring player names and a portrait of The Big Unit. Backs have additional color photos in a filmstrip design and a few words about the player.

NM/M
Complete Set (15): 6.50
Common Player: .15
1 Cal Ripken Jr. 2.00
2 Alex Rodriguez 1.25
3 Cal Ripken Jr.,
  Alex Rodriguez 1.25
4 Edgar Martinez .15
5 Ivan Rodriguez .50
6 Mark McGwire 1.25
7 Tim Salmon .15
8 Chili Davis .15
9 Joe Carter .15
10 Frank Thomas .60
11 Will Clark .15
12 Mo Vaughn .15
13 Wade Boggs .75
14 Ken Griffey Jr. 1.00
15 Randy Johnson .60

Stand & Deliver

This 24-card insert was printed on a silver foil background, with the series name and team logo in gold foil across the bottom. Cards were found in Series 2 packs at the rate of one per 71 retail, one per 41 hobby. Card numbers 21-24 (Wild Card) were the winning group in a World Series contest, allowing the first 225 collectors that mailed in those four cards to receive a gold upgrade version of the set framed in glass. The gold cards have a gold foil background and red foil highlights.

NM/M
Complete Set (24): 50.00
Common Player: .50
Gold: 4X
1 Andruw Jones 3.00
2 Greg Maddux 4.00
3 Chipper Jones 4.00
4 John Smoltz .50
5 Ken Griffey Jr. 5.00
6 Alex Rodriguez 6.00
7 Jay Buhner .50
8 Randy Johnson 3.00
9 Derek Jeter 7.50
10 Andy Pettitte .75
11 Bernie Williams .50
12 Mariano Rivera .50
13 Mike Piazza 5.00
14 Hideo Nomo 1.50
15 Raul Mondesi .50
16 Todd Hollandsworth .50
17 Manny Ramirez 3.00
18 Jim Thome 2.00
19 David Justice .50
20 Matt Williams .50
21 Juan Gonzalez 1.50
22 Jeff Bagwell 3.00
23 Cal Ripken Jr. 7.50
24 Frank Thomas 3.00

Stellar Season

These 1997 Score Series 1 inserts were seeded one per every 17 magazine packs.

NM/M
Complete Set (18): 15.00
Common Player: .50
1 Juan Gonzalez .75
2 Chuck Knoblauch .50
3 Jeff Bagwell 1.50
4 John Smoltz .50
5 Mark McGwire 3.00
6 Ken Griffey Jr. 2.50
7 Frank Thomas 1.50
8 Alex Rodriguez 3.00
9 Mike Piazza 2.50
10 Albert Belle .50
11 Roberto Alomar .60
12 Sammy Sosa 2.00
13 Mo Vaughn .50
14 Brady Anderson .50
15 Henry Rodriguez .50
16 Eric Young .50
17 Gary Sheffield .75
18 Ryan Klesko .50

The Franchise

There were two versions made for these 1997 Score Series 1 inserts - regular and The Glowing Franchise, which has glow-in-the-dark highlights. The regular version is seeded one per 72 packs; glow-in-the-dark cards are seeded one per 240 packs. Each regular card can also be found in a promo version with a large, black "SAMPLE" on front and back.

NM/M
Complete Set (9): 5.00
Common Player: .15
Glowing: 2.5X
Samples: 2.5X
1 Ken Griffey Jr. 1.00
2 John Smoltz .15
3 Cal Ripken Jr. 2.00
4 Chipper Jones .75
5 Mike Piazza 1.00
6 Albert Belle .15
7 Frank Thomas .60
8 Sammy Sosa .75
9 Roberto Alomar .30

Titanic Taters

Some of the game's most powerful hitters are featured on these Series 1 inserts, found on average of one per 35 retail packs.

NM/M
Complete Set (18): 25.00
Common Player: .35
1 Mark McGwire 4.00
2 Mike Piazza 3.50
3 Ken Griffey Jr. 3.50
4 Juan Gonzalez 1.00
5 Frank Thomas 1.50
6 Albert Belle .35
7 Sammy Sosa 2.50
8 Jeff Bagwell 1.50
9 Todd Hundley .35
10 Ryan Klesko .35
11 Brady Anderson .35
12 Mo Vaughn .35
13 Jay Buhner .35
14 Chipper Jones 3.00
15 Barry Bonds 6.00
16 Gary Sheffield .75
17 Alex Rodriguez 4.00
18 Cecil Fielder .35

Team Collection

Team sets consisting of 15 players each were produced for 10 different teams. Each card is similar in design to the regular 1997 Score set except for a special foil stamping at the bottom of the card that corresponds with team colors. In a parallel "Platinum" version, seeded one per six packs, the background and team foil on front are replaced with silver prismatic foil. A top of the line parallel set, "Premier" utilizes gold foil highlights on fronts and is found one per 31 packs. Team Collection was sold in five-card, single-team packs with a suggested retail price of about $1.29. It was reported that 100 cases of each team were issued.

NM/M
Complete Set (150): 30.00
Common Player: .10
Platinums: 4X
Premiers: 15X
Braves Wax Box: 7.50
Orioles Wax Box: 6.00
Red Sox Wax Box: 6.00
White Sox Wax Box: 6.00
Indians Wax Box: 6.00
Rockies Wax Box: 5.00
Dodgers Wax Box: 6.00
Yankees Wax Box: 7.50
Mariners Wax Box: 7.50
Rangers Wax Box: 5.00
Atlanta Braves 5.00
1 Ryan Klesko .10
2 David Justice .10
3 Terry Pendleton .10
4 Tom Glavine .35
5 Javier Lopez .10
6 John Smoltz .10
7 Jermaine Dye .10
8 Mark Lemke .10
9 Fred McGriff .10
10 Chipper Jones 1.50
11 Terrell Wade .10
12 Greg Maddux 1.50
13 Mark Wohlers .10
14 Marquis Grissom .10
15 Andruw Jones 1.00
Baltimore Orioles 4.50
1 Rafael Palmeiro .75
2 Eddie Murray 1.00
3 Roberto Alomar .40
4 Rocky Coppinger .10
5 Brady Anderson .10
6 Bobby Bonilla .10
7 Cal Ripken Jr. 2.50
8 Mike Mussina .45
9 Nerio Rodriguez .10
10 Randy Myers .10
11 B.J. Surhoff .10
12 Jeffrey Hammonds .10
13 Chris Hoiles .10
14 Jimmy Haynes .10
15 David Wells .10
Boston Red Sox 3.00
1 Wil Cordero .10
2 Mo Vaughn .10
3 John Valentin .10
4 Reggie Jefferson .10
5 Tom Gordon .10
6 Mike Stanley .10
7 Jose Canseco .45
8 Roger Clemens 1.75
9 Darren Bragg .10
10 Jeff Frye .10
11 Jeff Suppan .10
12 Mike Greenwell .10
13 Arquimedez Pozo .10
14 Tim Naehring .10
15 Troy O'Leary .10
Chicago White Sox 2.25
1 Frank Thomas 1.00
2 James Baldwin .10
3 Danny Tartabull .10
4 Jeff Darwin .10
5 Harold Baines .10
6 Roberto Hernandez .10
7 Ray Durham .10
8 Robin Ventura .10
9 Wilson Alvarez .10
10 Lyle Mouton .10
11 Alex Fernandez .10
12 Ron Karkovice .10
13 Kevin Tapani .10
14 Tony Phillips .10
15 Mike Cameron .10
Cleveland Indians 2.25
1 Albert Belle .10
2 Jack McDowell .10
3 Jim Thome .75
4 Dennis Martinez .10
5 Julio Franco .10
6 Omar Vizquel .10
7 Kenny Lofton .10
8 Manny Ramirez 1.00
9 Sandy Alomar Jr. .10
10 Charles Nagy .10
11 Kevin Seitzer .10
12 Mark Carreon .10
13 Jeff Kent .10
14 Danny Graves .10
15 Brian Giles .10
Colorado Rockies 1.75
1 Dante Bichette .10
2 Kevin Ritz .10
3 Walt Weiss .10
4 Ellis Burks .10
5 Jamey Wright .10
6 Andres Galarraga .10
7 Eric Young .10
8 Larry Walker .10
9 Vinny Castilla .10
10 Quinton McCracken .10
11 Armando Reynoso .10
12 Jayhawk Owens .10
13 Mark Thompson .10
14 John Burke .10
15 Bruce Ruffin .10
Los Angeles Dodgers 4.00
1 Ismael Valdez .10
2 Mike Piazza 2.00
3 Todd Hollandsworth .10
4 Delino DeShields .10
5 Chan Ho Park .10
6 Roger Cedeno .10
7 Raul Mondesi .10
8 Darren Dreifort .10
9 Jim Bruske .10
10 Greg Gagne .10
11 Chad Curtis .10
12 Ramon Martinez .10
13 Brett Butler .10
14 Eric Karros .10
15 Hideo Nomo .50
New York Yankees 4.50
1 Bernie Williams .10
2 Cecil Fielder .10
3 Derek Jeter 2.50
4 Darryl Strawberry .10
5 Andy Pettitte .20
6 Ruben Rivera .10
7 Mariano Rivera .15
8 John Wetteland .10
9 Paul O'Neill .10
10 Wade Boggs 1.50
11 Dwight Gooden .10
12 David Cone .10
13 Tino Martinez .10
14 Kenny Rogers .10
15 Andy Fox .10
Seattle Mariners 5.00
1 Chris Bosio .10
2 Edgar Martinez .10
3 Alex Rodriguez 2.25
4 Paul Sorrento .10
5 Bob Wells .10
6 Ken Griffey Jr. 2.00
7 Jay Buhner .10
8 Dan Wilson .10
9 Randy Johnson 1.00
10 Joey Cora .10
11 Mark Whiten .10
12 Rich Amaral .10
13 Raul Ibanez .10
14 Jamie Moyer .10
15 Makoto Suzuki .10
Texas Rangers 2.25
1 Mickey Tettleton .10
2 Will Clark .10
3 Ken Hill .10
4 Rusty Greer .10
5 Kevin Elster .10
6 Darren Oliver .10
7 Mark McLemore .10
8 Roger Pavlik .10
9 Dean Palmer .10
10 Bobby Witt .10
11 Juan Gonzalez .75
12 Ivan Rodriguez .50
13 Darryl Hamilton .10
14 John Burkett .10
15 Warren Newson .10

Team Collection Platinum Team

Team sets consisting of 15 players each were produced for 10 different teams. Each card is similar in design to the regular 1997 Score set except for a special foil stamping at the bottom of the card that corresponds with team colors. In a parallel "Platinum" version, seeded one per six packs, the background and team foil on front are replaced with silver prismatic foil. Backs are overprinted in gold script, "Platinum Team." Team Collection was sold in five-card, single-team packs with a suggested retail price of about $1.29. It was reported that 100 cases of each team were issued.

	NM/M
Common Player:	2.00
Platinum Stars:	3X

Team Collection Premier Club

Team sets consisting of 15 players each were produced for 10 different teams. Each card is similar in design to the regular 1997 Score set except for a special foil stamping at the bottom of the card that corresponds with team colors. In a top of the line parallel "Premier Club" version, seeded one per 31 packs, the background and team foil on front are replaced with gold prismatic foil, and backs are overprinted "Premier Club" in gold script. Team Collection was sold in five-card, single-team packs with a suggested retail price of about $1.29. It was reported that 100 cases of each team were issued.

	NM/M
Common Player:	5.00
Premier Club Stars:	15X

1998 Score Samples

Half a dozen top stars were picked to introduce 1998 Score in this series of promo cards. Cards are virtually identical to the issued version except for the large black overprinted "SAMPLE" on back and the use of zeroes to replace 1997 stats.

	NM/M
Complete Set (6):	7.50
Common Player:	1.00
10 Alex Rodriguez	1.50
24 Mike Piazza	1.50
34 Ken Griffey Jr.	1.50
43 Cal Ripken Jr.	2.00
51 Chipper Jones	1.50
60 Carlos Delgado	1.00

1998 Score

The cards in the 270-card base set feature a color photo inside a black and white border. The player's

name is printed in the left border. The entire base set is paralleled in the silver-foil Showcase Series (1:5). The Artist's Proof partial parallel gives a prismatic foil treatment to 165 base cards and was seeded 1:23. Inserts included All-Stars, Complete Players and Epix.

	NM/M
Complete Set (270):	12.00
Common Player:	.05
Showcases:	3X
Artist's Proofs:	6X
Pack (10):	.75
Wax Box (36):	15.00
All-Star Edition Box (36/10):	10.00
Jumbo Pack (20):	1.00
Jumbo Box (24):	15.00
1 Andruw Jones	.50
2 Dan Wilson	.05
3 Hideo Nomo	.30
4 Chuck Carr	.05
5 Barry Bonds	1.50
6 Jack McDowell	.05
7 Albert Belle	.05
8 Francisco Cordova	.05
9 Greg Maddux	.65
10 Alex Rodriguez	1.00
11 Steve Avery	.05
12 Chuck McElroy	.05
13 Larry Walker	.05
14 Hideki Irabu	.05
15 Roberto Alomar	.20
16 Neifi Perez	.05
17 Jim Thome	.40
18 Rickey Henderson	.50
19 Andres Galarraga	.05
20 Jeff Fassero	.05
21 Kevin Young	.05
22 Derek Jeter	1.50
23 Andy Benes	.05
24 Mike Piazza	.05
25 Todd Stottlemyre	.05
26 Michael Tucker	.05
27 Denny Neagle	.05
28 Javier Lopez	.05
29 Aaron Sele	.05
30 Ryan Klesko	.05
31 Dennis Eckersley	.40
32 Quinton McCracken	.05
33 Brian Anderson	.05
34 Ken Griffey Jr.	.75
35 Shawn Estes	.05
36 Tim Wakefield	.05
37 Jimmy Key	.05
38 Jeff Bagwell	.05
39 Edgardo Alfonzo	.05
40 Mike Cameron	.05
41 Mark McGwire	1.00
42 Tino Martinez	.05
43 Cal Ripken Jr.	1.50
44 Curtis Goodwin	.05
45 Bobby Ayala	.05
46 Sandy Alomar Jr.	.05
47 Bobby Jones	.05
48 Omar Vizquel	.05
49 Roger Clemens	.70
50 Tony Gwynn	.75
51 Chipper Jones	.75
52 Ron Coomer	.05
53 Dmitri Young	.05
54 Brian Giles	.05
55 Steve Finley	.05
56 David Cone	.05
57 Andy Pettitte	.20
58 Wilton Guerrero	.05
59 Deion Sanders	.30
60 Carlos Delgado	.30
61 Jason Giambi	.30
62 Ozzie Guillen	.05
63 Jay Bell	.05
64 Barry Larkin	.05
65 Sammy Sosa	.65
66 Bernie Williams	.05
67 Terry Steinbach	.05
68 Scott Rolen	.40
69 Melvin Nieves	.05
70 Craig Biggio	.05
71 Todd Greene	.05
72 Greg Gagne	.05
73 Shigetosi Hasegawa	.05
74 Mark McLemore	.05
75 Darren Bragg	.05
76 Brett Butler	.05
77 Ron Gant	.05
78 Mike Difelice	.05

79 Charles Nagy	.05
80 Scott Hatteberg	.05
81 Brady Anderson	.05
82 Jay Buhner	.05
83 Todd Hollandsworth	.05
84 Geronimo Berroa	.05
85 Jeff Suppan	.05
86 Pedro Martinez	.50
87 Roger Cedeno	.05
88 Ivan Rodriguez	.40
89 Jaime Navarro	.05
90 Chris Hoiles	.05
91 Nomar Garciaparra	.65
92 Rafael Palmeiro	.40
93 Darin Erstad	.15
94 Kenny Lofton	.05
95 Mike Timlin	.05
96 Chris Clemons	.05
97 Vinny Castilla	.05
98 Charlie Hayes	.05
99 Lyle Mouton	.05
100 Jason Dickson	.05
101 Justin Thompson	.05
102 Pat Kelly	.05
103 Chan Ho Park	.05
104 Ray Lankford	.05
105 Frank Thomas	.50
106 Jermaine Allensworth	.05
107 Doug Drabek	.05
108 Todd Hundley	.05
109 Carl Everett	.05
110 Edgar Martinez	.05
111 Robin Ventura	.05
112 John Wetteland	.05
113 Mariano Rivera	.10
114 Jose Rosado	.05
115 Ken Caminiti	.05
116 Paul O'Neill	.05
117 Tim Salmon	.05
118 Eduardo Perez	.05
119 Mike Jackson	.05
120 John Smoltz	.05
121 Brant Brown	.05
122 John Mabry	.05
123 Chuck Knoblauch	.05
124 Reggie Sanders	.05
125 Ken Hill	.05
126 Mike Mussina	.25
127 Chad Curtis	.05
128 Todd Worrell	.05
129 Chris Widger	.05
130 Damon Mashore	.05
131 Kevin Brown	.05
132 Bip Roberts	.05
133 Tim Naehring	.05
134 Dave Martinez	.05
135 Jeff Blauser	.05
136 David Justice	.05
137 Dave Hollins	.05
138 Pat Hentgen	.05
139 Darren Daulton	.05
140 Ramon Martinez	.05
141 Raul Casanova	.05
142 Tom Glavine	.30
143 J.T. Snow	.05
144 Tony Graffanino	.05
145 Randy Johnson	.50
146 Orlando Merced	.05
147 Jeff Juden	.05
148 Darryl Kile	.05
149 Ray Durham	.05
150 Alex Fernandez	.05
151 Joey Cora	.05
152 Royce Clayton	.05
153 Randy Myers	.05
154 Charles Johnson	.05
155 Alan Benes	.05
156 Mike Bordick	.05
157 Heathcliff Slocumb	.05
158 Roger Bailey	.05
159 Reggie Jefferson	.05
160 Ricky Bottalico	.05
161 Scott Erickson	.05
162 Matt Williams	.05
163 Robb Nen	.05
164 Matt Stairs	.05
165 Ismael Valdes	.05
166 Lee Stevens	.05
167 Gary DiSarcina	.05
168 Brad Radke	.05
169 Mike Lansing	.05
170 Armando Benitez	.05
171 Mike James	.05
172 Russ Davis	.05
173 Lance Johnson	.05
174 Joey Hamilton	.05
175 John Valentin	.05
176 David Segui	.05
177 David Wells	.05
178 Delino DeShields	.05
179 Eric Karros	.05
180 Jim Leyritz	.05
181 Raul Mondesi	.05
182 Travis Fryman	.05
183 Todd Zeile	.05
184 Brian Jordan	.05
185 Rey Ordonez	.05
186 Jim Edmonds	.05
187 Terrell Wade	.05
188 Marquis Grissom	.05
189 Chris Snopek	.05
190 Shane Reynolds	.05
191 Jeff Frye	.05
192 Paul Sorrento	.05
193 James Baldwin	.05
194 Brian McRae	.05
195 Fred McGriff	.05
196 Troy Percival	.05

197 Rich Amaral	.05
198 Juan Guzman	.05
199 Cecil Fielder	.05
200 Willie Blair	.05
201 Chili Davis	.05
202 Gary Gaetti	.05
203 B.J. Surhoff	.05
204 Steve Cooke	.05
205 Chuck Finley	.05
206 Jeff Kent	.05
207 Ben McDonald	.05
208 Jeffrey Hammonds	.05
209 Tom Goodwin	.05
210 Billy Ashley	.05
211 Wil Cordero	.05
212 Shawon Dunston	.05
213 Tony Phillips	.05
214 Jamie Moyer	.05
215 John Jaha	.05
216 Troy O'Leary	.05
217 Brad Ausmus	.05
218 Garret Anderson	.05
219 Wilson Alvarez	.05
220 Kent Mercker	.05
221 Wade Boggs	.65
222 Mark Wohlers	.05
223 Kevin Appier	.05
224 Tony Fernandez	.05
225 Ugueth Urbina	.05
226 Gregg Jefferies	.05
227 Mo Vaughn	.05
228 Arthur Rhodes	.05
229 Jorge Fabregas	.05
230 Mark Gardner	.05
231 Shane Mack	.05
232 Jorge Posada	.05
233 Jose Cruz Jr.	.05
234 Paul Konerko	.15
235 Derek Lee	.30
236 Steve Woodard RC	.15
237 Todd Dunwoody	.05
238 Fernando Tatis	.05
239 Jacob Cruz	.05
240 Pokey Reese RC	.25
241 Mark Kotsay	.05
242 Matt Morris	.05
243 Antone Williamson RC	.05
244 Ben Grieve	.05
245 Ryan McGuire	.05
246 Lou Collier RC	.05
247 Shannon Stewart	.05
248 Brett Tomko RC	.10
249 Bobby Estalella	.05
250 Livan Hernandez RC	.15
251 Todd Helton	.40
252 Jaret Wright	.05
253 Darryl Hamilton (Interleague Moments)	.05
254 Stan Javier (Interleague Moments)	.05
255 Glenallen Hill (Interleague Moments)	.05
256 Mark Gardner (Interleague Moments)	.05
257 Cal Ripken Jr. (Interleague Moments)	.75
258 Mike Mussina (Interleague Moments)	.15
259 Mike Piazza (Interleague Moments)	.45
260 Sammy Sosa (Interleague Moments)	.35
261 Todd Hundley (Interleague Moments)	.05
262 Eric Karros (Interleague Moments)	.05
263 Denny Neagle (Interleague Moments)	.05
264 Jeromy Burnitz (Interleague Moments)	.05
265 Greg Maddux (Interleague Moments)	.35
266 Tony Clark (Interleague Moments)	.05
267 Vladimir Guerrero (Interleague Moments)	.25
268 Checklist	.05
269 Checklist	.05
270 Checklist	.05

Artist's Proofs

This partial parallel reprinted 160 of the 270 cards in Score Baseball on a foil background with an Artist's Proof logo on the front. The cards were renumbered within the

160-card set and inserted one per 35 packs. Cards have a "PP" prefix to the number on back.

	NM/M
Complete Set (160):	125.00
Common Player:	.50
Inserted 1:35	
1 Andruw Jones	1.25
2 Dan Wilson	.50
3 Hideo Nomo	.75
4 Neifi Perez	.50
5 Jim Thome	1.00
7 Jeff Fassero	.50
7 Derek Jeter	4.00
8 Andy Benes	.50
9 Michael Tucker	.50
10 Ryan Klesko	.50
11 Dennis Eckersley	1.00
12 Jimmy Key	.50
13 Edgardo Alfonzo	.50
14 Mike Cameron	.50
15 Omar Vizquel	.50
16 Ron Coomer	.50
17 Dmitri Young	.50
18 Brian Giles	.50
19 Steve Finley	.50
20 Andy Pettitte	.75
21 Wilton Guerrero	.50
22 Deion Sanders	.50
23 Carlos Delgado	.75
24 Jason Giambi	.75
25 David Cone	.50
26 Jay Bell	.50
27 Sammy Sosa	2.00
28 Barry Larkin	.50
29 Scott Rolen	1.00
30 Todd Greene	.50
31 Bernie Williams	.50
32 Brett Butler	.50
33 Ron Gant	.50
34 Brady Anderson	.50
35 Craig Biggio	.50
36 Charles Nagy	.50
37 Jay Buhner	.50
38 Geronimo Berroa	.50
39 Jeff Suppan	.50
40 Rafael Palmeiro	1.00
41 Darin Erstad	.65
42 Mike Timlin	.50
43 Vinny Castilla	.50
44 Carl Everett	.50
45 Robin Ventura	.50
46 John Wetteland	.50
47 Paul O'Neill	.50
48 Tim Salmon	.50
49 Mike Jackson	.50
50 John Smoltz	.50
51 Brant Brown	.50
52 Reggie Sanders	.50
53 Ken Hill	.50
54 Todd Worrell	.50
55 Bip Roberts	.50
56 Tim Naehring	.50
57 Darren Daulton	.50
58 Ramon Martinez	.50
59 Raul Casanova	.50
60 J.T. Snow	.50
61 Jeff Juden	.50
62 Royce Clayton	.50
63 Charles Johnson	.50
64 Alan Benes	.50
65 Reggie Jefferson	.50
66 Ricky Bottalico	.50
67 Scott Erickson	.50
68 Matt Williams	.50
69 Robb Nen	.50
70 Matt Stairs	.50
71 Ismael Valdes	.50
72 Brad Radke	.50
73 Armando Benitez	.50
74 Russ Davis	.50
75 Lance Johnson	.50
76 Joey Hamilton	.50
77 John Valentin	.50
78 David Segui	.50
79 David Wells	.50
80 Eric Karros	.50
81 Raul Mondesi	.50
82 Travis Fryman	.50
83 Todd Zeile	.50
84 Brian Jordan	.50
85 Rey Ordonez	.50
86 Jim Edmonds	.50
87 Marquis Grissom	.50
88 Shane Reynolds	.50
89 Paul Sorrento	.50
90 Brian McRae	.50
91 Fred McGriff	.50
92 Troy Percival	.50
93 Juan Guzman	.50
94 Cecil Fielder	.50
95 Chili Davis	.50
96 B.J. Surhoff	.50
97 Chuck Finley	.50
98 Jeff Kent	.50
99 Ben McDonald	.50
100 Jeffrey Hammonds	.50
101 Tom Goodwin	.50
102 Wil Cordero	.50
103 Tony Phillips	.50
104 John Jaha	.50
105 Garret Anderson	.50
106 Wilson Alvarez	.50
107 Wade Boggs	2.00
108 Mark Wohlers	.50
109 Kevin Appier	.50
110 Mo Vaughn	.50

111 Ray Durham	.50
112 Alex Fernandez	.50
113 Barry Bonds	4.00
114 Albert Belle	.50
115 Greg Maddux	2.00
116 Alex Rodriguez	3.00
117 Larry Walker	.50
118 Roberto Alomar	.60
119 Andres Galarraga	.50
120 Mike Piazza	2.50
121 Denny Neagle	.50
122 Javier Lopez	.50
123 Ken Griffey Jr.	2.50
124 Shawn Estes	.50
125 Jeff Bagwell	1.25
126 Mark McGwire	3.00
127 Tino Martinez	.50
128 Cal Ripken Jr.	4.00
129 Sandy Alomar Jr.	.50
130 Bobby Jones	.50
131 Roger Clemens	2.25
132 Tony Gwynn	2.00
133 Chipper Jones	2.00
134 Orlando Merced	.50
135 Todd Stottlemyre	.50
136 Delino DeShields	.50
137 Pedro Martinez	1.25
138 Ivan Rodriguez	1.00
139 Nomar Garciaparra	2.00
140 Kenny Lofton	.50
141 Jason Dickson	.50
142 Justin Thompson	.50
143 Ray Lankford	.50
144 Frank Thomas	1.25
145 Todd Hundley	.50
146 Edgar Martinez	.50
147 Mariano Rivera	.50
148 Jose Rosado	.50
149 Ken Caminiti	.50
150 Chuck Knoblauch	.50
151 Mike Mussina	.65
152 Kevin Brown	.50
153 Jeff Blauser	.50
154 David Justice	.50
155 Pat Hentgen	.50
156 Tom Glavine	.65
157 Randy Johnson	1.25
158 Darryl Kile	.50
159 Joey Cora	.50
160 Randy Myers	.50

Showcase Series

This partial parallel reprinted 160 of the 270 cards in Score Baseball on silver foil. They were marked on the back and renumbered within the 160-card set. Showcase parallels were inserted one per seven packs. All Showcase Series cards except #1 have a "PP" prefix to the number.

	NM/M
Complete Set (160):	40.00
Common Player:	.25
Inserted 1:7	
1 Andruw Jones	.75
2 Dan Wilson	.25
3 Hideo Nomo	.40
4 Neifi Perez	.25
5 Jim Thome	.60
6 Jeff Fassero	.25
7 Derek Jeter	2.00
8 Andy Benes	.25
9 Michael Tucker	.25
10 Ryan Klesko	.25
11 Dennis Eckersley	.65
12 Jimmy Key	.25
13 Edgardo Alfonzo	.25
14 Mike Cameron	.25
15 Omar Vizquel	.25
16 Ron Coomer	.25
17 Dmitri Young	.25
18 Brian Giles	.25
19 Steve Finley	.25
20 Andy Pettitte	.40
21 Wilton Guerrero	.25
22 Deion Sanders	.25
23 Carlos Delgado	.50
24 Jason Giambi	.25
25 David Cone	.25
26 Jay Bell	.25
27 Sammy Sosa	1.00
28 Barry Larkin	.25
29 Scott Rolen	.60
30 Todd Greene	.25
31 Bernie Williams	.25
32 Brett Butler	.25

33	Ron Gant	.25
34	Brady Anderson	.25
35	Craig Biggio	.25
36	Charles Nagy	.25
37	Jay Buhner	.25
38	Geronimo Berroa	.25
39	Jeff Suppan	.25
40	Rafael Palmeiro	.65
41	Darin Erstad	.35
42	Mike Timlin	.25
43	Vinny Castilla	.25
44	Carl Everett	.25
45	Robin Ventura	.25
46	John Wetteland	.25
47	Paul O'Neill	.25
48	Tim Salmon	.25
49	Mike Jackson	.25
50	John Smoltz	.25
51	Brant Brown	.25
52	Reggie Sanders	.25
53	Ken Hill	.25
54	Todd Worrell	.25
55	Bip Roberts	.25
56	Tim Naehring	.25
57	Darren Daulton	.25
58	Ramon Martinez	.25
59	Raul Casanova	.25
60	J.T. Snow	.25
61	Jeff Juden	.25
62	Royce Clayton	.25
63	Charles Johnson	.25
64	Alan Benes	.25
65	Reggie Jefferson	.25
66	Ricky Bottalico	.25
67	Scott Erickson	.25
68	Matt Williams	.25
69	Robb Nen	.25
70	Matt Stairs	.25
71	Ismael Valdes	.25
72	Brad Radke	.25
73	Armando Benitez	.25
74	Russ Davis	.25
75	Lance Johnson	.25
76	Joey Hamilton	.25
77	John Valentin	.25
78	David Segui	.25
79	David Wells	.25
80	Eric Karros	.25
81	Raul Mondesi	.25
82	Travis Fryman	.25
83	Todd Zeile	.25
84	Brian Jordan	.25
85	Rey Ordonez	.25
86	Jim Edmonds	.25
87	Marquis Grissom	.25
88	Shane Reynolds	.25
89	Paul Sorrento	.25
90	Brian McRae	.25
91	Fred McGriff	.25
92	Troy Percival	.25
93	Juan Guzman	.25
94	Cecil Fielder	.25
95	Chili Davis	.25
96	B.J. Surhoff	.25
97	Chuck Finley	.25
98	Jeff Kent	.25
99	Ben McDonald	.25
100	Jeffrey Hammonds	.25
101	Tom Goodwin	.25
102	Wil Cordero	.25
103	Tony Phillips	.25
104	John Jaha	.25
105	Garret Anderson	.25
106	Wilson Alvarez	.25
107	Wade Boggs	1.00
108	Mark Wohlers	.25
109	Kevin Appier	.25
110	Mo Vaughn	.25
111	Ray Durham	.25
112	Alex Fernandez	.25
113	Barry Bonds	2.00
114	Albert Belle	.25
115	Greg Maddux	1.00
116	Alex Rodriguez	1.50
117	Larry Walker	.25
118	Roberto Alomar	.35
119	Andres Galarraga	.25
120	Mike Piazza	1.25
121	Denny Neagle	.25
122	Javier Lopez	.25
123	Ken Griffey Jr.	1.25
124	Shawn Estes	.25
125	Jeff Bagwell	.75
126	Mark McGwire	1.50
127	Tino Martinez	.25
128	Cal Ripken Jr.	2.00
129	Sandy Alomar Jr.	.25
130	Bobby Jones	.25
131	Roger Clemens	1.00
132	Tony Gwynn	1.00
133	Chipper Jones	1.00
134	Orlando Merced	.25
135	Todd Stottlemyre	.25
136	Delino DeShields	.25
137	Pedro Martinez	.75
138	Ivan Rodriguez	.65
139	Nomar Garciaparra	1.00
140	Kenny Lofton	.25
141	Jason Dickson	.25
142	Justin Thompson	.25
143	Ray Lankford	.25
144	Frank Thomas	.75
145	Todd Hundley	.25
146	Edgar Martinez	.25
147	Mariano Rivera	.25
148	Jose Rosado	.25
149	Ken Caminiti	.25
150	Chuck Knoblauch	.25

151	Mike Mussina	.40
152	Kevin Brown	.25
153	Jeff Blauser	.25
154	David Justice	.25
155	Pat Hentgen	.25
156	Tom Glavine	.40
157	Randy Johnson	.75
158	Darryl Kile	.25
159	Joey Cora	.25
160	Randy Myers	.25

All Score Team

For its 10th anniversary Score selected an all-star team and issued this insert set. Cards have player action photos on a silver-foil background with an anniversary logo at bottom. Backs have a portrait photo and a career summary. The cards were inserted one per 35 packs.

		NM/M
Complete Set (20):		15.00
Common Player:		.25
Inserted 1:35		
1	Mike Piazza	1.50
2	Ivan Rodriguez	.65
3	Frank Thomas	.75
4	Mark McGwire	2.00
5	Ryne Sandberg	1.00
6	Roberto Alomar	.35
7	Cal Ripken Jr.	2.50
8	Barry Larkin	.25
9	Paul Molitor	.75
10	Travis Fryman	.25
11	Kirby Puckett	1.00
12	Tony Gwynn	1.00
13	Ken Griffey Jr.	1.50
14	Juan Gonzalez	.45
15	Barry Bonds	2.50
16	Andruw Jones	.75
17	Roger Clemens	1.25
18	Randy Johnson	.75
19	Greg Maddux	1.00
20	Dennis Eckersley	.65

All Score Team - Gold

The purpose for which this variation of the regular All Score Team insert was created will likely remain unknown. A small number of the Gold version have turned up in the hobby market since Score's bankruptcy in mid-1998. This apparently premium version differs from the issued silver version only in its use of gold metallic foil background on front.

		NM/M
Complete Set (20):		115.00
Common Player:		2.00
1	Mike Piazza	10.00
2	Ivan Rodriguez	5.00
3	Frank Thomas	6.00
4	Mark McGwire	12.00
5	Ryne Sandberg	7.50
6	Roberto Alomar	2.50
7	Cal Ripken Jr.	15.00
8	Barry Larkin	2.00
9	Paul Molitor	6.00
10	Travis Fryman	2.00
11	Kirby Puckett	7.50
12	Tony Gwynn	7.50
13	Ken Griffey Jr.	10.00
14	Juan Gonzalez	3.00
15	Barry Bonds	15.00
16	Andruw Jones	6.00
17	Roger Clemens	8.00
18	Randy Johnson	6.00
19	Greg Maddux	7.50
20	Dennis Eckersley	5.00

All Score Team Andruw Jones Autograph

This special version of Jones' All Score Team was a prize in a random hobby-shop drawing. Instead of the silver foil seen on regular All Score Team inserts, this version has a gold-foil background and an "AUTHENTIC SIGNATURE" notation at right-center. Only 500 of the cards were produced.

		NM/M
16	Andruw Jones	25.00

Complete Players

Complete Players is a 30-card insert featuring 10 players who can do it all. Each player had three cards displaying their variety of skills. The cards feature holographic foil highlights on fronts. Backs form a three-piece vertical picture of the player. The cards were inserted about one per 23 packs. Cards can be found with either gold or silver holographic foil. The gold version was found in packs of Score Team Collection at a 1:11 pack ratio. Because of these looser odds, the gold cards are valued lower than the silver.

		NM/M
Complete Set (30):		75.00
Common Player:		1.00
Inserted 1:23		
Golds: 75 Percent		
1A-1C	Ken Griffey Jr.	3.25
2A-2C	Mark McGwire	3.75
3A-3C	Derek Jeter	5.00
4A-4C	Cal Ripken Jr.	5.00
5A-5C	Mike Piazza	3.25
6A-6C	Darin Erstad	1.00
7A-7C	Frank Thomas	2.00
8A-8C	Andruw Jones	2.00
9A-9C	Nomar Garciaparra	3.00
10A-10C	Manny Ramirez	2.00

Epix

Epix is a cross-brand insert, with 24 cards appearing in Score. The cards are printed on 20-point stock with holographic foil technology. The cards honor the top Play, Game, Season and Moment in a player's career and come in Orange, Purple and Emerald versions. Game cards were inserted 1:141, Plays 1:171, Seasons 1:437 and Moments 1:757.

		NM/M
Common Card:		.50
Purple:		2X
Emeralds:		3X
1	Ken Griffey Jr./P	2.50
2	Juan Gonzalez/P	.75
3	Jeff Bagwell/P	1.25

4	Ivan Rodriguez/P	1.00
5	Nomar Garciaparra/P	2.00
6	Ryne Sandberg/P	1.50
7	Frank Thomas/G	1.25
8	Derek Jeter/G	3.50
9	Tony Gwynn/G	2.00
10	Albert Belle/G	.50
11	Scott Rolen/G	1.00
12	Barry Larkin/G	.50
13	Alex Rodriguez/S	6.00
14	Cal Ripken Jr./S	7.50
15	Chipper Jones/S	4.00
16	Roger Clemens/S	4.50
17	Mo Vaughn/S	1.50
18	Mark McGwire/S	6.00
19	Mike Piazza/M	8.00
20	Andruw Jones/M	1.50
21	Greg Maddux/M	6.00
22	Barry Bonds/M	12.00
23	Paul Molitor/M	4.00
24	Eddie Murray/M	4.00

First Pitch

These inserts were a 1:11 pack find in Score's All-Star edition. Fronts have portrait photos printed in the center of textured foil background of red and silver. The basic design is repeated on back, with career highlights and team logo instead of a photo.

		NM/M
Complete Set (20):		25.00
Common Player:		.50
Inserted 1:11 All-Star Edition.		
1	Ken Griffey Jr.	2.00
2	Frank Thomas	1.25
3	Alex Rodriguez	2.50
4	Cal Ripken Jr.	3.25
5	Chipper Jones	1.50
6	Juan Gonzalez	.75
7	Derek Jeter	3.25
8	Mike Piazza	2.00
9	Andruw Jones	1.25
10	Nomar Garciaparra	1.50
11	Barry Bonds	3.25
12	Jeff Bagwell	1.25
13	Scott Rolen	.50
14	Hideo Nomo	.75
15	Roger Clemens	1.75
16	Mark McGwire	2.50
17	Greg Maddux	1.50
18	Albert Belle	.50
19	Ivan Rodriguez	1.00
20	Mo Vaughn	.50

Andruw Jones Icon Order Card

This special card was the pack-topper on retail 27-card blister packs of 1998 Score. The front is identical to the regular Jones card in the set, but the back carries an ad for Pinnacle's Icon card display mail-in offer.

		NM/M
	Andruw Jones	2.50

Loaded Lineup

This insert series was packaged on average of one card per 45 packs of Score's All-Star edition. Fronts have action photos printed on a copper and silver textured metallic-foil background. Backs have

a portrait photo, career highlights, the Loaded Lineup batting order and stats for the player's best season. Cards have an "LL" prefix to their number.

		NM/M
Complete Set (10):		20.00
Common Player:		.50
Inserted 1:45 All-Star Edition.		
LL1	Chuck Knoblauch	.50
LL2	Tony Gwynn	2.25
LL3	Frank Thomas	1.50
LL4	Ken Griffey Jr.	3.00
LL5	Mike Piazza	3.00
LL6	Barry Bonds	4.50
LL7	Cal Ripken Jr.	4.50
LL8	Paul Molitor	1.50
LL9	Nomar Garciaparra	2.25
LL10	Greg Maddux	2.25

New Season

Found only in Score All-Star Edition, at an average rate of one per 23 packs, this insert series mixes veteran stars with hot young players. Fronts have a large portrait photo. Horizontal backs have an action photo.

		NM/M
Complete Set (15):		18.00
Common Player:		.50
Inserted 1:23 All-Star Edition.		
NS1	Kenny Lofton	.50
NS2	Nomar Garciaparra	2.00
NS3	Todd Helton	1.00
NS4	Miguel Tejada	.75
NS5	Jaret Wright	.50
NS6	Alex Rodriguez	3.00
NS7	Vladimir Guerrero	1.25
NS8	Ken Griffey Jr.	2.50
NS9	Ben Grieve	.50
NS10	Travis Lee	.50
NS11	Jose Cruz Jr.	.50
NS12	Paul Konerko	.75
NS13	Frank Thomas	1.25
NS14	Chipper Jones	2.00
NS15	Cal Ripken Jr.	4.00

1998 Score Rookie & Traded

Score Rookie/Traded consists of a 270-card base set. The base cards have a white and gray border with the player's name on the left. Cards are printed on a slightly glossier stock. Cards #1-50 were short-printed and inserted at a rate of one per pack. Ten-card packs carried an SRP of 99 cents. The Showcase Series parallels 110 base cards and was inserted 1:7. Artist's Proofs is a 50-card partial parallel done on prismatic foil and inserted 1:35. Inserts included All-Star Epix, Complete Players and Star Gazing.

		NM/M
Complete Set (270):		10.00
Common SP (1-50):		.10
Common Player (51-270):		.05
Artist's Proofs:		4X
Inserted 1:35		
Paul Konerko Auto. (500):		15.00
Pack (10):		.65
Wax Box (36):		15.00

Jumbo Pack (20):		1.50
Jumbo Box (24):		25.00
1	Tony Clark	.10
2	Juan Gonzalez	.35
3	Frank Thomas	.60
4	Greg Maddux	.75
5	Barry Larkin	.10
6	Derek Jeter	1.50
7	Randy Johnson	.60
8	Roger Clemens	.85
9	Tony Gwynn	.75
10	Barry Bonds	1.50
11	Jim Edmonds	.10
12	Bernie Williams	.10
13	Ken Griffey Jr.	1.00
14	Tim Salmon	.10
15	Mo Vaughn	.10
16	David Justice	.10
17	Jose Cruz Jr.	.10
18	Andruw Jones	.60
19	Sammy Sosa	.75
20	Jeff Bagwell	.60
21	Scott Rolen	.50
22	Darin Erstad	.30
23	Andy Pettitte	.35
24	Mike Mussina	.30
25	Mark McGwire	1.25
26	Hideo Nomo	.35
27	Chipper Jones	.75
28	Cal Ripken Jr.	1.50
29	Chuck Knoblauch	.10
30	Alex Rodriguez	1.25
31	Jim Thome	.30
32	Mike Piazza	1.00
33	Ivan Rodriguez	.50
34	Roberto Alomar	.40
35	Nomar Garciaparra	.75
36	Albert Belle	.30
37	Vladimir Guerrero	.60
38	Raul Mondesi	.10
39	Larry Walker	.10
40	Manny Ramirez	.60
41	Tino Martinez	.10
42	Craig Biggio	.10
43	Jay Buhner	.10
44	Kenny Lofton	.30
45	Pedro Martinez	.60
46	Edgar Martinez	.10
47	Gary Sheffield	.45
48	Jose Guillen	.10
49	Ken Caminiti	.10
50	Bobby Higginson	.05
51	Alan Benes	.05
52	Shawn Green	.15
53	Ron Coomer	.05
54	Charles Nagy	.05
55	Steve Karsay	.05
56	Matt Morris	.05
57	Bobby Jones	.05
58	Jason Kendall	.05
59	Jeff Conine	.05
60	Joe Girardi	.05
61	Mark Kotsay	.05
62	Eric Karros	.05
63	Bartolo Colon	.05
64	Mariano Rivera	.10
65	Alex Gonzalez	.05
66	Scott Spiezio	.05
67	Luis Castillo	.05
68	Joey Cora	.05
69	Mark McLemore	.05
70	Reggie Jefferson	.05
71	Lance Johnson	.05
72	Damian Jackson	.05
73	Jeff D'Amico	.05
74	David Ortiz	.30
75	J.T. Snow	.05
76	Todd Hundley	.05
77	Billy Wagner	.05
78	Vinny Castilla	.05
79	Ismael Valdes	.05
80	Neifi Perez	.05
81	Derek Bell	.05
82	Ryan Klesko	.05
83	Rey Ordonez	.05
84	Carlos Garcia	.05
85	Curt Schilling	.30
86	Robin Ventura	.05
87	Pat Hentgen	.05
88	Glendon Rusch	.05
89	Hideki Irabu	.05
90	Antone Williamson	.05
91	Denny Neagle	.05
92	Kevin Orie	.05
93	Reggie Sanders	.05
94	Brady Anderson	.05
95	Andy Benes	.05
96	John Valentin	.05
97	Bobby Bonilla	.05
98	Walt Weiss	.05
99	Robin Jennings	.05
100	Marty Cordova	.05
101	Brad Ausmus	.05
102	Brian Rose	.05
103	Calvin Maduro	.05
104	Raul Casanova	.05
105	Jeff King	.05
106	Sandy Alomar	.05
107	Tim Naehring	.05
108	Mike Cameron	.05
109	Omar Vizquel	.05
110	Brad Radke	.05
111	Jeff Fassero	.05
112	Deivi Cruz	.05
113	Dave Hollins	.05
114	Dean Palmer	.05
115	Esteban Loaiza	.05
116	Brian Giles	.05

117	Steve Finley	.05
118	Jose Canseco	.30
119	Al Martin	.05
120	Eric Young	.05
121	Curtis Goodwin	.05
122	Ellis Burks	.05
123	Mike Hampton	.05
124	Lou Collier	.05
125	John Olerud	.05
126	Ramon Martinez	.05
127	Todd Dunwoody	.05
128	Jermaine Allensworth	.05
129	Eduardo Perez	.05
130	Dante Bichette	.05
131	Edgar Renteria	.05
132	Bob Abreu	.10
133	Rondell White	.05
134	Michael Coleman	.05
135	Jason Giambi	.30
136	Brant Brown	.05
137	Michael Tucker	.05
138	Dave Nilsson	.05
139	Benito Santiago	.05
140	Ray Durham	.05
141	Jeff Kent	.05
142	Matt Stairs	.05
143	Kevin Young	.05
144	Eric Davis	.05
145	John Wetteland	.05
146	Esteban Yan	.05
147	Wilton Guerrero	.05
148	Moises Alou	.05
149	Edgardo Alfonzo	.05
150	Andy Ashby	.05
151	Todd Walker	.05
152	Jermaine Dye	.05
153	Brian Hunter	.05
154	Shawn Estes	.05
155	Bernard Gilkey	.05
156	Tony Womack	.05
157	John Smoltz	.05
158	Delino DeShields	.05
159	Jacob Cruz	.05
160	Javier Valentin	.05
161	Chris Hoiles	.05
162	Garret Anderson	.05
163	Dan Wilson	.05
164	Paul O'Neill	.05
165	Matt Williams	.05
166	Travis Fryman	.05
167	Javier Lopez	.05
168	Ray Lankford	.05
169	Bobby Estalella	.05
170	Henry Rodriguez	.05
171	Quinton McCracken	.05
172	Jaret Wright	.05
173	Darryl Kile	.05
174	Wade Boggs	.65
175	Orel Hershiser	.05
176	B.J. Surhoff	.05
177	Fernando Tatis	.05
178	Carlos Delgado	.30
179	Jorge Fabregas	.05
180	Tony Saunders	.05
181	Devon White	.05
182	Dmitri Young	.05
183	Ryan McGuire	.05
184	Mark Bellhorn	.05
185	Joe Carter	.05
186	Kevin Stocker	.05
187	Mike Lansing	.05
188	Jason Dickson	.05
189	Charles Johnson	.05
190	Will Clark	.05
191	Shannon Stewart	.05
192	Johnny Damon	.20
193	Todd Greene	.05
194	Carlos Baerga	.05
195	David Cone	.05
196	Pokey Reese	.05
197	Livan Hernandez	.05
198	Tom Glavine	.25
199	Geronimo Berroa	.05
200	Darryl Hamilton	.05
201	Terry Steinbach	.05
202	Robb Nen	.05
203	Ron Gant	.05
204	Rafael Palmeiro	.40
205	Rickey Henderson	.40
206	Justin Thompson	.05
207	Jeff Suppan	.05
208	Kevin Brown	.05
209	Jimmy Key	.05
210	Brian Jordan	.05
211	Aaron Sele	.05
212	Fred McGriff	.05
213	Jay Bell	.05
214	Andres Galarraga	.05
215	Mark Grace	.05
216	Brett Tomko	.05
217	Francisco Cordova	.05
218	Rusty Greer	.05
219	Bubba Trammell	.05
220	Derek Lee	.35
221	Brian Anderson	.05
222	Mark Grudzielanek	.05
223	Marquis Grissom	.05
224	Gary DiSarcina	.05
225	Jim Leyritz	.05
226	Jeffrey Hammonds	.05
227	Karim Garcia	.05
228	Chan Ho Park	.05
229	Brooks Kieschnick	.05
230	Trey Beamon	.05
231	Kevin Appier	.05
232	Wally Joyner	.05
233	Richie Sexson	.05
234	Frank Catalanotto RC	.15

235	Rafael Medina	.05
236	Travis Lee	.05
237	Eli Marrero	.05
238	Carl Pavano	.05
239	Enrique Wilson	.05
240	Richard Hidalgo	.05
241	Todd Helton	.40
242	Ben Grieve	.05
243	Mario Valdez	.05
244	Magglio Ordonez RC	.75
245	Juan Encarnacion	.05
246	Russell Branyan	.05
247	Sean Casey	.10
248	Abraham Nunez	.05
249	Brad Fullmer	.05
250	Paul Konerko	.20
251	Miguel Tejada	.15
252	Mike Lowell RC	.50
253	Ken Griffey Jr. (Spring Training)	.35
254	Frank Thomas (Spring Training)	.25
255	Alex Rodriguez (Spring Training)	.45
256	Jose Cruz Jr. (Spring Training)	.05
257	Jeff Bagwell (Spring Training)	.20
258	Chipper Jones (Spring Training)	.30
259	Mo Vaughn (Spring Training)	.05
260	Nomar Garciaparra (Spring Training)	.30
261	Jim Thome (Spring Training)	.05
262	Derek Jeter (Spring Training)	.50
263	Mike Piazza (Spring Training)	.45
264	Tony Gwynn (Spring Training)	.30
265	Scott Rolen (Spring Training)	.15
266	Andruw Jones (Spring Training)	.20
267	Cal Ripken Jr. (Spring Training)	.50
268	Checklist (Ken Griffey Jr.)	.30
269	Checklist (Cal Ripken Jr.)	.45
270	Checklist (Jose Cruz Jr.)	.05

Artist's Proofs

This partial parallel reprints 160 (the same cards as the Showcase Series) of the 270 cards in Score Rookie & Traded. The cards are printed on a foil surface and feature an Artist's Proof logo on front. The cards were renumbered within the 160-card set and inserted one per 35 packs.

	NM/M
Common Player:	1.00
AP Stars:	4X

Artist's Proofs 1 of 1

Printed on primatic gold metallic foil background and featuring a gold "001/001 One of One" seal on front, these were random inserts in hobby packs. More than one "1/1" from this issue are known for some players, probably having been produced for use as replacements for damaged cards pulled from packs, then entering the hobby with the company's demise in mid-1998.

	NM/M
Common Player:	40.00

Showcase Series

The Showcase Series is a partial parallel reprint of 160 of the 270 cards in Rookie & Traded. The cards are printed on a silver-foil surface, marked on the back and renumbered (with an "RTPP" prefix) within the 160-card set. Showcase parallels were inserted one per seven packs.

		NM/M
Complete Set (160):		10.00
Common Player:		.15
1	Tony Clark	.15
2	Juan Gonzalez	.30
3	Frank Thomas	.60
4	Greg Maddux	.75
5	Barry Larkin	.15
6	Derek Jeter	1.50
7	Randy Johnson	.60
8	Roger Clemens	.85
9	Tony Gwynn	.75
10	Barry Bonds	1.50
11	Jim Edmonds	.15
12	Bernie Williams	.15
13	Ken Griffey Jr.	1.00
14	Tim Salmon	.15
15	Mo Vaughn	.15
16	David Justice	.15
17	Jose Cruz Jr.	.15
18	Andruw Jones	.60
19	Sammy Sosa	.75
20	Jeff Bagwell	.60
21	Scott Rolen	.50
22	Darin Erstad	.25
23	Andy Pettitte	.30
24	Mike Mussina	.30
25	Mark McGwire	1.25
26	Hideo Nomo	.30
27	Chipper Jones	.75
28	Cal Ripken Jr.	1.50
29	Chuck Knoblauch	.15
30	Alex Rodriguez	1.25
31	Jim Thome	.50
32	Mike Piazza	1.00
33	Ivan Rodriguez	.50
34	Roberto Alomar	.25
35	Nomar Garciaparra	1.00
36	Albert Belle	.15
37	Vladimir Guerrero	.60
38	Raul Mondesi	.15
39	Larry Walker	.15
40	Manny Ramirez	.60
41	Tino Martinez	.15
42	Craig Biggio	.15
43	Jay Buhner	.15
44	Kenny Lofton	.15
45	Pedro Martinez	.60
46	Edgar Martinez	.15
47	Gary Sheffield	.40
48	Jose Guillen	.15
49	Ken Caminiti	.15
50	Bobby Higginson	.15
51	Alan Benes	.15
52	Shawn Green	.35
53	Matt Morris	.15
54	Jason Kendall	.15
55	Mark Kotsay	.15
56	Bartolo Colon	.15
57	Damian Jackson	.15
58	David Ortiz	.35
59	J.T. Snow	.15
60	Todd Hundley	.15
61	Neifi Perez	.15
62	Ryan Klesko	.15
63	Robin Ventura	.15
64	Pat Hentgen	.15
65	Antone Williamson	.15
66	Kevin Orie	.15
67	Brady Anderson	.15
68	Bobby Bonilla	.15
69	Brian Rose	.15
70	Sandy Alomar Jr.	.15
71	Mike Cameron	.15
72	Omar Vizquel	.15
73	Steve Finley	.15
74	Jose Canseco	.40
75	Al Martin	.15
76	Eric Young	.15
77	Ellis Burks	.15

78	Todd Dunwoody	.15
79	Dante Bichette	.15
80	Edgar Renteria	.15
81	Bobby Abreu	.15
82	Rondell White	.15
83	Michael Coleman	.15
84	Jason Giambi	.50
85	Wilton Guerrero	.15
86	Moises Alou	.15
87	Todd Walker	.15
88	Shawn Estes	.15
89	John Smoltz	.15
90	Jacob Cruz	.15
91	Javier Valentin	.15
92	Garret Anderson	.15
93	Paul O'Neill	.15
94	Matt Williams	.15
95	Travis Fryman	.15
96	Javier Lopez	.15
97	Ray Lankford	.15
98	Bobby Estalella	.15
99	Jaret Wright	.15
100	Wade Boggs	.75
101	Fernando Tatis	.15
102	Carlos Delgado	.50
103	Joe Carter	.15
104	Jason Dickson	.15
105	Charles Johnson	.15
106	Will Clark	.15
107	Shannon Stewart	.15
108	Todd Greene	.15
109	Pokey Reese	.15
110	Livan Hernandez	.15
111	Tom Glavine	.35
112	Rafael Palmeiro	.15
113	Justin Thompson	.15
114	Jeff Suppan	.15
115	Kevin Brown	.15
116	Brian Jordan	.15
117	Fred McGriff	.15
118	Andres Galarraga	.15
119	Mark Grace	.15
120	Rusty Greer	.15
121	Bubba Trammell	.15
122	Derek Lee	.40
123	Brian Anderson	.15
124	Karim Garcia	.15
125	Chan Ho Park	.15
126	Richie Sexson	.15
127	Frank Catalanotto	.15
128	Rafael Medina	.15
129	Travis Lee	.15
130	Eli Marrero	.15
131	Carl Pavano	.15
132	Enrique Wilson	.15
133	Richard Hidalgo	.15
134	Todd Helton	.40
135	Ben Grieve	.15
136	Mario Valdez	.15
137	Magglio Ordonez	.25
138	Juan Encarnacion	.15
139	Russell Branyan	.15
140	Sean Casey	.25
141	Abraham Nunez	.15
142	Brad Fullmer	.15
143	Paul Konerko	.25
144	Miguel Tejada	.30
145	Mike Lowell	.15
146	Ken Griffey Jr. (Spring Training)	.50
147	Frank Thomas (Spring Training)	.35
148	Alex Rodriguez (Spring Training)	.65
149	Jose Cruz Jr. (Spring Training)	.15
150	Jeff Bagwell (Spring Training)	.35
151	Chipper Jones (Spring Training)	.40
152	Mo Vaughn (Spring Training)	.15
153	Nomar Garciaparra (Spring Training)	.40
154	Jim Thome (Spring Training)	.30
155	Derek Jeter (Spring Training)	.75
156	Mike Piazza (Spring Training)	.50
157	Tony Gwynn (Spring Training)	.40
158	Scott Rolen (Spring Training)	.25
159	Andruw Jones (Spring Training)	.35
160	Cal Ripken Jr. (Spring Training)	.75

Complete Players

Complete Players is a 30-card insert seeded one per 11 packs. The set highlights 10 players who can do it all on the field. Each player has three cards showcasing one of their talents. The cards feature holographic foil stamping. Each card can also be found in a promo version with a large, black "SAMPLE" overprinted on front and back.

		NM/M
Complete Set (30):		65.00
Common Player:		1.00
Inserted 1:11		
Samples:		1X
1A-1C	Ken Griffey Jr.	3.50

2A-2C	Larry Walker	1.00
3A-3C	Alex Rodriguez	4.00
4A-4C	Jose Cruz Jr.	1.00
5A-5C	Jeff Bagwell	2.00
6A-6C	Greg Maddux	2.75
7A-7C	Ivan Rodriguez	1.75
8A-8C	Roger Clemens	3.00
9A-9C	Chipper Jones	2.75
10A-10C	Hideo Nomo	1.50

Epix All-Star Moment

All-Star Epix is a 1:61 insert. The cards honor the top All-Star Game moments of 12 star players. The dot matrix hologram cards were printed in orange, purple and emerald versions. This series was continued with cards numbered 13-24 in Pinnacle Plus.

		NM/M
Complete Set (12):		25.00
Common Player:		1.00
Purples:		1.5X
Emeralds:		2.5X
1	Ken Griffey Jr.	4.00
2	Juan Gonzalez	1.50
3	Jeff Bagwell	2.50
4	Ivan Rodriguez	2.00
5	Nomar Garciaparra	3.00
6	Ryne Sandberg	3.00
7	Frank Thomas	2.50
8	Derek Jeter	5.00
9	Tony Gwynn	3.00
10	Albert Belle	1.00
11	Scott Rolen	2.00
12	Barry Larkin	1.00

Star Gazing

Printed on micro-etched foil board, Star Gazing features 20 top players and was seeded 1:35.

		NM/M
Complete Set (20):		12.00
Common Player:		.25
Inserted 1:35		
1	Ken Griffey Jr.	1.00
2	Frank Thomas	.60
3	Chipper Jones	.75
4	Mark McGwire	1.25
5	Cal Ripken Jr.	1.50
6	Mike Piazza	1.00
7	Nomar Garciaparra	.75
8	Derek Jeter	1.50
9	Juan Gonzalez	.35
10	Vladimir Guerrero	.60
11	Alex Rodriguez	1.25
12	Tony Gwynn	.75
13	Andruw Jones	.60
14	Scott Rolen	.40
15	Jose Cruz Jr.	.25
16	Mo Vaughn	.25
17	Bernie Williams	.25
18	Greg Maddux	.75
19	Tony Clark	.25
20	Ben Grieve	.25

1998 Score Team Collection

Team sets of 15 players each were produced for 10 different teams. Each card is similar in design to the regular 1998 Score set except for a special silver-foil team logo stamped at the bottom of the card. On back, this version has a "Team Collection" underprinted and each card is numbered "_ of 15." In a parallel "Platinum" version, seeded one per six packs, the front background is replaced with silver prismatic foil. A gold highlighted version of the three-card Complete Players inserts were found one per 11 packs. Team Collection was sold in five-card, single-team packs (32 per box).

		NM/M
Complete Set (150):		25.00
Common Player:		.10
ANAHEIM ANGELS TEAM SET		2.00
1	Rickey Henderson	.60
2	Todd Greene	.10
3	Shigetoshi Hasegawa	.10
4	Darin Erstad	.20
5	Jason Dickson	.10
6	Tim Salmon	.10
7	Ken Hill	.10
8	Dave Hollins	.10
9	Gary DiSarcina	.10
10	Mike James	.10
11	Jim Edmonds	.10
12	Troy Percival	.10
13	Chuck Finley	.10
14	Tony Phillips	.10
15	Garret Anderson	.10
ATLANTA BRAVES TEAM SET		2.75
1	Andruw Jones	.60
2	Greg Maddux	.75
3	Michael Tucker	.10
4	Denny Naegle	.10
5	Javier Lopez	.10
6	Ryan Klesko	.10
7	Chipper Jones	.75
8	Kenny Lofton	.10
9	John Smoltz	.10
10	Jeff Blauser	.10
11	Tom Glavine	.30
12	Tony Graffanino	.10
13	Terrell Wade	.10
14	Fred McGriff	.10
15	Mark Wohlers	.10
BALTIMORE ORIOLES TEAM SET		3.25
1	Roberto Alomar	.20
2	Jimmy Key	.10
3	Cal Ripken Jr.	1.75
4	Brady Anderson	.10
5	Geronimo Berroa	.10
6	Chris Hoiles	.10
7	Rafael Palmeiro	.50
8	Mike Mussina	.30
9	Randy Myers	.10
10	Mike Bordick	.10
11	Scott Erickson	.10
12	Armando Benitez	.10
13	B.J. Surhoff	.10
14	Jeffrey Hammonds	.10
15	Arthur Rhodes	.10
BOSTON RED SOX TEAM SET		2.25
1	Steve Avery	.10
2	Aaron Sele	.10
3	Tim Wakefield	.10
4	Darren Bragg	.10
5	Scott Hatteberg	.10
6	Jeff Suppan	.10
7	Nomar Garciaparra	.75
8	Tim Naehring	.10
9	Reggie Jefferson	.10
10	John Valentin	.10
11	Jeff Frye	.10
12	Wil Cordero	.10

13	Troy O'Leary	.10
14	Mo Vaughn	.10
15	Shane Mack	.10

CHICAGO WHITE SOX

	TEAM SET	2.00
1	Albert Belle	.10
2	Chuck McElroy	.10
3	Mike Cameron	.10
4	Ozzie Guillen	.10
5	Jaime Navarro	.10
6	Chris Clemons	.10
7	Lyle Mouton	.10
8	Frank Thomas	.60
9	Doug Drabek	.10
10	Robin Ventura	.10
11	Dave Martinez	.10
12	Ray Durham	.10
13	Chris Snopek	.10
14	James Baldwin	.10
15	Jorge Fabregas	.10

CLEVELAND INDIANS

	TEAM SET	1.25
1	Jack McDowell	.10
2	Jim Thome	.50
3	Brian Anderson	.10
4	Sandy Alomar Jr.	.10
5	Omar Vizquel	.10
6	Brian Giles	.10
7	Charles Nagy	.10
8	Mike Jackson	.10
9	David Justice	.10
10	Jeff Juden	.10
11	Matt Williams	.10
12	Marquis Grissom	.10
13	Tony Fernandez	.10
14	Bartolo Colon	.10
15	Jaret Wright	.10

LOS ANGELES DODGERS

	TEAM SET	2.75
1	Hideo Nomo	.30
2	Mike Piazza	1.00
3	Wilton Guerrero	.10
4	Greg Gagne	.10
5	Brett Butler	.10
6	Todd Hollandsworth	.10
7	Roger Cedeno	.10
8	Chan Ho Park	.10
9	Todd Worrell	.10
10	Ramon Martinez	.10
11	Ismael Valdes	.10
12	Eric Karros	.10
13	Raul Mondesi	.10
14	Todd Zeile	.10
15	Billy Ashley	.10

NEW YORK YANKEES

	TEAM SET	3.25
1	Hideki Irabu	.10
2	Derek Jeter	1.75
3	Tino Martinez	.10
4	David Cone	.10
5	Andy Pettitte	.25
6	Bernie Williams	.10
7	Charlie Hayes	.10
8	Pat Kelly	.10
9	Mariano Rivera	.15
10	Paul O'Neill	.10
11	Chad Curtis	.10
12	David Wells	.10
13	Cecil Fielder	.10
14	Wade Boggs	.75
15	Jorge Posada	.10

SEATTLE MARINERS TEAM SET 3.25

1	Dan Wilson	.10
2	Alex Rodriguez	1.25
3	Jeff Fassero	.10
4	Ken Griffey Jr.	1.00
5	Bobby Ayala	.10
6	Jay Buhner	.10
7	Mike Timlin	.10
8	Edgar Martinez	.10
9	Randy Johnson	.60
10	Joey Cora	.10
11	Heathcliff Slocumb	.10
12	Russ Davis	.10
13	Paul Sorrento	.10
14	Rich Amaral	.10
15	Jamie Moyer	.10

ST. LOUIS CARDINALS

	TEAM SET	2.25
1	Andy Benes	.10
2	Todd Stottlemyre	.10
3	Dennis Eckersley	.45
4	Mark McGwire	1.25
5	Dmitri Young	.10
6	Ron Gant	.10
7	Mike Difelice	.10
8	Ray Lankford	.10
9	John Mabry	.10
10	Royce Clayton	.10
11	Alan Benes	.10
12	Delino DeShields	.10
13	Brian Jordan	.10
14	Gary Gaetti	.10
15	Matt Morris	.10

Platinum

Each of the Team Collection cards was also issued in a Platinum Team version, inserted on average of one card per six packs. The front has a background of star-studded refractive silver foil and a "PLATINUM TEAM" designation at the right edge of the photo. That designation is repeated on back as an underprint.

NM/M	
Common Player:	.50
Stars:	4X

Complete Players

(See 1998 Score Complete Players.)

1996-97 Score Board All Sport PPF

Stars and prospects, Past, Present and Future (PPF), in the four major team sports are featued in this two series set whose issue spanned late 1996 and early 1997. Borderless action photos and gold-foil graphic highlights are featured on front. Another photo, stats and personal data can be found on back. Only the baseball players from the 200-card set are listed here. A gold parallel edition was also issued.

	NM/M	
Common Player:		.10
Gold:		2X
Wax Pack (6):		.65
Wax Box (18):		7.50
Wax Box (36):		15.00
21	Ryan Minor	.10
60	Rey Ordonez	.10
61	Todd Greene	.10
62	Jermaine Dye	.10
63	Karim Garcia	.10
64	Todd Walker	.10
65	Calvin Reese	.10
66	Roger Cedeno	.10
67	Ben Davis	.10
68	Chad Hermansen	.10
69	Vladimir Guerrero	.50
70	Billy Wagner	.10
93	Barry Bonds	.50
95	Vladimir Guerrero	.50
96	Livan Hernandez	.10
160	Barry Bonds	.50
161	Jay Payton	.10
162	Jose Cruz Jr.	.10
163	Richard Hidalgo	.10
164	Bartolo Colon	.10
165	Matt Drews	.10
166	Kerry Wood	.35
167	Ben Grieve	.10
168	Wes Helms	.10
169	Livan Hernandez	.10
196	Todd Walker	.10
197	Rey Ordonez	.10
198	Todd Greene	.10

Retro

Current and potential stars in the format of classic sports cards are featured in this Series 2 insert found at an announced rate of one per 35 packs. Only a single baseball player is included among the 10 cards in the set.

	NM/M	
R10	Rey Ordonez	.50

Revivals

Current and potential stars in the format of classic sports cards are featured in this Series 1 insert found at an announced rate of one per 35 packs. Only a single baseball player is included among the 10 cards in the set.

	NM/M	
REV10	Barry Bonds	1.00

1997 Score Board Mickey Mantle Shoe Box Collection

Yet another collectors' issue of Mickey Mantle cards, the Score Board "Shoe Box Collection" offered packs containing two of the 75 Mantle cards or seven-card insert set, along with a genuine - usually a low-grade common - Topps card from 1951-69. Several designs of Mantle cards are featured in the set, including color photos as well as blue-and-white duotones. Five of the cards are printed with gold-foil backgrounds and die-cut. Cards #51-69 are short-printed at a ratio of about 1-to-3 with #1-50. Suggested retail price was $6.50 per pack.

	NM/M	
Complete Set (75):		60.00
Common Card:		.75
1	Summary Of The Legend (Foil die-cut.)	3.00
1p	Summary of the Legend (Promo Card)	3.00
2	Triple Crown 1956	.75
3	MVP 1956	.75
4	MVP 1957	.75
5	MVP 1962	.75
6	Uniform #6 (Foil die-cut)	3.00
6p	Uniform #6 (Promo Card)	3.00
7	Uniform #7 (Foil die-cut)	3.00
7p	Uniform #7 (Promo Card)	3.00
8	Gold Glove Winner	.75
9	17-time All-Star	.75
10	4-time HR Champion	.75
11	World Series Records	.75
12	The Dirty Dozen (Post-Seasons)	.75
13	World Champion-1951	.75
14	World Champion-1952	.75
15	World Champion-1953	.75
16	World Champion-1956	.75
17	World Champion-1958	.75
18	World Champion-1961	.75
19	World Champion-1962	.75
20	Replacing A Legend	.75
21	Casey On Mantle	.75
22	Mickey & The Media	.75
23	Family Man	.75
24	Fan Favorite	.75
25	Playing Injured	.75
26	Clubhouse Leader	.75
27	Team Leader	.75
28	M & M Boys	.75
29	Legendary Friendships	.75
30	Time Out	.75
31	Mantle Is Born	.75
32	Mutt Mantle	.75
33	Growing Up	.75
34	5-tool player-Arm	.75
35	5-tool player-Defense	.75
36	5-tool player-Average	.75
37	5-tool player-Speed	.75
38	5-tool player-Power	.75
39	First Homer	.75
40	100th Homer	.75
41	200th Homer	.75
42	300th Homer	.75
43	400th Homer	.75
44	500th Homer	.75
45	536 Career Homers	.75
46	Yankee Stadium Blasts	.75
47	Switch-hit Home Runs	.75
48	565-ft. Home Run	.75
49	Signs 1st Pro Contract	.75
50	Mickey In The Minors	.75
51	1951 Trading Card	3.00
52	1952 Trading Card	3.00
53	1953 Trading Card	3.00
54	1954 Trading Card	3.00
55	1955 Trading Card	3.00
56A	1956 Trading Card	3.00
56B	1956 Trading Card	3.00
57	1957 Trading Card	3.00
58	1958 Trading Card	3.00
59	1959 Trading Card	3.00
60	1960 Trading Card	3.00
61	1961 Trading Card	3.00
62	1962 Trading Card	3.00
63	1963 Trading Card	3.00
64	1964 Trading Card	3.00
65	1965 Trading Card	3.00
66	1966 Trading Card	3.00
67	1967 Trading Card	3.00
68	1968 Trading Card	3.00
69	1969 Trading Card	3.00
70	Number Retired By Yankees (Foil die-cut.)	3.00
70p	Number Retired By Yankees (Promo Card)	3.00
71	Mickey Mantle Day/1965	.75
72	Mickey Mantle Day/1969	.75
73	Life After Baseball	.75
74	Hall Of Fame Induction (Foil die-cut.)	3.00
74p	Hall of Fame Induction (Promo Card)	3.00

Mickey Mantle Shoe Box Inserts

A set of seven insert cards, found on average of one per 16 packs, was part of the Mickey Mantle Shoe Box Collection. The inserts have a photo of Mantle on front, with blue metallic foil highlights. Contest rules on the back specify that the first seven persons to redeem a complete set of the seven insert cards will win a $7,000 Mantle phone card. All others redeeming the set of seven prior to July 7, 1998, received a $700 Mantle phone card. The #7 insert card was short-printed to limit the number of phone card winners.

	NM/M	
Complete Set (7):		70.00
Common Card:		6.00
$700 Phone Card:		115.00
$7,000 Phone Card:		850.00
1	Mickey Mantle Insert #1	6.00
2	Mickey Mantle Insert #2	6.00
3	Mickey Mantle Insert #3	6.00
4	Mickey Mantle Insert #4	6.00
5	Mickey Mantle Insert #5	25.00
6	Mickey Mantle Insert #6	6.00
7	Mickey Mantle Insert #7 (Short-Print)	40.00

Players Club

Seven baseball players are among the cards in this multi-sport issue. Card fronts feature borderless action photos from which uniform logos have been removed. The player's name and the city in which he plays are in gold-foil in a baseball strip at bottom. Backs

have another photo, biographical data and stats, including projected 1998 figures. Only the baseball players in the set are listed here.

	NM/M	
Common Player:		.25
3	Barry Bonds	.50
7	Jose Cruz Jr.	.25
17	Matt Drews	.25
27	Wes Helms	.25
37	Richard Hidalgo	.25
48	Jay Payton	.25
69	Kerry Wood	.35

Players Club #1 Die-Cuts

Former #1 draft picks from all four major sports are included in this insert set. Highlighted in gold foil, cards are die-cut into the shape of a numeral 1. Backs have biographical information and stats. Cards are numbered with a "D" prefix. Only the baseball players are listed here. They were a 1:32 pack insert.

	NM/M	
D10	Jose Cruz Jr.	1.00
D11	Barry Bonds	5.00

Talk N' Sports

Insert phone cards with talk time worth up to $1,000, along with trivia contests to win memorabilia were among the incentives to purchase this four-sport issue. The base card set features 50 stars and prospects, all of whom are also found, along with a few other superstars, in the inserts. Fronts of the base cards have action photos on which uniform logos have been airbrushed away. Backs have a couple more photos, some player bio and stats. Only the baseball players from the set are listed here.

	NM/M	
Common Player:		.10
40	Barry Bonds	.50
41	Jay Payton	.10
42	Todd Walker	.10
43	Jose Cruz Jr.	.10
44	Kerry Wood	.30
45	Wes Helms	.10

Talk N' Sports Essentials

See-through plastic and action photos are combined on this 1:20 pack insert. Only a single

baseball player is included among the four-sport stars and prospects.

	NM/M	
E3	Barry Bonds	7.50

Visions Signings

Stars and prospects from all four major team sports are included in this issue. Fronts have borderless action photos with professional logos removed as necessary to meet licensing regulations. Front graphics feature holographic foil highlights. Backs have another photo along with stats, personal data and career notes. Cards were sold in five-card packs, each of which contained either an autographed card or an insert card. Only the seven baseball players from the 50-card set are listed here.

	NM/M	
Common Player:		.25
Gold Parallel:		2X
1	Barry Bonds	1.50
5	Jose Cruz Jr.	.25
6	Ben Grieve	.25
7	Kerry Wood	.75
44	Wes Helms	.25
45	Richard Hidalgo	.25
46	Jay Payton	.25

Visions Signings Autographs

Each five-card pack of Score Board Vision Signings contained either an authentically autographed card or an insert card. Only the baseball players from the 63 autographed cards in the multi-sports set of stars and prospects are listed here. Barry Bonds autographs can be found on other companies' cards, with a Score Board authenticity seal.

	NM/M	
9	Jose Cruz Jr.	2.00
20	Ben Grieve	2.00
21	Vladimir Guerrero	30.00
26	Wes Helms	2.00
27	Richard Hidalgo	2.00
34	Jason Kendall	2.00
44	Jay Payton	2.00
62	Paul Wilson	2.00

63 Kerry Wood 20.00
Barry Bonds 45.00

Visions Signings Artistry

These specially printed cards were a one-in-six packs insert (regular version; 1:18 autographed) in five-card Visions Signings packs. Only a single baseball player is represented among the 20 cards in the set.

	NM/M
1 Jose Cruz Jr.	1.00
1 Jose Cruz Jr./Auto.	3.00

Autographed Collection

JOSE CRUZ JR.

A handful of baseball players are among the four-sport stars and prospects in this set. Luring collectors was the presence of autographed cards at the rate of one per 4-1/2 packs, Blue Ribbon serially numbered autographs and memorabilia redemption cards (many of which became worthless when Score Board went bankrupt shortly after the set was issued). Because the cards are licensed only by the players, and not leagues, there are no uniform logos on the photos, nor mention of team names, only cities. Only the baseball players are listed here.

	NM/M
Common Player:	.25
3 J.D. Drew	1.50
11 Matt White	.25
12 Jay Payton	.25
23 Brandon Larson	.25
28 Jose Cruz Jr.	.25
49 Adrian Beltre	.50

Autographed Collection Strongbox

As part of a special $125 television offer, a parallel version of Score Board's Autographed Collection was offered featuring special inserts, autographs and memorabilia. The parallel cards are marked with an embossed "Strongbox" logo.

	NM/M
Common Player:	.25
3 J.D. Drew	2.00
11 Matt White	.50
12 Jay Payton	.50
23 Brandon Larson	.50
28 Jose Cruz Jr.	.50
49 Adrian Beltre	1.50

Autographed Collection Autographs

Authentically autographed cards were inserted in this issue at the rate of about four per 18-pack box. Cards have a round player photo at center with the signature in a white oval below. Backs have a congratulatory message. Only the

JAY PAYTON 1st Rounder

baseball players among the four-sport stars and prospects are listed here. Cards are unnumbered.

	NM/M
Ben Grieve	2.00
Wes Helms	2.00
Jay Payton	2.00
Kerry Wood	20.00

Autographed Collection Blue Ribbon

These one-per-box inserts are similar in format to the autographed cards, but have a blue ribbon beneath the player photo on which the signature has been penned. Each card is individually serial numbered from within editions which vary from fewer than 100 to nearly 2,000. Only one baseball player was among the four-sport stars and prospects.

	NM/M
Jose Cruz Jr. /1,600	3.00

Autographed Collection Sports City USA

Players whose teams share a common city are featured in this insert series, found on average one per nine packs. A parallel version, embossed "Strongbox" was issued in special $125 television-offer packages of Autographed Collection. The parallels are individually serial numbered to 600. Only cards with baseball players are listed here.

	NM/M
Common Card:	1:00
Embossed:	2X
SC3 Richard Hidalgo (Olajuwan, Drexler)	1.00
SC4 Kerry Wood (Pippen, Autry)	2.50
SC6 Adrian Beltre (Bryant)	1.50
SC7 J.D. Drew (Thomas, Staley)	2.50
SC12 Wes Helms (Hanspard, Gray)	1.00
SC14 Jay Payton (Barber, Van Horn)	1.00
SC15 Matt Drews (Westbrook, Pollard)	1.00

1981 Seattle Mariners Police

These 2-5/8" x 4-1/8" cards were co-sponsored by the Washington State Crime Prevention Assoc., Coca-Cola, Kiawanis and Ernst Home Centers. Fronts have a color photo, player name and posi-

FLOYD BANNISTER Pitcher
Seattle Mariners

tion and a team logo. Card backs are printed in blue and red and offer a "Tip from the Mariners" along with the four sponsor logos.

	NM/M
Complete Set (16):	3.00
Common Player:	.25
1 Jeff Burroughs	.25
2 Floyd Bannister	.25
3 Glenn Abbott	.25
4 Jim Anderson	.25
5 Danny Meyer	.25
6 Dave Edler	.25
7 Julio Cruz	.25
8 Kenny Clay	.25
9 Lenny Randle	.25
10 Mike Parrott	.25
11 Tom Paciorek	.25
12 Jerry Narron	.25
13 Richie Zisk	.25
14 Maury Wills	.50
15 Joe Simpson	.25
16 Shane Rawley	.25

1993 Select Promos

MITCH WILLIAMS

Zeroes in the career stats line on the back of the card distinguish the promo cards for Score's premiere issue of its Select brand name. The promo cards were distributed to introduce dealers and collectors to the new mid-range set.

	NM/M
Complete Set (8):	12.00
Common Player:	1.00
22 Robin Yount	3.00
24 Don Mattingly	5.00
26 Sandy Alomar Jr.	1.00
41 Gary Sheffield	2.00
56 Brady Anderson	1.00
65 Rob Dibble	1.00
75 John Smiley	1.00
79 Mitch Williams	1.00

1993 Select Dufex Proofs

DAVE FLEMING P

To test the Dufex textured foil printing technology which was used on its Stars, Rookies and Triple Crown insert sets, Select produced a very limited number of blank-back proof cards.

Select Rookies:	15X
Select Stars:	20X
Select Triple Crown:	20X

1993 Select

This 400-card set from Score is designed for the mid-priced card market. The card fronts feature green borders on two sides of the card with the photo filling the remaining portion of the card front. The backs feature an additional photo, player information and statistics. Cards numbered 271-360 are devoted to rookies and draft picks.

	NM/M
Complete Set (405):	15.00
Common Player:	.05
Pack (15):	.75
Wax Box (36):	22.50
1 Barry Bonds	1.50
2 Ken Griffey Jr.	1.00
3 Will Clark	.05
4 Kirby Puckett	.75
5 Tony Gwynn	.75
6 Frank Thomas	.65
7 Tom Glavine	.35
8 Roberto Alomar	.25
9 Andre Dawson	.25
10 Ron Darling	.05
11 Bobby Bonilla	.05
12 Danny Tartabull	.05
13 Darren Daulton	.05
14 Roger Clemens	.85
15 Ozzie Smith	.75
16 Mark McGwire	1.25
17 Terry Pendleton	.05
18 Cal Ripken, Jr.	1.50
19 Fred McGriff	.05
20 Cecil Fielder	.05
21 Darryl Strawberry	.05
22 Robin Yount	.65
23 Barry Larkin	.05
24 Don Mattingly	.85
25 Craig Biggio	.05
26 Sandy Alomar Jr.	.05
27 Larry Walker	.05
28 Junior Felix	.05
29 Eddie Murray	.65
30 Robin Ventura	.05
31 Greg Maddux	.75
32 Dave Winfield	.65
33 John Kruk	.05
34 Wally Joyner	.05
35 Andy Van Slyke	.05
36 Chuck Knoblauch	.05
37 Tom Pagnozzi	.05
38 Dennis Eckersley	.60
39 Dave Justice	.05
40 Juan Gonzalez	.35
41 Gary Sheffield	.40
42 Paul Molitor	.65
43 Delino DeShields	.05
44 Travis Fryman	.05
45 Hal Morris	.05
46 Gregg Olson	.05
47 Ken Caminiti	.05
48 Wade Boggs	.75
49 Orel Hershiser	.05
50 Albert Belle	.05
51 Bill Swift	.05
52 Mark Langston	.05
53 Joe Girardi	.05
54 Keith Miller	.05
55 Gary Carter	.65
56 Brady Anderson	.05
57 Dwight Gooden	.05
58 Julio Franco	.05
59 Len Dykstra	.05
60 Mickey Tettleton	.05
61 Randy Tomlin	.05
62 B.J. Surhoff	.05
63 Todd Zeile	.05
64 Roberto Kelly	.05
65 Rob Dibble	.05
66 Leo Gomez	.05
67 Doug Jones	.05
68 Ellis Burks	.05
69 Mike Scioscia	.05
70 Charles Nagy	.05
71 Cory Snyder	.05
72 Devon White	.05
73 Mark Grace	.05
74 Luis Polonia	.05
75 John Smiley	.05
76 Carlton Fisk	.65
77 Luis Sojo	.05
78 George Brett	.50
79 Mitch Williams	.05
80 Kent Hrbek	.05
81 Jay Bell	.05
82 Edgar Martinez	.05
83 Lee Smith	.05
84 Deion Sanders	.05
85 Bill Gullickson	.05
86 Paul O'Neill	.05
87 Kevin Seitzer	.05
88 Steve Finley	.05
89 Mel Hall	.05
90 Nolan Ryan	1.50
91 Eric Davis	.05
92 Mike Mussina	.35
93 Tony Fernandez	.05
94 Frank Viola	.05
95 Matt Williams	.05
96 Joe Carter	.05
97 Ryne Sandberg	.75
98 Jim Abbott	.05
99 Marquis Grissom	.05
100 George Bell	.05
101 Howard Johnson	.05
102 Kevin Appier	.05
103 Dale Murphy	.20
104 Shane Mack	.05
105 Jose Lind	.05
106 Rickey Henderson	.65
107 Bob Tewksbury	.05
108 Kevin Mitchell	.05
109 Steve Avery	.05
110 Candy Maldonado	.05
111 Bip Roberts	.05
112 Lou Whitaker	.05
113 Jeff Bagwell	.65
114 Dante Bichette	.05
115 Brett Butler	.05
116 Melido Perez	.05
117 Andy Benes	.05
118 Randy Johnson	.65
119 Willie McGee	.05
120 Jody Reed	.05
121 Shawon Dunston	.05
122 Carlos Baerga	.05
123 Bret Saberhagen	.05
124 John Olerud	.05
125 Ivan Calderon	.05
126 Bryan Harvey	.05
127 Terry Mulholland	.05
128 Ozzie Guillen	.05
129 Steve Buechele	.05
130 Kevin Tapani	.05
131 Felix Jose	.05
132 Terry Steinbach	.05
133 Ron Gant	.05
134 Harold Reynolds	.05
135 Chris Sabo	.05
136 Ivan Rodriguez	.60
137 Eric Anthony	.05
138 Mike Henneman	.05
139 Robby Thompson	.05
140 Scott Fletcher	.05
141 Bruce Hurst	.05
142 Kevin Maas	.05
143 Tom Candiotti	.05
144 Chris Hoiles	.05
145 Mike Morgan	.05
146 Mark Whiten	.05
147 Dennis Martinez	.05
148 Tony Pena	.05
149 Dave Magadan	.05
150 Mark Lewis	.05
151 Mariano Duncan	.05
152 Gregg Jefferies	.05
153 Doug Drabek	.05
154 Brian Harper	.05
155 Ray Lankford	.05
156 Carney Lansford	.05
157 Mike Sharperson	.05
158 Jack Morris	.05
159 Otis Nixon	.05
160 Steve Sax	.05
161 Mark Lemke	.05
162 Rafael Palmeiro	.60
163 Jose Rijo	.05
164 Omar Vizquel	.05
165 Sammy Sosa	.75
166 Milt Cuyler	.05
167 John Franco	.05
168 Darryl Hamilton	.05
169 Ken Hill	.05
170 Mike Devereaux	.05
171 Don Slaught	.05
172 Steve Farr	.05
173 Bernard Gilkey	.05
174 Mike Fetters	.05
175 Vince Coleman	.05
176 Kevin McReynolds	.05
177 John Smoltz	.05
178 Greg Gagne	.05
179 Greg Swindell	.05
180 Juan Guzman	.05
181 Kal Daniels	.05
182 Rick Sutcliffe	.05
183 Orlando Merced	.05
184 Bill Wegman	.05
185 Mark Gardner	.05
186 Rob Deer	.05
187 Dave Hollins	.05
188 Jack Clark	.05
189 Brian Hunter	.05
190 Tim Wallach	.05
191 Tim Belcher	.05
192 Walt Weiss	.05
193 Kurt Stillwell	.05
194 Charlie Hayes	.05
195 Willie Randolph	.05
196 Jack McDowell	.05
197 Jose Offerman	.05
198 Chuck Finley	.05
199 Darrin Jackson	.05
200 Kelly Gruber	.05
201 John Wetteland	.05
202 Jay Buhner	.05
203 Mike LaValliere	.05
204 Kevin Brown	.05
205 Luis Gonzalez	.05
206 Rick Aguilera	.05
207 Norm Charlton	.05
208 Mike Bordick	.05
209 Charlie Leibrandt	.05
210 Tom Brunansky	.05
211 Tom Henke	.05
212 Randy Milligan	.05
213 Ramon Martinez	.05
214 Mo Vaughn	.05
215 Randy Myers	.05
216 Greg Hibbard	.05
217 Wes Chamberlain	.05
218 Tony Phillips	.05
219 Pete Harnisch	.05
220 Mike Gallego	.05
221 Bud Black	.05
222 Greg Vaughn	.05
223 Milt Thompson	.05
224 Ben McDonald	.05
225 Billy Hatcher	.05
226 Paul Sorrento	.05
227 Mark Gubicza	.05
228 Mike Greenwell	.05
229 Curt Schilling	.35
230 Alan Trammell	.05
231 Zane Smith	.05
232 Bobby Thigpen	.05
233 Greg Olson	.05
234 Joe Orsulak	.05
235 Joe Oliver	.05
236 Tim Raines	.05
237 Juan Samuel	.05
238 Chili Davis	.05
239 Spike Owen	.05
240 Dave Stewart	.05
241 Jim Eisenreich	.05
242 Phil Plantier	.05
243 Sid Fernandez	.05
244 Dan Gladden	.05
245 Mickey Morandini	.05
246 Tino Martinez	.05
247 Kirt Manwaring	.05
248 Dean Palmer	.05
249 Tom Browning	.05
250 Brian McRae	.05
251 Scott Leius	.05
252 Bert Blyleven	.05
253 Scott Erickson	.05
254 Bob Welch	.05
255 Pat Kelly	.05
256 Felix Fermin	.05
257 Harold Baines	.05
258 Duane Ward	.05
259 Bill Spiers	.05
260 Jaime Navarro	.05
261 Scott Sanderson	.05
262 Gary Gaetti	.05
263 Bob Ojeda	.05
264 Jeff Montgomery	.05
265 Scott Bankhead	.05
266 Lance Johnson	.05
267 Rafael Belliard	.05
268 Kevin Reimer	.05
269 Benito Santiago	.05
270 Mike Moore	.05
271 Dave Fleming	.05
272 Moises Alou	.05
273 Pat Listach	.05
274 Reggie Sanders	.05
275 Kenny Lofton	.05
276 Donovan Osborne	.05
277 Rusty Meacham	.05
278 Eric Karros	.05
279 Andy Stankiewicz	.05
280 Brian Jordan	.05
281 Gary DiSarcina	.05
282 Mark Wohlers	.05
283 Dave Nilsson	.05
284 Anthony Young	.05
285 Jim Bullinger	.05
286 Derek Bell	.05
287 Brian Williams	.05
288 Julio Valera	.05
289 Dan Walters	.05
290 Chad Curtis	.05
291 Michael Tucker	.05
292 Bob Zupcic	.05
293 Todd Hundley	.05
294 Jeff Tackett	.05
295 Greg Colbrunn	.05
296 Cal Eldred	.05
297 Chris Roberts	.05
298 John Doherty	.05
299 Denny Neagle	.05
300 Arthur Rhodes	.05
301 Mark Clark	.05
302 Scott Cooper	.05
303 Jamie Arnold RC	.05
304 Jim Thome	.60
305 Frank Seminara	.05
306 Kurt Knudsen	.05
307 Tim Wakefield	.05
308 John Jaha	.05
309 Pat Hentgen	.05
310 B.J. Wallace	.05
311 Roberto Hernandez	.05
312 Hipolito Pichardo	.05
313 Eric Fox	.05
314 Willie Banks	.05
315 Sam Militello	.05

316	Vince Horsman	.05
317	Carlos Hernandez	.05
318	Jeff Kent	.05
319	Mike Perez	.05
320	Scott Livingstone	.05
321	Jeff Conine	.05
322	James Austin	.05
323	John Vander Wal	.05
324	Pat Mahomes	.05
325	Pedro Astacio	.05
326	Bret Boone	.05
327	Matt Stairs	.05
328	Damion Easley	.05
329	Ben Rivera	.05
330	Reggie Jefferson	.05
331	Luis Mercedes	.05
332	Kyle Abbott	.05
333	Eddie Taubensee	.05
334	Tim McIntosh	.05
335	Phil Clark	.05
336	Wil Cordero	.05
337	Russ Springer	.05
338	Craig Colbert	.05
339	Tim Salmon	.05
340	Braulio Castillo	.05
341	Donald Harris	.05
342	Eric Young	.05
343	Bob Wickman	.05
344	John Valentin	.05
345	Dan Wilson	.05
346	Steve Hosey	.05
347	Mike Piazza	1.00
348	Willie Greene	.05
349	Tom Goodwin	.05
350	Eric Hillman	.05
351	Steve Reed RC	.05
352	Dan Serafini RC	.05
353	Todd Steverson RC	.05
354	Benji Grigsby	.05
355	Shannon Stewart RC	1.00
356	Sean Lowe	.05
357	Derek Wallace	.05
358	Rick Helling	.05
359	Jason Kendall RC	1.00
360	Derek Jeter RC	10.00
361	David Cone	.05
362	Jeff Reardon	.05
363	Bobby Witt	.05
364	Jose Canseco	.40
365	Jeff Russell	.05
366	Ruben Sierra	.05
367	Alan Mills	.05
368	Matt Nokes	.05
369	Pat Borders	.05
370	Pedro Munoz	.05
371	Danny Jackson	.05
372	Geronimo Pena	.05
373	Craig Lefferts	.05
374	Joe Grahe	.05
375	Roger McDowell	.05
376	Jimmy Key	.05
377	Steve Olin	.05
378	Glenn Davis	.05
379	Rene Gonzales	.05
380	Manuel Lee	.05
381	Ron Karkovice	.05
382	Sid Bream	.05
383	Gerald Williams	.05
384	Lenny Harris	.05
385	J.T. Snow RC	.75
386	Dave Stieb	.05
387	Kirk McCaskill	.05
388	Lance Parrish	.05
389	Craig Greback	.05
390	Rick Wilkins	.05
391	Manny Alexander	.05
392	Mike Schooler	.05
393	Bernie Williams	.05
394	Kevin Koslofski	.05
395	Willie Wilson	.05
396	Jeff Parrett	.05
397	Mike Harkey	.05
398	Frank Tanana	.05
399	Doug Henry	.05
400	Royce Clayton	.05
401	Eric Wedge	.05
402	Derrick May	.05
403	Carlos Garcia	.05
404	Henry Rodriguez	.05
405	Ryan Klesko	.05

Aces

Cards from this set feature 24 of the top pitchers from 1992 and were included one per every 27-card Super Pack. The fronts have a picture of the player in action against an Ace card background. Backs have text and a portrait in the middle of a card suit for an Ace.

		NM/M
Complete Set (24):		20.00
Common Player:		1.00
1	Roger Clemens	6.00
2	Tom Glavine	3.00
3	Jack McDowell	1.00
4	Greg Maddux	4.50
5	Jack Morris	1.00
6	Dennis Martinez	1.00
7	Kevin Brown	1.00
8	Dwight Gooden	1.00
9	Kevin Appier	1.00
10	Mike Morgan	1.00
11	Juan Guzman	1.00
12	Charles Nagy	1.00
13	John Smiley	1.00
14	Ken Hill	1.00
15	Bob Tewksbury	1.00
16	Doug Drabek	1.00
17	John Smoltz	1.00
18	Greg Swindell	1.00
19	Bruce Hurst	1.00
20	Mike Mussina	2.00
21	Cal Eldred	1.00
22	Melido Perez	1.00
23	Dave Fleming	1.00
24	Kevin Tapani	1.00

Rookies

Top newcomers in 1992 are featured in this 21-card insert set. Cards were randomly inserted in 15-card hobby packs. The fronts, printed on metallic foil, have a Score Select Rookies logo on the front. The backs have text and a player portrait.

		NM/M
Complete Set (21):		4.00
Common Player:		.50
1	Pat Listach	.50
2	Moises Alou	.50
3	Reggie Sanders	.50
4	Kenny Lofton	.50
5	Eric Karros	.50
6	Brian Williams	.50
7	Donovan Osborne	.50
8	Sam Militello	.50
9	Chad Curtis	.50
10	Bob Zupcic	.50
11	Tim Salmon	1.50
12	Jeff Conine	.50
13	Pedro Astacio	.50
14	Arthur Rhodes	.50
15	Cal Eldred	.50
16	Tim Wakefield	.50
17	Andy Stankiewicz	.50
18	Wil Cordero	.50
19	Todd Hundley	.50
20	Dave Fleming	.50
21	Bret Boone	1.00

Stars

The top 24 players from 1992 are featured in this insert set. Cards were randomly inserted in 15-card retail packs. Fronts are printed on metallic foil.

		NM/M
Complete Set (24):		40.00
Common Player:		.60
1	Fred McGriff	.60
2	Ryne Sandberg	4.00
3	Ozzie Smith	4.00
4	Gary Sheffield	1.25
5	Darren Daulton	.60
6	Andy Van Slyke	.60
7	Barry Bonds	7.50
8	Tony Gwynn	4.00
9	Greg Maddux	4.00
10	Tom Glavine	1.00
11	John Franco	.60
12	Lee Smith	.60
13	Cecil Fielder	.60
14	Roberto Alomar	1.00
15	Cal Ripken, Jr. (Blank-back simple card)	7.50
16	Edgar Martinez	.60
17	Ivan Rodriguez	2.50
18	Kirby Puckett	4.00
19	Ken Griffey Jr.	6.00
20	Joe Carter	.60
21	Roger Clemens	4.50
22	Dave Fleming	.60
(22)	Dave Fleming (Blank-back sample card.)	1.00
23	Paul Molitor	3.00
(23)	Paul Molitor (Blank-back sample card.)	2.75
24	Dennis Eckersley	2.50

Stat Leaders

This 90-card set features 1992 American League and National League leaders in various statistical categories. Each card front indicates the league and the category in which the player finished at or near the top. The backs have a list of the leaders; the pictured player's name is in larger type size. Cards were inserted one per foil pack.

		NM/M
Complete Set (90):		8.00
Common Player:		.05
1	Edgar Martinez	.05
2	Kirby Puckett	.30
3	Frank Thomas	.25
4	Gary Sheffield	.15
5	Andy Van Slyke	.05
6	John Kruk	.05
7	Kirby Puckett	.30
8	Carlos Baerga	.05
9	Paul Molitor	.25
10	Andy Van Slyke, Terry Pendleton	.05
11	Ryne Sandberg	.30
12	Mark Grace	.05
13	Frank Thomas	.25
14	Don Mattingly	.05
15	Ken Griffey Jr.	.45
16	Andy Van Slyke	.05
17	Mariano Duncan, Jerald Clark, Ray Lankford	.05
18	Marquis Grissom, Terry Pendleton	.05
19	Lance Johnson	.05
20	Mike Devereaux	.05
21	Brady Anderson	.05
22	Deion Sanders	.05
23	Steve Finley	.05
24	Andy Van Slyke	.05
25	Juan Gonzalez	.15
26	Mark McGwire	.50
27	Cecil Fielder	.05
28	Fred McGriff	.05
29	Barry Bonds	.60
30	Gary Sheffield	.05
31	Cecil Fielder	.05
32	Joe Carter	.05
33	Frank Thomas	.25
34	Darren Daulton	.05
35	Terry Pendleton	.05
36	Fred McGriff	.05
37	Tony Phillips	.05
38	Frank Thomas	.25
39	Roberto Alomar	.15
40	Barry Bonds	.60
41	Dave Hollins	.05
42	Andy Van Slyke	.05
43	Mark McGwire	.50
44	Edgar Martinez	.05
45	Frank Thomas	.25
46	Barry Bonds	.60
47	Gary Sheffield	.15
48	Fred McGriff	.05
49	Frank Thomas	.25
50	Danny Tartabull	.05
51	Roberto Alomar	.15
52	Barry Bonds	.60
53	John Kruk	.05
54	Brett Butler	.05
55	Kenny Lofton	.05
56	Pat Listach	.05
57	Brady Anderson	.05
58	Marquis Grissom	.05
59	Delino DeShields	.05
60	Steve Finley, Bip Roberts	.05
61	Jack McDowell	.05
62	Kevin Brown	.05
63	Melido Perez	.05
64	Terry Mulholland	.05
65	Curt Schilling	.20
66	John Smoltz, Doug Drabek, Greg Maddux	.05
67	Dennis Eckersley	.20
68	Rick Aguilera	.05
69	Jeff Montgomery	.05
70	Lee Smith	.05
71	Randy Myers	.05
72	John Wetteland	.05
73	Randy Johnson	.25
74	Melido Perez	.05
75	Roger Clemens	.35
76	John Smoltz	.05
77	David Cone	.05
78	Greg Maddux	.30
79	Roger Clemens	.35
80	Kevin Appier	.05
81	Mike Mussina	.15
82	Bill Swift	.05
83	Bob Tewksbury	.05
84	Greg Maddux	.30
85	Kevin Brown	.05
86	Jack McDowell	.05
87	Roger Clemens	.35
88	Tom Glavine	.10
89	Ken Hill, Bob Tewksbury	.05
90	Dennis Martinez, Mike Morgan	.05

Triple Crown

This three-card set commemorates the Triple Crown seasons of Hall of Famers Mickey Mantle, Frank Robinson and Carl Yastrzemski. Cards were randomly inserted in 15-card hobby packs. Card fronts have a green metallic-look textured border, with the player's name at top in gold, and "Triple Crown" in gold at bottom. There are other silver and green highlights around the photo, which feature the player set against a metallized background. Dark green backs have a player photo and information on his Triple Crown season.

		NM/M
Complete Set (3):		35.00
Common Player:		10.00
1	Mickey Mantle	22.50
2	Frank Robinson	10.00
3	Carl Yastrzemski	12.50

Rookie/Traded

Production of this 150-card set was limited to 1,950 numbered cases. Several future Hall of Famers and six dozen top rookies are featured in the set. Cards were available in packs rather than collated sets and include randomly inserted FX cards, which feature Nolan Ryan (two per 24-box case), Tim Salmon and Mike Piazza (one per 576 packs) and All-Star Rookie Team members (one per 58 packs).

		NM/M
Complete Set (150):		11.00
Common Player:		.05
Pack (12):		1.25
Wax Box (24):		20.00
1	Rickey Henderson	.75
2	Rob Deer	.05
3	Tim Belcher	.05
4	Gary Sheffield	.35
5	Fred McGriff	.05
6	Mark Whiten	.05
7	Jeff Russell	.05
8	Harold Baines	.05
9	Dave Winfield	.75
10	Ellis Burks	.05
11	Andre Dawson	.25
12	Gregg Jefferies	.05
13	Jimmy Key	.05
14	Harold Reynolds	.05
15	Tom Henke	.05
16	Paul Molitor	.75
17	Wade Boggs	1.00
18	David Cone	.05
19	Tony Fernandez	.05
20	Roberto Kelly	.05
21	Paul O'Neill	.05
22	Jose Lind	.05
23	Barry Bonds	2.00
24	Dave Stewart	.05
25	Randy Myers	.05
26	Benito Santiago	.05
27	Tim Wallach	.05
28	Greg Gagne	.05
29	Kevin Mitchell	.05
30	Jim Abbott	.05
31	Lee Smith	.05
32	Bobby Munoz RC	.05
33	Mo Sanford RC	.05
34	John Roper RC	.05
35	David Hulse RC	.05
36	Pedro Martinez	.75
37	Chuck Carr RC	.05
38	Armando Reynoso RC	.10
39	Ryan Thompson	.05
40	Carlos Garcia RC	.05
41	Matt Whiteside	.05
42	Benji Gil	.05
43	Rodney Bolton RC	.05
44	J.T. Snow	.05
45	David McCarty	.05
46	Paul Quantrill RC	.05
47	Al Martin	.05
48	Lance Painter	.05
49	Lou Frazier RC	.05
50	Eduardo Perez	.05
51	Kevin Young	.05
52	Mike Trombley	.05
53	Sterling Hitchcock RC	.10
54	Tim Bogar RC	.05
55	Hilly Hathaway RC	.05
56	Wayne Kirby RC	.05
57	Craig Paquette RC	.05
58	Bret Boone	.05
59	Greg McMichael RC	.05
60	Mike Lansing RC	.35
61	Brent Gates	.05
62	Rene Arocha	.05
63	Ricky Gutierrez	.05
64	Kevin Rogers RC	.05
65	Ken Ryan RC	.05
66	Phil Hiatt	.05
67	Pat Meares RC	.05
68	Troy Neel	.05
69	Steve Cooke	.05
70	Sherman Obando RC	.05
71	Blas Minor RC	.05
72	Angel Miranda RC	.05
73	Tom Kramer RC	.05
74	Chip Hale RC	.05
75	Brad Pennington RC	.05
76	Graeme Lloyd RC	.05
77	Darrell Whitmore RC	.05
78	David Nied	.05
79	Todd Van Poppel	.05
80	Chris Gomez RC	.10
81	Jason Bere	.05
82	Jeffrey Hammonds	.05
83	Brad Ausmus RC	.10
84	Kevin Stocker	.05
85	Jeromy Burnitz	.05
86	Aaron Sele	.05
87	Roberto Mejia RC	.05
88	Kirk Rueter RC	.10
89	Kevin Roberson RC	.05
90	Allen Watson RC	.05
91	Charlie Leibrandt	.05
92	Eric Davis	.05
93	Jody Reed	.05
94	Danny Jackson	.05
95	Gary Gaetti	.05
96	Norm Charlton	.05
97	Doug Drabek	.05
98	Scott Fletcher	.05
99	Greg Swindell	.05
100	John Smiley	.05
101	Kevin Reimer	.05
102	Andres Galarraga	.05
103	Greg Hibbard	.05
104	Chris Hammond	.05
105	Darnell Coles	.05
106	Mike Felder	.05
107	Jose Guzman	.05
108	Chris Bosio	.05
109	Spike Owen	.05
110	Felix Jose	.05
111	Cory Snyder	.05
112	Craig Lefferts	.05
113	David Wells	.05
114	Pete Incaviglia	.05
115	Mike Pagliarulo	.05
116	Dave Magadan	.05
117	Charlie Hough	.05
118	Ivan Calderon	.05
119	Manuel Lee	.05
120	Bob Patterson	.05
121	Bob Ojeda	.05
122	Scott Bankhead	.05
123	Greg Maddux	1.00
124	Chili Davis	.05
125	Milt Thompson	.05
126	Dave Martinez	.05
127	Frank Tanana	.05
128	Phil Plantier	.05
129	Juan Samuel	.05
130	Eric Young	.05
131	Joe Orsulak	.05
132	Derek Bell	.05
133	Darrin Jackson	.05
134	Tom Brunansky	.05
135	Jeff Reardon	.05
136	Kevin Higgins RC	.05
137	Joel Johnston RC	.05
138	Rick Trlicek RC	.05
139	Richie Lewis RC	.05
140	Jeff Gardner RC	.05
141	Jack Voigt RC	.05
142	Rod Correia RC	.05
143	Billy Brewer RC	.05
144	Terry Jorgensen RC	.05
145	Rich Amaral RC	.05
146	Sean Berry RC	.05
147	Dan Peltier RC	.05
148	Paul Wagner RC	.05
149	Damon Buford RC	.05
150	Wil Cordero	.05

Rookie/Traded All-Star Rookies

These cards were randomly inserted into the Score Select Rookie/Traded packs, making them among the scarcest of the year's many "chase" cards. Card fronts feature metallic foil printing. Backs have a few words about the player. Stated odds of finding an All-Star Rookie Team insert card are one per 58 packs.

		NM/M
Complete Set (10):		30.00
Common Player:		1.00
1	Jeff Conine	1.00
2	Brent Gates	1.00
3	Mike Lansing	1.00
4	Kevin Stocker	1.00
5	Mike Piazza	25.00
6	Jeffrey Hammonds	1.00
7	David Hulse	1.00
8	Tim Salmon	2.00
9	Rene Arocha	1.00
10	Greg McMichael	1.00

Rookie/Traded Inserts

Three cards honoring the 1993 Rookies of the Year and retiring superstar Nolan Ryan were issued as random inserts in the Select Rookie/Traded packs. Cards are printed with metallic foil front backgrounds. Stated odds of finding a Piazza or

Salmon card are about one per 24-box case; Ryan cards are found on average two per case.

	NM/M
Complete Set (3):	60.00
Common Player:	6.00
1NR Nolan Ryan	40.00
1ROY Tim Salmon	6.00
2ROY Mike Piazza	20.00

1994 Select Promos

To introduce its 1994 offering to dealers and collectors, Score Select created an eight-card promo set. Cards are identical in format to regular-issue cards with the exception of the word "SAMPLE" overprinted diagonally on front and back. The promos included five of the regular-run cards, a Rookie Prospect card and one each of its Rookie Surge '94 and Crown Contenders insert sets. The promos were cellopackaged with a header card describing the set and chase cards.

		NM/M
Complete Set (8):		7.50
Common Player:		.75
3	Paul Molitor	1.50
17	Kirby Puckett	2.50
19	Randy Johnson	1.50
24	John Kruk	.75
51	Jose Lind	.75
197	Ryan Klesko (Rookie Prospect)	1.00
1CC	Lenny Dykstra (Crown Contenders)	1.00
1RS	Cliff Floyd (Rookie Surge)	1.00
---	Header Card	.05

1994 Select

Both series of this premium brand from the Score/Pinnacle lineup offered 210 regular cards for a combined 420 cards, and seven insert sets. The announced press run for each series was 4,950 20-box cases. Cards have a horizontal format with a color action photo at right and a second photo at left done in a single team color-coded hue. The player's last name is dropped out of a vertical gold-foil strip between the two photos, with his first name in white at top-center. Backs are vertical with yet another color action photo at center. In a vertical bar at right, matching the color-coding on front and printed over the photo are 1993 and career stats, a "Select Stat," and a few sentences about the player. The appropriate logos and Pinnacle's optical-variable anti-counterfeiting device are at bottom-center. Thirty of the final 33 cards in the first series are a "1994 Rookie Prospect" subset, so noted in a special gold-foil logo on front.

		NM/M
Complete Set (420):		12.50
Common Player:		.05
Pack (12):		1.25
Wax Box (24):		16.00
1	Ken Griffey Jr.	1.50
2	Greg Maddux	1.00
3	Paul Molitor	.75
4	Mike Piazza	1.50
5	Jay Bell	.05
6	Frank Thomas	.75
7	Barry Larkin	.05
8	Paul O'Neill	.05
9	Darren Daulton	.05
10	Mike Greenwell	.05
11	Chuck Carr	.05
12	Joe Carter	.05
13	Lance Johnson	.05
14	Jeff Blauser	.05
15	Chris Hoiles	.05
16	Rick Wilkins	.05
17	Kirby Puckett	1.00
18	Larry Walker	.05
19	Randy Johnson	.75
20	Bernard Gilkey	.05
21	Devon White	.05
22	Randy Myers	.05
23	Don Mattingly	1.25
24	John Kruk	.05
25	Ozzie Guillen	.05
26	Jeff Conine	.05
27	Mike Macfarlane	.05
28	Dave Hollins	.05
29	Chuck Knoblauch	.05
30	Ozzie Smith	1.00
31	Harold Baines	.05
32	Ryne Sandberg	1.00
33	Ron Karkovice	.05
34	Terry Pendleton	.05
35	Wally Joyner	.05
36	Mike Mussina	.35
37	Felix Jose	.05
38	Derrick May	.05
39	Scott Cooper	.05
40	Jose Rijo	.05
41	Robin Ventura	.05
42	Charlie Hayes	.05
43	Jimmy Key	.05
44	Eric Karros	.05
45	Ruben Sierra	.05
46	Ryan Thompson	.05
47	Brian McRae	.05
48	Pat Hentgen	.05
49	John Valentin	.05
50	Al Martin	.05
51	Jose Lind	.05
52	Kevin Stocker	.05
53	Mike Gallego	.05
54	Dwight Gooden	.05
55	Brady Anderson	.05
56	Jeff King	.05
57	Mark McGwire	1.75
58	Sammy Sosa	1.00
59	Ryan Bowen	.05
60	Mark Lemke	.05
61	Roger Clemens	1.25
62	Brian Jordan	.05
63	Andres Galarraga	.05
64	Kevin Appier	.05
65	Don Slaught	.05
66	Mike Blowers	.05
67	Wes Chamberlain	.05
68	Troy Neel	.05
69	John Wetteland	.05
70	Joe Girardi	.05
71	Reggie Sanders	.05
72	Edgar Martinez	.05
73	Todd Hundley	.05
74	Pat Borders	.05
75	Roberto Mejia	.05
76	David Cone	.05
77	Tony Gwynn	1.00
78	Jim Abbott	.05
79	Jay Buhner	.05
80	Mark McLemore	.05
81	Wil Cordero	.05
82	Pedro Astacio	.05
83	Bob Tewksbury	.05
84	Dave Winfield	.75
85	Jeff Kent	.05
86	Todd Van Poppel	.05
87	Steve Avery	.05
88	Mike Lansing	.05
89	Len Dykstra	.05
90	Jose Guzman	.05
91	Brian Hunter	.05
92	Tim Raines	.05
93	Andre Dawson	.25
94	Joe Orsulak	.05
95	Ricky Jordan	.05
96	Billy Hatcher	.05
97	Jack McDowell	.05
98	Tom Pagnozzi	.05
99	Darryl Strawberry	.05
100	Mike Stanley	.05
101	Bret Saberhagen	.05
102	Willie Greene	.05
103	Bryan Harvey	.05
104	Tim Bogar	.05
105	Jack Voight	.05
106	Brad Ausmus	.05
107	Ramon Martinez	.05
108	Mike Perez	.05
109	Jeff Montgomery	.05
110	Danny Darwin	.05
111	Wilson Alvarez	.05
112	Kevin Mitchell	.05
113	David Nied	.05
114	Rich Amaral	.05
115	Stan Javier	.05
116	Mo Vaughn	.05
117	Ben McDonald	.05
118	Tom Gordon	.05
119	Carlos Garcia	.05
120	Phil Plantier	.05
121	Mike Morgan	.05
122	Pat Meares	.05
123	Kevin Young	.05
124	Jeff Fassero	.05
125	Gene Harris	.05
126	Bob Welch	.05
127	Walt Weiss	.05
128	Bobby Witt	.05
129	Andy Van Slyke	.05
130	Steve Cooke	.05
131	Mike Devereaux	.05
132	Joey Cora	.05
133	Bret Barberie	.05
134	Orel Hershiser	.05
135	Ed Sprague	.05
136	Shawon Dunston	.05
137	Alex Arias	.05
138	Archi Cianfrocco	.05
139	Tim Wallach	.05
140	Bernie Williams	.05
141	Karl Rhodes	.05
142	Pat Kelly	.05
143	Dave Magadan	.05
144	Kevin Tapani	.05
145	Eric Young	.05
146	Derek Bell	.05
147	Dante Bichette	.05
148	Geronimo Pena	.05
149	Joe Oliver	.05
150	Orestes Destrade	.05
151	Tim Naehring	.05
152	Ray Lankford	.05
153	Phil Clark	.05
154	David McCarty	.05
155	Tommy Greene	.05
156	Wade Boggs	1.00
157	Kevin Gross	.05
158	Hal Morris	.05
159	Moises Alou	.05
160	Rick Aguilera	.05
161	Curt Schilling	.35
162	Chip Hale	.05
163	Tino Martinez	.05
164	Mark Whiten	.05
165	Dave Stewart	.05
166	Steve Buechele	.05
167	Bobby Jones	.05
168	Darrin Fletcher	.05
169	John Smiley	.05
170	Cory Snyder	.05
171	Scott Erickson	.05
172	Kirk Rueter	.05
173	Dave Fleming	.05
174	John Smoltz	.05
175	Ricky Gutierrez	.05
176	Mike Bordick	.05
177	Chan Ho Park RC	1.00
178	Alex Gonzalez	.05
179	Steve Karsay	.05
180	Jeffrey Hammonds	.05
181	Manny Ramirez	.75
182	Salomon Torres	.05
183	Raul Mondesi	.05
184	James Mouton	.05
185	Cliff Floyd	.05
186	Danny Bautista	.05
187	Kurt Abbott RC	.05
188	Javier Lopez	.05
189	John Patterson	.05
190	Greg Blosser	.05
191	Bob Hamelin	.05
192	Tony Eusebio	.05
193	Carlos Delgado	.50
194	Chris Gomez	.05
195	Kelly Stinnett	.05
196	Shane Reynolds	.05
197	Ryan Klesko	.05
198	Jim Edmonds	.05
199	James Hurst	.05
200	Dave Staton	.05
201	Rondell White	.05
202	Keith Mitchell	.05
203	Darren Oliver	.05
204	Mike Matheny	.05
205	Chris Turner	.05
206	Matt Mieske	.05
207	N.L. Team Checklist	.05
208	N.L. Team Checklist	.05
209	A.L. Team Checklist	.05
210	A.L. Team Checklist	.05
211	Barry Bonds	2.00
212	Juan Gonzalez	.40
213	Jim Eisenreich	.05
214	Ivan Rodriguez	.65
215	Tony Phillips	.05
216	John Jaha	.05
217	Lee Smith	.05
218	Bip Roberts	.05
219	Dave Hansen	.05
220	Pat Listach	.05
221	Willie McGee	.05
222	Damion Easley	.05
223	Dean Palmer	.05
224	Mike Moore	.05
225	Brian Harper	.05
226	Gary DiSarcina	.05
227	Delino DeShields	.05
228	Otis Nixon	.05
229	Roberto Alomar	.30
230	Mark Grace	.05
231	Kenny Lofton	.05
232	Gregg Jefferies	.05
233	Cecil Fielder	.05
234	Jeff Bagwell	.75
235	Albert Belle	.05
236	Dave Justice	.05
237	Tom Henke	.05
238	Bobby Bonilla	.05
239	John Olerud	.05
240	Robby Thompson	.05
241	Dave Valle	.05
242	Marquis Grissom	.05
243	Greg Swindell	.05
244	Todd Zeile	.05
245	Dennis Eckersley	.65
246	Jose Offerman	.05
247	Greg McMichael	.05
248	Tim Belcher	.05
249	Cal Ripken, Jr.	2.00
250	Tom Glavine	.05
251	Luis Polonia	.05
252	Bill Swift	.05
253	Juan Guzman	.05
254	Rickey Henderson	.75
255	Terry Mulholland	.05
256	Gary Sheffield	.40
257	Terry Steinbach	.05
258	Brett Butler	.05
259	Jason Bere	.05
260	Doug Strange	.05
261	Kent Hrbek	.05
262	Graeme Lloyd	.05
263	Lou Frazier	.05
264	Charles Nagy	.05
265	Bret Boone	.05
266	Kirk Gibson	.05
267	Kevin Brown	.05
269	Matt Williams	.05
270	Greg Gagne	.05
271	Mariano Duncan	.05
272	Jeff Russell	.05
273	Eric Davis	.05
274	Shane Mack	.05
275	Jose Vizcaino	.05
276	Jose Canseco	.45
277	Roberto Hernandez	.05
278	Royce Clayton	.05
279	Carlos Baerga	.05
280	Pete Incaviglia	.05
281	Brent Gates	.05
282	Jeromy Burnitz	.05
283	Chili Davis	.05
284	Pete Harnisch	.05
285	Alan Trammell	.05
286	Eric Anthony	.05
287	Ellis Burks	.05
288	Julio Franco	.05
289	Jack Morris	.05
290	Erik Hanson	.05
291	Chuck Finley	.05
292	Reggie Jefferson	.05
293	Kevin McReynolds	.05
294	Greg Hibbard	.05
295	Travis Fryman	.05
296	Craig Biggio	.05
297	Kenny Rogers	.05
298	Dave Henderson	.05
299	Jim Thome	.50
300	Rene Arocha	.05
301	Pedro Munoz	.05
302	David Hulse	.05
303	Greg Vaughn	.05
304	Darren Lewis	.05
305	Deion Sanders	.05
306	Danny Tartabull	.05
307	Darryl Hamilton	.05
308	Andujar Cedeno	.05
309	Tim Salmon	.05
310	Tony Fernandez	.05
311	Alex Fernandez	.05
312	Roberto Kelly	.05
313	Harold Reynolds	.05
314	Chris Sabo	.05
315	Howard Johnson	.05
316	Mark Portugal	.05
317	Rafael Palmeiro	.65
318	Pete Smith	.05
319	Will Clark	.05
320	Henry Rodriguez	.05
321	Omar Vizquel	.05
322	David Segui	.05
323	Lou Whitaker	.05
324	Felix Fermin	.05
325	Spike Owen	.05
326	Darryl Kile	.05
327	Chad Kreuter	.05
328	Rod Beck	.05
329	Eddie Murray	.75
330	B.J. Surhoff	.05
331	Mickey Tettleton	.05
332	Pedro Martinez	.75
333	Roger Pavlik	.05
334	Eddie Taubensee	.05
335	John Doherty	.05
336	Jody Reed	.05
337	Aaron Sele	.05
338	Leo Gomez	.05
339	Dave Nilsson	.05
340	Rob Dibble	.05
341	John Burkett	.05
342	Wayne Kirby	.05
343	Dan Wilson	.05
344	Armando Reynoso	.05
345	Chad Curtis	.05
346	Dennis Martinez	.05
347	Cal Eldred	.05
348	Luis Gonzalez	.05
349	Doug Drabek	.05
350	Jim Leyritz	.05
351	Mark Langston	.05
352	Darrin Jackson	.05
353	Sid Fernandez	.05
354	Benito Santiago	.05
355	Kevin Seitzer	.05
356	Bo Jackson	.05
357	David Wells	.05
358	Paul Sorrento	.05
359	Ken Caminiti	.05
360	Eduardo Perez	.05
361	Orlando Merced	.05
362	Steve Finley	.05
363	Andy Benes	.05
364	Manuel Lee	.05
365	Todd Benzinger	.05
366	Sandy Alomar Jr.	.05
367	Rex Hudler	.05
368	Mike Henneman	.05
369	Vince Coleman	.05
370	Kirt Manwaring	.05
371	Ken Hill	.05
372	Glenallen Hill	.05
373	Sean Berry	.05
374	Geronimo Berroa	.05
375	Duane Ward	.05
376	Allen Watson	.05
377	Marc Newfield	.05
378	Dan Miceli	.05
379	Denny Hocking	.05
380	Mark Kiefer	.05
381	Tony Tarasco	.05
382	Tony Longmire	.05
383	Brian Anderson RC	.05
384	Fernando Vina	.05
385	Hector Carrasco	.05
386	Mike Kelly	.05
387	Greg Colbrunn	.05
388	Roger Salkeld	.05
389	Steve Trachsel	.05
390	Rich Becker	.05
391	Billy Taylor RC	.05
392	Rich Rowland	.05
393	Carl Everett	.05
394	Johnny Ruffin	.05
395	Keith Lockhart RC	.05
396	J.R. Phillips	.05
397	Sterling Hitchcock	.05
398	Jorge Fabregas	.05
399	Jeff Granger	.05
400	Eddie Zambrano RC	.05
401	Rikkert Faneyte RC	.05
402	Gerald Williams	.05
403	Joey Hamilton	.05
404	Joe Hall RC	.05
405	John Hudek RC	.05
406	Roberto Petagine	.05
407	Charles Johnson	.05
408	Mark Smith	.05
409	Jeff Juden	.05
410	Carlos Pulido RC	.05
411	Paul Shuey	.05
412	Rob Butler	.05
413	Mark Acre	.05
414	Greg Pirkl	.05
415	Melvin Nieves	.05
416	Tim Hyers RC	.05
417	N.L. Checklist	.05
418	N.L. Checklist	.05
419	A.L. Checklist	.05
420	A.L. Checklist	.05

Crown Contenders

Candidates for the major baseball annual awards are featured in this subset. Horizontal-format cards have a color player photo printed on a holographic foil background. Backs are vertically oriented with a player portrait photo and justification for the player's inclusion in the set. Cards are numbered with a "CC" prefix and feature a special optical-variable anti-counterfeiting device at bottom-center. According to stated odds of one card on average in every 24 packs it has been estimated that fewer than 12,000 of each Crown Contenders card was produced.

		NM/M
Complete Set (10):		12.50
Common Player:		.50
1	Len Dykstra	.50
2	Greg Maddux	1.75
3	Roger Clemens	2.00
4	Randy Johnson	1.50
5	Frank Thomas	1.50
6	Barry Bonds	3.00
7	Juan Gonzalez	1.00
8	John Olerud	.50
9	Mike Piazza	2.50
10	Ken Griffey Jr.	2.50

MVP

Paul Molitor was the 1994 Select MVP and is featured in this one card set. Molitor is pictured in front of three distinct foil designs across the rest of the card.

	NM/M
MVP1 Paul Molitor	5.00

Rookie of the Year

Carlos Delgado was the 1994 Select Rookie of the Year. Delgado is pictured on top of a glowing foil background with his initials in large capital letters in the background and Rookie of the Year printed across the bottom.

	NM/M
RY1 Carlos Delgado	7.50

Rookie Surge

Each series of 1994 Score Select offered a chase card set of nine top rookies. Fronts feature action photos set against a rainbow-colored metallic foil background. Backs have a portrait photo and a few words about the player. Cards are numbered with an "RS" prefix and were inserted at an average rate of one per 48 packs.

		NM/M
Complete Set (18):		10.00
Common Player:		.75
1	Cliff Floyd	.75
2	Bob Hamelin	.75
3	Ryan Klesko	.75
4	Carlos Delgado	3.00
5	Jeffrey Hammonds	.75
6	Rondell White	.75
7	Salomon Torres	.75
8	Steve Karsay	.75
9	Javier Lopez	.75
10	Manny Ramirez	3.00
11	Tony Tarasco	.75
12	Kurt Abbott	.75
13	Chan Ho Park	.75
14	Rich Becker	.75
15	James Mouton	.75
16	Alex Gonzalez	.75
17	Raul Mondesi	.75
18	Steve Trachsel	.75

Salute

With odds of finding one of these cards stated at one per 360 packs, it is estimated that only about 4,000 of each of this two-card chase set were produced.

		NM/M
Complete Set (2):		15.00
1	Cal Ripken, Jr.	12.50
2	Dave Winfield	5.00

Skills

Select Skills is a 10-card insert that was randomly inserted into every 24 packs. Ten specific skills were designated and matched with the player whom, in the opinion of Select officials, demonstrated that particular skill the best in baseball. Each card is printed on a foil background with the player name vertically on left side of the card and the skill that they are being featured for along the bottom.

		NM/M
Complete Set (10):		15.00
Common Player:		.75
1	Randy Johnson	3.00
2	Barry Larkin	.75
3	Len Dykstra	.75
4	Kenny Lofton	.75
5	Juan Gonzalez	1.50
6	Barry Bonds	6.00
7	Marquis Grissom	.75
8	Ivan Rodriguez	2.50
9	Larry Walker	.75
10	Travis Fryman	.75

1995 Select Samples

Pinnacle's hobby-only Select brand issue for 1995 was previewed with this four-card cello-packed sample set. Three player cards are in the basic format of the regular-issue Select cards, except they have a large white "SAMPLE" printed diagonally across the front and back. The fourth card in the sample pack is a header card advertising the features of the issue.

		NM/M
Complete Set (4):		4.00
Common Player:		.50
34	Roberto Alomar	.50
37	Jeff Bagwell	.75
241	Alex Rodriguez	4.00
--	Header Card	.05

1995 Select

The 250 regular-issue cards in Pinnacle's mid-price brand feature three basic formats. Veteran players' cards are presented horizontally and feature an action photo at left. At right is a portrait in a trapezoidal gold-foil frame set against a team color-coordinated marbled background. The team logo beneath the portrait and the player's name below that are printed in gold foil. Backs feature a black-and-

white photo with a few career highlights, 1994 and career stats, and a "Select Stat" printed in red. The colored marble effect is carried over from the front. The Select Rookie cards, which are grouped toward the end of the set, are vertical in format and feature a borderless player photo with a gold-foil band at bottom which includes the player name and team logo, along with waves of gold emanating from the logo. Backs have a small, narrow color photo at left, with a large sepia version of the same photo ghosted at center and overprinted with a career summary. At bottom are 1994 and career stats. Ending the set are a series of "Show Time" cards of top prospects. Cards feature large gold-foil "Show Time" and team logos at bottom, with a facsimile autograph printed above. The player photo is shown as if at a curtain raising, with spotlight effects behind. Backs repeat the curtain and spotlight motif and feature another player photo, with autograph above. Production of this hobby-only product was stated as 4,950 cases, which translates to about 110,000 of each regular-issue card. A special card (#251) of Hideo Nomo was added to the set later. It was not issued in foil packs, but distributed to dealers who had purchased Select cases.

		NM/M
Complete Set (251):		9.00
Common Player:		.05
Artist's Proofs:		10X
Pack (12):		1.50
Wax Box (24):		17.50
1	Cal Ripken Jr.	1.50
2	Robin Ventura	.05
3	Al Martin	.05
4	Jeff Frye	.05
5	Darryl Strawberry	.05
6	Chan Ho Park	.05
7	Steve Avery	.05
8	Bret Boone	.05
9	Danny Tartabull	.05
10	Dante Bichette	.05
11	Rondell White	.05
12	Dave McCarty	.05
13	Bernard Gilkey	.05
14	Mark McGwire	1.25
15	Ruben Sierra	.05
16	Wade Boggs	.75
17	Mike Piazza	1.00
18	Jeffrey Hammonds	.05
19	Mike Mussina	.35
20	Darryl Kile	.05
21	Greg Maddux	.75
22	Frank Thomas	.65
23	Kevin Appier	.05
24	Jay Bell	.05
25	Kirk Gibson	.05
26	Pat Hentgen	.05
27	Joey Hamilton	.05
28	Bernie Williams	.05
29	Aaron Sele	.05
30	Delino DeShields	.05
31	Danny Bautista	.05
32	Jim Thome	.45
33	Rikkert Faneyte	.05
34	Roberto Alomar	.20
35	Paul Molitor	.65
36	Allen Watson	.05
37	Jeff Bagwell	.65
38	Jay Buhner	.05
39	Marquis Grissom	.05
40	Jim Edmonds	.05
41	Ryan Klesko	.05
42	Fred McGriff	.05
43	Tony Tarasco	.05
44	Darren Daulton	.05
45	Marc Newfield	.05
46	Barry Bonds	1.50
47	Bobby Bonilla	.05
48	Greg Pirkl	.05
49	Steve Karsay	.05
50	Bob Hamelin	.05
51	Javier Lopez	.05
52	Barry Larkin	.05
53	Kevin Young	.05
54	Sterling Hitchcock	.05
55	Tom Glavine	.05
56	Carlos Delgado	.40
57	Darren Oliver	.05
58	Cliff Floyd	.05
59	Tim Salmon	.05
60	Albert Belle	.35
61	Salomon Torres	.05
62	Gary Sheffield	.35
63	Ivan Rodriguez	.50
64	Charles Nagy	.05
65	Eduardo Perez	.05
66	Terry Steinbach	.05
67	Dave Justice	.05
68	Jason Bere	.05
69	Dave Nilsson	.05
70	Brian Anderson	.05
71	Billy Ashley	.05
72	Roger Clemens	.85
73	Jimmy Key	.05
74	Wally Joyner	.05
75	Andy Benes	.05
76	Ray Lankford	.05
77	Jeff Kent	.05
78	Moises Alou	.05
79	Kirby Puckett	.75
80	Joe Carter	.05
81	Manny Ramirez	.65
82	J.R. Phillips	.05
83	Matt Mieske	.05
84	John Olerud	.05
85	Andres Galarraga	.05
86	Juan Gonzalez	.35
87	Pedro Martinez	.05
88	Dean Palmer	.05
89	Ken Griffey Jr.	1.00
90	Brian Jordan	.05
91	Hal Morris	.05
92	Lenny Dykstra	.05
93	Wil Cordero	.05
94	Tony Gwynn	.75
95	Alex Gonzalez	.05
96	Cecil Fielder	.05
97	Mo Vaughn	.05
98	John Valentin	.05
99	Will Clark	.05
100	Geronimo Pena	.05
101	Don Mattingly	.85
102	Charles Johnson	.05
103	Raul Mondesi	.05
104	Reggie Sanders	.05
105	Royce Clayton	.05
106	Reggie Jefferson	.05
107	Craig Biggio	.05
108	Jack McDowell	.05
109	James Mouton	.05
110	Mike Greenwell	.05
111	David Cone	.05
112	Matt Williams	.05
113	Garret Anderson	.05
114	Carlos Garcia	.05
115	Alex Fernandez	.05
116	Deion Sanders	.05
117	Chili Davis	.05
118	Mike Kelly	.05
119	Jeff Conine	.05
120	Kenny Lofton	.05
121	Rafael Palmeiro	.50
122	Chuck Knoblauch	.05
123	Ozzie Smith	.75
124	Carlos Baerga	.05
125	Brett Butler	.05
126	Sammy Sosa	.75
127	Ellis Burks	.05
128	Bret Saberhagen	.05
129	Doug Drabek	.05
130	Dennis Martinez	.05
131	Paul O'Neill	.05
132	Travis Fryman	.05
133	Brent Gates	.05
134	Rickey Henderson	.65
135	Randy Johnson	.65
136	Mark Langston	.05
137	Greg Colbrunn	.05
138	Jose Rijo	.05
139	Bryan Harvey	.05
140	Dennis Eckersley	.50
141	Ron Gant	.05
142	Carl Everett	.05
143	Jeff Granger	.05
144	Ben McDonald	.05
145	Kurt Abbott	.05
146	Jim Abbott	.05
147	Jason Jacome	.05
148	Rico Brogna	.05
149	Cal Eldred	.05
150	Rich Becker	.05
151	Pete Harnisch	.05
152	Roberto Petagine	.05
153	Jacob Brumfield	.05
154	Todd Hundley	.05
155	Roger Cedeno	.05
156	Harold Baines	.05
157	Steve Dunn	.05
158	Tim Belk	.05
159	Marty Cardova	.05
160	Russ Davis	.05
161	Jose Malave	.05
162	Brian Hunter	.05
163	Andy Pettitte	.20
164	Brooks Kieschnick	.05
165	Midre Cummings	.05
166	Frank Rodriguez	.05
167	Chad Mottola	.05
168	Brian Barber	.05
169	Tim Unroe	.05
170	Shane Andrews	.05
171	Kevin Flora	.05
172	Ray Durham	.05
173	Chipper Jones	.75
174	Butch Huskey	.05
175	Ray McDavid	.05
176	Jeff Cirillo	.05
177	Terry Pendleton	.05
178	Scott Ruffcorn	.05
179	Ray Holbert	.05
180	Joe Randa	.05
181	Jose Oliva	.05
182	Andy Van Slyke	.05
183	Albie Lopez	.05
184	Chad Curtis	.05
185	Ozzie Guillen	.05
186	Chad Ogea	.05
187	Dan Wilson	.05
188	Tony Fernandez	.05
189	John Smoltz	.05
190	Willie Greene	.05
191	Darren Lewis	.05
192	Orlando Miller	.05
193	Kurt Miller	.05
194	Andrew Lorraine	.05
195	Ernie Young	.05
196	Jimmy Haynes	.05
197	Raul Casanova RC	.05
198	Joe Vitiello	.05
199	Brad Woodall	.05
200	Juan Acevedo	.05
201	Michael Tucker	.05
202	Shawn Green	.05
203	Alex Rodriguez	1.25
204	Julian Tavarez	.05
205	Jose Lima	.05
206	Wilson Alvarez	.05
207	Rich Aude	.05
208	Armando Benitez	.05
209	Dwayne Hosey	.05
210	Gabe White	.05
211	Joey Eischen	.05
212	Bill Pulsipher	.05
213	Robby Thompson	.05
214	Toby Borland	.05
215	Rusty Greer	.05
216	Fausto Cruz	.05
217	Luis Ortiz	.05
218	Duane Singleton	.05
219	Troy Percival	.05
220	Gregg Jefferies	.05
221	Mark Grace	.05
222	Mickey Tettleton	.05
223	Phil Plantier	.05
224	Larry Walker	.05
225	Ken Caminiti	.05
226	Dave Winfield	.65
227	Brady Anderson	.05
228	Kevin Brown	.05
229	Andujar Cedeno	.05
230	Roberto Kelly	.05
231	Jose Canseco	.35
231	Scott Ruffcorn (Showtime)	.05
232	Billy Ashley (Showtime)	.05
234	J.R. Phillips (Showtime)	.05
235	Chipper Jones (Showtime)	.40
236	Charles Johnson (Showtime)	.05
237	Midre Cummings (Showtime)	.05
238	Brian Hunter (Showtime)	.05
239	Garret Anderson (Showtime)	.05
240	Shawn Green (Showtime)	.10
241	Alex Rodriguez (Showtime)	.65
242	Checklist #1 (Frank Thomas)	.35
243	Checklist #2 (Ken Griffey Jr.)	.50
244	Checklist #3 (Albert Belle)	.05
245	Checklist #4 (Cal Ripken Jr.)	.65
246	Checklist #5 (Barry Bonds)	.75
247	Checklist #6 (Raul Mondesi)	.05
248	Checklist #7 (Mike Piazza)	.65
249	Checklist #8 (Jeff Bagwell)	.30
250	Checklist #9 (Jeff Bagwell, Frank Thomas, Ken Griffey Jr., Mike Piazza)	.25
251	Hideo Nomo	.35

Artist's Proofs

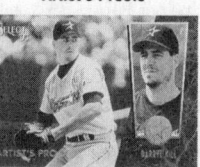

Among the scarcest and most valuable of 1995's baseball card inserts are the Select Artist's Proof parallel set. While an AP card is found on average once per 24 packs, the limited print run of the basic Select set means that only about 475 of each of the 250 regular-issue cards in the Select set were made in this edition. The AP inserts have a gold-foil "ARTIST'S PROOF" line at bottom, and other gold-foil highlights are embossed, rather than merely stamped on, as on regular Select cards.

	NM/M
Complete Set (250):	100.00
Common Player:	1.00
AP Stars:	10X

Big Sticks

With fronts printed in what Pinnacle describes as "holographic Gold Rush technology," the Big Sticks

chase card issue offers a dozen of the game's big hitters in action photos superimposed over their team's logo. Conventionally printed backs have another player photo, along with a summary of career highlights and description of the player's power potential. Stated odds of pulling a Big Sticks chase card are one per 48 packs, on average. Cards are numbered with a "BS" prefix.

		NM/M
Complete Set (12):		40.00
Common Player:		1.50
1	Frank Thomas	4.00
2	Ken Griffey Jr.	7.50
3	Cal Ripken Jr.	10.00
4	Mike Piazza	7.50
5	Don Mattingly	6.00
6	Will Clark	1.50
7	Tony Gwynn	5.00
8	Jeff Bagwell	4.00
9	Barry Bonds	10.00
10	Paul Molitor	4.00
11	Matt Williams	1.50
12	Albert Belle	1.50

Can't Miss

A mix of rookies and sophomore standouts, along with a few players of slightly longer service are presented in this chase set. Cards feature color player action photos printed on a metallic red background, with their last name in gold foil at lower-left. An umpire on the "Can't Miss" logo is at upper-left. Backs repeat the logo, have a tall, narrow player photo, a few biographical details and a paragraph of career summary. Cards are numbered with a "CM" prefix.

		NM/M
Complete Set (12):		10.00
Common Player:		.35
1	Cliff Floyd	.35
2	Ryan Klesko	.35
3	Charles Johnson	.35
4	Raul Mondesi	.35
5	Manny Ramirez	2.00
6	Billy Ashley	.35
7	Alex Gonzalez	.35
8	Carlos Delgado	.75
9	Garret Anderson	.35
10	Alex Rodriguez	5.00
11	Chipper Jones	3.00
12	Shawn Green	.75

Sure Shots

Ten of Select's picks for future stardom are featured in this chase set, the toughest find of any of the 1995 Select inserts, at an average rate of one per 90 packs. Card fronts feature player action photos set against a gold "Dufex" foil printed background with a Sure Shots logo vertically at left. Backs have a blue background with a few words

about the player and a portrait photo at left. Cards are numbered with a "SS" prefix.

		NM/M
Complete Set (10):		10.00
Common Player:		1.00
1	Ben Grieve	1.00
2	Kevin Witt	1.00
3	Mark Farris	1.00
4	Paul Konerko	3.00
5	Dustin Hermanson	1.00
6	Ramon Castro	1.00
7	McKay Christensen	1.00
8	Brian Buchanan	1.00
9	Paul Wilson	1.00
10	Terrence Long	1.00

Certified Samples

Pinnacle's hobby-only Select brand issue for 1995 was previewed with this four-card cello-packed sample set. Three player cards are in the basic format of the regular-issue Select cards, except they have a large "SAMPLE" printed diagonally across the front and back. The fourth card in the sample pack is a header card advertising the features of the issue.

		NM/M
Complete Set (8):		7.50
Common Player:		.50
2	Reggie Sanders	.50
10	Mo Vaughn	.50
39	Mike Piazza	2.00
50	Mark McGwire	2.50
75	Roberto Alomar	.65
89	Larry Walker	.50
110	Ray Durham	.50
3 of 12	Cal Ripken Jr. (Gold Team)	4.00

1995 Select Certified

The concepts of hobby-only distribution and limited production, which were the hallmarks of Pinnacle's Select brand, were carried a step further with the postseason release of Select Certified baseball. Printed on double-thick cardboard stock card fronts feature all metallic-foil printing protected by a double laminated gloss coat.

Backs have key player stats against each team in the league. The final 44 cards in the set are distinguished with a special Rookie logo and with gold added to the silver foil in the photo background.

		NM/M
Complete Set (135):		10.00
Common Player:		.05
Mirror Gold Stars:		5X
Pack (6):		2.00
Wax Box (20):		25.00
1	Barry Bonds	2.50
2	Reggie Sanders	.05
3	Terry Steinbach	.05
4	Eduardo Perez	.05
5	Frank Thomas	.75
6	Wil Cordero	.05
7	John Olerud	.05
8	Deion Sanders	.05
9	Mike Mussina	.40
10	Mo Vaughn	.05
11	Will Clark	.05
12	Chili Davis	.05
13	Jimmy Key	.05
14	Eddie Murray	.75
15	Bernard Gilkey	.05
16	David Cone	.05
17	Tim Salmon	.05
19	Steve Ontiveros	.05
20	Andres Galarraga	.05
21	Don Mattingly	1.25
22	Kevin Appier	.05
23	Paul Molitor	.75
24	Edgar Martinez	.05
25	Andy Benes	.05
26	Rafael Palmeiro	.65
27	Barry Larkin	.05
28	Gary Sheffield	.25
29	Wally Joyner	.05
30	Wade Boggs	1.00
31	Rico Brogna	.05
32	Eddie Murray (Murray Tribute)	.40
33	Kirby Puckett	1.00
34	Bobby Bonilla	.05
35	Hal Morris	.05
36	Moises Alou	.05
37	Javier Lopez	.05
38	Chuck Knoblauch	.05
39	Mike Piazza	1.50
40	Travis Fryman	.05
41	Rickey Henderson	.75
42	Jim Thome	.60
43	Carlos Baerga	.05
44	Dean Palmer	.05
45	Kirk Gibson	.05
46	Bret Saberhagen	.05
47	Cecil Fielder	.05
48	Manny Ramirez	.75
49	Derek Bell	.05
50	Mark McGwire	2.00
51	Jim Edmonds	.05
52	Robin Ventura	.05
53	Ryan Klesko	.05
54	Jeff Bagwell	.75
55	Ozzie Smith	1.00
56	Albert Belle	.05
57	Darren Daulton	.05
58	Jeff Conine	.05
59	Greg Maddux	1.00
60	Lenny Dykstra	.05
61	Randy Johnson	.75
62	Fred McGriff	.05
63	Ray Lankford	.05
64	Dave Justice	.05
65	Paul O'Neill	.05
66	Tony Gwynn	1.00
67	Matt Williams	.05
68	Dante Bichette	.05
69	Craig Biggio	.05
70	Ken Griffey Jr.	1.50
71	J.T. Snow	.05
72	Cal Ripken Jr.	2.50
73	Jay Bell	.05
74	Joe Carter	.05
75	Roberto Alomar	.30
76	Benji Gil	.05
77	Ivan Rodriguez	.65
78	Raul Mondesi	.05
79	Cliff Floyd	.05
80	Eric Karros, Mike Piazza, Raul Mondesi (Dodger Dynasty)	.30
81	Royce Clayton	.05
82	Billy Ashley	.05
83	Joey Hamilton	.05
84	Sammy Sosa	1.00
85	Jason Bere	.05
86	Dennis Martinez	.05
87	Greg Vaughn	.05
88	Roger Clemens	1.25
89	Larry Walker	.05
90	Mark Grace	.05
91	Kenny Lofton	.05
92	Carlos Perez RC	.05
93	Roger Cedeno	.05
94	Scott Ruffcorn	.05
95	Jim Pittsley	.05
96	Andy Pettitte	.20
97	James Baldwin	.05
98	Hideo Nomo RC	1.50
99	Ismael Valdes	.05
100	Armando Benitez	.05
101	Jose Malave	.05
102	Bobby Higginson RC	.25

103	LaTroy Hawkins	.05
104	Russ Davis	.05
105	Shawn Green	.40
106	Joe Vitiello	.05
107	Chipper Jones	1.00
108	Shane Andrews	.05
109	Jose Oliva	.05
110	Ray Durham	.05
111	Jon Nunnally	.05
112	Alex Gonzalez	.05
113	Vaughn Eshelman	.05
114	Marty Cordova	.05
115	Mark Grudzielanek RC	.25
116	Brian Hunter	.05
117	Charles Johnson	.05
118	Alex Rodriguez	2.00
119	David Bell	.05
120	Todd Hollandsworth	.05
121	Joe Randa	.05
122	Derek Jeter	2.50
123	Frank Rodriguez	.05
124	Curtis Goodwin	.05
125	Bill Pulsipher	.05
126	John Mabry	.05
127	Julian Tavarez	.05
128	Edgardo Alfonzo	.05
129	Orlando Miller	.05
130	Juan Acevedo	.05
131	Jeff Cirillo	.05
132	Roberto Petagine	.05
133	Antonio Osuna	.05
134	Michael Tucker	.05
135	Garret Anderson	.05
2131	Cal Ripken Jr. (Consecutive Game Record)	1.00

Mirror Gold

Inserted at an average rate of one per nine packs, this parallel set is a gold-foil version of the regular Select Certified set. Backs have a "MIRROR GOLD" notation at bottom.

		NM/M
Complete Set (135):		150.00
Common Player:		1.00
Mirror Gold Stars:		5X

Checklists

The seven checklists issued with Select Certified are not numbered as part of the set. They are found one per foil pack and are printed on much thinner card stock than the regular-issue cards.

		NM/M
Complete Set (7):		2.00
Common Player:		.40
1	Ken Griffey Jr. (A.L., #3-41)	.50
2	Frank Thomas (A.L., #42-95)	.40
3	Cal Ripken Jr. (A.L., #96-135)	.65
4	Jeff Bagwell (N.L., #1-58)	.40
5	Mike Piazza (N.L., #59-92)	.50
6	Barry Bonds (N.L., #93-133)	.65
7	Manny Ramirez, Raul Mondesi (Chase Cards)	.40

Future

A striking new all-metal, brushed-foil printing technology was used in the production of this chase set of 10 rookie players with "unlimited future potential." Stated

odds of finding a Certified Future insert card were one in 19 packs.

		NM/M
Complete Set (10):		10.00
Common Player:		.50
1	Chipper Jones	2.00
2	Curtis Goodwin	.50
3	Hideo Nomo	1.00
4	Shawn Green	1.00
5	Ray Durham	.50
6	Todd Hollandsworth	.50
7	Brian Hunter	.50
8	Carlos Delgado	1.00
9	Michael Tucker	.50
10	Alex Rodriguez	4.00

Gold Team

A dozen of the top position players in the league were selected for appearance in this insert set. Cards are printed in a special double-sided, all-gold Dufex technology. An action photo is featured on the front, a portrait on back. Odds of picking a Gold Team card were stated as one in 41 packs.

		NM/M
Complete Set (12):		40.00
Common Player:		2.00
1	Ken Griffey Jr.	7.50
2	Frank Thomas	4.00
3	Cal Ripken Jr.	10.00
4	Jeff Bagwell	4.00
5	Mike Piazza	7.50
6	Barry Bonds	10.00
7	Matt Williams	4.00
8	Don Mattingly	6.00
9	Will Clark	2.00
10	Tony Gwynn	5.00
11	Kirby Puckett	5.00
12	Jose Canseco	2.50

Potential Unlimited

Dufex printing with textured foil highlights and transparent inks is featured in this chase set, produced in an edition of 1,975, as witnessed by the numbering on card backs. Approximate odds of finding a Potential Unlimited card are one per 29 packs. A super-scarce edition of 903 cards each featuring "microetch" foil printing technology was issued at the rate of one per 70 packs.

		NM/M
Complete Set (20):		35.00
Common Player:		1.00
903s:		2.5X
1	Cliff Floyd	1.00
2	Manny Ramirez	4.50
3	Raul Mondesi	1.00
4	Scott Ruffcorn	1.00
5	Billy Ashley	1.00
6	Alex Gonzalez	1.00
7	Midre Cummings	1.00
8	Charles Johnson	1.00
9	Garret Anderson	1.00
10	Hideo Nomo	2.00
11	Chipper Jones	8.00
12	Curtis Goodwin	1.00
13	Frank Rodriguez	1.00
14	Shawn Green	2.00
15	Ray Durham	1.00
16	Todd Hollandsworth	1.00
17	Brian Hunter	1.00
18	Carlos Delgado	1.00
19	Michael Tucker	1.00
20	Alex Rodriguez	1.00

1996 Select

Select's 1996 baseball set has 200 cards in it, including 35 rookies, five checklists and 10 Lineup Leaders subset cards. All 200 cards are also reprinted as part of an Artist's Proof parallel set, using a holographic Artist's Proof logo. Cards were seeded one per every 35 packs; there were approximately 435 sets produced. Three insert sets were also created: Claim to Fame, En Fuego and Team Nucleus.

		NM/M
Complete Set (200):		9.00
Common Player:		.05
Artist's Proofs:		7X
Pack (10):		1.00
Wax Box (24):		16.00
1	Wade Boggs	1.00
2	Shawn Green	.35
3	Andres Galarraga	.05
4	Bill Pulsipher	.05
5	Chuck Knoblauch	.05
6	Ken Griffey Jr.	1.25
7	Greg Maddux	1.00
8	Manny Ramirez	.75
9	Ivan Rodriguez	.65
10	Tim Salmon	.05
11	Frank Thomas	.75
12	Jeff Bagwell	.75
13	Travis Fryman	.05
14	Kenny Lofton	.05
15	Matt Williams	.05
16	Jay Bell	.05
17	Ken Caminiti	.05
18	Ray Lankford	.05
19	Cal Ripken Jr.	2.00
20	Roger Clemens	1.00
21	Carlos Baerga	.05
22	Mike Piazza	1.25
23	Gregg Jefferies	.05
24	Reggie Sanders	.05
25	Rondell White	.05
26	Sammy Sosa	1.00
27	Kevin Appier	.05
28	Kevin Seitzer	.05
29	Gary Sheffield	.40
30	Mike Mussina	.35
31	Mark McGwire	1.50
32	Barry Larkin	.05
33	Marc Newfield	.05
34	Ismael Valdes	.05
35	Marty Cordova	.05
36	Albert Belle	.05
37	Johnny Damon	.35
38	Garret Anderson	.05
39	Cecil Fielder	.05
40	John Mabry	.05
41	Chipper Jones	1.00
42	Omar Vizquel	.05
43	Jose Rijo	.05
44	Charles Johnson	.05
45	Alex Rodriguez	1.50
46	Rico Brogna	.05
47	Joe Carter	.05
48	Mo Vaughn	.05
49	Moises Alou	.05
50	Raul Mondesi	.05
51	Robin Ventura	.05
52	Jim Thome	.60
53	Dave Justice	.05
54	Jeff King	.05
55	Brian Hunter	.05
56	Juan Gonzalez	.40
57	John Olerud	.05
58	Rafael Palmeiro	.65
59	Tony Gwynn	1.00
60	Eddie Murray	.75
61	Jason Isringhausen	.05

62	Dante Bichette	.05
63	Randy Johnson	.75
64	Kirby Puckett	1.00
65	Jim Edmonds	.05
66	David Cone	.05
67	Ozzie Smith	1.00
68	Fred McGriff	.05
69	Darren Daulton	.05
70	Edgar Martinez	.05
71	J.T. Snow	.05
72	Butch Huskey	.05
73	Hideo Nomo	.40
74	Pedro Martinez	.75
75	Bobby Bonilla	.05
76	Jeff Conine	.05
77	Ryan Klesko	.05
78	Bernie Williams	.25
79	Andre Dawson	.05
80	Trevor Hoffman	.05
81	Mark Grace	.05
82	Benji Gil	.05
83	Eric Karros	.05
84	Pete Schourek	.05
85	Edgardo Alfonzo	.05
86	Jay Buhner	.05
87	Vinny Castilla	.05
88	Bret Boone	.05
89	Ray Durham	.05
90	Brian Jordan	.05
91	Jose Canseco	.40
92	Paul O'Neill	.05
93	Chili Davis	.05
94	Tom Glavine	.30
95	Julian Tavarez	.05
96	Derek Bell	.05
97	Will Clark	.05
98	Larry Walker	.05
99	Denny Neagle	.05
100	Alex Fernandez	.05
101	Barry Bonds	2.00
102	Ben McDonald	.05
103	Andy Pettitte	.25
104	Tino Martinez	.05
105	Sterling Hitchcock	.05
106	Royce Clayton	.05
107	Jim Abbott	.05
108	Rickey Henderson	.75
109	Ramon Martinez	.05
110	Paul Molitor	.75
111	Dennis Eckersley	.65
112	Alex Gonzalez	.05
113	Marquis Grissom	.05
114	Greg Vaughn	.05
115	Lance Johnson	.05
116	Todd Stottlemyre	.05
117	Jack McDowell	.05
118	Ruben Sierra	.05
119	Brady Anderson	.05
120	Julio Franco	.05
121	Brooks Kieshnick	.05
122	Roberto Alomar	.20
123	Greg Gagne	.05
124	Wally Joyner	.05
125	John Smoltz	.05
126	John Valentin	.05
127	Russ Davis	.05
128	Joe Vitiello	.05
129	Shawon Dunston	.05
130	Frank Rodriguez	.05
131	Charlie Hayes	.05
132	Andy Benes	.05
133	B.J. Surhoff	.05
134	Dave Nilsson	.05
135	Carlos Delgado	.50
136	Walt Weiss	.05
137	Mike Stanley	.05
138	Greg Colbrunn	.05
139	Mike Kelly	.05
140	Ryne Sandberg	1.00
141	Lee Smith	.05
142	Dennis Martinez	.05
143	Bernard Gilkey	.05
144	Lenny Dykstra	.05
145	Danny Tartabull	.05
146	Dean Palmer	.05
147	Craig Biggio	.05
148	Juan Acevedo	.05
149	Michael Tucker	.05
150	Bobby Higginson	.05
151	Ken Griffey Jr. (Line Up Leaders)	.65
152	Frank Thomas (Line Up Leaders)	.45
153	Cal Ripken Jr. (Line Up Leaders)	1.00
154	Albert Belle (Line Up Leaders)	.05
155	Mike Piazza (Line Up Leaders)	.65
156	Barry Bonds (Line Up Leaders)	1.00
157	Sammy Sosa (Line Up Leaders)	.60
158	Mo Vaughn (Line Up Leaders)	.05
159	Greg Maddux (Line Up Leaders)	.50
160	Jeff Bagwell (Line Up Leaders)	.40
161	Derek Jeter	2.00
162	Paul Wilson	.05
163	Chris Snopek	.05
164	Jason Schmidt	.05
165	Jimmy Haynes	.05
166	George Arias	.05
167	Steve Gibralter	.05
168	Bob Wolcott	.05
169	Jason Kendall	.05

170	Gregg Zaun	.05
171	Quinton McCracken	.05
172	Alan Benes	.05
173	Rey Ordonez	.05
174	Ugueth Urbina	.05
175	Osvaldo Fernandez RC	.10
176	Marc Barcelo	.05
177	Sal Fasano	.05
178	Mike Grace RC	.05
179	Chan Ho Park	.05
180	Robert Perez	.05
181	Todd Hollandsworth	.05
182	Wilton Guerrero RC	.05
183	John Wasdin	.05
184	Jim Pittsley	.05
185	LaTroy Hawkins	.05
186	Jay Powell	.05
187	Felipe Crespo	.05
188	Jermaine Dye	.05
189	Bob Abreu	.05
190	Matt Luke RC	.05
191	Richard Hidalgo	.05
192	Karim Garcia	.05
193	Tavo Alvarez	.05
194	Andy Fox RC	.05
195	Terrell Wade	.05
196	Frank Thomas (Checklist)	.40
197	Ken Griffey Jr. (Checklist)	.65
198	Greg Maddux (Checklist)	.50
199	Mike Piazza (Checklist)	.65
200	Cal Ripken Jr. (Checklist)	.75

Artist's Proofs

Approximately once per 35 packs, a card from this parallel chase set is encountered among 1996 Select. Reported production was 435 sets. The Artist's Proof cards are distinguished by a holographic logo testifying to their status on the front of the card.

		NM/M
Complete Set (200):		200.00
Common Player:		1.00
AP Stars:		7X

Claim to Fame

Twenty different stars are featured on these 1996 Select insert cards. Each card is numbered "1 of 2100" and uses an external die-cut design. The cards were seeded one per every 72 packs.

		NM/M
Complete Set (20):		45.00
Common Player:		.75
1	Cal Ripken Jr.	7.50
2	Greg Maddux	4.50
3	Ken Griffey Jr.	6.00
4	Frank Thomas	3.50
5	Mo Vaughn	.75
6	Albert Belle	.75
7	Jeff Bagwell	3.50
8	Sammy Sosa	4.50
8s	Sammy Sosa (Overprinted "SAMPLE.")	2.50
9	Reggie Sanders	.75
10	Hideo Nomo	2.00
11	Chipper Jones	4.50
12	Mike Piazza	6.00
13	Matt Williams	.75
14	Tony Gwynn	4.50
15	Johnny Damon	1.50
16	Dante Bichette	.75
17	Kirby Puckett	4.50
18	Barry Bonds	7.50
19	Randy Johnson	3.50
20	Eddie Murray	3.50

En Fuego

ESPN announcer Dan Patrick is featured on his own card in this set, inspired by his Sportscenter catch phrase "en fuego," which means "on fire." Patrick's teammate, Keith Ol-berman, wrote the card backs. The 25 cards, printed on all-foil Dufex stock, are seeded one per every 48 packs of 1996 Select baseball.

		NM/M
Complete Set (25):		35.00
Common Player:		.75
1	Ken Griffey Jr.	3.50
2	Frank Thomas	2.00
3	Cal Ripken Jr.	5.00
4	Greg Maddux	3.00
5	Jeff Bagwell	2.00
6	Barry Bonds	5.00
7	Mo Vaughn	.75
8	Albert Belle	.75
9	Sammy Sosa	.75
10	Reggie Sanders	.75
11	Mike Piazza	3.50
12	Chipper Jones	3.00
13	Tony Gwynn	3.00
14	Kirby Puckett	3.00
15	Wade Boggs	3.00
16	Dan Patrick	.75
17	Gary Sheffield	1.25
18	Dante Bichette	.75
19	Randy Johnson	2.00
20	Matt Williams	.75
21	Alex Rodriguez	4.00
22	Tim Salmon	.75
23	Johnny Damon	1.25
24	Manny Ramirez	2.00
25	Hideo Nomo	1.25

Team Nucleus

This 1996 Select insert set pays tribute to the three top players from each Major League Baseball team; each card features the three team-mates on it. The cards are printed on a clear plastic, utilizing a holographic micro-etched design. They are seeded one per every 18 packs.

		NM/M
Complete Set (28):		20.00
Common Player:		.50
1	Albert Belle, Manny Ramirez, Carlos Baerga	1.25
2	Ray Lankford, Brian Jordan, Ozzie Smith	1.25
3	Jay Bell, Jeff King, Denny Neagle	.50
4	Dante Bichette, Andres Galarraga, Larry Walker	.50
5	Mark McGwire, Mike Bordick, Terry Steinbach	1.75
6	Bernie Williams, Wade Boggs, David Cone	1.25
7	Joe Carter, Alex Gonzalez, Shawn Green	.50
8	Roger Clemens, Mo Vaughn, Jose Canseco	1.25
9	Ken Griffey Jr., Edgar Martinez, Randy Johnson	1.50
10	Gregg Jefferies, Darren Daulton, Lenny Dykstra	.50
11	Mike Piazza, Raul Mondesi, Hideo Nomo	1.50
12	Greg Maddux, Chipper Jones, Ryan Klesko	1.25
13	Cecil Fielder, Travis Fryman, Phil Nevin	.50
14	Ivan Rodriguez, Will Clark, Juan Gonzalez	1.00
15	Ryne Sandberg, Sammy Sosa, Mark Grace	1.50
16	Gary Sheffield, Charles Johnson, Andre Dawson	.60

17	Johnny Damon, Michael Tucker, Kevin Appier	.65
18	Barry Bonds, Matt Williams, Rod Beck	2.00
19	Kirby Puckett, Chuck Knoblauch, Marty Cordova	1.25
20	Cal Ripken Jr., Bobby Bonilla, Mike Mussina	2.00
21	Jason Isringhausen, Bill Pulsipher, Rico Brogna	.50
22	Tony Gwynn, Ken Caminiti, Marc Newfield	1.25
23	Tim Salmon, Garret Anderson, Jim Edmonds	.50
24	Moises Alou, Rondell White, Cliff Floyd	.50
25	Barry Larkin, Reggie Sanders, Bret Boone	.50
26	Jeff Bagwell, Craig Biggio, Derek Bell	1.00
27	Frank Thomas, Robin Ventura, Alex Fernandez	1.00
28	John Jaha, Greg Vaughn, Kevin Seitzer	.50

1996 Select Certified

This hobby-exclusive set has 144 cards in its regular issue, plus six parallel versions and two insert sets. The parallel sets are: Certified Red (one per five packs), Certified Blue (one per 50), Artist's Proofs (one per 12), Mirror Red (one per 100), Mirror Blue (one per 200), and Mirror Gold (one per 300). Breaking down the numbers, there are 1,800 Certified Red sets, 180 Certified Blue, 500 Artist's Proofs, 90 Mirror Red 45 Mirror Blue and 30 Mirror Gold sets. The insert sets are Interleague Preview cards and Select Few. Cards #135-144 are a "Pastime Power" subset.

		NM/M
Complete Set (144):		20.00
Common Player:		.15
Pack (6):		2.50
Wax Box (20):		40.00
1	Frank Thomas	1.25
2	Tino Martinez	.15
3	Gary Sheffield	.50
4	Kenny Lofton	.15
5	Joe Carter	.15
6	Alex Rodriguez	2.50
7	Chipper Jones	1.50
8	Roger Clemens	1.75
9	Jay Bell	.15
10	Eddie Murray	1.00
11	Will Clark	.35
12	Mike Mussina	.35
13	Hideo Nomo	.50
14	Andres Galarraga	.15
15	Marc Newfield	.15
16	Jason Isringhausen	.15
17	Randy Johnson	1.00
18	Chuck Knoblauch	.15
19	J.T. Snow	.15
20	Mark McGwire	2.50
21	Tony Gwynn	1.50
22	Albert Belle	.15
23	Gregg Jefferies	.15
24	Reggie Sanders	.15
25	Bernie Williams	.15
26	Ray Lankford	.15
27	Johnny Damon	.40
28	Ryne Sandberg	1.50
29	Rondell White	.15
30	Mike Piazza	2.00
31	Barry Bonds	3.00
32	Greg Maddux	1.50
33	Craig Biggio	.35
34	John Valentin	.15
35	Ivan Rodriguez	.75
36	Rico Brogna	.15
37	Tim Salmon	.35
38	Sterling Hitchcock	.15
39	Charles Johnson	.15
40	Travis Fryman	.15
41	Barry Larkin	.15
42	Tom Glavine	.15
43	Marty Cordova	.15

44	Shawn Green	.40
45	Ben McDonald	.15
46	Robin Ventura	.15
47	Ken Griffey Jr.	2.00
48	Orlando Merced	.15
49	Paul O'Neill	.15
50	Ozzie Smith	1.50
51	Manny Ramirez	1.00
52	Ismael Valdes	.15
53	Cal Ripken Jr.	3.00
54	Jeff Bagwell	1.00
55	Greg Vaughn	.15
56	Juan Gonzalez	.50
57	Raul Mondesi	.15
58	Carlos Baerga	.15
59	Sammy Sosa	1.50
60	Mike Kelly	.15
61	Edgar Martinez	.15
62	Kirby Puckett	1.50
63	Cecil Fielder	.15
64	David Cone	.15
65	Moises Alou	.15
66	Fred McGriff	.15
67	Mo Vaughn	.15
68	Edgardo Alfonzo	.15
69	Jim Thome	.75
70	Rickey Henderson	1.00
71	Dante Bichette	.15
72	Lenny Dykstra	.15
73	Benji Gil	.15
74	Wade Boggs	1.50
75	Jim Edmonds	.15
76	Michael Tucker	.15
77	Carlos Delgado	.65
78	Butch Huskey	.15
79	Billy Ashley	.15
80	Dean Palmer	.15
81	Paul Molitor	1.00
82	Ryan Klesko	.15
83	Brian Hunter	.15
84	Jay Buhner	.15
85	Larry Walker	.15
86	Mike Bordick	.15
87	Matt Williams	.15
88	Jack McDowell	.15
89	Hal Morris	.15
90	Brian Jordan	.15
91	Andy Pettitte	.35
92	Melvin Nieves	.15
93	Pedro Martinez	1.00
94	Mark Grace	.15
95	Garret Anderson	.15
96	Andre Dawson	.30
97	Ray Durham	.15
98	Jose Canseco	.50
99	Roberto Alomar	.30
100	Derek Jeter	3.00
101	Alan Benes	.15
102	Karim Garcia	.15
103	Robin Jennings RC	.15
104	Bob Abreu	.15
105	Sal Fasano (Livan Hernandez' name on front.)	.15
106	Steve Gibralter	.15
107	Jermaine Dye	.15
108	Jason Kendall	.15
109	Mike Grace RC	.15
110	Jason Schmidt	.15
111	Paul Wilson	.15
112	Rey Ordonez	.15
113	Wilton Guerrero RC	.15
114	Brooks Kieschnick	.15
115	George Arias	.15
116	Osvaldo Fernandez RC	.15
117	Todd Hollandsworth	.15
118	John Wasdin	.15
119	Eric Owens	.15
120	Chan Ho Park	.15
121	Mark Loretta	.15
122	Richard Hidalgo	.15
123	Jeff Suppan	.15
124	Jim Pittsley	.15
125	LaTroy Hawkins	.15
126	Chris Snopek	.15
127	Justin Thompson	.15
128	Jay Powell	.15
129	Alex Ochoa	.15
130	Felipe Crespo	.15
131	Matt Lawton RC	.15
132	Jimmy Haynes	.15
133	Terrell Wade	.15
134	Ruben Rivera	.15
135	Frank Thomas (Pastime Power)	.55
136	Ken Griffey Jr. (Pastime Power)	1.00
137	Greg Maddux (Pastime Power)	.65
138	Mike Piazza (Pastime Power)	.75
139	Cal Ripken Jr. (Pastime Power)	1.50
140	Albert Belle (Pastime Power)	.15
141	Mo Vaughn (Pastime Power)	.15
142	Chipper Jones (Pastime Power)	.75
143	Hideo Nomo (Pastime Power)	.25
144	Ryan Klesko (Pastime Power)	.15

Artist's Proofs

Only 500 cards each of this parallel issue were produced, seeded one in every dozen packs. The

cards are identical to the regular-issue Select Certified except for the presence on front of a prismatic gold Artist's Proof logo.

	NM/M
Complete Set (144):	200.00
Common Player:	1.00
AP Stars:	7X

Red, Blue

These 1996 Select Certified insert cards were the most common of the parallel cards issued; they were seeded one per five packs. There were 1,800 Certified Red sets produced, with the number of Certified Blue sets at 180. Cards are essentially the same as regular-issue Select Certified except for the color of the foil background on front.

	NM/M
Common Red:	.50
Red Stars:	3X
Common Blue:	2.50
Blue Stars:	10X

Mirror Red, Blue, Gold

These 1996 Select Certified inserts are the scarcest of the set. Only 30 Mirror Gold sets were made, with 60 Mirror Blue sets and 90 Mirror Red. Due to the improbability of completing the collection, no complete set price is given.

	NM/M
Common Mirror Red:	6.00
Mirror Red Stars:	20X
Common Mirror Blue:	12.00
Mirror Blue Stars:	30X
Common Mirror Gold:	20.00
Mirror Gold Stars:	100X

Interleague Preview

These 1996 Select Certified insert cards feature 21 prospective matchups from interleague play's beginnings. The cards were seeded one per 42 packs. Each card can also be found in a promo version with a large, black "SAMPLE" over-print on front and back.

		NM/M
Complete Set (25):		45.00
Common Card:		.75
Promos:		1X
1	Ken Griffey Jr., Hideo Nomo	3.50
2	Greg Maddux, Mo Vaughn	3.00
3	Frank Thomas, Sammy Sosa	3.00
4	Mike Piazza, Jim Edmonds	3.50
5	Ryan Klesko, Roger Clemens	3.25
6	Derek Jeter, Rey Ordonez	4.50
7	Johnny Damon, Ray Lankford	1.00
8	Manny Ramirez, Reggie Sanders	2.50
9	Barry Bonds, Jay Buhner	4.50
10	Jason Isringhausen, Wade Boggs	3.00
11	David Cone, Chipper Jones	3.00
12	Jeff Bagwell, Will Clark	2.50
13	Tony Gwynn, Randy Johnson	3.00
14	Cal Ripken Jr., Tom Glavine	4.50
15	Kirby Puckett, Alan Benes	3.00
16	Gary Sheffield, Mike Mussina	1.00
17	Raul Mondesi, Tim Salmon	.75
18	Rondell White, Carlos Delgado	1.00
19	Cecil Fielder, Ryne Sandberg	3.00
20	Kenny Lofton, Brian Hunter	.75
21	Paul Wilson, Paul O'Neill	.75
22	Ismael Valdes, Edgar Martinez	.75
23	Matt Williams, Mark McGwire	4.00
24	Albert Belle, Barry Larkin	.75
25	Brady Anderson, Marquis Grissom	.75

Select Few

Eighteen top players are featured on these 1996 Select Certified inserts, which utilize holographic technology with a dot matrix hologram. Cards were seeded one per every 60 packs.

		NM/M
Complete Set (18):		40.00
Common Player:		1.00
1	Sammy Sosa	3.00
2	Derek Jeter	5.00
3	Ken Griffey Jr.	5.00
4	Albert Belle	1.00
5	Cal Ripken Jr.	5.00
6	Greg Maddux	3.00
7	Frank Thomas	2.50
8	Mo Vaughn	1.00
9	Chipper Jones	3.00
10	Mike Piazza	3.50
11	Ryan Klesko	1.00
12	Hideo Nomo	1.50
13	Alan Benes	1.00
14	Manny Ramirez	2.50
15	Gary Sheffield	1.50
16	Barry Bonds	5.00
17	Matt Williams	1.00
18	Johnny Damon	2.00

1997 Select Samples

The 1997 edition of Select was previewed with the issue of several regular-issue and Select Co. cards carrying a large black "SAMPLE" overprint on front and back. The Rodriguez sample, untrimmed and

larger than standard size, was not distributed in three-card cello packs like the other cards. This checklist may not be complete.

		NM/M
Common Player:		1.00
1	Tony Gwynn	2.00
8	Frank Thomas	1.50
9	Paul Molitor	1.50
23	Greg Maddux	2.00
28	Javy Lopez	1.00
47	Ken Griffey Jr.	3.00
53	Alex Rodriguez	4.00
94	Will Clark	1.00

1997 Select

The Series 1 base set is made up of 150 cards printed on thick 16-point stock. Each card features a distinctive silver-foil treatment and either red (100 cards) or blue (50 cards) foil accent. Blue-foiled cards were short-printed at a ratio of 1:2 compared to the red-foil cards. Blue-foil cards are indicated with a (B) in the checklist. Subsets include 40 Rookies, eight Super Stars and two checklists. Inserts include two parallel sets, (Artist's Proof and Registered Gold), Tools of the Trade, Mirror Blue Tools of the Trade, and Rookie Revolution. The cards were sold only at hobby shops in six-card packs for $2.99 each. A high-number series was issued with each card bearing a "Select Company" notation.

		NM/M
Complete Set (200):		30.00
Series 1 (#1-150):		20.00
Common Red Player:		.10
Common Blue Player:		.25
Registered Golds:		2X
Artist's Proofs:		5X
High Series (#151-200):		10.00
Common High Series:		.25
Pack (6):		1.50
Wax Box (24):		25.00
1	Juan Gonzalez (B)	2.00
2	Mo Vaughn (B)	.25
3	Tony Gwynn	1.50
4	Manny Ramirez (B)	2.00
5	Jose Canseco	.50
6	David Cone	.10
7	Chan Ho Park	.10
8	Frank Thomas (B)	2.50
9	Todd Hollandsworth	.10
10	Marty Cordova	.10
11	Gary Sheffield (B)	.75
12	John Smoltz	.25
13	Mark Grudzielanek	.10
14	Sammy Sosa (B)	3.00
15	Paul Molitor	1.00
16	Kevin Brown	.10
17	Albert Belle (B)	.25
18	Eric Young	.10
19	John Wetteland	.10
20	Ryan Klesko (B)	.25
21	Joe Carter	.10
22	Alex Ochoa	.10
23	Greg Maddux (B)	3.00
24	Roger Clemens (B)	2.00
25	Ivan Rodriguez (B)	1.50
26	Barry Bonds (B)	1.50

27	Kenny Lofton (B)	.25
28	Javy Lopez	.10
29	Hideo Nomo (B)	1.00
30	Rusty Greer	.10
31	Rafael Palmeiro	.75
32	Mike Piazza (B)	3.50
33	Ryne Sandberg	1.50
34	Wade Boggs	1.50
35	Jim Thome (B)	1.50
36	Ken Caminiti (B)	.25
37	Mark Grace	.10
38	Brian Jordan (B)	.25
39	Craig Biggio	.10
40	Henry Rodriguez	.10
41	Dean Palmer	.10
42	Jason Kendall	.10
43	Bill Pulsipher	.10
44	Tim Salmon (B)	.25
45	Marc Newfield	.10
46	Pat Hentgen	.10
47	Ken Griffey Jr. (B)	4.00
48	Paul Wilson	.10
49	Jay Buhner (B)	.25
50	Rickey Henderson	1.00
51	Jeff Bagwell (B)	2.00
52	Cecil Fielder	.10
53	Alex Rodriguez (B)	4.00
54	John Jaha	.10
55	Brady Anderson (B)	.25
56	Andres Galarraga	.10
57	Raul Mondesi	.10
58	Andy Pettitte	.30
59	Roberto Alomar (B)	1.00
60	Derek Jeter (B)	5.00
61	Charles Johnson	.10
62	Travis Fryman	.10
63	Chipper Jones (B)	3.00
64	Edgar Martinez	.10
65	Bobby Bonilla	.10
66	Greg Vaughn	.10
67	Bobby Higginson	.10
68	Garret Anderson	.10
69	Chuck Knoblauch (B)	.25
70	Jermaine Dye	.10
71	Cal Ripken Jr. (B)	5.00
72	Jason Giambi	.60
73	Trey Beamon	.10
74	Shawn Green	.35
75	Mark McGwire (B)	4.00
76	Carlos Delgado	.60
77	Jason Isringhausen	.10
78	Randy Johnson (B)	2.00
79	Troy Percival (B)	.25
80	Ron Gant	.10
81	Ellis Burks	.10
82	Mike Mussina (B)	1.00
83	Todd Hundley	.10
84	Jim Edmonds	.10
85	Charles Nagy	.10
86	Dante Bichette (B)	.25
87	Mariano Rivera	.20
88	Matt Williams (B)	.25
89	Rondell White	.10
90	Steve Finley	.10
91	Alex Fernandez	.10
92	Barry Larkin	.10
93	Tom Goodwin	.10
94	Will Clark	.10
95	Michael Tucker	.10
96	Derek Bell	.10
97	Larry Walker	.10
98	Alan Benes	.10
99	Tom Glavine	.35
100	Darin Erstad (B)	.35
101	Andruw Jones (B)	2.00
102	Scott Rolen	.65
103	Todd Walker (B)	.25
104	Dmitri Young	.10
105	Vladimir Guerrero (B)	2.00
106	Nomar Garciaparra	1.50
107	Danny Patterson RC	.10
108	Karim Garcia	.10
109	Todd Greene	.10
110	Ruben Rivera	.10
111	Raul Casanova	.10
112	Mike Cameron	.10
113	Bartolo Colon	.10
114	Rod Myers RC	.10
115	Todd Dunn	.10
116	Torii Hunter	.10
117	Jason Dickson	.10
118	Gene Kingsale RC	.10
119	Rafael Medina	.10
120	Raul Ibanez	.10
121	Bobby Henley RC	.10
122	Scott Spiezio	.10
123	Bobby Smith RC	.10
124	J.J. Johnson	.10
125	Bubba Trammell RC	.50
126	Jeff Abbott	.10
127	Neifi Perez	.10
128	Derrek Lee	.65
129	Kevin Brown RC	.10
130	Mendy Lopez	.10
131	Kevin Orie	.10
132	Ryan Jones	.10
133	Juan Encarnacion	.10
134	Jose Guillen (B)	.25
135	Greg Norton	.10
136	Richie Sexson	.10
137	Jay Payton	.10
138	Bob Abreu	.15
139	Ronnie Belliard RC	.10
140	Wilton Guerrero (B)	.25
141	Alex Rodriguez (Select Stars)(B)	2.00
142	Juan Gonzalez (Select Stars)(B)	.50
143	Ken Caminiti (Select Stars)(B)	.25

144	Frank Thomas (Select Stars)(B)	1.25
145	Ken Griffey Jr. (Select Stars)(B)	1.75
146	John Smoltz (Select Stars)(B)	.25
147	Mike Piazza (Select Stars)(B)	1.75
148	Derek Jeter (Select Stars)(B)	3.00
149	Frank Thomas (Checklist)	.75
150	Ken Griffey Jr. (Checklist)	1.00
151	Jose Cruz Jr. RC	1.00
152	Moises Alou	.25
153	Hideki Irabu RC	.50
154	Glendon Rusch	.25
155	Ron Coomer	.25
156	Jeremi Gonzalez RC	.25
157	Fernando Tatis RC	.40
158	John Olerud	.25
159	Rickey Henderson	1.00
160	Shannon Stewart	.25
161	Kevin Polcovich	.25
162	Jose Rosado	.25
163	Ray Lankford	.25
164	David Justice	.25
165	Mark Kotsay RC	.50
166	Deivi Cruz RC	.25
167	Billy Wagner	.25
168	Jacob Cruz	.25
169	Matt Morris	.25
170	Brian Banks	.25
171	Brett Tomko	.25
172	Todd Helton	.75
173	Eric Young	.25
174	Bernie Williams	.25
175	Jeff Fassero	.25
176	Ryan McGuire	.25
177	Darryl Kile	.25
178	Kelvim Escobar RC	.50
179	Dave Nilsson	.25
180	Geronimo Berroa	.25
181	Livan Hernandez	.25
182	Tony Womack RC	.50
183	Deion Sanders	.25
184	Jeff Kent	.25
185	Brian Hunter	.25
186	Jose Malave	.25
187	Steve Woodard RC	.50
188	Brad Radke	.25
189	Todd Dunwoody	.25
190	Joey Hamilton	.25
191	Denny Naegle	.25
192	Bobby Jones	.25
193	Tony Clark	.25
194	Jaret Wright RC	.50
195	Matt Stairs	.25
196	Francisco Cordova	.25
197	Justin Thompson	.25
198	Pokey Reese	.25
199	Garrett Stephenson	.25
200	Carl Everett	.25

Artist's Proofs

Featuring a holographic foil background and special Artist's Proof logo on front, this parallel of the 150-card Series 1 Select was a random pack insert at an average pull rate of 1:71 for reds and 1:355 for blues.

	NM/M
Complete Set (150):	450.00
Common Red:	1.25
Red Stars:	5X
Common Blue:	2.50
Blue Stars:	1.5X

Company

Select Company was intended to be a one-per-pack parallel found in '97 high series. The cards have the front background photo replaced with textured silver metallic foil and "Select Company" printed vertically at right-center. While all high-number (151-200) cards have the "Select Company" notation erroneously printed on front, only those cards with silver-foil backgrounds are true parallels. All Select Company cards can also be found in a promo version with a large black "SAMPLE" overprinted on back.

	NM/M
Complete Set (200):	150.00
Common Player:	.50
Red Stars:	3X
Blue Stars:	1.5X
High-Series Stars:	1.5X
Samples:	10X

Registered Gold

This parallel insert set, like the regular issue, can be found with 100 red-foil and 50 blue-foil enhanced cards. They differ from the regular issue in the use of gold foil instead of silver on the right side of the front. Also, the inserts have "Registered Gold" printed vertically on the right side of the photo. Backs are identical to the regular issue. Red-foil Registered Gold cards are found on average of once every 11 packs; blue-foiled cards are a 1-in-47 pick.

	NM/M
Complete Set (150):	300.00
Common Red Gold:	.75
Common Blue Gold:	1.50
Registered Gold Stars:	2X

Autographs

Four top candidates for the 1997 Rookie of the Year Award - Wilton Guerrero, Jose Guillen, Andruw Jones and Todd Walker - each signed a limited number of their Select Rookie cards. Jones signed 2,500 cards while each of the other players signed 3,000 each.

	NM/M
Complete Set (4):	15.00
Common Autograph:	3.00
AU1	Wilton Guerrero	3.00
AU2	Jose Guillen	3.00
AU3	Andruw Jones	10.00
AU4	Todd Walker	3.00

Rookie Revolution

This 20-card insert highlights some of the top young stars in the game. Cards feature a silver microetched mylar design on front. Backs are sequentially numbered and contain a few words about the player. Odds of finding a card are 1:56 packs.

	NM/M
Complete Set (20):	21.00
Common Player:	.50
1	Andruw Jones	2.50
2	Derek Jeter	6.00
3	Todd Hollandsworth	.50
4	Edgar Renteria	.50
5	Jason Kendall	.50
6	Rey Ordonez	.50
7	F.P. Santangelo	.50
8	Jermaine Dye	.50
9	Alex Ochoa	.50
10	Vladimir Guerrero	2.50
11	Dmitri Young	.50
12	Todd Walker	.50
13	Scott Rolen	1.50
14	Nomar Garciaparra	3.50
15	Ruben Rivera	.50
16	Darin Erstad	1.00
17	Todd Greene	.50
18	Mariano Rivera	1.00
19	Trey Beamon	.50
20	Karim Garcia	.50

Tools of the Trade

A 25-card insert featuring a double-front design salutes a top veteran player on one side and a promising youngster on the other. Cards feature a silver-foil card stock with gold-foil stamping. Cards were inserted 1:9 packs. A parallel to this set - Blue Mirror Tools of the Trade - features blue-foil stock with an insert ratio of 1:240 packs.

	NM/M
Complete Set (25):	25.00
Common Player:	.40
Mirror Blues:	2.5X
1	Ken Griffey Jr., Andruw Jones	2.00
2	Greg Maddux, Andy Pettitte	1.50
3	Cal Ripken Jr., Chipper Jones	2.50
4	Mike Piazza, Jason Kendall	2.00
5	Albert Belle, Karim Garcia	.40
6	Mo Vaughn, Dmitri Young	.40
7	Juan Gonzalez, Vladimir Guerrero	1.00
8	Tony Gwynn, Jermaine Dye	1.50
9	Barry Bonds, Alex Ochoa	2.50
10	Jeff Bagwell, Jason Giambi	1.00
11	Kenny Lofton, Darin Erstad	.50
12	Gary Sheffield, Manny Ramirez	1.00
13	Tim Salmon, Todd Hollandsworth	.40
14	Sammy Sosa, Ruben Rivera	1.50
15	Paul Molitor, George Arias	1.00
16	Jim Thome, Todd Walker	.75
17	Wade Boggs, Scott Rolen	1.50
18	Ryne Sandberg, Chuck Knoblauch	1.50
19	Mark McGwire, Frank Thomas	2.25
20	Ivan Rodriguez, Charles Johnson	.75
21	Brian Jordan, Trey Beamon	.40
22	Roger Clemens, Troy Percival	1.75
23	John Smoltz, Mike Mussina	.65
24	Alex Rodriguez, Rey Ordonez	2.25
25	Derek Jeter, Nomar Garciaparra	2.50

1998 Select

Select was intended to be a four-tier, 100-player, 250-card base set based on the "Quasar System." One hundred players were to appear as one-star cards; two-star cards comprised a shortened checklist of 75 of those players, and so on through three- and four-star subsets. Besides an increase in player popularity, each level featured enhanced technical bells and whistles on the cards themselves. Each five-card $3.99 pack was to have three one-star cards and two two-star cards, unless one or more were replaced with three- or four-star cards or one of several insert series. The set was never officially released due to the mid-year collapse and subsequent bankruptcy of Select's parent firm, Pinnacle.

	NM/M
Common Player:	10.00

Numbers

Five players from each of four major statistical categories were selected for inclusion in this all-numbered insert issue. Each player in the chase set was intended to have cards numbered to his 1997 performance in the category for which he was chosen. While distribution of the cards was halted by Pinnacle's bankruptcy, limited quantities of these insert cards have found their way into the hobby. Those cards seen thus far do not bear sequential numbers. The number of cards intended for each player is listed, although it is unknown how many of each player were actually released.

	NM/M
Complete Set (20):	1,150
Common Player:	20.00
1	Mark McGwire/58	225.00
2	Juan Gonzalez/42	40.00
3	Ken Griffey Jr./56	225.00
4	Jeff Bagwell/43	60.00
5	Andres Galarraga/41	40.00
6	Frank Thomas/347	30.00
7	Mike Piazza/362	100.00
8	Tony Gwynn/372	35.00
9	Larry Walker/366	40.00
10	Kenny Lofton/333	20.00
11	Barry Bonds/446	50.00
12	Chuck Knoblauch/390	20.00
13	Derek Jeter/370	150.00
14	Nomar Garciaparra/342	75.00
15	Chipper Jones/371	60.00
16	Pedro Martinez/305	40.00
17	Hideo Nomo/233	65.00
18	Randy Johnson/291	30.00
19	Roger Clemens/292	75.00
20	Greg Maddux/177	75.00

Jersey Numbers

Whatever the intended scope and manner of distribution for this parallel insert may never be known because Pinnacle's bankruptcy interrupted the issue. Only a few specimens have made their way into the hobby. The gold-foil highlighted numbers on back correspond to the extent of the player's uniform number.

	NM/M
116	Ken Griffey Jr./24	65.00

1998 Select Selected Samples

Selected promos were released in two-card cello packs prior to Pinnacle's bankruptcy. Fronts have color action photos on bright metallic-foil backgrounds was a large "S." Backs have a smaller version of the front photo along with career highlights and a large overprinted "SAMPLE."

	NM/M
Complete Set (10):	30.00
Common Player:	2.50
1	Vladimir Guerrero	4.00
2	Nomar Garciaparra	5.00
3	Ben Grieve	2.50
4	Travis Lee	2.50
5	Jose Cruz Jr.	2.50
6	Alex Rodriguez	6.00
7	Todd Helton	3.50
8	Derek Jeter	7.00
9	Scott Rolen	3.50
10	Jaret Wright	2.50

1998 Select Selected

Intended as a 1:23 pack insert for a set which was never released due to Pinnacle's bankruptcy, Selected cards later leaked out into the hobby market. Fronts have color action photos on bright metallic-foil backgrounds with a large "S." Backs have a smaller version of the front photo along with career highlights.

	NM/M
Complete Set (10):	135.00
Common Player:	10.00
1	Vladimir Guerrero	15.00
2	Nomar Garciaparra	20.00
3	Ben Grieve	10.00
4	Travis Lee	10.00
5	Jose Cruz Jr.	10.00
6	Alex Rodriguez	22.50
7	Todd Helton	12.50
8	Derek Jeter	25.00
9	Scott Rolen	12.50
10	Jaret Wright	10.00

2002 Select Rookies & Prospects Autographs

		NM/M
Common Player:		3.00
Retail-Exclusive		
1	Abraham Nunez	5.00
2	Adam Bernero	3.00
3	Adam Pettyjohn	3.00
4	Alex Escobar	4.00
5	Allan Simpson	4.00
6	Andres Torres	3.00
7	Andy Pratt	4.00
8	Bert Snow	3.00
9	Bill Ortega	3.00
10	Billy Sylvester	3.00
11	Brad Voyles	3.00
12	Brandon Backe	3.00
13	Brent Abernathy	3.00
14	Brian Mallette	3.00
15	Brian Rogers	3.00
16	Cam Esslinger	3.00
17	Carlos Garcia	3.00
18	Carlos Valderrama	3.00
19	Cesar Izturis	6.00
20	Chad Durbin	3.00
21	Chris Baker	3.00
22	Claudio Vargas	3.00
23	Cory Aldridge	3.00
24	Craig Monroe	5.00
25	David Elder	3.00
26	David Brous	3.00
27	David Espinosa	3.00
28	Derrick Lewis	3.00
29	Elio Serrano	3.00
30	Elpidio Guzman	3.00
31	Eric Cyr	3.00
32	Eric Valent	4.00
33	Erik Bedard	5.00
34	Esix Snead	3.00
35	Francis Beltran	3.00
36	George Perez	3.00
37	Gene Altman	3.00
38	Greg Miller	4.00
39	Horacio Ramirez	3.00
40	Jason Hart	4.50
41	Jason Karnuth	3.00
42	Jason Romano	3.00
43	Jeff Deardorff	3.00
44	Jeremy Affeldt	3.00
45	Jeremy Lambert	3.00
46	John Ennis	3.00
47	John Grabow	3.00
48	Jose Cueto	3.00
49	Jose Mieses	3.00
50	Jose Ortiz	3.00
51	Josh Pearce	3.00
52	Josue Perez	3.00
53	Juan Diaz	3.00
54	Juan Pena	3.00
55	Keith Ginter	3.00
56	Kevin Frederick	3.00
57	Kevin Joseph	3.00
58	Kevin Olsen	3.00
59	Kris Keller	3.00
60		
61	Larry Bigbie	3.00
62	Les Walrond	3.00
63	Luis Pineda	3.00
64	Luis Rivas	3.00
65	Luis Rivera	4.50
66	Luke Hudson	3.00
67	Marcus Giles	8.00
68	Mark Ellis	3.00
69	Martin Vargas	3.00
70	Matt Childers	3.00
71	Matt Guerrier	3.00
72	Matt Thornton	3.00
73	Matt White	3.00
74	Mike Penney	3.00
75	Nate Teut	3.00
76	Nick Maness	3.00
77	Orlando Woodards	3.00
78	Paul Phillips	3.00
79	Pedro Feliz	3.00
80	Ramon Vazquez	3.00
81	Raul Chavez	3.00
82	Reed Johnson	3.00
83	Ryan Freel	4.50
84	Ryan Jamison	3.00
85	Ryan Ludwick	10.00
86	Saul Rivera	3.00
87	Steve Bechler	3.00
88	Steve Green	3.00
89	Steve Smyth	3.00
90	Tike Redman	3.00
91	Tom Shearn	3.00
92	Tomas de la Rosa	3.00
93	Tony Cogan	3.00
94	Travis Hafner	25.00
95	Travis Hughes	3.00
96	Wilkin Ruan	3.00
97	Will Ohman	3.00
98	Wilmy Caceres	3.00
99	Wilson Guzman	3.00
100	Winston Abreu	3.00

1992 Sentry Robin Yount

At the Sept. 25, 1992, Brewers home game, the first 25,000 fans through the turnstile received a four-card set commemorating Robin Yount's 3,000th career hit. The 2-1/2" x 3-1/2" cards feature on front a gold-foil framed action photo set against a purple marbled border. Backs have a write-up about the career milestone hit and include the grocery store logo at bottom. The cards are unnumbered and were issued in a heavy paper wrapper.

		NM/M
Complete Set (4):		15.00
Common Card:		5.00
(1)	Hit #1, April 12, 1974 (Robin Yount)	5.00
(2)	Hit #1,000, Aug. 16, 1980 (Robin Yount)	5.00
(3)	Hit #2,000, Sept. 6, 1986 (Robin Yount)	5.00
(4)	Hit #3,000, Sept. 9, 1992 (Robin Yount)	5.00

1993 Sentry Brewers Memorable Moments

Fans at a special Brewer home game were given this set of team highlight cards. Fronts have a color photo of the highlight with a brief description and date printed in gold foil. The photo is framed in dark blue, which is also used for the border of the card. The territory between the photo and border is printed in light blue and includes the Brewers logo and "Memorable Moments" headline. Backs have a description of the action shown on front, and the sponsor's logo. Cards are numbered according to player uniform number printed on back.

		NM/M
Complete Set (4):		8.00
Common Card:		1.00
4	Paul Molitor	3.50
7	Dale Sveum	1.00
19	Robin Yount	3.50
20	Juan Nieves	1.00

1993 Sentry Milwaukee Brewers

This set of a dozen coupon/card combos was distributed at Milwaukee area Sentry grocery stores during the 1993 season. A new card was issued every week or two between April 27 and September 28. Each piece measures 12-1/2" x 7" and has a 5" x 7" Brewer player photo attached to six perforated coupons, each of which has a postage stamp-size Brewer

photo at lower-right. Backs are blank. Cards #11 and 12 were never officially issued and have blank coupons.

		NM/M
Complete Set (12):		7.00
Common Player:		.60
1	Pat Listach	.50
2	Tom Brunansky	.50
3	B.J. Surhoff	.50
4	Kevin Reimer	.50
5	Darryl Hamilton	.50
6	Greg Vaughn	.50
7	Robin Yount	4.00
8	Phil Garner	.50
9	Bill Spiers	.50
10	Dave Nilsson	.50
11	Bill Wegman	.50
12	Cal Eldred	.50

1994 Sentry Brewer Highlights

This eight-card set featuring highlights from Brewers history was issued in the team's 25th anniversary season. Sponsored by Sentry Foods, the cards were available on a one-per-week basis, attached to an 8-1/2" x 11" sheet of coupons, from May through August. (The last two cards were never officially issued due to the strike.) In standard 2-1/2" x 3-1/2", cards feature wide violet borders highlighted by green and gold geometric shapes. The team's 25th anniversary logo is at top-left, with the featured highlight at upper-right in gold. The player's name appears in white in a black ribbon beneath the color photo. Backs describe the highlight and are printed in blue and black. There is no sponsor's logo or card number. Cards are checklisted here alphabetically.

		NM/M
Complete Set (8):		14.00
Common Player:		1.00
(1)	Hank Aaron (Final Home Run)	5.00
(2)	Rollie Fingers (Cy Young/MVP Season)	1.50
(3)	Pat Listach (Rookie of the Year)	1.00
(4)	Paul Molitor (39-game Hitting Streak)	3.50
(5)	Juan Nieves (No-hitter)	1.00
(6)	Don Sutton (3,000th Strikeout)	1.00
(7)	Robin Yount (3,000 Hit)	3.50
(8)	Triumphant Trio (Jim Gantner, Paul Molitor, Robin Yount)	2.50

1983 7-11 Slurpee Coins

This first production of player coins by 7-Eleven stores was distributed only in the Los Angeles area. The test promotion, which awarded a coin to every purchaser of a large Slurpee drink, must have proved successful, as it was expanded nationally in subsequent

years. Six California Angels and six Los Angeles Dodgers are included in the full-color set, with Angels players in red backgrounds and the Dodgers in blue. The 1-3/4" diameter plastic coins feature both an action and a portrait photo of the player, which can be alternately seen by moving the coin slightly from side to side. The 12 coin backs are numbered and include brief statistics and the company logo.

		NM/M
Complete Set (12):		6.00
Common Player:		.50
1	Rod Carew	2.00
2	Steve Sax	.50
3	Fred Lynn	.50
4	Pedro Guerrero	.50
5	Reggie Jackson	3.00
6	Dusty Baker	.50
7	Doug DeCinces	.50
8	Fernando Valenzuela	.50
9	Tommy John	.50
10	Rick Monday	.50
11	Bobby Grich	.50
12	Greg Brock	.50

1984 7-11 Slurpee Coins Central Region

The 7-Eleven/Slurpee coins were distributed nationally in 1984 with 60 different players in three regional issues of 24 pieces each. Coins of Brett, Dawson, Murphy, Murray, Schmidt and Yount were common to all three regions. The 1-3/4" diameter plastic coins feature an action and a portrait photo on front which change when the viewing angle is altered. Statistics and coin numbers are found on the backs, along with the 7-Eleven logo.

		NM/M
Complete Set (24):		7.50
Common Player:		.25
1	Andre Dawson	.40
2	Robin Yount	.75
3	Dale Murphy	.50
4	Mike Schmidt	1.25
5	George Brett	1.25
6	Eddie Murray	.75
7	Bruce Sutter	.65
8	Cecil Cooper	.25
9	Willie McGee	.25
10	Mike Hargrove	.25
11	Kent Hrbek	.25
12	Carlton Fisk	.75
13	Mario Soto	.25
14	Lonnie Smith	.25
15	Gary Carter	.75
16	Lou Whitaker	.25
17	Ron Kittle	.25
18	Paul Molitor	.75
19	Ozzie Smith	1.00
20	Fergie Jenkins	.40
21	Ted Simmons	.25
22	Pete Rose	1.50
23	LaMarr Hoyt	.25
24	Dan Quisenberry	.25

Eastern Region

		NM/M
Complete Set (24):		10.00
Common Player:		.25
1	Andre Dawson	.40
2	Robin Yount	.75
3	Dale Murphy	.50
4	Mike Schmidt	1.25
5	George Brett	1.25
6	Eddie Murray	.75
7	Dave Winfield	.75
8	Tom Seaver	.75

9	Mike Boddicker	.25
10	Wade Boggs	1.00
11	Bill Madlock	.25
12	Steve Carlton	.50
13	Dave Stieb	.25
14	Cal Ripken, Jr.	3.00
15	Jim Rice	.40
16	Ron Guidry	.25
17	Darryl Strawberry	.25
18	Tony Pena	.25
19	John Denny	.25
20	Tim Raines	.25
21	Rick Dempsey	.25
22	Rich Gossage	.25
23	Gary Matthews	.25
24	Keith Hernandez	.25

Western Region

		NM/M
Complete Set (24):		9.00
Common Player:		.25
1	Andre Dawson	.40
2	Robin Yount	.75
3	Dale Murphy	.50
4	Mike Schmidt	1.25
5	George Brett	1.25
6	Eddie Murray	.75
7	Steve Garvey	.35
8	Rod Carew	.75
9	Fernando Valenzuela	.25
10	Bob Horner	.25
11	Buddy Bell	.25
12	Reggie Jackson	1.00
13	Nolan Ryan	2.00
14	Pedro Guerrero	.25
15	Atlee Hammaker	.25
16	Fred Lynn	.25
17	Terry Kennedy	.25
18	Dusty Baker	.25
19	Jose Cruz	.25
20	Steve Rogers	.25
21	Rickey Henderson	.75
22	Steve Sax	.25
23	Dickie Thon	.25
24	Matt Young	.25

Jumbo Coin

Dale Murphy, the MVP of the National League in 1983 was featured on a jumbo-format (4-1/2" diameter) "3D" disc distributed by 7-11 stores in conjunction with their Slurpee fountain drink. Like the smaller Slurpee coins, the photos on the disc change as the viewing angle is changed.

	NM/M
Dale Murphy	15.00

1985 7-11 Slurpee Coins Eastern Region

In 1985, the "Slurpee Disc" promotion was further expanded to a total of 94 full-color coins. The formats were very similar to the previous two years, but there were six different regional sets. Five of these regional series contain 16 coins, with a Detroit series totaling 14. The other five regions are: East, West, Great Lakes, Central and Southeast. The coins are again 1-1/4" in diameter, printed on plastic with double-image photos. All coins are numbered. No player appears in all regions, although several are in two or more.

		NM/M
Complete Set (16):		10.00
Common Player:		.25
1	Eddie Murray	1.00
2	George Brett	2.50
3	Steve Carlton	1.00
4	Jim Rice	.45
5	Dave Winfield	1.00
6	Mike Boddicker	.25
7	Wade Boggs	2.00
8	Dwight Evans	.25
9	Dwight Gooden	.25
10	Keith Hernandez	.25
11	Bill Madlock	.25
12	Don Mattingly	2.50
13	Dave Righetti	.25
14	Cal Ripken, Jr.	4.00
15	Juan Samuel	.25
16	Mike Schmidt	2.50

Great Lakes Region

		NM/M
Complete Set (16):		10.00
Common Player:		.25

1	Willie Hernandez	.25
2	George Brett	2.50
3	Dave Winfield	1.00
4	Eddie Murray	1.00
5	Bruce Sutter	.75
6	Harold Baines	.25
7	Bert Blyleven	.25
8	Leon Durham	.25
9	Chet Lemon	.25
10	Pete Rose	3.00
11	Ryne Sandberg	2.00
12	Tom Seaver	1.00
13	Mario Soto	.25
14	Rick Sutcliffe	.25
15	Alan Trammell	.25
16	Robin Yount	1.00

Southeastern Region

		NM/M
Complete Set (16):		7.50
Common Player:		.25
1	Dale Murphy	.75
2	Steve Carlton	1.00
3	Nolan Ryan	4.00
4	Bruce Sutter	.75
5	Dave Winfield	1.00
6	Steve Bedrosian	.25
7	Andre Dawson	.50
8	Kirk Gibson	.25
9	Fred Lynn	.25
10	Gary Matthews	.25
11	Phil Niekro	1.00
12	Tim Raines	.25
13	Darryl Strawberry	.25
14	Dave Stieb	.25
15	Willie Upshaw	.25
16	Lou Whitaker	.25

Southwest/Central Region

		NM/M
Complete Set (16):		10.00
Common Player:		.25
1	Nolan Ryan	4.00
2	George Brett	2.50
3	Dave Winfield	1.00
4	Mike Schmidt	2.50
5	Bruce Sutter	.75
6	Joaquin Andujar	.25
7	Willie Hernandez	.25
8	Wade Boggs	1.50
9	Gary Carter	1.00
10	Jose Cruz	.25
11	Kent Hrbek	.25
12	Reggie Jackson	1.50
13	Lance Parrish	.25
14	Terry Puhl	.25
15	Dan Quisenberry	.25
16	Ozzie Smith	1.50

Western Region

		NM/M
Complete Set (16):		7.50
Common Player:		.25
1	Mike Schmidt	2.50
2	Jim Rice	.45
3	Dale Murphy	.50
4	Eddie Murray	1.00
5	Dave Winfield	1.00
6	Rod Carew	1.00
7	Alvin Davis	.25
8	Steve Garvey	.35
9	Rich Gossage	.25
10	Pedro Guerrero	.25
11	Tony Gwynn	1.50
12	Rickey Henderson	1.00
13	Reggie Jackson	2.00
14	Jeff Leonard	.25
15	Alejandro Pena	.25
16	Fernando Valenzuela	.25

Tigers

		NM/M
Complete Set (14):		7.50
Common Player:		.75
1	Sparky Anderson	1.00
2	Darrell Evans	1.00
3	Kirk Gibson	1.00
4	Willie Hernandez	.75
5	Larry Herndon	.75
6	Chet Lemon	.75
7	Aurelio Lopez	.75
8	Jack Morris	.75
9	Lance Parrish	.75
10	Dan Petry	.75
11	Dave Rozema	.75
12	Alan Trammell	1.00
13	Lou Whitaker	1.00
14	Milt Wilcox	.75

Test Coins

These 3-D "Magic Motion" coins are identical to the regional issues in all aspects except size. These test coins are 2-1/4" diameter, an inch bigger than the issued versions.

		NM/M
Complete Set (3):		4.00
Common Player:		1.00
4	Mike Schmidt	2.50
5	Bruce Sutter	1.00
5	Dave Winfield	1.50

Jumbo Coins

World Series MVP Alan Trammell and Yankees slugger Dave Winfield were featured on jumbo-format (4-1/2" diameter) "3D" discs distributed by 7-11 stores in conjunction with their Slurpee fountain drink. Like the smaller Slurpee coins, the photos on the disc change as the viewing angle is changed.

		NM/M
Complete Set (2):		15.00
(1)	Alan Trammell	5.00
(2)	Dave Winfield	10.00

Twins

The Minnesota Twins, in cooperation with 7-Eleven and the Fire Marshall's Association, issued this set of 13 baseball fire safety cards. The card fronts feature full-color pictures of Twins players. A fire safety tip and short player history appear on the back. The cards were given out at all 7-Eleven stores in the state and at the Twins June 3 baseball game. Each fan received one baseball card with a poster which told how to collect the other cards in the set. Twelve cards feature players and the 13th card has an artist's rendering of Twins players on the front and a checklist of the set on the back. A group of 50,000 cards was distributed to fifth graders throughout the state by the fire departments.

		NM/M
Complete Set (13):		6.00
Common Player:		.35
1	Kirby Puckett	5.00
2	Frank Viola	.35
3	Mickey Hatcher	.35
4	Kent Hrbek	.35
5	John Butcher	.35
6	Roy Smalley	.35
7	Tom Brunansky	.35
8	Ron Davis	.35
9	Gary Gaetti	.35
10	Tim Teufel	.35
11	Mike Smithson	.35
12	Tim Laudner	.35
---	Checklist	.10

1986 7-11 Slurpee Coins
Eastern Region

This marked the fourth year of production for these coins, issued with the purchase of a large Slurpee drink at 7-Eleven stores. Once again, there are different regional issues, with 16 coins issued for four different regions in 1986. The 1-3/4" diameter plastic coins each feature three different players' pictures, which can be seen alternately by tilting from side to side. Eight of the coins are the same in every region. Each coin is numbered on the back, along with brief player information.

		NM/M
Complete Set (16):		7.50
Common Coin:		.25
1	Dwight Gooden	.25
2	Batting Champs (Wade Boggs, George Brett, Pete Rose)	2.50
3	MVP's (Keith Hernandez, Don Mattingly, Cal Ripken, Jr.)	2.50
4	Slugging Champs (Harold Baines, Pedro Guerrero, Dave Parker)	.25
5	Home Run Champs (Dale Murphy, Jim Rice, Mike Schmidt)	2.00
6	Cy Young Winners (Ron Guidry, Bret Saberhagen, Fernando Valenzuela)	.25
7	Bullpen Aces (Rich Gossage, Dan Quisenberry, Bruce Sutter)	.50
8	Strikeout Kings (Steve Carlton, Nolan Ryan, Tom Seaver)	2.50
9	1985 Rookies (Steve Lyons, Rick Schu, Larry Sheets)	.25
10	Bullpen Aces (Jeff Reardon, Dave Righetti, Bob Stanley)	.25
11	Power Hitters (George Bell, Darryl Strawberry, Dave Winfield)	.75
12	Base Stealers (Rickey Henderson, Tim Raines, Juan Samuel)	.75
13	Home Run Hitters (Andre Dawson, Dwight Evans, Eddie Murray)	.75
14	Ace Pitchers (Mike Boddicker, Ron Darling, Dave Stieb)	.25
15	1985 Bullpen Rookies (Tim Burke, Brian Fisher, Roger McDowell)	.25
16	Sluggers (Jesse Barfield, Gary Carter, Fred Lynn)	.75

Mideastern Region

		NM/M
Complete Set (16):		7.50
Common Coin:		.25
1	Dwight Gooden	.25
2	Batting Champs (Wade Boggs, George Brett, Pete Rose)	2.50
3	MVP's (Keith Hernandez, Don Mattingly, Cal Ripken)	2.50
4	Slugging Champs (Harold Baines, Pedro Guerrero, Dave Parker)	.25
5	Home Run Champs (Dale Murphy, Jim Rice, Mike Schmidt)	2.00
6	Cy Young Winners (Ron Guidry, Bret Saberhagen, Fernando Valenzuela)	.25
7	Bullpen Aces (Rich Gossage, Dan Quisenberry, Bruce Sutter)	.50
8	Strikeout Kings (Steve Carlton, Nolan Ryan, Tom Seaver)	2.50
9	MVP's (Willie Hernandez, Ryne Sandberg, Robin Yount)	1.50
10	Ace Pitchers (Bert Blyleven, Jack Morris, Rick Sutcliffe)	.25
11	Bullpen Aces (Rollie Fingers, Bob James, Lee Smith)	.50
12	All-Star Catchers (Carlton Fisk, Lance Parrish, Tony Pena)	.75
13	1985 Rookies (Shawon Dunston, Ozzie Guillen, Ernest Riles)	.25

Midwestern Region

		NM/M
Complete Set (16):		7.50
Common Coin:		.25
1	Dwight Gooden	.25
2	Batting Champs (Wade Boggs, George Brett, Pete Rose)	2.50
3	MVP's (Keith Hernandez, Don Mattingly, Cal Ripken, Jr.)	2.50
4	Slugging Champs (Harold Baines, Pedro Guerrero, Dave Parker)	.25
5	Home Run Champs (Dale Murphy, Jim Rice, Mike Schmidt)	2.00
6	Cy Young Winners (Ron Guidry, Bret Saberhagen, Fernando Valenzuela)	.25
7	Bullpen Aces (Rich Gossage, Dan Quisenberry, Bruce Sutter)	.50
8	Strikeout Kings (Steve Carlton, Nolan Ryan, Tom Seaver)	2.50
9	1985 Rookies (Vince Coleman, Glenn Davis, Oddibe McDowell)	.25
10	Gold Glovers (Buddy Bell, Ozzie Smith, Lou Whitaker)	1.00
11	Ace Pitchers (Mike Scott, Mario Soto, John Tudor)	.25
12	Bullpen Aces (Jeff Lahti, Ted Power, Dave Smith)	.25
13	Big Hitters (Jack Clark, Jose Cruz, Bob Horner)	.25
14	Star Second Basemen (Bill Doran, Tommy Herr, Ron Oester)	.25
15	1985 Rookie Pitchers (Tom Browning, Joe Hesketh, Todd Worrell)	.25
16	Top Switch-Hitters (Willie McGee, Jerry Mumphrey, Pete Rose)	2.00

Western Region

		NM/M
Complete Set (16):		7.50
Common Coin:		.25
1	Dwight Gooden	.25
2	Batting Champs (Wade Boggs, George Brett, Pete Rose)	2.50
3	MVP's (Keith Hernandez, Don Mattingly, Cal Ripken, Jr.)	2.50
4	Slugging Champs (Harold Baines, Pedro Guerrero, Dave Parker)	.25
5	Home Run Champs (Dale Murphy, Jim Rice, Mike Schmidt)	2.00
6	Cy Young Winners (Ron Guidry, Bret Saberhagen, Fernando Valenzuela)	.25
7	Bullpen Aces (Rich Gossage, Dan Quisenberry, Bruce Sutter)	.50
8	Strikeout Kings (Steve Carlton, Nolan Ryan, Tom Seaver)	2.50
9	Home Run Champs (Reggie Jackson, Dave Kingman, Gorman Thomas)	1.00
10	Batting Champs (Rod Carew, Tony Gwynn, Carney Lansford)	1.00
11	Sluggers (Phil Bradley, Mike Marshall, Graig Nettles)	.25
12	Ace Pitchers (Andy Hawkins, Orel Hershiser, Mike Witt)	.25
13	1985 Rookies (Chris Brown, Ivan Calderon, Mariano Duncan)	.25
14	Big Hitters (Steve Garvey, Bill Madlock, Jim Presley)	.25
15	Bullpen Aces (Jay Howell, Donnie Moore, Ed Nunez)	.25
16	1985 Bullpen Rookies (Karl Best, Stewart Cliburn, Steve Ontiveros)	.25

Jumbo Coin

Three of the game's top stars were featured on a jumbo-format (4-1/2" diameter) "3D" disc distributed by 7-11 stores in conjunction

---

14	Star Outfielders (Brett Butler, Chet Lemon, Willie Wilson)	.25
15	Home Run Hitters (Tom Brunansky, Cecil Cooper, Darrell Evans)	.25
16	Big Hitters (Kirk Gibson, Paul Molitor, Greg Walker)	.75

with their Slurpee fountain drink. Like the smaller Slurpee coins, the photos on the disc change as the viewing angle is changed.

		NM/M
Wade Boggs, George Brett, Pete Rose		10.00

1987 7-11 Slurpee Coins
Eastern Region

Continuing with a tradition started in 1983, 7-Eleven stores offered a free "Super Star Sports Coin" with the purchase of a Slurpee drink. Five different regional sets of Slurpee coins were issued for 1987, a total of 75 coins. Each coin measures 1-3/4" in diameter and features a multiple image effect which allows three different pictures to be seen, depending on how the coin is tilted. The coin reverses contain career records and personal player information.

		NM/M
Complete Set (15):		7.50
Common Player:		.25
1	Gary Carter	1.00
2	Don Baylor	.25
3	Rickey Henderson	1.00
4	Lenny Dykstra	.25
5	Wade Boggs	1.50
6	Mike Pagliarulo	.25
7	Dwight Gooden	.25
8	Roger Clemens	2.00
9	Dave Righetti	.25
10	Keith Hernandez	.25
11	Pat Dodson	.25
12	Don Mattingly	2.00
13	Darryl Strawberry	.25
14	Jim Rice	.45
15	Dave Winfield	1.00

Great Lakes Region

		NM/M
Complete Set (16):		6.00
Common Player:		.25
1	Harold Baines	.25
2	Jody Davis	.25
3	John Cangelosi	.25
4	Shawon Dunston	.25
5	Dave Cochrane	.25
6	Leon Durham	.25
7	Carlton Fisk	1.50
8	Dennis Eckersley	1.00
9	Ozzie Guillen	.25
10	Gary Matthews	.25
11	Ron Karkovice	.25
12	Keith Moreland	.25
13	Bobby Thigpen	.25
14	Ryne Sandberg	2.50
15	Greg Walker	.25
16	Lee Smith	.25

Mideastern Region

		NM/M
Complete Set (16):		7.50
Common Player:		.25
1	Gary Carter	1.00
2	Marty Barrett	.25
3	Jody Davis	.25
4	Don Aase	.25
5	Lenny Dykstra	.25
6	Wade Boggs	1.50
7	Keith Moreland	.25
8	Mike Boddicker	.25
9	Dwight Gooden	.25
10	Roger Clemens	1.50
11	Ryne Sandberg	1.50
12	Eddie Murray	1.00
13	Keith Hernandez	.25
14	Jim Rice	.45
15	Lee Smith	.25
16	Cal Ripken, Jr.	4.00

Western Region

		NM/M
Complete Set (16):		2.00
Common Player:		.25
1	Doug DeCinces	.25
2	Mariano Duncan	.25
3	Wally Joyner	.25
4	Pedro Guerrero	.25
5	Kirk McCaskill	.25
6	Orel Hershiser	.25
7	Gary Pettis	.25
8	Mike Marshall	.25
9	Dick Schofield	.25
10	Steve Sax	.25
11	Don Sutton	1.00
12	Mike Scioscia	.25

13	Devon White	.25
14	Franklin Stubbs	.25
15	Mike Witt	.25
16	Fernando Valenzuela	.25

Tigers Coins

		NM/M
Complete Set (12):		6.00
Common Player:		.50
1	Darnell Coles	.50
2	Darrell Evans	.60
3	Kirk Gibson	.60
4	Willie Hernandez	.50
5	Larry Herndon	.50
6	Chet Lemon	.50
7	Dwight Lowry	.50
8	Jack Morris	.60
9	Dan Petry	.50
10	Frank Tanana	.50
11	Alan Trammell	.75
12	Lou Whitaker	.65

1991 7-11 Slurpee Coins
Atlantic Region

After a three-year hiatus, "3-D" magic-motion coins returned to 7-11 stores in the form of regional sets produced by Score under the name Superstar Sports Coins and given away with the purchase of Slurpee fountain drinks. In the familiar 1-3/4" diameter, the discs have alternating portrait and action images on the front with the player name at top, the team at bottom, the uniform number at left and position at right. Each regional set has a different border color. Backs have 7-11 and Score logos along with career stats and a short career summary. The 120 coins in the sets feature 81 different major leaguers.

		NM/M
Complete Set (15):		7.50
Common Player:		.25
1	Glenn Davis	.25
2	Dwight Evans	.25
3	Leo Gomez	.25
4	Ken Griffey Jr.	1.50
5	Rickey Henderson	.75
6	Jose Canseco	.60
7	Dave Justice	.25
8	Ben McDonald	.25
9	Randy Milligan	.25
10	Gregg Olson	.25
11	Kirby Puckett	1.00
12	Bill Ripken	.25
13	Cal Ripken Jr.	2.50
14	Nolan Ryan	2.50
15	David Segui	.25

Florida Region

		NM/M
Complete Set (15):		10.00
Common Player:		.25
1	Barry Bonds	2.50
2	George Brett	1.50
3	Roger Clemens	1.50
4	Glenn Davis	.25
5	Alex Fernandez	.25
6	Cecil Fielder	.25
7	Ken Griffey Jr.	2.00
8	Dwight Gooden	.25
9	Dave Justice	.25
10	Barry Larkin	.25
11	Ramon Martinez	.25
12	Jose Offerman	.25
13	Kirby Puckett	1.00
14	Nolan Ryan	2.50
15	Terry Schumpert	.25

Metro Northeast Region

		NM/M
Complete Set (15):		9.00
Common Player:		.25
1	Wade Boggs	1.00
2	Barry Bonds	2.50
3	Roger Clemens	1.50
4	Len Dykstra	.25
5	Dwight Gooden	.25
6	Ken Griffey Jr.	2.00
7	Rickey Henderson	.75
8	Gregg Jefferies	.25
9	Roberto Kelly	.25
10	Kevin Maas	.25
11	Don Mattingly	1.50
12	Mickey Morandini	.25
13	Dale Murphy	.50
14	Darryl Strawberry	.25
15	Frank Viola	.25

Midwest

		NM/M
Complete Set (15):		6.00
Common Player:		.25
1	George Brett	1.50
2	Andre Dawson	.40
3	Cecil Fielder	.25
4	Carlton Fisk	.75
5	Travis Fryman	.25
6	Mark Grace	.25
7	Ken Griffey Jr.	2.00
8	Ozzie Guillen	.25
9	Alex Fernandez	.25
10	Ray Lankford	.25

11	Ryne Sandberg	1.00
12	Ozzie Smith	1.00
13	Bobby Thigpen	.25
14	Frank Thomas	.75
15	Alan Trammell	.25

Northern California Region

		NM/M
Complete Set (15):		9.00
Common Player:		.25
1	John Burkett	.25
2	Jose Canseco	.65
3	Will Clark	.25
4	Steve Decker	.25
5	Dennis Eckersley	.25
6	Ken Griffey Jr.	2.00
7	Rickey Henderson	.75
8	Nolan Ryan	3.00
9	Mark McGwire	2.50
10	Kevin Mitchell	.25
11	Terry Steinbach	.25
12	Dave Stewart	.25
13	Todd Van Poppel	.25
14	Bob Welch	.25
15	Matt Williams	.25

Northwest Region

		NM/M
Complete Set (15):		9.00
Common Player:		.25
1	George Brett	1.50
2	Jose Canseco	.60
3	Alvin Davis	.25
4	Ken Griffey Jr.	
	Ken Griffey Sr.	1.00
5	Ken Griffey Jr.	2.00
6	Erik Hanson	.25
7	Rickey Henderson	.25
8	Ryne Sandberg	1.00
9	Randy Johnson	.75
10	Dave Justice	.25
11	Edgar Martinez	.25
12	Tino Martinez	.25
13	Harold Reynolds	.25
14	Nolan Ryan	3.00
15	Mike Schooler	.25

Southern California Region

		NM/M
Complete Set (15):		7.00
Common Player:		.25
1	Jim Abbott	.25
2	Jose Canseco	.60
3	Ken Griffey Jr.	2.00
4	Tony Gwynn	1.00
5	Orel Hershiser	.25
6	Eric Davis	.25
7	Wally Joyner	.25
8	Ramon Martinez	.25
9	Fred McGriff	.25
10	Eddie Murray	.75
11	Jose Offerman	.25
12	Nolan Ryan	3.00
13	Benito Santiago	.25
14	Darryl Strawberry	.25
15	Fernando Valenzuela	.25

Texas Region

		NM/M
Complete Set (15):		10.00
Common Player:		.25
1	Craig Biggio	.25
2	Barry Bonds	3.00
3	Jose Canseco	.50
4	Roger Clemens	1.50
5	Glenn Davis	.25
6	Julio Franco	.25
7	Juan Gonzalez	.50
8	Ken Griffey Jr.	2.00
9	Mike Scott	.25
10	Rafael Palmeiro	.75
11	Nolan Ryan	3.00
12	Ryne Sandberg	1.00
13	Ruben Sierra	.25
14	Todd Van Poppel	.25
15	Bobby Witt	.25

1992 7-11 Slurpee
Superstar Action Coins

Score baseball 3-D coins returned to 7-11 stores on a very limited basis in 1992. A 26-piece set of the plastic coins (one for each major league team) was produced by Score in the familiar 1-3/4" diameter format. The coins feature a maroon border on which is printed in white the player's name, team, position and uniform number. At center is a 1-1/4" circle with "flasher" portrait and action photos of the player. Backs have a black border with the player name in yellow at the top, a few career stats, 7-11 and Score logos and a coin number in a pale yellow center circle. At bottom in green is "Superstar Action Coin."

		NM/M
Complete Set (26):		10.00
Common Player:		.25
1	Dwight Gooden	.25
2	Don Mattingly	1.00
3	Roger Clemens	1.00
4	Ivan Calderon	.25
5	Roberto Alomar	.40
6	Sandy Alomar, Jr.	.25
7	Andy Van Slyke	.25
8	Lenny Dykstra	.25
9	Cal Ripken, Jr.	2.00
10	Dave Justice	.25
11	Nolan Ryan	2.00
12	Craig Biggio	.25
13	Barry Larkin	.25
14	Ozzie Smith	.75
15	Ryne Sandberg	.75
16	Frank Thomas	.60
17	Robin Yount	.60
18	Kirby Puckett	.75
19	Cecil Fielder	.25
20	Will Clark	.25
21	Jose Canseco	.45
22	Jim Abbott	.25
23	Tony Gwynn	.75
24	Darryl Strawberry	.25
25	George Brett	1.00
26	Ken Griffey Jr.	1.50

2000 7-11 Slurpee Coins

Returning after a long hiatus, lenticular-motion player discs were once again affixed to the bottoms of Super Big Gulp and 32-oz. Slurpee cups at 20,000 convenience stores nationwide. A step up in quality from the "flicker image" coins of the 1980s, this generation was produced by Pacific Trading Cards and licensed by MLB and the Players Union. The 1-3/4" plastic discs have three photos at center with player identification at top and bottom; uniform numbers and logos are at the sides. On back, conventionally printed, is a color portrait photo, a few stats and vital data and appropriate copyright and licensing notices. There is one player coin from each major league team. An album was available to house the set.

		NM/M
Complete Set (30):		10.00
Common Player:		.25
Album:		3.00
In-Store Ad Sheet:		6.00
1	Tim Salmon	.25
2	Erubiel Durazo	.25
3	Chipper Jones	.65
4	Cal Ripken Jr.	2.00
5	Nomar Garciaparra	.65
6	Mark Grace	.25
7	Frank Thomas	.50
8	Sean Casey	.25
9	Manny Ramirez	.50
10	Larry Walker	.25
11	Dean Palmer	.25
12	Alex Gonzalez	.25
13	Jeff Bagwell	.50
14	Carlos Beltran	.45
15	Gary Sheffield	.40
16	Jeromy Burnitz	.25
17	Corey Koskie	.25
18	Vladimir Guerrero	.75
19	Mike Piazza	1.00
20	Roger Clemens	.75
21	Ben Grieve	.25
22	Scott Rolen	.45

23	Jason Kendall	.25
24	Mark McGwire	1.50
25	Tony Gwynn	.65
26	Jeff Kent	.25
27	Jay Buhner	.25
28	Jose Canseco	.40
29	Ivan Rodriguez	.45
30	Carlos Delgado	.45

1981 7-Up

These 5-1/2" x 8-1/2" color photocards are part of a multi-sport series. Fronts have a borderless photo, a facsimile autograph and, at lower-right, a 7-Up logo and slogan. Back is printed in black, red and green on white and features a career summary through the 1980 season, and a large version of the soda logo. Posters in 19" x 25" size were also issued.

		NM/M
Common Player:		3.00
(1)	George Brett	6.00
(3)	Dave Parker	3.00
(5)	Mike Schmidt	6.00

1984 7-Up Cubs

The Chicago Cubs and 7-Up issued this 28-card set featuring full-color game-action photos on a 2-1/4" x 3-1/2" borderless front. The backs have the player's stats and personal information. This was the third consecutive year the Cubs issued this type of set as a giveaway at a "Baseball Card Day" promotional game.

		NM/M
Complete Set (28):		13.50
Common Player:		.25
1	Larry Bowa	.25
6	Keith Moreland	.25
7	Jody Davis	.25
10	Leon Durham	.25
11	Ron Cey	.25
15	Ron Hassey	.25
18	Richie Hebner	.25
19	Dave Owen	.25
20	Bob Dernier	.25
21	Jay Johnstone	.25
23	Ryne Sandberg	9.00
24	Scott Sanderson	.25
25	Gary Woods	.25
27	Thad Bosley	.25
28	Henry Cotto	.25
34	Steve Trout	.25
36	Gary Matthews	.25
39	George Frazier	.25
40	Rick Sutcliffe	.25
41	Warren Brusstar	.25
42	Rich Bordi	.25
43	Dennis Eckersley	3.00
44	Dick Ruthven	.25
46	Lee Smith	.25
47	Rick Reuschel	.25
49	Tim Stoddard	.25
---	Jim Frey	.25
---	Cubs Coaches	
	(Ruben Amaro,	
	Billy Connors,	

	Johnny Oates,	
	John Vukovich,	
	Don Zimmer)	.25

1985 7-Up Cubs

(7) JODY DAVIS C

This was the second year a Chicago Cubs card set was released with 7-Up as the sponsor. The set has 28 unnumbered cards in the standard 2-1/2" x 3-1/2" size. They were distributed to fans attending the Cubs game on August 14 at Wrigley Field. They feature full-color game-action photos of the players. Card backs contain the player's professional stats.

		NM/M
Complete Set (28):		10.00
Common Player:		.25
1	Larry Bowa	.25
6	Keith Moreland	.25
7	Jody Davis	.25
10	Leon Durham	.25
11	Ron Cey	.25
15	Davey Lopes	.25
16	Steve Lake	.25
18	Richie Hebner	.25
20	Bob Dernier	.25
21	Scott Sanderson	.25
22	Billy Hatcher	.25
23	Ryne Sandberg	7.50
24	Brian Dayett	.25
25	Gary Woods	.25
27	Thad Bosley	.25
28	Chris Speier	.25
31	Ray Fontenot	.25
34	Steve Trout	.25
36	Gary Matthews	.25
39	George Frazier	.25
40	Rick Sutcliffe	.25
41	Warren Brusstar	.25
42	Lary Sorensen	.25
43	Dennis Eckersley	2.00
44	Dick Ruthven	.25
46	Lee Smith	.25
---	Jim Frey	.25
---	Coaching Staff	
	(Ruben Amaro, Billy Connors,	
	Johnny Oates,	
	John Vukovich,	
	Don Zimmer)	.25

1995 Skin Bracer

BILL MAZEROSKI

This three-card set was included in several packagings of Mennen skin care products for men. Three sepia-toned 3-1/2" x 2-1/2" cards feature great moments in post-season play. Fronts are trimmed in gold ink and feature the player's name in a green box. Backs are printed in black, green and gold and describe the highlight. Logos of the sponsor and Major League Baseball Players Alumni Association are also printed on back. A related offer allowed collectors to purchase autographed 8" x 10" photos of the events for $7.99 each via a coupon.

		NM/M
Complete Set (3):		6.00
Common Player:		2.00
(1)	The Perfect Game (Don Larsen)	2.00
(2)	The Series Ender (Bill Mazeroski)	2.00
(3)	The Shot Heard 'Round the World (Bobby Thomson)	2.00

2001 Skippy Peanut Butter Derek Jeter

Specially marked jars Skippy Peanut Butter had a Derek Jeter "Dig-

ital Card" under the cap, enclosed in protective plastic. The 2-1/2" diameter discs are printed on thin cardboard and have portrait and action photos of the spokesman on front (Yankees team logos have been removed) along with a facsimile autograph and logos of Skippy and CyberAction. Backs are in red and blue with information on the company's website and a card title.

		NM/M
Complete Set (4):		6.00
Common Card:		2.00
1	1,000 Hits Club/Btg (Derek Jeter)	2.00
2	1998 Runs Leader/Running (Derek Jeter)	2.00
3	Three Time All-Star/Leaping (Derek Jeter)	2.00
4	World Champion MVP/ Throwing (Derek Jeter)	2.00

1995 SkyBox E-Motion Promo

To introduce its new super-premium baseball card line, SkyBox debuted a Cal Ripken promo card at the 1995 National Sports Collectors Convention. The card is virtually identical to Ripken's card in the regular issue, except for diagonal overprinting on each side which reads, "Promotional Sample."

		NM/M
8	Cal Ripken Jr. (Class)	2.50

1995 SkyBox E-Motion

PRESENCE

This is a super-premium debut issue from the newly merged Fleer/SkyBox company. Printed on double-thick cardboard, card fronts have borderless photos marred by the presence of four gold-foil "viewfinder" corner marks. The player's last name and team are printed in gold foil near the bottom. On each card there is a large silver-foil word printed in block letters; either a nickname or an emotion or attribute associated with the player. Backs have two more player photos, 1994 and career stats and a few biographical bits. Eight-cards packs were issued with a suggested retail price of $4.99.

		NM/M
Complete Set (200):		15.00

Common Player:		.05
Pack (8):		1.00
Wax Box (36):		20.00
1	Brady Anderson	.05
2	Kevin Brown	.05
3	Curtis Goodwin	.05
4	Jeffrey Hammonds	.05
5	Ben McDonald	.05
6	Mike Mussina	.35
7	Rafael Palmeiro	.65
8	Cal Ripken Jr.	2.00
9	Jose Canseco	.45
10	Roger Clemens	1.00
11	Vaughn Eshelman	.05
12	Mike Greenwell	.05
13	Erik Hanson	.05
14	Tim Naehring	.05
15	Aaron Sele	.05
16	John Valentin	.05
17	Mo Vaughn	.05
18	Chili Davis	.05
19	Gary DiSarcina	.05
20	Chuck Finley	.05
21	Tim Salmon	.05
22	Lee Smith	.05
23	J.T. Snow	.05
24	Jim Abbott	.05
25	Jason Bere	.05
26	Ray Durham	.05
27	Ozzie Guillen	.05
28	Tim Raines	.05
29	Frank Thomas	.75
30	Robin Ventura	.05
31	Carlos Baerga	.05
32	Albert Belle	.05
33	Orel Hershiser	.05
34	Kenny Lofton	.05
35	Dennis Martinez	.05
36	Eddie Murray	.75
37	Manny Ramirez	.75
38	Julian Tavarez	.05
39	Jim Thome	.60
40	Dave Winfield	.75
41	Chad Curtis	.05
42	Cecil Fielder	.05
43	Travis Fryman	.05
44	Kirk Gibson	.05
45	Bob Higginson RC	.25
46	Alan Trammell	.05
47	Lou Whitaker	.05
48	Kevin Appier	.05
49	Gary Gaetti	.05
50	Jeff Montgomery	.05
51	Jon Nunnally	.05
52	Ricky Bones	.05
53	Cal Eldred	.05
54	Joe Oliver	.05
55	Kevin Seitzer	.05
56	Marty Cordova	.05
57	Chuck Knoblauch	.05
58	Kirby Puckett	1.00
59	Wade Boggs	1.00
60	Derek Jeter	2.00
61	Jimmy Key	.05
62	Don Mattingly	1.00
63	Jack McDowell	.05
64	Paul O'Neill	.05
65	Andy Pettitte	.30
66	Ruben Rivera	.05
67	Mike Stanley	.05
68	John Wetteland	.05
69	Geronimo Berroa	.05
70	Dennis Eckersley	.65
71	Rickey Henderson	.75
72	Mark McGwire	1.50
73	Steve Ontiveros	.05
74	Ruben Sierra	.05
75	Terry Steinbach	.05
76	Jay Buhner	.05
77	Ken Griffey Jr.	1.25
78	Randy Johnson	.75
79	Edgar Martinez	.05
80	Tino Martinez	.05
81	Marc Newfield	.05
82	Alex Rodriguez	1.50
83	Will Clark	.05
84	Benji Gil	.05
85	Juan Gonzalez	.40
86	Rusty Greer	.05
87	Dean Palmer	.05
88	Ivan Rodriguez	.65
89	Kenny Rogers	.05
90	Roberto Alomar	.30
91	Joe Carter	.05
92	David Cone	.05
93	Alex Gonzalez	.05
94	Shawn Green	.40
95	Pat Hentgen	.05
96	Paul Molitor	.75
97	John Olerud	.05
98	Devon White	.05
99	Steve Avery	.05
100	Tom Glavine	.35
101	Marquis Grissom	.05
102	Chipper Jones	1.00
103	Dave Justice	.05
104	Ryan Klesko	.05
105	Javier Lopez	.05
106	Greg Maddux	1.00
107	Fred McGriff	.05
108	John Smoltz	.05
109	Shawon Dunston	.05
110	Mark Grace	.05
111	Brian McRae	.05
112	Randy Myers	.05
113	Sammy Sosa	1.00
114	Steve Trachsel	.05
115	Bret Boone	.05

116	Ron Gant	.05
117	Barry Larkin	.05
118	Deion Sanders	.05
119	Reggie Sanders	.05
120	Pete Schourek	.05
121	John Smiley	.05
122	Jason Bates	.05
123	Dante Bichette	.05
124	Vinny Castilla	.05
125	Andres Galarraga	.05
126	Larry Walker	.05
127	Greg Colbrunn	.05
128	Jeff Conine	.05
129	Andre Dawson	.30
130	Chris Hammond	.05
131	Charles Johnson	.05
132	Gary Sheffield	.45
133	Quilvio Veras	.05
134	Jeff Bagwell	.75
135	Derek Bell	.05
136	Craig Biggio	.05
137	Jim Dougherty	.05
138	John Hudek	.05
139	Orlando Miller	.05
140	Phil Plantier	.05
141	Eric Karros	.05
142	Ramon Martinez	.05
143	Raul Mondesi	.05
144	Hideo Nomo RC	2.00
145	Mike Piazza	1.25
146	Ismael Valdes	.05
147	Todd Worrell	.05
148	Moises Alou	.05
149	Yamil Benitez RC	.05
150	Wil Cordero	.05
151	Jeff Fassero	.05
152	Cliff Floyd	.05
153	Pedro Martinez	.75
154	Carlos Perez RC	.05
155	Tony Tarasco	.05
156	Rondell White	.05
157	Edgardo Alfonzo	.05
158	Bobby Bonilla	.05
159	Rico Brogna	.05
160	Bobby Jones	.05
161	Bill Pulsipher	.05
162	Bret Saberhagen	.05
163	Ricky Bottalico	.05
164	Darren Daulton	.05
165	Lenny Dykstra	.05
166	Charlie Hayes	.05
167	Dave Hollins	.05
168	Gregg Jefferies	.05
169	Michael Mimbs RC	.05
170	Curt Schilling	.35
171	Heathcliff Slocumb	.05
172	Jay Bell	.05
173	Micah Franklin RC	.05
174	Mark Johnson RC	.05
175	Jeff King	.05
176	Al Martin	.05
177	Dan Miceli	.05
178	Denny Neagle	.05
179	Bernard Gilkey	.05
180	Ken Hill	.05
181	Brian Jordan	.05
182	Ray Lankford	.05
183	Ozzie Smith	1.00
184	Andy Benes	.05
185	Ken Caminiti	.05
186	Steve Finley	.05
187	Tony Gwynn	1.00
188	Joey Hamilton	.05
189	Melvin Nieves	.05
190	Scott Sanders	.05
191	Rod Beck	.05
192	Barry Bonds	2.00
193	Royce Clayton	.05
194	Glenallen Hill	.05
195	Darren Lewis	.05
196	Mark Portugal	.05
197	Matt Williams	.05
198	Checklist	.05
199	Checklist	.05
200	Checklist	.05

Masters

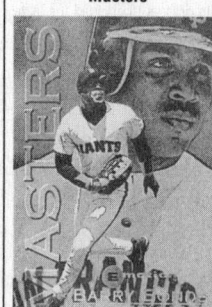

Ten of the game's top veterans are featured in this chase card set. A large close-up photo in a single team-related color in the background, with a color action photo in the foreground. Backs have a borderless color photo and a top to bottom color bar with some good words about the player. The Masters inserts are found at an average rate of one per eight packs.

		NM/M
Complete Set (10):		12.00
Common Player:		.50
1	Barry Bonds	2.50
2	Juan Gonzalez	.65
3	Ken Griffey Jr.	2.00
4	Tony Gwynn	1.50
5	Kenny Lofton	.50
6	Greg Maddux	1.50
7	Raul Mondesi	.50
8	Cal Ripken Jr.	2.50
9	Frank Thomas	1.00
10	Matt Williams	.50

N-Tense

A colored wave-pattern printed on metallic foil is the background for the action photo of one of baseball's top sluggers in this chase card set. A huge rainbow prismatic foil "N" appears in an upper corner. The player's name and team are at lower-right in gold foil. Backs are conventionally printed and repeat the front's patterned background, with another color player photo and a shaded box with a few career highlights.

		NM/M
Complete Set (12):		16.00
Common Player:		.50
1	Jeff Bagwell	2.00
2	Albert Belle	.50
3	Barry Bonds	4.00
4	Cecil Fielder	.50
5	Ron Gant	.50
6	Ken Griffey Jr.	2.50
7	Mark McGwire	3.00
8	Mike Piazza	2.50
9	Manny Ramirez	2.00
10	Frank Thomas	2.00
11	Mo Vaughn	.50
12	Matt Williams	.50

Cal Ripken Jr. Timeless

A white background with a clockface and gold-foil "TIMELESS" logo are the standard elements of this insert tribute to Cal Ripken, Jr. Fronts also feature a large color photo and a smaller sepia photo contemporary to some phase of his career. The first 10 cards in the set chronicle Ripken's career through 1994. A special mail-in offer provided five more cards featuring highlights of his 1995 season.

		NM/M
Complete Set (15):		20.00
Common Player:		1.50
1	High School Pitcher	1.50
2	Role Model	1.50
3	Rookie of the Year	1.50
4	1st MVP Season	1.50
5	95 Consecutive Errorless Games	1.50
6	All-Star MVP	1.50
7	Conditioning	1.50

8	Shortstop HR Record	1.50
9	Literacy Work	1.50
10	2000th Consecutive Game	1.50
11	All-Star Selection	2.25
12	Record-tying Game	2.25
13	Record-breaking Game	2.25
14	2,153 and Counting	2.25
15	Birthday	2.25

Rookies

A bold colored background with outline white letters repeating the word "ROOKIE" is the frame for the central action photo in this insert series. The top of the photo is vignetted with a white circle that has the player's name in gold at left, and his team in white at right. Backs repeat the front background and include a player portrait photo and a few sentences about his potential. Rookie inserts are found at an average rate of one per five packs.

		NM/M
Complete Set (10):		6.50
Common Player:		.25
1	Edgardo Alfonzo	.25
2	Jason Bates	.25
3	Marty Cordova	.25
4	Ray Durham	.25
5	Alex Gonzalez	.25
6	Shawn Green	.75
7	Charles Johnson	.25
8	Chipper Jones	1.50
9	Hideo Nomo	1.00
10	Alex Rodriguez	3.00

1996 SkyBox E-Motion XL

Each card in SkyBox's 1996 E-Motion XL Baseball arrives on two layers of stock - a die-cut matte frame over a UV-coated card. The frames come in three colors - blue, green and maroon (but each player has only one color version). The 300-card set also includes four insert sets: Legion of Boom, D-Fense, N-Tense and Rare Breed.

		NM/M
Complete Set (300):		10.00
Common Player:		.05
Pack (7):		1.00
Wax Box (24):		20.00
1	Roberto Alomar	.15
2	Brady Anderson	.05
3	Bobby Bonilla	.05
4	Jeffrey Hammonds	.05
5	Chris Hoiles	.05
6	Mike Mussina	.30
7	Randy Myers	.05
8	Rafael Palmeiro	.50
9	Cal Ripken Jr.	2.00
10	B.J. Surhoff	.05
11	Jose Canseco	.25
12	Roger Clemens	1.00
13	Wil Cordero	.05
14	Mike Greenwell	.05
15	Dwayne Hosey	.05
16	Tim Naehring	.05
17	Troy O'Leary	.05
18	Mike Stanley	.05
19	John Valentin	.05
20	Mo Vaughn	.05

21	Jim Abbott	.05
22	Garret Anderson	.05
23	George Arias	.05
24	Chili Davis	.05
25	Jim Edmonds	.05
26	Chuck Finley	.05
27	Todd Greene	.05
28	Mark Langston	.05
29	Troy Percival	.05
30	Tim Salmon	.05
31	Lee Smith	.05
32	J.T. Snow	.05
33	Harold Baines	.05
34	Jason Bere	.05
35	Ray Durham	.05
36	Alex Fernandez	.05
37	Ozzie Guillen	.05
38	Darren Lewis	.05
39	Lyle Mouton	.05
40	Tony Phillips	.05
41	Danny Tartabull	.05
42	Frank Thomas	.60
43	Robin Ventura	.05
44	Sandy Alomar	.05
45	Carlos Baerga	.05
46	Albert Belle	.05
47	Julio Franco	.05
48	Orel Hershiser	.05
49	Kenny Lofton	.05
50	Dennis Martinez	.05
51	Jack McDowell	.05
52	Jose Mesa	.05
53	Eddie Murray	.60
54	Charles Nagy	.05
55	Manny Ramirez	.60
55p	Manny Ramirez/OPS	.60
56	Jim Thome	.45
57	Omar Vizquel	.05
58	Chad Curtis	.05
59	Cecil Fielder	.05
60	Travis Fryman	.05
61	Chris Gomez	.05
62	Felipe Lira	.05
63	Alan Trammell	.05
64	Kevin Appier	.05
65	Johnny Damon	.35
66	Tom Goodwin	.05
67	Mark Gubicza	.05
68	Jeff Montgomery	.05
69	Jon Nunnally	.05
70	Bip Roberts	.05
71	Ricky Bones	.05
72	Chuck Carr	.05
73	John Jaha	.05
74	Ben McDonald	.05
75	Matt Mieske	.05
76	Dave Nilsson	.05
77	Kevin Seitzer	.05
78	Greg Vaughn	.05
79	Rick Aguilera	.05
80	Marty Cordova	.05
81	Roberto Kelly	.05
82	Chuck Knoblauch	.05
83	Pat Meares	.05
84	Paul Molitor	.60
85	Kirby Puckett	.75
86	Brad Radke	.05
87	Wade Boggs	.75
88	David Cone	.05
89	Dwight Gooden	.05
90	Derek Jeter	2.00
91	Tino Martinez	.05
92	Paul O'Neill	.05
93	Andy Pettitte	.15
94	Tim Raines	.05
95	Ruben Rivera	.05
96	Kenny Rogers	.05
97	Ruben Sierra	.05
98	John Wetteland	.05
99	Bernie Williams	.05
100	Allen Battle	.05
101	Geronimo Berroa	.05
102	Brent Gates	.05
103	Doug Johns	.05
104	Mark McGwire	1.50
105	Pedro Munoz	.05
106	Ariel Prieto	.05
107	Terry Steinbach	.05
108	Todd Van Poppel	.05
109	Chris Bosio	.05
110	Jay Buhner	.05
111	Joey Cora	.05
112	Russ Davis	.05
113	Ken Griffey Jr.	1.25
114	Sterling Hitchcock	.05
115	Randy Johnson	.60
116	Edgar Martinez	.05
117	Alex Rodriguez	1.50
118	Paul Sorrento	.05
119	Dan Wilson	.05
120	Will Clark	.05
121	Juan Gonzalez	.30
122	Rusty Greer	.05
123	Kevin Gross	.05
124	Ken Hill	.05
125	Dean Palmer	.05
126	Roger Pavlik	.05
127	Ivan Rodriguez	.50
128	Mickey Tettleton	.05
129	Joe Carter	.05
130	Carlos Delgado	.40
131	Alex Gonzalez	.05
132	Shawn Green	.25
133	Erik Hanson	.05
134	Pat Hentgen	.05
135	Otis Nixon	.05
136	John Olerud	.05
137	Ed Sprague	.05

138	Steve Avery	.05
139	Jermaine Dye	.05
140	Tom Glavine	.35
141	Marquis Grissom	.05
142	Chipper Jones	.75
143	David Justice	.05
144	Ryan Klesko	.05
145	Javier Lopez	.05
146	Greg Maddux	.75
147	Fred McGriff	.05
148	Jason Schmidt	.05
149	John Smoltz	.05
150	Mark Wohlers	.05
151	Jim Bullinger	.05
152	Frank Castillo	.05
153	Kevin Foster	.05
154	Luis Gonzalez	.05
155	Mark Grace	.05
156	Brian McRae	.05
157	Jaime Navarro	.05
158	Rey Sanchez	.05
159	Ryne Sandberg	.75
160	Sammy Sosa	.75
161	Bret Boone	.05
162	Jeff Brantley	.05
163	Vince Coleman	.05
164	Steve Gibralter	.05
165	Barry Larkin	.05
166	Hal Morris	.05
167	Mark Portugal	.05
168	Reggie Sanders	.05
169	Pete Schourek	.05
170	John Smiley	.05
171	Jason Bates	.05
172	Dante Bichette	.05
173	Ellis Burks	.05
174	Vinny Castilla	.05
175	Andres Galarraga	.05
176	Kevin Ritz	.05
177	Bill Swift	.05
178	Larry Walker	.05
179	Walt Weiss	.05
180	Eric Young	.05
181	Kurt Abbott	.05
182	Kevin Brown	.05
183	John Burkett	.05
184	Greg Colbrunn	.05
185	Jeff Conine	.05
186	Chris Hammond	.05
187	Charles Johnson	.05
188	Terry Pendleton	.05
189	Pat Rapp	.05
190	Gary Sheffield	.25
191	Quilvio Veras	.05
192	Devon White	.05
193	Jeff Bagwell	.05
194	Derek Bell	.05
195	Sean Berry	.05
196	Craig Biggio	.05
197	Doug Drabek	.05
198	Tony Eusebio	.05
199	Mike Hampton	.05
200	Brian Hunter	.05
201	Derrick May	.05
202	Orlando Miller	.05
203	Shane Reynolds	.05
204	Mike Blowers	.05
205	Tom Candiotti	.05
206	Delino DeShields	.05
207	Greg Gagne	.05
208	Karim Garcia	.05
209	Todd Hollandsworth	.05
210	Eric Karros	.05
211	Ramon Martinez	.05
212	Raul Mondesi	.05
213	Hideo Nomo	.30
214	Chan Ho Park	.05
215	Mike Piazza	1.25
216	Ismael Valdes	.05
217	Todd Worrell	.05
218	Moises Alou	.05
219	Yamil Benitez	.05
220	Jeff Fassero	.05
221	Darrin Fletcher	.05
222	Cliff Floyd	.05
223	Pedro Martinez	.60
224	Carlos Perez	.05
225	Mel Rojas	.05
226	David Segui	.05
227	Rondell White	.05
228	Rico Brogna	.05
229	Carl Everett	.05
230	John Franco	.05
231	Bernard Gilkey	.05
232	Todd Hundley	.05
233	Jason Isringhausen	.05
234	Lance Johnson	.05
235	Bobby Jones	.05
236	Jeff Kent	.05
237	Rey Ordonez	.05
238	Bill Pulsipher	.05
239	Jose Vizcaino	.05
240	Paul Wilson	.05
241	Ricky Bottalico	.05
242	Darren Daulton	.05
243	Lenny Dykstra	.05
244	Jim Eisenreich	.05
245	Sid Fernandez	.05
246	Gregg Jefferies	.05
247	Mickey Morandini	.05
248	Benito Santiago	.05
249	Curt Schilling	.35
250	Mark Whiten	.05
251	Todd Zeile	.05
252	Jay Bell	.05
253	Carlos Garcia	.05
254	Charlie Hayes	.05
255	Jason Kendall	.05

256	Jeff King	.05
257	Al Martin	.05
258	Orlando Merced	.05
259	Dan Miceli	.05
260	Denny Neagle	.05
261	Alan Benes	.05
262	Andy Benes	.05
263	Royce Clayton	.05
264	Dennis Eckersley	.50
265	Gary Gaetti	.05
266	Ron Gant	.05
267	Brian Jordan	.05
268	Ray Lankford	.05
269	John Mabry	.05
270	Tom Pagnozzi	.05
271	Ozzie Smith	.75
272	Todd Stottlemyre	.05
273	Andy Ashby	.05
274	Brad Ausmus	.05
275	Ken Caminiti	.05
276	Steve Finley	.05
277	Tony Gwynn	.75
278	Joey Hamilton	.05
279	Rickey Henderson	.60
280	Trevor Hoffman	.05
281	Wally Joyner	.05
282	Jody Reed	.05
283	Bob Tewksbury	.05
284	Fernando Valenzuela	.05
285	Rod Beck	.05
286	Barry Bonds	2.00
287	Mark Carreon	.05
288	Shawon Dunston	.05
289	Osvaldo Fernandez RC	.10
290	Glenallen Hill	.05
291	Stan Javier	.05
292	Mark Leiter	.05
293	Kirt Manwaring	.05
294	Robby Thompson	.05
295	William Van Landingham	.05
296	Allen Watson	.05
297	Matt Williams	.05
298	Checklist	.05
299	Checklist	.05
300	Checklist	.05

XL D-Fense

Ten top defensive players are featured on these 1996 SkyBox E-Motion XL insert cards. The cards were seeded at a rate of one per every four packs.

		NM/M
Complete Set (10):		9.00
Common Player:		.50
1	Roberto Alomar	.65
2	Barry Bonds	3.50
3	Mark Grace	.50
4	Ken Griffey Jr.	2.50
5	Kenny Lofton	.50
6	Greg Maddux	1.50
7	Raul Mondesi	.50
8	Cal Ripken Jr.	3.50
9	Ivan Rodriguez	1.00
10	Matt Williams	.50

XL Legion of Boom

The top power hitters in baseball are featured on these 1996 SkyBox E-Motion XL insert cards. The cards, exclusive to hobby packs at a ratio of one per every 36 packs, have translucent card backs.

		NM/M
Complete Set (12):		27.50
Common Player:		2.00

1	Albert Belle	2.00
2	Barry Bonds	6.00
3	Juan Gonzalez	2.50
4	Ken Griffey Jr.	4.00
5	Mark McGwire	5.00
6	Mike Piazza	4.00
7	Manny Ramirez	3.00
8	Tim Salmon	2.00
9	Sammy Sosa	3.50
10	Frank Thomas	2.00
11	Mo Vaughn	2.00
12	Matt Williams	2.00

XL N-Tense

Ten top clutch performers are featured on these 1996 SkyBox E-Motion XL insert cards. The cards, which use an N-shaped die-cut design, were included one per every 12 packs.

		NM/M
Complete Set (10):		17.50
Common Player:		.50
1	Albert Belle	.50
2	Barry Bonds	3.50
3	Jose Canseco	1.00
4	Ken Griffey Jr.	3.00
5	Tony Gwynn	2.50
6	Randy Johnson	2.50
7	Greg Maddux	2.50
8	Cal Ripken Jr.	3.50
9	Frank Thomas	2.00
10	Matt Williams	.50

XL Rare Breed

These 1996 E-Motion XL inserts are the most difficult to find; they are seeded one per every 100 packs. The cards showcase top young stars on a 3-D lenticular-motion design.

		NM/M
Complete Set (10):		50.00
Common Player:		3.00
1	Garret Anderson	3.00
2	Marty Cordova	3.00
3	Brian Hunter	3.00
4	Jason Isringhausen	3.00
5	Charles Johnson	3.00
6	Chipper Jones	16.00
7	Raul Mondesi	3.00
8	Hideo Nomo	6.00
9	Manny Ramirez	12.00
10	Rondell White	3.00

E-X2000 Sample

To introduce its innovative high-tech premium brand, SkyBox released this promo card. It is identical in format to the issued version, except it carries a "SAMPLE" notation instead of a card number on back.

	NM/M
Alex Rodriguez	4.00

1997 SkyBox E-X2000

The premiere issue of E-X2000 consists of 100 base cards designed with "SkyView" technology, utilizing a die-cut holofoil border and the player silhouetted in front of a transparent "window" featuring a variety of sky patterns. Inserts include two sequentially-numbered parallel sets - Credentials (1:50 packs) and Essential Credentials (1:200 packs) - as well as Emerald Autograph Exchange Cards, A Cut Above, Hall of Nothing, and Star Date. Cards were sold in two-card packs for $3.99 each.

		NM/M
Complete Set (100):		20.00
Common Player:		.15
Credentials Stars:		6X
Essential Credentials:		10X
Pack (2):		1.25
Wax Box (24):		20.00
1	Jim Edmonds	.15
2	Darin Erstad	.25
3	Eddie Murray	1.00
4	Roberto Alomar	.25
5	Brady Anderson	.15
6	Mike Mussina	.45
7	Rafael Palmeiro	.75
8	Cal Ripken Jr.	3.00
9	Steve Avery	.15
10	Nomar Garciaparra	1.50
11	Mo Vaughn	.15
12	Albert Belle	.15
13	Mike Cameron	.15
14	Ray Durham	.15
15	Frank Thomas	1.00
16	Robin Ventura	.15
17	Manny Ramirez	1.00
18	Jim Thome	.65
19	Matt Williams	.15
20	Tony Clark	.15
21	Travis Fryman	.15
22	Bob Higginson	.15
23	Kevin Appier	.15
24	Johnny Damon	.45
25	Jermaine Dye	.15
26	Jeff Cirillo	.15
27	Ben McDonald	.15
28	Chuck Knoblauch	.15
29	Paul Molitor	1.00
30	Todd Walker	.15
31	Wade Boggs	1.50
32	Cecil Fielder	.15
33	Derek Jeter	3.00
34	Andy Pettitte	.25
35	Ruben Rivera	.15
36	Bernie Williams	.15
37	Jose Canseco	.50
38	Mark McGwire	2.50
39	Jay Buhner	.15
40	Ken Griffey Jr.	2.00
41	Randy Johnson	1.00
42	Edgar Martinez	.15
43	Alex Rodriguez	2.50
44	Dan Wilson	.15
45	Will Clark	.40
46	Juan Gonzalez	.50
47	Ivan Rodriguez	.75
48	Joe Carter	.15
49	Roger Clemens	1.75
50	Juan Guzman	.15
51	Pat Hentgen	.15
52	Tom Glavine	.35
53	Andruw Jones	1.00
54	Chipper Jones	2.00
55	Ryan Klesko	.15
56	Kenny Lofton	.15
57	Greg Maddux	1.50
58	Fred McGriff	.15
59	John Smoltz	.15
60	Mark Wohlers	.15
61	Mark Grace	.15
62	Ryne Sandberg	1.50

63	Sammy Sosa	1.50
64	Barry Larkin	.15
65	Deion Sanders	.15
66	Reggie Sanders	.15
67	Dante Bichette	.15
68	Ellis Burks	.15
69	Andres Galarraga	.15
70	Moises Alou	.15
71	Kevin Brown	.15
72	Cliff Floyd	.15
73	Edgar Renteria	.15
74	Gary Sheffield	.50
75	Bob Abreu	.15
76	Jeff Bagwell	1.00
77	Craig Biggio	.15
78	Todd Hollandsworth	.15
79	Eric Karros	.15
80	Raul Mondesi	.15
81	Hideo Nomo	.50
82	Mike Piazza	2.00
83	Vladimir Guerrero	1.00
84	Henry Rodriguez	.15
85	Todd Hundley	.15
86	Rey Ordonez	.15
87	Alex Ochoa	.15
88	Gregg Jefferies	.15
89	Scott Rolen	.65
90	Jermaine Allensworth	.15
91	Jason Kendall	.15
92	Ken Caminiti	.15
93	Tony Gwynn	1.50
94	Rickey Henderson	1.00
95	Barry Bonds	3.00
96	J.T. Snow	.15
97	Dennis Eckersley	.75
98	Ron Gant	.15
99	Brian Jordan	.15
100	Ray Lankford	.15

Credentials

This parallel set features different colored foils from the base cards, as well as different images on the "window." Cards are sequentially numbered on back within an issue of 299. Cards were inserted 1:50 packs.

	NM/M
Common Player:	1.00
Credentials Stars:	6X

Essential Credentials

A sequentially-numbered parallel set, found one per 200 packs, and limited to 99 total sets.

	NM/M
Common Player:	3.00
Essential Credentials Stars:	10X

A Cut Above

Some of the game's elite players are featured in this 1:288 pack insert that features a die-cut design resembling a saw blade. Printed on silver-foil stock, the player's name and Cut Above logo are embossed on front. On back is another color photo and a few words about the player.

		NM/M
Complete Set (10):		55.00
Common Player:		2.00
1	Frank Thomas	7.50
2	Ken Griffey Jr.	9.00
3	Alex Rodriguez	12.00

4	Albert Belle	2.00
5	Juan Gonzalez	4.00
6	Mark McGwire	10.00
7	Mo Vaughn	2.00
8	Manny Ramirez	7.50
9	Barry Bonds	12.00
10	Fred McGriff	2.00

Emerald Autograph Redemptions

Inserted 1:480 packs, these cards could be exchanged by mail prior to May 1, 1998 for autographed cards or memorabilia from one of six major leaguers.

		NM/M
Complete Set (6):		17.50
Common Player:		1.00
(1)	Darin Erstad	2.50
(2)	Todd Hollandsworth	1.00
(3)	Alex Ochoa	1.00
(4)	Alex Rodriguez	10.00
(5)	Scott Rolen	3.00
(6)	Todd Walker	1.00

Emerald Autographs

These authentically autographed versions of the players' E-X2000 cards were available (until May 1, 1998) by a mail-in exchange of redemption cards. The autographed cards are authenticated by the presence of an embossed Sky-Box logo seal.

		NM/M
Complete Set (6):		75.00
Common Player:		3.00
2	Darin Erstad	12.00
30	Todd Walker	5.00
43	Alex Rodriguez	60.00
78	Todd Hollandsworth	3.00
86	Alex Ochoa	3.00
89	Scott Rolen	25.00

Hall or Nothing

This 20-card insert, featuring players who are candidates for the Hall of Fame, utilizes a die-cut design on plastic stock. Stately architectural details and brush bronze highlights frame the player picture on front. The player silhouette on back contains career information. Cards were inserted 1:20 packs.

		NM/M
Complete Set (20):		55.00
Common Player:		1.00
1	Frank Thomas	2.50
2	Ken Griffey Jr.	5.00
3	Eddie Murray	2.50
4	Cal Ripken Jr.	7.00
5	Ryne Sandberg	4.00
6	Wade Boggs	4.00
7	Roger Clemens	4.50
8	Tony Gwynn	4.00
9	Alex Rodriguez	6.00
10	Mark McGwire	6.00
11	Barry Bonds	7.00
12	Greg Maddux	4.00
13	Juan Gonzalez	1.25
14	Albert Belle	1.00
15	Mike Piazza	5.00
16	Jeff Bagwell	2.50
17	Dennis Eckersley	1.50
18	Mo Vaughn	1.00
19	Roberto Alomar	1.00
20	Kenny Lofton	1.00

Alex Rodriguez Jumbo

This 8" x 10" version of A-Rod's SkyBox E-X2000 card was given to dealers who ordered case quantities of the new product. The card is identical in design to the standard-sized issued version, but is numbered on back from within an edition of 3,000.

	NM/M
Alex Rodriguez	12.00

Star Date 2000

A 15-card set highlighting young stars that are likely to be the game's top players in the year 2000. Cards were inserted 1:9 packs.

		NM/M
Complete Set (15):		10.00
Common Player:		.40
1	Alex Rodriguez	2.00
2	Andruw Jones	1.25
3	Andy Pettitte	.60
4	Brooks Kieschnick	.40
5	Chipper Jones	1.50
6	Darin Erstad	.60
7	Derek Jeter	2.50
8	Jason Kendall	.40
9	Jermaine Dye	.40
10	Neifi Perez	.40
11	Scott Rolen	.90
12	Todd Hollandsworth	.40
13	Todd Walker	.40
14	Tony Clark	.40
15	Vladimir Guerrero	1.25

1998 SkyBox E-X2001 Sample

To preview its high-tech E-X2001 brand for 1998, SkyBox issued this sample card of A-Rod. Similar in format to the issued version, it is numbered "SAMPLE" on back and has a "PROMOTIONAL SAMPLE" overprint on back.

	NM/M
Alex Rodriguez	2.00

1998 SkyBox E-X2001

This super-premium set featured 100 players on a layered, die-cut design utilizing mirror-image

silhouetted photography and etched holofoil treatment over a clear, 20-point plastic card.

		NM/M
Complete Set (100):		25.00
Common Player:		.15
Pack (2):		1.50
Wax Box (24):		25.00
1	Alex Rodriguez	2.50
2	Barry Bonds	3.00
3	Greg Maddux	1.50
4	Roger Clemens	1.75
5	Juan Gonzalez	.50
6	Chipper Jones	1.50
7	Derek Jeter	3.00
8	Frank Thomas	1.00
9	Cal Ripken Jr.	3.00
10	Ken Griffey Jr.	2.00
11	Mark McGwire	2.50
12	Hideo Nomo	.50
13	Tony Gwynn	1.50
14	Ivan Rodriguez	.75
15	Mike Piazza	2.00
16	Roberto Alomar	.30
17	Jeff Bagwell	1.00
18	Andruw Jones	1.00
19	Albert Belle	.15
20	Mo Vaughn	.15
21	Kenny Lofton	.15
22	Gary Sheffield	.40
23	Tony Clark	.15
24	Mike Mussina	.30
25	Barry Larkin	.15
26	Moises Alou	.15
27	Brady Anderson	.15
28	Andy Pettitte	.25
29	Sammy Sosa	1.50
30	Raul Mondesi	.15
31	Andres Galarraga	.15
32	Chuck Knoblauch	.15
33	Jim Thome	.65
34	Craig Biggio	.15
35	Jay Buhner	.15
36	Rafael Palmeiro	.75
37	Curt Schilling	.35
38	Tino Martinez	.15
39	Pedro Martinez	1.00
40	Jose Canseco	.50
41	Jeff Cirillo	.15
42	Dean Palmer	.15
43	Tim Salmon	.15
44	Jason Giambi	.50
45	Bobby Higginson	.15
46	Jim Edmonds	.15
47	David Justice	.15
48	John Olerud	.15
49	Ray Lankford	.15
50	Al Martin	.15
51	Mike Lieberthal	.15
52	Henry Rodriguez	.15
53	Edgar Renteria	.15
54	Eric Karros	.15
55	Marquis Grissom	.15
56	Wilson Alvarez	.15
57	Darryl Kile	.15
58	Jeff King	.15
59	Shawn Estes	.15
60	Tony Womack	.15
61	Willie Greene	.15
62	Ken Caminiti	.15
63	Vinny Castilla	.15
64	Mark Grace	.15
65	Ryan Klesko	.15
66	Robin Ventura	.15
67	Todd Hundley	.15
68	Travis Fryman	.15
69	Edgar Martinez	.15
70	Matt Williams	.15
71	Paul Molitor	1.00
72	Kevin Brown	.15
73	Randy Johnson	1.00
74	Bernie Williams	.10
75	Manny Ramirez	1.00
76	Fred McGriff	.15
77	Tom Glavine	.35
78	Carlos Delgado	.60
79	Larry Walker	.15
80	Hideki Irabu	.15
81	Ryan McGuire	.15
82	Justin Thompson	.15
83	Kevin Orie	.15
84	Jon Nunnally	.15
85	Mark Kotsay	.15
86	Todd Walker	.15
87	Jason Dickson	.15
88	Fernando Tatis	.15
89	Karim Garcia	.15

90	Ricky Ledee	.15
91	Paul Konerko	.25
92	Jaret Wright	.15
93	Darin Erstad	.30
94	Livan Hernandez	.15
95	Nomar Garciaparra	1.50
96	Jose Cruz Jr.	.15
97	Scott Rolen	.65
98	Ben Grieve	.15
99	Vladimir Guerrero	.15
100	Travis Lee	.15

Essential Credentials Future

Essential Credentials Future, along with Essential Credentials Now, paralleled all 100 cards in the base set. Production varied depending on the card number, with the exact production number of each player determined by subtracting his card number from 101. Number issued for each card is shown in parentheses.

		NM/M
Common Player:		5.00
1	Alex Rodriguez/100	55.00
2	Barry Bonds/99	60.00
3	Greg Maddux/98	40.00
4	Roger Clemens/97	45.00
5	Juan Gonzalez/96	15.00
6	Chipper Jones/95	40.00
7	Derek Jeter/94	55.00
8	Frank Thomas/93	35.00
9	Cal Ripken Jr./92	65.00
10	Ken Griffey Jr./91	45.00
11	Mark McGwire/90	55.00
12	Hideo Nomo/89	15.00
13	Tony Gwynn/88	25.00
14	Ivan Rodriguez/87	25.00
15	Mike Piazza/86	40.00
16	Roberto Alomar/85	15.00
17	Jeff Bagwell/84	25.00
18	Andruw Jones/83	25.00
19	Albert Belle/82	5.00
20	Mo Vaughn/81	5.00
21	Kenny Lofton/80	5.00
22	Gary Sheffield/79	12.00
23	Tony Clark/78	5.00
24	Mike Mussina/77	25.00
25	Barry Larkin/76	5.00
26	Moises Alou/75	5.00
27	Brady Anderson/74	5.00
28	Andy Pettitte/73	7.50
29	Sammy Sosa/72	40.00
30	Raul Mondesi/71	5.00
31	Andres Galarraga/70	6.00
32	Chuck Knoblauch/69	6.00
33	Jim Thome/68	20.00
34	Craig Biggio/67	6.00
35	Jay Buhner/66	6.00
36	Rafael Palmeiro/65	30.00
37	Curt Schilling/64	20.00
38	Tino Martinez/63	6.00
39	Pedro Martinez/62	32.50
40	Jose Canseco/61	30.00
41	Jeff Cirillo/60	6.00
42	Dean Palmer/59	6.00
43	Tim Salmon/58	7.50
44	Jason Giambi/57	25.00
45	Bobby Higginson/56	6.00
46	Jim Edmonds/55	6.00
47	David Justice/54	6.00
48	John Olerud/53	6.00
49	Ray Lankford/52	6.00
50	Al Martin/51	6.00
51	Mike Lieberthal/50	6.00
52	Henry Rodriguez/49	6.00
53	Edgar Renteria/48	6.00
54	Eric Karros/47	6.00
55	Marquis Grissom/46	6.00
56	Wilson Alvarez/45	6.00
57	Darryl Kile/44	6.00
58	Jeff King/43	6.00
59	Shawn Estes/42	6.00
60	Tony Womack/41	6.00
61	Willie Greene/40	6.00
62	Ken Caminiti/39	6.00
63	Vinny Castilla/38	6.00
64	Mark Grace/37	6.00
65	Ryan Klesko/36	6.00
66	Robin Ventura/35	6.00
67	Todd Hundley/34	6.00
68	Travis Fryman/33	6.00
69	Edgar Martinez/32	7.50
70	Matt Williams/31	7.50
71	Paul Molitor/30	45.00

#	Player	NM/M
72	Kevin Brown/29	7.50
73	Randy Johnson/28	40.00
74	Bernie Williams/27	20.00
75	Manny Ramirez/26	45.00
76	Fred McGriff/25	20.00
77	Tom Glavine/24	35.00
78	Carlos Delgado/23	35.00
79	Larry Walker/22	9.00
80	Hideki Irabu/21	9.00
81	Ryan McGuire/20	9.00
82	Justin Thompson/19	9.00
83	Kevin Orie/18	9.00
84	Jon Nunnally/17	9.00
85	Mark Kotsay/16	9.00

Essential Credentials Now

Essential Credentials Now parallels all 100 cards in the E-X2001 base set. Production for each card was limited to that player's card number, as shown in parentheses.

		NM/M
	Common Player:	5.00
21	Kenny Lofton/21	10.00
22	Gary Sheffield/22	20.00
23	Tony Clark/23	10.00
24	Mike Mussina/24	30.00
25	Barry Larkin/25	10.00
26	Moises Alou/26	10.00
27	Brady Anderson/27	10.00
28	Andy Pettitte/28	15.00
29	Sammy Sosa/29	30.00
30	Raul Mondesi/30	10.00
31	Andres Galarraga/31	10.00
32	Chuck Knoblauch/32	10.00
33	Jim Thome/33	25.00
34	Craig Biggio/34	10.00
35	Jay Buhner/35	10.00
36	Rafael Palmeiro/36	25.00
37	Curt Schilling/37	20.00
38	Tino Martinez/38	10.00
39	Pedro Martinez/39	30.00
40	Jose Canseco/40	20.00
41	Jeff Cirillo/41	5.00
42	Dean Palmer/42	5.00
43	Tim Salmon/43	5.00
44	Jason Giambi/44	15.00
45	Bobby Higginson/45	5.00
46	Jim Edmonds/46	5.00
47	David Justice/47	5.00
48	John Olerud/48	5.00
49	Ray Lankford/49	5.00
50	Al Martin/50	5.00
51	Mike Lieberthal/51	5.00
52	Henry Rodriguez/52	5.00
53	Edgar Renteria/53	5.00
54	Eric Karros/54	5.00
55	Marquis Grissom/55	5.00
56	Wilson Alvarez/56	5.00
57	Darryl Kile/57	5.00
58	Jeff King/58	5.00
59	Shawn Estes/59	5.00
60	Tony Womack/60	5.00
61	Willie Greene/61	5.00
62	Ken Caminiti/62	5.00
63	Vinny Castilla/63	5.00
64	Mark Grace/64	5.00
65	Ryan Klesko/65	5.00
66	Robin Ventura/66	5.00
67	Todd Hundley/67	5.00
68	Travis Fryman/68	5.00
69	Edgar Martinez/69	5.00
70	Matt Williams/70	5.00
71	Paul Molitor/71	15.00
72	Kevin Brown/72	5.00
73	Randy Johnson/73	20.00
74	Bernie Williams/74	5.00
75	Manny Ramirez/75	20.00
76	Fred McGriff/76	5.00
77	Tom Glavine/77	12.00
78	Carlos Delgado/78	10.00
79	Larry Walker/79	5.00
80	Hideki Irabu/80	5.00
81	Ryan McGuire/81	5.00
82	Justin Thompson/82	5.00
83	Kevin Orie/83	5.00
84	Jon Nunnally/84	5.00
85	Mark Kotsay/85	5.00
86	Todd Walker/86	5.00
87	Jason Dickson/87	5.00
88	Fernando Tatis/88	5.00
89	Karim Garcia/89	5.00
90	Ricky Ledee/90	5.00
91	Paul Konerko/91	7.50
92	Jaret Wright/92	5.00
93	Darin Erstad/93	5.00
94	Livan Hernandez/94	5.00
95	Nomar Garciaparra/95	20.00
96	Jose Cruz Jr./96	5.00
97	Scott Rolen/97	10.00
98	Ben Grieve/98	5.00
99	Vladimir Guerrero/99	12.00
100	Travis Lee/100	5.00

Cheap Seat Treats

This 20-card die-cut insert arrived in the shape of a stadium seat. Inserted at one per 24 packs, Cheap Seat Treats included some of the top home run hitters and were numbered with a "CS" prefix.

		NM/M
	Complete Set (20):	30.00
	Common Player:	1.00
	Inserted 1:24	

#	Player	NM/M
1	Frank Thomas	2.00
2	Ken Griffey Jr.	3.00
3	Mark McGwire	4.00
4	Tino Martinez	1.00
5	Larry Walker	1.00
6	Juan Gonzalez	1.50
7	Mike Piazza	3.00
8	Jeff Bagwell	2.00
9	Tony Clark	1.00
10	Albert Belle	1.00
11	Andres Galarraga	1.00
12	Jim Thome	1.50
13	Mo Vaughn	1.00
14	Barry Bonds	5.00
15	Vladimir Guerrero	2.00
16	Scott Rolen	1.25
17	Travis Lee	1.00
18	David Justice	1.00
19	Jose Cruz Jr.	1.00
20	Andruw Jones	2.00

Destination: Cooperstown

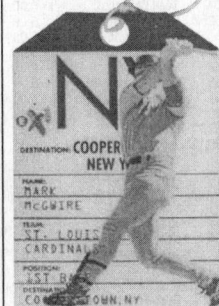

Destination: Cooperstown captures a mixture of rising young stars and top veterans on die-cut cards that were inserted one per 720 packs. Cards resemble a luggage tag and have a string through a hole at top. Fronts have an action photo, backs have a portrait. Cards are numbered with a "DC" prefix.

		NM/M
	Complete Set (15):	375.00
	Common Player:	8.00
	Inserted 1:720	
1	Alex Rodriguez	40.00
2	Frank Thomas	20.00
3	Cal Ripken Jr.	50.00
4	Roger Clemens	30.00
5	Greg Maddux	25.00
6	Chipper Jones	25.00
7	Ken Griffey Jr.	35.00
8	Mark McGwire	40.00
9	Tony Gwynn	25.00
10	Mike Piazza	35.00
11	Jeff Bagwell	20.00
12	Jose Cruz Jr.	8.00
13	Derek Jeter	50.00
14	Hideo Nomo	10.00
15	Ivan Rodriguez	15.00

Signature 2001

Seventeen top young and future stars signed cards for Signature 2001 inserts in E-X2001. The

cards featured the player over a blue and white, sky-like background, with an embossed SkyBox seal of authenticity. Backs were horizontal and also included a Certificate of Authenticity. These cards were unnumbered and inserted one per 60 packs.

		NM/M
	Complete Set (17):	100.00
	Common Player:	3.00
	Inserted 1:60	
1	Ricky Ledee	3.00
2	Derrick Gibson	3.00
3	Mark Kotsay	3.00
4	Kevin Millwood	10.00
5	Brad Fullmer	3.00
6	Todd Walker	4.00
7	Ben Grieve	3.00
8	Tony Clark	3.00
9	Jaret Wright	4.00
10	Randall Simon	3.00
11	Paul Konerko	15.00
12	Todd Helton	15.00
13	David Ortiz	30.00
14	Alex Gonzalez	4.00
15	Bobby Estalella	3.00
16	Alex Rodriguez	50.00
17	Mike Lowell	10.00

Star Date 2001

Star Date 2001 displays 15 of the top rising stars on an acetate space/planet background with gold-foil printing on front. This insert was seeded one per 12 packs and was numbered with a "SD" suffix.

		NM/M
	Complete Set (15):	5.00
	Common Player:	.25
	Inserted 1:12	
1	Travis Lee	.25
2	Jose Cruz Jr.	.25
3	Paul Konerko	1.00
4	Bobby Estalella	.25
5	Magglio Ordonez	.25
6	Juan Encarnacion	.25
7	Richard Hidalgo	.25
8	Abraham Nunez	.25
9	Sean Casey	.50
10	Todd Helton	1.50
11	Brad Fullmer	.25
12	Ben Grieve	.25
13	Livan Hernandez	.25
14	Jaret Wright	.25
15	Todd Dunwoody	.25

Kerry Wood

In an effort to get rookie pitching phenom Kerry Wood into its E-X2001 set, SkyBox created a cardboard, rather than plastic, trade card and inserted it at a rate of one per 50 packs. The trade card could be exchanged by mail for a plastic version.

		NM/M
	Complete Set (2):	2.00
---	Kerry Wood (Cardboard trade card.)	1.00
101	Kerry Wood (Plastic redemption card.)	4.00

1998 SkyBox Dugout Axcess Promo

This introduction to SkyBox's new brand is labeled front and back as a "PROMOTIONAL SAMPLE."

		NM/M
15	Alex Rodriguez	3.00

1998 SkyBox Dugout Axcess

Dugout Axcess was a 150-card set that attempted to provide collectors with an inside look at baseball. The cards were printed on "playing card" quality stock and used unique information and photography. The product arrived in 12-card packs with an Inside Axcess parallel set that was individually numbered to 50 sets. Six different inserts sets were available, including Double Header, Frequent Flyers, Dishwashers, Superheroes, Gronks and Autograph Redemptions.

		NM/M
	Complete Set (150):	12.00
	Common Player:	.05
	Inside Axcess Stars:	25X
	Production 50 Sets	
	Pack (12):	1.00
	Wax Box (36):	20.00
1	Travis Lee	.05
2	Matt Williams	.05
3	Andy Benes	.05
4	Chipper Jones	.75
5	Ryan Klesko	.05
6	Greg Maddux	.75
7	Sammy Sosa	.05
8	Henry Rodriguez	.05
9	Mark Grace	.05
10	Barry Larkin	.05
11	Bret Boone	.05
12	Reggie Sanders	.05
13	Vinny Castilla	.05
14	Larry Walker	.05
15	Darryl Kile	.05
16	Charles Johnson	.05
17	Edgar Renteria	.05
18	Gary Sheffield	.40
19	Jeff Bagwell	.65
20	Craig Biggio	.05
21	Moises Alou	.05
22	Mike Piazza	1.00
23	Hideo Nomo	.35
24	Raul Mondesi	.05
25	John Jaha	.05
26	Jeff Cirillo	.05
27	Jeromy Burnitz	.05
28	Mark Grudzielanek	.05
29	Vladimir Guerrero	.65
30	Rondell White	.05
31	Edgardo Alfonzo	.05
32	Rey Ordonez	.05
33	Bernard Gilkey	.05
34	Scott Rolen	.50
35	Curt Schilling	.35
36	Ricky Bottalico	.05
37	Tony Womack	.05
38	Al Martin	.05
39	Jason Kendall	.05
40	Ron Gant	.05
41	Mark McGwire	1.25
42	Ray Lankford	.05
43	Tony Gwynn	.75
44	Ken Caminiti	.05
45	Kevin Brown	.05
46	Barry Bonds	1.50
47	J.T. Snow	.05
48	Shawn Estes	.05
49	Jim Edmonds	.05
50	Tim Salmon	.05

#	Player	NM/M
51	Jason Dickson	.05
52	Cal Ripken Jr.	1.50
53	Mike Mussina	.35
54	Roberto Alomar	.20
55	Mo Vaughn	.65
56	Pedro Martinez	.65
57	Nomar Garciaparra	.75
58	Albert Belle	.05
59	Frank Thomas	.65
60	Robin Ventura	.05
61	Jim Thome	.60
62	Sandy Alomar Jr.	.05
63	Jaret Wright	.05
64	Bobby Higginson	.05
65	Tony Clark	.05
66	Justin Thompson	.05
67	Dean Palmer	.05
68	Kevin Appier	.05
69	Johnny Damon	.05
70	Paul Molitor	.65
71	Marty Cordova	.05
72	Brad Radke	.05
73	Derek Jeter	1.50
74	Bernie Williams	.25
75	Andy Pettitte	.25
76	Matt Stairs	.05
77	Ben Grieve	.05
78	Jason Giambi	.50
79	Randy Johnson	.65
80	Ken Griffey Jr.	1.00
81	Alex Rodriguez	1.25
82	Fred McGriff	.05
83	Wade Boggs	.75
84	Wilson Alvarez	.05
85	Juan Gonzalez	.35
86	Ivan Rodriguez	.50
87	Fernando Tatis	.05
88	Roger Clemens	.85
89	Jose Cruz Jr.	.05
90	Shawn Green	.30
91	Jeff Suppan (Little Dawgs)	.05
92	Eli Marrero (Little Dawgs)	.05
93	Mike Lowell RC (Little Dawgs)	1.00
94	Ben Grieve (Little Dawgs)	.05
95	Cliff Politte (Little Dawgs)	.05
96	Rolando Arrojo RC (Little Dawgs)	.25
97	Mike Caruso (Little Dawgs)	.05
98	Miguel Tejada (Little Dawgs)	.15
99	Rod Myers (Little Dawgs)	.05
100	Juan Encarnacion (Little Dawgs)	.05
101	Enrique Wilson (Little Dawgs)	.05
102	Brian Giles (Little Dawgs)	.05
103	Magglio Ordonez RC (Little Dawgs)	1.00
104	Brian Rose (Little Dawgs)	.05
105	Ryan Jackson RC (Little Dawgs)	.05
106	Mark Kotsay (Little Dawgs)	.05
107	Desi Relaford (Little Dawgs)	.05
108	A.J. Hinch (Little Dawgs)	.05
109	Eric Milton (Little Dawgs)	.05
110	Ricky Ledee (Little Dawgs)	.05
111	Karim Garcia (Little Dawgs)	.05
112	Derrek Lee (Little Dawgs)	.60
113	Brad Fullmer (Little Dawgs)	.05
114	Travis Lee (Little Dawgs)	.05
115	Greg Norton (Little Dawgs)	.05
116	Rich Butler (Little Dawgs)	.05
117	Masato Yoshii RC (Little Dawgs)	.25
118	Paul Konerko (Little Dawgs)	.20
119	Richard Hidalgo (Little Dawgs)	.05
120	Todd Helton (Little Dawgs)	.60
121	Nomar Garciaparra (7th Inning Sketch)	.40
122	Scott Rolen (7th Inning Sketch)	.20
123	Cal Ripken Jr. (7th Inning Sketch)	.75
124	Derek Jeter (7th Inning Sketch)	.75
125	Mike Piazza (7th Inning Sketch)	.45
126	Tony Gwynn (7th Inning Sketch)	.05
127	Mark McGwire (7th Inning Sketch)	.65
128	Kenny Lofton (7th Inning Sketch)	.05
129	Greg Maddux (7th Inning Sketch)	.40
130	Jeff Bagwell (7th Inning Sketch)	.30
131	Randy Johnson (7th Inning Sketch)	.30
132	Alex Rodriguez (7th Inning Sketch)	.65
133	Mo Vaughn (Name Plates)	.05
134	Chipper Jones (Name Plates)	.40
135	Juan Gonzalez (Name Plates)	.15
136	Tony Clark (Name Plates)	.05

#	Player	NM/M
137	Fred McGriff (Name Plates)	.05
138	Roger Clemens (Name Plates)	.45
139	Ken Griffey Jr. (Name Plates)	.65
140	Ivan Rodriguez (Name Plates)	.25
141	Vinny Castilla (Trivia Card)	.05
142	Livan Hernandez (Trivia Card)	.05
143	Jose Cruz Jr. (Trivia Card)	.05
144	Andruw Jones (Trivia Card)	.30
145	Rafael Palmeiro (Trivia Card)	.50
146	Chuck Knoblauch (Trivia Card)	.05
147	Jay Buhner (Trivia Card)	.05
148	Andres Galarraga (Trivia Card)	.05
149	Frank Thomas (Trivia Card)	.35
150	Todd Hundley (Trivia Card)	.05

Inside Axcess

This 150-card parallel set was sequentially numbered to 50 sets, with each card containing a stamped logo on the front and serial numbering on the back.

		NM/M
	Common Player:	4.00
	Inside Axcess Stars:	25X

Autograph Redemption Cards

These scarce - one per 96 packs - inserts were redeemable (until March 31, 1999) for autographed baseballs or gloves from more than a dozen established stars and promising youngsters. Because the cards do not picture the player involved, having a generic photo of a person's arm signing an autograph, the exchange cards don't have tremendous collector value now that the redemption period has expired. The autographed balls and gloves would be valued according to supply and demand in the memorabilia marketplace.

		NM/M
	Complete Set (15):	37.00
	Common Card:	1.50
(1)	Jay Buhner/Ball	1.50
(2)	Roger Clemens/Ball	3.00
(3)	Jose Cruz Jr./Ball	2.25
(4)	Darin Erstad/Glv	4.50
(5)	Nomar Garciaparra/Ball	3.00
(6)	Tony Gwynn/Ball	2.75
(7)	Roberto Hernandez/Ball	1.50
(8)	Todd Hollandsworth/Glv	3.00
(9)	Greg Maddux/Ball	3.00
(10)	Alex Ochoa/Ball	3.00
(11)	Alex Rodriguez/Ball	4.50
(12)	Scott Rolen/Glv	4.50
(13)	Scott Rolen/Ball	2.50
(14)	Todd Walker/Glv	1.50
(15)	Tony Womack/Ball	1.50

Dishwashers

This 10-card set was a tribute to the game's best pitchers who "clean the home plate of opposing batters." Cards were inserted one per eight packs.

	NM/M
Complete Set (10):	7.00
Common Player:	.50
Inserted 1:8	
D1 Greg Maddux	2.00
D2 Kevin Brown	.50
D3 Pedro Martinez	1.00
D4 Randy Johnson	1.00
D5 Curt Schilling	.75
D6 John Smoltz	.50
D7 Darryl Kile	.50
D8 Roger Clemens	2.25
D9 Andy Pettitte	.60
D10 Mike Mussina	.65

Double Header

Double Header featured 20 players on cards that doubled as game pieces. The game instructions were on the card and required two dice to play. These were inserted at a rate of two per pack.

	NM/M
Complete Set (20):	2.00
Common Player:	.05
Inserted 2:1	
DH1 Jeff Bagwell	.15
DH2 Albert Belle	.05
DH3 Barry Bonds	.40
DH4 Derek Jeter	.40
DH5 Tony Clark	.05
DH6 Nomar Garciaparra	.20
DH7 Juan Gonzalez	.10
DH8 Ken Griffey Jr.	.25
DH9 Chipper Jones	.20
DH10 Kenny Lofton	.05
DH11 Mark McGwire	.30
DH12 Mo Vaughn	.25
DH13 Mike Piazza	.25
DH14 Cal Ripken Jr.	.40
DH15 Ivan Rodriguez	.10
DH16 Scott Rolen	.10
DH17 Frank Thomas	.15
DH18 Tony Gwynn	.20
DH19 Travis Lee	.05
DH20 Jose Cruz Jr.	.05

Frequent Flyers

The game's top 10 base stealers were included in Frequent Flyers. This insert was designed to look like airline frequent flyer cards and was inserted one per four packs. Fronts have player action photos on a metallic-foil background of a cloudy sky. Backs have a portrait photo and a few words about the player's base-stealing ability. Cards are numbered with an "FF" prefix.

	NM/M
Complete Set (10):	2.50
Common Player:	.25
Inserted 1:4	
FF1 Brian Hunter	.25
FF2 Kenny Lofton	.25
FF3 Chuck Knoblauch	.25
FF4 Tony Womack	.25
FF5 Marquis Grissom	.25
FF6 Craig Biggio	.25
FF7 Barry Bonds	2.00
FF8 Tom Goodwin	.25
FF9 Delino DeShields	.25
FF10 Eric Young	.25

Gronks

Gronks featured 10 of the top home run hitters and was a hobby

exclusive insert. The name of the insert originated from shortstop Greg Gagne, and the cards were inserted in one per 72 packs.

	NM/M
Complete Set (10):	30.00
Common Player:	1.50
Inserted 1:72	
G1 Jeff Bagwell	3.50
G2 Albert Belle	1.50
G3 Juan Gonzalez	2.00
G4 Ken Griffey Jr.	6.00
G5 Mark McGwire	7.50
G6 Mike Piazza	6.00
G7 Frank Thomas	3.50
G8 Mo Vaughn	1.50
G9 Ken Caminiti	1.50
G10 Tony Clark	1.50

SuperHeroes

SuperHeroes combined 10 top superstars with the Marvel Comics superhero with whom they share a common trait in this 10-card insert set. Cards were inserted at a rate of one per 20 packs.

	NM/M
Complete Set (10):	10.00
Common Player:	.15
Inserted 1:20	
SH1 Barry Bonds	3.00
SH2 Andres Galarraga	.50
SH3 Ken Griffey Jr.	5.00
SH4 Chipper Jones	1.00
SH5 Andruw Jones	.75
SH6 Hideo Nomo	.60
SH7 Cal Ripken Jr.	3.00
SH8 Alex Rodriguez	2.00
SH9 Frank Thomas	.75
SH10 Mo Vaughn	.50

Todd Helton Autograph

For use in various promotions, Fleer arranged to have Todd Helton autograph 800 of his SkyBox Dugout Axcess Little Dawgs subset cards. Besides the signature, the cards feature an embossed authentication logo.

	NM/M
120 Todd Helton	15.00

SportsFest

As part of its participation at SportsFest in Philadelphia in May

1998, SkyBox issued a special card of hometown hero Scott Rolen. The card was available only as a wrapper redemption at the show and was limited to 5,000. Front has an action photo of Rolen on a colorful background with the team and show logos at bottom. Back has a portrait photo and stats.

	NM/M
SF1 Scott Rolen	3.00

1999 SkyBox E-X Century

The 120-card base set features a clear plastic stock with the player name, logo and position stamped in holographic foil. Card backs have the featured player's vital information along with his '98 statistics and his major league totals. Cards 91-120 are part of a prospects subset and are short-printed seeded 1:2 packs. Three-card packs have a SRP of $5.99.

	NM/M
Complete Set (120):	35.00
Common Player:	.15
Common SP (91-120):	.60
Inserted 1:2	
Pack (3):	3.00
Wax Box (18):	40.00
1 Scott Rolen	.75
2 Nomar Garciaparra	1.50
3 Mike Piazza	2.00
4 Tony Gwynn	1.50
5 Sammy Sosa	1.50
6 Alex Rodriguez	2.50
7 Vladimir Guerrero	1.50
8 Chipper Jones	1.50
9 Derek Jeter	3.00
10 Kerry Wood	.50
11 Juan Gonzalez	.50
12 Frank Thomas	1.00
13 Mo Vaughn	.15
14 Greg Maddux	1.50
15 Jeff Bagwell	1.00
16 Mark McGwire	2.50
17 Ken Griffey Jr.	2.00
18 Roger Clemens	1.75
19 Cal Ripken Jr.	3.00
20 Travis Lee	.15
21 Todd Helton	.75
22 Darin Erstad	.30
23 Pedro Martinez	.75
24 Barry Bonds	3.00
25 Andruw Jones	1.00
26 Larry Walker	.15
27 Albert Belle	.15
28 Ivan Rodriguez	.75
29 Magglio Ordonez	.25
30 Andres Galarraga	.15
31 Mike Mussina	.15
32 Randy Johnson	1.00
33 Tom Glavine	.35
34 Barry Larkin	.15
35 Jim Thome	.75
36 Gary Sheffield	.45
37 Bernie Williams	.15
38 Carlos Delgado	.60
39 Rafael Palmeiro	.75
40 Edgar Renteria	.15
41 Brad Fullmer	.15
42 David Wells	.15
43 Dante Bichette	.15
44 Jaret Wright	.15

45 Ricky Ledee	.15
46 Ray Lankford	.15
47 Mark Grace	.15
48 Jeff Cirillo	.15
49 Rondell White	.15
50 Jeromy Burnitz	.15
51 Sean Casey	.25
52 Rolando Arrojo	.15
53 Jason Giambi	.65
54 John Olerud	.15
55 Will Clark	.15
56 Raul Mondesi	.15
57 Scott Brosius	.15
58 Bartolo Colon	.15
59 Steve Finley	.15
60 Javy Lopez	.15
61 Tim Salmon	.15
62 Roberto Alomar	.30
63 Vinny Castilla	.15
64 Craig Biggio	.15
65 Jose Guillen	.15
66 Greg Vaughn	.15
67 Jose Canseco	.40
68 Shawn Green	.50
69 Curt Schilling	.35
70 Orlando Hernandez	.15
71 Jose Cruz Jr.	.15
72 Alex Gonzalez	.15
73 Tino Martinez	.15
74 Todd Hundley	.15
75 Brian Giles	.15
76 Cliff Floyd	.15
77 Paul O'Neill	.15
78 Ken Caminiti	.15
79 Ron Gant	.15
80 Juan Encarnacion	.15
81 Ben Grieve	.15
82 Brian Jordan	.15
83 Rickey Henderson	1.00
84 Tony Clark	.15
85 Shannon Stewart	.15
86 Robin Ventura	.15
87 Todd Walker	.15
88 Kevin Brown	.15
89 Moises Alou	.15
90 Manny Ramirez	1.00
91 Gabe Alvarez	.60
92 Jeremy Giambi	.60
93 Adrian Beltre	.75
94 George Lombard	.60
95 Ryan Minor	.60
96 Kevin Witt	.60
97 Scott Hunter RC	.60
98 Carlos Guillen	.60
99 Derrick Gibson	.60
100 Trot Nixon	.75
101 Troy Glaus	3.00
102 Armando Rios	.60
103 Preston Wilson	.60
104 Pat Burrell RC	3.00
105 J.D. Drew	1.50
106 Bruce Chen	.60
107 Matt Clement	.60
108 Carlos Beltran	1.50
109 Carlos Febles	.60
110 Rob Fick	.60
111 Russell Branyan	.60
112 Roosevelt Brown RC	.60
113 Corey Koskie	.60
114 Mario Encarnacion	.60
115 Peter Tucci RC	.60
116 Eric Chavez	.75
117 Gabe Kapler	.60
118 Marlon Anderson	.60
119 A.J. Burnett RC	.75
120 Ryan Bradley	.60
--- Checklist 1-96	.05
--- Checklist 97-120/Inserts	.05

Essential Credentials Future

A glossy silver design replaces the clear plastic portions seen on the base cards. Production varied depending on the card number, with the exact production number of each player determined by subtracting his card number from 121. Quantity issued is listed in parentheses.

	NM/M
Common Player:	5.00
1 Scott Rolen/120	15.00
2 Nomar Garciaparra/119	15.00
3 Mike Piazza/118	25.00
4 Tony Gwynn/117	20.00
5 Sammy Sosa/116	15.00
6 Alex Rodriguez/115	20.00

7 Vladimir Guerrero/114	15.00
8 Chipper Jones/113	20.00
9 Derek Jeter/112	50.00
10 Kerry Wood/111	10.00
11 Juan Gonzalez/110	10.00
12 Frank Thomas/109	25.00
13 Mo Vaughn/108	5.00
14 Greg Maddux/107	25.00
15 Jeff Bagwell/106	15.00
16 Mark McGwire/105	20.00
17 Ken Griffey Jr./104	25.00
18 Roger Clemens/103	25.00
19 Cal Ripken Jr./102	40.00
20 Travis Lee/101	5.00
21 Todd Helton/100	15.00
22 Darin Erstad/99	5.00
23 Pedro Martinez/98	15.00
24 Barry Bonds/97	40.00
25 Andruw Jones/96	10.00
26 Larry Walker/95	5.00
27 Albert Belle/94	5.00
28 Ivan Rodriguez/93	15.00
29 Magglio Ordonez/92	10.00
30 Andres Galarraga/91	5.00
31 Mike Mussina/90	10.00
32 Randy Johnson/89	20.00
33 Tom Glavine/88	15.00
34 Barry Larkin/87	8.00
35 Jim Thome/86	15.00
36 Gary Sheffield/85	15.00
37 Bernie Williams/84	5.00
38 Carlos Delgado/83	15.00
39 Rafael Palmeiro/82	10.00
40 Edgar Renteria/81	5.00
41 Brad Fullmer/80	5.00
42 David Wells/79	5.00
43 Dante Bichette/78	5.00
44 Jaret Wright/77	5.00
45 Ricky Ledee/76	5.00
46 Ray Lankford/75	5.00
47 Mark Grace/74	8.00
48 Jeff Cirillo/73	5.00
49 Rondell White/72	5.00
50 Jeromy Burnitz/71	5.00
51 Sean Casey/70	5.00
52 Rolando Arrojo/69	5.00
53 Jason Giambi/68	10.00
54 John Olerud/67	5.00
55 Will Clark/66	8.00
56 Raul Mondesi/65	5.00
57 Scott Brosius/64	5.00
58 Bartolo Colon/63	5.00
59 Steve Finley/62	5.00
60 Javy Lopez/61	5.00
61 Tim Salmon/60	5.00
62 Roberto Alomar/59	10.00
63 Vinny Castilla/58	5.00
64 Craig Biggio/57	8.00
65 Jose Guillen/56	5.00
66 Greg Vaughn/55	5.00
67 Jose Canseco/54	10.00
68 Shawn Green/53	5.00
69 Curt Schilling/52	15.00
70 Orlando Hernandez/51	5.00
71 Jose Cruz Jr./50	5.00
72 Alex Gonzalez/49	5.00
73 Tino Martinez/48	8.00
74 Todd Hundley/47	5.00
75 Brian Giles/46	5.00
76 Cliff Floyd/45	5.00
77 Paul O'Neill/44	10.00
78 Ken Caminiti/43	5.00
79 Ron Gant/42	5.00
80 Juan Encarnacion/41	8.00
81 Ben Grieve/40	5.00
82 Brian Jordan/39	5.00
83 Rickey Henderson/38	15.00
84 Tony Clark/37	5.00
85 Shannon Stewart/36	5.00
86 Robin Ventura /35	5.00
87 Todd Walker/34	5.00
88 Kevin Brown/33	5.00
89 Moises Alou/32	10.00
90 Manny Ramirez/31	25.00
91 Gabe Alvarez/30	5.00
92 Jeremy Giambi/29	5.00
93 Adrian Beltre/28	8.00
94 George Lombard/27	5.00
95 Ryan Minor/26	5.00
96 Kevin Witt/25	5.00
97 Scott Hunter/24	5.00
98 Carlos Guillen/23	10.00
99 Derrick Gibson/22	5.00
100 Trot Nixon/21	8.00

Essential Credentials Now

Like Future, this is a parallel of the base set, with production of each card limited to that player's card number. These cards have a glossy gold look.

	NM/M
Common Player:	5.00
21 Todd Helton/21	15.00
22 Darin Erstad/22	5.00
23 Pedro Martinez/23	20.00
24 Barry Bonds/24	50.00
25 Andruw Jones/25	10.00
26 Larry Walker/26	8.00
27 Albert Belle/27	5.00
28 Ivan Rodriguez/28	10.00
29 Magglio Ordonez/29	5.00
30 Andres Galarraga/30	5.00
31 Mike Mussina/31	5.00
32 Randy Johnson/32	15.00
33 Tom Glavine/33	10.00
34 Barry Larkin/34	5.00
35 Jim Thome/35	10.00
36 Gary Sheffield/36	10.00
37 Bernie Williams/37	10.00
38 Carlos Delgado/38	10.00
39 Rafael Palmeiro/39	10.00
40 Edgar Renteria/40	5.00
41 Brad Fullmer/41	5.00
42 David Wells/42	5.00
43 Dante Bichette/43	5.00
44 Jaret Wright/44	5.00
45 Ricky Ledee/45	5.00
46 Ray Lankford/46	5.00
47 Mark Grace/47	8.00
48 Jeff Cirillo/48	5.00
49 Rondell White/49	5.00
50 Jeromy Burnitz/50	5.00
51 Sean Casey/51	5.00
52 Rolando Arrojo/52	5.00
53 Jason Giambi/53	10.00
54 John Olerud/54	5.00
55 Will Clark/55	8.00
56 Raul Mondesi/56	5.00
57 Scott Brosius/57	5.00
58 Bartolo Colon/58	5.00
59 Steve Finley/59	5.00
60 Javy Lopez/60	5.00
61 Tim Salmon/61	5.00
62 Roberto Alomar/62	8.00
63 Vinny Castilla/63	5.00
64 Craig Biggio/64	8.00
65 Jose Guillen/65	5.00
66 Greg Vaughn/66	5.00
67 Jose Canseco/67	10.00
68 Shawn Green/68	5.00
69 Curt Schilling/69	15.00
70 Orlando Hernandez/70	5.00
71 Jose Cruz Jr./71	5.00
72 Alex Gonzalez/72	5.00
73 Tino Martinez/73	8.00
74 Todd Hundley/74	5.00
75 Brian Giles/75	5.00
76 Cliff Floyd/76	5.00
77 Paul O'Neill/77	8.00
78 Ken Caminiti/78	5.00
79 Ron Gant/79	5.00
80 Juan Encarnacion/80	5.00
81 Ben Grieve/81	5.00
82 Brian Jordan/82	5.00
83 Rickey Henderson/83	10.00
84 Tony Clark/84	5.00
85 Shannon Stewart/85	5.00
86 Robin Ventura/86	5.00
87 Todd Walker/87	5.00
88 Kevin Brown/88	5.00
89 Moises Alou/89	5.00
90 Manny Ramirez/90	15.00
91 Gabe Alvarez/91	5.00
92 Jeremy Giambi/92	5.00
93 Adrian Beltre/93	5.00
94 George Lombard/94	5.00
95 Ryan Minor/95	5.00
96 Kevin Witt/96	5.00
97 Scott Hunter/97	5.00
98 Carlos Guillen/98	8.00
99 Derrick Gibson/99	5.00
100 Trot Nixon/100	5.00
101 Troy Glaus/101	8.00
102 Armando Rios/102	5.00
103 Preston Wilson/103	5.00
104 Pat Burrell/104	5.00
105 J.D. Drew/105	5.00
106 Bruce Chen/106	5.00
107 Matt Clement/107	5.00
108 Carlos Beltran/108	10.00
109 Carlos Febles/109	5.00
110 Rob Fick/110	5.00
111 Russell Branyan/111	5.00
112 Roosevelt Brown/112	5.00
113 Corey Koskie/113	5.00
114 Mario Encarnacion/114	5.00
115 Peter Tucci/115	5.00
116 Eric Chavez/116	8.00
117 Gabe Kapler/117	5.00
118 Marlon Anderson/118	5.00
119 A.J. Burnett/119	5.00
120 Ryan Bradley/120	5.00

Authen-Kicks

Travis Lee

Authen-Kicks is a game-used insert that embeds game-worn shoe swatches from the featured player. Each is done in a horizontal format and is sequentially hand-numbered. The number of swatch cards differs from player to player, and is indicated here in parentheses. Autographed versions of two colors of J.D. Drew shoes were also produced.

		NM/M
Common Player:		4.00
(1)	J.D. Drew/160	8.00
(1ab)	J.D. Drew/8 (Autographed black.)	75.00
(1ar)	J.D. Drew/8 (Autographed red.)	75.00
(2)	Travis Lee/175	4.00
(3)	Kevin Millwood/160	6.00
(4)	Bruce Chen/205	4.00
(5)	Troy Glaus/205	10.00
(6)	Todd Helton/205	15.00
(7)	Ricky Ledee/180	4.00
(8)	Scott Rolen/205	15.00
(9)	Jeremy Giambi/205	4.00

E-X Quisite

15 of baseball's top young players are showcased, with a black background and interior die-cutting around the player image. These are seeded 1:18 packs.

		NM/M
Complete Set (15):		15.00
Common Player:		.50
Inserted 1:18		
1	Troy Glaus	3.00
2	J.D. Drew	2.00
3	Pat Burrell	2.00
4	Russell Branyan	.50
5	Kerry Wood	1.50
6	Eric Chavez	1.00
7	Ben Grieve	.50
8	Gabe Kapler	.50
9	Adrian Beltre	1.00
10	Todd Helton	4.00
11	Roosevelt Brown	.50
12	Marlon Anderson	.50
13	Jeremy Giambi	.50
14	Magglio Ordonez	1.50
15	Travis Lee	.50

Favorites for Fenway

This 20-card set pays tribute to one of baseball's favorite ballparks, Fenway Park the venue for the 1999 All-Star Game. These have a photo of the featured player with an image of Fenway Park in the background on a horizontal format. These are seeded 1:36 packs.

		NM/M
Complete Set (20):		45.00
Common Player:		1.00
Inserted 1:36		
1	Mo Vaughn	1.00
2	Nomar Garciaparra	2.00
3	Frank Thomas	2.00
4	Ken Griffey Jr.	3.00
5	Roger Clemens	2.50
6	Alex Rodriguez	4.00
7	Derek Jeter	5.00
8	Juan Gonzalez	1.50
9	Cal Ripken Jr.	5.00
10	Ivan Rodriguez	1.50
11	J.D. Drew	1.50
12	Barry Bonds	5.00
13	Tony Gwynn	2.00
14	Vladimir Guerrero	2.00
15	Chipper Jones	2.00
16	Kerry Wood	1.50
17	Mike Piazza	3.00
18	Sammy Sosa	2.00

19	Scott Rolen	1.50
20	Mark McGwire	4.00

Milestones of the Century

This 10-card set spotlights the top statistical performances from the 1998 season, sequentially numbered to that performance in a multi-layered design.

		NM/M
Common Player:		5.00
Numbered to featured milestone.		
1	Kerry Wood/20	15.00
2	Mark McGwire/70	20.00
3	Sammy Sosa/66	15.00
4	Ken Griffey Jr./350	15.00
5	Roger Clemens/98	25.00
6	Cal Ripken Jr./17	100.00
7	Alex Rodriguez/40	40.00
8	Barry Bonds/400	25.00
9	N.Y. Yankees/114	15.00
10	Travis Lee/98	5.00

1999 SkyBox Molten Metal

Distributed exclusively to the hobby, the 150-card set consists of three subsets: Metal Smiths, Heavy Metal and Supernatural. Metal Smiths (1-100) show baseball's top players, Heavy Metal (101-130) focus on power hitters and Supernatural (131-150) focus on rookies. Base cards feature silver foil stamping on a 24-point stock with holofoil and wet-laminate overlays. Molten Metal was released in six-card packs with a SRP of $4.99. A special version of the issue was sold only at the 20th Nat'l Sports Collectors Convention in Atlanta, July 19-24. The show version includes autograph redemption cards for show guests and a die-cut series of 30 current and former Braves favorites. Each of the show version cards has a small National Convention logo printed on back; they currently carry no premium.

		NM/M
Complete Set (150):		35.00
Common Metalsmiths (1-100):		.15
Inserted 4:1		
Common Heavy Metal (101-130):		.25
Inserted 1:1		
Common Supernatural (131-150):		.50
Inserted 1:2		
Pack (6):		1.00
Wax Box (24):		20.00
1	Larry Walker	.15
2	Jose Canseco	.50
3	Brian Jordan	.15
4	Rafael Palmeiro	.65
5	Edgar Renteria	.15
6	Dante Bichette	.15
7	Mark Kotsay	.15
8	Denny Neagle	.15
9	Ellis Burks	.15
10	Paul O'Neill	.15
11	Miguel Tejada	.30
12	Ken Caminiti	.15
13	David Cone	.15
14	Jason Kendall	.15
15	Ruben Rivera	.15

16	Todd Walker	.15
17	Bobby Higginson	.15
18	Derrek Lee	.60
19	Rondell White	.15
20	Pedro J. Martinez	.75
21	Jeff Kent	.15
22	Randy Johnson	.75
23	Matt Williams	.15
24	Sean Casey	.25
25	Eric Davis	.15
26	Ryan Klesko	.15
27	Curt Schilling	.35
28	Geoff Jenkins	.15
29	Armand Abreu	.15
30	Vinny Castilla	.15
31	Will Clark	.15
32	Ray Durham	.15
33	Ray Lankford	.15
34	Richie Sexson	.15
35	Derrick Gibson	.15
36	Mark Grace	.15
37	Greg Vaughn	.15
38	Bartolo Colon	.15
39	Steve Finley	.15
40	Chuck Knoblauch	.15
41	Ricky Ledee	.15
42	John Smoltz	.15
43	Moises Alou	.15
44	Jim Edmonds	.15
45	Cliff Floyd	.15
46	Javy Lopez	.15
47	Jim Thome	.65
48	J.T. Snow	.15
49	Sandy Alomar Jr.	.15
50	Andy Pettitte	.25
51	Juan Encarnacion	.15
52	Travis Fryman	.15
53	Eli Marrero	.15
54	Jeff Cirillo	.15
55	Brady Anderson	.15
56	Jose Cruz Jr.	.15
57	Edgar Martinez	.15
58	Garret Anderson	.15
59	Paul Konerko	.30
60	Eric Milton	.15
61	Jason Giambi	.45
62	Tom Glavine	.35
63	Justin Thompson	.15
64	Brad Fullmer	.15
65	Marquis Grissom	.15
66	Fernando Tatis	.15
67	Carlos Beltran	.45
68	Charles Johnson	.15
69	Raul Mondesi	.15
70	Richard Hildalgo	.15
71	Barry Larkin	.15
72	David Wells	.15
73	Jay Buhner	.15
74	Matt Clement	.15
75	Eric Karros	.15
76	Carl Pavano	.15
77	Mariano Rivera	.15
78	Livan Hernandez	.15
79	A.J. Hinch	.15
80	Tino Martinez	.15
81	Rusty Greer	.15
82	Jose Guillen	.15
83	Robin Ventura	.15
84	Kevin Brown	.15
85	Chan Ho Park	.15
86	John Olerud	.15
87	Johnny Damon	.35
88	Todd Hundley	.15
89	Fred McGriff	.15
90	Wade Boggs	1.00
91	Mike Cameron	.15
92	Gary Sheffield	.50
93	Rickey Henderson	.75
94	Pat Hentgen	.15
95	Omar Vizquel	.15
96	Craig Biggio	.15
97	Mike Caruso	.15
98	Neifi Perez	.15
99	Mike Mussina	.50
100	Carlos Delgado	.45
101	Andruw Jones (Heavy Metal)	1.00
102	Pat Burrell RC (Heavy Metal)	3.00
103	Orlando Hernandez (Heavy Metal)	.25
104	Darin Erstad (Heavy Metal)	.40
105	Roberto Alomar (Heavy Metal)	.35
106	Tim Salmon (Heavy Metal)	.25
107	Albert Belle (Heavy Metal)	.25
108	Chad Allen RC (Heavy Metal)	.25
109	Travis Lee (Heavy Metal)	.25
110	Jesse Garcia RC (Heavy Metal)	.25
111	Tony Clark (Heavy Metal)	.25
112	Ivan Rodriguez (Heavy Metal)	.75
113	Troy Glaus (Heavy Metal)	1.00
114	A.J. Burnett RC (Heavy Metal)	1.50
115	David Justice (Heavy Metal)	.25
116	Adrian Beltre (Heavy Metal)	.50
117	Eric Chavez (Heavy Metal)	.35
118	Kenny Lofton (Heavy Metal)	.25
119	Michael Barrett (Heavy Metal)	.25

120	Jeff Weaver RC (Heavy Metal)	1.50
121	Manny Ramirez (Heavy Metal)	1.00
122	Barry Bonds (Heavy Metal)	2.00
123	Bernie Williams (Heavy Metal)	.25
124	Freddy Garcia RC (Heavy Metal)	1.50
125	Scott Hunter RC (Heavy Metal)	.25
126	Jeremy Giambi (Heavy Metal)	.25
127	Masao Kida RC (Heavy Metal)	.25
128	Todd Helton (Heavy Metal)	1.00
129	Mike Figga (Heavy Metal)	.25
130	Mo Vaughn (Heavy Metal)	.25
131	J.D. Drew (Supernaturals)	.65
132	Cal Ripken Jr. (Supernaturals)	3.00
133	Ken Griffey Jr. (Supernaturals)	1.50
134	Mark McGwire (Supernaturals)	2.00
135	Nomar Garciaparra (Supernaturals)	1.00
136	Greg Maddux (Supernaturals)	1.00
137	Mike Piazza (Supernaturals)	1.50
138	Alex Rodriguez (Supernaturals)	2.00
139	Frank Thomas (Supernaturals)	.85
140	Juan Gonzalez (Supernaturals)	.65
141	Tony Gwynn (Supernaturals)	1.00
142	Derek Jeter (Supernaturals)	3.00
143	Chipper Jones (Supernaturals)	1.00
144	Scott Rolen (Supernaturals)	.65
145	Sammy Sosa (Supernaturals)	1.00
146	Kerry Wood (Supernaturals)	.50
147	Roger Clemens (Supernaturals)	1.25
148	Jeff Bagwell (Supernaturals)	.75
149	Vladimir Guerrero (Supernaturals)	.75
150	Ben Grieve (Supernaturals)	.50

Fusion

Fusion is a 50-card partial parallel that is paralleled three times: Fusion, Sterling Fusion and Titanium Fusion. The three parallels consist of the two subsets Heavy Metal and Supernatural. Fusion Heavy Metals (1-30) are seeded 1:12 packs and Supernatural Fusions are seeded 1:24 packs. Fusions are laser die-cut with additional silver-foil stamping. Sterling Fusions are limited to 500 numbered sets with each card laser die-cut on a blue background with blue foil stamping. Titanium Fusions are limited to 50 sequentially numbered sets with gold background and enhanced with gold foil highlights.

		NM/M
Complete Set (50):		100.00
Common Heavy Metal (1-30):		1.00
Inserted 1:12		
Common Supernatural (31-50):		2.50
Inserted 1:24		
Sterling (31-50):		1.5X
Production 500 Sets		
Titanium (31-50):		6X
Production 50 Sets		
1	Andruw Jones	4.00
2	Pat Burrell	2.00
3	Orlando Hernandez	1.00
4	Darin Erstad	1.50
5	Roberto Alomar	1.00
6	Tim Salmon	1.00

7	Albert Belle	1.00
8	Chad Allen	1.00
9	Travis Lee	1.00
10	Jesse Garcia	1.00
11	Tony Clark	1.00
12	Ivan Rodriguez	3.00
13	Troy Glaus	3.00
14	A.J. Burnett	1.00
15	David Justice	1.00
16	Adrian Beltre	1.00
17	Eric Chavez	1.50
18	Kenny Lofton	1.00
19	Michael Barrett	1.00
20	Jeff Weaver	1.00
21	Manny Ramirez	4.00
22	Barry Bonds	10.00
23	Bernie Williams	1.00
24	Freddy Garcia	1.00
25	Scott Hunter	1.00
26	Jeremy Giambi	1.00
27	Masao Kida	1.00
28	Todd Helton	3.00
29	Mike Figga	1.00
30	Mo Vaughn	1.00
31	J.D. Drew	2.00
32	Cal Ripken Jr.	10.00
33	Ken Griffey Jr.	6.00
34	Mark McGwire	7.50
35	Nomar Garciaparra	5.00
36	Greg Maddux	5.00
37	Mike Piazza	6.00
38	Alex Rodriguez	7.50
39	Frank Thomas	3.00
40	Juan Gonzalez	1.50
41	Tony Gwynn	5.00
42	Derek Jeter	10.00
43	Chipper Jones	5.00
44	Scott Rolen	3.00
45	Sammy Sosa	5.00
46	Kerry Wood	2.00
47	Roger Clemens	5.50
48	Jeff Bagwell	4.00
49	Vladimir Guerrero	4.00
50	Ben Grieve	4.00

Fusion - Sterling

Sterling Fusions are limited to 500 numbered sets with each card laser die-cut on a blue background with blue foil graphic highlights. A special version of the issue was sold only at the 20th Nat'l Sports Collectors Convention in Atlanta, July 19-24. Each of the show-version cards has a small National Convention logo printed on back; they currently carry no premium.

	NM/M
Common Player:	1.50
Sterling Stars:	1.5X

Fusion - Titanium

Titanium Fusions are limited to 50 sequentially numbered sets with gold background and enhanced with gold foil highlights. A special version of the issue was sold only at the 20th Nat'l Sports Collectors Convention in Atlanta, July 19-24. Each of the show-version cards has a small National Convention logo printed on back; they currently carry no premium.

	NM/M
Common Player:	4.00
Titanium Stars:	6X

Oh Atlanta!

This 30-card set features players who are either current or former Atlanta Braves like Chipper Jones and Dave Justice. These inserts are seeded one per pack and was produced in conjunction with the 20th annual National Sports Collectors Convention in Atlanta.

		NM/M
Complete Set (30):		30.00
Common Player:		.60
Inserted 1:1		
1	Kenny Lofton	.60
2	Kevin Millwood	.60
3	Bret Boone	.60
4	Otis Nixon	.60
5	Vinny Castilla	.60
6	Brian Jordan	.60
7	Chipper Jones	8.00
8	Dave Justice	.60
9	Micah Bowie	.60
10	Fred McGriff	.60
11	Ron Gant	.60
12	Andruw Jones	4.00
13	Kent Mercker	.60
14	Greg McMichael	.60
15	Steve Avery	.60
16	Marquis Grissom	.60
17	Jason Schmidt	.60
18	Ryan Klesko	.60
19	Charlie O'Brien	.60
20	Terry Pendleton	.60
21	Denny Neagle	.60
22	Greg Maddux	8.00
23	Tom Glavine	1.50
24	Javy Lopez	.60
25	John Rocker	.60
26	Walt Weiss	.60
27	John Smoltz	.60
28	Michael Tucker	.60
29	Odalis Perez	.60
30	Andres Galarraga	.60

Xplosion Sample

This sample card was issued to preview SkyBox's Xplosion metal inserts. Etched and printed on metal stock, the card is identical in format to the issued versions, except for sample notations on back.

	NM/M
Kerry Wood	3.00

Xplosion

This is a 150-card parallel set, which is seeded 1:2 packs. These are made of actual metal that have added etching and some foil stamping.

	NM/M
Complete Set (150):	300.00
Common Player:	1.00

Stars: 3X
Inserted 1:2

1999 SkyBox Premium

The base set consists of 300 cards, base cards feature full bleed fronts with gold-foil stamped player and team names. Card backs have complete year-by-year stats along with a close-up photo. The Rookie subset (223-272) also have a short-printed parallel version as well. Different photos are used but they have the same card number and card back. The short-print versions are seeded 1:8 packs and have an action photo front while the non-seeded cards have a close-up photo.

	NM/M
Complete Set (300):	20.00
Complete Set w/SP's (350):	40.00
Common Player:	.10
Common SP (223-272):	.60
SP's inserted 1:8	
Star Rubies:	50X
Production 50 Sets	
SP Star Rubies:	15X
Production 15 Sets	
Pack (8):	1.50
Wax Box (24):	25.00
1	Alex Rodriguez	2.00
2	Sidney Ponson	.10
3	Shawn Green	.35
4	Dan Wilson	.10
5	Rolando Arrojo	.10
6	Roberto Alomar	.30
7	Matt Anderson	.10
8	David Segui	.10
9	Alex Gonzalez	.10
10	Edgar Renteria	.10
11	Benito Santiago	.10
12	Todd Stottlemyre	.10
13	Rico Brogna	.10
14	Troy Glaus	.65
15	Al Leiter	.10
16	Pedro J. Martinez	.75
17	Paul O'Neill	.25
18	Manny Ramirez	.75
19	Scott Rolen	.65
20	Curt Schilling	.35
21	Bobby Abreu	.15
22	Robb Nen	.10
23	Andy Pettitte	.25
24	John Wetteland	.10
25	Bobby Bonilla	.10
26	Darin Erstad	.20
27	Shawn Estes	.10
28	John Franco	.10
29	Nomar Garciaparra	1.00
30	Rick Helling	.10
31	David Justice	.10
32	Chuck Knoblauch	.10
33	Quinton McCracken	.10
34	Kenny Rogers	.10
35	Brian Giles	.10
36	Armando Benitez	.10
37	Trevor Hoffman	.10
38	Charles Johnson	.10
39	Travis Lee	.10
40	Tom Glavine	.35
41	Rondell White	.10
42	Orlando Hernandez	.10
43	Mickey Morandini	.10
44	Darryl Kile	.10
45	Greg Vaughn	.10
46	Gregg Jefferies	.10

47	Mark McGwire	2.00
48	Kerry Wood	.40
49	Jeromy Burnitz	.10
50	Ron Gant	.10
51	Vinny Castilla	.10
52	Doug Glanville	.10
53	Juan Guzman	.10
54	Dustin Hermanson	.10
55	Jose Hernandez	.10
56	Bob Higginson	.10
57	A.J. Hinch	.10
58	Randy Johnson	.75
59	Eli Marrero	.10
60	Rafael Palmeiro	.65
61	Carl Pavano	.10
62	Brett Tomko	.10
63	Jose Guillen	.10
64	Mike Lieberthal	.10
65	Jim Abbott	.10
66	Dante Bichette	.10
67	Jeff Cirillo	.10
68	Eric Davis	.10
69	Delino DeShields	.10
70	Steve Finley	.10
71	Mark Grace	.10
72	Jason Kendall	.10
73	Jeff Kent	.10
74	Desi Relaford	.10
75	Ivan Rodriguez	.65
76	Shannon Stewart	.10
77	Geoff Jenkins	.10
78	Ben Grieve	.10
79	Cliff Floyd	.10
80	Jason Giambi	.50
81	Rod Beck	.10
82	Derek Bell	.10
83	Will Clark	.10
84	David Dellucci	.10
85	Joey Hamilton	.10
86	Livan Hernandez	.10
87	Barry Larkin	.10
88	Matt Mantei	.10
89	Dean Palmer	.10
90	Chan Ho Park	.10
91	Jim Thome	.65
92	Miguel Tejada	.20
93	Justin Thompson	.10
94	David Wells	.10
95	Bernie Williams	.10
96	Jeff Bagwell	.75
97	Derek Lee	.50
98	Devon White	.10
99	Jeff Shaw	.10
100	Brad Radke	.10
101	Mark Grudzielanek	.10
102	Javy Lopez	.10
103	Mike Sirotka	.10
104	Robin Ventura	.10
105	Andy Ashby	.10
106	Juan Gonzalez	.40
107	Albert Belle	.10
108	Andy Benes	.10
109	Jay Buhner	.10
110	Ken Caminiti	.10
111	Roger Clemens	1.25
112	Mike Hampton	.10
113	Pete Harnisch	.10
114	Mike Piazza	1.50
115	J.T. Snow	.10
116	John Olerud	.10
117	Tony Womack	.10
118	Todd Zeile	.10
119	Tony Gwynn	1.00
120	Brady Anderson	.10
121	Sean Casey	.20
122	Jose Cruz Jr.	.10
123	Carlos Delgado	.50
124	Edgar Martinez	.10
125	Jose Mesa	.10
126	Shane Reynolds	.10
127	John Valentin	.10
128	Mo Vaughn	.10
129	Kevin Young	.10
130	Jay Bell	.10
131	Aaron Boone	.10
132	John Smoltz	.10
133	Mike Stanley	.10
134	Bret Saberhagen	.10
135	Tim Salmon	.10
136	Mariano Rivera	.15
137	Ken Griffey Jr.	1.50
138	Jose Offerman	.10
139	Troy Percival	.10
140	Greg Maddux	1.00
141	Frank Thomas	.75
142	Steve Avery	.10
143	Kevin Millwood	.10
144	Sammy Sosa	1.00
145	Larry Walker	.10
146	Matt Williams	.10
147	Mike Caruso	.10
148	Todd Helton	.65
149	Andruw Jones	.75
150	Ray Lankford	.10
151	Craig Biggio	.10
152	Ugueth Urbina	.10
153	Wade Boggs	1.00
154	Derek Jeter	2.50
155	Wally Joyner	.10
156	Mike Mussina	.30
157	Gregg Olson	.10
158	Henry Rodriguez	.10
159	Reggie Sanders	.10
160	Fernando Tatis	.10
161	Dmitri Young	.10
162	Rick Aguilera	.10
163	Marty Cordova	.10
164	Johnny Damon	.30

165	Ray Durham	.10
166	Brad Fullmer	.10
167	Chipper Jones	1.00
168	Bobby Smith	.10
169	Omar Vizquel	.10
170	Todd Hundley	.10
171	David Cone	.10
172	Royce Clayton	.10
173	Ryan Klesko	.10
174	Jeff Montgomery	.10
175	Magglio Ordonez	.10
176	Billy Wagner	.10
177	Masato Yoshii	.10
178	Jason Christiansen	.10
179	Chuck Finley	.10
180	Tom Gordon	.10
181	Wilton Guerrero	.10
182	Rickey Henderson	.75
183	Sterling Hitchcock	.10
184	Kenny Lofton	.10
185	Tino Martinez	.10
186	Fred McGriff	.10
187	Matt Stairs	.10
188	Neifi Perez	.10
189	Bob Wickman	.10
190	Barry Bonds	2.50
191	Jose Canseco	.40
192	Damion Easley	.10
193	Jim Edmonds	.10
194	Juan Encarnacion	.50
195	Travis Fryman	.10
196	Tom Goodwin	.10
197	Rusty Greer	.10
198	Roberto Hernandez	.10
199	B.J. Surhoff	.10
200	Scott Brosius	.10
201	Brian Jordan	.10
202	Paul Konerko	.20
203	Ismael Valdes	.10
204	Eric Milton	.10
205	Adrian Beltre	.25
206	Tony Clark	.10
207	Bartolo Colon	.10
208	Cal Ripken Jr.	2.50
209	Moises Alou	.10
210	Wilson Alvarez	.10
211	Kevin Brown	.10
212	Orlando Cabrera	.10
213	Vladimir Guerrero	.75
214	Jose Rosado	.10
215	Raul Mondesi	.10
216	Dave Nilsson	.10
217	Carlos Perez	.10
218	Jason Schmidt	.10
219	Richie Sexson	.10
220	Gary Sheffield	.40
221	Fernando Vina	.10
222	Todd Walker	.10
223	Scott Sauerbeck RC	.10
223	Scott Sauerbeck/SP RC	.60
224	Pascual Matos RC	.10
224	Pascual Matos/SP RC	.60
225	Kyle Farnsworth RC	.15
225	Kyle Farnsworth/SP RC	.60
226	Freddy Garcia RC	.75
226	Freddy Garcia/SP RC	1.50
227	David Lundquist RC	.10
227	David Lundquist/SP RC	.60
228	Jolbert Cabrera RC	.10
228	Jolbert Cabrera/SP RC	.60
229	Dan Perkins RC	.10
229	Dan Perkins/SP RC	.60
230	Warren Morris RC	.10
230	Warren Morris/SP	.60
231	Carlos Febles RC	.10
231	Carlos Febles/SP	.60
232	Brett Hinchliffe RC	.10
232	Brett Hinchliffe/SP RC	.60
233	Jason Phillips RC	.10
233	Jason Phillips/SP RC	.60
234	Glen Barker RC	.10
234	Glen Barker/SP RC	.60
235	Jose Macias RC	.25
235	Jose Macias/SP RC	1.00
236	Joe Mays RC	.10
236	Joe Mays/SP RC	.60
237	Chad Allen RC	.10
237	Chad Allen/SP RC	.60
238	Miguel Del Toro RC	.10
238	Miguel Del Toro/SP RC	.60
239	Chris Singleton RC	.10
239	Chris Singleton/SP	.60
240	Jesse Garcia RC	.10
240	Jesse Garcia/SP RC	.60
241	Kris Benson RC	.10
241	Kris Benson/SP	.60
242	Clay Bellinger RC	.10
242	Clay Bellinger/SP RC	.60
243	Scott Williamson RC	.10
243	Scott Williamson/SP	.60
244	Masao Kida RC	.10
244	Masao Kida/SP RC	.60
245	Guillermo Garcia RC	.10
245	Guillermo Garcia/SP RC	.60
246	A.J. Burnett RC	.25
246	A.J. Burnett/SP RC	1.50
247	Bo Porter RC	.10
247	Bo Porter/SP RC	.60
248	Pat Burrell RC	1.50
248	Pat Burrell/SP RC	4.00
249	Carlos Lee	.50
249	Carlos Lee/SP	1.50
250	Jeff Weaver RC	.50
250	Jeff Weaver/SP RC	1.50
251	Ruben Mateo	.10
251	Ruben Mateo/SP	.60
252	J.D. Drew	.40
252	J.D. Drew/SP	.10

253	Jeremy Giambi	.10
253	Jeremy Giambi/SP	.60
254	Gary Bennett RC	.10
254	Gary Bennett/SP RC	.60
255	Edwards Guzman RC	.10
255	Edwards Guzman/SP RC	.60
256	Ramon Martinez	.10
256	Ramon Martinez/SP	.60
257	Giomar Guevara RC	.10
257	Giomar Guevara/SP RC	.60
258	Joe McEwing RC	.10
258	Joe McEwing/SP RC	.60
259	Tom Davey RC	.10
259	Tom Davey/SP RC	.60
260	Gabe Kapler	.10
260	Gabe Kapler/SP	.60
261	Ryan Rupe RC	.10
261	Ryan Rupe/SP RC	.60
262	Kelly Dransfeldt RC	.10
262	Kelly Dransfeldt/SP RC	.60
263	Michael Barrett	.10
263	Michael Barrett/SP	.60
264	Eric Chavez	.25
264	Eric Chavez/SP	1.00
265	Orber Moreno RC	.10
265	Orber Moreno/SP RC	.60
266	Marlon Anderson	.10
266	Marlon Anderson/SP	.60
267	Carlos Beltran	.50
267	Carlos Beltran/SP	1.50
268	Doug Mientkiewicz	.10
268	Doug Mientkiewicz/SP	.60
269	Roy Halladay	.10
269	Roy Halladay/SP	.60
270	Torii Hunter	.10
270	Torii Hunter/SP	.60
271	Stan Spencer	.10
271	Stan Spencer/SP	.60
272	Alex Gonzalez	.10
272	Alex Gonzalez/SP	.60
273	Mark McGwire (Spring Fling)	1.00
274	Scott Rolen (Spring Fling)	.30
275	Jeff Bagwell (Spring Fling)	.40
276	Derek Jeter (Spring Fling)	1.50
277	Tony Gwynn (Spring Fling)	.50
278	Frank Thomas (Spring Fling)	.40
279	Sammy Sosa (Spring Fling)	.50
280	Nomar Garciaparra (Spring Fling)	.50
281	Cal Ripken Jr. (Spring Fling)	1.50
282	Albert Belle (Spring Fling)	.10
283	Kerry Wood (Spring Fling)	.20
284	Greg Maddux (Spring Fling)	.50
285	Barry Bonds (Spring Fling)	1.50
286	Juan Gonzalez (Spring Fling)	.25
287	Ken Griffey Jr. (Spring Fling)	.75
288	Alex Rodriguez (Spring Fling)	1.00
289	Ben Grieve (Spring Fling)	.10
290	Travis Lee (Spring Fling)	.10
291	Mo Vaughn (Spring Fling)	.10
292	Mike Piazza (Spring Fling)	.85
293	Roger Clemens (Spring Fling)	.60
294	J.D. Drew (Spring Fling)	.20
295	Randy Johnson (Spring Fling)	.40
296	Chipper Jones (Spring Fling)	.50
297	Vladimir Guerrero (Spring Fling)	.40
298	Checklist (Nomar Garciaparra)	.40
299	Checklist (Ken Griffey Jr.)	.50
300	Checklist (Mark McGwire)	.60

Star Rubies

Star Rubies are a parallel of the base set and are limited to 50 sequentially numbered sets. SP Rookie parallels are limited to 15 numbered sets. Rubies feature a complete prism foil front with red-foil stamping.

Star Rubies:	50X
Production 50 Sets	
SP Star Rubies:	15X
Production 15 Sets	

Autographics

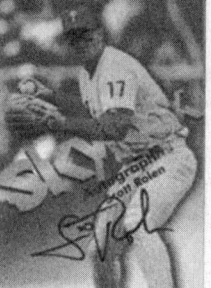

This 54-card autographed set feature an embossed SkyBox Seal of Authenticity stamp and are seeded 1:68 packs. Cards are commonly found signed in black ink. Blue-ink versions, serially numbered to 50 each, were also produced.

	NM/M
Common Player:	3.00
Inserted 1:68	
Blue Ink:	1.5X
Production 50 Sets	
	Roberto Alomar	15.00
	Paul Bako	3.00
	Michael Barrett	8.00
	Kris Benson	8.00
	Micah Bowie	3.00
	Roosevelt Brown	3.00
	A.J. Burnett	8.00
	Pat Burrell	15.00
	Ken Caminiti	15.00
	Royce Clayton	3.00
	Edgard Clemente	3.00
	Bartolo Colon	10.00
	J.D. Drew	15.00
	Damion Easley	5.00
	Derrin Ebert	3.00
	Mario Encarnacion	3.00
	Juan Encarnacion	5.00
	Troy Glaus	15.00
	Tom Glavine	20.00
	Juan Gonzalez/SP	50.00
	Shawn Green	10.00
	Wilton Guerrero	3.00
	Jose Guillen	8.00
	Tony Gwynn	30.00
	Mark Harriger	3.00
	Bobby Higginson	3.00
	Todd Hollandsworth	3.00
	Scott Hunter	3.00
	Gabe Kapler	3.00
	Scott Karl	3.00
	Mike Kinkade	3.00
	Ray Lankford	3.00
	Barry Larkin	15.00
	Matt Lawton	5.00
	Ricky Ledee	3.00
	Travis Lee	5.00
	Eli Marrero	5.00
	Ruben Mateo	3.00
	Joe McEwing	3.00
	Doug Mientkiewicz	4.00
	Russ Ortiz	5.00
	Jim Parque	3.00
	Robert Person	3.00
	Alex Rodriguez	80.00
	Scott Rolen	20.00
	Benj Sampson	3.00
	Luis Saturria	3.00
	Curt Schilling	35.00
	David Segui	3.00
	Fernando Tatis	3.00
	Peter Tucci	3.00
	Javier Vasquez	6.00
	Robin Ventura	10.00
	Checklist	.05

Diamond Debuts

SP Star Rubies: 15X
Production 15 Sets

This 15-card set features the best rookies of 1999 on a silver rainbow holo-foil card stock. These are seeded 1:49 packs. Card backs are numbered with a "DD" suffix.

	NM/M
Complete Set (15):	17.50
Common Player:	2.00
Inserted 1:49	
1	Eric Chavez	3.00
2	Kyle Farnsworth	2.00
3	Ryan Rupe	2.00
4	Jeremy Giambi	2.00
5	Marlon Anderson	2.00
6	J.D. Drew	4.00
7	Carlos Febles	2.00
8	Joe McEwing	2.00
9	Jeff Weaver	2.00
10	Alex Gonzalez	2.00
11	Chad Allen	2.00
12	Michael Barrett	2.00
13	Gabe Kapler	2.00
14	Carlos Lee	2.00
15	Edwards Guzman	2.00

Intimidation Nation

This 15-card set highlights the top performers in baseball and features gold rainbow holo-foil stamping. These are limited to 99 sequentially numbered sets. Card backs are numbered with a "IN" suffix.

	NM/M
Complete Set (15):	280.00
Common Player:	12.00
Production 99 Sets	
1	Cal Ripken Jr.	40.00
2	Tony Gwynn	20.00
3	Nomar Garciaparra	20.00
4	Frank Thomas	15.00
5	Mike Piazza	25.00
6	Mark McGwire	30.00
7	Scott Rolen	12.00
8	Chipper Jones	20.00
9	Greg Maddux	20.00
10	Ken Griffey Jr.	25.00
11	Juan Gonzalez	12.00
12	Derek Jeter	40.00
13	J.D. Drew	12.00
14	Roger Clemens	22.50
15	Alex Rodriguez	30.00

Live Bats

This 15-card set spotlights baseball's top hitters and feature red foil stamping. Card backs are numbered with a "LB" suffix and are seeded 1:7 packs.

	NM/M
Complete Set (15):	10.00
Common Player:	.25
Inserted 1:7	
1	Juan Gonzalez	.35
2	Mark McGwire	1.50
3	Jeff Bagwell	.50
4	Frank Thomas	.50
5	Mike Piazza	1.00
6	Nomar Garciaparra	.75
7	Alex Rodriguez	1.50
8	Scott Rolen	.40
9	Travis Lee	.25
10	Tony Gwynn	.75
11	Derek Jeter	2.00
12	Ben Grieve	.25
13	Chipper Jones	.75
14	Ken Griffey Jr.	1.00
15	Cal Ripken Jr.	2.00

Show Business

This 15-card set features some of the best players in the "show" on double foil-stamped card fronts. Card backs are numbered with a "SB" suffix and are seeded 1:70 packs.

	NM/M
Complete Set (15):	60.00
Common Player:	2.00
Inserted 1:70	
1	Mark McGwire	7.50
2	Tony Gwynn	5.00
3	Nomar Garciaparra	5.00
4	Juan Gonzalez	2.50

(25 sets), which are both hobby exclusive. The Rant parallel set is retail exclusive (1:2).

	NM/M
Complete Set (300):	15.00
Common Player (1-240):	.05
Common Player (241-300):	.15
Raves:	15X
Production 150 Sets	
SuperRaves:	45X
Production 25 Sets	
Rants:	8X
Inserted 1:2 R	
Pack (8):	1.50
Wax Box (36):	25.00

5	Roger Clemens	5.00
6	Chipper Jones	5.00
7	Cal Ripken Jr.	10.00
8	Alex Rodriguez	7.50
9	Orlando Hernandez	2.00
10	Greg Maddux	5.00
11	Mike Piazza	6.00
12	Frank Thomas	4.00
13	Ken Griffey Jr.	6.00
14	Scott Rolen	3.00
15	Derek Jeter	10.00

Soul of The Game

This 15-card set features rainbow foil stamping and the name Soul of the Game prominently stamped, covering the entire card behind the player photo. Card backs are numbered with a "SG" suffix and are seeded 1:14 packs.

		NM/M
Complete Set (15):		15.00
Common Player:		.60
Inserted 1:14		
1	Alex Rodriguez	2.00
2	Vladimir Guerrero	.90
3	Chipper Jones	1.25
4	Derek Jeter	2.50
5	Tony Gwynn	1.25
6	Scott Rolen	.60
7	Juan Gonzalez	.60
8	Mark McGwire	2.00
9	Ken Griffey Jr.	1.50
10	Jeff Bagwell	.90
11	Cal Ripken Jr.	2.50
12	Frank Thomas	.90
13	Mike Piazza	1.50
14	Nomar Garciaparra	1.25
15	Sammy Sosa	1.25

1999 SkyBox Thunder

Skybox Thunder consists of a 300-card base set with three parallels and six inserts. The base set is inserted at varying odds. In hobby packs, regular-player cards #1-140 come 4-5 per pack, veteran stars on cards #141-240 come two per pack, and superstars on cards #241-300 are seeded one per pack. For retail packs the odds were: #1-141 (3-4 per pack), #141-240 (two per pack), and #241-300 (one per pack). Parallels include Rave (numbered to 150 sets) and Super Rave

1	John Smoltz	.05
2	Garret Anderson	.05
3	Matt Williams	.05
4	Daryle Ward	.05
5	Andy Ashby	.05
6	Miguel Tejada	.15
7	Dmitri Young	.05
8	Roberto Alomar	.25
9	Kevin Brown	.05
10	Eric Young	.05
11	Odalis Perez	.05
12	Preston Wilson	.05
13	Jeff Abbott	.05
14	Bret Boone	.05
15	Mendy Lopez	.05
16	B.J. Surhoff	.05
17	Steve Woodard	.05
18	Ron Coomer	.05
19	Rondell White	.05
20	Edgardo Alfonzo	.05
21	Kevin Millwood	.05
22	Jose Canseco	.45
23	Blake Stein	.05
24	Quilvio Veras	.05
25	Chuck Knoblauch	.05
26	David Segui	.05
27	Eric Davis	.05
28	Francisco Cordova	.05
29	Randy Winn	.05
30	Will Clark	.05
31	Billy Wagner	.05
32	Kevin Witt	.05
33	Jim Edmonds	.05
34	Todd Stottlemyre	.05
35	Shane Andrews	.05
36	Michael Tucker	.05
37	Sandy Alomar Jr.	.05
38	Neifi Perez	.05
39	Jaret Wright	.05
40	Devon White	.05
41	Edgar Renteria	.05
42	Shane Reynolds	.05
43	Jeff King	.05
44	Darren Dreifort	.05
45	Fernando Vina	.05
46	Marty Cordova	.05
47	Ugueth Urbina	.05
48	Bobby Bonilla	.05
49	Omar Vizquel	.05
50	Tom Gordon	.05
51	Ryan Christenson	.05
52	Aaron Boone	.05
53	Jamie Moyer	.05
54	Brian Giles	.05
55	Kevin Tapani	.05
56	Scott Brosius	.05
57	Ellis Burks	.05
58	Al Leiter	.05
59	Royce Clayton	.05
60	Chris Carpenter	.05
61	Bubba Trammell	.05
62	Tom Glavine	.35
63	Shannon Stewart	.05
64	Todd Zeile	.05
65	J.T. Snow	.05
66	Matt Clement	.05
67	Matt Stairs	.05
68	Ismael Valdes	.05
69	Todd Walker	.05
70	Jose Lima	.05
71	Mike Caruso	.05
72	Brett Tomko	.05
73	Mike Lansing	.05
74	Justin Thompson	.05
75	Damion Easley	.05
76	Derek Lee	.50
77	Derek Bell	.05
78	Brady Anderson	.05
79	Charles Johnson	.05
80	Rafael Roque RC	.05
81	Corey Koskie	.05
82	Fernando Seguignol	.05
83	Jay Tessmer	.05
84	Jason Giambi	.50
85	Mike Lieberthal	.05
86	Jose Guillen	.05
87	Jim Leyritz	.05
88	Shawn Estes	.05
89	Ray Lankford	.05
90	Paul Sorrento	.05
91	Javy Lopez	.05
92	John Wetteland	.05
93	Sean Casey	.15
94	Chuck Finley	.05
95	Trot Nixon	.05
96	Ray Durham	.05
97	Reggie Sanders	.05
98	Bartolo Colon	.05
99	Henry Rodriguez	.05
100	Rolando Arrojo	.05
101	Geoff Jenkins	.05
102	Darryl Kile	.05

103	Mark Kotsay	.05
104	Craig Biggio	.05
105	Omar Daal	.05
106	Carlos Febles	.05
107	Eric Karros	.05
108	Matt Lawton	.05
109	Carl Pavano	.05
110	Brian McRae	.05
111	Mariano Rivera	.15
112	Jay Buhner	.05
113	Doug Glanville	.05
114	Jason Kendall	.05
115	Wally Joyner	.05
116	Jeff Kent	.05
117	Shane Monahan	.05
118	Eli Marrero	.05
119	Bobby Smith	.05
120	Shawn Green	.20
121	Kirk Rueter	.05
122	Tom Goodwin	.05
123	Andy Benes	.05
124	Ed Sprague	.05
125	Mike Mussina	.25
126	Jose Offerman	.05
127	Mickey Morandini	.05
128	Paul Konerko	.20
129	Denny Neagle	.05
130	Travis Fryman	.05
131	John Rocker	.05
132	Rob Fick RC	.05
133	Livan Hernandez	.05
134	Ken Caminiti	.05
135	Johnny Damon	.30
136	Jeff Kubenka	.05
137	Marquis Grissom	.05
138	Doug Mientkiewicz	.05
139	Dustin Hermanson	.05
140	Carl Everett	.05
141	Hideo Nomo	.40
142	Jorge Posada	.05
143	Rickey Henderson	.75
144	Robb Nen	.05
145	Ron Gant	.05
146	Aramis Ramirez	.05
147	Trevor Hoffman	.05
148	Bill Mueller	.05
149	Edgar Martinez	.05
150	Fred McGriff	.05
151	Rusty Greer	.05
152	Tom Evans	.05
153	Todd Greene	.05
154	Jay Bell	.05
155	Mike Lowell	.05
156	Orlando Cabrera	.05
157	Troy O'Leary	.05
158	Jose Hernandez	.05
159	Magglio Ordonez	.05
160	Barry Larkin	.05
161	David Justice	.05
162	Derrick Gibson	.05
163	Luis Gonzalez	.05
164	Alex Gonzalez	.05
165	Scott Elarton	.05
166	Dermal Brown	.05
167	Eric Milton	.05
168	Raul Mondesi	.05
169	Jeff Cirillo	.05
170	Benj Sampson	.05
171	John Olerud	.05
172	Andy Pettitte	.20
173	A.J. Hinch	.05
174	Rico Brogna	.05
175	Jason Schmidt	.05
176	Dean Palmer	.05
177	Matt Morris	.05
178	Quinton McCracken	.05
179	Rick Helling	.05
180	Walt Weiss	.05
181	Troy Percival	.05
182	Tony Batista	.05
183	Brian Jordan	.05
184	Jerry Hairston Jr.	.05
185	Bret Saberhagen	.05
186	Mark Grace	.05
187	Brian Simmons	.05
188	Pete Harnisch	.05
189	Kenny Lofton	.05
190	Vinny Castilla	.05
191	Bobby Higginson	.05
192	Joey Hamilton	.05
193	Cliff Floyd	.05
194	Andres Galarraga	.05
195	Chan Ho Park	.05
196	Jeromy Burnitz	.05
197	David Ortiz	.35
198	Wilton Guerrero	.05
199	Rey Ordonez	.05
200	Paul O'Neill	.05
201	Kenny Rogers	.05
202	Marlon Anderson	.05
203	Tony Womack	.05
204	Robin Ventura	.05
205	Russ Ortiz	.05
206	Mike Frank	.05
207	Fernando Tatis	.05
208	Miguel Cairo	.05
209	Ivan Rodriguez	.65
210	Carlos Delgado	.50
211	Tim Salmon	.15
212	Brian Anderson	.05
213	Ryan Klesko	.05
214	Scott Erickson	.05
215	Mike Stanley	.05
216	Brant Brown	.05
217	Rod Beck	.05
218	Guillermo Garcia RC	.05
219	David Wells	.05
220	Dante Bichette	.05

221	Armando Benitez	.05
222	Todd Dunwoody	.05
223	Kelvim Escobar	.05
224	Richard Hidalgo	.05
225	Angel Pena	.05
226	Ronnie Belliard	.05
227	Brad Radke	.05
228	Brad Fullmer	.05
229	Jay Payton	.05
230	Tino Martinez	.05
231	Scott Spiezio	.05
232	Bobby Abreu	.05
233	John Valentin	.05
234	Kevin Young	.05
235	Steve Finley	.05
236	David Cone	.05
237	Armando Rios	.05
238	Russ Davis	.05
239	Wade Boggs	1.00
240	Aaron Sele	.05
241	Jose Cruz Jr.	.15
242	George Lombard	.05
243	Todd Helton	.65
244	Andruw Jones	.75
245	Troy Glaus	.65
246	Manny Ramirez	.75
247	Ben Grieve	.15
247p	Ben Grieve ("PROMOTIONAL SAMPLE")	1.00
248	Richie Sexson	.15
249	Juan Encarnacion	.15
250	Randy Johnson	.75
251	Gary Sheffield	.45
252	Rafael Palmeiro	.15
253	Roy Halladay	.15
254	Mike Piazza	1.50
255	Tony Gwynn	1.00
256	Juan Gonzalez	.40
257	Jeremy Giambi	.15
258	Ben Davis	.15
259	Russ Branyan	.15
260	Pedro Martinez	.75
261	Frank Thomas	1.00
262	Calvin Pickering	.15
263	Chipper Jones	1.00
264	Ryan Minor	.15
265	Roger Clemens	1.25
266	Sammy Sosa	1.00
267	Mo Vaughn	.15
268	Carlos Beltran	.50
269	Jim Thome	.65
270	Mark McGwire	2.00
271	Travis Lee	.15
272	Darin Erstad	.30
273	Derek Jeter	2.50
274	Greg Maddux	1.00
275	Ricky Ledee	.15
276	Alex Rodriguez	2.00
277	Vladimir Guerrero	.75
278	Greg Vaughn	.15
279	Scott Rolen	.60
280	Carlos Guillen	.15
281	Jeff Bagwell	.75
282	Bruce Chen	.15
283	Tony Clark	.15
284	Albert Belle	.05
285	Cal Ripken Jr.	2.50
286	Barry Bonds	2.50
287	Curt Schilling	.35
288	Eric Chavez	.30
289	Larry Walker	.15
290	Orlando Hernandez	.15
291	Moises Alou	.15
292	Ken Griffey Jr.	1.50
293	Kerry Wood	.50
294	Nomar Garciaparra	1.00
295	Gabe Kapler	.15
296	Bernie Williams	.05
297	Matt Anderson	.05
298	Adrian Beltre	.35
299	J.D. Drew	.40
300	Ryan Bradley	.15
---	Checklist 1-230	.05
---	Checklist 231-300 and Inserts	.05
---	Video Game Sweepstakes Form (Derek Jeter)	.05

Dial 1

Designed to look like a mobile phone, this insert set features 10 cards of long distance hitters. The format consists of black plastic cards with rounded corners.

	NM/M
Complete Set (10):	70.00

Rant

A retail-only parallel of the 300-card base set, Rant substitutes purple metallic foil highlights for the regular-issue's silver on front, and a has a "RANT" notation at upper-right on back, also in purple. The stated insertion rate for the parallel is one per two retail packs.

		NM/M
Common Player:		.50
Rant Stars:		8X

Todd Helton Autograph

An unknown number of Helton's regular card (#243) were autographed and received an embossed seal of authenticity for use in various promotional endeavors.

		NM/M
243	Todd Helton	15.00

Hip-No-Tized

This insert set consisted of 15 cards, featuring both hitters and pitchers. The cards were seeded one card in every 36 packs, and consist of mesmerizing patterned holo-foil stamping.

		NM/M
Complete Set (15):		20.00
Common Player:		1.25
Inserted 1:36		
1H	J.D. Drew	1.25
2H	Nomar Garciaparra	2.00
3H	Juan Gonzalez	1.25
4H	Ken Griffey Jr.	2.50
5H	Derek Jeter	3.00
6H	Randy Johnson	1.50
7H	Chipper Jones	2.00
8H	Mark McGwire	3.00

9H	Mike Piazza	2.50
10H	Cal Ripken Jr.	4.00
11H	Alex Rodriguez	3.00
12H	Sammy Sosa	2.00
13H	Frank Thomas	1.50
14H	Jim Thome	1.25
15H	Kerry Wood	1.25

In Depth

This insert set consists of 10 cards, featuring baseball's elite players. The cards are highlighted with gold rainbow holo-foil and gold metallic ink. The insertion rate for this insert was one card in every 24 packs.

		NM/M
Complete Set (10):		17.50
Common Player:		1.00
Inserted 1:24		
1ID	Albert Belle	1.00
2ID	Barry Bonds	5.00
3ID	Roger Clemens	1.50
4ID	Juan Gonzalez	1.25
5ID	Ken Griffey Jr.	3.00
6ID	Mark McGwire	4.00
7ID	Mike Piazza	3.00
8ID	Sammy Sosa	2.50
9ID	Mo Vaughn	1.00
10ID	Kerry Wood	1.25

Turbo Charged

This 10-card insert set consisted of the top home run hitters. The players were featured on plastic see-through cards with rainbow holofoil.

		NM/M
Complete Set (10):		35.00
Common Player:		2.00
Inserted 1:72		
1TC	Jose Canseco	2.50
2TC	Juan Gonzalez	2.00
3TC	Ken Griffey Jr.	5.00
4TC	Vladimir Guerrero	3.00
5TC	Mark McGwire	6.00
6TC	Mike Piazza	5.00
7TC	Manny Ramirez	3.00
8TC	Alex Rodriguez	6.00
9TC	Sammy Sosa	4.00
10TC	Mo Vaughn	2.00

Unleashed

This insert set contained 15 cards designed to resemble a cereal box. The players featured included the best young talent in baseball. The cards were silver-foil stamped,

Common Player: 2.50
Inserted 1:300
1D	Nomar Garciaparra	7.50
2D	Juan Gonzalez	3.40
3D	Ken Griffey Jr.	10.00
4D	Chipper Jones	7.50
5D	Mark McGwire	12.50
6D	Mike Piazza	10.00
7D	Manny Ramirez	6.00
8D	Alex Rodriguez	12.50
9D	Sammy Sosa	7.50
10D	Mo Vaughn	2.50

and offered facsimile signatures of each player. One card was included with every six packs.

		NM/M
Complete Set (15):		10.00
Common Player:		.50
Inserted 1:6		
1U	Carlos Beltran	1.50
2U	Adrian Beltre	1.00
3U	Eric Chavez	.75
4U	J.D. Drew	1.00
5U	Juan Encarnacion	.50
6U	Jeremy Giambi	.50
7U	Troy Glaus	2.00
8U	Ben Grieve	.50
9U	Todd Helton	2.00
10U	Orlando Hernandez	.50
11U	Gabe Kapler	.50
12U	Travis Lee	.50
13U	Calvin Pickering	.50
14U	Richie Sexson	.50
15U	Kerry Wood	1.00

www.Batterz.com

www.batterz.com is a 10-card insert set that was seeded one card per every 18 packs. The game's best hitters are in their own home site in this computer-inspired set.

		NM/M
Complete Set (10):		12.00
Common Player:		.50
Inserted 1:18		
1WB	J.D. Drew	.60
2WB	Nomar Garciaparra	1.00
3WB	Ken Griffey Jr.	1.50
4WB	Tony Gwynn	1.00
5WB	Derek Jeter	3.00
6WB	Mark McGwire	2.00
7WB	Alex Rodriguez	2.00
8WB	Scott Rolen	.65
9WB	Sammy Sosa	1.00
10WB	Bernie Williams	.50

2000 SkyBox National Covention Promos

Six-card cello packs of specially marked (printed logo in top corner) cards were distributed at the 2000 National Sports Collectors Convention in Anaheim, Calif., to promote Fleer's SkyBox brand. Cards are numbered "X of 6" on back.

		NM/M
Complete Set (6):		8.00
Common Player:		1.25
1	Cal Ripken Jr.	2.00
2	Ken Griffey Jr.	1.25
3	Derek Jeter	2.00
4	Alex Rodriguez	1.50
5	Mark McGwire	1.50
6	Mike Piazza	1.25

2000 SkyBox

		NM/M
Complete Set (250):		25.00
Comp. Set w/SPs (300):		60.00
Common Player:		.10
Common SP (201-240):		.10
Inserted 1:8		
Common SP (241-250):		.50
Inserted 1:12		
Pack (10):		1.50
Wax Box (24):		30.00
1	Cal Ripken Jr.	2.00

2	Ivan Rodriguez	.65
3	Chipper Jones	1.00
4	Dean Palmer	.10
5	Devon White	.10
6	Ugueth Urbina	.10
7	Doug Glanville	.10
8	Damian Jackson	.10
9	Jose Canseco	.40
10	Billy Koch	.10
11	Brady Anderson	.10
12	Vladimir Guerrero	.75
13	Dan Wilson	.10
14	Kevin Brown	.10
15	Eddie Taubensee	.10
16	Jose Lima	.10
17	Greg Maddux	1.00
18	Manny Ramirez	.75
19	Brad Fullmer	.10
20	Ron Gant	.10
21	Edgar Martinez	.10
22	Pokey Reese	.10
23	Jason Varitek	.25
24	Neifi Perez	.10
25	Shane Reynolds	.10
26	Robin Ventura	.10
27	Scott Rolen	.65
28	Trevor Hoffman	.10
29	John Valentin	.10
30	Shannon Stewart	.10
31	Troy Glaus	.75
32	Kerry Wood	.65
33	Jim Thome	.65
34	Rafael Roque	.10
35	Tino Martinez	.10
36	Jeffrey Hammonds	.10
37	Orlando Hernandez	.10
38	Kris Benson	.10
39	Fred McGriff	.10
40	Brian Jordan	.10
41	Trot Nixon	.10
42	Matt Clement	.10
43	Ray Durham	.10
44	Johnny Damon	.30
45	Todd Hollandsworth	.10
46	Edgardo Alfonzo	.10
47	Tim Hudson	.25
48	Tony Gwynn	1.00
49	Barry Bonds	2.00
50	Andruw Jones	.75
51	Pedro Martinez	.75
52	Mike Hampton	.10
53	Miguel Tejada	.25
54	Kevin Young	.10
55	J.T. Snow	.10
56	Carlos Delgado	.50
57	Bobby Howry	.10
58	Andres Galarraga	.10
59	Paul Konerko	.20
60	Mike Cameron	.10
61	Jeremy Giambi	.10
62	Todd Hundley	.10
63	Al Leiter	.10
64	Matt Stairs	.10
65	Edgar Renteria	.10
66	Jeff Kent	.10
67	John Wetteland	.10
68	Nomar Garciaparra	1.25
69	Jeff Weaver	.10
70	Matt Williams	.10
71	Kyle Farnsworth	.10
72	Brad Radke	.10
73	Eric Chavez	.25
74	J.D. Drew	.25
75	Steve Finley	.10
76	Pete Harnisch	.10
77	Chad Kreuter	.10
78	Todd Pratt	.10
79	John Jaha	.10
80	Armando Rios	.10
81	Luis Gonzalez	.25
82	Ryan Minor	.10
83	Juan Gonzalez	.75
84	Rickey Henderson	.25
85	Jason Giambi	.50
86	Shawn Estes	.10
87	Chad Curtis	.10
88	Jeff Cirillo	.10
89	Juan Encarnacion	.10
90	Tony Womack	.10
91	Mike Mussina	.35
92	Jeff Bagwell	.75
93	Rey Ordonez	.10
94	Joe McEwing	.10
95	Robb Nen	.10
96	Will Clark	.10
97	Chris Singleton	.10
98	Jason Kendall	.10
99	Ken Griffey Jr.	1.25

100	Rusty Greer	.10
101	Charles Johnson	.10
102	Carlos Lee	.10
103	Brad Ausmus	.10
104	Preston Wilson	.10
105	Ronnie Belliard	.10
106	Mike Lieberthal	.10
107	Alex Rodriguez	1.50
108	Jay Bell	.10
109	Frank Thomas	.75
110	Adrian Beltre	.30
111	Ron Coomer	.10
112	Ben Grieve	.10
113	Darryl Kile	.10
114	Erubiel Durazo	.10
115	Magglio Ordonez	.10
116	Gary Sheffield	.40
117	Joe Mays	.10
118	Fernando Tatis	.10
119	David Wells	.10
120	Tim Salmon	.20
121	Troy O'Leary	.10
122	Roberto Alomar	.40
123	Damion Easley	.10
124	Brant Brown	.10
125	Carlos Beltran	.45
126	Eric Karros	.10
127	Geoff Jenkins	.10
128	Roger Clemens	1.00
129	Warren Morris	.10
130	Eric Owens	.10
131	Jose Cruz Jr.	.10
132	Mo Vaughn	.10
133	Eric Young	.10
134	Kenny Lofton	.10
135	Marquis Grissom	.10
136	A.J. Burnett	.10
137	Bernie Williams	.25
138	Javy Lopez	.10
139	Jose Offerman	.10
140	Sean Casey	.25
141	Alex Gonzalez	.10
142	Carlos Febles	.10
143	Mike Piazza	1.25
144	Curt Schilling	.35
145	Ben Davis	.10
146	Rafael Palmeiro	.65
147	Scott Williamson	.10
148	Darin Erstad	.25
149	Joe Girardi	.10
150	Gerald Williams	.10
151	Richie Sexson	.10
152	Corey Koskie	.10
153	Paul O'Neill	.10
154	Chad Hermansen	.10
155	Randy Johnson	.75
156	Henry Rodriguez	.10
157	Bartolo Colon	.10
158	Tony Clark	.10
159	Mike Lowell	.10
160	Moises Alou	.10
161	Todd Walker	.10
162	Mariano Rivera	.20
163	Mark McGwire	1.50
164	Roberto Hernandez	.10
165	Larry Walker	.10
166	Albert Belle	.15
167	Barry Larkin	.10
168	Rolando Arrojo	.10
169	Mark Kotsay	.10
170	Ken Caminiti	.10
171	Dermal Brown	.10
172	Michael Barrett	.10
173	Jay Buhner	.10
174	Ruben Mateo	.10
175	Jim Edmonds	.10
176	Sammy Sosa	1.25
177	Omar Vizquel	.10
178	Todd Helton	.75
179	Kevin Barker	.10
180	Derek Jeter	2.00
181	Brian Giles	.10
182	Greg Vaughn	.10
183	Roy Halladay	.10
184	Tom Glavine	.35
185	Craig Biggio	.10
186	Jose Vidro	.10
187	Andy Ashby	.10
188	Freddy Garcia	.10
189	Garret Anderson	.10
190	Mark Grace	.20
191	Travis Fryman	.10
192	Jeromy Burnitz	.10
193	Jacque Jones	.10
194	David Cone	.10
195	Ryan Rupe	.10
196	John Smoltz	.10
197	Daryle Ward	.10
198	Rondell White	.10
199	Bobby Abreu	.10
200	Justin Thompson	.10
201	Norm Hutchins (Prospect)	.10
201	Norm Hutchins/SP	1.00
202	Ramon Ortiz (Prospect)	.10
202	Ramon Ortiz/SP	1.00
203	Dan Wheeler (Prospect)	.10
203	Dan Wheeler/SP	1.00
204	Matt Riley (Prospect)	.10
204	Matt Riley/SP	1.00
205	Steve Lomasney (Prospect)	.10
205	Steve Lomasney/SP	1.00
206	Chad Meyers (Prospect)	.10
206	Chad Meyers/SP	1.00
207	Gary Glover RC (Prospect)	.20
207	Gary Glover/SP	1.00
208	Joe Crede (Prospect)	.10
208	Joe Crede/SP	1.00

209	Kip Wells (Prospect)	.10
209	Kip Wells/SP	1.00
210	Travis Dawkins (Prospect)	.10
210	Travis Dawkins/SP	1.00
211	Denny Stark RC (Prospect)	.20
211	Denny Stark/SP	1.00
212	Ben Petrick (Prospect)	.10
212	Ben Petrick/SP	1.00
213	Eric Munson (Prospect)	.10
213	Eric Munson/SP	1.00
214	Josh Beckett (Prospect)	.25
214	Josh Beckett/SP	1.50
215	Pablo Ozuna (Prospect)	.10
215	Pablo Ozuna/SP	1.00
216	Brad Penny (Prospect)	.10
216	Brad Penny/SP	1.00
217	Julio Ramirez (Prospect)	.10
217	Julio Ramirez/SP	1.00
218	Danny Peoples (Prospect)	.10
218	Danny Peoples/SP	1.00
219	Wilfredo Rodriguez RC (Prospect)	.10
219	Wilfredo Rodriguez/ SP RC	1.00
220	Julio Lugo (Prospect)	.10
220	Julio Lugo/SP	1.00
221	Mark Quinn (Prospect)	.10
221	Mark Quinn/SP	1.00
222	Eric Gagne (Prospect)	.10
222	Eric Gagne/SP	1.00
223	Chad Green (Prospect)	.10
223	Chad Green/SP	1.00
224	Tony Armas Jr. (Prospect)	.10
224	Tony Armas Jr/SP	1.00
225	Milton Bradley (Prospect)	.10
225	Milton Bradley/SP	1.00
226	Rob Bell (Prospect)	.10
226	Rob Bell/SP	1.00
227	Alfonso Soriano (Prospect)	1.00
227	Alfonso Soriano/SP	4.00
228	Wily Pena (Prospect)	.10
228	Wily Pena/SP	1.00
229	Nick Johnson (Prospect)	.10
229	Nick Johnson/SP	1.50
230	Ed Yarnall (Prospect)	.10
230	Ed Yarnall/SP	1.00
231	Ryan Bradley (Prospect)	.10
231	Ryan Bradley/SP	1.00
232	Adam Piatt (Prospect)	.10
232	Adam Piatt/SP	1.00
233	Chad Harville (Prospect)	.10
233	Chad Harville/SP	1.00
234	Alex Sanchez (Prospect)	.10
234	Alex Sanchez/SP	1.00
235	Michael Coleman (Prospect)	.10
235	Michael Coleman/SP	1.00
236	Pat Burrell (Prospect)	.25
236	Pat Burrell/SP	1.50
237	Wascar Serrano RC (Prospect)	.10
237	Wascar Serrano/SP RC	1.00
238	Rick Ankiel (Prospect)	.25
238	Rick Ankiel/SP	1.00
239	Mike Lamb RC (Prospect)	.10
239	Mike Lamb/SP RC	1.00
240	Vernon Wells (Prospect)	.10
240	Vernon Wells/SP	1.00
241	Jorge Toca, Goefrey Tomlinson (Premium Pairs)	.10
241	Jorge Toca, Goefrey Tomlinson/SP	.50
242	Shea Hillenbrand, Josh Phelps RC (Premium Pairs)	2.00
242	Shea Hillenbrand, Josh Phelps/SP RC	4.00
243	Aaron Myette, Doug Davis (Premium Pairs)	.10
243	Aaron Myette, Doug Davis/SP	.50
244	Brett Laxton, Robert Ramsay (Premium Pairs)	.10
244	Brett Laxton, Robert Ramsay/SP	.50
245	B.J. Ryan, Corey Lee (Premium Pairs)	.10
245	B.J. Ryan, Corey Lee/SP	.50
246	Chris Haas, Wilton Veras (Premium Pairs)	.10
246	Chris Haas, Wilton Veras/SP	.50
247	Jimmy Anderson, Kyle Peterson (Premium Pairs)	.10
247	Jimmy Anderson, Kyle Peterson/SP	.50
248	Jason Dewey, Giuseppe Chiaramonte (Premium Pairs)	.10
248	Jason Dewey, Giuseppe Chiaramonte/SP	.50
249	Guillermo Mota, Orber Moreno (Premium Pairs)	.10
249	Guillermo Mota, Orber Moreno/SP	1.00
250	Steve Cox, Julio Zuleta RC (Premium Pairs)	.15
250	Steve Cox, Julio Zuleta/SP RC	.50

Star Rubies

This parallel of the 250-card SkyBox base set shares the same format and photos. On front, however, the player identification and SkyBox logo are in red foil. On back, an SR has been added beneath the card number. Insertion rate was one per 12 packs.

	NM/M
Complete Set (250):	200.00
Common Player (1-200):	.50
Common SP Prospect (201-250):	3.00
Stars:	6X
Star SP's:	3X

Star Rubies Extreme

This parallel of the 250-card SkyBox base set shares the same format and photos. On front, however, the player identification and SkyBox logo are in red foil, and the metallic-foil background has an optical variable layer of stars. On back, an SRE has been added beneath the card number, as well as a strip with a red-foil serial number from within an edition of 50 cards each.

	NM/M
Common Player (1-200):	3.00
Common SP Prospect (201-250):	4.50
Stars:	25X
Star SP's:	15X

Autographics

	NM/M
Common Player:	5.00
Rick Ankiel	15.00
Michael Barrett	5.00
Josh Beckett	25.00
Rob Bell	5.00
Adrian Beltre	15.00
Peter Bergeron	5.00
Lance Berkman	20.00
Rico Brogna	5.00
Pat Burrell	20.00
Orlando Cabrera	15.00
Mike Cameron	8.00
Roger Cedeno	5.00
Eric Chavez	15.00
Bruce Chen	5.00
Johnny Damon	20.00
Ben Davis	5.00
Jason Dewey	5.00
Octavio Dotel	6.00
J.D. Drew	15.00
Erubiel Durazo	15.00
Jason Giambi	20.00
Doug Glanville	5.00
Troy Glaus	20.00
Alex Gonzalez	8.00
Shawn Green	15.00
Jason Grilli	5.00
Tony Gwynn	40.00
Mike Hampton	8.00
Tim Hudson	15.00
Norm Hutchins	5.00
John Jaha	5.00
Derek Jeter	100.00
D'Angelo Jimenez	5.00
Randy Johnson	60.00
Andruw Jones	20.00

Gabe Kapler	8.00
Jason Kendall	10.00
Adam Kennedy	8.00
Cesar King	5.00
Paul Konerko	8.00
Mark Kotsay	6.00
Carlos Lee	8.00
Mike Lieberthal	8.00
Steve Lomasney	5.00
Greg Maddux	60.00
Edgar Martinez	15.00
Aaron McNeal	5.00
Kevin Millwood	10.00
Raul Mondesi	8.00
Joe Nathan	5.00
Magglio Ordonez	15.00
Eric Owens	5.00
Rafael Palmeiro	25.00
Angel Pena	5.00
Wily Pena	15.00
Cal Ripken Jr.	85.00
Scott Rolen	20.00
Jimmy Rollins	15.00
B.J. Ryan	5.00
Tim Salmon	10.00
Chris Singleton	5.00
J.T. Snow	6.00
Mike Sweeney	8.00
Jose Vidro	8.00
Rondell White	8.00
Jaret Wright	5.00

E-Ticket

		NM/M
Complete Set (14):		15.00
Common Player:		.50
Inserted 1:4		
Star Ruby:		4-8X
Production 100 Sets		
1	Alex Rodriguez	2.50
2	Derek Jeter	3.00
3	Nomar Garciaparra	1.50
4	Cal Ripken Jr.	3.00
5	Sean Casey	.50
6	Mark McGwire	2.50
7	Sammy Sosa	1.50
8	Ken Griffey Jr.	2.00
9	Tony Gwynn	1.50
10	Pedro Martinez	1.50
11	Chipper Jones	1.50
12	Vladimir Guerrero	1.00
13	Roger Clemens	1.75
14	Mike Piazza	2.00

Genuine Coverage

		NM/M
Common Player:		8.00
Inserted 1:399		
1	Troy Glaus	15.00
2	Cal Ripken Jr.	40.00
3	Alex Rodriguez	25.00
4	Mike Mussina	10.00
5	J.D. Drew	8.00
6	Robin Ventura	8.00
7	Matt Williams	8.00

Genuine Coverage HOBBY

		NM/M
Common Player:		10.00
Inserted 1:144		
1	Ivan Rodriguez	12.00
2	Jose Canseco	10.00
3	Frank Thomas	15.00
4	Manny Ramirez	15.00

Higher Level

		NM/M
Complete Set (10):		20.00
Common Player:		1.00
Inserted 1:24		
Star Ruby:		5-10X
Production 50 Sets		
1	Cal Ripken Jr.	4.00
2	Derek Jeter	4.00
3	Nomar Garciaparra	2.00
4	Chipper Jones	2.00

Higher Level

#	Player	NM/M
5	Mike Piazza	2.50
6	Ivan Rodriguez	1.00
7	Ken Griffey Jr.	2.50
8	Sammy Sosa	2.00
9	Alex Rodriguez	3.00
10	Mark McGwire	3.00

Preeminence

		NM/M
Complete Set (10):		15.00
Common Player:		.50
Inserted 1:24		
Star Ruby:		5-10X
Production 50 Sets		
1	Pedro Martinez	1.25
2	Derek Jeter	4.00
3	Nomar Garciaparra	1.50
4	Alex Rodriguez	3.00
5	Mark McGwire	3.00
6	Sammy Sosa	1.50
7	Sean Casey	.50
8	Mike Piazza	2.00
9	Chipper Jones	1.50
10	Ivan Rodriguez	1.00

SkyLines

		NM/M
Complete Set (10):		10.00
Common Player:		.50
Inserted 1:11		
Star Ruby:		10-20X
Production 50 Sets		
1	Cal Ripken Jr.	2.00
2	Mark McGwire	1.50
3	Alex Rodriguez	1.50
4	Sammy Sosa	.75
5	Derek Jeter	2.00
6	Mike Piazza	1.00
7	Nomar Garciaparra	.75
8	Chipper Jones	.75
9	Ken Griffey Jr.	1.00
10	Manny Ramirez	.50

Speed Merchants

		NM/M
Complete Set (10):		12.00
Common Player:		.50
Inserted 1:8		
Star Ruby:		3-6X
Production 100 Sets		
1	Derek Jeter	3.00
2	Sammy Sosa	1.25
3	Nomar Garciaparra	1.25
4	Alex Rodriguez	2.50
5	Randy Johnson	1.00
6	Ken Griffey Jr.	1.50
7	Pedro Martinez	1.00
8	Pat Burrell	.50
9	Barry Bonds	3.00
10	Mark McGwire	2.50

The Technique

		NM/M
Complete Set (15):		20.00
Common Player:		.50
Inserted 1:11		
Star Ruby:		3-6X
Production 50 Sets		
1	Alex Rodriguez	3.00
2	Tony Gwynn	1.50
3	Sean Casey	.50
4	Mark McGwire	3.00
5	Sammy Sosa	1.50
6	Ken Griffey Jr.	2.00
7	Mike Piazza	2.00
8	Nomar Garciaparra	1.50
9	Derek Jeter	4.00
10	Vladimir Guerrero	1.00
11	Cal Ripken Jr.	4.00
12	Chipper Jones	1.50
13	Frank Thomas	1.00
14	Manny Ramirez	1.00
15	Jeff Bagwell	1.00

2000 SkyBox Dominion

#	Player	NM/M
Complete Set (300):		20.00
Common Player:		.10
Pack (10):		1.50
Wax Box (36):		30.00
1	Mark McGwire, Ken Griffey Jr. (League Leaders)	.40
2	Mark McGwire, Manny Ramirez (League Leaders)	.40
3	Larry Walker, Nomar Garciaparra (League Leaders)	.25
4	Tony Womack, Brian Hunter (League Leaders)	.10
5	Mike Hampton, Pedro Martinez (League Leaders)	.20
6	Randy Johnson, Pedro Martinez (League Leaders)	.20
7	Randy Johnson, Pedro Martinez (League Leaders)	.20
8	Ugueth Urbina, Mariano Rivera (League Leaders)	.10
9	Vinny Castilla (Highlights)	.10
10	Orioles host Cuban National Team (Highlights)	.10
11	Jose Canseco (Highlights)	.10
12	Fernando Tatis (Highlights)	.10
13	Robin Ventura (Highlights)	.10
14	Roger Clemens (Highlights)	.50
15	Jose Jimenez (Highlights)	.10
16	David Cone (Highlights)	.10
17	Mark McGwire (Highlights)	.65
18	Cal Ripken Jr. (Highlights)	.75
19	Tony Gwynn (Highlights)	.30
20	Wade Boggs (Highlights)	.25
21	Ivan Rodriguez (Highlights)	.20
22	Chuck Finley (Highlights)	.10
23	Eric Milton (Highlights)	.10
24	Adrian Beltre (Highlights)	.10
25	Brad Radke	.10
26	Derek Bell	.10
27	Garret Anderson	.10
28	Ivan Rodriguez	.40
29	Jeff Kent	.10
30	Jeremy Giambi	.10
31	John Franco	.10
32	Jose Hernandez	.10
33	Jose Offerman	.10
34	Jose Rosado	.10
35	Kevin Appier	.10
36	Kris Benson	.10
37	Mark McGwire	1.00
38	Matt Williams	.10
39	Paul O'Neill	.10
40	Rickey Henderson	.50
41	Todd Greene	.10
42	Russ Ortiz	.10
43	Sean Casey	.20
44	Tony Womack	.10
45	Troy O'Leary	.10
46	Ugueth Urbina	.10
47	Tom Glavine	.25
48	Mike Mussina	.30
49	Carlos Febles	.10
50	Jon Lieber	.10
51	Juan Gonzalez	.30
52	Matt Clement	.10
53	Moises Alou	.10
54	Ray Durham	.10
55	Robb Nen	.10
56	Tino Martinez	.10
57	Troy Glaus	.40
58	Curt Schilling	.15
59	Mike Sweeney	.10
60	Steve Finley	.10
61	Roger Cedeno	.10
62	Bobby Jones	.10
63	John Smoltz	.10
64	Darin Erstad	.25
65	Carlos Delgado	.35
66	Ray Lankford	.10
67	Todd Stottlemyre	.10
68	Andy Ashby	.10
69	Bobby Abreu	.15
70	Chuck Finley	.10
71	Damion Easley	.10
72	Dustin Hermanson	.10
73	Frank Thomas	.50
74	Kevin Brown	.10
75	Kevin Millwood	.10
76	Mark Grace	.10
77	Matt Stairs	.10
78	Mike Hampton	.10
79	Omar Vizquel	.10
80	Preston Wilson	.10
81	Robin Ventura	.10
82	Todd Helton	.40
83	Tony Clark	.10
84	Al Leiter	.10
85	Alex Fernandez	.10
86	Bernie Williams	.10
87	Edgar Martinez	.10
88	Edgar Renteria	.10
89	Fred McGriff	.10
90	Jermaine Dye	.10
91	Joe McEwing	.10
92	John Halama	.10
93	Lee Stevens	.10
94	Matt Lawton	.10
95	Mike Piazza	.75
96	Pete Harnisch	.10
97	Scott Karl	.10
98	Tony Fernandez	.10
99	Sammy Sosa	.60
100	Bobby Higginson	.10
101	Tony Gwynn	.60
102	J.D. Drew	.19
103	Roberto Hernandez	.10
104	Rondell White	.10
105	David Nilsson	.10
106	Shane Reynolds	.10
107	Jaret Wright	.10
108	Jeff Bagwell	.50
109	Jay Bell	.10
110	Kevin Tapani	.10
111	Michael Barrett	.10
112	Neifi Perez	.10
113	Pat Hentgen	.10
114	Roger Clemens	.65
115	Travis Fryman	.10
116	Aaron Sele	.10
117	Eric Davis	.10
118	Trevor Hoffman	.10
119	Chris Singleton	.10
120	Ryan Klesko	.10
121	Scott Rolen	.10
122	Jorge Posada	.10
123	Abraham Nunez	.10
124	Alex Gonzalez	.10
125	B.J. Surhoff	.10
126	Barry Bonds	1.50
127	Billy Koch	.10
128	Billy Wagner	.10
129	Brad Ausmus	.10
130	Bret Boone	.10
131	Cal Ripken Jr.	1.50
132	Chad Allen	.10
133	Chris Carpenter	.10
134	Craig Biggio	.10
135	Dante Bichette	.10
136	Dean Palmer	.10
137	Derek Jeter	1.50
138	Ellis Burks	.10
139	Freddy Garcia	.10
140	Gabe Kapler	.10
141	Greg Maddux	.60
142	Greg Vaughn	.10
143	Jason Kendall	.10
144	Jim Parque	.10
145	John Valentin	.10
146	Jose Vidro	.10
147	Ken Griffey Jr.	.75
148	Kenny Lofton	.10
149	Kenny Rogers	.10
150	Kent Bottenfield	.10
151	Chuck Knoblauch	.10
152	Larry Walker	.10
153	Manny Ramirez	.50
154	Mickey Morandini	.10
155	Mike Cameron	.10
156	Mike Lieberthal	.10
157	Mo Vaughn	.10
158	Randy Johnson	.50
159	Rey Ordonez	.10
160	Roberto Alomar	.20
161	Scott Williamson	.10
162	Shawn Estes	.10
163	Tim Wakefield	.10
164	Tony Batista	.10
165	Will Clark	.10
166	Wade Boggs	.60
167	David Cone	.10
168	Doug Glanville	.10
169	Jeff Cirillo	.10
170	John Jaha	.10
171	Mariano Rivera	.20
172	Tom Gordon	.10
173	Wally Joyner	.10
174	Alex Gonzalez	.10
175	Andruw Jones	.50
176	Barry Larkin	.10
177	Bartolo Colon	.10
178	Brian Giles	.10
179	Carlos Lee	.10
180	Darren Dreifort	.10
181	Eric Chavez	.20
182	Henry Rodriguez	.10
183	Ismael Valdes	.10
184	Jason Giambi	.40
185	John Wetteland	.10
186	Juan Encarnacion	.10
187	Luis Gonzalez	.10
188	Reggie Sanders	.10
189	Richard Hidalgo	.10
190	Ryan Rupe	.10
191	Sean Berry	.10
192	Rick Helling	.10
193	Randy Wolf	.10
194	Cliff Floyd	.10
195	Jose Lima	.10
196	Chipper Jones	.60
197	Charles Johnson	.10
198	Nomar Garciaparra	.60
199	Magglio Ordonez	.10
200	Shawn Green	.25
201	Travis Lee	.10
202	Jose Canseco	.35
203	Fernando Tatis	.10
204	Bruce Aven	.10
205	Johnny Damon	.35
206	Gary Sheffield	.25
207	Ken Caminiti	.10
208	Ben Grieve	.10
209	Sidney Ponson	.10
210	Vinny Castilla	.10
211	Alex Rodriguez	1.00
212	Chris Widger	.10
213	Carl Pavano	.10
214	J.T. Snow	.10
215	Jim Thome	.40
216	Kevin Young	.10
217	Mike Sirotka	.10
218	Rafael Palmeiro	.40
219	Rico Brogna	.10
220	Todd Walker	.10
221	Todd Zelle	.10
222	Brian Rose	.10
223	Chris Fussell	.10
224	Corey Koskie	.10
225	Rich Aurilia	.10
226	Geoff Jenkins	.10
227	Pedro Martinez	.50
228	Todd Hundley	.10
229	Brian Jordan	.10
230	Cristian Guzman	.10
231	Raul Mondesi	.10
232	Tim Hudson	.20
233	Albert Belle	.10
234	Andy Pettitte	.25
235	Brady Anderson	.10
236	Brian Bohannon	.10
237	Carlos Beltran	.35
238	Doug Mientkiewicz	.10
239	Jason Schmidt	.10
240	Jeff Zimmerman	.10
241	John Olerud	.10
242	Paul Byrd	.10
243	Vladimir Guerrero	.50
244	Warren Morris	.10
245	Eric Karros	.10
246	Jeff Weaver	.10
247	Jeromy Burnitz	.10
248	David Bell	.10
249	Rusty Greer	.10
250	Kevin Stocker	.10
251	Shea Hillenbrand (Prospect)	.15
252	Alfonso Soriano (Prospect)	.50
253	Micah Bowie (Prospect)	.10
254	Gary Matthews Jr. (Prospect)	.10
255	Lance Berkman (Prospect)	.10
256	Pat Burrell (Prospect)	.25
257	Ruben Mateo (Prospect)	.10
258	Kip Wells (Prospect)	.10
259	Wilton Veras (Prospect)	.10
260	Ben Davis (Prospect)	.10
261	Eric Munson (Prospect)	.10
262	Ramon Hernandez (Prospect)	.10
263	Tony Armas Jr. (Prospect)	.10
264	Erubiel Durazo (Prospect)	.10
265	Chad Meyers (Prospect)	.10
266	Rick Ankiel (Prospect)	.10
267	Ramon Ortiz (Prospect)	.10
268	Adam Kennedy (Prospect)	.10
269	Vernon Wells (Prospect)	.10
270	Chad Hermansen (Prospect)	.10
271	Norm Hutchins, Trent Durrington (Prospects)	.10
272	Gabe Molina, B.J. Ryan (Prospects)	.10
273	Juan Pena, Tomokazu Ohka RC (Prospects)	.25
274	Pat Daneker, Aaron Myette (Prospects)	.15
275	Jason Rakers, Russell Branyan (Prospects)	.10
276	Beiker Graterol, Dave Borkowski (Prospects)	.10
277	Mark Quinn, Dan Reichert (Prospects)	.15
278	Mark Redman, Jacque Jones (Prospects)	.15
279	Ed Yarnall, Wily Pena (Prospects)	.10
280	Chad Harville, Brett Laxton (Prospects)	.10
281	Aaron Scheffer, Gil Meche (Prospects)	.10
282	Jim Morris, Dan Wheeler (Prospects)	.10
283	Danny Kolb, Kelly Dransfeldt (Prospects)	.10
284	Peter Munro, Casey Blake (Prospects)	.10
285	Rob Ryan, Byung-Hyun Kim (Prospects)	.10
286	Derrin Ebert, Pascual Matos (Prospects)	.10
287	Richard Barker, Kyle Farnsworth (Prospects)	.10
288	Jason LaRue, Travis Dawkins (Prospects)	.10
289	Chris Sexton, Edgard Clemente (Prospects)	.10
290	Amaury Garcia, A.J. Burnett (Prospects)	.10
291	Carlos Hernandez, Daryle Ward (Prospects)	.10
292	Eric Gagne, Jeff Williams (Prospects)	.10
293	Kyle Peterson, Kevin Barker (Prospects)	.10
294	Fernando Seguignol, Guillermo Mota (Prospects)	.10
295	Melvin Mora, Octavio Dotel (Prospects)	.10
296	Anthony Shumaker, Cliff Politte (Prospects)	.10
297	Yamid Haad, Jimmy Anderson (Prospects)	.10
298	Rick Heiserman, Chad Hutchinson (Prospects)	.10
299	Mike Darr, Wiki Gonzalez (Prospects)	.10
300	Joe Nathan, Calvin Murray (Prospects)	.10

Autographics

		NM/M
Common Player:		5.00
Inserted 1:144		
1	Rick Ankiel	15.00
2	Peter Bergeron	5.00
3	Wade Boggs	25.00
4	Barry Bonds	200.00
5	Pat Burrell	20.00
6	Miguel Cairo	5.00
7	Mike Cameron	8.00
8	Ben Davis	5.00
9	Russ Davis	5.00
10	Einar Diaz	5.00
11	Scott Elarton	5.00
12	Jeremy Giambi	5.00
13	Todd Greene	5.00
14	Vladimir Guerrero	25.00
15	Tony Gwynn	30.00
16	Bobby Howry	5.00
17	Tim Hudson	15.00
18	Randy Johnson	50.00
19	Andruw Jones	20.00
20	Jacque Jones	8.00
21	Jason LaRue	5.00
22	Matt Lawton	6.00
23	Greg Maddux	50.00
24	Pedro Martinez	50.00
25	Pokey Reese	5.00
26	Alex Rodriguez	75.00
27	Ryan Rupe	5.00
28	J.T. Snow	6.00
29	Jose Vidro	6.00
30	Tony Womack	5.00
31	Ed Yarnall	5.00
32	Kevin Young	5.00

Double Play

		NM/M
Complete Set (10):		10.00
Common Player:		1.00
Inserted 1:9		
Plus:		2-4X
Inserted 1:90		
WarpTek:		10-20X
Inserted 1:900		
1	Nomar Garciaparra	1.50
2	Pedro Martinez	1.25
3	Chipper Jones	1.50
4	Mark McGwire	2.50
5	Cal Ripken Jr.	3.00
6	Roger Clemens	1.75
7	Juan Gonzalez	1.00
8	Tony Gwynn	1.50
9	Sammy Sosa	1.50
10	Mike Piazza	2.00

Eye on October

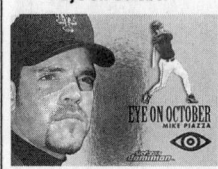

		NM/M
Complete Set (15):		25.00
Common Player:		1.00
Inserted 1:24		
Plus:		2-4X
Inserted 1:240		
1	Ken Griffey Jr.	2.50
2	Mark McGwire	3.00
3	Derek Jeter	4.00
4	Juan Gonzalez	1.00
5	Chipper Jones	2.00
6	Sammy Sosa	2.00
7	Greg Maddux	2.00
8	Frank Thomas	1.50
9	Nomar Garciaparra	2.00
10	Shawn Green	1.00
11	Cal Ripken Jr.	4.00
12	Manny Ramirez	1.50
13	Scott Rolen	1.25
14	Mike Piazza	2.50
15	Alex Rodriguez	3.00

Hats Off

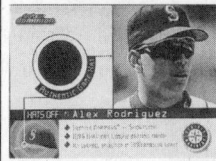

		NM/M
Common Player:		15.00
Inserted 1:468 H		
1	Wade Boggs	25.00
2	Barry Bonds	75.00
3	J.D. Drew	15.00
4	Shawn Green	15.00
5	Vladimir Guerrero	25.00
6	Randy Johnson	30.00
7	Andruw Jones	20.00
8	Greg Maddux	40.00
9	Pedro Martinez	25.00
10	Mike Mussina	15.00
11	Rafael Palmeiro	20.00
12	Alex Rodriguez	50.00
13	Scott Rolen	15.00
14	Tim Salmon	15.00
15	Robin Ventura	15.00

Milestones

		NM/M
Common Player:		15.00
Inserted 1:1,999		
1	Mark McGwire	60.00
2	Roger Clemens	40.00
3	Tony Gwynn	25.00
4	Wade Boggs	25.00
5	Cal Ripken Jr.	75.00
6	Jose Canseco	15.00

New Era

	NM/M
Complete Set (20):	5.00
Common Player:	.25

Inserted 1:3
Plus: 2-4X
Inserted 1:30
WarpTek: 5-10X
Inserted 1:300

1	Pat Burrell	.75
2	Ruben Mateo	.25
3	Wilton Veras	.25
4	Eric Munson	.25
5	Jeff Weaver	.25
6	Tim Hudson	.50
7	Carlos Beltran	1.00
8	Chris Singleton	.25
9	Lance Berkman	.25
10	Freddy Garcia	.25
11	Erubiel Durazo	.25
12	Randy Wolf	.25
13	Shea Hillenbrand	.25
14	Kip Wells	.25
15	Alfonso Soriano	1.50
16	Rick Ankiel	.25
17	Ramon Ortiz	.25
18	Adam Kennedy	.25
19	Vernon Wells	.25
20	Chad Hermansen	.25

2000 E-X

Released as a 90-card set the card fronts have a holo-foil card front, with the E-X logo and player name stamped in silver foil. Card backs have a player image, 1999 stats and the featured player's career totals.

		NM/M
Complete Set (90):		80.00
Common Player:		.25
Common Prospect (61-90):		3.00
Production 3,499 Sets		
Pack:		2.75
Box:		50.00
1	Alex Rodriguez	2.50
2	Jeff Bagwell	1.00
3	Mike Piazza	2.00
4	Tony Gwynn	1.50
5	Ken Griffey Jr.	2.00
6	Juan Gonzalez	.40
7	Vladimir Guerrero	1.00
8	Cal Ripken Jr.	3.00
9	Mo Vaughn	.25
10	Chipper Jones	1.50
11	Derek Jeter	3.00
12	Nomar Garciaparra	1.50
13	Mark McGwire	2.50
14	Sammy Sosa	1.50
15	Pedro Martinez	1.00
16	Greg Maddux	1.50
17	Frank Thomas	.75
18	Shawn Green	.50
19	Carlos Beltran	.50
20	Roger Clemens	1.75
21	Randy Johnson	1.00
22	Bernie Williams	.25
23	Carlos Delgado	.50
24	Manny Ramirez	.75
25	Freddy Garcia	.25
26	Barry Bonds	3.00
27	Tim Hudson	.40
28	Larry Walker	.25
29	Raul Mondesi	.25
30	Ivan Rodriguez	.65
31	Magglio Ordonez	.25
32	Scott Rolen	.65
33	Mike Mussina	.40
34	J.D. Drew	.40
35	Tom Glavine	.50
36	Barry Larkin	.25
37	Jim Thome	.65
38	Erubiel Durazo	.25
39	Curt Schilling	.50
40	Orlando Hernandez	.50
41	Rafael Palmeiro	.65
42	Gabe Kapler	.25
43	Mark Grace	.25
44	Jeff Cirillo	.25
45	Jeromy Burnitz	.25
46	Sean Casey	.35
47	Kevin Millwood	.25

48	Vinny Castilla	.25
49	Jose Canseco	.50
50	Roberto Alomar	.30
51	Craig Biggio	.25
52	Preston Wilson	.25
53	Jeff Weaver	.25
54	Robin Ventura	.25
55	Ben Grieve	.25
56	Troy Glaus	.65
57	Jacque Jones	.25
58	Brian Giles	.25
59	Kevin Brown	.25
60	Todd Helton	.65
61	Ben Petrick (Prospects)	3.00
62	Chad Hermansen (Prospects)	3.00
63	Kevin Barker (Prospects)	3.00
64	Matt LeCroy (Prospects)	3.00
65	Brad Penny (Prospects)	4.00
66	D.T. Cromer (Prospects)	3.00
67	Steve Lomasney (Prospects)	3.00
68	Cole Liniak (Prospects)	3.00
69	B.J. Ryan (Prospects)	3.00
70	Wilton Veras (Prospects)	3.00
71	Aaron McNeal RC (Prospects)	4.00
72	Nick Johnson (Prospects)	4.00
73	Adam Piatt (Prospects)	3.00
74	Adam Kennedy (Prospects)	3.00
75	Cesar King (Prospects)	3.00
76	Peter Bergeron (Prospects)	3.00
77	Rob Bell (Prospects)	3.00
78	Wily Pena (Prospects)	4.00
79	Ruben Mateo (Prospects)	3.00
80	Kip Wells (Prospects)	3.00
81	Alex Escobar (Prospects)	3.00
82	Danys Baez RC (Prospects)	5.00
83	Travis Dawkins (Prospects)	3.00
84	Mark Quinn (Prospects)	3.00
85	Jimmy Anderson (Prospects)	3.00
86	Rick Ankiel (Prospects)	4.00
87	Alfonso Soriano (Prospects)	5.00
88	Pat Burrell (Prospects)	4.00
89	Eric Munson (Prospects)	3.00
90	Josh Beckett (Prospects)	4.00

Autographics

	NM/M
Common Player:	5.00
Inserted 1:24	

	Bob Abreu	15.00
	Moises Alou	15.00
	Rick Ankiel	20.00
	Michael Barrett	5.00
	Josh Beckett	25.00
	Rob Bell	5.00
	Adrian Beltre	15.00
	Carlos Beltran	15.00
	Wade Boggs	25.00
	Barry Bonds	150.00
	Kent Bottenfield	5.00
	Milton Bradley	10.00
	Pat Burrell	15.00
	Chris Carpenter	20.00
	Sean Casey	8.00
	Eric Chavez	8.00
	Will Clark	25.00
	Johnny Damon	20.00
	Mike Darr	5.00
	Ben Davis	5.00
	Russ Davis	5.00
	Carlos Delgado	20.00
	Jason Dewey	5.00
	Octavio Dotel	5.00
	J.D. Drew	10.00
	Ray Durham	5.00
	Damion Easley	6.00
	Kelvim Escobar	5.00
	Carlos Febles	5.00
	Freddy Garcia	5.00
	Jeremy Giambi	5.00
	Todd Greene	5.00
	Jason Grilli	5.00
	Vladimir Guerrero	30.00
	Tony Gwynn	40.00
	Jerry Hairston Jr.	5.00
	Mike Hampton	8.00
	Todd Helton	20.00
	Trevor Hoffman	10.00

	Tim Hudson	15.00
	John Jaha	5.00
	Derek Jeter	100.00
	D'Angelo Jimenez	5.00
	Randy Johnson	60.00
	Jason Kendall	8.00
	Adam Kennedy	8.00
	Cesar King	5.00
	Paul Konerko	10.00
	Mark Kotsay	6.00
	Ray Lankford	6.00
	Jason LaRue	6.00
	Matt Lawton	8.00
	Carlos Lee	8.00
	Mike Lieberthal	8.00
	Cole Liniak	5.00
	Steve Lomasney	5.00
	Jose Macias	5.00
	Greg Maddux	60.00
	Edgar Martinez	15.00
	Pedro Martinez	60.00
	Ruben Mateo	5.00
	Gary Matthews Jr.	8.00
	Aaron McNeal	5.00
	Raul Mondesi	8.00
	Orber Moreno	5.00
	Warren Morris	5.00
	Eric Munson	5.00
	Heath Murray	5.00
	Mike Mussina	30.00
	Joe Nathan	5.00
	Rafael Palmeiro	25.00
	Jim Parque	6.00
	Angel Pena	8.00
	Wily Pena	8.00
	Pokey Reese	6.00
	Matt Riley	5.00
	Cal Ripken Jr.	85.00
	Alex Rodriguez	75.00
	Scott Rolen	20.00
	Jimmy Rollins	20.00
	B.J. Ryan	5.00
	Randall Simon	5.00
	Chris Singleton	5.00
	Alfonso Soriano	30.00
	Shannon Stewart	8.00
	Mike Sweeney	8.00
	Miguel Tejada	20.00
	Frank Thomas	25.00
	Wilton Veras	5.00
	Billy Wagner	8.00
	Jeff Weaver	5.00
	Rondell White	8.00
	Scott Williamson	8.00
	Randy Wolf	5.00
	Jaret Wright	5.00
	Ed Yarnall	5.00
	Kevin Young	5.00

Essential Credentials Future

Production varied for these parallel inserts depending on the card number, with the exact production number for cards 1-60 determined by subtracting the card number from 61. Cards 61-90 are determined by subtracting the card number from 91. Quantity issued is listed in paranthesis.

		NM/M
Common Player:		10.00
1	Alex Rodriguez/60	75.00
2	Jeff Bagwell/59	30.00
3	Mike Piazza/58	50.00
4	Tony Gwynn/57	50.00
5	Ken Griffey Jr./56	50.00
6	Juan Gonzalez/55	15.00
7	Vladimir Guerrero/54	20.00
8	Cal Ripken Jr./53	85.00
9	Mo Vaughn/52	10.00
10	Chipper Jones/51	30.00
11	Derek Jeter/50	85.00
12	Nomar Garciaparra/49	45.00
13	Mark McGwire/48	75.00
14	Sammy Sosa/47	50.00
15	Pedro Martinez/46	30.00
16	Greg Maddux/45	50.00
17	Frank Thomas/44	20.00
18	Shawn Green/43	10.00
19	Carlos Beltran/42	10.00
20	Roger Clemens/41	60.00
21	Randy Johnson/40	30.00
22	Bernie Williams/39	10.00
23	Carlos Delgado/38	15.00
24	Manny Ramirez/37	25.00
25	Freddy Garcia/36	10.00
26	Barry Bonds/35	90.00
27	Tim Hudson/34	20.00
28	Larry Walker/33	10.00
29	Raul Mondesi/32	10.00
30	Ivan Rodriguez/31	15.00
31	Magglio Ordonez/30	10.00
32	Scott Rolen/29	20.00
33	Mike Mussina/28	25.00
34	J.D. Drew/27	20.00
35	Tom Glavine/26	25.00
36	Barry Larkin/25	15.00
37	Jim Thome/24	15.00
38	Erubiel Durazo/23	15.00
39	Curt Schilling/22	15.00
40	Orlando Hernandez/21	15.00
41	Rafael Palmeiro/20	40.00
42	Gabe Kapler/19	15.00
43	Mark Grace/18	15.00
44	Jeff Cirillo/17	15.00
45	Jeromy Burnitz/16	15.00

46	Sean Casey/15	15.00
47	Kevin Millwood/14	20.00
48	Vinny Castilla/13	20.00
49	Jose Canseco/12	40.00
50	Roberto Alomar/11	50.00
51	Craig Biggio/10	50.00
61	Ben Petrick/30 (Prospects)	10.00
62	Chad Hermansen/29 (Prospects)	10.00
63	Kevin Barker/28 (Prospects)	10.00
64	Matt LeCroy/27 (Prospects)	10.00
65	Brad Penny/26 (Prospects)	10.00
66	D.T. Cromer/25 (Prospects)	10.00
67	Steve Lomasney/24 (Prospects)	10.00
68	Cole Liniak/23 (Prospects)	10.00
69	B.J. Ryan/22 (Prospects)	10.00
70	Wilton Veras/21 (Prospects)	10.00
71	Aaron McNeal/20 (Prospects)	15.00
72	Nick Johnson/19 (Prospects)	25.00
73	Adam Piatt/18 (Prospects)	15.00
74	Adam Kennedy/17 (Prospects)	15.00
75	Cesar King/16 (Prospects)	15.00
76	Peter Bergeron/15 (Prospects)	15.00
77	Rob Bell/14 (Prospects)	15.00
78	Wily Pena/13 (Prospects)	15.00
79	Ruben Mateo/12 (Prospects)	15.00
80	Kip Wells/11 (Prospects)	15.00
81	Alex Escobar/10 (Prospects)	20.00

Essential Credentials Now

Like Future, this is a parallel of the base set, with the production of cards 1-60 limited to that player's card number. Production for cards 61-90 can be determined by subtracting 60 from the card number. Quantity issued is listed in paranthesis.

		NM/M
Common Player:		8.00
20	Roger Clemens/20	50.00
21	Randy Johnson/21	30.00
22	Bernie Williams/22	10.00
23	Carlos Delgado/23	25.00
24	Manny Ramirez/24	10.00
25	Freddy Garcia/25	10.00
26	Barry Bonds/26	75.00
27	Tim Hudson/27	15.00
28	Larry Walker/28	10.00
29	Raul Mondesi/29	10.00
30	Ivan Rodriguez/30	15.00
31	Magglio Ordonez/31	10.00
32	Scott Rolen/32	20.00
33	Mike Mussina/33	15.00
34	J.D. Drew/34	10.00
35	Tom Glavine/35	20.00
36	Barry Larkin/36	15.00
37	Jim Thome/37	25.00
38	Erubiel Durazo/38	8.00
39	Curt Schilling/39	20.00
40	Orlando Hernandez/40	8.00
41	Rafael Palmeiro/41	15.00
42	Gabe Kapler/42	8.00
43	Mark Grace/43	10.00
44	Jeff Cirillo/44	8.00
45	Jeromy Burnitz/45	8.00
46	Sean Casey/46	8.00
47	Kevin Millwood/47	8.00
48	Vinny Castilla/48	8.00
49	Jose Canseco/49	15.00
50	Roberto Alomar/50	12.00
51	Craig Biggio/51	15.00
52	Preston Wilson/52	8.00
53	Jeff Weaver/53	8.00
54	Robin Ventura/54	8.00
55	Ben Grieve/55	8.00
56	Troy Glaus/56	15.00
57	Jacque Jones/57	12.00

58	Brian Giles/58	8.00
59	Kevin Brown/59	8.00
60	Todd Helton/60	20.00
74	Adam Kennedy/14 (Prospects)	15.00
75	Cesar King/15 (Prospects)	15.00
76	Peter Bergeron/16 (Prospects)	15.00
77	Rob Bell/17 (Prospects)	15.00
78	Wily Pena/18 (Prospects)	15.00
79	Ruben Mateo/19 (Prospects)	15.00
80	Kip Wells/20 (Prospects)	15.00
81	Alex Escobar/21 (Prospects)	15.00
82	Danys Baez/22 (Prospects)	15.00
83	Travis Dawkins/23 (Prospects)	15.00
84	Mark Quinn/24 (Prospects)	15.00
85	Jimmy Anderson/25 (Prospects)	15.00
86	Rick Ankiel/26 (Prospects)	15.00
87	Alfonso Soriano/27 (Prospects)	60.00
88	Pat Burrell/28 (Prospects)	30.00
89	Eric Munson/29 (Prospects)	15.00
90	Josh Beckett/30 (Prospects)	20.00

E-Xceptional Red

Die-cut in a shape similar to an oval, these inserts have a cloth like feel with silver foil stamping with a red background. Card backs are numbered consecutively "1 of 15XC" and so on. These are seeded 1:14 packs. Two parallels are also inserted: Blues are seeded 1:288 packs and Greens are limited to 999 serial numbered sets.

	NM/M
Complete Set (15):	100.00
Common Player:	4.00
Inserted 1:14	
Blue:	
Inserted 1:288	2-3X
Green:	1-1.5X
Production 999 Sets	
1	Ken Griffey Jr.	8.00
2	Derek Jeter	15.00
3	Nomar Garciaparra	6.00
4	Mark McGwire	10.00
5	Sammy Sosa	6.00
6	Mike Piazza	8.00
7	Alex Rodriguez	10.00
8	Cal Ripken Jr.	15.00
9	Chipper Jones	6.00
10	Pedro Martinez	4.00
11	Jeff Bagwell	4.00
12	Greg Maddux	6.00
13	Roger Clemens	7.00
14	Tony Gwynn	5.00
15	Frank Thomas	4.00

E-Xciting

Die-cut in the shape of a jersey card fronts have a holograpic appearance with silver foil stamping. These were seeded 1:24 packs. Card backs are numbered with an "XT" suffix.

	NM/M
Complete Set (10):	25.00
Common Player:	1.00
Inserted 1:24	
1	Mark McGwire	6.00
2	Ken Griffey Jr.	4.00
3	Randy Johnson	2.00
4	Sammy Sosa	3.00
5	Manny Ramirez	2.00
6	Jose Canseco	1.00
7	Derek Jeter	6.00
8	Scott Rolen	1.50
9	Juan Gonzalez	1.25
10	Barry Bonds	6.00

E-Xplosive

These inserts have a traditional format, with a holographic star like image in the background and "explosive" running down the top left side. Card backs are numbered with an "XP" suffix and are serial numbered on the bottom portion in an edition of 2,499 sets.

	NM/M
Complete Set (20):	90.00
Common Player:	2.00
Production 2,499 Sets	
1	Tony Gwynn	6.00
2	Alex Rodriguez	10.00
3	Pedro Martinez	5.00
4	Sammy Sosa	6.00
5	Cal Ripken Jr.	15.00
6	Adam Piatt	2.00
7	Pat Burrell	2.50
8	J.D. Drew	2.50
9	Mike Piazza	8.00
10	Shawn Green	2.50
11	Troy Glaus	4.00
12	Randy Johnson	5.00
13	Juan Gonzalez	2.50
14	Chipper Jones	6.00
15	Ivan Rodriguez	4.00
16	Nomar Garciaparra	6.00
17	Ken Griffey Jr.	8.00
18	Nick Johnson	2.50
19	Mark McGwire	10.00
20	Frank Thomas	5.00

Generation E-X

This 15-card set spotlights the top young players in the game and were seeded 1:8 packs. Card fronts have silver foil stamping over a background resembling a sky. These were seeded 1:8 packs. Card backs are numbered with a "GX" suffix.

	NM/M
Complete Set (15):	20.00
Common Player:	1.00
Inserted 1:8	
1	Rick Ankiel	1.00
2	Josh Beckett	1.50
3	Carlos Beltran	2.00
4	Pat Burrell	2.00
5	Freddy Garcia	1.00
6	Alex Rodriguez	5.00
7	Derek Jeter	6.00
8	Tim Hudson	1.50

9	Shawn Green	1.50
10	Eric Munson	1.00
11	Adam Piatt	1.00
12	Adam Kennedy	1.00
13	Nick Johnson	1.00
14	Alfonso Soriano	2.00
15	Nomar Garciaparra	4.00

Genuine Coverage

NM/M

Common Player:		5.00
Inserted 1:144		
1	Alex Rodriguez	40.00
2	Tom Glavine	10.00
3	Cal Ripken Jr.	50.00
4	Edgar Martinez	5.00
5	Raul Mondesi	5.00
6	Carlos Beltran	5.00
7	Chipper Jones	25.00
8	Barry Bonds	50.00
9	Heath Murray	5.00
10	Tim Hudson	10.00
11	Mike Mussina	10.00
12	Derek Jeter	50.00

1992 Snyder's Bread Washington Sports Heroes

This set was sponsored by Snyder's, a Northwest baker, and produced by Little Sun, which had earlier done a number of amateur baseball card sets. Two baseball players are included in the set: Ryne Sandberg (in a high school football jersey) and John Olerud (pitching for WSU). Cards picture the athletes against a pine tree border photo. Backs are printed in blue and yellow on white and feature a summary of the athlete's days in Washington.

NM/M

Complete Set (8):		15.00
1	Ryne Sandberg	12.00
6	John Olerud	3.00

2004 SkyBox Autographics

NM/M

Complete Set (100):		
Common Player:		.40
Hobby Box (4):		75.00
1	Albert Pujols	2.50
2	Richie Sexson	.75
3	Scott Rolen	1.00
4	Rafael Palmeiro	.75
5	Ichiro Suzuki	2.00
6	Craig Biggio	.50
7	Todd Helton	.75
8	Miguel Cabrera	.75
9	Ken Griffey Jr.	1.50
10	Pat Burrell	.50
11	Jose Reyes	.50
12	Hideki Matsui	2.50
13	Geoff Jenkins	.50
14	Mark Prior	.75
15	Gary Sheffield	.50
16	Nomar Garciaparra	2.00
17	Luis Gonzalez	.50
18	Troy Glaus	.50
19	Rocco Baldelli	.75
20	Hank Blalock	.50
21	Bret Boone	.40
22	Mike Sweeney	.40
23	Dmitri Young	.40
24	Dontrelle Willis	.50
25	Austin Kearns	.50
26	Jason Kendall	.40
27	Derek Jeter	3.00
28	Miguel Tejada	.50
29	Torii Hunter	.50
30	Sammy Sosa	2.00
31	Chipper Jones	1.50
32	Pedro J. Martinez	1.00
33	Curt Schilling	.75
34	Roy Halladay	.50
35	Jim Edmonds	.50
36	Alex Rodriguez	2.50
37	Jason Schmidt	.50
38	Jeff Bagwell	.75
39	Omar Vizquel	.40
40	Ivan Rodriguez	.75
41	Magglio Ordonez	.50
42	Jim Thome	1.00
43	Mike Piazza	2.00
44	Alfonso Soriano	1.00
45	Hideo Nomo	.50
46	Kerry Wood	.50
47	Greg Maddux	1.50
48	Tony Batista	.40
49	Randy Johnson	1.00
50	Garret Anderson	.50
51	Mark Teixeira	.50
52	Carlos Delgado	.75
53	Darin Erstad	.50
54	Shawn Green	.50
55	Josh Beckett	.75
56	Lance Berkman	.50
57	Adam Dunn	.50
58	Brian Giles	.50
59	Jason Giambi	1.00
60	Barry Zito	.50
61	Vladimir Guerrero	1.00
62	Frank Thomas	.75
63	Jay Gibbons	.40
64	Manny Ramirez	.75
65	Andruw Jones	.75
66	Rickie Weeks	4.00
67	Chad Bentz RC	4.00
68	Bobby Crosby	4.00
69	Greg Dobbs RC	5.00
70	John Gall RC	3.00
71	Kazuo Matsui RC	5.00
72	Dallas McPherson	3.00
73	Brandon Watson	3.00
74	Jerry Gil RC	3.00
75	Garrett Atkins	3.00
76	Cory Sullivan RC	3.00
77	Khalil Greene	5.00
78	Shawn Hill RC	3.00
79	Graham Koonce	3.00
80	Chien-Ming Wang	3.00
81	Josh Labandeira RC	3.00
82	Jonny Gomes	3.00
83	Edwin Jackson	3.00
84	Alfredo Simon RC	4.00
85	Delmon Young	6.00
86	Jason Bartlett RC	5.00
87	Angel Chavez RC	3.00
88	Angel Guzman	3.00
89	Ryan Howard	3.00
90	Scott Hairston	3.00
91	Ronny Cedeno RC	3.00
92	Donald Kelly RC	3.00
93	Ivan Ochoa RC	3.00
94	Edwin Encarnacion	3.00
95	Byron Gettis	3.00
96	Kevin Youkilis	4.00
97	Grady Sizemore	3.00
98	Mariano Gomez RC	3.00
99	Hector Gimenez RC	3.00
100	Ruddy Yan RC	3.00

Insignia

Cards (1-65):	3-5X
Rookies (66-100):	1-2X
Production 150 Sets	

Royal Insignia

No Pricing
Production 25 Sets

Autoclassics

NM/M

Complete Set (15):	25.00
Common Player:	1.50
Johnny Bench	4.00
Wade Boggs	2.00
Steve Carlton	2.00
Albert Chandler	1.50
Ty Cobb	4.00
Carlton Fisk	1.50
George Kelly	1.50
Sal Maglie	1.50
Bill Mazeroski	1.50
Jim Palmer	2.00
Nolan Ryan	6.00
Mike Schmidt	3.00
Joe Sewell	1.50
Duke Snider	3.00
Warren Spahn	4.00

Autographics

NM/M

Common Player:	5.00
Silver:	.75-1.5X
Production 100 Sets	
Gold:	1.5-2X
Production 25 Sets	
Purple:	No Pricing
Production One Set	
Garrett Atkins/175	5.00
Rocco Baldelli/255	15.00
Josh Beckett/100	25.00
Angel Berroa/182	10.00
Hank Blalock/205	15.00
A.J. Burnett/485	10.00
Marlon Byrd/240	8.00
Edwin Encarnacion/188	10.00
Eric Gagne/225	25.00
Jonny Gomes/265	15.00
Khalil Greene/190	25.00
Rich Harden/185	10.00
Dan Haren/176	10.00
Koyie Hill/24	15.00
Shea Hillenbrand/213	10.00
Ryan Howard/170	75.00
Tim Hudson/169	15.00
Aubrey Huff/296	10.00
Torii Hunter/215	10.00
Edwin Jackson/224	10.00
Bobby Jenks/307	10.00
Matt Kata/197	10.00
Austin Kearns/275	8.00
Graham Koonce/190	10.00
Barry Larkin/195	25.00
Dallas McPherson/179	8.00
Aaron Miles/140	15.00
Mark Mulder/186	15.00
Laynce Nix/185	8.00
Trot Nixon/210	15.00
Corey Patterson/220	12.00
Juan Pierre/220	15.00
Scott Podsednik/210	25.00
Albert Pujols/103	160.00
Jose Reyes/195	30.00
Juan Richardson/345	5.00
Gary Sheffield/210	20.00
Chris Snelling/200	5.00
Shannon Stewart/340	10.00
Cory Sullivan/170	15.00
Javier Vazquez/210	15.00
Billy Wagner/180	25.00
Chien-Ming Wang/195	100.00
Brandon Webb/310	12.00
Rickie Weeks/187	25.00
Dontrelle Willis/225	25.00
Kerry Wood/191	25.00
Delmon Young/205	20.00

Jerseygraphics Blue

NM/M

Common Player:	4.00
Silver:	1-2X
Production 100 Sets	
Gold:	No Pricing
Production 25 Sets	
Bobby Abreu	6.00
Rocco Baldelli	6.00

Josh Beckett	10.00
Lance Berkman	6.00
Craig Biggio	6.00
Hank Blalock	4.00
Pat Burrell	6.00
Miguel Cabrera	10.00
Carlos Delgado	6.00
Adam Dunn	8.00
Jim Edmonds	4.00
Darin Erstad	4.00
Nomar Garciaparra	8.00
Jason Giambi	8.00
Jay Gibbons	4.00
Troy Glaus	4.00
Shawn Green	4.00
Vladimir Guerrero	8.00
Roy Halladay	6.00
Todd Helton	8.00
Torii Hunter	6.00
Derek Jeter	15.00
Andruw Jones	8.00
Chipper Jones	10.00
Austin Kearns	4.00
Greg Maddux	15.00
Pedro J. Martinez	10.00
Kevin Millwood	4.00
Hideo Nomo	8.00
David Ortiz	10.00
Rafael Palmeiro	6.00
Mike Piazza	10.00
Mark Prior	6.00
Albert Pujols	15.00
Manny Ramirez	8.00
Jose Reyes	10.00
Alex Rodriguez	15.00
Ivan Rodriguez	8.00
Scott Rolen	8.00
Curt Schilling	6.00
Alfonso Soriano	8.00
Sammy Sosa	8.00
Mark Teixeira	8.00
Miguel Tejada	6.00
Frank Thomas	10.00
Jim Thome	8.00
Dontrelle Willis	6.00
Kerry Wood	4.00
Barry Zito	4.00

Prospects Endorsed

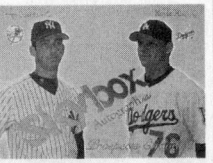

NM/M

Complete Set (15):		10.00
Common Duo:		.50
1	Albert Pujols, Delmon Young	3.00
2	Eric Gagne, Bobby Jenks	.50
3	Barry Larkin, Kazuo Matsui	2.00
4	Andruw Jones, Jonny Gomes	1.00
5	Hideo Nomo, Chien-Ming Wang	.50
6	Gary Sheffield, Cory Sullivan	.75
7	Billy Wagner, Ryan Howard	1.00
8	Jorge Posada, Koyie Hill	.75
9	Curt Schilling, Ryan Wagner	.75
10	Jose Reyes, Rickie Weeks	1.50
11	Alfonso Soriano, Matt Kata	1.50
12	Barry Zito, Rich Harden	.75
13	Randy Johnson, Brandon Webb	1.50
14	Alex Rodriguez, Angel Berroa	3.00
15	Dontrelle Willis, Edwin Jackson	.50

2004 SkyBox LE

NM/M

Complete Set (160):		
Common Player (1-110):		.25
Common SP (111-160):		4.00
Production 299 unless noted.		
Pack (3):		5.00
Box (18):		80.00
1	Juan Pierre	.25
2	Derek Jeter	3.00
3	Brandon Webb	.25
4	Jeff Bagwell	.75
5	Jason Schmidt	.40
6	Marlon Byrd	.25
7	Garret Atkins	.50
8	Miguel Cabrera	.75
9	Jose Reyes	.50
10	Rocco Baldelli	.50
11	Tony Batista	.25
12	Carlos Beltran	.50
13	Nomar Garciaparra	.50
14	Shawn Green	.50
15	Albert Pujols	2.50
16	Magglio Ordonez	.50
17	Kip Wells	.25
18	Andruw Jones	.50
19	Ryan Wagner	.25
20	Alex Rodriguez	3.00
21	Vernon Wells	.50
22	Todd Helton	.75
23	David Ortiz	.25
24	Troy Glaus	.25
25	Jim Thome	1.00
26	Greg Maddux	1.50
27	Roberto Alomar	.25
28	Edgardo Alfonzo	.25
29	Hee Seop Choi	.25
30	Ken Griffey Jr.	1.50
31	Tim Hudson	.50
32	Shannon Stewart	.25
33	Ichiro Suzuki	2.00
34	Luis Gonzalez	.50
35	Darin Erstad	.25
36	Dmitri Young	.25
37	Ivan Rodriguez	.75
38	Scott Podsednik	.50
39	Jose Vidro	.25
40	Mark Prior	2.00
41	Mike Mussina	.75
42	Gary Sheffield	.50
43	Manny Ramirez	.75
44	C.C. Sabathia	.40
45	Curt Schilling	.75
46	Scott Rolen	1.00
47	Hideo Nomo	.50
48	Torii Hunter	.50
49	Aubrey Huff	.25
50	Javy Lopez	.50
51	Austin Kearns	.25
52	Mike Piazza	1.50
53	Sean Burroughs	.25
54	Kerry Wood	.75
55	Marquis Grissom	.25
56	Preston Wilson	.25
57	Angel Berroa	.25
58	Jason Kendall	.25
59	Rafael Palmeiro	.75
60	Mike Lowell	.50
61	Eric Chavez	.50
62	Bartolo Colon	.50
63	Adam Dunn	.50
64	Pedro J. Martinez	1.00
65	Lance Berkman	.50
66	Bret Boone	.40
67	Eric Gagne	.40
68	Vladimir Guerrero	1.00
69	Jay Gibbons	.25
70	Larry Walker	.40
71	Orlando Cabrera	.40
72	Jorge Posada	.50
73	Jamie Moyer	.25
74	Carl Crawford	.25
75	Hank Blalock	.50
76	Josh Beckett	.75
77	Jody Gerut	.25
78	Kevin Brown	.25
79	Sammy Sosa	2.00
80	Chipper Jones	1.00
81	Tom Glavine	.50
82	Barry Zito	.50
83	Edgar Renteria	.25
84	Esteban Loaiza	.25
85	Jason Giambi	1.00
86	Miguel Tejada	.50
87	Randy Johnson	1.00
88	A.J. Burnett	.25
89	Richie Sexson	.75
90	Reggie Sanders	.25
91	Carlos Delgado	.75
92	Pat Burrell	.25
93	Jacque Jones	.25
94	Roy Oswalt	.50
95	Frank Thomas	.75
96	Melvin Mora	.25
97	Jeremy Bonderman	.25
98	Mike Sweeney	.25
99	Brian Giles	.50
100	Edgar Martinez	.40
101	Mark Teixeira	.50
102	Sean Casey	.25
103	Javier Vazquez	.50
104	Hideki Matsui	2.50
105	Jim Edmonds	.40
106	Roy Halladay	.50
107	Craig Biggio	.40
108	Geoff Jenkins	.25
109	Alfonso Soriano	1.00
110	Barry Larkin	.50
111	Chris Bootcheck	4.00
112	Dallas McPherson/99	6.00
113	Matt Kata/99	6.00
114	Scott Hairston	.50
115	Bobby Crosby	8.00
116	Adam Wainright/99	4.00
117	Daniel Cabrera	4.00
118	Kevin Youkilis	4.00
119	Ronny Cedeno RC	6.00
120	Ruddy Yan RC	4.00
121	Ryan Wing	4.00
122	William Bergolla RC	5.00
123	Edwin Encarnacion	4.00
124	Jonny Gomes	4.00
125	Garrett Atkins	4.00
126	Clint Barmes	4.00
127	Wilfredo Ledezma	4.00
128	Cody Ross	6.00
129	Josh Willingham/99	4.00
130	Chin-Hui Tsao	4.00
131	Hector Gimenez RC	4.00
132	David DeJesus	4.00
133	Jimmy Gobble	4.00
134	Edwin Jackson/99	6.00
135	Koyie Hill	4.00
136	Rickie Weeks/99	5.00
137	Graham Koonce	4.00
138	Rob Bowen	4.00
139	Shawn Hill RC	4.00
140	Craig Brazell	4.00
141	Mike Hessman	4.00
142	Jorge DePaula	4.00
143	Chien-Ming Wang/99	6.00
144	Rich Harden	4.00
145	Ryan Howard/99	6.00
146	Alfredo Simon RC	4.00
147	Ian Snell RC	6.00
148	Ryan Doumit	4.00
149	Khalil Greene/99	6.00
150	Angel Chavez RC	4.00
151	Dan Haren	6.00
152	Chris Snelling	4.00
153	Aaron Miles	4.00
154	John Gall RC	8.00
155	Chris Narveson	4.00
156	Delmon Young/99	8.00
157	Chad Gaudin	4.00
158	Gerald Laird	4.00
159	Alexis Rios	4.00
160	Jason Arnold	4.00

Artist's Proof

Cards (1-110):	3-6X
SP's (110-160):	1-1.5X
Production 50 Sets	

Executive Proof

No Pricing
Production One Set

Gold Proof

Cards (1-110):	3-5X
SP's (111-160):	1X
Production 150 Sets	

Photographer Proof

Cards (1-110):	6-12X
SP's (110-160):	2-3X
Production 25 Sets	

History of the Draft Autographs

NM/M

Common Autograph:	10.00
Production 199 Sets	
Draft Year:	1-1.25X
#'d to last 2 digits of draft year.	
Silver Proof:	1-1.5X
Production 50 Sets	
Gold Proof:	No Pricing
Production 10 Sets	
Hank Blalock	10.00
A.J. Burnett	10.00
Marlon Byrd	10.00
Roy Halladay	20.00
Tim Hudson	15.00
Aubrey Huff	10.00
Torii Hunter	15.00
Austin Kearns	10.00
Mike Lowell	15.00
Corey Patterson	15.00
Juan Pierre	15.00
Scott Podsednik	20.00
Albert Pujols	125.00
Scott Rolen	25.00
Shannon Stewart	10.00
Javier Vazquez	15.00
Vernon Wells	15.00

History of the Draft Game-Used

NM/M

Common Player:	4.00
Numbered to last 2 digits of draft yr.	
Silver Proof:	1-1.5X
Production 50 Sets	
Gold Proof:	No Pricing
Production 10 Sets	
Garret Anderson	4.00
Josh Beckett	10.00
Carlos Beltran	8.00
Lance Berkman	6.00
Hank Blalock	4.00
Bret Boone	4.00
A.J. Burnett	4.00
Pat Burrell	4.00
Marlon Byrd	4.00
Eric Chavez	4.00
Adam Dunn	8.00
Darin Erstad	8.00
Nomar Garciaparra	8.00
Jason Giambi	8.00
Shawn Green	4.00
Roy Halladay	8.00
Todd Helton	8.00
Tim Hudson	8.00
Aubrey Huff	4.00
Torii Hunter	8.00
Derek Jeter	15.00
Chipper Jones	10.00
Austin Kearns	4.00
Mike Lowell	5.00
Mike Mussina	8.00
Corey Patterson	4.00

	Juan Pierre	4.00
	Scott Podsednik	4.00
	Jorge Posada	8.00
	Albert Pujols	20.00
	Manny Ramirez	8.00
	Alex Rodriguez	15.00
	Scott Rolen	8.00
	Jason Schmidt	6.00
	Richie Sexson	6.00
	Shannon Stewart	4.00
	Javier Vazquez	4.00
	Vernon Wells	6.00
	Kerry Wood	6.00
	Barry Zito	6.00

Jersey Proof

		NM/M
	Common Player:	4.00
	Production 299 Sets	
	Silver Proof:	1.5-2X
	Production 50 Sets	
	Gold Proof:	No Pricing
	Production 10 Sets	
1	Troy Glaus	6.00
2	Curt Schilling	6.00
3	Randy Johnson	8.00
4	Brandon Webb	6.00
5	Gary Sheffield	6.00
6	Greg Maddux	15.00
7	Chipper Jones	10.00
8	David Ortiz	10.00
9	Nomar Garciaparra	15.00
10	Pedro J. Martinez	8.00
11	Manny Ramirez	8.00
12	Kerry Wood	6.00
13	Mark Prior	6.00
14	Sammy Sosa	10.00
15	Frank Thomas	8.00
16	Austin Kearns	4.00
17	Todd Helton	8.00
18	Preston Wilson	4.00
19	Juan Pierre	4.00
20	Josh Beckett	8.00
21	Ivan Rodriguez	6.00
22	Miguel Cabrera	8.00
23	Mike Lowell	6.00
24	Lance Berkman	6.00
25	Jeff Bagwell	8.00
26	Angel Berroa	4.00
27	Hideo Nomo	10.00
28	Eric Gagne	4.00
29	Scott Podsednik	10.00
30	Richie Sexson	6.00
31	Torii Hunter	6.00
32	Mike Piazza	10.00
33	Jose Reyes	10.00
34	Tom Glavine	6.00
35	Derek Jeter	25.00
36	Jorge Posada	6.00
37	Jason Giambi	8.00
38	Alfonso Soriano	6.00
39	Eric Chavez	4.00
40	Miguel Tejada	6.00
41	Jim Thome	8.00
42	Albert Pujols	15.00
43	Scott Rolen	6.00
44	Rocco Baldelli	6.00
45	Alex Rodriguez	15.00
46	Hank Blalock	6.00
47	Mark Teixeira	6.00
48	Rafael Palmeiro	6.00
49	Carlos Delgado	6.00
50	Roy Halladay	6.00

L.E.ague L.E.aders

		NM/M
	Complete Set (10):	10.00
	Common Player:	.50
	Inserted 1:18	
1LL	Alex Rodriguez	3.00
2LL	Jim Thome	1.50
3LL	Albert Pujols	3.00
4LL	Pedro J. Martinez	1.50
5LL	Roy Halladay	.75
6LL	Jason Schmidt	.50
7LL	Kerry Wood	1.00
8LL	Juan Pierre	.50
9LL	Preston Wilson	.50
10LL	Carlos Delgado	1.00

L.E.ague L.E.aders Game-Used

		NM/M
	Common Player:	4.00
	Production 75 Sets	
	Silver Proof:	1-1.5X
	Production 50 Sets	
	Gold Proof:	No Pricing

JUAN PIERRE/OF

	Production 10 Sets	
	Alex Rodriguez	15.00
	Jim Thome	8.00
	Albert Pujols	20.00
	Pedro J. Martinez	10.00
	Roy Halladay	6.00
	Jason Schmidt	4.00
	Kerry Wood	4.00
	Juan Pierre	4.00
	Preston Wilson	4.00
	Carlos Delgado	6.00

Rare Form

		NM/M
	Common Player:	5.00
	Inserted 1:288	
1	Albert Pujols	20.00
2	Miguel Cabrera	5.00
3	Jim Thome	10.00
4	Derek Jeter	30.00
5	Nomar Garciaparra	15.00
6	Mike Piazza	15.00
7	Alex Rodriguez	20.00
8	Delmon Young	15.00
9	Chipper Jones	12.00
10	Rickie Weeks	8.00

Rare Form Autographs

		NM/M
	Common Autograph:	10.00
	Production 299 Sets	
	Level 2:	1-1.5X
	Production 99 Sets	
	Silver Proof:	1.5X
	Production 50 Sets	
	Gold Proof:	No Pricing
	Production 10 Sets	
	Rocco Baldelli	25.00
	Angel Berroa	15.00
	Rich Harden	20.00
	Edwin Jackson	20.00
	Matt Kata	10.00
	Dallas McPherson	15.00
	Brandon Webb	15.00
	Rickie Weeks	20.00
	Delmon Young	25.00

Rare Form Game-Used Silver Proof

		NM/M
	Common Player:	5.00
	Production 50 Sets	
	Gold Proof:	No Pricing
	Production 10 Sets	
	Rocco Baldelli	5.00
	Miguel Cabrera	10.00
	Nomar Garciaparra	15.00
	Derek Jeter	25.00
	Chipper Jones	12.00
	Mike Piazza	15.00
	Albert Pujols	25.00
	Alex Rodriguez	20.00
	Jim Thome	10.00

Rare Form Memorabilia Jersey Number

		NM/M
	Numbered to jersey number.	
	Most not priced due to scarcity.	
	Mike Piazza/31	30.00
	Jim Thome/25	25.00

Sky's the Limit

		NM/M
	Complete Set (20):	20.00
	Common Player:	.50
	Inserted 1:6	
1SL	Dontrelle Willis	1.00
2SL	Rocco Baldelli	1.00
3SL	Miguel Cabrera	1.00
4SL	Mark Prior	3.00
5SL	Hideki Matsui	4.00
6SL	Kerry Wood	1.50
7SL	Alfonso Soriano	1.50
8SL	Ichiro Suzuki	2.50
9SL	Brandon Webb	.50
10SL	Alex Rodriguez	3.00
11SL	Barry Zito	1.00
12SL	Hank Blalock	1.00
13SL	Jose Reyes	.75
14SL	Torii Hunter	.75
15SL	Josh Beckett	1.00
16SL	Manny Ramirez	1.00
17SL	Andruw Jones	1.00
18SL	Vladimir Guerrero	1.50
19SL	Miguel Tejada	.75
20SL	Carlos Delgado	1.00

Sky's the Limit Game-Used

		NM/M
	Common Player:	4.00
	Production 99 Sets	
	Silver Proof:	1X
	Production 50 Sets	
	Gold Proof:	No Pricing
	Production 10 Sets	
	Rocco Baldelli	4.00
	Josh Beckett	10.00
	Hank Blalock	6.00
	Miguel Cabrera	8.00
	Carlos Delgado	6.00
	Vladimir Guerrero	6.00
	Torii Hunter	6.00
	Andruw Jones	6.00
	Mark Prior	6.00
	Manny Ramirez	8.00
	Jose Reyes	10.00
	Alex Rodriguez	15.00
	Alfonso Soriano	6.00
	Miguel Tejada	6.00
	Brandon Webb	4.00
	Dontrelle Willis	4.00
	Kerry Wood	4.00
	Barry Zito	4.00

2005 SkyBox Autographics

CARLOS BELTRAN 15

		NM/M
	Complete Set (115):	
	Common Player (1-60):	.15
	Common (61-115):	1.50
	Production 750	
	Pack (5):	8.00
	Box (12):	85.00
1	Vladimir Guerrero	.75
2	Garret Anderson	.25
3	Troy Glaus	.25
4	Shawn Green	.25
5	Chipper Jones	.75
6	Andruw Jones	.40
7	Miguel Tejada	.50
8	Melvin Mora	.15
9	Manny Ramirez	.75
10	Curt Schilling	.75
11	Nomar Garciaparra	.50
12	Mark Prior	.50
13	Sammy Sosa	1.00
14	Frank Thomas	.40
15	Paul Konerko	.25
16	Adam Dunn	.50
17	Ken Griffey Jr.	1.50
18	Victor Martinez	.25
19	Travis Hafner	.25
20	Todd Helton	.50
21	Ivan Rodriguez	.50
22	Carlos Guillen	.15
23	Miguel Cabrera	.75
24	Juan Pierre	.25

25	Roger Clemens	2.00
26	Jeff Bagwell	.50
27	Lance Berkman	.25
28	Mike Sweeney	.15
29	Eric Gagne	.15
30	J.D. Drew	.15
31	Ben Sheets	.25
32	Lyle Overbay	.15
33	Johan Santana	.50
34	Torii Hunter	.15
35	Mike Piazza	1.00
36	Pedro Martinez	.75
37	Carlos Beltran	.50
38	Derek Jeter	2.00
39	Alex Rodriguez	2.00
40	Hideki Matsui	1.50
41	Randy Johnson	.75
42	Eric Chavez	.25
43	Jim Thome	.50
44	Craig Wilson	.15
45	Khalil Greene	.25
46	Jake Peavy	.25
47	Jason Schmidt	.15
48	Ichiro Suzuki	1.50
49	Adrian Beltre	.25
50	Albert Pujols	2.00
51	Scott Rolen	.50
52	Carl Crawford	.15
53	Rocco Baldelli	.15
54	Alfonso Soriano	.50
55	Hank Blalock	.25
56	Vernon Wells	.15
57	Jose Vidro	.15
58	David Ortiz	.75
59	Bobby Abreu	.25
60	Gary Sheffield	.40
61	Nolan Ryan	15.00
62	Mike Schmidt	10.00
63	Johnny Bench	8.00
64	Lou Brock	3.00
65	Dennis Eckersley	2.00
66	Carlton Fisk	3.00
67	Bob Gibson	4.00
68	Reggie Jackson	4.00
69	Al Kaline	3.00
70	Bill Mazeroski	3.00
71	Willie McCovey	3.00
72	Jim Palmer	3.00
73	Phil Rizzuto	2.00
74	Warren Spahn	4.00
75	Brooks Robinson	3.00
76	Willie Stargell	3.00
77	Jim "Catfish" Hunter	2.00
78	Tony Perez	2.00
79	George Kell	2.00
80	Robin Yount	4.00
81	Fergie Jenkins	2.00
82	Tom Seaver	3.00
83	Eddie Mathews	3.00
84	Enos Slaughter	2.00
85	Pee Wee Reese	2.00
86	Harmon Killebrew	3.00
87	Eddie Murray	3.00
88	Orlando Cepeda	2.00
89	Billy Williams	2.00
90	Ralph Kiner	2.00
91	Ryan Raburn	1.50
92	Justin Morneau	2.00
93	Zack Greinke	1.50
94	David Aardsma	1.50
95	B.J. Upton	2.00
96	Gavin Floyd	1.50
97	David Wright	8.00
98	Russ Adams	1.50
99	Jose Lopez	2.00
100	Scott Kazmir	1.50
101	Mike Gosling	1.50
102	Jeff Keppinger	1.50
103	David Krynzel	1.50
104	Jeff Niemann RC	6.00
105	Ruben Gotay	1.50
106	Dioner Navarro	1.50
107	Nick Swisher	1.50
108	Yadier Molina	1.50
109	Joey Gathright	1.50
110	Jon Knott	1.50
111	J.D. Durbin	1.50
112	Andres Blanco	1.50
113	Charlton Jimerson	1.50
114	Sean Burnett	1.50
115	Justin Verlander RC	6.00

Insignia

	Insignia (1-60):	2-3X
	Insignia (61-115):	1X
	Production 150 Sets	

Royal Insignia

	Royal Insignia (1-60):	4-6X
	Royal Insignia (61-115):	1.5-2X
	Production 25 Sets	

Future Signs

		NM/M
	Common Player:	.50
	Inserted 1:6	
1	Bobby Crosby	.50
2	David Aardsma	.50
3	Russ Adams	.50
4	J.D. Durbin	.50
5	Johnny Estrada	.50
6	Chone Figgins	.50
7	Jason Bay	.75
8	Gavin Floyd	.50
9	Lew Ford	.50
10	Victor Martinez	.50
11	Joe Mauer	.75
12	Justin Morneau	.50

13	Laynce Nix	.50
14	Sean Burnett	.50
15	B.J. Upton	.75
16	Justin Verlander	1.50
17	David Wright	3.00
18	Delmon Young	1.00
19	Michael Young	.50
20	Zack Greinke	.50

Future Signs Autograph Blue

		NM/M
	Production 8-505	
	Cards not serial numbered.	
JB	Jason Bay/264	15.00
ZG	Zack Greinke/264	20.00
VM	Victor Martinez/500	12.00
JM	Justin Morneau/224	20.00
AO	Akinori Otsuka/639	10.00
JV	Justin Verlander/505	25.00

Future Signs Autograph Gold

		NM/M
	Production 65 Sets	
JB	Jason Bay	15.00
SB	Sean Burnett	10.00
JD	J.D. Durbin	5.00
EE	Edwin Encarnacion	10.00
ZG	Zack Greinke	20.00
SH	Scott Hairston	8.00
VMJ	Val Majewski	15.00
VM	Victor Martinez	15.00
JM	Justin Morneau	20.00
AO	Akinori Otsuka	10.00
AS	Alfredo Simon	5.00
BU	B.J. Upton	15.00
JV	Justin Verlander	30.00
RW	Rickie Weeks	15.00
DW	David Wright	50.00

Future Signs Auto. Gold Embossed

		NM/M
	Production 45 Sets	
JB	Jason Bay	15.00
SB	Sean Burnett	10.00
JD	J.D. Durbin	5.00
EE	Edwin Encarnacion	10.00
ZG	Zack Greinke	20.00
SH	Scott Hairston	8.00
VMJ	Val Majewski	15.00
VM	Victor Martinez	15.00
JM	Justin Morneau	20.00
AO	Akinori Otsuka	10.00
AS	Alfredo Simon	5.00
BU	B.J. Upton	15.00
JV	Justin Verlander	30.00
RW	Rickie Weeks	15.00
DW	David Wright	50.00
DY	Delmon Young	20.00

Future Signs Auto. Platinum

		NM/M
	Production 25 Sets	
	Gold Embossed:	No Pricing
	Production 5 Sets	
JB	Jason Bay	20.00
SB	Sean Burnett	10.00
JD	J.D. Durbin	8.00
EE	Edwin Encarnacion	10.00
ZG	Zack Greinke	20.00
SH	Scott Hairston	10.00
VMJ	Val Majewski	15.00
VM	Victor Martinez	20.00
JM	Justin Morneau	25.00
AO	Akinori Otsuka	15.00
AS	Alfredo Simon	5.00
BU	B.J. Upton	20.00
JV	Justin Verlander	35.00
RW	Rickie Weeks	20.00
DW	David Wright	60.00
DY	Delmon Young	20.00

Future Signs Autograph Silver

J.D. DURBIN
MINNESOTA TWINS

		NM/M
	Production 100 Sets	
	Silver Embossed:	1X
	Production 85 Sets	
JB	Jason Bay	15.00
SB	Sean Burnett	10.00
JD	J.D. Durbin	5.00
EE	Edwin Encarnacion	10.00
ZG	Zack Greinke	20.00
VMJ	Val Majewski	15.00
VM	Victor Martinez	15.00
JM	Justin Morneau	15.00
AO	Akinori Otsuka	10.00
AS	Alfredo Simon	5.00
BU	B.J. Upton	15.00

JV	Justin Verlander	30.00
RW	Rickie Weeks	15.00
DW	David Wright	50.00

Jerseygraphics Blue

		NM/M
	Common Player:	4.00
	Inserted 1:40 Retail	
	Gold:	1-2X
	Inserted 1:240 Retail	
	Silver:	1X
	Inserted 1:80 Retail	
GA	Garret Anderson	4.00
JB	Jeff Bagwell	6.00
RB	Rocco Baldelli	4.00
JBE	Josh Beckett	4.00
AB	Adrian Beltre	4.00
HB	Hank Blalock	4.00
MB	Marlon Byrd	4.00
MC	Miguel Cabrera	8.00
CD	Carlos Delgado	4.00
AD	Adam Dunn	6.00
EG	Eric Gagne	4.00
BG	Brian Giles	4.00
TG	Troy Glaus	4.00
TGL	Tom Glavine	4.00
TH	Torii Hunter	4.00
AK	Austin Kearns	4.00
MO	Magglio Ordonez	4.00
JR	Jose Reyes	6.00
BS	Ben Sheets	4.00
MT	Mark Teixeira	6.00

Master Collection

	Production 25 Sets	
	All are Jsy/Jsy/Patch combos.	
	One of a Kind:	No Pricing
	Production One Set	

Signature Blue

		NM/M
	Print run info provided by UD.	
	Cards are not serial #'d.	
	Jsy Gold:	1-1.5X
	Production 45 Sets	
	Jsy Gold Embossed:	1-2X
	Production 30 Sets	
	Jsy Silver:	1X
	Production 100 Sets	
	Jsy Silver Embossed:	1X
	Production 75 Sets	
EP	Jeremy Bonderman/369	12.00
MC	Miguel Cabrera/250	30.00
MCA	Mike Cameron/200	10.00
CC	Carl Crawford/150	15.00
DE	David Eckstein/546	20.00
AE	Adam Everett/590	6.00
LG	Luis Gonzalez/187	6.00
THA	Travis Hafner/246	15.00
TH	Trevor Hoffman/590	12.00
OH	Orlando Hudson/231	8.00
CK	Casey Kotchman/227	10.00
JK	Jason Kubel/137	8.00
BL	Brad Lidge/164	20.00
JO	John Olerud/446	15.00
CP	Corey Patterson/329	8.00
EP	Eduardo Perez/584	6.00
JS	Johan Santana/200	30.00

Signatures Game Patch Gold

	No Pricing	
	Production 5 Sets	
	Gold Embossed	
	Production 15 Sets	
	Masterpiece Embossed:	No Pricing
	Production One Set	

Signatures Game Patch Silver

		NM/M
	Production 25 Sets	
RB	Rocco Baldelli	40.00
JB	Jeremy Bonderman	40.00
SS	Shannon Stewart	20.00

Signature Moments

REGGIE JACKSON / NEW YORK YANKEES / 1977 WORLD SERIES MVP

		NM/M
	Complete Set (10):	15.00
	Common Player:	1.00
	Inserted 1:12	
1	Manny Ramirez	1.50
2	Derek Jeter	4.00
3	Ichiro Suzuki	3.00
4	Roger Clemens	4.00
5	Albert Pujols	4.00
6	Nolan Ryan	4.00
7	Reggie Jackson	1.50
8	Carlton Fisk	1.00
9	Mike Schmidt	1.50
10	Johnny Bench	1.50

1995 Sonic/Coke Heroes of Baseball

In a promotion with the Sonic chain of Southern drive-in restaurants, Upper Deck issued a 20-card set of baseball greats. Cards featured vintage sepia photos on the front, with player biographies and stats on the back. The Coca-Cola and Sonic logos also appear on back.

		NM/M
Complete Set (20):		5.00
Common Player:		.25
1	Whitey Ford	.25
2	Cy Young	.25
3	Babe Ruth	1.50
4	Lou Gehrig	1.00
5	Mike Schmidt	.35
6	Nolan Ryan	1.00
7	Robin Yount	.25
8	Gary Carter	.25
9	Tom Seaver	.25
10	Reggie Jackson	.25
11	Bob Gibson	.25
12	Gil Hodges	.25
13	Monte Irvin	.25
14	Minnie Minoso	.25
15	Willie Stargell	.25
16	Al Kaline	.25
17	Joe Jackson	1.50
18	Walter Johnson	.25
19	Ty Cobb	.50
20	Satchel Paige	.25

1995 Sonic/Pepsi Baseball Greats

While some Sonic drive-in restaurants (basically a Southern chain) featured a baseball card promotion using Upper Deck cards with a Coca-Cola logo on back, other drive-ins in the chain featured a 12-card set sponsored by Pepsi. Cards have a red border on front and a color photo of a player on which team logos have been airbrushed away. Backs have career data and the Pepsi logo, along with that of the Major League Baseball Players Alumni, and are printed in red and blue. The cards were issued in three-card cello packs with a meal purchase. The unnumbered cards are checklisted here in alphabetical order.

		NM/M
Complete Set (12):		4.00
Common Player:		.25
(1)	Bert Campaneris	.25
(2)	George Foster	.25
(3)	Steve Garvey	.40
(4)	Fergie Jenkins	.25
(5)	Tommy John	.25
(6)	Harmon Killebrew	.75
(7)	Sparky Lyle	.25
(8)	Fred Lynn	.25
(9)	Joe Morgan	.25
(10)	Graig Nettles	.25
(11)	Warren Spahn	.75
(12)	Maury Wills	.25

1987 Sonshine Industries 19th Century Baseball

A. C. ANSON

There is no indication of the origins of this collectors' issue on the cards themselves. Fronts feature black-and-white reproductions of vintage woodcuts of the players with an ornate orange framework. Backs of the 2-1/2" x 3-1/2" cards are printed in black on blue-gray with lengthy biographical information. The unnumbered cards are checklisted here in alphabetical order.

		NM/M
Complete Set (20):		20.00
Common Player:		1.00
(1)	A.C. Anson	2.00
(2)	Cap Anson	2.00
(3)	D. Brouthers	1.00
(4)	Alexander Cartwright	1.50
(5)	Alexander Cartwright	1.50
(6)	L.N. David	1.00
(7)	Wes Fisler	1.00
(8)	F.E. Goldsmith	1.00
(9)	T.J. Keefe	1.00
(10)	M.J. Kelly	2.00
(11)	Robert T. Mathews	1.00
(12)	Wm. McLean	1.00
(13)	C.A. McVey	1.00
(14)	James Mutrie	1.00
(15)	Lipman Pike	1.50
(16)	John J. Smith	1.00
(17)	A.G. Spalding	1.50
(18)	M. Welch	1.50
(19)	N.E. Young	1.00
(20)	Going to the game	1.00

1995 South Carolina Athletic Hall of Fame

Sports stars from around the state were honored in this 108-card issue. Fronts feature borderless color or sepia photos with the S.C. Athletic Hall of Fame logo in an upper corner and a gold-foil seal at bottom-right. A colored stripe has the athlete's name in gold foil. On back are a few personal and career stats and highlights. Only the baseball players are listed here. Issue price of the set was $40.

		NM/M
Complete Set (108):		40.00
Common (Baseball) Player:		.50
5	Frank Howard	.75
6	Bobby Richardson	1.00
13	Shoeless Joe Jackson	4.00
27	Van Lingle Mungo	.50
35	Earl Wooten	.50
54	Marty Marion	.50
55	Frank Howard	.75
72	Jim Rice	.75
74	Danny Ford	.50
83	Lou Brissie	.50
84	Billy O'Dell	.50
97	B.J. Surhoff	1.00
100	Frank Howard	.75

1993 SP

Upper Deck's first super-premium baseball card issue features 290 cards in the single-series set; 252 are

individual player cards, while the remainder includes a Premier Prospects subset featuring top prospects (20 cards), 18 All-Stars and a Platinum Power insert set of 20 top home run hitters. Cards, which were available in 12-card foil packs, feature borderless color photos and UV coating on the front, plus a special logo using lenticular printing. Foil is also used intricately in the design. Backs have a large color photo and statistics. Cards are numbered and color-coded by team.

		NM/M
Complete Set (290):		75.00
Common Player:		.10
Pack (12):		10.00
Wax Box (24):		220.00
1	Roberto Alomar	.30
2	Wade Boggs	2.00
3	Joe Carter	.10
4	Ken Griffey Jr.	2.50
5	Mark Langston	.10
6	John Olerud	.10
7	Kirby Puckett	2.00
8	Cal Ripken, Jr.	4.00
9	Ivan Rodriguez	1.25
10	Barry Bonds	4.00
11	Darren Daulton	.10
12	Marquis Grissom	.10
13	Dave Justice	.10
14	John Kruk	.10
15	Barry Larkin	.10
16	Terry Mulholland	.10
17	Ryne Sandberg	2.00
18	Gary Sheffield	.10
19	Chad Curtis	.10
20	Chili Davis	.10
21	Gary DiSarcina	.10
22	Damion Easley	.10
23	Chuck Finley	.10
24	Luis Polonia	.10
25	Tim Salmon	.10
26	J.T. Snow RC	1.00
27	Russ Springer	.10
28	Jeff Bagwell	1.50
29	Craig Biggio	.10
30	Ken Caminiti	.10
31	Andujar Cedeno	.10
32	Doug Drabek	.10
33	Steve Finley	.10
34	Luis Gonzalez	.10
35	Pete Harnisch	.10
36	Darryl Kile	.10
37	Mike Bordick	.10
38	Dennis Eckersley	1.25
39	Brent Gates	.10
40	Rickey Henderson	1.50
41	Mark McGwire	3.00
42	Craig Paquette	.10
43	Ruben Sierra	.10
44	Terry Steinbach	.10
45	Todd Van Poppel	.10
46	Pat Borders	.10
47	Tony Fernandez	.10
48	Juan Guzman	.10
49	Pat Hentgen	.10
50	Paul Molitor	1.50
51	Jack Morris	.10
52	Ed Sprague	.10
53	Duane Ward	.10
54	Devon White	.10
55	Steve Avery	.10
56	Jeff Blauser	.10
57	Ron Gant	.10
58	Tom Glavine	.40
59	Greg Maddux	2.00
60	Fred McGriff	.50
61	Terry Pendleton	.10
62	Deion Sanders	.50
63	John Smoltz	.10
64	Cal Eldred	.10
65	Darryl Hamilton	.10
66	John Jaha	.10
67	Pat Listach	.10
68	Jaime Navarro	.10
69	Kevin Reimer	.10
70	B.J. Surhoff	.10
71	Greg Vaughn	.10
72	Robin Yount	1.50
73	Rene Arocha RC	.10
74	Bernard Gilkey	.10
75	Gregg Jefferies	.10
76	Ray Lankford	.10

77	Tom Pagnozzi	.10
78	Lee Smith	.10
79	Ozzie Smith	2.00
80	Bob Tewksbury	.10
81	Mark Whiten	.10
82	Steve Buechele	.10
83	Mark Grace	.10
84	Jose Guzman	.10
85	Derrick May	.10
86	Mike Morgan	.10
87	Randy Myers	.10
88	Kevin Roberson RC	.10
89	Sammy Sosa	2.00
90	Rick Wilkins	.10
91	Brett Butler	.10
92	Eric Davis	.10
93	Orel Hershiser	.10
94	Eric Karros	.10
95	Ramon Martinez	.10
96	Raul Mondesi	.10
97	Jose Offerman	.10
98	Mike Piazza	2.50
99	Darryl Strawberry	.10
100	Moises Alou	.10
101	Wil Cordero	.10
102	Delino DeShields	.10
103	Darrin Fletcher	.10
104	Ken Hill	.10
105	Mike Lansing RC	.40
106	Dennis Martinez	.10
107	Larry Walker	.10
108	John Wetteland	.10
109	Rod Beck	.10
110	John Burkett	.10
111	Will Clark	.10
112	Royce Clayton	.10
113	Darren Lewis	.10
114	Willie McGee	.10
115	Bill Swift	.10
116	Robby Thompson	.10
117	Matt Williams	.10
118	Sandy Alomar Jr.	.10
119	Carlos Baerga	.10
120	Albert Belle	.10
121	Reggie Jefferson	.10
122	Kenny Lofton	.10
123	Wayne Kirby	.10
124	Carlos Martinez	.10
125	Charles Nagy	.10
126	Paul Sorrento	.10
127	Rich Amaral	.10
128	Jay Buhner	.10
129	Norm Charlton	.10
130	Dave Fleming	.10
131	Erik Hanson	.10
132	Randy Johnson	1.50
133	Edgar Martinez	.10
134	Tino Martinez	.10
135	Omar Vizquel	.10
136	Bret Barberie	.10
137	Chuck Carr	.10
138	Jeff Conine	.10
139	Orestes Destrade	.10
140	Chris Hammond	.10
141	Bryan Harvey	.10
142	Benito Santiago	.10
143	Walt Weiss	.10
144	Darrell Whitmore RC	.10
145	Tim Bolger RC	.10
146	Bobby Bonilla	.10
147	Jeromy Burnitz	.10
148	Vince Coleman	.10
149	Dwight Gooden	.10
150	Todd Hundley	.10
151	Howard Johnson	.10
152	Eddie Murray	1.50
153	Bret Saberhagen	.10
154	Brady Anderson	.10
155	Mike Devereaux	.10
156	Jeffrey Hammonds	.10
157	Chris Hoiles	.10
158	Ben McDonald	.10
159	Mark McLemore	.10
160	Mike Mussina	.50
161	Gregg Olson	.10
162	David Segui	.10
163	Derek Bell	.10
164	Andy Benes	.10
165	Archi Cianfrocco	.10
166	Ricky Gutierrez	.10
167	Tony Gwynn	2.00
168	Gene Harris	.10
169	Trevor Hoffman	.10
170	Ray McDavid RC	.10
171	Phil Plantier	.10
172	Mariano Duncan	.10
173	Len Dykstra	.10
174	Tommy Greene	.10
175	Dave Hollins	.10
176	Pete Incaviglia	.10
177	Mickey Morandini	.10
178	Curt Schilling	.40
179	Kevin Stocker	.10
180	Mitch Williams	.10
181	Stan Belinda	.10
182	Jay Bell	.10
183	Steve Cooke	.10
184	Carlos Garcia	.10
185	Jeff King	.10
186	Orlando Merced	.10
187	Don Slaught	.10
188	Andy Van Slyke	.10
189	Kevin Young	.10
190	Kevin Brown	.10
191	Jose Canseco	.60
192	Julio Franco	.10
193	Benji Gil	.10
194	Juan Gonzalez	.75

195	Tom Henke	.10
196	Rafael Palmeiro	1.25
197	Dean Palmer	.10
198	Nolan Ryan	4.00
199	Roger Clemens	2.25
200	Scott Cooper	.10
201	Andre Dawson	.35
202	Mike Greenwell	.10
203	Carlos Quintana	.10
204	Jeff Russell	.10
205	Aaron Sele	.10
206	Mo Vaughn	.10
207	Frank Viola	.10
208	Rob Dibble	.10
209	Roberto Kelly	.10
210	Kevin Mitchell	.10
211	Hal Morris	.10
212	Joe Oliver	.10
213	Jose Rijo	.10
214	Bip Roberts	.10
215	Chris Sabo	.10
216	Reggie Sanders	.10
217	Dante Bichette	.10
218	Jerald Clark	.10
219	Alex Cole	.10
220	Andres Galarraga	.10
221	Joe Girardi	.10
222	Charlie Hayes	.10
223	Robert Mejia RC	.10
224	Armando Reynoso	.10
225	Eric Young	.10
226	Kevin Appier	.10
227	George Brett	2.25
228	David Cone	.10
229	Phil Hiatt	.10
230	Felix Jose	.10
231	Wally Joyner	.10
232	Mike Macfarlane	.10
233	Brian McRae	.10
234	Jeff Montgomery	.10
235	Rob Deer	.10
236	Cecil Fielder	.10
237	Travis Fryman	.10
238	Mike Henneman	.10
239	Tony Phillips	.10
240	Mickey Tettleton	.10
241	Alan Trammell	.10
242	David Wells	.10
243	Lou Whitaker	.10
244	Rick Aguilera	.10
245	Scott Erickson	.10
246	Brian Harper	.10
247	Kent Hrbek	.10
248	Chuck Knoblauch	.10
249	Shane Mack	.10
250	David McCarty	.10
251	Pedro Munoz	.10
252	Dave Winfield	1.50
253	Alex Fernandez	.10
254	Ozzie Guillen	.10
255	Bo Jackson	.20
256	Lance Johnson	.10
257	Ron Karkovice	.10
258	Jack McDowell	.10
259	Tim Raines	.10
260	Frank Thomas	1.50
261	Robin Ventura	.10
262	Jim Abbott	.10
263	Steve Farr	.10
264	Jimmy Key	.10
265	Don Mattingly	2.25
266	Paul O'Neill	.10
267	Mike Stanley	.10
268	Danny Tartabull	.10
269	Bob Wickman	.10
270	Bernie Williams	.10
271	Jason Bere	.10
272	Roger Cedeno RC	.10
273	Johnny Damon RC	12.00
274	Russ Davis RC	.25
275	Carlos Delgado RC	.75
276	Carl Everett	.10
277	Cliff Floyd	.10
278	Alex Gonzalez	.10
279	Derek Jeter RC	75.00
280	Chipper Jones	2.00
281	Javier Lopez	.10
282	Chad Mottola RC	.10
283	Marc Newfield	.10
284	Eduardo Perez	.10
285	Manny Ramirez	1.50
286	Todd Steverson RC	.10
287	Michael Tucker	.10
288	Allen Watson	.10
289	Rondell White	.10
290	Dmitri Young	.10

Platinum Power

This 20-card insert set features 20 of the game's top home run hitters. The top of each insert card features a special die cut treatment. Backs are numbered with a PP prefix.

		NM/M
Complete Set (20):		27.50
Common Player:		.50
1	Albert Belle	.50
2	Barry Bonds	5.00
3	Joe Carter	.50
4	Will Clark	.50
5	Darren Daulton	.50
6	Cecil Fielder	.50
7	Ron Gant	.50
8	Juan Gonzalez	1.00
9	Ken Griffey Jr.	3.00
10	Dave Hollins	.50

11	Dave Justice	.50
12	Fred McGriff	.50
13	Mark McGwire	5.00
14	Dean Palmer	.50
15	Mike Piazza	3.00
16	Tim Salmon	.50
17	Ryne Sandberg	2.50
18	Gary Sheffield	.75
19	Frank Thomas	2.00
20	Matt Williams	.50

Jumbos

These jumbo-size (8-1/2" x 11") versions of the players' 1993 SP cards were sold through Upper Deck Authenticated. Each player's jumbo card was produced in a limited edition of 1,000, except for Frank Thomas, whose jumbo card was an edition of 1,993. The jumbos were sold in heavy plastic screwdown holders.

		NM/M
Complete Set (5):		35.00
Common Player:		5.00
10	Barry Bonds	12.50
58	Tom Glavine	6.00
173	Lenny Dykstra	5.00
199	Roger Clemens	10.00
260	Frank Thomas	7.50

1994 SP Promo

Virtually identical to the issued version of Ken Griffey, Jr.'s card in the regular SP set (#105) this differs in the card number on the back (#24) and the inclusion on front and back of the notice, "For Promotional Use Only."

		NM/M
24	Ken Griffey Jr.	3.00

1994 SP

The second edition of Upper Deck's top-shelf SP brand features each card with a front background printed on metallic foil; the first 20 cards in the set, a series of "Prospects," have front backgrounds of textured metallic foil. Backs are printed with standard processes and include a color player photo a few stats and typical copyright notice and logos. Each foil pack contains one card featuring a special die-cut treatment at top.

		NM/M
Complete Set (200):		125.00
Common Player:		.10
Die-Cut:		1-2X
Pack (8):		15.00
Wax Box (32):		450.00
1	Mike Bell RC	.10
2	D.J. Boston	.10
3	Johnny Damon	.45
4	Brad Fullmer RC	.75
5	Joey Hamilton	.10
6	Todd Hollandsworth	.10
7	Brian Hunter	.10
8	LaTroy Hawkins RC	.25
9	Brooks Kieschnick RC	.10
10	Derek Lee RC	15.00
11	Trot Nixon RC	3.00
12	Alex Ochoa	.10
13	Chan Ho Park RC	1.50
14	Kirk Presley RC	.10
15	Alex Rodriguez RC	100.00
16	Jose Silva RC	.10
17	Terrell Wade RC	.10
18	Billy Wagner RC	1.00
19	Glenn Williams RC	.10
20	Preston Wilson	.10
21	Brian Anderson	.10
22	Chad Curtis	.10
23	Chili Davis	.10
24	Bo Jackson	.25
25	Mark Langston	.10
26	Tim Salmon	.10
27	Jeff Bagwell	1.00
28	Craig Biggio	.10
29	Ken Caminiti	.10
30	Doug Drabek	.10
31	John Hudek	.10
32	Greg Swindell	.10
33	Brent Gates	.10
34	Rickey Henderson	1.00
35	Steve Karsay	.10
36	Mark McGwire	2.50
37	Ruben Sierra	.10
38	Terry Steinbach	.10
39	Roberto Alomar	.30
40	Joe Carter	.10
41	Carlos Delgado	.50
42	Alex Gonzalez	.10
43	Juan Guzman	.10
44	Paul Molitor	1.00
45	John Olerud	.10
46	Devon White	.10
47	Steve Avery	.10
48	Jeff Blauser	.10
49	Tom Glavine	.35
50	Dave Justice	.10
51	Roberto Kelly	.10
52	Ryan Klesko	.10
53	Javier Lopez	.10
54	Greg Maddux	1.25
55	Fred McGriff	.10
56	Ricky Bones	.10
57	Cal Eldred	.10
58	Brian Harper	.10
59	Pat Listach	.10
60	B.J. Surhoff	.10
61	Greg Vaughn	.10
62	Bernard Gilkey	.10
63	Gregg Jefferies	.10
64	Ray Lankford	.10
65	Ozzie Smith	1.25
66	Bob Tewksbury	.10
67	Mark Whiten	.10
68	Todd Zeile	.10
69	Mark Grace	.10
70	Randy Myers	.10
71	Ryne Sandberg	1.25
72	Sammy Sosa	1.25
73	Steve Trachsel	.10
74	Rick Wilkins	.10
75	Brett Butler	.10
76	Delino DeShields	.10
77	Orel Hershiser	.10
78	Eric Karros	.10
79	Raul Mondesi	.10
80	Mike Piazza	2.00
81	Tim Wallach	.10
82	Moises Alou	.10
83	Cliff Floyd	.10
84	Marquis Grissom	.10
85	Pedro Martinez	1.00
86	Larry Walker	.10
87	John Wetteland	.10
88	Rondell White	.10
89	Rod Beck	.10
90	Barry Bonds	3.00
91	John Burkett	.10
92	Royce Clayton	.10
93	Billy Swift	.10
94	Robby Thompson	.10
95	Matt Williams	.10
96	Carlos Baerga	.10
97	Albert Belle	.10
98	Kenny Lofton	.10
99	Dennis Martinez	.10
100	Eddie Murray	1.00
101	Manny Ramirez	1.00
102	Eric Anthony	.10
103	Chris Bosio	.10
104	Jay Buhner	.10
105	Ken Griffey Jr.	2.00
106	Randy Johnson	1.00
107	Edgar Martinez	.10
108	Chuck Carr	.10

109	Jeff Conine	.10
110	Carl Everett	.10
111	Chris Hammond	.10
112	Bryan Harvey	.10
113	Charles Johnson	.10
114	Gary Sheffield	.45
115	Bobby Bonilla	.10
116	Dwight Gooden	.10
117	Todd Hundley	.10
118	Bobby Jones	.10
119	Jeff Kent	.10
120	Bret Saberhagen	.10
121	Jeffrey Hammonds	.10
122	Chris Hoiles	.10
123	Ben McDonald	.10
124	Mike Mussina	.40
125	Rafael Palmeiro	.10
126	Cal Ripken, Jr.	3.00
127	Lee Smith	.10
128	Derek Bell	.10
129	Andy Benes	.10
130	Tony Gwynn	1.25
131	Trevor Hoffman	.10
132	Phil Plantier	.10
133	Bip Roberts	.10
134	Darren Daulton	.10
135	Len Dykstra	.10
136	Dave Hollins	.10
137	Danny Jackson	.10
138	John Kruk	.10
139	Kevin Stocker	.10
140	Jay Bell	.10
141	Carlos Garcia	.10
142	Jeff King	.10
143	Orlando Merced	.10
144	Andy Van Slyke	.10
145	Paul Wagner	.10
146	Jose Canseco	.50
147	Will Clark	.10
148	Juan Gonzalez	.10
149	Rick Helling	.10
150	Dean Palmer	.10
151	Ivan Rodriguez	.75
152	Roger Clemens	1.50
153	Scott Cooper	.10
154	Andre Dawson	.30
155	Mike Greenwell	.10
156	Aaron Sele	.10
157	Mo Vaughn	.10
158	Bret Boone	.10
159	Barry Larkin	.10
160	Kevin Mitchell	.10
161	Jose Rijo	.10
162	Deion Sanders	.10
163	Reggie Sanders	.10
164	Dante Bichette	.10
165	Ellis Burks	.10
166	Andres Galarraga	.10
167	Charlie Hayes	.10
168	David Nied	.10
169	Walt Weiss	.10
170	Kevin Appier	.10
171	David Cone	.10
172	Jeff Granger	.10
173	Felix Jose	.10
174	Wally Joyner	.10
175	Brian McRae	.10
176	Cecil Fielder	.10
177	Travis Fryman	.10
178	Mike Henneman	.10
179	Tony Phillips	.10
180	Mickey Tettleton	.10
181	Alan Trammell	.10
182	Rick Aguilera	.10
183	Rich Becker	.10
184	Scott Erickson	.10
185	Chuck Knoblauch	.10
186	Kirby Puckett	1.25
187	Dave Winfield	1.00
188	Wilson Alvarez	.10
189	Jason Bere	.10
190	Alex Fernandez	.10
191	Julio Franco	.10
192	Jack McDowell	.10
193	Frank Thomas	1.00
194	Robin Ventura	.10
195	Jim Abbott	.10
196	Wade Boggs	1.25
197	Jimmy Key	.10
198	Don Mattingly	1.50
199	Paul O'Neill	.10
200	Danny Tartabull	.10

Die-Cut

Upper Deck SP Die-cuts are a 200-card parallel set inserted at the rate of one per foil pack. Each card

has a die-cut top instead of the flat-top found on regular SP cards. Die-cuts also have a silver-foil Upper Deck hologram logo on back, in contrast to the gold-tone hologram found on regular SP; this is an effort to prevent fraudulent replication by any crook with a pair of scissors.

Holoview Blue

Holoview F/X Blue is a 38-card set utilizing Holoview printing technology, which uses 200 frames of video to produce a three-dimensional image on the bottom third of each card. The hologram is bordered in blue and there is a blue stripe running down the right side of the card. Backs are done with a blue background and feature a player photo over top of bold letters reading "Holoview FX." This insert could be found in one per five packs of SP baseball.

		NM/M
Common Player:		1.50
1	Roberto Alomar	2.00
2	Kevin Appier	1.50
3	Jeff Bagwell	3.00
4	Jose Canseco	3.00
5	Roger Clemens	6.00
6	Carlos Delgado	2.00
7	Cecil Fielder	1.50
8	Cliff Floyd	1.50
9	Travis Fryman	1.50
10	Andres Galarraga	1.50
11	Juan Gonzalez	3.00
12	Ken Griffey Jr.	6.00
13	Tony Gwynn	3.00
14	Jeffrey Hammonds	1.50
15	Bo Jackson	3.00
16	Michael Jordan	15.00
17	Dave Justice	1.50
18	Steve Karsay	1.50
19	Jeff Kent	2.00
20	Brooks Kieschnick	1.50
21	Ryan Klesko	1.50
22	John Kruk	1.50
23	Barry Larkin	2.00
24	Pat Listach	1.50
25	Don Mattingly	5.00
26	Mark McGwire	8.00
27	Raul Mondesi	1.50
28	Trot Nixon	1.50
29	Mike Piazza	6.00
30	Kirby Puckett	4.00
31	Manny Ramirez	3.00
32	Cal Ripken, Jr.	10.00
33	Alex Rodriguez	75.00
34	Tim Salmon	1.50
35	Gary Sheffield	2.00
36	Ozzie Smith	4.00
37	Sammy Sosa	4.00
38	Andy Van Slyke	1.50

Holoview Blue Mismatches

Some Holoview Blue inserts are known on which the player photograph and data do not match the player shown in the horizontal hologram at bottom front.

Holoview Red

Holoview F/X Red is a parallel set to the Blue insert. Once again,

this 38-card set utilizes Holoview printing technology. However, these cards have a red border surrounding the hologram and along the right side, as well as a red background on the back and a large "SPECIAL FX" under the player photo. Holoview red cards also have die-cut tops. Red cards are much scarcer than blue; the red being inserted once per 75 packs of SP baseball.

		NM/M
Common Player:		12.00
1	Roberto Alomar	15.00
2	Kevin Appier	12.00
3	Jeff Bagwell	30.00
4	Jose Canseco	20.00
5	Roger Clemens	50.00
6	Carlos Delgado	20.00
7	Cecil Fielder	12.00
8	Cliff Floyd	12.00
9	Travis Fryman	12.00
10	Andres Galarraga	12.00
11	Juan Gonzalez	20.00
12	Ken Griffey Jr.	50.00
13	Tony Gwynn	40.00
14	Jeffrey Hammonds	12.00
15	Bo Jackson	20.00
16	Michael Jordan	120.00
17	Dave Justice	12.00
18	Steve Karsay	12.00
19	Jeff Kent	12.00
20	Brooks Kieschnick	12.00
21	Ryan Klesko	12.00
22	John Kruk	12.00
23	Barry Larkin	12.00
24	Pat Listach	12.00
25	Don Mattingly	45.00
26	Mark McGwire	60.00
27	Raul Mondesi	12.00
28	Trot Nixon	20.00
29	Mike Piazza	50.00
30	Kirby Puckett	30.00
31	Manny Ramirez	40.00
32	Cal Ripken, Jr.	80.00
33	Alex Rodriguez	1,200.
34	Tim Salmon	12.00
35	Gary Sheffield	15.00
36	Ozzie Smith	40.00
37	Sammy Sosa	40.00
38	Andy Van Slyke	12.00

Alex Rodriguez Autographed Jumbo

This 3-1/2" x 5" version of A-Rod's SP rookie card was produced in an authentically autographed edition of 500. The card has serial numbers on front and back and a numbered UD Authenticated hologram sticker on front. The card was sold sealed in a heavy plastic holder and velour drawstring bag.

		NM/M
15	Alex Rodriguez	250.00

1995 SP

Foil highlights and die-cut specialty cards are once again featured in Upper Deck's premium-brand SP baseball card issue. The 207-card set opens with four die-cut tribute cards,

followed by 20 Premier Prospect die-cuts printed on metallic foil backgrounds with copper-foil highlights. Three checklists follow, also die-cut. The regular player cards in the set are arranged in team-alphabetical order within league. Card fronts feature photos which are borderless at top, bottom and right. On the left is a gold-highlighted metallic foil border of blue for N.L., red for A.L. Backs have a large photo at top, with a few stats and career highlights at bottom, along with a gold infield-shaped hologram. The SP insert program consists of a "SuperbaFoil" parallel set, in which each card's normal foil highlights are replaced with silver foil; a 48-card Special F/X set utilizing holographic portraits, and, a 20-card Platinum Power set. The hobby-only SP was issued in eight-card foil packs with a $3.99 suggested retail price.

		NM/M
Complete Set (207):		12.50
Common Player:		.05
Pack (8):		1.25
Wax Box (32):		25.00
1	Cal Ripken Jr. (Salute)	2.00
2	Nolan Ryan (Salute)	2.00
3	George Brett (Salute)	1.25
4	Mike Schmidt (Salute)	1.25
5	Dustin Hermanson (Premier Prospects)	.05
6	Antonio Osuna (Premier Prospects)	.05
7	Mark Grudzielanek RC (Premier Prospects)	.35
8	Ray Durham (Premier Prospects)	.05
9	Ugueth Urbina (Premier Prospects)	.05
10	Ruben Rivera (Premier Prospects)	.05
11	Curtis Goodwin (Premier Prospects)	.05
12	Jimmy Hurst (Premier Prospects)	.05
13	Jose Malave (Premier Prospects)	.05
14	Hideo Nomo RC (Premier Prospects)	1.50
15	Juan Acevedo (Premier Prospects)	.05
16	Tony Clark (Premier Prospects)	.05
17	Jim Pittsley (Premier Prospects)	.05
18	Freddy Garcia RC (Premier Prospects)	.05
19	Carlos Perez RC (Premier Prospects)	.05
20	Raul Casanova RC (Premier Prospects)	.05
21	Quilvio Veras (Premier Prospects)	.05
22	Edgardo Alfonzo (Premier Prospects)	.05
23	Marty Cordova (Premier Prospects)	.05
24	C.J. Nitkowski (Premier Prospects)	.05
25	Checklist 1-69 (Wade Boggs)	.30
26	Checklist 70-138 (Dave Winfield)	.25
27	Checklist 139-207 (Eddie Murray)	.25
28	Dave Justice	.05
29	Marquis Grissom	.05
30	Fred McGriff	.05
31	Greg Maddux	1.00
32	Tom Glavine	.35
33	Steve Avery	.05
34	Chipper Jones	1.00
35	Sammy Sosa	1.00
36	Jaime Navarro	.05
37	Randy Myers	.05
38	Mark Grace	.05
39	Todd Zeile	.05
40	Brian McRae	.05
41	Reggie Sanders	.05
42	Ron Gant	.05
43	Deion Sanders	.05
44	Barry Larkin	.05

45	Bret Boone	.05
46	Jose Rijo	.05
47	Jason Bates	.05
48	Andres Galarraga	.05
49	Bill Swift	.05
50	Larry Walker	.05
51	Vinny Castilla	.05
52	Dante Bichette	.05
53	Jeff Conine	.05
54	John Burkett	.05
55	Gary Sheffield	.40
56	Andre Dawson	.30
57	Terry Pendleton	.05
58	Charles Johnson	.05
59	Brian L. Hunter	.05
60	Jeff Bagwell	.75
61	Craig Biggio	.05
62	Phil Nevin	.05
63	Doug Drabek *	.05
64	Derek Bell	.05
65	Raul Mondesi	.05
66	Eric Karros	.05
67	Roger Cedeno	.05
68	Delino DeShields	.05
69	Ramon Martinez	.05
70	Mike Piazza	1.50
71	Billy Ashley	.05
72	Jeff Fassero	.05
73	Shane Andrews	.05
74	Wil Cordero	.05
75	Tony Tarasco	.05
76	Rondell White	.05
77	Pedro Martinez	.75
78	Moises Alou	.05
79	Rico Brogna	.05
80	Bobby Bonilla	.05
81	Jeff Kent	.05
82	Brett Butler	.05
83	Bobby Jones	.05
84	Bill Pulsipher	.05
85	Bret Saberhagen	.05
86	Gregg Jefferies	.05
87	Lenny Dykstra	.05
88	Dave Hollins	.05
89	Charlie Hayes	.05
90	Darren Daulton	.05
91	Curt Schilling	.35
92	Heathcliff Slocumb	.05
93	Carlos Garcia	.05
94	Denny Neagle	.05
95	Jay Bell	.05
96	Orlando Merced	.05
97	Dave Clark	.05
98	Bernard Gilkey	.05
99	Scott Cooper	.05
100	Ozzie Smith	1.00
100	Ken Griffey Jr. (Promo Card)	2.00
101	Tom Henke	.05
102	Ken Hill	.05
103	Brian Jordan	.05
104	Ray Lankford	.05
105	Tony Gwynn	1.00
106	Andy Benes	.05
107	Ken Caminiti	.05
108	Steve Finley	.05
109	Joey Hamilton	.05
110	Bip Roberts	.05
111	Eddie Williams	.05
112	Rod Beck	.05
113	Matt Williams	.05
114	Glenallen Hill	.05
115	Barry Bonds	2.50
116	Robby Thompson	.05
117	Mark Portugal	.05
118	Brady Anderson	.05
119	Mike Mussina	.35
120	Rafael Palmeiro	.65
121	Chris Hoiles	.05
122	Harold Baines	.05
123	Jeffrey Hammonds	.05
124	Tim Naehring	.05
125	Mo Vaughn	.05
126	Mike Macfarlane	.05
127	Roger Clemens	1.25
128	John Valentin	.05
129	Aaron Sele	.05
130	Jose Canseco	.50
131	J.T. Snow	.05
132	Mark Langston	.05
133	Chili Davis	.05
134	Chuck Finley	.05
135	Tim Salmon	.05
136	Tony Phillips	.05
137	Jason Bere	.05
138	Robin Ventura	.05
139	Tim Raines	.05
140a	Frank Thomas (5-yr. BA .326)	.75
140b	Frank Thomas (5-yr. BA .303)	.75
141	Alex Fernandez	.05
142	Jim Abbott	.05
143	Wilson Alvarez	.05
144	Carlos Baerga	.05
145	Albert Belle	.05
146	Jim Thome	.65
147	Dennis Martinez	.05
148	Eddie Murray	.75
149	Dave Winfield	.75
150	Kenny Lofton	.75
151	Manny Ramirez	.75
152	Chad Curtis	.05
153	Lou Whitaker	.05
154	Alan Trammell	.05
155	Cecil Fielder	.05
156	Kirk Gibson	.05
157	Michael Tucker	.05
158	Jon Nunnally	.05
159	Wally Joyner	.05
160	Kevin Appier	.05

#	Player	Price
161	Jeff Montgomery	.05
162	Greg Gagne	.05
163	Ricky Bones	.05
164	Cal Eldred	.05
165	Greg Vaughn	.05
166	Kevin Seitzer	.05
167	Jose Valentin	.05
168	Joe Oliver	.05
169	Rick Aguilera	.05
170	Kirby Puckett	1.00
171	Scott Stahoviak	.05
172	Kevin Tapani	.05
173	Chuck Knoblauch	.05
174	Rich Becker	.05
175	Don Mattingly	1.25
176	Jack McDowell	.05
177	Jimmy Key	.05
178	Paul O'Neill	.05
179	John Wetteland	.05
180	Wade Boggs	1.00
181	Derek Jeter	2.50
182	Rickey Henderson	.75
183	Terry Steinbach	.05
184	Ruben Sierra	.05
185	Mark McGwire	2.00
186	Todd Stottlemyre	.05
187	Dennis Eckersley	.65
188	Alex Rodriguez	2.00
189	Randy Johnson	.75
190	Ken Griffey Jr.	1.50
191	Tino Martinez	.05
192	Jay Buhner	.05
193	Edgar Martinez	.05
194	Mickey Tettleton	.05
195	Juan Gonzalez	.40
196	Benji Gil	.05
197	Dean Palmer	.05
198	Ivan Rodriguez	.65
199	Kenny Rogers	.05
200	Will Clark	.05
201	Roberto Alomar	.20
202	David Cone	.05
203	Paul Molitor	.75
204	Shawn Green	.40
205	Joe Carter	.05
206	Alex Gonzalez	.05
207	Pat Hentgen	.05

SuperbaFoil

This chase set parallels the 207 regular cards in the SP issue. Cards were found at the rate of one per eight-card foil pack. SuperbaFoil cards feature a silver-rainbow metallic foil in place of the gold, copper, red or blue foil highlights on regular-issue SP cards. On back, the SuperbaFoil inserts have a silver hologram instead of the gold version found on standard cards.

NM/M
Complete Set (207): 30.00
Common Player: .10
SuperbaFoil Stars: 1.5X

Platinum Power

This die-cut insert set features the game's top power hitters in color action photos set against a background of two-toned gold rays emanating from the SP logo at lower-right. Player name, team and position are printed in white in a black band at bottom. Backs repeat the golden ray effect in the background and have a color photo at center. Career and 1994 stats are presented. An infield-shaped gold foil hologram is at lower-right. Cards have a "PP" prefix. Stated odds of finding one of the 20 Platinum Power inserts are one per five packs.

NM/M
Complete Set (20): 10.00
Common Player: .20

#	Player	Price
1	Jeff Bagwell	.75
2	Barry Bonds	2.00
3	Ron Gant	.20
4	Fred McGriff	.20
5	Raul Mondesi	.20
6	Mike Piazza	1.25
7	Larry Walker	.20
8	Matt Williams	.20
9	Albert Belle	.20
10	Cecil Fielder	.20
11	Juan Gonzalez	.40
12	Ken Griffey Jr.	1.25
13	Mark McGwire	1.50
14	Eddie Murray	.75
15	Manny Ramirez	.75
16	Cal Ripken Jr.	2.00
17	Tim Salmon	.20
18	Frank Thomas	.65
19	Jim Thome	.65
20	Mo Vaughn	.20

Special F/X

By far the preferred pick of the '95 SP insert program is the Special F/X set of 48. The cards have a color action photo on front, printed on a metallic foil background. A 3/4" square holographic portrait is printed on the front. Backs are printed in standard technology and include another photo and a few stats and career highlights. Stated odds of finding a Special F/X card are 1 per 75 packs, or about one per two boxes.

NM/M
Complete Set (48): 200.00
Common Player: 2.00

#	Player	Price
1	Jose Canseco	6.00
2	Roger Clemens	20.00
3	Mo Vaughn	2.00
4	Tim Salmon	2.00
5	Chuck Finley	2.00
6	Robin Ventura	2.00
7	Jason Bere	2.00
8	Carlos Baerga	2.00
9	Albert Belle	4.00
10	Kenny Lofton	3.00
11	Manny Ramirez	8.00
12	Jeff Montgomery	2.00
13	Kirby Puckett	15.00
14	Wade Boggs	5.00
15	Don Mattingly	15.00
16	Cal Ripken Jr.	25.00
17	Ruben Sierra	2.00
18	Ken Griffey Jr.	20.00
19	Randy Johnson	8.00
20	Alex Rodriguez	25.00
21	Will Clark	5.00
22	Juan Gonzalez	4.00
23	Roberto Alomar	4.00
24	Joe Carter	3.00
25	Alex Gonzalez	2.00
26	Paul Molitor	6.00
27	Ryan Klesko	2.00
28	Fred McGriff	3.00
29	Greg Maddux	15.00
30	Sammy Sosa	10.00
31	Bret Boone	2.00
32	Barry Larkin	5.00
33	Reggie Sanders	2.00
34	Dante Bichette	2.00
35	Andres Galarraga	2.00
36	Charles Johnson	2.00
37	Gary Sheffield	5.00
38	Jeff Bagwell	8.00
39	Craig Biggio	4.00
40	Eric Karros	2.00
41	Billy Ashley	2.00
42	Raul Mondesi	2.00
43	Mike Piazza	10.00
44	Rondell White	2.00
45	Bret Saberhagen	2.00
46	Tony Gwynn	8.00
47	Melvin Nieves	2.00
48	Matt Williams	2.00

Griffey Gold Signature

A specially autographed version of Griffey's card from 1995 SP was made available from Upper Deck Authenticated. These cards are signed and numbered in gold ink from within an edition of 1,000.

NM/M
190 Ken Griffey Jr. 65.00

1995 SP/Championship

Championship was a version of Upper Deck's popular SP line designed for sale in retail outlets. The first 20 cards in the set are a "Diamond in the Rough" subset featuring hot rookies printed on textured metallic foil background. Regular player cards are arranged by team within league, alphabetically by city name. Each team set is led off with a "Pro Files" card of a star player; those card backs feature team season and post-season results. Each of the regular player cards has a borderless action photo on front, highlighted with a gold-foil SP Championship logo. The team name is in a blue-foil oval on National Leaguers' cards; red on American Leaguers'. Backs have a portrait photo, a few stats and career highlights. Situated between the N.L. and A.L. cards in the checklist are a subset of 15 October Legends. A parallel set of cards with die-cut tops was inserted into the six-card foil packs at the rate of one per pack. A special card honoring Cal Ripken's consecutive-game record was issued as a super-scarce insert.

NM/M
Complete Set (200): 25.00
Common Player: .05
Die-Cuts: 1.5X
Wax Pack (6): 1.00
Wax Box (44): 30.00

#	Player	Price
1	Hideo Nomo RC (Diamonds in the Rough)	1.50
2	Roger Cedeno (Diamonds in the Rough)	.05
3	Curtis Goodwin (Diamonds in the Rough)	.05
4	Jon Nunnally (Diamonds in the Rough)	.05
5	Bill Pulsipher (Diamonds in the Rough)	.05
6	C.J. Nitkowski (Diamonds in the Rough)	.05
7	Dustin Hermanson (Diamonds in the Rough)	.05
8	Marty Cordova (Diamonds in the Rough)	.05
9	Ruben Rivera (Diamonds in the Rough)	.05
10	Ariel Prieto RC (Diamonds in the Rough)	.05
11	Edgardo Alfonzo (Diamonds in the Rough)	.05
12	Ray Durham (Diamonds in the Rough)	.05
13	Quilvio Veras (Diamonds in the Rough)	.05
14	Ugueth Urbina (Diamonds in the Rough)	.05
15	Carlos Perez RC (Diamonds in the Rough)	.05
16	Glenn Dishman RC (Diamonds in the Rough)	.05
17	Jeff Suppan (Diamonds in the Rough)	.05
18	Jason Bates (Diamonds in the Rough)	.05
19	Jason Isringhausen (Diamonds in the Rough)	.05
20	Derek Jeter (Diamonds in the Rough)	2.00
21	Fred McGriff (Major League Profiles)	.05
22	Marquis Grissom	.05
23	Fred McGriff	.05
24	Tom Glavine	.35
25	Greg Maddux	1.00
26	Chipper Jones	1.00
27	Sammy Sosa (Major League Profiles)	.50
28	Randy Myers	.05
29	Mark Grace	.05
30	Sammy Sosa	1.00
31	Todd Zeile	.05
32	Brian McRae	.05
33	Ron Gant (Major League Profiles)	.05
34	Reggie Sanders	.05
35	Ron Gant	.05
36	Barry Larkin	.05
37	Bret Boone	.05
38	John Smiley	.05
39	Larry Walker (Major League Profiles)	.05
40	Andres Galarraga	.05
41	Bill Swift	.05
42	Larry Walker	.05
43	Vinny Castilla	.05
44	Dante Bichette	.05
45	Jeff Conine (Major League Profiles)	.05
46	Charles Johnson	.05
47	Gary Sheffield	.45
48	Andre Dawson	.25
49	Jeff Conine	.05
50	Jeff Bagwell (Major League Profiles)	.40
51	Phil Nevin	.05
52	Craig Biggio	.05
53	Brian L. Hunter	.05
54	Doug Drabek	.05
55	Jeff Bagwell	.75
56	Derek Bell	.05
57	Mike Piazza (Major League Profiles)	.65
58	Raul Mondesi	.05
59	Eric Karros	.05
60	Mike Piazza	1.25
61	Ramon Martinez	.05
62	Billy Ashley	.05
63	Rondell White (Major League Profiles)	.05
64	Jeff Fassero	.05
65	Moises Alou	.05
66	Tony Tarasco	.05
67	Rondell White	.05
68	Pedro Martinez	.75
69	Bobby Jones (Major League Profiles)	.05
70	Bobby Bonilla	.05
71	Bobby Jones	.05
72	Bret Saberhagen	.05
73	Darren Daulton (Major League Profiles)	.05
74	Darren Daulton	.05
75	Gregg Jefferies	.05
76	Tyler Green	.05
77	Heathcliff Slocumb	.05
78	Lenny Dykstra	.05
79	Jay Bell (Major League Profiles)	.05
80	Denny Neagle	.05
81	Orlando Merced	.05
82	Jay Bell	.05
83	Ozzie Smith (Major League Profiles)	.50
84	Ken Hill	.05
85	Ozzie Smith	1.00
86	Bernard Gilkey	.05
87	Ray Lankford	.05
88	Tony Gwynn (Major League Profiles)	.50
89	Ken Caminiti	.05
90	Tony Gwynn	1.00
91	Joey Hamilton	.05
92	Bip Roberts	.05
93	Deion Sanders (Major League Profiles)	.05
94	Glenallen Hill	.05
95	Matt Williams	.05
96	Barry Bonds	2.00
97	Rod Beck	.05
98	Eddie Murray (Checklist)	.35
99	Cal Ripken Jr. (Checklist)	1.00
100	Roberto Alomar (October Legends)	.10
101	George Brett (October Legends)	.60
102	Joe Carter (Ocober Legends)	.05
103	Will Clark (October Legends)	.05
104	Dennis Eckersley (October Legends)	.40
105	Whitey Ford (October Legends)	.40
106	Steve Garvey (October Legends)	.05
107	Kirk Gibson (October Legends)	.05
108	Orel Hershiser (October Legends)	.05
109	Reggie Jackson (October Legends)	.50
110	Paul Molitor (October Legends)	.40
111	Kirby Puckett (October Legends)	.05
112	Mike Schmidt (October Legends)	.60
113	Dave Stewart (October Legends)	.05
114	Alan Trammell (October Legends)	.05
115	Cal Ripken Jr. (Major League Profiles)	1.00
116	Brady Anderson	.05
117	Mike Mussina	.30
118	Rafael Palmeiro	.65
119	Chris Hoiles	.05
120	Cal Ripken Jr.	2.00
121	Mo Vaughn (Major League Profiles)	.05
122	Roger Clemens	1.25
123	Tim Naehring	.05
124	John Valentin	.05
125	Mo Vaughn	.05
126	Tim Wakefield	.05
127	Jose Canseco	.40
128	Rick Aguilera	.05
129	Chili Davis (Major League Profiles)	.05
130	Lee Smith	.05
131	Jim Edmonds	.05
132	Chuck Finley	.05
133	Chili Davis	.05
134	J.T. Snow	.05
135	Tim Salmon	.05
136	Frank Thomas (Major League Profiles)	.45
137	Jason Bere	.05
138	Robin Ventura	.05
139	Tim Raines	.05
140	Frank Thomas	.75
141	Alex Fernandez	.05
142	Eddie Murray (Major League Profiles)	.40
143	Carlos Baerga	.05
144	Eddie Murray	.75
145	Albert Belle	.05
146	Jim Thome	.65
147	Dennis Martinez	.05
148	Dave Winfield	.75
149	Kenny Lofton	.05
150	Manny Ramirez	.75
151	Cecil Fielder (Major League Profiles)	.05
152	Lou Whitaker	.05
153	Alan Trammell	.05
154	Kirk Gibson	.05
155	Cecil Fielder	.05
156	Bobby Higginson RC	.25
157	Kevin Appier (Major League Profiles)	.05
158	Wally Joyner	.05
159	Jeff Montgomery	.05
160	Kevin Appier	.05
161	Gary Gaetti	.05
162	Greg Gagne	.05
163	Ricky Bones (Major League Profiles)	.05
164	Greg Vaughn	.05
165	Kevin Seitzer	.05
166	Ricky Bones	.05
167	Kirby Puckett (Major League Profiles)	.50
168	Pedro Munoz	.05
169	Chuck Knoblauch	.05
170	Kirby Puckett	1.00
171	Don Mattingly (Major League Profiles)	.60
172	Wade Boggs	1.00
173	Paul O'Neill	.05
174	John Wetteland	.05
175	Don Mattingly	1.25
176	Jack McDowell	.05
177	Mark McGwire (Major League Profiles)	.05
178	Rickey Henderson	.75
179	Terry Steinbach	.05
180	Ruben Sierra	.05
181	Mark McGwire	1.50
182	Dennis Eckersley	.05
183	Ken Griffey Jr. (Major League Profiles)	.65
184	Alex Rodriguez	1.50
185	Ken Griffey Jr.	1.25
186	Randy Johnson	.75
187	Jay Buhner	.05
188	Edgar Martinez	.05
189	Will Clark (Major League Profiles)	.05
190	Juan Gonzalez	.40
191	Benji Gil	.05
192	Ivan Rodriguez	.65
193	Kenny Rogers	.05
194	Will Clark	.05
195	Paul Molitor (Major League Profiles)	.40
196	Roberto Alomar	.20
197	David Cone	.05
198	Paul Molitor	.75
199	Shawn Green	.30
200	Joe Carter	.05
CR1	Cal Ripken Jr. (2,131 games tribute)	5.00
CR1	Cal Ripken Jr. Die-Cut	7.50

Die-Cuts

Each of the 200 cards in the regular SP championship issue, plus the 20 insert cards, can also be found in a parallel chase card set with die-cut tops. One die-cut card was found in each six-card foil pack, making them five times scarcer than the regular cards. To prevent regular cards from being fraudulently cut, factory-issue die-cuts have the Upper Deck hologram on back in silver tone, rather than the gold holograms found on regular cards.

NM/M
Complete Set (200): 50.00
Common Player: .25
Die-Cut Stars: 1.5X

Classic Performances

Vintage action photos are featured in this chase set marking great post-season performances of modern times. The cards have a wide red strip at top with "CLASSIC PERFORMANCES" in gold-foil; the player's name, team and the SP Championship embossed logo at bottom are also in gold. Backs have a portrait photo and description of the highlight along with stats from that series. Regular Classic Performances cards are found at a stated rate of one per 15 foil packs, with die-cut versions in every 75 packs, on average. The die-cuts have silver UD holograms on back as opposed to the gold hologram found on regular versions of the chase cards.

NM/M
Complete Set (10): 8.00
Common Player: .50
Complete Die-Cut Set (10): 16.00
Common Die-Cuts: 1.00

#	Player	Price
CP1	Reggie Jackson (Game 6 of '77 WS)	.60
CP1	Reggie Jackson (Die-Cut)	2.00
CP2	Nolan Ryan (Game 3 of '69 WS)	4.00
CP2	Nolan Ryan (Die-Cut)	8.00
CP3	Kirk Gibson (Game 1 of '88 WS)	.50
CP3	Kirk Gibson (Die-Cut)	1.00
CP4	Joe Carter (Game 6 of '93 WS)	.50
CP4	Joe Carter (Die-Cut)	1.00
CP5	George Brett (Game 3 of '80 ALCS)	1.25
CP5	George Brett (Die-Cut)	2.50
CP6	Roberto Alomar (Game 4 of '92 ALCS)	.50
CP6	Roberto Alomar (Die-Cut)	1.00
CP7	Ozzie Smith (Game 5 of '85 NLCS)	.75
CP7	Ozzie Smith (Die-Cut)	1.00

CP8	Kirby Puckett (Game 6 of '91 WS)	1.25
CP8	Kirby Puckett (Die-Cut)	2.00
CP9	Bret Saberhagen (Game 7 of '85 WS)	.50
CP9	Bret Saberhagen (Die-Cut)	1.00
CP10	Steve Garvey (Game 4 of '84 NLCS)	.50
CP10	Steve Garvey (Die-Cut)	1.00

Destination: Fall Classic

Colored foil background printing and copper-foil graphic highlights are featured on this insert set picturing players who, for the most part, had yet to make a post-season appearance prior to 1995's expanded playoffs. Found at a stated average rate of one per 40 foil packs, the cards have short career summaries and another photo on back. A die-cut version of the cards was also issued, with a silver UD hologram on back rather than the gold found on the standard chase cards. The die-cut Fall Classic cards were inserted at a rate of one per 75 packs.

		NM/M
Complete Set (9):		18.00
Common Player:		1.00
Complete Die-Cut Set (9):		36.00
Common Die-Cut:		2.00
1	Ken Griffey Jr.	3.00
1	Ken Griffey Jr. (Die-Cut)	6.00
2	Frank Thomas	2.00
2	Frank Thomas (Die-Cut)	4.00
3	Albert Belle	1.00
3	Albert Belle (Die-Cut)	2.00
4	Mike Piazza	3.00
4	Mike Piazza (Die-Cut)	6.00
5	Don Mattingly	2.75
5	Don Mattingly (Die-Cut)	5.50
6	Hideo Nomo	1.50
6	Hideo Nomo (Die-Cut)	3.00
7	Greg Maddux	2.50
7	Greg Maddux (Die-Cut)	5.00
8	Fred McGriff	1.00
8	Fred McGriff (Die-Cut)	2.00
9	Barry Bonds	4.00
9	Barry Bonds (Die-Cut)	8.00

Ripken Tribute Jumbo

A special super-size (3" x 5") version of the SP/Championship edition Cal Ripken Jr. 2,131 Games tribute card insert was created for sale by Upper Deck Authentic on home shopping programs. The card is die-cut and serially numbered on back from within an edition of 2,131 pieces.

		NM/M
CR1	Cal Ripken Jr.	12.00

1996 SP FanFest Promos

To introduce its SP product, Upper Deck prepared an eight-card promo set for distribution at the All-Star FanFest in Philadelphia. The promos are identical in format to the issued versions except for the pres-

ence of a bright silver-foil FanFest logo in the lower-left corner of each card's front. The cards lack the overprint which has become standard on promo cards in the recent years.

		NM/M
Complete Set (8):		8.00
Common Player:		.60
1	Ken Griffey Jr.	1.50
2	Frank Thomas	1.00
3	Albert Belle	.60
4	Mo Vaughn	.60
5	Barry Bonds	2.50
6	Mike Piazza	1.50
7	Matt Williams	.60
8	Sammy Sosa	1.25

1996 SP

This 188-card set, distributed through hobby-only channels, features tremendous photography, including two photos on the front, and six insert sets. The inserts sets are Heroes, Marquee Matchups Blue and Die-Cut Marquee Matchups Red, Holoview Special F/X Blue and Die-Cut Holoview Special F/X Red, and the continuation of the Cal Ripken Collection.

		NM/M
Complete Set (188):		12.50
Common Player:		.05
Pack (8):		1.25
Wax Box (30):		25.00
1	Rey Ordonez (Premier Prospects)	.05
2	George Arias (Premier Prospects)	.05
3	Osvaldo Fernandez RC (Premier Prospects)	.25
4	Darin Erstad RC (Premier Prospects)	2.00
5	Paul Wilson (Premier Prospects)	.05
6	Richard Hidalgo (Premier Prospects)	.05
7	Bob Wolcott (Premier Prospects)	.05
8	Jimmy Haynes (Premier Prospects)	.05
9	Edgar Renteria (Premier Prospects)	.05
10	Alan Benes (Premier Prospects)	.05
11	Chris Snopek (Premier Prospects)	.05
12	Billy Wagner (Premier Prospects)	.05
13	Mike Grace RC (Premier Prospects)	.05
14	Todd Greene (Premier Prospects)	.05
15	Karim Garcia (Premier Prospects)	.05
16	John Wasdin (Premier Prospects)	.05
17	Jason Kendall (Premier Prospects)	.05
18	Bob Abreu (Premier Prospects)	.15
19	Jermaine Dye (Premier Prospects)	.05
20	Jason Schmidt (Premier Prospects)	.05
21	Javy Lopez	.05
22	Ryan Klesko	.05
23	Tom Glavine	.35
24	John Smoltz	.05
25	Greg Maddux	1.00
26	Chipper Jones	.05
27	Fred McGriff	.05
28	David Justice	.05
29	Roberto Alomar	.20
30	Cal Ripken Jr.	2.00
31	Jeffrey Hammonds	.05
32	Bobby Bonilla	.05
33	Mike Mussina	.30
34	Randy Myers	.05
35	Rafael Palmeiro	.65
36	Brady Anderson	.05
37	Tim Naehring	.05
38	Jose Canseco	.40
39	Roger Clemens	1.00
40	Mo Vaughn	.05
41	Jose Valentin RC	.05
42	Kevin Mitchell	.05
43	Chili Davis	.05
44	Garret Anderson	.05
45	Tim Salmon	.05
46	Chuck Finley	.05
47	Mark Langston	.05
48	Jim Abbott	.05
49	J.T. Snow	.05
50	Jim Edmonds	.05
51	Sammy Sosa	1.00
52	Brian McRae	.05
53	Ryne Sandberg	1.00
54	Mark Grace	.05
55	Jaime Navarro	.05
56	Harold Baines	.05
57	Robin Ventura	.05
58	Tony Phillips	.05
59	Alex Fernandez	.05
60	Frank Thomas	.75
61	Ray Durham	.05
62	Bret Boone	.05
63	Barry Larkin	.05
64	Pete Schourek	.05
65	Reggie Sanders	.05
66	John Smiley	.05
67	Carlos Baerga	.05
68	Jim Thome	.65
69	Eddie Murray	.75
70	Albert Belle	.05
71	Dennis Martinez	.05
72	Jack McDowell	.05
73	Kenny Lofton	.05
74	Manny Ramirez	.75
75	Dante Bichette	.05
76	Vinny Castilla	.05
77	Andres Galarraga	.05
78	Walt Weiss	.05
79	Ellis Burks	.05
80	Larry Walker	.05
81	Cecil Fielder	.05
82	Melvin Nieves	.05
83	Travis Fryman	.05
84	Chad Curtis	.05
85	Alan Trammell	.05
86	Gary Sheffield	.45
87	Charles Johnson	.05
88	Andre Dawson	.30
89	Jeff Conine	.05
90	Greg Colbrunn	.05
91	Derek Bell	.05
92	Brian Hunter	.05
93	Doug Drabek	.05
94	Craig Biggio	.05
95	Jeff Bagwell	.75
96	Kevin Appier	.05
97	Jeff Montgomery	.05
98	Michael Tucker	.05
99	Bip Roberts	.05
100	Johnny Damon	.35
101	Eric Karros	.05
102	Raul Mondesi	.05
103	Ramon Martinez	.05
104	Ismael Valdes	.05
105	Mike Piazza	1.25
106	Hideo Nomo	.40
107	Chan Ho Park	.05
108	Ben McDonald	.05
109	Kevin Seitzer	.05
110	Greg Vaughn	.05
111	Jose Valentin	.05
112	Rick Aguilera	.05
113	Marty Cordova	.05
114	Brad Radke	.05
115	Kirby Puckett	1.00
116	Chuck Knoblauch	.05
117	Paul Molitor	.75
118	Pedro Martinez	.75
119	Mike Lansing	.05
120	Rondell White	.05
121	Moises Alou	.05
122	Mark Grudzielanek	.05
123	Jeff Fassero	.05
124	Rico Brogna	.05
125	Jason Isringhausen	.05
126	Jeff Kent	.05
127	Bernard Gilkey	.05
128	Todd Hundley	.05
129	David Cone	.05
130	Andy Pettitte	.25
131	Wade Boggs	1.00
132	Paul O'Neill	.05
133	Ruben Sierra	.05
134	John Wetteland	.05
135	Derek Jeter	2.00
136	Geronimo Pena	.05
137	Terry Steinbach	.05
138	Ariel Prieto	.05
139	Scott Brosius	.05
140	Mark McGwire	1.50
141	Lenny Dykstra	.05
142	Todd Zeile	.05
143	Benito Santiago	.05
144	Mickey Morandini	.05
145	Gregg Jefferies	.05
146	Denny Neagle	.05
147	Orlando Merced	.05
148	Charlie Hayes	.05
149	Carlos Garcia	.05
150	Jay Bell	.05
151	Ray Lankford	.05
152	Alan Benes	.05
153	Dennis Eckersley	.65
154	Gary Gaetti	.05
155	Ozzie Smith	1.00
156	Ron Gant	.05
157	Brian Jordan	.05
158	Ken Caminiti	.05
159	Rickey Henderson	.75
160	Tony Gwynn	1.00
161	Wally Joyner	.05
162	Andy Ashby	.05
163	Steve Finley	.05
164	Glenallen Hill	.05
165	Matt Williams	.05
166	Barry Bonds	2.00
167	William Van Landingham	.05
168	Rod Beck	.05
169	Randy Johnson	.75
170	Ken Griffey Jr.	1.25
170p	Ken Griffey Jr. (Unmarked promo; bio on back says, ". . .against Cleveland" as opposed to ". . . against the Indians.")	4.00
171	Alex Rodriguez	1.50
172	Edgar Martinez	.05
173	Jay Buhner	.05
174	Russ Davis	.05
175	Juan Gonzalez	.40
176	Mickey Tettleton	.05
177	Will Clark	.05
178	Ken Hill	.05
179	Dean Palmer	.05
180	Ivan Rodriguez	.65
181	Carlos Delgado	.50
182	Alex Gonzalez	.05
183	Shawn Green	.30
184	Erik Hanson	.05
185	Joe Carter	.05
186	Checklist (Hideo Nomo)	.20
187	Checklist (Cal Ripken Jr.)	1.00
188	Checklist (Ken Griffey Jr.)	.65

Baseball Heroes

This 1996 insert set is a continuation of the series which began in 1990. These cards, numbered 81-90, feature nine of today's top stars, plus a Ken Griffey Jr. header card (#81). The cards were seeded one per every 96 packs.

		NM/M
Complete Set (10):		65.00
Common Player:		4.00
81	Ken Griffey Jr. Header	8.00
82	Frank Thomas	6.50
83	Albert Belle	4.00
84	Barry Bonds	12.00
85	Chipper Jones	8.00
86	Hideo Nomo	8.00
87	Mike Piazza	10.00
88	Manny Ramirez	6.50
89	Greg Maddux	8.00
90	Ken Griffey Jr.	10.00

Marquee Matchups Blue

This 20-card Upper Deck SP insert set contains cards that allow collectors to match up the game's top players against each other, such as Greg Maddux against Cal Ripken Jr. The design and stadiums in the background match together when the two cards are next to each other. Blue versions are seeded one per five packs. Cards are numbered with a "MM" prefix.

		NM/M
Complete Set (20):		15.00
Common Player:		.50

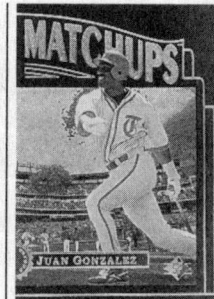

1	Ken Griffey Jr.	2.00
2	Hideo Nomo	.50
3	Derek Jeter	3.00
4	Rey Ordonez	.50
5	Tim Salmon	.50
6	Mike Piazza	1.50
7	Mark McGwire	1.50
8	Barry Bonds	2.00
9	Cal Ripken Jr.	3.00
10	Greg Maddux	1.50
11	Albert Belle	.50
12	Barry Larkin	1.00
13	Jeff Bagwell	.75
14	Juan Gonzalez	.75
15	Frank Thomas	1.00
16	Sammy Sosa	.75
17	Mike Mussina	.75
18	Chipper Jones	1.00
19	Roger Clemens	2.00
20	Fred McGriff	.50

Marquee Matchups Red

A parallel set to the blue Marquee Matchups, the red cards are found on average of one per 61 packs. Besides the red background printing, this version is distinguished from the more common blue version by the die-cutting around the top. Cards are numbered with a "MM" prefix.

		NM/M
Common Player:		1.50
1	Ken Griffey Jr.	10.00
2	Hideo Nomo	2.00
3	Derek Jeter	15.00
4	Rey Ordonez	1.50
5	Tim Salmon	1.50
6	Mike Piazza	8.00
7	Mark McGwire	8.00
8	Barry Bonds	15.00
9	Cal Ripken Jr.	15.00
10	Greg Maddux	10.00
11	Albert Belle	1.50
12	Barry Larkin	4.00
13	Jeff Bagwell	4.00
14	Juan Gonzalez	3.00
15	Frank Thomas	5.00
16	Sammy Sosa	5.00
17	Mike Mussina	4.00
18	Chipper Jones	5.00
19	Roger Clemens	10.00
20	Fred McGriff	5.00

Ripken Collection

The last five cards of the Cal Ripken Jr. Collection, which began in Collector's Choice Series I, are featured in this Upper Deck SP product. These five cards, numbered 18-22, cover Ripken's early days, including his 1982 Rookie of the Year Award, his Major League debut, and photos of him playing third base. Ripken Collection inserts are found one per every 45 packs.

		NM/M
Complete Set (5):		25.00

Common Card:		5.00
18-22	Cal Ripken Jr.	5.00

SpecialFX

These 48 cards capture Upper Deck Holoview technology. Blue versions were seeded one per every five packs of 1996 Upper Deck SP baseball.

		NM/M
Complete Set (48):		50.00
Common Player:		.60
1	Greg Maddux	2.50
2	Eric Karros	.60
3	Mike Piazza	3.00
4	Raul Mondesi	.60
5	Hideo Nomo	1.00
6	Jim Edmonds	.60
7	Jason Isringhausen	.60
8	Jay Buhner	.60
9	Barry Larkin	.60
10	Ken Griffey Jr.	3.00
11	Gary Sheffield	1.25
12	Craig Biggio	.60
13	Paul Wilson	.60
14	Rondell White	.60
15	Chipper Jones	2.50
16	Kirby Puckett	2.50
17	Ron Gant	.60
18	Wade Boggs	2.50
19	Fred McGriff	.60
20	Cal Ripken Jr.	5.00
21	Jason Kendall	.60
22	Johnny Damon	.90
23	Kenny Lofton	.60
24	Roberto Alomar	1.00
25	Barry Bonds	5.00
26	Dante Bichette	.60
27	Mark McGwire	4.00
28	Rafael Palmeiro	1.50
29	Juan Gonzalez	1.00
30	Albert Belle	.60
31	Randy Johnson	1.75
32	Jose Canseco	1.25
33	Sammy Sosa	2.50
34	Eddie Murray	1.75
35	Frank Thomas	1.75
36	Tom Glavine	.90
37	Matt Williams	.60
38	Roger Clemens	2.75
39	Paul Molitor	1.75
40	Tony Gwynn	2.50
41	Mo Vaughn	.60
42	Tim Salmon	.60
43	Manny Ramirez	1.75
44	Jeff Bagwell	1.75
45	Edgar Martinez	.60
46	Rey Ordonez	.60
47	Osvaldo Fernandez	.60
48	Derek Jeter	4.00

SpecialFX Red

These 1996 Upper Deck SP red die-cut cards use Upper Deck's Holoview technology. They are scarcer than the blue versions; these being seeded one per every 75 packs.

		NM/M
Common Player:		3.00
Inserted 1:75		
1	Greg Maddux	20.00
2	Eric Karros	3.00
3	Mike Piazza	10.00
4	Raul Mondesi	3.00
5	Hideo Nomo	4.00

6	Jim Edmonds	4.00
7	Jason Isringhausen	4.00
8	Jay Buhner	3.00
9	Barry Larkin	5.00
10	Ken Griffey Jr.	20.00
11	Gary Sheffield	8.00
12	Craig Biggio	5.00
13	Paul Wilson	3.00
14	Rondell White	3.00
15	Chipper Jones	15.00
16	Kirby Puckett	20.00
17	Ron Gant	3.00
18	Wade Boggs	6.00
19	Fred McGriff	4.00
20	Cal Ripken Jr.	25.00
21	Jason Kendall	3.00
22	Johnny Damon	8.00
23	Kenny Lofton	4.00
24	Roberto Alomar	5.00
25	Barry Bonds	25.00
26	Dante Bichette	3.00
27	Mark McGwire	15.00
28	Rafael Palmeiro	6.00
29	Juan Gonzalez	5.00
30	Albert Belle	3.00
31	Randy Johnson	10.00
32	Jose Canseco	5.00
33	Sammy Sosa	10.00
34	Eddie Murray	8.00
35	Frank Thomas	10.00
36	Tom Glavine	10.00
37	Matt Williams	4.00
38	Roger Clemens	20.00
39	Paul Molitor	8.00
40	Tony Gwynn	10.00
41	Mo Vaughn	5.00
42	Tim Salmon	4.00
43	Manny Ramirez	10.00
44	Jeff Bagwell	8.00
45	Edgar Martinez	3.00
46	Rey Ordonez	3.00
47	Osvaldo Fernandez	3.00
48	Derek Jeter	25.00

1996 SPx

Upper Deck's 1996 SPx set has 60 players in it, which are each paralleled as a Gold version (one per every seven packs). Base cards feature a new look with a different perimeter die-cut design from those used in the past for basketball and football sets. A 10-card insert set, Bound for Glory, was also produced. Tribute cards were also made for Ken Griffey Jr. and Mike Piazza, with scarcer autographed versions also produced for each player.

		NM/M
Complete Set (60):		17.50
Common Player:		.15
Golds:		1.5X
Pack (1):		1.25
Wax Box (36):		25.00
1	Greg Maddux	1.50
2	Chipper Jones	1.50
3	Fred McGriff	.50
4	Tom Glavine	.50
5	Cal Ripken Jr.	3.00
6	Roberto Alomar	.50
7	Rafael Palmeiro	.50
8	Jose Canseco	.65
9	Roger Clemens	1.75
10	Mo Vaughn	.15
11	Jim Edmonds	.15
12	Tim Salmon	.15
13	Sammy Sosa	1.50
14	Ryne Sandberg	1.50
15	Mark Grace	.15
16	Frank Thomas	1.25
17	Barry Larkin	.15
18	Kenny Lofton	.15
19	Albert Belle	.15
20	Eddie Murray	1.25
21	Manny Ramirez	1.25
22	Dante Bichette	.15
23	Larry Walker	.15
24	Vinny Castilla	.15
25	Andres Galarraga	.15
26	Cecil Fielder	.15
27	Gary Sheffield	.75
28	Craig Biggio	.15
29	Jeff Bagwell	1.25
30	Derek Bell	.15
31	Johnny Damon	.60
32	Eric Karros	.15
33	Mike Piazza	2.00
34	Raul Mondesi	.15
35	Hideo Nomo	.65
36	Kirby Puckett	1.50
37	Paul Molitor	1.25
38	Marty Cordova	.15
39	Rondell White	.15
40	Jason Isringhausen	.15
41	Paul Wilson	.15
42	Rey Ordonez	.15
43	Derek Jeter	3.00
44	Wade Boggs	1.50
45	Mark McGwire	2.50
46	Jason Kendall	.15
47	Ron Gant	.15
48	Ozzie Smith	.15
49	Tony Gwynn	1.50
50	Ken Caminiti	.15
51	Barry Bonds	3.00
52	Matt Williams	.15
53	Osvaldo Fernandez RC	.25
54	Jay Buhner	.15
55	Ken Griffey Jr.	2.00
55p	Ken Griffey Jr./OPS	2.00
56	Randy Johnson	1.25
57	Alex Rodriguez	2.50
58	Juan Gonzalez	.65
59	Joe Carter	.15
60	Carlos Delgado	.75

Bound for Glory

Some of baseball's best players are highlighted on these 1996 Upper Deck SPx insert cards. The cards were seeded one per every 24 packs. Fronts of the die-cut cards feature a color photograph on a background of silver-foil holographic portrait and action photos. Backs have another portrait photo, stats, career highlights and logos.

		NM/M
Complete Set (10):		18.00
Common Player:		1.00
1	Ken Griffey Jr.	3.00
2	Frank Thomas	1.50
3	Barry Bonds	4.00
4	Cal Ripken Jr.	4.00
5	Greg Maddux	2.00
6	Chipper Jones	2.00
7	Roberto Alomar	1.00
8	Manny Ramirez	1.50
9	Tony Gwynn	2.00
10	Mike Piazza	3.00

Ken Griffey Jr. Commemorative

Seattle Mariners' star Ken Griffey Jr. has this tribute card in Upper Deck's 1996 SPx set. The card was seeded one per every 75 packs. Autographed versions were also produced; these cards were seeded one per every 2,000 packs.

		NM/M
KG1	Ken Griffey Jr.	2.50
KGA1	Ken Griffey Jr./Auto.	100.00

Mike Piazza Tribute

Los Angeles Dodgers' star catcher Mike Piazza is featured on this 1996 Upper Deck SPx insert card. Normal versions of the card are found one per every 95 packs, making it scarcer than the Ken Griffey Jr. inserts. Autographed Piazza cards are seeded one per every 2,000 packs.

		NM/M
MP1	Mike Piazza	2.00
MP1	Mike Piazza/Auto.	125.00

1997 SP Sample

To preview its SP brand for 1997, Upper Deck issued a sample card of Ken Griffey Jr. Similar in format to the issued cards, the promo bears card number 1 and is overprinted "SAMPLE" on back.

		NM/M
1	Ken Griffey Jr.	3.00

1997 SP

The fifth anniversary edition of SP Baseball features 184 regular cards sold in eight-card packs for $4.39. Card fronts feature the player's name in gold foil-stamping at bottom. Team name and position are vertically at one edge. Backs have two more photos along with "Best Year" and career stats. Inserts include Marquee Matchups, Special FX, Inside Info, Baseball Heroes, Game Film, SPx Force, and Autographed Vintage SP cards.

		NM/M
Complete Set (184):		12.00
Common Player:		.05
Pack (8):		2.00
Wax Box (30):		45.00
1	Andruw Jones (Great Futures)	.75
2	Kevin Orie (Great Futures)	.05
3	Nomar Garciaparra (Great Futures)	1.00
4	Jose Guillen (Great Futures)	.05
5	Todd Walker (Great Futures)	.05
6	Derrick Gibson (Great Futures)	.05
7	Aaron Boone (Great Futures)	.05
8	Bartolo Colon (Great Futures)	.05
9	Derrek Lee (Great Futures)	.50
10	Vladimir Guerrero (Great Futures)	.75
11	Wilton Guerrero (Great Futures)	.05
12	Luis Castillo (Great Futures)	.05
13	Jason Dickson (Great Futures)	.05
14	Bubba Trammell RC (Great Futures)	.25
15	Jose Cruz Jr. RC (Great Futures)	.50
16	Eddie Murray	.75
17	Darin Erstad	.20
18	Garret Anderson	.05
19	Jim Edmonds	.05
20	Tim Salmon	.05
21	Chuck Finley	.05
22	John Smoltz	.05
23	Greg Maddux	1.00
24	Kenny Lofton	1.00
25	Chipper Jones	1.00
26	Ryan Klesko	.05
27	Javier Lopez	.05
28	Fred McGriff	.05
29	Roberto Alomar	.20
30	Rafael Palmeiro	.65
31	Mike Mussina	.30
32	Brady Anderson	.05
33	Rocky Coppinger	.05
34	Cal Ripken Jr.	2.00
35	Mo Vaughn	.05
36	Steve Avery	.05
37	Tom Gordon	.05
38	Tim Naehring	.05
39	Troy O'Leary	.05
40	Sammy Sosa	1.00
41	Brian McRae	.05
42	Mel Rojas	.05
43	Ryne Sandberg	1.00
44	Mark Grace	.05
45	Albert Belle	.05
46	Robin Ventura	.05
47	Roberto Hernandez	.05
48	Ray Durham	.05
49	Harold Baines	.05
50	Frank Thomas	.75
51	Bret Boone	.05
52	Reggie Sanders	.05
53	Deion Sanders	.05
54	Hal Morris	.05
55	Barry Larkin	.05
56	Jim Thome	.65
57	Marquis Grissom	.05
58	David Justice	.05
59	Charles Nagy	.05
60	Manny Ramirez	.75
61	Matt Williams	.05
62	Jack McDowell	.05
63	Vinny Castilla	.05
64	Dante Bichette	.05
65	Andres Galarraga	.05
66	Ellis Burks	.05
67	Larry Walker	.05
68	Eric Young	.05
69	Brian L. Hunter	.05
70	Travis Fryman	.05
71	Tony Clark	.05
72	Bobby Higginson	.05
73	Melvin Nieves	.05
74	Jeff Conine	.05
75	Gary Sheffield	.40
76	Moises Alou	.05
77	Edgar Renteria	.05
78	Alex Fernandez	.05
79	Charles Johnson	.05
80	Bobby Bonilla	.05
81	Darryl Kile	.05
82	Derek Bell	.05
83	Shane Reynolds	.05
84	Craig Biggio	.05
85	Jeff Bagwell	.75
86	Billy Wagner	.05
87	Chili Davis	.05
88	Kevin Appier	.05
89	Jay Bell	.05
90	Johnny Damon	.35
91	Jeff King	.05
92	Hideo Nomo	.40
93	Todd Hollandsworth	.05
94	Eric Karros	.05
95	Mike Piazza	1.25
96	Ramon Martinez	.05
97	Todd Worrell	.05
98	Raul Mondesi	.05
99	Dave Nilsson	.05
100	John Jaha	.05
101	Jose Valentin	.05
102	Jeff Cirillo	.05
103	Jeff D'Amico	.05
104	Ben McDonald	.05
105	Paul Molitor	.75
106	Rich Becker	.05
107	Frank Rodriguez	.05
108	Marty Cordova	.05
109	Terry Steinbach	.05
110	Chuck Knoblauch	.05
111	Mark Grudzielanek	.05
112	Mike Lansing	.05
113	Pedro Martinez	.75
114	Henry Rodriguez	.05
115	Rondell White	.05
116	Rey Ordonez	.05
117	Carlos Baerga	.05
118	Lance Johnson	.05
119	Bernard Gilkey	.05
120	Todd Hundley	.05
121	John Franco	.05
122	Bernie Williams	.75
123	David Cone	.05
124	Cecil Fielder	.05
125	Derek Jeter	2.00
126	Tino Martinez	.05
127	Mariano Rivera	.15
128	Andy Pettitte	.15
129	Wade Boggs	1.00
130	Mark McGwire	1.50
131	Jose Canseco	.50
132	Geronimo Berroa	.05
133	Jason Giambi	.45
134	Ernie Young	.05
135	Scott Rolen	.65
136	Ricky Bottalico	.05
137	Curt Schilling	.35
138	Gregg Jefferies	.05
139	Mickey Morandini	.05
140	Jason Kendall	.05
141	Kevin Elster	.05
142	Al Martin	.05
143	Joe Randa	.05
144	Jason Schmidt	.05
145	Ray Lankford	.05
146	Brian Jordan	.05
147	Andy Benes	.05
148	Alan Benes	.05
149	Gary Gaetti	.05
150	Ron Gant	.05
151	Dennis Eckersley	.65
152	Rickey Henderson	.75
153	Joey Hamilton	.05
154	Ken Caminiti	.05
155	Tony Gwynn	1.00
156	Steve Finley	.05
157	Trevor Hoffman	.05
158	Greg Vaughn	.05
159	J.T. Snow	.05
160	Barry Bonds	2.00
161	Glenallen Hill	.05
162	William Van Landingham	.05
163	Jeff Kent	.05
164	Jay Buhner	.05
165	Ken Griffey Jr.	1.25
166	Alex Rodriguez	1.50
167	Randy Johnson	.75
168	Edgar Martinez	.05
169	Dan Wilson	.05
170	Ivan Rodriguez	.65
171	Roger Pavlik	.05
172	Will Clark	.05
173	Dean Palmer	.05
174	Rusty Greer	.05
175	Juan Gonzalez	.40
176	John Wetteland	.05
177	Joe Carter	.05
178	Ed Sprague	.05
179	Carlos Delgado	.45
180	Roger Clemens	1.00
181	Juan Guzman	.05
182	Pat Hentgen	.05
183	Ken Griffey Jr. (Checklist)	.65
184	Hideki Irabu RC	.25

Buy-Back Autographed Inserts

To celebrate the fifth anniversary of its premium SP brand, Upper Deck went into the hobby market to buy nearly 3,000 previous years' cards for a special insert program in 1997 SP packs. Various SP cards from 1993-96 issues and inserts were autographed by star players and a numbered holographic seal added on back. The number of each particular card signed ranged widely from fewer than 10 to more than 100. Numbers in parentheses in the checklist are the quantity reported signed for that card. All cards were inserted into foil packs except those of Mo Vaughn, which were a mail-in redemption.

		NM/M
Common Autograph:		7.50
4	Ken Griffey Jr./16	600.00
28	Jeff Bagwell/7	100.00
167	Tony Gwynn/17	250.00
280	Chipper Jones/34	110.00
PP9	Ken Griffey Jr./5	800.00
6	Todd Hollandsworth/167	7.50
15	Alex Rodriguez/94	1,200
105	Ken Griffey Jr./103	125.00
114	Gary Sheffield/130	25.00
130	Tony Gwynn/367	25.00
13	Tony Gwynn/31	150.00
35	Gary Sheffield/4	60.00
34	Chipper Jones/60	125.00
60	Jeff Bagwell/173	40.00
75	Gary Sheffield/221	20.00
105	Tony Gwynn/64	60.00
188	Alex Rodriguez/63	200.00
190	Ken Griffey Jr./38	200.00
195	Jay Buhner/57	15.00
6	Rey Ordonez/111	7.50
18	Gary Sheffield/58	30.00
26	Chipper Jones/102	50.00
95	Jeff Bagwell/292	20.00
160	Tony Gwynn/20	200.00
170	Ken Griffey Jr./312	65.00
171	Alex Rodriguez/73	125.00
173	Jay Buhner/79	30.00
MM13	Jeff Bagwell/23	65.00
MM4	Rey Ordonez/40	15.00
8	Jay Buhner/27	30.00

Game Film

A 10-card insert utilizing pieces of actual game footage to highlight the top stars in the game. Only 500 of each card were available. Cards are numbered with a "GF" prefix.

		NM/M
Complete Set (10):		175.00
Common Player:		12.00
1	Alex Rodriguez	25.00
2	Frank Thomas	12.00
3	Andruw Jones	10.00
4	Cal Ripken Jr.	30.00
5	Mike Piazza	15.00
6	Derek Jeter	15.00
7	Mark McGwire	20.00
8	Chipper Jones	15.00
9	Barry Bonds	30.00
10	Ken Griffey Jr.	20.00

Griffey Baseball Heroes

First started in 1990, this single-player insert continues with a salute to Ken Griffey Jr. Each card in the set is numbered to 2,000.

		NM/M
Complete Set (10):		75.00
Common Griffey Jr.:		10.00
91-100	Ken Griffey Jr.	10.00

Inside Info

Each of the 25 cards in this insert feature a pull-out panel describing the player's major accomplishments. Both front and back are printed on metallic-foil stock. Cards were inserted one per box.

		NM/M
Complete Set (25):		75.00
Common Player:		1.00
1	Ken Griffey Jr.	5.00
2	Mark McGwire	6.00
3	Kenny Lofton	1.00
4	Paul Molitor	3.00
5	Frank Thomas	3.00
6	Greg Maddux	3.50
7	Mo Vaughn	1.00
8	Cal Ripken Jr.	7.50
9	Jeff Bagwell	3.00
10	Alex Rodriguez	6.00
11	John Smoltz	1.00
12	Manny Ramirez	3.00
13	Sammy Sosa	3.50
14	Vladimir Guerrero	3.00
15	Albert Belle	1.00
16	Mike Piazza	5.00
17	Derek Jeter	7.50
18	Scott Rolen	2.00
19	Tony Gwynn	3.50

20	Barry Bonds	7.50
21	Ken Caminiti	1.00
22	Chipper Jones	4.00
23	Juan Gonzalez	1.50
24	Roger Clemens	4.00
25	Andruw Jones	3.00

Marquee Matchups

A 20-card die-cut set designed to highlight top interleague matchups, when the matching cards are put together, a third player is highlighted in the background. Cards were inserted 1:5 packs and have an "MM" card-number prefix.

		NM/M
Complete Set (20):		20.00
Common Player:		.25
1	Ken Griffey Jr.	1.50
2	Andres Galarraga	.25
3	Barry Bonds	3.00
4	Mark McGwire	2.00
5	Mike Piazza	1.50
6	Tim Salmon	1.00
7	Tony Gwynn	1.00
8	Alex Rodriguez	2.00
9	Chipper Jones	1.00
10	Derek Jeter	3.00
11	Manny Ramirez	.75
12	Jeff Bagwell	.75
13	Greg Maddux	1.00
14	Cal Ripken Jr.	3.00
15	Mo Vaughn	.25
16	Gary Sheffield	.45
17	Jim Thome	.65
18	Barry Larkin	.25
19	Frank Thomas	.75
20	Sammy Sosa	1.00

Special FX

Color 3-D motion portraits are front and center on these cards that also feature a die-cut design. The rest of the front includes color action photos printed on silver-foil stock. Backs have another color photo. One of the Alex Rodriguez cards (#49) features the 1996 die-cut design. Special FX were inserted 1:9 packs.

		NM/M
Common Player:		.75
1	Ken Griffey Jr.	6.00
2	Frank Thomas	3.00
3	Barry Bonds	8.00
4	Albert Belle	.75
5	Mike Piazza	4.00
6	Greg Maddux	5.00
7	Chipper Jones	4.00
8	Cal Ripken Jr.	8.00
9	Jeff Bagwell	2.00
10	Alex Rodriguez	8.00
11	Mark McGwire	5.00
12	Kenny Lofton	.75
13	Juan Gonzalez	1.50
14	Mo Vaughn	.75
15	John Smoltz	1.00
16	Derek Jeter	8.00
17	Tony Gwynn	3.00
18	Ivan Rodriguez	2.00
19	Barry Larkin	1.00
20	Sammy Sosa	3.00
21	Mike Mussina	1.50
22	Gary Sheffield	2.00
23	Brady Anderson	.75
24	Roger Clemens	6.00

25	Ken Caminiti	.75
26	Roberto Alomar	1.50
27	Hideo Nomo	1.00
28	Bernie Williams	1.00
29	Todd Hundley	.75
30	Manny Ramirez	3.00
31	Eric Karros	.75
32	Tim Salmon	.75
33	Jay Buhner	.75
34	Andy Pettitte	1.50
35	Jim Thome	2.00
36	Ryne Sandberg	3.00
37	Matt Williams	1.00
38	Ryan Klesko	.75
39	Jose Canseco	1.50
40	Paul Molitor	2.00
41	Eddie Murray	2.00
42	Darin Erstad	.75
43	Todd Walker	.75
44	Wade Boggs	2.50
45	Andruw Jones	2.00
46	Scott Rolen	2.00
47	Vladimir Guerrero	3.00
49	Alex Rodriguez (1996 design)	8.00

SPx Force

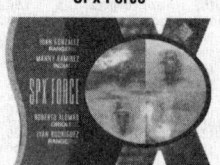

Each of the 10 cards in this set feature four different players. Cards are individually numbered to 500. In addition, a number of players signed 100 versions of their SPx Force cards that are also randomly inserted into packs.

		NM/M
Complete Set (10):		60.00
Common Player:		6.00
1	Ken Griffey Jr., Jay Buhner, Andres Galarraga, Dante Bichette	7.50
2	Albert Belle, Brady Anderson, Mark McGwire, Cecil Fielder	9.00
3	Mo Vaughn, Ken Caminiti, Frank Thomas, Jeff Bagwell	9.00
4	Gary Sheffield, Sammy Sosa, Barry Bonds, Jose Canseco	12.00
5	Greg Maddux, Roger Clemens, John Smoltz, Randy Johnson	6.00
6	Alex Rodriguez, Derek Jeter, Chipper Jones, Rey Ordonez	12.00
7	Todd Hollandsworth, Mike Piazza, Raul Mondesi, Hideo Nomo	7.50
8	Juan Gonzalez, Manny Ramirez, Roberto Alomar, Ivan Rodriguez	6.00
9	Tony Gwynn, Wade Boggs, Eddie Murray, Paul Molitor	6.00
10	Andruw Jones, Vladimir Guerrero, Todd Walker, Scott Rolen	6.00

SPx Force Autographs

Ten players signed cards for this insert, which was serially numbered to 100. The cards were randomly seeded in packs except the Mo Vaughn card which was available by redemption.

		NM/M
Common Player:		20.00
1	Ken Griffey Jr.	125.00
2	Albert Belle	25.00
3	Mo Vaughn	20.00
4	Gary Sheffield	25.00
5	Greg Maddux	100.00
6	Alex Rodriguez	160.00
7	Todd Hollandsworth	20.00
8	Roberto Alomar	30.00
9	Tony Gwynn	75.00
10	Andruw Jones	40.00

1997 SPx

Fifty cards, each featuring a perimeter die-cut design and a 3-D holoview photo, make up the SPx base set. Five different parallel sets - Steel (1:1 pack), Bronze (1:1), Silver (1:1), Gold (1:17) and Grand Finale (50 per card) - are found as inserts, as are Cornerstones of the Game, Bound for Glory and Bound for Glory Signature cards. Packs contain three cards and carried a suggested retail price of $5.99.

		NM/M
Complete Set (50):		20.00
Common Player:		.15
Steel:		1.5X
Bronze:		1.5X
Silver:		1.5X
Gold:		3X
Grand Finale:		4X
Pack (3):		2.00
Wax Box (18):		30.00
1	Eddie Murray	1.00
2	Darin Erstad	.35
3	Tim Salmon	.15
4	Andruw Jones	1.00
5	Chipper Jones	1.50
6	John Smoltz	.15
7	Greg Maddux	1.50
8	Kenny Lofton	.15
9	Roberto Alomar	.30
10	Rafael Palmeiro	.75
11	Brady Anderson	.15
12	Cal Ripken Jr.	3.00
13	Nomar Garciaparra	1.50
14	Mo Vaughn	.15
15	Ryne Sandberg	1.50
16	Sammy Sosa	1.50
17	Frank Thomas	1.00
18	Albert Belle	.15
19	Barry Larkin	.15
20	Deion Sanders	.15
21	Manny Ramirez	1.00
22	Jim Thome	.65
23	Dante Bichette	.15
24	Andres Galarraga	.15
25	Larry Walker	.15
26	Gary Sheffield	.50
27	Jeff Bagwell	1.00
28	Raul Mondesi	.50
29	Hideo Nomo	.50
30	Mike Piazza	2.00
31	Paul Molitor	1.00
32	Todd Walker	.15
33	Vladimir Guerrero	1.00
34	Todd Hundley	.15
35	Andy Pettitte	.25
36	Derek Jeter	3.00
37	Jose Canseco	.50
38	Mark McGwire	2.50
39	Scott Rolen	.65
40	Ron Gant	.15
41	Ken Caminiti	.15
42	Tony Gwynn	1.50
43	Barry Bonds	3.00
44	Jay Buhner	.15
45	Ken Griffey Jr.	2.00
45s	Ken Griffey Jr. (Overprinted "SAMPLE" on back.)	2.00
46	Alex Rodriguez	2.50
47	Jose Cruz Jr. RC	1.00
48	Juan Gonzalez	.50
49	Ivan Rodriguez	.75
50	Roger Clemens	1.75

SPx Bound for Glory

This 20-card insert utilizes holoview technology and is sequentially numbered to 1,500 per card.

		NM/M
Complete Set (20):		60.00
Common Player:		1.00
1	Andruw Jones	3.00
2	Chipper Jones	4.00
3	Greg Maddux	4.00
4	Kenny Lofton	1.00
5	Cal Ripken Jr.	7.50
6	Mo Vaughn	1.00
7	Frank Thomas	3.00
8	Albert Belle	1.00
9	Manny Ramirez	3.00
10	Gary Sheffield	1.50
11	Jeff Bagwell	3.00
12	Mike Piazza	5.00
13	Derek Jeter	7.50
14	Mark McGwire	6.00
15	Tony Gwynn	4.00
16	Ken Caminiti	1.00
17	Barry Bonds	7.50
18	Alex Rodriguez	6.00
19	Ken Griffey Jr.	5.00
20	Juan Gonzalez	1.50

SPx Bound for Glory Supreme Signatures

This five-card set featured autographs from the players and was sequentially numbered to 250.

		NM/M
Complete Set (5):		250.00
Common Player:		30.00
1	Jeff Bagwell	40.00
2	Ken Griffey Jr.	120.00
3	Andruw Jones	40.00
4	Alex Rodriguez	160.00
5	Gary Sheffield	30.00

SPx Cornerstones of the Game

A 20-card insert utilizing a double-front design highlighting 40 of the top players in the game. Each card is sequentially numbered to 500.

		NM/M
Complete Set (10):		150.00
Common Player:		12.00
1	Ken Griffey Jr., Barry Bonds	25.00
2	Frank Thomas, Albert Belle	12.00
3	Chipper Jones, Greg Maddux	15.00
4	Tony Gwynn, Paul Molitor	15.00
5	Andruw Jones, Vladimir Guerrero	12.00
6	Jeff Bagwell, Ryne Sandberg	15.00
7	Mike Piazza, Ivan Rodriguez	20.00
8	Cal Ripken Jr., Eddie Murray	20.00
9	Mo Vaughn, Mark McGwire	20.00
10	Alex Rodriguez, Derek Jeter	25.00

1998 SP Authentic Sample

This card of Upper Deck spokesman Ken Griffey, Jr., was issued to preview the new SP Authentic line. Design is similar to the issued version but the sample displays different photos, a different the card number and the word "SAMPLE" printed in large letters on back.

	NM/M
Ken Griffey Jr.	3.00

1998 SP Authentic

The SP Authentic base set consists of 198 cards, including the 30-card Future Watch subset and one checklist card. The base cards have a color photo inside a thick white border. Inserts include Chirography, Sheer Dominance and SP Authentics.

	NM/M
Complete Set (198):	15.00

		NM/M
Common Player:		.05
Pack (5):		2.00
Wax Box (24):		35.00
1	Travis Lee (Future Watch)	.10
2	Mike Caruso (Future Watch)	.05
3	Kerry Wood (Future Watch)	.65
4	Mark Kotsay (Future Watch)	.05
5	Magglio Ordonez RC (Future Watch)	5.00
6	Scott Elarton (Future Watch)	.05
7	Carl Pavano (Future Watch)	.10
8	A.J. Hinch (Future Watch)	.05
9	Rolando Arrojo RC (Future Watch)	.40
10	Ben Grieve (Future Watch)	.05
11	Gabe Alvarez (Future Watch)	.05
12	Mike Kinkade RC (Future Watch)	.40
13	Bruce Chen (Future Watch)	.05
14	Juan Encarnacion (Future Watch)	.05
15	Todd Helton (Future Watch)	.75
16	Aaron Boone (Future Watch)	.05
17	Sean Casey (Future Watch)	.15
18	Ramon Hernandez (Future Watch)	.05
19	Daryle Ward (Future Watch)	.05
20	Paul Konerko (Future Watch)	.15
21	David Ortiz (Future Watch)	.50
22	Derrek Lee (Future Watch)	.50
23	Brad Fullmer (Future Watch)	.05
24	Javier Vazquez (Future Watch)	.05
25	Miguel Tejada (Future Watch)	.15
26	David Dellucci (Future Watch)	.05
27	Alex Gonzalez (Future Watch)	.05
28	Matt Clement (Future Watch)	.05
29	Eric Milton (Future Watch)	.05
30	Russell Branyan (Future Watch)	.05
31	Chuck Finley	.05
32	Jim Edmonds	.05
33	Jason Dickson	.05
34	Darin Erstad	.20
35	Tim Salmon	.05
36	Cecil Fielder	.05
37	Todd Greene	.05
38	Andy Benes	.05
39	Jay Bell	.05
40	Matt Williams	.05
41	Brian Anderson	.05
42	Karim Garcia	.05
43	Javy Lopez	.05
44	Tom Glavine	.35
45	Greg Maddux	1.50
46	Andruw Jones	1.00
47	Chipper Jones	1.50
48	Ryan Klesko	.05
49	John Smoltz	.05
50	Andres Galarraga	.05
51	Rafael Palmeiro	.75
52	Mike Mussina	.30
53	Roberto Alomar	.20
54	Joe Carter	.05
55	Cal Ripken Jr.	3.00
56	Brady Anderson	.05
57	Mo Vaughn	.05
58	John Valentin	.05
59	Dennis Eckersley	.75
60	Nomar Garciaparra	1.50
61	Pedro J. Martinez	1.00
62	Jeff Blauser	.05
63	Kevin Orie	.05
64	Henry Rodriguez	.05
65	Mark Grace	.05
66	Albert Belle	.05
67	Mike Cameron	.05
68	Robin Ventura	.05
69	Frank Thomas	1.00
70	Barry Larkin	.05
71	Brett Tomko	.05
72	Willie Greene	.05
73	Reggie Sanders	.05
74	Sandy Alomar Jr.	.05
75	Kenny Lofton	.05
76	Jaret Wright	.05
77	David Justice	.05
78	Omar Vizquel	.05
79	Manny Ramirez	1.00
80	Jim Thome	.75
81	Travis Fryman	.05
82	Neifi Perez	.05
83	Mike Lansing	.05
84	Vinny Castilla	.05
85	Larry Walker	.05
86	Dante Bichette	.05
87	Darryl Kile	.05
88	Justin Thompson	.05
89	Damion Easley	.05
90	Tony Clark	.05
91	Bobby Higginson	.05
92	Brian L. Hunter	.05
93	Edgar Renteria	.05
94	Craig Counsell	.05
95	Mike Piazza	2.00
96	Livan Hernandez	.05
97	Todd Zeile	.05
98	Richard Hidalgo	.05
99	Moises Alou	.05
100	Jeff Bagwell	1.00
101	Mike Hampton	.05
102	Craig Biggio	.05
103	Dean Palmer	.05
104	Tim Belcher	.05
105	Jeff King	.05
106	Jeff Conine	.05
107	Johnny Damon	.30
108	Hideo Nomo	.50
109	Raul Mondesi	.05
110	Gary Sheffield	.45
111	Ramon Martinez	.05
112	Chan Ho Park	.05
113	Eric Young	.05
114	Charles Johnson	.05
115	Eric Karros	.05
116	Bobby Bonilla	.05
117	Jeromy Burnitz	.05
118	Carl Eldred	.05
119	Jeff D'Amico	.05
120	Marquis Grissom	.05
121	Dave Nilsson	.05
122	Brad Radke	.05
123	Marty Cordova	.05
124	Ron Coomer	.05
125	Paul Molitor	1.00
126	Todd Walker	.05
127	Rondell White	.05
128	Mark Grudzielanek	.05
129	Carlos Perez	.05
130	Vladimir Guerrero	1.00
131	Dustin Hermanson	.05
132	Butch Huskey	.05
133	John Franco	.05
134	Rey Ordonez	.05
135	Todd Hundley	.05
136	Edgardo Alfonzo	.05
137	Bobby Jones	.05
138	John Olerud	.05
139	Chili Davis	.05
140	Tino Martinez	.05
141	Andy Pettitte	.15
142	Chuck Knoblauch	.05
143	Bernie Williams	.05
144	David Cone	.05
145	Derek Jeter	3.00
146	Paul O'Neill	.05
147	Rickey Henderson	1.00
148	Jason Giambi	.50
149	Kenny Rogers	.05
150	Scott Rolen	.75
151	Curt Schilling	.35
152	Ricky Bottalico	.05
153	Mike Lieberthal	.05
154	Francisco Cordova	.05
155	Jose Guillen	.05
156	Jason Schmidt	.05
157	Jason Kendall	.05
158	Kevin Young	.05
159	Delino DeShields	.05
160	Mark McGwire	2.50
161	Ray Lankford	.05
162	Brian Jordan	.05
163	Ron Gant	.05
164	Todd Stottlemyre	.05
165	Ken Caminiti	.05
166	Kevin Brown	.05
167	Trevor Hoffman	.05
168	Steve Finley	.05
169	Wally Joyner	.05
170	Tony Gwynn	1.50
171	Shawn Estes	.05
172	J.T. Snow	.05
173	Jeff Kent	.05
174	Robb Nen	.05
175	Barry Bonds	3.00
176	Randy Johnson	1.00
177	Edgar Martinez	.05
178	Jay Buhner	.05
179	Alex Rodriguez	2.50
180	Ken Griffey Jr.	2.00
181	Ken Cloude	.05
182	Wade Boggs	1.50
183	Tony Saunders	.05
184	Wilson Alvarez	.05
185	Fred McGriff	.05
186	Roberto Hernandez	.05
187	Kevin Stocker	.05
188	Fernando Tatis	.05
189	Will Clark	.05

190	Juan Gonzalez	.50
191	Rusty Greer	.05
192	Ivan Rodriguez	.75
193	Jose Canseco	.45
194	Carlos Delgado	.50
195	Roger Clemens	1.75
196	Pat Hentgen	.05
197	Randy Myers	.05
198	Checklist (Ken Griffey Jr.)	.85

Chirography

Chirography insert are seeded one per 25 packs. The featured player signed his cards in the white border at the bottom.

		NM/M
Common Card:		4.00
Inserted 1:25		
RA	Roberto Alomar	15.00
RB	Russell Branyan	4.00
SC	Sean Casey	10.00
TC	Tony Clark	4.00
RC	Roger Clemens/SP/400	80.00
JC	Jose Cruz Jr.	4.00
DE	Darin Erstad	7.50
NG	Nomar Garciaparra/SP/400	30.00
BG	Ben Grieve	4.00
KG	Ken Griffey Jr./SP/400	60.00
VG	Vladimir Guerrero	30.00
TG	Tony Gwynn/SP/850	30.00
TH	Todd Helton	15.00
LH	Livan Hernandez	6.00
CJ	Charles Johnson	6.00
AJ	Andruw Jones	17.50
CHIP	Chipper Jones/SP/800	40.00
PK	Paul Konerko	15.00
MK	Mark Kotsay	6.00
RL	Ray Lankford	6.00
TL	Travis Lee	6.00
PM	Paul Molitor/SP/700	20.00
MM	Mike Mussina	20.00
AR	Alex Rodriguez/SP/800	80.00
IR	Ivan Rodriguez	30.00
SR	Scott Rolen	20.00
GS	Gary Sheffield	15.00
MT	Miguel Tejada	20.00
JW	Jaret Wright	6.00
MV	Mo Vaughn/SP/800	12.50

Ken Griffey Jr. 300th HR Redemption

This 5" x 7" version of Ken Griffey Jr.'s SP Authentic card was issued as a redemption for one of the 1000 Trade Cards which were foil-pack inserts.

		NM/M
KG300	Ken Griffey Jr.	30.00

Jersey Swatch

These 5" x 7" redemption cards were issued in exchange for Trade Cards found as random foil-packs inserts. Fronts have a player action photo on a white background. Backs have a congratulatory message of authenticity. Sandwiched between is a swatch of that player's uniform jersey. The large-format jersey cards were available in limited editions which are listed in parentheses, though all might not have been redeemed prior to the August 1, 1999, cut-off date.

		NM/M
Complete Set (6):		130.00
Common Player:		7.50
(1)	Jay Buhner/125	7.50
(2)	Ken Griffey Jr./125	50.00
(3)	Tony Gwynn/415	10.00
(4)	Greg Maddux/125	30.00
(5)	Alex Rodriguez/125	60.00
(6)	Gary Sheffield/125	12.00

Trade Cards

Cards which could be traded (prior to the Aug. 1, 1999 cut-off) for special cards and autographed memorabilia were inserted into SP Authentic foil packs at an announced rate of one per 291 packs. Trade cards have a white background on front with a color player action photo and the name of the redemption item. Backs gives details for redemption. In some cases, because of their insertion-rate rarity, the cards are worth more than the redemption items. The unnumbered cards are listed here alphabetically.

		NM/M
Common Card:		5.00
(1)	Roberto Alomar/ Auto. Ball/100	15.00
(2)	Albert Belle/ Auto. Ball/100	7.50
(3)	Jay Buhner/ Jersey Card 125	5.00
(4)	Ken Griffey Jr./ Auto. Glv/30	200.00
(5)	Ken Griffey Jr./ Auto. Jsy/30	200.00
(6)	Ken Griffey Jr./ Jsy Card 125	25.00
(7)	Ken Griffey Jr./ Standee/200	15.00
(8)	Ken Griffey Jr./ 300th HR Card 1000	5.00
(9)	Tony Gwynn/ Jsy Card 415	15.00
(10)	Brian Jordan/ Auto. Ball/50	10.00
(11)	Greg Maddux/ Jsy Card/125	20.00
(12)	Raul Mondesi/ Auto. Ball/100	5.00
(13)	Alex Rodriguez/ Jsy Card/125	40.00
(14)	Gary Sheffield/ Jsy Card/125	5.00
(15)	Robin Ventura/ Auto. Ball/50	10.00

Sheer Dominance

Sheer Dominance is a 42-card insert. The base set is inserted one per three packs. The Sheer Dominance Gold parallel is sequentially numbered to 2,000 and the Titanium parallel is numbered to 100. The cards feature a player photo inside a white border. The background color corresponds to the level of the insert.

		NM/M
Complete Set (42):		32.50
Common Player:		.25
Inserted 1:3		
Gold (2,000 Sets):		2X
Titanium (100 Sets):		12X
SD1	Ken Griffey Jr.	1.75
SD2	Rickey Henderson	1.00
SD3	Jaret Wright	.25
SD4	Craig Biggio	.25
SD5	Travis Lee	.25
SD6	Kenny Lofton	.25
SD7	Raul Mondesi	.25
SD8	Cal Ripken Jr.	2.50
SD9	Matt Williams	.25
SD10	Mark McGwire	2.00
SD11	Alex Rodriguez	2.00
SD12	Fred McGriff	.25
SD13	Scott Rolen	.75
SD14	Paul Molitor	1.00
SD15	Nomar Garciaparra	1.50
SD16	Vladimir Guerrero	1.00
SD17	Andruw Jones	1.00
SD18	Manny Ramirez	1.00
SD19	Tony Gwynn	1.50
SD20	Barry Bonds	2.50
SD21	Ben Grieve	.25
SD22	Ivan Rodriguez	.75
SD23	Jose Cruz Jr.	.25
SD24	Pedro J. Martinez	1.00
SD25	Chipper Jones	1.50
SD26	Albert Belle	.25
SD27	Todd Helton	.75
SD28	Paul Konerko	.35
SD29	Sammy Sosa	1.50
SD30	Frank Thomas	1.00
SD31	Greg Maddux	1.50
SD32	Randy Johnson	1.00
SD33	Larry Walker	.25
SD34	Roberto Alomar	.45
SD35	Roger Clemens	1.50
SD36	Mo Vaughn	.25
SD37	Jim Thome	.75
SD38	Jeff Bagwell	1.00
SD39	Tino Martinez	.25
SD40	Mike Piazza	1.75
SD41	Derek Jeter	2.50
SD42	Juan Gonzalez	.50

Sheer Dominance Gold

Identical in format and using the same photos as the Silver version, the scarcer Sheer Dominance Gold card differs on front in its use of a gold-metallic foil background within the white border. Backs of the gold version are individually serial numbered within an edition of 2,000 each.

	NM/M
Common Player:	.50
Gold Stars:	2X

Sheer Dominance Titanium

Sheer Dominance Titanium is a parallel of the 42-card Sheer Dominance insert. The cards are numbered to 100 and have a gray background with "Titanium" printed across it.

	NM/M
Common Player:	4.00
Titanium Stars:	12X

1998 SPx Finite Sample

This card was issued to promote SPx's all-numbered Finite issue. The serial number on the card's back is "0000/0000." The card is overprinted "SAMPLE" on back.

		NM/M
1	Ken Griffey Jr.	3.00

1998 SPx Finite

SPx Finite is an all-sequentially numbered set issued in two 180-card series. The Series 1 base set consists of five subsets: 90 regular cards (numbered to 9,000), 30 Star Focus (7,000), 30 Youth Movement (5,000), 20 Power Explosion (4,000) and 10 Heroes of the Game (2,000). The set is paralleled in the Radiance and Spectrum sets. Radiance regular cards are numbered to 4,500, Star Focus to 3,500, Youth Movement to 2,500, Power Explosion to 1,000 and Heroes of the Game to 100. Spectrum regular cards are numbered to 2,250, Star Focus to 1,750, Youth Movement to 1,250, Power Explosion to 50 and Heroes of the Game to 1. The Series 2 base set has 90 regular cards (numbered to 9,000), 30 Power Passion (7,000), 30 Youth Movement (5,000), 20 Tradewinds (4,000) and 10 Cornerstones of the Game (2,000). Series 2 also has Radiance and Spectrum parallels. Radiance regular cards are numbered to 4,500, Power Passion to 3,500, Youth Movement to 2,500, Tradewinds to 1,000 and Cornerstones of the Game to 100. Spectrum regular cards are numbered to 2,250, Power Passion to 1,750, Youth Movement to 1,250, Tradewinds to 50 and Cornerstones of the Game to 1. The 1-of-1 cards are not valued due to scarcity and fluctuating demand. The only insert is Home Run Hysteria.

	NM/M
Complete Set (360):	200.00
Common Youth Movement:	
(#1-30, 181-210):	.50
Radiance YM (2,500):	1.5X
Spectrum YM (1,250):	2X
Common Power Explosion:	
(#31-50):	.50
Radiance PE (1,000):	2X
Spectrum PE (50):	25X
Common Base Card	
(#51-140, 241-330):	.15
Radiance Base Card (4,500):	1X
Spectrum Base Card (2,250):	2X
Common Star Focus:	
(#141-170):	.35
Radiance SF (3,500):	1X
Spectrum SF (1,750):	2X
Common Heroes of the Game:	
(#171-180):	2.50
Radiance HG (100):	15X
Common Power Passion:	
(#211-240):	.50
Radiance PP (3,500):	1X
Spectrum PP (1,750):	2X
Common Tradewinds:	
(#331-350):	.75
Radiance TW (1,000):	2X
Spectrum TW (50):	25X
Common Cornerstones/Game:	
(#351-360):	2.50
Radiance CG (100):	15X
Pack (3):	2.00
Wax Box:	25.00

#	Player	Value
1	Nomar Garciaparra (Youth Movement)	3.00
2	Miguel Tejada (Youth Movement)	.75
3	Mike Cameron (Youth Movement)	.50
4	Ken Cloude (Youth Movement)	.50
5	Jaret Wright (Youth Movement)	.50
6	Mark Kotsay (Youth Movement)	.50
7	Craig Counsell (Youth Movement)	.50
8	Jose Guillen (Youth Movement)	.50
9	Neifi Perez (Youth Movement)	.50
10	Jose Cruz Jr. (Youth Movement)	.50
11	Brett Tomko (Youth Movement)	.50
12	Matt Morris (Youth Movement)	.50
13	Justin Thompson (Youth Movement)	.50
14	Jeremi Gonzalez (Youth Movement)	.50
15	Scott Rolen (Youth Movement)	1.50
16	Vladimir Guerrero (Youth Movement)	2.00
17	Brad Fullmer (Youth Movement)	.50
18	Brian Giles (Youth Movement)	.50
19	Todd Dunwoody (Youth Movement)	.50
20	Ben Grieve (Youth Movement)	.50
21	Juan Encarnacion (Youth Movement)	.50
22	Aaron Boone (Youth Movement)	.50
23	Richie Sexson (Youth Movement)	.50
24	Richard Hidalgo (Youth Movement)	.50
25	Andruw Jones (Youth Movement)	2.00
26	Todd Helton (Youth Movement)	1.50
27	Paul Konerko (Youth Movement)	.75
28	Dante Powell (Youth Movement)	.50
29	Elieser Marrero (Youth Movement)	.50
30	Derek Jeter (Youth Movement)	5.00
31	Mike Piazza (Power Explosion)	3.00
32	Tony Clark (Power Explosion)	.50
33	Larry Walker (Power Explosion)	.50
34	Jim Thome (Power Explosion)	1.50
35	Juan Gonzalez (Power Explosion)	1.00
36	Jeff Bagwell (Power Explosion)	2.00
37	Jay Buhner (Power Explosion)	.50
38	Tim Salmon (Power Explosion)	.50
39	Albert Belle (Power Explosion)	1.00
40	Mark McGwire (Power Explosion)	4.00
41	Sammy Sosa (Power Explosion)	2.50
42	Mo Vaughn (Power Explosion)	.50
43	Manny Ramirez (Power Explosion)	2.00
44	Tino Martinez (Power Explosion)	.50
45	Frank Thomas (Power Explosion)	2.00
46	Nomar Garciaparra (Power Explosion)	2.50
47	Alex Rodriguez (Power Explosion)	4.00
48	Chipper Jones (Power Explosion)	2.50
49	Barry Bonds (Power Explosion)	5.00
50	Ken Griffey Jr. (Power Explosion)	3.00
51	Jason Dickson	.15
52	Jim Edmonds	.35
53	Darin Erstad	.35
54	Tim Salmon	.15
55	Chipper Jones	2.00
56	Ryan Klesko	.15
57	Tom Glavine	.15
58	Denny Neagle	.15
59	John Smoltz	.15
60	Javy Lopez	.15
61	Roberto Alomar	.30
62	Rafael Palmeiro	1.25
63	Mike Mussina	.35
64	Cal Ripken Jr.	4.00
65	Mo Vaughn	.15
66	Tim Naehring	.15
67	John Valentin	.15
68	Mark Grace	.15
69	Kevin Orie	.15
70	Sammy Sosa	2.50
71	Albert Belle	.15
72	Frank Thomas	1.50
73	Robin Ventura	.15
74	David Justice	.15
75	Kenny Lofton	.15
76	Omar Vizquel	.15
77	Manny Ramirez	1.50
78	Jim Thome	.65
79	Dante Bichette	.15
80	Larry Walker	.15
81	Vinny Castilla	.15
82	Ellis Burks	.15
83	Bobby Higginson	.15
84	Brian L. Hunter	.15
85	Tony Clark	.15
86	Mike Hampton	.15
87	Jeff Bagwell	1.50
88	Craig Biggio	.15
89	Derek Bell	.15
90	Mike Piazza	3.00
91	Ramon Martinez	.15
92	Raul Mondesi	.15
93	Hideo Nomo	.75
94	Eric Karros	.15
95	Paul Molitor	1.50
96	Marty Cordova	.15
97	Brad Radke	.15
98	Mark Grudzielanek	.15
99	Carlos Perez	.15
100	Rondell White	.15
101	Todd Hundley	.15
102	Edgardo Alfonzo	.15
103	John Franco	.15
104	John Olerud	.15
105	Tino Martinez	.15
106	David Cone	.15
107	Paul O'Neill	.15
108	Andy Pettitte	.25
109	Bernie Williams	.15
110	Rickey Henderson	1.50
111	Jason Giambi	.75
112	Matt Stairs	.15
113	Gregg Jefferies	.15
114	Rico Brogna	.15
115	Curt Schilling	.35
116	Jason Schmidt	.15
117	Jose Guillen	.15
118	Kevin Young	.15
119	Ray Lankford	.15
120	Mark McGwire	3.00
121	Delino DeShields	.15
122	Ken Caminiti	.15
123	Tony Gwynn	2.00
124	Trevor Hoffman	.15
125	Barry Bonds	4.00
126	Jeff Kent	.15
127	Shawn Estes	.15
128	J.T. Snow	.15
129	Jay Buhner	.15
130	Ken Griffey Jr.	2.50
131	Dan Wilson	.15
132	Edgar Martinez	.15
133	Alex Rodriguez	3.00
134	Rusty Greer	.15
135	Juan Gonzalez	.75
136	Fernando Tatis	.15
137	Ivan Rodriguez	1.00
138	Carlos Delgado	.75
139	Pat Hentgen	.15
140	Roger Clemens	2.25
141	Chipper Jones (Star Focus)	2.00
142	Greg Maddux (Star Focus)	2.00
143	Rafael Palmeiro (Star Focus)	1.25
144	Mike Mussina (Star Focus)	.65
145	Cal Ripken Jr. (Star Focus)	4.00
146	Nomar Garciaparra (Star Focus)	2.00
147	Mo Vaughn (Star Focus)	.35
148	Sammy Sosa (Star Focus)	2.00
149	Albert Belle (Star Focus)	.35
150	Frank Thomas (Star Focus)	1.50
151	Jim Thome (Star Focus)	1.25
152	Kenny Lofton (Star Focus)	.35
153	Manny Ramirez (Star Focus)	1.50
154	Larry Walker (Star Focus)	.35
155	Jeff Bagwell (Star Focus)	1.50
156	Craig Biggio (Star Focus)	.35
157	Mike Piazza (Star Focus)	2.50
158	Paul Molitor (Star Focus)	1.50
159	Derek Jeter (Star Focus)	4.00
160	Tino Martinez (Star Focus)	.35
161	Curt Schilling (Star Focus)	.50
162	Mark McGwire (Star Focus)	3.00
163	Tony Gwynn (Star Focus)	2.00
164	Barry Bonds (Star Focus)	4.00
165	Ken Griffey Jr. (Star Focus)	2.50
166	Randy Johnson (Star Focus)	1.50
167	Alex Rodriguez (Star Focus)	3.00
168	Juan Gonzalez (Star Focus)	.75
169	Ivan Rodriguez (Star Focus)	1.25
170	Roger Clemens (Star Focus)	2.25
171	Greg Maddux (Heroes of the Game)	3.00
172	Cal Ripken Jr. (Heroes of the Game)	6.50
173	Frank Thomas (Heroes of the Game)	2.00
174	Jeff Bagwell (Heroes of the Game)	2.00
175	Mike Piazza (Heroes of the Game)	4.00
176	Mark McGwire (Heroes of the Game)	5.00
177	Barry Bonds (Heroes of the Game)	6.50
178	Ken Griffey Jr. (Heroes of the Game)	4.00
179	Alex Rodriguez (Heroes of the Game)	5.00
180	Roger Clemens (Heroes of the Game)	3.25
181	Mike Caruso (Youth Movement)	.50
182	David Ortiz (Youth Movement)	1.00
183	Gabe Alvarez (Youth Movement)	.50
184	Gary Matthews Jr. (Youth Movement)	.50
185	Kerry Wood (Youth Movement)	1.25
186	Carl Pavano (Youth Movement)	.50
187	Alex Gonzalez (Youth Movement)	.50
188	Masato Yoshii (Youth Movement)	.50
189	Larry Sutton (Youth Movement)	.50
190	Russell Branyan (Youth Movement)	.50
191	Bruce Chen (Youth Movement)	.50
192	Rolando Arrojo (Youth Movement)	.50
193	Ryan Christenson (Youth Movement)	.50
194	Cliff Politte (Youth Movement)	.50
195	A.J. Hinch (Youth Movement)	.50
196	Kevin Witt (Youth Movement)	.50
197	Daryle Ward (Youth Movement)	.50
198	Corey Koskie (Youth Movement)	.50
199	Mike Lowell RC (Youth Movement)	3.00
200	Travis Lee (Youth Movement)	.50

#	Player	Price
201	Kevin Millwood RC (Youth Movement)	1.00
202	Robert Smith (Youth Movement)	.50
203	Magglio Ordonez RC (Youth Movement)	10.00
204	Eric Milton (Youth Movement)	.50
205	Geoff Jenkins (Youth Movement)	.50
206	Rich Butler (Youth Movement)	.50
207	Mike Kinkade RC (Youth Movement)	.75
208	Braden Looper (Youth Movement)	.50
209	Matt Clement (Youth Movement)	.50
210	Derrek Lee (Youth Movement)	1.50
211	Randy Johnson (Power Passion)	1.50
212	John Smoltz (Power Passion)	.50
213	Roger Clemens (Power Passion)	2.25
214	Curt Schilling (Power Passion)	.75
215	Pedro J. Martinez (Power Passion)	1.50
216	Vinny Castilla (Power Passion)	.50
217	Jose Cruz Jr. (Power Passion)	.50
218	Jim Thome (Power Passion)	1.20
219	Alex Rodriguez (Power Passion)	3.00
220	Frank Thomas (Power Passion)	1.50
221	Tim Salmon (Power Passion)	.50
222	Larry Walker (Power Passion)	.50
223	Albert Belle (Power Passion)	.50
224	Manny Ramirez (Power Passion)	1.50
225	Mark McGwire (Power Passion)	3.00
226	Mo Vaughn (Power Passion)	.50
227	Andres Galarraga (Power Passion)	.50
228	Scott Rolen (Power Passion)	1.25
229	Travis Lee (Power Passion)	.50
230	Mike Piazza (Power Passion)	2.50
231	Nomar Garciaparra (Power Passion)	2.00
232	Andruw Jones (Power Passion)	1.50
233	Barry Bonds (Power Passion)	4.00
234	Jeff Bagwell (Power Passion)	1.50
235	Juan Gonzalez (Power Passion)	.75
236	Tino Martinez (Power Passion)	.50
237	Vladimir Guerrero (Power Passion)	1.50
238	Rafael Palmeiro (Power Passion)	1.25
239	Russell Branyan (Power Passion)	.50
240	Ken Griffey Jr. (Power Passion)	2.50
241	Cecil Fielder	.15
242	Chuck Finley	.15
243	Jay Bell	.15
244	Andy Benes	.15
245	Matt Williams	.15
246	Brian Anderson	.15
247	David Dellucci	.15
248	Andres Galarraga	.15
249	Andruw Jones	1.50
250	Greg Maddux	2.00
251	Brady Anderson	.15
252	Joe Carter	.15
253	Eric Davis	.15
254	Pedro J. Martinez	1.50
255	Nomar Garciaparra	2.00
256	Dennis Eckersley	1.25
257	Henry Rodriguez	.15
258	Jeff Blauser	.15
259	Jaime Navarro	.15
260	Ray Durham	.15
261	Chris Stynes	.15
262	Willie Greene	.15
263	Reggie Sanders	.15
264	Bret Boone	.15
265	Barry Larkin	.15
266	Travis Fryman	.15
267	Charles Nagy	.15
268	Sandy Alomar Jr.	.15
269	Darryl Kile	.15
270	Mike Lansing	.15
271	Pedro Astacio	.15
272	Damion Easley	.15
273	Joe Randa	.15
274	Luis Gonzalez	.15
275	Mike Piazza	2.50
276	Todd Zeile	.15
277	Edgar Renteria	.15
278	Livan Hernandez	.15
279	Cliff Floyd	.15
280	Moises Alou	.15
281	Billy Wagner	.15
282	Jeff King	.15
283	Hal Morris	.15
284	Johnny Damon	.35
285	Dean Palmer	.15
286	Tim Belcher	.15
287	Eric Young	.15
288	Bobby Bonilla	.15
289	Gary Sheffield	.60
290	Chan Ho Park	.15
291	Charles Johnson	.15
292	Jeff Cirillo	.15
293	Jeromy Burnitz	.15
294	Jose Valentin	.15
295	Marquis Grissom	.15
296	Todd Walker	.15
297	Terry Steinbach	.15
298	Rick Aguilera	.15
299	Vladimir Guerrero	1.50
300	Rey Ordonez	.15
301	Butch Huskey	.15
302	Bernard Gilkey	.15
303	Mariano Rivera	.25
304	Chuck Knoblauch	.15
305	Derek Jeter	4.00
306	Ricky Bottalico	.15
307	Bob Abreu	.15
308	Scott Rolen	1.25
309	Al Martin	.15
310	Jason Kendall	.15
311	Brian Jordan	.15
312	Ron Gant	.15
313	Todd Stottlemyre	.15
314	Greg Vaughn	.15
315	J. Kevin Brown	.15
316	Wally Joyner	.15
317	Robb Nen	.15
318	Orel Hershiser	.15
319	Russ Davis	.15
320	Randy Johnson	1.50
321	Quinton McCracken	.15
322	Tony Saunders	.15
323	Wilson Alvarez	.15
324	Wade Boggs	2.00
325	Fred McGriff	.15
326	Lee Stevens	.15
327	Jim Wetteland	.15
328	Jose Canseco	.60
329	Randy Myers	.15
330	Jose Cruz Jr.	.15
331	Matt Williams (Tradewinds)	.50
332	Andres Galarraga (Tradewinds)	.50
333	Walt Weiss (Tradewinds)	.50
334	Joe Carter (Tradewinds)	.50
335	Pedro J. Martinez (Tradewinds)	2.00
336	Henry Rodriguez (Tradewinds)	.50
337	Travis Fryman (Tradewinds)	.50
338	Darryl Kile (Tradewinds)	.50
339	Mike Lansing (Tradewinds)	.50
340	Mike Piazza (Tradewinds)	4.00
341	Moises Alou (Tradewinds)	.50
342	Charles Johnson (Tradewinds)	.50
343	Chuck Knoblauch (Tradewinds)	.50
344	Rickey Henderson (Tradewinds)	2.00
345	J. Kevin Brown (Tradewinds)	.50
346	Orel Hershiser (Tradewinds)	.50
347	Wade Boggs (Tradewinds)	3.00
348	Fred McGriff (Tradewinds)	.50
349	Jose Canseco (Tradewinds)	1.00
350	Gary Sheffield (Tradewinds)	1.00
351	Travis Lee (Cornerstones)	2.50
352	Nomar Garciaparra (Cornerstones)	5.00
353	Frank Thomas (Cornerstones)	4.00
354	Cal Ripken Jr. (Cornerstones)	10.00
355	Mark McGwire (Cornerstones)	8.00
356	Mike Piazza (Cornerstones)	6.00
357	Alex Rodriguez (Cornerstones)	8.00
358	Barry Bonds (Cornerstones)	10.00
359	Tony Gwynn (Cornerstones)	5.00
360	Ken Griffey Jr. (Cornerstones)	6.00

Home Run Hysteria

Home Run Hysteria is a 10-card insert in SPx Finite Series Two. The cards were sequentially numbered to 62.

		NM/M
Complete Set (10):		400.00
Common Player:		15.00
Production 62 Sets		
HR1	Ken Griffey Jr.	75.00

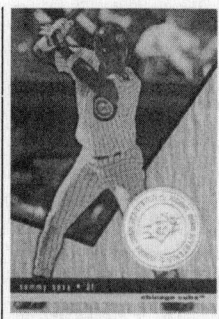

HR2	Mark McGwire	100.00
HR3	Sammy Sosa	60.00
HR4	Albert Belle	15.00
HR5	Alex Rodriguez	100.00
HR6	Greg Vaughn	15.00
HR7	Andres Galarraga	15.00
HR8	Vinny Castilla	15.00
HR9	Juan Gonzalez	25.00
HR10	Chipper Jones	60.00

1999 SP Authentic Sample

UD spokesman Ken Griffey Jr. is featured on the promo card for '99 SP Authentic. In the same format as the issued version, the sample card has different photos on front and back, a different season summary on back and a large, black "SAMPLE" overprint on back.

		NM/M
1	Ken Griffey Jr.	3.00

1999 SP Authentic

SP Authentic was a 135-card set that sold in packs of five cards for $4.99. The set includes a 30-card Future Watch subset and a 15-card Season to Remember subset. Both subsets were shorted-printed, with each card sequentially numbered to 2,700. The insert lineup included Ernie Banks 500 Club "Piece of History" bat cards. Other insert sets included SP Chirography, The Home Run Chronicles, Epic Figures, Reflections, and SP Authentics.

		NM/M
Complete Set (135):		100.00
Common Player (1-90):		.10
Common Future Watch (91-120):		2.00
Production: (2,700)		
Common Season to Remember (121-135):		2.00
Production: (2,700)		
Pack (5):		3.50
Wax Box (24):		75.00
1	Mo Vaughn	.10
2	Jim Edmonds	.10
3	Darin Erstad	.25
4	Travis Lee	.10
5	Matt Williams	.10
6	Randy Johnson	1.50
7	Chipper Jones	1.75
8	Greg Maddux	1.75
9	Andruw Jones	1.50
10	Andres Galarraga	.10
11	Tom Glavine	.35
12	Cal Ripken Jr.	3.00
13	Brady Anderson	.10
14	Albert Belle	.10
15	Nomar Garciaparra	1.75
16	Donnie Sadler	.10
17	Pedro Martinez	1.50
18	Sammy Sosa	1.75
19	Kerry Wood	.60
20	Mark Grace	.10
21	Mike Caruso	.10
22	Frank Thomas	1.50
23	Paul Konerko	.20
24	Sean Casey	.20
25	Barry Larkin	.10
26	Kenny Lofton	.10
27	Manny Ramirez	1.50
28	Jim Thome	1.25
29	Bartolo Colon	.10
30	Jaret Wright	.10
31	Larry Walker	.10
32	Todd Helton	1.25
33	Tony Clark	.10
34	Dean Palmer	.10
35	Mark Kotsay	.10
36	Cliff Floyd	.10
37	Ken Caminiti	.10
38	Craig Biggio	.10
39	Jeff Bagwell	1.50
40	Moises Alou	.10
41	Johnny Damon	.35
42	Larry Sutton	.10
43	Kevin Brown	.10
44	Gary Sheffield	.40
45	Raul Mondesi	.10
46	Jeromy Burnitz	.10
47	Jeff Cirillo	.10
48	Todd Walker	.10
49	David Ortiz	.50
50	Brad Radtke	.10
51	Vladimir Guerrero	1.50
52	Rondell White	.10
53	Brad Fullmer	.10
54	Mike Piazza	2.00
55	Robin Ventura	.10
56	John Olerud	.10
57	Derek Jeter	3.00
58	Tino Martinez	.10
59	Bernie Williams	.10
60	Roger Clemens	1.75
61	Ben Grieve	.10
62	Miguel Tejada	.20
63	A.J. Hinch	.10
64	Scott Rolen	1.00
65	Curt Schilling	.35
66	Doug Glanville	.10
67	Aramis Ramirez	.10
68	Tony Womack	.10
69	Jason Kendall	.10
70	Tony Gwynn	1.75
71	Wally Joyner	.10
72	Greg Vaughn	.10
73	Barry Bonds	3.00
74	Ellis Burks	.10
75	Jeff Kent	.10
76	Ken Griffey Jr.	2.00
77	Alex Rodriguez	2.50
78	Edgar Martinez	.10
79	Mark McGwire	2.50
80	Eli Marrero	.10
81	Matt Morris	.10
82	Rolando Arrojo	.10
83	Quinton McCracken	.10
84	Jose Canseco	.50
85	Ivan Rodriguez	1.25
86	Juan Gonzalez	.75
87	Royce Clayton	.10
88	Shawn Green	.30
89	Jose Cruz Jr.	.10
90	Carlos Delgado	.60
91	Troy Glaus/Future Watch	6.00
92	George Lombard/Future Watch	2.00
93	Ryan Minor/Future Watch	2.00
94	Calvin Pickering/Future Watch	2.00
95	Jin Ho Cho (Future Watch)	2.00
96	Russ Branyon (Future Watch)	2.00
97	Derrick Gibson (Future Watch)	2.00
98	Gabe Kapler (Future Watch)	2.00
99	Matt Anderson (Future Watch)	2.00
100	Preston Wilson (Future Watch)	2.00
101	Alex Gonzalez (Future Watch)	2.00
102	Carlos Beltran (Future Watch)	6.00
103	Dee Brown (Future Watch)	2.00
104	Jeremy Giambi (Future Watch)	2.00
105	Angel Pena (Future Watch)	2.00
106	Geoff Jenkins (Future Watch)	2.00
107	Corey Koskie (Future Watch)	2.00
108	A.J. Pierzynski (Future Watch)	2.00
109	Michael Barrett (Future Watch)	2.00
110	Fernando Seguignol (Future Watch)	2.00
111	Mike Kinkade (Future Watch)	2.00
112	Ricky Ledee (Future Watch)	2.00
113	Mike Lowell (Future Watch)	2.00
114	Eric Chavez (Future Watch)	2.50
115	Matt Clement (Future Watch)	2.00
116	Shane Monahan (Future Watch)	2.00
117	J.D. Drew (Future Watch)	4.00
118	Bubba Trammell (Future Watch)	2.00
119	Kevin Witt (Future Watch)	2.00
120	Roy Halladay (Future Watch)	2.50
121	Mark McGwire (Season to Remember)	5.00
122	Mark McGwire, Sammy Sosa (Season to Remember)	4.00
123	Sammy Sosa (Season to Remember)	2.50
124	Ken Griffey Jr. (Season to Remember)	3.00
125	Cal Ripken Jr. (Season to Remember)	6.00
126	Juan Gonzalez (Season to Remember)	2.50
127	Kerry Wood (Season to Remember)	2.50
128	Trevor Hoffman (Season to Remember)	2.00
129	Barry Bonds (Season to Remember)	5.00
130	Alex Rodriguez (Season to Remember)	4.00
131	Ben Grieve (Season to Remember)	2.00
132	Tom Glavine (Season to Remember)	2.00
133	David Wells (Season to Remember)	2.00
134	Mike Piazza (Season to Remember)	3.00
135	Scott Brosius (Season to Remember)	2.00

Chirography

Baseball's top players and future stars are included in this 39-card autograph insert set. The set was split into Level 1 and Level 2 versions. Level 1 cards are not numbered and were inserted one card per 24 packs. Level 2 (gold) cards are sequentially numbered to the featured player's jersey number.

		NM/M
Common Player:		4.00
Inserted 1:24		
EC	Eric Chavez	8.00
GK	Gabe Kapler	4.00
GMj	Gary Matthews Jr.	4.00
CP	Calvin Pickering	4.00
CK	Corey Koskie	6.00
SM	Shane Monahan	4.00
RH	Richard Hidalgo	4.00
MK	Mike Kinkade	4.00
CB	Carlos Beltran	35.00
AG	Alex Gonzalez	4.00
BC	Bruce Chen	4.00
MA	Matt Anderson	4.00
RM	Ryan Minor	4.00
RL	Ricky Ledee	4.00
RR	Ruben Rivera	4.00
BF	Brad Fullmer	4.00
RB	Russ Branyan	4.00
ML	Mike Lowell	15.00
JG	Jeremy Giambi	4.00
GL	George Lombard	4.00
KW	Kevin Witt	4.00
TW	Todd Walker	4.00
SR	Scott Rolen	20.00
KW	Kerry Wood	25.00
BG	Ben Grieve	4.00
JR	Ken Griffey Jr.	75.00
CJ	Chipper Jones	40.00
IR	Ivan Rodriguez	25.00
TGI	Troy Glaus	15.00
TL	Travis Lee	4.00
VG	Vladimir Guerrero	30.00
GV	Greg Vaughn	4.00
JT	Jim Thome	25.00
JD	J.D. Drew	15.00
TH	Todd Helton	15.00
GM	Greg Maddux	75.00
NG	Nomar Garciaparra	40.00
TG	Tony Gwynn	30.00
CR	Cal Ripken Jr.	125.00

Chirography Gold

These Chirography parallels can be identified by the gold tint on the card front and their sequential numbering; each featured player signed to his jersey number.

		NM/M
Common Player:		5.00
Inserted 1:24		
EC	Eric Chavez/30	40.00
GK	Gabe Kapler/51	10.00
GMj	Gary Matthews Jr./68	10.00
CP	Calvin Pickering/6	40.00
CK	Corey Koskie/47	15.00
SM	Shane Monahan/12	20.00
RH	Richard Hidalgo/15	30.00
MK	Mike Kinkade/33	10.00
CB	Carlos Beltran/36	75.00
AG	Alex Gonzalez/22	20.00
BC	Bruce Chen/48	10.00
MA	Matt Anderson/14	20.00
RM	Ryan Minor/10	35.00
RL	Ricky Ledee/38	10.00
RR	Ruben Rivera/28	10.00
BF	Brad Fullmer/20	10.00
RB	Russ Branyon/66	10.00
ML	Mike Lowell/60	15.00
JG	Jeremy Giambi/15	20.00
GL	George Lombard/26	10.00
KW	Kevin Witt/6	20.00
TW	Todd Walker/12	40.00
SR	Scott Rolen/17	75.00
KW	Kerry Wood/34	60.00
BG	Ben Grieve/14	35.00
JR	Ken Griffey Jr./24	250.00
CJ	Chipper Jones/10	200.00
IR	Ivan Rodriguez/7	125.00
TGI	Troy Glaus/14	90.00
TL	Travis Lee/16	35.00
VG	Vladimir Guerrero/27	75.00
GV	Greg Vaughn/23	75.00
JT	Jim Thome/25	40.00
JD	J.D. Drew/8	125.00
TH	Todd Helton/17	75.00
GM	Greg Maddux/31	150.00
NG	Nomar Garciaparra/5	375.00
TG	Tony Gwynn/19	125.00
CR	Cal Ripken Jr./8	650.00

Epic Figures

This 30-card set highlights baseball's biggest talents, including Mark McGwire and Derek Jeter. The card fronts have two photos, with the larger photo done with a shadow look in the background. Fronts also feature a holographic look, while the card backs feature the player's career highlights. These are seeded one per seven packs.

	NM/M
Complete Set (30):	30.00
Common Player:	1.00
Inserted 1:7	

E01	Mo Vaughn	.50
E02	Travis Lee	.50
E03	Andres Galarraga	.50
E04	Andruw Jones	1.00
E05	Chipper Jones	1.50
E06	Greg Maddux	1.25
E07	Cal Ripken Jr.	3.00
E08	Nomar Garciaparra	1.25
E09	Sammy Sosa	1.25
E10	Frank Thomas	1.00
E11	Kerry Wood	.60
E12	Kenny Lofton	.50
E13	Manny Ramirez	1.00
E14	Larry Walker	.50
E15	Jeff Bagwell	1.00
E16	Paul Molitor	1.00
E17	Vladimir Guerrero	1.00
E18	Derek Jeter	3.00
E19	Tino Martinez	.50
E20	Mike Piazza	1.50
E21	Ben Grieve	.50
E22	Scott Rolen	.75
E23	Mark McGwire	2.00
E24	Tony Gwynn	1.25
E25	Barry Bonds	3.00
E26	Ken Griffey Jr.	1.50
E27	Alex Rodriguez	2.00
E28	J.D. Drew	.65
E29	Juan Gonzalez	.60
E30	Kevin Brown	.50

Home Run Chronicles

This two-tiered 70-card set focuses on the amazing seasons of McGwire and Sammy Sosa. Other players help round out the 70-card set, but special emphasis has been placed on the duo. These are seeded one per pack. A die-cut version also exists, with each card serially numbered to 70.

		NM/M
Complete Set (70):		50.00
Common Player:		.15
Inserted 1:1		
Die-Cuts:		10X
Production 70 Sets		
HR01	Mark McGwire	1.50
HR02	Sammy Sosa	1.25
HR03	Ken Griffey Jr.	1.00
HR04	Mark McGwire	1.50
HR05	Mark McGwire	1.50
HR06	Albert Belle	.15
HR07	Jose Canseco	.30
HR08	Juan Gonzalez	.45
HR09	Manny Ramirez	.65
HR10	Rafael Palmeiro	.50
HR11	Mo Vaughn	.15
HR12	Carlos Delgado	.45
HR13	Nomar Garciaparra	.75
HR14	Barry Bonds	1.50
HR15	Alex Rodriguez	1.25
HR16	Tony Clark	.15
HR17	Jim Thome	.50
HR18	Edgar Martinez	.15
HR19	Frank Thomas	.75
HR20	Greg Vaughn	.15
HR21	Vinny Castilla	.15
HR22	Andres Galarraga	.15
HR23	Moises Alou	.15
HR24	Jeromy Burnitz	.15
HR25	Vladimir Guerrero	.65
HR26	Jeff Bagwell	.65
HR27	Chipper Jones	.75
HR28	Javier Lopez	.15
HR29	Mike Piazza	1.00
HR30	Andruw Jones	.65
HR31	Henry Rodriguez	.15
HR32	Jeff Kent	.15
HR33	Ray Lankford	.15
HR34	Scott Rolen	.50
HR35	Raul Mondesi	.15
HR36	Ken Caminiti	.15
HR37	J.D. Drew	.40
HR38	Troy Glaus	.50
HR39	Gabe Kapler	.15
HR40	Alex Rodriguez	1.25
HR41	Ken Griffey Jr.	1.00
HR42	Sammy Sosa	1.25
HR43	Mark McGwire	1.50
HR44	Sammy Sosa	1.25
HR45	Mark McGwire	1.50
HR46	Vinny Castilla	.15
HR47	Sammy Sosa	1.25
HR48	Mark McGwire	1.50
HR49	Sammy Sosa	1.25

HR50	Greg Vaughn	.15
HR51	Sammy Sosa	1.25
HR52	Mark McGwire	1.50
HR53	Sammy Sosa	1.25
HR54	Mark McGwire	1.50
HR55	Sammy Sosa	1.25
HR56	Ken Griffey Jr.	1.00
HR57	Sammy Sosa	1.25
HR58	Mark McGwire	1.50
HR59	Sammy Sosa	1.25
HR60	Mark McGwire	1.50
HR61	Mark McGwire	2.50
HR62	Mark McGwire	1.50
HR63	Mark McGwire	1.50
HR64	Mark McGwire	1.50
HR65	Mark McGwire	1.50
HR66	Sammy Sosa	2.50
HR67	Mark McGwire	1.50
HR68	Mark McGwire	1.50
HR69	Mark McGwire	1.50
HR70	Mark McGwire	4.00

Home Run Chronicles Die-Cuts

Each of the 70 cards in the Home Run Chronicles insert set was also issued in a die-cut version. The die-cuts share the basic front and back design of the regular HR Chronicle cards but have portions of the upper-left and lower-right cut away. On back, each of the die-cuts features an ink-jetted serial number from within an edition of 70.

HR Chronicle Die-Cuts: 10X

Reflections

Dot Matrix technology is utilized to provide a unique look at 30 of the best players in the game. Card fronts are horizontal with two small and one large photo. These are seeded 1:23 packs.

		NM/M
Complete Set (30):		60.00
Common Player:		.75
Inserted 1:23		
R01	Mo Vaughn	.75
R02	Travis Lee	.75
R03	Andres Galarraga	.75
R04	Andruw Jones	2.50
R05	Chipper Jones	3.00
R06	Greg Maddux	3.00
R07	Cal Ripken Jr.	6.00
R08	Nomar Garciaparra	3.00
R09	Sammy Sosa	3.00
R10	Frank Thomas	2.50
R11	Kerry Wood	1.50
R12	Kenny Lofton	.75
R13	Manny Ramirez	2.50
R14	Larry Walker	.75
R15	Jeff Bagwell	2.50
R16	Paul Molitor	2.50
R17	Vladimir Guerrero	2.50
R18	Derek Jeter	6.00
R19	Tino Martinez	.75
R20	Mike Piazza	3.50
R21	Ben Grieve	.75
R22	Scott Rolen	2.00
R23	Mark McGwire	4.50
R24	Tony Gwynn	3.00
R25	Barry Bonds	6.00
R26	Ken Griffey Jr.	3.50
R27	Alex Rodriguez	4.50
R28	J.D. Drew	1.25
R29	Juan Gonzalez	1.25
R30	Roger Clemens	3.25

SP Authentics

These 1:864 pack inserts are redemption cards that could be redeemed for special pieces of memorabilia from either Ken Griffey Jr. or Mark McGwire. The redemption period ended March 1, 2000. Because of rarity any surviving unredeemed McGwire home run-game autographed tickets cannot be valued.

		NM/M
Common Card:		10.00
(1)	K.Griffey Jr./ Auto. Ball/75	60.00
(2)	Ken Griffey Jr./Glv/200	20.00
(3)	K. Griffey Jr./ HR Cel Card/346	10.00
(4)	Ken Griffey Jr./ Auto. Jsy/25	125.00
(5)	K. Griffey Jr./ Auto. Mini Helmet/75	80.00
(6)	Ken Griffey Jr./ SI Cover/200	15.00
(7)	K. Griffey Jr./ SI Cover Auto./75	75.00
(8)	K. Griffey Jr./ Standee/300	10.00

500 Club Piece of History

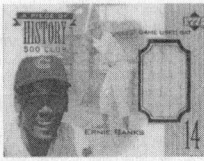

These cards feature a piece of game-used bat once swung by Ernie Banks. Approximately 350 cards exist. An autographed version of this card also exists, only 14 were produced.

		NM/M
EB	Ernie Banks	120.00
EB	Ernie Banks/Auto./14	325.00

1999 SP Signature Edition

Even with one autograph per three-card pack, this single-series issue's price of $19.99 per pack shocked the hobby when it was introduced. Horizontal cards have a color or black-and-white photo at the left end with foil highlights and airbrushed geometric designs on a white background. Backs repeat the portrait portion of the front photo and add player data and some stats.

		NM/M
Complete Set (180):		60.00
Common Player:		.15
Pack (3):		15.00
Wax Box (12):		150.00
1	Nomar Garciaparra	2.00
2	Ken Griffey Jr.	2.50
3	J.D. Drew	.50
4	Alex Rodriguez	3.00
5	Juan Gonzalez	.60
6	Mo Vaughn	.15
7	Greg Maddux	2.00
8	Chipper Jones	2.00
9	Frank Thomas	1.50
10	Vladimir Guerrero	1.50
11	Mike Piazza	2.50
12	Eric Chavez	.25
13	Tony Gwynn	2.00
14	Orlando Hernandez	.25
15	Pat Burrell RC	6.00
16	Darin Erstad	.30
17	Greg Vaughn	.15
18	Russ Branyan	.15
19	Gabe Kapler	.15
20	Craig Biggio	.15
21	Troy Glaus	1.25
22	Pedro J. Martinez	1.50
23	Carlos Beltran	.50
24	Derrek Lee	.50
25	Manny Ramirez	1.50
26	Shea Hillenbrand RC	1.00
27	Carlos Lee	.15
28	Angel Pena	.15
29	Rafael Roque	.15
30	Octavio Dotel	.15
31	Jeromy Burnitz	.15
32	Jeremy Giambi	.15
33	Andruw Jones	1.50
34	Todd Helton	1.25
35	Scott Rolen	1.25
36	Jason Kendall	.15
37	Trevor Hoffman	.15
38	Barry Bonds	4.00
.39	Ivan Rodriguez	1.25
40	Roy Halladay	1.25
41	Rickey Henderson	1.50
42	Ryan Minor	.15
43	Brian Jordan	.15
44	Alex Gonzalez	.15
45	Raul Mondesi	.15
46	Corey Koskie	.15
47	Paul O'Neill	.15
48	Todd Walker	.15
49	Carlos Febles	.15
50	Travis Fryman	.15
51	Albert Belle	.15
52	Travis Lee	.15
53	Bruce Chen	.15
54	Reggie Taylor	.15
55	Jerry Hairston Jr.	.15
56	Carlos Guillen	.15
57	Michael Barrett	.15
58	Jason Conti	.15
59	Joe Lawrence	.15
60	Jeff Cirillo	.15
61	Juan Melo	.15
62	Chad Hermansen	.15
63	Ruben Mateo	.15
64	Ben Davis	.15
65	Mike Caruso	.15
66	Jason Giambi	.50
67	Jose Canseco	.50
68	Chad Hutchinson RC	.15
69	Mitch Meluskey	.15
70	Adrian Beltre	.25
71	Mark Kotsay	.15
72	Juan Encarnacion	.15
73	Dermal Brown	.15
74	Kevin Witt	.15
75	Vinny Castilla	.15
76	Aramis Ramirez	.15
77	Marlon Anderson	.15
78	Mike Kinkade	.15
79	Kevin Barker	.15
80	Ron Belliard	.15
81	Chris Haas	.15
82	Bob Henley	.15
83	Fernando Seguignol	.15
84	Damon Minor	.15
85	A.J. Burnett RC	1.00
86	Calvin Pickering	.15
87	Mike Darr	.15
88	Cesar King	.15
89	Rob Bell	.15
90	Derrick Gibson	.15
91	Ober Moreno RC	.15
92	Robert Fick	.15
93	Doug Mientkiewicz RC	.75
94	A.J. Pierzynski	.15
95	Orlando Palmeiro	.15
96	Sidney Ponson	.15
97	Ivanon Coffie RC	.15
98	Juan Pena RC	1.00
99	Mark Karchner	.15
100	Carlos Castillo	.15
101	Bryan Ward	.15
102	Mario Valdez	.15
103	Billy Wagner	.15
104	Miguel Tejada	.25
105	Jose Cruz Jr.	.15
106	George Lombard	.15
107	Geoff Jenkins	.15
108	Ray Lankford	.15
109	Todd Stottlemyre	.15
110	Mike Lowell	.15
111	Matt Clement	.15
112	Scott Brosius	.15
113	Preston Wilson	.15
114	Bartolo Colon	.15
115	Rolando Arrojo	.15
116	Jose Guillen	.15
117	Ron Gant	.15
118	Ricky Ledee	.15
119	Carlos Delgado	.50
120	Abraham Nunez	.15
121	John Olerud	.15
122	Chan Ho Park	.15
123	Brad Radke	.15
124	Al Leiter	.15
125	Gary Matthews Jr.	.15
126	F.P. Santangelo	.15
127	Brad Fullmer	.15
128	Matt Anderson	.15
129	A.J. Hinch	.15
130	Sterling Hitchcock	.15
131	Edgar Martinez	.15
132	Fernando Tatis	.15
133	Bobby Smith	.15
134	Paul Konerko	.25
135	Sean Casey	.25
136	Donnie Sadler	.15
137	Denny Neagle	.15
138	Sandy Alomar	.15
139	Mariano Rivera	.25
140	Emil Brown	.15
141	J.T. Snow	.15
142	Eli Marrero	.15
143	Rusty Greer	.15
144	Johnny Damon	.35
145	Damion Easley	.15
146	Eric Milton	.15
147	Rico Brogna	.15
148	Ray Durham	.15
149	Wally Joyner	.15
150	Royce Clayton	.15
151	David Ortiz	.50
152	Wade Boggs	2.00
153	Ugueth Urbina	.15
154	Richard Hidalgo	.15
155	Bobby Abreu	.15
156	Robb Nen	.15
157	David Segui	.15
158	Sean Berry	.15
159	Kevin Tapani	.15
160	Jason Varitek	.15
161	Fernando Vina	.15
162	Jim Leyritz	.15
163	Enrique Wilson	.15
164	Jim Parque	.15
165	Doug Glanville	.15
166	Jesus Sanchez	.15
167	Nolan Ryan	4.00
168	Robin Yount	.50
169	Stan Musial	1.00
170	Tom Seaver	.50
171	Mike Schmidt	1.00
172	Willie Stargell	.50
173	Rollie Fingers	.45
174	Willie McCovey	.50
175	Harmon Killebrew	.50
176	Eddie Mathews	.50
177	Reggie Jackson	1.00
178	Frank Robinson	.50
179	Ken Griffey Sr.	.15
180	Eddie Murray	1.50

Autographs

Authentically autographed cards of nearly 100 current stars, top prospects and Hall of Famers were featured as one-per-pack inserts in SP Signature Edition. Some players did not return their signed cards in time for pack inclusion and had to be obtained by returning an exchange card prior to the May 12, 2000, deadline.

		NM/M
Common Player:		3.00
Inserted 1:1		
BA	Bobby Abreu	15.00
SA	Sandy Alomar	5.00
MA	Marlon Anderson	4.00
KB	Kevin Barker	3.00
MB	Michael Barrett	4.00
RoB	Rob Bell	3.00
AB	Albert Belle	15.00
RBe	Ron Belliard	3.00
CBe	Carlos Beltran	50.00
ABe	Adrian Beltre	25.00
BB	Barry Bonds	180.00
RB	Russ Branyan	3.00
SB	Scott Brosius/SP	30.00
DB	Dermal Brown	3.00
EB	Emil Brown	3.00
AJB	A.J. Burnett (Exchange Card)	3.00
AJB	A.J. Burnett/Auto.	20.00
PB	Pat Burrell	25.00
JoC	Jose Canseco	30.00
MC	Mike Caruso	3.00
SC	Sean Casey (Exchange Card)	3.00
SC	Sean Casey/Auto.	15.00
VC	Vinny Castilla (Exchange Card)	3.00
VC	Vinny Castilla/Auto.	8.00
CC	Carlos Castillo	3.00
EC	Eric Chavez	10.00
BC	Bruce Chen	3.00
JCi	Jeff Cirillo	3.00
RC	Royce Clayton	3.00
MCl	Matt Clement	6.00
IC	Ivanon Coffie	3.00
BCo	Bartolo Colon (Exchange Card)	3.00
BCo	Bartolo Colon/Auto.	8.00
JC	Jason Conti	3.00
JDa	Johnny Damon	25.00
BD	Ben Davis	3.00
CD	Carlos Delgado	20.00
OD	Octavio Dotel	3.00
JD	J.D. Drew	15.00
RD	Ray Durham	3.00
DEa	Damion Easley	3.00
JE	Juan Encarnacion	3.00
DE	Darin Erstad	8.00
CF	Carlos Febles	3.00
Rob	Robert Fick	3.00
Rol	Rollie Fingers	8.00
BF	Brad Fullmer	3.00
RGa	Ron Gant	8.00
NG	Nomar Garciaparra	30.00
JaG	Jason Giambi	20.00
DG	Derrick Gibson	3.00
DGl	Doug Glanville	3.00
TGl	Troy Glaus	15.00
AG	Alex Gonzalez	3.00
RGr	Rusty Greer	3.00
Jr.	Ken Griffey Jr.	80.00
1	Ken Griffey Jr. (Facsimile autographed "SAMPLE.")	
Sr.	Ken Griffey Sr.	8.00
VG	Vladimir Guerrero	30.00
JG	Jose Guillen	10.00
TG	Tony Gwynn	35.00
CHa	Chris Haas	3.00
HHj	Jerry Hairston Jr.	4.00
RH	Roy Halladay	15.00
THe	Todd Helton	20.00
BH	Bob Henley	3.00
ED	Orlando Hernandez	40.00
CH	Chad Hermansen	3.00
ShH	Shea Hillenbrand	8.00
StH	Sterling Hitchcock	3.00
THo	Trevor Hoffman	8.00
CHu	Chad Hutchinson	3.00
RJ	Reggie Jackson/SP	40.00
GJ	Geoff Jenkins	5.00
AJ	Andruw Jones	20.00
CJ	Chipper Jones	50.00
WJ	Wally Joyner	8.00
GK	Gabe Kapler	3.00
MKa	Mark Karchner	3.00
JK	Jason Kendall	6.00
HK	Harmon Killebrew	40.00
CKi	Cesar King	3.00
MKi	Mike Kinkade	3.00
PK	Paul Konerko	15.00
CK	Corey Koskie	6.00
MK	Mark Kotsay	4.00
RL	Ray Lankford	5.00
JLa	Joe Lawrence	3.00
CL	Carlos Lee	20.00
DL	Derrek Lee	25.00
AL	Al Leiter	6.00
JLe	Jim Leyritz	6.00
GL	George Lombard	3.00
GM	Greg Maddux	80.00
Eli	Eli Marrero	3.00
EM	Edgar Martinez	20.00
PM	Pedro J. Martinez (Exchange Card)	5.00
PM	Pedro J. Martinez (Autographed)	100.00
RMa	Ruben Mateo (Exchange Card)	3.00
RMa	Ruben Mateo/Auto.	8.00
EMa	Eddie Mathews	60.00
GMj	Gary Matthews Jr.	3.00
WMc	Willie McCovey	35.00
JM	Juan Melo	3.00
MMe	Mitch Meluskey	3.00
DoM	Doug Mientkiewicz	6.00
EMi	Eric Milton	3.00
DaM	Damon Minor	3.00
RM	Ryan Minor	3.00
EMu	Eddie Murray	20.00
SM	Stan Musial	50.00
RN	Robb Nen	3.00
AN	Abraham Nunez	3.00
JO	John Olerud	10.00
PO	Paul O'Neill	20.00
DO	David Ortiz	40.00
OP	Orlando Palmeiro	3.00
JP	Jim Parque	3.00
AP	Angel Pena	3.00
MP	Mike Piazza (Exchange Card)	6.00
MP	Mike Piazza/Auto.	150.00
CP	Calvin Pickering	3.00
AJP	A.J. Pierzynski	5.00
SP	Sidney Ponson	8.00
BR	Brad Radke	4.00
ARa	Aramis Ramirez	20.00
MR	Manny Ramirez	50.00
MRi	Mariano Rivera	25.00
FR	Frank Robinson	25.00
AR	Alex Rodriguez	120.00
PG		25.00
SR	Scott Rolen (Exchange Card)	3.00
SR	Scott Rolen/Auto.	25.00
RR	Rafael Roque	3.00
NR	Nolan Ryan	120.00
DS	Donnie Sadler	3.00
JS	Jesus Sanchez	3.00
MS	Mike Schmidt	60.00
TSe	Tom Seaver	35.00
DSe	David Segui	3.00
FS	Fernando Seguignol	3.00
BS	Bobby Smith	3.00
JT	J.T. Snow (Exchange Card)	3.00
JT	J.T. Snow/Auto.	6.00
POP	Willie Stargell (Exchange Card)	3.00
POP	Willie Stargell/Auto.	60.00
TSt	Todd Stottlemyre	3.00
FTa	Fernando Tatis	3.00
RT	Reggie Taylor	3.00
MT	Miguel Tejada	20.00
FT	Frank Thomas	50.00
MV	Mario Valdez	3.00
JV	Jason Varitek	30.00
GV	Greg Vaughn	3.00
MO	Mo Vaughn	8.00
FV	Fernando Vina	3.00
BWa	Billy Wagner	10.00
TW	Todd Walker	3.00
BW	Bryan Ward	3.00
EW	Enrique Wilson	3.00
KW	Kevin Witt	3.00
RY	Robin Yount	40.00

Autographs Gold

This parallel edition of the Signature Series Autographs features special gold graphic highlights on front and cards serially numbered within an edition of 50 each (except A.J. Burnett). Cards of 11 players were never signed, while cards of several others had to be obtained by sending in an exchange card, valid through May 12, 2000.

NM/M
Common Player: 12.00
Production 50 Sets

Code	Player	NM/M
MA	Marlon Anderson	12.00
KB	Kevin Barker	12.00
MB	Michael Barrett	12.00
RoB	Rob Bell	12.00
AB	Albert Belle	20.00
RBe	Ron Belliard	12.00
CBe	Carlos Beltran	75.00
ABe	Adrian Beltre	40.00
CB	Craig Biggio (Unsigned)	3.00
BB	Barry Bonds	250.00
RB	Russ Branyan	12.00
DB	Dermal Brown	12.00
AJB	A.J. Burnett (Exchange Card)	4.00
AJB	A.J. Burnett (Autographed edition of 20.)	40.00
JB	Jeromy Burnitz (Unsigned)	3.00
PB	Pat Burrell	40.00
JoC	Jose Canseco	50.00
MC	Mike Caruso	12.00
VC	Vinny Castilla (Exchange Card)	3.00
VC	Vinny Castilla/Auto.	20.00
CC	Carlos Castillo	12.00
EC	Eric Chavez	20.00
BC	Bruce Chen	12.00
JCi	Jeff Cirillo	12.00
JC	Jason Conti	12.00
MD	Mike Darr (Unsigned)	3.00
BD	Ben Davis	12.00
OD	Octavio Dotel	12.00
JD	J.D. Drew	30.00
JE	Juan Encarnacion	12.00
DE	Darin Erstad	20.00
CF	Carlos Febles	12.00
TF	Travis Fryman (Unsigned)	3.00
BF	Brad Fullmer	12.00
NG	Nomar Garciaparra	100.00
JaG	Jason Giambi	40.00
JeG	Jeremy Giambi (Unsigned)	3.00
DG	Derrick Gibson	12.00
DGl	Doug Glanville	12.00
TGl	Troy Glaus	30.00
AG	Alex Gonzalez	12.00
JG	Juan Gonzalez (Unsigned)	6.00
Jr.	Ken Griffey Jr.	150.00
Sr.	Ken Griffey Sr.	12.00
VG	Vladimir Guerrero	75.00
JG	Jose Guillen (Unsigned)	3.00
TG	Tony Gwynn	60.00
CHa	Chris Haas	12.00
JHj	Jerry Hairston Jr.	12.00
RH	Roy Halladay	25.00
THe	Todd Helton	30.00
RH	Rickey Henderson (Unsigned)	6.00
BH	Bob Henley	12.00
ED	Orlando Hernandez	25.00
CH	Chad Hermansen	12.00
ShH	Shea Hillenbrand	20.00
StH	Sterling Hitchcock	12.00
THo	Trevor Hoffman	30.00
CHu	Chad Hutchinson	12.00
GJ	Geoff Jenkins	12.00
AJ	Andruw Jones	40.00
CJ	Chipper Jones	80.00
BJ	Brian Jordan (Unsigned)	3.00
WJ	Wally Joyner	25.00
GK	Gabe Kapler	12.00
MKa	Mark Karchner	12.00
JK	Jason Kendall	20.00
CKi	Cesar King	12.00
MKi	Mike Kinkade	12.00
PK	Paul Konerko	15.00
CK	Corey Koskie	20.00
MK	Mark Kotsay	12.00
RL	Ray Lankford	12.00
JLa	Joe Lawrence	12.00
CL	Carlos Lee	25.00
DL	Derrek Lee	50.00
TL	Travis Lee (Unsigned)	3.00
AL	Al Leiter	12.00
JLe	Jim Leyritz	12.00
GL	George Lombard	12.00
GM	Greg Maddux	150.00
PM	Pedro Martinez (Exchange Card)	6.00
PM	Pedro Martinez/Auto.	200.00
RMa	Ruben Mateo (Exchange Card)	3.00
RMa	Ruben Mateo/Auto.	15.00
GMj	Gary Matthews Jr.	12.00
JM	Juan Melo	12.00
MMe	Mitch Meluskey	12.00
DoM	Doug Mientkiewicz	12.00
EMi	Eric Milton	12.00
DaM	Damon Minor	12.00
RM	Ryan Minor	12.00
PO	Paul O'Neill	30.00
DO	David Ortiz	75.00
OP	Orlando Palmeiro	12.00
AP	Angel Pena	12.00
MP	Mike Piazza (Exchange Card)	10.00
MP	Mike Piazza/Auto.	250.00
CP	Calvin Pickering	12.00
ARa	Aramis Ramirez	30.00
MR	Manny Ramirez	80.00
AR	Alex Rodriguez	185.00
PG	Ivan Rodriguez	45.00
SR	Scott Rolen (Exchange Card)	4.00
SR	Scott Rolen/Auto.	75.00
RR	Rafael Roque	12.00
DSe	David Segui	12.00
FS	Fernando Seguignol	12.00
BS	Bobby Smith	12.00
RT	Reggie Taylor	12.00
FT	Frank Thomas	70.00
MV	Mario Valdez	12.00
GV	Greg Vaughn	12.00
MO	Mo Vaughn	20.00
TW	Todd Walker	12.00
KW	Kevin Witt	12.00

Legendary Cuts

Each of the cards in this one-of-one insert series is unique, thus catalog values are impossible to assign.

No Pricing
Production One Set

500 Club Piece of History

NM/M
MO Mel Ott/350 100.00

1999 SPx

Formerly SPx Finite, this super-premium product showcases 80 of baseball's veteran players on regular cards and a 40-card rookie subset, which are serially numbered to 1,999. Two top rookies, J.D. Drew and Gabe Kapler autographed all 1,999 of their rookie subset cards. There are two parallels, SPx Radiance and SPx Spectrum. Radiance are serially numbered to 100 with Drew and Kapler signing all 100 of their cards. They are exclusive to Finite Radiance Hot Packs. Spectrums are limited to only one set and available only in Finite Spectrum Hot Packs. Packs consist of three cards with a S.R.P. of $5.99.

NM/M
Complete Set (120): 100.00
Common Player: .50
Common SPx Rookie (81-120): 2.00
Production 1,999 Sets
Radiance (1-80): 7X
Radiance SP (81-120): 1.5X
Spectrum (1-of-1): Value Undetermined
Pack (3): 3.00
Wax Box (18): 40.00

1 Mark McGwire #61 2.50
2 Mark McGwire #62 1.00
3 Mark McGwire #63 1.00
4 Mark McGwire #64 1.00
5 Mark McGwire #65 1.00
6 Mark McGwire #66 1.00
7 Mark McGwire #67 1.00
8 Mark McGwire #68 1.00
9 Mark McGwire #69 1.00
10 Mark McGwire #70 2.50
11 Mo Vaughn .50
12 Darin Erstad .75
13 Travis Lee .50
14 Randy Johnson 1.50
15 Matt Williams .50
16 Chipper Jones 2.00
17 Greg Maddux 2.00
18 Andruw Jones 1.50
19 Andres Galarraga .50
20 Cal Ripken Jr. 4.00
21 Albert Belle .50
22 Mike Mussina .75
23 Nomar Garciaparra 2.00
24 Pedro Martinez 1.50
25 John Valentin .50
26 Kerry Wood 1.00
27 Sammy Sosa 2.00
28 Mark Grace .50
29 Frank Thomas 1.50
30 Mike Caruso .50
31 Barry Larkin .50
32 Sean Casey .50
33 Jim Thome 1.25
34 Kenny Lofton .50
35 Manny Ramirez 1.50
36 Larry Walker .50
37 Todd Helton 1.25
38 Vinny Castilla .50
39 Tony Clark .50
40 Derrek Lee 1.00
41 Mark Kotsay .50
42 Jeff Bagwell 1.50
43 Craig Biggio .50
44 Moises Alou .50
45 Larry Sutton .50
46 Johnny Damon 1.00
47 Gary Sheffield 1.00
48 Raul Mondesi .50
49 Jeromy Burnitz .50
50 Todd Walker .50
51 David Ortiz 1.00
52 Vladimir Guerrero 1.50
53 Rondell White .50
54 Mike Piazza 2.50
55 Derek Jeter 4.00
56 Tino Martinez .50
57 David Wells .50
58 Ben Grieve .50
59 A.J. Hinch .50
60 Scott Rolen 1.25
61 Doug Glanville .50
62 Aramis Ramirez .50
63 Jose Guillen .50
64 Tony Gwynn 2.00
65 Greg Vaughn .50
66 Ruben Rivera .50
67 Barry Bonds 4.00
68 J.T. Snow .50
69 Alex Rodriguez 3.00
70 Ken Griffey Jr. 2.50
71 Jay Buhner .50
72 Mark McGwire 3.00
73 Fernando Tatis .50
74 Quinton McCracken .50
75 Wade Boggs 2.00
76 Ivan Rodriguez 1.25
77 Juan Gonzalez 1.00
78 Rafael Palmeiro 1.25
79 Jose Cruz Jr. .50
80 Carlos Delgado 1.00
81 Troy Glaus 5.00
82 Vladimir Nunez 2.00
83 George Lombard 2.00
84 Bruce Chen 2.00
85 Ryan Minor 2.00
86 Calvin Pickering 2.00
87 Jin Ho Cho 2.00
88 Russ Branyan 2.00
89 Derrick Gibson 2.00
90 Gabe Kapler/Auto 6.00
91 Matt Anderson 2.00
92 Robert Fick 2.00
93 Juan Encarnacion 2.00
94 Preston Wilson 2.00
95 Alex Gonzalez 2.00
96 Carlos Beltran 5.00
97 Jeremy Giambi 2.00
98 Dee Brown 2.00
99 Adrian Beltre 4.00
100 Alex Cora 2.00
101 Angel Pena 2.00
102 Geoff Jenkins 2.00
103 Ronnie Belliard 2.00
104 Corey Koskie 2.00
105 A.J. Pierzynski 2.00
106 Michael Barrett 2.00
107 Fernando Seguignol 2.00
108 Mike Kinkade 2.00
109 Mike Lowell 2.00
110 Ricky Ledee 2.00
111 Eric Chavez 2.00
112 Abraham Nunez 2.00
113 Matt Clement 2.00
114 Ben Davis 2.00
115 Mike Darr 2.00
116 Ramon Martinez 2.00
117 Carlos Guillen 2.00
118 Shane Monahan 2.00
119 J.D. Drew/Auto. 15.00
120 Kevin Witt 2.00

Dominance

This 20-card set showcases the most dominant MLB superstars, including Derek Jeter and Alex Rodriguez. These are seeded 1:17 packs and numbered with a FB prefix.

NM/M
Complete Set (20): 35.00
Common Player: 1.00
Inserted 1:17

1 Chipper Jones 2.00
2 Greg Maddux 2.00
3 Cal Ripken Jr. 4.00
4 Nomar Garciaparra 2.00
5 Mo Vaughn 1.00
6 Sammy Sosa 2.00
7 Albert Belle 1.00
8 Frank Thomas 1.50
9 Jim Thome 1.25
10 Jeff Bagwell 1.50
11 Vladimir Guerrero 1.50
12 Mike Piazza 2.50
13 Derek Jeter 4.00
14 Tony Gwynn 2.00
15 Barry Bonds 4.00
16 Ken Griffey Jr. 2.50
17 Alex Rodriguez 3.00
18 Mark McGwire 3.00
19 J.D. Drew 1.25
20 Juan Gonzalez 1.25

Premier Stars

This 30-card set captures baseball's most dominant players, including Randy Johnson and Ken Griffey Jr. Featured on a rainbow-foil design, these are numbered with a PS prefix.

NM/M
Complete Set (30): 45.00
Common Player: 1.00
Inserted 1:17

1 Mark McGwire 3.00
2 Sammy Sosa 2.00
3 Frank Thomas 1.50
4 J.D. Drew 1.25
5 Kerry Wood 1.25
6 Moises Alou 1.00
7 Kenny Lofton 1.00
8 Jeff Bagwell 1.50
9 Tony Clark 1.00
10 Roberto Alomar 1.00
11 Cal Ripken Jr. 4.00
12 Derek Jeter 4.00
13 Mike Piazza 2.50
14 Jose Cruz Jr. 1.00
15 Chipper Jones 2.00
16 Nomar Garciaparra 2.00
17 Greg Maddux 2.00
18 Scott Rolen 1.25
19 Vladimir Guerrero 1.50
20 Albert Belle 1.00
21 Ken Griffey Jr. 2.50
22 Alex Rodriguez 2.00
23 Ben Grieve 1.00
24 Juan Gonzalez 1.25
25 Barry Bonds 4.00
26 Larry Walker 1.00
27 Tony Gwynn 2.00
28 Randy Johnson 1.50
29 Travis Lee 1.00
30 Mo Vaughn 1.00

Power Explosion

This 30-card set salutes the top power hitters in the game today, including Mark McGwire and Sammy Sosa. These are numbered with a PE prefix.

NM/M
Complete Set (30): 15.00
Common Player: .20
Inserted 1:3

1 Troy Glaus .65
2 Mo Vaughn .20
3 Travis Lee .20
4 Chipper Jones 1.00
5 Andres Galarraga .20
6 Brady Anderson .20
7 Albert Belle .20
8 Nomar Garciaparra 1.00
9 Sammy Sosa 1.00
10 Frank Thomas .75
11 Jim Thome .65
12 Manny Ramirez .75
13 Larry Walker .20
14 Tony Clark .20
15 Jeff Bagwell .75
16 Moises Alou .20
17 Ken Caminiti .20
18 Vladimir Guerrero .75
19 Mike Piazza 1.25
20 Tino Martinez .20
21 Ben Grieve .20
22 Scott Rolen .60
23 Greg Vaughn .20
24 Barry Bonds 2.00
25 Ken Griffey Jr. 1.25
26 Alex Rodriguez 1.50
27 Mark McGwire 1.50
28 J.D. Drew .35
29 Juan Gonzalez .45
30 Ivan Rodriguez .60

Star Focus

This 30-card set focuses on the 30 brightest stars in the game. These are numbered with a SF prefix.

NM/M
Complete Set (30): 50.00
Common Player: .75
Inserted 1:8

1 Chipper Jones 2.25
2 Greg Maddux 2.25
3 Cal Ripken Jr. 4.50
4 Nomar Garciaparra 2.25
5 Mo Vaughn .75
6 Sammy Sosa 2.25
7 Albert Belle .75
8 Frank Thomas 1.50
9 Jim Thome 1.25
10 Kenny Lofton .75
11 Manny Ramirez 1.50
12 Larry Walker .75
13 Jeff Bagwell 1.50
14 Craig Biggio .75
15 Randy Johnson 1.50
16 Vladimir Guerrero 1.50
17 Mike Piazza 3.00
18 Derek Jeter 4.50
19 Tino Martinez .75
20 Bernie Williams .75
21 Curt Schilling 1.00
22 Tony Gwynn 2.25
23 Barry Bonds 4.50
24 Ken Griffey Jr. 3.00
25 Alex Rodriguez 3.00
26 Mark McGwire 4.00
27 J.D. Drew 1.00
28 Juan Gonzalez 1.50
29 Ivan Rodriguez 1.25
30 Ben Grieve .75

Winning Materials

This eight-card set includes a piece of the featured player's game-worn jersey and game-used bat on each card. These are seeded 1:251 packs.

NM/M
Complete Set (8): 90.00
Common Player: 5.00
Inserted 1:251

VC Vinny Castilla 5.00
JD J.D. Drew 7.50
JR Ken Griffey Jr. 20.00
VG Vladimir Guerrero 12.00
TG Tony Gwynn 15.00
TH Todd Helton 10.00
TL Travis Lee 5.00
IR Ivan Rodriguez 10.00

500 Club Piece of History

Each of these approximately 350 cards include a piece of game-used Louisville Slugger once swung by Willie Mays. Mays also signed 24 of his Piece of History cards.

NM/M
WM Willie Mays/350 275.00
WM Willie Mays/Auto./24 1,700

2000 SP Authentic

The 135-card base set is composed of 90 regular cards, 30 Future Watch subset cards (serial numbered to 2,500) and 15 SP Superstars (serial numbered to 2,500). The regular cards have a gold foiled stamped line around the player image with a matte finished white border around the player image. The player name is stamped in gold foil in the top portion and the SP Authentic logo is stamped in silver foil. Card backs have a small photo, a brief career note and up to the past five seasons of complete statistics. Five-card packs carried a $4.99 SRP.

NM/M
Complete Set (135): 150.00
Common Player: .15
Common (91-105): 2.00
Production 2,500 Sets
Common (106-135): 2.00
Production 2,500 Sets
Pack (5): 3.00
Box (24): 60.00

1 Mo Vaughn .15
2 Troy Glaus .50
3 Jason Giambi .75
4 Tim Hudson .40
5 Eric Chavez .25
6 Shannon Stewart .15
7 Raul Mondesi .15
8 Carlos Delgado .50
9 Jose Canseco .50
10 Vinny Castilla .15
11 Greg Vaughn .15
12 Manny Ramirez 1.00
13 Roberto Alomar .40
14 Jim Thome .75
15 Richie Sexson .40
16 Alex Rodriguez 2.50
17 Fred Garcia .15
18 John Olerud .25
19 Albert Belle .25
20 Cal Ripken Jr. 3.00
21 Mike Mussina .50
22 Ivan Rodriguez .75
23 Gabe Kapler .15
24 Rafael Palmeiro .75
25 Nomar Garciaparra 1.00
26 Pedro Martinez 1.00
27 Carl Everett .25
28 Carlos Beltran .50
29 Jermaine Dye .25
30 Juan Gonzalez .50
31 Dean Palmer .15
32 Corey Koskie .15
33 Jacque Jones .15
34 Frank Thomas .75
35 Paul Konerko .40
36 Magglio Ordonez .40
37 Bernie Williams .40
38 Derek Jeter 2.50
39 Roger Clemens 2.00
40 Mariano Rivera .40
41 Jeff Bagwell .40
42 Craig Biggio .40
43 Jose Lima .15
44 Moises Alou .25
45 Chipper Jones 1.00
46 Greg Maddux 1.50
47 Andruw Jones 1.00

48	Kevin Millwood	.15
49	Jeromy Burnitz	.15
50	Geoff Jenkins	.15
51	Mark McGwire	1.50
52	Fernando Tatis	.15
53	J.D. Drew	.25
54	Sammy Sosa	1.00
55	Kerry Wood	.50
56	Mark Grace	.25
57	Matt Williams	.15
58	Randy Johnson	1.00
59	Erubiel Durazo	.15
60	Gary Sheffield	.50
61	Kevin Brown	.15
62	Shawn Green	.40
63	Vladimir Guerrero	1.00
64	Michael Barrett	.15
65	Barry Bonds	2.50
66	Jeff Kent	.25
67	Russ Ortiz	.15
68	Preston Wilson	.15
69	Mike Lowell	.15
70	Mike Piazza	1.00
71	Mike Hampton	.15
72	Robin Ventura	.15
73	Edgardo Alfonzo	.15
74	Tony Gwynn	1.50
75	Ryan Klesko	.15
76	Trevor Hoffman	.15
77	Scott Rolen	1.00
78	Bob Abreu	.40
79	Mike Lieberthal	.15
80	Curt Schilling	.75
81	Jason Kendall	.15
82	Brian Giles	.15
83	Kris Benson	.15
84	Ken Griffey Jr.	2.00
85	Sean Casey	.25
86	Pokey Reese	.15
87	Barry Larkin	.40
88	Larry Walker	.25
89	Todd Helton	.75
90	Jeff Cirillo	.15
91	Ken Griffey Jr. (SP Superstars)	4.00
92	Mark McGwire (SP Superstars)	4.00
93	Chipper Jones (SP Superstars)	3.00
94	Derek Jeter (SP Superstars)	6.00
95	Shawn Green (SP Superstars)	2.00
96	Pedro Martinez (SP Superstars)	4.00
97	Mike Piazza (SP Superstars)	4.00
98	Alex Rodriguez (SP Superstars)	5.00
99	Jeff Bagwell (SP Superstars)	2.50
100	Cal Ripken Jr. (SP Superstars)	6.00
101	Sammy Sosa (SP Superstars)	3.00
102	Barry Bonds (SP Superstars)	5.00
103	Jose Canseco (SP Superstars)	2.00
104	Nomar Garciaparra (SP Superstars)	4.00
105	Ivan Rodriguez (SP Superstars)	2.50
106	Rick Ankiel (Future Watch)	2.00
107	Pat Burrell (Future Watch)	2.50
108	Vernon Wells (Future Watch)	2.50
109	Nick Johnson (Future Watch)	2.00
110	Kip Wells (Future Watch)	2.00
111	Matt Riley (Future Watch)	2.00
112	Alfonso Soriano (Future Watch)	8.00
113	Josh Beckett (Future Watch)	4.00
114	Danys Baez **RC** (Future Watch)	6.00
115	Travis Dawkins (Future Watch)	2.50
116	Eric Gagne (Future Watch)	4.00
117	Mike Lamb **RC** (Future Watch)	4.00
118	Eric Munson (Future Watch)	2.50
119	Wilfredo Rodriguez **RC** (Future Watch)	2.00
120	Kazuhiro Sasaki **RC** (Future Watch)	3.00
121	Chad Hutchinson (Future Watch)	2.00
122	Peter Bergeron (Future Watch)	2.00
123	Wascar Serrano **RC** (Future Watch)	2.00
124	Tony Armas Jr. (Future Watch)	2.00
125	Ramon Ortiz (Future Watch)	2.00
126	Adam Kennedy (Future Watch)	2.00
127	Joe Crede (Future Watch)	5.00
128	Roosevelt Brown (Future Watch)	2.00

129	Mark Mulder (Future Watch)	2.50
130	Brad Penny (Future Watch)	2.00
131	Terrence Long (Future Watch)	2.00
132	Ruben Mateo (Future Watch)	2.00
133	Wily Mo Pena (Future Watch)	2.00
134	Rafael Furcal (Future Watch)	2.00
135	Mario Encarnacion (Future Watch)	2.00

Limited

A parallel to the 135-card base set these have "SP Limited" printed down the right side of the front and are serial numbered on the card front in an edition of 100 sets.

Cards (1-90):	4-8X
Cards (91-105):	2-3X
Cards (106-135):	1-2X
Production 100 Sets	

Chirography

This autographed insert set has a horizontal format with two player images on the card front. The player signature appears in the top right portion over a silver, checkered background. The insert name and logo have a silver tint. Card backs are numbered with the featured players first and last initial. Chirographies are seeded 1:23 packs.

		NM/M
Common Player:		5.00
Inserted 1:23		
RA	Rick Ankiel	25.00
CBe	Carlos Beltran	30.00
BB	Barry Bonds	200.00
PB	Pat Burrell	15.00
JC	Jose Canseco	25.00
SC	Sean Casey	8.00
RC	Roger Clemens	80.00
ED	Erubiel Durazo	5.00
TGl	Troy Glaus	20.00
VG	Vladimir Guerrero	30.00
TG	Tony Gwynn	40.00
DJ	Derek Jeter	120.00
NJ	Nick Johnson	10.00
CJ	Chipper Jones	40.00
AJ	Andruw Jones	20.00
SK	Sandy Koufax	250.00
BP	Ben Petrick	5.00
MQ	Mark Quinn	5.00
MR	Manny Ramirez	40.00
CR	Cal Ripken Jr.	100.00
AR	Alex Rodriguez	90.00
IR	Ivan Rodriguez	25.00
SR	Scott Rolen	25.00
AS	Alfonso Soriano	30.00
MV	Mo Vaughn	8.00
EY	Ed Yarnall	5.00

Chirography Gold

Golds use the same photos as the regular Chirography inserts and can be differentiated by the gold checkered background of the player signature in the upper right portion as well as the gold tint in the insert

---

name and logo. Golds are also hand-numbered to the player's jersey number on the card front and are numbered with a "G" prefix on the card back before the players initials.

		NM/M
Common Player:		
RA	Rick Ankiel/66 EXCH	50.00
CBe	Carlos Beltran/15	65.00
BB	Barry Bonds/25	300.00
PB	Pat Burrell/33 EXCH	50.00
JC	Jose Canseco/33	75.00
SC	Sean Casey/21	65.00
RC	Roger Clemens/22	300.00
ED	Erubiel Durazo/44	25.00
VG	Vladimir Guerrero/27	100.00
TG	Tony Gwynn/19	200.00
NJ	Nick Johnson/63	15.00
BP	Ben Petrick/15	30.00
MR	Manny Ramirez/24 EXCH	100.00
AS	Alfonso Soriano/53	60.00
MV	Mo Vaughn/42	25.00
EY	Ed Yarnall/41	15.00

Joe DiMaggio Game Jersey

This is DiMaggio's first Game Jersey insert and has three different versions. The first is limited to 500 total cards, the second version is Gold and numbered to 56. The rarest version has a DiMaggio cut signature along with a piece of his game-used jersey and is limited to only five total cards.

		NM/M
JD	Joe DiMaggio/Jsy/500	120.00
JD	Joe DiMaggio/Jsy Gold/56	200.00

Midsummer Classics

This 10-card set spotlights perennial All-Stars and has a silver holo-foiled front with gold foil etching and stamping. These are found 1:12 packs and are numbered on the card back with an "MC" prefix.

		NM/M
Complete Set (10):		10.00
Common Player:		.50
Inserted 1:12		
1	Cal Ripken Jr.	3.00
2	Roger Clemens	1.75
3	Jeff Bagwell	.75
4	Barry Bonds	3.00
5	Jose Canseco	.50
6	Frank Thomas	.75
7	Mike Piazza	2.00
8	Tony Gwynn	1.50
9	Juan Gonzalez	.75
10	Greg Maddux	1.50

Premier Performers

This 10-card set spotlights baseball's best on a silver holo-foiled card front with the player name, insert name and logo stamped in gold foil. Card backs are numbered with a "PP" prefix and are found 1:12 packs.

		NM/M
Complete Set (10):		10.00
Common Player:		.75
Inserted 1:12		
1	Mark McGwire	2.00
2	Alex Rodriguez	2.50
3	Cal Ripken Jr.	3.00
4	Nomar Garciaparra	1.50
5	Ken Griffey Jr.	2.00
6	Chipper Jones	1.50
7	Derek Jeter	3.00
8	Ivan Rodriguez	.75
9	Vladimir Guerrero	.75
10	Sammy Sosa	1.50

SP Buyback

This autographed set features previously issued SP cards that were re-purchased by Upper Deck. The cards are autographed by the featured player and hand-numbered on the card front. The number autographed and released by Upper Deck is listed after the player name. Buybacks are found 1:95 packs.

		NM/M
Common Player:		
1	Jeff Bagwell Exch.	50.00
2	Craig Biggio '93/59	50.00
3	Craig Biggio '94/69	50.00
4	Craig Biggio '95/171	40.00
5	Craig Biggio '96/71	50.00
6	Craig Biggio '97/46	50.00
7	Craig Biggio '98/40	50.00
8	Craig Biggio '99/125	40.00
15	Barry Bonds '99/520	150.00
16	Jose Canseco '93/29	60.00
17	Jose Canseco '94/20	60.00
19	Jose Canseco '96/23	60.00
20	Jose Canseco '97/23	60.00
21	Jose Canseco '98/24	60.00
22	Jose Canseco '99/502	30.00
24	Sean Casey '99/139	20.00
25	Roger Clemens '93/68	85.00
26	Roger Clemens '94/68	85.00
27	Roger Clemens '95/68	85.00
28	Roger Clemens '96/68	85.00
30	Roger Clemens '98/25	200.00
31	Roger Clemens '99/134	75.00
32	Jason Giambi '97/34	50.00
33	Jason Giambi '98/25	50.00
34	Tom Glavine '93/60	40.00
35	Tom Glavine '94/107	40.00
36	Tom Glavine '95/97	40.00
37	Tom Glavine '96/42	50.00
38	Tom Glavine '98/40	50.00
39	Tom Glavine '99/138	40.00
40	Shawn Green '96/55	30.00
41	Shawn Green '99/530	20.00
42	Ken Griffey Jr. '96/12	275.00
48	Tony Gwynn '97/24	150.00
49	Tony Gwynn '99/129	50.00
50	Tony Gwynn '99/369	40.00
56	Derek Jeter '99/119	200.00
57	Randy Johnson '93/60	75.00
58	Randy Johnson '94/45	80.00
59	Randy Johnson '95/70	75.00
60	Randy Johnson '96/60	75.00
63	Randy Johnson '99/113	75.00
64	Andruw Jones Exch.	40.00
65	Chipper Jones Exch.	40.00
66	Kenny Lofton '94/100	25.00
67	Kenny Lofton '95/84	25.00
68	Kenny Lofton '96/34	40.00
69	Kenny Lofton '97/82	25.00
70	Kenny Lofton '98/21	40.00
71	Kenny Lofton '99/99	20.00
72	Javy Lopez '93/106	15.00
73	Javy Lopez '94/160	20.00
74	Javy Lopez '96/99	15.00
75	Javy Lopez '97/61	20.00
77	Greg Maddux '93/22	275.00
78	Greg Maddux '94/19	25.00
83	Greg Maddux '99/504	75.00
84	Paul O'Neill '93/110	25.00
85	Paul O'Neill '94/97	30.00
86	Paul O'Neill '95/142	25.00

87	Paul O'Neill '96/70	30.00
88	Paul O'Neill '98/23	40.00
89	Manny Ramirez/Redemp	50.00
91	Cal Ripken Jr. '94/22	300.00
96	Cal Ripken Jr. '99/510	125.00
97	Alex Rodriguez Exch.	150.00
98	Ivan Rodriguez '93/29	15.00
100	Ivan Rodriguez '95/18	125.00
101	Ivan Rodriguez '96/22	125.00
103	Ivan Rodriguez '98/27	125.00
109	Frank Thomas '97/20	75.00
111	Frank Thomas '99/100	50.00
112	Greg Vaughn '93/79	20.00
113	Greg Vaughn '94/75	20.00
114	Greg Vaughn '95/155	15.00
115	Greg Vaughn '96/113	15.00
117	Greg Vaughn '99/527	10.00
118	Mo Vaughn '93/119	20.00
119	Mo Vaughn '94/96	20.00
120	Mo Vaughn '95/121	20.00
121	Mo Vaughn '96/114	20.00
122	Mo Vaughn '97/61	25.00
124	Mo Vaughn '99/537	15.00
125	Robin Ventura '93/59	25.00
126	Robin Ventura '94/49	25.00
127	Robin Ventura '95/125	20.00
128	Robin Ventura '96/55	25.00
129	Robin Ventura '97/44	30.00
130	Robin Ventura '98/28	30.00
131	Robin Ventura '99/370	15.00
133	Matt Williams '94/50	40.00
134	Matt Williams '95/137	40.00
135	Matt Williams '96/77	40.00
136	Matt Williams '97/54	40.00
137	Matt Williams '98/29	60.00
138	Matt Williams '99/529	15.00
139	Preston Wilson '94/249	15.00
140	Preston Wilson '99/195	15.00

SP Cornerstones

Printed on a silver holo-foiled card front a close-up image of the player appears in a baseball diamond shaped enclosed by gold foil etching. Another shadow image of the featured player appears in the background. The player name, insert name and logo are stamped in gold foil. These are seeded 1:23 packs and are numbered with a "C" prefix on the card back.

		NM/M
Complete Set (7):		15.00
Common Player:		2.00
Inserted 1:23		
1	Ken Griffey Jr.	2.00
2	Cal Ripken Jr.	4.00
3	Mike Piazza	2.00
4	Derek Jeter	4.00
5	Mark McGwire	3.00
6	Nomar Garciaparra	2.00
7	Sammy Sosa	2.00

SP Supremacy

This seven-card set has a silver foiled card front with the insert name and logo stamped in gold foil. The inserts are found on the average of 1:23 packs and are numbered with a "S" prefix.

		NM/M
Complete Set (7):		8.00
Common Player:		.75
Inserted 1:23		

1	Alex Rodriguez	3.00
2	Shawn Green	.75
3	Pedro Martinez	1.00
4	Chipper Jones	2.00
5	Tony Gwynn	2.00
6	Ivan Rodriguez	1.00
7	Jeff Bagwell	1.00

United Nations

Done on a horizontal format this 10-card set salutes the top international stars of the game. The featured player's country of origin flag is in the background of the player image. The card design features silver holofoil and silver foil etching and stamping. These are seeded 1:4 packs and are numbered with an "UN" prefix on the card back.

		NM/M
Complete Set (10):		5.00
Common Player:		.50
Inserted 1:4		
1	Sammy Sosa (Dominican Rep.)	1.50
2	Ken Griffey Jr. (USA)	2.00
3	Orlando Hernandez (Cuba)	.50
4	Andres Galarraga (Venezuela)	.50
5	Kazuhiro Sasaki (Japan)	.50
6	Larry Walker (Canada)	.50
7	Vinny Castilla (Mexico)	.50
8	Andruw Jones (Neth. Antilles)	.75
9	Ivan Rodriguez (Puerto Rico)	.75
10	Chan Ho Park (So. Korea)	.50

3,000 Hit Club

A continuation of Upper Deck's cross brand salute to players who have reached the magical 3,000 hit milestone. 350 game-used bat cards and five bat/cut signature combos were issued for each player.

		NM/M
PW	Paul Waner/Bat/350	50.00
TS	Tris Speaker/Bat/350	100.00

2000 SPx

The base set consists of 120-cards including 30 Rookie/ Young Star subset cards which has three tiers. The first five are numbered to 1,000, the next 22 autographed and numbered to 1,500 and the final three are autographed and numbered to 500. Each base card has a holo-foiled front with the SPx logo, player name, team name stamped in gold foil.

	NM/M
Complete Set (120):	400.00
Common Player:	.15
Common Rookie (91-120):	10.00
Pack (4):	6.00
Box (18):	80.00
1	Troy Glaus	.50
2	Mo Vaughn	.15
3	Ramon Ortiz	.15
4	Jeff Bagwell	.75
5	Moises Alou	.25
6	Craig Biggio	.40

7	Jose Lima	.15
8	Jason Giambi	.75
9	John Jaha	.15
10	Matt Stairs	.15
11	Chipper Jones	1.00
12	Greg Maddux	1.50
13	Andres Galarraga	.15
14	Andruw Jones	1.00
15	Jeromy Burnitz	.15
16	Ron Belliard	.15
17	Carlos Delgado	.75
18	David Wells	.15
19	Tony Batista	.15
20	Shannon Stewart	.15
21	Sammy Sosa	1.00
22	Mark Grace	.50
23	Henry Rodriguez	.15
24	Mark McGwire	2.00
25	J.D. Drew	.25
26	Luis Gonzalez	.25
27	Randy Johnson	1.00
28	Matt Williams	.15
29	Steve Finley	.15
30	Shawn Green	.25
31	Kevin Brown	.15
32	Gary Sheffield	.50
33	Jose Canseco	.50
34	Greg Vaughn	.15
35	Vladimir Guerrero	1.00
36	Michael Barrett	.15
37	Russ Ortiz	.15
38	Barry Bonds	3.00
39	Jeff Kent	.25
40	Richie Sexson	.40
41	Manny Ramirez	1.00
42	Jim Thome	1.00
43	Roberto Alomar	.50
44	Edgar Martinez	.15
45	Alex Rodriguez	2.50
46	John Olerud	.15
47	Alex Gonzalez	.15
48	Cliff Floyd	.15
49	Mike Piazza	1.50
50	Al Leiter	.15
51	Robin Ventura	.15
52	Edgardo Alfonzo	.15
53	Albert Belle	.15
54	Cal Ripken Jr.	3.00
55	B.J. Surhoff	.15
56	Tony Gwynn	1.50
57	Trevor Hoffman	.15
58	Brian Giles	.15
59	Jason Kendall	.15
60	Kris Benson	.15
61	Bob Abreu	.50
62	Scott Rolen	1.00
63	Curt Schilling	.75
64	Mike Lieberthal	.15
65	Sean Casey	.25
66	Dante Bichette	.15
67	Ken Griffey Jr.	2.00
68	Pokey Reese	.15
69	Mike Sweeney	.15
70	Carlos Febles	.15
71	Ivan Rodriguez	1.00
72	Ruben Mateo	.15
73	Rafael Palmeiro	1.00
74	Larry Walker	.40
75	Todd Helton	.75
76	Nomar Garciaparra	1.00
77	Pedro Martinez	1.00
78	Troy O'Leary	.15
79	Jacque Jones	.15
80	Corey Koskie	.15
81	Juan Gonzalez	.50
82	Dean Palmer	.15
83	Juan Encarnacion	.15
84	Frank Thomas	1.00
85	Magglio Ordonez	.25
86	Paul Konerko	.50
87	Bernie Williams	.50
88	Derek Jeter	3.00
89	Roger Clemens	2.50
90	Orlando Hernandez	.15
91	Vernon Wells AU-1,000	25.00
92	Rick Ankiel AU-1,000	40.00
93	Eric Chavez AU-1,000	15.00
94	Alfonso Soriano AU-1,000	40.00
95	Eric Gagne AU-1,000	15.00
96	Rob Bell AU-1,500	10.00
97	Matt Riley AU-1,500	10.00
98	Josh Beckett AU-1,500	40.00
99	Ben Petrick AU-1,500	10.00
100	Rob Ramsay AU-1,500 RC	10.00
101	Scott Williamson AU-1,500	10.00
102	Doug Davis AU-1,500	15.00
103	Eric Munson AU-1,500	10.00
104	Pat Burrell AU-500	20.00
105	Jim Morris AU-1,500	10.00
106	Gabe Kapler AU-500	15.00
107	Lance Berkman 1,500	30.00
108	Erubiel Durazo AU-1,500	10.00
109	Tim Hudson AU-1,500	30.00
110	Ben Davis AU-1,500	10.00
111	Nick Johnson AU-1,500	15.00
112	Octavio Dotel AU-1,500	10.00
113	Jerry Hairston Jr. 1,500	10.00
114	Ruben Mateo 1,500	10.00
115	Chris Singleton AU-1,500	10.00
116	Bruce Chen AU-1,500	10.00
117	Derrick Gibson AU-1,500	10.00
118	Carlos Beltran AU-500	40.00
119	Fred Garcia AU-500	10.00
120	Preston Wilson AU-500	15.00

Radiance

A parallel to the 120-card base set these are serially numbered to 100. A one-of-one Spectrum parallel of each base card is also randomly seeded.

NM/M
Stars (1-90): 4-8X
Common Young Star (91-120): 10.00
Production 100 Sets

Foundations

This 10-card set features a holo-foiled front with gold foil stamping. Three miniature action shots appear to the right of a close-up shot of the featured player. Card backs are numbered with an "F" prefix and inserted 1:32 packs.

		NM/M
Complete Set (10):		15.00
Common Player:		.50
Inserted 1:32		
1	Ken Griffey Jr.	3.00
2	Nomar Garciaparra	3.00
3	Cal Ripken Jr.	4.00
4	Chipper Jones	2.00
5	Mike Piazza	3.00
6	Derek Jeter	4.00
7	Manny Ramirez	1.00
8	Jeff Bagwell	1.00
9	Tony Gwynn	2.00
10	Larry Walker	.50

Heart of the Order

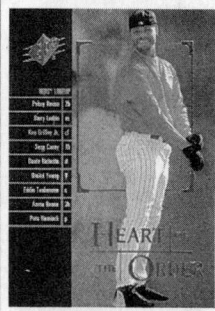

This 20-card set features a top hitter with his teams batting order to the left of his photo. The SPx logo and insert name are stamped in gold foil. Card backs are numbered with an "H" prefix and seeded 1:8 packs.

		NM/M
Complete Set (20):		10.00
Common Player:		.40
Inserted 1:8		
1	Bernie Williams	.50
2	Mike Piazza	2.00
3	Ivan Rodriguez	.75
4	Mark McGwire	2.50
5	Manny Ramirez	1.00
6	Ken Griffey Jr.	2.00
7	Matt Williams	.40
8	Sammy Sosa	2.00
9	Mo Vaughn	.40
10	Carlos Delgado	.75
11	Brian Giles	.40
12	Chipper Jones	1.50
13	Sean Casey	.40
14	Tony Gwynn	1.50
15	Barry Bonds	3.00
16	Carlos Beltran	.65
17	Scott Rolen	.75
18	Juan Gonzalez	1.00
19	Larry Walker	.40
20	Vladimir Guerrero	1.00

Highlight Heroes

This 10-card set has a horizontal format on a holo-foiled front with gold foil stamping. Card backs are numbered with an "HH" prefix and inserted 1:16 packs.

		NM/M
Complete Set (10):		10.00
Common Player:		.50
Inserted 1:16		
1	Pedro Martinez	1.00
2	Ivan Rodriguez	.75
3	Carlos Beltran	.65
4	Nomar Garciaparra	2.00
5	Ken Griffey Jr.	2.00
6	Randy Johnson	1.00
7	Chipper Jones	1.50
8	Scott Williamson	.50
9	Larry Walker	.50
10	Mark McGwire	2.50

Power Brokers

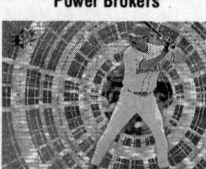

This 20-card set has a horizontal format with the background of the player photo having a kaleidoscope effect. The SPx logo is stamped in gold foil. Card backs are numbered with an "PB" prefix and are inserted 1:8 packs.

		NM/M
Complete Set (20):		10.00
Common Player:		.25
Inserted 1:8		
1	Rafael Palmeiro	.75
2	Carlos Delgado	.65
3	Ken Griffey Jr.	2.00
4	Matt Stairs	.25
5	Mike Piazza	2.00
6	Vladimir Guerrero	1.00
7	Chipper Jones	1.50
8	Mark McGwire	2.50
9	Matt Williams	.25
10	Juan Gonzalez	1.00
11	Shawn Green	.50
12	Sammy Sosa	2.00
13	Brian Giles	.25
14	Jeff Bagwell	1.00
15	Alex Rodriguez	2.50
16	Frank Thomas	1.00
17	Larry Walker	.25
18	Albert Belle	.25
19	Dean Palmer	.25
20	Mo Vaughn	.25

SPxcitement

This 20-card set features a holo-foiled front with gold foil stamping. Card backs are numbered with an "XC" prefix and are inserted 1:4 packs.

		NM/M
Complete Set (20):		15.00
Common Player:		.25
Inserted 1:4		
1	Nomar Garciaparra	1.25
2	Mark McGwire	1.50
3	Derek Jeter	2.00
4	Cal Ripken Jr.	2.00
5	Barry Bonds	2.00
6	Alex Rodriguez	1.50
7	Scott Rolen	.75
8	Pedro Martinez	.75
9	Sean Casey	.25
10	Sammy Sosa	1.25
11	Randy Johnson	.75
12	Ivan Rodriguez	.75
13	Frank Thomas	.75
14	Greg Maddux	1.00
15	Tony Gwynn	1.00
16	Ken Griffey Jr.	1.25
17	Carlos Beltran	.50
18	Mike Piazza	1.25
19	Chipper Jones	1.00
20	Craig Biggio	.25

SPx Signatures

These autographed inserts are seeded 1:112 packs.

		NM/M
Common Player:		10.00
Inserted 1:179		
JB	Jeff Bagwell	25.00
BB	Barry Bonds	150.00
JC	Jose Canseco	25.00
SC	Sean Casey	15.00
RC	Roger Clemens	85.00
KG	Ken Griffey Jr.	100.00
VG	Vladimir Guerrero	35.00
TG	Tony Gwynn	40.00
OH	Orlando Hernandez	20.00
DJ	Derek Jeter	125.00
CJ	Chipper Jones	60.00
MR	Manny Ramirez	40.00
CR	Cal Ripken Jr.	125.00
IR	Ivan Rodriguez	25.00
SR	Scott Rolen	30.00

Untouchable Talents

These inserts have a holo-foiled front and are numbered with an "UT" prefix. They are found on the average of 1:96 packs.

		NM/M
Complete Set (10):		30.00
Common Player:		1.50
Inserted 1:96		
1	Mark McGwire	8.00
2	Ken Griffey Jr.	6.00
3	Shawn Green	2.00
4	Ivan Rodriguez	2.50
5	Sammy Sosa	6.00
6	Derek Jeter	10.00
7	Sean Casey	1.50
8	Chipper Jones	5.00
9	Pedro Martinez	3.00
10	Vladimir Guerrero	3.00

Winning Materials

Five different tiers make up this memorabilia insert set with players having varying levels of their inserts in the set. Each insert has two pieces of memorabilia, combinations include Jersey/Bat, Jersey/Bat numbered to player's jersey number, Jersey/Cap, Jersey/Ball and Ball/Bat.

		NM/M
Common Bat/Jsy		6.00
AR	Alex Rodriguez/Bat/Jsy	25.00
AR	Alex Rodriguez/Cap/Jsy/100	40.00
AR	Alex Rodriguez/Jsy/Bat/Auto./50	50.00
DJ	Derek Jeter/Bat/Jsy	40.00
DJ	Derek Jeter/Ball/Jsy/50	75.00
BB	Barry Bonds/Bat/Jsy	30.00
BB	Barry Bonds/Cap/Jsy	50.00
BB	Barry Bonds/Ball/Jsy/Auto./25	350.00
JB	Jeff Bagwell/Bat/Jsy	8.00
JB	Jeff Bagwell/Cap/Jsy/100	15.00
JB	Jeff Bagwell/Ball/Jsy/50	25.00
KG	Ken Griffey Jr./Bat/Jsy	20.00
KG	Ken Griffey Jr./Ball/Jsy/50	50.00
KG	Ken Griffey Jr./Jsy/Bat/Auto./24	225.00
TG	Tony Gwynn/Bat/Jsy	10.00
TG	Tony Gwynn/Ball/Jsy/50	40.00
TG	Tony Gwynn/Cap/Jsy/100	30.00
BW	Bernie Williams/Bat/Jsy	8.00
EC	Eric Chavez/Bat/Jsy	8.00
EC	Eric Chavez/Cap/Jsy/100	15.00
GM	Greg Maddux/Bat/Jsy	25.00
IR	Ivan Rodriguez/Bat/Jsy	8.00
JC	Jose Canseco/Bat/Jsy	8.00
JL	Javy Lopez/Bat/Jsy	6.00
JL	Javy Lopez/Cap/Jsy/100	8.00
MM	Mark McGwire/Base/Ball/500	50.00
MR	Manny Ramirez/Bat/Jsy	10.00
MW	Matt Williams/Bat/Jsy	6.00
PM	Pedro Martinez/Bat/Jsy	25.00
PO	Paul O'Neill/Bat/Jsy	6.00
VG	Vladimir Guerrero/Bat/Jsy	10.00
VG	Vladimir Guerrero/Cap/Jsy/100	20.00
VG	Vladimir Guerrero/Ball/Jsy/50	30.00
TG	Troy Glaus/Bat/Jsy	

3,000 Hit Club

A continuation of Upper Deck's cross-brand insert program, this set pays tribute to Ty Cobb with three variations. The collection includes 350 bat cards, three cut signatures and one bat/cut signature card.

		NM/M
TC-B	Ty Cobb/Bat/350	130.00

2001 SP Authentic Sample

Base cards in the forthcoming SP Authentic issue were previewed with this card. In a format identical to the regularly issued version, the promo card has a large black "SAMPLE" overprinted diagonally on back.

		NM/M
90	Ken Griffey Jr.	3.00

2001 SP Authentic

		NM/M
Common Player:		.25
Common SP (91-135):		4.00
Production 1,250		
Common SP (136-180):		2.00
Production 1,250		
Pack (5):		12.00
Box (24):		240.00
1	Troy Glaus	.40
2	Darin Erstad	.25
3	Jason Giambi	.75
4	Tim Hudson	.50
5	Eric Chavez	.25
6	Miguel Tejada	.25
7	Jose Ortiz	.25
8	Carlos Delgado	.25
9	Tony Batista	.25
10	Raul Mondesi	.25
11	Aubrey Huff	.25
12	Greg Vaughn	.25
13	Roberto Alomar	.50
14	Juan Gonzalez	.50
15	Jim Thome	.25
16	Omar Vizquel	.25
17	Edgar Martinez	.25
18	Fred Garcia	.25
19	Cal Ripken Jr.	3.00
20	Ivan Rodriguez	.75
21	Rafael Palmeiro	.75
22	Alex Rodriguez	2.00
23	Manny Ramirez	1.00
24	Pedro Martinez	.75
25	Nomar Garciaparra	.75
26	Mike Sweeney	.25
27	Jermaine Dye	.25
28	Bobby Higginson	.25
29	Dean Palmer	.25
30	Matt Lawton	.25
31	Eric Milton	.25
32	Frank Thomas	.75
33	Magglio Ordonez	.40
34	David Wells	.25
35	Paul Konerko	.50
36	Derek Jeter	3.00
37	Bernie Williams	.50
38	Roger Clemens	.50
39	Mike Mussina	.50
40	Jorge Posada	.50
41	Jeff Bagwell	.50
42	Richard Hidalgo	.25
43	Craig Biggio	.50
44	Greg Maddux	2.00
45	Chipper Jones	.50
46	Andruw Jones	.50
47	Rafael Furcal	.40
48	Tom Glavine	.50
49	Jeromy Burnitz	.25
50	Jeffrey Hammonds	.25
51	Mark McGwire	1.50
52	Jim Edmonds	.50
53	Rick Ankiel	.50
54	J.D. Drew	.40
55	Sammy Sosa	.75
56	Corey Patterson	.25
57	Kerry Wood	.50
58	Randy Johnson	1.00
59	Luis Gonzalez	.40
60	Curt Schilling	.50
61	Gary Sheffield	.50
62	Shawn Green	.50
63	Kevin Brown	.25
64	Vladimir Guerrero	.75
65	Jose Vidro	.25
66	Barry Bonds	3.00
67	Jeff Kent	.50
68	Livan Hernandez	.25
69	Preston Wilson	.25
70	Charles Johnson	.25
71	Ryan Dempster	.25
72	Mike Piazza	1.00
73	Al Leiter	.25
74	Edgardo Alfonzo	.25
75	Robin Ventura	.25
76	Tony Gwynn	1.00
77	Phil Nevin	.25
78	Trevor Hoffman	.25
79	Scott Rolen	.50
80	Pat Burrell	.50
81	Bob Abreu	.25
82	Jason Kendall	.25
83	Brian Giles	.25
84	Kris Benson	.25
85	Ken Griffey Jr.	.50
86	Barry Larkin	.50
87	Sean Casey	.25
88	Todd Helton	.50

#	Player	Price
89	Mike Hampton	.25
90	Larry Walker	.25
91	Ichiro Suzuki RC (Future Watch)	100.00
92	Wilson Betemit RC (Future Watch)	6.00
93	Adrian Hernandez RC (Future Watch)	4.00
94	Juan Uribe RC (Future Watch)	4.00
95	Travis Hafner RC (Future Watch)	15.00
96	Morgan Ensberg RC (Future Watch)	6.00
97	Sean Douglass RC (Future Watch)	4.00
98	Juan Diaz RC (Future Watch)	4.00
99	Erick Almonte RC (Future Watch)	4.00
100	Ryan Freel RC (Future Watch)	8.00
101	Elpidio Guzman RC (Future Watch)	4.00
102	Christian Parker RC (Future Watch)	4.00
103	Josh Fogg RC (Future Watch)	4.00
104	Bert Snow RC (Future Watch)	4.00
105	Horacio Ramirez RC (Future Watch)	4.00
106	Ricardo Rodriguez RC (Future Watch)	4.00
107	Tyler Walker RC (Future Watch)	4.00
108	Jose Mieses RC (Future Watch)	4.00
109	Billy Sylvester RC (Future Watch)	4.00
110	Martin Vargas RC (Future Watch)	4.00
111	Andres Torres RC (Future Watch)	4.00
112	Greg Miller RC (Future Watch)	4.00
113	Alexis Gomez RC (Future Watch)	4.00
114	Grant Balfour RC (Future Watch)	4.00
115	Henry Mateo RC (Future Watch)	4.00
116	Esix Snead RC (Future Watch)	4.00
117	Jackson Mellan RC (Future Watch)	4.00
118	Nate Teut RC (Future Watch)	4.00
119	Tsuyoshi Shinjo RC (Future Watch)	4.00
120	Carlos Valderrama RC (Future Watch)	4.00
121	Johnny Estrada RC (Future Watch)	6.00
122	Jason Michaels RC (Future Watch)	4.00
123	William Ortega RC (Future Watch)	4.00
124	Jason Smith RC (Future Watch)	4.00
125	Brian Lawrence RC (Future Watch)	4.00
126	Albert Pujols RC (Future Watch)	250.00
127	Wilken Ruan RC (Future Watch)	4.00
128	Josh Towers RC (Future Watch)	4.00
129	Kris Keller RC (Future Watch)	4.00
130	Nick Maness RC (Future Watch)	4.00
131	Jack Wilson RC (Future Watch)	6.00
132	Brandon Duckworth RC (Future Watch)	4.00
133	Mike Penney RC (Future Watch)	4.00
134	Jay Gibbons RC (Future Watch)	4.00
135	Cesar Crespo RC (Future Watch)	4.00
136	Ken Griffey Jr. (SP Superstars)	8.00
137	Mark McGwire (SP Superstars)	8.00
138	Derek Jeter (SP Superstars)	10.00
139	Alex Rodriguez (SP Superstars)	10.00
140	Sammy Sosa (SP Superstars)	4.00
141	Carlos Delgado (SP Superstars)	3.00
142	Cal Ripken Jr. (SP Superstars)	12.00
143	Pedro Martinez (SP Superstars)	5.00
144	Frank Thomas (SP Superstars)	5.00
145	Juan Gonzalez (SP Superstars)	2.00
146	Troy Glaus (SP Superstars)	3.00
147	Jason Giambi (SP Superstars)	4.00
148	Ivan Rodriguez (SP Superstars)	4.00

#	Player	Price
149	Chipper Jones (SP Superstars)	5.00
150	Vladimir Guerrero (SP Superstars)	5.00
151	Mike Piazza (SP Superstars)	5.00
152	Jeff Bagwell (SP Superstars)	4.00
153	Randy Johnson (SP Superstars)	5.00
154	Todd Helton (SP Superstars)	4.00
155	Gary Sheffield (SP Superstars)	3.00
156	Tony Gwynn (SP Superstars)	5.00
157	Barry Bonds (SP Superstars)	10.00
158	Nomar Garciaparra (SP Superstars)	3.00
159	Bernie Williams (SP Superstars)	3.00
160	Greg Vaughn (SP Superstars)	2.00
161	David Wells (SP Superstars)	2.00
162	Roberto Alomar (SP Superstars)	3.00
163	Jermaine Dye (SP Superstars)	2.00
164	Rafael Palmeiro (SP Superstars)	4.00
165	Andruw Jones (SP Superstars)	3.00
166	Preston Wilson (SP Superstars)	2.00
167	Edgardo Alfonzo (SP Superstars)	2.00
168	Pat Burrell (SP Superstars)	3.00
169	Jim Edmonds (SP Superstars)	3.00
170	Mike Hampton (SP Superstars)	2.00
171	Jeff Kent (SP Superstars)	2.00
172	Kevin Brown (SP Superstars)	2.00
173	Manny Ramirez (SP Superstars)	5.00
174	Magglio Ordonez (SP Superstars)	2.00
175	Roger Clemens (SP Superstars)	8.00
176	Jim Thome (SP Superstars)	4.00
177	Barry Zito (SP Superstars)	2.00
178	Brian Giles (SP Superstars)	2.00
179	Rick Ankiel (SP Superstars)	4.00
180	Corey Patterson (SP Superstars)	2.00

Limited

Stars (1-90):		8-15X
SP (91-135):		1-2X
SP (136-180):		1-30X
Production 50 Sets		

Buyback Autographs

Inserted 1:144
Some not priced due to scarcity.

4	Ken Griffey '93/SP/34	125.00
105	Ken Griffey '94/SP/182	80.00
190	Ken Griffey '95/SP/116	80.00
170	Ken Griffey '95/SP/53	100.00
84	Ken Griffey '00/SP/333	70.00
188	Alex Rodriguez '95/SP Red/117	100.00
171	Alex Rodriguez '96/SP/72	120.00
16	Alex Rodriguez '00/SP/332	100.00
260	Frank Thomas '93/SP/79	40.00
193	Frank Thomas '94/SP/165	35.00
50	Frank Thomas '97/SP/34	75.00
34	Frank Thomas '00/SP/302	35.00
34	Chipper Jones '95/SP/118	40.00
26	Chipper Jones '96/SP/72	50.00

#	Player	Price
45	Chipper Jones '00/SP/303	40.00
132	Randy Johnson '93/SP/97	60.00
106	Randy Johnson '94/SP/146	40.00
189	Randy Johnson '95/SP/121	40.00
169	Randy Johnson '96/SP/78	50.00
58	Randy Johnson '00/SP/213	40.00
41	Carlos Delgado '94/SP/279	15.00
181	Carlos Delgado '96/SP/83	20.00
8	Carlos Delgado '00/SP/174	
50	Jim Edmonds '96/SP/74	20.00
167	Tony Gwynn '93/SP/101	40.00
130	Tony Gwynn '94/SP/88	40.00
105	Tony Gwynn '95/SP/179	30.00
160	Tony Gwynn '96/SP/92	40.00
74	Tony Gwynn '00/SP/95	40.00
3	Jason Giambi '00/SP/290	30.00
9	Ivan Rodriguez '93/SP/89	40.00
180	Ivan Rodriguez '96/SP/64	40.00
22	Ivan Rodriguez '00/SP/163	30.00
47	Andruw Jones '00/SP/336	25.00
10	Barry Bonds '93/SP/75	150.00
90	Barry Bonds '94/SP/103	
166	Barry Bonds '96/SP/49	150.00
65	Barry Bonds '00/SP/146	150.00
18	Gary Sheffield '93/SP/83	20.00
114	Gary Sheffield '94/SP/70	20.00
86	Gary Sheffield '96/SP/69	20.00
60	Gary Sheffield '00/SP/133	15.00
89	Sammy Sosa '93/SP/73	100.00
126	Cal Ripken '94/SP/99	100.00
1	Cal Ripken '95/SP/37	150.00
20	Cal Ripken '00/SP/266	100.00
89	Todd Helton '00/SP/194	25.00
4	Tim Hudson '00/SP/291	20.00
62	Shawn Green '00/SP/340	20.00
52	Fernando Tatis '00/SP/267	8.00
57	Matt Williams '00/SP/340	10.00
72	Robin Ventura '00/SP/340	10.00
2	Troy Glaus '00/SP/340	15.00
39	Roger Clemens '00/SP/145	100.00

Chirography

NM/M
Common Player: 5.00
Inserted 1:72

EA	Edgardo Alfonzo	5.00
AB	Albert Belle	15.00
CB	Carlos Beltran	35.00
MB	Milton Bradley	12.00
PB	Pat Burrell	15.00
JC	Jose Canseco	30.00
CD	Carlos Delgado	12.00
DD	Darren Dreifort/206	5.00
JD	J.D. Drew	15.00
JE	Jim Edmonds	20.00
DEr	Darin Erstad	10.00
DEs	David Espinosa	5.00
CF	Cliff Floyd	10.00
RF	Rafael Furcal/222	10.00
JG	Jason Giambi	15.00
TrG	Troy Glaus	15.00
LG	Luis Gonzalez/271	15.00
SG	Shawn Green/82	20.00
KG	Ken Griffey Jr/126	80.00
ToG	Tony Gwynn/76	40.00
RH	Rick Helling/211	5.00
ToH	Todd Helton/152	30.00
TiH	Tim Hudson	15.00
RJ	Randy Johnson/143	50.00
AJ	Andruw Jones	20.00
CJ	Chipper Jones/184	50.00
DJ	David Justice	8.00
MK	Mark Kotsay/228	5.00
TL	Travis Lee/226	5.00
AP	Albert Pujols	400.00
CR	Cal Ripken/109	125.00
AR	Alex Rodriguez/229	100.00
DS	Dane Sardinha	5.00
BS	Ben Sheets	20.00
SS	Sammy Sosa/76	100.00
MS	Mike Sweeney	8.00
MV	Mo Vaughn/103	8.00
RV	Robin Ventura/92	10.00
DW	David Wells	8.00
RW	Rondell White	8.00
MW	Matt Williams	8.00

Chirography Gold

NM/M
Common Player:

AB	Albert Belle/88	15.00
CD	Carlos Delgado/25	50.00

NM/M
		Complete Set (30):	50.00
		Common Player:	1.00
		One Pack/Hobby Box	
RS1	Ichiro Suzuki, Tsuyoshi Shinjo	5.00
RS2	Shigetoshi Hasegawa, Hideki Irabu	1.00
RS3	Tomokazu Ohka, Mac Suzuki	1.00
RS4	Tsuyoshi Shinjo, Hideki Irabu	1.00
RS5	Ichiro Suzuki, Hideo Nomo	5.00
RS6	Tsuyoshi Shinjo, Mac Suzuki	1.00
RS7	Tsuyoshi Shinjo, Kazuhiro Sasaki	1.00
RS8	Hideo Nomo, Masato Yoshii	1.50
RS9	Ichiro Suzuki, Mac Suzuki	5.00
RS10	Hideo Nomo, Tsuyoshi Shinjo	1.50
RS11	Hideo Nomo, Masato Yoshii	1.50
RS12	Hideo Nomo, Hideki Irabu	1.50
RS13	Shigetoshi Hasegawa, Kazuhiro Sasaki	1.00
RS14	Shigetoshi Hasegawa, Mac Suzuki	1.00
RS15	Tsuyoshi Shinjo, Hideo Nomo	1.50
RS16	Tsuyoshi Shinjo, Tomokazu Ohka	1.00
RS17	Ichiro Suzuki, Kazuhiro Sasaki	5.00
RS18	Masato Yoshii, Hideki Irabu	1.00
RS19	Ichiro Suzuki, Tomokazu Ohka	5.00
RS20	Hideki Irabu, Kazuhiro Sasaki	1.00
RS21	Tsuyoshi Shinjo, Masato Yoshii	1.00
RS22	Ichiro Suzuki, Shigetoshi Hasegawa	5.00
RS23	Mac Suzuki, Kazuhiro Sasaki	1.00
RS24	Ichiro Suzuki, Hideki Irabu	5.00
RS25	Tomokazu Ohka, Kazuhiro Sasaki	1.00
RS26	Tsuyoshi Shinjo, Shigetoshi Hasegawa	1.00
RS27	Masato Yoshii, Kazuhiro Sasaki	1.00
RS28	Hideo Nomo, Kazuhiro Sasaki	1.50
RS29	Ichiro Suzuki, Masato Yoshii	5.00
RS30	Hideo Nomo, Ichiro Suzuki	5.00

Cooperstown Calling Game Jersey

NM/M
Common Player: 5.00
Overall jersey odds 1:24

JB	Jeff Bagwell	8.00
WB	Wade Boggs	8.00
GC	Gary Carter	5.00
RC	Roger Clemens	30.00
AD	Andre Dawson	5.00
SG	Steve Garvey	5.00
GG	Goose Gossage	5.00
TG	Tony Gwynn	10.00
RM	Roger Maris/243	75.00
PM	Pedro Martinez/SP	15.00
DM	Don Mattingly	30.00
BM	Bill Mazeroski	5.00
PM	Paul Molitor	8.00
EM	Eddie Murray	5.00
MP	Mike Piazza/SP	25.00
KP	Kirby Puckett	10.00
MR	Manny Ramirez/SP	15.00
CR	Cal Ripken Jr.	30.00
RS	Ryne Sandberg	20.00
OS	Ozzie Smith	10.00
DW	Dave Winfield	5.00

Game Jersey

NM/M
Common Player: 5.00
Overall jersey odds 1:24.

JD	Joe DiMaggio/243	100.00
KG	Ken Griffey Jr.	15.00
MM	Mickey Mantle/243	150.00
AR	Alex Rodriguez	15.00
GS	Gary Sheffield	5.00
SS	Sammy Sosa	10.00

Combo Game Jersey

NM/M
Overall jersey odds 1:24

SD	Sammy Sosa, Andre Dawson	25.00
RS	Alex Rodriguez, Ozzie Smith	35.00
GD	Ken Griffey Jr., Joe DiMaggio/98	120.00
SW	Gary Sheffield, Dave Winfield	15.00
MD	Mickey Mantle, Joe DiMaggio/98	300.00
MG	Mickey Mantle, Ken Griffey /98	160.00

Stars of Japan

STARS OF JAPAN

Inserted 1:576

HI-KS	Hideki Irabu, Kazuhiro Sasaki/SP/30	25.00
HN-KS	Hideo Nomo, Kazuhiro Sasaki/SP/50	75.00
HN-SH	Hideo Nomo, Shigetoshi Hasegawa	20.00

Tsuyoshi Shinjo

Stars of Japan Game Ball

NM/M
Common Player: 8.00

SH	Shigetoshi Hasegawa/SP/30	15.00
HI	Hideki Irabu	8.00
KS	Kazuhiro Sasaki	10.00
TS	Tsuyoshi Shinjo/SP/50	20.00
IS	Ichiro Suzuki	75.00
MY	Masato Yoshii	10.00

Stars of Japan Game Ball Gold

NM/M
Production 25 Sets

SH	Shigetoshi Hasegawa	40.00
HI	Hideki Irabu	20.00
KS	Kazuhiro Sasaki	40.00

Stars of Japan Game Ball-Base Combos

NM/M
Inserted 1:576

HI-KS	Hideki Irabu, Kazuhiro Sasaki/SP/30	25.00
HN-KS	Hideo Nomo, Kazuhiro Sasaki/SP/50	75.00
HN-SH	Hideo Nomo, Shigetoshi Hasegawa	20.00

IS-KS	Ichiro Suzuki, Kazuhiro Sasaki/SP/30	120.00
IS-MY	Ichiro Suzuki, Masato Yoshii	50.00
IS-SH	Ichiro Suzuki, Shigetoshi Hasegawa/SP/72	75.00
IS-TS	Ichiro Suzuki, Tsuyoshi Shinjo/SP/40	125.00
MS-KS	Mac Suzuki, Kazuhiro Sasaki/SP/30	20.00
MY-KS	Masato Yoshii, Kazuhiro Sasaki/SP/30	25.00
SH-KS	Shigetoshi Hasegawa, Kazuhiro Sasaki/SP/30	25.00
TO-KS	Tomokazu Ohka, Kazuhiro Sasaki	20.00
TS-HI	Tsuyoshi Shinjo, Hideki Irabu/SP/30	25.00
TS-KS	Tsuyoshi Shinjo, Kazuhiro Sasaki	25.00
TS-SH	Tsuyoshi Shinjo, Shigetosi Hasegawa	25.00

Stars of Japan Game Ball-Base Combos Gold

NM/M
Common Card: 20.00
Production 25 Sets

HI-KS	Hideki Irabu, Kazuhiro Sasaki	25.00
HN-KS	Hideo Nomo, Kazuhiro Sasaki	65.00
HN-SH	Hideo Nomo, Shigetosi Hasegawa	65.00
IS-KS	Ichiro Suzuki, Kazuhiro Sasaki	150.00
IS-MY	Ichiro Suzuki, Masato Yoshii	150.00
IS-SH	Ichiro Suzuki, Shigetosi Hasegawa	150.00
IS-TS	Ichiro Suzuki, Tsuyoshi Shinjo	150.00
MS-KS	Mac Suzuki, Kazuhiro Sasaki	20.00
MY-KS	Masato Yoshii, Kazuhiro Sasaki	20.00
SH-KS	Shigetosi Hasegawa, Kazuhiro Sasaki	20.00
TO-KS	Tomokazu Ohka, Kazuhiro Sasaki	20.00
TS-HI	Tsuyoshi Shinjo, Hideki Irabu	25.00
TS-KS	Tsuyoshi Shinjo, Kazuhiro Sasaki	25.00
TS-SH	Tsuyoshi Shinjo, Shigetosi Hasegawa	25.00

Stars of Japan Game Ball-Base Trio

NM/M
Complete Set (1):

RS	Kazuhiro Sasaki, Ichiro Suzuki, Hideo Nomo	175.00

Stars of Japan Game Ball-Base Trio Gold

Production 25

Stars of Japan Game Base

NM/M
Common Player: 15.00

SH	Shigetosi Hasegawa/SP/33	20.00
HI	Hideki Irabu/SP/33	20.00
TO	Tomokazu Ohka/SP/33	15.00
KS	Kazuhiro Sasaki/SP/33	25.00
TS	Tsuyoshi Shinjo/SP/33	25.00
MS	Mac Suzuki/SP/23	20.00
MY	Masato Yoshii/SP/33	20.00

Stars of Japan Game Base Gold

NM/M
Common Player: 25.00
Production 25 Sets

SH	Shigetosi Hasegawa	25.00
HI	Hideki Irabu	25.00
TO	Tomokazu Ohka	25.00
KS	Kazuhiro Sasaki	30.00
TS	Tsuyoshi Shinjo	35.00
MS	Mac Suzuki	25.00
MY	Masato Yoshii	25.00

Stars of Japan Game Bat Gold

NM/M
Common Player: 10.00
Production 25 Sets

HN	Hideo Nomo	80.00
TS	Tsuyoshi Shinjo	30.00
MY	Masato Yoshii	10.00

Stars of Japan Game Jersey

		NM/M
Common Player:		5.00
Inserted 1:12		
SH	Shigetosi Hasegawa	5.00
HN	Hideo Nomo	40.00
KS	Kazuhiro Sasaki	8.00
TS	Tsuyoshi Shinjo	8.00
IS	Ichiro Suzuki/SP/260 EXCH	100.00
MY	Masato Yoshii	5.00

Stars of Japan Game Jersey Gold

		NM/M
Common Player:		10.00
Production 25 Sets		
SH	Shigetosi Hasegawa	10.00
HN	Hideo Nomo	60.00
KS	Kazuhiro Sasaki	15.00
TS	Tsuyoshi Shinjo	15.00
MY	Masato Yoshii	10.00

Stars of Japan Game Jersey-Bat Combos

		NM/M
Common Player:		15.00
HS	Shigetosi Hasegawa, Tsuyoshi Shinjo	15.00
NN	Hideo Nomo	60.00
SN	Kazuhiro Sasaki, Hideo Nomo	40.00
SH	Kazuhiro Sasaki, Shigetosi Hasegawa	15.00

Stars of Japan Game Bat-Jersey Combo Gold

	NM/M
Production 25 Sets	
BB-HS Shigetosi Hasegawa, Tsuyoshi Shinjo	40.00

Stars of Japan Game Bat

		NM/M
Inserted 1:12		
HN	Hideo Nomo/SP/30	60.00
TS	Tsuyoshi Shinjo/SP/30	20.00
MY	Masato Yoshii	5.00

Sultan of Swatch Jersey or Pants

	NM/M
Quantity produced listed.	
SOS2 Babe Ruth/29	350.00
SOS3 Babe Ruth/94	300.00
SOS4 Babe Ruth/54	350.00
SOS5 Babe Ruth/59	350.00
SOS6 Babe Ruth/26	350.00
SOS7 Babe Ruth/26	350.00
SOS8 Babe Ruth/32	350.00
SOS9 Babe Ruth/20	350.00
SOS10 Babe Ruth/21	350.00
SOS11 Babe Ruth/23	350.00
SOS12 Babe Ruth/24	350.00
SOS13 Babe Ruth/26	350.00

	NM/M
SOS14 Babe Ruth/27	350.00
SOS15 Babe Ruth/28	350.00
SOS16 Babe Ruth/29	350.00
SOS17 Babe Ruth/30	350.00
SOS18 Babe Ruth/31	350.00
SOS19 Babe Ruth/33	350.00
SOS20 Babe Ruth/36	350.00
SOS21 Babe Ruth/48	350.00

Sultan of Swatch Jersey/Cut

No Pricing
Production One Set

2001 SP Game Bat

		NM/M
Complete Set (90):		40.00
Common Player:		.25
Pack (4):		10.00
Box (16):		150.00
1	Troy Glaus	.50
2	Darin Erstad	.50
3	Mo Vaughn	.25
4	Jason Giambi	.75
5	Ben Grieve	.25
6	Eric Chavez	.50
7	Carlos Delgado	.75
8	Tony Batista	.25
9	Shannon Stewart	.25
10	Jose Cruz Jr.	.25
11	Fred McGriff	.25
12	Greg Vaughn	.25
13	Roberto Alomar	.50
14	Manny Ramirez	1.00
15	Jim Thome	.75
16	Russ Branyan	.25
17	Alex Rodriguez	2.00
18	John Olerud	.25
19	Edgar Martinez	.25
20	Cal Ripken Jr.	3.00
21	Albert Belle	.25
22	Ivan Rodriguez	.75
23	Rafael Palmeiro	.50
24	Nomar Garciaparra	1.00
25	Carl Everett	.25
26	Dante Bichette	.25
27	Mike Sweeney	.25
28	Jermaine Dye	.25
29	Carlos Beltran	.75
30	Juan Gonzalez	.50
31	Dean Palmer	.25
32	Bobby Higginson	.25
33	Matt Lawton	.25
34	Jacque Jones	.25
35	Frank Thomas	1.00
36	Magglio Ordonez	.25
37	Paul Konerko	.50
38	Carlos Lee	.40
39	Bernie Williams	.50
40	Derek Jeter	3.00
41	Paul O'Neill	.40
42	Jose Canseco	.50
43	Ken Caminiti	.25
44	Jeff Bagwell	.75
45	Craig Biggio	.40
46	Richard Hidalgo	.25
47	Andruw Jones	1.00
48	Chipper Jones	1.00
49	Andres Galarraga	.25
50	B.J. Surhoff	.25
51	Jeromy Burnitz	.25
52	Geoff Jenkins	.25
53	Richie Sexson	.40
54	Mark McGwire	2.50
55	Jim Edmonds	.50
56	J.D. Drew	.40
57	Fernando Tatis	.25
58	Sammy Sosa	1.50
59	Mark Grace	.50
60	Eric Young	.25
61	Matt Williams	.25
62	Luis Gonzalez	.40
63	Steve Finley	.25
64	Shawn Green	.40
65	Gary Sheffield	.50
66	Eric Karros	.25
67	Vladimir Guerrero	1.00
68	Jose Vidro	.25

69	Barry Bonds	3.00
70	Jeff Kent	.40
71	Preston Wilson	.25
72	Mike Lowell	.25
73	Luis Castillo	.25
74	Mike Piazza	1.50
75	Robin Ventura	.25
76	Edgardo Alfonzo	.25
77	Tony Gwynn	1.00
78	Eric Owens	.25
79	Ryan Klesko	.25
80	Scott Rolen	.75
81	Bobby Abreu	.50
82	Pat Burrell	.50
83	Brian Giles	.25
84	Jason Kendall	.25
85	Aaron Boone	.25
86	Ken Griffey Jr.	2.00
87	Barry Larkin	.50
88	Todd Helton	1.00
89	Larry Walker	.25
90	Jeffrey Hammonds	.25

Big League Hit Parade

		NM/M
Complete Set (6):		15.00
Common Player:		1.50
Inserted 1:15		
1	Nomar Garciaparra	1.50
2	Ken Griffey Jr.	3.00
3	Sammy Sosa	2.00
4	Alex Rodriguez	4.00
5	Mark McGwire	4.00
6	Ivan Rodriguez	1.50

In the Swing

		NM/M
Complete Set (15):		25.00
Common Player:		1.00
Inserted 1:7		
1	Ken Griffey Jr.	2.50
2	Jim Edmonds	1.00
3	Carlos Delgado	1.00
4	Frank Thomas	1.50
5	Barry Bonds	4.00
6	Nomar Garciaparra	2.00
7	Gary Sheffield	1.00
8	Vladimir Guerrero	1.50
9	Alex Rodriguez	3.00
10	Todd Helton	1.50
11	Darin Erstad	1.00
12	Derek Jeter	4.00
13	Sammy Sosa	2.50
14	Mark McGwire	3.00
15	Jason Giambi	1.00

Lineup Time

		NM/M
Complete Set (11):		20.00
Common Player:		1.00
Inserted 1:8		
1	Mark McGwire	3.00
2	Roberto Alomar	1.00
3	Alex Rodriguez	3.00
4	Chipper Jones	2.00
5	Ivan Rodriguez	1.00
6	Ken Griffey Jr.	2.50
7	Sammy Sosa	2.50
8	Barry Bonds	4.00
9	Frank Thomas	1.50
10	Pedro Martinez	1.50
11	Derek Jeter	4.00

Piece of the Game

	NM/M
Common Player:	4.00
Inserted 1:1	
SP production 1,500 or fewer.	
Golds:	2-5X
Production 25 Sets	
EA	Edgardo Alfonzo/SP	10.00
RA	Roberto Alomar	8.00
SA	Sandy Alomar	4.00
RA	Rick Ankiel	10.00
JB	Jeff Bagwell/SP	15.00
TB	Tony Batista	5.00
CB	Carlos Beltran	4.00
JB	Johnny Bench/SP	25.00
BB	Barry Bonds	25.00
KB	Kevin Brown/SP	10.00
PB	Pat Burrell	8.00
JC	Jose Canseco	6.00
WC	Will Clark	8.00
CD	Carlos Delgado	6.00
JoD	Joe DiMaggio/SP	100.00
JD	J.D. Drew	6.00
JE	Jim Edmonds	6.00
DE	Darin Erstad/SP	10.00
RF	Rafael Furcal	6.00
BG	Bob Gibson/SP	20.00
TGI	Tom Glavine/SP	15.00
MG	Mark Grace	8.00
SG	Shawn Green	6.00
KG	Ken Griffey Jr.	15.00
TGw	Tony Gwynn	10.00
TH	Todd Helton	8.00
TH	Todd Hundley/SP	10.00

RJ	Reggie Jackson/SP	20.00
RJ	Randy Johnson	10.00
AJ	Andruw Jones	8.00
CJ	Chipper Jones	10.00
DJ	David Justice	5.00
KL	Kenny Lofton	4.00
GM	Greg Maddux	15.00
EM	Edgar Martinez	6.00
TM	Tino Martinez	6.00
FM	Fred McGrift/SP	10.00
PN	Phil Nevin/SP	10.00
JO	John Olerud	6.00
PO	Paul O'Neill	6.00
MO	Magglio Ordonez/SP	10.00
MQ	Mark Quinn/SP	10.00
MR	Manny Ramirez	8.00
CR	Cal Ripken Jr./SP	40.00
AR	Alex Rodriguez	10.00
IR	Ivan Rodriguez	8.00
SR	Scott Rolen	8.00
NR	Nolan Ryan/SP	35.00
TS	Tim Salmon/SP	10.00
GS	Gary Sheffield	5.00
SS	Sammy Sosa/SP	25.00
SS	Shannon Stewart	4.00
FT	Frank Thomas	8.00
GV	Greg Vaughn	4.00
MV	Mo Vaughn	4.00
RV	Robin Ventura	4.00
BW	Bernie Williams	6.00
MW	Matt Williams	4.00
PW	Preston Wilson	4.00

Piece of the Game Autograph

		NM/M
Common Autograph:		30.00
Inserted 1:96		
BB	Barry Bonds	150.00
JC	Jose Canseco	40.00
KG	Ken Griffey Jr.	100.00
TGw	Tony Gwynn	50.00
AJ	Andruw Jones	30.00
AR	Alex Rodriguez	120.00
NR	Nolan Ryan	125.00
FT	Frank Thomas	50.00

The Lumber Yard

		NM/M
Complete Set (10):		15.00
Common Player:		.50
Inserted 1:10		
1	Jason Giambi	1.00
2	Chipper Jones	1.50
3	Carl Everett	.50
4	Alex Rodriguez	3.00
5	Frank Thomas	1.50
6	Barry Bonds	4.00
7	Jeff Bagwell	1.50
8	Sammy Sosa	2.50
9	Carlos Delgado	1.00
10	Mike Piazza	2.50

2001 SP Game Bat - Milestone

Tony Gwynn

		NM/M
Complete Set (96):		
Common Player:		.40
Common Rookie (91-96):		5.00
Production 500		
Pack (4):		15.00
Box (10):		125.00
1	Troy Glaus	.50
2	Darin Erstad	.50
3	Jason Giambi	.50
4	Jermaine Dye	.40
5	Eric Chavez	.50
6	Carlos Delgado	.50
7	Raul Mondesi	.40
8	Shannon Stewart	.40
9	Greg Vaughn	.40
10	Aubrey Huff	.40
11	Juan Gonzalez	.50
12	Roberto Alomar	.50
13	Jim Thome	.75
14	Omar Vizquel	.40
15	Mike Cameron	.40

16	Edgar Martinez	.40
17	John Olerud	.40
18	Bret Boone	.40
19	Cal Ripken Jr.	3.00
20	Tony Batista	.40
21	Alex Rodriguez	2.50
22	Ivan Rodriguez	.75
23	Rafael Palmeiro	.75
24	Manny Ramirez	1.00
25	Pedro Martinez	1.00
26	Nomar Garciaparra	.50
27	Carl Everett	.50
28	Mike Sweeney	.40
29	Neifi Perez	.40
30	Mark Quinn	.40
31	Bobby Higginson	.40
32	Tony Clark	.40
33	Doug Mientkiewicz	.40
34	Cristian Guzman	.40
35	Joe Mays	.40
36	David Ortiz	.40
37	Frank Thomas	1.00
38	Magglio Ordonez	.40
39	Carlos Lee	.50
40	Alfonso Soriano	.75
41	Bernie Williams	.50
42	Derek Jeter	3.00
43	Roger Clemens	2.00
44	Jeff Bagwell	.75
45	Richard Hidalgo	.40
46	Moises Alou	.40
47	Chipper Jones	1.00
48	Greg Maddux	2.00
49	Rafael Furcal	.50
50	Andruw Jones	.50
51	Jeromy Burnitz	.40
52	Geoff Jenkins	.40
53	Richie Sexson	.40
54	Edgar Renteria	.40
55	Mark McGwire	2.00
56	Jim Edmonds	.50
57	J.D. Drew	.40
58	Sammy Sosa	1.00
59	Bill Mueller	.40
60	Luis Gonzalez	.50
61	Randy Johnson	1.00
62	Gary Sheffield	.50
63	Shawn Green	.40
64	Kevin Brown	.40
65	Vladimir Guerrero	1.00
66	Jose Vidro	.40
67	Fernando Tatis	.40
68	Barry Bonds	3.00
69	Jeff Kent	.50
70	Rich Aurilia	.40
71	Preston Wilson	.40
72	Charles Johnson	.40
73	Cliff Floyd	.40
74	Mike Piazza	1.00
75	Matt Lawton	.40
76	Edgardo Alfonzo	.40
77	Tony Gwynn	1.50
78	Phil Nevin	.40
79	Scott Rolen	.50
80	Pat Burrell	.50
81	Bobby Abreu	.50
82	Brian Giles	.40
83	Jason Kendall	.40
84	Aramis Ramirez	.50
85	Sean Casey	.40
86	Ken Griffey Jr.	2.50
87	Barry Larkin	.50
88	Todd Helton	.75
89	Mike Hampton	.40
90	Larry Walker	.50
91	Ichiro Suzuki RC	50.00
92	Albert Pujols RC	120.00
93	Tsuyoshi Shinjo RC	5.00
94	Jack Wilson RC	8.00
95	Donaldo Mendez RC	5.00
96	Junior Spivey RC	5.00

Slugging Sensations

		NM/M
Complete Set (12):		12.00
Common Player:		.50
Inserted 1:5		
SS1	Troy Glaus	.50
SS2	Mark McGwire	2.00
SS3	Sammy Sosa	1.50
SS4	Juan Gonzalez	.50
SS5	Barry Bonds	3.00
SS6	Jeff Bagwell	.75
SS7	Jason Giambi	.50
SS8	Ivan Rodriguez	.75
SS9	Mike Piazza	1.50
SS10	Chipper Jones	1.00
SS11	Ken Griffey Jr.	2.50
SS12	Gary Sheffield	.50

The Art of Hitting

		NM/M
Complete Set (12):		10.00
Common Player:		.50
Inserted 1:5		
AH1	Tony Gwynn	1.50
AH2	Manny Ramirez	1.00
AH3	Todd Helton	1.00
AH4	Nomar Garciaparra	1.00
AH5	Vladimir Guerrero	1.00
AH6	Ichiro Suzuki	1.50
AH7	Darin Erstad	.50
AH8	Alex Rodriguez	2.50
AH9	Carlos Delgado	.75
AH10	Edgar Martinez	.50
AH11	Luis Gonzalez	.50
AH12	Barry Bonds	3.00

The Trophy Room

The Trophy Room

		NM/M
Complete Set (6):		8.00
Common Player:		1.00
Inserted 1:10		
TR1	Sammy Sosa	1.50
TR2	Jason Giambi	1.00
TR3	Todd Helton	1.00
TR4	Alex Rodriguez	2.50
TR5	Mark McGwire	2.50
TR6	Ken Griffey Jr.	2.00

P.O.A. Milestone Bat

Piece of Action MILESTONE

	NM/M
Common Player:	5.00
Golds:	3-5X
Production 35 Sets	
JB	Jeff Bagwell	8.00
BB	Barry Bonds	20.00
RB	Russell Branyan	5.00
JB	Jeromy Burnitz	5.00
RC	Roger Clemens	20.00
DE	Darin Erstad	5.00
LG	Luis Gonzalez	5.00
KG	Ken Griffey Jr.	12.00
TH	Todd Helton	8.00
Chj	Chipper Jones	10.00
MP	Mike Piazza	10.00
CR	Cal Ripken Jr.	30.00
AR	Alex Rodriguez	15.00
GS	Gary Sheffield	5.00
IS	Ichiro Suzuki/203	80.00
FT	Frank Thomas	8.00
JT	Jim Thome	8.00

P.O.A. Autograph Bat

	NM/M
Common Autograph:	15.00
Inserted 1:5	

RB	Russell Branyan	15.00
CD	Carlos Delgado/97	30.00
JDr	J.D. Drew	20.00
JDy	Jermaine Dye	15.00
LG	Luis Gonzalez	15.00
JK	Jason Kendall	15.00
JK	Jeff Kent/194	30.00
AR	Alex Rodriguez/97	120.00
GS	Gary Sheffield/194	40.00
IS	Ichiro Suzuki/53	800.00
MT	Miguel Tejada	15.00
JV	Jose Vidro	15.00
PW	Preston Wilson	15.00

P.O.A. BFH Bat

NM/M
Common Player: 5.00
Golds: 2-3X
Production 35 Sets

BB	Barry Bonds	20.00
RC	Roger Clemens/203	25.00
CD	Carlos Delgado	5.00
JG	Jason Giambi	5.00
KG	Ken Griffey Jr.	15.00
TGw	Tony Gwynn	15.00
GM	Greg Maddux	12.00
EM	Edgar Martinez	6.00
FM	Fred McGriff	8.00
RP	Rafael Palmeiro	8.00
MP	Mike Piazza	10.00
CR	Cal Ripken Jr.	30.00
AR	Alex Rodriguez	15.00
IR	Ivan Rodriguez	8.00
SS	Sammy Sosa	10.00

P.O.A. Int. Conn. Bat

NM/M
Common Player: 5.00
Golds: 3-5X
Production 35 Sets

RA	Roberto Alomar	6.00
AB	Adrian Beltre	5.00
RF	Rafael Furcal	5.00
JG	Juan Gonzalez	6.00
AJ	Andruw Jones	8.00
PM	Pedro Martinez	10.00
HN	Hideo Nomo/203	25.00
MO	Magglio Ordonez	5.00
CP	Chan Ho Park	5.00
JP	Jorge Posada	10.00
AP	Albert Pujols	60.00
MR	Manny Ramirez	8.00
TS	Tsuyoshi Shinjo	8.00
IS	Ichiro Suzuki/273	80.00
MT	Miguel Tejada	6.00
OV	Omar Vizquel	5.00

P.O.A. Triple Bat

NM/M
Common Card: 15.00

Inserted 1:50

GRS	Ken Griffey Jr., Alex Rodriguez, Sammy Sosa	40.00
JJF	Chipper Jones, Andruw Jones, Rafael Furcal	15.00
RRP	Alex Rodriguez, Ivan Rodriguez, Rafael Palmeiro	35.00
SGB	Gary Sheffield, Shawn Green, Adrian Beltre	15.00
TVA	Jim Thome, Omar Vizquel, Roberto Alomar	15.00
KGR	Jason Kendall, Brian Giles, Aramis Ramirez	15.00
OJC	Paul O'Neill, David Justice, Roger Clemens	35.00
CMG	Roger Clemens, Greg Maddux, Tom Glavine	40.00
VSA	Robin Ventura, Tsuyoshi Shinjo, Edgardo Alfonzo	15.00
OTA	Magglio Ordonez, Frank Thomas, Sandy Alomar	15.00
PWS	Kirby Puckett, Dave Winfield, Ozzie Smith	25.00
GRB	Tony Gwynn, Cal Ripken Jr., Barry Bonds	60.00
GBM	Ken Griffey Jr., Barry Bonds, Fred McGriff	35.00
SFR	Alfonso Soriano, Rafael Furcal, Alex Ramirez	25.00

P.O.A. Quad Bat

Common Card: 15.00
Inserted 1:50

TVAL	Jim Thome, Omar Vizquel, Roberto Alomar, Kenny Lofton	25.00
RRPM	Alex Rodriguez, Ivan Rodriguez, Rafael Palmeiro, Ruben Mateo	50.00
OJCP	Paul O'Neill, David Justice, Roger Clemens, Jorge Posada	60.00
JJFM	Chipper Jones, Andruw Jones, Rafael Furcal, Greg Maddux	50.00
PWSG	Kirby Puckett, Dave Winfield, Ozzie Smith, Steve Garvey	30.00
GRSB	Ken Griffey Jr., Alex Rodriguez, Sammy Sosa, Barry Bonds	80.00
SGBP	Gary Sheffield, Shawn Green, Adrian Beltre, Chan Ho Park	15.00
GGRR	Ken Griffey Jr., Ken Griffey Jr., Alex Rodriguez, Alex Rodriguez	65.00
GRBM	Tony Gwynn, Cal Ripken Jr., Barry Bonds, Fred McGriff	70.00
TDTA	Frank Thomas, Jermaine Dye, Jim Thome, Roberto Alomar	25.00
GHSK	Luis Gonzalez, Todd Helton, Gary Sheffield, Jeff Kent	20.00
GDBS	Ken Griffey Jr., J.D. Drew, Jeromy Burnitz, Sammy Sosa	50.00
JVBW	Chipper Jones, Robin Ventura, Pat Burrell, Preston Wilson	30.00
RGGM	Alex Rodriguez, Troy Glaus, Jason Giambi, Edgar Martinez	40.00
ONRD	Paul O'Neill, Hideo Nomo, Cal Ripken Jr., Carlos Delgado	80.00

2001 SP Game-Used Edition

NM/M
Common Player: .50
Common SP (61-90): 5.00
Production 500
Pack (3): 30.00
Box (6): 150.00

1	Garret Anderson	.50
2	Troy Glaus	1.00
3	Darin Erstad	.75
4	Jason Giambi	1.50
5	Tim Hudson	.75
6	Johnny Damon	2.00
7	Carlos Delgado	1.00
8	Greg Vaughn	.50
9	Juan Gonzalez	.75
10	Roberto Alomar	1.00
11	Jim Thome	1.50
12	Edgar Martinez	.50

13	Cal Ripken Jr.	5.00
14	Andres Galarraga	.50
15	Alex Rodriguez	4.00
16	Rafael Palmeiro	1.00
17	Ivan Rodriguez	1.50
18	Manny Ramirez	1.50
19	Nomar Garciaparra	1.00
20	Pedro Martinez	2.00
21	Jermaine Dye	.50
22	Dean Palmer	.50
23	Matt Lawton	.50
24	Frank Thomas	1.50
25	David Wells	.50
26	Magglio Ordonez	.50
27	Derek Jeter	5.00
28	Bernie Williams	.50
29	Roger Clemens	3.00
30	Jeff Bagwell	1.50
31	Richard Hidalgo	.50
32	Chipper Jones	2.00
33	Andruw Jones	1.00
34	Greg Maddux	3.00
35	Jeffrey Hammonds	.50
36	Mark McGwire	3.00
37	Jim Edmonds	.75
38	Sammy Sosa	1.50
39	Corey Patterson	.50
40	Randy Johnson	1.50
41	Luis Gonzalez	.50
42	Gary Sheffield	.75
43	Shawn Green	.75
44	Kevin Brown	.50
45	Vladimir Guerrero	1.50
46	Barry Bonds	5.00
47	Jeff Kent	.75
48	Preston Wilson	.50
49	Charles Johnson	.50
50	Mike Piazza	2.00
51	Edgardo Alfonzo	.50
52	Tony Gwynn	2.00
53	Scott Rolen	1.50
54	Pat Burrell	1.00
55	Brian Giles	.50
56	Jason Kendall	.50
57	Ken Griffey Jr.	3.00
58	Mike Hampton	.50
59	Todd Helton	1.50
60	Larry Walker	.75
61	Wilson Betemit RC	10.00
62	Travis Hafner RC	15.00
63	Ichiro Suzuki RC	50.00
64	Juan Diaz RC	5.00
65	Morgan Ensberg RC	5.00
66	Horacio Ramirez RC	8.00
67	Ricardo Rodriguez RC	5.00
68	Sean Douglass RC	5.00
69	Brandon Duckworth RC	5.00
70	Jackson Melian RC	5.00
71	Adrian Hernandez RC	5.00
72	Kyle Kessel RC	5.00
73	Jason Michaels RC	5.00
74	Esix Snead RC	5.00
75	Jason Smith RC	5.00
76	Tyler Walker RC	5.00
77	Juan Uribe RC	8.00
78	Adam Pettyjohn RC	5.00
79	Tsuyoshi Shinjo RC	5.00
80	Mike Penney RC	5.00
81	Josh Towers RC	5.00
82	Erick Almonte RC	5.00
83	Ryan Freel RC	10.00
84	Juan Pena RC	5.00
85	Albert Pujols RC	200.00
86	Henry Mateo RC	5.00
87	Greg Miller RC	5.00
88	Jose Mieses RC	5.00
89	Jack Wilson RC	10.00
90	Carlos Valderrama RC	5.00

Authentic Fabric Jersey

NM/M
Common Player: 4.00
Inserted 1:1

EA	Edgardo Alfonso	4.00
RA	Roberto Alomar	6.00
RA	Rick Ankiel	8.00
TB	Tony Batista/SP	8.00
BB	Barry Bonds	25.00
KB	Kevin Brown	5.00
JB	Jeromy Burnitz	4.00
PB	Pat Burrell	5.00
JC(B)	Jose Canseco BLC	
JC(H)	Jose Canseco/Yanks	8.00
EC	Eric Chavez	5.00
JCi	Jeff Cirillo	4.00
RC	Roger Clemens	20.00
CD	Carlos Delgado/SP	10.00
JDi	Joe DiMaggio/SP/50	125.00

JDr	J.D. Drew	5.00
JDy	Jermaine Dye/SP	8.00
JE	Jim Edmonds	5.00
DE	Darin Erstad	5.00
JG	Jason Giambi	8.00
BG	Brian Giles/SP	8.00
TGl	Troy Glaus	5.00
ToG	Tom Glavine	6.00
LG	Luis Gonzalez	5.00
MG	Mark Grace	8.00
SG	Shawn Green	6.00
KG(H)	Ken Griffey/Reds	12.00
KG(M)	Ken Griffey/M's	12.00
KG(R)	Ken Griffey/Reds	12.00
TGw	Tony Gwynn	10.00
MH	Mike Hampton	4.00
THe	Todd Helton	8.00
TrH	Trevor Hoffman	4.00
TH	Tim Hudson	6.00
AH	Aubrey Huff	4.00
JI	J. Isringhausen/SP	8.00
CJo	Charles Johnson	4.00
RJ	Randy Johnson	10.00
AJ	Andruw Jones	8.00
CJ	Chipper Jones	10.00
JK	Jason Kendall	4.00
JK	Jeff Kent	5.00
BL	Barry Larkin	6.00
AL	Al Leiter	4.00
KL	Kenny Lofton	4.00
TL	Terrence Long	4.00
GM	Greg Maddux	10.00
MM	Mickey Mantle/SP/50	250.00
RM	Roger Maris/SP	75.00
EM	Edgar Martinez	5.00
TM	Tino Martinez	5.00
FM	Fred McGriff	5.00
KM	Kevin Millwood	5.00
PN	Phil Nevin	4.00
JO	John Olerud	5.00
MO	Magglio Ordonez	5.00
AP	Adam Piatt	4.00
CR	Cal Ripken Jr.	25.00
MR	Mariano Rivera	6.00
AR(R)	Alex Rodriguez/Rangers	10.00
AR(M)	Alex Rodriguez/M's	8.00
IR	Ivan Rodriguez	8.00
SR	Scott Rolen	5.00
NR	Nolan Ryan/SP/50	50.00
TS	Tom Seaver/SP/50	30.00
GS	Gary Sheffield	5.00
SS(H)	Sammy Sosa	15.00
SS(R)	Sammy Sosa	15.00
FTa	Fernando Tatis	4.00
MT	Miguel Tejada	6.00
FTh	Frank Thomas	8.00
JT	Jim Thome	4.00
GV	Greg Vaughn	4.00
RV	Robin Ventura	4.00
JV	Jose Vidro	4.00
DW	David Wells/SP	8.00
MW	Matt Williams	5.00
PW	Preston Wilson	5.00
DY	Dmitri Young	4.00
TZ	Todd Zeile	4.00

2-Player Auth. Fabric Jersey

NM/M
Common Card: 25.00
Production 50 Sets

R-R	Alex Rodriguez, Ivan Rodriguez	50.00
M-D	Mickey Mantle, Joe DiMaggio	400.00
M-M	Mickey Mantle, Roger Maris	400.00
R-S	Nolan Ryan, Tom Seaver	100.00
B-C	Barry Bonds, Jose Canseco	60.00
S-G	Gary Sheffield, Shawn Green	25.00
J-J	Chipper Jones, Andruw Jones	40.00
C-W	Roger Clemens, Bernie Williams	40.00
J-R	Randy Johnson, Nolan Ryan	75.00
S-T	Sammy Sosa, Frank Thomas	30.00
G-S	Ken Griffey Jr., Sammy Sosa	50.00
G-R	Ken Griffey Jr., Alex Rodriguez	50.00
S-R	Sammy Sosa, Alex Rodriguez	40.00
H-G	Tim Hudson, Jason Giambi	30.00

3-Player Auth. Fabric Jersey

NM/M
Production 25 Sets

GRS	Ken Griffey Jr., Alex Rodriguez, Sammy Sosa	100.00
MJJ	Greg Maddux, Chipper Jones, Andruw Jones	80.00
JBS	Andruw Jones, Barry Bonds, Sammy Sosa	100.00
JSM	Randy Johnson, Tom Seaver, Greg Maddux	80.00

Authentic Fabric Jersey Auto.

NM/M
Production 50 Sets

EA	Edgardo Alfonzo	25.00
RA	Rick Ankiel	40.00
BB	Barry Bonds/50	200.00
JC	Jose Canseco	40.00
CD	Carlos Delgado/50	40.00
JDr	J.D. Drew/50	40.00
JG	Jason Giambi/50	40.00
TGl	Troy Glaus/50	50.00
KG	Ken Griffey Jr.	150.00
TH	Tim Hudson/50	50.00
RJ	Randy Johnson	100.00
AJ	Andruw Jones	40.00
CJ	Chipper Jones	80.00
CR	Cal Ripken /50	200.00
AR	Alex Rodriguez	150.00
IR	Ivan Rodriguez	75.00
NR	Nolan Ryan /50	200.00
TS	Tom Seaver /50	80.00
SS	Sammy Sosa /50	120.00
FTh	Frank Thomas	75.00
DW	David Wells/50	25.00

2001 SP Legendary Cuts

NM/M
Complete Set (90): 25.00
Common Player: .40
Pack (4): 16.00
Box (18): 250.00

1	Al Simmons	.40
2	Jimmie Foxx (Height, weight and birthplace incorrect.)	1.00
3	Mickey Cochrane	.40
4	Phil Niekro	.40
5	Eddie Mathews	1.00
6	Gary Matthews	.40
7	Hank Aaron	2.50
8	Joe Adcock	.40
9	Warren Spahn	.75
10	George Sisler	.40
11	Stan Musial	1.00
12	Dizzy Dean	.75
13	Frankie Frisch	.40
14	Harvey Haddix	.40
15	Johnny Mize	.40
16	Ken Boyer	.40
17	Rogers Hornsby	.75
18	Cap Anson	.40
19	Andre Dawson	.40
20	Billy Williams	.40
21	Billy Herman	.40
22	Hack Wilson	.40
23	Ron Santo	.40
24	Ryne Sandberg	1.50
25	Ernie Banks	1.50
26	Burleigh Grimes	.40
27	Don Drysdale	.75
28	Gil Hodges	.40
29	Jackie Robinson	2.00
30	Tommy Lasorda	.40
31	Pee Wee Reese	1.00
32	Roy Campanella	.75
33	Tommy Davis	.40
34	Branch Rickey	.40
35	Leo Durocher	.75
36	Walt Alston	.40
37	Bill Terry	.40
38	Carl Hubbell	.40
39	Eddie Stanky	.40
40	George Kelly	.40
41	Mel Ott	.75
42	Juan Marichal	.40
43	Rube Marquard	.40
44	Travis Jackson	.40
45	Bob Feller	.40
46	Earl Averill	.40
47	Elmer Flick	.40
48	Ken Keltner	.40
49	Lou Boudreau	.40
50	Early Wynn	.40
51	Satchel Paige	1.50
52	Ron Hunt	.40
53	Tom Seaver	1.00
54	Richie Ashburn	.40
55	Mike Schmidt	1.00
56	Honus Wagner	1.00
57	Lloyd Waner	.40
58	Max Carey	.40
59	Paul Waner	.40
60	Roberto Clemente	2.50
61	Nolan Ryan	3.00
62	Bobby Doerr	.40
63	Carlton Fisk	.75
64	Joe Cronin	.40
65	Smokey Joe Wood	.40
66	Tony Conigliaro	.40
67	Edd Roush	.40
68	Johnny Vander Meer	.40
69	Walter Johnson	.75
70	Charlie Gehringer	.40
71	Al Kaline	1.00
72	Ty Cobb	2.00
73	Tony Oliva	.40
74	Luke Appling	.40
75	Minnie Minoso	.40
76	Nellie Fox	.40
77	Shoeless Joe Jackson	2.00
78	Babe Ruth	3.00
79	Bill Dickey	.40
80	Elston Howard	.40
81	Joe DiMaggio	2.50
82	Lefty Gomez	.40
83	Lou Gehrig	2.50
84	Mickey Mantle	3.00
85	Reggie Jackson	1.00
86	Roger Maris	1.00
87	Whitey Ford	.40
88	Waite Hoyt	.40
89	Yogi Berra	1.00
90	Casey Stengel	.40

Bat

NM/M
Common Player: 4.00
Inserted 1:18

HA	Hank Aaron/SP	40.00
YB	Yogi Berra	10.00
WB	Wade Boggs	8.00
GB	George Brett	15.00
RCa	Roy Campanella/SP	40.00
RC	Rico Carty	4.00
RCl	Roberto Clemente	60.00
TC	Ty Cobb/SP	125.00
KC	Kiki Cuyler	8.00
TD	Tommy Davis/SP	40.00
AD	Andre Dawson	8.00
JD	Joe DiMaggio/SP	100.00
DD	Don Drysdale	25.00
CF	Carlton Fisk	10.00
NF	Nellie Fox	10.00
JF	Jimmie Foxx	40.00
GH	Gil Hodges/SP	40.00
THo	Tommy Holmes (Photo on front is Eddie Mathews.)	8.00
RJ	Reggie Jackson	15.00
DJ	Davey Johnson	4.00
MM	Mickey Mantle/SP	120.00
RM	Roger Maris/SP	60.00
EM	Eddie Mathews	25.00
WMc	Willie McCovey	8.00
PM	Paul Molitor	15.00
MM	Manny Mota	4.00
MO	Mel Ott/SP	50.00
VP	Vada Pinson	4.00
JR	Jackie Robinson/SP	50.00
BR	Babe Ruth/SP	165.00
NR	Nolan Ryan/SP	40.00
RS	Ryne Sandberg	20.00
AS	Al Simmons/SP	25.00
BT	Bill Terry/SP	40.00
MW	Maury Wills	8.00
RY	Robin Yount	15.00

Combo Bat

No pricing due to scarcity.
Production 25 Sets

Debut Bat

		NM/M
	Common Player:	5.00
	Inserted 1:18	
JA	Joe Adcock/SP	15.00
LA	Luke Appling/SP	25.00
RA	Richie Ashburn/SP	25.00
BB	Bobby Bonds	5.00
LB	Lou Boudreau	10.00
KB	Ken Boyer/SP	15.00
BB	Bill Buckner	5.00
MC	Mickey Cochrane	60.00
TC	Tony Conigliaro/SP	15.00
JC	Joe Cronin	10.00
BD	Bobby Doerr/SP	15.00
BF	Bob Feller/SP	15.00
BF	Bill Freehan	5.00
FF	Frankie Frisch/SP	15.00
CG	Charlie Gehringer	15.00
BH	Billy Herman/SP	15.00
WH	Willie Horton	6.00
EH	Elston Howard/SP	15.00
RH	Ron Hunt	5.00
JJ	Joe Jackson	300.00
GL	Greg Luzinski	5.00
GM	Gary Matthews	5.00
MM	Minnie Minoso/SP	15.00
TO	Tony Oliva	8.00
WP	Wes Parker	5.00
BR	Bobby Richardson/SP	15.00
SS	Steve Sax	5.00
GS	George Sisler	20.00
ES	Eddie Stanky	5.00
AT	Alan Trammell	5.00
PW	Paul Waner/SP	60.00
HW	Hack Wilson/SP	70.00
SY	Steve Yeager	5.00

Game Jersey

		NM/M
	Common Player:	5.00
	Inserted 1:18	
YB	Yogi Berra	15.00
WB	Wade Boggs	5.00
RC	Roberto Clemente	80.00
TC	Tony Conigliaro	8.00
BD	Bill Dickey	25.00
JD	Joe DiMaggio/SP	350.00
LD	Leo Durocher	4.00
WF	Whitey Ford	15.00
NF	Nellie Fox	8.00
JF	Jim Fregosi	5.00
GH	Gil Hodges	10.00
THo	Tommy Holmes	5.00
RJ	Reggie Jackson	15.00
TK	Ted Kluszewski	5.00
BL	Bob Lemon	5.00
VL	Vic Lombardi	5.00
MM	Mickey Mantle/SP	275.00
JM	Juan Marichal	10.00
RM	Roger Maris/SP	150.00
WM	Willie McCovey	15.00
JN	Joe Nuxhall	8.00
GP	Gaylord Perry	5.00
BR	Bobby Richardson	5.00
BRo	Brooks Robinson	15.00
BR	Babe Ruth/SP	600.00
NR	Nolan Ryan	40.00
TS	Tom Seaver/SP	100.00
CS	Casey Stengel	15.00
BT	Bobby Thomson	5.00
HW	Honus Wagner/SP	750.00
BW	Billy Williams	6.00
MW	Maury Wills	5.00
RY	Robin Yount	15.00

Signatures

		NM/M
	Inserted 1:252	
WA	Walt Alston/34	175.00
CA	Cap Anson/2	
	(11/01 Auction)	10,000

LA	Luke Appling/45	205.00
EA	Earl Averill/189	100.00
EB	E.G. Barrow/16	600.00
MC	Max Carey/73	145.00
TC	Ty Cobb/24	2,500
JC	Jocko Conlan/12	1,200
SC	Stanley Coveleski/42	315.00
JC	Joe Cronin/12	1,200
KC	Kiki Cuyler/6	4,000
DDe	Dizzy Dean/56	410.00
BD	Bill Dickey/28	275.00
JD	Joe DiMaggio/25	650.00
JD	Joe DiMaggio/50	400.00
JD	Joe DiMaggio/150	400.00
JD	Joe DiMaggio/275	350.00
DDr	Don Drysdale/12	1,500
LD	Leo Durocher/45	260.00
RF	Rick Ferrell/8	750.00
EF	Elmer Flick/22	400.00
NF	Nellie Fox/9	750.00
JF	Jimmie Foxx/16	2,500
FF	Ford Frick/21	750.00
FF	Frankie Frisch/3	3,500
LGe	Lou Gehrig/7	6,000
WG	Warren Giles/10	800.00
LGo	Lefty Gomez/85	195.00
BG	Burleigh Grimes/18	500.00
LG	Lefty Grove/34	600.00
HH	Harvey Haddix/4	3,000
BH	Bucky Harris/10	500.00
GH	Gabby Hartnett/32	380.00
BH	Billy Herman/88	140.00
GH	Gil Hodges/6	1,050
HH	Harry Hooper/14	800.00
WH	Waite Hoyt/38	245.00
CH	Carl Hubbell/30	375.00
TJ	Travis Jackson/35	225.00
JJ	Judy Johnson/9	650.00
WJ	Walter Johnson/113	510.00
CK	Charlie Keller/16	365.00
GK	George Kelly/52	140.00
KK	Ken Keltner/11	500.00
MK	Mark Koenig/30	275.00
BL	Bob Lemon/23	225.00
EL	Eddie Lopat/22	275.00
TL	Ted Lyons/59	185.00
SM	Sal Maglie/19	400.00
MM	Mickey Mantle/8	5,000
HM	Heinie Manush/50	185.00
RoM	Roger Maris/73	1,675
RuM	Rube Marquard/23	375.00
JMc	Joe McCarthy/40	340.00
JM	Joe Medwick/18	750.00
BM	Bob Meusel/23	400.00
JMi	Johnny Mize/84	160.00
MO	Mel Ott/8	4,000
SP	Satchel Paige/36	900.00
RP	Roger Peckinpaugh/45	200.00
VR	Vic Raschi/26	175.00
BRi	Branch Rickey/16	1,350
JR	Jackie Robinson/147	700.00
ER	Edd Roush/83	170.00
RR	Red Ruffing/5	2,250
BRu	Babe Ruth/7	9,000
GS	George Selkirk/15	450.00
JS	Joe Sewell/55	130.00
RS	Rip Sewell/39	155.00
BS	Bob Shawkey/39	165.00
CS	Casey Stengel/10	1,500
BT	Bill Terry/184	125.00
VM	Johnny Vander Meer/65	125.00
HW	Honus Wagner/24	2,200
BW	Bucky Walters/13	400.00
LW	Lloyd Waner/217	105.00
PW	Paul Waner/4	2,250
HW	Hack Wilson/4	6,000
JW	Smokey Joe Wood/43	215.00

2001 SPx Sample

To introduce the annual SPx brand, Upper Deck issued this sample card of spokesman Ken Griffey Jr. The card is in the same format as the later-issued version, but has a large red "SAMPLE" overprinted diagonally on back.

		NM/M
001	Ken Griffey Jr.	5.00

2001 SPx

		NM/M
	Complete Set (150):	
	Common Player:	.25
	Common Young Star (91-120):	4.00
	Production 2,000	
	Common Prospect Jersey (121-135):	6.00
	Common Prosp. Auto. Jersey (136-150):	10.00
	Pack (4):	10.00
	Box (18):	160.00
1	Darin Erstad	.50
2	Troy Glaus	.50
3	Mo Vaughn	.25
4	Johnny Damon	1.00
5	Jason Giambi	.75
6	Tim Hudson	.50
7	Miguel Tejada	.50
8	Carlos Delgado	.75
9	Raul Mondesi	.25
10	Tony Batista	.25
11	Ben Grieve	.25
12	Greg Vaughn	.25
13	Juan Gonzalez	.50
14	Jim Thome	.75
15	Roberto Alomar	.50
16	John Olerud	.25
17	Edgar Martinez	.25
18	Albert Belle	.25
19	Cal Ripken Jr.	3.00
20	Ivan Rodriguez	.75
21	Rafael Palmeiro	.75
22	Alex Rodriguez	2.50
23	Nomar Garciaparra	1.00
24	Pedro J. Martinez	1.00
25	Manny Ramirez	1.00
26	Jermaine Dye	.25
27	Mark Quinn	.25
28	Carlos Beltran	.75
29	Tony Clark	.25
30	Bobby Higginson	.25
31	Eric Milton	.25
32	Matt Lawton	.25
33	Frank Thomas	1.00
34	Magglio Ordonez	.50
35	Ray Durham	.25
36	David Wells	.25
37	Derek Jeter	3.00
38	Bernie Williams	.50
39	Roger Clemens	2.00
40	David Justice	.25
41	Jeff Bagwell	.75
42	Richard Hidalgo	.25
43	Moises Alou	.40
44	Chipper Jones	1.00
45	Andruw Jones	.50
46	Greg Maddux	2.00
47	Rafael Furcal	.50
48	Jeromy Burnitz	.25
49	Geoff Jenkins	.25
50	Mark McGwire	2.00
51	Jim Edmonds	.50
52	Rick Ankiel	.50
53	Edgar Renteria	.25
54	Sammy Sosa	1.50
55	Kerry Wood	.50
56	Rondell White	.25
57	Randy Johnson	1.00
58	Steve Finley	.25
59	Matt Williams	.25
60	Luis Gonzalez	.25
61	Kevin Brown	.25
62	Gary Sheffield	.50
63	Shawn Green	.50
64	Vladimir Guerrero	1.00
65	Jose Vidro	.25
66	Barry Bonds	3.00
67	Jeff Kent	.40
68	Livan Hernandez	.25
69	Preston Wilson	.25
70	Charles Johnson	.25
71	Cliff Floyd	.25
72	Mike Piazza	1.50
73	Edgardo Alfonzo	.25
74	Jay Payton	.25
75	Robin Ventura	.25
76	Tony Gwynn	1.50
77	Phil Nevin	.25
78	Ryan Klesko	.25
79	Scott Rolen	.75
80	Pat Burrell	.50
81	Bob Abreu	.25
82	Brian Giles	.25
83	Kris Benson	.25
84	Jason Kendall	.25
85	Ken Griffey Jr.	2.00
86	Barry Larkin	.50
87	Sean Casey	.40
88	Todd Helton	.75
89	Larry Walker	.25
90	Mike Hampton	.25
91	Billy Sylvester RC	4.00
92	Josh Towers RC	4.00
93	Zach Day RC	4.00
94	Martin Vargas RC	4.00
95	Adam Pettyjohn RC	4.00
96	Andres Torres RC	4.00
97	Kris Keller RC	4.00
98	Blaine Neal RC	4.00
99	Kyle Kessel RC	4.00
100	Greg Miller RC	4.00
101	Shawn Sonnier RC	4.00
102	Alexis Gomez RC	4.00
103	Grant Balfour RC	4.00
104	Henry Mateo RC	4.00
105	Wilkin Ruan RC	4.00
106	Nick Maness RC	4.00
107	Jason Michaels RC	4.00
108	Esix Snead RC	4.00
109	William Ortega RC	4.00
110	David Elder RC	4.00
111	Jackson Melian RC	4.00
112	Nate Teut RC	4.00
113	Jason Smith RC	4.00
114	Mike Penney RC	4.00
115	Jose Mieses RC	4.00
116	Juan Pena	4.00
117	Brian Lawrence RC	6.00
118	Jeremy Owens RC	4.00
119	Carlos Valderrama RC	4.00
120	Rafael Soriano RC	6.00
121	Horacio Ramirez RC	10.00
122	Ricardo Rodriguez RC	6.00
123	Juan Diaz RC	6.00
124	Donnie Bridges	6.00
125	Tyler Walker RC	6.00
126	Erick Almonte RC	6.00
127	Jesus Colome RC	6.00
128	Ryan Freel RC	8.00
129	Elpidio Guzman RC	6.00
130	Jack Cust	8.00
131	Eric Hinske RC	10.00
132	Josh Fogg RC	6.00
133	Juan Uribe RC	10.00
134	Bert Snow RC	6.00
135	Pedro Feliz	6.00
136	Wilson Betemit RC	25.00
137	Sean Douglass RC	10.00
138	Dernell Stenson RC	10.00
139	Brandon Inge	6.00
140	Morgan Ensberg RC	15.00
141	Brian Cole	6.00
142	Adrian Hernandez RC	10.00
143	Brandon Duckworth RC	10.00
144	Jack Wilson RC	15.00
145	Travis Hafner RC	25.00
146	Carlos Pena	20.00
147	Corey Patterson	10.00
148	Xavier Nady	10.00
149	Jason Hart	10.00
150	Ichiro Suzuki RC	750.00

Spectrum

Stars (1-90):	10-20X
SP's (91-120):	1-1.5X
Production 50 Sets	

Foundations

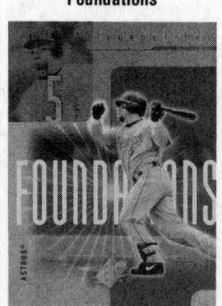

		NM/M
	Complete Set (12):	15.00
	Common Player:	1.00
	Inserted 1:8	
F1	Mark McGwire	3.00
F2	Jeff Bagwell	1.00
F3	Alex Rodriguez	3.00
F4	Ken Griffey Jr.	2.00
F5	Andruw Jones	1.00
F6	Cal Ripken Jr.	4.00
F7	Barry Bonds	4.00
F8	Derek Jeter	4.00
F9	Frank Thomas	1.00
F10	Sammy Sosa	1.50
F11	Tony Gwynn	1.50
F12	Vladimir Guerrero	1.50

SPXcitement

		NM/M
	Complete Set (12):	15.00
	Common Player:	.75
	Inserted 1:8	
X1	Alex Rodriguez	3.00
X2	Jason Giambi	.75
X3	Ken Griffey Jr.	2.00
X4	Sammy Sosa	1.50
X5	Frank Thomas	1.00
X6	Todd Helton	1.00
X7	Mark McGwire	2.00
X8	Mike Piazza	1.50
X9	Derek Jeter	3.00
X10	Vladimir Guerrero	1.50
X11	Carlos Delgado	.75
X12	Chipper Jones	1.50

Untouchable Talents

		NM/M
	Complete Set (6):	10.00
	Inserted 1:15	
UT1	Ken Griffey Jr.	2.00
UT2	Mike Piazza	2.00
UT3	Mark McGwire	2.50

UT4	Alex Rodriguez	2.50
UT5	Sammy Sosa	1.50
UT6	Derek Jeter	3.00

Winning Materials Base

		NM/M
	Common Duo:	40.00
	Production 50	
	Trios:	No Pricing
	Production 25	
MG	Mark McGwire, Ken Griffey Jr.	40.00
MS	Mark McGwire, Sammy Sosa	50.00
MR	Mark McGwire, Alex Rodriguez	40.00
GJ	Nomar Garciaparra, Derek Jeter	50.00
TR	Frank Thomas, Alex Rodriguez	40.00
JG	Derek Jeter, Jason Giambi	40.00
PB	Mike Piazza, Barry Bonds	40.00
RJ	Alex Rodriguez, Derek Jeter	50.00
PM	Mike Piazza, Mark McGwire	40.00
JP	Derek Jeter, Mike Piazza	40.00
MGS	Mark McGwire, Ken Griffey Jr., Sammy Sosa	80.00
JRG	Derek Jeter, Alex Rodriguez, Nomar Garciaparra	100.00
PJW	Mike Piazza, Derek Jeter, Bernie Williams	80.00
BMS	Barry Bonds, Mark McGwire, Sammy Sosa	100.00
GJR	Ken Griffey Jr., Derek Jeter, Alex Rodriguez	100.00

Winning Materials Base/Ball

		NM/M
	Common Player:	10.00
	Production 250 Sets	
BB	Barry Bonds	50.00
NG	Nomar Garciaparra	20.00
KG	Ken Griffey Jr.	30.00
VG	Vladimir Guerrero	15.00
DJ	Derek Jeter	50.00
AJ	Andruw Jones	10.00
CJ	Chipper Jones	15.00
PM	Pedro Martinez	15.00
MM	Mark McGwire	75.00
MP	Mike Piazza	20.00
AR	Alex Rodriguez	20.00
SS	Sammy Sosa	20.00
FT	Frank Thomas	15.00

Winning Materials Jersey Combo

		NM/M
	Common Duo:	25.00
	Production 50	
	Common Trio:	

	Production 25	
KG-AR	Ken Griffey Jr., Alex Rodriguez	50.00
KG-BB	Ken Griffey Jr., Barry Bonds	50.00
KG-RJ	Ken Griffey Jr., Randy Johnson	50.00
CJ-DW	Chipper Jones, David Wells	25.00
BB-SS	Barry Bonds, Sammy Sosa	50.00
KG-JD	Ken Griffey Jr., Joe DiMaggio	180.00
KG-SS	Ken Griffey Jr., Sammy Sosa	50.00
SS-CD	Sammy Sosa, Carlos Delgado	25.00
SS-FT	Sammy Sosa, Frank Thomas	25.00
IR-AR	Ivan Rodriguez, Alex Rodriguez	40.00
AR-CR	Alex Rodriguez, Cal Ripken Jr.	60.00
AJ-CJ	Andruw Jones, Chipper Jones	25.00
KG-KG	Ken Griffey Jr., Ken Griffey Jr.	40.00
G-R-B	Alex Rodriguez, Alex Rodriguez, Barry Bonds	100.00
S-G-C	Sammy Sosa, Ken Griffey Jr., Chipper Jones	60.00
B-G-J	Barry Bonds, Ken Griffey Jr., Andruw Jones	100.00
R-R-D	Alex Rodriguez, Ivan Rodriguez, Carlos Delgado	60.00
D-B-S	Carlos Delgado, Barry Bonds, Sammy Sosa	60.00
R-J-D	Cal Ripken Jr., Chipper Jones, Carlos Delgado	100.00

Winning Materials Jersey/Bat

		NM/M
	Common Player:	8.00
	Inserted 1:18	
RA	Rick Ankiel	8.00
BB1	Barry Bonds	25.00
BB2	Barry Bonds	25.00
CD	Carlos Delgado	10.00
JD	Joe DiMaggio	150.00
JE	Jim Edmonds	8.00
KG1	Ken Griffey Jr.	15.00
KG2	Ken Griffey Jr.	15.00
RJ1	Randy Johnson	15.00
RJ2	Randy Johnson	15.00
AJ1	Andruw Jones	10.00
AJ2	Andruw Jones	10.00
CJ1	Chipper Jones	15.00
CJ2	Chipper Jones	15.00
CR	Cal Ripken Jr.	40.00
AR1	Alex Rodriguez	15.00
AR2	Alex Rodriguez	15.00
IR1	Ivan Rodriguez	10.00
IR2	Ivan Rodriguez	10.00
SS	Sammy Sosa	15.00
FT	Frank Thomas	10.00

2002 SP Authentic

		NM/M
	Complete Set (170):	
	Common Player:	.25
	Common SP (91-135):	4.00
	Production 1,999	
	Common SP Auto. (136-170):	10.00
	Production 999	
	Pack (5):	3.50
	Box (24):	75.00
1	Troy Glaus	.40
2	Darin Erstad	.40
3	Barry Zito	.40
4	Eric Chavez	.40
5	Tim Hudson	.50
6	Miguel Tejada	.50
7	Carlos Delgado	.60
8	Shannon Stewart	.25
9	Ben Grieve	.25

#	Player	Price
10	Jim Thome	.75
11	C.C. Sabathia	.50
12	Ichiro Suzuki	2.00
13	Freddy Garcia	.25
14	Edgar Martinez	.25
15	Bret Boone	.25
16	Jeff Conine	.25
17	Alex Rodriguez	2.00
18	Juan Gonzalez	.50
19	Ivan Rodriguez	.50
20	Rafael Palmeiro	.75
21	Hank Blalock	.50
22	Pedro J. Martinez	1.00
23	Manny Ramirez	1.00
24	Nomar Garciaparra	1.00
25	Carlos Beltran	.75
26	Mike Sweeney	.25
27	Randall Simon	.25
28	Dmitri Young	.25
29	Bobby Higginson	.25
30	Corey Koskie	.25
31	Eric Milton	.25
32	Torii Hunter	.50
33	Joe Mays	.25
34	Frank Thomas	.75
35	Mark Buehrle	.40
36	Magglio Ordonez	.25
37	Kenny Lofton	.25
38	Roger Clemens	2.00
39	Derek Jeter	2.50
40	Jason Giambi	1.00
41	Bernie Williams	.50
42	Alfonso Soriano	.75
43	Lance Berkman	.50
44	Roy Oswalt	.50
45	Jeff Bagwell	.75
46	Craig Biggio	.50
47	Chipper Jones	1.00
48	Greg Maddux	1.50
49	Gary Sheffield	.50
50	Andruw Jones	.75
51	Ben Sheets	.40
52	Richie Sexson	.50
53	Albert Pujols	2.50
54	Matt Morris	.25
55	J.D. Drew	.40
56	Sammy Sosa	1.00
57	Kerry Wood	.50
58	Corey Patterson	.25
59	Mark Prior	.75
60	Randy Johnson	.75
61	Luis Gonzalez	.75
62	Curt Schilling	.75
63	Shawn Green	.50
64	Kevin Brown	.25
65	Hideo Nomo	.75
66	Vladimir Guerrero	.75
67	Jose Vidro	.25
68	Barry Bonds	2.50
69	Jeff Kent	.40
70	Rich Aurilia	.25
71	Preston Wilson	.25
72	Josh Beckett	.40
73	Mike Lowell	.25
74	Roberto Alomar	.40
75	Mo Vaughn	.25
76	Jeromy Burnitz	.25
77	Mike Piazza	1.50
78	Sean Burroughs	.25
79	Phil Nevin	.25
80	Bobby Abreu	.50
81	Pat Burrell	.40
82	Scott Rolen	.75
83	Jason Kendall	.25
84	Brian Giles	.25
85	Ken Griffey Jr.	1.50
86	Adam Dunn	.75
87	Sean Casey	.25
88	Todd Helton	.75
89	Larry Walker	.25
90	Mike Hampton	.25
91	Brandon Puffer RC	4.00
92	Tom Shearn RC	4.00
93	Chris Baker RC	4.00
94	Gustavo Chacin RC	6.00
95	Joe Orloski RC	4.00
96	Mike Smith RC	4.00
97	John Ennis RC	4.00
98	John Foster RC	4.00
99	Kevin Gryboski RC	4.00
100	Brian Mallette RC	4.00
101	Takahito Nomura RC	4.00
102	So Taguchi RC	6.00
103	Jeremy Lambert RC	4.00
104	Jason Simontacchi RC	4.00
105	Jorge Sosa RC	4.00
106	Brandon Backe RC	4.00
107	P.J. Bevis RC	4.00
108	Jeremy Ward RC	4.00
109	Doug DeVore RC	4.00
110	Ron Chiavacci RC	4.00
111	Ron Calloway RC	4.00
112	Nelson Castro RC	4.00
113	Deivis Santos RC	4.00
114	Earl Snyder RC	4.00
115	Julio Mateo RC	4.00
116	J.J. Putz RC	4.00
117	Allan Simpson RC	4.00
118	Satoru Komiyama RC	4.00
119	Adam Walker RC	4.00
120	Oliver Perez RC	8.00
121	Clifford Bartosh RC	4.00
122	Todd Donovan RC	4.00
123	Elio Serrano RC	4.00
124	Peter Zamora RC	4.00
125	Mike Gonzalez RC	4.00
126	Travis Hughes RC	4.00
127	Jorge de la Rosa RC	4.00
128	Anastacio Martinez RC	4.00
129	Colin Young RC	4.00
130	Nate Field RC	4.00
131	Tim Kalita RC	4.00
132	Julius Matos RC	4.00
133	Terry Pearson RC	4.00
134	Kyle Kane RC	4.00
135	Mitch Wylie RC	4.00
136	Rodrigo Rosario RC	10.00
137	Franklyn German RC	10.00
138	Reed Johnson RC	10.00
139	Luis Martinez RC	10.00
140	Michael Crudale RC	10.00
141	Francis Beltran RC	10.00
142	Steve Kent RC	10.00
143	Felix Escalona RC	10.00
144	Jose Valverde RC	15.00
145	Victor Alvarez RC	10.00
146	Kazuhisa Ishii/249 RC	25.00
147	Jorge Nunez RC	10.00
148	Eric Good RC	10.00
149	Luis Ugueto RC	10.00
150	Matt Thornton RC	10.00
151	Wilson Valdez RC	10.00
152	Hansel Izquierdo/249 RC	25.00
153	Jaime Cerda RC	10.00
154	Mark Corey RC	10.00
155	Tyler Yates RC	10.00
156	Steve Bechler RC	10.00
157	Ben Howard/249 RC	20.00
158	Anderson Machado RC	15.00
159	Jorge Padilla RC	15.00
160	Eric Junge RC	10.00
161	Adrian Burnside RC	10.00
162	Josh Hancock RC	10.00
163	Chris Booker RC	10.00
164	Cam Esslinger RC	10.00
165	Rene Reyes RC	10.00
166	Aaron Cook RC	10.00
167	Juan Brito RC	10.00
168	Miguel Ascencio RC	10.00
169	Kevin Frederick RC	10.00
170	Edwin Almonte RC	10.00

Limited

Stars (1-90):	5-10X
Cards (91-135):	.5-1X
Cards (136-170):	.5-1X
Production 125 Sets	
Golds (1-90):	10-20X
Golds (91-135):	.75-1.5X
Golds (136-170):	.75-1.5X
Production 50 Sets	

Chirography

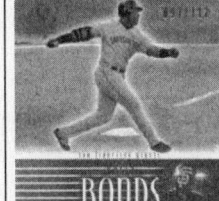

NM/M
Common Autograph: 10.00
Inserted 1:72

Code	Player	Price
HB	Hank Blalock/282	25.00
BB	Barry Bonds/112	180.00
BBo	Bret Boone/500	15.00
MB	Milton Bradley/470	15.00
JB	John Buck/427	15.00
MB	Mark Buehrle/438	15.00
SB	Sean Burroughs/275	15.00
AD	Adam Dunn/348	30.00
DE	Darin Erstad/80	15.00
CF	Cliff Floyd/313	10.00
FG	Freddy Garcia/456	15.00
JG	Jason Giambi/244	25.00
TG	Tom Glavine/376	25.00
AG	Alex Graman/418	10.00
KG	Ken Griffey Jr/238	100.00
TG	Tony Gwynn/75	40.00
JL	Jon Lieber/462	15.00
JM	Joe Mays/469	15.00
MM	Mark McGwire/50	300.00
DM	Doug Mientkiewicz/478	15.00
AR	Alex Rodriguez/391	90.00
CS	C.C. Sabathia/442	15.00
RS	Richie Sexson/483	15.00
SS	Sammy Sosa/247	100.00
IS	Ichiro Suzuki/78	350.00
MS	Mike Sweeney/265	15.00
BZ	Barry Zito/419	20.00

Chirography Gold

NM/M
Quantity produced listed.

Code	Player	Price
MB	Mark Buehrle/56	25.00
AD	Adam Dunn/44	40.00
CF	Cliff Floyd/30	20.00
FG	Freddy Garcia/34	35.00
TG	Tom Glavine/47	50.00
AG	Alex Graman/76	15.00
KG	Ken Griffey Jr./30	200.00
JL	Jon Lieber/32	20.00

Excellence

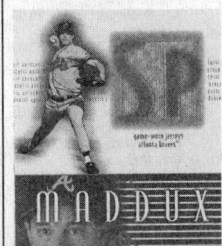

NM/M
Production 25
AE-1 Ken Griffey Jr., Sammy Sosa, Cal Ripken Jr., Jason Giambi, Mark McGwire, Ichiro Suzuki, 1,500

Future USA Watch

NM/M
Common Player: 5.00
Production 1,999 Sets

Code	Player	Price
USA1	Chad Cordero	5.00
USA2	Philip Humber	10.00
USA3	Grant Johnson	5.00
USA4	Wes Littleton	5.00
USA5	Kyle Sleeth	10.00
USA6	Huston Street	5.00
USA7	Brad Sullivan	5.00
USA8	Bob Zimmermann	5.00
USA9	Abe Alvarez	5.00
USA10	Kyle Bakker	5.00
USA11	Landon Powell	5.00
USA12	Clint Sammons	5.00
USA13	Michael Aubrey	10.00
USA14	Aaron Hill	5.00
USA15	Conor Jackson	20.00
USA16	Eric Patterson	5.00
USA17	Dustin Pedroia	10.00
USA18	Rickie Weeks	20.00
USA19	Shane Costa	5.00
USA20	Mark Jurich	5.00
USA21	Sam Fuld	10.00
USA22	Carlos Quentin	20.00

Game Jerseys

NM/M
Common Player: 5.00
Inserted 1:24

Code	Player	Price
RA	Roberto Alomar	8.00
JB	Jeff Bagwell	10.00
JB	Jeromy Burnitz/SP	5.00
RC	Roger Clemens	15.00
CD	Carlos Delgado	6.00
JE	Jim Edmonds	8.00
JGi	Jason Giambi	8.00
JGo	Juan Gonzalez	8.00
SG	Shawn Green	6.00
KG	Ken Griffey Jr/95	40.00
TH	Todd Helton	10.00
KI	Kazuhisa Ishii	10.00
RJ	Randy Johnson	10.00
AJ	Andruw Jones	8.00
CJ	Chipper Jones	10.00
JK	Jason Kendall	5.00
GM	Greg Maddux	15.00
MM	Mark McGwire/SP	30.00
MO	Magglio Ordonez	8.00
AP	Andy Pettitte	10.00
MP	Mike Piazza	15.00
MR	Manny Ramirez	15.00
AR	Alex Rodriguez	15.00
IR	Ivan Rodriguez	8.00
SR	Scott Rolen	10.00
CC	C.C. Sabathia	5.00
CS	Curt Schilling	10.00
GS	Gary Sheffield	6.00
TS	Tsuyoshi Shinjo	5.00
SS	Sammy Sosa	15.00
IS	Ichiro Suzuki/SP	50.00
JT	Jim Thome	10.00
RV	Robin Ventura	5.00
OV	Omar Vizquel	5.00
BW	Bernie Williams	8.00
PW	Preston Wilson	5.00
BZ	Barry Zito	5.00

Game Jersey Gold

NM/M
Quantity produced listed.

Code	Player	Price
KG	Ken Griffey Jr./30	65.00
RJ	Randy Johnson/51	25.00
GM	Greg Maddux/31	50.00
MO	Magglio Ordonez/30	15.00
AP	Andy Pettitte/46	20.00
MP	Mike Piazza/31	50.00
CC	C.C. Sabathia/52	10.00
CS	Curt Schilling/38	30.00
CS	C.C. Sabathia/52	25.00
MS	Mike Sweeney/29	40.00
BZ	Barry Zito/75	25.00

Prospect Signatures

NM/M
Common Autograph: 5.00
Inserted 1:36

Code	Player	Price
JC	Jose Cueto	5.00
JDe	Jeff Deardorff	5.00
JDi	Jose Diaz	5.00
AG	Alex Graman	8.00
MG	Matt Guerrier	5.00
BH	Bill Hall	5.00
KH	Ken Huckaby	5.00
DM	Dustan Mohr	5.00
XN	Xavier Nady	8.00
MS	Marco Scutaro	5.00
ST	Steve Torrealba	6.00
DW	Danny Wright	5.00

Big Mac Missing Link

Production 25 Sets

Signed SP Big Mac

NM/M
Quantity signed listed.
MM6 Mark McGwire/70 250.00

Signs of Greatness

Only one example of this card exists. The card is actually a 3-1/2" x 2-1/2" folder. On front are pictures of the players and a 1/1 designation. On back is a certification of authenticity. Inside are cut signatures of each of the players.

NM/M
Babe Ruth, Joe DiMaggio, Mickey Mantle, Ken Griffey Jr., Sammy Sosa (2/03 Auction) 30,000

2002 SP Legendary Cuts

NM/M
Complete Set (90): 30.00
Common Player: .40
Pack (4): 10.00
Box (12): 100.00

#	Player	Price
1	Al Kaline	.75
2	Alvin Dark	.40
3	Andre Dawson	.75
4	Babe Ruth	4.00
5	Ernie Banks	1.00
6	Bob Lemon	.40
7	Bobby Bonds	.40
8	Carl Erskine	.40
9	Carl Hubbell	.40
10	Casey Stengel	.40
11	Charlie Gehringer	.40
12	Christy Mathewson	.75
13	Dale Murphy	.75
14	Dave Concepcion	.40
15	Dave Parker	.40
16	Dazzy Vance	.40
17	Dizzy Dean	.75
18	Don Baylor	.40
19	Don Drysdale	.75
20	Duke Snider	1.00
22	Earl Averill	.40
23	Early Wynn	.40
24	Edd Roush	.40
25	Elston Howard	.40
26	Ferguson Jenkins	.40
27	Frank Crosetti	.40
28	Frankie Frisch	.40
29	Gaylord Perry	.40
30	George Foster	.40
31	George Kell	.40
32	Gil Hodges	.75
33	Hank Greenberg	.75
34	Phil Niekro	.40
35	Harvey Haddix	.40
36	Harvey Kuenn	.40
37	Honus Wagner	1.50
38	Jackie Robinson	2.00
39	Orlando Cepeda	.40
40	Joe Adcock	.40
41	Joe Cronin	.40
42	Joe DiMaggio	2.50
43	Joe Morgan	.40
44	Johnny Mize	.40
45	Lefty Gomez	.75
46	Lefty Grove	.40
47	Jim Palmer	.75
48	Lou Boudreau	.40
49	Lou Gehrig	2.50
50	Luke Appling	.40
51	Mark McGwire	2.00
52	Mel Ott	.75
53	Mickey Cochrane	.40
54	Mickey Mantle	3.00
55	Minnie Minoso	.40
56	Brooks Robinson	1.00
57	Nellie Fox	.40
58	Nolan Ryan	3.00
59	Rollie Fingers	.40
60	Pee Wee Reese	.40
61	Phil Rizzuto	.75
62	Ralph Kiner	.75
63	Ray Dandridge	.40
64	Richie Ashburn	.40
65	Robin Yount	.75
66	Rocky Colavito	.40
67	Roger Maris	2.00
68	Rogers Hornsby	.75
69	Ron Santo	.40
70	Ryne Sandberg	1.50
71	Stan Musial	1.50
72	Sam McDowell	.40
73	Satchel Paige	1.00
74	Willie McCovey	.40
75	Steve Garvey	.40
76	Ted Kluszewski	.40
77	Catfish Hunter	.40
78	Terry Moore	.40
79	Thurman Munson	1.00
80	Tom Seaver	1.00
81	Tommy John	.40
82	Tony Gwynn	1.00
83	Tony Kubek	.40
84	Tony Lazzeri	.40
85	Ty Cobb	2.00
86	Wade Boggs	1.00
87	Waite Hoyt	.40
88	Walter Johnson	1.00
89	Willie Stargell	.75
90	Yogi Berra	1.00
91	Zack Wheat	.40

(Prospect Signatures / parallel column)

Code	Player	Price
IS	Ichiro Suzuki/51	85.00
BW	Bernie Williams/51	20.00
PW	Preston Wilson/44	10.00
BZ	Barry Zito/75	10.00

Bat

NM/M
Common Player: 6.00
Inserted 1:8

Code	Player	Price
DBa	Don Baylor	6.00
YBe	Yogi Berra/SP	20.00
BBo	Bobby Bonds	6.00
RCo	Rocky Colavito	12.00
ADa	Alvin Dark	6.00
AnD	Andre Dawson	8.00
GFo	George Foster	6.00
NFo	Nellie Fox	15.00
SGa	Steve Garvey	6.00
HGr	Hank Greenberg/SP	40.00
LGr	Lefty Grove	15.00
TGw	Tony Gwynn	12.00
EHo	Elston Howard/SP	15.00
GKe	George Kell	8.00
RKi	Ralph Kiner	.40
TKu	Tonk (Tony) Kubek	8.00
TLa	Tony Lazzeri	.40
MMa	Mickey Mantle/SP	120.00
RMa	Roger Maris/SP	50.00
MMc	Mark McGwire	60.00
JMi	Johnny Mize	12.00
TMu	Thurman Munson	25.00
DMu	Dale Murphy	10.00
DPa	Dave Parker	6.00
GPe	Gaylord Perry	8.00
PWe	Pee Wee Reese	10.00
CRi	Cal Ripken Jr.	25.00
JaR	Jackie Robinson/SP	50.00
BRu	Babe Ruth/SP	150.00
NRy	Nolan Ryan	30.00
RSa	Ryne Sandberg	12.00
TSe	Tom Seaver/SP	20.00
DSn	Duke Snider	12.00
RYo	Robin Yount	10.00
EWy	Early Wynn	8.00

Bat Barrel

NM/M
Many not priced due to scarcity.

Code	Player	Price
BB-ADa	Alvin Dark/4	800.00
BB-AnD	Andre Dawson/4	750.00
BB-GFo	George Foster/5	250.00
BB-LGr	Lefty Grove/1 (8/03 Auction)	10,000
BB-TGw	Tony Gwynn/11	650.00
BB-MMa	Mickey Mantle/7 (8/04 Auction)	3,000
BB-MMc	Mark McGwire/4	2,000
BB-JMi	Johnny Mize/2	1,275
BB-DMu	Dale Murphy/3	600.00
BB-PWe	Pee Wee Reese/4	1,500
BB-BRu	Babe Ruth/3 (8/05 Auction)	9,500
BB-NRy	Nolan Ryan/9	1,500
BB-RSa	Ryne Sandberg/3	2,250
BB-DSn	Duke Snider/2	1,500
BB-RYo	Robin Yount/8	750.00

Jersey

NM/M
Common Player: 6.00
Inserted 1:24

Code	Player	Price
DBa	Don Baylor	8.00
YBe	Yogi Berra	20.00
BBo	Bobby Bonds	6.00
FCr	Frank Crosetti	10.00
AnD	Andre Dawson	8.00
GFo	George Foster	6.00
SGa	Steve Garvey	8.00
MMa	Mickey Mantle/SP	100.00
RMa	Roger Maris	40.00
DPa	Dave Parker	6.00
PWe	Pee Wee Reese	12.00
JRo	Jackie Robinson/SP	45.00
NRy	Nolan Ryan	30.00
RSa	Ryne Sandberg	25.00
TSe	Tom Seaver	10.00

Signatures

NM/M
Quantity signed listed

Code	Player	Price
JAd	Joe Adcock/48	150.00
LAp	Luke Appling/53	150.00
RAs	Richie Ashburn/10	550.00
EAv	Earl Averill/22	275.00
JBe	Johnny Berardino/12	450.00
LBo	Lou Boudreau/85	120.00
GBu	Guy Bush/38	125.00
GCa	George Case/36	180.00
HCh	Happy Chandler/96	100.00
SCh	Spud Chandler/17	350.00
TyC	Ty Cobb/2	5,500
MCo	Mickey Cochrane/5	5,000
JCo	Johnny Cooney/64	75.00
SCo	Stan Coveleski/85	150.00
JCr	Joe Cronin/185	120.00
BDa	Babe Dahlgren/51	180.00
RDa	Ray Dandridge/179	85.00
DDe	Dizzy Dean/4	2,000
JDi	Joe DiMaggio/103	175.00
DDo	Dick Donovan/23	200.00
TDo	Taylor Douthit/60	165.00
DDr	Don Drysdale/14	650.00
JDu	Joe Dugan/39	140.00
BFa	Bibb Falk/44	150.00
RFe	Rick Ferrell/19	225.00
NFo	Nellie Fox/1 (12/02 Auction)	3,100
FoF	Ford Frick/1 (10/03 Auction)	4,000
LGe	Lou Gehrig/3 (6/04 Auction)	7,500
CGe	Charlie Gehringer/3	700.00
LGo	Lefty Gomez/3	750.00
BGo	Billy Goodman/53	140.00
HGr	Hank Greenberg/94	425.00
LGr	Lefty Grove/190	240.00
SHa	Stan Hack/36	200.00
HHa	Harvey Haddix/37	250.00
BHa	Buddy Hassett/56	200.00
WHo	Waite Hoyt/62	250.00
CHu	Carl Hubbell/17	475.00
LJa	Larry Jackson/37	125.00
NJa	Newton "Bucky" Jacobs/44	150.00
EJo	Earl Johnson/31	200.00
JJo	Judy Johnson/86	150.00
WJo	Walter Johnson/20	2,000
BKa	Bob Kahle/53	150.00
WKa	Willie Kamm/57	110.00
CKe	Charlie Keller/29	280.00
KKe	Ken Keltner/11	415.00
TKl	Ted Kluszewski/23	300.00
MKo	Mark Koenig/22	260.00
HKu	Harvey Kuenn/23	230.00
CLa	Cookie Lavagetto/22	200.00
BiL	Billy Lee/40	150.00

BoL	Bob Lemon/91	110.00
ELo	Ed Lopat/58	150.00
SMa	Sal Maglie/29	200.00
HMa	Hank Majeski/21	300.00
MMa	Mickey Mantle/2 (10/04 Auction)	6,000
ChrM	Christy Mathewson/2 (5/03 Auction)	2,000
RMc	Roy McMillan/18	250.00
JMi	Johnny Mize/3	2,500
JMo	Johnny Moore/22	250.00
TMo	Terry Moore/86	95.00
ChM	Chet Morgan/27	185.00
HNe	Hal Newhouser/81	135.00
VRa	Vic Raschi/98	110.00
PWe	Pee Wee Reese/23	450.00
PRe	Pete Reiser/73	140.00
RRe	Rip Repulski/19	275.00
LRi	Lance Richbourg/3	1,800
ORo	Oscar Roettger/9	700.00
ERo	Edd Roush/101	100.00
ERo2	Edd Roush/99	100.00
BRu	Babe Ruth/3 (6/04 Auction)	12,500
BSc	Bob Scheffing/19	200.00
WSc	Willard Schmidt/10	350.00
HSc	Hal Schumacher/17	300.00
BSe	Bill Serena/16	275.00
JSe	Joe Sewell/136	125.00
BSh	Bob Shawkey/10	120.00
BSh	Bill Sherdel/10	450.00
BSz	Bill Shantz/17	300.00
WSt	Willie Stargell/153	95.00
CSt	Casey Stengel/8	750.00
BVe	Bill Veeck/11	500.00
HWa	Honus Wagner/6 (2/05 Auction)	5,000
BWa	Bucky Walters/31	165.00
VWe	Vic Wertz/17	300.00
ZWh	Zack Wheat/127	150.00
PWi	Pete Whisenant/13	300.00
EWy	Early Wynn/4	1,650

Swatches

Common Player:		6.00
Inserted 1:24		
DBa	Don Baylor	6.00
WBo	Wade Boggs	8.00
FCr	Frank Crosetti	8.00
DDr	Don Drysdale	20.00
CEr	Carl Erskine	6.00
TGw	Tony Gwynn	10.00
FJe	Ferguson Jenkins	8.00
TJo	Tommy John	6.00
SMc	Sam McDowell	6.00
MMi	Minnie Minoso	8.00
JMo	Joe Morgan	8.00
MOt	Mel Ott	25.00
DPa	Dave Parker	6.00
CRj	Cal Ripken Jr.	25.00
RSa	Ron Santo	10.00

2002 SPx

NM/M
Common Player: .25
Common SP (91-120): 4.00
Production 1,800
Common SP Auto. (121-150): 10.00
Common Star Swatch (151-190): 5.00
Production 800
Pack (4): 4.00
Box (18): 60.00

#		
1	Troy Glaus	.50
2	Darin Erstad	.40
3	David Justice	.25
4	Tim Hudson	.50
5	Miguel Tejada	.75
6	Barry Zito	.40
7	Carlos Delgado	.50
8	Shannon Stewart	.25
9	Greg Vaughn	.25
10	Toby Hall	.25
11	Jim Thome	.75
12	C.C. Sabathia	.50
13	Ichiro Suzuki	2.00
14	Edgar Martinez	.25
15	Freddy Garcia	.25
16	Mike Cameron	.25
17	Jeff Conine	.25
18	Tony Batista	.25
19	Alex Rodriguez	2.00
20	Rafael Palmeiro	.75
21	Ivan Rodriguez	.75
22	Carl Everett	.25
23	Pedro J. Martinez	1.00
24	Manny Ramirez	1.00
25	Nomar Garciaparra	1.00
26	Johnny Damon	1.00
27	Mike Sweeney	.25
28	Carlos Beltran	.75
29	Dmitri Young	.25
30	Joe Mays	.25
31	Doug Mientkiewicz	.25
32	Cristian Guzman	.25
33	Corey Koskie	.25
34	Frank Thomas	.75
35	Magglio Ordonez	.25
36	Mark Buehrle	.25
37	Bernie Williams	.50
38	Roger Clemens	2.00
39	Derek Jeter	2.50
40	Jason Giambi	.50
41	Mike Mussina	.50
42	Lance Berkman	.50
43	Jeff Bagwell	.50
44	Roy Oswalt	.50
45	Greg Maddux	2.00
46	Chipper Jones	1.00
47	Andruw Jones	.75
48	Gary Sheffield	.25
49	Geoff Jenkins	.25
50	Richie Sexson	.50
51	Ben Sheets	.40
52	Albert Pujols	2.50
53	J.D. Drew	.40
54	Jim Edmonds	.50
55	Sammy Sosa	1.50
56	Moises Alou	.25
57	Kerry Wood	.25
58	Jon Lieber	.25
59	Fred McGriff	.40
60	Randy Johnson	.75
61	Luis Gonzalez	.35
62	Curt Schilling	.75
63	Kevin Brown	.25
64	Hideo Nomo	.25
65	Shawn Green	.40
66	Vladimir Guerrero	1.00
67	Jose Vidro	.25
68	Barry Bonds	2.50
69	Jeff Kent	.40
70	Rich Aurilia	.25
71	Cliff Floyd	.25
72	Josh Beckett	.40
73	Preston Wilson	.25
74	Mike Piazza	1.00
75	Mo Vaughn	.25
76	Jeromy Burnitz	.25
77	Roberto Alomar	.50
78	Phil Nevin	.25
79	Ryan Klesko	.25
80	Scott Rolen	.75
81	Bobby Abreu	.50
82	Jimmy Rollins	.50
83	Brian Giles	.50
84	Aramis Ramirez	.50
85	Ken Griffey Jr.	1.50
86	Sean Casey	.40
87	Barry Larkin	.50
88	Mike Hampton	.50
89	Larry Walker	.40
90	Todd Helton	.75
91	Ron Calloway RC	4.00
92	Joe Orloski RC	4.00
93	Anderson Machado RC	6.00
94	Eric Good RC	4.00
95	Reed Johnson RC	8.00
96	Brendan Donnelly RC	4.00
97	Chris Baker RC	4.00
98	Wilson Valdez RC	4.00
99	Scotty Layfield RC	4.00
100	P.J. Bevis RC	4.00
101	Edwin Almonte RC	4.00
102	Francis Beltran RC	4.00
103	Valentino Pasucci RC	4.00
104	Nelson Castro RC	4.00
105	Michael Crudale RC	4.00
106	Colin Young RC	4.00
107	Todd Donovan RC	4.00
108	Felix Escalona RC	4.00
109	Brandon Backe RC	8.00
110	Corey Thurman RC	4.00
111	Kyle Kane RC	4.00
112	Allan Simpson RC	4.00
113	Jose Valverde RC	4.00
114	Chris Booker RC	4.00
115	Brandon Puffer RC	4.00
116	John Foster RC	4.00
117	Clifford Bartosh RC	4.00
118	Gustavo Chacin RC	8.00
119	Steve Kent RC	4.00
120	Nate Field RC	4.00
121	Victor Alvarez RC	10.00
122	Steve Bechler RC	10.00
123	Adrian Burnside RC	10.00
124	Marlon Byrd RC	15.00
125	Jaime Cerda RC	10.00
126	Brandon Claussen RC	10.00
127	Mark Corey RC	10.00
128	Doug DeVore RC	10.00
129	Kazuhisa Ishii RC	15.00
130	John Ennis RC	10.00
131	Kevin Frederick RC	10.00
132	Josh Hancock RC	10.00
133	Ben Howard RC	10.00
134	Orlando Hudson RC	15.00
135	Hansel Izquierdo RC	10.00
136	Eric Junge RC	10.00
137	Austin Kearns RC	15.00
138	Victor Martinez	25.00
139	Luis Martinez RC	10.00
140	Danny Mota RC	10.00
141	Jorge Padilla RC	10.00
142	Andy Pratt RC	10.00
143	Rene Reyes RC	10.00
144	Rodrigo Rosario RC	10.00
145	Tom Shearn RC	10.00
146	So Taguchi RC	30.00
147	Dennis Tankersley	15.00
148	Matt Thornton	10.00
149	Jeremy Ward RC	10.00
150	Mitch Wylie RC	10.00
151	Pedro Martinez	8.00
152	Cal Ripken Jr.	25.00
153	Roger Clemens	15.00
154	Bernie Williams	6.00
155	Jason Giambi	8.00
156	Robin Ventura	5.00
157	Carlos Delgado	6.00
158	Frank Thomas	8.00
159	Magglio Ordonez	5.00
160	Jim Thome	10.00
161	Darin Erstad	5.00
162	Tim Salmon	5.00
163	Tim Hudson	5.00
164	Barry Zito	5.00
165	Ichiro Suzuki	30.00
166	Edgar Martinez	8.00
167	Alex Rodriguez	15.00
168	Ivan Rodriguez	8.00
169	Juan Gonzalez	6.00
170	Greg Maddux	12.00
171	Chipper Jones	10.00
172	Andruw Jones	8.00
173	Tom Glavine	6.00
174	Mike Piazza	15.00
175	Roberto Alomar	8.00
176	Scott Rolen	12.00
177	Sammy Sosa	15.00
178	Moises Alou	8.00
179	Ken Griffey Jr.	15.00
180	Jeff Bagwell	8.00
181	Jim Edmonds	6.00
182	J.D. Drew	5.00
183	Brian Giles	5.00
184	Randy Johnson	10.00
185	Curt Schilling	10.00
186	Luis Gonzalez	5.00
187	Todd Helton	8.00
188	Shawn Green	5.00
189	David Wells	5.00
190	Jeff Kent	5.00

SuperStar Swatch Silver
Jersey (151-190): .5-1X
Production 400

SuperStar Swatch Gold
Jersey (151-190): .75-1.5X
Production 150

Sweet Spot Bat Barrel
No Pricing

Winning Materials Ball/Patch Combo

No Pricing
Production 25 Sets

Winning Materials Base Combo

NM/M
Common Card: 15.00
Production 200

PE	Mike Piazza, Jim Edmonds	20.00
RJ	Alex Rodriguez, Derek Jeter	40.00
BG	Barry Bonds, Shawn Green	20.00
IM	Ichiro Suzuki, Edgar Martinez	50.00
SG	Sammy Sosa, Luis Gonzalez	25.00
GR	Troy Glaus, Alex Rodriguez	20.00
WJ	Bernie Williams, Derek Jeter	30.00
GS	Ken Griffey Jr., Sammy Sosa	30.00
PI	Albert Pujols, Ichiro Suzuki	60.00
SR	Kazuhiro Sasaki, Mariano Rivera	20.00

Winning Materials Base/Patch Combo
No Pricing
Production 25 Sets

Winning Materials Jersey Combo

NM/M
Common Card: 8.00
Inserted 1:18

AR	Alex Rodriguez, Ivan Rodriguez	20.00
GC	Ken Griffey Jr., Sean Casey/SP	20.00
BR	Jeff Bagwell, Alex Rodriguez	15.00
WG	Bernie Williams, Jason Giambi	10.00
JS	Randy Johnson, Curt Schilling	15.00
MJ	Greg Maddux, Chipper Jones	20.00
MC	Edgar Martinez, Mike Cameron	10.00
SP	Sammy Sosa, Corey Patterson	20.00
ED	Jim Edmonds, J.D. Drew	15.00
PA	Mike Piazza, Roberto Alomar	15.00
DH	Jermaine Dye, Tim Hudson	8.00
RA	Scott Rolen, Bobby Abreu	15.00
TO	Frank Thomas, Magglio Ordonez	15.00
HW	Mike Hampton, Larry Walker	8.00
TS	Jim Thome, C.C. Sabathia	15.00
GK	Shawn Green, Eric Karros	10.00
KG	Jason Kendall, Brian Giles	8.00
WP	David Wells, Jorge Posada	10.00
NM	Hideo Nomo, Pedro Martinez/SP	20.00
RP	Ivan Rodriguez, Chan Ho Park	10.00
LH	Al Leiter, Mike Hampton	8.00
BA	Jeromy Burnitz, Edgardo Alfonzo	8.00
DS	Carlos Delgado, Shannon Stewart	10.00
BG	Jeff Bagwell, Juan Gonzalez	10.00
GR	Juan Gonzalez, Ivan Rodriguez	10.00
VR	Omar Vizquel, Alex Rodriguez	15.00
SE	Aaron Sele, Darin Erstad	8.00
JJ	Chipper Jones, Andruw Jones	15.00
SH	Kazuhiro Sasaki, Shigetoshi Hasegawa	8.00

Winning Materials USA Jersey Combo
NM/M
Common Card: 10.00
Production 150

AH	Brent Abernathy, Orlando Hudson	8.00
BT	Sean Burroughs, Mark Teixeira	25.00
GB	Jason Giambi, Sean Burroughs	15.00
HD	Orlando Hudson, Jeff Deardorff	10.00
GT	Jason Giambi, Mark Teixeira	20.00
HOU	Roy Oswalt, Adam Everett	10.00
HP	Dustin Hermanson, Mark Prior	15.00
JC	Jacque Jones, Michael Cuddyer	10.00
KB	Austin Kearns, Sean Burroughs	15.00
KC	Austin Kearns, Michael Cuddyer	15.00
MG	Doug Mientkiewicz, Jason Giambi	15.00
MIN	Doug Mientkiewicz, Michael Cuddyer	10.00
MO	Matt Morris, Roy Oswalt	15.00
MP	Matt Morris, Mark Prior	15.00
AW	Matt Anderson, Jeff Weaver	10.00
MW	Matt Morris, Jeff Weaver	10.00
PB	Mark Prior, Dewon Brazelton	15.00
RE	Brian Roberts, Adam Everett	10.00
SD	Mark Kotsay, Sean Burroughs	10.00
TB	Brent Abernathy, Dewon Brazelton	10.00
TP	Mark Teixeira, Mark Prior	25.00
WB	Jeff Weaver, Dewon Brazelton	10.00
WH	Jeff Weaver, Dustin Hermanson	10.00

2003 SP Authentic

NM/M
Complete Set (189):
Common Player: .25
Common Rk Archives (91-123): 1.00
Production 2,500
Common Back to '93 (124-150): 1.50
Production 1,993
Common Future Watch (150-180): 4.00
Production 2,003
Pack (5): 3.50
Box (24): 70.00

#		
1	Darin Erstad	.40
2	Garret Anderson	.40
3	Troy Glaus	.50
4	Eric Chavez	.50
5	Barry Zito	.50
6	Miguel Tejada	.75
7	Eric Hinske	.25
8	Carlos Delgado	.50
9	Josh Phelps	.25
10	Ben Grieve	.25
11	Carl Crawford	.25
12	Omar Vizquel	.40
13	Matt Lawton	.25
14	C.C. Sabathia	.25
15	Ichiro Suzuki	1.50
16	John Olerud	.40
17	Freddy Garcia	.25
18	Jay Gibbons	.25
19	Tony Batista	.25
20	Melvin Mora	.25
21	Alex Rodriguez	2.00
22	Rafael Palmeiro	.50
23	Hank Blalock	.50
24	Nomar Garciaparra	1.00
25	Pedro J. Martinez	.75
26	Johnny Damon	.75
27	Mike Sweeney	.25
28	Carlos Febles	.25
29	Carlos Beltran	.50
30	Carlos Pena	.25
31	Eric Munson	.25
32	Bobby Higginson	.25
33	Torii Hunter	.40
34	Doug Mientkiewicz	.25
35	Jacque Jones	.25
36	Paul Konerko	.50
37	Bartolo Colon	.25
38	Magglio Ordonez	.50
39	Derek Jeter	2.00
40	Bernie Williams	.50
41	Jason Giambi	.50
42	Alfonso Soriano	.75
43	Roger Clemens	1.00
44	Jeff Bagwell	.50
45	Jeff Kent	.40
46	Lance Berkman	.40
47	Chipper Jones	.75
48	Andruw Jones	.50
49	Gary Sheffield	.50
50	Ben Sheets	.40
51	Richie Sexson	.50
52	Geoff Jenkins	.40
53	Jim Edmonds	.40
54	Albert Pujols	2.00
55	Scott Rolen	.75
56	Sammy Sosa	1.00
57	Kerry Wood	.75
58	Eric Karros	.25
59	Luis Gonzalez	.40
60	Randy Johnson	.75
61	Curt Schilling	.75
62	Fred McGriff	.40
63	Shawn Green	.40
64	Paul LoDuca	.25
65	Vladimir Guerrero	.75
66	Jose Vidro	.25
67	Barry Bonds	2.00
68	Rich Aurilia	.25
69	Edgardo Alfonzo	.25
70	Ivan Rodriguez	.50
71	Mike Lowell	.40
72	Derrek Lee	.50
73	Tom Glavine	.50
74	Mike Piazza	1.00
75	Roberto Alomar	.50
76	Ryan Klesko	.25
77	Phil Nevin	.25
78	Mark Kotsay	.25
79	Jim Thome	.75
80	Pat Burrell	.40
81	Bobby Abreu	.40
82	Jason Kendall	.25
83	Brian Giles	.40
84	Aramis Ramirez	.25
85	Austin Kearns	.40
86	Ken Griffey Jr.	1.00
87	Adam Dunn	.50
88	Larry Walker	.40
89	Todd Helton	.50
90	Preston Wilson	.40
91	Derek Jeter	6.00
92	Johnny Damon	3.00
93	Chipper Jones	3.00
94	Manny Ramirez	3.00
95	Trot Nixon	1.00
96	Alex Rodriguez	5.00
97	Chan Ho Park	1.00
98	Brad Fullmer	1.00
99	Billy Wagner	1.00
100	Hideo Nomo	2.00
101	Freddy Garcia	1.00
102	Darin Erstad	1.00
103	Jose Cruz Jr.	1.00
104	Nomar Garciaparra	4.00
105	Magglio Ordonez	1.50
106	Kerry Wood	1.50
107	Troy Glaus	1.50
108	J.D. Drew	1.00
109	Alfonso Soriano	3.00
110	Danys Baez	1.00
111	Kazuhiro Sasaki	1.00
112	Barry Zito	2.00
113	Brent Abernathy	1.00
114	Ben Diggins	1.00
115	Ben Sheets	1.00
116	Brad Wilkerson	1.00
117	Juan Pierre	1.00
118	Jon Rauch	1.00
119	Ichiro Suzuki	6.00
120	Albert Pujols	6.00
121	Mark Prior	2.00
122	Mark Teixeira	4.00
123	Kazuhisa Ishii	1.00
124	Troy Glaus	1.50
125	Randy Johnson	3.00
126	Curt Schilling	3.00
127	Chipper Jones	3.00
128	Greg Maddux	4.00
129	Nomar Garciaparra	4.00
130	Pedro J. Martinez	3.00
131	Sammy Sosa	3.00
132	Mark Prior	2.00
133	Ken Griffey Jr.	4.00
134	Adam Dunn	2.00
135	Jeff Bagwell	2.00
136	Vladimir Guerrero	4.00
137	Mike Piazza	4.00
138	Tom Glavine	1.50
139	Derek Jeter	8.00
140	Roger Clemens	6.00
141	Jason Giambi	3.00
142	Alfonso Soriano	3.00
143	Miguel Tejada	1.50
144	Barry Zito	1.50
145	Jim Thome	3.00
146	Barry Bonds	8.00
147	Ichiro Suzuki	8.00
148	Albert Pujols	8.00
149	Alex Rodriguez	6.00
150	Carlos Delgado	2.00
151	Richard Fischer RC	4.00
152	Brandon Webb RC	25.00
153	Rob Hammock RC	4.00
154	Matt Kata RC	4.00
155	Tim Olson RC	4.00
156	Oscar Villarreal RC	4.00
157	Michael Hessman RC	4.00
158	Daniel Cabrera RC	6.00
159	Jon Leicester RC	4.00
160	Todd Wellemeyer RC	6.00
161	Felix Sanchez RC	4.00
162	David Sanders RC	4.00
163	Josh Stewart RC	4.00
164	Arnie Munoz RC	4.00
165	Ryan Cameron RC	4.00
166	Clint Barmes RC	4.00
167	Josh Willingham RC	10.00

169	Willie Eyre **RC**	4.00
170	Brent Hoard **RC**	4.00
171	Termmel Sledge **RC**	4.00
172	Phil Seibel **RC**	4.00
173	Craig Brazell **RC**	4.00
174	Jeff Duncan **RC**	5.00
176	Bernie Castro **RC**	4.00
177	Mike Nicolas **RC**	4.00
178	Rett Johnson **RC**	4.00
179	Bobby Madritsch **RC**	4.00
180	Chris Capuano **RC**	6.00
181	Hideki Matsui/ Auto./500 **RC**	240.00
181	H. Matsui/Bronze/ Auto./75	275.00
182	Jose Contreras/ Auto./500 **RC**	35.00
183	Lew Ford/Auto./500 **RC**	10.00
184	Jeremy Griffiths/ Auto./500	10.00
185	Guillermo Quiroz/ Auto./500 **RC**	10.00
186	Alejandro Machado/ Auto./500 **RC**	10.00
187	Francisco Cruceta/ Auto./500 **RC**	10.00
188	Prentice Redman/ Auto./500 **RC**	10.00
189	Shane Bazzell/ Auto./500 **RC**	10.00

Simply Splendid

	NM/M
Complete Set (30):	200.00
Common Williams:	8.00
Production 406 Sets	
TW1-30 Ted Williams	8.00

Chirography

	NM/M
Common Autograph:	10.00
Varying quantities produced.	
Bronze Autos.:	1X
Production 100	
Silver Autos.:	1-1.5X
Production 50	
Gold Autos.:	No Pricing
Production 10	
GA1	Garret Anderson/245	15.00
BA	Jeff Bagwell/175	40.00
JD	Johnny Damon/245	35.00
AD	Adam Dunn/170	25.00
JE2	Jim Edmonds/350	20.00
FL	Cliff Floyd/125	12.00
FC	Rafael Furcal/150	15.00
FG	Freddy Garcia/345	15.00
GI	Jason Giambi/250	15.00
GL	Brian Giles/225	15.00
LG1	Luis Gonzalez/195	15.00
GJ	Ken Griffey Jr./350	85.00
JR	Ken Griffey Jr./350	85.00
TO	Torii Hunter/245	15.00
KE	Jason Kendall/145	10.00
MM	Mark McGwire/50	200.00
MP	Mark Prior/150	20.00
CR	Cal Ripken Jr./250	100.00
RO	Scott Rolen/345	30.00
TS	Tim Salmon/350	15.00
RS	Richie Sexson/245	15.00
SA	Sammy Sosa/335	75.00
SO	Sammy Sosa/335	75.00
IC	Ichiro Suzuki/85	350.00
IS	Ichiro Suzuki/75	350.00
SW	Mike Sweeney/125	15.00
JT1	Jim Thome/250	30.00

Chirography Dodger Stars

	NM/M
Common Autograph:	8.00
Bronze Autos.:	1X
Production 100	
Silver Autos.:	1-1.5X
Production 50	
Gold Autos.:	No Pricing
Production 10	
BB	Bill Buckner/245	10.00
CE	Ron Cey/345	8.00
SG	Steve Garvey/320	20.00
JN	Tommy John/170	15.00
DL	Davey Lopes/245	8.00
DN	Don Newcombe/345	15.00
BI	Bill Russell/245	8.00
DS	Duke Snider/345	30.00
SU	Don Sutton/245	15.00
MW	Maury Wills/320	10.00
SY	Steve Yeager/345	15.00

Chirography Double

		NM/M
Common Duo Auto.:		40.00
FB	Yogi Berra, Whitey Ford/75	150.00
FE	Carlton Fisk, Dwight Evans/75	65.00
FM	Carlton Fisk, Bill Mazeroski/75	40.00
GG	Jason Giambi, Ken Griffey Jr.	125.00
GR	Steve Garvey, Ron Cey/75	50.00
JI	Ken Griffey Jr., Ichiro Suzuki	350.00
KR	Tony Kubek, Bobby Richardson/75	80.00
KT	Tom Seaver, Jerry Koosman/75	80.00
MG	Don Mattingly, Jason Giambi/25	150.00
MS	Mark McGwire, Sammy Sosa/15	500.00
SJ	Sammy Sosa, Jason Giambi/25	125.00
WB	Bill Buckner, Mookie Wilson,/150	40.00

Chirography Flash Backs

		NM/M
Common Autograph:		8.00
Bronze Autos.:		1X
Production 100		
Silver Autos.:		1-1.5X
Production 50		
Gold Autos.:		No Pricing
No Pricing		
JE1	Jim Edmonds/350	15.00
CF1	Cliff Floyd/350	8.00
JA	Jason Giambi/350	15.00
BN	Brian Giles/245	10.00
LA	Luis Gonzalez/200	15.00
GM	Ken Griffey Jr./350	80.00
MA	Mark McGwire/55	280.00
SR	Sammy Sosa/245	100.00

Chirography Hall of Famers

		NM/M
Common Autograph:		15.00
Bronze Autos.:		1X
Production 100		
Silver Autos.:		1-1.5X
Production 50		
Gold Autos.:		No Pricing
Production 10		
JB1	Johnny Bench/350	40.00
GC1	Gary Carter/350	20.00
OC	Orlando Cepeda/245	20.00
RF	Rollie Fingers/170	15.00
CF	Carlton Fisk/240	35.00
WF	Whitey Ford/150	40.00
BG	Bob Gibson/245	35.00
TP	Tony Perez/320	20.00
RR	Robin Roberts/170	30.00
NR	Nolan Ryan/170	140.00
TS	Tom Seaver/170	40.00
DS	Duke Snider/250	30.00
DW2	Dave Winfield/350	25.00

Chirography Triple

		NM/M
Quantity produced listed		
BKR	Bobby Richardson, Yogi Berra, Tony Kubek/75	120.00
FCG	Carlton Fisk, Gary Carter, Kirk Gibson/75	75.00

GIS	Sammy Sosa, Ichiro Suzuki, Ken Griffey Jr./75	400.00
GLC	Davey Lopes, Ron Cey, Steve Garvey/75	65.00
GRC	Steve Garvey, Ron Cey, Bill Russell/75	60.00
GSG	Sammy Sosa, Jason Giambi, Ken Griffey Jr./75	250.00
GSJ	Ken Griffey Jr., Jason Giambi, Sammy Sosa/75	250.00
ISG	Sammy Sosa, Jason Giambi, Ichiro Suzuki/75	300.00
SEA	Tim Salmon, Garret Anderson, Darin Erstad/75	100.00
SKM	Tom Seaver, Tug McGraw, Jerry Koosman/75	125.00

Chirography World Series Heroes

		NM/M
Common Autograph:		10.00
Bronze Autos.:		1X
Production 100		
Silver Autos.:		1-1.5X
Production 50		
Gold Autos.:		No Pricing
Production 10		
GA	Garret Anderson/245	15.00
GC	Gary Carter/345	20.00
DE	Darin Erstad/245	15.00
CF	Carlton Fisk/200	40.00
KG	Kirk Gibson/145	15.00
GO	Luis Gonzalez/225	15.00
GS	Ken Griffey Sr./295	10.00
AJ1	Andruw Jones/350	20.00
DJ	David Justice/170	20.00
JK	Jerry Koosman/170	15.00
BM	Bill Mazeroski/245	30.00
TM	Tug McGraw/170	25.00
JP	Jorge Posada/350	35.00
ER	Edgar Renteria/220	15.00
CR	Cal Ripken Jr./295	100.00
TI	Tim Salmon/245	15.00
CS	Curt Schilling/345	30.00

Chirography Yankee Stars

		NM/M
Common Autograph:		10.00
Bronze Autos.:		1X
Production 100		
Silver Autos.:		1-1.5X
Production 50		
Gold Autos.:		No Pricing
Production 10		
YB	Yogi Berra/320	35.00
JB	Jim Bouton/345	10.00
RC	Roger Clemens/210	100.00
JG	Jason Giambi/275	15.00
KS	Ken Griffey Sr./350	10.00
TH	Tommy Henrich/345	15.00
HK	Ralph Houk/245	12.00
TJ	Tommy John/245	15.00
TK	Tony Kubek/345	20.00
SL	Sparky Lyle/345	10.00
DM	Don Mattingly/295	60.00
BR	Bobby Richardson/320	20.00
ST	Mel Stottlemyre/345	10.00
DW1	Dave Winfield/350	25.00

Chirography Young Stars

		NM/M
Common Autograph:		6.00
Bronze Autos.:		1X
Production 100		
Silver Autos.:		1-1.5X
Production 50		
Gold Autos.:		No Pricing
Production 10		
HB	Hank Blalock/245	25.00
BO	Joe Borchard/245	8.00
SB	Sean Burroughs/245	8.00
MB	Marlon Byrd/245	8.00
HC	Hee Seop Choi/245	20.00
DI1	Ben Diggins/350	8.00
DH	Drew Henson/245	15.00
EH	Eric Hinske/245	10.00
OH	Orlando Hudson/245	10.00
JJ	Jacque Jones/245	15.00
JJ1	Jimmy Journell/350	10.00
JL	Jason Lane/245	6.00
JO	Joe Mays/245	8.00
MI	Doug Mientkiewicz/245	15.00
MY	Brett Myers/245	10.00
CP	Corey Patterson/245	10.00
PE	Carlos Pena/245	10.00
OP	Oliver Perez/245	10.00
JP	Josh Phelps/245	10.00
BP1	Brandon Phillips/350	15.00
AP	A.J. Pierzynski/245	15.00
FS1	Freddy Sanchez/350	15.00
TX	Mark Teixeira/245	25.00
BZ	Barry Zito/350	20.00

Splendid Jerseys

		NM/M
Production 406 Sets		
TW	Mickey Mantle, Ted Williams	180.00

SJ-TW	Ted Williams	100.00
TW-IS	Ted Williams, Ichiro Suzuki	100.00
TW-JG	Ted Williams, Jason Giambi	60.00
TW-KG	Ted Williams, Ken Griffey Jr.	75.00
TW-MM	Mark McGwire, Ted Williams	110.00
TW-SS	Ted Williams, Sammy Sosa	80.00
TW-NM1	Ted Williams, Nomar Garciaparra	80.00
TW-NM2	Nomar Garciaparra, Ted Williams	80.00

Splendid Signatures

		NM/M
Hand Numbered to five or three.		
GA	Nomar Garciaparra/ 406	100.00
TW-NM3	Ted Williams, Nomar Garciaparra/3 (10/03 Auction)	2,400

Spotlight "Godzilla"

Complete Set (15):	
Common Matsui:	
Production 500 Sets	

Superstar Flashback

		NM/M
Complete Set (60):		65.00
Common Player:		1.00
Production 2,003 Sets		
SF1	Tim Salmon	1.00
SF2	Darin Erstad	1.00
SF3	Troy Glaus	1.50
SF4	Randy Johnson	2.00
SF5	Curt Schilling	1.50
SF6	Steve Finley	1.00
SF7	Greg Maddux	3.00
SF8	Chipper Jones	3.00
SF9	Andruw Jones	1.50
SF10	Gary Sheffield	1.00
SF11	Manny Ramirez	2.00
SF12	Pedro J. Martinez	2.00
SF13	Nomar Garciaparra	2.50
SF14	Sammy Sosa	3.00
SF15	Frank Thomas	1.50
SF16	Kerry Wood	1.50
SF17	Paul Konerko	1.00
SF18	Corey Patterson	1.00
SF19	Mark Prior	2.00
SF20	Ken Griffey Jr.	3.00
SF21	Adam Dunn	1.50
SF22	Larry Walker	1.00
SF23	Preston Wilson	1.00
SF24	Todd Helton	1.50
FS1	Ivan Rodriguez	1.50
SF26	Josh Beckett	1.00
SF27	Jeff Bagwell	1.50
SF28	Jeff Kent	1.00
SF29	Lance Berkman	1.00
SF30	Carlos Beltran	1.50
SF31	Shawn Green	1.00
SF32	Richie Sexson	1.00
SF33	Vladimir Guerrero	1.50

SF34	Mike Piazza	4.00
SF35	Roberto Alomar	1.50
SF36	Roger Clemens	4.00
SF37	Derek Jeter	6.00
SF38	Jason Giambi	1.50
SF39	Bernie Williams	1.50
SF40	Nick Johnson	1.00
SF41	Alfonso Soriano	3.00
SF42	Miguel Tejada	1.50
SF43	Eric Chavez	1.50
SF44	Barry Zito	1.50
SF45	Jim Thome	1.50
SF46	Pat Burrell	1.00
SF47	Marlon Byrd	1.00
SF48	Jason Kendall	1.50
SF49	Aramis Ramirez	1.50
SF50	Brian Giles	1.00
SF51	Phil Nevin	1.00
SF52	Barry Bonds	6.00
SF53	Ichiro Suzuki	4.00
SF54	Scott Rolen	2.00
SF55	J.D. Drew	1.00
SF56	Albert Pujols	6.00
SF57	Mark Teixeira	1.50
SF58	Hank Blalock	2.00
SF59	Carlos Delgado	1.50
SF60	Roy Halladay	1.00

500 Home Run Club

	NM/M
Production 25	
500HR Ted Williams, Barry Bonds, Mark McGwire, Sammy Sosa, Mickey Mantle	325.00

2003 SP Legendary Cuts

	NM/M
Complete Set (130):	
Common Player:	.25
Common SP:	3.00
Production 1,299	
Pack (4):	8.00
Box (12):	85.00
1	Luis Aparicio	.25
2	Al Barlick	.25
3	Al Lopez	.25
4	Ernie Banks	1.00
5	Alexander Cartwright	.25
6	Lou Brock	.50
7	Babe Ruth/SP	10.00
8	Bill Dickey	.50
9	Bill Mazeroski	.25
10	Bob Feller	.50
11	Billy Herman	.25
12	Billy Williams	.25
13	Bob Gibson/SP	4.00
14	Bob Lemon	.25
15	Bobby Doerr	.25
16	Branch Rickey	.25
17	Gary Carter	.50
18	Burleigh Grimes	.25
19	Cap Anson	.25
20	Carl Hubbell	.25
21	Carlton Fisk	.50
22	Casey Stengel	.50
23	Charlie Gehringer	.25
24	Chief Bender	.25
25	Christy Mathewson/SP	5.00
26	Cy Young	1.00
27	Dave Winfield	.50
28	Dazzy Vance	.25
29	Dizzy Dean/SP	4.00
30	Don Drysdale/SP	4.00
31	Duke Snider/SP	4.00
32	Earl Averill	.25
33	Earle Combs	.25
34	Edd Roush	.25
35	Earl Weaver	.25

36	Eddie Collins	.25
37	Eddie Plank	.25
38	Elmer Flick	.25
39	Enos Slaughter	.25
40	Ernie Lombardi	.25
41	Ford Frick	.25
42	Jim "Catfish" Hunter	.25
43	Frankie Frisch	.25
44	Gabby Hartnett	.25
45	George Kell	.25
46	Early Wynn	.25
47	Ferguson Jenkins	.25
48	Al Kaline	1.00
49	Harmon Killebrew	1.00
50	Hal Newhouser	.25
51	Hank Greenberg/SP	5.00
52	Harry Caray	.25
53	Tommy Lasorda	.25
54	Honus Wagner/SP	6.00
55	Hoyt Wilhelm/SP	3.00
56	Jackie Robinson/SP	6.00
57	Jim Bottomley	.25
58	Jim Bunning/SP	3.00
59	Jimmie Foxx/SP	6.00
60	Eddie Mathews	1.00
61	Joe Cronin	.25
62	Joe DiMaggio/SP	8.00
63	Joe McCarthy/SP	3.00
64	Joe Morgan/SP	3.00
65	Willie McCovey	.50
66	Joe Tinker	.25
67	Johnny Bench/SP	6.00
68	Johnny Evers/SP	3.00
69	Johnny Mize/SP	3.00
70	Josh Gibson/SP	5.00
71	Juan Marichal	.50
72	Judy Johnson	.25
73	Stan Musial	1.50
74	Kiki Cuyler	.25
75	Larry Doby	.75
76	Nap Lajoie	.25
77	Larry MacPhail	.25
78	Phil Niekro	.25
79	Lefty Gomez/SP	3.00
80	Lefty Grove/SP	3.00
81	Leo Durocher/SP	3.00
82	Leon Day	.25
83	Gaylord Perry/SP	3.00
84	Lou Boudreau	.25
85	Lou Gehrig	3.00
86	Luke Appling	.25
87	Max Carey	.25
88	Mel Allen/SP	3.00
89	Mel Ott/SP	5.00
90	Mickey Cochrane	.50
91	Mickey Mantle	4.00
92	Brooks Robinson	1.00
93	Monte Irvin	.50
94	Nellie Fox	.50
95	Nolan Ryan/SP	10.00
96	Ozzie Smith/SP	6.00
97	Mike Schmidt	2.00
98	Pee Wee Reese/SP	3.00
99	Phil Rizzuto	.75
100	Ralph Kiner	.50
101	Ray Dandridge	.25
102	Richie Ashburn	.25
103	Rick Ferrell	.25
104	Roberto Clemente	2.00
105	Robin Roberts	.25
106	Robin Yount	1.00
107	Rogers Hornsby	.50
108	Rollie Fingers	.25
109	Roy Campanella	.50
110	Rube Marquard	.25
111	Sam Crawford	.25
112	Steve Carlton	.50
113	Satchel Paige/SP	5.00
114	Sparky Anderson	.25
115	Stan Coveleski	.25
116	Red Schoendienst	.25
117	Ted Williams	3.00
118	Tom Seaver	1.00
119	Tom Yawkey	.25
120	Tony Lazzeri	.25
121	Tony Perez	.25
122	Tris Speaker	.25
123	Ty Cobb	2.00
124	Waite Hoyt/SP	3.00
125	Walter Alston	.25
126	Walter Johnson	.75
127	Warren Spahn	1.00
128	Whitey Ford	.50
129	Willie Stargell	.50
130	Yogi Berra	.75

Blue

Non SP's (1-130):	2-4X
SP's:	1-2X
Production 275 Sets	

Green

No pricing due to scarcity.	
Production 25 Sets	

Autographs

	NM/M
Common Player:	
Inserted 1:196	
Many not priced due to scarcity.	
AL	Alexander Cartwright/1 (6/05 Auction)	7,800
BG	Burleigh Grimes/34	250.00
BI	Billy Herman/30	150.00
BL	Bob Lemon/34	150.00
BL1	Bob Lemon/41	150.00
CH	Carl Hubbell/47	300.00
CH1	Carl Hubbell/63	300.00

EA	Earl Averill/96	125.00
EC	Earle Combs/45	150.00
ES	Enos Slaughter/30	200.00
HC	Harry Caray/29	225.00
HC1	Harry Caray/35	225.00
HG	Hank Greenberg/30	375.00
JD	Joe DiMaggio/30	375.00
JD1	Joe DiMaggio/28	400.00
LB	Lou Boudreau/82	110.00
LB1	Lou Boudreau/49	120.00
LU	Luke Appling/52	150.00
RM	Rube Marquard/40	200.00

Autographs Blue

NM/M
Many not priced due to scarcity.

EA	Earl Averill/50	125.00
HC1	Harry Caray/35	240.00
HN1	Hal Newhouser B2B/29	
		125.00
JD1	Joe DiMaggio/40	375.00

Combo Cuts

No Pricing
Production One Set

Etched in Time

NM/M
Common Player: 3.00
Production 400 Sets
Etched 300: .5-1X
Production 300
Etched 175: .75-1.5X
Production 175

ME	Mel Allen	3.00
RA	Richie Ashburn	4.00
AB	Al Barlick	3.00
LB	Lou Boudreau	3.00
RO	Roy Campanella	4.00
AC	Alexander Cartwright	3.00
HC	Harry Caray	3.00
RC	Roberto Clemente	10.00
TC	Ty Cobb	6.00
EC	Eddie Collins	3.00
DD	Dizzy Dean	3.00
JD	Joe DiMaggio	8.00
DO	Don Drysdale	3.00
LD	Leo Durocher	3.00
JF	Jimmie Foxx	5.00
LO	Lou Gehrig	8.00
CG	Charlie Gehringer	3.00
JG	Josh Gibson	5.00
LG	Lefty Gomez	3.00
HG	Hank Greenberg	5.00
LE	Lefty Grove	3.00
GH	Gabby Hartnett	3.00
RH	Rogers Hornsby	4.00
CH	Carl Hubbell	3.00
TL	Tony Lazzeri	3.00
EL	Ernie Lombardi	3.00
MM	Mickey Mantle	15.00
CM	Christy Mathewson	8.00
JM	Joe McCarthy	3.00
JO	Johnny Mize	3.00
MO	Mel Ott	4.00
SP	Satchel Paige	5.00
PR	Pee Wee Reese	3.00
JR	Jackie Robinson	5.00
BR	Babe Ruth	10.00
TS	Tris Speaker	3.00
CS	Casey Stengel	5.00
HW	Honus Wagner	5.00
TW	Ted Williams	8.00
CY	Cy Young	5.00

Hall Marks Autographs

NM/M
Inserted 1:196
Many not priced due to scarcity.

Greens:		No Pricing
Production 10		
BD1	Bobby Doerr/Black/50	40.00
BM1	Bill Mazeroski/Black/50	40.00
CF1	Carlton Fisk/Black/50	50.00
CY1	Carl Yastrzemski/ Black/45	75.00
DS1	Duke Snider/Black/50	40.00
GC1	Gary Carter/Black/50	30.00
GK1	George Kell/Black/50	20.00
JM1	Juan Marichal/Black/50	35.00
JO1	Joe Morgan/Black/75	30.00
LA1	Luis Aparicio/Black/45	30.00
MI1	Monte Irvin/Black/85	30.00
OS1	Ozzie Smith/Black/45	75.00
PR1	Phil Rizzuto/Black/50	40.00
RF1	Rollie Fingers/Black/99	20.00
RK1	Ralph Kiner/Black/50	30.00
RR1	Robin Roberts/Black/55	40.00
RY1	Robin Yount/Black/45	75.00
TP1	Tony Perez/Black/50	30.00
WS1	Warren Spahn/Black/35	70.00
YB1	Yogi Berra/Black/50	60.00

Historic Impressions

NM/M
Common Player: 3.00
Production 350 Sets
Golds: 1X
Production 200 Sets
Golds 75: 1.5-2X
Production 75
Silvers: 1X
Production 250 Sets

MA	Mel Allen	3.00
RA	Richie Ashburn	5.00
LB	Lou Boudreau	3.00
RO	Roy Campanella	3.00
AC	Alexander Cartwright	3.00
HC	Harry Caray	4.00
RC	Roberto Clemente	15.00
TY	Ty Cobb	8.00
MC	Mickey Cochrane	3.00
EC	Eddie Collins	3.00
DD	Dizzy Dean	5.00
JD	Joe DiMaggio	8.00
DO	Don Drysdale	3.00
LD	Leo Durocher	3.00
JF	Jimmie Foxx	5.00
LO	Lou Gehrig	10.00
CG	Charlie Gehringer	3.00
LG	Lefty Gomez	3.00
HG	Hank Greenberg	6.00
LE	Lefty Grove	3.00
GH	Gabby Hartnett	3.00
RH	Rogers Hornsby	6.00
CH	Carl Hubbell	6.00
TL	Tony Lazzeri	3.00
MM	Mickey Mantle	25.00
CM	Christy Mathewson	6.00
JM	Joe McCarthy	3.00
JM	Johnny Mize	3.00
MO	Mel Ott	6.00
SP	Satchel Paige	6.00
PR	Pee Wee Reese	3.00
JR	Jackie Robinson	8.00
BR	Babe Ruth	15.00
ES	Enos Slaughter	3.00
TS	Tris Speaker	5.00
CS	Casey Stengel	3.00
HW	Honus Wagner	8.00
HO	Hoyt Wilhelm	3.00
TW	Ted Williams	15.00
CY	Cy Young	8.00

Historic Lumber

NM/M
Common Player: 6.00
Inserted 1:12

BR	Babe Ruth/Away/150	125.00
BR1	Babe Ruth/Home/150	125.00
CF	Carlton Fisk/R.Sox/50	15.00
CF1	Carlton Fisk/W.Sox/50	15.00
CY	Carl Yastrzemski. w/Bat/300	20.00
CY1	Carl Yastrzemski. w/Cap/350	20.00
CY2	Carl Yastrzemski. w/Helmet/350	20.00
DW	Dave Winfield/ Padres/350	10.00
DW1	Dave Winfield/ Yanks/350	10.00
FR	Frank Robinson/O's/300	10.00
FR1	Frank Robinson/ Reds/350	10.00
FR2	Frank Robinson/ Angels/350	10.00

GC	Gary Carter/Mets/300	6.00
GC1	Gary Carter/ Helmet/Expos/100	6.00
GC2	Gary Carter/Cap/ Expos/100	6.00
HK	Harmon Killebrew/350	10.00
JB	Johnny Bench. w/Bat/350	10.00
JB1	Johnny Bench/ Swing/350	10.00
JM	Joe Morgan/Reds/350	6.00
JM1	Joe Morgan/Astros/350	6.00
MM	Mickey Mantle/300	100.00
NR	Nolan Ryan/Rgr./225	25.00
OS	Ozzie Smith/Cards/300	15.00
OS1	Ozzie Smith/Cards/350	15.00
RS	Red Schoendienst/ Look Right/165	6.00
RS1	Red Schoendienst/ Look Left/165	6.00
SC	Steve Carlton/350	8.00
TP	Tony Perez/Swing/350	6.00
TP1	Tony Perez/Portrait/350	6.00
TS	Tom Seaver/100	10.00
TW	Ted Williams/ w/3 Bats/150	75.00
TW1	Ted Williams/ Portrait/150	75.00
WS	Willie Stargell/ Arms Down/150	8.00
WS1	Willie Stargell/ Arms Up/150	8.00
YB	Yogi Berra/Shout/350	10.00
YB1	Yogi Berra w/Bat/350	10.00

Historic Lumber Green

NM/M
Common Player:

BR	Babe Ruth/Away/75	140.00
BR1	Babe Ruth/Home/75	140.00
CY	Carl Yastrzemski. w/Bat/125	25.00
CY1	Carl Yastrzemski. w/Cap/125	25.00
CY2	Carl Yastrzemski. w/Helmet/125	25.00
DW	Dave Winfield/ Padres/125	10.00
DW1	Dave Winfield/ Yanks/125	10.00
FR	Frank Robinson/O's/125	10.00
FR1	Frank Robinson/ Reds/125	10.00
FR2	Frank Robinson/ Angels/125	10.00
GC	Gary Carter/Mets/125	6.00
GC1	Gary Carter/Helmet/ Expos/125	6.00
GC2	Gary Carter/ Cap/Expos/125	6.00
HK	Harmon Killebrew/125	10.00
JB	Johnny Bench. w/Bat/125	10.00
JB1	Johnny Bench/ Swing/125	10.00
JM	Joe Morgan/Reds/125	6.00
JM1	Joe Morgan/Astros/125	6.00
MM	Mickey Mantle/75	120.00
NR	Nolan Ryan/Astros/50	50.00
OS	Ozzie Smith/Cards/125	20.00
OS1	Ozzie Smith/ Padres/125	20.00
RS	Red Schoendienst/ Look Right/125	8.00
RS1	Red Schoendienst/ Look Left/125	8.00
SC	Steve Carlton/125	10.00
TP	Tony Perez/Swing/125	6.00
TP1	Tony Perez/Portrait/125	6.00
TS	Tom Seaver/50	15.00
TW	Ted Williams. w/3 Bats/75	75.00
TW1	Ted Williams/ Portrait/75	75.00
WS	Willie Stargell/ Arms Down/125	10.00
WS1	Willie Stargell/ Arms Up/125	10.00
YB	Yogi Berra/Shout/125	10.00
YB1	Yogi Berra w/Bat/125	10.00

Historic Swatches

NM/M
Common Player: 5.00
Inserted 1:12
Blues: .75-1.5X
Production 50 Sets
Greens: .75-1X
Production 160 to 250
Purples: .75-1.5X
Production 75 to 150

BG	Bob Gibson CO/Jsy/350	10.00
BM	Bill Mazeroski/Pants/50	15.00
BW	Billy Williams/Jsy/190	5.00
CF	Carlton Fisk/Pants/350	8.00
CM	Christy Mathewson/ Pants/300	100.00

CS	Casey Stengel/Jsy/275	10.00
CY	Carl Yastrzemski/ Jsy/350	20.00
CY1	Carl Yastrzemski/ Pants/350	20.00
DS	Duke Snider/Jsy/350	10.00
DW1	Dave Winfield/ Twins Jsy/300	8.00
FR	Frank Robinson/ O's Jsy/350	10.00
FR1	Frank Robinson/ Angels Jsy/350	10.00
GC	Gary Carter/Mets Jsy/350	5.00
GC1	Gary Carter/ Expos Jsy/350	5.00
HW	Honus Wagner/ Pants/275	120.00
JB	Johnny Bench/Jsy/150	10.00
JM	Joe Morgan/Jsy/350	5.00
JN	Juan Marichal/Pants/225	5.00
JN1	Juan Marichal/Jsy/48	5.00
LA	Luis Aparicio/Jsy/230	5.00
LB	Lou Boudreau/Jsy/265	5.00
MM	Mickey Mantle/ Pants/350	100.00
NR	Nolan Ryan/ Rgr. Pants/350	25.00
NR1	Nolan Ryan/ Astro Pants/350	25.00
OS	Ozzie Smith/Jsy/85	25.00
RF	Rollie Fingers/Jsy/105	5.00
RY	Robin Yount/ Portrait/Jsy/350	10.00
RY1	Robin Yount/ Swing/Jsy/350	10.00
SA	Sparky Anderson/ Jsy/350	5.00
SC	Steve Carlton/Jsy/350	10.00
SM	Stan Musial/Jsy/350	25.00
TC	Ty Cobb/Pants/350	90.00
TP	Tony Perez/Jsy/350	5.00
TS	Tom Seaver/Jsy/350	10.00
TS1	Tom Seaver/Pants/350	10.00
TW	Ted Williams/Jsy/250	85.00
WA	Walter Alston/ Look Left/Jsy/350	5.00
WA1	Walter Alston/ Ahead/Jsy/350	5.00
WI	Willie Stargell/Jsy/55	15.00
WS	Warren Spahn/ CO/Jsy/350	15.00
YB	Yogi Berra/Jsy/300	10.00

2003 SPx

NM/M
Complete Set (178):
Common Player: .25
Common SP (126-160): 4.00
Production 999
Common Jsy Auto. (161-178): 10.00
Production 1,224 unless noted.
Pack (4): 6.00
Box (18): 90.00

1	Darin Erstad	.50
2	Garret Anderson	.50
3	Tim Salmon	.50
4	Troy Glaus/SP	2.00
5	Luis Gonzalez	.50
6	Randy Johnson	1.50
7	Curt Schilling	.75
8	Lyle Overbay	.25
9	Andruw Jones/SP	3.00
10	Gary Sheffield	.75
11	Rafael Furcal	.40
12	Greg Maddux	2.00
13	Chipper Jones/SP	3.00
14	Tony Batista	.25
15	Rodrigo Lopez	.25
16	Jay Gibbons	.25
17	Byung-Hyun Kim	.25
18	Johnny Damon	1.00
19	Derek Lowe	.50
20	Nomar Garciaparra/SP	4.00
21	Pedro J. Martinez	1.50
22	Manny Ramirez/SP	4.00
23	Mark Prior	1.00
24	Kerry Wood	.50
25	Corey Patterson	.50
26	Sammy Sosa/SP	4.00
27	Moises Alou	.50
28	Magglio Ordonez	.50
29	Frank Thomas	1.00
30	Paul Konerko	.50
31	Bartolo Colon	.25
32	Adam Dunn	1.00
33	Austin Kearns	.50
34	Aaron Boone	.25
35	Ken Griffey Jr./SP	.50
36	Omar Vizquel	.50
37	C.C. Sabathia	.25
38	Jason Davis	.25
39	Travis Hafner	.75
40	Brandon Phillips	.25
41	Larry Walker	.50
42	Preston Wilson	.25
43	Jay Payton	.25
44	Todd Helton	.75

45	Carlos Pena	.25
46	Eric Munson	.25
47	Ivan Rodriguez	1.00
48	Josh Beckett	.50
49	Alex Gonzalez	.25
50	Roy Oswalt	.50
51	Craig Biggio	.50
52	Jeff Bagwell	.75
53	Dontrelle Willis/SP	2.00
54	Mike Sweeney	.25
55	Carlos Beltran	1.00
56	Brent Mayne	.25
57	Hideo Nomo	.75
58	Rickey Henderson	.75
59	Adrian Beltre	.25
60	Miguel Cabrera/SP	4.00
61	Kazuhisa Ishii	.25
62	Ben Sheets	.50
63	Richie Sexson	.25
64	Torii Hunter/SP	2.00
65	Jacque Jones	.25
66	Joe Mays	.25
67	Corey Koskie	.25
68	A.J. Pierzynski	.25
69	Jose Vidro	.25
70	Vladimir Guerrero/SP	4.00
71	Tom Glavine	.50
72	Jose Reyes/SP	4.00
73	Aaron Heilman	.25
74	Mike Piazza	2.00
75	Jorge Posada	.75
76	Mike Mussina	.75
77	Robin Ventura	.25
78	Mariano Rivera	.75
79	Roger Clemens/SP	6.00
80	Jason Giambi	.75
81	Bernie Williams	.75
82	Alfonso Soriano/SP	4.00
83	Derek Jeter	3.00
84	Miguel Tejada/SP	.50
85	Eric Chavez	.50
86	Tim Hudson	.50
87	Barry Zito	.50
88	Mark Mulder	.50
89	Erubiel Durazo	.25
90	Pat Burrell	.50
91	Jim Thome/SP	4.00
92	Bobby Abreu	.50
93	Brian Giles	.50
94	Reggie Sanders/SP	2.00
95	Kenny Lofton	.50
96	Ryan Klesko	.25
97	Sean Burroughs	.25
98	Edgardo Alfonzo	.25
99	Rich Aurilia	.25
100	Jose Cruz Jr.	.25
101	Barry Bonds/SP	8.00
102	Mike Cameron	.25
103	Kazuhiro Sasaki	.25
104	Bret Boone	.25
105	Ichiro Suzuki/SP	5.00
106	J.D. Drew	.50
107	Jim Edmonds	.50
108	Scott Rolen/SP	3.00
109	Matt Morris	.25
110	Tino Martinez	.50
111	Albert Pujols/SP	8.00
112	Damian Rolls	.25
113	Carl Crawford	.50
114	Rocco Baldelli/SP	2.00
115	Hank Blalock	.50
116	Alex Rodriguez/SP	5.00
117	Kevin Mench	.25
118	Rafael Palmeiro	.75
119	Mark Teixeira	.75
120	Shannon Stewart	.25
121	Vernon Wells	.50
122	Josh Phelps	.25
123	Eric Hinske	.25
124	Orlando Hudson	.25
125	Carlos Delgado/SP	3.00
126	Jason Roach RC	4.00
127	Dan Haren	10.00
128	Luis Ayala RC	4.00
129	Bo Hart RC	4.00
130	Wilfredo Ledezma RC	4.00
131	Rick Roberts RC	4.00
132	Miguel Ojeda RC	4.00
133	Aquilino Lopez RC	4.00
134	Roger Deago RC	4.00
135	Arnie Munoz RC	4.00
136	Brent Hoard RC	4.00
137	Terrmel Sledge RC	4.00
138	Ryan Cameron RC	4.00
139	Prentice Redman RC	4.00
140	Clint Barmes RC	5.00
141	Jeremy Griffiths	4.00
142	Jon Leicester RC	4.00
143	Brandon Webb RC	20.00
144	Todd Wellemeyer RC	6.00
145	Felix Sanchez RC	4.00
146	Anthony Ferrari RC	4.00
147	Ian Ferguson RC	4.00
148	Micheal Nakamura RC	4.00
149	Lew Ford RC	8.00
150	Nate Bland RC	4.00
151	Dave Matranga RC	4.00
152	Edgar Gonzalez RC	4.00
153	Carlos Mendez RC	4.00
154	Jason Gilfillan RC	4.00
155	Mike Neu RC	4.00
156	Jason Shiell RC	4.00
157	Jeff Duncan RC	4.00
158	Oscar Villarreal RC	4.00
159	Diegomar Markwell RC	4.00
160	Joe Valentine RC	4.00
161	Hideki Matsui/864 RC	275.00
162	Jose Contreras/800 RC	20.00

163	Willie Eyre RC	10.00
164	Matt Bruback RC	10.00
165	Rett Johnson RC	10.00
166	Jeremy Griffiths	10.00
167	Francisco Cruceta RC	10.00
168	Fernando Cabrera RC	10.00
169	Jhonny Peralta	20.00
170	Shane Bazzell RC	10.00
171	Bobby Madritsch RC	10.00
172	Phil Seibel RC	10.00
173	Josh Willingham RC	20.00
174	Robby Hammock RC	10.00
175	Alejandro Machado RC	10.00
176	David Sanders RC	10.00
177	Matt Kata RC	10.00
178	Heath Bell RC	10.00

Spectrum

Stars (1-125) print run 51-99: 3-6X
Stars (1-125) p/r 26-50: 6-12X
Print run 25 or less not priced.
Numbered to jersey number.
SP's (126-160): .75-1.5X
Production 125

SPX Combos

NM/M
Common Duo: 20.00
Quantity produced listed.

MJ	Hideki Matsui, Derek Jeter/90	100.00
RC	Nolan Ryan, Roger Clemens/90	120.00
SJ	Curt Schilling, Randy Johnson/90	30.00
EG	Darin Erstad, Troy Glaus/90	20.00
GC	Greg Maddux, Chipper Jones/90	50.00
GS	Jason Giambi, Alfonso Soriano/90	30.00
BK	Jeff Bagwell, Jeff Kent/90	25.00
GD	Ken Griffey Jr., Adam Dunn/90	50.00
GR	Ken Griffey Jr., Sammy Sosa/90	50.00
SP	Sammy Sosa, Rafael Palmeiro/90	40.00
MG	Pedro Martinez, Nomar Garciaparra/90	40.00
RG	Alex Rodriguez, Nomar Garciaparra/90	40.00
CM	Jose Contreras, Pedro Martinez/90	40.00
FC	Carlton Fisk, Gary Carter/90	30.00
RR	Cal Ripken Jr., Scott Rolen/90	80.00
JJ	Chipper Jones, Andruw Jones/90	30.00
PM	Rafael Palmeiro, Fred McGriff/90	30.00
RT	Alex Rodriguez, Miguel Tejada/90	30.00
SB	Sammy Sosa, Barry Bonds/90	50.00
SN	Ichiro Suzuki, Hideo Nomo/90	175.00
MS	Hideki Matsui, Ichiro Suzuki/50	350.00
MW	Mickey Mantle, Ted Williams/50	300.00
CC	Jose Contreras, Roger Clemens/50	40.00
CL	Cal Ripken Jr., Lou Gehrig/300	300.00
HJ	Hideki Matsui, Jason Giambi/50	75.00
CA	Cal Ripken Jr., Alex Rodriguez/50	150.00
IA	Ichiro Suzuki, Albert Pujols/50	250.00
NI	Hideo Nomo, Kazuhisa Ishii/50	50.00
MD	Mickey Mantle, Derek Jeter/50	180.00
BT	Barry Bonds, Ted Williams/50	180.00
BM	Barry Bonds, Roger Maris/50	80.00
MB	Mickey Mantle, Barry Bonds/50	150.00
PS	Rafael Palmeiro, Sammy Sosa/90	40.00
RS	Nolan Ryan, Tom Seaver/90	110.00

Stars

NM/M
Common Player: 20.00
Quantity produced listed.

LB	Lance Berkman/590	30.00
PB	Pat Burrell/590	25.00
NM	Nomar Garciaparra/195	80.00
JG	Jason Giambi/315	30.00
TG	Troy Glaus/490	25.00

LG Luis Gonzalez/790 20.00
KG Ken Griffey Jr./690 80.00
VG Vladimir Guerrero/390 50.00
CJ Chipper Jones/195 50.00
MP Mark Prior/490 40.00
CS Curt Schilling/490 40.00

Winning Materials

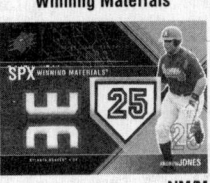

NM/M
Common Player: 5.00
Version 1 Production 375
Golds: 1X
Production 250
Version 2 Production 175
Golds: 1-2X
Production 50
RA1 Roberto Alomar 8.00
RA2 Roberto Alomar 10.00
JB1 Jeff Bagwell 6.00
JB2 Jeff Bagwell 8.00
LB1 Lance Berkman 5.00
LB2 Lance Berkman 5.00
PB1 Pat Burrell 6.00
PB2 Pat Burrell 8.00
RC1 Roger Clemens 15.00
RC2 Roger Clemens 15.00
CD1 Carlos Delgado 6.00
CD2 Carlos Delgado 8.00
RF1 Rafael Furcal 6.00
RF2 Rafael Furcal 8.00
JG1 Jason Giambi 8.00
JG2 Jason Giambi 8.00
TR1 Troy Glaus 6.00
TG2 Troy Glaus 8.00
TG1 Tom Glavine 6.00
TG2 Tom Glavine 5.00
LG1 Luis Gonzalez 5.00
LG2 Luis Gonzalez 5.00
SG1 Shawn Green 5.00
SG2 Shawn Green 5.00
KG1 Ken Griffey Jr. 15.00
KG2 Ken Griffey Jr. 15.00
VG1 Vladimir Guerrero 10.00
VG2 Vladimir Guerrero 12.00
TO1 Todd Helton 8.00
TH2 Todd Helton 10.00
TH1 Torii Hunter 8.00
RJ1 Randy Johnson 10.00
RJ2 Randy Johnson 12.00
AJ1 Andruw Jones 8.00
AJ2 Andruw Jones 8.00
CJ1 Chipper Jones 10.00
CJ2 Chipper Jones 15.00
JK1 Jeff Kent 5.00
JK2 Jeff Kent 5.00
GM1 Greg Maddux 15.00
GM2 Greg Maddux 15.00
MM2 Mickey Mantle 120.00
PM1 Pedro Martinez 10.00
PM2 Pedro Martinez 15.00
HM1 Hideki Matsui 30.00
HM2 Hideki Matsui 30.00
HN1 Hideo Nomo 15.00
HN2 Hideo Nomo 20.00
MP1 Mike Piazza 10.00
MP2 Mike Piazza 15.00
MA1 Mark Prior 10.00
MP2 Mark Prior 10.00
AP1 Albert Pujols 20.00
AP2 Albert Pujols 20.00
MR1 Manny Ramirez 10.00
MR2 Manny Ramirez 10.00
AR1 Alex Rodriguez 10.00
AR2 Alex Rodriguez 12.00
IR1 Ivan Rodriguez 8.00
IR2 Ivan Rodriguez 10.00
CS1 Curt Schilling 8.00
CS2 Curt Schilling 10.00
GS1 Gary Sheffield 6.00
GS2 Gary Sheffield 8.00
AS1 Alfonso Soriano 10.00
AS2 Alfonso Soriano 12.00
SS1 Sammy Sosa 10.00
SS2 Sammy Sosa 15.00
IS1 Ichiro Suzuki 25.00
IS2 Ichiro Suzuki 35.00
MT1 Miguel Tejada 6.00
MT2 Miguel Tejada 8.00
FT1 Frank Thomas 8.00
FT2 Frank Thomas 10.00
JT1 Jim Thome 8.00
JT2 Jim Thome 10.00
BW1 Bernie Williams 8.00
BW2 Bernie Williams 8.00
TW2 Ted Williams 80.00
TW2 Ted Williams/Gold/50 200.00
BZ1 Barry Zito 6.00
BZ2 Barry Zito 8.00

Young Stars

NM/M
Common Player: 8.00
1,295 unless noted.
KA Kurt Ainsworth/1,460 6.00
RB Rocco Baldelli 10.00
JBa Josh Bard 8.00
HB Hank Blalock 10.00

SB Sean Burroughs 8.00
MD Michael Cuddyer/1,156 10.00
AD Adam Dunn 20.00
CG Chris George/1,260 8.00
EH Eric Hinske 8.00
JA Jason Jennings 8.00
NJ Nick Johnson 8.00
JJ Jacque Jones/1,260 12.00
AK Austin Kearns/964 15.00
MK Mike Kinkade 8.00
BM Brett Myers 8.00
RO Roy Oswalt 15.00
JP Josh Phelps 10.00
BP Brandon Phillips 8.00
KS Kirk Saarloos 8.00
MT Mark Teixeira 25.00

2004 SP Authentic

NM/M
Complete Set (191):
Common (1-90): .25
Common RC (91-132, 178-191): 4.00
Production 999
Common SP (133-177): 2.00
Production 999
Pack (5): 5.00
Box (24): 100.00
1 Bret Boone .25
2 Gary Sheffield .50
3 Rafael Palmeiro .75
4 Jorge Posada .50
5 Derek Jeter 3.00
6 Garret Anderson .50
7 Bartolo Colon .40
8 Kevin Brown .40
9 Shea Hillenbrand .25
10 Ryan Klesko .25
11 Bobby Abreu .50
12 Scott Rolen 1.00
13 Alfonso Soriano .75
14 Jason Giambi 1.00
15 Tom Glavine .50
16 Hideo Nomo .50
17 Johan Santana 1.00
18 Sammy Sosa 1.00
19 Rickie Weeks .50
20 Barry Zito .50
21 Kerry Wood .50
22 Austin Kearns .40
23 Shawn Green .40
24 Miguel Cabrera 1.00
25 Richard Hidalgo .25
26 Andruw Jones .75
27 Randy Wolf .25
28 David Ortiz 1.00
29 Roy Oswalt .50
30 Vernon Wells .50
31 Ben Sheets .50
32 Mike Lowell .25
33 Todd Helton .75
34 Jacque Jones .25
35 Mike Sweeney .25
36 Hank Blalock .50
37 Jason Schmidt .50
38 Jeff Kent .40
39 Josh Beckett .50
40 Manny Ramirez 1.00
41 Torii Hunter .50
42 Brian Giles .40
43 Javier Vazquez .25
44 Jim Edmonds .50
45 Dmitri Young .25
46 Preston Wilson .25
47 Jeff Bagwell .75
48 Pedro J. Martinez 1.00
49 Eric Chavez .40
50 Ken Griffey Jr. 2.00
51 Shannon Stewart .25
52 Rafael Furcal .40
53 Brandon Webb .25
54 Juan Pierre .25
55 Roger Clemens 2.00
56 Geoff Jenkins .25
57 Lance Berkman .50
58 Albert Pujols 3.00
59 Frank Thomas .75
60 Edgar Martinez .40
61 Tim Hudson .50
62 Eric Gagne .50
63 Richie Sexson .50
64 Corey Patterson .25
65 Nomar Garciaparra 1.00
66 Hideki Matsui 2.00
67 Mark Teixeira .75
68 Troy Glaus .50
69 Carlos Lee .40
70 Mike Mussina .75
71 Magglio Ordonez .50
72 Roy Halladay .50
73 Ichiro Suzuki 2.00
74 Randy Johnson 1.00
75 Luis Gonzalez .40
76 Mark Prior .75
77 Carlos Beltran .50
78 Ivan Rodriguez .75
79 Alex Rodriguez 2.50
80 Dontrelle Willis .50
81 Mike Piazza 1.00
82 Curt Schilling .75
83 Vladimir Guerrero 1.00
84 Greg Maddux 1.50
85 Jim Thome 1.00
86 Miguel Tejada .50
87 Carlos Delgado .50
88 Jose Reyes .75
89 Matt Morris .25
90 Mark Mulder .40
91 Angel Chavez RC 4.00
92 Brandon Medders RC 4.00
93 Carlos Vasquez RC 4.00
94 Chris Aguila RC 4.00
95 Colby Miller RC 4.00
96 David Crouthers RC 4.00
97 Dennis Sarfate RC 4.00
98 Donnie Kelly RC 4.00
99 Merkin Valdez RC 6.00
100 Eddy Rodriguez RC 4.00
101 Edwin Moreno RC 4.00
102 Enemencio Pacheco RC 4.00
103 Roberto Novoa RC 4.00
104 Greg Dobbs RC 4.00
105 Hector Gimenez RC 4.00
106 Ian Snell RC 6.00
107 Jake Woods RC 4.00
108 Jamie Brown RC 4.00
109 Jason Frasor RC 4.00
110 Jerome Gamble RC 4.00
111 Jerry Gil RC 6.00
112 Jesse Harper RC 4.00
113 Jorge Vasquez RC 4.00
114 Jose Capellan RC 4.00
115 Josh Labandeira RC 4.00
116 Justin Hampson RC 4.00
117 Justin Huisman RC 4.00
118 Justin Leone RC 6.00
119 Lincoln Holdzkom RC 4.00
120 Lino Urdaneta RC 4.00
121 Mike Gosling RC 4.00
122 Mike Johnston RC 4.00
123 Mike Rouse RC 4.00
124 Scott Proctor RC 4.00
125 Roman Colon RC 4.00
126 Ronny Cedeno RC 6.00
127 Ryan Meaux RC 4.00
128 Scott Dohmann RC 4.00
129 Sean Henn RC 6.00
130 Tim Bausher RC 4.00
131 Tim Bittner RC 4.00
132 William Bergolla RC 6.00
133 Rick Ferrell 2.00
134 Joe DiMaggio 6.00
135 Bob Feller 3.00
136 Ted Williams 6.00
137 Stan Musial 5.00
138 Larry Doby 2.00
139 Red Schoendienst 2.00
140 Enos Slaughter 2.00
141 Stan Musial 5.00
142 Mickey Mantle 8.00
143 Ted Williams 6.00
144 Mickey Mantle 8.00
145 Stan Musial 5.00
146 Tom Seaver 3.00
147 Willie McCovey 2.00
148 Bob Gibson 3.00
149 Frank Robinson 3.00
150 Joe Morgan 2.00
151 Billy Williams 2.00
152 Catfish Hunter 2.00
153 Joe Morgan 2.00
154 Joe Morgan 2.00
155 Mike Schmidt 5.00
156 Tommy Lasorda 2.00
157 Robin Yount 4.00
158 Nolan Ryan 8.00
159 John Franco 2.00
160 Nolan Ryan 8.00
161 Ken Griffey Jr. 4.00
162 Cal Ripken Jr. 8.00
163 Ken Griffey Jr. 5.00
164 Gary Sheffield 2.00
165 Fred McGriff 2.00
166 Hideo Nomo 2.00
167 Mike Piazza 2.00
168 Sandy Alomar Jr. 2.00
169 Roberto Alomar 2.00
170 Ted Williams 6.00
171 Pedro J. Martinez 2.00
172 Derek Jeter 8.00
173 Cal Ripken Jr. 8.00
174 Torii Hunter 2.00
175 Alfonso Soriano 3.00
176 Hank Blalock 2.00
177 Ichiro Suzuki 4.00
178 Orlando Rodriguez RC 4.00
179 Ramon Ramirez RC 4.00
180 Kazuo Matsui RC 6.00
181 Kevin Cave RC 4.00
182 John Gall RC 4.00
183 Freddy Guzman RC 4.00
184 Chris Oxspring RC 4.00
185 Rusty Tucker RC 4.00
186 Jorge Sequea RC 4.00
187 Carlos Hines RC 4.00
188 Luis Gonzalez 4.00
189 Ryan Wing 4.00
190 Jeff Bennett RC 4.00
191 Luis Gonzalez 4.00

Silver

Stars (1-90): 2-4X
Production 499
SP (91-132, 178-191): 1X
Production 249

Gold

Stars (1-90): 4-8X
Gold SP,(91-132, 178-191): 2X
Production 99
Gold (133-177): 1-1.5X
Production 499

Chirography

NM/M
Bronze: 1X
Production 65
Bronze Duo Tone: 1X
Production 60
Gold: 1-1.5X
Production 40
Gold Duo Tone: No Pricing
Production 20
Silver: 1X
Production 60
Silver Duo Tone: 1.5-2X
Production 30
Duo Tone: 1X
Production 75
AB Bobby Abreu 15.00
GA Garret Anderson 15.00
RB Rocco Baldelli 20.00
JB Josh Beckett 20.00
CB Carlos Beltran 30.00
HB Hank Blalock 20.00
BB Bret Boone 20.00
MC Miguel Cabrera 40.00
EC Eric Chavez 20.00
DE Dennis Eckersley 30.00
WE Willie Eyre 8.00
EG Eric Gagne 30.00
JG Juan Gonzalez 20.00
KG Ken Griffey Jr. 120.00
TH Travis Hafner 15.00
HY Roy Halladay 20.00
RH Robby Hammock 10.00
BH Bo Hart 8.00
HE Runelvys Hernandez 8.00
HI Bobby Hill 10.00
DJ Derek Jeter 150.00
JL Jacque Jones 15.00
AK Austin Kearns 15.00
CL Cliff Lee 15.00
AL Al Leiter 15.00
PL Paul LoDuca 15.00
JL Javy Lopez 15.00
ML Mike Lowell 15.00
EM Edgar Martinez 25.00
RO Roy Oswalt 20.00
PA Corey Patterson 15.00
PI Mike Piazza 125.00
CP Colin Porter 10.00
JP Jorge Posada 25.00
MP Mark Prior 30.00
HR Horacio Ramirez 15.00
JR Jose Reyes 35.00
CR Cal Ripken Jr. 100.00
JS Jae Weong Seo 15.00
BS Ben Sheets 20.00
SM John Smoltz 60.00
MT Mark Teixeira 25.00
JV Javier Vazquez 20.00
CW Chien-Ming Wang 125.00
RW Rickie Weeks 15.00
BW Brandon Webb 15.00
VW Vernon Wells 15.00
JW Jerome Williams 10.00
DW Dontrelle Willis 30.00
KW Kerry Wood 25.00
DY Delmon Young 20.00
BZ Barry Zito 20.00

Chirography Dual

NM/M
Common Duo 40.00
Production 50 Sets
BC Bret Boone, Eric Chavez 50.00
BL Mike Lowell, Josh Beckett 50.00
BP Corey Patterson, Carlos Beltran 50.00
BT Hank Blalock, Mark Teixeira 50.00
EG Dennis Eckersley, Eric Gagne 50.00
HW Vernon Wells, Roy Halladay 40.00
JM Johnny Bench, Mike Piazza 200.00
KG Ken Griffey Jr., Austin Kearns 100.00
PB Yogi Berra, Jorge Posada 100.00
RR Alex Rodriguez, Cal Ripken Jr. 400.00
SG Ken Griffey Jr., Ichiro Suzuki 375.00
SM Stan Musial, Ozzie Smith 175.00
WC Miguel Cabrera, Dontrelle Willis 70.00
WJ Chien-Ming Wang, Derek Jeter 350.00
WR Nolan Ryan, Kerry Wood 225.00
WW Dontrelle Willis, Brandon Webb 50.00
YW Delmon Young, Rickie Weeks 40.00
ZC Eric Chavez, Barry Zito 50.00

Chirography Triple

NM/M
Production 25 Sets
BWR Kerry Wood, Nolan Ryan, Josh Beckett 250.00
FBB Johnny Bench, Carlton Fisk, Yogi Berra 300.00
GSM Bob Gibson, Stan Musial, Ozzie Smith 220.00
JVB Derek Jeter, Yogi Berra, Javier Vazquez 250.00
PRC Jose Reyes, Miguel Cabrera, Colin Porter 100.00
RBT Hank Blalock, Mark Teixeira, Alex Rodriguez 250.00
RRR Alex Rodriguez, Cal Ripken Jr., Phil Rizzuto 400.00
SJB Rocco Baldelli, Jacque Jones, Ichiro Suzuki 275.00
WLE Chien-Ming Wang, Willie Eyre, Cliff Lee 275.00
WPB Mark Prior, Josh Beckett, Brandon Webb 250.00
YYM Robin Yount, Carl Yastrzemski, Stan Musial 300.00
ZHO Barry Zito, Roy Oswalt, Roy Halladay 200.00

Chirography Quad

No Pricing
Production 10 Sets

Chirography Hall of Famers

NM/M
Production 40 Sets
Duo Tone: No Pricing
Production 25
LA Luis Aparicio 20.00
JB Johnny Bench 60.00
YB Yogi Berra 50.00
BD Bob Doerr 30.00
DE Dennis Eckersley 30.00
CF Carlton Fisk 30.00
BG Bob Gibson 40.00
MI Monte Irvin 20.00
AK Al Kaline 50.00
HK Harmon Killebrew 65.00
RK Ralph Kiner 25.00
PM Paul Molitor 30.00
SM Stan Musial 100.00
TP Tony Perez 30.00
KP Kirby Puckett 100.00
PR Phil Rizzuto 40.00
RR Robin Roberts 40.00
BR Brooks Robinson 40.00
NR Nolan Ryan 120.00
MS Mike Schmidt 120.00
TS Tom Seaver 40.00
OS Ozzie Smith 65.00
DS Duke Snider 30.00
CY Carl Yastrzemski 75.00
RY Robin Yount 75.00

Future Watch Autograph

NM/M
Production 295
91 Angel Chavez 8.00
92 Brandon Medders 8.00
93 Carlos Vasquez 10.00
94 Chris Aguila 8.00
95 Colby Miller 10.00
96 David Crouthers 10.00
97 Dennis Sarfate 8.00
98 Donnie Kelly 15.00
99 Merkin Valdez 15.00
100 Eddy Rodriguez 15.00
101 Edwin Moreno 10.00
102 Enemencio Pacheco 8.00
103 Roberto Novoa 8.00
104 Greg Dobbs 8.00
105 Hector Gimenez 8.00
106 Ian Snell 30.00
107 Jake Woods 10.00
108 Jamie Brown 10.00
109 Jason Frasor 10.00
110 Jerome Gamble 8.00
111 Jerry Gil 12.00
112 Jesse Harper 8.00
113 Jorge Vasquez 12.00
114 Jose Capellan 10.00
115 Josh Labandeira 10.00
116 Justin Hampson 8.00
117 Justin Huisman 8.00
118 Justin Leone 15.00
119 Lincoln Holdzkom 8.00
120 Lino Urdaneta 10.00
121 Mike Gosling 10.00
122 Mike Johnston 10.00
123 Mike Rouse 10.00
124 Scott Proctor 15.00
125 Roman Colon 15.00
126 Ronny Cedeno 15.00
127 Ryan Meaux 15.00
128 Scott Dohmann 8.00
129 Sean Henn 15.00
130 Tim Bausher 10.00
131 Tim Bittner 8.00
132 William Bergolla 10.00
178 Orlando Rodriguez 10.00
179 Ramon Ramirez 10.00
181 Kevin Cave 10.00
182 John Gall 15.00
183 Freddy Guzman 10.00
184 Chris Oxspring 8.00
185 Rusty Tucker 10.00
186 Jorge Sequea 10.00
187 Carlos Hines 8.00
188 Luis Gonzalez 10.00
189 Ryan Wing 10.00
190 Jeff Bennett 10.00
191 Luis Gonzalez 10.00

USA Signature

NM/M
Production 445 Sets
Reds: 1.5X
Production 50
USA-1 Ernie Young 6.00
USA-2 Chris Burke 12.00
USA-3 Jesse Crain 15.00
USA-4 Justin Duchscherer 15.00
USA-5 J.D. Durbin 10.00
USA-6 Gerald Laird 8.00
USA-7 John Grabow 8.00
USA-8 Gabe Gross 15.00
USA-9 J.J. Hardy 15.00
USA-10 Jeremy Reed 15.00
USA-11 Graham Koonce 10.00
USA-12 Mike Lamb 10.00
USA-13 Justin Leone 15.00
USA-14 Ryan Madson 12.00
USA-15 Joe Mauer 50.00
USA-16 Todd Williams 6.00
USA-17 Horacio Ramirez 15.00
USA-18 Mike Rouse 6.00
USA-19 Jason Stanford 8.00
USA-20 John Van Benschoten 10.00
USA-21 Grady Sizemore 40.00

2004 SP Game-Used Patch

NM/M
Complete Set (119):
Common (1-60): 2.00
Common (61-90): 2.00
Quantity produced listed.
Common (91-119): 6.00
Production 375
Box (1:Pack): 125.00
1 Miguel Cabrera 4.00
2 Alex Rodriguez 10.00
3 Edgar Renteria 2.50
4 Juan Gonzalez 2.50
5 Mike Lowell 2.50
6 Andruw Jones 3.00
7 Eric Chavez 2.00
8 Jim Edmonds 2.00
9 Mike Piazza 5.00

10	Angel Berroa	2.00
11	Eric Gagne	3.00
12	Jody Gerut	2.00
13	Orlando Cabrera	2.00
14	Austin Kearns	3.00
15	Frank Thomas	3.00
16	Johan Santana	3.00
17	Randy Johnson	4.00
18	Preston Wilson	2.00
19	Garret Anderson	2.50
20	Jorge Posada	3.00
21	Rich Harden	2.00
22	Barry Zito	2.50
23	Gary Sheffield	3.00
24	Jose Reyes	3.00
25	Roy Halladay	2.00
26	Ben Sheets	2.00
27	Geoff Jenkins	2.00
28	Josh Beckett	3.00
29	Roy Oswalt	2.50
30	Bobby Abreu	2.50
31	Hank Blalock	2.50
32	Kerry Wood	2.50
33	Ryan Klesko	2.00
34	Rafael Furcal	2.00
35	Tom Glavine	2.50
36	Kevin Brown	2.50
37	Scott Rolen	3.00
38	Bret Boone	2.50
39	Ichiro Suzuki	6.00
40	Lance Berkman	3.00
41	Tim Hudson	2.50
42	Carlos Delgado	3.00
43	Ivan Rodriguez	3.00
44	Luis Gonzalez	2.00
45	Torii Hunter	2.00
46	Carlos Lee	2.00
47	Jacque Jones	2.00
48	Manny Ramirez	3.00
49	Troy Glaus	2.50
50	Corey Patterson	2.00
51	Jason Schmidt	2.50
52	Mark Mulder	2.00
53	Vernon Wells	2.00
54	Curt Schilling	4.00
55	Javy Lopez	2.50
56	Mark Prior	3.00
57	Dontrelle Willis	2.50
58	Derek Jeter	10.00
59	Jeff Bagwell	3.00
60	Marlon Byrd	2.00
61	Rafael Palmeiro/500	3.00
62	Kevin Millwood/165	2.00
63	Greg Maddux/273	6.00
64	Adam Dunn/400	3.00
65	Richie Sexson/469	3.00
66	Magglio Ordonez/567	2.00
67	Hideo Nomo/236	2.00
68	Albert Pujols/194	10.00
69	Rocco Baldelli/368	3.00
70	Mark Teixeira/86	4.00
71	Jason Giambi/660	3.00
72	Alfonso Soriano/230	4.00
73	Roger Clemens/300	8.00
74	Miguel Tejada/359	2.00
75	Jeff Kent/684	3.00
76	Bernie Williams/342	3.00
77	Sammy Sosa/470	6.00
78	Mike Mussina/641	3.00
79	Jim Thome/334	4.00
80	Brian Giles/506	2.00
81	Shawn Green/234	2.00
82	Mike Sweeney/340	2.00
83	John Smoltz/262	3.00
84	Carlos Beltran/319	3.00
85	Todd Helton/384	3.00
86	Nomar Garciaparra/372	4.00
87	Ken Griffey Jr./481	8.00
88	Chipper Jones/633	4.00
89	Vladimir Guerrero/226	4.00
90	Pedro Martinez/313	6.00
91	Brandon Medders RC	6.00
92	Colby Miller RC	6.00
93	David Crouthers RC	6.00
94	Dennis Sarfate RC	8.00
95	Donald Kelly RC	6.00
96	Alec Zumwalt RC	6.00
97	Chris Aguila RC	6.00
98	Greg Dobbs RC	6.00
99	Ian Snell RC	8.00
100	Jake Woods RC	6.00
101	Jamie Brown RC	6.00
102	Jason Frasor RC	6.00
103	Jerome Gamble RC	6.00
104	Jesse Harper RC	6.00
105	Josh Labandeira RC	6.00
106	Justin Hampson RC	6.00
107	Justin Huisman RC	6.00
108	Justin Leone RC	6.00
109	Lincoln Holdzkom RC	6.00
110	Mike Bumatay RC	6.00
111	Mike Gosling	6.00
112	Mike Johnston RC	6.00
113	Mike Rouse	6.00
114	Nick Regilio RC	6.00
115	Ryan Meaux RC	6.00
116	Scott Dohmann RC	6.00
117	Sean Henn	8.00
118	Tim Bausher RC	6.00
119	Tim Bittner RC	6.00

Logo Threads
No Pricing
Production One Set

Logo Threads Autograph

No Pricing
Production One Set

"All-Star Patch Autograph"
Production 10 Sets

All-Star Patch Auto-Dual
Production 10 Sets

All-Star Patch Gold
NM/M
Production 50 Sets

AP	Albert Pujols	75.00
AR	Alex Rodriguez	50.00
AS	Alfonso Soriano	25.00
BZ	Barry Zito	25.00
CD	Carlos Delgado	20.00
CJ	Chipper Jones	30.00
CS	Curt Schilling	35.00
DJ	Derek Jeter	85.00
EC	Eric Chavez	20.00
FT	Frank Thomas	35.00
GS	Gary Sheffield	20.00
HE	Todd Helton	25.00
HN	Hideo Nomo	50.00
IS	Ichiro Suzuki	80.00
JG	Juan Gonzalez	20.00
JT	Jim Thome	30.00
KG	Ken Griffey Jr.	50.00
MP	Mark Prior	30.00
SS	Sammy Sosa	40.00
TH	Tim Hudson	25.00
VW	Vernon Wells	20.00

All-Star Patch Number
NM/M
Quantity produced listed.

AJ	Andruw Jones/25	30.00
AP	Andy Pettitte/46	25.00
BZ	Barry Zito/50	30.00
CD	Carlos Delgado/25	25.00
CS	Curt Schilling/38	30.00
FT	Frank Thomas/35	40.00
GM	Greg Maddux/31	50.00
IS	Ichiro Suzuki/50	65.00
JG	Juan Gonzalez/19	35.00
JP	Jorge Posada/20	30.00
JT	Jim Thome/25	30.00
KG	Ken Griffey Jr./30	60.00
MM	Mike Mussina/35	30.00
MO	Magglio Ordonez/30	25.00
PM	Pedro Martinez/45	35.00
RC	Roger Clemens/22	50.00
RH	Roy Halladay/32	25.00
RP	Rafael Palmeiro/25	30.00
SG	Shawn Green/15	30.00
SR	Scott Rolen/27	35.00
SS	Sammy Sosa/21	50.00

Famous Nicknames
NM/M
Quantity produced listed

BR	Brooks Robinson/23	25.00
CR	Cal Ripken Jr./21	140.00
CY	Carl Yastrzemski/23	70.00
DM	Don Mattingly/14	50.00
DS	Darryl Strawberry/23	25.00
ES	Duke Snider/18	45.00
FT	Frank Thomas/14	40.00
GA	Sparky Anderson/27	25.00
GC	Gary Carter/19	30.00
HK	Harmon Killebrew/22	25.00
JF	Nellie Fox/19	120.00
JG	Juan Gonzalez/15	35.00
JH	"Catfish" Hunter/15	35.00
KG	Ken Griffey Jr./15	80.00
LB	Yogi Berra/19	50.00
MM	Mike Mussina/13	35.00
NR	Nolan Ryan/27	60.00
OC	Orlando Cepeda/17	25.00
OS	Ozzie Smith/19	60.00
PN	Phil Niekro/24	25.00
RC	Roger Clemens/20	60.00
RI	Phil Rizzuto/13	50.00
RJ	Randy Johnson/16	40.00
RY	Robin Yount/20	40.00
TS	Tom Seaver/20	60.00
SM	Stan Musial/22	85.00
SS	Sammy Sosa/15	50.00
WS	Willie Stargell/21	40.00

Famous Nicknames Autograph
NM/M
Production 50 Sets

AD	Andre Dawson	45.00
AR	Alex Rodriguez	150.00
BM	Bill Mazeroski	65.00
BR	Brooks Robinson	60.00
DM	Don Mattingly	120.00
FT	Frank Thomas	70.00
HK	Harmon Killebrew	70.00
HM	Hideki Matsui	350.00
JB	Jeff Bagwell	80.00
JG	Juan Gonzalez	50.00
KG	Ken Griffey Jr.	160.00
LJ	Chipper Jones	80.00
MM	Mike Mussina	60.00
NR	Nolan Ryan	125.00
OS	Ozzie Smith	90.00
PN	Phil Niekro	45.00
RC	Roger Clemens	150.00
RY	Robin Yount	80.00
TS	Tom Seaver	65.00
WI	Dontrelle Willis	60.00

Hall of Fame Numbers
NM/M
Quantity produced listed.

AJ	Andruw Jones/25	30.00
BG	Bob Gibson/45	35.00
BW	Billy Williams/26	20.00
CD	Carlos Delgado/25	25.00
CH	Jim "Catfish" Hunter/27	40.00
CL	Roger Clemens/22	50.00
CS	Curt Schilling/38	25.00
DD	Don Drysdale/50	35.00
DS	Don Sutton/25	25.00
EG	Eric Gagne/38	25.00
EM	Eddie Mathews/41	50.00
FR	Frank Robinson/20	25.00
FT	Frank Thomas/35	40.00
GL	Tom Glavine/47	25.00
GM	Greg Maddux/31	45.00
GO	Juan Gonzalez/35	35.00
GP	Gaylord Perry/36	25.00
HE	Todd Helton/17	35.00
IS	Ichiro Suzuki/50	65.00
JC	Jose Canseco/33	25.00
JG	Jason Giambi/25	30.00
JI	Jim Thome/25	30.00
JP	Jim Palmer/22	35.00
KG	Ken Griffey Jr./30	60.00
MA	Juan Marichal/27	25.00
MP	Mike Piazza/31	40.00
MR	Manny Ramirez/24	30.00
MS	Mike Schmidt/20	60.00
MZ	Pedro Martinez/45	25.00
NR	Nolan Ryan/34	70.00
OC	Orlando Cepeda/30	20.00
OM	Mark Prior/22	40.00
RC	Roberto Clemente/21	200.00
RF	Rollie Fingers/34	25.00
RH	Rickey Henderson/25	40.00
RP	Rafael Palmeiro/25	30.00
RY	Robin Yount/19	45.00
SC	Steve Carlton/32	30.00
SG	Shawn Green/15	25.00
SR	Scott Rolen/27	30.00
SS	Sammy Sosa/21	50.00
TG	Tony Gwynn/19	45.00
TH	Tim Hudson/15	25.00
TS	Tom Seaver/41	25.00
WB	Wade Boggs/26	30.00
WS	Warren Spahn/21	65.00

Hall of Fame Numbers Autograph
Production 10 Sets

Hall of Fame Numbers Auto. Dual
Production 10 Sets

Historic Cut Signatures
Production One Set

Legendary Fabrics
NM/M
Production 50 unless noted.

BE	Johnny Bench	20.00
BG	Bob Gibson	30.00
BW	Billy Williams	25.00
CH	"Catfish" Hunter	25.00
CR	Cal Ripken Jr.	60.00
CY	Carl Yastrzemski/31	45.00
EM	Eddie Mathews	35.00
FR	Frank Robinson	25.00
GP	Gaylord Perry	20.00
HK	Harmon Killebrew	40.00
JC	Jose Canseco	40.00
JM	Joe Morgan	20.00
JT	Joe Torre	25.00
LA	Luis Aparicio	20.00
LD	Leo Durocher	30.00
MS	Mike Schmidt	40.00
NR	Nolan Ryan	50.00
OC	Orlando Cepeda	20.00
OS	Ozzie Smith	35.00
PO	Paul O'Neill	20.00
RF	Rollie Fingers	20.00
RY	Robin Yount	35.00
SC	Steve Carlton	25.00
TS	Tom Seaver	30.00
WS	Warren Spahn	40.00

Legendary Fabrics Auto. Dual
NM/M
Production 25 unless noted.

AD	Andre Dawson	60.00
BE	Johnny Bench	90.00
BR	Brooks Robinson	90.00
BW	Billy Williams	65.00
CR	Cal Ripken Jr.	275.00
CY	Carl Yastrzemski/17	125.00
DE	Dwight Evans	60.00
DM	Don Mattingly	150.00
DS	Don Sutton	65.00
FL	Fred Lynn	70.00
FR	Frank Robinson	75.00
GP	Gaylord Perry	40.00
HK	Harmon Killebrew	100.00
JC	Jose Canseco	100.00
JM	Joe Morgan	50.00
JP	Jim Palmer	60.00
JT	Joe Torre	70.00
KP	Kirby Puckett	100.00
LA	Luis Aparicio	70.00
LB	Lou Brock/13	125.00
NR	Nolan Ryan	200.00
OC	Orlando Cepeda	50.00
OS	Ozzie Smith	100.00
PM	Paul Molitor	75.00
PO	Paul O'Neill	70.00
RC	Roger Clemens	150.00
RF	Rollie Fingers	65.00
RY	Robin Yount	120.00
SG	Steve Garvey	60.00
ST	Darryl Strawberry	65.00
TG	Tony Gwynn	120.00
TS	Tom Seaver	85.00
WB	Wade Boggs	100.00
WI	Maury Wills	50.00

Legendary Combo Cuts
Production One Set

Masters
NM/M
Quantity produced listed.

AJ	Andruw Jones/25	25.00
BE	Josh Beckett/25	40.00
CD	Carlos Delgado/25	25.00
CS	Curt Schilling/38	25.00
FT	Frank Thomas/35	30.00
GM	Greg Maddux/31	45.00
GO	Juan Gonzalez/19	30.00
HE	Todd Helton/17	35.00
IS	Ichiro Suzuki/50	65.00
JG	Jason Giambi/25	30.00
JP	Jorge Posada/20	30.00
JT	Jim Thome/25	30.00
KG	Ken Griffey Jr./30	60.00
MO	Magglio Ordonez/30	20.00
MP	Mark Prior/22	40.00
MR	Manny Ramirez/24	25.00
PI	Mike Piazza/31	40.00
PM	Pedro Martinez/45	25.00
RC	Roger Clemens/22	50.00
RH	Roy Halladay/32	25.00
SG	Shawn Green/15	25.00
SR	Scott Rolen/27	30.00
SS	Sammy Sosa/21	50.00
TH	Tim Hudson/15	25.00

MVP Patch
NM/M
Production 25 Sets

AR	Alex Rodriguez	60.00
BR	Brooks Robinson	50.00
BW	Bernie Williams	35.00
CJ	Chipper Jones	40.00
CR	Cal Ripken Jr.	90.00
CS	Curt Schilling	35.00
DJ	Derek Jeter	75.00
FT	Frank Thomas	40.00
GA	Garret Anderson	30.00
IS	Ichiro Suzuki	75.00
IV	Ivan Rodriguez	40.00
JB	Josh Beckett	30.00
JG	Jason Giambi	30.00
KG	Ken Griffey Jr.	60.00
MP	Mike Piazza	50.00
MT	Miguel Tejada	40.00
PM	Pedro Martinez	45.00
RC	Roger Clemens	60.00
RJ	Randy Johnson	50.00
SS	Sammy Sosa	40.00
TG	Troy Glaus	25.00

Premium Patch
NM/M
Production 50 unless noted.

AD	Adam Dunn	30.00
AP	Albert Pujols	50.00
AR	Alex Rodriguez	50.00
AR1	Alex Rodriguez/Yankees	65.00
AS	Alfonso Soriano/34	35.00
BE	Josh Beckett	25.00
BW	Bernie Williams	25.00
BZ	Barry Zito	25.00
CD	Carlos Delgado	20.00
CJ	Chipper Jones	35.00
CS	Curt Schilling	25.00
DJ	Derek Jeter	60.00
DW	Dontrelle Willis	20.00
EC	Eric Chavez	20.00
FT	Frank Thomas	40.00
GM	Greg Maddux	40.00
GO	Juan Gonzalez	25.00
HM	Hideki Matsui/17	120.00
IR	Ivan Rodriguez	30.00
IS	Ichiro Suzuki	65.00
JB	Jeff Bagwell	30.00
JG	Jason Giambi	30.00
JP	Jorge Posada	30.00
JT	Jim Thome	30.00
KB	Kevin Brown	30.00
KG	Ken Griffey Jr.	50.00
MO	Magglio Ordonez	30.00
MP	Mark Prior	30.00
MR	Manny Ramirez	30.00
MT	Miguel Tejada	20.00
PI	Mike Piazza	35.00
NR	Nolan Ryan	50.00
PM	Pedro Martinez	30.00
RC	Roger Clemens	30.00
RH	Roy Halladay	20.00
RI	Mariano Rivera	30.00
RJ	Randy Johnson	30.00
RP	Rafael Palmeiro	30.00
SG	Shawn Green	20.00
SR	Scott Rolen	30.00
SS	Sammy Sosa	35.00
TE	Mark Teixeira	20.00
TG	Tom Glavine	25.00
TH	Tim Hudson	25.00

Premium Patch Autograph
NM/M
Production 50 unless noted.

AK	Austin Kearns	45.00
AR	Alex Rodriguez	150.00
BZ	Barry Zito	60.00
CD	Carlos Delgado	50.00
DW	Dontrelle Willis	60.00
EC	Eric Chavez	40.00
EG	Eric Gagne	60.00
HM	Hideki Matsui	350.00
IR	Ivan Rodriguez	80.00
IS	Ichiro Suzuki	300.00
KB	Kevin Brown	45.00
KG	Ken Griffey Jr.	160.00
MP	Mark Prior	60.00
MT	Miguel Tejada	50.00
NG	Nomar Garciaparra/33	140.00
RC	Roger Clemens	150.00
SG	Shawn Green	50.00
TH	Tim Hudson	50.00
TG	Troy Glaus	50.00
VG	Vladimir Guerrero	75.00

Significant Numbers
NM/M
Quantity produced listed.

CR	Cal Ripken Jr./21	120.00
CS	Curt Schilling/16	40.00
CY	Carl Yastrzemski/23	65.00
DS	Darryl Strawberry/17	25.00
EM	Eddie Mathews/18	50.00
FT	Frank Thomas/14	50.00
GM	Greg Maddux/18	50.00
GO	Juan Gonzalez/15	40.00
GS	Gary Sheffield/16	50.00
JB	Jeff Bagwell/13	50.00
KG	Ken Griffey Jr./15	75.00
NR	Nolan Ryan/27	50.00
PO	Paul O'Neill/17	25.00
RC	Roger Clemens/20	50.00
RF	Rollie Fingers/17	25.00
RJ	Randy Johnson/16	25.00
RP	Rafael Palmeiro/18	40.00
SN	Duke Snider/18	50.00
SS	Sammy Sosa/15	50.00
TG	Tom Glavine/17	30.00
TS	Tom Seaver/20	40.00

Significant Numbers Autograph
NM/M
Production 50 unless noted.

AR	Alex Rodriguez	150.00
BA	Bobby Abreu	40.00
BG	Brian Giles	40.00
BW	Bernie Williams	100.00
BZ	Barry Zito	60.00
CD	Carlos Delgado	50.00
CJ	Chipper Jones	90.00
EC	Eric Chavez	40.00
EG	Eric Gagne	40.00
GM	Greg Maddux	110.00
HE	Todd Helton	60.00
GO	Juan Gonzalez	50.00
HM	Hideki Matsui	350.00
KB	Kevin Brown	45.00
KG	Ken Griffey Jr.	160.00
LB	Lou Brock/16	50.00
LG	Luis Gonzalez	50.00
MM	Mike Mussina	60.00
MP	Mike Piazza	185.00
MS	Mike Schmidt	200.00
MT	Miguel Tejada	50.00
NR	Nolan Ryan	140.00
PB	Pat Burrell	50.00
PO	Paul O'Neill	65.00
PR	Mark Prior	65.00
RA	Roberto Alomar	60.00
RB	Rocco Baldelli	55.00
RF	Rollie Fingers	40.00
RO	Roy Oswalt	40.00
RP	Rafael Palmeiro	70.00
RS	Ryne Sandberg	90.00
SG	Shawn Green	50.00
TG	Tom Glavine	60.00
TH	Tim Hudson	50.00
VG	Vladimir Guerrero	75.00

Significant Numbers Auto. Dual

NM/M
Production 25 unless noted.

AR	Alex Rodriguez	200.00
BA	Bobby Abreu	50.00
BG	Brian Giles	50.00
BW	Bernie Williams	120.00
BZ	Barry Zito	80.00
CD	Carlos Delgado	70.00
CJ	Chipper Jones	100.00
DW	Dontrelle Willis	60.00
EC	Eric Chavez	65.00
EG	Eric Gagne	80.00
GI	Bob Gibson	100.00
GL	Troy Glaus	70.00
GM	Greg Maddux	90.00
HE	Todd Helton	85.00
GO	Juan Gonzalez	60.00
HM	Hideki Matsui	500.00
KB	Kevin Brown	65.00
KG	Ken Griffey Jr.	200.00
KP	Kirby Puckett	100.00
LB	Lou Brock/14	50.00
LG	Luis Gonzalez	50.00
MM	Mike Mussina	80.00
MP	Mike Piazza	200.00
MS	Mike Schmidt	160.00
MT	Miguel Tejada	50.00
NR	Nolan Ryan	200.00
PB	Pat Burrell	50.00
PO	Paul O'Neill	80.00
RA	Roberto Alomar	80.00
RF	Rollie Fingers	65.00
RP	Rafael Palmeiro	100.00
RS	Ryne Sandberg	150.00
SG	Shawn Green	60.00
TG	Tom Glavine	50.00
TH	Tim Hudson	75.00
VG	Vladimir Guerrero	100.00
TO	Tony Gwynn	120.00
TS	Tom Seaver	85.00

Star Potential Patch
NM/M
Quantity produced listed

BW	Brandon Webb/50	25.00
CP	Corey Patterson/20	25.00
DW	Dontrelle Willis/35	30.00
HA	Roy Halladay/32	30.00
IS	Ichiro Suzuki/50	65.00
HB	Josh Beckett/21	30.00
LB	Lance Berkman/17	30.00
MM	Mark Mulder/20	30.00
MP	Mark Prior/22	30.00
MT	Mark Teixeira/23	25.00
RH	Rich Harden/40	25.00
RO	Roy Oswalt/44	25.00
RW	Rickie Weeks/23	20.00
TG	Troy Glaus/25	25.00
TH	Tim Hudson/15	30.00

Stellar Combos
NM/M
Production 25 unless noted.

AD	Derek Jeter, Alfonso Soriano	75.00
AJ	Alex Rodriguez, Jim Thome, Bobby Abreu	40.00
BK	Jeff Bagwell, Jeff Kent	30.00
BT	Mark Teixeira, Hank Blalock	40.00
CA	Roberto Alomar, Joe Carter	50.00
CO	Roger Clemens, Roy Oswalt	60.00
CR	Randy Johnson, Curt Schilling	40.00
DG	Jason Giambi, Carlos Delgado	40.00

DK	Austin Kearns, Adam Dunn	40.00
GH	Eric Gagne, Trevor Hoffman	40.00
GT	Greg Maddux, Tom Glavine	65.00
JJ	Andruw Jones, Chipper Jones	50.00
KR	Nolan Ryan, Jerry Koosman	100.00
LP	Mike Piazza, Al Leiter	50.00
LS	Fred Lynn, Ichiro Suzuki	75.00
MG	Don Mattingly, Jason Giambi	80.00
MT	Frank Thomas, Edgar Martinez	50.00
MY	Paul Molitor, Robin Yount	60.00
NB	Hideo Nomo, Kevin Brown	40.00
NY	Alfonso Soriano, Jose Reyes	40.00
PC	Mark Prior, Roger Clemens	60.00
PE	Albert Pujols, Jim Edmonds	80.00
PM	Mike Mussina, Andy Pettitte	50.00
PP	Mike Piazza, Jorge Posada	60.00
PS	Sammy Sosa, Rafael Palmeiro	50.00
RB	Ivan Rodriguez, Josh Beckett	50.00
RJ	Alex Rodriguez, Derek Jeter	100.00
RR	Alex Rodriguez, Cal Ripken Jr.	180.00
RS	Mike Schmidt, Brooks Robinson	85.00
SG	Shawn Green, Duke Snider	40.00
SJ	Randy Johnson, Gary Sheffield	40.00
SM	Pedro Martinez, Curt Schilling	50.00
SR	Nolan Ryan, Curt Schilling	75.00
TO	Frank Thomas, Magglio Ordonez	60.00
WC	Roger Clemens, David Wells	50.00
WH	Larry Walker, Todd Helton	45.00
WS	Sammy Sosa, Billy Williams	60.00
ZH	Barry Zito, Tim Hudson	50.00
RJ	Alex Rodriguez, Derek Jeter	100.00
RG	Cal Ripken Jr., Lou Gehrig	350.00
SC	Ty Cobb, Ichiro Suzuki	180.00

Team Threads
Production 10 unless noted.

Triple Authentic
Production 10

World Series Stars
NM/M
Production 50 unless noted.

AJ	Andruw Jones	25.00
AP	Andy Pettitte/15	40.00
AS	Alfonso Soriano/15	35.00
BL	Barry Larkin	25.00
BW	Bernie Williams	25.00
CA	Jose Canseco	30.00
CJ	Chipper Jones	30.00
CS	Curt Schilling	25.00
CY	Carl Yastrzemski/31	50.00
DW	Dontrelle Willis	40.00
GA	Garret Anderson	25.00
GL	Troy Glaus	30.00
GM	Greg Maddux	50.00
HM	Hideki Matsui/17	140.00
IR	Ivan Rodriguez	30.00
JB	Josh Beckett	25.00
JE	Derek Jeter	60.00
JM	Joe Morgan	25.00
JP	Jorge Posada	30.00
JT	Jim Thome	25.00
KB	Kevin Brown	20.00
MM	Mike Mussina/43	50.00
MP	Mike Piazza	35.00
MR	Mariano Rivera	30.00
MS	Mike Schmidt	40.00
PM	Paul Molitor	30.00
PO	Paul O'Neill	20.00
RC	Roger Clemens	40.00
RF	Rollie Fingers	25.00
RJ	Randy Johnson	30.00
TG	Tom Glavine	25.00

World Series Stars Autograph
No Pricing
Production One Set

300 Win Club
Production 10 Sets

Autographed 300 Win Club
Production 10 Sets

500 HR Club
Production 10 Sets

Autographed 500 HR Club
Production 10 Sets

500 HR Club Triple Patches
Production 10 Sets

3000 Hit Club
Production 10 Sets

3000 Hit Club Autograph
Production 10 Sets

2004 SP Legendary Cuts

NM/M

Complete Set (126):		.40
Common Player:		.40
Pack (4):		12.00
Box (12):		120.00
1	Al Kaline	1.00
2	Al Lopez	.40
3	Alan Trammell	.40
4	Andre Dawson	.40
5	Babe Ruth	3.00
6	Bert Campaneris	.40
7	Bill Mazeroski	.40
8	Bill Russell	.40
9	Billy Williams	.40
10	Bob Feller	.50
11	Bob Gibson	.75
12	Bob Lemon	.40
13	Bobby Doerr	.40
14	Brooks Robinson	1.00
15	Cal Ripken Jr.	3.00
16	Carl Yastrzemski	1.00
17	Carlton Fisk	.40
18	Jim "Catfish" Hunter	.40
19	Dale Murphy	.40
20	Darryl Strawberry	.40
21	Dave Concepcion	.40
22	Dave Winfield	.50
23	Dennis Eckersley	.40
24	Denny McLain	.40
25	Don Drysdale	.50
26	Don Larsen	.50
27	Don Mattingly	2.00
28	Don Sutton	.40
29	Duke Snider	1.00
30	Dusty Baker	.40
31	Dwight Gooden	.40
32	Earl Weaver	.40
33	Early Wynn	.40
34	Eddie Mathews	1.00
35	Eddie Murray	.75
36	Enos Slaughter	.40
37	Ernie Banks	1.50
38	Fergie Jenkins	.40
39	Frank Robinson	.75
40	Fred Lynn	.40
41	Gary Carter	.50
42	Gaylord Perry	.40
43	George Brett	2.00
44	George Foster	.40
45	George Kell	.40
46	Greg Luzinski	.40
47	Hal Newhouser	.40
48	Hank Greenberg	1.00
49	Harmon Killebrew	1.00
50	Honus Wagner	1.00
51	Hoyt Wilhelm	.40
52	Jackie Robinson	1.50
53	Jim Bunning	.40
54	Jim Palmer	.75
55	Jimmie Foxx	1.00
56	Joe Carter	.40
57	Joe DiMaggio	2.00
58	Joe Morgan	.40
59	Joe Torre	.40
60	Johnny Bench	1.00
61	Johnny Podres	.40
62	John Roseboro	.40
63	Johnny Sain	.40
64	Juan Marichal	.50
65	Keith Hernandez	.40
66	Kirby Puckett	.75
67	Kirk Gibson	.40
68	Will Clark	.40
69	Jim Rice	.40
70	Larry Doby	.40
71	Lou Boudreau	.40
72	Lou Brock	.50
73	Lou Gehrig	2.50
74	Lou Piniella	.40
75	Luis Aparicio	.40
76	Mark Grace	.40
77	Mel Ott	.40
78	Mickey Lolich	.40
79	Mickey Mantle	3.00
80	Mike Greenwell	.40
81	Mike Schmidt	2.00
82	Monte Irvin	.40
83	Nellie Fox	.50
84	Nolan Ryan	3.00
85	Orlando Cepeda	.40
86	Ozzie Smith	1.00
87	Paul Molitor	.75
88	Pee Wee Reese	.40
89	Phil Niekro	.40
90	Phil Rizzuto	.75
91	Ralph Kiner	.75
92	Red Rolfe	.40
93	Red Schoendienst	.40
94	Reggie Smith	.40
95	Rich "Goose" Gossage	.40
96	Richie Ashburn	.40
97	Rick Ferrell	.40
98	Elston Howard	.40
99	Roberto Clemente	2.00
100	Robin Roberts	.40
101	Robin Yount	1.00
102	Roger Maris	2.00
103	Rollie Fingers	.40
104	Ron Santo	.40
105	Roy Campanella	.75
106	Ryne Sandberg	1.50
107	Sparky Anderson	.40
108	Sparky Lyle	.40
109	Stan Musial	2.00
110	Steve Carlton	.50
111	Steve Garvey	.40
112	Ted Williams	2.50
113	Thurman Munson	1.00
114	Tom Seaver	1.00
115	Tommy Henrich	.40
116	Tommy Lasorda	.40
117	Tony Gwynn	1.00
118	Tony Perez	.40
119	Ty Cobb	1.50
120	Wade Boggs	.50
121	Warren Spahn	.75
122	Whitey Ford	.75
123	Willie McCovey	.40
124	Willie Randolph	.40
125	Willie Stargell	.50
126	Yogi Berra	.75

All-Time Autographs
NM/M
Production 50 Sets

LA	Luis Aparicio	20.00
YB	Yogi Berra	65.00
WB	Wade Boggs	40.00
SC	Steve Carlton	20.00
GC	Gary Carter	25.00
JC	Joe Carter	20.00
OC	Orlando Cepeda	25.00
WC	Will Clark	20.00
BD	Bobby Doerr	20.00
DE	Dennis Eckersley	20.00
RF	Rollie Fingers	20.00
CF	Carlton Fisk	30.00
WF	Whitey Ford	50.00
TG	Tony Gwynn	50.00
MI	Monte Irvin	20.00
FJ	Fergie Jenkins	20.00
AK	Al Kaline	25.00
GK	George Kell	20.00
HK	Harmon Killebrew	40.00
FL	Fred Lynn	20.00
MA	Don Mattingly	60.00
BM	Bill Mazeroski	40.00
WM	Willie McCovey	50.00
MC	Denny McLain	30.00
DM	Dale Murphy	30.00
SM	Stan Musial	80.00
DN	Don Newcombe	20.00
PN	Phil Niekro	20.00
TP	Tony Perez	25.00
GP	Gaylord Perry	20.00
JP	Johnny Podres	20.00
CR	Cal Ripken Jr.	125.00
RR	Robin Roberts	30.00
NR	Nolan Ryan	125.00
SA	Ryne Sandberg	75.00
RS	Red Schoendienst	25.00
TS	Tom Seaver	50.00
DS	Don Sutton	15.00
BW	Billy Williams	20.00
MW	Maury Wills	20.00
RY	Robin Yount	75.00

Game Graphs
NM/M
Production 25 Sets
Gold: No Pricing
Production 10 Sets

LA	Luis Aparicio	25.00
EB	Ernie Banks	75.00
JB	Johnny Bench	80.00
YB	Yogi Berra	80.00
WB	Wade Boggs	50.00
GB	George Brett	100.00
LB	Lou Brock	40.00
SC	Steve Carlton	30.00
GC	Gary Carter	35.00
JC	Joe Carter	30.00
RF	Rollie Fingers	25.00
CF	Carlton Fisk	40.00
BG	Bob Gibson	40.00
TG	Tony Gwynn	65.00
AK	Al Kaline	50.00
HK	Harmon Killebrew	50.00
JM	Juan Marichal	35.00
MA	Don Mattingly	80.00
BM	Bill Mazeroski	50.00
WM	Willie McCovey	50.00
PM	Paul Molitor	40.00
MO	Joe Morgan	40.00
DM	Dale Murphy	40.00
EM	Eddie Murray	85.00
SM	Stan Musial	100.00
PN	Phil Niekro	30.00
KP	Kirby Puckett	75.00
CR	Cal Ripken Jr.	180.00
PR	Phil Rizzuto	50.00
FR	Frank Robinson	50.00
NR	Nolan Ryan	175.00
RS	Ryne Sandberg	85.00
MS	Mike Schmidt	80.00
TS	Tom Seaver	60.00
OS	Ozzie Smith	75.00
SN	Duke Snider	50.00
DS	Don Sutton	20.00
BW	Billy Williams	25.00
DW	Dave Winfield	30.00
CY	Carl Yastrzemski	85.00
RY	Robin Yount	85.00

Historic Patches
NM/M
Production 25 Sets

EB	Ernie Banks	50.00
GB	George Brett	60.00
DD	Don Drysdale	25.00
BG	Bob Gibson	25.00
TG	Tony Gwynn	50.00
EM	Eddie Mathews	30.00
SM	Stan Musial	60.00
CR	Cal Ripken Jr.	100.00
NR	Nolan Ryan	75.00
TS	Tom Seaver	50.00
DS	Duke Snider	30.00
CY	Carl Yastrzemski	60.00
RY	Robin Yount	50.00

Historic Quads
No Pricing
Production 10 Sets

Historic Swatches

NM/M
Common Swatch: 4.00
Golds: 2X-3X
Production 25 Sets

AN	Sparky Anderson	4.00
JB	Johnny Bench/SP	10.00
GB	George Brett	12.00
LB	Lou Brock	8.00
GC	Gary Carter	6.00
JC	Joe Carter	6.00
DC	Dave Concepcion	4.00
DD	Don Drysdale	8.00
RF	Rollie Fingers	6.00
CF	Carlton Fisk	8.00
GF	George Foster	4.00
SG	Steve Garvey	4.00
CH	Jim "Catfish" Hunter	6.00
FJ	Fergie Jenkins	8.00
HK	Harmon Killebrew	10.00
DL	Don Larsen/SP	10.00
ML	Mickey Lolich	4.00
SL	Sparky Lyle	4.00
MA	Eddie Mathews	10.00
DM	Don Mattingly	15.00
PM	Paul Molitor	6.00
JM	Joe Morgan	6.00
TM	Thurman Munson	12.00
MU	Dale Murphy	8.00
EM	Eddie Murray/SP	10.00
SM	Stan Musial	20.00
PN	Phil Niekro	6.00
GP	Gaylord Perry	6.00
JP	Johnny Podres	6.00
KP	Kirby Puckett	10.00
JR	Jim Rice	8.00
CR	Cal Ripken Jr.	20.00
BR	Brooks Robinson	8.00
NR	Nolan Ryan	20.00
TS	Tom Seaver	8.00
OS	Ozzie Smith	10.00
DS	Don Sutton	4.00
HW	Hoyt Wilhelm	4.00
DW	Dave Winfield	6.00
RY	Robin Yount	8.00

Legendary Cuts
NM/M
Quantity produced listed.

WA	Walter Alston/74	200.00
LU	Luke Appling/108	150.00
RA	Richie Ashburn/31	350.00
LB	Lou Boudreau/199	125.00
EC	Earle Combs/27	350.00
ST	Stan Covelski/102	150.00
RD	Ray Dandridge/199	125.00
DD	Dizzy Dean/33	650.00
BD	Bill Dickey/82	250.00
JD	Joe DiMaggio/111	500.00
DO	Larry Doby/14	400.00
DR	Don Drysdale/66	450.00
LD	Leo Durocher/175	400.00
RF	Rick Ferrell/44	160.00
WF	Wes Ferrell/36	200.00
FF	Frankie Frisch/57	450.00
CG	Charlie Gehringer/171	200.00
LG	Lefty Gomez/98	325.00
HG	Hank Greenberg/37	500.00
BU	Burleigh Grimes/83	200.00
GR	Lefty Grove/75	375.00
GH	Gabby Hartnett/19	475.00
BH	Billy Herman/134	125.00
WH	Waite Hoyt/106	200.00
CH	Carl Hubbell/199	180.00
JH	Jim "Catfish" Hunter/25	220.00
BJ	"Indian" Bob Johnson/32	200.00
HK	Harvey Kuenn/49	150.00
BL	Bob Lemon/199	100.00
EL	Ernie Lombardi/39	450.00
TL	Ted Lyons/199	150.00
RU	Rube Marquard/59	220.00
JM	Joe Medwick/32	450.00
MI	Johnny Mize/118	140.00
HN	Hal Newhouser/51	140.00
KN	Kid Nichols/4	2,500
SP	Satchel Paige/28	1,325
GP	George Pipgras/46	200.00
PR	Pee Wee Reese/35	350.00
SR	Sam Rice/28	500.00
ER	Edd Roush/129	125.00
RR	Red Ruffing/30	500.00
JS	Joe Sewell/199	140.00
GS	George Sisler/32	850.00
ES	Enos Slaughter/147	125.00
WS	Willie Stargell/39	220.00
WM	Hoyt Wilhelm/115	100.00
SW	"Smokey" Joe Wood/79	400.00
EW	Early Wynn/54	200.00

Legendary Duels
NM/M
Production 25 Sets

BG	George Brett, Rich "Goose" Gossage	40.00
DW	Joe DiMaggio, Ted Williams	150.00
EG	Dennis Eckersley, Kirk Gibson	25.00
FM	Joe Morgan, Carlton Fisk	30.00
GL	Bob Gibson, Mickey Lolich	30.00
MW	Mickey Mantle, Ted Williams	200.00
PL	Johnny Podres, Don Larsen	30.00
RM	Juan Marichal, John Roseboro	25.00
RR	Pee Wee Reese, Phil Rizzuto	35.00
SM	Duke Snider, Mickey Mantle	125.00
SS	Ryne Sandberg, Ozzie Smith	80.00
WB	Ernie Banks, Honus Wagner	125.00

Legendary Duels Patch
No Pricing
Production 15 Sets

Legendary Duos
NM/M
Production 25 Sets

CM	Joe Morgan, Dave Concepcion	20.00
DM	Joe DiMaggio, Mickey Mantle	200.00
LB	Yogi Berra, Don Larsen	60.00
MB	Yogi Berra, Mickey Mantle	200.00
MM	Mickey Mantle, Roger Maris	200.00
MY	Paul Molitor, Robin Yount	30.00
PJ	Jackie Robinson, Pee Wee Reese	75.00
RR	Cal Ripken Jr., Brooks Robinson	65.00
RS	Tom Seaver, Nolan Ryan	75.00
SC	Roy Campanella, Duke Snider	40.00
SS	Johnny Sain, Warren Spahn	40.00
WB	Ernie Banks, Billy Williams	40.00

Legendary Duos Patch
No Pricing
Production 15 Sets

Legendary Sigs
NM/M
Production 50 Sets

LA	Luis Aparicio	20.00
EB	Ernie Banks	60.00
JB	Johnny Bench	60.00
WB	Wade Boggs	40.00
GC	Gary Carter	25.00
JC	Joe Carter	20.00
WC	Will Clark	40.00
BD	Bobby Doerr	20.00
DE	Dennis Eckersley	25.00
BF	Bob Feller	30.00
RF	Rollie Fingers	20.00
BG	Bob Gibson	35.00
TG	Tony Gwynn	50.00
MI	Monte Irvin	25.00
AK	Al Kaline	40.00
GK	George Kell	25.00
HK	Harmon Killebrew	40.00
RK	Ralph Kiner	30.00
FL	Fred Lynn	15.00
JM	Juan Marichal	30.00
MA	Don Mattingly	60.00
WM	Willie McCovey	40.00
DM	Denny McLain	30.00
DM	Dale Murphy	30.00
EM	Eddie Murray	80.00
DN	Don Newcombe	25.00
PA	Jim Palmer	30.00
GP	Gaylord Perry	20.00
JP	Johnny Podres	20.00
CR	Cal Ripken Jr.	125.00
PR	Phil Rizzuto	25.00
RR	Robin Roberts	30.00
BR	Brooks Robinson	40.00
SA	Ryne Sandberg	75.00
MS	Mike Schmidt	60.00
RS	Red Schoendienst	25.00
OS	Ozzie Smith	65.00
SN	Duke Snider	40.00
DS	Don Sutton	15.00
MW	Maury Wills	20.00
CY	Carl Yastrzemski	75.00

Legendary Swatches

NM/M
Common Swatch: 4.00
Golds: No Pricing
Production 15 Sets

EB	Ernie Banks/SP	15.00
JB	Johnny Bench	10.00
YB	Yogi Berra	12.00
WB	Wade Boggs	6.00
GB	George Brett	12.00
RC	Roy Campanella	8.00
SC	Steve Carlton	6.00
OC	Orlando Cepeda	6.00
BD	Bobby Doerr	6.00
DD	Don Drysdale	8.00
CF	Carlton Fisk	8.00
NF	Nellie Fox	10.00
BG	Bob Gibson	8.00
TG	Tony Gwynn	10.00
EH	Elston Howard	8.00
CH	Jim "Catfish" Hunter	8.00
AK	Al Kaline	10.00
HK	Harmon Killebrew	10.00
MA	Juan Marichal	10.00
EM	Eddie Mathews	10.00
DM	Don Mattingly	15.00
WM	Willie McCovey	6.00
TM	Thurman Munson	12.00
SM	Stan Musial	15.00
TP	Tony Perez	4.00
PO	Johnny Podres	8.00
PR	Pee Wee Reese	8.00
JR	Jim Rice	8.00
CR	Cal Ripken Jr.	20.00
RI	Phil Rizzuto	10.00
FR	Frank Robinson	6.00
NR	Nolan Ryan	20.00
MS	Mike Schmidt	15.00
TS	Tom Seaver	8.00
DS	Duke Snider	10.00
WS	Warren Spahn	10.00
ST	Willie Stargell	8.00
BW	Billy Williams	4.00
DW	Dave Winfield	6.00
CY	Carl Yastrzemski	10.00
RY	Robin Yount	8.00

Marked for the Hall
NM/M
Production 50 Sets

LA	Luis Aparicio	20.00
EB	Ernie Banks	60.00
JB	Johnny Bench	60.00
YB	Yogi Berra	65.00
GB	George Brett	75.00
LB	Lou Brock	30.00
SC	Steve Carlton	20.00
GC	Gary Carter	25.00
OC	Orlando Cepeda	25.00
BD	Bobby Doerr	30.00
BF	Bob Feller	30.00
CF	Carlton Fisk	35.00
WF	Whitey Ford	40.00
BG	Bob Gibson	35.00
AK	Al Kaline	40.00
HK	Harmon Killebrew	40.00
RK	Ralph Kiner	40.00
MA	Juan Marichal	30.00
BM	Bill Mazeroski	50.00
WM	Willie McCovey	40.00

Code	Player	Price
PM	Paul Molitor	40.00
JM	Joe Morgan	35.00
EM	Eddie Murray	80.00
SM	Stan Musial	80.00
PN	Phil Niekro	20.00
JP	Jim Palmer	30.00
TP	Tony Perez	25.00
GP	Gaylord Perry	20.00
KP	Kirby Puckett	60.00
PR	Phil Rizzuto	25.00
RR	Robin Roberts	30.00
BR	Brooks Robinson	40.00
FR	Frank Robinson	30.00
NR	Nolan Ryan	125.00
MS	Mike Schmidt	60.00
TS	Tom Seaver	65.00
OS	Ozzie Smith	50.00
DS	Duke Snider	40.00
BW	Billy Williams	20.00
DW	Dave Winfield	30.00
CY	Carl Yastrzemski	75.00
RY	Robin Yount	75.00

Marks of Greatness

NM/M
Production 50 Sets

Code	Player	Price
EB	Ernie Banks	60.00
JB	Johnny Bench	60.00
YB	Yogi Berra	65.00
WB	Wade Boggs	40.00
GB	George Brett	75.00
LB	Lou Brock	30.00
SC	Steve Carlton	20.00
JC	Joe Carter	20.00
OC	Orlando Cepeda	25.00
WC	Will Clark	40.00
RF	Rollie Fingers	20.00
CF	Carlton Fisk	35.00
WF	Whitey Ford	40.00
BG	Bob Gibson	35.00
TG	Tony Gwynn	50.00
FJ	Fergie Jenkins	20.00
AK	Al Kaline	40.00
HK	Harmon Killebrew	40.00
FL	Fred Lynn	15.00
MA	Don Mattingly	60.00
MC	Denny McLain	30.00
PM	Paul Molitor	40.00
JM	Joe Morgan	35.00
DM	Dale Murphy	30.00
SM	Stan Musial	80.00
DN	Don Newcombe	25.00
PN	Phil Niekro	20.00
JP	Jim Palmer	30.00
TP	Tony Perez	25.00
KP	Kirby Puckett	60.00
CR	Cal Ripken Jr.	125.00
BR	Brooks Robinson	40.00
FR	Frank Robinson	30.00
NR	Nolan Ryan	125.00
RS	Ryne Sandberg	75.00
MS	Mike Schmidt	60.00
TS	Tom Seaver	50.00
OZ	Ozzie Smith	65.00
DS	Duke Snider	40.00
BW	Billy Williams	20.00
DW	Dave Winfield	30.00
RY	Robin Yount	75.00

Significant Swatches

NM/M
Common Swatch: 4.00
Golds: 2-3X
Production 25 Sets

Code	Player	Price
SA	Sparky Anderson	4.00
EB	Ernie Banks/SP	10.00
LB	Lou Brock/SP	8.00
GC	Gary Carter	4.00
JC	Joe Carter	4.00
OC	Orlando Cepeda	6.00
DC	Dave Concepcion	4.00
BD	Bobby Doerr	8.00
DD	Don Drysdale	6.00
RF	Rollie Fingers	6.00
CF	Carlton Fisk	8.00
GF	George Foster	4.00
SG	Steve Garvey	4.00
CH	Jim "Catfish" Hunter	8.00
FJ	Fergie Jenkins	4.00
SL	Sparky Lyle	4.00
RM	Roger Maris	30.00
ED	Eddie Mathews	10.00
MA	Don Mattingly	15.00
BM	Bill Mazeroski	8.00
WM	Willie McCovey	6.00
PM	Paul Molitor	6.00
TM	Thurman Munson	12.00
DM	Dale Murphy	8.00
EM	Eddie Murray/SP	8.00
PN	Phil Niekro	6.00
TP	Tony Perez	4.00
GP	Gaylord Perry	6.00
JP	Johnny Podres	6.00
CR	Cal Ripken Jr.	20.00
FR	Frank Robinson	6.00
NR	Nolan Ryan	20.00
MS	Mike Schmidt	15.00
TS	Tom Seaver	8.00
SN	Duke Snider	10.00
WS	Warren Spahn	10.00
ST	Willie Stargell	8.00
DS	Don Sutton	4.00
HW	Hoyt Wilhelm	4.00
DW	Dave Winfield	6.00
CY	Carl Yastrzemski	10.00
RY	Robin Yount	8.00

Significant Trips

No Pricing
Production 15 Sets

Significant Trips Patch

No Pricing
Production 10 Sets

Ultimate Autos.

NM/M
Production 25 Sets

Code	Player	Price
EB	Ernie Banks	60.00
JB	Johnny Bench	60.00
YB	Yogi Berra	60.00
GB	George Brett	90.00
LB	Lou Brock	35.00
SC	Steve Carlton	25.00
DE	Dennis Eckersley	25.00
BF	Bob Feller	35.00
WF	Whitey Ford	40.00
BG	Bob Gibson	40.00
MI	Monte Irvin	30.00
FJ	Fergie Jenkins	30.00
AK	Al Kaline	50.00
GK	George Kell	25.00
HK	Harmon Killebrew	50.00
RK	Ralph Kiner	40.00
MA	Juan Marichal	30.00
DM	Don Mattingly	75.00
BM	Bill Mazeroski	40.00
PM	Paul Molitor	40.00
JM	Joe Morgan	35.00
EM	Eddie Murray	80.00
SM	Stan Musial	80.00
PA	Jim Palmer	40.00
JP	Johnny Podres	25.00
KP	Kirby Puckett	70.00
PR	Phil Rizzuto	35.00
BR	Brooks Robinson	40.00
FR	Frank Robinson	40.00
NR	Nolan Ryan	120.00
SA	Ryne Sandberg	80.00
MS	Mike Schmidt	75.00
RS	Red Schoendienst	25.00
TS	Tom Seaver	50.00
OS	Ozzie Smith	60.00
SN	Duke Snider	50.00
DS	Don Sutton	20.00
MW	Maury Wills	25.00
DW	Dave Winfield	30.00
CY	Carl Yastrzemski	80.00
RY	Robin Yount	60.00

Ultimate Swatches

NM/M
Common Swatch: 6.00
Golds: No Pricing
Production 10 Sets

Code	Player	Price
EB	Ernie Banks	12.00
JB	Johnny Bench	10.00
YB	Yogi Berra	12.00
WB	Wade Boggs	6.00
GB	George Brett	12.00
RC	Roy Campanella	10.00
SC	Steve Carlton	6.00
JD	Joe DiMaggio/SP	75.00
DD	Don Drysdale	8.00
NF	Nellie Fox	12.00
BG	Bob Gibson	8.00
HG	Hank Greenberg	20.00
TG	Tony Gwynn	10.00
CH	Jim "Catfish" Hunter	6.00
HK	Harmon Killebrew	10.00
MM	Mickey Mantle/SP	125.00
MA	Juan Marichal	8.00
RM	Roger Maris	30.00
EM	Eddie Mathews	10.00
DM	Don Mattingly	15.00
WM	Willie McCovey	6.00
TM	Thurman Munson	10.00
SM	Stan Musial	15.00
KP	Kirby Puckett	10.00
PR	Pee Wee Reese	8.00
CR	Cal Ripken Jr.	20.00
BR	Brooks Robinson	8.00
FR	Frank Robinson	6.00
JR	Jackie Robinson	40.00
NR	Nolan Ryan	20.00
MS	Mike Schmidt	15.00
TS	Tom Seaver	10.00
OS	Ozzie Smith	10.00
DS	Duke Snider/SP	10.00
WS	Warren Spahn	10.00
HW	Honus Wagner/SP	140.00
BW	Billy Williams	6.00
TW	Ted Williams	60.00
DW	Dave Winfield	6.00
CY	Carl Yastrzemski	10.00
RY	Robin Yount	8.00

2004 SP Prospects

NM/M

Complete Set (447):
Common SP (1-90): .50 / 1:Pack
Common Rookie (91-290): 1.00
Common Rookie Auto. (291-447): 8.00
Production 400 unless noted.
Overall Autos. 1:5
Pack (5): 8.00
Box (24): 180.00

#	Player	Price
1	Roger Clemens	3.00
2	Melvin Mora	.50
3	Dontrelle Willis	.50
4	Jose Vidro	.50
5	Oliver Perez	.50
6	Carlos Zambrano	.50
7	Chipper Jones	1.00
8	Greg Maddux	1.50
9	Curt Schilling	1.00
10	Jose Reyes	.75
11	David Ortiz	1.00
12	Mike Piazza	2.00
13	Jason Schmidt	.50
14	Randy Johnson	1.00
15	Magglio Ordonez	.50
16	Mike Mussina	1.00
17	Jake Peavy	.50
18	Jim Edmonds	.75
19	Ken Griffey Jr.	1.50
20	Jason Giambi	.75
21	Mike Sweeney	.50
22	Carlos Lee	.50
23	Craig Wilson	.50
24	Pedro Martinez	1.00
25	Bobby Abreu	.50
26	Mike Lowell	.50
27	Miguel Cabrera	1.00
28	Hank Blalock	.50
29	Frank Thomas	.75
30	Manny Ramirez	1.00
31	Mark Mulder	.50
32	Scott Podsednik	.50
33	Albert Pujols	3.00
34	Preston Wilson	.50
35	Todd Helton	.75
36	Victor Martinez	.50
37	Kerry Wood	.50
38	Carlos Beltran	1.00
39	Vernon Wells	.50
40	Sammy Sosa	1.00
41	Pat Burrell	.50
42	Tim Hudson	.50
43	Eric Gagne	.75
44	Jim Thome	1.00
45	Vladimir Guerrero	1.00
46	Travis Hafner	.75
47	Rickie Weeks	.50
48	Miguel Tejada	.75
49	Ivan Rodriguez	.75
50	J.D. Drew	.50
51	Ben Sheets	.50
52	Garret Anderson	.50
53	Aubrey Huff	.50
54	Nomar Garciaparra	1.00
55	Luis Gonzalez	.50
56	Lance Berkman	.50
57	Ichiro Suzuki	2.00
58	Torii Hunter	.50
59	Adam Dunn	.75
60	Mark Teixeira	.75
61	Bret Boone	.50
62	Roy Oswalt	.50
63	Joe Mauer	.75
64	Scott Rolen	1.00
65	Hideki Matsui	2.00
66	Richie Sexson	.50
67	Jeff Kent	.50
68	Barry Zito	.50
69	C.C. Sabathia	.50
70	Carlos Delgado	.50
71	Gary Sheffield	.75
72	Shawn Green	.50
73	Jason Bay	.50
74	Andruw Jones	.75
75	Jeff Bagwell	.75
76	Rafael Palmeiro	.75
77	Alex Rodriguez	3.00
78	Adrian Beltre	.50
79	Troy Glaus	.50
80	Tom Glavine	.50
81	Paul Konerko	.50
82	Alfonso Soriano	1.00
83	Roy Halladay	.50
84	Derek Jeter	3.00
85	Josh Beckett	.50
86	Delmon Young	.50
87	Brian Giles	.50
88	Eric Chavez	.50
89	Lyle Overbay	.50
90	Mark Prior	.75
91	Shawn Camp RC	1.00
92	Travis Smith	1.00
93	Juan Padilla RC	1.00
94	Brad Halsey RC	1.00
95	Scott Kazmir	6.00
96	Sam Narron RC	1.00
97	Frank Francisco RC	1.00
98	Mike Johnston RC	1.00
99	Sam McConnell RC	1.00
100	Josh Labandeira RC	1.00
101	Kazuhito Tadano RC	1.00
102	Hector Gimenez RC	1.00
103	David Aardsma RC	1.00
104	Charles Thomas RC	2.00
105	Ian Snell RC	1.50
106	Jeff Keppinger RC	3.00
107	Michael Vento RC	2.00
108	Jerry Gil RC	1.00
109	Marty McLeary RC	1.00
110	Donnie Kelly RC	1.00
111	Roman Colon RC	1.00
112	Travis Blackley RC	1.00
113	Edwardo Sierra RC	1.00
114	Chris Shelton RC	1.00
115	Bartolome Fortunato RC	1.00
116	Brandon Medders RC	1.00
117	Merkin Valdez RC	2.00
118	Carlos Vasquez RC	1.00
119	Shingo Takatsu RC	1.50
120	Aarom Baldiris RC	1.00
121	Chris Aguila RC	1.00
122	Jimmy Serrano RC	1.00
123	Mike Gosling RC	1.00
124	Brian Dallimore RC	1.00
125	Ronald Belisario RC	1.00
126	George Sherrill RC	1.00
127	Fernando Nieve RC	1.00
128	Abe Alvarez RC	1.50
129	Jeff Bennett RC	1.00
130	Ryan Meaux RC	1.00
131	Edwin Moreno RC	1.00
132	Jesse Crain RC	2.00
133	Scott Dohmann RC	1.00
134	Ronny Cedeno RC	1.00
135	Orlando Rodriguez RC	1.00
136	Mike Wuertz RC	1.00
137	Justin Hampson RC	1.00
138	Matt Treanor RC	1.00
139	Andy Green RC	1.00
140	Yadier Molina RC	3.00
141	Joe Nelson RC	1.00
142	Justin Lehr RC	1.00
143	Ryan Wing RC	1.00
144	Kevin Cave RC	1.50
145	Evan Rust RC	1.00
146	Mike Rouse RC	1.00
147	Lance Cormier RC	1.00
148	Eduardo Villacis RC	1.00
149	Justin Knoedler RC	1.00
150	Freddy Guzman RC	1.00
151	Casey Daigle RC	1.00
152	Joey Gathright RC	2.00
153	Tim Bittner RC	1.00
154	Scott Atchison RC	1.00
155	Ivan Ochoa RC	1.50
156	Lincoln Holdzkom RC	1.00
157	Onil Joseph RC	1.00
158	Jason Bartlett RC	1.00
159	Jon Knott RC	1.00
160	Jake Woods RC	1.00
161	Jerome Gamble RC	1.00
162	Sean Henn	1.50
163	Kazuo Matsui RC	1.50
164	Roberto Novoa RC	1.00
165	Eddy Rodriguez RC	1.00
166	Ramon Ramirez RC	1.00
167	Enemencio Pacheco RC	1.00
168	Chad Bentz RC	1.00
169	Chris Oxspring RC	1.00
170	Justin Leone RC	1.00
171	Joe Horgan RC	1.00
172	Jose Capellan RC	1.50
173	Greg Dobbs RC	1.00
174	Jason Frasor RC	1.00
175	Shawn Hill RC	1.00
176	Carlos Hines RC	1.00
177	John Gall RC	1.00
178	Steve Andrade RC	1.00
179	Scott Proctor RC	1.00
180	Rusty Tucker RC	1.00
181	David Crouthers RC	1.00
182	Franklyn Gracesqui RC	1.00
183	Justin Germano RC	1.00
184	Alfredo Simon RC	1.00
185	Jorge Sequea RC	1.00
186	Nick Regilio RC	1.00
187	Justin Huisman RC	1.00
188	Akinori Otsuka RC	1.00
189	Luis Gonzalez RC	1.00
190	Renyel Pinto RC	1.00
191	Josh LeBlanc RC	1.50
192	Devin Ivany RC	1.00
193	Chad Blackwell RC	1.50
194	Brandon Burgess RC	1.50
195	Cory Patton RC	1.50
196	Daniel Batz RC	1.50
197	Adam Russell RC	1.00
198	Jarrett Hoffpauir RC	1.00
199	Patrick Bryant RC	1.00
200	Sean Gamble RC	1.50
201	Jermaine Brock RC	1.50
202	Benjamin Zobrist RC	1.50
203	Cla Meredith RC	1.50
204	Derek Tharpe RC	1.00
205	Brad McCann RC	2.00
206	Justin Hedrick RC	1.00
207	Clint Sammons RC	2.50
208	Richard Steik RC	1.00
209	Fernando Perez RC	1.00
210	Mark Jecmen RC	1.00
211	Benjamin Harrison RC	1.00
212	Jason Quarles RC	1.00
213	William Layman RC	1.00
214	Koley Kolberg RC	1.00
215	Randy Dicken RC	1.00
216	Barry Richmond RC	1.00
217	Timothy Murphey RC	1.50
218	John Hardy RC	1.00
219	Sebastien Boucher RC	1.00
220	Andrew Alvarado RC	1.00
221	Patrick Perry RC	1.00
222	Jarod McAuliff RC	1.00
223	Jared Gaston RC	1.00
224	William Thompson RC	1.50
225	Lucas French RC	1.00
226	Brandon Parillo RC	1.00
227	Greg Goetz RC	1.00
228	David Haehnel RC	1.50
229	James Miller RC	1.00
230	Mark Roberts RC	1.00
231	Eric Ridener RC	1.00
232	Freddy Sandoval RC	1.00
234	Carlos Medero-Stullz RC	1.00
235	Matt Shepherd RC	1.00
236	Thomas Hubbard RC	1.00
238	Kyle Bono RC	1.50
239	Craig Moldrem RC	1.00
239	Brandon Timm RC	1.00
241	Mike Carp RC	2.50
242	Joseph Muro RC	1.00
243	Derek Decarlo RC	1.00
244	Chris Niesel RC	1.50
245	Trevor Lawhorn RC	1.50
246	Joey Howell RC	1.00
247	Dustin Hahn RC	1.00
248	Jim Fasano RC	2.00
249	Hainley Statia RC	1.00
250	Brandon Conway RC	1.00
251	Christopher McConnell RC	2.00
252	Austin Shappi RC	1.50
253	Joey Metropoulos RC	2.00
254	David Nicholson RC	1.00
255	Ryan McCarthy RC	2.00
256	Michael Parisi RC	1.00
257	Andrew Macfarlane RC	1.00
258	Jeffery Dominguez RC	1.50
259	Troy Patton RC	4.00
260	Ryan Norwood RC	1.50
261	Chad Boyd RC	1.00
262	Grant Plumley RC	1.00
263	Jeffrey Katz RC	1.00
264	Cory Middleton RC	1.00
265	Andrew Moffitt RC	1.00
266	Jarrett Grube RC	1.00
267	Derek Hankins RC	1.00
268	Douglas Reinhardt RC	1.00
269	Duron Legrande RC	1.00
270	Steven Jackson RC	1.00
271	Brian Hall RC	2.00
272	Cory Wade RC	1.50
273	John Grogan RC	1.00
274	Robert Asanovich RC	1.50
275	Kevin Hart RC	1.00
276	Matt Guillory RC	1.00
277	Cliff Remole RC	1.00
278	David Trahan RC	1.00
279	Kristian Bell RC	1.00
280	Chris Westervelt RC	1.00
281	Garry Bakker RC	1.00
282	Jonny Ash RC	1.00
283	Ryan Phillips RC	1.00
284	Wes Letson RC	1.00
285	Jeff Landing RC	1.00
286	Mark Worrell RC	1.00
287	Sean Gallagher RC	5.00
288	Nick Blasi RC	2.00
289	Kevin Frandsen RC	2.00
290	Richard Mercado RC	1.00
291	Matt Bush RC	15.00
292	Mark Rogers RC	15.00
293	Homer Bailey RC	30.00
294	Chris Nelson RC	20.00
295	Thomas Diamond RC	15.00
296	Neil Walker RC	20.00
297	Bill Bray RC	15.00
298	David Purcey RC	15.00
299	Scott Elbert RC	25.00
300	Josh Fields RC	15.00
301	Chris Lambert RC	15.00
302	Trevor Plouffe RC	25.00
303	Greg Golson RC	25.00
304	Phillip Hughes RC	120.00
305	Kyle Waldrop RC	25.00
306	Richie Robnett/350 RC	30.00
307	Taylor Tankersley RC	15.00
308	Blake Dewitt RC	20.00
309	Eric Hurley RC	20.00
310	James Howell RC	15.00
311	Zachary Jackson RC	15.00
312	Justin Orenduff RC	15.00
313	Tyler Lumsden RC	20.00
314	Matt Fox/600 RC	10.00
315	Dan Putnam/450 RC	20.00
316	Jon Poterson RC	15.00
317	Gio Gonzalez RC	25.00
318	Jay Rainville/475 RC	20.00
319	Huston Street RC	25.00
320	Jeff Marquez RC	20.00
321	Eric Beattie/500 RC	20.00
322	Reid Brignac/325 RC	40.00
323	Yovani Gallardo RC	60.00
324	Justin Hoyman RC	15.00
325	Brandon Szymanski RC	20.00
326	Seth Smith/600 RC	35.00
327	Karl Herren/600 RC	20.00
328	Brian Bixler/600 RC	15.00
329	Wes Whisler/600 RC	15.00
330	Erick San Pedro RC	15.00
331	Billy Buckner RC	20.00
332	Jon Zeringue RC	20.00
333	Curtis Thigpen RC	20.00
334	Blake Johnson RC	15.00
335	Donny Lucy RC	15.00
336	Mike Ferris/600 RC	15.00
337	Anthony Swarzak/600 RC	30.00
338	Jason Jaramillo RC	15.00
339	Hunter Pence/600 RC	50.00
340	Dustin Pedroia RC	120.00
341	Grant Johnson RC	15.00
342	Kurt Suzuki RC	30.00
343	Jason Vargas/600 RC	15.00
344	Ray Liotta RC	15.00
346	Eric Campbell RC	40.00
347	Jeff Frazier RC	15.00
348	Gaby Hernandez RC	20.00
349	Wade Davis/600 RC	50.00
350	Josh Wahpepah RC	15.00
351	Scott Lewis RC	15.00
352	Jeff Fiorentino RC	15.00
353	Steven Register/600 RC	10.00
354	Michael Schlact RC	15.00
355	Eddie Prasch RC	15.00
356	Adam Lind RC	50.00
357	Ian Desmond RC	40.00
358	Josh Johnson/575 RC	25.00
359	Garrett Mock/600 RC	15.00
360	Danny Hill/600 RC	10.00
361	Cory Dunlap/600 RC	15.00
362	Grant Hansen/600 RC	12.00
363	Eric Haberer RC	15.00
364	Eduardo Morlan RC	20.00
365	James Happ/600 RC	15.00
366	Matt Tuiasosopo/600 RC	15.00
367	Jordan Parraz RC	15.00
368	Andrew Dobies RC	15.00
369	Mark Reed RC	15.00
370	Jason Windsor RC	15.00
371	Gregory Burns/600 RC	15.00
372	Christian Garcia/600 RC	15.00
373	John Bowker/575 RC	20.00
374	John Holt/550 RC	15.00
375	Daryl Jones RC	15.00
376	Colin Mahoney RC	15.00
377	Aaron Hathaway RC	15.00
378	Matt Spring RC	10.00
379	Josh Baker RC	10.00
380	Charles Lofgren RC	15.00
381	Rafael Gonzalez RC	15.00
382	Bradley Bergesen/575 RC	10.00
383	Brandon Boggs RC	20.00
384	Joseph Bauserman RC	15.00
385	Collin Balester/500 RC	20.00
386	James Moore RC	15.00
387	Robert Janssen RC	15.00
388	Luis Guerra RC	15.00
389	Lucas Harrell/550 RC	15.00
390	Donnie Smith/500 RC	15.00
391	Mark Robinson/525 RC	15.00
392	Louis Marson/550 RC	20.00
393	Robert Johnson/600 RC	15.00
394	Lou Santangelo/600 RC	15.00
395	Tommy Hottovy RC	10.00
396	Ryan Webb RC	10.00
397	Jamar Walton RC	10.00
398	Jason Jones RC	10.00
399	Clay Timpner/600 RC	10.00

#	Player	Price
400	James Parr RC	15.00
401	Sean Kazmar RC	15.00
402	Andrew Kown RC	10.00
403	Jacob McGee/600 RC	30.00
404	Mike Butia/600 RC	10.00
405	Paul Janish/500 RC	15.00
406	Matt Macri RC	10.00
407	Mike Nickeas/500 RC	10.00
408	Kyle Bloom/550 RC	10.00
409	Luis Rivera/500 RC	10.00
410	William Bunn/600 RC	10.00
411	Enrique Barrera RC	10.00
412	Ryan Klosterman RC	10.00
413	John Raglani/515 RC	10.00
414	Brandon Allen/500 RC	30.00
415	Andy Baldwin/600 RC	10.00
416	Mark Lowe RC	20.00
417	Mitch Einertson RC	20.00
418	Ryan Schroyer/600 RC	15.00
419	Brad Davis RC	15.00
420	Jesse Hoover/500 RC	10.00
421	Garrett Broshuis RC	15.00
422	Peter Pope RC	15.00
423	Brent Dlugach RC	15.00
424	Ryan Coultas RC	15.00
425	Ryan Royster RC	20.00
426	Stephen Chapman RC	15.00
427	Bryce Chamberlin RC	15.00
428	Joe Koshansky/550 RC	20.00
429	William Susdorf RC	15.00
430	A.J. Johnson RC	15.00
431	Jeremy Sowers RC	10.00
432	Justin Pekarek RC	10.00
433	Brett Smith RC	10.00
434	Matt Durkin RC	10.00
435	Daniel Barone RC	10.00
436	Scott Hyde RC	15.00
437	Thomas Everidge RC	15.00
444	Mark Trumbo RC	20.00
446	Eric Patterson RC	15.00
447	Mike Rozier RC	15.00

Gold
Gold (291-447): No Pricing
Production 10 Sets

Platinum
No Pricing
Production One Set

Draft Class
No Pricing
Production 10 Sets

Draft Duos

		NM/M
	Common Dual Autograph:	15.00
	Production 175 Sets	
LK	Adam Lind, Ryan Klosterman	40.00
BB	Bill Bray, Collin Balester	15.00
BI	Bill Bray, Ian Desmond	25.00
BM	William Buckner, James Moore	15.00
JH	James Howell, Josh Johnson	25.00
DB	Blake Dewitt, Daniel Batz	20.00
SJ	Brandon Szymanski, Paul Janish	15.00
SH	Brett Smith, Phillip Hughes	40.00
LS	Chris Lambert, Donnie Smith	15.00
LF	Chris Lambert, Mike Ferris	15.00
NS	Chris Nelson, Seth Smith	25.00
NM	Chris Nelson, Matt Macri	20.00
DG	Cory Dunlap, Luis Guerra	30.00
BN	Matt Bush, Chris Nelson	20.00
TH	Curtis Thigpen, Danny Hill	15.00
PT	Dan Putnam, Derek Tharpe	15.00
PJ	David Purcey, Robert Janssen	15.00
DZ	David Purcey, Zachary Jackson	15.00
LH	Donny Lucy, Grant Hansen	15.00
PD	Dustin Pedroia, Andrew Dobies	40.00
MR	Eduardo Morlan, Mark Robinson	15.00
PB	Eddie Prasch, Joseph Bauserman	15.00
EA	Eric Beattie, Andrew Kown	15.00
EJ	Eric Campbell, John Holt	20.00
EM	Eric Hurley, Mike Nickeas	20.00
PI	Erick San Pedro, Devin Ivany	15.00
HH	Gaby Hernandez, Aaron Hathaway	20.00
SK	Seth Smith, Joe Koshansky	20.00
GM	Gio Gonzalez, Timothy Murphey	25.00
BH	Matt Bush, Phillip Hughes	40.00
JR	Grant Johnson, Mark Reed	20.00
GH	Greg Golson, James Happ	20.00
GG	Greg Golson, Sean Gamble	15.00
BS	Homer Bailey, Brandon Szymanski	20.00
BG	Homer Bailey, Rafael Gonzalez	40.00
HJ	Hunter Pence, Jordan Parraz	30.00
SS	Huston Street, Kurt Suzuki	30.00
SW	Huston Street, Ryan Webb	20.00
HB	James Howell, Chad Blackwell	20.00
JM	Jason Jaramillo, Louis Marson	15.00
RS	Jay Rainville, Anthony Swarzak	20.00
JP	Jay Rainville, Patrick Bryant	15.00
FM	Jeff Frazier, Colin Mahoney	15.00
MS	Jeff Marquez, Brett Smith	15.00
MH	Jeff Marquez, Jesse Hoover	15.00
SL	Jeremy Sowers, Charles Lofgren	15.00
JS	Jeremy Sowers, Scott Lewis	15.00
JJ	Jon Poterson, Jason Jones	15.00
ZM	Jon Zeringue, Garrett Mock	20.00
FH	Josh Fields, Lucas Harrell	20.00
FW	Josh Fields, Wes Whisler	20.00
WB	Josh Wahpepah, Josh Baker	15.00
CL	Justin Hoyman, Jeremy Sowers	15.00
OJ	Justin Orenduff, Blake Johnson	15.00
OG	Justin Orenduff, Luis Guerra	20.00
HS	Karl Herren, Michael Schlact	15.00
WF	Kyle Waldrop, Matt Fox	15.00
KB	Kyle Waldrop, Patrick Bryant	15.00
RW	Richie Robnett, Jason Windsor	15.00
SR	Richie Robnett, Kurt Suzuki	25.00
RB	Mark Rogers, Josh Baker	20.00
RG	Mark Rogers, Yovani Gallardo	40.00
BK	Matt Bush, Sean Kazmar	15.00
WE	William Buckner, Enrique Barrera	15.00
WJ	William Buckner, James Howell	15.00
KH	Matt Durkin, Aaron Hathaway	15.00
NB	Neil Walker, Brian Bixler	15.00
NK	Neil Walker, Kyle Bloom	15.00
HG	Phillip Hughes, Christian Garcia	30.00
HP	Phillip Hughes, Jon Poterson	40.00
LA	Ray Liotta, Brandon Allen	25.00
BR	Reid Brignac, Ryan Royster	25.00
RP	Richie Robnett, Dan Putnam	20.00
RH	Richie Robnett, Huston Street	30.00
CO	Steven Register, Seth Smith	15.00
TD	Taylor Tankersley, Brad Davis	15.00
TV	Taylor Tankersley, Jason Vargas	20.00
BT	Thomas Diamond, Brandon Boggs	20.00
DH	Thomas Diamond, Eric Hurley	20.00
ED	Scott Elbert, Blake Dewitt	25.00
ER	Scott Elbert, John Raglani	15.00
PW	Trevor Plouffe, Kyle Waldrop	20.00
PR	Trevor Plouffe, Mark Robinson	15.00
LR	Tyler Lumsden, Adam Russell	15.00
LG	Tyler Lumsden, Gio Gonzalez	15.00
JB	William Buckner, Josh Johnson	20.00
BJ	Matt Bush, Daryl Jones	30.00
GW	Yovani Gallardo, Josh Wahpepah	40.00
JK	Zachary Jackson, Ryan Klosterman	15.00
DR	Blake Dewitt, John Raglani	25.00
GB	Homer Bailey, Greg Goetz	30.00
WR	Reid Brignac, Wade Davis	30.00
HM	Jeff Marquez, Phillip Hughes	40.00
PZ	Jordan Parraz, Benjamin Zobrist	15.00
RL	Luis Rivera, William Layman	15.00
EC	Eric Beattie, Collin Mahoney	15.00
JE	Jeff Frazier, Eric Beattie	15.00
BP	Matt Bush, Trevor Plouffe	20.00
CH	Ryan Coultas, Aaron Hathaway	15.00
SB	Jeremy Sowers, Homer Bailey	25.00
FB	Jeff Fiorentino, Bradley Bergesen	15.00
CF	Bryce Chamberlin, Jeff Fiorentino	15.00
RD	Cory Dunlap, John Raglani	15.00
ZP	Hunter Pence, Benjamin Zobrist	30.00

Draft Generations
No Pricing
Production 25 Sets

Draft Generations Triple Autograph
No Pricing
Production 25 Sets

Draft Picks Autographs

		NM/M
	Common Autograph:	8.00
	Golds:	No Pricing
	Production 10 Sets	
	Platinum:	No Pricing
	Production One Set	
AA	Andrew Alvarado/400	8.00
RA	Robert Asanovich/400	10.00
JA	Jonny Ash/400	10.00
GB	Garry Bakker/400	10.00
DB	Daniel Batz/400	10.00
KB	Kristian Bell/400	8.00
BL	Chad Blackwell/400	10.00
NB	Nick Blasi/400	10.00
BO	Kyle Bono/400	10.00
SB	Sebastien Boucher/325	10.00
CB	Chad Boyd/475	8.00
JB	Jermaine Brock/400	10.00
PB	Patrick Bryant/400	10.00
BB	Brandon Burgess/400	10.00
CA	Mike Carp/400	15.00
BC	Brandon Conway/400	8.00
DD	Derek Decarlo/400	10.00
RD	Randy Dicken/475	8.00
JD	Jeffery Dominguez/400	15.00
JF	Jim Fasano/400	15.00
KF	Kevin Frandsen/400	20.00
LF	Lucas French/400	15.00
SE	Sean Gallagher/400	20.00
SG	Sean Gamble/400	15.00
GA	Jared Gaston/400	10.00
GG	Greg Goetz/400	15.00
GR	John Grogan/475	10.00
JG	Jarrett Grube/400	8.00
MG	Matt Guillory/400	10.00
DA	David Haehnel/475	12.00
HA	Dustin Hahn/400	8.00
BH	Brian Hall/400	15.00
DH	Derek Hankins/400	10.00
JO	John Hardy/475	10.00
BE	Benjamin Harrison/387	10.00
KH	Kevin Hart/400	10.00
HE	Justin Hedrick/400	10.00
JH	Jarrett Hoffpauir/400	10.00
HO	Joey Howell/400	10.00
TH	Thomas Hubbard/400	10.00
DI	Devin Ivany/550	10.00
SJ	Steven Jackson/475	15.00
MJ	Mark Jecmen/600	10.00
JK	Jeffrey Katz/400	10.00
KK	Koley Kolberg/400	10.00
LA	Jeff Landing/400	10.00
TL	Trevor Lawhorn/475	10.00
WL	William Layman/400	8.00
JL	Josh LeBlanc/400	10.00
DL	Duron Legrande/400	8.00
LE	Wes Letson/400	10.00
MA	Andrew Macfarlane/400	8.00
MC	Jarod McAuliff/400	15.00
BM	Brad McCann/400	20.00
RM	Ryan McCarthy/400	15.00
CH	Christopher McConnell/400	25.00
ME	Carlos Medero-Stullz/400	8.00
RI	Richard Mercado/475	12.00
CL	Cla Meredith/400	15.00
JM	Joey Metropoulos/400	15.00
CM	Cory Middleton/400	10.00
MI	James Miller/475	10.00
AM	Andrew Moffitt/400	10.00
MO	Craig Molldrem/400	10.00
MU	Joseph Muro/400	8.00
TM	Timothy Murphey/400	10.00
DN	David Nicholson/475	10.00
CN	Chris Niesel/475	15.00
RN	Ryan Norwood/400	10.00
BP	Brandon Parillo/475	15.00
MP	Michael Parisi/475	15.00
CP	Cory Patton/400	15.00
TP	Troy Patton/400	25.00
FP	Fernando Perez/400	15.00
PP	Patrick Perry/475	15.00
RP	Ryan Phillips/400	10.00
GP	Grant Plumley/475	15.00
JQ	Jason Quarles/400	8.00
DR	Douglas Reinhardt/400	8.00
CR	Cliff Remole/400	15.00
BR	Barry Richmond/400	15.00
ER	Eric Ridener/475	10.00
MR	Mark Roberts/400	8.00
AR	Adam Russell/550	10.00
CS	Clint Sammons/400	10.00
FS	Freddy Sandoval/400	10.00
AS	Austin Shappi/475	10.00
MS	Matt Shepherd/400	10.00
HS	Hainley Statia/400	10.00
RS	Richard Steik/400	8.00
DT	Derek Tharpe/400	8.00
WT	William Thompson/475	10.00
BT	Brandon Timm/475	10.00
TR	David Trahan/400	8.00
CW	Cory Wade/400	15.00
WE	Chris Westervelt/400	10.00
MW	Mark Worrell/400	15.00
BZ	Ben Zobrist/600	25.00

Link to the Future Dual Auto.

		NM/M
	Common Dual Auto.	10.00
	Production 100 Sets	
BD	Adrian Beltre, Blake Dewitt	20.00
RF	Scott Rolen, Mike Ferris	25.00
JR	Andruw Jones, Richie Robnett	20.00
KB	Scott Kazmir, Reid Brignac	20.00
JB	Jason Kendall, Brian Bixler	20.00
SR	Ben Sheets, Mark Rogers	30.00
GP	Brian Giles, Dan Putnam	20.00
BG	Carlos Beltran, Greg Golson	20.00
SJ	Johan Santana, Jay Rainville	40.00
WT	Dontrelle Willis, Taylor Tankersley	15.00
JJ	Edwin Jackson, Blake Johnson	15.00
EJ	Eric Chavez, Josh Fields	20.00
QT	Guillermo Quiroz, Curtis Thigpen	10.00
KW	Jason Kendall, Neil Walker	20.00
VM	Javier Vazquez, Jeff Marquez	20.00
MP	Joe Mauer, Trevor Plouffe	50.00
SW	Johan Santana, Kyle Waldrop	40.00
VP	Javier Vazquez, Jon Poterson	20.00
GS	Ken Griffey Jr., Brandon Szymanski	75.00
WB	Kerry Wood, Homer Bailey	30.00
MS	Mike Mussina, Brett Smith	30.00
HS	Todd Helton, Seth Smith	30.00
GZ	Luis Gonzalez, Jon Zeringue	20.00
OH	Magglio Ordonez, Karl Herren	15.00
MB	Mark Mulder, Bill Bray	20.00
PJ	Mark Prior, Grant Johnson	20.00
CF	Matt Clement, Matt Fox	15.00
TN	Miguel Tejada, Chris Nelson	20.00
MH	Mike Mussina, Phillip Hughes	75.00
GB	Nomar Garciaparra, Matt Bush	50.00
PE	Odalis Perez, Scott Elbert	20.00
LS	Paul LoDuca, Erick San Pedro	20.00
HW	Rich Harden, Kyle Waldrop	15.00
CD	Roger Clemens, Thomas Diamond	100.00
RP	Alexis Rios, David Purcey	25.00
RE	Roy Oswalt, Eric Hurley	25.00
RL	Scott Rolen, Chris Lambert	30.00
TS	Tim Hudson, Huston Street	30.00
TJ	Tom Glavine, Jeremy Sowers	25.00
VD	Victor Martinez, Donny Lucy	25.00
BH	Angel Berroa, James Howell	15.00

Link to the Future Triple Auto.

		NM/M
	Common Triple Auto.	
	Production 50 Sets	
BHH	Hank Blalock, Eric Hurley, Benjamin Harrison	30.00
KBS	Scott Kazmir, Reid Brignac, Matt Spring	30.00
SRB	Ben Sheets, Mark Rogers, Josh Baker	30.00
JJB	Edwin Jackson, Blake Johnson, Daniel Batz	20.00
SWM	Johan Santana, Kyle Waldrop, Eduardo Morlan	60.00
VBB	Jose Vidro, Bill Bray, Collin Balester	30.00
GSJ	Ken Griffey Jr., Brandon Szymanski, Paul Janish	60.00
MSH	Mike Mussina, Brett Smith, Jesse Hoover	50.00
OFA	Magglio Ordonez, Josh Fields, Brandon Allen	30.00
PJR	Mark Prior, Grant Johnson, Mark Reed	25.00
GHM	Juan Gonzalez, James Howell, James Moore	40.00
HSW	Rich Harden, Huston Street, Jason Windsor	30.00
GMZ	Luis Gonzalez, Garrett Mock, Jon Zeringue	50.00
HRW	Tim Hudson, Richie Robnett, Ryan Webb	40.00
GTR	Vladimir Guerrero, Mark Trumbo, Luis Rivera	50.00

Link to the Past

		NM/M
	Common Dual Autograph	
	Production 50 Sets	
MB	Bill Mazeroski, Brian Bixler	35.00
FL	Carlton Fisk, Tyler Lumsden	35.00
WJ	Dave Winfield, Zachary Jackson	35.00
BW	Johnny Bench, Neil Walker	40.00
JD	Jose Canseco, Dan Putnam	50.00
AS	Billy Williams, Richie Robnett	40.00
RB	Nolan Ryan, Homer Bailey	180.00
PD	Gaylord Perry, Thomas Diamond	50.00
WR	Wade Boggs, Reid Brignac	60.00
WB	Whitey Ford, Brett Smith	30.00
WP	Whitey Ford, Phillip Hughes	80.00

Link to the Past Dual Autograph

		NM/M
	Common Dual Autograph	
	Production 50 Sets	
MB	Bill Mazeroski, Brian Bixler	25.00
FL	Carlton Fisk, Tyler Lumsden	35.00
WJ	Dave Winfield, Zachary Jackson	35.00
BW	Johnny Bench, Neil Walker	50.00
JD	Jose Canseco, Dan Putnam	40.00
AS	Billy Williams, Richie Robnett	40.00
RB	Nolan Ryan, Homer Bailey	180.00
PD	Gaylord Perry, Thomas Diamond	40.00
WR	Wade Boggs, Reid Brignac	40.00
WB	Whitey Ford, Brett Smith	30.00
WP	Whitey Ford, Phillip Hughes	100.00

National Honors

		NM/M
	Common Player:	4.00
	Inserted 1:12	
DB	Daniel Bard	8.00
TB	Travis Buck	8.00
JC	Jeff Clement	8.00
BC	Brent Cox	8.00
TC	Trevor Crowe	4.00
JD	Joey Devine	4.00
AG	Alex Gordon	20.00
BH	Brett Hayes	4.00
LH	Luke Hochevar	8.00
SK	Stephen Kahn	4.00
IK	Ian Kennedy	8.00
JL	Jed Lowrie	4.00
JM	John Mayberry Jr.	8.00
MP	Mike Pelfrey	15.00
CR	Cesar Ramos	8.00
MR	Mark Romanczuk	4.00
RR	Ricky Romero	8.00
DS	Drew Stubbs	8.00
TE	Taylor Teagarden	6.00
TT	Troy Tulowitzki	15.00
CV	Chris Valaika	4.00
RZ	Ryan Zimmerman	10.00

2004 SPX

		NM/M
	Complete Set (202):	
	Common Player:	.25
	Common SP (111-145):	3.00
	Production 1,599	
	Common SP (146-154):	5.00
	Production 499	
	Common SP (155-160):	8.00
	Production 299	
	Common Jersey Auto. (161-202):	
	Production 799	
	Pack (4):	5.00
	Box (18):	75.00
1	Alfonso Soriano	1.00
2	Todd Helton	.75
3	Andruw Jones	.75
4	Eric Gagne	.50
5	Craig Wilson	.25
6	Brian Giles	.25
7	Miguel Tejada	.50
8	Kevin Brown	.25
9	Shawn Green	.50
10	Ben Sheets	.50
11	John Smoltz	.50
12	Tim Hudson	.50
13	Jason Schmidt	.50
14	Paul Konerko	.50
15	Randy Johnson	1.00
16	Roy Oswalt	.50
17	Mike Lowell	.25
18	Carlos Lee	.25
19	Sean Burroughs	.25
20	Edgar Renteria	.50
21	Michael Young	.25
22	Jose Vidro	.25
23	Scott Rolen	1.00
24	Rafael Furcal	.50
25	Tom Glavine	.75
26	Scott Podsednik	.25
27	Gary Sheffield	.75
28	Eric Chavez	.50
29	Mark Prior	.75
30	Chipper Jones	1.00
31	Frank Thomas	1.00
32	Victor Martinez	.50
33	Jake Peavy	.50
34	Carlos Beltran	1.00
35	Roy Halladay	.50
36	Mark Teixeira	.75
37	Jacque Jones	.25
38	Mike Sweeney	.25
39	Troy Glaus	.50
40	Pat Burrell	.50
41	Ichiro Suzuki	2.00
42	Vladimir Guerrero	1.00
43	Bobby Abreu	.50
44	Jim Edmonds	.50
45	Garret Anderson	.40
46	J.D. Drew	.40
47	C.C. Sabathia	.25
48	Joe Mauer	.75
49	Phil Nevin	.25
50	Hank Blalock	.50

51	Carlos Zambrano	.50
52	Mike Piazza	1.50
53	Manny Ramirez	1.00
54	Lance Berkman	.50
55	Delmon Young	.50
56	Nomar Garciaparra	1.00
57	Alex Rodriguez	2.50
58	Rickie Weeks	.50
59	Adrian Beltre	.50
60	Albert Pujols	2.50
61	Richie Sexson	.50
62	Magglio Ordonez	.50
63	Derrek Lee	.75
64	Sammy Sosa	1.50
65	Jason Giambi	.75
66	Curt Schilling	1.00
67	Jorge Posada	.50
68	Rafael Palmeiro	.75
69	Jeff Kent	.50
70	Jose Reyes	.50
71	David Ortiz	1.00
72	Aubrey Huff	.25
73	Jim Thome	1.00
74	Andy Pettitte	.50
75	Barry Zito	.50
76	Carlos Delgado	.50
77	Hideki Matsui	2.00
78	Sean Casey	.25
79	Luis Gonzalez	.25
80	Marcus Giles	.25
81	Preston Wilson	.25
82	Javy Lopez	.25
83	Mark Mulder	.50
84	Derek Jeter	2.50
85	Miguel Cabrera	1.00
86	Vernon Wells	.50
87	Roger Clemens	2.50
88	Lyle Overbay	.25
89	Bret Boone	.25
90	Melvin Mora	.25
91	Greg Maddux	2.00
92	Kerry Wood	.50
93	Ivan Rodriguez	.75
94	Pedro J. Martinez	1.00
95	Jeff Bagwell	.75
96	Torii Hunter	.50
97	Ken Griffey Jr.	2.00
98	Mike Mussina	.75
99	Oliver Perez	.25
100	Josh Beckett	.50
101	Bob Gibson	4.00
102	Cal Ripken Jr.	8.00
103	Ted Williams	8.00
104	Nolan Ryan	8.00
105	Mickey Mantle	10.00
106	Ernie Banks	5.00
107	Joe DiMaggio	6.00
108	Stan Musial	5.00
109	Tom Seaver	4.00
110	Mike Schmidt	6.00
111	Jerry Gil RC	3.00
112	Dioner Navarro RC	3.00
113	Bartolome Fortunato RC	3.00
114	Carlos Hines RC	3.00
115	Franklyn Gracesqui RC	3.00
116	Aarom Baldiris RC	5.00
117	Casey Daigle RC	3.00
118	Joey Gathright RC	3.00
119	William Bergolla RC	3.00
120	Jeff Bennett RC	3.00
121	Lincoln Holdzkom RC	3.00
122	Jorge Vasquez RC	3.00
123	Donnie Kelly RC	3.00
124	Yadier Molina RC	12.00
125	Ryan Wing RC	3.00
126	Justin Germano RC	3.00
127	Freddy Guzman RC	3.00
128	Onil Joseph RC	3.00
129	Roman Colon RC	3.00
130	Roberto Novoa RC	5.00
131	Renyel Pinto RC	5.00
132	Evan Rust RC	3.00
133	Orlando Rodriguez RC	3.00
134	Edwardo Sierra RC	5.00
135	Mike Rose RC	3.00
136	Phil Stockman RC	3.00
137	Greg Dobbs RC	3.00
138	Brad Halsey RC	3.00
139	David Aardsma RC	5.00
140	Joe Hietpas RC	3.00
141	Josh Labandeira RC	3.00
142	Mariano Gomez RC	3.00
143	Jeff Bajenaru RC	3.00
144	Travis Blackley RC	3.00
145	Abe Alvarez RC	5.00
146	Ramon Ramirez RC	5.00
147	Edwin Moreno RC	5.00
148	Ronny Cedeno RC	8.00
149	Hector Gimenez RC	5.00
150	Carlos Vasquez RC	8.00
151	Jesse Crain RC	8.00
152	Logan Kensing RC	5.00
153	Sean Henn RC	5.00
154	Rusty Tucker RC	5.00
155	Justin Lehr RC	5.00
156	Ian Snell RC	8.00
157	Merkin Valdez RC	8.00
158	Scott Proctor RC	8.00
159	Jose Capellan RC	8.00
160	Kazuo Matsui RC	8.00
161	Chris Oxspring RC	8.00
162	Jimmy Serrano RC	8.00
163	Jeff Keppinger RC	12.00
164	Brandon Medders RC	8.00
165	Brian Dallimore RC	8.00
166	Chad Bentz RC	8.00
167	Chris Aguila RC	8.00
168	Chris Saenz RC	8.00
169	Frank Francisco RC	8.00
170	Colby Miller RC	8.00
171	David Crouthers RC	8.00
172	Charles Thomas RC	8.00
173	Dennis Sarfate RC	8.00
174	Lance Cormier RC	8.00
175	Joe Horgan RC	8.00
176	Fernando Nieve RC	8.00
177	Jake Woods RC	8.00
178	Matt Treanor RC	8.00
179	Jerome Gamble RC	8.00
180	John Gall RC	8.00
181	Jorge Sequea RC	8.00
182	Justin Hampson RC	8.00
183	Justin Huisman RC	8.00
184	Justin Knoedler RC	8.00
185	Justin Leone RC	10.00
186	Scott Atchison RC	10.00
187	Jon Knott RC	10.00
188	Kevin Cave RC	10.00
189	Jason Frasor RC	10.00
190	George Sherrill RC	10.00
191	Mike Gosling	10.00
192	Mike Johnston RC	10.00
193	Mike Rouse	10.00
194	Nick Regilio RC	10.00
195	Ryan Meaux RC	10.00
196	Scott Dohmann RC	10.00
197	Shawn Camp RC	10.00
198	Shawn Hill RC	10.00
199	Shingo Takatsu RC	10.00
200	Tim Bausher RC	10.00
201	Tim Bittner RC	10.00
202	Scott Kazmir	15.00

Master Player Prints
No Pricing
Production One Set

Spectrum
Stars (1-100): 5-10X
SP's (101-202): 2-3X
Production 25 Sets

Superscripts
		NM/M
Common Player:		8.00
Inserted 1:18		
JB	Josh Beckett	20.00
MC	Miguel Cabrera	25.00
EC	Eric Chavez	10.00
BC	Bobby Crosby	8.00
BF	Bartolome Fortunato	8.00
NG	Nomar Garciaparra/SP	50.00
MG	Mariano Gomez	8.00
KG	Ken Griffey Jr.	75.00
RH	Rich Harden	10.00
SH	Sean Henn	8.00
CH	Carlos Hines	8.00
LH	Lincoln Holdzkom	8.00
EJ	Edwin Jackson	10.00
DJ	Derek Jeter/SP	200.00
DK	Donnie Kelly	8.00
LA	Josh Labandeira	8.00
JL	Justin Lehr	8.00
JM	Joe Mauer	40.00
IO	Juan Uchoa	8.00
RO	Roy Oswalt	20.00
MP	Mark Prior	10.00
SP	Scott Proctor	10.00
AP	Albert Pujols/SP	240.00
RR	Ramon Ramirez	10.00
JR	Jose Reyes	30.00
CR	Cal Ripken Jr./SP	125.00
RU	Evan Rust	8.00
ES	Edwardo Sierra	8.00
AS	Alfredo Simon	8.00
IS	Ian Snell	8.00
PS	Phil Stockman	8.00
TE	Miguel Tejada	15.00
MT	Mark Teixeira	30.00
MV	Merkin Valdez	8.00
CV	Carlos Vasquez	8.00
VE	Michael Vento	8.00
BW	Brandon Webb	12.00
RW	Rickie Weeks	15.00
DW	Dontrelle Willis	10.00
DY	Delmon Young	12.00

Swatch Supremacy Cut Signatures
No pricing due to scarcity.

Swatch Supremacy Signatures
		NM/M
Common Player:		8.00
Production 999 unless noted.		
Spectrum:		1.5-3X
Production 25 Sets		
GA	Garret Anderson/275	12.00
RB	Rocco Baldelli	10.00
JB	Josh Beckett	15.00
AB	Angel Berroa	10.00
HB	Hank Blalock	10.00
SB	Sean Burroughs	10.00
MC	Miguel Cabrera	30.00
EC	Eric Chavez/275	15.00
CC	Chad Cordero	15.00
BC	Bobby Crosby	10.00
AE	Adam Eaton	10.00
NG	Nomar Garciaparra/275	50.00
MG	Marcus Giles	10.00
GR	Khalil Greene	10.00
KG	Ken Griffey Jr/275	85.00
RH	Rich Harden	10.00
DJ	Derek Jeter/275	180.00
CK	Casey Kotchman	10.00
CL	Cliff Lee	15.00
DL	Derrek Lee/275	30.00
JM	Joe Mauer	40.00
RO	Roy Oswalt	20.00
LO	Lyle Overbay	15.00
CP	Corey Patterson	12.00
JP	Jake Peavy	35.00
SP	Scott Podsednik	15.00
MP	Mark Prior/275	10.00
AP	Albert Pujols/275	240.00
HR	Horacio Ramirez	10.00
JR	Jose Reyes	15.00
CR	Cal Ripken Jr./275	140.00
NR	Nolan Ryan/275	120.00
BS	Ben Sheets	15.00
MT	Mark Teixeira	30.00
BW	Brandon Webb	15.00
RW	Rickie Weeks	15.00
DW	Dontrelle Willis	15.00
JW	Jerome Williams	10.00
MY	Michael Young	15.00

Winning Materials

		NM/M
Common Player:		8.00
Inserted 1:18		
Spectrum:		2-3X
Production 25 Sets		
JB	Jeff Bagwell	10.00
BE	Josh Beckett	10.00
HB	Hank Blalock	10.00
KB	Kevin Brown	8.00
EC	Eric Chavez	8.00
RC	Roger Clemens	20.00
CD	Carlos Delgado	10.00
JG	Jason Giambi	12.00
TG	Troy Glaus	8.00
SG	Shawn Green	8.00
VG	Vladimir Guerrero	12.00
DJ	Derek Jeter	35.00
CJ	Chipper Jones	10.00
GM	Greg Maddux	15.00
HM	Hideki Matsui	30.00
MM	Mike Mussina	10.00
RP	Rafael Palmeiro	10.00
PI	Mike Piazza	15.00
JP	Jorge Posada	10.00
MP	Mark Prior	8.00
AP	Albert Pujols	30.00
MR	Manny Ramirez	15.00
JR	Jose Reyes	15.00
SR	Scott Rolen	8.00
GS	Gary Sheffield	10.00
SS	Sammy Sosa	15.00
IS	Ichiro Suzuki	30.00
TE	Miguel Tejada	10.00
JT	Jim Thome	12.00

2005 SP Collection

		NM/M
Complete SPx Set (100):		25.00
Common Player:		.25
Pack (5):		6.00
Box (20):		100.00
1	Aaron Harang	.25
2	Aaron Rowand	.25
3	Aaron Miles	.25
4	Adrian Gonzalez	.25
5	Alex Rios	.25
6	Angel Berroa	.25
7	B.J. Upton	.25
8	Brandon Claussen	.25
9	Andy Marte	.25
10	Brandon Webb	.25
11	Bronson Arroyo	.25
12	Casey Kotchman	.25
13	Cesar Izturis	.25
14	Chad Cordero	.25
15	Chad Tracy	.25
16	Charles Thomas	.25
17	Chase Utley	.50
18	Chone Figgins	.25
19	Chris Burke	.25
20	Cliff Lee	.25
21	Clint Barmes	.25
22	Coco Crisp	.25
23	Bill Hall	.25
24	Dallas McPherson	.25
25	Brad Halsey	.25
26	Daniel Cabrera	.25
27	Danny Haren	.25
28	David Bush	.25
29	David DeJesus	.25
30	D.J. Houlton	.25
31	Derek Jeter	3.00
32	Dewon Brazelton	.25
33	Edwin Jackson	.25
34	Brad Hawpe	.25
35	Brandon Inge	.25
36	Brett Myers	.25
37	Garrett Atkins	.25
38	Gavin Floyd	.25
39	Grady Sizemore	.50
40	Guillermo Mota	.25
41	Carlos Guillen	.25
42	Gustavo Chacin	.25
43	Huston Street	.25
44	Chris Duffy	.25
45	J.D. Closser	.25
46	J.J. Hardy	.25
47	Jason Bartlett	.25
48	Jason Dubois	.25
49	Chris Shelton	.25
50	Jason Lane	.25
51	Jayson Werth	.25
52	Jeff Baker	.25
53	Jeff Francis	.25
54	Jeremy Bonderman	.25
55	Jeremy Reed	.25
56	Jerome Williams	.25
57	Jesse Crain	.25
58	Chris Young	.25
59	Jhonny Peralta	.25
60	Joe Blanton	.25
61	Joe Crede	.25
62	Joel Pineiro	.25
63	Joey Gathright	.25
64	John Buck	.25
65	Jonny Gomes	.25
66	Jorge Cantu	.25
67	Dan Johnson	.25
68	Jose Valverde	.25
69	Ervin Santana	.25
70	Justin Morneau	.50
71	Keiichi Yabu	.25
72	Ken Griffey Jr.	2.00
73	Jason Repko	.25
74	Kevin Youkilis	.25
75	Koyie Hill	.25
76	Laynce Nix	.25
77	Luke Scott RC	1.00
78	Juan Rivera	.25
79	Justin Duchscherer	.25
80	Mark Teahen	.25
81	Lance Niekro	.25
82	Michael Cuddyer	.25
83	Nick Swisher	.25
84	Noah Lowry	.25
85	Matt Holliday	.50
86	Reed Johnson	.25
87	Rich Harden	.25
88	Robb Quinlan	.25
89	Nick Johnson	.25
90	Ryan Howard	1.00
91	Nook Logan	.25
92	Steve Schmoll	.25
93	Tadahito Iguchi	.25
94	Willy Taveras	.25
95	Wily Mo Pena	.25
96	Xavier Nady	.25
97	Yadier Molina	.25
98	Yhency Brazoban	.25
99	Ryan Freel	.25
100	Zack Greinke	.25

Complete SP Authentic Set (100): 25.00
Common Player: .25

1	A.J. Burnett	.25
2	Aaron Rowand	.25
3	Adam Dunn	.75
4	Adrian Beltre	.25
5	Adrian Gonzalez	.25
6	Akinori Otsuka	.25
7	Albert Pujols	3.00
8	Andre Dawson	.50
9	Andruw Jones	.50
10	Aramis Ramirez	.50
11	Barry Larkin	.50
12	Ben Sheets	.50
13	Bo Jackson	.50
14	Bobby Abreu	.50
15	Bobby Crosby	.25
16	Bronson Arroyo	.25
17	Cal Ripken Jr.	4.00
18	Carl Crawford	.50
19	Carlos Zambrano	.50
20	Casey Kotchman	.25
21	Cesar Izturis	.25
22	Chone Figgins	.25
23	Corey Patterson	.25
24	Craig Biggio	.50
25	Dale Murphy	.50
26	Dallas McPherson	.25
27	Danny Haren	.25
28	Darryl Strawberry	.25
29	David Ortiz	1.00
30	David Wright	1.00
31	Derek Jeter	3.00
32	Derrek Lee	.50
33	Don Mattingly	1.50
34	Dwight Gooden	.50
35	Edgar Renteria	.50
36	Eric Chavez	.25
37	Eric Gagne	.25
38	Gary Sheffield	.50
39	Gavin Floyd	.25
40	Pedro Martinez	1.00
41	Greg Maddux	2.00
42	Hank Blalock	.50
43	Huston Street	.25
44	J.D. Drew	.25
45	Jake Peavy	.50
46	Jake Westbrook	.25
47	Jason Bay	.25
48	Austin Kearns	.25
49	Jeremy Reed	.25
50	Jim Rice	.50
51	Jimmy Rollins	.50
52	Joe Blanton	.25
53	Joe Mauer	.50
54	Johan Santana	1.00
55	John Smoltz	.25
56	Johnny Estrada	.25
57	Jose Reyes	.50
58	Ken Griffey Jr.	2.00
59	Kerry Wood	.50
60	Khalil Greene	.25
61	Marcus Giles	.25
62	Melvin Mora	.25
63	Mark Grace	.50
64	Mark Mulder	.25
65	Mark Prior	1.00
66	Mark Teixeira	.50
67	Matt Clement	.25
68	Michael Young	.50
69	Miguel Cabrera	1.00
70	Miguel Tejada	.75
71	Mike Piazza	1.50
72	Mike Schmidt	2.00
73	Nolan Ryan	3.00
74	Oliver Perez	.25
75	Nick Johnson	.25
76	Paul Molitor	.75
77	Rafael Palmeiro	.50
78	Randy Johnson	1.00
79	Reggie Jackson	1.00
80	Rich Harden	.25
81	Rickie Weeks	.25
82	Robin Yount	1.00
83	Roger Clemens	3.00
84	Roy Oswalt	.50
85	Ryan Howard	1.00
86	Ryne Sandberg	2.00
87	Scott Kazmir	.50
88	Scott Rolen	1.00
89	Sean Burroughs	.25
90	Sean Casey	.25
91	Shingo Takatsu	.25
92	Tim Hudson	.50
93	Tony Gwynn	1.00
94	Torii Hunter	.25
95	Travis Hafner	.25
96	Victor Martinez	.25
97	Vladimir Guerrero	1.00
98	Wade Boggs	.50
99	Will Clark	.25
100	Yadier Molina	.25

SP Authentic Chirography
No Pricing
Production 15 Sets

SP Authentic Chirography Triple
No Pricing
Production Five Sets

SP Authentic Honors
		NM/M
Common Player:		1.00
Production 299 Sets		
JB	Jason Bay	1.50
AB	Adrian Beltre	1.50
WB	Wade Boggs	3.00
BO	Jeremy Bonderman	1.00
CA	Miguel Cabrera	3.00
WC	Will Clark	1.50
RC	Roger Clemens	6.00
CC	Carl Crawford	1.50
BC	Bobby Crosby	1.50
MG	Marcus Giles	1.00
DG	Dwight Gooden	1.50
GR	Khalil Greene	2.00
ZG	Zack Greinke	1.50
KG	Ken Griffey Jr.	4.00
TG	Tony Gwynn	3.00
TH	Travis Hafner	1.00
RH	Rich Harden	1.00
BJ	Bo Jackson	2.00
DJ	Derek Jeter	6.00
SK	Scott Kazmir	1.50
BL	Barry Larkin	1.50
VM	Victor Martinez	1.00
JM	Joe Mauer	1.50
MC	Dallas McPherson	1.00
PM	Paul Molitor	2.00
MO	Justin Morneau	1.00
DM	Dale Murphy	1.50
DO	David Ortiz	2.00
CP	Corey Patterson	1.00
JP	Jake Peavy	1.50
OP	Oliver Perez	1.00
AP	Albert Pujols	6.00
AR	Aramis Ramirez	1.50
RE	Jose Reyes	1.50
CR	Cal Ripken Jr.	8.00
JR	Jimmy Rollins	1.50
NR	Nolan Ryan	6.00
RS	Ryne Sandberg	4.00
JS	Johan Santana	2.00
MS	Mike Schmidt	4.00
BS	Ben Sheets	1.50
SM	John Smoltz	1.50
ST	Shingo Takatsu	1.00
MT	Mark Teixeira	1.50
TE	Miguel Tejada	2.00
BU	B.J. Upton	1.00
JW	Jake Westbrook	1.00
DW	David Wright	3.00
MY	Michael Young	1.00
CZ	Carlos Zambrano	1.50

SP Authentic Honors Jersey
		NM/M
Common Player:		4.00
Production 130 Sets		
JB	Jason Bay	4.00
AB	Adrian Beltre	6.00
WB	Wade Boggs	8.00
BO	Jeremy Bonderman	4.00
CA	Miguel Cabrera	8.00
WC	Will Clark	4.00
RC	Roger Clemens	10.00
CC	Carl Crawford	4.00
BC	Bobby Crosby	4.00
MG	Marcus Giles	4.00
DG	Dwight Gooden	4.00
GR	Khalil Greene	8.00
ZG	Zack Greinke	4.00
KG	Ken Griffey Jr.	15.00
TG	Tony Gwynn	8.00
TH	Travis Hafner	4.00
RH	Rich Harden	4.00
BJ	Bo Jackson	10.00
DJ	Derek Jeter	15.00
SK	Scott Kazmir	4.00
BL	Barry Larkin	4.00
VM	Victor Martinez	4.00
JM	Joe Mauer	6.00
MC	Dallas McPherson	4.00
PM	Paul Molitor	4.00
MO	Justin Morneau	4.00
DM	Dale Murphy	8.00
DO	David Ortiz	8.00
CP	Corey Patterson	4.00
JP	Jake Peavy	6.00
OP	Oliver Perez	4.00
AP	Albert Pujols	15.00
AR	Aramis Ramirez	6.00
RE	Jose Reyes	6.00
CR	Cal Ripken Jr.	20.00
JR	Jimmy Rollins	6.00
NR	Nolan Ryan	15.00
RS	Ryne Sandberg	10.00
JS	Johan Santana	4.00
MS	Mike Schmidt	6.00
BS	Ben Sheets	4.00
SM	John Smoltz	4.00
ST	Shingo Takatsu	4.00
MT	Mark Teixeira	6.00
TE	Miguel Tejada	6.00
BU	B.J. Upton	6.00
JW	Jake Westbrook	4.00
DW	David Wright	15.00
MY	Michael Young	6.00
CZ	Carlos Zambrano	6.00

SP Authentic Honors Signatures
No Pricing
Production Five Sets

SP Authentic Materials
		NM/M
Common Player:		
Production 199 Sets		
Gold:		1X
Production 99 Sets		
1	A.J. Burnett	4.00
2	Aaron Rowand	4.00
3	Adam Dunn	6.00
4	Adrian Beltre	4.00
5	Adrian Gonzalez	4.00
6	Akinori Otsuka	4.00
7	Albert Pujols	15.00
8	Andre Dawson	6.00
9	Andruw Jones	6.00
10	Aramis Ramirez	6.00
11	Barry Larkin	6.00
12	Ben Sheets	4.00
13	Bo Jackson	8.00
14	Bobby Abreu	4.00
15	Bobby Crosby	4.00
16	Bronson Arroyo	6.00
17	Cal Ripken Jr.	20.00
18	Carl Crawford	6.00
19	Carlos Zambrano	4.00
20	Casey Kotchman	4.00
21	Cesar Izturis	4.00
22	Chone Figgins	4.00
23	Corey Patterson	4.00
24	Craig Biggio	6.00
25	Dale Murphy	6.00
26	Dallas McPherson	4.00
27	Danny Haren	4.00
28	Darryl Strawberry	4.00
29	David Ortiz	10.00
30	David Wright	10.00
31	Derek Jeter	15.00
32	Derrek Lee	6.00
33	Don Mattingly	10.00
34	Dwight Gooden	6.00
35	Edgar Renteria	6.00
36	Eric Chavez	4.00
37	Eric Gagne	6.00
38	Gary Sheffield	6.00
39	Gavin Floyd	4.00
40	Pedro Martinez	8.00
41	Greg Maddux	10.00
42	Hank Blalock	4.00

43	Huston Street	6.00
44	J.D. Drew	4.00
45	Jake Peavy	6.00
46	Jake Westbrook	4.00
47	Jason Bay	4.00
48	Austin Kearns	4.00
49	Jeremy Reed	4.00
50	Jim Rice	6.00
51	Jimmy Rollins	6.00
52	Joe Blanton	4.00
53	Joe Mauer	6.00
54	Johan Santana	6.00
55	John Smoltz	6.00
56	Johnny Estrada	4.00
57	Jose Reyes	6.00
58	Ken Griffey Jr.	12.00
59	Kerry Wood	6.00
60	Khalil Greene	6.00
61	Marcus Giles	4.00
62	Melvin Mora	4.00
63	Mark Grace	6.00
64	Mark Mulder	4.00
65	Mark Prior	8.00
66	Mark Teixeira	6.00
67	Matt Clement	4.00
68	Michael Young	4.00
69	Miguel Cabrera	6.00
70	Miguel Tejada	6.00
71	Mike Piazza	8.00
72	Mike Schmidt	8.00
73	Nolan Ryan	15.00
74	Oliver Perez	4.00
75	Nick Johnson	4.00
76	Paul Molitor	8.00
77	Rafael Palmeiro	8.00
78	Randy Johnson	8.00
79	Reggie Jackson	8.00
80	Rich Harden	6.00
81	Rickie Weeks	5.00
82	Robin Yount	8.00
83	Roger Clemens	10.00
84	Roy Oswalt	4.00
85	Ryan Howard	15.00
86	Ryne Sandberg	8.00
87	Scott Kazmir	4.00
88	Scott Rolen	6.00
89	Sean Burroughs	4.00
90	Sean Casey	4.00
91	Shingo Takatsu	4.00
92	Tim Hudson	6.00
93	Tony Gwynn	8.00
94	Torii Hunter	6.00
95	Travis Hafner	4.00
96	Victor Martinez	4.00
97	Vladimir Guerrero	8.00
98	Wade Boggs	6.00
99	Will Clark	6.00
100	Yadier Molina	4.00

SP Authentic Signatures

NM/M

Production 25-550
Gold: No Pricing
Production 10 Sets

2	Aaron Rowand/550	15.00
3	Adam Dunn/25	20.00
4	Adrian Beltre/125	15.00
5	Adrian Gonzalez/550	20.00
6	Akinori Otsuka/475	10.00
7	Andre Dawson/125	20.00
10	Aramis Ramirez/475	15.00
11	Barry Larkin/125	20.00
12	Ben Sheets/350	12.00
15	Bobby Crosby/350	8.00
16	Bronson Arroyo/550	15.00
18	Carl Crawford/475	15.00
20	Casey Kotchman/550	8.00
21	Cesar Izturis/550	8.00
22	Chone Figgins/550	15.00
23	Corey Patterson/350	10.00
24	Craig Biggio/350	30.00
25	Dale Murphy/350	20.00
26	Dallas McPherson/550	10.00
27	Danny Haren/550	10.00
28	Darryl Strawberry/125	12.00
30	David Wright/350	60.00
31	Derek Jeter/150	140.00
32	Derrek Lee/350	15.00
35	Dwight Gooden/475	15.00
36	Eric Chavez/75	15.00
37	Gavin Floyd/550	8.00
43	Huston Street/550	25.00
45	Jake Peavy/475	15.00
46	Jake Westbrook/550	8.00
47	Jason Bay/475	12.00
48	Austin Kearns/75	10.00
49	Jeremy Reed/550	15.00
50	Jim Rice/350	15.00
52	Joe Blanton/550	8.00
53	Joe Mauer/350	20.00
57	Jose Reyes/475	35.00
60	Khalil Greene/350	8.00
62	Melvin Mora/475	10.00
64	Mark Mulder/350	8.00
66	Mark Teixeira/125	25.00
67	Matt Clement/350	10.00
68	Michael Young/350	15.00
69	Miguel Cabrera/125	25.00
72	Oliver Perez/475	10.00
75	Nick Johnson/350	10.00
84	Roy Oswalt/125	20.00
85	Ryan Howard/550	70.00
86	Ryne Sandberg/25	125.00
87	Scott Kazmir/475	15.00
89	Sean Burroughs/475	10.00
91	Shingo Takatsu/550	10.00

SP Authentic Signature Materials

No Pricing
Production 10 Sets

SP Collection of Stars

Common Player: 1.00
Production 299 Sets

BR	Bronson Arroyo	1.00
GA	Garrett Atkins	1.00
JE	Jeff Baker	1.00
BA	Clint Barmes	1.00
JB	Jason Bartlett	1.00
JA	Jason Bay	1.00
BE	Adrian Beltre	1.50
BL	Joe Blanton	1.00
BO	Jeremy Bonderman	1.00
YB	Yhency Brazoban	1.00
CB	Chris Burke	1.50
AB	A.J. Burnett	1.00
DB	David Bush	1.00
DC	Daniel Cabrera	1.00
MC	Miguel Cabrera	2.00
CA	Jorge Cantu	1.00
GC	Gustavo Chacin	1.00
RC	Roger Clemens	6.00
JD	J.D. Closser	1.00
CH	Chad Cordero	1.00
JC	Jesse Crain	1.00
CC	Carl Crawford	1.00
CO	Coco Crisp	1.00
DD	David DeJesus	1.00
DU	Jason Dubois	1.00
CD	Chris Duffy	1.00
CF	Chone Figgins	1.00
GF	Gavin Floyd	1.00
JF	Jeff Francis	1.00
RF	Ryan Freel	1.00
JG	Joey Gathright	1.00
GO	Jonny Gomes	1.00
AG	Adrian Gonzalez	1.00
GR	Khalil Greene	2.00
ZG	Zack Greinke	1.00
KG	Ken Griffey Jr.	4.00
CG	Carlos Guillen	1.00
TR	Travis Hafner	1.00
BH	Bill Hall	1.00
RH	Rich Harden	1.50
DH	Danny Haren	1.00
MH	Matt Holliday	1.00
HO	Ryan Howard	2.00
BI	Brandon Inge	1.00
CI	Cesar Izturis	1.00
EJ	Edwin Jackson	1.00
DJ	Derek Jeter	6.00
NJ	Nick Johnson	1.00
RJ	Reed Johnson	1.00
SK	Scott Kazmir	1.00
CK	Casey Kotchman	1.00
JL	Jason Lane	1.00
LE	Brandon League	1.00
CL	Cliff Lee	1.00
GM	Greg Maddux	4.00
AM	Andy Marte	1.00
JM	Joe Mauer	1.50
DM	Dallas McPherson	1.00
YM	Yadier Molina	1.00
MM	Melvin Mora	1.00
MO	Guillermo Mota	1.00
BM	Brett Myers	1.00
DO	David Ortiz	2.00
CP	Corey Patterson	1.00
JP	Jake Peavy	1.50
WM	Wily Mo Pena	1.00
OP	Oliver Perez	1.00
PI	Joel Pineiro	1.00
MP	Mark Prior	2.00
AP	Albert Pujols	6.00
RQ	Robb Quinlan	1.00
RA	Aramis Ramirez	1.50
JR	Jeremy Reed	1.00
RE	Jose Reyes	1.50
RI	Alex Rios	1.00
CR	Cal Ripken Jr.	8.00
RO	Jimmy Rollins	1.00
AR	Aaron Rowand	1.00
JS	Johan Santana	2.00
MS	Mike Schmidt	10.00
LS	Luke Scott	1.00
CS	Chris Shelton	1.00
GS	Grady Sizemore	1.50
SM	John Smoltz	1.50
HS	Huston Street	1.00
NS	Nick Swisher	1.00
ST	Shingo Takatsu	1.00
WT	Willy Taveras	1.00
MT	Mark Teahen	1.00
TE	Mark Teixeira	1.50
MI	Miguel Tejada	1.50
TH	Charles Thomas	1.00
CT	Chad Tracy	1.00
BU	B.J. Upton	1.50
WE	Jayson Werth	1.00
JW	Jake Westbrook	1.00
DW	David Wright	3.00
KY	Kevin Youkilis	1.00
MY	Michael Young	1.00
CZ	Carlos Zambrano	1.50

SP Collection of Stars Jersey

NM/M
Production 130 Sets

BR	Bronson Arroyo	4.00
GA	Garrett Atkins	4.00
JE	Jeff Baker	4.00
BA	Clint Barmes	6.00
JB	Jason Bartlett	4.00
JA	Jason Bay	4.00
BE	Adrian Beltre	4.00
BL	Joe Blanton	4.00
BO	Jeremy Bonderman	4.00
YB	Yhency Brazoban	4.00
CB	Chris Burke	4.00
AB	A.J. Burnett	4.00
DB	David Bush	4.00
DC	Daniel Cabrera	4.00
MC	Miguel Cabrera	8.00
CA	Jorge Cantu	4.00
GC	Gustavo Chacin	4.00
RC	Roger Clemens	10.00
JD	J.D. Closser	4.00
CH	Chad Cordero	4.00
JC	Jesse Crain	4.00
CC	Carl Crawford	4.00
CO	Coco Crisp	4.00
DD	David DeJesus	4.00
DU	Jason Dubois	4.00
CD	Chris Duffy	6.00
CF	Chone Figgins	4.00
GF	Gavin Floyd	4.00
JF	Jeff Francis	4.00
RF	Ryan Freel	4.00
JG	Joey Gathright	4.00
GO	Jonny Gomes	6.00
AG	Adrian Gonzalez	4.00
GR	Khalil Greene	6.00
ZG	Zack Greinke	4.00
KG	Ken Griffey Jr.	15.00
CG	Carlos Guillen	4.00
TR	Travis Hafner	4.00
BH	Bill Hall	4.00
RH	Rich Harden	4.00
DH	Danny Haren	4.00
MH	Matt Holliday	8.00
HO	Ryan Howard	15.00
BI	Brandon Inge	4.00
CI	Cesar Izturis	4.00
EJ	Edwin Jackson	4.00
DJ	Derek Jeter	15.00
NJ	Nick Johnson	4.00
RJ	Reed Johnson	4.00
SK	Scott Kazmir	4.00
CK	Casey Kotchman	4.00
JL	Jason Lane	4.00
LE	Brandon League	4.00
CL	Cliff Lee	4.00
GM	Greg Maddux	10.00
AM	Andy Marte	4.00
JM	Joe Mauer	6.00
DM	Dallas McPherson	4.00
YM	Yadier Molina	4.00
MM	Melvin Mora	4.00
MO	Guillermo Mota	4.00
BM	Brett Myers	4.00
DO	David Ortiz	8.00
CP	Corey Patterson	4.00
JP	Jake Peavy	6.00
WM	Wily Mo Pena	4.00
OP	Oliver Perez	4.00
PI	Joel Pineiro	4.00
MP	Mark Prior	6.00
AP	Albert Pujols	15.00
RQ	Robb Quinlan	4.00
RA	Aramis Ramirez	4.00
JR	Jeremy Reed	4.00
RE	Jose Reyes	6.00
RI	Alex Rios	4.00
CR	Cal Ripken Jr.	20.00
RO	Jimmy Rollins	4.00
AR	Aaron Rowand	6.00
JS	Johan Santana	8.00
MS	Mike Schmidt	10.00
LS	Luke Scott	4.00
CS	Chris Shelton	4.00
GS	Grady Sizemore	6.00
SM	John Smoltz	6.00
HS	Huston Street	6.00
NS	Nick Swisher	4.00
ST	Shingo Takatsu	4.00
WT	Willy Taveras	4.00
MT	Mark Teahen	4.00
TE	Mark Teixeira	6.00
MI	Miguel Tejada	6.00
TH	Charles Thomas	4.00
CT	Chad Tracy	4.00
BU	B.J. Upton	4.00
WE	Jayson Werth	4.00
JW	Jake Westbrook	4.00
DW	David Wright	10.00
KY	Kevin Youkilis	4.00
CZ	Carlos Zambrano	4.00

SP Collection of Stars Signatures

No Pricing
Production Five Sets

SPx Materials

NM/M
Common Player: 3.00
Production 199 Sets
Spectrum: 1X
Production 99 Sets

1	Aaron Harang	3.00
2	Aaron Rowand	5.00
3	Adrian Miles	3.00
4	Adrian Gonzalez	3.00
5	Alex Rios	3.00
6	Angel Berroa	3.00
7	B.J. Upton	5.00
8	Brandon Claussen	3.00
9	Andy Marte	3.00
10	Brandon Webb	5.00
11	Bronson Arroyo	3.00
12	Casey Kotchman	3.00
13	Cesar Izturis	3.00
14	Chad Cordero	3.00
15	Chad Tracy	3.00
16	Charles Thomas	3.00
17	Chase Utley	8.00
18	Chone Figgins	3.00
19	Chris Burke	5.00
20	Cliff Lee	3.00
21	Clint Barmes	5.00
22	Coco Crisp	3.00
23	Bill Hall	3.00
24	Dallas McPherson	3.00
25	Brad Halsey	3.00
26	Daniel Cabrera	3.00
27	Danny Haren	3.00
28	David Bush	3.00
29	David DeJesus	3.00
30	D.J. Houlton	3.00
31	Derek Jeter	20.00
32	Dewon Brazelton	3.00
33	Edwin Jackson	3.00
34	Brad Hawpe	3.00
35	Brandon Inge	3.00
36	Brett Myers	3.00
37	Garrett Atkins	3.00
38	Gavin Floyd	3.00
39	Grady Sizemore	10.00
40	Guillermo Mota	3.00
41	Carlos Guillen	3.00
42	Gustavo Chacin	3.00
43	Huston Street	5.00
44	Chris Duffy	3.00
45	J.D. Closser	3.00
46	J.J. Hardy	3.00
47	Jason Bartlett	3.00
48	Jason Dubois	3.00
49	Chris Shelton	3.00
50	Jason Lane	3.00
51	Jayson Werth	3.00
52	Jeff Baker	3.00
53	Jeff Francis	3.00
54	Jeremy Bonderman	3.00
55	Jeremy Reed	3.00
56	Jerome Williams	3.00
57	Jesse Crain	3.00
58	Chris Young	3.00
59	Jhonny Peralta	3.00
60	Joe Blanton	3.00
61	Joe Crede	3.00
62	Joel Pineiro	3.00
63	Joey Gathright	3.00
64	John Buck	3.00
65	Jonny Gomes	8.00
66	Jorge Cantu	3.00
67	Dan Johnson	3.00
68	Jose Valverde	3.00
69	Ervin Santana	3.00
70	Justin Morneau	3.00
71	Keiichi Yabu	3.00
72	Ken Griffey Jr.	15.00
73	Jason Repko	3.00
74	Kevin Youkilis	3.00
75	Koyie Hill	3.00
76	Laynce Nix	3.00
77	Luke Scott	3.00
78	Juan Rivera	3.00
79	Justin Duchscherer	3.00
80	Mark Teahen	3.00
81	Lance Niekro	3.00
82	Michael Cuddyer	3.00
83	Nick Swisher	3.00
84	Noah Lowry	3.00
85	Matt Holliday	8.00
86	Reed Johnson	3.00
87	Rich Harden	5.00
88	Robb Quinlan	3.00
89	Nick Johnson	3.00
90	Ryan Howard	20.00
91	Nook Logan	3.00
92	Steve Schmoll	3.00
93	Tadahito Iguchi	20.00
94	Willy Taveras	3.00
95	Wily Mo Pena	3.00
96	Xavier Nady	3.00
97	Yadier Molina	3.00
98	Yhency Brazoban	3.00
99	Ryan Freel	3.00
100	Zack Greinke	3.00

SPx Signatures

NM/M
Production 50-350
Spectrum: No Pricing
Production 10 Sets

Jersey Auto: No Pricing
Production 10 Sets

1	Aaron Harang/350	8.00
2	Aaron Rowand/150	12.00
4	Adrian Gonzalez/225	20.00
6	Angel Berroa/150	8.00
7	B.J. Upton/50	12.00
8	Brandon Claussen/350	8.00
9	Andy Marte/350	8.00
11	Bronson Arroyo/350	15.00
12	Casey Kotchman/350	8.00
13	Cesar Izturis/150	8.00
14	Chad Cordero/350	8.00
15	Chad Tracy/350	8.00
16	Charles Thomas/350	8.00
17	Chase Utley/350	50.00
18	Chone Figgins/150	8.00
19	Chris Burke/350	8.00
20	Cliff Lee/225	20.00
21	Clint Barmes/350	10.00
22	Coco Crisp/225	8.00
23	Bill Hall/350	8.00
24	Dallas McPherson/150	8.00
25	Brad Halsey/350	8.00
27	Daniel Cabrera/350	10.00
28	Danny Haren/225	8.00
29	David Bush/350	8.00
30	David DeJesus/225	8.00
31	Derek Jeter/50	150.00
32	Dewon Brazelton/225	8.00
33	Edwin Jackson/150	8.00
34	Brad Hawpe/350	12.00
35	Brandon Inge/350	10.00
36	Brett Myers/150	8.00
37	Garrett Atkins/350	10.00
38	Gavin Floyd/150	8.00
39	Grady Sizemore/350	30.00
40	Guillermo Mota/350	8.00
41	Carlos Guillen/150	8.00
42	Gustavo Chacin/350	10.00
43	Huston Street/350	15.00
44	Chris Duffy/225	10.00
45	J.D. Closser/350	8.00
46	J.J. Hardy/350	10.00
47	Jason Bartlett/350	8.00
48	Jason Dubois/350	8.00
51	Jayson Werth/350	30.00
53	Jeff Baker/350	8.00
54	Jeff Francis/150	8.00
55	Jeremy Bonderman/50	10.00
57	Jeremy Reed/150	10.00
59	Jhonny Peralta/350	15.00
60	Joe Blanton/350	10.00
61	Joe Crede/350	8.00
62	Joel Pineiro/150	15.00
63	Joey Gathright/350	8.00
64	John Buck/350	8.00
66	Jorge Cantu/350	15.00
67	Dan Johnson/350	8.00
68	Jose Valverde/350	8.00
69	Ervin Santana/350	15.00
71	Keiichi Yabu/350	10.00
73	Jason Repko/350	10.00
74	Kevin Youkilis/225	8.00
75	Koyie Hill/350	10.00
77	Luke Scott/350	15.00
78	Juan Rivera/225	8.00
79	Justin Duchscherer/350	10.00
80	Mark Teahen/350	8.00
81	Lance Niekro/350	10.00
82	Michael Cuddyer/350	12.00
84	Noah Lowry/150	8.00
85	Matt Holliday/225	35.00
87	Reed Johnson/350	8.00
88	Robb Quinlan/350	5.00
89	Nick Johnson/350	8.00
90	Ryan Howard/225	80.00
91	Nook Logan/350	8.00
92	Steve Schmoll/350	5.00
93	Tadahito Iguchi/50	50.00
95	Wily Mo Pena/150	8.00
96	Xavier Nady/150	12.00
99	Ryan Freel/350	8.00
100	Yhency Brazoban/350	8.00

SPx Superscripts Signatures

No Pricing
Production 15 Sets

SPx Superscripts Triple Signature

No Pricing
Production Five Sets

SPx Winning Materials Dual

No Pricing
Production 20 Sets
Dual Auto: No Pricing
Production Five Sets

SPXtreme Stats

NM/M
Common Player: 1.00
Production 299 Sets

BA	Bobby Abreu	1.50
AB	Adrian Beltre	1.50
CB	Craig Biggio	1.50
HB	Hank Blalock	1.50
MC	Miguel Cabrera	3.00
SC	Sean Casey	1.00
EC	Eric Chavez	1.00
RC	Roger Clemens	6.00
CC	Carl Crawford	1.00
BC	Bobby Crosby	1.00
JD	J.D. Drew	1.00
AD	Adam Dunn	1.50
EG	Eric Gagne	1.00
GR	Khalil Greene	1.50
KG	Ken Griffey Jr.	4.00
VG	Vladimir Guerrero	2.00
TH	Tim Hudson	1.50
HU	Torii Hunter	1.00
DJ	Derek Jeter	6.00
RJ	Randy Johnson	2.00
AJ	Andruw Jones	1.50
DL	Derrek Lee	1.50
GM	Greg Maddux	4.00
VM	Victor Martinez	1.00
JM	Joe Mauer	1.50
MO	Melvin Mora	1.00
MM	Mark Mulder	1.50
DO	David Ortiz	2.00
RO	Roy Oswalt	1.50
RP	Rafael Palmeiro	1.50
CP	Corey Patterson	1.00
JP	Jake Peavy	1.50
OP	Oliver Perez	1.00
PI	Mike Piazza	3.00
MP	Mark Prior	2.00
AP	Albert Pujols	6.00
AR	Aramis Ramirez	1.50
ER	Edgar Renteria	1.00
JR	Jose Reyes	1.00
SR	Scott Rolen	2.00
SA	Johan Santana	1.50
BS	Ben Sheets	1.00
GS	Gary Sheffield	1.50
SM	John Smoltz	1.50
MT	Mark Teixeira	1.50
TE	Miguel Tejada	1.50
KW	Kerry Wood	1.50
MY	Michael Young	1.50
DW	David Wright	3.00
CZ	Carlos Zambrano	1.50

SPXtreme Stats Jersey

NM/M

BA	Bobby Abreu	6.00
AB	Adrian Beltre	6.00
CB	Craig Biggio	6.00
HB	Hank Blalock	4.00
MC	Miguel Cabrera	8.00
SC	Sean Casey	4.00
EC	Eric Chavez	4.00
RC	Roger Clemens	10.00
CC	Carl Crawford	4.00
BC	Bobby Crosby	4.00
JD	J.D. Drew	4.00
AD	Adam Dunn	6.00
EG	Eric Gagne	4.00
GR	Khalil Greene	4.00
KG	Ken Griffey Jr.	15.00
VG	Vladimir Guerrero	8.00
TH	Tim Hudson	4.00
HU	Torii Hunter	4.00
DJ	Derek Jeter	15.00
RJ	Randy Johnson	8.00
AJ	Andruw Jones	6.00
DL	Derrek Lee	6.00
GM	Greg Maddux	10.00
VM	Victor Martinez	4.00
JM	Joe Mauer	6.00
MO	Melvin Mora	4.00
MM	Mark Mulder	4.00
DO	David Ortiz	8.00
RO	Roy Oswalt	4.00
RP	Rafael Palmeiro	4.00
CP	Corey Patterson	4.00
JP	Jake Peavy	6.00
OP	Oliver Perez	4.00
PI	Mike Piazza	8.00
MP	Mark Prior	8.00
AP	Albert Pujols	15.00
AR	Aramis Ramirez	4.00
ER	Edgar Renteria	4.00
JR	Jose Reyes	66.00
SR	Scott Rolen	6.00
SA	Johan Santana	6.00
BS	Ben Sheets	4.00
GS	Gary Sheffield	6.00
SM	John Smoltz	6.00
MT	Mark Teixeira	6.00
TE	Miguel Tejada	6.00
KW	Kerry Wood	6.00
DW	David Wright	8.00
MY	Michael Young	6.00
CZ	Carlos Zambrano	6.00

SPXtreme Stats Signatures

No Pricing
Production Five Sets

2005 SP Legendary Cuts

NM/M
Complete Set (90): 25.00
Common Player: .25
Pack (4): 14.00
Box (12): 150.00

1	Al Kaline	1.00
2	Babe Ruth	3.00
3	Bill Mazeroski	.25
4	Billy Williams	.50
5	Bob Feller	.50
6	Bob Gibson	1.00
7	Bob Lemon	.25
8	Bobby Doerr	.25
9	Brooks Robinson	.50
10	Carl Yastrzemski	1.50
11	Carlton Fisk	.75
12	Casey Stengel	.25
13	Jim "Catfish" Hunter	.25
14	Christy Mathewson	1.00

#	Player	NM/M
15	Cy Young	.50
16	Dennis Eckersley	.25
17	Dizzy Dean	.50
18	Don Drysdale	.25
19	Don Sutton	.25
20	Duke Snider	.75
21	Early Wynn	.25
22	Eddie Mathews	1.00
23	Eddie Murray	.75
24	Enos Slaughter	.25
25	Ernie Banks	1.00
26	Fergie Jenkins	.25
27	Frank Robinson	1.00
28	Gary Carter	.25
29	Gaylord Perry	.25
30	Reggie Jackson	1.00
31	George Kell	.25
32	George Sisler	.25
33	Hal Newhouser	.25
34	Harmon Killebrew	1.00
35	Honus Wagner	1.00
36	Jackie Robinson	
37	Jim Bunning	.25
38	Jim Palmer	.50
39	Jimmie Foxx	.75
40	Joe DiMaggio	2.00
41	Joe Morgan	.50
42	Johnny Bench	1.00
43	Johnny Mize	.25
44	Juan Marichal	.50
45	Kirby Puckett	.75
46	Larry Doby	.25
47	Lefty Grove	.25
48	Lou Boudreau	.25
49	Lou Brock	.50
50	Lou Gehrig	2.00
51	Luis Aparicio	.25
52	Mel Ott	.50
53	Mickey Cochrane	.25
54	Mickey Mantle	4.00
55	Mike Schmidt	1.50
56	Monte Irvin	.50
57	Nolan Ryan	2.00
58	Orlando Cepeda	.25
59	Ozzie Smith	1.00
60	Paul Molitor	.50
61	Pee Wee Reese	.25
62	Phil Niekro	.25
63	Phil Rizzuto	.50
64	Ralph Kiner	.25
65	Red Schoendienst	.25
66	Richie Ashburn	.25
67	Rick Ferrell	.25
68	Robin Roberts	.25
69	Robin Yount	1.00
70	Rod Carew	.50
71	Rogers Hornsby	.50
72	Rollie Fingers	.25
73	Roy Campanella	.50
74	Ryne Sandberg	1.00
75	Satchel Paige	1.00
76	Stan Musial	1.00
77	Steve Carlton	.25
78	Ted Williams	2.00
79	Thurman Munson	1.00
80	Tom Seaver	1.00
81	Tony Gwynn	1.00
82	Tony Perez	.25
83	Ty Cobb	1.50
84	Wade Boggs	.50
85	Walter Johnson	1.00
86	Warren Spahn	1.00
87	Whitey Ford	1.00
88	Willie McCovey	.50
89	Willie Stargell	.75
90	Yogi Berra	1.00

Holofoil
Holofoil: 3-5X
Production 50 Sets

Classic Careers
NM/M
Common Player: 2.00
Production 399 Sets
Gold: 1-2X
Production 75 Sets
Platinum: No Pricing
Production One Set

Code	Player	NM/M
LA	Luis Aparicio	2.00
HB	Harold Baines	2.00
JB	Jay Buhner	2.00
CA	Jose Canseco	3.00
GC	Gary Carter	2.00
OC	Orlando Cepeda	2.00
JC	Jack Clark	2.00
WC	Will Clark	3.00
DC	David Cone	2.00
AD	Andre Dawson	2.00
BD	Bobby Doerr	2.00
LD	Lenny Dykstra	2.00
CE	Carl Erskine	2.00
SF	Sid Fernandez	2.00
CF	Carlton Fisk	3.00
GF	George Foster	2.00
BF	Bill Freehan	2.00
DG	Dwight Gooden	2.00
GG	Rich "Goose" Gossage	2.00
MG	Mark Grace	3.00
RG	Ron Guidry	2.00
GU	Don Gullett	2.00
KH	Keith Hernandez	2.00
BH	Bob Horner	2.00
FJ	Fergie Jenkins	2.00
BL	Barry Larkin	3.00
SL	Sparky Lyle	2.00
BM	Bill Madlock	2.00
DE	Dennis Martinez	2.00
GM	Gary Mathews	2.00
MA	Don Mattingly	5.00
JM	Jack Morris	2.00
MU	Bobby Murcer	2.00
DM	Dale Murphy	3.00
GN	Graig Nettles	2.00
PN	Phil Niekro	2.00
TO	Tony Oliva	2.00
GP	Gaylord Perry	2.00
JP	Johnny Podres	2.00
TR	Tim Raines	2.00
JR	Jim Rice	2.00
CR	Cal Ripken Jr.	8.00
AR	Al Rosen	2.00
ST	Dave Stewart	2.00
DS	Darryl Strawberry	2.00
SU	Bruce Sutter	2.00
DO	Don Sutton	2.00
LT	Luis Tiant	2.00
AV	Andy Van Slyke	2.00
CY	Carl Yastrzemski	4.00

Classic Careers Autograph
NM/M
Common Player: 15.00
Production 25 Sets
Gold: No Pricing
Production 10 Sets
Platinum: No Pricing
Production One Set

Code	Player	NM/M
LA	Luis Aparicio	20.00
HB	Harold Baines	25.00
JB	Jay Buhner	30.00
CA	Jose Canseco	40.00
GC	Gary Carter	20.00
OC	Orlando Cepeda	30.00
JC	Jack Clark	20.00
WC	Will Clark	25.00
DC	David Cone	20.00
AD	Andre Dawson	20.00
BD	Bobby Doerr	20.00
LD	Lenny Dykstra	20.00
CE	Carl Erskine	20.00
SF	Sid Fernandez	15.00
CF	Carlton Fisk	35.00
GF	George Foster	25.00
BF	Bill Freehan	25.00
DG	Dwight Gooden	15.00
GG	Rich "Goose" Gossage	20.00
MG	Mark Grace	30.00
RG	Ron Guidry	35.00
GU	Don Gullett	15.00
KH	Keith Hernandez	20.00
BH	Bob Horner	15.00
FJ	Fergie Jenkins	25.00
BL	Barry Larkin	40.00
SL	Sparky Lyle	20.00
BM	Bill Madlock	20.00
DE	Dennis Martinez	15.00
GM	Gary Mathews	15.00
MA	Don Mattingly	60.00
JM	Jack Morris	20.00
MU	Bobby Murcer	30.00
DM	Dale Murphy	35.00
PN	Phil Niekro	20.00
GN	Graig Nettles	20.00
TO	Tony Oliva	20.00
GP	Gaylord Perry	20.00
JP	Johnny Podres	15.00
TR	Tim Raines	20.00
JR	Jim Rice	25.00
CR	Cal Ripken Jr.	125.00
AR	Al Rosen	20.00
ST	Dave Stewart	15.00
DS	Darryl Strawberry	20.00
SU	Bruce Sutter	25.00
DO	Don Sutton	20.00
LT	Luis Tiant	20.00
AV	Andy Van Slyke	30.00
CY	Carl Yastrzemski	50.00

Classic Careers Jersey
NM/M
Common Player: 4.00
Gold: 1X
Production 75 Sets
Platinum: No Pricing
Production One Set

Code	Player	NM/M
LA	Luis Aparicio	6.00
HB	Harold Baines	6.00
JB	Jay Buhner	6.00
CA	Jose Canseco	8.00
GC	Gary Carter	4.00
OC	Orlando Cepeda	6.00
JC	Jack Clark	4.00
WC	Will Clark	6.00
DC	David Cone	4.00
AD	Andre Dawson	6.00
BD	Bobby Doerr	6.00
LD	Lenny Dykstra	6.00
CE	Carl Erskine	6.00
SF	Sid Fernandez	4.00
CF	Carlton Fisk	6.00
GF	George Foster	4.00
BF	Bill Freehan	6.00
DG	Dwight Gooden	6.00
GG	Rich "Goose" Gossage	6.00
MG	Mark Grace	8.00
RG	Ron Guidry	6.00
GU	Don Gullett	4.00
KH	Keith Hernandez	6.00
BH	Bob Horner	4.00
FJ	Fergie Jenkins	6.00
BL	Barry Larkin	6.00
SL	Sparky Lyle	4.00
BM	Bill Madlock	4.00
DE	Dennis Martinez	4.00
GM	Gary Mathews	4.00
MA	Don Mattingly	12.00
JM	Jack Morris	4.00
MU	Bobby Murcer	4.00
DM	Dale Murphy	8.00
PN	Phil Niekro	4.00
GN	Graig Nettles	4.00
TO	Tony Oliva	4.00
GP	Gaylord Perry	4.00
JP	Johnny Podres	6.00
TR	Tim Raines	4.00
JR	Jim Rice	6.00
CR	Cal Ripken Jr.	20.00
AR	Al Rosen	6.00
ST	Dave Stewart	4.00
DS	Darryl Strawberry	6.00
SU	Bruce Sutter	4.00
DO	Don Sutton	4.00
LT	Luis Tiant	4.00
AV	Andy Van Slyke	4.00
CY	Carl Yastrzemski	15.00

Classic Careers Jersey Autograph
NM/M
Production 25 Sets
Gold: No Pricing
Production 10 Sets
Platinum: No Pricing
Production One Set

Code	Player	NM/M
LA	Luis Aparicio	20.00
HB	Harold Baines	25.00
JB	Jay Buhner	30.00
GC	Gary Carter	20.00
OC	Orlando Cepeda	30.00
JC	Jack Clark	20.00
WC	Will Clark	25.00
DC	David Cone	20.00
AD	Andre Dawson	20.00
BD	Bobby Doerr	20.00
LD	Lenny Dykstra	20.00
CE	Carl Erskine	20.00
SF	Sid Fernandez	15.00
BF	Bill Freehan	25.00
DG	Dwight Gooden	15.00
GG	Rich "Goose" Gossage	12.00
MG	Mark Grace	20.00
KH	Keith Hernandez	12.00
BL	Barry Larkin	25.00
DE	Dennis Martinez	10.00
GM	Gary Mathews	10.00
JM	Jack Morris	10.00
GN	Graig Nettles	10.00
GP	Gaylord Perry	12.00
TR	Tim Raines	10.00
JR	Jim Rice	15.00
CR	Cal Ripken Jr.	40.00
AV	Andy Van Slyke	15.00
ST	Dave Stewart	10.00
DS	Darryl Strawberry	12.00

Classic Careers Patch
NM/M
Production 50 Sets
Gold: No Pricing
Production 10 Sets
Platinum: No Pricing
Production One Set

Code	Player	NM/M
HB	Harold Baines	10.00
CA	Jose Canseco	15.00
JC	Jack Clark	10.00
WC	Will Clark	20.00
DC	David Cone	15.00
AD	Andre Dawson	15.00
BD	Bobby Doerr	15.00
LD	Lenny Dykstra	15.00
SF	Sid Fernandez	10.00
BF	Bill Freehan	12.00
DG	Dwight Gooden	15.00
GG	Rich "Goose" Gossage	12.00
MG	Mark Grace	20.00
KH	Keith Hernandez	12.00
BL	Barry Larkin	25.00
DE	Dennis Martinez	10.00
GM	Gary Mathews	10.00

Classic Careers Patch Autograph
NM/M
Production 25 Sets
Gold: No Pricing
Production Five Sets
Platinum: No Pricing
Production One Set

Code	Player	NM/M
HB	Harold Baines	40.00
JB	Jay Buhner	50.00
JC	Jack Clark	35.00
WC	Will Clark	40.00
DC	David Cone	35.00
AD	Andre Dawson	35.00
BD	Bobby Doerr	35.00
LD	Lenny Dykstra	35.00
SF	Sid Fernandez	25.00
GF	George Foster	40.00
BF	Bill Freehan	40.00
DG	Dwight Gooden	25.00
GG	Rich "Goose" Gossage	35.00
MG	Mark Grace	50.00
GU	Don Gullett	25.00
KH	Keith Hernandez	35.00
BL	Barry Larkin	40.00
DE	Dennis Martinez	25.00
GM	Gary Mathews	25.00
JM	Jack Morris	20.00
GN	Graig Nettles	35.00
TO	Tony Oliva	35.00
GP	Gaylord Perry	30.00
TR	Tim Raines	30.00
JR	Jim Rice	40.00
CR	Cal Ripken Jr.	200.00
ST	Dave Stewart	25.00
DS	Darryl Strawberry	30.00
AV	Andy Van Slyke	40.00

Dual Legendary Cuts
Production 1-10

Glory Days
NM/M
Common Player: 2.00
Production 399 Sets
Gold: 1X-2X
Production 75 Sets
Platinum: No Pricing
Production One Set

Code	Player	NM/M
HB	Harold Baines	2.00
YB	Yogi Berra	4.00
LB	Lou Brock	2.00
JB	Jay Buhner	2.00
CA	Jose Canseco	3.00
JC	Jack Clark	2.00
WC	Will Clark	2.00
DC	David Cone	2.00
AD	Andre Dawson	2.00
BD	Bobby Doerr	2.00
LD	Lenny Dykstra	2.00
SF	Sid Fernandez	2.00
WF	Whitey Ford	3.00
GF	George Foster	2.00
BF	Bill Freehan	2.00
KG	Kirk Gibson	2.00
DG	Dwight Gooden	2.00
RG	Ron Guidry	2.00
GU	Don Gullett	2.00
TG	Tony Gwynn	4.00
KH	Keith Hernandez	2.00
BH	Bob Horner	2.00
FJ	Fergie Jenkins	2.00
BL	Barry Larkin	3.00
SL	Sparky Lyle	2.00
FL	Fred Lynn	2.00
BM	Bill Madlock	2.00
MA	Juan Marichal	3.00
DE	Dennis Martinez	2.00
GM	Gary Mathews	2.00
PM	Paul Molitor	4.00
JM	Jack Morris	2.00
MU	Bobby Murcer	2.00
DM	Dale Murphy	3.00
GN	Graig Nettles	2.00
TO	Tony Oliva	2.00
JP	Jim Palmer	3.00
TR	Tim Raines	2.00
JR	Jim Rice	2.00
CR	Cal Ripken Jr.	8.00
AR	Al Rosen	2.00
NR	Nolan Ryan	15.00
RS	Red Schoendienst	2.00
SN	Duke Snider	3.00
ST	Dave Stewart	2.00
DS	Darryl Strawberry	2.00
BS	Bruce Sutter	2.00
LT	Luis Tiant	2.00
AV	Andy Van Slyke	2.00
RY	Robin Yount	4.00

Glory Days Autograph
NM/M
Common Player: 15.00
Production 25 Sets
Gold: No Pricing
Production 10 Sets
Platinum: No Pricing
Production One Set

Code	Player	NM/M
HB	Harold Baines	25.00
YB	Yogi Berra	50.00
LB	Lou Brock	30.00
JB	Jay Buhner	30.00
CA	Jose Canseco	40.00
JC	Jack Clark	20.00
WC	Will Clark	25.00
DC	David Cone	20.00
AD	Andre Dawson	20.00
BD	Bobby Doerr	20.00
LD	Lenny Dykstra	20.00
SF	Sid Fernandez	15.00
WF	Whitey Ford	40.00
GF	George Foster	25.00
BF	Bill Freehan	25.00
KG	Kirk Gibson	20.00
DG	Dwight Gooden	15.00
RG	Ron Guidry	35.00
GU	Don Gullett	15.00
TG	Tony Gwynn	40.00
KH	Keith Hernandez	20.00
FJ	Fergie Jenkins	25.00
BL	Barry Larkin	40.00
SL	Sparky Lyle	20.00
FL	Fred Lynn	15.00
BM	Bill Madlock	20.00
DE	Dennis Martinez	15.00
GM	Gary Mathews	15.00
JM	Jack Morris	20.00
MU	Bobby Murcer	25.00
DM	Dale Murphy	35.00
GN	Graig Nettles	20.00
TO	Tony Oliva	25.00
JP	Jim Palmer	25.00
TR	Tim Raines	25.00
JR	Jim Rice	25.00
AR	Al Rosen	20.00
NR	Nolan Ryan	100.00
RS	Red Schoendienst	20.00
SN	Duke Snider	40.00
ST	Dave Stewart	15.00
DS	Darryl Strawberry	20.00
BS	Bruce Sutter	25.00
LT	Luis Tiant	20.00
AV	Andy Van Slyke	30.00
RY	Robin Yount	50.00

Glory Days Jersey
NM/M
Common Player: 4.00
Gold: 1X
Production 75 Sets
Platinum: No Pricing
Production One Set

Code	Player	NM/M
HB	Harold Baines	6.00
YB	Yogi Berra	10.00
LB	Lou Brock	6.00
JB	Jay Buhner	6.00
CA	Jose Canseco	8.00
JC	Jack Clark	6.00
WC	Will Clark	6.00
DC	David Cone	6.00
AD	Andre Dawson	6.00
BD	Bobby Doerr	6.00
LD	Lenny Dykstra	6.00
SF	Sid Fernandez	4.00
WF	Whitey Ford	10.00
GF	George Foster	4.00
BF	Bill Freehan	6.00
KG	Kirk Gibson	4.00
DG	Dwight Gooden	4.00
RG	Ron Guidry	4.00
GU	Don Gullett	4.00
TG	Tony Gwynn	8.00
KH	Keith Hernandez	4.00
BH	Bob Horner	4.00
FJ	Fergie Jenkins	6.00
BL	Barry Larkin	6.00
SL	Sparky Lyle	4.00
FL	Fred Lynn	4.00
BM	Bill Madlock	4.00
MA	Juan Marichal	6.00
DE	Dennis Martinez	4.00
GM	Gary Mathews	4.00
PM	Paul Molitor	6.00
JM	Jack Morris	4.00
MU	Bobby Murcer	4.00
DM	Dale Murphy	8.00
GN	Graig Nettles	4.00
TO	Tony Oliva	4.00
JP	Jim Palmer	6.00
TR	Tim Raines	4.00
JR	Jim Rice	6.00
CR	Cal Ripken Jr.	20.00
AR	Al Rosen	6.00
NR	Nolan Ryan	15.00
RS	Red Schoendienst	4.00
SN	Duke Snider	8.00
ST	Dave Stewart	4.00
DS	Darryl Strawberry	4.00
BS	Bruce Sutter	4.00
LT	Luis Tiant	4.00
AV	Andy Van Slyke	4.00
RY	Robin Yount	10.00

Glory Days Memorabilia Autograph
NM/M
Production 25 Sets
Gold: No Pricing
Production 10 Sets
Platinum: No Pricing
Production One Set

Code	Player	NM/M
HB	Harold Baines	25.00
YB	Yogi Berra	50.00
JB	Jay Buhner	30.00
JC	Jack Clark	20.00
WC	Will Clark	25.00
DC	David Cone	20.00
AD	Andre Dawson	20.00
BD	Bobby Doerr	20.00
LD	Lenny Dykstra	20.00
SF	Sid Fernandez	15.00
WF	Whitey Ford	40.00
GF	George Foster	25.00
BF	Bill Freehan	25.00
KG	Kirk Gibson	20.00
DG	Dwight Gooden	15.00
BG	Ron Guidry	35.00
GU	Don Gullett	15.00
TG	Tony Gwynn	40.00
KH	Keith Hernandez	20.00
BH	Bob Horner	15.00
FJ	Fergie Jenkins	25.00
BL	Barry Larkin	40.00
SL	Sparky Lyle	20.00
FL	Fred Lynn	15.00
BM	Bill Madlock	20.00
MA	Juan Marichal	25.00
DE	Dennis Martinez	15.00
GM	Gary Mathews	15.00
JM	Jack Morris	20.00
MU	Bobby Murcer	25.00
DM	Dale Murphy	35.00
GN	Graig Nettles	20.00
TO	Tony Oliva	25.00
JP	Jim Palmer	25.00
TR	Tim Raines	25.00
JR	Jim Rice	25.00
AR	Al Rosen	20.00
NR	Nolan Ryan	100.00
RS	Red Schoendienst	20.00
SN	Duke Snider	40.00
ST	Dave Stewart	15.00
DS	Darryl Strawberry	20.00
BS	Bruce Sutter	25.00
LT	Luis Tiant	20.00
AV	Andy Van Slyke	30.00
RY	Robin Yount	50.00

Glory Days Patch
NM/M
Production 50 Sets
Gold: No Pricing
Production 10 Sets
Platinum: No Pricing
Production One Set

Code	Player	NM/M
HB	Harold Baines	10.00
JC	Jack Clark	10.00
DC	David Cone	15.00
AD	Andre Dawson	15.00
BD	Bobby Doerr	15.00
LD	Lenny Dykstra	15.00
SF	Sid Fernandez	10.00
GF	George Foster	10.00
DG	Dwight Gooden	15.00
KH	Keith Hernandez	12.00
BH	Bob Horner	10.00
FJ	Fergie Jenkins	15.00
BL	Barry Larkin	25.00
GM	Gary Mathews	10.00
JM	Jack Morris	10.00
DM	Dale Murphy	15.00
GN	Graig Nettles	10.00
JP	Jim Palmer	15.00
TR	Tim Raines	10.00
RS	Red Schoendienst	15.00
DS	Darryl Strawberry	12.00
BS	Bruce Sutter	15.00
LT	Luis Tiant	15.00
AV	Andy Van Slyke	15.00

Glory Days Patch Autograph
NM/M
Production 25 Sets
Gold: No Pricing
Production Five Sets
Platinum: No Pricing
Production One Set

Code	Player	NM/M
HB	Harold Baines	40.00
JB	Jay Buhner	50.00
JC	Jack Clark	35.00
DC	David Cone	35.00
AD	Andre Dawson	35.00
BD	Bobby Doerr	35.00
LD	Lenny Dykstra	35.00
SF	Sid Fernandez	25.00
GF	George Foster	40.00
DG	Dwight Gooden	25.00
KH	Keith Hernandez	35.00
BH	Bob Horner	25.00
FJ	Fergie Jenkins	40.00
BL	Barry Larkin	60.00
BM	Bill Madlock	25.00
DE	Dennis Martinez	25.00
GM	Gary Mathews	25.00
JM	Jack Morris	25.00
DM	Dale Murphy	40.00
GN	Graig Nettles	35.00
TO	Tony Oliva	35.00
JP	Jim Palmer	40.00
TR	Tim Raines	30.00
JR	Jim Rice	25.00
RS	Red Schoendienst	30.00
DS	Darryl Strawberry	30.00
BS	Bruce Sutter	25.00
LT	Luis Tiant	25.00
AV	Andy Van Slyke	40.00

Historic Cuts
No Pricing
Production One Set

Historic Quads Autograph
No Pricing
Production Five Sets

SHistoric Quads Material
No Pricing
Production Five Sets
Patch: No Pricing
Production One Set

Lasting Legends
NM/M
Common Player: 2.00

Production 399 Sets
Gold: 1-2X
Production 75 Sets
Platinum: No Pricing
Production One Set

LA	Luis Aparicio	2.00
EB	Ernie Banks	4.00
BE	Johnny Bench	4.00
YB	Yogi Berra	4.00
WB	Wade Boggs	3.00
LB	Lou Brock	3.00
RC	Rod Carew	3.00
SC	Steve Carlton	2.00
GC	Gary Carter	2.00
OC	Orlando Cepeda	2.00
BD	Bobby Doerr	2.00
DE	Dennis Eckersley	2.00
RF	Rollie Fingers	2.00
CF	Carlton Fisk	3.00
WF	Whitey Ford	3.00
BG	Bob Gibson	3.00
DG	Dwight Gooden	2.00
TG	Tony Gwynn	3.00
KH	Keith Hernandez	2.00
FJ	Fergie Jenkins	2.00
AK	Al Kaline	3.00
BL	Barry Larkin	3.00
MA	Juan Marichal	2.00
DM	Don Mattingly	5.00
BM	Bill Mazeroski	2.00
PM	Paul Molitor	3.00
JM	Joe Morgan	2.00
MU	Dale Murphy	3.00
EM	Eddie Murray	3.00
SM	Stan Musial	4.00
PN	Phil Niekro	2.00
GN	Graig Nettles	2.00
JP	Jim Palmer	3.00
TP	Tony Perez	2.00
GP	Gaylord Perry	2.00
KP	Kirby Puckett	3.00
JR	Jim Rice	2.00
CR	Cal Ripken Jr.	8.00
BR	Brooks Robinson	3.00
FR	Frank Robinson	3.00
NR	Nolan Ryan	6.00
SA	Ryne Sandberg	4.00
MS	Mike Schmidt	4.00
RS	Red Schoendienst	3.00
OS	Ozzie Smith	4.00
SN	Duke Snider	3.00
BS	Bruce Sutter	2.00
DS	Don Sutton	2.00
CY	Carl Yastrzemski	4.00
RY	Robin Yount	4.00

Lasting Legends Autograph
NM/M
Common Player:
Production 25 Sets
Gold: No Pricing
Production 10 Sets
Platinum: No Pricing
Production One Set

LA	Luis Aparicio	20.00
EB	Ernie Banks	60.00
BE	Johnny Bench	50.00
YB	Yogi Berra	60.00
WB	Wade Boggs	40.00
LB	Lou Brock	25.00
RC	Rod Carew	35.00
SC	Steve Carlton	25.00
GC	Gary Carter	25.00
OC	Orlando Cepeda	25.00
BD	Bobby Doerr	20.00
DE	Dennis Eckersley	25.00
RF	Rollie Fingers	20.00
CF	Carlton Fisk	35.00
WF	Whitey Ford	40.00
BG	Bob Gibson	40.00
DG	Dwight Gooden	15.00
TG	Tony Gwynn	50.00
KH	Keith Hernandez	20.00
FG	Fergie Jenkins	25.00
AK	Al Kaline	40.00
BL	Barry Larkin	40.00
MA	Juan Marichal	25.00
DM	Don Mattingly	60.00
BM	Bill Mazeroski	35.00
PM	Paul Molitor	40.00
JM	Joe Morgan	25.00
MU	Dale Murphy	40.00
EM	Eddie Murray	50.00
SM	Stan Musial	60.00
GN	Graig Nettles	20.00
PN	Phil Niekro	25.00
JP	Jim Palmer	25.00
TP	Tony Perez	20.00
GP	Gaylord Perry	20.00
KP	Kirby Puckett	50.00
JR	Jerry Rice	25.00
CR	Cal Ripken Jr.	125.00
BR	Brooks Robinson	40.00
FR	Frank Robinson	25.00
NR	Nolan Ryan	100.00
SA	Ryne Sandberg	50.00
MS	Mike Schmidt	50.00
RS	Red Schoendienst	20.00
OS	Ozzie Smith	60.00
SN	Duke Snider	40.00
BS	Bruce Sutter	25.00
DS	Don Sutton	
CY	Carl Yastrzemski	50.00
RY	Robin Yount	50.00

Lasting Legends Material
NM/M
Common Player: 4.00
Gold: 1-1.5X

Production 75 Sets
Platinum: No Pricing
Production One Set

LA	Luis Aparicio	4.00
EB	Ernie Banks	10.00
BE	Johnny Bench	8.00
YB	Yogi Berra	8.00
WB	Wade Boggs	6.00
LB	Lou Brock	6.00
RC	Rod Carew	6.00
SC	Steve Carlton	4.00
GC	Gary Carter	4.00
OC	Orlando Cepeda	4.00
BD	Bobby Doerr	6.00
DE	Dennis Eckersley	6.00
RF	Rollie Fingers	4.00
CF	Carlton Fisk	6.00
WF	Whitey Ford	6.00
BG	Bob Gibson	8.00
DG	Dwight Gooden	6.00
TG	Tony Gwynn	8.00
KH	Keith Hernandez	4.00
FJ	Fergie Jenkins	4.00
AK	Al Kaline	10.00
BL	Barry Larkin	6.00
MA	Juan Marichal	6.00
DM	Don Mattingly	10.00
BM	Bill Mazeroski	6.00
PM	Paul Molitor	6.00
JM	Joe Morgan	4.00
MU	Dale Murphy	6.00
EM	Eddie Murray	6.00
SM	Stan Musial	10.00
GN	Graig Nettles	4.00
PN	Phil Niekro	4.00
JP	Jim Palmer	6.00
TP	Tony Perez	4.00
GP	Gaylord Perry	4.00
KP	Kirby Puckett	8.00
JR	Jim Rice	4.00
CR	Cal Ripken Jr.	20.00
BR	Brooks Robinson	6.00
FR	Frank Robinson	6.00
NR	Nolan Ryan	15.00
SA	Ryne Sandberg	8.00
MS	Mike Schmidt	10.00
RS	Red Schoendienst	4.00
SN	Duke Snider	6.00
BS	Bruce Sutter	4.00
DS	Don Sutton	4.00
CY	Carl Yastrzemski	15.00
RY	Robin Yount	8.00

Lasting Legends Jersey Autograph
NM/M
Production 25 Sets
Gold: No Pricing
Production 10 Sets
Platinum: No Pricing
Production One Set

LA	Luis Aparicio	20.00
EB	Ernie Banks	60.00
BE	Johnny Bench	50.00
YB	Yogi Berra	60.00
WB	Wade Boggs	40.00
LB	Lou Brock	25.00
RC	Rod Carew	40.00
SC	Steve Carlton	25.00
GC	Gary Carter	25.00
OC	Orlando Cepeda	25.00
BD	Bobby Doerr	20.00
DE	Dennis Eckersley	25.00
RF	Rollie Fingers	20.00
CF	Carlton Fisk	40.00
WF	Whitey Ford	40.00
BG	Bob Gibson	40.00
DG	Dwight Gooden	15.00
TG	Tony Gwynn	50.00
KH	Keith Hernandez	20.00
FG	Fergie Jenkins	25.00
AK	Al Kaline	50.00
BL	Barry Larkin	40.00
MA	Juan Marichal	25.00
DM	Don Mattingly	60.00
BM	Bill Mazeroski	40.00
PM	Paul Molitor	40.00
JM	Joe Morgan	25.00
MU	Dale Murphy	40.00
SM	Stan Musial	60.00
GN	Graig Nettles	20.00
PN	Phil Niekro	25.00
JP	Jim Palmer	25.00
TP	Tony Perez	20.00
GP	Gaylord Perry	20.00
JR	Jim Rice	25.00
CR	Cal Ripken Jr.	140.00
BR	Brooks Robinson	40.00
FR	Frank Robinson	25.00
NR	Nolan Ryan	100.00
SA	Ryne Sandberg	50.00
MS	Mike Schmidt	50.00
RS	Red Schoendienst	20.00
OS	Ozzie Smith	60.00
SN	Duke Snider	40.00
BS	Bruce Sutter	25.00
CY	Carl Yastrzemski	50.00
RY	Robin Yount	50.00

Lasting Legends Patch
NM/M
Production 50 Sets
Gold: No Pricing
Production 10 Sets
Platinum: No Pricing
Production One Set

WB	Wade Boggs	20.00
LB	Lou Brock	15.00
RC	Rod Carew	15.00
SC	Steve Carlton	15.00
GC	Gary Carter	12.00
OC	Orlando Cepeda	15.00
DE	Dennis Eckersley	15.00
RF	Rollie Fingers	10.00
CF	Carlton Fisk	15.00
DG	Dwight Gooden	10.00
KH	Keith Hernandez	10.00
FJ	Fergie Jenkins	15.00
BL	Barry Larkin	25.00
MA	Juan Marichal	15.00
JM	Joe Morgan	15.00
PN	Phil Niekro	15.00
JP	Jim Palmer	15.00
TP	Tony Perez	15.00
GP	Gaylord Perry	12.00
KP	Kirby Puckett	25.00
JR	Jim Rice	15.00
BR	Brooks Robinson	20.00
FR	Frank Robinson	15.00
SA	Ryne Sandberg	25.00
OS	Ozzie Smith	25.00
BS	Bruce Sutter	15.00
DS	Don Sutton	12.00
RY	Robin Yount	25.00

Lasting Legends Patch Autograph
NM/M
Production 25 Sets
Gold: No Pricing
Production Five Sets
Platinum: No Pricing
Production One Set

WB	Wade Boggs	50.00
RC	Rod Carew	50.00
SC	Steve Carlton	35.00
GC	Gary Carter	35.00
OC	Orlando Cepeda	35.00
DE	Dennis Eckersley	35.00
RF	Rollie Fingers	35.00
DG	Dwight Gooden	25.00
KH	Keith Hernandez	25.00
FJ	Fergie Jenkins	35.00
BL	Barry Larkin	50.00
MA	Juan Marichal	35.00
PM	Paul Molitor	50.00
JM	Joe Morgan	35.00
PN	Phil Niekro	35.00
JP	Jim Palmer	40.00
TP	Tony Perez	30.00
GP	Gaylord Perry	30.00
JR	Jim Rice	35.00
BR	Brooks Robinson	50.00
NR	Nolan Ryan	140.00
SA	Ryne Sandberg	80.00
OS	Ozzie Smith	75.00
BS	Bruce Sutter	30.00
RY	Robin Yount	65.00

Legendary Cuts
NM/M
Production 1-108

LA	Luke Appling/55	125.00
RI	Richie Ashburn/83	150.00
EA	Earl Averill/91	90.00
JB	Cool Papa Bell/78	300.00
LB	Lou Boudreau/99	125.00
MC	Max Carey/84	140.00
HC	Happy Chandler/39	125.00
JC	Jocko Conlan/40	140.00
ST	Stan Coveleski/71	140.00
CR	Joe Cronin/76	140.00
RD	Ray Dandridge/76	100.00
BD	Bill Dickey/95	150.00
JD	Joe DiMaggio/56	500.00
LD	Larry Doby/32	200.00
DD	Don Drysdale/50	200.00
DU	Leo Durocher/57	150.00
FE	Rick Ferrell/80	125.00
CF	Carl Furillo/25	200.00
CG	Charlie Gehringer/97	120.00
GO	Lefty Gomez/68	150.00
HG	Hank Greenberg/44	280.00
BU	Burleigh Grimes/99	125.00
GR	Lefty Grove/41	150.00
HA	Chick Hafey/52	150.00
JH	Jesse Haines/99	125.00
GH	Gabby Hartnett/50	180.00
BH	Billy Herman/99	90.00
WH	Waite Hoyt/99	140.00
CH	Carl Hubbell/99	150.00
HU	Jim "Catfish" Hunter/65	140.00
JJ	Jackie Jensen/48	180.00
JO	Judy Johnson/39	150.00
CK	Charlie Keller/98	140.00
HK	Harvey Kuenn/33	165.00
BL	Bob Lemon/108	100.00
LE	Buck Leonard/71	140.00
LI	Freddie Lindstrom/19	250.00
LO	Ernie Lombardi/29	150.00
HM	Heinie Manush/25	175.00
RU	Rube Marquard/80	150.00
EM	Eddie Mathews/80	150.00
RO	Roy McMillan/23	140.00
MI	Johnny Mize/90	125.00
HN	Hal Newhouser/96	125.00
PR	Pee Wee Reese/69	180.00
SR	Sam Rice/41	180.00
ER	Edd Roush/99	100.00
JS	Joe Sewell/76	140.00
ES	Enos Slaughter/99	100.00
WA	Warren Spahn/92	140.00

WS	Willie Stargell/63	165.00
CS	Casey Stengel/61	250.00
BW	Bucky Walters/34	150.00
JW	Hoyt Wilhelm/48	100.00
EW	Early Wynn/89	120.00

Legendary Cuts Material
Production 75 unless noted.
Gold: No Pricing
Production 15 Sets

CA	Roy Campanella	40.00
RC	Roberto Clemente	80.00
TC	Ty Cobb	140.00
CO	Mickey Cochrane	50.00
CR	Joe Cronin	15.00
DE	Dizzy Dean	60.00
BD	Bill Dickey	35.00
JD	Joe DiMaggio	120.00
DD	Don Drysdale	15.00
JF	Jimmie Foxx	60.00
LG	Lou Gehrig	175.00
HG	Hank Greenberg	35.00
HO	Gil Hodges	40.00
RH	Rogers Hornsby	80.00
HU	Jim "Catfish" Hunter	20.00
TK	Ted Kluszewski	20.00
TL	Tony Lazerri	40.00
BL	Bob Lemon	25.00
MM	Mickey Mantle	150.00
RM	Roger Maris	60.00
EM	Eddie Mathews	30.00
CM	Christy Mathewson	125.00
MI	Johnny Mize	25.00
TM	Thurman Munson	35.00
MO	Mel Ott	50.00
SP	Satchel Paige	75.00
PR	Pee Wee Reese	25.00
JR	Jackie Robinson	65.00
BR	Babe Ruth	180.00
SI	George Sisler	15.00
ES	Enos Slaughter	15.00
WA	Warren Spahn	40.00
CS	Casey Stengel	40.00
HW	Honus Wagner/22	140.00
JW	Hoyt Wilhelm	15.00
TW	Ted Williams	75.00
EW	Early Wynn	10.00

Legendary Cuts Quad
No Pricing
Production One Set

Legendary Battery Cuts
NM/M
Production 6-99

SC	Stan Coveleski/25	140.00
BD	Bill Dickey/22	200.00
DD	Don Drysdale/31	200.00
LG	Lefty Gomez/77	160.00
JH	Jesse Haines/28	200.00
WH	Waite Hoyt/58	140.00
CH	Carl Hubbell/99	140.00
HN	Hal Newhouser/32	140.00
WS	Warren Spahn/43	150.00
EW	Early Wynn/32	125.00

Legendary Cornerstone Cuts
NM/M
Production 1-79

DC	Dolph Camilli/79	125.00
RD	Ray Dandridge/27	125.00
EM	Eddie Mathews/50	150.00
JM	Johnny Mize/44	175.00
WS	Willie Stargell/36	150.00

Legendary Duels Material
NM/M
Production 25 Sets
Patch: No Pricing
Production 10 Sets

BM	Ernie Banks, Stan Musial	50.00
CC	Jose Canseco, Will Clark	40.00
DM	Paul Molitor, Lenny Dykstra	25.00
EG	Dennis Eckersley, Kirk Gibson	25.00
FB	Carlton Fisk, Johnny Bench	25.00
FR	George Foster, Jim Rice	15.00
JY	Reggie Jackson, Carl Yastrzemski	40.00
MC	Rod Carew, Paul Molitor	25.00
MH	Don Mattingly, Keith Hernandez	35.00
SF	Duke Snider, Whitey Ford	35.00
SG	Ron Guidry, Don Sutton	15.00
SS	Ozzie Smith, Ryne Sandberg	60.00
YS	Mike Schmidt, Robin Yount	35.00

Legendary Duels Autograph
No Pricing
Production 15 Sets

Legendary Duos Material
NM/M
Production 25 Sets
Patch: No Pricing
Production 10 Sets

CO	Tony Oliva, Rod Carew	20.00
ES	Duke Snider, Carl Erskine	15.00

FB	Yogi Berra, Whitey Ford	40.00
GS	Ryne Sandberg, Mark Grace	50.00
JG	Reggie Jackson, Ron Guidry	25.00
MB	Joe Morgan, Johnny Bench	35.00
MY	Robin Yount, Paul Molitor	40.00
RB	Wade Boggs, Jim Rice	20.00
RC	Will Clark, Cal Ripken Jr.	50.00
RM	Cal Ripken Jr., Eddie Murray	50.00
RR	Brooks Robinson, Frank Robinson	25.00
SC	Mike Schmidt, Steve Carlton	30.00
SG	Darryl Strawberry, Dwight Gooden	15.00

Legendary Duos Autograph
No Pricing
Production 15 Sets

Legendary Glovemen Cuts
NM/M

EA	Earl Averill/39	120.00
CP	Cool Papa Bell/29	350.00
MC	Max Carey/50	140.00
JD	Joe DiMaggio/99	400.00
ES	Enos Slaughter/65	120.00

Middlemen Cuts
NM/M
Production 2-99

LA	Luke Appling/32	150.00
LB	Lou Boudreau/99	100.00
JC	Joe Cronin/30	140.00
CG	Charlie Gehringer/95	140.00
BH	Billy Herman/99	140.00
PW	Pee Wee Reese/39	200.00
JS	Joe Sewell/76	140.00

Legendary Lineage
NM/M
Common Player: 2.00
Production 399 Sets
Gold: 1-2X
Production 75 Sets
Platinum: No Pricing
Production One Set

HB	Harold Baines	2.00
JB	Jay Buhner	2.00
CA	Jose Canseco	3.00
SC	Steve Carlton	2.00
JC	Jack Clark	2.00
WC	Will Clark	3.00
DC	David Cone	2.00
AD	Andre Dawson	2.00
BD	Bobby Doerr	2.00
LD	Lenny Dykstra	2.00
EC	Dennis Eckersley	2.00
SF	Sid Fernandez	2.00
BF	Bill Freehan	2.00
DG	Dwight Gooden	2.00
GG	Rich "Goose" Gossage	2.00
MG	Mark Grace	3.00
RG	Ron Guidry	2.00
GU	Don Gullett	2.00
TG	Tony Gwynn	4.00
KH	Keith Hernandez	2.00
BH	Bob Horner	2.00
RJ	Reggie Jackson	3.00
FJ	Fergie Jenkins	2.00
BL	Barry Larkin	3.00
SL	Sparky Lyle	2.00
BM	Bill Madlock	2.00
DE	Dennis Martinez	2.00
GM	Gary Matthews	2.00
MA	Don Mattingly	5.00
PM	Paul Molitor	2.00
JM	Jack Morris	2.00
MU	Bobby Murcer	2.00
MU	Dale Murphy	3.00
GN	Graig Nettles	2.00
TO	Tony Oliva	2.00
JP	Jim Palmer	3.00
KP	Kirby Puckett	4.00
TR	Tim Raines	2.00
JR	Jim Rice	2.00
CR	Cal Ripken Jr.	8.00
BR	Brooks Robinson	3.00
AR	Al Rosen	2.00
MS	Mike Schmidt	5.00
OS	Ozzie Smith	3.00
SN	Duke Snider	3.00
DS	Dave Stewart	2.00
ST	Darryl Strawberry	2.00
SU	Bruce Sutter	2.00
LT	Luis Tiant	2.00
AV	Andy Van Slyke	2.00

Legendary Lineage Auto
NM/M
Common Player: 15.00
Production 25 Sets
Gold: No Pricing
Production 10 Sets
Platinum: No Pricing
Production One Set

HB	Harold Baines	25.00
JB	Jay Buhner	30.00
CA	Jose Canseco	40.00
SC	Steve Carlton	25.00
JC	Jack Clark	25.00
WC	Will Clark	25.00
DC	David Cone	20.00

AD	Andre Dawson	20.00
BD	Bobby Doerr	20.00
LD	Lenny Dykstra	20.00
EC	Dennis Eckersley	25.00
SF	Sid Fernandez	15.00
BF	Bill Freehan	15.00
DG	Dwight Gooden	15.00
GG	Rich "Goose" Gossage	20.00
MG	Mark Grace	30.00
RG	Ron Guidry	35.00
GU	Don Gullett	15.00
TG	Tony Gwynn	40.00
KH	Keith Hernandez	20.00
BH	Bob Horner	15.00
RJ	Reggie Jackson	40.00
FJ	Fergie Jenkins	20.00
BL	Barry Larkin	40.00
SL	Sparky Lyle	20.00
BM	Bill Madlock	20.00
DE	Dennis Martinez	15.00
GM	Gary Matthews	15.00
MA	Don Mattingly	60.00
PM	Paul Molitor	20.00
JM	Jack Morris	20.00
MU	Bobby Murcer	25.00
DM	Dale Murphy	35.00
GN	Graig Nettles	20.00
TO	Tony Oliva	20.00
JP	Jim Palmer	20.00
KP	Kirby Puckett	50.00
TR	Tim Raines	20.00
JR	Jim Rice	20.00
CR	Cal Ripken Jr.	125.00
BR	Brooks Robinson	40.00
AR	Al Rosen	20.00
MS	Mike Schmidt	60.00
OS	Ozzie Smith	50.00
SN	Duke Snider	40.00
DS	Dave Stewart	15.00
ST	Darryl Strawberry	20.00
SU	Bruce Sutter	25.00
LT	Luis Tiant	20.00
AV	Andy Van Slyke	30.00

Legendary Lineage Jersey

NM/M
Common Player: 4.00
Gold: 1-1.5X
Production 75 Sets
Platinum: No Pricing
Production One Set

HB	Harold Baines	4.00
JB	Jay Buhner	4.00
CA	Jose Canseco	8.00
SC	Steve Carlton	6.00
JC	Jack Clark	4.00
WC	Will Clark	6.00
DC	David Cone	4.00
AD	Andre Dawson	6.00
BD	Bobby Doerr	6.00
LD	Lenny Dykstra	6.00
EC	Dennis Eckersley	6.00
SF	Sid Fernandez	4.00
BF	Bill Freehan	6.00
DG	Dwight Gooden	6.00
GG	Rich "Goose" Gossage	4.00
MG	Mark Grace	8.00
RG	Ron Guidry	4.00
GU	Don Gullett	4.00
TG	Tony Gwynn	8.00
KH	Keith Hernandez	4.00
BH	Bob Horner	4.00
RJ	Reggie Jackson	8.00
FJ	Fergie Jenkins	6.00
BL	Barry Larkin	4.00
SL	Sparky Lyle	4.00
BM	Bill Madlock	4.00
DE	Dennis Martinez	4.00
GM	Gary Matthews	4.00
MA	Don Mattingly	12.00
PM	Paul Molitor	6.00
JM	Jack Morris	4.00
MU	Bobby Murcer	4.00
DM	Dale Murphy	6.00
GN	Graig Nettles	4.00
TO	Tony Oliva	6.00
JP	Jim Palmer	6.00
KP	Kirby Puckett	8.00
TR	Tim Raines	4.00
JR	Jim Rice	4.00
CR	Cal Ripken Jr.	20.00
BR	Brooks Robinson	6.00
AR	Al Rosen	4.00
MS	Mike Schmidt	10.00
OS	Ozzie Smith	8.00
SN	Duke Snider	4.00
DS	Dave Stewart	4.00
ST	Darryl Strawberry	4.00
SU	Bruce Sutter	4.00
LT	Luis Tiant	4.00
AV	Andy Van Slyke	4.00

Legendary Lineage Jersey Autographs
NM/M
Production 25 Sets
Gold: No Pricing

Production 10 Sets		
Platinum:	No Pricing	
Production One Set		
HB	Harold Baines	20.00
JB	Jay Buhner	20.00
CA	Jose Canseco	40.00
SC	Steve Carlton	25.00
JC	Jack Clark	20.00
WC	Will Clark	25.00
DC	David Cone	20.00
AD	Andre Dawson	20.00
BD	Bobby Doerr	25.00
LD	Lenny Dykstra	20.00
EC	Dennis Eckersley	25.00
SF	Sid Fernandez	15.00
BF	Bill Freehan	25.00
DG	Dwight Gooden	15.00
GG	Rich "Goose" Gossage	20.00
MG	Mark Grace	30.00
RG	Ron Guidry	35.00
GU	Don Gullett	15.00
TG	Tony Gwynn	40.00
KH	Keith Hernandez	20.00
BH	Bob Horner	15.00
RJ	Reggie Jackson	40.00
FJ	Fergie Jenkins	25.00
BL	Barry Larkin	40.00
SL	Sparky Lyle	20.00
BM	Bill Madlock	20.00
DE	Dennis Martinez	15.00
GM	Gary Matthews	15.00
MA	Don Mattingly	60.00
PM	Paul Molitor	40.00
JM	Jack Morris	20.00
MU	Bobby Murcer	25.00
DM	Dale Murphy	35.00
GN	Graig Nettles	20.00
TO	Tony Oliva	20.00
JP	Jim Palmer	25.00
KP	Kirby Puckett	50.00
TR	Tim Raines	20.00
JR	Jim Rice	25.00
CR	Cal Ripken Jr.	150.00
BR	Brooks Robinson	40.00
AR	Al Rosen	20.00
MS	Mike Schmidt	60.00
OS	Ozzie Smith	50.00
SN	Duke Snider	40.00
DS	Dave Stewart	20.00
ST	Darryl Strawberry	20.00
SU	Bruce Sutter	25.00
LT	Luis Tiant	20.00
AV	Andy Van Slyke	30.00

Legendary Lineage Patch

NM/M

Production 50 Sets		
Gold:	No Pricing	
Production 10 Sets		
Platinum:	No Pricing	
Production One Set		
HB	Harold Baines	10.00
JB	Jay Buhner	15.00
JC	Jack Clark	10.00
WC	Will Clark	20.00
DC	David Cone	15.00
AD	Andre Dawson	15.00
BD	Bobby Doerr	15.00
BF	Bill Freehan	12.00
DG	Dwight Gooden	15.00
GG	Rich "Goose" Gossage	12.00
MG	Mark Grace	20.00
TG	Tony Gwynn	20.00
KH	Keith Hernandez	12.00
BH	Bob Horner	10.00
BL	Barry Larkin	25.00
BM	Bill Madlock	10.00
DE	Dennis Martinez	10.00
JM	Jack Morris	10.00
DM	Dale Murphy	20.00
GN	Graig Nettles	10.00
TR	Tim Raines	10.00
CR	Cal Ripken Jr.	40.00
MS	Mike Schmidt	25.00
DS	Dave Stewart	10.00
ST	Darryl Strawberry	12.00
LT	Luis Tiant	10.00
AV	Andy Van Slyke	15.00

Legendary Lineage Patch Autographs

NM/M

Production 25 Sets		
Gold:	No Pricing	
Production Five Sets		
Platinum:	No Pricing	
Production One Set		
HB	Harold Baines	40.00
JB	Jay Buhner	50.00
JC	Jack Clark	35.00
WC	Will Clark	40.00
DC	David Cone	35.00
AD	Andre Dawson	35.00
BD	Bobby Doerr	35.00
BF	Bill Freehan	40.00
DG	Dwight Gooden	25.00
GG	Rich "Goose" Gossage	35.00
MG	Mark Grace	50.00
TG	Tony Gwynn	70.00
KH	Keith Hernandez	35.00
BH	Bob Horner	25.00
BL	Barry Larkin	60.00
BM	Bill Madlock	25.00
DE	Dennis Martinez	25.00
PM	Paul Molitor	50.00
JM	Jack Morris	35.00
DM	Dale Murphy	40.00

GN	Graig Nettles	35.00
TR	Tim Raines	30.00
JR	Jim Rice	40.00
CR	Cal Ripken Jr.	200.00
MS	Mike Schmidt	90.00
DS	Dave Stewart	25.00
ST	Darryl Strawberry	30.00
LT	Luis Tiant	25.00
AV	Andy Van Slyke	40.00

Significant Tips

No Pricing		
Production 10 Sets		
Patch:	No Pricing	
Production Five Sets		

Significant Trips Auto.

No Pricing	
Production 10 Sets	

2006 SP Authentic

NM/M

Complete Set (300):		
Common Player (1-100):		.25
Common SP (101-200):		2.00
Production 899		
Common Auto. (201-300):		8.00
Production 125-899		
Pack (5):		5.00
Box (24):		110.00
1	Erik Bedard	.50
2	Corey Patterson	.25
3	Ramon Hernandez	.25
4	Kris Benson	.25
5	Shawn Green	.25
6	Orlando Hudson	.25
7	Jeff Francoeur	.50
8	Marcus Giles	.25
9	Edgar Renteria	.25
10	Tim Hudson	.50
11	Tim Wakefield	.25
12	Mark Loretta	.25
13	Kevin Youkilis	.50
14	Mike Lowell	.50
15	Coco Crisp	.25
16	Tadahito Iguchi	.25
17	Scott Podsednik	.25
18	Jermaine Dye	.40
19	Jose Contreras	.25
20	Carlos Zambrano	.50
21	Aramis Ramirez	.50
22	Jacque Jones	.25
23	Austin Kearns	.25
24	Felipe Lopez	.25
25	Brandon Phillips	.25
26	Aaron Harang	.40
27	Cliff Lee	.25
28	Jhonny Peralta	.25
29	Jason Michaels	.25
30	Clint Barmes	.25
31	Brad Hawpe	.40
32	Aaron Cook	.25
33	Kenny Rogers	.25
34	Carlos Guillen	.40
35	Brian Moehler	.25
36	Andy Pettitte	.50
37	Wandy Rodriguez	.25
38	Morgan Ensberg	.25
39	Preston Wilson	.25
40	Mark Grudzielanek	.25
41	Angel Berroa	.25
42	Jeremy Affeldt	.25
43	Zack Greinke	.50
44	Orlando Cabrera	.25
45	Garret Anderson	.25
46	Ervin Santana	.40
47	Derek Lowe	.25
48	Nomar Garciaparra	.50
49	J.D. Drew	.50
50	Rafael Furcal	.50
51	Rickie Weeks	.50
52	Geoff Jenkins	.25
53	Bill Hall	.25
54	Chris Capuano	.25
55	Derrick Turnbow	.25
56	Justin Morneau	.50
57	Michael Cuddyer	.25
58	Luis Castillo	.25
59	Hideki Matsui	1.00
60	Jason Giambi	.50
61	Jorge Posada	.50
62	Mariano Rivera	.50
63	Billy Wagner	.25
64	Carlos Delgado	.50
65	Jose Reyes	.75
66	Nick Swisher	.40
67	Bobby Crosby	.25

69	*Frank Thomas	.50
70	Ryan Howard	2.00
71	Pat Burrell	.50
72	Jimmy Rollins	.75
73	Craig Wilson	.25
74	Freddy Sanchez	.25
75	Sean Casey	.25
76	Mike Piazza	1.00
77	Dave Roberts	.25
78	Chris Young	.25
79	Noah Lowry	.25
80	Armando Benitez	.25
81	Pedro Feliz	.25
82	Jose Lopez	.25
83	Adrian Beltre	.40
84	Jamie Moyer	.25
85	Jason Isringhausen	.25
86	Jason Marquis	.25
87	David Eckstein	.25
88	Juan Encarnacion	.25
89	Julio Lugo	.25
90	Ty Wigginton	.25
91	Jorge Cantu	.25
92	Akinori Otsuka	.25
93	Hank Blalock	.40
94	Kevin Mench	.25
95	Lyle Overbay	.25
96	Shea Hillenbrand	.25
97	B.J. Ryan	.25
98	Tony Armas	.25
99	Chad Cordero	.25
100	Jose Guillen	.25
101	Miguel Tejada	3.00
102	Brian Roberts	2.00
103	Melvin Mora	2.00
104	Brandon Webb	3.00
105	Chad Tracy	2.00
106	Luis Gonzalez	2.00
107	Andruw Jones	4.00
108	Chipper Jones	5.00
109	John Smoltz	3.00
110	Curt Schilling	4.00
111	Josh Beckett	4.00
112	David Ortiz	5.00
113	Manny Ramirez	4.00
114	Jason Varitek	4.00
115	Jim Thome	4.00
116	Paul Konerko	4.00
117	Javier Vazquez	2.00
118	Mark Prior	3.00
119	Derrek Lee	4.00
120	Greg Maddux	6.00
121	Ken Griffey Jr.	6.00
122	Adam Dunn	3.00
123	Bronson Arroyo	2.00
124	Travis Hafner	3.00
125	Victor Martinez	2.00
126	Grady Sizemore	3.00
127	C.C. Sabathia	3.00
128	Todd Helton	3.00
129	Matt Holliday	3.00
130	Garrett Atkins	2.00
131	Jeff Francis	2.00
132	Jeremy Bonderman	3.00
133	Ivan Rodriguez	3.00
134	Chris Shelton	2.00
135	Magglio Ordonez	2.00
136	Dontrelle Willis	2.00
137	Miguel Cabrera	5.00
138	Roger Clemens	8.00
139	Roy Oswalt	3.00
140	Lance Berkman	3.00
141	Reggie Sanders	2.00
142	Vladimir Guerrero	5.00
143	Bartolo Colon	2.00
144	Chone Figgins	3.00
145	Francisco Rodriguez	3.00
146	Brad Penny	2.00
147	Jeff Kent	3.00
148	Eric Gagne	2.00
149	Carlos Lee	3.00
150	Ben Sheets	2.00
151	Johan Santana	4.00
152	Torii Hunter	2.00
153	Joe Nathan	2.00
154	Alex Rodriguez	8.00
155	Derek Jeter	8.00
156	Randy Johnson	4.00
157	Johnny Damon	3.00
158	Mike Mussina	3.00
159	Pedro Martinez	4.00
160	Tom Glavine	3.00
161	David Wright	5.00
162	Carlos Beltran	3.00
163	Rich Harden	3.00
164	Barry Zito	3.00
165	Eric Chavez	2.00
166	Huston Street	2.00
167	Bobby Abreu	3.00
168	Chase Utley	4.00
169	Brett Myers	2.00
170	Jason Bay	2.00
171	Zachary Duke	2.00
172	Jake Peavy	2.00
173	Brian Giles	2.00
174	Khalil Greene	2.00
175	Trevor Hoffman	2.00
176	Jason Schmidt	2.00
177	Randy Winn	2.00
178	Omar Vizquel	2.00
179	Kenji Johjima	2.00
180	Ichiro Suzuki	6.00
181	Richie Sexson	3.00
182	Felix Hernandez	3.00
183	Albert Pujols	8.00
184	Chris Carpenter	3.00
185	Jim Edmonds	2.00
186	Scott Rolen	4.00

187	Carl Crawford	3.00
188	Scott Kazmir	2.00
189	Jonny Gomes	2.00
190	Mark Teixeira	3.00
191	Michael Young	2.00
192	Kevin Millwood	2.00
193	Vernon Wells	2.00
194	Troy Glaus	3.00
195	Roy Halladay	3.00
196	Alex Rios	3.00
197	Nick Johnson	2.00
198	Livan Hernandez	2.00
199	Alfonso Soriano	4.00
200	Jose Vidro	2.00
201	Aaron Rakers/399 RC	8.00
202	Angel Pagan/399 RC	2.00
203	Ben Hendrickson/399 RC	8.00
204	Bobby Livingston/399 RC	8.00
205	Darrell Rasner/399 RC	10.00
206	Brian Bannister/399 RC	15.00
207	Brian Wilson/899 RC	8.00
208	Bobby Keppel/199 RC	8.00
209	Choo Freeman/399 RC	8.00
210	Chris Booker/899 RC	8.00
211	Chris Britton/399 RC	10.00
212	Chris Demaria/329 RC	8.00
213	Chris Resop/899 RC	8.00
214	Tony Gwynn Jr./399 RC	20.00
215	Eric Reed/399 RC	8.00
216	Fabio Castro/399 RC	15.00
217	Fernando Nieve/299 RC	8.00
218	Freddie Bynum/899 RC	8.00
219	Guillermo Quiroz/399 RC	8.00
220	Hong-Chih Kuo/899 RC	30.00
221	Ryan Theriot/399 RC	8.00
222	Jack Taschner/899 RC	8.00
223	Jason Bergmann/899 RC	10.00
224	Jason Hammel/899 RC	8.00
225	Jeff Harris/399 RC	8.00
226	Jeremy Accardo/399 RC	8.00
227	Ty Taubenheim/399 RC	15.00
228	Joel Zumaya/399 RC	15.00
229	John Koronka/399 RC	8.00
230	Erick Aybar/399 RC	15.00
231	Jordan Tata/399 RC	8.00
232	Russell Martin/399 RC	15.00
233	Josh Rupe/399 RC	8.00
234	Kevin Frandsen/399 RC	15.00
235	Martin Prado/399 RC	20.00
236	Matt Capps/399 RC	15.00
237	Agustin Montero/199 RC	10.00
238	Mike Thompson/399 RC	8.00
239	Nate McLouth/399 RC	15.00
240	Peter Moylan/399 RC	8.00
241	Reggie Abercrombie/399 RC	8.00
242	Carlos Quentin/399 RC	20.00
243	Ron Flores/399 RC	8.00
244	Ryan Shealy/399 RC	15.00
245	Mike Rouse/399 RC	10.00
246	Santiago Ramirez/399 RC	8.00
247	Clay Hensley/899 RC	8.00
248	Skip Schumaker/399 RC	8.00
249	Eliezer Alfonzo/899 RC	8.00
250	Steve Stemle/399 RC	8.00
251	Tim Hamulack/399 RC	8.00
252	Tony Pena/299 RC	10.00
253	Emiliano Fruto/899 RC	8.00
254	Wilbert Nieves/399 RC	8.00
255	Joey Devine/399 RC	15.00
256	Adam Wainwright/399 RC	30.00
257	Andre Ethier/399 RC	40.00
258	Ben Johnson/399 RC	8.00
259	Boone Logan/399 RC	8.00
260	Chris Denorfia/899 RC	8.00
261	Alay Soler/399 RC	8.00
262	Cody Ross/899 RC	8.00
263	Dave Gassner/399 RC	8.00
264	Fausto Carmona/399 RC	20.00
265	Jeremy Sowers/299 RC	10.00
266	Jason Kubel/399 RC	15.00
267	John Van Benschoten/399 RC	10.00
268	Jose Capellan/399 RC	8.00
269	Josh Wilson/399 RC	8.00
270	Kelly Shoppach/399 RC	8.00
271	Macay McBride/399 RC	8.00
272	Matt Cain/399 RC	25.00
273	Mike Jacobs/399 RC	15.00
274	Paul Maholm/399 RC	15.00
275	Chad Billingsley/399 RC	25.00
276	Ruddy Lugo/399 RC	8.00
277	Jon Lester/399 RC	50.00
278	Sean Marshall/383 RC	15.00
279	Melky Cabrera/399 RC	20.00
280	Yusmeiro Petit/399 RC	15.00
281	Anderson Hernandez/299 RC	8.00
282	Brian Anderson/699 RC	8.00
283	Cole Hamels/299 RC	50.00
284	Boof Bonser/299 RC	8.00
285	Dan Uggla/199 RC	30.00
286	Francisco Liriano/299 RC	25.00
287	Hanley Ramirez/199 RC	60.00
288	Ian Kinsler/299 RC	40.00
289	Jeremy Hermida/299 RC	15.00
290	Jonathan Papelbon/199 RC	25.00
291	Jered Weaver/199 RC	30.00
292	Josh Johnson/299 RC	25.00

293	Josh Willingham/199 RC	15.00
294	Justin Verlander/199 RC	60.00
295	Stephen Drew/299 RC	25.00
296	Prince Fielder/125 RC	120.00
297	Ryan Zimmerman/199 RC	50.00
298	Takashi Saito/283 RC	50.00
299	Taylor Buchholz/299 RC	10.00
300	Conor Jackson/299 RC	15.00

Rookie Signatures Platinum

No Pricing	
Production One Set	

By The Letter

NM/M

Production 4-200		
BA	Bronson Arroyo/80	40.00
JB	Jason Bay/110	50.00
JB2	Jason Bay/50	50.00
CB	Craig Biggio/55	100.00
BI	Chad Billingsley/75	50.00
HB	Hank Blalock/50	40.00
AB	A.J. Burnett/50	40.00
MC	Miguel Cabrera/35	85.00
EC	Eric Chavez/75	50.00
AD	Adam Dunn/50	60.00
MG	Marcus Giles/136	20.00
JG	Jonny Gomes/175	30.00
KH	Khalil Greene/75	20.00
KG	Ken Griffey Jr./25	200.00
KG2	Ken Griffey Jr./25	200.00
KG3	Ken Griffey Jr./25	200.00
KG4	Ken Griffey Jr./25	200.00
VG	Vladimir Guerrero/25	120.00
AG	Tony Gwynn Jr./150	35.00
CO	Cole Hamels/120	65.00
CH	Craig Hansen/30	40.00
DH	Dan Haren/180	35.00
JH	Jeremy Hermida/125	35.00
FH	Felix Hernandez/40	50.00
FH2	Felix Hernandez/25	50.00
MH	Matt Holliday/37	80.00
HU	Tim Hudson/50	50.00
TI	Tadahito Iguchi/20	60.00
IK	Ian Kinsler/125	50.00
DL	Derrek Lee/200	50.00
FL	Francisco Liriano/100	50.00
GM	Greg Maddux/25	140.00
GM2	Greg Maddux/25	140.00
VM	Victor Martinez/75	35.00
JM	Joe Mauer/25	100.00
MO	Justin Morneau/75	30.00
MM	Mark Mulder/50	30.00
JN	Joe Nathan/100	20.00
RO	Roy Oswalt/50	40.00
JP	Jonathan Papelbon/100	50.00
PE	Jake Peavy/100	40.00
HR	Hanley Ramirez/125	75.00
JR	Jose Reyes/75	65.00
AR	Alex Rios/100	40.00
CS	C.C. Sabathia/40	50.00
BS	Ben Sheets/125	35.00
SM	John Smoltz/75	50.00
JS	Jeremy Sowers/60	25.00
HS	Huston Street/75	30.00
NS	Nick Swisher/170	30.00
TE	Miguel Tejada/25	50.00
JT	Jim Thome/30	75.00
DU	Dan Uggla/100	50.00
BU	B.J. Upton/20	50.00
CU	Chase Utley/25	100.00
JW	Jered Weaver/40	60.00
RW	Rickie Weeks/100	30.00
WI	Josh Willingham/75	40.00
DW	Dontrelle Willis/150	40.00
MY	Michael Young/40	45.00
CZ	Carlos Zambrano/17	50.00
RZ	Ryan Zimmerman/17	50.00
JZ	Joel Zumaya/125	30.00

Chirography Dual Signatures

NM/M

Production 25 Sets		
CE	Eric Reed, Cody Ross	25.00
FJ	Conor Jackson, Prince Fielder	40.00
GB	Khalil Greene, Josh Barfield	15.00
HA	Jeremy Hermida, Reggie Abercrombie	15.00
HK	Cole Hamels, Scott Kazmir	40.00
KH	Anderson Hernandez, Ian Kinsler	30.00
KS	Takashi Saito, Hong-Chih Kuo	100.00
LB	Francisco Liriano, Boof Bonser	15.00
MH	Rich Hill, Sean Marshall	20.00
MW	Josh Willingham, Victor Martinez	25.00
PB	Freddie Bynum, Angel Pagan	15.00
PG	Ken Griffey Jr., Albert Pujols	350.00
PP	Tony Pena, Martin Prado	25.00
RC	Hanley Ramirez, Miguel Cabrera	60.00
RR	Jose Reyes, Hanley Ramirez	60.00

SC	Jose Capellan, Ben Sheets	25.00
UH	Cole Hamels, Chase Utley	65.00
WS	Josh Wilson, Ryan Shealy	15.00

Chirography

NM/M

Production 75 unless noted.		
AN	Brian Anderson	8.00
GA	Garret Anderson	10.00
BB	Brandon Backe	8.00
BA	Brian Bannister	12.00
DB	Denny Bautista	10.00
CB	Craig Biggio	60.00
BI	Chad Billingsley	25.00
HB	Hank Blalock	15.00
JB	Joe Blanton	12.00
BO	Boof Bonser	8.00
TB	Taylor Buchholz	8.00
MC	Matt Cain	30.00
JC	Jose Capellan	8.00
FC	Fausto Carmona	15.00
SC	Sean Casey	15.00
BC	Bobby Crosby	8.00
DD	David DeJesus	10.00
CD	Chris Denorfia	10.00
JD	Joey Devine	10.00
SD	Stephen Drew	20.00
JE	Johnny Estrada	8.00
AE	Andre Ethier	25.00
KF	Keith Foulke	8.00
JF	Jeff Francis	8.00
CF	Choo Freeman	8.00
DG	Dave Gassner	8.00
KG	Khalil Greene	10.00
GR	Ken Griffey Jr.	80.00
CG	Carlos Guillen	10.00
AG	Tony Gwynn Jr.	15.00
TH	Travis Hafner	15.00
CH	Cole Hamels	40.00
RH	Rich Harden	10.00
HA	Jeff Harris	8.00
JH	Jeremy Hermida	15.00
AH	Anderson Hernandez	10.00
FH	Felix Hernandez/25	40.00
CJ	Conor Jackson	15.00
DJ	Derek Jeter	160.00
JJ	Josh Johnson	15.00
JQ	Jacque Jones	10.00
SK	Scott Kazmir/25	20.00
IK	Ian Kinsler	25.00
CK	Casey Kotchman	8.00
JK	Jason Kubel	15.00
HK	Hong-Chih Kuo	15.00
CL	Cliff Lee	15.00
JL	Jon Lester	30.00
LI	Francisco Liriano	15.00
BL	Boone Logan	10.00
FL	Felipe Lopez	10.00
ML	Mark Loretta	10.00
PM	Paul Maholm	15.00
SM	Sean Marshall	8.00
VM	Victor Martinez	15.00
MM	Macay McBride	8.00
KM	Kevin Mench	8.00
JN	Joe Nathan	8.00
LO	Lyle Overbay/40	15.00
VP	Vicente Padilla	8.00
JP	Jonathan Papelbon	40.00
CP	Corey Patterson	8.00
TP	Tony Pena	8.00
WM	Wily Mo Pena	8.00
OP	Oliver Perez	15.00
YP	Yusmeiro Petit	8.00
MP	Mark Prior/25	40.00
HR	Hanley Ramirez	40.00
RE	Eric Reed	10.00
ER	Edgar Renteria	8.00
AR	Alex Rios	15.00
IR	Ivan Rodriguez	25.00
CR	Cody Ross	8.00
JR	Josh Rupe	10.00
CS	C.C. Sabathia	25.00
TS	Takashi Saito	20.00
BS	Ben Sheets	25.00
SH	Chris Shelton	8.00
KS	Kelly Shoppach	8.00
SO	Alay Soler	8.00
AS	Alfonso Soriano	40.00
JS	Jeremy Sowers	10.00
NS	Nick Swisher	20.00
FT	Frank Thomas	65.00
DU	Dan Uggla	25.00
CU	Chase Utley	50.00
VA	John Van Benschoten	8.00
JV	Jason Varitek	50.00
VE	Justin Verlander	40.00
AW	Adam Wainwright	30.00
WE	Jered Weaver	30.00
JW	Josh Willingham	15.00
DW	Dontrelle Willis	10.00
WI	Josh Wilson	8.00
KY	Kevin Youkilis	20.00
RZ	Ryan Zimmerman	30.00

Chirography Triple Signatures

No Pricing	
Production 15 Sets	

Sign of the Times

NM/M

Production 75 Sets		
RA	Reggie Abercrombie	8.00
BA	Bobby Abreu	35.00

AN	Brian Anderson	10.00
BR	Brian Bannister	15.00
AB	Adrian Beltre	15.00
YB	Yuniesky Betancourt	15.00
BI	Chad Billingsley	25.00
BB	Boof Bonser	10.00
CB	Chris Booker	8.00
TB	Taylor Buchholz	8.00
ME	Melky Cabrera	10.00
MC	Miguel Cabrera	30.00
CA	Matt Cain	30.00
JC	Jose Capellan	8.00
FC	Fausto Carmona	10.00
CC	Carl Crawford	15.00
CD	Chris Demaria	8.00
DE	Chris Denorfia	8.00
JD	J.D. Drew	15.00
SD	Stephen Drew	30.00
AE	Andre Ethier	30.00
FR	Ron Flores	10.00
RF	Rafael Furcal	15.00
EG	Eric Gagne	15.00
DG	Dave Gassner	8.00
ZG	Zack Greinke	25.00
KG	Ken Griffey Jr.	80.00
VG	Vladimir Guerrero	50.00
JG	Jose Guillen	8.00
AG	Tony Gwynn Jr.	35.00
CH	Cole Hamels	50.00
JH	Jason Hammel	8.00
HA	Tim Hamulack	10.00
CY	Clay Hensley	8.00
HE	Jeremy Hermida	15.00
AH	Anderson Hernandez	8.00
RH	Ramon Hernandez	10.00
TH	Tim Hudson	15.00
JA	Conor Jackson	10.00
MJ	Mike Jacobs	10.00
DJ	Derek Jeter	160.00
BJ	Ben Johnson	10.00
JJ	Josh Johnson	15.00
RJ	Randy Johnson	50.00
AJ	Andruw Jones	15.00
JK	Jason Kendall	10.00
IK	Ian Kinsler	25.00
MK	Mark Kotsay	10.00
KU	Jason Kubel	15.00
CL	Carlos Lee	15.00
DL	Derek Lee	25.00
FL	Francisco Liriano	35.00
BL	Boone Logan	10.00
LO	Derek Lowe	25.00
GM	Greg Maddux	140.00
PM	Paul Maholm	15.00
SM	Sean Marshall	10.00
RM	Russell Martin	10.00
JM	Joe Mauer	35.00
MA	Macay McBride	10.00
MO	Justin Morneau	25.00
MM	Mark Mulder	10.00
PA	Jonathan Papelbon	20.00
JP	Tony Pena	8.00
PE	Joel Peralta	10.00
YP	Yusmeiro Petit	10.00
SP	Scott Podsednik	15.00
AR	Aramis Ramirez	20.00
HR	Hanley Ramirez	35.00
SA	Santiago Ramirez	10.00
ER	Eric Reed	10.00
JR	Jose Reyes	40.00
SR	Scott Rolen	25.00
CR	Cody Ross	10.00
TS	Takashi Saito	30.00
CS	Curt Schilling	50.00
SS	Skip Schumaker	10.00
RS	Ryan Shealy	15.00
JS	John Smoltz	40.00
AS	Alay Soler	10.00
JY	Jeremy Sowers	8.00
ST	Steve Stemle	8.00
MT	Mark Teixeira	20.00
TE	Miguel Tejada	15.00
MI	Mike Thompson	10.00
DU	Dan Uggla	25.00
JV	John Van Benschoten	10.00
VE	Justin Verlander	40.00
AW	Adam Wainwright	30.00
JE	Jered Weaver	40.00
RW	Rickie Weeks	15.00
VW	Vernon Wells	15.00
JW	Josh Willingham	15.00
WI	Josh Wilson	10.00
RZ	Ryan Zimmerman	30.00

Sign of the Times Dual
NM/M

Production 25 Sets

BM	Nate McLouth, Jason Bay	25.00
CH	Jose Capellan, Ben Hendrickson	10.00
FW	Prince Fielder, Rickie Weeks	60.00
GP	Ken Griffey Jr., Albert Pujols	300.00
HD	Tim Hudson, Joey Devine	30.00
HF	Rich Harden, Ron Flores	15.00
KN	Michael Napoli, Howie Kendrick	30.00
LG	Dave Gassner, Francisco Liriano	30.00
MM	Sean Marshall, Greg Maddux	120.00
OB	Roy Oswalt, Taylor Buchholz	25.00

PB	Angel Pagan, Freddie Bynum	15.00
PT	Jake Peavy, Mike Thompson	20.00
RW	Josh Willingham, Hanley Ramirez	40.00
SC	Fausto Carmona, C.C. Sabathia	30.00
WM	Kendry Morales, Jered Weaver	40.00
ZH	Ryan Zimmerman, Brendan Harris	40.00

Signs of the Times Triple
No Pricing

Production 15 Sets

Heroes
NM/M

Common Player: .50

1	Albert Pujols	3.00
2	Andruw Jones	1.00
3	Aramis Ramirez	.75
4	Brian Roberts	.50
5	Carl Crawford	.75
6	Carlos Lee	.75
7	Vladimir Guerrero	1.00
8	Chris Carpenter	.75
9	Craig Biggio	.75
10	David Ortiz	1.50
11	David Wright	2.00
12	Derek Lee	.75
13	Dontrelle Willis	.75
14	Felix Hernandez	.75
15	Garrett Atkins	.50
16	Grady Sizemore	.75
17	Huston Street	.50
18	Jake Peavy	.75
19	Jason Bay	.75
20	Joe Mauer	1.00
21	John Smoltz	.75
22	Jonny Gomes	.50
23	Jorge Cantu	.50
24	Ken Griffey Jr.	2.00
25	Marcus Giles	.50
26	Mark Teixeira	.75
27	Matt Cain	.75
28	Michael Young	.50
29	Miguel Cabrera	1.00
30	Johan Santana	1.00
31	Nick Swisher	.50
32	Prince Fielder	1.00
33	Joe Blanton	.50
34	Roy Oswalt	.75
35	Ryan Howard	3.00
36	Scott Kazmir	.50
37	Tadahito Iguchi	.50
38	Travis Hafner	.75
39	Victor Martinez	.75
40	Jose Reyes	1.00
41	Chris Carpenter, Albert Pujols	3.00
42	Albert Pujols, Miguel Cabrera	3.00
43	Andruw Jones, Ken Griffey Jr.	2.00
44	Derek Lee, Aramis Ramirez	.75
45	Ryan Howard, Prince Fielder	3.00
46	Jake Peavy, Roy Oswalt	.75
47	Morgan Ensberg, Craig Biggio	.75
48	David Ortiz, Travis Hafner	1.50
49	Derek Jeter, David Wright	3.00
50	Derek Jeter, Ken Griffey Jr.	3.00
51	Derek Jeter, Michael Young	3.00
52	Scott Kazmir, Dontrelle Willis	.50
53	Jason Bay, Grady Sizemore	.75
54	Michael Young, Mark Teixeira	.75
55	Brian Roberts, Tadahito Iguchi	.50
56	Matt Cain, Felix Hernandez, Chien-Ming Wang	2.00
57	Mark Teixeira, Derek Lee, Albert Pujols	3.00
58	Albert Pujols, Ken Griffey Jr., Miguel Cabrera	3.00
59	Marcus Giles, Andruw Jones, John Smoltz	1.00
60	Derek Lee, Kerry Wood, Aramis Ramirez	1.00
61	Aramis Ramirez, Morgan Ensberg, David Wright	2.00
62	Carl Crawford, Jorge Cantu, Jonny Gomes	.50
63	Jake Peavy, Chris Carpenter, John Smoltz	1.00
64	Travis Hafner, Grady Sizemore, Victor Martinez	3.00
65	Ryan Howard, Prince Fielder, David Ortiz	3.00
66	Chris Carpenter, John Smoltz, Jake Peavy, Dontrelle Willis	.75
67	Ken Griffey Jr., Derek Jeter, David Ortiz, Albert Pujols	3.00
68	David Ortiz, Andruw Jones, Derek Lee, Mark Teixeira	1.50
69	Brian Roberts, Marcus Giles, Craig Biggio, Tadahito Iguchi	.50
70	Jason Bay, David Wright, Mark Teixeira, Miguel Cabrera	2.00

WBC Future Watch
NM/M

Common Player: 3.00

Production 999 Sets

1	Adrian Burnside	3.00
2	Gavin Fingleson	3.00
3	Bradley Harman	3.00
4	Brendan Kingman	3.00
5	Brett Roneberg	3.00
6	Paul Rutgers	3.00
7	Phil Stockman	3.00
8	Stubby Clapp	3.00
9	Steve Green	3.00
10	Pete LaForest	5.00
11	Adam Loewen	5.00
12	Ryan Radmanovich	3.00
13	Chenhao Li	3.00
14	Guangbiao Liu	3.00
15	Guogang Yang	3.00
16	Jinghao Wang	3.00
17	Lei Li	3.00
18	Lingfeng Sun	3.00
19	Nan Wang	3.00
20	Shuo Yang	3.00
21	Tao Bu	3.00
22	Wei Wang	3.00
23	Yi Feng	3.00
24	Chien-Ming Chiang	15.00
25	Yung-Chi Chen	20.00
26	Chia-Hsien Hseih	15.00
27	Chin-Lung Hu	15.00
28	En-Yu Lin	20.00
29	Wei-Lun Pan	10.00
30	Ariel Borrero	3.00
31	Yadel Marti	3.00
32	Yulieski Gourriel	15.00
33	Frederich Cepeda	3.00
34	Yadier Pedroso	3.00
35	Elier Sanchez	3.00
36	Elier Sanchez	3.00
37	Norberto Gonzalez	3.00
38	Carlos Tabares	3.00
39	Eduardo Paret	3.00
40	Osmany Urrutia	3.00
41	Alexei Ramirez	40.00
42	Yoandy Garbobo	3.00
43	Vicyohandry Odelin	3.00
44	Michel Enriquez	3.00
45	Ormari Romero	3.00
46	Ariel Pestano	3.00
47	Francisco Liriano	5.00
48	Dustin Dellucchi	3.00
49	Tony Giarratano	3.00
50	Tom Gregorio	3.00
51	Mark Saccomanno	3.00
52	Takahiro Arai	8.00
53	Akinori Iwamura	10.00
54	Munenori Kawasaki	10.00
55	Nobuhiko Matsunaka	10.00
56	Daisuke Matsuzaka	60.00
57	Shinya Miyamoto	10.00
58	Tsuyoshi Nishioka	10.00
59	Tomoya Satozaki	3.00
60	Koji Uehara	10.00
61	Shunsuke Watanabe	3.00
62	Sadaharu Oh	20.00
63	Byung Kyu Lee	3.00
64	Ji Man Song	3.00
65	Jin Man Park	3.00
66	Jong Beom Lee	3.00
67	Jong Kook Kim	3.00
68	Min Han Son	3.00
69	Min Jae Kim	3.00
70	Seung-Yeop Lee	10.00
71	Luis A. Garcia	3.00
72	Mario Valenzuela	3.00
73	Sharnol Adriana	3.00
74	Rob Cordemans	3.00
75	Michael Duursma	3.00
76	Percy Isenia	3.00
77	Sidney de Jong	3.00
78	Dirk Klooster	3.00
79	Raylinoe Legito	3.00
80	Shairon Martis	3.00
81	Harvey Monte	3.00
82	Hainley Statia	3.00
83	Roger Deago	5.00
84	Audes De Leon	3.00
85	Freddy Herrera	3.00
86	Yoni Lasso	5.00
87	Orlando Miller	3.00
88	Len Picota	3.00
89	Federico Baez	3.00
90	Dicky Gonzalez	3.00
91	Josue Matos	3.00
92	Orlando Roman	3.00
93	Paul Bell	3.00
94	Kyle Botha	3.00
95	Jason Cook	3.00
96	Nicholas Dempsey	3.00
97	Victor Moreno	3.00
98	Ricardo Rima	3.00
99	Huston Street	3.00
100	Chase Utley	3.00

2006 SP Legendary Cuts
NM/M

Complete Set (200):

Common Player: .25

Common SP (101-200): 2.00

Production 550

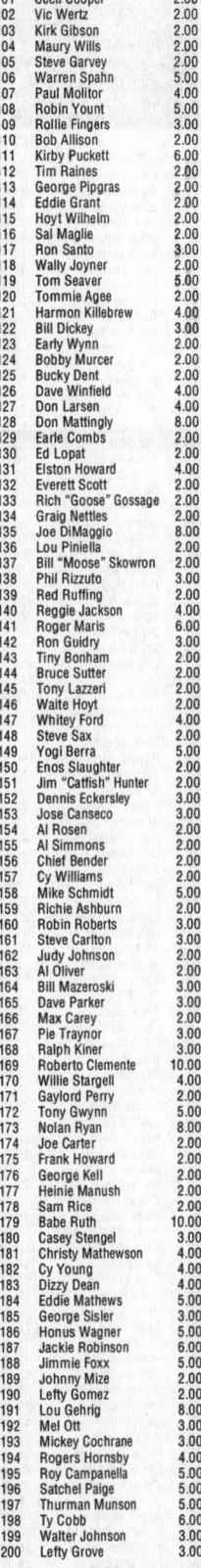

Pack (4):		10.00
Box (12):		100.00
1	Juan Marichal	.50
2	Monte Irvin	.75
3	Will Clark	.75
4	Willie McCovey	.75
5	Eddie Gaedel	.25
6	Ken Williams	.25
7	Earl Battey	.25
8	Rick Ferrell	.25
9	Bob Gibson	1.00
10	Elmer Flick	.25
11	Joe Medwick	.25
12	Lou Brock	.75
13	Ozzie Smith	1.00
14	Red Schoendienst	.25
15	Stan Musial	2.00
16	Tony Oliva	.50
17	Phil Niekro	.25
18	Boog Powell	.25
19	Brooks Robinson	1.00
20	Cal Ripken Jr.	3.00
21	Eddie Murray	.75
22	Frank Robinson	1.00
23	Jim Palmer	.50
24	Jocko Conlon	.25
25	Carlton Fisk	.50
26	Dwight Evans	.25
27	Fred Lynn	.25
28	Jim Rice	.50
29	Ted Williams	2.00
30	Wade Boggs	.75
31	Hugh Duffy	.25
32	Kid Nichols	.25
33	Johnny Vander Meer	.25
34	Dolph Camilli	.25
35	Carl Yastrzemski	1.00
36	Chick Hafey	.25
37	Kirby Higbe	.25
38	Pee Wee Reese	.50
39	Pete Reiser	.25
40	Don Sutton	.25
41	Rod Carew	.75
42	Andre Dawson	.50
43	Billy Herman	.25
44	Billy Williams	.25
45	Charlie Root	.25
46	Hack Wilson	.25
47	Ernie Banks	1.00
48	Fergie Jenkins	.50
49	Gabby Hartnett	.25
50	Ken Hubbs	.25
51	Kiki Cuyler	.25
52	Mark Grace	.25
53	Ryne Sandberg	1.50
54	Harold Newhouser	.25
55	Charlie Robertson	.25
56	Harold Baines	.25
57	Luis Aparicio	.25
58	Luke Appling	.25
59	Nellie Fox	.50
60	Ray Schalk	.25
61	Red Faber	.25
62	Sloppy Thurston	.25
63	Freddie Lindstrom	.25
64	Vern Kennedy	.25
65	Barry Larkin	.50
66	Bucky Walters	.25
67	Dolf Luque	.25
68	Al Campanis	.25
69	Ernie Lombardi	.25
70	George Foster	.25
71	Joe Morgan	.75
72	Johnny Bench	1.00
73	Ken Griffey Sr.	.25
74	Ted Kluszewski	.25
75	Tony Perez	.50
76	Wally Post	.25
77	Bob Feller	.50
78	Bob Lemon	.25
79	Earl Averill	.25
80	Joe Sewell	.25
81	Johnny Hodapp	.25
82	Larry Doby	.50
83	Lou Boudreau	.25
84	Rocky Colavito	.25
85	Stan Coveleski	.25
86	Nap Lajoie	.50
87	Al Kaline	1.00
88	Alan Trammell	.25
89	Charlie Gehringer	.25
90	Denny McLain	.50
91	Hank Greenberg	.50
92	Jack Morris	.25
93	Mark Fidrych	.25
94	Ray Boone	.25
95	Rudy York	.25
96	Buck Leonard	.25

97	Bo Jackson	1.00
98	Zoilo Versalles	.25
99	John Kruk	.25
100	Don Drysdale	.50
101	Cecil Cooper	2.00
102	Vic Wertz	2.00
103	Kirk Gibson	2.00
104	Maury Wills	2.00
105	Steve Garvey	2.00
106	Warren Spahn	5.00
107	Paul Molitor	4.00
108	Robin Yount	5.00
109	Rollie Fingers	3.00
110	Bob Allison	2.00
111	Kirby Puckett	6.00
112	Tim Raines	2.00
113	George Pipgras	2.00
114	Eddie Grant	2.00
115	Hoyt Wilhelm	2.00
116	Sal Maglie	2.00
117	Ron Santo	3.00
118	Wally Joyner	2.00
119	Tom Seaver	5.00
120	Tommie Agee	2.00
121	Harmon Killebrew	4.00
122	Bill Dickey	3.00
123	Early Wynn	2.00
124	Bobby Murcer	2.00
125	Bucky Dent	2.00
126	Dave Winfield	4.00
127	Don Larsen	4.00
128	Don Mattingly	8.00
129	Earle Combs	2.00
130	Ed Lopat	2.00
131	Elston Howard	2.00
132	Everett Scott	2.00
133	Rich "Goose" Gossage	2.00
134	Graig Nettles	2.00
135	Joe DiMaggio	8.00
136	Lou Piniella	2.00
137	Bill "Moose" Skowron	2.00
138	Phil Rizzuto	3.00
139	Red Ruffing	2.00
140	Reggie Jackson	4.00
141	Roger Maris	6.00
142	Ron Guidry	3.00
143	Tiny Bonham	2.00
144	Bruce Sutter	2.00
145	Tony Lazzeri	2.00
146	Waite Hoyt	2.00
147	Whitey Ford	4.00
148	Steve Sax	2.00
149	Yogi Berra	5.00
150	Enos Slaughter	2.00
151	Jim "Catfish" Hunter	2.00
152	Dennis Eckersley	2.00
153	Jose Canseco	3.00
154	Al Rosen	2.00
155	Al Simmons	2.00
156	Chief Bender	2.00
157	Cy Williams	2.00
158	Mike Schmidt	5.00
159	Richie Ashburn	2.00
160	Robin Roberts	3.00
161	Steve Carlton	3.00
162	Judy Johnson	2.00
163	Al Oliver	2.00
164	Bill Mazeroski	2.00
165	Dave Parker	3.00
166	Max Carey	2.00
167	Pie Traynor	3.00
168	Ralph Kiner	2.00
169	Roberto Clemente	10.00
170	Willie Stargell	4.00
171	Gaylord Perry	2.00
172	Tony Gwynn	5.00
173	Nolan Ryan	8.00
174	Joe Carter	2.00
175	Frank Howard	2.00
176	George Kell	2.00
177	Heinie Manush	2.00
178	Sam Rice	2.00
179	Babe Ruth	10.00
180	Casey Stengel	3.00
181	Christy Mathewson	4.00
182	Cy Young	4.00
183	Dizzy Dean	4.00
184	Eddie Mathews	5.00
185	George Sisler	3.00
186	Honus Wagner	5.00
187	Jackie Robinson	6.00
188	Jimmie Foxx	5.00
189	Lefty Gomez	2.00
190	Lou Gehrig	8.00
191	Mel Ott	3.00
192	Mickey Cochrane	3.00
193	Rogers Hornsby	4.00
194	Babe Ruth/99	225.00
195	Roy Campanella	5.00
196	Satchel Paige	5.00
197	Thurman Munson	3.00
198	Ty Cobb	6.00
199	Walter Johnson	5.00
200	Lefty Grove	2.00

Gold
Gold (101-200): 2-4X

Production 99 Sets

Legendary Materials
NM/M

Production 225 unless noted.

Tier 1:	.75-1.5X
Production 50-199	
Tier 2:	1-2X
Production 25-99	
Tier 3:	No Pricing
Production 5-15	

HB	Harold Baines	6.00
EB	Ernie Banks	20.00
JB	Johnny Bench	15.00
YB	Yogi Berra	15.00
WB	Wade Boggs	10.00
LB	Lou Brock	10.00
LB2	Lou Brock	10.00
JC	Jose Canseco	10.00
CW	Rod Carew	10.00
SC	Steve Carlton	8.00
SC2	Steve Carlton	8.00
WC	Will Clark	10.00
WC2	Will Clark	10.00
RC	Rocky Colavito	20.00
DC	Dave Concepcion	6.00
CC	Cecil Cooper	10.00
AD	Andre Dawson	8.00
BD	Bucky Dent	8.00
JD	Joe DiMaggio/99	75.00
DE	Dennis Eckersley	8.00
DE2	Dennis Eckersley	8.00
EV	Dwight Evans	8.00
BF	Bob Feller	10.00
RF	Rollie Fingers	8.00
CF	Carlton Fisk	8.00
GF	George Foster	6.00
SG	Steve Garvey	8.00
BG	Bob Gibson	10.00
KI	Kirk Gibson	8.00
GG	Rich "Goose" Gossage	8.00
MG	Mark Grace	10.00
KG	Ken Griffey Sr.	8.00
GU	Ron Guidry	10.00
TG	Tony Gwynn	15.00
FH	Frank Howard	8.00
BO	Bo Jackson	15.00
RJ	Reggie Jackson	8.00
FJ	Fergie Jenkins	8.00
WJ	Wally Joyner	8.00
AK	Al Kaline	12.00
RK	Ralph Kiner	8.00
JK	John Kruk	8.00
BL	Barry Larkin	8.00
DL	Don Larsen	12.00
FL	Fred Lynn	6.00
JU	Juan Marichal	8.00
MA	Don Mattingly	20.00
BM	Bill Mazeroski	8.00
WM	Willie McCovey	10.00
PM	Paul Molitor	8.00
JO	Joe Morgan	10.00
JM	Jack Morris	6.00
MU	Bobby Murcer	8.00
EM	Eddie Murray	10.00
SM	Stan Musial	20.00
GN	Graig Nettles	8.00
PN	Phil Niekro	8.00
PN2	Phil Niekro	8.00
TO	Tony Oliva	8.00
AO	Al Oliver	8.00
JP	Jim Palmer	10.00
JP2	Jim Palmer	10.00
DP	Dave Parker	8.00
TP	Tony Perez	8.00
GP	Gaylord Perry	8.00
GP2	Gaylord Perry	8.00
LP	Lou Piniella	8.00
BP	Boog Powell	8.00
KP	Kirby Puckett	15.00
JR	Jim Rice	8.00
CR	Cal Ripken Jr.	25.00
PR	Phil Rizzuto/99	10.00
RR	Robin Roberts	8.00
RO	Brooks Robinson/175	10.00
FR	Frank Robinson	10.00
FR2	Frank Robinson	10.00
AR	Al Rosen	8.00
BR	Babe Ruth/99	225.00
NR	Nolan Ryan	20.00
RS	Ryne Sandberg	15.00
RN	Ron Santo/125	12.00
RN2	Ron Santo/125	12.00
SS	Steve Sax	6.00
MS	Mike Schmidt	15.00
RE	Red Schoendienst/99	15.00
TS	Tom Seaver	12.00
SK	Bill "Moose" Skowron	8.00
OS	Ozzie Smith	15.00
SU	Don Sutton	8.00
BS	Bruce Sutter	8.00
JT	Joe Torre	10.00
BW	Billy Williams	8.00
MW	Maury Wills	6.00
DW	Dave Winfield	8.00
CY	Carl Yastrzemski	15.00
RY	Robin Yount	6.00
MW		6.00

Baseball Chronology

NM/M

Production 550 Sets
Platinum: 1.5-2X
Production 99 Sets

		NM/M
EB	Ernie Banks	5.00
EB2	Ernie Banks	5.00
JB	Johnny Bench	4.00
YB	Yogi Berra	4.00
WB	Wade Boggs	4.00
WB2	Wade Boggs	4.00
LB	Lou Boudreau	2.00
LO	Lou Brock	4.00
RC	Roy Campanella	4.00
CA	Rod Carew	3.00
SC	Steve Carlton	3.00
SC2	Steve Carlton	3.00
JC	Joe Carter	2.00
WC	Will Clark	4.00
CL	Roberto Clemente	10.00
TC	Ty Cobb	6.00
TC2	Ty Cobb	6.00
MC	Mickey Cochrane	3.00
CN	Joe Cronin	2.00
AD	Andre Dawson	3.00
DZ	Dizzy Dean	3.00
BD	Bucky Dent	2.00
JD	Joe DiMaggio	8.00
DD	Don Drysdale	3.00
DE	Dennis Eckersley	3.00
BF	Bob Feller	3.00
MF	Mark Fidrych	2.00
RF	Rollie Fingers	3.00
CF	Carlton Fisk	3.00
WF	Whitey Ford	4.00
JF	Jimmie Foxx	5.00
JF2	Jimmie Foxx	5.00
SG	Steve Garvey	2.00
LG	Lou Gehrig	8.00
LG2	Lou Gehrig	8.00
BG	Bob Gibson	4.00
KG	Kirk Gibson	3.00
HG	Hank Greenberg	3.00
TG	Tony Gwynn	4.00
GH	Gil Hodges	3.00
RH	Rogers Hornsby	4.00
CH	Jim "Catfish" Hunter	4.00
BO	Bo Jackson	3.00
RJ	Reggie Jackson	4.00
WJ	Walter Johnson	4.00
AK	Al Kaline	4.00
RK	Ralph Kiner	2.00
NL	Nap Lajoie	3.00
DL	Don Larsen	3.00
BL	Bob Lemon	2.00
FL	Fred Lynn	2.00
RM	Roger Maris	6.00
CM	Christy Mathewson	4.00
DM	Don Mattingly	6.00
BM	Bill Mazeroski	3.00
WM	Willie McCovey	3.00
JM	Johnny Mize	3.00
PM	Paul Molitor	3.00
JO	Joe Morgan	3.00
TM	Thurman Munson	5.00
EM	Eddie Murray	3.00
SM	Stan Musial	6.00
PN	Phil Niekro	2.00
MO	Mel Ott	3.00
SP	Satchel Paige	5.00
GP	Gaylord Perry	2.00
KP	Kirby Puckett	5.00
PW	Pee Wee Reese	3.00
RI	Jim Rice	3.00
CR	Cal Ripken Jr.	8.00
RO	Brooks Robinson	4.00
FR	Frank Robinson	4.00
JR	Jackie Robinson	6.00
BR	Babe Ruth	10.00
BR2	Babe Ruth	10.00
BR3	Babe Ruth	10.00
NR	Nolan Ryan	8.00
NR2	Nolan Ryan	8.00
NR3	Nolan Ryan	8.00
RS	Ryne Sandberg	5.00
MS	Mike Schmidt	5.00
TS	Tom Seaver	4.00
GS	George Sisler	3.00
ES	Enos Slaughter	2.00
OS	Ozzie Smith	5.00
WS	Warren Spahn	4.00
ST	Willie Stargell	4.00
CS	Casey Stengel	3.00
CS2	Casey Stengel	3.00
DS	Don Sutton	2.00
AT	Alan Trammell	3.00
HW	Honus Wagner	5.00
HY	Hoyt Wilhelm	2.00
BW	Billy Williams	2.00
TW	Ted Williams	8.00
TW2	Ted Williams	8.00
MW	Maury Wills	2.00
YZ	Carl Yastrzemski	4.00
CY	Cy Young	3.00
RY	Robin Yount	4.00

Baseball Chronology Materials

NM/M

Common Player:

		NM/M
EB	Ernie Banks	15.00
EB2	Ernie Banks/SP	20.00
JB	Johnny Bench	15.00
YB	Yogi Berra	20.00
WB	Wade Boggs	10.00
WB2	Wade Boggs	10.00
LB	Lou Boudreau	12.00
LO	Lou Brock	10.00
RC	Roy Campanella	20.00
CA	Rod Carew	10.00
SC	Steve Carlton	8.00
SC2	Steve Carlton	8.00
JC	Joe Carter	6.00
WC	Will Clark	10.00
CL	Roberto Clemente/SP	60.00
TC	Ty Cobb/SP	150.00
TC2	Ty Cobb/SP	150.00
CN	Joe Cronin	15.00
AD	Andre Dawson	8.00
DZ	Dizzy Dean/SP	60.00
BD	Bucky Dent	6.00
JD	Joe DiMaggio/SP	75.00
DD	Don Drysdale/SP	25.00
DE	Dennis Eckersley	10.00
BF	Bob Feller	10.00
MF	Mark Fidrych	8.00
RF	Rollie Fingers	8.00
CF	Carlton Fisk	10.00
JF	Jimmie Foxx/SP	40.00
JF2	Jimmie Foxx/SP	40.00
SG	Steve Garvey	6.00
LG	Lou Gehrig/SP	175.00
LG2	Lou Gehrig	175.00
BG	Bob Gibson	10.00
HG	Hank Greenberg	25.00
TG	Tony Gwynn	12.00
GH	Gil Hodges/SP	40.00
RH	Rogers Hornsby/SP	50.00
CH	Jim "Catfish" Hunter	10.00
BO	Bo Jackson	12.00
RJ	Reggie Jackson	12.00
AK	Al Kaline	15.00
RK	Ralph Kiner	12.00
DL	Don Larsen	12.00
BL	Bob Lemon	10.00
FL	Fred Lynn	8.00
RM	Roger Maris	30.00
CM	Christy Mathewson/SP	240.00
DM	Don Mattingly	15.00
BM	Bill Mazeroski/SP	20.00
WM	Willie McCovey	12.00
JM	Johnny Mize	15.00
PM	Paul Molitor	8.00
JO	Joe Morgan	10.00
TM	Thurman Munson	25.00
EM	Eddie Murray	10.00
SM	Stan Musial	20.00
PN	Phil Niekro	10.00
MO	Mel Ott/SP	35.00
SP	Satchel Paige/SP	75.00
GP	Gaylord Perry	8.00
KP	Kirby Puckett	15.00
PW	Pee Wee Reese	10.00
RI	Jim Rice	8.00
CR	Cal Ripken Jr.	25.00
RO	Brooks Robinson	12.00
FR	Frank Robinson	10.00
JR	Jackie Robinson/SP	60.00
BR	Babe Ruth/SP	250.00
BR2	Babe Ruth/SP	250.00
BR3	Babe Ruth/SP	250.00
NR	Nolan Ryan	20.00
NR2	Nolan Ryan	20.00
NR3	Nolan Ryan	20.00
RS	Ryne Sandberg	15.00
MS	Mike Schmidt	12.00
TS	Tom Seaver	15.00
GS	George Sisler/SP	35.00
ES	Enos Slaughter	15.00
OS	Ozzie Smith	12.00
WS	Warren Spahn	15.00
ST	Willie Stargell	15.00
CS	Casey Stengel	25.00
CS2	Casey Stengel	35.00
DS	Don Sutton	8.00
AT	Alan Trammell	8.00
HW	Honus Wagner/SP	160.00
HY	Hoyt Wilhelm/SP	15.00
BW	Billy Williams	8.00
TW	Ted Williams	40.00
TW2	Ted Williams	40.00
MW	Maury Wills	8.00
YZ	Carl Yastrzemski	15.00
RY	Robin Yount	12.00

When It Was A Game

NM/M

Production 550 Sets
Gold: 1.5-2X
Production 99 Sets

		NM/M
LA	Luis Aparicio	2.00
HB	Harold Baines	2.00
EB	Ernie Banks	5.00
JB	Johnny Bench	4.00
YB	Yogi Berra	4.00
WB	Wade Boggs	4.00
LB	Lou Brock	4.00
CA	Rod Carew	3.00
SC	Steve Carlton	3.00
SC2	Steve Carlton	3.00
WC	Will Clark	4.00
RC	Roberto Clemente	10.00
MC	Mickey Cochrane	3.00
CO	Rocky Colavito	3.00
AD	Andre Dawson	3.00
JD	Joe DiMaggio	8.00
DD	Don Drysdale	3.00
DE	Dennis Eckersley	3.00
EV	Dwight Evans	2.00
BF	Bob Feller	3.00
RF	Rollie Fingers	3.00
CF	Carlton Fisk	3.00
WF	Whitey Ford	4.00
JF	Jimmie Foxx	5.00
SG	Steve Garvey	2.00
LG	Lou Gehrig	8.00
BG	Bob Gibson	4.00
KI	Kirk Gibson	3.00
GG	Rich "Goose" Gossage	2.00
HG	Hank Greenberg	3.00
KG	Ken Griffey Sr.	2.00
GU	Ron Guidry	3.00
TG	Tony Gwynn	4.00
HO	Rogers Hornsby	4.00
FH	Frank Howard	2.00
RJ	Reggie Jackson	3.00
FJ	Fergie Jenkins	3.00
WJ	Wally Joyner	2.00
AK	Al Kaline	4.00
RK	Ralph Kiner	2.00
JK	John Kruk	2.00
DL	Don Larsen	3.00
FL	Fred Lynn	2.00
JU	Juan Marichal	3.00
EM	Eddie Mathews	3.00
MA	Don Mattingly	6.00
BM	Bill Mazeroski	3.00
WM	Willie McCovey	3.00
DY	Denny McLain	3.00
MZ	Johnny Mize	2.00
PM	Paul Molitor	2.00
JO	Joe Morgan	3.00
JM	Jack Morris	2.00
TM	Thurman Munson	5.00
MU	Bobby Murcer	2.00
ED	Eddie Murray	3.00
SM	Stan Musial	6.00
GN	Graig Nettles	2.00
PN	Phil Niekro	2.00
TO	Tony Oliva	3.00
TO2	Tony Oliva	3.00
MO	Mel Ott	3.00
SP	Satchel Paige	5.00
JP	Jim Palmer	3.00
DP	Dave Parker	2.00
TP	Tony Perez	2.00
GP	Gaylord Perry	2.00
LP	Lou Piniella	2.00
PS	Johnny Podres	2.00
KP	Kirby Puckett	5.00
TR	Tim Raines	2.00
RI	Jim Rice	2.00
CR	Cal Ripken Jr.	8.00
PR	Phil Rizzuto	2.00
RR	Robin Roberts	2.00
RO	Brooks Robinson	4.00
RO2	Brooks Robinson	4.00
FR	Frank Robinson	4.00
FR2	Frank Robinson	4.00
JR	Jackie Robinson	6.00
AR	Al Rosen	2.00
BR	Babe Ruth	10.00
NR	Nolan Ryan	8.00
SA	Ryne Sandberg	5.00
RN	Ron Santo	2.00
MS	Mike Schmidt	5.00
RS	Red Schoendienst	2.00
TS	Tom Seaver	4.00
GS	George Sisler	3.00
SK	Bill "Moose" Skowron	2.00
OS	Ozzie Smith	5.00
BS	Bruce Sutter	2.00
SU	Don Sutton	2.00
JT	Joe Torre	3.00
HW	Honus Wagner	5.00
BW	Billy Williams	2.00
MW	Maury Wills	2.00
YZ	Carl Yastrzemski	4.00
CY	Cy Young	3.00
RY	Robin Yount	4.00

When It Was A Game Used

NM/M

Production 75 unless noted.

		NM/M
LA	Luis Aparicio/25	10.00
HB	Harold Baines/25	10.00
EB	Ernie Banks	20.00
JB	Johnny Bench	15.00
YB	Yogi Berra	20.00
WB	Wade Boggs	10.00
LB	Lou Brock/25	12.00
CA	Rod Carew	12.00
SC	Steve Carlton	10.00
SC2	Steve Carlton	10.00
WC	Will Clark	12.00
RC	Roberto Clemente	80.00
MC	Mickey Cochrane/25	75.00
CO	Rocky Colavito	25.00
AD	Andre Dawson	10.00
JD	Joe DiMaggio	80.00
DD	Don Drysdale	15.00
DE	Dennis Eckersley	15.00
EV	Dwight Evans/25	15.00
BF	Bob Feller	10.00
RF	Rollie Fingers	10.00
CF	Carlton Fisk	12.00
JF	Jimmie Foxx	50.00
SG	Steve Garvey	8.00
LG	Lou Gehrig	140.00
BG	Bob Gibson	12.00
KI	Kirk Gibson	10.00
GG	Rich "Goose" Gossage/25	10.00
HG	Hank Greenberg	30.00
KG	Ken Griffey Sr.	8.00
GU	Ron Guidry	15.00
TG	Tony Gwynn	15.00
HO	Rogers Hornsby	50.00
FH	Frank Howard	20.00
RJ	Reggie Jackson/25	15.00
FJ	Fergie Jenkins	15.00
WJ	Wally Joyner	8.00
RK	Ralph Kiner	12.00
JK	John Kruk	10.00
DL	Don Larsen	15.00
FL	Fred Lynn	8.00
JU	Juan Marichal	10.00
EM	Eddie Mathews	15.00
MA	Don Mattingly	15.00
BM	Bill Mazeroski	25.00
WM	Willie McCovey	10.00
MZ	Johnny Mize	15.00
PM	Paul Molitor	10.00
JO	Joe Morgan	10.00
JM	Jack Morris/25	15.00
TM	Thurman Munson	25.00
MU	Bobby Murcer	10.00
ED	Eddie Murray	12.00
SM	Stan Musial	25.00
GN	Graig Nettles	10.00
PN	Phil Niekro	10.00
TO	Tony Oliva	10.00
TO2	Tony Oliva	10.00
MO	Mel Ott	30.00
JP	Jim Palmer	10.00
DP	Dave Parker	8.00
TP	Tony Perez	10.00
GP	Gaylord Perry	10.00
LP	Lou Piniella	12.00
KP	Kirby Puckett	20.00
TR	Tim Raines	10.00
RI	Jim Rice	10.00
CR	Cal Ripken Jr.	25.00
PR	Phil Rizzuto/25	25.00
RR	Robin Roberts	15.00
RO	Brooks Robinson/25	20.00
RO2	Brooks Robinson/25	20.00
FR	Frank Robinson	15.00
FR2	Frank Robinson	15.00
JR	Jackie Robinson	50.00
AR	Al Rosen	10.00
BR	Babe Ruth/25	350.00
NR	Nolan Ryan/25	30.00
SA	Ryne Sandberg/25	20.00
RN	Ron Santo	15.00
MS	Mike Schmidt	20.00
RS	Red Schoendienst	15.00
TS	Tom Seaver	15.00
GS	George Sisler	30.00
SK	Bill "Moose" Skowron	15.00
OS	Ozzie Smith	15.00
BS	Bruce Sutter	15.00
SU	Don Sutton	8.00
JT	Joe Torre	10.00
BW	Billy Williams	10.00
MW	Maury Wills	10.00
YZ	Carl Yastrzemski	15.00
RY	Robin Yount	12.00

Place In History Signatures

NM/M

Production 99 unless noted.

		NM/M
LA	Luis Aparicio	25.00
LA2	Luis Aparicio	25.00
HB	Harold Baines/35	25.00
EB	Ernie Banks/25	75.00
JB	Johnny Bench/42	50.00
WB	Wade Boggs/50	35.00
LB	Lou Brock	25.00
LB2	Lou Brock	25.00
JC	Jose Canseco	40.00
CA	Rod Carew/50	25.00
SC	Steve Carlton	25.00
SC2	Steve Carlton	25.00
WC	Will Clark/92	25.00
WC2	Will Clark	25.00
CC	Cecil Cooper	20.00
AD	Andre Dawson	20.00
BD	Bucky Dent	25.00
DE	Dennis Eckersley	25.00
DE2	Dennis Eckersley	20.00
EV	Dwight Evans	20.00
BF	Bob Feller/35	40.00
RF	Rollie Fingers/77	20.00
CF	Carlton Fisk	30.00
WF	Whitey Ford/35	60.00
GF	George Foster/56	15.00
SG	Steve Garvey	25.00
MG	Mark Grace	25.00
KG	Ken Griffey Sr.	15.00
TG	Tony Gwynn/26	60.00
FH	Frank Howard	25.00
BO	Bo Jackson	50.00
RJ	Reggie Jackson/25	60.00
FJ	Fergie Jenkins	25.00
WJ	Wally Joyner	25.00
BL	Barry Larkin/49	40.00
FL	Fred Lynn	15.00
JU	Juan Marichal/29	25.00
MA	Don Mattingly/50	100.00
BM	Bill Mazeroski	35.00
MC	Denny McLain/31	25.00
PM	Paul Molitor	35.00
JO	Joe Morgan/50	30.00
JM	Jack Morris/82	15.00
SM	Stan Musial/45	70.00
GN	Graig Nettles	20.00
PN	Phil Niekro/52	20.00
PN2	Phil Niekro/52	20.00
TO	Tony Oliva	20.00
TO2	Tony Oliva	20.00
JP	Jim Palmer	25.00
GP	Gaylord Perry	20.00
GP2	Gaylord Perry	20.00
LP	Lou Piniella	20.00
JY	Johnny Podres/38	20.00
BP	Boog Powell	20.00
KP	Kirby Puckett	25.00
TR	Tim Raines	20.00
JR	Jim Rice	20.00
CR	Cal Ripken Jr./50	140.00
PR	Phil Rizzuto	40.00
RR	Robin Roberts/55	25.00
BR	Brooks Robinson/50	40.00
BR2	Brooks Robinson/50	40.00
FR	Frank Robinson	40.00
FR2	Frank Robinson	40.00
AR	Al Rosen	20.00
RO	Ron Santo	60.00
RO2	Ron Santo	60.00
SS	Steve Sax	20.00
MS	Mike Schmidt/25	75.00
RD	Red Schoendienst	35.00
TS	Tom Seaver/55	50.00
SK	Bill "Moose" Skowron	25.00
OS	Ozzie Smith	50.00
BS	Bruce Sutter	25.00
JT	Joe Torre	40.00
BW	Billy Williams	20.00
MW	Maury Wills/96	20.00
CY	Carl Yastrzemski	60.00
RY	Robin Yount	40.00

Legendary Cuts

NM/M

Production 1-90

		NM/M
JA	Joe Adcock/47	120.00
MA	Mel Allen/67	175.00
WA	Walter Alston/27	160.00
LA	Luke Appling/84	100.00
RA	Richie Ashburn/22	200.00
EA	Earl Averill/50	100.00
EB	Ed Barrow/35	250.00
RB	Ray Boone/51	120.00
LB	Lou Boudreau/86	100.00
DC	Dolph Camilli/58	100.00
MC	Max Carey/79	140.00
EC	Earle Combs/65	200.00
ST	Stan Coveleski/81	120.00
JO	Joe Cronin/30	125.00
RD	Ray Dandridge/35	120.00
DD	Dizzy Dean/21	600.00
BD	Bill Dickey/34	240.00
DR	Don Drysdale/45	200.00
DU	Joe Dugan/25	150.00
DL	Leo Durocher/22	150.00
CG	Charlie Gehringer/76	100.00
LG	Lefty Gomez/44	125.00
HG	Hank Greenberg/60	250.00
BG	Burleigh Grimes/33	150.00
HE	Billy Herman/87	100.00
WH	Waite Hoyt/49	125.00
CH	Jim "Catfish" Hunter/24	150.00
JJ	Judy Johnson/40	150.00
HK	Harvey Kuenn/89	120.00
BL	Bob Lemon/77	80.00
LO	Ernie Lombardi/25	160.00
EL	Ed Lopat/32	140.00
EM	Eddie Mathews/59	150.00
JM	Joe McCarthy/67	180.00
ME	Joe Medwick/82	180.00
MI	Johnny Mize/90	140.00
WP	Wally Post/66	120.00
PR	Pee Wee Reese/47	180.00
SR	Sam Rice/31	180.00
ER	Edd Roush/90	80.00
RR	Red Ruffing/72	200.00
JS	Joe Sewell/83	120.00
WS	Warren Spahn/52	120.00
CS	Casey Stengel/35	300.00
PT	Pie Traynor/26	500.00
BW	Bucky Walters/52	100.00
WI	Hoyt Wilhelm/47	100.00

Place In History Cut Signatures

NM/M

Production 1-98

		NM/M
BA	Bob Allison/94	140.00
LA	Luke Appling/94	100.00
EA	Earl Averill/75	80.00
LB	Lou Boudreau/88	100.00
HC	Happy Chandler/61	70.00
CO	Chuck Connors/450	450.00
JC	Joe Cronin/30	125.00
RD	Ray Dandridge/43	120.00
BD	Bill Dickey/29	200.00
DL	Leo Durocher/42	140.00
JD	Joe Dugan/25	150.00
FF	Ford Frick/30	150.00
CG	Charlie Gehringer/57	120.00
WG	Warren Giles/45	200.00
LG	Lefty Gomez/30	125.00
HG	Hank Greenberg/31	260.00
BG	Burleigh Grimes/43	150.00
HI	Kirby Higbe/59	140.00
JH	Johnny Hodapp/26	125.00
DH	Dick Howser/28	160.00
JJ	Judy Johnson/30	180.00
VK	Vern Kennedy/61	120.00
BL	Bob Lemon/47	90.00
SM	Sal Maglie/73	120.00
EM	Eddie Mathews/34	150.00
JM	Joe McCarthy/58	200.00
ME	Joe Medwick/60	200.00
PR	Pee Wee Reese/57	180.00
RE	Pete Reiser/75	125.00
RO	Charlie Robertson/42	150.00
ER	Edd Roush/98	100.00
JS	Joe Sewell/87	100.00
GS	George Sisler/42	450.00
WS	Warren Spahn/41	140.00
WI	Hoyt Wilhelm/65	100.00
CW	Cy Williams/29	180.00
EW	Early Wynn/36	100.00

Dual Legendary Cuts
Production One Set

Quadruple Legendary Cuts
Production One Set

Historical Cut Signatures
Production One Set

Memorable Moments Swatch

NM/M

Common Player:
Production 225 Sets

		NM/M
JB	Johnny Bench	15.00
CC	Cesar Cedeno	8.00
RC	Rocky Colavito	20.00
DC	David Cone	8.00
CE	Cecil Cooper	10.00
AD	Andre Dawson	10.00
DE	Dwight Evans	8.00
BF	Bob Feller	12.00
RF	Rollie Fingers	8.00
CF	Carlton Fisk	10.00
GF	George Foster	8.00
SG	Steve Garvey	8.00
KG	Kirk Gibson	10.00
GG	Rich "Goose" Gossage	10.00
RG	Ron Guidry	12.00
TG	Tony Gwynn	15.00
BJ	Bo Jackson	15.00
RJ	Reggie Jackson	10.00
JK	John Kruk	10.00
BL	Barry Larkin	10.00
MA	Juan Marichal	10.00
EM	Eddie Mathews	15.00
DM	Don Mattingly	20.00
JM	Johnny Mize	10.00
MO	Joe Morgan	10.00
BM	Bobby Murcer	10.00
MU	Eddie Murray	10.00
SM	Stan Musial	20.00
PO	Paul O'Neill	8.00
DP	Dave Parker	8.00
GP	Gaylord Perry	8.00
TR	Tim Raines	8.00
PR	Phil Rizzuto	10.00
RS	Ron Santo	10.00
SS	Steve Sax	8.00
MS	Mike Schmidt	15.00
TS	Tom Seaver	15.00
OS	Ozzie Smith	12.00
BS	Bruce Sutter	10.00
DS	Don Sutton	8.00
RY	Robin Yount	12.00

Memorable Moments Auto.

NM/M

Production 1-99

		NM/M
CC	Cesar Cedeno/99	20.00
RC	Rocky Colavito/25	80.00
DC	David Cone/99	15.00
CE	Cecil Cooper/99	20.00
AD	Andre Dawson/99	25.00
DE	Dwight Evans/25	25.00
BF	Bob Feller/25	40.00
RF	Rollie Fingers/47	20.00
CF	Carlton Fisk/25	30.00
GF	George Foster/25	25.00
SG	Steve Garvey/25	35.00
KG	Kirk Gibson/25	25.00
TG	Tony Gwynn/25	75.00
BJ	Bo Jackson/25	50.00
JK	John Kruk/99	20.00
BL	Barry Larkin/50	40.00
MA	Juan Marichal/25	30.00
DM	Don Mattingly/50	100.00
MO	Joe Morgan/20	25.00
MU	Eddie Murray/45	20.00
GP	Gaylord Perry/99	20.00
TR	Tim Raines/50	30.00
PR	Phil Rizzuto/25	40.00
RS	Ron Santo/25	65.00
TS	Tom Seaver/44	40.00
OS	Ozzie Smith/25	50.00
RY	Robin Yount/25	60.00

When It Was a Game Cut Signature

Production 2-99

		NM/M
JA	Joe Adcock/18	150.00
LA	Luke Appling/83	100.00
EA	Earl Averill/67	80.00
EB	Earl Battey/25	175.00
RB	Ray Boone/68	120.00
LB	Lou Boudreau/50	100.00
AC	Al Campanis/30	250.00
MC	Max Carey/71	140.00
HC	Happy Chandler/64	100.00
SC	Stan Coveleski/91	100.00
CR	Joe Cronin/34	120.00
RD	Ray Dandridge/75	120.00
JD	Joe Dugan/30	150.00
DU	Leo Durocher/25	160.00
RF	Rick Ferrell/25	150.00
EF	Elmer Flick/25	150.00
FF	Ford Frick/30	150.00
CG	Charlie Gehringer/64	120.00
LG	Lefty Gomez/36	125.00
HG	Hank Greenberg/21	260.00
BG	Burleigh Grimes/56	140.00
HE	Billy Herman/99	100.00
WH	Waite Hoyt/70	100.00
CH	Carl Hubbell/80	140.00
HU	Jim "Catfish" Hunter/34	150.00
JJ	Judy Johnson/20	180.00
VK	Vern Kennedy/58	120.00
TK	Ted Kluszewski/50	140.00
BL	Bob Lemon/79	90.00
FL	Freddie Lindstrom/25	200.00
EL	Ernie Lombardi/24	175.00
LO	Ed Lopat/28	140.00
SM	Sal Maglie/68	100.00
EM	Eddie Mathews/33	150.00
JM	Joe McCarthy/51	200.00
ME	Joe Medwick/57	200.00
MI	Johnny Mize/70	120.00
GP	George Pipgras/25	180.00
WP	Wally Post/66	120.00
PR	Pee Wee Reese/52	180.00
SR	Sam Rice/33	175.00
ER	Edd Roush/98	100.00
RR	Red Ruffing/44	180.00
SE	George Selkirk/175	175.00
JS	Joe Sewell/78	100.00
GS	George Sisler/37	450.00
WS	Warren Spahn/78	100.00
ST	Willie Stargell/27	160.00
JV	Johnny Vander Meer/45	150.00
VW	Vic Wertz/30	160.00
HW	Hoyt Wilhelm/56	100.00
EW	Early Wynn/40	100.00

2006 SPx

Complete Set (160):
Common Player (1-100): .25
Common Auto. (101-160): 10.00
Production 190-999
Pack (4): 7.00
Box (18): 100.00

		NM/M
1	Luis Gonzalez	.25
2	Chad Tracy	.25
3	Brandon Webb	.50
4	Andruw Jones	.75
5	Chipper Jones	1.00
6	John Smoltz	.75
7	Tim Hudson	.50
8	Miguel Tejada	.75
9	Brian Roberts	.25
10	Ramon Hernandez	.25
11	Curt Schilling	1.00
12	David Ortiz	1.50
13	Manny Ramirez	1.00
14	Jason Varitek	1.00
15	Josh Beckett	.75
16	Greg Maddux	2.00
17	Derrek Lee	.75
18	Mark Prior	.50
19	Aramis Ramirez	.50
20	Jim Thome	.75
21	Paul Konerko	.75
22	Scott Podsednik	.25
23	Jose Contreras	.25
24	Ken Griffey Jr.	2.00
25	Adam Dunn	.75
26	Felipe Lopez	.25
27	Travis Hafner	.75
28	Victor Martinez	.50
29	Grady Sizemore	.75
30	Jhonny Peralta	.25
31	Todd Helton	.75
32	Garrett Atkins	.50
33	Clint Barmes	.25
34	Ivan Rodriguez	.75
35	Chris Shelton	.25
36	Jeremy Bonderman	.50
37	Miguel Cabrera	1.00
38	Dontrelle Willis	.50
39	Lance Berkman	.50

40	Morgan Ensberg	.25
41	Roy Oswalt	.50
42	Reggie Sanders	.25
43	Mike Sweeney	.25
44	Vladimir Guerrero	1.00
45	Bartolo Colon	.25
46	Chone Figgins	.50
47	Nomar Garciaparra	.75
48	Jeff Kent	.50
49	J.D. Drew	.25
50	Carlos Lee	.50
51	Ben Sheets	.50
52	Rickie Weeks	.50
53	Johan Santana	1.00
54	Torii Hunter	.50
55	Joe Mauer	.50
56	Pedro Martinez	1.00
57	David Wright	2.00
58	Carlos Beltran	.75
59	Carlos Delgado	.75
60	Jose Reyes	1.00
61	Derek Jeter	3.00
62	Alex Rodriguez	3.00
63	Randy Johnson	1.00
64	Hideki Matsui	2.00
65	Gary Sheffield	.75
66	Rich Harden	.50
67	Eric Chavez	.25
68	Huston Street	.50
69	Bobby Crosby	.25
70	Bobby Abreu	.50
71	Ryan Howard	2.00
72	Chase Utley	.75
73	Pat Burrell	.50
74	Jason Bay	.50
75	Sean Casey	.25
76	Mike Piazza	1.00
77	Jake Peavy	.75
78	Brian Giles	.25
79	Milton Bradley	.25
80	Omar Vizquel	.25
81	Jason Schmidt	.25
82	Ichiro Suzuki	2.00
83	Felix Hernandez	.50
84	Richie Sexson	.25
85	Albert Pujols	3.00
86	Chris Carpenter	.50
87	Scott Rolen	.50
88	Jim Edmonds	.25
89	Carl Crawford	.50
90	Jonny Gomes	.25
91	Scott Kazmir	.50
92	Mark Teixeira	.75
93	Michael Young	.50
94	Phil Nevin	.25
95	Vernon Wells	.50
96	Roy Halladay	.50
97	Troy Glaus	.50
98	Alfonso Soriano	.75
99	Nick Johnson	.25
100	Jose Vidro	.25
101	Conor Jackson/999 RC	10.00
102	Jered Weaver/299 RC	25.00
103	Macay McBride/999 RC	10.00
104	Aaron Rakers/499 RC	10.00
105	Jonathan Papelbon/499 RC	20.00
106	Jason Bergmann/999 RC	10.00
107	Stephen Drew/350 RC	25.00
108	Chris Denorfia/999 RC	10.00
109	Kelly Shoppach/999 RC	10.00
110	Ryan Shealy/999 RC	10.00
111	Josh Wilson/999 RC	10.00
112	Brian Anderson/999 RC	10.00
113	Justin Verlander/749 RC	40.00
114	Jeremy Hermida/999 RC	15.00
115	Mike Jacobs/999 RC	12.00
116	Josh Johnson/999 RC	35.00
117	Hanley Ramirez/659 RC	40.00
118	Chris Resop/999 RC	10.00
119	Josh Willingham/999 RC	15.00
120	Cole Hamels/499 RC	40.00
121	Matt Cain/999 RC	25.00
122	Steve Stemle/999 RC	10.00
123	Tim Hamulack/999 RC	10.00
124	Choo Freeman/999 RC	10.00
125	Hong-Chih Kuo/999 RC	20.00
126	Cody Ross/999 RC	10.00
127	Jose Capellan/999 RC	10.00
128	Prince Fielder/190 RC	80.00
129	David Gassner/999 RC	10.00
130	Jason Kubel/999 RC	20.00
131	Francisco Liriano/299 RC	30.00
132	Anderson Hernandez/999 RC	10.00
133	Joey Devine/499 RC	10.00
134	Chris Booker/999 RC	10.00
135	Matt Capps/999 RC	15.00
136	Paul Maholm/999 RC	10.00
137	Nate McLouth/999 RC	10.00
138	John Van Benschoten/999 RC	10.00
139	Jeff Harris/999 RC	10.00
140	Ben Johnson/999 RC	10.00
141	Wilbert Nieves/999 RC	10.00
142	Guillermo Quiroz/999 RC	10.00
143	Josh Rupe/500 RC	10.00
144	Skip Schumaker/999 RC	20.00
145	Jack Taschner/999 RC	10.00
146	Adam Wainwright/999 RC	35.00

147	Alay Soler/499 RC	15.00
148	Kendry Morales/999 RC	30.00
149	Ian Kinsler/999 RC	30.00
150	Jason Hammel/999 RC	10.00
151	Chad Billingsley/499 RC	25.00
152	Boof Bonser/999 RC	10.00
153	Peter Moylan/999 RC	10.00
154	Chris Britton/999 RC	10.00
155	Takashi Saito/999 RC	30.00
156	Scott Dunn RC	10.00
157	Joel Zumaya/299 RC	15.00
158	Dan Uggla/999 RC	35.00
159	Taylor Buchholz/999 RC	10.00
160	Melky Cabrera/499 RC	20.00

Rookie Signature Printing Plates

No Pricing
Production one set per color.

Rookie Signature Platinum

No Pricing
Production One Set

Rookie Signature Gold

No Pricing
Production Five Sets

Spectrum

Stars (1-100): 2-3X
Inserted 1:3

Next in Line

		NM/M
	Common Player:	1.00
BA	Brian Anderson	1.00
BB	Brian Bannister	1.00
JB	Josh Barfield	1.00
TB	Taylor Buchholz	1.00
MC	Matt Cain	1.50
RC	Ryan Church	1.00
PF	Prince Fielder	3.00
JH	Jeremy Hermida	1.00
FH	Felix Hernandez	1.50
RH	Ryan Howard	3.00
TI	Travis Ishikawa	1.00
CJ	Conor Jackson	1.00
MJ	Mike Jacobs	1.00
BJ	Ben Johnson	1.00
IK	Ian Kinsler	1.00
LE	Jon Lester	3.00
FL	Francisco Liriano	3.00
JL	James Loney	1.00
SO	Scott Olsen	1.00
JP	Jonathan Papelbon	3.00
HR	Hanley Ramirez	1.50
NM	Alay Soler	1.00
JS	Jeremy Sowers	1.00
HS	Huston Street	1.00
DU	Dan Uggla	1.00
JV	Justin Verlander	1.00
AW	Adam Wainwright	1.00
JW	Jered Weaver	3.00
JW	Josh Willingham	1.00
RZ	Ryan Zimmerman	3.00

SPxciting Signatures

Production 30 unless noted.

		NM/M
JA	Jeremy Accardo	10.00
BA	Brian Anderson	10.00
BY	Jason Bay	20.00
BI	Craig Biggio	40.00
CH	Chad Billingsley	35.00
HB	Hank Blalock	20.00
BR	Chris Britton	15.00
MI	Miguel Cabrera	40.00
MC	Matt Cain	30.00
CA	Matt Capps	15.00
RC	Roger Clemens	165.00
CW	Carl Crawford	30.00
SD	Scott Dunn	10.00
EG	Eric Gagne	20.00
GR	Khalil Greene	25.00
KG	Ken Griffey Jr.	100.00
HT	Travis Hafner	25.00
HA	Jason Hammel	15.00
TH	Tim Hamulack	15.00
JH	Jeff Harris	12.00
HE	Jeremy Hermida	25.00
TR	Trevor Hoffman	40.00
CJ	Conor Jackson	20.00
KU	Jason Kubel	15.00
HK	Hong-Chih Kuo	180.00
CL	Cliff Lee	15.00
PM	Paul Maholm	15.00
VM	Victor Martinez	20.00
MM	Macay McBride	20.00

NM	Nate McLouth	15.00
MU	Mark Mulder	20.00
WN	Wilbert Nieves	20.00
JP	Jonathan Papelbon	100.00
CP	Corey Patterson	20.00
PE	Jake Peavy	25.00
OP	Oliver Perez	10.00
HR	Hanley Ramirez	40.00
CR	Chris Resop	10.00
CR	Cody Ross	20.00
TS	Takashi Saito	140.00
SS	Skip Schumaker	30.00
RS	Ryan Shealy	20.00
KS	Kelly Shoppach	25.00
DU	Dan Uggla	75.00
JV	John Van Benschoten	15.00
VE	Justin Verlander	90.00
AW	Adam Wainwright	50.00
JW	Josh Willingham	20.00
WI	Josh Wilson	15.00

SPxtra Info

		NM/M
	Common Player:	.50
BA	Bobby Abreu	.75
JB	Jason Bay	.75
EC	Eric Chavez	.75
CC	Carl Crawford	.75
BG	Brian Giles	.50
LG	Luis Gonzalez	.50
KG	Ken Griffey Jr.	2.00
VG	Vladimir Guerrero	1.00
TH	Travis Hafner	.75
HE	Todd Helton	.75
DJ	Derek Jeter	3.00
NJ	Nick Johnson	.50
AJ	Andruw Jones	.75
JK	Jeff Kent	.50
CL	Carlos Lee	.75
DL	Derrek Lee	1.00
PM	Pedro Martinez	.75
DO	David Ortiz	1.50
RO	Roy Oswalt	.75
AP	Albert Pujols	3.00
IR	Ivan Rodriguez	.75
RS	Reggie Sanders	.50
JS	Johan Santana	1.00
SC	Jason Schmidt	.50
IS	Ichiro Suzuki	2.00
TE	Mark Teixeira	.75
MT	Miguel Tejada	.75
JT	Jim Thome	1.00
VW	Vernon Wells	.50
DW	Dontrelle Willis	.75

SPxtreme Team

		NM/M
	Common Player:	.50
BA	Bobby Abreu	.75
JB	Jason Bay	.75
LB	Lance Berkman	.75
MC	Miguel Cabrera	1.00
CC	Chris Carpenter	.75
CR	Carl Crawford	.75
CD	Carlos Delgado	.75
AD	Adam Dunn	.75
PF	Prince Fielder	3.00
KG	Ken Griffey Jr.	2.00
VG	Vladimir Guerrero	1.00
HA	Travis Hafner	.75
RH	Todd Helton	.75
HO	Ryan Howard	2.00
DJ	Derek Jeter	3.00
AJ	Andruw Jones	.50
JK	Jeff Kent	.50
PK	Paul Konerko	.75
CL	Carlos Lee	.75
DL	Derrek Lee	1.00
PM	Pedro Martinez	.75
VM	Victor Martinez	.50
HM	Hideki Matsui	1.50
DO	David Ortiz	1.50
JP	Jake Peavy	.50
AP	Albert Pujols	3.00
MR	Manny Ramirez	1.00
JR	Jose Reyes	.75

Winning Materials

		NM/M
	Common Player:	5.00
BA	Bobby Abreu	6.00
JB	Jason Bay	10.00
CB	Carlos Beltran	10.00
MC	Miguel Cabrera	10.00
FC	Frederich Cepeda	5.00
RC	Roger Clemens	15.00
JD	Johnny Damon	10.00
CD	Carlos Delgado	6.00
ME	Michel Enriquez	5.00
MF	Maikel Folch	5.00
YG	Yulieski Gourriel	8.00
KG	Ken Griffey Jr.	20.00
AI	Akinori Iwamura	20.00
AJ	Andruw Jones	8.00
MK	Munenori Kawasaki	20.00
PL	Pedro Luis Lazo	5.00
DL	Derrek Lee	8.00
JL	Jong Beom Lee	5.00
VM	Victor Martinez	5.00
NM	Nobuhiko Matsunaka	20.00
YM	Tsuyoshi Nishioka	25.00
VO	Vicyohandry Odelin	5.00
MO	Michichi Ogasawara	5.00
DO	David Ortiz	15.00
EP	Eduardo Paret	5.00
AP	Ariel Pestano	5.00
MP	Mike Piazza	15.00

AR	Alex Rodriguez	3.00
JS	Johan Santana	1.00
GS	Grady Sizemore	.75
AS	Alfonso Soriano	1.00
IS	Ichiro Suzuki	2.00
MT	Mark Teixeira	.75
TE	Miguel Tejada	.75
JT	Jim Thome	1.00
VW	Vernon Wells	.50
DW	David Wright	2.00
MY	Michael Young	.50

WBC All-World Team

(image area)

Winning Big Materials

Production 5-55

		NM/M
BA	Bobby Abreu/40	75.00
MA	Moises Alou/53	50.00
JB	Jason Bay/40	80.00
EB	Erik Bedard/40	50.00
CB	Carlos Beltran/40	75.00
AB	Adrian Beltre/40	50.00
MC	Miguel Cabrera/40	80.00
FC	Frederich Cepeda/20	65.00
HC	Hee Seop Choi/32	75.00
JD	Johnny Damon/40	100.00
CD	Carlos Delgado/40	65.00
ME	Michel Enriquez/30	50.00
MF	Maikel Folch/30	50.00
JF	Jeff Francis/40	50.00
YG	Yulieski Gourriel/30	100.00
AI	Akinori Iwamura/30	275.00
AJ	Andruw Jones/40	80.00
MK	Munenori Kawasaki/30	350.00
PL	Pedro Luis Lazo/30	80.00
CL	Carlos Lee/40	60.00
DL	Derrek Lee/40	75.00
JL	Jong Beom Lee/20	75.00
WL	Wei-Chu Lin/45	350.00
LO	Javy Lopez/40	60.00
VM	Victor Martinez/40	75.00
NM	Nobuhiko Matsunaka/30	300.00
YM	Yuneiski Maya/30	60.00
JM	Justin Morneau/25	60.00
TN	Tsuyoshi Nishioka/30	375.00
VO	Vicyohandry Odelin/30	75.00
MO	Michichi Ogasawara/30	350.00
DO	David Ortiz/30	150.00
WP	Wei-Lun Pan/38	300.00
EP	Eduardo Paret/30	50.00
PE	Wily Mo Pena/60	50.00
AP	Ariel Pestano/30	60.00
MP	Mike Piazza/40	100.00
AR	Alex Rios/55	50.00
IR	Ivan Rodriguez/40	60.00
JS	Johan Santana/40	75.00
NS	Naoyuki Shimizu/30	50.00
AS	Alfonso Soriano/40	90.00
HT	Hitoshi Tamura/30	300.00
MT	Miguel Tejada/40	300.00
KU	Koji Uehara/30	300.00
OU	Osmany Urrutia/30	65.00
JV	Jason Varitek/40	120.00
TW	Tsuyoshi Wada/30	250.00
SW	Shunsuke Watanabe/30	260.00
BW	Bernie Williams/40	75.00
GY	Guogang Yang/52	50.00
CZ	Carlos Zambrano/40	50.00

2007 SP Authentic

Complete Set (162):
Common Player: .25
Common RC Letter Auto.: 15.00
Pack (5): 5.00
Box (24): 100.00

		NM/M
1	Chipper Jones	1.00
2	Andruw Jones	.50
3	John Smoltz	.50
4	Carlos Quentin	.25
5	Randy Johnson	1.00
6	Brandon Webb	.50
7	Alfonso Soriano	1.00
8	Derrek Lee	.75
9	Aramis Ramirez	.50
10	Carlos Zambrano	.50
11	Ken Griffey Jr.	2.00
12	Adam Dunn	.50
13	Josh Hamilton	.50
14	Todd Helton	.75
15	Jeff Francis	.25
16	Matt Holliday	.75
17	Hanley Ramirez	1.00
18	Dontrelle Willis	.25

NM	Common Player:	.50
1	Brett Willemburg	.50
2	Bradley Harman	.50
3	Adam Stern	1.00
4	Jason Bay	1.00
5	Adam Loewen	.50
6	Wei Wang	2.00
7	Yi Feng	1.00
8	Yung-Chi Chen	6.00
9	Chin-Lung Hu	6.00
10	Wei-Lun Pan	5.00
11	Yoandy Garlobo	.50
12	Frederich Cepeda	.50
13	Osmany Urrutia	1.00
14	Yulieski Gourriel	2.00
15	Yadel Marti	.50
16	Pedro Luis Lazo	.50
17	Adrian Beltre	.50
18	David Ortiz	2.00
19	Albert Pujols	4.00
20	Bartolo Colon	1.00
21	Miguel Tejada	1.00
22	Mike Piazza	1.50
23	Jason Grilli	.50
24	Nobuhiko Matsunaka	3.00
25	Tomoya Satozaki	3.00
26	Ichiro Suzuki	3.00
27	Hitoshi Tamura	3.00
28	Daisuke Matsuzaka	8.00
29	Koji Uehara	3.00
30	Jong Beom Lee	.50
31	Seung-Yeop Lee	.50
32	Jae Weong Seo	.50
33	Min Han Son	.50
34	Chan Ho Park	.50
35	Jorge Cantu	.50
36	Miguel Ojeda	.50
37	Andruw Jones	1.00
38	Shairon Martis	.50
39	Carlos Lee	.75
40	Carlos Beltran	.50
41	Javy Lopez	.50
42	Javier Vazquez	.50
43	Ken Griffey Jr.	3.00
44	Derek Jeter	4.00
45	Alex Rodriguez	4.00
46	Derek Lee	.50
47	Roger Clemens	3.00
48	Miguel Cabrera	1.50
49	Victor Martinez	1.50
50	Johan Santana	1.50

PU	Albert Pujols	20.00
AR	Alex Rodriguez	20.00
JS	Johan Santana	10.00
NS	Min Han Son	25.00
MS	Min Han Son	8.00
AS	Alfonso Soriano	10.00
IS	Ichiro Suzuki	75.00
HT	Hitoshi Tamura	20.00
MT	Miguel Tejada	20.00
KU	Koji Uehara	20.00
OU	Osmany Urrutia	8.00
TW	Tsuyoshi Wada	20.00
SW	Shunsuke Watanabe	20.00

#	Player	Price
19	Miguel Cabrera	1.00
20	Lance Berkman	.50
21	Roy Oswalt	.50
22	Carlos Lee	.50
23	Nomar Garciaparra	.50
24	Derek Lowe	.25
25	Juan Pierre	.50
26	Rafael Furcal	.50
27	Rickie Weeks	.50
28	Prince Fielder	1.50
29	Ben Sheets	.50
30	David Wright	1.50
31	Jose Reyes	1.00
32	Tom Glavine	.50
33	Carlos Beltran	.75
34	Cole Hamels	.75
35	Jimmy Rollins	.75
36	Ryan Howard	2.00
37	Jason Bay	.50
38	Freddy Sanchez	.25
39	Ian Snell	.25
40	Jake Peavy	.50
41	Greg Maddux	2.00
42	Trevor Hoffman	.50
43	Matt Cain	.50
44	Barry Zito	.50
45	Ray Durham	.25
46	Albert Pujols	3.00
47	Chris Carpenter	.50
48	Jim Edmonds	.50
49	Scott Rolen	.50
50	Ryan Zimmerman	.50
51	Felipe Lopez	.25
52	Austin Kearns	.25
53	Miguel Tejada	.50
54	Erik Bedard	.25
55	Daniel Cabrera	.25
56	David Ortiz	1.00
57	Curt Schilling	.75
58	Manny Ramirez	1.00
59	Jonathan Papelbon	.75
60	Jim Thome	.75
61	Paul Konerko	.50
62	Bobby Jenks	.25
63	Grady Sizemore	.75
64	Victor Martinez	.50
65	Travis Hafner	.50
66	Ivan Rodriguez	.75
67	Justin Verlander	1.00
68	Joel Zumaya	.25
69	Jeremy Bonderman	.50
70	Gil Meche	.25
71	Mike Sweeney	.25
72	Mark Teahen	.25
73	Vladimir Guerrero	1.00
74	Howie Kendrick	.25
75	Francisco Rodriguez	.25
76	Johan Santana	1.00
77	Justin Morneau	.50
78	Joe Mauer	.50
79	Joe Nathan	.25
80	Alex Rodriguez	3.00
81	Derek Jeter	4.00
82	Johnny Damon	.75
83	Chien-Ming Wang	1.00
84	Rich Harden	.25
85	Mike Piazza	1.00
86	Danny Haren	.25
87	Ichiro Suzuki	2.00
88	Felix Hernandez	.50
89	Kenji Johjima	.50
90	Adrian Beltre	.50
91	Carl Crawford	.50
92	Scott Kazmir	.50
93	Delmon Young	.50
94	Michael Young	.50
95	Mark Teixeira	.50
96	Eric Gagne	.25
97	Hank Blalock	.25
98	Vernon Wells	.50
99	Roy Halladay	.50
100	Frank Thomas	.75
101	Joaquin Arias/75 (RC)	15.00
102	Jeff Baker/Redemp. (RC)	15.00
103	Michael Bourn/75 (RC)	20.00
104	Brian Burres/75 (RC)	15.00
105	Jared Burton/75 RC	15.00
106	Ryan Braun/50 (RC)	100.00
107	Yovani Gallardo/75 (RC)	40.00
107	Yovani Gallardo/35 (RC)	40.00
108	Hector Gimenez/75 (RC)	15.00
108	Hector Gimenez/50 (RC)	15.00
109	Alex Gordon/50 RC	20.00
110	Josh Hamilton/50 (RC)	50.00
110	Josh Hamilton/35 (RC)	50.00
111	Justin Hampson/50 (RC)	15.00
111	Justin Hampson/75 (RC)	15.00
112	Sean Henn/75 (RC)	15.00
113	Phil Hughes/Redemp. (RC)	50.00
114	Kei Igawa/25 RC	30.00
115	Akinori Iwamura/20 RC	30.00
116	Mark Reynolds/75 RC	30.00
116	Mark Reynolds/35 RC	35.00
117	Homer Bailey/75 (RC)	20.00
117	Homer Bailey/50 (RC)	20.00
118	Kevin Kouzmanoff/75 (RC)	20.00
118	Kevin Kouzmanoff/40 (RC)	20.00
119	Adam Lind/75 (RC)	15.00
120	Carlos Gomez/75 RC	15.00
120	Carlos Gomez/50 RC	15.00
121	Glen Perkins/75 (RC)	20.00
121	Glen Perkins/50 (RC)	20.00
122	Rick Vanden Hurk/75 RC	20.00
122	Rick Vanden Hurk/35 RC	20.00
123	Brad Salmon/75 RC	15.00
124	Zack Segovia/75 (RC)	20.00
124	Zack Segovia/50 (RC)	25.00
125	Kurt Suzuki/75 (RC)	25.00
125	Kurt Suzuki/50 (RC)	25.00
126	Chris Stewart/75 (RC)	15.00
126	Chris Stewart/50 (RC)	15.00
127	Cesar Jimenez/75 RC	15.00
128	Ryan Sweeney/50 (RC)	20.00
128	Ryan Sweeney/40 (RC)	20.00
129	Troy Tulowitzki/Redmp. (RC)	40.00
130	Chase Wright/75 RC	20.00
131	Delmon Young/20 (RC)	30.00
132	Tony Abreu/75 (RC)	20.00
132	Tony Abreu/50 (RC)	20.00
133	Brian Barden/75 RC	15.00
134	Curtis Thigpen/75 (RC)	20.00
134	Curtis Thigpen/40 (RC)	20.00
135	Jon Coutlangus/75 (RC)	15.00
135	Jon Coutlangus/55 (RC)	15.00
136	Kevin Cameron/75 RC	15.00
136	Kevin Cameron/50 RC	15.00
137	Billy Butler/75 (RC)	30.00
138	Alexi Casilla/75 RC	15.00
138	Alexi Casilla/50 RC	20.00
139	Kory Casto/75 (RC)	20.00
140	Matt Chico/75 (RC)	20.00
141	John Danks/75 (RC)	30.00
142	Andrew Miller/50 (RC)	20.00
143	Ben Francisco/75 (RC)	15.00
143	Ben Francisco/40 (RC)	15.00
144	Andy Gonzalez/75 (RC)	15.00
144	Andy Gonzalez/50 RC	15.00
145	Devern Hansack/Redemp. RC	20.00
146	Mike Rabelo/75 RC	15.00
147	Tim Lincecum/50 RC	150.00
147	Tim Lincecum/25 RC	150.00
148	Matt Lindstrom/75 (RC)	15.00
148	Matt Lindstrom/40 (RC)	15.00
149	Jay Marshall/75 RC	15.00
149	Jay Marshall/50 RC	15.00
150	Daisuke Matsuzaka/Redemp. RC	200.00
151	Miguel Montero/75 (RC)	20.00
151	Miguel Montero/50 (RC)	20.00
152	Micah Owings/75 (RC)	20.00
153	Hunter Pence/75 (RC)	30.00
154	Brandon Wood/75 (RC)	20.00
155	Felix Pie/75 (RC)	15.00
155	Felix Pie/70 (RC)	15.00
156	Danny Putnam/75 (RC)	15.00
157	Andy LaRoche/50 (RC)	20.00
157	Andy LaRoche/40 (RC)	20.00
158	Jarrod Saltalamacchia/75 (RC)	20.00
158	Jarrod Saltalamacchia/25 (RC)	20.00
159	Doug Slaten/75 RC	15.00
160	Joe Smith/75 (RC)	20.00
161	Justin Upton/120 RC	80.00
162	Joba Chamberlain/60 RC	60.00

Authentic Power

NM/M

#	Player	Price
	Common Player:	.50
1	Adam Dunn	1.00
2	Albert Pujols	4.00
3	Alex Rodriguez	4.00
4	Alfonso Soriano	1.50
5	Andruw Jones	.75
6	Aramis Ramirez	.75
7	Bill Hall	.50
8	Carlos Beltran	1.00
9	Carlos Delgado	.75
10	Carlos Lee	.75
11	Chase Utley	1.50
12	Chipper Jones	1.50
13	Dan Uggla	.50
14	David Ortiz	1.50
15	David Wright	2.00
16	Derek Lee	.75
17	Eric Chavez	.50
18	Frank Thomas	1.00
19	Garrett Atkins	.50
20	Gary Sheffield	1.00
21	Hideki Matsui	2.50
22	J.D. Drew	.50
23	Jason Bay	.75
24	Jason Giambi	1.00
25	Jeff Francoeur	1.50
26	Jermaine Dye	.50
27	Jim Thome	1.00
28	Justin Morneau	1.00
29	Ken Griffey Jr.	3.00
30	Lance Berkman	.75
31	Magglio Ordonez	.75
32	Manny Ramirez	1.00
33	Mark Teixeira	1.00
34	Matt Holliday	1.00
35	Miguel Cabrera	1.50
36	Miguel Tejada	.75
37	Mike Piazza	1.50
38	Nick Swisher	.75
39	Pat Burrell	.75
40	Paul Konerko	1.00
41	Prince Fielder	2.00
42	Richie Sexson	.75
43	Ryan Howard	2.50
44	Sammy Sosa	1.00
45	Todd Helton	1.00
46	Travis Hafner	.75
47	Troy Glaus	.75
48	Vernon Wells	.75
49	Victor Martinez	.75
50	Vladimir Guerrero	1.50

Authentic Speed

NM/M

#	Player	Price
	Common Player:	.50
1	Alex Rios	.75
2	Alex Rodriguez	4.00
3	Alfonso Soriano	1.50
4	B.J. Upton	.75
5	Bobby Abreu	.75
6	Brandon Phillips	.50
7	Brian Roberts	.75
8	Carl Crawford	.75
9	Carlos Beltran	1.00
10	Chase Utley	1.50
11	Chone Figgins	.75
12	Chris Burke	.50
13	Chris Duffy	.50
14	Coco Crisp	.50
15	Corey Patterson	.50
16	Dave Roberts	.50
17	David Wright	2.00
18	Derek Jeter	4.00
19	Edgar Renteria	.50
20	Eric Byrnes	.75
21	Felipe Lopez	.50
22	Gary Matthews	.50
23	Grady Sizemore	2.00
24	Hanley Ramirez	1.50
25	Ian Kinsler	.75
26	Ichiro Suzuki	3.00
27	Jacque Jones	.50
28	Jimmy Rollins	1.00
29	Johnny Damon	1.00
30	Jose Reyes	2.00
31	Juan Pierre	.50
32	Julio Lugo	.50
33	Kenny Lofton	.50
34	Luis Castillo	.50
35	Marcus Giles	.50
36	Melky Cabrera	1.00
37	Mike Cameron	.50
38	Orlando Cabrera	.75
39	Rafael Furcal	.75
40	Randy Winn	.50
41	Rickie Weeks	.50
42	Rocco Baldelli	.50
43	Ryan Freel	.50
44	Ryan Theriot	1.00
45	Scott Podsednik	.50
46	Shane Victorino	.50
47	Tadahito Iguchi	.50
48	Torii Hunter	.75
49	Vernon Wells	.75
50	Willy Taveras	.50

By The Letter Signatures

NM/M

#	Player	Price
	Common Player:	.50
1	Derek Jeter/Redemp.	250.00
2	Ken Griffey Jr./25	150.00
2	Ken Griffey Jr./20	150.00
4	Justin Verlander/25	50.00
4	Justin Verlander/15	50.00
5	Adrian Gonzalez/60	25.00
5	Adrian Gonzalez/50	25.00
8	Josh Beckett/15	60.00
9	Aramis Ramirez/25	50.00
11	Austin Kearns/50	15.00
12	B.J. Upton/25	25.00
12	B.J. Upton/25	25.00
13	Boof Bonser/75	15.00
13	Boof Bonser/50	15.00
14	Bronson Arroyo/75	20.00
15	Troy Tulowitzki/Redemp.	40.00
16	Felix Pie/25	25.00
17	Alex Gordon/25	50.00
18	Chris Duffy/Redemp.	15.00
19	Chris Young/75	20.00
19	Chris Young/50	20.00
20	Cliff Lee/75	15.00
20	Cliff Lee/50	30.00
21	Cole Hamels/25	50.00
21	Cole Hamels/15	50.00
22	Adam Lind/75	25.00
23	Akinori Iwamura/40	40.00
23	Akinori Iwamura/15	30.00
24	Dan Uggla/25	30.00
25	Danny Haren/25	30.00
26	David Ortiz/10	125.00
27	Felix Hernandez/10	75.00
28	Tony Gwynn Jr./Redemp.	25.00
29	Josh Hamilton/75	50.00
29	Josh Hamilton/50	50.00
30	Phil Hughes/Redemp.	60.00
32	Khalil Greene/25	15.00
32	Dontrelle Willis/25	50.00
32	Dontrelle Willis/20	50.00
33	Hanley Ramirez/50	50.00
33	Hanley Ramirez/25	50.00
34	Howie Kendrick/60	20.00
34	Howie Kendrick/50	20.00
35	Huston Street/50	20.00
35	Huston Street/25	20.00
36	Ian Kinsler/Redmp.	30.00
37	Jason Bay/25	25.00
37	Jason Bay/25	25.00
40	Joe Mauer/Redemp.	75.00
41	Jonathan Papelbon/40	30.00
42	Tim Lincecum/50	120.00
42	Tim Lincecum/40	120.00
43	Matt Cain/75	30.00
43	Matt Cain/40	30.00
44	Victor Martinez/25	50.00
46	Ryan Zimmerman/25	50.00
47	Stephen Drew/25	30.00
48	Travis Hafner/25	25.00
49	Josh Willingham/50	15.00
49	Josh Willingham/Redemp.	15.00
50	Torii Hunter/25	30.00
51	Billy Butler/50	40.00
52	Justin Morneau/25	40.00
52	Justin Morneau/15	40.00
53	Andy LaRoche/75	20.00
53	Andy LaRoche/60	20.00
53	Andy LaRoche/50	20.00
54	Brandon Wood/75	20.00
54	Brandon Wood/50	20.00
55	Hunter Pence/50	25.00
56	Devern Hansack/Redemp.	20.00
56	Devern Hansack/75	20.00
57	Derek Lee/25	40.00
59	Prince Fielder/25	60.00
60	Kevin Kouzmanoff/50	20.00

Chirography Dual Signatures

NM/M

	Players	Price
CG	Eric Chavez, Alex Gordon/75	20.00
CL	Matt Cain, Tim Lincecum/175	100.00
DR	Stephen Drew, Hanley Ramirez/75	40.00
HD	Travis Hafner, Adam Dunn/75	20.00
HW	Danny Haren, Jered Weaver/175	30.00
KH	Scott Kazmir, Cole Hamels/175	40.00
MI	Daisuke Matsuzaka, Akinori Iwamura/75	200.00
ML	Andrew Miller, Tim Lincecum/175	100.00
MZ	Nicholas Markakis, Ryan Zimmerman/75	40.00
RJ	Cal Ripken Jr., Derek Jeter/75	200.00
VH	Justin Verlander, Felix Hernandez/175	50.00
WH	Vernon Wells, Torii Hunter/75	25.00
WK	Rickie Weeks, Ian Kinsler/175	20.00

Chirography Quad Signatures

Production Five Sets

Sign of the Times Dual Signatures

NM/M

	Players	Price
	Common Dual Auto.:	20.00
BP	Josh Beckett, Jonathan Papelbon/75	50.00
CH	Eric Chavez, Rich Harden/75	20.00
CJ	Roger Clemens, Derek Jeter/75	200.00
CL	Matt Cain, Tim Lincecum/175	100.00
FL	Rafael Furcal, Andy LaRoche/175	20.00
GD	Ken Griffey Jr., Adam Dunn/75	100.00
HM	Travis Hafner, Victor Martinez/75	30.00
SW	Ben Sheets, Rickie Weeks/75	15.00
TK	Mark Teixeira, Ian Kinsler/75	40.00
UY	B.J. Upton, Delmon Young/75	25.00
VM	Justin Verlander, Andrew Miller/75	40.00

Sign of the Times Quad Signatures

Production Five Sets

Sign of the Times Triple Signatures

No Pricing

By The Letter RC Signatures Full Redm

No Pricing

By The Letter Signatures Full Redemption

No Pricing

Autograph Parallel

Production Five Sets

2007 SP Legendary Cuts

NM/M

Complete Set (200):
Common Player (1-100): .25
Common SP (101-200): 3.00
Production 550 Sets
Pack (4): 10.00
Box (12): 100.00

#	Player	Price
1	Phil Niekro	.25
2	Brooks Robinson	1.00
3	Frank Robinson	1.00
4	Jim Palmer	.50
5	Cal Ripken Jr.	3.00
6	Warren Spahn	1.00
7	Cy Young	1.00
8	Carl Yastrzemski	1.00
9	Wade Boggs	1.00
10	Carlton Fisk	.50
11	Joe Cronin	.25
12	Bobby Doerr	.50
13	Roy Campanella	1.00
14	Pee Wee Reese	1.00
15	Rod Carew	.75
16	Ernie Banks	1.00
17	Fergie Jenkins	.50
18	Billy Williams	.25
19	Gabby Hartnett	.25
20	Luis Aparicio	.25
21	Nellie Fox	.25
22	Luke Appling	.25
23	Joe Morgan	.50
24	Johnny Bench	1.00
25	Tony Perez	.25
26	George Foster	.25
27	Johnny Vander Meer	.25
28	Bob Feller	.25
29	Bob Lemon	.25
30	Lou Boudreau	.25
31	Early Wynn	.25
32	Charlie Gehringer	.25
33	George Kell	.25
34	Hal Newhouser	.25
35	Al Kaline	1.00
36	Ted Kluszewski	.25
37	Maury Wills	.25
39	Don Drysdale	.50
40	Don Sutton	.50
41	Eddie Mathews	1.00
42	Joe Adcock	.25
43	Paul Molitor	.75
44	Kirby Puckett	1.50
45	Harmon Killebrew	1.00
46	Monte Irvin	.50
47	Ralph Kiner	.50
48	Christy Mathewson	.25
49	Hoyt Wilhelm	.25
50	Tom Seaver	1.00
51	Allie Reynolds	.25
52	Joe DiMaggio	2.00
53	Lou Gehrig	2.00
54	Babe Ruth	3.00
55	Casey Stengel	1.00
56	Phil Rizzuto	.50
57	Thurman Munson	1.00
58	Johnny Mize	.50
59	Yogi Berra	1.00
61	Don Mattingly	1.00
62	Ray Dandridge	.25
63	Rollie Fingers	.50
64	Roberto Clemente	2.00
65	Reggie Jackson	1.00
66	Dennis Eckersley	.50
67	Robin Yount	1.00
68	Jimmie Foxx	1.00
69	Lefty Grove	.50
70	Richie Ashburn	.25
71	Jim Bunning	.25
72	Steve Carlton	.50
73	Robin Roberts	.50
74	Mike Schmidt	1.00
75	Willie Stargell	1.00
76	Ozzie Smith	1.00
77	Bill Mazeroski	.50
78	Honus Wagner	1.00
79	Pie Traynor	.50
80	Tony Gwynn	1.00
81	Willie McCovey	.25
82	Gaylord Perry	.25
83	Juan Marichal	.50
84	Orlando Cepeda	.50
85	Satchel Paige	1.00
86	George Sisler	.25
87	Ken Boyer	.25
88	Joe Medwick	.25
89	Travis Jackson	.25
90	Stan Musial	1.50
91	Dizzy Dean	1.00
92	Bob Gibson	1.00
93	Red Schoendienst	.50
94	Lou Brock	.75
95	Enos Slaughter	.25
96	Nolan Ryan	3.00
97	Smoky Burgess	.25
98	Mickey Vernon	.25
99	Vern Stephens	.25
100	Rick Ferrell	.25
101	Phil Niekro	3.00
102	Brooks Robinson	6.00
103	Frank Robinson	6.00
104	Jim Palmer	5.00
105	Cal Ripken Jr.	15.00
106	Warren Spahn	6.00
107	Cy Young	5.00
108	Nellie Fox	6.00
109	Carl Yastrzemski	6.00
110	Joe Sewell	4.00
111	Wade Boggs	5.00
112	Carlton Fisk	5.00
113	Jackie Robinson	8.00
114	Roy Campanella	6.00
115	Pee Wee Reese	5.00
116	Earl Averill	5.00
117	Rod Carew	5.00
118	Ernie Banks	6.00
119	Fergie Jenkins	3.00
120	Billy Williams	5.00
121	Al Lopez	3.00
122	Luis Aparicio	5.00
123	Luke Appling	5.00
124	Joe Morgan	5.00
125	Johnny Bench	6.00
126	Tony Perez	5.00
127	George Foster	3.00
128	Bob Feller	5.00
129	Bob Lemon	5.00
130	Larry Doby	5.00
131	George Kell	3.00
132	Hal Newhouser	3.00
133	Al Kaline	8.00
134	Ty Cobb	5.00
135	Buck Leonard	5.00
136	Maury Wills	3.00
137	Don Drysdale	5.00
138	Don Sutton	5.00
139	Eddie Mathews	6.00
140	Paul Molitor	5.00
141	Kirby Puckett	8.00
142	Harmon Killebrew	5.00
143	Monte Irvin	5.00
144	Mel Ott	5.00
145	Charlie Gehringer	5.00
146	Hoyt Wilhelm	3.00
147	Tom Seaver	6.00
148	Ted Kluszewski	3.00
149	Joe DiMaggio	8.00
150	Lou Gehrig	5.00
151	Babe Ruth	10.00
152	Casey Stengel	5.00
153	Phil Rizzuto	5.00
154	Thurman Munson	5.00
155	Johnny Mize	5.00
156	Yogi Berra	6.00
157	Roger Maris	5.00
158	Early Wynn	3.00
159	Bobby Doerr	5.00
160	Joe Cronin	5.00
161	Don Mattingly	8.00
162	Ray Dandridge	3.00
163	Rollie Fingers	5.00
164	Christy Mathewson	5.00
165	Reggie Jackson	5.00
166	Dennis Eckersley	3.00
167	Mickey Cochrane	3.00
168	Jimmie Foxx	5.00
169	Lefty Gomez	3.00
170	Jim Bunning	3.00
171	Steve Carlton	5.00
172	Robin Roberts	3.00
173	Richie Ashburn	5.00
174	Mike Schmidt	5.00
175	Ralph Kiner	3.00
176	Willie Stargell	5.00
177	Roberto Clemente	10.00
178	Bill Mazeroski	5.00
179	Honus Wagner	8.00
180	Pie Traynor	3.00
181	Tony Gwynn	5.00
182	Willie McCovey	3.00
183	Gaylord Perry	3.00
184	Juan Marichal	5.00
185	Orlando Cepeda	3.00
186	Satchel Paige	5.00
187	George Sisler	3.00
188	Rogers Hornsby	5.00
189	Stan Musial	8.00
190	Dizzy Dean	5.00
191	Bob Gibson	5.00
192	Red Schoendienst	5.00
193	Lou Brock	5.00
194	Enos Slaughter	3.00

#	Player	Price
197	Nolan Ryan	8.00
198	Mickey Vernon	3.00
199	Walter Johnson	5.00
200	Rick Ferrell	3.00

A Stitch In Time

PAUL MOLITOR 3B • BREWERS — STITCH IN TIME

		NM/M
	Common Player:	5.00
BG	Bob Gibson	8.00
BR	Brooks Robinson	10.00
BW	Billy Williams	5.00
CR	Cal Ripken Jr.	20.00
DE	Dwight Evans	5.00
DM	Don Mattingly	10.00
EM	Eddie Murray	8.00
GP	Gaylord Perry	5.00
HK	Harmon Killebrew	10.00
JB	Johnny Bench	10.00
JR	Jim Rice	8.00
KP	Kirby Puckett	15.00
MS	Mike Schmidt	10.00
PM	Paul Molitor	8.00
RC	Rod Carew	8.00
RJ	Reggie Jackson	10.00
TG	Tony Gwynn	10.00

Cut Signatures

		NM/M
	Production 1-133	
AB	Al Barlick/49	75.00
AH	Happy Chandler/44	75.00
AR	Allie Reynolds/40	150.00
BA	Bob Allison/31	90.00
BD	Bill Dickey/50	125.00
BG	Burleigh Grimes/52	125.00
BH	Babe Herman/99	100.00
BV	Bill Veeck/47	250.00
CA	Max Carey/40	80.00
CG	Charlie Gehringer/50	75.00
CH	Carl Hubbell/54	100.00
DC	Dolph Camilli/25	75.00
DI	Joe DiMaggio/52	400.00
DU	Leo Durocher/84	140.00
EA	Earl Averill/62	80.00
EL	Ed Lopat/66	100.00
EM	Eddie Mathews/69	125.00
ER	Edd Roush/50	60.00
ES	Enos Slaughter/47	80.00
EW	Early Wynn/40	100.00
FF	Ford Frick/88	140.00
FL	Freddy Lindstrom/45	200.00
GH	Gabby Hartnett/56	160.00
GP	George Pipgras/70	90.00
GR	Lefty Grove/66	220.00
HG	Hank Greenberg/59	200.00
HO	Gil Hodges/25	450.00
JA	Joe Adcock/49	100.00
JD	Joe Dugan/46	120.00
JO	Judy Johnson/54	150.00
JS	Joe Sewell/110	80.00
JV	Johnny Vander Meer/49	140.00
KB	Ken Boyer/19	275.00
LA	Luke Appling/92	80.00
LD	Larry Doby/50	100.00
MI	Johnny Mize/133	100.00
PR	Pee Wee Reese/39	160.00
RA	Richie Ashburn/50	150.00
RD	Ray Dandridge/50	85.00
RS	Ray Schalk/44	275.00
SC	Stan Coveleski/84	80.00
SW	Warren Spahn/95	100.00
WA	Walter Alston/48	140.00
WH	Waite Hoyt/79	90.00
WI	Hoyt Wilhelm/60	80.00
WS	Willie Stargell/71	180.00

Hall of Fame Cuts

		NM/M
	Production 1-86	
AB	Al Barlick/44	100.00
BL	Bob Lemon/53	75.00
CG	Charlie Gehringer/65	85.00
CH	Carl Hubbell/31	100.00
EC	Earle Combs/27	250.00
ER	Edd Roush/65	80.00
GH	Gabby Hartnett/31	180.00
HN	Hal Newhouser/40	80.00
JC	Joe Cronin/86	90.00
LA	Luke Appling/45	80.00
LB	Lou Boudreau/30	80.00
WH	Waite Hoyt/33	100.00
WS	Warren Spahn/35	125.00

Historical Cuts

Production One Set

Snside the Numbers Cuts

		NM/M
	Production 4-119	
BD	Bill Dickey/28	150.00
BH	Babe Herman/99	100.00
BL	Bob Lemon/75	75.00
CG	Charlie Gehringer/60	120.00
CH	Carl Hubbell/70	100.00
EA	Earl Averill/57	65.00
EL	Ernie Lombardi/52	200.00
EM	Eddie Mathews/70	125.00
ES	Enos Slaughter/69	80.00
EW	Early Wynn/34	100.00
FS	Fred Snodgrass/75	150.00
GH	Gabby Hartnett/50	160.00
GR	Lefty Grove/73	220.00
HG	Hank Greenberg/25	250.00
JC	Joe Cronin/29	100.00
JM	Joe Medwick/119	140.00
JV	Johnny Vander Meer/39	140.00
LA	Luke Appling/59	80.00
LG	Lefty Gomez/75	125.00
SC	Stan Coveleski/72	65.00
WH	Waite Hoyt/65	100.00
WI	Hoyt Wilhelm/55	80.00
WS	Warren Spahn/55	100.00

Legendary Americana

		NM/M
	Common Card:	5.00
	Production 550 Sets	
1	George Washington Carver	5.00
3	Frederick Douglass	5.00
4	Crazy Horse	5.00
6	Abraham Lincoln	5.00
7	Thomas Edison	5.00
8	Andrew Carnegie	5.00
9	Eli Whitney	5.00
11	Davy Crockett	5.00
12	Robert E. Lee	5.00
13	John D. Rockefeller	5.00
14	Billy the Kid	5.00
15	Ulysses S. Grant	5.00
18	Kit Carson	5.00
19	Francis Scott Key	5.00
20	Franklin D. Roosevelt	5.00
21	Mark Twain	5.00
24	Alexander Graham Bell	5.00
27	Eleanor Roosevelt	5.00
28	John F. Kennedy	8.00
30	Frank Lloyd Wright	5.00
34	Henry Ford	5.00
35	Dwight D. Eisenhower	5.00
36	Daniel Boone	5.00
38	William Randolph Hearst	5.00
42	Wyatt Earp	5.00
47	Abner Doubleday	5.00
48	Harry S. Truman	5.00
53	Amelia Earhart	5.00
55	Orville Wright	5.00
55	Jack London	5.00
59	Andrew Jackson	5.00
60	Zachary Taylor	5.00
62	Jefferson Davis	5.00
63	Sitting Bull	10.00
65	Clara Barton	5.00
66	Booker T. Washington	5.00
68	Samuel F. B. Morse	5.00
69	Alexander Cartwright	5.00
72	Andrew Johnson	5.00
74	Rutherford B. Hayes	5.00
74	James A. Garfield	5.00
75	Chester Arthur	5.00
76	Grover Cleveland	5.00
78	William McKinley	5.00
79	William H. Taft	5.00
80	Woodrow Wilson	5.00
81	Warren G. Harding	5.00
82	Calvin Coolidge	5.00
83	Herbert Hoover	5.00
84	Lyndon B. Johnson	5.00
85	Richard M. Nixon	5.00
86	Gerald Ford	5.00
88	Ronald Reagan	5.00
92	Babe Ruth	10.00
93	Jackie Robinson	8.00

Legendary Dual Cuts

Production One Set

Legendary Materials

SD — LEGENDARY MATERIALS CUTS — STEVE GARVEY

		NM/M
	Common Player:	5.00
	Production 199 Sets	
AO	Al Oliver	5.00
BJ	Bo Jackson	15.00
BL	Barry Larkin	8.00
BS	Bruce Sutter	5.00
BW	Billy Williams	15.00
CA	Roy Campanella	10.00
DD	Don Drysdale	8.00
DE	Dwight Evans	5.00
DP	Dave Parker	5.00
DS	Don Sutton	5.00
EC	Dennis Eckersley	5.00
FJ	Fergie Jenkins	5.00
FR	Frank Robinson	10.00
GF	George Foster	5.00
GG	Rich "Goose" Gossage	5.00
HB	Harold Baines	5.00
JP	Jim Palmer	8.00
JT	Joe Torre	10.00
KG	Ken Griffey Sr.	5.00
LA	Luis Aparicio	5.00
MA	Bill Madlock	5.00
MG	Mark Grace	10.00
PN	Phil Niekro	5.00
PO	Paul O'Neill	10.00
PW	Pee Wee Reese	5.00
RA	Roberto Alomar	10.00
RC	Roberto Clemente	50.00
RF	Rollie Fingers	8.00
RG	Ron Guidry	20.00
RM	Roger Maris	25.00
RS	Ryne Sandberg	15.00
SC	Red Schoendienst	10.00
TO	Tony Oliva	8.00
TP	Tony Perez	8.00
AD1	Andre Dawson	8.00
AD2	Andre Dawson	8.00
AK1-2	Al Kaline	15.00
BR1-2	Brooks Robinson	15.00
CF1-2	Carlton Fisk	10.00
CR1-2	Cal Ripken Jr.	25.00
CY1-2	Carl Yastrzemski	15.00
DM1-2	Don Mattingly	20.00
DW1-2	Dave Winfield	8.00
EM1-2	Eddie Murray	8.00
FL1-2	Fred Lynn	5.00
GP1-2	Gaylord Perry	5.00
HK1-2	Harmon Killebrew	15.00
JB1-2	Johnny Bench	15.00
JM1-2	Jack Morris	5.00
JR1	Jim Rice	8.00
J2	Jim Rice	8.00
KG1-2	Kirk Gibson	5.00
KP1-2	Kirby Puckett	25.00
LB1-2	Lou Brock	10.00
MS1-2	Mike Schmidt	15.00
NR1-2	Nolan Ryan	25.00
OS1-2	Ozzie Smith	20.00
PM1-2	Paul Molitor	8.00
RC1-2	Rod Carew	8.00
RJ1-2	Reggie Jackson	10.00
RY1-2	Robin Yount	20.00
SC1-2	Steve Carlton	5.00
SG1-2	Steve Garvey	5.00
TG1-2	Tony Gwynn	15.00
WB1-2	Wade Boggs	8.00
WC1-2	Will Clark	8.00

Legendary Quad Cuts

Production One Set

Legendary Signatures

		NM/M
	Production 15-199	
JT	Joe Torre/99	40.00
KG	Kirk Gibson/199	15.00
AD1-2	Andre Dawson/199	20.00
AK1-2	Al Kaline/199	25.00
BF1-2	Bob Feller/199	20.00
BF3	Bob Feller/189	20.00
BG1-2	Bob Gibson/199	25.00
BG3	Bob Gibson/40	25.00
BJ1-2	Bo Jackson/100	50.00
BM1	Bill Mazeroski/189	30.00
BM2	Bill Mazeroski/199	30.00
BR1	Brooks Robinson/150	30.00
BR2	Brooks Robinson/140	30.00
BW1	Billy Williams/199	20.00
BW2	Billy Williams/189	20.00
CF1-2	Carlton Fisk/75	25.00
CF3	Carlton Fisk/65	25.00
CR1	Cal Ripken Jr./99	100.00
CR2	Cal Ripken Jr./50	120.00
DM1-2	Don Mattingly/75	75.00
EB1-2	Ernie Banks/35	60.00
EM1-2	Eddie Murray/25	50.00
FJ1-3	Fergie Jenkins/125	20.00
FR1-2	Frank Robinson/50	25.00
FR3	Frank Robinson/40	25.00
GP1-2	Gaylord Perry/199	15.00
HK1	Harmon Killebrew/100	75.00
HK2	Harmon Killebrew/90	75.00
JM1-2	Juan Marichal/199	20.00
JM3	Juan Marichal/189	20.00
JP1-3	Jim Palmer/199	20.00
LA1	Luis Aparicio/199	20.00
LA2	Luis Aparicio/186	20.00
MS1-2	Mike Schmidt/35	50.00
MS3	Mike Schmidt/60	60.00
NR1-2	Nolan Ryan/25	100.00
OS1-3	Ozzie Smith/100	40.00
PM1	Paul Molitor/100	25.00
PM2	Paul Molitor/90	25.00
RC1-2	Rod Carew/35	60.00
RJ1	Reggie Jackson/25	60.00
RS1-3	Ryne Sandberg/25	60.00
RY1-2	Robin Yount/35	60.00
RY3	Robin Yount/25	60.00
SC1-2	Steve Carlton/199	20.00
SC3	Steve Carlton/189	20.00
TP1-2	Tony Perez/199	20.00
WB1-3	Wade Boggs/35	50.00
WC1-2	Will Clark/199	20.00
WM1-2	Willie McCovey/25	50.00

Legendary Team Cuts

Production One Set

Masterful Material

		NM/M
	Common Player:	5.00
AD	Andre Dawson	5.00
BJ	Bo Jackson	10.00
BL	Barry Larkin	8.00
BM	Bill Madlock	5.00
BR	Brooks Robinson	8.00
BS	Bruce Sutter	8.00
CF	Carlton Fisk	8.00
CR	Cal Ripken Jr.	20.00
CY	Carl Yastrzemski	10.00
DE	Dwight Evans	5.00
DM	Don Mattingly	15.00
DP	Dave Parker	5.00
DS	Don Sutton	5.00
DW	Dave Winfield	8.00
EM	Eddie Mathews	10.00
FL	Fred Lynn	5.00
FR	Frank Robinson	5.00
GP	Gaylord Perry	5.00
JB	Johnny Bench	10.00
JR	Jim Rice	5.00
KG	Ken Griffey Sr.	5.00
KP	Kirby Puckett	15.00
MS	Mike Schmidt	10.00
MU	Eddie Murray	8.00
NR	Nolan Ryan	20.00
PM	Paul Molitor	8.00
RJ	Reggie Jackson	10.00
RS	Ryne Sandberg	8.00
RY	Robin Yount	10.00
SC	Steve Carlton	8.00
SG	Steve Garvey	5.00
TG	Tony Gwynn	10.00
WB	Wade Boggs	8.00
WC	Will Clark	8.00
WM	Willie McCovey	8.00
YB	Yogi Berra	15.00

Material Cuts

No Pricing
Production 1-5

Material Signatures

No Pricing
Production 10 Sets

Quotation Cuts

		NM/M
	Production 1-109	
BL	Bob Lemon/80	75.00
CS	Casey Stengel/36	275.00
HC	Happy Chandler/44	75.00
JM	Joe McCarthy/109	140.00
LB	Lou Boudreau/28	60.00
MI	Johnny Mize/45	80.00
RA	Richie Ashburn/48	175.00
RD	Ray Dandridge/72	90.00
SC	Stan Coveleski/71	75.00
WA	Walter Alston/31	80.00
WI	Hoyt Wilhelm/37	90.00
WS	Warren Spahn/60	100.00

Reel History Film Frame

Cards are serial numbered 1/1.

BR	Babe Ruth	125.00
LG	Lou Gehrig	120.00

Signature Cuts

Production One Set

When It Was A Game - Memorabilia

		NM/M
	Common Player:	5.00
AT	Alan Trammell	5.00
BF	Bob Feller	8.00
BG	Bob Gibson	10.00
BM	Bill Mazeroski	8.00
BW	Billy Williams	5.00
CF	Carlton Fisk	8.00
CY	Carl Yastrzemski	10.00
DE	Dennis Eckersley	5.00
DM	Don Mattingly	15.00
DW	Dave Winfield	8.00
EM	Eddie Murray	8.00
FJ	Fergie Jenkins	5.00
FL	Fred Lynn	5.00
FR	Frank Robinson	8.00
GP	Gaylord Perry	5.00
HK	Harmon Killebrew	10.00
JP	Jim Palmer	8.00
JR	Jim Rice	5.00
KG	Kirk Gibson	5.00
KP	Kirby Puckett	15.00
LB	Lou Brock	8.00
MS	Mike Schmidt	10.00
NR	Nolan Ryan	20.00
PM	Paul Molitor	8.00
PW	Pee Wee Reese	8.00
RF	Rollie Fingers	5.00
RJ	Reggie Jackson	10.00
RM	Roger Maris	25.00
RS	Red Schoendienst	8.00
TG	Tony Gwynn	10.00

2007 SPX

	NM/M
Complete Set (150):	
Common Player (1-100):	.25

rookie signAABURES — SPX

	NM/M
Common RC Auto. (101-150):	10.00
Pack (3):	15.00
Box (10):	140.00

#	Player	Price
1	Miguel Tejada	.50
2	Brian Roberts	.50
3	Melvin Mora	.25
4	David Ortiz	1.00
5	Manny Ramirez	.50
6	Jason Varitek	.50
7	Curt Schilling	1.00
8	Jim Thome	.50
9	Paul Konerko	.50
10	Jermaine Dye	.50
11	Travis Hafner	.50
12	Victor Martinez	.25
13	Grady Sizemore	.75
14	C.C. Sabathia	.50
15	Ivan Rodriguez	.25
16	Magglio Ordonez	.50
17	Carlos Guillen	.25
18	Justin Verlander	.75
19	Shane Costa	.25
20	Emil Brown	.25
21	Mark Teahen	.25
22	Vladimir Guerrero	1.00
23	Jered Weaver	.75
24	Juan Rivera	.25
25	Justin Morneau	.75
26	Joe Mauer	.75
27	Torii Hunter	.50
28	Johan Santana	.75
29	Derek Jeter	3.00
30	Alex Rodriguez	3.00
31	Johnny Damon	1.00
32	Jason Giambi	.75
33	Bobby Crosby	.25
34	Nick Swisher	.50
35	Eric Chavez	.25
36	Ichiro Suzuki	2.00
37	Raul Ibanez	.25
38	Richie Sexson	.50
39	Carl Crawford	.50
40	Rocco Baldelli	.25
41	Scott Kazmir	.50
42	Michael Young	.50
43	Mark Teixeira	.75
44	Ian Kinsler	.50
45	Troy Glaus	.50
46	Vernon Wells	.50
47	Roy Halladay	.50
48	Lyle Overbay	.25
49	Brandon Webb	.50
50	Conor Jackson	.25
51	Stephen Drew	.50
52	Chipper Jones	1.00
53	Andruw Jones	.50
54	Adam LaRoche	.25
55	John Smoltz	.50
56	Derrek Lee	.75
57	Aramis Ramirez	.50
58	Carlos Zambrano	.50
59	Ken Griffey Jr.	2.00
60	Adam Dunn	.50
61	Aaron Harang	.25
62	Todd Helton	.75
63	Matt Holliday	.50
64	Garrett Atkins	.50
65	Miguel Cabrera	1.00
66	Hanley Ramirez	1.00
67	Dontrelle Willis	.50
68	Lance Berkman	.50
69	Roy Oswalt	.50
70	Craig Biggio	.50
71	J.D. Drew	.25
72	Nomar Garciaparra	.50
73	Rafael Furcal	.50
74	Jeff Kent	.50
75	Prince Fielder	1.00
76	Bill Hall	.50
77	Rickie Weeks	.50
78	Jose Reyes	.50
79	David Wright	1.00
80	Carlos Delgado	.50
81	Carlos Beltran	.50
82	Ryan Howard	2.00
83	Chase Utley	1.00
84	Jimmy Rollins	.50
85	Jason Bay	.50
86	Freddy Sanchez	.50
87	Zachary Duke	.25
88	Trevor Hoffman	.25
89	Adrian Gonzalez	.50
90	Chris Young	.50
91	Ray Durham	.25
92	Omar Vizquel	.25
93	Jason Schmidt	.50
94	Albert Pujols	3.00
95	Scott Rolen	.75
96	Jim Edmonds	.50
97	Chris Carpenter	.50
98	Alfonso Soriano	.50
99	Ryan Zimmerman	.50
100	Nick Johnson	.25
101	Delmon Young (RC)	15.00
102	Andrew Miller RC	10.00
103	Troy Tulowitzki (RC)	30.00
104	Jeff Fiorentino (RC)	10.00
105	David Murphy (RC)	10.00
106	Tim Lincecum RC	150.00
107	Phil Hughes RC	40.00
108	Kevin Kouzmanoff (RC)	10.00
109	Adam Lind (RC)	15.00
110	Mark Reynolds RC	30.00
111	Kevin Hooper (RC)	10.00
112	Mitch Maier RC	10.00
113	Homer Bailey (RC)	15.00
114	Dennis Sarfate (RC)	10.00
115	Drew Anderson (RC)	10.00
116	Miguel Montero (RC)	10.00
117	Glen Perkins (RC)	10.00
118	Kevin Slowey (RC)	15.00
119	Tim Gradoville RC	10.00
120	Ryan Braun (RC)	75.00
121	Chris Narveson (RC)	10.00
122	Patrick Misch (RC)	10.00
123	Juan Salas (RC)	10.00
124	Beltran Perez (RC)	10.00
125	Joaquin Arias (RC)	10.00
126	Philip Humber (RC)	15.00
127	Kei Igawa RC	15.00
128	Daisuke Matsuzaka RC	100.00
129	Andy Cannizaro (RC)	10.00
130	Ubaldo Jimenez (RC)	60.00
131	Fred Lewis (RC)	10.00
132	Ryan Sweeney (RC)	10.00
133	Jeff Baker (RC)	10.00
134	Michael Bourn (RC)	20.00
135	Akinori Iwamura (RC)	20.00
136	Oswaldo Navarro (RC)	10.00
137	Hunter Pence (RC)	20.00
138	Jon Knott (RC)	10.00
139	Justin Hampson (RC)	10.00
140	Jeff Salazar (RC)	10.00
141	Juan Morillo (RC)	10.00
142	Delwyn Young (RC)	10.00
143	Brian Burres (RC)	10.00
144	Chris Stewart RC	10.00
145	Eric Stults RC	10.00
146	Carlos Maldonado (RC)	10.00
147	Angel Sanchez RC	10.00
148	Cesar Jimenez RC	10.00
149	Shawn Riggans (RC)	10.00
150	John Nelson (RC)	10.00

Printing Plates

No Pricing
Production one set per color.

Spectrum

Spectrum (101-150):	No Pricing
Production 25 Sets	

Autofacts Preview

		NM/M
	Common Autograph:	10.00
	1:Hobby Box	
AI	Akinori Iwamura	20.00
AL	Adam Lind	10.00
AM	Andrew Miller/SP	20.00
AS	Angel Sanchez	10.00
BP	Beltran Perez	10.00
BR	Jeremy Brown	10.00
CM	Carlos Maldonado	10.00
CN	Chris Narveson	10.00
CR	Cal Ripken Jr./SP	150.00
DS	Dennis Sarfate	10.00
DW	Dewayne Wise	10.00
DY	Delmon Young	15.00
ES	Eric Stults	15.00
FL	Fred Lewis	15.00
GP	Glen Perkins	15.00
JA	Joaquin Arias	10.00
JB	Jeff Baker	10.00
JH	Justin Hampson	10.00
JK	Jon Knott	15.00
JM	Juan Morillo	10.00
JS	Juan Salas	10.00
JW	Jason Wood	10.00
KG	Ken Griffey Jr./SP	80.00
KH	Kevin Hooper	10.00
KI	Kei Igawa	20.00
KK	Kevin Kouzmanoff	15.00
MB	Michael Bourn	15.00
MM	Miguel Montero	10.00
PH	Philip Humber	15.00
PM	Patrick Misch	10.00
SA	Jeff Salazar	10.00
SR	Shawn Riggans	10.00
ST	Chris Stewart	10.00
TT	Troy Tulowitzki	20.00
YO	Delwyn Young	10.00

Iron Man

	NM/M
Common Ripken (1-100):	5.00
Production 699 Sets	
Platinum:	No Pricing
Production One Set	
Printing Plates:	No Pricing
Production One Set	

Iron Man Memorabilia

	NM/M
Common Ripken:	40.00
Production 25 Sets	

Iron Man Autograph

NM/M

Young Star Signatures

		NM/M
	Common Autograph:	10.00
	Spectrum:	1-2X
	Production 25 Sets	
AE	Andre Ethier	20.00

Code	Player	Price
AG	Adrian Gonzalez	20.00
AS	Anibal Sanchez	10.00
BU	B.J. Upton	20.00
CA	Matt Cain/SP	15.00
CH	Cole Hamels/SP	30.00
CQ	Carlos Quentin	15.00
DJ	Derek Jeter	125.00
DU	Dan Uggla	20.00
DY	Delmon Young	15.00
FH	Felix Hernandez	25.00
FL	Francisco Liriano	15.00
HA	Rich Harden	15.00
HI	Rich Hill/SP	15.00
HK	Howie Kendrick	20.00
HR	Hanley Ramirez	30.00
JB	Jeremy Brown	10.00
JJ	Josh Johnson	15.00
JL	Jon Lester	30.00
JM	Joe Mauer	40.00
JP	Jonathan Papelbon	20.00
JR	Jose Reyes	40.00
JS	Jeremy Sowers	10.00
JV	Justin Verlander	25.00
JW	Jered Weaver/SP	20.00
JZ	Joel Zumaya	15.00
KG	Ken Griffey Jr.	75.00
KU	Hong-Chih Kuo	20.00
LO	James Loney	20.00
MO	Justin Morneau	25.00
NM	Nick Markakis	25.00
PH	Philip Humber	10.00
RW	Rickie Weeks	15.00
RZ	Ryan Zimmerman	20.00
SD	Stephen Drew	20.00
ST	Scott Thorman	10.00
TT	Troy Tulowitzki	20.00
WI	Josh Willingham	15.00

Winning Materials Bronze 199

	NM/M
Common Player:	5.00
Gold 199:	1X
Silver 199:	1X
Production 199 Sets	
Blue 175:	1X
Green 175:	1X
Production 175 Sets	
Gold 99:	1-1.5X
Silver 99:	1-1.5X
Production 99 Sets	
Dual Bronze:	No Pricing
Production 25 Sets	
Dual Gold:	1-1.5X
Dual Silver:	1-1.5X
Production 50 Sets	
Dual Green:	No Pricing
Production 15 Sets	
AB A.J. Burnett	5.00
AD Adam Dunn	6.00
AE Andre Ethier	6.00
AJ Andruw Jones	8.00
AL Adam LaRoche	5.00
AP Albert Pujols	20.00
AR Aramis Ramirez	8.00
AS Anibal Sanchez	6.00
BA Bobby Abreu	6.00
BG Brian Giles	5.00
BL Joe Blanton	5.00
BM Brian McCann	5.00
BO Jeremy Bonderman	6.00
BR Brian Roberts	5.00
BS Ben Sheets	5.00
BU B.J. Upton	5.00
CA Miguel Cabrera	8.00
CB Craig Biggio	5.00
CC Chris Carpenter	8.00
CF Chone Figgins	5.00
CH Cole Hamels	10.00
CJ Chipper Jones	8.00
CL Roger Clemens	15.00
CN Robinson Cano	10.00
CR Carl Crawford	5.00
CU Chase Utley	10.00
CW Chien-Ming Wang	35.00
DJ Derek Jeter	20.00
DJ2 Derek Jeter	20.00
DL Derek Lee	8.00
DO David Ortiz	10.00
DU Dan Uggla	5.00
DW Dontrelle Willis	5.00
EC Eric Chavez	5.00
FH Felix Hernandez	6.00
FL Francisco Liriano	6.00
FS Freddy Sanchez	5.00
FT Frank Thomas	8.00
GA Garrett Atkins	5.00
HA Travis Hafner	6.00
HE Todd Helton	8.00
HK Howie Kendrick	5.00
HN Rich Harden	5.00
HR Hanley Ramirez	8.00
HS Huston Street	5.00
IK Ian Kinsler	5.00
IR Ivan Rodriguez	8.00
JB Jason Bay	6.00
JE Jim Edmonds	5.00
JF Jeff Francoeur	8.00
JJ Josh Johnson	5.00
JL Chad Billingsley	5.00
JM Joe Mauer	8.00
JN Joe Nathan	5.00
JP Jake Peavy	5.00
JR Jose Reyes	10.00
JS Jeremy Sowers	5.00
JT Jim Thome	8.00
JV Justin Verlander	8.00
JW Jered Weaver	8.00
JZ Joel Zumaya	5.00
KG Ken Griffey Jr.	15.00
KG2 Ken Griffey Jr.	15.00
KH Khalil Greene	5.00
KU Hong-Chih Kuo	20.00
LE Jon Lester	5.00
LG Luis Gonzalez	5.00
MC Matt Cain	5.00
ME Melky Cabrera	6.00
MH Matt Holliday	8.00
MO Justin Morneau	8.00
MT Mark Teixeira	8.00
NM Nicholas Markakis	8.00
NS Nick Swisher	5.00
PA Jonathan Papelbon	15.00
PF Prince Fielder	10.00
PL Paul LoDuca	5.00
RC Cal Ripken Jr.	20.00
RI Alex Rios	5.00
RJ Randy Johnson	5.00
RO Roy Oswalt	6.00
RW Rickie Weeks	5.00
RZ Ryan Zimmerman	8.00
SA Alfonso Soriano	8.00
SD Stephen Drew	5.00
SH James Shields	5.00
SK Scott Kazmir	5.00
SM John Smoltz	8.00
SO Scott Olsen	5.00
SR Scott Rolen	8.00
TE Miguel Tejada	6.00
TG Tom Glavine	5.00
TH Trevor Hoffman	5.00
TO Torii Hunter	6.00
VG Vladimir Guerrero	8.00
VM Victor Martinez	5.00
WE David Wells	5.00
WI Josh Willingham	5.00
YB Yuniesky Betancourt	5.00

Winning Materials Patch Gold

	NM/M
Common Player:	10.00
Production 99 unless noted.	
Patch Silver:	1X
Production 3-99	
Patch Bronze:	1X
Production 50 Sets	
Triple Patch:	No Pricing
Production 25 Sets	
AB A.J. Burnett	10.00
AD Adam Dunn	15.00
AE Andre Ethier	10.00
AJ Andruw Jones	10.00
AL Adam LaRoche	10.00
AP Albert Pujols	40.00
AR Aramis Ramirez	10.00
AS Anibal Sanchez/54	10.00
BA Bobby Abreu	10.00
BG Brian Giles	10.00
BL Joe Blanton	10.00
BM Brian McCann	10.00
BO Jeremy Bonderman	15.00
BR Brian Roberts	10.00
BS Ben Sheets	10.00
BU B.J. Upton	10.00
CA Miguel Cabrera	20.00
CB Craig Biggio	15.00
CC Chris Carpenter	20.00
CF Chone Figgins	10.00
CH Cole Hamels	20.00
CJ Chipper Jones	20.00
CL Roger Clemens	25.00
CN Robinson Cano	20.00
CR Carl Crawford	10.00
CU Chase Utley	20.00
CW Chien-Ming Wang	60.00
DJ Derek Jeter	40.00
DJ2 Derek Jeter	40.00
DL Derek Lee	20.00
DO David Ortiz	20.00
DU Dan Uggla	10.00
DW Dontrelle Willis	10.00
EC Eric Chavez	10.00
FH Felix Hernandez	15.00
FL Francisco Liriano	15.00
FS Freddy Sanchez	10.00
FT Frank Thomas	20.00
GA Garrett Atkins	10.00
HA Travis Hafner	15.00
HE Todd Helton	20.00
HK Howie Kendrick/34	15.00
HN Rich Harden	10.00
HR Hanley Ramirez	20.00
HS Huston Street	10.00
IK Ian Kinsler	10.00
IR Ivan Rodriguez	20.00
JB Jason Bay	15.00
JE Jim Edmonds	10.00
JF Jeff Francoeur	20.00
JJ Josh Johnson	10.00
JL Chad Billingsley	10.00
JM Joe Mauer	20.00
JN Joe Nathan	10.00
JP Jake Peavy	10.00
JR Jose Reyes	25.00
JS Jeremy Sowers	10.00
JT Jim Thome	20.00
JW Jered Weaver	20.00
JZ Joel Zumaya	10.00
KG Ken Griffey Jr.	30.00
KG2 Ken Griffey Jr.	30.00
KH Khalil Greene	10.00
KU Hong-Chih Kuo	40.00
LE Jon Lester	20.00
LG Luis Gonzalez	10.00
MC Matt Cain	15.00
ME Melky Cabrera	20.00
MH Matt Holliday	20.00
MO Justin Morneau	15.00
MT Mark Teixeira	15.00
NM Nicholas Markakis	15.00
NS Nick Swisher	10.00
PA Jonathan Papelbon	20.00
PF Prince Fielder	20.00
PL Paul LoDuca	10.00
RC Cal Ripken Jr.	40.00
RI Alex Rios	10.00
RJ Randy Johnson	15.00
RO Roy Oswalt	15.00
RW Rickie Weeks	15.00
RZ Ryan Zimmerman	15.00
SA Alfonso Soriano	15.00
SD Stephen Drew	15.00
SH James Shields	10.00
SK Scott Kazmir	15.00
SM John Smoltz	20.00
SO Scott Olsen	10.00
SR Scott Rolen	15.00
TE Miguel Tejada	15.00
TG Tom Glavine	15.00
TH Trevor Hoffman	10.00
TO Torii Hunter	15.00
VG Vladimir Guerrero	20.00
VM Victor Martinez	10.00
WE David Wells	10.00
WI Josh Willingham	15.00
YB Yuniesky Betancourt	10.00

Winning Materials Triple Signatures

	NM/M
Production 15-35	5.00
Platinum:	No Pricing
Production 3-10	
BR Brian Roberts/35	35.00
EC Eric Chavez/35	30.00
FH Felix Hernandez/35	50.00
GA Garrett Atkins/35	25.00
HA Travis Hafner/35	35.00
HK Howie Kendrick/35	30.00
JJ Josh Johnson/35	35.00
JM Joe Mauer/35	40.00
JP Jake Peavy/35	35.00
JR Jose Reyes/35	75.00
KU Hong-Chih Kuo/35	120.00
LE Jon Lester/35	40.00
TE Miguel Tejada/35	40.00
TG Tom Glavine/35	60.00

Winning Trios Gold

	NM/M
Common Trio:	15.00
Production 75 Sets	
Silver:	1X
Production 50 Sets	
Bronze:	1-1.5X
Production 30 Sets	
Patch:	No Pricing
Production 8-25	
1 Ken Griffey Jr., Derek Jeter, Albert Pujols	40.00
2 Josh Willingham, Hanley Ramirez, Dan Uggla	15.00
3 Josh Johnson, Dontrelle Willis, Anibal Sanchez	15.00
4 Travis Hafner, David Ortiz, Lance Berkman	25.00
5 Ben Sheets, Roy Oswalt, Jake Peavy	15.00
6 Ivan Rodriguez, Jeremy Bonderman, Justin Verlander	25.00
7 Jose Reyes, Stephen Drew, Hanley Ramirez	25.00
8 Miguel Cabrera, Ryan Zimmerman, B.J. Upton	15.00
9 Justin Verlander, Jonathan Papelbon, Jered Weaver	40.00
10 Randy Johnson, Derek Jeter, Bobby Abreu	40.00
11 Craig Biggio, Lance Berkman, Morgan Ensberg	15.00
12 Brian McCann, Jeff Francoeur, Adam LaRoche	30.00
13 Victor Martinez, Joe Mauer, Brian McCann	20.00
14 Carl Crawford, Grady Sizemore, Jose Reyes	30.00
15 Freddy Garcia, Carlos Zambrano, Johan Santana	20.00
16 Vladimir Guerrero, Bobby Abreu, Alfonso Soriano	20.00
17 Justin Morneau, Johan Santana, Joe Mauer	25.00
18 Carlos Delgado, Carlos Beltran, Jose Reyes	25.00
19 Andre Ethier, Chad Billingsley, Matthew Kemp	25.00
20 Jim Thome, Jermaine Dye, Tadahito Iguchi	20.00
21 Jimmy Rollins, Chase Utley, Aaron Rowand	30.00
22 Ivan Rodriguez, Magglio Ordonez, Curtis Granderson	20.00
23 Chris Carpenter, Scott Rolen, Albert Pujols	30.00
24 Carl Crawford, B.J. Upton, James Shields	15.00
25 Howie Kendrick, Mike Napoli, Jered Weaver	15.00
26 Ian Kinsler, Dan Uggla, Howie Kendrick	15.00
27 Miguel Tejada, Brian Roberts, Nicholas Markakis	15.00
28 Justin Verlander, Jered Weaver, Mike Pelfrey	20.00
30 Randy Johnson, Derek Lowe, Anibal Sanchez	15.00
31 Prince Fielder, Ryan Zimmerman, Dan Uggla	20.00
32 Trevor Hoffman, Joe Nathan, Huston Street	15.00
33 Vernon Wells, Alex Rios, A.J. Burnett	15.00
34 Ben Sheets, Rickie Weeks, Prince Fielder	15.00
35 Adrian Beltre, Felix Hernandez, Yuniesky Betancourt	15.00
36 Jeremy Bonderman, Justin Verlander, Joel Zumaya	20.00
37 Billy Wagner, Paul LoDuca, Jose Reyes	15.00
38 Victor Martinez, Jeremy Sowers, C.C. Sabathia	15.00
39 Conor Jackson, Brandon Webb, Stephen Drew	20.00
40 Justin Verlander, Felix Hernandez, Jered Weaver	20.00
41 Ken Griffey Jr., Frank Thomas, Ivan Rodriguez	20.00
42 Cal Ripken Jr., Derek Jeter, Jose Reyes	50.00

2008 SP Authentic

	NM/M
Common Player (1-100):	.25
Common RC Auto.: (101-191):	8.00
Production 149-999	
Pack (5):	4.00
Box (24):	80.00
1 Ken Griffey Jr.	2.00
2 Derek Jeter	3.00
3 Albert Pujols	3.00
4 Ichiro Suzuki	2.00
5 Daisuke Matsuzaka	2.00
6 Vladimir Guerrero	1.00
7 Magglio Ordonez	.50
8 Eric Chavez	.25
9 Randy Johnson	1.00
10 Ryan Braun	1.50
11 Phil Hughes	.75
12 Joba Chamberlain	2.00
13 B.J. Upton	.50
14 Frank Thomas	1.00
15 Greg Maddux	2.00
16 Delmon Young	.25
17 Carlos Beltran	.75
18 Derek Lee	.75
19 Aramis Ramirez	.50
20 Miguel Tejada	.50
21 Manny Ramirez	1.00
22 Justin Upton	.75
23 Miguel Cabrera	1.00
24 Prince Fielder	1.00
25 Adam Dunn	.75
26 Jose Reyes	1.00
27 Chase Utley	1.00
28 Jimmy Rollins	.75
29 Joe Blanton	.25
30 Mark Teixeira	.50
31 Brian McCann	.50
32 Russell Martin	.75
33 Ian Kinsler	.50
34 Travis Hafner	.50
35 Victor Martinez	.50
36 Grady Sizemore	1.00
37 Alex Rodriguez	3.00
38 David Wright	2.00
39 Ryan Howard	2.00
40 Carlos Lee	.50
41 Lance Berkman	.50
42 Hunter Pence	.50
43 John Lackey	.50
44 C.C. Sabathia	.75
45 Michael Young	.25
46 Carl Crawford	.50
47 Carlos Pena	.50
48 Justin Verlander	.50
49 Cole Hamels	.75
50 Carlos Zambrano	.50
51 Jake Peavy	.75
52 Khalil Greene	.25
53 Chris Young	.50
54 Vernon Wells	.50
55 Alex Rios	.50
56 Roy Halladay	.50
57 Roy Oswalt	.50
58 Ben Sheets	.25
59 J.J. Hardy	.50
60 Pedro Martinez	.50
61 Nick Swisher	.25
62 Curtis Granderson	.75
63 Johnny Damon	.75
64 Mariano Rivera	.50
65 Josh Beckett	.75
66 Erik Bedard	.25
67 Johan Santana	1.00
68 Joe Mauer	.50
69 Justin Morneau	.50
70 Torii Hunter	.50
71 Alex Gordon	.50
72 Jose Guillen	.25
73 Jim Thome	.75
74 Paul Konerko	.50
75 Josh Hamilton	1.00
76 Hanley Ramirez	1.00
77 Dontrelle Willis	.25
78 Dan Uggla	.50
79 Brandon Phillips	.50
80 Rick Ankiel	.50
81 Nick Markakis	.75
82 Ryan Zimmerman	.50
83 Brian Roberts	.25
84 Lastings Milledge	.25
85 Freddy Sanchez	.25
86 Barry Zito	.25
87 Matt Cain	.50
88 Andruw Jones	.25
89 Dan Haren	.50
90 Chien-Ming Wang	1.00
91 Jonathan Papelbon	.50
92 Felix Hernandez	.50
93 David Ortiz	1.00
94 Jason Bay	.50
95 Matt Holliday	.50
96 Troy Tulowitzki	.50
97 Hideki Matsui	.75
98 Jeff Francoeur	.25
99 Alfonso Soriano	.75
100 Curt Schilling	.50
101 Alex Romero/ Jsy Auto./799 (RC)	10.00
102 Matt Tolbert/ Jsy Auto./699 RC	10.00
103 Bobby Wilson/ Auto./699 RC	10.00
104 Brent Lillibridge/ Auto./599 (RC)	10.00
105 Brian Barton/ Auto./698 RC	10.00
106 Brian Bass/ Jsy Auto./799 (RC)	10.00
107 Brian Bixler/ Auto./698 (RC)	8.00
108 Brian Bocock/ Jsy Auto./799 RC	8.00
109 Burke Badenhop/ Auto./798 RC	8.00
110 Chin-Lung Hu/ Jsy Auto./999 (RC)	20.00
111 Chris Perez/ Auto./699 RC	10.00
112 Clay Buchholz/ Jsy Auto./999 (RC)	20.00
113 Clayton Kershaw/ Jsy Auto./699 RC	30.00
114 Colt Morton/ Auto./574 RC	8.00
115 Daric Barton/ Jsy Auto./999 (RC)	10.00
116 Darren O'Day/ Auto./798 RC	8.00
117 David Purcey/ Auto./599 (RC)	8.00
118 Denard Span/ Jsy Auto./299 (RC)	15.00
119 Elliot Johnson/ Auto./798 (RC)	8.00
120 Emmanuel Burriss/ Auto./799 RC	8.00
121 Evan Longoria/ Jsy Auto./499 RC	120.00
122 Evan Meek/ Jsy Auto./649 RC	10.00
123 Felipe Paulino/ Jsy Auto./799 (RC)	8.00
124 Carlos Gonzalez/ Jsy Auto./599 (RC)	25.00
125 German Duran/ Auto./699 RC	8.00
126 Greg Reynolds/ Auto./149 RC	8.00
127 Greg Smith/ Jsy Auto./799 RC	10.00
128 Harvey Garcia/ Auto./699 (RC)	15.00
129 Hernan Iribarren/ Jsy Auto./799 (RC)	10.00
130 Ian Kennedy/ Jsy Auto./699 RC	15.00
131 J.R. Towles/ Jsy Auto./499 RC	10.00
132 Jay Bruce/ Jsy Auto./549 (RC)	30.00
133 Jayson Nix/ Jsy Auto./299 (RC)	8.00
134 Jed Lowrie/ Auto./499 (RC)	20.00
135 Jeff Clement/ Auto./399 (RC)	10.00
136 Jonathan Herrera/ Auto./699 RC	8.00
137 Joey Votto/ Jsy Auto./999 (RC)	40.00
138 Johnny Cueto/ Auto./999 RC	20.00
139 Jonathan Albaladejo/ Jsy Auto./79 9 (RC)	10.00
140 Justin Masterson/ Auto./699 (RC)	20.00
141 Justin Ruggiano/ Auto./149 (RC)	8.00
142 Kevin Hart/ Jsy Auto./749 (RC)	8.00
143 Kosuke Fukudome/ Jsy/799 RC	15.00
144 Luis Mendoza/ Jsy Auto./299 (RC)	8.00
145 Luke Carlin/ Auto./699 RC	15.00
146 Luke Hochevar/ Auto./799 RC	12.00
147 Max Scherzer/ Jsy Auto./799 RC	30.00
148 Micah Hoffpauir/ Auto./699 RC	20.00
149 Mike Parisi/ Auto./699 RC	15.00
150 Nick Adenhart/ Auto./699 (RC)	15.00
151 Nick Blackburn/ Jsy Auto./799 RC	15.00
152 Nyjer Morgan/ Jsy Auto./999 (RC)	10.00
153 Ramon Troncoso/ Jsy Auto./399 RC	10.00
154 Randor Bierd/ Jsy Auto./799 RC	10.00
155 Rich Thompson/ Auto./399 RC	10.00
156 Rico Washington/ Jsy Auto./799 (RC)	8.00
157 Ross Ohlendorf/ Jsy Auto./999 RC	10.00
158 Steve Holm/ Jsy Auto./999 RC	8.00
159 Wesley Wright/ Jsy Auto./849 RC	10.00
160 Wladimir Balentien/ Auto./599 (RC)	10.00
161 Alex Hinshaw/ Auto./699 RC	15.00
162 Bobby Korecky/ Auto./999 RC	15.00
163 Bradley Harman/ Auto./999 RC	12.00
164 Brandon Boggs/ Auto./799 (RC)	10.00
165 Callix Crabbe/ Auto./325 (RC)	10.00
166 Clay Timpner/ Auto./849 (RC)	10.00
167 Clete Thomas/ Auto./849 RC	15.00
168 Cory Wade/ Auto./999 (RC)	8.00
169 Doug Mathis/ Auto./999 RC	8.00
170 Eider Torres/ Auto./699 (RC)	15.00
171 Gregorio Petit/ Auto./999 RC	15.00
172 Michael Aubrey/ Auto./699 RC	10.00
173 Jesse Carlson/ Auto./999 RC	8.00
174 Billy Buckner/ Auto./699 (RC)	10.00
175 Josh Newman/ Auto./699 RC	8.00
176 Matt Tupman/ Auto./999 RC	15.00
177 Matt Joyce/ Auto./999 RC	20.00
178 Paul Janish/ Auto./999 (RC)	15.00
179 Robinzon Diaz/ Auto./999 RC	10.00
180 Fernando Hernandez/ Auto./999 RC	10.00
181 Brandon Jones/ Auto./499 RC	10.00
182 Eddie Bonine/ Auto./899 (RC)	15.00
183 Chris Smith/ Auto./385 (RC)	10.00
184 Jonathan Van Every/ Auto./999 RC	10.00
185 Marino Salas/ Auto./999 RC	8.00
186 Mike Aviles/ Auto./699 (RC)	20.00
187 Mitch Boggs/ Auto./699 (RC)	15.00

188	Chris Carter/ Auto./699 (RC)	10.00
189	Travis Denker/ Auto./699 RC	8.00
190	Carlos Rosa/ Auto./699 RC	10.00
191	Evan Longoria/ Auto./350 (RC)	120.00

Gold

Gold (1-100): 5-10X
Gold RC Auto.: 1-2X
Gold RC Jsy Auto.: 1-2X
Production 50 Sets

Authentic Achievements

		NM/M
Common Player:		.50
Inserted 1:2		
1	Derek Jeter	4.00
2	Ken Griffey Jr.	3.00
3	Randy Johnson	1.50
4	Frank Thomas	1.00
5	Tom Glavine	1.00
6	Matt Holliday	1.00
7	Justin Verlander	1.00
8	Manny Ramirez	1.50
9	Scott Rolen	1.00
10	Brandon Webb	.75
11	Erik Bedard	.50
12	Daisuke Matsuzaka	2.50
13	Johan Santana	1.50
14	Carlos Lee	.75
15	Alfonso Soriano	1.00
16	Grady Sizemore	1.50
17	Jose Reyes	1.50
18	Chase Utley	2.00
19	Roy Oswalt	.75
20	David Ortiz	1.50
21	Jake Peavy	1.00
22	Hanley Ramirez	1.50
23	Alex Rodriguez	4.00
24	Ryan Howard	2.50
25	David Wright	3.00
26	Trevor Hoffman	.50
27	Prince Fielder	1.50
28	Ichiro Suzuki	2.50
29	Jimmy Rollins	1.00
30	Mariano Rivera	1.00
31	Pedro Martinez	.75
32	Torii Hunter	.75
33	Ivan Rodriguez	.75
34	Jim Thome	.75
35	Chipper Jones	2.00
36	John Smoltz	1.00
37	Jeff Kent	.50
38	Albert Pujols	4.00
39	Lance Berkman	1.00
40	Justin Morneau	1.00
41	Andruw Jones	.50
42	Adam Dunn	1.00
43	Greg Maddux	2.50
44	Billy Wagner	.50
45	Vladimir Guerrero	1.50
46	C.C. Sabathia	1.50
47	Mark Teixeira	1.00
48	Mark Buehrle	.50
49	Miguel Cabrera	1.50
50	Josh Beckett	1.50

By The Letter Autographs

RUSSELL MARTIN Catcher

		NM/M
Common Letter Auto.:		15.00
Varying numbering for each Letter		
AD	Adam Dunn/140	25.00
AG	Adrian Gonzalez/110	35.00
BH	Bill Hall/1570	15.00
BP	Brandon Phillips/1259	25.00
BW	Billy Wagner/125	40.00
CB	Chad Billingsley/1306	25.00
CJ	Chipper Jones/100	125.00
CL	Carlos Lee/160	40.00
CW	Chien-Ming Wang/80	80.00
DA	David Murphy/1837	25.00
DJ	Derek Jeter/240	150.00
DM	Daisuke Matsuzaka/125	120.00
EE	Edwin Encarnacion/1570	15.00
FC	Fausto Carmona/844	20.00
GA	Garrett Atkins/588	15.00
GJ	Geoff Jenkins/1200	15.00
GS	Grady Sizemore/240	40.00
JB	Joe Blanton/580	20.00
JE	Jeff Francoeur/275	20.00
JF	Jeff Francis/335	15.00
JG	Jeremy Guthrie/985	20.00
JL	James Loney/1275	20.00
JN	Joe Nathan/365	25.00
JO	John Lackey/187	25.00
JP	Jonathan Papelbon/550	30.00
JS	Jon Lester/235	100.00
KE	Kevin Youkilis/365	25.00
KG	Ken Griffey Jr./275	150.00
KJ	Kelly Johnson/1399	20.00
LB	Lance Berkman/165	50.00
ME	Mark Ellis/995	15.00
MG	Matt Garza/235	40.00
MK	Matt Kemp/1369	35.00
MM	Melvin Mora/490	20.00
NL	Noah Lowry/1440	15.00
NS	Nick Swisher/1150	20.00
PF	Prince Fielder/245	50.00
PH	Phil Hughes/385	40.00
PK	Paul Konerko/175	30.00
RH	Rich Hill/220	15.00
RM	Russell Martin/265	40.00
RO	Roy Halladay/160	100.00
SB	Scott Baker/1248	20.00
TG	Tom Gorzelanny/1082	20.00
TT	Troy Tulowitzki/252	50.00

Chirography Dual Signatures

		NM/M
Production 10-99		
GB	Chad Billingsley, Tom Gorzelanny/96	15.00
HK	Phil Hughes, Ian Kennedy/99	40.00
MK	Nick Markakis, Matt Kemp/99	25.00
PE	Brandon Phillips, Edwin Encarnacion/99	20.00

Chirography Quad Signatures

Production 5-15

Chirography Triple Signatures

Production 25-50

Marquee Matchups

MARQUEE MATCHUPS

		NM/M
Common Duo:		.50
Inserted 1:2		
1	Derek Jeter, Curt Schilling	4.00
2	Derek Jeter, Josh Beckett	4.00
3	Albert Pujols, Brad Lidge	4.00
4	Alex Rodriguez, Daisuke Matsuzaka	3.00
5	Ken Griffey Jr., John Smoltz	3.00
6	John Smoltz, David Wright	2.50
7	Gary Sheffield, Jonathan Papelbon	1.00
8	Roy Oswalt, Ryan Braun	2.00
9	Mariano Rivera, David Ortiz	1.50
10	Albert Pujols, Carlos Zambrano	4.00
11	Travis Hafner, Dontrelle Willis	.50
12	Victor Martinez, Felix Hernandez	1.00
13	Carlos Lee, Carlos Zambrano	.75
14	Manny Ramirez, Chien-Ming Wang	2.50
15	Justin Morneau, Felix Hernandez	1.00
16	Francisco Rodriguez, Ichiro Suzuki	2.50
17	Erik Bedard, Grady Sizemore	1.50
18	Vladimir Guerrero, Justin Verlander	1.50
19	Ichiro Suzuki, Daisuke Matsuzaka	3.00
20	Chris Carpenter, Alfonso Soriano	1.50
21	Pedro Martinez, Hanley Ramirez	1.50
22	Randy Johnson, Chase Utley	2.00
23	Ken Griffey Jr., Roy Oswalt	3.00
24	Ken Griffey Jr., Randy Johnson	3.00
25	Jimmy Rollins, Johan Santana	1.50
26	Andruw Jones, Matt Cain	.50
27	Pedro Martinez, Ryan Howard	2.50
39	David Wright, Cole Hamels	2.50
29	Chipper Jones, Johan Santana	2.00
30	Billy Wagner, Mark Teixeira	1.00
31	Magglio Ordonez, C.C. Sabathia	1.00
32	Tom Glavine, Jose Reyes	1.50
33	Derek Jeter, Jonathan Papelbon	4.00
34	Alex Rodriguez, Johan Santana	4.00
35	Alfonso Soriano, Jake Peavy	1.00
36	Ryan Howard, Johan Santana	2.50
37	Jake Peavy, Russell Martin	1.00
38	Carlos Zambrano, Prince Fielder	1.50
39	Carlos Beltran, Cole Hamels	1.50
40	Alex Rodriguez, Josh Beckett	3.00
41	Derek Jeter, Roy Halladay	4.00
42	Hideki Matsui, Daisuke Matsuzaka	2.50
43	Joe Mauer, C.C. Sabathia	1.00
44	Manny Ramirez, Francisco Rodriguez	1.50
45	Miguel Cabrera, Jered Weaver	1.50
46	David Wright, Jake Peavy	3.00
47	Greg Maddux, Ken Griffey Jr.	3.00
48	John Smoltz, Hanley Ramirez	1.50
49	Alex Rodriguez, Pedro Martinez	4.00
50	Trevor Hoffman, Matt Holliday	1.00

Presidential Predictors

		NM/M
Both are SP's		
15	Sarah Palin	100.00
16	Joseph Biden	125.00

Rookie Exclusives

		NM/M
Common Player:		2.00
Autographs:		No Pricing
AH	Alex Hinshaw	2.00
AR	Alex Romero	2.00
BA	Brian Barton	2.00
BB	Brandon Boggs	2.00
BH	Bradley Harman	2.00
BI	Brian Bixler	2.00
BK	Bobby Korecky	2.00
BO	Brian Bocock	2.00
BR	Brian Bass	2.00
BU	Burke Badenhop	2.00
BW	Bobby Wilson	2.00
CB	Clay Buchholz	2.00
CC	Callix Crabbe	2.00
CM	Colt Morton	3.00
CT	Clay Timpner	2.00
CU	Johnny Cueto	2.00
CW	Cory Wade	2.00
DB	Daric Barton	2.00
DM	Doug Mathis	2.00
DS	Denard Span	3.00
EB	Emmanuel Burriss	2.00
EJ	Elliot Johnson	2.00
EM	Evan Meek	2.00
ET	Eider Torres	2.00
FH	Fernando Hernandez	2.00
FP	Felipe Paulino	2.00
GD	German Duran	2.00
GP	Gregorio Petit	2.00
GS	Greg Smith	2.00
HI	Hernan Iribarren	2.00
IK	Ian Kennedy	3.00
JA	Jonathan Albaladejo	2.00
JB	Jay Bruce	5.00
JC	Jesse Carlson	3.00
JH	Jonathan Herrera	2.00
JL	Jed Lowrie	3.00
JN	Jayson Nix	2.00
JT	J.R. Towles	3.00
KH	Kevin Hart	2.00
LC	Luke Carlin	2.00
LM	Luis Mendoza	2.00
MA	Matt Tolbert	2.00
MH	Micah Hoffpauir	2.00
MJ	Matt Joyce	2.00
MP	Mike Parisi	2.00
MT	Matt Tupman	2.00
NA	Nick Adenhart	2.00
NB	Nick Blackburn	3.00
NE	Josh Newman	2.00
NM	Nyjer Morgan	2.00
RA	Alexei Ramirez	15.00
RB	Randor Bierd	2.00
RD	Robinzon Diaz	2.00
RI	Rich Thompson	2.00
RO	Ross Ohlendorf	2.00
RT	Ramon Troncoso	2.00
RW	Rico Washington	2.00
SH	Steve Holm	2.00
TH	Clete Thomas	2.00
WB	Wladimir Balentien	2.00
WW	Wesley Wright	2.00

Sign of the Times Dual Signatures

		NM/M
Production 10-99		
BB	Chad Billingsley, Clay Buchholz/99	40.00
GL	Yovani Gallardo, Tim Lincecum/99	50.00
NW	Billy Wagner, Joe Nathan/74	25.00
PW	Josh Willingham, Felix Pie/99	15.00

Sign of the Times Quad Signatures

No Pricing

Sign of the Times Triple Signatures

Production 10-50

USA 18U Jr. Team Jersey Autographs

		NM/M
Production 120 Sets		
Patch:		1.5-2X
Production 50 Sets		
AA	Andrew Aplin	20.00
AM	Austin Maddox	30.00
CC	Colton Cain	8.00
CG	Cameron Garfield	10.00
CT	Cecil Tanner	8.00
DN	David Nick	8.00
DT	Donavan Tate	20.00
FR	Nick Franklin	10.00
HM	Harold Martinez	20.00
JB	Jake Barrett	15.00
MA	Jeff Malm	10.00
ME	Jonathan Meyer	15.00
MP	Matt Purke	15.00
MS	Max Stassi	15.00
TU	Jacob Turner	15.00
WH	Wes Hatton	20.00

USA National Team By the Letter Auto.

		NM/M
Production 50-181		
AG	A.J. Griffin/105	15.00
BS	Blake Smith/105	15.00
CC	Christian Colon/105	20.00
CH	Chris Hernandez/180	25.00
DD	Derek Dietrich/105	25.00
KD	Kentrail Davis/103	40.00
KG	Kyle Gibson/181	20.00
KR	Kevin Rhoderick/171	15.00
KV	Kendal Volz/105	20.00
MD	Matt den Dekker/105	15.00
MG	Micah Gibbs/180	15.00
ML	Mike Leake/180	35.00
MM	Mike Minor/105	20.00
RJ	Ryan Jackson/104	15.00
SS	Stephen Strasburg/105	250.00
TL	Tyler Lyons/104	15.00

2008 SP Legendary Cuts

		NM/M
Common Player (1-100):		.25
Common SP (101-200):		4.00
Production 550		
Pack (4):		2.00
Box (12):		110.00
1	Ken Griffey Jr.	1.50
2	Derek Jeter	2.00
3	Albert Pujols	2.00
4	Ichiro Suzuki	1.50
5	Ryan Braun	.75
6	Manny Ramirez	.75
7	David Ortiz	.75
8	Greg Maddux	1.50
9	Roger Clemens	1.00
10	Chase Utley	.75
11	Vladimir Guerrero	.50
12	Johan Santana	.50
13	Chipper Jones	.75
14	Tom Glavine	.50
15	Ryan Howard	.75
16	Hunter Pence	.40
17	Prince Fielder	.40
18	Jeff Francoeur	.40
19	David Wright	.75
20	Carlos Beltran	.50
21	Carlos Lee	.40
22	Cole Hamels	.40
23	Jered Weaver	.40
24	B.J. Upton	.40
25	Akinori Iwamura	.40
26	Daisuke Matsuzaka	1.00
27	Curt Schilling	.50
28	Adam Dunn	.50
29	Jose Reyes	.75
30	Nomar Garciaparra	.40
31	Hideki Matsui	1.00
32	Matt Holliday	.50
33	Jason Bay	.40
34	Grady Sizemore	.75
35	Travis Hafner	.40
36	Victor Martinez	.40
37	C.C. Sabathia	.50
38	Justin Morneau	.40
39	Torii Hunter	.40
40	Joe Mauer	.40
41	Russell Martin	.40
42	Frank Thomas	.75
43	Miguel Tejada	.50
44	Brian Roberts	.40
45	Justin Verlander	.40
46	Gary Sheffield	.40
47	Magglio Ordonez	.40
48	Alex Rodriguez	2.00
49	Bobby Abreu	.40
50	Mark Teixeira	.50
51	Andruw Jones	.40
52	Derek Lee	.40
53	Aramis Ramirez	.40
54	Carlos Zambrano	.40
55	Alfonso Soriano	.50
56	Omar Vizquel	.25
57	Lance Berkman	.40
58	Roy Oswalt	.40
59	Jake Peavy	.40
60	Chris Young	.40
61	Khalil Greene	.25
62	Troy Tulowitzki	.50
63	Todd Helton	.50
64	Josh Beckett	.50
65	Miguel Cabrera	.75
66	Hanley Ramirez	.75
67	Dan Uggla	.40
68	Scott Kazmir	.40
69	Delmon Young	.25
70	Erik Bedard	.25
71	Alex Gordon	.40
72	Felix Hernandez	.50
73	Kenji Johjima	.25
74	John Lackey	.40
75	Ryan Zimmerman	.40
76	Jeremy Bonderman	.25
77	Chien-Ming Wang	.75
78	Jim Thome	.40
79	Jimmy Rollins	.75
80	Mariano Rivera	.50
81	Curtis Granderson	.40
82	Nick Markakis	.40
83	Trevor Hoffman	.25
84	Barry Zito	.25
85	Yovani Gallardo	.40
86	Dan Haren	.25
87	Vernon Wells	.40
88	Ian Kennedy RC	2.00
89	Phil Hughes	.40
90	Brian McCann	.40
91	J.J. Hardy	.25
92	Roy Halladay	.40
93	Mike Piazza	.75
94	Ivan Rodriguez	.40
95	Dontrelle Willis	.25
96	Brandon Webb	.40
97	Carl Crawford	.40
98	Tim Lincecum	.50
99	Jason Varitek	.40
100	Freddy Sanchez	.25
101	Abraham Lincoln	8.00
102	Ulysses S. Grant	5.00
103	Andrew Johnson	4.00
104	George Washington	8.00
105	Thomas Jefferson	6.00
106	Andrew Jackson	5.00
107	James Madison	4.00
108	James Monroe	4.00
109	Benjamin Franklin	8.00
110	Alexander Graham Bell	4.00
111	Thomas Edison	4.00
112	Red Baron	4.00
113	Robert E. Lee	6.00
114	Mark Twain	5.00
115	Arthur Conan Doyle	4.00
116	Bram Stoker	4.00
117	Jules Verne	4.00
118	Billy the Kid	4.00
119	Harriet Beecher Stowe	4.00
120	Andrew Carnegie	4.00
121	Lewis Carroll	4.00
122	Cornelius Vanderbilt	4.00
123	Brigham Young	4.00
124	Charles Dickens	4.00
125	Vincent Van Gogh	4.00
126	Claude Monet	4.00
127	Jesse James	4.00
128	John D. Rockefeller	4.00
129	Harry Longabaugh	4.00
130	John F. Kennedy	8.00
131	Richard Nixon	4.00
132	Lyndon B. Johnson	4.00
133	Dwight D. Eisenhower	5.00
134	Franklin D. Roosevelt	4.00
135	Harry S. Truman	5.00
136	Ronald Reagan	4.00
137	Bill Clinton	5.00
138	George H.W. Bush	5.00
139	Jimmy Carter	4.00
140	Gerald Ford	4.00
141	Herbert Hoover	4.00
142	Calvin Coolidge	4.00
143	Warren G. Harding	4.00
144	Woodrow Wilson	4.00
145	William Taft	4.00
146	Theodore Roosevelt	5.00
147	Phil Niekro	4.00
148	Brooks Robinson	4.00
149	Cal Ripken Jr.	10.00
150	Eddie Murray	5.00
151	Jim Palmer	4.00
152	Abner Doubleday	4.00
153	Wade Boggs	4.00
154	Carl Yastrzemski	6.00
155	Bobby Doerr	4.00
156	Carlton Fisk	4.00
157	Pee Wee Reese	4.00
158	Ernie Banks	6.00
159	Fergie Jenkins	4.00
160	Billy Williams	4.00
161	Ryne Sandberg	6.00
162	Luis Aparicio	4.00
163	Joe Morgan	4.00
164	Johnny Bench	6.00
165	Tony Perez	4.00
166	Bob Feller	4.00
167	Larry Doby	4.00
168	Bob Lemon	4.00
169	Al Kaline	5.00
170	Warren Spahn	4.00
171	Robin Yount	5.00
172	Rollie Fingers	4.00
173	Harmon Killebrew	5.00
174	Rod Carew	4.00
175	Babe Ruth	12.00
176	Monte Irvin	4.00
177	Tom Seaver	5.00
178	Phil Rizzuto	4.00
179	Jack Chesbro	4.00
180	"Catfish" Hunter	4.00
181	Babe Ruth	12.00
182	Reggie Jackson	5.00
183	Dennis Eckersley	4.00
184	Steve Carlton	4.00
185	Ed Delahanty	4.00
186	Mike Schmidt	6.00
187	Jim Bunning	4.00
188	Robin Roberts	4.00
189	Willie Stargell	5.00
190	Bill Mazeroski	4.00
191	Ralph Kiner	4.00
192	Tony Gwynn	5.00
193	Juan Marichal	4.00
194	Willie McCovey	4.00
195	Orlando Cepeda	4.00
196	Stan Musial	5.00
197	Ozzie Smith	6.00
198	Bob Gibson	5.00
199	Bruce Sutter	4.00
200	Nolan Ryan	8.00

Baseball Headlines Cut Signature

No Pricing

Classic Signatures

		NM/M
Production 25 Sets		
BD	Bucky Dent	15.00
BR	Brooks Robinson	50.00
BT	Bobby Thomson	30.00
BW	Billy Williams	20.00
CF	Carlton Fisk	25.00
DL	Don Larsen	50.00
EB	Ernie Banks	60.00
FL	Fred Lynn	20.00
JB	Johnny Bench	50.00
JC	Joe Carter	50.00
JP	Johnny Pesky	30.00
JP2	Jim Palmer	30.00
JR	Jim Rice	25.00
JR	Lou Brock	40.00
MS	Mike Schmidt	70.00
NR	Nolan Ryan	90.00
OS	Ozzie Smith	50.00
PM	Paul Molitor	35.00
RC	Rod Carew	25.00
RS2	Ron Santo	40.00
RY	Robin Yount	50.00
SC	Steve Carlton	40.00
TG	Tony Gwynn	50.00
TM	Tino Martinez	50.00
TP	Tony Perez	40.00

Destination Stardom Memorabilia

		NM/M
Common Player:		4.00
AG	Alex Gordon	8.00
AI	Akinori Iwamura	4.00
AM	Andrew Miller	4.00
AR	Alex Rios	4.00
BB	Billy Butler	4.00
BM	Brian McCann	6.00
BU	B.J. Upton	6.00
CB	Chad Billingsley	4.00
CD	Chris Duncan	4.00
CG	Curtis Granderson	6.00
CH	Cole Hamels	6.00
DH	Dan Haren	4.00
DM	Daisuke Matsuzaka	15.00
DU	Dan Uggla	6.00
DY	Delmon Young	4.00
FH	Felix Hernandez	6.00
FI	Josh Fields	4.00
GA	Garrett Atkins	4.00
GS	Grady Sizemore	8.00
HA	Corey Hart	4.00
HK	Howie Kendrick	4.00
HP	Hunter Pence	6.00
HR	Hanley Ramirez	8.00
JF	Jeff Francoeur	4.00
JH	J.J. Hardy	6.00
JL	James Loney	6.00
JM	John Maine	4.00
JO	Josh Hamilton	10.00
JP	Jonathan Papelbon	8.00

JV	Justin Verlander	6.00
JW	Jered Weaver	4.00
KG	Khalil Greene	4.00
LE	Jon Lester	8.00
MH	Matt Holliday	6.00
NM	Nick Markakis	6.00
PF	Prince Fielder	8.00
PH	Phil Hughes	8.00
RB	Ryan Braun	8.00
RG	Ryan Garko	4.00
RH	Rich Hill	4.00
RM	Russell Martin	6.00
RZ	Ryan Zimmerman	6.00
SD	Stephen Drew	6.00
TB	Travis Buck	4.00
TL	Tim Lincecum	15.00
TT	Troy Tulowitzki	4.00
YG	Yovani Gallardo	6.00

Destined for History Memorabilia
NM/M

Common Player:		4.00
AD	Adam Dunn	6.00
AJ	Andruw Jones	4.00
AP	Albert Pujols	15.00
AP	Andy Pettitte	6.00
AR	Alex Rodriguez	15.00
AS	Alfonso Soriano	6.00
BW	Brandon Webb	6.00
CB	Carlos Beltran	6.00
CD	Carlos Delgado	4.00
CJ	Chipper Jones	6.00
CL	Carlos Lee	6.00
CM	Chien-Ming Wang	10.00
CS	Curt Schilling	6.00
CZ	Carlos Zambrano	6.00
DJ	Derek Jeter	20.00
DL	Derrek Lee	6.00
DO	David Ortiz	6.00
DW	Dontrelle Willis	4.00
FT	Frank Thomas	8.00
GM	Greg Maddux	10.00
GS	Gary Sheffield	6.00
HA	Travis Hafner	4.00
IR	Ivan Rodriguez	6.00
JM	Justin Morneau	8.00
JR	Jimmy Rollins	6.00
JS	John Smoltz	8.00
JT	Jim Thome	8.00
MC	Miguel Cabrera	8.00
MO	Magglio Ordonez	4.00
MP	Mike Piazza	10.00
MR	Manny Ramirez	8.00
MT	Mark Teixeira	6.00
MY	Michael Young	4.00
OV	Omar Vizquel	4.00
PM	Pedro Martinez	6.00
RA	Aramis Ramirez	6.00
RC	Roger Clemens	10.00
RE	Jose Reyes	8.00
RH	Roy Halladay	4.00
RJ	Randy Johnson	8.00
RO	Roy Oswalt	4.00
SA	Johan Santana	6.00
SS	Sammy Sosa	6.00
TE	Miguel Tejada	6.00
TG	Tom Glavine	6.00
TH	Todd Helton	6.00
TH	Trevor Hoffman	4.00
VG	Vladimir Guerrero	4.00

Fall Classic Cut Signatures
NM/M
Production 7-15

CH	"Catfish" Hunter/15	60.00
SC	Stan Coveleski/15	60.00

Future Legends Signatures
NM/M
Production 99 Sets

BM	Brian McCann	20.00
BU	B.J. Upton	20.00
BW	Brandon Wood	10.00
CB	Clay Buchholz	25.00
CD	Chris Duncan	15.00
CH	Chin-Lung Hu	25.00
CH	Cole Hamels	30.00
CH	Corey Hart	15.00
DB	Daric Barton	10.00
DU	Dan Uggla	15.00
FC	Fausto Carmona	15.00
FH	Felix Hernandez	30.00
GA	Garrett Atkins	15.00
HK	Hong-Chih Kuo	35.00
HR	Hanley Ramirez	25.00
IK	Ian Kennedy	20.00
IK2	Ian Kinsler	15.00
JF	Jeff Francis	10.00
JH	Josh Hamilton	50.00
JL	Jon Lester	25.00
JM	John Maine	15.00
JP	Jonathan Papelbon	20.00
KG	Ken Griffey Jr.	90.00
KY	Kevin Youkilis	20.00
LH	Luke Hochevar	15.00
MC	Matt Cain	15.00
MG	Matt Garza	15.00
NM	Nick Markakis	20.00
PH	Phil Hughes	20.00
RH	Rich Hill	10.00
TH	Travis Hafner	10.00
YG	Yovani Gallardo	15.00

Generations Dual Autographs
NM/M
Production 75 Sets

CH	Steve Carlton, Cole Hamels	60.00
GG	Tony Gwynn, Tony Gwynn Jr.	50.00
GM	Ken Griffey Jr., Stan Musial	220.00
MB	Willie McCovey, Lance Berkman	60.00
PC	Gaylord Perry, Fausto Carmona	30.00
PK	Jim Palmer, Ian Kennedy	40.00
RC	Brooks Robinson, Eric Chavez	40.00

Generations Dual Memorabilia
NM/M

Common Duo:		10.00
AR	Luis Aparicio, Hanley Ramirez	10.00
BC	Lou Brock, Carl Crawford	15.00
BL	Ernie Banks, Derrek Lee	25.00
BM	Johnny Bench, Victor Martinez	10.00
BM	Johnny Bench, Joe Mauer	10.00
BP	Lance Berkman, Hunter Pence	10.00
BY	Wade Boggs, Kevin Youkilis	15.00
CD	Cal Ripken Jr., Derek Jeter	30.00
CG	Roberto Clemente, Vladimir Guerrero	30.00
CH	Roger Clemens, Phil Hughes	15.00
CK	Rod Carew, Howie Kendrick	15.00
CM	Will Clark, Justin Morneau	10.00
CP	Orlando Cepeda, Albert Pujols	20.00
CS	Steve Carlton, Johan Santana	10.00
DC	Don Sutton, Chad Billingsley	10.00
DD	Don Mattingly, Derek Jeter	25.00
DJ	Joe DiMaggio, Derek Jeter	80.00
DP	Bill Dickey, Jorge Posada	20.00
DS	Andre Dawson, Alfonso Soriano	20.00
DT	Don Mattingly, Todd Helton	15.00
EA	Enos Slaughter, Albert Pujols	25.00
EC	Eddie Murray, Chipper Jones	20.00
FF	Frank Robinson, Frank Thomas	15.00
FP	Carlton Fisk, Mike Piazza	10.00
FS	Rollie Fingers, Huston Street	10.00
FV	Carlton Fisk, Jason Varitek	15.00
GC	Bob Gibson, Chris Carpenter	15.00
GF	Tony Gwynn, Prince Fielder	15.00
GG	Gaylord Perry, Greg Maddux	15.00
GH	Ken Griffey Jr., Josh Hamilton	20.00
GL	Tom Glavine, Jon Lester	10.00
GP	"Goose" Gossage, Jonathan Papelbon	15.00
GR	Rich "Goose" Gossage, Mariano Rivera	15.00
HH	"Catfish" Hunter, Phil Hughes	15.00
HU	Rogers Hornsby, Chase Utley	30.00
JD	Jim Rice, David Ortiz	15.00
JG	Frank Robinson, Ken Griffey Jr.	20.00
JG	Reggie Jackson, Ken Griffey Jr.	20.00
JH	Reggie Jackson, Travis Hafner	10.00
KB	Ralph Kiner, Jason Bay	15.00
KD	Ted Kluszewski, Adam Dunn	15.00
KH	Harmon Killebrew, Travis Hafner	15.00
KK	Ken Griffey Jr., Ken Griffey Sr.	15.00
KT	Harmon Killebrew, Frank Thomas	15.00
LM	Fred Lynn, Nick Markakis	10.00
MA	Mike Schmidt, Albert Pujols	20.00
MB	Paul Molitor, Ryan Braun	20.00
MG	Stan Musial, Ken Griffey Jr.	25.00
MJ	Roger Maris, Derek Jeter	35.00
MM	Juan Marichal, Pedro Martinez	15.00
MS	Bill Mazeroski, Ryne Sandberg	20.00
NW	Phil Niekro, Tim Wakefield	10.00
OJ	Ozzie Smith, Jose Reyes	15.00
PB	Jim Palmer, Erik Bedard	10.00
PH	Gaylord Perry, Roy Halladay	10.00
PL	Gaylord Perry, Tim Lincecum	15.00
PM	Mike Piazza, Russell Martin	15.00
PO	Dave Parker, David Ortiz	10.00
PY	Gaylord Perry, Chris Young	10.00
RC	Nolan Ryan, Roger Clemens	20.00
RD	Ryne Sandberg, Dan Uggla	15.00
RJ	Phil Rizzuto, Derek Jeter	25.00
RM	Cal Ripken Jr., Nick Markakis	20.00
RO	Nolan Ryan, Roy Oswalt	20.00
RR	Randy Johnson, Rich Hill	10.00
RT	Cal Ripken Jr., Troy Tulowitzki	20.00
RV	Nolan Ryan, Justin Verlander	15.00
RW	Nolan Ryan, Jered Weaver	15.00
SA	Stan Musial, Albert Pujols	25.00
SB	Mike Schmidt, Ryan Braun	20.00
SC	Steve Carlton, Cole Hamels	10.00
SG	Ben Sheets, Yovani Gallardo	10.00
SJ	Mike Schmidt, Chipper Jones	20.00
SL	John Smoltz, Tim Lincecum	15.00
SM	Tom Seaver, John Maine	10.00
SP	Tom Seaver, Jake Peavy	10.00
SR	Ron Santo, Aramis Ramirez	15.00
SU	Ryne Sandberg, Chase Utley	15.00
SY	Gary Sheffield, Delmon Young	10.00
SZ	Mike Schmidt, Ryan Zimmerman	15.00
TM	Todd Helton, Matt Holliday	15.00
TR	Cal Ripken Jr., Miguel Tejada	15.00
YH	Robin Yount, J.J. Hardy	15.00
YJ	Robin Yount, Derek Jeter	20.00
YO	Carl Yastrzemski, David Ortiz	20.00

Headliners and Heroes Cut Signatures
NM/M
Production 4-122

AB	Al Barlick/32	60.00
AL	Al Lopez/45	50.00
BH	Babe Herman/44	50.00
BH	Billy Herman/76	50.00
BL	Bob Lemon/39	50.00
BL	Buck Leonard/58	50.00
BT	Bill Terry/94	70.00
CG	Charlie Gehringer/40	70.00
EL	Ed Lopat/46	70.00
ER	Edd Roush/122	60.00
ES	Enos Slaughter/36	60.00
EW	Eugene Woodling/72	50.00
GK	George Kelly/77	75.00
HC	Happy Chandler/75	60.00
HH	Harry Hooper/34	350.00
JB	James "Cool Papa" Bell/23	225.00
JH	Jesse Haines/37	125.00
JJ	Judy Johnson/38	70.00
JM	Johnny Mize/47	70.00
JM	Johnny Mize/50	70.00
JS	Joe Sewell/50	50.00
JS	Joe Sewell/47	50.00
JS	Johnny Sain/59	70.00
LA	Luke Appling/45	50.00
MC	Max Carey/31	85.00
PR	Pee Wee Reese/52	100.00
RC	Roy Campanella/37	450.00
TL	Ted Lyons/34	65.00

Legendary Cut Signatures
NM/M
Production 2-108

AB	Al Barlick/52	60.00
BH	Babe Herman/30	60.00
BH	Billy Herman/79	50.00
BL	Bob Lemon/40	50.00
BL	Buck Leonard/62	50.00
CG	Charlie Gehringer/45	60.00
CH	Carl Hubbell/31	75.00
CK	Charlie Keller/34	60.00
EA	Earl Averill/44	60.00
ES	Enos Slaughter/30	60.00
HC	Happy Chandler/55	60.00
HN	Hal Newhouser/52	75.00
HW	Hoyt Wilhelm/32	60.00
JC	Jocko Conlan/40	60.00
JH	Jesse Haines/40	125.00
JJ	Judy Johnson/29	70.00
JM	Johnny Mize/41	70.00
JS	Joe Sewell/46	50.00
LB	Lou Boudreau/54	50.00
LB	Lou Boudreau/50	50.00
LW	Lloyd Waner/60	150.00
RC	Roy Campanella/26	450.00
RF	Rick Ferrell/108	60.00
RM	Rube Marquard/40	60.00
SC	Stan Coveleski/45	50.00
TL	Ted Lyons/32	70.00
WH	Waite Hoyt/18	65.00
WS	Warren Spahn/39	80.00

Legendary Cut Signatures Dual
No Pricing

Legendary Memorabilia
NM/M

Common Player:		5.00
Production 99 Sets		
Parallel 75:		1X
Production 75 Sets		
Parallel 50:		1X
Production 50 Sets		
Parallel 35:		1-1.5X
Production 35 Sets		
Parallel 25:		1-2X
Production 25 Sets		
Parallel 15:		No Pricing
Production 15 Sets		
Parallel 10:		No Pricing
Production 10 Sets		
AD	Andre Dawson	6.00
BF	Bob Feller	10.00
BL	Bob Lemon	5.00
BM	Bill Mazeroski	10.00
BR	Brooks Robinson	5.00
BS	Bruce Sutter	5.00
BW	Billy Williams	6.00
CA	Rod Carew	6.00
CF2	Carlton Fisk	6.00
CR	Cal Ripken Jr.	15.00
CY	Carl Yastrzemski	10.00
DM	Don Mattingly	7.00
DP	Dave Parker	5.00
DP2	Dave Parker	5.00
DS	Don Sutton	5.00
DW	Dave Winfield	6.00
EB	Ernie Banks	10.00
EH	Elston Howard	8.00
EW	Early Wynn	6.00
FJ	Fergie Jenkins	6.00
FL	Fred Lynn	6.00
FR	Frank Robinson	8.00
GG	"Goose" Gossage	5.00
GP	Gaylord Perry	5.00
HK	Harmon Killebrew	10.00
JB	Johnny Bench	10.00
JB	Jim Bunning	5.00
JC	Joe Carter	5.00
JM	Juan Marichal	6.00
JM	Joe Morgan	6.00
JT	Joe Torre	6.00
LA	Luis Aparicio	5.00
MA	Edgar Martinez	5.00
MG	Mark Grace	6.00
MS	Mike Schmidt	10.00
NR	Nolan Ryan	15.00
OC	Orlando Cepeda	5.00
OS	Ozzie Smith	8.00
OS2	Ozzie Smith	8.00
PM	Paul Molitor	5.00
PN	Phil Niekro	5.00
PO	Paul O'Neill	5.00
RC	Roberto Clemente	35.00
RF	Rollie Fingers	5.00
RG	Ron Guidry	15.00
RI	Jim Rice	5.00
RM	Roger Maris	25.00
RS	Red Schoendienst	5.00
RY	Robin Yount	10.00
SA	Ron Santo	10.00
SM	Stan Musial	15.00
ST	Steve Carlton	5.00
TG	Tony Gwynn	10.00
TP	Tony Perez	6.00
TR	Tim Raines	5.00
TS	Tom Seaver	8.00
WB	Wade Boggs	6.00
WC	Will Clark	6.00
WF	Whitey Ford	10.00

Midsummer Classic Cut Signatures
NM/M
Production 14-16

BD	Bill Dickey/15	150.00
EL	Ernie Lombardi/14	160.00
LD	Larry Doby/14	125.00

Mystery Cut Signatures
No Pricing

2008 SPX

NM/M

Common Player (1-100):		.25
Common RC Auto. (101-151):		10.00
Pack (3):		18.00
Box (10):		160.00
1	Brandon Webb	.50
2	Chris B. Young	.50
3	Eric Byrnes	.25
4	Dan Haren	.50
5	Mark Teixeira	.75
6	Chipper Jones	1.50
7	John Smoltz	.50
8	Erik Bedard	.50
9	Nick Markakis	.50
10	Brian Roberts	.50
11	David Ortiz	1.00
12	Curt Schilling	.50
13	Manny Ramirez	.50
14	Daisuke Matsuzaka	1.00
15	Josh Beckett	.75
16	Derek Lee	.75
17	Alfonso Soriano	1.00
18	Carlos Zambrano	.50
19	Aramis Ramirez	.50
20	Jermaine Dye	.50
21	Jim Thome	.50
22	Nick Swisher	.50
23	Ken Griffey Jr.	2.00
24	Adam Dunn	.50
25	Brandon Phillips	.50
26	Grady Sizemore	.75
27	Victor Martinez	.50
28	C.C. Sabathia	.50
29	Travis Hafner	.50
30	Matt Holliday	.50
31	Todd Helton	.75
32	Troy Tulowitzki	.50
33	Magglio Ordonez	.50
34	Gary Sheffield	.50
35	Justin Verlander	.50
36	Curtis Granderson	.50
37	Miguel Cabrera	.75
38	Hanley Ramirez	1.00
39	Dan Uggla	.50
40	Miguel Tejada	.50
41	Lance Berkman	.50
42	Hunter Pence	.50
43	Carlos Lee	.50
44	Alex Gordon	.50
45	David DeJesus	.25
46	Vladimir Guerrero	1.00
47	Jered Weaver	.25
48	Torii Hunter	.50
49	Andruw Jones	.25
50	Rafael Furcal	.50
51	Russell Martin	.50
52	Brad Penny	.25
53	Ryan Braun	.75
54	Prince Fielder	1.00
55	J.J. Hardy	.50
56	Justin Morneau	.50
57	Johan Santana	.75
58	Joe Mauer	.75
59	Delmon Young	.50
60	Jose Reyes	.75
61	David Wright	1.00
62	Carlos Beltran	.75
63	Pedro Martinez	.75
64	Chien-Ming Wang	.75
65	Alex Rodriguez	3.00
66	Derek Jeter	3.00
67	Robinson Cano	.50
68	Hideki Matsui	1.00
69	Joe Blanton	.25
70	Jack Cust	.25
71	Cole Hamels	.50
72	Jimmy Rollins	.75
73	Ryan Howard	1.00
74	Chase Utley	1.00
75	Jason Bay	.50
76	Freddy Sanchez	.25
77	Jake Peavy	.50
78	Greg Maddux	2.00
79	Adrian Gonzalez	.50
80	Barry Zito	.25
81	Omar Vizquel	.25
82	Tim Lincecum	.50
83	Ichiro Suzuki	2.00
84	Felix Hernandez	.50
85	Kenji Johjima	.25
86	Albert Pujols	3.00
87	Scott Rolen	.50
88	Chris Carpenter	.50
89	Rick Ankiel	.50
90	Scott Kazmir	.50
91	Carl Crawford	.50
92	B.J. Upton	.50
93	Michael Young	.25
94	Josh Hamilton	.50
95	Hank Blalock	.50
96	Roy Halladay	.50
97	Vernon Wells	.50
98	Alex Rios	.50
99	Ryan Zimmerman	.50
100	Dmitri Young	.25
101	Bill Murphy/Auto. (RC)	10.00
102	Emilio Bonifacio/ Auto. RC	10.00
103	Brandon Jones/ Auto. RC	15.00
104	Clint Sammons/ Auto. (RC)	10.00
105	Clay Buchholz/ Auto. (RC)	25.00
106	Kevin Hart/Auto. (RC)	10.00
107	Donny Lucy/Auto. (RC)	10.00
108	Lance Broadway/ Auto. RC	10.00
109	Joey Votto/Auto. (RC)	40.00
110	Ryan Hanigan/Auto. RC	10.00
111	Joe Koshansky/ Auto. (RC)	10.00
112	Josh Newman/Auto. RC	10.00
113	Seth Smith/Auto. (RC)	15.00
114	Chris Seddon/ Auto. (RC)	10.00
115	Harvey Garcia/ Auto. (RC)	10.00
116	Felipe Paulino/Auto. RC	10.00
117	J.R. Towles/Auto. RC	10.00
118	Josh Anderson/ Auto. (RC)	10.00
119	Troy Patton/Auto. (RC)	10.00
120	Billy Buckner/ Auto. (RC)	10.00
121	Luke Hochevar/ Auto. RC	15.00
122	Chin-Lung Hu/ Auto. (RC)	15.00
123	Jonathan Meloan/ Auto. (RC)	10.00
124	Jose Morales/ Auto. (RC)	10.00
126	Alberto Gonzalez/ Auto. (RC)	10.00
127	Bronson Sardinha/ Auto. (RC)	10.00
128	Ian Kennedy/Auto. RC	15.00
129	Ross Ohlendorf/ Auto. (RC)	10.00
130	Daric Barton/Auto. (RC)	15.00
131	Jerry Blevins/Auto. RC	10.00
132	David Davidson/ Auto. RC	10.00
133	Nyjer Morgan/ Auto. (RC)	10.00
134	Steve Pearce/Auto. RC	15.00
135	Colt Morton/Auto. RC	10.00
136	Eugenio Velez/Auto. RC	10.00
138	Rob Johnson/ Auto. (RC)	10.00
139	Wladimir Balentien/ Auto. (RC)	15.00
140	Justin Ruggiano/ Auto. (RC)	10.00
141	Bill White/Auto. RC	10.00
142	Luis Mendoza/ Auto. (RC)	10.00
143	Jonathan Albaladejo/ Auto. (RC)	10.00
145	Ross Detwiler/Auto. RC	10.00
146	Jay Bruce/Auto. RC	50.00
147	Carlos Gonzalez/ Auto. RC	40.00
148	Evan Longoria/ Auto. RC	100.00
151	Clayton Kershaw/ Auto. RC	30.00
152	Alexei Ramirez/ Auto. RC	25.00

Babe Ruth American Legend
Production One Set

Ken Griffey Jr. American Hero
NM/M

Common Griffey (1-100):	5.00
Production 725 Sets	
Boxscore:	No Pricing
Production One Set	

Ken Griffey Jr. American Hero - Memorabilia
NM/M

Common Griffey (1-100):	20.00
Production 25 Sets	
Auto.:	No Pricing
Production Three Sets	

Superstar Signatures
NM/M

Common Player:		15.00
BW	Brandon Webb	20.00
DJ	Derek Jeter	100.00
DM	Daisuke Matsuzaka	80.00
DU	Dan Uggla	20.00
HR	Hanley Ramirez	25.00
KG	Ken Griffey Jr.	80.00
MH	Matt Holliday	25.00
MT	Mark Teixeira	25.00
PF	Prince Fielder	30.00
SR	Scott Rolen	15.00
TG	Tom Glavine	30.00
TH	Travis Hafner	15.00
VG	Vladimir Guerrero	30.00
VM	Victor Martinez	15.00

Winning Materials
NM/M

Common Player:	5.00
Production 150 Sets	
Parallels:	1X
Production 75, 99 or 125	
Jersey #:	1.5X
Production 35 Sets	
Position:	No Pricing
Production 20 Sets	
Team Letters:	1.5-2X
Production 25 Sets	
Patch 50:	2X
Production 50 Sets	
Patch 25:	No Pricing
Production 25 Sets	
Patch 99:	1.5-2X
Production 99 Sets	
Patch 15:	No Pricing
Production 15 Sets	

AB	A.J. Burnett	5.00
AE	Andre Ethier	5.00
AG	Adrian Gonzalez	8.00
AH	Aaron Harang	5.00
AJ	Andruw Jones	5.00
AK	Austin Kearns	5.00
AL	Adam LaRoche	5.00
AP	Albert Pujols	15.00
AR	Aaron Rowand	5.00
AS	Alfonso Soriano	10.00
AT	Garrett Atkins	8.00
BA	Bobby Abreu	5.00
BC	Bartolo Colon	5.00
BE	Adrian Beltre	5.00
BG	Brian Giles	5.00
BM	Brian McCann	10.00
BS	Ben Sheets	5.00
BU	B.J. Upton	8.00
BW	Billy Wagner	5.00
CA	Chris Carpenter	5.00
CB	Carlos Beltran	5.00
CC	Chad Cordero	5.00
CD	Carlos Delgado	5.00
CG	Carlos Guillen	5.00
CH	Chris Burke	5.00
CJ	Chipper Jones	10.00
CK	Casey Kotchman	5.00
CL	Carlos Lee	5.00
CS	Curt Schilling	8.00
CU	Chase Utley	10.00
CZ	Carlos Zambrano	8.00
DH	Dan Haren	5.00
DJ	Derek Jeter	20.00
DL	Derrek Lee	8.00
DO	David Ortiz	10.00
DU	Dan Uggla	5.00
DW	Dontrelle Willis	5.00
DY	Jermaine Dye	5.00
EC	Eric Chavez	5.00
FH	Felix Hernandez	8.00
FL	Francisco Liriano	5.00
GA	Garret Anderson	5.00
GJ	Geoff Jenkins	5.00
GM	Greg Maddux	10.00
GO	Alex Gordon	8.00
GR	Curtis Granderson	8.00
GS	Grady Sizemore	8.00
HA	Cole Hamels	5.00
HB	Hank Blalock	5.00
HE	Todd Helton	5.00
HO	Trevor Hoffman	5.00
HR	Hanley Ramirez	8.00
HU	Torii Hunter	5.00
IR	Ivan Rodriguez	5.00
J.	J.J. Hardy	5.00
JA	Conor Jackson	5.00
JB	Josh Barfield	5.00
JD	J.D. Drew	5.00
JE	Jim Edmonds	5.00
JF	Jeff Francoeur	5.00
JG	Jason Giambi	5.00
JH	Jhonny Peralta	5.00
JK	Jeff Kent	5.00
JM	Joe Mauer	5.00
JN	Joe Nathan	5.00
JO	Josh Beckett	8.00
JP	Jake Peavy	5.00
JR	Jose Reyes	8.00
JS	Johan Santana	8.00
JT	Jim Thome	5.00
JV	Jason Varitek	8.00
KG	Ken Griffey Jr.	10.00
KJ	Kenji Johjima	5.00
KY	Kevin Youkilis	5.00
LB	Lance Berkman	8.00
LG	Luis Gonzalez	5.00
MC	Miguel Cabrera	8.00
MH	Matt Holliday	8.00
MO	Justin Morneau	8.00
MR	Manny Ramirez	8.00
MT	Mark Teixeira	5.00
MY	Michael Young	5.00
OR	Magglio Ordonez	5.00
PA	Jonathan Papelbon	8.00
PE	Andy Pettitte	5.00
PF	Prince Fielder	10.00
PM	Pedro Martinez	8.00
PO	Jorge Posada	5.00
RA	Aramis Ramirez	8.00
RF	Rafael Furcal	5.00
RH	Roy Halladay	5.00
RJ	Randy Johnson	8.00
RO	Roy Oswalt	5.00
SM	John Smoltz	8.00
TE	Miguel Tejada	5.00
TH	Tim Hudson	5.00
TR	Travis Hafner	5.00
VE	Justin Verlander	8.00
VG	Vladimir Guerrero	8.00
VW	Vernon Wells	5.00

Winning Materials - Team Letters
No Pricing
Production 15 Sets

Winning Materials - Autograph
Production 20 sets unless noted.

Winning Materials Auto
No Pricing
Production Five Sets

Winning Trios
NM/M
Production 75 Sets
Parallel: 1.5X
Production 25 Sets

Patch:		2X
Production 25 Sets		
AGK	Garret Anderson, Vladimir Guerrero, Casey Kotchman	10.00
BHJ	Adrian Beltre, Felix Hernandez, Kenji Johjima	15.00
BSS	Josh Beckett, Johan Santana, C.C. Sabathia	15.00
CRP	Chris Carpenter, Scott Rolen, Albert Pujols	25.00
CRU	Miguel Cabrera, Hanley Ramirez, Dan Uggla	15.00
DBR	Carlos Delgado, Carlos Beltran, Jose Reyes	15.00
DOP	Carlos Delgado, David Ortiz, Albert Pujols	20.00
GHL	Yovani Gallardo, Phil Hughes, Tim Lincecum	15.00
GIB	Alex Gordon, Akinori Iwamura, Ryan Braun	15.00
GJP	Ken Griffey Jr., Derek Jeter, Albert Pujols	35.00
GMW	Tom Glavine, Pedro Martinez, Billy Wagner	20.00
HAH	Todd Helton, Garrett Atkins, Matt Holliday	15.00
HDF	Travis Hafner, Adam Dunn, Prince Fielder	10.00
HFB	J.J. Hardy, Prince Fielder, Ryan Braun	25.00
HRR	J.J. Hardy, Jose Reyes, Hanley Ramirez	15.00
HSS	Travis Hafner, Grady Sizemore, C.C. Sabathia	10.00
JBH	Andruw Jones, Carlos Beltran, Torii Hunter	15.00
JRR	Chipper Jones, Scott Rolen, Aramis Ramirez	20.00
JST	Chipper Jones, John Smoltz, Mark Teixeira	15.00
KFE	Jeff Kent, Rafael Furcal, Andre Ethier	10.00
KUY	Scott Kazmir, B.J. Upton, Delmon Young	15.00
LBO	Carlos Lee, Lance Berkman, Roy Oswalt	10.00
LCL	Noah Lowry, Matt Cain, Tim Lincecum	15.00
LSZ	Derrek Lee, Alfonso Soriano, Carlos Zambrano	20.00
MGS	Greg Maddux, Tom Glavine, John Smoltz	20.00
MHP	Greg Maddux, Trevor Hoffman, Jake Peavy	20.00
MPB	Victor Martinez, Jhonny Peralta, Josh Barfield	10.00
MSM	Justin Morneau, Johan Santana, Joe Mauer	15.00
OGV	Magglio Ordonez, Curtis Granderson, Justin Verlander	15.00
PJP	Andy Pettitte, Derek Jeter, Jorge Posada	30.00
RJC	Alex Rodriguez, Derek Jeter, Robinson Cano	40.00
RMM	Ivan Rodriguez, Victor Martinez, Joe Mauer	10.00
SBP	Curt Schilling, Josh Beckett, Jonathan Papelbon	20.00
SOH	Ben Sheets, Roy Oswalt, Aaron Harang	10.00
SRG	Gary Sheffield, Ivan Rodriguez, Carlos Guillen	10.00
TDB	Jim Thome, Jermaine Dye, Mark Buehrle	10.00
UHR	Chase Utley, Cole Hamels, Aaron Rowand	15.00
UKU	Chase Utley, Ian Kinsler, Dan Uggla	15.00
VOY	Jason Varitek, David Ortiz, Kevin Youkilis	20.00
WHB	Vernon Wells, Roy Halladay, A.J. Burnett	15.00
ZPH	Carlos Zambrano, Jake Peavy, Aaron Harang	15.00

Young Star Signatures
NM/M

	Common Auto.:	10.00
AC	Alexi Casilla	10.00
AE	Andre Ethier	20.00
BB	Brian Bannister	10.00
BM	Brian McCann	20.00
BU	Brian Burres	10.00
CD	Chris Duncan	15.00
CH	Cole Hamels	20.00
CY	Chris B. Young	15.00
FC	Fausto Carmona	15.00
FL	Francisco Liriano	10.00
IK	Ian Kinsler	20.00
JA	Joaquin Arias	10.00
JD	Josh Danks	15.00
JL	James Loney	20.00
JS	Jarrod Saltalamacchia	10.00
JW	Josh Willingham	10.00

JZ	Joel Zumaya	15.00
KK	Kevin Kouzmanoff	10.00
MA	Nick Markakis	15.00
MC	Matt Chico	8.00
MF	Mike Fontenot	15.00
MO	Micah Owings	10.00
MR	Mark Reynolds	15.00
NM	Nate McLouth	15.00
PH	Phil Hughes	30.00
RB	Ryan Braun	40.00
RG	Ryan Garko	10.00
RM	Russell Martin	10.00
SD	Stephen Drew	15.00
SH	James Shields	10.00
TB	Travis Buck	10.00
TG	Tom Gorzelanny	8.00
TT	Troy Tulowitzki	15.00

Joe DiMaggio's Career Highlights

NM/M
Common DiMaggio: 5.00
Production 425 Sets
1-100 Joe DiMaggio 5.00

Winning Materials

NM/M

Common Player:		6.00
Patch:		1.5X
Production 99 Sets		
AS	Alfonso Soriano	6.00
CJ	Chipper Jones	10.00
CW	Chien-Ming Wang	12.00
DJ	Derek Jeter	15.00
DM	Daisuke Matsuzaka	12.00
JB	Josh Beckett	8.00
JM	Justin Morneau	6.00
JP	Jake Peavy	6.00
JR	Jose Reyes	8.00
LB	Lance Berkman	6.00
MC	Miguel Cabrera	8.00
MH	Matt Holliday	6.00
MR	Mariano Rivera	10.00
MT	Mark Teixeira	6.00
PF	Prince Fielder	10.00
RA	Manny Ramirez	8.00
RB	Ryan Braun	10.00
RL	Ryan Ludwick	10.00
SK	Scott Kazmir	8.00
TL	Tim Lincecum	15.00

Winning Materials Dual

NM/M

Common Player:		6.00
BH	Roy Halladay, A.J. Burnett	6.00
GE	Ken Griffey Jr., Jim Edmonds	15.00
GR	Khalil Greene, Jose Reyes	15.00
GS	Jason Giambi, Richie Sexson	6.00
HB	Matt Holliday, Jeff Baker	8.00
JD	Derek Jeter, Joe DiMaggio	75.00
JY	Randy Johnson, Chris B. Young	10.00
KT	Jim Thome, Paul Konerko	8.00
LL	Adam LaRoche, Andy LaRoche	10.00
ML	Daisuke Matsuzaka, Tim Lincecum	15.00
PS	Jake Peavy, C.C. Sabathia	10.00
RB	Manny Ramirez, Jason Bay	10.00
RO	Manny Ramirez, David Ortiz	15.00
RP	Mariano Rivera, Jonathan Papelbon	10.00

2009 SP Authentic

		NM/M
Common Player (1-128):		.25
Common RC (129-170):		1.50
Common SP (171-200):		1.00
Common (201-225):		2.00
Production 495		
Common Auto. (226-250):		10.00
Production 100-500		
Pack (4):		5.00
Box (24):		110.00
1	Kosuke Fukudome	.50
2	Derek Jeter	2.00
3	Evan Longoria	1.00
4	Yadier Molina	.25
5	Albert Pujols	2.00
6	Ryan Howard	1.00
7	Joe Mauer	1.00
8	Ryan Braun	1.00
9	Hunter Pence	.50
10	Gary Sheffield	.50
11	Ryan Zimmerman	.50
12	Alfonso Soriano	.50
13	Alex Rodriguez	1.50
14	Paul Konerko	.25
15	Dustin Pedroia	1.00
16	Brian McCann	.50
17	Lance Berkman	.50
18	Daisuke Matsuzaka	1.00
19	Josh Beckett	.50
20	Carlos Quentin	.40
21	Carlos Delgado	.25
22	Clayton Kershaw	.50
23	Zack Greinke	.50
24	Ken Griffey Jr.	1.50
25	Mark Teixeira	.75
26	Chase Utley	1.00
27	Vladimir Guerrero	.50
28	Prince Fielder	1.00
29	Adrian Beltre	.40
30	Magglio Ordonez	.50
31	Jon Lester	.50
32	Josh Hamilton	.75
33	Justin Morneau	.50
34	Felix Hernandez	.50
35	Cole Hamels	.50
36	Edinson Volquez	.25
37	Hideki Okajima	.25
38	Carlos Zambrano	.40
39	Aaron Harang	.25
40	Chien-Ming Wang	.50
41	Shin-Soo Cho	.50
42	Mariano Rivera	.75
43	Josh Johnson	.50
44	Roy Oswalt	.50
45	Carlos Lee	.50
46	Ryan Dempster	.25
47	Ryan Ludwick	.25
48	Joakim Soria	.25
49	Jair Jurrjens	.25
50	John Danks	.25
51	Ichiro Suzuki	1.50
52	C.C. Sabathia	.75
53	Yovani Gallardo	.50
54	Ervin Santana	.25
55	Tim Lincecum	1.00
56	Mark Buehrle	.25
57	Johan Santana	.75
58	Chad Billingsley	.50
59	Francisco Liriano	.40
60	Joey Votto	.50
61	Matt Kemp	.75
62	Joba Chamberlain	.75
63	Hiroki Kuroda	.25
64	Brian Roberts	.50
65	Randy Johnson	.75
66	Jay Bruce	.50
67	Curtis Granderson	.75
68	Hideki Matsui	.75
69	Todd Helton	.50
70	Nick Markakis	.50
71	Andy Pettitte	.50
72	Ian Kinsler	.75
73	Brandon Inge	.25
74	Adrian Gonzalez	.50
75	Francisco Rodriguez	.50
76	Derek Lowe	.25
77	Carlos Beltran	.50
78	Matt Holliday	.50
79	Jake Peavy	.50
80	Scott Kazmir	.25
81	David Ortiz	.75
82	Dan Haren	.50
83	Hanley Ramirez	1.00
84	Jim Thome	.50
85	Brad Hawpe	.40
86	Vernon Wells	.25
87	B.J. Upton	.50
88	James Shields	.50
89	Jason Giambi	.50
90	Adam Dunn	.50
91	Brandon Webb	.50
92	Roy Halladay	.50
93	Miguel Cabrera	.75
94	Jose Reyes	.75
95	Chipper Jones	1.00
96	Grady Sizemore	.75
97	Jason Varitek	.25
98	David Wright	1.00
99	Manny Ramirez	.75
100	Kevin Youkilis	.50
101	Bengie Molina	.25
102	Ivan Rodriguez	.40
103	Andruw Jones	.25
104	Jorge Cantu	.25
105	Corey Hart	.25
106	Adam Wainwright	.50
107	Raul Ibanez	.50
108	Jason Bay	.50
109	Chris Volstad	.25
110	Jermaine Dye	.50
111	Torii Hunter	.40
112	Brad Ziegler	.25
113	Carl Crawford	.50
114	Troy Tulowitzki	.50
115	Aramis Ramirez	.50
116	Nomar Garciaparra	.40
117	Pedro Martinez	.50
118	Ryan Theriot	.40
119	Matt Cain	.50
120	Carlos Pena	.50
121	Nick Swisher	.25
122	Javier Vazquez	.40
123	John Lackey	.40
124	Jack Cust	.25
125	Justin Upton	.50
126	Michael Young	.40
127	Jeff Samardzija	.50
128	John Smoltz	.50
129	Josh Reddick RC	4.00
130	Chris Tillman RC	4.00
131	Aaron Cunningham RC	1.50
132	Andrew McCutchen (RC)	5.00
133	Anthony Ortega RC	1.50
134	Anthony Swarzak (RC)	1.50
135	Antonio Bastardo RC	1.50
136	Brad Bergesen (RC)	1.50
137	Brett Cecil RC	1.50
138	Neftali Feliz RC	5.00
139	Chris Coghlan RC	4.00
140	Daniel Bard RC	1.50
141	Dan Schlereth RC	1.50
142	Donald Veal RC	1.50
143	Brad Mills RC	1.50
144	David Huff RC	2.50
145	Elvis Andrus RC	5.00
146	Everth Cabrera RC	3.00
147	Mat Latos RC	5.00
148	Shairon Martis RC	2.00
149	Jess Todd RC	1.50
150	Jon Niese RC	3.00
151	Jose Mijares RC	1.50
152	Jhoulys Chacin RC	3.00
153	Kyle Blanks RC	1.50
154	Kris Medlen RC	1.50
155	Fu-Te Ni RC	6.00
156	Bud Norris RC	1.50
157	Julio Borbon RC	5.00
158	Mat Gamel RC	1.50
159	Matt LaPorta RC	5.00
160	Michael Bowden (RC)	3.00
161	Michael Saunders RC	1.50
162	Ricky Romero (RC)	2.50
163	Marc Rzepczynski RC	1.50
164	Ryan Perry RC	4.00
165	Sean O'Sullivan RC	1.50
166	Sean West (RC)	1.50
167	Trevor Cahill RC	4.00
168	Mike Carp (RC)	1.50
169	Vin Mazzaro RC	1.50
170	Wilkin Ramirez RC	3.00
171	Albert Pujols	5.00
172	Alfonso Soriano	1.00
173	Brandon Webb	1.00
174	Carlos Quentin	1.00
175	Carlos Zambrano	1.00
176	C.C. Sabathia	1.50
177	Chase Utley	2.00
178	Chipper Jones	2.00
179	Cole Hamels	1.50
180	Daisuke Matsuzaka	2.50
181	David Wright	3.00
182	Derek Jeter	5.00
183	Derek Lowe	1.00
184	Dustin Pedroia	3.00
185	Felix Hernandez	1.50
186	Grady Sizemore	2.00
187	Jason Giambi	1.00
188	Joba Chamberlain	2.50
189	Joe Mauer	2.00
190	Johan Santana	2.00
191	Jose Reyes	2.50
192	Josh Beckett	1.50
193	Josh Hamilton	2.50
194	Ken Griffey Jr.	4.00
195	Manny Ramirez	2.00
196	Prince Fielder	2.00
197	Randy Johnson	1.50
198	Ryan Braun	2.50
199	Ryan Howard	3.00
200	Tim Lincecum	2.50
201	A.J. Burnett	2.00
202	Adam Dunn	2.50
203	Alex Rodriguez	6.00
204	Alfonso Soriano	2.50
205	Andy Pettitte	2.00
206	Bobby Abreu	2.00
207	Carlos Beltran	2.50
208	Chipper Jones	4.00
209	Dan Haren	2.00
210	Derek Jeter	8.00
211	Derek Lowe	2.00
212	Gary Sheffield	2.50
213	Ivan Rodriguez	2.00
214	Jamie Moyer	2.00
215	Jason Giambi	2.00
216	Jim Thome	2.50
217	Johan Santana	3.00
218	John Smoltz	2.50
219	Johnny Damon	3.00
220	Josh Beckett	3.00
221	Ken Griffey Jr.	6.00
222	Manny Ramirez	3.00
223	Mark Teixeira	3.00
224	Randy Johnson	3.00
225	Tim Wakefield	2.00
226	Aaron Poreda 300/Auto. RC	10.00
227	Brett Anderson 371/Auto. RC	15.00
228	Matt LaPorta 225/Auto. RC	15.00
229	Colby Rasmus 300/Auto. (RC)	30.00
230	David Price 222/Auto. RC	30.00
231	Derek Holland 195/Auto. RC	15.00
232	Dexter Fowler 500/Auto. RC	15.00
233	Fernando Martinez 243/Auto. RC	15.00
234	Gerardo Parra 299/Auto. RC	15.00
235	Gordon Beckham 136/Auto. RC	50.00
236	James McDonald 500/Auto. RC	10.00
237	James Parr 500/Auto. (RC)	10.00
238	Jason Motte 415/Auto. (RC)	15.00
239	Jordan Schafer 475/Auto. (RC)	12.00
240	Jordan Zimmermann 417/Auto. RC	15.00
241	Kenshin Kawakami 425/Auto. RC	20.00
242	Koji Uehara 200/Auto. RC	20.00
243	Luis Perdomo 275/Auto. RC	10.00
244	Matt Tuiasosopo 500/Auto. RC	10.00
245	Matt Wieters 500/Auto. RC	60.00
246	Nolan Reimold 135/Auto. (RC)	15.00
247	Pablo Sandoval 230/Auto. (RC)	30.00
248	Rick Porcello 225/Auto. RC	30.00
249	Tommy Hanson 198/Auto. RC	60.00
250	Travis Snider 100/Auto. RC	25.00

Silver
	NM/M
Silver (1-128):	4-6X
Silver (129-200):	2-3X
(1-200) Production 59	
Silver (201-225):	No Pricing
Production 19	
Autos. (226-250) listed below	
226 Aaron Poreda/Auto./25	20.00
227 Brett Anderson/Auto./25	30.00
228 Matt LaPorta/Auto./25	40.00
229 Colby Rasmus/Auto./25	40.00
230 David Price/Auto./25	50.00
232 Dexter Fowler/Auto./25	20.00
233 Fernando Martinez/Auto./25	25.00
236 James McDonald/Auto./25	25.00
237 James Parr/Auto./25	15.00
238 Jason Motte/Auto./25	20.00
239 Jordan Schafer/Auto./25	20.00
240 Jordan Zimmermann/Auto./25	25.00
241 Kenshin Kawakami/Auto./25	75.00
247 Pablo Sandoval/Auto./25	125.00

Titanium
	NM/M
Titanium (1-200):	No Pricing
Production 19	
(201-225) Production 9	
Autos. (226-250) production 1-10.	

Copper
	NM/M
Copper (1-128):	3-5X
Copper (129-200):	1-2X
(1-200) Production 99	

Copper (201-225): 2-4X
Production 29
Autos. (226-250) listed below

226	Aaron Poreda/Auto./50	15.00
227	Brett Anderson/ Auto./50	25.00
228	Matt LaPorta/Auto./50	35.00
229	Colby Rasmus/ Auto./50	40.00
230	David Price/Auto./50	40.00
231	Derek Holland/ Auto./35	20.00
232	Dexter Fowler/Auto./50	20.00
233	Fernando Martinez/ Auto./50	20.00
234	Gerardo Parra/Auto./50	20.00
235	Gordon Beckham/ Auto./40	150.00
236	James McDonald/ Auto./50	20.00
237	James Parr/Auto./50	15.00
238	Jason Motte/Auto./50	15.00
239	Jordan Schafer/ Auto./50	20.00
240	Jordan Zimmermann/ Auto./50	20.00
241	Kenshin Kawakami/ Auto./50	60.00
243	Luis Perdomo/ Auto./50	15.00
244	Matt Tuiasosopo/ Auto./50	20.00
245	Matt Wieters/Auto./25	175.00
246	Nolan Reimold/ Auto./25	40.00
247	Pablo Sandoval/ Auto./50	90.00
248	Rick Porcello/Auto./25	80.00
249	Tommy Hanson/ Auto./35	120.00
250	Travis Snider/Auto./25	60.00

Gold

NM/M
Gold (1-128): 2-4X
Gold (129-200): 1-1.5X
(1-200) Production 299
Gold (201-225): 1-1.5X
Production 99
Autos (226-250) listed below

226	Aaron Poreda/ Auto./124	12.00
227	Brett Anderson/ Auto./125	20.00
228	Matt LaPorta/ Auto./125	30.00
229	Colby Rasmus/ Auto./100	30.00
230	David Price/Auto./125	35.00
231	Derek Holland/Auto./90	15.00
232	Dexter Fowler/ Auto./125	15.00
233	Fernando Martinez/ Auto./125	15.00
234	Gerardo Parra/ Auto./125	15.00
235	Gordon Beckham/ Auto./85	120.00
236	James McDonald/ Auto./125	15.00
237	James Parr/Auto./125	12.00
238	Jason Motte/Auto./125	12.00
239	Jordan Schafer/ Auto./125	15.00
240	Jordan Zimmermann/ Auto./125	15.00
241	Kenshin Kawakami/ Auto./125	60.00
242	Koji Uehara/Auto./25	75.00
243	Luis Perdomo/ Auto./125	10.00
244	Matt Tuiasosopo/ Auto./125	15.00
245	Matt Wieters/ Auto./50	125.00
246	Nolan Reimold/ Auto./65	30.00
247	Pablo Sandoval/ Auto./75	65.00
248	Rick Porcello/ Auto./60	80.00
249	Tommy Hanson/ Auto./65	85.00
250	Travis Snider/Auto./50	40.00

By the Letter Rookie Autographs

NM/M
Common Auto.:
#'d 11-100
Total print run listed

BA	Brett Anderson/599	15.00
CR	Colby Rasmus/450	30.00
DF	David Freese/450	15.00
DH	Derek Holland/270	15.00
DP	David Patton/600	8.00
DV	Donald Veal/715	12.00
EA	Elvis Andrus/660	20.00
EC	Everth Cabrera/715	15.00
FO	Dexter Fowler/715	15.00
GK	George Kottaras/715	15.00
JM	James McDonald/715	10.00
JS	Jordan Schafer/510	15.00
JZ	Jordan Zimmermann/ 297	12.00
KJ	Kevin Jepsen/600	10.00
KK	Kenshin Kawakami/ 600	25.00
KU	Koji Uehara/400	25.00
MO	Jason Motte/600	25.00
MW	Matt Wieters/165	65.00
PC	Phil Coke/709	15.00
PD	David Price/168	35.00
PE	Ryan Perry/300	25.00
PR	David Price/140	30.00
PS	Pablo Sandoval/308	40.00
RP	Rick Porcello/510	30.00
RR	Ricky Romero/715	15.00
SM	Shairon Martis/715	15.00
TC	Trevor Cahill/510	15.00
TR	Trevor Crowe/715	10.00
TS	Travis Snider/540	30.00
UE	Koji Uehara/190	30.00

By the Letter Autographs

NM/M
#'d 2-60
Total print run listed

AH	Alex Hinshaw/473	12.00
AR	Alex Romero/400	15.00
BJ	Brandon Jones/360	20.00
BM	Brian McCann/220	35.00
BR	Jay Bruce/350	25.00
BU	B.J. Upton/26	15.00
CG	Carlos Gonzalez/495	15.00
CH	Chin-Lung Hu/120	30.00
CJ	Chipper Jones/24	180.00
CK	Clayton Kershaw/140	40.00
CV	Chris Volstad/300	10.00
CW	Chien-Ming Wang/60	125.00
DJ	Derek Jeter/200	250.00
DM	Daniel Murphy/360	25.00
DP	David Purcey/341	15.00
DU	Dustin Pedroia/390	40.00
EB	Emmanuel Burriss/375	15.00
EC	Eric Chavez/54	25.00
EL	Evan Longoria/60	120.00
FH	Felix Hernandez/80	35.00
GA	Garrett Atkins/65	15.00
GF	Gavin Floyd/400	15.00
GP	Glen Perkins/385	10.00
GS	Geovany Soto/40	40.00
HA	Cole Hamels/100	40.00
HP	Hunter Pence/48	15.00
HR	Hanley Ramirez/52	60.00
HU	Chin-Lung Hu/270	25.00
JB	Jay Bruce/494	25.00
JC	Joba Chamberlain/150	40.00
JJ	Josh Johnson/297	25.00
JN	Joe Nathan/324	15.00
JT	J.R. Towles/400	10.00
JV	Jason Varitek/30	125.00
KG	Ken Griffey Jr./144	100.00
KM	Kyle McClellan/390	10.00
KS	Kelly Shoppach/494	10.00
KY	Kevin Youkilis/260	40.00
LE	Jon Lester/270	40.00
LJ	Jed Lowrie/297	20.00
MA	Mike Aviles/500	10.00
MC	Matt Cain/400	25.00
MD	Daniel Murphy/385	25.00
MG	Matt Garza/450	12.00
MN	Nick Markakis/315	25.00
MO	Nyjer Morgan/385	15.00
MR	Nick Markakis/360	25.00
NA	Joe Nathan/350	15.00
NM	Nate McLouth/495	15.00
PE	Dustin Pedroia/408	40.00
RB	Ryan Braun/90	60.00
RH	Roy Halladay/110	65.00
RJ	Randy Johnson/21	150.00
TT	Troy Tulowitzki/420	25.00
UB	B.J. Upton/210	15.00
WA	Cory Wade/400	15.00

'93 Jeter SP RC Auto. Buyback

NM/M
Production 93

279	Derek Jeter/93	1,500

Pennant Run Heroes

NM/M
Common Player: 1.00
Inserted 1:20

1	Alfonso Soriano	1.50
2	B.J. Upton	1.00
3	Brad Lidge	1.00
4	Brandon Webb	1.00
5	Carlos Quentin	1.00
6	Chad Billingsley	1.00
7	Chase Utley	3.00
8	Chris Young	1.00
9	Clayton Kershaw	2.00
10	Cole Hamels	2.00
11	David Ortiz	2.00
12	David Price	6.00
13	Derek Jeter	6.00
14	Evan Longoria	4.00
15	John Lackey	1.00
16	Jonathan Papelbon	1.50
17	Kevin Youkilis	1.50
18	Lance Berkman	1.50
19	Magglio Ordonez	1.00
20	Mariano Rivera	1.50

Platinum Power

NM/M
Common Player: 1.00
Inserted 1:10

1	A.J. Burnett	1.00
2	Adam Dunn	1.50
3	Adrian Gonzalez	1.00
4	Albert Pujols	8.00
5	Alex Rodriguez	6.00
6	Alfonso Soriano	1.50
7	Brandon Webb	1.50
8	Bronson Arroyo	1.00
9	Carlos Delgado	1.50
10	Carlos Lee	1.50
11	Carlos Pena	1.00
12	Carlos Quentin	1.50
13	C.C. Sabathia	2.00
14	Chad Billingsley	1.00
15	Chase Utley	3.00
16	Cole Hamels	2.50
17	Dan Haren	1.00
18	David Wright	3.00
19	Edinson Volquez	1.00
20	Evan Longoria	4.00
21	Felix Hernandez	1.50
22	Grady Sizemore	2.00
23	Ian Kinsler	2.00
24	Jack Cust	1.00
25	Jake Peavy	1.50
26	James Shields	1.50
27	Jason Bay	1.50
28	Jason Giambi	1.00
29	Javier Vazquez	1.00
30	Jermaine Dye	1.00
31	Jim Thome	1.50
32	Joey Votto	1.50
33	Johan Santana	1.50
34	Josh Beckett	2.00
35	Josh Hamilton	2.00
36	Josh Johnson	1.00
37	Justin Verlander	1.50
38	Lance Berkman	1.00
39	Manny Ramirez	2.00
40	Mark Teixeira	2.00
41	Matt Cain	1.50
42	Miguel Cabrera	2.00
43	Mike Jacobs	1.00
44	Nick Markakis	1.50
45	Prince Fielder	1.50
46	Randy Johnson	2.00
47	Ricky Nolasco	1.50
48	Roy Halladay	1.50
49	Roy Oswalt	1.50
50	Ryan Braun	3.00
51	Ryan Dempster	1.00
52	Ryan Howard	4.00
53	Ryan Ludwick	1.50
54	Scott Kazmir	1.50
55	Tim Lincecum	3.00
56	Ubaldo Jimenez	1.00
57	Vladimir Guerrero	1.50
58	Wandy Rodriguez	1.00
59	Yovani Gallardo	1.50
60	Zack Greinke	1.50

Signatures

NM/M
Common Auto:
Inserted 1:8

DS	Denard Span	15.00
EB	Emilio Bonifacio	12.00
HA	Corey Hart	12.00
JH	J.A. Happ	15.00
JL	Jed Lowrie	12.00
JM	James McDonald	12.00
JS	Joe Smith	10.00
KM	Kyle McClellan	10.00
KO	Kevin Kouzmanoff	12.00
NB	Nick Blackburn	10.0
RA	Alexei Ramirez	20.00
SH	Steve Holm	8.00
SM	Sean Marshall	8.00
AN	Andy LaRoche/SP	20.00
AR	Aaron Rowand/SP	15.00
AS	Anibal Sanchez/SP	10.00
CB	Chad Billingsley/SP	12.00
CH	Chase Headley/SP	8.00
CW	Cory Wade/SP	10.00
DB	Daric Barton/SP	15.00
DE	David Eckstein/SP	15.00
DJ	Derek Jeter/SP	200.00
DL	Derek Lowe/SP	15.00
DU	Dan Uggla/SP	12.00
EJ	Edwin Jackson/SP	12.00
FC	Fausto Carmona/SP	10.00
FJ	Jeff Francoeur/SP	10.00
GG	Greg Golson/SP	8.00
GP	Glen Perkins/SP	10.00
HE	Jeremy Hermida/SP	10.00
HJ	Josh Hamilton/SP	30.00
JD	John Danks/SP	10.00
JG	Josh Geer/SP	10.00
JM	Justin Masterson/SP	15.00
JP	Jonathan Papelbon/SP	20.00
JS	James Shields/SP	15.00
KG	Ken Griffey Jr./SP	125.00
KS	Kurt Suzuki/SP	10.00
KY	Kevin Youkilis/SP	20.00
LA	Adam Lind/SP	12.00
MA	Daisuke Matsuzaka/SP	150.00
ME	Mark Ellis/SP	8.00
MG	Matt Garza/SP	10.00
MU	David Murphy/SP	8.00
NM	Nick Markakis/SP	25.00
NS	Nick Swisher/SP	10.00
RC	Ryan Church/SP	10.00
RM	Russell Martin/SP	15.00
SA	Jarrod Saltalamacchia/ SP	8.00
SO	Joakim Soria/SP	10.00
VM	Victor Martinez/SP	15.00

Signatures Dual

NM/M
Production 15 Sets

BL	Jason Bay, Jed Lowrie	50.00
BP	Fernando Perez, Michael Bourn	15.00
BS	Chad Billingsley, James Shields	25.00
CL	Aaron Laffey, Fausto Carmona	15.00
DN	Denard Span, Nick Blackburn	20.00
DZ	Elijah Dukes, Ryan Zimmerman	20.00
ES	Kurt Suzuki, Mark Ellis	20.00
FW	Chone Figgins, Jered Weaver	30.00
HH	Jeremy Hermida, Josh Hamilton	30.00
HL	Adam Lind, Roy Halladay	50.00
JM	James Shields, Matt Garza	25.00
JP	Derek Jeter, Dustin Pedroia	250.00
JR	Joe Blanton, Rich Harden	20.00
JS	Derek Jeter, Nick Swisher	250.00
KD	Daric Barton, Kurt Suzuki	20.00
LK	James Loney, Matt Kemp	60.00
LR	Andy LaRoche, Aramis Ramirez	30.00
LY	Jon Lester, Kevin Youkilis	75.00
MB	Chad Billingsley, John Maine	25.00
MP	John Maine, Mike Pelfrey	40.00
ND	Denard Span, Nick Blackburn	20.00
PN	Fernando Perez, Nyjer Morgan	15.00
PP	Dustin Pedroia, Jonathan Papelbon	75.00
TA	Aaron Rowand, Tim Lincecum	75.00
WH	Corey Hart, Rickie Weeks	20.00
WY	Brandon Webb, Chris Young	40.00

Signatures Quad

Production 10 Sets
No Pricing

Signatures Triple

Production 10 Sets
No Pricing

2009 SP Legendary Cuts

NM/M
Common (1-100): .25
Common (101-200): 3.00
(101-200) production 550.
Pack (5): 10.00
Box (12): 100.00

1	Brian Roberts	.25
2	Derek Jeter	2.00
3	Evan Longoria	1.50
4	Brandon Phillips	.25
5	David Wright	.75
6	Ryan Howard	.75
7	Jose Reyes	.75
8	Ryan Braun	.75
9	Jim Thome	.40
10	Chipper Jones	.75
11	Jimmy Rollins	.50
12	Alfonso Soriano	.50
13	Alex Rodriguez	1.50
14	David Price RC	3.00
15	Carlos Beltran	.50
16	Aramis Ramirez	.40
17	Ken Griffey Jr.	1.50
18	Daisuke Matsuzaka	.75
19	Josh Beckett	.50
20	Kevin Youkilis	.50
21	Carlos Delgado	.40
22	Clayton Kershaw	.40
23	Adrian Gonzalez	.50
24	Grady Sizemore	.75
25	Mark Teixeira	.50
26	Chase Utley	.75
27	Vladimir Guerrero	.50
28	Prince Fielder	.50
29	Jeff Samardzija	.25
30	Magglio Ordonez	.40
31	Cliff Lee	.50
32	Josh Hamilton	.75
33	Justin Morneau	.50
34	David Ortiz	.50
35	Cole Hamels	.50
36	Edinson Volquez	.25
37	Nick Markakis	.40
38	Carlos Zambrano	.40
39	Max Scherzer	.25
40	Rich Harden	.25
41	Ryan Doumit	.25
42	Mariano Rivera	.40
43	Alexei Ramirez	.40
44	Jake Peavy	.40
45	Trevor Hoffman	.25
46	Ryan Dempster	.25
47	Francisco Liriano	.25
48	Travis Hafner	.25
49	Joakim Soria	.25
50	Albert Pujols	2.00
51	Ichiro Suzuki	1.50
52	C.C. Sabathia	.50
53	Ryan Ludwick	.40
54	Mike Lowell	.40
55	Tim Lincecum	.75
56	Francisco Rodriguez	.40
57	Johan Santana	.75
58	Jonathan Papelbon	.40
59	Geovany Soto	.40
60	Jacoby Ellsbury	.75
61	Jon Lester	.50
62	Joba Chamberlain	.75
63	Rick Ankiel	.25
64	Chad Billingsley	.40
65	Chien-Ming Wang	.40
66	Stephen Drew	.40
67	Roy Halladay	.50
68	Ian Kinsler	.50
69	Scott Kazmir	.40
70	Miguel Tejada	.40
71	Carlos Lee	.50
72	Hanley Ramirez	.75
73	Carlos Pena	.40
74	Alex Gordon	.40
75	Pat Burrell	.40
76	Dan Uggla	.40
77	Joe Mauer	.50
78	Felix Hernandez	.50
79	Jermaine Dye	.40
80	Carlos Quentin	.40
81	Lance Berkman	.40
82	Randy Johnson	.50
83	Matt Holliday	.40
84	Curtis Granderson	.50
85	Miguel Cabrera	.50
86	Matt Cain	.40
87	Troy Tulowitzki	.25
88	Brian McCann	.40
89	Adam Dunn	.40
90	Matt Kemp	.50
91	B.J. Upton	.40
92	A.J. Burnett	.25
93	Carl Crawford	.40
94	Nate McLouth	.40
95	Derrek Lee	.50
96	Dustin Pedroia	.75
97	Russell Martin	.25
98	John Lackey	.25
99	Manny Ramirez	.50
100	Jay Bruce	.75
101	Ozzie Smith	6.00
102	Luis Aparicio	3.00
103	Johnny Bench	6.00
104	Yogi Berra	6.00
105	Lou Brock	5.00
106	Rod Carew	4.00
107	Whitey Ford	5.00
108	Dennis Eckersley	3.00
109	Bob Feller	5.00
110	Rollie Fingers	3.00
111	Carlton Fisk	4.00
112	Bob Gibson	5.00
113	Jim "Catfish" Hunter	3.00
114	Reggie Jackson	5.00
115	Fergie Jenkins	4.00
116	Al Kaline	6.00
117	Harmon Killebrew	6.00
118	Ralph Kiner	4.00
119	Juan Marichal	4.00
120	Vince Coleman	3.00
121	Bill Mazeroski	4.00
122	Don Newcombe	3.00
123	Joe Morgan	4.00
124	Eddie Murray	5.00
125	Phil Niekro	4.00
126	Mike Schmidt	6.00
127	John Kruk	4.00
128	Steve Carlton	4.00
129	Brooks Robinson	4.00
130	Nolan Ryan	10.00
131	Dave Winfield	4.00
132	Bo Jackson	5.00
133	Paul Molitor	5.00
134	Billy Williams	4.00
135	Robin Yount	6.00
136	Don Mattingly	6.00
137	Cal Ripken Jr.	10.00
138	Bobby Doerr	3.00
139	Rich "Goose" Gossage	3.00
140	Wade Boggs	5.00
141	Jim Palmer	5.00
142	Carl Yastrzemski	6.00
143	Frank Robinson	4.00
144	Joe Carter	3.00
145	Dennis "Oil Can" Boyd	3.00
146	Tony Perez	3.00
147	Gaylord Perry	3.00
148	Jules Verne	3.00
149	James K. Polk	3.00
150	William Henry Harrison	3.00
151	Manfred von Richthofen	3.00
152	William Jennings Bryan	3.00
153	Susan B. Anthony	3.00
154	Gentleman Jim Corbett	3.00
155	Cornelius Vanderbilt	3.00
156	John L. Sullivan	3.00
157	Daniel Boone	5.00
158	Davy Crockett	5.00
159	Edgar Allen Poe	3.00
160	George Custer	3.00
161	Harriet Tubman	3.00
162	Adolphus Busch	3.00
163	Bonnie Parker	3.00
164	Clyde Barrow	3.00
165	Winston Churchill	3.00
166	Sir Isaac Newton	3.00
167	Christopher Columbus	3.00
168	Doc Holliday	3.00
169	Wyatt Earp	3.00
170	Sam Houston	3.00
171	Francis Scott Key	3.00
172	Betsy Ross	3.00
173	John Hancock	3.00
174	Vincent Van Gogh	3.00
175	Charles Dickens	3.00
176	Pope John Paul II	5.00
177	Woodrow Wilson	3.00
178	James A. Garfield	3.00
179	Robert E. Lee	3.00
180	Julius Caesar	3.00
181	Napoleon Bonaparte	3.00
182	Alexander Hamilton	3.00
183	Frederick Douglass	3.00
184	Booker T. Washington	3.00
185	Paul Revere	3.00
186	Grover Cleveland	3.00
187	Andrew Johnson	3.00
188	Billy the Kid	3.00
189	Samuel Adams	3.00
190	Dwight D. Eisenhower	3.00
191	Theodore Roosevelt	3.00
192	Ulysses S. Grant	3.00
193	George Washington	8.00
194	John D. Rockefeller	3.00
195	Martin Van Buren	3.00
196	John Adams	3.00
197	Andrew Jackson	3.00
198	Jesse James	3.00
199	Thomas Jefferson	5.00
200	Abraham Lincoln	8.00

Classic Signatures

NM/M
Production 10-25

CF	Carlton Fisk/25	30.00
DE	Dennis Eckersley/25	30.00
DM	Don Mattingly/25	70.00
FR	Frank Robinson/25	40.00
LB	Lou Brock/25	40.00
MS	Mike Schmidt/25	50.00
PM	Paul Molitor/25	30.00
SL	Sparky Lyle/25	20.00
TG	Tony Gwynn/25	50.00

Destination Stardom Memorabilia

NM/M
Common Player: 5.00

BP	Brandon Phillips	5.00
BS	Ben Sheets	5.00
BU	B.J. Upton	5.00
BW	Brandon Webb	5.00
CB	Carlos Beltran	6.00
CU	Chase Utley	10.00
CZ	Carlos Zambrano	5.00
DL	Derrek Lee	5.00
DS	Denard Span	5.00
EV	Edinson Volquez	5.00
FH	Felix Hernandez	5.00
FL	Francisco Liriano	5.00
GS	Grady Sizemore	6.00
JB	Josh Beckett	6.00
JC	Joba Chamberlain	5.00
JE	Jacoby Ellsbury	10.00

		NM/M
JH	Josh Hamilton	8.00
JM	Joe Mauer	6.00
JP	Jonathan Papelbon	6.00
JV	Justin Verlander	5.00
MH	Matt Holliday	5.00
MO	Justin Morneau	5.00
MT	Mark Teixeira	5.00
PE	Jake Peavy	5.00
PF	Prince Fielder	6.00
RC	Robinson Cano	5.00
RM	Russell Martin	5.00
SK	Scott Kazmir	5.00

Destined for History Memorabilia

		NM/M
	Common Jersey:	5.00
AP	Albert Pujols	15.00
AR	Aramis Ramirez	5.00
AS	Alfonso Soriano	5.00
CD	Carlos Delgado	5.00
CH	Cole Hamels	8.00
CJ	Chipper Jones	8.00
CS	Curt Schilling	5.00
DJ	Derek Jeter	15.00
DO	David Ortiz	8.00
FT	Frank Thomas	6.00
GS	Gary Sheffield	5.00
HE	Todd Helton	5.00
JG	Jason Giambi	5.00
JP	Jorge Posada	5.00
JS	John Smoltz	5.00
JT	Jim Thome	5.00
JV	Jason Varitek	5.00
KG	Ken Griffey Jr.	15.00
LB	Lance Berkman	5.00
MO	Magglio Ordonez	5.00
MR	Mariano Rivera	10.00
PE	Andy Pettitte	5.00
PM	Pedro Martinez	5.00
RA	Manny Ramirez	8.00
RH	Roy Halladay	5.00
RJ	Randy Johnson	6.00
RO	Roy Oswalt	5.00
TG	Tom Glavine	5.00
TH	Trevor Hoffman	5.00
VG	Vladimir Guerrero	6.00

Dual Cut Signatures

Production One Set
No Pricing

Future Legends Signatures

		NM/M
	Production 10-125	
AG	Adrian Gonzalez/125	15.00
BM	Brian McCann/125	25.00
BP	Brandon Phillips/125	15.00
BU	B.J. Upton/125	20.00
BZ	Clay Buchholz/125	20.00
CG	Carlos Gonzalez/125	12.00
CK	Clayton Kershaw/25	30.00
CL	Carlos Lee/125	15.00
CW	Chien-Ming Wang/25	180.00
CY	Chris B. Young/34	20.00
DJ	Derek Jeter/45	150.00
DP	Dustin Pedroia/125	100.00
EE	Edwin Encarnacion/125	10.00
FH	Felix Hernandez/125	30.00
IK	Ian Kennedy/125	10.00
JC	Johnny Cueto/125	15.00
JF	Jeff Francoeur/125	15.00
JL	John Lackey/125	15.00
JN	Joe Nathan/125	15.00
JP	Jonathan Papelbon/125	25.00
JW	Josh Willingham/125	15.00
KG	Ken Griffey Jr./125	85.00
MK	Matt Kemp/125	15.00
MU	David Murphy/125	15.00
RZ	Ryan Zimmerman/125	20.00
TT	Troy Tulowitzki/125	12.00
VM	Victor Martinez/125	15.00
YG	Yovani Gallardo/125	20.00

Generations Dual Signatures

	Production 5-25	
BL	Derek Lee, Lou Brock/25	75.00
GB	Bob Gibson, Josh Beckett/25	85.00
RL	Brooks Robinson, Evan Longoria/25	80.00
SK	Clayton Kershaw, Don Sutton/25	65.00
SL	Evan Longoria, Mike Schmidt/25	80.00

Generations Dual Memorabilia

		NM/M
	Common Duo:	5.00
1B	Don Mattingly, Jason Giambi	12.00
AV	Jason Varitek, Luis Aparicio	8.00
BC	Carlos Beltran, Roberto Clemente	30.00
BJ	Derek Jeter, Ernie Banks	25.00
BL	Evan Longoria, Wade Boggs	15.00
BO	David Ortiz, Wade Boggs	10.00
BP	Bob Gibson, Pedro Martinez	12.00
BR	Ernie Banks, Hanley Ramirez	10.00
BS	Brooks Robinson, Scott Rolen	10.00
BY	Robin Yount, Ryan Braun	15.00
CG	Roberto Clemente, Vladimir Guerrero	25.00
CH	Cole Hamels, Steve Carlton	12.00
CM	Cal Ripken Jr., Miguel Tejada	15.00
CP	Andy Pettitte, Steve Carlton	8.00
DB	Carlos Beltran, Joe DiMaggio	40.00
DD	Daisuke Matsuzaka, Don Sutton	10.00
DJ	Bucky Dent, Derek Jeter	20.00
DM	Carlos Delgado, Eddie Murray	8.00
DS	Grady Sizemore, Joe DiMaggio	40.00
EA	Aramis Ramirez, Ernie Banks	10.00
ED	Derek Lee, Ernie Banks	10.00
EH	Dennis Eckersley, Trevor Hoffman	8.00
EJ	Edgar Martinez, Jason Bay	8.00
EP	Dennis Eckersley, Jonathan Papelbon	10.00
ES	Dennis Eckersley, Huston Street	8.00
FM	Carlton Fisk, Joe Mauer	8.00
FP	Carlton Fisk, Jorge Posada	8.00
FV	Carlton Fisk, Jason Varitek	8.00
GG	Brian Giles, Tony Gwynn	8.00
GJ	Rich "Goose" Gossage, Jonathan Papelbon	8.00
GM	Jason Giambi, Tino Martinez	8.00
GP	Bob Gibson, Jake Peavy	10.00
GR	Rich "Goose" Gossage, Mariano Rivera	10.00
GY	Carl Yastrzemski, Ken Griffey Jr.	15.00
HG	Mark Grace, Todd Helton	10.00
HJ	Josh Hamilton, Reggie Jackson	15.00
HY	J.J. Hardy, Robin Yount	10.00
JB	Brian McCann, Johnny Bench	10.00
JH	Bo Jackson, Josh Hamilton	15.00
JJ	Derek Jeter, Reggie Jackson	20.00

JO	David Ortiz, Reggie Jackson	10.00
JP	Albert Pujols, Bo Jackson	20.00
JR	Nolan Ryan, Randy Johnson	20.00
JS	Chipper Jones, Mike Schmidt	12.00
JV	Johnny Bench, Victor Martinez	10.00
LA	Chad Billingsley, Don Sutton	8.00
LG	Derek Lee, Mark Grace	10.00
LH	Phil Hughes, Sparky Lyle	8.00
LR	Mariano Rivera, Sparky Lyle	10.00
MB	Paul Molitor, Ryan Braun	10.00
MH	Edgar Martinez, Matt Holliday	8.00
MJ	Derek Jeter, Don Mattingly	25.00
MK	Ian Kinsler, Joe Morgan	10.00
MM	Justin Morneau, Paul Molitor	10.00
MP	Jack Morris, Jake Peavy	8.00
MR	Brooks Robinson, Melvin Mora	8.00
MT	Eddie Murray, Mark Teixeira	10.00
MU	Chase Utley, Joe Morgan	10.00
MV	Jack Morris, Justin Verlander	8.00
NC	Graig Nettles, Robinson Cano	10.00
NY	Derek Jeter, Joe DiMaggio	60.00
PB	Jake Peavy, Josh Beckett	10.00
PF	Dave Parker, Prince Fielder	10.00
PG	Ken Griffey Jr., Kirby Puckett	20.00
PL	Gaylord Perry, John Lackey	8.00
PM	Jorge Posada, Tino Martinez	8.00
PP	Gaylord Perry, Jake Peavy	8.00
PV	Jason Varitek, Tony Perez	8.00
RA	Aramis Ramirez, Ron Santo	15.00
RB	Ivan Rodriguez, Johnny Bench	8.00
RK	Nolan Ryan, Scott Kazmir	15.00
RL	Brooks Robinson, Evan Longoria	20.00
RN	Aramis Ramirez, Graig Nettles	8.00
RO	Nolan Ryan, Roy Oswalt	15.00
RR	Cal Ripken Jr., Hanley Ramirez	15.00
RT	Cal Ripken Jr., Troy Tulowitzki	15.00
SA	Albert Pujols, Stan Musial	30.00
SB	Mike Schmidt, Pat Burrell	15.00
SD	Jake Peavy, Tony Gwynn	10.00
SG	Khalil Greene, Ozzie Smith	12.00
SJ	Derek Jeter, Ozzie Smith	25.00
SL	Evan Longoria, Mike Schmidt	15.00
SP	Albert Pujols, Ozzie Smith	25.00
SR	Aramis Ramirez, Mike Schmidt	8.00
SS	Cal Ripken Jr., Derek Jeter	30.00
ST	Steve Carlton, Tom Glavine	8.00
SW	Brandon Webb, Don Sutton	10.00
TA	Adrian Gonzalez, Tino Martinez	8.00
TB	Chad Billingsley, Tom Glavine	8.00
TC	Carlos Beltran, Tony Perez	8.00
TJ	Jose Reyes, Tim Raines	8.00
TX	Josh Beckett, Nolan Ryan	15.00
WK	Kevin Youkilis, Wade Boggs	10.00
WM	Mike Lowell, Wade Boggs	8.00
YE	Carl Yastrzemski, Jacoby Ellsbury	20.00
YO	Carl Yastrzemski, David Ortiz	10.00

Legendary Cut Signatures

		NM/M
	Production 5-55	
	Overall odds approx. 2:Case	
6	Wally Berger/50	75.00
27	Bob O'Farrell/26	100.00
109	Bill Stafford/26	50.00

122	Ed Barrow/16	200.00
147	Jack Kramer/16	75.00
148	Lew Burdette/16	65.00
155	Mike Garcia/15	75.00
162	Ossie Bluege/16	50.00
178	Tug McGraw/17	50.00
193	Mace Brown/14	60.00
199	Smead Jolley/14	60.00
201	Al Barlick/50	50.00
202	Luke Appling/33	60.00
203	Allie Reynolds/39	85.00
204	Aurelio Rodriguez/50	50.00
205	Bibb Falk/36	75.00
206	Bob Grim/37	60.00
207	Bill Hallahan/21	70.00
208	Billy Herman/50	75.00
210	Bob Lemon/50	60.00
211	Barney McCosky/43	60.00
213	Bob Buhl/44	35.00
214	Bucky Walters/42	60.00
215	Clete Boyer/42	60.00
216	Charlie Gehringer/36	60.00
218	Del Ennis/27	65.00
219	Harry Danning/37	60.00
220	Dick Donovan/31	50.00
221	Doc Cramer/39	70.00
223	Dick Sisler/27	125.00
227	Frank Crosetti/50	90.00
228	Freddie Fitzsimmons/32	60.00
229	Frank McCormick/50	70.00
230	Charlie Grimm/50	60.00
231	George Kelly/26	60.00
232	Gus Suhr/55	50.00
233	Gene Woodling/47	50.00
234	Hank Borowy/33	60.00
235	Happy Chandler/28	50.00
237	Harvey Kuenn/32	70.00
238	Hank Sauer/33	60.00
239	Hal Trosky/34	100.00
240	Joe Adcock/30	80.00
241	Joe Black/23	125.00
242	Joe DiMaggio/27	350.00
244	Joe Niekro/28	60.00
245	Joe Sewell/50	50.00
246	Jim Turner/32	40.00
247	Johnny Vander Meer/42	70.00
248	Ken Keltner/19	65.00
249	Clem Labine/26	60.00
250	Lew Fonseca/29	65.00
252	Lloyd Waner/50	120.00
253	Ted Lyons/30	100.00
254	Mel Harder/41	50.00
255	Marius Russo/21	60.00
256	Mickey Owen/16	100.00
257	Pete Runnels/28	60.00
258	Paul Waner/17	300.00
259	Ray Boone/37	60.00
260	Ray Dandridge/31	50.00
262	Roger Peckinpaugh/41	100.00
263	Rip Repulski/48	60.00
265	Stan Coveleski/42	60.00
266	Riggs Stephenson/39	50.00
267	Birdie Tebbetts/20	65.00
269	Vic Wertz/43	60.00
270	Walker Cooper/44	60.00
273	Willie Stargell/23	80.00
276	Buck Leonard/52	70.00
277	Cool Papa Bell/30	120.00
278	Jim "Catfish" Hunter/40	70.00
280	Dutch Leonard/27	65.00
281	Ewell Blackwell/48	60.00
284	Hoyt Wilhelm/35	65.00
285	Harry Walker/45	60.00
287	Johnny Callison/26	60.00
288	Johnny Hopp/23	60.00
289	Lou Boudreau/50	50.00
290	Larry French/45	65.00
291	Phil Rizzuto/50	80.00
292	Richie Ashburn/24	120.00
295	Spec Shea/22	60.00
296	Tony Cuccinello/37	60.00
297	Tommy Holmes/41	65.00
298	Terry Moore/50	60.00
299	Sammy White/28	80.00
300	Warren Spahn/39	110.00
302	Billy Martin/15	180.00
304	Carl Hubbell/22	80.00
309	Edd Roush/31	60.00
311	Enos Slaughter/43	60.00

Legendary Memorabilia

		NM/M
	Production 125 unless noted	
	Blue:	1X
	Production 30-100	
	Brown:	1-1.5X
	Production 20-50	
	Red:	1-1.5X
	Production 25-75	
	Violet:	1-2X
	Production 25 Sets	
BD	Bucky Dent	10.00
BG	Bob Gibson/40	10.00
BO	Bo Jackson	8.00

BR	Brooks Robinson	8.00
BW	Billy Williams	5.00
CA	Rod Carew	5.00
CF	Carlton Fisk	6.00
CR	Cal Ripken Jr.	20.00
CY	Carl Yastrzemski	10.00
DE	Dennis Eckersley	5.00
DM	Don Mattingly	10.00
DS	Don Sutton	5.00
DW	Dave Winfield	6.00
EB	Ernie Banks	8.00
EM	Edgar Martinez	5.00
FR	Frank Robinson	6.00
GG	Rich "Goose" Gossage	5.00
GK	Kirk Gibson	5.00
GP	Gaylord Perry	5.00
JB	Johnny Bench	8.00
JC	Joe Carter	5.00
JM	Joe Morgan	5.00
JP	Jim Palmer	6.00
JR	Jim Rice	5.00
KG	Ken Griffey Sr.	5.00
LA	Luis Aparicio	5.00
LB	Lou Brock	5.00
MG	Mark Grace	5.00
MO	Jack Morris	5.00
MS	Mike Schmidt	10.00
NR	Nolan Ryan	15.00
OS	Ozzie Smith	10.00
PM	Paul Molitor	6.00
RJ	Reggie Jackson	8.00
RS	Ryne Sandberg	10.00
RY	Robin Yount	5.00
SA	Ron Santo	15.00
SC	Steve Carlton	5.00
SL	Sparky Lyle	5.00
SM	Stan Musial/100	20.00
TG	Tony Gwynn	8.00
TM	Tino Martinez	6.00
TP	Tony Perez	5.00
TR	Tim Raines	5.00
TW	Ted Williams/50	40.00
WB	Wade Boggs	5.00
BG2	Bob Gibson/40	10.00
BO2	Bo Jackson	8.00
BR2	Brooks Robinson	8.00
BW2	Billy Williams	5.00
BW3	Billy Williams	5.00
CA2	Rod Carew	5.00
CA3	Rod Carew	5.00
CF2	Carlton Fisk	6.00
CF3	Carlton Fisk	6.00
CR2	Cal Ripken Jr.	20.00
CR3	Cal Ripken Jr.	20.00
CY2	Carl Yastrzemski	10.00
DE2	Dennis Eckersley	5.00
DM2	Don Mattingly	10.00
DM3	Don Mattingly	10.00
DS2	Don Sutton	5.00
EB2	Ernie Banks	8.00
GG2	Rich "Goose" Gossage	5.00
GK2	Kirk Gibson	5.00
GP2	Gaylord Perry	5.00
GP3	Gaylord Perry	5.00
GP4	Gaylord Perry	5.00
JB2	Johnny Bench	8.00
JC2	Joe Carter	5.00
JM2	Joe Morgan	5.00
JP2	Jim Palmer	5.00
JR2	Jim Rice	5.00
LB2	Lou Brock	5.00
MG2	Mark Grace	5.00
MO2	Jack Morris	5.00
MS2	Mike Schmidt	10.00
NR2	Nolan Ryan	15.00
OS2	Ozzie Smith	10.00
OS3	Ozzie Smith	10.00
PM2	Paul Molitor	6.00
RJ2	Reggie Jackson	8.00
RS2	Ryne Sandberg	10.00
RY2	Robin Yount	8.00
SA2	Ron Santo	15.00
SC2	Steve Carlton	5.00
SL2	Sparky Lyle	5.00
SM2	Stan Musial/100	20.00
SM3	Stan Musial/100	20.00
TG2	Tony Gwynn	8.00
TM2	Tino Martinez	5.00
TP2	Tony Perez	5.00
TR2	Tim Raines	5.00
TW2	Ted Williams/50	40.00
WB2	Wade Boggs	8.00

Mystery Cuts

		NM/M
	Inserted 1:Case	
	Exchange Card	250.00

Quad Cut Signatures

Production One Set
No Pricing

2009 SPX

		NM/M
	Common Player (1-100):	.50
	Common RC Auto. (101-123):	15.00
	Pack (4):	8.00
	Box (18):	120.00
1	Ichiro Suzuki	2.50
2	Rick Ankiel	1.00
3	Garrett Atkins	.50
4	Jason Bay	.75
5	Josh Beckett	1.50
6	Erik Bedard	.50
7	Carlos Beltran	1.50
8	Lance Berkman	1.00
9	Ryan Braun	2.50
10	Jay Bruce	2.00
11	Miguel Cabrera	1.50
12	Matt Cain	.75
13	Joba Chamberlain	2.50
14	Carl Crawford	.75
15	Jack Cust	.50
16	Joe DiMaggio	4.00
17	Ryan Doumit	.50
18	Justin Duchscherer	.50
19	Adam Dunn	1.00
20	Prince Fielder	1.50
21	Kosuke Fukudome	1.50
22	Troy Glaus	.75
23	Tom Glavine	1.00
24	Adrian Gonzalez	1.00
25	Alex Gordon	.75
26	Zack Greinke	.75
27	Ken Griffey Jr.	3.00
28	Vladimir Guerrero	1.50
29	Travis Hafner	.50
30	Roy Halladay	1.50
31	Cole Hamels	1.50
32	Josh Hamilton	2.50
33	Rich Harden	.75
34	Dan Haren	.75
35	Felix Hernandez	1.00
36	Trevor Hoffman	.50
37	Matt Holliday	1.00
38	Ryan Howard	2.50
39	Torii Hunter	.75
40	Derek Jeter	4.00
41	Randy Johnson	1.50
42	Chipper Jones	2.00
43	Scott Kazmir	.75
44	Matt Kemp	1.00
45	Clayton Kershaw	1.00
46	Ian Kinsler	1.00
47	John Lackey	.75
48	Carlos Lee	1.00
49	Derrek Lee	.75
50	Tim Lincecum	2.50
51	Evan Longoria	2.50
52	Nick Markakis	1.00
53	Russell Martin	.75
54	Victor Martinez	.75
55	Hideki Matsui	1.00
56	Daisuke Matsuzaka	1.50
57	Joe Mauer	2.00
58	Brian McCann	1.00
59	Nate McLouth	.75
60	Lastings Milledge	1.00
61	Justin Morneau	1.00
62	Magglio Ordonez	.75
63	David Ortiz	1.50
64	Roy Oswalt	.75
65	Jonathan Papelbon	1.00
66	Jake Peavy	1.00
67	Dustin Pedroia	1.50
68	Brandon Phillips	.75
69	Albert Pujols	4.00
70	Carlos Quentin	1.00
71	Aramis Ramirez	1.00
72	Hanley Ramirez	1.50
73	Manny Ramirez	1.50
74	Jose Reyes	1.50
75	Alex Rios	.75
76	Mariano Rivera	1.50
77	Brian Roberts	75.00
78	Alex Rodriguez	3.00
79	Ivan Rodriguez	1.00
80	Jimmy Rollins	1.00
81	C.C. Sabathia	1.50
82	Johan Santana	1.50
83	Grady Sizemore	1.50
84	John Smoltz	1.00
85	Alfonso Soriano	1.00
86	Mark Teixeira	1.00
87	Miguel Tejada	.75
88	Jim Thome	.75

89	Troy Tulowitzki	.75
90	Dan Uggla	.75
91	B.J. Upton	.75
92	Chase Utley	1.50
93	Edinson Volquez	.75
94	Chien-Ming Wang	1.00
95	Brandon Webb	1.00
96	Vernon Wells	.75
97	David Wright	2.00
98	Michael Young	.50
99	Carlos Zambrano	.75
100	Ryan Zimmerman	.75
101	David Price/ Auto./99 **RC**	60.00
102	Aaron Cunningham/ Auto./99 **RC**	20.00
103	Angel Salome/ Auto./99 **RC**	25.00
104	Conor Gillaspie/ Auto./99 **RC**	30.00
105	Chris Lambert/ Auto./99 **RC**	25.00
106	Dexter Fowler/ Auto./99 **RC**	30.00
107	Francisco Cervelli/ Auto./99 **RC**	20.00
108	Greg Golson/ Auto./99 **RC**	20.00
109	Josh Geer/Auto./99 **RC**	15.00
110	Josh Outman/ Auto./99 **RC**	15.00
111	James Parr/Auto./99 **RC**	15.00
112	Kila Ka'aihue/ Auto./99 **RC**	20.00
113	Luis Cruz/Auto./99 **RC**	25.00
114	Lou Marson/ Auto./99 **RC**	25.00
115	Matt Antonelli/ Auto./99 **RC**	25.00
116	Michael Bowden/ Auto./99 **RC**	35.00
117	Mat Gamel/Auto./99 **RC**	20.00
118	Matt Tuiasosopo/ Auto./99 **RC**	20.00
119	Phil Coke/Auto./99 **RC**	20.00
120	James McDonald/ Auto./99 **RC**	25.00
121	Shairon Martis/ Auto./99 **RC**	15.00
122	Travis Snider/ Auto./99 **RC**	75.00
123	Wade LeBlanc/ Auto./99 **RC**	15.00

Winning Materials Triple

		NM/M
Common Trio:		8.00
AKD	Garrett Atkins, Kevin Kouzmanoff, Blake DeWitt	8.00
BCM	Mark Mulder, Chris Carpenter, Brian Barton	10.00
CGV	Miguel Cabrera, Curtis Granderson, Justin Verlander	15.00
DOF	Jermaine Dye, Magglio Ordonez, Jeff Francoeur	8.00
FJH	J.J. Hardy, Bill Hall, Prince Fielder	10.00
KCM	Paul Konerko, Justin Morneau, Miguel Cabrera	15.00
KIB	Scott Kazmir, Rocco Baldelli, Akinori Iwamura	8.00
KSB	Jeff Kent, Freddy Sanchez, Josh Barfield	8.00
KSK	Hong-Chih Kuo, Takashi Saito, Hiroki Kuroda	15.00
MBK	Kevin Millwood, Hank Blalock, Ian Kinsler	10.00
MLY	Joe Mauer, Francisco Liriano, Delmon Young	15.00
NLB	Joe Nathan, Francisco Liriano, Scott Baker	10.00
PCS	Chad Cordero, Jonathan Papelbon, Joakim Soria	10.00
PJG	Andy Pettitte, Randy Johnson, Tom Glavine	10.00
PKD	Brad Penny, Jeff Kent, Blake DeWitt	8.00
RBE	Manny Ramirez, Jason Bay, Jacoby Ellsbury	15.00
RMD	Johnny Damon, Manny Ramirez, Pedro Martinez	15.00
SBM	Curt Schilling, Josh Beckett, Daisuke Matsuzaka	15.00
TCB	Frank Thomas, Bobby Crosby, Travis Buck	15.00
TGB	Mark Teahen, Zack Greinke, Billy Butler	10.00
WNP	Kerry Wood, Joe Nathan, Jonathan Papelbon	10.00

Flashback Fabrics

		NM/M
Common Player:		5.00
AG	Adrian Gonzalez	5.00
AJ	Andruw Jones	5.00
AP	Andy Pettitte	8.00
BA	Bobby Abreu	6.00
CC	Coco Crisp	5.00

CD	Carlos Delgado	6.00
CL	Carlos Lee	5.00
CS	Curt Schilling	8.00
DA	Johnny Damon	8.00
FT	Frank Thomas	8.00
GJ	Geoff Jenkins	5.00
IR	Ivan Rodriguez	5.00
JE	Jim Edmonds	5.00
JV	Jose Valverde	5.00
KM	Kevin Millwood	5.00
LG	Luis Gonzalez	5.00
MA	Moises Alou	5.00
MG	Magglio Ordonez	5.00
MR	Manny Ramirez	10.00
MT	Mark Teixeira	8.00
OC	Orlando Cabrera	5.00
PM	Pedro Martinez	6.00
RJ	Randy Johnson	8.00
SR	Scott Rolen	5.00
VG	Vladimir Guerrero	6.00

Game Jersey Autos

	NM/M
Common Jersey Autos.:	10.00
Patch Autos.:	
Production 2-23	
No pricing prod. less than 20.	

AE	Andre Ethier	20.00
AK	Austin Kearns	10.00
AL	Adam LaRoche	15.00
AM	Andrew Miller	15.00
AR	Aaron Rowand	20.00
AX	Alex Romero	8.00
BA	Brian Barton	15.00
BC	Bobby Crosby	15.00
BE	Josh Beckett	30.00
BG	Brian Giles	15.00
BH	Bill Hall	15.00
BM	Brian McCann	20.00
BP	Brandon Phillips	25.00
BR	Brian Roberts	15.00
BW	Brandon Webb	15.00
CB	Chad Billingsley	20.00
CC	Chris Carpenter	35.00
CD	Chris Duncan	25.00
CF	Chone Figgins	15.00
CH	Cole Hamels	30.00
CJ	Chipper Jones	85.00
CL	Clay Buchholz	25.00
CR	Coco Crisp	10.00
DL	Derrek Lee	25.00
DS	Denard Span	20.00
DU	Dan Uggla	20.00
DW	Dontrelle Willis	10.00
EC	Eric Chavez	15.00
EM	Evan Meek	15.00
EV	Edinson Volquez	20.00
FC	Fausto Carmona	15.00
FH	Felix Hernandez	30.00
FL	Francisco Liriano	15.00
FP	Felix Pie	15.00
FT	Frank Thomas	60.00
GJ	Geoff Jenkins	15.00
HK	Howie Kendrick	20.00
HR	Hanley Ramirez	35.00
IK	Ian Kinsler	25.00
JB	Jason Bay	25.00
JC	Johnny Cueto	25.00
JH	Jeremy Hermida	15.00
JJ	Josh Johnson	15.00
JL	John Lackey	25.00
JN	Joe Nathan	15.00
JP	Jonathan Papelbon	25.00
JR	J.R. Towles	10.00
JV	Joey Votto	40.00
JZ	Joel Zumaya	15.00
LA	Andy LaRoche	10.00
LE	Jon Lester	50.00
LS	Luke Scott	10.00
ML	Mark Loretta	10.00
MO	Justin Morneau	25.00
NS	Nick Swisher	15.00
PH	Phil Hughes	30.00
RA	Aramis Ramirez	20.00
RH	Ramon Hernandez	15.00
SD	Stephen Drew	20.00
TH	Travis Hafner	15.00
TT	Troy Tulowitzki	15.00
VE	Justin Verlander	20.00
VM	Victor Martinez	15.00
WI	Josh Willingham	10.00
ZG	Zack Greinke	25.00

Winning Materials Quad

	NM/M
Common Quad:	10.00
BDBM	Rocco Baldelli, Nick Markakis, Chris Duncan, Ryan Braun 20.00
BUUB	Lance Berkman, Chase Utley, Dan Uggla, Ryan Braun 20.00
DJCP	Derek Jeter, Joe DiMaggio, Jorge Posada, Robinson Cano 65.00
DTGS	Ken Griffey Jr., Jim Thome, Jermaine Dye, Nick Swisher 20.00

HFBS	Ben Sheets, J.J. Hardy, Bill Hall, Prince Fielder	15.00
HHBN	Todd Helton, Jayson Nix, Matt Holliday, Jeff Baker	15.00
HRBB	Manny Ramirez, Pat Burrell, Matt Holliday, Ryan Braun	20.00
HRNB	Mariano Rivera, Trevor Hoffman, Joe Nathan, Brad Lidge	10.00
HSLC	Trevor Hoffman, Brad Lidge, Chad Cordero, Takashi Saito	10.00
JTJF	Andruw Jones, Chipper Jones, Rafael Furcal, Mark Teixeira	15.00
KFSK	Rafael Furcal, Hong-Chih Kuo, Takashi Saito, Matt Kemp	25.00
MMPV	Jason Varitek, Jorge Posada, Joe Mauer, Brian McCann	15.00
OEYV	Jason Varitek, David Ortiz, Kevin Youkilis, Jacoby Ellsbury	25.00
OGDF	Jason Giambi, Carlos Delgado, David Ortiz, Prince Fielder	15.00
OGTS	Jim Thome, Jason Giambi, Gary Sheffield, David Ortiz	15.00
PCLZ	Derrek Lee, Chris Carpenter, Albert Pujols, Carlos Zambrano	25.00
PLKL	Francisco Liriano, Scott Kazmir, Jake Peavy, Tim Lincecum	20.00
PMSL	Curt Schilling, Jon Lester, Jonathan Papelbon, Daisuke Matsuzaka	20.00
PRMV	Ivan Rodriguez, Jason Varitek, Jorge Posada, Joe Mauer	10.00
RGBN	Ken Griffey Jr., Manny Ramirez, Xavier Nady, Jason Bay	15.00
RLZW	Kerry Wood, Derrek Lee, Aramis Ramirez, Carlos Zambrano	15.00
RRTD	Jose Reyes, Stephen Drew, Hanley Ramirez, Troy Tulowitzki	20.00
RUJC	Derek Jeter, Robinson Cano, Hanley Ramirez, Dan Uggla	20.00
SZCO	Chris Carpenter, Ben Sheets, Roy Oswalt, Carlos Zambrano	10.00
UPRI	Brian Roberts, Brandon Phillips, Chase Utley, Akinori Iwamura	15.00
VGSZ	Gary Sheffield, Curtis Granderson, Justin Verlander, Joel Zumaya	15.00

Game Jerseys

	NM/M
Common Jersey:	4.00
Patch:	1.5X
Production 50-99	

BU	B.J. Upton	6.00
CZ	Carlos Zambrano	6.00
DJ	Derek Jeter	15.00
DL	Derrek Lee	6.00
DO	David Ortiz	8.00
FL	Francisco Liriano	6.00
GJ	Geoff Jenkins	4.00
HR	Hanley Ramirez	8.00
JD	Jermaine Dye	4.00
JL	John Lackey	6.00
JS	John Smoltz	6.00
JT	Jim Thome	8.00
JV	Justin Verlander	8.00
KF	Kosuke Fukudome	8.00
KW	Kerry Wood	8.00
MR	Manny Ramirez	8.00
MT	Miguel Tejada	6.00
RH	Roy Halladay	6.00
SA	Johan Santana	6.00
TH	Travis Hafner	4.00
TT	Troy Tulowitzki	6.00

Rookie Redemption Autographs

	NM/M
1 Koji Uehara	60.00

1993 Spectrum Diamond Club Promo Set

Ten Hall of Famers are featured in this promo card set. Fronts of the 2-1/2" x 3-1/2" cards have borderless player action or posed photos. The issuer's logo, player's

name and striping are printed in gold. Backs have a color ghost-image photo of the player along with personal data and career summary. A box near the bottom indicates the set's serial number from within an edition of 10,000. A "Pure Gold" parallel edition of 5,000 each was also produced.

	NM/M
Complete Set (10):	8.00
Common Player:	1.00
Pure Gold:	2X
1 Carl Yastrzemski	1.50
2 Johnny Bench (Numbered promo.)	1.00
-- Johnny Bench ("For Promotional Use Only" on back.)	1.00
3 Al Kaline	1.00
4 Ernie Banks	2.00
5 Catfish Hunter	1.00
6 Rod Carew	1.00
7 Mike Schmidt	2.00
8 Harmon Killebrew	1.00
9 Frank Robinson	1.50
10 Rollie Fingers	1.00

Diamond Club Red Sox

This collectors' issue features five stars of the Boston Red Sox from the 1940s-1970s. Fronts have action photos on which uniform logos are eliminated. A pinstripe around the photo, the issuer's logo and player name are printed in gold. Horizontal backs have a color Fenway Park photo ghosted in the background. Player career highlights and stats are overprinted.

	NM/M
Complete Set (5):	1.00
Common Player:	.25
1 Carl Yastrzemski	.50
2 Bobby Doerr	.25
3 Dwight Evans	.25
4 Fred Lynn	.25
5 Luis Tiant	.25

Legends of Baseball

This collectors' edition of 10 of baseball's greatest players was issued in two versions, with and

without a gold facsimile autograph on the cards' fronts. The gold-signature cards were limited to an edition of 5,000 numbered cards of each sport. Fronts have black-and-white photos with gold-foil graphic highlights. Backs have another photo subdued in the background with career history and stats and personal data overprinted in black. Copyright information is at bottom. Cards were issued in two series of five each and are checklisted here alphabetically.

	NM/M
Complete Set (10):	7.50
Common Player:	.50
Gold Signature:	2X
(1) Grover Alexander	.50
(2) Ty Cobb	.75
(3) Dizzy Dean	.50
(4) Lou Gehrig	1.00
(5) Rogers Hornsby	.50
(6) Satchel Paige	.75
(7) Babe Ruth	2.00
(8) Casey Stengel	.50
(9) Honus Wagner	.75
(10) Cy Young	.50

Nolan Ryan

Produced in the same format as its Legends of Baseball 10-card sets, this issue honors the career of Nolan Ryan. Each set comes with a numbered certificate of authenticity. There were 5,000 regular sets produced and 5,000 with gold-foil facsimile autographs on fronts. Each card can also be found in a promotional overprinted version.

	NM/M
Complete Set (10):	3.00
Common Card:	.50
Gold:	2X
Promo:	2X

Nolan Ryan 23K

A "pure gold" background on front offsets the color action photo of Ryan in action (team logos have been removed for licensing reasons). Backs of the 2-1/2" x 3-1/2" cards have career highlights and stats. Each set was issued with a certificate of authenticity numbered from an edition of 10,000.

	NM/M
Complete Set (3):	3.00
Common Card:	1.00
1-3 Nolan Ryan	1.00

1994 Spectrum 1969 Miracle Mets

The 1969 Miracle Mets card set, produced by Spectrum Holdings Group of Birmingham, Mich., was part of what the company called "an integrated memorabilia program, with the 1969 Mets card set as the centerpiece." The 70-card set measures the standard 2-1/2" x 3-1/2",

with UV coating on both sides and gold foil on fronts. It was sold complete at $24.95, and limited to 25,000 sets. A reported 1,000 numbered sets were signed by all 25 living players, including Hall of Famer Tom Seaver and future Cooperstown resident Nolan Ryan.

		NM/M
Complete Set (70):		20.00
Common Player:		.25
Autographed Set:		500.00
1	Commemorative Card	.25
2	Team Photo	.25
3	Tom Seaver	4.00
4	Jerry Koosman	.35
5	Tommie Agee	.25
6	Bud Harrelson	.25
7	Nolan Ryan	6.00
8	Jerry Grote	.25
9	Ron Swoboda	.25
10	Donn Clendenon	.25
11	Art Shamsky	.25
12	Tug McGraw	.25
13	Ed Kranepool	.25
14	Cleon Jones	.25
15	Ron Taylor	.25
16	Gary Gentry	.25
17	Ken Boswell	.25
18	Ed Charles	.25
19	J.C. Martin	.25
20	Al Weis	.25
21	Jack DiLauro	.25
22	Duffy Dyer	.25
23	Wayne Garrett	.25
24	Jim McAndrew	.25
25	Rod Gaspar	.25
26	Don Cardwell	.25
27	Bob Pfeil	.25
28	Cal Koonce	.25
29	Gil Hodges	1.50
30	Yogi Berra	2.00
31	Joe Pignatano	.25
32	Rube Walker	.25
33	Eddie Yost	.25
34	First-ever Met Game	.25
35	Opening Day 1969	.25
36	Kranepool Breaks Home Run Record	.25
37	Koosman Sets Club Strikeout Record	.25
38	Mets Trade for Clendenon	.25
39	Koosman's 23 Scoreless Innings	.25
40	Mets Begin 7-Game Winning Streak	.25
41	Mets vs. Division Leading Cubs	.25
42	Seaver's Near Perfect Game	.25
43	Mets Trail by 3-1/2	.25
44	All-Star Break	.25
45	All-Star Game	.25
46	Mets Sweep Atlanta	.25
47	Mets Sweep Padres	.25
48	Mets Defeat Cubs, Koosman Strikes Out 1	.25
49	Mets Defeat Cubs 1/2 Game Back	.25
50	First Place!	.25
51	Mets Continue Nine Game Winning Streak	.25
52	Seaver Earns 22nd Victory	.25
53	Mets Win, Carlton Strikes Out 19	.25
54	Koosman Pitches 15th Complete Game	.25
55	Eastern Division Champs!	.25
56	100th Victory	.25
57	Final Game, Mets Prepare for Braves	.25
58	N.L. Championship Series, Game 1	.25
59	N.L. Championship Series, Game 2	.25
60	N.L. Championship Series, Game 3	.25
61	World Series, Game 1	.25
62	World Series, Game 2	.25
63	World Series, Game 3	.25
64	World Series, Game 4	.25
65	World Series, Game 5	.25
66	World Champions	.25
67	World Champions	.25
68	World Champions	.25
69	World Champions	.25
----	Checklist	.25

1986 Sportflics Prototype Cards

This six-card set was apparently produced as a prototype as part of the licensing process. Similar in format to the 1986 Sportflics issue the cards have stats through the 1984 season. The prototype cards are much rarer than the promo cards. The Schmidt, Sutter and Winfield cards are standard 2-1/2" x 3-1/2" in size while the DiMaggio card is 1-5/16" square and the MLB logo card is 1-3/4" x 2".

		NM/M
Complete Set (7):		175.00
Common Card:		2.00
(1)	Joe DiMaggio (Black-and-white.)	100.00
(2)	Mike Schmidt	20.00
(3)	Bruce Sutter	5.00
(4)	Dave Winfield (Biographical back.)	50.00
(5)	Dave Winfield (Statistical back.)	37.50
(6)	Mike Schmidt, Bruce Sutter, Dave Winfield (Blank-back.)	10.00
(7)	Major League Baseball Logo	2.00

1986 Sportflics Promo Cards

Though they carry stats only through 1984, and have a 1986 copyright date, these promo cards were issued late in 1985 to preview the "Triple Action Sportflics" concept. They were the first really widely distributed promo cards. Each of the promo cards differs slightly from the issued version. The RBI Sluggers card in the issued set, for instance, was #126 and pictured Gary Carter, George Foster and Al Oliver. In the regular set, Pete Rose's card was #50 while Tom Seaver was #25. The regular-issue 1986 Sportflics cards, of course, include complete 1985 stats on back. Promo cards were distributed in three-card cello packs.

		NM/M
Complete Set (3):		12.50
Common Player:		3.00
1	RBI Sluggers (Dale Murphy, Jim Rice, Mike Schmidt)	3.00
43	Pete Rose	10.00
45	Tom Seaver	4.00

1986 Sportflics

The premiere issue from Sportflics was distributed nationally by Amurol Division of Wrigley Gum Co. The three-phase "Magic Motion" cards depict three different photos per card, with each visible separately as the card is tilted. The 1986 issue features 200 full-color baseball cards plus 133 trivia cards. The cards are in the standard 2-1/2" x 3-1/2" size with the backs

containing player stats and personal information. There are three different types of picture cards: 1) Tri-Star cards - 50 cards feature three players on one card; 2) Big Six cards - 10 cards which have six players in special categories; and 3) the Big Twelve card of 12 World Series players from the Kansas City Royals. The trivia cards are 1-3/4" x 2" and do not have player photos.

		NM/M
Unopened Factory Set (200):		10.00
Complete Set (200):		7.50
Common Player:		.10
Foil Pack (3+2):		.50
Foil Box (36):		9.00
1	George Brett	2.25
2	Don Mattingly	2.25
3	Wade Boggs	2.00
4	Eddie Murray	1.00
5	Dale Murphy	.65
6	Rickey Henderson	1.00
7	Harold Baines	.10
8	Cal Ripken, Jr.	3.00
9	Orel Hershiser	.10
10	Bret Saberhagen	.10
11	Tim Raines	.10
12	Fernando Valenzuela	.10
13	Tony Gwynn	2.00
14	Pedro Guerrero	.10
15	Keith Hernandez	.10
16	Ernest Riles	.10
17	Jim Rice	.20
18	Ron Guidry	.10
19	Willie McGee	.10
20	Ryne Sandberg	2.00
21	Kirk Gibson	.10
22	Ozzie Guillen	.10
23	Dave Parker	.10
24	Vince Coleman	.10
25	Tom Seaver	1.00
26	Brett Butler	.10
27	Steve Carlton	1.00
28	Gary Carter	1.00
29	Cecil Cooper	.10
30	Jose Cruz	.10
31	Alvin Davis	.10
32	Dwight Evans	.10
33	Julio Franco	.10
34	Damaso Garcia	.10
35	Steve Garvey	.60
36	Kent Hrbek	.10
37	Reggie Jackson	2.25
38	Fred Lynn	.10
39	Paul Molitor	1.00
40	Jim Presley	.10
41	Dave Righetti	.10
42a	Robin Yount (Yankees logo on back.)	400.00
42b	Robin Yount (Brewers logo.)	1.00
43	Nolan Ryan	3.00
44	Mike Schmidt	2.25
45	Lee Smith	.10
46	Rick Sutcliffe	.10
47	Bruce Sutter	.75
48	Lou Whitaker	.10
49	Dave Winfield	1.00
50	Pete Rose	2.50
51	N.L. MVPs (Steve Garvey, Pete Rose, Ryne Sandberg)	1.00
52	Slugging Stars (Harold Baines, George Brett, Jim Rice)	.35
53	No-Hitters (Phil Niekro, Jerry Reuss, Mike Witt)	.25
54	Big Hitters (Don Mattingly, Cal Ripken, Jr., Robin Yount)	2.00
55	Bullpen Aces (Goose Gossage, Dan Quisenberry, Lee Smith)	.10
56	Rookies of the Year (Pete Rose, Steve Sax, Darryl Strawberry)	1.00
57	A.L. MVPs (Don Baylor, Reggie Jackson, Cal Ripken, Jr.)	.50
58	Repeat Batting Champs (Bill Madlock, Dave Parker, Pete Rose)	.45
59	Cy Young Winners (Mike Flanagan, Ron Guidry, LaMarr Hoyt)	.10
60	Double Award Winners (Tom Seaver, Rick Sutcliffe, Fernando Valenzuela)	.20
61	Home Run Champs (Tony Armas, Reggie Jackson, Jim Rice)	.25
62	N.L. MVPs (Keith Hernandez, Dale Murphy, Mike Schmidt)	.40
63	A.L. MVPs (George Brett, Fred Lynn, Robin Yount)	.30
64	Comeback Players (Bert Blyleven, John Denny, Jerry Koosman)	.10
65	Cy Young Relievers (Rollie Fingers, Willie Hernandez, Bruce Sutter)	.10
66	Rookies of the Year (Andre Dawson, Bob Horner, Gary Matthews)	.20
67	Rookies of the Year (Carlton Fisk, Ron Kittle, Tom Seaver)	.25
68	Home Run Champs (George Foster, Dave Kingman, Mike Schmidt)	.25
69	Double Award Winners (Rod Carew, Cal Ripken, Jr., Pete Rose)	2.00
70	Cy Young Winners (Steve Carlton, Tom Seaver, Rick Sutcliffe)	.25
71	Top Sluggers (Reggie Jackson, Fred Lynn, Robin Yount)	.30
72	Rookies of the Year (Dave Righetti, Rick Sutcliffe, Fernando Valenzuela)	.10
73	Rookies of the Year (Fred Lynn, Eddie Murray, Cal Ripken, Jr.)	.50
74	Rookies of the Year (Rod Carew, Alvin Davis, Lou Whitaker)	.20
75	Batting Champs (Wade Boggs, Carney Lansford, Don Mattingly)	1.00
76	Jesse Barfield	.10
77	Phil Bradley	.10
78	Chris Brown	.10
79	Tom Browning	.10
80	Tom Brunansky	.10
81	Bill Buckner	.10
82	Chili Davis	.10
83	Mike Davis	.10
84	Rich Gedman	.10
85	Willie Hernandez	.10
86	Ron Kittle	.10
87	Lee Lacy	.10
88	Bill Madlock	.10
89	Mike Marshall	.10
90	Keith Moreland	.10
91	Graig Nettles	.10
92	Lance Parrish	.10
93	Kirby Puckett	2.00
94	Juan Samuel	.10
95	Steve Sax	.10
96	Dave Stieb	.10
97	Darryl Strawberry	.10
98	Willie Upshaw	.10
99	Frank Viola	.10
100	Dwight Gooden	.10
101	Joaquin Andujar	.10
102	George Bell	.10
103	Bert Blyleven	.10
104	Mike Boddicker	.10
105	Britt Burns	.10
106	Rod Carew	1.00
107	Jack Clark	.10
108	Danny Cox	.10
109	Ron Darling	.10
110	Andre Dawson	.45
111	Leon Durham	.10
112	Tony Fernandez	.10
113	Tom Herr	.10
114	Teddy Higuera	.10
115	Bob Horner	.10
116	Dave Kingman	.10
117	Jack Morris	.10
118	Dan Quisenberry	.10
119	Jeff Reardon	.10
120	Bryn Smith	.10
121	Ozzie Smith	2.00
122	John Tudor	.10
123	Tim Wallach	.10
124	Willie Wilson	.10
125	Carlton Fisk	1.00
126	RBI Sluggers (Gary Carter, George Foster, Al Oliver)	.10
127	Run Scorers (Keith Hernandez, Tim Raines, Ryne Sandberg)	.25
128	Run Scorers (Paul Molitor, Cal Ripken, Jr., Willie Wilson)	.50
129	No-Hitters (John Candelaria, Dennis Eckersley, Bob Forsch)	.10
130	World Series MVPs (Ron Cey, Rollie Fingers, Pete Rose)	.35
131	All-Star Game MVPs (Dave Concepcion, George Foster, Bill Madlock)	.10
132	Cy Young Winners (Vida Blue, John Denny, Fernando Valenzuela)	.10
133	Comeback Players (Doyle Alexander, Joaquin Andujar, Richard Dotson)	.10
134	Big Winners (John Denny, Tom Seaver, Rick Sutcliffe)	.10
135	Veteran Pitchers (Phil Niekro, Tom Seaver, Don Sutton)	.25
136	Rookies of the Year (Vince Coleman, Dwight Gooden, Alfredo Griffin)	.20
137	All-Star Game MVPs (Gary Carter, Steve Garvey, Fred Lynn)	.20
138	Veteran Hitters (Tony Perez, Pete Rose, Rusty Staub)	.50
139	Power Hitters (George Foster, Jim Rice, Mike Schmidt)	.30
140	Batting Champs (Bill Buckner, Tony Gwynn, Al Oliver)	.15
141	No-Hitters (Jack Morris, Dave Righetti, Nolan Ryan)	.50
142	No-Hitters (Vida Blue, Bert Blyleven, Tom Seaver)	.10
143	Strikeout Kings (Dwight Gooden, Nolan Ryan, Fernando Valenzuela)	1.25
144	Base Stealers (Dave Lopes, Tim Raines, Willie Wilson)	.10
145	RBI Sluggers (Tony Armas, Cecil Cooper, Eddie Murray)	.15
146	A.L. MVPs (Rod Carew, Rollie Fingers, Jim Rice)	.15
147	World Series MVPs (Rick Dempsey, Reggie Jackson, Alan Trammell)	.25
148	World Series MVPs (Pedro Guerrero, Darrell Porter, Mike Schmidt)	.20
149	ERA Leaders (Mike Boddicker, Ron Guidry, Rick Sutcliffe)	.10
150	Comeback Players (Reggie Jackson, Dave Kingman, Fred Lynn)	.20
151	Buddy Bell	.10
152	Dennis Boyd	.10
153	Dave Concepcion	.10
154	Brian Downing	.10
155	Shawon Dunston	.10
156	John Franco	.10
157	Scott Garrelts	.10
158	Bob James	.10
159	Charlie Leibrandt	.10
160	Oddibe McDowell	.10
161	Roger McDowell	.10
162	Mike Moore	.10
163	Phil Niekro	.75
164	Al Oliver	.10
165	Tony Pena	.10
166	Ted Power	.10
167	Mike Scioscia	.10
168	Mario Soto	.10
169	Bob Stanley	.10
170	Garry Templeton	.10
171	Andre Thornton	.10
172	Alan Trammell	.10
173	Doug DeCinces	.10
174	Greg Walker	.10
175	Don Sutton	.75
176	1985 Award Winners (Vince Coleman, Dwight Gooden, Ozzie Guillen, Don Mattingly, Willie McGee, Bret Saberhagen)	.50
177	1985 Hot Rookies (Stewart Cliburn, Brian Fisher, Joe Hesketh, Joe Orsulak, Mark Salas, Larry Sheets)	.10
178a	Future Stars (Jose Canseco RC, Mark Funderburk, Mike Greenwell, Steve Lombardozzi, Billy Joe Robidoux, Danny Tartabull)	2.00
178b	Future Stars (Jose Canseco, Mike Greenwell, Steve Lombardozzi, Billy Jo Robidoux, Danny Tartabull, Jim Wilson)	30.00
179	Gold Glove (George Brett, Ron Guidry, Keith Hernandez, Don Mattingly, Willie McGee, Dale Murphy)	1.00
180	.300 (Wade Boggs, George Brett, Rod Carew, Cecil Cooper, Don Mattingly, Willie Wilson)	1.00
181	.300 (Pedro Guerrero, Tony Gwynn, Keith Hernandez, Bill Madlock, Dave Parker, Pete Rose)	.50
182	1985 Milestones (Rod Carew, Phil Niekro, Pete Rose, Nolan Ryan, Tom Seaver, Matt Tallman)	1.50
183	1985 Triple Crown (Wade Boggs, Darrell Evans, Don Mattingly, Willie McGee, Dave Parker)	1.00
184	1985 HL (Wade Boggs, Dwight Gooden, Rickey Henderson, Don Mattingly, Willie McGee, John Tudor)	1.00
185	1985 20-Game Winners (Joaquin Andujar, Tom Browning, Dwight Gooden, Ron Guidry, Bret Saberhagen, John Tudor)	.10
186	World Series Champs (Steve Balboni, George Brett, Dane Iorg, Danny Jackson, Charlie Leibrandt, Darryl Motley, Dan Quisenberry, Bret Saberhagen, Lonnie Smith, Jim Sundberg, Frank White, Willie Wilson)	.40
187	Hubie Brooks	.10
188	Glenn Davis	.10
189	Darrell Evans	.10
190	Rich Gossage	.10
191	Andy Hawkins	.10
192	Jay Howell	.10
193	LaMarr Hoyt	.10
194	Davey Lopes	.10
195	Mike Scott	.10
196	Ted Simmons	.10
197	Gary Ward	.10
198	Bob Welch	.10
199	Mike Young	.10
200	Buddy Biancalana	.10

Decade Greats Sample Cards

To promote its Decade Greats set of current and former cards, Sportflics issued this two-card promo set. Card fronts are identical to the issued versions. Backs are printed in blue on white: "DECADE GREATS/SAMPLE CARD." The players are not identified on the cards.

		NM/M
Complete Set (2):		2.00
(1)	Dwight Gooden	1.00
(2)	Mel Ott	1.00

Decade Greats

This set, produced by Sportflics, features outstanding players, by position, from the 1930s through the 1980s by decades. The card fronts are printed in sepia-toned photos or full-color with the Sportflics three-phase "Magic Motion" animation. The complete set contains 75 cards with 59 single player cards and 16 multi-

player cards. Biographies appear on the card backs which are printed in full-color and color-coded by decade. The set was distributed only through hobby dealers and is in the popular 2-1/2" x 3-1/2" size.

		NM/M
Complete Set (75):		9.00
Common Player:		.10
1	Babe Ruth	2.00
2	Jimmie Foxx	.15
3	Lefty Grove	.10
4	Hank Greenberg	.25
5	Al Simmons	.10
6	Carl Hubbell	.10
7	Joe Cronin	.10
8	Mel Ott	.10
9	Lefty Gomez	.10
10	Lou Gehrig	1.25
11	Pie Traynor	.10
12	Charlie Gehringer	.10
13	Catchers (Mickey Cochrane, Bill Dickey, Gabby Hartnett)	.10
14	Pitchers (Dizzy Dean, Paul Derringer, Red Ruffing)	.10
15	Outfielders (Earl Averill, Joe Medwick, Paul Waner)	.10
16	Bob Feller	.40
17	Lou Boudreau	.10
18	Enos Slaughter	.15
19	Hal Newhouser	.10
20	Joe DiMaggio	1.25
21	Pee Wee Reese	.25
22	Phil Rizzuto	.15
23	Ernie Lombardi	.10
24	Infielders (Joe Cronin, George Kell, Johnny Mize)	.10
25	Ted Williams	1.25
26	Mickey Mantle	3.00
27	Warren Spahn	.15
28	Jackie Robinson	1.00
29	Ernie Banks	.20
30	Stan Musial	.75
31	Yogi Berra	.40
32	Duke Snider	.50
33	Roy Campanella	.50
34	Eddie Mathews	.15
35	Ralph Kiner	.15
36	Early Wynn	.10
37	Double Play Duo (Luis Aparicio, Nellie Fox)	.35
38	First Basemen (Gil Hodges, Ted Kluszewski, Mickey Vernon)	.25
40	Henry Aaron	.75
41	Frank Robinson	.20
42	Bob Gibson	.20
43	Roberto Clemente	1.75
44	Whitey Ford	.25
45	Brooks Robinson	.35
46	Juan Marichal	.15
47	Carl Yastrzemski	.40
48	First Basemen (Orlando Cepeda, Harmon Killebrew, Willie McCovey)	.15
49	Catchers (Bill Freehan, Elston Howard, Joe Torre)	.10
50	Willie Mays	.75
51	Outfielders (Al Kaline, Tony Oliva, Billy Williams)	.15
52	Tom Seaver	.40
53	Reggie Jackson	.50
54	Steve Carlton	.25
55	Mike Schmidt	.50
56	Joe Morgan	.20
57	Jim Rice	.20
58	Jim Palmer	.20
59	Lou Brock	.20
60	Pete Rose	1.00
61	Steve Garvey	.25
62	Catchers (Carlton Fisk, Thurman Munson, Ted Simmons)	.15
63	Pitchers (Vida Blue, Catfish Hunter, Nolan Ryan)	.20
64	George Brett	.50
65	Don Mattingly	1.00
66	Fernando Valenzuela	.10
67	Dale Murphy	.10
68	Wade Boggs	.40
69	Rickey Henderson	.40
70	Eddie Murray	.40
71	Ron Guidry	.10
72	Catchers (Gary Carter, Lance Parrish, Tony Pena)	.15
73	Infielders (Cal Ripken, Jr., Lou Whitaker, Robin Yount)	.35
74	Outfielders (Pedro Guerrero, Tim Raines, Dave Winfield)	.15
75	Dwight Gooden	.10

Rookies

The 1986 Rookies set offers 50 cards and features 47 individual rookie players. In addition, there are two Tri-Star cards; one highlights former Rookies of the Year and the other features three prominent players. There is one "Big Six" card featuring six superstars. The full-color photos on the 2-1/2" x 3-1/2" cards use Sportflics three-phase "Magic Motion" animation. The set was packaged in a collector box which also contained 34 trivia cards that measure 1-3/4" x 2". The set was distributed only by hobby dealers.

		NM/M
Complete Set (50):		17.50
Common Player:		.10
1	John Kruk	.10
2	Edwin Correa	.10
3	Pete Incaviglia	.10
4	Dale Sveum	.10
5	Juan Nieves	.10
6	Will Clark	.25
7	Wally Joyner	.25
8	Lance McCullers	.10
9	Scott Bailes	.10
10	Dan Plesac	.10
11	Jose Canseco	1.50
12	Bobby Witt	.10
13	Barry Bonds	15.00
14	Andres Thomas	.10
15	Jim Deshaies	.10
16	Ruben Sierra	.10
17	Steve Lombardozzi	.10
18	Cory Snyder	.10
19	Reggie Williams	.10
20	Mitch Williams	.10
21	Glenn Braggs	.10
22	Danny Tartabull	.10
23	Charlie Kerfeld	.10
24	Paul Assenmacher	.10
25	Robby Thompson	.10
26	Bobby Bonilla	.10
27	Andres Galarraga	.10
28	Billy Jo Robidoux	.10
29	Bruce Ruffin	.10
30	Greg Swindell	.10
31	John Cangelosi	.10
32	Jim Traber	.10
33	Russ Morman	.10
34	Barry Larkin	.10
35	Todd Worrell	.10
36	John Cerutti	.10
37	Mike Kingery	.10
38	Mark Eichhorn	.10
39	Scott Bankhead	.10
40	Bo Jackson	.25
41	Greg Mathews	.10
42	Eric King	.10
43	Kal Daniels	.10
44	Calvin Schiraldi	.10
45	Mickey Brantley	.10
46	Outstanding Rookie Seasons (Fred Lynn, Willie Mays, Pete Rose)	.60
47	Outstanding Rookie Seasons (Dwight Gooden, Tom Seaver, Fernando Valenzuela)	.25
48	Outstanding Rookie Seasons (Eddie Murray, Dave Righetti, Cal Ripken, Jr., Steve Sax, Darryl Strawberry, Lou Whitaker)	.25
49	Kevin Mitchell	.10
50	Mike Diaz	.10

Dwight Gooden Discs

As the viewing angle changes on these 3-D simulated motion plastic discs, three different pictures of "Dr. K" can be seen, two action and one portrait. The discs are found in two diameters, 2-1/4" and 4-1/2". Fronts have team-color borders of blue with orange lettering. Backs are blank.

		NM/M
Complete Set (2):		3.00
(1)	Dwight Gooden (2-1/4")	1.00
(2)	Dwight Gooden (4-1/2")	2.00

Jumbo Discs

A portrait and two action pictures of the players are featured in these large-format (4-1/2" diameter) "Magic Motion" discs. Fronts have the player's name below the photos, with a title above. Backs are printed in purple, red, black and white. Discs were available for $5 each with a paper coupon found in Sportflics packs.

		NM/M
Complete Set (6):		13.50
Common Player:		1.50
(1)	Wade Boggs	4.00
(2)	Roger Clemens	5.00
(3)	Wally Joyner	1.50
(4)	Mickey Mantle	6.00
(5)	Don Mattingly	5.00
(6)	Dave Winfield	3.00
(1)	Wade Boggs	1.00
(2)	Roger Clemens	1.25
(3)	Wally Joyner	.40
(4)	Mickey Mantle	2.00
(5)	Don Mattingly	1.25
(6)	Dave Winfield	.75

1987 Sportflics

In its second year in the national market, Sportflics' basic issue was again a 200-card set of 2-1/2" x 3-1/2" "Magic Motion" cards, which offer three different photos on the same card, each visible in turn as the card is moved from top to bottom or side to side. Besides single-player cards, the '87 Sportflics set includes several three- and six-player cards, though not as many as in the 1986 set. The card backs feature a small player portrait photo on the single-player cards, an innovation for 1987. The cards were issued with a series of 136 team logo trivia cards. Most cards exist in two variations, carrying 1986 or 1987 copyright dates on back.

		NM/M
Factory Set (200+136):		12.00
Complete Set (200):		7.50
Common Player:		.10
Foil Pack (3+2):		.50
Foil Box (36):		10.00
1	Don Mattingly	1.25
2	Wade Boggs	1.00
3	Dale Murphy	.50
4	Rickey Henderson	.75
5	George Brett	1.25
6	Eddie Murray	.75
7	Kirby Puckett	1.00
8	Ryne Sandberg	.75
9	Cal Ripken, Jr.	2.00
10	Roger Clemens	1.25
11	Ted Higuera	.10
12	Steve Sax	.10
13	Chris Brown	.10
14	Jesse Barfield	.10
15	Kent Hrbek	.10
16	Robin Yount	.75
17	Glenn Davis	.10
18	Hubie Brooks	.10
19	Mike Scott	.10
20	Darryl Strawberry	.40
21	Alvin Davis	.10
22	Eric Davis	.10
23	Danny Tartabull	.10
24a	Cory Snyder (Pat Tabler photo on back.)	1.50
24b	Cory Snyder (Pat Tabler photo on back.)(Facing front, 1/4 swing on front.)	1.50
24c	Cory Snyder (Snyder photo on back.)(Facing to side.)	.50
25	Pete Rose	1.50
26	Wally Joyner	.10
27	Pedro Guerrero	.10
28	Tom Seaver	.75
29	Bob Knepper	.10
30	Mike Schmidt	1.25
31	Tony Gwynn	1.00
32	Don Slaught	.10
33	Todd Worrell	.10
34	Tim Raines	.10
35	Dave Parker	.10
36	Bob Ojeda	.10
37	Pete Incaviglia	.10
38	Bruce Hurst	.10
39	Bobby Witt	.10
40	Steve Garvey	.40
41	Dave Winfield	.75
42	Jose Cruz	.10
43	Orel Hershiser	.10
44	Reggie Jackson	.75
45	Chili Davis	.10
46	Robby Thompson	.10
47	Dennis Boyd	.10
48	Kirk Gibson	.10
49	Fred Lynn	.10
50	Gary Carter	.75
51	George Bell	.10
52	Pete O'Brien	.10
53	Ron Darling	.10
54	Paul Molitor	.75
55	Mike Pagliarulo	.10
56	Mike Boddicker	.10
57	Dave Righetti	.10
58	Len Dykstra RC	.10
59	Mike Witt	.10
60	Tony Bernazard	.10
61	John Kruk	.10
62	Mike Krukow	.10
63	Sid Fernandez	.10
64	Gary Gaetti	.10
65	Vince Coleman	.10
66	Pat Tabler	.10
67	Mike Scioscia	.10
68	Scott Garrelts	.10
69	Brett Butler	.10
70	Bill Buckner	.10
71a	Dennis Rasmussen (John Montefusco photo on back; mustache.)	.25
71b	Dennis Rasmussen (Correct photo on back, no mustache.)	.10
72	Tim Wallach	.10
73	Bob Horner	.10
74	Willie McGee	.10
75	A.L. First Basemen (Wally Joyner, Don Mattingly, Eddie Murray)	.50
76	Jesse Orosco	.10
77	N.L. Relief Pitchers (Jeff Reardon, Dave Smith, Todd Worrell)	.10
78	Candy Maldonado	.10
79	N.L. Shortstops (Hubie Brooks, Shawon Dunston, Ozzie Smith)	.10
80	A.L. Left Fielders (George Bell, Jose Canseco, Jim Rice)	.25
81	Bert Blyleven	.60
82	Mike Marshall	.10
83	Ron Guidry	.10
84	Julio Franco	.10
85	Willie Wilson	.10
86	Lee Lacy	.10
87	Jack Morris	.10
88	Ray Knight	.10
89	Phil Bradley	.10
90	Jose Canseco	.60
91	Gary Ward	.10
92	Mike Easler	.10
93	Tony Pena	.10
94	Dave Smith	.10
95	Will Clark	.10
96	Lloyd Moseby	.10
97	Jim Rice	.25
98	Shawon Dunston	.10
99	Don Sutton	.50
100	Dwight Gooden	.10
101	Lance Parrish	.10
102	Mark Langston	.10
103	Floyd Youmans	.10
104	Lee Smith	.10
105	Willie Hernandez	.10
106	Doug DeCinces	.10
107	Ken Schrom	.10
108	Don Carman	.10
109	Brook Jacoby	.10
110	Steve Bedrosian	.10
111	A.L. Pitchers (Roger Clemens, Teddy Higuera, Jack Morris)	.25
112	A.L. Second Basemen (Marty Barrett, Tony Bernazard, Lou Whitaker)	.10
113	A.L. Shortstops (Tony Fernandez, Scott Fletcher, Cal Ripken, Jr.)	.25
114	A.L. Third Basemen (Wade Boggs, George Brett, Gary Gaetti)	.25
115	N.L. Third Basemen (Chris Brown, Mike Schmidt, Tim Wallach)	.20
116	N.L. Second Basemen (Bill Doran, Johnny Ray, Ryne Sandberg)	.10
117	N.L. Right Fielders (Kevin Bass, Tony Gwynn, Dave Parker)	.10
118	Hot Rookie Prospects (David Clark, Pat Dodson, Ty Gainey, Phil Lombardi, Benito Santiago, Terry Steinbach RC)	.25
119	1986 Season Highlights (Dave Righetti, Mike Scott, Fernando Valenzuela)	.10
120	N.L. Pitchers (Dwight Gooden, Mike Scott, Fernando Valenzuela)	.10
121	Johnny Ray	.10
122	Keith Moreland	.10
123	Juan Samuel	.10
124	Wally Backman	.10
125	Nolan Ryan	2.00
126	Greg Harris	.10
127	Kirk McCaskill	.10
128	Dwight Evans	.10
129	Rick Rhoden	.10
130	Bill Madlock	.10
131	Oddibe McDowell	.10
132	Darrell Evans	.10
133	Keith Hernandez	.10
134	Tom Brunansky	.10
135	Kevin McReynolds	.10
136	Scott Fletcher	.10
137	Lou Whitaker	.10
138	Carney Lansford	.10
139	Andre Dawson	.45
140	Carlton Fisk	.75
141	Buddy Bell	.10
142	Ozzie Smith	1.00
143	Dan Pasqua	.10
144	Kevin Mitchell	.10
145	Bret Saberhagen	.10
146	Charlie Kerfeld	.10
147	Phil Niekro	.50
148	John Candelaria	.10
149	Rich Gedman	.10
150	Fernando Valenzuela	.10
151	N.L. Catchers (Gary Carter, Tony Pena, Mike Scioscia)	.10
152	N.L. Left Fielders (Vince Coleman, Jose Cruz, Tim Raines)	.10
153	A.L. Right Fielders (Harold Baines, Jesse Barfield, Dave Winfield)	.10
154	A.L. Catchers (Rich Gedman, Lance Parrish, Don Slaught)	.10
155	N.L. Center Fielders (Kevin McReynolds, Dale Murphy, Eric Davis)	.10
156	'86 Highlights (Jim Deshaies, Mike Schmidt, Don Sutton)	.10
157	A.L. Speedburners (John Cangelosi, Rickey Henderson, Gary Pettis)	.10
158	Hot Rookie Prospects (Randy Asadoor, Casey Candaele, Dave Cochrane, Rafael Palmeiro, Tim Pyznarski, Kevin Seitzer)	.75
159	The Best of the Best (Roger Clemens, Dwight Gooden, Rickey Henderson, Don Mattingly, Dale Murphy, Eddie Murray)	.75
160	Roger McDowell	.10
161	Brian Downing	.10
162	Bill Doran	.10
163	Don Baylor	.10
164	Alfredo Griffin	.10
165	Don Aase	.10
166	Glenn Wilson	.10
167	Dan Quisenberry	.10
168	Frank White	.10
169	Cecil Cooper	.10
170	Jody Davis	.10
171	Harold Baines	.10
172	Rob Deer	.10
173	John Tudor	.10
174	Larry Parrish	.10
175	Kevin Bass	.10
176	Joe Carter	.10
177	Mitch Webster	.10
178	Dave Kingman	.10
179	Jim Presley	.10
180	Mel Hall	.10
181	Shane Rawley	.10
182	Marty Barrett	.10
183	Damaso Garcia	.10
184	Bobby Grich	.10
185	Leon Durham	.10
186	Ozzie Guillen	.10
187	Tony Fernandez	.10
188	Alan Trammell	.10
189	Jim Clancy	.10
190	Bo Jackson	.15
191	Bob Forsch	.10
192	John Franco	.10
193	Von Hayes	.10
194	A.L. Relief Pitchers (Don Aase, Mark Eichhorn, Dave Righetti)	.10
195	N.L. First Basemen (Will Clark, Glenn Davis, Keith Hernandez)	.10
196	'86 Highlights (Roger Clemens, Joe Cowley, Bob Horner)	.10
197	The Best of the Best (Wade Boggs, George Brett, Hubie Brooks, Tony Gwynn, Tim Raines, Ryne Sandberg)	.75
198	A.L. Center Fielders (Rickey Henderson, Fred Lynn, Kirby Puckett)	.50
199	N.L. Speedburners (Vince Coleman, Tim Raines, Eric Davis)	.10
200	Steve Carlton	.75

Rookie Discs

The 1987 Sportflics Rookie Discs set consists of seven discs which measure 4" in diameter. The front of the discs offer three "Magic Motion" photos in full color, encompassed by a blue border. The disc backs are printed in color and include the team logo, player statistics, biography and the disc number. The set was issued with Cooperstown Timeless Trivia Cards.

		NM/M
Complete Set (7):		8.00
Common Player:		1.00
1	Casey Candaele	1.00
2	Mark McGwire	6.00
3	Kevin Seitzer	1.00
4	Joe Magrane	1.00
5	Benito Santiago	1.00
6	Dave Magadan	1.00
7	Devon White	1.00

Rookie Prospects

The Rookie Prospects set consists of 10 cards in standard 2-1/2" x 3-1/2" size. The card fronts feature Sportflics' "Magic Motion" process. Card backs contain a player photo plus a short biography and player personal and statistical information. The set was offered in two separately wrapped mylar packs of five cards to hobby dealers purchasing cases of Sportflics' Team Preview set. Twenty-four packs of "Rookie Prospects" cards were included with each case.

		NM/M
Complete Set (10):		4.00
Common Player:		.25
1	Terry Steinbach	.25
2	Rafael Palmeiro	3.00
3	Dave Magadan	.25
4	Marvin Freeman	.25
5	Brick Smith	.25
6	B.J. Surhoff	.25
7	John Smiley	.25
8	Alonzo Powell	.25
9	Benny Santiago	.25
10	Devon White	.25

Rookies

The Rookies set was issued in two boxed series of 25 cards. The first was released in July with the second series following in October. The cards, which are the standard 2-1/2" x 3-1/2", feature Sportflics' special "Magic Motion" process. The card fronts contain a full-color photo and present three different pictures, depending on how the card is held. The backs also contain a full-color photo along with player statistics and a biography.

		NM/M
Complete Set One (1-25):		4.00
Complete Set Two (26-50):		2.00
Common Player:		.10
1	Eric Bell	.10
2	Chris Bosio	.10
3	Bob Brower	.10
4	Jerry Browne	.10
5	Ellis Burks	.10
6	Casey Candaele	.10
7	Ken Gerhart	.10
8	Mike Greenwell	.10
9	Stan Jefferson	.10
10	Dave Magadan	.10
11	Joe Magrane	.10
12	Fred McGriff	.25
13	Mark McGwire	3.00
14	Mark McLemore	.10
15	Jeff Musselman	.10
16	Matt Nokes	.10
17	Paul O'Neill	.10
18	Luis Polonia	.10
19	Benny Santiago	.10
20	Kevin Seitzer	.10
21	John Smiley	.10
22	Terry Steinbach	.10
23	B.J. Surhoff	.10
24	Devon White	.10
25	Matt Williams	.25
26	DeWayne Buice	.10
27	Willie Fraser	.10
28	Bill Ripken	.10
29	Mike Henneman	.10
30	Shawn Hillegas	.10
31	Shane Mack	.10
32	Rafael Palmeiro	1.50
33	Mike Jackson	.10
34	Gene Larkin	.10
35	Jimmy Jones	.10
36	Gerald Young	.10
37	Ken Caminiti	.10
38	Sam Horn	.10
39	David Cone	.10
40	Mike Dunne	.10
41	Ken Williams	.10
42	John Morris	.10
43	Jim Lindeman	.10
44	Mike Stanley	.10
45	Les Straker	.10
46	Jeff Robinson	.10
47	Todd Benzinger	.10
48	Jeff Blauser	.10
49	John Marzano	.10
50	Keith Miller	.10

Superstar Discs

Released in three series of six discs, the Superstar Disc set features the special "Magic Motion" process. Each disc, which measures 4-1/2" in diameter, contains three different player photos, depending which way it is tilted. A red border, containing 11 stars, the player's name and uniform number, surrounds the photo. The backs have a turquoise border which carries the words "Superstar Disc Collector Series." The backs also include the team logo, player statistics, biography and the disc number. The discs were issued with 18 1-3/4" x 2-1/2" Cooperstown Timeless Trivia Cards.

		NM/M
Complete Set (18):		35.00
Common Player:		1.50
1	Jose Canseco	2.50
2	Mike Scott	1.50
3	Ryne Sandberg	3.50
4	Mike Schmidt	4.00
5	Dale Murphy	2.00
6	Fernando Valenzuela	1.50
7	Tony Gwynn	3.50
8	Cal Ripken, Jr.	6.00
9	Gary Carter	3.00
10	Cory Snyder	1.50
11	Kirby Puckett	3.50
12	George Brett	3.50
13	Keith Hernandez	1.50
14	Rickey Henderson	3.00
15	Tim Raines	1.50
16	Bo Jackson	2.00
17	Pete Rose	4.50
18	Eric Davis	1.50

Team Previews

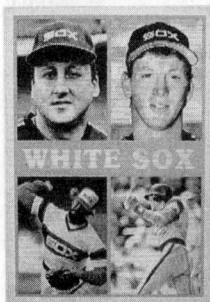

The 1987 Sportflics Team Preview appeared to be a good idea, but never caught on with collectors. The intent of the set is to provide a pre-season look at each of the 26 major league clubs. The card backs contain three categories of the team preview: Outlook, Newcomers to Watch and Summary. Using the "Magic Motion" process, 12 different players are featured on the card fronts. Four of the different player photos can be made visible at once. The cards, which measure 2-1/2" x 3-1/2", were issued with team logo/trivia cards in a specially designed box.

		NM/M
Complete Set (26):		15.00
Common Team:		.50
1	Texas Rangers	
	(Scott Fletcher, Greg Harris,	
	Charlie Hough,	
	Pete Incaviglia, Mike Loynd,	
	Oddibe McDowell,	
	Pete O'Brien, Larry Parrish,	
	Ruben Sierra, Don Slaught,	
	Mitch Williams,	
	Bobby Witt)	.50
2	New York Mets	
	(Wally Backman, Gary Carter,	
	Ron Darling, Lenny Dykstra,	
	Sid Fernandez,	
	Dwight Gooden,	
	Keith Hernandez,	
	Dave Magadan,	
	Kevin McReynolds,	
	Randy Myers, Bob Ojeda,	
	Darryl Strawberry)	.75
3	Cleveland Indians	
	(Tony Bernazard, Brett Butler,	
	Tom Candiotti, Joe Carter,	
	Julio Franco, Mel Hall,	
	Brook Jacoby, Phil Niekro,	
	Ken Schrom, Cory Snyder,	
	Greg Swindell, Pat Tabler)	.50
4	Cincinnati Reds (Buddy Bell,	
	Tom Browning, Kal Daniels,	
	John Franco, Bill Gullickson,	
	Tracy Jones, Barry Larkin,	
	Rob Murphy, Paul O'Neill,	
	Dave Parker, Pete Rose,	
	Eric Davis)	1.00
5	Toronto Blue Jays	
	(Jesse Barfield, George Bell,	
	John Cerutti, Mark Eichhorn,	
	Tony Fernandez, Tom Henke,	
	Glenallen Hill, Jimmy Key,	
	Fred McGriff, Lloyd Moseby,	
	Dave Stieb,	
	Willie Upshaw)	.50

6	Philadelphia Phillies	
	(Steve Bedrosian,	
	Don Carman,	
	Marvin Freeman, Kevin Gross,	
	Von Hayes, Shane Rawley,	
	Bruce Ruffin, Juan Samuel,	
	Mike Schmidt, Kent Tekulve,	
	Milt Thompson,	
	Glenn Wilson)	.75
7	New York Yankees	
	(Rickey Henderson,	
	Phil Lombardi, Don Mattingly,	
	Mike Pagliarulo, Dan Pasqua,	
	Willie Randolph,	
	Dennis Rasmussen,	
	Rick Rhoden, Dave Righetti,	
	Joel Skinner, Bob Tewksbury,	
	Dave Winfield)	1.25
8	Houston Astros (Kevin Bass,	
	Jose Cruz, Glenn Davis,	
	Jim Deshaies, Bill Doran,	
	Ty Gainey, Charlie Kerfeld,	
	Bob Knepper, Nolan Ryan,	
	Mike Scott, Dave Smith,	
	Robby Wine)	1.50
9	Boston Red Sox	
	(Marty Barrett, Don Baylor,	
	Wade Boggs, Dennis Boyd,	
	Roger Clemens, Pat Dodson,	
	Dwight Evans,	
	Mike Greenwell,	
	Dave Henderson,	
	Bruce Hurst, Jim Rice,	
	Calvin Schiraldi)	1.00
10	San Francisco Giants	
	(Bob Brenly, Chris Brown,	
	Will Clark, Chili Davis,	
	Kelly Downs, Scott Garrelts,	
	Mark Grant, Mike Krukow,	
	Jeff Leonard,	
	Candy Maldonado,	
	Terry Mulholland,	
	Robby Thompson)	.50
11	California Angels	
	(John Candelaria,	
	Doug DeCinces,	
	Brian Downing,	
	Ruppert Jones, Wally Joyner,	
	Kirk McCaskill, Darrell Miller,	
	Donnie Moore, Gary Pettis,	
	Don Sutton, Devon White,	
	Mike Witt)	.50
12	St. Louis Cardinals	
	(Jack Clark, Vince Coleman,	
	Danny Cox, Bob Forsch,	
	Tom Herr, Joe Magrane,	
	Willie McGee,	
	Terry Pendleton, Ozzie Smith,	
	John Tudor, Andy Van Slyke,	
	Todd Worrell)	.75
13	Kansas City Royals	
	(George Brett, Mark Gubicza,	
	Bo Jackson,	
	Charlie Leibrandt, Hal McRae,	
	Dan Quisenberry,	
	Bret Saberhagen,	
	Kevin Seitzer, Lonnie Smith,	
	Danny Tartabull, Frank White,	
	Willie Wilson)	.75
14	Los Angeles Dodgers	
	(Ralph Bryant,	
	Mariano Duncan,	
	Jose Gonzalez,	
	Pedro Guerrero,	
	Orel Hershiser,	
	Mike Marshall, Steve Sax,	
	Mike Scioscia,	
	Franklin Stubbs,	
	Fernando Valenzuela,	
	Reggie Williams,	
	Matt Young)	.50
15	Detroit Tigers (Darnell Coles,	
	Darrell Evans, Kirk Gibson,	
	Willie Hernandez, Eric King,	
	Chet Lemon, Dwight Lowry,	
	Jack Morris, Dan Petry,	
	Frank Tanana, Alan Trammell,	
	Lou Whitaker)	.50
16	San Diego Padres	
	(Randy Asadoor,	
	Steve Garvey, Tony Gwynn,	
	Andy Hawkins, Jim Jones,	
	John Kruk, Craig Lefferts,	
	Shane Mack,	
	Lance McCullers,	
	Kevin Mitchell,	
	Benny Santiago,	
	Ed Wojna)	.75
17	Minnesota Twins	
	(Bert Blyleven,	
	Tom Brunansky, Gary Gaetti,	
	Greg Gagne, Kent Hrbek,	
	Joe Klink, Steve Lombardozzi,	
	Kirby Puckett, Jeff Reardon,	
	Mark Salas, Roy Smalley,	
	Frank Viola)	.75
18	Pittsburgh Pirates	
	(Barry Bonds, Bobby Bonilla,	
	Sid Bream, Mike Diaz,	
	Brian Fisher, Jim Morrison,	
	Joe Orsulak, Bob Patterson,	
	Tony Pena, Johnny Ray,	
	R.J. Reynolds,	
	John Smiley)	1.50
19	Milwaukee Brewers	
	(Glenn Braggs, Rob Deer,	
	Teddy Higuera, Paul Molitor,	
	Juan Nieves, Dan Plesac,	

	Tim Pyznarski, Ernest Riles,	
	Billy Jo Robidoux,	
	B.J. Surhoff, Dale Sveum,	
	Robin Yount)	.75
20	Montreal Expos	
	(Hubie Brooks, Tim Burke,	
	Casey Candaele, Dave Collins,	
	Mike Fitzgerald,	
	Andres Galarraga,	
	Billy Moore, Alonzo Powell,	
	Randy St. Claire,	
	Tim Wallach, Mitch Webster,	
	Floyd Youmans)	.50
21	Baltimore Orioles (Don Aase,	
	Eric Bell, Mike Boddicker,	
	Ken Gerhardt, Terry Kennedy,	
	Ray Knight, Lee Lacy,	
	Fred Lynn, Eddie Murray,	
	Cal Ripken, Jr., Larry Sheets,	
	Jim Traber)	1.50
22	Chicago Cubs (Jody Davis,	
	Shawon Dunston,	
	Leon Durham,	
	Dennis Eckersley,	
	Greg Maddux, Dave Martinez,	
	Keith Moreland,	
	Jerry Mumphrey,	
	Rafael Palmeiro,	
	Ryne Sandberg,	
	Scott Sanderson,	
	Lee Smith)	1.00
23	Oakland Athletics	
	(Jose Canseco, Mike Davis,	
	Alfredo Griffin,	
	Reggie Jackson,	
	Carney Lansford,	
	Mark McGwire,	
	Dwayne Murphy, Rob Nelson,	
	Tony Phillips, Jose Rijo,	
	Terry Steinbach,	
	Curt Young)	1.50
24	Atlanta Braves	
	(Paul Assenmacher,	
	Gene Garber, Tom Glavine,	
	Ken Griffey, Glenn Hubbard,	
	Dion James, Rick Mahler,	
	Dale Murphy, Ken Oberkfell,	
	David Palmer, Zane Smith,	
	Andres Thomas)	.50
25	Seattle Mariners	
	(Scott Bankhead,	
	Phil Bradley, Scott Bradley,	
	Mickey Brantley, Alvin Davis,	
	Steve Fireovid,	
	Mark Langston, Mike Moore,	
	Donell Nixon, Ken Phelps,	
	Jim Presley, Dave Valle)	.50
26	Chicago White Sox	
	(Harold Baines,	
	John Cangelosi,	
	Dave Cochrane, Joe Cowley,	
	Carlton Fisk, Ozzie Guillen,	
	Ron Hassey, Bob James,	
	Ron Karkovice,	
	Russ Mormon,	
	Bobby Thigpen,	
	Greg Walker)	.50

4-in-1 Panels

These 4-in-1 player and team logo panels were given to dealers who made quantity purchases of Sportflics products. The player panels measure 4-7/8" x 6-7/8", making each of the four cards slightly smaller than the regular-issue versions. Otherwise the cards are identical to the standard version, right down to the card numbers. The team-logo panels correspond to the players on the player panels, but they are smaller, at 3-3/8" x 3-7/8". The logo cards have two views of each logo on front and on back display various team stats. Each of the panels carries a 1986 copyright.

		NM/M
Complete Set (8):		15.00
Common Panel:		1.00
(1)	Don Mattingly,	
	10 Roger Clemens,	
	30 Mike Schmidt,	
	34 Tim Raines	5.00
(2)	2 Wade Boggs,	
	6 Eddie Murray,	
	26 Wally Joyner,	
	150 Fernando Valenzuela	2.50
(3)	3 Dale Murphy,	
	31 Tony Gwynn, 97 Jim Rice,	
	133 Keith Hernandez	2.50
(4)	4 Rickey Henderson,	
	5 George Brett,	
	9 Cal Ripken Jr.,	
	100 Dwight Gooden	6.50
(5)	Yankees, Expos, Red Sox,	
	Phillies	1.00
(6)	Red Sox, Dodgers, Angels,	
	Orioles	1.00
(7)	Braves, Mets, Red Sox,	
	Padres	1.00
(8)	Mets, Orioles, Yankees,	
	Royals	1.00

1988 Sportflics

The design of the 1988 Sportflics set differs greatly from the pre-

RYNE SANDBERG 23 — SECOND BASE

vious two years. Besides increasing the number of cards in the set to 225, Sportflics included the player name, team and uniform number on the card front. The triple-action color photos are surrounded by a red border. The backs are re-designed, also. Full-color action photos, plus extensive statistics and informative biographies are utilized. Three highlights cards and three rookie prospects card are included in the set. The cards are the standard 2-1/2" x 3-1/2".

		NM/M
Factory Set (225+136):		17.50
Complete Set (225):		10.00
Common Player:		.10
Foil Pack (3+2):		.50
Foil Box (36):		9.00
1	Don Mattingly	1.25
2	Tim Raines	.10
3	Andre Dawson	.25
4	George Bell	.10
5	Joe Carter	.10
6	Matt Nokes	.10
7	Dave Winfield	.75
8	Kirby Puckett	1.00
9	Will Clark	.10
10	Eric Davis	.10
11	Rickey Henderson	.75
12	Ryne Sandberg	1.00
13	Jesse Barfield	.10
14	Ozzie Guillen	.10
15	Bret Saberhagen	.10
16	Tony Gwynn	1.00
17	Kevin Seitzer	.10
18	Jack Clark	.10
19	Danny Tartabull	.10
20	Ted Higuera	.10
21	Charlie Leibrandt, Jr.	.10
22	Benny Santiago	.10
23	Fred Lynn	.10
24	Rob Thompson	.10
25	Alan Trammell	.10
26	Tony Fernandez	.10
27	Rick Sutcliffe	.10
28	Gary Carter	.25
29	Cory Snyder	.10
30	Lou Whitaker	.10
31	Keith Hernandez	.10
32	Mike Witt	.10
33	Harold Baines	.10
34	Robin Yount	.75
35	Mike Schmidt	1.25
36	Dion James	.10
37	Tom Candiotti	.10
38	Tracy Jones	.10
39	Nolan Ryan	2.00
40	Fernando Valenzuela	.10
41	Vance Law	.10
42	Roger McDowell	.10
43	Carlton Fisk	.75
44	Scott Garrelts	.10
45	Lee Guetterman	.10
46	Mark Langston	.10
47	Willie Randolph	.10
48	Bill Doran	.10
49	Larry Parrish	.10
50	Wade Boggs	1.00
51	Shane Rawley	.10
52	Alvin Davis	.10
53	Jeff Reardon	.10
54	Jim Presley	.10
55	Kevin Bass	.10
56	Kevin McReynolds	.10
57	B.J. Surhoff	.10
58	Julio Franco	.10
59	Eddie Murray	.75
60	Jody Davis	.10
61	Todd Worrell	.10
62	Von Hayes	.10
63	Billy Hatcher	.10
64	John Kruk	.10
65	Tom Henke	.10
66	Mike Scott	.10
67	Vince Coleman	.10
68	Ozzie Smith	1.00
69	Ken Williams	.10
70	Steve Bedrosian	.10
71	Luis Polonia	.10
72	Brook Jacoby	.10
73	Ron Darling	.10
74	Lloyd Moseby	.10
75	Wally Joyner	.10

76	Dan Quisenberry	.10
77	Scott Fletcher	.10
78	Kirk McCaskill	.10
79	Paul Molitor	.75
80	Mike Aldrete	.10
81	Neal Heaton	.10
82	Jeffrey Leonard	.10
83	Dave Magadan	.10
84	Danny Cox	.10
85	Lance McCullers	.10
86	Jay Howell	.10
87	Charlie Hough	.10
88	Gene Garber	.10
89	Jesse Orosco	.10
90	Don Robinson	.10
91	Willie McGee	.10
92	Bert Blyleven	.10
93	Phil Bradley	.10
94	Terry Kennedy	.10
95	Kent Hrbek	.10
96	Juan Samuel	.10
97	Pedro Guerrero	.10
98	Sid Bream	.10
99	Devon White	.10
100	Mark McGwire	1.50
101	Dave Parker	.10
102	Glenn Davis	.10
103	Greg Walker	.10
104	Rick Rhoden	.10
105	Mitch Webster	.10
106	Lenny Dykstra	.10
107	Gene Larkin	.10
108	Floyd Youmans	.10
109	Andy Van Slyke	.10
110	Mike Scioscia	.10
111	Kirk Gibson	.10
112	Kal Daniels	.10
113	Ruben Sierra	.10
114	Sam Horn	.10
115	Ray Knight	.10
116	Jimmy Key	.10
117	Bo Diaz	.10
118	Mike Greenwell	.10
119	Barry Bonds	2.00
120	Reggie Jackson	1.25
121	Mike Pagliarulo	.10
122	Tommy John	.10
123	Bill Madlock	.10
124	Ken Caminiti	.10
125	Gary Ward	.10
126	Candy Maldonado	.10
127	Harold Reynolds	.10
128	Joe Magrane	.10
129	Mike Henneman	.10
130	Jim Gantner	.10
131	Bobby Bonilla	.10
132	John Farrell	.10
133	Frank Tanana	.10
134	Zane Smith	.10
135	Dave Righetti	.10
136	Rick Reuschel	.10
137	Dwight Evans	.10
138	Howard Johnson	.10
139	Terry Leach	.10
140	Casey Candaele	.10
141	Tom Herr	.10
142	Tony Pena	.10
143	Lance Parrish	.10
144	Ellis Burks	.10
145	Pete O'Brien	.10
146	Mike Boddicker	.10
147	Buddy Bell	.10
148	Bo Jackson	.15
149	Frank White	.10
150	George Brett	1.25
151	Tim Wallach	.10
152	Cal Ripken, Jr.	2.00
153	Brett Butler	.10
154	Gary Gaetti	.10
155	Darryl Strawberry	.10
156	Alfredo Griffin	.10
157	Marty Barrett	.10
158	Jim Rice	.25
159	Terry Pendleton	.10
160	Orel Hershiser	.10
161	Larry Sheets	.10
162	Dave Stewart	.10
163	Shawon Dunston	.10
164	Keith Moreland	.10
165	Ken Oberkfell	.10
166	Ivan Calderon	.10
167	Bob Welch	.10
168	Fred McGriff	.10
169	Pete Incaviglia	.10
170	Dale Murphy	.25
171	Mike Dunne	.10
172	Chili Davis	.10
173	Milt Thompson	.10
174	Terry Steinbach	.10
175	Oddibe McDowell	.10
176	Jack Morris	.10
177	Sid Fernandez	.10
178	Ken Griffey	.10
179	Lee Smith	.10
180	1987 Highlights	
	(Juan Nieves, Kirby Puckett,	
	Mike Schmidt)	.25
181	Brian Downing	.10
182	Andres Galarraga	.10
183	Rob Deer	.10
184	Greg Brock	.10
185	Doug DeCinces	.10
186	Johnny Ray	.10
187	Hubie Brooks	.10
188	Darrell Evans	.10
189	Mel Hall	.10
190	Jim Deshaies	.10
191	Dan Plesac	.10

192	Willie Wilson	.10
193	Mike LaValliere	.10
194	Tom Brunansky	.10
195	John Franco	.10
196	Frank Viola	.10
197	Bruce Hurst	.10
198	John Tudor	.10
199	Bob Forsch	.10
200	Dwight Gooden	.10
201	Jose Canseco	.65
202	Carney Lansford	.10
203	Kelly Downs	.10
204	Glenn Wilson	.10
205	Pat Tabler	.10
206	Mike Davis	.10
207	Roger Clemens	1.25
208	Dave Smith	.10
209	Curt Young	.10
210	Mark Eichhorn	.10
211	Juan Nieves	.10
212	Bob Boone	.10
213	Don Sutton	.50
214	Willie Upshaw	.10
215	Jim Clancy	.10
216	Bill Ripken	.10
217	Ozzie Virgil	.10
218	Dave Concepcion	.10
219	Alan Ashby	.10
220	Mike Marshall	.10
221	'87 Highlights	
	(Vince Coleman,	
	Mark McGwire,	
	Paul Molitor)	.75
222	'87 Highlights	
	(Steve Bedrosian,	
	Don Mattingly,	
	Benito Santiago)	.40
223	Hot Rookie Prospects	
	(Shawn Abner,	
	Jay Buhner RC,	
	Gary Thurman)	.25
224	Hot Rookie Prospects	
	(Tim Crews, John Davis,	
	Vincente Palacios)	.10
225	Hot Rookie Prospects	
	(Keith Miller, Jody Reed,	
	Jeff Treadway)	.10

Gamewinners

GAMEWINNERS — DON MATTINGLY 23 1B

This set of 25 standard-size cards (2-1/2" x 3-1/2"), featuring star players in the Sportflics patented 3-D Magic Motion design, was issued by Weiser Card Co. of Plainsboro, N.J., for use as a youth organizational fundraiser. (Weiser's president was former Yankees outfielder Bobby Murcer.) A limited number of sets was produced for test marketing in the Northwestern U.S., with plans for a 1989 set to be marketed nationwide. A green-and-yellow Gamewinners logo banner spans the upper border of the cards face, with a matching player name (with uniform number and position) below the full-color triple photo. The card backs carry large full-color player photos along with stats, personal information and career highlights.

		NM/M
Complete Set (25):		7.50
Common Player:		.25
1	Don Mattingly	1.50
2	Mark McGwire	3.50
3	Wade Boggs	1.25
4	Will Clark	.25
5	Eric Davis	.25
6	Willie Randolph	.25
7	Dave Winfield	.75
8	Rickey Henderson	.75
9	Dwight Gooden	.25
10	Benny Santiago	.25
11	Keith Hernandez	.25
12	Juan Samuel	.25
13	Kevin Seitzer	.25
14	Gary Carter	.75
15	Darryl Strawberry	.25
16	Rick Rhoden	.25
17	Howard Johnson	.25
18	Matt Nokes	.25
19	Dave Righetti	.25
20	Roger Clemens	1.50
21	Mike Schmidt	1.50

22	Kevin McReynolds	.25
23	Mike Pagliarulo	.25
24	Kevin Elster	.25
25	Jack Clark	.25

1989 Sportflics

GEORGE BRETT
KANSAS CITY ROYALS

This basic issue includes 225 standard-size player cards (2-1/2 x 3-1/2) and 153 trivia cards, all featuring the patented Magic Motion design. A five-card sub-set of "Tri-Star" cards features a mix of veterans and rookies. The card fronts feature a white outer border and double color inner border in one of six color schemes. The inner border color changes when the card is tilted and the bottom border carries a double stripe of colors. The player name appears in the top border, player position and uniform number appear, alternately, in the bottom border. The card backs contain crisp 1-7/8 by 1-3/4 player-action shots, along with personal information, stats and career highlights. "The Unforgettables" trivia cards in this set salute members of the Hall of Fame.

		NM/M
Factory Set (225+153):		17.50
Complete Set (225):		12.00
Common Player:		.10
Foil Pack (3+2):		.50
Foil Box (36):		10.00
1	Jose Canseco	.60
2	Wally Joyner	.10
3	Roger Clemens	1.25
4	Greg Swindell	.10
5	Jack Morris	.10
6	Mickey Brantley	.10
7	Jim Presley	.10
8	Pete O'Brien	.10
9	Jesse Barfield	.10
10	Frank Viola	.10
11	Kevin Bass	.10
12	Glenn Wilson	.10
13	Chris Sabo	.10
14	Fred McGriff	.20
15	Mark Grace	.20
16	Devon White	.10
17	Juan Samuel	.10
18	Lou Whitaker	.10
19	Greg Walker	.10
20	Roberto Alomar	.20
21	Mike Schmidt	1.25
22	Benny Santiago	.10
23	Dave Stewart	.10
24	Dave Winfield	.75
25	George Bell	.10
26	Jack Clark	.10
27	Doug Drabek	.10
28	Ron Gant	.10
29	Glenn Braggs	.10
30	Rafael Palmeiro	.65
31	Brett Butler	.10
32	Ron Darling	.10
33	Alvin Davis	.10
34	Bob Walk	.10
35	Dave Stieb	.10
36	Orel Hershiser	.10
37	John Farrell	.10
38	Doug Jones	.10
39	Kelly Downs	.10
40	Bob Boone	.10
41	Gary Sheffield	.35
42	Doug Dascenzo	.10
43	Chad Krueter	.10
44	Ricky Jordan	.10
45	Dave West	.10
46	Danny Tartabull	.10
47	Teddy Higuera	.10
48	Gary Gaetti	.10
49	Dave Parker	.10
50	Don Mattingly	1.25
51	David Cone	.10
52	Kal Daniels	.10
53	Carney Lansford	.10
54	Mike Marshall	.10
55	Kevin Seitzer	.10
56	Mike Henneman	.10
57	Bill Doran	.10
58	Steve Sax	.10
59	Lance Parrish	.10
60	Keith Hernandez	.10
61	Jose Uribe	.10
62	Jose Lind	.10
63	Steve Bedrosian	.10
64	George Brett	1.25
65	Kirk Gibson	.10
66	Cal Ripken, Jr.	2.00
67	Mitch Webster	.10
68	Fred Lynn	.10
69	Eric Davis	.10
70	Bo Jackson	.15
71	Kevin Elster	.10
72	Rick Reuschel	.10
73	Tim Burke	.10
74	Mark Davis	.10
75	Claudell Washington	.10
76	Lance McCullers	.10
77	Mike Moore	.10
78	Robby Thompson	.10
79	Roger McDowell	.10
80	Danny Jackson	.10
81	Tim Leary	.10
82	Bobby Witt	.10
83	Jim Gott	.10
84	Andy Hawkins	.10
85	Ozzie Guillen	.10
86	John Tudor	.10
87	Todd Burns	.10
88	Dave Gallagher	.10
89	Jay Buhner	.10
90	Gregg Jefferies	.75
91	Bob Welch	.10
92	Charlie Hough	.10
93	Tony Fernandez	.10
94	Ozzie Virgil	.10
95	Andre Dawson	.25
96	Hubie Brooks	.10
97	Kevin McReynolds	.10
98	Mike LaValliere	.10
99	Terry Pendleton	.10
100	Wade Boggs	1.00
101	Dennis Eckersley	.65
102	Mark Gubicza	.10
103	Frank Tanana	.10
104	Joe Carter	.10
105	Ozzie Smith	1.00
106	Dennis Martinez	.10
107	Jeff Treadway	.10
108	Greg Maddux	1.00
109	Bret Saberhagen	.10
110	Dale Murphy	.20
111	Rob Deer	.10
112	Pete Incaviglia	.10
113	Vince Coleman	.10
114	Tim Wallach	.10
115	Nolan Ryan	2.00
116	Walt Weiss	.10
117	Brian Downing	.10
118	Melido Perez	.10
119	Terry Steinbach	.10
120	Mike Scott	.10
121	Tim Belcher	.10
122	Mike Boddicker	.10
123	Len Dykstra	.10
124	Fernando Valenzuela	.10
125	Gerald Young	.10
126	Tom Henke	.10
127	Dave Henderson	.10
128	Dan Plesac	.10
129	Chili Davis	.10
130	Bryan Harvey	.10
131	Don August	.10
132	Mike Harkey	.10
133	Luis Polonia	.10
134	Craig Worthington	.10
135	Joey Meyer	.10
136	Barry Larkin	.10
137	Glenn Davis	.10
138	Mike Scioscia	.10
139	Andres Galarraga	.10
140	Doc Gooden	.10
141	Keith Moreland	.10
142	Kevin Mitchell	.10
143	Mike Greenwell	.10
144	Mel Hall	.10
145	Rickey Henderson	.75
146	Barry Bonds	2.00
147	Eddie Murray	.75
148	Lee Smith	.10
149	Julio Franco	.10
150	Tim Raines	.10
151	Mitch Williams	.10
152	Tim Laudner	.10
153	Mike Pagliarulo	.10
154	Floyd Bannister	.10
155	Gary Carter	.75
156	Kirby Puckett	1.00
157	Harold Baines	.10
158	Dave Righetti	.10
159	Mark Langston	.10
160	Tony Gwynn	1.00
161	Tom Brunansky	.10
162	Vance Law	.10
163	Kelly Gruber	.10
164	Gerald Perry	.10
165	Harold Reynolds	.10
166	Andy Van Slyke	.10
167	Jimmy Key	.10
168	Jeff Reardon	.10
169	Milt Thompson	.10
170	Will Clark	.10
171	Chet Lemon	.10
172	Pat Tabler	.10
173	Jim Rice	.25
174	Billy Hatcher	.10
175	Bruce Hurst	.10
176	John Franco	.10
177	Van Snider	.10
178	Ron Jones	.10
179	Jerald Clark	.10
180	Tom Browning	.10
181	Von Hayes	.10
182	Bobby Bonilla	.10
183	Todd Worrell	.10
184	John Kruk	.10
185	Scott Fletcher	.10
186	Willie Wilson	.10
187	Jody Davis	.10
188	Kent Hrbek	.10
189	Ruben Sierra	.10
190	Shawon Dunston	.10
191	Ellis Burks	.10
192	Brook Jacoby	.10
193	Jeff Robinson	.10
194	Rich Dotson	.10
195	Johnny Ray	.10
196	Cory Snyder	.10
197	Mike Witt	.10
198	Marty Barrett	.10
199	Robin Yount	.75
200	Mark McGwire	1.50
201	Ryne Sandberg	1.00
202	John Candelaria	.10
203	Matt Nokes	.10
204	Dwight Evans	.10
205	Darryl Strawberry	.10
206	Willie McGee	.10
207	Bobby Thigpen	.10
208	B.J. Surhoff	.10
209	Paul Molitor	.75
210	Jody Reed	.10
211	Doyle Alexander	.10
212	Dennis Rasmussen	.10
213	Kevin Gross	.10
214	Kirk McCaskill	.10
215	Alan Trammell	.10
216	Damon Berryhill	.10
217	Rick Sutcliffe	.10
218	Don Slaught	.10
219	Carlton Fisk	.75
220	Allan Anderson	.10
221	'88 Highlights (Wade Boggs, Jose Canseco, Mike Greenwell)	.15
222	'88 Highlights (Tom Browning, Dennis Eckersley, Orel Hershiser)	.20
223	Hot Rookie Prospects (Sandy Alomar, Gregg Jefferies, Gary Sheffield)	.50
224	Hot Rookie Prospects (Randy Johnson, Ramon Martinez, Bob Milacki)	.75
225	Hot Rookie Prospects (Geronimo Berroa, Cameron Drew, Ron Jones)	.10

1990 Sportflics

ROBIN VENTURA
CHICAGO WHITE SOX

The Sportflics set for 1990 again contains 225 cards. The cards feature the unique "Magic Motion" effect which displays either of two different photos depending on how the card is tilted. (Previous years' sets had used three photos per card.) The two-photo "Magic Motion" sequence is designed to depict sequential game-action, showing a batter following through on his swing, a pitcher completing his motion, etc. Sportflics also added a moving red and yellow "marquee" border on the cards to complement the animation effect. The player's name, which appears below the animation, remains stationary. The set includes 19 special rookie cards. The backs contain a color player photo, team logo, player information and stats. The cards were distributed in non-transparent mylar packs with small MVP trivia cards.

		NM/M
Factory Set (225+153):		15.00
Complete Set (225):		12.00
Common Player:		.10
Foil Pack (3+2):		.75
Foil Box (36):		20.00
1	Kevin Mitchell	.10
2	Wade Boggs	1.00
3	Cory Snyder	.10
4	Paul O'Neill	.10
5	Will Clark	.10
6	Tony Fernandez	.10
7	Ken Griffey Jr.	1.50
8	Nolan Ryan	2.00
9	Rafael Palmeiro	.65
10	Jesse Barfield	.10
11	Kirby Puckett	1.00
12	Steve Sax	.10
13	Fred McGriff	.10
14	Gregg Jefferies	.10
15	Mark Grace	.10
16	Devon White	.10
17	Juan Samuel	.10
18	Robin Yount	.75
19	Glenn Davis	.10
20	Jeffrey Leonard	.10
21	Chili Davis	.10
22	Craig Biggio	.10
23	Jose Canseco	.50
24	Derek Lilliquist	.10
25	Chris Bosio	.10
26	Dave Steib	.10
27	Bobby Thigpen	.10
28	Jack Clark	.10
29	Kevin Ritz	.10
30	Tom Gordon	.10
31	Bryan Harvey	.10
32	Jim Deshaies	.10
33	Terry Steinbach	.10
34	Tom Glavine	.35
35	Bob Welch	.10
36	Charlie Hayes	.10
37	Jeff Reardon	.10
38	Joe Orsulak	.10
39	Scott Garrelts	.10
40	Bob Boone	.10
41	Scott Bankhead	.10
42	Tom Henke	.10
43	Greg Briley	.10
44	Teddy Higuera	.10
45	Pat Borders	.10
46	Kevin Seitzer	.10
47	Bruce Hurst	.10
48	Ozzie Guillen	.10
49	Wally Joyner	.10
50	Mike Greenwell	.10
51	Gary Gaetti	.10
52	Gary Sheffield	.30
53	Dennis Martinez	.10
54	Ryne Sandberg	1.00
55	Mike Scott	.10
56	Todd Benzinger	.10
57	Kelly Gruber	.10
58	Jose Lind	.10
59	Allan Anderson	.10
60	Robby Thompson	.10
61	John Smoltz	.10
62	Mark Davis	.10
63	Tom Herr	.10
64	Randy Johnson	.75
65	Lonnie Smith	.10
66	Pedro Guerrero	.10
67	Jerome Walton	.10
68	Ramon Martinez	.10
69	Tim Raines	.10
70	Matt Williams	.10
71	Joe Oliver	.10
72	Nick Esasky	.10
73	Kevin Brown	.10
74	Walt Weiss	.10
75	Roger McDowell	.10
76	Jose DeLeon	.10
77	Brian Downing	.10
78	Jay Howell	.10
79	Jose Uribe	.10
80	Ellis Burks	.10
81	Sammy Sosa	7.50
82	Johnny Ray	.10
83	Danny Darwin	.10
84	Carney Lansford	.10
85	Jose Oquendo	.10
86	John Cerutti	.10
87	Dave Winfield	.75
88	Dave Righetti	.10
89	Danny Jackson	.10
90	Andy Benes	.10
91	Tom Browning	.10
92	Pete O'Brien	.10
93	Roberto Alomar	.20
94	Bret Saberhagen	.10
95	Phil Bradley	.10
96	Doug Jones	.10
97	Eric Davis	.10
98	Tony Gwynn	1.00
99	Jim Abbott	.10
100	Cal Ripken, Jr.	2.00
101	Andy Van Slyke	.10
102	Dan Plesac	.10
103	Lou Whitaker	.10
104	Steve Bedrosian	.10
105	Dave Gallagher	.10
106	Keith Hernandez	.10
107	Duane Ward	.10
108	Andre Dawson	.10
109	Howard Johnson	.35
110	Mark Langston	.10
111	Jerry Browne	.10
112	Alvin Davis	.10
113	Sid Fernandez	.10
114	Mike Devereaux	.10
115	Benny Santiago	.10
116	Bip Roberts	.10
117	Craig Worthington	.10
118	Kevin Elster	.10
119	Harold Reynolds	.10
120	Joe Carter	.10
121	Brian Harper	.10
122	Frank Viola	.10
123	Jeff Ballard	.10
124	John Kruk	.10
125	Harold Baines	.10
126	Tom Candiotti	.10
127	Kevin McReynolds	.10
128	Mookie Wilson	.10
129	Danny Tartabull	.10
130	Craig Lefferts	.10
131	Jose DeJesus	.10
132	John Orton	.10
133	Curt Schilling	.35
134	Marquis Grissom	.10
135	Greg Vaughn	.10
136	Brett Butler	.10
137	Rob Deer	.10
138	John Franco	.10
139	Keith Moreland	.10
140	Dave Smith	.10
141	Mark McGwire	1.50
142	Vince Coleman	.10
143	Barry Bonds	2.00
144	Mike Henneman	.10
145	Doc Gooden	.10
146	Darryl Strawberry	.10
147	Von Hayes	.10
148	Andres Galarraga	.10
149	Roger Clemens	1.25
150	Don Mattingly	1.25
151	Joe Magrane	.10
152	Dwight Smith	.10
153	Ricky Jordan	.10
154	Alan Trammell	.10
155	Brook Jacoby	.10
156	Lenny Dykstra	.10
157	Mike LaValliere	.10
158	Julio Franco	.10
159	Joey Belle	.25
160	Barry Larkin	.10
161	Rick Reuschel	.10
162	Nelson Santovenia	.10
163	Mike Scioscia	.10
164	Damon Berryhill	.10
165	Todd Worrell	.10
166	Jim Eisenreich	.10
167	Ivan Calderon	.10
168	Goose Gozzo	.10
169	Kirk McCaskill	.10
170	Dennis Eckersley	.65
171	Mickey Tettleton	.10
172	Chuck Finley	.10
173	Dave Magadan	.10
174	Terry Pendleton	.10
175	Willie Randolph	.10
176	Jeff Huson	.10
177	Todd Zeile	.10
178	Steve Olin	.10
179	Eric Anthony	.10
180	Scott Coolbaugh	.10
181	Rick Sutcliffe	.10
182	Tim Wallach	.10
183	Paul Molitor	.75
184	Roberto Kelly	.10
185	Mike Moore	.10
186	Junior Felix	.10
187	Mike Schooler	.10
188	Ruben Sierra	.10
189	Dale Murphy	.30
190	Dan Gladden	.10
191	John Smiley	.10
192	Jeff Russell	.10
193	Bert Blyleven	.10
194	Dave Stewart	.10
195	Bobby Bonilla	.10
196	Mitch Williams	.10
197	Orel Hershiser	.10
198	Kevin Bass	.10
199	Tim Burke	.10
200	Bo Jackson	.15
201	David Cone	.10
202	Gary Pettis	.10
203	Kent Hrbek	.10
204	Carlton Fisk	.75
205	Bob Geren	.10
206	Bill Spiers	.10
207	Oddibe McDowell	.10
208	Rickey Henderson	.75
209	Ken Caminiti	.10
210	Devon White	.10
211	Greg Maddux	1.00
212	Ed Whitson	.10
213	Carlos Martinez	.10
214	George Brett	1.25
215	Gregg Olson	.10
216	Kenny Rogers	.10
217	Dwight Evans	.10
218	Pat Tabler	.10
219	Jeff Treadway	.10
220	Scott Fletcher	.10
221	Deion Sanders	.15
222	Robin Ventura	.10
223	Chip Hale	.10
224	Tommy Greene	.10
225	Dean Palmer	.10

1994 Sportflics 2000 Promos

To reintroduce its "Magic Motion" baseball cards to the hobby (last produced by Score in 1990), Pinnacle Brands produced a three-card promo set which it sent to dealers along with a header card explaining the issue. In the same format as the regular issue, though some different photos were used, the promos feature on front what Sportflics calls "state-of-the-art lenticular technology" to create an action effect when the card is moved. Backs are produced by standard printing techniques and are gold-foil highlighted and UV-coated. Each of the promo cards has a large black "SAMPLE" overprinted diagonally across front and back.

		NM/M
Complete Set (4):		5.00
Common Player:		1.00
1a	Lenny Dykstra ("SAMPLE" front only.)	1.00
1b	Lenny Dykstra ("SAMPLE" back and front.)	1.00
7	Javy Lopez (Shakers)	1.00
193	Greg Maddux (Starflics)	3.00
	Header Card	.25

1994 Sportflics 2000

STANLEY

The concept of "Magic Motion" baseball cards returned to the hobby in 1994 after a three-year hiatus. Pinnacle refined its "state-of-the-art lenticular technology" to produce cards which show alternating pictures when viewed from different angles on the basic cards, and to create a striking 3-D effect on its "Starflics" A.L. and N.L. All-Star team subset. Backs are conventionally printed, UV-coated and gold-foil highlighted, featuring a player photo and recent stats. Cards were sold in eight-card foil packs with a suggested retail price of $2.49.

		NM/M
Complete Set (193):		15.00
Common Player:		.10
Pack (8):		.50
Wax Box (36):		15.00
1	Len Dykstra	.10
2	Mike Stanley	.10
3	Alex Fernandez	.10
4	Mark McGuire (McGwire)	1.50
5	Eric Karros	.10
6	Dave Justice	.10
7	Jeff Bagwell	.65
8	Darren Lewis	.10
9	David McCarty	.10
10	Albert Belle	.65
11	Ben McDonald	.10
12	Joe Carter	.10
13	Benito Santiago	.10
14	Rob Dibble	.10
15	Roger Clemens	.85
16	Travis Fryman	.10
17	Doug Drabek	.10
18	Jay Buhner	.10
19	Orlando Merced	.10
20	Ryan Klesko	.10
21	Chuck Finley	.10
22	Dante Bichette	.10
23	Wally Joyner	.10
24	Robin Yount	.65
25	Tony Gwynn	.75
26	Allen Watson	.10
27	Rick Wilkins	.10
28	Gary Sheffield	.40

29	John Burkett	.10
30	Randy Johnson	.65
31	Roberto Alomar	.25
32	Fred McGriff	.10
33	Ozzie Guillen	.10
34	Jimmy Key	.10
35	Juan Gonzalez	.35
36	Wil Cordero	.10
37	Aaron Sele	.10
38	Mark Langston	.10
39	David Cone	.10
40	John Jaha	.10
41	Ozzie Smith	.75
42	Kirby Puckett	.75
43	Kenny Lofton	.10
44	Mike Mussina	.40
45	Ryne Sandberg	.75
46	Robby Thompson	.10
47	Bryan Harvey	.10
48	Marquis Grissom	.10
49	Bobby Bonilla	.10
50	Dennis Eckersley	.60
51	Curt Schilling	.35
52	Andy Benes	.10
53	Greg Maddux	.75
54	Bill Swift	.10
55	Andres Galarraga	.10
56	Tony Phillips	.10
57	Darryl Hamilton	.10
58	Duane Ward	.10
59	Bernie Williams	.10
60	Steve Avery	.10
61	Eduardo Perez	.10
62	Jeff Conine	.10
63	Dave Winfield	.65
64	Phil Plantier	.10
65	Ray Lankford	.10
66	Robin Ventura	.10
67	Mike Piazza	1.00
68	Jason Bere	.10
69	Cal Ripken, Jr.	2.00
70	Frank Thomas	.65
71	Carlos Baerga	.10
72	Darryl Kile	.10
73	Ruben Sierra	.10
74	Gregg Jefferies	.10
75	John Olerud	.10
76	Andy Van Slyke	.10
77	Larry Walker	.10
78	Cecil Fielder	.10
79	Andre Dawson	.25
80	Tom Glavine	.35
81	Sammy Sosa	.75
82	Charlie Hayes	.10
83	Chuck Knoblauch	.10
84	Kevin Appier	.10
85	Dean Palmer	.10
86	Royce Clayton	.10
87	Moises Alou	.10
88	Ivan Rodriguez	.60
89	Tim Salmon	.10
90	Ron Gant	.10
91	Barry Bonds	2.00
92	Jack McDowell	.10
93	Alan Trammell	.10
94	Dwight Gooden	.10
95	Jay Bell	.10
96	Devon White	.10
97	Wilson Alvarez	.10
98	Jim Thome	.60
99	Ramon Martinez	.10
100	Kent Hrbek	.10
101	John Kruk	.10
102	Wade Boggs	.75
103	Greg Vaughn	.10
104	Tom Henke	.10
105	Brian Jordan	.10
106	Paul Molitor	.65
107	Cal Eldred	.10
108	Deion Sanders	.10
109	Barry Larkin	.10
110	Mike Greenwell	.10
111	Jeff Blauser	.10
112	Jose Rijo	.10
113	Pete Harnisch	.10
114	Chris Hoiles	.10
115	Edgar Martinez	.10
116	Juan Guzman	.10
117	Todd Zeile	.10
118	Danny Tartabull	.10
119	Chad Curtis	.10
120	Mark Grace	.10
121	J.T. Snow	.10
122	Mo Vaughn	.10
123	Lance Johnson	.10
124	Eric Davis	.10
125	Orel Hershiser	.10
126	Kevin Mitchell	.10
127	Don Mattingly	.85
128	Darren Daulton	.10
129	Rod Beck	.10
130	Charles Nagy	.10
131	Mickey Tettleton	.10
132	Kevin Brown	.10
133	Pat Hentgen	.10
134	Terry Mulholland	.10
135	Steve Finley	.10
136	John Smoltz	.10
137	Frank Viola	.10
138	Jim Abbott	.10
139	Matt Williams	.10
140	Bernard Gilkey	.10
141	Jose Canseco	.45
142	Mark Whiten	.10
143	Ken Griffey Jr.	1.00
144	Rafael Palmeiro	.60
145	Dave Hollins	.10
146	Will Clark	.10

147	Paul O'Neill	.10
148	Bobby Jones	.10
149	Butch Huskey	.10
150	Jeffrey Hammonds	.10
151	Manny Ramirez	.65
152	Bob Hamelin	.10
153	Kurt Abbott	.10
154	Scott Stahoviak	.10
155	Steve Hosey	.10
156	Salomon Torres	.10
157	Sterling Hitchcock	.10
158	Nigel Wilson	.10
159	Luis Lopez	.10
160	Chipper Jones	.75
161	Norberto Martin	.10
162	Raul Mondesi	.10
163	Steve Karsay	.10
164	J.R. Phillips	.10
165	Marc Newfield	.10
166	Mark Hutton	.10
167	Curtis Pride	.10
168	Carl Everett	.10
169	Scott Ruffcorn	.10
170	Turk Wendell	.10
171	Jeff McNeely	.10
172	Javier Lopez	.10
173	Cliff Floyd	.10
174	Rondell White	.10
175	Scott Lydy	.10
176	Frank Thomas/AS	.35
177	Roberto Alomar/AS	.20
178	Travis Fryman/AS	.10
179	Cal Ripken, Jr./AS	1.00
180	Chris Hoiles/AS	.10
181	Ken Griffey Jr./AS	.60
182	Juan Gonzalez/AS	.20
183	Joe Carter/AS	.10
184	Jack McDowell/AS	.10
185	Fred McGriff/AS	.10
186	Robby Thompson/AS	.10
187	Matt Williams/AS	.10
188	Jay Bell/AS	.10
189	Mike Piazza/AS	.60
190	Barry Bonds/AS	1.00
191	Len Dykstra/AS	.10
192	Dave Justice/AS	.10
193	Greg Maddux/AS	.45

Commemoratives

A pair of extra-rare commemorative chase cards was produced for the Sportflics 2000 set honoring Canada's veteran superstar Paul Molitor and its hottest rookie, Cliff Floyd. Cards, utilizing Magic Motion technology to alternate card-front pictures when the viewing angle changes, were inserted on average once in every 360 packs.

		NM/M
Complete Set (2):		5.00
1	Paul Molitor	4.50
2	Cliff Floyd	1.25

Movers

A dozen top veteran ballplayers were featured in the "Movers" insert set produced for inclusion in retail packaging of Sportflics 2000. The inserts feature the same Magic Motion features as the regular cards, showing different images on the card front when the card is viewed from different angles. The UV-coated, gold-foil highlighted backs are printed conventionally. A special "Movers" logo is found on both front and back. Stated odds of finding a Movers card are one in 24 packs.

		NM/M
Complete Set (12):		12.00
Common Player:		.60
1	Gregg Jefferies	.60
2	Ryne Sandberg	2.00
3	Cecil Fielder	.60
4	Kirby Puckett	2.00
5	Tony Gwynn	2.00
6	Andres Galarraga	.60
7	Sammy Sosa	2.00
8	Rickey Henderson	1.00
9	Don Mattingly	2.50
10	Joe Carter	.60
11	Carlos Baerga	.60
12	Len Dykstra	.60

Shakers

Hobby packs are the exclusive source for this 12-card insert set of top rookies, found on average once every 24 packs. The chase cards utilize the Sportflics Magic Motion technology to create two different images on the card front when the card is viewed from different angles. Backs are printed conventionally but feature UV-coating and gold-foil highlights. The "Shakers" logo appears on both front and back.

		NM/M
Complete Set (12):		12.00
Common Player:		.60
1	Kenny Lofton	.60
2	Tim Salmon	.60
3	Jeff Bagwell	2.50
4	Jason Bere	.60
5	Salomon Torres	.60
6	Rondell White	.60
7	Javier Lopez	.60
8	Dean Palmer	.60
9	Jim Thome	2.00
10	J.T. Snow	.60
11	Mike Piazza	4.00
12	Manny Ramirez	2.50

1994 Sportflics 2000 Rookie/Traded Promos

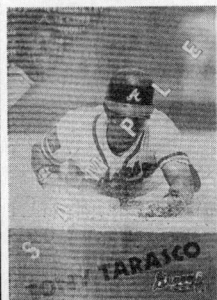

This nine-card set was issued to promote the Sportflics Rookie/Traded update set which was released as a hobby-only product. Cards are virtually identical to the corresponding cards in the R/T set except for the overprinted "SAMPLE" in white on front and back.

		NM/M
Complete Set (9):		5.00
Common Player:		1.00
1	Will Clark	1.00
14	Bret Boone	1.00
20	Ellis Burks	1.00
25	Deion Sanders	1.00
62	Chris Turner	1.00
82	Tony Tarasco	1.00
102	Rich Becker	1.00
GG1	Gary Sheffield (Going, Going, Gone)	2.00
---	Header Card	.25

1994 Sportflics 2000 Rookie/Traded

Each of the 150 regular cards in the Sportflics 2000 Rookie & Traded issue was also produced in a parallel chase card set designated on front with a black and gold "Artist's Proof" logo. Stated odds of finding an AP cards were one per 24 packs. Fewer than 1,000 of each AP card were reportedly produced.

		NM/M
Complete Set (150):		20.00
Common Player:		.10
Pack (5):		3.00
Wax Box (24):		60.00
1	Will Clark	
2	Sid Fernandez	.10

3	Joe Magrane	.10
4	Pete Smith	.10
5	Roberto Kelly	.10
6	Delino DeShields	.10
7	Brian Harper	.10
8	Darrin Jackson	.10
9	Omar Vizquel	.10
10	Luis Polonia	.10
11	Reggie Jefferson	.10
12	Geronimo Berroa	.10
13	Mike Harkey	.10
14	Bret Boone	.10
15	Dave Henderson	.10
16	Pedro Martinez	.75
17	Jose Vizcaino	.10
18	Xavier Hernandez	.10
19	Eddie Taubensee	.10
20	Ellis Burks	.10
21	Turner Ward	.10
22	Terry Mulholland	.10
23	Howard Johnson	.10
24	Vince Coleman	.10
25	Deion Sanders	.10
26	Rafael Palmeiro	.65
27	Dave Weathers	.10
28	Kent Mercker	.10
29	Gregg Olson	.10
30	Cory Bailey	.10
31	Brian Hunter	.10
32	Garey Ingram	.10
33	Daniel Smith	.10
34	Denny Hocking	.10
35	Charles Johnson	.10
36	Otis Nixon	.10
37	Hector Fajardo	.10
38	Lee Smith	.10
39	Phil Stidham	.10
40	Melvin Nieves	.10
41	Julio Franco	.10
42	Greg Gohr	.10
43	Steve Dunn	.10
44	Tony Fernandez	.10
45	Toby Borland	.10
46	Paul Shuey	.10
47	Shawn Hare	.10
48	Shawn Green	.50
49	Julian Tavarez RC	.10
50	Ernie Young	.10
51	Chris Sabo	.10
52	Greg O'Halloran	.10
53	Donnie Elliott	.10
54	Jim Converse	.10
55	Ray Holbert	.10
56	Keith Lockhart	.10
57	Tony Longmire	.10
58	Jorge Fabregas	.10
59	Ravelo Manzanillo	.10
60	Marcus Moore	.10
61	Carlos Rodriguez	.10
62	Mark Portugal	.10
63	Yorkis Perez	.10
64	Dan Miceli	.10
65	Chris Turner	.10
66	Mike Oquist	.10
67	Tom Quinlan	.10
68	Matt Walbeck	.10
69	Dave Staton	.10
70	Bill Van Landingham RC	.10
71	Dave Stevens	.10
72	Domingo Cedeno	.10
73	Alex Diaz	.10
74	Darren Bragg	.10
75	James Hurst	.10
76	Alex Gonzalez	.10
77	Steve Dreyer	.10
78	Robert Eenhoorn	.10
79	Derek Parks	.10
80	Jose Valentin	.10
81	Wes Chamberlain	.10
82	Tony Tarasco	.10
83	Steve Trachsel	.10
84	Willie Banks	.10
85	Rob Butler	.10
86	Miguel Jimenez	.10
87	Gerald Williams	.10
88	Aaron Small	.10
89	Matt Mieske	.10
90	Tim Hyers	.10
91	Eddie Murray	.75
92	Dennis Martinez	.10
93	Tony Eusebio	.10
94	Brian Anderson RC	.25
95	Blaise Ilsley	.10
96	Johnny Ruffin	.10
97	Carlos Reyes	.10
98	Greg Pirkl	.10
99	Jack Morris	.10
100	John Mabry	.10

101	Mike Kelly	.10
102	Rich Becker	.10
103	Chris Gomez	.10
104	Jim Edmonds	.10
105	Rich Rowland	.10
106	Damon Buford	.10
107	Mark Kiefer	.10
108	Matias Carrillo	.10
109	James Mouton	.10
110	Kelly Stinnett	.10
111	Billy Ashley	.10
112	Fausto Cruz RC	.10
113	Roberto Petagine	.10
114	Joe Hall	.10
115	Brian Johnson RC	.10
116	Kevin Jarvis	.10
117	Tim Davis	.10
118	John Patterson	.10
119	Stan Royer	.10
120	Jeff Juden	.10
121	Bryan Eversgerd	.10
122	Chan Ho Park RC	1.00
123	Shane Reynolds	.10
124	Danny Bautista	.10
125	Rikkert Faneyte	.10
126	Carlos Pulido	.10
127	Mike Matheny	.10
128	Hector Carrasco	.10
129	Eddie Zambrano	.10
130	Lee Tinsley	.10
131	Roger Salkeld	.10
132	Carlos Delgado	1.00
133	Troy O'Leary	.10
134	Keith Mitchell	.10
135	Lance Painter	.10
136	Nate Minchey	.10
137	Eric Anthony	.10
138	Rafael Bournigal	.10
139	Joey Hamilton	.10
140	Bobby Munoz	.10
141	Rex Hudler	.10
142	Alex Cole	.10
143	Stan Javier	.10
144	Jose Oliva	.10
145	Tom Brunansky	.10
146	Greg Colbrunn	.10
147	Luis Lopez	.10
148	Alex Rodriguez RC	10.00
149	Darryl Strawberry	.10
150	Bo Jackson	.15

Artist's Proof

Each of the 150 regular cards in the Sportflics 2000 Rookie & Traded issue was also produced in a parallel chase set designated on front with a black and gold "Artist's Proof" logo. Stated odds of finding an AP card were one per 24 packs. Fewer than 1,000 of each AP card were reportedly produced.

	NM/M
Complete Set (150):	300.00
Common Player:	1.00
Stars:	25X
148 Alex Rodriguez:	

Going, Going, Gone

A dozen of the game's top home run hitters are featured in this insert set. On front, simulated 3-D action photos depict the player's swing for the fences. Backs have a portrait photo and information about the player's home run prow-

ess. A crossed bats and "Going, Going Gone" logo appear on both front and back. Cards are numbered with a "GG" prefix. Stated odds of finding one of these inserts were once in 18 packs.

		NM/M
Complete Set (12):		10.00
Common Player:		.50
1	Gary Sheffield	.75
2	Matt Williams	.50
3	Juan Gonzalez	.90
4	Ken Griffey Jr.	2.00
5	Mike Piazza	2.00
6	Frank Thomas	1.50
7	Tim Salmon	.50
8	Barry Bonds	3.00
9	Fred McGriff	.50
10	Cecil Fielder	.50
11	Albert Belle	.50
12	Joe Carter	.50

Rookies of the Year

Sportflics' choices for Rookies of the Year were featured on this one-card insert set. Ryan Klesko (National League) and Manny Ramirez (American League) are shown on the card when viewed from different angles. Sportflics batted .000 in their guesses, however, as Raul Mondesi and Bob Hamelin were the actual R.O.Y. selections. This card was inserted at the average rate of once per 360 packs.

		NM/M
Complete Set (1):		
RO1	Ryan Klesko, Manny Ramirez	3.00

3-D Rookies

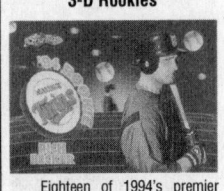

Eighteen of 1994's premier rookies are featured in this insert set. Combining a 3-D look and Sportflics' "Magic Motion" technology, the horizontal-format Starflics rookie cards present a striking appearance. Backs feature a full-bleed color photo overprinted with gold foil. A notice on back gives the production run of the chase cards as "No more than 5,000 sets." Stated odds of finding a Starflics Rookie card were given as one per 36 packs. Cards are numbered with a "TR" prefix.

		NM/M
Complete Set (18):		65.00
Common Player:		2.00
1	John Hudek	2.00
2	Manny Ramirez	15.00
3	Jeffrey Hammonds	2.00
4	Carlos Delgado	7.50
5	Javier Lopez	2.00
6	Alex Gonzalez	2.00
7	Raul Mondesi	2.00
8	Bob Hamelin	2.00
9	Ryan Klesko	2.00
10	Brian Anderson	2.00
11	Alex Rodriguez	40.00
12	Cliff Floyd	2.00
13	Chan Ho Park	2.00
14	Steve Karsay	2.00
15	Rondell White	2.00
16	Shawn Green	6.00
17	Rich Becker	2.00
18	Charles Johnson	2.00

FanFest All-Stars

An American and a National League player at each position share the fronts of these "Magic Motion" cards. Cards were available by redeeming coupons acquired at various locations around the Pittsburgh All-Star FanFest celebration in July, 1994. Action photos of the players alternate on the fronts of the cards when the viewing angle is changed. The N.L. player's name appears at upper-left; the A.L. All-Star at lower-right. Backs have portrait photos of the players and a few stats and comments. The players' names, teams, position and card number are printed in gold foil, along with the notation "1 of 10,000." Cards are numbered with an "AS" prefix.

	NM/M
Complete Set (9):	25.00
Common Card:	2.50
1 Fred McGriff,	
Frank Thomas	3.00
2 Ryne Sandberg,	
Roberto Alomar	3.50
3 Matt Williams,	
Travis Fryman	2.50
4 Ozzie Smith,	
Cal Ripken Jr.	5.00
5 Mike Piazza,	
Ivan Rodriguez	4.00
6 Barry Bonds,	
Juan Gonzalez	5.00
7 Len Dykstra,	
Ken Griffey Jr.	4.00
8 Gary Sheffield,	
Kirby Puckett	3.50
9 Greg Maddux,	
Mike Mussina	3.50

1995 Sportflix Samples

This nine-card promo pack was sent to Pinnacle's dealer network to introduce its revamped (new logo, spelling) magic-motion card set for 1995. The sample cards are identical in format to the regular-issue Sportflix cards except that a large white "SAMPLE" is printed diagonally on front and back of the promos.

	NM/M
Complete Set (9):	20.00
Common Player:	2.00
3 Fred McGriff	2.00
20 Frank Thomas	3.50
105 Manny Ramirez	3.00
122 Cal Ripken Jr.	5.00
128 Roberto Alomar	2.25
152 Russ Davis (Rookie)	2.00
162 Chipper Jones (Rookie)	4.00
DE2 Matt Williams	
(Detonators)	2.00
---- Advertising Card	.10

1995 Sportflix

With only 170 cards in the set, only the biggest stars and hottest rookies (25 of them in a specially designed subset) are included in this simulated 3-D issue. Fronts feature two borderless action photos which are alternately visible as the card's viewing angle is changed. Backs are conventionally printed and have a portrait photo, a few career stats and a couple of sentences about the player. The basic packaging options for '95 Sportflix were five- and eight card foils at $1.89 and $2.99, respectively.

	NM/M
Complete Set (170):	13.50
Common Player:	.10
Artist's Proofs:	12X
Pack (5):	1.50
Wax Box (36):	30.00
1 Ken Griffey Jr.	1.25
2 Jeffrey Hammonds	.10
3 Fred McGriff	.10
4 Rickey Henderson	.75
5 Derrick May	.10
6 Robin Ventura	.10
7 Royce Clayton	.10
8 Paul Molitor	.75
9 Charlie Hayes	.10
10 David Nied	.10
11 Ellis Burks	.10
12 Bernard Gilkey	.10
13 Don Mattingly	1.00
14 Albert Belle	.10
15 Doug Drabek	.10
16 Tony Gwynn	1.00
17 Delino DeShields	.10
18 Bobby Bonilla	.10
19 Cliff Floyd	.10
20 Frank Thomas	.75
21 Raul Mondesi	.10
22 Dave Nilsson	.10
23 Todd Zeile	.10
24 Bernie Williams	.10
25 Kirby Puckett	1.00
26 David Cone	.10
27 Darren Daulton	.10
28 Marquis Grissom	.10
29 Randy Johnson	.75
30 Jeff Kent	.10
31 Orlando Merced	.10
32 Dave Justice	.10
33 Ivan Rodriguez	.65
34 Kirk Gibson	.10
35 Alex Fernandez	.10
36 Rick Wilkins	.10
37 Andy Benes	.10
38 Bret Saberhagen	.10
39 Billy Ashley	.10
40 Jose Rijo	.10
41 Matt Williams	.10
42 Lenny Dykstra	.10
43 Jay Bell	.10
44 Reggie Jefferson	.10
45 Greg Maddux	1.00
46 Gary Sheffield	.35
47 Bret Boone	.10
48 Jeff Bagwell	.75
49 Ben McDonald	.10
50 Eric Karros	.10
51 Roger Clemens	1.00
52 Sammy Sosa	1.00
53 Barry Bonds	2.00
54 Joey Hamilton	.10
55 Brian Jordan	.10
56 Wil Cordero	.10
57 Aaron Sele	.10
58 Paul O'Neill	.10
59 Carlos Garcia	.10
60 Mike Mussina	.40
61 John Olerud	.10
62 Kevin Appier	.10
63 Matt Mieske	.10
64 Carlos Baerga	.10
65 Ryan Klesko	.10
66 Jimmy Key	.10
67 James Mouton	.10
68 Tim Salmon	.10
69 Hal Morris	.10
70 Albie Lopez	.10
71 Dave Hollins	.10
72 Greg Colbrunn	.10
73 Juan Gonzalez	.40
74 Wally Joyner	.10
75 Bob Hamelin	.10
76 Brady Anderson	.10
77 Deion Sanders	.10
78 Javier Lopez	.10
79 Brian McRae	.10
80 Craig Biggio	.10
81 Kenny Lofton	.10
82 Cecil Fielder	.10
83 Mike Piazza	1.25
84 Rafael Palmeiro	.65
85 Jim Thome	.65
86 Ruben Sierra	.10
87 Mark Langston	.10
88 John Valentin	.10
89 Shawon Dunston	.10
90 Travis Fryman	.10
91 Chuck Knoblauch	.10
92 Dean Palmer	.10
93 Robby Thompson	.10
94 Barry Larkin	.10
95 Darren Lewis	.10
96 Andres Galarraga	.10
97 Tony Phillips	.10
98 Mo Vaughn	.10
99 Pedro Martinez	.75
100 Chad Curtis	.10
101 Brent Gates	.10
102 Pat Hentgen	.10
103 Rico Brogna	.10
104 Carlos Delgado	.50
105 Manny Ramirez	.75
106 Mike Greenwell	.10
107 Wade Boggs	1.00
108 Ozzie Smith	1.00
109 Rusty Greer	.10
110 Willie Greene	.10
111 Chili Davis	.10
112 Reggie Sanders	.10
113 Roberto Kelly	.10
114 Tom Glavine	.35
115 Moises Alou	.10
116 Dennis Eckersley	.65
117 Danny Tartabull	.10
118 Jeff Conine	.10
119 Will Clark	.10
120 Joe Carter	.10
121 Mark McGwire	1.50
122 Cal Ripken Jr.	2.00
123 Danny Jackson	.10
124 Phil Plantier	.10
125 Dante Bichette	.10
126 Jack McDowell	.10
127 Jose Canseco	.40
128 Roberto Alomar	.20
129 Rondell White	.10
130 Ray Lankford	.10
131 Ryan Thompson	.10
132 Ken Caminiti	.10
133 Gregg Jefferies	.10
134 Omar Vizquel	.10
135 Mark Grace	.10
136 Derek Bell	.10
137 Mickey Tettleton	.10
138 Wilson Alvarez	.10
139 Larry Walker	.10
140 Bo Jackson	.15
141 Alex Rodriguez	1.50
142 Orlando Miller	.10
143 Shawn Green	.35
144 Steve Dunn	.10
145 Midre Cummings	.10
146 Chan Ho Park	.10
147 Jose Oliva	.10
148 Armando Benitez	.10
149 J.R. Phillips	.10
150 Charles Johnson	.10
151 Garret Anderson	.10
152 Russ Davis	.10
153 Brian Hunter	.10
154 Ernie Young	.10
155 Marc Newfield	.10
156 Greg Pirkl	.10
157 Scott Ruffcorn	.10
158 Rikkert Faneyte	.10
159 Duane Singleton	.10
160 Gabe White	.10
161 Alex Gonzalez	.10
162 Chipper Jones	1.00
163 Mike Kelly	.10
164 Kurt Miller	.10
165 Roberto Petagine	.10
166 Checklist (Jeff Bagwell)	.40
167 Checklist (Mike Piazza)	.65
168 Checklist (Ken Griffey Jr.)	.65
169 Checklist (Frank Thomas)	.40
170 Checklist (Barry Bonds, Cal Ripken Jr.)	.75

Artist's Proofs

Each of the 170 cards in the regular Sportflix set can be found with a special tombstone shaped black-and-gold "Artist's Proof" seal designating it as one of a parallel edition of 700 cards each. Cards are otherwise identical to the regular-issue version. AP cards were inserted at an average rate of one per 36 packs.

	NM/M
Complete Set (170):	200.00
Common Player:	.75
Stars:	12X

Double Take

A see-through plastic background and A.L. and N.L. stars at the same position sharing the card with their shadows marks this chase set as the top of the line for '95 Sportflix. Found at an average rate of one per 48 packs, the Double Take inserts represent a new level in "magic motion" card technology.

	NM/M
Complete Set (12):	25.00
Common Player:	1.00
1 Frank Thomas,	
Jeff Bagwell	1.50
2 Will Clark, Fred McGriff	1.00
3 Roberto Alomar,	
Jeff Kent	1.00
4 Wade Boggs,	
Matt Williams	2.00
5 Cal Ripken Jr.,	
Ozzie Smith	6.00
6 Alex Rodriguez,	
Wil Cordero	4.00
7 Carlos Delgado,	
Mike Piazza	3.00
8 Kenny Lofton,	
Dave Justice	1.00
9 Ken Griffey Jr.,	
Barry Bonds	6.00
10 Albert Belle,	
Raul Mondesi	1.00
11 Kirby Puckett,	
Tony Gwynn	2.50
12 Jimmy Key,	
Greg Maddux	2.00

ProMotion

Twelve of baseball's biggest stars morph into team logos on a bright team-color background in this chase series. Backs have a portrait photo and a few words about the players. The ProMotion inserts are a one per 18 pack pick in jumbo packs only.

	NM/M
Complete Set (12):	30.00
Common Player:	1.50
1 Ken Griffey Jr.	4.00
2 Frank Thomas	2.50
3 Cal Ripken Jr.	5.00
4 Jeff Bagwell	2.50
5 Mike Piazza	4.00
6 Matt Williams	1.50
7 Albert Belle	1.50
8 Jose Canseco	2.00
9 Don Mattingly	3.50
10 Barry Bonds	5.00
11 Will Clark	1.50
12 Kirby Puckett	3.00

3D Detonators

With the players on a pedestal and fireworks in the background, this chase set lives up to its name, "Detonators." The cards feature a deep 3-D look on front. Backs have a close-up photo of the player in the pedestal's column. Detonator cards are pulled at an average rate of one per 16 packs.

3D Hammer Team

Sledge hammers flying in formation through a cloud-studded sky are the background for this insert set featuring the game's heavy hitters. Backs have a portrait photo and a few words about the player's power hitting prowess. Hammer Team cards are picked on an average of once per four packs.

	NM/M
Complete Set (18):	7.50
Common Player:	.20
1 Ken Griffey Jr.	1.50
2 Frank Thomas	.65
3 Jeff Bagwell	.65
4 Mike Piazza	1.50
5 Cal Ripken Jr.	2.00
6 Albert Belle	.20
7 Barry Bonds	2.00
8 Don Mattingly	1.00
9 Will Clark	.20
10 Tony Gwynn	.75
11 Matt Williams	.20
12 Kirby Puckett	.75
13 Manny Ramirez	.65
14 Fred McGriff	.20
15 Juan Gonzalez	.35
16 Kenny Lofton	.20
17 Raul Mondesi	.20
18 Tim Salmon	.20

1995 Sportflix/UC3 Samples

To introduce the new technology it was bringing to the insert cards in the Sportflix UC3 issue, the company sent a sample of the Clear Shots insert, along with a header card describing the entire UC3 issue, to card dealers and the media in June 1995. A large, black, "SAMPLE" is over-

printed diagonally on the front. A similarly marked Fred McGriff previewed the set's regular cards.

	NM/M
Complete Set (3):	5.00
3 Fred McGriff	2.00
CS8 Cliff Floyd	2.00
CS10 Alex Gonzalez	2.00
-- Header Card	.05

1995 Sportflix/UC3

Using advanced technology to create a premium 3-D card brand and inserts, UC3 offers three distinctly different card formats in the base 147-card set, plus a parallel set and three insert sets. All cards have borderless fronts and feature a heavy ribbed plastic top layer. The first 95 cards are veteran players in a horizontal format. A central action photo is flanked at left by a large gold glove (National Leaguers) or baseball (A.L.), and at right by a blue and green vista from which flies one (N.L.) or three (A.L.) baseballs. Player identification is in red at upper-left, the UC3 logo at lower-left. Backs have another color photo and a few stats set against a background of the team logo. Cards #96-122 are a vertical-format Rookie subset. Player photos are set against a purple and green vista with a large bat, ball and glove behind the player. His name is at upper-right; team logo at lower-right. Horizontal backs are similar to the other cards. The final 25 cards of the set are a subset titled, "In-Depth." These vertically formatted cards feature eye-popping graphics on front in which the main player photo almost jumps from the background. The only graphics are the player's name at left and the UC3 logo at upper-left. Backs have a portrait photo at top, bathed in golden rays. A team logo is at center and an outer space design at bottom. There is a short paragraph describing the player at right.

	NM/M
Complete Set (147):	12.50
Common Player:	.10
Artist's Proofs:	12X
Pack (5):	1.00
Wax Box (36):	25.00
1 Frank Thomas	.75
2 Wil Cordero	.10
3 John Olerud	.10
4 Deion Sanders	.10
5 Mike Mussina	.30
6 Mo Vaughn	.10
7 Will Clark	.10
8 Chili Davis	.10
9 Jimmy Key	.10
10 John Valentin	.10
11 Tony Tarasco	.10
12 Alan Trammell	.10
13 David Cone	.10
14 Tim Salmon	.10
15 Danny Tartabull	.10
16 Aaron Sele	.10
17 Alex Fernandez	.10
18 Barry Bonds	2.00
19 Andres Galarraga	.10
20 Don Mattingly	1.00
21 Kevin Appier	.10
22 Paul Molitor	.75
23 Omar Vizquel	.10
24 Andy Benes	.10
25 Rafael Palmeiro	.65
26 Barry Larkin	.10
27 Bernie Williams	.10
28 Gary Sheffield	.40
29 Wally Joyner	.10
30 Wade Boggs	1.00
31 Rico Brogna	.10
32 Ken Caminiti	.10
33 Kirby Puckett	1.00
34 Bobby Bonilla	.10
35 Hal Morris	.10
36 Moises Alou	.10
37 Jim Thome	.65
38 Chuck Knoblauch	.10
39 Mike Piazza	1.25
40 Travis Fryman	.10
41 Rickey Henderson	.75

42	Jack McDowell	.10
43	Carlos Johnson	.10
44	Gregg Jeffries	.10
45	Kirk Gibson	.10
46	Bret Saberhagen	.10
47	Cecil Fielder	.10
48	Manny Ramirez	.75
49	Marquis Grissom	.10
50	Dave Winfield	.75
51	Mark McGwire	1.50
52	Dennis Eckersley	.65
53	Robin Ventura	.10
54	Ryan Klesko	.10
55	Jeff Bagwell	.75
56	Ozzie Smith	1.00
57	Brian McRae	.10
58	Albert Belle	.10
59	Darren Daulton	.10
60	Jose Canseco	.40
61	Greg Maddux	1.00
62	Ben McDonald	.10
63	Lenny Dykstra	.10
64	Randy Johnson	.75
65	Fred McGriff	.10
66	Ray Lankford	.10
67	Dave Justice	.10
68	Paul O'Neill	.10
69	Tony Gwynn	1.00
70	Matt Williams	.10
71	Dante Bichette	.10
72	Craig Biggio	.10
73	Ken Griffey Jr.	1.25
74	Juan Gonzalez	.40
75	Cal Ripken Jr.	2.00
76	Jay Bell	.10
77	Joe Carter	.10
78	Roberto Alomar	.20
79	Mark Langston	.10
80	Dave Hollins	.10
81	Tom Glavine	.35
82	Ivan Rodriguez	.65
83	Mark Whiten	.10
84	Raul Mondesi	.10
85	Kenny Lofton	.10
86	Ruben Sierra	.10
87	Mark Grace	.10
88	Royce Clayton	.10
89	Billy Ashley	.10
90	Larry Walker	.10
91	Sammy Sosa	1.00
92	Jason Bere	.10
93	Bob Hamelin	.10
94	Greg Vaughn	.10
95	Roger Clemens	1.00
96	Scott Ruffcorn	.10
97	Hideo Nomo **RC**	1.50
98	Michael Tucker	.10
99	J.R. Phillips	.10
100	Roberto Petagine	.10
101	Chipper Jones	1.00
102	Armando Benitez	.10
103	Orlando Miller	.10
104	Carlos Delgado	.50
105	Jeff Cirillo	.10
106	Shawn Green	.30
107	Joe Rando	.10
108	Vaughn Eshelman	.10
109	Frank Rodriguez	.10
110	Russ Davis	.10
111	Todd Hollandsworth	.10
112	Mark Grudzielanek	.10
113	Jose Oliva	.10
114	Ray Durham	.10
115	Alex Rodriguez	1.50
116	Alex Gonzalez	.10
117	Midre Cummings	.10
118	Marty Cordova	.10
119	John Mabry	.10
120	Jason Jacome	.10
121	Joe Vitiello	.10
122	Charles Johnson	.10
123	Cal Ripken Jr. (In Depth)	1.00
124	Ken Griffey Jr. (In Depth)	.65
125	Frank Thomas (In Depth)	.40
126	Mike Piazza (In Depth)	.65
127	Matt Williams (In Depth)	.10
128	Barry Bonds (In Depth)	1.00
129	Greg Maddux (In Depth)	.50
130	Randy Johnson (In Depth)	.40
131	Albert Belle (In Depth)	.10
132	Will Clark (In Depth)	.10
133	Tony Gwynn (In Depth)	.50
134	Manny Ramirez (In Depth)	.40
135	Raul Mondesi (In Depth)	.10
136	Mo Vaughn (In Depth)	.10
137	Mark McGwire (In Depth)	.75
138	Kirby Puckett (In Depth)	.50
139	Don Mattingly (In Depth)	.60
140	Carlos Baerga (In Depth)	.10
141	Roger Clemens (In Depth)	.60
142	Fred McGriff (In Depth)	.10
143	Kenny Lofton (In Depth)	.10
144	Jeff Bagwell (In Depth)	.10
145	Larry Walker (In Depth)	.10
146	Joe Carter (In Depth)	.10
147	Rafael Palmeiro (In Depth)	.30

UC3 Artist's Proof

This chase set parallels the 147 regular cards in the UC3 set with a version on which a round, gold "ARTIST'S PROOF" seal is printed on the front of the card. The AP cards are on the average of one per box (36 packs).

		NM/M
Complete Set (147):		200.00
Common Player:		.75
Stars:		12X

Clear Shots

Seeded at the rate of about one per 24 packs, the 12 cards in this chase set feature top rookies in a technologically advanced format. The left two-thirds of the card are clear plastic, the right third is blue (American League) or red-purple (N.L.). At center is a circle which features the player photos, portrait and action, depending on the viewing angle. Also changing with the viewpoint are the words "CLEAR" and "SHOT" at top-right, and team and UC3 logos at bottom-right. The player's last name is in black at lower-left and appears to change size as the card is moved. Backs have a gray strip vertically at left with the card number, manufacturer and licensor logos and copyright information. Card numbers have a "CS" prefix.

		NM/M
Complete Set (12):		12.00
Common Player:		.25
1	Alex Rodriguez	5.00
2	Shawn Green	.75
3	Hideo Nomo	1.25
4	Charles Johnson	.25
5	Orlando Miller	.25
6	Billy Ashley	.25
7	Carlos Delgado	1.50
8	Cliff Floyd	.25
9	Chipper Jones	4.00
10	Alex Gonzalez	.25
11	J.R. Phillips	.25
12	Michael Tucker	.25

Cyclone Squad

The most commonly encountered (one per four packs, on average) of the UC3 chase cards are the 20-card Cyclone Squad, featuring the game's top batsmen. Cards have a player in a batting pose set against a dark copper background with two golden pinwheels behind him which

appear to spin when the card is moved. Horizontal backs have a green toned photo of the player in his follow-through swing, with shock waves radiating from the lower-left corner. Cards have a CS prefix.

		NM/M
Complete Set (20):		10.00
Common Player:		.25
1	Frank Thomas	.65
2	Ken Griffey Jr.	1.00
3	Jeff Bagwell	.65
4	Cal Ripken Jr.	2.00
5	Barry Bonds	2.00
6	Mike Piazza	1.00
7	Matt Williams	.25
8	Kirby Puckett	.75
9	Jose Canseco	.45
10	Will Clark	.25
11	Don Mattingly	.85
12	Albert Belle	.25
13	Tony Gwynn	.75
14	Raul Mondesi	.25
15	Bobby Bonilla	.25
16	Rafael Palmeiro	.60
17	Fred McGriff	.25
18	Tim Salmon	.25
19	Kenny Lofton	.25
20	Joe Carter	.25

In Motion

Found on an average of once per 18 packs, the cards in this chase set feature maximim motion. When the card is held almost vertically a small eight-piece jigsaw puzzle photo of the player is visible against a light blue background. As the card is moved toward a horizontal position, the pieces appear to become large and move together until the picture fills most of the card. The player's name is in orange at lower-left, with manufacturer's logos at top. Horizontal backs have a green background, two color player photos and a few words of career highlights. The In Motion card numbers are preceded by an "IM" prefix.

		NM/M
Complete Set (10):		7.00
Common Player:		.25
1	Cal Ripken Jr.	1.50
2	Ken Griffey Jr.	1.00
3	Frank Thomas	.50
4	Mike Piazza	1.00
5	Barry Bonds	1.50
6	Matt Williams	.25
7	Kirby Puckett	.75
8	Greg Maddux	.75
9	Don Mattingly	.85
10	Will Clark	.25

1996 Sportflix

Distributed in only retail locations, this 1996 Sportflix set has 144 cards, including 24-card UC3 and 21-card Rookies subsets. The set also has a parallel set, Artist's Proof; these cards are seeded one per every 48 packs. Four insert sets

were also produced: Double Take, Hit Parade, Power Surge and ProMotion.

	NM/M
Complete Set (144):	17.50
Common Player:	.10
Common Artist's Proof:	1.00
AP Stars:	12X
Pack (5):	1.00
Wax Box (36):	30.00

1	Wade Boggs	1.00
2	Tim Salmon	.10
3	Will Clark	.10
4	Dante Bichette	.10
5	Barry Bonds	2.00
6	Kirby Puckett	1.00
7	Albert Belle	.10
8	Greg Maddux	1.00
9	Tony Gwynn	1.00
10	Mike Piazza	1.25
11	Ivan Rodriguez	.65
12	Marty Cordova	.10
13	Frank Thomas	.75
14	Raul Mondesi	.10
15	Johnny Damon	.35
16	Mark McGwire	1.50
17	Lenny Dykstra	.10
18	Ken Griffey Jr.	1.25
19	Chipper Jones	1.00
20	Alex Rodriguez	1.50
21	Jeff Bagwell	.75
22	Jim Edmonds	.10
23	Edgar Martinez	.10
24	David Cone	.10
25	Tom Glavine	.35
26	Eddie Murray	.75
27	Paul Molitor	.75
28	Ryan Klesko	.10
29	Rafael Palmeiro	.65
30	Manny Ramirez	.75
31	Mo Vaughn	.10
32	Rico Brogna	.10
33	Marc Newfield	.10
34	J.T. Snow	.10
35	Reggie Sanders	.10
36	Fred McGriff	.10
37	Craig Biggio	.10
38	Jeff King	.10
39	Kenny Lofton	.10
40	Gary Gaetti	.10
41	Eric Karros	.10
42	Jason Isringhausen	.10
43	B.J. Surhoff	.10
44	Michael Tucker	.10
45	Gary Sheffield	.45
46	Chili Davis	.10
47	Bobby Bonilla	.10
48	Hideo Nomo	.40
49	Ray Durham	.10
50	Phil Nevin	.10
51	Randy Johnson	.75
52	Bill Pulsipher	.10
53	Ozzie Smith	1.00
54	Cal Ripken Jr.	2.00
55	Cecil Fielder	.10
56	Matt Williams	.10
57	Sammy Sosa	1.00
58	Roger Clemens	1.00
59	Brian Hunter	.10
60	Barry Larkin	.10
61	Charles Johnson	.10
62	Dave Justice	.10
63	Garret Anderson	.10
64	Rondell White	.10
65	Derek Bell	.10
66	Andres Galarraga	.10
67	Moises Alou	.10
68	Travis Fryman	.10
69	Pedro Martinez	.75
70	Carlos Baerga	.10
71	John Valentin	.10
72	Larry Walker	.10
73	Roberto Alomar	.20
74	Mike Mussina	.30
75	Kevin Appier	.10
76	Bernie Williams	.10
77	Ray Lankford	.10
78	Gregg Jefferies	.10
79	Robin Ventura	.10
80	Kenny Rogers	.10
81	Paul O'Neill	.10
82	Mark Grace	.10
83	Deion Sanders	.10
84	Tino Martinez	.10
85	Joe Carter	.10
86	Pete Schourek	.10
87	Jack McDowell	.10
88	John Mabry	.10
89	Darren Daulton	.10
90	Jim Thome	.65
91	Jay Buhner	.10
92	Jay Bell	.10
93	Kevin Seitzer	.10
94	Jose Canseco	.40
95	Juan Gonzalez	.40
96	Jeff Conine	.10
97	Chipper Jones (UC3)	.50
98	Ken Griffey Jr. (UC3)	.65
99	Frank Thomas (UC3)	.40
100	Cal Ripken Jr. (UC3)	1.00
101	Albert Belle (UC3)	.10
102	Mike Piazza (UC3)	.65
103	Dante Bichette (UC3)	.10
104	Sammy Sosa (UC3)	.50
105	Mo Vaughn (UC3)	.10
106	Tim Salmon (UC3)	.10
107	Reggie Sanders (UC3)	.10

108	Gary Sheffield (UC3)	.25
109	Ruben Rivera (UC3)	.10
110	Rafael Palmeiro (UC3)	.35
111	Edgar Martinez (UC3)	.10
112	Barry Bonds (UC3)	1.00
113	Manny Ramirez (UC3)	.40
114	Larry Walker (UC3)	.40
115	Jeff Bagwell (UC3)	.40
116	Matt Williams (UC3)	.75
117	Mark McGwire (UC3)	.75
118	Johnny Damon (UC3)	.30
119	Eddie Murray (UC3)	.40
120	Jay Buhner (UC3)	.10
121	Tim Unroe (Rookie)	.10
122	Todd Hollandsworth (Rookie)	.10
123	Tony Clark (Rookie)	.10
124	Roger Cedeno (Rookie)	.10
125	Jim Pittsley (Rookie)	.10
126	Ruben Rivera (Rookie)	.10
127	Bob Wolcott (Rookie)	.10
128	Chan Ho Park (Rookie)	.10
129	Chris Snopek (Rookie)	.10
130	Alex Ochoa (Rookie)	.10
131	Yamil Benitez (Rookie)	.10
132	Jimmy Haynes (Rookie)	.10
133	Dustin Hermanson (Rookie)	.10
134	Shawn Estes (Rookie)	.10
135	Howard Battle (Rookie)	.10
136	Matt Lawton **RC** (Rookie)	.25
137	Terrell Wade (Rookie)	.10
138	Jason Schmidt (Rookie)	.10
139	Derek Jeter (Rookie)	2.50
140	Shannon Stewart (Rookie)	.10
141	Chris Stynes (Rookie)	.10
142	Ken Griffey Jr. (Checklist)	.65
143	Greg Maddux (Checklist)	.50
144	Cal Ripken Jr. (Checklist)	1.00

Artist's Proofs

Artist's Proof parallels to 1996 Sportflix are a 1:48 find and are distinctively marked with an AP seal on front.

	NM/M
Complete Set (144):	200.00
Common Player:	1.00
AP Stars:	12X

Double Take

These 1996 Sportflix insert cards each feature two players who are tops at a particular position. Tilting the card to change the angle of view brings each player into focus. The cards were seeded one per 22 packs.

		NM/M
Complete Set (12):		30.00
Common Player:		1.50
1	Barry Larkin, Cal Ripken Jr.	6.00
2	Roberto Alomar, Craig Biggio	1.50
3	Chipper Jones, Matt Williams	2.50
4	Ken Griffey Jr., Ruben Rivera	3.50
5	Greg Maddux, Hideo Nomo	3.00
6	Frank Thomas, Mo Vaughn	2.00
7	Mike Piazza, Ivan Rodriguez	3.50
8	Albert Belle, Barry Bonds	6.00
9	Alex Rodriguez, Derek Jeter	8.00
10	Kirby Puckett, Tony Gwynn	3.00
11	Manny Ramirez, Sammy Sosa	3.00
12	Jeff Bagwell, Rico Brogna	2.00

Hit Parade

Sixteen of baseball's most productive hitters are featured on these

inserts. Horizontal fronts have a player portrait at right. In the background is a lenticular-motion scene of a generic player swinging the bat. Backs have an action photo and a few career highlights. The cards were seeded one per every 35 packs.

		NM/M
Complete Set (16):		24.00
Common Player:		.50
1	Ken Griffey Jr.	2.50
2	Cal Ripken Jr.	4.00
3	Frank Thomas	1.50
4	Mike Piazza	2.50
5	Mo Vaughn	.50
6	Albert Belle	.50
7	Jeff Bagwell	1.50
8	Matt Williams	.50
9	Sammy Sosa	2.00
9p	Sammy Sosa (Overprinted "SAMPLE.")	2.00
10	Kirby Puckett	2.00
11	Dante Bichette	.50
12	Gary Sheffield	1.00
13	Tony Gwynn	2.00
14	Wade Boggs	2.00
15	Chipper Jones	2.00
16	Barry Bonds	4.00

Power Surge

This 1996 Sportflix insert set showcases 24 sluggers on a clear 3-D parallel rendition of the UC3 subset in the main issue. These cards are seeded one per every 35 packs.

		NM/M
Complete Set (24):		30.00
Common Player:		.50
1	Chipper Jones	2.00
2	Ken Griffey Jr.	2.50
3	Frank Thomas	1.50
4	Cal Ripken Jr.	4.00
5	Albert Belle	.50
6	Mike Piazza	2.50
7	Dante Bichette	.50
8	Sammy Sosa	2.00
9	Mo Vaughn	.50
10	Tim Salmon	.50
11	Reggie Sanders	.50
12	Gary Sheffield	1.00
13	Ruben Rivera	.50
14	Rafael Palmeiro	1.25
15	Edgar Martinez	.50
16	Barry Bonds	4.00
17	Manny Ramirez	1.50
18	Larry Walker	.50
19	Jeff Bagwell	1.50
20	Matt Williams	.50
21	Mark McGwire	3.00
22	Johnny Damon	.90
23	Eddie Murray	1.50
24	Jay Buhner	.50

ProMotion

These 1996 Sportflix inserts were seeded one per every 17 packs. The cards' "morphing" technology turns baseball equipment, such as bats, balls and gloves, into 20 of the top veteran superstars using multi-phase animation.

	NM/M
Complete Set (20):	22.50

	Common Player:	.50
1	Cal Ripken Jr.	5.00
2	Greg Maddux	2.00
3	Mo Vaughn	.50
4	Albert Belle	.50
5	Mike Piazza	3.00
6	Ken Griffey Jr.	3.00
7	Frank Thomas	1.50
8	Jeff Bagwell	1.50
9	Hideo Nomo	1.00
10	Chipper Jones	2.00
11	Tony Gwynn	2.00
12	Don Mattingly	2.50
13	Dante Bichette	.50
14	Matt Williams	.50
15	Manny Ramirez	1.50
16	Barry Bonds	5.00
17	Reggie Sanders	.50
18	Tim Salmon	.50
19	Ruben Rivera	.50
20	Garret Anderson	.50

Rookie Supers

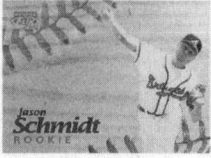

Eight of the young players included in the Sportflix Rookies subset are featured in an enlarged version which was issued one per retail box. The cards measure 3" x 5" and are numbered "X of 8," on back, but are otherwise identical to the smaller version.

		NM/M
	Complete Set (8):	12.50
	Common Player:	1.00
1	Jason Schmidt	1.00
2	Chris Snopek	1.00
3	Tony Clark	1.00
4	Todd Hollandsworth	1.00
5	Alex Ochoa	1.00
6	Derek Jeter	10.00
7	Howard Battle	1.00
8	Bob Wolcott	1.00

1981 Sporting News Conlon Collection

This set of 100 cards was sold directly into the hobby by The Sporting News in a slip-cover case for $50. The blank-backed cards measure 4" x 5" and feature a sepitoned photo surrounded by a 1/4" white border. The photos were the first of several uses on baseball cards of TSN's archives of ballplayer photos taken by Charles Martin Conlon between 1915-1935. The paper's logo appears at the top of the card. At bottom are the player's or players' names(s), team at the time the photo was taken, and position or positions played for the season indicated. A card number appears at lower-right.

		NM/M
	Complete Set (100):	90.00
	Common Player:	1.00
1	Ty Cobb	10.00
2	Hughie Jennings	1.00
3	Miller Huggins	1.00
4	Babe Ruth	12.50
5	Lou Gehrig	10.00
6	John McGraw	1.00
7	Bill Terry	1.00
8	Stan Baumgartner	1.00
9	Christy Mathewson	1.00
10	Grover Alexander	2.00
11	Tony Lazzeri	1.00
12	Frank Chance, Joe Tinker	2.00
13	Johnny Evers	1.00
14	Tris Speaker	1.00
15	Harry Hooper	1.00
16	Duffy Lewis	1.00
17	Joe Wood	1.00
18	Hugh Duffy	1.00
19	Rogers Hornsby	4.00
20	Earl Averill	1.00
21	Dizzy Dean	2.00
22	Daffy Dean	1.00
23	Frankie Frisch	1.00
24	Pepper Martin	1.00
25	Blondie Ryan	1.00
26	Hank Gowdy	1.00
27	Fred Merkle	1.00
28	Ernie Lombardi	1.00
29	Greasy Neale	1.00
30	Morris "Red" Badgro	1.00
31	Jim Thorpe	9.00
32	Roy Johnson	1.00
33	Bob Johnson	1.00
34	Mule Solters	1.00
35	Specs Toporcer	1.00
36	Jackie Hayes	1.00
37	Walter Johnson	5.00
38	Lefty Grove	1.00
39	Eddie Collins	1.00
40	Buck Weaver	7.50
41	Cozy Dolan	1.00
42	Emil Meusel	1.00
43	Bob Meusel	1.00
44	Lefty Gomez	1.00
45	Rube Marquard	1.00
46	Jeff Tesreau	1.00
47	Joe Heving	1.00
48	John Heving	1.00
49	Rick Ferrell	1.00
50	Wes Ferrell	1.00
51	Bill Wambsganss	1.00
52	Ben Chapman	1.00
53	Joe Sewell	1.00
54	Luke Sewell	1.00
55	Odell Hale	1.00
56	Sammy Hale	1.00
57	Earle Mack	1.00
58	Connie Mack	1.00
59	Rube Walberg	1.00
60	Mule Haas	1.00
61	Paul Waner	1.00
62	Lloyd Waner	1.00
63	Pie Traynor	1.00
64	Honus Wagner	2.00
65	Joe Cronin	1.00
66	Joe Harris	1.00
67	Dave Harris	1.00
68	Bucky Harris	1.00
69	Alex Gaston	1.00
70	Milt Gaston	1.00
71	Casey Stengel	1.00
72	Amos Rusie	1.00
73	Mickey Welch	1.00
74	Roger Bresnahan	1.00
75	Jesse Burkett	1.00
76	Harry Heilmann	1.00
77	Heinie Manush	1.00
78	Charlie Gehringer	1.00
79	Hank Greenberg	2.00
80	Jimmie Foxx	4.00
81	Al Simmons	1.00
82	Eddie Plank	1.00
83	George Sisler	1.00
84	Joe Medwick	1.00
85	Mel Ott	1.00
86	Hack Wilson	1.00
87	Jimmy Wilson	1.00
88	Chuck Klein	1.00
89	Gabby Hartnett	1.00
90	Henie Groh	1.00
91	Ping Bodie	1.00
92	Ted Lyons	1.00
93	Jack Quinn	1.00
94	Oscar Roettger	1.00
95	Wally Roettger	1.00
96	Bubbles Hargrave	1.00
97	Pinky Hargrave	1.00
98	Sam Crawford	1.00
99	Gee Walker	1.00
100	Homer Summa	1.00

1983 Sporting News Conlon Collection Prototypes

Walter (Barney) Johnson
Pitcher, Senators 1926

Unlike the issued cards which were in a large format, these prototypes are in standard 2-1/2" x 3-1/2" size. Fronts are printed in sepia. Black-and-white backs have player data, career summary and stats up to the date the photo was taken. Backs also have the TSN Conlon Collection logo and a Marketcom copyright.

		NM/M
	Complete Set (5):	7.50
	Common Player:	2.00
83-1	Lewis (Hack) Wilson	2.00
83-2	Joe Cronin	2.00
82-3	Walter (Barney) Johnson	3.00
83-4	Paul (Daffy) Dean	2.00
83-5	Connie Mack	2.00

1983 Sporting News Conlon Collection

This set was issued to mark the 50th anniversary of the first All-Star game in 1933. Besides the American and National League players who made up those teams, the set includes a group of all-stars from the Negro Leagues. The oversize (4-1/2" x 6-1/8") cards were sold only as complete sets. The cards feature sepia player photos on front, with a facsimile autograph and appropriate commemorative labeling. Black-and-white backs feature 1933 stats, an anecdote about the player, and the logos of appropriate parties in the set's marketing. The major leaguers' photos were the work of Charles M. Conlon, while the Black ballplayers' pictures were garnered from a variety of sources.

		NM/M
	Complete Set (60):	20.00
	Common Player:	.25
1	Jimmie Foxx	.50
2	Heinie Manush	.25
3	Lou Gehrig	2.50
4	Al Simmons	.25
5	Charlie Gehringer	.25
6	Luke Appling	.25
7	Mickey Cochrane	.25
8	Joe Kuhel	.25
9	Bill Dickey	.40
10	Pinky Higgins	.25
11	Roy Johnson	.25
12	Ben Chapman	.25
13	Johnny Hodapp	.25
14	Joe Cronin	.25
15	Evar Swanson	.25
16	Earl Averill	.25
17	Babe Ruth	4.00
18	Tony Lazzeri	.40
19	Alvin Crowder	.25
20	Lefty Grove	.25
21	Earl Whitehill	.25
22	Lefty Gomez	.25
23	Mel Harder	.25
24	Tommy Bridges	.25
25	Chuck Klein	.25
26	Spud Davis	.25
27	Riggs Stephenson	.25
28	Tony Piet	.25
29	Bill Terry	.25
30	Wes Schulmerich	.25
31a	Pepper Martin (Teeth don't show.)	.25
31b	Pepper Martin (Teeth show.)	.25
32	Arky Vaughan	.25
33	Wally Berger	.25
34	Rip Collins	.25
35	Fred Lindstrom	.25
36	Chick Fullis	.25
37	Paul Waner	.25
38	Johnny Frederick	.25
39	Joe Medwick	.25
40	Pie Traynor	.25
41	Frank Frisch	.25
42	Chick Hafey	.25
43	Carl Hubbell	.25
44	Guy Bush	.25
45	Dizzy Dean	.40
46	Hal Schumacher	.25
47	Larry French	.25
48	Lon Warneke	.25
49	Cool Papa Bell	.25
50	Oscar Charleston	.50
51	Josh Gibson	.50
52	Satchel Paige	1.00
53	Dave Malarcher	.25
54	Pop Lloyd	.25
55	Rube Foster	.25
56	Buck Leonard	.40
57	Smoky Joe Williams	.40
58	Willie Wells	.40
59	Judy Johnson	.25
60	Martin DiHigo	.25

1984 Sporting News Conlon Collection

Tyrus Raymond Cobb

This 60-card set, mostly Hall of Famers, was produced in conjunction with the Smithsonian Institution's "Baseball Immortals" photo exhibition of the work of Charles Martin Conlon. The oversize (4-1/2" x 6-1/8") cards have sepia-toned photos on front; backs are printed in black-and-white. The issue was initially sold only as a complete set.

		NM/M
	Complete Set (60):	35.00
	Common Player:	.25
1	Grover Cleveland Alexander	.60
2	Chief Bender	.25
3a	Fred Clarke (Jack Coombs front.)	1.50
3b	Fred Clarke (Correct front.)	.40
4-7	Ty Cobb	1.25
8	Mickey Cochrane	.25
9a	Jack Coombs (Fred Clarke front.)	1.50
9b	Jack Coombs (Correct front.)	.25
10	Charles & Margie Conlon	.25
11	Charles Conlon	.25
12	Joe Cronin	.25
13	Dizzy Dean	.60
14	Leo Durocher	.25
15	Jimmie Foxx	.40
16	The Gashouse Gang (Frank Frisch, Mike Gonzalez, Buzzy Wares)	.25
17	Lou Gehrig	1.75
18	Lou Gehrig	1.75
19	Lou Gehrig	1.75
20	Lou Gehrig	1.75
21	Charlie Gehringer	.25
22	Lefty Gomez	.25
23	Lefty Grove	.25
24	Bucky Harris	.25
25	Harry Heilmann	.25
26	Rogers Hornsby	.40
27	Waite Hoyt	.25
28	Carl Hubbell	.25
29	Miller Huggins	.25
30	Walter Johnson	.60
31	Bill Klem	.25
32	Connie Mack	.25
33	Heinie Manush	.25
34	Rube Marquard	.25
35	Pepper Martin	.25
36	Christy Mathewson	.60
37	Christy Mathewson	.60
38	Christy Mathewson	.60
39	Joe McCarthy	.25
40	John McGraw	.25
41	Fred Merkle	.25
42	Mel Ott	.25
43	Roger Peckinpaugh	.25
44	Herb Pennock	.25
45-50	Babe Ruth	2.25
51	Al Simmons	.25
52	Tris Speaker	.40
53	Casey Stengel	.25
54	Bill Terry	.25
55	Pie Traynor	.25
56	Rube Waddell	.25
57	Honus Wagner	1.00
58	Lloyd Waner, Paul Waner	.25
59	Paul Waner	.25
60	Hack Wilson	.25

1981 Sportrait Hall of Fame

This collectors' issue feature portrait art by Stan Sypulski in a blank-back 3-1/2" x 5" format. Portraits have a color frame line and are numbered.

		NM/M
	Complete Set (25):	55.00
	Common Player:	2.00
1	Honus Wagner	4.00
2	Miller Huggins	2.00
3	Babe Ruth	6.00
4	Connie Mack	2.00
5	Ty Cobb	5.00
6	Lou Gehrig	5.00
7	Eddie Collins	2.00
8	Chuck Klein	2.00
9	Ted Williams	5.00
10	Jimmy Foxx	3.00
11	Frank Baker	2.00
12	Nap Lajoie	2.00
13	Casey Stengel	2.00
14	Joe DiMaggio	5.00
15	Mickey Mantle	6.00
16	Frank Frisch	2.00
17	Bill Terry	2.00
18	Jackie Robinson	5.00
19	Sam Rice	2.00
20	Mickey Cochrane	2.00
21	George Sisler	2.00
22	Bob Feller	3.00
23	Walter Johnson	3.00
24	Tris Speaker	3.00
---	Checklist	2.00

1984 Sports Design Products Doug West

CARL YASTRZEMSKI OF

The art of Doug West is featured in portrait and action pictures on each card in this collectors set. The player art is on a blue background. In the white border at bottom a red box displays the player name and position in white. The producer's logo is in black at bottom-right. Backs are printed in red and blue on white with personal data, career summary and stats. Production was reported as 5,000 sets, including 250 uncut sheets. Issue price was about $10.

		NM/M
	Complete Set (24):	15.00
	Common Player:	.50
1	Jackie Robinson	1.25
2	Luis Aparicio	.50
3	Roberto Clemente	3.00
4	Mickey Mantle	5.00
5	Joe DiMaggio	3.00
6	Willie Stargell	.50
7	Brooks Robinson	.60
8	Ty Cobb	1.50
9	Don Drysdale	.50
10	Bob Feller	.50
11	Stan Musial	1.00
12	Al Kaline	.50
13	Willie Mays	1.75
14	Willie McCovey	.50
15	Thurman Munson	.75
16	Charlie Gehringer	.50
17	Eddie Mathews	.50
18	Carl Yastrzemski	.50
19	Warren Spahn	.50
20	Ted Williams	2.00
21	Ernie Banks	.60
22	Roy Campanella	.75
23	Harmon Killebrew	.50
24	Duke Snider	.75

1985 Sports Design Products Doug West

TED KLUSZEWSKI FIRST BASE

The art of Doug West is featured in portrait and action pictures on each card in this collectors' set. In the white border at bottom a blue box displays the player name and position in white. The producer's logo is in black at bottom-right. Backs are printed in red and blue on white with personal data, career summary and stats. Cards are numbered sequentially from the previous year's issue. Besides 5,000 complete sets (issued at $8), 250 uncut sheets were also sold.

		NM/M
	Complete Set (24):	7.50
	Common Player:	.25
25	Lou Gehrig	1.00
26	Hoyt Wilhelm	.25
27	Enos Slaughter	.25
28	Lou Brock	.25
29	Mickey Cochrane	.25
30	Gil Hodges	.50
31	Yogi Berra	.50
32	Carl Hubbell	.50
33	Hank Greenberg	.50
34	Casey Stengel	.25
35	Pee Wee Reese	.35
36	Ralph Kiner	.50
37	Satchel Paige	.50
38	Richie Ashburn	.35
39	Connie Mack	.25
40	Dick Groat	.25
41	Tony Oliva	.25
42	Honus Wagner	.40
43	Denny McLain	.25
44	Johnny Mize	.25
45	Bob Lemon	.25
46	Fergie Jenkins	.25
47	Babe Ruth	2.00
48	Ted Kluszewski	.35

1997 Sports Illustrated

Fleer teamed up with Sports Illustrated to produce a 180-card World Series Fever set. The regular set is divided into six different subsets: 96 Player Cards, 27 Fresh Faces, 18 Inside Baseball, 18 Silber Vision, 12 covers and 9 Newsmakers. Inserts included the Extra Edition parallel set, Great Shots, Cooperstown Collection and Autographed Mini-Cover Redemption Cards. Cards were sold in six-card packs for $1.99 each.

		NM/M
	Complete Set (180):	20.00
	Common Player:	.05
	Extra Edition Stars:	8X
	Pack (6):	1.25
	Wax Box (24):	20.00
1	Bob Abreu (Fresh Faces)	.10
2	Jaime Bluma (Fresh Faces)	.05
3	Emil Brown (Fresh Faces)	.05
4	Jose Cruz, Jr. (Fresh Faces)	.05
5	Jason Dickson (Fresh Faces)	.05
6	Nomar Garciaparra (Fresh Faces)	1.00
7	Todd Greene (Fresh Faces)	.05
8	Vladimir Guerrero (Fresh Faces)	.75
9	Wilton Guerrero (Fresh Faces)	.05
10	Jose Guillen (Fresh Faces)	.05
11	Hideki Irabu (Fresh Faces)	.05
12	Russ Johnson (Fresh Faces)	.05
13	Andruw Jones (Fresh Faces)	.75
14	Damon Mashore (Fresh Faces)	.05
15	Jason McDonald (Fresh Faces)	.05
16	Ryan McGuire (Fresh Faces)	.05
17	Matt Morris (Fresh Faces)	.05
18	Kevin Orie (Fresh Faces)	.05
19	Dante Powell (Fresh Faces)	.05
20	Pokey Reese (Fresh Faces)	.05
21	Joe Roa (Fresh Faces)	.05
22	Scott Rolen (Fresh Faces)	.65
23	Glendon Rusch (Fresh Faces)	.05
24	Scott Spiezio (Fresh Faces)	.05
25	Bubba Trammell (Fresh Faces)	.05

26	Todd Walker (Fresh Faces)	.05	
27	Jamey Wright (Fresh Faces)	.05	
28	Ken Griffey Jr. (Season Highlights)	.75	
29	Tino Martinez (Season Highlights)	.05	
30	Roger Clemens (Season Highlights)	.65	
31	Hideki Irabu (Season Highlights)	.05	
32	Kevin Brown (Season Highlights)		
33	Chipper Jones, Cal Ripken Jr. (Season Highlights)	.65	
34	Sandy Alomar (Season Highlights)		
35	Ken Caminiti (Season Highlights)	.05	
36	Randy Johnson (Season Highlights)	.40	
37	Andy Ashby (Inside Baseball)		
38	Jay Buhner (Inside Baseball)	.05	
39	Joe Carter (Inside Baseball)	.05	
40	Darren Daulton (Inside Baseball)		
41	Jeff Fassero (Inside Baseball)	.05	
42	Andres Galarraga (Inside Baseball)	.05	
43	Rusty Greer (Inside Baseball)		
44	Marquis Grissom (Inside Baseball)	.05	
45	Joey Hamilton (Inside Baseball)	.05	
46	Jimmy Key (Inside Baseball)		
47	Ryan Klesko (Inside Baseball)	.05	
48	Eddie Murray (Inside Baseball)	.75	
49	Charles Nagy (Inside Baseball)		
50	Dave Nilsson (Inside Baseball)	.05	
51	Ricardo Rincon (Inside Baseball)	.05	
52	Billy Wagner (Inside Baseball)	.05	
53	Dan Wilson (Inside Baseball)	.05	
54	Dmitri Young (Inside Baseball)	.05	
55	Roberto Alomar (S.I.BER Vision)	.30	
56	Sandy Alomar Jr. (S.I.BER Vision)	.05	
57	Scott Brosius (S.I.BER Vision)	.05	
58	Tony Clark (S.I.BER Vision)	.05	
59	Carlos Delgado (S.I.BER Vision)	.45	
60	Jermaine Dye (S.I.BER Vision)	.05	
61	Darin Erstad (S.I.BER Vision)	.20	
62	Derek Jeter (S.I.BER Vision)	1.00	
63	Jason Kendall (S.I.BER Vision)	.05	
64	Hideo Nomo (S.I.BER Vision)	.20	
65	Rey Ordonez (S.I.BER Vision)	.05	
66	Andy Pettitte (S.I.BER Vision)	.10	
67	Manny Ramirez (S.I.BER Vision)	.75	
68	Edgar Renteria (S.I.BER Vision)	.05	
69	Shane Reynolds (S.I.BER Vision)	.05	
70	Alex Rodriguez (S.I.BER Vision)	1.00	
71	Ivan Rodriguez (S.I.BER Vision)	.65	
72	Jose Rosado (S.I.BER Vision)	.05	
73	John Smoltz	.05	
74	Tom Glavine	.35	
75	Greg Maddux	1.00	
76	Chipper Jones	1.00	
77	Kenny Lofton	.05	
78	Fred McGriff	.05	
79	Kevin Brown	.05	
80	Alex Fernandez	.05	
81	Al Leiter	.05	
82	Bobby Bonilla	.05	
83	Gary Sheffield	.40	
84	Moises Alou	.05	
85	Henry Rodriguez	.05	
86	Mark Grudzielanek	.05	
87	Pedro Martinez	.75	
88	Todd Hundley	.05	
89	Bernard Gilkey	.05	
90	Bobby Jones	.05	
91	Curt Schilling	.35	
92	Ricky Bottalico	.05	
93	Mike Lieberthal	.05	
94	Sammy Sosa	1.00	
95	Ryne Sandberg	1.00	
96	Mark Grace	.25	
97	Deion Sanders	.05	

98	Reggie Sanders	.05	
99	Barry Larkin	.05	
100	Craig Biggio	.75	
101	Jeff Bagwell	.75	
102	Derek Bell	.05	
103	Brian Jordan	.05	
104	Ray Lankford	.05	
105	Ron Gant	.05	
106	Al Martin	.05	
107	Kevin Elster	.05	
108	Jermaine Allensworth	.05	
109	Vinny Castilla	.05	
110	Dante Bichette	.05	
111	Larry Walker	.05	
112	Mike Piazza	1.25	
113	Eric Karros	.05	
114	Todd Hollandsworth	.05	
115	Raul Mondesi	.05	
116	Hideo Nomo	.40	
117	Ramon Martinez	.05	
118	Ken Caminiti	.05	
119	Tony Gwynn	1.00	
120	Steve Finley	.05	
121	Barry Bonds	2.00	
122	J.T. Snow	.05	
123	Rod Beck	.05	
124	Cal Ripken Jr.	2.00	
125	Mike Mussina	.30	
126	Brady Anderson	.05	
127	Bernie Williams	.05	
128	Derek Jeter	2.00	
129	Tino Martinez	.05	
130	Andy Pettitte	.30	
131	David Cone	.05	
132	Mariano Rivera	.15	
133	Roger Clemens	1.00	
134	Pat Hentgen	.05	
135	Juan Guzman	.05	
136	Bob Higginson	.05	
137	Tony Clark	.05	
138	Travis Fryman	.05	
139	Mo Vaughn	.05	
140	Tim Naehring	.05	
141	John Valentin	.05	
142	Matt Williams	.05	
143	David Justice	.05	
144	Jim Thome	.65	
145	Chuck Knoblauch	.05	
146	Paul Molitor	.75	
147	Marty Cordova	.05	
148	Frank Thomas	.85	
149	Albert Belle	.05	
150	Robin Ventura	.05	
151	John Jaha	.05	
152	Jeff Cirillo	.05	
153	Jose Valentin	.05	
154	Jay Bell	.05	
155	Jeff King	.05	
156	Kevin Appier	.05	
157	Ken Griffey Jr.	1.25	
158	Alex Rodriguez	1.50	
158p	Alex Rodriguez/OPS	1.50	
159	Randy Johnson	.75	
160	Juan Gonzalez	.40	
161	Will Clark	.05	
162	Dean Palmer	.05	
163	Tim Salmon	.05	
164	Jim Edmonds	.05	
165	Jim Leyritz	.05	
166	Jose Canseco	.40	
167	Jason Giambi	.50	
168	Mark McGwire	1.50	
169	Barry Bonds (Classic Covers)	1.00	
170	Alex Rodriguez (Classic Covers)	.75	
171	Roger Clemens (Classic Covers)	.65	
172	Ken Griffey Jr. (Classic Covers)	.65	
173	Greg Maddux (Classic Covers)	.50	
174	Mike Piazza (Classic Covers)	.65	
175	Will Clark, Mark McGwire (Classic Covers)	1.00	
176	Hideo Nomo (Classic Covers)	.20	
177	Cal Ripken Jr. (Classic Covers)	1.00	
178	Ken Griffey Jr., Frank Thomas (Classic Covers)	.50	
179	Alex Rodriguez, Derek Jeter (Classic Covers)	1.50	
180	John Wetteland (Classic Covers)	.05	
---	Checklist (Jose Cruz Jr.)	.05	

Extra Edition

Each of the regular cards in the premiere Fleer SI issue is also found in a parallel set designated on front in gold holographic foil as "Extra Edition." Backs of the cards carry a serial number from within a production of 500 of each card.

	NM/M
Complete Set (180):	150.00
Common Player:	1.00
Extra Edition Stars:	8X

Autographed Mini-Covers

Six different players autographed 250 magazine mini-covers that were available through randomly seeded redemption cards. The players who autographed cards were Hank Aaron, Willie Mays, Frank Robinson, Kirby Puckett, Cal Ripken Jr., and Alex Rodriguez.

	NM/M
Complete Set (6):	300.00
Common Player:	30.00
Alex Rodriguez	100.00
Cal Ripken Jr.	100.00
Kirby Puckett	80.00
Willie Mays	125.00
Frank Robinson	30.00
Hank Aaron	200.00

Box Topper

This special version of A-Rod's card was packaged one per box of foil packs. It was intended to be inserted into die-cuts on the box to create a sample display for the new issue. The card measures 2-1/2" x 4-1/16". The back is in black-and-white with instructions on how to insert the card into the box.

	NM/M
Alex Rodriguez	4.50

Cooperstown Collection

This 12-card insert (found in 1:12 packs) lets collectors relive classic SI baseball covers with a description of each issue on the back.

		NM/M
Complete Set (12):		27.50
Common Player:		2.00
1	Hank Aaron	6.00
2	Yogi Berra	3.00
3	Lou Brock	2.00
4	Rod Carew	2.00
5	Juan Marichal	2.00
6	Al Kaline	2.50
7	Joe Morgan	2.00
8	Brooks Robinson	3.00
9	Willie Stargell	2.00
10	Kirby Puckett	4.00
11	Willie Mays	6.00
12	Frank Robinson	3.00

Great Shots

A 25-card insert, found one per pack, designed to highlight Sports Illustrated's classic photography. Each card in the set folds out to a 5" x 7" format to showcase a larger photo.

		NM/M
Complete Set (25):		10.00
Common Player:		.20
(1)	Roberto Alomar	.30
(2)	Andy Ashby	.20
(3)	Albert Belle	.20
(4)	Barry Bonds	2.00
(5)	Jay Buhner	.20
(6)	Vinny Castilla, Andres Galarraga	.20
(7)	Darren Daulton	.20
(8)	Juan Gonzalez	.40
(9)	Ken Griffey Jr.	1.25
(10)	Derek Jeter	2.00
(11)	Randy Johnson	.75
(12)	Chipper Jones	1.00
(13)	Eric Karros	.20
(14)	Ryan Klesko	.20
(15)	Kenny Lofton	.20
(16)	Greg Maddux	1.00
(17)	Mark McGwire	1.50
(18)	Mike Piazza	1.25
(19)	Cal Ripken Jr.	2.00
(20)	Alex Rodriguez	1.50
(21)	Ryne Sandberg	1.00
(22)	Deion Sanders	.30
(23)	John Smoltz	.20
(24)	Frank Thomas	.75
(25)	Mo Vaughn	.20

1998 Sports Illustrated Promo

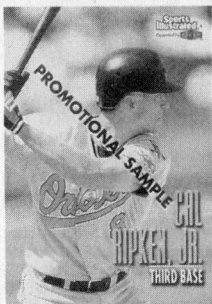

This sample card was issued to preview the 1998 Sports Illustrated set presented by Fleer. The card is in the same format as the regular issue, but has a different card number and is overprinted "PROMOTIONAL SAMPLE" on front and back.

		NM/M
8	Cal Ripken Jr.	3.00

1998 Sports Illustrated

The second of three Sports Illustrated releases of 1998 from Fleer contained 200 cards and featured exclusive Sports Illustrated photography and commentary. Cards arrived in six-card packs and carried a Sports Illustrated logo in a top corner. The set included a

Travis Lee One to Watch cards (#201) that was inserted just before going to press. Subsets included: Baseball's Best (129-148), One to Watch (149-176), and '97 in Review (177-200). Inserts sets include: Extra Edition and First Edition parallels, Autographs, Covers, Editor's Choice and Opening Day Mini Posters.

	NM/M
Complete Set (201):	20.00
Common Player:	.05
Pack (6):	1.50
Wax Box (24):	25.00

1	Edgardo Alfonzo	.05	
2	Roberto Alomar	.20	
3	Sandy Alomar	.05	
4	Moises Alou	.05	
5	Brady Anderson	.05	
6	Garret Anderson	.05	
7	Kevin Appier	.05	
8	Jeff Bagwell	.75	
9	Jay Bell	.05	
10	Albert Belle	.05	
11	Dante Bichette	.05	
12	Craig Biggio	.05	
13	Barry Bonds	2.00	
14	Bobby Bonilla	.05	
15	Kevin Brown	.05	
16	Jay Buhner	.05	
17	Ellis Burks	.05	
18	Mike Cameron	.05	
19	Ken Caminiti	.05	
20	Jose Canseco	.45	
21	Joe Carter	.05	
22	Vinny Castilla	.05	
23	Jeff Cirillo	.05	
24	Tony Clark	.05	
25	Will Clark	.05	
26	Roger Clemens	1.00	
27	David Cone	.05	
28	Jose Cruz Jr.	.05	
29	Carlos Delgado	.50	
30	Jason Dickson	.05	
31	Dennis Eckersley	.65	
32	Jim Edmonds	.05	
33	Scott Erickson	.05	
34	Darin Erstad	.20	
35	Shawn Estes	.05	
36	Jeff Fassero	.05	
37	Alex Fernandez	.05	
38	Chuck Finley	.05	
39	Steve Finley	.05	
40	Travis Fryman	.05	
41	Andres Galarraga	.05	
42	Ron Gant	.05	
43	Nomar Garciaparra	1.00	
44	Jason Giambi	.50	
45	Tom Glavine	.35	
46	Juan Gonzalez	.40	
47	Mark Grace	.05	
48	Willie Green	.05	
49	Rusty Greer	.05	
50	Ben Grieve	.05	
51	Ken Griffey Jr.	1.25	
52	Mark Grudzielanek	.05	
53	Vladimir Guerrero	.75	
54	Juan Guzman	.05	
55	Tony Gwynn	1.00	
56	Joey Hamilton	.05	
57	Rickey Henderson	.75	
58	Pat Hentgen	.05	
59	Livan Hernandez	.05	
60	Bobby Higginson	.05	
61	Todd Hundley	.05	
62	Hideki Irabu	.05	
63	John Jaha	.05	
64	Derek Jeter	2.00	
65	Charles Johnson	.05	
66	Randy Johnson	.75	
67	Andruw Jones	.75	
68	Bobby Jones	.05	
69	Chipper Jones	1.00	
70	Brian Jordan	.05	
71	David Justice	.05	
72	Eric Karros	.05	
73	Jeff Kent	.05	
74	Jimmy Key	.05	
75	Darryl Kile	.05	
76	Jeff King	.05	
77	Ryan Klesko	.05	
78	Chuck Knoblauch	.05	
79	Ray Lankford	.05	
80	Barry Larkin	.05	
81	Kenny Lofton	.05	

82	Greg Maddux	1.00	
83	Al Martin	.05	
84	Edgar Martinez	.05	
85	Pedro Martinez	.75	
86	Tino Martinez	.05	
87	Mark McGwire	1.50	
88	Paul Molitor	.75	
89	Raul Mondesi	.05	
90	Jamie Moyer	.05	
91	Mike Mussina	.30	
92	Tim Naehring	.05	
93	Charles Nagy	.05	
94	Denny Neagle	.05	
95	Dave Nilsson	.05	
96	Hideo Nomo	.40	
97	Rey Ordonez	.05	
98	Dean Palmer	.05	
99	Rafael Palmeiro	.65	
100	Andy Pettitte	.30	
101	Mike Piazza	1.25	
102	Brad Radke	.05	
103	Manny Ramirez	.75	
104	Edgar Renteria	.05	
105	Cal Ripken Jr.	2.00	
106	Alex Rodriguez	1.50	
106p	Alex Rodriguez ("PROMOTIONAL SAMPLE")	1.50	
107	Henry Rodriguez	.05	
108	Ivan Rodriguez	.65	
109	Scott Rolen	.65	
110	Tim Salmon	.05	
111	Curt Schilling	.35	
112	Gary Sheffield	.45	
113	John Smoltz	.05	
114	J.T. Snow	.05	
115	Sammy Sosa	1.00	
116	Matt Stairs	.05	
117	Shannon Stewart	.05	
118	Frank Thomas	.75	
119	Jim Thome	.65	
120	Justin Thompson	.05	
121	Mo Vaughn	.05	
122	Robin Ventura	.05	
123	Larry Walker	.05	
124	Rondell White	.05	
125	Bernie Williams	.05	
126	Matt Williams	.05	
127	Tony Womack	.05	
128	Jaret Wright	.05	
129	Edgar Renteria (Baseball's Best)	.05	
130	Kenny Lofton (Baseball's Best)	.05	
131	Tony Gwynn (Baseball's Best)	.50	
132	Mark McGwire (Baseball's Best)	.75	
133	Craig Biggio (Baseball's Best)	.05	
134	Charles Johnson (Baseball's Best)		
135	J.T. Snow (Baseball's Best)		
136	Ken Caminiti (Baseball's Best)		
137	Vladimir Guerrero (Baseball's Best)	.40	
138	Jim Edmonds (Baseball's Best)		
139	Randy Johnson (Baseball's Best)	.40	
140	Darryl Kile (Baseball's Best)		
141	John Smoltz (Baseball's Best)		
142	Greg Maddux (Baseball's Best)	.50	
143	Andy Pettitte (Baseball's Best)		
144	Ken Griffey Jr. (Baseball's Best)	.65	
145	Mike Piazza (Baseball's Best)	.65	
146	Todd Greene (Baseball's Best)		
147	Vinny Castilla (Baseball's Best)		
148	Derek Jeter (Baseball's Best)	1.00	
149	Robert Machado (One to Watch)	.05	
150	Mike Gulan (One to Watch)	.05	
151	Randall Simon (One to Watch)	.05	
152	Michael Coleman (One to Watch)	.05	
153	Brian Rose (One to Watch)	.05	
154	Scott Eyre RC (One to Watch)	.05	
155	Magglio Ordonez RC (One to Watch)	1.50	
156	Todd Helton (One to Watch)	.65	
157	Juan Encarnacion (One to Watch)	.05	
158	Mark Kotsay (One to Watch)	.05	
159	Josh Booty (One to Watch)	.05	
160	Melvin Rosario RC (One to Watch)	.05	
161	Shane Halter (One to Watch)	.05	
162	Paul Konerko (One to Watch)	.25	

163	Henry Blanco RC (One to Watch)	.05
164	Antone Williamson (One to Watch)	.05
165	Brad Fullmer (One to Watch)	.05
166	Ricky Ledee (One to Watch)	.05
167	Ben Grieve (One to Watch)	.05
168	Frank Catalanotto RC (One to Watch)	.25
169	Bobby Estalella (One to Watch)	.05
170	Dennis Reyes (One to Watch)	.05
171	Kevin Polcovich (One to Watch)	.05
172	Jacob Cruz (One to Watch)	.05
173	Ken Cloude (One to Watch)	.05
174	Eli Marrero (One to Watch)	.05
175	Fernando Tatis (One to Watch)	.05
176	Tom Evans (One to Watch)	.05
177	Carl Everett, Nomar Garciaparra (97 in Review)	.35
178	Eric Davis (97 in Review)	.05
179	Roger Clemens (97 in Review)	.60
180	Brett Butler, Eddie Murray (97 in Review)	.30
181	Frank Thomas (97 in Review)	.45
182	Curt Schilling (97 in Review)	.15
183	Jeff Bagwell (97 in Review)	.40
184	Mark McGwire, Ken Griffey Jr. (97 in Review)	.75
185	Kevin Brown (97 in Review)	.05
186	Marty Cordova, Ricardo Rincon (97 in Review)	.05
187	Charles Johnson (97 in Review)	.05
188	Hideki Irabu (97 in Review)	.05
189	Tony Gwynn (97 in Review)	.50
190	Sandy Alomar (97 in Review)	.05
191	Ken Griffey Jr. (97 in Review)	.65
192	Larry Walker (97 in Review)	.05
193	Roger Clemens (97 in Review)	.60
194	Pedro Martinez (97 in Review)	.40
195	Nomar Garciaparra (97 in Review)	.60
196	Scott Rolen (97 in Review)	.40
197	Brian Anderson (97 in Review)	.05
198	Tony Saunders (97 in Review)	.05
199	Florida Celebration (97 in Review)	.05
200	Livan Hernandez (97 in Review)	.05
201	Travis Lee/SP (One to Watch)	2.00

Extra Edition

Extra Edition is a 201-card parallel set that includes a holofoil stamp on the front and sequential numbering to 250 on the back. There is also a First Edition version of these that was identical on the front, but contains the text "The Only 1 of 1 First Edition" in purple lettering on the card back.

	NM/M
Common Player:	2.00
Extra Edition Stars:	8X

Autographs

This six-card insert features autographs of players. The Konerko and Grieve cards were available through redemptions until Nov. 1, 1999.

	NM/M
Common Player:	7.50
Lou Brock/500	40.00
Jose Cruz Jr./250	10.00
Rollie Fingers/500	10.00

PAUL KO... 025/250

Ben Grieve/250 (Exchange Card)		3.00
Ben Grieve (Signed Card)		7.50
Paul Konerko/250 (Exchange Card)		3.00
Paul Konerko (Signed Card)		20.00
Brooks Robinson/250		50.00

Covers

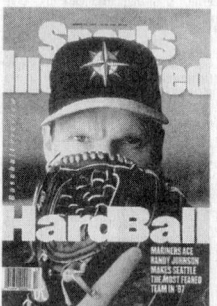

This 10-card insert set pictures actual Sports Illustrated covers on trading cards. The cards are numbered with a "C" prefix and inserted one per nine packs.

		NM/M
Complete Set (10):		15.00
Common Player:		1.00
Inserted 1:9		
1	Ken Griffey Jr., Mike Piazza	2.00
2	Derek Jeter	3.00
3	Ken Griffey Jr.	2.50
4	Cal Ripken Jr.	3.00
5	Manny Ramirez	1.50
6	Jay Buhner	1.00
7	Matt Williams	1.00
8	Randy Johnson	1.50
9	Deion Sanders	1.00
10	Jose Canseco	1.50

Editor's Choice

Editor's Choice includes 10 top players in 1998 as profiled by the editors of Sports Illustrated. Cards are numbered with an "EC" prefix and seeded one per 24 packs.

		NM/M
Complete Set (10):		20.00
Common Player:		1.00
Inserted 1:24		
1	Ken Griffey Jr.	3.00
2	Alex Rodriguez	4.00
3	Frank Thomas	1.50
4	Mark McGwire	4.00
5	Greg Maddux	2.00
6	Derek Jeter	5.00
7	Cal Ripken Jr.	5.00
8	Nomar Garciaparra	2.50
9	Jeff Bagwell	2.00
10	Jose Cruz Jr.	1.00

Mini-Posters

Thirty 5" x 7" mini-posters were available at a rate of one per pack. The posters took the top play-

er or two from each team and added their 1998 schedule. Backs were blank so the cards are numbered on the front with an "OD" prefix.

		NM/M
Complete Set (30):		8.00
Common Player:		.10
Inserted 1:1		
1	Tim Salmon	.10
2	Travis Lee	.10
3	John Smoltz, Greg Maddux	.50
4	Cal Ripken Jr.	1.00
5	Nomar Garciaparra	.50
6	Sammy Sosa	.50
7	Frank Thomas	.45
8	Barry Larkin	.10
9	David Justice	.10
10	Larry Walker	.10
11	Tony Clark	.10
12	Livan Hernandez	.10
13	Jeff Bagwell	.45
14	Kevin Appier	.10
15	Mike Piazza	.65
16	Fernando Vina	.10
17	Chuck Knoblauch	.10
18	Vladimir Guerrero	.45
19	Rey Ordonez	.10
20	Bernie Williams	.10
21	Matt Stairs	.10
22	Curt Schilling	.30
23	Tony Womack	.10
24	Mark McGwire	.75
25	Tony Gwynn	.50
26	Barry Bonds	1.00
27	Ken Griffey Jr.	.65
28	Fred McGriff	.10
29	Juan Gonzalez, Alex Rodriguez	.50
30	Roger Clemens	.60

1998 Sports Illustrated Then & Now

Then and Now was the first of three Sports Illustrated baseball releases in 1998. It contained 150 cards and sold in six-card packs, with five cards and a mini-poster. Fronts carried photos of active and retired players, as well as rookies. There was only one subset - A Place in History (#37-53) - which compares statistics between current players and retired greats. The product arrived with an Extra Edition parallel set, Art of the Game, Autograph Redemptions, Covers and Great Shots inserts. There was also an Alex Rodriguez checklist/mini-poster seeded every 12th pack.

		NM/M
Complete Set (150):		15.00
Common Player:		.05
Extra Edition Stars:		6X
Production 500 Sets		
Pack (5):		
Wax Box (24):		16.00
1	Luis Aparicio (Legends of the Game)	.05
2	Richie Ashburn (Legends of the Game)	.05
3	Ernie Banks (Legends of the Game)	.50
4	Yogi Berra (Legends of the Game)	.50
5	Lou Boudreau (Legends of the Game)	.05
6	Lou Brock (Legends of the Game)	.15
7	Jim Bunning (Legends of the Game)	.05
8	Rod Carew (Legends of the Game)	.15
9	Bob Feller (Legends of the Game)	.25
10	Rollie Fingers (Legends of the Game)	.05
11	Bob Gibson (Legends of the Game)	.15
12	Fergie Jenkins (Legends of the Game)	.05
13	Al Kaline (Legends of the Game)	.25
14	George Kell (Legends of the Game)	.05
15	Harmon Killebrew (Legends of the Game)	.25
16	Ralph Kiner (Legends of the Game)	.05
17	Tommy Lasorda (Legends of the Game)	.05
18	Juan Marichal (Legends of the Game)	.05
19	Eddie Mathews (Legends of the Game)	.25
20	Willie Mays (Legends of the Game)	1.00
21	Willie McCovey (Legends of the Game)	.05
22	Joe Morgan (Legends of the Game)	.15
23	Gaylord Perry (Legends of the Game)	.05
24	Kirby Puckett (Legends of the Game)	1.00
25	Pee Wee Reese (Legends of the Game)	.25
26	Phil Rizzuto (Legends of the Game)	.05
27	Robin Roberts (Legends of the Game)	.05
28	Brooks Robinson (Legends of the Game)	.35
29	Frank Robinson (Legends of the Game)	.35
30	Red Schoendienst (Legends of the Game)	.05
31	Enos Slaughter (Legends of the Game)	.05
32	Warren Spahn (Legends of the Game)	.25
33	Willie Stargell (Legends of the Game)	.15
34	Earl Weaver (Legends of the Game)	.05
35	Billy Williams (Legends of the Game)	.15
36	Early Wynn (Legends of the Game)	.05
37	Rickey Henderson (A Place in History)	.75
38	Greg Maddux (A Place in History)	1.00
39	Mike Mussina (A Place in History)	.40
40	Cal Ripken Jr. (A Place in History)	2.00
41	Albert Belle (A Place in History)	.05
42	Frank Thomas (A Place in History)	.75
43	Jeff Bagwell (A Place in History)	.75
44	Paul Molitor (A Place in History)	.75
45	Chuck Knoblauch (A Place in History)	.05
46	Todd Hundley (A Place in History)	.05
47	Bernie Williams (A Place in History)	.05
48	Tony Gwynn (A Place in History)	1.00
49	Barry Bonds (A Place in History)	2.00
50	Ken Griffey Jr. (A Place in History)	1.25
51	Randy Johnson (A Place in History)	.75
52	Mark McGwire (A Place in History)	1.50
53	Roger Clemens (A Place in History)	1.00
54	Jose Cruz Jr. (A Place in History)	.05
55	Roberto Alomar (Legends of Today)	.20
56	Sandy Alomar (Legends of Today)	.05
57	Brady Anderson (Legends of Today)	.05
58	Kevin Appier (Legends of Today)	.05
59	Jeff Bagwell (Legends of Today)	.75
60	Albert Belle (Legends of Today)	.05
61	Dante Bichette (Legends of Today)	.05
62	Craig Biggio (Legends of Today)	.05
63	Barry Bonds (Legends of Today)	2.00
64	Kevin Brown (Legends of Today)	.05
65	Jay Buhner (Legends of Today)	.05
66	Ellis Burks (Legends of Today)	.05
67	Ken Caminiti (Legends of Today)	.05
68	Jose Canseco (Legends of Today)	.50
69	Joe Carter (Legends of Today)	.05
70	Vinny Castilla (Legends of Today)	.05
71	Tony Clark (Legends of Today)	.05
72	Roger Clemens (Legends of Today)	1.00
73	David Cone (Legends of Today)	.05
74	Jose Cruz Jr. (Legends of Today)	.05
75	Jason Dickson (Legends of Today)	.05
76	Jim Edmonds (Legends of Today)	.05
77	Scott Erickson (Legends of Today)	.05
78	Darin Erstad (Legends of Today)	.20
79	Alex Fernandez (Legends of Today)	.05
80	Steve Finley (Legends of Today)	.05
81	Travis Fryman (Legends of Today)	.05
82	Andres Galarraga (Legends of Today)	.05
83	Nomar Garciaparra (Legends of Today)	1.00
84	Tom Glavine (Legends of Today)	.35
85	Juan Gonzalez (Legends of Today)	.40
86	Mark Grace (Legends of Today)	.05
87	Willie Greene (Legends of Today)	.05
88	Ken Griffey Jr. (Legends of Today)	1.25
89	Vladimir Guerrero (Legends of Today)	.75
90	Tony Gwynn (Legends of Today)	1.00
91	Livan Hernandez (Legends of Today)	.05
92	Bobby Higginson (Legends of Today)	.05
93	Derek Jeter (Legends of Today)	2.00
94	Charles Johnson (Legends of Today)	.05
95	Randy Johnson (Legends of Today)	.75
96	Andruw Jones (Legends of Today)	.75
97	Chipper Jones (Legends of Today)	1.00
98	David Justice (Legends of Today)	.05
99	Eric Karros (Legends of Today)	.05
100	Jason Kendall (Legends of Today)	.05
101	Jimmy Key (Legends of Today)	.05
102	Darryl Kile (Legends of Today)	.05
103	Chuck Knoblauch (Legends of Today)	.05
104	Ray Lankford (Legends of Today)	.05
105	Barry Larkin (Legends of Today)	.05
106	Kenny Lofton (Legends of Today)	.05
107	Greg Maddux (Legends of Today)	1.00
108	Al Martin (Legends of Today)	.05
109	Edgar Martinez (Legends of Today)	.05
110	Pedro Martinez (Legends of Today)	.75
111	Ramon Martinez (Legends of Today)	.05
112	Tino Martinez (Legends of Today)	.05
113	Mark McGwire (Legends of Today)	1.50
114	Raul Mondesi (Legends of Today)	.05
115	Matt Morris (Legends of Today)	.05
116	Charles Nagy (Legends of Today)	.05
117	Denny Neagle (Legends of Today)	.05
118	Hideo Nomo (Legends of Today)	.40
119	Dean Palmer (Legends of Today)	.05
120	Andy Pettitte (Legends of Today)	.25
121	Mike Piazza (Legends of Today)	1.25
122	Manny Ramirez (Legends of Today)	.75
123	Edgar Renteria (Legends of Today)	.05
124	Cal Ripken Jr. (Legends of Today)	2.00
125	Alex Rodriguez (Legends of Today)	1.50
126	Henry Rodriguez (Legends of Today)	.05
127	Ivan Rodriguez (Legends of Today)	.65
128	Scott Rolen (Legends of Today)	.65
129	Tim Salmon (Legends of Today)	.05
130	Curt Schilling (Legends of Today)	.35
131	Gary Sheffield (Legends of Today)	.45
132	John Smoltz (Legends of Today)	.05
133	Sammy Sosa (Legends of Today)	1.00
134	Frank Thomas (Legends of Today)	.75
135	Jim Thome (Legends of Today)	.65
136	Mo Vaughn (Legends of Today)	.05
137	Robin Ventura (Legends of Today)	.05
138	Larry Walker (Legends of Today)	.05
139	Bernie Williams (Legends of Today)	.05
140	Matt Williams (Legends of Today)	.05
141	Jaret Wright (Legends of Today)	.05
142	Michael Coleman (Legends of the Future)	.05
143	Juan Encarnacion (Legends of the Future)	.05
144	Brad Fullmer (Legends of the Future)	.05
145	Ben Grieve (Legends of the Future)	.05
146	Todd Helton (Legends of the Future)	.75
147	Paul Konerko (Legends of the Future)	.20
148	Derrek Lee (Legends of the Future)	.50
149	Magglio Ordonez RC (Legends of the Future)	1.50
150	Enrique Wilson (Legends of the Future)	.05
---	Alex Rodriguez (Checklist)	1.00

Then & Now Extra Edition

This 150-card set paralleled the base set and was distinguished by an "Extra Edition" foil stamp on the front. There were 500 sets of Extra Edition and the cards were individually numbered on the back.

	NM/M
Common Extra Edition:	1.00
Extra Edition Stars:	6X
Production 500 Sets	

Then & Now Art of the Game

"Brooks"

Art of the Game was an eight-card insert featuring reproductions of original artwork of current and retired baseAll-Stars done by eight popular sports artists. Cards are numbered with a "AG" prefix and inserted one per nine packs.

		NM/M
Complete Set (8):		11.00
Common Player:		1.00
Inserted 1:9		
1	It's Gone (Ken Griffey Jr.)	1.50
2	Alex Rodriguez	2.00
3	Mike Piazza	1.50
4	Brooks Robinson	1.00
5	David Justice/AS	1.00
6	Cal Ripken Jr.	3.00
7	The Prospect and the Prospector	
8	Barry Bonds	3.00

Then & Now Autographs

Six autograph redemption cards were randomly inserted into packs of Then & Now and could be exchanged prior to Nov. 1, 1999. The signed cards were produced in the following quantities: Clemens 250, Gibson 500, Gwynn 250, Killebrew 500, Mays 250 and Rolen 150. Four of the six cards use the same fronts as the Covers insert; Gibson and Rolen cards each feature unique card fronts.

	NM/M
Common Autograph:	15.00
Redemption Cards: 10 Percent	
Bob Gibson/500	15.00
Tony Gwynn/250	35.00
Roger Clemens/250	120.00
Scott Rolen/150	20.00
Willie Mays/250	90.00
Harmon Killebrew/500	25.00

Then & Now Covers

This 12-card insert features color shots of six actual Sports Illustrated covers, including six current players and six retired players. The cards are numbered with a "C" prefix and were seeded one per 18 packs.

		NM/M
Complete Set (12):		22.00
Common Player:		1.00
Inserted 1:18		
1	Lou Brock (10/16/67)	1.00
2	Kirby Puckett (4/6/92)	2.50
3	Harmon Killebrew (4/8/63 - inside)	1.00
4	Eddie Mathews (8/16/54)	1.00
5	Willie Mays (5/22/72)	2.00
6	Frank Robinson (10/6/69)	1.00
7	Cal Ripken Jr. (9/11/95)	2.50
8	Roger Clemens (5/12/86)	2.50
9	Ken Griffey Jr. (10/16/95)	3.00
10	Mark McGwire (6/1/92)	4.00
11	Tony Gwynn (7/28/97)	2.50
12	Ivan Rodriguez (8/11/97)	1.50

Then & Now Great Shots!

This 25-card set featured 5" x 7" fold-out mini-posters using Sports Illustrated photos. Great

Shots were inserted one per pack and contained a mix of retired and current players.

		NM/M
Complete Set (25):		7.50
Common Player:		.10
Inserted 1:1		
1	Ken Griffey Jr.	.65
2	Frank Thomas	.45
3	Alex Rodriguez	.75
4	Andruw Jones	.45
5	Chipper Jones	.50
6	Cal Ripken Jr.	1.00
7	Mark McGwire	.75
8	Derek Jeter	1.00
9	Greg Maddux	.50
10	Jeff Bagwell	.45
11	Mike Piazza	.65
12	Scott Rolen	.35
13	Nomar Garciaparra	.50
14	Jose Cruz Jr.	.10
15	Charles Johnson	.10
16	Fergie Jenkins	.10
17	Lou Brock	.10
18	Bob Gibson	.10
19	Harmon Killebrew	.10
20	Juan Marichal	.10
21	Brooks Robinson	.10
22	Rod Carew	.10
23	Yogi Berra	.25
24	Willie Mays	.50
25	Kirby Puckett	.50

Then & Now Road to Cooperstown

Road to Cooperstown features 10 current players who are having Hall of Fame careers. The insert name is printed across the back in bold, gold letters. Cards are numbered with a "RC" prefix and were inserted one per 24 packs.

		NM/M
Complete Set (10):		10.00
Common Player:		.75
Inserted 1:24		
1	Barry Bonds	2.50
2	Roger Clemens	1.25
3	Ken Griffey Jr.	1.50
4	Tony Gwynn	1.00
5	Rickey Henderson	.75
6	Greg Maddux	1.00
7	Paul Molitor	.75
8	Mike Piazza	1.50
9	Cal Ripken Jr.	2.50
10	Frank Thomas	.75

World Series Fever

The third and final Sports Illustrated release of 1998 contained 150 cards and focused on the World Series while recapping memorable moments from the season. The set also included many stars of tomorrow, like Kerry Wood, Orlando Hernandez, Ben Grieve and Travis Lee. Once again, all the photos were taken from Sports Illustrated archives. The set has two subsets - 10 Magnificent Moments and 20 Cover Collection. The set is paralleled twice in Extra and First Edi-

tion parallel sets, and has three insert sets - MVP Collection, Reggie Jackson's Picks and Autumn Excellence.

		NM/M
Complete Set (150):		10.00
Common Player:		.05
Pack (6):		1.00
Wax Box (24):		17.50
1	Mickey Mantle (Covers)	1.50
2	1957 World Series Preview (Covers)	.15
3	1958 World Series Preview (Covers)	.15
4	1959 World Series Preview (Covers)	.15
5	1962 World Series (Covers)	.10
6	Lou Brock (Covers)	.10
7	Brooks Robinson (Covers)	.25
8	Frank Robinson (Covers)	.25
9	1974 World Series (Covers)	.10
10	Reggie Jackson (Covers)	.60
11	1985 World Series (Covers)	.10
12	1987 World Series (Covers)	.05
13	Orel Hershiser (Covers)	.05
14	Rickey Henderson (Covers)	.40
15	1991 World Series (Covers)	.10
16	1992 World Series (Covers)	.05
17	Joe Carter (Covers)	.05
18	1995 World Series (Covers)	.10
19	1996 World Series (Covers)	.15
20	Edgar Renteria (Covers)	.05
21	Bill Mazeroski (Magnificent Moments)	.15
22	Joe Carter (Magnificent Moments)	.05
23	Carlton Fisk (Magnificent Moments)	.40
24	Bucky Dent (Magnificent Moments)	.15
25	Mookie Wilson (Magnificent Moments)	.05
26	Enos Slaughter (Magnificent Moments)	.05
27	Mickey Lolich (Magnificent Moments)	.05
28	Bobby Richardson (Magnificent Moments)	.05
29	Kirk Gibson (Magnificent Moments)	.05
30	Edgar Renteria (Magnificent Moments)	.05
31	Albert Belle	.05
32	Kevin Brown	.05
33	Brian Rose	.05
34	Ron Gant	.05
35	Jeromy Burnitz	.05
36	Andres Galarraga	.05
37	Jim Edmonds	.05
38	Jose Cruz Jr.	.05
39	Mark Grudzielanek	.05
40	Shawn Estes	.05
41	Mark Grace	.05
42	Nomar Garciaparra	.50
43	Juan Gonzalez	.50
44	Tom Glavine	.25
45	Brady Anderson	.05
46	Tony Clark	.05
47	Jeff Cirillo	.05
48	Dante Bichette	.05
49	Ben Grieve	.05
50	Ken Griffey Jr.	.65
51	Edgardo Alfonzo	.05
52	Roger Clemens	.60
53	Pat Hentgen	.05
54	Todd Helton	.30
55	Andy Benes	.05
56	Tony Gwynn	.50
57	Andruw Jones	.40
58	Bobby Higginson	.05
59	Bobby Jones	.05
60	Darryl Kile	.05
61	Chan Ho Park	.05
62	Charles Johnson	.05
63	Rusty Greer	.05
64	Travis Fryman	.05
65	Derek Jeter	1.00
66	Jay Buhner	.05
67	Chuck Knoblauch	.05
68	David Justice	.05
69	Brian Hunter	.05
70	Eric Karros	.05
71	Edgar Martinez	.05
72	Chipper Jones	.50
73	Barry Larkin	.05
74	Mike Lansing	.05
75	Craig Biggio	.05
76	Al Martin	.05
77	Barry Bonds	1.00
78	Randy Johnson	.40
79	Ryan Klesko	.05
80	Mark McGwire	.75
81	Fred McGriff	.05
82	Javy Lopez	.05
83	Kenny Lofton	.05
84	Sandy Alomar Jr.	.05
85	Matt Morris	.05
86	Paul Konerko	.10
87	Ray Lankford	.05
88	Kerry Wood	.30
89	Roberto Alomar	.20
90	Greg Maddux	.50
91	Travis Lee	.05
92	Moises Alou	.05
93	Dean Palmer	.05
94	Hideo Nomo	.20
95	Ken Caminiti	.05
96	Pedro Martinez	.40
97	Raul Mondesi	.05
98	Denny Neagle	.05
99	Tino Martinez	.05
100	Mike Mussina	.20
101	Kevin Appier	.05
102	Vinny Castilla	.05
103	Jeff Bagwell	.40
104	Paul O'Neill	.05
105	Rey Ordonez	.05
106	Vladimir Guerrero	.40
107	Rafael Palmeiro	.35
108	Alex Rodriguez	.75
109	Andy Pettitte	.15
110	Carl Pavano	.05
111	Henry Rodriguez	.05
112	Gary Sheffield	.40
113	Curt Schilling	.25
114	John Smoltz	.05
115	Reggie Sanders	.05
116	Scott Rolen	.35
117	Mike Piazza	.65
118	Manny Ramirez	.40
119	Cal Ripken Jr.	1.00
120	Brad Radke	.05
121	Tim Salmon	.05
122	Brett Tomko	.05
123	Robin Ventura	.05
124	Mo Vaughn	.05
125	A.J. Hinch	.05
126	Derek Lee	.45
127	Orlando Hernandez RC	.40
128	Aramis Ramirez	.40
129	Frank Thomas	.40
130	J.T. Snow	.05
131	Magglio Ordonez RC	1.00
132	Bobby Bonilla	.05
133	Marquis Grissom	.05
134	Jim Thome	.45
135	Justin Thompson	.05
136	Matt Williams	.05
137	Matt Stairs	.05
138	Wade Boggs	.50
139	Chuck Finley	.05
140	Jaret Wright	.05
141	Ivan Rodriguez	.35
142	Brad Fullmer	.05
143	Bernie Williams	.05
144	Jason Giambi	.30
145	Larry Walker	.05
146	Tony Womack	.05
147	Sammy Sosa	.50
148	Rondell White	.05
149	Todd Stottlemyre	.05
150	Shane Reynolds	.05

WS Fever Extra Edition

Extra Edition parallels the entire 150-card base set and is identified by a gold-foil stamp on the card front and sequential numbering to 98 sets on the back. World Series Fever also includes one-of-one parallel versions called First Edition. These have a purple-foil identifier on front, with the legend on back, "THE ONLY 1 OF 1 FIRST EDITION," also in purple foil.

	NM/M
Common EE Player:	2.00
EE Stars:	15X
Production: 98 Sets	
Common FE Player:	100.00
FE Stars: Values Undetermined	
1 of 1	

WS Fever Autumn Excellence

Autumn Excellence honors players with the most select World Series records. The 10-card set was seeded one per 24 packs, while rarer Gold versions were seeded one per 240 packs.

		NM/M
Complete Set (10):		15.00
Common Player:		.50
Inserted 1:24		
Golds:		2X
Inserted 1:240		
AE1	Willie Mays	2.50
AE2	Kirby Puckett	2.00
AE3	Babe Ruth	4.00
AE4	Reggie Jackson	1.50
AE5	Whitey Ford	.50
AE6	Lou Brock	.50
AE7	Mickey Mantle	4.00
AE8	Yogi Berra	.75
AE9	Bob Gibson	.50
AE10	Don Larsen	1.00

WS Fever Reggie Jackson Picks

Reggie Jackson's Picks contains top players that Jackson believes have what it takes to perform on center stage in the World Series. Fronts have a shot of the player with his name in the background, and a head shot of Reggie Jackson in the bottom right corner. These were numbered with a "RP" prefix and inserted one per 12 packs.

		NM/M
Complete Set (15):		12.50
Common Player:		.25
Inserted 1:12		
1	Paul O'Neill	.25
2	Barry Bonds	2.50
3	Ken Griffey Jr.	1.50
4	Juan Gonzalez	.40
5	Greg Maddux	1.00
6	Mike Piazza	1.50
7	Larry Walker	.25
8	Mo Vaughn	.25
9	Roger Clemens	1.25
10	John Smoltz	.25
11	Alex Rodriguez	2.00
12	Frank Thomas	.75
13	Mark McGwire	2.00
14	Jeff Bagwell	.75
15	Randy Johnson	.75

WS Fever MVP Collection

This 10-card insert set features select MVPs from the World Series. Card fronts contain a shot of the player over a white border with the year in black letters and the insert and player's name in blue foil.

MVP Collection inserts were seeded one per four packs and numbered with a "MC" prefix.

		NM/M
Complete Set (10):		1.00
Common Player:		.10
Inserted 1:4		
1	Frank Robinson	.25
2	Brooks Robinson	.25
3	Willie Stargell	.10
4	Bret Saberhagen	.10
5	Rollie Fingers	.10
6	Orel Hershiser	.10
7	Paul Molitor	.50
8	Tom Glavine	.90
9	John Wetteland	.10
10	Livan Hernandez	.10

1999 Sports Illustrated

The Sports Illustrated set from Fleer consists of 180 base cards composed of 107 player cards, and four subsets. They include Team 2000, Postseason Review, Award Winners, and Season Highlights. Cards came in six-card packs with an SRP of $1.99. The set also includes five insert sets, along with hobby exclusive autographed J.D. Drew cards numbered to 250.

		NM/M
Complete Set (180):		15.00
Common Player:		.05
Wax Pack (6):		1.00
Hobby Box (24):		15.00
Retail Box (12):		10.00
1	Yankees (Postseason Review)	.25
2	Scott Brosius (Postseason Review)	.05
3	David Wells (Postseason Review)	.05
4	Sterling Hitchcock (Postseason Review)	.05
5	David Justice (Postseason Review)	.05
6	David Cone (Postseason Review)	.05
7	Greg Maddux (Postseason Review)	.50
8	Jim Leyritz (Postseason Review)	.05
9	Gary Gaetti (Postseason Review)	.05
10	Mark McGwire (Award Winners)	.75
11	Sammy Sosa (Award Winners)	.50
12	Larry Walker (Award Winners)	.05
13	Tony Womack (Award Winners)	.05
14	Tom Glavine (Award Winners)	.10
15	Curt Schilling (Award Winners)	.05
16	Greg Maddux (Award Winners)	.50
17	Trevor Hoffman (Award Winners)	.05
18	Kerry Wood (Award Winners)	.20
19	Tom Glavine (Award Winners)	.10

#	Player	Price
20	Sammy Sosa (Award Winners)	.50
21	Travis Lee (Season Highlights)	.05
22	Roberto Alomar (Season Highlights)	.05
23	Roger Clemens (Season Highlights)	.60
24	Barry Bonds (Season Highlights)	1.00
25	Paul Molitor (Season Highlights)	.45
26	Todd Stottlemyre (Season Highlights)	.05
27	Chris Hoiles (Season Highlights)	.05
28	Albert Belle (Season Highlights)	.05
29	Tony Clark (Season Highlights)	.05
30	Kerry Wood (Season Highlights)	.20
31	David Wells (Season Highlights)	.05
32	Dennis Eckersley (Season Highlights)	.40
33	Mark McGwire (Season Highlights)	.75
34	Cal Ripken Jr. (Season Highlights)	1.00
35	Ken Griffey Jr. (Season Highlights)	.65
36	Alex Rodriguez (Season Highlights)	.75
37	Craig Biggio (Season Highlights)	.05
38	Sammy Sosa (Season Highlights)	.50
39	Dennis Martinez (Season Highlights)	.05
40	Curt Schilling (Season Highlights)	.10
41	Orlando Hernandez (Season Highlights)	.05
42	Troy Glaus, Ben Molina RC, Todd Greene ("Team" 2000)	.45
43	Mitch Meluskey, Daryle Ward, Mike Grzanich ("Team" 2000)	.05
44	Eric Chavez, Mike Neill, Steve Connelly RC ("Team" 2000)	.10
45	Roy Halladay, Tom Evans, Kevin Witt ("Team" 2000)	.05
46	George Lombard, Adam Butler, Bruce Chen ("Team" 2000)	.05
47	Ronnie Belliard, Valerio de los Santos, Rafael Roque RC ("Team" 2000)	.05
48	J.D. Drew, Placido Polanco, Mark Little RC ("Team" 2000)	.50
49	Jason Maxwell, Jose Nieves RC, Jeremi Gonzalez ("Team" 2000)	.05
50	Scott McClain, Kerry Robinson, Mike Duvall RC ("Team" 2000)	.05
51	Ben Ford, Bryan Corey RC, Danny Klassen ("Team" 2000)	.05
52	Angel Pena, Jeff Kubenka, Paul LoDuca ("Team" 2000)	.05
53	Kirk Bullinger, Fernando Seguignol, Tim Young ("Team" 2000)	.05
54	Ramon Martinez, Wilson Delgado, Armando Rios ("Team" 2000)	.05
55	Russ Branyon, Jolbert Cabrera RC, Jason Rakers ("Team" 2000)	.05
56	Carlos Guillen RC, David Holdridge RC, Giomar Guevara RC ("Team" 2000)	.10
57	Alex Gonzalez, Joe Fontenot, Preston Wilson ("Team" 2000)	.05
58	Mike Kinkade, Jay Payton, Masato Yoshii ("Team" 2000)	.05
59	Willis Otanez, Ryan Minor, Calvin Pickering ("Team" 2000)	.05
60	Ben Davis, Matt Clement, Stan Spencer ("Team" 2000)	.05
61	Marlon Anderson, Mike Welch, Gary Bennett RC ("Team" 2000)	.05
62	Abraham Nunez, Sean Lawrence RC, Aramis Ramirez ("Team" 2000)	.05
63	Jonathan Johnson, Rob Sasser RC, Scott Sheldon RC ("Team" 2000)	.05
64	Keith Glauber RC, Guillermo Garcia RC, Eddie Priest ("Team" 2000)	.05
65	Brian Barkley, Jin Ho Cho, Donnie Sadler ("Team" 2000)	.05
66	Derrick Gibson, Mark Strittmatter, Edgard Clemente RC ("Team" 2000)	.05
67	Jeremy Giambi, Dermal Brown, Chris Hatcher RC ("Team" 2000)	.05
68	Rob Fick RC, Gabe Kapler, Marino Santana ("Team" 2000)	.05
69	Corey Koskie, A.J. Pierzynski, Benj Sampson ("Team" 2000)	.05
70	Brian Simmons, Mark Johnson, Craig Wilson ("Team" 2000)	.05
71	Ryan Bradley, Mike Lowell, Jay Tessmer ("Team" 2000)	.05
72	Ben Grieve	.05
73	Shawn Green	.45
74	Rafael Palmeiro	.65
75	Juan Gonzalez	.40
76	Mike Piazza	1.25
77	Devon White	.05
78	Jim Thome	.65
79	Barry Larkin	.05
80	Scott Rolen	.65
81	Raul Mondesi	.05
82	Jason Giambi	.50
83	Jose Canseco	.45
84	Tony Gwynn	1.00
85	Cal Ripken Jr.	2.00
86	Andy Pettitte	.15
87	Carlos Delgado	.50
88	Jeff Cirillo	.05
89	Bret Saberhagen	.05
90	John Olerud	.05
91	Ron Coomer	.05
92	Todd Helton	.65
93	Ray Lankford	.05
94	Tim Salmon	.05
95	Fred McGriff	.05
96	Matt Stairs	.05
97	Ken Griffey Jr.	1.25
98	Chipper Jones	1.00
99	Mark Grace	.05
100	Ivan Rodriguez	.65
101	Jeromy Burnitz	.05
102	Kenny Rogers	.05
103	Kevin Millwood	.05
104	Vinny Castilla	.05
105	Jim Edmonds	.05
106	Craig Biggio	.05
107	Andres Galarraga	.05
108	Sammy Sosa	1.00
109	Juan Encarnacion	.05
110	Larry Walker	.05
111	John Smoltz	.05
112	Randy Johnson	.75
113	Bobby Higginson	.05
114	Albert Belle	.05
115	Jaret Wright	.05
116	Edgar Renteria	.05
117	Andruw Jones	.75
118	Barry Bonds	2.00
119	Rondell White	.05
120	Jamie Moyer	.05
121	Darin Erstad	.20
122	Al Leiter	.05
123	Mark McGwire	1.50
124	Mo Vaughn	.05
125	Livan Hernandez	.05
126	Jason Kendall	.05
127	Frank Thomas	.75
128	Denny Neagle	.05
129	Johnny Damon	.35
130	Derek Bell	.05
131	Jeff Kent	.05
132	Tony Womack	.05
133	Trevor Hoffman	.05
134	Gary Sheffield	.40
135	Tino Martinez	.05
136	Travis Fryman	.05
137	Rolando Arrojo	.05
138	Dante Bichette	.05
139	Nomar Garciaparra	1.00
140	Moises Alou	.05
141	Chuck Knoblauch	.05
142	Robin Ventura	.05
143	Scott Erickson	.05
144	David Cone	.05
145	Greg Vaughn	.05
146	Wade Boggs	1.00
147	Mike Mussina	.30
148	Tony Clark	.05
149	Alex Rodriguez	1.50
150	Javy Lopez	.05
151	Bartolo Colon	.05
152	Derek Jeter	2.00
153	Greg Maddux	1.00
154	Kevin Brown	.05
155	Curt Schilling	.35
156	Jeff King	.05
157	Bernie Williams	.05
158	Roberto Alomar	.20
159	Travis Lee	.05
160	Kerry Wood	.50
160p	Kerry Wood ("PROMOTIONAL SAMPLE")	1.00
161	Jeff Bagwell	.75
162	Roger Clemens	1.00
163	Matt Williams	.05
164	Chan Ho Park	.05
165	Damion Easley	.05
166	Manny Ramirez	.75
167	Quinton McCracken	.05
168	Todd Walker	.05
169	Eric Karros	.05
170	Will Clark	.05
171	Edgar Martinez	.05
172	Cliff Floyd	.05
173	Vladimir Guerrero	.75
174	Tom Glavine	.35
175	Pedro Martinez	.75
176	Chuck Finley	.05
177	Dean Palmer	.05
178	Omar Vizquel	.05
179	Checklist	.05
180	Checklist	.05

Diamond Dominators

This 10-card insert set features five hitters and five pitchers on embossed cards. The hitters are seeded 1 in every 180 packs, while the pitchers are seeded 1 in every 90 packs.

		NM/M
	Complete Set (10):	30.00
	Common Player:	1.50
	Pitchers inserted 1:90	
	Hitters inserted 1:180	
1DD	Kerry Wood	1.50
2DD	Roger Clemens	3.00
3DD	Randy Johnson	2.00
4DD	Greg Maddux	2.50
5DD	Pedro Martinez	2.00
6DD	Ken Griffey Jr.	5.00
7DD	Sammy Sosa	2.50
8DD	Nomar Garciaparra	2.50
9DD	Mark McGwire	6.00
10DD	Alex Rodriguez	6.00

Fabulous 40s

This 13-card insert set consists of the players that hit 40 or more homers during the 1998 season. The cards are sculpture embossed and foil-stamped, with the player's home run total also on the card. One card comes with every 20 packs.

		NM/M
	Complete Set (13):	9.00
	Common Player:	.25
	Inserted 1:20	
1FF	Mark McGwire	2.00
2FF	Sammy Sosa	1.25
3FF	Ken Griffey Jr.	1.50
4FF	Greg Vaughn	.25
5FF	Albert Belle	.25
6FF	Jose Canseco	.50
7FF	Vinny Castilla	.25
8FF	Juan Gonzalez	.50
9FF	Manny Ramirez	1.00
10FF	Andres Galarraga	.25
11FF	Rafael Palmeiro	.25
12FF	Alex Rodriguez	2.00
13FF	Mo Vaughn	.25

Fabulous 40s Extra

The insert set parallels the 13 cards in the Fabulous 40s set. The cards are hobby exclusive, highlighted with silver patterned holofoil. Each player's cards are hand-numbered to the total number of home runs he hit in 1998.

		NM/M
	Common Player:	12.00
	Numbered to amount of HRs.	
1FF	Mark McGwire/70	60.00
2FF	Sammy Sosa/66	40.00
3FF	Ken Griffey Jr./56	35.00
4FF	Greg Vaughn/50	12.00
5FF	Albert Belle/49	12.00
6FF	Jose Canseco/46	25.00
7FF	Vinny Castilla/46	12.00
8FF	Juan Gonzalez/45	20.00
9FF	Manny Ramirez/45	30.00
10FF	Andres Galarraga/44	12.00
11FF	Rafael Palmeiro/43	25.00
12FF	Alex Rodriguez/42	45.00
13FF	Mo Vaughn/40	12.00

Headliners

Headliners is a 25-card insert set that features silver foil stamped, team-color coded cards. One card comes with every four packs.

		NM/M
	Complete Set (25):	10.00
	Common Player:	.25
	Inserted 1:4	
1H	Vladimir Guerrero	.40
2H	Randy Johnson	.40
3H	Mo Vaughn	.25
4H	Chipper Jones	.50
5H	Jeff Bagwell	.40
6H	Juan Gonzalez	.30
7H	Mark McGwire	.75
8H	Cal Ripken Jr.	1.00
9H	Frank Thomas	.40
10H	Manny Ramirez	.40
11H	Ken Griffey Jr.	.65
12H	Scott Rolen	.35
13H	Alex Rodriguez	.75
14H	Barry Bonds	1.00
15H	Roger Clemens	.55
16H	Darin Erstad	.30
17H	Nomar Garciaparra	.50
18H	Mike Piazza	.65
19H	Greg Maddux	.50
20H	Ivan Rodriguez	.35
21H	Derek Jeter	.75
22H	Sammy Sosa	.50
23H	Andruw Jones	.40
24H	Pedro Martinez	.40
25H	Kerry Wood	.25

Ones To Watch

ERIC CHAVEZ-3B

This 15-card insert set features the game's top rookies and young stars. The cards have 100 percent foil background and are team-color coded. One card was inserted in every 12 packs.

		NM/M
	Complete Set (15):	5.00
	Common Player:	.25
	Inserted 1:12	
1OW	J.D. Drew	.65
2OW	Marlon Anderson	.25
3OW	Roy Halladay	.35
40W	Ben Grieve	.25
50W	Todd Helton	.75
60W	Gabe Kapler	.25
70W	Troy Glaus	.75
80W	Ben Davis	.25
90W	Eric Chavez	.35
100W	Richie Sexson	.25
110W	Fernando Seguignol	.25
120W	Kerry Wood	.50
130W	Bobby Smith	.25
140W	Ryan Minor	.25
150W	Jeremy Giambi	.25
	J.D. Drew autograph/250	15.00

1999 Sports Illustrated Greats of the Game

The 90-card base set includes many legendary major-leaguers including Babe Ruth and Cy Young. Card fronts feature a full bleed photo with the player name across the bottom and Greats of the Game printed on the bottom left portion of the card. Card backs have the player's vital information, along with career statistics and a few career highlights. Seven-card packs were issued with a SRP of $15.

		NM/M
	Complete Set (90):	12.00
	Common Player:	.05
	Pack (7):	15.00
	Wax Box (12):	150.00
1	Jimmie Foxx	.25
2	Red Schoendienst	.05
3	Babe Ruth	3.00
4	Lou Gehrig	2.00
5	Mel Ott	.05
6	Stan Musial	.25
7	Mickey Mantle	3.00
8	Carl Yastrzemski	.15
9	Enos Slaughter	.05
10	Andre Dawson	.05
11	Luis Aparicio	.05
12	Ferguson Jenkins	.05
13	Christy Mathewson	.25
14	Ernie Banks	.15
15	Johnny Podres	.05
16	George Foster	.05
17	Jerry Koosman	.05
18	Curt Simmons	.05
19	Bob Feller	.05
20	Frank Robinson	.05
21	Gary Carter	.05
22	Frank Thomas	.05
23	Bill Lee	.05
24	Willie Mays	1.00
25	Tommie Agee	.05
26	Boog Powell	.05
27	Jimmy Wynn	.05
28	Sparky Lyle	.05
29	Bo Belinsky	.05
30	Maury Wills	.05
31	Bill Buckner	.05
32	Steve Carlton	.05
33	Harmon Killebrew	.05
34	Nolan Ryan	1.00
35	Randy Jones	.05
36	Robin Roberts	.05
37	Al Oliver	.05
38	Rico Petrocelli	.05
39	Dave Parker	.05
40	Eddie Mathews	.05
41	Earl Weaver	.05
42	Jackie Robinson	1.50
43	Lou Brock	.05
44	Reggie Jackson	.15
45	Bob Gibson	.05
46	Jeff Burroughs	.05
47	Jim Bouton	.05
48	Bob Forsch	.05
49	Ron Guidry	.05
50	Ty Cobb	2.00
51	Roy White	.05
52	Joe Rudi	.05
53	Moose Skowron	.05
54	Goose Gossage	.05
55	Ed Kranepool	.05
56	Paul Blair	.05
57	Kent Hrbek	.05
58	Orlando Cepeda	.05
59	Buck O'Neil	.05
60	Al Kaline	.05
61	Vida Blue	.05
62	Sam McDowell	.05
63	Jesse Barfield	.05
64	Dave Kingman	.05
65	Ron Santo	.05
66	Steve Garvey	.05
67	Gaylord Perry	.05
68	Darrell Evans	.05
69	Rollie Fingers	.25
70	Walter Johnson	.25
71	Al Hrabosky	.05
72	Mickey Rivers	.05
73	Mike Torrez	.05
74	Hank Bauer	.05
75	Tug McGraw	.05
76	David Clyde	.05
77	Jim Lonborg	.05
78	Clete Boyer	.05
79	Harry Walker	.05
80	Cy Young	.25
81	Bud Harrelson	.05
82	Paul Splittorff	.05
83	Bert Campaneris	.05
84	Joe Niekro	.05
85	Bob Horner	.05
86	Jerry Royster	.05
87	Tommy John	.05
88	Mark Fidrych	.05
89	Dick Williams	.05
90	Graig Nettles	.05

Greats/Game Autographs

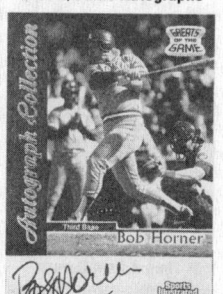

Each Greats of the Game pack has one autograph from the 80 card autograph checklist. Each card is autographed on the white portion on the bottom of the card, and is stamped "seal of authenticity." Card backs certify the autograph is authentic and "has been embossed with the Fleer Mark of Authenticity." The unnumbered cards are checklisted here in alphabetical order.

		NM/M
	Common Player:	4.00
	Inserted 1:1	
(1)	Tommie Agee	8.00
(2)	Luis Aparicio	12.00
(3)	Ernie Banks	25.00
(4)	Jesse Barfield	6.00
(5)	Hank Bauer	10.00
(6)	Bo Belinsky	6.00
(7)	Paul Blair	6.00
(8)	Vida Blue	10.00
(9)	Jim Bouton	10.00
(10)	Clete Boyer	10.00
(11)	Lou Brock	15.00
(12)	Bill Buckner	10.00
(13)	Jeff Burroughs	5.00
(14)	Bert Campaneris	8.00
(15)	Steve Carlton	20.00
(16)	Gary Carter	10.00
(17)	Orlando Cepeda	12.00
(18)	David Clyde	10.00
(19)	Andre Dawson	10.00
(20)	Darrell Evans	10.00
(21)	Bob Feller	15.00
(22)	Mark Fidrych	15.00
(23)	Rollie Fingers	10.00
(24)	Bob Forsch	6.00
(25)	George Foster	10.00
(26)	Steve Garvey	10.00
(27)	Bob Gibson	15.00
(28)	Goose Gossage	10.00
(29)	Ron Guidry	20.00
(30)	Bud Harrelson	10.00
(31)	Bob Horner	10.00
(32)	Al Hrabosky	10.00
(33)	Kent Hrbek	10.00

(34a)	Reggie Jackson	150.00
(34b)	Reggie Jackson ("Mr. October")	200.00
(34c)	Reggie Jackson ("HoF 93")	200.00
(35)	Ferguson Jenkins	10.00
(36)	Tommy John	8.00
(37)	Randy Jones	4.00
(38)	Al Kaline	25.00
(39)	Harmon Killebrew	25.00
(40)	Dave Kingman	8.00
(41)	Jerry Koosman	8.00
(42)	Ed Kranepool	8.00
(43)	Bill Lee	10.00
(44)	Jim Lonborg	5.00
(45)	Sparky Lyle	8.00
(46)	Eddie Mathews	60.00
(47)	Willie Mays	125.00
(48)	Sam McDowell	8.00
(49)	Tug McGraw	25.00
(50)	Stan Musial	100.00
(51)	Graig Nettles	10.00
(52)	Joe Niekro	8.00
(53)	Buck O'Neil	20.00
(54)	Al Oliver	10.00
(55)	Dave Parker	10.00
(56)	Gaylord Perry	10.00
(57)	Rico Petrocelli	8.00
(58)	Johnny Podres	20.00
(59)	Boog Powell	10.00
(60)	Mickey Rivers	8.00
(61)	Robin Roberts	20.00
(62)	Frank Robinson	20.00
(63)	Jerry Royster	4.00
(64)	Joe Rudi	8.00
(65)	Nolan Ryan	200.00
(66)	Ron Santo	15.00
(67)	Red Schoendienst	12.00
(68)	Curt Simmons	6.00
(69)	Moose Skowron	15.00
(70)	Enos Slaughter	25.00
(71)	Paul Splittorff	6.00
(72)	Frank Thomas	4.00
(73)	Mike Torrez	4.00
(74)	Harry Walker	10.00
(75)	Earl Weaver	10.00
(76)	Roy White	8.00
(77)	Dick Williams	10.00
(78)	Maury Wills	10.00
(79)	Jimmy Wynn	10.00
(80)	Carl Yastrzemski	50.00

Greats/ Game Cover Collection

Each pack features one of the 50 chosen baseball covers from the Sports Illustrated archives. Card fronts are a reprint of the actual cover, while the backs give a brief description of the cover article and date of the magazine cover. Each card is numbered with a "C" suffix.

NM/M
Complete Set (50): 25.00
Common Player: .50
Inserted 1:1

1	Johnny Podres	.50
2	Mickey Mantle	5.00
3	Stan Musial	.50
4	Eddie Mathews	.50
5	Frank Thomas	.50
6	Willie Mays	1.00
7	Red Schoendienst	.50
8	Luis Aparicio	.50
9	Mickey Mantle	3.00
10	Al Kaline	.50
11	Maury Wills	.50
12	Sam McDowell	.50
13	Harry Walker	.50
14	Carl Yastrzemski	.50
15	Carl Yastrzemski	.50
16	Lou Brock	.50
17	Ron Santo	.50
18	Reggie Jackson	.50
19	Frank Robinson	.50
20	Jerry Koosman	.50
21	Bud Harrelson	.50
22	Vida Blue	.50
23	Ferguson Jenkins	.50
24	Sparky Lyle	.50
25	Steve Carlton	.50
26	Bert Campaneris	.50
27	Jimmy Wynn	.50
28	Steve Garvey	.50
29	Nolan Ryan	1.00
30	Randy Jones	.50
31	Reggie Jackson	.50
32	Joe Rudi	.50
33	Reggie Jackson	.50
34	Dave Parker	.50
35	Mark Fidrych	.50
36	Earl Weaver	.50
37	Nolan Ryan	1.00
38	Steve Carlton	.50
39	Reggie Jackson	.50
40	Rollie Fingers	.50
41	Gary Carter	.50
42	Graig Nettles	.50
43	Gaylord Perry	.50
44	Kent Hrbek	.50
45	Gary Carter	.50
46	Steve Garvey	.50
47	Steve Carlton	.50
48	Nolan Ryan	1.00
49	Nolan Ryan	1.00
50	Mickey Mantle	3.00

Greats/ Game Record Breakers

This 10-card set spotlights the top record breakers in the past century from Christy Mathewson to Nolan Ryan. Card fronts are full foiled with an oblong stamp on the bottom portion detailing the player's respective record. Card backs are numbered with a "RB" suffix and gives more detail on the featured player's record. These are seeded 1:12 packs. A Gold parallel is also randomly seeded 1:120 packs and have gold holo-foil.

NM/M
Complete Set (10): 40.00
Common Player: 2.00
Inserted 1:12
Golds: 6X
Inserted 1:120

1	Mickey Mantle	8.00
2	Stan Musial	3.50
3	Babe Ruth	8.00
4	Christy Mathewson	2.00
5	Cy Young	2.00
6	Nolan Ryan	7.50
7	Jackie Robinson	6.00
8	Lou Gehrig	7.00
9	Ty Cobb	3.50
10	Walter Johnson	2.00

1989-91 Sports Illustrated For Kids

Beginning with its January 1989 issue and continuing for three years, the magazine "Sports Illustrated For Kids" produced a set of sportscards featuring many professional and amateur stars in more than a dozen sports. Generally issued in a nine-card panel, cards were perforated so they could be removed from the magazine and separated from each other. A variety of designs and formats were used in that period. Only the pro baseball cards from the series are checklisted here.

NM/M
Complete Set (60): 55.00
Common Player: .50

5	Orel Hershiser	.50
11	Jose Canseco	1.00
20	Darryl Strawberry	.50
31	Mike Greenwell	.50
33	Tony Gwynn	2.00
35	Frank Viola	.50
37	Don Mattingly	2.25
43	Ozzie Smith	2.00
46	Rickey Henderson	1.50
48	Chris Sabo	.50
52	Andre Dawson	.75
56	Alan Trammell	.50
60	Roger Clemens	2.25
63	Andres Galarraga	.50
64	John Franco	.50
69	Cal Ripken Jr.	4.00
70	Will Clark	.50
75	Bo Jackson	.75
81	Nolan Ryan	4.00
90	Mike Schmidt	2.25
112	Kevin Mitchell	.50
121	Ryne Sandberg	2.00
127	Robin Yount	1.50
133	Dave Stewart	.50
140	Eric Davis	.50
144	Mike Scott	.50
145	Mark McGwire	3.00
151	Dwight Gooden	.50
158	Ken Griffey Jr.	2.50
162	George Brett	2.25
165	Ruben Sierra	.50
171	Kirby Puckett	2.00
172	Carlton Fisk	1.50
176	Fred McGriff	.50
	Wade Boggs	2.00
181	Tim Raines	.50
189	Bobby Bonilla	.50
	Kelly Gruber	.50
197	Dennis Eckersley	1.00
205	Cecil Fielder	.50
212	Jackie Robinson	2.00
216	Babe Ruth	3.00
229	Barry Bonds	4.00
240	Jose Rijo	.50
248	Sandy Alomar Jr.	.50
251	Ron Gant	.50
259	David Justice	.50
261	Bob Welch	.50
268	Doug Drabek	.50
271	Rafael Palmeiro	1.25
275	Paul Molitor	1.50
279	Bobby Thigpen	.50
282	Edgar Martinez	.50
283	Dave Winfield	1.50
289	Mark Grace	.50
294	Dwight Evans	.50
303	Dave Henderson	.50
321	Lee Smith	.50
	Ramon Martinez	.50
	Ty Cobb	1.50

1992-2000 Sports Illustrated For Kids

A new series, with cards numbered consecutively from #1, of magazine insert cards was begun with SI For Kids' in its January 1992 issue. Like the earlier series, cards are 2-1/2 x 3-1/2 inches and most often found as a nine-card panel, with each card perforated for removal from the magazine and separation from the other cards. As before, the cards feature a number of different designs, formats and back treatments. Backs usually include a few personal details and a trivia question. Only the cards of pro baseball players are checklisted here.

NM/M
Complete Set (157): 150.00
Common Player: .25

24	Terry Pendleton	.25
29	Kirby Puckett	2.00
36	Roger Clemens	2.25
40	Tom Glavine	.45
45	Frank Thomas	1.50
50	Jim Abbott	.25
54	Roberto Alomar	.35
64	Matt Williams	.25
68	Bobby Bonilla	.25
72	Chuck Finley	.25
75	Danny Tartabull	.25
81	Jack Morris	.25
86	Will Clark	.25
108	Lou Gehrig	2.50
132	Juan Gonzalez	.75
136	Cal Ripken Jr.	4.00
144	Jack McDowell	.25
145	Marquis Grissom	.25
157	Andy Van Slyke	.25
168	Dennis Eckersley	1.00
173	Barry Bonds	4.00
178	Greg Maddux	2.00
185	Nolan Ryan	4.00
187	Dave Winfield	1.50
190	Ken Griffey Jr.	2.50
196	Wade Boggs	2.00
199	Kirk Gibson	.25
204	Albert Belle	.25
212	John Burkett	.25
234	John Kruk	.25
244	Randy Johnson	1.50
254	Lou Whitaker	.25
268	Yogi Berra	.50
	Lenny Dykstra	.25
	Carlos Baerga	.25
	Joe Carter	.25
	Chuck Carr	.25
	Julie Croteau (Colorado Silver Bullets)	.25
270	Michael Jordan	3.00
274	Andres Galarraga	.25
278	Jeff Bagwell	1.50
281	John Olerud	.25
288	Tony Gwynn	2.00
292	Gregg Jefferies	.25
297	Mo Vaughn	.25
301	Moises Alou	.25
305	Jimmy Key	.25
313	Mike Mussina	.40
321	Mike Piazza	2.50
327	Stan Musial	2.00
343	Matt Williams	.25
	Frank Thomas (Boyhood photo.)	1.00
349	Michael Jordan (Boyhood photo.)	2.00
359	Kenny Lofton	.25
362	Raul Mondesi	.25
381	David Cone	.25
386	Brady Anderson	.25
390	Eric Karros	.25
391	Paul O'Neil	.25
398	Eddie Murray	1.50
402	Barry Larkin	.25
407	Edgar Martinez	.25
411	Mark McGwire	3.00
416	Albert Belle (Cartoon)	.25
433	Mark Grace	.25
	Chuck Knoblauch	.25
447	Chipper Jones	2.00
451	Tom Glavine (Boyhood photo.)	.25
455	Cal Ripken Jr. (Boyhood photo.)	3.00
462	Jeff Conine	.25
470	Hideo Nomo	.75
475	Bernie Williams	.25
478	Craig Biggio	.25
485	Jose Mesa	.25
497	Roberto Alomar	.35
503	John Smoltz	.25
505	Henry Rodriguez	.25
513	Rey Ordonez	.25
516	Ellis Burks	.25
518	Ivan Rodriguez	1.25
543	Alex Rodriguez	3.00
553	Mo Vaughn	.25
561	Andy Pettitte	.25
562	Barry Bonds	4.00
582	Andruw Jones	.25
570	Randy Johnson (April Fool card as L.A. Laker.)	1.50
572	Ken Griffey Jr. (April Fool card as Orlando Magic.)	2.50
588	Brian Jordan	.25
589	Derek Jeter	4.00
596	Juan Gonzalez	.75
598	Andres Galarraga	.25
608	Mark McGwire	3.00
611	Pat Hentgen	.25
627	Cal Ripken Jr. (Cartoon as Tin Man.)	4.00
634	Sandy Alomar Jr.	.25
641	Brady Anderson	.25
652	Jeff Bagwell	1.50
669	Larry Walker	.25
673	Roger Clemens	2.25
685	Frank Thomas	1.50
693	Denny Neagle	.25
695	Tony Gwynn	2.00
697	Mike Piazza	2.50
703	Kenny Lofton	.25
708	Moises Alou	.25
712	Dante Bichette	.25
720	John Wetteland	.25
721	Curt Schilling	.45
725	Nomar Garciaparra	.25
734	Ken Griffey Jr. (Cartoon as The Cat in the Hat.)	2.50
737	Greg Maddux (Cartoon as Encyclopedia Brown.)	2.00
743	Sammy Sosa	.25
749	David Wells	.25
No#	Mark McGwire (The Best of 1998)	2.50
758	Pedro Martinez	1.50
768	Ila Borders	.25
770	David Cone	.25
784	Mike Piazza (April Fool's - hockey player.)	2.50
790	Mark McGwire (April Fool's - Chicago Cub.)	3.00
795	Craig Biggio	.25
796	Tom Glavine	.45
802	Alex Rodriguez	3.00
804	Trevor Hoffman	.25
813	Rickey Henderson	1.50
815	Mo Vaughn	.25
817	Vinny Castilla	.25
825	John Smoltz	.25
831	Jose Canseco	.65
831	Matt Williams	.25
833	Derek Jeter	4.00
840	Ivan Rodriguez (As Darth Vader.)	1.25
841	Roger Clemens (As lion.)	2.25
846	Ken Caminiti (As Ghoul.)	.25
849	Roberto Alomar	.35
No#	Greg Maddux (Fall/Winter 1999)	2.00
No#	Ken Griffey Jr. (Fall/Winter 1999)	2.50
856	Randy Johnson	1.50
866	Babe Ruth	3.00
869	Mickey Mantle	5.00
870	Jackie Robinson	2.00
882	Mark McGwire (Kid photo.)	3.00
884	Mariano Rivera	.35
892	Billy the Marlin (Mascot)	.25
896	The Phillie Phanatic (Mascot)	.25
901	Kevin Millwood	.25
906	Manny Ramirez	1.50
910	Bernie Williams	.25
914	Larry Walker	.25
920	Ken Griffey Jr.	2.50
922	David Wells	.25
929	Chipper Jones	2.00
935	Carlos Beltran	.25
941	Vladimir Guerrero	1.50
945	Andres Galarraga	.25
953	Jason Kendall (As Pokemon's Ash Ketchum.)	.40
955	Pedro Martinez	.25
962	Todd Helton	1.25

1996-98 Sports Illustrated For Kids Legends

Unlike the nine-card panels which appear in every issue of SI For Kids, the Legends series appeared sporadically as a four-card panel honoring the past greats of many sports. While designs vary from issue to issue, the format of the cards has remained a consistent 2-9/16" x 4". Only the baseball players are listed here.

NM/M
Complete Set (7): 9.00
Common Player: .25

45	Sadaharu Oh	1.00
52	Willie Mays	2.00
66	Mike Schmidt	1.50
(1)	Mickey Mantle	3.00
(2)	Bob Feller	.50
(3)	Lou Brock	.50
(4)	Honus Wagner	.50

1999 SI for Kids 10th Anniversary Sheet

Saluting Sports Illustrated for Kids on its 10th anniversary, Major League Baseball, the Players' Association and the four card licensees created a a special eight-card insert sheet which appears in the magazine's July 1999 issue. The sheet consists of nine 2-1/2" x 3-1/2" cards printed on thin cardboard and perforated for easy separation. The Fleer and Upper Deck cards are very similar to those companies' regular 1999 issues, except for the absence of foil printing and UV coating. The Topps and Pacific offerings are new designs. All player cards feature action photos on front along with card company and SI for Kids logos. Backs have another photo plus stats, biographical data and copyright notice.

NM/M
Complete Sheet: 6.00
Complete Set (9): 5.00
Common Player: .50

7	J.D. Drew (Fleer Tradition)	.50
49	Cal Ripken Jr. (Upper Deck)	1.00
205	Ken Griffey Jr. (Upper Deck)	.65
266	Sammy Sosa (SkyBox Thunder)	.65
---	Roger Clemens (Topps)	.50
---	Tony Gwynn (Pacific)	.50
---	Mark McGwire (Pacific)	.75
---	Mike Piazza (Topps)	.65
---	Sponsors' card	.10

1981 Spot-Bilt George Brett

This one-card set was released in both 1981 and 1982 (see stats on back to differentiate) in boxes of turf baseball shoes, for which Brett served on the athletic advisory staff. Cards are standard 2-1/2" x 3-1/2". Despite the card number 5 on the back, there are no other players in the series. Brett wore uniform #5.

NM/M
George Brett 2.50

1981 Squirt

These cards, issued in conjunction with Topps, were issued as two-card panels in eight-pack cartons of the soft drink. Individual cards measure the standard 2-1/2" x 3-1/2", while the vertical panels measure 2-1/2" x 10-1/2", with a promotional card reading "Free Topps 1981 Baseball Cards" attached. The promotional card is blank-backed, while the player card backs are similar to Topps' regular issue, though re-numbered for inclusion in this 33-card set. Most of the game's top players are included. There are only 22 different two-card panels, as card numbers 1-11 appear in two different bottom panel combinations. Card fronts feature a color player portrait photo within a baseball design, team and position designation, and the Squirt logo.

		NM/M
Complete Panel Set (22):		20.00
Complete Singles Set (33):		20.00
Common Panel:		.50
Common Player:		.15
Panel (1)		2.00
1	George Brett	1.50
12	Garry Templeton	.15
Panel (2)		2.00
1	George Brett	1.50
23	Jerry Mumphrey	.15
Panel (3)		.50
2	George Foster	.15
13	Rick Burleson	.15
Panel (4)		.50
2	George Foster	.15
24	Tony Armas	.15
Panel (5)		.50
3	Ben Oglivie	.15
14	Dave Kingman	.15
Panel (6)		.15
3	Ben Oglivie	.15
25	Fred Lynn	.15
Panel (7)		1.50
4	Steve Garvey	.50
15	Eddie Murray	.75
Panel (8)		.75
4	Steve Garvey	.75
26	Ron LeFlore	.15
Panel (9)		2.00
5	Reggie Jackson	1.50
16	Don Sutton	.50
Panel (10)		2.00
5	Reggie Jackson	1.50
27	Steve Kemp	.15
Panel (11)		.75
6	Bill Buckner	.15
17	Dusty Baker	.15
Panel (12)		1.50
6	Bill Buckner	.15
28	Rickey Henderson	.75
Panel (13)		.50
7	Jim Rice	.25
18	Jack Clark	.15
Panel (14)		.50
7	Jim Rice	.25
29	John Castino	.15
Panel (15)		3.00
8	Mike Schmidt	1.50
19	Dave Winfield	.75
Panel (16)		2.00
8	Mike Schmidt	1.50
30	Cecil Cooper	.15
Panel (17)		2.50
9	Rod Carew	1.00
20	Johnny Bench	1.00
Panel (18)		1.00
9	Rod Carew	1.00
31	Bruce Bochte	.15
Panel (19)		.50
10	Dave Parker	.15
21	Lee Mazzilli	.15
Panel (20)		.65
10	Dave Parker	.15
32	Joe Charboneau	.25
Panel (21)		3.00
11	Pete Rose	2.00
22	Al Oliver	.15
Panel (22)		3.00
11	Pete Rose	2.00
33	Chet Lemon	.15

1982 Squirt

This set was again prepared in conjunction with Topps, but the 1982 Squirt cards are completely different from Topps' regular issue. Only 22 players are included in the full-color set, with the 2-1/2" x 3-1/2" player cards available in one- or two-player panels. Card panels come in four variations, with free grocery contest and scratch-off game cards taking one or two of the positions on the three-card panels. Card backs are numbered and list player statistics.

		NM/M
Complete Set (22):		12.00
Common Player:		.15

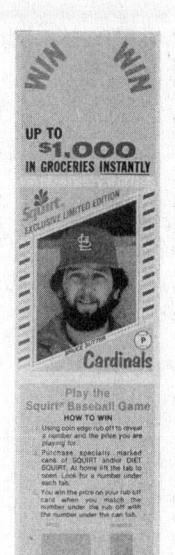

1	Cecil Cooper	.15
2	Jerry Remy	.15
3	George Brett	2.00
4	Alan Trammell	.15
5	Reggie Jackson	2.00
6	Kirk Gibson	.15
7	Dave Winfield	.75
8	Carlton Fisk	.75
9	Ron Guidry	.15
10	Dennis Leonard	.15
11	Rollie Fingers	.60
12	Pete Rose	2.50
13	Phil Garner	.15
14	Mike Schmidt	2.00
15	Dave Concepcion	.15
16	George Hendrick	.15
17	Andre Dawson	.35
18	George Foster	.15
19	Gary Carter	.75
20	Fernando Valenzuela	.15
21	Tom Seaver	1.00
22	Bruce Sutter	.60

1996 St. Louis Browns Historical Society

This collectors issue honoring the 1944 American League Champion St. Louis Browns was issued in conjunction with a reunion of that team in 1996, sponsored by the St. Louis Browns Historical Society. Every player on the '44 team is included in the set, representing the first-ever baseball card for some of them. Fronts of the 2-5/8" x 3-3/4" cards feature color portraits by artist Ronnie Joyner. Shades of brown form the border. Backs are also printed in brown tones and include a cartoon, 1944 season and World Series stats, lifetime stats, personal data, a career summary and part of a team "Timeline" of the 1944 season. It was reported 2,500 sets were issued at $10 retail.

		NM/M
Complete Set (36):		10.00
Common Player:		.50
1	Team Logo Card	.50
2	Don Gutteridge	.50
3	Milt Byrnes	.50
4	Al Hollingsworth	.50
5	Willis Hudlin	.50
6	Sig Jakucki	.50
7	Nelson Potter	.50
8	Len Schulte	.50
9	Vern Stephens	.50
10	Frank Demaree	.50

11	Al Zarilla	.50
12	Bob Muncrief	.50
13	Steve Sundra	.50
14	Jack Kramer	.50
15	Lefty West	.50
16	Denny Galehouse	.50
17	Luke Sewell	.50
18	Joe Schultz	.50
19	George McQuinn	.50
20	Ellis Clary	.50
21	Babe Martin	.50
22	Red Hayworth	.50
23	Frank Mancuso	.50
24	Tex Shirley	.50
25	Mike Chartak	.50
26	Mark Christman	.50
27	Tom Hafey	.50
28	Tom Turner	.50
29	Floyd Baker	.50
30	Mike Kreevich	.50
31	George Caster	.50
32	Gene Moore	.50
33	Chet Laabs	.50
34	Sam Zoldak	.50
35	Hal Epps	.50
36	Team Composite/ Checklist Card	.50

1987 St. Louis Cardinals Fire Safety

Approximately 25,000 fans in attendance at Busch Stadium on August 24 received this set produced by the U.S. Forestry Service. The cards measure 4" x 6". Fronts feature a full-color photo set inside an oval frame. Only the player's last name appears on front. Backs carry the player's name, position and personal data plus a Smokey Bear cartoon fire prevention message.

		NM/M
Complete Set (25):		6.00
Common Player:		.25
1	Ray Soff	.25
2	Todd Worrell	.25
3	John Tudor	.25
4	Pat Perry	.25
5	Rick Horton	.25
6	Dan Cox	.25
7	Bob Forsch	.25
8	Greg Mathews	.25
9	Bill Dawley	.25
10	Steve Lake	.25
11	Tony Pena	.25
12	Tom Pagnozzi	.25
13	Jack Clark	.25
14	Jim Lindeman	.25
15	Mike Laga	.25
16	Terry Pendleton	.25
17	Ozzie Smith	3.50
18	Jose Oquendo	.25
19	Tom Lawless	.25
20	Tom Herr	.25
21	Curt Ford	.25
22	Willie McGee	.25
23	Tito Landrum	.25
24	Vince Coleman	.25
25	Whitey Herzog	.25

1988 St. Louis Cardinals Fire Safety

This set of oversized (3" x 5") cards features full-color action photos that fill the entire front. A thin white line frames the player photo. The player name, team logo and Smokey Bear picture logo are printed in the lower-right corner. Black-and-white backs contain player information and a Smokey Bear fire prevention cartoon. The sets were distributed to young St. Louis fans as part of a U.S. Forest Service fire prevention campaign. The National Association of State Foresters co-sponsored this set.

		NM/M
Complete Set (25):		6.00
Common Player:		.25
1	Whitey Herzog	.25

2	Danny Cox	.25
3	Ken Dayley	.25
4	Jose DeLeon	.25
5	Bob Forsch	.25
6	Joe Magrane	.25
7	Greg Mathews	.25
8	Scott Terry	.25
9	John Tudor	.25
10	Todd Worrell	.25
11	Steve Lake	.25
12	Tom Pagnozzi	.25
13	Tony Pena	.25
14	Bob Horner	.25
15	Tom Lawless	.25
16	Jose Oquendo	.25
17	Terry Pendleton	.25
18	Ozzie Smith	3.50
19	Vince Coleman	.25
20	Curt Ford	.25
21	Willie McGee	.25
22	Larry McWilliams	.25
23	Steve Peters	.25
24	Luis Alicea	.25
25	Tom Brunansky	.25

1989 St. Louis Cardinals Fire Safety

This set featuring action player photos was issued by the U.S. Forest Service to promote fire safety. The cards measure 4" x 6" and include the player's name, team logo and a small picture of Smokey Bear beneath the player photo.

		NM/M
Complete Set (25):		6.00
Common Player:		.25
(1)	Tom Brunansky	.25
(2)	Cris Carpenter	.25
(3)	Vince Coleman	.25
(4)	John Costello	.25
(5)	Ken Dayley	.25
(6)	Jose DeLeon	.25
(7)	Frank DiPino	.25
(8)	Whitey Herzog	.25
(9)	Ken Hill	.25
(10)	Pedro Guerrero	.25
(11)	Tim Jones	.25
(12)	Jim Lindeman	.25
(13)	Joe Magrane	.25
(14)	Willie McGee	.25
(15)	John Morris	.25
(16)	Jose Oquendo	.25
(17)	Tom Pagnozzi	.25
(18)	Tony Pena	.25
(19)	Terry Pendleton	.25
(20)	Dan Quisenberry	.25
(21)	Ozzie Smith	3.50
(22)	Scott Terry	.25
(23)	Milt Thompson	.25
(24)	Denny Walling	.25
(25)	Todd Worrell	.25

1990 St. Louis Cardinals Fire Safety

Player photos dominate the fronts of this large-format (3"x5") set sponsored by the U.S. Forest Service. Backs have a cartoon fire safety tip plus a few stats and personal data. The unnumbered cards are checklisted here in alphabetical order.

		NM/M
Complete Set (27):		6.00
Common Player:		.25
(1)	Vince Coleman	.25
(2)	Dave Collins	.25
(3)	Danny Cox	.25
(4)	Ken Dayley	.25
(5)	Frank DiPino	.25
(6)	Jose DeLeon	.25
(7)	Pedro Guerrero	.25
(8)	Whitey Herzog	.25
(9)	Rick Horton	.25
(10)	Rex Hudler	.25
(11)	Tim Jones	.25
(12)	Joe Magrane	.25
(13)	Greg Mathews	.25
(14)	Willie McGee	.25
(15)	John Morris	.25
(16)	Tom Niedenfuer	.25

(17)	Jose Oquendo	.25
(18)	Tom Pagnozzi	.25
(19)	Terry Pendleton	.25
(20)	Bryn Smith	.25
(21)	Lee Smith	.35
(22)	Ozzie Smith	3.50
(23)	Scott Terry	.25
(24)	Milt Thompson	.25
(25)	John Tudor	.25
(26)	Denny Walling	.25
(27)	Todd Zeile	.25

1991 St. Louis Cardinals Police

Cardinals #34 Felix Jose

Color action photos are featured prominently on these large-format (2-5/8" x 4-1/16") cards. In the white border at bottom, the team name is printed in red, with the player name and uniform number printed in black. Backs feature a large cartoon safety message, career stats, some biographical data and the logos of the set's sponsors, Kansas City Life Insurance and the Greater St. Louis Law Enforcement Agencies. Backs are printed in red on white.

		NM/M
Complete Set (24):		7.50
Common Player:		.15
1	Ozzie Smith	5.00
9	Geronimo Pena	.15
9	Joe Torre	.50
10	Rex Hudler	.15
12	Jose Oquendo	.15
12	Craig Wilson	.15
16	Ray Lankford	.25
19	Tom Pagnozzi	.15
21	Gerald Perry	.15
23	Bernard Gilkey	.15
25	Milt Thompson	.15
27	Todd Zeile	.15
28	Pedro Guerrero	.15
29	Rich Gedman	.15
34	Felix Jose	.15
35	Frank DiPino	.15
36	Bryn Smith	.15
37	Scott Terry	.15
38	Todd Worrell	.15
39	Bob Tewksbury	.15
43	Ken Hill	.15
47	Lee Smith	.25
48	Jose DeLeon	.15
49	Juan Agosto	.15

1992 St. Louis Cardinals Police

Cardinals #1 Ozzie Smith

The Cardinals were the subject of this set given out at Busch Stadium on April 25. Sponsored by Kansas City Life Insurance and distributed by Greater St. Louis law enforcement agencies, the cards are 2-1/2" x 4", and contain a special logo on the front which commemorates the team's 100th anniversary.

		NM/M
Complete Set (27):		7.50
Common Player:		.25

(17)	Jose Oquendo	.25
(18)	Tom Pagnozzi	.25
(19)	Terry Pendleton	.25
(20)	Bryn Smith	.25
(21)	Lee Smith	.35
(22)	Ozzie Smith	3.50
(23)	Scott Terry	.25
(24)	Milt Thompson	.25
(25)	John Tudor	.25
(26)	Denny Walling	.25
(27)	Todd Zeile	.25

1993 St. Louis Cardinals Police

BERNARD GILKEY OF • 23

This Cardinals/Kansas City Life police set features 2-5/8" x 4" cards with a blue border and "Cardinals" printed in red at top. The team logo appears in the lower-left corner, while the player's name, position and number appear lower-right. Backs are printed in red on a white background with the player's biography and statistics listed above a safety message.

		NM/M
Complete Set (25):		7.50
Common Player:		.25
1	Ozzie Smith	5.00
3	Brian Jordan	.35
5	Stan Royer	.25
9	Joe Torre	.50
11	Jose Oquendo	.25
16	Ray Lankford	.25
19	Luis Alicea	.25
19	Tom Pagnozzi	.25
23	Geronimo Pena	.25
23	Bernard Gilkey	.25
25	Gregg Jefferies	.25
27	Rob Murphy	.25
27	Todd Zeile	.25
29	Gerald Perry	.25
29	Hector Villanueva	.25
31	Donovan Osborne	.25
33	Rod Brewer	.25
39	Bob Tewksbury	.25
42	Mike Perez	.25
43	Rene Arocha	.25
46	Ozzie Canseco	.25
47	Lee Smith	.25
52	Rheal Cormier	.25
54	Tracy Woodson	.25
---	Checklist	.25

1994 St. Louis Cardinals Police

Cardinals

Gregg Jefferies 1st Base

1	Ozzie Smith	5.00
9	Geronimo Pena	.25
9	Joe Torre	.50
10	Rex Hudler	.25
12	Jose Oquendo	.25
12	Craig Wilson	.25
12	Ray Lankford	.25
19	Tom Pagnozzi	.25
21	Gerald Perry	.25
23	Bernard Gilkey	.25
25	Milt Thompson	.25
26	Omar Olivares	.25
27	Todd Zeile	.25
28	Pedro Guerrero	.25
29	Rich Gedman	.25
32	Joe Magrane	.25
34	Felix Jose	.25
36	Bryn Smith	.25
37	Scott Terry	.25
38	Todd Worrell	.25
39	Bob Tewksbury	.25
41	Andres Galarraga	.25
44	Cris Carpenter	.25
47	Lee Smith	.30
48	Jose DeLeon	.25
49	Juan Agosto	.25
---	Checklist	.25

An emphasis on border graphics marks the perennial Cardinals safety set for 1994. The 2-5/8" x 4" cards have a cream colored border. Near the left edge is a vertical red stripe with a team logo at top. Above the color photo at center is the team name. The player name and position are at lower-left. A baseball zooms out of the photo at lower-right carrying the uniform number. Backs are printed in red on white and feature a large cartoon safety message at center. Career stats and biographical data are at top. At bottom are sponsors' logos for the Kansas City Life Insurance Co., and Greater St. Louis Law Enforcement Agencies.

		NM/M
Complete Set (26):		7.50
Common Player:		.15
1	Ozzie Smith	5.00
3	Brian Jordan	.25
5	Stan Royer	.15
9	Joe Torre	.50
11	Jose Oquendo	.15
12	Erik Pappas	.15
16	Ray Lankford	.15
18	Luis Alicea	.15
19	Tom Pagnozzi	.15
21	Geronimo Pena	.15
22	Mark Whiten	.15
23	Bernard Gilkey	.15
25	Gregg Jefferies	.15
26	Omar Olivares	.15
27	Todd Zeile	.15
28	Gerald Perry	.15
34	Tom Urbani	.15
36	Paul Kilgus	.15
38	Allen Watson	.15
39	Bob Tewksbury	.15
40	Rick Sutcliffe	.15
42	Mike Perez	.15
43	Rene Arocha	.15
46	Rob Murphy	.15
48	Rich Batchelor	.15
52	Rheal Cormier	.15

1995 St. Louis Cardinals Police

In 1995, the Cardinals safety set was sponsored by Kansas City Life Insurance Co., and distributed by law enforcement agencies in the greater St. Louis area. The cards measure about 2-5/8" x 4" and feature action photos on front. The team name is scripted at bottom and the player's last name and "1995" are vertically at right. Backs have a few vital data, a career stats line, a safety message and sponsor's logo. Cards are listed here in alphabetical order.

		NM/M
Complete Set (12):		7.50
Common Player:		.50
(1)	Rene Arocha	.50
(2)	Scott Cooper	.50
(3)	Tripp Cromer	.50
(4)	Bernard Gilkey	.50
(5)	Tom Henke	.50
(6)	Ken Hill	.50
(7)	Danny Jackson	.50
(8)	Brian Jordan	.50
(9)	Ray Lankford	.50
(10)	Jose Oquendo	.50
(11)	Tom Pagnozzi	.50
(12)	Ozzie Smith	5.00

1996 St. Louis Cardinals Police

Once again for 1996, the Cardinals safety set was sponsored by Kansas City Life Insurance Co., and distributed by law enforcement agencies in the greater St. Louis area. The cards measure about 2-5/8" x 4" and feature action photos on front. The team name is vertically in a ghosted strip at left. At bottom, beneath a "torn" photo edge are the player's last name, uniform number and the team logo. Backs have a few vital data, a career stats line, a safety message and sponsor's logo.

		NM/M
Complete Set (26):		10.00
Common Player:		.25
1	Ozzie Smith	5.00
3	Brian Jordan	.25
5	Ron Gant	.25
8	Gary Gaetti	.25
12	Tony LaRussa	.25
13	Royce Clayton	.25
16	Ray Lankford	.25
19	Tom Pagnozzi	.25
22	Mike Gallego	.25
23	Mark Sweeney	.25
24	Tom Urbani	.25
29	Danny Jackson	.25
30	Todd Stottlemyre	.25
31	Donovan Osborne	.25
32	Rick Honeycutt	.25
33	T.J. Mathews	.25
35	Mike Morgan	.25
36	Pat Borders	.25
40	Andy Benes	.25
41	Alan Benes	.25
43	Dennis Eckersley	3.00
46	Mark Petkovsek	.25
47	John Mabry	.25
48	Tony Fossas	.25
51	Willie McGee	.25
---	Fredbird/Checklist (Mascot)	.25

1998 St. Louis Cardinals Police

Similar in format to those used in the preceding years, this safety issue is printed on a 2-1/4" x 4" format. Fronts have color action photos surrounded by busy borders in predominantly yellow and green. A blue strip at bottom has player name and uniform number and team logo. Backs are in red-and-white with a few biographical details and stats, a cartoon baseball figure, safety message and sponsors' credits. Cards are checklisted here by uniform number.

		NM/M
Complete Set (26):		8.00
Common Player:		.25
3	Brian Jordan	.25
5	Ron Gant	.25
7	Delino DeShields	.25
8	Gary Gaetti	.25
10	Tony LaRussa	.25
11	Royce Clayton	.25
13	David Howard	.25
16	Ray Lankford	.25
19	Tom Pagnozzi	.25
25	Mark McGwire	6.00
28	Eli Marrero	.25
29	Lance Painter	.25
30	Todd Stottlemyre	.25
35	Matt Morris	.25
37	Kent Bottenfield	.25
39	Manny Aybar	.25
41	Alan Benes	.25
44	Kent Mercker	.25
45	Jeff Brantley	.25
46	Mark Petkovsek	.25
47	John Mabry	.25
49	Tom Lampkin	.25
50	John Frascatore	.25
51	Willie McGee	.25
57	Curtis King	.25
---	Fredbird (Mascot)	.25

2000 St. Louis Cardinals Police

The Cardinals issued this safety set to fans 15 and under at the April 22 game in Busch Stadium. The 2-5/8" x 4" cards have game-action color photos bordered in white. Backs are in red on white with a few bits of personal data, a cartoon safety message and the logo of sponsoring Kansas City Life Insurance, which provided the cards for distribution by the Metropolitan Chiefs and Sheriffs Assn. Cards are checklisted here by uniform number. The checklist of actually-issued cards does not correspond with the checklist on the Fredbird card due to the trades which sent away Kent Bottenfield, Joe McEwing, Brian McRae and Paul Spoljaric.

		NM/M
Complete Set (23):		6.00
Common Player:		.25
3	Edgar Renteria	.45
4	Fernando Vina	.25
5	Thomas Howard	.25
7	J.D. Drew	1.50
10	Tony LaRussa	.25
12	Shawon Dunston	.25
16	Ray Lankford	.25
21	Craig Paquette	.25
22	Mike Matheny	.25
23	Fernando Tatis	.25
24	Eric Davis	.25
25	Mark McGwire	3.00
26	Eli Marrero	.25
31	Alan Benes	.25
36	Scott Radinsky	.25
40	Andy Benes	.25
41	Pat Hentgen	.25
43	Dave Veres	.25
57	Garrett Stephenson	.25
	Darryl Kile	.25
58	Heathcliff Slocumb	.25
66	Rick Ankiel	.25
	Fredbird/Checklist	.25

1991 Stadium Club Promos

Topps' response to the upscale Leaf baseball card issue was a new brand labeled Stadium Club. To introduce the premium cards, a set of 50 promo cards was produced with single cards distributed to employees and candy companies. Production has been reported in the area of 600 of each card. The promos differ from the issued cards in front in that there are four horizontal gold-foil stripes on the promos, instead of three. The back of each promo card is identical, showing a 1986 Topps Traded Jose Canseco card. The unnumbered cards are checklisted here in alphabetical order.

		NM/M
Complete Set (50):		150.00
Common Player:		2.50
(1)	Allan Anderson	2.50
(2)	Steve Balboni	2.50
(3)	Jeff Ballard	2.50
(4)	Jesse Barfield	2.50
(5)	Andy Benes	2.50
(6)	Bobby Bonilla	2.50
(7)	Chris Bosio	2.50
(8)	Daryl Boston	2.50
(9)	Chuck Cary	2.50
(10)	Pat Combs	2.50
(11)	Delino DeShields	2.50
(12)	Shawon Dunston	2.50
(13)	Alvaro Espinoza	2.50
(14)	Sid Fernandez	2.50
(15)	Bob Geren	2.50
(16)	Brian Holman	2.50
(17)	Jay Howell	2.50
(18)	Stan Javier	2.50
(19)	Dave Johnson	2.50
(20)	Howard Johnson	2.50
(21)	Kevin Maas	2.50
(22)	Shane Mack	2.50
(23)	Joe Magrane	2.50
(24)	Denny Martinez	2.50
(25)	Don Mattingly	30.00
(26)	Ben McDonald	2.50
(27)	Eddie Murray	15.00
(28)	Matt Nokes	2.50
(29)	Greg Olson	2.50
(30)	Gregg Olson	2.50
(31)	Jose Oquendo	2.50
(32)	Tony Phillips	2.50
(33)	Rafael Ramirez	2.50
(34)	Dennis Rasmussen	2.50
(35)	Billy Ripken	2.50
(36)	Nolan Ryan	65.00
(37)	Bill Sampen	2.50
(38)	Steve Sax	2.50
(39)	Mike Scioscia	2.50
(40)	David Segui	2.50
(41)	Zane Smith	2.50
(42)	B.J. Surhoff	2.50
(43)	Bobby Thigpen	2.50
(44)	Alan Trammell	2.50
(45)	Fernando Valenzuela	2.50
(46)	Andy Van Slyke	2.50
(47)	Hector Villanueva	2.50
(48)	Larry Walker	2.50
(49)	Walt Weiss	2.50
(50)	Bob Welch	2.50

1991 Stadium Club

One of the most popular sets of 1991, this 600-card issue was released in two 300-card series. The cards were available in foil packs only. No factory sets were available. The cards feature borderless high gloss photos on the front and a player evaluation and card photo on the back. Each card can be found with two different letters preceding the copyright cymbol on back. A special Stadium Club membership package was made available for $29.95 with 10 proof of purchase seals from wrappers.

		NM/M
Complete Set (600):		20.00
Common Player:		.05
Series 1 or 2 Pack (13):		.60
Series 1 or 2 Box (36):		15.00
1	Dave Stewart	.05
2	Wally Joyner	.05
3	Shawon Dunston	.05
4	Darren Daulton	.05
5	Will Clark	.05
6	Sammy Sosa	1.00
7	Dan Plesac	.05
8	Marquis Grissom	.05
9	Erik Hanson	.05
10	Geno Petralli	.05
11	Jose Rijo	.05
12	Carlos Quintana	.05
13	Junior Ortiz	.05
14	Bob Walk	.05
15	Mike Macfarlane	.05
16	Eric Yelding	.05
17	Bryn Smith	.05
18	Bip Roberts	.05
19	Mike Scioscia	.05
20	Mark Williamson	.05
21	Don Mattingly	1.00
22	John Franco	.05
23	Chet Lemon	.05
24	Tom Henke	.05
25	Jerry Browne	.05
26	Dave Justice	.05
27	Mark Langston	.05
28	Damon Berryhill	.05
29	Kevin Bass	.05
30	Scott Fletcher	.05
31	Moises Alou	.05
32	Dave Valle	.05
33	Jody Reed	.05
34	Dave West	.05
35	Kevin McReynolds	.05
36	Pat Combs	.05
37	Eric Davis	.05
38	Bret Saberhagen	.05
39	Stan Javier	.05
40	Chuck Cary	.05
41	Tony Phillips	.05
42	Lee Smith	.05
43	Tim Teufel	.05
44	Lance Dickson	.05
45	Greg Litton	.05
46	Teddy Higuera	.05
47	Edgar Martinez	.05
48	Steve Avery	.05
49	Walt Weiss	.05
50	David Segui	.05
51	Andy Benes	.05
52	Karl Rhodes	.05
53	Neal Heaton	.05
54	Dan Gladden	.05
55	Luis Rivera	.05
56	Kevin Brown	.05
57	Frank Thomas	.75
58	Terry Mulholland	.05
59	Dick Schofield	.05
60	Ron Darling	.05
61	Sandy Alomar, Jr.	.05
62	Dave Stieb	.05
63	Alan Trammell	.05
64	Matt Nokes	.05
65	Lenny Harris	.05
66	Milt Thompson	.05
67	Storm Davis	.05
68	Joe Oliver	.05
69	Andres Galarraga	.05
70	Ozzie Guillen	.05
71	Ken Howell	.05
72	Garry Templeton	.05
73	Derrick May	.05
74	Xavier Hernandez	.05
75	Dave Parker	.05
76	Rick Aguilera	.05
77	Robby Thompson	.05
78	Pete Incaviglia	.05
79	Bob Welch	.05
80	Randy Milligan	.05
81	Chuck Finley	.05
82	Alvin Davis	.05
83	Tim Naehring	.05
84	Jay Bell	.05
85	Joe Magrane	.05
86	Howard Johnson	.05
87	Jack McDowell	.05
88	Kevin Seitzer	.05
89	Bruce Ruffin	.05
90	Fernando Valenzuela	.05
91	Terry Kennedy	.05
92	Barry Larkin	.05
93	Larry Walker	.05
94	Luis Salazar	.05
95	Gary Sheffield	.45
96	Bobby Witt	.05
97	Lonnie Smith	.05
98	Bryan Harvey	.05
99	Mookie Wilson	.05
100	Dwight Gooden	.05
101	Lou Whitaker	.05
102	Ron Karkovice	.05
103	Jesse Barfield	.05
104	Jose DeJesus	.05
105	Benito Santiago	.05
106	Brian Holman	.05
107	Rafael Ramirez	.05
108	Ellis Burks	.05
109	Mike Bielecki	.05
110	Kirby Puckett	1.00
111	Terry Shumpert	.05
112	Chuck Crim	.05
113	Todd Benzinger	.05
114	Brian Barnes	.05
115	Carlos Baerga	.05
116	Kal Daniels	.05
117	Dave Johnson	.05
118	Andy Van Slyke	.05
119	John Burkett	.05
120	Rickey Henderson	.75
121	Tim Jones	.05
122	Daryl Irvine	.05
123	Ruben Sierra	.05
124	Jim Abbott	.05
125	Daryl Boston	.05
126	Greg Maddux	1.00
127	Von Hayes	.05
128	Mike Fitzgerald	.05
129	Wayne Edwards	.05
130	Greg Briley	.05
131	Rob Dibble	.05
132	Gene Larkin	.05
133	David Wells	.05
134	Steve Balboni	.05
135	Greg Vaughn	.05
136	Mark Davis	.05
137	Dave Rohde	.05
138	Eric Show	.05
139	Bobby Bonilla	.05
140	Dana Kiecker	.05
141	Gary Pettis	.05
142	Dennis Boyd	.05
143	Mike Benjamin	.05
144	Luis Polonia	.05
145	Doug Jones	.05
146	Al Newman	.05
147	Alex Fernandez	.05
148	Bill Doran	.05
149	Kevin Elster	.05
150	Len Dykstra	.05
151	Mike Gallego	.05
152	Tim Belcher	.05
153	Jay Buhner	.05
154	Ozzie Smith	1.00
155	Jose Canseco	.50
156	Gregg Olson	.05
157	Charlie O'Brien	.05
158	Frank Tanana	.05
159	George Brett	1.00
160	Jeff Huson	.05
161	Kevin Tapani	.05
162	Jerome Walton	.05
163	Charlie Hayes	.05
164	Chris Bosio	.05
165	Chris Sabo	.05
166	Lance Parrish	.05
167	Don Robinson	.05
168	Manuel Lee	.05
169	Dennis Rasmussen	.05
170	Wade Boggs	1.00
171	Bob Geren	.05
172	Mackey Sasser	.05
173	Julio Franco	.05
174	Otis Nixon	.05
175	Bert Blyleven	.05
176	Craig Biggio	.05
177	Eddie Murray	.75
178	Randy Tomlin	.05
179	Tino Martinez	.05
180	Carlton Fisk	.75
181	Dwight Smith	.05
182	Scott Garrelts	.05
183	Jim Gantner	.05
184	Dickie Thon	.05
185	John Farrell	.05
186	Cecil Fielder	.05
187	Glenn Braggs	.05
188	Allan Anderson	.05
189	Kurt Stillwell	.05
190	Jose Oquendo	.05
191	Joe Orsulak	.05
192	Ricky Jordan	.05
193	Kelly Downs	.05
194	Delino DeShields	.05
195	Omar Vizquel	.05
196	Mark Carreon	.05
197	Mike Harkey	.05
198	Jack Howell	.05
199	Lance Johnson	.05
200	Nolan Ryan	2.00
201	John Marzano	.05
202	Doug Drabek	.05
203	Mark Lemke	.05
204	Steve Sax	.05
205	Greg Harris	.05
206	B.J. Surhoff	.05
207	Todd Burns	.05
208	Jose Gonzalez	.05
209	Mike Scott	.05
210	Dave Magadan	.05
211	Dante Bichette	.05
212	Trevor Wilson	.05
213	Hector Villanueva	.05
214	Dan Pasqua	.05
215	Greg Colbrunn	.05
216	Mike Jeffcoat	.05
217	Harold Reynolds	.05
218	Paul O'Neill	.05
219	Mark Guthrie	.05
220	Barry Bonds	2.00
221	Jimmy Key	.05
222	Billy Ripken	.05
223	Tom Pagnozzi	.05
224	Bo Jackson	.10
225	Sid Fernandez	.05
226	Mike Marshall	.05
227	John Kruk	.05
228	Mike Fetters	.05
229	Eric Anthony	.05
230	Ryne Sandberg	1.00
231	Carney Lansford	.05
232	Melido Perez	.05
233	Jose Lind	.05
234	Darryl Hamilton	.05
235	Tom Browning	.05
236	Spike Owen	.05
237	Juan Gonzalez	.40
238	Felix Fermin	.05
239	Keith Miller	.05
240	Mark Gubicza	.05
241	Kent Anderson	.05
242	Alvaro Espinoza	.05
243	Dale Murphy	.20
244	Orel Hershiser	.05
245	Paul Molitor	.75
246	Eddie Whitson	.05
247	Joe Girardi	.05
248	Kent Hrbek	.05
249	Bill Sampen	.05
250	Kevin Mitchell	.05
251	Mariano Duncan	.05
252	Scott Bradley	.05
253	Mike Greenwell	.05
254	Tom Gordon	.05
255	Todd Zeile	.05
256	Bobby Thigpen	.05
257	Gregg Jefferies	.05
258	Kenny Rogers	.05
259	Shane Mack	.05
260	Zane Smith	.05
261	Mitch Williams	.05
262	Jim DeShaies	.05
263	Dave Winfield	.75
264	Ben McDonald	.05
265	Randy Ready	.05
266	Pat Borders	.05
267	Jose Uribe	.05
268	Derek Lilliquist	.05
269	Greg Brock	.05
270	Ken Griffey Jr.	1.25
271	Jeff Gray	.05
272	Danny Tartabull	.05
273	Dennis Martinez	.05
274	Robin Ventura	.05
275	Randy Myers	.05
276	Jack Daugherty	.05
277	Greg Gagne	.05
278	Jay Howell	.05
279	Mike LaValliere	.05
280	Rex Hudler	.05
281	Mike Simms	.05
282	Kevin Maas	.05
283	Jeff Ballard	.05
284	Dave Henderson	.05
285	Pete O'Brien	.05
286	Brook Jacoby	.05
287	Mike Henneman	.05
288	Greg Olson	.05

289	Greg Myers	.05
290	Mark Grace	.05
291	Shawn Abner	.05
292	Frank Viola	.05
293	Lee Stevens	.05
294	Jason Grimsley	.05
295	Matt Williams	.05
296	Ron Robinson	.05
297	Tom Brunansky	.05
298	Checklist	.05
299	Checklist	.05
300	Checklist	.05
301	Darryl Strawberry	.05
302	Bud Black	.05
303	Harold Baines	.05
304	Roberto Alomar	.20
305	Norm Charlton	.05
306	Gary Thurman	.05
307	Mike Felder	.05
308	Tony Gwynn	1.00
309	Roger Clemens	1.00
310	Andre Dawson	.25
311	Scott Radinsky	.05
312	Bob Melvin	.05
313	Kirk McCaskill	.05
314	Pedro Guerrero	.05
315	Walt Terrell	.05
316	Sam Horn	.05
317	Wes Chamberlain RC	.05
318	Pedro Munoz RC	.05
319	Roberto Kelly	.05
320	Mark Portugal	.05
321	Tim McIntosh	.05
322	Jesse Orosco	.05
323	Gary Green	.05
324	Greg Harris	.05
325	Hubie Brooks	.05
326	Chris Nabholz	.05
327	Terry Pendleton	.05
328	Eric King	.05
329	Chili Davis	.05
330	Anthony Telford	.05
331	Kelly Gruber	.05
332	Dennis Eckersley	.65
333	Mel Hall	.05
334	Bob Kipper	.05
335	Willie McGee	.05
336	Steve Olin	.05
337	Steve Buechele	.05
338	Scott Leius	.05
339	Hal Morris	.05
340	Jose Offerman	.05
341	Kent Mercker	.05
342	Ken Griffey	.05
343	Pete Harnisch	.05
344	Kirk Gibson	.05
345	Dave Smith	.05
346	Dave Martinez	.05
347	Atlee Hammaker	.05
348	Brian Downing	.05
349	Todd Hundley	.05
350	Candy Maldonado	.05
351	Dwight Evans	.05
352	Steve Searcy	.05
353	Gary Gaetti	.05
354	Jeff Reardon	.05
355	Travis Fryman	.05
356	Dave Righetti	.05
357	Fred McGriff	.05
358	Don Slaught	.05
359	Gene Nelson	.05
360	Billy Spiers	.05
361	Lee Guetterman	.05
362	Darren Lewis	.05
363	Duane Ward	.05
364	Lloyd Moseby	.05
365	John Smoltz	.05
366	Felix Jose	.05
367	David Cone	.05
368	Wally Backman	.05
369	Jeff Montgomery	.05
370	Rich Garces	.05
371	Billy Hatcher	.05
372	Bill Swift	.05
373	Jim Eisenreich	.05
374	Rob Ducey	.05
375	Tim Crews	.05
376	Steve Finley	.05
377	Jeff Blauser	.05
378	Willie Wilson	.05
379	Gerald Perry	.05
380	Jose Mesa	.05
381	Pat Kelly	.05
382	Matt Merullo	.05
383	Ivan Calderon	.05
384	Scott Chiamparino	.05
385	Lloyd McClendon	.05
386	Dave Bergman	.05
387	Ed Sprague	.05
388	Jeff Bagwell RC	3.00
389	Brett Butler	.05
390	Larry Andersen	.05
391	Glenn Davis	.05
392	Alex Cole	
	(Photo is Otis Nixon.)	.05
393	Mike Heath	.05
394	Danny Darwin	.05
395	Steve Lake	.05
396	Tim Layana	.05
397	Terry Leach	.05
398	Bill Wegman	.05
399	Mark McGwire	1.50
400	Mike Boddicker	.05
	Steve Howe	.05
	Bernard Gilkey	.05
	Thomas Howard	.05
	Rafael Belliard	.05
	Tom Candiotti	.05

406	Rene Gonzalez	.05
407	Chuck McElroy	.05
408	Paul Sorrento	.05
409	Randy Johnson	.75
410	Brady Anderson	.05
411	Dennis Cook	.05
412	Mickey Tettleton	.05
413	Mike Stanton	.05
414	Ken Oberkfell	.05
415	Rick Honeycutt	.05
416	Nelson Santovenia	.05
417	Bob Tewksbury	.05
418	Brent Mayne	.05
419	Steve Farr	.05
420	Phil Stephenson	.05
421	Jeff Russell	.05
422	Chris James	.05
423	Tim Leary	.05
424	Gary Carter	.75
425	Glenallen Hill	.05
426	Matt Young	.05
427	Sid Bream	.05
428	Greg Swindell	.05
429	Scott Aldred	.05
430	Cal Ripken, Jr.	2.00
431	Bill Landrum	.05
432	Ernie Riles	.05
433	Danny Jackson	.05
434	Casey Candaele	.05
435	Ken Hill	.05
436	Jaime Navarro	.05
437	Lance Blankenship	.05
438	Randy Velarde	.05
439	Frank DiPino	.05
440	Carl Nichols	.05
441	Jeff Robinson	.05
442	Deion Sanders	.05
443	Vincente Palacios	.05
444	Devon White	.05
445	John Cerutti	.05
446	Tracy Jones	.05
447	Jack Morris	.05
448	Mitch Webster	.05
449	Bob Ojeda	.05
450	Oscar Azocar	.05
451	Luis Aquino	.05
452	Mark Whiten	.05
453	Stan Belinda	.05
454	Ron Gant	.05
455	Jose DeLeon	.05
456	Mark Salas	.05
457	Junior Felix	.05
458	Wally Whitehurst	.05
459	Phil Plantier RC	.05
460	Juan Berenguer	.05
461	Franklin Stubbs	.05
462	Joe Boever	.05
463	Tim Wallach	.05
464	Mike Moore	.05
465	Albert Belle	.05
466	Mike Witt	.05
467	Craig Worthington	.05
468	Jerald Clark	.05
469	Scott Terry	.05
470	Milt Cuyler	.05
471	John Smiley	.05
472	Charles Nagy	.05
473	Alan Mills	.05
474	John Russell	.05
475	Bruce Hurst	.05
476	Andujar Cedeno	.05
477	Dave Eiland	.05
478	Brian McRae RC	.10
479	Mike LaCoss	.05
480	Chris Gwynn	.05
481	Jamie Moyer	.05
482	John Olerud	.05
483	Efrain Valdez	.05
484	Sil Campusano	.05
485	Pascual Perez	.05
486	Gary Redus	.05
487	Andy Hawkins	.05
488	Cory Snyder	.05
489	Chris Hoiles	.05
490	Ron Hassey	.05
491	Gary Wayne	.05
492	Mark Lewis	.05
493	Scott Coolbaugh	.05
494	Gerald Young	.05
495	Juan Samuel	.05
496	Willie Fraser	.05
497	Jeff Treadway	.05
498	Vince Coleman	.05
499	Cris Carpenter	.05
500	Jack Clark	.05
501	Kevin Appier	.05
502	Rafael Palmeiro	.65
503	Hensley Meulens	.05
504	George Bell	.05
505	Tony Pena	.05
506	Roger McDowell	.05
507	Luis Sojo	.05
508	Mike Schooler	.05
509	Robin Yount	.75
510	Jack Armstrong	.05
511	Rick Cerone	.05
512	Curt Wilkerson	.05
513	Joe Carter	.05
514	Tim Burke	.05
515	Tony Fernandez	.05
516	Ramon Martinez	.05
517	Tim Hulett	.05
518	Terry Steinbach	.05
519	Pete Smith	.05
520	Ken Caminiti	.05
521	Shawn Boskie	.05
522	Mike Pagliarulo	.05
523	Tim Raines	.05

524	Alfredo Griffin	.05
525	Henry Cotto	.05
526	Mike Stanley	.05
527	Charlie Leibrandt	.05
528	Jeff King	.05
529	Eric Plunk	.05
530	Tom Lampkin	.05
531	Steve Bedrosian	.05
532	Tom Herr	.05
533	Craig Lefferts	.05
534	Jeff Reed	.05
535	Mickey Morandini	.05
536	Greg Cadaret	.05
537	Ray Lankford	.05
538	John Candelaria	.05
539	Rob Deer	.05
540	Brad Arnsberg	.05
541	Mike Sharperson	.05
542	Jeff Robinson	.05
543	Mo Vaughn	.05
544	Jeff Parrett	.05
545	Willie Randolph	.05
546	Herm Winningham	.05
547	Jeff Innis	.05
548	Chuck Knoblauch	.05
549	Tommy Greene	.05
550	Jeff Hamilton	.05
551	Barry Jones	.05
552	Ken Dayley	.05
553	Rick Dempsey	.05
554	Greg Smith	.05
555	Mike Devereaux	.05
556	Keith Comstock	.05
557	Paul Faries	.05
558	Tom Glavine	.35
559	Craig Grebeck	.05
560	Scott Erickson	.05
561	Joel Skinner	.05
562	Mike Morgan	.05
563	Dave Gallagher	.05
564	Todd Stottlemyre	.05
565	Rich Rodriguez	.05
566	Craig Wilson RC	.05
567	Jeff Brantley	.05
568	Scott Kamieniecki	.05
569	Steve Decker	.05
570	Juan Agosto	.05
571	Tommy Gregg	.05
572	Kevin Wickander	.05
573	Jamie Quirk	.05
574	Jerry Don Gleaton	.05
575	Chris Hammond	.05
576	Luis Gonzalez RC	1.00
577	Russ Swan	.05
578	Jeff Conine RC	.50
579	Charlie Hough	.05
580	Jeff Kunkel	.05
581	Darrel Akerfelds	.05
582	Jeff Manto	.05
583	Alejandro Pena	.05
584	Mark Davidson	.05
585	Bob MacDonald	.05
586	Paul Assenmacher	.05
587	Dan Wilson	.05
588	Tom Bolton	.05
589	Brian Harper	.05
590	John Habyan	.05
591	John Orton	.05
592	Mark Gardner	.05
593	Turner Ward	.05
594	Bob Patterson	.05
595	Edwin Nunez	.05
596	Gary Scott	.05
597	Scott Bankhead	.05
598	Checklist	.05
599	Checklist	.05
600	Checklist	.05

Charter Members

Charter members of Topps Stadium Club received a package which included a 50-card multi-sport set unavailable in any other fashion. Cards are similar in format to S.C. regular issues, with full-bleed photos on front, UV coating and gold-foil highlights. This special edition has a gold foil "Charter Member" notation at the bottom of each card front. Backs have a simulated newspaper page describing a career highlight. The cards are unnumbered and the checklist here includes only the baseball cards from the set.

	NM/M
Complete Set (50):	12.50

Common Player:		.15
(1)	Sandy Alomar, Jr.	.15
(2)	George Brett	1.00
(3)	Barry Bonds	2.50
(4)	Ellis Burks	.15
(5)	Eric Davis	.15
(6)	Delino DeShields	.15
(7)	Doug Drabek	.15
(8)	Cecil Fielder	.15
(9)	Carlton Fisk	.50
(10)	Ken Griffey Jr.,	
	Ken Griffey Sr.	1.50
(11)	Billy Hatcher	.15
(12)	Andy Hawkins	.15
(13)	Rickey Henderson (A.L. MVP)	.50
(14)	Rickey Henderson (A.L. base-stealing leader.)	.15
(15)	Randy Johnson	.50
(16)	Dave Justice	.15
(17)	Mark Langston, Mike Witt	.15
(18)	Kevin Maas	.15
(19)	Ramon Martinez	.15
(20)	Willie McGee	.15
(21)	Terry Mulholland	.15
(22)	Jose Offerman	.15
(23)	Melido Perez	.15
(24)	Nolan Ryan (No-hitter).	2.50
(25)	Nolan Ryan (300th win)	2.50
(26)	Ryne Sandberg	.75
(27)	Dave Stewart	.15
(28)	Dave Stieb	.15
(29)	Bobby Thigpen	.15
(30)	Fernando Valenzuela	.15
(31)	Frank Viola	.15
(32)	Bob Welch	.15

Members Only

Each member of Topps Stadium Club during 1991 received three packages of multi-sport cards bearing a special design and stamped "Members Only" in gold foil on the front. Cards followed the basic Stadium Club format of full-bleed action photos on front. Backs have a facsimile newspaper page - the "Stadium Club Herald" - which gives details of a career highlight. Cards are unnumbered and the baseball-only checklist here is arranged alphabetically.

		NM/M
Complete Set (30):		9.00
Common Player:		.15
(1)	A.L. Home Run Leaders (Jose Canseco, Cecil Fielder)	.15
(2)	Wilson Alvarez	.15
(3)	Andy Ashby	.15
(4)	Jeff Bagwell	1.00
(5)	Braves no-hitter (Kent Mercker, Mark Wohlers, Alejandro Pena)	.15
(6)	Roger Clemens	.75
(7)	David Cone	.15
(8)	Carlton Fisk	.50
(9)	Julio Franco	.15
(10)	Tom Glavine	.35
(11)	Tommy Greene	.15
(12)	Pete Harnisch	.15
(13)	Rickey Henderson (All-time theft leader.)	.50
(14)	Rickey Henderson (11th time A.L. theft leader.)	.50
(15)	Howard Johnson	.15
(16)	Chuck Knoblauch	.15
(17)	Ray Lankford	.15
(18)	Denny Martinez	.15
(19)	Paul Molitor	.50
(20)	Jack Morris	.15
(21)	Orioles No-Hitter (Bob Milacki, Mike Flanagan, Mark Williamson, Gregg Olson, Chris Hoiles)	.15
(22)	Terry Pendleton (N.L. leading hitter)	.15
(23)	Terry Pendleton (MVP)	.15
(24)	Jeff Reardon	.15
(25)	Cal Ripken, Jr.	2.50
(26)	Nolan Ryan (7th no-hitter)	2.50
(27)	Nolan Ryan (22nd 100-K season)	2.50
(28)	Bret Saberhagen	.15
(29)	Robby Thompson	.15
(30)	Dave Winfield	.50

Nolan Ryan Bronze

One of the premiums included with charter membership in the Topps Stadium Club was a bronze replica of the Nolan Ryan card from the Charter Member's card set. The replica measures 2-1/2" x 3-1/2" and reproduces both front and back of the Ryan card on a 10-oz. metal slab.

	NM/M
Nolan Ryan (Bronze)	15.00

1992 Stadium Club

This 900-card set was released in three 100-card series. Like the 1991 issue, the cards feature borderless high-gloss photos on the front. The flip sides feature the player's first Topps card and a player evaluation. Topps released updated cards in the third series for traded player and free agents. Several players appear on two cards. Special Members Choice cards are included in the set. Series III features special inserts of the last three number one draft picks: Phil Nevin, Brien Taylor and Chipper Jones.

		NM/M
Complete Set (900):		20.00
Common Player:		.05
Series 1, 2, 3 Pack (15):		.75
Series 1, 2, 3 Box (36):		15.00
1	Cal Ripken, Jr.	1.50
2	Eric Yelding	.05
3	Geno Petralli	.05
4	Wally Backman	.05
5	Milt Cuyler	.05
6	Kevin Bass	.05
7	Dante Bichette	.05
8	Ray Lankford	.05
9	Mel Hall	.05
10	Joe Carter	.05
11	Juan Samuel	.05
12	Jeff Montgomery	.05
13	Glenn Braggs	.05
14	Henry Cotto	.05
15	Deion Sanders	.05
16	Dick Schofield	.05
17	David Cone	.05
18	Chili Davis	.05
19	Tom Foley	.05
20	Ozzie Guillen	.05
21	Luis Salazar	.05
22	Terry Steinbach	.05
23	Chris James	.05
24	Jeff King	.05
25	Carlos Quintana	.05
26	Mike Maddux	.05
27	Tommy Greene	.05
28	Jeff Russell	.05
29	Steve Finley	.05
30	Mike Flanagan	.05
31	Darren Lewis	.05
32	Mark Lee	.05
33	Willie Fraser	.05
34	Mike Henneman	.05
35	Kevin Maas	.05
36	Dave Hansen	.05
37	Erik Hanson	.05
38	Bill Doran	.05

39	Mike Boddicker	.05
40	Vince Coleman	.05
41	Devon White	.05
42	Mark Gardner	.05
43	Scott Lewis	.05
44	Juan Berenguer	.05
45	Carney Lansford	.05
46	Curt Wilkerson	.05
47	Shane Mack	.05
48	Bip Roberts	.05
49	Greg Harris	.05
50	Ryne Sandberg	.75
51	Mark Whiten	.05
52	Jack McDowell	.05
53	Jimmy Jones	.05
54	Steve Lake	.05
55	Bud Black	.05
56	Dave Valle	.05
57	Kevin Reimer	.05
58	Rich Gedman	.05
59	Travis Fryman	.05
60	Steve Avery	.05
61	Francisco de la Rosa	.05
62	Scott Hemond	.05
63	Hal Morris	.05
64	Hensley Meulens	.05
65	Frank Castillo	.05
66	Gene Larkin	.05
67	Jose DeLeon	.05
68	Al Osuna	.05
69	Dave Cochrane	.05
70	Robin Ventura	.05
71	John Cerutti	.05
72	Kevin Gross	.05
73	Ivan Calderon	.05
74	Mike Macfarlane	.05
75	Stan Belinda	.05
76	Shawn Hillegas	.05
77	Pat Borders	.05
78	Jim Vatcher	.05
79	Bobby Rose	.05
80	Roger Clemens	.85
81	Craig Worthington	.05
82	Jeff Treadway	.05
83	Jamie Quirk	.05
84	Randy Bush	.05
85	Anthony Young	.05
86	Trevor Wilson	.05
87	Jaime Navarro	.05
88	Les Lancaster	.05
89	Pat Kelly	.05
90	Alvin Davis	.05
91	Larry Andersen	.05
92	Rob Deer	.05
93	Mike Sharperson	.05
94	Lance Parrish	.05
95	Cecil Espy	.05
96	Tim Spehr	.05
97	Dave Stieb	.05
98	Terry Mulholland	.05
99	Dennis Boyd	.05
100	Barry Larkin	.05
101	Ryan Bowen	.05
102	Felix Fermin	.05
103	Luis Alicea	.05
104	Tim Hulett	.05
105	Rafael Belliard	.05
106	Mike Gallego	.05
107	Dave Righetti	.05
108	Jeff Schaefer	.05
109	Ricky Bones	.05
110	Scott Erickson	.05
111	Matt Nokes	.05
112	Bob Scanlan	.05
113	Tom Candiotti	.05
114	Sean Berry	.05
115	Kevin Morton	.05
116	Scott Fletcher	.05
117	B.J. Surhoff	.05
118	Dave Magadan	.05
119	Bill Gullickson	.05
120	Marquis Grissom	.05
121	Lenny Harris	.05
122	Wally Joyner	.05
123	Kevin Brown	.05
124	Braulio Castillo	.05
125	Eric King	.05
126	Mark Portugal	.05
127	Calvin Jones	.05
128	Mike Heath	.05
129	Todd Van Poppel	.05
130	Benny Santiago	.05
131	Gary Thurman	.05
132	Joe Girardi	.05
133	Dave Eiland	.05
134	Orlando Merced	.05
135	Joe Orsulak	.05
136	John Burkett	.05
137	Ken Dayley	.05
138	Ken Hill	.05
139	Walt Terrell	.05
140	Mike Scioscia	.05
141	Junior Felix	.05
142	Ken Caminiti	.05
143	Carlos Baerga	.05
144	Tony Fossas	.05
145	Craig Grebeck	.05
146	Scott Bradley	.05
147	Kent Mercker	.05
148	Derrick May	.05
149	Jerald Clark	.05
150	George Brett	.85
151	Luis Quinones	.05
152	Mike Pagliarulo	.05
153	Jose Guzman	.05
154	Charlie O'Brien	.05
155	Darren Holmes	.05
156	Joe Boever	.05

#	Player	$
157	Rich Monteleone	.05
158	Reggie Harris	.05
159	Roberto Alomar	.20
160	Robby Thompson	.05
161	Chris Hoiles	.05
162	Tom Pagnozzi	.05
163	Omar Vizquel	.05
164	John Candelaria	.05
165	Terry Shumpert	.05
166	Andy Mota	.05
167	Scott Bailes	.05
168	Jeff Blauser	.05
169	Steve Olin	.05
170	Doug Drabek	.05
171	Dave Bergman	.05
172	Eddie Whitson	.05
173	Gilberto Reyes	.05
174	Mark Grace	.05
175	Paul O'Neill	.05
176	Greg Cadaret	.05
177	Mark Williamson	.05
178	Casey Candaele	.05
179	Candy Maldonado	.05
180	Lee Smith	.05
181	Harold Reynolds	.05
182	Dave Justice	.05
183	Lenny Webster	.05
184	Donn Pall	.05
185	Gerald Alexander	.05
186	Jack Clark	.05
187	Stan Javier	.05
188	Ricky Jordan	.05
189	Franklin Stubbs	.05
190	Dennis Eckersley	.60
191	Danny Tartabull	.35
192	Pete O'Brien	.05
193	Mark Lewis	.05
194	Mike Felder	.05
195	Mickey Tettleton	.05
196	Dwight Smith	.05
197	Shawn Abner	.05
198	Jim Leyritz	.05
199	Mike Devereaux	.05
200	Craig Biggio	.05
201	Kevin Elster	.05
202	Rance Mulliniks	.05
203	Tony Fernandez	.05
204	Allan Anderson	.05
205	Herm Winningham	.05
206	Tim Jones	.05
207	Ramon Martinez	.05
208	Teddy Higuera	.05
209	John Kruk	.05
210	Jim Abbott	.05
211	Dean Palmer	.05
212	Mark Davis	.05
213	Jay Buhner	.05
214	Jesse Barfield	.05
215	Kevin Mitchell	.05
216	Mike LaValliere	.05
217	Mark Wohlers	.05
218	Dave Henderson	.05
219	Dave Smith	.05
220	Albert Belle	.05
221	Spike Owen	.05
222	Jeff Gray	.05
223	Paul Gibson	.05
224	Bobby Thigpen	.05
225	Mike Mussina	.30
226	Darrin Jackson	.05
227	Luis Gonzalez	.05
228	Greg Briley	.05
229	Brent Mayne	.05
230	Paul Molitor	.65
231	Al Leiter	.05
232	Andy Van Slyke	.05
233	Ron Tingley	.05
234	Bernard Gilkey	.05
235	Kent Hrbek	.05
236	Eric Karros	.05
237	Randy Velarde	.05
238	Andy Allanson	.05
239	Willie McGee	.05
240	Juan Gonzalez	.35
241	Karl Rhodes	.05
242	Luis Mercedes	.05
243	Billy Swift	.05
244	Tommy Gregg	.05
245	David Howard	.05
246	Dave Hollins	.05
247	Kip Gross	.05
248	Walt Weiss	.05
249	Mackey Sasser	.05
250	Cecil Fielder	.05
251	Jerry Browne	.05
252	Doug Dascenzo	.05
253	Darryl Hamilton	.05
254	Dann Bilardello	.05
255	Luis Rivera	.05
256	Larry Walker	.05
257	Ron Karkovice	.05
258	Bob Tewksbury	.05
259	Jimmy Key	.05
260	Bernie Williams	.05
261	Gary Wayne	.05
262	Mike Simms	.05
263	John Orton	.05
264	Marvin Freeman	.05
265	Mike Jeffcoat	.05
266	Roger Mason	.05
267	Edgar Martinez	.05
268	Henry Rodriguez	.05
269	Sam Horn	.05
270	Brian McRae	.05
271	Kirt Manwaring	.05
272	Mike Bordick	.05
273	Chris Sabo	.05
274	Jim Olander	.05
275	Greg Harris	.05
276	Dan Gakeler	.05
277	Bill Sampen	.05
278	Joel Skinner	.05
279	Curt Schilling	.35
280	Dale Murphy	.25
281	Lee Stevens	.05
282	Lonnie Smith	.05
283	Manuel Lee	.05
284	Shawn Boskie	.05
285	Kevin Seitzer	.05
286	Stan Royer	.05
287	John Dopson	.05
288	Scott Bullett	.05
289	Ken Patterson	.05
290	Todd Hundley	.05
291	Tim Leary	.05
292	Brett Butler	.05
293	Gregg Olson	.05
294	Jeff Brantley	.05
295	Brian Holman	.05
296	Brian Harper	.05
297	Brian Bohanon	.05
298	Checklist 1-100	.05
299	Checklist 101-200	.05
300	Checklist 201-300	.05
301	Frank Thomas	.65
302	Lloyd McClendon	.05
303	Brady Anderson	.05
304	Julio Valera	.05
305	Mike Aldrete	.05
306	Joe Oliver	.05
307	Todd Stottlemyre	.05
308	Rey Sanchez	.05
309	Gary Sheffield	.35
310	Andujar Cedeno	.05
311	Kenny Rogers	.05
312	Bruce Hurst	.05
313	Mike Schooler	.05
314	Mike Benjamin	.05
315	Chuck Finley	.05
316	Mark Lemke	.05
317	Scott Livingstone	.05
318	Chris Nabholz	.05
319	Mike Humphreys	.05
320	Pedro Guerrero	.05
321	Willie Banks	.05
322	Tom Goodwin	.05
323	Hector Wagner	.05
324	Wally Ritchie	.05
325	Mo Vaughn	.05
326	Joe Klink	.05
327	Cal Eldred	.05
328	Daryl Boston	.05
329	Mike Huff	.05
330	Jeff Bagwell	.65
331	Bob Milacki	.05
332	Tom Prince	.05
333	Pat Tabler	.05
334	Ced Landrum	.05
335	Reggie Jefferson	.05
336	Mo Sanford	.05
337	Kevin Ritz	.05
338	Gerald Perry	.05
339	Jeff Hamilton	.05
340	Tim Wallach	.05
341	Jeff Huson	.05
342	Jose Melendez	.05
343	Willie Wilson	.05
344	Mike Stanton	.05
345	Joel Johnston	.05
346	Lee Guetterman	.05
347	Francisco Olivares	.05
348	Dave Burba	.05
349	Tim Crews	.05
350	Scott Leius	.05
351	Danny Cox	.05
352	Wayne Housie	.05
353	Chris Donnels	.05
354	Chris George	.05
355	Gerald Young	.05
356	Roberto Hernandez	.05
357	Neal Heaton	.05
358	Todd Frohwirth	.05
359	Jose Vizcaino	.05
360	Jim Thome	.60
361	Craig Wilson	.05
362	Dave Haas	.05
363	Billy Hatcher	.05
364	John Barfield	.05
365	Luis Aquino	.05
366	Charlie Leibrandt	.05
367	Howard Farmer	.05
368	Bryn Smith	.05
369	Mickey Morandini	.05
370	Jose Canseco (Members Choice, should have been #597.)	.35
371	Jose Uribe	.05
372	Bob MacDonald	.05
373	Luis Sojo	.05
374	Craig Shipley	.05
375	Scott Bankhead	.05
376	Greg Gagne	.05
377	Scott Cooper	.05
378	Jose Offerman	.05
379	Billy Spiers	.05
380	John Smiley	.05
381	Jeff Carter	.05
382	Heathcliff Slocumb	.05
383	Jeff Tackett	.05
384	John Kiely	.05
385	John Vander Wal	.05
386	Omar Olivares	.05
387	Ruben Sierra	.05
388	Tom Gordon	.05
389	Charles Nagy	.05
390	Dave Stewart	.05
391	Pete Harnisch	.05
392	Tim Burke	.05
393	Roberto Kelly	.05
394	Freddie Benavides	.05
395	Tom Glavine	.35
396	Wes Chamberlain	.05
397	Eric Gunderson	.05
398	Dave West	.05
399	Ellis Burks	.05
400	Ken Griffey Jr.	1.00
401	Thomas Howard	.05
402	Juan Guzman	.05
403	Mitch Webster	.05
404	Matt Merullo	.05
405	Steve Buechele	.05
406	Danny Jackson	.05
407	Felix Jose	.05
408	Doug Piatt	.05
409	Jim Eisenreich	.05
410	Bryan Harvey	.05
411	Jim Austin	.05
412	Jim Poole	.05
413	Glenallen Hill	.05
414	Gene Nelson	.05
415	Ivan Rodriguez	.60
416	Frank Tanana	.05
417	Steve Decker	.05
418	Jason Grimsley	.05
419	Tim Layana	.05
420	Don Mattingly	.85
421	Jerome Walton	.05
422	Rob Ducey	.05
423	Andy Benes	.05
424	John Marzano	.05
425	Gene Harris	.05
426	Tim Raines	.05
427	Bret Barberie	.05
428	Harvey Pulliam	.05
429	Cris Carpenter	.05
430	Howard Johnson	.05
431	Orel Hershiser	.05
432	Brian Hunter	.05
433	Kevin Tapani	.05
434	Rick Reed	.05
435	Ron Witmeyer	.05
436	Gary Gaetti	.05
437	Alex Cole	.05
438	Chito Martinez	.05
439	Greg Litton	.05
440	Julio Franco	.05
441	Mike Munoz	.05
442	Erik Pappas	.05
443	Pat Combs	.05
444	Lance Johnson	.05
445	Ed Sprague	.05
446	Mike Greenwell	.05
447	Milt Thompson	.05
448	Mike Magnante	.05
449	Chris Haney	.05
450	Robin Yount	.65
451	Rafael Ramirez	.05
452	Gino Minutelli	.05
453	Tom Lampkin	.05
454	Tony Perezchica	.05
455	Dwight Gooden	.05
456	Mark Guthrie	.05
457	Jay Howell	.05
458	Gary DiSarcina	.05
459	John Smoltz	.05
460	Will Clark	.05
461	Dave Otto	.05
462	Rob Maurer	.05
463	Dwight Evans	.05
464	Tom Brunansky	.05
465	Shawn Hare RC	.05
466	Geronimo Pena	.05
467	Alex Fernandez	.05
468	Greg Myers	.05
469	Jeff Fassero	.05
470	Len Dykstra	.05
471	Jeff Johnson	.05
472	Russ Swan	.05
473	Archie Corbin	.05
474	Chuck McElroy	.05
475	Mark McGwire	1.25
476	Wally Whitehurst	.05
477	Tim McIntosh	.05
478	Sid Bream	.05
479	Jeff Juden	.05
480	Carlton Fisk	.65
481	Jeff Plympton	.05
482	Carlos Martinez	.05
483	Jim Gott	.05
484	Bob McClure	.05
485	Tim Teufel	.05
486	Vicente Palacios	.05
487	Jeff Reed	.05
488	Tony Phillips	.05
489	Mel Rojas	.05
490	Ben McDonald	.05
491	Andres Santana	.05
492	Chris Beasley	.05
493	Mike Timlin	.05
494	Brian Downing	.05
495	Kirk Gibson	.05
496	Scott Sanderson	.05
497	Nick Esasky	.05
498	Johnny Guzman RC	.05
499	Mitch Williams	.05
500	Kirby Puckett	.75
501	Mike Harkey	.05
502	Jim Gantner	.05
503	Bruce Egloff	.05
504	Josias Manzanillo	.05
505	Delino DeShields	.05
506	Rheal Cormier	.05
507	Jay Bell	.05
508	Rich Rowland	.05
509	Scott Servais	.05
510	Terry Pendleton (Members Choice)	.50
511	Rich DeLucia	.05
512	Warren Newson	.05
513	Paul Faries	.05
514	Kal Daniels	.05
515	Jarvis Brown	.05
516	Rafael Palmeiro	.60
517	Kelly Downs	.05
518	Steve Chitren	.05
519	Moises Alou	.05
520	Wade Boggs	.75
521	Pete Schourek	.05
522	Scott Terry	.05
523	Kevin Appier	.05
524	Gary Redus	.05
525	George Bell	.05
526	Jeff Kaiser	.05
527	Alvaro Espinoza	.05
528	Luis Polonia	.05
529	Darren Daulton	.05
530	Norm Charlton	.05
531	John Olerud	.05
532	Dan Plesac	.05
533	Billy Ripken	.05
534	Rod Nichols	.05
535	Joey Cora	.05
536	Harold Baines	.05
537	Bob Ojeda	.05
538	Mark Leonard	.05
539	Danny Darwin	.05
540	Shawon Dunston	.05
541	Pedro Munoz	.05
542	Mark Gubicza	.05
543	Kevin Baez	.05
544	Todd Zeile	.05
545	Don Slaught	.05
546	Tony Eusebio	.05
547	Alonzo Powell	.05
548	Gary Pettis	.05
549	Brian Barnes	.05
550	Lou Whitaker	.05
551	Keith Mitchell	.05
552	Oscar Azocar	.05
553	Stu Cole	.05
554	Steve Wapnick	.05
555	Derek Bell	.05
556	Luis Lopez	.05
557	Anthony Telford	.05
558	Tim Mauser	.05
559	Glenn Sutko	.05
560	Darryl Strawberry	.05
561	Tom Bolton	.05
562	Cliff Young	.05
563	Bruce Walton	.05
564	Chico Walker	.05
565	John Franco	.05
566	Paul McClellan	.05
567	Paul Abbott	.05
568	Gary Varsho	.05
569	Carlos Maldonado	.05
570	Kelly Gruber	.05
571	Jose Oquendo	.05
572	Steve Frey	.05
573	Tino Martinez	.05
574	Bill Haselman	.05
575	Eric Anthony	.05
576	John Habyan	.05
577	Jeffrey McNeely	.05
578	Chris Bosio	.05
579	Joe Grahe	.05
580	Fred McGriff	.05
581	Rick Honeycutt	.05
582	Matt Williams	.05
583	Cliff Brantley	.05
584	Rob Dibble	.05
585	Skeeter Barnes	.05
586	Greg Hibbard	.05
587	Randy Milligan	.05
588	Checklist 301-400	.05
589	Checklist 401-500	.05
590	Checklist 501-600	.05
591	Frank Thomas (Members Choice)	.35
592	Dave Justice (Members Choice)	.05
593	Roger Clemens (Members Choice)	.45
594	Steve Avery (Members Choice)	.05
595	Cal Ripken, Jr. (Members Choice)	.75
596	Barry Larkin (Members Choice)	.05
597	Not issued (See #370)	.05
598	Will Clark (Members Choice)	.05
599	Cecil Fielder (Members Choice)	.05
600	Ryne Sandberg (Members Choice)	.40
601	Chuck Knoblauch (Members Choice)	.05
602	Dwight Gooden (Members Choice)	.05
603	Ken Griffey Jr. (Members Choice)	.65
604	Barry Bonds (Members Choice)	.75
605	Nolan Ryan (Members Choice)	.75
606	Jeff Bagwell (Members Choice)	.35
607	Robin Yount (Members Choice)	.30
608	Bobby Bonilla (Members Choice)	.05
609	George Brett (Members Choice)	.50
610	Howard Johnson (Members Choice)	.05
611	Esteban Beltre	.05
612	Mike Christopher	.05
613	Troy Afenir	.05
614	Mariano Duncan	.05
615	Doug Henry	.05
616	Doug Jones	.05
617	Alvin Davis	.05
618	Craig Lefferts	.05
619	Kevin McReynolds	.05
620	Barry Bonds	1.50
621	Turner Ward	.05
622	Joe Magrane	.05
623	Mark Parent	.05
624	Tom Browning	.05
625	John Smiley	.05
626	Steve Wilson	.05
627	Mike Gallego	.05
628	Sammy Sosa	.75
629	Rico Rossy	.05
630	Royce Clayton	.05
631	Clay Parker	.05
632	Pete Smith	.05
633	Jeff McKnight	.05
634	Jack Daugherty	.05
635	Steve Sax	.05
636	Joe Hesketh	.05
637	Vince Horsman	.05
638	Eric King	.05
639	Joe Boever	.05
640	Jack Morris	.05
641	Arthur Rhodes	.05
642	Bob Melvin	.05
643	Rick Wilkins	.05
644	Scott Scudder	.05
645	Bip Roberts	.05
646	Julio Valera	.05
647	Kevin Campbell	.05
648	Steve Searcy	.05
649	Scott Kamieniecki	.05
650	Kurt Stillwell	.05
651	Bob Welch	.05
652	Andres Galarraga	.05
653	Mike Jackson	.05
654	Bo Jackson	.10
655	Sid Fernandez	.05
656	Mike Bielecki	.05
657	Jeff Reardon	.05
658	Wayne Rosenthal	.05
659	Eric Bullock	.05
660	Eric Davis	.05
661	Randy Tomlin	.05
662	Tom Edens	.05
663	Rob Murphy	.05
664	Leo Gomez	.05
665	Greg Maddux	.75
666	Greg Vaughn	.05
667	Wade Taylor	.05
668	Brad Arnsberg	.05
669	Mike Moore	.05
670	Mark Langston	.05
671	Barry Jones	.05
672	Bill Landrum	.05
673	Greg Swindell	.05
674	Wayne Edwards	.05
675	Greg Olson	.05
676	Bill Pulsipher RC	.05
677	Bobby Witt	.05
678	Mark Carreon	.05
679	Patrick Lennon	.05
680	Ozzie Smith	.75
681	John Briscoe	.05
682	Matt Young	.05
683	Jeff Conine	.05
684	Phil Stephenson	.05
685	Ron Darling	.05
686	Bryan Hickerson	.05
687	Dale Sveum	.05
688	Kirk McCaskill	.05
689	Rich Amaral	.05
690	Danny Tartabull	.05
691	Donald Harris	.05
692	Doug Davis	.05
693	John Farrell	.05
694	Paul Gibson	.05
695	Kenny Lofton	.05
696	Mike Fetters	.05
697	Rosario Rodriguez	.05
698	Chris Jones	.05
699	Jeff Manto	.05
700	Rick Sutcliffe	.05
701	Scott Bankhead	.05
702	Donnie Hill	.05
703	Todd Worrell	.05
704	Rene Gonzales	.05
705	Rick Cerone	.05
706	Tony Pena	.05
707	Paul Sorrento	.05
708	Gary Scott	.05
709	Junior Noboa	.05
710	Wally Joyner	.05
711	Charlie Hayes	.05
712	Rich Rodriguez	.05
713	Rudy Seanez	.05
714	Jim Bullinger	.05
715	Jeff Robinson	.05
716	Jeff Robinson	.05
717	Andy Ashby	.05
718	Dave Burba	.05
719	Rich Gossage	.05
720	Randy Johnson	.65
721	David Wells	.05
722	Paul Kilgus	.05
723	Dave Martinez	.05
724	Denny Neagle	.05
725	Andy Stankiewicz	.05
726	Rick Aguilera	.05
727	Junior Ortiz	.05
728	Storm Davis	.05
729	Don Robinson	.05
730	Ron Gant	.05
731	Paul Assenmacher	.05
732	Mark Gardiner	.05
733	Milt Hill	.05
734	Jeremy Hernandez	.05
735	Ken Hill	.05
736	Xavier Hernandez	.05
737	Gregg Jefferies	.05
738	Dick Schofield	.05
739	Ron Robinson	.05
740	Sandy Alomar	.05
741	Mike Stanley	.05
742	Butch Henry	.05
743	Floyd Bannister	.05
744	Brian Drahman	.05
745	Dave Winfield	.65
746	Bob Walk	.05
747	Chris James	.05
748	Don Prybylinski	.05
749	Dennis Rasmussen	.05
750	Rickey Henderson	.65
751	Chris Hammond	.05
752	Bob Kipper	.05
753	Dave Rohde	.05
754	Hubie Brooks	.05
755	Bret Saberhagen	.05
756	Jeff Robinson	.05
757	Pat Listach RC	.05
758	Bill Wegman	.05
759	John Wetteland	.05
760	Phil Plantier	.05
761	Wilson Alvarez	.05
762	Scott Aldred	.05
763	Armando Reynoso RC	.05
764	Todd Benzinger	.05
765	Kevin Mitchell	.05
766	Gary Sheffield	.35
767	Allan Anderson	.05
768	Rusty Meacham	.05
769	Rick Parker	.05
770	Nolan Ryan	1.50
771	Jeff Ballard	.05
772	Cory Snyder	.05
773	Denis Boucher	.05
774	Jose Gonzales	.05
775	Juan Guerrero	.05
776	Ed Nunez	.05
777	Scott Ruskin	.05
778	Terry Leach	.05
779	Carl Willis	.05
780	Bobby Bonilla	.05
781	Duane Ward	.05
782	Joe Slusarski	.05
783	David Segui	.05
784	Kirk Gibson	.05
785	Frank Viola	.05
786	Keith Miller	.05
787	Mike Morgan	.05
788	Kim Batiste	.05
789	Sergio Valdez	.05
790	Eddie Taubensee	.05
791	Jack Armstrong	.05
792	Scott Fletcher	.05
793	Steve Farr	.05
794	Dan Pasqua	.05
795	Eddie Murray	.65
796	John Morris	.05
797	Francisco Cabrera	.05
798	Mike Perez	.05
799	Ted Wood	.05
800	Jose Rijo	.05
801	Danny Gladden	.05
802	Arci Cianfrocco	.05
803	Monty Fariss	.05
804	Roger McDowell	.05
805	Randy Myers	.05
806	Kirk Dressendorfer	.05
807	Zane Smith	.05
808	Glenn Davis	.05
809	Torey Lovullo	.05
810	Andre Dawson	.25
811	Bill Pecota	.05
812	Ted Power	.05
813	Willie Blair	.05
814	Dave Fleming	.05
815	Chris Gwynn	.05
816	Jody Reed	.05
817	Mark Dewey	.05
818	Kyle Abbott	.05
819	Tom Henke	.05
820	Kevin Seitzer	.05
821	Al Newman	.05
822	Tim Sherrill	.05
823	Chuck Crim	.05
824	Darren Reed	.05
825	Tony Gwynn	.75
826	Steve Foster	.05
827	Steve Howe	.05
828	Brook Jacoby	.05
829	Rodney McCray	.05
830	Chuck Knoblauch	.05
831	John Wehner	.05
832	Scott Garrelts	.05
833	Alejandro Pena	.05
834	Jeff Parrett	.05
835	Juan Bell	.05
836	Lance Dickson	.05
837	Darryl Kile	.05
838	Efrain Valdez	.05
839	Bob Zupcic RC	.05
840	George Bell	.05
841	Dave Gallagher	.05
842	Tim Belcher	.05

843	Jeff Shaw	.05
844	Mike Fitzgerald	.05
845	Gary Carter	.65
846	John Russell	.05
847	Eric Hillman RC	.05
848	Mike Witt	.05
849	Curt Wilkerson	.05
850	Alan Trammell	.05
851	Rex Hudler	.05
852	Michael Walkden RC	.05
853	Kevin Ward	.05
854	Tim Naehring	.05
855	Bill Swift	.05
856	Damon Berryhill	.05
857	Mark Eichhorn	.05
858	Hector Villanueva	.05
859	Jose Lind	.05
860	Denny Martinez	.05
861	Bill Krueger	.05
862	Mike Kingery	.05
863	Jeff Innis	.05
864	Derek Lilliquist	.05
865	Reggie Sanders	.05
866	Ramon Garcia	.05
867	Bruce Ruffin	.05
868	Dickie Thon	.05
869	Melido Perez	.05
870	Ruben Amaro	.05
871	Alan Mills	.05
872	Matt Sinatro	.05
873	Eddie Zosky	.05
874	Pete Incaviglia	.05
875	Tom Candiotti	.05
876	Bob Patterson	.05
877	Neal Heaton	.05
878	Terrel Hansen RC	.05
879	Dave Eiland	.05
880	Von Hayes	.05
881	Tim Scott	.05
882	Otis Nixon	.05
883	Herm Winningham	.05
884	Dion James	.05
885	Dave Wainhouse	.05
886	Frank DiPino	.05
887	Dennis Cook	.05
888	Jose Mesa	.05
889	Mark Leiter	.05
890	Willie Randolph	.05
891	Craig Colbert	.05
892	Dwayne Henry	.05
893	Jim Lindeman	.05
894	Charlie Hough	.05
895	Gil Heredia	.05
896	Scott Chiamparino	.05
897	Lance Blankenship	.05
898	Checklist 601-700	.05
899	Checklist 701-800	.05
900	Checklist 801-900	.05

First Draft Picks

Issued as inserts with Stadium Club Series 3, this three-card set features the No. 1 draft picks of 1990-92. Fronts have a full-bleed photo with S.C. logo and player name in the lower-right corner. At bottom-left in a red strip is a gold-foil stamping, "#1 Draft Pick of the '90's." An orange circle at upper-right has the year the player was the No. 1 choice. The basic red-and-black back has a color photo, a few biographical and draft details and a gold facsimile autograph among other gold-foil highlights.

		NM/M
Complete Set (3):		4.50
Common Player:		.25
1	Chipper Jones	4.00
2	Brien Taylor	.25
3	Phil Nevin	.25

Master Photos

Uncropped versions of the photos which appear on regular Stadium Club cards are featured on these large-format (5" x 7") cards. The photos are set against a white [bac]kground and trimmed with ho- [lo]graphic foil. Backs are blank and [the] cards are unnumbered. Mem- [bers] of Topps' Stadium Club re- [ceive]d a Master Photo in their

members' packs for 1992. The cards were also available as inserts in special boxes of Stadium Club cards sold at Wal-Mart stores.

		NM/M
Complete Set (15):		20.00
Common Player:		.50
(1)	Wade Boggs	2.25
(2)	Barry Bonds	4.00
(3)	Jose Canseco	1.00
(4)	Will Clark	.50
(5)	Cecil Fielder	.50
(6)	Dwight Gooden	.50
(7)	Ken Griffey Jr.	3.00
(8)	Rickey Henderson	2.00
(9)	Lance Johnson	.50
(10)	Cal Ripken, Jr.	4.00
(11)	Nolan Ryan	4.00
(12)	Deion Sanders	.50
(13)	Darryl Strawberry	.50
(14)	Danny Tartabull	.50
(15)	Frank Thomas	2.00

East Coast National

In conjunction with its appearance at the August 1992 East Coast National card show, Topps distributed 22,000 five-card cello packs of its 1992 Stadium Club series bearing a special gold-foil show commemorative overprint. The cards are in all other respects identical to regular issue '92 S.C. Only 100 cards from Series III can be found with the overprint. Production of each card thus totals 1,100.

		NM/M
Complete Set (100):		40.00
Common Player:		.60
601	Chuck Knoblauch	.60
602	Dwight Gooden	.60
603	Ken Griffey Jr.	6.00
604	Barry Bonds	6.50
605	Nolan Ryan	7.50
606	Jeff Bagwell	2.50
607	Robin Yount	2.50
608	Bobby Bonilla	.60
609	George Brett	5.50
610	Howard Johnson	.60
611	Esteban Beltre	.60
612	Mike Christopher	.60
613	Troy Afenir	.60
619	Kevin McReynolds	.60
620	Barry Bonds	7.50
622	Joe Magrane	.60
623	Mark Parent	.60
626	Steve Wilson	.60
629	Rico Rossy	.60
630	Clay Parker	.60
633	Jeff McKnight	.60
637	Vince Horsman	.60
638	Eric King	.60
639	Joe Boever	.60
642	Arthur Rhodes	.60
647	Kevin Campbell	.60

653	Mike Jackson	.60
661	Randy Tomlin	.60
665	Greg Maddux	3.00
668	Brad Arnsberg	.60
671	Barry Jones	.60
672	Bill Landrum	.60
673	Greg Swindell	.60
676	Bill Pulsipher	.60
679	Patrick Lennon	.60
681	John Briscoe	.60
684	Phil Stephenson	.60
685	Ron Darling	.60
686	Bryan Hickerson	.60
688	Kirk McCaskill	.60
689	Rich Amaral	.60
692	Doug Davis	.60
693	John Farrell	.60
700	Rick Sutcliffe	.60
704	Rene Gonzalez	.60
713	Rudy Seanez	.60
714	Jim Bullinger	.60
716	Jeff Branson	.60
717	Andy Ashby	.60
725	Andy Stankiewicz	.60
733	Milt Hill	.60
739	Ron Robinson	.60
742	Butch Henry	.60
747	Chris James	.60
749	Dennis Rasmussen	.60
753	Dave Rohde	.60
757	Pat Listach	.60
758	Bill Wegman	.60
762	Armando Reynoso	.60
765	Kevin Mitchell	.60
766	Gary Sheffield	.90
769	Rick Parker	.60
771	Jeff Ballard	.60
772	Cory Snyder	.60
774	Jose Gonzalez	.60
776	Juan Guerrero	.60
776	Edwin Nunez	.60
777	Terry Leach	.60
782	Joe Slusarski	.60
784	Kirk Gibson	.60
788	Kim Batiste	.60
802	Arci Cianfrocco	.60
806	Kirk Dressendorfer	.60
807	Zane Smith	.60
814	Dave Fleming	.60
815	Chris Gwynn	.60
817	Mark Dewey	.60
819	Tom Henke	.60
822	Tim Sherrill	.60
826	Steve Foster	.60
831	John Wehner	.60
832	Scott Garrelts	.60
840	George Bell	.60
841	Dave Gallagher	.60
846	John Russell	.60
847	Eric Hillman	.60
852	Michael Walkden	.60
855	Bill Swift	.60
876	Derek Lilliquist	.60
876	Bob Patterson	.60
878	Terrel Hansen	.60
881	Tim Scott	.60
886	Frank DiPino	.60
891	Craig Colbert	.60
892	Dwayne Henry	.60
893	Jim Lindeman	.60
895	Gil Heredia	.60
898	Checklist 601-700	.05
899	Checklist 701-800	.05
900	Checklist 801-900	.05

National Convention

To promote its Stadium Club baseball card brand to dealers, Topps distributed sample cards during the National Sports Collectors Convention in Atlanta, Ga. The sample cards are regular-issue S.C. cards which have received a gold-foil overprint of the 1992 National logo. Only 100 cards from the third series can be found with the overprint. Only 5,000 four-card packs were distributed, thus only 200 of each card were made.

		NM/M
Complete Set (100):		135.00
Common Player:		1.50
616	Doug Jones	1.50
618	Alvin Davis	1.50
618	Craig Lefferts	1.50
621	Turner Ward	1.50
624	John Smiley	1.50
627	Mike Gallego	1.50
631	Royce Clayton	1.50
634	Jack Daugherty	1.50
635	Steve Sax	1.50
636	Joe Hesketh	1.50
643	Rick Wilkins	1.50
643	Scott Scudder	1.50
645	Bip Roberts	1.50

650	Kurt Stillwell	1.50
652	Andres Galarraga	1.50
657	Jeff Reardon	1.50
660	Eric Davis	1.50
675	Tom Edens	1.50
675	Greg Olson	1.50
677	Mark Carreon	1.50
680	Ozzie Smith	15.00
682	Matt Young	1.50
690	Danny Tartabull	1.50
691	Donald Harris	1.50
695	Kenny Lofton	1.50
697	Rosario Rodriguez	1.50
705	Scott Bankhead	1.50
705	Rick Cerone	1.50
708	Tony Pena	1.50
709	Junior Noboa	1.50
710	Wally Joyner	1.50
711	Charlie Hayes	1.50
712	Rich Rodriguez	1.50
723	David Wells	1.50
724	Dave Martinez	1.50
726	Rick Aguilera	1.50
728	Junior Ortiz	1.50
729	Don Robinson	1.50
730	Ron Gant	1.50
731	Paul Assenmacher	1.50
732	Mark Gardiner	1.50
735	Ken Hill	1.50
736	Xavier Hernandez	1.50
737	Gregg Jefferies	1.50
740	Sandy Alomar, Jr.	1.50
741	Mike Stanley	1.50
744	Brian Drahman	1.50
745	Bob Walk	1.50
751	Chris Hammond	1.50
759	John Wetteland	1.50
760	Phil Plantier	1.50
761	Wilson Alvarez	1.50
773	Denis Boucher	1.50
777	Scott Ruskin	1.50
779	Carl Willis	1.50
783	David Segui	1.50
786	Keith Miller	1.50
790	Eddie Taubensee	1.50
792	Jack Armstrong	1.50
792	Scott Fletcher	1.50
793	Steve Farr	1.50
794	Dan Pasqua	1.50
797	Francisco Cabrera	1.50
798	Mike Perez	1.50
801	Danny Gladden	1.50
803	Monty Fariss	1.50
804	Roger McDowell	1.50
805	Randy Myers	1.50
808	Glenn Davis	1.50
809	Torey Lovullo	1.50
816	Jody Reed	1.50
825	Tony Gwynn	15.00
827	Steve Howe	1.50
828	Brook Jacoby	1.50
829	Rodney McCray	1.50
830	Chuck Knoblauch	1.50
835	Juan Bell	1.50
836	Lance Dickson	1.50
837	Darryl Kile	1.50
842	Tim Belcher	1.50
843	Jeff Shaw	1.50
844	Mike Fitzgerald	1.50
845	Gary Carter	6.00
851	Rex Hudler	1.50
856	Damon Berryhill	1.50
857	Mark Eichhorn	1.50
858	Hector Villanueva	1.50
860	Denny Martinez	1.50
865	Reggie Sanders	1.50
869	Melido Perez	1.50
874	Pete Incaviglia	1.50
875	Tom Candiotti	1.50
877	Neal Heaton	1.50
879	Dave Eiland	1.50
882	Otis Nixon	1.50
883	Herm Winningham	1.50
884	Dion James	1.50
887	Dennis Cook	1.50
894	Charlie Hough	1.50

Members Only

A multi-sport set of 50 cards was sent in four installments to members of Topps' Stadium Club as part of their 1992 benefits package. Cards are similar in format to regular Stadium Club cards, 2-1/2" x 3-1/2", UV coated on front. Fronts

have a special gold foil "Members Only" logo on front. Backs have a stadium scoreboard design with details of a career highlight. The un-numbered cards (baseball only) are checklisted here alphabetically.

		NM/M
Complete Set (36):		18.00
Common Player:		.15
(1)	Carlos Baerga	.15
(2)	Wade Boggs	1.00
(3)	Barry Bonds	2.50
(4)	Bret Boone	.15
(5)	Pat Borders	.15
(6)	George Brett	1.00
(7)	George Brett (3,000 hits)	1.00
(8)	Jim Bullinger	.15
(9)	Gary Carter	.75
(10)	Andujar Cedeno	.15
(11)	Roger Clemens, Matt Young	.45
(12)	Dennis Eckersley (Cy Young Award)	.60
(13)	Dennis Eckersley (MVP)	.60
(14)	Dave Eiland	.15
(15)	Dwight Gooden, Gary Sheffield	.25
(16)	Ken Griffey Jr.	1.50
(17)	Kevin Gross	.15
(18)	Bo Jackson	.25
(19)	Eric Karros	.15
(20)	Pat Listach	.15
(21)	Greg Maddux	1.00
(22)	Fred McGriff, Gary Sheffield	.25
(23)	Mickey Morandini	.15
(24)	Jack Morris	.15
(25)	Eddie Murray	.75
(26)	Eddie Murray	.75
(27)	Bip Roberts	.15
(28)	Nolan Ryan (27 seasons)	2.50
(29)	Nolan Ryan (1993 finale)	2.50
(30)	Lee Smith	.15
(31)	Ozzie Smith (2,000 hits)	1.00
(32)	Ozzie Smith (7,000 assists)	1.00
(33)	Ozzie Smith (Stolen base record.)	1.00
(34)	Bobby Thigpen	.15
(35)	Dave Winfield	.75
(36)	Robin Yount	.75

1992 Stadium Club SkyDome

This 200-card special Stadium Club set from Topps was uniquely packaged in a plastic replica of the Toronto SkyDome, the home of the 1991 All-Star Game. Featured in the set are members of Team USA, All-Stars, draft picks, top prospects and eight cards from the World Series between the Twins and Braves. The cards are styled much like the regular Stadium Club cards. Some cards have been found with incorrect gold-foil identifiers as well as the correct version.

		NM/M
Unopened Factory Set (200):		15.00
Complete Set (200):		10.00
Common Player:		.05
1	Terry Adams RC	.05
2	Tommy Adams	.05
3	Rick Aguilera	.05
4	Ron Allen	.05
5	Roberto Alomar/AS	.20
6	Sandy Alomar	.05
7	Greg Anthony	.05
8	James Austin	.05
9	Steve Avery	.05
10	Harold Baines	.05
11	Brian Barber RC	.05
12	Jon Barnes	.05
13	George Bell	.05
14	Doug Bennett	.05
15	Sean Bergman	.05
16	Craig Biggio	.05
17	Bill Bliss	.05
18	Wade Boggs/AS	.60
19	Bobby Bonilla/AS	.05
20	Russell Brock	.05
21	Tarrik Brock	.05
22	Tom Browning	.05
23	Brett Butler	.05

24	Ivan Calderon	.05
25	Joe Carter	.05
26	Joe Caruso	.05
27	Dan Cholowsky	.05
28	Will Clark/AS	.05
29	Roger Clemens/AS	.65
30	Shawn Curran	.05
31	Chris Curtis	.05
32	Chili Davis	.05
33	Andre Dawson	.25
34	Joe DeBerry	.05
35	John Dettmer	.05
36	Rob Dibble	.05
37	John Donati RC	.05
38	Dave Doorneweerd	.05
39	Darren Dreifort	.05
40	Mike Durant	.05
41	Chris Durkin	.05
42	Dennis Eckersley	.40
43	Brian Edmondson RC	.05
44	Vaughn Eshelman RC	.05
45	Shawn Estes RC	.50
46	Jorge Fabregas RC	.10
47	Jon Farrell	.05
48	Cecil Fielder/AS	.05
49	Carlton Fisk	.50
50	Tim Flannelly	.05
51	Cliff Floyd RC	.50
52	Julio Franco	.05
53	Greg Gagne	.05
54	Chris Gambs RC	.05
55	Ron Gant	.05
56	Brent Gates	.05
57	Dwayne Gerald	.05
58	Jason Giambi	1.50
59	Benji Gil RC	.05
60	Mark Gipner	.05
61	Danny Gladden	.05
62	Tom Glavine	.35
63	Jimmy Gonzalez	.05
64	Jeff Granger	.05
65	Dan Grapenthien	.05
66	Dennis Gray	.05
67	Shawn Green RC	2.00
68	Tyler Green	.05
69	Todd Greene	.05
70	Ken Griffey Jr./AS	.75
71	Kelly Gruber	.05
72	Ozzie Guillen	.05
73	Tony Gwynn/AS	.60
74	Shane Halter	.05
75	Jeffrey Hammonds	.05
76	Larry Hanlon	.05
77	Pete Harnisch	.05
78	Mike Harrison	.05
79	Bryan Harvey	.05
80	Scott Hatteberg	.05
81	Rick Helling	.05
82	Dave Henderson	.05
83	Rickey Henderson/AS	.50
84	Tyrone Hill	.05
85	Todd Hollandsworth RC	.10
86	Brian Holliday	.05
87	Terry Horn	.05
88	Jeff Hostetler	.05
89	Kent Hrbek	.05
90	Mark Hubbard	.05
91	Charles Johnson	.05
92	Howard Johnson	.05
93	Todd Johnson	.05
94	Bobby Jones RC	.10
95	Dan Jones	.05
96	Felix Jose	.05
97	Dave Justice	.05
98	Jimmy Key	.05
99	Marc Kroom RC	.05
100	John Kruk	.05
101	Mark Langston	.05
102	Barry Larkin	.05
103	Mike LaValliere	.05
104a	Scott Leius (1991 N.L. All-Star - Error)	
104b	Scott Leius (1991 World Series - Correct)	.25
105	Mark Lemke	.05
106	Donnie Leshnock	.05
107	Jimmy Lewis	.05
108	Shawn Livesy	.05
109	Ryan Long	.05
110	Trevor Mallory	.05
111	Denny Martinez	.05
112	Justin Mashore	.05
113	Jason McDonald	.05
114	Jack McDowell	.05
115	Tom McKinnon	.05
116	Billy McKinnon	.05
117	Buck McNabb RC	.05
118	Jim Mecir	.05
119	Dan Melendez	.05
120	Shawn Miller RC	.05
121	Trever Miller	.05
122	Paul Molitor	.50
123	Vincent Moore	.05
124	Mike Morgan	.05
125	Jack Morris (World Series)	.05
126	Jack Morris/AS	.05
127	Sean Mulligan	.05
128	Eddie Murray	.50
129	Mike Neill	.05
130	Phil Nevin	.05
131	Mark O'Brien	.05
132	Alex Ochoa RC	.05
133	Chad Ogea RC	.05
134	Greg Olson	.05
135	Paul O'Neill	.05
136a	Jared Osentowski (1991 World Series - Error)	.05

No.	Player	Price
136b	Jared Osentowski (Draft Pick - Correct)	.25
137	Mike Pagliarulo	.05
138	Rafael Palmeiro	.40
139	Rodney Pedraza	.05
140	Tony Phillips	.05
141	Scott Pisciotta RC	.05
142	Chris Pritchett	.05
143	Jason Pruitt	.05
144a	Kirby Puckett (1991 N.L. All-Star - Error)	.60
144b	Kirby Puckett (1991 World Series - Correct)	3.00
145	Kirby Puckett/AS	.60
146	Manny Ramirez RC	5.00
147	Eddie Ramos	.05
148	Mark Ratekin	.05
149	Jeff Reardon	.05
150	Sean Rees	.05
151	Calvin Reese RC	.50
152	Desmond Relaford RC	.10
153	Eric Richardson	.05
154	Cal Ripken, Jr./AS	1.50
155	Chris Roberts	.05
156	Mike Robertson	.05
157	Steve Rodriguez	.05
158	Mike Rossiter	.05
159	Scott Ruffcorn	.05
160a	Chris Sabo (1991 World Series - Error)	.05
160b	Chris Sabo (1991 N.L. All-Star - Correct)	.25
161	Juan Samuel	.05
162	Ryne Sandberg/AS	.60
163	Scott Sanderson	.05
164	Benito Santiago	.05
165	Gene Schall RC	.05
166	Chad Schoenvogel	.05
167	Chris Seelbach RC	.05
168	Aaron Sele RC	.50
169	Basil Shabazz	.05
170	Al Shirley RC	.05
171	Paul Shuey	.05
172	Ruben Sierra	.05
173	John Smiley	.05
174	Lee Smith	.05
175	Ozzie Smith	.60
176	Tim Smith	.05
177	Zane Smith	.05
178	John Smoltz	.05
179	Scott Stahoviak	.05
180	Kennie Steenstra	.05
181	Kevin Stocker	.05
182	Chris Stynes RC	.05
183	Danny Tartabull	.05
184	Brien Taylor	.05
185	Todd Taylor	.05
186	Larry Thomas	.05
187a	Ozzie Timmons RC	.05
187b	David Tuttle (Should be #188.)	.05
188	Not issued	.05
189	Andy Van Slyke	.05
190a	Frank Viola (1991 World Series - Error)	.05
190b	Frank Viola (1991 N.L. All-Star - Correct)	.25
191	Michael Walkden	.05
192	Jeff Ware	.05
193	Allen Watson RC	.05
194	Steve Whitaker	.05
195a	Jerry Willard (1991 Draft Pick - Error)	.05
195b	Jerry Willard (1991 World Series - Correct)	.25
196	Craig Wilson	.05
197	Chris Wimmer	.05
198	Steve Wojciechowski RC	.05
199	Joel Wolfe	.05
200	Ivan Zweig	.05

1993 Stadium Club

JEFF BAGWELL

Topps' premium set for 1993 was issued in three series, two 300-card series and a final series of 150. Boxes contained 24 packs this year, compared to 36 in the past. Packs had 14 cards and an insert card. Each box had a 5" x 7" Master Photo card.

	NM/M
Complete Set (750):	25.00
Common Player:	.05
First Day:	8X
Pack (15):	.75
Wax Box (24):	10.00

No.	Player	Price
1	Pat Borders	.05
2	Greg Maddux	.85
3	Daryl Boston	.05
4	Bob Ayrault	.05
5	Tony Phillips	.05
6	Damion Easley	.05
7	Kip Gross	.05
8	Jim Thome	.65
9	Tim Belcher	.05
10	Gary Wayne	.05
11	Sam Militello	.05
12	Mike Magnante	.05
13	Tim Wakefield	.05
14	Tim Hulett	.05
15	Rheal Cormier	.05
16	Juan Guerrero	.05
17	Rich Gossage	.05
18	Tim Laker	.05
19	Darrin Jackson	.05
20	Jack Clark	.05
21	Roberto Hernandez	.05
22	Dean Palmer	.05
23	Harold Reynolds	.05
24	Dan Plesac	.05
25	Brent Mayne	.05
26	Pat Hentgen	.05
27	Luis Sojo	.05
28	Ron Gant	.05
29	Paul Gibson	.05
30	Bip Roberts	.05
31	Mickey Tettleton	.05
32	Randy Velarde	.05
33	Brian McRae	.05
34	Wes Chamberlain	.05
35	Wayne Kirby	.05
36	Rey Sanchez	.05
37	Jesse Orosco	.05
38	Mike Stanton	.05
39	Royce Clayton	.05
40	Cal Ripken, Jr.	2.50
41	John Dopson	.05
42	Gene Larkin	.05
43	Tim Raines	.05
44	Randy Myers	.05
45	Clay Parker	.05
46	Mike Scioscia	.05
47	Pete Incaviglia	.05
48	Todd Van Poppel	.05
49	Ray Lankford	.05
50	Eddie Murray	.75
51	Barry Bonds	2.50
52	Gary Thurman	.05
53	Bob Wickman	.05
54	Joey Cora	.05
55	Kenny Rogers	.05
56	Mike Devereaux	.05
57	Kevin Seitzer	.05
58	Rafael Belliard	.05
59	David Wells	.05
60	Mark Clark	.05
61	Carlos Baerga	.05
62	Scott Brosius	.05
63	Jeff Grotewold	.05
64	Rick Wrona	.05
65	Kurt Knudsen	.05
66	Lloyd McClendon	.05
67	Omar Vizquel	.05
68	Jose Vizcaino	.05
69	Rob Ducey	.05
70	Casey Candaele	.05
71	Ramon Martinez	.05
72	Todd Hundley	.05
73	John Marzano	.05
74	Derek Parks	.05
75	Jack McDowell	.05
76	Tim Scott	.05
77	Mike Mussina	.40
78	Delino DeShields	.05
79	Chris Bosio	.05
80	Mike Bordick	.05
81	Rod Beck	.05
82	Ted Power	.05
83	John Kruk	.05
84	Steve Shifflett	.05
85	Danny Tartabull	.05
86	Mike Greenwell	.05
87	Jose Melendez	.05
88	Craig Wilson	.05
89	Melvin Nieves	.05
90	Ed Sprague	.05
91	Willie McGee	.05
92	Joe Orsulak	.05
93	Jeff King	.05
94	Dan Pasqua	.05
95	Brian Harper	.05
96	Joe Oliver	.05
97	Shane Turner	.05
98	Lenny Harris	.05
99	Jeff Parrett	.05
100	Luis Polonia	.05
101	Kent Bottenfield	.05
102	Albert Belle	.05
103	Mike Maddux	.05
104	Randy Tomlin	.05
105	Andy Stankiewicz	.05
106	Rico Rossy	.05
107	Joe Hesketh	.05
108	Dennis Powell	.05
109	Derrick May	.05
110	Pete Harnisch	.05
111	Kent Mercker	.05
112	Scott Fletcher	.05
113	Rex Hudler	.05
114	Chico Walker	.05
115	Rafael Palmeiro	.65
116	Mark Leiter	.05
117	Pedro Munoz	.05
118	Jim Bullinger	.05
119	Ivan Calderon	.05
120	Mike Timlin	.05
121	Rene Gonzales	.05
122	Greg Vaughn	.05
123	Mike Flanagan	.05
124	Mike Hartley	.05
125	Jeff Montgomery	.05
126	Mike Gallego	.05
127	Don Slaught	.05
128	Charlie O'Brien	.05
129a	Jose Offerman (Home: (Blank))	2.00
129b	Jose Offerman (Home: S.P. de MACORIS, D.R.)	.05
130	Mark Wohlers	.05
131	Eric Fox	.05
132	Doug Strange	.05
133	Jeff Frye	.05
134	Wade Boggs	.85
135	Lou Whitaker	.05
136	Craig Grebeck	.05
137	Rich Rodriguez	.05
138	Jay Bell	.05
139	Felix Fermin	.05
140	Denny Martinez	.05
141	Eric Anthony	.05
142	Roberto Alomar	.20
143	Darren Lewis	.05
144	Mike Blowers	.05
145	Scott Bankhead	.05
146	Jeff Reboulet	.05
147	Frank Viola	.05
148	Bill Pecota	.05
149	Carlos Hernandez	.05
150	Bobby Witt	.05
151	Sid Bream	.05
152	Todd Zeile	.05
153	Dennis Cook	.05
154	Brian Bohanon	.05
155	Pat Kelly	.05
156	Milt Cuyler	.05
157	Juan Bell	.05
158	Randy Milligan	.05
159	Mark Gardner	.05
160	Pat Tabler	.05
161	Jeff Reardon	.05
162	Ken Patterson	.05
163	Bobby Bonilla	.05
164	Tony Pena	.05
165	Greg Swindell	.05
166	Kirk McCaskill	.05
167	Doug Drabek	.05
168	Franklin Stubbs	.05
169	Ron Tingley	.05
170	Willie Banks	.05
171	Sergio Valdez	.05
172	Mark Lemke	.05
173	Robin Yount	.75
174	Storm Davis	.05
175	Dan Walters	.05
176	Steve Farr	.05
177	Curt Wilkerson	.05
178	Luis Alicea	.05
179	Russ Swan	.05
180	Mitch Williams	.05
181	Wilson Alvarez	.05
182	Carl Willis	.05
183	Craig Biggio	.05
184	Sean Berry	.05
185	Trevor Wilson	.05
186	Jeff Tackett	.05
187	Ellis Burks	.05
188	Jeff Branson	.05
189	Matt Nokes	.05
190	John Smiley	.05
191	Danny Gladden	.05
192	Mike Boddicker	.05
193	Roger Pavlik	.05
194	Paul Sorrento	.05
195	Vince Coleman	.05
196	Gary DiSarcina	.05
197	Rafael Bournigal	.05
198	Mike Schooler	.05
199	Scott Ruskin	.05
200	Frank Thomas	.75
201	Kyle Abbott	.05
202	Mike Perez	.05
203	Andre Dawson	.25
204	Bill Swift	.05
205	Alejandro Pena	.05
206	Dave Winfield	.75
207	Andujar Cedeno	.05
208	Terry Steinbach	.05
209	Chris Hammond	.05
210	Todd Burns	.05
211	Hipolito Pichardo	.05
212	John Kiely	.05
213	Tim Teufel	.05
214	Lee Guetterman	.05
215	Geronimo Pena	.05
216	Brett Butler	.05
217	Bryan Hickerson	.05
218	Rick Trlicek	.05
219	Lee Stevens	.05
220	Roger Clemens	1.25
221	Carlton Fisk	.75
222	Chili Davis	.05
223	Walt Terrell	.05
224	Jim Eisenreich	.05
225	Ricky Bones	.05
226	Henry Rodriguez	.05
227	Ken Hill	.05
228	Rick Wilkins	.05
229	Ricky Jordan	.05
230	Bernard Gilkey	.05
231	Tim Fortugno	.05
232	Geno Petralli	.05
233	Jose Rijo	.05
234	Jim Leyritz	.05
235	Kevin Campbell	.05
236	Al Osuna	.05
237	Pete Smith	.05
238	Pete Schourek	.05
239	Moises Alou	.05
240	Donn Pall	.05
241	Denny Neagle	.05
242	Dan Peltier	.05
243	Scott Scudder	.05
244	Juan Guzman	.05
245	Dave Burba	.05
246	Rick Sutcliffe	.05
247	Tony Fossas	.05
248	Mike Munoz	.05
249	Tim Salmon	.05
250	Rob Murphy	.05
251	Roger McDowell	.05
252	Lance Parrish	.05
253	Cliff Brantley	.05
254	Scott Leius	.05
255	Carlos Martinez	.05
256	Vince Horsman	.05
257	Oscar Azocar	.05
258	Craig Shipley	.05
259	Ben McDonald	.05
260	Jeff Brantley	.05
261	Damon Berryhill	.05
262	Joe Grahe	.05
263	Dave Hansen	.05
264	Rich Amaral	.05
265	Tim Pugh RC	.05
266	Dion James	.05
267	Frank Tanana	.05
268	Stan Belinda	.05
269	Jeff Kent	.05
270	Bruce Ruffin	.05
271	Xavier Hernandez	.05
272	Darrin Fletcher	.05
273	Tino Martinez	.05
274	Benny Santiago	.05
275	Scott Radinsky	.05
276	Mariano Duncan	.05
277	Kenny Lofton	.05
278	Dwight Smith	.05
279	Joe Carter	.05
280	Tim Jones	.05
281	Jeff Huson	.05
282	Phil Plantier	.05
283	Kirby Puckett	.85
284	Johnny Guzman	.05
285	Mike Morgan	.05
286	Chris Sabo	.05
287	Matt Williams	.05
288	Checklist 1-100	.05
289	Checklist 101-200	.05
290	Checklist 201-300	.05
291	Dennis Eckersley	.05
292	Eric Karros (Members Choice)	.30
293	Pat Listach (Members Choice)	.05
294	Andy Van Slyke (Members Choice)	.05
295	Robin Ventura (Members Choice)	.05
296	Tom Glavine (Members Choice)	.05
297	Juan Gonzalez (Members Choice)	.20
298	Travis Fryman (Members Choice)	.05
299	Larry Walker (Members Choice)	.05
300	Gary Sheffield (Members Choice)	.20
301	Chuck Finley	.05
302	Luis Gonzalez	.05
303	Darryl Hamilton	.05
304	Bien Figueroa	.05
305	Ron Darling	.05
306	Jonathan Hurst	.05
307	Mike Sharperson	.05
308	Mike Christopher	.05
309	Marvin Freeman	.05
310	Jay Buhner	.05
311	Butch Henry	.05
312	Greg Harris	.05
313	Darren Daulton	.05
314	Chuck Knoblauch	.05
315	Greg Harris	.05
316	John Franco	.05
317	John Wehner	.05
318	Donald Harris	.05
319	Benny Santiago	.05
320	Larry Walker	.05
321	Randy Knorr	.05
322	Ramon D. Martinez RC	.05
323	Mike Stanley	.05
324	Bill Wegman	.05
325	Tom Candiotti	.05
326	Glenn Davis	.05
327	Chuck Crim	.05
328	Scott Livingstone	.05
329	Eddie Taubensee	.05
330	George Bell	.05
331	Edgar Martinez	.05
332	Paul Assenmacher	.05
333	Steve Hosey	.05
334	Mo Vaughn	.05
335	Bret Saberhagen	.05
336	Mike Trombley	.05
337	Mark Lewis	.05
338	Terry Pendleton	.05
339	Dave Hollins	.05
340	Jeff Conine	.05
341	Bob Tewksbury	.05
342	Billy Ashley	.05
343	Zane Smith	.05
344	John Wetteland	.05
345	Chris Hoiles	.05
346	Frank Castillo	.05
347	Bruce Hurst	.05
348	Kevin McReynolds	.05
349	Dave Henderson	.05
350	Ryan Bowen	.05
351	Sid Fernandez	.05
352	Mark Whiten	.05
353	Nolan Ryan	2.50
354	Rick Aguilera	.05
355	Mark Langston	.05
356	Jack Morris	.05
357	Rob Deer	.05
358	Dave Fleming	.05
359	Lance Johnson	.05
360	Joe Millette	.05
361	Wil Cordero	.05
362	Chito Martinez	.05
363	Scott Servais	.05
364	Bernie Williams	.05
365	Pedro Martinez	.75
366	Ryne Sandberg	.85
367	Brad Ausmus	.05
368	Scott Cooper	.05
369	Rob Dibble	.05
370	Walt Weiss	.05
371	Mark Davis	.05
372	Orlando Merced	.05
373	Mike Jackson	.05
374	Kevin Appier	.05
375	Esteban Beltre	.05
376	Joe Slusarski	.05
377	William Suero	.05
378	Pete O'Brien	.05
379	Alan Embree	.05
380	Lenny Webster	.05
381	Eric Davis	.05
382	Duane Ward	.05
383	John Habyan	.05
384	Jeff Bagwell	.75
385	Ruben Amaro	.05
386	Julio Valera	.05
387	Robin Ventura	.05
388	Archi Cianfrocco	.05
389	Skeeter Barnes	.05
390	Tim Costo	.05
391	Luis Mercedes	.05
392	Jeremy Hernandez	.05
393	Shawon Dunston	.05
394	Andy Van Slyke	.05
395	Kevin Maas	.05
396	Kevin Brown	.05
397	J.T. Bruett	.05
398	Darryl Strawberry	.05
399	Tom Pagnozzi	.05
400	Sandy Alomar	.05
401	Keith Miller	.05
402	Rich DeLucia	.05
403	Shawn Abner	.05
404	Howard Johnson	.05
405	Mike Benjamin	.05
406	Roberto Mejia RC	.05
407	Mike Butcher	.05
408	Deion Sanders	.05
409	Todd Stottlemyre	.05
410	Scott Kamieniecki	.05
411	Doug Jones	.05
412	John Burkett	.05
413	Lance Blankenship	.05
414	Jeff Parrett	.05
415	Barry Larkin	.05
416	Alan Trammell	.05
417	Mark Kiefer	.05
418	Gregg Olson	.05
419	Mark Grace	.05
420	Shane Mack	.05
421	Bob Walk	.05
422	Curt Schilling	.25
423	Erik Hanson	.05
424	George Brett	1.25
425	Reggie Jefferson	.05
426	Mark Portugal	.05
427	Ron Karkovice	.05
428	Matt Young	.05
429	Troy Neel	.05
430	Hector Fajardo	.05
431	Dave Righetti	.05
432	Pat Listach	.05
433	Jeff Innis	.05
434	Bob MacDonald	.05
435	Brian Jordan	.05
436	Jeff Blauser	.05
437	Mike Myers RC	.05
438	Frank Seminara	.05
439	Rusty Meacham	.05
440	Greg Briley	.05
441	Derek Lilliquist	.05
442	John Vander Wal	.05
443	Scott Erickson	.05
444	Bob Scanlan	.05
445	Todd Frohwirth	.05
446	Tom Goodwin	.05
447	William Pennyfeather	.05
448	Travis Fryman	.05
449	Mickey Morandini	.05
450	Greg Olson	.05
451	Trevor Hoffman	.05
452	Dave Magadan	.05
453	Shawn Jeter	.05
454	Andres Galarraga	.05
455	Ted Wood	.05
456	Freddie Benavides	.05
457	Junior Felix	.05
458	Alex Cole	.05
459	John Orton	.05
460	Eddie Zosky	.05
461	Dennis Eckersley	.65
462	Lee Smith	.05
463	John Smoltz	.05
464	Ken Caminiti	.05
465	Melido Perez	.05
466	Tom Marsh	.05
467	Jeff Nelson	.05
468	Jesse Levis	.05
469	Chris Nabholz	.05
470	Mike Mcfarlane	.05
471	Reggie Sanders	.05
472	Chuck McElroy	.05
473	Kevin Gross	.05
474	Matt Whiteside RC	.05
475	Cal Eldred	.05
476	Dave Gallagher	.05
477	Len Dykstra	.05
478	Mark McGwire	2.00
479	David Segui	.05
480	Mike Henneman	.05
481	Bret Barberie	.05
482	Steve Sax	.05
483	Dave Valle	.05
484	Danny Darwin	.05
485	Devon White	.05
486	Eric Plunk	.05
487	Jim Gott	.05
488	Scooter Tucker	.05
489	Omar Oliveres	.05
490	Greg Myers	.05
491	Brian Hunter	.05
492	Kevin Tapani	.05
493	Rich Monteleone	.05
494	Steve Buechele	.05
495	Bo Jackson	.10
496	Mike LaValliere	.05
497	Mark Leonard	.05
498	Daryl Boston	.05
499	Jose Canseco	.45
500	Brian Barnes	.05
501	Randy Johnson	.75
502	Tim McIntosh	.05
503	Cecil Fielder	.05
504	Derek Bell	.05
505	Kevin Koslofski	.05
506	Darren Holmes	.05
507	Brady Anderson	.05
508	John Valentin	.05
509	Jerry Browne	.05
510	Fred McGriff	.05
511	Pedro Astacio	.05
512	Gary Gaetti	.05
513	John Burke RC	.05
514	Dwight Gooden	.05
515	Thomas Howard	.05
516	Darrell Whitmore RC	.05
517	Ozzie Guillen	.05
518	Darryl Kile	.05
519	Rich Rowland	.05
520	Carlos Delgado	.50
521	Doug Henry	.05
522	Greg Colbrunn	.05
523	Tom Gordon	.05
524	Ivan Rodriguez	.65
525	Kent Hrbek	.05
526	Eric Young	.05
527	Rod Brewer	.05
528	Eric Karros	.05
529	Marquis Grissom	.05
530	Rico Brogna	.05
531	Sammy Sosa	1.00
532	Bret Boone	.05
533	Luis Rivera	.05
534	Hal Morris	.05
535	Monty Fariss	.05
536	Leo Gomez	.05
537	Wally Joyner	.05
538	Tony Gwynn	.85
539	Mike Williams	.05
540	Juan Gonzalez	.40
541	Ryan Klesko	.05
542	Ryan Thompson	.05
543	Chad Curtis	.05
544	Orel Hershiser	.05
545	Carlos Garcia	.05
546	Bob Welch	.05
547	Vinny Castilla	.05
548	Ozzie Smith	.85
549	Luis Salazar	.05
550	Mark Guthrie	.05
551	Charles Nagy	.05
552	Alex Fernandez	.05
553	Mel Rojas	.05
554	Orestes Destrade	.05
555	Mark Gubicza	.05
556	Steve Finley	.05
557	Don Mattingly	1.25
558	Rickey Henderson	.75
559	Tommy Greene	.05
560	Arthur Rhodes	.05
561	Alfredo Griffin	.05
562	Will Clark	.05
563	Bob Zupcic	.05
564	Chuck Carr	.05
565	Henry Cotto	.05
566	Billy Spiers	.05
567	Jack Armstrong	.05
568	Kurt Stillwell	.05
569	David McCarty	.05
570	Joe Vitiello	.05
571	Gerald Williams	.05
572	Dale Murphy	.25
573	Scott Aldred	.05
574	Bill Gullickson	.05
575	Bobby Thigpen	.05
576	Glenallen Hill	.05
577	Dwayne Henry	.05
578	Calvin Jones	.05

579	Al Martin	.05
580	Ruben Sierra	.05
581	Andy Benes	.05
582	Anthony Young	.05
583	Shawn Boskie	.05
584	Scott Pose RC	.05
585	Mike Piazza	1.50
586	Donovan Osborne	.05
587	James Austin	.05
588	Checklist 301-400	.05
589	Checklist 401-500	.05
590	Checklist 501-600	.05
591	Ken Griffey Jr. (Members Choice)	.75
592	Ivan Rodriguez (Members Choice)	.40
593	Carlos Baerga (Members Choice)	.05
594	Fred McGriff (Members Choice)	.05
595	Mark McGwire (Members Choice)	1.00
596	Roberto Alomar (Members Choice)	.10
597	Kirby Puckett (Members Choice)	.45
598	Marquis Grissom (Members Choice)	.05
599	John Smoltz (Members Choice)	.05
600	Ryne Sandberg (Members Choice)	.45
601	Wade Boggs	.85
602	Jeff Reardon	.05
603	Billy Ripken	.05
604	Bryan Harvey	.05
605	Carlos Quintana	.05
606	Greg Hibbard	.05
607	Ellis Burks	.05
608	Greg Swindell	.05
609	Dave Winfield	.75
610	Charlie Hough	.05
611	Chili Davis	.05
612	Jody Reed	.05
613	Mark Williamson	.05
614	Phil Plantier	.05
615	Jim Abbott	.05
616	Dante Bichette	.05
617	Mark Eichhorn	.05
618	Gary Sheffield	.45
619	Richie Lewis RC	.05
620	Joe Girardi	.05
621	Jaime Navarro	.05
622	Willie Wilson	.05
623	Scott Fletcher	.05
624	Bud Black	.05
625	Tom Brunansky	.05
626	Steve Avery	.05
627	Paul Molitor	.75
628	Gregg Jefferies	.05
629	Dave Stewart	.05
630	Javier Lopez	.05
631	Greg Gagne	.05
632	Bobby Kelly	.05
633	Mike Fetters	.05
634	Ozzie Canseco	.05
635	Jeff Russell	.05
636	Pete Incaviglia	.05
637	Tom Henke	.05
638	Chipper Jones	1.00
639	Jimmy Key	.05
640	Dave Martinez	.05
641	Dave Stieb	.05
642	Milt Thompson	.05
643	Alan Mills	.05
644	Tony Fernandez	.05
645	Randy Bush	.05
646	Joe Magrane	.05
647	Ivan Calderon	.05
648	Jose Guzman	.05
649	John Olerud	.25
650	Tom Glavine	.25
651	Julio Franco	.05
652	Armando Reynoso	.05
653	Felix Jose	.05
654	Ben Rivera	.05
655	Andre Dawson	.25
656	Mike Harkey	.05
657	Kevin Seitzer	.05
658	Lonnie Smith	.05
659	Norm Charlton	.05
660	Dave Justice	.05
661	Fernando Valenzuela	.05
662	Dan Wilson	.05
663	Mark Gardner	.05
664	Doug Dascenzo	.05
665	Greg Maddux	.85
666	Harold Baines	.05
667	Randy Myers	.05
668	Harold Reynolds	.05
669	Candy Maldonado	.05
670	Al Leiter	.05
671	Jerald Clark	.05
672	Doug Drabek	.05
673	Kirk Gibson	.05
674	Steve Reed RC	.05
675	Mike Felder	.05
676	Ricky Gutierrez	.05
677	Spike Owen	.05
678	Otis Nixon	.05
679	Scott Sanderson	.05
680	Mark Carreon	.05
681	Troy Percival	.05
682	Kevin Stocker	.05
683	Jim Converse RC	.05
684	Barry Bonds	2.50
685	Greg Gohr	.05
686	Tim Wallach	.05

687	Matt Mieske	.05
688	Robby Thompson	.05
689	Brien Taylor	.05
690	Kirt Manwaring	.05
691	Mike Lansing RC	.25
692	Steve Decker	.05
693	Mike Moore	.05
694	Kevin Mitchell	.05
695	Phil Hiatt	.05
696	Tony Tarasco RC	.05
697	Benji Gil	.05
698	Jeff Juden	.05
699	Kevin Reimer	.05
700	Andy Ashby	.05
701	John Jaha	.05
702	Tim Bogar RC	.05
703	David Cone	.05
704	Willie Greene	.05
705	David Hulse RC	.05
706	Cris Carpenter	.05
707	Ken Griffey Jr.	1.50
708	Steve Bedrosian	.05
709	Dave Nilsson	.05
710	Paul Wagner	.05
711	B.J. Surhoff	.05
712	Rene Arocha RC	.05
713	Manny Lee	.05
714	Brian Williams	.05
715	Sherman Obando RC	.05
716	Terry Mulholland	.05
717	Paul O'Neill	.05
718	David Nied	.05
719	J.T. Snow RC	.50
720	Nigel Wilson	.05
721	Mike Bielecki	.05
722	Kevin Young	.05
723	Charlie Leibrandt	.05
724	Frank Bolick	.05
725	Jon Shave RC	.05
726	Steve Cooke	.05
727	Domingo Martinez RC	.05
728	Todd Worrell	.05
729	Jose Lind	.05
730	Jim Tatum RC	.05
731	Mike Hampton	.05
732	Mike Draper	.05
733	Henry Mercedes	.05
734	John Johnstone RC	.05
735	Mitch Webster	.05
736	Russ Springer	.05
737	Rob Natal	.05
738	Steve Howe	.05
739	Darrell Sherman RC	.05
740	Pat Mahomes	.05
741	Alex Arias	.05
742	Damon Buford	.05
743	Charlie Hayes	.05
744	Guillermo Velasquez	.05
745	Checklist 601-750	.05
746	Frank Thomas (Members Choice)	.40
747	Barry Bonds (Members Choice)	1.50
748	Roger Clemens (Members Choice)	.50
749	Joe Carter (Members Choice)	.05
750	Greg Maddux (Members Choice)	.45

1st Day Production

Inserted at the rate of about one per box, with an estimated production of 2,000 apiece, 1st Day Production cards are a parallel of 1993 TSC on which an embossed silver holographic foil logo has been added. Because of the considerably higher value of the 1st Day parallels, collectors should be aware that fakes can be created by cutting the logo off a common player's card and attaching it to a superstar card.

	NM/M
Common Player:	1.00
1st Day Stars:	8X

Series 1 Inserts

Four bonus cards were produced as special inserts in Series I Stadium Club packs. Two of the full-bleed, gold-foil enhanced cards honor Robin Yount and George Brett

for achieving the 3,000-hit mark, while the other two commemorate the first picks in the 1993 expansion draft by the Colorado Rockies (David Nied) and Marlins (Nigel Wilson).

		NM/M
Complete Set (4):		3.00
Common Player:		.25
1	Robin Yount (3,000 hits)	1.00
2	George Brett (3,000 hits)	2.00
3	David Nied (#1 pick)	.25
4	Nigel Wilson (#1 pick)	.25

Series 2 Inserts

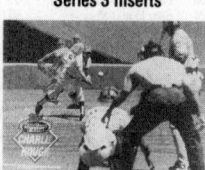

Cross-town and regional rivals were featured in this four-card insert set found, on average, one per 24 packs of Series II Stadium Club. Each of the two-faced cards is typical S.C. quality with gold-foil stamping and UV coating front and back.

		NM/M
Complete Set (4):		5.00
Common Player:		1.50
1	Pacific Terrific (Will Clark, Mark McGwire)	2.00
2	Broadway Stars (Dwight Gooden, Don Mattingly)	1.50
3	Second City Sluggers (Ryne Sandberg, Frank Thomas)	1.50
4	Pacific Terrific (Ken Griffey Jr., Darryl Strawberry)	1.50

Series 3 Inserts

Team "firsts" - first game, first pitch, first batter, etc. - for the 1993 expansion Florida Marlins and Colorado Rockies are featured on this pair of inserts found in Series III Stadium Club packs. Fronts featured game-action photos with the player's name in gold foil. On back is a stadium scene with the team first overprinted in black. At top the team name and Stadium Club logo are in gold foil.

		NM/M
Complete Set (2):		.50
Common Player:		.25
1	David Nied	.25
2	Charlie Hough	.25

Master Photos

Each box of 1993 Stadium Club packs included one Master Photo premium insert. Prize cards good for three Master Photos in a mail-in offer were also included in each of the three series. The 5" x 7" Master Photos feature wide white borders and a

large Stadium Club logo at top, highlighted by prismatic foil. The same foil is used as a border for a larger-format version of the player's regular S.C. card at the center of the Master Photo. A "Members Only" version of each of the 1993 Master Photos was available as a premium with the purchase of a Members Only Stadium Club set. the Members Only Master Photos have a gold-foil seal in the upper-right corner.

		NM/M
Complete Set (30):		15.00
Common Player:		.20
Series 1		
(1)	Carlos Baerga	.20
(2)	Delino DeShields	.20
(3)	Brian McRae	.20
(4)	Sam Militello	.20
(5)	Joe Oliver	.20
(6)	Kirby Puckett	1.50
(7)	Cal Ripken Jr.	4.00
(8)	Bip Roberts	.20
(9)	Mike Scioscia	.20
(10)	Rick Sutcliffe	.20
(11)	Danny Tartabull	.20
(12)	Tim Wakefield	.20
Series 2		
(13)	George Brett	3.00
(14)	Jose Canseco	.50
(15)	Will Clark	.20
(16)	Travis Fryman	.20
(17)	Dwight Gooden	.20
(18)	Mark Grace	.30
(19)	Rickey Henderson	1.00
(20)	Mark McGwire	2.50
(21)	Nolan Ryan	4.00
(22)	Ruben Sierra	.20
(23)	Darryl Strawberry	.20
(24)	Larry Walker	.20
Series 3		
(25)	Barry Bonds	5.00
(26)	Ken Griffey Jr.	2.50
(27)	Greg Maddux	2.00
(28)	David Nied	.20
(29)	J.T. Snow	.20
(30)	Brien Taylor	.20
Redemption Card:		3X

Members Only

A special version of the Topps' 1993 Stadium Club set was made available exclusively to members of the company's Stadium Club program. The set is a parallel of the regular-issue SC set (plus insert) on which a gold-foil "Members Only" shield logo has been added to the card front. In all other respects the cards are identical to the regular SC issue. Production was a reported 12,000 sets.

		NM/M
Complete Set (750):		100.00
Common Player:		.50
Members Only Stars:		8X

Members Only Baseball

As a benefit of membership in Topps' Stadium Club, each member received a 59-card set in four separate shipments. The cards featured highlights of the 1993 baseball, hockey, football and basketball seasons. Besides the 28 baseball player cards checklisted here there were nine football cards, six hockey card and 16 basketball cards. Each sport's cards came separately in a heat-sealed cello wrap in a special box. Cards were typical S.C. quality, featuring full-bleed action photos on the front, with the Stadium Club log and player name enhanced with gold-foil stamping and a gold-foil "Members Only" notice beneath the player's name. Backs feature a parti-color background with a colorized, stylized player figure at right. At left is the story of the player's season or career highlight. The cards are unnumbered and are checklisted alphabetically.

		NM/M
Complete Set (28):		9.00
Common Player:		.10
(1)	Jim Abbott	.10
(2)	Barry Bonds	2.50
(3)	Chris Bosio	.10
(4)	George Brett	.75
(5)	Jay Buhner	.10
(6)	Joe Carter (3 HR in game 5th time)	.10
(7)	Joe Carter (World Series-winning HR)	.10
(8)	Carlton Fisk	.60
(9)	Travis Fryman	.10
(10)	Mark Grace	.20
(11)	Ken Griffey Jr.	1.50
(12)	Darryl Kile	.10
(13)	Darren Lewis	.10
(14)	Greg Maddux	.65
(15)	Jack McDowell	.10
(16)	Paul Molitor	.60
(17)	Eddie Murray	.60
(18)	Mike Piazza (Rookie catcher HR record)	1.50
(19)	Mike Piazza (N.L. Rookie of the Year)	1.50
(20)	Kirby Puckett	.65
(21)	Jeff Reardon	.10
(22)	Tim Salmon	.20
(23)	Curt Schilling	.35
(24)	Lee Smith	.10
(25)	Dave Stewart	.10
(26)	Frank Thomas	.60
(27)	Mark Whiten	.10
(28)	Dave Winfield	.60

1993 Stadium Club Special

Though the packaging and the cards themselves identify this 200-card set as a 1992 issue, it was not released until 1993 and is thought of by the hobby at large as a 1993 set. The set is sold in a plastic replica of Jack Murphy Stadium in San Diego, venue for the 1993 All-Star Game. Fifty-six of the eighty-six

players from that contest and are so identified by a line of gold-foil on the card front and an All-Star logo on back. Twenty-five members of the 1992 Team U.S.A. Olympic baseball squad are also included in the set, with appropriate logos and notations front and back. There are 19 cards depicting action and stars of the the 1992 League Championships and World Series. The other 100 cards in the set are 1992 draft picks. All cards have the same basic format as the regular-issue 1992 Topps Stadium Club cards, full-bleed photos on front and back, UV coating on both sides and gold-foil highlights on front. Besides the 200 standard-size cards, the Special Edition set included a dozen "Master Photos," 5" x 7" white-bordered premium cards.

		NM/M
Unopened Set (200):		45.00
Complete Set (200):		40.00
Common Player:		.05
1	Dave Winfield	.75
2	Juan Guzman	.05
3	Tony Gwynn	.85
4	Chris Roberts	.05
5	Benny Santiago	.05
6	Sherard Clinkscales	.05
7	Jonathan Nunnally RC	.05
8	Chuck Knoblauch	.05
9	Bob Wolcott RC	.05
10	Steve Rodriguez	.05
11	Mark Williams RC	.05
12	Danny Clyburn RC	.05
13	Darren Dreifort	.05
14	Andy Van Slyke	.05
15	Wade Boggs	.85
16	Scott Patton	.05
17	Gary Sheffield	.45
18	Ron Villone	.05
19	Roberto Alomar	.20
20	Marc Valdes	.05
21	Daron Kirkreit	.05
22	Jeff Granger	.05
23	Levon Largusa	.05
24	Jimmy Key	.05
25	Kevin Pearson	.05
26	Michael Moore	.05
27	Preston Wilson RC	1.00
28	Kirby Puckett	.85
29	Tim Crabtree RC	.05
30	Bip Roberts	.05
31	Kelly Gruber	.05
32	Tony Fernandez	.05
33	Jason Angel	.05
34	Calvin Murray	.05
35	Chad McConnell	.05
36	Jason Moler	.05
37	Mark Lemke	.05
38	Tom Knauss	.05
39	Larry Mitchell	.05
40	Doug Mirabelli	.05
41	Everett Stull II	.05
42	Chris Wimmer	.05
43	Dan Serafini RC	.05
44	Ryne Sandberg	.85
45	Steve Lyons	.05
46	Ryan Freeburg	.05
47	Ruben Sierra	.05
48	David Mysel	.05
49	Joe Hamilton	.05
50	Steve Rodriguez	.05
51	Tim Wakefield	.05
52	Scott Gentile	.05
53	Doug Jones	.05
54	Willie Brown	.05
55	Chad Mottola RC	.05
56	Ken Griffey Jr.	1.50
57	Jon Lieber RC	.50
58	Denny Martinez	.05
59	Joe Petcka	.05
60	Benji Simonton	.05
61	Brett Backlund	.05
62	Damon Berryhill	.05
63	Juan Guzman	.05
64	Doug Hecker	.05
65	Jamie Arnold	.05
66	Bob Tewksbury	.05
67	Tim Leger	.05
68	Todd Etler	.05
69	Lloyd McClendon	.05
70	Kurt Ehmann	.05
71	Rick Magdaleno	.05
72	Tom Pagnozzi	.05
73	Jeffrey Hammonds	.05
74	Joe Carter	.05
75	Chris Holt	.05
76	Charles Johnson	.05
77	Bob Walk	.05
78	Fred McGriff	.05
79	Tom Evans	.05
80	Scott Klingenbeck	.05
81	Chad McConnell	.05
82	Chris Eddy	.05
83	Phil Nevin	.05
84	John Kruk	.05
85	Tony Sheffield	.05
86	John Smoltz	.05
87	Trevor Humphry	.05

88 Charles Nagy .05
89 Sean Runyan .05
90 Mike Gulan .05
91 Darren Daulton .05
92 Otis Nixon .05
93 Nomar Garciaparra 8.00
94 Larry Walker .05
95 Hut Smith .05
96 Rick Helling .05
97 Roger Clemens 1.00
98 Ron Gant .05
99 Kenny Felder .05
100 Steve Murphy .05
101 Mike Smith .05
102 Terry Pendleton .05
103 Tim Davis .05
104 Jeff Patzke .05
105 Craig Wilson .05
106 Tom Glavine .35
107 Mark Langston .05
108 Mark Thompson .05
109 Mark Owens RC .05
110 Keith Johnson .05
111 Robin Ventura .05
112 Ed Sprague .05
113 Jeff Schmidt RC .05
114 Don Wengert .05
115 Craig Biggio .05
116 Kenny Carlyle .05
117 Derek Jeter RC 80.00
118 Manuel Lee .05
119 Jeff Haas .05
120 Roger Bailey .05
121 Sean Lowe .05
122 Rick Aguilera .05
123 Sandy Alomar .05
124 Derek Wallace .05
125 B.J. Wallace .05
126 Greg Maddux .85
127 Tim Moore .05
128 Lee Smith .05
129 Todd Steverson .05
130 Chris Widger .05
131 Paul Molitor .75
132 Chris Smith .05
133 Chris Gomez RC .05
134 Jimmy Baron .05
135 John Smoltz .05
136 Pat Borders .05
137 Donnie Leshnock .05
138 Gus Gandarillas .05
139 Will Clark .05
140 Ryan Luzinski RC .05
141 Cal Ripken, Jr. 2.50
142 B.J. Wallace .05
143 Trey Beamon RC .05
144 Norm Charlton .05
145 Mike Mussina .30
146 Billy Owens .05
147 Ozzie Smith .85
148 Jason Kendall RC 1.00
149 Mike Matthews RC .05
150 David Spykstra .05
151 Benji Grigsby .05
152 Sean Smith .05
153 Mark McGwire 2.00
154 David Cone .05
155 Shon Walker RC .05
156 Jason Giambi .50
157 Jack McDowell .05
158 Paxton Briley .05
159 Edgar Martinez .05
160 Brian Sackinsky .05
161 Barry Bonds 2.50
162 Roberto Kelly .05
163 Jeff Alkire .05
164 Mike Sharperson .05
165 Jamie Taylor .05
166 John Saffer .05
167 Jerry Browne .05
168 Travis Fryman .05
169 Brady Anderson .05
170 Chris Roberts .05
171 Lloyd Peever .05
172 Francisco Cabrera .05
173 Ramiro Martinez .05
174 Jeff Alkire .05
175 Ivan Rodriguez .65
176 Kevin Brown .05
177 Chad Roper .05
178 Rod Henderson .05
179 Dennis Eckersley .65
180 Shannon Stewart RC 1.00
181 DeShawn Warren .05
182 Lonnie Smith .05
183 Willie Adams .05
184 Jeff Montgomery .05
185 Damon Hollins .05
186 Byron Matthews .05
187 Harold Baines .05
188 Rick Greene .05
189 Carlos Baerga .05
190 Brandon Cromer .05
191 Roberto Alomar .20
192 Rich Ireland .05
193 Steve Montgomery .05
194 Brant Brown .05
195 Ritchie Moody .05
196 Michael Tucker .05
197 Jason Varitek RC 6.00
198 David Manning .05
199 Marquis Riley .05
200 Jason Giambi .60

Special Master Photos

Each 1993 Stadium Club Special (Jack Murphy Stadium) set included 12 Master Photos replicating cards from the set. There were nine All-Stars, two '92 rookies and a Team USA player among the Master Photos. Gold-tone prismatic foil highlights the 5" x 7" cards, decorating the large logo at top and separating the card photo from the wide white border. Backs have Stadium Club and MLB logos and copyright information printed in black. The unnumbered cards are checklisted here in alphabetical order.

		NM/M
Complete Set (12):		5.00
Common Player:		.20
(1)	Sandy Alomar	.20
(2)	Tom Glavine	.65
(3)	Ken Griffey Jr.	2.00
(4)	Tony Gwynn	1.50
(5)	Chuck Knoblauch	.20
(6)	Chad Mottola	.20
(7)	Kirby Puckett	1.50
(8)	Chris Roberts	.20
(9)	Ryne Sandberg	1.50
(10)	Gary Sheffield	.40
(11)	Larry Walker	.20
(12)	Preston Wilson	.20

Team Sets

This special edition of Stadium Club cards consists of 16 separate team sets of 30 cards each. Each blister-packed team set was priced around $6 and sold exclusively at Wal-Mart. Fronts of the UV coated cards have a player photo that is borderless at the top, bottom and left. At right is a green stripe, at top of which is a partial baseball design and some other striping in gold-foil. Backs are basically green, with a light blue box at lower-right containing personal information and stats, along with the S.C. logo. A player photo is at upper-left, with his name superimposed on a bat. Cards are checklisted here within team set. Several of the Braves cards were authentically autographed as pack-toppers on specially marked sets.

	NM/M
Complete Set (480):	30.00
Common Player:	.10

ATLANTA BRAVES
Team Set: 3.00
1 Tom Glavine .35
2 Bill Pecota .10
3 David Justice .10
4 Mark Lemke .10
5 Jeff Blauser .10
6 Ron Gant .10
7 Greg Olson .10
8 Francisco Cabrera .10
9 Chipper Jones 1.00
9a Chipper Jones/Auto. 20.00
10 Steve Avery .10
11 Kent Mercker .10
12 John Smoltz .10
12a John Smoltz/Auto. 6.00
13 Pete Smith .10
14 Damon Berryhill .10
15 Sid Bream .10
16 Otis Nixon .10
17 Mike Stanton .10
18 Greg Maddux 1.00
19 Jay Howell .10
20 Rafael Belliard .10
21 Terry Pendleton .10
22 Deion Sanders .15
23 Brian Hunter .10
24 Marvin Freeman .10
25 Mark Wohlers .10
26 Ryan Klesko .10
26a Ryan Klesko/Auto. 4.00
27a Javy Lopez/Auto. 4.00
27 Javy Lopez .10
28 Melvin Nieves .10
29 Tony Tarasco .10
30 Ramon Caraballo .10

CHICAGO CUBS
Team Set: 2.50
1 Ryne Sandberg 1.50
2 Sammy Sosa 1.50
3 Greg Hibbard .10
4 Candy Maldonado .10
5 Willie Wilson .10
6 Dan Plesac .10
7 Steve Buechele .10
8 Mark Grace .25
9 Shawon Dunston .10
10 Steve Lake .10
11 Dwight Smith .10
12 Derrick May .10
13 Paul Assenmacher .10
14 Mike Harkey .10
15 Lance Dickson .10
16 Randy Myers .10
17 Mike Morgan .10
18 Chuck McElroy .10
19 Jose Guzman .10
20 Jose Vizcaino .10
21 Frank Castillo .10
22 Bob Scanlon .10
23 Rick Wilkins .10
24 Rey Sanchez .10
25 Phil Dauphin .10
26 Jim Bullinger .10
27 Jessie Hollins .10
28 Matt Walbeck .10
29 Fernando Ramsey .10
30 Jose Bautista .10

CALIFORNIA ANGELS
Team Set: 1.50
1 J.T. Snow .25
2 Chuck Crim .10
3 Chili Davis .10
4 Mark Langston .10
5 Ron Tingley .10
6 Eduardo Perez .10
7 Scott Sanderson .10
8 Jorge Fabregas .10
9 Troy Percival .10
10 Rod Correia .10
11 Greg Myers .10
12 Steve Frey .10
13 Tim Salmon .25
14 Scott Lewis .10
15 Rene Gonzales .10
16 Chuck Finley .10
17 John Orton .10
18 Joe Grahe .10
19 Luis Polonia .10
20 John Farrell .10
21 Damion Easley .10
22 Gene Nelson .10
23 Chad Curtis .10
24 Russ Springer .10
25 De Shawn Warren .10
26 Darryl Scott .10
27 Gary DiSarcina .10
28 Jerry Nielson .10
29 Torey Lovullo .10
30 Julio Valera .10

CHICAGO WHITE SOX
Team Set: 2.50
1 Frank Thomas 1.00
2 Bo Jackson .25
3 Rod Bolton .10
4 Dave Stieb .10
5 Tim Raines .10
6 Joey Cora .10
7 Warren Newson .10
8 Roberto Hernandez .10
9 Brandon Wilson .10
10 Wilson Alvarez .10
11 Dan Pasqua .10
12 Ozzie Guillen .10
13 Robin Ventura .25
14 Craig Grebeck .10
15 Lance Johnson .10
16 Carlton Fisk .75
17 Ron Karkovice .10
18 Jack McDowell .10
19 Scott Radinsky .10
20 Bobby Thigpen .10
21 Donn Pall .10
22 George Bell .10
23 Alex Fernandez .10
24 Mike Huff .10
25 Jason Bere .10
26 Johnny Ruffin .10
27 Ellis Burks .10
28 Kirk McCaskill .10
29 Terry Leach .10
30 Shawn Gilbert .10

COLORADO ROCKIES
Team Set: 1.50
1 David Nied .10
2 Quinton McCracken .10
3 Charlie Hayes .10
4 Bryn Smith .10
5 Dante Bichette .10
6 Alex Cole .10
7 Scott Aldred .10
8 Roberto Mejia .10
9 Jeff Parrett .10
10 Joe Girardi .10
11 Andres Galarraga .10
12 Daryl Boston .10
13 Jerald Clark .10
14 Gerald Young .10
15 Bruce Ruffin .10
16 Rudy Seanez .10
17 Darren Holmes .10
18 Andy Ashby .10
19 Chris Jones .10
20 Mark Thompson .10
21 Freddie Benavides .10
22 Eric Wedge .10
23 Vinny Castilla .10
24 Butch Henry .10
25 Jim Tatum .10
26 Steve Reed .10
27 Eric Young .10
28 Danny Sheaffer .10
29 Roger Bailey .10
30 Brad Ausmus .10

FLORIDA MARLINS
Team Set: 1.50
1 Nigel Wilson .10
2 Bryan Harvey .10
3 Bob McClure .10
4 Alex Arias .10
5 Walt Weiss .10
6 Charlie Hough .10
7 Scott Chiamparino .10
8 Junior Felix .10
9 Jack Armstrong .10
10 Dave Magadan .10
11 Cris Carpenter .10
12 Benny Santiago .10
13 Jeff Conine .10
14 Jerry Don Gleaton .10
15 Steve Decker .10
16 Ryan Bowen .10
17 Ramon Martinez .10
18 Bret Barberie .10
19 Monty Fariss .10
20 Trevor Hoffman .25
21 Scott Pose .10
22 Mike Myers .10
23 Geronimo Berroa .10
24 Darrell Whitmore .10
25 Chuck Carr .10
26 Dave Weathers .10
27 Matt Turner .10
28 Jose Martinez .10
29 Orestes Destrade .10
30 Carl Everett .10

HOUSTON ASTROS
Team Set: 1.50
1 Doug Drabek .10
2 Eddie Taubensee .10
3 James Mouton .10
4 Ken Caminiti .10
5 Chris James .10
6 Jeff Juden .10
7 Eric Anthony .10
8 Jeff Bagwell 1.00
9 Greg Swindell .10
10 Steve Finley .10
11 Al Osuna .10
12 Gary Mota .10
13 Scott Servais .10
14 Craig Biggio .50
15 Doug James .10
16 Rob Mallicoat .10
17 Darryl Kile .10
18 Kevin Bass .10
19 Pete Harnisch .10
20 Andujar Cedeno .10
21 Brian Hunter .10
22 Brian Williams .10
23 Chris Donnels .10
24 Xavier Hernandez .10
25 Todd Jones .10
26 Luis Gonzalez .10
27 Rick Parker .10
28 Casey Candaele .10
29 Tony Eusebio .10
30 Mark Portugal .10

KANSAS CITY ROYALS
Team Set: 1.50
1 George Brett 1.00
2 Mike MacFarlane .10
3 Tom Gordon .15
4 Wally Joyner .10
5 Kevin Appier .10
6 Phil Hiatt .10
7 Keith Miller .10
8 Hipolito Pichardo .10
9 Chris Gwynn .10
10 Jose Lind .10
11 Mark Gubicza .10
12 Dennis Rasmussen .10
13 Mike Magnante .10
14 Joe Vitiello .10
15 Kevin McReynolds .10
16 Greg Gagne .10
17 David Cone .15
18 Brent Mayne .10
19 Jeff Montgomery .10
20 Joe Randa .10
21 Felix Jose .10
22 Bill Sampen .10
23 Curt Wilkerson .10
24 Mark Gardner .10
25 Brian McRae .10
26 Hubie Brooks .10
27 Chris Eddy .10
28 Harvey Pulliam .10
29 Rusty Meacham .10
30 Danny Miceli .10

LOS ANGELES DODGERS
Team Set: 3.00
1 Darryl Strawberry .10
2 Pedro Martinez .75
3 Jody Reed .10
4 Carlos Hernandez .10
5 Kevin Gross .10
6 Mike Piazza 1.50
7 Jim Gott .10
8 Eric Karros .10
9 Mike Sharperson .10
10 Ramon Martinez .10
11 Tim Wallach .10
12 Pedro Astacio .10
13 Lenny Harris .10
14 Brett Butler .10
15 Raul Mondesi .10
16 Todd Worrell .10
17 Jose Offerman .10
18 Mitch Webster .10
19 Tom Candiotti .10
20 Eric Davis .10
21 Michael Moore .10
22 Billy Ashley .10
23 Orel Hershiser .15
24 Roger Cedeno .10
25 Roger McDowell .10
26 Mike James .10
27 Steve Wilson .10
28 Todd Hollandsworth .10
29 Cory Snyder .10
30 Todd Williams .10

NEW YORK YANKEES
Team Set: 2.50
1 Don Mattingly 1.25
2 Jim Abbott .10
3 Matt Nokes .10
4 Danny Tartabull .10
5 Wade Boggs 1.00
6 Melido Perez .10
7 Steve Farr .10
8 Kevin Maas .10
9 Randy Velarde .10
10 Mike Humphreys .10
11 Mike Gallego .10
12 Mike Stanley .10
13 Jimmy Key .10
14 Paul O'Neill .10
15 Spike Owen .10
16 Pat Kelly .10
17 Sterling Hitchcock .10
18 Mike Witt .10
19 Scott Kamieniecki .10
20 John Habyan .10
21 Bernie Williams .20
22 Brien Taylor .10
23 Rich Monteleone .10
24 Mark Hutton .10
25 Robert Eenhoorn .10
26 Gerald Williams .10
27 Sam Militello .10
28 Bob Wickman .10
29 Andy Stankiewicz .10
30 Domingo Jean .10

OAKLAND A'S
Team Set: 3.00
1 Dennis Eckersley .75
2 Lance Blankenship .10
3 Mike Mohler .10
4 Jerry Browne .10
5 Kevin Seitzer .10
6 Storm Davis .10
7 Mark McGwire 2.00
8 Rickey Henderson .75
9 Terry Steinbach .10
10 Ruben Sierra .10
11 Dave Henderson .10
12 Bob Welch .10
13 Rick Honeycutt .10
14 Ron Darling .10
15 Joe Boever .10
16 Bobby Witt .10
17 Izzy Molina .10
18 Mike Bordick .10
19 Brent Gates .10
20 Shawn Hillegas .10
21 Scott Hammond .10
22 Todd Van Poppel .10
23 Johnny Guzman .10
24 Scott Lydy .10
25 Scott Baker .10
26 Todd Revenig .10
27 Scott Brosius .10
28 Troy Neel .10
29 Dale Sveum .10
30 Walt Weiss .10

PHILADELPHIA PHILLIES
Team Set: 1.50
1 Darren Daulton .10
2 Larry Andersen .10
3 Kyle Abbott .10
4 Chad McConnell .10
5 Danny Jackson .10
6 Kevin Stocker .10
7 Jim Eisenreich .10
8 Mickey Morandini .10
9 Bob Ayrault .10
10 Doug Lindsey .10
11 Dave Hollins .10
12 Dave West .10
13 Wes Chamberlain .10
14 Curt Schilling .35
15 Len Dykstra .10
16 Trevor Humphry .10
17 Terry Mulholland .10
18 Gene Schall .10
19 Mike Lieberthal .15
20 Ben Rivera .10
21 Mariano Duncan .10
22 Pete Incaviglia .10
23 Ron Blazier .10
24 Jeff Jackson .10
25 Jose DeLeon .10
26 Ron Lockett .10
27 Tommy Greene .10
28 Milt Thompson .10
29 Mitch Williams .10
30 John Kruk .10

ST. LOUIS CARDINALS
Team Set: 1.50
1 Ozzie Smith 1.00
2 Rene Arocha .10
3 Bernard Gilkey .10
4 Jose Oquendo .10
5 Mike Perez .10
6 Tom Pagnozzi .10
7 Rod Brewer .10
8 Joe Magrane .10
9 Todd Zeile .10
10 Bob Tewksbury .10
11 Darrel Deak .10
12 Gregg Jefferies .25
13 Lee Smith .25
14 Ozzie Canseco .10
15 Tom Urbani .10
16 Donovan Osborne .10
17 Ray Lankford .10
18 Rheal Cormier .10
19 Allen Watson .10
20 Geronimo Pena .10
21 Rob Murphy .10
22 Tracy Woodson .10
23 Basil Shabazz .10
24 Omar Olivares .10
25 Brian Jordan .10
26 Les Lancaster .10
27 Sean Lowe .10
28 Hector Villanueva .10
29 Brian Barber .10
30 Aaron Holbert .10

SAN FRANCISCO GIANTS
Team Set: 2.50
1 Barry Bonds 2.00
2 Dave Righetti .10
3 Matt Williams .10
3a Matt Williams/Auto. 10.00
4 Royce Clayton .10
5 Salomon Torres .10
6 Kirt Manwaring .10
7 J.R. Phillips .10
8 Kevin Rogers .10
9 Will Clark .10
10 John Burkett .10
11 Willie McGee .10
12 Rod Beck .10
13 Jeff Reed .10
14 Jeff Brantley .10
15 Steve Hosey .10
16 Chris Hancock .10
17 Adell Davenport .10
18 Mike Jackson .10
19 Dave Martinez .10
20 Bill Swift .10
21 Steve Scarsone .10
22 Trevor Wilson .10
23 Mark Carreon .10
24 Bud Black .10
25 Darren Lewis .10
26 Dan Carlson .10
27 Craig Colbert .10
28 Greg Brummet .10
29 Bryan Hickerson .10
30 Robby Thompson .10

SEATTLE MARINERS
Team Set: 3.00
1 Ken Griffey Jr. 1.50
2 Desi Relaford .10
3 Dave Weinhouse .10
4 Rich Amaral .10
5 Brian Deak .10
6 Bret Boone .10
7 Bill Haselman .10
8 Dave Fleming .10
9 Fernando Vina .10
10 Greg Litton .10
11 Mackey Sasser .10
12 Lee Tinsley .10
13 Norm Charlton .10
14 Russ Swan .10
15 Brian Holman .10
16 Randy Johnson .75
17 Erik Hanson .10
18 Tino Martinez .10
19 Marc Newfield .10
20 Dave Valle .10
21 John Cummings .10
22 Mike Hampton .10
23 Jay Buhner .10
24 Edgar Martinez .10
25 Omar Vizquel .10
26 Pete O'Brien .10
27 Brian Turang .10
28 Chris Bosio .10
29 Mike Felder .10
30 Shawn Estes .10

TEXAS RANGERS

Team Set: 5.00

#	Player	Price
1	Nolan Ryan	2.50
2	Ritchie Moody	.10
3	Matt Whiteside	.10
4	David Hulse	.10
5	Roger Pavlik	.10
6	Dan Smith	.10
7	Donald Harris	.10
8	Butch Davis	.10
9	Benji Gil	.10
10	Ivan Rodriguez	.65
11	Dean Palmer	.10
12	Jeff Huson	.10
13	Rob Mauer	.10
14	Gary Redus	.10
15	Doug Dascenzo	.10
16	Charlie Liebrandt	.10
17	Tom Henke	.10
18	Manuel Lee	.10
19	Kenny Rogers	.10
20	Kevin Brown	.10
21	Juan Gonzalez	.50
22	Geno Petralli	.10
23	John Russell	.10
24	Robb Nen	.10
25	Julio Franco	.10
26	Rafael Palmeiro	.65
27	Todd Burns	.10
28	Jose Canseco	.50
29	Billy Ripken	.10
30	Dan Peltier	.10

Ultra Pro

Special packages of plastic sheets and sleeves carrying the "Topps Stadium Club UltraPro" brand name included one of 10 special Stadium Club cards of Barry Bonds, Bobby Bonds and/or Willie Mays. Cards are typical UV coated, gold-foil quality, but because the cards were not licensed by Major League Baseball, team logos were removed from the photos.

NM/M
Complete Set (10): 7.00
Common Card: .50

#	Player	Price
1	Barry Bonds, Willie Mays, Bobby Bonds	.50
2	Willie Mays	1.00
3	Bobby Bonds	.50
4	Barry Bonds	1.00
5	Barry Bonds, Bobby Bonds	.50
6	Willie Mays	1.00
7	Barry Bonds (Business suit.)	1.00
8	Willie Mays, Bobby Bonds	1.00
9	Willie Mays	1.00
10	Barry Bonds (Tuxedo)	1.00

1994 Stadium Club Pre-Production

These sample cards introducing the 1994 Stadium Club set differ from their regular-issue counterparts only in the inclusion of a line of type vertically on the back-right, "Pre-Production Sample."

NM/M
Complete Set (9): 5.00
Common Player: .50

#	Player	Price
6	Al Martin	.50
15	Junior Ortiz	.50
36	Tim Salmon	.75
56	Jerry Spradlin	.50
122	Tom Pagnozzi	.50
123	Ron Gant	.50
125	Dennis Eckersley	1.50
135	Jose Lind	.50
238	Barry Bonds	4.00

1994 Stadium Club

[card image: Cecil Fielder]

Issued in three series to a total of 720 cards, Topps' mid-price brand features a hip look and a wide range of insert specials. The regular cards feature a borderless photo with the player's name presented in a unique typewriter/label maker style at bottom. The player's last name and Topps Stadium Club logo at top are in red foil. Backs feature another player photo, some personal data and a headlined career summary. Various stats and skills rankings complete the data. Subsets within the issue include cards annotated with Major League debut dates, 1993 awards won, home run club cards, cards featuring two or three players, and Final Tribute cards for George Brett and Nolan Ryan.

NM/M
Complete Set (720): 20.00
Common Player: .05
1st Day: 8X
Golden Rainbow: 2X
Series 1, 2, 3 Pack (12): 1.00
Series 1, 2, 3 Wax Box (24): 15.00

#	Player	Price
1	Robin Yount	.65
2	Rick Wilkins	.05
3	Steve Scarsone	.05
4	Gary Sheffield	.40
5	George Brett	1.00
6	Al Martin	.05
7	Joe Oliver	.05
8	Stan Belinda	.05
9	Denny Hocking	.05
10	Roberto Alomar	.20
11	Luis Polonia	.05
12	Scott Hemond	.05
13	Joey Reed	.05
14	Mel Rojas	.05
15	Junior Ortiz	.05
16	Harold Baines	.05
17	Brad Pennington	.05
18	Jay Bell	.05
19	Tom Henke	.05
20	Jeff Branson	.05
21	Roberto Mejia	.05
22	Pedro Munoz	.05
23	Matt Nokes	.05
24	Jack McDowell	.05
25	Cecil Fielder	.05
26	Tony Fossas	.05
27	Jim Eisenreich	.05
28	Anthony Young	.05
29	Chuck Carr	.05
30	Jeff Treadway	.05
31	Chris Nabholz	.05
32	Tom Candiotti	.05
33	Mike Maddux	.05
34	Nolan Ryan	2.00
35	Luis Gonzalez	.05
36	Tim Salmon	.05
37	Mark Whiten	.05
38	Roger McDowell	.05
39	Royce Clayton	.05
40	Troy Neel	.05
41	Mike Harkey	.05
42	Darrin Fletcher	.05
43	Wayne Kirby	.05
44	Rich Amaral	.05
45	Robb Nen	.05
46	Tim Teufel	.05
47	Steve Cooke	.05
48	Jeff McNeely	.05
49	Jeff Montgomery	.05
50	Skeeter Barnes	.05
51	Scott Stahoviak	.05
52	Pat Kelly	.05
53	Brady Anderson	.05
54	Mariano Duncan	.05
55	Brian Bohanon	.05
56	Jerry Spradlin	.05
57	Ron Karkovice	.05
58	Jeff Gardner	.05
59	Bobby Bonilla	.05
60	Tino Martinez	.05
61	Todd Benzinger	.05
62	Steve Trachsel RC	.25
63	Brian Jordan	.05
64	Steve Bedrosian	.05
65	Brent Gates	.05
66	Shawn Green	.05
67	Sean Berry	.05
68	Joe Klink	.05
69	Fernando Valenzuela	.05
70	Andy Tomberlin	.05
71	Tony Pena	.05
72	Eric Young	.05
73	Chris Gomez	.05
74	Paul O'Neill	.05
75	Ricky Gutierrez	.05
76	Brad Holman	.05
77	Lance Painter	.05
78	Mike Butcher	.05
79	Sid Bream	.05
80	Sammy Sosa	.75
81	Felix Fermin	.05
82	Todd Hundley	.05
83	Kevin Higgins	.05
84	Todd Pratt	.05
85	Ken Griffey Jr.	1.25
86	John O'Donoghue	.05
87	Rick Renteria	.05
88	John Burkett	.05
89	Jose Vizcaino	.05
90	Kevin Seitzer	.05
91	Bobby Witt	.05
92	Chris Turner	.05
93	Omar Vizquel	.05
94	Dave Justice	.05
95	David Segui	.05
96	Dave Hollins	.05
97	Doug Strange	.05
98	Jerald Clark	.05
99	Mike Moore	.05
100	Joey Cora	.05
101	Scott Kamieniecki	.05
102	Andy Benes	.05
103	Chris Bosio	.05
104	Rey Sanchez	.05
105	John Jaha	.05
106	Otis Nixon	.05
107	Rickey Henderson	.65
108	Jeff Bagwell	.65
109	Gregg Jefferies	.05
110	Topps Trios (Roberto Alomar, Paul Molitor, John Olerud)	.25
111	Topps Trios (Ron Gant, David Justice, Fred McGriff)	.05
112	Topps Trios (Juan Gonzalez, Rafael Palmeiro, Dean Palmer)	.25
113	Greg Swindell	.05
114	Bill Hasleman	.05
115	Phil Plantier	.05
116	Ivan Rodriguez	.60
117	Kevin Tapani	.05
118	Mike LaValliere	.05
119	Tim Costo	.05
120	Mickey Morandini	.05
121	Brett Butler	.05
122	Tom Pagnozzi	.05
123	Ron Gant	.05
124	Damion Easley	.05
125	Dennis Eckersley	.60
126	Matt Mieske	.05
127	Cliff Floyd	.05
128	Julian Tavarez RC	.05
129	Arthur Rhodes	.05
130	Dave West	.05
131	Tim Naehring	.05
132	Freddie Benavides	.05
133	Paul Assenmacher	.05
134	David McCarty	.05
135	Jose Lind	.05
136	Reggie Sanders	.05
137	Don Slaught	.05
138	Andujar Cedeno	.05
139	Rob Deer	.05
140	Mike Piazza	1.25
141	Moises Alou	.05
142	Tom Foley	.05
143	Benny Santiago	.05
144	Sandy Alomar	.05
145	Carlos Hernandez	.05
146	Luis Alicea	.05
147	Tom Lampkin	.05
148	Ryan Klesko	.05
149	Juan Guzman	.05
150	Scott Servais	.05
151	Tony Gwynn	.75
152	Tim Wakefield	.05
153	David Nied	.05
154	Chris Haney	.05
155	Danny Bautista	.05
156	Randy Velarde	.05
157	Darrin Jackson	.05
158	J.R. Phillips RC	.05
159	Greg Gagne	.05
160	Luis Aquino	.05
161	John Vander Wal	.05
162	Randy Myers	.05
163	Ted Power	.05
164	Scott Brosius	.05
165	Len Dykstra	.05
166	Jacob Brumfield	.05
167	Bo Jackson	.10
168	Eddie Taubensee	.05
169	Carlos Baerga	.05
170	Tim Bogar	.05
171	Jose Canseco	.50
172	Greg Blosser	.05
173	Chili Davis	.05
174	Randy Knorr	.05
175	Mike Perez	.05
176	Henry Rodriguez	.05
177	Brian Turang RC	.05
178	Roger Pavlik	.05
179	Aaron Sele	.05
180	Tale of 2 Players (Fred McGriff, Gary Sheffield)	.05
181	Tale of 2 Players (J.T. Snow, Tim Salmon)	.05
182	Roberto Hernandez	.05
183	Jeff Reboulet	.05
184	John Doherty	.05
185	Danny Sheaffer	.05
186	Bip Roberts	.05
187	Denny Martinez	.05
188	Darryl Hamilton	.05
189	Eduardo Perez	.05
190	Pete Harnisch	.05
191	Rick Gossage	.05
192	Mickey Tettleton	.05
193	Lenny Webster	.05
194	Lance Johnson	.05
195	Don Mattingly	1.00
196	Gregg Olson	.05
197	Mark Gubicza	.05
198	Scott Fletcher	.05
199	Jon Shave	.05
200	Tim Mauser	.05
201	Jeromy Burnitz	.05
202	Rob Dibble	.05
203	Will Clark	.05
204	Steve Buechele	.05
205	Brian Williams	.05
206	Carlos Garcia	.05
207	Mark Clark	.05
208	Rafael Palmeiro	.60
209	Eric Davis	.05
210	Pat Meares	.05
211	Chuck Finley	.05
212	Jason Bere	.05
213	Gary DiSarcina	.05
214	Tony Fernandez	.05
215	B.J. Surhoff	.05
216	Lee Guetterman	.05
217	Tim Wallach	.05
218	Kirt Manwaring	.05
219	Albert Belle	.05
220	Dwight Gooden	.05
221	Archi Cianfrocco	.05
222	Terry Mulholland	.05
223	Hipolito Pichardo	.05
224	Kent Hrbek	.05
225	Criag Grebeck	.05
226	Todd Jones	.05
227	Mike Bordick	.05
228	John Olerud	.05
229	Jeff Blauser	.05
230	Alex Arias	.05
231	Bernard Gilkey	.05
232	Denny Neagle	.05
233	Pedro Borbon RC	.05
234	Dick Schofield	.05
235	Matias Carrillo	.05
236	Juan Bell	.05
237	Mike Hampton	.05
238	Barry Bonds	2.00
239	Cris Carpenter	.05
240	Eric Karros	.05
241	Greg McMichael	.05
242	Pat Hentgen	.05
243	Tim Pugh	.05
244	Vinny Castilla	.05
245	Charlie Hough	.05
246	Bobby Munoz	.05
247	Kevin Baez	.05
248	Todd Frohwirth	.05
249	Charlie Hayes	.05
250	Mike Macfarlane	.05
251	Danny Darwin	.05
252	Ben Rivera	.05
253	Dave Henderson	.05
254	Steve Avery	.05
255	Tim Belcher	.05
256	Dan Plesac	.05
257	Jim Thome	.60
258	Albert Belle (35+ HR Hitter)	.05
259	Barry Bonds (35+ HR Hitter)	1.00
260	Ron Gant (35+ HR Hitter)	.05
261	Juan Gonzalez (35+ HR Hitter)	.20
262	Ken Griffey Jr. (35+ HR Hitter)	.65
263	Dave Justice (35+ HR Hitter)	.05
264	Fred McGriff (35+ HR Hitter)	.05
265	Rafael Palmeiro (35+ HR Hitter)	.20
266	Mike Piazza (35+ HR Hitter)	.05
267	Frank Thomas (35+ HR Hitter)	.35
268	Matt Williams (35+ HR Hitter)	.05
269a	Checklist 1-135	.05
269b	Checklist 271-408	.05
270a	Checklist 136-270	.05
270b	Checklist 409-540	.05
271	Mike Stanley	.05
272	Tony Tarasco	.05
273	Teddy Higuera	.05
274	Ryan Thompson	.05
275	Rick Aguilera	.05
276	Ramon Martinez	.05
277	Orlando Merced	.05
278	Guillermo Velasquez	.05
279	Mark Hutton	.05
280	Larry Walker	.05
281	Kevin Gross	.05
282	Jose Offerman	.05
283	Jim Leyritz	.05
284	Jamie Moyer	.05
285	Frank Thomas	.65
286	Derek Bell	.05
287	Derrick May	.05
288	Dave Winfield	.65
289	Curt Schilling	.35
290	Carlos Quintana	.05
291	Bob Natal	.05
292	David Cone	.05
293	Al Osuna	.05
294	Bob Hamelin	.05
295	Chad Curtis	.05
296	Danny Jackson	.05
297	Bob Welch	.05
298	Felix Jose	.05
299	Jay Buhner	.05
300	Joe Carter	.05
301	Kenny Lofton	.05
302	Kirk Rueter RC	.15
303	Kim Batiste	.05
304	Mike Morgan	.05
305	Pat Borders	.05
306	Rene Arocha	.05
307	Ruben Sierra	.05
308	Steve Finley	.05
309	Travis Fryman	.05
310	Zane Smith	.05
311	Willie Wilson	.05
312	Trevor Hoffman	.05
313	Terry Pendleton	.05
314	Salomon Torres	.05
315	Robin Ventura	.05
316	Randy Tomlin	.05
317	Dave Stewart	.05
318	Mike Benjamin	.05
319	Matt Turner	.05
320	Manny Ramirez	.65
321	Kevin Young	.05
322	Ken Caminiti	.05
323	Joe Girardi	.05
324	Jeff McKnight	.05
325	Gene Harris	.05
326	Devon White	.05
327	Darryl Kile	.05
328	Craig Paquette	.05
329	Cal Eldred	.05
330	Bill Swift	.05
331	Alan Trammell	.05
332	Armando Reynoso	.05
333	Brent Mayne	.05
334	Chris Donnels	.05
335	Darryl Strawberry	.05
336	Dean Palmer	.05
337	Frank Castillo	.05
338	Jeff King	.05
339	John Franco	.05
340	Kevin Appier	.05
341	Lance Blankenship	.05
342	Mark McLemore	.05
343	Pedro Astacio	.05
344	Rich Batchelor	.05
345	Ryan Bowen	.05
346	Terry Steinbach	.05
347	Troy O'Leary	.05
348	Willie Blair	.05
349	Wade Boggs	.75
350	Tim Raines	.05
351	Scott Livingstone	.05
352	Rod Correia	.05
353	Ray Lankford	.05
354	Pat Listach	.05
355	Milt Thompson	.05
356	Miguel Jimenez	.05
357	Marc Newfield	.05
358	Mark McGwire	1.50
359	Kirby Puckett	.75
360	Kent Mercker	.05
361	John Kruk	.05
362	Jeff Kent	.05
363	Hal Morris	.05
364	Edgar Martinez	.05
365	Dave Magadan	.05
366	Dante Bichette	.05
367	Chris Hammond	.05
368	Bret Saberhagen	.05
369	Billy Ripken	.05
370	Bill Gullickson	.05
371	Andre Dawson	.35
372	Bobby Kelly	.05
373	Cal Ripken, Jr.	2.00
374	Craig Biggio	.05
375	Dan Pasqua	.05
376	Dave Nilsson	.05
377	Duane Ward	.05
378	Greg Vaughn	.05
379	Jeff Fassero	.05
380	Jerry Dipoto	.05
381	John Patterson	.05
382	Kevin Brown	.05
383	Kevin Roberson	.05
384	Joe Orsulak	.05
385	Hilly Hathaway	.05
386	Mike Greenwell	.05
387	Orestes Destrade	.05
388	Mike Gallego	.05
389	Ozzie Guillen	.05
390	Raul Mondesi	.05
391	Scott Lydy	.05
392	Tom Urbani	.05
393	Wil Cordero	.05
394	Tony Longmire	.05
395	Todd Zeile	.05
396	Scott Cooper	.05
397	Ryne Sandberg	.75
398	Ricky Bones	.05
399	Phil Clark	.05
400	Orel Hershiser	.05
401	Mike Henneman	.05
402	Mark Lemke	.05
403	Mark Grace	.05
404	Ken Ryan	.05
405	John Smoltz	.05
406	Jeff Conine	.05
407	Greg Harris	.05
408	Doug Drabek	.05
409	Dave Fleming	.05
410	Danny Tartabull	.05
411	Chad Kreuter	.05
412	Brad Ausmus	.05
413	Ben McDonald	.05
414	Barry Larkin	.05
415	Bret Barberie	.05
416	Chuck Knoblauch	.05
417	Ozzie Smith	.75
418	Ed Sprague	.05
419	Matt Williams	.05
420	Jeremy Hernandez	.05
421	Jose Bautista	.05
422	Kevin Mitchell	.05
423	Manuel Lee	.05
424	Mike Devereaux	.05
425	Omar Olivares	.05
426	Rafael Belliard	.05
427	Richie Lewis	.05
428	Ron Darling	.05
429	Shane Mack	.05
430	Tim Hulett	.05
431	Wally Joyner	.05
432	Wes Chamberlain	.05
433	Tom Browning	.05
434	Scott Radinsky	.05
435	Rondell White	.05
436	Rod Beck	.05
437	Rheal Cormier	.05
438	Randy Johnson	.65
439	Pete Schourek	.05
440	Mo Vaughn	.05
441	Mike Timlin	.05
442	Mark Langston	.05
443	Lou Whitaker	.05
444	Kevin Stocker	.05
445	Ken Hill	.05
446	John Wetteland	.05
447	J.T. Snow	.05
448	Erik Pappas	.05
449	David Hulse	.05
450	Darren Daulton	.05
451	Chris Hoiles	.05
452	Bryan Harvey	.05
453	Darren Lewis	.05
454	Andres Galarraga	.05
455	Joe Hesketh	.05
456	Jose Valentin	.05
457	Dan Peltier	.05
458	Joe Boever	.05
459	Kevin Rogers	.05
460	Craig Shipley	.05
461	Alvaro Espinoza	.05
462	Wilson Alvarez	.05
463	Cory Snyder	.05
464	Candy Maldonado	.05
465	Blas Minor	.05
466	Rod Bolton	.05
467	Kenny Rogers	.05
468	Greg Myers	.05
469	Jimmy Key	.05
470	Tony Castillo	.05
471	Mike Stanton	.05
472	Deion Sanders	.05
473	Tito Navarro	.05
474	Mike Gardiner	.05
475	Steve Reed	.05
476	John Roper	.05
477	Mike Trombley	.05
478	Charles Nagy	.05
479	Larry Casian	.05
480	Eric Hillman	.05
481	Bill Wertz	.05
482	Jeff Schwarz	.05
483	John Valentin	.05
484	Carl Willis	.05
485	Gary Gaetti	.05
486	Bill Pecota	.05
487	John Smiley	.35
488	Mike Mussina	.35
489	Mike Ignasiak RC	.05
490	Billy Brewer	.05
491	Jack Voigt	.05
492	Mike Munoz	.05
493	Lee Tinsley	.05
494	Bob Wickman	.05
495	Roger Salkeld	.05
496	Thomas Howard	.05
497	Mark Davis	.05
498	Dave Clark	.05
499	Turk Wendell	.05
500	Rafael Bournigal	.05
501	Chip Hale	.05
502	Matt Whiteside	.05
503	Brian Koelling	.05
504	Jeff Reed	.05
505	Paul Wagner	.05
506	Torey Lovullo	.05
507	Curtis Leskanic	.05
508	Derek Lilliquist	.05
509	Joe Magrane	.05

510	Mackey Sasser	.05
511	Lloyd McClendon	.05
512	Jayhawk Owens RC	.05
513	Woody Williams RC	.05
514	Gary Redus	.05
515	Tim Spehr	.05
516	Jim Abbott	.05
517	Lou Frazier	.05
518	Erik Plantenberg	.05
519	Tim Worrell	.05
520	Brian McRae	.05
521	Chan Ho Park RC	1.00
522	Mark Wohlers	.05
523	Geronimo Pena	.05
524	Andy Ashby	.05
525	Tale of 2 Players (Tim Raines, Andre Dawson)	.05
526	Tale of 2 Players (Paul Molitor, Dave Winfield)	.40
527	Joe Carter (RBI Leader)	.05
528	Frank Thomas (HR Leader)	.35
529	Ken Griffey Jr. (TB Leader)	.65
530	Dave Justice (HR Leader)	.05
531	Gregg Jefferies (AVG Leader)	.05
532	Barry Bonds (HR Leader)	1.00
533	John Kruk (Quick Start)	.05
534	Roger Clemens (Quick Start)	.50
535	Cecil Fielder (Quick Start)	.05
536	Ruben Sierra (Quick Start)	.05
537	Tony Gwynn (Quick Start)	.40
538	Tom Glavine (Quick Start)	.10
541	Ozzie Smith (Career Leader)	.40
542	Eddie Murray (Career Leader)	.30
543a	Lee Smith (Career Leader)	.05
543b	Lonnie Smith (Should be #643.)	
544	Greg Maddux	.75
545	Denis Boucher	.05
546	Mark Gardner	.05
547	Bo Jackson	.10
548	Eric Anthony	.05
549	Delino DeShields	.05
550	Turner Ward	.05
551	Scott Sanderson	.05
552	Hector Carrasco	.05
553	Tony Phillips	.05
554	Melido Perez	.05
555	Mike Felder	.05
556	Jack Morris	.05
557	Rafael Palmeiro	.60
558	Shane Reynolds	.05
559	Pete Incaviglia	.05
560	Greg Harris	.05
561	Matt Walbeck	.05
562	Todd Van Poppel	.05
563	Todd Stottlemyre	.05
564	Ricky Bones	.05
565	Mike Jackson	.05
566	Kevin McReynolds	.05
567	Melvin Nieves	.05
568	Juan Gonzalez	.35
569	Frank Viola	.05
570	Vince Coleman	.05
571	Brian Anderson RC	.25
572	Omar Vizquel	.05
573	Bernie Williams	.05
574	Tom Glavine	.35
575	Mitch Williams	.05
576	Shawon Dunston	.05
577	Mike Lansing	.05
578	Greg Pirkl	.05
579	Sid Fernandez	.05
580	Doug Jones	.05
581	Walt Weiss	.05
582	Tim Belcher	.05
583	Alex Fernandez	.05
584	Alex Cole	.05
585	Greg Cadaret	.05
586	Bob Tewksbury	.05
587	Dave Hansen	.05
588	Kurt Abbott RC	.25
589	Rick White RC	.05
590	Kevin Bass	.05
591	Geronimo Berroa	.05
592	Jaime Navarro	.05
593	Steve Farr	.05
594	Jack Armstrong	.05
595	Steve Howe	.05
596	Jose Rijo	.05
597	Otis Nixon	.05
598	Robby Thompson	.05
599	Kelly Stinnett	.05
600	Carlos Delgado	.50
601	Brian Johnson RC	.05
602	Gregg Olson	.05
603	Jim Edmonds	.05
604	Mike Blowers	.05
605	Lee Smith	.05
606	Pat Rapp	.05
607	Mike Magnante	.05
608	Karl Rhodes	.05
609	Jeff Juden	.05
610	Rusty Meacham	.05
611	Pedro Martinez	.65
612	Todd Worrell	.05
613	Stan Javier	.05
614	Mike Hampton	.05
615	Jose Guzman	.05
616	Xavier Hernandez	.05
617	David Wells	.05
618	John Habyan	.05
619	Chris Nabholz	.05

620	Bobby Jones	.05
621	Chris James	.05
622	Ellis Burks	.05
623	Erik Hanson	.05
624	Pat Meares	.05
625	Harold Reynolds	.05
626	Bob Hamelin (Rookie Rocker)	.05
627	Manny Ramirez (Rookie Rocker)	.30
628	Ryan Klesko (Rookie Rocker)	
629	Carlos Delgado (Rookie Rocker)	.30
630	Javier Lopez (Rookie Rocker)	.05
631	Steve Karsay (Rookie Rocker)	.05
632	Rick Helling (Rookie Rocket)	.05
633	Steve Trachsel (Rookie Rocket)	.05
634	Hector Carrasco (Rookie Rocket)	.05
635	Andy Stankiewicz	.05
636	Paul Sorrento	.05
637	Scott Erickson	.05
638	Chipper Jones	.75
639	Luis Polonia	.05
640	Howard Johnson	.05
641	John Dopson	.05
642	Jody Reed	.05
644	Mark Portugal	.05
645	Paul Molitor	.65
646	Paul Assenmacher	.05
647	Hubie Brooks	.05
648	Gary Wayne	.05
649	Sean Berry	.05
650	Roger Clemens	1.00
651	Brian Hunter	.05
652	Wally Whitehurst	.05
653	Allen Watson	.05
654	Rickey Henderson	.65
655	Sid Bream	.05
656	Dan Wilson	.05
657	Ricky Jordan	.05
658	Sterling Hitchcock	.05
659	Darrin Jackson	.05
660	Junior Felix	.05
661	Tom Brunansky	.05
662	Jose Vizcaino	.05
663	Mark Leiter	.05
664	Gil Heredia	.05
665	Fred McGriff	.05
666	Will Clark	.05
667	Al Leiter	.05
668	James Mouton	.05
669	Billy Bean	.05
670	Scott Leius	.05
671	Bret Boone	.05
672	Darren Holmes	.05
673	Dave Weathers	.05
674	Eddie Murray	.65
675	Felix Fermin	.05
676	Chris Sabo	.05
677	Billy Spiers	.05
678	Aaron Sele	.05
679	Juan Samuel	.05
680	Julio Franco	.05
681	Heathcliff Slocumb	.05
682	Denny Martinez	.05
683	Jerry Browne	.05
684	Pedro A. Martinez RC	.05
685	Rex Hudler	.05
686	Willie McGee	.05
687	Andy Van Slyke	.05
688	Pat Mahomes	.05
689	Dave Henderson	.05
690	Tony Eusebio	.05
691	Rick Sutcliffe	.05
692	Willie Banks	.05
693	Alan Mills	.05
694	Jeff Treadway	.05
695	Alex Gonzalez	.05
696	David Segui	.05
697	Rick Helling	.05
698	Bip Roberts	.05
699	Jeff Cirillo RC	.25
700	Terry Mulholland	.05
701	Marvin Freeman	.05
702	Jason Bere	.05
703	Javier Lopez	.05
704	Greg Hibbard	.05
705	Tommy Greene	.05
706	Marquis Grissom	.05
707	Brian Harper	.05
708	Steve Karsay	.05
709	Jeff Brantley	.05
710	Jeff Russell	.05
711	Bryan Hickerson	.05
712	Jim Pittsley RC	.05
713	Bobby Ayala	.05
714	John Smoltz (Fantastic Finisher)	.05
715	Jose Rijo (Fantastic Finisher)	.05
716	Greg Maddux (Fantastic Finisher)	.40
717	Matt Williams (Fantastic Finisher)	.05
718	Frank Thomas (Fantastic Finisher)	.35
719	Ryne Sandberg (Fantastic Finisher)	.40
720	Checklist	.05

Golden Rainbow

Found at the rate of one per pack, Stadium Club "Golden Rainbow" cards were issued for each of the 720 cards in the regular set. These inserts are distinguished by the use of gold prismatic foil highlights for the S.C. logo and box with the player's last name, instead of the red foil found on regular S.C. cards.

	NM/M
Complete Set (720):	60.00
Common Player:	.25
Stars:	2X

1st Day Issue

A special silver-foil embossment designating "1st Day Issue" was placed on fewer than 2,000 of each of the 720 regular cards in the '94 Stadium Club set. Inserted at the rate of one per 24 foil packs and one per 15 jumbo packs, the cards are otherwise identical to the regular TSC cards.

	NM/M
Common Player:	1.00
Stars:	8X

Dugout Dirt

Cartoons of some of baseball's top stars are featured on the backs of this 12-card insert set. Fronts are virtually identical in format to regular S.C. cards, except the logo and box with the player's last name are in gold-foil, rather than red. Stated odds of finding a Dugout Dirt insert card were one per six packs, on average. Cards can also be found with a gold "Members Only" seal on front.

		NM/M
Complete Set (12):		5.00
Common Player:		.25
1	Mike Piazza (Catch of the Day)	1.00
2	Dave Winfield (The Road to 3,000)	.65
3	John Kruk (From Coal Mine to Gold Mine)	.25

4	Cal Ripken, Jr. (On Track)	2.00
5	Jack McDowell (Chin Music)	.25
6	Barry Bonds (The Bonds Market)	2.00
7	Ken Griffey Jr./AS (Gold Gloves)	1.00
8	Tim Salmon (The Salmon Run)	.25
9	Frank Thomas (Big Hurt)	.65
10	Jeff Kent (Super Kent)	.25
11	Randy Johnson (High Heat)	.65
12	Darren Daulton (Daulton's Gym)	.25

Finest

This insert set was included only in Series III packs of Topps Stadium Club, at the rate of one card per six packs, on average. Cards utilize Topps Finest technology and feature a player action photo on front, set against a red-and-gold sunburst background. Backs have a player portrait photo, a few stats and appropriate logos. Cards can also be found with a "Members Only" logo on front.

		NM/M
Complete Set (10):		11.00
Common Player:		.50
1	Jeff Bagwell	1.25
2	Albert Belle	.50
3	Barry Bonds	3.00
4	Juan Gonzalez	.75
5	Ken Griffey Jr.	2.00
6	Marquis Grissom	.50
7	David Justice	.50
8	Mike Piazza	2.00
9	Tim Salmon	.50
10	Frank Thomas	1.50

Finest Jumbo

Found only as a one per tub insert in special Wal-Mart repackaging of baseball packs, these 5" x 7" versions of the Series III Stadium Club inserts are identical to the smaller version. Cards utilize Topps Finest technology and feature a player action photo on front, set against a red-and-gold sunburst background. Backs have a player portrait photo, a few stats and appropriate logos.

		NM/M
Complete Set (10):		30.00
Common Player:		2.00
1	Jeff Bagwell	4.00
2	Albert Belle	2.00
3	Barry Bonds	6.50
4	Juan Gonzalez	3.00
5	Ken Griffey Jr.	5.00
6	Marquis Grissom	2.00
7	David Justice	2.00
8	Mike Piazza	5.00
9	Tim Salmon	2.00
10	Frank Thomas	4.00

Super Teams

Super Team cards were issued for each of the 28 major league teams and inserted at the rate of one per 24 regular packs and one per 15 jumbo packs. At the end of the 1995 season (the promotion was carried over when the 1994 season was ended prematurely by the players' strike), persons holding Super Team cards of the division winners, league champions and World Champions could redeem the cards for prizes. Division winning team cards could be redeemed for a set of 10 S.C. cards of that team with a special division winner embossed logo. League champion cards could be redeemed for a set of 10 Master Photos of the team with a special league logo embossed. Persons with a Super Team card of the eventual World Series champion could trade the card in for a complete set of Stadium Club cards embossed with a World's Champion logo. Each of the Super Team cards features a small group of players on the front with the Super Team Card and S.C. logos in gold foil, and the team name in prismatic foil. Backs contain redemption rules. A version of the Super Team cards was distributed with "Members Only" sets containing such an indicia on front and team roster on back.

		NM/M
Complete Set (28):		25.00
Common Team:		.70
Expired Jan. 31, 1996.		
1	Atlanta Braves	5.00
2	Chicago Cubs	.70
3	Cincinnati Reds	1.25
4	Colorado Rockies	1.00
5	Florida Marlins	.70
6	Houston Astros	1.00
7	Los Angeles Dodgers	1.75
8	Montreal Expos	1.00
9	New York Mets	.70
10	Philadelphia Phillies	.70
11	Pittsburgh Pirates	.70
12	St. Louis Cardinals	.70
13	San Diego Padres	.70
14	San Francisco Giants	1.25
15	Baltimore Orioles	1.25
16	Boston Red Sox	1.00
17	California Angels	.70
18	Chicago White Sox	1.50
19	Cleveland Indians	2.00
20	Detroit Tigers	.70
21	Kansas City Royals	1.00
22	Milwaukee Brewers	.70
23	Minnesota Twins	1.00
24	New York Yankees	1.50
25	Oakland Athletics	1.00
26	Seattle Mariners	2.00
27	Texas Rangers	1.00
28	Toronto Blue Jays	1.00

Members Only

This special gold-seal embossed version of the 1994 Topps Stadium Club set was available by a mail-in offer to club members for $230. The set includes all regular Stadium Club cards from Series I, II and III, along with the Dugout Dirt, Finest, and Super Teams insert cards. The Super Team cards, which were not eligible for the contest, have team rosters on back, rather than contest rules. All other cards are identical to the regular-issue S.C. cards except for the present of the 1/2" round gold-foil "Members Only" seal beneath or alongside of the red-foil Topps Stadium Club logo on front. There are two different checklists each numbered 269 and 270. Only 5,000 sets were produced.

	NM/M
Complete Set (770):	150.00
Common Player:	.50
Stars:	8X

Members Only Baseball

Available for purchase by Topps Stadium Club members as a 50-card boxed set (football and basketball sets were also available), this issue features top stars, performances and career highlights from the 1993 season. Cards feature borderless action photos on front with the Topps logo and player's last name in gold-foil. Backs are horizontal and feature a black background on which the player's achievement is detailed in blue and gold. A second player photo appears on the card back. Cards #46-50 were produced in the Topps Finest-style foil-printing technology.

		NM/M
Complete Set (50):		6.00
Common Player:		.10
1	Juan Gonzalez	.25
2	Tom Henke	.10
3	John Kruk	.10
4	Paul Molitor	.50
5	Dave Justice	.10
6	Rafael Palmeiro	.45
7	John Smoltz	.10
8	Matt Williams	.10
9	John Olerud	.10
10	Mark Grace	.10
11	Joe Carter	.10
12	Wilson Alvarez	.10
13	Lenny Dykstra	.10
14	Kevin Appier	.10
15	Andres Galarraga	.10
16	Mark Langston	.10
17	Ken Griffey Jr.	.75
18	Albert Belle	.10
19	Gregg Jefferies	.10
20	Duane Ward	.10
21	Jack McDowell	.10
22	Randy Johnson	.50
23	Tom Glavine	.35
24	Barry Bonds	1.50
25	Chuck Carr	.10
26	Ron Gant	.10
27	Kenny Lofton	.10
28	Mike Piazza	.75
29	Frank Thomas	.55
30	Fred McGriff	.10
31	Bryan Harvey	.10
32	John Burkett	.10
33	Roberto Alomar	.10
34	Cecil Fielder	.10
35	Marquis Grissom	.10
36	Randy Myers	.10
37	Tony Phillips	.10
38	Rickey Henderson	.50
39	Luis Polonia	.10
40	Jose Rijo	.10
41	Jeff Montgomery	.10
42	Greg Maddux	.60
43	Tony Gwynn	.60
44	Rod Beck	.10

45	Carlos Baerga	.10
46	Wil Cordero	.10
47	Tim Salmon	.10
48	Mike Lansing	.10
49	J.T. Snow	.10
50	Jeff Conine	.10

Superstar Sampler

A small, round black-and-white "Topps Superstar Sampler" logo printed on the back is all that distinguishes these cards from regular-issue S.C. cards. This version of 45 of the top stars from the Stadium Club set was issued only in three-card cello packs inserted into 1994 Topps retail factory sets. The packs also contained the same player's cards from the Bowman and Finest sets, similarly marked.

		NM/M
Complete Set (45):		275.00
Common Player:		2.00
4	Gary Sheffield	3.00
10	Roberto Alomar	4.00
24	Jack McDowell	2.00
25	Cecil Fielder	2.00
36	Tim Salmon	2.00
59	Bobby Bonilla	2.00
85	Ken Griffey Jr.	20.00
94	Dave Justice	2.00
108	Jeff Bagwell	12.00
109	Gregg Jefferies	2.00
127	Cliff Floyd	2.00
140	Mike Piazza	20.00
151	Tony Gwynn	12.50
165	Len Dykstra	2.00
169	Carlos Baerga	2.00
171	Jose Canseco	8.00
195	Don Mattingly	15.00
203	Will Clark	2.00
208	Rafael Palmeiro	10.00
219	Albert Belle	2.00
228	John Olerud	2.00
238	Barry Bonds	30.00
280	Larry Walker	2.00
285	Frank Thomas	12.00
300	Joe Carter	2.00
320	Manny Ramirez	12.00
359	Kirby Puckett	12.50
373	Cal Ripken Jr.	30.00
390	Raul Mondesi	2.00
397	Ryne Sandberg	12.50
403	Mark Grace	2.00
414	Barry Larkin	2.00
419	Matt Williams	2.00
438	Randy Johnson	12.00
440	Mo Vaughn	2.00
450	Darren Daulton	2.00
454	Andres Galarraga	2.00
544	Greg Maddux	12.50
568	Juan Gonzalez	6.00
574	Tom Glavine	3.00
645	Paul Molitor	12.00
650	Roger Clemens	15.00
665	Fred McGriff	2.00
687	Andy Van Slyke	2.00
706	Marquis Grissom	2.00

Team Series

Only 12 of the 28 major league teams are included in this special issue marketed in both team-set blister packs and foil packs at Wal-Mart stores around the country. Card fronts feature a player action photo bordered in the lower-right corner by a dark green mottled effect. The player's name, team and "Team Stadium Club" logo are in gold foil. Backs have a second player photo set against a

background in mottled shades of green. There are a few stats and player biographical details.

		NM/M
Complete Set (360):		25.00
Common Player:		.10
Wax Box (24):		15.00
1	Barry Bonds	3.50
2	Royce Clayton	.10
3	Kirt Manwaring	.10
4	J.R. Phillips	.10
5	Robby Thompson	.10
6	Willie McGee	.10
7	Steve Hosey	.10
8	Dave Burba	.10
9	Steve Scarsone	.10
10	Salomon Torres	.10
11	Bryan Hickerson	.10
12	Mike Benjamin	.10
13	Mark Carreon	.10
14	Rich Monteleone	.10
15	Dave Martinez	.10
16	Bill Swift	.10
17	Jeff Reed	.10
18	John Patterson	.10
19	Darren Lewis	.10
20	Mark Portugal	.10
21	Trevor Wilson	.10
22	Matt Williams	.10
23	Kevin Rogers	.10
24	Luis Mercedes	.10
25	Mike Jackson	.10
26	Steve Frey	.10
27	Tony Menendez	.10
28	John Burkett	.10
29	Todd Benzinger	.10
30	Rod Beck	.10
31	Greg Maddux	1.50
32	Steve Avery	.10
33	Milt Hill	.10
34	Charlie O'Brien	.10
35	John Smoltz	.10
36	Jarvis Brown	.10
37	Dave Gallagher	.10
38	Ryan Klesko	.10
39	Kent Mercker	.10
40	Terry Pendleton	.10
41	Ron Gant	.10
42	Pedro Borbon	.10
43	Steve Bedrosian	.10
44	Ramon Caraballo	.10
45	Tyler Houston	.10
46	Mark Lemke	.10
47	Fred McGriff	.10
48	Jose Oliva	.10
49	David Justice	.10
50	Chipper Jones	1.50
51	Tony Tarasco	.10
52	Javy Lopez	.10
53	Mark Wohlers	.10
54	Deion Sanders	.10
55	Greg McMichael	.10
56	Tom Glavine	.35
57	Bill Pecota	.10
58	Mike Stanton	.10
59	Rafael Belliard	.10
60	Jeff Blauser	.10
61	Bryan Harvey	.10
62	Bret Barberie	.10
63	Rick Renteria	.10
64	Chris Hammond	.10
65	Pat Rapp	.10
66	Nigel Wilson	.10
67	Gary Sheffield	.30
68	Jerry Browne	.10
69	Charlie Hough	.10
70	Orestes Destrade	.10
71	Mario Diaz	.10
72	Ryan Bowen	.10
73	Carl Everett	.10
74	Richie Lewis	.10
75	Bob Natal	.10
76	Rich Rodriguez	.10
77	Darrell Whitmore	.10
78	Matt Turner	.10
79	Benny Santiago	.10
80	Robb Nen	.10
81	Dave Magadan	.10
82	Brian Drahman	.10
83	Mark Gardner	.10
84	Chuck Carr	.10
85	Alex Arias	.10
86	Kurt Abbott	.10
87	Joe Klink	.10
88	Jeff Mutis	.10
89	Dave Weathers	.10
90	Jeff Conine	.10
91	Andres Galarraga	.10
92	Vinny Castilla	.10
93	Roberto Mejia	.10
94	Darrell Sherman	.10
95	Mike Harkey	.10
96	Danny Sheaffer	.10
97	Pedro Castellano	.10
98	Walt Weiss	.10
99	Greg Harris	.10
100	Jayhawk Owens	.10
101	Bruce Ruffin	.10
102	Mike Munoz	.10
103	Armando Reynoso	.10
104	Eric Young	.10
105	Dante Bichette	.10
106	Marvin Freeman	.10
107	Joe Girardi	.10
108	Kent Bottenfield	.10
109	Howard Johnson	.10
110	Nelson Liriano	.10

111	David Nied	.10
112	Steve Reed	.10
113	Eric Wedge	.10
114	Charlie Hayes	.10
115	Ellis Burks	.10
116	Willie Blair	.10
117	Darren Holmes	.10
118	Curtis Leskanic	.10
119	Lance Painter	.10
120	Jim Tatum	.10
121	Frank Thomas	1.00
122	Jack McDowell	.10
123	Ron Karkovice	.10
124	Mike LaValliere	.10
125	Scott Radinsky	.10
126	Robin Ventura	.10
127	Scott Ruffcorn	.10
128	Steve Sax	.10
129	Roberto Hernandez	.10
130	Jose DeLeon	.10
131	Rod Bolton	.10
132	Wilson Alvarez	.10
133	Craig Grebeck	.10
134	Lance Johnson	.10
135	Kirk McCaskill	.10
136	Tim Raines	.10
137	Jeff Schwarz	.10
138	Warren Newson	.10
139	Norberto Martin	.10
140	Mike Huff	.10
141	Ozzie Guillen	.10
142	Alex Fernandez	.10
143	Joey Cora	.10
144	Jason Bere	.10
145	James Baldwin	.10
146	Esteban Beltre	.10
147	Julio Franco	.10
148	Matt Merullo	.10
149	Dan Pasqua	.10
150	Darrin Jackson	.10
151	Joe Carter	.10
152	Danny Cox	.10
153	Roberto Alomar	.20
154	Woody Williams	.10
155	Duane Ward	.10
156	Ed Sprague	.10
157	Domingo Martinez	.10
158	Pat Hentgen	.10
159	Shawn Green	.30
160	Dick Schofield	.10
161	Paul Molitor	1.00
162	Darnell Coles	.10
163	Willie Canate	.10
164	Domingo Cedeno	.10
165	Pat Borders	.10
166	Greg Cadaret	.10
167	Tony Castillo	.10
168	Carlos Delgado	.45
169	Scott Brow	.10
170	Juan Guzman	.10
171	Al Leiter	.10
172	John Olerud	.10
173	Todd Stottlemyre	.10
174	Devon White	.10
175	Paul Spoljaric	.10
176	Randy Knorr	.10
177	Huck Flener **RC**	.10
178	Rob Butler	.10
179	Dave Stewart	.10
180	Mike Timlin	.10
181	Don Mattingly	2.00
182	Mark Hutton	.10
183	Mike Gallego	.10
184	Jim Abbott	.10
185	Paul Gibson	.10
186	Scott Kamieniecki	.10
187	Sam Horn	.10
188	Melido Perez	.10
189	Randy Velarde	.10
190	Gerald Williams	.10
191	Dave Silvestri	.10
192	Jim Leyritz	.10
193	Steve Howe	.10
194	Russ Davis	.10
195	Paul Assenmacher	.10
196	Pat Kelly	.10
197	Mike Stanley	.15
198	Bernie Williams	.80
199	Paul O'Neill	.10
200	Donn Pall	.10
201	Xavier Hernandez	.10
202	James Austin	.10
203	Sterling Hitchcock	.10
204	Wade Boggs	1.50
205	Jimmy Key	.10
206	Matt Nokes	.10
207	Terry Mulholland	.10
208	Luis Polonia	.10
209	Danny Tartabull	.10
210	Bob Wickman	.10
211	Len Dykstra	.10
212	Kim Batiste	.10
213	Tony Longmire	.10
214	Bobby Munoz	.10
215	Pete Incaviglia	.10
216	Doug Jones	.10
217	Mariano Duncan	.10
218	Jeff Juden	.10
219	Milt Thompson	.10
220	Dave West	.10
221	Roger Mason	.10
222	Tommy Greene	.10
223	Larry Andersen	.10
224	Jim Eisenreich	.10
225	Dave Hollins	.10
226	John Kruk	.10
227	Todd Pratt	.10
228	Ricky Jordan	.10

229	Curt Schilling	.35
230	Mike Williams	.10
231	Heathcliff Slocumb	.10
232	Ben Rivera	.10
233	Mike Lieberthal	.10
234	Mickey Morandini	.10
235	Danny Jackson	.10
236	Kevin Foster	.10
237	Darren Daulton	.10
238	Wes Chamberlain	.10
239	Tyler Green	.10
240	Kevin Stocker	.10
241	Juan Gonzalez	.50
242	Rick Honeycutt	.10
243	Bruce Hurst	.10
244	Steve Dreyer	.10
245	Brian Bohanon	.10
246	Benji Gil	.10
247	Jon Shave	.10
248	Manuel Lee	.10
249	Donald Harris	.10
250	Jose Canseco	.50
251	David Hulse	.10
252	Kenny Rogers	.10
253	Jeff Huson	.10
254	Dan Peltier	.10
255	Mike Scioscia	.10
256	Jack Armstrong	.10
257	Rob Ducey	.10
258	Will Clark	.10
259	Cris Carpenter	.10
260	Kevin Brown	.10
261	Jeff Frye	.10
262	Jay Howell	.10
263	Roger Pavlik	.10
264	Gary Redus	.10
265	Ivan Rodriguez	.75
266	Matt Whiteside	.10
267	Doug Strange	.10
268	Billy Ripken	.10
269	Dean Palmer	.10
270	Tom Henke	.10
271	Cal Ripken Jr.	3.50
272	Mark McLemore	.10
273	Sid Fernandez	.10
274	Sherman Obando	.10
275	Paul Carey	.10
276	Mike Oquist	.10
277	Alan Mills	.10
278	Harold Baines	.10
279	Mike Mussina	.30
280	Arthur Rhodes	.10
281	Kevin McGehee	.10
282	Mark Eichhorn	.10
283	Damon Buford	.10
284	Ben McDonald	.10
285	David Segui	.10
286	Brad Pennington	.10
287	Jamie Moyer	.10
288	Chris Hoiles	.10
289	Mike Cook	.10
290	Brady Anderson	.10
291	Chris Sabo	.10
292	Jack Voigt	.10
293	Jim Poole	.10
294	Jeff Tackett	.10
295	Rafael Palmeiro	.75
296	Alex Ochoa	.10
297	John O'Donoghue	.10
298	Tim Hulett	.10
299	Mike Devereaux	.10
300	Manny Alexander	.10
301	Ozzie Smith	1.50
302	Omar Olivares	.10
303	Rheal Cormier	.10
304	Donovan Osborne	.10
305	Mark Whiten	.10
306	Todd Zeile	.10
307	Geronimo Pena	.10
308	Brian Jordan	.10
309	Luis Alicea	.10
310	Ray Lankford	.10
311	Stan Royer	.10
312	Bob Tewksbury	.10
313	Jose Oquendo	.10
314	Steve Dixon	.10
315	Rene Arocha	.10
316	Bernard Gilkey	.10
317	Gregg Jefferies	.10
318	Rob Murphy	.10
319	Tom Pagnozzi	.10
320	Mike Perez	.10
321	Tom Urbani	.10
322	Allen Watson	.10
323	Erik Pappas	.10
324	Paul Kilgus	.10
325	John Habyan	.10
326	Rod Brewer	.10
327	Rich Batchelor	.10
328	Tripp Cromer	.10
329	Gerald Perry	.10
330	Les Lancaster	.10
331	Ryne Sandberg	1.50
332	Derrick May	.10
333	Steve Buechele	.10
334	Willie Banks	.10
335	Larry Luebbers	.10
336	Tommy Shields	.10
337	Eric Yelding	.10
338	Rey Sanchez	.10
339	Mark Grace	.10
340	Jose Bautista	.10
341	Frank Castillo	.10
342	Jose Guzman	.10
343	Rafael Novoa	.10
344	Karl Rhodes	.10
345	Steve Trachsel	.10
346	Rick Wilkins	.10

347	Sammy Sosa	1.50
348	Kevin Roberson	.10
349	Mark Parent	.10
350	Randy Myers	.10
351	Glenallen Hill	.10
352	Lance Dickson	.10
353	Shawn Boskie	.10
354	Shawon Dunston	.10
355	Dan Plesac	.10
356	Jose Vizcaino	.10
357	Willie Wilson	.10
358	Turk Wendell	.10
359	Mike Morgan	.10
360	Jim Bullinger	.10

Team Series 1st Day Issue

Each of the cards in the Stadium Club Team Series can be found with a speial embossed silver-foil "1st Day Issue" seal on front. Cards are otherwise identical to the regular issue.

		NM/M
Complete Set (360):		200.00
Common Player:		.50
Stars:		8X

Team Series Finest

One player from each of the 12 teams in the Stadium Club Team Series issue was printed in a chromium-metallic technology reminiscent of Topps Finest cards. These special cards are labeled "Team Stadium Club Finest." Other than the printing, the cards are in the same format as the rest of the issue.

		NM/M
Complete Set (12):		12.00
Common Player:		.50
1	Roberto Alomar	.50
2	Barry Bonds	3.00
3	Len Dykstra	.50
4	Andres Galarraga	.50
5	Juan Gonzalez	.50
6	Dave Justice	.50
7	Don Mattingly	2.00
8	Cal Ripken Jr.	3.00
9	Ryne Sandberg	1.50
10	Gary Sheffield	.65
11	Ozzie Smith	1.50
12	Frank Thomas	1.00

1995 Stadium Club

Topps' upscale brand was issued for 1995 in three series of, respectively, 270, 225 and 135 cards. Fronts have borderless color photos with a gold-foil device at bottom holding the team logo. Also in gold are the player's name at bottom and the Stadium Club logo at top. Backs have another player photo at left within a pair of computer-enhanced close-ups above it. At right are bar graphs

detailing the player's '94 stats and his skills rankings. A number of specially designed subsets - "Best Seat in the House, Cover Story, MLB Debut," etc., are spread throughout the issue, which also includes a full slate of chase cards depending on the series and packaging.

		NM/M
Complete Set (630):		25.00
Common Player:		.05
Common First Day Production:		.50
First Day Stars:		7X
Series 1 or 2 Pack (14):		1.25
Series 1 or 2 Wax Box (24):		20.00
Series 3 Pack (13):		1.25
Series 3 Wax Box (24):		20.00
1	Cal Ripken Jr.	2.50
2	Bo Jackson	.10
3	Bryan Harvey	.05
4	Curt Schilling	.35
5	Bruce Ruffin	.05
6	Travis Fryman	.05
7	Jim Abbott	.05
8	David McCarty	.05
9	Gary Gaetti	.05
10	Roger Clemens	1.25
11	Carlos Garcia	.05
12	Lee Smith	.05
13	Bobby Ayala	.05
14	Charles Nagy	.05
15	Lou Frazier	.05
16	Rene Arocha	.05
17	Carlos Delgado	.50
18	Steve Finley	.05
19	Ryan Klesko	.05
20	Cal Eldred	.05
21	Rey Sanchez	.05
22	Ken Hill	.05
23	Benny Santiago	.05
24	Julian Tavarez	.05
25	Jose Vizcaino	.05
26	Andy Benes	.05
27	Mariano Duncan	.05
28	Checklist A	.05
29	Shawon Dunston	.05
30	Rafael Palmeiro	.65
31	Dean Palmer	.05
32	Andres Galarraga	.05
33	Joey Cora	.05
34	Mickey Tettleton	.05
35	Barry Larkin	.05
36	Carlos Baerga	.05
37	Orel Hershiser	.05
38	Jody Reed	.05
39	Paul Molitor	.25
40	Jim Edmonds	.05
41	Bob Tewksbury	.05
42	John Patterson	.05
43	Ray McDavid	.05
44	Zane Smith	.05
45	Bret Saberhagen	.05
46	Greg Maddux	1.00
47	Frank Thomas	.75
48	Carlos Baerga	.05
49	Billy Spiers	.05
50	Stan Javier	.05
51	Rex Hudler	.05
52	Denny Hocking	.05
53	Todd Worrell	.05
54	Mark Clark	.05
55	Hipilito Pichardo	.05
56	Bob Wickman	.05
57	Raul Mondesi	.05
58	Steve Cooke	.05
59	Rod Beck	.05
60	Tim Davis	.05
61	Jeff Kent	.05
62	John Valentin	.05
63	Alex Arias	.05
64	Steve Reed	.05
65	Ozzie Smith	1.00
66	Terry Pendleton	.05
67	Kenny Rogers	.05
68	Vince Coleman	.05
69	Tom Pagnozzi	.05
70	Roberto Alomar	.20
71	Darrin Jackson	.05
72	Dennis Eckersley	.65
73	Jay Buhner	.05
74	Darren Lewis	.05
75	Dave Weathers	.05
76	Matt Walbeck	.05
77	Brad Ausmus	.05
78	Danny Bautista	.05
79	Bob Hamelin	.05
80	Steve Traschel	.05
81	Ken Ryan	.05
82	Chris Turner	.05
83	David Segui	.05
84	Ben McDonald	.05
85	Wade Boggs	1.00
86	John Vander Wal	.05
87	Sandy Alomar	.05
88	Ron Karkovice	.05
89	Doug Jones	.05
90	Gary Sheffield	.40
91	Ken Caminiti	.05
92	Chris Bosio	.05
93	Kevin Tapani	.05
94	Walt Weiss	.05
95	Erik Hanson	.05
96	Ruben Sierra	.05
97	Nomar Garciaparra	1.00
98	Terrence Long	.05
99	Jacob Shumate	.05

#	Player	Price
100	Paul Wilson	.05
101	Kevin Witt	.05
102	Paul Konerko	.15
103	Ben Grieve	.05
104	Mark Johnson RC	.05
105	Cade Gaspar RC	.05
106	Mark Farris	.05
107	Dustin Hermanson RC	.05
108	Scott Elarton RC	.15
109	Doug Million	.05
110	Matt Smith	.05
111	Brian Buchanan RC	.05
112	Jayson Peterson RC	.05
113	Bret Wagner	.05
114	C.J. Nitkowski	.05
115	Ramon Castro RC	.05
116	Rafael Bournigal	.05
117	Jeff Fassero	.05
118	Bobby Bonilla	.05
119	Ricky Gutierrez	.05
120	Roger Pavlik	.05
121	Mike Greenwell	.05
122	Deion Sanders	.05
123	Charlie Hayes	.05
124	Paul O'Neill	.05
125	Jay Bell	.05
126	Royce Clayton	.05
127	Willie Banks	.05
128	Mark Wohlers	.05
129	Todd Jones	.05
130	Todd Stottlemyre	.05
131	Will Clark	.05
132	Wilson Alvarez	.05
133	Chili Davis	.05
134	Dave Burba	.05
135	Chris Hoiles	.05
136	Jeff Blauser	.05
137	Jeff Reboulet	.05
138	Bret Saberhagen	.05
139	Kirk Rueter	.05
140	Dave Nilsson	.05
141	Pat Borders	.05
142	Ron Darling	.05
143	Derek Bell	.05
144	Dave Hollins	.05
145	Juan Gonzalez	.40
146	Andre Dawson	.25
147	Jim Thome	.65
148	Larry Walker	.05
149	Mike Piazza	1.50
150	Mike Perez	.05
151	Steve Avery	.05
152	Dan Wilson	.05
153	Andy Van Slyke	.05
154	Junior Felix	.05
155	Jack McDowell	.05
156	Danny Tartabull	.05
157	Willie Blair	.05
158	William Van Landingham	.05
159	Robb Nen	.05
160	Lee Tinsley	.05
161	Ismael Valdes	.05
162	Juan Guzman	.05
163	Scott Servais	.05
164	Cliff Floyd	.05
165	Allen Watson	.05
166	Eddie Taubensee	.05
167	Scott Hemond	.05
168	Jeff Tackett	.05
169	Chad Curtis	.05
170	Rico Brogna	.05
171	Luis Polonia	.05
172	Checklist B	.05
173	Lance Johnson	.05
174	Sammy Sosa	1.00
175	Mike MacFarlane	.05
176	Darryl Hamilton	.05
177	Rick Aguilera	.05
178	Dave West	.05
179	Mike Gallego	.05
180	Marc Newfield	.05
181	Steve Buechele	.05
182	David Wells	.05
183	Tom Glavine	.35
184	Joe Girardi	.05
185	Craig Biggio	.05
186	Eddie Murray	.75
187	Kevin Gross	.05
188	Sid Fernandez	.05
189	John Franco	.05
190	Bernard Gilkey	.05
191	Matt Williams	.05
192	Darrin Fletcher	.05
193	Jeff Conine	.05
194	Ed Sprague	.05
195	Eduardo Perez	.05
196	Scott Livingstone	.05
197	Ivan Rodriguez	.65
198	Orlando Merced	.05
199	Ricky Bones	.05
200	Javier Lopez	.05
201	Miguel Jimenez	.05
202	Terry McGriff	.05
203	Mike Lieberthal	.05
204	David Cone	.05
205	Todd Hundley	.05
206	Ozzie Guillen	.05
207	Alex Cole	.05
208	Tony Phillips	.05
209	Jim Eisenreich	.05
210	Greg Vaughn	.05
211	Barry Larkin	.05
212	Don Mattingly	1.00
213	Mark Grace	.05
214	Jose Canseco	.50
215	Joe Carter	.05
216	David Cone	.05
217	Sandy Alomar	.05
218	Al Martin	.05
219	Roberto Kelly	.05
220	Paul Sorrento	.05
221	Tony Fernandez	.05
222	Stan Belinda	.05
223	Mike Stanley	.05
224	Doug Drabek	.05
225	Todd Van Poppel	.05
226	Matt Mieske	.05
227	Tino Martinez	.05
228	Andy Ashby	.05
229	Midre Cummings	.05
230	Jeff Frye	.05
231	Hal Morris	.05
232	Jose Lind	.05
233	Shawn Green	.30
234	Rafael Belliard	.05
235	Randy Myers	.05
236	Frank Thomas	.45
237	Darren Daulton	.05
238	Sammy Sosa	.65
239	Cal Ripken Jr.	1.00
240	Jeff Bagwell	.40
241	Ken Griffey Jr.	1.50
242	Brett Butler	.05
243	Derrick May	.05
244	Pat Listach	.05
245	Mike Bordick	.05
246	Mark Langston	.05
247	Randy Velarde	.05
248	Julio Franco	.05
249	Chuck Knoblauch	.05
250	Bill Gullickson	.05
251	Dave Henderson	.05
252	Bret Boone	.05
253	Al Martin	.05
254	Armando Benitez	.05
255	Wil Cordero	.05
256	Al Leiter	.05
257	Luis Gonzalez	.05
258	Charlie O'Brien	.05
259	Tim Wallach	.05
260	Scott Sanders	.05
261	Tom Henke	.05
262	Otis Nixon	.05
263	Darren Daulton	.05
264	Manny Ramirez	.75
265	Bret Barberie	.05
266	Mel Rojas	.05
267	John Burkett	.05
268	Brady Anderson	.05
269	John Roper	.05
270	Shane Reynolds	.05
271	Barry Bonds	2.50
272	Alex Fernandez	.05
273	Brian McRae	.05
274	Todd Zeile	.05
275	Greg Swindell	.05
276	Johnny Ruffin	.05
277	Troy Neel	.05
278	Eric Karros	.05
279	John Hudek	.05
280	Thomas Howard	.05
281	Joe Carter	.05
282	Mike Devereaux	.05
283	Butch Henry	.05
284	Reggie Jefferson	.05
285	Mark Lemke	.05
286	Jeff Montgomery	.05
287	Ryan Thompson	.05
288	Paul Shuey	.05
289	Mark McGwire	2.00
290	Bernie Williams	.05
291	Mickey Morandini	.05
292	Scott Leius	.05
293	David Hulse	.05
294	Greg Gagne	.05
295	Moises Alou	.05
296	Geronimo Berroa	.05
297	Eddie Zambrano	.05
298	Alan Trammell	.05
299	Don Slaught	.05
300	Jose Rijo	.05
301	Joe Ausanio	.05
302	Tim Raines	.05
303	Melido Perez	.05
304	Kent Mercker	.05
305	James Mouton	.05
306	Luis Lopez	.05
307	Mike Kingery	.05
308	Willie Greene	.05
309	Cecil Fielder	.05
310	Scott Kamieniecki	.05
311	Mike Greenwell (Best Seat in the House)	.05
312	Bobby Bonilla (Best Seat in the House)	.05
313	Andres Galarraga (Best Seat in the House)	.05
314	Cal Ripken Jr. (Best Seat in the House)	1.25
315	Matt Williams (Best Seat in the House)	.05
316	Tom Pagnozzi (Best Seat in the House)	.05
317	Len Dykstra (Best Seat in the House)	.05
318	Frank Thomas (Best Seat in the House)	.40
319	Kirby Puckett (Best Seat in the House)	.50
320	Mike Piazza (Best Seat in the House)	1.00
321	Jason Jacome	.05
322	Brian Hunter	.05
323	Brent Gates	.05
324	Jim Converse	.05
325	Damion Easley	.05
326	Dante Bichette	.05
327	Kurt Abbott	.05
328	Scott Cooper	.05
329	Mike Henneman	.05
330	Orlando Miller	.05
331	John Kruk	.05
332	Jose Oliva	.05
333	Reggie Sanders	.05
334	Omar Vizquel	.05
335	Devon White	.05
336	Mike Morgan	.05
337	J.R. Phillips	.05
338	Gary DiSarcina	.05
339	Joey Hamilton	.05
340	Randy Johnson	.75
341	Jim Leyritz	.05
342	Bobby Jones	.05
343	Jaime Navarro	.05
344	Bip Roberts	.05
345	Steve Karsay	.05
346	Kevin Stocker	.05
347	Jose Canseco	.50
348	Bill Wegman	.05
349	Rondell White	.05
350	Mo Vaughn	.05
351	Joe Orsulak	.05
352	Pat Meares	.05
353	Albie Lopez	.05
354	Edgar Martinez	.05
355	Brian Jordan	.05
356	Tommy Greene	.05
357	Chuck Carr	.05
358	Pedro Astacio	.05
359	Russ Davis	.05
360	Chris Hammond	.05
361	Gregg Jefferies	.05
362	Shane Mack	.05
363	Fred McGriff	.05
364	Pat Rapp	.05
365	Bill Swift	.05
366	Checklist	.05
367	Robin Ventura	.05
368	Bobby Witt	.05
369	Karl Rhodes	.05
370	Eddie Williams	.05
371	John Jaha	.05
372	Steve Howe	.05
373	Leo Gomez	.05
374	Hector Fajardo	.05
375	Jeff Bagwell	.75
376	Mark Acre	.05
377	Wayne Kirby	.05
378	Mark Portugal	.05
379	Jesus Tavarez	.05
380	Jim Lindeman	.05
381	Don Mattingly	1.25
382	Trevor Hoffman	.05
383	Chris Gomez	.05
384	Garret Anderson	.05
385	Bobby Munoz	.05
386	Jon Lieber	.05
387	Rick Helling	.05
388	Marvin Freeman	.05
389	Juan Castillo	.05
390	Jeff Cirillo	.05
391	Sean Berry	.05
392	Hector Carrasco	.05
393	Mark Grace	.05
394	Pat Kelly	.05
395	Tim Naehring	.05
396	Greg Pirkl	.05
397	John Smoltz	.05
398	Robby Thompson	.05
399	Rick White	.05
400	Frank Thomas	.75
401	Jeff Conine (Cover Story)	.05
402	Jose Valentin (Cover Story)	.05
403	Carlos Baerga (Cover Story)	.05
404	Rick Aguilera (Cover Story)	.05
405	Wilson Alvarez (Cover Story)	.05
406	Juan Gonzalez (Cover Story)	.20
407	Barry Larkin (Cover Story)	.05
408	Ken Hill (Cover Story)	.05
409	Chuck Carr (Cover Story)	.05
410	Tim Raines (Cover Story)	.05
411	Bryan Eversgerd	.05
412	Phil Plantier	.05
413	Josias Manzanillo	.05
414	Roberto Kelly	.05
415	Rickey Henderson	.75
416	John Smiley	.05
417	Kevin Brown	.05
418	Jimmy Key	.05
419	Wally Joyner	.05
420	Roberto Hernandez	.05
421	Felix Fermin	.05
422	Checklist	.05
423	Greg Vaughn	.05
424	Ray Lankford	.05
425	Greg Maddux	1.00
426	Mike Mussina	.30
427	Geronimo Pena	.05
428	David Nied	.05
429	Scott Erickson	.05
430	Kevin Mitchell	.05
431	Mike Lansing	.05
432	Brian Anderson	.05
433	Jeff King	.05
434	Ramon Martinez	.05
435	Kevin Seitzer	.05
436	Salomon Torres	.05
437	Brian Hunter	.05
438	Melvin Nieves	.05
439	Mike Kelly	.05
440	Marquis Grissom	.05
441	Chuck Finley	.05
442	Len Dykstra	.05
443	Ellis Burks	.05
444	Harold Baines	.05
445	Kevin Appier	.05
446	Dave Justice	.05
447	Darryl Kile	.05
448	John Olerud	.05
449	Greg McMichael	.05
450	Kirby Puckett	1.00
451	Jose Valentin	.05
452	Rick Wilkins	.05
453	Arthur Rhodes	.05
454	Pat Hentgen	.05
455	Tom Gordon	.05
456	Tom Candiotti	.05
457	Jason Bere	.05
458	Wes Chamberlain	.05
459	Greg Colbrunn	.05
460	John Doherty	.05
461	Kevin Foster	.05
462	Mark Whiten	.05
463	Terry Steinbach	.05
464	Aaron Sele	.05
465	Kirt Manwaring	.05
466	Darren Hall	.05
467	Delino DeShields	.05
468	Andujar Cedeno	.05
469	Billy Ashley	.05
470	Kenny Lofton	.05
471	Pedro Munoz	.05
472	John Wetteland	.05
473	Tim Salmon	.05
474	Denny Neagle	.05
475	Tony Gwynn	1.00
476	Vinny Castilla	.05
477	Steve Dreyer	.05
478	Jeff Shaw	.05
479	Chad Ogea	.05
480	Scott Ruffcorn	.05
481	Lou Whitaker	.05
482	J.T. Snow	.05
483	Rich Rowland	.05
484	Dennis Martinez	.05
485	Pedro Martinez	.75
486	Rusty Greer	.05
487	Dave Fleming	.05
488	John Dettmer	.05
489	Albert Belle	.05
490	Ravelo Manzanillo	.05
491	Henry Rodriguez	.05
492	Andrew Lorraine	.05
493	Dwayne Hosey	.05
494	Mike Blowers	.05
495	Turner Ward	.05
496	Fred McGriff (Extreme Corps)	.05
497	Sammy Sosa (Extreme Corps)	.50
498	Barry Larkin (Extreme Corps)	.05
499	Andres Galarraga (Extreme Corps)	.05
500	Gary Sheffield (Extreme Corps)	.15
501	Jeff Bagwell (Extreme Corps)	.40
502	Mike Piazza (Extreme Corps)	1.00
503	Moises Alou (Extreme Corps)	.05
504	Bobby Bonilla (Extreme Corps)	.05
505	Darren Daulton (Extreme Corps)	.05
506	Jeff King (Extreme Corps)	.05
507	Ray Lankford (Extreme Corps)	.05
508	Tony Gwynn (Extreme Corps)	.50
509	Barry Bonds (Extreme Corps)	1.25
510	Cal Ripken Jr. (Extreme Corps)	1.25
511	Mo Vaughn (Extreme Corps)	.05
512	Tim Salmon (Extreme Corps)	.05
513	Frank Thomas (Extreme Corps)	.45
514	Albert Belle (Extreme Corps)	.05
515	Cecil Fielder (Extreme Corps)	.05
516	Kevin Appier (Extreme Corps)	.05
517	Greg Vaughn (Extreme Corps)	.05
518	Kirby Puckett (Extreme Corps)	.50
519	Paul O'Neill (Extreme Corps)	.05
520	Ruben Sierra (Extreme Corps)	.05
521	Ken Griffey Jr. (Extreme Corps)	.75
522	Will Clark (Extreme Corps)	.05
523	Joe Carter (Extreme Corps)	.05
524	Antonio Osuna	.05
525	Glenallen Hill	.05
526	Alex Gonzalez	.05
527	Dave Stewart	.05
528	Ron Gant	.05
529	Jason Bates	.05
530	Mike Macfarlane	.05
531	Esteban Loaiza	.05
532	Joe Randa	.05
533	Dave Winfield	.75
534	Danny Darwin	.05
535	Pete Harnisch	.05
536	Joey Cora	.05
537	Jaime Navarro	.05
538	Marty Cordova	.05
539	Andujar Cedeno	.05
540	Mickey Tettleton	.05
541	Andy Van Slyke	.05
542	Carlos Perez RC	.05
543	Chipper Jones	1.00
544	Tony Fernandez	.05
545	Tom Henke	.05
546	Pat Borders	.05
547	Chad Curtis	.05
548	Ray Durham	.05
549	Joe Oliver	.05
550	Jose Mesa	.05
551	Steve Finley	.05
552	Otis Nixon	.05
553	Jacob Brumfield	.05
554	Bill Swift	.05
555	Quilvio Veras	.05
556	Hideo Nomo RC	1.50
557	Joe Vitiello	.05
558	Mike Perez	.05
559	Charlie Hayes	.05
560	Brad Radke RC	.25
561	Darren Bragg	.05
562	Orel Hershiser	.05
563	Edgardo Alfonzo	.05
564	Doug Jones	.05
565	Andy Pettitte	.05
566	Benito Santiago	.05
567	John Burkett	.05
568	Brad Clontz	.05
569	Jim Abbott	.05
570	Joe Rosselli	.05
571	Mark Grudzielanek RC	.25
572	Dustin Hermanson	.05
573	Benji Gil	.05
574	Mark Whiten	.05
575	Mike Ignasiak	.05
576	Kevin Ritz	.05
577	Paul Quantrill	.05
578	Andre Dawson	.25
579	Jerald Clark	.05
580	Frank Rodriguez	.05
581	Mark Kiefer	.05
582	Trevor Wilson	.05
583	Gary Wilson RC	.05
584	Andy Stankiewicz	.05
585	Felipe Lira	.05
586	Mike Mimbs RC	.05
587	Jon Nunnally	.05
588	Tomas Perez RC	.05
589	Checklist	.05
590	Todd Hollandsworth	.05
591	Roberto Petagine	.05
592	Mariano Rivera	.15
593	Mark McLemore	.05
594	Bobby Witt	.05
595	Jose Offerman	.05
596	Jason Christiansen	.05
597	Jeff Manto	.05
598	Jim Dougherty	.05
599	Juan Acevedo	.05
600	Troy O'Leary	.05
601	Ron Villone	.05
602	Tripp Cromer	.05
603	Steve Scarsone	.05
604	Lance Parrish	.05
605	Ozzie Timmons	.05
606	Ray Holbert	.05
607	Tony Phillips	.05
608	Phil Plantier	.05
609	Shane Andrews	.05
610	Heathcliff Slocumb	.05
611	Bobby Higginson RC	.25
612	Bob Tewksbury	.05
613	Terry Pendleton	.05
614	Scott Cooper (Trans-Action)	.05
615	John Wetteland (Trans-Action)	.05
616	Ken Hill (Trans-Action)	.05
617	Marquis Grissom (Trans-Action)	.05
618	Larry Walker (Trans-Action)	.05
619	Derek Bell (Trans-Action)	.05
620	David Cone (Trans-Action)	.05
621	Ken Caminiti (Trans-Action)	.05
622	Jack McDowell (Trans-Action)	.05
623	Vaughn Eshelman (Trans-Action)	.05
624	Brian McRae (Trans-Action)	.05
625	Gregg Jefferies (Trans-Action)	.05
626	Kevin Brown (Trans-Action)	.05
627	Lee Smith (Trans-Action)	.05
628	Tony Tarasco (Trans-Action)	.05
629	Brett Butler (Trans-Action)	.05
630	Jose Canseco (Trans-Action)	.35

1st Day Pre-Production

Stadium Club 1st Day Preproduction cards were randomly packed into one every 36 packs of Topps Series I baseball. The set of nine cards is only found in hobby packs.

		NM/M
Complete Set (9):		7.50
Common Player:		.50
29	Shawon Dunston	.50
39	Paul Molitor	1.50
79	Bob Hamelin	.50
96	Ruben Sierra	.50
131	Will Clark	.50
149	Mike Piazza	3.00
153	Andy Van Slyke	.50
166	Jeff Tackett	.50
197	Ivan Rodriguez	1.00

1st Day Issue

Series II hobby packs of Topps baseball featured a chase set of Stadium Club 1st Day Issue cards, #1-270. The FDI cards have a small gold embossed seal on front. Cards were seeded on an average of one per six packs. Ten FDI cards were also randomly inserted in each Factory set.

	NM/M
Common Player:	.50
Stars:	7X

Clear Cut

Among the most technically advanced of 1995's insert cards is the Clear Cut chase set found in Series I and II packs. Cards feature a color player action photo printed on see-through plastic. There is a rainbow-hued trapezoid behind the player with an overall background tinted in blue, green and gold. The player's name is in white in a vertical bar at right. Backs have a few stats and data in a blue bar vertically at left. Each of the cards can also be found in a version with the round Members Only seal embossed into the plastic at lower-left.

		NM/M
Complete Set (28):		20.00
Common Player:		.65
1	Mike Piazza	3.00
2	Ruben Sierra	.65
3	Tony Gwynn	2.50
4	Frank Thomas	2.00
5	Fred McGriff	.65
6	Rafael Palmeiro	1.50
7	Bobby Bonilla	.65
8	Chili Davis	.65
9	Hal Morris	.65
10	Jose Canseco	1.00
11	Jay Bell	.65
12	Kirby Puckett	2.50
13	Gary Sheffield	1.00
14	Bob Hamelin	.65
15	Jeff Bagwell	2.00
16	Albert Belle	.65
17	Sammy Sosa	2.50
18	Ken Griffey Jr.	3.00
19	Todd Zeile	.65

20	Mo Vaughn	.65
21	Moises Alou	.65
22	Paul O'Neill	.65
23	Andres Galarraga	.65
24	Greg Vaughn	.65
25	Len Dykstra	.65
26	Joe Carter	.65
27	Barry Bonds	4.50
28	Cecil Fielder	.65

Crunch Time

Series 1 rack packs were the exclusive provenance of these cards featuring baseball's top run creators. Fronts are printed on rainbow prismatic foil. The central color action photo is repeated as an enlarged background photo, along with a team logo. At bottom in gold foil are the player name and Crunch Time logo. Backs have a positive and a negative image of the same photo as background to a pie chart and stats relative to the player's runs-created stats.

		NM/M
Complete Set (20):		15.00
Common Player:		1.00
1	Jeff Bagwell	2.50
2	Kirby Puckett	3.00
3	Frank Thomas	2.50
4	Albert Belle	1.00
5	Julio Franco	1.00
6	Jose Canseco	1.50
7	Paul Molitor	2.50
8	Joe Carter	1.00
9	Ken Griffey Jr.	4.00
10	Larry Walker	1.00
11	Dante Bichette	1.00
12	Carlos Baerga	1.00
13	Fred McGriff	1.00
14	Ruben Sierra	1.00
15	Will Clark	1.00
16	Moises Alou	1.00
17	Rafael Palmeiro	2.00
18	Travis Fryman	1.00
19	Barry Bonds	5.00
20	Cal Ripken Jr.	5.00

Crystal Ball

Multi-colored swirls around a clear central circle with the player's photo, all printed on foil, are the front design for this Series 3 insert. Backs have a portrait photo in a floating crystal ball image at one side. At the other end are year-by-year minor league stats and a few words about each of the player's seasons. This insert was also produced in an edition of 4,000 bearing a gold-foil "Members Only" seal, sold in complete Stadium Club Members Only factory sets.

		NM/M
Complete Set (15):		15.00
Common Player:		.75
1	Chipper Jones	5.00
2	Dustin Hermanson	.75
3	Ray Durham	.75
4	Phil Nevin	.75
5	Billy Ashley	.75
6	Shawn Green	2.50

7	Jason Bates	.75
8	Benji Gil	.75
9	Marty Cordova	.75
10	Quilvio Veras	.75
11	Mark Grudzielanek	.75
12	Ruben Rivera	.75
13	Bill Pulsipher	.75
14	Derek Jeter	7.50
15	LaTroy Hawkins	.75

Power Zone

The performance in several parks around the league is chronicled on the back of these Series 3 inserts. Fronts are printed on foil and feature a player swinging into an exploding asteroid. His name is printed vertically down one side in prismatic glitter foil. Backs also have a portrait photo and a baseball with a weird red and green vapor trail. A special edition of 4,000 each of these inserts was included with the purchase of Stadium Club Members Only factory sets; those cards have an embossed gold-foil seal on front.

		NM/M
Complete Set (12):		9.00
Common Player:		.50
1	Jeff Bagwell	1.00
2	Albert Belle	.50
3	Barry Bonds	3.00
4	Joe Carter	.50
5	Cecil Fielder	.50
6	Andres Galarraga	.50
7	Ken Griffey Jr.	2.00
8	Paul Molitor	1.00
9	Fred McGriff	.50
10	Rafael Palmeiro	.75
11	Frank Thomas	1.00
12	Matt Williams	.50

Ring Leaders

With a background that looks like an explosion at a jewelry factory, these cards feature players who have won championship, All-Star or other award rings. Fronts are foil-printed with a player action photo on a background of flying rings and stars, and, - for some reason - an attacking eagle. Backs repeat the background motif, have a player portrait in an oval frame at top-left, photos of some of his rings and a list of rings won. Cards were random inserts in both Series 1 and 2; complete sets could also be won in Stadium Club's phone card insert contest. A version with the Members Only gold seal was also issued for each.

		NM/M
Complete Set (40):		70.00
Common Player:		.75
1	Jeff Bagwell	3.00
2	Mark McGwire	7.50
3	Ozzie Smith	4.00
4	Paul Molitor	3.00
5	Darryl Strawberry	.75
6	Eddie Murray	3.00
7	Tony Gwynn	4.00
8	Jose Canseco	2.00
9	Howard Johnson	.75
10	Andre Dawson	1.25
11	Matt Williams	.75
12	Tim Raines	.75
13	Fred McGriff	.75
14	Ken Griffey Jr.	6.00
15	Gary Sheffield	2.00
16	Dennis Eckersley	2.50
17	Kevin Mitchell	.75
18	Will Clark	.75
19	Darren Daulton	.75
20	Paul O'Neill	.75
21	Julio Franco	.75
22	Albert Belle	.75
23	Juan Gonzalez	1.50
24	Kirby Puckett	4.00
25	Joe Carter	.75
26	Frank Thomas	3.00
27	Cal Ripken Jr.	9.00

28	John Olerud	.75
29	Ruben Sierra	.75
30	Barry Bonds	9.00
31	Cecil Fielder	.75
32	Roger Clemens	5.00
33	Don Mattingly	5.00
34	Terry Pendleton	.75
35	Rickey Henderson	3.00
36	Dave Winfield	3.00
37	Edgar Martinez	.75
38	Wade Boggs	4.00
39	Willie McGee	.75
40	Andres Galarraga	.75

Ring Leaders Phone Cards

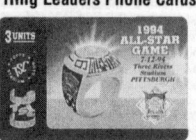

An interactive contest carrying through the "Ring Leaders" insert card set theme featured randomly inserted phone cards picturing All-Star Game players' rings. The 2-1/8" x 3/3/8" plastic cards could be found in regular, silver and gold editions. By using the card for a long distance call, the holder could determine if it was a further winner. Regular card winners received a set of Stadium Club Ring Leaders insert cards. Winners on a silver card received a complete set of the 13 different phone cards in all three versions. Gold card winners received the genuine All-Star ring pictured on the card. Approximately 217,000 phone cards were inserted in the program; odds of finding a regular card were about one per 40 packs; silver, one per 237 packs, and, gold, one per 2,955 packs. Cards picturing the 1988 and 1989 All-Star rings were not issued. Phone cards with the number panel on back scratched off are worth 50 percent of the values quoted.

		NM/M
Complete Set, Regular (13):		10.00
Complete Set, Silver (13):		25.00
Complete Set, Gold (13):		50.00
Common Card, Regular:		1.00
Common Card, Silver:		2.50
Common Card, Gold:		5.00
(1)	1980 All-Star Game, Los Angeles	1.00
(1s)	1980 All-Star Game, Los Angeles/Silver	2.50
(1g)	1980 All-Star Game, Los Angeles/Gold	5.00
(2)	1981 All-Star Game, Cleveland	1.00
(2s)	1981 All-Star Game, Cleveland/Silver	2.50
(2g)	1981 All-Star Game, Cleveland/Gold	5.00
(3)	1982 All-Star Game, Montreal	1.00
(3s)	1982 All-Star Game, Montreal/Silver	2.50
(3g)	1982 All-Star Game, Montreal/Gold	5.00
(4)	1983 All-Star Game, Chicago A.L.	1.00
(4s)	1983 All-Star Game, Chicago A.L./Silver	2.50
(4g)	1983 All-Star Game, Chicago/Gold	5.00
(5)	1984 All-Star Game, San Francisco	1.00
(5s)	1984 All-Star Game, San Francisco/Silver	2.50
(5g)	1984 All-Star Game, San Francisco/Gold	5.00
(6)	1985 All-Star Game, Minneapolis	1.00
(6s)	1985 All-Star Game, Minneapolis (Silver)	2.50
(6g)	1985 All-Star Game, Minneapolis/Gold	5.00
(7)	1986 All-Star Game, Houston	1.00
(7s)	1986 All-Star Game, Houston/Silver	2.50
(7g)	1986 All-Star Game, Houston/Gold	5.00
(8)	1987 All-Star Game, Oakland	1.00
(8s)	1987 All-Star Game, Oakland/Silver	2.50
(8g)	1987 All-Star Game, Oakland/Gold	5.00
(9)	1990 All-Star Game, Chicago N.L.	1.00
(9s)	1990 All-Star Game, Chicago N.L./Silver	2.50
(9g)	1990 All-Star Game, Chicago N.L./Gold	5.00

(10)	1991 All-Star Game, Toronto	1.00
(10s)	1991 All-Star Game, Toronto/Silver	2.50
(10g)	1991 All-Star Game, Toronto/Gold	5.00
(11)	1992 All-Star Game, San Diego	1.00
(11s)	1992 All-Star Game, San Diego/Silver	2.50
(11g)	1992 All-Star Game, San Diego/Gold	5.00
(12)	1993 All-Star Game, Baltimore	1.00
(12s)	1993 All-Star Game, Baltimore/Silver	2.50
(12g)	1993 All-Star Game, Baltimore/Gold	5.00
(13)	1994 All-Star Game, Pittsburgh	1.00
(13s)	1994 All-Star Game, Pittsburgh/Silver	2.50
(13g)	1994 All-Star Game, Pittsburgh/Gold	5.00

Super Skills

These random hobby pack inserts in both Series 1 and 2 are printed on rainbow prismatic foil which features as a background an enlarged version of the front photo. The S.C. and Super Skills logos are printed in gold foil in opposite corners, while the player's name is in blue at bottom-right. Backs repeat the enlarged background image of a close-up foreground photo, while a few words about the player's particular specialties are in white at left. Each card can also be found in a version featuring the Members Only gold-foil seal on front.

		NM/M
Complete Set (20):		30.00
Common Player:		.75
1	Roberto Alomar	1.00
2	Barry Bonds	10.00
3	Jay Buhner	.75
4	Chuck Carr	.75
5	Don Mattingly	5.00
6	Raul Mondesi	.75
7	Tim Salmon	.75
8	Deion Sanders	.75
9	Devon White	.75
10	Mark Whiten	.75
11	Ken Griffey Jr.	7.50
12	Marquis Grissom	.75
13	Paul O'Neill	.75
14	Kenny Lofton	.75
15	Larry Walker	.75
16	Scott Cooper	.75
17	Barry Larkin	.75
18	Matt Williams	.75
19	John Wetteland	.75
20	Randy Johnson	2.50

Virtual Reality

A partial parallel set found one per foil pack, two per rack pack, these cards share the basic front and back with the corresponding card in the regular S.C. issue. On front, however, is a "Virtual Reality" seal around the team logo at bottom (gold foil in Series 1, silver-foil in Series 2). Backs differ in that instead of actual 1994 season stats, they present a bar graph of computer projected stats representing a full 162-game season stats versus the strike-shortened reality. Each of these inserts can also be found in

a version bearing the round gold- (Series 1) or silver-foil (Series 2) Members Only seal on the front.		

		NM/M
Complete Set (270):		35.00
Common Player:		.10
1	Cal Ripken Jr.	2.50
2	Travis Fryman	.10
3	Jim Abbott	.10
4	Gary Gaetti	.10
5	Roger Clemens	1.25
6	Carlos Garcia	.10
7	Lee Smith	.10
8	Bobby Ayala	.10
9	Charles Nagy	.10
10	Rene Arocha	.10
11	Carlos Delgado	.50
12	Steve Finley	.10
13	Ryan Klesko	.10
14	Cal Eldred	.10
15	Rey Sanchez	.10
16	Ken Hill	.10
17	Jose Vizcaino	.10
18	Andy Benes	.10
19	Shawon Dunston	.10
20	Rafael Palmeiro	.65
21	Dean Palmer	.10
22	Joey Cora	.10
23	Mickey Tettleton	.10
24	Barry Larkin	.10
25	Carlos Baerga	.10
26	Orel Hershiser	.10
27	Jody Reed	.10
28	Paul Molitor	.75
29	Jim Edmonds	.10
30	Bob Tewksbury	.10
31	Ray McDavid	.10
32	Stan Javier	.10
33	Todd Worrell	.10
34	Bob Wickman	.10
35	Raul Mondesi	.10
36	Rod Beck	.10
37	Jeff Kent	.10
38	John Valentin	.10
39	Ozzie Smith	1.00
40	Terry Pendleton	.10
41	Kenny Rogers	.10
42	Vince Coleman	.10
43	Roberto Alomar	.20
44	Darrin Jackson	.10
45	Dennis Eckersley	.65
46	Jay Buhner	.10
47	Dave Weathers	.10
48	Danny Bautista	.10
49	Bob Hamelin	.10
50	Steve Trachsel	.10
51	Ben McDonald	.10
52	Wade Boggs	1.00
53	Sandy Alomar	.10
54	Ron Karkovice	.10
55	Doug Jones	.10
56	Gary Sheffield	.40
57	Ken Caminiti	.10
58	Kevin Tapani	.10
59	Ruben Sierra	.10
60	Bobby Bonilla	.10
61	Deion Sanders	.10
62	Charlie Hayes	.10
63	Paul O'Neill	.10
64	Jay Bell	.10
65	Todd Jones	.10
66	Todd Stottlemyre	.10
67	Will Clark	.10
68	Wilson Alvarez	.10
69	Chili Davis	.10
70	Chris Hoiles	.10
71	Bret Saberhagen	.10
72	Dave Nilsson	.10
73	Derek Bell	.10
74	Juan Gonzalez	.40
75	Andre Dawson	.30
76	Jim Thome	.65
77	Larry Walker	.10
78	Mike Piazza	1.50
79	Dan Wilson	.10
80	Junior Felix	.10
81	Jack McDowell	.10
82	Danny Tartabull	.10
83	William Van Landingham	.10
84	Robb Nen	.10
85	Ismael Valdes	.10
86	Juan Guzman	.10
87	Cliff Floyd	.10
88	Rico Brogna	.10
89	Luis Polonia	.10
90	Lance Johnson	.10
91	Sammy Sosa	1.00
92	Dave West	.10
93	Tom Glavine	.35
94	Joe Girardi	.10
95	Craig Biggio	.10
96	Eddie Murray	.75
97	Kevin Gross	.10
98	John Franco	.10
99	Matt Williams	.10
100	Darrin Fletcher	.10
101	Jeff Conine	.10
102	Ed Sprague	.10
103	Ivan Rodriguez	.65
104	Orlando Merced	.10
105	Ricky Bones	.10
106	David Cone	.10
107	Todd Hundley	.10
108	Alex Cole	.10
109	Tony Phillips	.10
110	Jim Eisenreich	.10
111	Paul Sorrento	.10

112	Mike Stanley	.10
113	Doug Drabek	.10
114	Matt Mieske	.10
115	Tino Martinez	.10
116	Midre Cummings	.10
117	Hal Morris	.10
118	Shawn Green	.40
119	Randy Myers	.10
120	Ken Griffey Jr.	1.50
121	Brett Butler	.10
122	Julio Franco	.10
123	Chuck Knoblauch	.10
124	Bret Boone	.10
125	Wil Cordero	.10
126	Luis Gonzalez	.10
127	Tim Wallach	.10
128	Scott Sanders	.10
129	Tom Henke	.10
130	Otis Nixon	.10
131	Darren Daulton	.10
132	Manny Ramirez	.75
133	Bret Barberie	.10
134	Brady Anderson	.10
135	Shane Reynolds	.10
136	Barry Bonds	2.50
137	Alex Fernandez	.10
138	Brian McRae	.10
139	Todd Zeile	.10
140	Greg Swindell	.10
141	Troy Neel	.10
142	Eric Karros	.10
143	John Hudek	.10
144	Joe Carter	.10
145	Mike Devereaux	.10
146	Butch Henry	.10
147	Mark Lemke	.10
148	Jeff Montgomery	.10
149	Ryan Thompson	.10
150	Bernie Williams	.10
151	Scott Leius	.10
152	Greg Gagne	.10
153	Moises Alou	.10
154	Geronimo Berroa	.10
155	Alan Trammell	.10
156	Don Slaught	.10
157	Jose Rijo	.10
158	Tim Raines	.10
159	Melido Perez	.10
160	Kent Mercker	.10
161	James Mouton	.10
162	Luis Lopez	.10
163	Mike Kingery	.10
164	Cecil Fielder	.10
165	Scott Kamieniecki	.10
166	Brent Gates	.10
167	Jason Jacome	.10
168	Dante Bichette	.10
169	Kurt Abbott	.10
170	Mike Henneman	.10
171	John Kruk	.10
172	Jose Oliva	.10
173	Reggie Sanders	.10
174	Omar Vizquel	.10
175	Devon White	.10
176	Mark McGwire	2.00
177	Gary DiSarcina	.10
178	Joey Hamilton	.10
179	Randy Johnson	.75
180	Jim Leyritz	.10
181	Bobby Jones	.10
182	Bip Roberts	.10
183	Jose Canseco	.40
184	Mo Vaughn	.10
185	Edgar Martinez	.10
186	Tommy Greene	.10
187	Chuck Carr	.10
188	Pedro Astacio	.10
189	Shane Mack	.10
190	Fred McGriff	.10
191	Pat Rapp	.10
192	Bill Swift	.10
193	Robin Ventura	.10
194	Bobby Witt	.10
195	Steve Howe	.10
196	Leo Gomez	.10
197	Hector Fajardo	.10
198	Jeff Bagwell	.75
199	Rondell White	.10
200	Don Mattingly	1.25
201	Trevor Hoffman	.10
202	Chris Gomez	.10
203	Bobby Munoz	.10
204	Marvin Freeman	.10
205	Sean Berry	.10
206	Mark Grace	.10
207	Pat Kelly	.10
208	Eddie Williams	.10
209	Frank Thomas	.75
210	Bryan Eversgerd	.10
211	Phil Plantier	.10
212	Roberto Kelly	.10
213	Rickey Henderson	.75
214	John Smiley	.10
215	Kevin Brown	.10
216	Jimmy Key	.10
217	Wally Joyner	.10
218	Roberto Hernandez	.10
219	Felix Fermin	.10
220	Greg Vaughn	.10
221	Ray Lankford	.10
222	Greg Maddux	1.00
223	Mike Mussina	.30
224	David Nied	.10
225	Scott Erickson	.10
226	Kevin Mitchell	.10
227	Brian Anderson	.10
228	Jeff King	.10
229	Ramon Martinez	.10

No.	Player	Price
230	Kevin Seitzer	.10
231	Marquis Grissom	.10
232	Chuck Finley	.10
233	Len Dykstra	.10
234	Ellis Burks	.10
235	Harold Baines	.10
236	Kevin Appier	.10
237	Dave Justice	.10
238	Darryl Kile	.10
239	John Olerud	.10
240	Greg McMichael	.10
241	Kirby Puckett	1.00
242	Jose Valentin	.10
243	Rick Wilkins	.10
244	Pat Hentgen	.10
245	Tom Gordon	.10
246	Tom Candiotti	.10
247	Jason Bere	.10
248	Wes Chamberlain	.10
249	Jeff Cirillo	.10
250	Kevin Foster	.10
251	Mark Whiten	.10
252	Terry Steinbach	.10
253	Aaron Sele	.10
254	Kirt Manwaring	.10
255	Delino DeShields	.10
256	Andujar Cedeno	.10
257	Kenny Lofton	.10
258	John Wetteland	.10
259	Tim Salmon	.10
260	Denny Neagle	.10
261	Tony Gwynn	1.00
262	Lou Whitaker	.10
263	J.T. Snow	.10
264	Dennis Martinez	.10
265	Pedro Martinez	.75
266	Rusty Greer	.10
267	Dave Fleming	.10
268	John Dettmer	.10
269	Albert Belle	.10
270	Henry Rodriguez	.10

VR Extremist

A huge silver-blue metallic baseball separates the player from the background of the photo in this Series 2 insert found only in rack packs. A blue sky and clouds provides the front border. The player rises out of the clouds in a back photo in the foreground of which are some pie-in-the-sky stats. The metallic baseball is also repeated on the back, with the player's name in orange script on the sweet spot. Each card was also issued in the Members Only boxed set in a version with a round silver-foil Members Only seal on front. Cards are numbered with a "VRE" prefix.

		NM/M
Complete Set (10):		25.00
Common Player:		1.50
1	Barry Bonds	7.50
2	Ken Griffey Jr.	6.00
3	Jeff Bagwell	3.50
4	Albert Belle	1.50
5	Frank Thomas	3.50
6	Tony Gwynn	4.50
7	Kenny Lofton	1.50
8	Deion Sanders	1.50
9	Ken Hill	1.50
10	Jimmy Key	1.50

Super Team Division Winners

Persons who saved 1994 Topps Stadium Club Super Team cards for the 1995 divisional winners in Major League Baseball's new playoff format were able to redeem them for a set of 10 SC cards of that team's players with a special gold-foil division series logo on front. The cards are otherwise identical to the regular-issue '95 SC versions. Included in the cello-wrapped team set was a Super Team card with the gold logo on front and a white "REDEEMED" across the back.

	NM/M
Complete Set (66):	25.00
Common Player:	.15

No.	Player	Price
	Atlanta Braves Team Set	7.00
1	Atlanta Braves Super Team	.30
19	Ryan Klesko	.15
128	Mark Wohlers	.15
151	Steve Avery	.15
183	Tom Glavine	.60
200	Javy Lopez	.15
393	Fred McGriff	.15
397	John Smoltz	.15
425	Greg Maddux	3.00
446	David Justice	.15
543	Chipper Jones	3.00
	Boston Red Sox Team Set	4.50
16	Boston Red Sox Super Team	.30
10	Roger Clemens	3.25
62	John Valentin	.15
121	Mike Greenwell	.15
160	Lee Tinsley	.15
347	Jose Canseco	1.25
350	Mo Vaughn	.15
395	Tim Naehring	.15
464	Aaron Sele	.15
530	Mike MacFarlane	.15
600	Troy O;Leary	.15
	Cincinnati Red Team Set	1.50
3	Cincinnati Reds Super Team	.30
35	Barry Larkin	.15
231	Hal Morris	.15
252	Bret Boone	.15
280	Thomas Howard	.15
300	Jose Rijo	.15
333	Reggie Sanders	.15
392	Hector Carrasco	.15
416	John Smiley	.15
528	Ron Gant	.15
566	Benito Santiago	.15
	Cleveland Indians Team Set	4.50
19	Cleveland Indians Super Team	2.00
36	Carlos Baerga	.15
147	Jim Thome	1.50
186	Eddie Murray	2.00
264	Manny Ramirez	2.00
334	Omar Vizquel	.15
470	Kenny Lofton	.15
484	Dennis Martinez	.15
	Albert Belle	.15
	Jose Mesa	.15
562	Orel Hershiser	.15
	Los Angeles Dodgers Team Set	7.00
7	Los Angeles Dodgers Super Team	.30
57	Raul Mondesi	.15
149	Mike Piazza	4.00
161	Ismael Valdez	.15
242	Brett Butler	.15
259	Tim Wallach	.15
278	Eric Karros	.15
434	Ramon Martinez	.15
456	Tom Candiotti	.15
467	Delino DeShields	.15
556	Hideo Nomo	1.00
	Seattle Mariners Team Set	6.50
26	Seattle Mariners Super Team	.30
73	Jay Buhner	.15
92	Chris Bosio	.15
152	Dan Wilson	.15
227	Tino Martinez	.15
241	Ken Griffey Jr.	4.00
340	Randy Johnson	2.00
354	Edgar Martinez	.15
421	Felix Fermin	.15
494	Mike Blowers	.15
536	Joey Cora	.15

League Champion Master Photos

Persons who held onto Braves and Indians Super Team insert cards from the 1994 Stadium Club issue could redeem them following the 1995 season for special Master Photos team sets of the League Champions. Each team set included 10 player cards and a Super Team card with special gold-foil League Champion logos on the fronts. The player cards are in 5" x

7" format with the player's 1995 SC card in the center of a blue background. Backs are in black-and-white with a card number and appropriate logos and copyright. The Super Team card is 2-1/2" x 3-1/2" with a white "REDEEMED" notice overprinted on back.

		NM/M
Complete Set (22):		15.00
Common Player:		.35
	Atlanta Braves Team Set	9.00
1	Steve Avery	.40
2	Tom Glavine	.75
3	Chipper Jones	3.00
4	David Justice	.40
5	Ryan Klesko	.40
6	Javy Lopez	.40
7	Greg Maddux	3.00
8	Fred McGriff	.40
9	John Smoltz	.40
10	Mark Wohlers	.40
1	Atlanta Braves Super Team	.40
	Cleveland Indians Team Set	7.50
11	Carlos Baerga	.40
12	Albert Belle	.40
13	Orel Hershiser	.40
14	Kenny Lofton	.40
15	Dennis Martinez	.40
16	Jose Mesa	.40
17	Eddie Murray	2.50
18	Manny Ramirez	2.50
19	Jim Thome	2.00
20	Omar Vizquel	.40
19	Cleveland Indians Super Team	.40

World Series Winners

Persons who redeemed a 1994 Stadium Club Atlanta Braves Super Team insert following the Tribe's 1995 World Series victory received a set of 1995 Stadium Club cards, each of which bears a gold-foil World's Series logo on front. The cards are otherwise identical to the regular-issue SC cards. The prize "set" contains only 585 cards, a note sent with the set explains 45 of the TSC cards - #496-523 (the Extreme Corps subset) and cards #614-630 (the TransAction subset) were not printed in the parallel version.

	NM/M
Complete Set (585):	40.00
Common Player:	.25
Stars:	3X

Members Only

A special version of all of the regular cards from Stadium Club Series I-III, as well as many of the insert sets was offered to members of Topps' Stadium Club. Virtually identical to the regular S.C. cards, the specially boxed set differs in the presence on each card front of an embossed round 1/2" gold-foil "Members Only" seal. Even the plastic Clear Cut inserts have the

members' seal embossed directly into the plastic. The edition was limited to 4,000 sets.

	NM/M
Complete Set (630):	150.00
Common Player:	.25
Stars:	6X
Inserts:	50-100 Percent

Members Only Baseball

This boxed set was sold exclusively through the newsletter for Topps Stadium Club members. Cards feature noteworthy performances and achievements of the 1994 baseball season. Borderless card fronts have a player action photo on which the background has been quartered in colors of blue, green, orange and magenta. The Members Only logo, and player name and position are presented in gold foil. Backs have another player photo at left and a description of the highlight printed in white on a blue background at right. Both front and back of each card are UV coated. The final five cards in the set are printed in Topps Finest technology and feature the company's choice of the top rookies of 1994.

		NM/M
Complete Set (50):		9.00
Common Player:		.20
1	Moises Alou	.20
2	Jeff Bagwell	.75
3	Albert Belle	.20
4	Andy Benes	.20
5	Dante Bichette	.20
6	Craig Biggio	.20
7	Wade Boggs	1.00
8	Barry Bonds	3.00
9	Brett Butler	.20
10	Jose Canseco	.50
11	Joe Carter	.20
12	Vince Coleman	.20
13	Jeff Conine	.20
14	Cecil Fielder	.20
15	John Franco	.20
16	Julio Franco	.20
17	Travis Fryman	.20
18	Andres Galarraga	.20
19	Ken Griffey Jr.	1.50
20	Marquis Grissom	.20
21	Tony Gwynn	1.00
22	Ken Hill	.20
23	Randy Johnson	.75
24	Lance Johnson	.20
25	Jimmy Key	.20
26	Chuck Knoblauch	.20
27	Ray Lankford	.20
28	Darren Lewis	.20
29	Kenny Lofton	.20
30	Greg Maddux	1.00
31	Fred McGriff	.20
32	Kevin Mitchell	.20
33	Paul Molitor	.75
34	Hal Morris	.20
35	Paul O'Neill	.20
36	Rafael Palmeiro	.65
37	Tony Phillips	.20
38	Mike Piazza	1.50
39	Kirby Puckett	1.00

40	Cal Ripken Jr.	3.00
41	Deion Sanders	.20
42	Lee Smith	.20
43	Frank Thomas	.75
44	Larry Walker	.20
45	Matt Williams	.20
46	Manny Ramirez (Rookie Picks)	1.00
47	Joey Hamilton (Rookie Picks)	.20
48	Raul Mondesi (Rookie Picks)	.20
49	Bob Hamelin (Rookie Picks)	.20
50	Ryan Klesko (Rookie Picks)	.20

1996 Stadium Club

Consisting of 450 cards in a pair of 225-card series, Stadium Club continued Topps' 1996 tribute to Mickey Mantle with 19 Retrospective inserts. Cards feature full-bleed photos with gold-foil graphic highlights. Backs offer a TSC Skills Matrix along with another player photo, some biographical data and stats. Team TSC is the only subset with 45 cards each in Series 1 and 2. Stadium Club was issued in retail and hobby packs, with inserts found at differing ratios in each type of packaging.

		NM/M
Complete Set (450):		25.00
Common Player:		.05
Series 1 or 2 Pack (10):		1.00
Series 1 or 2 Wax Box (24):		20.00
1	Hideo Nomo (Extreme Player)	.40
2	Paul Molitor	.75
3	Garret Anderson (Extreme Player)	.05
4	Jose Mesa (Extreme Player)	.05
5	Vinny Castilla (Extreme Player)	.05
6	Mike Mussina (Extreme Player)	.30
7	Ray Durham (Extreme Player)	.05
8	Jack McDowell (Extreme Player)	.05
9	Juan Gonzalez (Extreme Player)	.40
10	Chipper Jones (Extreme Player)	1.00
11	Deion Sanders (Extreme Player)	.05
12	Rondell White (Extreme Player)	.05
13	Tom Henke (Extreme Player)	.05
14	Derek Bell (Extreme Player)	.05
15	Randy Myers (Extreme Player)	.05
16	Randy Johnson (Extreme Player)	.75
17	Len Dykstra (Extreme Player)	.05
18	Bill Pulsipher (Extreme Player)	.05
19	Greg Colbrunn (Extreme Player)	.05
20	David Wells (Extreme Player)	.05
21	Chad Curtis (Extreme Player)	.05
22	Roberto Hernandez (Extreme Player)	.05
23	Kirby Puckett (Extreme Player)	1.00
24	Joe Vitiello (Extreme Player)	.05
25	Roger Clemens (Extreme Player)	1.25
26	Al Martin (Extreme Player)	.05
27	Chad Ogea (Extreme Player)	.05
28	David Segui (Extreme Player)	.05
29	Joey Hamilton (Extreme Player)	.05
30	Dan Wilson (Extreme Player)	.05
31	Chad Fonville (Extreme Player)	.05
32	Bernard Gilkey (Extreme Player)	.05
33	Kevin Seitzer (Extreme Player)	.05
34	Shawn Green (Extreme Player)	.35

35	Rick Aguilera (Extreme Player)	.05
36	Gary DiSarcina	.05
37	Jaime Navarro	.05
38	Doug Jones	.05
39	Brent Gates	.05
40	Dean Palmer (Extreme Player)	.05
41	Pat Rapp	.05
42	Tony Clark	.05
43	Bill Swift	.05
44	Randy Velarde	.05
45	Matt Williams (Extreme Player)	.05
46	John Mabry	.05
47	Mike Fetters	.05
48	Orlando Miller	.05
49	Tom Glavine (Extreme Player)	.35
50	Delino DeShields (Extreme Player)	.05
51	Scott Erickson	.05
52	Andy Van Slyke	.05
53	Jim Bullinger	.05
54	Lyle Mouton	.05
55	Bret Saberhagen	.05
56	Benito Santiago (Extreme Player)	.05
57	Dan Miceli	.05
58	Carl Everett	.05
59	Rod Beck (Extreme Player)	.05
60	Phil Nevin	.05
61	Jason Giambi	.50
62	Paul Menhart	.05
63	Eric Karros (Extreme Player)	.05
64	Allen Watson	.05
65	Jeff Cirillo	.05
66	Lee Smith (Extreme Player)	.05
67	Sean Berry	.05
68	Luis Sojo	.05
69	Jeff Montgomery (Extreme Player)	.05
70	Todd Hundley	.05
71	John Burkett	.05
72	Mark Gubicza	.05
73	Don Mattingly (Extreme Player)	1.25
74	Jeff Brantley	.05
75	Matt Walbeck	.05
76	Steve Parris	.05
77	Ken Caminiti (Extreme Player)	.05
78	Kirt Manwaring	.05
79	Greg Vaughn	.05
80	Pedro Martinez (Extreme Player)	.75
81	Benji Gil	.05
82	Heathcliff Slocumb (Extreme Player)	.05
83	Joe Girardi (Extreme Player)	.05
84	Sean Bergman	.05
85	Matt Karchner	.05
86	Butch Huskey	.05
87	Mike Morgan	.05
88	Todd Worrell (Extreme Player)	.05
89	Mike Bordick	.05
90	Bip Roberts (Extreme Player)	.05
91	Mike Hampton	.05
92	Troy O'Leary	.05
93	Wally Joyner	.05
94	Dave Stevens	.05
95	Cecil Fielder (Extreme Player)	.05
96	Wade Boggs (Extreme Player)	1.00
97	Hal Morris	.05
98	Mickey Tettleton (Extreme Player)	.05
99	Jeff Kent (Extreme Player)	.05
100	Denny Martinez (Extreme Player)	.05
101	Luis Gonzalez	.05
102	John Jaha	.05
103	Javy Lopez (Extreme Player)	.05
104	Mark McGwire (Extreme Player)	2.00
105	Ken Griffey Jr. (Extreme Player)	1.50
106	Darren Daulton (Extreme Player)	.05
107	Bryan Rekar	.05
108	Mike Macfarlane (Extreme Player)	.05
109	Gary Gaetti	.05
110	Shane Reynolds	.05
111	Pat Meares	.05
112	Jason Schmidt	.05
113	Otis Nixon	.05
114	John Franco	.05
115	Marc Newfield	.05
116	Andy Benes (Extreme Player)	.05
117	Ozzie Guillen	.05
118	Brian Jordan	.05
119	Terry Pendleton (Extreme Player)	.05

120	Chuck Finley		
	(Extreme Player)	.05	
121	Scott Stahoviak	.05	
122	Sid Fernandez	.05	
123	Derek Jeter		
	(Extreme Player)	3.00	
124	John Smiley	.05	
125	David Bell	.05	
126	Brett Butler		
	(Extreme Player)	.05	
127	Doug Drabek	.05	
128	J.T. Snow		
	(Extreme Player)	.05	
129	Joe Carter		
	(Extreme Player)	.05	
130	Dennis Eckersley		
	(Extreme Player)	.65	
131	Marty Cordova		
	(Extreme Player)	.05	
132	Greg Maddux		
	(Extreme Player)	1.00	
133	Tom Goodwin	.05	
134	Andy Ashby	.05	
135	Paul Sorrento		
	(Extreme Player)	.05	
136	Ricky Bones	.05	
137	Shawon Dunston	.05	
138	Moises Alou		
	(Extreme Player)	.05	
139	Mickey Morandini	.05	
140	Ramon Martinez		
	(Extreme Player)	.05	
141	Royce Clayton	.05	
142	Brad Ausmus	.05	
143	Kenny Rogers		
	(Extreme Player)	.05	
144	Tim Naehring		
	(Extreme Player)	.05	
145	Chris Gomez		
	(Extreme Player)	.05	
146	Bobby Bonilla		
	(Extreme Player)	.05	
147	Wilson Alvarez	.05	
148	Johnny Damon		
	(Extreme Player)	.35	
149	Pat Hentgen	.05	
150	Andres Galarraga		
	(Extreme Player)	.05	
151	David Cone		
	(Extreme Player)	.05	
152	Lance Johnson		
	(Extreme Player)	.05	
153	Carlos Garcia	.05	
154	Doug Johns	.05	
155	Midre Cummings	.05	
156	Steve Sparks	.05	
157	Sandy Martinez RC	.05	
158	William Van Landingham	.05	
159	Dave Justice		
	(Extreme Player)	.05	
160	Mark Grace		
	(Extreme Player)	.05	
161	Robb Nen		
	(Extreme Player)	.05	
162	Mike Greenwell		
	(Extreme Player)	.05	
163	Brad Radke	.05	
164	Edgardo Alfonzo	.05	
165	Mark Leiter	.05	
166	Walt Weiss	.05	
167	Mel Rojas		
	(Extreme Player)	.05	
168	Bret Boone		
	(Extreme Player)	.05	
169	Ricky Bottalico	.05	
170	Bobby Higginson	.05	
171	Trevor Hoffman	.05	
172	Jay Bell (Extreme Player)	.05	
173	Gabe White	.05	
174	Curtis Goodwin	.05	
175	Tyler Green	.05	
176	Roberto Alomar		
	(Extreme Player)	.20	
177	Sterling Hitchcock	.05	
178	Ryan Klesko		
	(Extreme Player)	.05	
179	Donne Wall RC	.05	
180	Brian McRae	.05	
181	Will Clark (Team TSC)	.05	
182	Frank Thomas (Team TSC)	.60	
183	Jeff Bagwell (Team TSC)	.60	
184	Mo Vaughn (Team TSC)	.05	
185	Tino Martinez (Team TSC)	.05	
186	Craig Biggio (Team TSC)	.05	
187	Chuck Knoblauch		
	(Team TSC)	.05	
188	Carlos Baerga (Team TSC)	.05	
189	Quilvio Veras (Team TSC)	.05	
190	Luis Alicea (Team TSC)	.05	
191	Jim Thome (Team TSC)	.40	
192	Mike Blowers (Team TSC)	.05	
193	Robin Ventura		
	(Team TSC)	.05	
194	Jeff King (Team TSC)	.05	
195	Tony Phillips (Team TSC)	.05	
196	John Valentin (Team TSC)	.05	
197	Barry Larkin (Team TSC)	.05	
198	Cal Ripken Jr.		
	(Team TSC)	2.00	
199	Omar Vizquel (Team TSC)	.05	
200	Kurt Abbott (Team TSC)	.05	
201	Albert Belle (Team TSC)	.05	
202	Barry Bonds (Team TSC)	2.00	
203	Ron Gant (Team TSC)	.05	

204	Dante Bichette (Team TSC)	.05
205	Jeff Conine (Team TSC)	.05
206	Jim Edmonds (Team TSC)	.05
207	Stan Javier (Team TSC)	.05
208	Kenny Lofton (Team TSC)	.05
209	Ray Lankford (Team TSC)	.05
210	Bernie Williams (Team TSC)	.05
211	Jay Buhner (Team TSC)	.05
212	Paul O'Neill (Team TSC)	.05
213	Tim Salmon (Team TSC)	.05
214	Reggie Sanders (Team TSC)	.05
215	Manny Ramirez (Team TSC)	.60
216	Mike Piazza (Team TSC)	1.50
217	Mike Stanley (Team TSC)	.05
218	Tony Eusebio (Team TSC)	.05
219	Chris Hoiles (Team TSC)	.05
220	Ron Karkovice (Team TSC)	.05
221	Edgar Martinez (Team TSC)	.05
222	Chili Davis (Team TSC)	.05
223	Jose Canseco (Team TSC)	.35
224	Eddie Murray (Team TSC)	.60
225	Geronimo Berroa (Team TSC)	.05
226	Chipper Jones (Team TSC)	.75
227	Garret Anderson (Team TSC)	.05
228	Marty Cordova (Team TSC)	.05
229	Jon Nunnally (Team TSC)	.05
230	Brian Hunter (Team TSC)	.05
231	Shawn Green (Team TSC)	.20
232	Ray Durham (Team TSC)	.05
233	Alex Gonzalez (Team TSC)	.05
234	Bobby Higginson	.05
235	Randy Johnson (Team TSC)	.60
236	Al Leiter (Team TSC)	.05
237	Tom Glavine (Team TSC)	.10
238	Kenny Rogers (Team TSC)	.05
239	Mike Hampton (Team TSC)	.05
240	David Wells (Team TSC)	.05
241	Jim Abbott (Team TSC)	.05
242	Denny Neagle (Team TSC)	.05
243	Wilson Alvarez (Team TSC)	.05
244	John Smiley (Team TSC)	.05
245	Greg Maddux (Team TSC)	.75
246	Andy Ashby (Team TSC)	.05
247	Hideo Nomo (Team TSC)	.30
248	Pat Rapp (Team TSC)	.05
249	Tim Wakefield (Team TSC)	.05
250	John Smoltz (Team TSC)	.10
251	Joey Hamilton (Team TSC)	.05
252	Frank Castillo (Team TSC)	.05
253	Denny Martinez (Team TSC)	.05
254	Jaime Navarro (Team TSC)	.05
255	Karim Garcia (Team TSC)	.05
256	Bob Abreu (Team TSC)	.05
257	Butch Huskey (Team TSC)	.05
258	Ruben Rivera (Team TSC)	.05
259	Johnny Damon (Team TSC)	.20
260	Derek Jeter (Team TSC)	2.00
261	Dennis Eckersley (Team TSC)	.50
262	Jose Mesa (Team TSC)	.05
263	Tom Henke (Team TSC)	.05
264	Rick Aguilera (Team TSC)	.05
265	Randy Myers (Team TSC)	.05
266	John Franco (Team TSC)	.05
267	Jeff Brantley (Team TSC)	.05
268	John Wetteland (Team TSC)	.05
269	Mark Wohlers (Team TSC)	.05
270	Rod Beck (Team TSC)	.05
271	Barry Larkin	.05
272	Paul O'Neill	.05
273	Bobby Jones (Team TSC)	.05
274	Will Clark	.05
275	Steve Avery	.05
276	Jim Edmonds	.05
277	John Olerud	.05
278	Carlos Perez	.05
279	Chris Hoiles	.05
280	Jeff Conine	.05
281	Jim Eisenreich	.05
282	Jason Jacome	.05
283	Ray Lankford	.05
284	John Wasdin	.05
285	Frank Thomas	.75
286	Jason Isringhausen	.05
287	Glenallen Hill	.05
288	Esteban Loaiza	.05
289	Bernie Williams	.05
290	Curtis Leskanic	.05
291	Scott Cooper	.05
292	Curt Schilling	.35
293	Eddie Murray	.75
294	Rick Krivda	.05
295	Domingo Cedeno	.05
296	Jeff Fassero	.05
297	Albert Belle	.05
298	Craig Biggio	.05
299	Fernando Vina	.05
300	Edgar Martinez	.05
301	Tony Gwynn	1.00

302	Felipe Lira	.05
303	Mo Vaughn	.05
304	Alex Fernandez	.05
305	Keith Lockhart	.05
306	Roger Pavlik	.05
307	Lee Tinsley	.05
308	Omar Vizquel	.05
309	Scott Servais	.05
310	Danny Tartabull	.05
311	Chili Davis	.05
312	Cal Eldred	.05
313	Roger Cedeno	.05
314	Chris Hammond	.05
315	Rusty Greer	.05
316	Brady Anderson	.05
317	Ron Villone	.05
318	Mark Carreon	.05
319	Larry Walker	.05
320	Pete Harnisch	.05
321	Robin Ventura	.05
322	Tim Belcher	.05
323	Tony Tarasco	.05
324	Juan Guzman	.05
325	Kenny Lofton	.05
326	Kevin Foster	.05
327	Wil Cordero	.05
328	Troy Percival	.05
329	Turk Wendell	.05
330	Thomas Howard	.05
331	Carlos Baerga	.05
332	B.J. Surhoff	.05
333	Jay Buhner	.05
334	Andujar Cedeno	.05
335	Jeff King	.05
336	Dante Bichette	.05
337	Alan Trammell	.05
338	Scott Leius	.05
339	Chris Snopek	.05
340	Roger Bailey	.05
341	Jacob Brumfield	.05
342	Jose Canseco	.50
343	Rafael Palmeiro	.05
344	Quilvio Veras	.05
345	Darrin Fletcher	.05
346	Carlos Delgado	.50
347	Tony Eusebio	.05
348	Ismael Valdes	.05
349	Terry Steinbach	.05
350	Orel Hershiser	.05
351	Kurt Abbott	.05
352	Jody Reed	.05
353	David Howard	.05
354	Ruben Sierra	.05
355	John Ericks	.05
356	Buck Showalter	.05
357	Jim Thome	.65
358	Geronimo Berroa	.05
359	Robby Thompson	.05
360	Jose Vizcaino	.05
361	Jeff Frye	.05
362	Kevin Appier	.05
363	Pat Kelly	.05
364	Ron Gant	.05
365	Luis Alicea	.05
366	Armando Benitez	.05
367	Rico Brogna	.05
368	Manny Ramirez	.75
369	Mike Lansing	.05
370	Sammy Sosa	1.00
371	Don Wengert	.05
372	Dave Nilsson	.05
373	Sandy Alomar	.05
374	Joey Cora	.05
375	Larry Thomas	.05
376	John Valentin	.05
377	Kevin Ritz	.05
378	Steve Finley	.05
379	Frank Rodriguez	.05
380	Ivan Rodriguez	.65
381	Alex Ochoa	.05
382	Mark Lemke	.05
383	Scott Brosius	.05
384	James Mouton	.05
385	Mark Langston	.05
386	Ed Sprague	.05
387	Joe Oliver	.05
388	Steve Ontiveros	.05
389	Rey Sanchez	.05
390	Mike Henneman	.05
391	Jose Valentin RC	.05
392	Tom Candiotti	.05
393	Damon Buford	.05
394	Erik Hanson	.05
395	Mark Smith	.05
396	Pete Schourek	.05
397	John Flaherty	.05
398	Dave Martinez	.05
399	Tommy Greene	.05
400	Gary Sheffield	.45
401	Glenn Dishman	.05
402	Barry Bonds	3.00
403	Tom Pagnozzi	.05
404	Todd Stottlemyre	.05
405	Tim Salmon	.05
406	John Hudek	.05
407	Fred McGriff	.05
408	Orlando Merced	.05
409	Brian Barber	.05
410	Ryan Thompson	.05
411	Mariano Rivera	.10
412	Eric Young	.05
413	Chris Bosio	.05
414	Chuck Knoblauch	.05
415	Jamie Moyer	.05
416	Chan Ho Park	.05
417	Mark Portugal	.05
418	Tim Raines	.05
419	Antonio Osuna	.05

420	Todd Zeile	.05
421	Steve Wojciechowski	.05
422	Marquis Grissom	.05
423	Norm Charlton	.05
424	Cal Ripken Jr.	3.00
425	Gregg Jefferies	.05
426	Mike Stanton	.05
427	Tony Fernandez	.05
428	Jose Rijo	.05
429	Jeff Bagwell	.75
430	Raul Mondesi	.05
431	Travis Fryman	.05
432	Ron Karkovice	.05
433	Alan Benes	.05
434	Tony Phillips	.05
435	Reggie Sanders	.05
436	Andy Pettitte	.25
437	Matt Lawton RC	.25
438	Jeff Blauser	.05
439	Michael Tucker	.05
440	Mark Loretta	.05
441	Charlie Hayes	.05
442	Mike Piazza	1.50
443	Shane Andrews	.05
444	Jeff Suppan	.05
445	Steve Rodriguez	.05
446	Mike Matheny	.05
447	Trenidad Hubbard	.05
448	Denny Hocking	.05
449	Mark Grudzielanek	.05
450	Joe Randa	.05

Mickey Mantle "Cereal Box" Set

This factory-set version of TSC was packaged in boxes which resembled single-serving cereal boxes. The cards are identical to the regular TSC version except for the use of silver-foil, rather than gold-foil, highlights on front.

	NM/M
Unopened Set:	30.00
Common Player:	.10

Extreme Player

A special interactive version of 179 players' cards in 1996 Stadium Club was issued as an insert set across Series 1 and 2. Specially stamped with an "Extreme Player" logo in bronze (1 per 12 packs average), silver (1:24) or gold (1:48), the cards have backs which detail a contest by which the player's on-field performance was used to rank each by position. At season's end, cards of the winning players at each position could be redeemed for special prizes. The contest cards do not have card numbers on back and are numbered here based on the regular version.

		NM/M
Complete Bronze Set (179):		40.00
Common Bronze:		.10
Silvers:		1.5X
Golds:		2.5X
1	Hideo Nomo	.50
3	Garret Anderson	.10
4	Jose Mesa	.10
5	Vinny Castilla	.10
6	Mike Mussina	.30
7	Ray Durham	.10
8	Jack McDowell	.10
9	Juan Gonzalez	.50
10	Chipper Jones	1.50
11	Deion Sanders	.10
12	Rondell White	.10
13	Tom Henke	.10
14	Derek Bell	.10
15	Randy Myers	.10
16	Randy Johnson	1.00
17	Len Dykstra	.10
18	Bill Pulsipher	.10
21	Chad Curtis	.10
22	Roberto Hernandez	.10
23	Kirby Puckett	1.50
26	Roger Clemens	1.75
31	Chad Fonville	.10
32	Bernard Gilkey	.10
34	Shawn Green	.35
35	Rick Aguilera	.10

40	Dean Palmer	.10
45	Matt Williams	.10
47	Tom Glavine	.35
50	Delino DeShields	.10
56	Benito Santiago	.10
59	Rod Beck	.10
63	Eric Karros	.10
66	Lee Smith	.10
69	Jeff Montgomery	.10
70	Todd Hundley	.10
73	Don Mattingly	1.75
77	Ken Caminiti	.10
80	Pedro Martinez	1.00
82	Heathcliff Slocumb	.10
83	Joe Girardi	.10
88	Todd Worrell	.10
90	Bip Roberts	.10
95	Cecil Fielder	.10
96	Wade Boggs	1.50
98	Mickey Tettleton	.10
99	Jeff Kent	.10
101	Luis Gonzalez	.10
103	Javier Lopez	.10
104	Mark McGwire	3.00
105	Ken Griffey Jr.	2.00
106	Darren Daulton	.10
108	Mike Macfarlane	.10
109	Gary Gaetti	.10
110	Shane Reynolds	.10
114	John Franco	.10
116	Andy Benes	.10
118	Brian Jordan	.10
119	Terry Pendleton	.10
120	Chuck Finley	.10
123	Derek Jeter	4.00
124	John Smiley	.10
126	Brett Butler	.10
127	Doug Drabek	.10
128	J.T. Snow	.10
129	Joe Carter	.10
130	Dennis Eckersley	.75
131	Marty Cordova	.10
132	Greg Maddux	1.50
135	Paul Sorrento	.10
137	Shawon Dunston	.10
138	Moises Alou	.10
140	Ramon Martinez	.10
141	Royce Clayton	.10
143	Kenny Rogers	.10
144	Tim Naehring	.10
145	Chris Gomez	.10
146	Bobby Bonilla	.10
148	Johnny Damon	.40
150	Andres Galarraga	.10
151	David Cone	.10
152	Lance Johnson	.10
159	Dave Justice	.10
160	Mark Grace	.10
161	Robb Nen	.10
162	Mike Greenwell	.10
167	Mel Rojas	.10
168	Bret Boone	.10
172	Jay Bell	.10
176	Roberto Alomar	.25
178	Ryan Klesko	.10
271	Barry Larkin	.10
272	Paul O'Neill	.10
274	Will Clark	.10
275	Steve Avery	.10
276	Jim Edmonds	.10
277	John Olerud	.10
279	Chris Hoiles	.10
280	Jeff Conine	.10
283	Ray Lankford	.10
285	Frank Thomas	1.00
286	Jason Isringhausen	.10
287	Glenallen Hill	.10
289	Bernie Williams	.10
290	Eddie Murray	1.00
296	Jeff Fassero	.10
297	Albert Belle	.10
298	Craig Biggio	.10
300	Edgar Martinez	.10
301	Tony Gwynn	1.50
303	Mo Vaughn	.10
304	Alex Fernandez	.10
308	Omar Vizquel	.10
310	Danny Tartabull	.10
316	Brady Anderson	.10
319	Larry Walker	.10
321	Robin Ventura	.10
325	Kenny Lofton	.10
327	Wil Cordero	.10
328	Troy Percival	.10
331	Carlos Baerga	.10
333	Jay Buhner	.10
335	Jeff King	.10
336	Dante Bichette	.10
337	Alan Trammell	.10
342	Jose Canseco	.50
343	Rafael Palmeiro	.10
344	Quilvio Veras	.10
345	Darrin Fletcher	.10
347	Tony Eusebio	.10
348	Ismael Valdes	.10
349	Terry Steinbach	.10
350	Orel Hershiser	.10
351	Kurt Abbott	.10
354	Ruben Sierra	.10
357	Jim Thome	.75
358	Geronimo Berroa	.10
359	Robby Thompson	.10
360	Jose Vizcaino	.10
362	Kevin Appier	.10
364	Ron Gant	.10
367	Rico Brogna	.10
368	Manny Ramirez	1.00
370	Sammy Sosa	1.50

373	Sandy Alomar	.10
378	Steve Finley	.10
380	Ivan Rodriguez	.75
382	Mark Lemke	.10
385	Mark Langston	.10
386	Ed Sprague	.10
388	Steve Ontiveros	.10
392	Tom Candiotti	.10
394	Erik Hanson	.10
396	Pete Schourek	.10
400	Gary Sheffield	.35
402	Barry Bonds	4.00
403	Tom Pagnozzi	.10
404	Todd Stottlemyre	.10
405	Tim Salmon	.10
407	Fred McGriff	.10
408	Orlando Merced	.10
412	Eric Young	.10
414	Chuck Knoblauch	.10
417	Mark Portugal	.10
418	Tim Raines	.10
420	Todd Zeile	.10
422	Marquis Grissom	.10
423	Norm Charlton	.10
424	Cal Ripken Jr.	4.00
425	Gregg Jefferies	.10
428	Jose Rijo	.10
429	Jeff Bagwell	1.00
430	Raul Mondesi	.10
431	Travis Fryman	.10
434	Tony Phillips	.10
435	Reggie Sanders	.10
436	Andy Pettitte	.25
438	Jeff Blauser	.10
441	Charlie Hayes	.10
442	Mike Piazza	2.00

Extreme Player - Bronze Winner

Ten-card sets of these special bronze-foil highlighted cards were the prize for those who redeemed bronze statistical winners' cards from the Stadium Club Extreme Player interactive series. Backs have statistical ratings pertinent to the game and scoring rules. Cards have an "EW" prefix to the number. The same photos and back design were used in different technologies in the bronze, silver and gold winners cards.

		NM/M
Complete Set (10):		6.00
Common Player:		.40
1	Greg Maddux	1.50
2	Mike Piazza	1.50
3	Andres Galarraga	.40
4	Chuck Knoblauch	.40
5	Ken Caminiti	.40
6	Barry Larkin	.40
7	Barry Bonds	3.00
8	Ken Griffey Jr.	2.00
9	Gary Sheffield	.75
10	Todd Worrell	.40

Extreme Player - Silver Winner

Ten-card sets of these Finest technology cards were the prize for those who redeemed statistical winners' cards from the Stadium Club Extreme Player interactive series. Backs have statistical ratings pertinent to the game and scoring rules. Cards have an "EW" prefix to the number.

		NM/M
Complete Set (10):		17.50
Common Player:		.75
1	Greg Maddux	3.00
2	Mike Piazza	4.00
3	Andres Galarraga	.75
4	Chuck Knoblauch	.75
5	Ken Caminiti	.75
6	Barry Larkin	.75
7	Barry Bonds	5.00
8	Ken Griffey Jr.	4.00
9	Gary Sheffield	1.50
10	Todd Worrell	.75

Extreme Player - Gold Winner

One of these large (2-3/4" x 3-3/4"), heavy, acrylic-coated bronze refractor cards was the prize for those who redeemed the same player's gold statistical winners' card from the Stadium Club Extreme Player interactive series. Backs have statistical ratings pertinent to the game and scoring rules. Cards have an "EW" prefix to the number. The same photos and back design were used in different technologies in the bronze, silver and gold winners cards.

		NM/M
Complete Set (10):		45.00
Common Player:		2.00
1	Greg Maddux	8.00
2	Mike Piazza	10.00
3	Andres Galarraga	2.00
4	Chuck Knoblauch	2.00
5	Ken Caminiti	2.00
6	Barry Larkin	2.00
7	Barry Bonds	15.00
8	Ken Griffey Jr.	10.00
9	Gary Sheffield	3.50
10	Todd Worrell	2.00

Bash & Burn

Inserted in one per 24 retail packs and one per 48 hobby packs of Series II, Bash & Burn includes 10 players on double-fronted cards. Both sides are foil-etched with the Bash side highlighting home runs and runs batted in for 1995 and career, and the Burn side featured stolen base and runs scored leaders for 1995 and career. Cards are numbered with a "B&B" prefix.

		NM/M
Complete Set (10):		10.00
Common Player:		.75
1	Sammy Sosa	3.50
2	Barry Bonds	6.00
3	Reggie Sanders	.75
4	Craig Biggio	.75
5	Raul Mondesi	.75
6	Ron Gant	.75
7	Ray Lankford	.75
8	Glenallen Hill	.75
9	Chad Curtis	.75
10	John Valentin	.75

Mickey Mantle Retrospective

Following the success of the Mantle reprints in Topps baseball, Stadium Club produced a series of 19 Mickey Mantle Retrospective inserts; nine black-and-white cards in Series 1 and 10 color cards in Series 2. The cards chronicle Mantle's career and provide insights from baseball contemporaries. The Mantle cards are found on an average of once per 24 Series 1 packs and once per 12 Series 2 packs. Cards are numbered with an "MM" prefix.

		NM/M
Complete Set (19):		35.00
Common Series 1:		4.00
Common Series 2:		2.00
1	Mickey Mantle/1950 (Minor league)	4.00
2	Mickey Mantle/1951	4.00
3	Mickey Mantle/1951	4.00
4	Mickey Mantle/1953	4.00
5	Mickey Mantle/1954 (W/Yogi Berra.)	4.00
6	Mickey Mantle/1956	4.00
7	Mickey Mantle/1957	4.00
8	Mickey Mantle/1958 (W/Casey Stengel.)	4.00
9	Mickey Mantle/1959	4.00
10	Mickey Mantle/1960 (W/Elston Howard.)	2.00
11	Mickey Mantle/1961	2.00
12	Mickey Mantle/1961 (W/Roger Maris.)	4.00
13	Mickey Mantle/1962	2.00
14	Mickey Mantle/1963	2.00
15	Mickey Mantle/1964	2.00
16	Mickey Mantle	2.00
17	Mickey Mantle/1968	2.00
18	Mickey Mantle/1969	2.00
19	Mickey Mantle (In Memoriam)	3.50

Mega Heroes

Ten heroic players are matched with a comic book-style illustration depicting their nicknames in the Mega Heroes insert set. Printed on foilboard in a defraction technology, the cards are found, on average, once per 48 Series 1 hobby packs and twice as often in retail packs.

		NM/M
Complete Set (10):		10.00
Common Player:		.75
1	Frank Thomas	1.50
2	Ken Griffey Jr.	3.00
3	Hideo Nomo	1.25
4	Ozzie Smith	1.75
5	Will Clark	1.00
6	Jack McDowell	1.00
7	Andres Galarraga	1.00
8	Roger Clemens	2.00
9	Deion Sanders	1.00
10	Mo Vaughn	1.00

Metalists

Eight players who have won two or more major awards in their careers are featured in this Series II insert. Cards are printed on foilboard and feature intricate laser-cut designs that depict the player's face. Metalist inserts are found one per 96 retail and one per 48 hobby packs, on average. Cards are numbered with a "M" prefix.

		NM/M
Complete Set (8):		12.00
Common Player:		1.00
1	Jeff Bagwell	1.25
2	Barry Bonds	3.50
3	Jose Canseco	1.00
4	Roger Clemens	2.50
5	Dennis Eckersley	1.00
6	Greg Maddux	2.00
7	Cal Ripken Jr.	3.50
8	Frank Thomas	1.25

Midsummer Matchups

These inserts salute 1995 National League and American League All-Stars on back-to-back etched-foil cards. Players are matched by position in the 10-card set. Average insertion rate is one per 48 hobby packs and one per 24 retail packs in Series 1. Cards are numbered with an "M" prefix.

		NM/M
Complete Set (10):		20.00
Common Player:		1.00
1	Hideo Nomo, Randy Johnson	2.00
2	Mike Piazza, Ivan Rodriguez	4.00
3	Fred McGriff, Frank Thomas	2.00
4	Craig Biggio, Carlos Baerga	1.00
5	Vinny Castilla, Wade Boggs	2.50
6	Barry Larkin, Cal Ripken Jr.	5.00
7	Barry Bonds, Albert Belle	5.00
8	Len Dykstra, Kenny Lofton	1.00
9	Tony Gwynn, Kirby Puckett	3.00
10	Ron Gant, Edgar Martinez	1.00

Power Packed

Topps' Power Matrix technology is used to showcase 15 of the biggest, strongest players in this Series 2 insert set. Card backs fea-ture a diagram of the player's home park with baseball graphics measuring his home runs during the 1995 season. The inserts are a one in 48 packs pick, on average, both hobby and retail. Cards are numbered with a "PP" prefix.

		NM/M
Complete Set (15):		15.00
Common Player:		1.00
1	Albert Belle	1.00
2	Mark McGwire	4.00
3	Jose Canseco	1.75
4	Mike Piazza	3.00
5	Ron Gant	1.00
6	Ken Griffey Jr.	3.00
7	Mo Vaughn	1.00
8	Cecil Fielder	1.00
9	Tim Salmon	1.00
10	Frank Thomas	2.50
11	Juan Gonzalez	1.50
12	Andres Galarraga	1.00
13	Fred McGriff	1.00
14	Jay Buhner	1.00
15	Dante Bichette	1.00

Power Streak

The best power hitters in baseball are featured in Power Matrix technology on these Series I inserts. Average insertion rate is one per 24 hobby and 48 retail packs. Cards are numbered with a "PS" prefix.

		NM/M
Complete Set (15):		20.00
Common Player:		1.00
1	Randy Johnson	2.00
2	Hideo Nomo	1.25
3	Albert Belle	1.00
4	Dante Bichette	1.00
5	Jay Buhner	1.00
6	Frank Thomas	4.00
7	Mark McGwire	2.00
8	Rafael Palmeiro	1.00
9	Mo Vaughn	1.00
10	Sammy Sosa	3.00
11	Larry Walker	1.00
12	Gary Gaetti	1.00
13	Tim Salmon	1.00
14	Barry Bonds	5.00
15	Jim Edmonds	1.00

Prime Cuts

The purest swings in baseball are the focus on these laser-cut, defraction-foil inserts found in Series 1 packs at an average rate of one per 36 hobby and 72 retail packs. Cards are numbered with a "PC" prefix.

		NM/M
Complete Set (8):		20.00
Common Player:		1.50
1	Albert Belle	1.50
2	Barry Bonds	6.00
3	Ken Griffey Jr.	4.00
4	Tony Gwynn	3.00
5	Edgar Martinez	1.50
6	Rafael Palmeiro	1.00
7	Mike Piazza	4.00
8	Frank Thomas	2.50

TSC Awards

TSC Awards insert cards allowed Topps' experts to honor best performances, newcomer, comeback, etc. The cards are found in Series 2 packs at an average rate of one per 24 retail and 48 hobby packs.

		NM/M
Complete Set (10):		15.00
Common Player:		.50
1	Cal Ripken Jr.	5.00
2	Albert Belle	.60
3	Tom Glavine	1.00
4	Jeff Conine	.50
5	Ken Griffey Jr.	4.00
6	Hideo Nomo	1.25
7	Greg Maddux	3.00
8	Chipper Jones	3.00
9	Randy Johnson	2.00
10	Jose Mesa	.50

Members Only

For the fourth year Topps offered a special edition of its high-end Stadium Club issue to members of its mail-order family. Each of the regular and insert cards was stamped with a gold- or silver-foil "MEMBERS ONLY" seal. The '96 edition was the scarcest ever produced, with only 750 sets offered at $200. Single "Members Only" cards paralleling the regular-issue Stadium Club cards sell for a premium while the M.O. versions of the inserts usually sell at par or even a discount from the issued cards.

	NM/M
Complete Set (660):	150.00
Common Player:	.50
Stars:	6X
Inserts: 50-100 Percent	

Members Only Baseball

This 50-card boxed set was offered to members of Topps Stadium Club at about $15 retail. The first 45 cards in the set represent Topps' choice of 1995's top players in each league. The final five cards, printed in Topps Finest technology, honor hot rookies. The basic cards feature borderless action photos on which the background has been posterized and darkened to make the color photo stand out in the foreground. A gold-foil strip at bottom has the player name and position; a "Members Only" logo is in gold foil in an upper corner. Horizontal backs once again have much of the photo background darkened with a close-up photo at right and a few sentences about the player at left. "Member's Choice" Finest rookie cards have a stylized baseball diamond in red tones as background to the action photos. Backs have a large red-shaded baseball with player write-up at bottom and - honest - a pea-green portrait photo at upper-left. Each of the Finest cards has a peel-off protective layer on front.

		NM/M
Complete Set (50):		6.00
Common Player:		.10
1	Carlos Baerga	.10
2	Derek Bell	.10
3	Albert Belle	.10
4	Dante Bichette	.10
5	Craig Biggio	.10
6	Wade Boggs	.65
7	Barry Bonds	1.50
8	Jay Buhner	.10
9	Vinny Castilla	.10
10	Jeff Conine	.10
11	Jim Edmonds	.10
12	Steve Finley	.10
13	Andres Galarraga	.10
14	Mark Grace	.10
15	Tony Gwynn	.65
16	Lance Johnson	.10
17	Randy Johnson	.50
18	Eric Karros	.10
19	Chuck Knoblauch	.10
20	Barry Larkin	.10
21	Kenny Lofton	.50
22	Greg Maddux	.65
23	Edgar Martinez	.10
24	Tino Martinez	.10
25	Mark McGwire	1.00
26	Brian McRae	.10
27	Jose Mesa	.10
28	Eddie Murray	.50
29	Mike Mussina	.30
30	Randy Myers	.10
31	Hideo Nomo	.25
32	Rafael Palmeiro	.50
33	Tony Phillips	.10
34	Mike Piazza	.75
35	Kirby Puckett	.65
36	Manny Ramirez	.50
37	Tim Salmon	.10
38	Reggie Sanders	.10
39	Sammy Sosa	.65
40	Frank Thomas	.50
41	Jim Thome	.45
42	John Valentin	.10
43	Mo Vaughn	.10
44	Quilvio Veras	.10
45	Larry Walker	.10
46	Hideo Nomo (Finest)	.50
47	Marty Cordova (Finest)	.50
48	Chipper Jones (Finest)	1.50
49	Garret Anderson (Finest)	.50
50	Andy Pettitte (Finest)	.50

1997 Stadium Club Pre-Production

These specially marked promo cards were issued in a cello wrapper.

		NM/M
Complete Set (3):		4.00
Common Player:		1.00
PP1	Chipper Jones	3.00
PP2	Kenny Lofton	1.00
PP3	Gary Sheffield	1.50

1997 Stadium Club

Stadium Club totalled 390 cards in 1997, issued in two series of 195 cards each. In Series 1 (Feb.), cards #181-195 are a rookie subset called TSC 2000. In Series 2 (April), cards #376-390 form a subset called Stadium Slugger. Each of these subsets was short-printed and inserted about one per two packs. TSC is printed on an improved 20-point stock with Topps' Super Color process.

		NM/M
Complete Set (390):		35.00
Common Player:		.05
Series 1 or 2 Pack (9):		1.50
Series 1 or 2 Wax Box (24):		27.50

No.	Player	Price
1	Chipper Jones	1.50
2	Gary Sheffield	.50
3	Kenny Lofton	.05
4	Brian Jordan	.05
5	Mark McGwire	2.50
6	Charles Nagy	.05
7	Tim Salmon	.05
8	Cal Ripken Jr.	3.00
9	Jeff Conine	.05
10	Paul Molitor	1.00
11	Mariano Rivera	.15
12	Pedro Martinez	1.00
13	Jeff Bagwell	1.00
14	Bobby Bonilla	.05
15	Barry Bonds	3.00
16	Ryan Klesko	.05
17	Barry Larkin	.05
18	Jim Thome	.65
19	Jay Buhner	.05
20	Juan Gonzalez	.50
21	Mike Mussina	.30
22	Kevin Appier	.05
23	Eric Karros	.05
24	Steve Finley	.05
25	Ed Sprague	.05
26	Bernard Gilkey	.05
27	Tony Phillips	.05
28	Henry Rodriguez	.05
29	John Smoltz	.05
30	Dante Bichette	.05
31	Mike Piazza	2.00
32	Paul O'Neill	.05
33	Billy Wagner	.05
34	Reggie Sanders	.05
35	John Jaha	.05
36	* Eddie Murray	1.00
37	Eric Young	.05
38	Roberto Hernandez	.05
39	Pat Hentgen	.05
40	Sammy Sosa	1.50
41	Todd Hundley	.05
42	Mo Vaughn	.05
43	Robin Ventura	.05
44	Mark Grudzielanek	.05
45	Shane Reynolds	.05
46	Andy Pettitte	.25
47	Fred McGriff	.05
48	Rey Ordonez	.05
49	Will Clark	.05
50	Ken Griffey Jr.	2.00
51	Todd Worrell	.05
52	Rusty Greer	.05
53	Mark Grace	.05
54	Tom Glavine	.35
55	Derek Jeter	3.00
56	Rafael Palmeiro	.75
57	Bernie Williams	.05
58	Marty Cordova	.05
59	Andres Galarraga	.05
60	Ken Caminiti	.05
61	Garret Anderson	.05
62	Denny Martinez	.05
63	Mike Greenwell	.05
64	David Segui	.05
65	Julio Franco	.05
66	Rickey Henderson	1.00
67	Ozzie Guillen	.05
68	Pete Harnisch	.05
69	Chan Ho Park	.05
70	Harold Baines	.05
71	Mark Clark	.05
72	Steve Avery	.05
73	Brian Hunter	.05
74	Pedro Astacio	.05
75	Jack McDowell	.05
76	Gregg Jefferies	.05
77	Jason Kendall	.05
78	Todd Walker	.05
79	B.J. Surhoff	.05
80	Moises Alou	.05
81	Fernando Vina	.05
82	Darryl Strawberry	.05
83	Jose Rosado	.05
84	Chris Gomez	.05
85	Chili Davis	.05
86	Alan Benes	.05
87	Todd Hollandsworth	.05
88	Jose Vizcaino	.05
89	Edgardo Alfonzo	.05
90	Ruben Rivera	.05
91	Donovan Osborne	.05
92	Doug Glanville	.05
93	Gary DiSarcina	.05
94	Brooks Kieschnick	.05
95	Bobby Jones	.05
96	Raul Casanova	.05
97	Jermaine Allensworth	.05
98	Kenny Rogers	.05
99	Mark McLemore	.05
100	Jeff Fassero	.05
101	Sandy Alomar	.05
102	Chuck Finley	.05
103	Eric Owens	.05
104	Billy McMillon	.05
105	Dwight Gooden	.05
106	Sterling Hitchcock	.05
107	Doug Drabek	.05
108	Paul Wilson	.05
109	Chris Snopek	.05
110	Al Leiter	.05
111	Bob Tewksbury	.05
112	Todd Greene	.05
113	Jose Valentin	.05
114	Delino DeShields	.05
115	Mike Bordick	.05
116	Pat Meares	.05
117	Mariano Duncan	.05
118	Steve Trachsel	.05
119	Luis Castillo	.05
120	Andy Benes	.05
121	Donne Wall	.05
122	Alex Gonzalez	.05
123	Dan Wilson	.05
124	Omar Vizquel	.05
125	Devon White	.05
126	Darryl Hamilton	.05
127	Orlando Merced	.05
128	Royce Clayton	.05
129	William Van Landingham	.05
130	Terry Steinbach	.05
131	Jeff Blauser	.05
132	Jeff Cirillo	.05
133	Roger Pavlik	.05
134	Danny Tartabull	.05
135	Jeff Montgomery	.05
136	Bobby Higginson	.05
137	Mike Grace	.05
138	Kevin Elster	.05
139	Brian Giles RC	1.00
140	Rod Beck	.05
141	Ismael Valdes	.05
142	Scott Brosius	.05
143	Mike Fetters	.05
144	Gary Gaetti	.05
145	Mike Lansing	.05
146	Glenallen Hill	.05
147	Shawn Green	.35
148	Mel Rojas	.05
149	Joey Cora	.05
150	John Smiley	.05
151	Marvin Benard	.05
152	Curt Schilling	.35
153	Dave Nilsson	.05
154	Edgar Renteria	.05
155	Joey Hamilton	.05
156	Carlos Garcia	.05
157	Nomar Garciaparra	2.00
158	Kevin Ritz	.05
159	Keith Lockhart	.05
160	Justin Thompson	.05
161	Terry Adams	.05
162	Jamey Wright	.05
163	Otis Nixon	.05
164	Michael Tucker	.05
165	Mike Stanley	.05
166	Ben McDonald	.05
167	John Mabry	.05
168	Troy O'Leary	.05
169	Mel Nieves	.05
170	Bret Boone	.05
171	Mike Timlin	.05
172	Scott Rolen	.75
173	Reggie Jefferson	.05
174	Neifi Perez	.05
175	Brian McRae	.05
176	Tom Goodwin	.05
177	Aaron Sele	.05
178	Benny Santiago	.05
179	Frank Rodriguez	.05
180	Eric Davis	.05
181	Andruw Jones (TSC 2000)	.75
182	Todd Walker (TSC 2000)	.15
183	Wes Helms (TSC 2000)	.15
184	Nelson Figueroa RC (TSC 2000)	.15
185	Vladimir Guerrero (TSC 2000)	.75
186	Billy McMillon (TSC 2000)	.15
187	Todd Helton (TSC 2000)	.65
188	Nomar Garciaparra (TSC 2000)	2.00
189	Katsuhiro Maeda (TSC 2000)	.15
190	Russell Branyan (TSC 2000)	.15
191	Glendon Rusch (TSC 2000)	.15
192	Bartolo Colon (TSC 2000)	.15
193	Scott Rolen (TSC 2000)	.50
194	Angel Echevarria (TSC 2000)	.15
195	Bob Abreu (TSC 2000)	.20
196	Greg Maddux	1.50
197	Joe Carter	.05
198	Alex Ochoa	.05
199	Ellis Burks	.05
200	Ivan Rodriguez	.75
201	Marquis Grissom	.05
202	Trevor Hoffman	.05
203	Matt Williams	.05
204	Carlos Delgado	.50
205	Ramon Martinez	.05
206	Chuck Knoblauch	.05
207	Juan Guzman	.05
208	Derek Bell	.05
209	Roger Clemens	1.75
210	Vladimir Guerrero	1.00
211	Cecil Fielder	.05
212	Hideo Nomo	.50
213	Frank Thomas	1.00
214	Greg Vaughn	.05
215	Javy Lopez	.05
216	Raul Mondesi	.05
217	Wade Boggs	1.50
218	Carlos Baerga	.05
219	Tony Gwynn	1.50
220	Tino Martinez	.05
221	Vinny Castilla	.05
222	Lance Johnson	.05
223	David Justice	.05
224	Rondell White	.05
225	Dean Palmer	.05
226	Jim Edmonds	.05
227	Albert Belle	.05
228	Alex Fernandez	.05
229	Ryne Sandberg	1.50
230	Jose Mesa	.05
231	David Cone	.05
232	Troy Percival	.05
233	Edgar Martinez	.05
234	Jose Canseco	.50
235	Kevin Brown	.05
236	Ray Lankford	.05
237	Karim Garcia	.05
238	J.T. Snow	.05
239	Dennis Eckersley	.75
240	Roberto Alomar	.35
241	John Valentin	.05
242	Ron Gant	.05
243	Geronimo Berroa	.05
244	Manny Ramirez	1.00
245	Travis Fryman	.05
246	Denny Neagle	.05
247	Randy Johnson	1.00
248	Darin Erstad	.15
249	Mark Wohlers	.05
250	Ken Hill	.05
251	Larry Walker	.05
252	Craig Biggio	.05
253	Brady Anderson	.05
254	John Wetteland	.05
255	Andruw Jones	1.00
256	Turk Wendell	.05
257	Jason Isringhausen	.05
258	Jaime Navarro	.05
259	Sean Berry	.05
260	Albie Lopez	.05
261	Jay Bell	.05
262	Bobby Witt	.05
263	Tony Clark	.05
264	Tim Wakefield	.05
265	Brad Radke	.05
266	Tim Belcher	.05
267	Mark Lewis	.05
268	Roger Cedeno	.05
269	Tim Naehring	.05
270	Kevin Tapani	.05
271	Joe Randa	.05
272	Randy Myers	.05
273	Dave Burba	.05
274a	Mike Sweeney	.05
274b	Tom Pagnozzi (Should be #374.)	.05
275	Danny Graves	.05
276	Chad Mottola	.05
277	Ruben Sierra	.05
278	Norm Charlton	.05
279	Scott Servais	.05
280	Jacob Cruz	.05
281	Mike Macfarlane	.05
282	Rich Becker	.05
283	Shannon Stewart	.05
284	Gerald Williams	.05
285	Jody Reed	.05
286	Jeff D'Amico	.05
287	Walt Weiss	.05
288	Jim Leyritz	.05
289	Francisco Cordova	.05
290	F.P. Santangelo	.05
291	Scott Erickson	.05
292	Hal Morris	.05
293	Ray Durham	.05
294	Andy Ashby	.05
295	Darryl Kile	.05
296	Jose Paniagua	.05
297	Mickey Tettleton	.05
298	Joe Girardi	.05
299	Rocky Coppinger	.05
300	Bob Abreu	.05
301	John Olerud	.05
302	Paul Shuey	.05
303	Jeff Brantley	.05
304	Bob Wells	.05
305	Kevin Seitzer	.05
306	Shawon Dunston	.05
307	Jose Herrera	.05
308	Butch Huskey	.05
309	Jose Offerman	.05
310	Rick Aguilera	.05
311	Greg Gagne	.05
312	John Burkett	.05
313	Mark Thompson	.05
314	Alvaro Espinoza	.05
315	Todd Stottlemyre	.05
316	Al Martin	.05
317	James Baldwin	.05
318	Cal Eldred	.05
319	Sid Fernandez	.05
320	Mickey Morandini	.05
321	Robb Nen	.05
322	Mark Lemke	.05
323	Pete Schourek	.05
324	Marcus Jensen	.05
325	Rich Aurilia	.05
326	Jeff King	.05
327	Scott Stahoviak	.05
328	Ricky Otero	.05
329	Antonio Osuna	.05
330	Chris Hoiles	.05
331	Luis Gonzalez	.05
332	Wil Cordero	.05
333	Johnny Damon	.35
334	Mark Langston	.05
335	Orlando Miller	.05
336	Jason Giambi	.50
337	Damian Jackson	.05
338	David Wells	.05
339	Bip Roberts	.05
340	Matt Ruebel	.05
341	Tom Candiotti	.05
342	Wally Joyner	.05
343	Jimmy Key	.05
344	Tony Batista	.05
345	Paul Sorrento	.05
346	Ron Karkovice	.05
347	Wilson Alvarez	.05
348	John Flaherty	.05
349	Rey Sanchez	.05
350	John Vander Wal	.05
351a	Jermaine Dye	.05
351b	Brant Brown (Should be #361.)	.05
352	Mike Hampton	.05
353	Greg Colbrunn	.05
354	Heathcliff Slocumb	.05
355	Ricky Bottalico	.05
356	Marty Janzen	.05
357	Orel Hershiser	.05
358	Rex Hudler	.05
359	Amaury Telemaco	.05
360	Darrin Fletcher	.05
361	Not Issued - See #351	
362	Russ Davis	.05
363	Allen Watson	.05
364	Mike Lieberthal	.05
365	Dave Stevens	.05
366	Jay Powell	.05
367	Tony Fossas	.05
368	Bob Wolcott	.05
369	Mark Loretta	.05
370	Shawn Estes	.05
371	Sandy Martinez	.05
372	Wendell Magee Jr.	.05
373	John Franco	.05
374	Not Issued - See #274	.05
375	Willie Adams	.05
376	Chipper Jones (Stadium Sluggers)	2.00
377	Mo Vaughn (Stadium Sluggers)	.15
378	Frank Thomas (Stadium Sluggers)	1.50
379	Albert Belle (Stadium Sluggers)	.15
380	Andres Galarraga (Stadium Sluggers)	.15
381	Gary Sheffield (Stadium Sluggers)	.85
382	Jeff Bagwell (Stadium Sluggers)	1.50
383	Mike Piazza (Stadium Sluggers)	3.00
384	Mark McGwire (Stadium Sluggers)	3.00
385	Ken Griffey Jr. (Stadium Sluggers)	2.50
386	Barry Bonds (Stadium Sluggers)	3.50
387	Juan Gonzalez (Stadium Sluggers)	.40
388	Brady Anderson (Stadium Sluggers)	.15
389	Ken Caminiti (Stadium Sluggers)	.15
390	Jay Buhner (Stadium Sluggers)	.15

Co-Signers

Each series of Stadium Club included five different Co-Signers, with an insertion ratio of one per 168 hobby packs. These double-sided cards featured authentic autographs from each star, one per side.

		NM/M
Complete Set (10):		200.00
Common Card:		5.00
CO1	Andy Pettitte, Derek Jeter	100.00
CO2	Paul Wilson, Todd Hundley	5.00
CO3	Jermaine Dye, Mark Wohlers	6.00
CO4	Scott Rolen, Gregg Jefferies	15.00
CO5	Todd Hollandsworth, Jason Kendall	8.00
CO6	Alan Benes, Robin Ventura	8.00
CO7	Eric Karros, Raul Mondesi	15.00
CO8	Rey Ordonez, Nomar Garciaparra	45.00
CO9	Rondell White, Marty Cordova	6.00
CO10	Tony Gwynn, Karim Garcia	30.00

Firebrand Redemption

Because of production problems with its "Laser-Etched Wood" technology, Stadium Club was unable to package the Firebrand insert cards with the rest of the issue. Instead, a redemption card was substituted. The redemption card pictures the Firebrand card on its horizontal front; the back has details for exchanging the redemption card for the actual wood-printed, die-cut version. The exchange offer ended Sept. 30, 1997.

		NM/M
Complete Set (12):		15.00
Common Player:		.60
F1	Jeff Bagwell	1.25
F2	Albert Belle	.60
F3	Barry Bonds	4.00
F4	Andres Galarraga	.60
F5	Ken Griffey Jr.	2.50
F6	Brady Anderson	.60
F7	Mark McGwire	3.25
F8	Chipper Jones	2.00
F9	Frank Thomas	1.25
F10	Mike Piazza	2.50
F11	Mo Vaughn	.60
F12	Juan Gonzalez	.85

Firebrand

This 12-card insert was found only in packs sold at retail chains. Cards were inserted 1:36 packs. The hortizontal format cards are printed on thin wood stock, die-cut at top. Fronts are trimmed in gold foil. Cards are numbered with a "F" prefix.

		NM/M
Complete Set (12):		25.00
Common Player:		1.00
1	Jeff Bagwell	2.50
2	Albert Belle	1.00
3	Barry Bonds	6.50
4	Andres Galarraga	1.00
5	Ken Griffey Jr.	4.50
6	Brady Anderson	1.00
7	Mark McGwire	5.50
8	Chipper Jones	4.00
9	Frank Thomas	2.50
10	Mike Piazza	4.50
11	Mo Vaughn	1.00
12	Juan Gonzalez	1.50

Instavision

Instavision features holographic cards with exciting moments from the 1996 playoffs and World Series. Inserted one per 24 hobby packs and one per 36 retail packs, these cards are printed horizontally on plastic stock. Cards carry an "I" prefix, with the first 10 found in Series 1 and the final 12 in Series 2.

		NM/M
Complete Set (22):		10.00
Common Player:		.35
11	Eddie Murray	.75
12	Paul Molitor	.75
13	Todd Hundley	.35
14	Roger Clemens	1.50
15	Barry Bonds	3.00
16	Mark McGwire	2.00

No.	Player	Price
17	Brady Anderson	.35
18	Barry Larkin	.35
19	Ken Caminiti	.35
110	Hideo Nomo	.45
111	Bernie Williams	.35
112	Juan Gonzalez	.45
113	Andy Pettitte	.35
114	Albert Belle	.35
115	John Smoltz	.35
116	Brian Jordan	.35
117	Derek Jeter	3.00
118	Ken Caminiti	.35
119	John Wetteland	.35
120	Brady Anderson	.35
121	Andruw Jones	.75
122	Jim Leyritz	.35

Millennium

Millennium was a 40-card insert that was released with 20 cards in Series I and Series II. The set featured 40 top prospects and rookies on a silver foil, holographic front, with a Future Forecast section on the back. Cards carried an "M" prefix and were numbered consecutively M1-M40. Millennium inserts were found every 24 hobby packs and every 36 retail packs.

		NM/M
Complete Set (40):		12.50
Common Player:		.25
1	Derek Jeter	5.00
2	Mark Grudzielanek	.25
3	Jacob Cruz	.25
4	Ray Durham	.25
5	Tony Clark	.25
6	Chipper Jones	2.50
7	Luis Castillo	.25
8	Carlos Delgado	.50
9	Brant Brown	.25
10	Jason Kendall	.25
11	Alan Benes	.25
12	Rey Ordonez	.25
13	Justin Thompson	.25
14	Jermaine Allensworth	.25
15	Brian Hunter	.25
16	Marty Cordova	.25
17	Edgar Renteria	.25
18	Karim Garcia	.25
19	Todd Greene	.25
20	Paul Wilson	.25
21	Andruw Jones	1.50
22	Todd Walker	.25
23	Alex Ochoa	.25
24	Bartolo Colon	.25
25	Wendell Magee Jr.	.25
26	Jose Rosado	.25
27	Katsuhiro Maeda	.25
28	Bob Abreu	.25
29	Brooks Kieschnick	.25
30	Derrick Gibson	.25
31	Mike Sweeney	.25
32	Jeff D'Amico	.25
33	Chad Mottola	.25
34	Chris Snopek	.25
35	Jaime Bluma	.25
36	Vladimir Guerrero	1.50
37	Nomar Garciaparra	2.50
38	Scott Rolen	1.25
39	Dmitri Young	.25
40	Neifi Perez	.25

Patent Leather

Patent Leather featured 13 of the top gloves in baseball on a leather, die-cut card. The cards carry a "PL" prefix and are inerted one per 36 retail packs.

		NM/M
Complete Set (13):		25.00
Common Player:		1.00
1	Ivan Rodriguez	3.00
2	Ken Caminiti	1.00
3	Barry Bonds	6.00
4	Ken Griffey Jr.	5.00
5	Greg Maddux	4.00
6	Craig Biggio	1.00
7	Andres Galarraga	1.00
8	Kenny Lofton	1.00
9	Barry Larkin	1.00
10	Mark Grace	1.00
11	Rey Ordonez	1.00
12	Roberto Alomar	1.25
13	Derek Jeter	6.00

Pure Gold

Pure Gold featured 20 of the top players in baseball on gold, embossed foil cards. Cards carry a "PG" prefix and were inserted every 72 hobby packs and every 108 retail packs. The first 10 cards were in Series I packs, while the final 10 cards are exclusive to Series II.

		NM/M
Complete Set (20):		60.00
Common Player:		1.25
1	Brady Anderson	1.25
2	Albert Belle	1.25
3	Dante Bichette	1.25
4	Barry Bonds	12.00
5	Jay Buhner	1.25
6	Tony Gwynn	6.00
7	Chipper Jones	6.00
8	Mark McGwire	9.00
9	Gary Sheffield	2.25
10	Frank Thomas	4.50
11	Juan Gonzalez	2.50
12	Ken Caminiti	1.25
13	Kenny Lofton	1.25
14	Jeff Bagwell	4.50
15	Ken Griffey Jr.	7.50
16	Cal Ripken Jr.	12.00
17	Mo Vaughn	1.25
18	Mike Piazza	7.50
19	Derek Jeter	12.00
20	Andres Galarraga	1.25

TSC Matrix

TSC Matrix consists of 120 cards from Series I and II reprinted with Power Matrix technology. In each Series, 60 of the 190 cards were selected for inclusion in TSC Matrix and inserted every 12 hobby packs and every 18 retail packs. Each insert carries the TSC Matrix logo in a top corner of the card.

		NM/M
Complete Set (120):		70.00
Common Player:		.50
1	Chipper Jones	2.50
2	Gary Sheffield	1.00
3	Kenny Lofton	.50
4	Brian Jordan	.50
5	Mark McGwire	4.25

6	Charles Nagy	.50
7	Tim Salmon	.50
8	Cal Ripken Jr.	5.00
9	Jeff Conine	.50
10	Paul Molitor	1.75
11	Mariano Rivera	.65
12	Pedro Martinez	1.75
13	Jeff Bagwell	1.75
14	Bobby Bonilla	.50
15	Barry Bonds	5.00
16	Ryan Klesko	.50
17	Barry Larkin	.50
18	Jim Thome	1.50
19	Jay Buhner	.50
20	Juan Gonzalez	1.00
21	Mike Mussina	.75
22	Kevin Appier	.50
23	Eric Karros	.50
24	Steve Finley	.50
25	Ed Sprague	.50
26	Bernard Gilkey	.50
27	Tony Phillips	.50
28	Henry Rodriguez	.50
29	John Smoltz	.50
30	Dante Bichette	.50
31	Mike Piazza	3.25
32	Paul O'Neill	.50
33	Billy Wagner	.50
34	Reggie Sanders	.50
35	John Jaha	.50
36	Eddie Murray	1.75
37	Eric Young	.50
38	Roberto Hernandez	.50
39	Pat Hentgen	.50
40	Sammy Sosa	2.50
41	Todd Hundley	.50
42	Mo Vaughn	.50
43	Robin Ventura	.50
44	Mark Grudzielanek	.50
45	Shane Reynolds	.50
46	Andy Pettitte	.65
47	Fred McGriff	.50
48	Rey Ordonez	.50
49	Will Clark	.50
50	Ken Griffey Jr.	3.25
51	Todd Worrell	.50
52	Rusty Greer	.50
53	Mark Grace	.50
54	Tom Glavine	.75
55	Derek Jeter	5.00
56	Rafael Palmeiro	1.50
57	Bernie Williams	.50
58	Marty Cordova	.50
59	Andres Galarraga	.50
60	Ken Caminiti	.50
196	Greg Maddux	2.50
197	Joe Carter	.50
198	Alex Ochoa	.50
199	Ellis Burks	.50
200	Ivan Rodriguez	1.50
201	Marquis Grissom	.50
202	Trevor Hoffman	.50
203	Matt Williams	.50
204	Carlos Delgado	1.25
205	Ramon Martinez	.50
206	Chuck Knoblauch	.50
207	Juan Guzman	.50
208	Derek Bell	.50
209	Roger Clemens	3.00
210	Vladimir Guerrero	1.75
211	Cecil Fielder	.50
212	Hideo Nomo	1.00
213	Frank Thomas	1.75
214	Greg Vaughn	.50
215	Javy Lopez	.50
216	Raul Mondesi	.50
217	Wade Boggs	2.50
218	Carlos Baerga	.50
219	Tony Gwynn	2.50
220	Tino Martinez	.50
221	Vinny Castilla	.50
222	Lance Johnson	.50
223	David Justice	.50
224	Rondell White	.50
225	Dean Palmer	.50
226	Jim Edmonds	.50
227	Albert Belle	.50
228	Alex Fernandez	.50
229	Ryne Sandberg	2.50
230	Jose Mesa	.50
231	David Cone	.50
232	Troy Percival	.50
233	Edgar Martinez	.50
234	Jose Canseco	1.25
235	Kevin Brown	.50
236	Ray Lankford	.50
237	Karim Garcia	.50
238	J.T. Snow	.50
239	Dennis Eckersley	1.50
240	Roberto Alomar	.75
241	John Valentin	.50
242	Ron Gant	.50
243	Geronimo Berroa	.50
244	Manny Ramirez	1.75
245	Travis Fryman	.50
246	Denny Neagle	.50
247	Randy Johnson	1.75
248	Darin Erstad	.65
249	Mark Wohlers	.50
250	Ken Hill	.50
251	Larry Walker	.50
252	Craig Biggio	.50
253	Brady Anderson	.50
254	John Wetteland	.50
255	Andruw Jones	1.75

Members Only

Production was reported at just 750 complete sets of these

specially marked Stadium Club cards and inserts. Sold only as complete sets through Topps' Stadium Club program, each card differs from the regular-issue TSC version only in the presence of a subdued "MEMBERS ONLY" repeated all across the cards' backs. Star players' cards sell for a significant premium over regular-issue TSC version; inserts, depending on the scarcity of the regular version, usually sell for a significant discount in the Members Only version.

	NM/M
Complete Set:	250.00
Common Player:	.50
Stars:	5X
Inserts: 50-100 Percent	

Members Only Baseball

This boxed set was available only to members of Topps' Stadium Club for a price of $15, which included a year's membership in the club. Fronts feature action photos with a 2-1/2" circle behind the player, a gold-foil Members Only seal and the player's name, also in gold-foil. Backs feature another photo and a career summary on a red background which has the Members Only seal in a repeating pattern. Cards #51-55 are rookie stars and are printed in Topps Finest technologies.

		NM/M
Complete Set (55):		12.00
Common Player:		.10
1	Brady Anderson	.10
2	Carlos Baerga	.10
3	Jeff Bagwell	.75
4	Albert Belle	.10
5	Dante Bichette	.10
6	Craig Biggio	.10
7	Wade Boggs	1.00
8	Barry Bonds	2.50
9	Jay Buhner	.10
10	Ellis Burks	.10
11	Ken Caminiti	.10
12	Jose Canseco	.50
13	Joe Carter	.10
14	Roger Clemens	1.25
15	Jeff Conine	.10
16	Andres Galarraga	.10
17	Ron Gant	.10
18	Juan Gonzalez	.40
19	Mark Grace	.10
20	Ken Griffey Jr.	1.50
21	Tony Gwynn	1.00
22	Pat Hentgen	.10
23	Todd Hollandsworth	.10
24	Todd Hundley	.10
25	Derek Jeter	2.50
26	Randy Johnson	.75
27	Chipper Jones	1.00
28	Ryan Klesko	.10
29	Chuck Knoblauch	.10
30	Barry Larkin	.10
31	Kenny Lofton	.10
32	Greg Maddux	1.00
33	Mark McGwire	2.00
34	Paul Molitor	.75

35	Raul Mondesi	.10
36	Hideo Nomo	.40
37	Rafael Palmeiro	.65
38	Mike Piazza	1.50
39	Manny Ramirez	.75
40	Cal Ripken Jr.	2.50
41	Ivan Rodriguez	.65
42	Tim Salmon	.10
43	Gary Sheffield	.45
44	John Smoltz	.10
45	Sammy Sosa	1.00
46	Frank Thomas	.75
47	Jim Thome	.65
48	Mo Vaughn	.10
49	Bernie Williams	.10
50	Matt Williams	.10
51	Darin Erstad (Finest)	1.00
52	Vladimir Guerrero (Finest)	2.50
53	Andruw Jones (Finest)	2.00
54	Scott Rolen (Finest)	1.00
55	Todd Walker (Finest)	1.00

1998 Stadium Club

Stadium Club was issued in two series for 1998, with 200 odd-numbered cards in Series 1 and 200 even-numbered cards in Series 2. Retail packs contain six cards and carried an SRP of $2; hobby packs have nine cards and an SRP of $3 and HTA packs offered 15 cards at an SRP of $5. Three subsets were included: Future Stars (361-379) and Draft Picks (381-399), both being odd-numbered, and Traded (356-400) being even-numbered. Inserts in Series 1 include: First Day Issue parallels (retail), One of a Kind parallels (hobby), Printing Plates parallels (HTA), Bowman Previews, Co-Signers (hobby), In the Wings, Never Comprimise, and Triumvirates (retail). Inserts in Series 2 include: First Day Issue parallels (retail), One of a Kind parallels (hobby), Printing Plates parallels (HTA), Bowman Prospect Previews, Co-Signers (hobby), Playing with Passion, Royal Court and Triumvirates (retail).

		NM/M
Complete Set (400):		30.00
Common Player:		.05
Hobby Pack (10):		1.50
Retail Pack (7):		1.50
Home Team Adv. Pack (16):		4.00
Hobby Box (24):		30.00
1	Chipper Jones	1.00
2	Frank Thomas	.75
3	Vladimir Guerrero	.75
4	Ellis Burks	.05
5	John Franco	.05
6	Paul Molitor	.75
7	Rusty Greer	.05
8	Todd Hundley	.05
9	Brett Tomko	.05
10	Eric Karros	.05
11	Mike Cameron	.05
12	Jim Edmonds	.05
13	Bernie Williams	.05
14	Denny Neagle	.05
15	Jason Dickson	.05
16	Sammy Sosa	1.00
17	Brian Jordan	.05
18	Jose Vidro	.05
19	Scott Spiezio	.05
20	Jay Buhner	.05
21	Jim Thome	.65
22	Sandy Alomar	.05
23	Devon White	.05
24	Roberto Alomar	.20
25	John Flaherty	.05
26	John Wetteland	.05
27	Willie Greene	.05
28	Gregg Jefferies	.05
29	Johnny Damon	.35
30	Barry Larkin	.05
31	Chuck Knoblauch	.05
32	Mo Vaughn	.05
33	Tony Clark	.05
34	Marty Cordova	.05
35	Vinny Castilla	.05
36	Jeff King	.05

37	Reggie Jefferson	.05
38	Mariano Rivera	.15
39	Jermaine Allensworth	.05
40	Livan Hernandez	.05
41	Heathcliff Slocumb	.05
42	Jacob Cruz	.05
43	Barry Bonds	2.50
44	Dave Magadan	.05
45	Chan Ho Park	.05
46	Jeremi Gonzalez	.05
47	Jeff Cirillo	.05
48	Delino DeShields	.05
49	Craig Biggio	.05
50	Benito Santiago	.05
51	Mark Clark	.05
52	Fernando Vina	.05
53	F.P. Santangelo	.05
54	Pep Harris **RC**	.05
55	Edgar Renteria	.05
56	Jeff Bagwell	.74
57	Jimmy Key	.05
58	Bartolo Colon	.05
59	Curt Schilling	.35
60	Steve Finley	.05
61	Andy Ashby	.05
62	John Burkett	.05
63	Orel Hershiser	.05
64	Pokey Reese	.05
65	Scott Servais	.05
66	Todd Jones	.05
67	Javy Lopez	.05
68	Robin Ventura	.05
69	Miguel Tejada	.15
70	Raul Casanova	.05
71	Reggie Sanders	.05
72	Edgardo Alfonzo	.05
73	Dean Palmer	.05
74	Todd Stottlemyre	.05
75	David Wells	.05
76	Troy Percival	.05
77	Albert Belle	.05
78	Pat Hentgen	.05
79	Brian Hunter	.05
80	Richard Hidalgo	.05
81	Darren Oliver	.05
82	Mark Wohlers	.05
83	Cal Ripken Jr.	2.50
84	Hideo Nomo	.40
85	Derrek Lee	.50
86	Stan Javier	.05
87	Rey Ordonez	.05
88	Randy Johnson	.75
89	Jeff Kent	.05
90	Brian McRae	.05
91	Manny Ramirez	.75
92	Trevor Hoffman	.05
93	Doug Glanville	.05
94	Todd Walker	.05
95	Andy Benes	.05
96	Jason Schmidt	.05
97	Mike Matheny	.05
98	Tim Naehring	.05
99	Jeff Blauser	.05
100	Jose Rosado	.05
101	Roger Clemens	1.25
102	Pedro Astacio	.05
103	Mark Bellhorn	.05
104	Paul O'Neill	.05
105	Darin Erstad	.15
106	Mike Lieberthal	.05
107	Wilson Alvarez	.05
108	Mike Mussina	.30
109	George Williams	.05
110	Cliff Floyd	.05
111	Shawn Estes	.05
112	Mark Grudzielanek	.05
113	Tony Gwynn	1.00
114	Alan Benes	.05
115	Terry Steinbach	.05
116	Greg Maddux	1.00
117	Andy Pettitte	.25
118	Dave Nilsson	.05
119	Deivi Cruz	.05
120	Carlos Delgado	.50
121	Scott Hatteberg	.05
122	John Olerud	.05
123	Moises Alou	.05
124	Garret Anderson	.05
125	Royce Clayton	.05
126	Dante Powell	.05
127	Tom Glavine	.35
128	Gary DiSarcina	.05
129	Terry Adams	.05
130	Raul Mondesi	.05
131	Dan Wilson	.05
132	Al Martin	.05
133	Mickey Morandini	.05
134	Rafael Palmeiro	.65
135	Juan Encarnacion	.05
136	Jim Pittsley	.05
137	Magglio Ordonez **RC**	1.00
138	Will Clark	.05
139	Todd Helton	.65
140	Kelvim Escobar	.05
141	Esteban Loaiza	.05
142	John Jaha	.05
143	Jeff Fassero	.05
144	Harold Baines	.05
145	Butch Huskey	.05
146	Pat Meares	.05
147	Brian Giles	.05
148	Ramiro Mendoza	.05
149	John Smoltz	.05
150	Felix Martinez	.05
151	Jose Valentin	.05
152	Brad Rigby	.05
153	Ed Sprague	.05
154	Mike Hampton	.05

155	Mike Lansing	.05
156	Ray Lankford	.05
157	Bobby Bonilla	.05
158	Bill Mueller	.05
159	Jeffrey Hammonds	.05
160	Charles Nagy	.05
161	Rich Loiselle	.05
162	Al Leiter	.05
163	Larry Walker	.05
164	Chris Hoiles	.05
165	Jeff Montgomery	.05
166	Francisco Cordova	.05
167	James Baldwin	.05
168	Mark McLemore	.05
169	Kevin Appier	.05
170	Jamey Wright	.05
171	Nomar Garciaparra	1.00
172	Matt Franco	.05
173	Armando Benitez	.05
174	Jeromy Burnitz	.05
175	Ismael Valdes	.05
176	Lance Johnson	.05
177	Paul Sorrento	.05
178	Rondell White	.05
179	Kevin Elster	.05
180	Jason Giambi	.50
181	Carlos Baerga	.05
182	Russ Davis	.05
183	Ryan McGuire	.05
184	Eric Young	.05
185	Ron Gant	.05
186	Manny Alexander	.05
187	Scott Karl	.05
188	Brady Anderson	.05
189	Randall Simon	.05
190	Tim Belcher	.05
191	Jaret Wright	.05
192	Dante Bichette	.05
193	John Valentin	.05
194	Darren Bragg	.05
195	Mike Sweeney	.05
196	Craig Counsell	.05
197	Jaime Navarro	.05
198	Todd Dunn	.05
199	Ken Griffey Jr.	1.50
200	Juan Gonzalez	.40
201	Billy Wagner	.05
202	Tino Martinez	.05
203	Mark McGwire	2.00
204	Jeff D'Amico	.05
205	Rico Brogna	.05
206	Todd Hollandsworth	.05
207	Chad Curtis	.05
208	Tom Goodwin	.05
209	Neifi Perez	.05
210	Derek Bell	.05
211	Quilvio Veras	.05
212	Greg Vaughn	.05
213	Roberto Hernandez	.05
214	Arthur Rhodes	.05
215	Cal Eldred	.05
216	Bill Taylor	.05
217	Todd Greene	.05
218	Mario Valdez	.05
219	Ricky Bottalico	.05
220	Frank Rodriguez	.05
221	Rich Becker	.05
222	Roberto Duran	.05
223	Ivan Rodriguez	.65
224	Mike Jackson	.05
225	Deion Sanders	.05
226	Tony Womack	.05
227	Mark Kotsay	.05
228	Steve Trachsel	.05
229	Ryan Klesko	.05
230	Ken Cloude	.05
231	Luis Gonzalez	.05
232	Gary Gaetti	.05
233	Michael Tucker	.05
234	Shawn Green	.35
235	Ariel Prieto	.05
236	Kirt Manwaring	.05
237	Omar Vizquel	.05
238	Matt Beech	.05
239	Justin Thompson	.05
240	Bret Boone	.05
241	Derek Jeter	2.50
242	Ken Caminiti	.05
243	Jay Bell	.05
244	Kevin Tapani	.05
245	Jason Kendall	.05
246	Jose Guillen	.05
247	Mike Bordick	.05
248	Dustin Hermanson	.05
249	Darrin Fletcher	.05
250	Dave Hollins	.05
251	Ramon Martinez	.05
252	Hideki Irabu	.05
253	Mark Grace	.05
254	David Segui	.05
255	Jason Isringhausen	.05
256	Jose Cruz Jr.	.05
257	Brian Johnson	.05
258	Brad Ausmus	.05
259	Andruw Jones	.75
260	Doug Jones	.05
261	Jeff Shaw	.05
262	Chuck Finley	.05
263	Gary Sheffield	.45
264	David Segui	.05
265	John Smiley	.05
266	Tim Salmon	.05
267	J.T. Snow Jr.	.05
268	Alex Fernandez	.05
269	Matt Stairs	.05
270	B.J. Surhoff	.05
271	Keith Foulke	.05
272	Edgar Martinez	.05
273	Shannon Stewart	.05

273	Eduardo Perez	.05
274	Wally Joyner	.05
275	Kevin Young	.05
276	Eli Marrero	.05
277	Brad Radke	.05
278	Jamie Moyer	.05
279	Joe Girardi	.05
280	Troy O'Leary	.05
281	Aaron Sele	.05
282	Jose Offerman	.05
283	Scott Erickson	.05
284	Sean Berry	.05
285	Shigetosi Hasegawa	.05
286	Felix Heredia	.05
287	Willie McGee	.05
288	Alex Rodriguez	2.00
289	Ugueth Urbina	.05
290	Jon Lieber	.05
291	Fernando Tatis	.05
292	Chris Stynes	.05
293	Bernard Gilkey	.05
294	Joey Hamilton	.05
295	Matt Karchner	.05
296	Paul Wilson	.05
297	Mel Nieves	.05
298	Kevin Millwood **RC**	.75
299	Quinton McCracken	.05
300	Jerry DiPoto	.05
301	Jermaine Dye	.05
302	Travis Lee	.05
303	Ron Coomer	.05
304	Matt Williams	.05
305	Bobby Higginson	.05
306	Jorge Fabregas	.05
307	Hal Morris	.05
308	Jay Bell	.05
309	Joe Randa	.05
310	Andy Benes	.05
311	Sterling Hitchcock	.05
312	Jeff Suppan	.05
313	Shane Reynolds	.05
314	Willie Blair	.05
315	Scott Rolen	.65
316	Wilson Alvarez	.05
317	David Justice	.05
318	Fred McGriff	.05
319	Bobby Jones	.05
320	Wade Boggs	1.00
321	Tim Wakefield	.05
322	Tony Saunders	.05
323	David Cone	.05
324	Roberto Hernandez	.05
325	Jose Canseco	.45
326	Kevin Stocker	.05
327	Gerald Williams	.05
328	Quinton McCracken	.05
329	Mark Gardner	.05
330	Ben Grieve (Prime Rookie)	.05
331	Kevin Brown	.05
332	Mike Lowell **RC** (Prime Rookie)	1.00
333	Jed Hansen	.05
334	Abraham Nunez (Prime Rookie)	.05
335	John Thomson	.05
336	Derrek Lee (Prime Rookie)	.05
337	Mike Piazza	1.50
338	Brad Fullmer (Prime Rookie)	.05
339	Ray Durham	.05
340	Kerry Wood (Prime Rookie)	.50
341	Kevin Polcovich **RC**	.05
342	Russ Johnson (Prime Rookie)	.05
343	Darryl Hamilton	.05
344	David Ortiz (Prime Rookie)	.45
345	Kevin Orie	.05
346	Sean Casey (Prime Rookie)	.25
347	Juan Guzman	.05
348	Ruben Rivera (Prime Rookie)	.05
349	Rick Aguilera	.05
350	Bobby Estalella (Prime Rookie)	.05
351	Bobby Witt	.05
352	Paul Konerko (Prime Rookie)	.25
353	Matt Morris (Prime Rookie)	.05
354	Carl Pavano (Prime Rookie)	.05
355	Todd Zeile	.05
356	Kevin Brown (Transaction)	.05
357	Alex Gonzalez	.05
358	Chuck Knoblauch (Transaction)	.05
359	Joey Cora	.05
360	Mike Lansing (Transaction)	.05
361	Adrian Beltre (Future Stars)	.45
362	Dennis Eckersley (Transaction)	.65
363	A.J. Hinch (Future Stars)	.05
364	Kenny Lofton (Transaction)	.05
365	Alex Gonzalez (Future Stars)	.05
366	Henry Rodriguez (Transaction)	.05
367	Mike Stoner **RC** (Future Stars)	.05
368	Darryl Kile (Transaction)	.05
369	Carl Pavano (Future Stars)	.05
370	Walt Weiss (Transaction)	.05
371	Kris Benson (Future Stars)	.05
372	Cecil Fielder (Transaction)	.05

373	Dermal Brown (Future Stars)	.05
374	Rod Beck (Transaction)	.05
375	Eric Milton (Future Stars)	.05
376	Travis Fryman (Transaction)	.05
377	Preston Wilson (Future Stars)	.10
378	Chili Davis (Transaction)	.05
379	Travis Lee (Future Stars)	.10
380	Jim Leyritz (Transaction)	.05
381	Vernon Wells (Draft Picks)	.05
382	Joe Carter (Transaction)	.05
383	J.J. Davis (Draft Picks)	.05
384	Marquis Grissom (Transaction)	.05
385	Mike Cuddyer **RC** (Draft Picks)	.50
386	Rickey Henderson (Transaction)	.75
387	Chris Enochs **RC** (Draft Picks)	.10
388	Andres Galarraga (Transaction)	.05
389	Jason Dellaero (Draft Picks)	.05
390	Robb Nen (Transaction)	.05
391	Mark Mangum (Draft Picks)	.05
392	Jeff Blauser (Transaction)	.05
393	Adam Kennedy (Draft Picks)	.05
394	Bob Abreu (Transaction)	.05
395	Jack Cust **RC** (Draft Picks)	1.00
396	Jose Vizcaino (Transaction)	.05
397	Jon Garland (Draft Picks)	.05
398	Pedro Martinez (Transaction)	.75
399	Aaron Akin (Draft Picks)	.05
400	Jeff Conine (Transaction)	.05

First Day Issue

	NM/M
Common Player:	2.00
Stars:	10X
Production 200 Sets	

One of a Kind

This hobby-only parallel set includes all 400 cards from Series 1 and 2 printed on a silver mirrorboard stock. Cards are sequentially numbered to 150 and inserted one per 21 Series 1 packs and one per 24 Series 2 packs.

	NM/M
Common Player:	2.00
Stars:	12X
Production 150 Sets	

Bowman Preview

This Series I insert gave collectors a sneak peak at Bowman's 50th anniversary set, with 10 top veterans displayed on the 1998 Bowman design. The cards were inserted one per 12 packs and numbered with a "BP" prefix.

	NM/M
Complete Set (10):	10.00
Common Player:	.25
Inserted 1:12	
BP1 Nomar Garciaparra	1.00
BP2 Scott Rolen	.65
BP3 Ken Griffey Jr.	1.50
BP4 Frank Thomas	.75
BP5 Larry Walker	.25
BP6 Mike Piazza	1.50
BP7 Chipper Jones	1.00
BP8 Tino Martinez	.25
BP9 Mark McGwire	2.00
BP10 Barry Bonds	2.50

Bowman Prospect Preview

Bowman Prospect Previews were inserted into Series 2 retail and hobby packs at a rate of one per 12 and HTA packs at one per four. The 10-card insert previews the upcoming 1998 Bowman set and includes top prospects that were expected to make an impact in 1998.

	NM/M
Complete Set (10):	3.00
Common Player:	.25
Inserted 1:12	
BP1 Ben Grieve	.25
BP2 Brad Fullmer	.25
BP3 Ryan Anderson	.25
BP4 Mark Kotsay	.25
BP5 Bobby Estalella	.25
BP6 Juan Encarnacion	.25
BP7 Todd Helton	2.00
BP8 Mike Lowell	.50
BP9 A.J. Hinch	.25
BP10 Richard Hidalgo	.25

Co-Signers

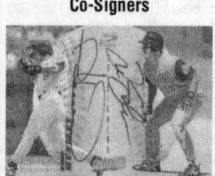

Co-Signers were inserted into both Series 1 and 2 hobby and HTA packs. The complete set is 36 cards, each featuring two top players along with both autographs. They were available in three levels of scarcity: Series 1 Group A 1:4,372 hobby and 1:2,623 HTA; Series 1 Group B 1:1,457 hobby and HTA 1:874; Series 1 Group C 1:121 hobby and 1:73 HTA; Series 2 Group A 1:4,702 hobby and 1:2,821 HTA; Series 2 Group B 1:1,567 hobby and 1:940 HTA, Series 2 Group C 1:1,131 hobby and 1:78 HTA. Some cards are known to bear fake autographs, despite having the Topps seal of authenticity. Those cards are believed to have been released in unsigned form in an unauthorized manner, and then signed with counterfeit signatures.

	NM/M
Common Card:	10.00
Group A 1:4,372	
Group B 1:1,457	
Group C 1:121	
CS1 Nomar Garciaparra, Scott Rolen (A)	120.00
CS2 Nomar Garciaparra, Derek Jeter (B)	250.00
CS3 Nomar Garciaparra, Eric Karros (C)	60.00
CS4 Scott Rolen, Derek Jeter (C)	100.00
CS5 Scott Rolen, Eric Karros (B)	40.00
CS6 Derek Jeter, Eric Karros (A)	150.00
CS7 Travis Lee, Jose Cruz Jr. (B)	15.00
CS8 Travis Lee, Mark Kotsay (C)	10.00
CS9 Travis Lee, Paul Konerko (A)	25.00
CS10 Jose Cruz Jr., Mark Kotsay (A)	25.00
CS11 Jose Cruz Jr., Paul Konerko (C)	12.00
CS12 Mark Kotsay, Paul Konerko (B)	20.00
CS13 Tony Gwynn, Larry Walker (A)	120.00
CS14 Tony Gwynn, Mark Grudzielanek (C)	30.00
CS15 Tony Gwynn, Andres Galarraga (B)	60.00

CS16 Larry Walker, Mark Grudzielanek (B)	40.00
CS17 Larry Walker, Andres Galarraga (C)	30.00
CS18 Mark Grudzielanek, Andres Galarraga (A)	25.00
CS19 Sandy Alomar, Roberto Alomar (A)	75.00
CS20 Sandy Alomar, Andy Pettitte (C)	20.00
CS21 Sandy Alomar, Tino Martinez (B)	40.00
CS22 Roberto Alomar, Andy Pettitte (B)	50.00
CS23 Roberto Alomar, Tino Martinez (C)	25.00
CS24 Andy Pettitte, Tino Martinez (A)	75.00
CS25 Tony Clark, Todd Hundley (A)	25.00
CS26 Tony Clark, Tim Salmon (B)	30.00
CS27 Tony Clark, Robin Ventura (C)	10.00
CS28 Todd Hundley, Tim Salmon (C)	15.00
CS29 Todd Hundley, Robin Ventura (B)	12.00
CS30 Tim Salmon, Robin Ventura (A)	50.00
CS31 Roger Clemens, Randy Johnson (B)	175.00
CS32 Roger Clemens, Jaret Wright (A)	140.00
CS33 Roger Clemens, Matt Morris (C)	100.00
CS34 Randy Johnson, Jaret Wright (C)	50.00
CS35 Randy Johnson, Matt Morris (A)	85.00
CS36 Jaret Wright, Matt Morris (B)	20.00

In the Wings

In the Wings was a Series I insert found every 36 packs. It included 15 future stars on uniluster technology.

	NM/M
Complete Set (15):	6.00
Common Player:	.50
Inserted 1:36	
W1 Juan Encarnacion	.50
W2 Brad Fullmer	.50
W3 Ben Grieve	.50
W4 Todd Helton	3.00
W5 Richard Hidalgo	.50
W6 Russ Johnson	.50
W7 Paul Konerko	.75
W8 Mark Kotsay	.50
W9 Derek Lee	1.00
W10 Travis Lee	.50
W11 Eli Marrero	.50
W12 David Ortiz	.75
W13 Randall Simon	.50
W14 Shannon Stewart	.50
W15 Fernando Tatis	.50

Never Compromise

Never Compromise was a 20-card insert found in packs of Series I. Cards were inserted one per 12 packs and numbered with a "NC" prefix.

	NM/M
Complete Set (20):	10.00
Common Player:	.15

Inserted 1:12	
NC1 Cal Ripken Jr.	2.00
NC2 Ivan Rodriguez	.50
NC3 Ken Griffey Jr.	1.00
NC4 Frank Thomas	.60
NC5 Tony Gwynn	.75
NC6 Mike Piazza	1.00
NC7 Randy Johnson	.60
NC8 Greg Maddux	.75
NC9 Roger Clemens	.85
NC10 Derek Jeter	2.00
NC11 Chipper Jones	.75
NC12 Barry Bonds	2.00
NC13 Larry Walker	.15
NC14 Jeff Bagwell	.60
NC15 Barry Larkin	.15
NC16 Ken Caminiti	.15
NC17 Mark McGwire	1.50
NC18 Manny Ramirez	.60
NC19 Tim Salmon	.15
NC20 Paul Molitor	.60

Playing with Passion

This Series II insert displayed 10 players with a strong desire to win. The cards are numbered with a "P" prefix.

	NM/M
Complete Set (10):	10.00
Common Player:	.35
Inserted 1:12	
P1 Bernie Williams	.35
P2 Jim Edmonds	.35
P3 Chipper Jones	1.00
P4 Cal Ripken Jr.	3.00
P5 Craig Biggio	.35
P6 Juan Gonzalez	.45
P7 Alex Rodriguez	2.25
P8 Tino Martinez	.35
P9 Mike Piazza	1.50
P10 Ken Griffey Jr.	1.50

Printing Plates

Inserted only in Home Team Advantage boxes at a rate of approximately one per 90 packs were the actual aluminum plates used to print the fronts of the base cards. Unlike some printing plate issues, the plates used for the card backs were not inserted. Each card's plate can be found in four different colors: Cyan, magenta, yellow and black. Because of their unique nature, pricing of individual player's plates cannot be provided.

	NM/M
Common Player:	25.00

Royal Court

Fifteen players were showcased on uniluster technology for this Series II insert. The set is broken up into 10 Kings (veterans) and five Princes (rookies) and inserted one per 36 packs.

	NM/M
Complete Set (15):	15.00
Common Player:	.50
Inserted 1:36	
RC1 Ken Griffey Jr.	2.00
RC2 Frank Thomas	1.25
RC3 Mike Piazza	2.00

RC4 Chipper Jones	1.50
RC5 Mark McGwire	2.50
RC6 Cal Ripken Jr.	3.00
RC7 Jeff Bagwell	1.25
RC8 Barry Bonds	3.00
RC9 Juan Gonzalez	.85
RC10 Alex Rodriguez	2.50
RC11 Travis Lee	.50
RC12 Paul Konerko	.75
RC13 Todd Helton	1.00
RC14 Ben Grieve	.50
RC15 Mark Kotsay	.50

Screen Plays Sound Chips

One of the packs in each Home Team Advantage box of TSC "Odd Series" cards contained this special "card" commemorating the home run hit by Cal Ripken, Jr. in his historic 2,131st game on Sept. 6, 1995. The item is 3-1/2" x 2-1/2" x 3/8" deep. Glued to the top is a magic motion card showing Ripken hitting the blast. When a corner of the card is squeezed, a sound chip replays the radio call of the home run by Jon Miller and President Bill Clinton. The top of the package opens to reveal a newspaper-like presentation with a picture of Ripken, details of his home run and the technology used to produce the item.

	NM/M
SC1 Cal Ripken Jr.	5.00

Triumvirate

Triumvirates were included in both series of Stadium Club and were available only in retail packs. Series 1 has 24 players, with three players from eight different teams, while Series 2 has 30 players, with three players from 10 different positions. The cards are all die-cut and fit together to form three-card panels. Three different versions of each card were available - Luminous (regular) versions were seeded one per 48 packs, Luminescent versions were seeded one per 192 packs and Illuminator versions were seeded one per 384 packs.

	NM/M
Complete Set (54):	70.00
Complete Series 1 (24):	30.00
Complete Series 2 (30):	40.00
Common Player:	.50
Luminous 1:48	
Luminescents 1:192:	1.5X
Illuminators 1:384:	3X
T1a Chipper Jones	2.50

T1b	Andruw Jones	2.00
T1c	Kenny Lofton	.50
T2a	Derek Jeter	5.00
T2b	Bernie Williams	.50
T2c	Tino Martinez	.50
T3a	Jay Buhner	.50
T3b	Edgar Martinez	.50
T3c	Ken Griffey Jr.	3.00
T4a	Albert Belle	.50
T4b	Robin Ventura	.50
T4c	Frank Thomas	2.00
T5a	Brady Anderson	.50
T5b	Cal Ripken Jr.	5.00
T5c	Rafael Palmeiro	1.50
T6a	Mike Piazza	3.00
T6b	Raul Mondesi	.50
T6c	Eric Karros	.50
T7a	Vinny Castilla	.50
T7b	Andres Galarraga	.50
T7c	Larry Walker	.50
T8a	Jim Thome	1.50
T8b	Manny Ramirez	2.00
T8c	David Justice	.50
T9a	Mike Mussina	.75
T9b	Greg Maddux	2.50
T9c	Randy Johnson	2.00
T10a	Mike Piazza	3.00
T10b	Sandy Alomar	.50
T10c	Ivan Rodriguez	1.50
T11a	Mark McGwire	4.00
T11b	Tino Martinez	.50
T11c	Frank Thomas	2.00
T12a	Roberto Alomar	.75
T12b	Chuck Knoblauch	.50
T12c	Craig Biggio	.50
T13a	Cal Ripken Jr.	5.00
T13b	Chipper Jones	2.50
T13c	Ken Caminiti	.50
T14a	Derek Jeter	5.00
T14b	Nomar Garciaparra	2.50
T14c	Alex Rodriguez	4.00
T15a	Barry Bonds	5.00
T15b	David Justice	.50
T15c	Albert Belle	.50
T16a	Bernie Williams	.50
T16b	Ken Griffey Jr.	3.00
T16c	Ray Lankford	.50
T17a	Tim Salmon	.50
T17b	Larry Walker	.50
T17c	Tony Gwynn	2.50
T18a	Paul Molitor	2.00
T18b	Edgar Martinez	.50
T18c	Juan Gonzalez	1.00

1999 Stadium Club

Released in two series, base cards feature a full bleed design on 20-pt. stock with an embossed holographic logo. Draft Pick, Prospect and Series 2 Future Star subset cards are short-printed, seeded in every three packs. Card backs have 1998 statistics and personal information. Hobby packs consist of six cards with an S.R.P. of $2.

		NM/M
Complete Set (355):		40.00
Complete Series 1 (170):		20.00
Complete Series 2 (185):		20.00
Common Player:		.05
Common SP (141-160; 336-355):		.50
Inserted 1:3		
Pack (6):		1.25
Wax Box (24):		25.00
1	Alex Rodriguez	2.00
2	Chipper Jones	1.50
3	Rusty Greer	.05
4	Jim Edmonds	.05
5	Ron Gant	.05
6	Kevin Polcovich	.05
7	Darryl Strawberry	.05
8	Bill Mueller	.05
9	Vinny Castilla	.05
10	Wade Boggs	1.50
11	Jose Lima	.05
12	Darren Dreifort	.05
13	Jay Bell	.05
14	Ben Grieve	.05
15	Shawn Green	.35
16	Andres Galarraga	.05
17	Bartolo Colon	.05
18	Francisco Cordova	.05
19	Paul O'Neill	.05
20	Trevor Hoffman	.05
21	Darren Oliver	.05
22	John Franco	.05
23	Eli Marrero	.05
24	Roberto Hernandez	.05
25	Craig Biggio	.05
26	Brad Fullmer	.05
27	Scott Erickson	.05
28	Tom Gordon	.05
29	Brian Hunter	.05
30	Raul Mondesi	.05
31	Rick Reed	.05
32	Jose Canseco	.50
33	Robb Nen	.05
34	Turner Ward	.05
35	Bret Boone	.05
36	Jose Offerman	.05
37	Matt Lawton	.05
38	David Wells	.05
39	Bob Abreu	.10
40	Jeromy Burnitz	.05
41	Deivi Cruz	.05
42	Mike Cameron	.05
43	Rico Brogna	.05
44	Dmitri Young	.05
45	Chuck Knoblauch	.05
46	Johnny Damon	.35
47	Brian Meadows	.05
48	Jeremi Gonzalez	.05
49	Gary DiSarcina	.05
50	Frank Thomas	1.00
51	F.P. Santangelo	.05
52	Tom Candiotti	.05
53	Shane Reynolds	.05
54	Rod Beck	.05
55	Rey Ordonez	.05
56	Todd Helton	.75
57	Mickey Morandini	.05
58	Jorge Posada	.05
59	Mike Mussina	.30
60	Bobby Bonilla	.05
61	David Segui	.05
62	Brian McRae	.05
63	Fred McGriff	.05
64	Brett Tomko	.05
65	Derek Jeter	2.50
66	Sammy Sosa	1.50
67	Kenny Rogers	.05
68	Dave Nilsson	.05
69	Eric Young	.05
70	Mark McGwire	2.00
71	Kenny Lofton	.35
72	Tom Glavine	.35
73	Joey Hamilton	.05
74	John Valentin	.05
75	Mariano Rivera	.15
76	Ray Durham	.05
77	Tony Clark	.05
78	Livan Hernandez	.05
79	Rickey Henderson	1.00
80	Vladimir Guerrero	1.00
81	J.T. Snow Jr.	.05
82	Juan Guzman	.05
83	Darryl Hamilton	.05
84	Matt Anderson	.05
85	Travis Lee	.05
86	Joe Randa	.05
87	Dave Dellucci	.05
88	Moises Alou	.05
89	Alex Gonzalez	.05
90	Tony Womack	.05
91	Neifi Perez	.05
92	Travis Fryman	.05
93	Masato Yoshii	.05
94	Woody Williams	.05
95	Ray Lankford	.05
96	Roger Clemens	1.50
97	Dustin Hermanson	.05
98	Joe Carter	.05
99	Jason Schmidt	.05
100	Greg Maddux	1.50
101	Kevin Tapani	.05
102	Charles Johnson	.05
103	Derrek Lee	.50
104	Pete Harnisch	.05
105	Dante Bichette	.05
106	Scott Brosius	.05
107	Mike Caruso	.05
108	Eddie Taubensee	.05
109	Jeff Fassero	.05
110	Marquis Grissom	.05
111	Jose Hernandez	.05
112	Chan Ho Park	.05
113	Wally Joyner	.05
114	Bobby Estalella	.05
115	Pedro Martinez	1.00
116	Shawn Estes	.05
117	Walt Weiss	.05
118	John Mabry	.05
119	Brian Johnson	.05
120	Jim Thome	.65
121	Bill Spiers	.05
122	John Olerud	.05
123	Jeff King	.05
124	Tim Belcher	.05
125	John Wetteland	.05
126	Tony Gwynn	1.50
127	Brady Anderson	.05
128	Randy Winn	.05
129	Devon White	.05
130	Eric Karros	.05
131	Kevin Millwood	.05
132	Andy Benes	.05
133	Andy Ashby	.05
134	Ron Comer	.05
135	Juan Gonzalez	.50
136	Randy Johnson	1.00
137	Aaron Sele	.05
138	Edgardo Alfonzo	.05
139	B.J. Surhoff	.05
140	Jose Vizcaino	.05
141	Chad Moeller RC (Prospect)	.75
142	Mike Zwicka RC (Prospect)	.50
143	Angel Pena (Prospect)	.50
144	Nick Johnson RC (Prospect)	2.00
145	Giuseppe Chiaramonte RC (Prospect)	.50
146	Kit Pellow RC (Prospect)	.50
147	Clayton Andrews RC (Prospect)	.50
148	Jerry Hairston Jr. RC (Prospect)	.75
149	Jason Tyner RC (Draft Pick)	.50
150	Chip Ambres RC (Draft Pick)	.50
151	Pat Burrell RC (Draft Pick)	2.00
152	Josh McKinley RC (Draft Pick)	.75
153	Choo Freeman RC (Draft Pick)	.75
154	Rick Elder RC (Draft Pick)	.50
155	Eric Valent RC (Draft Pick)	.75
156	Jeff Winchester RC (Draft Pick)	.50
157	Mike Nannini RC (Draft Pick)	.50
158	Mamon Tucker RC (Draft Pick)	.50
159	Nate Bump RC (Draft Pick)	.50
160	Andy Brown RC (Draft Pick)	.50
161	Troy Glaus (Future Star)	1.00
162	Adrian Beltre (Future Star)	.45
163	Mitch Meluskey (Future Star)	.05
164	Alex Gonzalez (Future Star)	.05
165	George Lombard (Future Star)	.05
166	Eric Chavez (Future Star)	.25
167	Ruben Mateo (Future Star)	.05
168	Calvin Pickering (Future Star)	.05
169	Gabe Kapler (Future Star)	.05
170	Bruce Chen (Future Star)	.05
171	Darin Erstad	.15
172	Sandy Alomar	.05
173	Miguel Cairo	.05
174	Jason Kendall	.05
175	Cal Ripken Jr.	2.50
176	Darryl Kile	.05
177	David Cone	.05
178	Mike Sweeney	.05
179	Royce Clayton	.05
180	Curt Schilling	.25
181	Barry Larkin	.05
182	Eric Milton	.05
183	Ellis Burks	.05
184	A.J. Hinch	.05
185	Garret Anderson	.05
186	Sean Bergman	.05
187	Shannon Stewart	.05
188	Bernard Gilkey	.05
189	Jeff Blauser	.05
190	Andruw Jones	1.00
191	Omar Daal	.05
192	Jeff Kent	.05
193	Mark Kotsay	.05
194	Dave Burba	.05
195	Bobby Higginson	.05
196	Hideki Irabu	.05
197	Jamie Moyer	.05
198	Doug Glanville	.05
199	Quinton McCracken	.05
200	Ken Griffey Jr.	1.75
201	Mike Lieberthal	.05
202	Carl Everett	.05
203	Omar Vizquel	.05
204	Mike Lansing	.05
205	Manny Ramirez	1.00
206	Ryan Klesko	.05
207	Jeff Montgomery	.05
208	Chad Curtis	.05
209	Rick Helling	.05
210	Justin Thompson	.05
211	Tom Goodwin	.05
212	Todd Dunwoody	.05
213	Kevin Young	.05
214	Tony Saunders	.05
215	Gary Sheffield	.45
216	Jaret Wright	.05
217	Quilvio Veras	.05
218	Marty Cordova	.05
219	Tino Martinez	.05
220	Scott Rolen	.75
221	Fernando Tatis	.05
222	Damion Easley	.05
223	Aramis Ramirez	.05
224	Brad Radke	.05
225	Nomar Garciaparra	1.50
226	Magglio Ordonez	.05
227	Andy Pettitte	.20
228	David Ortiz	.45
229	Todd Jones	.05
230	Larry Walker	.05
231	Tim Wakefield	.05
232	Jose Guillen	.05
233	Gregg Olson	.05
234	Ricky Gutierrez	.05
235	Todd Walker	.05
236	Abraham Nunez	.05
237	Sean Casey	.15
238	Greg Norton	.05
239	Bret Saberhagen	.05
240	Bernie Williams	.05
241	Tim Salmon	.05
242	Jason Giambi	.50
243	Fernando Vina	.05
244	Darrin Fletcher	.05
245	Greg Vaughn	.05
246	Dennis Reyes	.05
247	Hideo Nomo	.05
248	Reggie Sanders	.05
249	Mike Hampton	.05
250	Kerry Wood	.50
251	Ismael Valdes	.05
252	Pat Hentgen	.05
253	Scott Spiezio	.05
254	Chuck Finley	.05
255	Troy Glaus	.75
256	Bobby Jones	.05
257	Wayne Gomes	.05
258	Rondell White	.05
259	Todd Zeile	.05
260	Matt Williams	.05
261	Henry Rodriguez	.05
262	Matt Stairs	.05
263	Jose Valentin	.05
264	David Justice	.05
265	Javy Lopez	.05
266	Matt Morris	.05
267	Steve Trachsel	.05
268	Edgar Martinez	.05
269	Al Martin	.05
270	Ivan Rodriguez	.75
271	Carlos Delgado	.50
272	Mark Grace	.50
273	Ugueth Urbina	.05
274	Jay Buhner	.05
275	Mike Piazza	1.75
276	Rick Aguilera	.05
277	Javier Valentin	.05
278	Brian Anderson	.05
279	Cliff Floyd	.05
280	Barry Bonds	2.50
281	Troy O'Leary	.05
282	Seth Greisinger	.05
283	Mark Grudzielanek	.05
284	Jose Cruz Jr.	.05
285	Jeff Bagwell	1.00
286	John Smoltz	.05
287	Jeff Cirillo	.05
288	Richie Sexson	.05
289	Charles Nagy	.05
290	Pedro Martinez	1.00
291	Juan Encarnacion	.05
292	Phil Nevin	.05
293	Terry Steinbach	.05
294	Miguel Tejada	.15
295	Dan Wilson	.05
296	Chris Peters	.05
297	Brian Moehler	.05
298	Jason Christiansen	.05
299	Kelly Stinnett	.05
300	Dwight Gooden	.05
301	Randy Velarde	.05
302	Kirt Manwaring	.05
303	Jeff Abbott	.05
304	Dave Hollins	.05
305	Kerry Ligtenberg	.05
306	Aaron Boone	.05
307	Carlos Hernandez	.05
308	Mike DiFelice	.05
309	Brian Meadows	.05
310	Tim Bogar	.05
311	Greg Vaughn (Transaction)	.05
312	Brant Brown (Transaction)	.05
313	Steve Finley (Transaction)	.05
314	Bret Boone (Transaction)	.05
315	Albert Belle (Transaction)	.05
316	Robin Ventura (Transaction)	.05
317	Eric Davis (Transaction)	.05
318	Todd Hundley (Transaction)	.05
319	Jose Offerman (Transaction)	.05
320	Kevin Brown (Transaction)	.05
321	Denny Neagle (Transaction)	.05
322	Brian Jordan (Transaction)	.05
323	Brian Giles (Transaction)	.05
324	Bobby Bonilla (Transaction)	.05
325	Roberto Alomar (Transaction)	.20
326	Ken Caminiti (Transaction)	.05
327	Todd Stottlemyre (Transaction)	.05
328	Randy Johnson (Transaction)	1.00
329	Luis Gonzalez (Transaction)	.05
330	Rafael Palmeiro (Transaction)	.75
331	Devon White (Transaction)	.05
332	Will Clark (Transaction)	.05
333	Dean Palmer (Transaction)	.05
334	Gregg Jefferies (Transaction)	.05
335	Mo Vaughn (Transaction)	.05
336	Brad Lidge RC (Draft Pick)	2.00
337	Chris George RC (Draft Pick)	.75
338	Austin Kearns RC (Draft Pick)	1.50
339	Matt Belisle RC (Draft Pick)	.75
340	Nate Cornejo RC (Draft Pick)	.75
341	Matt Holliday RC (Draft Pick)	5.00
342	J.M. Gold RC (Draft Pick)	.50
343	Matt Roney RC (Draft Pick)	.50
344	Seth Etherton RC (Draft Pick)	.75
345	Adam Everett RC (Draft Pick)	.75
346	Marlon Anderson (Future Star)	.05
347	Ron Belliard (Future Star)	.05
348	Fernando Seguignol (Future Star)	.05
349	Michael Barrett (Future Star)	.05
350	Dernell Stenson (Future Star)	.05
351	Ryan Anderson (Future Star)	.50
352	Ramon Hernandez (Future Star)	.05
353	Jeremy Giambi (Future Star)	.05
354	Ricky Ledee (Future Star)	.50
355	Carlos Lee (Future Star)	1.00

First Day Issue

A parallel of the 355-card set inserted exclusively in retail packs, Series I (1-170) are serially numbered to 170 at a rate of 1:75 packs. Series 2 (171-355) are serially numbered to 200 and inserted at a rate of 1:60 packs.

	NM/M
Common Player:	2.00
Stars:	8X
SP Stars:	4X

One of a Kind

This insert set parallels the 355-card base set. Cards feature a mirror-board look and are serially numbered to 150. Inserted exclusively in hobby packs, insertion rate for Series 1 is 1:53 and Series 2 is 1:48 packs.

	NM/M
Common Player:	2.00
Stars:	8X
SP Stars:	4X

Autographs

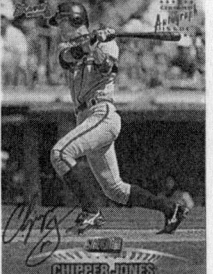

This 10-card autographed set was issued in Series 1 and 2 with five players signing in each series. Available exclusively in retail chains, Series 1 autographs were seeded 1:1,107 packs, while series 2 were inserted in every 877 packs. Each autograph is marked with the Topps Certified Autograph Issue stamp. Card numbers have an "SCA" prefix.

		NM/M
Common Player:		10.00
Inserted 1:1,107		
1	Alex Rodriguez	75.00
2	Chipper Jones	30.00
3	Barry Bonds	150.00
4	Tino Martinez	25.00
5	Ben Grieve	10.00
6	Juan Gonzalez	15.00
7	Vladimir Guerrero	30.00
8	Albert Belle	15.00
9	Kerry Wood	25.00
10	Todd Helton	20.00

Chrome

This 40-card set was inserted in Series 1 and 2 packs, with 1-20 in first series packs and 21-40 in Series 2. Chrome appropriately utilizes chromium technology. Card numbers have an "SCC" prefix.

		NM/M
Complete Set (40):		45.00
Common Player:		.50
Inserted 1:24		
Refractors:		2X
Inserted 1:96		
1	Nomar Garciaparra	2.00
2	Kerry Wood	1.00
3	Jeff Bagwell	1.50
4	Ivan Rodriguez	1.25
5	Albert Belle	.50
6	Gary Sheffield	1.00
7	Andruw Jones	1.50
8	Kevin Brown	.50
9	David Cone	.50
10	Darin Erstad	.75
11	Manny Ramirez	1.50
12	Larry Walker	.50
13	Mike Piazza	2.50
14	Cal Ripken Jr.	4.00
15	Pedro Martinez	1.50
16	Greg Vaughn	.50
17	Barry Bonds	4.00
18	Mo Vaughn	.50
19	Bernie Williams	.50
20	Ken Griffey Jr.	2.50
21	Alex Rodriguez	3.00
22	Chipper Jones	2.00
23	Ben Grieve	.50
24	Frank Thomas	1.50
25	Derek Jeter	4.00
26	Sammy Sosa	2.00
27	Mark McGwire	3.00
28	Vladimir Guerrero	1.50
29	Greg Maddux	2.00
30	Juan Gonzalez	.75
31	Troy Glaus	1.25
32	Adrian Beltre	1.25
33	Mitch Meluskey	.50
34	Alex Gonzalez	.50
35	George Lombard	.50
36	Eric Chavez	.75
37	Ruben Mateo	.50
38	Calvin Pickering	.50
39	Gabe Kapler	.50
40	Bruce Chen	.50

Co-Signers

Co-Signers feature two autographs on each card and also for the first time includes one level of four autographs per card. Co-Signers are grouped into categories A, B, C and D. Group A Co-Signers are autographed by four players, while

B-D are signed by two players. Each card features the Topps Certified Autograph Issue stamp.

	NM/M
Common Group A:	90.00
Inserted 1:18,085	
Common Group B:	20.00
Inserted 1:9043	
Common Group C:	9.00
Inserted 1:3014	
Common Group D:	6.00
Inserted 1:254	
CS1 Ben Grieve, Richie Sexson (D)	15.00
CS2 Todd Helton, Troy Glaus (D)	50.00
CS3 Alex Rodriguez, Scott Rolen (D)	85.00
CS4 Derek Jeter, Chipper Jones (D)	150.00
CS5 Cliff Floyd, Eli Marrero (D)	6.00
CS6 Jay Buhner, Kevin Young (D)	8.00
CS7 Ben Grieve, Troy Glaus (C)	40.00
CS8 Todd Helton, Richie Sexson (C)	40.00
CS9 Alex Rodriguez, Chipper Jones (C)	125.00
CS10 Derek Jeter, Scott Rolen (C)	125.00
CS11 Cliff Floyd, Kevin Young (C)	10.00
CS12 Jay Buhner, Eli Marrero (B)	10.00
CS13 Ben Grieve, Todd Helton (B)	50.00
CS14 Richie Sexson, Troy Glaus (B)	40.00
CS15 Alex Rodriguez, Derek Jeter (B)	350.00
CS16 Chipper Jones, Scott Rolen (B)	150.00
CS17 Cliff Floyd, Jay Buhner (B)	15.00
CS18 Eli Marrero, Kevin Young (B)	20.00
CS19 Ben Grieve, Todd Helton, Richie Sexson, Troy Glaus (A)	180.00
CS20 Alex Rodriguez, Derek Jeter, Chipper Jones, Scott Rolen (A)	2,500
CS21 Cliff Floyd, Jay Buhner, Eli Marrero, Kevin Young (A)	100.00
CS22 Edgardo Alfonzo, Jose Guillen (D)	15.00
CS23 Mike Lowell, Ricardo Rincon (D)	10.00
CS24 Juan Gonzalez, Vinny Castilla (D)	20.00
CS25 Moises Alou, Roger Clemens (D)	60.00
CS26 Scott Spezio, Tony Womack (D)	10.00
CS27 Fernando Vina, Quilvio Veras (D)	10.00
CS28 Edgardo Alfonzo, Ricardo Rincon (C)	10.00
CS29 Jose Guillen, Mike Lowell (C)	10.00
CS30 Juan Gonzalez, Moises Alou (C)	25.00
CS31 Roger Clemens, Vinny Castilla (C)	85.00
CS32 Scott Spezio, Fernando Vina (C)	10.00
CS33 Tony Womack, Quilvio Veras (B)	20.00
CS34 Edgardo Alfonzo, Mike Lowell (B)	30.00
CS35 Jose Guillen, Ricardo Rincon (B)	30.00
CS36 Juan Gonzalez, Roger Clemens (B)	135.00
CS37 Moises Alou, Vinny Castilla (B)	30.00
CS38 Scott Spezio, Quilvio Veras (B)	20.00
CS39 Tony Womack, Fernando Vina (B)	20.00
CS40 Edgardo Alfonzo, Jose Guillen, Mike Lowell, Ricardo Rincon (A)	90.00
CS41 Juan Gonzalez, Moises Alou, Roger Clemens, Vinny Castilla (A)	900.00
CS42 Scott Spezio, Tony Womack, Fernando Vina, Quilvio Veras (A)	90.00

Never Compromise

Topps selected players who bring hard work and devotion to the field every game. The first 10 cards in the set are inserted in Series 1 packs while the remaining 10 are inserted in Series 2 at a rate of 1:12 packs.

	NM/M
Complete Set (20):	10.00
Common Player:	.25
Inserted 1:12	
NC1 Mark McGwire	1.00

NOMAR GARCIAPARRA

NC2 Sammy Sosa	.65
NC3 Ken Griffey Jr.	.75
NC4 Greg Maddux	.65
NC5 Barry Bonds	1.50
NC6 Alex Rodriguez	1.00
NC7 Darin Erstad	.35
NC8 Roger Clemens	.65
NC9 Nomar Garciaparra	.65
NC10 Derek Jeter	1.50
NC11 Cal Ripken Jr.	1.50
NC12 Mike Piazza	.75
NC13 Greg Vaughn	.25
NC14 Andres Galarraga	.25
NC15 Vinny Castilla	.25
NC16 Jeff Bagwell	.50
NC17 Chipper Jones	.75
NC18 Eric Chavez	.35
NC19 Orlando Hernandez	.25
NC20 Troy Glaus	.40

Printing Plates

Inserted only in Home Team Advantage boxes at a rate of approximately one per 175 packs were the actual aluminum plates used to print the fronts of the base cards. Unlike some printing plate issues, the plates used for the card backs were not inserted. Each card's plate can be found in four different colors: Cyan, magenta, yellow and black. Because of their unique nature, pricing of individual player's plates cannot be provided.

	NM/M
Common Player:	25.00

Triumvirate

KERRY WOOD

Three of these inserts "fuse" together to form a set of three cards, forming a Triumvirate. 48 players, 24 from each series, are available in three different technologies, Luminous, Luminescent and Illuminator.

	NM/M
Complete Set (48):	75.00
Common Player:	.50
Inserted 1:36	
Luminescents	1.5X
Inserted 1:144	
Illuminators	2.5X
Inserted 1:288	
T1A Greg Vaughn	.50
T1B Ken Caminiti	.50
T1C Tony Gwynn	2.50

T2A Andruw Jones	2.00
T2B Chipper Jones	2.50
T2C Andres Galarraga	.50
T3A Jay Buhner	.50
T3B Ken Griffey Jr.	3.00
T3C Alex Rodriguez	4.00
T4A Derek Jeter	6.00
T4B Tino Martinez	.50
T4C Bernie Williams	.50
T5A Brian Jordan	.50
T5B Ray Lankford	.50
T5C Mark McGwire	4.00
T6A Jeff Bagwell	2.00
T6B Craig Biggio	.50
T6C Randy Johnson	1.50
T7A Nomar Garciaparra	2.50
T7B Pedro Martinez	2.00
T7C Mo Vaughn	.50
T8A Mark Grace	.50
T8B Sammy Sosa	2.50
T8C Kerry Wood	1.00
T9A Alex Rodriguez	4.00
T9B Nomar Garciaparra	2.50
T9C Derek Jeter	6.00
T10A Todd Helton	1.50
T10B Travis Lee	.50
T10C Pat Burrell	1.50
T11A Greg Maddux	2.50
T11B Kerry Wood	1.00
T11C Tom Glavine	.75
T12A Chipper Jones	2.50
T12B Vinny Castilla	.50
T12C Scott Rolen	1.50
T13A Juan Gonzalez	1.00
T13B Ken Griffey Jr.	3.00
T13C Ben Grieve	.50
T14A Sammy Sosa	3.00
T14B Vladimir Guerrero	2.00
T14C Barry Bonds	6.00
T15A Frank Thomas	2.00
T15B Jim Thome	1.50
T15C Tino Martinez	.50
T16A Mark McGwire	4.00
T16B Andres Galarraga	.50
T16C Jeff Bagwell	2.00

Video Replay

Utilizing lenticular technology, these inserts capture highlights, such as McGwire's 70th home run, from the '98 season. By tilting the card, successive images show the selected highlight almost come to life. Video Replays are inserted in Series 2 packs at a rate of 1:12.

	NM/M
Complete Set (5):	4.50
Common Player:	.75
Inserted 1:12	
VR1 Mark McGwire	1.50
VR2 Sammy Sosa	1.00
VR3 Ken Griffey Jr.	1.25
VR4 Kerry Wood	.75
VR5 Alex Rodriguez	1.50

Photography

The photos used on some Stadium Club Series 1 cards was available as a special issue in the format of a framed 11" x 14" color photo. The borderless action photos could be ordered from a form found in TSC packs. With a $4 shipping charge, the initial cost per picture was $23.99. The numbers here are as given on the order form.

	NM/M
Complete Set (10):	200.00
Common Player:	20.00
1 Alex Rodriguez	20.00
65 Derek Jeter	20.00
66 Sammy Sosa	20.00
135 Juan Gonzalez	20.00
NC1 Mark McGwire	20.00
NC3 Ken Griffey Jr.	20.00
SCA5 Ben Grieve	20.00
SCC1 Nomar Garciaparra	20.00
SCC2 Kerry Wood	20.00
SCC13 Mike Piazza	20.00

2000 Stadium Club

Released in one series, the base set consists of 250 cards, embossed and printed on 20-pt. stock with silver holo-foil stamping. Card backs have a small photo, with the player's vital information and 1999 season statistical breakdown. The 20-card Draft Pick subset (#231-250) are short-printed, seeded 1:5 packs.

	NM/M
Complete Set (250):	80.00

BARRY LARKIN

Common Player:	.15
Common SP (201-250):	2.00
Inserted 1:5	
Pack (6):	1.50
Wax Box (24):	30.00
1 Nomar Garciaparra	1.25
2 Brian Jordan	.15
3 Mark Grace	.15
4 Jeromy Burnitz	.15
5 Shane Reynolds	.15
6 Alex Gonzalez	.15
7 Jose Offerman	.15
8 Orlando Hernandez	.15
9 Mike Caruso	.15
10 Tony Clark	.15
11 Sean Casey	.25
12 Johnny Damon	.15
13 Dante Bichette	.15
14 Kevin Young	.15
15 Juan Gonzalez	.75
16 Chipper Jones	1.00
17 Quilvio Veras	.15
18 Trevor Hoffman	.15
19 Roger Cedeno	.15
20 Ellis Burks	.15
21 Richie Sexson	.15
22 Gary Sheffield	.40
23 Delino DeShields	.15
24 Wade Boggs	1.00
25 Ray Lankford	.15
26 Kevin Appier	.15
27 Roy Halladay	.15
28 Harold Baines	.15
29 Todd Zeile	.15
30 Barry Larkin	.15
31 Ron Coomer	.15
32 Jorge Posada	.15
33 Magglio Ordonez	.15
34 Brian Giles	.15
35 Jeff Kent	.15
36 Henry Rodriguez	.15
37 Fred McGriff	.25
38 Shawn Green	.50
39 Derek Bell	.15
40 Ben Grieve	.15
41 Dave Nilsson	.15
42 Mo Vaughn	.15
43 Rondell White	.15
44 Doug Glanville	.15
45 Paul O'Neill	.15
46 Carlos Lee	.15
47 Vinny Castilla	.15
48 Mike Sweeney	.15
49 Rico Brogna	.15
50 Alex Rodriguez	1.50
51 Luis Castillo	.15
52 Kevin Brown	.15
53 Jose Vidro	.15
54 John Smoltz	.15
55 Garret Anderson	.15
56 Matt Stairs	.15
57 Omar Vizquel	.15
58 Tom Goodwin	.15
59 Scott Brosius	.15
60 Robin Ventura	.15
61 B.J. Surhoff	.15
62 Andy Ashby	.15
63 Chris Widger	.15
64 Tim Hudson	.40
65 Javy Lopez	.15
66 Tim Salmon	.25
67 Warren Morris	.15
68 John Wetteland	.15
69 Gabe Kapler	.15
70 Bernie Williams	.30
71 Rickey Henderson	.75
72 Andruw Jones	.75
73 Eric Young	.15
74 Bob Abreu	.15
75 David Cone	.15
76 Rusty Greer	.15
77 Ron Belliard	.15
78 Troy Glaus	.75
79 Mike Hampton	.15
80 Miguel Tejada	.30
81 Jeff Cirillo	.15
82 Todd Hundley	.15
83 Roberto Alomar	.40
84 Charles Johnson	.15
85 Rafael Palmeiro	.65
86 Doug Mientkiewicz	.15
87 Mariano Rivera	.25
88 Neifi Perez	.15
89 Jermaine Dye	.15
90 Ivan Rodriguez	.65
91 Jay Buhner	.15
92 Pokey Reese	.15
93 John Olerud	.15

94 Brady Anderson	.15
95 Manny Ramirez	.75
96 Keith Osik	.15
97 Mickey Morandini	.15
98 Matt Williams	.15
99 Eric Karros	.15
100 Ken Griffey Jr.	1.25
101 Bret Boone	.15
102 Ryan Klesko	.15
103 Craig Biggio	.15
104 John Jaha	.15
105 Vladimir Guerrero	.75
106 Devon White	.15
107 Tony Womack	.15
108 Marvin Benard	.15
109 Kenny Lofton	.15
110 Preston Wilson	.15
111 Al Leiter	.15
112 Reggie Sanders	.15
113 Scott Williamson	.15
114 Deivi Cruz	.15
115 Carlos Beltran	.50
116 Ray Durham	.15
117 Ricky Ledee	.15
118 Torii Hunter	.15
119 John Valentin	.15
120 Scott Rolen	.65
121 Jason Kendall	.15
122 Dave Martinez	.15
123 Jim Thome	.65
124 David Bell	.15
125 Jose Canseco	.45
126 Jose Lima	.15
127 Carl Everett	.15
128 Kevin Millwood	.15
129 Bill Spiers	.15
130 Omar Daal	.15
131 Miguel Cairo	.15
132 Mark Grudzielanek	.15
133 David Justice	.15
134 Russ Ortiz	.15
135 Mike Piazza	1.25
136 Brian Meadows	.15
137 Tony Gwynn	1.00
138 Cal Ripken Jr.	2.00
139 Kris Benson	.15
140 Larry Walker	.15
141 Cristian Guzman	.15
142 Tino Martinez	.25
143 Chris Singleton	.15
144 Lee Stevens	.15
145 Rey Ordonez	.15
146 Russ Davis	.15
147 J.T. Snow Jr.	.15
148 Luis Gonzalez	.25
149 Marquis Grissom	.15
150 Greg Maddux	1.00
151 Fernando Tatis	.15
152 Jason Giambi	.50
153 Carlos Delgado	.50
154 Joe McEwing	.15
155 Raul Mondesi	.15
156 Rich Aurilia	.15
157 Alex Fernandez	.15
158 Albert Belle	.25
159 Pat Meares	.15
160 Mike Lieberthal	.15
161 Mike Cameron	.15
162 Juan Encarnacion	.15
163 Chuck Knoblauch	.15
164 Pedro Martinez	.75
165 Randy Johnson	.75
166 Shannon Stewart	.15
167 Jeff Bagwell	.75
168 Edgar Renteria	.15
169 Barry Bonds	2.00
170 Steve Finley	.15
171 Brian Hunter	.15
172 Tom Glavine	.35
173 Mark Kotsay	.15
174 Tony Fernandez	.15
175 Sammy Sosa	1.25
176 Geoff Jenkins	.15
177 Adrian Beltre	.15
178 Jay Bell	.15
179 Mike Bordick	.15
180 Ed Sprague	.15
181 Dave Roberts	.15
182 Greg Vaughn	.15
183 Brian Daubach	.15
184 Damion Easley	.15
185 Carlos Febles	.15
186 Kevin Tapani	.15
187 Frank Thomas	.75
188 Roger Clemens	1.00
189 Mike Benjamin	.15
190 Curt Schilling	.40
191 Edgardo Alfonzo	.15
192 Mike Mussina	.40
193 Todd Helton	.75
194 Todd Jones	.15
195 Dean Palmer	.15
196 John Flaherty	.15
197 Derek Jeter	2.00
198 Todd Walker	.15
199 Brad Ausmus	.15
200 Mark McGwire	1.50
201 Erubiel Durazo (Future Stars)	2.00
202 Nick Johnson (Future Stars)	2.50
203 Ruben Mateo (Future Stars)	2.00
204 Lance Berkman (Future Stars)	2.50
205 Pat Burrell (Future Stars)	3.00
206 Pablo Ozuna (Future Stars)	2.00

207 Roosevelt Brown (Future Stars)	2.00
208 Alfonso Soriano (Future Stars)	4.00
209 A.J. Burnett (Future Stars)	2.00
210 Rafael Furcal (Future Stars)	2.00
211 Scott Morgan (Future Stars)	2.00
212 Adam Piatt (Future Stars)	2.00
213 Dee Brown (Future Stars)	2.00
214 Corey Patterson (Future Stars)	2.50
215 Mickey Lopez (Future Stars)	2.00
216 Rob Ryan (Future Stars)	2.00
217 Sean Burroughs (Future Stars)	2.00
218 Jack Cust (Future Stars)	2.00
219 John Patterson (Future Stars)	2.00
220 Kit Pellow (Future Stars)	2.00
221 Chad Hermansen (Future Stars)	2.00
222 Daryle Ward (Future Stars)	2.00
223 Jayson Werth (Future Stars)	2.00
224 Jason Standridge (Future Stars)	2.00
225 Mark Mulder (Future Stars)	2.50
226 Peter Bergeron (Future Stars)	2.00
227 Willi Mo Pena (Future Stars)	2.00
228 Aramis Ramirez (Future Stars)	2.00
229 John Sneed RC (Future Stars)	2.00
230 Wilton Veras (Future Stars)	2.00
231 Josh Hamilton (Draft Picks)	2.00
232 Eric Munson (Draft Picks)	2.00
233 Bobby Bradley RC (Draft Picks)	2.00
234 Larry Bigbie RC (Draft Picks)	2.00
235 B.J. Garbe RC (Draft Picks)	2.00
236 Brett Myers RC (Draft Picks)	6.00
237 Jason Stumm RC (Draft Picks)	2.00
238 Corey Myers RC (Draft Picks)	2.00
239 Ryan Christianson RC (Draft Picks)	2.00
240 David Walling (Draft Picks)	2.00
241 Josh Girdley (Draft Picks)	2.00
242 Omar Ortiz (Draft Picks)	2.00
243 Jason Jennings (Draft Picks)	2.00
244 Kyle Snyder RC (Draft Picks)	2.00
245 Jay Gehrke (Draft Picks)	2.00
246 Mike Paradis RC (Draft Picks)	2.00
247 Chance Caple RC (Draft Picks)	2.00
248 Ben Christiansen RC (Draft Picks)	2.00
249 Brad Baker RC (Draft Picks)	2.00
250 Rick Asadoorian RC (Draft Picks)	2.00
--- Checklist (Nomar Garciaparra)	.25

First Day Issue

Identifiable by the "First Day Issue" stamp, this retail exclusive parallel set is limited to 150 sequentially numbered sets.

Stars:	5-10X
Short-Prints:	2-3X
Production 150 Sets R	

One of a Kind

JOSH GIRDLEY

This 250-card set is a parallel to the base set, is hobby exclusive and limited to 150 serially numbered sets.

Stars: 5-10X
Short-prints: 2-3X
Production 150 Sets H

Bats of Brilliance

This insert set focused on 10 of baseball's top hitters. Card fronts have a silver foil border over a black backdrop. Backs highlight the player's statistics from 1999 and his career statistics. They are numbered with a "BB" prefix and are seeded 1:12 packs. A die-cut parallel is also randomly seeded 1:60 packs.

	NM/M
Complete Set (10):	10.00
Common Player:	.50
Inserted 1:12	
1 Mark McGwire	2.50
2 Sammy Sosa	1.50
3 Jose Canseco	.50
4 Jeff Bagwell	.75
5 Ken Griffey Jr.	1.50
6 Nomar Garciaparra	1.50
7 Mike Piazza	1.50
8 Alex Rodriguez	2.50
9 Vladimir Guerrero	.75
10 Chipper Jones	1.50

Capture The Action

This 20-card set is divided into categories of Rookies, Stars, and Legends. These were seeded 1:12 packs and have the insert title, player name and logo stamped in silver foil. They are numbered with a "CA" prefix on the backs. A hobby-exclusive parallel version was also available, serially numbered to 100 and featuring a replica of the actual photo slide used to create the card.

	NM/M
Complete Set (20):	20.00
Common Player:	.50
Inserted 1:12	
Game View Stars:	3-6X
Production 100 Sets H	
1 Josh Hamilton	.50
2 Pat Burrell	.75
3 Erubiel Durazo	.50
4 Alfonso Soriano	1.00
5 A.J. Burnett	.50
6 Alex Rodriguez	3.00
7 Sean Casey	.50
8 Derek Jeter	4.00
9 Vladimir Guerrero	1.00
10 Nomar Garciaparra	2.00
11 Mike Piazza	2.00
12 Ken Griffey Jr.	2.00
13 Sammy Sosa	2.00
14 Juan Gonzalez	1.00
15 Mark McGwire	3.00
16 Ivan Rodriguez	.75
17 Barry Bonds	4.00
18 Wade Boggs	1.50
19 Tony Gwynn	1.50
20 Cal Ripken Jr.	4.00

Co-Signers

This 15-card hobby exclusive set features two signatures on the card front, with the Topps "Certified Autograph Issue" stamp as well as the Topps 3M sticker to ensure its authenticity. The cards are divided into three groupings with the following odds: Group A - 1:10,184; Group B - 1:5,092; and Group C - 1:508.

	NM/M
Common Card:	15.00
Group A 1:10,184	
Group B 1:5,092	
Group C 1:508	
1 Alex Rodriguez, Derek Jeter	400.00
2 Derek Jeter, Omar Vizquel	150.00
3 Alex Rodriguez, Rey Ordonez	100.00
4 Derek Jeter, Rey Ordonez	150.00
5 Omar Vizquel, Alex Rodriguez	100.00
6 Rey Ordonez, Omar Vizquel	15.00
7 Wade Boggs, Robin Ventura	30.00
8 Randy Johnson, Mike Mussina	90.00
9 Pat Burrell, Magglio Ordonez	40.00
10 Chad Hermansen, Pat Burrell	20.00
11 Magglio Ordonez, Chad Hermansen	20.00
12 Josh Hamilton, Corey Myers	25.00
13 B.J. Garbe, Josh Hamilton	25.00
14 Corey Myers, B.J. Garbe	15.00
15 Tino Martinez, Fred McGriff	60.00

Lone Star Signatures

This 16-card autographed set features the Topps "Certified Autograph Issue" stamp to verify its authenticity. The cards are divided into four groupings with the following odds: Group 1, 1:1,979 hobby; Group 2, 1:2,374 hobby; Group 3, 1:1,979; and Group 4, 1:424 hobby.

	NM/M
Common Player:	8.00
Group 1 1:1,979	
Group 2 1:2,374	
Group 3 1:1,979	
Group 4 1:424	
1 Derek Jeter	100.00
2 Alex Rodriguez	100.00
3 Wade Boggs	25.00
4 Robin Ventura	15.00
5 Randy Johnson	60.00
6 Mike Mussina	25.00
7 Tino Martinez	35.00
8 Fred McGriff	25.00
9 Omar Vizquel	15.00
10 Rey Ordonez	8.00
11 Pat Burrell	15.00
12 Chad Hermansen	8.00
13 Magglio Ordonez	10.00
14 Josh Hamilton	35.00
15 Corey Myers	8.00
16 B.J. Garbe	8.00

Onyx Extreme

This 10-card set features black styrene technology with silver foil stamping and are seeded 1:12 packs. A die-cut parallel is also randomly inserted 1:60 hobby packs.

	NM/M
Complete Set (10):	10.00
Common Player:	.40
Inserted 1:12	
Die-Cuts:	2-3X
Inserted 1:60	
1 Ken Griffey Jr.	1.50
2 Derek Jeter	3.00
3 Vladimir Guerrero	1.00
4 Nomar Garciaparra	1.50
5 Barry Bonds	3.00
6 Alex Rodriguez	2.50
7 Sammy Sosa	1.50
8 Ivan Rodriguez	.75
9 Larry Walker	.40
10 Andruw Jones	1.00

Printing Plates

Inserted only in Home Team boxes at a rate of approximately one per 100 packs were the actual aluminum plates used to print the fronts of the base cards. Unlike some printing plate issues, the plates used for the card backs were not inserted. Each card's plate can be found in four different colors: Cyan, magenta, yellow and black. Because of their unique nature, pricing of individual player's plates cannot be provided.

	NM/M
Common Player:	60.00

Scenes

Available only in hobby and Home Team Advantage boxes, these broaden the view of the featured player and have a format sized 2-1/2" x 4-11/16". These are boxtoppers, seeded one per box.

	NM/M
Complete Set (9):	10.00
Common Player:	.50
Inserted 1:Box	
1 Mark McGwire	2.50
2 Alex Rodriguez	2.50
3 Cal Ripken Jr.	3.00
4 Sammy Sosa	2.00
5 Derek Jeter	3.00
6 Ken Griffey Jr.	2.00
7 Raul Mondesi	.50
8 Chipper Jones	1.50
9 Nomar Garciaparra	2.00

Souvenirs

These memorabilia inserts feature die-cut technology that incorporates an actual piece of a game-used uniform. Each card back contains the Topps 3M sticker to ensure its authenticity. The insert rate is 2:339 hobby packs and 2:136 HTA packs.

	NM/M
Complete Set (3):	35.00
Common Player:	8.00
Inserted 2:339	
1 Wade Boggs	20.00
2 Randy Johnson	20.00
3 Robin Ventura	8.00

3 X 3

Ten groups of three top-notch players are arranged by position on three different laser-cut technologies. The three players can be "fused" together to form one oversize card. The three versions are Luminous (1:18), Luminescent (1:72) and Illuminator (1:144).

	NM/M
Complete Set (30):	40.00
Common Player:	.75
Inserted 1:18	
Luminescent:	2X
Inserted 1:72	
Illuminator:	3-4X
Inserted 1:144	
1A Randy Johnson	1.50
1B Pedro Martinez	1.50
1C Greg Maddux	2.00
2A Mike Piazza	3.00
2B Ivan Rodriguez	1.25
2C Mike Lieberthal	.75
3A Mark McGwire	4.50
3B Jeff Bagwell	1.50
3C Sean Casey	.75
4A Craig Biggio	.75
4B Roberto Alomar	1.00
4C Jay Bell	.75
5A Chipper Jones	2.00
5B Matt Williams	.75
5C Robin Ventura	.75
6A Alex Rodriguez	4.50
6B Derek Jeter	6.00
6C Nomar Garciaparra	3.00
7A Barry Bonds	6.00
7B Luis Gonzalez	1.00
7C Dante Bichette	.75
8A Ken Griffey Jr.	3.00
8B Bernie Williams	1.00
8C Andruw Jones	1.50
9A Manny Ramirez	1.50
9B Sammy Sosa	3.00
9C Juan Gonzalez	1.50
10A Jose Canseco	1.00
10B Frank Thomas	1.50
10C Rafael Palmeiro	1.00

2000 Stadium Club Chrome Preview

This 20-card set features Topps Chromium technology, previewing the debut of Stadium Club Chrome, a later release. The insertion odds are 1:24 packs. A Refractor parallel version is also available seeded 1:120 packs.

	NM/M
Complete Set (20):	40.00
Common Player:	1.00
Inserted 1:24	
Refractors:	2-3X
Inserted 1:120	
1 Nomar Garciaparra	3.00
2 Juan Gonzalez	1.50
3 Chipper Jones	2.00
4 Alex Rodriguez	4.50
5 Ivan Rodriguez	1.25
6 Manny Ramirez	1.50
7 Ken Griffey Jr.	3.00
8 Vladimir Guerrero	1.50
9 Mike Piazza	3.00
10 Pedro Martinez	2.00
11 Jeff Bagwell	1.50
12 Barry Bonds	6.00
13 Sammy Sosa	3.00
14 Derek Jeter	6.00
15 Mark McGwire	4.50
16 Erubiel Durazo	1.00
17 Nick Johnson	1.00
18 Pat Burrell	1.00
19 Alfonso Soriano	1.00
20 Adam Piatt	1.00

2000 Stadium Club Chrome

The 250-card base set uses the same photography and is identical to 2000 Stadium Club besides the utilization of Chromium technology. Five-card packs had a $4 SRP.

	NM/M
Complete Set (250):	40.00
Common Player:	.15
Pack (11):	1.50
Wax Box (36):	40.00
1 Nomar Garciaparra	1.50
2 Brian Jordan	.15
3 Mark Grace	.25
4 Jeromy Burnitz	.15
5 Shane Reynolds	.15
6 Alex Gonzalez	.15
7 Jose Offerman	.15
8 Orlando Hernandez	.15
9 Mike Caruso	.15
10 Tony Clark	.15
11 Sean Casey	.25
12 Johnny Damon	.25
13 Dante Bichette	.15
14 Kevin Young	.15
15 Juan Gonzalez	.75
16 Chipper Jones	1.00
17 Quivio Veras	.15
18 Trevor Hoffman	.15
19 Roger Cedeno	.15
20 Ellis Burks	.15
21 Richie Sexson	.15
22 Gary Sheffield	.45
23 Delino DeShields	.15
24 Wade Boggs	1.00
25 Ray Lankford	.15
26 Kevin Appier	.15
27 Roy Halladay	.15
28 Harold Baines	.15
29 Todd Zeile	.15
30 Barry Larkin	.15
31 Ron Coomer	.15
32 Jorge Posada	.15
33 Magglio Ordonez	.15
34 Brian Giles	.15
35 Jeff Kent	.15
36 Henry Rodriguez	.15
37 Fred McGriff	.15
38 Shawn Green	.50
39 Derek Bell	.15
40 Ben Grieve	.15
41 Dave Nilsson	.15
42 Mo Vaughn	.15
43 Rondell White	.15
44 Doug Glanville	.15
45 Paul O'Neill	.15
46 Carlos Lee	.15
47 Vinny Castilla	.15
48 Mike Sweeney	.15
49 Rico Brogna	.15
50 Alex Rodriguez	2.50
51 Luis Castillo	.15
52 Kevin Brown	.15
53 Jose Vidro	.15
54 John Smoltz	.15
55 Garret Anderson	.15
56 Matt Stairs	.15
57 Omar Vizquel	.15
58 Tom Goodwin	.15
59 Scott Brosius	.15
60 Robin Ventura	.15
61 B.J. Surhoff	.15
62 Andy Ashby	.15
63 Chris Widger	.15
64 Tim Hudson	.40
65 Javy Lopez	.15
66 Tim Salmon	.25
67 Warren Morris	.15
68 John Wetteland	.15
69 Gabe Kapler	.15
70 Bernie Williams	.25
71 Rickey Henderson	.75
72 Andruw Jones	.75
73 Eric Young	.15
74 Bobby Abreu	.15
75 David Cone	.15
76 Rusty Greer	.15
77 Ron Belliard	.15
78 Troy Glaus	.15
79 Mike Hampton	.15
80 Miguel Tejada	.30
81 Jeff Cirillo	.15
82 Todd Hundley	.15
83 Roberto Alomar	.35
84 Charles Johnson	.15
85 Rafael Palmeiro	.65
86 Doug Mientkiewicz	.15
87 Mariano Rivera	.25
88 Neifi Perez	.15
89 Jermaine Dye	.15
90 Ivan Rodriguez	.65
91 Jay Buhner	.15
92 Pokey Reese	.15
93 John Olerud	.15
94 Brady Anderson	.15
95 Manny Ramirez	.75
96 Keith Osik	.15
97 Mickey Morandini	.15
98 Matt Williams	.15
99 Eric Karros	.15
100 Ken Griffey Jr.	1.50
101 Bret Boone	.15
102 Ryan Klesko	.15
103 Craig Biggio	.15
104 John Jaha	.15
105 Vladimir Guerrero	.75
106 Devon White	.15
107 Tony Womack	.15
108 Marvin Benard	.15
109 Kenny Lofton	.15
110 Preston Wilson	.15
111 Al Leiter	.15
112 Reggie Sanders	.15
113 Scott Williamson	.15
114 Deivi Cruz	.15
115 Carlos Beltran	.50
116 Ray Durham	.15
117 Ricky Ledee	.15
118 Torii Hunter	.15
119 John Valentin	.15
120 Scott Rolen	.65
121 Jason Kendall	.15
122 Dave Martinez	.15
123 Jim Thome	.65
124 David Bell	.15
125 Jose Canseco	.50
126 Jose Lima	.15
127 Carl Everett	.15
128 Kevin Millwood	.15
129 Bill Spiers	.15
130 Omar Daal	.15
131 Miguel Cairo	.15
132 Mark Grudzielanek	.15
133 David Justice	.15
134 Russ Ortiz	.15
135 Mike Piazza	1.50
136 Brian Meadows	.15
137 Tony Gwynn	1.00
138 Cal Ripken Jr.	3.00
139 Kris Benson	.15
140 Larry Walker	.15
141 Cristian Guzman	.15
142 Tino Martinez	.15
143 Chris Singleton	.15
144 Lee Stevens	.15
145 Rey Ordonez	.15
146 Russ Davis	.15
147 J.T. Snow Jr.	.15
148 Luis Gonzalez	.25
149 Marquis Grissom	.15
150 Greg Maddux	1.00
151 Fernando Tatis	.15
152 Jason Giambi	.50
153 Carlos Delgado	.15
154 Joe McEwing	.15
155 Raul Mondesi	.15
156 Rich Aurilia	.15
157 Alex Fernandez	.15
158 Albert Belle	.25
159 Pat Meares	.15
160 Mike Lieberthal	.15
161 Mike Cameron	.15
162 Juan Encarnacion	.15
163 Chuck Knoblauch	.15
164 Pedro Martinez	.75
165 Randy Johnson	.75
166 Shannon Stewart	.15
167 Jeff Bagwell	.75
168 Edgar Renteria	.15
169 Barry Bonds	3.00
170 Steve Finley	.15
171 Brian Hunter	.15
172 Tom Glavine	.40
173 Mark Kotsay	.15
174 Tony Fernandez	.15
175 Sammy Sosa	1.50
176 Geoff Jenkins	.15
177 Adrian Beltre	.45
178 Jay Bell	.15
179 Mike Bordick	.15
180 Ed Sprague	.15
181 Dave Roberts	.15
182 Greg Vaughn	.15
183 Brian Daubach	.15
184 Damion Easley	.15
185 Carlos Febles	.15
186 Kevin Tapani	.15
187 Frank Thomas	.75
188 Roger Clemens	1.25
189 Mike Benjamin	.15
190 Curt Schilling	.40
191 Edgardo Alfonzo	.15
192 Mike Mussina	.45
193 Todd Helton	.75
194 Todd Jones	.15
195 Dean Palmer	.15
196 John Flaherty	.15
197 Derek Jeter	3.00
198 Todd Walker	.15
199 Brad Ausmus	.15
200 Mark McGwire	2.50
201 Erubiel Durazo	.15
(Future Stars)	.15

202	Nick Johnson (Future Stars)	.15
203	Ruben Mateo (Future Stars)	.15
204	Lance Berkman (Future Stars)	.15
205	Pat Burrell (Future Stars)	.65
206	Pablo Ozuna (Future Stars)	.15
207	Roosevelt Brown (Future Stars)	.15
208	Alfonso Soriano (Future Stars)	1.00
209	A.J. Burnett (Future Stars)	.15
210	Rafael Furcal (Future Stars)	.15
211	Scott Morgan (Future Stars)	.15
212	Adam Piatt (Future Stars)	.15
213	Dee Brown (Future Stars)	.15
214	Corey Patterson (Future Stars)	.15
215	Mickey Lopez (Future Stars)	.15
216	Rob Ryan (Future Stars)	.15
217	Sean Burroughs (Future Stars)	.15
218	Jack Cust (Future Stars)	.15
219	John Patterson (Future Stars)	.15
220	Kit Pellow (Future Stars)	.15
221	Chad Hermansen (Future Stars)	.15
222	Daryle Ward (Future Stars)	.15
223	Jayson Werth (Future Stars)	.15
224	Jason Standridge (Future Stars)	.15
225	Mark Mulder (Future Stars)	.15
226	Peter Bergeron (Future Stars)	.15
227	Willi Mo Pena (Future Stars)	.15
228	Aramis Ramirez (Future Stars)	.15
229	John Sneed (Future Stars)	.15
230	Wilton Veras (Future Stars)	.15
231	Josh Hamilton (Draft Picks)	.50
232	Eric Munson (Draft Picks)	.15
233	Bobby Bradley RC (Draft Picks)	1.00
234	Larry Bigbie RC (Draft Picks)	1.00
235	B.J. Garbe RC (Draft Picks)	1.00
236	Brett Myers RC (Draft Picks)	4.00
237	Jason Stumm RC (Draft Picks)	1.00
238	Corey Myers RC (Draft Picks)	1.00
239	Ryan Christianson RC (Draft Picks)	1.00
240	David Walling (Draft Picks)	.15
241	Josh Girdley (Draft Picks)	.15
242	Omar Ortiz (Draft Picks)	.15
243	Jason Jennings (Draft Picks)	.15
244	Kyle Snyder (Draft Picks)	.15
245	Jay Gehrke (Draft Picks)	.15
246	Mike Paradis (Draft Picks)	.15
247	Chance Caple RC (Draft Picks)	1.00
248	Ben Christensen RC (Draft Picks)	1.00
249	Brad Baker RC (Draft Picks)	1.00
250	Rick Asadoorian RC (Draft Picks)	1.00

Refractor

A parallel to the 250-card base set these utilize Refractor technology and have a mirror sheen to them when held up to a light source. "Refractor" is also written under the card number on the card back. Refractors are seeded 1:12 packs.

Stars: 2-4X
Rookies: 1-2X
Inserted 1:12

First Day Issue

A parallel to the 250-card base set. Card fronts are identical besides "First Day Issue" printed three times over the player name and Stadium Club Chrome logo. Card backs are serial numbered in an edition of 100. A Refractor First Day Issue parallel is also randomly inserted, limited to 25 serial-numbered sets.

Stars: 4-8X
Rookies: 1-30X
Production 100 Sets
Refractor: 25-40X
Rookies: 5-10X
Production 25 Sets

Capture The Action

This 20-card set is divided into three groups: Rookies, Stars and Legends. Card backs are numbered with a "CA" prefix. These are found 1:18 packs. A Refractor parallel version is also randomly seeded 1:90 packs and also have "Refractor" written under the card number on the back.

		NM/M
Complete Set (20):		40.00
Common Player:		1.00
Inserted 1:18		
Refractors:		2-3X
Inserted 1:90		
1	Josh Hamilton	1.00
2	Pat Burrell	1.50
3	Erubiel Durazo	1.00
4	Alfonso Soriano	1.50
5	A.J. Burnett	1.00
6	Alex Rodriguez	5.00
7	Sean Casey	1.00
8	Derek Jeter	6.00
9	Vladimir Guerrero	1.50
10	Nomar Garciaparra	3.00
11	Mike Piazza	3.00
12	Ken Griffey Jr.	3.00
13	Sammy Sosa	3.00
14	Juan Gonzalez	1.50
15	Mark McGwire	5.00
16	Ivan Rodriguez	1.50
17	Barry Bonds	6.00
18	Wade Boggs	2.00
19	Tony Gwynn	2.00
20	Cal Ripken Jr.	6.00

Clear Shots

Printed on a clear, acetate stock this 10-card insert set will depict the front of the player on the card front and the back on the card back. Card backs are numbered with a "CS" prefix. Clear Shots are inserted 1:24 packs. A die-cut Refractor parallel version is also randomly seeded 1:120 packs.

		NM/M
Complete Set (10):		10.00
Common Player:		.50
Inserted 1:24		
Refractor:		2-3X
Inserted 1:120		
1	Derek Jeter	4.00
2	Bernie Williams	.50
3	Roger Clemens	2.50
4	Chipper Jones	2.00
5	Greg Maddux	2.00
6	Andruw Jones	1.00
7	Juan Gonzalez	1.00
8	Manny Ramirez	1.00
9	Ken Griffey Jr.	3.00
10	Josh Hamilton	.50

Eyes of the Game

Printed on a clear, acetate stock this 10-card set focuses on the facial expression of the featured player. Two images are on the front with the background image a close-up shot of the player's facial expression. These were seeded 1:16. Card backs are numbered with an "EG" prefix. A Refractor parallel is randomly inserted in 1:80 packs and has "Refractor" written under the card number on the back.

		NM/M
Complete Set (10):		10.00
Common Player:		.50
Inserted 1:16		
Refractors:		2-3X
Inserted 1:80		
1	Randy Johnson	1.00
2	Mike Piazza	1.50
3	Nomar Garciaparra	1.50
4	Mark McGwire	2.50
5	Alex Rodriguez	2.50
6	Derek Jeter	3.00
7	Tony Gwynn	1.00
8	Sammy Sosa	1.50
9	Larry Walker	.50
10	Ken Griffey Jr.	1.50

True Colors

This 10-card set focuses on players Topps deemed that performed best when the game's on the line. These were inserted 1:32 and are numbered with a "TC" prefix on the card back. A Refractor parallel is randomly inserted 1:160 packs.

		NM/M
Complete Set (10):		15.00
Common Player:		1.00
Inserted 1:32		
Refractors:		2-3X
Inserted 1:160		
1	Sammy Sosa	2.00
2	Nomar Garciaparra	2.00
3	Alex Rodriguez	3.00

4	Derek Jeter	4.00
5	Mark McGwire	3.00
6	Chipper Jones	1.50
7	Mike Piazza	2.00
8	Ken Griffey Jr.	2.00
9	Manny Ramirez	1.00
10	Vladimir Guerrero	1.00

Visionaries

This 20-card set spotlights young prospects who are deemed destined for stardom. Card backs are numbered with a "V" prefix. These are found 1:18 packs. A Refractor parallel version is also seeded 1:90 packs. "Refractor" is written under the card number on the back.

		NM/M
Complete Set (20):		17.50
Common Player:		1.00
Inserted 1:18		
Refractors:		2X
Inserted 1:90		
1	Alfonso Soriano	3.00
2	Josh Hamilton	1.00
3	A.J. Burnett	1.50
4	Pat Burrell	2.50
5	Ruben Salazar	1.00
6	Aaron Rowand	1.00
7	Adam Piatt	1.00
8	Nick Johnson	1.00
9	Rafael Furcal	1.00
10	Jack Cust	1.00
11	Corey Patterson	1.00
12	Sean Burroughs	1.50
13	Pablo Ozuna	1.00
14	Dee Brown	1.00
15	John Patterson	1.00
16	Willi Mo Pena	1.00
17	Mark Mulder	1.00
18	Eric Munson	1.00
19	Alex Escobar	1.00
20	Rob Ryan	1.00

2001 Stadium Club

		NM/M
Complete Set (200):		65.00
Common Player:		.15
Common SP:		1.50
Inserted 1:6		
Pack (7):		2.00
Box (24):		35.00
1	Nomar Garciaparra	1.25
2	Chipper Jones	.75
3	Jeff Bagwell	.75
4	Chad Kreuter	.15
5	Randy Johnson	.75
6	Mike Hampton	.15
7	Barry Larkin	.15
8	Bernie Williams	.30
9	Chris Singleton	.15
10	Larry Walker	.15
11	Brad Ausmus	.15
12	Ron Coomer	.15
13	Edgardo Alfonzo	.15
14	Delino DeShields	.15
15	Tony Gwynn	1.00
16	Andruw Jones	.75
17	Raul Mondesi	.15
18	Troy Glaus	.75
19	Ben Grieve	.15
20	Sammy Sosa	1.25
21	Fernando Vina	.15
22	Jeromy Burnitz	.15
23	Jay Bell	.15
24	Pete Harnisch	.15
25	Barry Bonds	2.00

4	Derek Jeter	4.00
5	Mark McGwire	3.00
6	Chipper Jones	1.50
7	Mike Piazza	2.00
8	Ken Griffey Jr.	2.00
9	Manny Ramirez	1.00
10	Vladimir Guerrero	1.00
26	Eric Karros	.15
27	Alex Gonzalez	.15
28	Mike Lieberthal	.15
29	Juan Encarnacion	.15
30	Derek Jeter	2.00
31	Bruce Aven	.15
32	Eric Milton	.15
33	Aaron Boone	.15
34	Roberto Alomar	.40
35	John Olerud	.15
36	Orlando Cabrera	.15
37	Shawn Green	.45
38	Roger Cedeno	.15
39	Garret Anderson	.15
40	Jim Thome	.65
41	Gabe Kapler	.15
42	Mo Vaughn	.15
43	Sean Casey	.25
44	Preston Wilson	.15
45	Javy Lopez	.15
46	Ryan Klesko	.15
47	Ray Durham	.15
48	Dean Palmer	.15
49	Jorge Posada	.15
50	Alex Rodriguez	1.50
51	Tom Glavine	.40
52	Ray Lankford	.15
53	Jose Canseco	.40
54	Tim Salmon	.25
55	Cal Ripken Jr.	2.00
56	Bob Abreu	.15
57	Robin Ventura	.15
58	Damion Easley	.15
59	Paul O'Neill	.15
60	Ivan Rodriguez	.65
61	Carl Everett	.15
62	Doug Glanville	.15
63	Jeff Kent	.15
64	Jay Buhner	.15
65	Cliff Floyd	.15
66	Rick Ankiel	.25
67	Mark Grace	.25
68	Brian Jordan	.15
69	Craig Biggio	.15
70	Carlos Delgado	.50
71	Brad Radke	.15
72	Greg Maddux	1.00
73	Al Leiter	.15
74	Pokey Reese	.15
75	Todd Helton	.75
76	Mariano Rivera	.25
77	Shane Spencer	.15
78	Jason Kendall	.15
79	Chuck Knoblauch	.15
80	Scott Rolen	.65
81	Jose Offerman	.15
82	J.T. Snow Jr.	.15
83	Pat Meares	.15
84	Quilvio Veras	.15
85	Edgar Renteria	.15
86	Luis Matos	.15
87	Adrian Beltre	.15
88	Luis Gonzalez	.25
89	Rickey Henderson	.75
90	Brian Giles	.15
91	Carlos Febles	.15
92	Tino Martinez	.15
93	Magglio Ordonez	.15
94	Rafael Furcal	.15
95	Mike Mussina	.30
96	Gary Sheffield	.40
97	Kenny Lofton	.15
98	Fred McGriff	.15
99	Ken Caminiti	.15
100	Mark McGwire	1.50
101	Tom Goodwin	.15
102	Mark Grudzielanek	.15
103	Derek Bell	.15
104	Mike Lowell	.15
105	Jeff Cirillo	.15
106	Orlando Hernandez	.15
107	Jose Valentin	.15
108	Warren Morris	.15
109	Mike Williams	.15
110	Gregg Zaun	.15
111	Jose Vidro	.15
112	Omar Vizquel	.15
113	Vinny Castilla	.15
114	Gregg Jefferies	.15
115	Kevin Brown	.15
116	Shannon Stewart	.15
117	Marquis Grissom	.15
118	Manny Ramirez	.75
119	Albert Belle	.15
120	Bret Boone	.15
121	Johnny Damon	.25
122	Juan Gonzalez	.75
123	David Justice	.15
124	Jeffrey Hammonds	.15
125	Ken Griffey Jr.	1.25
126	Mike Sweeney	.15
127	Tony Clark	.15
128	Todd Zeile	.15
129	Mark Johnson	.15
130	Matt Williams	.15
131	Geoff Jenkins	.15
132	Jason Giambi	.50
133	Steve Finley	.15
134	Derrek Lee	.15
135	Royce Clayton	.15
136	Joe Randa	.15
137	Rafael Palmeiro	.65
138	Kevin Young	.15
139	Curt Schilling	.40
140	Vladimir Guerrero	.75
141	Greg Vaughn	.15
142	Jermaine Dye	.15
143	Roger Clemens	1.00

144	Denny Hocking	.15
145	Frank Thomas	.75
146	Carlos Beltran	.50
147	Eric Young	.15
148	Pat Burrell	.50
149	Pedro Martinez	.75
150	Mike Piazza	1.25
151	Adrian Gonzalez	.50
152	Adam Johnson	.15
153	Luis Montanez RC	1.50
154	Mike Stodolka	.15
155	Phil Dumatrait	.15
156	Sean Burnett	1.50
157	Dominic Rich RC	1.50
158	Adam Wainwright	.50
159	Scott Thorman	.15
160	Scott Heard	.25
161	Chad Petty RC	1.50
162	Matt Wheatland	2.00
163	Brad Digby	.15
164	Rocco Baldelli	1.00
165	Grady Sizemore	1.00
166	Brian Sellier RC	1.50
167	Rick Brosseau RC	1.50
168	Shawn Fagan RC	1.50
169	Sean Smith	1.50
170	Chris Bass RC	1.50
171	Corey Patterson (Future Stars)	.25
172	Sean Burroughs (Future Stars)	.25
173	Ben Petrick (Future Stars)	.15
174	Mike Glendenning (Future Stars)	.15
175	Barry Zito (Future Stars)	.50
176	Milton Bradley (Future Stars)	.15
177	Bobby Bradley (Future Stars)	.15
178	Jason Hart (Future Stars)	.15
179	Ryan Anderson (Future Stars)	.15
180	Ben Sheets (Future Stars)	.25
181	Adam Everett (Future Stars)	.15
182	Alfonso Soriano (Future Stars)	.75
183	Josh Hamilton (Future Stars)	.50
184	Eric Munson (Future Stars)	.15
185	Chin-Feng Chen (Future Stars)	.25
186	Tim Christman RC	1.50
187	J.R. House	2.00
188	Brandon Parker RC	1.50
189	Sean Fesh RC	1.50
190	Joel Pieniero RC	2.00
191	Oscar Ramirez RC	1.50
192	Alex Santos RC	1.50
193	Eddy Reyes RC	1.50
194	Mike Jacobs RC	1.50
195	Erick Almonte RC	2.00
196	Brandon Claussen RC	2.00
197	Kris Keller RC	1.50
198	Wilson Betemit RC	1.50
199	Andy Phillips RC	1.50
200	Adam Pettyjohn RC	1.50
---	Derek Jeter (Checklist)	.25

Beam Team

		NM/M
Complete Set (30):		100.00
Common Player:		1.50
Production 500 Sets		
1	Sammy Sosa	6.00
2	Mark McGwire	8.00
3	Vladimir Guerrero	3.00
4	Chipper Jones	4.50
5	Manny Ramirez	3.00
6	Derek Jeter	10.00
7	Alex Rodriguez	8.00
8	Cal Ripken Jr.	10.00
9	Ken Griffey Jr.	6.00
10	Greg Maddux	4.50
11	Barry Bonds	10.00
12	Pedro Martinez	3.00
13	Nomar Garciaparra	6.00
14	Randy Johnson	3.00
15	Frank Thomas	3.00
16	Ivan Rodriguez	2.50
17	Jeff Bagwell	3.00
18	Mike Piazza	6.00
19	Todd Helton	3.00
20	Shawn Green	2.00
21	Juan Gonzalez	3.00
22	Larry Walker	1.50
23	Tony Gwynn	4.50
24	Pat Burrell	2.00
25	Rafael Furcal	1.50
26	Corey Patterson	1.50
27	Chin-Feng Chen	1.50
28	Sean Burroughs	1.50
29	Ryan Anderson	1.50
30	Josh Hamilton	5.00

Capture The Action

		NM/M
Complete Set (15):		15.00
Common Player:		1.00
Inserted 1:8		
1	Cal Ripken Jr.	3.00
2	Alex Rodriguez	2.50
3	Mike Piazza	2.00
4	Mark McGwire	2.50
5	Greg Maddux	1.50
6	Derek Jeter	3.00
7	Chipper Jones	1.50

#	Player	Price
8	Pedro Martinez	1.00
9	Ken Griffey Jr.	2.00
10	Nomar Garciaparra	2.00
11	Randy Johnson	1.00
12	Sammy Sosa	2.00
13	Vladimir Guerrero	1.00
14	Barry Bonds	3.00
15	Ivan Rodriguez	1.00

Capture The Action Game View

Common Player: 10.00
Production 100 Sets

#	Player	Price
1	Cal Ripken Jr.	30.00
2	Alex Rodriguez	25.00
3	Mike Piazza	20.00
4	Mark McGwire	25.00
5	Greg Maddux	15.00
6	Derek Jeter	30.00
7	Chipper Jones	15.00
8	Pedro Martinez	10.00
9	Ken Griffey Jr.	20.00
10	Nomar Garciaparra	20.00
11	Randy Johnson	10.00
12	Sammy Sosa	20.00
13	Vladimir Guerrero	10.00
14	Barry Bonds	30.00
15	Ivan Rodriguez	10.00

Co-Signers

Common Duo: 15.00
Inserted 1:1,117

#	Players	Price
1	Nomar Garciaparra, Derek Jeter	400.00
2	Roberto Alomar, Edgardo Alfonzo	50.00
3	Rick Ankiel, Kevin Millwood	15.00
4	Chipper Jones, Troy Glaus	65.00
5	Magglio Ordonez, Bobby Abreu	20.00
6	Adam Piatt, Sean Burroughs	20.00
7	Corey Patterson, Nick Johnson	40.00
8	Adrian Gonzalez, Rocco Baldelli	40.00
9	Adam Johnson, Mike Stodolka	15.00

Diamond Pearls

Complete Set (20): 20.00
Common Player: .65
Inserted 1:8

#	Player	Price
1	Ken Griffey Jr.	2.00
2	Alex Rodriguez	2.50
3	Derek Jeter	3.00
4	Chipper Jones	1.50
5	Nomar Garciaparra	2.00
6	Vladimir Guerrero	1.00
7	Jeff Bagwell	1.00
8	Cal Ripken Jr.	3.00
9	Sammy Sosa	2.00
10	Mark McGwire	2.50
11	Frank Thomas	2.00
12	Pedro Martinez	1.00
13	Manny Ramirez	1.00
14	Randy Johnson	1.00
15	Barry Bonds	3.00
16	Ivan Rodriguez	.75
17	Greg Maddux	1.50
18	Mike Piazza	2.00
19	Todd Helton	1.00
20	Shawn Green	.65

Game-Used Cards

Common Player: 5.00
Inserted 1:285

#	Player	Price
1	Chin-Feng Chen	20.00
2	Bobby Bradley	5.00
3	Tomokazu Ohka	5.00
4	Kurt Ainsworth	5.00
5	Craig Anderson	5.00
6	Josh Hamilton	10.00
7	Felipe Lopez	5.00
8	Ryan Anderson	5.00
9	Alex Escobar	5.00
10	Ben Sheets	8.00
11	Ntema Ndungidi	5.00
12	Eric Munson	5.00
13	Aaron Myette	5.00
14	Jack Cust	5.00
15	Julio Zuleta	5.00
16	Corey Patterson	10.00
17	Carlos Pena	5.00
18	Marcus Giles	5.00
19	Travis Wilson	5.00
20	Barry Zito	8.00

King of the Hill

Complete Set (5): 30.00
Common Player: 3.00
Inserted 1:21

#	Player	Price
1	Pedro Martinez	10.00
2	Randy Johnson	10.00
3	Greg Maddux	15.00
4	Rick Ankiel	3.00
5	Kevin Brown	3.00

Lone Star Signatures

Common Player: 6.00
Inserted 1:196

#	Player	Price
1	Nomar Garciaparra	100.00
2	Derek Jeter	120.00
3	Edgardo Alfonzo	20.00
4	Roberto Alomar	40.00
5	Magglio Ordonez	20.00
6	Bobby Abreu	40.00
7	Chipper Jones	50.00
8	Troy Glaus	30.00
9	Nick Johnson	15.00
10	Adam Piatt	6.00
11	Sean Burroughs	8.00
12	Corey Patterson	15.00
13	Rick Ankiel	15.00
14	Kevin Millwood	10.00
15	Adrian Gonzalez	15.00
16	Adam Johnson	6.00
17	Rocco Baldelli	25.00
18	Mike Stodolka	6.00

Play at the Plate

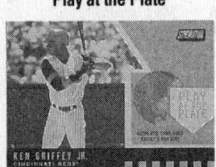

Common Player: 10.00
Inserted 1:11

#	Player	Price
1	Mark McGwire	20.00
2	Sammy Sosa	15.00
3	Vladimir Guerrero	8.00
4	Ken Griffey Jr.	15.00
5	Mike Piazza	15.00
6	Chipper Jones	10.00
7	Barry Bonds	25.00
8	Alex Rodriguez	20.00
9	Jeff Bagwell	8.00
10	Nomar Garciaparra	15.00

Souvenirs

Common Player:	4.00
1 Scott Rolen/Bat	8.00
2 Larry Walker/Bat	5.00
3 Rafael Furcal/Bat	5.00
4 Darin Erstad/Bat	5.00
5 Mike Sweeney/Jsy	4.00
6 Matt Lawton/Jsy	4.00
7 Jose Vidro/Jsy	4.00
8 Pat Burrell/Jsy	6.00

Super Teams

These scarce exchange cards were seeded at an average rate of about one per 875 packs of TSC Hobby and Retail and one per 340 packs of Home Team Advantage. Prior to the cards' redemption deadline which expired Dec. 1, 2001, they could be entered into drawings for various prizes including specially marked card sets, game tickets, autographs, etc.

Common Card: 1.00

#	Team	Price
STP1	Anaheim Angels (Troy Glaus)	2.00
STP2	Houston Astros (Jeff Bagwell)	2.00
STP3	Oakland A's (Jason Giambi)	1.25
STP4	Toronto Blue Jays (Carlos Delgado)	1.00
STP5	Atlanta Braves (Chipper Jones)	2.50
STP6	Milwaukee Brewers (Geoff Jenkins)	1.00
STP7	St. Louis Cardinals (Mark McGwire)	4.00
STP8	Chicago Cubs (Sammy Sosa)	3.00
STP9	Tampa Bay Devil Rays (Greg Vaughn)	1.00
STP10	Arizona Diamondbacks (Luis Gonzalez)	1.00
STP11	L.A. Dodgers (Shawn Green)	1.00
STP12	Montreal Expos (Vladimir Guerrero)	1.50
STP13	S.F. Giants (Barry Bonds)	5.00
STP14	Cleveland Indians (Roberto Alomar)	1.00
STP15	Seattle Mariners (Alex Rodriguez)	4.00
STP16	Florida Marlins (Preston Wilson)	1.00
STP17	N.Y. Mets (Mike Piazza)	3.00
STP18	Baltimore Orioles (Mike Mussina)	1.00
STP19	S.D. Padres (Tony Gwynn)	2.00
STP20	Philadelphia Phillies (Scott Rolen)	1.25
STP21	Pittsburgh Pirates (Jason Kendall)	1.00
STP22	Texas Rangers (Ivan Rodriguez)	1.25
STP23	Boston Red Sox (Nomar Garciaparra)	3.00
STP24	Cincinnati Reds (Ken Griffey Jr.)	3.00
STP25	Colorado Rockies (Todd Helton)	1.50
STP26	K.C. Royals (Mike Sweeney)	1.00
STP27	Detroit Tigers (Juan Gonzalez)	1.50
STP28	Minnesota Twins (Brad Radke)	1.00
STP29	Chicago White Sox (Frank Thomas)	1.50
STP30	N.Y. Yankees (Derek Jeter)	5.00

2002 Stadium Club Relic Edition

Complete Set (125): —
Common Player: .15
Common SP (101-125): 5.00
Production 2,999
Pack (6): 1.50
Box (24): 30.00

#	Player	Price
1	Pedro Martinez	.75
2	Derek Jeter	2.00
3	Chipper Jones	.75
4	Roberto Alomar	.40
5	Albert Pujols	1.50
6	Bret Boone	.15
7	Alex Rodriguez	1.50
8	Jose Cruz	.15
9	Mike Hampton	.15
10	Vladimir Guerrero	.75
11	Jim Edmonds	.25
12	Luis Gonzalez	.25
13	Jeff Kent	.15
14	Mike Piazza	1.25
15	Ben Sheets	.15
16	Tsuyoshi Shinjo	.15
17	Pat Burrell	.40
18	Jermaine Dye	.15
19	Rafael Furcal	.15
20	Randy Johnson	.75
21	Carlos Delgado	.50
22	Roger Clemens	1.50
23	Eric Chavez	.25
24	Nomar Garciaparra	1.25
25	Ivan Rodriguez	.65
26	Juan Gonzalez	.75
27	Reggie Sanders	.15
28	Jeff Bagwell	.75
29	Kazuhiro Sasaki	.15
30	Larry Walker	.15
31	Ben Grieve	.15
32	David Justice	.15
33	David Wells	.15
34	Kevin Brown	.15
35	Miguel Tejada	.25
36	Jorge Posada	.15
37	Javy Lopez	.15
38	Cliff Floyd	.15
39	Carlos Lee	.15
40	Manny Ramirez	.75
41	Jim Thome	.65
42	Pokey Reese	.15
43	Scott Rolen	.65
44	Richie Sexson	.15
45	Dean Palmer	.15
46	Rafael Palmeiro	.65
47	Alfonso Soriano	.75
48	Craig Biggio	.25
49	Troy Glaus	.15
50	Andruw Jones	.75
51	Ichiro Suzuki	1.50
52	Kenny Lofton	.15
53	Hideo Nomo	.75
54	Magglio Ordonez	.15
55	Brad Penny	.15
56	Omar Vizquel	.15
57	Mike Sweeney	.15
58	Gary Sheffield	.25
59	Ken Griffey Jr.	1.25
60	Curt Schilling	.40
61	Bobby Higginson	.15
62	Terrence Long	.15
63	Moises Alou	.15
64	Sandy Alomar	.15
65	Cristian Guzman	.15
66	Sammy Sosa	1.25
67	Jose Vidro	.15
68	Edgar Martinez	.15
69	Jason Giambi	.50
70	Mark McGwire	1.50
71	Barry Bonds	2.00
72	Greg Vaughn	.15
73	Phil Nevin	.15
74	Jason Kendall	.15
75	Greg Maddux	1.00
76	Jeromy Burnitz	.15
77	Mike Mussina	.40
78	Johnny Damon	.25
79	Shawn Green	.40
80	Jimmy Rollins	.25
81	Edgardo Alfonzo	.15
82	Barry Larkin	.15
83	Raul Mondesi	.15
84	Preston Wilson	.15
85	Mike Lieberthal	.15
86	J.D. Drew	.40
87	Ryan Klesko	.15
88	David Segui	.15
89	Derek Bell	.15
90	Bernie Williams	.40
91	Doug Mientkiewicz	.15
92	Rich Aurilia	.15
93	Ellis Burks	.15
94	Placido Polanco	.15
95	Darin Erstad	.25
96	Brian Giles	.15
97	Geoff Jenkins	.15
98	Kerry Wood	.65
99	Mariano Rivera	.40
100	Todd Helton	.75
101	Adam Dunn	15.00
102	Grant Balfour	5.00
103	Jae Weong Seo	5.00
104	Hank Blalock	8.00
105	Chris George	5.00
106	Jack Cust	5.00
107	Juan Cruz	5.00
108	Adrian Gonzalez	8.00
109	Nick Johnson	5.00
110	Jeff Devanon RC	5.00
111	Juan Diaz	5.00
112	Brandon Duckworth	5.00
113	Jason Lane	5.00
114	Seung Jun Song	5.00
115	Morgan Ensberg	5.00
116	Marlyn Tisdale RC	5.00
117	Jason Botts RC	5.00
118	Henry Pichardo RC	5.00
119	John Rodriguez RC	5.00
120	Mike Peeples RC	5.00
121	Rob Bowen RC	5.00
122	Jeremy Affeldt	5.00
123	Jorge Buret RC	5.00
124	Manny Ravelo RC	5.00
125	Eudy Lajara RC	5.00

All-Star Relics

Common Player: 5.00

Code	Player	Price
RA	Roberto Alomar	7.50
MA	Moises Alou	5.00
BB	Barry Bonds	40.00
BRB	Bret Boone	5.00
MC	Mike Cameron	5.00
SC	Sean Casey	7.50
CF	Cliff Floyd	5.00
BG	Brian Giles	5.00
JG	Juan Gonzalez	12.00
LG3	Luis Gonzalez	5.00
CG	Cristian Guzman	5.00
TG	Tony Gwynn	15.00

Code	Player	Price
MH	Mike Hampton	5.00
TH	Todd Helton	12.00
RJ	Randy Johnson	12.00
CJ	Chipper Jones	15.00
JK	Jeff Kent	5.00
RK	Ryan Klesko	5.00
EM	Edgar Martinez	5.00
ERM	Eric Milton	5.00
JO	John Olerud	5.00
MO	Magglio Ordonez	20.00
MP	Mike Piazza	20.00
JP	Jorge Posada	5.00
AP	Albert Pujols	30.00
MR	Manny Ramirez	12.00
IR	Ivan Rodriguez	10.00
KS	Kazuhiro Sasaki	5.00
MS	Mike Sweeney	5.00
LW	Larry Walker	5.00

Chasing 500-500

Common Player: —

Code	Player	Price
BB1	Barry Bonds/Dual	40.00
BB2	Barry Bonds/Jsy/600	30.00
BB3	Barry Bonds/Mult/200	75.00

Passport to the Majors

Common Player: 5.00
Jsy 1:84
Bat 1:795

Code	Player	Price
BA	Bobby Abreu/400	6.00
EA	Edgardo Alfonzo	5.00
RA	Roberto Alomar	6.00
WB	Wilson Betemit/325	5.00
BC	Bartolo Colon	5.00
RF	Rafael Furcal	5.00
AG	Andres Galarraga	5.00
JG	Juan Gonzalez	8.00
SH	Shigetoshi Hasegawa	5.00
AJ	Andruw Jones	8.00
CL	Carlos Lee	5.00
JL	Javy Lopez	5.00
PM	Pedro Martinez	10.00
RM	Raul Mondesi	5.00
MO	Magglio Ordonez	5.00
RP	Rafael Palmeiro	8.00
CP	Chan Ho Park	5.00
AP	Albert Pujols/450	40.00
MR	Manny Ramirez	5.00
IR	Ivan Rodriguez	10.00
KS	Kazuhiro Sasaki	5.00
TS	Tsuyoshi Shinjo/400	5.00
AS	Alfonso Soriano/400	10.00
MT	Miguel Tejada/375	5.00
LW	Larry Walker	5.00

Reel Time

Common Player: .50

Inserted 1:8

Code	Player	Price
RT1	Luis Gonzalez	.50
RT2	Derek Jeter	5.00
RT3	Ken Griffey Jr.	2.50
RT4	Alex Rodriguez	5.00
RT5	Barry Bonds	4.00
RT6	Ichiro Suzuki	2.50
RT7	Carlos Delgado	1.00
RT8	Manny Ramirez	1.50
RT9	Mike Piazza	2.50
RT10	Mark McGwire	3.00
RT11	Todd Helton	1.50
RT12	Vladimir Guerrero	1.50
RT13	Jim Thome	1.50
RT14	Rich Aurilia	.50
RT15	Bret Boone	.50
RT16	Roberto Alomar	.75
RT17	Jason Giambi	1.00
RT18	Chipper Jones	2.00
RT19	Albert Pujols	3.00
RT20	Sammy Sosa	2.50

Stadium Shots

Complete Set (10): 15.00
Common Player: 1.00
Inserted 1:12

Code	Player	Price
SS1	Sammy Sosa	2.00
SS2	Manny Ramirez	1.50
SS3	Jason Giambi	1.00
SS4	Mike Piazza	2.00
SS5	Barry Bonds	4.00
SS6	Ken Griffey Jr.	2.00
SS7	Juan Gonzalez	1.50
SS8	Jeff Bagwell	1.50
SS9	Jim Thome	1.00
SS10	Mark McGwire	3.00

Stadium Slices Barrel

Common Player: 15.00

Code	Player	Price
BB	Barry Bonds	75.00
LG	Luis Gonzalez	15.00
AP	Albert Pujols	75.00
IR	Ivan Rodriguez	35.00
BW	Bernie Williams	25.00

Stadium Slices Handle

Common Player: 15.00

Code	Player	Price
BB	Barry Bonds	50.00
LG	Luis Gonzalez	15.00
AP	Albert Pujols	50.00
IR	Ivan Rodriguez	20.00
BW	Bernie Williams	15.00

Stadium Slices Trademar

Common Player: 15.00

Code	Player	Price
BB	Barry Bonds	60.00
LG	Luis Gonzalez	15.00
AP	Albert Pujols	60.00
IR	Ivan Rodriguez	20.00
BW	Bernie Williams	15.00

World Champions Relics

Common Player: 4.00
Jersey 1:106
Bat 1:94
Pants 1:795
Spikes 1:38,400

Code	Player	Price
RA	Roberto Alomar	15.00
MA	Moises Alou	8.00
DB	Don Baylor	8.00
JB	Johnny Bench	20.00
BB	Bert Blyleven	8.00
WB	Wade Boggs	15.00
BRB	Bob Boone	4.00
GB	George Brett	50.00
SB	Scott Brosius	10.00
AB	Al Bumbry	4.00
JC1	Jose Canseco	15.00
JC2	Jose Canseco	15.00

GC1	Gary Carter	15.00
GC2	Gary Carter	15.00
JC	Joe Carter	10.00
RC	Ron Cey	10.00
CC	Chris Chambliss	8.00
DC	Dave Concepcion	8.00
ED	Eric Davis	10.00
BD	Bucky Dent	8.00
GF	George Foster	8.00
PG	Phil Garner	4.00
KG1	Kirk Gibson	10.00
KG2	Kirk Gibson	10.00
TG	Tom Glavine	15.00
KG	Ken Griffey Sr.	10.00
RH	Rickey Henderson/50	80.00
GH	George Hendrick	6.00
KH	Keith Hernandez	15.00
WH	Willie Hernandez	8.00
OH	Orel Hershiser	10.00
RJ	Reggie Jackson	15.00
CWJ	Chipper Jones	15.00
DJ	David Justice	8.00
CK	Chuck Knoblauch	4.00
AL	Al Leiter	8.00
DL	Davey Lopes	8.00
JL	Javy Lopez	8.00
GL	Greg Luzinski	6.00
GM	Greg Maddux	30.00
BM	Bill Madlock	8.00
TLM	Tino Martinez	15.00
HM	Hal McCrae	8.00
FM	Fred McGriff	10.00
PM	Paul Molitor	15.00
TM	Thurman Munson	50.00
EM1	Eddie Murray	15.00
EM2	Eddie Murray	15.00
JO	John Olerud	6.00
PO	Paul O'Neill	15.00
DP	Dave Parker	10.00
TP	Tony Perez	10.00
LVP	Lou Pinella	8.00
JP	Jorge Posada	10.00
KP	Kirby Puckett	20.00
WR	Willie Randolph	10.00
MJS	Mike Schmidt	50.00
MS	Mike Scoscia	10.00
OS	Ozzie Smith	30.00
JS	John Smoltz	10.00
ES	Ed Sprague	4.00
WS	Willie Stargell	15.00
AT	Alan Trammell	10.00
LW	Lou Whitaker	10.00
BW	Bernie Williams	15.00
MW	Mookie Wilson	10.00
DW	Dave Winfield	10.00
FV	Fernando Valenzuela	8.00
JV	Jose Vizcaino	4.00

2003 Stadium Club

		NM/M
Complete Set (125):		30.00
Common Player:		.15
Hobby Pack (6):		1.50
Hobby Box (24):		30.00
1	Rafael Furcal	.15
2	Randy Winn	.15
3	Eric Chavez	.15
4	Fernando Vina	.25
5	Pat Burrell	.25
6	Derek Jeter	2.00
7	Ivan Rodriguez	.65
8	Eric Hinske	.15
9	Roberto Alomar	.40
10	Tony Batista	.15
11	Jacque Jones	.15
12	Alfonso Soriano	.75
13	Omar Vizquel	.25
14	Paul Konerko	.25
15	Shawn Green	.45
16	Garret Anderson	.25
17	Darin Erstad	.25
18	Johnny Damon	.25
19	Juan Gonzalez	.75
20	Luis Gonzalez	.25
21	Sean Burroughs	.15
22	Mark Prior	.75
23	Javier Vazquez	.15
24	Shannon Stewart	.15
25	Jay Gibbons	.15
26	A.J. Pierzynski	.15
27	Vladimir Guerrero	.25
28	Austin Kearns	.25
29	Shea Hillenbrand	.15
30	Magglio Ordonez	.15
31	Mike Cameron	.15
32	Tim Salmon	.25
33	Brian Jordan	.15
34	Moises Alou	.15
35	Rich Aurilia	.15
36	Nick Johnson	.15
37	Junior Spivey	.15
38	Curt Schilling	.40
39	Jose Vidro	.15
40	Orlando Cabrera	.15
41	Jeff Bagwell	.75
42	Mo Vaughn	.15
43	Luis Castillo	.15
44	Vicente Padilla	.15
45	Pedro J. Martinez	.75
46	John Olerud	.15
47	Tom Glavine	.40
48	Torii Hunter	.25
49	J.D. Drew	.25
50	Alex Rodriguez	1.50
51	Randy Johnson	.75
52	Richie Sexson	.15
53	Jimmy Rollins	.25
54	Cristian Guzman	.15
55	Tim Hudson	.25
56	Mark Buehrle	.15
57	Paul LoDuca	.15
58	Aramis Ramirez	.15
59	Todd Helton	.75
60	Lance Berkman	.25
61	Josh Beckett	.25
62	Bret Boone	.15
63	Miguel Tejada	.35
64	Nomar Garciaparra	1.25
65	Albert Pujols	1.50
66	Chipper Jones	1.00
67	Scott Rolen	.65
68	Kerry Wood	.65
69	Jorge Posada	.15
70	Ichiro Suzuki	1.50
71	Jeff Kent	.15
72	David Eckstein	.15
73	Phil Nevin	.15
74	Brian Giles	.15
75	Barry Zito	.25
76	Andruw Jones	.75
77	Jim Thome	.65
78	Robert Fick	.15
79	Rafael Palmeiro	.15
80	Barry Bonds	2.00
81	Gary Sheffield	.40
82	Jim Edmonds	.15
83	Kazuhisa Ishii	.15
84	Jose Hernandez	.15
85	Jason Giambi	.40
86	Mark Mulder	.15
87	Roger Clemens	1.00
88	Troy Glaus	.75
89	Carlos Delgado	.50
90	Mike Sweeney	.15
91	Ken Griffey Jr.	1.25
92	Manny Ramirez	.15
93	Ryan Klesko	.15
94	Larry Walker	.65
95	Adam Dunn	.65
96	Raul Ibanez	.15
97	Preston Wilson	.15
98	Roy Oswalt	.15
99	Sammy Sosa	1.25
100	Mike Piazza	1.25
101	Jose Reyes	.50
102	Ed Rogers	.15
103	Hank Blalock	.75
104	Mark Teixeira	.65
105	Orlando Hudson	.15
106	Drew Henson	.25
107	Joe Mauer	.75
108	Carl Crawford	.15
109	Marlon Byrd	.15
110	Jason Stokes	.15
111	Miguel Cabrera	.50
112	Wilson Betemit	.15
113	Jerome Williams	.15
114	Walter Young	.15
115	Juan Camacho RC	.15
116	Chris Duncan RC	.50
117	Franklin Gutierrez RC	3.00
118	Adam LaRoche	.50
119	Manuel Ramirez RC	.50
120	Il Kim RC	.50
121	Wayne Lydon RC	.50
122	Daryl Clark RC	.50
123	Sean Pierce	.15
124	Andy Marte RC	3.00
125	Matthew Peterson RC	.75

Photographer's Proof

Stars (1-100):	4-8X
Cards (101-125):	2-4X
Production 299 Sets	

Royal Gold

Stars:	1-30X
Inserted 1:1	

Beam Team

		NM/M
Complete Set (20):		50.00
Common Player:		1.00
Inserted 1:12		
BT1	Larry Walker	1.00
BT2	Miguel Tejada	1.50
BT3	Ichiro Suzuki	5.00
BT4	Sammy Sosa	5.00
BT5	Ivan Rodriguez	2.50
BT6	Alex Rodriguez	6.00
BT7	Mike Piazza	5.00
BT8	Jeff Kent	1.00
BT9	Chipper Jones	4.00
BT10	Derek Jeter	8.00
BT11	Todd Helton	1.00
BT12	Vladimir Guerrero	3.00
BT13	Shawn Green	1.50
BT14	Brian Giles	1.00
BT15	Jason Giambi	2.00
BT16	Nomar Garciaparra	2.00
BT17	Adam Dunn	2.00
BT18	Carlos Delgado	1.50
BT19	Barry Bonds	8.00
BT20	Lance Berkman	1.00

Born In The USA

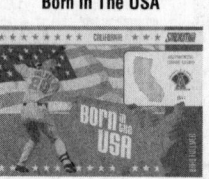

		NM/M
Common Player:		5.00
Jerseys Inserted 1:52		
Bats Inserted 1:76		
RA	Rich Aurilia/Jsy	5.00
JB	Jeff Bagwell/Jsy	12.00
CB	Craig Biggio/Jsy	8.00
BB	Bret Boone/Jsy	5.00
AB	A.J. Burnett/Jsy	5.00
JNB	Jeromy Burnitz/Bat	6.00
PB	Pat Burrell/Bat	10.00
SB	Sean Burroughs/Bat	6.00
EC	Eric Chavez/Jsy	6.00
TC	Tony Clark/Bat	5.00
JD	Johnny Damon/Bat	8.00
JDD	J.D. Drew/Bat	5.00
AD	Adam Dunn/Bat	12.00
JE	Jim Edmonds/Jsy	8.00
CF	Cliff Floyd/Bat	5.00
BF	Brad Fullmer/Bat	5.00
NG	Nomar Garciaparra/Bat	20.00
LG	Luis Gonzalez/Bat	12.00
MG	Mark Grace/Jsy	12.00
SG	Shawn Green/Bat	6.00
TJH	Toby Hall	5.00
JH	Josh Hamilton/Bat	10.00
TH	Todd Helton/Bat	8.00
RH	Rickey Henderson/Bat	12.00
RJ	Randy Johnson/Bat	8.00
CJ	Chipper Jones/Jsy	12.00
RK	Ryan Klesko/Bat	5.00
PK	Paul Konerko/Bat	8.00
BL	Barry Larkin/Jsy	10.00
TRL	Travis Lee/Bat	5.00
TL	Terrence Long/Jsy	5.00
GM	Greg Maddux/Jsy	15.00
TM	Tino Martinez/Bat	10.00
WM	Willie Mays/Bat	40.00
EM	Eric Milton/Jsy	6.00
JO	John Olerud/Jsy	6.00
CP	Corey Patterson/Bat	8.00
MP	Mike Piazza/Jsy	15.00
AR	Alex Rodriguez/Bat	15.00
SR	Scott Rolen/Bat	15.00
RS	Richie Sexson/Bat	6.00
GS	Gary Sheffield/Bat	8.00
JS	John Smoltz/Bat	8.00
FT	Frank Thomas/Bat	8.00
JT	Jim Thome/Jsy	15.00
MV	Mo Vaughn/Bat	6.00
RV	Robin Ventura/Bat	8.00
MW	Matt Williams/Bat	8.00
PW	Preston Wilson/Jsy	5.00
KW	Kerry Wood/Bat	10.00

Clubhouse Exclusive

		NM/M
Jersey Inserted 1:488		
Jersey & Bat 1:2,073		
Jersey, Bat & Spikes 1:2,750		
CE1	Albert Pujols/Jsy	15.00
CE2	Albert Pujols/Bat/Jsy	35.00
CE3	Albert Pujols/Jsy/ Bat/Spike	100.00

Co-Signers

		NM/M
HTA Exclusive		
MI	Masanori Murakami, Kazuhisa Ishii	180.00
AM	Hank Aaron, Willie Mays	400.00

License To Drive

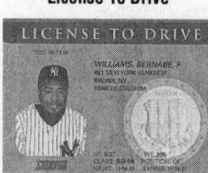

		NM/M
Common Player:		6.00
Inserted 1:98		
RA	Roberto Alomar	8.00
MA	Moises Alou	6.00
AB	Adrian Beltre	6.00
LB	Lance Berkman	6.00
EC	Eric Chavez	6.00
AD	Adam Dunn	8.00
NG	Nomar Garciaparra	15.00
JG	Juan Gonzalez	8.00
LG	Luis Gonzalez	6.00
SG	Shawn Green	8.00
TH	Todd Helton	10.00
AJ	Andruw Jones	10.00
CJ	Chipper Jones	12.00
TM	Tino Martinez	6.00
RP	Rafael Palmeiro	6.00
MP	Mike Piazza	15.00
AP	Albert Pujols	25.00
ANR	Aramis Ramirez	6.00
AR	Alex Rodriguez	20.00
IR	Ivan Rodriguez	8.00
SR	Scott Rolen	10.00
GS	Gary Sheffield	8.00
FT	Frank Thomas	10.00
LW	Larry Walker	6.00
BW	Bernie Williams	6.00

MLB Match-Ups

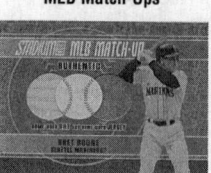

		NM/M
Inserted 1:485		
BB	Bret Boone	15.00
TH	Todd Helton	15.00
AJ	Andruw Jones	12.00
GM	Greg Maddux	15.00
AP	Albert Pujols	30.00

Stadium Shots

		NM/M
Complete Set (10):		25.00
Common Player:		1.00
Inserted 1:24		
SS1	Lance Berkman	1.00
SS2	Barry Bonds	6.00
SS3	Jason Giambi	2.50
SS4	Shawn Green	1.50
SS5	Vladimir Guerrero	3.00
SS6	Paul Konerko	1.00
SS7	Mike Piazza	4.50
SS8	Alex Rodriguez	6.00
SS9	Sammy Sosa	4.50
SS10	Jim Thome	2.00

Stadium Slices Handle

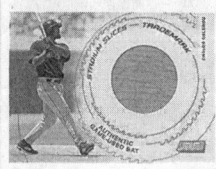

		NM/M
Common Player:		5.00
Inserted 1:237		
Trademarks:		1-1.5X
Inserted 1:415		
Barrels:		1.5-2X
Inserted 1:550		
RA	Roberto Alomar	15.00
CD	Carlos Delgado	8.00
NG	Nomar Garciaparra	20.00
TH	Todd Helton	8.00
AJ	Andruw Jones	8.00
RP	Rafael Palmeiro	8.00
MP	Mike Piazza	15.00
AP	Albert Pujols	25.00
AR	Alex Rodriguez	15.00
GS	Gary Sheffield	10.00

World Stage

		NM/M
Common Player:		5.00
Jerseys Inserted 1:118		
Bats Inserted 1:809		
AB	Adrian Beltre/Jsy	6.00
KI	Kazuhisa Ishii/Jsy	5.00
BK	Byung-Hyun Kim/Jsy	5.00
HN	Hideo Nomo/Bat	8.00
AP	Albert Pujols/Jsy	15.00
IR	Ivan Rodriguez/Jsy	8.00
KS	Kazuhiro Sasaki/Jsy	5.00
TS	Tsuyoshi Shinjo/Bat	5.00
AS	Alfonso Soriano/Bat	15.00
MT	Miguel Tejada/Jsy	8.00

2008 Stadium Club

Common Player (1-100):	1.00
Common SP 999:	2.00
Common RC (1-150):	1.50
Common RC SP 999:	2.00
Common RC Auto. (151-185):	8.00
Pack (5):	20.00
Box (12):	200.00

1	Chase Utley	2.50
2	Tim Lincecum	2.00
3	Ryan Zimmerman/999	2.50
4	Todd Helton	1.50
5	Russell Martin	1.00
6	Curtis Granderson/999	2.50
7	Torii Hunter	1.50
8	Mark Teixeira	1.50
9	Alfonso Soriano/999	2.50
10	C.C. Sabathia	2.00
11	David Ortiz	2.00
12	Miguel Tejada/999	2.00
13	Alex Rodriguez	4.00
14	Prince Fielder	2.00
15	Alex Gordon/999	3.00
16	Jake Peavy	1.50
17	B.J. Upton	2.00
18	Michael Young/999	2.00
19	Jason Bay	1.00
20	Jorge Posada	2.00
21	Jacoby Ellsbury/999	2.50
22	Nick Markakis	1.50
23	Tom Glavine	1.50
24	Justin Upton/999	3.00
25	Edinson Volquez	2.00
26	Miguel Cabrera	2.00
27	Carlos Lee/999	2.00
28	Ryan Church	1.00
29	Delmon Young	1.00
30	Carlos Quentin/999	2.50
31	Carl Crawford	1.50
32	Roy Halladay	1.50
33	Brandon Webb/999	2.50
34	Brian Roberts	1.50
35	Ken Griffey Jr.	4.00
36	Troy Tulowitzki/999	2.50
37	Hanley Ramirez	2.50
38	Hunter Pence	2.50
39	Johnny Damon/999	2.50
40	Eric Chavez	1.00
41	Adrian Gonzalez	1.50
42	Carlos Pena/999	2.50
43	Felix Hernandez	1.50
44	Magglio Ordonez	1.50
45	Josh Beckett/999	3.00
46	Fausto Carmona	1.00
47	Chris Young	1.00
48	John Lackey/999	2.00
49	John Smoltz	1.50
50	David Wright	3.00
51	Ichiro Suzuki/999	6.00
52	Vernon Wells	1.00
53	Josh Hamilton	3.00
54	Albert Pujols/999	8.00
55	Dustin Pedroia	3.00
56	Garrett Atkins	1.00
57	Roy Oswalt/999	2.00
58	Jose Reyes	2.50
59	Derek Jeter	5.00
60	Scott Kazmir/999	2.00
61	Vladimir Guerrero	1.50
62	Joba Chamberlain	3.00
63	Kevin Youkilis/999	3.00
64	Victor Martinez	2.00
65	Nick Swisher	1.00
66	Carlos Beltran/999	3.00
67	Joe Mauer	1.50
68	Gary Sheffield	1.50
69	Cole Hamels/999	3.00
70	Brian McCann	2.50
71	Grady Sizemore	2.50
72	Robinson Cano/999	2.50
73	Greg Maddux	3.00
74	Rich Harden	1.00
75	Ryan Howard/999	5.00
76	Johan Santana	2.00
77	Dan Uggla	1.00
78	Justin Verlander/999	3.00
79	Derrek Lee	1.50
80	Ryan Braun	3.00
81	Lance Berkman/999	2.50
82	Manny Ramirez	2.00
83	Chipper Jones	3.00
84	Daisuke Matsuzaka/999	5.00
85	Matt Holliday	1.50
86	Justin Morneau	1.50
87	Jimmy Rollins/999	3.00
88	Hideki Matsui	2.00
89	Pedro Martinez	1.50
90	Carlos Zambrano/999	2.50
91	Jackie Robinson	2.50
92	Mickey Mantle	6.00
93	Ty Cobb/999	5.00
94	Joe DiMaggio/Cut-out	50.00
95	Honus Wagner	2.00
96	Babe Ruth/999	5.00
97	Nolan Ryan	6.00
98	Roberto Clemente	5.00
99	Ted Williams/999	8.00
100	Tom Seaver	2.00
101	Luke Hochevar RC	2.00
101	Luke Hochevar/999 RC	4.00
102	Daric Barton (RC)	1.50
102	Daric Barton/999 (RC)	2.00
103	Nick Adenhart (RC)	1.50
103	Nick Adenhart/999 (RC)	2.00
104	Gregor Blanco (RC)	1.50
104	Gregor Blanco/999 (RC)	2.00
105	Chris Carter (RC)	1.50
105	Chris Carter/999 (RC)	2.00
106	Eric Hurley (RC)	1.50
106	Eric Hurley/999 (RC)	2.00
107	Clayton Kershaw RC	3.00
107	Clayton Kershaw/999 RC	5.00
108	Evan Longoria RC	10.00
108	Evan Longoria/999 RC	12.00
109	Garrett Mock (RC)	1.50
109	Garrett Mock/999 (RC)	2.00
110	David Purcey (RC)	1.50
110	David Purcey/999 (RC)	2.00
111	Ryan Tucker (RC)	1.50
111	Ryan Tucker/999 (RC)	2.00
112	Joey Votto (RC)	4.00
112	Joey Votto/999 (RC)	5.00
113	Jeff Clement (RC)	1.50
113	Jeff Clement/999 (RC)	2.00
114	Michael Aubrey (RC)	1.50
114	Michael Aubrey/999 RC	3.00
115	Brandon Boggs (RC)	1.50
115	Brandon Boggs/999 (RC)	2.00
116	Johnny Cueto (RC)	1.50
116	Johnny Cueto/999 RC	3.00
117	Hernan Iribarren (RC)	1.50
117	Hernan Iribarren/ 999 (RC)	
118	Masahide Kobayashi RC	1.50
118	Masahide Kobayashi/ 999 RC	
119	Jed Lowrie (RC)	2.00
119	Jed Lowrie/999 (RC)	4.00
120	Greg Reynolds (RC)	2.00
120	Greg Reynolds/999 RC	2.00
121	Matt Tolbert RC	1.50
121	Matt Tolbert/999 RC	2.00
122	Jonathan Herrera RC	1.50
122	Jonathan Herrera/999 RC	2.00
123	J.R. Towles (RC)	1.50
123	J.R. Towles/999 (RC)	3.00
124	Armando Galarraga (RC)	1.50
124	Armando Galarraga/ 999 RC	3.00
125	Josh Banks (RC)	1.50
125	Josh Banks/999 (RC)	2.00
126	Mitch Boggs RC	1.50
126	Mitch Boggs/999 RC	2.00
127	Blake DeWitt RC	1.50
127	Blake DeWitt/999 (RC)	4.00
128	Carlos Gonzalez (RC)	3.0
128	Carlos Gonzalez/ 999 (RC)	5.00
129	Elliot Johnson (RC)	1.50
129	Elliot Johnson/999 (RC)	2.00

130	Brian Barton RC	1.50
130	Brian Barton/999 RC	2.00
131	Sean Rodriguez (RC)	1.50
131	Sean Rodriguez/999 (RC)	2.00
132	Kosuke Fukudome RC	4.00
133	Kosuke Fukudome/999 RC	6.00
134	Wladimir Balentien (RC)	1.50
134	Wladimir Balentien/999 (RC)	2.00
135	Jeff Niemann (RC)	1.50
135	Jeff Niemann/999 (RC)	2.00
136	Jay Bruce (RC)	4.00
136	Jay Bruce/999 (RC)	6.00
137	Brandon Jones RC	2.00
137	Brandon Jones/999 RC	3.00
138	Justin Masterson RC	5.00
138	Justin Masterson/999 RC	8.00
139	Jayson Nix (RC)	1.50
139	Jayson Nix/999 (RC)	2.00
140	Max Scherzer RC	2.00
140	Max Scherzer/999 RC	3.00
141	Mike Aviles RC	2.00
141	Mike Aviles/999 RC	3.00
142	Greg Smith RC	1.50
142	Greg Smith/999 RC	2.00
143	Nick Blackburn RC	2.00
143	Nick Blackburn/999 RC	3.00
144	Justin Ruggiano RC	1.50
144	Justin Ruggiano/999 RC	2.00
145	Clay Buchholz (RC)	2.00
145	Clay Buchholz/999 (RC)	3.00
146	German Duran RC	2.00
146	German Duran/999 RC	3.00
147	Radhames Liz RC	1.50
147	Radhames Liz/999 RC	2.00
148	Chris Perez RC	1.50
148	Chris Perez/999 RC	2.50
149	Hiroki Kuroda RC	1.50
149	Hiroki Kuroda/999 RC	2.50
150	Gregorio Petit (RC)	1.50
150	Gregorio Petit/999 (RC)	2.50
151	Emmanuel Burriss/ Auto. RC	10.00
152	Elliot Johnson/Auto. (RC)	8.00
153	Jonathan Van Every/ Auto. RC	8.00
154	Darren O'Day/Auto. RC	8.00
155	Matt Joyce/Auto. RC	15.00
156	Burke Badenhop/ Auto. RC	8.00
157	Brent Lillibridge/ Auto. (RC)	8.00
158	Johnny Cueto/Auto. RC	15.00
159	Jeff Niemann/ Auto. (RC)	10.00
160	John Bowker/ Auto. (RC)	10.00
161	Brandon Boggs/ Auto. (RC)	8.00
162	Justin Masterson/ Auto. RC	25.00
163	Masahide Kobayashi/ Auto. RC	10.00
164	Nick Adenhart/ Auto. (RC)	10.00
165	Chris Perez/Auto. RC	10.00
166	Gregor Blanco/ Auto. (RC)	8.00
167	Travis Denker/Auto. RC	10.00
168	Jeff Clement/Auto. (RC)	10.00
169	Evan Longoria/Auto. RC	60.00
170	Greg Smith/Auto. RC	10.00
171	Jay Bruce/Auto. (RC)	30.00
172	Brian Barton/Auto. (RC)	10.00
173	Max Scherzer/Auto. RC	20.00
174	Blake DeWitt/Auto. (RC)	15.00
175	Jed Lowrie/Auto. RC	20.00
176	Clayton Kershaw/ Auto. RC	20.00
177	Jonathan Albaladejo/ Auto. (RC)	10.00
178	Josh Banks/Auto. (RC)	10.00
179	Brian Horwitz/Auto. RC	10.00
180	Micah Hoffpauir/ Auto. RC	15.00
181	Robinzon Diaz/ Auto. (RC)	8.00
182	Nick Evans/Auto. RC	15.00
183	Joe Mather/Auto. RC	15.00
184	Danny Herrera/Auto. RC	10.00
185	Eugenio Velez/Auto. RC	10.00

1st Day Issue

1st Day (1-100):	1-1.5X
1st Day RC (101-150):	1-1.5X
1st Day 999 SP:	.75-1X
Production 599 Sets	

Printing Plates

No Pricing
Production one set per color.

Beam Team Autographs

	NM/M
Common Auto.:	8.00
Black & White:	1-1.25X
Production 99 Sets	
Gold:	1-1.25X
Production 50 Sets	
Platinum:	No Pricing
Production One Set	
Printing Plates:	No Pricing
Production one set per color.	
AG	Adrian Gonzalez	15.00
BH	Brad Hawpe	10.00
BP	Brandon Phillips	8.00
BT	Brad Thompson	8.00

JJ	Jair Jurrjens	10.00
GC	Gary Carter	15.00
CCR	Callix Crabbe	8.00
CC	Carl Crawford	15.00
CD	Carlos Delgado	20.00
ME	Mark Ellis	8.00
TG	Tom Gorzelanny	8.00
JGU	Jeremy Guthrie	10.00
DH	Dan Haren	10.00
FL	Francisco Liriano	15.00
MK	Mark Kotsay	8.00
CM	Carlos Marmol	20.00
MN	Mike Napoli	8.00
JP	Jonathan Papelbon	25.00
JR	Jose Reyes	30.00
FS	Freddy Sanchez	10.00
GS	Gary Sheffield	15.00
GSM	Greg Smith	10.00
CP	Carlos Pena	15.00
JB	Jason Bartlett	12.00
JGA	Joey Gathright	8.00
MT	Marcus Thames	8.00
CV	Claudio Vargas	8.00
JC	Jack Cust	10.00
RC	Robinson Cano	15.00
GD	German Duran	8.00
CF	Chone Figgins	10.00
JH	Josh Hamilton	25.00
TJ	Todd Jones	10.00
JL	John Lackey	10.00
CM	Craig Monroe	8.00
RP	Ronny Paulino	8.00
FP	Felix Pie	10.00
JP	Johnny Podres	15.00
ER	Edwar Ramirez	8.00
NR	Nate Robertson	8.00
KS	Kevin Slowey	15.00
DS	Darryl Strawberry	15.00
CW	C.J. Wilson	8.00
WB	Wilson Betemit	8.00
GP	Glen Perkins	8.00
LM	Lastings Milledge	10.00
CVI	Carlos Villanueva	8.00
JCR	Jesse Crain	8.00
JN	Jayson Nix	8.00
YP	Yusmeiro Petit	10.00
JS	Jeff Salazar	8.00
MT	Matt Tolbert	10.00
DY	Delwyn Young	8.00

Ceremonial Cuts

	NM/M
Production 199 Sets	
Photographer's Proof Blue:	1-1.2X
Production 99 Sets	
Photo. Proof Gold:	1-1.2X
Production 50 Sets	
Photo. Proof Platinum:	No Pricing
Production One Set	
MO	Mel Ott	15.00
JR	Jackie Robinson	20.00
JF	Jimmie Foxx	20.00
TC	Ty Cobb	20.00
RH	Rogers Hornsby	15.00
TW	Ted Williams	20.00
GB	George Bush	15.00
BR	Babe Ruth	35.00
LG	Lou Gehrig	35.00

Photographer's Proof Blue

Blue (1-100):	1-2.5X
Blue SP 999:	1-1.5X
Blue RC (101-150):	1-1.5X
Blue Auto.:	1-1.2X
Production 99 Sets	

Photographer's Proof Gold

Gold (1-100):	2-3X
Gold SP 999:	1-2X
Gold RC (101-150):	2-3X
Gold Auto.:	1-1.5X
Production 50 Sets	

Photographer's Proof Platinum

Production One Set

Sketch Cards

No Pricing
Multiple versions of each card

Stadium Slices

	NM/M
Production 89-428	
Photo. Proof Blue:	1-1.2X
Production 25-99	
Photo. Proof Gold:	1-1.2X
Production 5-50	
No pricing prod. less than 25.	
Photo. Proof Platinum:	No Pricing
Production One Set	
MM	Mickey Mantle/89	60.00
TM	Thurman Munson/89	60.00
AR	Alex Rodriguez/89	50.00
RJ	Reggie Jackson/89	40.00
YB	Yogi Berra/89	40.00
MR	Mariano Rivera/428	30.00
HM	Hideki Matsui/428	20.00
IS	Ichiro Suzuki/428	20.00
DM	Daisuke Matsuzaka/428	20.00
AP	Albert Pujols/428	20.00
DO	David Ortiz/428	15.00
GG	"Goose" Gossage/89	30.00
JT	Joe Torre/89	40.00
LP	Lou Piniella/89	20.00
WF	Whitey Ford/89	35.00

Triumvirate Memorabilia Autographs

	NM/M
Common Auto.:	
Production 99 unless noted.	
Black:	No Pricing
Production One Set	
AP	Albert Pujols/99	200.00
DO	David Ortiz	50.00
MO	Magglio Ordonez/49	20.00
TH	Todd Helton	25.00
MH	Matt Holliday	40.00
CC	Carl Crawford	20.00
AD	Adam Dunn	20.00
JF	Jeff Francoeur	25.00
VG	Vladimir Guerrero	40.00
TH	Torii Hunter	25.00
SK	Scott Kazmir	25.00
CL	Carlos Lee	15.00
DL	Derrek Lee	25.00
RM	Russell Martin	20.00
JM	Justin Morneau	35.00
JP	Jake Peavy	25.00
AR	Aramis Ramirez	30.00
HR	Hanley Ramirez	40.00
ARI	Alex Rios	25.00
MR	Mariano Rivera	100.00
AS	Alfonso Soriano	35.00
MT	Miguel Tejada	15.00
TT	Troy Tulowitzki	20.00
BU	B.J. Upton	25.00
JU	Justin Upton	30.00
CW	Chien-Ming Wang	100.00
VW	Vernon Wells	20.00
JPA	Jonathan Papelbon	35.00

1983 Star '83

Star's first baseball card issue was a 15-card tribute to Mike Schmidt, subtitled "Ten Years of Excellence." On the cards' fronts, Schmidt is shown in various posed and game-action photos, surrounded by a red border. Backs tell his story in words and numbers. The cards are the standard 2-1/2" x 3-1/2" and were sold only as complete sets through hobby dealers. Single cards are not listed because the sets are seldom broken for individual card sales.

	NM/M
Complete Set:	6.00

1984 Star '84

YAZ CHECKLIST

Star broadened the selection of its single-player collectors' issues in 1984 and adopted a new design which it used with little variation for several years. Most cards were issued in panels of three, perforated for easy separation. Each set has posed and game-action photos surrounded by colorful borders. Team logos are in a circle at lower-left; "Star '84" is in an inset at the photo's upper-right. Backs within a set feature stats, career highlights personal information and, sometimes, puzzle pieces.

		NM/M
1-24	George Brett	7.50

1-24	Steve Carlton	6.00
1-36	Steve Garvey (7,500 Sets)	3.50
1-36	Darryl Strawberry	2.00
	(Not issued in panels.)	4.00
1-24	Carl Yastrzemski	
	(First card autographed, edition of 500.)	20.00

1985 Star Nolan Ryan Promo

NOLAN RYAN "Baseball's K-King"

Issued to promote a set that was never issued, this promo card has on back logos and copyright information for an NBA issue.

	NM/M
Nolan Ryan	15.00

1985 Star '85

OAKLAND ATHLETICS
WORLD SERIES RECORDS !

Star maintained the basic format of 1984 for its sole single-player issue of 1985. The 36-card set of Reggie Jackson has portrait and action photos surrounded by colorful borders. The logo of the A's, Orioles or Yankees appears in a circle at lower-left on front, with a "Star '85" logo at upper-right. Backs have a mix of stats, personal data and career highlights. Cards were issued in a dozen three-card panels, perforated between the cards. Production was reported as 6,000 sets, with 500 of them signed and numbered by Jackson.

	NM/M
Complete Set (36):	5.00

1986 Star Promos

Several of the 1986 Star single-player series were introduced with the issue of a promo card, different on their backs, but otherwise similar in appearance to the regular cards.

		NM/M
Complete Set (7):		55.00
Common Player:		2.50
(1)	Rod Carew (Ad back.)	1.50
(2)	Don Mattingly (White card.) (Blank back.)	2.50
(3)	Don Mattingly (Yellow sticker.) (Blank back.)	3.00
(4)	Dale Murphy (Ad back.)	3.50
(5)	Jim Rice (Blank back.)	2.50
(6)	Nolan Ryan (Ad back.)	15.00
(7)	Tom Seaver (Name on back.)	2.00

1986 Star '86

The basic format of previous years' issues was retained for Star's single-player sets of 1986. Player poses and game-action photos are presented on the front, bordered in a bright color usually associated with the player's team. In standard 2-1/2 x 3-1/2 size, the cards have a circle at lower-left with the player's name - first only or first and last. Infringing on the photo is the notation, "Star '86." Backs have stats, career highlights, personal data or puzzle

STAR '86
WALLY
WALLY JOYNER CHECKLIST

pieces. Most sets were issued in three-card perforated panels. Some of the player sets can also be found in a glossy edition and/or a blank-back sticker version. Single cards are seldom offered and are not listed here.

		NM/M
1-24	Wade Boggs	2.00
1-24	Wade Boggs (Glossy set.)	2.00
(1-24)	Wade Boggs (Sticker set.)	2.00
1-15	Jose Canseco (Not issued in panels.)	3.00
1-15	Jose Canseco/Auto. (Edition of 500.)	17.50
1-15	Jose Canseco (Glossy set.)	3.00
(1-15)	Jose Canseco (Sticker set.)	1.50
1-24	Rod Carew	1.50
1-15	Wally Joyner (Not issued in panels.)	1.00
1-15	Wally Joyner/Auto. (Edition of 500.)	15.00
1-15	Wally Joyner (Glossy set.)	1.50
(1-15)	Wally Joyner (Sticker set.)	2.50
1-24	Don Mattingly	5.00
1-24	Don Mattingly (Glossy set.)	7.50
(1-24)	Don Mattingly (Sticker set.)	5.00
1-24	Dale Murphy	5.00
1-20	Jim Rice (Four-card panels.)	1.00
1-20	Jim Rice/Auto. (Edition of 500.)	40.00
1-20	Jim Rice (Glossy set.)	1.50
(1-20)	Jim Rice (Sticker set.)	1.50
1-24	Nolan Ryan (4,000 Sets)	9.00
1-24	Tom Seaver (8,000 Sets)	3.50

1987 Star Promos

Most of Star's single-player sets issued for 1987 were preceded by the issue of blank-backed promo cards in a nearly identical format to the issued version.

		NM/M
Complete Set (6):		8.75
Common Player:		1.00
(1)	Steve Carlton	2.50
(2)	Gary Carter	2.00
(3)	Roger Clemens	4.00
(4)	Keith Hernandez	1.00
(5)	Tim Raines	1.00
(6)	Fernando Valenzuela	1.00

1987 Star '87

STAR '87
ROGER
ROGER CLEMENS COMPLETE 1986 STATS

The single-player sets issued by Star in 1987 retain the basic format used since 1984. Standard size (2-1/2" x 3-1/2") cards were printed singly, rather than in panels, but the design remained virtually unchanged. Posed and action photos are surrounded by a colorful border which protrudes into the photo at upper-right with the logo "Star '87." At lower-left is a circle with the player's first name, or, in the

case of Fernando Valenzuela, the team logo. Backs have stats, personal data or career highlights. Sets were also issued in a limited glossy version and/or as blank-back stickers. Single cards are usually not sold, so are not listed here.

		NM/M
		17.50
(1-5)	Wade Boggs, Jose Canseco (Unnumbered)	3.00
(1-5)	Wade Boggs, Jose Canseco (Glossy set.) (Unnumbered))	4.50
1-14	Steve Carlton (Glossy version only.)	3.50
1-14	Gary Carter	2.00
1-14	Gary Carter (Glossy set.)	2.25
(1-10)	Gary Carter (Sticker set.) (Different photos.)	2.50
1-12	Roger Clemens (8,500 Regular Sets; 500 Autographed)	2.00
1-12	Roger Clemens (Glossy; 1,000 Sets)	2.50
(1-5)	Roger Clemens (Update)(Unnumbered)	3.00
(1-5)	Roger Clemens (Update, glossy). (Unnumbered)	4.50
1-13	Keith Hernandez (8,500 Regular Sets, 500 Autographed)	1.25
1-13	Keith Hernandez (Glossy; 1,000 Sets)	2.25
(1-6)	Don Mattingly (Unnumbered, five blank-back cards, one w/1986 stats.)	3.00
(1-6)	Don Mattingly (Glossy) (Unnumbered, five cards blank-back, one w/1986 stats.)	4.50
1-12	Tim Raines (8,500 Regular Sets; 500 Autographed)	1.00
1-12	Tim Raines (Glossy; 1,000 Sets)	1.50
1-13	Fernando Valenzuela (8,500 Regular Sets, 500 Autographed)	1.50
1-13	Fernando Valenzuela (Glossy; 1,000 Sets)	2.25
(1-10)	Fernando Valenzuela (Sticker set.) (Different photos.)	

1988-89 Star Promos

STAR
TEXAS
NOLAN RYAN Promo

The lengthy series of 11-card sets issued by Star in 1988-89 in the company's "new" format included one promo card for nearly every player's set. The promos are blank-backed but otherwise similar in design to the regular cards.

		NM/M
Complete Set (40):		32.50
Common Player:		.75
(1)	Alomar Brothers (Roberto Alomar)	.75
(2)	Sandy Alomar Jr. (Alomar Brothers)	.75
(3)	Sandy Alomar Jr.	.75
(4)	Wade Boggs	2.00
(5)	Jose Canseco (Blue borders.)	1.50
(6)	Jose Conseco (Canseco) (Yellow borders.)	1.50
(7)	Jose Canseco (Bay Bombers Series)	1.50
(8)	Will Clark (Purple/Yellow)	1.50
(9)	Will Clark (Clark/Mitchell set, gold borders.)	.75
(10)	Will Clark (Bay Bombers Series)	1.50
(11)	David Cone	.75
(12)	Dwight Gooden	.75
(13)	Tom Gordon	.75
(14)	Mark Grace (1,300 issued)	1.00
(15)	Mike Greenwell (Blue borders.)	.75
(16)	Mike Greenwell (Pink borders.)	.75
(17)	Ken Griffey Jr. (White-back set, blue/white borders.)	2.50

(18) Ken Griffey Jr. (Yellow-back set, yellow borders.) 3.50
(19) Orel Hershiser .75
(20) Sam Horn .75
(21) Bo Jackson .75
(22) Gregg Jefferies (Blue-border set, orange borders.) .75
(23) Gregg Jefferies (Orange-border set, dark blue borders, misspelled Greg.) .75
(24) Gregg Jefferies (Pink-border set, light blue borders, misspelled Greg.) .75
(25) Ricky Jordan .75
(26) Don Mattingly 2.00
(27) Kevin McReynolds .75
(28) Kevin Mitchell (Clark/Mitchell set, gold borders.) .75
(29) Kevin Mitchell (Orange borders.) .75
(30) Matt Nokes (Yellow borders, glossy.) .75
(31) Kirby Puckett 1.75
(32) Nolan Ryan 2.50
(33) Benito Santiago .75
(34) Gary Sheffield .75
(35) Darryl Strawberry (Blue-border set, pink borders.) .75
(36) Darryl Strawberry (Purple-border set, orange borders.) .75
(37) Alan Trammell .75
(38) Robin Ventura .75
(39) Jerome Walton (Regular set, borders in two shades of blue.) .75
(40) Jerome Walton/Portrait (Glossy set, solid blue borders.) .75

1988-1989 Star

KIRBY PUCKETT HIT MACHINE

Late in 1988 Star introduced a new format for its single-player card sets, which it carried forward into 1989. Sets were standardized at 11 cards in the 2-1/2" x 3-1/2" format. Fronts feature posed and game-action photos that are bordered by graduating shades of a particular color, or two different colors, going from dark at top to light at bottom, or vice versa. (The first Gregg Jefferies set is an exception, having the same shade of blue on all borders.) Backs may be printed in any of a variety of colors on white, yellow, pink or green backgrounds. Stats, personal data, career highlights and team logos are found on back. Sets may carry either a 1988 or 1989 copyright date. Because the sets are seldom broken up for singles sales, individual cards are not listed here. The number of player sets for which glossy versions were issued is uncertain. Existing glossy sets should retail for 2-5X the regular version, depending on player popularity.

		NM/M
1-11	Alomar Brothers (Roberto Alomar, Sandy Alomar Jr.)	1.50
1-11	Sandy Alomar Jr.	1.50
1-11	Bay Bombers Series (Jose Canseco) (Solid green borders.)	3.00
1-11	Bay Bombers Series (Will Clark) (Solid orange borders.)	1.75
1-11	Wade Boggs (Solid red borders.)	4.00
1-11	Jose Canseco (Error set - "Conseco.")	5.00
1-11	Jose Canseco (Correct, dark green borders, white name.)	3.00
1-11	Jose Canseco (Correct, light green borders, green name.)	3.00
1-11	Will Clark	3.00
1-11	Will Clark, Kevin Mitchell	1.50
1-11	David Cone	1.50
1-11	Dwight Gooden	1.50
1-11	Tom Gordon	1.50
1-11	Mark Grace (Solid orange borders; 6,500 sets.)	1.00
1-11	Mark Grace/Auto. (500 sets.)	5.00
1-11	Mike Greenwell (Purple borders.)	1.50
1-11	Mike Greenwell (Red borders.)	1.50
1-11	Ken Griffey Jr. (White backs.)	7.50
1-11	Ken Griffey Jr. (Yellow backs, different photos.)	7.50
1-11	Orel Hershiser (8,000 Regular Sets)	1.50
1-11	Orel Hershiser (Glossy - 250 sets.)	2.25
1-11	Sam Horn (Solid blue borders; 4,000 sets.)	1.00
1-11	Sam Horn (Glossy - 1,000 sets.)	1.50
1-11	Bo Jackson	1.50
1-11	Gregg Jefferies (Blue borders; 8,000 sets.)	1.50
1-11	Gregg Jefferies (Orange borders.)	1.50
1-11	Gregg Jefferies (Pink borders.)	1.50
1-11	Ron Jones	1.00
1-11	Ricky Jordan (8,000 Sets)	1.00
1-11	Ricky Jordan (Glossy - 250 sets.)	2.00
1-11	Ricky Jones/Auto. (500 sets.)	3.00
1-11	Kevin McReynolds (8,000 Sets)	1.50
1-11	Kevin McReynolds (Glossy - 250 sets.)	2.25
1-11	Kevin Mitchell	1.50
1-11	Matt Nokes (3,500 sets, each bag serial numbered)	1.25
1-11	Kirby Puckett	4.50
---	Pete Rose (Blank-back, Reds.)	15.00
1-11	Nolan Ryan (Pink backs only.)	6.00
1-11	Benito Santiago	1.50
1-11	Gary Sheffield	1.50
1-11	Darryl Strawberry (Blue borders.)	1.00
1-11	Darryl Strawberry (Purple borders.)	1.00
1-11	Alan Trammell (#4 Misspelled Trammel.)	1.50
1-11	Robin Ventura	1.50
1-11	Jerome Walton	1.50
1-11	Jerome Walton (Glossy, borders one shade of blue.)	1.50

1988-92 Star Ad Cards

KEVIN MAAS NEW YORK Ad Card

These cards were distributed to give dealers and collectors basic information about Star's baseball issues. Fronts look like contemporary Star cards, but most (not all) have the notation "Ad Card" beneath the city name at lower-right. Backs have an advertising message with general information except for Horn and Jefferies, whose ads are specific to ordering those player sets. Some cards exist in both regular and glossy finish. Except for the 1992s, the Ad Cards are undated and some of the dates on this possibly incomplete checklist are only best estimates. The unnumbered cards are checklisted here alphabetically.

		NM/M
	Complete Set (45):	70.00
	Common Player:	1.50
(1)	Sandy Alomar Jr./1989 (Regular gray.)	1.50
(1g)	Sandy Alomar Jr./1989 (Glossy gray.)	1.50
(2)	Steve Avery/1992 (Regular red/blue.)	1.50
(3)	Jeff Bagwell/1992 (Plastic orange/green.)	1.50
(4)	Wade Boggs/1989 (Regular pink.)	3.25
(5)	Bobby Bonilla/1991 (Regular purple.)	1.50
(5g)	Bobby Bonilla/1991 (Glossy purple.)	1.50
(6)	Will Clark/1988 (Regular green.)	1.50
(6g)	Will Clark/1988 (Glossy green.)	1.50
(7)	Roger Clemens/1988 (Regular)	2.50
(8)	Eric Davis/1989 (Glossy red.)	1.50
(9)	Ken Griffey Jr./1989 (Regular purple.)	3.50
(10)	Ken Griffey Jr./1990 (Regular green.)	2.50
(10g)	Ken Griffey Jr./1990 (Glossy green.)	3.50
(11)	Rickey Henderson/1991 (Regular green/yellow.)	1.50
(11g)	Rickey Henderson/1991 (Glossy green/yellow.)	1.50
(12)	Keith Hernandez/1989 (Regular orange.)	1.50
(13)	Orel Hershiser/1989 (Regular purple.)	1.50
(14)	Sam Horn/1988 (Regular purple.)	1.50
(15)	Bo Jackson/1990 (Regular blue.)	1.50
(16)	Bo Jackson/1992 (Regular green.)	1.50
(17)	Gregg Jefferies/1988 (Regular blue.)	1.50
(18)	Howard Johnson/1990 (Regular orange.)	1.50
(19)	David Justice/1992 (Plastic blue/yellow.)	1.50
(20)	Eric Karros/1992 (Glossy white.)	1.50
(21)	Barry Larkin/1990 (Regular red.)	1.50
(22)	Kevin Maas/1990 (Regular white.)	1.50
(23)	Don Mattingly/1988 (Regular green.)	3.50
(24)	Don Mattingly/1989 (Regular blue.)	3.50
(25)	Don Mattingly/1989 (Regular gray.)	3.50
(26)	Kevin Mitchell/1990 (Regular white/black.)	1.50
(27)	Phil Plantier/1990 (Plastic blue/purple.)	1.50
(28)	Kirby Puckett/1989 (Regular red.)	6.50
(29)	Kirby Puckett/1992 (Plastic purple/blue.)	3.25
(30)	Cal Ripken Jr./1992 (Regular black/orange.)	3.50
(31)	Reggie Sanders/1992 (Glossy white.)	1.50
(32)	Benito Santiago/1990 (Regular purple.)	1.50
(33)	Mike Scott/1989 (Regular green.)	1.50
(34)	Darryl Strawberry/1991 (Regular red.)	1.50
(35g)	Frank Thomas/1991 (Glossy blue/red.)	3.25
(35p)	Frank Thomas/1991 (Plastic blue/red.)	3.25
(36)	Frank Thomas/1992 (Plastic red/yellow.)	3.25
(37)	Alan Trammell/1989 (Glossy blue.)	1.50
(38)	Robin Ventura/1990 (Glossy gold.)	3.25
(39)	Jerome Walton/1990 (Regular blue/red.)	1.50

1988-89 Star Gold Edition

KIRBY PUCKETT GOLD EDITION

This 180-card set was released from late 1988 into 1989 (though all cards bear 1988 copyright date) in a format matching the regular-issue player sets of the 1988-89 issue. Eighteen single-player sets of 10 cards each are included. The high quality photographs on front feature a special gold embossing. The cards devoted to each player are noted by number in the corresponding listings. Single cards are not checklisted because the issue is usually sold only as complete single-player sets. Fifteen hundred of each set were produced, plus 300 black-bordered, blank-back "promo" cards of each player.

		NM/M
	Complete Set (180):	22.50
	Common Player Set (10):	1.00
	Complete Promo Set:	32.50
	Common Promo Card:	1.50
1-10	Gregg Jefferies	1.00
	Gregg Jefferies (Promo card.)	1.50
11-20	Sam Horn	1.00
	Sam Horn (Promo card.)	1.50
21-30	Don Mattingly	6.00
	Don Mattingly (Promo card.)	7.50
31-40	Matt Nokes	1.00
	Matt Nokes (Promo card.)	1.50
41-50	Darryl Strawberry	1.00
	Darryl Strawberry (Promo card.)	1.50
51-60	Will Clark	2.00
	Will Clark (Promo card.)	3.00
61-70	Wade Boggs	3.00
	Wade Boggs (Promo card.)	3.00
71-80	Mark Grace	1.50
	Mark Grace (Promo card.)	1.00
81-90	Bo Jackson	1.00
	Bo Jackson (Promo card.)	1.50
91-100	Jose Canseco	2.00
	Jose Canseco (Promo card.)	3.00
101-110	Eric Davis	1.00
	Eric Davis (Promo card.)	1.50
110-119	Orel Hershiser (#120 Misnumbered #110)	1.00
	Orel Hershiser (Promo card.)	1.50
121-130	Mike Greenwell	1.00
	Mike Greenwell (Promo card.)	1.50
131-140	Dave Winfield	2.00
	Dave Winfield (Promo card.)	3.00
141-150	Alan Trammell	1.00
	Alan Trammell (Promo card.)	1.50
151-160	Roger Clemens	4.00
	Roger Clemens (Promo card.)	3.50
161-170	Kirby Puckett	2.50
	Kirby Puckett (Promo card.)	3.50
171-180	Kevin Seitzer	1.00
	Kevin Seitzer (Promo card.)	1.50

1988-89 Star Nova Edition

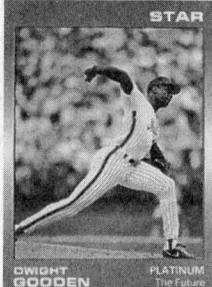

NOVA
JOSE CANSECO Major League Stats

With production limited to just 500 sets and 40 promo cards of each player, these are the most limited of the regular Star issues of 1989. Cards follow the format of the regular-issue Star single-player sets of the 1988-89 issue. Each of the nine-card player sets is listed here in alphabetical order. Single cards are not listed because complete player sets are seldom broken for individual card sales. The Nova promo cards have blue borders at the top and red at bottom. Cards #109-117 were not issued. Ryne Sandberg cards #154-161 have his name misspelled Sanberg on front and back.

		NM/M
	Complete Set (153):	85.00
	Common Player Set (9):	3.00
	Complete Promo Card Set (17):	225.00
	Common Promo Card:	7.50
1-9	Mike Greenwell	3.00
	Mike Greenwell (Promo card.)	7.50
10-18	Darryl Strawberry	3.00
	Darryl Strawberry (Promo card.)	7.50
19-27	Don Mattingly	11.00
	Don Mattingly (Promo card.)	30.00
28-36	Eric Davis	3.00
	Eric Davis (Promo)	7.50
37-45	Jose Canseco	7.50
	Jose Canseco (Promo card.)	22.50
46-54	Sandy Alomar Jr.	3.00
	Sandy Alomar Jr. (Promo card.)	7.50
55-63	Kirby Puckett	9.00
	Kirby Puckett (Promo card.)	25.00
64-72	Orel Hershiser	3.00
	Orel Hershiser (Promo card.)	7.50
73-81	Wade Boggs	7.50
	Wade Boggs (Promo card.)	17.50
82-90	Rickey Henderson	5.00
	Rickey Henderson (Promo card.)	9.00
91-99	Will Clark	3.50
	Will Clark (Promo card.)	15.00
100-108	Bo Jackson	3.50
	Bo Jackson (Promo card.)	12.50
118-126	Ken Griffey Jr.	15.00
	Ken Griffey Jr. (Promo card.)	30.00
127-135	Mike Schmidt	11.00
	Mike Schmidt (Promo card.)	30.00
136-144	Gary Sheffield	3.50
	Gary Sheffield (Promo card.)	9.00
145-153	Cal Ripken Jr.	12.50
	Cal Ripken Jr. (Promo card.)	35.00
154-162	Ryne Sandberg	7.50
	Ryne Sandberg (Promo card.)	20.00

1988 Star Platinum Edition

DWIGHT GOODEN PLATINUM The Future

Twelve single-player sets make up the 1988 Star Platinum series. Ten cards were devoted to each player. While the cards were sold as individual player sets, they were numbered continuously. Fronts feature color photos with various colorful borders (by player), highlighted in silver foil. No single card prices are quoted because the cards are usually sold only as complete player sets. One thousand sets of each player were issued, along with 200 gold-bordered promo cards per player.

		NM/M
	Complete Set (120):	27.50
	Common Player Set (10):	1.50
	Complete Promo Set (12):	32.50
	Common Promo Player:	2.00
1-10	Don Mattingly	6.00
	Don Mattingly (Promo card.)	10.00
11-20	Dwight Gooden	1.50
	Dwight Gooden (Promo card.)	2.00
21-30	Roger Clemens	3.50
	Roger Clemens (Promo card.)	3.50
31-40	Mike Schmidt	3.50
	Mike Schmidt (Promo card.)	4.00
41-50	Wade Boggs	2.50
	Wade Boggs (Promo card.)	3.00
51-60	Mark McGwire	6.00
	Mark McGwire (Promo card.)	5.00
61-70	Andre Dawson	1.50
	Andre Dawson (Promo card.)	2.50
71-80	Jose Canseco	2.50
	Jose Canseco (Promo card.)	4.00
81-90	Eric Davis	1.50
	Eric Davis (Promo card.)	2.00
91-100	George Brett	4.00
	George Brett/Throwing (Promo card.)	4.00
101-110	Darryl Strawberry	1.50
	Darryl Strawberry (Promo card.)	2.00
111-120	Dale Murphy	1.50
	Dale Murphy (Promo card.)	2.00

1988-89 Star Platinum

GEORGE BRETT PLATINUM 1980 MVP

Fourteen of baseball's top players are featured in 10-card single-player sets within this issue. Cards #21-30 were devoted to Gregg Jefferies, but a contract dispute prevented their release. While sold as single-player sets, the cards are numbered contiguously. Card numbers are provided for each player in the checklist below. Single cards are not checklisted because the issue is generally sold only as complete player sets. A thousand sets of each player were produced, along with 200 promo cards of each player. The cards follow the format of the regular-issue Star 1988-89 player sets.

		NM/M
	Complete Set (140):	17.50
	Common Player Set (10):	1.00
	Complete Promo Set (14):	22.50
	Common Promo Card:	1.50
1-10	Jose Canseco	2.00
	Jose Canseco (Promo card.)	2.00
11-20	Mike Greenwell	1.00
	Mike Greenwell (Promo card.)	1.50
31-40	Wade Boggs	2.50
	Wade Boggs (Promo card.)	3.00
41-50	Don Mattingly	3.25
	Don Mattingly (Promo card.)	3.75
51-60	Kirby Puckett	2.50
	Kirby Puckett (Promo card.)	3.00
61-70	Dwight Gooden	1.50
	Dwight Gooden (Promo card.)	1.00
71-80	Alan Trammell	1.00
	Alan Trammell (Promo card.)	1.50
81-90	Darryl Strawberry	1.00
	Darryl Strawberry (White uniform.)	1.50
91-100	Orel Hershiser	1.00
	Orel Hershiser (Promo card.)	1.50
101-110	Will Clark	1.50
	Will Clark (Promo card.)	2.50
111-120	Roger Clemens	2.00
	Roger Clemens (Promo card.)	3.50
121-130	Eric Davis	1.00
	Eric Davis (Promo card.)	1.50
131-140	George Brett	3.00
	George Brett/Btg (Promo card.)	3.50
141-150	Frank Viola	1.00
	Frank Viola (Promo card.)	1.50

1988-89 Star Silver Edition

RICKY JORDAN SILVER SERIES Career Stats

This 90-card issue features 10 single-player sets. Only Only 2,000 serial numbered sets were printed (plus 400 "promo" cards of each player, featuring black borders fading to white at the middle). Single-card values are not quoted because the player sets are seldom broken for individual card sales. Cards follow the format of the regular-issue 1988-89 Star player sets.

	NM/M
Complete Set (90):	35.00
Common Player Set:	1.50
Complete Promo Card Set (10):	37.50
Common Promo Card:	3.00
1-9 Ken Griffey Jr.	17.50
Ken Griffey Jr. (Promo card.)	9.00
10-18 Wade Boggs	5.00
Wade Boggs (Promo card.)	6.00
19-27 Ricky Jordan	1.50
Ricky Jordan (Promo card.)	3.00
28-36 Mike Greenwell	1.50
Mike Greenwell (Promo card.)	3.00
37-45 Sandy Alomar Jr.	1.50
Sandy Alomar Jr. (Promo card.)	3.00
46-54 Mike Schmidt	6.00
Mike Schmidt (Promo card.)	7.50
55-63 Gary Sheffield	2.25
Gary Sheffield (Promo card.)	3.00
64-72 Will Clark	2.25
Will Clark (Promo card.)	3.50
73-81 Ron Jones	1.50
Ron Jones (Promo card.)	3.00
82-90 Kirby Puckett	6.00
Kirby Puckett (Promo card.)	6.00

1988 Star '88 Promos

Most of the Star '88 single- and dual-player card sets also had a promo card issued; blank-backed but otherwise nearly identical to the regular cards.

	NM/M
Complete Set (23):	35.00
Common Player:	1.00
(1) George Bell	1.00
(2) Wade Boggs	2.00
(3) Wade Boggs, Tony Gwynn	1.50
(4) Gary Carter	1.50
(5) Will Clark	1.50
(6) Roger Clemens, Dwight Gooden	1.50
(7) Eric Davis	1.00
(8) Andre Dawson	1.50
(9) Dwight Gooden	1.00
(10) Tony Gwynn	2.00
(11) Bo Jackson	1.50
(12) Don Mattingly	3.00
(13) Don Mattingly, Mike Schmidt	1.75
(14) Mark McGwire (Yellow-border set, green-border promo.)	4.00
(15) Mark McGwire (Aqua-border set, yellow-border promo.)	2.50
(16) Mark McGwire (Green-border set, white-border promo.)	4.00
(17) Eddie Murray	2.00
(18) Cal Ripken Jr.	3.50
(19) Mike Schmidt	2.50
(20) Mike Scott	1.00
(21) Kevin Seitzer	1.00
(22) Cory Snyder	1.00
(23) Dave Winfield	2.50

1988 Star '88

ANDRE DAWSON "THE HAWK"

For the fifth straight year Star utilized the same basic format for its single-player card sets of 1988. Fronts have player posed and game-action photos surrounded by a brightly colored border. Pushing

into the top-right of the photo is a "Star '88" logo. A circle at the lower-left contains the player name or logo. Backs have stats, personal data, career highlights or a checklist. Single cards are not listed here because sets are seldom broken. Many player sets were also issued in a more limited glossy edition, and some sets were produced with the first card authentically autographed.

	NM/M
1-11 George Bell (7,500 Sets)	1.50
(1-10) George Bell (Sticker set.)	2.00
1-11 Wade Boggs (10,000 Sets)	2.50
1-11 Wade Boggs (#1 Autographed)	25.00
1-11 Wade Boggs (Glossy - 1,000 sets.)	4.00
1-11 Wade Boggs, Tony Gwynn	2.50
1-11 Gary Carter (6,000 Sets)	2.00
1-11 Gary Carter (Glossy - 1,000 sets.)	3.00
1-11 Will Clark (7,500 Sets)	1.75
1-11 Will Clark (#1 Autographed)	15.00
1-11 Roger Clemens, Dwight Gooden	2.00
1-12 Eric Davis	1.50
1-12 Eric Davis (Glossy - 1,000 sets.)	1.50
1-11 Eric Davis, Mark McGwire	2.25
1-11 Andre Dawson (4,500 Sets)	1.50
1-11 Andre Dawson (Glossy - 1,000 sets.)	2.50
1-11 Andre Dawson (Autographed - 500 sets.)	12.50
1-12 Dwight Gooden (5,600 Sets)	1.50
1-12 Dwight Gooden (Glossy - 1,000 sets.)	2.25
1-12 Dwight Gooden (Autographed - 400 sets.)	10.00
1-11 Tony Gwynn (5,000 Sets)	2.50
1-11 Tony Gwynn (Glossy - 1,000 sets.)	4.50
1-11 Tony Gwynn (Autographed - 500 sets.)	15.00
1-16 Bo Jackson (Set includes four blank-back cards as Auburn football player; 6,000 sets.)	3.00
1-16 Bo Jackson (Glossy - 1,000 sets.)	4.50
1-11 Don Mattingly (Card #3 exists with fielding or batting pose, 10,000 sets.)	6.00
1-11 Don Mattingly (Glossy - 1,000 sets.)	7.00
1-11 Don Mattingly, Mike Schmidt (2,000 Sets)	4.00
1-11 Don Mattingly, Mike Schmidt (Glossy - 1,000 sets.)	4.50
1-12 Mark McGwire (Yellow borders; 12,000 sets.)	3.50
1-12 Mark McGwire (Yellow borders; glossy - 1,000 sets.)	4.50
1-12 Mark McGwire (Yellow borders; autographed - 500 sets.)	50.00
1-11 Mark McGwire (Aqua borders.)	7.50
1-11 Mark McGwire (Green borders; 6,000 sets.)	3.00
1-11 Mark McGwire (Green borders; glossy - 1,000 sets.)	4.50
1-12 Eddie Murray (Glossy version only.)	2.00
1-12 Cal Ripken Jr.	6.00
1-12 Mike Schmidt (Glossy version only.)	4.00
1-11 Mike Scott	1.50
1-11 Kevin Seitzer (6,000 Sets)	1.50
1-11 Kevin Seitzer (Glossy - 1,000 sets.)	2.25
1-11 Cory Snyder (8,500 Sets)	1.50
1-11 Cory Snyder (Glossy - 1,000 sets.)	2.25
1-11 Cory Snyder (Autographed - 500 sets.)	5.00
(1-8) Cory Snyder (Sticker set; 4,000 sets.)	2.00
1-12 Dave Winfield (5,000 Sets)	2.00
1-12 Dave Winfield (Glossy - 1,000 sets.)	3.00
1-12 Dave Winfield (Autographed - 500 sets.)	16.00
(1-10) Dave Winfield (Sticker set; 3,000.)	2.00

1989-90 Star Rookies

Two-card "sets" of each of 12 promising players were produced in an edition of 10,000 each as an exclusive for a New York comic

book dealer. Cards have player photos on front with a few stats on back. Cards #1-12 have borders of red and gold and backs printed in red and tan. The 1990 cards, #13-24, are bordered in purple and yellow with backs printed in purple on yellow. All cards have 1989 copyright dates. Unlike most other contemporary Star sets, no glossy or promo cards were made.

	NM/M
Complete Set (24):	2.50
Common Player:	.15
1 Eric Anthony	.15
2 Eric Anthony	.15
3 Mark Lewis	.15
4 Mark Lewis	.15
5 Pete Rose, Jr.	.25
6 Pete Rose, Jr.	.25
7 Robin Ventura	.40
8 Robin Ventura	.40
9 Beau Allred	.15
10 Beau Allred	.15
11 Pat Combs	.15
12 Pat Combs	.15
13 Deion Sanders	.25
14 Deion Sanders	.25
15 Bob Hamelin	.15
16 Bob Hamelin	.15
17 Andy Benes	.20
18 Andy Benes	.20
19 Bam Bam Muelens	.15
20 Bam Bam Muelens	.15
21 Trey McCoy	.15
22 Trey McCoy	.15
23 Sandy Alomar Jr.	.25
24 Sandy Alomar Jr.	.25

1990-91 Star Promos

FRANK THOMAS CHICAGO Promo

Most of the 1990-91 series of Star player sets feature a promo card in the same format. They are blank-backed and have the word "Promo" on front beneath the city name. Regular and glossy promos exist for most cards.

	NM/M
Complete Set (44):	75.00
Common Player:	1.50
(1) Jim Abbott	1.50
(2) Andy Benes	1.50
(3) Barry Bonds (Correct)	6.00
(4) Bobby Bonds (Photo actually Barry.)	6.00
(5) Bobby Bonilla	1.50
(6) Jose Canseco (Blue borders, from purple set.)	1.50
(7) Jose Canseco (Orange borders, from yellow set.)	1.50
(8) Jose Canseco (Green borders, from yellow set.)	1.50
(9) Will Clark (Black borders.)	1.50
(10) Will Clark (Purple)	1.50
(11) Will Clark (Orange, from Clark/Grace set.)	1.50
(12) Mark Davis	1.50
(13) Cecil Fielder (Purple, from blue set.)	1.50
(14) Cecil Fielder (Yellow glossy, from blue set.)	12.50

	NM/M
(15) Ken Griffey Jr. (Purple, from blue set.)	2.25
(16) Ken Griffey Jr. (Blue on yellow, from blue set.)	1.50
(17) Ken Griffey Jr. (Red, batting with "S" on helmet, from yellow set.)	1.50
(18) Ken Griffey Jr. (Red, no "S" on helmet, from aqua Jr./Sr. set.)	2.25
(19) Ken Griffey Jr. (Red on yellow, from red Jr./Sr. set.)	2.25
(20) Ken Griffey Sr. (Blue, from aqua set.)	1.50
(21) Ken Griffey Sr. (Yellow, from red set.)	1.50
(22) Rickey Henderson/1990/Blue	1.50
(23) Rickey Henderson/Running/1990 (Green)	1.50
(24) Rickey Henderson/Btg/1991 (Green)	1.50
(25) Bo Jackson/Running	1.50
(26) Bo Jackson/Portrait	1.50
(27) Bo Jackson (Diamond Terror, yellow.)	1.50
(28) David Justice	1.50
(29) Barry Larkin	1.50
(30) Kevin Maas	1.50
(31) Ben McDonald	1.50
(32) Kevin Mitchell	1.50
(33) Gregg Olson	1.50
(34) Cal Ripken Jr.	3.00
(35) Nolan Ryan (Blue, from Rangers set.)	4.00
(36) Nolan Ryan (Yellow, from all-team set.)	3.00
(37) Bret Saberhagen	1.50
(38) Ryne Sandberg	1.50
(39) Darryl Strawberry	1.50
(40) Frank Thomas	2.50
(41) Jerome Walton	1.50
(42) Matt Williams	1.50
(43) Robin Yount (Brown on yellow, from Mitchell/Yount set.)	1.50
(44) Robin Yount (Blue on yellow.)	1.50

1990-91 Star

NOLAN RYAN TEXAS Minor League Stats

Issued as single-player sets over the two-year span these sets maintain a design continuity despite the fact some have a 1990 copyright line on back and some have a 1991 date. Fronts of all cards have posed and game-action photos which are bordered in a single bright color, by player. That border color is darkest at top and bottom and fades to white at the center. Backs are printed in one of several colors on white cardboard and feature personal data, stats, career highlights, checklists and team logos. Single cards are not listed because sets are seldom broken for individual card sales. Glossy versions are known for most, but not all, player sets.

	NM/M
1-11 Jim Abbott	1.50
1-11 Andy Benes	1.50
1-11 Barry Bonds (Error, cards #2-11 say "Bobby Bonds.")	9.00
1-11 Barry Bonds (Corrected)	9.00
1-11 Bobby Bonilla	1.50
1-11 Jose Canseco (Purple borders.)	1.50
1-11 Jose Canseco (Yellow borders.)	1.50
1-11 Will Clark	1.50
1-11 Will Clark, Mark Grace	1.50
1-11 Cecil Fielder (Blue borders.)	1.50
1-11 Cecil Fielder (Orange borders.)	1.50
1-11 Ken Griffey Jr. (Blue borders.)	3.00
1-11 Ken Griffey Jr. (Yellow borders.)	2.00

		NM/M
1-11	Ken Griffey Jr., Ken Griffey Sr. (Aqua borders.)	2.00
1-11	Ken Griffey Jr., Ken Griffey Sr. (Red borders.)	2.00
1-11	Rickey Henderson/1990	4.00
1-11	Rickey Henderson (Glossy - 250 sets.)	4.50
1-11	Rickey Henderson/1991	4.00
1-11	Bo Jackson	1.50
1-11	Bo Jackson, Barry Larkin (Diamond Terror)	1.50
1	Howard Johnson (Autographed card numbered to 400.)	5.00
1-11	Dave Justice	1.50
1-11	Dave Justice, Kevin Maas	1.50
1-11	Barry Larkin	1.50
1-11	Kevin Maas	1.50
1-11	Ben McDonald	1.50
1-11	Kevin Mitchell, Robin Yount	1.50
1-11	Cal Ripken Jr.	6.00
1-11	Nolan Ryan (Card #1 pitching, all Rangers photos.)	2.50
1-11	Nolan Ryan (Card #1 portrait, all four teams.)	2.50
1-11	Bret Saberhagen, Mark Davis	1.50
1-11	Ryne Sandberg	2.00
1-11	Ryne Sandberg (Glossy)	10.00
1-11	Darryl Strawberry	1.50
1-11	Frank Thomas	1.50
1-11	Jerome Walton, Gregg Olson	1.50
1-11	Matt Williams	1.50
1-11	Robin Yount	1.50

1990-93 Star "Career Stats"

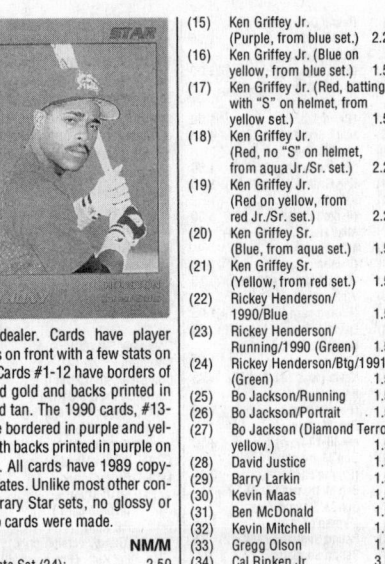

FRANK THOMAS CHICAGO Career Stats

These unnumbered cards are not part of any Star sets. They share a common design of two-color graduated borders on front, with color photos both front and back. The words "Career Stats" are prominently displayed on both front and back. Some players were sold in both autographed and unautographed versions, while some are known only in one version or the other.

	NM/M
Complete Set (26):	65.00
Common Player:	1.50
(1) Ken Griffey Jr./1990	3.50
(2) Barry Bonds/1991	4.00
(2a) Barry Bonds/1991/Auto.	15.00
(3) Bobby Bonilla/1991	1.50
(4) Scott Erickson/1991	1.50
(4a) Scott Erickson/1991/Auto.	3.00
(5) Chuck Knoblauch/1991	1.50
(5a) Chuck Knoblauch/1991/Auto	3.00
(6) Frank Thomas/1991	3.00
(6a) Frank Thomas/1991/Auto.	10.00
(7) Frank Thomas/1991 (Glossy)	10.00
(7a) Matt Williams/1991	1.50
(7a) Matt Williams/1991/Auto.	3.00
(8) Jeff Bagwell/1992	2.00
(9a) Pat Kelly/1992/Auto.	3.00
(10a) Mark Lewis/1992/Auto.	3.00
(11a) John Olerud/1992/Auto.	3.00
(12) Jim Abbott/1993	1.50
(12a) Jim Abbott/1993/Auto.	3.00
(13) Bret Barberie/1993	1.50
(13a) Bret Barberie/1993/Auto.	3.00
(14) Andy Benes/1993	1.50
(14a) Andy Benes/1993/Auto.	3.00
(15) Rickey Henderson/1993	2.00
(16a) Eric Karros/1993/Auto.	3.00
(17) Ryan Klesko/1993	1.50
(18) Kevin Mass/1993 (Maas)	1.50
(19) Dean Palmer/1993	1.50

1990-91 Star Gold Edition

Only 1,500 of each nine-card, single-player set was produced in Star's 1990 Gold Edition. Single cards are not listed or priced because the same issue is almost exclusively traded in complete player

STAR GOLD HOWARD JOHNSON New York Mets

sets. Cards are numbered contiguously as noted in the alphabetical checklist presented here. Suggested retail price at issue was $15-20 per set. An addition of 300 gray-bordered promo cards was issued for each player.

	NM/M
Complete Set (180):	40.00
Common Player Set:	1.50
Complete Promo Set (20):	50.00
Common Promo Card:	2.00
(1) Wade Boggs (#136-144)	2.25
(1) Wade Boggs (Promo card.)	4.00
(2) Bobby Bonilla (#145-153)	1.50
(2) Bobby Bonilla (Promo card.)	2.00
(3) Jose Canseco (#19-27)	2.25
(3) Jose Canseco (Promo card.)	3.00
(4) Will Clark (#64-72)	2.25
(4) Will Clark (Promo card.)	3.00
(5) Dwight Gooden (#109-117)	1.50
(5) Dwight Gooden (Promo card.)	2.00
(6) Mark Grace (#154-162)	1.50
(6) Mark Grace (Promo card.)	2.00
(7) Ken Griffey Jr. (#10-18)	7.50
(7) Ken Griffey Jr. (Promo card.)	10.00
(8) Rickey Henderson (#82-90)	3.00
(8) Rickey Henderson (Promo card.)	4.00
(9) Bo Jackson (#1-9)	1.50
(9) Bo Jackson (Promo card.)	2.00
(10) Howard Johnson (#163-171)	1.50
(10) Howard Johnson (Promo card.)	2.00
(11) David Justice (#118-126)	1.50
(11) David Justice (Promo card.)	2.00
(12) Barry Larkin (#91-99)	1.50
(12) Barry Larkin (Promo card.)	2.00
(13) Kevin Maas (#127-135)	1.50
(13) Kevin Maas (Promo card.)	2.00
(14) Don Mattingly (#100-108)	4.50
(14) Don Mattingly (Promo card.)	6.00
(15) Kirby Puckett (#55-63)	4.00
(15) Kirby Puckett (Promo card.)	6.00
(16) Tim Raines (#37-45)	1.50
(16) Tim Raines (Promo card.)	2.00
(17) Cal Ripken Jr. (#73-81)	7.50
(17) Cal Ripken Jr. (Promo card.)	10.00
(18) Ryne Sandberg (#46-54)	3.00
(18) Ryne Sandberg (Promo card.)	4.00
(19) Darryl Strawberry (#172-180)	1.50
(19) Darryl Strawberry (Promo card.)	2.00
(20) Robin Ventura (#28-36)	1.50
(20) Robin Ventura (Promo card.)	2.00

1990-91 Star Nova Edition

With just 500 of each nine-card single-player set produced, the Nova Edition was Star's top of the line in 1990. Player sets are listed alphabetically. Single cards are not listed because sets are seldom broken. Each set is also represented by an issue of 100 promo cards, featuring black borders at top and yellow at bottom.

	NM/M
Complete Set (180):	50.00
Common Player Set:	2.25
Complete Promo Set (20):	65.00
Common Promo Card:	3.00

(1) Wade Boggs (#28-36) 5.00
(1) Wade Boggs (Promo card.) 6.00
(2) Jose Canseco (#55-63) 3.75
(2) Jose Canseco (Promo card.) 5.00
(3) Joe Carter (#118-126) 2.25
(3) Joe Carter (Promo card.) 3.00
(4) Will Clark (#46-54) 3.00
(4) Will Clark (Promo card.) 4.00
(5) Roger Clemens (#109-117) 6.50
(5) Roger Clemens (Promo card.) 7.50
(6) Glenn Davis (#127-135) 2.25
(6) Glenn Davis (Promo card.) 3.00
(7) Len Dykstra (#163-171) 2.25
(7) Len Dykstra (Promo card.) 3.00
(8) Cecil Fielder (#154-162) 2.25
(8) Cecil Fielder (Promo card.) 3.00
(9) Ken Griffey Jr. (#172-180) 7.50
(9) Ken Griffey Jr. (Promo card.) 10.00
(10) Rickey Henderson (#73-81) 3.00
(10) Rickey Henderson (Promo card.) 4.00
(11) Bo Jackson (#64-72) 2.25
(11) Bo Jackson (Promo card.) 3.00
(12) Howard Johnson (#37-45) 2.25
(12) Howard Johnson (Promo card.) 3.00
(13) Barry Larkin (#100-108) 2.25
(13) Barry Larkin (Promo card.) 3.00
(14) Don Mattingly (#1-9) 6.50
(14) Don Mattingly (Promo card.) 9.00
(15) Kevin Mitchell (#145-153) 2.25
(15) Kevin Mitchell (Promo card.) 3.00
(16) Nolan Ryan (#19-27) 7.50
(16) Nolan Ryan (Promo card.) 10.00
(17) Ryne Sandberg (#136-144) 5.00
(17) Ryne Sandberg (Promo card.) 6.00
(18) Dave Stewart (#91-99) 2.25
(18) Dave Stewart (Promo card.) 3.00
(19) Darryl Strawberry (#82-90) 2.25
(19) Darryl Strawberry (Promo card.) 3.00
(20) Robin Yount (#10-18) 2.25
(20) Robin Yount (Promo card.) 3.00

1990-91 Star Platinum Edition

The stars in Star's Platinum Edition were featured in nine-card sets with production of 1,000 each (plus 200 black-bordered promo cards of each player). Suggested retail price at the time of issue was about $20. The player sets are checklisted here in alphabetical order. Single cards are not listed because the sets are almost never broken up. Cards are numbered contiguously as noted in the alphabetical checklisted.

NM/M
Complete Set (180): 40.00
Common Player Set: 1.50
Complete Promo Set (21): 50.00
Common Promo Card: 1.50
(1) Jim Abbott (#19-27) 1.50
(1) Jim Abbott (Promo card.) 2.00
(2) Wade Boggs (#145-153) 3.00
(2) Wade Boggs (Promo card.) 4.00
(3) Jose Canseco (#91-99) 3.50
(3) Jose Canseco (Promo card.) 4.00
(4) Will Clark (#1-9) 2.50
(4) Will Clark (Promo card.) 4.00
(5) Roger Clemens (#46-54) 3.50
(5) Roger Clemens (Promo card.) 7.50
(6) Eric Davis (#55-63) 1.50
(6) Eric Davis (Promo card.) 2.00
(7) Dwight Gooden (#82-90) 1.50
(7) Dwight Gooden (Promo card.) 2.00
(8) Mark Grace (#172-180) (#172 says "Silver Series") 2.25
(8) Mark Grace (Promo card.) 3.00
(9) Mike Greenwell (#64-72) 1.50
(9) Mike Greenwell (Promo card.) 2.00
(10) Ken Griffey Jr. (#100-108) 7.00
(10) Ken Griffey Jr. (Promo card.) 8.00
(11) Tony Gwynn (#28-36) 4.50
(11) Tony Gwynn (Promo card.) 6.00
(12) Bo Jackson (#136-144) 1.50
(12) Bo Jackson (Promo card.) 2.00
(13) Howard Johnson (#109-117) 1.50
(13) Howard Johnson (Promo card.) 2.00
(14) Don Mattingly (#73-81) 5.00
(14) Don Mattingly (Promo card.) 6.00
(15) Kevin Mitchell (#10-18) 1.50
(15) Kevin Mitchell/Btg (Promo card.) 1.50
(16) Kevin Mitchell (#154-162) 1.50
(16) Kevin Mitchell/Running (Promo card.) 2.00
(17) Kirby Puckett (#37-45) 4.50
(17) Kirby Puckett (Promo card.) 6.00
(18) Ryne Sandberg (#163-171) 3.00
(18) Ryne Sandberg (Promo card.) 4.00
(19) Darryl Strawberry (#118-126) 1.50
(19) Darryl Strawberry (Promo card.) 2.00
(20) Matt Williams (#127-135) 1.50
(20) Matt Williams (Promo card.) 2.00

1990-91 Star Silver Edition

Many of 1990's biggest stars are represented in nine-card single-player sets within Star Co.'s Silver Edition. Production of each silver-foil trimmed set was limited to 2,000. Because single cards are seldom offered, only complete player sets are priced. Cards are numbered contiguously as noted in the alphabetical checklist presented here. Retail price at issue was $10-15. Each player is also represented by an issue of 400 black-bordered promo cards.

NM/M
Complete Set (180): 17.50
Common Player Set: .75
Complete Promo Set: 22.50
Common Promo Card: 1.00
(1) Jim Abbott (#1-9) .75
(1) Jim Abbott (Promo card.) 1.00
(2) Sandy Alomar Jr. (#55-63).75
(2) Sandy Alomar Jr. (Promo card.) 1.00
(3) Andy Benes (#19-27) .75
(3) Andy Benes (Promo card.) 1.00
(4) Barry Bonds (#172-180) 3.00
(4) Barry Bonds (Promo card.) 4.00
(5) Bobby Bonilla (#154-162) .75
(5) Bobby Bonilla (Promo card.) 1.00
(6) Jose Canseco (#127-135) 1.25
(6) Jose Canseco (Promo card.) 1.50
(7) Will Clark (#73-81) 1.25
(7) Will Clark (Promo card.) 1.50
(8) Delino DeShields (#145-153) .75
(8) Delino DeShields (Promo card.) 1.00
(9) Tom Gordon (#37-45) .75
(9) Tom Gordon (Promo card.) 1.00
(10) Mark Grace (#10-18) 1.25
(10) Mark Grace (Promo card.) 1.50
(11) Ken Griffey Jr. (#91-99) 3.50
(11) Ken Griffey Jr. (Promo card.) 5.00
(12) Mike Harkey (#163-171) .75
(12) Mike Harkey (Promo card.) 1.00
(13) Wally Joyner (#28-36) .75
(13) Wally Joyner (Promo card.) 1.00
(14) David Justice (#118-126) .75
(14) David Justice (Promo card.) 1.00
(15) Kevin Maas (#109-117) .75
(15) Kevin Maas (Promo card.) 1.00
(16) Don Mattingly (#136-144) 2.50
(16) Don Mattingly (Promo card.) 3.00
(17) Ben McDonald (#100-108) .75
(17) Ben McDonald (Promo card.) 1.00
(18) Benito Santiago (#64-72) .75
(18) Benito Santiago (Promo card.) 1.00
(19) Alan Trammell (#46-54) (All cards misspelled "Allan.") .75
(19) Alan Trammell (Promo card.) 1.00
(20) Jerome Walton (#82-90) .75
(20) Jerome Walton (Promo card.) 1.00

1990 Star Sophomore Stars

This special six-card set was distributed only at the 1990 Arlington 11th National Sports Collectors Convention. The set came polybagged with a DC comic book in exchange for a $2 donation to the Arthritis Foundation. The 2-1/2" x 3-1/2" cards feature a border that changes from dark blue at the top to red at the bottom. Backs are printed in blue-on-white and include team and MLB logos along with major and minor league career stats. Production was reported as 10,000 sets.

NM/M
Complete Set (6): 4.50
Common Player: .15
1 Ken Griffey Jr. (Batting cage.) 2.00
2 Ken Griffey Jr./Sitting 2.00
3 Gary Sheffield/Portrait .30
4 Gary Sheffield/Btg .30
5 Jerome Walton/Portrait .15
6 Jerome Walton/Btg .15

1991 Star

A common design is again shared by the single-player card sets released by Star for 1991. Cards feature posed and action photos on front with borders that graduate from one color at top to another at bottom (yellow to blue; green to gray, etc.). The player name is at left beneath the photo, his city at right and the card name beneath that. Backs are printed in one of several colors on white stock and feature personal data, stats, career highlights, checklist or team logo. Each set was also produced in a high-gloss version, which carries a 4-5X premium today. Single cards are not listed here because player sets are seldom broken for individual card sales. All promo cards except Clemens have a solid-color border.

NM/M
Complete Set (88): 10.00
Common Player Set: 1.25
Complete Promo Set (6): 11.00
Common Promo Card: 1.50
1-11 Roger Clemens 1.50
Roger Clemens (Promo card.) 2.50
1-11 Rickey Henderson 1.50
1-11 Bo Jackson 1.25
Bo Jackson (Promo card.) 1.50
1-11 Pat Kelly (Glossy version only.) 1.25
Pat Kelly (Promo card.) 1.50
1-11 Cal Ripken Jr. 2.50
Cal Ripken Jr. (Promo card.) 3.25
1-11 Nolan Ryan 2.00
Nolan Ryan (Promo card.) 3.25
1-11 Darryl Strawberry 1.25
1-11 Frank Thomas (Glossy version only.) 2.50
Frank Thomas (Promo card.) 3.00

All-Stars

This Star issue is comprised of 500 sets and 100 promo cards of each player. (Except Jackson who has 200.) The checklist is arranged alphabetically.

NM/M
Complete Set (135): 80.00
Common Player Set: 3.75
Complete Promo Set (15): 110.00
Common Promo Card: 5.00
(1) Wade Boggs (#109-117) 7.50
(1) Wade Boggs (Promo card.) 10.00
(2) Jose Canseco (#37-45) 7.50
(2) Jose Canseco (Promo card.) 10.00
(3) Roger Clemens (#64-72) 7.50
(3) Roger Clemens (Promo card.) 10.00
(4) Lenny Dykstra (#91-99) 3.75
(4) Lenny Dykstra (Promo card.) 5.00
(5) Cecil Fielder (#118-126) 3.75
(5) Cecil Fielder (Promo card.) 5.00
(6) Dwight Gooden (#82-90) 3.75
(6) Dwight Gooden (Promo card.) 5.00
(7) Ken Griffey Jr. (#1-9) 10.00
(7) Ken Griffey Jr. (Promo card.) 15.00
(8) Rickey Henderson (#19-27) 7.50
(8) Rickey Henderson (Promo card.) 10.00
(9) Bo Jackson (#46-54) 3.75
(9) Bo Jackson (Promo card.) 5.00
(10) Don Mattingly (#73-81) 9.00
(10) Don Mattingly (Promo card.) 12.00
(11) Kirby Puckett (#100-108) 7.50
(11) Kirby Puckett (Promo card.) 12.00
(12) Cal Ripken Jr. (#55-63) 9.00
(12p) Cal Ripken Jr. (#55-63) (Plastic test issue.) 12.00
(12) Cal Ripken Jr. (Promo card.) 12.00
(12p) Cal Ripken Jr. (Promo card.) (Plastic) 16.00
(13) Nolan Ryan (#10-18) 9.00
(13) Nolan Ryan (Promo card.) 12.00
(14) Ryne Sandberg (#28-36) 7.50
(14) Ryne Sandberg (Promo card.) 10.00

Diamond Series

Production of these nine-card, single-player sets was limited to 2,000 of each (plus 400 promo cards each), with a suggested retail price at issue of $25. Players in the edition are listed here in alphabetical order. Cards are numbered contiguously throughout the issue, as noted in the

FRANK THOMAS — CHICAGO — 1989 Season

alpha-order listings here. Single cards are not priced because the sets are seldom broken up.

NM/M
Complete Set (126): 22.50
Common Player Set: 1.00
Complete Promo Set: 27.50
Common Promo Card: 1.50
(1) Barry Bonds (#10-18) 5.00
(1) Barry Bonds (Promo card.) 5.00
(2) Bobby Bonilla (#46-54) 1.00
(2) Bobby Bonilla (Promo card.) 1.50
(3) Jose Canseco (#37-45) 2.00
(3) Jose Canseco (Promo card.) 2.50
(4) Roger Clemens (#64-72) 2.50
(4) Roger Clemens (Promo card.) 2.50
(5) Cecil Fielder (#118-126) 1.00
(5) Cecil Fielder (Promo card.) 1.50
(6) Ken Griffey Jr (#55-63) 3.50
(6) Ken Griffey Jr. (Promo card.) 5.00
(7) Tony Gwynn (#100-108) 1.75
(7) Tony Gwynn (Promo card.) 2.50
(8) Bo Jackson (#1-9) 1.00
(8) Bo Jackson (Promo card.) 1.50
(9) Don Mattingly (#19-27) 5.00
(9) Don Mattingly (Promo card.) 6.00
(10) Kirby Puckett (#82-90) 2.50
(10) Kirby Puckett (Promo card.) 6.00
(11) Cal Ripken Jr. (#28-36) 7.50
(11) Cal Ripken Jr. (Promo card.) 3.50
(12) Nolan Ryan (#109-117) 6.00
(12) Nolan Ryan (Promo card.) 7.50
(13) Darryl Strawberry (#73-81) 1.00
(13) Darryl Strawberry (Promo card.) 1.50
(14) Frank Thomas (#91-99) 2.25
(14) Frank Thomas (Promo card.) 3.00

Gold Edition

Only 1,500 of each nine-card, single-player set was produced - along with 300 promo cards of each player - in Star's 1991 Gold Edition. Cards are numbered contiguously throughout the issue, as noted in the alphabetical checklist shown here. Single cards are not listed or priced because the issue is almost exclusively traded in complete-player sets.

NM/M
Complete Set (144): 40.00
Common Player Set: 2.00
Complete Promo Set (16): 40.00
Common Promo Card: 2.00
(1) Albert Belle (#118-126) 2.00
(1) Albert Belle (Promo card.) 2.00
(2) Barry Bonds (#73-81) 7.00
(2) Barry Bonds (Promo card.) 7.00
(3) Bobby Bonilla (#127-135) 2.00
(3) Bobby Bonilla (Promo card.) 2.00
(4) Jose Canseco (#55-63) 3.00
(4) Jose Canseco (Promo card.) 3.00
(5) Will Clark (#28-36) 2.00
(5) Will Clark (Promo card.) 2.00
(6) Roger Clemens (#64-72) 6.00
(6) Roger Clemens (Promo card.) 2.00
(7) Ken Griffey Jr. (#19-27) 5.00
(7) Ken Griffey Jr. (Promo card.) 5.00
(8) Bo Jackson (#37-45) 2.00
(8) Bo Jackson (Promo card.) 2.00
(9) David Justice (#82-90) 2.00
(9) David Justice (Promo card.) 2.00
(10) Don Mattingly (#91-99) 6.00
(10) Don Mattingly (Promo card.) 6.00
(11) Fred McGriff (#136-144) 2.00
(11) Fred McGriff (Promo card.) 2.00
(12) Kirby Puckett (#1-9) 4.50
(12) Kirby Puckett (Promo card.) 4.50
(13) Nolan Ryan (#109-117) 6.00
(13) Nolan Ryan (Promo card.) 6.00
(14) Ryne Sandberg (#10-18) 4.00
(14) Ryne Sandberg (Promo card.) 4.00
(15) Darryl Strawberry (#46-54) 2.00
(15) Darryl Strawberry (Promo card.) 2.00
(16) Frank Thomas (#100-108) 3.00
(16) Frank Thomas (Promo card.) 3.00

Home Run Series

BALTIMORE — CAL RIPKEN, Jr. — Honors & Awards - 2

With a suggested retail price at issue of $25 or so, and an edition limit of 1,500 each of the single-player, nine-card sets (plus 300 promo cards of each player), these are among the scarcer of the 1991 Star issues. Numbers on individual player cards run contiguously throughout the issue and are noted in the alphabetical checklist. Because sets are seldom available as singles, individual cards are not listed here.

NM/M
Complete Set (126): 65.00
Common Player Set: 3.75
Complete Promo Set (14): 85.00
Common Promo Card: 5.00
(1) Wade Boggs (#91-99) 5.50
(1) Wade Boggs (Promo card.) 7.50
(2) Barry Bonds (#64-72) 9.00
(2) Barry Bonds (Promo card.) 12.00
(3) Bobby Bonilla (#10-18) 3.75
(3) Bobby Bonilla (Promo card.) 5.00
(4) Jose Canseco (#1-9) 5.50
(4) Jose Canseco (Promo card.) 7.50
(5) Dwight Gooden (#73-81) 3.75
(5) Dwight Gooden (Promo card.) 5.00
(6) Ken Griffey Jr. (#37-45) 5.00
(6) Ken Griffey Jr. (Promo card.) 7.50
(7) Rickey Henderson (#19-27) 6.00
(7) Rickey Henderson (Promo card.) 8.00
(8) Bo Jackson (#82-90) 3.00
(8) Bo Jackson (Promo card.) 4.50
(9) Don Mattingly (#46-54) 9.00
(9) Don Mattingly (Promo card.) 10.00
(10) Cal Ripken Jr. (#109-117) 9.00
(10) Cal Ripken Jr. (Promo card.) 12.00
(11) Nolan Ryan (#55-63) 9.00
(11) Nolan Ryan (Promo card.) 12.00
(12) Ryne Sandberg (#100-108) 7.50
(12) Ryne Sandberg (Promo card.) 7.50
(13) Darryl Strawberry (#28-36) 3.75
(13) Darryl Strawberry (Promo card.) 5.00
(14) Frank Thomas (#118-126) 7.50
(14) Frank Thomas (Promo card.) 10.00

Millennium Edition

As the name suggests, production of each of these nine-card, single-player sets was pegged at 1,000 (plus 200 promo cards of each play-

MILLENNIUM

DON MATTINGLY NEW YORK Minor League Stats

er). Suggested retail price at issue was about $30. Cards are numbered contiguously throughout the issue, as noted in the alphabetical checklist (part of each Ripken and Gooden set are misnumbered). Individual cards are not listed or priced because the sets are almost never broken down for singles sales.

		NM/M
Complete Set (126):		50.00
Common Player Set:		1.50
Complete Promo Set (14):		50.00
Common Promo Card:		1.50
(1)	Wade Boggs (#55-63)	7.50
(1)	Wade Boggs (Promo card.)	7.50
(2)	Will Clark (#46-54)	3.00
(2)	Will Clark (Promo card.)	3.00
(3)	Cecil Fielder (#109-117)	1.50
(3)	Cecil Fielder (Promo card.)	1.50
(4)	Dwight Gooden (#10-14, 78-81)	1.50
(4)	Dwight Gooden (Promo card.)	1.50
(5)	Ken Griffey Jr. (#91-99)	6.00
(5)	Ken Griffey Jr. (Promo card.)	6.00
(6)	Howard Johnson (#64-72)	1.50
(6)	Howard Johnson (Promo card.)	1.50
(7)	Dave Justice (#100-108)	1.50
(7)	David Justice (Promo card.)	1.50
(8)	Kevin Maas (#82-90)	1.50
(8)	Kevin Maas (Promo card.)	1.50
(9)	Don Mattingly (#37-45)	7.50
(9)	Don Mattingly (Promo card.)	7.50
(10)	Kirby Puckett (#19-27)	7.50
(10)	Kirby Puckett (Promo card.)	7.50
(11)	Cal Ripken Jr. (#15-18, 73-77)	7.50
(11)	Cal Ripken Jr. (Promo card.)	7.50
(12)	Ryne Sandberg (#28-36)	6.00
(12)	Ryne Sandberg (Promo card.)	6.00
(13)	Frank Thomas (#118-126)	6.00
(13)	Frank Thomas (Promo card.)	6.00
(14)	Robin Yount (#1-9)	3.00
(14)	Robin Yount (Promo card.)	3.00

Nova Edition

Nova

Rickey Henderson OAKLAND Minor League Stats

Production of these nine-card, single-player sets was limited to 500 of each (plus 100 promo cards of each player). Sets are checklisted here in alphabetical order. Individual cards are numbered contiguously throughout the issue, as noted. Single cards are not priced because the sets are seldom broken up for sale of individual cards.

		NM/M
Complete Set (144):		60.00
Common Player Set:		2.50
Complete Promo Set (16):		60.00

			NM/M
Common Promo Card:			2.50
(1)	Wade Boggs (#82-90)		6.00
(1)	Wade Boggs (Promo card.)		6.00
(2)	Jose Canseco (#55-63)		5.00
(2)	Jose Canseco (Promo card.)		5.00
(3)	Vince Coleman (#127-135)		2.50
(3)	Vince Coleman (Promo card.)		2.50
(4)	Cecil Fielder (#136-144)		2.50
(4)	Cecil Fielder (Promo card.)		2.50
(5)	Dwight Gooden (#10-18)		2.50
(5)	Dwight Gooden (Promo card.)		2.50
(6)	Ken Griffey Jr. (#91-99)		7.50
(6)	Ken Griffey Jr. (Promo card.)		7.50
(7)	Tony Gwynn (#100-108)		5.00
(7)	Tony Gwynn (Promo card.)		5.00
(8)	Rickey Henderson (#1-9)		5.00
(8)	Rickey Henderson (Promo card.)		5.00
(9)	Bo Jackson (#28-36)		2.50
(9)	Bo Jackson (Promo card.)		2.50
(10)	Howard Johnson (#118-126)		2.50
(10)	Howard Johnson (Promo card.)		2.50
(11)	Don Mattingly (#64-72)		7.50
(11)	Don Mattingly (Promo card.)		7.50
(12)	Kirby Puckett (#109-117)		5.00
(12)	Kirby Puckett (Promo card.)		5.00
(13)	Cal Ripken Jr. (#46-54)		9.00
(13)	Cal Ripken Jr. (Promo card.)		9.00
(14)	Nolan Ryan (#19-27)		10.00
(14)	Nolan Ryan (Promo card.)		10.00
(15)	Ryne Sandberg (#73-81)		6.00
(15)	Ryne Sandberg (Promo card.)		6.00
(16)	Darryl Strawberry (#37-45)		2.50
(16)	Darryl Strawberry (Promo card.)		2.50

Platinum Edition

PLATINUM

TEXAS

These nine-card, single-player sets were produced in an edition of 1,000 each (plus 200 promo cards per player). Sets are checklisted here alphabetically, with individual card numbers shown for each player. Single cards are not listed because the sets are seldom offered as singles.

		NM/M
Complete Set (108):		45.00
Common Player Set:		2.00
Complete Promo Set (14):		60.00

			NM/M
Common Promo Card:			2.50
(1)	Wade Boggs (#109-117)		5.00
(1)	Wade Boggs (Promo card.)		5.00
(2)	Barry Bonds (#28-36)		5.00
(2)	Barry Bonds (Promo card.)		7.50
(3)	Bobby Bonilla (#73-81)		2.00
(3)	Bobby Bonilla (Promo card.)		6.00
(4)	Jose Canseco (#19-27)		5.00
(4)	Jose Canseco (Promo card.)		6.00
(5)	Will Clark (#118-126)		3.75
(5)	Will Clark (Promo card.)		6.00
(6)	Roger Clemens (#10-18)		6.00
(6)	Roger Clemens (Promo card.)		8.00
(7)	Mark Grace (#1-9)		2.00
(7)	Mark Grace (Promo card.)		2.50
(8)	Ken Griffey Jr. (#55-63)		3.75
(8)	Ken Griffey Jr. (Promo card.)		6.00
(9)	Rickey Henderson (#46-54)		3.75
(9)	Rickey Henderson (Promo card.)		5.00
(10)	Kevin Maas (#37-45)		2.00
(10)	Kevin Maas (Promo card.)		2.50

		NM/M
(11)	Don Mattingly (#82-90)	6.00
(11)	Don Mattingly (Promo card.)	6.50
(12)	Cal Ripken Jr. (#91-99)	7.50
(12)	Cal Ripken Jr. (Promo card.)	10.00
(13)	Nolan Ryan (#64-72)	7.50
(13)	Nolan Ryan (Promo card.)	10.00
(14)	Frank Thomas (#100-108)	3.75
(14)	Frank Thomas (Promo card.)	3.75

Cal Ripken Promo Set

This unusual Star set has five solid orange-bordered cards of Ripken. Unlike the other Star promo cards, which are blank-backed, the backs of these glossy-finish cards says "1 of 1,000 Promo Sets," and include stats and other information.

	NM/M
1-5 Cal Ripken Jr.	10.00

Rookie Guild Prototypes

THE ROOKIE GUILD

MARK LEWIS CLEVELAND Prototype

Labeled as "Prototype" cards, these unnumbered blank-back cards can be found in a confusing variety of regular, glossy and plastic finish for the six players in the Rookie Guild set. Only those cards confirmed to exist are listed here.

		NM/M
Complete Set, Regular (3):		4.00
Complete Set, Glossy (3):		6.00
Complete Set, Plastic (4):		8.00
(1g)	Jeff Bagwell/Glossy	2.00
(1p)	Jeff Bagwell/Plastic	2.50
(2)	Albert Belle	1.50
(3g)	Juan Gonzalez/Glossy	2.00
(3p)	Juan Gonzalez/Plastic	2.50
(4a)	Chris Knoblauch (Chuck)	2.50
(4bp)	Chuck Knoblauch/Plastic	2.00
(5)	Mark Lewis	1.00
(6g)	Frank Thomas/Glossy	3.75
(6p)	Frank Thomas/Plastic	4.50

Rookie Guild Promos

A confusing variety of regular, glossy and plastic finish promo cards were issued in different combinations for the six players in Star's 1991 Rookie Guild issue. The blank-back, unnumbered cards are checklisted here in alphabetical order. Only those cards confirmed to have been issued are listed.

		NM/M
Complete Set, Regular (3):		4.00
Complete Set, Glossy (6):		12.50
Complete Set, Plastic (4):		9.00
(1g)	Jeff Bagwell/Glossy	2.25
(1p)	Jeff Bagwell/Plastic	2.50
(2)	Albert Belle	1.50
(2g)	Albert Belle/Glossy	3.00
(3g)	Juan Gonzalez/Glossy	2.25
(3p)	Juan Gonzalez/Plastic	2.50
(4a)	Chris Knoblauch (Chuck)	1.75
(4ag)	Chris Knoblauch (Chuck)/Glossy	
(4bp)	Chuck Knoblauch/Plastic	2.00
(5)	Mark Lewis	.70
(5g)	Mark Lewis/Glossy	1.50
(6g)	Frank Thomas/Glossy	2.50
(6p)	Frank Thomas/Plastic	3.25

Rookie Guild

Late in the 1991 baseball season, Star introduced yet another series of single-player card sets. The emphasis was on young stars in 11-card sets. Most player sets were produced in some combination of regular and glossy finish, or glossy and plastic finish. Each player was also represented with some combination of 1,000 each promotional (border other than white) and prototype cards and 50 glossy and/or plastic

---

		NM/M
(11)	Don Mattingly (#82-90)	6.00
(11)	Don Mattingly (Promo card.)	6.50
(12)	Cal Ripken Jr. (#91-99)	7.50
(12)	Cal Ripken Jr. (Promo card.)	10.00
(13)	Nolan Ryan (#64-72)	7.50
(13)	Nolan Ryan (Promo card.)	10.00
(14)	Frank Thomas (#100-108)	3.75
(14)	Frank Thomas (Promo card.)	3.75

THE ROOKIE GUILD

ALBERT BELLE CLEVELAND Career Info - 1

promo cards. Single cards are not listed because sets are seldom broken for individual card sales.

		NM/M
Common Player Set, Regular:		1.00
Common Player Set, Glossy:		1.50
Common Player Set, Plastic:		4.00
(1)	Albert Belle (#1-11)	1.00
(1g)	Albert Belle (#1)/Glossy	3.00
(2a)	Chris Knoblauch (Chuck)	3.00
(2ag)	Chris Knoblauch (Chuck)/Glossy	4.50
(2bg)	Chuck Knoblauch (#12-22)(Glossy only.)	1.50
(3)	Mark Lewis (#23-33)	1.00
(3g)	Mark Lewis/Glossy	3.00
(4g)	Frank Thomas (#33-44)/Glossy	1.75
(4p)	Frank Thomas/Plastic	5.00
(5g)	Juan Gonzalez (#45-55)/Glossy	1.50
(5p)	Juan Gonzalez/Plastic	4.00
(6g)	Jeff Bagwell (#56-66)/Glossy	1.50
(6p)	Jeff Bagwell/Plastic	4.00

1991 Star Silver Edition

SILVER

VINCE COLEMAN NEW YORK Career Highlights

Two thousand of each nine-card player set was produced in Star's silver-enhanced set, along with 400 promo cards of each player. Players are listed here in alphabetical order. Individual cards are not listed because the sets are seldom offered as singles.

	NM/M
Complete Set (126):	35.00
Common Player Set:	1.50
Complete Promo Set (15):	45.00

		NM/M
Common Promo Card:		2.00
(1)	Wade Boggs (#10-18)	4.00
(1)	Wade Boggs (Promo card.)	4.00
(2)	Bobby Bonilla (#37-45)	1.50
(2)	Bobby Bonilla (Promo card.)	2.00
(3)	Jose Canseco (#109-117)	3.00
(3)	Jose Canseco (Promo card.)	3.00
(4)	Vince Coleman (#1-9)	1.50
(4)	Vince Coleman (Promo card.)	2.00
(5)	Dwight Gooden (#73-81)	1.50
(5)	Dwight Gooden (Promo card.)	2.00
(6)	Ken Griffey Jr. (#91-99)	6.00
(6)	Ken Griffey Jr. (Promo card.)	8.00
(7)	Tony Gwynn (#46-54)	4.00
(7)	Tony Gwynn (Promo card.)	4.00
(8)	Rickey Henderson (#82-90)	3.00
(8)	Rickey Henderson (Promo card.)	4.00
(9)	Bo Jackson (#100-108)	1.50
(9)	Bo Jackson (Promo card.)	2.00
(10)	Kevin Maas (#28-36)	1.50
(10)	Kevin Maas (Promo card.)	2.00
(11)	Don Mattingly (#19-27)	4.50
(11)	Don Mattingly (Promo card.)	6.00
(12)	Nolan Ryan (#55-63)	6.00

		NM/M
(12)	Nolan Ryan (Promo card.)	8.00
(13)	Ryne Sandberg (#64-72)	4.00
(13)	Ryne Sandberg (Promo card.)	5.00
(14)	Frank Thomas (#118-126)	3.75
(14)	Frank Thomas (Promo card.)	5.00
(15)	Albert Belle (Promo card only, produced in error.)	3.00

Stellar Edition

The same players who appear in other Star sets for 1991 are repackaged into this edition of 500 sets of each player. One hundred promo cards of each player were also issued.

		NM/M
Complete Set (126):		50.00
Common Player Set:		2.00
Complete Promo Set (14):		65.00
Common Promo Card:		2.50
(1)	Bobby Bonilla (#55-63)	2.00
(1)	Bobby Bonilla (Promo card.)	2.50
(2)	Will Clark (#37-45)	5.00
(2)	Will Clark (Promo card.)	5.00
(3)	Roger Clemens (#10-18)	6.50
(3)	Roger Clemens (Promo card.)	8.00
(4)	Vince Coleman (#73-81)	2.00
(4)	Vince Coleman (Promo card.)	2.50
(5)	Ken Griffey Jr. (#1-9)	7.50
(5)	Ken Griffey Jr. (Promo card.)	10.00
(6)	Tony Gwynn (#46-54)	6.50
(6)	Tony Gwynn (Promo card.)	6.50
(7)	Rickey Henderson (#118-126)	5.00
(7)	Rickey Henderson (Promo card.)	6.50
(8)	Howard Johnson (#100-108)	2.00
(8)	Rickey Henderson (Promo card.)	2.50
(9)	Don Mattingly (#109-117)	6.00
(9)	Don Mattingly (Promo card.)	8.00
(10)	Kirby Puckett (#64-72)	6.00
(10)	Kirby Puckett (Promo card.)	6.00
(11)	Cal Ripken Jr. (#82-90)	7.50
(11)	Cal Ripken Jr. (Promo card.)	8.00
(12)	Nolan Ryan (#19-27)	7.50
(12)	Nolan Ryan (Promo card.)	8.00
(13)	Ryne Sandberg (#91-99)	6.00
(13)	Ryne Sandberg (Promo card.)	6.50
(14)	Robin Yount (#28-36)	4.50
(14)	Robin Yount (Promo card.)	5.00

1991 Star The Future

The FUTURE

PAT KELLY NEW YORK Checklist

A few players who had not yet been included among the flood of 1991 Star issues joined the others in this post-season issue. Production was put at 1,000 nine-card sets per player, plus 200 promo cards of each. Players are listed here in alphabetical order. Individual cards are not listed because the sets are usually never sold as singles.

		NM/M
Complete Set (90):		15.00
Common Player Set:		1.50
Complete Promo Set (10):		20.00
Common Promo Card:		2.00
(1)	Jeff Bagwell (#28-36)	3.00
(1)	Jeff Bagwell (Promo card.)	4.00
(2)	Albert Belle (#55-63)	2.00
(2)	Albert Belle (Promo card.)	2.75
(3)	Scott Erickson (#82-90)	1.50
(3)	Scott Erickson (Promo card.)	2.00

		NM/M
(4)	Juan Gonzalez (#1-9)	2.25
(4)	Juan Gonzalez (Promo card.)	3.50
(5)	Pat Kelly (#10-18)	1.50
(5)	Pat Kelly (Promo card.)	2.00
(6)	Mark Lewis (#73-81)	1.50
(6)	Mark Lewis (Promo card.)	2.00
(7)	Ramon Martinez (#46-54)	1.50
(7)	Ramon Martinez (Promo card.)	2.00
(8)	Brian McRae (#64-72)	1.50
(8)	Brian McRae (Promo card.)	2.00
(9)	Frank Thomas (#37-45)	3.50
(9)	Frank Thomas (Promo card.)	5.00
(10)	Mo Vaughn (#19-27)	1.50
(10)	Mo Vaughn (Promo card.)	2.00

1991 Star '92

STAR '92

TODD VAN POPPEL OAKLAND A's

Though labeled "Star '92" on front, these single-player 11-card sets were produced in 1991. Fronts feature borders which fade from one color at top to gray at the bottom. The photos at center are a mix of poses and game-action shots. Backs have a small color portrait photo - at the same on all cards within a set - at upper-left. Stats, personal data, highlights, checklists and team logos are printed in color on yellow cardboard. The cards carry a 1991 copyright line at bottom center. Each set can be found in a glossy version, which carries a premium of 2X.

	NM/M
Complete Set (22):	5.00
Common Player Set:	2.50
Complete Promo Set (2):	4.00
Common Promo Card:	2.00
1-11 Scott Erickson	1.50
Scott Erickson (Promo card.)	2.00
1-11 Todd Van Poppel	1.50
Todd Van Poppel (Promo card.)	2.00

1992 Star '92

STAR '92

DAVE JUSTICE ATLANTA Career Stats

Utilizing a design introduced the previous year, the Star '92 single-player card sets produced in 1992 are printed on cardboard laminated with high-gloss plastic surfaces front and back. Each player's cards are bordered with a single bright color at top which fades to gray at bottom. Photos are a mix of poses and game-action shots. Backs have a yellow background with a small color portrait (the same throughout the player's set) at upper-left. Stats, personal data, career highlights, checklist or team logo are printed in colored ink. The cards carry a 1992 copyright date and each set has a large capital letter in the lower-right corner. It is not known whether sets were issued for the letters missing in the checklist below, though prototype cards are known for some. Production was reported as 4,000 of each player set and 800 of each promo and prototype card. Only confirmed cards are listed. Single cards are not listed because sets are seldom broken for individual card sales.

		NM/M
Common Player Set:		1.00
Common Promo Card:		1.75
Common Prototype Card:		1.75
A1-11	Jeff Bagwell	2.00
	Jeff Bagwell (Promo card.)	3.00
	Jeff Bagwell (Prototype)	3.00
B1-11	Albert Belle	1.50
	Albert Belle (Promo)	2.00
C1-11	Ron Gant	1.00
	Ron Gant (Promo card.)	1.75
	Ron Gant (Prototype)	1.75
D1-11	Bo Jackson	1.00
	Bo Jackson (Promo card.)	1.75
	Bo Jackson (Prototype)	1.75
E1-11	Dave Justice	1.00
	David Justice (Promo card.)	1.75
	David Justice (Prototype)	1.75
F1-11	Chuck Knoblauch	1.00
	Chuck Knoblauch (Promo card.)	1.75
	Chuck Knoblauch (Prototype)	1.75
G1-11	Kirby Puckett	2.50
	Kirby Puckett (Promo card.)	3.25
	Kirby Puckett (Prototype)	3.25
H1-11	Ryne Sandberg	2.50
	Ryne Sandberg (Promo)	3.25
	Ryne Sandberg (Prototype)	3.25
I1-11	Steve Avery	1.00
	Steve Avery (Promo)	1.75
	Steve Avery (Prototype)	1.75
J1-11	Phil Plantier	1.00
	Phil Plantier (Promo)	1.75
K	Wade Boggs (Prototype)	3.25
M1-11	Will Clark	1.50
	Will Clark (Promo card.)	3.25
N1-11	Ken Griffey Jr.	5.00
	Ken Griffey Jr. (Promo card.)	6.25
	Ken Griffey Jr. (Prototype)	6.25
O	Cal Ripken Jr. (Prototype)	3.75
P	Nolan Ryan (Prototype, regular finish.)	4.50
	Nolan Ryan (Plastic prototype.)	6.00
R	Frank Thomas (Prototype)	4.50
S	Bobby Bonilla (Prototype)	1.75
T	Kevin Mitchell (Prototype)	1.75
U1-11	Danny Tartabull	1.00
	Danny Tartabull (Promo card.)	1.75
V1-11	Dean Palmer	1.00
	Dean Palmer (Promo)	1.75
	Dean Palmer (Prototype)	1.75

Gold Edition

The 12 players in Star's 1992 Gold Edition are represented in an issue of 750 sets each, plus 150 promo cards. The checklist is arranged alphabetically. Single cards are not listed because sets are not often broken up for individual card sales.

		NM/M
Complete Set (108):		55.00
Common Player Set:		3.00
Complete Promo Set (12):		75.00
Common Promo Card:		5.00
(1)	Steve Avery (#91-99)	3.00
(1)	Steve Avery (Promo card.)	5.00
(2)	Jose Canseco (#19-27)	6.00

(2)	Jose Canseco (Promo card.)	8.00
(3)	Will Clark (#28-36)	5.00
(3)	Will Clark (Promo card.)	8.00
(4)	Ken Griffey Jr. (#82-90)	9.00
(4)	Ken Griffey Jr. (Promo card.)	12.00
(5)	Bo Jackson (#46-54)	3.00
(5)	Bo Jackson (Promo card.)	4.00
(6)	David Justice (#10-18)	3.50
(6)	David Justice (Promo card.)	5.00
(7)	Don Mattingly (#1-9)	7.50
(7)	Don Mattingly (Promo card.)	10.00
(8)	Cal Ripken Jr. (#64-72)	9.00
(8)	Cal Ripken Jr. (Promo card.)	12.00
(9)	Nolan Ryan (#37-45)	9.00
(9)	Nolan Ryan (Promo card.)	12.00
(10)	Ryne Sandberg (#55-63)	6.00
(10)	Ryne Sandberg (Promo card.)	8.00
(11)	Darryl Strawberry (#100-108)	3.50
(11)	Darryl Strawberry (Promo card.)	5.00
(12)	Frank Thomas (#73-81)	7.50
(12)	Frank Thomas (Promo card.)	10.00

Millenium Edition

Star's Millenium Edition for 1992 included an issue of 750 sets and 150 promo cards for each of 12 players, listed alphabetically in the checklist below. Single cards are not listed because player sets are seldom broken up for individual card sales.

		NM/M
Complete Set (108):		70.00
Common Player Set:		4.00
Complete Promo Set (12):		95.00
Common Promo Card:		5.00
(1)	Wade Boggs (#100-108)	7.50
(1)	Wade Boggs (Promo card.)	10.00
(2)	Jose Canseco (#10-18)	7.50
(2)	Jose Canseco (Promo card.)	10.00
(3)	Roger Clemens (#28-36)	7.50
(3)	Roger Clemens (Promo card.)	10.00
(4)	Ken Griffey Jr. (#1-9)	10.00
(4)	Ken Griffey Jr. (Promo card.)	12.50
(5)	Bo Jackson (#82-90)	4.00
(5)	Bo Jackson (Promo card.)	5.00
(6)	David Justice (#73-81)	4.00
(6)	David Justice (Promo card.)	5.00
(7)	Don Mattingly (#37-45)	9.00
(7)	Don Mattingly (Promo card.)	12.00
(8)	Kirby Puckett (#91-99)	9.00
(8)	Kirby Puckett (Promo card.)	12.00
(9)	Cal Ripken Jr. (#19-27)	10.00
(9)	Cal Ripken Jr. (Promo card.)	12.50
(10)	Nolan Ryan (#55-63)	10.00
(10)	Nolan Ryan (Promo card.)	12.50
(11)	Ryne Sandberg (#46-54)	7.50
(11)	Ryne Sandberg (Promo card.)	10.00
(12)	Frank Thomas (#64-72)	9.00
(12)	Frank Thomas (Promo card.)	12.00

Nova Edition

These nine-card, single-player sets were limited to an edition of 500 for each player, plus 100 promo cards. Numbering errors occurred on the Avery and Strawberry cards. The former were supposed to be numbered 10-18; the latter 64-72.

		NM/M
Complete Set (108):		75.00
Common Player Set:		4.50
Complete Promo Set:		100.00
Common Promo Card:		6.00
(1)	Nolan Ryan (#1-9)	12.00
(1)	Nolan Ryan (Promo card.)	15.00
(2)	Steve Avery (#10-14, 69-72)	4.50
(2)	Steve Avery (Promo card.)	6.00
(3)	Frank Thomas (#19-27)	9.00
(3)	Frank Thomas (Promo card.)	12.00
(4)	Don Mattingly (#28-36)	12.50
(4)	Don Mattingly (Promo card.)	15.00
(5)	Ken Griffey Jr. (#37-45)	12.50
(5)	Ken Griffey Jr. (Promo card.)	15.00
(6)	David Justice (#46-54)	4.50
(6)	David Justice (Promo card.)	6.00

(7)	Ryne Sandberg (#55-63)	9.00
(7)	Ryne Sandberg (Promo card.)	12.00
(8)	Darryl Strawberry (#64-68, 15-18)	4.50
(8)	Darryl Strawberry (Promo card.)	6.00
(9)	Cal Ripken Jr. (#73-81)	12.50
(9)	Cal Ripken Jr. (Promo card.)	15.00
(10)	Bo Jackson (#82-90)	4.50
(10)	Bo Jackson (Promo card.)	5.00
(11)	Jose Canseco (#91-99)	7.50
(11)	Jose Canseco (Promo card.)	10.00
(12)	Roger Clemens (#100-108)	9.00
(12)	Roger Clemens (Promo card.)	12.00

Platinum Edition

A dozen established stars are featured in the '92 Star Platinum issue, each in nine-card sets, contiguously numbered. One thousand sets of each player were issued, along with 200 promo cards. The cards are listed here in alphabetical order. Single cards are not listed because the player sets are not often broken up for individual sales.

		NM/M
Complete Set (108):		50.00
Common Player Set:		2.50
Complete Promo Set (12):		65.00
Common Promo Card:		3.00
(1)	Jeff Bagwell (#55-63)	5.00
(1)	Jeff Bagwell (Promo card.)	6.00
(2)	Jose Canseco (#73-81)	5.00
(2)	Jose Canseco (Promo card.)	6.50
(3)	Will Clark (#100-108)	5.00
(3)	Will Clark (Promo card.)	4.00
(4)	Roger Clemens (#91-99)	5.00
(4)	Roger Clemens (Promo card.)	6.50
(5)	Ken Griffey Jr. (#37-45)	7.50
(5)	Ken Griffey Jr. (Promo card.)	10.00
(6)	Bo Jackson (#28-36)	2.50
(6)	Bo Jackson (Promo card.)	3.00
(7)	David Justice (#10-18)	2.50
(7)	David Justice (Promo card.)	3.00
(8)	Don Mattingly (#64-72)	7.50
(8)	Don Mattingly (Promo card.)	10.00
(9)	Cal Ripken Jr. (#46-54)	7.50
(9)	Cal Ripken Jr. (Promo card.)	10.00
(10)	Nolan Ryan (#82-90)	7.50
(10)	Nolan Ryan (Promo card.)	10.00
(11)	Ryne Sandberg (#1-9)	5.00
(11)	Ryne Sandberg (Promo card.)	6.50
(12)	Frank Thomas (#19-27)	6.00
(12)	Frank Thomas (Promo card.)	8.00

Rookie Guild

ROOKIE GUILD '92

LOS ANGELES · ERIC
Ad Card · KARROS

Each of the four players in the '92 Rookie Guild issue is represented by an 11-card set, a promo card and a gold preview card. The first 10 cards in each player's set have blue borders, while the last card has white borders. Cards are seldom available as singles since the sets are rarely broken up.

		NM/M
Complete Set (44):		6.00
Complete Promo Set:		8.00
Complete Preview Set:		12.00
1-11	Reggie Sanders	1.50
	Reggie Sanders (Promo card.)	2.00
	Reggie Sanders (Gold preview.)	3.00
12-22	Phil Plantier	1.50

	Phil Plantier (Promo card.)	2.00
	Phil Plantier (Gold preview.)	3.00
23-33	Dean Palmer	1.50
	Dean Palmer (Promo card.)	2.00
	Dean Palmer (Gold preview.)	3.00
34-44	Eric Karros	1.50
	Eric Karros (Promo card.)	2.00
	Eric Karros (Gold preview.)	3.00
	Eric Karros (Ad card.)	3.00

Silver Edition

Nearly the same line-up as found in other special edition Star nine-card player sets is found in the silver version. Announced production was 1,000 sets of each player along with 200 promo cards. The cards are listed here in alphabetical order. Single cards are not listed because the player sets are not often broken up for individual sales.

		NM/M
Complete Set (108):		40.00
Common Player Set:		3.00
Complete Promo Set (12):		55.00
Common Promo Card:		3.00
(1)	Jeff Bagwell (#46-54)	4.50
(1)	Jeff Bagwell (Promo card.)	6.00
(2)	Jose Canseco (#64-72)	4.50
(2)	Jose Canseco (Promo card.)	5.00
(3)	Will Clark (#1-9)	4.50
(3)	Will Clark (Promo card.)	6.00
(4)	Ken Griffey Jr. (#28-36)	6.00
(4)	Ken Griffey Jr. (Promo card.)	8.00
(5)	Bo Jackson (#37-45)	3.00
(5)	Bo Jackson (Promo card.)	4.00
(6)	David Justice (#19-27)	3.00
(6)	David Justice (Promo card.)	4.00
(7)	Don Mattingly (#100-108)	6.00
(7)	Don Mattingly (Promo card.)	8.00
(8)	Cal Ripken Jr. (#82-90)	6.00
(8)	Cal Ripken Jr. (Promo card.)	8.00
(9)	Nolan Ryan (#73-81)	6.00
(9)	Nolan Ryan (Promo card.)	8.00
(10)	Ryne Sandberg (#10-18)	6.00
(10)	Ryne Sandberg (Promo card.)	7.50
(11)	Darryl Strawberry (#91-99)	3.00
(11)	Darryl Strawberry (Promo card.)	4.00
(12)	Frank Thomas (#55-63)	5.00
(12)	Frank Thomas (Promo card.)	6.00

Stellar Edition

Among the scarcer of Star's 1992 single-player, nine-card sets, the Stellar Edition was produced in an issue of 500 sets and 100 promo cards of each player, contiguously numbered. The cards are listed here in alphabetical order. Single cards are not listed because the player sets are not often broken up for individual sales.

		NM/M
Complete Set (108):		65.00
Common Player Set:		4.50
Complete Promo Set (12):		90.00
Common Promo Card:		6.00
(1)	Jeff Bagwell (#19-27)	6.00
(1)	Jeff Bagwell (Promo card.)	10.00
(2)	Jose Canseco (#100-108)	7.50
(2)	Jose Canseco (Promo card.)	7.50
(3)	Will Clark (#37-45)	6.00
(3)	Will Clark (Promo card.)	6.00
(4)	Roger Clemens (#10-18)	7.50
(4)	Roger Clemens (Promo card.)	6.00
(5)	Ken Griffey Jr. (#55-63)	7.50
(5)	Ken Griffey Jr. (Promo card.)	12.00
(6)	Bo Jackson (#73-81)	4.50
(6)	Bo Jackson (Promo card.)	6.00
(7)	David Justice (#64-72)	4.50
(7)	David Justice (Promo card.)	6.00
(8)	Don Mattingly (#91-99)	9.00
(8)	Don Mattingly (Promo card.)	12.00
(9)	Cal Ripken Jr. (#46-54)	9.00
(9)	Cal Ripken Jr. (Promo card.)	12.00
(10)	Nolan Ryan (#82-90)	9.00

(10)	Nolan Ryan (Promo card.)	12.00
(11)	Ryne Sandberg (#28-36)	7.50
(11)	Ryne Sandberg (Promo card.)	10.00
(12)	Frank Thomas (#1-9)	7.50
(12)	Frank Thomas (Promo card.)	10.00

The Kid

This five-card set was reportedly produced in an edition of 1,000 as a value-added with Star's porcelain statue of Ken Griffey, Jr. One card set was given with the purchase of five statues at $125 each. No promo cards or glossy version were issued.

		NM/M
Complete Set (5):		50.00
1-5	Ken Griffey Jr.	10.00

1993 Star '93 Andy Benes

STAR '93

ANDY BENES · Career Stats

It is unknown whether the usual 11-card set was produced for this continuation of the Star single-player series, or whether this represents a promotional card. In format similar to the Star '92 issues, the card has a red top border which morphs to yellow at bottom. Back repeats a detail of the front photo and has career stats printed in red on a yellow background. There is a 1993 copyright date, but no card number. The card does not have the high-gloss plastic coating found on the earlier series.

		NM/M
Andy Benes		2.00
Andy Benes (Auto. w/COA.)		3.00

1995 Star Cal Ripken, Jr.

Cal, Ripken, Jr.
They Pinch hit for Cal · Star

A major design fault apparently prevented this issue from being widely circulated. Each of the 80 cards in the boxed set has an extraneous comma between "Cal" and "Ripken." That fatal flaw aside, the set does a creditable job of detailing Ripken's major league career through his record 2,131st consecutive game in 1995. Glossy card fronts have color photos at center with orange and brown graphic highlights. Each card has him identified as "Cal, Ripken, Jr." at bottom, below which there is a card title. Backs have a baseball at center with career highlights, stats, personal information or trivia. The name error is repeated in orange script at bottom. The set was fully licensed by Ripken and Major League Baseball.

	NM/M
Complete Boxed Set (80):	10.00
Common Card:	.25

(10)	Nolan Ryan (Promo card.)	12.00
(11)	Ryne Sandberg (#28-36)	7.50
(11)	Ryne Sandberg (Promo card.)	10.00
(12)	Frank Thomas (#1-9)	7.50
(12)	Frank Thomas (Promo card.)	10.00

1989 Starline Prototypes

MARK GRACE

Prior to its first major baseball card issue, Starline produced six variations of a prototype issue. The seven-card sets feature game-action photos on the front, surrounded by colorful borders and with a combination of up to three logos in the bottom border. Cards were produced with just the Starline logo, with the Starline and Coca-Cola logos and with the card company and soft drink logos in conjunction with those of McDonald's, 7-11, Burger King or Dominos pizza. Backs repeat the logos at bottom, along with that of Major League Baseball. At top is a color player photo, along with biographical data, complete major and minor league stats and career highlights. The unnumbered cards are checklisted here alphabetically.

		NM/M
Complete Set (7):		45.00
Common Player:		6.00
(1)	Eric Davis	6.00
(2)	Mark Grace	6.00
(3)	Tony Gwynn	10.00
(4)	Gregg Jefferies	6.00
(5)	Don Mattingly	12.00
(6)	Mark McGwire	13.50
(7)	Darryl Strawberry	6.00

1990 Starline

MARK GRACE

Five-card cello packs of this Coca-Cola sponsored issue were given away with the purchase of dinner and a soft drink at Long John Silver fish restaurants. Cards feature game-action photos on front, bordered in team colors. Backs repeat the team-color scheme and feature a portrait photo along with major league stats and career highlights. Most of the players had two or more cards in the 40-card issue. A header card in each pack offered a 2' x 3' poster of one of 18 players in set for $3.99.

		NM/M
Complete Set (40):		3.00
Common Player:		.10
1	Don Mattingly	.40
2	Mark Grace	.10
3	Eric Davis	.10
4	Tony Gwynn	.30
5	Bobby Bonilla	.10
6	Wade Boggs	.30
7	Frank Viola	.10
8	Ruben Sierra	.10
9	Mark McGwire	.50
10	Alan Trammell	.10
11	Mark McGwire	.50
12	Gregg Jefferies	.10
13	Nolan Ryan	.60
14	John Smoltz	.10
15	Glenn Davis	.10
16	Mark Grace	.10
17	Wade Boggs	.30
18	Frank Viola	.10

19	Bret Saberhagen	.10
20	Chris Sabo	.10
21	Darryl Strawberry	.10
22	Wade Boggs	.30
23	Tim Raines	.10
24	Alan Trammell	.10
25	Chris Sabo	.10
26	Nolan Ryan	.60
27	Mark McGwire	.50
28	Don Mattingly	.40
29	Tony Gwynn	.30
30	Glenn Davis	.10
31	Bobby Bonilla	.10
32	Gregg Jefferies	.10
33	Ruben Sierra	.10
34	John Smoltz	.10
35	Don Mattingly	.40
36	Bret Saberhagen	.10
37	Darryl Strawberry	.10
38	Eric Davis	.10
39	Tim Raines	.10
40	Mark Grace	.10
---	Header Card/Poster Offer	.05

1990 Starline Americana

Several baseball players were among the subjects featured in a set of "Americana" quiz cards. The 2-1/2" x 3-1/2" cards are printed in full-color front and back. Backs repeat the front photo in miniature and provide "Historical Highlights" along with a trivia question and the answer to the question on another card.

NM/M

237	Jackie Robinson	2.00
245	Babe Ruth	2.00

1991 Starline Prototypes

These sample cards were produced for submission to baseball licensing authorities for approval, and to prospective sponsors. Only 60 of each card were reported produced. Card fronts have color action photos and a team logo set against a black background. The player's name appears in white and red at top and along the side. Backs have a smaller player photo at upper-right. All of the prototypes have back stats and biography of Nolan Ryan, with a gray diagonal "PROTOTYPE" across them. The Starline, MLB and Players' Associations logo appear across the bottom.

NM/M

	Complete Set (5):	50.00
	Common Player:	10.00
(1)	George Bell	10.00
(2)	Bobby Bonilla	10.00
(3)	Roger Clemens	20.00
(4)	Tim Raines	10.00
(5)	Darryl Strawberry	10.00

1983 Starliner Stickers

This unauthorized collector's issue is based on 16 of the cards issued by Dexter Press in 1967 as Coca-Cola premiums. In July 1983, a Midwestern card dealer produced these stickers by reprinting the 5-1/2"

x 7" Dexter Press cards in 2-7/16" x 3-1/4" format and eliminating the white border. The stickers can be found with either white ("Mactac Starliner") or tan ("Tuchdown Splitless") paper on back. By the early 1990s, the story of the true origins of these stickers had been largely forgotten within the hobby and some dealers were charging between $10-50 apiece for them. The unnumbered stickers are checklisted here in alphabetical order. Production of the white-back stickers was reported at 2,000 sets, with Mantle and Rose double printed.

NM/M

	Complete Set (16):	40.00
	Common Player:	1.00
(1)	Hank Aaron	7.50
(2)	Ernie Banks	1.50
(3)	Roberto Clemente	10.00
(4)	Rocky Colavito	1.00
(5)	Al Kaline	1.50
(6)	Harmon Killebrew	1.00
(7)	Mickey Mantle/DP	20.00
(8)	Willie Mays	7.50
(9)	Willie McCovey	1.00
(10)	Joe Morgan	1.00
(11)	Jim Palmer	1.00
(12)	Brooks Robinson	1.00
(13)	Frank Robinson	1.00
(14)	Pete Rose/DP	7.50
(15)	Willie Stargell	1.00
(16)	Carl Yastrzemski	1.50

1988 Starting Lineup Talking Baseball

Measuring 2-5/8" x 3", these cards were part of the Starting Lineup Talking Baseball game produced by Kenner Parker Toys Inc. The electronic game, with a computer memory and keyboard to respond to a particular baseball game situation, retailed for more than $100. However, several hobby dealers sold the cards separately from the game. The set includes seven instruction cards that do not picture players.

NM/M

	Complete Set (42):	25.00
	Common Player:	.25
11a	Terry Kennedy	.25
11b	Gary Carter	1.25
12a	Carlton Fisk	1.25
12b	Steve Sax	.25
13a	Eddie Murray	1.25
13b	Jack Clark	.25
14a	Don Mattingly	2.50
15a	Keith Hernandez	.25
15a	Willie Randolph	.25
15b	Buddy Bell	.25
16a	Cal Ripken	4.00
16b	Ryne Sandberg	2.00
17a	Lou Whitaker	.25
17b	Ozzie Smith	2.00
18a	Wade Boggs	2.00
18b	Dale Murphy	.75
19a	George Brett	2.50
19b	Mike Schmidt	2.50
20a	Alan Trammell	.25
20b	Eric Davis	.25
21a	Kirby Puckett	2.00
21b	Tony Gwynn	2.00
22a	George Bell	.25
22b	Darryl Strawberry	.25
23a	Rickey Henderson	1.25
23b	Tim Raines	.25
24a	Dave Winfield	1.25
24b	Andre Dawson	.75
25a	Jack Morris	.25
25b	Mike Scott	.25
26a	Robin Yount	1.25
26b	Jody Davis	.25
27a	Roger Clemens	2.50
27b	Todd Worrell	.25
28a	Bret Saberhagen	.25
28b	Fernando Valenzuela	.25
29a	Dave Righetti	.25
29b	Dwight Gooden	.25
30a	Dan Quisenberry	.25
30b	Nolan Ryan	4.00
---	American League Checklist	.25
---	National League Checklist	.25

Team Sets

Similar in format to the cards issued with the Parker Brothers game, these accessory cards could be purchased in groups of three team sets. The team-set cards share the format (2-5/8" x 3") and design of the boxed-set cards, but differ in that the player portraits are presented as colored drawings rather than photos. Because the issue was licensed only by the Players Union, and not MLB, the caps have no team logos. Backs are in black-and-white. Each team set has 20 player cards (the Indians have only 19) plus a batting order/checklist card. Several players appear in more than one set as a result of trades. The cards are checklisted here alphabetically within team.

NM/M

	Complete Set (545):	60.00
	Common Player:	.10

Atlanta Braves Team Set: 4.00

(1)	Jim Acker	.10
(2)	Paul Assenmacher	.10
(3)	Jeff Blauser	.10
(4)	Jeff Dedmon	.10
(5)	Ron Gant	.10
(6)	Tom Glavine	.75
(7)	Ken Griffey	.10
(8)	Albert Hall	.10
(9)	Glenn Hubbard	.10
(10)	Dion James	.10
(11)	Rick Mahler	.10
(12)	Dale Murphy	1.00
(13)	Ken Oberkfell	.10
(14)	Gerald Perry	.10
(15)	Gary Roenicke	.10
(16)	Paul Runge	.10
(17)	Ted Simmons	.10
(18)	Pete Smith	.10
(19)	Andres Thomas	.10
(20)	Ozzie Virgil	.10
(21)	Batting Order/Checklist	.05

Baltimore Orioles Team Set: 12.00

(1)	Eric Bell	.10
(2)	Mike Boddicker	.10
(3)	Jim Dwyer	.10
(4)	Ken Gerhart	.10
(5)	Rene Gonzalez	.10
(6)	Terry Kennedy	.10
(7)	Ray Knight	.10
(8)	Lee Lacy	.10
(9)	Fred Lynn	.10
(10)	Eddie Murray	3.00
(11)	Tom Niedenfuer	.10
(12)	Billy Ripken (Ripken)	.10
(13)	Cal Ripken Jr.	7.50
(14)	Dave Schmidt	.10
(15)	Larry Sheets	.10
(16)	Pete Stanicek	.10
(17)	Mark Thurmond	.10
(18)	Ron Washington	.10
(19)	Mark Williamson	.10
(20)	Mike Young	.10
(21)	Batting Order/Checklist	.05

Boston Red Sox Team Set: 7.50

(1)	Marty Barrett	.10
(2)	Todd Benzinger	.10
(3)	Wade Boggs	4.00
(4)	Dennis Boyd	.10
(5)	Ellis Burks	.10
(6)	Roger Clemens	4.50
(7)	Dwight Evans	.10
(8)	Wes Gardner	.10
(9)	Rich Gedman	.10
(10)	Mike Greenwell	.10
(11)	Sam Horn	.10
(12)	Bruce Hurst	.10
(13)	John Marzano	.10
(14)	Spike Owen	.10
(15)	Jody Reed	.10
(16)	Jim Rice	.35
(17)	Ed Romero	.10
(18)	Kevin Romine	.10
(19)	Lee Smith	.10
(20)	Bob Stanley	.10
(21)	Batting Order/Checklist	.05

California Angels Team Set: 2.25

(1)	Tony Armas	.10
(2)	Bob Boone	.10
(3)	Bill Buckner	.10
(4)	DeWayne Buice	.10
(5)	Brian Downing	.10
(6)	Chuck Finley	.10
(7)	Willie Fraser	.10
(8)	George Hendrick	.10
(9)	Jack Howell	.10
(10)	Ruppert Jones	.10
(11)	Wally Joyner	.10
(12)	Kirk McCaskill	.10
(13)	Mark McLemore	.10
(14)	Darrell Miller	.10
(15)	Greg Minton	.10
(16)	Gary Pettis	.10
(17)	Johnny Ray	.10
(18)	Dick Schofield	.10
(19)	Devon White	.10
(20)	Mike Witt	.10
(21)	Batting Order/Checklist	.05

Chicago Cubs Team Set: 6.00

(1)	Jody Davis	.10
(2)	Andre Dawson	.35
(3)	Bob Dernier	.10
(4)	Frank DiPino	.10
(5)	Shawon Dunston	.10
(6)	Leon Durham	.10
(7)	Dave Martinez	.10
(8)	Keith Moreland	.10
(9)	Jamie Moyer	.10
(10)	Jerry Mumphrey	.10
(11)	Paul Noce	.10
(12)	Rafael Palmeiro	2.50
(13)	Luis Quinones	.10
(14)	Ryne Sandberg	4.00
(15)	Scott Sanderson	.10
(16)	Calvin Schiraldi	.10
(17)	Lee Smith	.10
(18)	Jim Sundberg	.10
(19)	Rick Sutcliffe	.10
(20)	Manny Trillo	.10
(21)	Batting Order/Checklist	.05

Chicago White Sox Team Set: 4.00

(1)	Harold Baines	.10
(2)	Floyd Bannister	.10
(3)	Daryl Boston	.10
(4)	Ivan Calderon	.10
(5)	Jose DeLeon	.10
(6)	Rich Dotson	.10
(7)	Carlton Fisk	3.00
(8)	Ozzie Guillen	.10
(9)	Jerry Hairston Sr.	.10
(10)	Donnie Hill	.10
(11)	Dave LaPoint	.10
(12)	Steve Lyons	.10
(13)	Fred Manrique	.10
(14)	Dan Pasqua	.10
(15)	Gary Redus	.10
(16)	Mark Salas	.10
(17)	Ray Searage	.10
(18)	Bobby Thigpen	.10
(19)	Greg Walker	.10
(20)	Ken Williams	.10
(21)	Batting Order/Checklist	.05

Cincinnati Reds Team Set: 2.25

(1)	Buddy Bell	.10
(2)	Tom Browning	.10
(3)	Dave Collins	.10
(4)	Dave Concepcion	.10
(5)	Kal Daniels	.10
(6)	Eric Davis	.10
(7)	Bo Diaz	.10
(8)	Nick Esasky	.10
(9)	John Franco	.10
(10)	Terry Francona	.10
(11)	Tracy Jones	.10
(12)	Barry Larkin	.10
(13)	Rob Murphy	.10
(14)	Paul O'Neill	.10
(15)	Dave Parker	.10
(16)	Ted Power	.10
(17)	Dennis Rasmussen	.10
(18)	Kurt Stillwell	.10
(19)	Jeff Treadway	.10
(20)	Frank Williams	.10
(21)	Batting Order/Checklist	.05

Cleveland Indians Team Set: 2.25

(1)	Andy Allanson	.10
(2)	Scott Bailes	.10
(3)	Chris Bando	.10
(4)	Jay Bell	.10
(5)	Brett Butler	.10
(6)	Tom Candiotti	.10
(7)	Joe Carter	.10
(8)	Carmen Castillo	.10
(9)	Dave Clark	.10
(10)	John Farrell	.10
(11)	Julio Franco	.10
(12)	Mel Hall	.10
(13)	Tom Hinzo	.10
(14)	Brook Jacoby	.10
(15)	Doug Jones	.10
(16)	Junior Noboa	.10
(17)	Ken Schrom	.10
(18)	Cory Snyder	.10
(19)	Pat Tabler	.10
(20)	Batting Order/Checklist	.05

Detroit Tigers Team Set: 2.25

(1)	Doyle Alexander	.10
(2)	Dave Bergman	.10
(3)	Tom Brookens	.10
(4)	Darrell Evans	.10
(5)	Kirk Gibson	.10
(6)	Mike Heath	.10
(7)	Mike Henneman	.10
(8)	Willie Hernandez	.10
(9)	Larry Herndon	.10
(10)	Eric King	.10
(11)	Ray Knight	.10
(12)	Chet Lemon	.10
(13)	Bill Madlock	.10
(14)	Jack Morris	.10
(15)	Jim Morrison	.10
(16)	Matt Nokes	.10
(17)	Pat Sheridan	.10
(18)	Frank Tanana	.10
(19)	Alan Trammell	.10
(20)	Lou Whitaker	.10
(21)	Batting Order/Checklist	.05

Houston Astros Team Set: 6.00

(1)	Juan Agosto	.10
(2)	Larry Anderson	.10
(3)	Alan Ashby	.10
(4)	Kevin Bass	.10
(5)	Ken Caminiti	.10
(6)	Jose Cruz	.10
(7)	Danny Darwin	.10
(8)	Glenn Davis	.10
(9)	Bill Doran	.10
(10)	Billy Hatcher	.10
(11)	Jim Pankovitz	.10
(12)	Terry Puhl	.10
(13)	Rafael Ramirez	.10
(14)	Craig Reynolds	.10
(15)	Nolan Ryan	7.50
(16)	Mike Scott	.10
(17)	Dave Smith	.10
(18)	Marc Sullivan	.10
(19)	Dennis Walling	.10
(20)	Eric Young	.10
(21)	Batting Order/Checklist	.05

Kansas City Royals Team Set: 6.00

(1)	Steve Balboni	.10
(2)	George Brett	4.50
(3)	Jim Eisenreich	.10
(4)	Gene Garber	.10
(5)	Jerry Don Gleaton	.10
(6)	Mark Gubicza	.10
(7)	Bo Jackson	.50
(8)	Charlie Leibrandt	.10
(9)	Mike Macfarlane	.10
(10)	Larry Owen	.10
(11)	Bill Pecota	.10
(12)	Jamie Quirk	.10
(13)	Dan Quisenberry	.10
(14)	Bret Saberhagen	.10
(15)	Kevin Seitzer	.10
(16)	Kurt Stillwell	.10
(17)	Danny Tartabull	.10
(18)	Gary Thurman	.10
(19)	Frank White	.10
(20)	Willie Wilson	.10
(21)	Batting Order/Checklist	.05

Los Angeles Dodgers Team Set: 2.50

(1)	Dave Anderson	.10
(2)	Mike Davis	.10
(3)	Mariano Duncan	.10
(4)	Kirk Gibson	.10
(5)	Alfredo Griffin	.10
(6)	Pedro Guerrero	.10
(7)	Mickey Hatcher	.10
(8)	Orel Hershiser	.10
(9)	Glenn Hoffman	.10
(10)	Brian Holton	.10
(11)	Mike Marshall	.10
(12)	Jesse Orosco	.10
(13)	Alejandro Pena	.10
(14)	Steve Sax	.10
(15)	Mike Scioscia	.10
(16)	John Shelby	.10
(17)	Franklin Stubbs	.10
(18)	Don Sutton	2.00
(19)	Alex Trevino	.10
(20)	Fernando Valenzuela	.10
(21)	Batting Order/Checklist	.05

Milwaukee Brewers Team Set: 6.00

(1)	Chris Bosio	.10
(2)	Glenn Braggs	.10
(3)	Greg Brock	.10
(4)	Juan Castillo	.10
(5)	Chuck Crim	.10
(6)	Rob Deer	.10
(7)	Mike Felder	.10
(8)	Jim Gantner	.10
(9)	Teddy Higuera	.10
(10)	Steve Kiefer	.10
(11)	Paul Molitor	3.00
(12)	Juan Nieves	.10
(13)	Dan Plesac	.10
(14)	Ernie Riles	.10
(15)	Billy Jo Robidoux	.10
(16)	Bill Schroeder	.10
(17)	B.J. Surhoff	.10
(18)	Dale Sveum	.10
(19)	Bill Wegman	.10
(20)	Robin Yount	3.00
(21)	Batting Order/Checklist	.05

Minnesota Twins Team Set: 6.00

(1)	Don Baylor	.10
(2)	Juan Berenguer	.10
(3)	Bert Blyleven	.10
(4)	Tom Brunansky	.10
(5)	Randy Bush	.10
(6)	Mark Davidson	.10
(7)	Gary Gaetti	.10
(8)	Greg Gagne	.10
(9)	Dan Gladden	.10
(10)	Kent Hrbek	.10
(11)	Gene Larkin	.10
(12)	Tim Laudner	.10
(13)	Steve Lombardozzi	.10
(14)	Al Newman	.10
(15)	Kirby Puckett	4.00
(16)	Jeff Reardon	.10
(17)	Dan Schatzeder	.10
(18)	Roy Smalley	.10
(19)	Les Straker	.10
(20)	Frank Viola	.10
(21)	Batting Order/Checklist	.05

Montreal Expos Team Set: 9.00

(1)	Hubie Brooks	.10
(2)	Tim Burke	.10
(3)	Casey Candaele	.10
(4)	Mike Fitzgerald	.10
(5)	Tom Foley	.10
(6)	Andres Galarraga	.10
(7)	Neal Heaton	.10
(8)	Randy Johnson	7.50
(9)	Vance Law	.10
(10)	Bob McClure	.10
(11)	Andy McGaffigan	.10
(12)	Dennis Powell	.10
(13)	Tim Raines	.10
(14)	Jeff Reed	.10
(15)	Luis Rivera	.10
(16)	Bryn Smith	.10
(17)	Tim Wallach	.10
(18)	Mitch Webster	.10
(19)	Herm Winningham	.10
(20)	Floyd Youmans	.10
(21)	Batting Order/Checklist	.05

New York Mets Team Issue: 4.00

(1)	Bill Almon	.10
(2)	Wally Backman	.10
(3)	Gary Carter	3.00
(4)	David Cone	.10
(5)	Ron Darling	.10
(6)	Lenny Dykstra	.10
(7)	Sid Fernandez	.10
(8)	Dwight Gooden	.10
(9)	Keith Hernandez	.10
(10)	Howard Johnson	.10
(11)	Barry Lyons	.10
(12)	Dave Magadan	.10
(13)	Lee Mazzilli	.10
(14)	Roger McDowell	.10
(15)	Kevin McReynolds	.10
(16)	Jesse Orosco	.10
(17)	Rafael Santana	.10
(18)	Darryl Strawberry	.10
(19)	Tim Teufel	.10
(20)	Mookie Wilson	.10
(21)	Batting Order/Checklist	.05

New York Yankees Team Set: 9.00

(1)	Rick Cerone	.10
(2)	Jack Clark	.10
(3)	Pat Clements	.10
(4)	Mike Easler	.10
(5)	Ron Guidry	.10
(6)	Rickey Henderson	3.00
(7)	Tommy John	.10
(8)	Don Mattingly	4.50
(9)	Bobby Meacham	.10
(10)	Mike Pagliarulo	.10
(11)	Willie Randolph	.10
(12)	Rick Rhoden	.10
(13)	Dave Righetti	.10
(14)	Jerry Royster	.10
(15)	Don Slaught	.10
(16)	Tim Stoddard	.10
(17)	Wayne Tolleson	.10
(18)	Gary Ward	.10
(19)	Claudell Washington	.10
(20)	Dave Winfield	3.00
(21)	Batting Order/Checklist	.05

Oakland A's Team Set: 15.00

(1)	Tony Bernazard	.10
(2)	Jose Canseco	1.50
(3)	Mike Davis	.10
(4)	Dennis Eckersley	2.00
(5)	Mike Gallego	.10
(6)	Alfredo Griffin	.10
(7)	Rickey Henderson	3.00
(8)	Reggie Jackson	4.50
(9)	Carney Lansford	.10
(10)	Mark McGwire	6.00
(11)	Gene Nelson	.10
(12)	Steve Ontiveros	.10
(13)	Dave Parker	.10
(14)	Tony Phillips	.10
(15)	Luis Polonia	.10
(16)	Terry Steinbach	.10
(17)	Dave Stewart	.10
(18)	Mickey Tettleton	.10
(19)	Bob Welch	.10
(20)	Curt Young	.10
(21)	Batting Order/Checklist	.05

Philadelphia Phillies Team Set: 5.00

(1)	Luis Aguayo	.10
(2)	Steve Bedrosian	.10
(3)	Phil Bradley	.10
(4)	Jeff Calhoun	.10
(5)	Don Carman	.10
(6)	Darren Daulton	.10
(7)	Bob Dernier	.10
(8)	Greg Gross	.10
(9)	Chris James	.10
(10)	Von Hayes	.10
(11)	Steve Jeltz	.10
(12)	Lance Parrish	.10

(13)	Shane Rawley	.10
(14)	Bruce Ruffin	.10
(15)	Juan Samuel	.10
(16)	Mike Schmidt	4.50
(17)	Rick Schu	.10
(18)	Kent Tekulve	.10
(19)	Milt Thompson	.10
(20)	Glenn Wilson	.10
(21)	Batting Order/Checklist	.05

Pittsburgh Pirates Team Set: 9.00

(1)	Rafael Belliard	.10
(2)	Barry Bonds	7.50
(3)	Bobby Bonilla	.10
(4)	Sid Bream	.10
(5)	John Cangelosi	.10
(6)	Darnell Coles	.10
(7)	Mike Diaz	.10
(8)	Doug Drabek	.10
(9)	Mike Dunne	.10
(10)	Felix Fermin	.10
(11)	Brian Fisher	.10
(12)	Jim Gott	.10
(13)	Mike LaValliere	.10
(14)	Jose Lind	.10
(15)	Junior Ortiz	.10
(16)	Al Pedrique	.10
(17)	R.J. Reynolds	.10
(18)	Jeff Robinson	.10
(19)	John Smiley	.10
(20)	Andy Van Slyke	.10
(21)	Batting Order/Checklist	.05

San Diego Padres Team Set: 5.00

(1)	Shawn Abner	.10
(2)	Roberto Alomar	.25
(3)	Bobby Brown	.10
(4)	Joey Cora	.10
(5)	Mark Davis	.10
(6)	Tim Flannery	.10
(7)	Goose Gossage	.10
(8)	Mark Grant	.10
(9)	Tony Gwynn	4.00
(10)	Stan Jefferson	.10
(11)	John Kruk	.10
(12)	Shane Mack	.10
(13)	Carmelo Martinez	.10
(14)	Lance McCullers	.10
(15)	Randy Ready	.10
(16)	Benito Santiago	.10
(17)	Eric Show	.10
(18)	Garry Templeton	.10
(19)	Ed Whitson	.10
(20)	Marvell Wynne	.10
(21)	Batting Order/Checklist	.05

San Francisco Giants Team Set: 2.50

(1)	Mike Aldrete	.10
(2)	Bob Brenly	.10
(3)	Brett Butler	.10
(4)	Will Clark	.10
(5)	Chili Davis	.10
(6)	Dave Dravecky	.10
(7)	Scott Garrelts	.10
(8)	Atlee Hammaker	.10
(9)	Craig Lefferts	.10
(10)	Jeffrey Leonard	.10
(11)	Candy Maldonado	.10
(12)	Bob Melvin	.10
(13)	Kevin Mitchell	.10
(14)	Rick Reuschel	.10
(15)	Don Robinson	.10
(16)	Chris Speier	.10
(17)	Chris Spielman	.10
(18)	Robby Thompson	.10
(19)	Jose Uribe	.10
(20)	Matt Williams	.10
(21)	Batting Order/Checklist	.05

Seattle Mariners Team Set: 2.25

(1)	Phil Bradley	.10
(2)	Scott Bradley	.10
(3)	Mickey Brantley	.10
(4)	Mike Campbell	.10
(5)	Henry Cotto	.10
(6)	Alvin Davis	.10
(7)	Mike Kingery	.10
(8)	Mark Langston	.10
(9)	Mike Moore	.10
(10)	John Moses	.10
(11)	Donell Nixon	.10
(12)	Ed Nunez	.10
(13)	Ken Phelps	.10
(14)	Jim Presley	.10
(15)	Rey Quinones	.10
(16)	Jerry Reed	.10
(17)	Harold Reynolds	.10
(18)	Dave Valle	.10
(19)	Bill Wilkinson	.10
(20)	Glenn Wilson	.10
(21)	Batting Order/Checklist	.05

St. Louis Cardinals Team Set: 4.50

(1)	Greg Booker	.10
(2)	Jack Clark	.10
(3)	Vince Coleman	.10
(4)	Danny Cox	.10
(5)	Ken Dayley	.10
(6)	Curt Ford	.10
(7)	Tom Herr	.10
(8)	Bob Horner	.10
(9)	Ricky Horton	.10
(10)	Lance Johnson	.10
(11)	Steve Lake	.10
(12)	Jim Lindeman	.10
(13)	Greg Mathews	.10
(14)	Willie McGee	.10
(15)	Jose Oquendo	.10
(16)	Tony Pena	.10
(17)	Terry Pendleton	.10
(18)	Ozzie Smith	4.00
(19)	John Tudor	.10
(20)	Todd Worrell	.10

---

(21)	Batting Order/Checklist	.05

Texas Rangers Team Set: 2.25

(1)	Jerry Browne	.10
(2)	Bob Brower	.10
(3)	Steve Buechele	.10
(4)	Scott Fletcher	.10
(5)	Juan Guzman	.10
(6)	Charlie Hough	.10
(7)	Pete Incaviglia	.10
(8)	Oddibe McDowell	.10
(9)	Dale Mohorcic	.10
(10)	Pete O'Brien	.10
(11)	Tom O'Malley	.10
(12)	Larry Parrish	.10
(13)	Geno Petralli	.10
(14)	Jeff Russell	.10
(15)	Ruben Sierra	.10
(16)	Don Slaught	.10
(17)	Mike Stanley	.10
(18)	Curt Wilkerson	.10
(19)	Mitch Williams	.10
(20)	Bobby Witt	.10
(21)	Batting Order/Checklist	.05

Toronto Blue Jays Team Set: 2.25

(1)	Jesse Barfield	.10
(2)	George Bell	.10
(3)	Juan Beniquez	.10
(4)	Jim Clancy	.10
(5)	Mark Eichhorn	.10
(6)	Tony Fernandez	.10
(7)	Cecil Fielder	.10
(8)	Tom Henke	.10
(9)	Garth Iorg	.10
(10)	Jimmy Key	.10
(11)	Rick Leach	.10
(12)	Manny Lee	.10
(13)	Nelson Liriano	.10
(14)	Fred McGriff	.10
(15)	Lloyd Moseby	.10
(16)	Rance Mulliniks	.10
(17)	Jeff Musselman	.10
(18)	Dave Steib	.10
(19)	Willie Upshaw	.10
(20)	Ernie Whitt	.10
(21)	Batting Order/Checklist	.05

1995 Stouffer's Legends of Baseball

To promote its French bread frozen pizza, this Nestle's subsidiary issued a series of five three-dimensional cards featuring current and future Hall of Famers. The 2-1/2" x 3-1/2" cards have a die-cut action photo on front connected to a tab at the card top. When the tab is pulled, the player figure stands up. The back of the card has another player photo and a few career highlights. Because the promotion was licensed only by individuals, and not Major League Baseball, uniform and cap logos have been airbrushed off the photos.

		NM/M
Complete Set (6):		4.00
Common Player:		1.00
1	Yogi Berra	2.00
1a	Yogi Berra/Auto.	20.00
2	Gary Carter	1.50
3	Don Drysdale	2.00
4	Bob Feller	2.00
5	Willie Stargell	2.00

1983 Stuart Expos

This set of Montreal Expos players and coaches was issued by a Montreal area baking company for inclusion in packages of snack cakes. The 30 cards feature full-color player photos, with the player name, number and team logo also on the card fronts. The backs list brief player biographies in both English and French. Twenty-five players are pictured on the 2-1/2" x 3-1/2" cards.

		NM/M
Complete Set (30):		10.00
Common Player:		.25
1	Bill Virdon	.25
2	Woodie Fryman	.25
3	Vern Rapp	.25
4	Andre Dawson	2.00
5	Jeff Reardon	.35
6	Al Oliver	.50
7	Doug Flynn	.25
8	Gary Carter	5.00
9	Tim Raines	1.00
10	Steve Rogers	.25
11	Billy DeMars	.25
12	Tim Wallach	.25
13	Galen Cisco	.25
14	Terry Francona	.25
15	Bill Gullickson	.25
16	Ray Burris	.25
17	Scott Sanderson	.25
18	Warren Cromartie	.25
19	Jerry White	.25
20	Bobby Ramos	.25
21	Jim Wohlford	.25
22	Dan Schatzeder	.25
23	Charlie Lea	.25
24	Bryan Little	.25
25	Mel Wright	.25
26	Tim Blackwell	.25
27	Chris Speier	.25
28	Randy Lerch	.25
29	Bryn Smith	.25
30	Brad Mills	.25

1984 Stuart Expos

For the second year in a row, Stuart Cakes issued a full-color card set of the Montreal Expos. The 2-1/2" x 3-1/2" cards again list the player name and number along with the team and company logos on the card fronts. The backs are bilingual with biographical information in both English and French. The 40-card set was issued in two series. Card numbers 21-40, issued late in the summer, are more difficult to find than the first 20 cards. The 40 cards include players, the manager, coaches and team mascot.

		NM/M
Complete Set (40):		15.00
Common Player (1-20):		.25
Common Player (21-40):		.35
Album:		6.00
1	Youppi! (Mascot)	.25
2	Bill Virdon	.25
3	Billy DeMars	.25
4	Galen Cisco	.25
5	Russ Nixon	.25
6	Felipe Alou	.75
7	Dan Schatzeder	.25
8	Charlie Lea	.25
9	Bobby Ramos	.25
10	Bob James	.25
11	Andre Dawson	2.00
12	Gary Lucas	.25
13	Jeff Reardon	.35
14	Tim Wallach	.35
15	Gary Carter	5.00
16	Bill Gullickson	.25
17	Pete Rose	6.00
18	Terry Francona	.25
19	Steve Rogers	.25
20	Tim Raines	1.00
21	Bryn Smith	.35
22	Greg Harris	.35
23	David Palmer	.35
24	Jim Wohlford	.35
25	Miguel Dilone	.35
26	Mike Stenhouse	.35
27	Chris Speier	.35

28	Derrel Thomas	.35
29	Doug Flynn	.35
30	Bryan Little	.35
31	Argenis Salazar	.35
32	Mike Fuentes	.35
33	Joe Kerrigan	.35
34	Andy McGaffigan	.35
35	Fred Breining	.35
36	Expos 1983 All-Stars (Gary Carter, Andre Dawson, Tim Raines, Steve Rogers)	.75
37	Co-Players Of The Year (Andre Dawson, Tim Raines)	.75
38	Expos' Coaching Staff (Felipe Alou, Galen Cisco, Billy DeMars, Joe Kerrigan, Russ Nixon, Bill Virdon)	.35
39	Team Photo	.50
40	Checklist	.10

1987 Stuart

Twenty-eight four-part folding panels make up the 1987 Stuart Super Stars set, which was issued only in Canada. Three player cards and a sweepstakes entry form card comprise each panel. All 26 major league teams are included with the Montreal Expos and Toronto Blue Jays being represented twice. The cards, which are full color and measure 2-1/2" x 3-1/2", are written in both English and French. The card backs contain the player's previous year's statistics. All team insignias have been airbrushed away.

		NM/M
Complete Panel Set (28):		15.00
Complete Singles Set (84):		10.00
Common Panel:		.35
Common Single Player:		.05
Panel (New York Mets)		.60
1a	Gary Carter	.25
1b	Keith Hernandez	.05
1c	Darryl Strawberry	.05
Panel (Atlanta Braves)		.60
2a	Bruce Benedict	.05
2b	Ken Griffey	.05
2c	Dale Murphy	.25
Panel (Chicago Cubs)		.50
3a	Jody Davis	.05
3b	Andre Dawson	.35
3c	Leon Durham	.05
Panel (Cincinnati Reds)		.50
4a	Buddy Bell	.05
4b	Eric Davis	.05
4c	Dave Parker	.05
Panel (Houston Astros)		1.75
5a	Glenn Davis	.05
5b	Nolan Ryan	.75
5c	Mike Scott	.05
Panel (Los Angeles Dodgers)		.60
6a	Pedro Guerrero	.05
6b	Mike Marshall	.05
6c	Fernando Valenzuela	.05
Panel (Montreal Expos)		1.00
7a	Tim Raines	.25
7b	Tim Wallach	.05
7c	Mitch Webster	.10
Panel (Montreal Expos)		.75
8a	Hubie Brooks	.05
8b	Bryn Smith	.10
8c	Floyd Youmans	.05
Panel (Philadelphia Phillies)		1.25
9a	Shane Rawley	.05
9b	Juan Samuel	.05
9c	Mike Schmidt	.60
Panel (Pittsburgh Pirates)		.35
10a	Jim Morrison	.05
10b	Johnny Ray	.05
10c	R.J. Reynolds	.05
Panel (St. Louis Cardinals)		1.00
11a	Jack Clark	.05
11b	Vince Coleman	.05
11c	Ozzie Smith	.50
Panel (San Diego Padres)		1.00
12a	Steve Garvey	.15
12b	Tony Gwynn	.50
12c	John Kruk	.05
Panel (San Francisco Giants)		
13a	Chili Davis	.05
13b	Jeffrey Leonard	.05
13c	Robbie Thompson	.05
Panel (Baltimore Orioles)		2.50
14a	Fred Lynn	.05

14b	Eddie Murray	.50
14c	Cal Ripken, Jr.	1.00
Panel (Boston Red Sox)		1.75
15a	Don Baylor	.05
15b	Wade Boggs	.50
15c	Roger Clemens	.60
Panel (California Angels)		.40
16a	Doug DeCinces	.05
16b	Wally Joyner	.05
16c	Mike Witt	.05
Panel (Chicago White Sox)		.70
17a	Harold Baines	.05
17b	Carlton Fisk	.50
17c	Ozzie Guillen	.05
Panel (Cleveland Indians)		.35
18a	Joe Carter	.05
18b	Julio Franco	.05
18c	Pat Tabler	.05
Panel (Detroit Tigers)		.35
19a	Kirk Gibson	.05
19b	Jack Morris	.05
19c	Alan Trammell	.05
Panel (Kansas City Royals)		1.25
20a	George Brett	.50
20b	Bret Saberhagen	.05
20c	Willie Wilson	.05
Panel (Milwaukee Brewers)		1.50
21a	Cecil Cooper	.05
21b	Paul Molitor	.40
21c	Robin Yount	.40
Panel (Minnesota Twins)		.70
22a	Tom Brunansky	.05
22b	Kent Hrbek	.05
22c	Kirby Puckett	.50
Panel (New York Yankees)		2.50
23a	Rickey Henderson	.40
23b	Don Mattingly	.60
23c	Dave Winfield	.40
Panel (Oakland A's)		1.00
24a	Jose Canseco	.35
24b	Alfredo Griffin	.05
24c	Carney Lansford	.05
Panel (Seattle Mariners)		.35
25a	Phil Bradley	.05
25b	Alvin Davis	.05
25c	Mark Langston	.05
Panel (Texas Rangers)		.35
26a	Pete Incaviglia	.05
26b	Pete O'Brien	.05
26c	Larry Parrish	.05
Panel (Toronto Blue Jays)		.75
27a	Jesse Barfield	.10
27b	George Bell	.10
27c	Tony Fernandez	.10
Panel (Toronto Blue Jays)		.75
28a	Lloyd Moseby	.10
28b	Dave Stieb	.10
28c	Ernie Whitt	.10

1991 Studio Preview

Each 1991 Donruss set packaged for the retail trade included a pack of four cards previewing the debut Studio set. The cards are in the same format as the regular set, 2-1/2" x 3-1/2" with evocative black-and-white photos bordered in maroon on front, and a biographical write-up on the back.

		NM/M
Complete Set (18):		5.00
Common Player:		.50
1	Juan Bell	.50
2	Roger Clemens	3.00
3	Dave Parker	.50
4	Tim Raines	.50
5	Kevin Seitzer	.50
6	Teddy Higuera	.50
7	Bernie Williams	.50
8	Harold Baines	.50
9	Gary Pettis	.50
10	Dave Justice	.50
11	Eric Davis	.50
12	Andujar Cedeno	.50
13	Tom Foley	.50
14	Dwight Gooden	.50
15	Doug Drabek	.50
16	Steve Decker	.50
17	Joe Torre	.75
18	Header Card	.10

1991 Studio

Donruss introduced this 264-card set in 1991. The cards feature maroon borders surrounding black and white posed player photos. The card backs are printed in black and white and feature personal data, career highlights, hobbies and interests and the player's hero. The cards were released in foil packs only and feature a special Rod Carew puzzle.

		NM/M
Complete Set (264):		7.50
Common Player:		.05
Foil Pack (10):		.50
Foil Box (48):		12.50
1	Glenn Davis	.05
2	Dwight Evans	.05
3	Leo Gomez	.05
4	Chris Hoiles	.05
5	Sam Horn	.05
6	Ben McDonald	.05
7	Randy Milligan	.05
8	Gregg Olson	.05
9	Cal Ripken, Jr.	1.00
10	David Segui	.05
11	Wade Boggs	.40
12	Ellis Burks	.05
13	Jack Clark	.05
14	Roger Clemens	.45
15	Mike Greenwell	.05
16	Tim Naehring	.05
17	Tony Pena	.05
18	Phil Plantier RC	.05
19	Jeff Reardon	.05
20	Mo Vaughn	.05
21	Jimmy Reese	.05
22	Jim Abbott	.05
23	Bert Blyleven	.05
24	Chuck Finley	.05
25	Gary Gaetti	.05
26	Wally Joyner	.05
27	Mark Langston	.05
28	Kirk McCaskill	.05
29	Lance Parrish	.05
30	Dave Winfield	.30
31	Alex Fernandez	.05
32	Carlton Fisk	.30
33	Scott Fletcher	.05
34	Greg Hibbard	.05
35	Charlie Hough	.05
36	Jack McDowell	.05
37	Tim Raines	.05
38	Sammy Sosa	.40
39	Bobby Thigpen	.05
40	Frank Thomas	.30
41	Sandy Alomar	.05
42	John Farrell	.05
43	Glenallen Hill	.05
44	Brook Jacoby	.05
45	Chris James	.05
46	Doug Jones	.05
47	Eric King	.05
48	Mark Lewis	.05
49	Greg Swindell	.05
50	Mark Whiten	.05
51	Milt Cuyler	.05
52	Rob Deer	.05
53	Cecil Fielder	.05
54	Travis Fryman	.05
55	Bill Gullickson	.05
56	Lloyd Moseby	.05
57	Frank Tanana	.05
58	Mickey Tettleton	.05
59	Alan Trammell	.05
60	Lou Whitaker	.05
61	Mike Boddicker	.05
62	George Brett	.45
63	Jeff Conine	.05
64	Warren Cromartie	.05
65	Storm Davis	.05
66	Kirk Gibson	.05
67	Mark Gubicza	.05
68	Brian McRae RC	.05
69	Bret Saberhagen	.05
70	Kurt Stillwell	.05
71	Tim McIntosh	.05
72	Candy Maldonado	.05
73	Paul Molitor	.30
74	Willie Randolph	.05
75	Ron Robinson	.05
76	Gary Sheffield	.20
77	Franklin Stubbs	.05
78	B.J. Surhoff	.05

79	Greg Vaughn	.05
80	Robin Yount	.30
81	Rick Aguilera	.05
82	Steve Bedrosian	.05
83	Scott Erickson	.05
84	Greg Gagne	.05
85	Dan Gladden	.05
86	Brian Harper	.05
87	Kent Hrbek	.05
88	Shane Mack	.05
89	Jack Morris	.05
90	Kirby Puckett	.40
91	Jesse Barfield	.05
92	Steve Farr	.05
93	Steve Howe	.05
94	Roberto Kelly	.05
95	Tim Leary	.05
96	Kevin Maas	.05
97	Don Mattingly	.45
98	Hensley Meulens	.05
99	Scott Sanderson	.05
100	Steve Sax	.05
101	Jose Canseco	.20
102	Dennis Eckersley	.25
103	Dave Henderson	.05
104	Rickey Henderson	.30
105	Rick Honeycutt	.05
106	Mark McGwire	.75
107	Dave Stewart	.05
108	Eric Show	.05
109	Todd Van Poppel RC	.05
110	Bob Welch	.05
111	Alvin Davis	.05
112	Ken Griffey Jr.	.50
113	Ken Griffey Sr.	.05
114	Erik Hanson	.05
115	Brian Holman	.05
116	Randy Johnson	.30
117	Edgar Martinez	.05
118	Tino Martinez	.05
119	Harold Reynolds	.05
120	David Valle	.05
121	Kevin Belcher	.05
122	Scott Chiamparino	.05
123	Julio Franco	.05
124	Juan Gonzalez	.20
125	Rich Gossage	.05
126	Jeff Kunkel	.05
127	Rafael Palmeiro	.05
128	Nolan Ryan	1.00
129	Ruben Sierra	.05
130	Bobby Witt	.05
131	Roberto Alomar	.10
132	Tom Candiotti	.05
133	Joe Carter	.05
134	Ken Dayley	.05
135	Kelly Gruber	.05
136	John Olerud	.05
137	Dave Stieb	.05
138	Turner Ward	.05
139	Devon White	.05
140	Mookie Wilson	.05
141	Steve Avery	.05
142	Sid Bream	.05
143	Nick Esasky	.05
144	Ron Gant	.05
145	Tom Glavine	.20
146	Dave Justice	.05
147	Kelly Mann	.05
148	Terry Pendleton	.05
149	John Smoltz	.05
150	Jeff Treadway	.05
151	George Bell	.05
152	Shawn Boskie	.05
153	Andre Dawson	.20
154	Lance Dickson	.05
155	Shawon Dunston	.05
156	Joe Girardi	.05
157	Mark Grace	.05
158	Ryne Sandberg	.40
159	Gary Scott	.05
160	Dave Smith	.05
161	Tom Browning	.05
162	Eric Davis	.05
163	Rob Dibble	.05
164	Mariano Duncan	.05
165	Chris Hammond	.05
166	Billy Hatcher	.05
167	Barry Larkin	.05
168	Hal Morris	.05
169	Paul O'Neill	.05
170	Chris Sabo	.05
171	Eric Anthony	.05
172	Jeff Bagwell RC	1.50
173	Craig Biggio	.05
174	Ken Caminitti	.05
175	Jim Deshaies	.05
176	Steve Finley	.05
177	Pete Harnisch	.05
178	Darryl Kile	.05
179	Curt Schilling	.20
180	Mike Scott	.05
181	Brett Butler	.05
182	Gary Carter	.30
183	Orel Hershiser	.05
184	Ramon Martinez	.05
185	Eddie Murray	.30
186	Jose Offerman	.05
187	Bob Ojeda	.05
188	Juan Samuel	.05
189	Mike Scioscia	.05
190	Darryl Strawberry	.05
191	Moises Alou	.05
192	Brian Barnes	.05
193	Oil Can Boyd	.05
194	Ivan Calderon	.05
195	Delino DeShields	.05
196	Mike Fitzgerald	.05

197	Andres Galarraga	.05
198	Marquis Grissom	.05
199	Bill Sampen	.05
200	Tim Wallach	.05
201	Daryl Boston	.05
202	Vince Coleman	.05
203	John Franco	.05
204	Dwight Gooden	.05
205	Tom Herr	.05
206	Gregg Jefferies	.05
207	Howard Johnson	.05
208	Dave Magadan	.05
209	Kevin McReynolds	.05
210	Frank Viola	.05
211	Wes Chamberlain	.05
212	Darren Daulton	.05
213	Len Dykstra	.05
214	Charlie Hayes	.05
215	Ricky Jordan	.05
216	Steve Lake	.05
217	Roger McDowell	.05
218	Mickey Morandini	.05
219	Terry Mulholland	.05
220	Dale Murphy	.15
221	Jay Bell	.05
222	Barry Bonds	1.00
223	Bobby Bonilla	.05
224	Doug Drabek	.05
225	Bill Landrum	.05
226	Mike LaValliere	.05
227	Jose Lind	.05
228	Don Slaught	.05
229	John Smiley	.05
230	Andy Van Slyke	.05
231	Bernard Gilkey	.05
232	Pedro Guerrero	.05
233	Rex Hudler	.05
234	Ray Lankford	.05
235	Joe Magrane	.05
236	Jose Oquendo	.05
237	Lee Smith	.05
238	Ozzie Smith	.40
239	Milt Thompson	.05
240	Todd Zeile	.05
241	Larry Andersen	.05
242	Andy Benes	.05
243	Paul Faries	.05
244	Tony Fernandez	.05
245	Tony Gwynn	.40
246	Atlee Hammaker	.05
247	Fred McGriff	.05
248	Bip Roberts	.05
249	Benito Santiago	.05
250	Ed Whitson	.05
251	Dave Anderson	.05
252	Mike Benjamin	.05
253	John Burkett	.05
254	Will Clark	.05
255	Scott Garrelts	.05
256	Willie McGee	.05
257	Kevin Mitchell	.05
258	Dave Righetti	.05
259	Matt Williams	.05
260	Black & Decker (Bud Black, Steve Decker)	.10
261	Checklist	.03
262	Checklist	.03
263	Checklist	.03
---	Header Card	.03

1992 Studio Preview

To introduce its 1992 Studio brand, Leaf produced 22 preview cards in format virtually identical to the issued versions of the same cards. The only differences are the appearance of the word "PREVIEW" in the lower-right corner of the card front, and the player's position, and the number "X of 22 / Preview Card" on the back where regular cards have the card number in the upper-right corner. The cards were distributed on a very limited basis to members of the Donruss dealers' network.

		NM/M
Complete Set (22):		75.00
Common Player:		1.50
1	Ruben Sierra	1.50
2	Kirby Puckett	6.00
3	Ryne Sandberg	6.00
4	John Kruk	1.50
5	Cal Ripken, Jr.	12.00
6	Robin Yount	4.50

7	Dwight Gooden	1.50
8	David Justice	1.50
9	Don Mattingly	7.50
10	Wally Joyner	1.50
11	Will Clark	1.50
12	Rob Dibble	1.50
13	Roberto Alomar	2.50
14	Wade Boggs	6.00
15	Barry Bonds	12.00
16	Jeff Bagwell	4.50
17	Mark McGwire	9.00
18	Frank Thomas	6.00
19	Brett Butler	1.50
20	Ozzie Smith	6.00
21	Jim Abbott	1.50
22	Tony Gwynn	6.00

1992 Studio

PETE HARNISCH — RHP
Houston Astros

Donruss introduced the Studio line in 1991 and released another 264-card set entitled Leaf Studio for 1992. The cards feature a color player closeup with a large, rough-textured black-and-white photo of the player in the background. Tan borders surround the photos. The cards were only released in foil packs. Special Heritage insert cards featuring top players in vintage uniforms could be found in foil and jumbo packs.

	NM/M
Complete Set (264):	8.00
Common Player:	.05
Pack (10):	.65
Wax Box (48):	15.00

1	Steve Avery	.05
2	Sid Bream	.05
3	Ron Gant	.05
4	Tom Glavine	.25
5	Dave Justice	.05
6	Mark Lemke	.05
7	Greg Olson	.05
8	Terry Pendleton	.05
9	Deion Sanders	.05
10	John Smoltz	.05
11	Doug Dascenzo	.05
12	Andre Dawson	.25
13	Joe Girardi	.05
14	Mark Grace	.05
15	Greg Maddux	.50
16	Chuck McElroy	.05
17	Mike Morgan	.05
18	Ryne Sandberg	.50
19	Gary Scott	.05
20	Sammy Sosa	.50
21	Norm Charlton	.05
22	Rob Dibble	.05
23	Barry Larkin	.05
24	Hal Morris	.05
25	Paul O'Neill	.05
26	Jose Rijo	.05
27	Bip Roberts	.05
28	Chris Sabo	.05
29	Reggie Sanders	.05
30	Greg Swindell	.05
31	Jeff Bagwell	.45
32	Craig Biggio	.05
33	Ken Caminiti	.05
34	Andujar Cedeno	.05
35	Steve Finley	.05
36	Pete Harnisch	.05
37	Butch Henry	.05
38	Doug Jones	.05
39	Darryl Kile	.05
40	Eddie Taubensee	.05
41	Brett Butler	.05
42	Tom Candiotti	.05
43	Eric Davis	.05
44	Orel Hershiser	.05
45	Eric Karros	.05
46	Ramon Martinez	.05
47	Jose Offerman	.05
48	Mike Scioscia	.05
49	Mike Sharperson	.05
50	Darryl Strawberry	.05
51	Bret Barbarie	.05
52	Ivan Calderon	.05
53	Gary Carter	.45
54	Delino DeShields	.05
55	Marquis Grissom	.05
56	Ken Hill	.05
57	Dennis Martinez	.05
58	Spike Owen	.05
59	Larry Walker	.05

60	Tim Wallach	.05
61	Bobby Bonilla	.05
62	Tim Burke	.05
63	Vince Coleman	.05
64	John Franco	.05
65	Dwight Gooden	.05
66	Todd Hundley	.05
67	Howard Johnson	.05
68	Eddie Murray	.45
69	Bret Saberhagen	.05
70	Anthony Young	.05
71	Kim Batiste	.05
72	Wes Chamberlain	.05
73	Darren Daulton	.05
74	Mariano Duncan	.05
75	Len Dykstra	.05
76	John Kruk	.05
77	Mickey Morandini	.05
78	Terry Mulholland	.05
79	Dale Murphy	.20
80	Mitch Williams	.05
81	Jay Bell	.05
82	Barry Bonds	1.00
83	Steve Buechele	.05
84	Doug Drabek	.05
85	Mike LaValliere	.05
86	Jose Lind	.05
87	Denny Neagle	.05
88	Randy Tomlin	.05
89	Andy Van Slyke	.05
90	Gary Varsho	.05
91	Pedro Guerrero	.05
92	Rex Hudler	.05
93	Brian Jordan	.05
94	Felix Jose	.05
95	Donovan Osborne	.05
96	Tom Pagnozzi	.05
97	Lee Smith	.05
98	Ozzie Smith	.50
99	Todd Worrell	.05
100	Todd Zeile	.05
101	Andy Benes	.05
102	Jerald Clark	.05
103	Tony Fernandez	.05
104	Tony Gwynn	.50
105	Gary Harris	.05
106	Fred McGriff	.05
107	Benito Santiago	.05
108	Gary Sheffield	.30
109	Kurt Stillwell	.05
110	Tim Teufel	.05
111	Kevin Bass	.05
112	Jeff Brantley	.05
113	John Burkett	.05
114	Will Clark	.05
115	Royce Clayton	.05
116	Mike Jackson	.05
117	Darren Lewis	.05
118	Bill Swift	.05
119	Robby Thompson	.05
120	Matt Williams	.05
121	Brady Anderson	.05
122	Glenn Davis	.05
123	Mike Devereaux	.05
124	Chris Hoiles	.05
125	Sam Horn	.05
126	Ben McDonald	.05
127	Mike Mussina	.25
128	Gregg Olson	.05
129	Cal Ripken, Jr.	1.00
130	Rick Sutcliffe	.05
131	Wade Boggs	.05
132	Roger Clemens	.60
133	Greg Harris	.05
134	Tim Naehring	.05
135	Tony Pena	.05
136	Phil Plantier	.05
137	Jeff Reardon	.05
138	Jody Reed	.05
139	Mo Vaughn	.05
140	Frank Viola	.05
141	Jim Abbott	.05
142	Hubie Brooks	.05
143	Chad Curtis RC	.05
144	Gary DiSarcina	.05
145	Chuck Finley	.05
146	Bryan Harvey	.05
147	Von Hayes	.05
148	Mark Langston	.05
149	Lance Parrish	.05
150	Lee Stevens	.05
151	George Bell	.05
152	Alex Fernandez	.05
153	Greg Hibbard	.05
154	Lance Johnson	.05
155	Kirk McCaskill	.05
156	Tim Raines	.05
157	Steve Sax	.05
158	Bobby Thigpen	.05
159	Frank Thomas	.45
160	Robin Ventura	.05
161	Sandy Alomar, Jr.	.05
162	Jack Armstrong	.05
163	Carlos Baerga	.05
164	Albert Belle	.05
165	Alex Cole	.05
166	Glenallen Hill	.05
167	Mark Lewis	.05
168	Kenny Lofton	.05
169	Paul Sorrento	.05
170	Mark Whiten	.05
171	Milt Cuyler (Color photo is Lou Whitaker.)	.05
172	Rob Deer	.05
173	Cecil Fielder	.05
174	Travis Fryman	.05
175	Mike Henneman	.05
176	Tony Phillips	.05

177	Frank Tanana	.05
178	Mickey Tettleton	.05
179	Alan Trammell	.05
180	Lou Whitaker	.05
181	George Brett	.60
182	Tom Gordon	.05
183	Mark Gubicza	.05
184	Gregg Jefferies	.05
185	Wally Joyner	.05
186	Brent Mayne	.05
187	Brian McRae	.05
188	Kevin McReynolds	.05
189	Keith Miller	.05
190	Jeff Montgomery	.05
191	Dante Bichette	.05
192	Ricky Bones	.05
193	Scott Fletcher	.05
194	Paul Molitor	.45
195	Jaime Navarro	.05
196	Franklin Stubbs	.05
197	B.J. Surhoff	.05
198	Greg Vaughn	.05
199	Bill Wegman	.05
200	Robin Yount	.45
201	Rick Aguilera	.05
202	Scott Erickson	.05
203	Greg Gagne	.05
204	Brian Harper	.05
205	Kent Hrbek	.05
206	Scott Leius	.05
207	Shane Mack	.05
208	Pat Mahomes	.05
209	Kirby Puckett	.50
210	John Smiley	.05
211	Mike Gallego	.05
212	Charlie Hayes	.05
213	Pat Kelly	.05
214	Roberto Kelly	.05
215	Kevin Maas	.05
216	Don Mattingly	.60
217	Matt Nokes	.05
218	Melido Perez	.05
219	Scott Sanderson	.05
220	Danny Tartabull	.05
221	Harold Baines	.05
222	Jose Canseco	.30
223	Dennis Eckersley	.35
224	Dave Henderson	.05
225	Carney Lansford	.05
226	Mark McGwire	.75
227	Mike Moore	.05
228	Randy Ready	.05
229	Terry Steinbach	.05
230	Dave Stewart	.05
231	Jay Buhner	.05
232	Ken Griffey Jr.	.65
233	Erik Hanson	.05
234	Randy Johnson	.45
235	Edgar Martinez	.05
236	Tino Martinez	.05
237	Kevin Mitchell	.05
238	Pete O'Brien	.05
239	Harold Reynolds	.05
240	David Valle	.05
241	Julio Franco	.05
242	Juan Gonzalez	.25
243	Jose Guzman	.05
244	Rafael Palmeiro	.35
245	Dean Palmer	.05
246	Ivan Rodriguez	.35
247	Jeff Russell	.05
248	Nolan Ryan	1.00
249	Ruben Sierra	.05
250	Dickie Thon	.05
251	Roberto Alomar	.05
252	Derek Bell	.05
253	Pat Borders	.05
254	Joe Carter	.05
255	Kelly Gruber	.05
256	Juan Guzman	.05
257	Jack Morris	.05
258	John Olerud	.05
259	Devon White	.05
260	Dave Winfield	.45
261	Checklist	.05
262	Checklist	.05
263	Checklist	.05
264	History Card	.05

Heritage

HERITAGE SERIES
RYNE SANDBERG

Superstars of 1992 were photographed in vintage-style uniforms in this 14-card insert set found in packages of Studio's 1992 issue. Cards #1-8 could be found in standard foil packs while #9-14 were inserted in Studio jumbos. Cards fea-

tured a sepia-tone photo bordered in turquoise and highlighted with copper foil. Cards carry a "BC" prefix to the card number on back.

	NM/M
Complete Set (14):	6.00
Common Player:	.50
1	Ryne Sandberg	1.00
2	Carlton Fisk	.75
3	Wade Boggs	1.00
4	Jose Canseco	.65
5	Don Mattingly	1.25
6	Darryl Strawberry	.50
7	Cal Ripken, Jr.	1.50
8	Will Clark	.50
9	Andre Dawson	.50
10	Andy Van Slyke	.50
11	Paul Molitor	.75
12	Jeff Bagwell	.75
13	Darren Daulton	.50
14	Kirby Puckett	1.00

1993 Studio Promos

Though unmarked as such, a pair of promo cards was produced in advance of '93 Studio. At first glance the cards appear identical to the same players' issued versions, but there are noticeable cropping differences. On the back of the Thomas card, the promo has a smaller projection of his face, with much more of his hair showing at top and the last line of type about even with the bottom of his nose. The issued card shows almost no hair at top and has the last line even with his top lip. The Sandberg cropping difference appears on front. On the promo his right ear is well clear of the left border; on the issued version his ear touches the border.

	NM/M
Complete Set (2):	6.00
Common Player:	2.00
139	Frank Thomas	2.00
176	Ryne Sandberg	5.00

1993 Studio

This 220-card set features full-bleed photos. The player's portrait appears against one of several backgrounds featuring his team's uniform. His signature and the Studio logo are printed in gold foil. Backs have an extreme closeup partial portrait of the player and insights into his personality.

	NM/M
Complete Set (220):	15.00
Common Player:	.05
Pack (12):	.75
Wax Box (36):	12.50
1	Dennis Eckersley	.35
2	Chad Curtis	.05
3	Eric Anthony	.05
4	Roberto Alomar	.20
5	Steve Avery	.05
6	Cal Eldred	.05
7	Bernard Gilkey	.05
8	Steve Buechele	.05
9	Brett Butler	.05
10	Terry Mulholland	.05
11	Moises Alou	.05
12	Barry Bonds	1.00
13	Sandy Alomar Jr.	.05
14	Chris Bosio	.05
15	Scott Sanderson	.05
16	Bobby Bonilla	.05
17	Brady Anderson	.05
18	Derek Bell	.05
19	Wes Chamberlain	.05
20	Jay Bell	.05
21	Kevin Brown	.05
22	Roger Clemens	.60
23	Roberto Kelly	.05
24	Dante Bichette	.05
25	George Brett	.60
26	Rob Deer	.05
27	Brian Harper	.05
28	George Bell	.05

#	Player	Price
29	Jim Abbott	.05
30	Dave Henderson	.05
31	Wade Boggs	.50
32	Chili Davis	.05
33	Ellis Burks	.05
34	Jeff Bagwell	.40
35	Kent Hrbek	.05
36	Pat Borders	.05
37	Cecil Fielder	.05
38	Sid Bream	.05
39	Greg Gagne	.05
40	Darryl Hamilton	.05
41	Jerald Clark	.05
42	Mark Grace	.05
43	Barry Larkin	.05
44	John Burkett	.05
45	Scott Cooper	.05
46	Mike Lansing RC	.25
47	Jose Canseco	.30
48	Will Clark	.05
49	Carlos Garcia	.05
50	Carlos Baerga	.05
51	Darren Daulton	.05
52	Jay Buhner	.05
53	Andy Benes	.05
54	Jeff Conine	.05
55	Mike Devereaux	.05
56	Vince Coleman	.05
57	Terry Steinbach	.05
58	J.T. Snow RC	.40
59	Greg Swindell	.05
60	Devon White	.05
61	John Smoltz	.05
62	Todd Zeile	.05
63	Rick Wilkins	.05
64	Tim Wallach	.05
65	John Wetteland	.05
66	Matt Williams	.05
67	Paul Sorrento	.05
68	David Valle	.05
69	Walt Weiss	.05
70	John Franco	.05
71	Nolan Ryan	1.00
72	Frank Viola	.05
73	Chris Sabo	.05
74	David Nied	.05
75	Kevin McReynolds	.05
76	Lou Whitaker	.05
77	Dave Winfield	.40
78	Robin Ventura	.05
79	Spike Owen	.05
80	Cal Ripken, Jr.	1.00
81	Dan Walter	.05
82	Mitch Williams	.05
83	Tim Wakefield	.05
84	Rickey Henderson	.40
85	Gary DiSarcina	.05
86	Craig Biggio	.05
87	Joe Carter	.05
88	Ron Gant	.05
89	John Jaha	.05
90	Gregg Jefferies	.05
91	Jose Guzman	.05
92	Eric Karros	.05
93	Wil Cordero	.05
94	Royce Clayton	.05
95	Albert Belle	.05
96	Ken Griffey Jr.	.65
97	Orestes Destrade	.05
98	Tony Fernandez	.05
99	Leo Gomez	.05
100	Tony Gwynn	.50
101	Len Dykstra	.05
102	Jeff King	.05
103	Julio Franco	.05
104	Andre Dawson	.25
105	Randy Milligan	.05
106	Alex Cole	.05
107	Phil Hiatt	.05
108	Travis Fryman	.05
109	Chuck Knoblauch	.05
110	Bo Jackson	.10
111	Pat Kelly	.05
112	Bret Saberhagen	.05
113	Ruben Sierra	.05
114	Tim Salmon	.05
115	Doug Jones	.05
116	Ed Sprague	.05
117	Terry Pendleton	.05
118	Robin Yount	.40
119	Mark Whiten	.05
120	Checklist	.05
121	Sammy Sosa	.50
122	Darryl Strawberry	.05
123	Larry Walker	.05
124	Robby Thompson	.05
125	Carlos Martinez	.05
126	Edgar Martinez	.05
127	Benito Santiago	.05
128	Howard Johnson	.05
129	Harold Reynolds	.05
130	Craig Shipley	.05
131	Curt Schilling	.30
132	Andy Van Slyke	.05
133	Ivan Rodriguez	.35
134	Mo Vaughn	.05
135	Bip Roberts	.05
136	Charlie Hayes	.05
137	Brian McRae	.05
138	Mickey Tettleton	.05
139	Frank Thomas	.40
140	Paul O'Neill	.05
141	Mark McGwire	.75
142	Damion Easley	.05
143	Ken Caminiti	.05
144	Juan Guzman	.05
145	Tom Glavine	.25
146	Pat Listach	.05

#	Player	Price
147	Lee Smith	.05
148	Derrick May	.05
149	Ramon Martinez	.05
150	Delino DeShields	.05
151	Kirt Manwaring	.05
152	Reggie Jefferson	.05
153	Randy Johnson	.40
154	Dave Magadan	.05
155	Dwight Gooden	.05
156	Chris Hoiles	.05
157	Fred McGriff	.05
158	Dave Hollins	.05
159	Al Martin	.05
160	Juan Gonzalez	.20
161	Mike Greenwell	.05
162	Kevin Mitchell	.05
163	Andres Galarraga	.05
164	Wally Joyner	.05
165	Kirk Gibson	.05
166	Pedro Munoz	.05
167	Ozzie Guillen	.05
168	Jimmy Key	.05
169	Kevin Seitzer	.05
170	Luis Polonia	.05
171	Luis Gonzalez	.05
172	Paul Molitor	.40
173	Dave Justice	.05
174	B.J. Surhoff	.05
175	Ray Lankford	.05
176	Ryne Sandberg	.50
177	Jody Reed	.05
178	Marquis Grissom	.05
179	Willie McGee	.05
180	Kenny Lofton	.05
181	Junior Felix	.05
182	Jose Offerman	.05
183	John Kruk	.05
184	Orlando Merced	.05
185	Rafael Palmeiro	.35
186	Billy Hatcher	.05
187	Joe Oliver	.05
188	Joe Girardi	.05
189	Jose Lind	.05
190	Harold Baines	.05
191	Mike Pagliarulo	.05
192	Lance Johnson	.05
193	Don Mattingly	.60
194	Doug Drabek	.05
195	John Olerud	.05
196	Greg Maddux	.50
197	Greg Vaughn	.05
198	Tom Pagnozzi	.05
199	Willie Wilson	.05
200	Jack McDowell	.05
201	Mike Piazza	.65
202	Mike Mussina	.30
203	Charles Nagy	.05
204	Tino Martinez	.05
205	Charlie Hough	.05
206	Todd Hundley	.05
207	Gary Sheffield	.30
208	Mickey Morandini	.05
209	Don Slaught	.05
210	Dean Palmer	.05
211	Jose Rijo	.05
212	Vinny Castilla	.05
213	Tony Phillips	.05
214	Kirby Puckett	.50
215	Tim Raines	.05
216	Otis Nixon	.05
217	Ozzie Smith	.50
218	Jose Vizcaino	.05
220	Checklist	.05

Heritage

OZZIE SMITH

All types of 1993 Leaf Studio packs were candidates for having one of 12 Heritage cards inserted in them. The fronts feature the player posing in an old-time uniform, framed in turquoise with copper highlights. The backs have a mug shot surrounded by an ornate frame and describe the uniform on the front. Team trivia is also included.

		NM/M
Complete Set (12):		12.00
Common Player:		.50
1	George Brett	2.00
2	Juan Gonzalez	.75
3	Roger Clemens	2.00
4	Mark McGwire	4.00
5	Mark Grace	.50
6	Ozzie Smith	1.50
7	Barry Larkin	.50
8	Frank Thomas	1.00

#	Player	Price
9	Carlos Baerga	.50
10	Eric Karros	.50
11	J.T. Snow	.50
12	John Kruk	.50

Silhouettes

SILHOUETTES

These insert cards were randomly included in jumbo packs only. The card fronts feature a ghosted image of the player against an action silhouette on a gray background. The player's name is in bronze foil at bottom. Backs have a player action photo and description of career highlights.

		NM/M
Complete Set (10):		7.00
Common Player:		.15
1	Frank Thomas	.65
2	Barry Bonds	3.00
3	Jeff Bagwell	.65
4	Juan Gonzalez	.40
5	Travis Fryman	.15
6	J.T. Snow	.15
7	John Kruk	.15
8	Jeff Blauser	.15
9	Mike Piazza	2.00
10	Nolan Ryan	3.00

Superstars on Canvas

SUPERSTARS ON CANVAS

Ten players are featured on these insert cards, which were available in hobby and retail packs. The cards show player portraits which mix photography and artwork.

		NM/M
Complete Set (10):		8.00
Common Player:		.25
1	Ken Griffey Jr.	1.50
2	Jose Canseco	.60
3	Mark McGwire	2.00
4	Mike Mussina	.50
5	Joe Carter	.25
6	Frank Thomas	1.00
7	Darren Daulton	.25
8	Mark Grace	.25
9	Andres Galarraga	.25
10	Barry Bonds	2.50

Frank Thomas

FRANK THOMAS COLLECTION

This five-card set is devoted to Frank Thomas. Cards were randomly included in all types of 1993 Leaf Studio packs. Topics covered on the cards include Thomas' childhood, his baseball memories, his family, his performance and being a role model.

		NM/M
Complete Set (5):		5.00
Common Card:		1.00
1	Childhood	1.00
2	Baseball Memories	1.00
3	Importance of Family	1.00
4	Performance	1.00
5	On Being a Role Model	1.00

1994 Studio Samples

To introduce its "locker-room look" issue for 1994, Leaf's Studio brand produced these three-star sample set and distributed it to its hobby dealer network. The cards are basically the same as the regular-issue cards of those players except for the addition of a "Promotional Sample" overprinted diagonally on front and back. The "Up Close" biographies on the cards' backs are different between the promos and the regular cards and there is a slight difference in front photo cropping on the Gonzalez card.

		NM/M
Complete Set (3):		6.00
83	Barry Bonds	3.00
154	Juan Gonzalez	1.00
209	Frank Thomas	2.00

1994 Studio

Studio baseball from Donruss returned in mid-August, 1994, with a three-time MVP spokesman, several jazzy and short-printed inserts subsets and a reduced overall production figure that represents a sharp drop from 1993. Barry Bonds is the MVP whose mug adorns Studio counter boxes and advertisements. According to Donruss officials, production was limited to 8,000 cases of 20 boxes each, which represents a 35 percent decrease from 1993 and works out to about 315,000 of each card. Only 2,000 cases were earmarked for retail distribution and no jumbo packs were produced. Studio 1994 features 220 cards issued in one series, once again with close-up personal portraits of the top stars in the game. Each card is foil-stamped with a borderless design and UV coating front and back. The front of the card features the player in the foreground with his locker in the background. As in the previous three Studio offerings, the backs of the cards contain personal information about the players.

		NM/M
Complete Set (220):		7.50
Common Player:		.05
Pack (12):		.45

Wax Box (36):		10.00
1	Dennis Eckersley	.45
2	Brent Gates	.05
3	Rickey Henderson	.55
4	Mark McGwire	1.00
5	Troy Neel	.05
6	Ruben Sierra	.05
7	Terry Steinbach	.05
8	Chad Curtis	.05
9	Chili Davis	.05
10	Gary DiSarcina	.05
11	Damion Easley	.05
12	Bo Jackson	.10
13	Mark Langston	.05
14	Eduardo Perez	.05
15	Tim Salmon	.05
16	Jeff Bagwell	.55
17	Craig Biggio	.05
18	Ken Caminiti	.05
19	Andujar Cedeno	.05
20	Doug Drabek	.05
21	Steve Finley	.05
22	Luis Gonzalez	.05
23	Darryl Kile	.05
24	Roberto Alomar	.20
25	Pat Borders	.05
26	Joe Carter	.05
27	Carlos Delgado	.40
28	Pat Hentgen	.05
29	Paul Molitor	.55
30	John Olerud	.05
31	Ed Sprague	.05
32	Devon White	.05
33	Steve Avery	.05
34	Tom Glavine	.25
35	David Justice	.05
36	Roberto Kelly	.05
37	Ryan Klesko	.05
38	Javier Lopez	.05
39	Greg Maddux	.60
40	Fred McGriff	.05
41	Terry Pendleton	.05
42	Ricky Bones	.05
43	Darryl Hamilton	.05
44	Brian Harper	.05
45	John Jaha	.05
46	Dave Nilsson	.05
47	Kevin Seitzer	.05
48	Greg Vaughn	.05
49	Turner Ward	.05
50	Bernard Gilkey	.05
51	Gregg Jefferies	.05
52	Ray Lankford	.05
53	Tom Pagnozzi	.05
54	Ozzie Smith	.60
55	Bob Tewksbury	.05
56	Mark Whiten	.05
57	Todd Zeile	.05
58	Steve Buechele	.05
59	Shawon Dunston	.05
60	Mark Grace	.05
61	Derrick May	.05
62	Tuffy Rhodes	.05
63	Ryne Sandberg	.60
64	Sammy Sosa	.60
65	Rick Wilkins	.05
66	Brett Butler	.05
67	Delino DeShields	.05
68	Orel Hershiser	.05
69	Eric Karros	.05
70	Raul Mondesi	.05
71	Jose Offerman	.05
72	Mike Piazza	.75
73	Tim Wallach	.05
74	Moises Alou	.05
75	Sean Berry	.05
76	Wil Cordero	.05
77	Cliff Floyd	.05
78	Marquis Grissom	.05
79	Ken Hill	.05
80	Larry Walker	.05
81	John Wetteland	.05
82	Rod Beck	.05
83	Barry Bonds	1.50
84	Royce Clayton	.05
85	Darren Lewis	.05
86	Willie McGee	.05
87	Bill Swift	.05
88	Robby Thompson	.05
89	Matt Williams	.05
90	Sandy Alomar Jr.	.05
91	Carlos Baerga	.05
92	Albert Belle	.05
93	Kenny Lofton	.05
94	Eddie Murray	.55
95	Manny Ramirez	.55
96	Paul Sorrento	.05
97	Jim Thome	.45
98	Rich Amaral	.05
99	Eric Anthony	.05
100	Jay Buhner	.05
101	Ken Griffey Jr.	.75
102	Randy Johnson	.55
103	Edgar Martinez	.05
104	Tino Martinez	.05
105	Kurt Abbott RC	.05
106	Bret Barberie	.05
107	Chuck Carr	.05
108	Jeff Conine	.05
109	Chris Hammond	.05
110	Bryan Harvey	.05
111	Benito Santiago	.05
112	Gary Sheffield	.30
113	Bobby Bonilla	.05
114	Dwight Gooden	.05
115	Todd Hundley	.05
116	Bobby Jones	.05
117	Jeff Kent	.05

#	Player	Price
118	Kevin McReynolds	.05
119	Bret Saberhagen	.05
120	Ryan Thompson	.05
121	Harold Baines	.05
122	Mike Devereaux	.05
123	Jeffrey Hammonds	.05
124	Ben McDonald	.05
125	Mike Mussina	.25
126	Rafael Palmeiro	.45
127	Cal Ripken, Jr.	1.50
128	Lee Smith	.05
129	Brad Ausmus	.05
130	Derek Bell	.05
131	Andy Benes	.05
132	Tony Gwynn	.60
133	Trevor Hoffman	.05
134	Scott Livingstone	.05
135	Phil Plantier	.05
136	Darren Daulton	.05
137	Mariano Duncan	.05
138	Len Dykstra	.05
139	Dave Hollins	.05
140	Pete Incaviglia	.05
141	Danny Jackson	.05
142	John Kruk	.05
143	Kevin Stocker	.05
144	Jay Bell	.05
145	Carlos Garcia	.05
146	Jeff King	.05
147	Al Martin	.05
148	Orlando Merced	.05
149	Don Slaught	.05
150	Andy Van Slyke	.05
151	Kevin Brown	.05
152	Jose Canseco	.40
153	Will Clark	.05
154	Juan Gonzalez	.30
155	David Hulse	.05
156	Dean Palmer	.05
157	Ivan Rodriguez	.45
158	Kenny Rogers	.05
159	Roger Clemens	.65
160	Scott Cooper	.05
161	Andre Dawson	.25
162	Mike Greenwell	.05
163	Otis Nixon	.05
164	Aaron Sele	.05
165	John Valentin	.05
166	Mo Vaughn	.05
167	Bret Boone	.05
168	Barry Larkin	.05
169	Kevin Mitchell	.05
170	Hal Morris	.05
171	Jose Rijo	.05
172	Deion Sanders	.05
173	Reggie Sanders	.05
174	John Smiley	.05
175	Dante Bichette	.05
176	Ellis Burks	.05
177	Andres Galarraga	.05
178	Joe Girardi	.05
179	Charlie Hayes	.05
180	Roberto Mejia	.05
181	Walt Weiss	.05
182	David Cone	.05
183	Gary Gaetti	.05
184	Greg Gagne	.05
185	Felix Jose	.05
186	Wally Joyner	.05
187	Mike Macfarlane	.05
188	Brian McRae	.05
189	Eric Davis	.05
190	Cecil Fielder	.05
191	Travis Fryman	.05
192	Tony Phillips	.05
193	Mickey Tettleton	.05
194	Alan Trammell	.05
195	Lou Whitaker	.05
196	Kent Hrbek	.05
197	Chuck Knoblauch	.05
198	Shane Mack	.05
199	Pat Meares	.05
200	Kirby Puckett	.60
201	Matt Walbeck	.05
202	Dave Winfield	.55
203	Wilson Alvarez	.05
204	Alex Fernandez	.05
205	Julio Franco	.05
206	Ozzie Guillen	.05
207	Jack McDowell	.05
208	Tim Raines	.05
209	Frank Thomas	.55
210	Robin Ventura	.05
211	Jim Abbott	.05
212	Wade Boggs	.60
213	Pat Kelly	.05
214	Jimmy Key	.05
215	Don Mattingly	.65
216	Paul O'Neill	.05
217	Mike Stanley	.05
218	Danny Tartabull	.05
219	Checklist	.05
220	Checklist	.05

Editor's Choice

Printed in similitude to a strip of color slide film, each of the cards in this insert set feature a complete player photo at center, with partial "frames" at top and bottom. Printed on acetate, the back of the card shows a reversed image of the front. Stated odds of finding an Editor's Choice insert card are about one per box of 36 packs.

Editor's Choice

		NM/M
Complete Set (8):		12.00
Common Player:		.50
1	Barry Bonds	3.00
2	Frank Thomas	1.50
3	Ken Griffey Jr.	2.50
4	Andres Galarraga	.50
5	Juan Gonzalez	.75
6	Tim Salmon	.50
7	Paul O'Neill	.50
8	Mike Piazza	2.50

Heritage

Besides picturing today's players in vintage uniforms, the 1994 Studio Heritage inserts have the player portraits set against sepia-toned photos of old ballparks. Fronts are enhanced by copper-foil logos and by a round device at upper-left containing the player's name, team and year represented. Backs have a second color player photo and a short write-up about the team represented. Unlike the other cards in the set, the Heritage cards are printed on a porous cardboard stock to enhance the image of antiquity. Stated odds of finding a Heritage Collection insert card are one in nine packs.

		NM/M
Complete Set (8):		9.00
Common Player:		.50
1	Barry Bonds	4.00
2	Frank Thomas	1.50
3	Joe Carter	.50
4	Don Mattingly	3.00
5	Ryne Sandberg	2.00
6	Javier Lopez	.50
7	Gregg Jefferies	.50
8	Mike Mussina	.65

Silver Stars

Each of the 10 players in this insert set was produced in an edition of 10,000 cards. Printed on acetate, fronts feature action photos set against a clear plastic background with a silver-foil seal at bottom. Within the player silhouette on back, a second photo is printed. The back also features a black-and-white version of the seal, including the card's unique serial number. Stated odds of picking a Silver Series Star are one per 60 packs, on average.

		NM/M
Complete Set (10):		35.00
Common Player:		1.50
1	Tony Gwynn	3.50
2	Barry Bonds	7.50
3	Frank Thomas	2.50
4	Ken Griffey Jr.	4.50
5	Joe Carter	1.50
6	Mike Piazza	4.50
7	Cal Ripken, Jr.	7.50
8	Greg Maddux	3.50
9	Juan Gonzalez	2.00
10	Don Mattingly	4.00

Gold Stars

The scarcest of the 1994 Studio chase cards, only 5,000 cards of each of the 10 players were produced. Printed on acetate, fronts feature an action photo set against a clear plastic background. At bottom is a large gold-foil seal. Backs have another player photo, within the silhouette of the front photo, and a black-and-white version of the seal, including the card's unique serial number. According to the series wrapper, odds of finding a Gold Series Star card are one in 120 packs.

		NM/M
Complete Set (10):		80.00
Common Player:		4.50
1	Tony Gwynn	9.00
2	Barry Bonds	16.00
3	Frank Thomas	7.50
4	Ken Griffey Jr.	12.50
5	Joe Carter	4.50
6	Mike Piazza	12.50
7	Cal Ripken, Jr.	16.00
8	Greg Maddux	9.00
9	Juan Gonzalez	5.00
10	Don Mattingly	10.00

1995 Studio

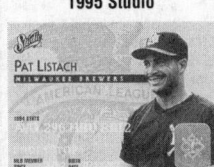

Known since its inception as a brand name for its innovative design, Studio did not disappoint in 1995, unveiling a baseball card with a credit card look. In horizontal format, the cards feature embossed stats and data on front, plus a team logo hologram. Backs have a color player photo, facsimile autograph and simulated magnetic data strip to carry through the credit card impression.

		NM/M
Complete Set (200):		25.00
Common Player:		.05
Pack (5):		1.00
Wax Box (36):		20.00
1	Frank Thomas	.75
2	Jeff Bagwell	.75
3	Don Mattingly	1.25
4	Mike Piazza	1.50
5	Ken Griffey Jr.	1.50
6	Greg Maddux	1.00
7	Barry Bonds	2.50
8	Cal Ripken Jr.	2.50
9	Jose Canseco	.40
10	Paul Molitor	.75
11	Kenny Lofton	.05
12	Will Clark	.05
13	Tim Salmon	.05
14	Joe Carter	.05
15	Albert Belle	1.25
16	Roger Clemens	1.25
17	Roberto Alomar	.30
18	Alex Rodriguez	2.00
19	Raul Mondesi	.05
20	Deion Sanders	.05
21	Juan Gonzalez	.40
22	Kirby Puckett	1.00
23	Fred McGriff	.05
24	Matt Williams	.05
25	Tony Gwynn	1.00
26	Cliff Floyd	.05
27	Travis Fryman	.05
28	Shawn Green	.30
29	Mike Mussina	.35
30	Bob Hamelin	.05
31	Dave Justice	.05
32	Manny Ramirez	.75
33	David Cone	.05
34	Marquis Grissom	.05
35	Moises Alou	.05
36	Carlos Baerga	.05
37	Barry Larkin	.05
38	Robin Ventura	.05
39	Mo Vaughn	.05
40	Jeffrey Hammonds	.05
41	Ozzie Smith	1.00
42	Andres Galarraga	.05
43	Carlos Delgado	.50
44	Lenny Dykstra	.05
45	Cecil Fielder	.05
46	Wade Boggs	1.00
47	Gregg Jefferies	.05
48	Randy Johnson	.75
49	Rafael Palmeiro	.65
50	Craig Biggio	.05
51	Steve Avery	.05
52	Ricky Bottalico	.05
53	Chris Gomez	.05
54	Carlos Garcia	.05
55	Brian Anderson	.05
56	Wilson Alvarez	.05
57	Roberto Kelly	.05
58	Larry Walker	.05
59	Dean Palmer	.05
60	Rick Aguilera	.05
61	Javy Lopez	.05
62	Shawon Dunston	.05
63	William Van Landingham	.05
64	Jeff Kent	.05
65	David McCarty	.05
66	Armando Benitez	.05
67	Brett Butler	.05
68	Bernard Gilkey	.05
69	Joey Hamilton	.05
70	Chad Curtis	.05
71	Dante Bichette	.05
72	Chuck Carr	.05
73	Pedro Martinez	.75
74	Ramon Martinez	.05
75	Rondell White	.05
76	Alex Fernandez	.05
77	Dennis Martinez	.05
78	Sammy Sosa	1.00
79	Bernie Williams	.05
80	Lou Whitaker	.05
81	Kurt Abbott	.05
82	Tino Martinez	.05
83	Willie Greene	.05
84	Garret Anderson	.05
85	Jose Rijo	.05
86	Jeff Montgomery	.05
87	Mark Langston	.05
88	Reggie Sanders	.05
89	Rusty Greer	.05
90	Delino DeShields	.05
91	Jason Bere	.05
92	Lee Smith	.05
93	Devon White	.05
94	John Wetteland	.05
95	Luis Gonzalez	.05
96	Greg Vaughn	.05
97	Lance Johnson	.05
98	Alan Trammell	.05
99	Bret Saberhagen	.05
100	Jack McDowell	.05
101	Trevor Hoffman	.05
102	Dave Nilsson	.05
103	Bryan Harvey	.05
104	Chuck Knoblauch	.05
105	Bobby Bonilla	.05
106	Hal Morris	.05
107	Mark Whiten	.05
108	Phil Plantier	.05
109	Ryan Klesko	.05
110	Greg Gagne	.05
111	Ruben Sierra	.05
112	J.R. Phillips	.05
113	Terry Steinbach	.05
114	Jay Buhner	.05
115	Ken Caminiti	.05
116	Gary DiSarcina	.05
117	Ivan Rodriguez	.65
118	Bip Roberts	.05
119	Jay Bell	.05
120	Ken Hill	.05
121	Mike Greenwell	.05
122	Rick Wilkins	.05
123	Rickey Henderson	.75
124	Dave Hollins	.05
125	Terry Pendleton	.05
126	Rich Becker	.05
127	Billy Ashley	.05
128	Derek Bell	.05
129	Dennis Eckersley	.65
130	Andujar Cedeno	.05
131	John Jaha	.05
132	Chuck Finley	.05
133	Steve Finley	.05
134	Danny Tartabull	.05
135	Jeff Conine	.05
136	Jon Lieber	.05
137	Jim Abbott	.05
138	Steve Traschel	.05
139	Bret Boone	.05
140	Charles Johnson	.05
141	Mark McGwire	2.00
142	Eddie Murray	.75
143	Doug Drabek	.05
144	Steve Cooke	.05
145	Kevin Seitzer	.05
146	Rod Beck	.05
147	Eric Karros	.05
148	Tim Raines	.05
149	Joe Girardi	.05
150	Aaron Sele	.05
151	Robby Thompson	.05
152	Chan Ho Park	.05
153	Ellis Burks	.05
154	Brian McRae	.05
155	Jimmy Key	.05
156	Rico Brogna	.05
157	Ozzie Guillen	.05
158	Chili Davis	.05
159	Darren Daulton	.05
160	Chipper Jones	1.00
161	Walt Weiss	.05
162	Paul O'Neill	.05
163	Al Martin	.05
164	John Valentin	.05
165	Tim Wallach	.05
166	Scott Erickson	.05
167	Ryan Thompson	.05
168	Todd Zeile	.05
169	Scott Cooper	.05
170	Matt Mieske	.05
171	Allen Watson	.05
172	Brian Hunter	.05
173	Kevin Stocker	.05
174	Cal Eldred	.05
175	Tony Phillips	.05
176	Ben McDonald	.05
177	Mark Grace	.05
178	Midre Cummings	.05
179	Orlando Merced	.05
180	Jeff King	.05
181	Gary Sheffield	.40
182	Tom Glavine	.35
183	Edgar Martinez	.05
184	Steve Karsay	.05
185	Pat Listach	.05
186	Wil Cordero	.05
187	Brady Anderson	.05
188	Bobby Jones	.05
189	Andy Benes	.05
190	Ray Lankford	.05
191	John Doherty	.05
192	Wally Joyner	.05
193	Jim Thome	.65
194	Royce Clayton	.05
195	John Olerud	.05
196	Steve Buechele	.05
197	Harold Baines	.05
198	Geronimo Berroa	.05
199	Checklist	.05
200	Checklist	.05

Gold

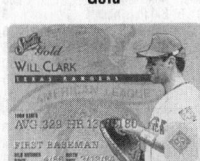

The chase cards in 1995 Studio are plastic versions of some of the regular cards. The round-cornered plastic format of the inserts gives them an even greater similitude to credit cards. The first 50 numbers in the regular set are reproduced in a parallel Studio Gold plastic version, found one per pack, except for those packs which have a platinum card.

		NM/M
Complete Set (50):		25.00
Common Player:		.15
1	Frank Thomas	1.00
2	Jeff Bagwell	1.00
3	Don Mattingly	1.75
4	Mike Piazza	2.00
5	Ken Griffey Jr.	2.00
6	Greg Maddux	1.50
7	Barry Bonds	3.00
8	Cal Ripken Jr.	3.00
9	Jose Canseco	.50
10	Paul Molitor	1.00
11	Kenny Lofton	.15
12	Will Clark	.15
13	Tim Salmon	.15
14	Joe Carter	.15
15	Albert Belle	.75
16	Roger Clemens	1.75
17	Roberto Alomar	.35
18	Alex Rodriguez	2.50
19	Raul Mondesi	.15
20	Deion Sanders	.15
21	Juan Gonzalez	.50
22	Kirby Puckett	1.50
23	Fred McGriff	.15
24	Matt Williams	.15
25	Tony Gwynn	1.50
26	Cliff Floyd	.15
27	Travis Fryman	.15
28	Shawn Green	.40
29	Mike Mussina	.35
30	Bob Hamelin	.15
31	Dave Justice	.15
32	Manny Ramirez	1.00
33	David Cone	.15
34	Marquis Grissom	.15
35	Moises Alou	.15
36	Carlos Baerga	.15
37	Barry Larkin	.15
38	Robin Ventura	.15
39	Mo Vaughn	.15
40	Jeffrey Hammonds	.15
41	Ozzie Smith	1.50
42	Andres Galarraga	.15
43	Carlos Delgado	.50
44	Lenny Dykstra	.15
45	Cecil Fielder	.15
46	Wade Boggs	1.50
47	Gregg Jefferies	.15
48	Randy Johnson	1.00
49	Rafael Palmeiro	.75
50	Craig Biggio	.15

Platinum

Found at the rate of one per 10 packs, Studio Platinum cards are silver-toned plastic versions of the first 25 cards from the regular set.

		NM/M
Complete Set (25):		25.00
Common Player:		.50
1	Frank Thomas	2.00
2	Jeff Bagwell	2.00
3	Don Mattingly	3.25
4	Mike Piazza	3.50
5	Ken Griffey Jr.	3.50
6	Greg Maddux	3.00
7	Barry Bonds	2.50
8	Cal Ripken Jr.	5.00
9	Jose Canseco	1.00
10	Paul Molitor	2.00
11	Kenny Lofton	.50
12	Will Clark	.50
13	Tim Salmon	.50
14	Joe Carter	.50
15	Albert Belle	.50
16	Roger Clemens	3.25
17	Roberto Alomar	.75
18	Alex Rodriguez	4.00
19	Raul Mondesi	.50
20	Deion Sanders	.50
21	Juan Gonzalez	1.00
22	Kirby Puckett	3.00
23	Fred McGriff	.50
24	Matt Williams	.50
25	Tony Gwynn	3.00

1996 Studio

The 1996 Studio set is the first Donruss product to be released under the Pinnacle Brands flagship. The 150-card set has three parallel sets - Bronze Press Proofs (2,000 sets), Silver Press Proofs (found only in magazine packs, 100 sets), and Gold Press Proofs (500 sets). Three insert sets were also made - Hit Parade, Masterstrokes and Stained Glass Stars.

		NM/M
Complete Set (150):		9.00
Common Player:		.05
Bronze Press Proofs:		3X
Gold Press Proofs:		7X
Silver Press Proofs:		25X
Pack (7):		1.25
Wax Box (24):		20.00
1	Cal Ripken Jr.	1.50
2	Alex Rodriguez	.05
3	Roger Cedeno	.05
4	Todd Hollandsworth	.05
5	Gregg Jefferies	.05
6	Ryne Sandberg	.65
7	Eric Karros	.05
8	Jeff Conine	.05
9	Rafael Palmeiro	.45
10	Bip Roberts	.05
11	Roger Clemens	.70
12	Tom Glavine	.30
13	Jason Giambi	.40
14	Rey Ordonez	.05
15	Chan Ho Park	.05
16	Vinny Castilla	.05
17	Butch Huskey	.05
18	Greg Maddux	.65
19	Bernard Gilkey	.05
20	Marquis Grissom	.05
21	Chuck Knoblauch	.05
22	Ozzie Smith	.65
23	Garret Anderson	.05
24	J.T. Snow	.05
25	John Valentin	.05
26	Barry Larkin	.05
27	Bobby Bonilla	.05
28	Todd Zeile	.05
29	Roberto Alomar	.20
30	Ramon Martinez	.05
31	Jeff King	.05
32	Dennis Eckersley	.45
33	Derek Jeter	1.50
34	Edgar Martinez	.05
35	Geronimo Berroa	.05
36	Hal Morris	.05
37	Troy Percival	.05
38	Jason Isringhausen	.05
39	Greg Vaughn	.05
40	Robin Ventura	.05
41	Craig Biggio	.05
42	Will Clark	.05
43	Sammy Sosa	.65
44	Bernie Williams	.05
45	Kenny Lofton	.05
46	Wade Boggs	.65
47	Javy Lopez	.05
48	Reggie Sanders	.55
49	Jeff Bagwell	.55
50	Fred McGriff	.05
51	Charles Johnson	.05
52	Darren Daulton	.05
53	Jose Canseco	.40
54	Cecil Fielder	.05
55	Hideo Nomo	.30
56	Tim Salmon	.05
57	Carlos Delgado	.40
58	David Cone	.05
59	Tim Raines	.05
60	Lyle Mouton	.05
61	Wally Joyner	.05
62	Bret Boone	.05
63	Raul Mondesi	.05
64	Gary Sheffield	.35
65	Alex Rodriguez	1.00
66	Russ Davis	.05
67	Checklist	.05
68	Marty Cordova	.05
69	Ruben Sierra	.05
70	Jose Mesa	.05
71	Matt Williams	.05
72	Chipper Jones	.75
73	Randy Johnson	.55
74	Kirby Puckett	.65
75	Jim Edmonds	.05
76	Barry Bonds	1.50
77	David Segui	.05
78	Larry Walker	.05
79	Jason Kendall	.05
80	Mike Piazza	.75
81	Brian Hunter	.05
82	Julio Franco	.05
83	Jay Bell	.05
84	Kevin Seitzer	.05
85	John Smoltz	.05
86	Joe Carter	.05
87	Ray Durham	.05
88	Carlos Baerga	.05
89	Ron Gant	.05
90	Orlando Merced	.05
91	Lee Smith	.05
92	Pedro Martinez	.55
93	Frank Thomas	.55
94	Al Martin	.05
95	Chad Curtis	.05
96	Eddie Murray	.55
97	Rusty Greer	.05
98	Jay Buhner	.05
99	Rico Brogna	.05
100	Todd Hundley	.05
101	Moises Alou	.05
102	Chili Davis	.05
103	Ismael Valdes	.05
104	Mo Vaughn	.05
105	Juan Gonzalez	.30
106	Mark Grudzielanek	.05
107	Derek Bell	.05
108	Shawn Green	.30
109	David Justice	.05
110	Paul O'Neill	.05
111	Kevin Appier	.05
112	Ray Lankford	.05
113	Travis Fryman	.05
114	Manny Ramirez	.55
115	Brooks Kieschnick	.05
116	Ken Griffey Jr.	.75
117	Jeffrey Hammonds	.05
118	Mark McGwire	1.00
119	Denny Neagle	.05
120	Quivilo Veras	.05
121	Alan Benes	.05
122	Rondell White	.05

123	Osvaldo Fernandez **RC**	.20
124	Andres Galarraga	.05
125	Johnny Damon	.35
126	Lenny Dykstra	.05
127	Jason Schmidt	.05
128	Mike Mussina	.30
129	Ken Caminiti	.05
130	Michael Tucker	.05
131	LaTroy Hawkins	.05
132	Checklist	.05
133	Delino DeShields	.05
134	Dave Nilsson	.05
135	Jack McDowell	.05
136	Joey Hamilton	.05
137	Dante Bichette	.05
138	Paul Molitor	.55
139	Ivan Rodriguez	.45
140	Mark Grace	.05
141	Paul Wilson	.05
142	Orel Hershiser	.05
143	Albert Belle	.05
144	Tino Martinez	.05
145	Tony Gwynn	.65
146	George Arias	.05
147	Brian Jordan	.05
148	Brian McRae	.05
149	Rickey Henderson	.55
150	Ryan Klesko	.05

Press Proofs

	NM/M
Common Player, Bronze:	.50
Bronze Stars:	3X
Common Player, Gold:	1.00
Gold Stars:	7X
Common Player, Silver:	4.00
Silver Stars:	25X

The basic 150-card 1996 Studio set was also produced in three parallel press proof versions. Each is basically identical to the regular-issue cards except for appropriately colored foil highlights on front and a notation of edition size in the circle around the portrait photo on back. Bronze press proofs were issued in an edition of 2,000 each and were inserted at an average rate of one per six packs. Gold press proofs were an edition of 500 with an average insertion rate of one per 24 packs. The silver press proofs were inserted only into magazine packs and limited to just 100 cards of each.

Hit Parade

These die-cut inserts resemble an album with half of the record pulled out of the sleeve. Hit Parade cards, which feature top long ball hitters, were seeded one per every 36 packs. The cards were individually numbered up to 7,500. Each card can also be found in a sample version which has a "XXXX/5000" serial number on back.

		NM/M
Complete Set (10):		10.00
Common Player:		.75
1	Tony Gwynn	1.50
2	Ken Griffey Jr.	2.00
3	Frank Thomas	1.00
4	Jeff Bagwell	1.00
5	Kirby Puckett	1.50
6	Mike Piazza	2.00
7	Barry Bonds	2.50
8	Albert Belle	.75
9	Tim Salmon	.75
10	Mo Vaughn	.75

Masterstrokes

Only 5,000 each of these 1996 Studio insert cards were made. The

cards simulate oil painting detail on an embossed canvas-feel front. Backs are glossy and individually serial numbered. They are found on average of once per 70 packs. Sample versions of each card overprinted as such on the back and numbered "PROMO/5000" were also issued.

		NM/M
Complete Set (8):		30.00
Common Player:		4.00
	Samples: 75 Percent	
1	Tony Gwynn	6.00
2	Mike Piazza	8.00
3	Jeff Bagwell	4.00
4	Manny Ramirez	4.00
5	Cal Ripken Jr.	12.00
6	Frank Thomas	4.00
7	Ken Griffey Jr.	8.00
8	Greg Maddux	6.00

Glass Stars

Twelve superstars are featured on these clear, die-cut plastic cards which resemble stained glass windows. These 1996 Studio inserts were seeded one per every 30 packs.

		NM/M
Complete Set (12):		24.00
Common Player:		1.00
1	Cal Ripken Jr.	5.00
2	Ken Griffey Jr.	3.50
3	Frank Thomas	2.00
4	Greg Maddux	2.50
5	Chipper Jones	2.50
6	Mike Piazza	3.50
7	Albert Belle	1.00
8	Jeff Bagwell	2.00
9	Hideo Nomo	1.50
10	Barry Bonds	5.00
11	Manny Ramirez	1.00
12	Kenny Lofton	1.00

1997 Studio

Innovations in both product and packaging marked the seventh annual issue of Donruss' Studio brand. As in the past, the 165 cards in the base set rely on high-quality front photos to bring out the players' personalities. For '97, the photos are set against a background of variously shaded gray horizontal stripes. Backs have a second player

photo, often an action shot, along with a short career summary. The "pack" for '97 Studio is something totally new to the hobby. An 8-1/2" x 12" cardboard envelope, complete with a zip strip opener in the style of an express-mail envelope, contains a cello pack of five standard-size cards plus either an 8" x 10" Studio Portrait card or an 8" x 10" version of the Master Strokes insert. Suggested retail price at issue was $2.49 per pack. Regular-size Master Strokes cards are one of several insert series which includes silver and gold press proofs and die-cut plastic Hard Hats.

	NM/M
Complete Set (165):	17.50
Common Player:	.05
Silver Press Proofs:	4X
Gold Press Proofs:	8X
Pack (5):	3.00
Wax Box (18):	40.00

1	Frank Thomas	.65
2	Gary Sheffield	.45
3	Jason Isringhausen	.05
4	Ron Gant	.05
5	Andy Pettitte	.25
6	Todd Hollandsworth	.05
7	Troy Percival	.05
8	Mark McGwire	1.50
9	Barry Larkin	.05
10	Ken Caminiti	.05
11	Paul Molitor	.65
12	Travis Fryman	.05
13	Kevin Brown	.05
14	Robin Ventura	.05
15	Andres Galarraga	.05
16	Ken Griffey Jr.	1.00
17	Roger Clemens	.85
18	Alan Benes	.05
19	David Justice	.05
20	Damon Buford	.05
21	Mike Piazza	1.00
22	Ray Durham	.05
23	Billy Wagner	.05
24	Dean Palmer	.05
25	David Cone	.05
26	Ruben Sierra	.05
27	Henry Rodriguez	.05
28	Ray Lankford	.05
29	Jamey Wright	.05
30	Brady Anderson	.05
31	Tino Martinez	.05
32	Manny Ramirez	.65
33	Jeff Conine	.05
34	Dante Bichette	.05
35	Jose Canseco	.50
36	Mo Vaughn	.05
37	Sammy Sosa	.75
38	Mark Grudzielanek	.05
39	Mike Mussina	.35
40	Bill Pulsipher	.05
41	Ryne Sandberg	.75
42	Rickey Henderson	.65
43	Alex Rodriguez	1.50
44	Eddie Murray	.65
45	Ernie Young	.05
46	Joey Hamilton	.05
47	Wade Boggs	.75
48	Rusty Greer	.05
49	Carlos Delgado	.50
50	Ellis Burks	.05
51	Cal Ripken Jr.	2.00
52	Alex Fernandez	.05
53	Wally Joyner	.05
54	James Baldwin	.05
55	Juan Gonzalez	.35
56	John Smoltz	.05
57	Omar Vizquel	.05
58	Shane Reynolds	.05
59	Barry Bonds	2.00
60	Jason Kendall	.05
61	Marty Cordova	.05
62	Charles Johnson	.05
63	John Jaha	.05
64	Chan Ho Park	.05
65	Jermaine Allensworth	.05
66	Mark Grace	.05
67	Tim Salmon	.05
68	Edgar Martinez	.05
69	Marquis Grissom	.05
70	Craig Biggio	.05
71	Bobby Higginson	.05
72	Kevin Seitzer	.05
73	Hideo Nomo	.35
74	Dennis Eckersley	.60
75	Bobby Bonilla	.05
76	Dwight Gooden	.05
77	Jeff Cirillo	.05
78	Brian McRae	.05
79	Chipper Jones	.75
80	Jeff Fassero	.05
81	Fred McGriff	.05
82	Garret Anderson	.05
83	Eric Karros	.05
84	Derek Bell	.05
85	Kenny Lofton	.05
86	John Mabry	.05
87	Pat Hentgen	.05
88	Greg Maddux	.75
89	Jason Giambi	.45
90	Al Martin	.05

91	Derek Jeter	2.00
92	Rey Ordonez	.05
93	Will Clark	.05
94	Kevin Appier	.05
95	Roberto Alomar	.30
96	Joe Carter	.05
97	Bernie Williams	.05
98	Albert Belle	.05
99	Greg Vaughn	.05
100	Tony Clark	.05
101	Matt Williams	.05
102	Jeff Bagwell	.65
103	Reggie Sanders	.05
104	Mariano Rivera	.15
105	Larry Walker	.05
106	Shawn Green	.30
107	Alex Ochoa	.05
108	Ivan Rodriguez	.60
109	Eric Young	.05
110	Javier Lopez	.05
111	Brian Hunter	.05
112	Raul Mondesi	.05
113	Randy Johnson	.65
114	Tony Phillips	.05
115	Carlos Garcia	.05
116	Moises Alou	.05
117	Paul O'Neill	.05
118	Jim Thome	.60
119	Jermaine Dye	.05
120	Wilson Alvarez	.05
121	Rondell White	.05
122	Michael Tucker	.05
123	Mike Lansing	.05
124	Tony Gwynn	.75
125	Ryan Klesko	.05
126	Jim Edmonds	.05
127	Chuck Knoblauch	.05
128	Rafael Palmeiro	.60
129	Jay Buhner	.05
130	Tom Glavine	.35
131	Julio Franco	.05
132	Cecil Fielder	.05
133	Paul Wilson	.05
134	Deion Sanders	.05
135	Alex Gonzalez	.05
136	Charles Nagy	.05
137	Andy Ashby	.05
138	Edgar Renteria	.05
139	Pedro Martinez	.65
140	Brian Jordan	.05
141	Todd Hundley	.05
142	Marc Newfield	.05
143	Darryl Strawberry	.05
144	Dan Wilson	.05
145	Brian Giles **RC**	.50
146	Bartolo Colon	.05
147	Shannon Stewart	.05
148	Scott Spiezio	.05
149	Andruw Jones	.65
150	Karim Garcia	.05
151	Vladimir Guerrero	.65
152	George Arias	.05
153	Brooks Kieschnick	.05
154	Todd Walker	.05
155	Scott Rolen	.60
156	Todd Greene	.05
157	Dmitri Young	.05
158	Ruben Rivera	.05
159	Trey Beamon	.05
160	Nomar Garciaparra	.75
161	Bob Abreu	.05
162	Darin Erstad	.15
163	Ken Griffey Jr. (Checklist)	.75
164	Frank Thomas (Checklist)	.35
165	Alex Rodriguez (Checklist)	.75

Press Proofs

Each of the 165 cards in the base set of '97 Studio was also produced in a pair of Press Proof versions as random pack inserts. Fronts of the Press Proofs have either silver or gold holographic foil replacing the silver foil graphics found on regular cards, as well as foil strips down each side. Backs are identical to the regular issue. The silver Press Proofs were issued in an edition of 1,500 of each player; the golds are limited to 500 of each.

	NM/M
Common Player, Silver:	.50
Silver Stars:	4X
Common Player, Gold:	1.00
Gold Stars:	8X

Hard Hats

Die-cut plastic is used to represent a player's batting helmet in this set of '97 Studio inserts. A player action photo appears in the foreground with his name and other graphic elements in silver foil. Backs feature a small portrait photo, short career summary and a serial number from within the edition of 5,000 of each card.

		NM/M
Complete Set (24):		50.00
Common Player:		1.50
1	Ivan Rodriguez	3.00
2	Albert Belle	1.50
3	Ken Griffey Jr.	6.00
4	Chuck Knoblauch	1.50
5	Frank Thomas	4.00
6	Cal Ripken Jr.	8.00
7	Todd Walker	1.50
8	Alex Rodriguez	7.00
9	Jim Thome	3.00
10	Mike Piazza	6.00
11	Barry Larkin	1.50
12	Chipper Jones	5.00
13	Derek Jeter	8.00
14	Jermaine Dye	1.50
15	Jason Giambi	2.00
16	Tim Salmon	1.50
17	Brady Anderson	1.50
18	Rondell White	1.50
19	Bernie Williams	1.50
20	Juan Gonzalez	2.00
21	Karim Garcia	1.50
22	Scott Rolen	3.00
23	Darin Erstad	2.00
24	Brian Jordan	1.50

Master Strokes

The look and feel of a painting on canvas is the effect presented by '97 Studio's Master Strokes inserts. Card fronts feature unique player action art and are highlighted by gold-foil graphics. Each card has a facsimile autograph on front. UV-coated backs are team-color coordinated and have a few sentences about the player. Gold-foil serial numbering identifies the card from an edition of 2,000 of each player.

		NM/M
Complete Set (24):		120.00
Common Player:		2.00
1	Derek Jeter	12.00
2	Jeff Bagwell	4.50
3	Ken Griffey Jr.	8.00
4	Barry Bonds	12.00
5	Frank Thomas	4.50
6	Andy Pettitte	2.25
7	Mo Vaughn	2.00
8	Alex Rodriguez	10.00
9	Andruw Jones	4.50
10	Kenny Lofton	2.00
11	Cal Ripken Jr.	12.00
12	Greg Maddux	6.00
13	Manny Ramirez	4.50
14	Mike Piazza	8.00
14p	Mike Piazza (Promo)	3.50
15	Vladimir Guerrero	4.50
16	Albert Belle	2.00
17	Chipper Jones	6.00
18	Hideo Nomo	2.50
19	Sammy Sosa	6.00
20	Tony Gwynn	4.50
21	Gary Sheffield	2.50
22	Mark McGwire	10.00
23	Juan Gonzalez	2.50
24	Paul Molitor	4.50

Master Strokes 8x10

The look and feel of a painting on canvas is the effect presented by

the 8" x 10" version of '97 Studio's Master Strokes inserts. Card fronts feature unique player action art and are highlighted by gold-foil graphics. Each card has a facsimile autograph on front. UV-coated backs are team-color coordinated and have a few sentences about the player. Gold-foil serial numbering identifies the card from an edition of 5,000 of each player - making the super-size version more than twice as common as the 2-1/2" x 3-1/2" version.

		NM/M
Complete Set (24):		45.00
Common Player:		.75
1	Derek Jeter	5.00
2	Jeff Bagwell	2.00
3	Ken Griffey Jr.	3.00
4	Barry Bonds	5.00
5	Frank Thomas	2.00
6	Andy Pettitte	1.00
7	Mo Vaughn	.75
8	Alex Rodriguez	4.00
9	Andruw Jones	2.00
10	Kenny Lofton	.75
11	Cal Ripken Jr.	5.00
12	Greg Maddux	2.50
13	Manny Ramirez	1.50
14	Mike Piazza	3.00
15	Vladimir Guerrero	2.00
16	Albert Belle	.75
17	Chipper Jones	2.50
18	Hideo Nomo	1.50
19	Sammy Sosa	2.50
20	Tony Gwynn	2.50
21	Gary Sheffield	1.50
22	Mark McGwire	4.00
23	Juan Gonzalez	1.50
24	Paul Molitor	2.00

Portraits

Perhaps the most innovative feature of '97 Studio is the 8" x 10" Portrait cards which come one per pack (except when a pack contains a Master Strokes 8x10). Virtually identical to the player's regular-size Studio card, the jumbo version has the word "PORTRAIT" in black beneath the team name on front. Backs have different card numbers than the same player's card in the regular set. The Portrait cards are produced with a special UV coating on front to facilitate autographing. Pre-autographed cards of three youngsters in the series were included as random pack inserts.

		NM/M
Complete Set (24):		10.00
Common Player:		.25
1	Ken Griffey Jr.	1.00
1s	Frank Thomas (Overprinted "SAMPLE.")	.75
2	Frank Thomas	.65
3	Alex Rodriguez	.75
4	Andruw Jones	.65
5	Cal Ripken Jr.	2.00
6	Greg Maddux	.75
7	Mike Piazza	1.00
8	Chipper Jones	.75
9	Albert Belle	.25
10	Derek Jeter	2.00
11	Juan Gonzalez	.50
12	Todd Walker	.25

#	Player	Price
12a	Todd Walker (Autographed edition of 1,250.)	10.00
13	Mark McGwire	1.50
14	Barry Bonds	2.00
15	Jeff Bagwell	.65
16	Manny Ramirez	.65
17	Kenny Lofton	.25
18	Mo Vaughn	.25
19	Hideo Nomo	.45
20	Tony Gwynn	.75
21	Vladimir Guerrero	.65
21a	Vladimir Guerrero (Autographed edition of 500.)	30.00
22	Gary Sheffield	.45
23	Ryne Sandberg	.75
24	Scott Rolen	.50
24a	Scott Rolen (Autographed edition of 1,000.)	12.00

Portrait Collection

In a departure from traditional sportscard marketing, the 1997 Studio program offered a pair of specially framed editions directly to consumers. The offer was made in a color brochure found in about half the packs advertising the "Portrait Collection." The offer includes one standard-size card and an 8" x 10" Portrait or Master card similar to those in the regular issue. These cards differ from the regular issue in that they are trimmed in platinum holographic foil, individually hand-numbered and signed by the photographer. The cards were sold framed with a metal plaque, also numbered, attesting to the limited-edition status. The framed Studio Portrait piece was produced in an edition of 500 of each player; the Master Strokes piece was limited to 100 for each player on the checklist. The former was issued at $159; the latter at $299.

		NM/M
Complete Set, Studio Portrait: (24)		2,850
Complete Set, Master Strokes: (24)		5,250
Common Plaque, Studio Portrait:		125.00
Common Plaque, Master Strokes:		225.00
P1	Ken Griffey Jr.	125.00
P2	Frank Thomas	125.00
P3	Alex Rodriguez	125.00
P4	Andruw Jones	125.00
P5	Cal Ripken Jr.	125.00
P6	Greg Maddux	125.00
P7	Mike Piazza	125.00
P8	Chipper Jones	125.00
P9	Albert Belle	125.00
P10	Derek Jeter	125.00
P11	Juan Gonzalez	125.00
P12	Todd Walker	125.00
P13	Mark McGwire	125.00
P14	Barry Bonds	125.00
P15	Jeff Bagwell	125.00
P16	Manny	125.00
P17	Kenny Lofton	125.00
P18	Mo Vaughn	125.00
P19	Hideo Nomo	125.00
P20	Tony Gwynn	125.00
P21	Vladimir Guerrero	125.00
P22	Gary Sheffield	125.00
P23	Ryne Sandberg	125.00
P24	Scott Rolen	125.00
M1	Derek Jeter	225.00
M2	Jeff Bagwell	225.00
M3	Ken Griffey Jr.	225.00
M4	Barry Bonds	225.00
M5	Frank Thomas	225.00
M6	Andy Pettitte	225.00
M7	Mo Vaughn	225.00
M8	Alex Rodriguez	225.00
M9	Andruw Jones	225.00
M10	Kenny Lofton	225.00
M11	Cal Ripken Jr.	225.00
M12	Greg Maddux	225.00
M13	Manny Ramirez	225.00
M14	Mike Piazza	225.00
M15	Vladimir Guerrero	225.00
M16	Albert Belle	225.00
M17	Chipper Jones	225.00
M18	Hideo Nomo	225.00
M19	Sammy Sosa	225.00
M20	Tony Gwynn	225.00
M21	Gary Sheffield	225.00
M22	Mark McGwire	225.00
M23	Juan Gonzalez	225.00
M24	Paul Molitor	225.00

1998 Studio

The Donruss Studio base set consists of 220 regular-sized cards and 36 8-x-10 portraits. The base cards feature a posed photo with an action shot in the background, surrounded by a white border. Silver Studio Proofs (numbered to 1,000) and Gold Studio Proofs (300) parallel the regular base set. Inserts included Freeze Frame, Hit Parade and Masterstrokes.

		NM/M
Complete Set (220):		25.00
Common Player:		.05
Silver Proofs:		3X
Gold Proofs:		6X
Proofs (5 Cards+8x10):		2.00
Pack (7 Cards):		2.00
Wax Box (18):		20.00
1	Tony Clark	.05
2	Jose Cruz Jr.	.05
3	Ivan Rodriguez	.65
4	Mo Vaughn	.05
5	Kenny Lofton	.05
6	Will Clark	.05
7	Barry Larkin	.05
8	Jay Bell	.05
9	Kevin Young	.05
10	Francisco Cordova	.05
11	Justin Thompson	.05
12	Paul Molitor	.75
13	Jeff Bagwell	.75
14	Jose Canseco	.45
15	Scott Rolen	.65
16	Wilton Guerrero	.05
17	Shannon Stewart	.05
18	Hideki Irabu	.05
19	Michael Tucker	.05
20	Joe Carter	.05
21	Gabe Alvarez	.05
22	Ricky Ledee	.05
23	Karim Garcia	.05
24	Eli Marrero	.05
25	Scott Elarton	.05
26	Mario Valdez	.05
27	Ben Grieve	.05
28	Paul Konerko	.15
29	Esteban Yan RC	.05
30	Esteban Loaiza	.05
31	Delino DeShields	.05
32	Bernie Williams	.05
33	Joe Randa	.05
34	Randy Johnson	.75
35	Brett Tomko	.05
36	Todd Erdos RC	.05
37	Bobby Higginson	.05
38	Jason Kendall	.05
39	Ray Lankford	.05
40	Mark Grace	.05
41	Andy Pettitte	.25
42	Alex Rodriguez	2.00
43	Hideo Nomo	.45
44	Sammy Sosa	1.00
45	J.T. Snow	.05
46	Jason Varitek	.05
47	Vinny Castilla	.05
48	Neifi Perez	.05
49	Todd Walker	.05
50	Mike Cameron	.05
51	Jeffrey Hammonds	.05
52	Deivi Cruz	.05
53	Brian Hunter	.05
54	Al Martin	.05
55	Ron Coomer	.05
56	Chan Ho Park	.05
57	Pedro Martinez	.75
58	Darin Erstad	.15
59	Albert Belle	.05
60	Nomar Garciaparra	1.00
61	Tony Gwynn	1.00
62	Mike Piazza	1.50
63	Todd Helton	.65
64	David Ortiz	.45
65	Todd Dunwoody	.05
66	Orlando Cabrera	.05
67	Ken Cloude	.05
68	Andy Benes	.05
69	Mariano Rivera	.15
70	Cecil Fielder	.05
71	Brian Jordan	.05
72	Darryl Kile	.05
73	Reggie Jefferson	.05
74	Shawn Estes	.05
75	Bobby Bonilla	.05
76	Denny Neagle	.05

#	Player	Price
77	Robin Ventura	.05
78	Omar Vizquel	.05
79	Craig Biggio	.05
80	Moises Alou	.05
81	Garret Anderson	.05
82	Eric Karros	.05
83	Dante Bichette	.05
84	Charles Johnson	.05
85	Rusty Greer	.05
86	Travis Fryman	.05
87	Fernando Tatis	.05
88	Wilson Alvarez	.05
89	Carl Pavano	.05
90	Brian Rose	.05
91	Geoff Jenkins	.05
92	Magglio Ordonez RC	1.50
93	David Segui	.05
94	David Cone	.05
95	John Smoltz	.05
96	Jim Thome	.65
97	Gary Sheffield	.45
98	Barry Bonds	2.50
99	Andres Galarraga	.05
100	Brad Fullmer	.05
101	Bobby Estalella	.05
102	Enrique Wilson	.05
103	Frank Catalanotto RC	.25
104	Mike Lowell RC	.05
105	Kevin Orie	.05
106	Matt Morris	.05
107	Pokey Reese	.05
108	Shawn Green	.35
109	Tony Womack	.05
110	Ken Caminiti	.05
111	Roberto Alomar	.05
112	Ken Griffey Jr.	1.50
113	Cal Ripken Jr.	2.50
114	Lou Collier	.05
115	Larry Walker	.05
116	Fred McGriff	.05
117	Jim Edmonds	.05
118	Edgar Martinez	.05
119	Matt Williams	.05
120	Ismael Valdes	.05
121	Bartolo Colon	.05
122	Jeff Cirillo	.05
123	Steve Woodard RC	.25
124	Kevin Millwood RC	1.00
125	Derrick Gibson	.05
126	Jacob Cruz	.05
127	Russell Branyan	.05
128	Sean Casey	.15
129	Derrek Lee	.50
130	Paul O'Neill	.05
131	Brad Radke	.05
132	Kevin Appier	.05
133	John Olerud	.05
134	Alan Benes	.05
135	Todd Greene	.05
136	Carlos Mendoza RC	.05
137	Wade Boggs	1.00
138	Jose Guillen	.05
139	Tino Martinez	.05
140	Aaron Boone	.05
141	Abraham Nunez	.05
142	Preston Wilson	.05
143	Randall Simon	.05
144	Dennis Reyes	.05
145	Mark Kotsay	.05
146	Richard Hidalgo	.05
147	Travis Lee	.05
148	Hanley Frias RC	.05
149	Ruben Rivera	.05
150	Rafael Medina	.05
151	Dave Nilsson	.05
152	Curt Schilling	.35
153	Brady Anderson	.05
154	Carlos Delgado	.50
155	Jason Giambi	.45
156	Pat Hentgen	.05
157	Tom Glavine	.35
158	Ryan Klesko	.05
159	Chipper Jones	1.00
160	Juan Gonzalez	.45
161	Mark McGwire	2.00
162	Vladimir Guerrero	.75
163	Derek Jeter	2.50
164	Manny Ramirez	.75
165	Mike Mussina	.30
166	Rafael Palmeiro	.65
167	Henry Rodriguez	.05
168	Jeff Suppan	.05
169	Eric Milton	.05
170	Scott Spiezio	.05
171	Wilson Delgado	.05
172	Bubba Trammell	.05
173	Ellis Burks	.05
174	Jason Dickson	.05
175	Butch Huskey	.05
176	Edgardo Alfonzo	.05
177	Eric Young	.05
178	Marquis Grissom	.05
179	Lance Johnson	.05
180	Kevin Brown	.05
181	Sandy Alomar Jr.	.05
182	Todd Hundley	.05
183	Rondell White	.05
184	Javier Lopez	.05
185	Damian Jackson	.05
186	Raul Mondesi	.05
187	Rickey Henderson	.75
188	David Justice	.05
189	Jay Buhner	.05
190	Jaret Wright	.05
191	Miguel Tejada	.25
192	Ron Wright	.05
193	Livan Hernandez	.05
194	A.J. Hinch	.05

#	Player	Price
195	Richie Sexson	.05
196	Bob Abreu	.05
197	Luis Castillo	.05
198	Michael Coleman	.05
199	Greg Maddux	1.00
200	Frank Thomas	.75
201	Andruw Jones	.75
202	Roger Clemens	1.25
203	Tim Salmon	.05
204	Chuck Knoblauch	.05
205	Wes Helms	.05
206	Juan Encarnacion	.05
207	Russ Davis	.05
208	John Valentin	.05
209	Tony Saunders	.05
210	Mike Sweeney	.05
211	Steve Finley	.05
212	David Dellucci RC	.25
213	Edgar Renteria	.05
214	Jeremi Gonzalez	.05
215	Checklist (Jeff Bagwell)	.40
216	Checklist (Mike Piazza)	1.00
217	Checklist (Greg Maddux)	.50
218	Checklist (Cal Ripken Jr.)	1.25
219	Checklist (Frank Thomas)	.45
220	Checklist (Ken Griffey Jr.)	.75

Silver Proofs

This parallel set includes all 220 cards in Studio baseball. Cards are identified by a silver holographic strip around the borders. Silver versions are limited to 1,000 sets.

	NM/M
Common Player:	1.00
Silver Stars:	3X

Gold Proofs

Gold proofs is a parallel of the 220-card base set. Card fronts feature gold holo-foil highlights. Backs are sequentially numbered to 300 each.

	NM/M
Common Player:	3.00
Stars:	6X

Autographs

Three top rookies signed a number of 8x10s for this product. Cards have a Donruss "Authentic Signature" stamp on front.

#	Player	NM/M
1	Travis Lee/500	20.00
2	Todd Helton/1,000	20.00
3	Ben Grieve/1,000	10.00

Freeze Frame

Freeze Frame is a 30-card insert sequentially numbered to 5,000. The cards are designed to look like a piece of film with a color action photo. The first 500 of each card are die-cut.

		NM/M
Complete Set (30):		75.00
Common Player:		1.25
Production 4,500 Sets		
Die-Cuts:		1.5X
Production 500 Sets		
1	Ken Griffey Jr.	5.00
2	Derek Jeter	7.50
3	Ben Grieve	1.25
4	Cal Ripken Jr.	7.50

5	Alex Rodriguez	6.00
6	Greg Maddux	4.00
7	David Justice	1.25
8	Mike Piazza	5.00
9	Chipper Jones	4.00
10	Randy Johnson	3.00
11	Jeff Bagwell	3.00
12	Nomar Garciaparra	4.00
13	Andruw Jones	3.00
14	Frank Thomas	3.00
15	Scott Rolen	2.50
16	Barry Bonds	7.50
17	Kenny Lofton	1.25
18	Ivan Rodriguez	2.50
19	Chuck Knoblauch	1.25
20	Jose Cruz Jr.	1.25
21	Bernie Williams	1.25
22	Tony Gwynn	4.00
23	Juan Gonzalez	2.00
24	Gary Sheffield	2.25
25	Roger Clemens	4.50
26	Travis Lee	1.25
27	Brad Fullmer	1.25
28	Tim Salmon	1.25
29	Raul Mondesi	1.25
30	Roberto Alomar	2.00

Hit Parade

These 20 cards are printed on micro-etched foil board. This set honors baseball's top hitters and is sequentially numbered to 5,000.

		NM/M
Complete Set (20):		30.00
Common Player:		1.00
Production 5,000 Sets		
1	Tony Gwynn	2.50
2	Larry Walker	1.00
3	Mike Piazza	3.00
4	Frank Thomas	2.00
5	Manny Ramirez	2.00
6	Ken Griffey Jr.	3.00
7	Todd Helton	1.50
8	Vladimir Guerrero	2.00
9	Albert Belle	1.00
10	Jeff Bagwell	2.00
11	Juan Gonzalez	2.00
12	Jim Thome	1.50
13	Scott Rolen	1.50
14	Tino Martinez	1.00
15	Mark McGwire	5.00
16	Barry Bonds	5.00
17	Tony Clark	1.00
18	Mo Vaughn	2.00
19	Darin Erstad	1.25
20	Paul Konerko	1.25

Masterstrokes

Printed on a canvas-like material, these 20 cards are numbered to 1,000.

		NM/M
Complete Set (20):		95.00
Common Player:		2.00
Production 1,000 Sets		
Samples:		3X
1	Travis Lee	2.00
2	Kenny Lofton	2.00
3	Mo Vaughn	2.00
4	Ivan Rodriguez	3.50
5	Roger Clemens	6.50
6	Mark McGwire	10.00
7	Hideo Nomo	2.50
8	Andruw Jones	4.50
9	Nomar Garciaparra	6.00
10	Juan Gonzalez	2.50
11	Jeff Bagwell	4.50
12	Derek Jeter	12.50
13	Tony Gwynn	6.00
14	Chipper Jones	6.00
15	Mike Piazza	7.50
16	Greg Maddux	6.00
17	Alex Rodriguez	10.00
18	Cal Ripken Jr.	12.50
19	Frank Thomas	4.50
20	Ken Griffey Jr.	7.50

Sony MLB 99

Twenty Sony MLB '99 sweepstakes cards were inserted one per two Studio packs. The fronts feature a color action shot and the backs have sweepstakes rules and a MLB '99 tip.

		NM/M
Complete Set (20):		8.00
Common Player:		.15
1	Cal Ripken Jr.	1.50
2	Nomar Garciaparra	.75
3	Barry Bonds	1.50
4	Mike Mussina	.35
5	Pedro Martinez	.60
6	Derek Jeter	1.50
7	Andruw Jones	.60
8	Kenny Lofton	.15
9	Gary Sheffield	.45
10	Raul Mondesi	.15
11	Jeff Bagwell	.60
12	Tim Salmon	.15
13	Tom Glavine	.35
14	Ben Grieve	.15
15	Matt Williams	.15
16	Juan Gonzalez	.35
17	Mark McGwire	1.00
18	Bernie Williams	.15
19	Andres Galarraga	.15
20	Jose Cruz Jr.	.15

8x10 Portraits Samples

Sample versions of the 8x10 cards which would be found in '98 Studio packs were also issued. They are identical in format to the issued cards, with UV coating and silver-foil graphics on fronts. Backs have a large black "SAMPLE" overprinted diagonally.

		NM/M
001	Travis Lee	2.00
002	Todd Helton	3.00

8x10 Portraits

One Studio 8-x-10 was included in each pack. The cards were blown-up versions of the regular-size base cards, which were inserted seven per pack. The large portraits are paralleled in the Gold Proofs set, which adds gold holo-foil to the cards. Gold Proofs are numbered to 300.

		NM/M
Complete Set (36):		65.00
Common Player:		.50
Inserted 1:1		
1	Travis Lee	.50
2	Todd Helton	1.50
3	Ben Grieve	.50
4	Paul Konerko	.65
5	Jeff Bagwell	2.00
6	Derek Jeter	7.00
7	Ivan Rodriguez	1.50
8	Cal Ripken Jr.	7.00
9	Mike Piazza	4.00
10	Chipper Jones	3.00
11	Frank Thomas	2.00
12	Tony Gwynn	3.00
13	Nomar Garciaparra	1.00
14	Juan Gonzalez	3.00
15	Greg Maddux	3.00
16	Hideo Nomo	1.00
17	Scott Rolen	1.50
18	Barry Bonds	7.00
19	Ken Griffey Jr.	4.00
20	Alex Rodriguez	5.00
21	Roger Clemens	3.50
22	Mark McGwire	5.00
23	Jose Cruz Jr.	.50
24	Andruw Jones	2.00
25	Tino Martinez	.50
26	Mo Vaughn	.50
27	Vladimir Guerrero	2.00
28	Tony Clark	.50
29	Andy Pettitte	.65
30	Jaret Wright	.65
31	Paul Molitor	2.00
32	Darin Erstad	.65
33	Larry Walker	.50
34	Chuck Knoblauch	.50
35	Barry Larkin	.50
36	Kenny Lofton	.50

Portraits Gold Proofs

This parallel of the 8x10 base set adds gold holo-foil treatments to the 36 cards, which are sequentially numbered to 300 and randomly inserted in packs.

	NM/M
Common Player:	5.00
Stars:	6X

1995 Summit Samples

Nine-card cello packs of Summit cards, including "Big Bang" inserts, were released to dealers to debut the new Score brand. Cards are specially marked as promotional samples.

		NM/M
Complete Set (9):		5.00
Common Player:		.50
10	Barry Larkin	.50
41	Albert Belle	.50
79	Cal Ripken Jr.	3.00
80	David Cone	.50

125	Alex Gonzalez (Rookie)	.50
130	Charles Johnson (Rookie)	.50
BB12	Jose Canseco (Big Bang)	1.00
BB17	Fred McGriff (Big Bang)	.50
---	Information Card	.05

1995 Summit

A late-season release, Summit introduced the Score label to a premium brand card. Printed on extra heavy cardboard stock and UV coated on both sides the veteran player cards (#1-111) feature horizontal or vertical action photos with the player's name and team logo printed in gold-foil on front. Backs have a player portrait photo along with his 1994 stats in monthly charted form. The rookie cards subset (#112-173) have a large black "ROOKIE" on top-front while the back has a short career summary instead of stats. Other subsets include "BAT SPEED" (#174-188), honoring top hitters, and "SPECIAL DELIVERY" (#189-193), featuring top pitchers. Each are designated on front with special gold-foil logos. Seven checklists close out the regular 200-card set. The Summit issued featured a four-tiered chase card program, including a parallel "Nth Degree" set. Summit was a hobby-only issue sold in 7-card foil packs.

		NM/M
Complete Set (200):		10.00
Common Player:		.05
Pack (7):		1.00
Wax Box (24):		12.50
1	Ken Griffey Jr.	1.00
2	Alex Fernandez	.05
3	Fred McGriff	.05
4	Ben McDonald	.05
5	Rafael Palmeiro	.60
6	Tony Gwynn	.75
7	Jim Thome	.60
8	Ken Hill	.05
9	Barry Bonds	2.00
10	Barry Larkin	.05
11	Albert Belle	.05
12	Billy Ashley	.05
13	Matt Williams	.05
14	Andy Benes	.05
15	Midre Cummings	.05
16	J.R. Phillips	.05
17	Edgar Martinez	.05
18	Manny Ramirez	.65
19	Jose Canseco	.40
20	Chili Davis	.05
21	Don Mattingly	.85
22	Bernie Williams	.05
23	Tom Glavine	.35
24	Robin Ventura	.05
25	Jeff Conine	.05
26	Mark Grace	.05
27	Mark McGwire	1.50
28	Carlos Delgado	.45
29	Greg Colbrunn	.05
30	Greg Maddux	.75
31	Craig Biggio	.05
32	Kirby Puckett	.75
33	Derek Bell	.05
34	Lenny Dykstra	.05
35	Tim Salmon	.05
36	Deion Sanders	.05
37	Moises Alou	.05
38	Ray Lankford	.05
39	Willie Greene	.05
40	Ozzie Smith	.75
41	Roger Clemens	.85
42	Andres Galarraga	.05
43	Gary Sheffield	.35
44	Sammy Sosa	.75
45	Larry Walker	.05
46	Kevin Appier	.05
47	Raul Mondesi	.05
48	Kenny Lofton	.05
49	Darryl Hamilton	.05
50	Roberto Alomar	.20
51	Hal Morris	.05
52	Cliff Floyd	.05
53	Brent Gates	.05

54	Rickey Henderson	.65
55	John Olerud	.05
56	Gregg Jefferies	.05
57	Cecil Fielder	.05
58	Paul Molitor	.65
59	Bret Boone	.05
60	Greg Vaughn	.05
61	Wally Joyner	.05
62	Jeffrey Hammonds	.05
63	James Mouton	.05
64	Omar Vizquel	.05
65	Wade Boggs	.75
66	Terry Steinbach	.05
67	Wil Cordero	.05
68	Joey Hamilton	.05
69	Rico Brogna	.05
70	Darren Daulton	.05
71	Chuck Knoblauch	.05
72	Bob Hamelin	.05
73	Carl Everett	.05
74	Joe Carter	.05
75	Dave Winfield	.65
76	Bobby Bonilla	.05
77	Paul O'Neill	.05
78	Javier Lopez	.05
79	Cal Ripken Jr.	2.00
80	David Cone	.05
81	Bernard Gilkey	.05
82	Ivan Rodriguez	.60
83	Dean Palmer	.05
84	Jason Bere	.05
85	Will Clark	.05
86	Scott Cooper	.05
87	Royce Clayton	.05
88	Mike Piazza	1.00
89	Ryan Klesko	.05
90	Juan Gonzalez	.35
91	Travis Fryman	.05
92	Frank Thomas	.65
93	Eduardo Perez	.05
94	Mo Vaughn	.05
95	Jay Bell	.05
96	Jeff Bagwell	.65
97	Randy Johnson	.05
98	Jimmy Key	.05
99	Dennis Eckersley	.60
100	Carlos Baerga	.05
101	Eddie Murray	.65
102	Mike Mussina	.30
103	Brian Anderson	.05
104	Jeff Cirillo	.05
105	Dante Bichette	.05
106	Bret Saberhagen	.05
107	Jeff Kent	.05
108	Ruben Sierra	.05
109	Kirk Gibson	.05
110	Reggie Sanders	.05
111	Dave Justice	.05
112	Benji Gil	.05
113	Vaughn Eshelman	.05
114	Carlos Perez **RC**	.05
115	Chipper Jones	.75
116	Shane Andrews	.05
117	Orlando Miller	.05
118	Scott Ruffcorn	.05
119	Jose Oliva	.05
120	Joe Vitiello	.05
121	Jon Nunnally	.05
122	Garret Anderson	.05
123	Curtis Goodwin	.05
124	Mark Grudzielanek **RC**	.25
125	Alex Gonzalez	.05
126	David Bell	.05
127	Dustin Hermanson	.05
128	Dave Nilsson	.05
129	Wilson Heredia	.05
130	Charles Johnson	.05
131	Frank Rodriguez	.05
132	Alex Ochoa	.05
133	Alex Rodriguez	1.50
134	Bobby Higginson **RC**	.25
135	Edgardo Alfonzo	.05
136	Armando Benitez	.05
137	Rich Aude	.05
138	Tim Naehring	.05
139	Joe Randa	.05
140	Quilvio Veras	.05
141	Hideo Nomo **RC**	1.00
142	Ray Holbert	.05
143	Michael Tucker	.05
144	Chad Mottola	.05
145	John Valentin	.05
146	James Baldwin	.05
147	Esteban Loaiza	.05
148	Marty Cordova	.05
149	Juan Acevedo **RC**	.05
150	Tim Unroe **RC**	.05
151	Brad Clontz	.05
152	Steve Rodriguez	.05
153	Rudy Pemberton	.05
154	Ozzie Timmons	.05
155	Ricky Otero	.05
156	Allen Battle	.05
157	Joe Roselli	.05
158	Roberto Petagine	.05
159	Todd Hollandsworth	.05
160	Shannon Penn	.05
161	Antonio Osuna	.05
162	Russ Davis	.05
163	Jason Giambi	.40
164	Terry Bradshaw	.05
165	Ray Durham	.05
166	Todd Steverson	.05
167	Tim Belk	.05
168	Andy Pettitte	.25
169	Roger Cedeno	.05
170	Jose Parra	.05
171	Scott Sullivan	.05

172	LaTroy Hawkins	.05
173	Jeff McCurry	.05
174	Ken Griffey Jr. (Bat Speed)	.50
175	Frank Thomas (Bat Speed)	.30
176	Cal Ripken Jr. (Bat Speed)	1.00
177	Jeff Bagwell (Bat Speed)	.30
178	Mike Piazza (Bat Speed)	.50
179	Barry Bonds (Bat Speed)	.05
180	Matt Williams (Bat Speed)	.05
181	Don Mattingly (Bat Speed)	.45
182	Will Clark (Bat Speed)	.05
183	Tony Gwynn (Bat Speed)	.40
184	Kirby Puckett (Bat Speed)	.40
185	Jose Canseco (Bat Speed)	.25
186	Paul Molitor (Bat Speed)	.30
187	Albert Belle (Bat Speed)	.05
188	Joe Carter (Bat Speed)	.05
189	Greg Maddux (Special Delivery)	.40
190	Roger Clemens (Special Delivery)	.45
191	David Cone (Special Delivery)	.05
192	Mike Mussina (Special Delivery)	.15
193	Randy Johnson (Special Delivery)	.30
194	Checklist (Frank Thomas)	.30
195	Checklist (Ken Griffey Jr.)	.30
196	Checklist (Cal Ripken Jr.)	.75
197	Checklist (Jeff Bagwell)	.30
198	Checklist (Mike Piazza)	.05
199	Checklist (Barry Bonds)	.75
200	Checklist (Mo Vaughn, Matt Williams)	.05

Big Bang

The game's top sluggers are featured in this insert set. The front is printed on prismatic metallic foil, a process which Score calls "Spectroetch," with large and small action photos. Backs are conventionally printed and have a large photo with a career highlight printed beneath. The toughest of the Summit chase cards, these are found on the average of once every two boxes (72 packs). Cards are numbered with a "BB" prefix.

		NM/M
Complete Set (20):		45.00
Common Player:		1.00
1	Ken Griffey Jr.	6.00
2	Frank Thomas	3.25
3	Cal Ripken Jr.	8.00
4	Jeff Bagwell	3.25
5	Mike Piazza	6.00
6	Barry Bonds	8.00
7	Matt Williams	4.50
8	Don Mattingly	4.50
9	Will Clark	1.00
10	Tony Gwynn	4.00
11	Kirby Puckett	4.00
12	Jose Canseco	2.00
13	Paul Molitor	3.25
14	Albert Belle	1.00
15	Joe Carter	1.00
16	Rafael Palmeiro	3.00
17	Fred McGriff	1.00
18	Dave Justice	1.00
19	Tim Salmon	1.00
20	Mo Vaughn	1.00

New Age

Printed on metallic foil in a horizontal format, the New Age inserts were seeded at a rate of about one per 18 packs. Red and silver colors predominate on front, while the backs are printed in standard technology and feature a second photo and career summary.

		NM/M
Complete Set (15):		10.00
Common Player:		.25
1	Cliff Floyd	.25
2	Manny Ramirez	2.00
3	Raul Mondesi	.25
4	Alex Rodriguez	5.00
5	Billy Ashley	.25
6	Alex Gonzalez	.25
7	Michael Tucker	.25
8	Charles Johnson	.25
9	Carlos Delgado	1.00
10	Benji Gil	.25
11	Chipper Jones	3.00
12	Todd Hollandsworth	.25
13	Frank Rodriguez	.25
14	Shawn Green	.60
15	Ray Durham	.25

Nth Degree

A prismatic foil background differentiates the Nth Degree parallel inserts from the Summit base cards. Nth Degree inserts are found on a 1:4 pack ratio.

	NM/M
Complete Set (200):	50.00
Common Player:	.25
Stars:	2X

21 Club

Metallic foil printing on front and back distinguishes this set of chase cards. A large red-foil "21 / CLUB" logo on each side identifies the theme of this set as players who professed to be that age during the 1955 baseball season. The players are pictured in action pose on front and a portrait on back. On average the 21 Club cards are seeded one per box (36 packs). Cards are numbered with a "TC" prefix.

		NM/M
Complete Set (9):		4.00
Common Player:		.50
1	Bob Abreu	.65
2	Pokey Reese	.50
3	Edgardo Alfonzo	.50
4	Jim Pittsley	.50
5	Ruben Rivera	.50
6	Chan Ho Park	.50
7	Julian Tavarez	.50
8	Ismael Valdes	.50
9	Dmitri Young	.50

1996 Summit

Pinnacle's 1996 Summit baseball has 200 cards, including 35 rookies, four checklists and 10 Deja Vu subset cards. Each card is also reprinted in three parallel versions - Above and Beyond (one per seven packs), Artist's Proofs (one in 36) and a retail-only silver foil-bordered version. Above and Beyond cards use an all-prismatic foil design; Artist's Proof cards have holographic foil stamping. Five insert sets were produced: Big Bang; Mirage (a parallel set to Big Bang); Hitters, Inc.; Ballparks; and Positions (found one per every 50 magazine packs).

		NM/M
Complete Set (200):		10.00
Common Player:		.05
Pack (7):		1.25
Wax Box (18):		15.00
1	Mike Piazza	1.25
2	Matt Williams	.05
3	Tino Martinez	.05
4	Reggie Sanders	.05
5	Ray Durham	.05
6	Brad Radke	.05
7	Jeff Bagwell	.65
8	Ron Gant	.05
9	Lance Johnson	.05
10	Kevin Seitzer	.05
11	Dante Bichette	.05
12	Ivan Rodriguez	.60
13	Jim Abbott	.05
14	Greg Colbrunn	.05
15	Rondell White	.05
16	Shawn Green	.40
17	Gregg Jefferies	.05
18	Omar Vizquel	.05
19	Cal Ripken Jr.	2.00
20	Mark McGwire	1.50
21	Wally Joyner	.05
22	Chili Davis	.05
23	Jose Canseco	.40
24	Royce Clayton	.05
25	Jay Bell	.05
26	Travis Fryman	.05
27	Jeff King	.05
28	Todd Hundley	.05
29	Joe Vitiello	.05
30	Russ Davis	.05
31	Mo Vaughn	.05
32	Raul Mondesi	.05
33	Ray Lankford	.05
34	Mike Stanley	.05
35	B.J. Surhoff	.05
36	Greg Vaughn	.05
37	Todd Stottlemyre	.05
38	Carlos Delgado	.50
39	Kenny Lofton	.05
40	Hideo Nomo	.35
41	Sterling Hitchcock	.05
42	Pete Schourek	.05
43	Edgardo Alfonzo	.05
44	Ken Hill	.05
45	Ken Caminiti	.05
46	Bobby Higginson	.05
47	Michael Tucker	.05
48	David Cone	.05
49	Cecil Fielder	.05
50	Brian Hunter	.05
51	Charles Johnson	.05
52	Bobby Bonilla	.05
53	Eddie Murray	.65
54	Kenny Rogers	.05
55	Jim Edmonds	.05
56	Trevor Hoffman	.05
57	Kevin Mitchell	.05
58	Ruben Sierra	.05
59	Benji Gil	.05
60	Juan Gonzalez	.35
61	Larry Walker	.05
62	Jack McDowell	.05
63	Shawon Dunston	.05
64	Andy Benes	.05
65	Jay Buhner	.05
66	Rickey Henderson	.65
67	Alex Gonzalez	.05
68	Mike Kelly	.05
69	Fred McGriff	.05
70	Ryne Sandberg	.75
71	Ernie Young	.05
72	Kevin Appier	.05
73	Moises Alou	.05
74	John Jaha	.05
75	J.T. Snow	.05
76	Jim Thome	.60
77	Kirby Puckett	.75
78	Hal Morris	.05
79	Robin Ventura	.05
80	Ben McDonald	.05
81	Tim Salmon	.05
82	Albert Belle	.05
83	Marquis Grissom	.05
84	Alex Rodriguez	1.50
85	Manny Ramirez	.05
86	Ken Griffey Jr.	1.25
87	Sammy Sosa	.75
88	Frank Thomas	.65
89	Lee Smith	.05
90	Marty Cordova	.05
91	Greg Maddux	.75
92	Lenny Dykstra	.05
93	Butch Huskey	.05
94	Garret Anderson	.05
95	Mike Bordick	.05
96	Dave Justice	.05
97	Chad Curtis	.05
98	Carlos Baerga	.05
99	Jason Isringhausen	.05
100	Gary Sheffield	.35

#	Player	Price
101	Roger Clemens	1.00
102	Ozzie Smith	.75
103	Ramon Martinez	.05
104	Paul O'Neill	.05
105	Will Clark	.05
106	Tom Glavine	.35
107	Barry Bonds	2.00
108	Barry Larkin	.05
109	Derek Bell	.05
110	Randy Johnson	.65
111	Jeff Conine	.05
112	John Mabry	.05
113	Julian Tavarez	.05
114	Gary DiSarcina	.05
115	Andres Galarraga	.05
116	Marc Newfield	.05
117	Frank Rodriguez	.05
118	Brady Anderson	.05
119	Mike Mussina	.30
120	Orlando Merced	.05
121	Melvin Nieves	.05
122	Brian Jordan	.05
123	Rafael Palmeiro	.60
124	Johnny Damon	.35
125	Wil Cordero	.05
126	Chipper Jones	.75
127	Eric Karros	.05
128	Darren Daulton	.05
129	Vinny Castilla	.05
130	Joe Carter	.05
131	Bernie Williams	.05
132	Bernard Gilkey	.05
133	Bret Boone	.05
134	Tony Gwynn	.75
135	Dave Nilsson	.05
136	Ryan Klesko	.05
137	Paul Molitor	.65
138	John Olerud	.05
139	Craig Biggio	.05
140	John Valentin	.05
141	Chuck Knoblauch	.05
142	Edgar Martinez	.05
143	Rico Brogna	.05
144	Dean Palmer	.05
145	Mark Grace	.05
146	Roberto Alomar	.20
147	Alex Fernandez	.05
148	Andre Dawson	.25
149	Wade Boggs	.75
150	Mark Lewis	.05
151	Gary Gaetti	.05
152	Paul Wilson, Roger Clemens (Deja Vu)	.45
153	Rey Ordonez, Ozzie Smith (Deja Vu)	.35
154	Derek Jeter, Cal Ripken Jr. (Deja Vu)	1.00
155	Alan Benes, Andy Benes (Deja Vu)	.05
156	Jason Kendall, Mike Piazza (Deja Vu)	.75
157	Ryan Klesko, Frank Thomas (Deja Vu)	.30
158	Johnny Damon, Ken Griffey Jr. (Deja Vu)	.65
159	Karim Garcia, Sammy Sosa (Deja Vu)	.40
160	Raul Mondesi, Tim Salmon (Deja Vu)	.05
161	Chipper Jones, Matt Williams (Deja Vu)	.40
162	Rey Ordonez	.05
163	Bob Wolcott	.05
164	Brooks Kieschnick	.05
165	Steve Gibralter	.05
166	Bob Abreu	.05
167	Gregg Zaun	.05
168	Tavo Alvarez	.05
169	Sal Fasano	.05
170	George Arias	.05
171	Derek Jeter	2.00
172	Livan Hernandez **RC**	.25
173	Alan Benes	.05
174	George Williams	.05
175	John Wasdin	.05
176	Chan Ho Park	.05
177	Paul Wilson	.05
178	Jeff Suppan	.05
179	Quinton McCracken	.05
180	Wilton Guerrero **RC**	.05
181	Eric Owens	.05
182	Felipe Crespo	.05
183	LaTroy Hawkins	.05
184	Jason Schmidt	.05
185	Terrell Wade	.05
186	Mike Grace **RC**	.05
187	Chris Snopek	.05
188	Jason Kendall	.05
189	Todd Hollandsworth	.05
190	Jim Pittsley	.05
191	Jermaine Dye	.05
192	Mike Busby **RC**	.05
193	Richard Hidalgo	.05
194	Tyler Houston	.05
195	Jimmy Haynes	.05
196	Karim Garcia	.05
197	Ken Griffey Jr. (Checklist)	.50
198	Frank Thomas (Checklist)	.30
199	Greg Maddux (Checklist)	.40
200	Cal Ripken Jr. (Checklist)	1.00

Artist's Proof

Holographic-foil highlights and an "ARTIST'S PROOF" notation on the front photo distinguish the cards in this parallel edition. The AP cards are found once per 36 packs.

	NM/M
Complete Set (200):	100.00
Common Player:	1.00
Stars:	8X

Foil

This parallel issue was an exclusive in Summit seven-card magazine retail packaging. The black borders of the regular Summit versions have been replaced on these cards by silver foil.

	NM/M
Complete Set (200):	30.00
Common Player:	.25
Stars:	3X

Above & Beyond

These 200 insert cards parallel Pinnacle's 1996 Summit set, using all-prismatic foil for each card. The cards were seeded one per every four packs.

	NM/M
Complete Set (200):	50.00
Common Player:	.25
Stars:	3X

Ballparks

These 18 cards feature images of players superimposed over their respective teams' ballparks. The cards were seeded one per every 18 packs of 1996 Pinnacle Summit baseball and are serially within an edition of 8,000 each.

	NM/M
Complete Set (18):	45.00
Common Player:	1.00
1	Cal Ripken Jr.	7.50
2	Albert Belle	1.00
3	Dante Bichette	1.00
4	Mo Vaughn	1.00
5	Ken Griffey Jr.	6.00
6	Derek Jeter	7.50
7	Juan Gonzalez	1.50
8	Greg Maddux	4.00
9	Frank Thomas	3.00
10	Ryne Sandberg	4.00
11	Mike Piazza	6.00
12	Johnny Damon	1.50
13	Barry Bonds	7.50
14	Jeff Bagwell	3.00
15	Paul Wilson	1.00
16	Tim Salmon	1.00
17	Kirby Puckett	4.00
18	Tony Gwynn	4.00

Big Bang

Sixteen of the biggest hitters are featured on these 1996 Pinnacle Summit insert cards. The cards, seeded one per every 72 packs, use Spectroetched backgrounds with foil highlights.

	NM/M
Complete Set (16):	60.00
Common Player:	1.50
1	Frank Thomas	4.00
2	Ken Griffey Jr.	7.50
3	Albert Belle	1.50
4	Mo Vaughn	1.50
5	Barry Bonds	12.00
6	Cal Ripken Jr.	12.00
7	Jeff Bagwell	4.00
8	Mike Piazza	7.50
9	Ryan Klesko	1.50
10	Manny Ramirez	4.00
11	Tim Salmon	1.50
12	Dante Bichette	1.50
13	Sammy Sosa	6.00
14	Raul Mondesi	1.50
15	Chipper Jones	6.00
16	Garret Anderson	1.50

Big Bang Mirage

These 16 cards form a parallel version to Summit's Big Bang inserts. The cards use an innovative technology that creates a floating background behind the player's image. By holding the card in direct sunlight or under an incandescent bulb, a collector can see three dimensions and a floating baseball that seems to levitate in the background. Mirage cards are serially numbered in an edition of 600 each.

	NM/M
Complete Set (16):	115.00
Common Player:	3.50
1	Frank Thomas	10.00
2	Ken Griffey Jr.	15.00
3	Albert Belle	3.50
4	Mo Vaughn	3.50
5	Barry Bonds	20.00
6	Cal Ripken Jr.	20.00
7	Jeff Bagwell	10.00
8	Mike Piazza	15.00
9	Ryan Klesko	3.50
10	Manny Ramirez	10.00
11	Tim Salmon	3.50
12	Dante Bichette	3.50
13	Sammy Sosa	12.50
14	Raul Mondesi	3.50
15	Chipper Jones	12.50
16	Garret Anderson	3.50

Hitters, Inc.

This 1996 Pinnacle Summit set honors 16 top hitters. The cards, seeded one per 36 packs, put an embossed highlight on an enlarged photo of the player's eyes. Backs are serially numbered within an edition of 4,000 each.

	NM/M
Complete Set (16):	40.00
Common Player:	1.25
1	Tony Gwynn	4.00
2	Mo Vaughn	1.25
3	Tim Salmon	1.25
4	Ken Griffey Jr.	5.00
5	Sammy Sosa	4.00
6	Frank Thomas	3.00
7	Wade Boggs	4.00
8	Albert Belle	1.25
9	Cal Ripken Jr.	8.00
10	Manny Ramirez	3.00
11	Ryan Klesko	1.25
11p	Ryan Klesko (Overprinted "SAMPLE.")	1.25
12	Dante Bichette	1.25
13	Mike Piazza	5.00
14	Chipper Jones	4.00
15	Ryne Sandberg	4.00
16	Matt Williams	1.25

Positions

This insert issue features top players at each position. It is an exclusive magazine pack find, seeded about one per 50 packs. Fronts have action photos of three top players at the position on a baseball infield background at top. Close-ups of those photos appear at bottom, separated by a gold-foil strip. Backs have narrow action photos of each player, a few stats and a serial number from within an edition of 1,500 each.

	NM/M
Complete Set (9):	100.00
Common Card:	6.00
1	Jeff Bagwell, Mo Vaughn, Frank Thomas (First Base)	10.00
2	Roberto Alomar, Craig Biggio, Chuck Knoblauch (Second Base)	6.00
3	Matt Williams, Jim Thome, Chipper Jones (Third Base)	12.50
4	Barry Larkin, Cal Ripken Jr., Alex Rodriguez (Short Stop)	20.00
5	Mike Piazza, Ivan Rodriguez, Charles Johnson (Catcher)	15.00
6	Hideo Nomo, Greg Maddux, Randy Johnson (Pitcher)	12.50
7	Barry Bonds, Albert Belle, Ryan Klesko (Left Field)	20.00
8	Johnny Damon, Jim Edmonds, Ken Griffey Jr. (Center Field)	15.00
9	Manny Ramirez, Gary Sheffield, Sammy Sosa (Right Field)	12.50

2001 Sunoco Dream Team

Twenty-four former stars are depicted two per card on this

"Dream Team" set. Horizontal format cards have action photos (or in the case of two cards, Jim Trusilo artwork) with a city name at top and player names at left and right. A gold-foil Sunoco Dream Team logo is at lower-right. Backs have career stats and highlights, a card title, Sunoco, Coca-Cola and MLB Players Alumni logos. Cards were available in three-card packs for 49 cents with a gasoline or Coke purchase.

	NM/M
Complete Set (12):	5.00
Common Card:	.50
1	Game Seven Slams (Bill Mazeroski, Willie Stargell)	1.00
2	Philly Phenoms (Mike Schmidt, Steve Carlton)	1.50
3	Red Hot Heroes (Tony Perez, Joe Morgan)	1.00
4	Bronx Legends (Yogi Berra, Don Mattingly)	1.50
5	Outstanding O's (Jim Palmer, Frank Robinson)	1.00
6	Dynamic Duo (Carlton Fisk, Luis Tiant)	1.00
7	Beantown Beginnings (Fred Lynn, Jim Rice)	1.00
8	Tiger Tough (Sparky Anderson, Al Kaline)	1.00
9	Whiz Kids (Robin Roberts, Richie Ashburn) (artwork)	1.00
10	Amazin' Championships (Tug McGraw, Gary Carter)	1.00
11	Top of the Tribe (Lou Boudreau, Bob Feller) (artwork)	1.00
12	In Tribute (Roger Maris, Catfish Hunter)	1.50

1987 Sun Foods Milwaukee Brewers

Though they are nowhere identified on the cards, Sun Foods was the sponsor of this team set, issuing four cards per week. Measuring 6" x 9", the cards were licensed only by the Players' Association and so do not feature team uniform logos. Bare-headed players were photographed against a blue background with a black facsimile autograph at bottom. An MLBPA logo appears in the upper-left. Backs are blank. The unnumbered cards are checklisted here in alphabetical order.

	NM/M
Complete Set (16):	15.00
Common Player:	.50
(1)	Glenn Braggs	.50
(2)	Greg Brock	.50
(3)	Mark Clear	.50
(4)	Cecil Cooper	.50
(5)	Rob Deer	.50
(6)	Jim Gantner	.50
(7)	Ted Higuera	.50
(8)	Paul Molitor	5.00
(9)	Juan Nieves	.50
(10)	Dan Plesac	.50
(11)	Billy Jo Robidoux	.50
(12)	Bill Schroeder	.50
(13)	B.J. Surhoff	.50
(14)	Dale Sveum	.50
(15)	Bill Wegman	.50
(16)	Robin Yount	5.00

1994 SuperSlam

An innovative issued felled by the 1994 baseball strike, SuperSlams are a 5-1/2" x 7-1/2" tent-fold display card. Front and back have a gridded silver metallic background. At center on front is a 3-3/4" x 5-1/4" color photo on which is superimposed a 3-D action pose of the player. Backs have extensive "This is my life" biographical information about the player. The cards are skip-numbered. Promo cards of Jack McDowell were issued with either silver or gold background. Cards were sold for $7.95 apiece with reported production between 2,000 and 50,000, depending on player.

	NM/M
Complete Set (18):	60.00
Common Player:	2.50
3	Greg Maddux	5.00
4	Fred McGriff	2.50
8	Moises Alou	2.50
19	Roberto Alomar	3.00
24	Cal Ripken Jr.	8.00
28	Roger Clemens	5.50
40	Mike Piazza	6.00
42	Barry Bonds	8.00
47	Tony Gwynn	5.00
53	Rickey Henderson	4.00
58	Tim Salmon	2.50
60	Ken Griffey Jr.	6.00
65	Juan Gonzalez	3.00
67	Jeff Bagwell	4.00
83	Albert Belle	2.50
84	Kenny Lofton	2.50
91	Kirby Puckett	5.00
95	Frank Thomas	4.00
P1	Jack McDowell/Gold	2.50
P2	Jack McDowell/Silver	2.50

1982 Superstar

A second series of Superstar collector cards was produced in 1982. Similar in format to the 1980 issue, they also feature black-and-white photos. Surrounding graphics on the second series are in red, white and blue. Backs are numbered from 45-90 in continuation of the first series and contain career narratives. Many players are again featured on multiple cards, and the second series contains sports stars other than baseball players. Issue price was again $3.50.

	NM/M
Complete Set (45):	10.00
Common Player:	.40
46	Duke Snider	.40
47	Al Kaline	.40
48	Stan Musial	.60
49	Frank Robinson	.40
50	Jim Brown	.80
51	Bobby Orr	.60
52	Roger Staubach	.40
53	Honus Wagner	.80
54	Willie Mays	.80
55	Roy Campanella	.40
56	Mickey Mantle	2.50
57	Hank Aaron	.80
58	Ernie Banks	.60

59	Babe Ruth, Lou Gehrig	1.50
60	Ted Williams	.80
61	Babe Ruth	1.50
62	Lou Gehrig	.80
63	Sandy Koufax	.80
64	Fran Tarkenton	.40
65	Gordie Howe	.60
66	Roberto Clemente	1.25
67	Ty Cobb	.60
68	Lou Brock	.60
69	Joe Namath	.60
70	O.J. Simpson	.60
71	Whitey Ford	.40
72	Jackie Robinson	.60
73	Bill Russell	.60
74	Johnny Unitas	.40
75	Bobby Hull	.60
76	Bob Cousy	.60
77	Walter Johnson	.60
78	Satchel Paige	.50
79	Joe DiMaggio	1.25
80	Yogi Berra	.40
81	Jerry West	.60
82	Rod Gilbert	.60
83	Sadaharu Oh	.40
84	Wilt Chamberlain	.60
85	Frank Gifford	.40
86	Casey Stengel	.40
87	Eddie Mathews	.40
88	Hank Aaron, Sandy Koufax	.80
89	Ted Williams, Mickey Mantle	1.25
90	Casey Stengel, Mickey Mantle	1.50

1987 Super Stars Discs

Produced by Mike Schecter Associates, the Super Stars disc set was released as part of a promotion for various brands of iced tea mixes in many parts of the country. Among the brands participating in the promotion were Acme, Alpha Beta, Bustelo, Key, King Kullen, Lady Lee, Our Own, and Weis. The discs were issued in three-part folding panels with each disc measuring 2-1/2" in diameter. Fronts feature a full-color photo inside a bright yellow border. Two player discs were included in each panel along with a coupon disc offering either an uncut press sheet of the set or a facsimile autographed ball. Because the series was licensed only by the players' union, and not MLB, cap logos were removed.

		NM/M
Complete Panel Set (10):		7.50
Complete Singles Set (20):		4.50
Common Panel:		.25
Common Single Player:		.10
Panel (1)		1.00
1	Darryl Strawberry	.10
2	Roger Clemens	.50
Panel (2)		.25
3	Ron Darling	.10
4	Keith Hernandez	.10
Panel (3)		1.00
5	Tony Pena	.10
6	Don Mattingly	.50
Panel (4)		.75
7	Eric Davis	.25
8	Gary Carter	.25
Panel (5)		.75
9	Dave Winfield	.10
10	Wally Joyner	.10
Panel (6)		1.00
11	Mike Schmidt	.50
12	Robby Thompson	.10
Panel (7)		2.00
13	Wade Boggs	.35
14	Cal Ripken Jr.	.75
Panel (8)		1.00
15	Dale Murphy	.10
16	Tony Gwynn	.35
Panel (9)		1.00
17	Jose Canseco	.20
18	Rickey Henderson	.25
Panel (10)		.25
19	Lance Parrish	.10
20	Leo Righetti	.10

1988 Super Stars Discs

The "Second Annual Collector's Edition" of Super Stars discs is similar to the 1987 issue. A set of 20 discs (2-1/2" diameter) featuring full-color player photos was inserted in specially marked cannisters of iced tea and fruit drinks. Each triple-fold insert consists of two player discs and one redemption card. Player discs are bright blue, yellow, red and green with a diamond design framing the player portrait. The player name appears upper left, the set logo appears upper right. Personalized disc series were issued for Tetley, Weis, Key Food and A&P supermarkets (untitled series were also sold at Lucky, Skaggs, Alpha Beta, Acme King Kullen, Laneco and Krasdale stores). The series name (i.e. Weis Winners) is printed below the player photo. Backs are in red with a few personal data and stats. Because the discs are licensed only through the players' union, cap logos have been airbrushed off the photos.

		NM/M
Complete Panel Set (10):		7.50
Complete Singles Set (20):		4.50
Common Panel:		.25
Common Single Player:		.10
Panel (1)		2.00
1	Wade Boggs	.50
9	Roger Clemens	.60
Panel (2)		1.25
3	Don Mattingly	.60
13	Dave Magadan	.10
Panel (3)		1.50
4	Mark McGwire	.65
10	Will Clark	.10
Panel (4)		.25
5	Matt Nokes	.10
11	Vince Coleman	.10
Panel (5)		.25
8	Kevin Seitzer	.10
2	Ellis Burks	.10
Panel (6)		1.25
6	Eric Davis	.10
6	Kirby Puckett	.50
Panel (7)		.25
15	Benito Santiago	.10
20	Fernando Valenzuela	.10
Panel (8)		1.50
16	Mike Schmidt	.25
14	Dale Murphy	.25
Panel (9)		.25
17	Darryl Strawberry	.10
10	Dwight Gooden	.25
Panel (10)		.25
18	Steve Bedrosian	.10
7	Billy Ripken	.10

1989 Super Stars Discs

The third annual series of Super Stars perforated disc folders again offered two players and an offer for a a facsimile autographed baseball or an uncut sheet of discs. The 2-3/4" diameter discs have a yellow border with a red star at center. A player portrait photo is in the star. Backs are printed in black and have a few previous season stats and biographical bits. As in previous years, the discs were produced by Michael Schechter Associates, which does business only with the Players Union, precluding the use of MLB logos on the player photos.

		NM/M
Complete Panel Set (10):		9.00
Complete Singles Set (20):		5.00
Common Panel:		.25
Common Player:		.10
Panel (1)		1.25
1	Don Mattingly	.50
2	David Cone	.10
Panel (2)		2.00
3	Mark McGwire	.65
4	Will Clark	.10
Panel (3)		.25
5	Darryl Strawberry	.10
6	Dwight Gooden	.10
Panel (4)		2.00
7	Wade Boggs	.45
8	Roger Clemens	.50
Panel (5)		.25
9	Benito Santiago	.10
10	Orel Hershiser	.10
Panel (6)		1.25
11	Eric Davis	.10
12	Kirby Puckett	.45
Panel (7)		1.25
13	Dave Winfield	.40
14	Andre Dawson	.25
Panel (8)		2.00
15	Steve Bedrosian	.10
16	Cal Ripken Jr.	.75
Panel (9)		1.00
17	Andy Van Slyke	.10
18	Jose Canseco	.35
Panel (10)		.75
19	Jose Oquendo	.10
20	Dale Murphy	.25

1990 Super Stars Discs

In its fourth annual edition the Super Stars discs continued the three-piece perforated folder format. Each panel consists of two player discs and a disc offering a 1990-1991 calendar at the center of an uncut sheet of the discs. Discs have a red border with a player portrait photo in the center of a tombstone-shaped yellow frame. A few 1989 stats and biographical notes are printed in black on the back. Because the discs are licensed only by the players' union, and not Major League Baseball, the player photos have had team logos excised.

		NM/M
Complete Panel Set (10):		9.00
Complete Set, Singles (20):		4.50
Common Panel:		.25
Common Player:		.10
Panel (1)		.50
1	Will Clark	.10
2	Howard Johnson	.10
Panel (2)		1.00
3	Chris Sabo	.10
4	Jose Canseco	.40
Panel (3)		.50
5	Bo Jackson	.15
6	Kevin Mitchell	.10
Panel (4)		2.25
7	Wade Boggs	.50
8	Ken Griffey Jr.	.65
Panel (5)		.25
9	George Bell	.15
10	Dwight Gooden	.10
Panel (6)		1.00
11	Bobby Bonilla	.10
12	Ryne Sandberg	.25
Panel (7)		2.00
13	Kirby Puckett	.50
14	Don Mattingly	.60
Panel (8)		1.50
15	Mark McGwire	.75
16	Frank Viola	.10
Panel (9)		.25
17	Bret Saberhagen	.10
18	Mike Greenwell	.15
Panel (10)		2.00
19	Steve Sax	.10
20	Nolan Ryan	.75

1989 Swell Baseball Greats

Collectors Marketing Corp. handled the distribution of Philadelphia Gum Company's debut "old-timers" set. Most cards featured color photos, though some of the older players were represented in sepia shots. Red-and-white backs featured career stats, a baseball biography and a few vital statistics.

		NM/M
Complete Set (135):		12.00
Common Player:		.15
Wax Pack (10):		.65
Wax Box (36):		15.00
1	Babe Ruth	3.50
2	Ty Cobb	1.50
3	Walter Johnson	.75
4	Honus Wagner	.75
5	Cy Young	.75
6	Joe Adcock	.15
7	Jim Bunning	.15
8	Orlando Cepeda	.15
9	Harvey Kuenn	.15
10	Catfish Hunter	.15
11	Johnny VanderMeer	.15
12	Tony Oliva	.15
13	Harvey Haddix (Reversed negative.)	.15
14	Dick McAuliffe	.15
15	Lefty Grove	.15
16	Bo Belinski	.15
17	Claude Osteen	.15
18	Doc Medich	.15
19	Del Ennis	.15
20	Rogers Hornsby	.40
21	Bob Buhl	.15
22	Phil Niekro	.15
23	Don Zimmer	.15
24	Greg Luzinski	.15
25	Lou Gehrig	2.50
26	Ken Singleton	.15
27	Bob Allison	.15
28	Ed Kranepool	.15
29	Manny Sanguillen	.15
30	Luke Appling	.15
31	Ralph Terry	.15
32	Smoky Burgess	.15
33	Gil Hodges	.40
34	Harry Walker	.15
35	Edd Roush	.15
36	Ron Santo	.15
37	Jim Perry	.15
38	Jose Morales	.15
39	Stan Bahnsen	.15
40	Al Kaline	.40
41	Mel Harder	.15
42	Ralph Houk	.15
43	Jack Billingham	.15
44	Carl Erskine	.15
45	Hoyt Wilhelm	.15
46	Dick Radatz	.15
47	Roy Sievers	.15
48	Jim Lonborg	.15
49	Bobby Richardson	.25
50	Whitey Ford	.40
51	Roy Face	.15
52	Tom Tresh	.15
53	Joe Nuxhall	.15
54	Mickey Vernon	.15
55	Johnny Mize	.15
56	Scott McGregor	.15
57	Billy Pierce	.15
58	Dave Giusti	.15
59	Minnie Minoso	.15
60	Early Wynn	.15
61	Jose Cardenal	.15
62	Sam Jethroe	.15
63	Sal Bando	.15
64	Elrod Hendricks	.15
65	Enos Slaughter	.15
66	Jim Bouton	.15
67	Bill Mazeroski	.25
68	Tony Kubek	.25
69	Joe Black	.15
70	Harmon Killebrew	.40
71	Sam McDowell	.15
72	Bucky Dent	.15
73	Virgil Trucks	.15
74	Andy Pafko	.15
75	Bob Feller	.40
76	Tito Francona	.15
77	Al Dark	.15
78	Larry Dierker	.15
79	Nellie Briles	.15
80	Lou Boudreau	.15
81	Wally Moon	.15
82	Hank Bauer	.15
83	Jim Piersall	.15
84	Jim Grant	.15
85	Richie Ashburn	.15
86	Bob Friend	.15
87	Ken Keltner	.15
88	Jim Kaat	.15
89	Dean Chance	.15
90	Al Lopez	.15
91	Dick Groat	.15
92	Johnny Blanchard	.15
93	Chuck Hinton	.15
94	Clete Boyer	.15
95	Steve Carlton	.40
96	Tug McGraw	.15
97	Mickey Lolich	.15
98	Earl Weaver	.15
99	Sal Maglie	.15
100	Ted Williams	2.25
101	Allie Reynolds (Photo actually Marius Russo.)	.15
102	Gene Woodling (Photo actually Irv Noren.)	.15
103	Moe Drabowsky	.15
104	Mickey Stanley	.15
105	Jim Palmer	.40
106	Bill Freehan	.15
107	Bob Robertson	.15
108	Walt Dropo	.15
109	Jerry Koosman	.15
110	Bobby Doerr	.15
111	Phil Rizzuto	.40
112	Don Kessinger	.15
113	Milt Pappas	.15
114	Herb Score	.15
115	Larry Doby	.15
116	Glenn Beckert	.15
117	Andre Thornton	.15
118	Gary Matthews	.15
119	Bill Virdon	.15
120	Billy Williams	.15
121	Johnny Sain	.15
122	Don Newcombe	.15
123	Rico Petrocelli	.15
124	Dick Bosman	.15
125	Roberto Clemente	3.00
126	Rocky Colavito	.15
127	Wilbur Wood	.15
128	Duke Sims	.15
129	Ken Holtzman	.15
130	Casey Stengel	.15
131	Bobby Shantz	.15
132	Del Crandall	.15
133	Bobby Thomson	.15
134	Brooks Robinson	.40
135	Checklist	.15

1990 Swell Baseball Greats

In its second year of "old-timers" set production, Swell moved its "Baseball Greats" banner to the card front, above a color player photo. Where color photos were unavailable, sepia pictures were used. Backs were virtually identical to the previous year, with a line of lifetime stats, a career highlights write-up and a few bits of personal data. Also nearly identical is player selection within the 135-card set.

		NM/M
Complete Set (135):		12.00
Common Player:		.15
Wax Pack (10):		.75
Wax Box (36):		12.50
1	Tom Seaver	.50
2	Hank Aaron	2.50
3	Mickey Cochrane	.15
4	Rod Carew	.15
5	Carl Yastrzemski	.40
6	Dizzy Dean	.50
7	Sal Bando	.15
8	Whitey Ford	.40
9	Bill White	.15
10	Babe Ruth	3.50
11	Robin Roberts	.15
12	Warren Spahn	.15
13	Billy Williams	.15
14	Joe Garagiola	.40
15	Ty Cobb	1.50
16	Boog Powell	.15
17	Tom Tresh	.15
18	Luke Appling	.15
19	Tommie Agee	.15
20	Roberto Clemente	3.00
21	Bobby Thomson	.15
22	Charlie Keller	.15
23	George Bamberger	.15
24	Eddie Lopat	.15
25	Lou Gehrig	2.50
26	Manny Mota	.15
27	Steve Stone	.15
28	Orlando Cepeda	.15
29	Al Bumbry	.15
30	Grover Alexander	.15
31	Lou Boudreau	.15
32	Herb Score	.15
33	Harry Walker	.15
34	Deron Johnson	.15
35	Edd Roush	.15
36	Carl Erskine	.15
37	Ken Forsch	.15
38	Sal Maglie	.15
39	Al Rosen	.15
40	Casey Stengel	.15
41	Cesar Cedeno	.15
42	Roy White	.15
43	Larry Doby	.15
44	Rod Kanehl	.15
45	Tris Speaker	.40
46	Ralph Garr	.15
47	Andre Thornton	.15
48	Frankie Crosetti	.15
49	Dick Groat	.15
50	Honus Wagner	.75
51	Rogers Hornsby	.40
52	Ken Brett	.15
53	Lenny Randle	.15
54	Enos Slaughter	.15
55	Mel Ott	.15
56	Rico Petrocelli	.15
57	Walt Dropo	.15
58	Bob Grich	.15
59	Billy Herman	.15
60	Bob Feller	.40
61	Davey Johnson	.15
62	Don Drysdale	.15
63	Larry Sorensen	.15
64	Ron Santo	.15
65	Eddie Mathews	.15
66	Gaylord Perry	.15
67	Lee May	.15
68	Johnnie LeMaster	.15
69	Don Kessinger	.15
70	Lefty Grove	.15
71	Lou Brock	.15
72	Don Cardwell	.15
73	Harvey Haddix	.15
74	Frank Torre	.15
75	Walter Johnson	.75
76	Don Newcombe	.15
77	Marv Throneberry	.15
78	Jim Northrup	.15
79	Fritz Peterson	.15
80	Ralph Kiner	.15
81	Mickey Lolich	.15
82	Donn Clendenon	.15
83	Pete Vuckovich	.15
84	Lefty Gomez	.15
85	Monte Irvin	.15
86	Rick Ferrell	.15
87	Tommy Hutton	.15
88	Julio Cruz	.15
89	Vida Blue	.15
90	Johnny Mize	.15
91	Rusty Staub	.15
92	Jimmy Piersall	.15
93	Bill Mazeroski	.15
94	Lee Lacy	.15
95	Ernie Banks	.40
96	Bobby Doerr	.15
97	George Foster	.15
98	Eric Soderholm	.15
99	Johnny VanderMeer	.15
100	Cy Young	.75
101	Jimmie Foxx	.40
102	Clete Boyer	.15
103	Steve Garvey	.15
104	Johnny Podres	.15
105	Yogi Berra	.40
106	Bill Monbouquette	.15
107	Milt Pappas	.15
108	Dave LaRoche	.15
109	Elliott Maddox	.15
110	Steve Carlton	.15
111	Bud Harrelson	.15
112	Mark Littell	.15
113	Frank J. Thomas	.15
114	Bill Robinson	.15
115	Satchel Paige	.75
116	John Denny	.15
117	Clyde King	.15
118	Billy Sample	.15
119	Rocky Colavito	.15
120	Bob Gibson	.15
121	Bert Campaneris	.15
122	Mark Fidrych	.15
123	Ed Charles	.15
124	Jim Lonborg	.15
125	Ted Williams	2.50
126	Manny Sanguillen	.15
127	Matt Keough	.15
128	Vern Ruhle	.15
129	Bob Skinner	.15
130	Joe Torre	.15
131	Ralph Houk	.15
132	Gil Hodges	.40
133	Ralph Branca	.15
134	Christy Mathewson	.75
135	Checklist	.15

1991 Swell Baseball Greats

The last of three "old-timers" sets issued by Philadelphia Gum Co., this 150-card set was marketed by Impel. Cards are 2-1/2" x 3-1/2" and feature red and yellow borders around color player photos. In the case of some older players, sepia-toned photos are used instead of color. Backs are printed in red and black and include career stats and a few vital statistics.

	NM/M
Complete Set (150):	17.50
Common Player:	.15

Wax Pack (10):		.75
Wax Box (36):		15.00
1	Tommie Agee	.15
2	Matty Alou	.15
3	Luke Appling	.15
4	Richie Ashburn	.15
5	Ernie Banks	.40
6	Don Baylor	.15
7	Buddy Bell	.15
8	Yogi Berra	.40
9	Joe Black	.15
10	Vida Blue	.15
11	Bobby Bonds	.15
12	Lou Boudreau	.15
13	Lou Brock	.15
14	Ralph Branca	.15
15	Bobby Brown	.15
16	Lou Burdette	.15
17	Steve Carlton	.25
18	Rico Carty	.15
19	Jerry Coleman	.15
20	Frankie Crosetti	.15
21	Julio Cruz	.15
22	Alvin Dark	.15
23	Doug DeCinces	.15
24	Larry Doby	.15
25	Bobby Doerr	.15
26	Don Drysdale	.15
27	Carl Erskine	.15
28	Elroy Face	.15
29	Rick Ferrell	.15
30	Rollie Fingers	.15
31	Joe Garagiola	.40
32	Steve Garvey	.15
33	Bob Gibson	.15
34	Mudcat Grant	.15
35	Dick Groat	.15
36	Jerry Grote	.15
37	Toby Harrah	.15
38	Bud Harrelson	.15
39	Billy Herman	.15
40	Ken Holtzman	.15
41	Willie Horton	.15
42	Ralph Houk	.15
43	Al Hrabosky	.15
44	Monte Irvin	.15
45	Fergie Jenkins	.15
46	Davey Johnson	.15
47	George Kell	.15
48	Charlie Keller	.15
49	Harmon Killebrew	.25
50	Ralph Kiner	.15
51	Clyde King	.15
52	Dave Kingman	.15
53	Al Kaline	.40
54	Clem Labine	.15
55	Vern Law	.15
56	Mickey Lolich	.15
57	Jim Lonborg	.15
58	Eddie Lopat	.15
59	Sal Maglie	.15
60	Bill Mazeroski	.25
61	Johnny VanderMeer	.15
62	Johnny Mize	.15
63	Manny Mota	.15
64	Wally Moon	.15
65	Rick Monday	.15
66	Tom Tresh	.15
67	Graig Nettles	.15
68	Don Newcombe	.15
69	Milt Pappas	.15
70	Gaylord Perry	.15
71	Rico Petrocelli	.15
72	Jimmy Piersall	.15
73	Johnny Podres	.15
74	Boog Powell	.15
75	Bobby Richardson	.25
76	Vern Ruhle	.15
77	Robin Roberts	.15
78	Al Rosen	.15
79	Billy Sample	.15
80	Manny Sanguillen	.15
81	Ron Santo	.15
82	Herb Score	.15
83	Bobby Shantz	.15
84	Enos Slaughter	.15
85	Eric Soderholm	.15
86	Warren Spahn	.15
87	Rusty Staub	.15
88	Bobby Thomson	.15
89	Marv Throneberry	.15
90	Luis Tiant	.15
91	Frank Torre	.15
92	Joe Torre	.25
93	Bill Virdon	.15
94	Harry Walker	.15
95	Earl Weaver	.15
96	Bill White	.15
97	Roy White	.15
98	Billy Williams	.15
99	Dick Williams	.15
100	Ted Williams	2.50
101	Gene Woodling	.15
102	Hank Aaron	2.50
103	Rod Carew	.15
104	Cesar Cedeno	.15
105	Orlando Cepeda	.15
106	Willie Mays	2.50
107	Tom Seaver	.40
108	Carl Yastrzemski	.40
109	Clete Boyer	.15
110	Bert Campaneris	.15
111	Walt Dropo	.15
112	George Foster	.15
113	Phil Garner	.15
114	Harvey Kuenn	.15
115	Don Kessinger	.15
116	Rocky Colavito	.15

117	Bobby Murcer	.15
118	Mel Parnell	.15
119	Ken Reitz	.15
120	Earl Wilson	.15
121	Wilbur Wood	.15
122	Ed Yost	.15
123	Jim Bouton	.15
124	Babe Ruth	3.50
125	Lou Gehrig	2.50
126	Honus Wagner	.75
127	Ty Cobb	1.50
128	Grover C. Alexander	.15
129	Lefty Gomez	.15
130	Walter Johnson	.75
131	Gil Hodges	.40
132	Roberto Clemente	3.00
133	Satchel Paige	.75
134	Edd Roush	.15
135	Cy Young	.75
136	Casey Stengel	.75
137	Rogers Hornsby	.40
138	Dizzy Dean	.50
139	Lefty Grove	.15
140	Tris Speaker	.40
141	Christy Mathewson	.75
142	Mickey Cochrane	.15
143	Jimmie Foxx	.40
144	Mel Ott	.25
145	Bob Feller	.25
146	Brooks Robinson	.40
147	Eddie Mathews	.15
148	Pie Traynor	.15
149	Thurman Munson	.25
150	Checklist	.15

2003 Sycuan Casino-Resort Tony Gwynn

This series of 3-1/2" x 5" cards commemorating the career of Padres icon Tony Gwynn was issued on a one-per-month basis between April-September by a San Diego area tribal entertainment complex. Cards are UV coated and feature silver-foil highlights on front. Posed or action photos are framed in dark green. Backs have a ghosted photo of the player, a few sentences about him and logos of the team and casino.

		NM/M
Complete Set (6):		50.00
Common Card:		10.00
1	Tony Gwynn (Twenty Great Years)	10.00
2	Tony Gwynn (Eight Batting Titles)	10.00
3	Tony Gwynn (Five Gold Gloves)	10.00
4	Tony Gwynn (3,000th Hit)	10.00
5	Tony Gwynn (Hitting Machine)	10.00
6	Tony Gwynn (Last At Bat)	10.00

T

1988 T & M Sports Umpires

8 DOUG HARVEY

The first umpires to be featured on baseball cards since the 1955 Bowman set are the arbiters included in this boxed set issued T & M and licensed by the umps' union. Cards have posed action photos framed in red (American League) green (National League) with a black border on front. The correct league logo is in a lower corner. The umpire's uniform number and

name are in white at bottom. The back has a blue background with personal data, career summary, service record and card number, along with licensor logos.

		NM/M
Complete Set (64):		5.00
Common Card:		.15
1	Doug Harvey	.15
2	Lee Weyer	.15
3	Billy Williams	.15
4	John Kibler	.15
5	Bob Engel	.15
6	Harry Wendelstedt	.15
7	Larry Barnett	.15
8	Don Denkinger	.15
9	Dave Phillips	.15
10	Larry McCoy	.15
11	Bruce Froemming	.15
12	John McSherry	.15
13	Jim Evans	.15
14	Frank Pulli	.15
15	Joe Brinkman	.15
16	Terry Tata	.15
17	Paul Runge	.15
18	Dutch Rennert	.15
19	Nick Bremigan	.15
20	Jim McKean	.15
21	Terry Cooney	.15
22	Rich Garcia	.15
23	Dale Ford	.15
24	Al Clark	.15
25	Greg Kosc	.15
26	Jim Quick	.15
27	Ed Montague	.15
28	Jerry Crawford	.15
29	Steve Palermo	.15
30	Durwood Merrill	.15
31	Ken Kaiser	.15
32	Vic Voltaggio	.15
33	Mike Reilly	.15
34	Eric Gregg	.15
35	Ted Hendry	.15
36	Joe West	.15
37	Dave Pallone	.15
38	Fred Brocklander	.15
39	John Shulock	.15
40	Derryl Cousins	.15
41	Charlie Williams	.15
42	Rocky Roe	.15
43	Randy Marsh	.15
44	Bob Davidson	.15
45	Drew Coble	.15
46	Tim McClelland	.15
47	Dan Morrison	.15
48	Rick Reed	.15
49	Steve Rippley	.15
50	John Hirschbeck	.15
51	Mark Johnson	.15
52	Gerry Davis	.15
53	Dana DeMuth	.15
54	Larry Young	.15
55	Tim Welke	.15
56	Greg Bonin	.15
57	Tom Hallion	.15
58	Dale Scott	.15
59	Tim Tschida	.15
60	Dick Stello	.15
61	1987 All-Star Game (Derryl Cousins, Bob Davidson, Don Denkinger, Dick Stello, Vic Voltaggio, Joe West)	.15
62	1987 World Series (Ken Kaiser, Greg Kosc, John McSherry, Dave Phillips, Terry Tata, Lee Weyer)	.15
63	Jocko Conlan	.30
64	Checklist	.15

1989 T & M Sports Senior League

ROLLIE FINGERS
PITCHER

The 120-card 1989-90 T&M Sports Senior League set features a full-color photo of the player on the front on a borderless card. A red stripe separates the photo from the black bottom with the player's name, team logo and position. The cards are printed on heavy, white cardboard stock and sold as a boxed set. The backs have a red border across the top and bio and career notes, along with a summary

of the player's career. Included in the set are eight static-cling puzzle pieces which, when put together, show a drawing of a prominent player from each team.		

		NM/M
Complete Set (120):		4.00
Common Player:		.05
1	Curt Flood (Commissioner)	.10
2	Willie Aikens	.05
3	Gary Allenson	.05
4	Stan Bahnsen	.05
5	Alan Bannister	.05
6	Juan Beniquez	.05
7	Jim Bibby	.05
8	Paul Blair	.05
9	Vida Blue	.10
10	Bobby Bonds	.15
11	Pedro Borbon	.05
12	Clete Boyer	.05
13	Gates Brown	.05
14	Al Bumbry	.05
15	Sal Butera	.05
16	Bert Campaneris	.10
17	Bill Campbell	.05
18	Bernie Carbo	.05
19	Dave Cash	.05
20	Cesar Cedeno	.05
21	Gene Clines	.05
22	Dave Collins	.05
23	Cecil Cooper	.05
24	Doug Corbett	.05
25	Al Cowens	.05
26	Jose Cruz	.05
27	Mike Cuellar	.10
28	Pat Dobson	.05
29	Dick Drago	.05
30	Dan Driessen	.05
31	Jamie Easterly	.05
32	Juan Eichelberger	.05
33	Dock Ellis	.05
34	Ed Figueroa	.05
35	Rollie Fingers	.50
36	George Foster	.15
37	Oscar Gamble	.05
38	Wayne Garland	.05
39	Wayne Garrett	.05
40	Ross Grimsley	.05
41	Jerry Grote	.05
42	Johnny Grubb	.05
43	Mario Guerrero	.05
44	Toby Harrah	.05
45	Steve Henderson	.05
46	George Hendrick	.05
47	Butch Hobson	.05
48	Roy Howell	.05
49	Al Hrabosky	.05
50	Clint Hurdle	.05
51	Garth Iorg	.05
52	Tim Ireland	.05
53	Grant Jackson	.05
54	Ron Jackson	.05
55	Ferguson Jenkins	.50
56	Odell Jones	.05
57	Mike Kekich	.05
58	Steve Kemp	.05
59	Dave Kingman	.10
60	Bruce Kison	.05
61	Lee Lacy	.05
62	Rafael Landestoy	.05
63	Ken Landreaux	.05
64	Tito Landrum	.05
65	Dave LaRoche	.05
66	Bill Lee	.05
67	Ron LeFlore	.05
68	Dennis Leonard	.05
69	Bill Madlock	.10
70	Mickey Mahler	.05
71	Rick Manning	.05
72	Tippy Martinez	.05
73	Jon Matlack	.05
74	Bake McBride	.05
75	Steve McCarty	.05
76	Hal McRae	.10
77	Dan Meyer	.05
78	Felix Millan	.05
79	Paul Mirabella	.05
80	Omar Moreno	.05
81	Jim Morrison	.05
82	Graig Nettles	.10
83	Al Oliver	.10
84	Amos Otis	.05
85	Tom Paciorek	.05
86	Lowell Plamer	.05
87	Pat Putnam	.05
88	Lenny Randle	.05
89	Ken Reitz	.05
90	Gene Richards	.05
91	Mickey Rivers	.05
92	Leon Roberts	.05
93	Joe Sambito	.05
94	Rodney Scott	.05
95	Bob Shirley	.05
96	Jim Slaton	.05
97	Elias Sosa	.05
98	Fred Stanley	.05
99	Bill Stein	.05
100	Rennie Stennett	.05
101	Sammy Stewart	.05
102	Tim Stoddard	.05
103	Champ Summers	.05
104	Derrell Thomas	.05
105	Luis Tiant	.10
106	Bobby Tolan	.05
107	Bill Travers	.05

108	Tom Underwood	.05
109	Rick Waits	.05
110	Ron Washington	.05
111	U.L. Washington	.05
112	Earl Weaver	.25
113	Jerry White	.05
114	Milt Wilcox	.05
115	Dick Williams	.05
116	Walt Williams	.05
117	Rick Wise	.05
118	Favorite Suns (Luis Tiant, Cesar Cedeno)	.05
119	Home Run Legends (George Foster, Bobby Bonds)	.05
120	Sunshine Skippers (Earl Weaver, Dick Williams)	.25

Umpires

LARRY McCOY 10

A second edition of umpires' cards from T & M was also sold as a boxed set. Fronts of the 2-1/2" x 3-1/2" cards have color photos which are borderless at top and sides. At bottom is a strip with the ump's name and uniform number at right and league logo at left. Backs have personal data and a career summary, along with logos of MLB and the Umpires' Association.

		NM/M
Complete Set (63):		7.50
Common Card:		.15
1	Doug Harvey	.25
2	John Kibler	.15
3	Bob Engel	.15
4	Harry Wendelstedt	.15
5	Larry Barnett	.15
6	Don Denkinger	.15
7	Dave Phillips	.15
8	Larry McCoy	.15
9	Bruce Froemming	.15
10	John McSherry	.20
11	Jim Evans	.15
12	Frank Pulli	.15
13	Joe Brinkman	.15
14	Terry Tata	.15
15	Nick Bremigan	.15
16	Jim McKean	.15
17	Paul Runge	.15
18	Dutch Rennert	.15
19	Terry Cooney	.15
20	Rich Garcia	.15
21	Dale Ford	.15
22	Al Clark	.15
23	Greg Kosc	.15
24	Jim Quick	.15
25	Ed Montague	.15
26	Jerry Crawford	.15
27	Steve Palermo	.35
28	Durwood Merrill	.15
29	Ken Kaiser	.20
30	Vic Voltaggio	.15
31	Mike Reilly	.15
32	Eric Gregg	.25
33	Ted Hendry	.15
34	Joe West	.15
35	Dave Pallone	.25
36	Fred Brocklander	.15
37	John Shulock	.15
38	Derryl Cousins	.15
39	Charlie Williams	.15
40	Rocky Roe	.15
41	Randy Marsh	.15
42	Bob Davidson	.15
43	Drew Coble	.15
44	Tim McClelland	.15
45	Dan Morrison	.15
46	Rick Reed	.15
47	Steve Rippley	.15
48	John Hirschbeck	.15
49	Mark Johnson	.15
50	Gerry Davis	.15
51	Dana DeMuth	.15
52	Larry Young	.15
53	Tim Welke	.15
54	Greg Bonin	.15
55	Tom Hallion	.15
56	Dale Scott	.15
57	Tim Tschida	.15
58	Gary Darling	.15
59	Mark Hirschbeck	.15
60	All-Star Crew	.15
61	World Series Crew	.15
62	Lee Weyer	.15
63	Tom Connolly, Bill Klem	.25

1990 T & M Sports Umpires

DUTCH RENNERT 16

Puzzle piece inserts and a send-away premium card are featured in the 1990 umpires set. Card fronts have action photos of the arbiters with league insignia in a home plate-shaped frame in a lower corner. Above the photo, the umpire's name and uniform number are printed in a banner. Backs have biographical data, a baseball rules trivia question and the logos of MLB and the Major League Umpires Association. Card #71, Hall of Fame umpire Al Barlick, was only available by sending in the four puzzle pieces overprinted with the National League logo.

		NM/M
Complete Set (70, No Barlick.):		6.00
Common Card:		.10
1	Doug Harvey	.10
2	John Kibler	.10
3	Bob Engel	.10
4	Harry Wendelstedt	.10
5	Larry Barnett	.10
6	Don Denkinger	.10
7	Dave Phillips	.10
8	Larry McCoy	.10
9	Bruce Froemming	.10
10	John McSherry	.10
11	Jim Evans	.10
12	Frank Pulli	.10
13	Joe Brinkman	.10
14	Terry Tata	.10
15	Jim McKean	.10
16	Dutch Rennert	.10
17	Paul Runge	.10
18	Terry Cooney	.10
19	Rich Garcia	.10
20	Dale Ford	.10
21	Al Clark	.10
22	Greg Kosc	.10
23	Jim Quick	.10
24	Eddie Montague	.10
25	Jerry Crawford	.10
26	Steve Palermo	.10
27	Durwood Merrill	.10
28	Ken Kaiser	.10
29	Vic Voltaggio	.10
30	Mike Reilly	.10
31	Eric Gregg	.10
32	Ted Hendry	.10
33	Joe West	.10
34	Fred Brocklander	.10
35	John Shulock	.10
36	Derryl Cousins	.10
37	Charlie Williams	.10
38	Rocky Roe	.10
39	Randy Marsh	.10
40	Bob Davidson	.10
41	Drew Coble	.10
42	Tim McClelland	.10
43	Dan Morrison	.10
44	Rick Reed	.10
45	Steve Rippley	.10
46	John Hirschbeck	.10
47	Mark Johnson	.10
48	Gerry Davis	.10
49	Dana DeMuth	.10
50	Larry Young	.10
51	Tim Welke	.10
52	Greg Bonin	.10
53	Tom Hallion	.10
54	Dale Scott	.10
55	Tim Tschida	.10
56	Gary Darling	.10
57	Mark Hirschbeck	.10
58	Jerry Layne	.10
59	Jim Joyce	.10
60	Bill Hohn	.10
61	All-Star Game	.10
62	World Series	.10
63	Nick Bremigan	.10
64	The Runges (Ed Runge, Paul Runge)	.10
65	A. Bartlett Giamatti	.10
66	Puzzle Piece #1	.10
66a	Puzzle Piece #1 (W/N.L. logo on back.)	.10
67	Puzzle Piece #2	.10
67a	Puzzle Piece #3 (N.L. logo.)	.10
68	Puzzle Piece #3	.10

No.	Player	Price
68a	Puzzle Piece #3 (N.L. logo.)	.10
69	Puzzle Piece #4	.10
69a	Puzzle piece #4 (N.L. logo.)	.10
70	Checklist	.05
71	Al Barlick	4.00

1990 Target Dodgers

CASEY STENGEL – MGR

TARGET

Virtually every player who appeared in the uniform of the Brooklyn or Los Angeles Dodgers between 1890-1990 was included in this 1,100-card issue. Quality of the photo varies wildly from sharp to barely identifiable. Cards measure 2-1/16" x 3" and are perforated on two, three or four sides, depending where they were positioned on the 15-card perforated sheets in which the cards were distributed at various Dodgers home games. Player photos are in dark blue and white, bordered in speckled blue. Name and position appear in black in a light blue banner at top. At lower-left is the Dodgers 100th anniversary logo, with the Target stores logo at lower-right. On back the player's name and position reappear at top, with the logos below and the card number in a banner at bottom. Cards were numbered roughly alphabetically, though many are out of order. Some cards have duplicated numbers and there were some numbers skipped in the issue. All back printing is in blue on white. Career major league stats and the years in which the player was with the Dodgers are also noted on back. According to figures released by the team, production was to be about 50,000 sets.

	NM/M
Complete Set (1,103):	150.00
Common Player:	.25

No.	Player	NM/M
1	Bert Abbey	.25
2	Cal Abrams	.50
3	Hank Aguirre	.25
4	Eddie Ainsmith	.25
5	Ed Albosta	.25
6	Luis Alcaraz	.25
7	Doyle Alexander	.25
8	Dick Allen	2.50
9	Frank Allen	.25
10	Johnny Allen	.25
11	Mel Almada	1.25
12	Walter Alston	1.25
13	Ed Amelung	.25
14	Sandy Amoros	1.25
15	Dave Anderson	.25
16	Ferrell Anderson	.25
17	John Anderson	.25
18	Stan Andrews	.25
19	Bill Antonello	.25
20	Jimmy Archer	.25
21	Bob Aspromonte	.25
22	Rick Auerbach	.25
23	Charlie Babb	.25
24	Johnny Babich	.25
25	Bob Bailey	.25
26	Bob Bailor	.25
27	Dusty Baker	1.25
28	Tom Baker	.25
29	Dave Bancroft	.75
30	Dan Bankhead	.25
31	Jack Banta	.25
32	Jim Barbieri	.25
33	Red Barkley	.25
34	Jesse Barnes	.25
35	Rex Barney	.75
36	Billy Barnie	.25
37	Bob Barrett	.25
38	Jim Baxes	.25
39	Billy Bean	.25
40	Boom Boom Beck	.25
41	Joe Beckwith	.25
42	Hank Behrman	.25
43	Mark Belanger	.25
44	Wayne Belardi	.25
45	Tim Belcher	.25
46	George Bell	.25
47	Ray Benge	.25
48	Moe Berg	4.00
49	Bill Bergen	.25
50	Ray Berres	.25
51	Don Bessent	.25
52	Steve Bilko	.25
53	Jack Billingham	.25
54	Babe Birrer	.25
55	Del Bissonette	.25
56	Joe Black	1.25
57	Lu Blue	.25
58	George Boehler	.25
59	Sammy Bohne	1.50
60	John Boiling	.25
61	Ike Boone	.25
62	Frenchy Bordagaray	.25
63	Ken Boyer	1.25
64	Buzz Boyle	.25
65	Mark Bradley	.25
66	Bobby Bragan	.25
67	Ralph Branca	1.25
68	Ed Brandt	.25
69	Sid Bream	.25
70	Marv Breeding	.25
71	Tom Brennan	.25
72	William Brennan	.25
73	Rube Bressler	.25
74	Ken Brett	.25
75	Jim Brewer	.25
76	Tony Brewer	.25
77	Rocky Bridges	.25
78	Greg Brock	.25
79	Dan Brouthers	.25
80	Eddie Brown	.25
81	Elmer Brown	.25
82	Lindsay Brown	.25
83	Lloyd Brown	.25
84	Mace Brown	.25
85	Tommy Brown	.25
86	Pete Browning	.25
87	Ralph Bryant	.25
88	Jim Bucher	.25
89	Bill Buckner	1.25
90	Jim Bunning	1.25
91	Jack Burdock	.25
92	Glenn Burke	.25
93	Buster Burrell	.25
94	Larry Burright	.25
95	Doc Bushong	.25
96	Max Butcher	.25
97	Johnny Butler	.25
98	Enos Cabell	.25
99	Leon Cadore	.25
100	Bruce Caldwell	.25
101	Dick Calmus	.25
102	Dolf Camilli	.25
103	Doug Camilli	.25
104	Roy Campanella	9.00
105	Al Campanis	.25
106	Jim Campanis	.25
107A	Leo Callahan	.25
107B	Gilly Campbell	.25
108	Jimmy Canavan	.25
109	Chris Cannizzaro	.25
110	Guy Cantrell	.25
111	Ben Cantwell	.25
112	Andy Carey	.25
113	Max Carey	.25
114	Tex Carleton	.25
115	Ownie Carroll	.25
116	Bob Caruthers	.25
117	Doc Casey	.25
118	Hugh Casey	.25
119	Bobby Castillo	.25
120	Cesar Cedeno	.25
121	Ron Cey	1.25
122	Ed Chandler	.25
123	Ben Chapman	.25
124	Larry Cheney	.25
125	Bob Chipman	.25
126	Chuck Churn	.25
127	Gino Cimoli	.50
128	Moose Clabaugh	.25
129	Bud Clancy	.25
130	Bob Clark	.25
131	Watty Clark	.25
132	Alta Cohen	.25
133	Rocky Colavito	5.00
134	Jackie Collum	.25
135	Chuck Connors	5.00
136	Jack Coombs	.25
137	Johnny Cooney	.25
138	Tommy Corcoran	.25
139	Pop Corkhill	.25
140	John Corriden	.25
141	Pete Coscarart	.25
142	Wes Covington	.25
143	Billy Cox	1.25
144	Roger Craig	.75
145	Cannonball Crane	.25
146	Willie Crawford	.25
147	Tim Crews	.25
148	John Cronin	.25
149	Lave Cross	.25
150	Bill Crouch	.25
151	Don Crow	.25
152	Henry Cruz	.25
153	Tony Cuccinello	.25
154	Roy Cullenbine	.25
155	George Culver	.25
156	Nick Cullop	.25
157	George Cutshaw	.25
158	Kiki Cuyler	.25
159	Bill Dahlen	.25
160	Babe Dahlgren	.25
161	Jack Dalton	.25
162	Tom Daly	.25
163	Cliff Dapper	.25
164	Bob Darnell	.25
165	Bobby Darwin	.25
166	Jake Daubert	.25
167	Vic Davalillo	.25
168	Curt Davis	.25
169	Mike Davis	.25
170	Ron Davis	.25
171	Tommy Davis	1.25
172	Willie Davis	1.25
173	Pea Ridge Day	.25
174	Tommy Dean	.25
175	Hank DeBerry	.25
176	Art Decatur	.25
177	Raoul Dedeaux	.25
178	Ivan DeJesus	.25
179	Don Demeter	.25
180	Gene DeMontreville	.25
181	Rick Dempsey	.25
182	Eddie Dent	.25
183	Mike Devereaux	.25
184	Carlos Diaz	.25
185	Dick Dietz	.25
186	Pop Dillon	.25
187	Bill Doak	.25
188	John Dobbs	.25
189	George Dockins	.25
190	Cozy Dolan	.25
191	Patsy Donovan	.25
192	Wild Bill Donovan	.25
193	Mickey Doolan	.25
194	Jack Doscher	.25
195	Phil Douglas	.25
196	Snooks Dowd	.25
197	Al Downing	.25
198	Red Downs	.25
199	Jack Doyle	.25
200	Solly Drake	.25
201	Tom Drake	.25
202	Chuck Dressen	.75
203	Don Drysdale	5.00
204	Clise Dudley	.25
205	Mariano Duncan	.25
206	Jack Dunn	.25
207	Bull Durham	.25
208	Leo Durocher	1.25
209	Billy Earle	.25
210	George Earnshaw	.25
211	Ox Eckhardt	.25
212	Bruce Edwards	.25
213	Hank Edwards	.25
214	Dick W. Egan	.25
215	Harry Eisenstat	.25
216	Kid Elberfeld	.25
217	Jumbo Elliot	.25
218	Don Elston	.25
219	Gil English	.25
220	Johnny Enzmann	.25
221	Al Epperly	.25
222	Carl Erskine	1.25
223	Tex Erwin	.25
224	Cecil Espy	.25
225	Chuck Essegian	.25
226	Dude Esterbrook	.25
227	Red Evans	.25
228	Bunny Fabrique	.25
229	Jim Fairey	.25
230	Ron Fairly	1.25
231	George Fallon	.25
232	Turk Farrell	.25
233	Duke Farrel	.25
234	Jim Faulkner	.25
235	Alex Ferguson	.25
236	Joe Ferguson	.25
237	Chico Fernandez	.25
238	Sid Fernandez	.25
239	Al Ferrara	.25
240	Wes Ferrell	.25
241	Lou Fette	.25
242	Chick Fewster	.25
243	Jack Fimple	.25
244	Neal "Mickey" Finn	.25
245	Bob Fisher	.25
246	Freddie Fitzsimmons	.25
247	Tim Flood	.25
248	Jake Flowers	.25
249	Hod Ford	.25
250	Terry Forster	.75
251	Alan Foster	.25
252	Jack Fournier	.25
253	Dave Foutz	.25
254	Art Fowler	.25
255	Fred Frankhouse	.25
256	Herman Franks	.25
257	Johnny Frederick	.25
258	Larry French	.25
259	Lonny Frey	.25
260	Pepe Frias	.25
261	Charlie Fuchs	.25
262	Carl Furillo	4.00
263	Len Gabrielson	.25
264	Augie Galan	.25
265	Joe Gallagher	.25
266	Phil Gallivan	.25
267	Balvino Galvez	.25
268	Mike Garman	.25
269	Phil Garner	.25
270	Steve Garvey	2.50
271	Ned Garvin	.25
272	Hank Gastright	.25
273	Sid Gautreaux	.25
274	Jim Gentile	.25
275	Greek George	.25
276	Ben Geraghty	.25
277	Gus Getz	.25
278	Bob Giallombardo	.25
279	Kirk Gibson	1.25
280	Charlie Gilbert	.25
281	Jim Gilliam	1.25
282	Al Gionfriddo	.50
283	Tony Giuliani	.25
284	Al Glossop	.25
285	John Gochnaur	.25
286	Jim Golden	.25
287	Dave Goltz	.25
288	Jose Gonzalez	.25
289	Johnny Gooch	.25
290	Ed Goodson	.25
291	Bill Grabarkewitz	.25
292	Jack Graham	.25
293	Mudcat Grant	.25
294	Dick Gray	.25
295	Kent Greenfield	.25
296	Hal Gregg	.25
297	Alfredo Griffin	.25
298	Mike Griffin	.25
299	Derrell Griffith	.25
300	Tommy Griffith	.25
301	Burleigh Grimes	.25
302	Lee Grissom	.25
303	Jerry Grote	.25
304	Pedro Guerrero	.75
305	Brad Gulden	.25
306	Ad Gumbert	.25
307	Chris Gwynn	.25
308	Bert Haas	.25
309	John Hale	.25
310	Tom Haller	.25
311	Bill Hallman	.25
312	Jeff Hamilton	.25
313	Luke Hamlin	.25
314	Ned Hanlon	.25
315	Gerald Hannahs	.25
316	Charlie Hargreaves	.25
317	Tim Harkness	.25
318	Harry Harper	.25
319	Joe Harris	.25
320	Lenny Harris	.25
321	Bill F. Hart	.25
322	Buddy Hassett	.25
323	Mickey Hatcher	.25
324	Joe Hatten	.25
325	Phil Haugstad	.25
326	Brad Havens	.25
327	Ray Hayworth	.25
328	Ed Head	.25
329	Danny Heep	.25
330	Fred Heimach	.25
331	Harvey Hendrick	.25
332	Weldon Henley	.25
333	Butch Henline	.25
334	Dutch Henry	.25
335	Roy Henshaw	.25
336	Babe Herman	.75
337	Billy Herman	.75
338	Gene Hermanski	.25
339	Enzo Hernandez	.25
340	Art Herring	.25
341	Orel Hershiser	1.25
342	Dave J. Hickman	.25
343	Jim Hickman	.25
344	Kirby Higbe	.25
345	Andy High	.25
346	George Hildebrand	.25
347	Hunkey Hines	.25
348	Don Hoak	.75
349	Oris Hockett	.25
350	Gil Hodges	5.00
351	Glenn Hoffman	.25
352	Al Hollingsworth	.25
353	Tommy Holmes	.25
354	Brian Holton	.25
355	Rick Honeycutt	.25
356	Burt Hooton	.25
357	Gail Hopkins	.25
358	Johnny Hopp	.25
359	Charlie Hough	.75
360	Frank Howard	1.25
361	Steve Howe	.75
362	Dixie Howell	.25
363	Harry Howell	.25
364	Jay Howell	.25
365	Ken Howell	.25
366	Waite Hoyt	.25
367	Johnny Hudson	.25
368	Jim J. Hughes	.25
369	Jim R. Hughes	.25
370	Mickey Hughes	.25
371	John Hummel	.25
372	Ron Hunt	.25
373	Willard Hunter	.25
374	Ira Hutchinson	.25
375	Tom Hutton	.25
376	Charlie Irwin	.25
377	Fred Jacklitsch	.25
378	Randy Jackson	.25
379	Merwin Jacobson	.25
380	Cleo James	.25
381	Hal Janvrin	.25
382	Roy Jarvis	.25
383	George Jeffcoat	.25
384	Jack Jenkins	.25
385	Hughie Jennings	.25
386	Tommy John	1.25
387	Fred Ivy Johnston	.25
388	Jimmy Johnston	.25
389	Jay Johnstone	.75
390	Fielder Jones	.25
391	Oscar Jones	.25
392	Tim Jordan	.25
393	Spider Jorgensen	.25
394	Von Joshua	.25
395	Bill Joyce	.25
396	—	
397	Joe Judge	.25
398	Alex Kampouris	.25
399	Willie Keeler	.25
400	Mike Kekich	.25
401	John Kelleher	.25
402	Frank Kellert	.25
403	Joe Kelley	.25
404	George Kelly	.25
405	Bob Kennedy	.25
406	Brickyard Kennedy	.25
407	John Kennedy	.25
408	Newt Kimball	.25
409	Clyde King	.25
410	Enos Kirkpatrick	.25
411	Frank Kitson	.25
412	Johnny Klippstein	.25
413	Elmer Klumpp	.25
414	Len Koenecke	.25
415	Ed Konetchy	.25
416	Andy Kosco	.25
417	Sandy Koufax	15.00
418	Ernie Koy	.25
419	Charlie Kress	.25
420	Bill Krueger	.25
421	Ernie Krueger	.25
422	Clem Labine	.75
423	Candy LaChance	.25
424	Lee Lacy	.25
425	Lerrin LaGrow	.25
426	Bill Lamar	.25
427	Wayne LaMaster	.25
428	Ray Lamb	.25
429	Rafael Landestoy	.25
430	Ken Landreaux	.25
431	Tito Landrum	.25
432	Norm Larker	.75
433	Lyn Lary	.25
434	Tom Lasorda	1.25
435	Cookie Lavagetto	.25
436	Rudy Law	.25
437	Tony Lazzeri	.25
438	Tim Leary	.25
439	Bob Lee	.25
440	Hall Lee	.25
441	Leron Lee	.25
442	Jim Lefebvre	.25
443	Ken Lehman	.25
444	Don LeJohn	.25
445	Steve Lembo	.25
446	Ed Lennox	.25
447	Dutch Leonard	.25
448	Jeffery Leonard	.25
449	Sam Leslie	.25
450	Dennis Lewallyn	.25
451	Bob Lillis	.25
452	Jim Lindsey	.25
453	Fred Lindstrom	.25
454	Billy Loes	.50
455	Bob Logan	.25
456	Bill Lohrman	.25
457	Vic Lombardi	.25
458	Davey Lopes	.75
459	Al Lopez	.25
460	Ray Lucas	.25
461	Harry Lumley	.25
462	Don Lund	.25
463	Dolf Luque	.25
464	Jim Lyttle	.25
465	Max Macon	.25
466	Bill Madlock	.75
467	Lee Magee	.25
468	Sal Maglie	.75
469	George Magoon	.25
470	Duster Mails	.25
471	Candy Maldonado	.25
472	Tony Malinosky	.25
473	Lew Malone	.25
474	Al Mamaux	.25
475	Gus Mancuso	.25
476	Charlie Manuel	.25
477	Heinie Manush	.25
478	Rabbit Maranville	.25
479	Juan Marichal	2.50
480	Rube Marquard	.25
481	Bill Marriott	.25
482	Buck Marrow	.25
483	Mike A. Marshall	.75
484	Mike G. Marshall	.75
485	Morrie Martin	.25
486	Ramon Martinez	1.25
487	Teddy Martinez	.25
488	Earl Mattingly	.25
489	Len Matuszek	.25
490	Gene Mauch	.25
491	Al Maul	.25
492	Carmen Mauro	.25
493	Alvin McBean	.25
494	Bill McCarren	.25
495	Jack McCarthy	.25
496	Tommy McCarthy	.25
497	Lew McCarty	.25
498	Mike J. McCormick	.25
499	Judge McCreedie	.25
500	Tom McCreery	.25
501	Danny McDevitt	.25
502	Chappie McFarland	.25
503	Joe McGinnity	.25
504	Bob McGraw	.25
505	Deacon McGuire	.25
506	Bill McGunnigle	.25
507	Harry McIntyre	.25
508	Cal McLish	.25
509	Ken McMullen	.25
510	Dough McWeeny	.25
511	Joe Medwick	.25
512	Rube Melton	.25
513	Fred Merkle	.25
514	Orlando Mercado	.25
518	Andy Messersmith	.25
519	Irish Meusel	.25
520	Benny Meyer	.25
521	Russ Meyer	.25
522	Chief Meyers	.25
523	Gene Michael	.25
524	Pete Mikkelsen	.25
525	Eddie Miksis	.25
526	Johnny Miljus	.25
527	Bob Miller	.25
528	Larry Miller	.25
529	Otto Miller	.25
530	Ralph Miller	.25
531	Walt Miller	.25
532	Wally Millies	.25
533	Bob Milliken	.25
534	Buster Mills	.25
535	Paul Minner	.25
536	Bobby Mitchell	.25
537	Clarence Mitchell	.25
538	Dale Mitchell	.25
539	Fred Mitchell	.25
540	Johnny Mitchell	.25
541	Joe Moeller	.25
542	Rick Monday	.75
543	Wally Moon	.75
544	Cy Moore	.25
545	Dee Moore	.25
546	Eddie Moore	.25
547	Gene Moore	.25
548	Randy Moore	.25
549	Ray Moore	.25
550	Jose Morales	.25
551	Bobby Morgan	.25
552	Eddie Morgan	.25
553	Mike Morgan	.25
554	Johnny Morrison	.25
555	Walt Moryn	.25
556	Ray Moss	.25
557	Manny Mota	.75
558	Joe Mulvey	.25
559	Van Lingle Mungo	.25
560	Les Munns	.25
561	Mike Munoz	.25
562	Simmy Murch	.25
563	Eddie Murray	4.00
564	Hy Myers	.25
565	Sam Nahem	.25
566	Earl Naylor	.25
567	Charlie Neal	.75
568	Ron Negray	.25
569	Bernie Neis	.25
570	Rocky Nelson	.25
571	Dick Nen	.25
572	Don Newcombe	2.50
573	Bobo Newsom	.25
574	Doc Newton	.25
575	Tom Niedenfuer	.25
576	Otho Nitcholas	.25
577	Al Nixon	.25
578	Jerry Nops	.25
579	Irv Noren	.25
580	Fred Norman	.25
581	Bill North	.25
582	Johnny Oates	.25
583	Bob O'Brien	.25
584	John O'Brien	.25
585	Lefty O'Doul	.25
586	Joe Oeschger	.25
587	Al Oliver	.75
588	Nate Oliver	.25
589	Luis Olmo	.25
590	Ivy Olson	.25
591	Mickey O'Neil	.25
592	Joe Orengo	.25
593	Jesse Orosco	.25
594	Frank O'Rourke	.25
595	Jorge Orta	.25
596	Phil Ortega	.25
597	Claude Osteen	.25
598	Fritz Ostermueller	.25
599	Mickey Owen	.25
600	Tom Paciorek	.25
601	Don Padgett	.25
602	Andy Pafko	.75
603	Erv Palica	.25
604	Ed Palmquist	.25
605	Wes Parker	.25
606	Jay Partridge	.25
607	Camilo Pascual	.25
608	Kevin Pasley	.25
609	Dave Patterson	.25
610	Harley Payne	.25
611	Johnny Peacock	.25
612	Hal Peck	.25
613	Stu Pederson	.25
614	Alejandro Pena	.25
615	Jose Pena	.25
616	Jack Perconte	.25
617	Charlie Perkins	.25
618	Ron Perranoski	.50
619	Jim Peterson	.25
620	Jesse Petty	.25
621	Jeff Pfeffer	.25
622	Babe Phelps	.25
623	Val Picinich	.25
624	Joe Pignatano	.25
625	George Pinckney	.25
626	Ed Pipgras	.25
627	Bud Podbielan	.25
628	Johnny Podres	.75
629	Boots Poffenberger	.25
630	Nick Polly	.25
631	Paul Popovich	.25
632	Bill Posedel	.25
633	Boog Powell	.50
634	Dennis Powell	.25
635	Paul Ray Powell	.25

No.	Player	Price
636	Ted Power	.25
637	Tot Pressnell	.25
638	John Purdin	.25
639	Jack Quinn	.25
640	Marv Rackley	.25
641	Jack Radtke	.25
642	Pat Ragan	.25
643	Ed Rakow	.25
644	Bob Ramazzotti	.25
645	Willie Ramsdell	.25
646	Mike James Ramsey	.25
647	Mike Jeffery Ramsey	.25
648	Willie Randolph	.25
649	Doug Rau	.25
650	Lance Rautzhan	.25
651	Howie Reed	.25
652	Pee Wee Reese	9.00
653	Phil Regan	.25
654	Bill Reidy	.25
655	Bobby Reis	.25
656	Pete Reiser	.75
657	Rip Repulski	.25
658	Ed Reulbach	.25
659	Jerry Reuss	.50
660	R.J. Reynolds	.25
661	Billy Rhiel	.25
662	Rick Rhoden	.25
663	Paul Richards	.25
664	Danny Richardson	.25
665	Pete Richert	.25
666	Harry Riconda	.25
667	Joe Riggert	.25
668	Lew Riggs	.25
669	Jimmy Ripple	.25
670	Lou Ritter	.25
671	German Rivera	.25
672	Johnny Rizzo	.25
673	Jim Roberts	.25
674	Earl Robinson	.25
675	Frank Robinson	5.00
676	Jackie Robinson	15.00
677a	Wilbert Robinson	.25
677b	Sergio Robles	.25
678	Rich Rodas	.25
679	Ellie Rodriguez	.25
680	Preacher Roe	.75
681	Ed Roebuck	.25
682	Ron Roenicke	.25
683	Oscar Roettger	.25
684	Lee Rogers	.25
685	Packy Rogers	.25
686	Stan Rojek	.25
687	Vicente Romo	.25
688	Johnny Roseboro	.75
689	Goody Rosen	.25
690	Don Ross	.25
691	Ken Rowe	.25
692	Schoolboy Rowe	.25
693	Luther Roy	.25
694	Jerry Royster	.50
695	Nap Rucker	.25
696	Dutch Ruether	.25
697	Bill Russell	.75
698	Jim Russell	.25
699	John Russell	.25
700	Johnny Rutherford	.25
701	John Ryan	.25
702	Rosy Ryan	.25
703	Mike Sandlock	.25
704	Ted Savage	.25
705	Dave Sax	.25
706	Steve Sax	.75
707	Bill Sayles	.25
708	Bill Schardt	.25
709	Johnny Schmitz	.25
710	Dick Schofield	.25
711	Howie Schultz	.25
712	Ferdie Schupp	.25
713	Mike Scioscia	.75
714	Dick Scott	.25
715	Tom Seats	.25
716	Jimmy Sebring	.25
717	Larry See	.25
718	Dave Sells	.25
719	Greg Shanahan	.25
720	Mike Sharperson	.25
721	Joe Shaute	.25
722	Merv Shea	.25
723	Jimmy Sheckard	.25
724	Jack Sheehan	.25
725	John Shelby	.25
726	Vince Sherlock	.25
727	Larry Sherry	.75
728	Norm Sherry	.75
729	Bill Shindle	.25
730	Craig Shipley	.25
731	Bart Shirley	.25
732	Steve Shirley	.25
733	Burt Shotton	.25
734	George Shuba	.50
735	Dick Siebert	.25
736	Joe Simpson	.25
737	Duke Sims	.25
738	Bill Singer	.25
739	Fred Sington	.25
740	Ted Sizemore	.25
741	Frank Skaff	.25
742	Bill Skowron	1.25
743	Gordon Slade	.25
744	Dwain Lefty Sloat	.25
745	Charley Smith	.25
746	Dick Smith	.25
747	George Smith	.25
748	Germany Smith	.25
749	Jack Smith	.25
750	Reggie Smith	.75
751	Sherry Smith	.25
752	Harry Smythe	.25
753	Duke Snider	9.00
754	Eddie Solomon	.25
755	Elias Sosa	.25
756	Daryl Spencer	.25
757	Roy Spencer	.25
758	Karl Spooner	.50
759	Eddie Stack	.25
760	Tuck Stainback	.25
761	George Stallings	.25
762	Jerry Standaert	.25
763	Don Stanhouse	.25
764	Eddie Stanky	.25
765	Dolly Stark	.25
766	Jigger Statz	.25
767	Casey Stengel	1.25
768	Jerry Stephenson	.25
769	Ed Stevens	.25
770	Dave Stewart	.75
771	Stuffy Stewart	.25
772	Bob Stinson	.25
773	Milt Stock	.25
774	Harry Stovey	.25
775	Mike Strahler	.25
776	Sammy Strang	.25
777	Elmer Stricklett	.25
778	Joe Stripp	.25
779	Dick Stuart	.50
780	Franklin Stubbs	.25
781	Bill Sudakis	.25
782	Clyde Sukeforth	.25
783	Billy Sullivan	.25
784	Tom Sunkel	.25
785	Rick Sutcliffe	.25
786	Don Sutton	4.00
787	Bill Swift	.25
788	Vito Tamulis	.25
789	Danny Taylor	.25
790	Harry Taylor	.25
791	Zack Taylor	.25
792	Chuck Templeton	.25
793	Wayne Terwilliger	.25
794	Derrel Thomas	.25
795	Fay Thomas	.25
796	Gary Thomasson	.25
797	Don Thompson	.25
798	Fresco Thompson	.25
799	Tim Thompson	.25
800	Hank Thormahlen	.25
801	Sloppy Thurston	.25
802	Cotton Tierney	.25
803	Al Todd	.25
804	Bert Tooley	.25
805	Jeff Torborg	.25
806	Dick Tracewski	.25
807	Nick Tremark	.25
808	Alex Trevino	.25
809	Tommy Tucker	.25
810	John Tudor	.25
811	Mike Vail	.25
812	Rene Valdes (Valdez)	.25
813	Bobby Valentine	.25
814	Fernando Valenzuela	.75
815	Elmer Valo	.25
816	Dazzy Vance	.75
817	Sandy Vance	.25
818	Chris Van Cuyk	.25
819	Ed VandeBerg	.25
820	Arky Vaughan	.25
821	Zoilo Versalles	.25
822	Joe Vosmik	.25
823	Ben Wade	.25
824	Dixie Walker	.50
825	Rube Walker	.25
826	Stan Wall	.25
827	Lee Walls	.25
828	Danny Walton	.25
829	Lloyd Waner	.25
830	Paul Waner	.25
831	Chuck Ward	.25
832	John Monte Ward	.25
833	Preston Ward	.25
834	Jack Warner	.25
835	Tommy Warren	.25
836	Carl Warwick	.25
837	Jimmy Wasdell	.25
838	Ron Washington	.25
839	Gene Watkins	.25
840	Hank Webb	.25
841	Les Webber	.25
842	Gary Weiss	.25
843	Bob Welch	.75
844	Brad Wellman	.25
845	John Werhas	.25
846	Max West	.25
847	Gus Weyhing	.25
848	Mack Wheat	.25
849	Zack Wheat	.25
850	Ed Wheeler	.25
851	Larry White	.25
852	Myron White	.25
853	Terry Whitfield	.25
854	Dick Whitman	.25
855	Possum Whitted	.25
856	Kemp Wicker	.25
857	Hoyt Wilhelm	.75
858	Kaiser Wilhelm	.25
859	Nick Willhite	.25
860	Dick Williams	.75
861	Reggie Williams	.25
862	Woody Williams	.25
863	Stan Williams	.25
864	Maury Wills	.75
865	Hack Wilson	.25
866	Robert Wilson	.25
867	Gordon Windhorn	.25
868	Jim Winford	.25
869	Lave Winham	.25
870	Tom Winsett	.25
871	Tom Winsett	.25
872	Hank Winston	.25
873	Whitey Witt	.25
874	Pete Wojey	.25
875	Tracy Woodson	.25
876	Clarence Wright	.25
877	Glenn Wright	.25
878	Ricky Wright	.25
879	Whit Wyatt	.25
880	Jimmy Wynn	.25
881	Joe Yeager	.25
882	Steve Yeager	.25
883	Matt Young	.25
884	Tom Zachary	.25
885	Pat Zachry	.25
886	Geoff Zahn	.25
887	Don Zimmer	.75
888	Morrie Aderholt	.25
889	Raleigh Aitchison	.25
890	Whitey Alperman	.25
891	Orlando Alvarez	.25
892	Pat Ankenman	.25
893	Ed Appleton	.25
894	Doug Baird	.25
895	Lady Baldwin	.25
896	Win Ballou	.25
897	Bob Barr	.25
898	Boyd Bartley	.25
899	Eddie Basinski	.25
900	Erve Beck	.25
901	Ralph Birkofer	.25
902	Joe Bradshaw	.25
904	Bruce Brubaker	.25
905	Oyster Burns	.25
906	John Butler	.25
907	Kid Carsey	.25
908	Pete Cassidy	.25
909	Pete Cassidy	.25
910	Tom Catterson	.25
911	Glenn Chapman	.25
912	Paul Chervinko	.25
913	George Cisar	.25
914	Wally Clement	.25
915	Bill Collins	.25
916	Chuck Corgan	.25
917	Dick Cox	.25
918	George Crable	.25
919	Sam Crane	.25
920	Cliff Curtis	.25
921	Fats Dantonio	.25
922	Con Daily	.25
923	Jud Daley	.25
924	Jake Daniel	.25
925	Kal Daniels	.25
926	Dan Daub	.25
927	Lindsay Deal	.25
928	Artie Dede	.25
929	Pat Deisel	.25
930	Bert Delmas	.25
931	Rube Dessau	.25
932	Leo Dickerman	.25
933	John Douglas	.25
934	Red Downey	.25
935	Carl Doyle	.25
936	John Duffie	.25
937	Dick Durning	.25
938	Red Durrett	.25
939	Mal Eason	.25
940	Charlie Ebbets	.75
941	Rube Ehardt	.25
942	Rowdy Elliot	.25
943	Bones Ely	.25
944	Woody English	.25
945	Roy Evans	.25
946	Gus Felix	.25
947	Bill Fischer	.25
948	Jeff Fischer	.25
949	Chauncey Fisher	.25
950	Tom Fitzsimmons	.25
951	Darrin Fletcher	.25
952	Wes Flowers	.25
953	Howard Freigau	.25
954	Nig Fuller	.25
955	John Gaddy	.25
956	Welcome Gaston	.25
957	Frank Gatins	.25
958	Pete Gilbert	.25
959	Wally Wilbert	.25
960	Carden Gillenwater	.25
961	Roy Gleason	.25
962	Harvey Green	.25
963	Nelson Greene	.25
964	John Grim	.25
965	Dan Griner	.25
966	Bill Hall	.25
967	Johnny Hall	.25
968	Pat Hanifin	.25
969	Bill Harris	.25
970	Bill W. Hart	.25
971	Chris Hartje	.25
972	Mike Hartley	.25
973	Gil Hatfield	.25
974	Chris Haughey	.25
975	Hugh Hearne	.25
976	Mike Hechinger	.25
977	Jake Hehl	.25
978	Bob Higgins	.25
979	Still Bill Hill	.25
980	Shawn Hillegas	.25
981	Wally Hood	.25
982	Lefty Hopper	.25
983	Ricky Horton	.25
984	Ed Householder	.25
985	Bill Hubbell	.25
986	Al Humphrey	.25
987	Bernie Hungling	.25
988	George Hunter	.25
989	Pat Hurley	.25
990	Joe Hutcheson	.25
991	Roy Hutson	.25
994	Bert Inks	.25
995	Dutch Jordan	.25
997	Frank Kane	.25
998	Chet Kehn	.25
999	Maury Kent	.25
1000	Tom Kinslow	.25
1001	Fred Kipp	.25
1002	Joe Klugman	.25
1003	Elmer Knetzer	.25
1004	Barney Koch	.25
1005	Jim Korwan	.25
1006	Joe Koukalik	.25
1007	Lou Koupal	.25
1008	Joe Kustus	.25
1009	Frank Lamanske	.25
1010	Tacks Latimer	.25
1011	Bill Leard	.25
1012	Phil Lewis	.25
1013	Mickey Livingston	.25
1014	Dick Loftus	.25
1015	Charlie Loudenslager	.25
1016	Tom Lovett	.25
1017	Charlie Malay	.25
1018	Mal Mallett	.25
1019	Ralph Mauriello	.25
1020	Bill McCabe	.25
1021	Gene McCann	.25
1022	Mike McCormick	.25
1023	Terry McDermott	.25
1024	John McDougal	.25
1025	Pryor McElveen	.25
1026	Dan McGann	.25
1027	Pat McGlothin	.25
1028	Doc McJames	.25
1029	Kit McKenna	.25
1030	Sadie McMahon	.25
1032	Tommy McMillan	.25
1033	Glenn Mickens	.25
1034	Don Miles	.25
1035	Hack Miller	.25
1036	John Miller	.25
1037	Lemmie Miller	.25
1038	George Mohart	.25
1039	Gary Moore	.25
1040	Herbie Moran	.25
1041	Earl Mossor	.25
1042	Glen Moulder	.25
1043	Billy Mullen	.25
1044	Hub Northen	.25
1045	Curly Onis	.25
1046	Tiny Osbourne	.25
1047	Jim Pastorius	.25
1048	Art Parks	.25
1049	Chink Outen	.25
1050	Jimmy Pattison	.25
1051	Norman Pitt	.25
1052	Doc Reisling	.25
1053	Gilberto Reyes	.25
1055	Lou Rochelli	.25
1056	Jim Romano	.25
1057	Max Rosenfeld	.25
1058	Andy Rush	.25
1059	Jack Ryan	.25
1060	Jack Savage	.25
1061	Ray Schmandt	.25
1062	Henry Schmidt	.25
1063	Charlie Schmutz	.25
1064	Joe Schultz	.25
1065	Ray Searage	.25
1066	Elmer Sexauer	.25
1067	George Sharrott	.25
1068	Tommy Sheehan	.25
1069	George Shoch	.25
1071	Broadway Aleck Smith	.25
1072	Hap Smith	.25
1073	Red Smith	.25
1074	Tony Smith	.25
1075	Gene Snyder	.25
1076	Denny Sothern	.25
1077	Bill Steele	.25
1078	Farmer Steelman	.25
1080	Dutch Stryker	.25
1081	Tommy Tatum	.25
1082	Adonis Terry	.25
1084	Ray Thomas	.25
1085	George Treadway	.25
1086	Overton Tremper	.25
1087	Ty Tyson	.25
1088	Rube Vickers	.25
1089	Jose Vizcaino	.25
1090	Bull Wagner	.25
1091	Butts Wagner	.25
1092	Rube Ward	.25
1093	John Wetteland	.25
1094	Eddie Wilson	.25
1095	Tex Wilson	.25
1096	Zeke Wrigley	.25
1097	Rube Yarrison	.25
1099	Earl Yingling	.25
1100	Chink Zachary	.25
1101	Lefty Davis	.25
1102	Bob Hall	.25
1103	Darby O'Brien	.25
1104	Larry LeJeune	.25

1989 Taystee Kansas City Royals

The 1989 Royals are featured on this set of discs distributed by a K.C. area bakery. The 2-3/4" discs have color player photos at center. The team logo has been airbrushed off the caps because the issue was licensed only by the players, and not by Major League Baseball. In the white border is the issuer's logo in red at top, player identification at bottom in a yellow banner and "AL STARS" in blue stars at each side. Backs are printed in blue with player data, 1988 stats and copyright information.

		NM/M
	Complete Set (12):	9.00
	Common Player:	.50
1	George Brett	4.00
2	Kevin Seitzer	.50
3	Pat Tabler	.50
4	Danny Tartabull	.50
5	Willie Wilson	.75
6	Bo Jackson	1.00
7	Frank White	.50
8	Kurt Stillwell	.50
9	Mark Gubicza	.50
10	Charlie Leibrandt	.50
11	Bret Saberhagen	.75
12	Steve Farr	.50

1981 TCMA The 1960's, Series 2

A second series of cards depicting major and minor league players of the 1960s was produced by TCMA in 1981. The cards continued in the same 2-1/2" x 3-1/2" format as the earlier series. Fronts are unadorned color photos, backs have player identification, data and career summary printed in green on white. The numbering of the cards continues at #294, where the first series concluded, but only about one-third the quantity was produced of this series, compared with the first series.

		NM/M
	Complete Set (189):	75.00
	Common Player:	.50
294	Fritzie Brickell	.50
295	Craig Anderson	.50
296	Cliff Cook	.50
297	Pumpsie Green	.50
298	Choo Choo Coleman	.50
299	Don Buford	.50
300	Sparky Anderson	1.00
301	John Anderson	.50
302	Ted Beard	.50
303	Mickey Mantle, Roger Maris	15.00
304	Gene Freese	.50
305	Don Wilkinson	.50
306	Walter Alston	1.00
307	George Bamberger	.50
308	Nelson Briles	.50
309	Dave Baldwin	.50
310	Bob Bailey	.50
311	Paul Blair	.50
312	Ken Boswell	.50
313	Sam Bowens	.50
314	Ray Barker	.50
315	Tommie Agee, Gil Hodges	.50
316	Elmer Valo	.50
317	Ken Walters	.50
318	Joel Horlen	.50
320	Charlie Maxwell	.50
321	Joe Foy	.50
322	Tommie Agee, Cleon Jones, Ron Swoboda	.50
323	Paul Foytack	.50
324	Ron Fairly	.50
325	Wilbur Wood	.50
327	Felix Mantilla	.50
328a	Ed Bouchee	.50
328b	Don Wilson	.50
329	Sandy Valdespino	.50
330	Al Ferrara	.50
331	Jose Tartabull	.50
332	Dick Kenworthy	.50
333	Don Pavletich	.50
334	Jim Fairey	.50
335	Rico Petrocelli	.50
336	Gary Roggenburk	.50
337	Rick Reichardt	.50
338	Ken McMullen	.50
339	Dooley Womack	.50
340	Joe Moock	.50
341	Lou Brock	1.00
342	Hector Torres	.50
343	Ted Savage	.50
344	Hobie Landrith	.50
345	Ed Lopat	.50
346	Mel Nelson	.50
347	Mickey Lolich	.50
348	Al Lopez	1.00
349	Frederico Olivo	.50
350	Bob Moose	.50
351	Bill McCool	.50
352	Ernie Bowman	.50
353	Tom McCraw	.50
354	Sam Mele	.50
355	Len Boehmer	.50
356	Hank Aaron	9.00
357	Ron Hunt	.50
358	Luis Aparicio	1.00
359	Gene Mauch	.50
360	Barry Moore	.50
361	John Buzhardt	.50
362	Spring Training (St. Louis Cardinals)	.50
363	Duke Snider	3.00
364	Billy Martin	1.00
365	Wes Parker	.50
366	Dick Stuart	.50
367	Glenn Beckert	.50
368	Ollie Brown	.50
369	Stan Bahnsen	.50
370	Lee Bales	.50
371	Johnny Keane	.50
372	Wally Moon	.50
373	Larry Miller	.50
374	Fred Newman	.50
375	John Orsino	.50
376	Joe Pactwa	.50
377	John O'Donoghue	.50
378	Jim Ollom	.50
379	Ray Oyler	.50
380	Ron Nischwitz	.50
381	Ron Paul	.50
382	Yogi Berra, John Blanchard, Roger Maris	2.00
383	Jim McKnight	.50
384	Gene Michael	.50
385	Dave May	.50
386	Tim McCarver	1.00
387	Larry Mason	.50
388	Don Hoak	.50
389	Nate Oliver	.50
390	Phil Ortega	.50
391	Billy Madden	.50
392	John Miller	.50
393	Danny Murtaugh	.50
394	Nelson Mathews	.50
395	Red Schoendienst	1.00
396	Roger Nelson	.50
397	Tom Matchick	.50
398	Dennis Musgraves	.50
399	Tommy Harper	.50
400	Fracis Peters	.50
401	Tony Pierce	.50
402	Billy Williams	1.00
403	Dave Boswell	.50
404	Ray Washburn	.50
405	Al Worthington	.50
406	Jesus Alou	.50
407	Yogi Berra, Gil Hodges, Joe Pignatano, Eddie Yost	1.00
408	Wally Bunker	.50
409	Jim Brenneman	.50
410	Bobby Bragan	.50
411	Cal McLish	.50
412	Curt Blefary	.50
413	Jim Bethke	.50
414	Infield 1964 (St. Louis Cardinals)	.50
415	Richie Allen	1.00
416	Larry Brown	.50
417	Mike Andrews	.50
418	Don Mossi	.50
419	J.C. Martin	.50
420	Dick Rusteck	.50
421	Elly Rodriguez	.50
422	Casey Stengel	1.00
423	Gil Hodges, Ed Vargo	.50
424	Johnny Briggs	.50
425	Bud Harrelson, Al Weis	.50
426	Doc Edwards	.50
427	Joe Hague	.50
428	Lee Elia	.50
429	Billy Moran	.50
431	Pete Mikkelsen	.50
432a	Al Moran (Should be #430.)	.50
432b	Aurelio Monteagudo	.50
433	Ken MacKenzie	.50
434	Dick Egan	.50
435	Al McBean	.50
436	Mike Ferraro	.50
437	Gary Wagner	.50
438	Jerry Grote, J.C. Martin	.50
439	Ted Kluszewski	1.00
440	Jerry Johnson	.50
441	Ross Moschitto	.50
442	Zoilo Versalles	.50

443	Dennis Ribant	.50
444	Ted Williams	9.00
445	Steve Whitaker	.50
446	Frank Bertaina	.50
447	Bo Belinsky	.50
448	Joe Moeller	.50
449	Don Shaw, Ron Taylor	.50
450	Al Downing, Whitey Ford, Fritz Peterson, Mel Stottlemyre	1.00
451	Jack Tracy	.50
452	Tony Curry	.50
453	Roy White	.50
454	Jim Bunning	1.00
455	Ralph Houk	.50
456	Bobby Shantz	.50
457	Bill Rigney	.50
458	Roger Repoz	.50
459	Robin Roberts, Bob Turley	.50
460	Gordon Richardson	.50
461	Dick Tracewski	.50
462	Thad Tillotson	.50
463	Larry Osborne	.50
464	Larry Burright	.50
465	Alan Foster	.50
466	Ron Taylor	.50
467	Fred Talbot	.50
468	Bob Miller	.50
469	Frank Tepedino	.50
470	Danny Frisella	.50
471	Cecil Perkins	.50
472	Danny Napoleon	.50
473	John Upham	.50
474	Yogi Berra, Elston Howard, Mickey Mantle, Roger Maris, Bill Skowron	6.00
475	Al Weis	.50
476	Rich Beck	.50
477	Clete Boyer, Tony Kubek, Joe Pepitone, Bobby Richardson	3.00
478	Jack Fisher	.50
479	Archie Moore	.50
480	Roger Craig	.50
481	Frank Crosetti, Mike Hegan, Ralph Houk, Wally Moses	.50
482	Roger Craig, Gil Hodges, Clem Labine, Cookie Lavagetto	.50

1981 TCMA 1959 Chicago White Sox

JIM McANANY OF.

The A.L. Champion Chicago White Sox are featured in this collectors' issue. The 2-1/2" x 3-1/2" cards have black-and-white player photos with dark blue borders. Backs are in black-and-white with a few bits of player data, career information, 1959 and lifetime stats, along with a TCMA copyright line.

		NM/M
Complete Set (45):		45.00
Common Player:		1.00
1	Earl Torgeson	1.00
2	Nellie Fox	5.00
3	Luis Aparicio	5.00
4	Bubba Phillips	1.00
5	Jim McAnany	1.00
6	Jim Landis	1.00
7	Al Smith	1.00
8	Sherman Lollar	1.00
9	Billy Goodman	1.00
10	Jim Rivera	1.00
11	Sammy Esposito	1.00
12	Norm Cash	2.50
13	Johnny Romano	1.00
14	Johnny Callison	1.00
15	Harry Simpson	1.00
16	Ted Kluszewski	4.00
17	Del Ennis	1.00
18	Earl Battey	1.00
19	Larry Doby	4.00
20	Ron Jackson	1.00
21	Ray Boone	1.00
22	Lou Skizas	1.00
23	Joe Hicks	1.00
24	Don Mueller	1.00
25	J.C. Martin	1.00
26	Cam Carreon	1.00
27	Early Wynn	3.00
28	Bob Shaw	1.00
29	Billy Pierce	1.50
30	Turk Lown	1.00
31	Dick Donovan	1.00
32	Gerry Staley	1.00

33	Barry Latman	1.00
34	Ray Moore	1.00
35	Rudy Arias	1.00
36	Joe Stanka	1.00
37	Ken McBride	1.00
38	Don Rudolph	1.00
39	Claude Raymond	1.00
40	Gary Peters	1.00
41	Al Lopez	1.50
42	Don Gutteridge	1.00
43	Ray Berres	1.00
44	Tony Cuccinello	1.00
45	John Cooney	1.00

1981 TCMA 1962 San Francisco Giants

CAP PETERSON IN

The National League Champions for 1962 are featured in this collector's edition card set. The 2-1/2" x 3-1/2" cards have orange borders on front, around black-and-white player photos. Backs are in black-and-white with personal data, career information and 1982 stats.

		NM/M
Complete Set (35):		45.00
Common Player:		1.00
1	Alvin Dark	1.00
2	Whitey Lockman	1.00
3	Larry Jansen	1.00
4	Wes Westrum	1.00
5	Ed Bailey	1.00
6	Tom Haller	1.00
7	Harvey Kuenn	1.00
8	Willie Mays	15.00
9	Felipe Alou	1.50
10	Orlando Cepeda	4.00
11	Chuck Hiller	1.00
12	Jose Pagan	1.00
13	Jim Davenport	1.00
14	Willie McCovey	4.00
15	Matty Alou	1.00
16	Manny Mota	1.50
17	Ernie Bowman	1.00
18	Carl Boles	1.00
19	John Orsino	1.00
20	Joe Pignatano	1.00
21	Gaylord Perry	2.50
22	Jim Duffalo	1.00
23	Dick LeMay	1.00
24	Bob Garibaldi	1.00
25	Bobby Bolin	1.00
26	Don Larsen	1.25
27	Mike McCormick	1.00
28	Stu Miller	1.00
29	Jack Sanford	1.00
30	Billy O'Dell	1.00
31	Juan Marichal	2.50
32	Billy Pierce	1.00
33	Dick Phillips	1.00
34	Cap Peterson	1.00
35	Bob Nieman	1.00

1982 TCMA Baseball's Greatest Hitters

BASEBALL'S GREATEST
HITTERS — JOE DiMAGGIO

Baseball's hit kings of the past are featured in this collectors set. Fronts of the 2-1/2" x 3-1/2" cards have a color or black-and-white photo surrounded by a colored frame. Backs are in black-and-white with a career summary, lifetime stats and Major League Baseball licensee logo.

		NM/M
Complete Set (45):		8.00
Common Player:		.25
1	Ted Williams	1.00
2	Stan Musial	1.00
3	Joe DiMaggio	2.00
4	Roberto Clemente	2.00
5	Jackie Robinson	1.00
6	Willie Mays	1.00
7	Lou Brock	.25
8	Al Kaline	.25
9	Richie Ashburn	.25
10	Tony Oliva	.25
11	Harvey Kuenn	.25
12	Mickey Vernon	.25
13	Tommy Davis	.25
14	Ty Cobb	.75
15	Rogers Hornsby	.25
16	Joe Jackson	2.00
17	Willie Keeler	.25
18	Tris Speaker	.25
19	Babe Ruth	2.50
20	Harry Heilmann	.25
21	Bill Terry	.25
22	George Sisler	.25
23	Lou Gehrig	1.00
24	Nap Lajoie	.25
25	Riggs Stephenson	.25
26	Al Simmons	.25
27	Cap Anson	.25
28	Paul Waner	.25
29	Eddie Collins	.25
30	Heinie Manush	.25
31	Honus Wagner	.50
32	Earle Combs	.25
33	Sam Rice	.25
34	Charlie Gehringer	.25
35	Chick Hafey	.25
36	Zack Wheat	.25
37	Frank Frisch	.25
38	Bill Dickey	.25
39	Ernie Lombardi	.25
40	Joe Cronin	.25
41	Lefty O'Doul	.25
42	Luke Appling	.25
43	Ferris Fain	.25
44	Arky Vaughan	.25
45	Joe Medwick	.25

1982 TCMA Baseball's Greatest Pitchers

BASEBALL'S GREATEST
PITCHERS — DON DRYSDALE

The best pitchers who were no longer active are featured in this collectors issue. Color or black-and-white photos are presented at center of the 2-1/2" x 3-1/2" cards, with a colored frame surrounding the title, name and position. Backs are printed in dark blue and have a career summary and lifetime stats.

		NM/M
Complete Set (45):		6.00
Common Player:		.25
1	Bob Feller	.35
2	Bob Lemon	.25
3	Whitey Ford	.75
4	Joe Page	.25
5	Wilbur Wood	.25
6	Robin Roberts	.25
7	Warren Spahn	.25
8	Sandy Koufax	3.00
9	Juan Marichal	.25
10	Don Newcombe	.25
11	Hoyt Wilhelm	.25
12	Roy Face	.25
13	Allie Reynolds	.25
14	Don Drysdale	.25
15	Bob Gibson	.25
16	Cy Young	.25
17	Walter Johnson	.25
18	Grover Alexander	.25
19	Jack Chesbro	.25
20	Lefty Gomez	.25
21	Wes Ferrell	.25
22	Hal Newhouser	.25
23	Early Wynn	.25
24	Denny McLain	.25
25	Catfish Hunter	.25
26	Jim Lonborg	.25
27	Frank Lary	.25
28	Red Ruffing	.25
29	Lefty Grove	.25
30	Herb Pennock	.25
31	Satchel Paige	1.50
32	Iron Man McGinnity	.25
33	Christy Mathewson	.50
34	Mordecai Brown	.25
35	Eppa Rixey	.25
36	Dizzy Dean	.40
37	Carl Hubbell	.25
38	Dazzy Vance	.25
39	Jim Bunning	.25
40	Smokey Joe Wood	.25
41	Freddie Fitzsimmons	.25
42	Rube Waddell	.25
43	Addie Joss	.25
44	Burleigh Grimes	.25
45	Chief Bender	.25

Baseball's Greatest Sluggers

BASEBALL'S GREATEST
SLUGGERS — BABE RUTH

The heaviest hitters in baseball history are featured in this collectors issue. The 2-1/2" x 3-1/2" cards have color or black-and-white photos on front framed in red or green and bordered in white. Backs have a few personal data, career stats and career summary along with a logo indicating licensing by Major League Baseball, all in black-and-white, or blue-and-white. Cards can be found printed on either white or gray cardboard.

		NM/M
Complete Set (45):		8.00
Common Player:		.25
1	Harmon Killebrew	.25
2	Roger Maris	.50
3	Mickey Mantle	3.00
4	Hank Aaron	1.50
5	Ralph Kiner	.25
6	Willie McCovey	.25
7	Eddie Mathews	.25
8	Ernie Banks	.50
9	Duke Snider	.50
10	Frank Howard	.25
11	Ted Kluszewski	.25
12	Frank Robinson	.25
13	Billy Williams	.25
14	Gil Hodges	.50
15	Yogi Berra	.50
16	Richie Allen	.25
17	Joe Adcock	.25
18	Babe Ruth	2.50
19	Lou Gehrig	2.00
20	Jimmie Foxx	.25
21	Rogers Hornsby	.25
22	Ted Williams	1.50
23	Hack Wilson	.25
24	Al Simmons	.25
25	John Mize	.25
26	Chuck Klein	.25
27	Hank Greenberg	.25
28	Babe Herman	.25
29	Norm Cash	.25
30	Rudy York	.25
31	Gavvy Cravath	.25
32	Mel Ott	.25
33	Orlando Cepeda	.25
34	Dolf Camilli	.25
35	Frank Baker	.25
36	Larry Doby	.25
37	Jim Gentile	.25
38	Harry Davis	.25
39	Rocco Colavito	.25
40	Cy Williams	.25
41	Roy Sievers	.25
42	Boog Powell	.25
43	Willie Mays	1.50
44	Joe DiMaggio	2.00
45	Earl Averill	.25

1982 TCMA Great Players of the 1950's & 60's: Series #1

These large-format (3-3/4" x 5-3/4") cards have white-bordered color poses on front, with no extraneous graphics. Backs have a black-and-white head shot of the player with lifetime stats, career highlights and personal data in a red border.

		NM/M
Complete Set (20):		15.00
Common Player:		.60
1	Roberto Clemente	3.00
2	Sandy Koufax	2.50

A find of player paintings evidently intended for use in Bowman's 1952 baseball card set allowed TCMA to produce this collectors' issue of 15 Bowman "high numbers that never were." The 2-1/8" x 3-1/8" cards approximate the size of the originals. Fronts have only the color picture with a white border around; the facsimile signatures found on original 1952 Bowmans are not present. Backs are printed in red and black and have layout and style similar to the 1952 cards, along with a 1982 TCMA copyright. The issue was numbered consecutively from #253, beginning where the original issue ended.

1982 TCMA "1952" Bowman

		NM/M
Complete Set (15):		12.00
Common Player:		1.00
253	Bob Kennedy	1.00
254	Barney McCosky	1.00
255	Chris Van Cuyk	1.00
256	Morrie Martin	1.00
257	Jim Wilson	1.00
258	Bob Thorpe	1.00
259	Bill Henry	1.00
260	Bob Addis	1.00
261	Terry Moore	1.00
262	Joe Dobson	1.00
263	Jack Merson	1.00
264	Virgil Trucks	1.00
265	Johnny Hopp	1.00
266	Cookie Lavagetto	1.00
267	George Shuba	1.00

1983 TCMA All-Time Athletics

This was one of several early 1980s collectors issues from TCMA depicting an All-Time team. The 2-1/2" x 3-1/2" cards have black-and-white photos on front with red graphics. Backs are printed in blue and offer personal data, a career summary and lifetime stats.

		NM/M
Complete Set (12):		12.00
Common Player:		.75
1	Jimmie Foxx	1.50

Mule Haas OF
ALL-TIME ATHLETICS

2	Eddie Collins	1.25
3	Frank Baker	1.25
4	Jack Barry	.75
5	Al Simmons	1.25
6	Mule Haas	.75
7	Bing Miller	.75
8	Mickey Cochrane	1.25
9	Chief Bender	1.25
10	Lefty Grove	1.25
11	John Wyatt	.75
12	Connie Mack	1.25

All-Time Cardinals

Jim Bottomley 1B
ALL-TIME CARDINALS

A picked team of Cardinal greats through the 1970s is featured on this collectors' issue. The 2-1/2" x 3-1/2" cards have black-and-white photos on front, with the set title printed in red in the white bottom border. Backs have player data and a career summary printed in purple on gray or blue on white.

		NM/M
Complete Set (12):		18.00
Common Player:		1.00
1	Jim Bottomley	1.00
2	Rogers Hornsby	1.25
3	Ken Boyer	1.50
4	Marty Marion	1.00
5	Ducky Medwick	1.00
6	Chick Hafey	1.00
7	Stan Musial	6.00
8	Tim McCarver	1.25
9	Robert "Bob" Gibson	1.50
10	Harry Brecheen	1.00
11	Alpha Brazle	1.00
12	Red Schoendienst	1.25

All-Time Pirates

DEACON PHILLIPPE P

This was one of several early 1980s collectors' issues from TCMA depicting an All-Time team. The 2-1/2" x 3-1/2" cards have black-and-white photos on front with blue graphics. Backs are printed in blue and offer personal data, a career summary and lifetime stats.

		NM/M
Complete Set (12):		12.00
Common Player:		1.00
1	Willie Stargell	2.00
2	Bill Mazeroski	1.50
3	Pie Traynor	1.00
4	Honus Wagner	2.00

Note (column for 1983 TCMA All-Time Athletics set listing):

3	Phil Rizzuto	1.00
4	Bob Feller	.60
5	Duke Snider	1.00
6	Hank Aaron	2.50
7	Eddie Mathews	.60
8	Roy Campanella	1.50
9	Willie Mays	2.50
10	Robin Roberts	.60
11	Nelson Fox	.60
12	Early Wynn	.60
13	Ted Williams	2.50
14	Warren Spahn	.60
15	Jackie Robinson	2.00
16	Joe DiMaggio	2.50
17	Frank Robinson	.60
18	Yogi Berra	1.25
19	Mickey Mantle	3.50
20	Stan Musial	2.00

5 Roberto Clemente 6.00
6 Lloyd Waner, Paul Waner 1.50
7 Ralph Kiner 1.00
8 Manny Sanguillen 1.00
9 Deacon Phillippe 1.00
10 Bob Veale 1.00
11 Elroy Face 1.00
12 Danny Murtaugh 1.00

Play Ball Postcards

These 5-1/2" x 3-1/2" postcards have vintage photos in sepia with white borders and player identification on front. The postcard-style backs have a write-up about the team represented.

NM/M
Complete Set (18): 25.00
Common Card: 2.00
1 1949 Indians (Lou Boudreau, Joe Gordon) 2.00
2 1948 Red Sox (Murrell Jones, Bobby Doerr, Junior Stephens, Johnny Pesky) 2.00
3 1948 Red Sox (Sam Mele, Ted Williams, Stan Spence, Dom DiMaggio) 4.00
4 1948 Yankees (Joe DiMaggio, Johnny Lindell, Charlie Keller, Tommy Henrich) 5.00
5 Pittsburgh 1947 (Happy Chandler, Hank Greenberg) 2.00
6 1948 Phillies (Eddie Miller, Emil Verban) 2.00
7 1948 Cardinals (Howie Pollett, Red Munger, Murry Dickson, Harry Brecheen, Ken Burkhart) 2.00
8 1948 Braves (Warren Spahn, Johnny Sain) 2.50
9 1948 Braves (Alvin Dark, Eddie Stanky) 2.00
10 1948 Braves (Bob Elliott, Tommy Holmes) 2.00
11 1941 Yankees Team Photo 3.00
12 1943 Yankees Team Photo 3.00
13 1947 Yankees Team Photo 3.00
14 1948 Spring Training (Yankees) (Eddie Lopat, Spec Shea, Vic Raschi, Red Embree, Bill Bevens) 3.00
15 1948 A's (Lou Brissie, Connie Mack) 2.00
16 1948 Tigers (Ted Gray, Hal Newhouser, Virgil Trucks, Art Houtteman, Fred Hutchinson, Dizzy Trout) 2.00
17 Yankees (Phil Rizzuto, Joe Gordon) 3.00
18 1944 Browns (Ellis Clary, Floyd Baker, Vern Stephens, Mark Christman, Don Gutteridge, George McQuinn) 2.00

50 Years of Yankees All-Stars

Yankees' players who participated in the first 50 years of All-Star Games (1933-1983) are featured in this collectors' issue. The 2-3/4" x 3-1/2" cards feature on front the art of Robert Stephen Simon.

NM/M
Complete Set (50): 12.50
Common Player: .40
1 Checklist (Mickey Mantle) 1.25
2 Luis Arroyo .40
3 Hank Bauer .40
4 Yogi Berra .75
5 Tommy Byrne .40
6 Spud Chandler .40
7 Ben Chapman .40
8 Jim Coates .40
9 Bill Dickey .50
10 Joe DiMaggio 3.00
11 Al Downing .40
12 Ryne Duren .40
13 Whitey Ford .75
14 Whitey Ford .75
15 Lou Gehrig 3.00
16 Lefty Gomez .40
17 Bob Grim .40
18 Tommy Henrich .40
19 Elston Howard .40
20 Catfish Hunter .40
21 Billy Johnson .40
22 Charlie Keller .40
23 Johnny Kucks .40
24 Ed Lopat .40
25 Sparky Lyle .40
26 Mickey Mantle 4.00
27 Roger Maris .75
28 Billy Martin .50
29 Johnny Mize .50
30 Bobby Murcer .40
31 Irv Noren .40
32 Joe Pepitone .40
33 Fritz Peterson .40
34 Vic Raschi .40
35 Allie Reynolds .40
36 Bobby Richardson .40
37 Phil Rizzuto .75
38 Marius Russo .40
39 Babe Ruth 3.50
40 Johnny Sain .40
41 George Selkirk .40
42 Bobby Shantz .40
43 Spec Shea .40
44 Moose Skowron .40
45 Casey Stengel .60
46 Mel Stottlemyre .40
47 Ralph Terry .40
48 Tom Tresh .40
49 Bob Turley .40
50 Roy White .40

1936-1939 Yankee Dynasty

Many of the players who participated in one or more of the Yankees' four consecutive World Champion seasons in the late 1930s are included in this collectors' edition. Cards are 2-3/4" x 4" and feature black-and-white photos on front. In the white borders at top and bottom, the set name and player identification are printed in blue. Backs have stats for each season and are printed in black-and-white on a brown background. This set is a virtual reprint of the set made in 1974, with two player cards added. The unnumbered cards are checklisted here alphabetically.

NM/M
Complete Set (56): 45.00
Common Player: 1.00
(1) "Poison Ivy" Andrews 1.00
(2) Joe Beggs 1.00
(3) Marv Breuer 1.00
(4) Johnny Broaca 1.00
(5) "Jumbo" Brown 1.00
(6) "Spud" Chandler 1.00
(7) Ben Chapman 1.00
(8) Earle Combs 1.00
(9) Frankie Crosetti 1.00
(10) "Babe" Dahlgren 1.00
(11) Bill Dickey 1.50
(12) Joe DiMaggio 8.00
(13) Atley Donald 1.00
(14) Wes Ferrell 1.00
(15) Artie Fletcher 1.00
(16) Joe Gallagher 1.00
(17) Lou Gehrig 8.00
(18) Joe Glenn 1.00
(19) "Lefty" Gomez 1.00
(20) Joe Gordon 1.00
(21) "Bump" Hadley 1.00
(22) Don Heffner 1.00
(23) Tommy Henrich 1.00
(24) Oral Hildebrand 1.00
(25) Myril Hoag 1.00
(26) Roy Johnson 1.00
(27) Arndt Jorgens 1.00
(28) Charlie Keller 1.00
(29) Ted Kleinhans 1.00
(30) Billy Knickerbocker 1.00
(31) Tony Lazzeri 1.00
(32) Frank Makosky 1.00
(33) "Pat" Malone 1.00
(34) Johnny Murphy 1.00
(35) "Monty" Pearson 1.00
(36) "Jake" Powell 1.00
(37) "Red" Rolfe 1.00
(38) "Buddy" Rosar 1.00
(39) "Red" Ruffing 1.00
(40) Marius Russo 1.00
(41) "Jack" Saltzgaver 1.00
(42) Paul Schreiber 1.00
(43) Johnny Schulte 1.00
(44) Bob Seeds 1.00
(45) "Twinkletoes" Selkirk 1.00
(46) Lee Stine 1.00
(47) Steve Sundra 1.00
(48) "Sandy" Vance 1.00
(49) Dixie Walker 1.00
(50) Kemp Wicker 1.00
(51) Joe McCarthy, Jacob Ruppert 1.00
(52) Joe DiMaggio, Frank Crosetti, Tony Lazzeri, Bill Dickey, Lou Gehrig, Jake Powell, George Selkirk 3.00
(53) Lou Gehrig, Joe DiMaggio 5.00
(54) Gehrig Hits Another 5.00
(55) Red Rolfe, Tony Lazzeri, Lou Gehrig, Frank Crosetti 3.00
(56) World Champions/1936 3.00

942-46 St. Louis Cardinals

This set is a virtual re-issue of the 1975 set, except for some minor changes in player selection, the use of a slightly smaller (2-1/2" x 3-1/2") format, gray cardboard backs instead of white and which include biographical information as well as stats and the appearance on a black line around the black-and-white player photos. Highlight printing on front is again in red. This version of the set includes card numbers.

NM/M
Complete Set (68): 24.00
Common Player: .25
1 Jimmy Brown .25
2 Jeff Cross .25
3 Lou Klein .25
4 Danny Litwhiler .25
5 Sam Narron .25
6 Estel Crabtree .25
7 Buzzy Wares .25
8 Ken O'Dea .25
9 Buddy Blattner .25
10 Erv Dusak .25
11 Ray Sanders .25
12 Harry Walker .25
13 Coaker Triplett .25
14 Stan Musial 4.00
15 Walker Cooper .25
16 Whitey Kurowski .25
17 Enos Slaughter 1.50
18 Terry Moore .35
19 Johnny Hopp .25
20 Creepy Crespi .25
21 Marty Marion .50
22 Debs Garms .25
23 Frank Demaree .25
24 George Fallon .25
25 Buster Adams .25
26 Emil Verban .50
27 Augie Bergamo .50
28 Pepper Martin .50
29 Mike Gonzalez .25
30 Leo Durocher, Eddie Dyer .50
31 Red Schoendienst 1.50
32 Del Rice .25
33 Joe Garagiola 2.00
34 Dick Sisler .25
35 Clyde Kluttz .25
36 Bill Endicott .25
37 Nippy Jones .25
38 Walt Sessi .25
39 Del Wilber .25
40 Mort Cooper .25
41 John Beazley .25
42 Howie Krist .25
43 Max Lanier .25
44 Harry Grumbert (Gumbert) .25
45 Howie Pollet .25
46 Ernie White .25
47 Murray Dickson (Murry) .25
48 Lon Warneke .25
49 Bill Lohrman .25
50 Clyde Shoun .25
51 Red Munger .25
52 Harry Brecheen .25
53 Al Brazle .25
54 Bud Byerly .25
55 Ted Wilks .25
56 Fred Schmidt .25
57 Al Jurisich .25
58 Red Barrett .25
59 Ken Burkhart .25
60 Blix Donnelly .25
61 Johnny Grodzicki .25
62 Billy Southworth .25
63 Eddie Dyer .25
64 Red Ruffing, Johnny Beazley .25
65 Stan Musial, Billy Southworth, Johnny Hopp 1.00
66 Sportsman's Park (5" x 3-1/2") 2.00
67 1942 St. Louis Cardinals (5" x 3-1/2") 2.00
68 Stan Musial, Billy Southworth, Ray Sanders 1.00

1942 Play Ball

Between 1983-85, TCMA produced eight sets of collectors' cards resurrecting the Play Ball brand name which had been active in the field from 1939-41. The TCMA sets attempt to replicate the style and substance of the earlier Play Ball cards as if the company had continued production through World War II and the end of the 1940s. The "1942" set features sepia-toned photos on front, with black graphics. Backs are printed on gray stock in blue ink. Size approximates the original Play Balls at 2-1/2" x 3-1/4".

NM/M
Complete Set (45): 30.00
Common Player: 1.50
1 Joe Gordon 1.50
2 Joe DiMaggio 6.50
3 Bill Dickey 2.00
4 Joe McCarthy 1.50
5 Tex Hughson 1.50
6 Ted Williams 5.00
7 Walt Judnich 1.50
8 Vern Stephens 1.50
9 Denny Galehouse 1.50
10 Lou Boudreau 1.50
11 Ken Keltner 1.50
12 Jim Bagby 1.50
13 Rudy York 1.50
14 Barney McCosky 1.50
15 Schoolboy Rowe 1.50
16 Luke Appling 1.50
17 Taft Wright 1.50
18 Ted Lyons 1.50
19 Mickey Vernon 1.50
20 George Case 1.50
21 Bobo Newsom 1.50
22 Bob Johnson 1.50
23 Buddy Blair 1.50
24 Pete Suder 1.50
25 Terry Moore 1.50
26 Stan Musial 5.00
27 Marty Marion 1.50
28 Pee Wee Reese 3.50
29 Arky Vaughan 1.50
30 Larry French 1.50
31 Johnny Mize 2.00
32 Mel Ott 2.00
33 Willard Marshall 1.50
34 Carl Hubbell 2.00
35 Frank McCormick 1.50
36 Linus Frey 1.50
37 Bob Elliott 1.50
38 Vince DiMaggio 1.50
39 Al Lopez 1.50
40 Stan Hack 1.50
41 Lou Novikoff 1.50
42 Casey Stengel 2.00
43 Tommy Holmes 1.50
44 Ron Northey 1.50
45 Rube Melton 1.50

1943 Play Ball

Between 1983-85, TCMA produced eight sets of collectors' cards resurrecting the Play Ball brand name which had been active in the field from 1939-41. The TCMA sets attempt to replicate the style and substance of the earlier Play Ball cards as if the company had continued production through World War II and the end of the 1940s. The "1943" set features sepia-toned photos on front, with black graphics. Backs are printed on gray stock in purple ink. Size approximates the original Play Balls at 2-1/2" x 3-1/4".

NM/M

Complete Set (45): 25.00
Common Player: 1.50
1 Spud Chandler 1.50
2 Frank Crosetti 1.50
3 Johnny Lindell 1.50
4 Emil "Dutch" Leonard 1.50
5 Stan Spence 1.50
6 Ray Mack 1.50
7 Hank Edwards 1.50
8 Al Smith 1.50
9 Mike Tresh 1.50
10 Don Kolloway 1.50
11 Orval Grove 1.50
12 Doc Cramer 1.50
13 Pinky Higgins 1.50
14 Dick Wakefield 1.50
15 Harland Clift (Harland) 1.50
16 Chet Laabs 1.50
17 George McQuinn 1.50
18 Tony Lupien 1.50
19 Oscar Judd 1.50
20 Roy Partee 1.50
21 Lum Harris 1.50
22 Roger Wolf 1.50
23 Dick Siebert 1.50
24 Walker Cooper 1.50
25 Mort Cooper 1.50
26 Whitey Kurowski 1.50
27 Eddie Miller 1.50
28 Elmer Riddle 1.50
29 Bucky Walters 1.50
30 Whitlow Wyatt 1.50
31 Dolf Camilli 1.50
32 Elbie Fletcher 1.50
33 Frank Gustine 1.50
34 Rip Sewell 1.50
35 Phil Cavarretta 1.50
36 Bill "Swish" Nicholson 1.50
37 Peanuts Lowrey 1.50
38 Phil Masi 1.50
39 Al Javery 1.50
40 Jim Tobin 1.50
41 Glen Stewart 1.50
42 Mickey Livingston 1.50
43 Ace Adams 1.50
44 Joe Medwick 2.50
45 Sid Gordon 1.50

1944 Play Ball

Between 1983-85, TCMA produced eight sets of collectors' cards resurrecting the Play Ball brand name which had been active in the field from 1939-41. The TCMA sets attempt to replicate the style and substance of the earlier Play Ball cards as if the company had continued production through World War II and the end of the 1940s. The "1944" set features black-and-white photos on front, with blue graphics. Backs are printed on gray stock in black ink. Size approximates the original Play Balls at 2-1/2" x 3-1/4".

NM/M
Complete Set (45): 25.00
Common Player: 1.50
1 Don Gutteridge 1.50
2 Mark Christman 1.50
3 Mike Kreevich 1.50
4 Jimmy Outlaw 1.50
5 Paul Richards 1.50
6 Hal Newhouser 2.50
7 Bud Metheny 1.50
8 Mike Garbark 1.50
9 Hersh Martin 1.50
10 Bob Johnson 1.50
11 Mike Ryba 1.50
12 Oris Hockett 1.50
13 Ed Klieman 1.50
14 Ford Garrison 1.50
15 Irv Hall 1.50
16 Ed Busch 1.50
17 Ralph Hogdin 1.50
18 Thurman Tucker 1.50
19 Bill Dietrich 1.50
20 Rick Ferrell 2.00
21 John Sullivan 1.50
22 Mickey Haefner 1.50
23 Ray Sanders 1.50
24 Johnny Hopp 1.50
25 Ted Wilks 1.50
26 John Barrett 1.50
27 Jim Russell 1.50
28 Nick Strincevich 1.50
29 Eric Tipton 1.50
30 Jim Konstanty 1.50
31 Gee Walker 1.50
32 Dom Dellessandro 1.50
33 Bob Chipman 1.50
34 Hank Wyse 1.50
35 Phil Weintraub 1.50
36 George Hausmann 1.50
37 Bill Voiselle 1.50
38 Whitey Wietelmann 1.50
39 Clyde Kluttz 1.50
40 Connie Ryan 1.50
41 Eddie Stanky 1.50
42 Augie Galan 1.50
43 Mickey Owen 1.50
44 Charlie Schanz 1.50
45 Bob Finley 1.50

1945 Play Ball

JOHNNY DICKSHOT

Between 1983-85, TCMA produced eight sets of collectors' cards resurrecting the Play Ball brand name which had been active in the field from 1939-41. The TCMA sets attempt to replicate the style and substance of the earlier Play Ball cards as if the company had continued production through World War II and the end of the 1940s. The "1945" set features black-and-white photos on front, with blue graphics. Backs are printed on gray stock in black ink. Size approximates the original Play Balls at 2-1/2" x 3-1/4".

NM/M
Complete Set (45): 25.00
Common Player: 1.50
1 Eddie Mayo 1.50
2 Dizzy Trout 1.50
3 Roy Cullenbine 1.50
4 Joe Kuhel 1.50
5 George Binks 1.50
6 Roger Wolff 1.50
7 Gene Moore 1.50
8 Frank Mancuso 1.50
9 Bob Muncrief 1.50
10 Tuck Stainback 1.50
11 Bill Bevens 1.50
12 Snuffy Stirnweiss 1.50
13 Don Ross 1.50
14 Felix Mackiewicz 1.50
15 Jeff Heath 1.50
16 John Dickshot 1.50
17 Ed Lopat 2.00
18 Skeeter Newsom (Newsome) 1.50
19 Eddie Lake 1.50
20 John Lazor 1.50
21 Hal Peck 1.50
22 Al Brancato 1.50
23 Paul Derringer 1.50
24 Stan Hack 1.50
25 Len Merullo 1.50
26 Emil Verban 1.50
27 Ken O'Dea 1.50
28 Red Barrett 1.50
29 Eddie Basinski 1.50
30 Dixie Walker 1.50
31 Goody Rosen 1.50
32 Preacher Roe 1.50
33 Pete Coscarat 1.50
34 Frankie Frisch 2.50
35 Napoleon Reyes 1.50
36 Dan Gardella 1.50
37 Buddy Kerr 1.50
38 Dick Culler 1.50
39 Tommy Holmes 1.50
40 Al Libke 1.50
41 Howie Fox 1.50
42 Johnny Riddle 1.50
43 Andy Seminick 1.50
44 Andy Karl 1.50
45 Rene Monteguedo 1.50

1984 TCMA American League All-Stars

The American League "players who compiled the greatest All-Star Game Records" are included in this collectors' edition - one at each position. In standard 2-1/2" x 3-1/2" size, the cards have black-and-white photos with blue frames. Backs have career All-Star Game stats and a copyright line. The unnumbered cards are listed here in alphabetical order.

LOU BOUDREAU

		NM/M
Complete Set (9):		6.00
Common Player:		.25
(1)	Lou Boudreau	.25
(2)	Rocky Colavito	.50
(3)	Bill Dickey	.50
(4)	Nellie Fox	.50
(5)	Jimmie Foxx	.50
(6)	Mel Harder	.25
(7)	Al Kaline	1.00
(8)	Brooks Robinson	1.00
(9)	Ted Williams	1.50

Roberto Clemente

This one-card set was produced in the same format as the four-card 1984 Hall of Fame Induction set and was probably printed on the same sheet in the same quantity (fewer than 500). Front has a black-and-white photo, back has lifetime stats.

	NM/M
Roberto Clemente	7.50

Great Players of the 1950's & 60's: Series #2

AL KALINE

These large-format (3-3/4" x 5-3/4") cards have color photos bordered in white with a green stripe at bottom bearing the player (or team) name. Backs have a black-and-white head shot of the player, his identification, personal data, career stats and a short biography, all framed in blue with decorative top corners.

		NM/M
Complete Set (33):		75.00
Common Player:		2.00
1	Brooks Robinson	6.00
2	Al Kaline	6.00
3	Tony Oliva	2.00
4	Frank Howard	2.00
5	Richie Ashburn	6.00
6	Harmon Killebrew	6.00
7	George Kell	6.00
8	Larry Doby	6.00
9	Ernie Banks	7.50
10	Maury Wills	4.00
11	Roger Maris	10.00
12	Al Rosen	2.00
13	Willie McCovey	6.00
14	Luis Aparicio	6.00
15	Ron Santo	4.00
16	Harvey Kuenn	2.00
17	Lou Brock	6.00
18	1960 Pittsburgh Pirates (Murtaugh on back)	7.50
19	1966 N.Y. Yankees (Westrum on back)	7.50
20	1950 Philadelphia Phillies (Sawyer on back)	6.00
21	1955 Brooklyn Dodgers (Alston on back)	7.50
22	1957 Milwaukee Braves (Haney on back)	7.50
23	Bob Gibson	6.00
24	Don Drysdale	6.00
25	Whitey Ford	7.50
26	Mickey Mantle, Roger Maris, Mrs. Babe Ruth	7.50

27	Harmon Killebrew, Willie Mays, Mickey Mantle	10.00
28	Willie Mays, Don Drysdale	7.50
29	1961 Yankees, Manager and Coaches	7.50
30	1964 Mets, Manager and Coaches	6.00
31	Ken Boyer, Stan Musial, Red Schoendienst	3.50
32	1952 Giants Pitching Staff	2.00
33	Vada Pinson	2.00

Hall of Fame Induction

While the production of Induction cards in the larger format continued for several years, TCMA's issue of standard 2-1/2" x 3-1/2" format cards was exclusive to 1984. The black-and-white cards have lifetime stats on back. It is reported that fewer than 500 sets were made.

		NM/M
Complete Set (4):		20.00
Common Player:		4.00
(1)	Luis Aparicio	6.00
(2)	Don Drysdale	8.00
(3)	Rick Ferrell	4.00
(4)	Harmon Killebrew	8.00

Hall of Fame Induction 8x10s

For four years TCMA produced 8" x 10" cards for the current inductees to the Baseball Hall of Fame. There are no TCMA markings on the cards, which were distributed by Baseball Nostalgia of Cooperstown, N.Y. The cards are blank-backed and unnumbered. They were printed in black-and-white in 1984, 1986-1987; the 1985 cards are blue-and-white. Only 500 of each card were issued.

		NM/M
Complete Set (18):		250.00
Common Player:		15.00
(1)	Luis Aparicio	15.00
(2)	Don Drysdale	15.00
(3)	Rick Ferrell	15.00
(4)	Harmon Killebrew	15.00
(5)	Pee Wee Reese	20.00
(6)	Composite (Luis Aparicio, Don Drysdale, Rick Ferrell, Harmon Killebrew, Pee Wee Reese)	20.00
(7)	Lou Brock	15.00
(8)	Enos Slaughter	15.00
(9)	Hoyt Wilhelm	15.00
(10)	Composite (Lou Brock, Enos Slaughter, Arky Vaughn (Vaughan), Hoyt Wilhelm)	20.00
(11)	Bobby Doerr	15.00
(12)	Willie McCovey	15.00
(13)	Composite (Bobby Doerr, Ernie Lombardi, Willie McCovey)	20.00
(14)	50th Anniversary Composite (Ty Cobb, Walter Johnson, Christy Mathewson, Babe Ruth, Honus Wagner (edition of 300))	75.00
(15)	Ray Dandridge	15.00
(16)	Jim "Catfish" Hunter	15.00
(17)	Billy Williams	15.00
(18)	Composite (Ray Dandridge, Jim "Catfish" Hunter, Billy Williams)	15.00

National League All-Stars

DICK GROAT

The National League "players who compiled the greatest All-Star Game Records" are included in this collectors' edition - one at each position. In standard 2-1/2" x 3-1/2" size, the cards have black-and-white photos with red frames. Backs have ca-

reer All-Star Game stats and a copyright line. The unnumbered cards are listed here in alphabetical order.

		NM/M
Complete Set (9):		6.00
Common Player:		.25
(1)	Ernie Banks	1.00
(2)	Ken Boyer	.25
(3)	Roberto Clemente	2.50
(4)	Dick Groat	.25
(5)	Billy Herman	.25
(6)	Ernie Lombardi	.25
(7)	Juan Marichal	.25
(8)	Willie Mays	2.00
(9)	Stan Musial	1.00

Bruce Stark Postcards

JOE DI MAGGIO

		NM/M
Complete Set (4):		20.00
Common Player:		4.00
(1)	Luis Aparicio	6.00
(2)	Don Ferrell	8.00
(3)	Rick Ferrell	4.00
(4)	Harmon Killebrew	8.00

Color artwork by Bruce Stark is featured on these 3-3/4" x 5-3/4" postcards.

		NM/M
Complete Set (5):		9.00
Common Player:		1.25
BS1	Joe DiMaggio	4.50
BS2	Ted Williams	3.00
BS3	Ted Kluzewski (Kluszewski)	1.75
BS4	Mickey Vernon	1.25
BS5	Stan Musial	2.50

1946 Play Ball

HANK GREENBERG

Between 1983-85, TCMA produced eight sets of collectors' cards which had been active in the field from 1939-41. The TCMA sets attempt to replicate the style and substance of the earlier Play Ball cards as if the company had continued production through World War II and the end of the 1940s. The "1946" set features black-and-white photos on front, with green graphics. Backs are printed on white stock in black ink. Size approximates the originals at 2-1/2" x 3-1/4".

		NM/M
Complete Set (45):		20.00
Common Player:		1.00
1	Dom DiMaggio	1.25
2	Boo Ferriss	1.00
3	Johnny Pesky	1.00
4	Hank Greenberg	2.00
5	George Kell	1.00
6	Virgil Trucks	1.00
7	Phil Rizzuto	1.75
8	Charlie Keller	1.25
9	Tommy Henrich	1.25
10	Cecil Travis	1.00
11	Al Evans	1.00
12	Buddy Lewis	1.00
13	Edgar Smith	1.00
14	Dario Lodigiani	1.00
15	Earl Caldwell	1.00
16	Jim Hegan	1.00
17	Bob Feller	1.75
18	John Berardino	1.25
19	Jack Kramer	1.00
20	John Lucadello	1.00
21	Hank Majeski	1.00
22	Elmer Valo	1.00
23	Buddy Rosar	1.00
24	Red Schoendienst	1.25
25	Dick Sisler	1.00
26	John Beazley	1.00
27	Vic Lombardi	1.00

28	Dick Whitman	1.00
29	Carl Furillo	1.75
30	Bill Jurges	1.00
31	Marv Rickert	1.00
32	Clyde McCullough	1.00
33	Johnny Hopp	1.00
34	Mort Cooper	1.00
35	Johnny Sain	1.25
36	Del Ennis	1.00
37	Roy Hughes	1.00
38	Bert Haas	1.00
39	Grady Hatton	1.00
40	Ed Bahr	1.00
41	Billy Cox	1.00
42	Lee Handley	1.00
43	Bill Rigney	1.00
44	Babe Young	1.00
45	Buddy Blattner	1.00

1985 TCMA Cy Young Award Winners

This polybagged set of 2-1/2" x 3-1/2" cards is formatted on two perforated strips. Fronts have color photos with orange borders while backs detail the player's CY season(s). The header card presents the history of the award. The unnumbered cards are listed here alphabetically.

		NM/M
Complete Set (10):		6.00
Common Player:		.25
(1)	Don Drysdale	.75
(2)	Whitey Ford	1.50
(3)	Bob Gibson	.50
(4)	Catfish Hunter	.40
(5)	Sandy Koufax	4.00
(6)	Vern Law	.25
(7)	Sparky Lyle	.25
(8)	Denny McLain	.35
(9)	Jim Palmer	.50
(10a)	Warren Spahn (Boston Braves)	.50
(10b)	Warren Spahn (Milwaukee Braves)	.50

Home Run Champs

This polybagged set of 2-1/2" x 3-1/2" cards is formatted on two perforated strips. Fronts have color photos with reddish-brown borders while backs detail the player's slugging prowess. The header card presents the history of the award. The unnumbered cards are listed here alphabetically.

		NM/M
Complete Set (10):		6.00
Common Player:		.30
(1)	Hank Aaron	1.50
(2)	Orlando Cepeda	.60
(3)	Joe DiMaggio	2.00
(4)	Larry Doby	.60
(5)	Ralph Kiner	.60
(6)	Eddie Mathews	.60
(7)	Willie McCovey	.60
(8)	Al Rosen	.30
(9)	Duke Snider	.60
(10)	Ted Williams	1.50

Most Valuable Players - A.L.

This polybagged set of 2-1/2" x 3-1/2" cards is formatted on two perforated strips. Fronts have color photos with green borders while backs detail the player's MVP season(s). The header card presents the history of the award. The unnumbered cards are listed here alphabetically.

		NM/M
Complete Set (10):		9.00
Common Player:		.40
(1)	Richie Allen	.40
(2)	Yogi Berra	.75
(3)	Elston Howard	.40
(4)	Jackie Jensen	.40
(5)	Harmon Killebrew	.75
(6)	Mickey Mantle	4.00
(7)	Roger Maris	1.50
(8)	Boog Powell	.40
(9)	Brooks Robinson	.75
(10)	Carl Yastrzemski	1.25

Most Valuable Players - N.L.

This polybagged set of 2-1/2" x 3-1/2" cards is formatted on two perforated strips. Fronts have color photos with blue borders while backs detail the player's MVP season(s). The header card presents the history of the award. The unnumbered cards are listed here alphabetically.

		NM/M
Complete Set (10):		9.00
Common Player:		.40
(1)	Ernie Banks	1.00
(2)	Johnny Bench	1.00
(3)	Roy Campanella	.90
(4)	Roberto Clemente	3.00
(5)	Dick Groat	1.00

(6)	Willie Mays	2.50
(7)	Stan Musial	1.50
(8)	Frank Robinson	1.00
(9)	Willie Stargell	.75
(10)	Maury Wills	.40

N.Y. Mets Postcards

A certain sameness of poses, generally belt-to-cap, marks the cards in this color player postcard issue produced by TCMA for team issue. The 3-1/2" x 5-1/2" cards have borderless color photos with a glossy finish and no extraneous graphics. Backs have a large, light blue team logo at left, with player ID at top and a line of 1984 stats at bottom. A TCMA copyright line is vertically at center. The postcard indicia at right includes a card number at the bottom of the stamp box; the number is preceded by an "NYM85-" prefix.

		NM/M
Complete Set (40):		12.50
Common Player:		.50
1	Davey Johnson	.75
2	Vern Hoscheit	.50
3	Bill Robinson	.50
4	Mel Stottlemyre	.75
5	Bobby Valentine	.50
6	Bruce Berenyi	.50
7	Jeff Bettendorf	.50
8	Ron Darling	.50
9	Sid Fernandez	.50
10	Brent Gaff	.50
11	Wes Gardner	.50
12	Dwight Gooden	1.50
13	Tom Gorman	.50
14	Ed Lynch	.50
15	Jesse Orosco	.50
16	Calvin Schiraldi	.50
17	Doug Sisk	.50
18	Gary Carter	2.00
19	John Gibbons	.50
20	Ronn Reynolds	.50
21	Wally Backman	.50
22	Kelvin Chapman	.50
23	Ron Gardenhire	.50
24	Keith Hernandez	1.00
25	Howard Johnson	.75
26	Ray Knight	.75
27	Kevin Mitchell	.50
28	Terry Blocker	.50
29	Rafael Santana	.50
30	Billy Beane	.50
31	John Christensen	.50
32	Len Dykstra	1.00
33	George Foster	1.00
34	Danny Heep	.50
35	Darryl Strawberry	1.00
36	Mookie Wilson	.75
37	Jeff Bittiger	.50
38	Clint Hurdle	.50
39	Laschelle Tarver	.50
40	Roger McDowell	.50

N.Y. Yankees Postcards

In 1985-86, TCMA produced color player postcard sets for the two New York teams. The 1985

Yankees set is 3-1/2" x 5-1/2" with borderless color poses on front. Backs have a light blue Yankees logo at left. Player identification and data is at top-left with 1984 stats at bottom. A TCMA copyright lines is vertically at center. Cards are numbered in the stamp box NYY85-1 through NYY85-40.

		NM/M
Complete Set (40):		12.50
Common Player:		.50
1	Yogi Berra	1.75
2	Mark Connor	.50
3	Stump Merrill	.50
4	Gene Michael	.50
5	Lou Piniella	.75
6	Jeff Torborg	.50
7	Mike Armstrong	.50
8	Rich Bordi	.50
9	Clay Christensen	.50
10	Joe Cowley	.50
11	Jim Deshaies	.50
12	Ron Guidry	.75
13	John Montefusco	.50
14	Dale Murray	.50
15	Phil Niekro	1.00
16	Alfonso Pulido	.50
17	Dennis Rasmussen	.50
18	Dave Righetti	.50
19	Bob Shirley	.50
20	Ed Whitson	.50
21	Scott Bradley	.50
22	Ron Hassey	.50
23	Butch Wynegar	.50
24	Dale Berra	.50
25	Billy Sample	.50
26	Rex Hudler	.50
27	Don Mattingly	3.00
28	Bobby Meacham	.50
29	Mike Pagliarulo	.50
30	Willie Randolph	.75
31	Andre Robertson	.50
32	Henry Cotto	.50
33	Don Baylor	.75
34	Ken Griffey	.50
35	Rickey Henderson	2.00
36	Vic Mata	.50
37	Omar Moreno	.50
38	Dan Pasqua	.50
39	Dave Winfield	2.00
40	Brian Fisher	.50

Photo Classics Postcards

Teammate pairings and other groupings are featured in this collector's issue set of black-and-white postcards. In 3-1/2" x 5-1/2" format, the postcard-style backs identify the players on front.

		NM/M
Complete Set (40):		45.00
Common Card:		1.00
1	Warren Spahn, Johnny Sain	1.50
2	Jackie Robinson	3.00
3	President Eisenhower w/Yankees	1.50
4	Babe Ruth	4.00
5	Joe McCarthy, Lou Gehrig, Joe DiMaggio	2.00
6	Bob Feller	1.50
7	Johnny Lindell, Johnny Murphy	1.00
8	Babe Ruth, Claire Ruth	1.50
9	Babe Ruth, Joe Cook	1.50
10	Bobo Newsom	1.00
11	Johnny Antonelli, Robin Roberts	1.00
12	Joe Adcock, Eddie Mathews	1.50
13	Al Lopez, Mike Garcia, Bob Lemon, Early Wynn	2.00
14	Gil McDougald, Roy Campanella	1.50
15	Ralph Branca, Bobby Thomson	2.00
16	Lou Gehrig	2.50
17	Johnny Mize, Bill Rigney, Mel Ott	1.50

18	Spider Jorgensen, Pee Wee Reese, Eddie Stanky, Jackie Robinson	2.00
19	Tommy Holmes, Earl Torgeson, Jeff Heath, Connie Ryan, Billy Southworth	1.00
20	Ted Williams, Bobby Doerr, Dom DiMaggio, Vern Stephens	1.50
21	Chuck Schilling, Carl Yastrzemski	1.50
22	Roger Maris, Mickey Mantle	3.00
23	Rogers Hornsby, Gil McDougald	1.00
24	Jim Gentile, Gus Triandos	1.00
25	Bobby Avila, Willie Mays	1.50
26	Joe Garagiola, Ralph Kiner	1.00
27	Jim Gentile, Willie Mays	1.50
28	Red Schoendienst, Marty Marion	1.00
29	Charlie Keller	1.00
30	House of David Team	1.00
31	Harvey Kuenn, Al Kaline	1.50
32	Hank Sauer	1.00
33	Enos Slaughter	1.00
34	Stan Musial	2.00
35	Willie Mays	2.00
36	William Bendix, Babe Ruth	1.50
37	Whitey Lockman, Davey Williams, Hank Thompson, Alvin Dark, Don Mueller, Willie Mays, Monte Irvin, Wes Westrum	1.00
38	Pete Runnels, Vic Wertz	1.00
39	Stan Musial	2.00
40	Dom DiMaggio	1.00

Rookies of the Year

ROOKIE OF THE YEAR
THURMAN MUNSON

This polybagged set of 2-1/2" x 3-1/2" cards is formatted on two perforated strips. Fronts have color photos while backs detail the player's ROY season. The header card presents the history of the award. The unnumbered cards are listed here alphabetically.

		NM/M
Complete Set (10):		6.00
Common Player:		.25
(1)	Tommy Agee	.25
(2)	Luis Aparicio	.50
(3)	Frank Howard	.25
(4)	Harvey Kuenn	.25
(5)	Thurman Munson	3.00
(6)	Don Newcombe	.25
(7)	Tony Oliva	.25
(8)	Jackie Robinson	3.00
(9)	Herb Score	.25
(10)	Billy Williams	.50

1947 Play Ball

JACKIE ROBINSON

Between 1983-85, TCMA produced eight sets of collectors' cards resurrecting the Play Ball brand name which had been active in the field from 1939-41. The TCMA sets attempt to replicate the style and substance of the earlier Play Ball cards as if the company had continued production through World War II and the end of

---

the 1940s. The "1947" set features black-and-white photos on front, with green graphics. Backs are printed on white stock in black ink. Size approximates the originals at 2-1/2" x 3-1/4".

		NM/M
Complete Set (45):		30.00
Common Player:		1.00
1	Hal Wagner	1.00
2	Jake Jones	1.00
3	Bobby Doerr	1.00
4	Fred Hutchinson	1.00
5	Bob Swift	1.00
6	Pat Mullin	1.00
7	Joe Page	1.00
8	Allie Reynolds	1.00
9	Billy Johnson	1.00
10	Early Wynn	1.00
11	Eddie Yost	1.00
12	Floyd Baker	1.00
13	Dave Philley	1.00
14	George Dickey	1.00
15	Dale Mitchell	1.00
16	Bob Lemon	1.00
17	Jerry Witte	1.00
18	Paul Lehner	1.00
19	Sam Zoldak	1.00
20	Sam Chapman	1.00
21	Eddie Joost	1.00
22	Ferris Fain	1.00
23	Erv Dusak	1.00
24	Joe Garagiola	1.00
25	Vernal "Nippy" Jones	1.00
26	Bobby Bragan	1.00
27	Jackie Robinson	6.00
28	Spider Jorgensen	1.00
29	Bob Scheffing	1.00
30	Johnny Schmitz	1.00
31	Doyle Lade	1.00
32	Earl Torgeson	1.00
33	Warren Spahn	1.00
34	Walt Lanfranconi	1.00
35	Johnny Wyrostek	1.00
36	Oscar Judd	1.00
37	Ewell Blackwell	1.00
38	Ed Lukon	1.00
39	Benny Zientara	1.00
40	Gene Woodling	1.00
41	Ernie Bonham	1.00
42	Hank Greenberg	3.00
43	Bobby Thomson	1.00
44	Jack "Lucky" Lohrke	1.00
45	Dave Koslo	1.00

1948 Play Ball

GIL HODGES

Between 1983-85, TCMA produced eight sets of collectors' cards resurrecting the Play Ball brand name which had been active in the field from 1939-41. The TCMA sets attempt to replicate the style and substance of the earlier Play Ball cards as if the company had continued production through World War II and the end of the 1940s. The "1948" set features black-and-white photos on front, with red graphics. Backs are printed on white stock in black ink. Size approximates the originals at 2-1/2" x 3-1/4".

		NM/M
Complete Set (45):		50.00
Common Player:		1.00
1	Murry Dickson	1.00
2	Enos Slaughter	1.50
3	Don Lang	1.00
4	Joe Hatten	1.00
5	Gil Hodges	2.00
6	Gene Hermanski	1.00
7	Eddie Waitkus	1.00
8	Jess Dobernic	1.00
9	Andy Pafko	1.00
10	Vern Bickford	1.00
11	Mike McCormick	1.00
12	Harry Walker	1.00
13	Putsy Caballero	1.00
14	Hubert "Dutch" Leonard	1.00
15	Frankie Baumholtz	1.00
16	Ted Kluszewski	1.50
17	Virgil Stallcup	1.00
18	Bob Chesnes	1.00
19	Ted Beard	1.00
20	Wes Westrum	1.00
21	Clint Hartung	1.00
22	Whitey Lockman	1.00
23	Billy Goodman	1.00
24	Jack Kramer	1.00

25	Mel Parnell	1.00
26	George Vico	1.00
27	Walter "Hoot" Evers	1.00
28	Vic Wertz	1.00
29	Yogi Berra	2.00
30	Joe DiMaggio	8.00
31	Tommy Byrne	1.00
32	Al Kozar	1.00
33	Jake Early	1.00
34	Gil Coan	1.00
35	Pat Seerey	1.00
36	Ralph Hodgin	1.00
37	Allie Clark	1.00
38	Gene Bearden	1.00
39	Steve Gromek	1.00
40	Al Zarilla	1.00
41	Fred Sanford	1.00
42	Les Moss	1.00
43	Don White	1.00
44	Carl Scheib	1.00
45	Lou Brissie	1.00

1949 Play Ball

LARRY DOBY

Between 1983-85, TCMA produced eight sets of collectors' cards resurrecting the Play Ball brand name which had been active in the field from 1939-41. The TCMA sets attempt to replicate the style and substance of the earlier Play Ball cards as if the company had continued production through World War II and the end of the 1940s. The "1949" set features black-and-white photos on front, with red graphics. Backs are printed on white stock in black ink. Size approximates the originals at 2-1/2" x 3-1/4".

		NM/M
Complete Set (45):		40.00
Common Player:		1.00
1	Al Brazle	1.00
2	Harry Brecheen	1.00
3	Howie Pollett	1.00
4	Cal Abrams	1.00
5	Ralph Branca	1.00
6	Duke Snider	2.50
7	Charlie Grimm	1.00
8	Clarence Maddern	1.00
9	Hal Jeffcoat	1.00
10	Johnny Antonelli	1.00
11	Alvin Dark	1.00
12	Nelson Potter	1.00
13	Granny Hamner	1.00
14	Willie Jones	1.00
15	Robin Roberts	1.50
16	Lloyd Merriman	1.00
17	Bobby Adams	1.00
18	Herman Wehmeier	1.00
19	Ralph Kiner	1.00
20	Dino Restelli	1.00
21	Larry Jansen	1.00
22	Sheldon Jones	1.00
23	Red Webb	1.00
24	Vern Stephens	1.00
25	Tex Hughson	1.00
26	Ellis Kinder	1.00
27	Neil Berry	1.00
28	Johnny Groth	1.00
29	Art Houtteman	1.00
30	Hank Bauer	1.00
31	Vic Raschi	1.00
32	Bobby Brown	1.00
33	Joe Haynes	1.00
34	Eddie Robinson	1.00
35	Sam Dente	1.00
36	Herb Adams	1.00
37	Don Wheeler	1.00
38	Randy Gumpert	1.00
39	Ray Boone	1.00
40	Larry Doby	1.50
41	Jack Graham	1.00
42	Bob Dillinger	1.00
43	Dick Kokos	1.00
44	Wally Moses	1.00
45	Mike Guerra	1.00

1986 TCMA All Time Teams

Similar to TCMA sets of 1980-83, these sets feature 11 all-time great players and a manager from each team. In standard 2-1/2"x3-1/2" format, most of the cards utilize black-and-white player photos, though some more recent stars are pictured in color. Several decorative

---

borders, varying by team, surround the front photos. On most team sets there is an "All Time" designation at top, with the player name and (usually) position at bottom. Backs are fairly uniform, printed in blue, and offering a few biographical details and career highlights. Besides hobby sales, these old-timers' sets were also sold in several major retails chains, originally priced at about $4.

All Time Angels

		NM/M
Complete Set (12):		4.50
Common Player:		.50
1-ANG	Rod Carew	2.00
2-ANG	Sandy Alomar	.50
3-ANG	Jim Fregosi	.50
4-ANG	Dave Chalk	.50
5-ANG	Leon Wagner	.50
6-ANG	Albie Pearson	.50
7-ANG	Rick Reichardt	.50
8-ANG	Bob Rodgers	.50
9-ANG	Dean Chance	.50
10-ANG	Clyde Wright	.50
11-ANG	Bob Lee	.50
12-ANG	Bill Rigney	.50

All Time Astros

		NM/M
Complete Set (12):		6.00
Common Player:		.50
1-AST	Bob Watson	.50
2-AST	Joe Morgan	1.75
3-AST	Roger Metzger	.50
4-AST	Doug Rader	.50
5-AST	Jimmy Wynn	.70
6-AST	Cesar Cedeno	.70
7-AST	Rusty Staub	.70
8-AST	Johnny Edwards	.50
9-AST	J.R. Richard	.80
10-AST	Dave Roberts	.50
11-AST	Fred Gladding	.50
12-AST	Bill Virdon	.50

All Time Blue Jays

		NM/M
Complete Set (12):		5.00
Common Player:		.50
1-BLU	John Mayberry	.50
2-BLU	Bob Bailor	.50
3-BLU	Luis Gomez	.50
4-BLU	Roy Howell	.50
5-BLU	Otto Velez	.50
6-BLU	Rick Bosetti	.50
7-BLU	Al Woods	.50
8-BLU	Rick Cerone	.50
9-BLU	Dave Lemanczyk	.50
10-BLU	Tom Underwood	.50
11-BLU	Joey McLaughlin	.50
12-BLU	Bobby Cox	.75

All Time Boston/Milwaukee Braves

ALL TIME BRAVES
JOE JACKSON OF

		NM/M
Complete Set (12):		7.50
Common Player:		.50
1B	Joe Adcock	.70
2B	Felix Millan	.50
3B	Rabbit Maranville	.50
4B	Eddie Mathews	2.00
5B	Hank Aaron	6.00
6B	Wally Berger	.50
7B	Tommy Holmes	.50
8B	Del Crandall	.50
9B	Warren Spahn	2.00
10B	Charles "Kid" Nichols	.50
11B	Cecil Upshaw	.50
12B	Fred Haney	.50

All Time Brewers

		NM/M
Complete Set (12):		6.00
Common Player:		.50
1-BRE	George Scott	.75
2-BRE	Pedro Garcia	.50
3-BRE	Tim Johnson	.50
4-BRE	Don Money	.50
5-BRE	Sixto Lezcano	.50
6-BRE	John Briggs	.50
7-BRE	Dave May	.50
8-BRE	Darrell Porter	.50
9-BRE	Jim Colborn	.50
10-BRE	Mike Caldwell	.50

ALL TIME BREWERS
HARVEY KUENN M

11-BRE	Rollie Fingers	1.50
12-BRE	Harvey Kuenn	.50

All Time Expos

ALL TIME EXPOS
JIM FANNING M

		NM/M
Complete Set (12):		5.00
Common Player:		.50
1-EXP	Ron Fairly	.50
2-EXP	Dave Cash	.50
3-EXP	Tim Foley	.50
4-EXP	Bob Bailey	.50
5-EXP	Ken Singleton	.75
6-EXP	Ellis Valentine	.50
7-EXP	Rusty Staub	.75
8-EXP	John Bateman	.50
9-EXP	Steve Rogers	.50
10-EXP	Woodie Fryman	.50
11-EXP	Mike Marshall	.50
12-EXP	Jim Fanning	.50

All Time Indians

ALL TIME INDIANS
DEL CRANDALL C

		NM/M
Complete Set (12):		7.00
Common Player:		.50
1-IND	Hal Trosky	.50
2-IND	Nap Lajoie	.50
3-IND	Lou Boudreau	.50
4-IND	Al Rosen	.50
5-IND	Joe Jackson	6.00
6-IND	Tris Speaker	.75
7-IND	Larry Doby	1.00
8-IND	Jim Hegan	.50
9-IND	Cy Young	.50
10-IND	Sam McDowell	.60
11-IND	Ray Narleski	.50
12-IND	Al Lopez	.50

All Time Mariners

		NM/M
Complete Set (12):		5.00
Common Player:		.50
1-MAR	Pat Putnam	.50
2-MAR	Larry Milbourne	.50
3-MAR	Todd Cruz	.50
4-MAR	Bill Stein	.50
5-MAR	Leon Roberts	.50
6-MAR	Leroy Stanton	.50
7-MAR	Dan Meyer	.50
8-MAR	Bob Stinson	.50
9-MAR	Glenn Abbott	.50
10-MAR	John Montague	.50
11-MAR	Bryan Clark	.50
12-MAR	Rene Lachemann	.50

All Time Mets

		NM/M
Complete Set (12):		7.50
Common Player:		.50
1M	Ed Kranepool	.50

2M	Ron Hunt	.50
3M	Bud Harrelson	.75
4M	Wayne Garrett	.50
5M	Cleon Jones	.75
6M	Tommie Agee	.75
7M	Rusty Staub	1.00
8M	Jerry Grote	.50
9M	Gary Gentry	.50
10M	Jerry Koosman	.75
11M	Tug McGraw	.75
12M	Gil Hodges	2.00

All Time Oakland A's

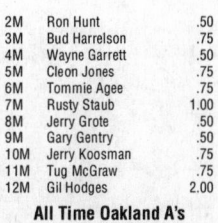

ALL TIME A's
JIM "CATFISH" HUNTER P

		NM/M
Complete Set (12):		7.00
Common Player:		.50
1-ATH	Gene Tenace	.50
2-ATH	Dick Green	.50
3-ATH	Bert Campaneris	.75
4-ATH	Sal Bando	.50
5-ATH	Joe Rudi	.75
6-ATH	Rick Monday	.50
7-ATH	Bill North	.50
8-ATH	Dave Duncan	.50
9-ATH	Jim "Catfish" Hunter	1.50
10-ATH	Ken Holtzman	.50
11-ATH	Rollie Fingers	1.50
12-ATH	Alvin Dark	.50

All Time Orioles

ALL TIME ORIOLES
FRANK ROBINSON OF

		NM/M
Complete Set (12):		14.00
Common Player:		.50
1BA	Hoyt Wilhelm	.50
2BA	Hank Bauer	.50
3BA	Jim Palmer	2.00
4BA	Dave McNally	.50
5BA	Paul Blair	.50
6BA	Gus Triandos	.50
7BA	Frank Robinson	3.00
8BA	Ken Singleton	.50
9BA	Luis Aparicio	2.50
10BA	Brooks Robinson	4.00
11BA	John "Boog" Powell	1.00
12BA	Dave Johnson	.50

All Time Padres

		NM/M
Complete Set (12):		6.00
Common Player:		.50
1-PAD	Nate Colbert	.50
2-PAD	Tito Fuentes	.50
3-PAD	Enzo Hernandez	.50
4-PAD	Dave Roberts	.50
5-PAD	Gene Richards	.50
6-PAD	Ollie Brown	.50
7-PAD	Clarence Gaston	.50
8-PAD	Fred Kendall	.50
9-PAD	Gaylord Perry	1.50
10-PAD	Randy Jones	.50
11-PAD	Rollie Fingers	1.50
12-PAD	Preston Gomez	.50

All Time Phillies

		NM/M
Complete Set (12):		7.00
Common Player:		.35
1PP	Chuck Klein	.35
2PP	Richie Ashburn	3.00
3PP	Del Ennis	.35
4PP	Spud Davis	.35
5PP	Grover Alexander	.35
6PP	Chris Short	.35
7PP	Jim Konstanty	.35
8PP	Danny Ozark	.35
9PP	Larry Bowa	.35

ALL TIME PHILLIES

RICHIE ALLEN 3B

10PP	Richie Allen	1.00
11PP	Don Hurst	.35
12PP	Tony Taylor	.35

All Time Pirates

		NM/M
Complete Set (12):		14.00
Common Player:		.50
1-PIR	Willie Stargell	2.50
2-PIR	Bill Mazeroski	2.50
3-PIR	Honus Wagner	2.50
4-PIR	Pie Traynor	.50
5-PIR	Ralph Kiner	.75
6-PIR	Paul Waner	.50
7-PIR	Roberto Clemente	5.00
8-PIR	Manny Sanguillen	.50
9-PIR	Vic Willis	.50
10-PIR	Wilbur Cooper	.50
11-PIR	Roy Face	.50
12-PIR	Danny Murtaugh	.50

All Time Rangers

		NM/M
Complete Set (12):		6.00
Common Player:		.50
1-RAN	Gaylord Perry	2.00
2-RAN	Jon Matlack	.50
3-RAN	Jim Kern	.50
4-RAN	Billy Hunter	.50
5-RAN	Mike Hargrove	.75
6-RAN	Bump Wills	.50
7-RAN	Toby Harrah	.75
8-RAN	Lenny Randle	.50
9-RAN	Al Oliver	.50
10-RAN	Mickey Rivers	.50
11-RAN	Jeff Burroughs	.50
12-RAN	Dick Billings	.50

All Time Reds

		NM/M
Complete Set (12):		9.00
Common Player:		.50
1CR	Clay Carroll	.50
2CR	Bill McKechnie	.50
3CR	Paul Derringer	.50
4CR	Eppa Rixey	.50
5CR	Frank Robinson	2.50
6CR	Vada Pinson	1.00
7CR	Leo Cardenas	.50
8CR	Heinie Groh	.50
9CR	Ted Kluszewski	2.00
10CR	Joe Morgan	1.50
11CR	Edd Roush	.50
12CR	Johnny Bench	3.00

All Time Red Sox

ALL TIME RED SOX

JIMMIE FOXX 1B

		NM/M
Complete Set (12):		10.00
Common Player:		.50
1BRS	Sammy White	.50
2BRS	Lefty Grove	.50
3BRS	Cy Young	1.00
4BRS	Jimmie Foxx	1.00
5BRS	Bobby Doerr	.50
6BRS	Joe Cronin	.50
7BRS	Frank Malzone	.50
8BRS	Ted Williams	6.00
9BRS	Carl Yastrzemski	4.00
10BRS	Tris Speaker	1.00
11BRS	Dick Radatz	.50
12BRS	Dick Williams	.50

All Time Royals

		NM/M
Complete Set (12):		5.00
Common Player:		.50
1-ROY	John Mayberry	.50
2-ROY	Cookie Rojas	.50

3-ROY	Fred Patek	.50
4-ROY	Paul Schall	.50
5-ROY	Lou Piniella	1.00
6-ROY	Amos Otis	.50
7-ROY	Tom Poquette	.50
8-ROY	Ed Kirkpatrick	.50
9-ROY	Steve Busby	.50
10-ROY	Paul Splittorff	.50
11-ROY	Mark Littell	.50
12-ROY	Jim Frey	.50

All Time Twins

		NM/M
Complete Set (12):		9.00
Common Player:		.50
1-TWI	Harmon Killebrew	2.50
2-TWI	Rod Carew	4.00
3-TWI	Zoilo Versalles	.50
4-TWI	Cesar Tovar	.50
5-TWI	Bob Allison	.50
6-TWI	Larry Hisle	.50
7-TWI	Tony Oliva	.50
8-TWI	Earl Battey	.50
9-TWI	Jim Perry	.50
10-TWI	Jim Kaat	.75
11-TWI	Allan Worthington	.50
12-TWI	Sam Mele	.50

N.Y. Mets Postcards

For a second, and final, year TCMA produced a set of color player postcards for the Mets. The 3-1/2" x 5-1/2" cards have borderless player poses on their glossy fronts; there are no other graphic elements. Backs have a large, light blue team 25th anniversary logo at left, with player ID above and a line of 1985 stats at right. There is a TCMA copyright line vertically at center. Among the postcard indicia at right, a card number pre-fixed with "NYM86-" appears within the stamp box. Cards were sold only as complete sets, for $7.95.

		NM/M
Complete Set (40):		7.50
Common Player:		.50
1	Rick Aguilera	.50
2	Bruce Berenyi	.50
3	Ron Darling	.50
4	Sid Fernandez	.50
5	Dwight Gooden	.75
6	Tom Gorman	.50
7	Ed Lynch	.50
8	Roger McDowell	.50
9	Randy Myers	.60
10	Bob Ojeda	.50
11	Jesse Orosco	.50
12	Doug Sisk	.50
13	Gary Carter	2.00
14	John Gibbons	.50
15	Barry Lyons	.50
16	Wally Backman	.50
17	Ron Gardenhire	.50
18	Keith Hernandez	.75
19	Howard Johnson	.75
20	Ray Knight	.75
21	Kevin Mitchell	.50
22	Rafael Santana	.50
23	Tim Teufel	.50
24	Lenny Dykstra	.75
25	George Foster	.75
26	Danny Heep	.50
27	Mel Stottlemyre	.50
28	Darryl Strawberry	.75
29	Mookie Wilson	.75
30	Randy Nieman	.50
31	Ed Hearn	.50
32	Stan Jefferson	.50
33	Bill Robinson	.50
34	Shawn Abner	.50
35	Terry Blocker	.50
36	Davey Johnson	.50
37	Bud Harrelson	.50
38	Vern Hoscheit	.50
39	Greg Pavlick	.50
40	Tim Corcoran	.50

N.Y. Yankees Postcards

For a second consecutive year, TCMA produced a set of color player postcards for team issue. Similar in

NEW YORK

format to the 1985 cards, the 1986 version is in 3-1/2" x 5-1/2" format. Fronts have borderless color poses with no other graphics and a high-gloss finish. Backs have a Yankee logo in light blue at left and (usually) a line of 1985 stats at lower-left. Player ID is at upper left. A TCMA copy-right line is vertically at center. Among the postcard indicia at right is a card number within the stamp box; cards are skip-numbered with an "NYY86-" prefix; there are two #18. The cards were sold only as complete sets, for $7.95.

		NM/M
Complete Set (40):		9.00
Common Player:		.50
1	Tommy John	.50
2	Brad Arnsburg (Arnsberg)	.50
3	Al Holland (Al)	.50
4	Mike Armstrong	.50
5	Marty Bystrom	.50
6	Doug Drabek	.50
7	Brian Fisher	.50
8	Stump Merrill	.50
9	Ron Guidry	.75
10	Joe Niekro	.50
11	Dennis Rasmussen	.50
12	Dave Righetti	.50
13	Rod Scurry	.50
14	Bob Shirley	.50
15	Bob Tewksbury	.50
16	Ed Whitson	.50
17		
18a	Britt Burns	.50
18b	Gene Michael	.50
19	Butch Wynegar	.50
20	Ron Hassey	.50
21	Dale Berra	.50
22	Jeff Torborg	.50
23	Mike Fischlin	.50
24	Don Mattingly	3.00
25	Bobby Meacham	.50
26	Mike Pagliarulo	.50
27	Willie Randolph	.75
28	Andre Robertson	.50
29	Roy White	.75
30	Henry Cotto	.50
31	Ken Griffey	.50
32	Rickey Henderson	2.00
33	Vic Mata	.50
34	Dan Pasqua	.50
35	Dave Winfield	2.00
36	Gary Roenicke	.50
37	Lou Piniella	.75
38	Joe Altobelli	.50
39	Sammy Ellis	.50
40	Mike Easler	.50

Premium Autographs

This three-card set was made available with the purchase of other items from TCMA. The 2-1/2" x 3-1/2" cards have a glossy front finish and each card is personally autographed by the player depicted. Backs have a message about card collecting from the player and 1985 stats, along with TCMA advertising.

		NM/M
Complete Set (3):		175.00
Common Player:		45.00
(1)	Gary Carter	60.00
(2)	Tony Gwynn	90.00
(3)	Bret Saberhagen	30.00

Simon's Super Stars

The paintings of sports artist Robert Stephen Simon are reproduced in an unusually sized (2-13/16" x 3-1/2") card issue marketed to collectors. Fronts have color pictures with no extraneous graphics, bordered in white. Backs, printed in blue and white, have biographical and career information.

		NM/M
Complete Set (50):		35.00
Common Player:		.50

1	Carl Erskine	.50
2	Babe Ruth, Henry Aaron	1.50
3	Ted Williams	1.50
4	Mickey Mantle	2.00
5	Gil Hodges	.75
6	Roberto Clemente	1.50
7	Mickey Mantle	2.00
8	Walter Johnson	.50
9	N.Y. Yankees Stars	1.50
10	Carl Yastrzemski, Ted Williams	1.50
11	Mickey Mantle	2.00
12	Harmon Killebrew	.50
13	Warren Spahn	.50
14	Ralph Kiner, Babe Ruth	1.00
15	Bob Gibson	.50
16	Pee Wee Reese	.50
17	Billy Martin	.50
18	Joe DiMaggio, Mickey Mantle	2.00
19	Phil Rizzuto	.50
20	Sandy Koufax	1.00
21	Jackie Robinson	1.00
22	Don Drysdale	.50
23	Mickey Mantle	2.00
24	Mickey Mantle	2.00
25	Joe DiMaggio	1.50
26	Robin Roberts	.50
27	Lou Brock	.50
28	Lou Gehrig	1.50
29	Willie Mays	1.00
30	Brooks Robinson	.50
31	Thurman Munson	.50
32	Roger Maris	1.00
33	Jim Palmer	.50
34	Stan Musial	.75
35	Roy Campanella	.50
36	Joe Pepitone	.50
37	Ebbets Field	.50
38	Honus Wagner	.50
39	Yogi Berra	.50
40	Eddie Mathews	.50
41	Carl Yastrzemski	.50
42	Babe Ruth	1.50
43	Babe Ruth	1.50
44	Pete Reiser	.50
45	Don Larsen	.50
46	Ernie Banks	.50
47	Casey Stengel	.50
48	Jackie Robinson	1.00
49	Duke Snider	.50
50	Checklist (Duke Snider)	.50

1987 TCMA All Time N.Y. Yankees

Mickey Mantle

Essentially a reprint of its 1980 team set, this TCMA collectors issue can be distinguished by the presence on back of a Major League Baseball logo. The earlier set has a TCMA date line on back. Fronts of the 2-1/2" x 3-1/2" cards have black-and-white player photos with an ornate blue frame and white border. Backs are in black-and-white and include the All Time team roster.

		NM/M
Complete Set (12):		33.00
Common Player:		.35
1	Lou Gehrig	7.00
2	Tony Lazzeri	.50
3	Red Rolfe	.40
4	Phil Rizzuto	1.25
5	Babe Ruth	7.50
6	Mickey Mantle	9.00
7	Joe DiMaggio	7.00
8	Bill Dickey	.70
9	Red Ruffing	.40

10	Whitey Ford	1.25
11	Johnny Murphy	.40
12	Casey Stengel	.60

Baseball's Greatest Teams

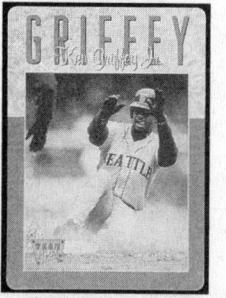

'69 Mets

TUG McGRAW P

Ten of the greatest line-ups in baseball history are featured in this collectors' series. Each of the nine-card team sets features a different front design while backs share a common format offering player biographical details. The earlier teams picture players in black-and-white photos, while the later sets have color photos. Original issue price was about $1 per set, retail.

		NM/M
Complete Set (90):		70.00
Common Team Set (9):		4.50
Common Player:		.25
1907 Chicago Cubs Team Set:		4.50
1	Harry Steinfeldt	.25
2	Three-Finger Brown	.25
3	Ed Reulbach	.25
4	Johnny Kling	.25
5	Orvie Overall	.25
6	Joe Tinker	.75
7	Wildfire Schulte	.25
8	Frank Chance	.75
9	Johnny Evers	.75
1927 N.Y. Yankees Team Set:		20.00
1	Miller Huggins	.25
2	Herb Pennock	.25
3	Tony Lazzeri	.25
4	Waite Hoyt	.25
5	Wilcy Moore	.25
6	Earle Combs	.25
7	Bob Meusel	.25
8	Lou Gehrig	6.00
9	Babe Ruth	9.00
1934 St. Louis Cardinals Team Set:		4.50
1	Dizzy Dean	1.50
2	Daffy Dean	.60
3	Pepper Martin	.50
4	Rip Collins	.25
5	Frank Frisch	.50
6	Leo Durocher	.50
7	Ducky Medwick	.50
8	Tex Carleton	.25
9	Spud Davis	.25
1946 Boston Red Sox Team Set:		7.50
1	Joe Cronin	.25
2	Rudy York	.25
3	Bobby Doerr	.25
4	Johnny Pesky	.25
5	Dom DiMaggio	.60
6	Ted Williams	4.50
7	Boo Ferriss	.25
8	Tex Hughson	.25
9	Mickey Harris	.25
1950 Philadelphia Phillies Team Set:		4.50
1	Eddie Sawyer	.25
2	Curt Simmons	.25
3	Jim Konstanty	.50
4	Eddie Waitkus	.25
5	Granny Hamner	.25
6	Del Ennis	.25
7	Richie Ashburn	.60
8	Dick Sisler	.25
9	Robin Roberts	.60
1955 Brooklyn Dodgers Team Set:		7.50
1	Duke Snider, Walt Alston	.75
2	Roy Campanella	1.50
3	Jackie Robinson	3.00
4	Carl Furillo	.60
5	Gil Hodges	.75
6	Pee Wee Reese, Jim Gilliam	.75
7	Don Newcombe	.50
8	Ed Roebuck, Clem Labine	.50
9	Carl Erskine	.25
1957 Milwaukee Braves Team Set:		7.50
1	Hank Aaron	4.50
2	Eddie Mathews	.60
3	Bob Hazle	.25
4	Johnny Logan	.25
5	Red Schoendienst	.50
6	Wes Covington	.25
7	Lew Burdette	.35
8	Warren Spahn	.60
9	Bob Buhl	.25

1960 Pittsburgh Pirates

Team Set:		7.50
1	Dick Stuart	.25
2	Bill Mazeroski	.75
3	Dick Groat	.35
4	Roberto Clemente	6.00
5	Bob Skinner	.25
6	Smoky Burgess	.35
7	Roy Face	.25
8	Bob Friend	.25
9	Vernon Law	.35
1961 N.Y. Yankees Team Set:		20.00
1	Bill Skowron	.50
2	Mickey Mantle	10.00
3	Bobby Richardson	.50
4	Tony Kubek	.50
5	Elston Howard	.50
6	Yogi Berra	2.25
7	Whitey Ford	2.25
8	Roger Maris	4.50
9	Ralph Houk	.25
1969 N.Y. Mets Team Set:		4.50
1	Ed Kranepool	.35
2	Bud Harrelson	.35
3	Cleon Jones, Tommie Agee, Ron Swoboda	.25
4	Jerry Koosman	.25
5	Gary Gentry	.25
6	Tug McGraw	.25
7	Ron Taylor	.25
8	Jerry Grote	.25
9	Ken Boswell	.25

1996 Team Metal Ken Griffey Jr.

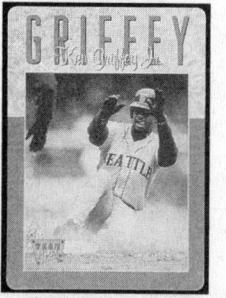

GRIFFEY

SEATTLE

CUI, the parent firm of the company that produces Metallic Images sports and non-sports cards, created this set of metal cards for sale in large retail chains. The four cards come packaged in a lithographed steel box about the size and shape of a Band-aid tin. The 2-5/8" x 3-9/16" cards have a blue and teal background with a color game-action photo at center. Backs have rolled metal edges with a photo at left. A few sentences about the player are printed at right. Logos and copyright data are at bottom. Issue price of the four-card set was just under $10.

		NM/M
Complete Set (4):		7.50
Common Card:		2.00
1	Ken Griffey Jr. (Home run trot.)	2.00
2	Ken Griffey Jr./Sliding	2.00
3	Ken Griffey Jr. (Batting follow-through.)	2.00
4	Ken Griffey Jr. (Batting follow-through.)	2.00

Cal Ripken, Jr.

RIPKEN
Cal Ripken Jr.

CUI, the parent firm of the company that produces Metallic Impressions sports and non-sports cards, created this set of metal cards for sale in large retail chains. The four cards come packaged in a lithographed steel box about the size and shape of a Band-aid tin. The 2-5/8" x 3-9/16" cards have a green and orange background with a color game-action photo at center. Backs have rolled metal edges with a photo at left. A few sentences about the player are printed at right. Logos and copyright data are at bottom. Issue price of the four-card set was just under $10.

		NM/M
Complete Set (4):		7.50
Common Card:		2.00
1	Cal Ripken Jr./Btg (Black jersey.)	2.00
2	Cal Ripken Jr. (Batting follow-through.)	2.00
3	Cal Ripken Jr./Fldng	2.00
4	Cal Ripken Jr./Btg (White jersey.)	2.00

1996 Team Out! Game

This baseball card game is sold as a boxed set containing 37 of the 91 different player cards, plus an assortment of 23 of the 10 cartoon "action" cards used to play the game. Cards are 2-1/4" x 3-1/2" with rounded corners and glossy surfaces. Backs have a close-up photo of a baseball with product and licensor logos and copyright information. Fronts of the player photo cards are bordered in black; the cartoon action cards have red or blue borders. The unnumbered cards are checklisted here in alphabetical order.

		NM/M
Complete Set (101):		40.00
Common Player:		.25
(1)	Roberto Alomar	.35
(2)	Brady Anderson	.25
(3)	Kevin Appier	.25
(4)	Carlos Baerga	.25
(5)	Jeff Bagwell	1.50
(6)	Albert Belle	.25
(7)	Dante Bichette	.25
(8)	Craig Biggio	.25
(9)	Wade Boggs	2.00
(10)	Barry Bonds	3.00
(11)	Kevin Brown	.25
(12)	Jay Buhner	.25
(13)	Ellis Burks	.25
(14)	Ken Caminiti	.25
(15)	Joe Carter	.25
(16)	Vinny Castilla	.25
(17)	Jeff Cirillo	.25
(18)	Will Clark	.25
(19)	Jeff Conine	.25
(20)	Joey Cora	.25
(21)	Marty Cordova	.25
(22)	Eric Davis	.25
(23)	Ray Durham	.25
(24)	Jim Edmonds	.25
(25)	Cecil Fielder	.25
(26)	Travis Fryman	.25
(27)	Jason Giambi	.60
(28)	Bernard Gilkey	.25
(29)	Tom Glavine	.45
(30)	Juan Gonzalez	.75
(31)	Mark Grace	.25
(32)	Ken Griffey Jr.	2.25
(33)	Marquis Grissom	.25
(34)	Mark Grudzielanek	.25
(35)	Ozzie Guillen	.25
(36)	Tony Gwynn	2.00
(37)	Bobby Higginson	.25
(38)	Todd Hundley	.25
(39)	Derek Jeter	3.00
(40)	Lance Johnson	.25
(41)	Randy Johnson	1.50
(42)	Chipper Jones	2.00
(43)	Brian Jordan	.25
(44)	Wally Joyner	.25
(45)	Jason Kendall	.25
(46)	Chuck Knoblauch	.25
(47)	Ray Lankford	.25
(48)	Mike Lansing	.25
(49)	Barry Larkin	.25
(50)	Kenny Lofton	.25
(51)	Javier Lopez	.25
(52)	Mike MacFarlane	.25
(53)	Greg Maddux	2.00
(54)	Al Martin	.25
(55)	Brian McRae	.25

(56)	Mark McGwire	2.50
(57)	Raul Mondesi	.25
(58)	Denny Neagle	.25
(59)	Hideo Nomo	.75
(60)	John Olerud	.25
(61)	Rey Ordonez	.25
(62)	Troy Percival	.25
(63)	Mike Piazza	2.25
(64)	Andy Pettitte	.35
(65)	Manny Ramirez	1.50
(66)	Cal Ripken Jr.	3.00
(67)	Alex Rodriguez	2.50
(68)	Ivan Rodriguez	1.00
(69)	Ryne Sandberg	2.00
(70)	Tim Salmon	.25
(71)	Benito Santiago	.25
(72)	Kevin Seitzer	.25
(73)	Scott Servais	.25
(74)	Gary Sheffield	.60
(75)	Ozzie Smith	2.00
(76)	John Smoltz	.25
(77)	Sammy Sosa	2.00
(78)	Mike Stanley	.25
(79)	Terry Steinbach	.25
(80)	Frank Thomas	1.50
(81)	Steve Trachsel	.25
(82)	Jose Valentin	.25
(83)	Mo Vaughn	.25
(84)	Jose Vizcaino	.25
(85)	Robin Ventura	.25
(86)	Larry Walker	.25
(87)	Walt Weiss	.25
(88)	Bernie Williams	.25
(89)	Matt Williams	.25
(90)	Eric Young	.25
(91)	Todd Zeile	.25
(92)	Double Play (Roberto Alomar)	.25
(93)	Free Agent Acquisition (Barry Bonds (Cartoon))	1.50
(94)	No Trade - Infield (Mark McGwire, Ozzie Smith, Mo Vaughn (Cartoon))	.75
(95)	No Trade - Outfield (Albert Belle, Raul Mondesi (Cartoon))	.75
(96)	Out! (Mike Piazza, Matt Williams (Cartoon))	.75
(97)	Pitcher Bombed (Cartoon)	.25
(98)	Pitcher Stays (Greg Maddux (Cartoon))	1.00
(99)	Safe! (Frank Thomas (Cartoon))	.75
(100)	Trade - Infield (Cal Ripken Jr., Alex Rodriguez (Cartoon))	.75
(101)	Trade - Outfield (Ken Griffey Jr., Sammy Sosa (Cartoon))	.65

1988 Tetley Tea Discs

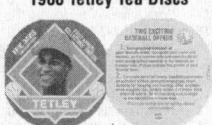

The Tetley iced tea discs are virtually identical in format to the 1988 Baseball Super Stars discs, but are labeled "FIRST ANNUAL COLLECTORS' EDITION," rather than Second and appear to have slight differences in the player pairs which make up each folder. Values for these can be extrapolated by combining the values of individual discs shown under the 1988 Baseball Super Stars listing.

1989 Tetley Tea Discs

The Tetley iced tea discs are virtually identical in format to the 1989 Baseball Super Stars discs, but are labeled "SECOND ANNUAL COLLECTORS' EDITION." The tri-fold panels were distributed in canisters of iced tea mix in the East.

1990 Tetley Tea Discs

The Tetley iced tea discs are virtually identical in format to the 1990 Baseball Super Stars discs, but are labeled "THIRD ANNUAL COLLECTORS' EDITION." The tri-fold panels were distributed in canisters of iced tea mix in the East.

1986 Texas Gold Ice Cream Reds

One of the last regional baseball card sets produced during the 1986 season was a 28-card team

(14) PETE ROSE MANAGER

set sponsored by a Cincinnati-area ice cream company and given to fans attending the September 19 game. Photos on the 2-1/2" x 3-1/2" cards are game-action shots, and include three different cards of playing manager Pete Rose. The set is also notable for the inclusion of first cards of some of the Reds' young prospects.

		NM/M
Complete Set (28):		16.00
Common Player:		.50
6	Bo Diaz	.50
9	Max Venable	.50
11	Kurt Stillwell	.50
12	Nick Esasky	.50
13	Dave Concepcion	.75
14a	Pete Rose (Commemorative)	4.00
14b	Pete Rose (Infield)	6.00
14c	Pete Rose (Manager)	4.00
16	Ron Oester	.50
20	Eddie Milner	.50
21	Sal Butera	.50
24	Tony Perez	1.50
25	Buddy Bell	.75
28	Kal Daniels	.50
29	Tracy Jones	.50
31	John Franco	.50
32	Tom Browning	.50
33	Ron Robinson	.50
34	Bill Gullickson	.50
36	Mario Soto	.50
38	Dave Parker	.75
40	John Denny	.50
44	Eric Davis	1.00
45	Chris Welsh	.50
48	Ted Power	.50
49	Joe Price	.50
---	Reds Coaches (Scott Breeden, Billy Demars, Tommy Helms, Bruce Kimm, Jim Lett, George Scherger)	.50
---	Logo/Coupon Card	.20

1987 Texas Rangers Fire Safety

Co-sponsored by the team, U.S. and Texas Forest Services, the set was given out to fans at special promotions at Arlington Stadium. Cards measure 4-1/4" x 6" and feature color action photos. Backs contain brief player personal information along with a Smokey the Bear wildfire prevention message. Cards of Mike Mason and Tom Paciorek were withdrawn from the sets given out by the Rangers and are quite scarce.

		NM/M
Complete Set (32):		45.00
Common Player:		.30
1	Charlie Hough	.30
2	Greg Harris	.30
3	Jose Guzman	.30
4	Mike Mason	20.00
5	Dale Mohorcic	.30
6	Bobby Witt	.30
7	Mitch Williams	.30
8	Geno Petralli	.30

9	Don Slaught	.30
10	Darrell Porter	.30
11	Steve Buechele	.30
12	Pete O'Brien	.30
13	Scott Fletcher	.30
14	Tom Paciorek	20.00
15	Pete Incaviglia	.30
16	Oddibe McDowell	.30
17	Ruben Sierra	.30
18	Larry Parrish	.30
19	Bobby Valentine	.30
20	Tom House	.30
21	Tom Robson	.30
22	Edwin Correa	.30
23	Mike Stanley	.30
24	Joe Ferguson	.30
25	Art Howe	.30
26	Bob Brower	.30
27	Mike Loynd	.30
28	Curtis Wilkerson	.30
29	Tim Foli	.30
30	Dave Oliver	.30
31	Jerry Browne	.30
32	Jeff Russell	.30

1988 Texas Rangers Fire Safety

This oversized (3-1/2" x 5") set was distributed to Rangers' fans at Smokey Bear Game Day on August 7. Fronts feature full-color action photos framed in an oval blue and red border on a white background. A nameplate above the photo identifies the player and a "Wildfire Prevention" logo is printed beneath the photo. Rangers (left) and Smokey (right) logos fill the upper corners of the card face. The card backs are black-and-white and include player info, U.S. and Texas Forest Service logos, and fire prevention tips.

		NM/M
Complete Set (21):		5.00
Common Player:		.30
1	Tom O'Malley	.30
2	Pete O'Brien	.30
3	Geno Petralli	.30
4	Pete Incaviglia	.30
5	Oddibe McDowell	.30
6	Dale Mohorcic	.30
7	Bobby Witt	.30
8	Bobby Valentine	.30
9	Ruben Sierra	.30
10	Scott Fletcher	.30
11	Mike Stanley	.30
12	Steve Buechele	.30
13	Charlie Hough	.30
14	Larry Parrish	.30
15	Jerry Browne	.30
16	Bob Brower	.30
17	Jeff Russell	.30
18	Edwin Correa	.30
19	Mitch Williams	.30
20	Jose Guzman	.30
21	Curtis Wilkerson	.30

1989 Texas Rangers Fire Safety

Given away at a Rangers home game in 1989, this large-format (4-1/4" x 6") set features player portrait photos within an oval frame on a white border. The team logo is

at upper-left; Smokey the Bear at upper-right. Backs have minimal biographical data and stats and a cartoon fire prevention tip. The unnumbered cards are checklisted here alphabetically.

		NM/M
Complete Set (34):		20.00
Common Player:		.25
(1)	Darrel Akerfelds	.25
(2)	Brad Arnsberg	.25
(3)	Buddy Bell	.25
(4)	Kevin Brown	.25
(5)	Steve Buechele	.25
(6)	Dick Egan	.25
(7)	Cecil Espy	.25
(8)	Scott Fletcher	.25
(9)	Julio Franco	.25
(10)	Cecilio Guante	.25
(11)	Jose Guzman	.25
(12)	Drew Hall	.25
(13)	Toby Harrah	.25
(14)	Charlie Hough	.25
(15)	Tom House	.25
(16)	Pete Incaviglia	.25
(17)	Chad Kreuter	.25
(18)	Jeff Kunkel	.25
(19)	Rick Leach	.25
(20)	Davey Lopes	.25
(21)	Craig McMurtry	.25
(22)	Jamie Moyer	.25
(23)	Dave Oliver	.25
(24)	Rafael Palmeiro	2.00
(25)	Geno Petralli	.25
(26)	Tom Robson	.25
(27)	Kenny Rogers	.25
(28)	Jeff Russell	.25
(29)	Nolan Ryan	15.00
(30)	Ruben Sierra	.25
(31)	Mike Stanley	.25
(32)	Jim Sundberg	.25
(33)	Bobby Valentine	.25
(34)	Bobby Witt	.25

1990 Texas Rangers Fire Safety

This oversized (3-1/2" x 5") set is identical in design to the 1989 issue, but at 3-1/2" x 5", is slightly smaller. Backs have a cartoon fire safety tip and a bit of player personal data.

		NM/M
Complete Set (24):		30.00
Common Player:		.50
(1)	Harold Baines	.50
(2)	Brian Bohannon	.50
(3)	Thad Bosley	.50
(4)	Kevin Brown	.75
(5)	Jack Daugherty	.50
(6)	Cecil Espy	.50
(7)	Julio Franco	.75
(8)	Jeff Huson	.50
(9)	Pete Incaviglia	.50
(10)	Mike Jeffcoat	.50
(11)	Chad Kreuter	.50
(12)	Jeff Kunkel	.50
(13)	Gary Mielke	.50
(14)	Jamie Moyer	.50
(15)	Rafael Palmeiro	3.00
(16)	Gary Pettis	.50
(17)	Kenny Rogers	.50
(18)	Jeff Russell	.50
(19)	John Russell	.50
(20)	Nolan Ryan	25.00
(21)	Ruben Sierra	.50
(22)	Bobby Valentine	.50
(23)	Bobby Witt	.50
(24)	Arlington Stadium	1.00

1983 Thorn Apple Valley Cubs

This set of 27 cards was issued in conjunction with a "Baseball Card Day" promotion at Wrigley Field in 1983. Thorn Apple Valley was the meat company which produced the hot dogs sold at the ballpark. The cards feature borderless color photos with the player's name, uniform number (also the card's number in the checklist) and an abbreviation for their position. Card backs feature advertising statis-

#33 JOE CARTER OF

tics. Of the 27 cards, which measure 2-1/4" x 3-1/2", 25 feature players, one is a team card, and one features the manager and coaches.

		NM/M
Complete Set (27):		25.00
Common Player:		.50
1	Larry Bowa	.50
6	Keith Moreland	.50
7	Jody Davis	.50
10	Leon Durham	.50
11	Ron Cey	.50
16	Steve Lake	.50
20	Thad Bosley	.50
22	Jay Johnstone	.50
22	Bill Buckner	1.00
23	Ryne Sandberg	15.00
24	Jerry Morales	.50
25	Gary Woods	.50
27	Mel Hall	.50
29	Tom Veryzer	.50
30	Chuck Rainey	.50
31	Fergie Jenkins	4.00
32	Craig Lefferts	.50
33	Joe Carter	2.00
34	Steve Trout	.50
36	Mike Proly	.50
39	Bill Campbell	.50
41	Warren Brusstar	.50
44	Dick Ruthven	.50
46	Lee Smith	1.50
48	Dickie Noles	.50
---	Coaching Staff (Ruben Amaro, Billy Connors, Duffy Dyer, Lee Elia, Fred Koenig, John Vukovich)	.50
---	Team Photo	.50

1994 Tombstone Pizza

'94 TOMBSTONE • SUPER-PRO SERIES

Mike Greenwell
BOSTON RED SOX

Score produced a special 30-card set which could be obtained by eating a lot of frozen pizzas (one card per pizza) or by sending in a dollar and five proofs of purchase. Titled "'94 Tombstone Super-Pro Series," the cards are black-bordered and UV coated on front and back. Because the set is licensed only by the Players Union and not by Major League Baseball, the uniform logos on the front action photos and back portraits have been airbrushed away. Cards feature the Tombstone logo on both front and back. Backs have recent and career stats, a facsimile autograph and a card number.

		NM/M
Complete Set (30):		4.00
Common Player:		.25
1	Jeff Bagwell	.50
2	Jay Bell	.25
3	Barry Bonds	1.50
4	Bobby Bonilla	.25
5	Andres Galarraga	.25
6	Mark Grace	.25
7	Marquis Grissom	.25
8	Tony Gwynn	.65
9	Bryan Harvey	.25
10	Gregg Jefferies	.25
11	David Justice	.25
12	John Kruk	.25

13	Barry Larkin	.25
14	Greg Maddux	.65
15	Mike Piazza	.75
16	Jim Abbott	.25
17	Albert Belle	.25
18	Cecil Fielder	.25
19	Juan Gonzalez	.35
20	Mike Greenwell	.25
21	Ken Griffey Jr.	.75
22	Jack McDowell	.25
23	Jeff Montgomery	.25
24	John Olerud	.25
25	Kirby Puckett	.65
26	Cal Ripken, Jr.	1.50
27	Tim Salmon	.25
28	Ruben Sierra	.25
29	Frank Thomas	.50
30	Robin Yount	.50

1995 Tombstone Pizza

TOMBSTONE '95 SUPER-PRO SERIES

Tombstone's second annual baseball card issue was available either singly in frozen pizza packages, or as a 30-card boxed set via a mail-in offer. Cards feature action player photos on front and portrait photos on back; both have had uniform logos airbrushed for lack of a MLB license. There is a graduated red to black border on each side. On front at lower-right are the player and team name and the Tombstone logo. Backs have biographical data, recent stats and career highlights. At bottom is a card number and the Players Association logo.

		NM/M
	Complete Set (30):	4.00
	Common Player:	.25
1	Frank Thomas	.50
2	David Cone	.25
3	Bob Hamelin	.25
4	Jeff Bagwell	.50
5	Greg Maddux	.65
6	Raul Mondesi	.25
7	Chili Davis	.25
8	Cecil Fielder	.25
9	Ken Griffey Jr.	.75
10	Jimmy Key	.25
11	Kenny Lofton	.50
12	Paul Molitor	.50
13	Kirby Puckett	.65
14	Cal Ripken Jr.	1.50
15	Ivan Rodriguez	.40
16	Kevin Seitzer	.25
17	Ruben Sierra	.25
18	Mo Vaughn	.25
19	Moises Alou	.25
20	Barry Bonds	1.50
21	Jeff Conine	.25
22	Lenny Dykstra	.25
23	Andres Galarraga	.25
24	Tony Gwynn	.65
25	Barry Larkin	.25
26	Fred McGriff	.25
27	Orlando Merced	.25
28	Bret Saberhagen	.25
29	Ozzie Smith	.65
30	Sammy Sosa	.65

1981 Topps

This is another 726-card set of 2-1/2" x 3-1/2" cards from Topps. The cards have the usual color photo with all cards from the same team sharing the same color borders. Player names appear under the photo with team and position on a baseball cap at lower-left. The Topps logo returned in a small baseball in the lower-right. Card backs include the usual stats along with a headline and a cartoon if there was room. Specialty cards include previous season record-breakers, highlights of the playoffs and World Series, along with the final appearance of team cards. Eleven cards on each of the six press sheets were double-printed.

		NM/M
	Complete Set (726):	45.00
	Common Player:	.10
	Wax Pack (15):	3.00
	Wax Box (36):	85.00
	Cello Pack (28):	3.00
	Cello Box (24):	75.00
	Rack Pack (48):	6.00
	Rack Box (24):	120.00
	Vending Box (500):	40.00
1	Batting Leaders (George Brett, Bill Buckner)	.75
2	Home Run Leaders (Reggie Jackson, Ben Oglivie, Mike Schmidt)	.75
3	RBI Leaders (Cecil Cooper, Mike Schmidt)	.25
4	Stolen Base Leaders (Rickey Henderson, Ron LeFlore)	.50
5	Victory Leaders (Steve Carlton, Steve Stone)	.15
6	Strikeout Leaders (Len Barker, Steve Carlton)	.15
7	ERA Leaders (Rudy May, Don Sutton)	.10
8	Leading Firemen (Rollie Fingers, Tom Hume, Dan Quisenberry)	.10
9	Pete LaCock/DP	.10
10	Mike Flanagan	.10
11	Jim Wohlford/DP	.10
12	Mark Clear	.10
13	Joe Charboneau RC	.50
14	John Tudor RC	.20
15	Larry Parrish	.10
16	Ron Davis	.10
17	Cliff Johnson	.10
18	Glenn Adams	.10
19	Jim Clancy	.10
20	Jeff Burroughs	.10
21	Ron Oester	.10
22	Danny Darwin	.10
23	Alex Trevino	.10
24	Don Stanhouse	.10
25	Sixto Lezcano	.10
26	U.L. Washington	.10
27	Champ Summers/DP	.10
28	Enrique Romo	.10
29	Gene Tenace	.10
30	Jack Clark	.10
31	Checklist 1-121/DP	.10
32	Ken Oberkfell	.10
33	Rick Honeycutt	.10
34	Aurelio Rodriguez	.10
35	Mitchell Page	.10
36	Ed Farmer	.10
37	Gary Roenicke	.10
38	Win Remmerswaal	.10
39	Tom Veryzer	.10
40	Tug McGraw	.10
41	Rangers Future Stars (Bob Babcock, John Butcher, Jerry Don Gleaton)	.10
42	Jerry White/DP	.10
43	Jose Morales	.10
44	Larry McWilliams	.10
45	Enos Cabell	.10
46	Rick Bosetti	.10
47	Ken Brett	.10
48	Dave Skaggs	.10
49	Bob Shirley	.10
50	Dave Lopes	.10
51	Bill Robinson/DP	.10
52	Hector Cruz	.10
53	Kevin Saucier	.10
54	Ivan DeJesus	.10
55	Mike Norris	.10
56	Buck Martinez	.10
57	Dave Roberts	.10
58	Joel Youngblood	.10
59	Dan Petry	.10
60	Willie Randolph	.10
61	Butch Wynegar	.10
62	Joe Pettini	.10
63	Steve Renko/DP	.10
64	Brian Asselstine	.10
65	Scott McGregor	.10
66	Royals Future Stars (Manny Castillo, Tim Ireland, Mike Jones)	.10
67	Ken Kravec	.10
68	Matt Alexander/DP	.10
69	Ed Halicki	.10
70	Al Oliver/DP	.10
71	Hal Dues	.10
72	Barry Evans/DP	.10
73	Doug Bair	.10
74	Mike Hargrove	.10
75	Reggie Smith	.10
76	Mario Mendoza	.10
77	Mike Barlow	.10
78	Steve Dillard	.10
79	Bruce Robbins	.10
80	Rusty Staub	.15
81	Dave Stapleton	.10
82	Astros Future Stars (Danny Heep, Alan Knicely, Bobby Sprowl/DP)	.10
83	Mike Proly	.10
84	Johnnie LeMaster	.10
85	Mike Caldwell	.10
86	Wayne Gross	.10
87	Rick Camp	.10
88	Joe Lefebvre	.10
89	Darrell Jackson	.10
90	Bake McBride	.10
91	Tim Stoddard/DP	.10
92	Mike Easler	.10
93	Ed Glynn/DP	.10
94	Harry Spilman/DP	.10
95	Jim Sundberg	.10
96	A's Future Stars (Dave Beard, Ernie Camacho RC, Pat Dempsey)	.10
97	Chris Speier	.10
98	Clint Hurdle	.10
99	Eric Wilkins	.10
100	Rod Carew	2.00
101	Benny Ayala	.10
102	Dave Tobik	.10
103	Jerry Martin	.10
104	Terry Forster	.10
105	Jose Cruz	.10
106	Don Money	.10
107	Rich Wortham	.10
108	Bruce Benedict	.10
109	Mike Scott	.10
110	Carl Yastrzemski	2.00
111	Greg Minton	.10
112	White Sox Future Stars (Rusty Kuntz, Fran Mullins, Leo Sutherland)	.10
113	Mike Phillips	.10
114	Tom Underwood	.10
115	Roy Smalley	.10
116	Joe Simpson	.10
117	Pete Falcone	.10
118	Kurt Bevacqua	.10
119	Tippy Martinez	.10
120	Larry Bowa	.10
121	Larry Harlow	.10
122	John Denny	.10
123	Al Cowens	.10
124	Jerry Garvin	.10
125	Andre Dawson	1.50
126	Charlie Leibrandt RC	.40
127	Rudy Law	.10
128	Gary Allenson/DP	.10
129	Art Howe	.10
130	Larry Gura	.10
131	Keith Moreland	.20
132	Tommy Boggs	.10
133	Jeff Cox	.10
134	Steve Mura	.10
135	Gorman Thomas	.10
136	Doug Capilla	.10
137	Hosken Powell	.10
138	Rich Dotson/DP RC	.20
139	Oscar Gamble	.10
140	Bob Forsch	.10
141	Miguel Dilone	.10
142	Jackson Todd	.10
143	Dan Meyer	.10
144	Allen Ripley	.10
145	Mickey Rivers	.10
146	Bobby Castillo	.10
147	Dale Berra	.10
148	Randy Niemann	.10
149	Joe Nolan	.10
150	Mark Fidrych	.15
151	Claudell Washington/DP	.10
152	John Urrea	.10
153	Tom Poquette	.10
154	Rick Langford	.10
155	Chris Chambliss	.10
156	Bob McClure	.10
157	John Wathan	.10
158	Fergie Jenkins	1.00
159	Brian Doyle	.10
160	Garry Maddox	.10
161	Dan Graham	.10
162	Doug Corbett	.10
163	Billy Almon	.10
164	Lamarr Hoyt (LaMarr) RC	.15
165	Tony Scott	.10
166	Floyd Bannister	.10
167	Terry Whitfield	.10
168	Don Robinson/DP	.10
169	John Mayberry	.10
170	Ross Grimsley	.10
171	Gene Richards	.10
172	Gary Woods	.10
173	Bump Wills	.10
174	Doug Rau	.10
175	Dave Collins	.10
176	Mike Krukow	.10
177	Rick Peters	.10
178	Jim Essian/DP	.10
179	Rudy May	.10
180	Pete Rose	5.00
181	Elias Sosa	.10
182	Bob Grich	.10
183	Dick Davis/DP	.10
184	Jim Dwyer	.10
185	Dennis Leonard	.10
186	Wayne Nordhagen	.10
187	Mike Parrott	.10
188	Doug DeCinces	.10
189	Craig Swan	.10
190	Cesar Cedeno	.10
191	Rick Sutcliffe	.10
192	Braves Future Stars (Terry Harper RC, Ed Miller, Rafael Ramirez RC)	.10
193	Pete Vuckovich	.10
194	Rod Scurry RC	.10
195	Rich Murray	.10
196	Duffy Dyer	.10
197	Jim Kern	.10
198	Jerry Dybzinski	.10
199	Chuck Rainey	.10
200	George Foster	.10
201	Johnny Bench (Record Breaker)	.45
202	Steve Carlton (Record Breaker)	.25
203	Bill Gullickson (Record Breaker)	.10
204	Ron LeFlore, Rodney Scott (Record Breaker)	.10
205	Pete Rose (Record Breaker)	1.50
206	Mike Schmidt (Record Breaker)	1.00
207	Ozzie Smith (Record Breaker)	1.00
208	Willie Wilson (Record Breaker)	.10
209	Dickie Thon/DP	.10
210	Jim Palmer	1.50
211	Derrel Thomas	.10
212	Steve Nicosia	.10
213	Al Holland RC	.10
214	Angels Future Stars (Ralph Botting, Jim Dorsey, John Harris)	.10
215	Larry Hisle	.10
216	John Henry Johnson	.10
217	Rich Hebner	.10
218	Paul Splittorff	.10
219	Ken Landreaux	.10
220	Tom Seaver	2.00
221	Bob Davis	.10
222	Jorge Orta	.10
223	Roy Lee Jackson	.10
224	Pat Zachry	.10
225	Ruppert Jones	.10
226	Manny Sanguillen/DP	.10
227	Fred Martinez	.10
228	Tom Paciorek	.10
229	Rollie Fingers	1.00
230	George Hendrick	.10
231	Joe Beckwith	.10
232	Mickey Klutts	.10
233	Skip Lockwood	.10
234	Lou Whitaker	.10
235	Scott Sanderson	.10
236	Mike Ivie	.10
237	Charlie Moore	.10
238	Willie Hernandez	.10
239	Rick Miller/DP	.10
240	Nolan Ryan	5.00
241	Checklist 122-242/DP	.10
242	Chet Lemon	.10
243	Sal Butera	.10
244	Cardinals Future Stars (Tito Landrum RC, Al Olmsted, Andy Rincon)	.10
245	Ed Figueroa	.10
246	Ed Ott/DP	.10
247	Glenn Hubbard/DP	.10
248	Joey McLaughlin	.10
249	Larry Cox	.10
250	Ron Guidry	.15
251	Tom Brookens	.10
252	Victor Cruz	.10
253	Dave Bergman	.10
254	Ozzie Smith	3.00
255	Mark Littell	.10
256	Bombo Rivera	.10
257	Rennie Stennett	.10
258	Joe Price RC	.10
259	Mets Future Stars (Juan Berenguer, Hubie Brooks RC, Mookie Wilson RC)	.75
260	Ron Cey	.10
261	Rickey Henderson	4.50
262	Sammy Stewart	.10
263	Brian Downing	.10
264	Jim Norris	.10
265	John Candelaria	.10
266	Tom Herr	.10
267	Stan Bahnsen	.10
268	Jerry Royster	.10
269	Ken Forsch	.10
270	Greg Luzinski	.10
271	Bill Castro	.10
272	Bruce Kimm	.10
273	Stan Papi	.10
274	Craig Chamberlain	.10
275	Dwight Evans	.10
276	Dan Spillner	.10
277	Alfredo Griffin	.10
278	Rick Sofield	.10
279	Bob Knepper	.10
280	Ken Griffey	.10
281	Fred Stanley	.10
282	Mariners Future Stars (Rick Anderson, Greg Biercevicz, Rodney Craig)	.10
283	Billy Sample	.10
284	Brian Kingman	.10
285	Jerry Turner	.10
286	Dave Frost	.10
287	Lenn Sakata	.10
288	Bob Clark	.10
289	Mickey Hatcher	.10
290	Bob Boone/DP	.10
291	Aurelio Lopez	.10
292	Mike Squires	.10
293	Charlie Lea RC	.15
294	Mike Tyson/DP	.10
295	Hal McRae	.10
296	Bill Nahorodny/DP	.10
297	Bob Bailor	.10
298	Buddy Solomon	.10
299	Elliott Maddox	.10
300	Paul Molitor	2.00
301	Matt Keough	.10
302	Dodgers Future Stars (Jack Perconte RC, Mike Scioscia RC, Fernando Valenzuela RC)	2.00
303	Johnny Oates	.10
304	John Castino	.10
305	Ken Clay	.10
306	Juan Beniquez/DP	.10
307	Gene Garber	.10
308	Rick Manning	.10
309	Luis Salazar RC	.10
310	Vida Blue/DP	.10
311	Freddie Patek	.10
312	Rick Rhoden	.10
313	Luis Pujols	.10
314	Rich Dauer	.10
315	Kirk Gibson RC	5.00
316	Craig Minetto	.10
317	Lonnie Smith	.10
318	Steve Yeager	.10
319	Rowland Office	.10
320	Tom Burgmeier	.10
321	Leon Durham RC	.15
322	Neil Allen	.10
323	Jim Morrison/DP	.10
324	Mike Willis	.10
325	Ray Knight	.10
326	Biff Pocoroba	.10
327	Moose Haas	.10
328	Twins Future Stars (Dave Engle RC, Greg Johnston, Gary Ward)	.15
329	Joaquin Andujar	.10
330	Frank White	.10
331	Dennis Lamp	.10
332	Lee Lacy/DP	.10
333	Sid Monge	.10
334	Dane Iorg	.10
335	Rick Cerone	.10
336	Eddie Whitson	.10
337	Lynn Jones	.10
338	Checklist 243-363	.10
339	John Ellis	.10
340	Bruce Kison	.10
341	Dwayne Murphy	.10
342	Eric Rasmussen/DP	.10
343	Frank Taveras	.10
344	Byron McLaughlin	.10
345	Warren Cromartie	.10
346	Larry Christenson/DP	.10
347	Harold Baines RC	4.00
348	Bob Sykes	.10
349	Glenn Hoffman	.10
350	J.R. Richard	.10
351	Otto Velez	.10
352	Dick Tidrow/DP	.10
353	Terry Kennedy	.10
354	Mario Soto	.10
355	Bob Horner	.10
356	Padres Future Stars (George Stablein, Craig Stimac, Tom Tellmann)	.10
357	Jim Slaton	.10
358	Mark Wagner	.10
359	Tom Hausman	.10
360	Willie Wilson	.10
361	Joe Strain	.10
362	Bo Diaz	.10
363	Geoff Zahn	.10
364	Mike Davis RC	.10
365	Graig Nettles/DP	.15
366	Mike Ramsey	.10
367	Denny Martinez	.10
368	Leon Roberts	.10
369	Frank Tanana	.10
370	Dave Winfield	2.00
371	Charlie Hough	.10
372	Jay Johnstone	.10
373	Pat Underwood	.10
374	Tom Hutton	.10
375	Dave Concepcion	.10
376	Ron Reed	.10
377	Jerry Morales	.10
378	Dave Rader	.10
379	Lary Sorensen	.10
380	Willie Stargell	2.00
381	Cubs Future Stars (Carlos Lezcano, Steve Macko, Randy Martz)	.10
382	Paul Mirabella RC	.10
383	Eric Soderholm/DP	.10
384	Mike Sadek	.10
385	Joe Sambito	.10
386	Dave Edwards	.10
387	Phil Niekro	1.00
388	Andre Thornton	.10
389	Marty Pattin	.10
390	Cesar Geronimo	.10
391	Dave Lemanczyk/DP	.10
392	Lance Parrish	.10
393	Broderick Perkins	.10
394	Woodie Fryman	.10
395	Scot Thompson	.10
396	Bill Campbell	.10
397	Julio Cruz	.10
398	Ross Baumgarten	.10
399	Orioles Future Stars (Mike Boddicker RC, Mark Corey, Floyd Rayford RC)	.20
400	Reggie Jackson	3.00
401	A.L. Championships (Royals Sweep Yankees)	.50
402	N.L. Championships (Phillies Squeak Past Astros)	.25
403	World Series (Phillies Beat Royals In 6)	.25
404	World Series Summary (Phillies Win First World Series)	.25
405	Nino Espinosa	.10
406	Dickie Noles	.10
407	Ernie Whitt	.10
408	Fernando Arroyo	.10
409	Larry Herndon	.10
410	Bert Campaneris	.10
411	Terry Puhl	.10
412	Britt Burns RC	.10
413	Tony Bernazard	.10
414	John Pacella/DP	.10
415	Ben Oglivie	.10
416	Gary Alexander	.10
417	Dan Schatzeder	.10
418	Bobby Brown	.10
419	Tom Hume	.10
420	Keith Hernandez	.10
421	Bob Stanley	.10
422	Dan Ford	.10
423	Shane Rawley	.10
424	Yankees Future Stars (Tim Lollar, Bruce Robinson, Dennis Werth)	.10
425	Al Bumbry	.10
426	Warren Brusstar	.10
427	John D'Acquisto	.10
428	John Stearns	.10
429	Mick Kelleher	.10
430	Jim Bibby	.10
431	Dave Roberts	.10
432	Len Barker	.10
433	Rance Mulliniks	.10
434	Roger Erickson	.10
435	Jim Spencer	.10
436	Gary Lucas	.10
437	Mike Heath/DP	.10
438	John Montefusco	.10
439	Denny Walling	.10
440	Jerry Reuss	.10
441	Ken Reitz	.10
442	Ron Pruitt	.10
443	Jim Beattie/DP	.10
444	Garth Iorg	.10
445	Ellis Valentine	.10
446	Checklist 364-484	.10
447	Junior Kennedy/DP	.10
448	Tim Corcoran	.10
449	Paul Mitchell	.10
450	Dave Kingman/DP	.10
451	Indians Future Stars (Chris Bando, Tom Brennan, Sandy Wihtol)	.10
452	Renie Martin	.10
453	Rob Wilfong/DP	.10
454	Andy Hassler	.10
455	Rick Burleson	.10
456	Jeff Reardon RC	1.50
457	Mike Lum	.10
458	Randy Jones	.10
459	Greg Gross	.10
460	Rich Gossage	.10
461	Dave McKay	.10
462	Jack Brohamer	.10
463	Milt May	.10
464	Adrian Devine	.10
465	Bill Russell	.10
466	Bob Molinaro	.10
467	Dave Stieb	.10
468	Johnny Wockenfuss	.10
469	Jeff Leonard	.10
470	Manny Trillo	.10
471	Mike Vail	.10
472	Dyar Miller/DP	.10
473	Jose Cardenal	.10
474	Mike LaCoss	.10
475	Buddy Bell	.10
476	Jerry Koosman	.10
477	Luis Gomez	.10
478	Juan Eichelberger	.10
479	Expos Future Stars (Bobby Pate RC, Tim Raines RC, Roberto Ramos RC)	3.00
480	Carlton Fisk	2.00
481	Bob Lacey/DP	.10
482	Jim Gantner	.10
483	Mike Griffin	.10
484	Max Venable/DP	.10
485	Garry Templeton	.10
486	Marc Hill	.10
487	Dewey Robinson	.10
488	Damaso Garcia RC	.10
489	John Littlefield (Photo actually Mark Riggins.)	.10
490	Eddie Murray	2.00

491	Gordy Pladson	.10
492	Barry Foote	.10
493	Dan Quisenberry	.10
494	Bob Walk RC	.20
495	Dusty Baker	.15
496	Paul Dade	.10
497	Fred Norman	.10
498	Pat Putnam	.10
499	Frank Pastore	.10
500	Jim Rice	.25
501	Tim Foli/DP	.10
502	Giants Future Stars (Chris Bourjos, Al Hargesheimer, Mike Rowland)	.10
503	Steve McCatty	.10
504	Dale Murphy	.75
505	Jason Thompson	.10
506	Phil Huffman	.10
507	Jamie Quirk	.10
508	Rob Dressler	.10
509	Pete Mackanin	.10
510	Lee Mazzilli	.10
511	Wayne Garland	.10
512	Gary Thomasson	.10
513	Frank LaCorte	.10
514	George Riley	.10
515	Robin Yount	2.00
516	Doug Bird	.10
517	Richie Zisk	.10
518	Grant Jackson	.10
519	John Tamargo/DP	.10
520	Steve Stone	.10
521	Sam Mejias	.10
522	Mike Colbern	.10
523	John Fulgham	.10
524	Willie Aikens	.10
525	Mike Torrez	.10
526	Phillies Future Stars (Marty Bystrom, Jay Loviglio, Jim Wright)	.10
527	Danny Goodwin	.10
528	Gary Matthews	.10
529	Dave LaRoche	.10
530	Steve Garvey	.75
531	John Curtis	.10
532	Bill Stein	.10
533	Jesus Figueroa	.10
534	Dave Smith RC	.10
535	Omar Moreno	.10
536	Bob Owchinko/DP	.10
537	Ron Hodges	.10
538	Tom Griffin	.10
539	Rodney Scott	.10
540	Mike Schmidt/DP	3.00
541	Steve Swisher	.10
542	Larry Bradford/DP	.10
543	Terry Crowley	.10
544	Rich Gale	.10
545	Johnny Grubb	.10
546	Paul Moskau	.10
547	Mario Guerrero	.10
548	Dave Goltz	.10
549	Jerry Remy	.10
550	Tommy John	.20
551	Pirates Future Stars (Vance Law RC, Tony Pena RC, Pascual Perez RC)	.75
552	Steve Trout	.10
553	Tim Blackwell	.10
554	Bert Blyleven	.10
555	Cecil Cooper	.10
556	Jerry Mumphrey	.10
557	Chris Knapp	.10
558	Barry Bonnell	.10
559	Willie Montanez	.10
560	Joe Morgan	2.00
561	Dennis Littlejohn	.10
562	Checklist 485-605	.10
563	Jim Kaat	.15
564	Ron Hassey/DP	.10
565	Burt Hooton	.10
566	Del Unser	.10
567	Mark Bomback	.10
568	Dave Revering	.10
569	Al Williams/DP	.10
570	Ken Singleton	.10
571	Todd Cruz	.10
572	Jack Morris	.10
573	Phil Garner	.10
574	Bill Caudill	.10
575	Tony Perez	1.00
576	Reggie Cleveland	.10
577	Blue Jays Future Stars (Luis Leal, Brian Milner, Ken Schrom RC)	.10
578	Bill Gullickson RC	.20
579	Tim Flannery	.10
580	Don Baylor	.15
581	Roy Howell	.10
582	Gaylord Perry	1.00
583	Larry Milbourne	.10
584	Randy Lerch	.10
585	Amos Otis	.10
586	Silvio Martinez	.10
587	Jeff Newman	.10
588	Gary Lavelle	.10
589	Lamar Johnson	.10
590	Bruce Sutter	1.00
591	John Lowenstein	.10
592	Steve Comer	.10
593	Steve Kemp	.10
594	Preston Hanna/DP	.10
595	Butch Hobson	.10
596	Jerry Augustine	.10
597	Rafael Landestoy	.10
598	George Vukovich/DP	.10

599	Dennis Kinney	.10
600	Johnny Bench	2.00
601	Don Aase	.10
602	Bobby Murcer	.10
603	John Verhoeven	.10
604	Rob Picciolo	.10
605	Don Sutton	1.00
606	Reds Future Stars (Bruce Berenyi, Geoff Combe, Paul Householder/DP)	.10
607	Dave Palmer	.10
608	Greg Pryor	.10
609	Lynn McGlothen	.10
610	Darrell Porter	.10
611	Rick Matula/DP	.10
612	Duane Kuiper	.10
613	Jim Anderson	.10
614	Dave Rozema	.10
615	Rick Dempsey	.10
616	Rick Wise	.10
617	Craig Reynolds	.10
618	John Milner	.10
619	Steve Henderson	.10
620	Dennis Eckersley	1.00
621	Tom Donohue	.10
622	Randy Moffitt	.10
623	Sal Bando	.10
624	Bob Welch	.10
625	Bill Buckner	.10
626	Tigers Future Stars (Dave Steffen, Jerry Ujdur, Roger Weaver)	.10
627	Luis Tiant	.10
628	Vic Correll	.10
629	Tony Armas	.10
630	Steve Carlton	2.00
631	Ron Jackson	.10
632	Alan Bannister	.10
633	Bill Lee	.10
634	Doug Flynn	.10
635	Bobby Bonds	.10
636	Al Hrabosky	.10
637	Jerry Narron	.10
638	Checklist 606	.10
639	Carney Lansford	.10
640	Dave Parker	.10
641	Mark Belanger	.10
642	Vern Ruhle	.10
643	Lloyd Moseby RC	.20
644	Ramon Aviles/DP	.10
645	Rick Reuschel	.10
646	Marvis Foley	.10
647	Dick Drago	.10
648	Darrell Evans	.10
649	Manny Sarmiento	.10
650	Bucky Dent	.10
651	Pedro Guerrero	.10
652	John Montague	.10
653	Bill Fahey	.10
654	Ray Burris	.10
655	Dan Driessen	.10
656	Jon Matlack	.10
657	Mike Cubbage/DP	.10
658	Milt Wilcox	.10
659	Brewers Future Stars (John Flinn, Ed Romero, Ned Yost)	.10
660	Gary Carter	2.00
661	Orioles Team (Earl Weaver)	.25
662	Red Sox Team (Ralph Houk)	.20
663	Angels Team (Jim Fregosi)	.10
664	White Sox Team (Tony LaRussa)	.25
665	Indians Team (Dave Garcia)	.10
666	Tigers Team (Sparky Anderson)	.25
667	Royals Team (Jim Frey)	.10
668	Brewers Team (Bob Rodgers)	.10
669	Twins Team (John Goryl)	.10
670	Yankees Team (Gene Michael)	.15
671	A's Team (Billy Martin)	.25
672	Mariners Team (Maury Wills)	.20
673	Rangers Team (Don Zimmer)	.20
674	Blue Jays Team (Bobby Mattick)	.10
675	Braves Team (Bobby Cox)	.25
676	Cubs Team (Joe Amalfitano)	.10
677	Reds Team (John McNamara)	.10
678	Astros Team (Bill Virdon)	.10
679	Dodgers Team (Tom Lasorda)	.25
680	Expos Team (Dick Williams)	.20
681	Mets Team (Joe Torre)	.25
682	Phillies Team (Dallas Green)	.15
683	Pirates Team (Chuck Tanner)	.10
684	Cardinals Team (Whitey Herzog)	.15
685	Padres Team (Frank Howard)	.20
686	Giants Team (Dave Bristol)	.10
687	Jeff Jones	.10
688	Kiko Garcia	.10

689	Red Sox Future Stars (Bruce Hurst RC, Keith MacWhorter, Reid Nichols RC)	.30
690	Bob Watson	.10
691	Dick Ruthven	.10
692	Lenny Randle	.10
693	Steve Howe RC	.20
694	Bud Harrelson/DP	.10
695	Kent Tekulve	.10
696	Alan Ashby	.10
697	Rick Waits	.10
698	Mike Jorgensen	.10
699	Glenn Abbott	.10
700	George Brett	3.50
701	Joe Rudi	.10
702	George Medich	.10
703	Alvis Woods	.10
704	Bill Travers/DP	.10
705	Ted Simmons	.10
706	Dave Ford	.10
707	Dave Cash	.10
708	Doyle Alexander	.10
709	Alan Trammell/DP	.10
710	Ron LeFlore/DP	.10
711	Joe Ferguson	.10
712	Bill Bonham	.10
713	Bill North	.10
714	Pete Redfern	.10
715	Bill Madlock	.10
716	Glenn Borgmann	.10
717	Jim Barr/DP	.10
718	Larry Biittner	.10
719	Sparky Lyle	.10
720	Fred Lynn	.10
721	Toby Harrah	.10
722	Joe Niekro	.10
723	Bruce Bochte	.10
724	Lou Piniella	.15
725	Steve Rogers	.10
726	Rick Monday	.10

Traded

The 132 cards in this extension set are numbered from 727 to 858, technically making them a high-numbered series of the regular Topps set. The set was not packaged in gum packs, but rather sold in a specially designed red box through baseball card dealers only. The set features not only mid-season trades, but also single-player rookie cards of some of the hottest prospects. The cards measure 2-1/2" x 3-1/2".

	NM/M
Complete Set (132):	15.00
Common Player:	.10

727	Danny Ainge RC	2.00
728	Doyle Alexander	.10
729	Gary Alexander	.10
730	Billy Almon	.10
731	Joaquin Andujar	.10
732	Bob Bailor	.10
733	Juan Beniquez	.10
734	Dave Bergman	.10
735	Tony Bernazard	.10
736	Larry Biittner	.10
737	Doug Bird	.10
738	Bert Blyleven	.25
739	Mark Bomback	.10
740	Bobby Bonds	.15
741	Rick Bosetti	.10
742	Hubie Brooks	.10
743	Rick Burleson	.10
744	Ray Burris	.10
745	Jeff Burroughs	.10
746	Enos Cabell	.10
747	Ken Clay	.10
748	Mark Clear	.10
749	Larry Cox	.10
750	Hector Cruz	.10
751	Victor Cruz	.10
752	Mike Cubbage	.10
753	Dick Davis	.10
754	Brian Doyle	.10
755	Dick Drago	.10
756	Leon Durham	.10
757	Jim Dwyer	.10
758	Dave Edwards	.10
759	Jim Essian	.10
760	Bill Fahey	.10
761	Rollie Fingers	.10
762	Carlton Fisk	2.00
763	Barry Foote	.10
764	Ken Forsch	.10

765	Kiko Garcia	.10
766	Cesar Geronimo	.10
767	Gary Gray	.10
768	Mickey Hatcher	.10
769	Steve Henderson	.10
770	Marc Hill	.10
771	Butch Hobson	.10
772	Rick Honeycutt	.10
773	Roy Howell	.10
774	Mike Ivie	.10
775	Roy Lee Jackson	.10
776	Cliff Johnson	.10
777	Randy Jones	.10
778	Ruppert Jones	.10
779	Mick Kelleher	.10
780	Terry Kennedy	.10
781	Dave Kingman	.10
782	Bob Knepper	.10
783	Ken Kravec	.10
784	Bob Lacey	.10
785	Dennis Lamp	.10
786	Rafael Landestoy	.10
787	Ken Landreaux	.10
788	Carney Lansford	.10
789	Dave LaRoche	.10
790	Joe Lefebvre	.10
791	Ron LeFlore	.10
792	Randy Lerch	.10
793	Sixto Lezcano	.10
794	John Littlefield	.10
795	Mike Lum	.10
796	Greg Luzinski	.10
797	Fred Lynn	.10
798	Jerry Martin	.10
799	Buck Martinez	.10
800	Gary Matthews	.10
801	Mario Mendoza	.10
802	Larry Milbourne	.10
803	Rick Miller	.10
804	John Montefusco	.10
805	Jerry Morales	.10
806	Jose Morales	.10
807	Joe Morgan	2.00
808	Jerry Mumphrey	.10
809	Gene Nelson RC	.10
810	Ed Ott	.10
811	Bob Owchinko	.10
812	Gaylord Perry	1.00
813	Mike Phillips	.10
814	Darrell Porter	.10
815	Mike Proly	.10
816	Tim Raines	3.00
817	Lenny Randle	.10
818	Doug Rau	.10
819	Jeff Reardon	.10
820	Ken Reitz	.10
821	Steve Renko	.10
822	Rick Reuschel	.10
823	Dave Revering	.10
824	Dave Roberts	.10
825	Leon Roberts	.10
826	Joe Rudi	.10
827	Kevin Saucier	.10
828	Tony Scott	.10
829	Bob Shirley	.10
830	Ted Simmons	.10
831	Lary Sorensen	.10
832	Jim Spencer	.10
833	Harry Spilman	.10
834	Fred Stanley	.10
835	Rusty Staub	.25
836	Bill Stein	.10
837	Joe Strain	.10
838	Bruce Sutter	1.00
839	Don Sutton	1.00
840	Steve Swisher	.10
841	Frank Tanana	.10
842	Gene Tenace	.10
843	Jason Thompson	.10
844	Dickie Thon	.10
845	Bill Travers	.10
846	Tom Underwood	.10
847	John Urrea	.10
848	Mike Vail	.10
849	Ellis Valentine	.10
850	Fernando Valenzuela	2.00
851	Pete Vuckovich	.10
852	Mark Wagner	.10
853	Bob Walk	.10
854	Claudell Washington	.10
855	Dave Winfield	4.00
856	Geoff Zahn	.10
857	Richie Zisk	.10
858	Checklist 727-858	.05

Team Card Sheet

Via a special mail-in offer, uncut sheets of team cards from the 1981 Topps issue were made available to collectors.

	NM/M
Team Card Sheet	20.00

Giant Photo Cards

Once again testing the popularity of large-format cards, Topps issued 4-7/8" x 6-7/8" cards in two different sets. The team-set cards feature a large color photo, facsimile autograph and white border on the front. Backs have the player's name, team, position and a checklist at the bottom. The 102 cards were sold in limited areas corresponding to the teams' geographic home. Cards

were sold in one-card wax packs with 36 packs per box. Boxes contained either the cards of a single team, or of two teams from the same city or state. It was also possible to order the whole set by mail. Ten teams are involved in the issue, with the number of players from each team ranging from 6 to 12.

	NM/M
Complete Set (102):	25.00
Common Player:	.25
Angels-Dodgers Wax Box:	6.00
Astros-Rangers Wax Box:	7.50
Cubs-White Sox Wax Box:	6.00
Mets-Yankees Wax Box:	9.00
Phillies Wax Box:	9.00
Reds Wax Box:	7.50
Red Sox Wax Box:	7.50

(1)	Tom Burgmeier	.25
(2)	Dennis Eckersley	1.00
(3)	Dwight Evans	.35
(4)	Carlton Fisk	1.00
(5)	Glenn Hoffman	.25
(6)	Carney Lansford	.25
(7)	Tony Perez	1.00
(8)	Jim Rice	.75
(9)	Bob Stanley	.25
(10)	Dave Stapleton	.25
(11)	Frank Tanana	.25
(12)	Carl Yastrzemski	1.50
(1)	Don Baylor	.35
(2)	Rick Burleson	.25
(3)	Rod Carew	1.00
(4)	Bobby Grich	.35
(5)	Butch Hobson	.25
(6)	Fred Lynn	.25
(1)	Tim Blackwell	.25
(2)	Bill Buckner	.35
(3)	Ivan DeJesus	.25
(4)	Leon Durham	.25
(5)	Dave Kingman	.40
(6)	Mike Krukow	.25
(7)	Ken Reitz	.25
(8)	Rick Reuschel	.25
(9)	Mike Tyson	.25
(1)	Britt Burns	.25
(2)	Rich Dotson	.25
(3)	Ed Farmer	.25
(4)	Lamar Johnson	.25
(5)	Ron LeFlore	.25
(6)	Chet Lemon	.25
(7)	Bob Molinaro	.25
(8)	Jim Morrison	.25
(9)	Wayne Nordhagen	.25
(1)	Johnny Bench	1.00
(2)	Dave Collins	.25
(3)	Dave Concepcion	.25
(4)	Dan Driessen	.25
(5)	George Foster	.35
(6)	Ken Griffey	.35
(7)	Tom Hume	.25
(8)	Ray Knight	.25
(9)	Joe Nolan	.25
(10)	Ron Oester	.25
(11)	Tom Seaver	1.00
(12)	Mario Soto	.25
(1)	Cesar Cedeno	.25
(2)	Jose Cruz	.25
(3)	Art Howe	.25
(4)	Terry Puhl	.25
(5)	Nolan Ryan	3.00
(6)	Don Sutton	1.00
(1)	Dusty Baker	.35
(2)	Ron Cey	.35
(3)	Steve Garvey	.75
(4)	Burt Hooton	.25
(5)	Steve Howe	.25
(6)	Davey Lopes	.25
(7)	Rick Monday	.25
(8)	Jerry Reuss	.25
(9)	Bill Russell	.25
(10)	Reggie Smith	.25
(11)	Bob Welch	.25
(12)	Steve Yeager	.25
(1)	Neil Allen	.25
(2)	Doug Flynn	.25
(3)	Lee Mazzilli	.25
(4)	Rusty Staub	.40
(5)	Alex Tavares	.25
(6)	Alex Trevino	.25
(1)	Rick Cerone	.25
(2)	Bucky Dent	.35
(3)	Rich Gossage	.50
(4)	Ron Guidry	.35
(5)	Reggie Jackson	1.50
(6)	Tommy John	.35
(7)	Ruppert Jones	.25

(8)	Rudy May	.25
(9)	Graig Nettles	.25
(10)	Willie Randolph	.25
(11)	Bob Watson	.25
(12)	Dave Winfield	1.00
(1)	Bob Boone	.35
(2)	Larry Bowa	.25
(3)	Steve Carlton	1.00
(4)	Greg Luzinski	.25
(5)	Garry Maddox	.25
(6)	Bake McBride	.25
(7)	Tug McGraw	.35
(8)	Pete Rose	3.00
(9)	Dick Ruthven	.25
(10)	Mike Schmidt	2.00
(11)	Manny Trillo	.25
(12)	Del Unser	.25
(1)	Buddy Bell	.25
(2)	Jon Matlack	.25
(3)	Al Oliver	.35
(4)	Mickey Rivers	.25
(5)	Jim Sundberg	.25
(6)	Bump Wills	.25

National 5x7 Photos

This set is the other half of Topps' efforts with large cards in 1981. Measuring 4-7/8" x 6-7/8", the National photo issue was limited to 15 cards. They were sold in areas not covered by the team-set issues. The set includes 10 cards which carry the same photos found in the team sets, but with no checklist on the backs. Five cards are unique to the National set: Brett, Cooper, Palmer, Parker and Simmons.

	NM/M
Complete Set (15):	4.00
Common Player:	.15

(1)	Buddy Bell	.15
(2)	Johnny Bench	.50
(3)	George Brett	.75
(4)	Rod Carew	.50
(5)	Cecil Cooper	.15
(6)	Steve Garvey	.35
(7)	Rich Gossage	.15
(8)	Reggie Jackson	.60
(9)	Jim Palmer	.50
(10)	Dave Parker	.15
(11)	Jim Rice	.30
(12)	Pete Rose	1.00
(13)	Mike Schmidt	.75
(14)	Tom Seaver	.50
(15)	Ted Simmons	.15

Mets Magic Memories

Celebrating 20 years of N.Y. Mets baseball, the team issued a set of "Magic Memories" cards. Topps produced 20,000 each of the 6-7/8" x 4-7/8" cards. The cards were individually cello wrapped. Cards #1-2 were distributed at the team's August 27 game; cards #3-4 at the September 22 contest. The first card is a sepia team photo of the 1962 Mets. Card #2-3 are color team photos from 1969 and 1973. The team photo cards have player stats on back. The fourth card depicts four of the Mets managers on front, with biographies on back.

	NM/M
Complete Set (4):	24.00
Common Player:	6.00

1	1962 Mets Team Photo	6.00
2	1969 Mets Team Photo	6.00
3	1973 Mets Team Photo	6.00
4	New York Mets Managers (Casey Stengel, Gil Hodges, Yogi Berra, Joe Torre)	12.00

Scratchoffs

Sold as a separate issue with bubble gum, this 108-card set was issued in three-card panels that measure 3-1/4" x 5-1/4". Each individual card measures 1-13/16" x 3-1/4" and contains a small player photo alongside a series of black dots designed to be scratched off as part of a baseball game. Cards of National League players have a green background, while American League players have a red background. While there are 108 different players in the set, there are 144 possible panel combinations. An intact panel of three cards is valued approximately 20-25 percent more than the sum of the individual cards.

	NM/M
Complete Set (108):	10.00
Common Player:	.15
Wax Pack:	.75
Wax Box (36):	15.00
1 George Brett	1.00
2 Cecil Cooper	.15
3 Reggie Jackson	.50
4 Al Oliver	.15
5 Fred Lynn	.15
6 Tony Armas	.15
7 Ben Oglivie	.15
8 Tony Perez	.25
9 Eddie Murray	.25
10 Robin Yount	.25
11 Steve Kemp	.15
12 Joe Charboneau	.25
13 Jim Rice	.20
14 Lance Parrish	.15
15 John Mayberry	.15
16 Richie Zisk	.15
17 Ken Singleton	.15
18 Rod Carew	.25
19 Rick Manning	.15
20 Willie Wilson	.15
21 Buddy Bell	.15
22 Dave Revering	.15
23 Tom Paciorek	.15
24 Champ Summers	.15
25 Carney Lansford	.15
26 Lamar Johnson	.15
27 Willie Aikens	.15
28 Rick Cerone	.15
29 Al Bumbry	.15
30 Bruce Bochte	.15
31 Mickey Rivers	.15
32 Mike Hargrove	.15
33 John Castino	.15
34 Chet Lemon	.15
35 Paul Molitor	.25
36 Willie Randolph	.15
37 Rick Burleson	.15
38 Alan Trammell	.15
39 Rickey Henderson	.25
40 Dan Meyer	.15
41 Ken Landreaux	.15
42 Damaso Garcia	.15
43 Roy Smalley	.15
44 Otto Velez	.15
45 Sixto Lezcano	.15
46 Toby Harrah	.15
47 Frank White	.15
48 Dave Stapleton	.15
49 Steve Stone	.15
50 Jim Palmer	.25
51 Larry Gura	.15
52 Tommy John	.15
53 Mike Norris	.15
54 Ed Farmer	.15
55 Bill Buckner	.15
56 Steve Garvey	.20
57 Reggie Smith	.15
58 Bake McBride	.15
59 Dave Parker	.15
60 Mike Schmidt	1.00
61 Bob Horner	.15
62 Pete Rose	2.00
63 Ted Simmons	.15
64 Johnny Bench	.25
65 George Foster	.15
66 Gary Carter	.25
67 Keith Hernandez	.15

Stickers

The 262 stickers in this full-color set measure 1-15/16" x 2-9/16" and are numbered on both the front and back. They were produced for Topps by the Panini Co. of Italy. The set includes a series of "All-Star" stickers printed on silver or gold "foil." An album to house the stickers was also available.

	NM/M
Complete Set (262):	9.00
Common Player:	.05
Sticker Album:	2.00
Wax Pack (5):	.40
Wax Box (100):	15.00
1 Steve Stone	.05
2 Tommy John, Mike Norris	.05
3 Rudy May	.05
4 Mike Norris	.05
5 Len Barker	.05
6 Mike Norris	.05
7 Dan Quisenberry	.05
8 Rich Gossage	.05
9 George Brett	.30
10 Cecil Cooper	.05
11 Reggie Jackson, Ben Oglivie	.05
12 Gorman Thomas	.05
13 Cecil Cooper	.05
14 George Brett, Ben Oglivie	.05
15 Rickey Henderson	.25
16 Willie Wilson	.05
17 Bill Buckner	.05
18 Keith Hernandez	.05
19 Mike Schmidt	.30
20 Bob Horner	.05
21 Mike Schmidt	.30
22 George Hendrick	.05
23 Ron LeFlore	.05
24 Omar Moreno	.05
25 Steve Carlton	.20
26 Joe Niekro	.05
27 Don Sutton	.05
28 Steve Carlton	.20
29 Steve Carlton	.20
30 Nolan Ryan	.50
31 Rollie Fingers, Tom Hume	.05
32 Bruce Sutter	.05
33 Ken Singleton	.05
34 Eddie Murray	.25
35 Al Bumbry	.05
36 Rich Dauer	.05
37 Scott McGregor	.05
38 Rick Dempsey	.05

39 Jim Palmer	.25
40 Steve Stone	.05
41 Jim Rice	.05
42 Fred Lynn	.05
43 Carney Lansford	.05
44 Tony Perez	.25
45 Carl Yastrzemski	.25
46 Carlton Fisk	.25
47 Dave Stapleton	.05
48 Dennis Eckersley	.05
49 Rod Carew	.25
50 Brian Downing	.05
51 Don Baylor	.05
52 Rick Burleson	.05
53 Bobby Grich	.05
54 Butch Hobson	.05
55 Andy Hassler	.05
56 Frank Tanana	.05
57 Chet Lemon	.05
58 Lamar Johnson	.05
59 Wayne Nordhagen	.05
60 Jim Morrison	.05
61 Bob Molinaro	.05
62 Rich Dotson	.05
63 Britt Burns	.05
64 Ed Farmer	.05
65 Toby Harrah	.05
66 Joe Charboneau	.25
67 Miguel Dilone	.05
68 Mike Hargrove	.05
69 Rick Manning	.05
70 Andre Thornton	.05
71 Ron Hassey	.05
72 Len Barker	.05
73 Lance Parrish	.05
74 Steve Kemp	.05
75 Alan Trammell	.05
76 Champ Summers	.05
77 Rick Peters	.05
78 Kirk Gibson	.05
79 Johnny Wockenfuss	.05
80 Jack Morris	.05
81 Willie Wilson	.05
82 George Brett	.30
83 Frank White	.05
84 Willie Aikens	.05
85 Clint Hurdle	.05
86 Hal McRae	.05
87 Dennis Leonard	.05
88 Larry Gura	.05
89 American League Pennant Winner (Kansas City Royals Team)	.05
90 American League Pennant Winner (Kansas City Royals Team)	.05
91 Paul Molitor	.25
92 Ben Oglivie	.05
93 Cecil Cooper	.05
94 Ted Simmons	.05
95 Robin Yount	.05
96 Gorman Thomas	.05
97 Mike Caldwell	.05
98 Moose Haas	.05
99 John Castino	.05
100 Roy Smalley	.05
101 Ken Landreaux	.05
102 Butch Wynegar	.05
103 Ron Jackson	.05
104 Jerry Koosman	.05
105 Roger Erickson	.05
106 Doug Corbett	.05
107 Reggie Jackson	.30
108 Willie Randolph	.05
109 Rick Cerone	.05
110 Bucky Dent	.05
111 Dave Winfield	.25
112 Ron Guidry	.10
113 Rich Gossage	.05
114 Tommy John	.10
115 Rickey Henderson	.25
116 Tony Armas	.05
117 Dave Revering	.05
118 Wayne Gross	.05
119 Dwayne Murphy	.05
120 Jeff Newman	.05
121 Rick Langford	.05
122 Mike Norris	.05
123 Bruce Bochte	.05
124 Tom Paciorek	.05
125 Dan Meyer	.05
126 Julio Cruz	.05
127 Richie Zisk	.05
128 Floyd Bannister	.05
129 Shane Rawley	.05
130 Buddy Bell	.05
131 Al Oliver	.05
132 Mickey Rivers	.05
133 Jim Sundberg	.05
134 Bump Wills	.05
135 Jon Matlack	.05
136 Danny Darwin	.05
137 Damaso Garcia	.05
138 Otto Velez	.05
139 John Mayberry	.05
140 Alfredo Griffin	.05
141 Alvis Woods	.05
142 Dave Stieb	.05
143 Jim Clancy	.05
144 Gary Matthews	.05
145 Bob Horner	.05
146 Dale Murphy	.25
147 Chris Chambliss	.05
148 Phil Niekro	.20
149 Glenn Hubbard	.05
150 Rick Camp	.05
151 Dave Kingman	.05
152 Bill Caudill	.05

153 Bill Buckner	.05
154 Barry Foote	.05
155 Mike Tyson	.05
156 Ivan DeJesus	.05
157 Rick Reuschel	.05
158 Ken Reitz	.05
159 George Foster	.05
160 Johnny Bench	.25
161 Dave Concepcion	.05
162 Dave Collins	.05
163 Ken Griffey	.05
164 Dan Driessen	.05
165 Tom Seaver	.25
166 Tom Hume	.05
167 Cesar Cedeno	.05
168 Rafael Landestoy	.05
169 Jose Cruz	.05
170 Art Howe	.05
171 Terry Puhl	.05
172 Joe Sambito	.05
173 Nolan Ryan	.50
174 Joe Niekro	.05
175 Dave Lopes	.05
176 Steve Garvey	.15
177 Ron Cey	.05
178 Reggie Smith	.05
179 Bill Russell	.05
180 Burt Hooton	.05
181 Jerry Reuss	.05
182 Dusty Baker	.05
183 Larry Parrish	.05
184 Gary Carter	.25
185 Rodney Scott	.05
186 Ellis Valentine	.05
187 Andre Dawson	.20
188 Warren Cromartie	.05
189 Chris Speier	.05
190 Steve Rogers	.05
191 Lee Mazzilli	.05
192 Doug Flynn	.05
193 Steve Henderson	.05
194 John Stearns	.05
195 Joel Youngblood	.05
196 Frank Taveras	.05
197 Pat Zachry	.05
198 Neil Allen	.05
199 Mike Schmidt	.30
200 Pete Rose	.50
201 Larry Bowa	.05
202 Bake McBride	.05
203 Bob Boone	.05
204 Garry Maddox	.05
205 Tug McGraw	.05
206 Steve Carlton	.20
207 National League Pennant Winner (Philadelphia Phillies Team)	.05
208 National League Pennant Winner (Philadelphia Phillies Team)	.05
209 Phil Garner	.05
210 Dave Parker	.05
211 Omar Moreno	.05
212 Mike Easler	.05
213 Bill Madlock	.05
214 Ed Ott	.05
215 Willie Stargell	.05
216 Jim Bibby	.05
217 Garry Templeton	.05
218 Sixto Lezcano	.05
219 Keith Hernandez	.05
220 George Hendrick	.05
221 Bruce Sutter	.20
222 Ken Oberkfell	.05
223 Tony Scott	.05
224 Darrell Porter	.05
225 Gene Richards	.05
226 Broderick Perkins	.05
227 Jerry Mumphrey	.05
228 Luis Salazar	.05
229 Jerry Turner	.05
230 Ozzie Smith	.30
231 John Curtis	.05
232 Rick Wise	.05
233 Terry Whitfield	.05
234 Jack Clark	.05
235 Darrell Evans	.05
236 Larry Herndon	.05
237 Milt May	.05
238 Greg Minton	.05
239 Vida Blue	.05
240 Eddie Whitson	.05
241 Cecil Cooper	.05
242 Willie Randolph	.05
243 George Brett	.30
244 Robin Yount	.25
245 Reggie Jackson	.30
246 Al Oliver	.05
247 Willie Wilson	.05
248 Rick Cerone	.05
249 Steve Stone	.05
250 Tommy John	.10
251 Rich Gossage	.05
252 Steve Garvey	.15
253 Phil Garner	.05
254 Mike Schmidt	.30
255 Garry Templeton	.05
256 George Hendrick	.05
257 Dave Parker	.05
258 Cesar Cedeno	.05
259 Gary Carter	.05
260 Jim Bibby	.05
261 Steve Carlton	.20
262 Tug McGraw	.05

Thirst Break Comics

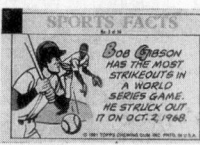

These 2-1/2" x 1-5/8" wax paper comics were the wrapper for Thirst Break Gum, a Topps test issue distributed to parts of Ohio and Pennsylvania. Each orange foil pack contained five comics (labeled as "Sport Facts") which were folded and wrapped around five soft gum pieces. A total of 56 different comics were produced, 20 of which were baseball players. The great majority of comics found today are slightly wrinkled and stained by the gum, but are usually considered to be in Near Mint condition.

	NM/M
Complete (Baseball) Set (20):	
Common Player:	1.00
Wax Pack (1):	4.00
Wax Box (48):	110.00
1 Shortest Game	.50
2 Lefty Gomez	1.00
3 Bob Gibson	1.00
4 Hoyt Wilhelm	1.00
5 Babe Ruth	5.00
6 Toby Harrah	1.00
7 Carl Hubbell	1.00
8 Harvey Haddix	1.00
9 Steve Carlton	1.50
10 Nolan Ryan, Tom Seaver, Steve Carlton	3.50
11 Lou Brock	1.00
12 Mickey Mantle	6.00
13 Tom Seaver	2.50
14 Don Drysdale	1.00
15 Billy Williams	1.00
20 Christy Mathewson	1.00
21 Hank Aaron	4.00
22 Ron Blomberg	1.00
23 Joe Nuxhall	1.00
24 Reggie Jackson	3.00

1982 Topps

At 792 cards, this was the largest issue produced up to that time, eliminating the need for double-printed cards. The 2-1/2" x 3-1/2" cards feature a front color photo with a pair of stripes down the left side. Under the player's photo are found his name, team and position. A facsimile autograph runs across the front of the picture. Specialty cards include great performances of the previous season, All-Stars, statistical leaders and "In Action" cards (indicated by "IA" in listings below). Managers and hitting/pitching leaders have cards, while rookies are shown as "Future Stars" on group cards.

	NM/M
Unopened Fact. Set (792):	180.00
Complete Set (792):	70.00
Common Player:	.10
Wax Pack (15):	5.00
Wax Box (36):	140.00
Cello Pack (28):	6.00
Cello Box (24):	130.00
Rack Pack (51):	8.00
Rack Box (24):	210.00
Vending Box (500):	60.00
1 Steve Carlton (1981 Highlight)	.25
2 Ron Davis (1981 Highlight)	.10
3 Tim Raines (1981 Highlight)	.10
4 Pete Rose (1981 Highlight)	.75
5 Nolan Ryan (1981 Highlight)	3.00

6 Fernando Valenzuela (1981 Highlight)	.10
7 Scott Sanderson	.10
8 Rich Dauer	.10
9 Ron Guidry	.15
10 Ron Guidry/IA	.10
11 Gary Alexander	.10
12 Moose Haas	.10
13 Lamar Johnson	.10
14 Steve Howe	.10
15 Ellis Valentine	.10
16 Steve Comer	.10
17 Darrell Evans	.10
18 Fernando Arroyo	.10
19 Ernie Whitt	.10
20 Garry Maddox	.10
21 Orioles Future Stars (Bob Bonner RC, Cal Ripken, Jr. RC, Jeff Schneider RC)	50.00
22 Jim Beattie	.10
23 Willie Hernandez	.10
24 Dave Frost	.10
25 Jerry Remy	.10
26 Jorge Orta	.10
27 Tom Herr	.10
28 John Urrea	.10
29 Dwayne Murphy	.10
30 Tom Seaver	1.50
31 Tom Seaver/IA	1.00
32 Gene Garber	.10
33 Jerry Morales	.10
34 Joe Sambito	.10
35 Willie Aikens	.10
36 Rangers Batting/Pitching Leaders (George Medich, Al Oliver)	.10
37 Dan Graham	.10
38 Charlie Lea	.10
39 Lou Whitaker	.10
40 Dave Parker	.10
41 Dave Parker/IA	.10
42 Rick Sofield	.10
43 Mike Cubbage	.10
44 Britt Burns	.10
45 Rick Cerone	.10
46 Jerry Augustine	.10
47 Jeff Leonard	.10
48 Bobby Castillo	.10
49 Alvis Woods	.10
50 Buddy Bell	.10
51 Chicago Cubs Future Stars (Jay Howell RC, Carlos Lezcano RC, Ty Waller RC)	.40
52 Larry Andersen	.10
53 Greg Gross	.10
54 Ron Hassey	.10
55 Rick Burleson	.10
56 Mark Littell	.10
57 Craig Reynolds	.10
58 John D'Acquisto	.10
59 Rich Gedman RC	.10
60 Tony Armas	.10
61 Tommy Boggs	.10
62 Mike Tyson	.10
63 Mario Soto	.10
64 Lynn Jones	.10
65 Terry Kennedy	.10
66 Astros Batting/Pitching Leaders (Art Howe, Nolan Ryan)	.75
67 Rich Gale	.10
68 Roy Howell	.10
69 Al Williams	.10
70 Tim Raines	.50
71 Roy Lee Jackson	.10
72 Rick Auerbach	.10
73 Buddy Solomon	.10
74 Bob Clark	.10
75 Tommy John	.20
76 Greg Pryor	.10
77 Miguel Dilone	.10
78 George Medich	.10
79 Bob Bailor	.10
80 Jim Palmer	1.00
81 Jim Palmer/IA	.30
82 Bob Welch	.10
83 Yankees Future Stars (Steve Balboni RC, Andy McGaffigan RC, Andre Robertson RC)	.15
84 Rennie Stennett	.10
85 Lynn McGlothen	.10
86 Dane Iorg	.10
87 Matt Keough	.10
88 Biff Pocoroba	.10
89 Steve Henderson	.10
90 Nolan Ryan	4.00
91 Carney Lansford	.10
92 Brad Havens	.10
93 Larry Hisle	.10
94 Andy Hassler	.10
95 Ozzie Smith	2.00
96 Royals Batting/Pitching Leaders (George Brett, Larry Gura)	.35
97 Paul Moskau	.10
98 Terry Bulling	.10
99 Barry Bonnell	.10
100 Mike Schmidt	3.00
101 Mike Schmidt/IA	1.50
102 Dan Briggs	.10
103 Bob Lacey	.10
104 Rance Mulliniks	.10
105 Kirk Gibson	.10
106 Enrique Romo	.10
107 Wayne Krenchicki	.10

No.	Player	Price
108	Bob Sykes	.10
109	Dave Revering	.10
110	Carlton Fisk	1.50
111	Carlton Fisk/IA	.65
112	Billy Sample	.10
113	Steve McCatty	.10
114	Ken Landreaux	.10
115	Gaylord Perry	1.00
116	Jim Wohlford	.10
117	Rawly Eastwick	.10
118	Expos Future Stars (Terry Francona RC, Brad Mills RC, Bryn Smith RC)	.20
119	Joe Pittman	.10
120	Gary Lucas	.10
121	Ed Lynch	.10
122	Jamie Easterly	.10
123	Danny Goodwin	.10
124	Reid Nichols	.10
125	Danny Ainge	1.00
126	Braves Batting/Pitching Leaders (Rick Mahler, Claudell Washington)	.10
127	Lonnie Smith	.10
128	Frank Pastore	.10
129	Checklist 1-132	.10
130	Julio Cruz	.10
131	Stan Bahnsen	.10
132	Lee May	.10
133	Pat Underwood	.10
134	Dan Ford	.10
135	Andy Rincon	.10
136	Lenn Sakata	.10
137	George Cappuzzello	.10
138	Tony Pena	.10
139	Jeff Jones	.10
140	Ron LeFlore	.10
141	Indians Future Stars (Chris Bando, Tom Brennan, Von Hayes RC)	.20
142	Dave LaRoche	.10
143	Mookie Wilson	.10
144	Fred Breining	.10
145	Bob Horner	.10
146	Mike Griffin	.10
147	Denny Walling	.10
148	Mickey Klutts	.10
149	Pat Putnam	.10
150	Ted Simmons	.10
151	Dave Edwards	.10
152	Ramon Aviles	.10
153	Roger Erickson	.10
154	Dennis Werth	.10
155	Otto Velez	.10
156	A's Batting/Pitching Leaders (Rickey Henderson, Steve McCatty)	.10
157	Steve Crawford	.10
158	Brian Downing	.10
159	Larry Biittner	.10
160	Luis Tiant	.10
161	Batting Leaders (Carney Lansford, Bill Madlock)	.10
162	Home Run Leaders (Tony Armas, Dwight Evans, Bobby Grich, Eddie Murray, Mike Schmidt)	.25
163	RBI Leaders (Eddie Murray, Mike Schmidt)	.40
164	Stolen Base Leaders (Rickey Henderson, Tim Raines)	.35
165	Victory Leaders (Denny Martinez, Steve McCatty, Jack Morris, Tom Seaver, Pete Vuckovich)	.10
166	Strikeout Leaders (Len Barker, Fernando Valenzuela)	.10
167	ERA Leaders (Steve McCatty, Nolan Ryan)	1.50
168	Leading Relievers (Rollie Fingers, Bruce Sutter)	.15
169	Charlie Leibrandt	.10
170	Jim Bibby	.10
171	Giants Future Stars (Bob Brenly RC, Chili Davis RC, Bob Tufts RC)	2.00
172	Bill Gullickson	.10
173	Jamie Quirk	.10
174	Dave Ford	.10
175	Jerry Mumphrey	.10
176	Dewey Robinson	.10
177	John Ellis	.10
178	Dyar Miller	.10
179	Steve Garvey	.75
180	Steve Garvey/IA	.10
181	Silvio Martinez	.10
182	Larry Herndon	.10
183	Mike Proly	.10
184	Mick Kelleher	.10
185	Phil Niekro	1.00
186	Cardinals Batting/Pitching Leaders (Bob Forsch, Keith Hernandez)	.10
187	Jeff Newman	.10
188	Randy Martz	.10
189	Glenn Hoffman	.10
190	J.R. Richard	.05
191	Tim Wallach RC	2.00
192	Broderick Perkins	.10
193	Darrell Jackson	.10
194	Mike Vail	.10
195	Paul Molitor	1.50
196	Willie Upshaw	.10
197	Shane Rawley	.10
198	Chris Speier	.10
199	Don Aase	.10
200	George Brett	3.00
201	George Brett/IA	2.00
202	Rick Manning	.10
203	Blue Jays Future Stars (Jesse Barfield RC, Brian Milner, Boomer Wells)	.50
204	Gary Roenicke	.10
205	Neil Allen	.10
206	Tony Bernazard	.10
207	Rod Scurry	.10
208	Bobby Murcer	.10
209	Gary Lavelle	.10
210	Keith Hernandez	.10
211	Dan Petry	.10
212	Mario Mendoza	.10
213	Dave Stewart RC	4.00
214	Brian Asselstine	.10
215	Mike Krukow	.10
216	White Sox Batting/Pitching Leaders (Dennis Lamp, Chet Lemon)	.10
217	Bo McLaughlin	.10
218	Dave Roberts	.10
219	John Curtis	.10
220	Manny Trillo	.10
221	Jim Slaton	.10
222	Butch Wynegar	.10
223	Lloyd Moseby	.10
224	Bruce Bochte	.10
225	Mike Torrez	.10
226	Checklist 133-264	.10
227	Ray Burris	.10
228	Sam Mejias	.10
229	Geoff Zahn	.10
230	Willie Wilson	.10
231	Phillies Future Stars (Mark Davis RC, Bob Dernier RC, Ozzie Virgil RC)	.20
232	Terry Crowley	.10
233	Duane Kuiper	.10
234	Ron Hodges	.10
235	Mike Easler	.10
236	John Martin	.10
237	Rusty Kuntz	.10
238	Kevin Saucier	.10
239	Jon Matlack	.10
240	Bucky Dent	.10
241	Bucky Dent/IA	.10
242	Milt May	.10
243	Bob Owchinko	.10
244	Rufino Linares	.10
245	Ken Reitz	.10
246	Mets Batting/Pitching Leaders (Hubie Brooks, Mike Scott)	.10
247	Pedro Guerrero	.10
248	Frank LaCorte	.10
249	Tim Flannery	.10
250	Tug McGraw	.10
251	Fred Lynn	.10
252	Fred Lynn/IA	.10
253	Chuck Baker	.10
254	George Bell RC	1.00
255	Tony Perez	1.00
256	Tony Perez/IA	.10
257	Larry Harlow	.10
258	Bo Diaz	.10
259	Rodney Scott	.10
260	Bruce Sutter	1.00
261	Tigers Future Stars (Howard Bailey, Marty Castillo, Dave Rucker)	.10
262	Doug Bair	.10
263	Victor Cruz	.10
264	Dan Quisenberry	.10
265	Al Bumbry	.10
266	Rick Leach	.10
267	Kurt Bevacqua	.10
268	Rickey Keeton	.10
269	Jim Essian	.10
270	Rusty Staub	.15
271	Larry Bradford	.10
272	Bump Wills	.10
273	Doug Bird	.10
274	Bob Ojeda RC	.50
275	Bob Watson	.10
276	Angels Batting/Pitching Leaders (Rod Carew, Ken Forsch)	.25
277	Terry Puhl	.10
278	John Littlefield	.10
279	Bill Russell	.10
280	Ben Oglivie	.10
281	John Verhoeven	.10
282	Ken Macha	.10
283	Brian Allard	.10
284	Bob Grich	.10
285	Sparky Lyle	.10
286	Bill Fahey	.10
287	Alan Bannister	.10
288	Garry Templeton	.10
289	Bob Stanley	.10
290	Ken Singleton	.10
291	Pirates Future Stars (Vance Law, Bob Long, Johnny Ray RC)	.15
292	Dave Palmer	.10
293	Rob Picciolo	.10
294	Mike LaCoss	.10
295	Jason Thompson	.10
296	Bob Walk	.10
297	Clint Hurdle	.10
298	Danny Darwin	.10
299	Steve Trout	.10
300	Reggie Jackson	2.00
301	Reggie Jackson/IA	1.50
302	Doug Flynn	.10
303	Bill Caudill	.10
304	Johnnie LeMaster	.10
305	Don Sutton	1.00
306	Don Sutton/IA	.20
307	Randy Bass	.10
308	Charlie Moore	.10
309	Pete Redfern	.10
310	Mike Hargrove	.10
311	Dodgers Batting/Pitching Leaders (Dusty Baker, Burt Hooton)	.10
312	Lenny Randle	.10
313	John Harris	.10
314	Buck Martinez	.10
315	Burt Hooton	.10
316	Steve Braun	.10
317	Dick Ruthven	.10
318	Mike Heath	.10
319	Dave Rozema	.10
320	Chris Chambliss	.10
321	Chris Chambliss/IA	.10
322	Garry Hancock	.10
323	Bill Lee	.10
324	Steve Dillard	.10
325	Jose Cruz	.10
326	Pete Falcone	.10
327	Joe Nolan	.10
328	Ed Farmer	.10
329	U.L. Washington	.10
330	Rick Wise	.10
331	Benny Ayala	.10
332	Don Robinson	.10
333	Brewers Future Stars (Frank DiPino RC, Marshall Edwards, Chuck Porter)	.10
334	Aurelio Rodriguez	.10
335	Jim Sundberg	.10
336	Mariners Batting/Pitching Leaders (Glenn Abbott, Tom Paciorek)	.10
337	Pete Rose/AS	1.50
338	Dave Lopes/AS	.10
339	Mike Schmidt/AS	1.00
340	Dave Concepcion/AS	.10
341	Andre Dawson/AS	.25
342a	George Foster/AS (No autograph.)	2.00
342b	George Foster/AS (Autograph on front.)	.10
343	Dave Parker/AS	.10
344	Gary Carter/AS	.60
345	Fernando Valenzuela/AS	.10
346	Tom Seaver/AS	.75
347	Bruce Sutter/AS	.50
348	Derrel Thomas	.10
349	George Frazier	.10
350	Thad Bosley	.10
351	Reds Future Stars (Scott Brown, Geoff Combe, Paul Householder)	.10
352	Dick Davis	.10
353	Jack O'Connor	.10
354	Roberto Ramos	.10
355	Dwight Evans	.10
356	Denny Lewallyn	.10
357	Butch Hobson	.10
358	Mike Parrott	.10
359	Jim Dwyer	.10
360	Len Barker	.10
361	Rafael Landestoy	.10
362	Jim Wright	.10
363	Bob Molinaro	.10
364	Doyle Alexander	.10
365	Bill Madlock	.10
366	Padres Batting/Pitching Leaders (Juan Eichelberger, Luis Salazar)	.10
367	Jim Kaat	.10
368	Alex Trevino	.10
369	Champ Summers	.10
370	Mike Norris	.10
371	Jerry Don Gleaton	.10
372	Luis Gomez	.10
373	Gene Nelson RC	.10
374	Tim Blackwell	.10
375	Dusty Baker	.15
376	Chris Welsh	.10
377	Kiko Garcia	.10
378	Mike Caldwell	.10
379	Rob Wilfong	.10
380	Dave Stieb	.10
381	Red Sox Future Stars (Bruce Hurst, Dave Schmidt, Julio Valdez)	.25
382	Joe Simpson	.10
383a	Pascual Perez (No position on front.)	20.00
383b	Pascual Perez ("Pitcher" on front)	.10
384	Keith Moreland	.10
385	Ken Forsch	.10
386	Jerry White	.10
387	Tom Veryzer	.10
388	Joe Rudi	.10
389	George Vukovich	.10
390	Eddie Murray	1.50
391	Dave Tobik	.10
392	Rick Bosetti	.10
393	Al Hrabosky	.10
394	Checklist 265-396	.10
395	Omar Moreno	.10
396	Twins Batting/Pitching Leaders (Fernando Arroyo, John Castino)	.10
397	Ken Brett	.10
398	Mike Squires	.10
399	Pat Zachry	.10
400	Johnny Bench	1.50
401	Johnny Bench/IA	.45
402	Bill Stein	.10
403	Jim Tracy	.10
404	Dickie Thon	.10
405	Rick Reuschel	.10
406	Al Holland	.10
407	Danny Boone	.10
408	Ed Romero	.10
409	Don Cooper	.10
410	Ron Cey	.10
411	Ron Cey/IA	.10
412	Luis Leal	.10
413	Dan Meyer	.10
414	Elias Sosa	.10
415	Don Baylor	.15
416	Marty Bystrom	.10
417	Pat Kelly	.10
418	Rangers Future Stars (John Butcher, Bobby Johnson, Dave Schmidt RC)	.10
419	Steve Stone	.10
420	George Hendrick	.10
421	Mark Clear	.10
422	Cliff Johnson	.10
423	Stan Papi	.10
424	Bruce Benedict	.10
425	John Candelaria	.10
426	Orioles Batting/Pitching Leaders (Eddie Murray, Sammy Stewart)	.25
427	Ron Oester	.10
428	Lamarr Hoyt (LaMarr)	.10
429	John Wathan	.10
430	Vida Blue	.10
431	Vida Blue/IA	.10
432	Mike Scott	.10
433	Alan Ashby	.10
434	Joe Lefebvre	.10
435	Robin Yount	1.50
436	Joe Strain	.10
437	Juan Berenguer	.10
438	Pete Mackanin	.10
439	Dave Righetti RC	.75
440	Jeff Burroughs	.10
441	Astros Future Stars (Danny Heep, Billy Smith, Bobby Sprowl)	.10
442	Bruce Kison	.10
443	Mark Wagner	.10
444	Terry Forster	.10
445	Larry Parrish	.10
446	Wayne Garland	.10
447	Darrell Porter	.10
448	Darrell Porter/IA	.10
449	Luis Aguayo RC	.10
450	Jack Morris	.10
451	Ed Miller	.10
452	Lee Smith RC	4.00
453	Art Howe	.10
454	Rick Langford	.10
455	Tom Burgmeier	.10
456	Cubs Batting & Pitching Ldrs. (Bill Buckner, Randy Martz)	.10
457	Tim Stoddard	.10
458	Willie Montanez	.10
459	Bruce Berenyi	.10
460	Jack Clark	.10
461	Rich Dotson	.10
462	Dave Chalk	.10
463	Jim Kern	.10
464	Juan Bonilla	.10
465	Lee Mazzilli	.10
466	Randy Lerch	.10
467	Mickey Hatcher	.10
468	Floyd Bannister	.10
469	Ed Ott	.10
470	John Mayberry	.10
471	Royals Future Stars (Atlee Hammaker RC, Mike Jones, Darryl Motley)	.15
472	Oscar Gamble	.10
473	Mike Stanton	.10
474	Ken Oberkfell	.10
475	Alan Trammell	.10
476	Brian Kingman	.10
477	Steve Yeager	.10
478	Ray Searage	.10
479	Rowland Office	.10
480	Steve Carlton	1.50
481	Steve Carlton/IA	.40
482	Glenn Hubbard	.10
483	Gary Woods	.10
484	Ivan DeJesus	.10
485	Kent Tekulve	.10
486	Yankees Batting & Pitching Ldrs. (Tommy John, Jerry Mumphrey)	.10
487	Bob McClure	.10
488	Ron Jackson	.10
489	Rick Dempsey	.10
490	Dennis Eckersley	1.00
491	Checklist 397-528	.10
492	Joe Price	.10
493	Chet Lemon	.10
494	Hubie Brooks	.10
495	Dennis Leonard	.10
496	Johnny Grubb	.10
497	Jim Anderson	.10
498	Dave Bergman	.10
499	Paul Mirabella	.10
500	Rod Carew	1.50
501	Rod Carew/IA	.40
502	Braves Future Stars (Steve Bedrosian RC, Brett Butler RC, Larry Owen)	2.00
503	Julio Gonzalez	.10
504	Rick Peters	.10
505	Graig Nettles	.10
506	Graig Nettles/IA	.10
507	Terry Harper	.10
508	Jody Davis RC	.15
509	Harry Spilman	.10
510	Fernando Valenzuela	.10
511	Ruppert Jones	.10
512	Jerry Dybzinski	.10
513	Rick Rhoden	.10
514	Joe Ferguson	.10
515	Larry Bowa	.10
516	Larry Bowa/IA	.10
517	Mark Brouhard	.10
518	Garth Iorg	.10
519	Glenn Adams	.10
520	Mike Flanagan	.10
521	Billy Almon	.10
522	Chuck Rainey	.10
523	Gary Gray	.10
524	Tom Hausman	.10
525	Ray Knight	.10
526	Expos Batting & Pitching Ldrs. (Warren Cromartie, Bill Gullickson)	.10
527	John Henry Johnson	.10
528	Matt Alexander	.10
529	Allen Ripley	.10
530	Dickie Noles	.10
531	A's Future Stars (Rich Bordi, Mark Budaska, Kelvin Moore)	.10
532	Toby Harrah	.10
533	Joaquin Andujar	.10
534	Dave McKay	.10
535	Lance Parrish	.10
536	Rafael Ramirez	.10
537	Doug Capilla	.10
538	Lou Piniella	.10
539	Vern Ruhle	.10
540	Andre Dawson	.75
541	Barry Evans	.10
542	Ned Yost	.10
543	Bill Robinson	.10
544	Larry Christenson	.10
545	Reggie Smith	.10
546	Reggie Smith/IA	.10
547	Rod Carew/AS	.25
548	Willie Randolph/AS	.10
549	George Brett/AS	1.50
550	Bucky Dent/AS	.10
551	Reggie Jackson/AS	.75
552	Ken Singleton/AS	.10
553	Dave Winfield/AS	.60
554	Carlton Fisk/AS	.25
555	Scott McGregor/AS	.10
556	Jack Morris/AS	.10
557	Rich Gossage/AS	.10
558	John Tudor	.10
559	Indians Batting & Pitching Ldrs. (Bert Blyleven, Mike Hargrove)	.10
560	Doug Corbett	.10
561	Cardinals Future Stars (Glenn Brummer, Luis DeLeon, Gene Roof)	.10
562	Mike O'Berry	.10
563	Ross Baumgarten	.10
564	Doug DeCinces	.10
565	Jackson Todd	.10
566	Mike Jorgensen	.10
567	Bob Babcock	.10
568	Joe Pettini	.10
569	Willie Randolph	.10
570	Willie Randolph/IA	.10
571	Glenn Abbott	.10
572	Juan Beniquez	.10
573	Rick Waits	.10
574	Mike Ramsey	.10
575	Al Cowens	.10
576	Giants Batting & Pitching Ldrs. (Vida Blue, Milt May)	.10
577	Rick Monday	.10
578	Shooty Babitt	.10
579	Rick Mahler RC	.10
580	Bobby Bonds	.10
581	Ron Reed	.10
582	Luis Pujols	.10
583	Tippy Martinez	.10
584	Hosken Powell	.10
585	Rollie Fingers	1.00
586	Rollie Fingers/IA	.15
587	Tim Lollar	.10
588	Dale Berra	.10
589	Dave Stapleton	.10
590	Al Oliver	.10
591	Al Oliver/IA	.10
592	Craig Swan	.10
593	Billy Smith	.10
594	Renie Martin	.10
595	Dave Collins	.10
596	Damaso Garcia	.10
597	Wayne Nordhagen	.10
598	Bob Galasso	.10
599	White Sox Future Stars (Jay Loviglio, Reggie Patterson, Leo Sutherland)	.10
600	Dave Winfield	1.50
601	Sid Monge	.10
602	Freddie Patek	.10
603	Rich Hebner	.10
604	Orlando Sanchez	.10
605	Steve Rogers	.10
606	Blue Jays Batting & Pitching Ldrs. (John Mayberry, Dave Stieb)	.10
607	Leon Durham	.10
608	Jerry Royster	.10
609	Rick Sutcliffe	.10
610	Rickey Henderson	1.50
611	Joe Niekro	.10
612	Gary Ward	.10
613	Jim Gantner	.10
614	Juan Eichelberger	.10
615	Bob Boone	.10
616	Bob Boone/IA	.10
617	Scott McGregor	.10
618	Tim Foli	.10
619	Bill Campbell	.10
620	Ken Griffey	.10
621	Ken Griffey/IA	.10
622	Dennis Lamp	.10
623	Mets Future Stars (Ron Gardenhire, Terry Leach RC, Tim Leary RC)	.20
624	Fergie Jenkins	1.00
625	Hal McRae	.10
626	Randy Jones	.10
627	Enos Cabell	.10
628	Bill Travers	.10
629	Johnny Wockenfuss	.10
630	Joe Charboneau	.10
631	Gene Tenace	.10
632	Bryan Clark	.10
633	Mitchell Page	.10
634	Checklist 529-660	.10
635	Ron Davis	.10
636	Phillies Batting & Pitching Ldrs. (Steve Carlton, Pete Rose)	.50
637	Rick Camp	.10
638	John Milner	.10
639	Ken Kravec	.10
640	Cesar Cedeno	.10
641	Steve Mura	.10
642	Mike Scioscia	.10
643	Pete Vuckovich	.10
644	John Castino	.10
645	Frank White	.10
646	Frank White/IA	.10
647	Warren Brusstar	.10
648	Jose Morales	.10
649	Ken Clay	.10
650	Carl Yastrzemski	1.50
651	Carl Yastrzemski/IA	.65
652	Steve Nicosia	.10
653	Angels Future Stars (Tom Brunansky RC, Luis Sanchez RC, Daryl Sconiers RC)	.40
654	Jim Morrison	.10
655	Joel Youngblood	.10
656	Eddie Whitson	.10
657	Tom Poquette	.10
658	Tito Landrum	.10
659	Fred Martinez	.10
660	Dave Concepcion	.10
661	Dave Concepcion/IA	.10
662	Luis Salazar	.10
663	Hector Cruz	.10
664	Dan Spillner	.10
665	Jim Clancy	.10
666	Tigers Batting & Pitching Ldrs. (Steve Kemp, Dan Petry)	.10
667	Jeff Reardon	.15
668	Dale Murphy	.75
669	Larry Milbourne	.10
670	Steve Kemp	.10
671	Mike Davis	.10
672	Bob Knepper	.10
673	Keith Drumright	.10
674	Dave Goltz	.10
675	Cecil Cooper	.10
676	Sal Butera	.10
677	Alfredo Griffin	.10
678	Tom Paciorek	.10
679	Sammy Stewart	.10
680	Gary Matthews	.10
681	Dodgers Future Stars (Mike Marshall RC, Ron Roenicke RC, Steve Sax RC)	.75
682	Jesse Jefferson	.10
683	Phil Garner	.10
684	Harold Baines	.05
685	Bert Blyleven	.10
686	Gary Allenson	.10
687	Greg Minton	.10
688	Leon Roberts	.10
689	Lary Sorensen	.10
690	Dave Kingman	.10
691	Dan Schatzeder	.10
692	Wayne Gross	.10
693	Cesar Geronimo	.10
694	Dave Wehrmeister	.10
695	Warren Cromartie	.10
696	Pirates Batting & Pitching Ldrs. (Bill Madlock, Buddy Solomon)	.10
697	John Montefusco	.10
698	Tony Scott	.10
699	Dick Tidrow	.10
700	George Foster	.10

Regular set (continued)

No.	Player	Price
701	George Foster/IA	.10
702	Steve Renko	.10
703	Brewers Batting & Pitching Ldrs. (Cecil Cooper, Pete Vuckovich)	.10
704	Mickey Rivers	.10
705	Mickey Rivers/IA	.10
706	Barry Foote	.10
707	Mark Bomback	.10
708	Gene Richards	.10
709	Don Money	.10
710	Jerry Reuss	.10
711	Mariners Future Stars (Dave Edler RC, Dave Henderson RC, Reggie Walton RC)	.25
712	Denny Martinez	.10
713	Del Unser	.10
714	Jerry Koosman	.10
715	Willie Stargell	1.50
716	Willie Stargell/IA	.30
717	Rick Miller	.10
718	Charlie Hough	.10
719	Jerry Narron	.10
720	Greg Luzinski	.10
721	Greg Luzinski/IA	.10
722	Jerry Martin	.10
723	Junior Kennedy	.10
724	Dave Rosello	.10
725	Amos Otis	.10
726	Amos Otis/IA	.10
727	Sixto Lezcano	.10
728	Aurelio Lopez	.10
729	Jim Spencer	.10
730	Gary Carter	1.50
731	Padres Future Stars (Mike Armstrong, Doug Gwosdz, Fred Kuhaulua)	.10
732	Mike Lum	.10
733	Larry McWilliams	.10
734	Mike Ivie	.10
735	Rudy May	.10
736	Jerry Turner	.10
737	Reggie Cleveland	.10
738	Dave Engle	.10
739	Joey McLaughlin	.10
740	Dave Lopes	.10
741	Dave Lopes/IA	.10
742	Dick Drago	.10
743	John Stearns	.10
744	Mike Witt RC	.25
745	Bake McBride	.10
746	Andre Thornton	.10
747	John Lowenstein	.10
748	Marc Hill	.10
749	Bob Shirley	.10
750	Jim Rice	.20
751	Rick Honeycutt	.10
752	Lee Lacy	.10
753	Tom Brookens	.10
754	Joe Morgan	1.50
755	Joe Morgan/IA	.25
756	Reds Batting & Pitching Ldrs. (Ken Griffey, Tom Seaver)	.25
757	Tom Underwood	.10
758	Claudell Washington	.10
759	Paul Splittorff	.10
760	Bill Buckner	.10
761	Dave Smith	.10
762	Mike Phillips	.10
763	Tom Hume	.10
764	Steve Swisher	.10
765	Gorman Thomas	.10
766	Twins Future Stars (Lenny Faedo RC, Kent Hrbek RC, Tim Laudner RC)	2.00
767	Roy Smalley	.10
768	Jerry Garvin	.10
769	Richie Zisk	.10
770	Rich Gossage	.10
771	Rich Gossage/IA	.10
772	Bert Campaneris	.10
773	John Denny	.10
774	Jay Johnstone	.10
775	Bob Forsch	.10
776	Mark Belanger	.10
777	Tom Griffin	.10
778	Kevin Hickey	.10
779	Grant Jackson	.10
780	Pete Rose	3.50
781	Pete Rose/IA	2.00
782	Frank Taveras	.10
783	Greg Harris RC	.10
784	Milt Wilcox	.10
785	Dan Driessen	.10
786	Red Sox Batting & Pitching Ldrs. (Carney Lansford, Mike Torrez)	.10
787	Fred Stanley	.10
788	Woodie Fryman	.10
789	Checklist 661-792	.10
790	Larry Gura	.10
791	Bobby Brown	.10
792	Frank Tanana	.10

"Blackless"

Whether through faulty pre-production work or the simple fact that the black ink may have run dry during printing, exactly half of the 1982 Topps cards can be found in a "blackless" version. All cards on the set's A, B and C press sheets can be found blackless. On regular player's

cards the lack of black printing is most obvious in the absence of the facsimile autograph on front. The thin black pinstripe around the player photo is also missing on those cards. On cards in which the position was supposed to be printed in black, it will be missing on these variations. All-Star cards affected by this error will be missing the player's name. It is estimated fewer than 100 of each "blackless" card were released. Originally cards from the A and B sheets were found in metro New York, while the C cards turned up most often in the Midwest. Cards from the C sheet are much scarcer than those from the A and B sheets, although limited collector demand for full sets has kept prices in relative parity.

NM/M

Complete Set (396): 5,500
Common Player: 12.50

No.	Player	Price
8	Rich Dauer	12.50
9	Ron Guidry	20.00
10	Ron Guidry/IA	12.50
11	Gary Alexander	12.50
12	Moose Haas	12.50
13	Lamar Johnson	12.50
14	Steve Howe	12.50
17	Darrell Evans	12.50
19	Fernando Arroyo	12.50
20	Garry Maddox	12.50
26	Dave Frost	12.50
28	Jorge Orta	12.50
28	John Urrea	12.50
35	Willie Aikens	12.50
37	Dan Graham	12.50
38	Charlie Lea	12.50
39	Lou Whitaker	12.50
40	Dave Parker	12.50
42	Rick Sofield	12.50
48	Bobby Castillo	12.50
49	Alvis Woods	12.50
51	Buddy Bell	12.50
52	Larry Andersen	12.50
54	Ron Hassey	12.50
55	Rick Burleson	12.50
60	Tony Armas	12.50
64	Lynn Jones	12.50
65	Terry Kennedy	12.50
67	Rich Gale	12.50
68	Roy Howell	12.50
70	Tim Raines	12.50
71	Roy Lee Jackson	12.50
72	Rick Auerbach	12.50
73	Buddy Solomon	12.50
74	Bob Clark	12.50
77	Miguel Dilone	12.50
78	George Medich	12.50
80	Jim Palmer	40.00
81	Jim Palmer/IA	15.00
84	Rennie Stennett	12.50
87	Matt Keough	12.50
88	Biff Pocoroba	12.50
89	Steve Henderson	12.50
90	Nolan Ryan	425.00
91	Carney Lansford	12.50
92	Brad Havens	12.50
94	Andy Hassler	12.50
95	Ozzie Smith	60.00
98	Terry Bulling	12.50
99	Barry Bonnell	12.50
100	Mike Schmidt	185.00
101	Mike Schmidt/IA	130.00
105	Kirk Gibson	12.50
107	Wayne Krenchicki	12.50
109	Dave Revering	12.50
110	Carlton Fisk	45.00
112	Billy Sample	12.50
113	Steve McCatty	12.50
114	Ken Landreaux	12.50
115	Gaylord Perry	35.00
116	Jim Wohlford	12.50
117	Rawly Eastwick	12.50
119	Joe Pittman	12.50
120	Gary Lucas	12.50
122	Jamie Easterly	12.50
123	Danny Goodwin	12.50
125	Danny Ainge	22.50
127	Lonnie Smith	12.50
128	Frank Pastore	12.50
130	Julio Cruz	12.50
131	Stan Bahnsen	12.50
132	Lee May	12.50
134	Dan Ford	12.50
135	Andy Rincon	12.50
136	Lenn Sakata	12.50
137	George Cappuzzello	12.50
138	Tony Pena	12.50
140	Ron LeFlore	12.50
143	Mookie Wilson	12.50
147	Denny Walling	12.50
150	Ted Simmons	12.50
155	Otto Velez	12.50
157	Steve Crawford	12.50
158	Brian Downing	12.50
159	Larry Biittner	12.50
160	Luis Tiant	12.50
170	Jim Bibby	12.50
172	Bill Gullickson	12.50
173	Jamie Quirk	12.50
174	Dave Ford	12.50
175	Jerry Mumphrey	12.50
177	John Ellis	12.50
178	Dyar Miller	12.50
179	Steve Garvey	30.00
181	Silvio Martinez	12.50
183	Mike Proly	12.50
185	Phil Niekro	35.00
189	Glenn Hoffman	12.50
190	J.R. Richard	12.50
192	Broderick Perkins	12.50
198	Chris Speier	12.50
200	George Brett	150.00
201	George Brett/IA	55.00
204	Gary Roenicke	12.50
209	Gary Lavelle	12.50
210	Keith Hernandez	12.50
211	Dan Petry	12.50
212	Mario Mendoza	12.50
215	Mike Krukow	12.50
220	Manny Trillo	12.50
221	Jim Slaton	12.50
222	Butch Wynegar	12.50
223	Lloyd Moseby	12.50
224	Bruce Bochte	12.50
225	Mike Torrez	12.50
228	Sam Mejias	12.50
230	Willie Wilson	12.50
232	Terry Crowley	12.50
233	Duane Kuiper	12.50
234	Ron Hodges	12.50
235	Mike Easler	12.50
237	Rusty Kuntz	12.50
238	Kevin Saucier	12.50
239	Jon Matlack	12.50
240	Bucky Dent	12.50
241	Bucky Dent/IA	12.50
245	Ken Reitz	12.50
249	Pedro Guerrero	12.50
251	Fred Lynn	12.50
255	Tony Perez	35.00
256	Tony Perez/IA	12.50
257	Larry Harlow	12.50
258	Bo Diaz	12.50
259	Rodney Scott	12.50
260	Bruce Sutter	35.00
262	Doug Bair	12.50
263	Dan Quisenberry	12.50
265	Al Bumbry	12.50
269	Kurt Bevacqua	12.50
270	Rusty Staub	15.00
272	Bump Wills	12.50
275	Bob Watson	12.50
278	John Littlefield	12.50
280	Ben Oglivie	12.50
281	John Verhoeven	12.50
282	Ken Macha	12.50
283	Brian Allard	12.50
285	Sparky Lyle	12.50
287	Alan Bannister	12.50
288	Garry Templeton	12.50
290	Bob Stanley	12.50
291	Ken Singleton	12.50
293	Clint Hurdle	12.50
299	Steve Trout	12.50
300	Reggie Jackson	65.00
303	Doug Flynn	12.50
305	Don Sutton	30.00
307	Randy Bass	12.50
308	Charlie Moore	12.50
310	Mike Hargrove	12.50
312	Lenny Randle	12.50
313	John Harris	12.50
316	Burt Hooton	12.50
317	Dick Ruthven	12.50
321	Bill Lee	12.50
324	Steve Dillard	12.50
325	Jose Cruz	12.50
328	Ed Farmer	12.50
329	U.L. Washington	12.50
331	Rick Wise	12.50
332	Don Robinson	12.50
335	Aurelio Rodriguez	12.50
336	Jim Sundberg	12.50
338	Mike Schmidt/AS	130.00
340	Dave Concepcion/AS	12.50
341	Andre Dawson/AS	15.00
342	George Foster/AS	12.50
343	Dave Parker/AS	12.50
344	Gary Carter/AS	15.00
345	Fernando Valenzuela/AS	12.50
349	George Frazier	12.50
352	Dick Davis	12.50
354	Roberto Ramos	12.50
355	Dwight Evans	12.50
358	Butch Hobson	12.50
359	Jim Dwyer	12.50
360	Len Barker	12.50
363	Bob Molinaro	12.50
365	Bill Madlock	12.50
370	Mike Norris	12.50
380	Dave Stieb	12.50
382	Joe Simpson	12.50
385	Ken Forsch	12.50
387	Tom Veryzer	12.50
388	Joe Rudi	12.50
390	Eddie Murray	45.00
397	Ken Brett	12.50
398	Mike Squires	12.50
399	Pat Zachry	12.50
400	Johnny Bench	50.00
406	Al Holland	12.50
409	Don Cooper	12.50
412	Luis Leal	12.50
413	Dan Meyer	12.50
415	Don Baylor	12.50
417	Pat Kelly	12.50
419	Steve Stone	12.50
420	George Hendrick	12.50
421	Mark Clear	12.50
422	Cliff Johnson	12.50
423	Stan Papi	12.50
424	Bruce Benedict	12.50
426	John Candelaria	12.50
430	Vida Blue	12.50
440	Jeff Burroughs	12.50
442	Bruce Kison	12.50
443	Mark Wagner	12.50
444	Larry Parrish	12.50
446	Wayne Garland	12.50
448	Darrell Porter/IA	12.50
450	Jack Morris	12.50
451	Ed Miller	12.50
459	Bruce Berenyi	12.50
460	Jack Clark	12.50
461	Rich Dotson	12.50
462	Dave Chalk	12.50
463	Jim Kern	12.50
464	Juan Bonilla	12.50
465	Lee Mazzilli	12.50
467	Mickey Hatcher	12.50
468	Floyd Bannister	12.50
472	Oscar Gamble	12.50
475	Alan Trammell	12.50
476	Brian Kingman	12.50
477	Steve Yeager	12.50
480	Steve Carlton	35.00
481	Steve Carlton/IA	15.00
490	Dennis Eckersley	35.00
492	Joe Price	12.50
493	Chet Lemon	12.50
494	Hubie Brooks	12.50
495	Dennis Leonard	12.50
496	Johnny Grubb	12.50
498	Dave Bergman	12.50
499	Paul Mirabella	12.50
500	Rod Carew	45.00
501	Rod Carew/IA	15.00
503	Julio Gonzalez	12.50
507	Terry Harper	12.50
510	Fernando Valenzuela	17.50
511	Ruppert Jones	12.50
512	Jerry Dybzinski	12.50
515	Larry Bowa	12.50
516	Garth Iorg	12.50
518	Glenn Adams	12.50
519	Mike Flanagan	12.50
521	Bill Almon	12.50
523	Gary Gray	12.50
527	Tom Hausman	12.50
532	Toby Harrah	12.50
534	Dave McKay	12.50
536	Rafael Ramirez	12.50
538	Andre Dawson	30.00
541	Barry Evans	12.50
542	Ned Yost	12.50
546	Bill Robinson	12.50
547	Rod Carew/AS	12.50
548	Willie Randolph/AS	12.50
549	George Brett/AS	150.00
550	Bucky Dent/AS	15.00
551	Reggie Jackson/AS	30.00
552	Ken Singleton/AS	12.50
553	Dave Winfield/AS	25.00
554	Carlton Fisk/AS	25.00
556	Scott McGregor/AS	12.50
556	Jack Morris/AS	12.50
558	Rich Gossage/AS	12.50
560	Doug Corbett	12.50
563	Ross Baumgarten	12.50
565	Doug DeCinces	12.50
565	Jackson Todd	12.50
568	Bob Babcock	12.50
568	Joe Pettini	12.50
569	Willie Randolph	12.50
573	Rick Waits	12.50
575	Mike Ramsey	12.50
575	Al Cowens	12.50
579	Rick Mahler	12.50
581	Bobby Bonds	12.50
581	Ron Reed	12.50
584	Rollie Fingers	35.00
585	Dale Berra	12.50
585	Luis Pujols	12.50
590	Al Oliver	12.50
594	Dave Winfield	50.00
594	Renie Martin	12.50
601	Sid Monge	12.50
602	Freddie Patek	12.50
603	Richie Hebner	12.50
608	Jerry Royster	12.50
610	Rickey Henderson	150.00
611	Joe Niekro	12.50
612	Gary Ward	12.50
613	Jim Gantner	12.50
615	Bob Boone	12.50
616	Bob Boone/IA	12.50
622	Dennis Lamp	12.50
624	Fergie Jenkins	35.00
625	Hal McRae	12.50
626	Randy Jones	12.50
627	Enos Cabell	12.50
629	Johnny Wockenfuss	12.50
630	Joe Charboneau	25.00
632	Bryan Clark	12.50
635	Ron Davis	12.50
637	Rick Camp	12.50
640	Cesar Cedeno	12.50
645	Frank White	12.50
646	Frank White/IA	12.50
648	Jose Morales	12.50
649	Ken Clay	12.50
654	Jim Morrison	12.50
655	Joel Youngblood	12.50
656	Eddie Whitson	12.50
661	Dave Concepcion/IA	12.50
663	Hector Cruz	12.50
664	Dan Spillner	12.50
665	Jim Clancy	12.50
668	Dale Murphy	35.00
669	Larry Milbourne	12.50
670	Steve Kemp	12.50
672	Bob Knepper	12.50
675	Cecil Cooper	12.50
677	Alfredo Griffin	12.50
678	Tom Paciorek	12.50
684	Harold Baines	12.50
685	Bert Blyleven	12.50
686	Gary Allenson	12.50
690	Dave Kingman	12.50
691	Dan Schatzeder	12.50
694	Dave Wehrmeister	12.50
695	Warren Cromartie	12.50
700	George Foster	12.50
702	Steve Renko	12.50
704	Mickey Rivers	12.50
705	Mickey Rivers/IA	12.50
706	Barry Foote	12.50
707	Mark Bomback	12.50
708	Gene Richards	12.50
710	Jerry Reuss	12.50
713	Del Unser	12.50
715	Willie Stargell	45.00
716	Willie Stargell/IA	15.00
718	Charlie Hough	12.50
720	Greg Luzinski	12.50
721	Greg Luzinski/IA	12.50
722	Jerry Martin	12.50
724	Dave Rosello	12.50
725	Amos Otis	12.50
730	Gary Carter	45.00
735	Rudy May	12.50
737	Reggie Cleveland	12.50
738	Dave Engle	12.50
739	Joey McLaughlin	12.50
740	Dave Lopes	12.50
741	Dave Lopes/IA	12.50
742	Dick Drago	12.50
743	John Stearns	12.50
745	Bake McBride	12.50
747	John Lowenstein	12.50
748	Marc Hill	12.50
751	Rick Honeycutt	12.50
753	Tom Brookens	12.50
754	Joe Morgan	45.00
757	Tom Underwood	12.50
760	Bill Buckner	12.50
761	Dave Smith	12.50
764	Steve Swisher	12.50
765	Gorman Thomas	12.50
767	Roy Smalley	12.50
768	Jerry Garvin	12.50
769	Richie Zisk	12.50
771	Rich Gossage/IA	12.50
775	Bob Forsch	12.50
776	Mark Belanger	12.50
777	Tom Griffin	12.50
778	Kevin Hickey	12.50
780	Pete Rose	225.00
781	Pete Rose/IA	100.00
782	Frank Taveras	12.50
784	Milt Wilcox	12.50
788	Woodie Fryman	12.50
790	Larry Gura	12.50
792	Frank Tanana	12.50

Traded

Topps released its second straight 132-card Traded set in September of 1982. Again, the 2-1/2" x 3-1/2" cards feature not only players who had been traded during the season, but also promising rookies who were given their first individual cards. The cards follow the basic design of the regular issues, but have their backs printed in red rather than the regular-issue green. As in 1981, the cards were not available in normal retail outlets and could only be purchased through regular baseball card dealers. Unlike the previous year, the cards are numbered 1-132 with the letter "T" following the number.

NM/M

Complete Set (132): 175.00
Common Player: .10

No.	Player	Price
1T	Doyle Alexander	.10
2T	Jesse Barfield	.10
3T	Ross Baumgarten	.10
4T	Steve Bedrosian	.10
5T	Mark Belanger	.10
6T	Kurt Bevacqua	.10
7T	Tim Blackwell	.10
8T	Vida Blue	.10
9T	Bob Boone	.30
10T	Larry Bowa	.10
11T	Dan Briggs	.10
12T	Bobby Brown	.10
13T	Tom Brunansky	.10
14T	Jeff Burroughs	.10
15T	Enos Cabell	.10
16T	Bill Campbell	.10
17T	Bobby Castillo	.10
18T	Bill Caudill	.10
19T	Cesar Cedeno	.10
20T	Dave Collins	.10
21T	Doug Corbett	.10
22T	Al Cowens	.10
23T	Chili Davis	.50
24T	Dick Davis	.10
25T	Ron Davis	.10
26T	Doug DeCinces	.10
27T	Ivan DeJesus	.10
28T	Bob Dernier	.10
29T	Bo Diaz	.10
30T	Roger Erickson	.10
31T	Jim Essian	.10
32T	Ed Farmer	.10
33T	Doug Flynn	.10
34T	Tim Foli	.10
35T	Dan Ford	.10
36T	George Foster	.10
37T	Dave Frost	.10
38T	Rich Gale	.10
39T	Ron Gardenhire	.10
40T	Ken Griffey	.10
41T	Greg Harris	.10
42T	Von Hayes	.10
43T	Larry Herndon	.10
44T	Kent Hrbek	2.00
45T	Mike Ivie	.10
46T	Grant Jackson	.10
47T	Reggie Jackson	5.00
48T	Ron Jackson	.10
49T	Fergie Jenkins	2.00
50T	Lamar Johnson	.10
51T	Randy Johnson	.10
52T	Jay Johnstone	.10
53T	Mick Kelleher	.10
54T	Steve Kemp	.10
55T	Junior Kennedy	.10
56T	Jim Kern	.10
57T	Ray Knight	.10
58T	Wayne Krenchicki	.10
59T	Mike Krukow	.10
60T	Duane Kuiper	.10
61T	Mike LaCoss	.10
62T	Chet Lemon	.10
63T	Sixto Lezcano	.10
64T	Dave Lopes	.10
65T	Jerry Martin	.10
66T	Renie Martin	.10
67T	John Mayberry	.10
68T	Lee Mazzilli	.10
69T	Bake McBride	.10
70T	Dan Meyer	.10
71T	Larry Milbourne	.10
72T	Eddie Milner RC	.10
73T	Sid Monge	.10
74T	John Montefusco	.10
75T	Jose Morales	.10
76T	Keith Moreland	.10
77T	Jim Morrison	.10
78T	Rance Mulliniks	.10
79T	Steve Mura	.10
80T	Gene Nelson	.10
81T	Joe Nolan	.10
82T	Dickie Noles	.10
83T	Al Oliver	.10
84T	Jorge Orta	.10
85T	Tom Paciorek	.10
86T	Larry Parrish	.10
87T	Jack Perconte	.10
88T	Gaylord Perry	2.00
89T	Rob Picciolo	.10
90T	Joe Pittman	.10
91T	Hosken Powell	.10
92T	Mike Proly	.10
93T	Greg Pryor	.10
94T	Charlie Puleo RC	.10
95T	Shane Rawley	.10
96T	Johnny Ray	.10
97T	Dave Revering	.10
98T	Cal Ripken, Jr.	140.00
99T	Allen Ripley	.10
100T	Bill Robinson	.10
101T	Aurelio Rodriguez	.10

102T	Joe Rudi	.10
103T	Steve Sax	.50
104T	Dan Schatzeder	.10
105T	Bob Shirley	.10
106T	Eric Show **RC**	.10
107T	Roy Smalley	.10
108T	Lonnie Smith	.10
109T	Ozzie Smith	20.00
110T	Reggie Smith	.10
111T	Lary Sorensen	.10
112T	Elias Sosa	.10
113T	Mike Stanton	.10
114T	Steve Stroughter	.10
115T	Champ Summers	.10
116T	Rick Sutcliffe	.10
117T	Frank Tanana	.10
118T	Frank Taveras	.10
119T	Garry Templeton	.10
120T	Alex Trevino	.10
121T	Jerry Turner	.10
122T	Ed Vande Berg **RC**	.10
123T	Tom Veryzer	.10
124T	Ron Washington	.10
125T	Bob Watson	.10
126T	Dennis Werth	.10
127T	Eddie Whitson	.10
128T	Rob Wilfong	.10
129T	Bump Wills	.10
130T	Gary Woods	.10
131T	Butch Wynegar	.10
132T	Checklist 1-132	.10

Team Leaders Sheet

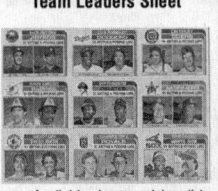

Available via a special mail-in offer, this 10-1/2" x 23" uncut sheet contained the 26 team batting and pitching leaders cards plus a card offering Topps collectors boxes. The team leader cards are identical to those issued in packs.

NM/M
Team Leaders Sheet 10.00

Insert Stickers

85
WILLIE STARGELL
1st Base
ALBUMS COMING SOON!
SAVE THIS STICKER... and place it in your new 1982 Topps Baseball Sticker Album. Albums and ALL stickers are sold where Topps Baseball cards are available.
IT'S Topps FOR SPORTS
© 1982 Topps Chewing Gum, Inc.

This 48-player set is actually an abbreviated version of the regular 1982 Topps sticker set with different backs. Used to promote the 1982 sticker set, Topps inserted these stickers in its baseball card wax packs. They are identical to the regular 1982 stickers, except for the backs, which advertise that the Topps sticker album will be "Coming Soon." The 48 stickers retain the same numbers used in the regular sticker set, resulting in the smaller set being skip-numbered.

NM/M
Complete Set (48):		3.00
Common Player:		.05
17	Chris Chambliss	.05
21	Bruce Benedict	.05
25	Leon Durham	.05
29	Bill Buckner	.05
33	Dave Collins	.05
37	Dave Concepcion	.05
41	Nolan Ryan	1.00
45	Bob Knepper	.05
49	Ken Landreaux	.05
53	Burt Hooton	.05
57	Andre Dawson	.15
61	Gary Carter	.25
65	Joel Youngblood	.05
69	Ellis Valentine	.05
73	Garry Maddox	.05
77	Bob Boone	.05
81	Omar Moreno	.05
85	Willie Stargell	.25
89	Ken Oberkfell	.05
93	Darrell Porter	.05
97	Juan Eichelberger	.05
101	Luis Salazar	.05
105	Enos Cabell	.05
109	Larry Herndon	.05
143	Scott McGregor	.05
148	Mike Flanagan	.05
151	Mike Torrez	.05
156	Carney Lansford	.05
161	Fred Lynn	.05
166	Rich Dotson	.05
171	Tony Bernazard	.05
176	Bo Diaz	.05
181	Alan Trammell	.05
186	Milt Wilcox	.05
191	Dennis Leonard	.05
196	Willie Aikens	.05
201	Ted Simmons	.05
206	Hosken Powell	.05
211	Roger Erickson	.05
215	Graig Nettles	.05
216	Reggie Jackson	.45
221	Rickey Henderson	.25
226	Cliff Johnson	.05
231	Jeff Burroughs	.05
236	Tom Paciorek	.05
241	Pat Putnam	.05
246	Lloyd Moseby	.05
251	Barry Bonnell	.05

Stickers

The 1982 Topps sticker set is complete at 260 stickers and includes another series of "foil" All-Stars. The stickers measure 1-15/16" x 2-9/16" and feature full-color photos surrounded by a red border for American League players or a blue border for National League players. They are numbered on both the front and back and were designed to be mounted in a special album.

NM/M
Complete Set (260):		7.50
Common Player:		.05
Sticker Album:		2.00
Wax Pack (5):		.25
Wax Box (100):		15.00
1	Bill Madlock	.05
2	Carney Lansford	.05
3	Mike Schmidt	.30
4	Tony Armas, Dwight Evans, Bobby Grich, Eddie Murray	.05
5	Mike Schmidt	.30
6	Eddie Murray	.25
7	Tim Raines	.05
8	Rickey Henderson	.25
9	Tom Seaver	.25
10	Denny Martinez, Steve McCatty, Jack Morris, Pete Vuckovich	.05
11	Fernando Valenzuela	.05
12	Len Barker	.05
13	Nolan Ryan	.50
14	Steve McCatty	.05
15	Bruce Sutter	.20
16	Rollie Fingers	.20
17	Chris Chambliss	.05
18	Bob Horner	.05
19	Dale Murphy	.15
20	Phil Niekro	.20
21	Bruce Benedict	.05
22	Claudell Washington	.05
23	Glenn Hubbard	.05
24	Rick Camp	.05
25	Leon Durham	.05
26	Ken Reitz	.05
27	Dick Tidrow	.05
28	Tim Blackwell	.05
29	Bill Buckner	.05
30	Steve Henderson	.05
31	Mike Krukow	.05
32	Ivan DeJesus	.05
33	Dave Collins	.05
34	Ron Oester	.05
35	Johnny Bench	.25
36	Tom Seaver	.25
37	Dave Concepcion	.05
38	Ken Griffey	.05
39	Ray Knight	.05
40	George Foster	.05
41	Nolan Ryan	.50
42	Terry Puhl	.05
43	Art Howe	.05
44	Jose Cruz	.05
45	Bob Knepper	.05
46	Craig Reynolds	.05
47	Cesar Cedeno	.05
48	Alan Ashby	.05
49	Ken Landreaux	.05
50	Fernando Valenzuela	.05
51	Ron Cey	.05
52	Dusty Baker	.05
53	Burt Hooton	.05
54	Steve Garvey	.15
55	Pedro Guerrero	.05
56	Jerry Reuss	.05
57	Andre Dawson	.20
58	Chris Speier	.05
59	Steve Rogers	.05
60	Warren Cromartie	.05
61	Gary Carter	.25
62	Tim Raines	.05
63	Scott Sanderson	.05
64	Larry Parrish	.05
65	Joel Youngblood	.05
66	Neil Allen	.05
67	Lee Mazzilli	.05
68	Hubie Brooks	.05
69	Ellis Valentine	.05
70	Doug Flynn	.05
71	Pat Zachry	.05
72	Dave Kingman	.05
73	Garry Maddox	.05
74	Mike Schmidt	.30
75	Steve Carlton	.25
76	Manny Trillo	.05
77	Bob Boone	.05
78	Pete Rose	.40
79	Gary Matthews	.05
80	Larry Bowa	.05
81	Omar Moreno	.05
82	Rick Rhoden	.05
83	Bill Madlock	.05
84	Mike Easler	.05
85	Willie Stargell	.25
86	Jim Bibby	.05
87	Dave Parker	.05
88	Tim Foli	.05
89	Ken Oberkfell	.05
90	Bob Forsch	.05
91	George Hendrick	.05
92	Keith Hernandez	.05
93	Darrell Porter	.05
94	Bruce Sutter	.20
95	Sixto Lezcano	.05
96	Garry Templeton	.05
97	Juan Eichelberger	.05
98	Broderick Perkins	.05
99	Ruppert Jones	.05
100	Terry Kennedy	.05
101	Luis Salazar	.05
102	Gary Lucas	.05
103	Gene Richards	.05
104	Ozzie Smith	.30
105	Enos Cabell	.05
106	Jack Clark	.05
107	Greg Minton	.05
108	Johnnie LeMaster	.05
109	Larry Herndon	.05
110	Milt May	.05
111	Vida Blue	.05
112	Darrell Evans	.05
113	Len Barker	.05
114	Julio Cruz	.05
115	Billy Martin	.05
116	Tim Raines	.05
117	Pete Rose	.40
118	Bill Stein	.05
119	Fernando Valenzuela	.05
120	Carl Yastrzemski	.25
121	Pete Rose	.40
122	Manny Trillo	.05
123	Mike Schmidt	.30
124	Dave Concepcion	.05
125	Andre Dawson	.20
126	George Foster	.05
127	Dave Parker	.05
128	Gary Carter	.25
129	Steve Carlton	.25
130	Bruce Sutter	.20
131	Rod Carew	.25
132	Jerry Remy	.05
133	George Brett	.30
134	Rick Burleson	.05
135	Dwight Evans	.05
136	Ken Singleton	.05
137	Dave Winfield	.25
138	Carlton Fisk	.25
139	Jack Morris	.05
140	Rich Gossage	.05
141	Al Bumbry	.05
142	Doug DeCinces	.05
143	Scott McGregor	.05
144	Ken Singleton	.05
145	Eddie Murray	.25
146	Jim Palmer	.20
147	Rich Dauer	.05
148	Mike Flanagan	.05
149	Jerry Remy	.05
150	Jim Rice	.15
151	Mike Torrez	.05
152	Tony Perez	.25
153	Dwight Evans	.05
154	Mark Clear	.05
155	Carl Yastrzemski	.25
156	Carney Lansford	.05
157	Rick Burleson	.05
158	Don Baylor	.10
159	Ken Forsch	.05
160	Rod Carew	.25
161	Fred Lynn	.05
162	Bob Grich	.05
163	Dan Ford	.05
164	Butch Hobson	.05
165	Greg Luzinski	.05
166	Rich Dotson	.05
167	Billy Almon	.05
168	Chet Lemon	.05
169	Steve Trout	.05
170	Carlton Fisk	.25
171	Tony Bernazard	.05
172	Ron LeFlore	.05
173	Bert Blyleven	.05
174	Andre Thornton	.05
175	Jorge Orta	.05
176	Bo Diaz	.05
177	Toby Harrah	.05
178	Len Barker	.05
179	Rick Manning	.05
180	Mike Hargrove	.05
181	Alan Trammell	.05
182	Al Cowens	.05
183	Jack Morris	.05
184	Kirk Gibson	.05
185	Steve Kemp	.05
186	Milt Wilcox	.05
187	Lou Whitaker	.05
188	Lance Parrish	.05
189	Willie Wilson	.05
190	George Brett	.30
191	Dennis Leonard	.05
192	John Wathan	.05
193	Frank White	.05
194	Amos Otis	.05
195	Larry Gura	.05
196	Willie Aikens	.05
197	Ben Oglivie	.05
198	Rollie Fingers	.20
199	Cecil Cooper	.05
200	Paul Molitor	.20
201	Ted Simmons	.05
202	Pete Vuckovich	.05
203	Robin Yount	.25
204	Gorman Thomas	.05
205	Rob Wilfong	.05
206	Hosken Powell	.05
207	Roy Smalley	.05
208	Butch Wynegar	.05
209	John Castino	.05
210	Doug Corbett	.05
211	Roger Erickson	.05
212	Mickey Hatcher	.05
213	Dave Winfield	.25
214	Tommy John	.10
215	Graig Nettles	.05
216	Reggie Jackson	.25
217	Rich Gossage	.05
218	Rick Cerone	.05
219	Willie Randolph	.05
220	Jerry Mumphrey	.05
221	Rickey Henderson	.25
222	Mike Norris	.05
223	Jim Spencer	.05
224	Tony Armas	.05
225	Matt Keough	.05
226	Cliff Johnson	.05
227	Dwayne Murphy	.05
228	Steve McCatty	.05
229	Richie Zisk	.05
230	Lenny Randle	.05
231	Jeff Burroughs	.05
232	Bruce Bochte	.05
233	Gary Gray	.05
234	Floyd Bannister	.05
235	Julio Cruz	.05
236	Tom Paciorek	.05
237	Danny Darwin	.05
238	Buddy Bell	.05
239	Al Oliver	.05
240	Jim Sundberg	.05
241	Pat Putnam	.05
242	Steve Comer	.05
243	Mickey Rivers	.05
244	Bump Wills	.05
245	Damaso Garcia	.05
246	Lloyd Moseby	.05
247	Ernie Whitt	.05
248	John Mayberry	.05
249	Otto Velez	.05
250	Dave Stieb	.05
251	Barry Bonnell	.05
252	Alfredo Griffin	.05
253	1981 N.L. Championship (Gary Carter)	.10
254	1981 A.L. Championship (Mike Heath, Larry Milbourne)	.05
255	1981 World Champions (Los Angeles Dodgers Team)	.05
256	1981 World Champions (Los Angeles Dodgers Team)	.05
257	1981 World Series - Game 3 (Fernando Valenzuela)	.05
258	1981 World Series - Game 4 (Steve Garvey)	.10
259	1981 World Series - Game 5 (Jerry Reuss, Steve Yeager)	.05
260	1981 World Series - Game 6 (Pedro Guerrero)	.05

1983 Topps

The 1983 Topps set totals 792 cards. Missing among the regular 2-1/2" x 3-1/2" cards are some form of future stars cards, as Topps was saving them for the now-established late season "Traded" set. The 1983 cards carry a large color photo as well as a smaller color photo on the front, quite similar in design to the 1963 set. Team colors frame the card, which, at

the bottom, have the player's name, position and team. At the upper right-hand corner is a Topps Logo. The backs are horizontal and include statistics, personal information and 1982 highlights. Specialty cards include record-breaking performances, league leaders, All-Stars, numbered checklists "Team Leaders" and "Super Veteran" cards which are horizontal with a current and first-season picture of the honored player.

NM/M
Complete Set (792):		60.00
Common Player:		.05
Wax Pack (15):		3.00
Wax Box (36):		110.00
Crimp-End Test Pack (15):		4.00
Crimp-end Test Box (36):		110.00
Cello Pack (28):		5.00
Cello Box (24):		125.00
Rack Pack (51):		7.50
Rack Box (24):		175.00
Vending Box (500):		65.00
1	Tony Armas (Record Breaker)	.05
2	Rickey Henderson (Record Breaker)	.75
3	Greg Minton (Record Breaker)	.05
4	Lance Parrish (Record Breaker)	.05
5	Manny Trillo (Record Breaker)	.05
6	John Wathan (Record Breaker)	.05
7	Gene Richards	.05
8	Steve Balboni	.05
9	Joey McLaughlin	.05
10	Gorman Thomas	.05
11	Billy Gardner	.05
12	Paul Mirabella	.05
13	Larry Herndon	.05
14	Frank LaCorte	.05
15	Ron Cey	.05
16	George Vukovich	.05
17	Kent Tekulve	.05
18	Kent Tekulve (Super Veteran)	.05
19	Oscar Gamble	.05
20	Carlton Fisk	2.00
21	Orioles Batting & Pitching Ldrs. (Eddie Murray, Jim Palmer)	.25
22	Randy Martz	.05
23	Mike Heath	.05
24	Steve Mura	.05
25	Hal McRae	.05
26	Jerry Royster	.05
27	Doug Corbett	.05
28	Bruce Bochte	.05
29	Randy Jones	.05
30	Jim Rice	.15
31	Bill Gullickson	.05
32	Dave Bergman	.05
33	Jack O'Connor	.05
34	Paul Householder	.05
35	Rollie Fingers	.75
36	Rollie Fingers (Super Veteran)	.15
37	Darrell Johnson	.05
38	Tim Flannery	.05
39	Terry Puhl	.05
40	Fernando Valenzuela	.05
41	Jerry Turner	.05
42	Dale Murray	.05
43	Bob Dernier	.05
44	Don Robinson	.05
45	John Mayberry	.05
46	Richard Dotson	.05
47	Dave McKay	.05
48	Lary Sorensen	.05
49	Willie McGee **RC**	1.50
50	Bob Horner	.05
51	Cubs Batting & Pitching Ldrs. (Leon Durham, Fergie Jenkins)	.05
52	Onix Concepcion **RC**	.05
53	Mike Witt	.05
54	Jim Maler	.05
55	Mookie Wilson	.05
56	Chuck Rainey	.05
57	Tim Blackwell	.05
58	Al Holland	.05
59	Benny Ayala	.05
60	Johnny Bench	2.00
61	Johnny Bench (Super Veteran)	.75
62	Bob McClure	.05
63	Rick Monday	.05
64	Bill Stein	.05
65	Jack Morris	.05
66	Bob Lillis	.05
67	Sal Butera	.05
68	Eric Show **RC**	.15
69	Lee Lacy	.05
70	Steve Carlton	2.00
71	Steve Carlton (Super Veteran)	.30
72	Tom Paciorek	.05
73	Allen Ripley	.05
74	Julio Gonzalez	.05
75	Amos Otis	.05
76	Rick Mahler	.05
77	Hosken Powell	.05
78	Bill Caudill	.05
79	Mick Kelleher	.05
80	George Foster	.05
81	Yankees Batting & Pitching Ldrs. (Jerry Mumphrey, Dave Righetti)	.05
82	Bruce Hurst	.05
83	Ryne Sandberg **RC**	15.00
84	Milt May	.05
85	Ken Singleton	.05
86	Tom Hume	.05
87	Joe Rudi	.05
88	Jim Gantner	.05
89	Leon Roberts	.05
90	Jerry Reuss	.05
91	Larry Milbourne	.05
92	Mike LaCoss	.05
93	John Castino	.05
94	Dave Edwards	.05
95	Alan Trammell	.05
96	Dick Howser	.05
97	Ross Baumgarten	.05
98	Vance Law	.05
99	Dickie Noles	.05
100	Pete Rose	4.00
101	Pete Rose (Super Veteran)	2.00
102	Dave Beard	.05
103	Darrell Porter	.05
104	Bob Walk	.05
105	Don Baylor	.15
106	Gene Nelson	.05
107	Mike Jorgensen	.05
108	Glenn Hoffman	.05
109	Luis Leal	.05
110	Ken Griffey	.05
111	Expos Batting & Pitching Ldrs. (Al Oliver, Steve Rogers)	.05
112	Bob Shirley	.05
113	Ron Roenicke	.05
114	Jim Slaton	.05
115	Chili Davis	.05
116	Dave Schmidt	.05
117	Alan Knicely	.05
118	Chris Welsh	.05
119	Tom Brookens	.05
120	Len Barker	.05
121	Mickey Hatcher	.05
122	Jimmy Smith	.05
123	George Frazier	.05
124	Marc Hill	.05
125	Leon Durham	.05
126	Joe Torre	.25
127	Preston Hanna	.05
128	Mike Ramsey	.05
129	Checklist 1-132	.05
130	Dave Stieb	.05
131	Ed Ott	.05
132	Todd Cruz	.05
133	Jim Barr	.05
134	Hubie Brooks	.05
135	Dwight Evans	.05
136	Willie Aikens	.05
137	Woodie Fryman	.05
138	Rick Dempsey	.05
139	Bruce Berenyi	.05
140	Willie Randolph	.05
141	Indians Batting & Pitching Ldrs. (Toby Harrah, Rick Sutcliffe)	.05
142	Mike Caldwell	.05
143	Joe Pettini	.05
144	Mark Wagner	.05
145	Don Sutton	.75
146	Don Sutton (Super Veteran)	.20
147	Rick Leach	.05
148	Dave Roberts	.05
149	Johnny Ray	.05
150	Bruce Sutter	.75
151	Bruce Sutter (Super Veteran)	.50
152	Jay Johnstone	.05
153	Jerry Koosman	.05
154	Johnnie LeMaster	.05
155	Dan Quisenberry	.05
156	Billy Martin	.15
157	Steve Bedrosian	.05
158	Rob Wilfong	.05
159	Mike Stanton	.05
160	Dave Kingman	.05
161	Dave Kingman (Super Veteran)	.05
162	Mark Clear	.05
163	Cal Ripken, Jr.	6.00
164	Dave Palmer	.05
165	Dan Driessen	.05

No.	Player	Price
166	John Pacella	.05
167	Mark Brouhard	.05
168	Juan Eichelberger	.05
169	Doug Flynn	.05
170	Steve Howe	.05
171	Giants Batting & Pitching Ldrs. (Bill Laskey, Joe Morgan)	.05
172	Vern Ruhle	.05
173	Jim Morrison	.05
174	Jerry Ujdur	.05
175	Bo Diaz	.05
176	Dave Righetti	.05
177	Harold Baines	.05
178	Luis Tiant	.05
179	Luis Tiant (Super Veteran)	.05
180	Rickey Henderson	2.00
181	Terry Felton	.05
182	Mike Fischlin	.05
183	Ed Vande Berg RC	.05
184	Bob Clark	.05
185	Tim Lollar	.05
186	Whitey Herzog	.05
187	Terry Leach	.05
188	Rick Miller	.05
189	Dan Schatzeder	.05
190	Cecil Cooper	.05
191	Joe Price	.05
192	Floyd Rayford	.05
193	Harry Spilman	.05
194	Cesar Geronimo	.05
195	Bob Stoddard	.05
196	Bill Fahey	.05
197	Jim Eisenreich RC	.50
198	Kiko Garcia	.05
199	Marty Bystrom	.05
200	Rod Carew	2.00
201	Rod Carew (Super Veteran)	.35
202	Blue Jays Batting & Pitching Ldrs. (Damaso Garcia, Dave Stieb)	.05
203	Mike Morgan	.05
204	Junior Kennedy	.05
205	Dave Parker	.05
206	Ken Oberkfell	.05
207	Rick Camp	.05
208	Dan Meyer	.05
209	Mike Moore RC	.15
210	Jack Clark	.05
211	John Denny	.05
212	John Stearns	.05
213	Tom Burgmeier	.05
214	Jerry White	.05
215	Mario Soto	.05
216	Tony LaRussa	.05
217	Tim Stoddard	.05
218	Roy Howell	.05
219	Mike Armstrong	.05
220	Dusty Baker	.05
221	Joe Niekro	.05
222	Damaso Garcia	.05
223	John Montefusco	.05
224	Mickey Rivers	.05
225	Enos Cabell	.05
226	Enrique Romo	.05
227	Chris Bando	.05
228	Joaquin Andujar	.05
229	Phillies Batting/Pitching Leaders (Steve Carlton, Bo Diaz)	.15
230	Fergie Jenkins	.75
231	Fergie Jenkins (Super Veteran)	.20
232	Tom Brunansky	.05
233	Wayne Gross	.05
234	Larry Andersen	.05
235	Claudell Washington	.05
236	Steve Renko	.05
237	Dan Norman	.05
238	Bud Black RC	.25
239	Dave Stapleton	.05
240	Rich Gossage	.05
241	Rich Gossage (Super Veteran)	.05
242	Joe Nolan	.05
243	Duane Walker	.05
244	Dwight Bernard	.05
245	Steve Sax	.05
246	George Bamberger	.05
247	Dave Smith	.05
248	Bake McBride	.05
249	Checklist 133-264	.05
250	Bill Buckner	.05
251	Alan Wiggins RC	.05
252	Luis Aguayo	.05
253	Larry McWilliams	.05
254	Rick Cerone	.05
255	Gene Garber	.05
256	Gene Garber (Super Veteran)	.05
257	Jesse Barfield	.05
258	Manny Castillo	.05
259	Jeff Jones	.05
260	Steve Kemp	.05
261	Tigers Batting & Pitching Ldrs. (Larry Herndon, Dan Petry)	.05
262	Ron Jackson	.05
263	Renie Martin	.05
264	Jamie Quirk	.05
265	Joel Youngblood	.05
266	Paul Boris	.05
267	Terry Francona	.05
268	Storm Davis RC	.05
269	Ron Oester	.05
270	Dennis Eckersley	.75
271	Ed Romero	.05
272	Frank Tanana	.05
273	Mark Belanger	.05
274	Terry Kennedy	.05
275	Ray Knight	.05
276	Gene Mauch	.05
277	Rance Mulliniks	.05
278	Kevin Hickey	.05
279	Greg Gross	.05
280	Bert Blyleven	.05
281	Andre Robertson	.05
282	Reggie Smith	.05
283	Reggie Smith (Super Veteran)	.05
284	Jeff Lahti	.05
285	Lance Parrish	.05
286	Rick Langford	.05
287	Bobby Brown	.05
288	Joe Cowley RC	.05
289	Jerry Dybzinski	.05
290	Jeff Reardon	.05
291	Pirates Batting & Pitching Ldrs. (John Candelaria, Bill Madlock)	.05
292	Craig Swan	.05
293	Glenn Gulliver	.05
294	Dave Engle	.05
295	Jerry Remy	.05
296	Greg Harris	.05
297	Ned Yost	.05
298	Floyd Chiffer	.05
299	George Wright	.05
300	Mike Schmidt	3.00
301	Mike Schmidt (Super Veteran)	1.50
302	Ernie Whitt	.05
303	Miguel Dilone	.05
304	Dave Rucker	.05
305	Larry Bowa	.05
306	Tom Lasorda	.25
307	Lou Piniella	.05
308	Jesus Vega	.05
309	Jeff Leonard	.05
310	Greg Luzinski	.05
311	Glenn Brummer	.05
312	Brian Kingman	.05
313	Gary Gray	.05
314	Ken Dayley RC	.05
315	Rick Burleson	.05
316	Paul Splittorff	.05
317	Gary Rajsich	.05
318	John Tudor	.05
319	Lenn Sakata	.05
320	Steve Rogers	.05
321	Brewers Batting & Pitching Ldrs. (Pete Vuckovich, Robin Yount)	.10
322	Dave Van Gorder	.05
323	Luis DeLeon	.05
324	Mike Marshall	.05
325	Von Hayes	.05
326	Garth Iorg	.05
327	Bobby Castillo	.05
328	Craig Reynolds	.05
329	Randy Niemann	.05
330	Buddy Bell	.05
331	Mike Krukow	.05
332	Glenn Wilson RC	.05
333	Dave LaRoche	.05
334	Dave LaRoche (Super Veteran)	.05
335	Steve Henderson	.05
336	Rene Lachemann	.05
337	Tito Landrum	.05
338	Bob Owchinko	.05
339	Terry Harper	.05
340	Larry Gura	.05
341	Doug DeCinces	.05
342	Atlee Hammaker	.05
343	Bob Bailor	.05
344	Roger LaFrancois	.05
345	Jim Clancy	.05
346	Joe Pittman	.05
347	Sammy Stewart	.05
348	Alan Bannister	.05
349	Checklist 265-396	.05
350	Robin Yount	2.00
351	Reds Batting & Pitching Ldrs. (Cesar Cedeno, Mario Soto)	.05
352	Mike Scioscia	.05
353	Steve Comer	.05
354	Randy S. Johnson	.05
355	Jim Bibby	.05
356	Gary Woods	.05
357	Len Matuszek RC	.05
358	Jerry Garvin	.05
359	Dave Collins	.05
360	Nolan Ryan	5.00
361	Nolan Ryan (Super Veteran)	4.00
362	Bill Almon	.05
363	John Stuper RC	.05
364	Brett Butler	.05
365	Dave Lopes	.05
366	Dick Williams	.05
367	Bud Anderson	.05
368	Richie Zisk	.05
369	Jesse Orosco	.05
370	Gary Carter	2.00
371	Mike Richardt	.05
372	Terry Crowley	.05
373	Kevin Saucier	.05
374	Wayne Krenchicki	.05
375	Pete Vuckovich	.05
376	Ken Landreaux	.05
377	Lee May	.05
378	Lee May (Super Veteran)	.05
379	Guy Sularz	.05
380	Ron Davis	.05
381	Red Sox Batting & Pitching Ldrs. (Jim Rice, Bob Stanley)	.05
382	Bob Knepper	.05
383	Ozzie Virgil	.05
384	Dave Dravecky RC	.50
385	Mike Easler	.05
386	Rod Carew/AS	.35
387	Bob Grich/AS	.05
388	George Brett/AS	1.50
389	Robin Yount/AS	1.00
390	Reggie Jackson/AS	1.00
391	Rickey Henderson/AS	.50
392	Fred Lynn/AS	.05
393	Carlton Fisk/AS	.35
394	Pete Vuckovich/AS	.05
395	Larry Gura/AS	.05
396	Dan Quisenberry/AS	.05
397	Pete Rose/AS	2.00
398	Manny Trillo/AS	.05
399	Mike Schmidt/AS	1.50
400	Dave Concepcion/AS	.05
401	Dale Murphy/AS	.20
402	Andre Dawson/AS	.35
403	Tim Raines/AS	.35
404	Gary Carter/AS	.35
405	Steve Rogers/AS	.05
406	Steve Carlton/AS	.30
407	Bruce Sutter/AS	.25
408	Rudy May	.05
409	Marvis Foley	.05
410	Phil Niekro	.75
411	Phil Niekro (Super Veteran)	.25
412	Rangers Batting & Pitching Ldrs. (Buddy Bell, Charlie Hough)	.05
413	Matt Keough	.05
414	Julio Cruz	.05
415	Bob Forsch	.05
416	Joe Ferguson	.05
417	Tom Hausman	.05
418	Greg Pryor	.05
419	Steve Crawford	.05
420	Al Oliver	.05
421	Al Oliver (Super Veteran)	.05
422	George Cappuzzello	.05
423	Tom Lawless RC	.05
424	Jerry Augustine	.05
425	Pedro Guerrero	.05
426	Earl Weaver	.25
427	Roy Lee Jackson	.05
428	Champ Summers	.05
429	Eddie Whitson	.05
430	Kirk Gibson	.05
431	Gary Gaetti RC	.75
432	Porfirio Altamirano	.05
433	Dale Berra	.05
434	Dennis Lamp	.05
435	Tony Armas	.05
436	Bill Campbell	.05
437	Rick Sweet	.05
438	Dave LaPoint RC	.05
439	Rafael Ramirez	.05
440	Ron Guidry	.20
441	Astros Batting & Pitching Ldrs. (Ray Knight, Joe Niekro)	.05
442	Brian Downing	.05
443	Don Hood	.05
444	Wally Backman RC	.05
445	Mike Flanagan	.05
446	Reid Nichols	.05
447	Bryn Smith	.05
448	Darrell Evans	.05
449	Eddie Milner RC	.05
450	Ted Simmons	.05
451	Ted Simmons (Super Veteran)	.05
452	Lloyd Moseby	.05
453	Lamar Johnson	.05
454	Bob Welch	.05
455	Sixto Lezcano	.05
456	Lee Elia	.05
457	Milt Wilcox	.05
458	Ron Washington	.05
459	Ed Farmer	.05
460	Roy Smalley	.05
461	Steve Trout	.05
462	Steve Nicosia	.05
463	Gaylord Perry	.75
464	Gaylord Perry (Super Veteran)	.20
465	Lonnie Smith	.05
466	Tom Underwood	.05
467	Rufino Linares	.05
468	Dave Goltz	.05
469	Ron Gardenhire	.05
470	Greg Minton	.05
471	Royals Batting & Pitching Ldrs. (Vida Blue, Willie Wilson)	.05
472	Gary Allenson	.05
473	John Lowenstein	.05
474	Ray Burris	.05
475	Cesar Cedeno	.05
476	Rob Picciolo	.05
477	Tom Niedenfuer RC	.05
478	Phil Garner	.05
479	Charlie Hough	.05
480	Toby Harrah	.05
481	Scot Thompson	.05
482	Tony Gwynn RC	25.00
483	Lynn Jones	.05
484	Dick Ruthven	.05
485	Omar Moreno	.05
486	Clyde King	.05
487	Jerry Hairston Sr.	.05
488	Alfredo Griffin	.05
489	Tom Herr	.05
490	Jim Palmer	1.50
491	Jim Palmer (Super Veteran)	.20
492	Paul Serna	.05
493	Steve McCatty	.05
494	Bob Brenly	.05
495	Warren Cromartie	.05
496	Tom Veryzer	.05
497	Rick Sutcliffe	.05
498	Wade Boggs RC	15.00
499	Jeff Little	.05
500	Reggie Jackson	2.00
501	Reggie Jackson (Super Veteran)	.75
502	Braves Batting & Pitching Ldrs. (Dale Murphy, Phil Niekro)	.20
503	Moose Haas	.05
504	Don Werner	.05
505	Garry Templeton	.05
506	Jim Gott RC	.25
507	Tony Scott	.05
508	Tom Filer	.05
509	Lou Whitaker	.05
510	Tug McGraw	.05
511	Tug McGraw (Super Veteran)	.05
512	Doyle Alexander	.05
513	Fred Stanley	.05
514	Rudy Law	.05
515	Gene Tenace	.05
516	Bill Virdon	.05
517	Gary Ward	.05
518	Bill Laskey	.05
519	Terry Bulling	.05
520	Fred Lynn	.05
521	Bruce Benedict	.05
522	Pat Zachry	.05
523	Carney Lansford	.05
524	Tom Brennan	.05
525	Frank White	.05
526	Checklist 397-528	.05
527	Larry Biittner	.05
528	Jamie Easterly	.05
529	Tim Laudner	.05
530	Eddie Murray	2.00
531	Athletics Batting & Pitching Ldrs. (Rickey Henderson, Rick Langford)	.15
532	Dave Stewart	.05
533	Luis Salazar	.05
534	John Butcher	.05
535	Manny Trillo	.05
536	Johnny Wockenfuss	.05
537	Rod Scurry	.05
538	Danny Heep	.05
539	Roger Erickson	.05
540	Ozzie Smith	2.00
541	Britt Burns	.05
542	Jody Davis	.05
543	Alan Fowlkes	.05
544	Larry Whisenton	.05
545	Floyd Bannister	.05
546	Dave Garcia	.05
547	Geoff Zahn	.05
548	Brian Giles	.05
549	Charlie Puleo RC	.05
550	Carl Yastrzemski	2.00
551	Carl Yastrzemski (Super Veteran)	.50
552	Tim Wallach	.05
553	Denny Martinez	.05
554	Mike Vail	.05
555	Steve Yeager	.05
556	Willie Upshaw	.05
557	Rick Honeycutt	.05
558	Dickie Thon	.05
559	Pete Redfern	.05
560	Ron LeFlore	.05
561	Cardinals Batting & Pitching Ldrs. (Joaquin Andujar, Lonnie Smith)	.05
562	Dave Rozema	.05
563	Juan Bonilla	.05
564	Sid Monge	.05
565	Bucky Dent	.05
566	Manny Sarmiento	.05
567	Joe Simpson	.05
568	Willie Hernandez	.05
569	Jack Perconte	.05
570	Vida Blue	.05
571	Mickey Klutts	.05
572	Bob Watson	.05
573	Andy Hassler	.05
574	Glenn Adams	.05
575	Neil Allen	.05
576	Frank Robinson	.25
577	Luis Aponte	.05
578	David Green	.05
579	Rich Dauer	.05
580	Tom Seaver	2.00
581	Tom Seaver (Super Veteran)	.50
582	Marshall Edwards	.05
583	Terry Forster	.05
584	Dave Hostetler	.05
585	Jose Cruz	.05
586	Frank Viola RC	1.50
587	Ivan DeJesus	.05
588	Pat Underwood	.05
589	Alvis Woods	.05
590	Tony Pena	.05
591	White Sox Batting & Pitching Ldrs. (LaMarr Hoyt, Greg Luzinski)	.05
592	Shane Rawley	.05
593	Broderick Perkins	.05
594	Eric Rasmussen	.05
595	Tim Raines	.05
596	Randy S. Johnson	.05
597	Mike Proly	.05
598	Dwayne Murphy	.05
599	Don Aase	.05
600	George Brett	3.00
601	Ed Lynch	.05
602	Rich Gedman	.05
603	Joe Morgan	2.00
604	Joe Morgan (Super Veteran)	.35
605	Gary Roenicke	.05
606	Bobby Cox	.05
607	Charlie Leibrandt	.05
608	Don Money	.05
609	Danny Darwin	.05
610	Steve Garvey	.50
611	Bert Roberge	.05
612	Steve Swisher	.05
613	Mike Ivie	.05
614	Ed Glynn	.05
615	Garry Maddox	.05
616	Bill Nahorodny	.05
617	Butch Wynegar	.05
618	LaMarr Hoyt	.05
619	Keith Moreland	.05
620	Mike Norris	.05
621	Mets Batting & Pitching Ldrs. (Craig Swan, Mookie Wilson)	.05
622	Dave Edler	.05
623	Luis Sanchez	.05
624	Glenn Hubbard	.05
625	Ken Forsch	.05
626	Jerry Martin	.05
627	Doug Bair	.05
628	Julio Valdez	.05
629	Charlie Lea	.05
630	Paul Molitor	2.00
631	Tippy Martinez	.05
632	Alex Trevino	.05
633	Vicente Romo	.05
634	Max Venable	.05
635	Graig Nettles	.05
636	Graig Nettles (Super Veteran)	.05
637	Pat Corrales	.05
638	Dan Petry	.05
639	Art Howe	.05
640	Andre Thornton	.05
641	Billy Sample	.05
642	Checklist 529-660	.05
643	Bump Wills	.05
644	Joe Lefebvre	.05
645	Bill Madlock	.05
646	Jim Essian	.05
647	Bobby Mitchell	.05
648	Jeff Burroughs	.05
649	Tommy Boggs	.05
650	George Hendrick	.05
651	Angels Batting & Pitching Ldrs. (Rod Carew, Mike Witt)	.05
652	Butch Hobson	.05
653	Ellis Valentine	.05
654	Bob Ojeda	.05
655	Al Bumbry	.05
656	Dave Frost	.05
657	Mike Gates	.05
658	Frank Pastore	.05
659	Charlie Moore	.05
660	Mike Hargrove	.05
661	Bill Russell	.05
662	Joe Sambito	.05
663	Tom O'Malley	.05
664	Bob Molinaro	.05
665	Jim Sundberg	.05
666	Sparky Anderson	.25
667	Dick Davis	.05
668	Larry Christenson	.05
669	Mike Squires	.05
670	Jerry Mumphrey	.05
671	Lenny Faedo	.05
672	Jim Kaat	.10
673	Jim Kaat (Super Veteran)	.05
674	Kurt Bevacqua	.05
675	Jim Beattie	.05
676	Biff Pocoroba	.05
677	Dave Revering	.05
678	Juan Beniquez	.05
679	Mike Scott	.05
680	Andre Dawson	.60
681	Dodgers Batting & Pitching Ldrs. (Pedro Guerrero, Fernando Valenzuela)	.05
682	Bob Stanley	.05
683	Dan Ford	.05
684	Rafael Landestoy	.05
685	Lee Mazzilli	.05
686	Randy Lerch	.05
687	U.L. Washington	.05
688	Jim Wohlford	.05
689	Ron Hassey	.05
690	Kent Hrbek	.60
691	Dave Tobik	.05
692	Denny Walling	.05
693	Sparky Lyle	.05
694	Sparky Lyle (Super Veteran)	.05
695	Ruppert Jones	.05
696	Chuck Tanner	.05
697	Barry Foote	.05
698	Tony Bernazard	.05
699	Lee Smith	.05
700	Keith Hernandez	.05
701	Batting Leaders (Al Oliver, Willie Wilson)	.05
702	Home Run Leaders (Reggie Jackson, Dave Kingman, Gorman Thomas)	.15
703	Runs Batted In Leaders (Hal McRae, Dale Murphy, Al Oliver)	.05
704	Stolen Base Leaders (Rickey Henderson, Tim Raines)	.10
705	Victory Leaders (Steve Carlton, LaMarr Hoyt)	.05
706	Strikeout Leaders (Floyd Bannister, Steve Carlton)	.05
707	Earned Run Average Leaders (Steve Rogers, Rick Sutcliffe)	.05
708	Leading Firemen (Dan Quisenberry, Bruce Sutter)	.10
709	Jimmy Sexton	.05
710	Willie Wilson	.05
711	Mariners Batting & Pitching Ldrs. (Jim Beattie, Bruce Bochte)	.05
712	Bruce Kison	.05
713	Ron Hodges	.05
714	Wayne Nordhagen	.05
715	Tony Perez	1.50
716	Tony Perez (Super Veteran)	.05
717	Scott Sanderson	.05
718	Jim Dwyer	.05
719	Rich Gale	.05
720	Dave Concepcion	.05
721	John Martin	.05
722	Jorge Orta	.05
723	Randy Moffitt	.05
724	Johnny Grubb	.05
725	Dan Spillner	.05
726	Harvey Kuenn	.05
727	Chet Lemon	.05
728	Ron Reed	.05
729	Jerry Morales	.05
730	Jason Thompson	.05
731	Al Williams	.05
732	Dave Henderson	.05
733	Buck Martinez	.05
734	Steve Braun	.05
735	Tommy John	.20
736	Tommy John	.05
737	Mitchell Page	.05
738	Tim Foli	.05
739	Rick Ownbey	.05
740	Rusty Staub	.05
741	Rusty Staub (Super Veteran)	.05
742	Padres Batting & Pitching Ldrs. (Terry Kennedy, Tim Lollar)	.05
743	Mike Torrez	.05
744	Brad Mills	.05
745	Scott McGregor	.05
746	John Wathan	.05
747	Fred Breining	.05
748	Derrel Thomas	.05
749	Jon Matlack	.05
750	Ben Oglivie	.05
751	Brad Havens	.05
752	Luis Pujols	.05
753	Elias Sosa	.05
754	Bill Robinson	.05
755	John Candelaria	.05
756	Russ Nixon	.05
757	Rick Manning	.05
758	Aurelio Rodriguez	.05
759	Doug Bird	.05
760	Dale Murphy	.60
761	Gary Lucas	.05
762	Cliff Johnson	.05
763	Al Cowens	.05
764	Pete Falcone	.05
765	Bob Boone	.05
766	Barry Bonnell	.05
767	Duane Kuiper	.05
768	Chris Speier	.05
769	Checklist 661-792	.05
770	Dave Winfield	2.00
771	Twins Batting & Pitching Ldrs. (Bobby Castillo, Kent Hrbek)	.05
772	Jim Kern	.05
773	Larry Hisle	.05
774	Alan Ashby	.05
775	Burt Hooton	.05
776	Larry Parrish	.05
777	John Curtis	.05
778	Rich Hebner	.05
779	Rick Waits	.05
780	Gary Matthews	.05
781	Rick Rhoden	.05
782	Bobby Murcer	.05
783	Bobby Murcer (Super Veteran)	.05
784	Jeff Newman	.05
785	Dennis Leonard	.05
786	Ralph Houk	.05
787	Dick Tidrow	.05
788	Dane Iorg	.05
789	Bryan Clark	.05
790	Bob Grich	.05
791	Gary Lavelle	.05
792	Chris Chambliss	.05

Traded

These 2-1/2" x 3-1/2" cards mark a continuation of the traded set introduced in 1981. The 132 cards retain the basic design of the year's regular issue, with their numbering being 1-132 with the "T" suffix. Cards in the set include traded players, new managers and promising rookies. Sold only through dealers, the set was in heavy demand as it contained the first cards of Darryl Strawberry, Ron Kittle, Julio Franco, and Mel Hall. While some of those cards were very hot in 1983, it seems likely that some of the rookies may not live up to their initial promise.

		NM/M
Complete Set (132):		20.00
Common Player:		.05
1T	Neil Allen	.05
2T	Bill Almon	.05
3T	Joe Altobelli	.05
4T	Tony Armas	.05
5T	Doug Bair	.05
6T	Steve Baker	.05
7T	Floyd Bannister	.05
8T	Don Baylor	.25
9T	Tony Bernazard	.05
10T	Larry Biittner	.05
11T	Dann Bilardello	.05
12T	Doug Bird	.05
13T	Steve Boros	.05
14T	Greg Brock RC	.05
15T	Mike Brown	.05
16T	Tom Burgmeier	.05
17T	Randy Bush RC	.05
18T	Bert Campaneris	.05
19T	Ron Cey	.25
20T	Chris Codiroli RC	.05
21T	Dave Collins	.05
22T	Terry Crowley	.05
23T	Julio Cruz	.05
24T	Mike Davis	.05
25T	Frank DiPino	.05
26T	Bill Doran RC	.05
27T	Jerry Dybzinski	.05
28T	Jamie Easterly	.05
29T	Juan Eichelberger	.05
30T	Jim Essian	.05
31T	Pete Falcone	.05
32T	Mike Ferraro	.05
33T	Terry Forster	.05
34T	Julio Franco RC	3.00
35T	Rich Gale	.05
36T	Kiko Garcia	.05
37T	Steve Garvey	1.00
38T	Johnny Grubb	.05
39T	Mel Hall RC	.05
40T	Von Hayes	.05
41T	Danny Heep	.05
42T	Steve Henderson	.05
43T	Keith Hernandez	.15
44T	Leo Hernandez	.05
45T	Willie Hernandez	.05
46T	Al Holland	.05
47T	Frank Howard	.05
48T	Bobby Johnson	.05
49T	Cliff Johnson	.05
50T	Odell Jones	.05
51T	Mike Jorgensen	.05
52T	Bob Kearney	.05
53T	Steve Kemp	.05
54T	Matt Keough	.05
55T	Ron Kittle RC	.05
56T	Mickey Klutts	.05
57T	Alan Knicely	.05
58T	Mike Krukow	.05
59T	Rafael Landestoy	.05
60T	Carney Lansford	.15
61T	Joe Lefebvre	.05
62T	Bryan Little	.05
63T	Aurelio Lopez	.05
64T	Mike Madden	.05
65T	Rick Manning	.05
66T	Billy Martin	.25
67T	Lee Mazzilli	.05
68T	Andy McGaffigan	.05
69T	Craig McMurtry RC	.05
70T	John McNamara	.05
71T	Orlando Mercado	.05
72T	Larry Milbourne	.05
73T	Randy Moffitt	.05

74T	Sid Monge	.05
75T	Jose Morales	.05
76T	Omar Moreno	.05
77T	Joe Morgan	4.00
78T	Mike Morgan	.05
79T	Dale Murray	.05
80T	Jeff Newman	.05
81T	Pete O'Brien RC	.05
82T	Jorge Orta	.05
83T	Alejandro Pena RC	.05
84T	Pascual Perez	.05
85T	Tony Perez	1.00
86T	Broderick Perkins	.05
87T	Tony Phillips RC	.15
88T	Charlie Puleo	.05
89T	Pat Putnam	.05
90T	Jamie Quirk	.05
91T	Doug Rader	.05
92T	Chuck Rainey	.05
93T	Bobby Ramos	.05
94T	Gary Redus	.05
95T	Steve Renko	.05
96T	Leon Roberts	.05
97T	Aurelio Rodriguez	.05
98T	Dick Ruthven	.05
99T	Daryl Sconiers	.05
100T	Mike Scott	.05
101T	Tom Seaver	6.00
102T	John Shelby RC	.05
103T	Bob Shirley	.05
104T	Joe Simpson	.05
105T	Doug Sisk RC	.05
106T	Mike Smithson RC	.05
107T	Elias Sosa	.05
108T	Darryl Strawberry RC	10.00
109T	Tom Tellmann	.05
110T	Gene Tenace	.05
111T	Gorman Thomas	.05
112T	Dick Tidrow	.05
113T	Dave Tobik	.05
114T	Wayne Tolleson RC	.05
115T	Mike Torrez	.05
116T	Manny Trillo	.05
117T	Steve Trout	.05
118T	Lee Tunnell RC	.05
119T	Mike Vail	.05
120T	Ellis Valentine	.05
121T	Tom Veryzer	.05
122T	George Vukovich	.05
123T	Rick Waits	.05
124T	Greg Walker RC	.05
125T	Chris Welsh	.05
126T	Len Whitehouse	.05
127T	Eddie Whitson	.05
128T	Jim Wohlford	.05
129T	Matt Young RC	.05
130T	Joel Youngblood	.05
131T	Pat Zachry	.05
132T	Checklist 1-132	.05

Traded Steve Carlton Bronze

The first in a series of 1/4-size metal replicas of Topps star cards was issued to dealers who purchased cases of 1983 Topps Traded sets. Each detail of the 1983 Steve Carlton card is reproduced on the 1-1/4" x 1-3/4" bronze metal mini-card, right down to the stats.

		NM/M
70	Steve Carlton	6.00

1982 League Leaders Sheet

The leaders in various major statistical categories in 1982 are featured on this 7-1/2" x 10-1/2" blank-back sheet. Most of the cards on the

sheet are identical to the players' regular 1983 Topps cards except for a white strip at upper-left identifying their statistical accomplishment. Reggie Jackson and Gorman Thomas who shared the A.L. home run record for 1982 share a card on this sheet. Available via a mail-in offer, huge quantities of these sheets are readily available.

NM/M

Uncut Sheet:
Willie Wilson,
Reggie Jackson,
Gorman Thomas, Al Oliver,
LaMarr Hoyt, Steve Carlton,
Dan Quisenberry,
Dave Kingman,
Bruce Sutter. 1.00

All-Star Glossy Set of 40

This set was a "consolation prize" in a scratch-off contest in regular packs of 1983 cards. The 2-1/2" x 3-1/2" cards have a large color photo surrounded by a yellow frame on the front. In very small type on a white border is printed the player's name. Backs carry the player's name, team, position and the card number along with a Topps identification. A major feature is that the surface of the front is glossy, which most collectors find very attractive. With many top stars, the set is a popular one, but the price has not moved too far above the issue price.

		NM/M
Complete Set (40):		3.00
Common Player:		.05
1	Carl Yastrzemski	.25
2	Mookie Wilson	.05
3	Andre Thornton	.05
4	Keith Hernandez	.05
5	Robin Yount	.25
6	Terry Kennedy	.05
7	Dave Winfield	.25
8	Mike Schmidt	.50
9	Buddy Bell	.05
10	Fernando Valenzuela	.05
11	Rich Gossage	.05
12	Bob Horner	.05
13	Toby Harrah	.05
14	Pete Rose	.75
15	Cecil Cooper	.05
16	Dale Murphy	.15
17	Carlton Fisk	.25
18	Ray Knight	.05
19	Jim Palmer	.25
20	Gary Carter	.25
21	Richard Zisk	.05
22	Dusty Baker	.05
23	Willie Wilson	.05
24	Bill Buckner	.05
25	Dave Stieb	.05
26	Bill Madlock	.05
27	Lance Parrish	.05
28	Nolan Ryan	1.00
29	Rod Carew	.25
30	Al Oliver	.05
31	George Brett	.50
32	Jack Clark	.05
33	Rickey Henderson	.25
34	Dave Concepcion	.05
35	Kent Hrbek	.05
36	Steve Carlton	.25
37	Eddie Murray	.25
38	Ruppert Jones	.05
39	Reggie Jackson	.30
40	Bruce Sutter	.20

Foldouts

Another Topps test issue, these 3-1/2" x 5-5/16" cards were printed in booklets like souvenir postcards. Each of the booklets have a theme of currently playing statistical leaders in a specific category such as home runs. The cards feature a color player photo on each side. A black strip at the

bottom gives the player's name, position and team along with statistics in the particular category. A facsimile autograph crosses the photograph. Booklets carry nine cards, with eight having players on both sides and one doubling as the back cover, for a total of 17 cards per booklet. There are 85 cards in the set, although some players appear in more than one category. Naturally, most of the players pictured are stars. Even so, the set is a problem as it seems to be most valuable when complete and unseparated, so the cards are difficult to display.

		NM/M
Complete Set (5):		9.00
Common Folder:		3.00
1	Pitching Leaders (Vida Blue, Bert Blyleven, Steve Carlton, Fergie Jenkins, Tommy John, Jim Kaat, Jerry Koosman, Joe Niekro, Phil Niekro, Jim Palmer, Gaylord Perry, Jerry Reuss, Nolan Ryan, Tom Seaver, Paul Splittorff, Don Sutton, Mike Torrez)	6.00
2	Home Run Leaders (Johnny Bench, Ron Cey, Darrell Evans, George Foster, Reggie Jackson, Dave Kingman, Greg Luzinski, John Mayberry, Rick Monday, Joe Morgan, Bobby Murcer, Graig Nettles, Tony Perez, Jim Rice, Mike Schmidt, Rusty Staub, Carl Yastrzemski)	4.50
3	Batting Leaders (George Brett, Rod Carew, Cecil Cooper, Steve Garvey, Ken Griffey, Pedro Guerrero, Keith Hernandez, Dane Iorg, Fred Lynn, Bill Madlock, Bake McBride, Al Oliver, Dave Parker, Jim Rice, Pete Rose, Lonnie Smith, Willie Wilson)	4.50
4	Relief Aces (Tom Burgmeier, Bill Campbell, Ed Farmer, Rollie Fingers, Terry Forster, Gene Garber, Rich Gossage, Jim Kern, Gary Lavelle, Tug McGraw, Greg Minton, Randy Moffitt, Dan Quisenberry, Ron Reed, Elias Sosa, Bruce Sutter, Kent Tekulve)	3.00
5	Stolen Base Leaders (Don Baylor, Larry Bowa, Al Bumbry, Rod Carew, Cesar Cedeno, Dave Concepcion, Jose Cruz, Julio Cruz, Rickey Henderson, Ron LeFlore, Davey Lopes, Garry Maddox, Omar Moreno, Joe Morgan, Amos Otis, Mickey Rivers, Willie Wilson)	3.00

Stickers

Topps increased the number of stickers in its set to 330 in 1983, but retained the same 1-15/16" x 2-9/16" size. The stickers are again numbered on both the front and back. Similar in style to previous sticker issues, the set includes 28 "foil" stickers, and various special stickers highlighting the 1982 season, playoffs and World Series. An album was also available.

		NM/M
Complete Set (330):		15.00
Common Player:		.05
Sticker Album:		2.00
Wax Pack (5):		.25
Wax Box (100):		16.00
1	Hank Aaron	1.00
2	Babe Ruth	2.00
3	Willie Mays	1.00
4	Frank Robinson	.15
5	Reggie Jackson	.50
6	Carl Yastrzemski	.25
7	Johnny Bench	.25
8	Tony Perez	.25
9	Lee May	.05
10	Mike Schmidt	.50
11	Dave Kingman	.05
12	Reggie Smith	.05
13	Graig Nettles	.05
14	Rusty Staub	.05
15	Willie Wilson	.05
16	LaMarr Hoyt	.05
17	Reggie Jackson, Gorman Thomas	.10
18	Floyd Bannister	.05
19	Hal McRae	.05
20	Rick Sutcliffe	.05
21	Rickey Henderson	.25
22	Dan Quisenberry	.05
23	Jim Palmer	.25
24	John Lowenstein	.05
25	Mike Flanagan	.05
26	Cal Ripken, Jr.	1.00
27	Rich Dauer	.05
28	Ken Singleton	.05
29	Eddie Murray	.25
30	Rick Dempsey	.05
31	Carl Yastrzemski	.25
32	Carney Lansford	.05
33	Jerry Remy	.05
34	Dennis Eckersley	.20
35	Dave Stapleton	.05
36	Mark Clear	.05
37	Jim Rice	.15
38	Dwight Evans	.05
39	Rod Carew	.25
40	Don Baylor	.10
41	Reggie Jackson	.50
42	Geoff Zahn	.05
43	Bobby Grich	.05
44	Fred Lynn	.05
45	Bob Boone	.05
46	Doug DeCinces	.05
47	Tom Paciorek	.05
48	Britt Burns	.05
49	Tony Bernazard	.05
50	Steve Kemp	.05
51	Greg Luzinski	.05
52	Harold Baines	.05
53	LaMarr Hoyt	.05
54	Carlton Fisk	.25
55	Andre Thornton	.05
56	Mike Hargrove	.05
57	Len Barker	.05
58	Toby Harrah	.05
59	Dan Spillner	.05
60	Rick Manning	.05
61	Rick Sutcliffe	.05
62	Ron Hassey	.05
63	Lance Parrish	.05
64	John Wockenfuss	.05
65	Lou Whitaker	.05
66	Alan Trammell	.05
67	Kirk Gibson	.05
68	Larry Herndon	.05
69	Jack Morris	.05
70	Dan Petry	.05
71	Frank White	.05
72	Amos Otis	.05
73	Willie Wilson	.05
74	Dan Quisenberry	.05
75	Hal McRae	.05
76	George Brett	.60
77	Larry Gura	.05
78	John Wathan	.05
79	Rollie Fingers	.20
80	Cecil Cooper	.05
81	Robin Yount	.20
82	Ben Oglivie	.05
83	Paul Molitor	.05
84	Gorman Thomas	.05
85	Ted Simmons	.05
86	Pete Vuckovich	.05
87	Gary Gaetti	.05
88	Kent Hrbek	.05
89	John Castino	.05
90	Tom Brunansky	.05
91	Bobby Mitchell	.05
92	Gary Ward	.05
93	Tim Laudner	.05
94	Ron Davis	.05
95	Willie Randolph	.05
96	Roy Smalley	.05
97	Jerry Mumphrey	.05

98	Ken Griffey	.05
99	Dave Winfield	.25
100	Rich Gossage	.05
101	Butch Wynegar	.05
102	Ron Guidry	.05
103	Rickey Henderson	.25
104	Mike Heath	.05
105	Dave Lopes	.05
106	Rick Langford	.05
107	Dwayne Murphy	.05
108	Tony Armas	.05
109	Matt Keough	.05
110	Dan Meyer	.05
111	Bruce Bochte	.05
112	Julio Cruz	.05
113	Floyd Bannister	.05
114	Gaylord Perry	.20
115	Al Cowens	.05
116	Richie Zisk	.05
117	Jim Essian	.05
118	Bill Caudill	.05
119	Buddy Bell	.05
120	Larry Parrish	.05
121	Danny Darwin	.05
122	Bucky Dent	.05
123	Johnny Grubb	.05
124	George Wright	.05
125	Charlie Hough	.05
126	Jim Sundberg	.05
127	Dave Stieb	.05
128	Willie Upshaw	.05
129	Alfredo Griffin	.05
130	Lloyd Moseby	.05
131	Ernie Whitt	.05
132	Jim Clancy	.05
133	Barry Bonnell	.05
134	Damaso Garcia	.05
135	Jim Kaat	.05
136	Jim Kaat	.05
137	Greg Minton	.05
138	Greg Minton	.05
139	Paul Molitor	.20
140	Paul Molitor	.20
141	Manny Trillo	.05
142	Manny Trillo	.05
143	Joel Youngblood	.05
144	Joel Youngblood	.05
145	Robin Yount	.20
146	Robin Yount	.20
147	Willie McGee	.05
148	Darrell Porter	.05
149	Darrell Porter	.05
150	Robin Yount	.20
151	Bruce Benedict	.05
152	Bruce Benedict	.05
153	George Hendrick	.05
154	Bruce Benedict	.05
155	Doug DeCinces	.05
156	Paul Molitor	.20
157	Charlie Moore	.05
158	Fred Lynn	.05
159	Rickey Henderson	.25
160	Dale Murphy	.15
161	Willie Wilson	.05
162	Jack Clark	.05
163	Reggie Jackson	.50
164	Andre Dawson	.15
165	Dan Quisenberry	.05
166	Bruce Sutter	.20
167	Robin Yount	.20
168	Ozzie Smith	.25
169	Frank White	.05
170	Phil Garner	.05
171	Doug DeCinces	.05
172	Mike Schmidt	.50
173	Cecil Cooper	.05
174	Al Oliver	.05
175	Jim Palmer	.25
176	Steve Carlton	.25
177	Carlton Fisk	.25
178	Gary Carter	.25
179	Joaquin Andujar	.05
180	Ozzie Smith	.25
181	Cecil Cooper	.05
182	Darrell Porter	.05
183	Darrell Porter	.05
184	Mike Caldwell	.05
185	Mike Caldwell	.05
186	Ozzie Smith	.25
187	Bruce Sutter	.20
188	Keith Hernandez	.05
189	Dane Iorg	.05
190	Dane Iorg	.05
191	Tony Armas	.05
192	Tony Armas	.05
193	Lance Parrish	.05
194	Lance Parrish	.05
195	John Wathan	.05
196	John Wathan	.05
197	Rickey Henderson	.20
198	Rickey Henderson	.20
199	Rickey Henderson	.20
200	Rickey Henderson	.20
201	Rickey Henderson	.20
202	Rickey Henderson	.20
203	Steve Carlton	.20
204	Steve Carlton	.20
205	Al Oliver	.05
206	Dale Murphy, Al Oliver	.05
207	Dave Kingman	.05
208	Steve Rogers	.05
209	Bruce Sutter	.20
210	Tim Raines	.05
211	Dale Murphy	.15
212	Chris Chambliss	.05
213	Gene Garber	.05
214	Bob Horner	.05
215	Glenn Hubbard	.05

No.	Player	Price
216	Claudell Washington	.05
217	Bruce Benedict	.05
218	Phil Niekro	.20
219	Leon Durham	.05
220	Jay Johnstone	.05
221	Larry Bowa	.05
222	Keith Moreland	.05
223	Bill Buckner	.05
224	Fergie Jenkins	.20
225	Dick Tidrow	.05
226	Jody Davis	.05
227	Dave Concepcion	.05
228	Dan Driessen	.05
229	Johnny Bench	.25
230	Ron Oester	.05
231	Cesar Cedeno	.05
232	Alex Trevino	.05
233	Tom Seaver	.25
234	Mario Soto	.05
235	Nolan Ryan	1.00
236	Art Howe	.05
237	Phil Garner	.05
238	Ray Knight	.05
239	Terry Puhl	.05
240	Joe Niekro	.05
241	Alan Ashby	.05
242	Jose Cruz	.05
243	Steve Garvey	.15
244	Ron Cey	.05
245	Dusty Baker	.05
246	Ken Landreaux	.05
247	Jerry Reuss	.05
248	Pedro Guerrero	.05
249	Bill Russell	.05
250	Fernando Valenzuela	.05
251	Al Oliver	.05
252	Andre Dawson	.15
253	Tim Raines	.05
254	Jeff Reardon	.05
255	Gary Carter	.25
256	Steve Rogers	.05
257	Tim Wallach	.05
258	Chris Speier	.05
259	Dave Kingman	.05
260	Bob Bailor	.05
261	Hubie Brooks	.05
262	Craig Swan	.05
263	George Foster	.05
264	John Stearns	.05
265	Neil Allen	.05
266	Mookie Wilson	.05
267	Steve Carlton	.20
268	Manny Trillo	.05
269	Gary Matthews	.05
270	Mike Schmidt	.50
271	Ivan DeJesus	.05
272	Pete Rose	.75
273	Bo Diaz	.05
274	Sid Monge	.05
275	Bill Madlock	.05
276	Jason Thompson	.05
277	Don Robinson	.05
278	Omar Moreno	.05
279	Dale Berra	.05
280	Dave Parker	.05
281	Tony Pena	.05
282	John Candelaria	.05
283	Lonnie Smith	.05
284	Bruce Sutter	.20
285	George Hendrick	.05
286	Tom Herr	.05
287	Ken Oberkfell	.05
288	Ozzie Smith	.25
289	Bob Forsch	.05
290	Keith Hernandez	.05
291	Garry Templeton	.05
292	Broderick Perkins	.05
293	Terry Kennedy	.05
294	Gene Richards	.05
295	Ruppert Jones	.05
296	Tim Lollar	.05
297	John Montefusco	.05
298	Sixto Lezcano	.05
299	Greg Minton	.05
300	Jack Clark	.05
301	Milt May	.05
302	Reggie Smith	.05
303	Joe Morgan	.25
304	John LeMaster	.05
305	Darrell Evans	.05
306	Al Holland	.05
307	Jesse Barfield	.05
308	Wade Boggs	.60
309	Tom Brunansky	.05
310	Storm Davis	.05
311	Von Hayes	.05
312	Dave Hostetler	.05
313	Kent Hrbek	.05
314	Tim Laudner	.05
315	Cal Ripken, Jr.	1.00
316	Andre Robertson	.05
317	Ed Vande Berg	.05
318	Glenn Wilson	.05
319	Chili Davis	.05
320	Bob Dernier	.05
321	Terry Francona	.05
322	Brian Giles	.05
323	David Green	.05
324	Atlee Hammaker	.05
325	Bill Laskey	.05
326	Willie McGee	.05
327	Johnny Ray	.05
328	Ryne Sandberg	.75
329	Steve Sax	.05
330	Eric Show	.05

Stickers Boxes

These eight cards were printed on the back panels of 1983 Topps sticker boxes, one card per box. The blank-backed cards measure the standard 2-1/2" x 3-1/2" and feature a full-color photo with the player's name at the top. The rest of the back panel advertises the sticker album, while the front of the box has an action photo of Reggie Jackson. The boxes are numbered on the front. Prices in the checklist that follows are for complete boxes.

		NM/M
	Complete Set (8):	6.50
	Common Player:	.75
1	Fernando Valenzuela	.75
2	Gary Carter	1.00
3	Mike Schmidt	1.50
4	Reggie Jackson	1.25
5	Jim Palmer	.75
6	Rollie Fingers	.75
7	Pete Rose	2.00
8	Rickey Henderson	1.00

1952 Reprint Set

The first of several reprint/retro sets in different sports issued by Topps, the 402-card reprinting of its classic 1952 baseball card set was controversial at the time of issue, but has since gained hobby acceptance and market value. To avoid possible confusion of the reprints for originals, the reprints were done in the now-standard 2-1/2" x 3-3/4" format instead of the original 2-5/8" x 3-3/4". Backs, printed in red, carry a line "Topps 1952 Reprint Series" at bottom, though there is no indication of the year of reprinting. Fronts have a semi-gloss finish, which also differs from the originals. Because of inability to come to terms with five of the players from the original 1952 Topps set, they were not included in the reprint series. Those cards which weren't issued are: #20 Billy Loes, #22 Dom DiMaggio, #159 Saul Rogovin, #196 Solly Hemus, and #289 Tommy Holmes. The '52 reprints were available only as a complete boxed set with a retail price of about $40 at issue.

	NM/M
Complete Sealed Boxed Set:	175.00
Complete Set (402):	150.00
Common Player:	.25
Minor Stars:	.35
Typical Hall of Famers:	2.00
Superstar Hall of Famers:	8.00
311 Mickey Mantle	30.00
407 Eddie Mathews (Sample card.)	8.00

1984 Topps

Another 792-card regular set from Topps. For the second straight year, the 2-1/2" x 3-1/2" cards featured a color action photo on the front along with a small portrait photo in the lower-left. The team name runs in big letters down the left side, while the player's name and position appear under the action photo. Backs have a team logo in the upper-right, along with statistics, personal information and a few highlights, all in a hard-to-read red and purple coloring. Specialty cards include past season highlights, team leaders, statistical leaders, All-Stars, active career leaders and numbered checklists. Again, promising rookies were saved for the traded set. The six 132-card uncut sheets which comprise the set were made available to collectors at about $30 for the set.

	NM/M
Complete Set (792):	40.00
Common Player:	.05
Wax Pack (15):	2.00
Wax Box (36):	50.00
Cello Pack (28):	2.50
Cello Box (24):	50.00
Rack Pack (54+1):	3.50
Rack Box (24):	60.00
Vending Box (500):	20.00

No.	Player	Price
1	Steve Carlton (1983 Highlight)	.25
2	Rickey Henderson (1983 Highlight)	.25
3	Dan Quisenberry (1983 Highlight)	.05
4	Steve Carlton, Gaylord Perry, Nolan Ryan (1983 Highlight)	.50
5	Bob Forsch, Dave Righetti, Mike Warren (1983 Highlight)	.05
6	Johnny Bench, Gaylord Perry, Carl Yastrzemski (1983 Highlight)	.25
7	Gary Lucas	.05
8	Don Mattingly RC	15.00
9	Jim Gott	.05
10	Robin Yount	1.00
11	Twins Batting & Pitching Leaders (Kent Hrbek, Ken Schrom)	.05
12	Billy Sample	.05
13	Scott Holman	.05
14	Tom Brookens	.05
15	Burt Hooton	.05
16	Omar Moreno	.05
17	John Denny	.05
18	Dale Berra	.05
19	Ray Fontenot RC	.05
20	Greg Luzinski	.05
21	Joe Altobelli	.05
22	Bryan Clark	.05
23	Keith Moreland	.05
24	John Martin	.05
25	Glenn Hubbard	.05
26	Bud Black	.05
27	Daryl Sconiers	.05
28	Frank Viola	.05
29	Danny Heep	.05
30	Wade Boggs	3.00
31	Andy McGaffigan	.05
32	Bobby Ramos	.05
33	Tom Burgmeier	.05
34	Eddie Milner	.05
35	Don Sutton	.65
36	Denny Walling	.05
37	Rangers Batting & Pitching Leaders (Buddy Bell, Rick Honeycutt)	.05
38	Luis DeLeon	.05
39	Garth Iorg	.05
40	Dusty Baker	.05
41	Tony Bernazard	.05
42	Johnny Grubb	.05
43	Ron Reed	.05
44	Jim Morrison	.05
45	Jerry Mumphrey	.05
46	Ray Smith	.05
47	Rudy Law	.05
48	Julio Franco	.05
49	John Stuper	.05
50	Chris Chambliss	.05
51	Jim Frey	.05
52	Paul Splittorff	.05
53	Juan Beniquez	.05
54	Jesse Orosco	.05
55	Dave Concepcion	.05
56	Gary Allenson	.05
57	Dan Schatzeder	.05
58	Max Venable	.05
59	Sammy Stewart	.05
60	Paul Molitor	1.00
61	Chris Codiroli RC	.05
62	Dave Hostetler	.05
63	Ed Vande Berg	.05
64	Mike Scioscia	.05
65	Kirk Gibson	.05
66	Astros Batting & Pitching Leaders (Jose Cruz, Nolan Ryan)	.05
67	Gary Ward	.05
68	Luis Salazar	.05
69	Rod Scurry	.05
70	Gary Matthews	.05
71	Leo Hernandez	.05
72	Mike Squires	.05
73	Jody Davis	.05
74	Jerry Martin	.05
75	Bob Forsch	.05
76	Alfredo Griffin	.05
77	Brett Butler	.05
78	Mike Torrez	.05
79	Rob Wilfong	.05
80	Steve Rogers	.05
81	Billy Martin	.15
82	Doug Bird	.05
83	Richie Zisk	.05
84	Lenny Faedo	.05
85	Atlee Hammaker	.05
86	John Shelby RC	.05
87	Frank Pastore	.05
88	Rob Picciolo	.05
89	Mike Smithson RC	.05
90	Pedro Guerrero	.05
91	Dan Spillner	.05
92	Lloyd Moseby	.05
93	Bob Knepper	.05
94	Mario Ramirez	.05
95	Aurelio Lopez	.05
96	Royals Batting & Pitching Leaders (Larry Gura, Hal McRae)	.05
97	LaMarr Hoyt	.05
98	Steve Nicosia	.05
99	Craig Lefferts RC	.25
100	Reggie Jackson	1.50
101	Porfirio Altamirano	.05
102	Ken Oberkfell	.05
103	Dwayne Murphy	.05
104	Ken Dayley	.05
105	Tony Armas	.05
106	Tim Stoddard	.05
107	Ned Yost	.05
108	Randy Moffitt	.05
109	Brad Wellman	.05
110	Ron Guidry	.05
111	Bill Virdon	.05
112	Tom Niedenfuer	.05
113	Kelly Paris	.05
114	Checklist 1-132	.05
115	Andre Thornton	.05
116	George Bjorkman	.05
117	Tom Veryzer	.05
118	Charlie Hough	.05
119	Johnny Wockenfuss	.05
120	Keith Hernandez	.05
121	Pat Sheridan RC	.05
122	Cecilio Guante RC	.05
123	Butch Wynegar	.05
124	Damaso Garcia	.05
125	Britt Burns	.05
126	Braves Batting & Pitching Leaders (Craig McMurtry, Dale Murphy)	.05
127	Mike Madden	.05
128	Rick Manning	.05
129	Bill Laskey	.05
130	Ozzie Smith	2.00
131	Batting Leaders (Wade Boggs, Bill Madlock)	.25
132	Home Run Leaders (Jim Rice, Mike Schmidt)	.25
133	RBI Leaders (Cecil Cooper, Dale Murphy, Jim Rice)	.10
134	Stolen Base Leaders (Rickey Henderson, Tim Raines)	.25
135	Victory Leaders (John Denny, LaMarr Hoyt)	.05
136	Strikeout Leaders (Steve Carlton, Jack Morris)	.05
137	Earned Run Average Leaders (Atlee Hammaker, Rick Honeycutt)	.05
138	Leading Firemen (Al Holland, Dan Quisenberry)	.05
139	Bert Campaneris	.05
140	Storm Davis	.05
141	Pat Corrales	.05
142	Rich Gale	.05
143	Jose Morales	.05
144	Brian Harper RC	.20
145	Gary Lavelle	.05
146	Ed Romero	.05
147	Dan Petry	.05
148	Joe Lefebvre	.05
149	Jon Matlack	.05
150	Dale Murphy	.50
151	Steve Trout	.05
152	Glenn Brummer	.05
153	Dick Tidrow	.05
154	Dave Henderson	.05
155	Frank White	.05
156	Athletics Batting & Pitching Leaders (Tim Conroy, Rickey Henderson)	.15
157	Gary Gaetti	.05
158	John Curtis	.05
159	Darryl Cias	.05
160	Mario Soto	.05
161	Junior Ortiz RC	.05
162	Bob Ojeda	.05
163	Lorenzo Gray	.05
164	Scott Sanderson	.05
165	Ken Singleton	.05
166	Jamie Nelson	.05
167	Marshall Edwards	.05
168	Juan Bonilla	.05
169	Larry Parrish	.05
170	Jerry Reuss	.05
171	Frank Robinson	.25
172	Frank DiPino	.05
173	Marvell Wynne RC	.05
174	Juan Berenguer	.05
175	Graig Nettles	.05
176	Lee Smith	.05
177	Jerry Hairston Sr.	.05
178	Bill Krueger	.05
179	Buck Martinez	.05
180	Manny Trillo	.05
181	Roy Thomas	.05
182	Darryl Strawberry	.25
183	Al Williams	.05
184	Mike O'Berry	.05
185	Sixto Lezcano	.05
186	Cardinals Batting & Pitching Leaders (Lonnie Smith, John Stuper)	.05
187	Luis Aponte	.05
188	Bryan Little	.05
189	Tim Conroy RC	.05
190	Ben Oglivie	.05
191	Mike Boddicker	.05
192	Nick Esasky RC	.05
193	Darrell Brown	.05
194	Domingo Ramos	.05
195	Jack Morris	.05
196	Don Slaught RC	.05
197	Garry Hancock	.05
198	Bill Doran RC	.05
199	Willie Hernandez	.05
200	Andre Dawson	.60
201	Bruce Kison	.05
202	Bobby Cox	.05
203	Matt Keough	.05
204	Bobby Meacham RC	.05
205	Greg Minton	.05
206	Andy Van Slyke RC	.75
207	Donnie Moore	.05
208	Jose Oquendo RC	.05
209	Manny Sarmiento	.05
210	Joe Morgan	1.00
211	Rick Sweet	.05
212	Broderick Perkins	.05
213	Bruce Hurst	.05
214	Paul Householder	.05
215	Tippy Martinez	.05
216	White Sox Batting & Pitching Leaders (Richard Dotson, Carlton Fisk)	.05
217	Alan Ashby	.05
218	Rick Waits	.05
219	Joe Simpson	.05
220	Fernando Valenzuela	.05
221	Cliff Johnson	.05
222	Rick Honeycutt	.05
223	Wayne Krenchicki	.05
224	Sid Monge	.05
225	Lee Mazzilli	.05
226	Juan Eichelberger	.05
227	Steve Braun	.05
228	John Rabb	.05
229	Paul Owens	.05
230	Rickey Henderson	1.00
231	Gary Woods	.05
232	Tim Wallach	.05
233	Checklist 133-264	.05
234	Rafael Ramirez	.05
235	Matt Young RC	.05
236	Ellis Valentine	.05
237	John Castino	.05
238	Reid Nichols	.05
239	Jay Howell	.05
240	Eddie Murray	1.00
241	Billy Almon	.05
242	Alex Trevino	.05
243	Pete Ladd	.05
244	Candy Maldonado RC	.05
245	Rick Sutcliffe	.05
246	Mets Batting & Pitching Leaders (Tom Seaver, Mookie Wilson)	.25
247	Onix Concepcion	.05
248	Bill Dawley RC	.05
249	Jay Johnstone	.05
250	Bill Madlock	.05
251	Tony Gwynn	4.00
252	Larry Christenson	.05
253	Jim Wohlford	.05
254	Shane Rawley	.05
255	Bruce Benedict	.05
256	Dave Geisel	.05
257	Julio Cruz	.05
258	Luis Sanchez	.05
259	Sparky Anderson	.15
260	Scott McGregor	.05
261	Bobby Brown	.05
262	Tom Candiotti RC	.25
263	Jack Fimple	.05
264	Doug Frobel	.05
265	Donnie Hill RC	.05
266	Steve Lubratich	.05
267	Carmelo Martinez RC	.05
268	Jack O'Connor	.05
269	Aurelio Rodriguez	.05
270	Jeff Russell RC	.05
271	Moose Haas	.05
272	Rick Dempsey	.05
273	Charlie Puleo	.05
274	Rick Monday	.05
275	Len Matuszek	.05
276	Angels Batting & Pitching Leaders (Rod Carew, Geoff Zahn)	.10
277	Eddie Whitson	.05
278	Jorge Bell	.05
279	Ivan DeJesus	.05
280	Floyd Bannister	.05
281	Larry Milbourne	.05
282	Jim Barr	.05
283	Larry Biittner	.05
284	Howard Bailey	.05
285	Darrell Porter	.05
286	Lary Sorensen	.05
287	Warren Cromartie	.05
288	Jim Beattie	.05
289	Randy S. Johnson	.05
290	Dave Dravecky	.05
291	Chuck Tanner	.05
292	Tony Scott	.05
293	Ed Lynch	.05
294	U.L. Washington	.05
295	Mike Flanagan	.05
296	Jeff Newman	.05
297	Bruce Berenyi	.05
298	Jim Gantner	.05
299	John Butcher	.05
300	Pete Rose	5.00
301	Frank LaCorte	.05
302	Barry Bonnell	.05
303	Marty Castillo	.05
304	Warren Brusstar	.05
305	Roy Smalley	.05
306	Dodgers Batting & Pitching Leaders (Pedro Guerrero, Bob Welch)	.05
307	Bobby Mitchell	.05
308	Ron Hassey	.05
309	Tony Phillips	.05
310	Willie McGee	.05
311	Jerry Koosman	.05
312	Jorge Orta	.05
313	Mike Jorgensen	.05
314	Orlando Mercado	.05
315	Bob Grich	.05
316	Mark Bradley	.05
317	Greg Pryor	.05
318	Bill Gullickson	.05
319	Al Bumbry	.05
320	Bob Stanley	.05
321	Harvey Kuenn	.05
322	Ken Schrom	.05
323	Alan Knicely	.05
324	Alejandro Pena RC	.05
325	Darrell Evans	.05
326	Bob Kearney	.05
327	Ruppert Jones	.05
328	Vern Ruhle	.05
329	Pat Tabler RC	.05
330	John Candelaria	.05
331	Bucky Dent	.05
332	Kevin Gross RC	.05
333	Larry Herndon	.05
334	Chuck Rainey	.05
335	Don Baylor	.15
336	Mariners Batting & Pitching Leaders (Pat Putnam, Matt Young)	.05
337	Kevin Hagen	.05
338	Mike Warren	.05
339	Roy Lee Jackson	.05
340	Hal McRae	.05
341	Dave Tobik	.05
342	Tim Foli	.05
343	Mark Davis	.05
344	Rick Miller	.05
345	Kent Hrbek	.05
346	Kurt Bevacqua	.05
347	Allan Ramirez	.05
348	Toby Harrah	.05
349	Bob L. Gibson	.05
350	George Foster	.05
351	Russ Nixon	.05
352	Dave Stewart	.05
353	Jim Anderson	.05
354	Jeff Burroughs	.05
355	Jason Thompson	.05
356	Glenn Abbott	.05
357	Ron Cey	.05
358	Bob Dernier	.05
359	Jim Acker RC	.05
360	Willie Randolph	.05
361	Dave Smith	.05
362	David Green	.05
363	Tim Laudner	.05
364	Scott Fletcher RC	.05
365	Steve Bedrosian	.05
366	Padres Batting & Pitching Leaders (Dave Dravecky, Terry Kennedy)	.05
367	Jamie Easterly	.05
368	Hubie Brooks	.05
369	Steve McCatty	.05
370	Tim Raines	.05
371	Dave Gumpert	.05

#	Player	Price
372	Gary Roenicke	.05
373	Bill Scherrer	.05
374	Don Money	.05
375	Dennis Leonard	.05
376	Dave Anderson RC	.05
377	Danny Darwin	.05
378	Bob Brenly	.05
379	Checklist 265-396	.05
380	Steve Garvey	.45
381	Ralph Houk	.05
382	Chris Nyman	.05
383	Terry Puhl	.05
384	Lee Tunnell RC	.05
385	Tony Perez	1.00
386	George Hendrick/AS	.05
387	Johnny Ray/AS	.05
388	Mike Schmidt/AS	.75
389	Ozzie Smith/AS	.50
390	Tim Raines/AS	.05
391	Dale Murphy/AS	.20
392	Andre Dawson/AS	.25
393	Gary Carter/AS	.30
394	Steve Rogers/AS	.05
395	Steve Carlton/AS	.25
396	Jesse Orosco/AS	.05
397	Eddie Murray/AS	.40
398	Lou Whitaker/AS	.05
399	George Brett/AS	.75
400	Cal Ripken, Jr./AS	4.00
401	Jim Rice/AS	.05
402	Dave Winfield/AS	.30
403	Lloyd Moseby/AS	.05
404	Ted Simmons/AS	.05
405	LaMarr Hoyt/AS	.05
406	Ron Guidry/AS	.05
407	Dan Quisenberry/AS	.05
408	Lou Piniella	.05
409	Juan Agosto RC	.05
410	Claudell Washington	.05
411	Houston Jimenez	.05
412	Doug Rader	.05
413	Spike Owen RC	.05
414	Mitchell Page	.05
415	Tommy John	.15
416	Dane Iorg	.05
417	Mike Armstrong	.05
418	Ron Hodges	.05
419	John Henry Johnson	.05
420	Cecil Cooper	.05
421	Charlie Lea	.05
422	Jose Cruz	.05
423	Mike Morgan	.05
424	Dann Bilardello	.05
425	Steve Howe	.05
426	Orioles Batting & Pitching Leaders (Mike Boddicker, Cal Ripken, Jr.)	.50
427	Rick Leach	.05
428	Fred Breining	.05
429	Randy Bush RC	.05
430	Rusty Staub	.05
431	Chris Bando	.05
432	Charlie Hudson RC	.05
433	Rich Hebner	.05
434	Harold Baines	.05
435	Neil Allen	.05
436	Rick Peters	.05
437	Mike Proly	.05
438	Biff Pocoroba	.05
439	Bob Stoddard	.05
440	Steve Kemp	.05
441	Bob Lillis	.05
442	Byron McLaughlin	.05
443	Benny Ayala	.05
444	Steve Renko	.05
445	Jerry Remy	.05
446	Luis Pujols	.05
447	Tom Brunansky	.05
448	Ben Hayes	.05
449	Joe Pettini	.05
450	Gary Carter	1.00
451	Bob Jones	.05
452	Chuck Porter	.05
453	Willie Upshaw	.05
454	Joe Beckwith	.05
455	Terry Kennedy	.05
456	Cubs Batting & Pitching Leaders (Fergie Jenkins, Keith Moreland)	.05
457	Dave Rozema	.05
458	Kiko Garcia	.05
459	Kevin Hickey	.05
460	Dave Winfield	1.00
461	Jim Maler	.05
462	Lee Lacy	.05
463	Dave Engle	.05
464	Jeff Jones	.05
465	Mookie Wilson	.05
466	Gene Garber	.05
467	Mike Ramsey	.05
468	Geoff Zahn	.05
469	Tom O'Malley	.05
470	Nolan Ryan	6.00
471	Dick Howser	.05
472	Mike Brown	.05
473	Jim Dwyer	.05
474	Greg Bargar	.05
475	Gary Redus RC	.05
476	Tom Tellmann	.05
477	Rafael Landestoy	.05
478	Alan Bannister	.05
479	Frank Tanana	.05
480	Ron Kittle RC	.05
481	Mark Thurmond RC	.05
482	Enos Cabell	.05
483	Fergie Jenkins	.65
484	Ozzie Virgil	.05
485	Rick Rhoden	.05

#	Player	Price
486	Yankees Batting & Pitching Leaders (Don Baylor, Ron Guidry)	.05
487	Ricky Adams	.05
488	Jesse Barfield	.05
489	Dave Von Ohlen	.05
490	Cal Ripken, Jr.	6.00
491	Bobby Castillo	.05
492	Tucker Ashford	.05
493	Mike Norris	.05
494	Chili Davis	.05
495	Rollie Fingers	.65
496	Terry Francona	.05
497	Bud Anderson	.05
498	Rich Gedman	.05
499	Mike Witt	.05
500	George Brett	2.00
501	Steve Henderson	.05
502	Joe Torre	.05
503	Elias Sosa	.05
504	Mickey Rivers	.05
505	Pete Vuckovich	.05
506	Ernie Whitt	.05
507	Mike LaCoss	.05
508	Mel Hall	.05
509	Brad Havens	.05
510	Alan Trammell	.05
511	Marty Bystrom	.05
512	Oscar Gamble	.05
513	Dave Beard	.05
514	Floyd Rayford	.05
515	Gorman Thomas	.05
516	Expos Batting & Pitching Leaders (Charlie Lea, Al Oliver)	.05
517	John Moses	.05
518	Greg Walker RC	.05
519	Ron Davis	.05
520	Bob Boone	.05
521	Pete Falcone	.05
522	Dave Bergman	.05
523	Glenn Hoffman	.05
524	Carlos Diaz	.05
525	Willie Wilson	.05
526	Ron Oester	.05
527	Checklist 397-528	.05
528	Mark Brouhard	.05
529	Keith Atherton RC	.05
530	Dan Ford	.05
531	Steve Boros	.05
532	Eric Show	.05
533	Ken Landreaux	.05
534	Pete O'Brien	.05
535	Bo Diaz	.05
536	Doug Bair	.05
537	Johnny Ray	.05
538	Kevin Bass	.05
539	George Frazier	.05
540	George Hendrick	.05
541	Dennis Lamp	.05
542	Duane Kuiper	.05
543	Craig McMurtry RC	.05
544	Cesar Geronimo	.05
545	Bill Buckner	.05
546	Indians Batting & Pitching Leaders (Mike Hargrove, Lary Sorensen)	.05
547	Mike Moore	.05
548	Ron Jackson	.05
549	Walt Terrell RC	.05
550	Jim Rice	.15
551	Scott Ullger	.05
552	Ray Burris	.05
553	Joe Nolan	.05
554	Ted Power RC	.05
555	Greg Brock	.05
556	Joey McLaughlin	.05
557	Wayne Tolleson	.05
558	Mike Davis	.05
559	Mike Scott	.05
560	Carlton Fisk	1.00
561	Whitey Herzog	.05
562	Manny Castillo	.05
563	Glenn Wilson	.05
564	Al Holland	.05
565	Leon Durham	.05
566	Jim Bibby	.05
567	Mike Heath	.05
568	Pete Filson	.05
569	Bake McBride	.05
570	Dan Quisenberry	.05
571	Bruce Bochy	.05
572	Jerry Royster	.05
573	Dave Kingman	.05
574	Brian Downing	.05
575	Jim Clancy	.05
576	Giants Batting & Pitching Leaders (Atlee Hammaker, Jeff Leonard)	.05
577	Mark Clear	.05
578	Lenn Sakata	.05
579	Bob James	.05
580	Lonnie Smith	.05
581	Jose DeLeon RC	.05
582	Bob McClure	.05
583	Derrel Thomas	.05
584	Dave Schmidt	.05
585	Dan Driessen	.05
586	Joe Niekro	.05
587	Von Hayes	.05
588	Milt Wilcox	.05
589	Mike Easler	.05
590	Dave Stieb	.05
591	Tony LaRussa	.05
592	Andre Robertson	.05
593	Jeff Lahti	.05
594	Gene Richards	.05
595	Jeff Reardon	.05

#	Player	Price
596	Ryne Sandberg	3.00
597	Rick Camp	.05
598	Rusty Kuntz	.05
599	Doug Sisk RC	.05
600	Rod Carew	1.00
601	John Tudor	.05
602	John Wathan	.05
603	Renie Martin	.05
604	John Lowenstein	.05
605	Mike Caldwell	.05
606	Blue Jays Batting & Pitching Leaders (Lloyd Moseby, Dave Stieb)	.05
607	Tom Hume	.05
608	Bobby Johnson	.05
609	Dan Meyer	.05
610	Steve Sax	.05
611	Chet Lemon	.05
612	Harry Spilman	.05
613	Greg Gross	.05
614	Len Barker	.05
615	Garry Templeton	.05
616	Don Robinson	.05
617	Rick Cerone	.05
618	Dickie Noles	.05
619	Jerry Dybzinski	.05
620	Al Oliver	.05
621	Frank Howard	.05
622	Al Cowens	.05
623	Ron Washington	.05
624	Terry Harper	.05
625	Larry Gura	.05
626	Bob Clark	.05
627	Dave LaPoint	.05
628	Ed Jurak	.05
629	Rick Langford	.05
630	Ted Simmons	.05
631	Denny Martinez	.05
632	Tom Foley	.05
633	Mike Krukow	.05
634	Mike Marshall	.05
635	Dave Righetti	.05
636	Pat Putnam	.05
637	Phillies Batting & Pitching Leaders (John Denny, Gary Matthews)	.05
638	George Vukovich	.05
639	Rick Lysander	.05
640	Lance Parrish	.05
641	Mike Richardt	.05
642	Tom Underwood	.05
643	Mike Brown	.05
644	Tim Lollar	.05
645	Tony Pena	.05
646	Checklist 529-660	.05
647	Ron Roenicke	.05
648	Len Whitehouse	.05
649	Tom Herr	.05
650	Phil Niekro	.65
651	John McNamara	.05
652	Rudy May	.05
653	Dave Stapleton	.05
654	Bob Bailor	.05
655	Amos Otis	.05
656	Bryn Smith	.05
657	Thad Bosley	.05
658	Jerry Augustine	.05
659	Duane Walker	.05
660	Ray Knight	.05
661	Steve Yeager	.05
662	Tom Brennan	.05
663	Johnnie LeMaster	.05
664	Dave Stegman	.05
665	Buddy Bell	.05
666	Tigers Batting & Pitching Leaders (Jack Morris, Lou Whitaker)	.05
667	Vance Law	.05
668	Larry McWilliams	.05
669	Dave Lopes	.05
670	Rich Gossage	.05
671	Jamie Quirk	.05
672	Ricky Nelson	.05
673	Mike Walters	.05
674	Tim Flannery	.05
675	Pascual Perez	.05
676	Brian Giles	.05
677	Doyle Alexander	.05
678	Chris Speier	.05
679	Art Howe	.05
680	Fred Lynn	.05
681	Tom Lasorda	.15
682	Dan Morogiello	.05
683	Marty Barrett RC	.05
684	Bob Shirley	.05
685	Willie Aikens	.05
686	Joe Price	.05
687	Roy Howell	.05
688	George Wright	.05
689	Mike Fischlin	.05
690	Jack Clark	.05
691	Steve Lake RC	.05
692	Dickie Thon	.05
693	Alan Wiggins	.05
694	Mike Stanton	.05
695	Lou Whitaker	.05
696	Pirates Batting & Pitching Leaders (Bill Madlock, Rick Rhoden)	.05
697	Dale Murray	.05
698	Marc Hill	.05
699	Dave Rucker	.05
700	Mike Schmidt	2.00
701	NL Active Career Batting Leaders (Bill Madlock, Dave Parker, Pete Rose)	.25

#	Player	Price
702	NL Active Career Hit Leaders (Tony Perez, Pete Rose, Rusty Staub)	.25
703	NL Active Career Home Run Leaders (Dave Kingman, Tony Perez, Mike Schmidt)	.15
704	NL Active Career RBI Leaders (Al Oliver, Tony Perez, Rusty Staub)	.05
705	NL Active Career Stolen Bases Leaders (Larry Bowa, Cesar Cedeno, Joe Morgan)	.05
706	NL Active Career Victory Leaders (Steve Carlton, Fergie Jenkins, Tom Seaver)	.05
707	NL Active Career Strikeout Leaders (Steve Carlton, Nolan Ryan, Tom Seaver)	.35
708	NL Active Career ERA Leaders (Steve Carlton, Steve Rogers, Tom Seaver)	.05
709	NL Active Career Save Leaders (Gene Garber, Tug McGraw, Bruce Sutter)	.10
710	AL Active Career Batting Leaders (George Brett, Rod Carew, Cecil Cooper)	.25
711	AL Active Career Hit Leaders (Bert Campaneris, Rod Carew, Reggie Jackson)	.15
712	AL Active Career Home Run Leaders (Reggie Jackson, Greg Luzinski, Graig Nettles)	.15
713	AL Active Career RBI Leaders (Reggie Jackson, Graig Nettles, Ted Simmons)	.05
714	AL Active Career Stolen Bases Leaders (Bert Campaneris, Dave Lopes, Omar Moreno)	.05
715	AL Active Career Victory Leaders (Tommy John, Jim Palmer, Don Sutton)	.05
716	AL Active Strikeout Leaders (Bert Blyleven, Jerry Koosman, Don Sutton)	.05
717	AL Active Career ERA Leaders (Rollie Fingers, Ron Guidry, Jim Palmer)	.05
718	AL Active Career Save Leaders (Rollie Fingers, Rich Gossage, Dan Quisenberry)	.05
719	Andy Hassler	.05
720	Dwight Evans	.05
721	Del Crandall	.05
722	Bob Welch	.05
723	Rich Dauer	.05
724	Eric Rasmussen	.05
725	Cesar Cedeno	.05
726	Brewers Batting & Pitching Leaders (Moose Haas, Ted Simmons)	.05
727	Joel Youngblood	.05
728	Tug McGraw	.05
729	Gene Tenace	.05
730	Bruce Sutter	.75
731	Lynn Jones	.05
732	Terry Crowley	.05
733	Dave Collins	.05
734	Odell Jones	.05
735	Rick Burleson	.05
736	Dick Ruthven	.05
737	Jim Essian	.05
738	Bill Schroeder RC	.05
739	Bob Watson	.05
740	Tom Seaver	1.00
741	Wayne Gross	.05
742	Dick Williams	.05
743	Don Hood	.05
744	Jamie Allen	.05
745	Dennis Eckersley	.65
746	Mickey Hatcher	.05
747	Pat Zachry	.05
748	Jeff Leonard	.05
749	Doug Flynn	.05
750a	Jim Palmer	.05
750b	Jim Palmer (Missing 1980-82 losses on back.)	3.00
750c	Jim Palmer (Missing 1979-83 losses on back.)	4.00
751	Charlie Moore	.05
752	Phil Garner	.05
753	Doug Gwosdz	.05
754	Kent Tekulve	.05
755	Garry Maddox	.05
756	Reds Batting & Pitching Leaders (Ron Oester, Mario Soto)	.05
757	Larry Bowa	.05
758	Bill Stein	.05
759	Richard Dotson	.05
760	Bob Horner	.05
761	John Montefusco	.05
762	Rance Mulliniks	.05
763	Craig Swan	.05
764	Mike Hargrove	.05
765	Ken Forsch	.05
766	Mike Vail	.05
767	Carney Lansford	.05
768	Champ Summers	.05
769	Bill Caudill	.05

#	Player	Price
770	Ken Griffey	.05
771	Billy Gardner	.05
772	Jim Slaton	.05
773	Todd Cruz	.05
774	Tom Gorman	.05
775	Dave Parker	.05
776	Craig Reynolds	.05
777	Tom Paciorek	.05
778	Andy Hawkins RC	.05
779	Jim Sundberg	.05
780	Steve Carlton	1.00
781	Checklist 661-792	.05
782	Steve Balboni	.05
783	Luis Leal	.05
784	Leon Roberts	.05
785	Joaquin Andujar	.05
786	Red Sox Batting & Pitching Leaders (Wade Boggs, Bob Ojeda)	.25
787	Bill Campbell	.05
788	Milt May	.05
789	Bert Blyleven	.05
790	Doug DeCinces	.05
791	Terry Forster	.05
792	Bill Russell	.05

Tiffany

In 1984 Topps introduced a specially boxed, limited edition version of its baseball card set. Sold only through hobby dealers, the cards differed from regular-issue 1984 Topps cards in their use of white cardboard stock and the application of a high-gloss finish to the front of the card. Production was limited to a reported 10,000 sets. The nickname "Tiffany" was coined by collectors to identify the glossy collectors edition.

	NM/M
Unopened Set (792):	250.00
Complete Set (792):	95.00
Common Player:	.15
Stars:	6X
8 Don Mattingly	80.00

Traded

The popular Topps Traded set returned for its fourth year in 1984 with another 132-card set. The 2-1/2" x 3-1/2" cards have an identical design to the regular Topps cards except that the back cardboard is white and card numbers carry a "T" suffix. As before, the set was sold only through hobby dealers. Also as before, players who changed teams, new managers and promising rookies are included in the set. A glossy-finish "Tiffany" version of the set was also issued.

	NM/M
Complete Set (132):	17.50
Common Player:	.05

#	Player	Price
1T	Willie Aikens	.05
2T	Luis Aponte	.05
3T	Mike Armstrong	.05
4T	Bob Bailor	.05
5T	Dusty Baker	.15
6T	Steve Balboni	.05
7T	Alan Bannister	.05
8T	Dave Beard	.05
9T	Joe Beckwith	.05
10T	Bruce Berenyi	.05
11T	Dave Bergman	.05
12T	Tony Bernazard	.05
13T	Yogi Berra	.25
14T	Barry Bonnell	.05
15T	Phil Bradley	.05
16T	Fred Breining	.05
17T	Bill Buckner	.05
18T	Ray Burris	.05
19T	John Butcher	.05
20T	Brett Butler	.05
21T	Enos Cabell	.05
22T	Bill Campbell	.05
23T	Bill Caudill	.05
24T	Bob Clark	.05
25T	Bryan Clark	.05
26T	Jaime Cocanower	.05
27T	Ron Darling RC	.50
28T	Alvin Davis RC	2X

#	Player	Price
29T	Ken Dayley	.05
30T	Jeff Dedmon	.05
31T	Bob Dernier	.05
32T	Carlos Diaz	.05
33T	Mike Easler	.05
34T	Dennis Eckersley	1.50
35T	Jim Essian	.05
36T	Darrell Evans	.05
37T	Mike Fitzgerald RC	.05
38T	Tim Foli	.05
39T	George Frazier	.05
40T	Rich Gale	.05
41T	Barbaro Garbey	.05
42T	Dwight Gooden RC	3.00
43T	Rich Gossage	.05
44T	Wayne Gross	.05
45T	Mark Gubicza RC	.25
46T	Jackie Gutierrez	.05
47T	Mel Hall	.05
48T	Toby Harrah	.05
49T	Ron Hassey	.05
50T	Rich Hebner	.05
51T	Willie Hernandez	.05
52T	Ricky Horton RC	.05
53T	Art Howe	.05
54T	Dane Iorg	.05
55T	Brook Jacoby RC	.05
56T	Mike Jeffcoat RC	.05
57T	Dave Johnson	.05
58T	Lynn Jones	.05
59T	Ruppert Jones	.05
60T	Mike Jorgensen	.05
61T	Bob Kearney	.05
62T	Jimmy Key RC	.50
63T	Dave Kingman	.05
64T	Jerry Koosman	.05
65T	Wayne Krenchicki	.05
66T	Rusty Kuntz	.05
67T	Rene Lachemann	.05
68T	Frank LaCorte	.05
69T	Dennis Lamp	.05
70T	Mark Langston RC	.50
71T	Rick Leach	.05
72T	Craig Lefferts	.05
73T	Gary Lucas	.05
74T	Jerry Martin	.05
75T	Carmelo Martinez	.05
76T	Mike Mason RC	.05
77T	Gary Matthews	.05
78T	Andy McGaffigan	.05
79T	Larry Milbourne	.05
80T	Sid Monge	.05
81T	Jackie Moore	.05
82T	Joe Morgan	2.00
83T	Graig Nettles	.05
84T	Phil Niekro	1.00
85T	Ken Oberkfell	.05
86T	Mike O'Berry	.05
87T	Al Oliver	.05
88T	Jorge Orta	.05
89T	Amos Otis	.05
90T	Dave Parker	.05
91T	Tony Perez	1.00
92T	Gerald Perry RC	.05
93T	Gary Pettis RC	.05
94T	Rob Picciolo	.05
95T	Vern Rapp	.05
96T	Floyd Rayford	.05
97T	Randy Ready RC	.05
98T	Ron Reed	.05
99T	Gene Richards	.05
100T	Jose Rijo RC	.25
101T	Jeff Robinson RC	.05
102T	Ron Romanick RC	.05
103T	Pete Rose	7.50
104T	Bret Saberhagen RC	3.00
105T	Juan Samuel RC	.05
106T	Scott Sanderson	.05
107T	Dick Schofield RC	.05
108T	Tom Seaver	3.00
109T	Jim Slaton	.05
110T	Mike Smithson	.05
111T	Lary Sorensen	.05
112T	Tim Stoddard	.05
113T	Champ Summers	.05
114T	Jim Sundberg	.05
115T	Rick Sutcliffe	.05
116T	Craig Swan	.05
117T	Tim Teufel RC	.05
118T	Derrel Thomas	.05
119T	Gorman Thomas	.05
120T	Alex Trevino	.05
121T	Manny Trillo	.05
122T	John Tudor	.05
123T	Tom Underwood	.05
124T	Mike Vail	.05
125T	Tom Waddell	.05
126T	Gary Ward	.05
127T	Curt Wilkerson	.05
128T	Frank Williams RC	.05
129T	Glenn Wilson	.05
130T	Johnny Wockenfuss	.05
131T	Ned Yost	.05
132T	Checklist 1-132	.05

Traded Tiffany

Following up on its inaugural Tiffany collectors' edition, Topps produced a special glossy version of its Traded set for 1984, as well. Cards in this special boxed set differ from regular Traded cards only in the use of white cardboard stock with a high-gloss finish coat on front.

	NM/M
Complete Set (132):	35.00
Common Player:	.25
Stars:	2X

Traded Darryl Strawberry Bronze

This 1/4-size metal replica of Strawberry's first-ever Topps card was issued to dealers who purchased cases of 1984 Topps Traded sets. Each detail of the 1983 Topps Traded Strawberry card is reproduced on the 1-1/4" x 1-3/4" bronze metal mini-card, right down to the stats.

		NM/M
108T	Darryl Strawberry	3.00

Proofs

Though still small in terms of actual numbers, the quantity of 1984 Topps proofs from the "A" sheet which have made their way into the hobby is relatively large. More precisely, 66 cards (half a production press sheet) are frequently seen in proof version. Like other true proofs, they are blank-backed but these have a very discernible difference from the issued 1984 Topps cards. On the proofs, the portrait photo at lower-left is completely within the black frame of the box. On issued cards, the cap extends above the box border. On the proofs, portrait photos of Steve Carlton and Gary Matthews are found on each other's cards and Manny Trillo is pictured in an Indians uniform, rather than the Expos livery on which he appears in the regularly issued version. Single proofs in the market have been cut from half-sheets.

		NM/M
Uncut Sheet (66):		650.00
Complete Set, Singles (66):		800.00
Common Player:		10.00
(1)	Buddy Bell	10.00
(2)	Wade Boggs	50.00
(3)	Bob Boone	12.50
(4)	Greg Brock	10.00
(5)	Hubie Brooks	10.00
(6)	Steve Carlton (Inset photo Gary Matthews.)	150.00
(7)	Gary Carter	20.00
(8)	Cecil Cooper	10.00
(9)	Andre Dawson	20.00
(10)	Storm Davis	10.00
(11)	Doug DeCinces	10.00
(12)	Ivan DeJesus	10.00
(13)	Rick Dempsey	10.00
(14)	Dwight Evans	10.00
(15)	Rollie Fingers	20.00
(16)	Carlton Fisk	50.00
(17)	Ken Forsch	10.00
(18)	George Foster	10.00
(19)	Julio Franco	10.00
(20)	Jim Gantner	10.00
(21)	Damaso Garcia	10.00
(22)	Ken Griffey	12.50
(23)	Alfredo Griffin	10.00
(24)	Bill Gullickson	10.00
(25)	Moose Haas	10.00
(26)	Rickey Henderson	50.00
(27)	Kent Hrbek	10.00
(28)	Reggie Jackson	50.00
(29)	Roy Lee Jackson	10.00
(30)	Cliff Johnson	10.00
(31)	Ron Kittle	10.00
(32)	Charlie Lea	10.00
(33)	Luis Leal	10.00
(34)	Bill Madlock	10.00
(35)	Buck Martinez	10.00
(36)	Gary Matthews (Inset photo is Steve Carlton.)	75.00
(37)	Willie McGee	12.50
(38)	Greg Minton	10.00
(39)	Paul Molitor	30.00
(40)	Joe Morgan	30.00
(41)	Lloyd Moseby	10.00
(42)	Rance Mulliniks	10.00
(43)	Graig Nettles	10.00
(44)	Al Oliver	15.00
(45)	Lou Piniella	15.00
(46)	Bobby Ramos	10.00
(47)	Johnny Ray	10.00
(48)	Jeff Reardon	10.00
(49)	Jim Rice	20.00
(50)	Andre Robertson	10.00
(51)	Nolan Ryan	300.00
(52)	Scott Sanderson	10.00
(53)	Steve Sax	10.00
(54)	Dan Schatzeder	10.00
(55)	Tom Seaver	60.00
(56)	Lee Smith	15.00
(57)	Don Sutton	20.00
(58)	Jason Thompson	10.00
(59)	Alan Trammell	15.00
(60)	Manny Trillo (Indians)	100.00
(61)	Willie Upshaw	10.00
(62)	Fernando Valenzuela	15.00
(63)	Tim Wallach	10.00
(64)	Ernie Whitt	10.00
(65)	Glenn Wilson	10.00
(66)	Robin Yount	30.00

All-Star Glossy Set of 22

These 2-1/2" x 3-1/2" cards were a result of the success of Topps' efforts the previous year with glossy cards on a mail-in basis. The set is divided evenly between the two leagues. Each All-Star Game starter for both leagues, the managers and the honorary team captains have an All-Star Glossy card. Cards feature a large color photo on the front with an All-Star banner across the top and the league emblem in the lower-left. Player identification appears below the photo. Backs have a name, team, position and card number along with the phrase "1983 All-Star Game Commemorative Set." The '84 Glossy All-Stars were distributed one card per rack pack.

		NM/M
Complete Set (22):		4.00
Common Player:		.10
1	Harvey Kuenn	.10
2	Rod Carew	.50
3	Manny Trillo	.10
4	George Brett	1.00
5	Robin Yount	.50
6	Jim Rice	.25
7	Fred Lynn	.10
8	Dave Winfield	.50
9	Ted Simmons	.10
10	Dave Stieb	.10
11	Carl Yastrzemski	.50
12	Whitey Herzog	.10
13	Al Oliver	.10
14	Steve Sax	.10
15	Mike Schmidt	1.00
16	Ozzie Smith	.50
17	Tim Raines	.25
18	Andre Dawson	.25
19	Dale Murphy	.25
20	Gary Carter	.50
21	Mario Soto	.10
22	Johnny Bench	.50

All-Star Glossy Set of 40

For the second straight year in 1984, Topps produced a 40-card All-Star "Collector's Edition" set as a "consolation prize" for its sweepstakes game. By collecting game cards and sending them in with a bit of cash, the collector could re-ceive one of eight different five-card series. As the previous year, the 2-1/2" x 3-1/2" cards feature a nearly full-frame color photo on its glossy finish front. Backs are printed in red and blue.

		NM/M
Complete Set (40):		6.00
Common Player:		.10
1	Pete Rose	1.00
2	Lance Parrish	.10
3	Steve Rogers	.10
4	Eddie Murray	.40
5	Johnny Ray	.10
6	Rickey Henderson	.40
7	Atlee Hammaker	.10
8	Wade Boggs	.50
9	Gary Carter	.40
10	Jack Morris	.10
11	Darrell Evans	.10
12	George Brett	1.00
13	Bob Horner	.10
14	Ron Guidry	.10
15	Nolan Ryan	1.50
16	Dave Winfield	.40
17	Ozzie Smith	.50
18	Ted Simmons	.10
19	Bill Madlock	.10
20	Tony Armas	.10
21	Al Oliver	.10
22	Jim Rice	.25
23	George Hendrick	.10
24	Dave Stieb	.10
25	Pedro Guerrero	.10
26	Rod Carew	.40
27	Steve Carlton	.40
28	Dave Righetti	.10
29	Darryl Strawberry	.10
30	Lou Whitaker	.10
31	Dale Murphy	.25
32	LaMarr Hoyt	.10
33	Jesse Orosco	.10
34	Cecil Cooper	.10
35	Andre Dawson	.25
36	Robin Yount	.40
37	Tim Raines	.10
38	Dan Quisenberry	.10
39	Mike Schmidt	1.00
40	Carlton Fisk	.40

Cereal Series

The Topps-produced 1984 Cereal Series set is identical to the Ralston Purina set from the same year in nearly all aspects. On the card fronts the words "Ralston Purina Company" were replaced by "Cereal Series" and Topps logos were substituted for Ralston checkerboard logos. The set is comprised of 33 cards, each measuring 2-1/2" x 3-1/2". The cards were inserted in unmarked boxes of Chex brand cereals.

		NM/M
Complete Set (33):		4.00
Common Player:		.05
1	Eddie Murray	.25
2	Ozzie Smith	.30
3	Ted Simmons	.05
4	Pete Rose	.75
5	Greg Luzinski	.05
6	Andre Dawson	.15
7	Dave Winfield	.25
8	Tom Seaver	.25
9	Jim Rice	.15
10	Fernando Valenzuela	.15
11	Wade Boggs	.30
12	Dale Murphy	.15
13	George Brett	.50
14	Nolan Ryan	1.00
15	Rickey Henderson	.25
16	Steve Carlton	.25
17	Rod Carew	.25
18	Steve Garvey	.15
19	Reggie Jackson	.35
20	Dave Concepcion	.05
21	Robin Yount	.25
22	Mike Schmidt	.25
23	Jim Palmer	.25
24	Bruce Sutter	.20
25	Dan Quisenberry	.05
26	Bill Madlock	.05
27	Cecil Cooper	.05
28	Gary Carter	.25
29	Fred Lynn	.05
30	Pedro Guerrero	.05
31	Ron Guidry	.05
32	Keith Hernandez	.05
33	Carlton Fisk	.25

"Darryl Palmer"

For use as a prop in the 1985 movie "The Slugger's Wife," Topps produced this 1984-style card of actor Michael O'Keefe as Darryl Palmer. (O'Keefe is better remembered as caddy Danny Noonan in "Caddyshack.") Front and back are in the '84T format, complete with personal data, stats and Topps copyrights.

		NM/M
801	Darryl Palmer	15.00

Gallery of Immortals

The Gallery of Immortals bronze and silver replicas were the first metal miniature set from Topps and the start of an annual tradition (in 1985, the name was changed to Gallery of Champions). Each mini is an exact one-quarter scale replica of the featured player's 1984 Topps baseball card, both front and back, in minute detail. The three-dimensional metal cards were packaged in a velvet-lined case that bears the title of the set in gold-embossed letters. A certificate of authenticity is included with each set. A Tom Seaver pewter metal mini-card was given as a premium to dealers who purchsed sets. Issue price was about $100 for the cased bronze set, $500 for the silver edition of 1,000.

		NM/M
Complete Bronze Set (12):		40.00
Complete Silver Set (12):		190.00
(1b)	George Brett/Bronze	12.50
(1s)	George Brett/Silver	45.00
(2b)	Rod Carew/Bronze	6.00
(2s)	Rod Carew/Silver	15.00
(3b)	Steve Carlton/Bronze	6.00
(3s)	Steve Carlton/Silver	15.00
(4b)	Rollie Fingers/Bronze	4.00
(4s)	Rollie Fingers/Silver	12.50
(5b)	Steve Garvey/Bronze	4.00
(5s)	Steve Garvey/Silver	12.50
(6b)	Reggie Jackson/Bronze	7.50
(6s)	Reggie Jackson/Silver	17.50
(7b)	Joe Morgan/Bronze	5.00
(7s)	Joe Morgan/Silver	12.50
(8b)	Jim Palmer/Bronze	5.00
(8s)	Jim Palmer/Silver	12.50
(9b)	Pete Rose/Bronze	20.00
(9s)	Pete Rose/Silver	50.00
(10b)	Nolan Ryan/Bronze	25.00
(10s)	Nolan Ryan/Silver	60.00
(11b)	Mike Schmidt/Bronze	20.00
(11s)	Mike Schmidt/Silver	45.00
(12b)	Tom Seaver/Bronze	6.00
(12s)	Tom Seaver/Silver	15.00
(12p)	Tom Seaver/Pewter	15.00

"Pewter" Gallery Ingots

All of the Topps Gallery of Immortals (1984) and Gallery of Champions (1985-1989) miniature ingots have been counterfeited in a pewter or pot metal alloy designed to look like the genuine silver pieces. The fakes are cast, rather than die-struck, have a porous surface upon magnification and sometimes the casting seam is visible despite the filing done to remove it. These are often sold on eBay as "pewter." Topps did did make one genuine pewter piece each year 1984-1991, as an ordering incentive; they are listed within each year's Gallery checklist.

Photo Rub Downs

This set consists of 32 "Rub Down" sheets featuring 112 different players. Each sheet measures 2-3/8" x 3-15/16" and includes small, color baseball player figures along with bats, balls and gloves. The pictures can be transferred to another surface by rubbing the paper backing. The sheets, which were sold as a separate issue, are somewhat reminiscent of earlier tattoo sets issued by Topps. The sheets are not numbered.

		NM/M
Complete Set (32):		7.50
Common Sheet:		.50
Pack (2):		.50
Box (36):		9.00
(1)	Steve Bedrosian, Bruce Benedict, Tony Armas, Harold Baines, Lonnie Smith	.50
(2)	Chris Chambliss, Bob Horner, Don Baylor, George Hendrick, Ron Kittle, Johnnie LeMaster	.50
(3)	Glenn Hubbard, Rafael Ramirez, Buddy Bell, Ray Knight, Lloyd Moseby	.50
(4)	Craig McMurtry, Bruce Benedict, Atlee Hammaker, Frank White	.50
(5)	Wade Boggs, Rick Dempsey, Keith Hernandez	.75
(6)	George Brett, Andre Dawson, Paul Molitor, Alan Wiggins	1.00
(7)	Tom Brunansky, Pedro Guerrero, Darryl Strawberry	.50
(8)	Bill Buckner, Rich Gossage, Dave Stieb, Rick Sutcliffe	.50
(9)	Rod Carew, Carlton Fisk, Johnny Ray, Matt Young	.60
(10)	Steve Carlton, Bob Horner, Dan Quisenberry	.60
(11)	Gary Carter, Phil Garner, Ron Guidry	.60
(12)	Ron Cey, Steve Kemp, Greg Luzinski, Kent Tekulve	.50
(13)	Chris Chambliss, Dwight Evans, Julio Franco	.50
(14)	Jack Clark, Damaso Garcia, Hal McRae, Lance Parrish	.50
(15)	Dave Concepcion, Cecil Cooper, Fred Lynn, Jesse Orosco	.50
(16)	Jose Cruz, Gary Matthews, Jack Morris, Jim Rice	.50
(17)	Ron Davis, Kent Hrbek, Tom Seaver	.60
(18)	John Denny, Carney Lansford, Mario Soto, Lou Whitaker	.50
(19)	Leon Durham, Dave Lopes, Steve Sax	.50
(20)	George Foster, Gary Gaetti, Bobby Grich, Gary Redus	.50
(21)	Steve Garvey, Bill Russell, Jerry Remy, George Wright	.50
(22)	Moose Haas, Bruce Sutter, Dickie Thon, Andre Thornton	.50
(23)	Toby Harrah, Pat Putnam, Tim Raines, Mike Schmidt	1.00
(24)	Rickey Henderson, Dave Righetti, Pete Rose	1.00
(25)	Steve Henderson, Bill Madlock, Alan Trammell	.50
(26)	LaMarr Hoyt, Larry Parrish, Nolan Ryan	1.50
(27)	Reggie Jackson, Eric Show, Jason Thompson	.60
(28)	Tommy John, Terry Kennedy, Eddie Murray, Ozzie Smith	.60
(29)	Jeff Leonard, Dale Murphy, Ken Singleton, Dave Winfield	.60
(30)	Craig McMurtry, Cal Ripken, Steve Rogers, Willie Upshaw	1.50
(31)	Ben Oglivie, Jim Palmer, Darrell Porter	.50
(32)	Tony Pena, Fernando Valenzuela, Robin Yount	.60

Stickers

The largest sticker set issued by Topps, the 1984 set consists of 386 stickers, each measuring 1-15/16" x 2-9/16". The full color photos have stars in each of the corners and are numbered on both the front and back. The back includes information about the sticker album and a promotion to order stickers through the mail. The back of the album is a tribute to Carl Yastrzemski, including a large photo and reproductions of his 1960-1983 cards in miniature.

		NM/M
Complete Set (386):		12.00
Common Player:		.05
Sticker Album:		3.00
Box (35):		6.00
1	Steve Carlton	.25
2	Steve Carlton	.25
3	Rickey Henderson	.25
4	Rickey Henderson	.25
5	Fred Lynn	.05
6	Fred Lynn	.05
7	Greg Luzinski	.05
8	Greg Luzinski	.05
9	Dan Quisenberry	.05
10	Dan Quisenberry	.05
11	1983 Championship (LaMarr Hoyt)	.05
12	1983 Championship (Mike Flanagan)	.05
13	1983 Championship (Mike Boddicker)	.05
14	1983 Championship (Tito Landrum)	.05
15	1983 Championship (Steve Carlton)	.10
16	1983 Championship (Fernando Valenzuela)	.05
17	1983 Championship (Charlie Hudson)	.05
18	1983 Championship (Gary Matthews)	.05

No.	Player	Price
19	1983 World Series (John Denny)	.05
20	1983 World Series (John Lowenstein)	.05
21	1983 World Series (Jim Palmer)	.10
22	1983 World Series (Benny Ayala)	.05
23	1983 World Series (Rick Dempsey)	.05
24	1983 World Series (Cal Ripken)	.50
25	1983 World Series (Sammy Stewart)	.05
26	1983 World Series (Eddie Murray)	.10
27	Dale Murphy	.15
28	Chris Chambliss	.05
29	Glenn Hubbard	.05
30	Bob Horner	.05
31	Phil Niekro	.20
32	Claudell Washington	.05
33	Rafael Ramirez	.05
34	Bruce Benedict	.05
35	Gene Garber	.05
36	Pascual Perez	.05
37	Jerry Royster	.05
38	Steve Bedrosian	.05
39	Keith Moreland	.05
40	Leon Durham	.05
41	Ron Cey	.05
42	Bill Buckner	.05
43	Jody Davis	.05
44	Lee Smith	.05
45	Ryne Sandberg	.30
46	Larry Bowa	.05
47	Chuck Rainey	.05
48	Fergie Jenkins	.20
49	Dick Ruthven	.05
50	Jay Johnstone	.05
51	Mario Soto	.05
52	Gary Redus	.05
53	Ron Oester	.05
54	Cesar Cedeno	.05
55	Dan Driessen	.05
56	Dave Concepcion	.05
57	Dann Bilardello	.05
58	Joe Price	.05
59	Tom Hume	.05
60	Eddie Milner	.05
61	Paul Householder	.05
62	Bill Scherrer	.05
63	Phil Garner	.05
64	Dickie Thon	.05
65	Jose Cruz	.05
66	Nolan Ryan	.60
67	Terry Puhl	.05
68	Ray Knight	.05
69	Joe Niekro	.05
70	Jerry Mumphrey	.05
71	Bill Dawley	.05
72	Alan Ashby	.05
73	Denny Walling	.05
74	Frank DiPino	.05
75	Pedro Guerrero	.05
76	Ken Landreaux	.05
77	Bill Russell	.05
78	Steve Sax	.05
79	Fernando Valenzuela	.05
80	Dusty Baker	.05
81	Jerry Reuss	.05
82	Alejandro Pena	.05
83	Rick Monday	.05
84	Rick Honeycutt	.05
85	Mike Marshall	.05
86	Steve Yeager	.05
87	Al Oliver	.05
88	Steve Rogers	.05
89	Jeff Reardon	.05
90	Gary Carter	.05
91	Tim Raines	.05
92	Andre Dawson	.15
93	Manny Trillo	.05
94	Tim Wallach	.05
95	Chris Speier	.05
96	Bill Gullickson	.05
97	Doug Flynn	.05
98	Charlie Lea	.05
99	Bill Madlock	.05
100	Wade Boggs	.25
101	Mike Schmidt	.40
102a	Jim Rice	.15
102b	Reggie Jackson	.25
103	Hubie Brooks	.05
104	Jesse Orosco	.05
105	George Foster	.05
106	Tom Seaver	.25
107	Keith Hernandez	.05
108	Mookie Wilson	.05
109	Bob Bailor	.05
110	Walt Terrell	.05
111	Brian Giles	.05
112	Jose Oquendo	.05
113	Mike Torrez	.05
114	Junior Ortiz	.05
115	Pete Rose	.50
116	Joe Morgan	.25
117	Mike Schmidt	.40
118	Gary Matthews	.05
119	Steve Carlton	.20
120	Bo Diaz	.05
121	Ivan DeJesus	.05
122	John Denny	.05
123	Garry Maddox	.05
124	Von Hayes	.05
125	Al Holland	.05
126	Tony Perez	.25
127	John Candelaria	.05

No.	Player	Price
128	Jason Thompson	.05
129	Tony Pena	.05
130	Dave Parker	.05
131	Bill Madlock	.05
132	Kent Tekulve	.05
133	Larry McWilliams	.05
134	Johnny Ray	.05
135	Marvell Wynne	.05
136	Dale Berra	.05
137	Mike Easler	.05
138	Lee Lacy	.05
139	George Hendrick	.05
140	Lonnie Smith	.05
141	Willie McGee	.05
142	Tom Herr	.05
143	Darrell Porter	.05
144	Ozzie Smith	.40
145	Bruce Sutter	.20
146	Dave LaPoint	.05
147	Neil Allen	.05
148	Ken Oberkfell	.05
149	David Green	.05
150	Andy Van Slyke	.05
151	Garry Templeton	.05
152	Juan Bonilla	.05
153	Alan Wiggins	.05
154	Terry Kennedy	.05
155	Dave Dravecky	.05
156	Steve Garvey	.10
157	Bobby Brown	.05
158	Ruppert Jones	.05
159	Luis Salazar	.05
160	Tony Gwynn	.40
161	Gary Lucas	.05
162	Eric Show	.05
163	Darrell Evans	.05
164	Gary Lavelle	.05
165	Atlee Hammaker	.05
166	Jeff Leonard	.05
167	Jack Clark	.05
168	Johnny LeMaster	.05
169	Duane Kuiper	.05
170	Tom O'Malley	.05
171	Chili Davis	.05
172	Bill Laskey	.05
173	Joel Youngblood	.05
174	Bob Brenly	.05
175	Atlee Hammaker	.05
176	Rick Honeycutt	.05
177	John Denny	.05
178	LaMarr Hoyt	.05
179	Tim Raines	.05
180	Dale Murphy	.15
181	Andre Dawson	.15
182	Steve Rogers	.05
183	Gary Carter	.25
184	Steve Carlton	.25
185	George Hendrick	.05
186	Johnny Ray	.05
187	Ozzie Smith	.40
188	Mike Schmidt	.40
189	Jim Rice	.15
190	Dave Winfield	.25
191	Lloyd Moseby	.05
192	LaMarr Hoyt	.05
193	Ted Simmons	.05
194	Ron Guidry	.05
195	Eddie Murray	.25
196	Lou Whitaker	.05
197	Cal Ripken, Jr.	.60
198	George Brett	.40
199	Dale Murphy	.15
200a	Cecil Cooper	.05
200b	Jim Rice	.15
201	Tim Raines	.05
202	Rickey Henderson	.25
203	Eddie Murray	.25
204	Cal Ripken	.60
205	Gary Roenicke	.05
206	Ken Singleton	.05
207	Scott McGregor	.05
208	Tippy Martinez	.05
209	John Lowenstein	.05
210	Mike Flanagan	.05
211	Jim Palmer	.25
212	Dan Ford	.05
213	Rick Dempsey	.05
214	Rich Dauer	.05
215	Jerry Remy	.05
216	Wade Boggs	.25
217	Jim Rice	.15
218	Tony Armas	.05
219	Dwight Evans	.05
220	Bob Stanley	.05
221	Dave Stapleton	.05
222	Rich Gedman	.05
223	Glenn Hoffman	.05
224	Dennis Eckersley	.20
225	John Tudor	.05
226	Bruce Hurst	.05
227	Rod Carew	.05
228	Bobby Grich	.05
229	Doug DeCinces	.05
230	Fred Lynn	.05
231	Reggie Jackson	.25
232	Tommy John	.05
233	Luis Sanchez	.05
234	Bob Boone	.05
235	Bruce Kison	.05
236	Brian Downing	.05
237	Ken Forsch	.05
238	Rick Burleson	.05
239	Dennis Lamp	.05
240	LaMarr Hoyt	.05
241	Richard Dotson	.05
242	Harold Baines	.05
243	Carlton Fisk	.25
244	Greg Luzinski	.05

No.	Player	Price
245	Rudy Law	.05
246	Tom Paciorek	.05
247	Floyd Bannister	.05
248	Julio Cruz	.05
249	Vance Law	.05
250	Scott Fletcher	.05
251	Toby Harrah	.05
252	Pat Tabler	.05
253	Gorman Thomas	.05
254	Rick Sutcliffe	.05
255	Andre Thornton	.05
256	Bake McBride	.05
257	Alan Bannister	.05
258	Jamie Easterly	.05
259	Lary Sorensen	.05
260	Mike Hargrove	.05
261	Bert Blyleven	.05
262	Ron Hassey	.05
263	Jack Morris	.05
264	Larry Herndon	.05
265	Lance Parrish	.05
266	Alan Trammell	.05
267	Lou Whitaker	.05
268	Aurelio Lopez	.05
269	Dan Petry	.05
270	Glenn Wilson	.05
271	Chet Lemon	.05
272	Kirk Gibson	.05
273	Enos Cabell	.05
274	Johnny Wockenfuss	.05
275	George Brett	.40
276	Willie Aikens	.05
277	Frank White	.05
278	Hal McRae	.05
279	Dan Quisenberry	.05
280	Willie Wilson	.05
281	Paul Splittorff	.05
282	U.L. Washington	.05
283	Bud Black	.05
284	John Wathan	.05
285	Larry Gura	.05
286	Pat Sheridan	.05
287a	Rusty Staub	.05
287b	Dave Righetti	.05
288a	Bob Forsch	.05
288b	Mike Warren	.05
289	Al Holland	.05
290	Dan Quisenberry	.05
291	Cecil Cooper	.05
292	Moose Haas	.05
293	Ted Simmons	.05
294	Paul Molitor	.25
295	Robin Yount	.25
296	Ben Oglivie	.05
297	Tom Tellmann	.05
298	Jim Gantner	.05
299	Rick Manning	.05
300	Don Sutton	.20
301	Charlie Moore	.05
302	Jim Slaton	.05
303	Gary Ward	.05
304	Tom Brunansky	.05
305	Kent Hrbek	.05
306	Gary Gaetti	.05
307	John Castino	.05
308	Ken Schrom	.05
309	Ron Davis	.05
310	Lenny Faedo	.05
311	Darrell Brown	.05
312	Frank Viola	.05
313	Dave Engle	.05
314	Randy Bush	.05
315	Dave Righetti	.05
316	Rich Gossage	.05
317	Ken Griffey	.05
318	Ron Guidry	.05
319	Dave Winfield	.25
320	Don Baylor	.10
321	Butch Wynegar	.05
322	Omar Moreno	.05
323	Andre Robertson	.05
324	Willie Randolph	.05
325	Don Mattingly	.60
326	Graig Nettles	.05
327	Rickey Henderson	.25
328	Carney Lansford	.05
329	Jeff Burroughs	.05
330	Chris Codiroli	.05
331	Dave Lopes	.05
332	Dwayne Murphy	.05
333	Wayne Gross	.05
334	Bill Almon	.05
335	Tom Underwood	.05
336	Dave Beard	.05
337	Mike Heath	.05
338	Mike Davis	.05
339	Pat Putnam	.05
340	Tony Bernazard	.05
341	Steve Henderson	.05
342	Richie Zisk	.05
343	Dave Henderson	.05
344	Al Cowens	.05
345	Bill Caudill	.05
346	Jim Beattie	.05
347	Ricky Nelson	.05
348	Roy Thomas	.05
349	Spike Owen	.05
350	Jamie Allen	.05
351	Buddy Bell	.05
352	Billy Sample	.05
353	George Wright	.05
354	Larry Parrish	.05
355	Jim Sundberg	.05
356	Charlie Hough	.05
357	Pete O'Brien	.05
358	Wayne Tolleson	.05
359	Danny Darwin	.05
360	Dave Stewart	.05

No.	Player	Price
361	Mickey Rivers	.05
362	Bucky Dent	.05
363	Willie Upshaw	.05
364	Damaso Garcia	.05
365	Lloyd Moseby	.05
366	Cliff Johnson	.05
367	Jim Clancy	.05
368	Dave Stieb	.05
369	Alfredo Griffin	.05
370	Barry Bonnell	.05
371	Luis Leal	.05
372	Jesse Barfield	.05
373	Ernie Whitt	.05
374	Rance Mulliniks	.05
375	Mike Boddicker	.05
376	Greg Brock	.05
377	Bill Doran	.05
378	Nick Esasky	.05
379	Julio Franco	.05
380	Mel Hall	.05
381	Bob Kearney	.05
382	Ron Kittle	.05
383	Carmelo Martinez	.05
384	Craig McMurtry	.05
385	Darryl Strawberry	.05
386	Matt Young	.05

Stickers Boxes

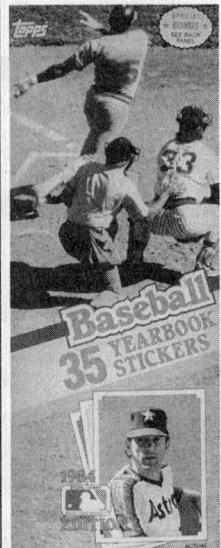

For the second straight year, Topps printed baseball cards on the back of its sticker boxes. The 1984 set, titled "The Super Bats" features 24 hitting leaders. The cards are blank-backed and measure 2-1/2" x 3-1/2". Two cards were printed on each of 12 different boxes. The player's name appears inside a bat above his photo. Prices listed are for complete boxes.

		NM/M
Complete Set (12):		8.50
Common Player:		.75
1	Al Oliver, Lou Whitaker	.75
2	Ken Oberkfell, Ted Simmons	.75
3	Hal McRae, Alan Wiggins	.75
4	Lloyd Moseby, Tim Raines	.75
5	Lonnie Smith, Willie Wilson	.75
6	Keith Hernandez, Robin Yount	1.00
7	Wade Boggs, Johnny Ray	1.00
8	Willie McGee, Ken Singleton	.75
9	Ray Knight, Alan Trammell	.75
11	Rod Carew, George Hendrick	1.00
12	Bill Madlock, Eddie Murray	1.00
13	Jose Cruz, Cal Ripken, Jr.	3.00

Super

A new generation in Topps' experiments to market large-format cards, these 4-7/8" x 6-7/8" cards were sold in single-card plastic-wrap packs with a complete set being 30 cards. Other than their size and the change in card number on the back, there is nothing to distinguish the Supers from the regular 1984 Topps cards of the same players. One plus is that the players are all big name stars, and are likely to remain in demand.

DARRYL STRAWBERRY OF

	NM/M
Complete Set (30):	10.00
Common Player:	.25
Wax Pack (1):	.50
Wax Box (36):	9.00
1 Cal Ripken, Jr.	3.00
2 Dale Murphy	.40
3 LaMarr Hoyt	.25
4 John Denny	.25
5 Jim Rice	.40
6 Mike Schmidt	1.00
7 Wade Boggs	.60
8 Bill Madlock	.25
9 Dan Quisenberry	.25
10 Al Holland	.25
11 Ron Kittle	.25
12 Darryl Strawberry	.35
13 George Brett	1.00
14 Bill Buckner	.25
15 Carlton Fisk	.50
16 Steve Carlton	.50
17 Ron Guidry	.25
18 Gary Carter	.50
19 Rickey Henderson	.50
20 Andre Dawson	.40
21 Reggie Jackson	.75
22 Steve Garvey	.30
23 Fred Lynn	.25
24 Pedro Guerrero	.25
25 Eddie Murray	.50
26 Keith Hernandez	.50
27 Dave Winfield	.50
28 Nolan Ryan	3.00
29 Robin Yount	.50
30 Fernando Valenzuela	.25

"1977" Topps Dale Murphy Aluminum

ROOKIES CATCHERS

GARY ALEXANDER GIANTS — RICK CERONE INDIANS — DALE MURPHY BRAVES — KEVIN PASLEY DODGERS

Authorized by Topps to be issued in 1984 as a fund raiser for Huntington's Disease research, this aluminum card is a full size replica of 1977 Topps card #476, Dale Murphy's rookie card. Front features rather crude black etchings of the player portraits found on the cardboard version, while back reproduces the biographical data and includes a serial number. The cards were originally sold for $10.

	NM/M
476 Rookie Catchers (Gary Alexander, Rick Cerone, Dale Murphy, Kevin Pasley)	10.00

7-Eleven/Pepsi Sheets

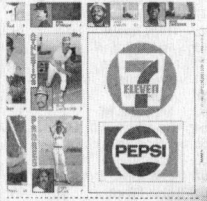

This test issue was reportedly limited to locations in the Midwest. About 28-1/2" x 43" the sheets have 128 regular '84 Topps cards and a 5" x 7" panel at lower-right with the sponsors' logos.

	NM/M
	10.00

1985 Topps

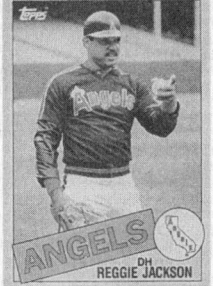

REGGIE JACKSON DH ANGELS

Holding the line at 792 cards, Topps initiated major design changes in its 2-1/2" x 3-1/2" cards in 1985. The use of two photos on the front was discontinued in favor of one large photo. The Topps logo appears in the upper-left corner. At bottom is a diagonal box with the team name. It joins a team logo, and below that point runs the player's position and name. The backs feature statistics, biographical information and a trivia question. Some interesting specialty sets were introduced in 1985, including the revival of the father/son theme from 1976, a subset of the 1984 U.S. Olympic Baseball Team members and a set featuring #1 draft choices since the inception of the baseball draft in 1965. Large numbers of uncut sheets were made available within the hobby, originally selling around $60 for a set of six.

	NM/M
Unopened Fact. Set (792):	140.00
Complete Set (792):	70.00
Common Player:	.05
Wax Pack (15):	4.50
Wax Box (36):	150.00
Cello Pack (28):	6.50
Cello Box (24):	150.00
Rack Pack (51+1):	9.00
Rack Box (24):	180.00
Vending Box (500):	60.00
1 Carlton Fisk (Record Breaker)	.25
2 Steve Garvey (Record Breaker)	.05
3 Dwight Gooden (Record Breaker)	.05
4 Cliff Johnson (Record Breaker)	.05
5 Joe Morgan (Record Breaker)	.10
6 Pete Rose (Record Breaker)	.50
7 Nolan Ryan (Record Breaker)	1.50
8 Juan Samuel RC (Record Breaker)	.05
9 Bruce Sutter (Record Breaker)	.10
10 Don Sutton (Record Breaker)	.05
11 Ralph Houk	.05
12 Dave Lopes	.05
13 Tim Lollar	.05
14 Chris Bando	.05
15 Jerry Koosman	.05
16 Bobby Meacham	.05
17 Mike Scott	.05
18 Mickey Hatcher	.05
19 George Frazier	.05
20 Chet Lemon	.05
21 Lee Tunnell	.05
22 Duane Kuiper	.05
23 Bret Saberhagen	.05
24 Jesse Barfield	.05
25 Steve Bedrosian	.05
26 Roy Smalley	.05
27 Bruce Berenyi	.05
28 Dann Bilardello	.05
29 Odell Jones	.05
30 Cal Ripken, Jr.	4.00
31 Terry Whitfield	.05
32 Chuck Porter	.05
33 Tito Landrum	.05
34 Ed Nunez RC	.05
35 Graig Nettles	.05
36 Fred Breining	.05
37 Reid Nichols	.05
38 Jackie Moore	.05
39 Johnny Wockenfuss	.05
40 Phil Niekro	.60
41 Mike Fischlin	.05

#	Player	Price		#	Player	Price		#	Player	Price
42	Luis Sanchez	.05		145	Alvin Davis	.05		263	Mel Hall	.05
43	Andre David	.05		146	Gary Redus	.05		264	Joe Sambito	.05
44	Dickie Thon	.05		147	Bill Swaggerty	.05		265	Juan Samuel RC	.05
45	Greg Minton	.05		148	Steve Yeager	.05		266	Frank Viola	.05
46	Gary Woods	.05		149	Dickie Noles	.05		267	Henry Cotto RC	.05
47	Dave Rozema	.05		150	Jim Rice	.15		268	Chuck Tanner	.05
48	Tony Fernandez RC	.05		151	Moose Haas	.05		269	Doug Baker RC	.05
49	Butch Davis	.05		152	Steve Braun	.05		270	Dan Quisenberry	.05
50	John Candelaria	.05		153	Frank LaCorte	.05		271	Tim Foli (#1 Draft Pick)	.05
51	Bob Watson	.05		154	Argenis Salazar RC	.05		272	Jeff Burroughs (#1 Draft Pick)	.05
52	Jerry Dybzinski	.05		155	Yogi Berra	.10		273	Bill Almon (#1 Draft Pick)	.05
53	Tom Gorman	.05		156	Craig Reynolds	.05		274	Floyd Bannister (#1 Draft Pick)	.05
54	Cesar Cedeno	.05		157	Tug McGraw	.05		275	Harold Baines (#1 Draft Pick)	.05
55	Frank Tanana	.05		158	Pat Tabler	.05		276	Bob Horner (#1 Draft Pick)	.10
56	Jim Dwyer	.05		159	Carlos Diaz	.05		277	Al Chambers (#1 Draft Pick)	.05
57	Pat Zachry	.05		160	Lance Parrish	.05		278	Darryl Strawberry (#1 Draft Pick)	.30
58	Orlando Mercado	.05		161	Ken Schrom	.05		279	Mike Moore RC (#1 Draft Pick)	.05
59	Rick Waits	.05		162	Benny Distefano RC	.05		280	Shawon Dunston RC (#1 Draft Pick)	.40
60	George Hendrick	.05		163	Dennis Eckersley	.60		281	Tim Belcher RC (#1 Draft Pick)	.30
61	Curt Kaufman	.05		164	Jorge Orta	.05		282	Shawn Abner RC (#1 Draft Pick)	.05
62	Mike Ramsey	.05		165	Dusty Baker	.05		283	Fran Mullins	.05
63	Steve McCatty	.05		166	Keith Atherton	.05		284	Marty Bystrom	.05
64	Mark Bailey RC	.05		167	Rufino Linares	.05		285	Dan Driessen	.05
65	Bill Buckner	.05		168	Garth Iorg	.05		286	Rudy Law	.05
66	Dick Williams	.05		169	Dan Spillner	.05		287	Walt Terrell	.05
67	Rafael Santana RC	.05		170	George Foster	.05		288	Jeff Kunkel RC	.05
68	Von Hayes	.05		171	Bill Stein	.05		289	Tom Underwood	.05
69	Jim Winn RC	.05		172	Jack Perconte	.05		290	Cecil Cooper	.05
70	Don Baylor	.10		173	Mike Young RC	.05		291	Bob Welch	.05
71	Tim Laudner	.05		174	Rick Honeycutt	.05		292	Brad Komminsk RC	.05
72	Rick Sutcliffe	.05		175	Dave Parker	.05		293	Curt Young RC	.05
73	Rusty Kuntz	.05		176	Bill Schroeder	.05		294	Tom Nieto RC	.05
74	Mike Krukow	.05		177	Dave Von Ohlen	.05		295	Joe Niekro	.05
75	Willie Upshaw	.05		178	Miguel Dilone	.05		296	Ricky Nelson	.05
76	Alan Bannister	.05		179	Tommy John	.10		297	Gary Lucas	.05
77	Joe Beckwith	.05		180	Dave Winfield	.75		298	Marty Barrett	.05
78	Scott Fletcher	.05		181	Roger Clemens	20.00		299	Andy Hawkins	.05
79	Rick Mahler	.05		182	Tim Flannery	.05		300	Rod Carew	.75
80	Keith Hernandez	.05		183	Larry McWilliams	.05		301	John Montefusco	.05
81	Lenn Sakata	.05		184	Carmen Castillo RC	.05		302	Tim Corcoran	.05
82	Joe Price	.05		185	Al Holland	.05		303	Mike Jeffcoat RC	.05
83	Charlie Moore	.05		186	Bob Lillis	.05		304	Gary Gaetti	.05
84	Spike Owen	.05		187	Mike Walters	.05		305	Dale Berra	.05
85	Mike Marshall	.05		188	Greg Pryor	.05		306	Rick Reuschel	.05
86	Don Aase	.05		189	Warren Brusstar	.05		307	Sparky Anderson	.10
87	David Green	.05		190	Rusty Staub	.05		308	John Wathan	.05
88	Bryn Smith	.05		191	Steve Nicosia	.05		309	Mike Witt	.05
89	Jackie Gutierrez	.05		192	Howard Johnson	.05		310	Manny Trillo	.05
90	Rich Gossage	.05		193	Jimmy Key	.02		311	Jim Gott	.05
91	Jeff Burroughs	.05		194	Dave Stegman	.05		312	Marc Hill	.05
92	Paul Owens	.05		195	Glenn Hubbard	.05		313	Dave Schmidt	.10
93	Don Schulze RC	.05		196	Pete O'Brien	.05		314	Ron Oester	.05
94	Toby Harrah	.05		197	Mike Warren	.05		315	Doug Sisk	.05
95	Jose Cruz	.05		198	Eddie Milner	.05		316	John Lowenstein	.05
96	Johnny Ray	.05		199	Denny Martinez	.05		317	Jack Lazorko RC	.05
97	Pete Filson	.05		200	Reggie Jackson	2.00		318	Ted Simmons	.05
98	Steve Lake	.05		201	Burt Hooton	.05		319	Jeff Jones	.05
99	Milt Wilcox	.05		202	Gorman Thomas	.05		320	Dale Murphy	.35
100	George Brett	3.00		203	Bob McClure	.05		321	Ricky Horton RC	.05
101	Jim Acker	.05		204	Art Howe	.05		322	Dave Stapleton	.05
102	Tommy Dunbar	.05		205	Steve Rogers	.05		323	Andy McGaffigan	.05
103	Randy Lerch	.05		206	Phil Garner	.05		324	Bruce Bochy	.05
104	Mike Fitzgerald	.05		207	Mark Clear	.05		325	John Denny	.05
105	Ron Kittle	.05		208	Champ Summers	.05		326	Kevin Bass	.05
106	Pascual Perez	.05		209	Bill Campbell	.05		327	Brook Jacoby	.05
107	Tom Foley	.05		210	Gary Matthews	.05		328	Bob Shirley	.05
108	Darnell Coles RC	.05		211	Clay Christiansen	.05		329	Ron Washington	.05
109	Gary Roenicke	.05		212	George Vukovich	.05		330	Leon Durham	.05
110	Alejandro Pena	.05		213	Billy Gardner	.05		331	Bill Laskey	.05
111	Doug DeCinces	.05		214	John Tudor	.05		332	Brian Harper	.05
112	Tom Tellmann	.05		215	Bob Brenly	.05		333	Willie Hernandez	.05
113	Tom Herr	.05		216	Jerry Don Gleaton	.05		334	Dick Howser	.05
114	Bob James	.05		217	Leon Roberts	.05		335	Bruce Benedict	.05
115	Rickey Henderson	.75		218	Doyle Alexander	.05		336	Rance Mulliniks	.05
116	Dennis Boyd RC	.05		219	Gerald Perry	.05		337	Billy Sample	.05
117	Greg Gross	.05		220	Fred Lynn	.05		338	Britt Burns	.05
118	Eric Show	.05		221	Ron Reed	.05		339	Danny Heep	.05
119	Pat Corrales	.05		222	Hubie Brooks	.05		340	Robin Yount	.75
120	Steve Kemp	.05		223	Tom Hume	.05		341	Floyd Rayford	.05
121	Checklist 1-132	.05		224	Al Cowens	.05		342	Ted Power	.05
122	Tom Brunansky	.05		225	Mike Boddicker	.05		343	Bill Russell	.05
123	Dave Smith	.05		226	Juan Beniquez	.05		344	Dave Henderson	.05
124	Rich Hebner	.05		227	Danny Darwin	.05		345	Charlie Lea	.05
125	Kent Tekulve	.05		228	Dion James RC	.05		346	Terry Pendleton RC	.75
126	Ruppert Jones	.05		229	Dave LaPoint	.05		347	Rick Langford	.05
127	Mark Gubicza	.05		230	Gary Carter	.75		348	Bob Boone	.05
128	Ernie Whitt	.05		231	Dwayne Murphy	.05		349	Domingo Ramos	.05
129	Gene Garber	.05		232	Dave Beard	.05		350	Wade Boggs	1.00
130	Al Oliver	.05		233	Ed Jurak	.05		351	Juan Agosto	.05
131	Father - Son (Buddy Bell, Gus Bell)	.05		234	Jerry Narron	.05		352	Joe Morgan	.75
132	Father - Son (Dale Berra, Yogi Berra)	.10		235	Garry Maddox	.05		353	Julio Solano	.05
133	Father - Son (Bob Boone, Ray Boone)	.05		236	Mark Thurmond	.05		354	Andre Robertson	.05
134	Father - Son (Terry Francona, Tito Francona)	.05		237	Julio Franco	.05		355	Bert Blyleven	.05
135	Father - Son (Bob Kennedy, Terry Kennedy)	.05		238	Jose Rijo	.05		356	Dave Meier	.05
136	Father - Son (Bill Kunkel, Jeff Kunkel RC)	.05		239	Tim Teufel	.05		357	Rich Bordi	.05
137	Father - Son (Vance Law, Vern Law)	.05		240	Dave Stieb	.05		358	Tony Pena	.05
138	Father - Son (Dick Schofield, Dick Schofield, Jr.)	.05		241	Jim Frey	.05		359	Pat Sheridan	.05
139	Father - Son (Bob Skinner, Joel Skinner)	.05		242	Greg Harris	.05		360	Steve Carlton	.75
140	Father - Son (Roy Smalley, Jr., Roy Smalley III)	.05		243	Barbaro Garbey	.05		361	Alfredo Griffin	.05
141	Father - Son (Dave Stenhouse, Mike Stenhouse)	.05		244	Mike Jones	.05		362	Craig McMurtry	.05
142	Father - Son (Dizzy Trout, Steve Trout)	.05		245	Chili Davis	.05		363	Ron Hodges	.05
143	Father - Son (Ozzie Virgil, Ozzie Virgil)	.05		246	Mike Norris	.05		364	Richard Dotson	.05
144	Ron Gardenhire	.05		247	Wayne Tolleson	.05		365	Danny Ozark	.05
				248	Terry Forster	.05		366	Todd Cruz	.05
				249	Harold Baines	.05		367	Keefe Cato	.05
				250	Jesse Orosco	.05		368	Dave Bergman	.05
				251	Brad Gulden	.05		369	R.J. Reynolds RC	.05
				252	Dan Ford	.05		370	Bruce Sutter	.65
				253	Sid Bream RC	.10		371	Mickey Rivers	.05
				254	Pete Vuckovich	.05				
				255	Lonnie Smith	.05				
				256	Mike Stanton	.05				
				257	Brian Little (Bryan)	.05				
				258	Mike Brown	.05				
				259	Gary Allenson	.05				
				260	Dave Righetti	.05				
				261	Checklist 133-264	.05				
				262	Greg Booker RC	.05				

#	Player	Price		#	Player	Price		#	Player	Price
372	Roy Howell	.05		479	Mike Madden	.05		597	Brad Lesley	.05
373	Mike Moore	.05		480	Lou Whitaker	.05		598	Jose Oquendo	.05
374	Brian Downing	.05		481	Dale Murray	.05		599	Storm Davis	.05
375	Jeff Reardon	.05		482	Harry Spilman	.05		600	Pete Rose	3.00
376	Jeff Newman	.05		483	Mike Smithson	.05		601	Tom Lasorda	.10
377	Checklist 265-396	.05		484	Larry Bowa	.05		602	Jeff Dedmon RC	.05
378	Alan Wiggins	.05		485	Matt Young	.05		603	Rick Manning	.05
379	Charles Hudson	.05		486	Steve Balboni	.05		604	Daryl Sconiers	.05
380	Ken Griffey	.05		487	Frank Williams RC	.05		605	Ozzie Smith	1.00
381	Roy Smith	.05		488	Joel Skinner RC	.05		606	Rich Gale	.05
382	Denny Walling	.05		489	Bryan Clark	.05		607	Bill Almon	.05
383	Rick Lysander	.05		490	Jason Thompson	.05		608	Craig Lefferts	.05
384	Jody Davis	.05		491	Rick Camp	.05		609	Broderick Perkins	.05
385	Jose DeLeon	.05		492	Dave Johnson	.05		610	Jack Morris	.05
386	Dan Gladden RC	.30		493	Orel Hershiser RC	2.00		611	Ozzie Virgil	.05
387	Buddy Biancalana RC	.05		494	Rich Dauer	.05		612	Mike Armstrong	.05
388	Bert Roberge	.05		495	Mario Soto	.05		613	Terry Puhl	.05
389	Rod Dedeaux (Team USA)	.05		496	Donnie Scott	.05		614	Al Williams	.05
390	Sid Akins (Team USA)	.05		497	Gary Pettis	.05		615	Marvell Wynne	.05
391	Flavio Alfaro (Team USA)	.05		498	Ed Romero	.05		616	Scott Sanderson	.05
392	Don August RC (Team USA)	.05		499	Danny Cox RC	.05		617	Willie Wilson	.05
393	Scott Bankhead RC (Team USA)	.10		500	Mike Schmidt	2.00		618	Pete Falcone	.05
394	Bob Caffrey RC (Team USA)	.05		501	Dan Schatzeder	.05		619	Jeff Leonard	.05
395	Mike Dunne RC (Team USA)	.05		502	Rick Miller	.05		620	Dwight Gooden	.50
396	Gary Green RC (Team USA)	.05		503	Tim Conroy	.05		621	Marvis Foley	.05
397	John Hoover (Team USA)	.05		504	Jerry Willard	.05		622	Luis Leal	.05
398	Shane Mack RC (Team USA)	.10		505	Jim Beattie	.05		623	Greg Walker	.05
399	John Marzano RC (Team USA)	.05		506	Franklin Stubbs RC	.05		624	Benny Ayala	.05
400	Oddibe McDowell RC (Team USA)	.05		507	Ray Fontenot	.05		625	Mark Langston	.05
401	Mark McGwire RC (Team USA)	20.00		508	John Shelby	.05		626	German Rivera	.05
402	Pat Pacillo RC (Team USA)	.05		509	Milt May	.05		627	Eric Davis RC	1.00
403	Cory Snyder RC (Team USA)	.30		510	Kent Hrbek	.05		628	Rene Lachemann	.05
404	Billy Swift RC (Team USA)	.40		511	Lee Smith	.05		629	Dick Schofield	.05
405	Tom Veryzer	.05		512	Tom Brookens	.05		630	Tim Raines	.05
406	Len Whitehouse	.05		513	Lynn Jones	.05		631	Bob Forsch	.05
407	Bobby Ramos	.05		514	Jeff Cornell	.05		632	Bruce Bochte	.05
408	Sid Monge	.05		515	Dave Concepcion	.05		633	Glenn Hoffman	.05
409	Brad Wellman	.05		516	Roy Lee Jackson	.05		634	Bill Dawley	.05
410	Bob Horner	.05		517	Jerry Martin	.05		635	Terry Kennedy	.05
411	Bobby Cox	.05		518	Chris Chambliss	.05		636	Shane Rawley	.05
412	Bud Black	.05		519	Doug Rader	.05		637	Brett Butler	.05
413	Vance Law	.05		520	LaMarr Hoyt	.05		638	Mike Pagliarulo RC	.10
414	Gary Ward	.05		521	Rick Dempsey	.05		639	Ed Hodge	.05
415	Ron Darling	.05		522	Paul Molitor	.75		640	Steve Henderson	.05
416	Wayne Gross	.05		523	Candy Maldonado	.05		641	Rod Scurry	.05
417	John Franco RC	.50		524	Rob Wilfong	.05		642	Dave Owen	.05
418	Ken Landreaux	.05		525	Darrell Porter	.05		643	Johnny Grubb	.05
419	Mike Caldwell	.05		526	Dave Palmer	.05		644	Mark Huismann RC	.05
420	Andre Dawson	.50		527	Checklist 397-528	.05		645	Damaso Garcia	.05
421	Dave Rucker	.05		528	Bill Krueger	.05		646	Scot Thompson	.05
422	Carney Lansford	.05		529	Rich Gedman	.05		647	Rafael Ramirez	.05
423	Barry Bonnell	.05		530	Dave Dravecky	.05		648	Bob Jones	.05
424	Al Nipper RC	.05		531	Joe Lefebvre	.05		649	Sid Fernandez RC	.05
425	Mike Hargrove	.05		532	Frank DiPino	.05		650	Greg Luzinski	.05
426	Verne Ruhle	.05		533	Tony Bernazard	.05		651	Jeff Russell	.05
427	Mario Ramirez	.05		534	Brian Dayett RC	.05		652	Joe Nolan	.05
428	Larry Andersen	.05		535	Pat Putnam	.05		653	Mark Brouhard	.05
429	Rick Cerone	.05		536	Kirby Puckett	10.00		654	Dave Anderson	.05
430	Ron Davis	.05		537	Don Robinson	.05		655	Joaquin Andujar	.05
431	U.L. Washington	.05		538	Keith Moreland	.05		656	Chuck Cottier	.05
432	Thad Bosley	.05		539	Aurelio Lopez	.05		657	Jim Slaton	.05
433	Jim Morrison	.05		540	Claudell Washington	.05		658	Mike Stenhouse	.05
434	Gene Richards	.05		541	Mark Davis	.05		659	Checklist 529-660	.05
435	Dan Petry	.05		542	Don Slaught	.05		660	Tony Gwynn	1.00
436	Willie Aikens	.05		543	Mike Squires	.05		661	Steve Crawford	.05
437	Al Jones	.05		544	Bruce Kison	.05		662	Mike Heath	.05
438	Joe Torre	.10		545	Lloyd Moseby	.05		663	Luis Aguayo	.05
439	Junior Ortiz	.05		546	Brent Gaff	.05		664	Steve Farr RC	.05
440	Fernando Valenzuela	.05		547	Pete Rose	1.50		665	Don Mattingly	3.00
441	Duane Walker	.05		548	Larry Parrish	.05		666	Mike LaCoss	.05
442	Ken Forsch	.05		549	Mike Scioscia	.05		667	Dave Engle	.05
443	George Wright	.05		550	Scott McGregor	.05		668	Steve Trout	.05
444	Tony Phillips	.05		551	Andy Van Slyke	.05		669	Lee Lacy	.05
445	Tippy Martinez	.05		552	Chris Codiroli	.05		670	Tom Seaver	.75
446	Jim Sundberg	.05		553	Bob Clark	.05		671	Dane Iorg	.05
447	Jeff Lahti	.05		554	Doug Flynn	.05		672	Juan Berenguer	.05
448	Derrel Thomas	.05		555	Bob Stanley	.05		673	Buck Martinez	.05
449	Phil Bradley RC	.10		556	Sixto Lezcano	.05		674	Atlee Hammaker	.05
450	Steve Garvey	.25		557	Len Barker	.05		675	Tony Perez	.75
451	Bruce Hurst	.05		558	Carmelo Martinez	.05		676	Albert Hall RC	.05
452	John Castino	.05		559	Jay Howell	.05		677	Wally Backman	.05
453	Tom Waddell	.05		560	Bill Madlock	.05		678	Joey McLaughlin	.05
454	Glenn Wilson	.05		561	Darryl Motley	.05		679	Bob Kearney	.05
455	Bob Knepper	.05		562	Houston Jimenez	.05		680	Jerry Reuss	.05
456	Tim Foli	.05		563	Dick Ruthven	.05		681	Ben Oglivie	.05
457	Cecilio Guante	.05		564	Alan Ashby	.05		682	Doug Corbett	.05
458	Randy S. Johnson	.05		565	Kirk Gibson	.05		683	Whitey Herzog	.05
459	Charlie Leibrandt	.05		566	Ed Vande Berg	.05		684	Bill Doran	.05
460	Ryne Sandberg	1.00		567	Joel Youngblood	.05		685	Bill Caudill	.05
461	Marty Castillo	.05		568	Cliff Johnson	.05		686	Mike Easler	.05
462	Gary Lavelle	.05		569	Ken Oberkfell	.05		687	Bill Gullickson	.05
463	Dave Collins	.05		570	Darryl Strawberry	.10		688	Len Matuszek	.05
464	Mike Mason RC	.05		571	Charlie Hough	.05		689	Luis DeLeon	.05
465	Bob Grich	.05		572	Tom Paciorek	.05		690	Alan Trammell	.05
466	Tony LaRussa	.10		573	Jay Tibbs RC	.05		691	Dennis Rasmussen RC	.05
467	Ed Lynch	.05		574	Joe Altobelli	.05		692	Randy Bush	.05
468	Wayne Krenchicki	.05		575	Pedro Guerrero	.05		693	Tim Stoddard	.05
469	Sammy Stewart	.05		576	Jaime Cocanower	.05		694	Joe Carter	.75
470	Steve Sax	.05		577	Chris Speier	.05		695	Rick Rhoden	.05
471	Pete Ladd	.05		578	Terry Francona	.05		696	John Rabb	.05
472	Jim Essian	.05		579	Ron Romanick RC	.05		697	Onix Concepcion	.05
473	Tim Wallach	.05		580	Dwight Evans	.05		698	Jorge Bell	.05
474	Kurt Kepshire	.05		581	Mark Wagner	.05		699	Donnie Moore	.05
475	Andre Thornton	.05		582	Ken Phelps RC	.05		700	Eddie Murray	.75
476	Jeff Stone RC	.05		583	Bobby Brown	.05		701	Eddie Murray/AS	.40
477	Bob Ojeda	.05		584	Kevin Gross	.05		702	Damaso Garcia/AS	.05
478	Kurt Bevacqua	.05		585	Butch Wynegar	.05		703	George Brett/AS	.25
				586	Bill Scherrer	.05		704	Cal Ripken, Jr./AS	1.50
				587	Doug Frobel	.05		705	Dave Winfield/AS	.40
				588	Bobby Castillo	.05		706	Rickey Henderson/AS	.40
				589	Bob Dernier	.05		707	Tony Armas/AS	.05
				590	Ray Knight	.05		708	Lance Parrish/AS	.05
				591	Larry Herndon	.05		709	Mike Boddicker/AS	.05
				592	Jeff Robinson RC	.05		710	Frank Viola/AS	.05
				593	Rick Leach	.05		711	Dan Quisenberry/AS	.05
				594	Curt Wilkerson RC	.05		712	Keith Hernandez/AS	.05
				595	Larry Gura	.05		713	Ryne Sandberg/AS	.40
				596	Jerry Hairston Sr.	.05		714	Mike Schmidt/AS	.05

715	Ozzie Smith/AS	.50
716	Dale Murphy/AS	.15
717	Tony Gwynn/AS	.75
718	Jeff Leonard/AS	.05
719	Gary Carter/AS	.40
720	Rick Sutcliffe/AS	.05
721	Bob Knepper/AS	.05
722	Bruce Sutter/AS	.30
723	Dave Stewart	.05
724	Oscar Gamble	.05
725	Floyd Bannister	.05
726	Al Bumbry	.05
727	Frank Pastore	.05
728	Bob Bailor	.05
729	Don Sutton	.60
730	Dave Kingman	.05
731	Neil Allen	.05
732	John McNamara	.05
733	Tony Scott	.05
734	John Henry Johnson	.05
735	Garry Templeton	.05
736	Jerry Mumphrey	.05
737	Bo Diaz	.05
738	Omar Moreno	.05
739	Ernie Camacho	.05
740	Jack Clark	.05
741	John Butcher	.05
742	Ron Hassey	.05
743	Frank White	.05
744	Doug Bair	.05
745	Buddy Bell	.05
746	Jim Clancy	.05
747	Alex Trevino	.05
748	Lee Mazzilli	.05
749	Julio Cruz	.05
750	Rollie Fingers	.60
751	Kelvin Chapman	.05
752	Bob Owchinko	.05
753	Greg Brock	.05
754	Larry Milbourne	.05
755	Ken Singleton	.05
756	Rob Picciolo	.05
757	Willie McGee	.05
758	Ray Burris	.05
759	Jim Fanning	.05
760	Nolan Ryan	4.00
761	Jerry Remy	.05
762	Eddie Whitson	.05
763	Kiko Garcia	.05
764	Jamie Easterly	.05
765	Willie Randolph	.05
766	Paul Mirabella	.05
767	Darrell Brown	.05
768	Ron Cey	.05
769	Joe Cowley	.05
770	Carlton Fisk	.75
771	Geoff Zahn	.05
772	Johnnie LeMaster	.05
773	Hal McRae	.05
774	Dennis Lamp	.05
775	Mookie Wilson	.05
776	Jerry Royster	.05
777	Ned Yost	.05
778	Mike Davis	.05
779	Nick Esasky	.05
780	Mike Flanagan	.05
781	Jim Gantner	.05
782	Tom Niedenfuer	.05
783	Mike Jorgensen	.05
784	Checklist 661-792	.05
785	Tony Armas	.05
786	Enos Cabell	.05
787	Jim Wohlford	.05
788	Steve Comer	.05
789	Luis Salazar	.05
790	Ron Guidry	.10
791	Ivan DeJesus	.05
792	Darrell Evans	.05

Tiffany

In its second year of producing a high-gloss collectors' edition of its regular baseball card set, Topps cut production to a reported 5,000 sets. Other than the use of white cardboard stock and the glossy front coating, the cards in this specially boxed set are identical to regular 1985 Topps cards.

	NM/M
Complete Unopened Set (792):	500.00
Complete Set, Opened (792):	325.00
Common Player:	.25
Stars:	4X
181 Roger Clemens	150.00
401 Mark McGwire	80.00

Traded

Topps continued the annual Traded set tradition with another 132-card set. The 2-1/2" x 3-1/2" cards follow the pattern of being virtually identical in design to the regular cards of that year. Sold only through hobby dealers, the set features traded veterans and promising rookies. A glossy-finish "Tiffany" edition of the set was also issued. Cards are numbered with a "T" suffix.

	NM/M
Complete Set (132):	10.00

	Common Player:	.05
	Wax Test Pack (8):	10.00
	Wax Test Wax Box (36):	150.00
1	Don Aase	.05
2	Bill Almon	.05
3	Benny Ayala	.05
4	Dusty Baker	.25
5	George Bamberger	.05
6	Dale Berra	.05
7	Rich Bordi	.05
8	Daryl Boston RC	.05
9	Hubie Brooks	.05
10	Chris Brown RC	.05
11	Tom Browning RC	.05
12	Al Bumbry	.05
13	Ray Burris	.05
14	Jeff Burroughs	.05
15	Bill Campbell	.05
16	Don Carman RC	.05
17	Gary Carter	1.50
18	Bobby Castillo	.05
19	Bill Caudill	.05
20	Rick Cerone	.05
21	Bryan Clark	.05
22	Jack Clark	.05
23	Pat Clements RC	.05
24	Vince Coleman RC	.50
25	Dave Collins	.05
26	Danny Darwin	.05
27	Jim Davenport	.05
28	Jerry Davis	.05
29	Brian Dayett	.05
30	Ivan DeJesus	.05
31	Ken Dixon	.05
32	Mariano Duncan RC	.05
33	John Felske	.05
34	Mike Fitzgerald	.05
35	Ray Fontenot	.05
36	Greg Gagne RC	.05
37	Oscar Gamble	.05
38	Scott Garrelts RC	.05
39	Bob L. Gibson	.05
40	Jim Gott	.05
41	David Green	.05
42	Alfredo Griffin	.05
43	Ozzie Guillen RC	3.00
44	Eddie Haas	.05
45	Terry Harper	.05
46	Toby Harrah	.05
47	Greg Harris	.05
48	Ron Hassey	.05
49	Rickey Henderson	2.50
50	Steve Henderson	.05
51	George Hendrick	.05
52	Joe Hesketh RC	.05
53	Teddy Higuera RC	.05
54	Donnie Hill	.05
55	Al Holland	.05
56	Burt Hooton	.05
57	Jay Howell	.05
58	Ken Howell RC	.05
59	LaMarr Hoyt	.05
60	Tim Hulett RC	.05
61	Bob James	.05
62	Steve Jeltz RC	.05
63	Cliff Johnson	.05
64	Howard Johnson	.05
65	Ruppert Jones	.05
66	Steve Kemp	.05
67	Bruce Kison	.05
68	Alan Knicely	.05
69	Mike LaCoss	.05
70	Lee Lacy	.05
71	Dave LaPoint	.05
72	Gary Lavelle	.05
73	Vance Law	.05
74	Johnnie LeMaster	.05
75	Sixto Lezcano	.05
76	Tim Lollar	.05
77	Fred Lynn	.05
78	Billy Martin	.25
79	Ron Mathis	.05
80	Len Matuszek	.05
81	Gene Mauch	.05
82	Oddibe McDowell	.05
83	Roger McDowell RC	.05
84	John McNamara	.05
85	Donnie Moore	.05
86	Gene Nelson	.05
87	Steve Nicosia	.05
88	Al Oliver	.05
89	Joe Orsulak RC	.05
90	Rob Picciolo	.05
91	Chris Pittaro	.05
92	Jim Presley RC	.05
93	Rick Reuschel	.05
94	Bert Roberge	.05
95	Bob Rodgers	.05
96	Jerry Royster	.05
97	Dave Rozema	.05
98	Dave Rucker	.05
99	Vern Ruhle	.05
100	Paul Runge RC	.05
101	Mark Salas RC	.05
102	Luis Salazar	.05
103	Joe Sambito	.05
104	Rick Schu RC	.05
105	Donnie Scott	.05
106	Larry Sheets RC	.05
107	Don Slaught	.05
108	Roy Smalley	.05
109	Lonnie Smith	.05
110	Nate Snell	.05
111	Chris Speier	.05
112	Mike Stenhouse	.05
113	Tim Stoddard	.05
114	Jim Sundberg	.05
115	Bruce Sutter	1.00
116	Don Sutton	.50
117	Kent Tekulve	.05
118	Tom Teilmann	.05
119	Walt Terrell	.05
120	Mickey Tettleton RC	1.00
121	Derrel Thomas	.05
122	Rich Thompson	.05
123	Alex Trevino	.05
124	John Tudor	.05
125	Jose Uribe RC	.05
126	Bobby Valentine	.05
127	Dave Von Ohlen	.05
128	U.L. Washington	.05
129	Earl Weaver	.30
130	Eddie Whitson	.05
131	Herm Winningham RC	.05
132	Checklist 1-132	.05

Traded Tiffany

This specially boxed collectors version of the Topps Traded sets features cards that differ only in the use of a high-gloss finish coat on the fronts.

	NM/M
Complete Set (132):	35.00
Common Player:	.25
Stars:	4X

Traded Pete Rose Bronze

This 1/4-size metal replica was issued to dealers who purchased cases of 1985 Topps Traded sets. Each detail of the 1985 Topps Pete Rose card is reproduced on the 1-3/4" x 1-3/4" bronze metal mini-card, right down to the stats.

	NM/M
600 Pete Rose	10.00

All-Star Glossy Set of 22

This was the second straight year for this set of 22 cards featuring the starting players, honorary captains and managers in the All-Star Game. The set is virtually identical to that of the previous year in design with a color photo, All-Star banner, league emblem, and player ID on the front. Fronts have a high-gloss finish. The cards were available as inserts in Topps rack packs.

	NM/M
Complete Set (22):	5.00

	Common Player:	.10
1	Paul Owens	.10
2	Steve Garvey	.30
3	Ryne Sandberg	.50
4	Mike Schmidt	1.00
5	Ozzie Smith	.50
6	Tony Gwynn	.50
7	Dale Murphy	.30
8	Darryl Strawberry	.10
9	Gary Carter	.40
10	Charlie Lea	.10
11	Willie McCovey	.30
12	Joe Altobelli	.10
13	Rod Carew	.40
14	Lou Whitaker	.10
15	George Brett	1.00
16	Cal Ripken, Jr.	1.50
17	Dave Winfield	.50
18	Chet Lemon	.10
19	Reggie Jackson	.50
20	Lance Parrish	.10
21	Dave Stieb	.10
22	Hank Greenberg	.25

All-Star Glossy Set of 40

Similar to previous years' glossy sets, the 1985 All-Star "Collector's Edition" set of 40 could be obtained through the mail in eight five-card subsets. To obtain the 2-1/2" x 3-1/2" cards, collectors had to accumulate sweepstakes insert cards from Topps packs, and pay 75¢ postage and handling. Under the circumstances, the complete set of 40 cards was not inexpensive.

	NM/M
Complete Set (40):	8.00
Common Player:	.10
1	Dale Murphy	.30
2	Jesse Orosco	.10
3	Bob Brenly	.10
4	Mike Boddicker	.10
5	Dave Kingman	.10
6	Jim Rice	.20
7	Frank Viola	.10
8	Alvin Davis	.10
9	Rick Sutcliffe	.10
10	Pete Rose	2.00
11	Leon Durham	.10
12	Joaquin Andujar	.10
13	Keith Hernandez	.10
14	Dave Winfield	.40
15	Reggie Jackson	.50
16	Alan Trammell	.10
17	Bert Blyleven	.10
18	Tony Armas	.10
19	Rich Gossage	.10
20	Jose Cruz	.10
21	Ryne Sandberg	.50
22	Bruce Sutter	.30
23	Mike Schmidt	1.00
24	Cal Ripken, Jr.	3.00
25	Dan Petry	.10
26	Jack Morris	.10
27	Don Mattingly	1.00
28	Eddie Murray	.40
29	Tony Gwynn	.50
30	Charlie Lea	.10
31	Juan Samuel	.10
32	Phil Niekro	.30
33	Alejandro Pena	.10
34	Harold Baines	.10
35	Dan Quisenberry	.10
36	Gary Carter	.40
37	Mario Soto	.10
38	Dwight Gooden	.10
39	Tom Brunansky	.10
40	Dave Stieb	.10

All-Time Record Holders

No Pricing

Gallery of Champions

This second annual metallic miniatures issue honors 12 award winners from the previous season (MVP, Cy Young, Rookie of Year, Fireman, etc.). Each mini is an exact reproduction at one-quarter scale of the player's 1985 Topps card, both front and back. The sets (editions of 1,000) were issued in a specially-designed velvet-like case.

A Dwight Gooden pewter replica was given as a premium to dealers who bought the sets.

	NM/M
Complete Bronze Set (12):	60.00
Complete Silver Set (12):	280.00
(1b)	Tony Armas/Bronze	3.00
(1s)	Tony Armas/Silver	10.00
(2b)	Alvin Davis/Bronze	3.00
(2s)	Alvin Davis/Silver	10.00
(3b)	Dwight Gooden/Bronze	15.00
(3s)	Dwight Gooden/Silver	15.00
(3p)	Dwight Gooden/Pewter	6.00
(4b)	Tony Gwynn/Bronze	15.00
(4s)	Tony Gwynn/Silver	50.00
(5b)	Willie Hernandez/Bronze	3.00
(5s)	Willie Hernandez/Silver	10.00
(6b)	Don Mattingly/Bronze	30.00
(6s)	Don Mattingly/Silver	75.00
(7b)	Dale Murphy/Bronze	15.00
(7s)	Dale Murphy/Silver	45.00
(8b)	Dan Quisenberry/Bronze	3.00
(8s)	Dan Quisenberry/Silver	10.00
(9b)	Ryne Sandberg/Bronze	15.00
(9s)	Ryne Sandberg/Silver	50.00
(10b)	Mike Schmidt/Bronze	25.00
(10s)	Mike Schmidt/Silver	60.00
(11b)	Rick Sutcliffe/Bronze	3.00
(11s)	Rick Sutcliffe/Silver	10.00
(12b)	Bruce Sutter/Bronze	6.00
(12s)	Bruce Sutter/Silver	20.00

Minis

Never released for public sale, quantities of these enigmatic sets nevertheless reached the hobby market. Smaller than the standard 2-1/2" x 3-1/2" Topps cards, the "mini" version measures 2-3/8" x 3-9/32", 10% smaller than regular cards. Printed in Canada, the minis use a whiter cardboard stock than the regular '85 Topps, making the color printing more vibrant. The minis were the result of a test of new printing equipment by O-Pee-Chee, Topps' Canadian licensee. Only 132 of the 792 cards in the '85 Topps set are found in mini version. Only about 100 of each mini card are known, including about 15% blank-backs.

	NM/M
Complete Set (132):	1,500
Common Player:	5.00
Blank-backs: 50 Percent	
12	Dave Lopes	5.00
15	Jerry Koosman	5.00
17	Mike Scott	5.00
25	Steve Bedrosian	5.00
44	Dickie Thon	5.00
65	Bill Buckner	5.00
68	Von Hayes	5.00
72	Rick Sutcliffe	5.00
75	Willie Upshaw	5.00
82	Joe Price	5.00
88	Bryn Smith	5.00
91	Jeff Burroughs	5.00
95	Jose Cruz	5.00
96	Johnny Ray	5.00
109	Gary Roenicke	5.00
113	Tom Herr	5.00
114	Bob James	5.00
118	Greg Gross	5.00
120	Steve Kemp	5.00

121	Checklist 1-132	3.00
128	Ernie Whitt	5.00
148	Steve Yaeger	5.00
150	Jim Rice	15.00
151	Moose Haas	5.00
154	Argenis Salazar	5.00
156	Craig Reynolds	5.00
160	Lance Parrish	5.00
165	Dusty Baker	5.00
170	George Foster	5.00
178	Miguel Dilone	5.00
185	Al Holland	5.00
190	Rusty Staub	5.00
198	Eddie Milner	5.00
201	Burt Hooton	5.00
205	Steve Rogers	5.00
209	Bill Campbell	5.00
210	Gary Matthews	5.00
218	Doyle Alexander	5.00
222	Hubie Brooks	5.00
223	Tom Hume	5.00
225	Mike Boddicker	5.00
229	Dave LaPoint	5.00
230	Gary Carter	45.00
235	Garry Maddox	5.00
236	Mark Thurmond	5.00
237	Julio Franco	5.00
239	Tim Teufel	5.00
248	Terry Forster	5.00
250	Jesse Orosco	5.00
251	Brad Gulden	5.00
255	Lonnie Smith	5.00
261	Checklist 133-264	3.00
263	Mel Hall	5.00
266	Frank Viola	5.00
287	Walt Terrell	5.00
306	Rick Reuschel	5.00
310	Manny Trillo	5.00
313	Dave Schmidt	5.00
325	John Denny	5.00
330	Leon Durham	5.00
333	Willie Hernandez	5.00
340	Robin Yount	45.00
343	Bill Russell	5.00
345	Charlie Lea	5.00
352	Joe Morgan	45.00
355	Bert Blyleven	5.00
358	Tony Pena	5.00
360	Steve Carlton	45.00
362	Craig McMurtry	5.00
375	Jeff Reardon	5.00
379	Charles Hudson	5.00
415	Ron Darling	5.00
445	Tippy Martinez	5.00
446	Jim Sundberg	5.00
450	Steve Garvey	7.50
452	John Castino	5.00
464	Mike Mason	5.00
470	Steve Sax	5.00
485	Matt Young	5.00
487	Frank Williams	5.00
489	Bryan Clark	5.00
491	Rick Camp	5.00
495	Mario Soto	5.00
500	Mike Schmidt	250.00
501	Dan Schatzeder	5.00
504	Jerry Willard	5.00
511	Lee Smith	5.00
515	Dave Concepcion	5.00
520	LaMarr Hoyt	5.00
526	Dave Palmer	5.00
530	Dave Dravecky	5.00
538	Keith Moreland	5.00
545	Lloyd Moseby	5.00
554	Andy Van Slyke	5.00
556	Doug Flynn	5.00
558	Sixto Lezcano	5.00
560	Bill Madlock	5.00
563	Dick Ruthven	5.00
568	Ed Vande Berg	5.00
568	Cliff Johnson	5.00
569	Ken Oberkfell	5.00
575	Pedro Guerrero	5.00
580	Dwight Evans	5.00
589	Bob Dernier	5.00
592	Jeff Robinson	5.00
603	Rick Manning	5.00
608	Craig Lefferts	5.00
610	Jack Morris	5.00
613	Terry Puhl	5.00
615	Marvell Wynne	5.00
619	Jeff Leonard	5.00
625	Mark Langston	5.00
630	Tim Raines	5.00
634	Bill Dawley	5.00
670	Tom Seaver	45.00
673	Buck Martinez	5.00
674	Atlee Hammaker	5.00
685	Bill Caudill	5.00
700	Eddie Murray	45.00
725	Floyd Bannister	5.00
729	Don Sutton	10.00
731	Neil Allen	5.00
736	Jerry Mumphrey	5.00
748	Lee Mazzilli	5.00
753	Greg Brock	5.00
755	Ken Singleton	5.00
757	Willie McGee	5.00
760	Nolan Ryan	650.00
762	Eddie Whitson	5.00
775	Mookie Wilson	5.00
780	Mike Flanagan	5.00
782	Tom Niedenfuer	5.00

Rub Downs

Similar in size and design to the Rub Downs of the previous

year, the 1985 set again consisted of 32 unnumbered sheets featuring 112 different players. The set was sold by Topps as a separate issue.

	NM/M
Complete Set (32):	5.00
Common Sheet:	.25
Pack (2):	.50
Wax Box (36):	7.50

(1) Tony Armas, Harold Baines, Lonnie Smith .25
(2) Don Baylor, George Hendrick, Ron Kittle, Johnnie LeMaster .25
(3) Buddy Bell, Tony Gwynn, Lloyd Moseby .75
(4) Bruce Benedict, Atlee Hammaker, Frank White .25
(5) Mike Boddicker, Rod Carew, Carlton Fisk, Johnny Ray .60
(6) Wade Boggs, Rick Dempsey, Keith Hernandez .60
(7) George Brett, Andre Dawson, Paul Molitor, Alan Wiggins 1.00
(8) Tom Brunansky, Pedro Guerrero, Darryl Strawberry .25
(9) Bill Buckner, Tim Raines, Ryne Sandberg, Mike Schmidt 1.00
(10) Steve Carlton, Bob Horner, Dan Quisenberry .60
(11) Gary Carter, Phil Garner, Ron Guidry .60
(12) Jack Clark, Damaso Garcia, Hal McRae, Lance Parrish .25
(13) Dave Concepcion, Cecil Cooper, Fred Lynn, Jesse Orosco .25
(14) Jose Cruz, Jack Morris, Jim Rice, Rick Sutcliffe .25
(15) Alvin Davis, Steve Kemp, Greg Luzinski, Kent Tekulve .25
(16) Ron Davis, Kent Hrbek, Juan Samuel .25
(17) John Denny, Carney Lansford, Mario Soto, Lou Whitaker .25
(18) Leon Durham, Willie Hernandez, Steve Sax .25
(19) Dwight Evans, Julio Franco, Dwight Gooden .25
(20) George Foster, Gary Gaetti, Bobby Grich, Gary Redus .25
(21) Steve Garvey, Jerry Remy, Bill Russell, George Wright .25
(22) Kirk Gibson, Rich Gossage, Don Mattingly, Dave Stieb 1.00
(23) Moose Haas, Bruce Sutter, Dickie Thon, Andre Thornton .25
(24) Rickey Henderson, Dave Righetti, Pete Rose 1.50
(25) Steve Henderson, Bill Madlock, Alan Trammell .25
(26) LaMarr Hoyt, Larry Parrish, Nolan Ryan 2.00
(27) Reggie Jackson, Eric Show, Jason Thompson .75
(28) Terry Kennedy, Eddie Murray, Tom Seaver, Ozzie Smith .75
(29) Mark Langston, Ben Oglivie, Darrell Porter .25
(30) Jeff Leonard, Gary Matthews, Dale Murphy, Dave Winfield .60
(31) Craig McMurtry, Cal Ripken, Jr., Steve Rogers, Willie Upshaw 2.00
(32) Tony Pena, Fernando Valenzuela, Robin Yount .60

Stickers

Topps went to a larger size for its stickers in 1985. Produced by Panini, each of the 376 stickers measures 2-1/8" x 3" and is numbered on both the front and the back. The backs contain either an offer to obtain an autographed team ball or a poster. An album was also available.

	NM/M
Complete Set (376):	12.50
Common Player:	.05
Sticker Album:	2.00
Pack (5):	.25
Box (100):	15.00

#	Player	Price
1	Steve Garvey	.15
2	Steve Garvey	.15
3	Dwight Gooden	.05
4	Dwight Gooden	.05
5	Joe Morgan	.30
6	Joe Morgan	.30
7	Don Sutton	.30
8	Don Sutton	.30
9	1984 A.L. Championships (Jack Morris)	.05
10	1984 A.L. Championships (Milt Wilcox)	.05
11	1984 A.L. Championships (Kirk Gibson)	.05
12	1984 N.L. Championships (Gary Matthews)	.05
13	1984 N.L. Championships (Steve Garvey)	.05
14	1984 N.L. Championships (Steve Garvey)	.05
15	1984 World Series (Jack Morris)	.05
16	1984 World Series (Kurt Bevacqua)	.05
17	1984 World Series (Milt Wilcox)	.05
18	1984 World Series (Alan Trammell)	.05
19	1984 World Series (Kirk Gibson)	.05
20	1984 World Series (Alan Trammell)	.05
21	1984 World Series (Chet Lemon)	.05
22	Dale Murphy	.25
23	Steve Bedrosian	.05
24	Bob Horner	.05
25	Claudell Washington	.05
26	Rick Mahler	.05
27	Rafael Ramirez	.05
28	Craig McMurtry	.05
29	Chris Chambliss	.05
30	Alex Trevino	.05
31	Bruce Benedict	.05
32	Ken Oberkfell	.05
33	Glenn Hubbard	.05
34	Ryne Sandberg	.40
35	Rick Sutcliffe	.05
36	Leon Durham	.05
37	Jody Davis	.05
38	Bob Dernier	.05
39	Keith Moreland	.05
40	Scott Sanderson	.05
41	Lee Smith	.05
42	Ron Cey	.05
43	Steve Trout	.05
44	Gary Matthews	.05
45	Larry Bowa	.05
46	Mario Soto	.05
47	Dave Parker	.05
48	Dave Concepcion	.05
49	Gary Redus	.05
50	Ted Power	.05
51	Nick Esasky	.05
52	Duane Walker	.05
53	Eddie Milner	.05
54	Ron Oester	.05
55	Cesar Cedeno	.05
56	Joe Price	.05
57	Pete Rose	.65
58	Nolan Ryan	.75
59	Jose Cruz	.05
60	Jerry Mumphrey	.05
61	Enos Cabell	.05
62	Bob Knepper	.05
63	Dickie Thon	.05
64	Phil Garner	.05
65	Craig Reynolds	.05
66	Frank DiPino	.05
67	Terry Puhl	.05
68	Bill Doran	.05
69	Joe Niekro	.05
70	Pedro Guerrero	.05
71	Fernando Valenzuela	.05
72	Mike Marshall	.05
73	Alejandro Pena	.05
74	Orel Hershiser	.10
75	Ken Landreaux	.05
76	Bill Russell	.05
77	Steve Sax	.05
78	Rick Honeycutt	.05
79	Mike Scioscia	.05
80	Tom Niedenfuer	.05
81	Candy Maldonado	.05
82	Tim Raines	.05
83	Gary Carter	.30
84	Charlie Lea	.05
85	Jeff Reardon	.05
86	Andre Dawson	.15
87	Tim Wallach	.05
88	Terry Francona	.05
89	Steve Rogers	.05
90	Bryn Smith	.05
91	Bill Gullickson	.05
92	Dan Driessen	.05
93	Doug Flynn	.05
94	Mike Schmidt	.50
95	Tony Armas	.05
96	Dale Murphy	.15
97	Rick Sutcliffe	.05
98	Keith Hernandez	.05
99	George Foster	.05
100	Darryl Strawberry	.05
101	Jesse Orosco	.05
102	Mookie Wilson	.05
103	Doug Sisk	.05
104	Hubie Brooks	.05
105	Ron Darling	.05
106	Wally Backman	.05
107	Dwight Gooden	.05
108	Mike Fitzgerald	.05
109	Walt Terrell	.05
110	Ozzie Virgil	.05
111	Mike Schmidt	.50
112	Steve Carlton	.30
113	Al Holland	.05
114	Juan Samuel	.05
115	Von Hayes	.05
116	Jeff Stone	.05
117	Jerry Koosman	.05
118	Al Oliver	.05
119	John Denny	.05
120	Charles Hudson	.05
121	Garry Maddox	.05
122	Bill Madlock	.05
123	John Candelaria	.05
124	Tony Pena	.05
125	Jason Thompson	.05
126	Lee Lacy	.05
127	Rick Rhoden	.05
128	Doug Frobel	.05
129	Kent Tekulve	.05
130	Johnny Ray	.05
131	Marvell Wynne	.05
132	Larry McWilliams	.05
133	Dale Berra	.05
134	George Hendrick	.05
135	Bruce Sutter	.20
136	Joaquin Andujar	.05
137	Ozzie Smith	.50
138	Andy Van Slyke	.05
139	Lonnie Smith	.05
140	Darrell Porter	.05
141	Willie McGee	.05
142	Tom Herr	.05
143	Dave LaPoint	.05
144	Neil Allen	.05
145	David Green	.05
146	Tony Gwynn	.50
147	Rich Gossage	.05
148	Terry Kennedy	.05
149	Steve Garvey	.15
150	Alan Wiggins	.05
151	Garry Templeton	.05
152	Ed Whitson	.05
153	Tim Lollar	.05
154	Dave Dravecky	.05
155	Graig Nettles	.05
156	Eric Show	.05
157	Carmelo Martinez	.05
158	Bob Brenly	.05
159	Gary Lavelle	.05
160	Jack Clark	.05
161	Jeff Leonard	.05
162	Chili Davis	.05
163	Mike Krukow	.05
164	Johnnie LeMaster	.05
165	Atlee Hammaker	.05
166	Dan Gladden	.05
167	Greg Minton	.05
168	Joel Youngblood	.05
169	Frank Williams	.05
170	Tony Gwynn	.50
171	Don Mattingly	.60
172	Bruce Sutter	.20
173	Dan Quisenberry	.05
174	Tony Gwynn	.50
175	Ryne Sandberg	.40
176	Steve Garvey	.15
177	Dale Murphy	.15
178	Mike Schmidt	.50
179	Darryl Strawberry	.05
180	Gary Carter	.30
181	Ozzie Smith	.50
182	Charlie Lea	.05
183	Lou Whitaker	.05
184	Rod Carew	.30
185	Cal Ripken, Jr.	.50
186	Dave Winfield	.40
187	Reggie Jackson	.50
188	George Brett	.50
189	Lance Parrish	.05
190	Chet Lemon	.05
191	Dave Stieb	.05
192	Gary Carter	.30
193	Mike Schmidt	.50
194	Tony Armas	.05
195	Mike Witt	.05
196	Eddie Murray	.05
197	Cal Ripken, Jr.	.75
198	Scott McGregor	.05
199	Rick Dempsey	.05
200	Tippy Martinez	.05
201	Ken Singleton	.05
202	Mike Boddicker	.05
203	Rich Dauer	.05
204	John Shelby	.05
205	Al Bumbry	.05
206	John Lowenstein	.05
207	Mike Flanagan	.05
208	Jim Rice	.10
209	Tony Armas	.05
210	Wade Boggs	.40
211	Bruce Hurst	.05
212	Dwight Evans	.05
213	Mike Easler	.05
214	Bill Buckner	.05
215	Bob Stanley	.05
216	Jackie Gutierrez	.05
217	Rich Gedman	.05
218	Jerry Remy	.05
219	Marty Barrett	.05
220	Reggie Jackson	.40
221	Geoff Zahn	.05
222	Doug DeCinces	.05
223	Rod Carew	.30
224	Brian Downing	.05
225	Fred Lynn	.05
226	Gary Pettis	.05
227	Mike Witt	.05
228	Bob Boone	.05
229	Tommy John	.05
230	Bobby Grich	.05
231	Ron Romanick	.05
232	Ron Kittle	.05
233	Richard Dotson	.05
234	Harold Baines	.05
235	Tom Seaver	.40
236	Greg Walker	.05
237	Roy Smalley	.05
238	Greg Luzinski	.05
239	Julio Cruz	.05
240	Scott Fletcher	.05
241	Rudy Law	.05
242	Vance Law	.05
243	Carlton Fisk	.30
244	Andre Thornton	.05
245	Julio Franco	.05
246	Brett Butler	.05
247	Bert Blyleven	.05
248	Mike Hargrove	.05
249	George Vukovich	.05
250	Pat Tabler	.05
251	Brook Jacoby	.05
252	Tony Bernazard	.05
253	Ernie Camacho	.05
254	Mel Hall	.05
255	Carmen Castillo	.05
256	Jack Morris	.05
257	Willie Hernandez	.05
258	Alan Trammell	.05
259	Lance Parrish	.05
260	Chet Lemon	.05
261	Lou Whitaker	.05
262	Howard Johnson	.05
263	Barbaro Garbey	.05
264	Dan Petry	.05
265	Aurelio Lopez	.05
266	Larry Herndon	.05
267	Kirk Gibson	.05
268	George Brett	.50
269	Dan Quisenberry	.05
270	Hal McRae	.05
271	Steve Balboni	.05
272	Pat Sheridan	.05
273	Jorge Orta	.05
274	Frank White	.05
275	Bud Black	.05
276	Darryl Motley	.05
277	Willie Wilson	.05
278	Larry Gura	.05
279	Don Slaught	.05
280	Dwight Gooden	.05
281	Mark Langston	.05
282	Tim Raines	.05
283	Rickey Henderson	.30
284	Robin Yount	.30
285	Rollie Fingers	.30
286	Jim Sundberg	.05
287	Cecil Cooper	.05
288	Jaime Cocanower	.05
289	Mike Caldwell	.05
290	Don Sutton	.30
291	Rick Manning	.05
292	Ben Oglivie	.05
293	Moose Haas	.05
294	Ted Simmons	.05
295	Jim Gantner	.05
296	Kent Hrbek	.05
297	Ron Davis	.05
298	Dave Engle	.05
299	Tom Brunansky	.05
300	Frank Viola	.05
301	Mike Smithson	.05
302	Gary Gaetti	.05
303	Tim Teufel	.05
304	Mickey Hatcher	.05
305	John Butcher	.05
306	Darrell Brown	.05
307	Kirby Puckett	.50
308	Dave Winfield	.40
309	Phil Niekro	.30
310	Don Mattingly	.60
311	Don Baylor	.05
312	Willie Randolph	.05
313	Ron Guidry	.05
314	Dave Righetti	.05
315	Bobby Meacham	.05
316	Butch Wynegar	.05
317	Mike Pagliarulo	.05
318	Joe Cowley	.05
319	John Montefusco	.05
320	Dave Kingman	.05
321	Rickey Henderson	.30
322	Bill Caudill	.05
323	Dwayne Murphy	.05
324	Steve McCatty	.05
325	Joe Morgan	.30
326	Mike Heath	.05
327	Chris Codiroli	.05
328	Ray Burris	.05
329	Tony Phillips	.05
330	Carney Lansford	.05
331	Bruce Bochte	.05
332	Alvin Davis	.05
333	Al Cowens	.05
334	Jim Beattie	.05
335	Bob Kearney	.05
336	Ed Vande Berg	.05
337	Mark Langston	.05
338	Dave Henderson	.05
339	Spike Owen	.05
340	Matt Young	.05
341	Jack Perconte	.05
342	Barry Bonnell	.05
343	Mike Stanton	.05
344	Pete O'Brien	.05
345	Charlie Hough	.05
346	Larry Parrish	.05
347	Buddy Bell	.05
348	Frank Tanana	.05
349	Curt Wilkerson	.05
350	Jeff Kunkel	.05
351	Billy Sample	.05
352	Danny Darwin	.05
353	Gary Ward	.05
354	Mike Mason	.05
355	Mickey Rivers	.05
356	Dave Stieb	.05
357	Damaso Garcia	.05
358	Willie Upshaw	.05
359	Lloyd Moseby	.05
360	George Bell	.05
361	Luis Leal	.05
362	Jesse Barfield	.05
363	Dave Collins	.05
364	Roy Lee Jackson	.05
365	Doyle Alexander	.05
366	Alfredo Griffin	.05
367	Cliff Johnson	.05
368	Alvin Davis	.05
369	Juan Samuel	.05
370	Brook Jacoby	.05
371	Dwight Gooden, Mark Langston	.05
372	Mike Fitzgerald	.05
373	Jackie Gutierrez	.05
374	Dan Gladden	.05
375	Carmelo Martinez	.05
376	Kirby Puckett	.50

Super

Still trying to sell collectors on the idea of jumbo-sized cards, Topps returned for a second year with its 4-7/8" x 6-7/8" "Super" set. In fact, the set size was doubled from the previous year, to 60 cards. The Supers are identical to the regular-issue 1985 cards of the same players, only the card numbers on back were changed. The cards were sold three per pack for 50 cents.

	NM/M
Complete Set (60):	12.00
Common Player:	.25
Wax Pack (1):	.25
Wax Box (24):	6.00

#	Player	Price
1	Ryne Sandberg	1.00
2	Willie Hernandez	.25
3	Rick Sutcliffe	.25
4	Don Mattingly	1.50
5	Tony Gwynn	1.00
6	Alvin Davis	.25
7	Dwight Gooden	.50
8	Dan Quisenberry	.25
9	Bruce Sutter	.65
10	Tony Armas	.25
11	Dale Murphy	.50
12	Mike Schmidt	1.50
13	Gary Carter	.75
14	Rickey Henderson	.75
15	Tim Raines	.25
16	Mike Boddicker	.25
17	Alejandro Pena	.25
18	Eddie Murray	.75
19	Gary Matthews	.25
20	Mark Langston	.25
21	Mario Soto	.25
22	Dave Stieb	.25
23	Nolan Ryan	3.00
24	Steve Carlton	.75
25	Alan Trammell	.25
26	Steve Garvey	.40
27	Kirk Gibson	.25
28	Juan Samuel	.25
29	Reggie Jackson	1.00
30	Darryl Strawberry	.25
31	Tom Seaver	.75
32	Pete Rose	2.00
33	Dwight Evans	.25
34	Jose Cruz	.25
35	Bert Blyleven	.25
36	Keith Hernandez	.25
37	Robin Yount	.75
38	Joaquin Andujar	.25
39	Lloyd Moseby	.25
40	Chili Davis	.25
41	Kent Hrbek	.25
42	Dave Parker	.25
43	Jack Morris	.25
44	Pedro Guerrero	.25
45	Mike Witt	.25
46	George Brett	1.50
47	Ozzie Smith	1.00
48	Cal Ripken, Jr.	3.00
49	Rich Gossage	.25
50	Jim Rice	.35
51	Harold Baines	.25
52	Fernando Valenzuela	.25
53	Buddy Bell	.25
54	Jesse Orosco	.25
55	Lance Parrish	.25
56	Jason Thompson	.25
57	Tom Brunansky	.25
58	Dave Righetti	.25
59	Dave Kingman	.25
60	Dave Winfield	.75

3-D

These 4-1/4" x 6" cards were something new. Printed on plastic, rather than paper, the player picture on the card is actually raised above the surface much like might be found on a relief map; a true 3-D baseball card. The plastic cards include the player's name, a Topps logo and card number across the top, and a team logo on the side. The backs are blank but have two peel-off adhesive strips so that the card may be attached to a flat surface. There are 30 cards in the set, mostly stars. Cards were sold one per pack for 50 cents.

	NM/M
Complete Set (30):	12.00
Common Player:	.25
Wax Pack (1):	.50
Wax Box (24):	12.50

#	Player	Price
1	Mike Schmidt	2.00
2	Eddie Murray	.75
3	Dale Murphy	.50
4	George Brett	2.00
5	Pete Rose	2.50
6	Jim Rice	.35
7	Ryne Sandberg	1.50
8	Don Mattingly	2.00
9	Darryl Strawberry	.25
10	Rickey Henderson	.75
11	Keith Hernandez	.25
12	Dave Kingman	.25
13	Tony Gwynn	1.50
14	Reggie Jackson	1.50
15	Gary Carter	.75
16	Cal Ripken, Jr.	3.00
17	Tim Raines	.25
18	Dave Winfield	.75
19	Dwight Gooden	.35
20	Dave Stieb	.25
21	Fernando Valenzuela	.25
22	Mark Langston	.25
23	Bruce Sutter	.65
24	Dan Quisenberry	.25
25	Steve Carlton	

1986 Topps

GARY CARTER

The 1986 Topps set consists of 792 cards. Fronts of the 2-1/2" x 3-1/2" cards feature color photos with the Topps logo in the upper right-hand corner while the player's position is in the lower left-hand corner. Above the picture is the team name, while below it is the player's name. The borders are a departure from previous practice, as the top 7/8" is black, while the remainder is white. Once again, a 5,000-set glossy-finish "Tiffany" edition was produced.

	NM/M
Unopened Fact. Set, Retail (792):	65.00
Unopened Fact. Set, Hobby (792):	30.00
Complete Set (792):	25.00
Common Player:	.05
Wax Pack (15):	.75
Wax Box (36):	20.00
Cello Pack (28):	1.00
Cello Box (24):	20.00
Rack Pack (51):	1.25
Rack Box (24):	25.00
Vending Box (500):	10.00

#	Player	NM/M
1	Pete Rose	1.50
2	Pete Rose (Special 1963-66)	.50
3	Pete Rose (Special 1967-70)	.50
4	Pete Rose (Special 1971-74)	.50
5	Pete Rose (Special 1975-78)	.50
6	Pete Rose (Special 1972-82)	.50
7	Pete Rose (Special 1983-85)	.50
8	Dwayne Murphy	.05
9	Roy Smith	.05
10	Tony Gwynn	.75
11	Bob Ojeda	.05
12	Jose Uribe RC	.05
13	Bob Kearney	.05
14	Julio Cruz	.05
15	Eddie Whitson	.05
16	Rick Schu RC	.05
17	Mike Stenhouse	.05
18	Brent Gaff	.05
19	Rich Hebner	.05
20	Lou Whitaker	.05
21	George Bamberger	.05
22	Duane Walker	.05
23	Manny Lee RC	.05
24	Len Barker	.05
25	Willie Wilson	.05
26	Frank DiPino	.05
27	Ray Knight	.05
28	Eric Davis	.05
29	Tony Phillips	.05
30	Eddie Murray	.50
31	Jamie Easterly	.05
32	Steve Yeager	.05
33	Jeff Lahti	.05
34	Ken Phelps RC	.05
35	Jeff Reardon	.05
36	Tigers Leaders (Lance Parrish)	.05
37	Mark Thurmond	.05
38	Glenn Hoffman	.05
39	Dave Rucker	.05
40	Ken Griffey	.05
41	Brad Wellman	.05
42	Geoff Zahn	.05
43	Dave Engle	.05
44	Lance McCullers RC	.05
45	Damaso Garcia	.05
46	Billy Hatcher RC	.05
47	Juan Berenguer	.05
48	Bill Almon	.05
49	Rick Manning	.05
50	Dan Quisenberry	.05
52	Chris Welsh	.05
53	Len Dykstra RC	.05
54	John Franco	.05
55	Fred Lynn	.05
56	Tom Niedenfuer	.05
57a	Bill Doran	.05
57b	Bobby Wine (Supposed to be #51.)	.05
58	Bill Krueger	.05
59	Andre Thornton	.05
60	Dwight Evans	.05
61	Karl Best	.05
62	Bob Boone	.05
63	Ron Roenicke	.05
64	Floyd Bannister	.05
65	Dan Driessen	.05
66	Cardinals Leaders (Bob Forsch)	.05
67	Carmelo Martinez	.05
68	Ed Lynch	.05
69	Luis Aguayo	.05
70	Dave Winfield	.50
71	Ken Schrom	.05
72	Shawon Dunston	.05
73	Randy O'Neal RC	.05
74	Rance Mulliniks	.05
75	Jose DeLeon	.05
76	Dion James	.05
77	Charlie Leibrandt	.05
78	Bruce Benedict	.05
79	Dave Schmidt	.05
80	Darryl Strawberry	.05
81	Gene Mauch	.05
82	Tippy Martinez	.05
83	Phil Garner	.05
84	Curt Young	.05
85	Tony Perez	.40
86	Tom Waddell	.05
87	Candy Maldonado	.05
88	Tom Nieto	.05
89	Randy St. Claire RC	.05
90	Garry Templeton	.05
91	Steve Crawford	.05
92	Al Cowens	.05
93	Scot Thompson	.05
94	Rich Bordi	.05
95	Ozzie Virgil	.05
96	Blue Jay Leaders (Jim Clancy)	.05
97	Gary Gaetti	.05
98	Dick Ruthven	.05
99	Buddy Biancalana	.05
100	Nolan Ryan	2.00
101	Dave Bergman	.05
102	Joe Orsulak RC	.15
103	Luis Salazar	.05
104	Sid Fernandez	.05
105	Gary Ward	.05
106	Ray Burris	.05
107	Rafael Ramirez	.05
108	Ted Power	.05
109	Len Matuszek	.05
110	Scott McGregor	.05
111	Roger Craig	.05
112	Bill Campbell	.05
113	U.L. Washington	.05
114	Mike Brown	.05
115	Jay Howell	.05
116	Brook Jacoby	.05
117	Bruce Kison	.05
118	Jerry Royster	.05
119	Barry Bonnell	.05
120	Steve Carlton	.50
121	Nelson Simmons	.05
122	Pete Filson	.05
123	Greg Walker	.05
124	Luis Sanchez	.05
125	Dave Lopes	.05
126	Mets Leaders (Mookie Wilson)	.05
127	Jack Howell RC	.05
128	John Wathan	.05
129	Jeff Dedmon RC	.05
130	Alan Trammell	.05
131	Checklist 1-132	.05
132	Razor Shines	.05
133	Andy McGaffigan	.05
134	Carney Lansford	.05
135	Joe Niekro	.05
136	Mike Hargrove	.05
137	Charlie Moore	.05
138	Mark Davis	.05
139	Daryl Boston	.05
140	John Candelaria	.05
141a	Chuck Cottier	.05
141b	Bob Rodgers (Supposed to be #171.)	.05
142	Bob Jones	.05
143	Dave Van Gorder	.05
144	Doug Sisk	.05
145	Pedro Guerrero	.05
146	Jack Perconte	.05
147	Larry Sheets	.05
148	Mike Heath	.05
149	Brett Butler	.05
150	Joaquin Andujar	.05
151	Dave Stapleton	.05
152	Mike Morgan	.05
153	Ricky Adams	.05
154	Bert Roberge	.05
155	Bob Grich	.05
156	White Sox Leaders (Richard Dotson)	.05
157	Ron Hassey	.05
158	Derrel Thomas	.05
159	Orel Hershiser	.05
160	Chet Lemon	.05
161	Lee Tunnell	.05
162	Greg Gagne	.05
163	Pete Ladd	.05
164	Steve Balboni	.05
165	Mike Davis	.05
166	Dickie Thon	.05
167	Zane Smith RC	.05
168	Jeff Burroughs	.05
169	George Wright	.05
170	Gary Carter	.50
171	Jerry Reed	.05
172	Wayne Gross	.05
173	Brian Snyder	.05
174	Steve Sax	.05
175	Jay Tibbs	.05
176	Joel Youngblood	.05
177	Ivan DeJesus	.05
178	Stu Cliburn RC	.05
179	Don Mattingly	1.00
180	Al Nipper	.05
181	Bobby Brown	.05
182	Larry Andersen	.05
183	Tim Laudner	.05
184	Rollie Fingers	.40
185	Astros Leaders (Jose Cruz)	.05
186	Scott Fletcher	.05
187	Bob Dernier	.05
188	Mike Mason	.05
189	George Hendrick	.05
190	Wally Backman	.05
191	Milt Wilcox	.05
192	Daryl Sconiers	.05
193	Craig McMurtry	.05
194	Dave Concepcion	.05
195	Doyle Alexander	.05
196	Doyle Alexander	.05
197	Enos Cabell	.05
198	Ken Dixon	.05
199	Dick Howser	.05
200	Mike Schmidt	1.00
201	Vince Coleman (Record Breaker)	.05
202	Dwight Gooden (Record Breaker)	.05
203	Keith Hernandez (Record Breaker)	.05
204	Phil Niekro (Record Breaker)	.05
205	Tony Perez (Record Breaker)	.05
206	Pete Rose (Record Breaker)	.25
207	Fernando Valenzuela (Record Breaker)	.05
208	Ramon Romero	.05
209	Randy Ready	.05
210	Calvin Schiraldi RC	.05
211	Ed Wojna	.05
212	Chris Speier	.05
213	Bob Shirley	.05
214	Randy Bush	.05
215	Frank White	.05
216	A's Leaders (Dwayne Murphy)	.05
217	Bill Scherrer	.05
218	Randy Hunt	.05
219	Dennis Lamp	.05
220	Bob Horner	.05
221	Dave Henderson	.05
222	Craig Gerber	.05
223	Atlee Hammaker	.05
224	Cesar Cedeno	.05
225	Ron Darling	.05
226	Lee Lacy	.05
227	Al Jones	.05
228	Tom Lawless	.05
229	Bill Gullickson	.05
230	Terry Kennedy	.05
231	Jim Frey	.05
232	Rick Rhoden	.05
233	Steve Lyons RC	.05
234	Doug Corbett	.05
235	Butch Wynegar	.05
236	Frank Eufemia	.05
237	Ted Simmons	.05
238	Larry Parrish	.05
239	Joel Skinner	.05
240	Tommy John	.10
241	Tony Fernandez	.05
242	Rich Thompson	.05
243	Johnny Grubb	.05
244	Craig Lefferts	.05
245	Jim Sundberg	.05
246	Phillies Leaders (Steve Carlton)	.10
247	Terry Harper	.05
248	Spike Owen	.05
249	Rob Deer RC	.05
250	Dwight Gooden	.05
251	Rich Dauer	.05
252	Bobby Castillo	.05
253	Dann Bilardello	.05
254	Ozzie Guillen RC	.30
255	Tony Armas	.05
256	Kurt Kepshire	.05
257	Doug DeCinces	.05
258	Tim Burke RC	.05
259	Dan Pasqua RC	.05
260	Tony Pena	.05
261	Bobby Valentine	.05
262	Mario Ramirez	.05
263	Checklist 133-264	.05
264	Darren Daulton	.05
265	Ron Davis	.05
266	Keith Moreland	.05
267	Paul Molitor	.50
268	Mike Scott	.05
269	Dane Iorg	.05
270	Jack Morris	.05
271	Dave Collins	.05
272	Tim Tolman	.05
273	Jerry Willard	.05
274	Ron Gardenhire	.05
275	Charlie Hough	.05
276	Yankees Leaders (Willie Randolph)	.05
277	Jaime Cocanower	.05
278	Sixto Lezcano	.05
279	Al Pardo	.05
280	Tim Raines	.05
281	Steve Mura	.05
282	Jerry Mumphrey	.05
283	Mike Fischlin	.05
284	Brian Dayett	.05
285	Buddy Bell	.05
286	Luis DeLeon	.05
287	John Christensen RC	.05
288	Don Aase	.05
289	Johnnie LeMaster	.05
290	Carlton Fisk	.50
291	Tom Lasorda	.10
292	Chuck Porter	.05
293	Chris Chambliss	.05
294	Danny Cox	.05
295	Kirk Gibson	.05
296	Geno Petralli RC	.05
297	Tim Lollar	.05
298	Craig Reynolds	.05
299	Bryn Smith	.05
300	George Brett	1.00
301	Dennis Rasmussen	.05
302	Greg Gross	.05
303	Curt Wardle	.05
304	Mike Gallego RC	.10
305	Phil Bradley	.05
306	Padres Leaders (Terry Kennedy)	.05
307	Dave Sax	.05
308	Ray Fontenot	.05
309	John Shelby	.05
310	Greg Minton	.05
311	Dick Schofield	.05
312	Tom Filer	.05
313	Joe DeSa	.05
314	Frank Pastore	.05
315	Mookie Wilson	.05
316	Sammy Khalifa	.05
317	Ed Romero	.05
318	Terry Whitfield	.05
319	Rick Camp	.05
320	Jim Rice	.15
321	Earl Weaver	.10
322	Bob Forsch	.05
323	Jerry Davis	.05
324	Dan Schatzeder	.05
325	Juan Beniquez	.05
326	Kent Tekulve	.05
327	Mike Pagliarulo	.05
328	Pete O'Brien	.05
329	Kirby Puckett	.75
330	Rick Sutcliffe	.05
331	Alan Ashby	.05
332	Darryl Motley	.05
333	Tom Henke RC	.05
334	Ken Oberkfell	.05
335	Don Sutton	.40
336	Indians Leaders (Andre Thornton)	.05
337	Darnell Coles	.05
338	Jorge Bell	.05
339	Bruce Berenyi	.05
340	Cal Ripken, Jr.	2.00
341	Frank Williams	.05
342	Gary Redus	.05
343	Carlos Diaz	.05
344	Jim Wohlford	.05
345	Donnie Moore	.05
346	Bryan Little	.05
347	Teddy Higuera RC	.10
348	Cliff Johnson	.05
349	Mark Clear	.05
350	Jack Clark	.05
351	Chuck Tanner	.05
352	Harry Spilman	.05
353	Keith Atherton	.05
354	Tony Bernazard	.05
355	Lee Smith	.05
356	Mickey Hatcher	.05
357	Ed Vande Berg	.05
358	Rick Dempsey	.05
359	Mike LaCoss	.05
360	Lloyd Moseby	.05
361	Shane Rawley	.05
362	Tom Paciorek	.05
363	Terry Forster	.05
364	Reid Nichols	.05
365	Mike Flanagan	.05
366	Reds Leaders (Dave Concepcion)	.05
367	Aurelio Lopez	.05
368	Greg Brock	.05
369	Al Holland	.05
370	Vince Coleman RC	.35
371	Bill Stein	.05
372	Ben Oglivie	.05
373	Urbano Lugo RC	.05
374	Terry Francona	.05
375	Rich Gedman	.05
376	Bill Dawley	.05
377	Joe Carter	.05
378	Bruce Bochte	.05
379	Bobby Meacham	.05
380	LaMarr Hoyt	.05
381	Ray Miller	.05
382	Ivan Calderon RC	.05
383	Chris Brown RC	.05
384	Steve Trout	.05
385	Cecil Cooper	.05
386	Cecil Fielder RC	.75
387	Steve Kemp	.05
388	Dickie Noles	.05
389	Glenn Davis RC	.05
390	Tom Seaver	.60
391	Julio Franco	.05
392	John Russell RC	.05
393	Chris Pittaro	.05
394	Checklist 265-396	.05
395	Scott Garrelts	.05
396	Red Sox Leaders (Dwight Evans)	.05
397	Steve Buechele RC	.10
398	Earnie Riles RC	.05
399	Bill Swift	.05
400	Rod Carew	.50
401	Fernando Valenzuela (Turn Back the Clock)	.05
402	Tom Seaver (Turn Back the Clock)	.25
403	Willie Mays (Turn Back the Clock)	.35
404	Frank Robinson (Turn Back the Clock)	.10
405	Roger Maris (Turn Back the Clock)	.30
406	Scott Sanderson	.05
407	Sal Butera	.05
408	Dave Smith	.05
409	Paul Runge RC	.05
410	Dave Kingman	.05
411	Sparky Anderson	.10
412	Jim Clancy	.05
413	Tim Flannery	.05
414	Tom Gorman	.05
415	Hal McRae	.05
416	Denny Martinez	.05
417	R.J. Reynolds	.05
418	Alan Knicely	.05
419	Frank Wills	.05
420	Von Hayes	.05
421	Dave Palmer	.05
422	Mike Jorgensen	.05
423	Dan Spillner	.05
424	Rick Miller	.05
425	Larry McWilliams	.05
426	Brewers Leaders (Charlie Moore)	.05
427	Joe Cowley	.05
428	Max Venable	.05
429	Greg Booker	.05
430	Kent Hrbek	.05
431	George Frazier	.05
432	Mark Bailey	.05
433	Chris Codiroli	.05
434	Curt Wilkerson	.05
435	Bill Caudill	.05
436	Doug Flynn	.05
437	Rick Mahler	.05
438	Clint Hurdle	.05
439	Rick Honeycutt	.05
440	Alvin Davis	.05
441	Whitey Herzog	.05
442	Ron Robinson RC	.05
443	Bill Buckner	.05
444	Alex Trevino	.05
445	Bert Blyleven	.05
446	Lenn Sakata	.05
447	Jerry Don Gleaton	.05
448	Herm Winningham RC	.05
449	Rod Scurry	.05
450	Graig Nettles	.05
451	Mark Brown	.05
452	Bob Clark	.05
453	Steve Jeltz	.05
454	Burt Hooton	.05
455	Willie Randolph	.05
456	Braves Leaders (Dale Murphy)	.10
457	Mickey Tettleton RC	.10
458	Kevin Bass	.05
459	Luis Leal	.05
460	Leon Durham	.05
461	Walt Terrell	.05
462	Domingo Ramos	.05
463	Jim Gott	.05
464	Ruppert Jones	.05
465	Jesse Orosco	.05
466	Tom Foley	.05
467	Bob James	.05
468	Mike Scioscia	.05
469	Storm Davis	.05
470	Bill Madlock	.05
471	Bobby Cox	.05
472	Joe Hesketh	.05
473	Mark Brouhard	.05
474	John Tudor	.05
475	Juan Samuel	.05
476	Ron Mathis	.05
477	Mike Easler	.05
478	Andy Hawkins	.05
479	Bob Melvin RC	.05
480	Oddibe McDowell RC	.05
481	Scott Bradley RC	.05
482	Rick Lysander	.05
483	George Vukovich	.05
484	Donnie Hill	.05
485	Gary Matthews	.05
486	Angels Leaders (Bob Grich)	.05
487	Bret Saberhagen	.05
488	Lou Thornton	.05
489	Jim Winn	.05
490	Jeff Leonard	.05
491	Pascual Perez	.05
492	Kelvin Chapman	.05
493	Gene Nelson	.05
494	Gary Roenicke	.05
495	Mark Langston	.05
496	Jay Johnstone	.05
497	John Stuper	.05
498	Tito Landrum	.05
499	Bob L. Gibson	.05
500	Rickey Henderson	.50
501	Dave Johnson	.05
502	Glen Cook	.05
503	Mike Fitzgerald	.05
504	Denny Walling	.05
505	Jerry Koosman	.05
506	Bill Russell	.05
507	Steve Ontiveros RC	.05
508	Alan Wiggins	.05
509	Ernie Camacho	.05
510	Wade Boggs	.75
511	Ed Nunez	.05
512	Thad Bosley	.05
513	Ron Washington	.05
514	Mike Jones	.05
515	Darrell Evans	.05
516	Giants Leaders (Greg Minton)	.05
517	Milt Thompson RC	.05
518	Buck Martinez	.05
519	Danny Darwin	.05
520	Keith Hernandez	.05
521	Nate Snell	.05
522	Bob Bailor	.05
523	Joe Price	.05
524	Darrell Miller RC	.05
525	Marvell Wynne	.05
526	Charlie Lea	.05
527	Checklist 397-528	.05
528	Terry Pendleton	.05
529	Marc Sullivan	.05
530	Rich Gossage	.05
531	Tony LaRussa	.05
532	Don Carman RC	.05
533	Billy Sample	.05
534	Jeff Calhoun	.05
535	Toby Harrah	.05
536	Jose Rijo	.05
537	Mark Salas	.05
538	Dennis Eckersley	.40
539	Glenn Hubbard	.05
540	Dan Petry	.05
541	Jorge Orta	.05
542	Don Schulze	.05
543	Jerry Narron	.05
544	Eddie Milner	.05
545	Jimmy Key	.05
546	Mariners Leaders (Dave Henderson)	.05
547	Roger McDowell	.05
548	Mike Young	.05
549	Bob Welch	.05
550	Tom Herr	.05
551	Dave LaPoint	.05
552	Marc Hill	.05
553	Jim Morrison	.05
554	Paul Householder	.05
555	Hubie Brooks	.05
556	John Denny	.05
557	Gerald Perry	.05
558	Tim Stoddard	.05
559	Tommy Dunbar	.05
560	Dave Righetti	.05
561	Bob Lillis	.05
562	Joe Beckwith	.05
563	Alejandro Sanchez	.05
564	Warren Brusstar	.05
565	Tom Brunansky	.05
566	Alfredo Griffin	.05
567	Jeff Barkley	.05
568	Donnie Scott	.05
569	Jim Acker	.05
570	Rusty Staub	.10
571	Mike Jeffcoat	.05
572	Paul Zuvella	.05
573	Tom Hume	.05
574	Ron Kittle	.05
575	Mike Boddicker	.05
576	Expos Leaders (Andre Dawson)	.05
577	Jerry Reuss	.05
578	Lee Mazzilli	.05
579	Jim Slaton	.05
580	Willie McGee	.05
581	Bruce Hurst	.05
582	Jim Gantner	.05
583	Al Bumbry	.05
584	Brian Fisher RC	.05
585	Garry Maddox	.05
586	Greg Harris	.05
587	Rafael Santana	.05
588	Steve Lake	.05
589	Sid Bream	.05
590	Bob Knepper	.05
591	Jackie Moore	.05
592	Frank Tanana	.05
593	Jesse Barfield	.05
594	Chris Bando	.05
595	Dave Parker	.05
596	Onix Concepcion	.05
597	Sammy Stewart	.05
598	Jim Presley	.05
599	Rick Aguilera RC	.25
600	Dale Murphy	.05
601	Gary Lucas	.05
602	Mariano Duncan	.05
603	Bill Laskey	.05
604	Gary Pettis	.05
605	Dennis Boyd	.05
606	Royals Leaders (Hal McRae)	.05
607	Ken Dayley	.05
608	Bruce Bochy	.05
609	Barbaro Garbey	.05
610	Ron Guidry	.05

#	Player	Price
611	Gary Woods	.05
612	Richard Dotson	.05
613	Roy Smalley	.05
614	Rick Waits	.05
615	Johnny Ray	.05
616	Glenn Brummer	.05
617	Lonnie Smith	.05
618	Jim Pankovits	.05
619	Danny Heep	.05
620	Bruce Sutter	.40
621	John Felske	.05
622	Gary Lavelle	.05
623	Floyd Rayford	.05
624	Steve McCatty	.05
625	Bob Brenly	.05
626	Roy Thomas	.05
627	Ron Oester	.05
628	Kirk McCaskill RC	.15
629	Mitch Webster RC	.05
630	Fernando Valenzuela	.05
631	Steve Braun	.05
632	Dave Von Ohlen	.05
633	Jackie Gutierrez	.05
634	Roy Lee Jackson	.05
635	Jason Thompson	.05
636	Cubs Leaders (Lee Smith)	.05
637	Rudy Law	.05
638	John Butcher	.05
639	Bo Diaz	.05
640	Jose Cruz	.05
641	Wayne Tolleson	.05
642	Ray Searage	.05
643	Tom Brookens	.05
644	Mark Gubicza	.05
645	Dusty Baker	.05
646	Mike Moore	.05
647	Mel Hall	.05
648	Steve Bedrosian	.05
649	Ronn Reynolds	.05
650	Dave Stieb	.05
651	Billy Martin	.10
652	Tom Browning	.05
653	Jim Dwyer	.05
654	Ken Howell	.05
655	Manny Trillo	.05
656	Brian Harper	.05
657	Juan Agosto	.05
658	Rob Wilfong	.05
659	Checklist 529-660	.05
660	Steve Garvey	.20
661	Roger Clemens	3.00
661	Roger Clemens (Blue streak upper-right.)	7.50
662	Bill Schroeder	.05
663	Neil Allen	.05
664	Tim Corcoran	.05
665	Alejandro Pena	.05
666	Rangers Leaders (Charlie Hough)	.05
667	Tim Teufel	.05
668	Cecilio Guante	.05
669	Ron Cey	.05
670	Willie Hernandez	.10
671	Lynn Jones	.05
672	Rob Picciolo	.05
673	Ernie Whitt	.05
674	Pat Tabler	.05
675	Claudell Washington	.05
676	Matt Young	.05
677	Nick Esasky	.05
678	Dan Gladden	.05
679	Britt Burns	.05
680	George Foster	.05
681	Dick Williams	.05
682	Junior Ortiz	.05
683	Andy Van Slyke	.05
684	Bob McClure	.05
685	Tim Wallach	.05
686	Jeff Stone	.05
687	Mike Trujillo	.05
688	Larry Herndon	.05
689	Dave Stewart	.05
690	Ryne Sandberg	.75
691	Mike Madden	.05
692	Dale Berra	.05
693	Tom Tellmann	.05
694	Garth Iorg	.05
695	Mike Smithson	.05
696	Dodgers Leaders (Bill Russell)	.05
697	Bud Black	.05
698	Brad Komminsk	.05
699	Pat Corrales	.05
700	Reggie Jackson	.75
701	Keith Hernandez/AS	.05
702	Tom Herr/AS	.05
703	Tim Wallach/AS	.05
704	Ozzie Smith/AS	.35
705	Dale Murphy/AS	.10
706	Pedro Guerrero/AS	.05
707	Willie McGee/AS	.05
708	Gary Carter/AS	.25
709	Dwight Gooden/AS	.05
710	John Tudor/AS	.05
711	Jeff Reardon/AS	.05
712	Don Mattingly/AS	.50
713	Damaso Garcia/AS	.05
714	George Brett/AS	.45
715	Cal Ripken, Jr./AS	1.00
716	Rickey Henderson/AS	.25
717	Dave Winfield/AS	.25
718	George Bell/AS	.20
719	Carlton Fisk/AS	.20
720	Bret Saberhagen/AS	.05
721	Ron Guidry/AS	.05
722	Dan Quisenberry/AS	.05
723	Marty Bystrom	.05
724	Tim Hulett	.05
725	Mario Soto	.05
726	Orioles Leaders (Rick Dempsey)	.05
727	David Green	.05
728	Mike Marshall	.05
729	Jim Beattie	.05
730	Ozzie Smith	.75
731	Don Robinson	.05
732	Floyd Youmans RC	.05
733	Ron Romanick	.05
734	Marty Barrett	.05
735	Dave Dravecky	.05
736	Glenn Wilson	.05
737	Pete Vuckovich	.05
738	Andre Robertson	.05
739	Dave Rozema	.05
740	Lance Parrish	.05
741	Pete Rose	1.00
742	Frank Viola	.05
743	Pat Sheridan	.05
744	Lary Sorensen	.05
745	Willie Upshaw	.05
746	Denny Gonzalez	.05
747	Rick Cerone	.05
748	Steve Henderson	.05
749	Ed Jurak	.05
750	Gorman Thomas	.05
751	Howard Johnson	.05
752	Mike Krukow	.05
753	Dan Ford	.05
754	Pat Clements RC	.05
755	Harold Baines	.05
756	Pirates Leaders (Rick Rhoden)	.05
757	Darrell Porter	.05
758	Dave Anderson	.05
759	Moose Haas	.05
760	Andre Dawson	.30
761	Don Slaught	.05
762	Eric Show	.05
763	Terry Puhl	.05
764	Kevin Gross	.05
765	Don Baylor	.05
766	Rick Langford	.05
767	Jody Davis	.05
768	Vern Ruhle	.05
769	Harold Reynolds RC	.25
770	Vida Blue	.05
771	John McNamara	.05
772	Brian Downing	.05
773	Greg Pryor	.05
774	Terry Leach	.05
775	Al Oliver	.05
776	Gene Garber	.05
777	Wayne Krenchicki	.05
778	Jerry Hairston Sr.	.05
779	Rick Reuschel	.05
780	Robin Yount	.50
781	Joe Nolan	.05
782	Ken Landreaux	.05
783	Ricky Horton	.05
784	Alan Bannister	.05
785	Bob Stanley	.05
786	Twins Leaders (Mickey Hatcher)	.05
787	Vance Law	.05
788	Marty Castillo	.05
789	Kurt Bevacqua	.05
790	Phil Niekro	.40
791	Checklist 661-792	.05
792	Charles Hudson	.05

Tiffany

A total of only 5,000 of these specially boxed collectors' edition sets was reported produced. Sold only through hobby dealers' the cards differ from the regular-issue 1986 Topps cards only in the use of white cardboard stock and the application of a high-gloss finish on the cards' fronts.

	NM/M
Unopened Set (792):	100.00
Complete Set (792):	45.00
Common Player:	.25

Traded

This 132-card set of 2-1/2" x 3-1/2" cards was, at issue, one of the most popular sets of recent times. As always, the set features traded veterans, and a better than usual crop of rookies. As in the pre-vious two years, a glossy-finish "Tiffany" edition of 5,000 Traded sets was produced.

	NM/M
Unopened Set (132):	30.00
Complete Set (132):	25.00
Common Player:	.05

#	Player	Price
1T	Andy Allanson RC	.05
2T	Neil Allen	.05
3T	Joaquin Andujar	.05
4T	Paul Assenmacher RC	.05
5T	Scott Bailes RC	.05
6T	Don Baylor	.15
7T	Steve Bedrosian	.05
8T	Juan Beniquez	.05
9T	Juan Berenguer	.05
10T	Mike Bielecki RC	.05
11T	Barry Bonds RC	20.00
12T	Bobby Bonilla RC	.50
13T	Juan Bonilla	.05
14T	Rich Bordi	.05
15T	Steve Boros	.05
16T	Rick Burleson	.05
17T	Bill Campbell	.05
18T	Tom Candiotti	.05
19T	John Cangelosi RC	.05
20T	Jose Canseco RC	4.00
21T	Carmen Castillo	.05
22T	Rick Cerone	.05
23T	John Cerutti RC	.05
24T	Will Clark RC	1.50
25T	Mark Clear	.05
26T	Darnell Coles	.05
27T	Dave Collins	.05
28T	Tim Conroy	.05
29T	Joe Cowley	.05
30T	Joel Davis RC	.05
31T	Rob Deer	.05
32T	John Denny	.05
33T	Mike Easler	.05
34T	Mark Eichhorn RC	.05
35T	Steve Farr	.05
36T	Scott Fletcher	.05
37T	Terry Forster	.05
38T	Terry Francona	.05
39T	Jim Fregosi	.05
40T	Andres Galarraga RC	.35
41T	Ken Griffey	.05
42T	Bill Gullickson	.05
43T	Jose Guzman RC	.05
44T	Moose Haas	.05
45T	Billy Hatcher	.05
46T	Mike Heath	.05
47T	Tom Hume	.05
48T	Pete Incaviglia RC	.20
49T	Dane Iorg	.05
50T	Bo Jackson RC	3.00
51T	Wally Joyner RC	.40
52T	Charlie Kerfeld RC	.05
53T	Eric King RC	.05
54T	Bob Kipper RC	.05
55T	Wayne Krenchicki	.05
56T	John Kruk RC	.35
57T	Mike LaCoss	.05
58T	Pete Ladd	.05
59T	Mike Laga	.05
60T	Hal Lanier	.05
61T	Dave LaPoint	.05
62T	Rudy Law	.05
63T	Rick Leach	.05
64T	Tim Leary	.05
65T	Dennis Leonard	.05
66T	Jim Leyland	.05
67T	Steve Lyons	.05
68T	Mickey Mahler	.05
69T	Candy Maldonado	.05
70T	Roger Mason RC	.05
71T	Bob McClure	.05
72T	Andy McGaffigan	.05
73T	Gene Michael	.05
74T	Kevin Mitchell RC	.25
75T	Omar Moreno	.05
76T	Jerry Mumphrey	.05
77T	Phil Niekro	.25
78T	Randy Niemann	.05
79T	Juan Nieves RC	.05
80T	Otis Nixon RC	.05
81T	Bob Ojeda	.05
82T	Jose Oquendo	.05
83T	Tom Paciorek	.05
84T	Dave Palmer	.05
85T	Frank Pastore	.05
86T	Lou Piniella	.05
87T	Dan Plesac RC	.05
88T	Darrell Porter	.05
89T	Rey Quinones RC	.05
90T	Gary Redus	.05
91T	Bip Roberts RC	.05
92T	Billy Jo Robidoux RC	.05
93T	Jeff Robinson	.05
94T	Gary Roenicke	.05
95T	Ed Romero	.05
96T	Argenis Salazar	.05
97T	Joe Sambito	.05
98T	Billy Sample	.05
99T	Dave Schmidt	.05
100T	Ken Schrom	.05
101T	Tom Seaver	.50
102T	Ted Simmons	.05
103T	Sammy Stewart	.05
104T	Kurt Stillwell RC	.05
105T	Franklin Stubbs	.05
106T	Dale Sveum RC	.05
107T	Chuck Tanner	.05
108T	Danny Tartabull RC	.05
109T	Tim Teufel	.05
110T	Bob Tewksbury RC	.05
111T	Andres Thomas RC	.05
112T	Milt Thompson	.05
113T	Robby Thompson RC	.05
114T	Jay Tibbs	.05
115T	Wayne Tolleson	.05
116T	Alex Trevino	.05
117T	Manny Trillo	.05
118T	Ed Vande Berg	.05
119T	Ozzie Virgil	.05
120T	Bob Walk	.05
121T	Gene Walter RC	.05
122T	Claudell Washington	.05
123T	Bill Wegman RC	.05
124T	Dick Williams	.05
125T	Mitch Williams RC	.05
126T	Bobby Witt RC	.05
127T	Todd Worrell RC	.05
128T	George Wright	.05
129T	Ricky Wright	.05
130T	Steve Yeager	.05
131T	Paul Zuvella	.05
132T	Checklist	.05

Traded Tiffany

This collectors' edition differs from the regular 1986 Topps Traded set only in the use of a high-gloss front finish. The set was sold only through hobby channels in a specially design box.

	NM/M
Unopened Set (132):	175.00
Complete Set (132):	125.00
Common Player:	.25
11T Barry Bonds	75.00

Traded Mickey Mantle Bronze

This 1/4-size metal replica of Mantle's first-ever Topps card was issued to dealers who purchased cases of 1986 Topps Traded sets. Each detail of the 1952 Topps Mantle card is reproduced on the 1-1/4" x 1-3/4" bronze metal mini-card, right down to the stats.

	NM/M
311 Mickey Mantle	9.00

Box Panels

Following the lead of Donruss, which introduced the concept in 1985, Topps produced special cards on the bottom panels of wax boxes. Individual cards measure 2-1/2" x 3-1/2", the same as regular cards. Design of the cards is virtually identical with regular '86 Topps, though the top border is in red, rather than black. The cards are lettered "A" through "P," rather than numbered on the back.

	NM/M
Complete Panel Set:	7.00
Complete Singles Set:	6.00
Common Panel:	1.00
Common Single Player:	.10
Panel	2.00
A Jorge Bell	.10
B Wade Boggs	.75
C George Brett	.25
D Vince Coleman	.25
Panel	1.00
E Carlton Fisk	.25
F Dwight Gooden	.10
G Pedro Guerrero	.10
H Ron Guidry	.10
Panel	2.00
I Reggie Jackson	.75
J Don Mattingly	.50
K Oddibe McDowell	.10
L Willie McGee	.10
Panel	2.50
M Dale Murphy	.35
N Pete Rose	1.50
O Bret Saberhagen	.10
P Fernando Valenzuela	.10

All-Star Glossy Set of 22

As in previous years, Topps continued to make the popular glossy-surfaced cards as an insert in rack packs. The All-Star Glossy set of 2-1/2" x 3-1/2" cards shows little design change from previous years. Cards feature a front color photo and All-Star banner at the top. The bottom has the player's name and position. The set includes the All-Star starting teams as well as the managers and honorary captains.

	NM/M
Complete Set (22):	2.50
Common Player:	.05
1 Sparky Anderson	.05
2 Eddie Murray	.35
3 Lou Whitaker	.05
4 George Brett	.50
5 Cal Ripken, Jr.	.65
6 Jim Rice	.25
7 Rickey Henderson	.35
8 Dave Winfield	.35
9 Carlton Fisk	.35
10 Jack Morris	.05
11 A.L. All-Star Team	.05
12 Dick Williams	.05
13 Steve Garvey	.15
14 Tom Herr	.05
15 Graig Nettles	.05
16 Ozzie Smith	.45
17 Tony Gwynn	.45
18 Dale Murphy	.25
19 Darryl Strawberry	.05
20 Terry Kennedy	.05
21 LaMarr Hoyt	.05
22 N.L. All-Star Team	.05

All-Star Glossy Set of 60

The Topps All-Star & Hot Prospects glossy set of 60 cards represents an expansion of a good idea. The 2-1/2" x 3-1/2" cards had a good following when they were limited to stars, but Topps realized that the addition of top young players would spice up the set even further, so in 1986 it was expanded from 40 to 60 cards. The cards themselves are basically all color glossy pictures with the player's name in very small print in the lower left-hand corner. To obtain the set, it was necessary to send $1 plus six special offer cards from wax packs to Topps for each series. At 60 cards, that meant the process had to be repeated six times as there were 10 cards in each series, making the set quite expensive from the outset.

	NM/M
Complete Set (60):	8.00
Common Player:	.10
1 Oddibe McDowell	.10
2 Reggie Jackson	.50
3 Fernando Valenzuela	.10
4 Jack Clark	.10
5 Rickey Henderson	.40
6 Steve Balboni	.10
7 Keith Hernandez	.10
8 Lance Parrish	.10
9 Willie McGee	.10
10 Chris Brown	.10
11 Darryl Strawberry	.10
12 Ron Guidry	.10
13 Dave Parker	.10
14 Cal Ripken	1.00
15 Tim Raines	.10
16 Rod Carew	.40
17 Mike Schmidt	.75
18 George Brett	.75
19 Joe Hesketh	.10
20 Dan Pasqua	.10
21 Vince Coleman	.40
22 Tom Seaver	.40
23 Gary Carter	.40
24 Orel Hershiser	.10
25 Pedro Guerrero	.10
26 Wade Boggs	.50
27 Bret Saberhagen	.10
28 Carlton Fisk	.40
29 Kirk Gibson	.10
30 Brian Fisher	.10
31 Don Mattingly	.75
32 Tom Herr	.10
33 Eddie Murray	.40
34 Ryne Sandberg	.50
35 Dan Quisenberry	.10
36 Jim Rice	.30
37 Dale Murphy	.30
38 Steve Garvey	.25
39 Roger McDowell	.10
40 Earnie Riles	.10
41 Dwight Gooden	.40
42 Dave Winfield	.40
43 Dave Stieb	.10
44 Bob Horner	.10
45 Nolan Ryan	1.00
46 Ozzie Smith	.50
47 Jorge Bell	.10
48 Gorman Thomas	.10
49 Tom Browning	.10
50 Larry Sheets	.10
51 Pete Rose	.90
52 Brett Butler	.10
53 John Tudor	.10
54 Phil Bradley	.10
55 Jeff Reardon	.10
56 Rich Gossage	.10
57 Tony Gwynn	.50
58 Ozzie Guillen	.10
59 Glenn Davis	.10
60 Darrell Evans	.10

Gallery of Champions

For the third consecutive year Topps issued 12 metal "mini cards," adding an aluminum version to the bronze and silver. The metal replicas were minted 1/4-size (approximately 1-1/4" x 1-3/4") of the regular cards. The bronze and silver sets were issued in leather-like velvet-lined display cases, the aluminum in individual cello packs. A pewter Don Mattingly was issued as a premium to those ordering the sets.

	NM/M
Complete Aluminum Set:	15.00
Complete Bronze Set:	50.00
Complete Silver Set:	200.00
(1a) Wade Boggs/Aluminum	2.00
(1b) Wade Boggs/Bronze	15.00
(1s) Wade Boggs/Silver	35.00
(2a) Vince Coleman/Aluminum	1.50
(2b) Vince Coleman/Bronze	4.00
(2s) Vince Coleman/Silver	12.00
(3a) Darrell Evans/Aluminum	1.50
(3b) Darrell Evans/Bronze	4.00

(3s)	Darrell Evans/Silver	12.00
(4a)	Dwight Gooden/ Aluminum	1.00
(4b)	Dwight Gooden/Bronze	4.00
(4s)	Dwight Gooden/Silver	12.00
(5a)	Ozzie Guillen/Aluminum	1.00
(5b)	Ozzie Guillen/Bronze	4.00
(5s)	Ozzie Guillen/Silver	12.00
(6a)	Don Mattingly/Aluminum	4.00
(6b)	Don Mattingly/Bronze	20.00
(6s)	Don Mattingly/Silver	75.00
(6p)	Don Mattingly/Pewter	45.00
(7a)	Willie McGee/Aluminum	1.00
(7b)	Willie McGee/Bronze	4.00
(7s)	Willie McGee/Silver	12.00
(8a)	Dale Murphy/Aluminum	1.50
(8b)	Dale Murphy/Bronze	7.50
(8s)	Dale Murphy/Silver	30.00
(9a)	Dan Quisenberry/ Aluminum	1.00
(9b)	Dan Quisenberry/Bronze	4.00
(9s)	Dan Quisenberry/Silver	12.00
(10a)	Jeff Reardon/Aluminum	1.00
(10b)	Jeff Reardon/Bronze	4.00
(10s)	Jeff Reardon/Silver	12.00
(11a)	Pete Rose/Aluminum	5.00
(11b)	Pete Rose/Bronze	25.00
(11s)	Pete Rose/Silver	90.00
(12a)	Bret Saberhagen/ Aluminum	1.00
(12b)	Bret Saberhagen/Bronze	4.00
(12s)	Bret Saberhagen/Silver	12.00

Mini League Leaders

MIKE SCHMIDT

Topps had long experimented with bigger cards, but in 1986, they also decided to try smaller ones. These 2-1/8" x 2-15/16" cards feature top players in a number of categories. Sold in plastic packs as a regular Topps issue, the 66-card set is attractive as well as innovative. The cards feature color photos and a minimum of added information on the fronts where only the player's name and Topps logo appear. Backs limited information as well, but do feature enough to justify the player's inclusion in a set of league leaders.

		NM/M
	Complete Set (66):	5.00
	Common Player:	.05
	Wax Pack (6):	.50
	Wax Box (36):	10.00
	Vend Box (500):	15.00
1	Eddie Murray	.35
2	Cal Ripken, Jr.	1.00
3	Wade Boggs	.45
4	Dennis Boyd	.05
5	Dwight Evans	.05
6	Bruce Hurst	.05
7	Gary Pettis	.05
8	Harold Baines	.05
9	Floyd Bannister	.05
10	Britt Burns	.05
11	Carlton Fisk	.35
12	Brett Butler	.05
13	Darrell Evans	.05
14	Jack Morris	.05
15	Lance Parrish	.05
16	Walt Terrell	.05
17	Steve Balboni	.05
18	George Brett	.75
19	Charlie Leibrandt	.05
20	Bret Saberhagen	.05
21	Lonnie Smith	.05
22	Willie Wilson	.05
23	Bert Blyleven	.05
24	Mike Smithson	.05
25	Frank Viola	.05
26	Ron Guidry	.05
27	Rickey Henderson	.05
28	Don Mattingly	.75
29	Dave Winfield	.35
30	Mike Moore	.05
31	Gorman Thomas	.05
32	Toby Harrah	.05
33	Charlie Hough	.05
34	Doyle Alexander	.05
35	Jimmy Key	.05
36	Dave Stieb	.05
37	Dale Murphy	.20
38	Keith Moreland	.05
39	Ryne Sandberg	.05
40	Tom Browning	.05

41	Dave Parker	.05
42	Mario Soto	.05
43	Nolan Ryan	1.00
44	Pedro Guerrero	.05
45	Orel Hershiser	.05
46	Mike Scioscia	.05
47	Fernando Valenzuela	.05
48	Bob Welch	.05
49	Tim Raines	.05
50	Gary Carter	.35
51	Sid Fernandez	.05
52	Dwight Gooden	.05
53	Keith Hernandez	.05
54	Juan Samuel	.05
55	Mike Schmidt	.75
56	Glenn Wilson	.05
57	Rick Reuschel	.05
58	Joaquin Andujar	.05
59	Jack Clark	.05
60	Vince Coleman	.05
61	Danny Cox	.05
62	Tom Herr	.05
63	Willie McGee	.05
64	John Tudor	.05
65	Tony Gwynn	.45
66	Checklist	.05

Stickers

The 1986 Topps stickers are 2-1/8" x 3". The 200-piece set features 316 different subjects, with some stickers including two or three players. Numbers run only to 315, however. The set includes some specialty stickers such as League Championships and World Series themes. Stickers are numbered both front and back and included a chance to win a trip to spring training as well as an offer to buy a complete 1986 Topps regular set. An album for the stickers was available in stores. It feautres Pete Rose in action on the front cover and reproductions of his Topps cards on back.

		NM/M
	Complete Set (315):	6.00
	Common Player:	.05
	Sticker Album:	1.50
	Wax Pack (5):	.30
	Wax Box (100):	11.00
1	Pete Rose	.60
2	Pete Rose	.60
3	George Brett	.50
4	Rod Carew	.40
5	Vince Coleman	.05
6	Dwight Gooden	.05
7	Phil Niekro	.20
8	Tony Perez	.30
9	Nolan Ryan	.75
10	Tom Seaver	.40
11	N.L. Championship Series (Ozzie Smith)	.10
12	N.L. Championship Series (Bill Madlock)	.05
13	N.L. Championship Series (Cardinals Celebrate)	.05
14	A.L. Championship Series (Al Oliver)	.05
15	A.L. Championship Series (Jim Sundberg)	.05
16	A.L. Championship Series (George Brett)	.10
17	World Series (Bret Saberhagen)	.05
18	World Series (Dane Iorg)	.05
19	World Series (Tito Landrum)	.05
20	World Series (John Tudor)	.05
21	World Series (Buddy Biancalana)	.05
22	World Series (Darryl Motley, Darrell Porter)	.05
23	World Series (George Brett, Frank White)	.05
24	Nolan Ryan	.75
25	Bill Doran	.05
26	Jose Cruz	.05
27	Mike Scott	.05
28	Kevin Bass	.05
29	Glenn Davis	.05
30	Mark Bailey	.05
31	Dave Smith	.05
32	Phil Garner	.05
33	Dickie Thon	.05
34	Bob Horner	.05
35	Dale Murphy	.25
36	Glenn Hubbard	.05
37	Bruce Sutter	.20
38	Ken Oberkfell	.05
39	Claudell Washington	.05
40	Steve Bedrosian	.05
41	Terry Harper	.05

42	Rafael Ramirez	.05
43	Rick Mahler	.05
44	Joaquin Andujar	.05
45	Willie McGee	.05
46	Ozzie Smith	.50
47	Vince Coleman	.05
48	Danny Cox	.05
49	Tom Herr	.05
50	Jack Clark	.05
51	Andy Van Slyke	.05
52	John Tudor	.05
53	Terry Pendleton	.05
54	Keith Moreland	.05
55	Ryne Sandberg	.40
56	Lee Smith	.05
57	Steve Trout	.05
58	Jody Davis	.05
59	Gary Matthews	.05
60	Leon Durham	.05
61	Rick Sutcliffe	.05
62	Dennis Eckersley	.30
63	Bob Dernier	.05
64	Fernando Valenzuela	.05
65	Pedro Guerrero	.05
66	Jerry Reuss	.05
67	Greg Brock	.05
68	Mike Scioscia	.05
69	Ken Howell	.05
70	Bill Madlock	.05
71	Mike Marshall	.05
72	Steve Sax	.05
73	Orel Hershiser	.05
74	Andre Dawson	.05
75	Tim Raines	.05
76	Jeff Reardon	.05
77	Hubie Brooks	.05
78	Bill Gullickson	.05
79	Bryn Smith	.05
80	Terry Francona	.05
81	Vance Law	.05
82	Tim Wallach	.05
83	Herm Winningham	.05
84	Jeff Leonard	.05
85	Chris Brown	.05
86	Scott Garrelts	.05
87	Jose Uribe	.05
88	Manny Trillo	.05
89	Dan Driessen	.05
90	Dan Gladden	.05
91	Mark Davis	.05
92	Bob Brenly	.05
93	Mike Krukow	.05
94	Dwight Gooden	.05
95	Darryl Strawberry	.05
96	Gary Carter	.40
97	Wally Backman	.05
98	Ron Darling	.05
99	Keith Hernandez	.05
100	George Foster	.05
101	Howard Johnson	.05
102	Rafael Santana	.05
103	Roger McDowell	.05
104	Steve Garvey	.15
105	Tony Gwynn	.05
106	Graig Nettles	.05
107	Rich Gossage	.05
108	Andy Hawkins	.05
109	Carmelo Martinez	.05
110	Garry Templeton	.05
111	Terry Kennedy	.05
112	Tim Flannery	.05
113	LaMarr Hoyt	.05
114	Mike Schmidt	.50
115	Ozzie Virgil	.05
116	Steve Carlton	.05
117	Garry Maddox	.05
118	Glenn Wilson	.05
119	Kevin Gross	.05
120	Von Hayes	.05
121	Juan Samuel	.05
122	Rick Schu	.05
123	Shane Rawley	.05
124	Johnny Ray	.05
125	Tony Pena	.05
126	Rick Reuschel	.05
127	Sammy Khalifa	.05
128	Marvell Wynne	.05
129	Jason Thompson	.05
130	Rick Rhoden	.05
131	Bill Almon	.05
132	Joe Orsulak	.05
133	Jim Morrison	.05
134	Pete Rose	.60
135	Dave Parker	.05
136	Mario Soto	.05
137	Dave Concepcion	.05
138	Ron Oester	.05
139	Buddy Bell	.05
140	Ted Power	.05
141	Tom Browning	.05
142	John Franco	.05
143	Tony Perez	.30
144	Willie McGee	.05
145	Dale Murphy	.25
146	Tony Gwynn	.50
147	Tom Herr	.05
148	Steve Garvey	.15
149	Dale Murphy	.25
150	Darryl Strawberry	.05
151	Graig Nettles	.05
152	Terry Kennedy	.05
153	Ozzie Smith	.50
154	LaMarr Hoyt	.05
155	Rickey Henderson	.40
156	Lou Whitaker	.05
157	George Brett	.50
158	Eddie Murray	.40
159	Cal Ripken, Jr.	.75

160	Dave Winfield	.40
161	Jim Rice	.15
162	Carlton Fisk	.40
163	Jack Morris	.05
164	Wade Boggs	.40
165	Darrell Evans	.05
166	Mike Davis	.05
167	Dave Kingman	.05
168	Alfredo Griffin	.05
169	Carney Lansford	.05
170	Bruce Bochte	.05
171	Dwayne Murphy	.05
172	Dave Collins	.05
173	Chris Codiroli	.05
174	Mike Heath	.05
175	Jay Howell	.05
176	Rod Carew	.05
177	Reggie Jackson	.50
178	Doug DeCinces	.05
179	Bob Boone	.05
180	Ron Romanick	.05
181	Bob Grich	.05
182	Donnie Moore	.05
183	Brian Downing	.05
184	Ruppert Jones	.05
185	Juan Beniquez	.05
186	Dave Stieb	.05
187	Jorge Bell	.05
188	Willie Upshaw	.05
189	Tom Henke	.05
190	Damaso Garcia	.05
191	Jimmy Key	.05
192	Jesse Barfield	.05
193	Dennis Lamp	.05
194	Tony Fernandez	.05
195	Lloyd Moseby	.05
196	Cecil Cooper	.05
197	Robin Yount	.40
198	Rollie Fingers	.20
199	Ted Simmons	.05
200	Ben Oglivie	.05
201	Moose Haas	.05
202	Jim Gantner	.05
203	Paul Molitor	.40
204	Charlie Moore	.05
205	Danny Darwin	.05
206	Brett Butler	.05
207	Brook Jacoby	.05
208	Andre Thornton	.05
209	Tom Waddell	.05
210	Tony Bernazard	.05
211	Julio Franco	.05
212	Pat Tabler	.05
213	Joe Carter	.05
214	George Vukovich	.05
215	Rich Thompson	.05
216	Gorman Thomas	.05
217	Phil Bradley	.05
218	Alvin Davis	.05
219	Jim Presley	.05
220	Matt Young	.05
221	Mike Moore	.05
222	Dave Henderson	.05
223	Ed Nunez	.05
224	Spike Owen	.05
225	Mark Langston	.05
226	Cal Ripken, Jr.	.75
227	Eddie Murray	.40
228	Fred Lynn	.05
229	Lee Lacy	.05
230	Scott McGregor	.05
231	Storm Davis	.05
232	Rick Dempsey	.05
233	Mike Boddicker	.05
234	Mike Young	.05
235	Sammy Stewart	.05
236	Pete O'Brien	.05
237	Oddibe McDowell	.05
238	Toby Harrah	.05
239	Gary Ward	.05
240	Larry Parrish	.05
241	Charlie Hough	.05
242	Burt Hooton	.05
243	Don Slaught	.05
244	Curt Wilkerson	.05
245	Greg Harris	.05
246	Jim Rice	.15
247	Wade Boggs	.40
248	Rich Gedman	.05
249	Dennis Boyd	.05
250	Marty Barrett	.05
251	Dwight Evans	.05
252	Bill Buckner	.05
253	Bob Stanley	.05
254	Tony Armas	.05
255	Mike Easler	.05
256	George Brett	.50
257	Dan Quisenberry	.05
258	Willie Wilson	.05
259	Jim Sundberg	.05
260	Bret Saberhagen	.05
261	Bud Black	.05
262	Charlie Leibrandt	.05
263	Frank White	.05
264	Lonnie Smith	.05
265	Steve Balboni	.05
266	Kirk Gibson	.05
267	Alan Trammell	.05
268	Jack Morris	.05
269	Darrell Evans	.05
270	Dan Petry	.05
271	Larry Herndon	.05
272	Lou Whitaker	.05
273	Lance Parrish	.05
274	Chet Lemon	.05
275	Willie Hernandez	.05
276	Tom Brunansky	.05
277	Kent Hrbek	.05

278	Mark Salas	.05
279	Bert Blyleven	.05
280	Tim Teufel	.05
281	Ron Davis	.05
282	Mike Smithson	.05
283	Gary Gaetti	.05
284	Frank Viola	.05
285	Kirby Puckett	.50
286	Carlton Fisk	.40
287	Tom Seaver	.40
288	Harold Baines	.05
289	Ron Kittle	.05
290	Bob James	.05
291	Rudy Law	.05
292	Britt Burns	.05
293	Greg Walker	.05
294	Ozzie Guillen	.05
295	Tim Hulett	.05
296	Don Mattingly	.50
297	Rickey Henderson	.40
298	Dave Winfield	.40
299	Butch Wynegar	.05
300	Don Baylor	.05
301	Eddie Whitson	.05
302	Ron Guidry	.05
303	Dave Righetti	.05
304	Bobby Meacham	.05
305	Willie Randolph	.05
306	Vince Coleman	.05
307	Oddibe McDowell	.05
308	Larry Sheets	.05
309	Ozzie Guillen	.05
310	Earnie Riles	.05
311	Chris Brown	.05
312	Brian Fisher, Roger McDowell	.05
313	Tom Browning	.05
314	Glenn Davis	.05
315	Mark Salas	.05

Super Sample

ORIOLES

EDDIE MURRAY

1B

To preview its oversize Super set for 1986, Topps issued a sample card of Eddie Murray. Front of the 4-7/8" x 6-7/8" card is the same as the issued version. On back, however, is this message: "topps / SPECIAL / COLLECTOR / SAMPLE / ACTUAL PRODUCT TO HAVE / STATISTICS PRINTED ON / WHITE-BOARD CARD BACK."

	NM/M
Eddie Murray	6.00

Super

ANGELS

REGGIE JACKSON

A third year of oversize (4-7/8" x 6-7/8") versions of Topps' regular issue cards saw the set once again hit the 60-card mark. Besides being four times the size of a normal card, the Supers differ only in the number on the back of the card.

		NM/M
	Complete Set (60):	9.00
	Common Player:	.05
1	Don Mattingly	1.00
2	Willie McGee	.25
3	Bret Saberhagen	.25
4	Dwight Gooden	.25
5	Dan Quisenberry	.25
6	Jeff Reardon	.25
7	Ozzie Guillen	.25
8	Vince Coleman	.25
9	Harold Baines	.25

10	Jorge Bell	.25
11	Bert Blyleven	.25
12	Wade Boggs	.60
13	Phil Bradley	.25
14	George Brett	1.00
15	Hubie Brooks	.25
16	Tom Browning	.25
17	Bill Buckner	.25
18	Brett Butler	.25
19	Gary Carter	.45
20	Cecil Cooper	.25
21	Darrell Evans	.25
22	Dwight Evans	.25
23	Carlton Fisk	.45
24	Steve Garvey	.35
25	Kirk Gibson	.25
26	Rich Gossage	.25
27	Pedro Guerrero	.25
28	Ron Guidry	.25
29	Tony Gwynn	.60
30	Rickey Henderson	.45
31	Keith Hernandez	.25
32	Tom Herr	.25
33	Orel Hershiser	.25
34	Jay Howell	.25
35	Reggie Jackson	.75
36	Bob James	.25
37	Charlie Leibrandt	.25
38	Jack Morris	.25
39	Dale Murphy	.35
40	Eddie Murray	.45
41	Dave Parker	.25
42	Tim Raines	.25
43	Jim Rice	.35
44	Dave Righetti	.25
45	Cal Ripken, Jr.	2.00
46	Pete Rose	1.50
47	Nolan Ryan	2.00
48	Ryne Sandberg	.60
49	Mike Schmidt	1.00
50	Tom Seaver	.45
51	Bryn Smith	.25
52	Lee Smith	.25
53	Ozzie Smith	.60
54	Dave Stieb	.25
55	Darryl Strawberry	.25
56	Gorman Thomas	.25
57	John Tudor	.25
58	Fernando Valenzuela	.25
59	Willie Wilson	.25
60	Dave Winfield	.45

Super Star

FRED LYNN

SUPER STAR

(See 1986 Woolworth.)

Tattoos

Topps returned to tattoos in 1986, marketing a set of 24 different tattoo sheets. Each sheet of tattoos measures 3-7/16" x 14" and includes both player and smaller action tattoos. As the action tattoos were uniform and not of any particular player, they add little value to the sheet. The player tattoos measure 1-1/2" x 2-1/2". With 24 sheets, eight players per sheet, there are 192 players represented in the set. The sheets are numbered.

NM/M
Complete Set (24): 9.00
Common Sheet: .40
Pack (1): .60
Wax Box (36): 13.50

1 Julio Franco, Rich Gossage, Keith Hernandez, Charlie Leibrandt, Jack Perconte, Lee Smith, Dickie Thon, Dave Winfield .60
2 Jesse Barfield, Shawon Dunston, Dennis Eckersley, Brian Fisher, Moose Haas, Mike Moore, Dale Murphy, Bret Saberhagen .50
3 George Bell, Bob Brenly, Steve Carlton, Jose DeLeon, Bob Horner, Bob James, Dan Quisenberry, Andre Thornton .60
4 Mike Davis, Leon Durham, Darrell Evans, Glenn Hubbard, Johnny Ray, Cal Ripken, Ted Simmons 1.50
5 John Candelaria, Rick Dempsey, Steve Garvey, Ozzie Guillen, Gary Matthews, Jesse Orosco, Tony Pena .45
6 Bruce Bochte, George Brett, Cecil Cooper, Sammy Khalifa, Ron Kittle, Scott McGregor, Pete Rose, Mookie Wilson 1.25
7 John Franco, Carney Lansford, Don Mattingly, Graig Nettles, Rick Reuschel, Mike Schmidt, Larry Sheets, Don Sutton 1.50
8 Cecilio Guante, Willie Hernandez, Mike Krukow, Fred Lynn, Phil Niekro, Ed Nunez, Ryne Sandberg, Pat Tabler .75
9 Brett Butler, Chris Codiroli, Jim Gantner, Charlie Hough, Dave Parker, Rick Rhoden, Glenn Wilson, Robin Yount .50
10 Tom Browning, Ron Darling, Von Hayes, Chet Lemon, Tom Seaver, Mike Smithson, Bruce Sutter, Alan Trammell .60
11 Tony Armas, Jose Cruz, Jay Howell, Rick Mahler, Jack Morris, Rafael Ramirez, Dave Righetti, Mike Young .40
12 Alvin Davis, Doug DeCinces, Andy Hawkins, Dennis Lamp, Keith Moreland, Jim Presley, Mario Soto, John Tudor .40
13 Hubie Brooks, Jody Davis, Dwight Evans, Ron Hassey, Charles Hudson, Kirby Puckett, Jose Uribe 1.00
14 Tony Bernazard, Phil Bradley, Bill Buckner, Brian Downing, Dan Driessen, Ron Guidry, LaMarr Hoyt, Garry Maddox .40
15 Buddy Bell, Joe Carter, Tony Fernandez, Tito Landrum, Jeff Leonard, Hal McRae, Willie Randolph, Juan Samuel .40
16 Dennis Boyd, Vince Coleman, Scott Garrelts, Alfredo Griffin, Donnie Moore, Tony Perez, Ozzie Smith, Frank White 1.00
17 Rich Gedman, Kent Hrbek, Reggie Jackson, Mike Marshall, Terry Pendleton, Tim Raines, Mark Salas, Claudell Washington 1.00
18 Chris Brown, Tom Brunansky, Glenn Davis, Ron Davis, Burt Hooton, Darryl Strawberry, Frank Viola, Tim Wallach .40
19 Jack Clark, Bill Doran, Toby Harrah, Bill Madlock, Pete O'Brien, Larry Parrish, Mike Scioscia, Garry Templeton .40
20 Gary Carter, Andre Dawson, Dwight Gooden, Orel Hershiser, Oddibe McDowell, Roger McDowell, Dwayne Murphy, Jim Rice .60
21 Steve Balboni, Mike Easler, Charlie Lea, Lloyd Moseby, Steve Sax, Rick Sutcliffe, Gary Ward, Willie Wilson .40
22 Wade Boggs, Dave Concepcion, Kirk Gibson, Tom Herr, Lance Parrish, Jeff Reardon, Bryn Smith, Gorman Thomas .75
23 Carlton Fisk, Bob Grich, Pedro Guerrero, Willie McGee, Paul Molitor, Mike Scott, Dave Stieb, Lou Whitaker .60
24 Bert Blyleven, Damaso Garcia, Phil Garner, Tony Gwynn, Rickey Henderson, Ben Oglivie, Nolan Ryan, Fernando Valenzuela 1.50

3-D

DON MATTINGLY

This set is a second effort in the production of over-size (4-1/2" x 6") plastic cards on which the player figure is embossed. Cards were sold one per pack for 50¢. The 30 players in the set are among the game's top stars. The embossed color photo is bordered at bottom by a strip of contrasting color on which the player name appears. At the top, a row of white baseballs each contain a letter of the team nickname. Backs have no printing, and contain two self-adhesive strips with which the cards can be attached to a hard surface.

NM/M
Complete Set (30): 9.00
Common Player: .25
Wax Pack (1): 1.00
Wax Box (24): 15.00
1 Bert Blyleven .25
2 Gary Carter .60
3 Wade Boggs .75
4 Dwight Gooden .25
5 George Brett 1.50
6 Rich Gossage .25
7 Darrell Evans .25
8 Pedro Guerrero .25
9 Ron Guidry .25
10 Keith Hernandez .25
11 Rickey Henderson .60
12 Orel Hershiser .25
13 Reggie Jackson 1.00
14 Willie McGee .25
15 Don Mattingly 1.50
16 Dale Murphy .45
17 Jack Morris .25
18 Dave Parker .25
19 Eddie Murray .60
20 Jeff Reardon .25
21 Dan Quisenberry .25
22 Pete Rose 2.00
23 Jim Rice .45
24 Mike Schmidt 1.50
25 Bret Saberhagen .25
26 Darryl Strawberry .25
27 Dave Stieb .25
28 John Tudor .25
29 Dave Winfield .60
30 Fernando Valenzuela .25

1987 Topps

The design of Topps' set of 792 2-1/2" x 3-1/2" cards is closely akin to the 1962 set in that the player photo is set against a woodgrain border. Instead of a rolling corner, as in 1962, the player photos in '87 feature a couple of clipped corners at top left and bottom right, where the team logo and player name appear. The player's position is not given on the front of the card. For the first time in several years, the trophy which designates members of Topps All-Star Rookie Team returned to the card design. As in the previous three years,

MARIANO DUNCAN

Topps issued a glossy-finish "Tiffany" edition of their 792-card set. However, it was speculated that as many as 30,000 sets were produced as opposed to the 5,000 sets printed in 1985 and 1986.

NM/M
Unopened Factory Set, Retail (792): 30.00
Unopened Factory Set, Hobby (792): 25.00
Complete Set (792): 20.00
Uncut Sheet Set (6): 45.00
Common Player: .05
Wax Pack (15): .75
Wax Box (36): 20.00
Cello Pack (31): 1.00
Cello Box (24): 20.00
Rack Pack (49): 1.50
Rack Box (24): 25.00
Vending Box (500): 12.00
1 Roger Clemens (Record Breaker) .45
2 Jim Deshaies (Record Breaker) .05
3 Dwight Evans (Record Breaker) .05
4 Dave Lopes (Record Breaker) .05
5 Dave Righetti (Record Breaker) .05
6 Ruben Sierra (Record Breaker) .05
7 Todd Worrell (Record Breaker) .05
8 Terry Pendleton .05
9 Jay Tibbs .05
10 Cecil Cooper .05
11 Indians Leaders (Jack Aker, Chris Bando, Phil Niekro) .05
12 Jeff Sellers .05
13 Nick Esasky .05
14 Dave Stewart .05
15 Claudell Washington .05
16 Pat Clements .05
17 Pete O'Brien .05
18 Dick Howser .05
19 Matt Young .05
20 Gary Carter .40
21 Mark Davis .05
22 Doug DeCinces .05
23 Lee Smith .05
24 Tony Walker .05
25 Bert Blyleven .05
26 Greg Brock .05
27 Joe Cowley .05
28 Rick Dempsey .05
29 Jimmy Key .05
30 Tim Raines .05
31 Braves Leaders (Glenn Hubbard, Rafael Ramirez) .05
32 Tim Leary .05
33 Andy Van Slyke .05
34 Jose Rijo .05
35 Sid Bream .05
36 Eric King RC .05
37 Marvell Wynne .05
38 Dennis Leonard .05
39 Marty Barrett .05
40 Dave Righetti .05
41 Bo Diaz .05
42 Gary Redus .05
43 Gene Michael .05
44 Greg Harris .05
45 Jim Presley .05
46 Danny Gladden .05
47 Dennis Powell .05
48 Wally Backman .05
49 Terry Harper .05
50 Dave Smith .05
51 Mel Hall .05
52 Keith Atherton .05
53 Ruppert Jones .05
54 Bill Dawley .05
55 Tim Wallach .05
56 Brewers Leaders (Jamie Cocanower, Paul Molitor, Charlie Moore, Herm Starrette) .10
57 Scott Nielsen RC .05
58 Thad Bosley .05
59 Ken Dayley .05
60 Tony Pena .05
61 Bobby Thigpen RC .05
62 Bobby Meacham .05
63 Fred Toliver RC .05
64 Harry Spilman .05
65 Tom Browning .05
66 Marc Sullivan .05
67 Bill Swift .05
68 Tony LaRussa .05
69 Lonnie Smith .05
70 Charlie Hough .05
71 Mike Aldrete RC .05
72 Walt Terrell .05
73 Dave Anderson .05
74 Dan Pasqua .05
75 Ron Darling .05
76 Rafael Ramirez .05
77 Bryan Oelkers .05
78 Tom Foley .05
79 Juan Nieves .05
80 Wally Joyner RC .35
81 Padres Leaders (Andy Hawkins, Terry Kennedy) .05
82 Rob Murphy RC .05
83 Mike Davis .05
84 Steve Lake .05
85 Kevin Bass .05
86 Nate Snell .05
87 Mark Salas .05
88 Ed Wojna .05
89 Ozzie Guillen .05
90 Dave Stieb .05
91 Harold Reynolds .05
92a Urbano Lugo (No trademark on front.) .10
92b Urbano Lugo (Trademark on front.) .05
93 Jim Leyland .05
94 Calvin Schiraldi .05
95 Oddibe McDowell .05
96 Frank Williams .05
97 Glenn Wilson .05
98 Bill Scherrer .05
99 Darryl Motley .05
100 Steve Garvey .15
101 Carl Willis RC .05
102 Paul Zuvella .05
103 Rick Aguilera .05
104 Billy Sample .05
105 Floyd Youmans .05
106 Blue Jays Leaders (George Bell, Willie Upshaw) .05
107 John Butcher .05
108 Jim Gantner (Photo reversed.) .05
109 R.J. Reynolds .05
110 John Tudor .05
111 Alfredo Griffin .05
112 Alan Ashby .05
113 Neil Allen .05
114 Billy Beane .05
115 Donnie Moore .05
116 Mike Stanley RC .05
117 Jim Beattie .05
118 Bobby Valentine .05
119 Ron Robinson .05
120 Eddie Murray .40
121 Kevin Romine RC .05
122 Jim Clancy .05
123 John Kruk .05
124 Ray Fontenot .05
125 Bob Brenly .05
126 Mike Loynd RC .05
127 Vance Law .05
128 Checklist 1-132 .05
129 Rick Cerone .05
130 Dwight Gooden .05
131 Pirates Leaders (Sid Bream, Tony Pena) .05
132 Paul Assenmacher RC .05
133 Jose Oquendo .05
134 Rich Yett RC .05
135 Mike Easler .05
136 Ron Romanick .05
137 Jerry Willard .05
138 Roy Lee Jackson .05
139 Devon White RC .40
140 Bret Saberhagen .05
141 Herm Winningham .05
142 Rick Sutcliffe .05
143 Steve Boros .05
144 Mike Scioscia .05
145 Charlie Kerfeld .05
146 Tracy Jones RC .05
147 Randy Niemann .05
148 Dave Collins .05
149 Ray Searage .05
150 Wade Boggs .45
151 Mike LaCoss .05
152 Toby Harrah .05
153 Duane Ward RC .05
154 Tom O'Malley .05
155 Eddie Whitson .05
156 Mariners Leaders (Bob Kearney, Phil Regan, Matt Young) .05
157 Danny Darwin .05
158 Tim Teufel .05
159 Ed Olwine .05
160 Julio Franco .05
161 Steve Ontiveros .05
162 Mike LaValliere RC .10
163 Kevin Gross .05
164 Sammy Khalifa .05
165 Jeff Reardon .05
166 Bob Boone .05
167 Jim Deshaies RC .10
168 Lou Piniella .05
169 Ron Washington .05
170 Bo Jackson (Future Stars) 1.50
171 Chuck Cary RC .05
172 Ron Oester .05
173 Alex Trevino .05
174 Henry Cotto .05
175 Bob Stanley .05
176 Steve Buechele .05
177 Keith Moreland .05
178 Cecil Fielder .05
179 Bill Wegman .05
180 Chris Brown .05
181 Cardinals Leaders (Mike LaValliere, Ozzie Smith, Ray Soff) .10
182 Lee Lacy .05
183 Andy Hawkins .05
184 Bobby Bonilla .05
185 Roger McDowell .05
186 Bruce Benedict .05
187 Mark Huismann .05
188 Tony Phillips .05
189 Joe Hesketh .05
190 Jim Sundberg .05
191 Charles Hudson .05
192 Cory Snyder RC .05
193 Roger Craig .05
194 Kirk McCaskill .05
195 Mike Pagliarulo .05
196 Randy O'Neal .05
197 Mark Bailey .05
198 Lee Mazzilli .05
199 Mariano Duncan .05
200 Pete Rose .75
201 John Cangelosi RC .05
202 Ricky Wright .05
203 Mike Kingery RC .05
204 Sammy Stewart .05
205 Graig Nettles .05
206 Twins Leaders (Tim Laudner, Frank Viola) .05
207 George Frazier .05
208 John Shelby .05
209 Rick Schu .05
210 Lloyd Moseby .05
211 John Morris RC .05
212 Mike Fitzgerald .05
213 Randy Myers RC .20
214 Omar Moreno .05
215 Mark Langston .05
216 B.J. Surhoff RC (Future Stars) .20
217 Chris Codiroli .05
218 Sparky Anderson .10
219 Cecilio Guante .05
220 Joe Carter .05
221 Vern Ruhle .05
222 Denny Walling .05
223 Charlie Leibrandt .05
224 Wayne Tolleson .05
225 Mike Smithson .05
226 Max Venable .05
227 Jamie Moyer RC .05
228 Curt Wilkerson .05
229 Mike Birkbeck RC .05
230 Don Baylor .05
231 Giants Leaders (Bob Brenly, Mike Krukow) .05
232 Reggie Williams RC .05
233 Russ Morman RC .05
234 Pat Sheridan .05
235 Alvin Davis .05
236 Tommy John .10
237 Jim Morrison .05
238 Bill Krueger .05
239 Juan Espino .05
240 Steve Balboni .05
241 Danny Heep .05
242 Rick Mahler .05
243 Whitey Herzog .05
244 Dickie Noles .05
245 Willie Upshaw .05
246 Jim Dwyer .05
247 Jeff Reed RC .05
248 Gene Walter .05
249 Jim Pankovits .05
250 Teddy Higuera .05
251 Rob Wilfong .05
252 Denny Martinez .05
253 Eddie Milner .05
254 Bob Tewksbury RC .20
255 Juan Samuel .05
256 Royals Leaders (George Brett, Frank White) .15
257 Bob Forsch .05
258 Steve Yeager .05
259 Mike Greenwell RC .25
260 Vida Blue .05
261 Ruben Sierra .05
262 Jim Winn .05
263 Stan Javier RC .05
264 Checklist 133-264 .05
265 Darrell Evans .05
266 Jeff Hamilton RC .05
267 Howard Johnson .05
268 Pat Corrales .05
269 Cliff Speck .05
270 Jody Davis .05
271 Mike Brown .05
272 Andres Galarraga RC .05
273 Gene Nelson .05
274 Jeff Hearron RC .05
275 LaMarr Hoyt .05
276 Jackie Gutierrez .05
277 Juan Agosto .05
278 Gary Pettis .05
279 Dan Plesac RC .05
280 Jeffrey Leonard .05
281 Reds Leaders (Bo Diaz, Bill Gullickson, Pete Rose) .10
282 Jeff Calhoun .05
283 Doug Drabek RC .25
284 John Moses .05
285 Dennis Boyd .05
286 Mike Woodard RC .05
287 Dave Von Ohlen .05
288 Tito Landrum .05
289 Bob Kipper .05
290 Leon Durham .05
291 Mitch Williams .05
292 Franklin Stubbs .05
293 Bob Rodgers .05
294 Steve Jeltz .05
295 Len Dykstra .05
296 Andres Thomas RC .05
297 Don Schulze .05
298 Larry Herndon .05
299 Joel Davis .05
300 Reggie Jackson .50
301 Luis Aquino RC .05
302 Bill Schroeder .05
303 Juan Berenguer .05
304 Phil Garner .05
305 John Franco .05
306 Red Sox Leaders (Rich Gedman, John McNamara, Tom Seaver) .10
307 Lee Guetterman RC .05
308 Don Slaught .05
309 Mike Young .05
310 Frank Viola .05
311 Rickey Henderson (Turn Back the Clock) .10
312 Reggie Jackson (Turn Back the Clock) .50
313 Roberto Clemente (Turn Back the Clock) .50
314 Carl Yastrzemski (Turn Back the Clock) .10
315 Maury Wills (Turn Back the Clock) .05
316 Brian Fisher .05
317 Clint Hurdle .05
318 Jim Fregosi .05
319 Greg Swindell RC .10
320 Barry Bonds 8.00
321 Mike Laga .05
322 Chris Bando .05
323 Al Newman RC .05
324 Dave Palmer .05
325 Garry Templeton .05
326 Mark Gubicza .05
327 Dale Sveum RC .05
328 Bob Welch .05
329 Ron Roenicke .05
330 Mike Scott .05
331 Mets Leaders (Gary Carter, Keith Hernandez, Dave Johnson, Darryl Strawberry) .10
332 Joe Price .05
333 Ken Phelps .05
334 Ed Correa RC .05
335 Candy Maldonado .05
336 Allan Anderson RC .05
337 Darrell Miller .05
338 Tim Conroy .05
339 Donnie Hill .05
340 Roger Clemens .65
341 Mike Brown .05
342 Bob James .05
343 Hal Lanier .05
344a Joe Niekro (Copyright outside yellow on back.) .25
344b Joe Niekro (Copyright inside yellow on back.) .05
345 Andre Dawson .25
346 Shawon Dunston .05
347 Mickey Brantley RC .05
348 Carmelo Martinez .05
349 Storm Davis .05
350 Keith Hernandez .05
351 Gene Garber .05
352 Mike Felder RC .05
353 Ernie Camacho .05
354 Jamie Quirk .05
355 Don Carman .05
356 White Sox Leaders (Ed Brinkman, Julio Cruz) .05
357 Steve Fireovid RC .05
358 Sal Butera .05
359 Doug Corbett .05
360 Pedro Guerrero .05
361 Mark Thurmond .05
362 Luis Quinones RC .05
363 Jose Guzman .05
364 Randy Bush .05
365 Rick Rhoden .05
366 Mark McGwire 3.00
367 Jeff Lahti .05
368 John McNamara .05
369 Brian Dayett .05
370 Fred Lynn .05
371 Mark Eichhorn RC .05
372 Jerry Mumphrey .05
373 Jeff Dedmon .05
374 Glenn Hoffman .05
375 Ron Guidry .10
376 Scott Bradley .05
377 John Henry Johnson .05
378 Rafael Santana .05
379 John Russell .05
380 Rich Gossage

381 Expos Leaders
(Mike Fitzgerald,
Bob Rodgers) .05
382 Rudy Law .05
383 Ron Davis .05
384 Johnny Grubb .05
385 Orel Hershiser .05
386 Dickie Thon .05
387 T.R. Bryden RC .05
388 Geno Petralli .05
389 Jeff Robinson .05
390 Gary Matthews .05
391 Jay Howell .05
392 Checklist 265-396 .05
393 Pete Rose .60
394 Mike Bielecki .05
395 Damaso Garcia .05
396 Tim Lollar .05
397 Greg Walker .05
398 Brad Havens .05
399 Curt Ford RC .05
400 George Brett .50
401 Billy Jo Robidoux .05
402 Mike Trujillo .05
403 Jerry Royster .05
404 Doug Sisk .05
405 Brook Jacoby .05
406 Yankees Leaders
(Rickey Henderson,
Don Mattingly) .25
407 Jim Acker .05
408 John Mizerock .05
409 Milt Thompson .05
410 Fernando Valenzuela .05
411 Darnell Coles .05
412 Eric Davis .05
413 Moose Haas .05
414 Joe Orsulak .05
415 Bobby Witt RC .05
416 Tom Nieto .05
417 Pat Perry RC .05
418 Dick Williams .05
419 Mark Portugal RC .10
420 Will Clark .40
421 Jose DeLeon .05
422 Jack Howell .05
423 Jaime Cocanower .05
424 Chris Speier .05
425 Tom Seaver .40
426 Floyd Rayford .05
427 Ed Nunez .05
428 Bruce Bochy .05
429 Tim Pyznarski RC
(Future Stars) .05
430 Mike Schmidt .50
431 Dodgers Leaders
(Tom Niedenfuer,
Ron Perranoski,
Alex Trevino) .05
432 Jim Slaton .05
433 Ed Hearn RC .05
434 Mike Fischlin .05
435 Bruce Sutter .35
436 Andy Allanson RC .05
437 Ted Power .05
438 Kelly Downs RC .05
439 Karl Best .05
440 Willie McGee .05
441 Dave Leiper RC .05
442 Mitch Webster .05
443 John Felske .05
444 Jeff Russell .05
445 Dave Lopes .05
446 Chuck Finley RC .25
447 Bill Almon .05
448 Chris Bosio RC .10
449 Pat Dodson RC
(Future Stars) .05
450 Kirby Puckett .45
451 Joe Sambito .05
452 Dave Henderson .05
453 Scott Terry RC .05
454 Luis Salazar .05
455 Mike Boddicker .05
456 A's Leaders (Carney Lansford,
Tony LaRussa,
Mickey Tettleton,
Dave Von Ohlen) .05
457 Len Matuszek .05
458 Kelly Gruber RC .05
459 Dennis Eckersley .35
460 Darryl Strawberry .05
461 Craig McMurtry .05
462 Scott Fletcher .05
463 Tom Candiotti .05
464 Butch Wynegar .05
465 Todd Worrell .05
466 Kal Daniels RC .05
467 Randy St. Claire .05
468 George Bamberger .05
469 Mike Diaz RC .05
470 Dave Dravecky .05
471 Ronn Reynolds .05
472 Bill Doran .05
473 Steve Farr .05
474 Jerry Narron .05
475 Scott Garrelts .05
476 Danny Tartabull .05
477 Ken Howell .05
478 Tim Laudner .05
479 Bob Sebra RC .05
480 Jim Rice .15
481 Phillies Leaders
(Von Hayes, Juan Samuel,
Glenn Wilson) .05
482 Daryl Boston .05
483 Dwight Lowry .05
484 Jim Traber RC .05

485 Tony Fernandez .05
486 Otis Nixon .05
487 Dave Gumpert .05
488 Ray Knight .05
489 Bill Gullickson .05
490 Dale Murphy .20
491 Ron Karkovice RC .05
492 Mike Heath .05
493 Tom Lasorda .10
494 Barry Jones RC .05
495 Gorman Thomas .05
496 Bruce Bochte .05
497 Dale Mohorcic RC .05
498 Bob Kearney .05
499 Bruce Ruffin RC .05
500 Don Mattingly .65
501 Craig Lefferts .05
502 Dick Schofield .05
503 Larry Andersen .05
504 Mickey Hatcher .05
505 Bryn Smith .05
506 Orioles Leaders
(Rich Bordi, Rick Dempsey,
Earl Weaver) .05
507 Dave Stapleton .05
508 Scott Bankhead RC .05
509 Enos Cabell .05
510 Tom Henke .05
511 Steve Lyons .05
512 Dave Magadan RC
(Future Stars) .20
513 Carmen Castillo .05
514 Orlando Mercado .05
515 Willie Hernandez .05
516 Ted Simmons .05
517 Mario Soto .05
518 Gene Mauch .05
519 Curt Young .05
520 Jack Clark .05
521 Rick Reuschel .05
522 Checklist 397-528 .05
523 Earnie Riles .05
524 Bob Shirley .05
525 Phil Bradley .05
526 Roger Mason .05
527 Jim Wohlford .05
528 Ken Dixon .05
529 Alvaro Espinoza RC .05
530 Tony Gwynn .45
531 Astros Leaders (Yogi Berra,
Hal Lanier, Denis Menke,
Gene Tenace) .05
532 Jeff Stone .05
533 Argenis Salazar .05
534 Scott Sanderson .05
535 Tony Armas .05
536 Terry Mulholland RC .15
537 Rance Mulliniks .05
538 Tom Niedenfuer .05
539 Reid Nichols .05
540 Terry Kennedy .05
541 Rafael Belliard RC .05
542 Ricky Horton .05
543 Dave Johnson .05
544 Zane Smith .05
545 Buddy Bell .05
546 Mike Morgan .05
547 Rob Deer .05
548 Bill Mooneyham RC .05
549 Bob Melvin .05
550 Pete Incaviglia .05
551 Frank Wills .05
552 Larry Sheets .05
553 Mike Maddux RC .05
554 Buddy Biancalana .05
555 Dennis Rasmussen .05
556 Angels Leaders (Bob Boone,
Marcel Lachemann,
Mike Witt) .05
557 John Cerutti RC .05
558 Greg Gagne .05
559 Lance McCullers .05
560 Glenn Davis .05
561 Rey Quinones RC .05
562 Bryan Clutterbuck RC .05
563 John Stefero .05
564 Larry McWilliams .05
565 Dusty Baker .05
566 Tim Hulett .05
567 Greg Mathews RC .05
568 Earl Weaver .10
569 Wade Rowdon RC .05
570 Sid Fernandez .05
571 Ozzie Virgil .05
572 Pete Ladd .05
573 Hal McRae .05
574 Manny Lee .05
575 Pat Tabler .05
576 Frank Pastore .05
577 Dann Bilardello .05
578 Billy Hatcher .05
579 Rick Burleson .05
580 Mike Krukow .05
581 Cubs Leaders
(Ron Cey, Steve Trout) .05
582 Bruce Berenyi .05
583 Junior Ortiz .05
584 Ron Kittle .05
585 Scott Bailes RC .05
586 Ben Oglivie .05
587 Eric Plunk RC .05
588 Wallace Johnson .05
589 Steve Crawford .05
590 Vince Coleman .05
591 Spike Owen .05
592 Chris Welsh .05
593 Chuck Tanner .05
594 Rick Anderson .05

595 Keith Hernandez/AS .05
596 Steve Sax/AS .05
597 Mike Schmidt/AS .35
598 Ozzie Smith/AS .30
599 Tony Gwynn/AS .30
600 Dave Parker/AS .05
601 Darryl Strawberry/AS .05
602 Gary Carter/AS .25
603a Dwight Gooden/AS
(No trademark on front.) .25
603b Dwight Gooden/AS
(Trademark on front.) .05
604 Fernando Valenzuela/AS .05
605 Todd Worrell/AS .05
606a Don Mattingly/AS
(No trademark on front.) .75
606b Don Mattingly/AS
(Trademark on front.) .35
607 Tony Bernazard/AS .05
608 Wade Boggs/AS .30
609 Cal Ripken, Jr./AS .45
610 Jim Rice/AS .05
611 Kirby Puckett/AS .30
612 George Bell/AS .05
613 Lance Parrish/AS .05
614 Roger Clemens/AS .35
615 Teddy Higuera/AS .05
616 Dave Righetti/AS .05
617 Al Nipper .05
618 Tom Kelly .05
619 Jerry Reed .05
620 Jose Canseco .60
621 Danny Cox .05
622 Glenn Braggs RC .05
623 Kurt Stillwell RC .05
624 Tim Burke .05
625 Mookie Wilson .05
626 Joel Skinner .05
627 Ken Oberkfell .05
628 Bob Walk .05
629 Larry Parrish .05
630 John Candelaria .05
631 Tigers Leaders
(Sparky Anderson,
Mike Heath,
Willie Hernandez) .05
632 Rob Woodward RC .05
633 Jose Uribe .05
634 Rafael Palmeiro RC 2.00
635 Ken Schrom .05
636 Darren Daulton .05
637 Bip Roberts RC .10
638 Rich Bordi .05
639 Gerald Perry .05
640 Mark Clear .05
641 Domingo Ramos .05
642 Al Pulido .05
643 Ron Shepherd .05
644 John Denny .05
645 Dwight Evans .05
646 Mike Mason .05
647 Tom Lawless .05
648 Barry Larkin RC .60
649 Mickey Tettleton .05
650 Hubie Brooks .05
651 Benny Distefano .05
652 Terry Forster .05
653 Kevin Mitchell .05
654 Checklist 529-660 .05
655 Jesse Barfield .05
656 Rangers Leaders
(Bobby Valentine,
Rickey Wright) .05
657 Tom Waddell .05
658 Robby Thompson RC .05
659 Aurelio Lopez .05
660 Bob Horner .05
661 Lou Whitaker .05
662 Frank DiPino .05
663 Cliff Johnson .05
664 Mike Marshall .05
665 Rod Scurry .05
666 Von Hayes .05
667 Ron Hassey .05
668 Juan Bonilla .05
669 Bud Black .05
670 Jose Cruz .05
671a Ray Soff (No "D*" before
copyright line.) .20
671b Ray Soff ("D*" before
copyright line.) .05
672 Chili Davis .05
673 Don Sutton .35
674 Bill Campbell .05
675 Ed Romero .05
676 Charlie Moore .05
677 Bob Grich .05
678 Carney Lansford .05
679 Kent Hrbek .05
680 Ryne Sandberg .45
681 George Bell .05
682 Jerry Reuss .05
683 Gary Roenicke .05
684 Kent Tekulve .05
685 Jerry Hairston Sr. .05
686 Doyle Alexander .05
687 Alan Trammell .05
688 Juan Beniquez .05
689 Darrell Porter .05
690 Dane Iorg .05
691 Dave Parker .05
692 Frank White .05
693 Terry Puhl .05
694 Phil Niekro .35
695 Chico Walker .05
696 Gary Lucas .05
697 Ed Lynch .05
698 Ernie Whitt .05

699 Ken Landreaux .05
700 Dave Bergman .05
701 Willie Randolph .05
702 Greg Gross .05
703 Dave Schmidt .05
704 Jesse Orosco .05
705 Bruce Hurst .05
706 Rick Manning .05
707 Bob McClure .05
708 Scott McGregor .05
709 Dave Kingman .05
710 Gary Gaetti .05
711 Ken Griffey .05
712 Don Robinson .05
713 Tom Brookens .05
714 Dan Quisenberry .05
715 Bob Dernier .05
716 Rick Leach .05
717 Ed Vande Berg .05
718 Steve Carlton .40
719 Tom Hume .05
720 Richard Dotson .05
721 Tom Herr .05
722 Bob Knepper .05
723 Brett Butler .05
724 Greg Minton .05
725 George Hendrick .05
726 Frank Tanana .05
727 Mike Moore .05
728 Tippy Martinez .05
729 Tom Paciorek .05
730 Eric Show .05
731 Dave Concepcion .05
732 Manny Trillo .05
733 Bill Caudill .05
734 Bill Madlock .05
735 Rickey Henderson .40
736 Steve Bedrosian .05
737 Floyd Bannister .05
738 Jorge Orta .05
739 Chet Lemon .05
740 Rich Gedman .05
741 Paul Molitor .40
742 Andy McGaffigan .05
743 Dwayne Murphy .05
744 Roy Smalley .05
745 Glenn Hubbard .05
746 Bob Ojeda .05
747 Johnny Ray .05
748 Mike Flanagan .05
749 Ozzie Smith .45
750 Steve Trout .05
751 Garth Iorg .05
752 Dan Petry .05
753 Rick Honeycutt .05
754 Dave LaPoint .05
755 Luis Aguayo .05
756 Carlton Fisk .40
757 Nolan Ryan .75
758 Tony Bernazard .05
759 Joel Youngblood .05
760 Mike Witt .05
761 Greg Pryor .05
762 Gary Ward .05
763 Tim Flannery .05
764 Bill Buckner .05
765 Kirk Gibson .05
766 Don Aase .05
767 Ron Cey .05
768 Dennis Lamp .05
769 Steve Sax .05
770 Dave Winfield .40
771 Shane Rawley .05
772 Harold Baines .05
773 Robin Yount .40
774 Wayne Krenchicki .05
775 Joaquin Andujar .05
776 Tom Brunansky .05
777 Chris Chambliss .05
778 Jack Morris .05
779 Craig Reynolds .05
780 Andre Thornton .05
781 Atlee Hammaker .05
782 Brian Downing .05
783 Willie Wilson .05
784 Cal Ripken, Jr. .75
785 Terry Francona .05
786 Jimy Williams .05
787 Alejandro Pena .05
788 Tim Stoddard .05
789 Dan Schatzeder .05
790 Julio Cruz .05
791 Lance Parrish .05
792 Checklist 661-792 .05

Tiffany

Produced in much greater quantity (reportedly 30,000 sets) than the previous years' sets, this specially boxed collectors' edition differs from the regular 1987 Topps cards only in its use of white cardboard stock and a high-gloss finish on the cards' fronts.

	NM/M
Unopened Set (792):	90.00
Complete Set (792):	50.00
Common Player:	.15
320 Barry Bonds	35.00

Traded

The Topps Traded set consists of 132 cards as did all Traded sets issued by Topps since 1981. Cards measure the standard 2-1/2" x 3-1/2"

KEVIN McREYNOLDS

and are identical in design to the regular edition set. The purpose of the set is to update player trades and feature rookies not included in the regular issue. As they had done the previous three years, Topps produced a glossy-coated "Tiffany" edition of the Traded set. Cards are numbered with a "T" suffix.

	NM/M
Complete Set (132):	4.00
Common Player:	.05

1 Bill Almon .05
2 Scott Bankhead .05
3 Eric Bell RC .05
4 Juan Beniquez .05
5 Juan Berenguer .05
6 Greg Booker .05
7 Thad Bosley .05
8 Larry Bowa .05
9 Greg Brock .05
10 Bob Brower RC .05
11 Jerry Browne RC .05
12 Ralph Bryant RC .05
13 DeWayne Buice RC .05
14 Ellis Burks RC .50
15 Ivan Calderon .05
16 Jeff Calhoun .05
17 Casey Candaele RC .05
18 John Cangelosi .05
19 Steve Carlton .25
20 Juan Castillo RC .05
21 Rick Cerone .05
22 Ron Cey .05
23 John Christensen .05
24 Dave Cone RC .15
25 Chuck Crim RC .05
26 Storm Davis .05
27 Andre Dawson .25
28 Rick Dempsey .05
29 Doug Drabek .05
30 Mike Dunne .05
31 Dennis Eckersley .25
32 Lee Elia .05
33 Brian Fisher .05
34 Terry Francona .05
35 Willie Fraser RC .05
36 Billy Gardner .05
37 Ken Gerhart RC .05
38 Danny Gladden .05
39 Jim Gott .05
40 Cecilio Guante .05
41 Albert Hall .05
42 Terry Harper .05
43 Mickey Hatcher .05
44 Brad Havens .05
45 Neal Heaton .05
46 Mike Henneman RC .20
47 Donnie Hill .05
48 Guy Hoffman .05
49 Brian Holton RC .05
50 Charles Hudson .05
51 Danny Jackson RC .05
52 Reggie Jackson .40
53 Chris James RC .05
54 Dion James .05
55 Stan Jefferson RC .05
56 Joe Johnson RC .05
57 Terry Kennedy .05
58 Mike Kingery .05
59 Ray Knight .05
60 Gene Larkin RC .05
61 Mike LaValliere .05
62 Jack Lazorko .05
63 Terry Leach .05
64 Tim Leary .05
65 Jim Lindeman RC .05
66 Steve Lombardozzi RC .05
67 Bill Long RC .05
68 Barry Lyons RC .05
69 Shane Mack RC .05
70 Greg Maddux RC 3.00
71 Bill Madlock .05
72 Joe Magrane RC .05
73 Dave Martinez RC .05
74 Fred McGriff RC .25
75 Mark McLemore RC .05
76 Kevin McReynolds RC .05
77 Dave Meads RC .05
78 Eddie Milner .05
79 Greg Minton .05
80 John Mitchell RC .05
81 Kevin Mitchell .05
82 Charlie Moore .05
83 Jeff Musselman RC .05
84 Gene Nelson .05

85 Graig Nettles .05
86 Al Newman .05
87 Reid Nichols .05
88 Tom Niedenfuer .05
89 Joe Niekro .05
90 Tom Nieto .05
91 Matt Nokes RC .10
92 Dickie Noles .05
93 Pat Pacillo .05
94 Lance Parrish .05
95 Tony Pena .05
96 Luis Polonia RC .05
97 Randy Ready .05
98 Jeff Reardon .05
99 Gary Redus .05
100 Jeff Reed .05
101 Rick Rhoden .05
102 Cal Ripken, Sr. .05
103 Wally Ritchie RC .05
104 Jeff Robinson RC .05
105 Gary Roenicke .05
106 Jerry Royster .05
107 Mark Salas .05
108 Luis Salazar .05
109 Benny Santiago RC .15
110 Dave Schmidt .05
111 Kevin Seitzer RC .05
112 John Shelby .05
113 Steve Shields RC .05
114 John Smiley RC .20
115 Chris Speier .05
116 Mike Stanley RC .05
117 Terry Steinbach RC .15
118 Les Straker RC .05
119 Jim Sundberg .05
120 Danny Tartabull .05
121 Tom Trebelhorn .05
122 Dave Valle .05
123 Ed Vande Berg .05
124 Andy Van Slyke .05
125 Gary Ward .05
126 Alan Wiggins .05
127 Bill Wilkinson RC .05
128 Frank Williams .05
129 Matt Williams RC .75
130 Jim Winn .05
131 Matt Young .05
132 Checklist 1T-132T .05

Traded Tiffany

The cards in this specially boxed limited edition version of the Traded set differ from the regular-issue cards only in the application of a high-gloss finish to the cards' fronts. Production was reported as 30,000 sets.

	NM/M
Complete Set (132):	30.00
Common Player:	.15

Traded Willie Mays Bronze

WILLIE MAYS — OUTFIELD — NEW YORK GIANTS

This 1/4-size metal replica was issued to dealers who purchased cases of 1987 Topps Traded sets. Each detail of the 1953 Topps Mays card is reproduced on the 1-1/4" x 1-3/4" bronze metal mini-card, right down to the stats.

	NM/M
244 Willie Mays	10.00

Box Panels

Offering baseball cards on retail boxes for a second straight year, Topps reduced the size of the cards to 2-1/8" x 3". Four different wax pack boxes were available, each featuring two cards that were placed on the sides of the boxes. The card fronts are identical in design to the regular issue cards. The backs are printed in blue and yellow and carry a commentary imitating a newspaper format. The cards are numbered A through H.

		NM/M
Complete Singles Set (8):		2.00
Complete Panel Set (4):		2.50
Common Panel:		.50
Common Single Player:		.15
Panel		.50
A	Don Baylor	.15
B	Steve Carlton	.30
Panel		
C	Ron Cey	.15
D	Cecil Cooper	.15
Panel		.75
E	Rickey Henderson	.40
F	Jim Rice	.20
Panel		.75
G	Don Sutton	.25
H	Dave Winfield	.40

All-Star Glossy Set of 22

For the fourth consecutive year, Topps produced an All-Star Game commemorative set of 22 cards. The glossy cards, 2-1/2"x3-1/2", were included in rack packs. Using the same basic design as in previous efforts with a few minor changes, the 1987 edition features American and National League logos on the card fronts. Cards #1-12 feature representatives from the American League, while #13-22 are National Leaguers.

		NM/M
Complete Set (22):		2.50
Common Player:		.05
1	Whitey Herzog	.05
2	Keith Hernandez	.05
3	Ryne Sandberg	.35
4	Mike Schmidt	.50
5	Ozzie Smith	.35
6	Tony Gwynn	.35
7	Dale Murphy	.20
8	Darryl Strawberry	.35
9	Gary Carter	.30
10	Dwight Gooden	.05
11	Fernando Valenzuela	.05
12	Dick Howser	.05
13	Wally Joyner	.35
14	Lou Whitaker	.05
15	Wade Boggs	.35
16	Cal Ripken, Jr.	.60
17	Dave Winfield	.30
18	Rickey Henderson	.30
19	Kirby Puckett	.35
20	Lance Parrish	.05
21	Roger Clemens	.40
22	Teddy Higuera	.05

All-Star Glossy Set of 60

Using the same design as the previous year, the 1987 Topps All-Star glossy set includes 48 All-Star performers plus 12 potential superstars branded as "Hot Prospects." The card fronts are uncluttered, save the player's name found in very small print at the bottom. The set was available via a mail-in offer. Six subsets make up the 60-card set, with each subset being available for $1.00 plus six special offer cards that were found in wax packs.

	NM/M
Complete Set (60):	15.00

		NM/M
Common Player:		.10
1	Don Mattingly	.75
2	Tony Gwynn	.50
3	Gary Gaetti	.10
4	Glenn Davis	.10
5	Roger Clemens	.65
6	Dale Murphy	.25
7	Lou Whitaker	.10
8	Roger McDowell	.10
9	Cory Snyder	.10
10	Todd Worrell	.10
11	Gary Carter	.40
12	Eddie Murray	.40
13	Bob Knepper	.10
14	Harold Baines	.10
15	Jeff Reardon	.10
16	Joe Carter	.10
17	Dave Parker	.10
18	Wade Boggs	.50
19	Danny Tartabull	.10
20	Jim Deshaies	.10
21	Rickey Henderson	.40
22	Rob Deer	.10
23	Ozzie Smith	.50
24	Dave Righetti	.10
25	Kent Hrbek	.10
26	Keith Hernandez	.10
27	Don Baylor	.10
28	Mike Schmidt	.85
29	Pete Incaviglia	.10
30	Barry Bonds	9.00
31	George Brett	.85
32	Darryl Strawberry	.10
33	Mike Witt	.10
34	Kevin Bass	.10
35	Jesse Barfield	.10
36	Bob Ojeda	.10
37	Cal Ripken, Jr.	2.00
38	Vince Coleman	.10
39	Wally Joyner	.10
40	Robby Thompson	.10
41	Pete Rose	1.00
42	Jim Rice	.25
43	Tony Bernazard	.10
44	Eric Davis	.10
45	George Bell	.10
46	Hubie Brooks	.10
47	Jack Morris	.10
48	Tim Raines	.10
49	Mark Eichhorn	.10
50	Kevin Mitchell	.10
51	Dwight Gooden	.10
52	Doug DeCinces	.10
53	Fernando Valenzuela	.10
54	Reggie Jackson	.50
55	Johnny Ray	.10
56	Mike Pagliarulo	.10
57	Kirby Puckett	.50
58	Lance Parrish	.10
59	Jose Canseco	.50
60	Greg Mathews	.10

Baseball Highlights

The "Baseball Highlights" boxed set of 33 cards was prepared by Topps for distribution at stores in the Woolworth's chain, although the retailer's name does not appear on the cards. Each card measures 2-1/2" x 3-1/2" in size and features a memorable baseball event that occurred during the 1986 season. The glossy set sold for $1.99.

Coins

For the first time since 1971, Topps issued a set of baseball "coins." Similar in design to the 1964 edition, the metal discs measure 1-1/2" in diameter. The aluminum coins were sold on a limited

basis in retail outlets. Three coins and three sticks of gum were found in a pack. The coin fronts feature a full-color photo along with the player's name, team and position in a white band at the bottom. Gold-colored rims are found for American League players; National League players have silver-colored rims. Backs are silvered and carry the coin number, player's name and personal and statistical information.

		NM/M
Complete Set (48):		7.50
Common Player:		.10
Wax Pack (3):		1.00
Wax Box (24):		15.00
1	Harold Baines	.10
2	Jesse Barfield	.10
3	George Bell	.10
4	Wade Boggs	.45
5	George Brett	1.00
6	Jose Canseco	.25
7	Joe Carter	.10
8	Roger Clemens	.60
9	Alvin Davis	.10
10	Rob Deer	.10
11	Kirk Gibson	.10
12	Rickey Henderson	.35
13	Kent Hrbek	.10
14	Pete Incaviglia	.10
15	Reggie Jackson	.60
16	Wally Joyner	.10
17	Don Mattingly	.75
18	Jack Morris	.10
19	Eddie Murray	.35
20	Kirby Puckett	.45
21	Jim Rice	.25
22	Dave Righetti	.10
23	Cal Ripken, Jr.	1.50
24	Cory Snyder	.10
25	Danny Tartabull	.10
26	Dave Winfield	.35
27	Hubie Brooks	.10
28	Gary Carter	.35
29	Vince Coleman	.10
30	Eric Davis	.10
31	Glenn Davis	.10
32	Steve Garvey	.15
33	Dwight Gooden	.10
34	Tony Gwynn	.45
35	Von Hayes	.10
36	Keith Hernandez	.10
37	Dale Murphy	.20
38	Dave Parker	.10
39	Tony Pena	.10
40	Nolan Ryan	1.50
41	Ryne Sandberg	.45
42	Steve Sax	.10
43	Mike Schmidt	1.00
44	Mike Scott	.10
45	Ozzie Smith	.45
46	Darryl Strawberry	.10
47	Fernando Valenzuela	.10
48	Todd Worrell	.10

Gallery of Champions

Designed as a tribute to 1986's winners of baseball's most prestigious awards, the Gallery of Champions are metal "cards" that are one-quarter size replicas of the regular issue Topps cards. The bronze and silver sets were issued in leather-like velvet-lined display cases; the aluminum sets came cello-wrapped. Hobby dealers who purchased one bronze set or a 16-set case of aluminum "cards" received one free Jose Canseco pewter metal mini-card. The purchase of a silver set included five Canseco pewters.

		NM/M
Complete Aluminum Set (12):		17.50
Complete Bronze Set (12):		75.00
Complete Silver Set (12):		250.00
(1a)	Jesse Barfield/Aluminum	2.00
(1b)	Jesse Barfield/Bronze	6.00
(1s)	Jesse Barfield/Silver	15.00
(2a)	Wade Boggs/Aluminum	4.50
(2b)	Wade Boggs/Bronze	15.00
(2s)	Wade Boggs/Silver	30.00

(3a)	Jose Canseco/Aluminum	3.50
(3b)	Jose Canseco/Bronze	10.00
(3s)	Jose Canseco/Silver	25.00
(3p)	Jose Canseco/Pewter	12.50
(4a)	Joe Carter/Aluminum	2.00
(4b)	Joe Carter/Bronze	6.00
(4s)	Joe Carter/Silver	15.00
(5a)	Roger Clemens/ Aluminum	5.00
(5b)	Roger Clemens/Bronze	16.00
(5s)	Roger Clemens/Silver	40.00
(6a)	Tony Gwynn/Aluminum	4.50
(6b)	Tony Gwynn/Bronze	15.00
(6s)	Tony Gwynn/Silver	30.00
(7a)	Don Mattingly/Aluminum	5.00
(7b)	Don Mattingly/Bronze	17.50
(7s)	Don Mattingly/Silver	45.00
(8a)	Tim Raines/Aluminum	2.00
(8b)	Tim Raines/Bronze	6.00
(8s)	Tim Raines/Silver	15.00
(9a)	Dave Righetti/Aluminum	2.00
(9b)	Dave Righetti/Bronze	6.00
(9s)	Dave Righetti/Silver	15.00
(10a)	Mike Schmidt/Aluminum	6.00
(10b)	Mike Schmidt/Bronze	20.00
(10s)	Mike Schmidt/Silver	50.00
(11a)	Mike Scott/Aluminum	2.00
(11b)	Mike Scott/Bronze	6.00
(11s)	Mike Scott/Silver	15.00
(12a)	Todd Worrell/Aluminum	2.00
(12b)	Todd Worrell/Bronze	6.00
(12s)	Todd Worrell/Silver	15.00

Glossy Rookies

The 1987 Topps Glossy Rookies set of 22 cards was introduced with Topps' new 100-card "Jumbo Packs." Intended for sale in supermarkets, the jumbo packs contained one glossy card. Measuring the standard 2-1/2" x 3-1/2" size, the special insert cards feature the top rookies from the previous season.

		NM/M
Complete Set (22):		3.00
Common Player:		.05
1	Andy Allanson	.05
2	John Cangelosi	.05
3	Jose Canseco	1.00
4	Will Clark	.25
5	Mark Eichhorn	.05
6	Pete Incaviglia	.05
7	Wally Joyner	.25
8	Eric King	.05
9	Dave Magadan	.05
10	John Morris	.05
11	Juan Nieves	.05
12	Rafael Palmeiro	2.50
13	Billy Jo Robidoux	.05
14	Bruce Ruffin	.05
15	Ruben Sierra	.50
16	Cory Snyder	.25
17	Kurt Stillwell	.05
18	Dale Sveum	.05
19	Danny Tartabull	.05
20	Andres Thomas	.05
21	Robby Thompson	.05
22	Todd Worrell	.05

Bobby Grich Night Sheet

In conjunction with a Bobby Grich Night sponsored by the California Angels on May 1, 1987, Sheraton Hotels of Los Angeles and radio station KLAC issued this sheet bearing reproductions of each of Grich's regular issue Topps cards from 1971-1987. The sheet measures 10" x 17-1/2", while the perforated cards, if removed from the sheet, measure the standard 2-1/2" x 3-1/2".

		NM/M
Complete Sheet:		10.00
Common Card:		.75
1971	Bob Grich #193	1.50
1972	Bob Grich #338	.75
1973	Bob Grich #418	.75
1974	Bob Grich #109	.75
1975	Bob Grich #225	.75
1976	Bob Grich #335	.75
1977	Bob Grich #521	.75
1978	Bob Grich #18	.75
1979	Bob Grich #477	.75

1980	Bob Grich #621	.75
1981	Bob Grich #182	.75
1982	Bob Grich #284	.75
1983	Bob Grich #790	.75
1984	Bob Grich #315	.75
1985	Bob Grich #465	.75
1986	Bob Grich #155	.75
1987	Bob Grich #677	.75

Mini League Leaders

DENNIS RASMUSSEN

Returning for 1987, the Topps "Major League Leaders" set was increased in size from 66 to 76 cards. The 2-1/8" x 3" cards feature woodgrain borders that encompass a white-bordered color photo. Backs are printed in yellow, orange and brown and list the player's official ranking based on his 1986 American or National League statistics. The players featured are those who finished the top five in their leagues' various batting and pitching categories. The cards were sold in plastic-wrapped packs, seven cards plus a game card per pack.

		NM/M
Complete Set (77):		4.00
Common Player:		.05
Wax Pack (7):		.50
Wax Box (36):		10.00
1	Bob Horner	.05
2	Dale Murphy	.15
3	Lee Smith	.05
4	Eric Davis	.05
5	John Franco	.05
6	Dave Parker	.05
7	Kevin Bass	.05
8	Glenn Davis	.05
9	Bill Doran	.05
10	Bob Knepper	.05
11	Mike Scott	.05
12	Dave Smith	.05
13	Mariano Duncan	.05
14	Orel Hershiser	.05
15	Steve Sax	.05
16	Fernando Valenzuela	.05
17	Tim Raines	.05
18	Jeff Reardon	.05
19	Floyd Youmans	.05
20	Gary Carter	.05
21	Ron Darling	.05
22	Sid Fernandez	.05
23	Dwight Gooden	.05
24	Keith Hernandez	.05
25	Bob Ojeda	.05
26	Darryl Strawberry	.05
27	Steve Bedrosian	.05
28	Von Hayes	.05
29	Juan Samuel	.05
30	Mike Schmidt	.75
31	Rick Rhoden	.05
32	Vince Coleman	.05
33	Danny Cox	.05
34	Todd Worrell	.05
35	Tony Gwynn	.35
36	Mike Krukow	.05
37	Candy Maldonado	.05
38	Don Aase	.05
39	Eddie Murray	.05
40	Cal Ripken, Jr.	1.00
41	Wade Boggs	.35
42	Roger Clemens	.40
43	Bruce Hurst	.05
44	Jim Rice	.15
45	Wally Joyner	.05
46	Donnie Moore	.05
47	Gary Pettis	.05
48	Mike Witt	.05
49	John Cangelosi	.05
50	Tom Candiotti	.05
51	Joe Carter	.05
52	Pat Tabler	.05
53	Kirk Gibson	.05
54	Willie Hernandez	.05
55	Jack Morris	.05
56	Alan Trammell	.05
57	George Brett	.75
58	Willie Wilson	.05
59	Rob Deer	.05
60	Teddy Higuera	.05
61	Bert Blyleven	.05
62	Gary Gaetti	.05
63	Kirby Puckett	.35
64	Rickey Henderson	.25

65	Don Mattingly	.50
66	Dennis Rasmussen	.05
67	Dave Righetti	.05
68	Jose Canseco	.20
69	Dave Kingman	.05
70	Phil Bradley	.05
71	Mark Langston	.05
72	Pete O'Brien	.05
73	Jesse Barfield	.05
74	George Bell	.05
75	Tony Fernandez	.05
76	Tom Henke	.05
77	Checklist	.05

Stickers - Hardback Test

In addition to its regular issue of Panini-produced paper-backed stickers, Topps in 1987 produced a very limited version of the same issue with a hard cardboard back. The Topps hard-back version is virtually identical to the more common Panini version except for the copyright line printed on back. Production of the hard-back version was reported to be 1/10 of 1% of the Panini version.

	NM/M
Complete Set (313):	75.00
Common Player:	.50
Wax Pack (5):	1.00
Wax Box (48):	25.00

Stickers - Panini

For the seventh consecutive year, Topps issued stickers produced by Panini in Italy for use in a special album or yearbook. The 2-1/8" x 3" stickers offer a full-color front with a peel-off paper back. Fronts feature either one full-size player picture or two half-size individual stickers. The yearbook contains 36 glossy, magazine-style pages, all printed in full color. Mike Schmidt, 1986 N.L. MVP, is featured on the covers. The yearbook sold in retail outlets for $.35, while stickers were sold five in a pack for $.25. The number in parentheses in this checklist is the sticker number the player shares the sticker with. Besides the common soft-back sticker made for Topps by Panini, there was a test issue of hard-back sticker cards.

		NM/M
Complete Set (313):		15.00
Common Player:		.05
Sticker Album:		1.50
Wax Pack (5):		.25
Wax Box (100):		15.00
1	1986 Highlights (Jim Deshaies/172)	.05
2	1986 Highlights (Roger Clemens/175)	.25
3	1986 Highlights (Roger Clemens/176)	.25
4	1986 Highlights (Dwight Evans/177)	.05
5	1986 Highlights (Dwight Gooden/178)	.05
6	1986 Highlights (Dwight Gooden/180)	.05
7	1986 Highlights (Dave Lopes/181)	.05

#	Player	Price
8	1986 Highlights (Dave Righetti/182)	.05
9	1986 Highlights (Dave Righetti/183)	.05
10	1986 Highlights (Ruben Sierra/185)	.05
11	1986 Highlights (Todd Worrell/186)	.05
12	1986 Highlights (Todd Worrell/187)	.05
13	N.L. Championship Series (Lenny Dykstra)	.05
14	N.L. Championship Series (Gary Carter)	.15
15	N.L. Championship Series (Mike Scott)	.05
16	A.L. Championship Series (Gary Pettis)	.05
17	A.L. Championship Series (Jim Rice)	.05
18	A.L. Championship Series (Bruce Hurst)	.05
19	1986 World Series (Bruce Hurst)	.05
20	1986 World Series (Wade Boggs)	.15
21	1986 World Series (Lenny Dykstra)	.05
22	1986 World Series (Gary Carter)	.15
23	1986 World Series (Dave Henderson)	.05
24	1986 World Series (Howard Johnson)	.05
25	1986 World Series (Mets Celebrate)	.05
26	Glenn Davis	.05
27	Nolan Ryan/188	.60
28	Charlie Kerfeld/189	.05
29	Jose Cruz/190	.05
30	Phil Garner/191	.05
31	Bill Doran/192	.05
32	Bob Knepper/195	.05
33	Denny Walling/196	.05
34	Kevin Bass/197	.05
35	Mike Scott	.05
36	Dale Murphy	.20
37	Paul Assenmacher/198	.05
38	Ken Oberkfell/200	.05
39	Andres Thomas/201	.05
40	Gene Garber/202	.05
41	Bob Horner	.05
42	Rafael Ramirez/203	.05
43	Rick Mahler/204	.05
44	Omar Moreno/205	.05
45	Dave Palmer/206	.05
46	Ozzie Smith	.35
47	Bob Forsch/207	.05
48	Willie McGee/209	.05
49	Tom Herr/210	.05
50	Vince Coleman/211	.05
51	Andy Van Slyke/212	.05
52	Jack Clark/215	.05
53	John Tudor/216	.05
54	Terry Pendleton/217	.05
55	Todd Worrell	.05
56	Lee Smith	.05
57	Leon Durham/218	.05
58	Jerry Mumphrey/219	.05
59	Shawon Dunston/220	.05
60	Scott Sanderson/221	.05
61	Ryne Sandberg	.35
62	Gary Matthews/222	.05
63	Dennis Eckersley/225	.25
64	Jody Davis/226	.05
65	Keith Moreland/227	.05
66	Mike Marshall/228	.05
67	Bill Madlock/229	.05
68	Greg Brock/230	.05
69	Pedro Guerrero/231	.05
70	Steve Sax	.05
71	Rick Honeycutt/232	.05
72	Franklin Stubbs/235	.05
73	Mike Scioscia/236	.05
74	Mariano Duncan/237	.05
75	Fernando Valenzuela	.05
76	Hubie Brooks	.05
77	Andre Dawson/238	.20
78	Tim Burke/240	.05
79	Floyd Youmans/241	.05
80	Tim Wallach/242	.05
81	Jeff Reardon/243	.05
82	Mitch Webster/244	.05
83	Bryn Smith/245	.05
84	Andres Galarraga/246	.05
85	Tim Raines	.05
86	Chris Brown	.05
87	Bob Brenly/247	.05
88	Will Clark/249	.10
89	Scott Garrelts/250	.05
90	Jeffrey Leonard/251	.05
91	Robby Thompson/252	.05
92	Mike Krukow/255	.05
93	Danny Gladden/256	.05
94	Candy Maldonado/257	.05
95	Chili Davis	.05
96	Dwight Gooden	.05
97	Sid Fernandez/258	.05
98	Len Dykstra/259	.05
99	Bob Ojeda/260	.05
100	Wally Backman/261	.05
101	Gary Carter	.30
102	Keith Hernandez/262	.05
103	Darryl Strawberry/264	.05
104	Roger McDowell/266	.05
105	Ron Darling/267	.05
106	Tony Gwynn	.35
107	Dave Dravecky/268	.05
108	Terry Kennedy/269	.05
109	Rich Gossage/270	.05
110	Garry Templeton/271	.05
111	Lance McCullers/272	.05
112	Eric Show/275	.05
113	John Kruk/276	.05
114	Tim Flannery/277	.05
115	Steve Garvey	.15
116	Mike Schmidt	.45
117	Glenn Wilson/278	.05
118	Kent Tekulve/280	.05
119	Gary Redus/281	.05
120	Shane Rawley/282	.05
121	Von Hayes	.05
122	Don Carman/283	.05
123	Bruce Ruffin/285	.05
124	Steve Bedrosian/286	.05
125	Juan Samuel/287	.05
126	Sid Bream/288	.05
127	Cecilio Guante/289	.05
128	Rick Reuschel/290	.05
129	Tony Pena/291	.05
130	Rick Rhoden	.05
131	Barry Bonds/292	5.00
132	Joe Orsulak/295	.05
133	Jim Morrison/296	.05
134	R.J. Reynolds/297	.05
135	Johnny Ray	.05
136	Eric Davis	.05
137	Tom Browning/298	.05
138	John Franco/300	.05
139	Pete Rose/301	.35
140	Bill Gullickson/302	.05
141	Ron Oester/303	.05
142	Bo Diaz/304	.05
143	Buddy Bell /305	.05
144	Eddie Milner/306	.05
145	Dave Parker	.05
146	Kirby Puckett	.05
147	Rickey Henderson	.30
148	Wade Boggs	.35
149	Lance Parrish	.05
150	Wally Joyner	.05
151	Cal Ripken, Jr.	.75
152	Dave Winfield	.30
153	Lou Whitaker	.05
154	Roger Clemens	.40
155	Tony Gwynn	.35
156	Ryne Sandberg	.35
157	Keith Hernandez	.05
158	Gary Carter	.30
159	Darryl Strawberry	.05
160	Mike Schmidt	.45
161	Dale Murphy	.15
162	Ozzie Smith	.35
163	Dwight Gooden	.05
164	Jose Canseco	.25
165	Curt Young/307	.05
166	Alfredo Griffin/30 8	.05
167	Dave Stewart/309	.05
168	Mike Davis/310	.05
169	Bruce Bochte/311	.05
170	Dwayne Murphy/312	.05
171	Carney Lansford/313	.05
172	Joaquin Andujar/1	.05
173	Dave Kingman	.05
174	Wally Joyner	.05
175	Gary Pettis/2	.05
176	Dick Schofield/3	.05
177	Donnie Moore/4	.05
178	Brian Downing/5	.05
179	Mike Witt	.05
180	Bob Boone/6	.05
181	Kirk McCaskill/7	.05
182	Doug DeCinces/8	.05
183	Don Sutton/9	.25
184	Jessie Barfield	.05
185	Tom Henke/10	.05
186	Willie Upshaw/11	.05
187	Mark Eichhorn/12	.05
188	Damaso Garcia/27	.05
189	Jim Clancy/28	.05
190	Lloyd Moseby/29	.05
191	Tony Fernandez/30	.05
192	Jimmy Key/31	.05
193	George Bell	.05
194	Rob Deer	.05
195	Mark Clear/32	.05
196	Robin Yount/33	.20
197	Jim Gantner/34	.05
198	Cecil Cooper/37	.05
199	Teddy Higuera	.05
200	Paul Molitor/38	.25
201	Dan Plesac/39	.05
202	Billy Jo Robidoux/40	.05
203	Earnie Riles/42	.05
204	Ken Schrom/43	.05
205	Pat Tabler/44	.05
206	Mel Hall/45	.05
207	Tony Bernazard/47	.05
208	Joe Carter	.05
209	Ernie Camacho/48	.05
210	Julio Franco/49	.05
211	Tom Candiotti/50	.05
212	Brook Jacoby/51	.05
213	Cory Snyder	.05
214	Jim Presley	.05
215	Mike Moore/52	.05
216	Harold Reynolds/53	.05
217	Scott Bradley/54	.05
218	Matt Young/57	.05
219	Mark Langston/58	.05
220	Alvin Davis/59	.05
221	Phil Bradley/60	.05
222	Ken Phelps/62	.05
223	Danny Tartabull	.05
224	Eddie Murray	.30
225	Rick Dempsey/63	.05
226	Fred Lynn/64	.05
227	Mike Boddicker/65	.05
228	Don Aase/66	.05
229	Larry Sheets/67	.05
230	Storm Davis/68	.05
231	Lee Lacy/69	.05
232	Jim Traber/71	.05
233	Cal Ripken, Jr.	.75
234	Larry Parrish	.05
235	Gary Ward/72	.05
236	Pete Incaviglia/73	.05
237	Scott Fletcher/74	.05
238	Greg Harris/77	.05
239	Pete O'Brien	.05
240	Charlie Hough/78	.05
241	Don Slaught/79	.05
242	Steve Buechele/80	.05
243	Oddibe McDowell/81	.05
244	Roger Clemens/82	.30
245	Bob Stanley/83	.05
246	Tom Seaver/84	.20
247	Rich Gedman/87	.05
248	Jim Rice	.15
249	Dennis Boyd/88	.05
250	Bill Buckner/89	.05
251	Dwight Evans/90	.05
252	Don Baylor/91	.05
253	Wade Boggs	.35
254	George Brett	.45
255	Steve Farr/92	.05
256	Jim Sundberg/93	.05
257	Dan Quisenberry/94	.05
258	Charlie Leibrandt/97	.05
259	Argenis Salazar/98	.05
260	Frank White/99	.05
261	Willie Wilson/100	.05
262	Lonnie Smith/102	.05
263	Steve Balboni	.05
264	Darrell Evans	.05
265	Johnny Grubb/103	.05
266	Jack Morris/104	.05
267	Lou Whitaker/105	.05
268	Chet Lemon/107	.05
269	Lance Parrish/108	.05
270	Alan Trammell/109	.05
271	Darnell Coles/110	.05
272	Willie Hernandez/111	.05
273	Kirk Gibson	.05
274	Kirby Puckett	.35
275	Mike Smithson/112	.05
276	Mickey Hatcher/113	.05
277	Frank Viola/114	.05
278	Bert Blyleven/117	.05
279	Gary Gaetti	.05
280	Tom Brunansky/118	.05
281	Kent Hrbek/119	.05
282	Roy Smalley/120	.05
283	Greg Gagne/122	.05
284	Harold Baines	.05
285	Ron Hassey/123	.05
286	Floyd Bannister/124	.05
287	Ozzie Guillen/125	.05
288	Carlton Fisk/126	.25
289	Tim Hulett/127	.05
290	Joe Cowley/128	.05
291	Greg Walker/129	.05
292	Neil Allen/131	.05
293	John Cangelosi	.05
294	Don Mattingly	.45
295	Mike Easler/132	.05
296	Rickey Henderson/133	.20
297	Dan Pasqua/134	.05
298	Dave Winfield/137	.20
299	Dave Righetti	.05
300	Mike Pagliarulo/138	.05
301	Ron Guidry/139	.05
302	Willie Randolph/140	.05
303	Dennis Rasmussen/141	.05
304	Jose Canseco/142	.20
305	Andres Thomas/143	.05
306	Danny Tartabull/144	.05
307	Robby Thompson/165	.05
308	Pete Incaviglia, Cory Snyder/166	.05
309	Dale Sveum/167	.05
310	Todd Worrell/168	.05
311	Andy Allanson/169	.05
312	Bruce Ruffin/170	.05
313	Wally Joyner/171	.05

1988 Topps

The 1988 Topps set features a clean, attractive design of a player photo surrounded by a thin colored frame which is encompassed by a white border. The player's name appears in the lower-right corner in a diagonal colored strip. The team nickname is in large letters at the top of the card. Backs feature black print on orange and gray stock and include the usual player personal and career statistics. Many of the cards contain a new feature titled "This Way To The Clubhouse," which explains how the player joined his current team. The 792-card set includes a number of special subsets including "Future Stars," "Turn Back The Clock," All-Star teams, All-Star rookie selections, and Record Breakers.

	NM/M
Unopened Factory Set, Retail (792):	15.00
Unopened Factory Set, Hobby (792):	15.00
Complete Set (792):	12.00
Common Player:	.05
Wax Pack (15):	.40
Wax Box (36):	15.00
Cello Pack (28):	.70
Cello Box (24):	13.50
Rack Pack (43):	.75
Rack Box (24):	15.00
Vending Box (500):	7.50

#	Player	Price
1	Vince Coleman (Record Breakers)	.05
2	Don Mattingly (Record Breakers)	.25
3a	Mark McGwire (Record Breakers, white triangle by left foot.)	1.00
3b	Mark McGwire (Record Breakers, no white triangle.)	.40
4a	Eddie Murray (Record Breakers, no mention of record on front.)	.25
4b	Eddie Murray (Record Breakers, record in box on front.)	.20
5	Joe Niekro, Phil Niekro (Record Breakers)	.05
6	Nolan Ryan (Record Breakers)	.40
7	Benito Santiago (Record Breakers)	.05
8	Kevin Elster RC (Future Stars)	.05
9	Andy Hawkins	.05
10	Ryne Sandberg	.50
11	Mike Young	.05
12	Bill Schroeder	.05
13	Andres Thomas	.05
14	Sparky Anderson	.10
15	Chili Davis	.05
16	Kirk McCaskill	.05
17	Ron Oester	.05
18a	Al Leiter RC (Future Stars, no "NY" on shirt, photo actually Steve George.)	.40
18b	Al Leiter (Future Stars, "NY" on shirt, correct photo.)	.20
19	Mark Davidson RC	.05
20	Kevin Gross	.05
21	Red Sox Leaders (Wade Boggs, Spike Owen)	.10
22	Greg Swindell	.05
23	Ken Landreaux	.05
24	Jim Deshaies	.05
25	Andres Galarraga	.05
26	Mitch Williams	.05
27	R.J. Reynolds	.05
28	Jose Nunez RC	.05
29	Argenis Salazar	.05
30	Sid Fernandez	.05
31	Bruce Bochy	.05
32	Mike Morgan	.05
33	Rob Deer	.05
34	Ricky Horton	.05
35	Harold Baines	.05
36	Jamie Moyer	.05
37	Ed Romero	.05
38	Jeff Calhoun	.05
39	Gerald Perry	.05
40	Orel Hershiser	.05
41	Bob Melvin	.05
42	Bill Landrum RC	.05
43	Dick Schofield	.05
44	Lou Piniella	.05
45	Kent Hrbek	.05
46	Darnell Coles	.05
47	Joaquin Andujar	.05
48	Alan Ashby	.05
49	Dave Clark RC	.05
50	Hubie Brooks	.05
51	Orioles Leaders (Eddie Murray, Cal Ripken, Jr.)	.25
52	Don Robinson	.05
53	Curt Wilkerson	.05
54	Jim Clancy	.05
55	Phil Bradley	.05
56	Ed Hearn	.05
57	Tim Crews RC	.05
58	Dave Magadan	.05
59	Danny Cox	.05
60	Rickey Henderson	.05
61	Mark Knudson RC	.05
62	Jeff Hamilton	.05
63	Jimmy Jones RC	.05
64	Ken Caminiti RC	.25
65	Leon Durham	.05
66	Shane Rawley	.05
67	Ken Oberkfell	.05
68	Dave Dravecky	.05
69	Mike Hart RC	.05
70	Roger Clemens	.60
71	Gary Pettis	.05
72	Dennis Eckersley	.30
73	Randy Bush	.05
74	Tom Lasorda	.05
75	Joe Carter	.05
76	Denny Martinez	.05
77	Tom O'Malley	.05
78	Dan Petry	.05
79	Ernie Whitt	.05
80	Mark Langston	.05
81	Reds Leaders (John Franco, Ron Robinson)	.05
82	Darrel Akerfelds RC	.05
83	Jose Oquendo	.05
84	Cecilio Guante	.05
85	Howard Johnson	.05
86	Ron Karkovice	.05
87	Mike Mason	.05
88	Earnie Riles	.05
89	Gary Thurman RC	.05
90	Dale Murphy	.20
91	Joey Cora RC	.10
92	Len Matuszek	.05
93	Bob Sebra	.05
94	Chuck Jackson RC	.05
95	Lance Parrish	.05
96	Todd Benzinger RC	.05
97	Scott Garrelts	.05
98	Rene Gonzales RC	.05
99	Chuck Finley	.05
100	Jack Clark	.05
101	Allan Anderson	.05
102	Barry Larkin	.05
103	Curt Young	.05
104	Dick Williams	.05
105	Jesse Orosco	.05
106	Jim Walewander RC	.05
107	Scott Bailes	.05
108	Steve Lyons	.05
109	Joel Skinner	.05
110	Teddy Higuera	.05
111	Expos Leaders (Hubie Brooks, Vance Law)	.05
112	Les Lancaster RC	.05
113	Kelly Gruber	.05
114	Jeff Russell	.05
115	Johnny Ray	.05
116	Jerry Don Gleaton	.05
117	James Steels RC	.05
118	Bob Welch	.05
119	Robbie Wine RC	.05
120	Kirby Puckett	.50
121	Checklist 1-132	.05
122	Tony Bernazard	.05
123	Tom Candiotti	.05
124	Ray Knight	.05
125	Bruce Hurst	.05
126	Steve Jeltz	.05
127	Jim Gott	.05
128	Johnny Grubb	.05
129	Greg Minton	.05
130	Buddy Bell	.05
131	Don Schulze	.05
132	Donnie Hill	.05
133	Greg Mathews	.05
134	Chuck Tanner	.05
135	Dennis Rasmussen	.05
136	Brian Dayett	.05
137	Chris Bosio	.05
138	Mitch Webster	.05
139	Jerry Browne	.05
140	Jesse Barfield	.05
141	Royals Leaders (George Brett, Bret Saberhagen)	.20
142	Andy Van Slyke	.05
143	Mickey Tettleton	.05
144	Don Gordon RC	.05
145	Bill Madlock	.05
146	Donell Nixon RC	.05
147	Bill Buckner	.05
148	Carmelo Martinez	.05
149	Ken Howell	.05
150	Eric Davis	.05
151	Bob Knepper	.05
152	Jody Reed RC	.10
153	John Habyan	.05
154	Jeff Stone	.05
155	Bruce Sutter	.30
156	Gary Matthews	.05
157	Atlee Hammaker	.05
158	Tim Hulett	.05
159	Brad Arnsberg RC	.05
160	Willie McGee	.05
161	Bryn Smith	.05
162	Mark McLemore	.05
163	Dale Mohorcic	.05
164	Dave Johnson	.05
165	Robin Yount	.40
166	Rick Rodriguez RC	.05
167	Rance Mulliniks	.05
168	Barry Jones	.05
169	Ross Jones RC	.05
170	Rich Gossage	.05
171	Cubs Leaders (Shawon Dunston, Manny Trillo)	.05
172	Lloyd McClendon RC	.05
173	Eric Plunk	.05
174	Phil Garner	.05
175	Kevin Bass	.05
176	Jeff Reed	.05
177	Frank Tanana	.05
178	Dwayne Henry RC	.05
179	Charlie Puleo	.05
180	Terry Kennedy	.05
181	Dave Cone	.05
182	Ken Phelps	.05
183	Tom Lawless	.05
184	Ivan Calderon	.05
185	Rick Rhoden	.35
186	Rafael Palmeiro	.35
187	Steve Kiefer RC	.05
188	John Russell	.05
189	Wes Gardner RC	.05
190	Candy Maldonado	.05
191	John Cerutti	.05
192	Devon White	.05
193	Brian Fisher	.05
194	Tom Kelly	.05
195	Dan Quisenberry	.05
196	Dave Engle	.05
197	Lance McCullers	.05
198	Franklin Stubbs	.05
199	Dave Meads RC	.05
200	Wade Boggs	.50
201	Rangers Leaders (Steve Buechele, Pete Incaviglia, Pete O'Brien, Bobby Valentine)	.05
202	Glenn Hoffman	.05
203	Fred Toliver	.05
204	Paul O'Neill RC	.05
205	Nelson Liriano RC	.05
206	Domingo Ramos	.05
207	John Mitchell RC	.05
208	Steve Lake	.05
209	Richard Dotson	.05
210	Willie Randolph	.05
211	Frank DiPino	.05
212	Greg Brock	.05
213	Albert Hall	.05
214	Dave Schmidt	.05
215	Von Hayes	.05
216	Jerry Reuss	.05
217	Harry Spilman	.05
218	Dan Schatzeder	.05
219	Mike Stanley	.05
220	Tom Henke	.05
221	Rafael Belliard	.05
222	Steve Farr	.05
223	Stan Jefferson	.05
224	Tom Trebelhorn	.05
225	Mike Scioscia	.05
226	Dave Lopes	.05
227	Ed Correa	.05
228	Wallace Johnson	.05
229	Jeff Musselman	.05
230	Pat Tabler	.05
231	Pirates Leaders (Barry Bonds, Bobby Bonilla)	.50
232	Bob James	.05
233	Rafael Santana	.05
234	Ken Dayley	.05
235	Gary Ward	.05
236	Ted Power	.05
237	Mike Heath	.05
238	Luis Polonia RC	.10
239	Roy Smalley	.05
240	Lee Smith	.05
241	Damaso Garcia	.05
242	Tom Niedenfuer	.05
243	Mark Ryal RC	.05
244	Jeff Robinson	.05
245	Rich Gedman	.05
246	Mike Campbell RC (Future Stars)	.05
247	Thad Bosley	.05
248	Storm Davis	.05
249	Mike Marshall	.05
250	Nolan Ryan	.75
251	Tom Foley	.05
252	Bob Brower	.05
253	Checklist 133-264	.05
254	Lee Elia	.05
255	Mookie Wilson	.05
256	Ken Schrom	.05
257	Jerry Royster	.05
258	Ed Nunez	.05
259	Ron Kittle	.05
260	Vince Coleman	.05
261	Giants Leaders (Will Clark, Candy Maldonado, Kevin Mitchell, Robby Thompson, Jose Uribe)	.05
262	Drew Hall RC	.05
263	Glenn Braggs	.05
264	Les Straker RC	.05
265	Bo Diaz	.05
266	Paul Assenmacher	.05
267	Billy Bean RC	.05
268	Bruce Ruffin	.05
269	Ellis Burks	.05
270	Mike Witt	.05
271	Ken Gerhart	.05
272	Steve Ontiveros	.05
273	Garth Iorg	.05
274	Junior Ortiz	.05
275	Kevin Seitzer	.05
276	Luis Salazar	.05
277	Alejandro Pena	.05
278	Jose Cruz	.05
279	Randy St. Claire	.05
280	Pete Incaviglia	.05
281	Jerry Hairston Sr.	.05
282	Pat Perry	.05
283	Phil Lombardi RC	.05
284	Larry Bowa	.05

No.	Player	Price
285	Jim Presley	.05
286	Chuck Crim RC	.05
287	Manny Trillo	.05
288	Pat Pacillo RC	.05
289	Dave Bergman	.05
290	Tony Fernandez	.05
291	Astros Leaders (Kevin Bass, Billy Hatcher)	.05
292	Carney Lansford	.05
293	Doug Jones RC	.05
294	Al Pedrique RC	.05
295	Bert Blyleven	.05
296	Floyd Rayford	.05
297	Zane Smith	.05
298	Milt Thompson	.05
299	Steve Crawford	.05
300	Don Mattingly	.60
301	Bud Black	.05
302	Jose Uribe	.05
303	Eric Show	.05
304	George Hendrick	.05
305	Steve Sax	.05
306	Billy Hatcher	.05
307	Mike Trujillo	.05
308	Lee Mazzilli	.05
309	Bill Long RC	.05
310	Tom Herr	.05
311	Scott Sanderson	.05
312	Joey Meyer RC (Future Stars)	.05
313	Bob McClure	.05
314	Jimy Williams	.05
315	Dave Parker	.05
316	Jose Rijo	.05
317	Tom Nieto	.05
318	Mel Hall	.05
319	Mike Loynd	.05
320	Alan Trammell	.05
321	White Sox Leaders (Harold Baines, Carlton Fisk)	.05
322	Vicente Palacios RC	.05
323	Rick Leach	.05
324	Danny Jackson	.05
325	Glenn Hubbard	.05
326	Al Nipper	.05
327	Larry Sheets	.05
328	Greg Cadaret RC	.05
329	Chris Speier	.05
330	Eddie Whitson	.05
331	Brian Downing	.05
332	Jerry Reed	.05
333	Wally Backman	.05
334	Dave LaPoint	.05
335	Claudell Washington	.05
336	Ed Lynch	.05
337	Jim Gantner	.05
338	Brian Holton	.05
339	Kurt Stillwell	.05
340	Jack Morris	.05
341	Carmen Castillo	.05
342	Larry Andersen	.05
343	Greg Gagne	.05
344	Tony LaRussa	.05
345	Scott Fletcher	.05
346	Vance Law	.05
347	Joe Johnson	.05
348	Jim Eisenreich	.05
349	Bob Walk	.05
350	Will Clark	.05
351	Cardinals Leaders (Tony Pena, Red Schoendienst)	.05
352	Billy Ripken RC	.05
353	Ed Olwine	.05
354	Marc Sullivan	.05
355	Roger McDowell	.05
356	Luis Aguayo	.05
357	Floyd Bannister	.05
358	Rey Quinones	.05
359	Tim Stoddard	.05
360	Tony Gwynn	.50
361	Greg Maddux	.50
362	Juan Castillo	.05
363	Willie Fraser	.05
364	Nick Esasky	.05
365	Floyd Youmans	.05
366	Chet Lemon	.05
367	Tim Leary	.05
368	Gerald Young RC	.05
369	Greg Harris	.05
370	Jose Canseco	.25
371	Joe Hesketh	.05
372	Matt Williams	.05
373	Checklist 265-396	.05
374	Doc Edwards	.05
375	Tom Brunansky	.05
376	Bill Wilkinson RC	.05
377	Sam Horn RC	.05
378	Todd Frohwirth RC	.05
379	Rafael Ramirez	.05
380	Joe Magrane RC	.05
381	Angels Leaders (Jack Howell, Wally Joyner)	.05
382	Keith Miller RC	.05
383	Eric Bell	.05
384	Neil Allen	.05
385	Carlton Fisk	.40
386	Don Mattingly/AS	.30
387	Willie Randolph/AS	.05
388	Wade Boggs/AS	.20
389	Alan Trammell/AS	.05
390	George Bell/AS	.05
391	Kirby Puckett/AS	.20
392	Dave Winfield/AS	.20
393	Matt Nokes/AS	.05
394	Roger Clemens/AS	.35
395	Jimmy Key/AS	.05
396	Tom Henke/AS	.05
397	Jack Clark/AS	.05
398	Juan Samuel/AS	.05
399	Tim Wallach/AS	.05
400	Ozzie Smith/AS	.25
401	Andre Dawson/AS	.15
402	Tony Gwynn/AS	.25
403	Tim Raines/AS	.05
404	Benny Santiago/AS	.05
405	Dwight Gooden/AS	.05
406	Shane Rawley/AS	.05
407	Steve Bedrosian/AS	.05
408	Dion James	.05
409	Joel McKeon RC	.05
410	Tony Pena	.05
411	Wayne Tolleson	.05
412	Randy Myers	.05
413	John Christensen	.05
414	John McNamara	.05
415	Don Carman	.05
416	Keith Moreland	.05
417	Mark Ciardi RC	.05
418	Joel Youngblood	.05
419	Scott McGregor	.05
420	Wally Joyner	.05
421	Ed Vande Berg	.05
422	Dave Concepcion	.05
423	John Smiley	.05
424	Dwayne Murphy	.05
425	Jeff Reardon	.05
426	Randy Ready	.05
427	Paul Kilgus RC	.05
428	John Shelby	.05
429	Tigers Leaders (Kirk Gibson, Alan Trammell)	.05
430	Glenn Davis	.05
431	Casey Candaele	.05
432	Mike Moore	.05
433	Bill Pecota RC	.05
434	Rick Aguilera	.05
435	Mike Pagliarulo	.05
436	Mike Bielecki	.05
437	Fred Manrique RC	.05
438	Rob Ducey RC	.05
439	Dave Martinez	.05
440	Steve Bedrosian	.05
441	Rick Manning	.05
442	Tom Bolton RC	.05
443	Ken Griffey	.05
444	Cal Ripken, Sr.	.05
445	Mark Krukow	.05
446	Doug DeCinces	.05
447	Jeff Montgomery RC	.20
448	Mike Davis	.05
449	Jeff Robinson RC	.05
450	Barry Bonds	.75
451	Keith Atherton	.05
452	Willie Wilson	.05
453	Dennis Powell	.05
454	Marvell Wynne	.05
455	Shawn Hillegas RC	.05
456	Dave Anderson	.05
457	Terry Leach	.05
458	Ron Hassey	.05
459	Yankees Leaders (Willie Randolph, Dave Winfield)	.05
460	Ozzie Smith	.50
461	Danny Darwin	.05
462	Don Slaught	.05
463	Fred McGriff	.05
464	Jay Tibbs	.05
465	Paul Molitor	.40
466	Jerry Mumphrey	.05
467	Don Aase	.05
468	Darren Daulton	.05
469	Jeff Dedmon	.05
470	Dwight Evans	.05
471	Donnie Moore	.05
472	Robby Thompson	.05
473	Joe Niekro	.05
474	Tom Brookens	.05
475	Pete Rose	.65
476	Dave Stewart	.05
477	Jamie Quirk	.05
478	Sid Bream	.05
479	Brett Butler	.05
480	Dwight Gooden	.05
481	Mariano Duncan	.05
482	Mark Davis	.05
483	Rod Booker RC	.05
484	Pat Clements	.05
485	Harold Reynolds	.05
486	Pat Keedy RC	.05
487	Jim Pankovits	.05
488	Andy McGaffigan	.05
489	Dodgers Leaders (Pedro Guerrero, Fernando Valenzuela)	.05
490	Larry Parrish	.05
491	B.J. Surhoff	.05
492	Doyle Alexander	.05
493	Mike Greenwell	.05
494	Wally Ritchie RC	.05
495	Eddie Murray	.40
496	Guy Hoffman	.05
497	Kevin Mitchell	.05
498	Bob Boone	.05
499	Eric King	.05
500	Andre Dawson	.25
501	Tim Birtsas RC	.05
502	Danny Gladden	.05
503	Junior Noboa RC	.05
504	Bob Rodgers	.05
505	Willie Upshaw	.05
506	John Cangelosi	.05
507	Mark Gubicza	.05
508	Tim Teufel	.05
509	Bill Dawley	.05
510	Dave Winfield	.40
511	Joel Davis	.05
512	Alex Trevino	.05
513	Tim Flannery	.05
514	Pat Sheridan	.05
515	Juan Nieves	.05
516	Jim Sundberg	.05
517	Ron Robinson	.05
518	Greg Gross	.05
519	Mariners Leaders (Phil Bradley, Harold Reynolds)	.05
520	Dave Smith	.05
521	Jim Dwyer	.05
522	Bob Patterson RC	.05
523	Gary Roenicke	.05
524	Gary Lucas	.05
525	Marty Barrett	.05
526	Juan Berenguer	.05
527	Steve Henderson	.05
528a	Checklist 397-528 (#455 is Steve Carlton)	.05
528b	Checklist 397-528 (#455 is Shawn Hillegas)	.05
529	Tim Burke	.05
530	Gary Carter	.40
531	Rich Yett	.05
532	Mike Kingery	.05
533	John Farrell RC	.05
534	John Wathan	.05
535	Ron Guidry	.05
536	John Morris	.05
537	Steve Buechele	.05
538	Bill Wegman	.05
539	Mike LaValliere	.05
540	Bret Saberhagen	.05
541	Juan Beniquez	.05
542	Paul Noce RC	.05
543	Kent Tekulve	.05
544	Jim Traber	.05
545	Don Baylor	.05
546	John Candelaria	.05
547	Felix Fermin RC	.05
548	Shane Mack	.05
549	Braves Leaders (Ken Griffey, Dion James, Dale Murphy, Gerald Perry)	.05
550	Pedro Guerrero	.05
551	Terry Steinbach	.05
552	Mark Thurmond	.05
553	Tracy Jones	.05
554	Mike Smithson	.05
555	Brook Jacoby	.05
556	Stan Clarke RC	.05
557	Craig Reynolds	.05
558	Bob Ojeda	.05
559	Ken Williams RC	.05
560	Tim Wallach	.05
561	Rick Cerone	.05
562	Jim Lindeman	.05
563	Jose Guzman	.05
564	Frank Lucchesi	.05
565	Lloyd Moseby	.05
566	Charlie O'Brien RC	.05
567	Mike Diaz	.05
568	Chris Brown	.05
569	Charlie Leibrandt	.05
570	Jeffrey Leonard	.05
571	Mark Williamson RC	.05
572	Chris James	.05
573	Bob Stanley	.05
574	Graig Nettles	.05
575	Don Sutton	.30
576	Tommy Hinzo RC	.05
577	Tom Browning	.05
578	Gary Gaetti	.05
579	Mets Leaders (Gary Carter, Kevin McReynolds)	.05
580	Mark McGwire	.65
581	Tito Landrum	.05
582	Mike Henneman	.05
583	Dave Valle	.05
584	Steve Trout	.05
585	Ozzie Guillen	.05
586	Bob Forsch	.05
587	Terry Puhl	.05
588	Jeff Parrett RC	.05
589	Geno Petralli	.05
590	George Bell	.05
591	Doug Drabek	.05
592	Dale Sveum	.05
593	Bob Tewksbury	.05
594	Bobby Valentine	.05
595	Frank White	.05
596	John Kruk	.05
597	Gene Garber	.05
598	Lee Lacy	.05
599	Calvin Schiraldi	.05
600	Mike Schmidt	.60
601	Jack Lazorko	.05
602	Mike Aldrete	.05
603	Rob Murphy	.05
604	Chris Bando	.05
605	Kirk Gibson	.05
606	Moose Haas	.05
607	Mickey Hatcher	.05
608	Charlie Kerfeld	.05
609	Twins Leaders (Gary Gaetti, Kent Hrbek)	.05
610	Keith Hernandez	.05
611	Tommy John	.05
612	Curt Ford	.05
613	Bobby Thigpen	.05
614	Herm Winningham	.05
615	Jody Davis	.05
616	Jay Aldrich RC	.05
617	Oddibe McDowell	.05
618	Cecil Fielder	.05
619	Mike Dunne RC	.05
620	Cory Snyder	.05
621	Gene Nelson	.05
622	Kal Daniels	.05
623	Mike Flanagan	.05
624	Jim Leyland	.05
625	Frank Viola	.05
626	Glenn Wilson	.05
627	Joe Boever RC	.05
628	Dave Henderson	.05
629	Kelly Downs	.05
630	Darrell Evans	.05
631	Jack Howell	.05
632	Steve Shields RC	.05
633	Barry Lyons RC	.05
634	Jose DeLeon	.05
635	Terry Pendleton	.05
636	Charles Hudson	.05
637	Jay Bell RC	.25
638	Steve Balboni	.05
639	Brewers Leaders (Glenn Braggs, Tony Muser)	.05
640	Garry Templeton	.05
641	Rick Honeycutt	.05
642	Bob Dernier	.05
643	Rocky Childress RC	.05
644	Terry McGriff RC	.05
645	Matt Nokes	.05
646	Checklist 529-660	.05
647	Pascual Perez	.05
648	Al Newman	.05
649	DeWayne Buice RC	.05
650	Cal Ripken, Jr.	.75
651	Mike Jackson RC	.05
652	Bruce Benedict	.05
653	Jeff Sellers	.05
654	Roger Craig	.05
655	Len Dykstra	.05
656	Lee Guetterman	.05
657	Gary Redus	.05
658	Tim Conroy	.05
659	Bobby Meacham	.05
660	Rick Reuschel	.05
661	Nolan Ryan (Turn Back the Clock)	.35
662	Jim Rice (Turn Back the Clock)	.05
663	Ron Blomberg (Turn Back the Clock)	.05
664	Bob Gibson (Turn Back the Clock)	.10
665	Stan Musial (Turn Back the Clock)	.20
666	Mario Soto	.05
667	Luis Quinones	.05
668	Walt Terrell	.05
669	Phillies Leaders (Lance Parrish, Mike Ryan)	.05
670	Dan Plesac	.05
671	Tim Laudner	.05
672	John Davis RC	.05
673	Tony Phillips	.05
674	Mike Fitzgerald	.05
675	Jim Rice	.20
676	Ken Dixon	.05
677	Eddie Milner	.05
678	Jim Acker	.05
679	Darrell Miller	.05
680	Charlie Hough	.05
681	Bobby Bonilla	.05
682	Jimmy Key	.05
683	Julio Franco	.05
684	Hal Lanier	.05
685	Ron Darling	.05
686	Terry Francona	.05
687	Mickey Brantley	.05
688	Jim Winn	.05
689	Tom Pagnozzi RC	.05
690	Jay Howell	.05
691	Dan Pasqua	.05
692	Mike Birkbeck	.05
693	Benny Santiago	.05
694	Eric Nolte RC	.05
695	Shawon Dunston	.05
696	Duane Ward	.05
697	Steve Lombardozzi	.05
698	Brad Havens	.05
699	Padres Leaders (Tony Gwynn, Benny Santiago)	.15
700	George Brett	.60
701	Sammy Stewart	.05
702	Mike Gallego	.05
703	Bob Brenly	.05
704	Dennis Boyd	.05
705	Juan Samuel	.05
706	Rick Mahler	.05
707	Fred Lynn	.05
708	Gus Polidor RC	.05
709	George Frazier	.05
710	Darryl Strawberry	.05
711	Bill Gullickson	.05
712	John Moses	.05
713	Willie Hernandez	.05
714	Jim Fregosi	.05
715	Todd Worrell	.05
716	Lenn Sakata	.05
717	Jay Baller RC	.05
718	Mike Felder	.05
719	Denny Walling	.05
720	Tim Raines	.05
721	Pete O'Brien	.05
722	Manny Lee	.05
723	Bob Kipper	.05
724	Danny Tartabull	.05
725	Mike Boddicker	.05
726	Alfredo Griffin	.05
727	Greg Booker	.05
728	Andy Allanson	.05
729	Blue Jays Leaders (George Bell, Fred McGriff)	.05
730	John Franco	.05
731	Rick Schu	.05
732	Dave Palmer	.05
733	Spike Owen	.05
734	Craig Lefferts	.05
735	Kevin McReynolds	.05
736	Matt Young	.05
737	Butch Wynegar	.05
738	Scott Bankhead	.05
739	Daryl Boston	.05
740	Rick Sutcliffe	.05
741	Mike Easler	.05
742	Mark Clear	.05
743	Larry Herndon	.05
744	Whitey Herzog	.05
745	Bill Doran	.05
746	Gene Larkin RC	.05
747	Bobby Witt	.05
748	Reid Nichols	.05
749	Mark Eichhorn	.05
750	Bo Jackson	.10
751	Jim Morrison	.05
752	Mark Grant	.05
753	Danny Heep	.05
754	Mike LaCoss	.05
755	Ozzie Virgil	.05
756	Mike Maddux	.05
757	John Marzano RC	.05
758	Eddie Williams RC	.05
759	A's Leaders (Jose Canseco, Mark McGwire)	.35
760	Mike Scott	.05
761	Tony Armas	.05
762	Scott Bradley	.05
763	Doug Sisk	.05
764	Greg Walker	.05
765	Neal Heaton	.05
766	Henry Cotto	.05
767	Jose Lind RC (Future Stars)	.10
768	Dickie Noles	.05
769	Cecil Cooper	.05
770	Lou Whitaker	.05
771	Ruben Sierra	.05
772	Sal Butera	.05
773	Frank Williams	.05
774	Gene Mauch	.05
775	Dave Stieb	.05
776	Checklist 661-792	.05
777	Lonnie Smith	.05
778a	Keith Comstock RC (White team letters.)	.40
778b	Keith Comstock RC (Blue team letters, white name.)	.10
778c	Keith Comstock RC (Blue team letters, yellow name.)	2.00
779	Tom Glavine RC	1.50
780	Fernando Valenzuela	.05
781	Keith Hughes RC	.05
782	Jeff Ballard RC	.05
783	Ron Roenicke	.05
784	Joe Sambito	.05
785	Alvin Davis	.05
786	Joe Price	.05
787	Bill Almon	.05
788	Ray Searage	.05
789	Indians Leaders (Joe Carter, Cory Snyder)	.05
790	Dave Righetti	.05
791	Ted Simmons	.05
792	John Tudor	.05

Tiffany

Sharing a checklist with the regular issue 1988 Topps baseball set, this specially boxed, limited-edition (25,000 sets) features cards printed on white cardboard stock with high-gloss front finish. Topps offered the sets directly to the public in ads in USA Today and Sporing News at a price of $99.

	NM/M
Complete Set (792):	40.00
Common Player:	.15

Traded

In addition to new players and traded veterans, 21 members of U.S.A. Olympic Baseball team are showcased in this 132-card set, numbered 1T-132T. The 2-1/2" x 3-1/2" cards follow the same design as the basic Topps issue - white borders, large full-color photos, team name (or U.S.A.) in large bold letters at the top of the card face, player name on a diagonal stripe across the lower-right corner. Topps had issued its traded series each year since 1981 in boxed complete sets available only through hobby dealers.

	NM/M
Complete Set (132):	5.00
Common Player:	.05

No.	Player	Price
1	Jim Abbott RC (USA)	.25
2	Juan Agosto	.05
3	Luis Alicea RC	.05
4	Roberto Alomar RC	1.50
5	Brady Anderson RC	.25
6	Jack Armstrong	.05
7	Don August	.05
8	Floyd Bannister	.05
9	Bret Barberie (USA)	.05
10	Jose Bautista RC	.05
11	Don Baylor	.05
12	Tim Belcher	.05
13	Buddy Bell	.05
14	Andy Benes RC (USA)	.25
15	Damon Berryhill	.05
16	Bud Black	.05
17	Pat Borders	.05
18	Phil Bradley	.05
19	Jeff Branson RC (USA)	.05
20	Tom Brunansky	.05
21	Jay Buhner RC	.75
22	Brett Butler	.05
23	Jim Campanis RC (USA)	.05
24	Sil Campusano RC	.05
25	John Candelaria	.05
26	Jose Cecena RC	.05
27	Rick Cerone	.05
28	Jack Clark	.05
29	Kevin Coffman RC	.05
30	Pat Combs (USA)	.05
31	Henry Cotto	.05
32	Chili Davis	.05
33	Mike Davis	.05
34	Jose DeLeon	.05
35	Richard Dotson	.05
36	Cecil Espy	.05
37	Tom Filer	.05
38	Mike Fiore RC (USA)	.05
39	Ron Gant RC	.25
40	Kirk Gibson	.05
41	Rich Gossage	.05
42	Mark Grace RC	1.00
43	Alfredo Griffin	.05
44	Ty Griffin RC (USA)	.05
45	Bryan Harvey	.05
46	Ron Hassey	.05
47	Ray Hayward RC	.05
48	Dave Henderson	.05
49	Tom Herr	.05
50	Bob Horner	.05
51	Ricky Horton	.05
52	Jay Howell	.05
53	Glenn Hubbard	.05
54	Jeff Innis RC	.05
55	Danny Jackson	.05
56	Darrin Jackson	.05
57	Roberto Kelly	.05
58	Ron Kittle	.05
59	Ray Knight	.05
60	Vance Law	.05
61	Jeffrey Leonard	.05
62	Mike Macfarlane RC	.05
63	Scotti Madison RC	.05
64	Kirt Manwaring RC	.05
65	Mark Marquess (USA)	.05
66	Tino Martinez RC (USA)	.75
67	Billy Masse RC (USA)	.05
68	Jack McDowell RC	.25
69	Jack McKeon	.05
70	Larry McWilliams	.05
71	Mickey Morandini (USA)	.05
72	Keith Moreland	.05
73	Mike Morgan	.05
74	Charles Nagy (USA)	.10
75	Al Nipper	.05
76	Russ Nixon	.05
77	Jesse Orosco	.05
78	Joe Orsulak	.05
79	Dave Palmer	.05
80	Mark Parent RC	.05
81	Dave Parker	.05
82	Dan Pasqua	.05
83	Melido Perez	.05
84	Steve Peters RC	.05
85	Dan Petry	.05
86	Gary Pettis	.05
87	Jeff Pico RC	.05
88	Jim Poole (USA)	.05
89	Ted Power	.05
90	Rafael Ramirez	.05
91	Dennis Rasmussen	.05
92	Jose Rijo	.05
93	Earnie Riles	.05
94	Luis Rivera RC	.05
95	Doug Robbins RC (USA)	.05
96	Frank Robinson	.05
97	Cookie Rojas	.05

98	Chris Sabo RC	.10
99	Mark Salas	.05
100	Luis Salazar	.05
101	Rafael Santana	.05
102	Nelson Santovenia RC	.05
103	Mackey Sasser RC	.05
104	Calvin Schiraldi	.05
105	Mike Schooler RC	.05
106	Scott Servais RC (USA)	.05
107	Dave Silvestri (USA)	.05
108	Don Slaught	.05
109	Joe Slusarski RC (USA)	.10
110	Lee Smith	.05
111	Pete Smith RC	.05
112	Jim Snyder	.05
113	Ed Sprague RC (USA)	.10
114	Pete Stanicek RC	.05
115	Kurt Stillwell	.05
116	Todd Stottlemyre	.05
117	Bill Swift	.05
118	Pat Tabler	.05
119	Scott Terry RC	.05
120	Mickey Tettleton	.05
121	Dickie Thon	.05
122	Jeff Treadway	.05
123	Willie Upshaw	.05
124	Robin Ventura RC	.25
125	Ron Washington	.05
126	Walt Weiss RC	.05
127	Bob Welch	.05
128	David Wells RC	.25
129	Glenn Wilson	.05
130	Ted Wood RC (USA)	.05
131	Don Zimmer	.05
132	Checklist 1T-132T	.05

Traded Tiffany

The high-gloss front surface is all that distinguishes this limited-edition, hobby-only collectors version from the regular Topps Traded boxed set.

	NM/M
Complete Set (132):	25.00
Common Player:	.15

Traded Duke Snider Bronze

This 1/4-size metal replica was issued to dealers who purchased cases of 1988 Topps Traded sets. Each detail of the 1955 Topps Snider card is reproduced on the 1-3/4" x 1-1/4" bronze metal mini-card, right down to the stats.

		NM/M
210	Duke Snider	7.50

Box Panels

After a one-year hiatus during which they appeared on the sides of Topps wax pack display boxes, Topps retail box cards returned to box bottoms in 1988. The series includes 16 standard-size baseball cards, four cards per each of four different display boxes. Card fronts follow the same design as the 1988 Topps basic issue; full-color player photos, framed in yellow, surrounded by a white border; diagonal player name lower-right; team name in large letters at the top. Card backs are "numbered" A through P and are printed in black and orange.

		NM/M
Complete Panel Set (4):		3.00
Complete Singles Set (16):		3.00
Common Panel:		.50
Common Single Player:		.10
Panel		.50
A	Don Baylor	.10
B	Steve Bedrosian	.10
C	Juan Beniquez	.10
D	Bob Boone	.10
Panel		.75
E	Darrell Evans	.10
F	Tony Gwynn	.50
G	John Kruk	.10
H	Marvell Wynne	.10
Panel		.60
I	Joe Carter	.10
J	Eric Davis	.10
K	Howard Johnson	.10
L	Darryl Strawberry	.10
Panel		2.00
M	Rickey Henderson	.40
N	Nolan Ryan	.75
O	Mike Schmidt	.75
P	Kent Tekulve	.10

All-Star Glossy Set of 22

1987 ALL-STAR DON MATTINGLY 1B

The fifth edition of Topps' special All-Star inserts was included in the company's 1988 rack packs. The 1987 American and National League All-Star lineup, plus honorary captains Jim Hunter and Billy Williams, are featured on the 2-1/2" x 3-1/2" cards. The glossy full-color fronts contain player photos centered between a red and yellow "1987 All-Star" logo at top and the player name (also red and yellow) which is printed in the bottom margin. A league logo is in the lower-left corner. Card backs are printed in red and blue on a white background, with the title and All-Star logo emblem printed above the player name and card number.

		NM/M
Complete Set (22):		3.00
Common Player:		.05
1	John McNamara	.05
2	Don Mattingly	.75
3	Willie Randolph	.05
4	Wade Boggs	.65
5	Cal Ripken, Jr.	1.00
6	George Bell	.05
7	Rickey Henderson	.50
8	Dave Winfield	.50
9	Terry Kennedy	.05
10	Bret Saberhagen	.05
11	Catfish Hunter	.05
12	Davey Johnson	.05
13	Jack Clark	.05
14	Ryne Sandberg	.65
15	Mike Schmidt	.75
16	Ozzie Smith	.65
17	Eric Davis	.05
18	Andre Dawson	.20
19	Darryl Strawberry	.05
20	Gary Carter	.50
21	Mike Scott	.05
22	Billy Williams	.05

All-Star Glossy Set of 60

This collectors' set includes 60 full-color glossy cards featuring All-Stars and Prospects in six separate 10-card sets. Card fronts have a white border and a thin red line framing the player photo, with the player's name in the lower-left corner. Backs, in red and blue, include basic player identification along with the set logo and card number. Sets were marketed via a special offer printed on a card packaged in all Topps wax packs. For six special offer cards and $1.25, collectors received one of the six 10-card sets; 18 special offer cards and $7.50 earned the entire 60-card collection.

		NM/M
Complete Set (60):		4.00
Common Player:		.10
1	Andre Dawson	.20
2	Jesse Barfield	.10
3	Mike Schmidt	.75
4	Ruben Sierra	.10
5	Mike Scott	.10
6	Cal Ripken, Jr.	1.00
7	Gary Carter	.50
8	Kent Hrbek	.10
9	Kevin Seitzer	.10
10	Mike Henneman	.10
11	Don Mattingly	.65
12	Tim Raines	.10
13	Roger Clemens	.65
14	Ryne Sandberg	.60
15	Tony Fernandez	.10
16	Eric Davis	.10
17	Jack Morris	.10
18	Tim Wallach	.10
19	Mike Dunne	.10
20	Mike Greenwell	.10
21	Dwight Evans	.10
22	Darryl Strawberry	.10
23	Cory Snyder	.10
24	Pedro Guerrero	.10
25	Rickey Henderson	.50
26	Dale Murphy	.20
27	Kirby Puckett	.60
28	Steve Bedrosian	.10
29	Devon White	.10
30	Benny Santiago	.10
31	George Bell	.10
32	Keith Hernandez	.10
33	Dave Stewart	.10
34	Dave Parker	.10
35	Tom Henke	.10
36	Willie McGee	.10
37	Alan Trammell	.10
38	Tony Gwynn	.60
39	Mark McGwire	.85
40	Joe Magrane	.10
41	Jack Clark	.10
42	Willie Randolph	.10
43	Juan Samuel	.10
44	Joe Carter	.10
45	Shane Rawley	.10
46	Dave Winfield	.50
47	Ozzie Smith	.60
48	Wally Joyner	.10
49	B.J. Surhoff	.10
50	Ellis Burks	.10
51	Wade Boggs	.60
52	Howard Johnson	.10
53	George Brett	.75
54	Dwight Gooden	.10
55	Jose Canseco	.35
56	Lee Smith	.10
57	Paul Molitor	.50
58	Andres Galarraga	.10
59	Matt Nokes	.10
60	Casey Candaele	.10

American Baseball

BOSTON RED SOX — DWIGHT EVANS OF/1B

This set, ostensibly issued for sale in the United Kingdom, was also made available for distribution by U.S. hobby dealers. Cards were packaged in checklist-backed boxes with an American flag on the top flap. The 2-1/4" x 3" cards feature full-color photos printed on white stock. The team name, printed in team colors, intersects the red frame at the top of the card. A yellow name banner appears below the photo. Backs have blue borders and cartoon-style horizontal layouts which include a team logo, stats, caricature of the player and a one-line caption. Below the cartoon, a short "Talkin' Baseball" paragraph provides elementary information, designed to acquaint soccer-playing European collectors with baseball rules and terminology. Uncut sheets of all 88 cards are not uncommon.

		NM/M
Complete Set (88):		6.00
Common Player:		.05
Uncut Sheet:		12.00
Wax Box (48):		7.50
1	Harold Baines	.05
2	Steve Bedrosian	.05
3	George Bell	.05
4	Wade Boggs	.60
5	Barry Bonds	1.00
6	Bob Boone	.05
7	George Brett	.75
8	Hubie Brooks	.05
9	Ivan Calderon	.05
10	Jose Canseco	.35
11	Gary Carter	.50
12	Joe Carter	.05
13	Jack Clark	.05
14	Will Clark	.05
15	Roger Clemens	.75
16	Vince Coleman	.05
17	Alvin Davis	.05
18	Eric Davis	.05
19	Glenn Davis	.05
20	Andre Dawson	.20
21	Mike Dunne	.05
22	Dwight Evans	.05
23	Tony Fernandez	.05
24	John Franco	.05
25	Gary Gaetti	.05
26	Kirk Gibson	.05
27	Dwight Gooden	.05
28	Pedro Guerrero	.05
29	Tony Gwynn	.60
30	Billy Hatcher	.05
31	Rickey Henderson	.50
32	Tom Henke	.05
33	Keith Hernandez	.05
34	Orel Hershiser	.05
35	Teddy Higuera	.05
36	Charlie Hough	.05
37	Kent Hrbek	.05
38	Brook Jacoby	.05
39	Dion James	.05
40	Wally Joyner	.05
41	John Kruk	.05
42	Mark Langston	.05
43	Jeffrey Leonard	.05
44	Candy Maldonaldo	.05
45	Don Mattingly	.75
46	Willie McGee	.05
47	Mark McGwire	.85
48	Kevin Mitchell	.05
49	Paul Molitor	.50
50	Jack Morris	.05
51	Lloyd Moseby	.05
52	Dale Murphy	.20
53	Eddie Murray	.50
54	Matt Nokes	.05
55	Dave Parker	.05
56	Larry Parrish	.05
57	Kirby Puckett	.60
58	Tim Raines	.05
59	Willie Randolph	.05
60	Harold Reynolds	.05
61	Cal Ripken, Jr.	1.00
62	Nolan Ryan	1.00
63	Bret Saberhagen	.05
64	Juan Samuel	.05
65	Ryne Sandberg	.60
66	Benny Santiago	.05
67	Mike Schmidt	.75
68	Mike Scott	.05
69	Kevin Seitzer	.05
70	Larry Sheets	.05
71	Ruben Sierra	.05
72	Ozzie Smith	.60
73	Zane Smith	.05
74	Cory Snyder	.05
75	Dave Stewart	.05
76	Darryl Strawberry	.05
77	Rick Sutcliffe	.05
78	Danny Tartabull	.05
79	Alan Trammell	.05
80	Fernando Valenzuela	.05
81	Andy Van Slyke	.05
82	Frank Viola	.05
83	Greg Walker	.05
84	Tim Wallach	.05
85	Dave Winfield	.50
86	Mike Witt	.05
87	Robin Yount	.50
88	Checklist	.05

American Baseball Tiffany

This glossy "Tiffany" edition of the Topps American Baseball set is a complete parallel of the regular-issue.

	NM/M
Complete Set (88):	15.00
Common Player:	.40

Big Baseball

ALAN TRAMMELL

Topps Big Baseball cards (2-5/8" x 3-3/4") were issued in three series, 88 cards per series (a total set of 264 cards) sold in seven-card packs. The glossy cards are similar in format, both front and back, to the 1956 Topps set. Each card features a portrait and a game-action photo on the front, framed by a wide white border. A white outline highlights the portrait. The player's name appears at bottom on a splash of color that fades from yellow to orange to red to pink. On the card back, the player's name is printed in large red letters across the top, followed by his team name and position in black. Personal info is printed in a red rectangle beside a Topps baseball logo bearing the card number. A triple cartoon strip, in full-color, illustrates career highlights, performance, personal background, etc. A red, white and blue statistics box (pitching, batting, fielding) is printed across the bottom.

		NM/M
Complete Set (264):		9.00
Common Player:		.05
Wax Box:		.05
Wax Pack (7):		.50
Wax Box, Series 1-3 (36):		9.00
1	Paul Molitor	.45
2	Milt Thompson	.05
3	Billy Hatcher	.05
4	Mike Witt	.05
5	Vince Coleman	.05
6	Dwight Evans	.05
7	Tim Wallach	.05
8	Alan Trammell	.05
9	Will Clark	.05
10	Jeff Reardon	.05
11	Dwight Gooden	.05
12	Benny Santiago	.05
13	Jose Canseco	.35
14	Dale Murphy	.20
15	George Bell	.05
16	Ryne Sandberg	.60
17	Brook Jacoby	.05
18	Fernando Valenzuela	.05
19	Scott Fletcher	.05
20	Eric Davis	.05
21	Willie Wilson	.05
22	B.J. Surhoff	.05
23	Steve Bedrosian	.05
24	Dave Winfield	.45
25	Bobby Bonilla	.05
26	Larry Sheets	.05
27	Ozzie Guillen	.05
28	Checklist 1-88	.05
29	Nolan Ryan	1.50
30	Bob Boone	.05
31	Tom Herr	.05
32	Wade Boggs	.60
33	Neal Heaton	.05
34	Doyle Alexander	.05
35	Candy Maldonado	.05
36	Kirby Puckett	.60
37	Gary Carter	.45
38	Lance McCullers	.05
39a	Terry Steinbach (Black Topps logo on front.)	.10
39b	Terry Steinbach (White Topps logo on front.)	.10
40	Gerald Perry	.05
41	Tom Henke	.05
42	Leon Durham	.05
43	Cory Snyder	.05
44	Dale Sveum	.05
45	Lance Parrish	.05
46	Steve Sax	.05
47	Charlie Hough	.05
48	Kal Daniels	.05
49	Bo Jackson	.10
50	Ron Guidry	.05
51	Bill Doran	.05
52	Wally Joyner	.05
53	Terry Pendleton	.05
54	Marty Barrett	.05
55	Andres Galarraga	.05
56	Larry Herndon	.05
57	Kevin Mitchell	.05
58	Greg Gagne	.05
59	Keith Hernandez	.05
60	John Kruk	.05
61	Mike LaValliere	.05
62	Cal Ripken, Jr.	1.50
63	Ivan Calderon	.05
64	Alvin Davis	.05
65	Luis Polonia	.05
66	Robin Yount	.45
67	Juan Samuel	.05
68	Andres Thomas	.05
69	Jeff Musselman	.05
70	Jerry Mumphrey	.05
71	Joe Carter	.05
72	Mike Scioscia	.05
73	Pete Incaviglia	.05
74	Barry Larkin	.05
75	Frank White	.05
76	Willie Randolph	.05
77	Kevin Bass	.05
78	Brian Downing	.05
79	Willie McGee	.05
80	Ellis Burks	.05
81	Hubie Brooks	.05
82	Darrell Evans	.05
83	Robby Thompson	.05
84	Kent Hrbek	.05
85	Ron Darling	.05
86	Stan Jefferson	.05
87	Teddy Higuera	.05
88	Mike Schmidt	.75
89	Barry Bonds	1.50
90	Jim Presley	.05
91	Orel Hershiser	.05
92	Jesse Barfield	.05
93	Tom Candiotti	.05
94	Bret Saberhagen	.05
95	Jose Uribe	.05
96	Tom Browning	.05
97	Johnny Ray	.05
98	Mike Morgan	.05
99	Jim Sundberg	.05
100	Roger McDowell	.05
101	Randy Ready	.05
102	Mike Gallego	.05
103	Steve Buechele	.05
104	Greg Walker	.05
105	Jose Lind	.05
106	Steve Trout	.05
107	Rick Rhoden	.05
108	Jim Pankovits	.05
109	Ken Griffey	.05
110	Danny Cox	.05
111	Franklin Stubbs	.05
112	Lloyd Moseby	.05
113	Mel Hall	.05
114	Kevin Seitzer	.05
115	Tim Raines	.05
116	Juan Castillo	.05
117	Roger Clemens	.75
118	Mike Aldrete	.05
119	Mario Soto	.05
120	Jack Howell	.05
121	Rick Schu	.05
122	Jeff Robinson	.05
123	Doug Drabek	.05
124	Henry Cotto	.05
125	Checklist 89-176	.05
126	Gary Gaetti	.05
127	Rick Sutcliffe	.05
128	Howard Johnson	.05
129	Chris Brown	.05
130	Dave Henderson	.05
131	Curt Wilkerson	.05
132	Mike Marshall	.05
133	Kelly Gruber	.05
134	Julio Franco	.05
135	Kurt Stillwell	.05
136	Donnie Hill	.05
137	Mike Pagliarulo	.05
138	Von Hayes	.05
139	Mike Scott	.05
140	Bob Kipper	.05
141	Harold Reynolds	.05
142	Bob Brenly	.05
143	Dave Concepcion	.05
144	Devon White	.05
145	Jeff Stone	.05
146	Chet Lemon	.05
147	Ozzie Virgil	.05
148	Todd Worrell	.05
149	Mitch Webster	.05
150	Rob Deer	.05
151	Rich Gedman	.05
152	Andre Dawson	.20
153	Mike Davis	.05
154	Nelson Liriano	.05
155	Greg Swindell	.05
156	George Brett	.75
157	Kevin McReynolds	.05
158	Brian Fisher	.05
159	Mike Kingery	.05
160	Tony Gwynn	.60
161	Don Baylor	.05
162	Jerry Browne	.05
163	Dan Pasqua	.05
164	Rickey Henderson	.45
165	Brett Butler	.05
166	Nick Esasky	.05
167	Kirk McCaskill	.05
168	Fred Lynn	.05
169	Jack Morris	.05
170	Pedro Guerrero	.05
171	Dave Stieb	.05
172	Pat Tabler	.05
173	Floyd Bannister	.05
174	Rafael Belliard	.05
175	Mark Langston	.05
176	Greg Mathews	.05
177	Claudell Washington	.05
178	Mark McGwire	1.00
179	Bert Blyleven	.05
180	Jim Rice	.15
181	Mookie Wilson	.05
182	Willie Fraser	.05
183	Andy Van Slyke	.05
184	Matt Nokes	.05
185	Eddie Whitson	.05
186	Tony Fernandez	.05
187	Rick Reuschel	.05
188	Ken Phelps	.05
189	Juan Nieves	.05
190	Kirk Gibson	.05
191	Glenn Davis	.05
192	Zane Smith	.05
193	Jose DeLeon	.05
194	Gary Ward	.05
195	Pascual Perez	.05
196	Carlton Fisk	.45
197	Oddibe McDowell	.05

199	Mark Gubicza	.05
200	Glenn Hubbard	.05
201	Frank Viola	.05
202	Jody Reed	.05
203	Len Dykstra	.05
204	Dick Schofield	.05
205	Sid Bream	.05
206	Guillermo Hernandez	.05
207	Keith Moreland	.05
208	Mark Eichhorn	.05
209	Rene Gonzales	.05
210	Dave Valle	.05
211	Tom Brunansky	.05
212	Charles Hudson	.05
213	John Farrell	.05
214	Jeff Treadway	.05
215	Eddie Murray	.45
216	Checklist 177-264	.05
217	Greg Brock	.05
218	John Shelby	.05
219	Craig Reynolds	.05
220	Dion James	.05
221	Carney Lansford	.05
222	Juan Berenguer	.05
223	Luis Rivera	.05
224	Harold Baines	.05
225	Shawon Dunston	.05
226	Luis Aguayo	.05
227	Pete O'Brien	.05
228	Ozzie Smith	.60
229	Don Mattingly	.75
230	Danny Tartabull	.05
231	Andy Allanson	.05
232	John Franco	.05
233	Mike Greenwell	.05
234	Bob Ojeda	.05
235	Chili Davis	.05
236	Mike Dunne	.05
237	Jim Morrison	.05
238	Carmelo Martinez	.05
239	Ernie Whitt	.05
240	Scott Garrelts	.05
241	Mike Moore	.05
242	Dave Parker	.05
243	Tim Laudner	.05
244	Bill Wegman	.05
245	Bob Horner	.05
246	Rafael Santana	.05
247	Alfredo Griffin	.05
248	Mark Bailey	.05
249	Ron Gant	.05
250	Bryn Smith	.05
251	Lance Johnson	.05
252	Sam Horn	.05
253	Darryl Strawberry	.05
254	Chuck Finley	.05
255	Darnell Coles	.05
256	Mike Henneman	.05
257	Andy Hawkins	.05
258	Jim Clancy	.05
259	Atlee Hammaker	.05
260	Glenn Wilson	.05
261	Larry McWilliams	.05
262	Jack Clark	.05
263	Walt Weiss	.05
264	Gene Larkin	.05

Cloth Experimental

This is a true experimental issue from Topps: Baseball cards printed on heavy textured paper, much like high-quality paper towels. The cloth cards are the standard 2-1/2" x 3-1/2" in size and feature the fronts as used on Topps' regular '88 baseball card issue. Overprinted across the fronts of some cards are parts of the legend, "SAMPLE ONLY NOT FOR SALE." Backs are blank, and unlike earlier Topps cloth issues, are not gummed for use as stickers. The checklist is presented here in alphabetical order.

		NM/M
Complete Set (121):		1,000
Uncut Sheet (121):		825.00
Common Player:		10.00
(1)	A's Team Leaders (Jose Canseco, Mark McGwire)	45.00
(2)	Rick Aguilera	10.00
(3)	Andy Allanson	10.00
(4)	Tony Armas	10.00
(5)	Keith Atherton	10.00
(6)	Steve Balboni	10.00
(7)	Billy Bean	10.00

(8)	Steve Bedrosian/AS	10.00
(9)	George Bell/AS	10.00
(10)	Bruce Benedict	10.00
(11)	Dave Bergman	10.00
(12)	Mike Bielecki	10.00
(13)	Tim Birtsas	10.00
(14)	Bruce Bochy	10.00
(15)	Wade Boggs/AS	60.00
(16)	Rod Booker	10.00
(17)	Dennis Boyd	10.00
(18)	Braves Leaders (Ken Griffey, Dion James, Dale Murphy, Gerald Perry)	25.00
(19)	Tom Browning	10.00
(20)	Carmen Castillo	10.00
(21)	Rick Cerone	10.00
(22)	Jack Clark/AS	10.00
(23)	Mark Clear	10.00
(24)	Roger Clemens/AS	110.00
(25)	Pat Clements	10.00
(26)	Keith Comstock	10.00
(27)	Cecil Cooper	10.00
(28)	Joey Cora	10.00
(29)	Ed Correa	10.00
(30)	Mark Davidson	10.00
(31)	Mark Davis	10.00
(32)	Jeff Dedmon	10.00
(33)	Jim Dwyer	10.00
(34)	Doc Edwards	10.00
(35)	John Farrell	10.00
(36)	Mike Felder	10.00
(37)	Curt Ford	10.00
(38)	Bob Forsch	10.00
(39)	Damaso Garcia	10.00
(40)	Tom Glavine	70.00
(41)	Mark Grant	10.00
(42)	Tony Gwynn/AS	60.00
(43)	Drew Hall	10.00
(44)	Jeff Hamilton	10.00
(45)	Mike Hart	10.00
(46)	Andy Hawkins	10.00
(47)	Ed Hearn	10.00
(48)	Tom Henke/AS	10.00
(49)	Whitey Herzog	10.00
(50)	Shawn Hillegas	10.00
(51)	Charles Hudson	10.00
(52)	Dave Johnson	10.00
(53)	Ron Karkovice	10.00
(54)	Pat Keedy	10.00
(55)	Jimmy Key/AS	10.00
(56)	Mark Kiefer	10.00
(57)	Bob Kipper	10.00
(58)	Les Lancaster	10.00
(59)	Ken Landreaux	10.00
(60)	Craig Lefferts	10.00
(61)	Jim Leyland	10.00
(62)	Jose Lind	10.00
(63)	Gary Lucas	10.00
(64)	Frank Lucchesi	10.00
(65)	Barry Lyons	10.00
(66)	John Marzano	10.00
(67)	Greg Mathews	10.00
(68)	Don Mattingly/AS	110.00
(69)	Len Matuszek	10.00
(70)	Kirk McCaskill	10.00
(71)	Terry McGriff	10.00
(72)	Joey Meyer	10.00
(73)	John Mitchell	10.00
(74)	Jeff Montgomery	10.00
(75)	John Morris	10.00
(76)	John Moses	10.00
(77)	Tom Nieto	10.00
(78)	Matt Nokes/AS	10.00
(79)	Charlie O'Brien	10.00
(80)	Ed Olwine	10.00
(81)	Paul O'Neill	10.00
(82)	Steve Ontiveros	10.00
(83)	Pat Pacillo	10.00
(84)	Tom Pagnozzi	10.00
(85)	Jim Pankovitz	10.00
(86)	Bill Pecota	10.00
(87)	Geno Petralli	10.00
(88)	Eric Plunk	10.00
(89)	Gus Polidor	10.00
(90)	Dennis Powell	10.00
(91)	Terry Puhl	10.00
(92)	Charlie Puleo	10.00
(93)	Shane Rawley/AS	10.00
(94)	Rick Rodriguez	10.00
(95)	Ron Roenicke	10.00
(96)	Pete Rose	300.00
(97)	Lenn Sakata	10.00
(98)	Joe Sambito	10.00
(99)	Juan Samuel/AS	10.00
(100)	Rafael Santana	10.00
(101)	Dan Schatzeder	10.00
(102)	Pat Sheridan	10.00
(103)	Steve Shields	10.00
(104)	Ted Simmons	10.00
(105)	Doug Sisk	10.00
(106)	Joel Skinner	10.00
(107)	Ozzie Smith/AS	60.00
(108)	Chris Speier	10.00
(109)	Jim Sundberg	10.00
(110)	Don Sutton	25.00
(111)	Chuck Tanner	10.00
(112)	Mickey Tettleton	10.00
(113)	Tim Teufel	10.00
(114)	Gary Thurman	10.00
(115)	Alex Trevino	10.00
(116)	Mike Trujillo	10.00
(117)	Twins Leaders (Gary Gaetti, Kent Hrbek)	30.00
(118)	Tim Wallach/AS	10.00
(119)	Frank Williams	10.00
(120)	Dave Winfield/AS	40.00
(121)	Butch Wynegar	10.00

Coins

This edition of 60 lightweight metal coins is similar in design to Topps' 1964 set. The 1988 coins are 1-1/2" in diameter and feature full-color player portraits under crimped edges in silver, gold and pink. Curved under the photo is a red and white player name banner pinned by two gold stars. Coin backs list the coin number, player name, personal information and career summary in black letters on a silver background.

		NM/M
Factory Boxed Set (60):		20.00
Complete Set (60):		10.00
Common Player:		.15
Wax Pack (3):		.45
Wax Box (36):		10.00
1	George Bell	.15
2	Roger Clemens	1.00
3	Mark McGwire	1.25
4	Wade Boggs	.75
5	Harold Baines	.15
6	Ivan Calderon	.15
7	Jose Canseco	.45
8	Joe Carter	.15
9	Jack Clark	.15
10	Alvin Davis	.15
11	Dwight Evans	.15
12	Tony Fernandez	.15
13	Gary Gaetti	.15
14	Mike Greenwell	.15
15	Charlie Hough	.15
16	Wally Joyner	.15
17	Jimmy Key	.15
18	Mark Langston	.15
19	Don Mattingly	1.00
20	Paul Molitor	.60
21	Jack Morris	.15
22	Eddie Murray	.60
23	Kirby Puckett	.75
24	Cal Ripken, Jr.	1.50
25	Bret Saberhagen	.15
26	Ruben Sierra	.15
27	Cory Snyder	.15
28	Terry Steinbach	.15
29	Danny Tartabull	.15
30	Alan Trammell	.15
31	Devon White	.15
32	Robin Yount	.60
33	Andre Dawson	.30
34	Steve Bedrosian	.15
35	Benny Santiago	.15
36	Tony Gwynn	.75
37	Bobby Bonilla	.15
38	Will Clark	.75
39	Eric Davis	.15
40	Mike Dunne	.15
41	John Franco	.15
42	Dwight Gooden	.15
43	Pedro Guerrero	.15
44	Dion James	.15
45	John Kruk	.15
46	Jeffrey Leonard	.15
47	Carmelo Martinez	.15
48	Dale Murphy	.30
49	Tim Raines	.15
50	Nolan Ryan	1.50
51	Juan Samuel	.15
52	Ryne Sandberg	.75
53	Mike Schmidt	1.00
54	Mike Scott	.15
55	Ozzie Smith	.15
56	Darryl Strawberry	.15
57	Rick Sutcliffe	.15
58	Fernando Valenzuela	.15
59	Tim Wallach	.15
60	Todd Worrell	.15

Gallery of Champions

These metal replicas are exact reproductions at one-quarter scale of Topps 1988 cards, both front and back. The set includes 12 three-dimensional raised metal cards packaged in a velvet-lined case that bears the title of the set in gold embossed letters. A deluxe limited edition of the set (1,000) was produced in in sterling silver and an economy version in aluminum. A Mark McGwire pewter replica was given as a premium to dealers ordering the aluminum, bronze and silver sets. The special pewter card is distinguished from the regular issue by a diagonal name banner in the lower-right corner; regular replicas have a rectangular name banner parallel to the lower edge of the card.

		NM/M
Complete Aluminum Set (12):		10.00
Complete Bronze Set (12):		60.00
Complete Silver Set (12):		140.00
(1a)	Steve Bedrosian/Aluminum	.50
(1b)	Steve Bedrosian/Bronze	1.50
(1s)	Steve Bedrosian/Silver	6.00
(2a)	George Bell/Aluminum	.50
(2b)	George Bell/Bronze	1.50
(2s)	George Bell/Silver	6.00
(3a)	Wade Boggs/Aluminum	1.50
(3b)	Wade Boggs/Bronze	6.00
(3s)	Wade Boggs/Silver	20.00
(4a)	Jack Clark/Aluminum	.50
(4b)	Jack Clark/Bronze	1.50
(4s)	Jack Clark/Silver	6.00
(5a)	Roger Clemens/Aluminum	2.00
(5b)	Roger Clemens/Bronze	10.00
(5s)	Roger Clemens/Silver	25.00
(6a)	Andre Dawson/Aluminum	1.00
(6b)	Andre Dawson/Bronze	2.50
(6s)	Andre Dawson/Silver	9.00
(7a)	Tony Gwynn/Aluminum	1.50
(7b)	Tony Gwynn/Bronze	6.00
(7s)	Tony Gwynn/Silver	20.00
(8a)	Mark Langston/Aluminum	.50
(8b)	Mark Langston/Bronze	1.50
(8s)	Mark Langston/Silver	6.00
(9a)	Mark McGwire/Aluminum	2.50
(9b)	Mark McGwire/Bronze	12.50
(9s)	Mark McGwire/Silver	25.00
(9p)	Mark McGwire/Pewter	13.50
(10a)	Dave Righetti/Aluminum	.50
(10b)	Dave Righetti/Bronze	1.50
(10s)	Dave Righetti/Silver	6.00
(11a)	Nolan Ryan/Aluminum	3.00
(11b)	Nolan Ryan/Bronze	15.00
(11s)	Nolan Ryan/Silver	30.00
(12a)	Benny Santiago/Aluminum	.50
(12b)	Benny Santiago/Bronze	1.50
(12s)	Benny Santiago/Silver	6.00

Glossy Rookies

The Topps 1988 Rookies special insert cards follow the same basic design as the All-Star inserts. The set consists of 22 standard-size cards found one per pack in 100-card jumbo cellos. Large, glossy color player photos are printed on a white background below a red, yellow and blue "1987 Rookies" banner. A red and yellow player name appears beneath the photo. Red, white and blue card backs bear the title of the special insert set, the Rookies logo emblem, player name and card number.

		NM/M
Complete Set (22):		3.00
Common Player:		.05
1	Billy Ripken	.05
2	Ellis Burks	.05
3	Mike Greenwell	.05
4	DeWayne Buice	.05
5	Devon White	.05
6	Fred Manrique	.05
7	Mike Henneman	.05
8	Matt Nokes	.05
9	Kevin Seitzer	.05

10	B.J. Surhoff	.05
11	Casey Candaele	.05
12	Randy Myers	.05
13	Mark McGwire	2.50
14	Luis Polonia	.05
15	Terry Steinbach	.05
16	Mike Dunne	.05
17	Al Pedrique	.05
18	Benny Santiago	.05
19	Kelly Downs	.05
20	Joe Magrane	.05
21	Jerry Browne	.05
22	Jeff Musselman	.05

Mini League Leaders

The third consecutive issue of Topps mini-cards (2-1/8" x 3") includes 77 cards spotlighting the top five ranked pitchers and batters. This set is unique in that it was the first time Topps included full-color player photos on both the front and back. Glossy action shots on the card fronts fade into a white border with a Topps logo in an upper corner. The player's name is printed in bold black letters beneath the photo. Horizontal reverses feature circular player photos on a blue and white background with the card number, player name, personal information, 1987 ranking and lifetime/1987 stats printed in red, black and yellow lettering.

		NM/M
Complete Set (77):		3.00
Common Player:		.05
Wax Pack (7):		.30
Wax Box (36):		6.00
1	Wade Boggs	.60
2	Roger Clemens	.65
3	Dwight Evans	.05
4	DeWayne Buice	.05
5	Brian Downing	.05
6	Wally Joyner	.05
7	Ivan Calderon	.05
8	Carlton Fisk	.50
9	Gary Redus	.05
10	Darrell Evans	.05
11	Jack Morris	.05
12	Alan Trammell	.05
13	Lou Whitaker	.05
14	Bret Saberhagen	.05
15	Kevin Seitzer	.05
16	Danny Tartabull	.05
17	Willie Wilson	.05
18	Teddy Higuera	.05
19	Paul Molitor	.50
20	Dan Plesac	.05
21	Robin Yount	.50
22	Kent Hrbek	.05
23	Kirby Puckett	.60
24	Jeff Reardon	.05
25	Frank Viola	.05
26	Rickey Henderson	.50
27	Don Mattingly	.65
28	Willie Randolph	.05
29	Dave Righetti	.05
30	Jose Canseco	.35
31	Mark McGwire	.75
32	Dave Stewart	.05
33	Phil Bradley	.05
34	Mark Langston	.05
35	Harold Reynolds	.05
36	Charlie Hough	.05
37	George Bell	.05
38	Tom Henke	.05
39	Jimmy Key	.05
40	Dion James	.05
41	Dale Murphy	.20
42	Zane Smith	.05
43	Andre Dawson	.20
44	Lee Smith	.05
45	Rick Sutcliffe	.05
46	Eric Davis	.05
47	John Franco	.05
48	Dave Parker	.05
49	Billy Hatcher	.05
50	Nolan Ryan	1.00
51	Mike Scott	.05
52	Pedro Guerrero	.05
53	Orel Hershiser	.05
54	Fernando Valenzuela	.05
55	Bob Welch	.05
56	Andres Galarraga	.05
57	Tim Raines	.05
58	Tim Wallach	.05
59	Len Dykstra	.05
60	Dwight Gooden	.05
61	Howard Johnson	.05
62	Roger McDowell	.05
63	Darryl Strawberry	.05
64	Steve Bedrosian	.05
65	Shane Rawley	.05
66	Juan Samuel	.05
67	Mike Schmidt	.65
68	Mike Dunne	.05
69	Jack Clark	.05
70	Vince Coleman	.05
71	Willie McGee	.05
72	Ozzie Smith	.50
73	Todd Worrell	.05
74	Tony Gwynn	.60
75	John Kruk	.05
76	Rick Rueschel	.05
77	Checklist	.05

Stickercards

Actually a part of the 1988 Topps Stickers issue, this set consists of 67 cards. The cards are the backs of the peel-off stickers and measure 2-1/8" x 3". To determine total value, combine the prices of the stickers (found in the 1988 Topps Stickers checklist) on the stickercard front with the value assigned to the stickercard in the following checklist.

		NM/M
Complete Set (67):		3.00
Common Player:		.05
1	Jack Clark	.05
2	Andres Galarraga	.05
3	Keith Hernandez	.05
4	Tom Herr	.05
5	Juan Samuel	.05
6	Ryne Sandberg	.50
7	Terry Pendleton	.05
8	Mike Schmidt	.60
9	Tim Wallach	.05
10	Hubie Brooks	.05
11	Shawon Dunston	.05
12	Ozzie Smith	.50
13	Andre Dawson	.20
14	Eric Davis	.05
15	Pedro Guerrero	.05
16	Tony Gwynn	.50
17	Jeffrey Leonard	.05
18	Dale Murphy	.20
19	Dave Parker	.05
20	Tim Raines	.05
21	Darryl Strawberry	.05
22	Gary Carter	.40
23	Jody Davis	.05
24	Ozzie Virgil	.05
25	Dwight Gooden	.05
26	Mike Scott	.05
27	Rick Sutcliffe	.05
28	Sid Fernandez	.05
29	Neal Heaton	.05
30	Fernando Valenzuela	.05
31	Steve Bedrosian	.05
32	John Franco	.05
33	Lee Smith	.05
34	Wally Joyner	.05
35	Don Mattingly	.60
36	Mark McGwire	.65
37	Willie Randolph	.05
38	Lou Whitaker	.05
39	Frank White	.05
40	Wade Boggs	.50
41	George Brett	.05
42	Paul Molitor	.40
43	Tony Fernandez	.05
44	Cal Ripken, Jr.	.75
45	Alan Trammell	.05
46	Jesse Barfield	.05
47	George Bell	.05
48	Jose Canseco	.35
49	Joe Carter	.05
50	Dwight Evans	.05
51	Rickey Henderson	.40
52	Kirby Puckett	.50
53	Cory Snyder	.05
54	Dave Winfield	.40
55	Terry Kennedy	.05
56	Matt Nokes	.05
57	B.J. Surhoff	.05
58	Roger Clemens	.60
59	Jack Morris	.05
60	Bret Saberhagen	.05
61	Ron Guidry	.05

		NM/M
62	Bruce Hurst	.05
63	Mark Langston	.05
64	Tom Henke	.05
65	Dan Plesac	.05
66	Dave Righetti	.05
67	Checklist	.05

Stickers

This set of 313 stickers (on 198 cards) offers an addition for 1988 - 66 different players are pictured on the backs of the sticker cards. The stickers come in two sizes (2-1/8" x 3" or 1-1/2" x 2-1/8"). Larger stickers fill an entire card, smaller ones are attached in pairs. A 36-page sticker yearbook with Mark McGwire on the cover has a designated space inside for each sticker, with one page per team and special pages of 1987 Highlights, World Series, All-Stars and Future Stars. No printing appears on the full-color action shot stickers except for a small black number in the lower left corner. Stickers were sold in packs of five (with gum) for 25 cents per pack. Unlike the 1987 Topps Stickers set, different pairings can be found, rather than the same two players/numbers always sharing the same sticker. To determine total value, combine the value of the stickercard (found in the 1988 Topps Stickercard checklist) with the values assigned the stickers in the following checklist.

		NM/M
Complete Set (313):		10.00
Common Player:		.05
Sticker Album:		1.50
Wax Pack (5):		.25
Wax Box (48):		7.00
1-263	1987 Highlights (Mark McGwire, Willie Wilson)	.25
2-304	1987 Highlights (Benny Santiago, Al Pedrique (Future Star))	.05
3-187	1987 Highlights (Don Mattingly, Ernie Whitt)	.20
4-223	1987 Highlights (Vince Coleman, Gary Matthews)	.05
5-272	1987 Highlights (Bob Boone, Jim Morrison)	.05
6-278	1987 Highlights (Steve Bedrosian, Tim Laudner)	.05
7-276	1987 Highlights (Nolan Ryan, Bert Blyleven)	.30
8-306	1987 Highlights (Darrell Evans, Kevin Seitzer (Future Star))	.05
9-255	1987 Highlights (Mike Schmidt, Frank White)	.15
10-256	1987 Highlights (Don Baylor, Dan Quisenberry)	.05
11-145	1987 Highlights (Eddie Murray, Dennis Rasmussen)	.10
12-237	1987 Highlights (Juan Beniquez, Oddibe McDowell)	.05
13	1987 Championship Series (John Tudor)	.05
14	1987 Championship Series (Jeff Reardon)	.05
15	1987 Championship Series (Tom Brunansky)	.05
16	1987 Championship Series (Jeffrey Leonard)	.05
17	1987 Championship Series (Gary Gaetti)	.05
18	1987 Championship Series (Cardinals Celebrate)	.05

		NM/M
19	1987 World Series (Danny Gladden)	.05
20	1987 World Series (Bert Blyleven)	.05
21	1987 World Series (John Tudor)	.05
22	1987 World Series (Tom Lawless)	.05
23	1987 World Series (Curt Ford)	.05
24	1987 World Series (Kent Hrbek)	.05
25	1987 World Series (Frank Viola)	.05
26-216	Dave Smith, Edwin Nunez	.05
27-240	Jim Deshaies, Pete O'Brien	.05
28-171	Billy Hatcher, Mike Davis	.05
29-196	Kevin Bass, Teddy Higuera	.05
30	Mike Scott	.05
31-224	Danny Walling, Eric Bell	.05
32-185	Alan Ashby, Willie Upshaw	.05
33-292	Ken Caminiti, Greg Walker	.05
34-245	Bill Doran, Dwight Evans	.05
35	Glenn Davis	.05
36	Ozzie Virgil	.05
37-260	Ken Oberkfell, Charlie Leibrandt	.05
38-183	Ken Griffey, Devon White	.05
39-287	Albert Hall, Ken Williams	.05
40-310	Zane Smith, Ellis Burks (Future Star)	.05
41-207	Andres Thomas, Julio Franco	.05
42-178	Dion James, Gary Pettis	.05
43-249	Jim Acker, Mike Greenwell	.05
44-226	Tom Glavine, Dave Schmidt	.20
45	Dale Murphy	.20
46	Jack Clark	.05
47-269	Vince Coleman, Matt Nokes	.05
48-221	Ricky Horton, Harold Reynolds	.05
49-303	Terry Pendleton, Gary Ward	.05
50-271	Tom Herr, Eric King	.05
51-265	Joe Magrane, Darrell Evans	.05
52-211	Tony Pena, Brook Jacoby	.05
53-298	Ozzie Smith, Rick Rhoden	.40
54-169	Todd Worrell, Alfredo Griffin	.05
55	Willie McGee	.05
56	Andre Dawson	.25
57-225	Ryne Sandberg, Terry Kennedy	.35
58-291	Keith Moreland, Richard Dotson	.05
59-198	Greg Maddux, Rob Deer	.40
60-290	Jody Davis, Carlton Fisk	.25
61	Rick Sutcliffe	.05
62-295	Jamie Moyer, Mike Pagliarulo	.05
63-172	Leon Durham, Luis Polonia	.05
64-313	Lee Smith, Devon White (Future Star)	.05
65-250	Shawon Dunston, Ellis Burks	.05
66-257	Franklin Stubbs, Danny Tartabull	.05
67-235	Mike Scioscia, Steve Buechele	.05
68-217	Orel Hershiser, Dick Schofield	.05
69-289	Mike Marshall, Bob James	.05
70	Fernando Valenzuela	.05
71-281	Mickey Hatcher, Danny Gladden	.05
72-166	Matt Young, Jay Howell	.05
73-236	Bob Welch, Charlie Hough	.05
74-170	Steve Sax, Dennis Eckersley	.25
75	Pedro Guerrero	.05
76	Tim Raines	.15
77-252	Casey Candaele, Rich Gedman	.05
78-248	Mike Fitzgerald, Marty Barrett	.05
79-301	Andres Galarraga, Claudell Washington	.05
80-212	Neal Heaton, Brett Butler	.05
81-296	Hubie Brooks, Ron Guidry	.05
82-258	Floyd Youmans, Bo Jackson	.10
83-201	Herm Winningham, Robin Yount	.25
84-307	Denny Martinez, Mike Dunne (Future Star)	.05
85	Tim Wallach	.05
86	Jeffrey Leonard	.05
87-251	Will Clark, Roger Clemens	.45
88-288	Kevin Mitchell, Jim Winn	.05

		NM/M
89-267	Mike Aldrete, Kirk Gibson	.05
90-191	Scott Garrelts, Dave Steib	.05
91-231	Jose Uribe, Mike Boddicker	.05
92-246	Bob Brenly, Sam Horn	.05
93-189	Robby Thompson, Lloyd Moseby	.05
94-217	Don Robinson, Jim Presley	.05
95	Candy Maldonado	.05
96	Darryl Strawberry	.05
97-192	Keith Hernandez, Jesse Barfield	.05
98-220	Ron Darling, Dave Valle	.05
99-218	Howard Johnson, Phil Bradley	.05
100-190	Roger McDowell, Jimmy Key	.05
101	Dwight Gooden	.05
102-165	Kevin McReynolds, Tony Phillips	.05
103-275	Sid Fernandez, Tom Brunansky	.05
104-241	Dave Magadan, Scott Fletcher	.05
105-167	Gary Carter, Carney Lansford	.25
106-302	Carmelo Martinez, Dave Winfield	.25
107-205	Eddie Whitson, Mel Hall	.05
108-180	Tim Flannery, DeWayne Buice	.05
109-266	Stan Jefferson, Bill Madlock	.05
110	John Kruk	.05
111-168	Chris Brown, Dave Stewart	.05
112-215	Benny Santiago, Rey Quinones	.05
113-270	Garry Templeton, Lou Whitaker	.05
114-186	Lance McCullers, Tom Henke	.05
115	Tony Gwynn	.50
116	Steve Bedrosian	.05
117-247	Von Hayes, Jim Rice	.10
118-279	Kevin Gross, Gene Larkin	.05
119-238	Bruce Ruffin, Mike Stanley	.05
120-184	Juan Samuel, Jim Clancy	.05
121-182	Shane Rawley, Bob Boone	.05
122-222	Chris James, Scott Bradley	.05
123-199	Lance Parrish, Dale Sveum	.05
124-181	Glenn Wilson, Brian Downing	.05
125	Mike Schmidt	.60
126	Andy Van Slyke	.05
127-297	Jose Lind, Rickey Henderson	.05
128-176	Al Pedrique, Greg Minton	.05
129-277	Bobby Bonilla, Gary Gaetti	.05
130-175	Sid Bream, Jack Howell	.05
131-230	Mike LaValliere, Larry Sheets	.05
132-197	Mike Dunne, Glenn Braggs	.05
133-232	Jeff Robinson, Tom Niedenfuer	.05
134-195	Doug Drabek, Jim Gantner	.05
135	Barry Bonds	.75
136	Dave Parker	.05
137-208	Nick Esasky, Cory Snyder	.05
138-280	Buddy Bell, Jeff Reardon	.05
139-239	Kal Daniels, Pete Incaviglia	.05
140-285	Barry Larkin, Ivan Calderon	.05
141	Eric Davis	.05
142-227	John Franco, Billy Ripken	.05
143-229	Bo Diaz, Ray Knight	.05
144-261	Ron Oester, Kevin Seitzer	.05
146	Eric Davis/AS	2.00
147	Ryne Sandberg/AS	.30
148	Andre Dawson/AS	.15
149	Mike Schmidt/AS	.40
150	Jack Clark/AS	.05
151	Darryl Strawberry/AS	.05
152	Gary Carter/AS	.35
153	Ozzie Smith/AS	.35
154	Mike Scott/AS	.05
155	Rickey Henderson/AS	.40
156	Don Mattingly/AS	.40
157	Wade Boggs/AS	.30
158	George Bell/AS	.35
159	Dave Winfield/AS	.35
160	Cal Ripken, Jr./AS	.50
161	Terry Kennedy/AS	.05
162	Willie Randolph/AS	.05
163	Bret Saberhagen/AS	.05
164	Mark McGwire	.65
173	Jose Canseco	.05
174	Mike Witt	.05
179	Wally Joyner	.05
188	George Bell	.05
193	Tony Fernandez	.05

		NM/M
194	Paul Molitor	.40
200-308	Bill Wegman, Jeff Musselman (Future Star)	.05
202-309	B.J. Surhoff, Mark McGwire (Future Star)	.50
203	Dan Plesac	.05
204	Pat Tabler	.05
206-305	Scott Bailes, Casey Candaele (Future Star)	.05
209-312	Chris Bando, Mike Greenwell (Future Star)	.05
210-311	Greg Swindell, Matt Nokes (Future Star)	.05
213	Joe Carter	.05
214	Mark Langston	.05
219	Alvin Davis	.05
228	Cal Ripken, Jr.	.75
233	Eddie Murray	.40
234	Ruben Sierra	.05
242-300	Dale Mohorcic, Dave Righetti	.05
243	Larry Parrish	.05
244	Wade Boggs	.40
253	Bruce Hurst	.05
254	Bret Saberhagen	.05
259	George Brett	.50
262-282	Mark Gubicza, Frank Viola	.05
264-286	Frank Tanana, Donnie Hill	.05
268	Jack Morris	.05
273	Alan Trammell	.05
274	Kent Hrbek	.05
283	Kirby Puckett	.50
284	Ozzie Guillen	.05
293	Harold Baines	.05
294	Willie Randolph	.05
299	Don Mattingly	.50

Campbell's Richie Ashburn Tribute Sheet

Longtime Phillies star, Hall of Famer and broadcaster Richie Ashburn was honored for his 40 years in baseball by the issue of a commemorative card set in the form of a 10" x 14" poster given away as a stadium promotion. A 5" x 7" card picturing the 61-year old Ashburn was at center, with his complete major league stats on back. Surrounding the center card and separated by perforations are reproductions of 12 of Ashburn's baseball cards. The cards are reduced to about 75 percent of actual size and shown on an American flag background. The back of each card is also reproduced, with a cartoon figure of the Campbell's Kid baseball player included on front and back.

	NM/M
Complete Set (Sheet):	25.00
Complete Set, Singles (13):	20.00
Common Card:	2.00
1952 Bowman	2.00
1952 Topps	2.00
1954 Topps	2.00
1956 Topps	2.00
1957 Topps	2.00
1958 Topps	2.00
1959 Topps	2.00
1959 Topps (N.L. Hitting Kings)	2.00
1960 Topps	2.00
1961 Topps	2.00
1962 Topps	2.00
1963 Topps	2.00
Richie Ashburn (1988 Portrait)	2.00

Sports Shots Portfolios

One hundred and thirty of the biggest names from Topps' 1988 baseball card set were reproduced in the form of 9-1/2" x 11-3/4" cardboard folders. The folders reproduce both front and back of the '88 Topps cards and open to offer two

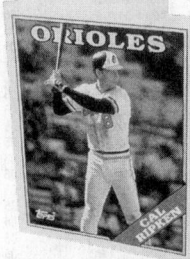

pockets for storage. Various manufacturer and licensor logos are the only printing inside. The folders carried a suggested retail price of $1 apiece and were distributed in either team packs or all-star assortments of 50 pieces each. By 1992, the folders were being wholesaled within the hobby at less than 30 cents apiece.

		NM/M
Complete Set (130):		60.00
Common Player:		.50
10	Ryne Sandberg	2.50
15	Chili Davis	.50
35	Andres Galarraga	.50
36	Harold Baines	.50
39	Gerald Perry	.50
40	Orel Hershiser	.50
45	Kent Hrbek	.50
50	Hubie Brooks	.50
55	Phil Bradley	.50
60	Rickey Henderson	2.00
70	Roger Clemens	3.00
75	Joe Carter	.50
80	Mark Langston	.50
90	Dale Murphy	1.00
95	Lance Parrish	.50
100	Jack Clark	.50
102	Barry Larkin	.50
110	Teddy Higuera	.50
118	Bob Welch	.50
120	Kirby Puckett	2.50
130	Buddy Bell	.50
138	Mitch Webster	.50
140	Jesse Barfield	.50
142	Andy Van Slyke	.50
150	Eric Davis	.50
165	Robin Yount	2.00
170	Goose Gossage	.50
180	Terry Kennedy	.50
184	Ivan Calderon	.50
192	Devon White	.50
193	Brian Fisher	.50
195	Dan Quisenberry	.50
197	Lance McCullers	.50
200	Wade Boggs	2.50
210	Willie Randolph	.50
215	Von Hayes	.50
230	Pat Tabler	.50
238	Luis Polonia	.50
240	Lee Smith	.50
250	Nolan Ryan	4.00
260	Vince Coleman	.50
265	Bo Diaz	.50
270	Mike Witt	.50
280	Pete Incaviglia	.50
285	Jim Presley	.50
297	Zane Smith	.50
300	Don Mattingly	3.00
305	Steve Sax	.50
306	Billy Hatcher	.50
320	Alan Trammell	.50
327	Larry Sheets	.50
331	Brian Downing	.50
340	Jack Morris	.50
343	Greg Gagne	.50
350	Will Clark	.50
360	Tony Gwynn	2.50
370	Jose Canseco	1.00
385	Carlton Fisk	2.00
408	Dion James	.50
410	Tony Pena	.50
420	Wally Joyner	.50
424	Dwayne Murphy	.50
430	Glenn Davis	.50
440	Steve Bedrosian	.50
450	Barry Bonds	4.00
452	Willie Wilson	.50
460	Ozzie Smith	2.50
465	Paul Molitor	2.00
470	Dwight Evans	.50
474	Dave Stewart	.50
477	Brett Butler	.50
480	Dwight Gooden	.50
485	Harold Reynolds	.50
490	Larry Parrish	.50
491	B.J. Surhoff	.50
495	Eddie Murray	2.00
497	Kevin Mitchell	.50
500	Andre Dawson	1.00
510	Dave Winfield	.50
525	Marty Barrett	.50
540	Bret Saberhagen	.50
550	Pedro Guerrero	.50

		NM/M
555	Brook Jacoby	.50
560	Tim Wallach	.50
565	Lloyd Moseby	.50
570	Jeffrey Leonard	.50
578	Gary Gaetti	.50
580	Mark McGwire	3.50
590	George Bell	.50
596	John Kruk	.50
600	Mike Schmidt	3.00
605	Kirk Gibson	.50
610	Keith Hernandez	.50
613	Bobby Thigpen	.50
615	Jody Davis	.50
619	Mike Dunne	.50
620	Cory Snyder	.50
625	Frank Viola	.50
645	Matt Nokes	.50
649	De Wayne Buice	.50
650	Cal Ripken Jr.	4.00
660	Rick Reuschel	.50
670	Dan Plesac	.50
675	Jim Rice	1.00
680	Charlie Hough	.50
681	Bobby Bonilla	.50
682	Jimmy Key	.50
685	Ron Darling	.50
693	Benito Santiago	.50
700	George Brett	3.00
705	Juan Samuel	.50
710	Darryl Strawberry	.50
715	Todd Worrell	.50
720	Tim Raines	.50
721	Pete O'Brien	.50
725	Mike Boddicker	.50
730	John Franco	.50
740	Rick Sutcliffe	.50
745	Bill Doran	.50
750	Bo Jackson	1.00
755	Ozzie Virgil	.50
760	Mike Scott	.50
764	Greg Walker	.50
770	Lou Whitaker	.50
771	Ruben Sierra	.50
775	Dave Steib	.50
780	Fernando Valenzuela	.50
785	Alvin Davis	.50
790	Dave Righetti	.50

1989 Topps

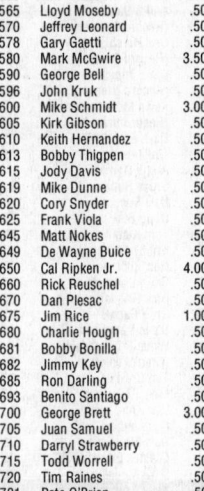

Ten top young players from the June 1988 draft are featured on "#1 Draft Pick" cards in this full-color basic set of 792 standard-size baseball cards. An additional five cards salute 1989 Future Stars, 22 cards highlight All-Stars, seven contain Record Breakers, five are designated Turn Back The Clock, and six contain checklists. This set features the familiar white borders, but upper-left and lower-right photo corners have been rounded off. A curved name banner in bright red or blue is beneath the team name in large script in the lower-right corner. The card backs are printed in black on a red background and include personal information and complete minor and major league stats. Another new addition in this set is the special Monthly Scoreboard chart that lists monthly stats (April through September) in two of several categories (hits, run, home runs, stolen bases, RBIs, wins, strikeouts, games or saves).

		NM/M
Unopened Factory Set, Retail (792):		25.00
Unopened Factory Set, Hobby (792):		25.00
Complete Set (792):		15.00
Common Player:		.05
Wax Pack (15):		.75
Wax Box (36):		12.00
Cello Pack (29):		1.00
Cello Box (24):		18.00
Rack Pack (43):		.75
Rack Box (24):		15.00
Vending Box (500):		6.00
1	George Bell (Record Breaker)	.05
2	Wade Boggs (Record Breaker)	.25

No.	Player	Price
3	Gary Carter (Record Breaker)	.20
4	Andre Dawson (Record Breaker)	.10
5	Orel Hershiser (Record Breaker)	.05
6	Doug Jones (Record Breaker)	.05
7	Kevin McReynolds (Record Breaker)	.05
8	Dave Eiland RC	.05
9	Tim Teufel	.05
10	Andre Dawson	.25
11	Bruce Sutter	.35
12	Dale Sveum	.05
13	Doug Sisk	.05
14	Tom Kelly	.05
15	Robby Thompson	.05
16	Ron Robinson	.05
17	Brian Downing	.05
18	Rick Rhoden	.05
19	Greg Gagne	.05
20	Steve Bedrosian	.05
21	White Sox Leaders (Greg Walker)	.05
22	Tim Crews	.05
23	Mike Fitzgerald	.05
24	Larry Andersen	.05
25	Frank White	.05
26	Dale Mohorcic	.05
27	Orestes Destrade RC	.05
28	Mike Moore	.05
29	Kelly Gruber	.05
30	Dwight Gooden	.05
31	Terry Francona	.05
32	Dennis Rasmussen	.05
33	B.J. Surhoff	.05
34	Ken Williams	.05
35	John Tudor	.05
36	Mitch Webster	.05
37	Bob Stanley	.05
38	Paul Runge	.05
39	Mike Maddux	.05
40	Steve Sax	.05
41	Terry Mulholland	.05
42	Jim Eppard RC	.05
43	Guillermo Hernandez	.05
44	Jim Snyder	.05
45	Kal Daniels	.05
46	Mark Portugal	.05
47	Carney Lansford	.05
48	Tim Burke	.05
49	Craig Biggio	.05
50	George Bell	.05
51	Angels Leaders (Mark McLemore)	.05
52	Bob Brenly	.05
53	Ruben Sierra	.05
54	Steve Trout	.05
55	Julio Franco	.05
56	Pat Tabler	.05
57	Alejandro Pena	.05
58	Lee Mazzilli	.05
59	Mark Davis	.05
60	Tom Brunansky	.05
61	Neil Allen	.05
62	Alfredo Griffin	.05
63	Mark Clear	.05
64	Alex Trevino	.05
65	Rick Reuschel	.05
66	Manny Trillo	.05
67	Dave Palmer	.05
68	Darrell Miller	.05
69	Jeff Ballard	.05
70	Mark McGwire	.65
71	Mike Boddicker	.05
72	John Moses	.05
73	Pascual Perez	.05
74	Nick Leyva	.05
75	Tom Henke	.05
76	Terry Blocker RC	.05
77	Doyle Alexander	.05
78	Jim Sundberg	.05
79	Scott Bankhead	.05
80	Cory Snyder	.05
81	Expos Leaders (Tim Raines)	.05
82	Dave Leiper	.05
83	Jeff Blauser RC	.05
84	Bill Bene RC (#1 Draft Pick)	.05
85	Kevin McReynolds	.05
86	Al Nipper	.05
87	Larry Owen	.05
88	Darryl Hamilton RC	.05
89	Dave LaPoint	.05
90	Vince Coleman	.05
91	Floyd Youmans	.05
92	Jeff Kunkel	.05
93	Ken Howell	.05
94	Chris Speier	.05
95	Gerald Young	.05
96	Rick Cerone	.05
97	Greg Mathews	.05
98	Larry Sheets	.05
99	Sherman Corbett RC	.05
100	Mike Schmidt	.50
101	Les Straker	.05
102	Mike Gallego	.05
103	Tim Birtsas	.05
104	Dallas Green	.05
105	Ron Darling	.05
106	Willie Upshaw	.05
107	Jose DeLeon	.05
108	Fred Manrique	.05
109	Hipolito Pena RC	.05
110	Paul Molitor	.40
111	Reds Leaders (Eric Davis)	.05
112	Jim Presley	.05
113	Lloyd Moseby	.05
114	Bob Kipper	.05
115	Jody Davis	.05
116	Jeff Montgomery	.05
117	Dave Anderson	.05
118	Checklist 1-132	.05
119	Terry Puhl	.05
120	Frank Viola	.05
121	Garry Templeton	.05
122	Lance Johnson RC	.05
123	Spike Owen	.05
124	Jim Traber	.05
125	Mike Krukow	.05
126	Sid Bream	.05
127	Walt Terrell	.05
128	Milt Thompson	.05
129	Terry Clark RC	.05
130	Gerald Perry	.05
131	Dave Otto RC	.05
132	Curt Ford	.05
133	Bill Long	.05
134	Don Zimmer	.05
135	Jose Rijo	.05
136	Joey Meyer	.05
137	Geno Petralli	.05
138	Wallace Johnson	.05
139	Mike Flanagan	.05
140	Shawon Dunston	.05
141	Indians Leaders (Brook Jacoby)	.05
142	Mike Diaz	.05
143	Mike Campbell	.05
144	Jay Bell	.05
145	Dave Stewart	.05
146	Gary Pettis	.05
147	DeWayne Buice	.05
148	Bill Pecota	.05
149	Doug Dascenzo RC	.05
150	Fernando Valenzuela	.05
151	Terry McGriff	.05
152	Mark Thurmond	.05
153	Jim Pankovits	.05
154	Don Carman	.05
155	Marty Barrett	.05
156	Dave Gallagher RC	.05
157	Tom Glavine	.25
158	Mike Aldrete	.05
159	Pat Clements	.05
160	Jeffrey Leonard	.05
161	Gregg Olson RC (Future Star)	.05
162	John Davis	.05
163	Bob Forsch	.05
164	Hal Lanier	.05
165	Mike Dunne	.05
166	Doug Jennings RC	.05
167	Steve Searcy RC (Future Star)	.05
168	Willie Wilson	.05
169	Mike Jackson	.05
170	Tony Fernandez	.05
171	Braves Leaders (Andres Thomas)	.05
172	Frank Williams	.05
173	Mel Hall	.05
174	Todd Burns RC	.05
175	John Shelby	.05
176	Jeff Parrett	.05
177	Monty Fariss RC (#1 Draft Pick)	.05
178	Mark Grant	.05
179	Ozzie Virgil	.05
180	Mike Scott	.05
181	Craig Worthington RC	.05
182	Bob McClure	.05
183	Oddibe McDowell	.05
184	John Costello RC	.05
185	Claudell Washington	.05
186	Pat Perry	.05
187	Darren Daulton	.05
188	Dennis Lamp	.05
189	Kevin Mitchell	.05
190	Mike Witt	.05
191	Sil Campusano	.05
192	Paul Mirabella	.05
193	Sparky Anderson	.05
194	Greg Harris	.05
195	Ozzie Guillen	.05
196	Denny Walling	.05
197	Neal Heaton	.05
198	Danny Heep	.05
199	Mike Schooler RC	.05
200	George Brett	.50
201	Blue Jays Leaders (Kelly Gruber)	.05
202	Brad Moore RC	.05
203	Rob Ducey	.05
204	Brad Havens	.05
205	Dwight Evans	.05
206	Roberto Alomar	.35
207	Terry Leach	.05
208	Tom Pagnozzi	.05
209	Jeff Bittiger RC	.05
210	Dale Murphy	.15
211	Mike Pagliarulo	.05
212	Scott Sanderson	.05
213	Rene Gonzales	.05
214	Charlie O'Brien	.05
215	Kevin Gross	.05
216	Jack Howell	.05
217	Joe Price	.05
218	Mike LaValliere	.05
219	Jim Clancy	.05
220	Gary Gaetti	.05
221	Cecil Espy	.05
222	Mark Lewis RC (#1 Draft Pick)	.05
223	Jay Buhner	.05
224	Tony LaRussa	.05
225	Ramon Martinez RC	.25
226	Bill Doran	.05
227	John Farrell	.05
228	Nelson Santovenia RC	.05
229	Jimmy Key	.05
230	Ozzie Smith	.45
231	Padres Leaders (Roberto Alomar)	.05
232	Ricky Horton	.05
233	Gregg Jefferies (Future Star)	.20
234	Tom Browning	.05
235	John Kruk	.05
236	Charles Hudson	.05
237	Glenn Hubbard	.05
238	Eric King	.05
239	Tim Laudner	.05
240	Greg Maddux	.45
241	Brett Butler	.05
242	Ed Vande Berg	.05
243	Bob Boone	.05
244	Jim Acker	.05
245	Jim Rice	.15
246	Rey Quinones	.05
247	Shawn Hillegas	.05
248	Tony Phillips	.05
249	Tim Leary	.05
250	Cal Ripken, Jr.	.75
251	John Dopson RC	.05
252	Billy Hatcher	.05
253	Jose Alvarez RC	.05
254	Tom LaSorda	.05
255	Ron Guidry	.10
256	Benny Santiago	.05
257	Rick Aguilera	.05
258	Checklist 133-264	.05
259	Larry McWilliams	.05
260	Dave Winfield	.40
261	Cardinals Leaders (Tom Brunansky)	.05
262	Jeff Pico RC	.05
263	Mike Felder	.05
264	Rob Dibble RC	.10
265	Kent Hrbek	.05
266	Luis Aquino	.05
267	Jeff Robinson	.05
268	Keith Miller	.05
269	Tom Bolton	.05
270	Wally Joyner	.05
271	Jay Tibbs	.05
272	Ron Hassey	.05
273	Jose Lind	.05
274	Mark Eichhorn	.05
275	Danny Tartabull	.05
276	Paul Kilgus	.05
277	Mike Davis	.05
278	Andy McGaffigan	.05
279	Scott Bradley	.05
280	Bob Knepper	.05
281	Gary Redus	.05
282	Cris Carpenter RC	.05
283	Andy Allanson	.05
284	Jim Leyland	.05
285	John Candelaria	.05
286	Darrin Jackson	.05
287	Juan Nieves	.05
288	Pat Sheridan	.05
289	Ernie Whitt	.05
290	John Franco	.05
291	Mets Leaders (Darryl Strawberry)	.05
292	Jim Corsi RC	.05
293	Glenn Wilson	.05
294	Juan Berenguer	.05
295	Scott Fletcher	.05
296	Ron Gant	.05
297	Oswald Peraza RC	.05
298	Chris James	.05
299	Steve Ellsworth RC	.05
300	Darryl Strawberry	.05
301	Charlie Leibrandt	.05
302	Gary Ward	.05
303	Felix Fermin	.05
304	Joel Youngblood	.05
305	Dave Smith	.05
306	Tracy Woodson RC	.05
307	Lance McCullers	.05
308	Ron Karkovice	.05
309	Mario Diaz RC	.05
310	Rafael Palmeiro	.35
311	Chris Bosio	.05
312	Tom Lawless	.05
313	Denny Martinez	.05
314	Bobby Valentine	.05
315	Greg Swindell	.05
316	Walt Weiss	.05
317	Jack Armstrong RC	.05
318	Gene Larkin	.05
319	Greg Booker	.05
320	Lou Whitaker	.05
321	Red Sox Leaders (Jody Reed)	.05
322	John Smiley	.05
323	Gary Thurman	.05
324	Bob Milacki RC	.05
325	Jesse Barfield	.05
326	Dennis Boyd	.05
327	Mark Lemke RC	.05
328	Rick Honeycutt	.05
329	Bob Melvin	.05
330	Eric Davis	.05
331	Curt Wilkerson	.05
332	Tony Armas	.05
333	Bob Ojeda	.05
334	Steve Lyons	.05
335	Dave Righetti	.05
336	Steve Balboni	.05
337	Calvin Schiraldi	.05
338	Jim Adduci RC	.05
339	Scott Bailes	.05
340	Kirk Gibson	.05
341	Jim Deshaies	.05
342	Tom Brookens	.05
343	Gary Sheffield RC (Future Star)	1.50
344	Tom Trebelhorn	.05
345	Charlie Hough	.05
346	Rex Hudler RC	.05
347	John Cerutti	.05
348	Ed Hearn	.05
349	Ron Jones RC	.05
350	Andy Van Slyke	.05
351	Giants Leaders (Bob Melvin)	.05
352	Rick Schu	.05
353	Marvell Wynne	.05
354	Larry Parrish	.05
355	Mark Langston	.05
356	Kevin Elster	.05
357	Jerry Reuss	.05
358	Ricky Jordan RC	.05
359	Tommy John	.10
360	Ryne Sandberg	.45
361	Kelly Downs	.05
362	Jack Lazorko	.05
363	Rich Yett	.05
364	Rob Deer	.05
365	Mike Henneman	.05
366	Herm Winningham	.05
367	Johnny Paredes RC	.05
368	Brian Holton	.05
369	Ken Caminiti	.05
370	Dennis Eckersley	.35
371	Manny Lee	.05
372	Craig Lefferts	.05
373	Tracy Jones	.05
374	John Wathan	.05
375	Terry Pendleton	.05
376	Steve Lombardozzi	.05
377	Mike Smithson	.05
378	Checklist 265-396	.05
379	Tim Flannery	.05
380	Rickey Henderson	.40
381	Orioles Leaders (Larry Sheets)	.05
382	John Smoltz	.50
383	Howard Johnson	.05
384	Mark Salas	.05
385	Von Hayes	.05
386	Andres Galarraga/AS	.05
387	Ryne Sandberg/AS	.20
388	Bobby Bonilla/AS	.05
389	Ozzie Smith/AS	.25
390	Darryl Strawberry/AS	.05
391	Andre Dawson/AS	.05
392	Andy Van Slyke/AS	.05
393	Gary Carter/AS	.05
394	Orel Hershiser/AS	.05
395	Danny Jackson/AS	.05
396	Kirk Gibson/AS	.05
397	Don Mattingly/AS	.30
398	Julio Franco/AS	.05
399	Wade Boggs/AS	.20
400	Alan Trammell/AS	.05
401	Jose Canseco/AS	.15
402	Mike Greenwell/AS	.05
403	Kirby Puckett/AS	.25
404	Bob Boone/AS	.05
405	Roger Clemens/AS	.30
406	Frank Viola/AS	.05
407	Dave Winfield/AS	.20
408	Greg Walker	.05
409	Ken Dayley	.05
410	Jack Clark	.05
411	Mitch Williams	.05
412	Barry Lyons	.05
413	Mike Kingery	.05
414	Jim Fregosi	.05
415	Rich Gossage	.05
416	Fred Lynn	.05
417	Mike LaCoss	.05
418	Bob Dernier	.05
419	Tom Filer	.05
420	Joe Carter	.05
421	Kirk McCaskill	.05
422	Bo Diaz	.05
423	Brian Fisher	.05
424	Luis Polonia	.05
425	Jay Howell	.05
426	Danny Gladden	.05
427	Eric Show	.05
428	Craig Reynolds	.05
429	Twins Leaders (Greg Gagne)	.05
430	Mark Gubicza	.05
431	Luis Rivera	.05
432	Chad Kreuter RC	.10
433	Albert Hall	.05
434	Ken Patterson RC	.05
435	Len Dykstra	.05
436	Bobby Meacham	.05
437	Andy Benes RC (#1 Draft Pick)	.05
438	Greg Gross	.05
439	Frank DiPino	.05
440	Bobby Bonilla	.05
441	Jerry Reed	.05
442	Jose Oquendo	.05
443	Rod Nichols RC	.05
444	Moose Stubing	.05
445	Matt Nokes	.05
446	Rob Murphy	.05
447	Donell Nixon	.05
448	Eric Plunk	.05
449	Carmelo Martinez	.05
450	Roger Clemens	.50
451	Mark Davidson	.05
452	Israel Sanchez RC	.05
453	Tom Prince RC	.05
454	Paul Assenmacher	.05
455	Johnny Ray	.05
456	Tim Belcher	.05
457	Mackey Sasser	.05
458	Donn Pall RC	.05
459	Mariners Leaders (Dave Valle)	.05
460	Dave Stieb	.05
461	Buddy Bell	.05
462	Jose Guzman	.05
463	Steve Lake	.05
464	Bryn Smith	.05
465	Mark Grace	.05
466	Chuck Crim	.05
467	Jim Walewander	.05
468	Henry Cotto	.05
469	Jose Bautista RC	.05
470	Lance Parrish	.05
471	Steve Curry RC	.05
472	Brian Harper	.05
473	Don Robinson	.05
474	Bob Rodgers	.05
475	Dave Parker	.05
476	Jon Perlman RC	.05
477	Dick Schofield	.05
478	Doug Drabek	.05
479	Mike Macfarlane	.05
480	Keith Hernandez	.05
481	Chris Brown	.05
482	Steve Peters RC	.05
483	Mickey Hatcher	.05
484	Steve Shields	.05
485	Hubie Brooks	.05
486	Jack McDowell	.05
487	Scott Lusader RC	.05
488	Kevin Coffman	.05
489	Phillies Leaders (Mike Schmidt)	.15
490	Chris Sabo	.05
491	Mike Birkbeck	.05
492	Alan Ashby	.05
493	Todd Benzinger	.05
494	Shane Rawley	.05
495	Candy Maldonado	.05
496	Dwayne Henry	.05
497	Pete Stanicek	.05
498	Dave Valle	.05
499	Don Heinkel RC	.05
500	Jose Canseco	.35
501	Vance Law	.05
502	Duane Ward	.05
503	Al Newman	.05
504	Bob Walk	.05
505	Pete Rose	.75
506	Kirt Manwaring	.05
507	Steve Farr	.05
508	Wally Backman	.05
509	Bud Black	.05
510	Bob Horner	.05
511	Richard Dotson	.05
512	Donnie Hill	.05
513	Jesse Orosco	.05
514	Chet Lemon	.05
515	Barry Larkin	.05
516	Eddie Whitson	.05
517	Greg Brock	.05
518	Bruce Ruffin	.05
519	Yankees Leaders (Willie Randolph)	.05
520	Rick Sutcliffe	.05
521	Mickey Tettleton	.05
522	Randy Kramer RC	.05
523	Andres Thomas	.05
524	Checklist 397-528	.05
525	Chili Davis	.05
526	Wes Gardner	.05
527	Dave Henderson	.05
528	Luis Medina RC	.05
529	Tom Foley	.05
530	Nolan Ryan	.75
531	Dave Hengel RC	.05
532	Jerry Browne	.05
533	Andy Hawkins	.05
534	Doc Edwards	.05
535	Todd Worrell	.05
536	Joel Skinner	.05
537	Pete Smith	.05
538	Juan Castillo	.05
539	Barry Jones	.05
540	Bo Jackson	.10
541	Cecil Fielder	.05
542	Todd Frohwirth	.05
543	Damon Berryhill	.05
544	Jeff Sellers	.05
545	Mookie Wilson	.05
546	Mark Williamson	.05
547	Mark McLemore	.05
548	Bobby Witt	.05
549	Cubs Leaders (Jamie Moyer)	.05
550	Orel Hershiser	.05
551	Randy Ready	.05
552	Greg Cadaret	.05
553	Luis Salazar	.05
554	Nick Esasky	.05
555	Bert Blyleven	.05
556	Bruce Fields RC	.05
557	Keith Miller RC	.05
558	Dan Pasqua	.05
559	Juan Agosto	.05
560	Tim Raines	.05
561	Luis Aguayo	.05
562	Danny Cox	.05
563	Bill Schroeder	.05
564	Russ Nixon	.05
565	Jeff Russell	.05
566	Al Pedrique	.05
567	David Wells	.05
568	Mickey Brantley	.05
569	German Jimenez RC	.05
570	Tony Gwynn	.45
571	Billy Ripken	.05
572	Atlee Hammaker	.05
573	Jim Abbott RC (#1 Draft Pick)	.10
574	Dave Clark	.05
575	Juan Samuel	.05
576	Greg Minton	.05
577	Randy Bush	.05
578	John Morris	.05
579	Astros Leaders (Glenn Davis)	.05
580	Harold Reynolds	.05
581	Gene Nelson	.05
582	Mike Marshall	.05
583	Paul Gibson RC	.05
584	Randy Velarde RC	.05
585	Harold Baines	.05
586	Joe Boever	.05
587	Mike Stanley	.05
588	Luis Alicea RC	.05
589	Dave Meads	.05
590	Andres Galarraga	.05
591	Jeff Musselman	.05
592	John Cangelosi	.05
593	Drew Hall	.05
594	Jimy Williams	.05
595	Teddy Higuera	.05
596	Kurt Stillwell	.05
597	Terry Taylor RC	.05
598	Ken Gerhart	.05
599	Tom Candiotti	.05
600	Wade Boggs	.45
601	Dave Dravecky	.05
602	Devon White	.05
603	Frank Tanana	.05
604	Paul O'Neill	.05
605a	Bob Welch (Missing Complete Major League Pitching Record line.)	3.00
605b	Bob Welch (Contains Complete Major League Pitching Record line.)	.05
606	Rick Dempsey	.05
607	Willie Ansley RC (#1 Draft Pick)	.05
608	Phil Bradley	.05
609	Tigers Leaders (Frank Tanana)	.05
610	Randy Myers	.05
611	Don Slaught	.05
612	Dan Quisenberry	.05
613	Gary Varsho RC	.05
614	Joe Hesketh	.05
615	Robin Yount	.40
616	Steve Rosenberg RC	.05
617	Mark Parent RC	.05
618	Rance Mulliniks	.05
619	Checklist 529-660	.05
620	Barry Bonds	.75
621	Rick Mahler	.05
622	Stan Javier	.05
623	Fred Toliver	.05
624	Jack McKeon	.05
625	Eddie Murray	.40
626	Jeff Reed	.05
627	Greg Harris	.05
628	Matt Williams	.05
629	Pete O'Brien	.05
630	Mike Greenwell	.05
631	Dave Bergman	.05
632	Bryan Harvey RC	.10
633	Daryl Boston	.05
634	Marvin Freeman RC	.05
635	Willie Randolph	.05
636	Bill Wilkinson	.05
637	Carmen Castillo	.05
638	Floyd Bannister	.05
639	Athletics Leaders (Walt Weiss)	.05
640	Willie McGee	.05
641	Curt Young	.05
642	Argenis Salazar	.05
643	Louie Meadows RC	.05
644	Lloyd McClendon	.05
645	Jack Morris	.05
646	Kevin Bass	.05
647	Randy Johnson RC	3.00
648	Sandy Alomar RC (Future Star)	.25
649	Stewart Cliburn	.05
650	Kirby Puckett	.45
651	Tom Niedenfuer	.05
652	Rich Gedman	.05
653	Tommy Barrett RC	.05
654	Whitey Herzog	.05
655	Dave Magadan	.05
656	Ivan Calderon	.05
657	Joe Magrane	.05
658	R.J. Reynolds	.05
659	Al Leiter	.05
660	Will Clark	.05
661	Dwight Gooden (Turn Back the Clock)	.05
662	Lou Brock (Turn Back the Clock)	.05
663	Hank Aaron (Turn Back the Clock)	.15
664	Gil Hodges (Turn Back the Clock)	.05
665a	Tony Oliva (No copyright line.)	12.50

665b	Tony Oliva (With copyright line.)	.05
666	Randy St. Claire	.05
667	Dwayne Murphy	.05
668	Mike Bielecki	.05
669	Dodgers Leaders (Orel Hershiser)	.05
670	Kevin Seitzer	.05
671	Jim Gantner	.05
672	Allan Anderson	.05
673	Don Baylor	.05
674	Otis Nixon	.05
675	Bruce Hurst	.05
676	Ernie Riles	.05
677	Dave Schmidt	.05
678	Dion James	.05
679	Willie Fraser	.05
680	Gary Carter	.40
681	Jeff Robinson	.05
682	Rick Leach	.05
683	Jose Cecena **RC**	.05
684	Dave Johnson	.05
685	Jeff Treadway	.05
686	Scott Terry	.05
687	Alvin Davis	.05
688	Zane Smith	.05
689a	Stan Jefferson (Pink triangle at bottom-left photo.)	.05
689b	Stan Jefferson (Pink/purple triangle.)	
689c	Stan Jefferson (Purple triangle.)	.05
690	Doug Jones	.05
691	Roberto Kelly	.05
692	Steve Ontiveros	.05
693	Pat Borders **RC**	.05
694	Les Lancaster	.05
695	Carlton Fisk	.40
696	Don August	.05
697	Franklin Stubbs	.05
698	Keith Atherton	.05
699	Pirates Leaders (Al Pedrique)	.05
700	Don Mattingly	.50
701	Storm Davis	.05
702	Jamie Quirk	.05
703	Scott Garrelts	.05
704	Carlos Quintana **RC**	.05
705	Terry Kennedy	.05
706	Pete Incaviglia	.05
707	Steve Jeltz	.05
708	Chuck Finley	.05
709	Tom Herr	.05
710	Dave Cone	.05
711	Candy Sierra **RC**	.05
712	Bill Swift	.05
713	Ty Griffin **RC** (#1 Draft Pick)	.05
714	Joe M. Morgan	.05
715	Tony Pena	.05
716	Wayne Tolleson	.05
717	Jamie Moyer	.05
718	Glenn Braggs	.05
719	Danny Darwin	.05
720	Tim Wallach	.05
721	Ron Tingley **RC**	.05
722	Todd Stottlemyre	.05
723	Rafael Belliard	.05
724	Jerry Don Gleaton	.05
725	Terry Steinbach	.05
726	Dickie Thon	.05
727	Joe Orsulak	.05
728	Charlie Puleo	.05
729	Rangers Leaders (Steve Buechele)	.05
730	Danny Jackson	.05
731	Mike Young	.05
732	Steve Buechele	.05
733	Randy Bockus **RC**	.05
734	Jody Reed	.05
735	Roger McDowell	.05
736	Jeff Hamilton	.05
737	Norm Charlton **RC**	.05
738	Darnell Coles	.05
739	Brook Jacoby	.05
740	Dan Plesac	.05
741	Ken Phelps	.05
742	Mike Harkey **RC** (Future Star)	.05
743	Mike Heath	.05
744	Roger Craig	.05
745	Fred McGriff	.05
746	German Gonzalez **RC**	.05
747	Wil Tejada **RC**	.05
748	Jimmy Jones	.05
749	Rafael Ramirez	.05
750	Bret Saberhagen	.05
751	Ken Oberkfell	.05
752	Jim Gott	.05
753	Jose Uribe	.05
754	Bob Brower	.05
755	Mike Scioscia	.05
756	Scott Medvin **RC**	.05
757	Brady Anderson	.05
758	Gene Walter	.05
759	Brewers Leaders (Rob Deer)	.05
760	Lee Smith	.05
761	Dante Bichette **RC**	.25
762	Bobby Thigpen	.05
763	Dave Martinez	.05
764	Robin Ventura (#1 Draft Pick)	.25
765	Glenn Davis	.05
766	Cecilio Guante	.05
767	Mike Capel **RC**	.05
768	Bill Wegman	.05
769	Junior Ortiz	.05

770	Alan Trammell	.05
771	Ron Kittle	.05
772	Ron Oester	.05
773	Keith Moreland	.05
774	Frank Robinson	.15
775	Jeff Reardon	.05
776	Nelson Liriano	.05
777	Ted Power	.05
778	Bruce Benedict	.05
779	Craig McMurtry	.05
780	Pedro Guerrero	.05
781	Greg Briley **RC**	.05
782	Checklist 661-792	.05
783	Trevor Wilson **RC**	.05
784	Steve Avery **RC** (#1 Draft Pick)	.15
785	Ellis Burks	.05
786	Melido Perez	.05
787	Dave West **RC**	.05
788	Mike Morgan	.05
789	Royals Leaders (Bo Jackson)	.05
790	Sid Fernandez	.05
791	Jim Lindeman	.05
792	Rafael Santana	.05

Tiffany

This special hobby-only edition shares the checklist with the regular 1989 Topps set. Cards are identical except for the use of white cardboard stock and the high-gloss front coating. Production has been reported as 25,000 sets.

	NM/M
Unopened Set (792):	75.00
Complete Set (792):	40.00
Common Player:	.10

Traded

For the ninth straight year, Topps issued its annual 132-card "Traded" set at the end of the 1989 baseball season. The set, which was packaged in a special box and sold by hobby dealers, includes traded players and rookies who were not in the regular 1989 Topps set.

	NM/M
Unopened Set, Retail (132):	12.50
Unopened Set, Hobby (132):	10.00
Complete Set (132):	7.50
Common Player:	.05

1T	Don Aase	.05
2T	Jim Abbott	.05
3T	Kent Anderson **RC**	.05
4T	Keith Atherton	.05
5T	Wally Backman	.05
6T	Steve Balboni	.05
7T	Jesse Barfield	.05
8T	Steve Bedrosian	.05
9T	Todd Benzinger	.05
10T	Geronimo Berroa	.05
11T	Bert Blyleven	.05
12T	Bob Boone	.05
13T	Phil Bradley	.05
14T	Jeff Brantley **RC**	.05
15T	Kevin Brown **RC**	.05
16T	Jerry Browne	.05
17T	Chuck Cary	.05
18T	Carmen Castillo	.05
19T	Jim Clancy	.05
20T	Jack Clark	.05
21T	Bryan Clutterbuck	.05
22T	Jody Davis	.05
23T	Mike Devereaux	.05
24T	Frank DiPino	.05
25T	Benny Distefano	.05
26T	John Dopson	.05
27T	Len Dykstra	.05
28T	Jim Eisenreich	.05
29T	Nick Esasky	.05
30T	Alvaro Espinoza	.05
31T	Darrell Evans	.05
32T	Junior Felix	.05
33T	Felix Fermin	.05
34T	Julio Franco	.05
35T	Terry Francona	.05
36T	Cito Gaston	.05
37T	Bob Geren **RC** (Photo actually Mike Fennell).	.05
38T	Tom Gordon **RC**	.10
39T	Tommy Gregg **RC**	.05
40T	Ken Griffey	.05
41T	Ken Griffey Jr. **RC**	6.00

42T	Kevin Gross	.05
43T	Lee Guetterman	.05
44T	Mel Hall	.05
45T	Erik Hanson **RC**	.05
46T	Gene Harris **RC**	.05
47T	Andy Hawkins	.05
48T	Rickey Henderson	.40
49T	Tom Herr	.05
50T	Ken Hill **RC**	.05
51T	Brian Holman **RC**	.05
52T	Brian Holton	.05
53T	Art Howe	.05
54T	Ken Howell	.05
55T	Bruce Hurst	.05
56T	Chris James	.05
57T	Randy Johnson	1.50
58T	Jimmy Jones	.05
59T	Terry Kennedy	.05
60T	Paul Kilgus	.05
61T	Eric King	.05
62T	Ron Kittle	.05
63T	John Kruk	.05
64T	Randy Kutcher **RC**	.05
65T	Steve Lake	.05
66T	Mark Langston	.05
67T	Dave LaPoint	.05
68T	Rick Leach	.05
69T	Terry Leach	.05
70T	Jim Levebvre	.05
71T	Al Leiter	.05
72T	Jeffrey Leonard	.05
73T	Derek Lilliquist **RC**	.05
74T	Rick Mahler	.05
75T	Tom McCarthy **RC**	.05
76T	Lloyd McClendon	.05
77T	Lance McCullers	.05
78T	Oddibe McDowell	.05
79T	Roger McDowell	.05
80T	Larry McWilliams	.05
81T	Randy Milligan	.05
82T	Mike Moore	.05
83T	Keith Moreland	.05
84T	Mike Morgan	.05
85T	Jamie Moyer	.05
86T	Rob Murphy	.05
87T	Eddie Murray	.40
88T	Pete O'Brien	.05
89T	Gregg Olson	.05
90T	Steve Ontiveros	.05
91T	Jesse Orosco	.05
92T	Spike Owen	.05
93T	Rafael Palmeiro	.35
94T	Clay Parker **RC**	.05
95T	Jeff Parrett	.05
96T	Lance Parrish	.05
97T	Dennis Powell	.05
98T	Rey Quinones	.05
99T	Doug Rader	.05
100T	Willie Randolph	.05
101T	Shane Rawley	.05
102T	Randy Ready	.05
103T	Bip Roberts	.05
104T	Kenny Rogers **RC**	.10
105T	Ed Romero	.05
106T	Nolan Ryan	1.00
107T	Luis Salazar	.05
108T	Juan Samuel	.05
109T	Alex Sanchez **RC**	.05
110T	Deion Sanders **RC**	.50
111T	Steve Sax	.05
112T	Rick Schu	.05
113T	Dwight Smith **RC**	.05
114T	Lonnie Smith	.05
115T	Billy Spiers **RC**	.05
116T	Kent Tekulve	.05
117T	Walt Terrell	.05
118T	Milt Thompson	.05
119T	Dickie Thon	.05
120T	Jeff Torborg	.05
121T	Jeff Treadway	.05
122T	Omar Vizquel **RC**	.50
123T	Jerome Walton **RC**	.05
124T	Gary Ward	.05
125T	Claudell Washington	.05
126T	Curt Wilkerson	.05
127T	Eddie Williams	.05
128T	Frank Williams	.05
129T	Ken Williams	.05
130T	Mitch Williams	.05
131T	Steve Wilson **RC**	.05
---	Topps Magazine Subscription Offer Card	.05

Traded Tiffany

The Topps Traded set was issued in a specially boxed, hobby-only edition. Cards are identical to the regular-issue Topps Traded cards except for the application of a high-gloss to the fronts. Production has been reported as 15,000 sets.

	NM/M
Unopened Set (132):	85.00
Complete Set (132):	50.00
Common Player:	.10

Traded Jackie Robinson Bronze

This 1/4-size metal replica of Robinson's first-ever Topps card was issued to dealers who purchased cases of 1989 Topps Traded sets. Each detail of the 1952 Topps Robinson card is reproduced on the 1-1/4" x 1-3/4" bronze metal mini-card, right down to the stats.

	NM/M
312	Jackie Robinson	10.00

Box Panels

Continuing its practice of printing baseball cards on the bottom panels of its wax pack boxes, Topps in 1989 issued a special 16-card set, printing four cards on each of four different box-bottom panels. The cards are identical in design to the regular 1989 Topps cards. They are designated by letter (from A through P) rather than by number.

	NM/M
Complete Panel Set (4):	7.50
Complete Singles Set: (16):	7.50
Common Panel:	1.50
Common Single Player:	.10

PANEL			NM/M
			1.50
A	George Bell		.10
B	Bill Buckner		.10
C	Darrell Evans		.10
D	Goose Gossage		.10
PANEL			1.50
E	Greg Gross		.10
F	Rickey Henderson		.60
G	Keith Hernandez		.10
H	Tommy Lasorda		.10
PANEL			7.50
I	Jim Rice		.20
J	Cal Ripken Jr.		2.00
K	Nolan Ryan		2.00
L	Mike Schmidt		.75
PANEL			2.00
M	Bruce Sutter		.30
N	Don Sutton		.30
O	Kent Tekulve		.10
P	Dave Winfield		.60

All-Star Glossy Set of 22

The glossy All-Stars were included in the Topps 1989 rack packs. Format was very similar to the sets produced since 1984. Besides the starting lineups of the 1988 All-Star Game, the set included the managers and honorary team captains, Bobby Doerr and Willie Stargell.

	NM/M
Complete Set (22):	3.00
Common Player:	.05
1	Tom Kelly	.05
2	Mark McGwire	.75
3	Paul Molitor	.40

4	Wade Boggs	.50
5	Cal Ripken, Jr.	1.00
6	Jose Canseco	.30
7	Rickey Henderson	.40
8	Dave Winfield	.40
9	Terry Steinbach	.05
10	Frank Viola	.05
11	Bobby Doerr	.05
12	Whitey Herzog	.05
13	Will Clark	.05
14	Ryne Sandberg	.50
15	Bobby Bonilla	.05
16	Ozzie Smith	.50
17	Vince Coleman	.05
18	Andre Dawson	.25
19	Darryl Strawberry	.05
20	Gary Carter	.40
21	Dwight Gooden	.05
22	Willie Stargell	.10

All-Star Glossy Set of 60

For the seventh straight year Topps issued this "send-away" glossy set. Divided into six 10-card sets, it was available only by sending in special offer cards from wax packs. The 2-1/2" x 3-1/2" cards feature full-color photos bordered in white with a thin yellow frame. The player's name appears in small print in the lower-right corner. Red-and-blue-printed flip sides provide basic information. Any of the six 10-card sets were available for $1.25 and six special offer cards. The set was also made available in its complete 60-card set form for $7.50 and 18 special offer cards.

	NM/M
Complete Set (60):	6.00
Common Player:	.05
1	Kirby Puckett	.60
2	Eric Davis	.05
3	Joe Carter	.05
4	Andy Van Slyke	.05
5	Wade Boggs	.60
6	Dave Cone	.05
7	Kent Hrbek	.05
8	Darryl Strawberry	.05
9	Jay Buhner	.05
10	Ron Gant	.05
11	Will Clark	.05
12	Jose Canseco	.35
13	Juan Samuel	.05
14	George Brett	.75
15	Benny Santiago	.05
16	Dennis Eckersley	.40
17	Gary Carter	.50
18	Frank Viola	.05
19	Roberto Alomar	.15
20	Paul Gibson	.05
21	Dave Winfield	.50
22	Howard Johnson	.05
23	Roger Clemens	.65
24	Bobby Bonilla	.05
25	Alan Trammell	.05
26	Kevin McReynolds	.05
27	George Bell	.05
28	Bruce Hurst	.05
29	Mark Grace	.05
30	Tim Belcher	.05
31	Mike Greenwell	.05
32	Glenn Davis	.05
33	Gary Gaetti	.05
34	Ryne Sandberg	.60
35	Rickey Henderson	.50
36	Dwight Evans	.05
37	Doc Gooden	.05
38	Robin Yount	.50
39	Damon Berryhill	.05
40	Chris Sabo	.05
41	Mark McGwire	1.00
42	Ozzie Smith	.60
43	Paul Molitor	.50
44	Andres Galarraga	.05
45	Dave Stewart	.05
46	Tom Browning	.05
47	Cal Ripken, Jr.	1.50
48	Orel Hershiser	.05
49	Dave Gallagher	.05
50	Walt Weiss	.05
51	Don Mattingly	.65
52	Tony Fernandez	.05
53	Tim Raines	.05
54	Jeff Reardon	.05

55	Kirk Gibson	.05
56	Jack Clark	.05
57	Danny Jackson	.05
58	Tony Gwynn	.60
59	Cecil Espy	.05
60	Jody Reed	.05

American Baseball

For the second consecutive year Topps released an 88-card set of baseball cards available in both the United States and the United Kingdom. The mini-sized cards (2-1/4" x 3") are printed on white stock with a low-gloss finish. The game-action color player photo is outlined in red, white and blue and framed in white. Backs are horizontal and include a characterization cartoon along with biographical information and statistics. The cards were sold in packs of five with a stick of bubble gum for 12 pence.

	NM/M
Complete Set (88):	6.00
Common Player:	.05
Wax Pack (5):	.50
Wax Box (48):	8.00
1	Brady Anderson	.05
2	Harold Baines	.05
3	George Bell	.05
4	Wade Boggs	.60
5	Barry Bonds	1.50
6	Bobby Bonilla	.05
7	George Brett	.75
8	Hubie Brooks	.05
9	Tom Brunansky	.05
10	Jay Buhner	.05
11	Brett Butler	.05
12	Jose Canseco	.30
13	Joe Carter	.05
14	Jack Clark	.05
15	Will Clark	.05
16	Roger Clemens	.65
17	Dave Cone	.05
18	Alvin Davis	.05
19	Eric Davis	.05
20	Glenn Davis	.05
21	Andre Dawson	.25
22	Bill Doran	.05
23	Dennis Eckersley	.35
24	Dwight Evans	.05
25	Tony Fernandez	.05
26	Carlton Fisk	.45
27	John Franco	.05
28	Andres Galarraga	.05
29	Ron Gant	.05
30	Kirk Gibson	.05
31	Dwight Gooden	.05
32	Mike Greenwell	.05
33	Mark Gubicza	.05
34	Pedro Gurrero	.05
35	Ozzie Guillen	.05
36	Tony Gwynn	.60
37	Rickey Henderson	.45
38	Orel Hershiser	.05
39	Teddy Higuera	.05
40	Charlie Hough	.05
41	Kent Hrbek	.05
42	Bruce Hurst	.05
43	Bo Jackson	.10
44	Gregg Jefferies	.05
45	Ricky Jordan	.05
46	Wally Joyner	.05
47	Mark Langston	.05
48	Mike Marshall	.05
49	Don Mattingly	.75
50	Fred McGriff	.05
51	Mark McGwire	1.00
52	Kevin McReynolds	.05
53	Paul Molitor	.45
54	Jack Morris	.05
55	Dale Murphy	.20
56	Eddie Murray	.05
57	Pete O'Brien	.05
58	Rafael Palmeiro	.05
59	Gerald Perry	.05
60	Kirby Puckett	.60
61	Tim Raines	.05
62	Johnny Ray	.05
63	Rick Reuschel	.05
64	Cal Ripken	1.50
65	Chris Sabo	.05
66	Juan Samuel	.05
67	Ryne Sandberg	.60

68	Benny Santiago	.05
69	Steve Sax	.05
70	Mike Schmidt	.75
71	Ruben Sierra	.05
72	Ozzie Smith	.60
73	Cory Snyder	.05
74	Dave Stewart	.05
75	Darryl Strawberry	.05
76	Greg Swindell	.05
77	Alan Trammell	.05
78	Fernando Valenzuela	.05
79	Andy Van Slyke	.05
80	Frank Viola	.05
81	Claudell Washington	.05
82	Walt Weiss	.05
83	Lou Whitaker	.05
84	Dave Winfield	.45
85	Mike Witt	.05
86	Gerald Young	.05
87	Robin Yount	.45
88	Checklist	.05

Batting Leaders

The active career batting leaders are showcased in this 22-card set. The 2-1/2" x 3-1/2" cards are printed on super glossy stock with full-color photos and bright red borders. A "Top Active Career Batting Leaders" cup is displayed in a lower corner. The player's name appears above the photo. This set is specially numbered in accordance to career batting average. Wade Boggs is featured on card #1 as the top active career batting leader. The flip sides present batting statistics. One batting leader card was included in each K-Mart blister pack, which also includes 100 cards from the 1989 regular Topps set.

		NM/M
Complete Set (22):		90.00
Common Player:		1.50
1	Wade Boggs	12.00
2	Tony Gwynn	12.00
3	Don Mattingly	16.00
4	Kirby Puckett	12.00
5	George Brett	16.00
6	Pedro Guerrero	1.50
7	Tim Raines	1.50
8	Keith Hernandez	1.50
9	Jim Rice	3.00
10	Paul Molitor	8.00
11	Eddie Murray	1.50
12	Willie McGee	1.50
13	Dave Parker	1.50
14	Julio Franco	1.50
15	Rickey Henderson	8.00
16	Kent Hrbek	1.50
17	Willie Wilson	1.50
18	Johnny Ray	1.50
19	Pat Tabler	1.50
20	Carney Lansford	1.50
21	Robin Yount	8.00
22	Alan Trammell	1.50

Big Baseball

Known by collectors as Topps "Big Baseball," the cards in this 330-card set measure 2-5/8" x 3-3/4" and are patterned after the 1956 Topps cards. The glossy card fronts are horizontally-designed and include two photos of each player, a portrait alongside an action photo. The backs include 1988 and career stats, but are dominated by a color cartoon featuring the player. Members of the 1988 Team U.S.A. Olympic baseball team are included in the set, which was issued in three series of 110 cards each.

		NM/M
Complete Set (330):		9.00
Common Player:		.05
Wax Pack:		.40
Wax Box (36):		7.50
1	Orel Hershiser	.05
2	Harold Reynolds	.05
3	Jody Davis	.05
4	Greg Walker	.05
5	Barry Bonds	1.00
6	Bret Saberhagen	.05
7	Johnny Ray	.05
8	Mike Fiore	.05
9	Juan Castillo	.05
10	Todd Burns	.05
11	Carmelo Martinez	.05
12	Geno Petralli	.05
13	Mel Hall	.05
14	Tom Browning	.05
15	Fred McGriff	.05
16	Kevin Elster	.05
17	Tim Leary	.05
18	Jim Rice	.20
19	Bret Barberie	.05
20	Jay Buhner	.05
21	Atlee Hammaker	.05
22	Lou Whitaker	.05
23	Paul Runge	.05
24	Carlton Fisk	.40
25	Jose Lind	.05
26	Mark Gubicza	.05
27	Billy Ripken	.05
28	Mike Pagliarulo	.05
29	Jim Deshaies	.05
30	Mark McLemore	.05
31	Scott Terry	.05
32	Franklin Stubbs	.05
33	Don August	.05
34	Mark McGwire	.75
35	Eric Show	.05
36	Cecil Espy	.05
37	Ron Tingley	.05
38	Mickey Brantley	.05
39	Paul O'Neill	.05
40	Ed Sprague	.05
41	Len Dykstra	.05
42	Roger Clemens	.60
43	Ron Gant	.05
44	Dan Pasqua	.05
45	Jeff Robinson	.05
46	George Brett	.65
47	Bryn Smith	.05
48	Mike Marshall	.05
49	Doug Robbins	.05
50	Don Mattingly	.65
51	Mike Scott	.05
52	Steve Jeltz	.05
53	Dick Schofield	.05
54	Tom Brunansky	.05
55	Gary Sheffield	.45
56	Dave Valle	.05
57	Carney Lansford	.05
58	Tony Gwynn	.50
59	Checklist	.05
60	Damon Berryhill	.05
61	Jack Morris	.05
62	Brett Butler	.05
63	Mickey Hatcher	.05
64	Bruce Sutter	.35
65	Robin Ventura	.05
66	Junior Ortiz	.05
67	Pat Tabler	.05
68	Greg Swindell	.05
69	Jeff Branson	.05
70	Manny Lee	.05
71	Dave Magadan	.05
72	Rich Gedman	.05
73	Tim Raines	.05
74	Mike Maddux	.05
75	Jim Presley	.05
76	Chuck Finley	.05
77	Jose Oquendo	.05
78	Rob Deer	.05
79	Jay Howell	.05
80	Terry Steinbach	.05
81	Eddie Whitson	.05
82	Ruben Sierra	.05
83	Bruce Benedict	.05
84	Fred Manrique	.05
85	John Smiley	.05
86	Mike Macfarlane	.05
87	Rene Gonzales	.05
88	Charles Hudson	.05
90	Les Straker	.05
91	Carmen Castillo	.05
92	Tracy Woodson	.05
93	Tino Martinez	.15
94	Herm Winningham	.05
95	Kelly Gruber	.05
96	Terry Leach	.05
97	Jody Reed	.05
98	Nelson Santovenia	.05
99	Tony Armas	.05
100	Greg Brock	.05
101	Dave Stewart	.05
102	Roberto Alomar	.20
103	Jim Sundberg	.05
104	Albert Hall	.05
105	Steve Lyons	.05
106	Sid Bream	.05
107	Danny Tartabull	.05
108	Rick Dempsey	.05
109	Rich Renteria	.05
110	Ozzie Smith	.50
111	Steve Sax	.05
112	Kelly Downs	.05
113	Larry Sheets	.05
114	Andy Benes	.05
115	Pete O'Brien	.05
116	Kevin McReynolds	.05
117	Juan Berenguer	.05
118	Billy Hatcher	.05
119	Rick Cerone	.05
120	Andre Dawson	.15
121	Storm Davis	.05
122	Devon White	.05
123	Alan Trammell	.05
124	Vince Coleman	.05
125	Al Leiter	.05
126	Dale Sveum	.05
127	Pete Incaviglia	.05
128	Dave Stieb	.05
129	Kevin Mitchell	.05
130	Dave Schmidt	.05
131	Gary Redus	.05
132	Ron Robinson	.05
133	Darnell Coles	.05
134	Benny Santiago	.05
135	John Farrell	.05
136	Willie Wilson	.05
137	Steve Bedrosian	.05
138	Don Slaught	.05
139	Darryl Strawberry	.05
140	Frank Viola	.05
141	Dave Silvestri	.05
142	Carlos Quintana	.05
143	Vance Law	.05
144	Dave Parker	.05
145	Tim Belcher	.05
146	Will Clark	.05
147	Mark Williamson	.05
148	Ozzie Guillen	.05
149	Kirk McCaskill	.05
150	Pat Sheridan	.05
151	Terry Pendleton	.05
152	Roberto Kelly	.05
153	Joey Meyer	.05
154	Mark Grant	.05
155	Joe Carter	.05
156	Steve Buechele	.05
157	Tony Fernandez	.05
158	Jeff Reed	.05
159	Bobby Bonilla	.05
160	Henry Cotto	.05
161	Kurt Stillwell	.05
162	Mickey Morandini	.05
163	Robby Thompson	.05
164	Rick Schu	.05
165	Stan Jefferson	.05
166	Ron Darling	.05
167	Kirby Puckett	.50
168	Bill Doran	.05
169	Dennis Lamp	.05
170	Ty Griffin	.05
171	Ron Hassey	.05
172	Dale Murphy	.15
173	Andres Galarraga	.05
174	Tim Flannery	.05
175	Cory Snyder	.05
176	Checklist	.05
177	Tommy Barrett	.05
178	Dan Petry	.05
179	Billy Masse	.05
180	Terry Kennedy	.05
181	Joe Orsulak	.05
182	Doyle Alexander	.05
183	Willie McGee	.05
184	Jim Gantner	.05
185	Keith Hernandez	.05
186	Greg Gagne	.05
187	Kevin Bass	.05
188	Mark Eichhorn	.05
189	Mark Grace	.15
190	Jose Canseco	.35
191	Bobby Witt	.05
192	Rafael Santana	.05
193	Dwight Evans	.05
194	Greg Booker	.05
195	Brook Jacoby	.05
196	Rafael Belliard	.05
197	Candy Maldonado	.05
198	Mickey Tettleton	.05
199	Barry Larkin	.05
200	Frank White	.05
201	Wally Joyner	.05
202	Chet Lemon	.05
203	Joe Magrane	.05
204	Glenn Braggs	.05
205	Scott Fletcher	.05
206	Gary Ward	.05
207	Nelson Liriano	.05
208	Howard Johnson	.05
209	Kent Hrbek	.05
210	Ken Caminiti	.05
211	Mike Greenwell	.05
212	Ryne Sandberg	.50
213	Joe Slusarski	.05
214	Donnell Nixon	.05
215	Tim Wallach	.05
216	John Kruk	.05
217	Charles Nagy	.05
218	Alvin Davis	.05
219	Oswald Peraza	.05
220	Mike Schmidt	.65
221	Spike Owen	.05
222	Mike Smithson	.05
223	Dion James	.05
224	Ernie Whitt	.05
225	Mike Davis	.05
226	Gene Larkin	.05
227	Pat Combs	.05
228	Jack Howell	.05
229	Ron Oester	.05
230	Paul Gibson	.05
231	Mookie Wilson	.05
232	Glenn Hubbard	.05
233	Shawon Dunston	.05
234	Otis Nixon	.05
235	Melido Perez	.05
236	Jerry Browne	.05
237	Rick Rhoden	.05
238	Bo Jackson	.10
239	Randy Velarde	.05
240	Jack Clark	.05
241	Wade Boggs	.50
242	Lonnie Smith	.05
243	Mike Flanagan	.05
244	Willie Randolph	.05
245	Oddibe McDowell	.05
246	Ricky Jordan	.05
247	Greg Briley	.05
248	Rex Hudler	.05
249	Robin Yount	.40
250	Lance Parrish	.05
251	Chris Sabo	.05
252	Mike Henneman	.05
253	Gregg Jefferies	.05
254	Curt Young	.05
255	Andy Van Slyke	.05
256	Rod Booker	.05
257	Rafael Palmeiro	.35
258	Jose Uribe	.05
259	Ellis Burks	.05
260	John Smoltz	.05
261	Tom Foley	.05
262	Lloyd Moseby	.05
263	Jim Poole	.05
264	Gary Gaetti	.05
265	Bob Dernier	.05
266	Harold Baines	.05
267	Tom Candiotti	.05
268	Rafael Ramirez	.05
269	Bob Boone	.05
270	Buddy Bell	.05
271	Rickey Henderson	.40
272	Willie Fraser	.05
273	Eric Davis	.05
274	Jeff Robinson	.05
275	Damaso Garcia	.05
276	Sid Fernandez	.05
277	Stan Javier	.05
278	Marty Barrett	.05
279	Gerald Perry	.05
280	Rob Ducey	.05
281	Mike Scioscia	.05
282	Randy Bush	.05
283	Tom Herr	.05
284	Glenn Wilson	.05
285	Pedro Guerrero	.05
286	Cal Ripken, Jr.	1.00
287	Randy Johnson	.50
288	Julio Franco	.05
289	Ivan Calderon	.05
290	Rich Yett	.05
291	Scott Servais	.05
292	Bill Pecota	.05
293	Ken Phelps	.05
294	Chili Davis	.05
295	Manny Trillo	.05
296	Mike Boddicker	.05
297	Geronimo Berroa	.05
298	Todd Stottlemyre	.05
299	Kirk Gibson	.05
300	Wally Backman	.05
301	Hubie Brooks	.05
302	Von Hayes	.05
303	Matt Nokes	.05
304	Dwight Gooden	.05
305	Walt Weiss	.05
306	Mike LaValliere	.05
307	Cris Carpenter	.05
308	Ted Wood	.05
309	Jeff Russell	.05
310	Dave Gallagher	.05
311	Andy Allanson	.05
312	Craig Reynolds	.05
313	Kevin Seitzer	.05
314	Dave Winfield	.40
315	Andy McGaffigan	.05
316	Nick Esasky	.05
317	Jeff Blauser	.05
318	George Bell	.05
319	Eddie Murray	.40
320	Mark Davidson	.05
321	Juan Samuel	.05
322	Jim Abbott	.05
323	Kal Daniels	.05
324	Mike Brumley	.05
325	Gary Carter	.40
326	Dave Henderson	.05
327	Checklist	.05
328	Garry Templeton	.05
329	Pat Perry	.05
330	Paul Molitor	.40

Coins

RUBEN SIERRA RANGERS

Similar in format to previous Topps coins, this 60-piece set features 1-1/2" diameter coins with rolled colored edges. A shooting star device printed over the player photo gives his name, team and position. Backs have a few biographical details and a summary of the player's previous season performance printed in black on silver. The coins were sold three per pack, with each pack including an offer card for an album to house the pieces.

		NM/M
Factory Boxed Set (60):		15.00
Complete Set (60):		7.50
Common Player:		.10
Wax Pack (3):		.10
Wax Box (36):		8.00
1	Kirk Gibson	.10
2	Orel Herhiser	.10
3	Chris Sabo	.10
4	Tony Gwynn	.50
5	Brett Butler	.10
6	Bobby Bonilla	.10
7	Jack Clark	.10
8	Will Clark	.50
9	Eric Davis	.10
10	Glenn Davis	.10
11	Andre Dawson	.15
12	John Franco	.10
13	Andres Galarraga	.10
14	Dwight Gooden	.10
15	Mark Grace	.10
16	Pedro Guerrero	.10
17	Ricky Jordan	.10
18	Mike Marshall	.10
19	Dale Murphy	.15
20	Eddie Murray	.40
21	Gerald Perry	.10
22	Tim Raines	.10
23	Juan Samuel	.10
24	Benito Santiago	.10
25	Ozzie Smith	.50
26	Darryl Strawberry	.10
27	Andy Van Slyke	.10
28	Gerald Young	.10
29	Jose Canseco	.35
30	Frank Viola	.10
31	Walt Weiss	.10
32	Wade Boggs	.50
33	Harold Baines	.10
34	George Brett	.75
35	Jay Buhner	.10
36	Joe Carter	.10
37	Roger Clemens	.60
38	Alvin Davis	.10
39	Tony Fernandez	.10
40	Carlton Fisk	.40
41	Mike Greenwell	.10
42	Kent Hrbek	.10
43	Don Mattingly	.75
44	Fred McGriff	.10
45	Mark McGwire	1.00
46	Paul Molitor	.10
47	Rafael Palmeiro	.35
48	Kirby Puckett	.50
49	Johnny Ray	.10
50	Cal Ripken, Jr.	1.50
51	Ruben Sierra	.10
52	Pete Stanicek	.10
53	Dave Stewart	.10
54	Greg Swindell	.10
55	Danny Tartabull	.10
56	Alan Trammell	.10
57	Lou Whitaker	.10
58	Dave Winfield	.40
59	Mike Witt	.10
60	Robin Yount	.40

Double Headers All-Stars

MIKE GREENWELL

This scarce test issue was produced in two versions, an All-Stars set and a set of exclusively Mets and Yankees players. The "cards" are two-sided miniature (1-5/8" x 2-1/4") reproductions of the player's 1989 Topps card and his Topps rookie card, encased in a clear plastic stand.

		NM/M
Complete Set (24):		9.00
Common Player:		.50
Wax Pack (1):		.50
Wax Box (24):		9.00
(1)	Alan Ashby	.50
(2)	Wade Boggs	1.00
(3)	Bobby Bonilla	.50
(4)	Jose Canseco	.65
(5)	Will Clark	.50
(6)	Roger Clemens	1.25
(7)	Andre Dawson	.60
(8)	Dennis Eckersley	.65
(9)	Carlton Fisk	.75
(10)	John Franco	.50
(11)	Julio Franco	.50
(12)	Kirk Gibson	.50
(13)	Mike Greenwell	.50
(14)	Orel Hershiser	.50
(15)	Danny Jackson	.50
(16)	Don Mattingly	1.25
(17)	Mark McGwire	2.00
(18)	Kirby Puckett	1.00
(19)	Ryne Sandberg	1.00
(20)	Ozzie Smith	1.00
(21)	Darryl Strawberry	.50
(22)	Alan Trammell	.50
(23)	Andy Van Slyke	.50
(24)	Frank Viola	.50

Double Headers Mets/Yankees Proofs

In advance of its special Mets/Yankees Double Headers novelty issue, Topps prepared a series of proof versions featuring four players from each of the New York teams. Like the later issues, these Double Headers feature miniature versions of the players' Topps rookie cards in a small plastic stand-up frame. However, the proof versions have the rookie cards back-to-back with the players' 1988 Topps cards, rather than 1989 as on the regularly issued pieces. Two different types of wrappers are found for the proofs, an opaque paper envelope picturing Gary Carter's piece and a cellophane wrapper with the proof issue's checklist.

		NM/M
Complete Set (8):		425.00
Common Player:		50.00
(1)	Gary Carter	125.00
(2)	Ron Darling	50.00
(3)	Dwight Gooden	50.00
(4)	Darryl Strawberry	50.00
(1)	Rickey Henderson	125.00
(2)	Don Mattingly	200.00
(3)	Dave Righetti	50.00
(4)	Dave Winfield	125.00

Double Headers Mets/Yankees

This was a regionally issued test for the concept of two "mini" baseball cards of a player encapsulated in clear plastic. Only New York players are represented in the set. Each double header plastic frame holds miniature (1-5/8" x 2-1/4") versions of the player's 1989 Topps card, and his first Topps card, printed on thin paper. The Double Headers of players who also appeared in the All-Star issue are indistinguishable in this version. The stand-ups were sold in boxes of 24 paper-wrapped pieces. It is reported that each box contains a full set. The unnumbered pieces are checklisted here in alphabetical order by team.

		NM/M
Complete Set (24):		150.00
Common Player:		10.00
New York Mets Team Set:		85.00
(1)	Gary Carter	25.00
(2)	David Cone	10.00
(3)	Ron Darling	10.00
(4)	Len Dykstra	10.00
(5)	Doc Gooden	10.00
(6)	Keith Hernandez	10.00
(7)	Gregg Jefferies	10.00
(8)	Howard Johnson	10.00
(9)	Kevin McReynolds	10.00
(10)	Randy Myers	10.00
(11)	Darryl Strawberry	.50
(12)	Tim Teufel	10.00
(13)	Mookie Wilson	10.00

New York Yankees Team Set: 65.00

(14)	Richard Dotson	10.00
(15)	Rickey Henderson	25.00
(16)	Don Mattingly	3.00
(17)	Mike Pagliarulo	10.00
(18)	Ken Phelps	10.00
(19)	Rick Rhoden	10.00
(20)	Dave Righetti	10.00
(21)	Rafael Santana	10.00
(22)	Steve Sax	10.00
(23)	Claudell Washington	10.00
(24)	Dave Winfield	25.00

Gallery of Champions

Topps continued its issue of 1/4-size metallic ingot reproductions of current-year baseball cards with aluminum, bronze and sterling silver sets in 1989. Again the players represented major award winners from the previous season. The metal mini-cards were sold only as complete sets. Dealers who ordered bronze and silver sets could receive as a bonus a pewter version of the Jose Canseco ingot.

		NM/M
Complete Aluminum Set (12):		12.50
Complete Bronze Set (12):		50.00
Complete Silver Set (12):		120.00
(1a)	Wade Boggs/Aluminum	3.50
(1b)	Wade Boggs/Bronze	12.00
(1s)	Wade Boggs/Silver	25.00
(2a)	Jose Canseco/Aluminum	2.00
(2b)	Jose Canseco/Bronze	5.00
(2s)	Jose Canseco/Silver	15.00
(2p)	Jose Canseco/Pewter	7.50
(3a)	Will Clark/Aluminum	3.50
(3b)	Will Clark/Bronze	3.50
(3s)	Will Clark/Silver	7.50
(4a)	Dennis Eckersley/Aluminum	1.50
(4b)	Dennis Eckersley/Bronze	5.00
(4s)	Dennis Eckersley/Silver	10.00
(5a)	John Franco/Aluminum	1.00
(5b)	John Franco/Bronze	3.50
(5s)	John Franco/Silver	7.50
(6a)	Kirk Gibson/Aluminum	1.00
(6b)	Kirk Gibson/Bronze	3.50
(6s)	Kirk Gibson/Silver	7.50
(7a)	Tony Gwynn/Aluminum	3.50
(7b)	Tony Gwynn/Bronze	10.00
(7s)	Tony Gwynn/Silver	25.00
(8a)	Orel Hershiser/Aluminum	1.00
(8b)	Orel Hershiser/Bronze	3.50
(8s)	Orel Hershiser/Silver	7.50
(9a)	Chris Sabo/Aluminum	1.00
(9b)	Chris Sabo/Bronze	3.50
(9s)	Chris Sabo/Silver	7.50
(10a)	Darryl Strawberry/Aluminum	1.00
(10b)	Darryl Strawberry/Bronze	3.50
(10s)	Darryl Strawberry/Silver	7.50
(11a)	Frank Viola/Aluminum	1.00
(11b)	Frank Viola/Bronze	3.50
(11s)	Frank Viola/Silver	7.50
(12a)	Walt Weiss/Aluminum	1.00
(12b)	Walt Weiss/Bronze	3.50
(12s)	Walt Weiss/Silver	7.50

Glossy Rookies Set of 22

DAVID WELLS

Bearing the same design and style of the past two years, Topps featured the top first-year players from the 1988 season in this glossy set. The full-color player photo appears beneath the "1988 Rookies" banner. The player's name is displayed beneath the photo. The flip side features the "1988 Rookies Commemorative Set" logo followed by the player ID and card number. Glossy rookies were found only in 100-card jumbo cello packs.

		NM/M
Complete Set (22):		5.00
Common Player:		.15
1	Roberto Alomar	.50
2	Brady Anderson	.15
3	Tim Belcher	.15
4	Damon Berryhill	.15
5	Jay Buhner	.25
6	Kevin Elster	.15
7	Cecil Espy	.15
8	Dave Gallagher	.15
9	Ron Gant	.25
10	Paul Gibson	.15
11	Mark Grace	.50
12	Darrin Jackson	.15
13	Gregg Jefferies	.25
14	Ricky Jordan	.15
15	Al Leiter	.15
16	Melido Perez	.15
17	Chris Sabo	.15
18	Nelson Santovenia	.15
19	Mackey Sasser	.15
20	Gary Sheffield	2.00
21	Walt Weiss	.15
22	David Wells	.15

Heads Up! Test Issue

Much rarer than the 1990 issue, this 24-card test debuted the bizarre "shrunken head" format of a die-cut player's head and cap printed on heavy cardboard, approximately 4-1/2" x 6-1/2" in size and sold one per pack. Backs feature both a small plastic suction cup and an adhesive strip for hanging the card. The player's name and team are printed in black on the back. Except for the copyright date on back, the cards of players from the 1989 test set which were repeated in the 1990 regular issue are virtually identical and often sell for much less than those players who were unique in the 1989 set.

		NM/M
Complete Set (24):		600.00
Common Player:		12.00
1	Tony Gwynn	65.00
2	Will Clark	17.50
3	Dwight Gooden	12.00
4	Ricky Jordan	12.00
5	Ken Griffey Jr.	150.00
6	Darryl Strawberry	17.50
7	Frank Viola	17.50
8	Bo Jackson	15.00
9	Ryne Sandberg	65.00
10	Gregg Jefferies	17.50
11	Wade Boggs	65.00
12	Ellis Burks	17.50
13	Gary Sheffield	25.00
14	Mark McGwire	150.00
15	Mark Grace	17.50
16	Jim Abbott	12.00
17	Ozzie Smith	65.00
18	Jose Canseco	25.00
19	Don Mattingly	75.00
20	Kirby Puckett	65.00
21	Eric Davis	17.50
22	Mike Greenwell	17.50
23	Dale Murphy	30.00
24	Mike Schmidt	125.00

Mini League Leaders

This 77-card set features baseball's statistical leaders from the 1988 season. It is referred to as a "mini" set because of the cards' small (2-1/8" x 3") size. The glossy cards feature action photos that have a soft focus on all edges. The player's team and name appear along the bottom of the card. The

back features a head-shot of the player along with his 1988 season ranking and stats.

		NM/M
Complete Set (77):		3.00
Common Player:		.05
Wax Pack (7):		.25
Wax Box (36):		6.00
1	Dale Murphy	.20
2	Gerald Perry	.05
3	Andre Dawson	.25
4	Greg Maddux	.65
5	Rafael Palmeiro	.45
6	Tom Browning	.05
7	Kal Daniels	.05
8	Eric Davis	.05
9	John Franco	.05
10	Danny Jackson	.05
11	Barry Larkin	.05
12	Jose Rijo	.05
13	Chris Sabo	.05
14	Nolan Ryan	1.00
15	Mike Scott	.05
16	Gerald Young	.05
17	Kirk Gibson	.05
18	Orel Hershiser	.05
19	Steve Sax	.05
20	John Tudor	.05
21	Hubie Brooks	.05
22	Andres Galarraga	.05
23	Otis Nixon	.05
24	Dave Cone	.05
25	Sid Fernandez	.05
26	Dwight Gooden	.05
27	Kevin McReynolds	.05
28	Darryl Strawberry	.05
29	Juan Samuel	.05
30	Bobby Bonilla	.05
31	Sid Bream	.05
32	Jim Gott	.05
33	Andy Van Slyke	.05
34	Vince Coleman	.05
35	Jose DeLeon	.05
36	Joe Magrane	.05
37	Ozzie Smith	.65
38	Todd Worrell	.05
39	Tony Gwynn	.65
40	Brett Butler	.05
41	Will Clark	.65
42	Rick Reuschel	.05
43	Checklist	
44	Eddie Murray	.50
45	Wade Boggs	.65
46	Roger Clemens	.70
47	Dwight Evans	.05
48	Mike Greenwell	.05
49	Bruce Hurst	.05
50	Johnny Ray	.05
51	Doug Jones	.05
52	Greg Swindell	.05
53	Gary Pettis	.05
54	George Brett	.70
55	Mark Gubicza	.05
56	Willie Wilson	.05
57	Teddy Higuera	.05
58	Paul Molitor	.50
59	Robin Yount	.50
60	Allan Anderson	.05
61	Gary Gaetti	.05
62	Kirby Puckett	.65
63	Jeff Reardon	.05
64	Frank Viola	.05
65	Jack Clark	.05
66	Rickey Henderson	.50
67	Dave Winfield	.50
68	Jose Canseco	.35
69	Dennis Eckersley	.45
70	Mark McGwire	.75
71	Dave Stewart	.05
72	Alvin Davis	.05
73	Mark Langston	.05
74	Harold Reynolds	.05
75	George Bell	.05
76	Tony Fernandez	.05
77	Fred McGriff	.05

Stickercards

Once again in 1989 Topps used a stickercard as cardboard backing for its paper sticker issue. Measuring 2-1/8" x 3", the cards are found with either one or two player stickers on back. The stickercards have a player photo on a background of graduated color. Minimal stats and biographic data are pre-

SUPER STAR RYNE SANDBERG 2B

sented at the bottom. Values shown are for complete stickercard/sticker(s), without regard to which stickers are on back.

		NM/M
Complete Set (66):		5.00
Common Player:		.05
Wax Pack (5):		.25
Wax Box (48):		6.00
1	George Brett	.65
2	Don Mattingly	.65
3	Mark McGwire	.75
4	Julio Franco	.05
5	Harold Reynolds	.05
6	Lou Whitaker	.05
7	Wade Boggs	.50
8	Gary Gaetti	.05
9	Paul Molitor	.45
10	Tony Fernandez	.05
11	Cal Ripken Jr.	1.00
12	Alan Trammell	.05
13	Jose Canseco	.30
14	Joe Carter	.05
15	Dwight Evans	.05
16	Mike Greenwell	.05
17	Dave Henderson	.05
18	Rickey Henderson	.45
19	Kirby Puckett	.45
20	Dave Winfield	.45
21	Robin Yount	.45
22	Bob Boone	.05
23	Carlton Fisk	.45
24	Geno Petralli	.05
25	Roger Clemens	.65
26	Mark Gubicza	.05
27	Dave Stewart	.05
28	Teddy Higuera	.05
29	Bruce Hurst	.05
30	Frank Viola	.05
31	Dennis Eckersley	.40
32	Doug Jones	.05
33	Jeff Reardon	.05
34	Will Clark	.05
35	Glenn Davis	.05
36	Andres Galarraga	.05
37	Juan Samuel	.05
38	Ryne Sandberg	.50
39	Steve Sax	.05
40	Bobby Bonilla	.05
41	Howard Johnson	.05
42	Vance Law	.05
43	Shawon Dunston	.05
44	Barry Larkin	.05
45	Ozzie Smith	.05
46	Barry Bonds	1.00
47	Eric Davis	.05
48	Andre Dawson	.25
49	Kirk Gibson	.05
50	Tony Gwynn	.05
51	Kevin McReynolds	.05
52	Rafael Palmeiro	.40
53	Darryl Strawberry	.05
54	Andy Van Slyke	.05
55	Gary Carter	.45
56	Mike LaValliere	.05
57	Benito Santiago	.05
58	David Cone	.05
59	Dwight Gooden	.05
60	Orel Hershiser	.05
61	Tom Browning	.05
62	Danny Jackson	.05
63	Bob Knepper	.05
64	Mark Davis	.05
65	John Franco	.05
66	Randy Myers	.05

Stickers

Topps' 1989 stickers were produced in two formats. Some measure 2-1/8" x 3" while there are 128 pairs of half-size (1-1/2" x 2-1/8") stickers. All stickers are attached to Super Star stickercards from which they can be peeled and affixed in a special Yearbook which was sold separately for 50 cents. Stickers have large center photos with white borders. Above and below are zipping fastball graphics trailing graduated color bars (blues for N.L., reds for A.L.). A tiny black sticker number is in the lower-right corner. There is no player name on the stickers; the albums have a box under each space with player data. The half-size stickers are printed in pairs and are checklisted in that fashion. Values given are for complete sticker(s)/stickercard combinations, but without regard to which stickercard is on back.

		NM/M
Complete Set (326):		11.00
Common Player/Pair:		.05
Album:		2.00
1-230	George Bell, Jeff Ballard	.05
2-272	Gary Carter, Steve Farr	.25
3-324	Doug Jones, Mark Grace	.05
4-320	John Franco, Cecil Espy	.05
5-322	Andre Dawson, Ron Gant	.15
6-326	Pat Tabler, Walt Weiss	.05
7-317	Tom Browning, Tim Belcher	.05
8-239	Jeff Reardon, Larry Sheets	.05
9-325	Wade Boggs, Chris Sabo	.30
10-319	Kevin McReynolds, Jay Buhner	.05
11-323	Jose Canseco, Paul Gibson	.20
12-318	Orel Hershiser, Damon Berryhill	.05
13-231	Dave Smith, Mickey Tettleton	.05
14-302	Kevin Bass, Jack McDowell	.05
15-232	Mike Scott, Pete Stanicek	.05
16-256	Bill Doran, Jim Rice	.10
17-207	Rafael Ramirez, Andy Allanson	.05
18-181	Buddy Bell, Jack Howell	.05
19-214	Billy Hatcher, John Farrell	.05
20-275	Nolan Ryan, Frank Tanana	.50
21	Glenn Davis	.05
22	Bob Knepper	.05
23-211	Gerald Young, Tom Candiotti	.05
24-208	Dion James, Julio Franco	.05
25-243	Bruce Sutter, Jeff Russell	.20
26-310	Andres Thomas, Tommy John	.05
27-200	Zane Smith, B.J. Surhoff	.05
28-198	Ozzie Virgil, Teddy Higuera	.05
29-269	Rick Mahler, Floyd Bannister	.05
30-219	Albert Hall, Mickey Brantley	.05
31-203	Pete Smith, Jim Gantner	.05
32	Dale Murphy	.20
33	Gerald Perry	.05
34-177	Ron Gant, Chili Davis	.05
35-244	Bob Horner, Mike Stanley	.05
36-313	Willie McGee, Rafael Santana	.05
37-288	Luis Alicea, Greg Gagne	.05
38-279	Tony Pena, Gary Pettis	.05
39-184	Todd Worrell, Kirk McCaskill	.05
40-228	Pedro Guerrero, Bill Swift	.05
41-174	Tom Brunansky, Dick Schofield	.05
42-262	Terry Pendleton, Frank White	.05
43	Vince Coleman	.05
44	Ozzie Smith	.60
45-240	Jose Oquendo, Cecil Espy	.05
46-191	Vance Law, Pat Borders	.05
47-258	Rafael Palmeiro, Bob Stanley	.25
48-213	Greg Maddux, Greg Swindell	.30
49-229	Shawon Dunston, Jose Bautista	.05
50-210	Mark Grace, Cory Snyder	.05
51-187	Damon Berryhill, Kelly Gruber	.05
52-192	Rick Sutcliffe, Rance Mulliniks	.05
53-291	Jamie Moyer, Juan Berenguer	.05
54	Andre Dawson	.05
55	Ryne Sandberg	.60
56-284	Calvin Schiraldi, Jeff Reardon	.05
57-308	Steve Sax, Jack Clark	.05
58-263	Mike Scioscia, Bret Saberhagen	.05
59-298	Alfredo Griffin, Steve Lyons	.05
60-202	Fernando Valenzuela, Rob Deer	.05
61-286	Jay Howell, Dan Gladden	.05
62-305	Tim Leary, Bobby Thigpen	.05
63-212	John Shelby, Brook Jacoby	.05
64-306	John Tudor, John Candelaria	.05
65	Orel Hershiser	.05
66	Kirk Gibson	.05
67-223	Mike Marshall, Jim Presley	.05
68-206	Luis Rivera, Dale Sveum	.05
69-311	Tim Burke, Mike Pagliarulo	.05
70-253	Tim Wallach, Rich Gedman	.05
71-265	Pascual Perez, Bo Jackson	.05
72-185	Hubie Brooks, Fred McGriff	.05
73-250	Jeff Parrett, Steve Buechele	.05
74-316	Dennis Martinez, Rich Dotson	.05
75-285	Andy McGaffigan, Bert Blyleven	.05
76	Andres Galarraga	.05
77	Rock Raines	.05
78-287	Nelson Santovenia, Kent Hrbek	.05
79-261	Rick Reuschel, Mike Boddicker	.05
80-276	Mike Aldrete, Luis Salazar	.05
81-247	Kelly Downs, Mitch Williams	.05
82-283	Jose Uribe, Chet Lemon	.05
83-190	Mike Krukow, Mike Flanagan	.05
84-179	Kevin Mitchell, Devon White	.05
85-195	Brett Butler, Tom Henke	.05
86-252	Don Robinson, Dwight Evans	.05
87	Robby Thompson	.05
88	Will Clark	.05
89-188	Candy Maldonado, Lloyd Moseby	.05
90-180	Len Dykstra, Bryan Harvey	.05
91-234	Howard Johnson, Rene Gonzalez	.05
92-266	Roger McDowell, Kurt Stillwell	.05
93-222	Keith Hernandez, Steve Balboni	.05
94-178	Gary Carter, Brian Downing	.05
95-277	Kevin McReynolds, Jack Morris	.05
96-307	David Cone, Dave Righetti	.05
97-175	Randy Myers, Bob Boone	.05
98	Darryl Strawberry	.05
99	Doc Gooden	.05
100-257	Ron Darling, Marty Barrett	.05
101-201	Benny Santiago, Greg Brock	.05
102-273	John Kruk, Mike Henneman	.05
103-242	Chris Brown, Ruben Sierra	.05
104-255	Roberto Alomar, Mike Greenwell	.10
105-290	Keith Moreland, Tim Laudner	.05
106-217	Randy Ready, Scott Bailes	.05
107-267	Marvell Wynne, Danny Tartabull	.05
108-176	Lance McCullers, Mike Witt	.05
109	Tony Gwynn	.60
110	Mark Davis	.05
111-186	Andy Hawkins, Tom Niedenfeur	.05
112-233	Steve Bedrosian, Jim Traber	.05
113-196	Phil Bradley, Glenn Braggs	.05
114-189	Steve Jeltz, Tony Fernandez	.05
115-209	Von Hayes, Bud Black	.05
116-245	Kevin Gross, Charlie Hough	.05
117-218	Juan Samuel, Henry Cotto	.05
118-274	Shane Rawley, Doyle Alexander	.05
119-186	Chris James, Jimmy Key	.05
120	Mike Schmidt	.65
121	Don Carman	.05
122-280	Bruce Ruffin, Matt Nokes	.05
123-246	Bob Walk, Scott Fletcher	.05

#	Player	Price
124-278	John Smiley, Tom Brookens	.05
125-301	Sid Bream, Dan Pasqua	.05
126-251	Jose Lind, Lee Smith	.05
127-309	Barry Bonds, Willie Randolph	.40
128-294	Mike LaValliere, Gene Larkin	.05
129-225	Jeff D. Robinson, Scott Bradley	.05
130-295	Mike Dunne, Dave Gallagher	.05
131	Bobby Bonilla	.05
132	Andy Van Slyke	.05
133-241	Rafael Belliard, Jose Guzman	.05
134-197	Nick Esasky, Dan Plesac	.05
135-300	Bo Diaz, Fred Manrique	.05
136-221	John Franco, Mark Langston	.05
137-312	Barry Larkin, Rickey Henderson	.25
138-173	Eric Davis, Ron Hassey	.05
139-299	Jeff Treadway, Carlton Fisk	.05
140-254	Jose Rijo, Ellis Burks	.05
141-220	Tom Browning, Mike Moore	.05
142	Chris Sabo	.05
143	Danny Jackson	.05
144-199	Kal Daniels, Jeffrey Leonard	.05
145	Rickey Henderson/AS	.50
146	Paul Molitor/AS	.25
147	Wade Boggs/AS	.35
148	Jose Canseco/AS	.20
149	Dave Winfield/AS	.30
150	Cal Ripken Jr./AS	.30
151	Mark McGwire/AS	.40
152	Terry Steinbach/AS	.05
153	Frank Viola/AS	.05
154	Vince Coleman/AS	.05
155	Ryne Sandberg/AS	.35
156	Andre Dawson/AS	.15
157	Darryl Strawberry/AS	.05
158	Bobby Bonilla/AS	.05
159	Will Clark/AS	.05
160	Gary Carter/AS	.05
161	Ozzie Smith/AS	.35
162	Doc Gooden/AS	.05
163-268	Dave Stewart, Willie Wilson	.05
164-297	Dave Henderson, Ivan Calderon	.05
165-321	Terry Steinbach, Dave Gallagher	.05
166-264	Bob Welch, Kevin Seitzer	.05
167-224	Dennis Eckersley, Rey Quinones	.30
168-235	Walt Weiss, Terry Kennedy	.05
169-296	Dave Parker, Melido Perez	.05
170-289	Carney Lansford, Gary Gaetti	.05
171	Jose Canseco	.35
172	Mark McGwire	.75
182	Johnny Ray	.05
183	Wally Joyner	.05
193	George Bell	.05
194	Dave Steib	.05
204	Paul Molitor	.50
205	Robin Yount	.50
215	Doug Jones	.05
216	Joe Carter	.05
226	Harold Reynolds	.05
227	Alvin Davis	.05
237	Cal Ripken Jr.	1.00
238	Eddie Murray	.50
248	Pete O'Brien	.05
249	Pete Incaviglia	.05
259	Roger Clemens	.65
260	Wade Boggs	.60
270	George Brett	.65
271	Mark Gubicza	.05
281	Alan Trammell	.05
282	Lou Whitaker	.05
292	Frank Viola	.05
293	Kirby Puckett	.60
303	Ozzie Guillen	.05
304	Harold Baines	.05
314	Don Mattingly	.50
315	Dave Winfield	.50

LJN Baseball Talk

Another generation of "talking baseball cards" was produced by Topps and the LJN Toy Co. in 1989. After purchasing a hand-held player, collectors could buy sets of four "Baseball Talk Collection" cards for about $4. The 3-1/4" x 5-1/4" cards have a plastic sheet laminated on their backs containing information about the player which could be heard by inserting the card into the player. Fronts of the cards of players active in 1989 reproduce their 1989 Topps cards. The cards of earlier stars reproduce various older Topps cards of those players. Narrators on the cards were Don Drysdale, Joe Torre and Mel Allen.

ANDRES GALARRAGA

	NM/M
Complete Set (164):	125.00
Common Player:	1.00
Record Player:	30.00

#	Player	Price
1	1975 World Series Game 6	1.00
2	1986 World Series Game 6	1.00
3	1986 ALCS Game 6	1.00
4	1956 World Series Game 5	1.00
5	1986 NLCS Game 6	1.00
6	1969 World Series Game 5	1.00
7	1984 World Series Game 5	1.00
8	1988 World Series Game 1	1.00
9	Reggie Jackson	4.00
10	Brooks Robinson	1.50
11	Billy Williams	1.50
12	Bobby Thomson	1.00
13	Harmon Killebrew	1.50
14	Johnny Bench	2.00
15	Tom Seaver	1.50
16	Willie Stargell	1.50
17	Ernie Banks	4.00
18	Gaylord Perry	1.50
19	Bill Mazeroski	1.50
20	Babe Ruth	7.50
21	Lou Gehrig	6.00
22	Ty Cobb	6.00
23	Bob Gibson	1.50
24	Al Kaline	1.50
25	Rod Carew	1.50
26	Lou Brock	1.50
27	Stan Musial	4.00
28	Joe Morgan	1.50
29	Willie McCovey	1.50
30	Duke Snider	4.00
31	Whitey Ford	4.00
32	Eddie Mathews	1.50
33	Carl Yastrzemski	2.00
34	Pete Rose	7.50
35	Hank Aaron (1976)	6.00
36	Ralph Kiner	1.50
37	Steve Carlton	1.50
38	Roberto Clemente	7.50
39	Don Drysdale	1.50
40	Robin Roberts	1.50
41	Hank Aaron (1954)	6.00
42	Dave Winfield	2.00
43	Alan Trammell	1.00
44	Darryl Strawberry	1.00
45	Ozzie Smith	3.00
46	Kirby Puckett	3.00
47	Will Clark	3.00
48	Keith Hernandez	1.00
49	Wally Joyner	1.00
50	Mike Scott	1.00
51	Eric Davis	1.00
52	George Brett	4.00
53	George Bell	1.00
54	Tommy Lasorda	1.00
55	Rickey Henderson	2.00
56	Robin Yount	3.00
57	Wade Boggs	3.00
58	Roger Clemens	4.00
59	Vince Coleman	1.00
60	Jose Canseco	1.50
61	Fernando Valenzuela	1.00
62	Tony Gwynn	3.00
63	Dwight Gooden	1.00
64	Mark McGwire	6.00
65	Jack Clark	1.00
66	Dale Murphy	1.25
67	Kirk Gibson	1.00
68	Jack Morris	1.00
69	Ryne Sandberg	3.00
70	Nolan Ryan	9.00
71	John Tudor	1.00
72	Mike Schmidt	4.00
73	Dave Righetti	1.00
74	Pedro Guerrero	1.00
75	Rick Sutcliffe	1.00
76	Gary Carter	2.00
77	Cal Ripken Jr.	9.00
78	Andre Dawson	1.00
79	Andy Van Slyke	1.00
80	Tim Raines	1.00
81	Frank Viola	1.00
82	Don Mattingly	4.00
83	Rick Reuschel	1.00
84	Willie McGee	1.00
85	Mark Langston	1.00
86	Ron Darling	1.00
87	Gregg Jefferies	1.00
88	Harold Baines	1.00
89	Eddie Murray	2.00
90	Barry Larkin	1.00
91	Gary Gaetti	1.00
92	Bret Saberhagen	1.00
93	Roger McDowell	1.00
94	Joe Magrane	1.00
95	Juan Samuel	1.00
96	Bert Blyleven	1.00
97	Kal Daniels	1.00
98	Kevin Bass	1.00
99	Glenn Davis	1.00
100	Steve Sax	1.00
101	Rich Gossage	1.00
102	Roger Craig	1.00
103	Carney Lansford	1.00
104	Joe Carter	1.00
105	Bruce Sutter	2.00
106	Barry Bonds	9.00
107	Danny Jackson	1.00
108	Mike Flanagan	1.00
109	Dwight Evans	1.00
110	Ron Guidry	1.00
111	Bruce Hurst	1.00
112	Jim Rice	1.25
113	Oddibe McDowell	1.00
114	Bobby Bonilla	1.00
115	Bob Welch	1.00
116	Dave Parker	1.00
117	Tim Wallach	1.00
118	Tom Henke	1.00
119	Mike Greenwell	1.00
120	Kevin Seitzer	1.00
121	Randy Myers	1.00
122	Andres Galarraga	1.00
123	Orel Hershiser	1.00
124	Cory Snyder	1.00
125	Mike Witt	1.00
126	Mike LaValliere	1.00
127	Pete Incaviglia	1.00
128	Dennis Eckersley	2.00
129	Jimmy Key	1.00
130	John Franco	1.00
131	Dan Plesac	1.00
132	Tony LaRussa	1.00
133	Hubie Brooks	1.00
134	Chili Davis	1.00
135	Bob Boone	1.00
136	Jeff Reardon	1.00
137	Candy Maldonado	1.00
138	Mike Marshall	1.00
139	Tommy John	1.00
140	Chris Sabo	1.00
141	Alvin Davis	1.00
142	Frank White	1.00
143	Harold Reynolds	1.00
144	Lee Smith	1.00
145	John Kruk	1.00
146	Tony Fernandez	1.00
147	Steve Bedrosian	1.00
148	Benito Santiago	1.00
149	Ozzie Guillen	1.00
150	Gerald Perry	1.00
151	Carlton Fisk	2.00
152	Tom Brunansky	1.00
153	Paul Molitor	2.00
154	Todd Worrell	1.00
155	Brett Butler	1.00
156	Sparky Anderson	1.00
157	Kent Hrbek	1.00
158	Frank Tanana	1.00
159	Kevin Mitchell	1.00
160	Charlie Hough	1.00
161	Doug Jones	1.00
162	Lou Whitaker	1.00
163	Fred Lynn	1.00
---	Checklist	.50

Sport Shots Portfolios

In its second year, the number of baseball card folders produced by Shaeffer Eaton reproducing current Topps baseball cards was drastically reduced, from 130 to 39. The format remains the same, a 9-1/2" x 11-3/4" cardboard two-pocket folder. The 1989 portfolios are considerably scarcer than the 1988s.

	NM/M
Complete Set (39):	40.00
Common Player:	1.00

#	Player	Price
10	Andre Dawson	1.25
30	Doc Gooden	1.00
70	Mark McGwire	4.00
85	Kevin McReynolds	1.00
110	Paul Molitor	1.50
120	Frank Viola	1.00
145	Dave Stewart	1.00
180	Mike Scott	1.00
200	George Brett	2.50
205	Dwight Evans	1.00
230	Ozzie Smith	1.00
233	Gregg Jefferies	1.00
260	Dave Winfield	1.50
300	Darryl Strawberry	1.00
330	Eric Davis	1.00
335	Dave Righetti	1.00
340	Kirk Gibson	1.00
370	Dennis Eckersley	1.25
380	Rickey Henderson	1.50
425	Jay Howell	1.00
450	Roger Clemens	2.50
480	Keith Hernandez	1.00
500	Jose Canseco	1.00
527	Dave Henderson	1.00
550	Orel Hershiser	1.00
570	Tony Gwynn	2.00
582	Mike A. Marshall	1.00
590	Andres Galarraga	1.00
600	Wade Boggs	2.00
630	Mike Greenwell	1.00
650	Kirby Puckett	2.00
660	Will Clark	1.00
700	Don Mattingly	2.50
710	David Cone	1.00
725	Terry Steinbach	1.00
730	Danny Jackson	1.00
755	Mike Scioscia	1.00
770	Alan Trammell	1.00
785	Ellis Burks	1.00

1990 Topps

INDIANS — JOEY BELLE

The 1990 Topps set again included 792 cards, and sported a newly-designed front that featured six different color schemes. The set led off with a special four-card salute to Nolan Ryan, and features other specials including All-Stars, Number 1 Draft Picks, Record Breakers, managers, rookies, and "Turn Back the Clock" cards. The set also includes a special card commemorating A. Bartlett Giamatti, the late baseball commissioner. Backs are printed in black on a chartreuse background. The set features 725 different individual player cards, the most ever, including 138 players' first appearance in a regular Topps set.

	NM/M
Unopened Factory Set, Retail (792):	25.00
Unopened Factory Set, Hobby (792):	20.00
Complete Set (792):	15.00
Common Player:	.05
Wax Pack (16):	.60
Wax Box (36):	12.00
Cello Pack (31):	1.00
Cello Box (24):	15.00
Rack Pack (45):	1.00
Rack Box (24):	16.00
Vending Box (500):	7.50

#	Player	Price
1	Nolan Ryan	.75
2	Nolan Ryan (Mets)	.35
3	Nolan Ryan (Angels)	.25
4	Nolan Ryan (Astros)	.25
5	Nolan Ryan (Rangers)	.25
6	Vince Coleman (Record Breaker)	.05
7	Rickey Henderson (Record Breaker)	.20
8	Cal Ripken, Jr. (Record Breaker)	.40
9	Eric Plunk	.05
10	Barry Larkin	.05
11	Paul Gibson	.05
12	Joe Girardi RC	.05
13	Mark Williamson	.05
14	Mike Fetters RC	.05
15	Teddy Higuera	.05
16	Kent Anderson RC	.05
17	Kelly Downs	.05
18	Carlos Quintana	.05
19	Al Newman	.05
20	Mark Gubicza	.05
21	Jeff Torborg	.05
22	Bruce Ruffin	.05
23	Randy Velarde	.05
24	Joe Hesketh	.05
25	Willie Randolph	.05
26	Don Slaught	.05
27	Rick Leach	.05
28	Duane Ward	.05
29	John Cangelosi	.05
30	David Cone	.05
31	Henry Cotto	.05
32	John Farrell	.05
33	Greg Walker	.05
34	Tony Fossas RC	.05
35	Benito Santiago	.05
36	John Costello	.05
37	Domingo Ramos	.05
38	Wes Gardner	.05
39	Curt Ford	.05
40	Jay Howell	.05
41	Matt Williams	.05
42	Jeff Robinson	.05
43	Dante Bichette	.05
44	Roger Salkeld RC (#1 Draft Pick)	.10
45	Dave Parker	.05
46	Rob Dibble	.05
47	Brian Harper	.05
48	Zane Smith	.05
49	Tom Lawless	.05
50	Glenn Davis	.05
51	Doug Rader	.05
52	Jack Daugherty RC	.05
53	Mike LaCoss	.05
54	Joel Skinner	.05
55	Darrell Evans	.05
56	Franklin Stubbs	.05
57	Greg Vaughn	.05
58	Keith Miller	.05
59	Ted Power	.05
60	George Brett	.50
61	Deion Sanders	.10
62	Ramon Martinez	.05
63	Mike Pagliarulo	.05
64	Danny Darwin	.05
65	Devon White	.05
66	Greg Litton RC	.05
67	Scott Sanderson	.05
68	Dave Henderson	.05
69	Todd Frohwirth	.05
70	Mike Greenwell	.05
71	Allan Anderson	.05
72	Jeff Huson RC	.05
73	Bob Milacki	.05
74	Jeff Jackson RC (#1 Draft Pick)	.05
75	Doug Jones	.05
76	Dave Valle	.05
77	Dave Bergman	.05
78	Mike Flanagan	.05
79	Ron Kittle	.05
80	Jeff Russell	.05
81	Bob Rodgers	.05
82	Scott Terry	.05
83	Hensley Meulens	.05
84	Ray Searage	.05
85	Juan Samuel	.05
86	Paul Kilgus	.05
87	Rick Luecken RC	.05
88	Glenn Braggs	.05
89	Clint Zavaras RC	.05
90	Jack Clark	.05
91	Steve Frey RC	.05
92	Mike Stanley	.05
93	Shawn Hillegas	.05
94	Herm Winningham	.05
95	Todd Worrell	.05
96	Jody Reed	.05
97	Curt Schilling	.25
98	Jose Gonzalez RC	.05
99	Rich Monteleone RC	.05
100	Will Clark	.05
101	Shane Rawley	.05
102	Stan Javier	.05
103	Marvin Freeman	.05
104	Bob Knepper	.05
105	Randy Myers	.05
106	Charlie O'Brien	.05
107	Fred Lynn	.05
108	Rod Nichols	.05
109	Roberto Kelly	.05
110	Tommy Helms	.05
111	Ed Whited	.05
112	Glenn Wilson	.05
113	Manny Lee	.05
114	Mike Bielecki	.05
115	Tony Pena	.05
116	Floyd Bannister	.05
117	Mike Sharperson RC	.05
118	Erik Hanson	.05
119	Billy Hatcher	.05
120	John Franco	.05
121	Robin Ventura	.05
122	Shawn Abner	.05
123	Rich Gedman	.05
124	Dave Dravecky	.05
125	Kent Hrbek	.05
126	Randy Kramer	.05
127	Mike Devereaux	.05
128	Checklist 1-132	.05
129	Ron Jones	.05
130	Bert Blyleven	.05
131	Matt Nokes	.05
132	Lance Blankenship RC	.05
133	Ricky Horton	.05
134	Earl Cunningham RC (#1 Draft Pick)	.05
135	Dave Magadan	.05
136	Kevin Brown	.05
137	Marty Pevey RC	.05
138	Al Leiter	.05
139	Greg Brock	.05
140	Andre Dawson	.25
141	John Hart	.05
141	John Hart (No black top-left corner.)	8.00
142	Jeff Wetherby RC	.05
143	Rafael Belliard	.05
144	Bud Black	.05
145	Terry Steinbach	.05
146	Rob Richie RC	.05
147	Chuck Finley	.05
148	Edgar Martinez RC	.05
149	Steve Farr	.05
150	Kirk Gibson	.05
151	Rick Mahler	.05
152	Lonnie Smith	.05
153	Randy Milligan	.05
154	Mike Maddux	.05
155	Ellis Burks	.05
156	Ken Patterson	.05
157	Craig Biggio	.05
158	Craig Lefferts	.05
159	Mike Felder	.05
160	Dave Righetti	.05
161	Harold Reynolds	.05
162	Todd Zeile RC	.20
163	Phil Bradley	.05
164	Jeff Juden RC (#1 Draft Pick)	.05
165	Walt Weiss	.05
166	Bobby Witt	.05
167	Kevin Appier RC	.05
168	Jose Lind	.05
169	Richard Dotson	.05
170	George Bell	.05
171	Russ Nixon	.05
172	Tom Lampkin RC	.05
173	Tim Belcher	.05
174	Jeff Kunkel	.05
175	Mike Moore	.05
176	Luis Quinones	.05
177	Mike Henneman	.05
178	Chris James	.05
179	Brian Holton	.05
180	Rock Raines	.05
181	Juan Agosto	.05
182	Mookie Wilson	.05
183	Steve Lake	.05
184	Danny Cox	.05
185	Ruben Sierra	.05
186	Dave LaPoint	.05
187	Rick Wrona RC	.05
188	Mike Smithson	.05
189	Dick Schofield	.05
190	Rick Reuschel	.05
191	Pat Borders	.05
192	Don August	.05
193	Andy Benes	.05
194	Glenallen Hill RC	.05
195	Tim Burke	.05
196	Gerald Young	.05
197	Doug Drabek	.05
198	Mike Marshall	.05
199	Sergio Valdez RC	.05
200	Don Mattingly	.50
201	Cito Gaston	.05
202	Mike Macfarlane	.05
203	Mike Roesler RC	.05
204	Bob Dernier	.05
205	Mark Davis	.05
206	Nick Esasky	.05
207	Bob Ojeda	.05
208	Brook Jacoby	.05
209	Greg Mathews	.05
210	Ryne Sandberg	.45
211	John Cerutti	.05
212	Joe Orsulak	.05
213	Scott Bankhead	.05
214	Terry Francona	.05
215	Kirk McCaskill	.05
216	Ricky Jordan	.05
217	Don Robinson	.05
218	Wally Backman	.05
219	Donn Pall	.05
220	Barry Bonds	.75
221	Gary Mielke RC	.05
222	Kurt Stillwell	.05
223	Tommy Gregg	.05
224	Delino DeShields RC	.15
225	Jim Deshaies	.05
226	Mickey Hatcher	.05
227	Kevin Tapani RC	.15
228	Dave Martinez	.05
229	David Wells	.05
230	Keith Hernandez	.05
231	Jack McKeon	.05
232	Darnell Coles	.05
233	Ken Hill RC	.05
234	Mariano Duncan	.05
235	Jeff Reardon	.05
236	Hal Morris RC	.05
237	Kevin Ritz RC	.05
238	Felix Jose RC	.05
239	Eric Show	.05
240	Mark Grace	.05
241	Mike Krukow	.05
242	Fred Manrique	.05
243	Barry Jones	.05
244	Bill Schroeder	.05
245	Roger Clemens	.50
246	Jim Eisenreich	.05
247	Jerry Reed	.05
248	Dave Anderson	.05
249	Mike Smith RC	.05
250	Jose Canseco	.25
251	Jeff Blauser	.05
252	Otis Nixon	.05
253	Mark Portugal	.05
254	Francisco Cabrera	.05
255	Bobby Thigpen	.05
256	Marvell Wynne	.05
257	Jose DeLeon	.05
258	Barry Lyons	.05
259	Lance McCullers	.05
260	Eric Davis	.05
261	Whitey Herzog	.05
262	Checklist 133-264	.05
263	Mel Stottlemyre, Jr. RC	.10
264	Bryan Clutterbuck	.05
265	Pete O'Brien	.05
266	German Gonzalez	.05
267	Mark Davidson	.05
268	Rob Murphy	.05
269	Dickie Thon	.05
270	Dave Stewart	.05
271	Chet Lemon	.05
272	Bryan Harvey	.05

#	Player	Price
273	Bobby Bonilla	.05
274	Goose Gozzo RC	.05
275	Mickey Tettleton	.05
276	Gary Thurman	.05
277	Lenny Harris RC	.05
278	Pascual Perez	.05
279	Steve Buechele	.05
280	Lou Whitaker	.05
281	Kevin Bass	.05
282	Derek Lilliquist	.05
283	Albert Belle	.15
284	Mark Gardner RC	.05
285	Willie McGee	.05
286	Lee Guetterman	.05
287	Vance Law	.05
288	Greg Briley	.05
289	Norm Charlton	.05
290	Robin Yount	.35
291	Dave Johnson	.05
292	Jim Gott	.05
293	Mike Gallego	.05
294	Craig McMurtry	.05
295	Fred McGriff	.05
296	Jeff Ballard	.05
297	Tom Herr	.05
298	Danny Gladden	.05
299	Adam Peterson RC	.05
300	Bo Jackson	.10
301	Don Aase	.05
302	Marcus Lawton RC	.05
303	Rick Cerone	.05
304	Marty Clary RC	.05
305	Eddie Murray	.35
306	Tom Niedenfuer	.05
307	Bip Roberts	.05
308	Jose Guzman	.05
309	Eric Yelding RC	.05
310	Steve Bedrosian	.05
311	Dwight Smith	.05
312	Dan Quisenberry	.05
313	Gus Polidor	.05
314	Donald Harris RC (#1 Draft Pick)	.05
315	Bruce Hurst	.05
316	Carney Lansford	.05
317	Mark Guthrie RC	.05
318	Wallace Johnson	.05
319	Dion James	.05
320	Dave Steib	.05
321	Joe M. Morgan	.05
322	Junior Ortiz	.05
323	Willie Wilson	.05
324	Pete Harnisch RC	.05
325	Robby Thompson	.05
326	Tom McCarthy RC	.05
327	Ken Williams	.05
328	Curt Young	.05
329	Oddibe McDowell	.05
330	Ron Darling	.05
331	Juan Gonzalez RC	1.50
332	Paul O'Neill	.05
333	Bill Wegman	.05
334	Johnny Ray	.05
335	Andy Hawkins	.05
336	Ken Griffey Jr.	.75
337	Lloyd McClendon	.05
338	Dennis Lamp	.05
339	Dave Clark	.05
340	Fernando Valenzuela	.05
341	Tom Foley	.05
342	Alex Trevino	.05
343	Frank Tanana	.05
344	George Canale RC	.05
345	Harold Baines	.05
346	Jim Presley	.05
347	Junior Felix RC	.05
348	Gary Wayne RC	.05
349	Steve Finley RC	.15
350	Bret Saberhagen	.05
351	Roger Craig	.05
352	Bryn Smith	.05
353	Sandy Alomar	.05
354	Stan Belinda RC	.05
355	Marty Barrett	.05
356	Randy Ready	.05
357	Dave West	.05
358	Andres Thomas	.05
359	Jimmy Jones	.05
360	Paul Molitor	.35
361	Randy McCament RC	.05
362	Damon Berryhill	.05
363	Dan Petry	.05
364	Rolando Roomes RC	.05
365	Ozzie Guillen	.05
366	Mike Heath	.05
367	Mike Morgan	.05
368	Bill Doran	.05
369	Todd Burns	.05
370	Tim Wallach	.05
371	Jimmy Key	.05
372	Terry Kennedy	.05
373	Alvin Davis	.05
374	Steve Cummings RC	.05
375	Dwight Evans	.05
376	Checklist 265-396	.05
377	Mickey Weston RC	.05
378	Luis Salazar	.05
379	Steve Rosenberg	.05
380	Dave Winfield	.35
381	Frank Robinson	.10
382	Jeff Musselman	.05
383	John Morris	.05
383	John Morris (No black top-right corner.)	8.00
384	Pat Combs RC	.05
385	Fred McGriff/AS	.05
386	Julio Franco/AS	.05
387	Wade Boggs/AS	.20

#	Player	Price
388	Cal Ripken, Jr./AS	.40
389	Robin Yount/AS	.20
390	Ruben Sierra/AS	.20
391	Kirby Puckett/AS	.25
392	Carlton Fisk/AS	.20
393	Bret Saberhagen/AS	.05
394	Jeff Ballard/AS	.05
395	Jeff Russell/AS	.05
396	A. Bartlett Giamatti	.20
397	Will Clark/AS	.20
398	Ryne Sandberg/AS	.20
399	Howard Johnson/AS	.05
400	Ozzie Smith/AS	.20
401	Kevin Mitchell/AS	.05
402	Eric Davis/AS	.05
403	Tony Gwynn/AS	.25
404	Craig Biggio/AS	.05
405	Mike Scott/AS	.05
406	Joe Magrane/AS	.05
407	Mark Davis/AS	.05
408	Trevor Wilson	.05
409	Tom Brunansky	.05
410	Joe Boever	.05
411	Ken Phelps	.05
412	Jamie Moyer	.05
413	Brian DuBois RC	.05
414a	Frank Thomas No Name RC (No name on front.)	650.00
414b	Frank Thomas (Name on front.)	3.00
415	Shawon Dunston	.05
416	Dave Johnson RC	.05
417	Jim Gantner	.05
418	Tom Browning	.05
419	Beau Allred RC	.05
420	Carlton Fisk	.35
421	Greg Minton	.05
422	Pat Sheridan	.05
423	Fred Toliver	.05
424	Jerry Reuss	.05
425	Bill Landrum	.05
426	Jeff Hamilton	.05
427	Carmen Castillo	.05
428	Steve Davis RC	.05
429	Tom Kelly	.05
430	Pete Incaviglia	.05
431	Randy Johnson	.35
432	Damaso Garcia	.05
433	Steve Olin RC	.05
434	Mark Carreon RC	.05
435	Kevin Seitzer	.05
436	Mel Hall	.05
437	Les Lancaster	.05
438	Greg Myers RC	.05
439	Jeff Parrett	.05
440	Alan Trammell	.05
441	Bob Kipper	.05
442	Jerry Browne	.05
443	Cris Carpenter	.05
444	Kyle Abbott RC (FDP)	.10
445	Danny Jackson	.05
446	Dan Pasqua	.05
447	Atlee Hammaker	.05
448	Greg Gagne	.05
449	Dennis Rasmussen	.05
450	Rickey Henderson	.35
451	Mark Lemke	.05
452	Luis de los Santos RC	.05
453	Jody Davis	.05
454	Jeff King (Correct use of white.)	.05
455	Jeffrey Leonard	.05
456	Chris Gwynn RC	.05
457	Gregg Jefferies	.05
458	Bob McClure	.05
459	Jim Lefebvre	.05
460	Mike Scott	.05
461	Carlos Martinez RC	.05
462	Denny Walling	.05
463	Drew Hall	.05
464	Jerome Walton RC	.05
465	Kevin Gross	.05
466	Rance Mulliniks	.05
467	Juan Nieves	.05
468	Billy Ripken	.05
469	John Kruk	.05
470	Frank Viola	.05
471	Mike Brumley	.05
472	Jose Uribe	.05
473	Joe Price	.05
474	Rich Thompson	.05
475	Bob Welch	.05
476	Brad Komminsk	.05
477	Willie Fraser	.05
478	Mike LaValliere	.05
479	Frank White	.05
480	Sid Fernandez	.05
481	Garry Templeton	.05
482	Steve Carter RC	.05
483	Alejandro Pena	.05
484	Mike Fitzgerald	.05
485	John Candelaria	.05
486	Jeff Treadway	.05
487	Steve Searcy	.05
488	Ken Oberkfell	.05
489	Nick Leyva	.05
490	Dan Plesac	.05
491	Dave Cochrane RC	.05
492	Ron Oester	.05
493	Jason Grimsley RC	.05
494	Terry Puhl	.05
495	Lee Smith	.05
496	Cecil Espy	.05
497	Dave Schmidt	.05
498	Rick Schu	.05
499	Bill Long	.05
500	Kevin Mitchell	.05
501	Matt Young	.05

#	Player	Price
502	Mitch Webster	.05
503	Randy St. Claire	.05
504	Tom O'Malley	.05
505	Kelly Gruber	.05
506	Tom Glavine	.25
507	Gary Redus	.05
508	Terry Leach	.05
509	Tom Pagnozzi	.05
510	Dwight Gooden	.05
511	Clay Parker	.05
512	Gary Pettis	.05
513	Mark Eichhorn	.05
514	Andy Allanson	.05
515	Len Dykstra	.05
516	Tim Leary	.05
517	Roberto Alomar	.15
518	Bill Krueger	.05
519	Bucky Dent	.05
520	Mitch Williams	.05
521	Craig Worthington	.05
522	Mike Dunne	.05
523	Jay Bell	.05
524	Daryl Boston	.05
525	Wally Joyner	.05
526	Checklist 397-528	.05
527	Ron Hassey	.05
528	Kevin Wickander RC	.05
529	Greg Harris	.05
530	Mark Langston	.05
531	Ken Caminiti	.05
532	Cecilio Guante	.05
533	Tim Jones RC	.05
534	Louie Meadows	.05
535	John Smoltz	.05
536	Bob Geren RC	.05
537	Mark Grant	.05
538	Billy Spiers RC	.05
539	Neal Heaton	.05
540	Danny Tartabull	.05
541	Pat Perry	.05
542	Darren Daulton	.05
543	Nelson Liriano	.05
544	Dennis Boyd	.05
545	Kevin McReynolds	.05
546	Kevin Hickey	.05
547	Jack Howell	.05
548	Pat Clements	.05
549	Don Zimmer	.05
550	Julio Franco	.05
551	Tim Crews	.05
552	Mike Smith RC	.05
553	Scott Scudder RC	.05
554	Jay Buhner	.05
555	Jack Morris	.05
556	Gene Larkin	.05
557	Jeff Innis RC	.05
558	Rafael Ramirez	.05
559	Andy McGaffigan	.05
560	Steve Sax	.05
561	Ken Dayley	.05
562	Chad Kreuter	.05
563	Alex Sanchez	.05
564	Tyler Houston RC (#1 Draft Pick)	.10
565	Scott Fletcher	.05
566	Mark Knudson	.05
567	Ron Gant	.05
568	John Smiley	.05
569	Ivan Calderon	.05
570	Cal Ripken, Jr.	.75
571	Brett Butler	.05
572	Greg Harris	.05
573	Danny Heep	.05
574	Bill Swift	.05
575	Lance Parrish	.05
576	Mike Dyer RC	.05
577	Charlie Hayes RC	.05
578	Joe Magrane	.05
579	Art Howe	.05
580	Joe Carter	.05
581	Ken Griffey	.05
582	Rick Honeycutt	.05
583	Bruce Benedict	.05
584	Phil Stephenson RC	.05
585	Kal Daniels	.05
586	Ed Nunez	.05
587	Lance Johnson	.05
588	Rick Rhoden	.05
589	Mike Aldrete	.05
590	Ozzie Smith	.45
591	Todd Stottlemyre	.05
592	R.J. Reynolds	.05
593	Scott Bradley	.05
594	Luis Sojo RC	.05
595	Greg Swindell	.05
596	Jose DeJesus RC	.05
597	Chris Bosio	.05
598	Brady Anderson	.05
599	Frank Williams	.05
600	Darryl Strawberry	.05
601	Luis Rivera	.05
602	Scott Garrelts	.05
603	Tony Armas	.05
604	Ron Robinson	.05
605	Mike Scioscia	.05
606	Storm Davis	.05
607	Steve Jeltz	.05
608	Eric Anthony RC	.10
609	Sparky Anderson	.10
610	Pedro Guerrero	.05
611	Walt Terrell	.05
612	Dave Gallagher	.05
613	Jeff Pico	.05
614	Nelson Santovenia	.05
615	Rob Deer	.05
616	Brian Holman	.05
617	Geronimo Berroa	.05
618	Eddie Whitson	.05

#	Player	Price
619	Rob Ducey	.05
620	Tony Castillo RC	.05
621	Melido Perez	.05
622	Sid Bream	.05
623	Jim Corsi	.05
624	Darrin Jackson	.05
625	Roger McDowell	.05
626	Bob Melvin	.05
627	Jose Rijo	.05
628	Candy Maldonado	.05
629	Eric Hetzel RC	.05
630	Gary Gaetti	.05
631	John Wetteland RC	.15
632	Scott Lusader	.05
633	Dennis Cook RC	.05
634	Luis Polonia	.05
635	Brian Downing	.05
636	Jesse Orosco	.05
637	Craig Reynolds	.05
638	Jeff Montgomery	.05
639	Tony LaRussa	.05
640	Rick Sutcliffe	.05
641	Doug Strange RC	.05
642	Jack Armstrong	.05
643	Alfredo Griffin	.05
644	Paul Assenmacher	.05
645	Jose Oquendo	.05
646	Checklist 529-660	.05
647	Rex Hudler	.05
648	Jim Clancy	.05
649	Dan Murphy RC	.05
650	Mike Witt	.05
651	Rafael Santana	.05
652	Mike Boddicker	.05
653	John Moses	.05
654	Paul Coleman RC (#1 Draft Pick)	.05
655	Gregg Olson	.05
656	Mackey Sasser	.05
657	Terry Mulholland	.05
658	Donell Nixon	.05
659	Greg Cadaret	.05
660	Vince Coleman	.05
661	Dick Howser (Turn Back the Clock)	.05
662	Mike Schmidt (Turn Back the Clock)	.10
663	Fred Lynn (Turn Back the Clock)	.05
664	Johnny Bench (Turn Back the Clock)	.05
665	Sandy Koufax (Turn Back the Clock)	.15
666	Brian Fisher	.05
667	Curt Wilkerson	.05
668	Joe Oliver RC	.05
669	Tom Lasorda	.05
670	Dennis Eckersley	.30
671	Bob Boone	.05
672	Roy Smith	.05
673	Joey Meyer	.05
674	Spike Owen	.05
675	Jim Abbott	.05
676	Randy Kutcher RC	.05
677	Jay Tibbs	.05
678	Kirt Manwaring	.05
679	Gary Ward	.05
680	Howard Johnson	.05
681	Mike Schooler	.05
682	Dann Bilardello	.05
683	Kenny Rogers	.05
684	Julio Machado RC	.05
685	Tony Fernandez	.05
686	Carmelo Martinez	.05
687	Tim Birtsas	.05
688	Milt Thompson	.05
689	Rich Yett	.05
690	Mark McGwire	.65
691	Chuck Cary	.05
692	Sammy Sosa RC	4.00
693	Calvin Schiraldi	.05
694	Mike Stanton RC	.05
695	Tom Henke	.05
696	B.J. Surhoff	.05
697	Mike Davis	.05
698	Omar Vizquel	.05
699	Jim Leyland	.05
700	Kirby Puckett	.45
701	Bernie Williams RC	1.00
702	Tony Phillips	.05
703	Jeff Brantley	.05
704	Chip Hale RC	.05
705	Claudell Washington	.05
706	Geno Petralli	.05
707	Luis Aquino	.05
708	Larry Sheets	.05
709	Juan Berneguer	.05
710	Von Hayes	.05
711	Rick Aguilera	.05
712	Todd Benzinger	.05
713	Tim Drummond RC	.05
714	Marquis Grissom RC	.45
715	Greg Maddux	.45
716	Steve Balboni	.05
717	Ron Kakovice	.05
718	Gary Sheffield	.30
719	Wally Whitehurst RC	.05
720	Andres Galarraga	.05
721	Lee Mazzilli	.05
722	Felix Fermin	.05
723	Jeff Robinson	.05
724	Juan Bell RC	.05
725	Terry Pendleton	.05
726	Gene Nelson	.05
727	Pat Tabler	.05
728	Jim Acker	.05
729	Bobby Valentine	.05
730	Tony Gwynn	.45

#	Player	Price
731	Don Carman	.05
732	Ernie Riles	.05
733	John Dopson	.05
734	Kevin Elster	.05
735	Charlie Hough	.05
736	Rick Dempsey	.05
737	Chris Sabo	.05
738	Gene Harris RC	.05
739	Dale Sveum	.05
740	Jesse Barfield	.05
741	Steve Wilson	.05
742	Ernie Whitt	.05
743	Tom Candiotti	.05
744	Kelly Mann RC	.05
745	Hubie Brooks	.05
746	Dave Smith	.05
747	Randy Bush	.05
748	Doyle Alexander	.05
749	Mark Parent	.05
750	Dale Murphy	.15
751	Steve Lyons	.05
752	Tom Gordon	.05
753	Chris Speier	.05
754	Bob Walk	.05
755	Rafael Palmeiro	.30
756	Ken Howell	.05
757	Larry Walker RC	.75
758	Mark Thurmond	.05
759	Tom Trebelhorn	.05
760	Wade Boggs	.45
761	Mike Jackson	.05
762	Doug Dascenzo	.05
763	Denny Martinez	.05
764	Tim Teufel	.05
765	Chili Davis	.05
766	Brian Meyer RC	.05
767	Tracy Jones	.05
768	Chuck Crim	.05
769	Greg Hibbard RC	.05
770	Cory Snyder	.05
771	Pete Smith	.05
772	Jeff Reed	.05
773	Dave Leiper	.05
774	Ben McDonald RC	.20
775	Andy Van Slyke	.05
776	Charlie Leibrandt	.05
777	Tim Laudner	.05
778	Mike Jeffcoat	.05
779	Lloyd Moseby	.05
780	Orel Hershiser	.05
781	Mario Diaz	.05
782	Jose Alvarez	.05
783	Checklist 661-792	.05
784	Scott Bailes	.05
785	Jim Rice	.15
786	Eric King	.05
787	Rene Gonzales	.05
788	Frank DiPino	.05
789	John Wathan	.05
790	Gary Carter	.35
791	Alvaro Espinoza	.05
792	Gerald Perry	.05

Tiffany

This specially boxed version of Topps' 1990 baseball card set was sold through hobby channels only. The checklist is identical to the regular-issue Topps set and the cards are nearly so. The Tiffany version features white cardboard stock and a high-gloss finish on the fronts.

	NM/M
Unopened Set (792):	115.00
Complete Set (792):	90.00
Common Player:	.10

Traded

TRAVIS FRYMAN

For the first time, Topps "Traded" series cards were made available nationwide in retail wax packs. The 132-card set was also sold in complete boxed form as it has been in recent years. The wax pack traded cards feature gray backs, while the boxed set cards feature white backs. Each of the gray-back wax-pack cards can be found with copyright lines preceded by one or two asterisks. The cards are numbered 1T-132T and showcase rookies, players who changed teams and new managers.

	NM/M
Complete Set, Retail (132):	6.00
Complete Set, Hobby (132):	4.00
Common Player:	.05
Wax Pack (7):	.75
Wax Box (36):	9.00

#	Player	Price
1	Darrel Akerfelds	.05
2	Sandy Alomar, Jr.	.05
3	Brad Arnsberg	.05
4	Steve Avery	.05
5	Wally Backman	.05
6	Carlos Baerga RC	.10
7	Kevin Bass	.05
8	Willie Blair RC	.05
9	Mike Blowers RC	.05
10	Shawn Boskie RC	.05
11	Daryl Boston	.05
12	Dennis Boyd	.05
13	Glenn Braggs	.05
14	Hubie Brooks	.05
15	Tom Brunansky	.05
16	John Burkett RC	.05
17	Casey Candaele	.05
18	John Candelaria	.05
19	Gary Carter	.75
20	Joe Carter	.05
21	Rick Cerone	.05
22	Scott Coolbaugh RC	.05
23	Bobby Cox	.05
24	Mark Davis	.05
25	Storm Davis	.05
26	Edgar Diaz RC	.05
27	Wayne Edwards RC	.05
28	Mark Eichhorn	.05
29	Scott Erickson RC	.05
30	Nick Esasky	.05
31	Cecil Fielder	.05
32	John Franco	.05
33	Travis Fryman RC	.25
34	Bill Gullickson	.05
35	Darryl Hamilton	.05
36	Mike Harkey	.05
37	Bud Harrelson	.05
38	Billy Hatcher	.05
39	Keith Hernandez	.05
40	Joe Hesketh	.05
41	Dave Hollins RC	.05
42	Sam Horn	.05
43	Steve Howard RC	.05
44	Todd Hundley RC	.15
45	Jeff Huson	.05
46	Chris James	.05
47	Stan Javier	.05
48	Dave Justice RC	.75
49	Jeff Kaiser RC	.05
50	Dana Kiecker RC	.05
51	Joe Klink RC	.05
52	Brent Knackert RC	.05
53	Brad Komminsk	.05
54	Mark Langston	.05
55	Tim Layana RC	.05
56	Rick Leach	.05
57	Terry Leach	.05
58	Tim Leary	.05
59	Craig Lefferts	.05
60	Charlie Leibrandt	.05
61	Jim Leyritz RC	.05
62	Fred Lynn	.05
63	Kevin Maas RC	.05
64	Shane Mack	.05
65	Candy Maldonado	.05
66	Fred Manrique	.05
67	Mike Marshall	.05
68	Carmelo Martinez	.05
69	John Marzano	.05
70	Ben McDonald	.05
71	Jack McDowell	.05
72	John McNamara	.05
73	Orlando Mercado	.05
74	Stump Merrill	.05
75	Alan Mills RC	.05
76	Hal Morris	.05
77	Lloyd Moseby	.05
78	Randy Myers	.05
79	Tim Naehring RC	.05
80	Junior Noboa	.05
81	Matt Nokes	.05
82	Pete O'Brien	.05
83	John Olerud RC	.75
84	Greg Olson RC	.05
85	Junior Ortiz	.05
86	Dave Parker	.05
87	Rick Parker RC	.05
88	Bob Patterson	.05
89	Alejandro Pena	.05
90	Tony Pena	.05
91	Pascual Perez	.05
92	Gerald Perry	.05
93	Dan Petry	.05
94	Gary Pettis	.05
95	Tony Phillips	.05
96	Lou Pinella	.05
97	Luis Polonia	.05
98	Jim Presley	.05
99	Scott Radinsky RC	.05
100	Willie Randolph	.05
101	Jeff Reardon	.05
102	Greg Riddoch	.05
103	Jeff Robinson	.05
104	Ron Robinson	.05
105	Kevin Romine	.05
106	Scott Ruskin RC	.05
107	John Russell	.05
108	Bill Sampen RC	.05
109	Juan Samuel	.05
110	Scott Sanderson	.05
111	Jack Savage RC	.05

112	Dave Schmidt	.05
113	Red Schoendienst	.10
114	Terry Shumpert RC	.05
115	Matt Sinatro	.05
116	Don Slaught	.05
117	Bryn Smith	.05
118	Lee Smith	.05
119	Paul Sorrento RC	.05
120	Franklin Stubbs	.05
121	Russ Swan RC	.05
122	Bob Tewksbury	.05
123	Wayne Tolleson	.05
124	John Tudor	.05
125	Randy Veres RC	.05
126	Hector Villanueva RC	.05
127	Mitch Webster	.05
128	Ernie Whitt	.05
129	Frank Wills	.05
130	Dave Winfield	.75
131	Matt Young	.05
132	Checklist	

Traded Tiffany

Identical to the regular Topps Traded issue except for the glossy front surface, this special hobby-only boxed set shares the same checklist.

	NM/M
Complete Set (132):	25.00
Common Player:	.15

Traded Hank Aaron Bronze

This 1/4-size metal replica of Aaron's first-ever Topps card was issued to dealers who purchased cases of 1990 Topps Traded sets. Each detail of the 1954 Topps Aaron card is reproduced on the 1-1/4" x 1-3/4" bronze metal mini-card, right down to the stats.

		NM/M
128	Hank Aaron	15.00

Box Panels

This special 16-card set features four cards on four different box-bottom panels. The cards are identical in design to the regular 1990 Topps cards. The cards are designated by letter.

		NM/M
Complete Panel Set (4):		7.00
Complete Singles Set (16):		6.00
Common Panel:		1.00
Common Player:		.10
Panel		2.00
A	Wade Boggs	.60
B	George Brett	.75
C	Andre Dawson	.15
D	Darrell Evans	.10
Panel		1.00
E	Dwight Gooden	.10
F	Rickey Henderson	.45
G	Tom Lasorda	.10
H	Fred Lynn	.10
Panel		1.50
I	Mark McGwire	1.00
J	Dave Parker	.10
K	Jeff Reardon	.10
L	Rick Reuschel	.10
Panel		4.00
M	Jim Rice	.20
N	Cal Ripken, Jr.	1.50
O	Nolan Ryan	1.50
P	Ryne Sandberg	.60

All-Star Glossy Set of 22

One glossy All-Star card was included in each 1990 Topps rack pack. The cards measure 2-1/2" x 3-1/2" and feature a similar style to past glossy All-Star cards. Special cards of All-Star team captains Carl Yastrzemski and Don Drysdale are included in the set.

		NM/M
Complete Set (22):		4.00
Common Player:		.05
1	Tom Lasorda	.05
2	Will Clark	.05
3	Ryne Sandberg	.50
4	Howard Johnson	.05
5	Ozzie Smith	.40
6	Kevin Mitchell	.05
7	Eric Davis	.05
8	Tony Gwynn	.50
9	Benny Santiago	.05
10	Rick Rueschel	.05
11	Don Drysdale	.10
12	Tony LaRussa	.05
13	Mark McGwire	.75
14	Julio Franco	.05
15	Wade Boggs	.50
16	Cal Ripken, Jr.	1.00
17	Bo Jackson	.10
18	Kirby Puckett	.50
19	Ruben Sierra	.05
20	Terry Steinbach	.05
21	Dave Stewart	.05
22	Carl Yastrzemski	.10

All-Star Glossy Set of 60

Sharp color photographs and a clutter-free design are features of the cards in this 60-card send away set. Topps initiated the redemption series in 1983. Six special offer cards, included in Topps baseball wax packs, were necessary to obtain each of the six 10-card sets in the series.

		NM/M
Complete Set (60):		9.00
Common Player:		.10
1	Ryne Sandberg	.75
2	Nolan Ryan	2.00
3	Glenn Davis	.10
4	Dave Stewart	.10
5	Barry Larkin	.10
6	Carney Lansford	.10
7	Darryl Strawberry	.10
8	Steve Sax	.10
9	Carlos Martinez	.10
10	Gary Sheffield	.50
11	Don Mattingly	1.00
12	Mark Grace	.10
13	Bret Saberhagen	.10
14	Mike Scott	.10
15	Robin Yount	.60
16	Ozzie Smith	.75
17	Jeff Ballard	.10
18	Rick Reuschel	.10
19	Greg Briley	.10
20	Ken Griffey Jr.	1.25
21	Kevin Mitchell	.10
22	Wade Boggs	.75
23	Dwight Gooden	.10
24	George Bell	.10
25	Eric Davis	.10
26	Ruben Sierra	.10
27	Roberto Alomar	.20
28	Gary Gaetti	.10
29	Gregg Olson	.10
30	Tom Gordon	.10
31	Jose Canseco	.45
32	Pedro Guerrero	.10
33	Joe Carter	.10
34	Mike Scioscia	.10
35	Julio Franco	.10
36	Joe Magrane	.10
37	Rickey Henderson	.60
38	Tim Raines	.10
39	Jerome Walton	.10
40	Bob Geren	.10
41	Andre Dawson	.10
42	Mark McGwire	1.50
43	Howard Johnson	.10
44	Bo Jackson	.20
45	Shawon Dunston	.10
46	Carlton Fisk	.60
47	Mitch Williams	.10
48	Kirby Puckett	.75
49	Craig Worthington	.10
50	Jim Abbott	.10
51	Cal Ripken, Jr.	2.00
52	Will Clark	.10
53	Dennis Eckersley	.55
54	Craig Biggio	.10
55	Fred McGriff	.10
56	Tony Gwynn	.75
57	Mickey Tettleton	.10
58	Mark Davis	.10
59	Omar Vizquel	.10
60	Gregg Jefferies	.10

Glossy Rookies

While the size of the annual glossy rookies set increased to 33 cards from previous years' issues of 22, the format remained identical in 1990. Above the player photo is a colored banner with "1989 Rookies." The player's name appears in red in a yellow bar beneath the photo. Backs are printed in red and blue and contain a shield design with the notation, "1989 Rookies Commemorative Set." The player's name, position and team are listed below, along with a card number. Cards are numbered alphabetically in the set. The glossy rookies were found one per pack in jumbo (100-card) cello packs.

		NM/M
Complete Set (33):		6.00
Common Player:		.10
1	Jim Abbott	.10
2	Joey Belle	.50
3	Andy Benes	.10
4	Greg Briley	.10
5	Kevin Brown	.10
6	Mark Carreon	.10
7	Mike Devereaux	.10
8	Junior Felix	.10
9	Bob Geren	.10
10	Tom Gordon	.10
11	Ken Griffey Jr.	5.00
12	Pete Harnisch	.10
13	Greg W. Harris	.10
14	Greg Hibbard	.10
15	Ken Hill	.10
16	Gregg Jefferies	.10
17	Jeff King	.10
18	Derek Lilliquist	.10
19	Carlos Martinez	.10
20	Ramon Martinez	.10
21	Bob Milacki	.10
22	Gregg Olson	.10
23	Donn Pall	.10
24	Kenny Rogers	.10
25	Gary Sheffield	1.50
26	Dwight Smith	.10
27	Billy Spiers	.10
28	Omar Vizquel	.10
29	Jerome Walton	.10
30	Dave West	.10
31	John Wetteland	.10
32	Steve Wilson	.10
33	Craig Worthington	.10

Glossy Rookies Foil-Test Cards

To test the use of metallic-foil highlights which it would debut on its 1991 Stadium Club and Desert Shield cards, Topps made a test run using as base cards the 33-piece "1989 Rookies Commemorative Set." The test consists of a 2-1/4" x 1/4" metallic strip with a "topps" logotype punched out of the center. Cards can be found with the strip in many different locations horizontally on the cards' fronts, and in many colors including silver, gold, red, green, blue and purple. Color of foil does not affect values, though a complete set in matching color might command a premium.

		NM/M
Complete Set (33):		40.00
Common Player:		1.00
1	Jim Abbott	1.00
2	Joey Belle	2.00
3	Andy Benes	1.00
4	Greg Briley	1.00
5	Kevin Brown	1.00
6	Mark Carreon	1.00
7	Mike Devereaux	1.00
8	Junior Felix	1.00
9	Bob Geren	1.00
10	Tom Gordon	1.00
11	Ken Griffey Jr.	20.00
12	Pete Harnisch	1.00
13	Greg W. Harris	1.00
14	Greg Hibbard	1.00
15	Ken Hill	1.00
16	Gregg Jefferies	1.00
17	Jeff King	1.00
18	Derek Lilliquist	1.00
19	Carlos Martinez	1.00
20	Ramon Martinez	1.00
21	Bob Milacki	1.00
22	Gregg Olson	1.00
23	Donn Pall	1.00
24	Kenny Rogers	1.00
25	Gary Sheffield	5.00
26	Dwight Smith	1.00
27	Billy Spiers	1.00
28	Omar Vizquel	1.00
29	Jerome Walton	1.00
30	Dave West	1.00
31	John Wetteland	1.00
32	Steve Wilson	1.00
33	Craig Worthington	1.00

Award Winners Commemorative Sheet

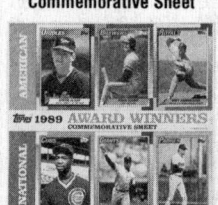

Six of 1989's top award winners are pictured in the style of 1990 Topps baseball cards on this sheet issued with blister packed sets of Topps baseball stickers. The cards are blank-backed and use photos which are different from those found on the same players' regular 1990 cards. Each player's award is noted in the panel beneath his name. The sheet measures 8-3/4" x 8-1/8" with individual cards measuring the standard 2-1/2" x 3-1/2".

		NM/M
Complete Set, Sheet:		3.00
Complete Set, Singles (6):		2.00
Common Player:		.10
(1)	Mark Davis (N.L. Cy Young)	.10
(2)	Kevin Mitchell (N.L. MVP)	.10
(3)	Gregg Olson (A.L. R.O.Y.)	.10
(4)	Bret Saberhagen (A.L. Cy Young)	.10
(5)	Jerome Walton (N.L. R.O.Y.)	.10
(6)	Robin Yount (A.L. MVP)	1.50

Batting Leaders

Once again produced as an exclusive insert in jumbo blister packs for K-Mart stores, the 1990 career batting leaders cards are similar in concept and design to the previous year's issue; in fact, some of the same player photos were used. The 22 cards in the set are arranged roughly in order of the players' standings in lifetime batting average. Cards fronts are bordered in bright green; backs are printed in red, white and dark green.

		NM/M
Complete Set (22):		110.00
Common Player:		1.50
1	Wade Boggs	12.50
2	Tony Gwynn	15.00
3	Kirby Puckett	15.00
4	Don Mattingly	20.00
5	George Brett	20.00
6	Pedro Guerrero	1.50
7	Tim Raines	1.50
8	Paul Molitor	12.50
9	Jim Rice	3.00
10	Keith Hernandez	1.50
11	Julio Franco	1.50
12	Carney Lansford	1.50
13	Dave Parker	1.50
14	Willie McGee	1.50
15	Robin Yount	12.50
16	Tony Fernandez	1.50
17	Eddie Murray	12.50
18	Johnny Ray	1.50
19	Lonnie Smith	1.50
20	Phil Bradley	1.50
21	Rickey Henderson	12.50
22	Kent Hrbek	1.50

Big Baseball

For the third consecutive year, Topps issued a 330-card set of oversized cards (2-5/8" x 3-3/4") in three 110-card series. The cards are reminiscent of Topps cards from the mid-1950s, featuring players in portrait and action shots. As in previous years, the cards are printed on white stock with a glossy front finish. Backs include 1989 and career hitting, fielding and pitching stats and a player cartoon. Series 3 cards (#221-330) are believed to have been somewhat scarcer than the first two series.

		NM/M
Complete Set (330):		15.00
Common Player:		.05
Wax Pack (8):		.50
Wax Box, Series 1-2 (36):		7.50
Wax Box, Series 3 (36):		20.00
1	Dwight Evans	.05
2	Kirby Puckett	.60
3	Kevin Gross	.05
4	Ron Hassey	.05
5	Lloyd McClendon	.05
6	Bo Jackson	.10
7	Lonnie Smith	.05
8	Alvaro Espinoza	.05
9	Roberto Alomar	.15
10	Glenn Braggs	.05
11	David Cone	.05
12	Claudell Washington	.05
13	Pedro Guerrero	.05
14	Todd Benzinger	.05
15	Jeff Russell	.05
16	Terry Kennedy	.05
17	Kelly Gruber	.05
18	Alfredo Griffin	.05
19	Mark Grace	.05
20	Dave Winfield	.50
21	Bret Saberhagen	.05
22	Roger Clemens	.65
23	Bob Walk	.05
24	Dave Magadan	.05
25	Spike Owen	.05
26	Jody Davis	.05
27	Kent Hrbek	.05
28	Mark McGwire	1.00
29	Eddie Murray	.50
30	Paul O'Neill	.05
31	Jose DeLeon	.05
32	Steve Lyons	.05
33	Dan Plesac	.05
34	Jack Howell	.05
35	Greg Briley	.05
36	Andy Hawkins	.05
37	Cecil Espy	.05
38	Rick Sutcliffe	.05
39	Jack Clark	.05
40	Dale Murphy	.15
41	Mike Henneman	.05
42	Rick Honeycutt	.05
43	Willie Randolph	.05
44	Marty Barrett	.05
45	Willie Wilson	.05
46	Wallace Johnson	.05
47	Greg Brock	.05
48	Tom Browning	.05
49	Gerald Young	.05
50	Dennis Eckersley	.40
51	Scott Garrelts	.05
52	Gary Redus	.05
53	Al Newman	.05
54	Darryl Boston	.05
55	Ron Oester	.05
56	Danny Tartabull	.05
57	Gregg Jefferies	.05
58	Tom Foley	.05
59	Robin Yount	.50
60	Pat Borders	.05
61	Mike Greenwell	.05
62	Shawon Dunston	.05
63	Steve Buechele	.05
64	Dave Stewart	.05
65	Jose Oquendo	.05
66	Ron Gant	.05
67	Mike Scioscia	.05
68	Randy Velarde	.05
69	Charlie Hayes	.05
70	Tim Wallach	.05
71	Eric Show	.05
72	Eric Davis	.05
73	Mike Gallego	.05
74	Rob Deer	.05
75	Ryne Sandberg	.60
76	Kevin Seitzer	.05
77	Wade Boggs	.60
78	Greg Gagne	.05
79	John Smiley	.05
80	Ivan Calderon	.05
81	Pete Incaviglia	.05
82	Orel Hershiser	.05
83	Carney Lansford	.05
84	Mike Fitzgerald	.05
85	Don Mattingly	.65
86	Chet Lemon	.05
87	Rolando Roomes	.05
88	Bill Spiers	.05
89	Pat Tabler	.05
90	Danny Heep	.05
91	Andre Dawson	.25
92	Randy Bush	.05
93	Tony Gwynn	.60
94	Tom Brunansky	.05
95	Johnny Ray	.05
96	Matt Williams	.05
97	Barry Lyons	.05
98	Jeff Hamilton	.05
99	Tom Glavine	.20
100	Ken Griffey Sr.	.05
101	Tom Henke	.05
102	Dave Righetti	.05
103	Paul Molitor	.50
104	Mike LaValliere	.05
105	Frank White	.05
106	Bob Welch	.05
107	Ellis Burks	.05
108	Andres Galarraga	.05
109	Mitch Williams	.05
110	Checklist	
111	Craig Biggio	.05
112	Dave Steib	.05
113	Ron Darling	.05
114	Bert Blyleven	.05
115	Dickie Thon	.05
116	Carlos Martinez	.05
117	Jeff King	.05
118	Terry Steinbach	.05
119	Frank Tanana	.05
120	Mark Lemke	.05
121	Chris Sabo	.05
122	Glenn Davis	.05
123	Mel Hall	.05
124	Jim Gantner	.05
125	Benito Santiago	.05
126	Milt Thompson	.05
127	Rafael Palmeiro	.40
128	Barry Bonds	1.50
129	Mike Bielecki	.05
130	Lou Whitaker	.05
131	Bob Ojeda	.05
132	Dion James	.05

133	Denny Martinez	.05
134	Fred McGriff	.05
135	Terry Pendleton	.05
136	Pat Combs	.05
137	Kevin Mitchell	.05
138	Marquis Grissom	.05
139	Chris Bosio	.05
140	Omar Vizquel	.05
141	Steve Sax	.05
142	Nelson Liriano	.05
143	Kevin Elster	.05
144	Dan Pasqua	.05
145	Dave Smith	.05
146	Craig Worthington	.05
147	Dan Gladden	.05
148	Oddibe McDowell	.05
149	Bip Roberts	.05
150	Randy Ready	.05
151	Dwight Smith	.05
152	Ed Whitson	.05
153	George Bell	.05
154	Tim Raines	.05
155	Sid Fernandez	.05
156	Henry Cotto	.05
157	Harold Baines	.05
158	Willie McGee	.05
159	Bill Doran	.05
160	Steve Balboni	.05
161	Pete Smith	.05
162	Frank Viola	.05
163	Gary Sheffield	.35
164	Bill Landrum	.05
165	Tony Fernandez	.05
166	Mike Heath	.05
167	Jody Reed	.05
168	Wally Joyner	.05
169	Robby Thompson	.05
170	Ken Caminiti	.05
171	Nolan Ryan	1.50
172	Ricky Jordan	.05
173	Lance Blankenship	.05
174	Dwight Gooden	.05
175	Ruben Sierra	.05
176	Carlton Fisk	.50
177	Garry Templeton	.05
178	Mike Devereaux	.05
179	Mookie Wilson	.05
180	Jeff Blauser	.05
181	Scott Bradley	.05
182	Luis Salazar	.05
183	Rafael Ramirez	.05
184	Vince Coleman	.05
185	Doug Drabek	.05
186	Darryl Strawberry	.05
187	Tim Burke	.05
188	Jesse Barfield	.05
189	Barry Larkin	.05
190	Alan Trammell	.05
191	Steve Lake	.05
192	Derek Lilliquist	.05
193	Don Robinson	.05
194	Kevin McReynolds	.05
195	Melido Perez	.05
196	Jose Lind	.05
197	Eric Anthony	.05
198	B.J. Surhoff	.05
199	John Olerud	.05
200	Mike Moore	.05
201	Mark Gubicza	.05
202	Phil Bradley	.05
203	Ozzie Smith	.60
204	Greg Maddux	.60
205	Julio Franco	.05
206	Tom Herr	.05
207	Scott Fletcher	.05
208	Bobby Bonilla	.05
209	Bob Geren	.05
210	Junior Felix	.05
211	Dick Schofield	.05
212	Jim Deshaies	.05
213	Jose Uribe	.05
214	John Kruk	.05
215	Ozzie Guillen	.05
216	Howard Johnson	.05
217	Andy Van Slyke	.05
218	Tim Laudner	.05
219	Manny Lee	.05
220	Checklist	.05
221	Cory Snyder	.05
222	Billy Hatcher	.05
223	Bud Black	.05
224	Will Clark	.05
225	Kevin Tapani	.05
226	Mike Pagliarulo	.05
227	Dave Parker	.05
228	Ben McDonald	.05
229	Carlos Baerga	.05
230	Roger McDowell	.05
231	Delino DeShields	.05
232	Mark Langston	.05
233	Wally Backman	.05
234	Jim Eisenreich	.05
235	Mike Schooler	.05
236	Kevin Bass	.05
237	John Farrell	.05
238	Kal Daniels	.05
239	Tony Phillips	.05
240	Todd Stottlemyre	.05
241	Greg Olson	.05
242	Charlie Hough	.05
243	Mariano Duncan	.05
244	Billy Ripken	.05
245	Joe Carter	.05
246	Tim Belcher	.05
247	Roberto Kelly	.05
248	Candy Maldonado	.05
249	Mike Scott	.05
250	Ken Griffey Jr.	.75

251	Nick Esasky	.05
252	Tom Gordon	.05
253	John Tudor	.05
254	Gary Gaetti	.05
255	Neal Heaton	.05
256	Jerry Browne	.05
257	Jose Rijo	.05
258	Mike Boddicker	.05
259	Brett Butler	.05
260	Andy Benes	.05
261	Kevin Brown	.05
262	Hubie Brooks	.05
263	Randy Milligan	.05
264	John Franco	.05
265	Sandy Alomar	.05
266	Dave Valle	.05
267	Jerome Walton	.05
268	Bob Boone	.05
269	Ken Howell	.05
270	Jose Canseco	.30
271	Joe Magrane	.05
272	Brian DuBois	.05
273	Carlos Quintana	.05
274	Lance Johnson	.05
275	Steve Bedrosian	.05
276	Brook Jacoby	.05
277	Fred Lynn	.05
278	Jeff Ballard	.05
279	Otis Nixon	.05
280	Chili Davis	.05
281	Joe Oliver	.05
282	Brian Holman	.05
283	Juan Samuel	.05
284	Rick Aguilera	.05
285	Jeff Reardon	.05
286	Sammy Sosa	3.00
287	Carmelo Martinez	.05
288	Greg Swindell	.05
289	Erik Hanson	.05
290	Tony Pena	.05
291	Pascual Perez	.05
292	Rickey Henderson	.50
293	Kurt Stillwell	.05
294	Todd Zeile	.05
295	Bobby Thigpen	.05
296	Larry Walker	.05
297	Rob Murphy	.05
298	Mitch Webster	.05
299	Devon White	.05
300	Len Dykstra	.05
301	Keith Hernandez	.05
302	Gene Larkin	.05
303	Jeffrey Leonard	.05
304	Jim Presley	.05
305	Lloyd Moseby	.05
306	John Smoltz	.05
307	Sam Horn	.05
308	Greg Litton	.05
309	Dave Henderson	.05
310	Mark McLemore	.05
311	Gary Pettis	.05
312	Mark Davis	.05
313	Cecil Fielder	.05
314	Jack Armstrong	.05
315	Alvin Davis	.05
316	Doug Jones	.05
317	Eric Yelding	.05
318	Joe Orsulak	.05
319	Chuck Finley	.05
320	Glenn Wilson	.05
321	Harold Reynolds	.05
322	Teddy Higuera	.05
323	Lance Parrish	.05
324	Bruce Hurst	.05
325	Dave West	.05
326	Kirk Gibson	.05
327	Cal Ripken, Jr.	1.50
328	Rick Reuschel	.05
329	Jim Abbott	.05
330	Checklist	

George Bush

GEORGE BUSH

As a favor to President George Bush, Topps produced a special run of 100 cards in its 1990 design featuring a photo of the president in his Yale University baseball uniform. At least a few of the cards reportedly were inadvertently included in regular Topps packages and made their way into the hobby.

	NM/M
USA1 George Bush (7/05 Auction)	2,000

Coins

Sixty top stars and promising rookies are featured in this fourth

annual coin set. Fronts of the 1-1/2" diameter coins feature a portrait photo with a symbolic infield. Player name and team appear below. Most coins feature natural aluminum coloring on the rolled edges and on the back. Special coins of major award winners have different colors in the background and edges. Backs feature a coin number, minimal biographical matter and a previous season career summary. Coins were sold three per pack which included an offer card for a coin holder and Topps magazine subscription offer.

	NM/M
Factory Set (60):	15.00
Complete Set (60):	7.50
Common Player:	.15
Wax Pack (3):	.75
Wax Box (36):	9.00
1 Robin Yount	.50
2 Bret Saberhagen	.15
3 Gregg Olson	.15
4 Kirby Puckett	.65
5 George Bell	.15
6 Wade Boggs	.65
7 Jerry Browne	.15
8 Ellis Burks	.15
9 Ivan Calderon	.15
10 Tom Candiotti	.15
11 Alvin Davis	.15
12 Chili Davis	.15
13 Chuck Finley	.15
14 Gary Gaetti	.15
15 Tom Gordon	.15
16 Ken Griffey Jr.	.75
17 Rickey Henderson	.50
18 Kent Hrbek	.15
19 Bo Jackson	.20
20 Carlos Martinez	.15
21 Don Mattingly	.75
22 Fred McGriff	.15
23 Paul Molitor	.50
24 Cal Ripken, Jr.	1.00
25 Nolan Ryan	1.00
26 Steve Sax	.15
27 Gary Sheffield	.30
28 Ruben Sierra	.15
29 Dave Stewart	.15
30 Mickey Tettleton	.15
31 Alan Trammell	.15
32 Lou Whitaker	.15
33 Kevin Mitchell	.15
34 Mark Davis	.15
35 Jerome Walton	.15
36 Tony Gwynn	.65
37 Roberto Alomar	.25
38 Tim Belcher	.15
39 Craig Biggio	.15
40 Barry Bonds	1.00
41 Bobby Bonilla	.15
42 Joe Carter	.15
43 Will Clark	.15
44 Eric Davis	.15
45 Glenn Davis	.15
46 Sid Fernandez	.15
47 Pedro Guerrero	.15
48 Von Hayes	.15
49 Tom Herr	.15
50 Howard Johnson	.15
51 Barry Larkin	.15
52 Joe Magrane	.15
53 Dale Murphy	.25
54 Tim Raines	.15
55 Willie Randolph	.15
56 Ryne Sandberg	.65
57 Dwight Smith	.15
58 Lonnie Smith	.15
59 Robby Thompson	.15
60 Tim Wallach	.15

Double Headers

For a second (and final) year, Topps produced an issue of mini cards encased in plastic stands and marketed as Double Headers. Each piece features a 1-5/8" x 2-1/4" reproduction of the player's Topps rookie card, backed by a reproduction of his card from the regular 1990 Topps set. The size of the DH set was increased from 24 in 1989 to 72 for 1990. The novelties were sold for 50 cents apiece. The unnumbered cards are checklisted here alphabetically.

White Sox

CARLTON FISK

	NM/M
Complete Set (72):	25.00
Common Player:	.25
Wax Pack (1):	.50
Wax Box (36):	15.00
(1) Jim Abbott	.25
(2) Jeff Ballard	.25
(3) George Bell	.25
(4) Wade Boggs	1.00
(5) Barry Bonds	2.50
(6) Bobby Bonilla	.25
(7) Ellis Burks	.25
(8) Jose Canseco	.50
(9) Joe Carter	.25
(10) Will Clark	.25
(11) Roger Clemens	1.25
(12) Vince Coleman	.25
(13) Alvin Davis	.25
(14) Eric Davis	.25
(15) Glenn Davis	.25
(16) Mark Davis	.25
(17) Andre Dawson	.40
(18) Shawon Dunston	.25
(19) Dennis Eckersley	.60
(20) Sid Fernandez	.25
(21) Tony Fernandez	.25
(22) Chuck Finley	.25
(23) Carlton Fisk	.75
(24) Julio Franco	.25
(25) Gary Gaetti	.25
(26) Dwight Gooden	.25
(27) Mark Grace	.25
(28) Mike Greenwell	.25
(29) Ken Griffey Jr.	1.50
(30) Pedro Guerrero	.25
(31) Tony Gwynn	1.00
(32) Von Hayes	.25
(33) Rickey Henderson	.75
(34) Orel Hershiser	.25
(35) Bo Jackson	.35
(36) Gregg Jefferies	.25
(37) Howard Johnson	.25
(38) Ricky Jordan	.25
(39) Carney Lansford	.25
(40) Barry Larkin	.25
(41) Greg Maddux	1.00
(42) Joe Magrane	.25
(43) Don Mattingly	1.25
(44) Fred McGriff	.25
(45) Mark McGwire	2.00
(46) Kevin McReynolds	.25
(47) Kevin Mitchell	.25
(48) Gregg Olson	.25
(49) Kirby Puckett	1.00
(50) Tim Raines	.25
(51) Harold Reynolds	.25
(52) Cal Ripken, Jr.	2.50
(53) Nolan Ryan	2.50
(54) Bret Saberhagen	.25
(55) Ryne Sandberg	1.00
(56) Benito Santiago	.25
(57) Steve Sax	.25
(58) Mike Scioscia	.25
(59) Mike Scott	.25
(60) Ruben Sierra	.25
(61) Lonnie Smith	.25
(62) Ozzie Smith	1.00
(63) Dave Stewart	.25
(64) Darryl Strawberry	.25
(65) Greg Swindell	.25
(66) Alan Trammell	.25
(67) Frank Viola	.25
(68) Tim Wallach	.25
(69) Jerome Walton	.25
(70) Lou Whitaker	.25
(71) Mitch Williams	.25
(72) Robin Yount	.75

Experimental Mylar Stickers

PADRES

JOE CARTER

For a second and final year, Topps produced a trial issue of mini cards encased in plastic stands and

Testing the concept of refractive printing, with stars in the background of these stickers, Topps produced a trial run of Mylar stickers using fronts from its 1990 Traded card set. Fronts of the 2-1/2" x 3-1/2" stickers are printed on metallic foil. Backs are blank.

	NM/M
Complete Set (6):	400.00
Common Player:	60.00
(1) Joe Carter	60.00
(2) Shane Mack	60.00
(3) Alan Mills	60.00
(4) Alejandro Pena	60.00
(5) Gerald Perry	60.00
(6) Dave Winfield	175.00

Gallery of Champions

BLUE JAYS

FRED McGRIFF

The 1990 Topps 1/4-size metal baseball mini-cards were issued only as complete sets in a special display case. As with earlier editions, the 1-1/4" x 1-3/4" ingots do a creditable job of reproducing the players' 1990 Topps cards, right down to the tiny stats on the back. Players in the set represent the winners of major awards and statistical leaders from the previous season. A pewter Nolan Ryan 1/4-size card was issued as a sales incentive for dealers purchasing the Gallery of Champions sets.

	NM/M
Complete Aluminum Set (12):	15.00
Complete Bronze Set (12):	50.00
Complete Silver Set (12):	100.00
(1a) Mark Davis/Aluminum	1.00
(1b) Mark Davis/Bronze	2.50
(1s) Mark Davis/Silver	5.00
(2a) Jose DeLeon/Aluminum	1.00
(2b) Jose DeLeon/Bronze	2.50
(2s) Jose DeLeon/Silver	5.00
(3a) Tony Gwynn/Aluminum	3.00
(3b) Tony Gwynn/Bronze	7.50
(3s) Tony Gwynn/Silver	20.00
(4a) Fred McGriff/Aluminum	1.00
(4b) Fred McGriff/Bronze	2.50
(4s) Fred McGriff/Silver	5.00
(5a) Kevin Mitchell/Aluminum	1.00
(5b) Kevin Mitchell/Bronze	2.50
(5s) Kevin Mitchell/Silver	5.00
(6a) Gregg Olson/Aluminum	1.00
(6b) Gregg Olson/Bronze	2.50
(6s) Gregg Olson/Silver	5.00
(7a) Kirby Puckett/Aluminum	3.00
(7b) Kirby Puckett/Bronze	7.50
(7s) Kirby Puckett/Silver	20.00
(8a) Jeff Russell/Aluminum	1.00
(8b) Jeff Russell/Bronze	2.50
(8s) Jeff Russell/Silver	5.00
(9a) Nolan Ryan/Aluminum	10.00
(9b) Nolan Ryan/Bronze	20.00
(9s) Nolan Ryan/Silver	40.00
(9p) Nolan Ryan/Pewter	35.00
(10a) Bret Saberhagen/Aluminum	1.00
(10b) Bret Saberhagen/Bronze	2.50
(10s) Bret Saberhagen/Silver	5.00
(11a) Jerome Walton/Aluminum	1.00
(11b) Jerome Walton/Bronze	2.50
(11s) Jerome Walton/Silver	5.00
(12a) Robin Yount/Aluminum	2.00
(12b) Robin Yount/Bronze	5.00
(12s) Robin Yount/Silver	15.00

Golden Spikes Award

This one-card "set" was given out at the United States Baseball Federation awards luncheon in New York City on Nov. 14, 1990, honoring Alex Fernandez as the outstanding amateur baseball player of the year and winner of the Golden Spikes Award. The rough borders found on many of these cards indicates they were cut from the press sheet by hand. Production was reported as 600 cards.

AUGUST 2, 1990 MAJOR LEAGUE DEBUT

ALEX FERNANDEZ

	NM/M
Alex Fernandez	85.00

Heads Up!

Following up a much rarer test issue of the previous year, the Heads Up! BasebAll-Stars of 1990 was a 24-piece set which received much wider distribution, but proved unpopular with collectors. On heavy cardboard, die-cut to approximately 5"x 6", these novelties featured only a head-and-cap photo of the player. Backs have the player's name and team, along with an adhesive strip and plastic suction cup which could be used to "hang" the player.

	NM/M
Complete Set (24):	10.00
Common Player:	.50
Wax Pack (1):	.75
Wax Box (24):	10.00
1 Tony Gwynn	2.00
2 Will Clark	.50
3 Dwight Gooden	.50
4 Dennis Eckersley	1.25
5 Ken Griffey Jr.	3.00
6 Craig Biggio	.50
7 Bret Saberhagen	.50
8 Bo Jackson	.75
9 Ryne Sandberg	2.00
10 Gregg Olson	.50
11 John Franco	.50
12 Rafael Palmeiro	1.25
13 Gary Sheffield	.50
14 Mark McGwire	4.00
15 Kevin Mitchell	.50
16 Jim Abbott	.50
17 Harold Reynolds	.50
18 Jose Canseco	1.00
19 Don Mattingly	2.50
20 Kirby Puckett	2.00
21 Tom Gordon	.50
22 Craig Worthington	.50
23 Dwight Smith	.50
24 Jerome Walton	.50

Magazine

ROYCE

GIANTS

Beginning with its debut issue dated Winter, 1990, Topps Magazine included sportscards in each quarterly issue. Generally printed on perforated panels which could be easily separated from the magazine and the other cards, six to eight cards were included in most issues. Most of the cards were original designs, but some depicted then-current players on Topps designs from previous years. For the duration of their issue, the cards were numbered consecutively with a "TM" prefix.

		NM/M
Complete Set (112):		50.00
Common Player:		.25
1	Dave Staton	.25
2	Dan Peltier	.25
3	Ken Griffey Jr.	2.00
4	Ruben Sierra	.25
5	Bret Saberhagen	.25
6	Jerome Walton	.25
7	Kevin Mitchell	.25
8	Mike Scott	.25
9	Bo Jackson	.30
10	Nolan Ryan	3.00
11	Will Clark	.25
12	Robin Yount	.75
13	Joe Morgan	.75
14	Jim Palmer	.75
15	Ben McDonald	.25
16	John Olerud	.25
17	Don Mattingly	1.50
18	Eric Davis, Barry Larkin, Chris Sabo	.25
19	Jim Abbott	.25
20	Sandy Alomar Jr.	.25
21	Jose Canseco	.50
22	Delino DeShields	.25
23	Wade Boggs	1.00
24	Kirby Puckett	1.00
25	Ryne Sandberg	1.00
26	Roger Clemens	1.25
27	Ken Griffey Jr., Ken Griffey Sr.	1.00
28	Cecil Fielder	.25
29	Steve Avery	.25
30	Rickey Henderson	.75
31	Kevin Maas	.25
32	Len Dykstra	.25
33	Darryl Strawberry	.25
34	Mark McGwire	2.25
35	Matt Williams	.25
36	David Justice	.25
37	Cincinnati Reds	.25
38	Todd Van Poppel	.25
39	Jose Offerman	.25
40	Alex Fernandez	.25
41	Carlton Fisk	.75
42	Barry Bonds	3.00
43	Bobby Bonilla	.25
44	Bob Welch	.25
45	Mo Vaughn	.25
46	Tino Martinez	.25
47	D.J. Dozier	.25
48	Frank Thomas	.75
49	Cal Ripken Jr. ('75 Topps Style)	3.00
50	Dave Winfield ('75 Topps Style)	.75
51	Dwight Gooden ('75 Topps Style)	.25
52	Bo Jackson ('75 Topps Style)	.30
53	Kirk Dressendorfer	.25
54	Gary Scott	.25
55	Steve Decker	.25
56	Ray Lankford	.25
57	Ozzie Smith ('86 Topps Style)	1.00
58	Joe Carter ('86 Topps Style)	.25
59	Dave Henderson ('86 Topps Style)	.25
60	Tony Gwynn ('86 Topps Style)	1.00
61	Jeff Bagwell	.75
62	Scott Erickson	.25
63	Pat Kelly	.25
64	Orlando Merced	.25
65	Andre Dawson	.40
66	Reggie Sanders	.25
67	Phil Plantier	.25
68	Paul Molitor	.75
69	Terry Pendleton	.25
70	Julio Franco	.25
71	Lee Smith	.25
72	'91 Minnesota Twins	.25
73	Royce Clayton	.25
74	Tom Glavine	.45
75	Roger Salkeld	.25
76	Robin Ventura	.25
77	John Goodman (As Babe Ruth.)	.25
78	Jack Morris	.25
79	Brien Taylor	.25
80	Howard Johnson	.25
81	Barry Larkin	.25
82	Deion Sanders	.30
83	Mike Mussina	.60
84	Juan Gonzalez	.50
85	Roberto Alomar	.50
86	Fred McGriff	.25
87	Doug Drabek	.25
88	George Brett	1.25
89	Otis Nixon	.25
90	Brady Anderson	.25
91	Gary Sheffield	.50
92	Dave Fleming	.25
93	Jeff Reardon	.25
94	Mark McGwire	2.25
95	Larry Walker	.25
96	John Kruk	.25
97	Carlos Baerga	.25
98	Pat Listach	.25
99	'92 Toronto Blue Jays	.25
100	Eric Karros	.25
101	Bret Boone	.25
102	Al Martin	.25
103	Wil Cordero	.25
104	Tim Salmon	.25
105	Danny Tartabull	.25
106	J.T. Snow	.25
107	Mike Piazza	1.50
108	Frank Viola	.25
109	Nolan Ryan (Mets)	2.25
110	Nolan Ryan (Angels)	2.25
111	Nolan Ryan (Astros)	2.25
112	Nolan Ryan (Rangers)	2.25

Mini League Leaders

The last in a five-year string of mini cards, the 1990 league leaders' set offers players who were in the top five in major batting and pitching stats during the 1989 season. Fronts of the 2-1/8" x 3" cards mimic the regular Topps' design for 1990; featuring an action photo with multi-colored borders. Backs offer a round player portrait photo and information about the statistical achievement, all printed in full color. Cards are numbered alphabetically within teams. The 1990 minis are considerably scarcer than the previous years' offerings.

		NM/M
Complete Set (88):		5.00
Common Player:		.05
1	Jeff Ballard	.05
2	Phil Bradley	.05
3	Wade Boggs	.65
4	Roger Clemens	.75
5	Nick Esasky	.05
6	Jody Reed	.05
7	Bert Blyleven	.05
8	Chuck Finley	.05
9	Kirk McCaskill	.05
10	Devon White	.05
11	Ivan Calderon	.05
12	Bobby Thigpen	.05
13	Joe Carter	.05
14	Gary Pettis	.05
15	Tom Gordon	.05
16	Bo Jackson	.10
17	Bret Saberhagen	.05
18	Kevin Seitzer	.05
19	Chris Bosio	.05
20	Paul Molitor	.50
21	Dan Plesac	.05
22	Robin Yount	.50
23	Kirby Puckett	.65
24	Don Mattingly	.75
25	Steve Sax	.05
26	Storm Davis	.05
27	Dennis Eckersley	.40
28	Rickey Henderson	.50
29	Carney Lansford	.05
30	Mark McGwire	1.00
31	Mike Moore	.05
32	Dave Stewart	.05
33	Alvin Davis	.05
34	Harold Reynolds	.05
35	Mike Schooler	.05
36	Cecil Espy	.05
37	Julio Franco	.05
38	Jeff Russell	.05
39	Nolan Ryan	1.50
40	Ruben Sierra	.05
41	George Bell	.05
42	Tony Fernandez	.05
43	Fred McGriff	.05
44	Dave Steib	.05
45	Checklist	.05
46	Lonnie Smith	.05
47	John Smoltz	.05
48	Mike Bielecki	.05
49	Mark Grace	.05
50	Greg Maddux	.65
51	Ryne Sandberg	.65
52	Mitch Williams	.05
53	Eric Davis	.05
54	John Franco	.05
55	Glenn Davis	.05
56	Mike Scott	.05
57	Tim Belcher	.05
58	Orel Hershiser	.05
59	Jay Howell	.05
60	Eddie Murray	.50
61	Tim Burke	.05
62	Mark Langston	.05
63	Tim Raines	.05
64	Tim Wallach	.05
65	David Cone	.05
66	Sid Fernandez	.05
67	Howard Johnson	.05
68	Juan Samuel	.05
69	Von Hayes	.05
70	Barry Bonds	1.50
71	Bobby Bonilla	.05
72	Andy Van Slyke	.05
73	Vince Coleman	.05
74	Jose DeLeon	.05
75	Pedro Guerrero	.05
76	Joe Magrane	.05
77	Roberto Alomar	.20
78	Jack Clark	.05
79	Mark Davis	.05
80	Tony Gwynn	.65
81	Bruce Hurst	.05
82	Eddie Whitson	.05
83	Brett Butler	.05
84	Will Clark	.05
85	Scott Garrelts	.05
86	Kevin Mitchell	.05
87	Rick Reuschel	.05
88	Robby Thompson	.05

Nolan Ryan Bronze

This full-size bronze reproduction of Ryan's 1990 Topps card was given to dealers who made early orders for Topps' 1991 "Tiffany" sets. A 2,500 piece limit was announced.

	NM/M
Nolan Ryan	50.00

Senior League

Topps was among several companies to produce a Senior League set in 1990. The set includes 132 cards and was sold as a boxed set. The card fronts have the Senior Baseball and Topps logo on top and the player's name and team logo on the bottom, with a woodgrain-like border surrounding the front photo. The backs of the card contain traditional biographical information, plus career major league statistics, career ML bests and stats from any Senior League experience.

		NM/M
Complete Set (132):		5.00
Common Player:		.05
1	George Foster	.15
2	Dwight Lowry	.05
3	Bob Jones	.05
4	Clete Boyer	.05
5	Rafael Landestoy	.05
6	Bob Shirley	.05
7	Ivan Murrell	.05
8	Jerry White	.05
9	Steve Henderson	.05
10	Marty Castillo	.05
11	Bruce Kison	.05
12	George Hendrick	.05
13	Bernie Carbo	.05
14	Jerry Martin	.05
15	Al Hrabosky	.05
16	Luis Gomez	.05
17	Dick Drago	.05
18	Bobby Ramos	.05
19	Joe Pittman	.05
20	Ike Blessitt	.05
21	Bill Travers	.05
22	Dick Williams	.05
23	Randy Lerch	.05
24	Tom Spencer	.05
25	Graig Nettles	.05
26	Jim Gideon	.05
27	Al Bumbry	.05
28	Tom Murphy	.05
29	Rodney Scott	.05
30	Alan Bannister	.05
31	John D'Acquisto	.05
32	Bert Campaneris	.05
33	Bill Lee	.05
34	Jerry Grote	.05
35	Ken Reitz	.05
36	Al Oliver	.15
37	Tim Stoddard	.05
38	Lenny Randle	.05
39	Rick Manning	.05
40	Bobby Bonds	.15
41	Rick Wise	.05
42	Sal Butera	.05
43	Ed Figueroa	.05
44	Ron Washington	.05
45	Elias Sosa	.05
46	Dan Driessen	.05
47	Wayne Nordhagen	.05
48	Vida Blue	.15
49	Butch Hobson	.05
50	Randy Bass	.05
51	Paul Mirabella	.05
52	Steve Kemp	.05
53	Kim Allen	.05
54	Stan Cliburn	.05
55	Derrel Thomas	.05
56	Pete Falcone	.05
57	Willie Aikens	.05
58	Toby Harrah	.05
59	Bob Tolan	.05
60	Rick Waits	.05
61	Jim Morrison	.05
62	Stan Bahnsen	.05
63	Gene Richards	.05
64	Dave Cash	.05
65	Rollie Fingers	.50
66	Butch Benton	.05
67	Tim Ireland	.05
68	Rick Lysander	.05
69	Cesar Cedeno	.05
70	Jim Willoughby	.05
71	Bill Madlock	.15
72	Lee Lacy	.05
73	Milt Wilcox	.05
74	Ron Pruitt	.05
75	Wayne Krenchicki	.05
76	Earl Weaver	.25
77	Pedro Borbon	.05
78	Jose Cruz	.05
79	Steve Ontiveros	.05
80	Mike Easler	.05
81	Amos Otis	.05
82	Mickey Mahler	.05
83	Orlando Gonzalez	.05
84	Doug Simunic	.05
85	Felix Millan	.05
86	Garth Iorg	.05
87	Pete Broberg	.05
88	Roy Howell	.05
89	Dave LaRoche	.05
90	Jerry Manuel	.05
91	Tony Scott	.05
92	Larvell Blanks	.05
93	Joaquin Andujar	.05
94	Tito Landrum	.05
95	Joe Sambito	.05
96	Pat Dobson	.05
97	Dan Meyer	.05
98	Clint Hurdle	.05
99	Pete LaCock	.05
100	Bob Galasso	.05
101	Dave Kingman	.15
102	Jon Matlack	.05
103	Larry Harlow	.05
104	Rick Peterson	.05
105	Joe Hicks	.05
106	Bill Campbell	.05
107	Tom Paciorek	.05
108	Ray Burris	.05
109	Ken Landreaux	.05
110	Steve McCatty	.05
111	Ron LeFlore	.05
112	Joe Decker	.05
113	Leon Roberts	.05
114	Doug Corbett	.05
115	Mickey Rivers	.05
116	Dock Ellis	.05
117	Ron Jackson	.05
118	Bob Molinaro	.05
119	Fergie Jenkins	.50
120	U.L. Washington	.05
121	Roy Thomas	.05
122	Hal McRae	.15
123	Juan Eichelberger	.05
124	Gary Rajsich	.05
125	Dennis Leonard	.05
126	Walt Williams	.05
127	Rennie Stennett	.05
128	Jim Bibby	.05
129	Dyar Miller	.05
130	Luis Pujols	.05
131	Juan Beniquez	.05
132	Checklist	.05

Stickercards

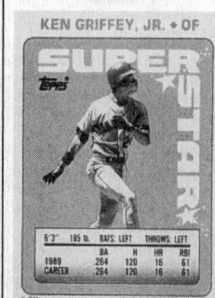

KEN GRIFFEY, JR. + OF

Topps' 1990 stickers were produced in two formats. Some measure 2-1/8" x 3" while there are many pairs of half-size (1-1/2" x 2-1/8") stickers. All stickers are attached to Super Star stickercards from which

Providing a cardboard backing for its annual series of player stickers, the stickercards are a collectible in themselves. Each 2-1/8" x 3" card is backed by one or two player stickers which could be removed and placed into a special album. The card portion features a player photo set against a solid-color background. A few vitae plus 1989 and career stats are presented in a graduated-color box toward the bottom. The stickercards are sequenced by position within league.

		NM/M
Complete Set (67):		5.00
Common Player:		.05
Wax Pack (5):		.25
Wax Box (48):		10.00
1	Will Clark	.05
2	Glenn Davis	.05
3	Pedro Guerrero	.05
4	Roberto Alomar	.15
5	Gregg Jefferies	.05
6	Ryne Sandberg	.60
7	Bobby Bonilla	.05
8	Howard Johnson	.05
9	Tim Wallach	.05
10	Shawon Dunston	.05
11	Barry Larkin	.05
12	Ozzie Smith	.60
13	Eric Davis	.05
14	Andre Dawson	.25
15	Tony Gwynn	.60
16	Von Hayes	.05
17	Kevin Mitchell	.05
18	Rock Raines	.05
19	Lonnie Smith	.05
20	Darryl Strawberry	.05
21	Jerome Walton	.05
22	Craig Biggio	.05
23	Benito Santiago	.05
24	Mike Scioscia	.05
25	Doc Gooden	.05
26	Rick Reuschel	.05
27	Mike Scott	.05
28	Sid Fernandez	.05
29	Mark Langston	.05
30	Joe Magrane	.05
31	Mark Davis	.05
32	Jay Howell	.05
33	Mitch Williams	.05
34	Don Mattingly	.65
35	Fred McGriff	.05
36	Mark McGwire	.85
37	Julio Franco	.05
38	Steve Sax	.05
39	Lou Whitaker	.05
40	Wade Boggs	.60
41	Gary Gaetti	.05
42	Carney Lansford	.05
43	Tony Fernandez	.05
44	Cal Ripken Jr.	1.00
45	Alan Trammell	.05
46	George Bell	.05
47	Jose Canseco	.35
48	Joe Carter	.05
49	Ken Griffey Jr.	.75
50	Rickey Henderson	.45
51	Bo Jackson	.05
52	Kirby Puckett	.60
53	Ruben Sierra	.05
54	Robin Yount	.45
55	Carlton Fisk	.45
56	Terry Steinbach	.05
57	Mickey Tettleton	.05
58	Nolan Ryan	1.00
59	Bret Saberhagen	.05
60	Dave Stewart	.05
61	Jeff Ballard	.05
62	Chuck Finley	.05
63	Greg Swindell	.05
64	Dennis Eckersley	.40
65	Gregg Olson	.05
66	Jeff Russell	.05
67	Checklist	.05

OPC Stickers

Topps' 1990 stickers were produced in two formats. Some measure 2-1/8" x 3" while there are many pairs of half-size (1-1/2" x 2-1/8") stickers. All stickers are attached to Super Star stickercards from which

they can be peeled and affixed in a special yearbook. Stickers have large center photos with a shadowbox effect in the borders, (blues for N.L., reds for A.L.). A tiny black sticker number is in the lower-right corner. There is no player name on the stickers; the albums have a box under each space with player data. The half-size stickers are printed in pairs and are checklisted in that fashion. Values given are for complete sticker(s)/stickercard combinations, but without regard for which stickercard is on back. The checklist and values for the O-Pee-Chee version of this set are identical to those for the Topps brand. Packs of five stickers sold for a quarter; the album with Don Mattingly on the cover retailed for 50 cents. Numbers in parentheses in this checklist indicate with which other sticker the named sticker is paired in the smaller format.

		NM/M
Complete Set (328):		7.50
Common Sticker:		.05
Album:		2.00
1	Rick Cerone/321 (Highlight)	.05
2	Kevin Elster/322 (Highlight)	.05
3	Nolan Ryan/323 (Highlight)	.45
4	Vince Coleman/319 (Highlight)	.05
5	Cal Ripken Jr./240 (Highlight)	.45
6	Jeff Reardon/328 (Highlight)	.05
7	Rickey Henderson/320 (Highlight)	.15
8	Wade Boggs/324 (Highlight)	.15
9	Barry Bonds/325 (Highlight)	.30
10	Gregg Olson/236 (Highlight)	.05
11	Tony Fernandez/327 (Highlight)	.30
12	Ryne Sandberg/326 (Highlight)	.30
13	Glenn Davis	.05
14	Danny Darwin/316	.05
15	Bill Doran/298	.05
16	Dave Smith/225	.05
17	Kevin Bass/278	.05
18	Rafael Ramirez/177	.05
19	Mike Scott	.05
20	Ken Caminiti/235	.05
21	Jim Deshaies/272	.05
22	Gerald Young/314	.05
23	Craig Biggio/186	.05
24	Lonnie Smith	.05
25	Dale Murphy/210	.10
26	Tom Glavine	.05
27	Gerald Perry/313	.05
28	Jeff Blauser/269	.05
29	Jeff Treadway/252	.05
30	John Smoltz/299	.05
31	Darrell Evans/295	.05
32	Oddibe McDowell/265	.05
33	Andres Thomas/304	.05
34	Joe Boever/191	.05
35	Pedro Guerrero	.05
36	Ken Dayley/226	.05
37	Milt Thompson/188	.05
38	Jose DeLeon/180	.05
39	Vince Coleman/293	.05
40	Terry Pendleton/225	.05
41	Joe Magrane	.05
42	Ozzie Smith/179	.30
43	Todd Worrell/195	.05
44	Jose Oquendo/238	.05
45	Tom Brunansky/287	.05
46	Ryne Sandberg	.60
47	Andre Dawson/268	.05
48	Mitch Williams	.05
49	Damon Berryhill/204	.05
50	Jerome Walton/274	.05
51	Greg Maddux/315	.30
52	Dwight Smith/248	.05
53	Shawon Dunston/194	.05
54	Mike Bielecki/239	.05
55	Rick Sutcliffe/305	.05
56	Mark Grace/228	.05
57	Eddie Murray	.40
58	Alfredo Griffin/197	.05
59	Fernando Valenzuela/277	.05
60	Kirk Gibson/201	.05
61	Ramon Martinez/190	.05
62	Mike Marshall/309	.05
63	Orel Hershiser	.05
64	Mike Scioscia/271	.05
65	Jay Howell/279	.05
66	Willie Randolph/283	.05
67	Jeff Hamilton/280	.05
68	Denny Martinez	.05
69	Tim Raines/184	.05
70	Mark Langston	.05
71	Dave Martinez/301	.05
72	Tim Burke/258	.05
73	Spike Owen/232	.05

74 Tim Wallach/254 .05
75 Andres Galarraga/208 .05
76 Kevin Gross/234 .05
77 Hubie Brooks/263 .05
78 Bryn Smith/207 .05
79 Kevin Mitchell .05
80 Craig Lefferts/256 .05
81 Ernest Riles/247 .05
82 Scott Garrelts/185 .05
83 Robby Thompson/251 .05
84 Don Robinson/282 .05
85 Will Clark .05
86 Steve Bedrosian/183 .05
87 Brett Butler/284 .05
88 Matt Williams/227 .05
89 Rick Reuschel/291 .05
90 Howard Johnson .05
91 Darryl Strawberry/246 .05
92 Sid Fernandez .05
93 David Cone/189 .05
94 Kevin McReynolds/311 .05
95 Frank Viola/229 .05
96 Dwight Gooden/206 .05
97 Kevin Elster/267 .05
98 Ron Darling/289 .05
99 Dave Magadan/257 .05
100 Randy Myers/192 .05
101 Tony Gwynn .60
102 Mark Davis/312 .05
103 Bip Roberts/212 .05
104 Jack Clark/205 .05
105 Chris James/211 .05
106 Mike Pagliarulo/199 .05
107 Ed Whitson .05
108 Bruce Hurst/245 .05
109 Roberto Alomar/202 .15
110 Benito Santiago/224 .05
111 Eric Show/307 .05
112 Ricky Jordan .05
113 Steve Jeltz/203 .05
114 Von Hayes .05
115 Dickie Thon/182 .05
116 Ken Howell/213 .05
117 John Kruk/306 .05
118 Lenny Dykstra/302 .05
119 Jeff Parrett/300 .05
120 Randy Ready/230 .05
121 Roger McDowell/262 .05
122 Tom Herr/250 .05
123 Barry Bonds .90
124 Andy Van Slyke/219 .05
125 Bob Walk/216 .05
126 R.J. Reynolds/243 .05
127 Gary Redus/249 .05
128 Bill Landrum/276 .05
129 Bobby Bonilla .05
130 Doug Drabek/218 .05
131 Jose Lind/221 .05
132 John Smiley/241 .05
133 Mike LaValliere/214 .05
134 Eric Davis .05
135 Tom Browning/270 .05
136 Barry Larkin .05
137 Jose Rijo/318 .05
138 Todd Benzinger/292 .05
139 Rick Mahler/217 .05
140 Chris Sabo/196 .05
141 Paul O'Neill/175 .05
142 Danny Jackson/273 .05
143 Rolando Roomes/261 .05
144 John Franco/231 .05
145 Ozzie Smith/AS .30
146 Tony Gwynn/AS .30
147 Will Clark/AS .05
148 Kevin Mitchell/AS .05
149 Eric Davis/AS .05
150 Howard Johnson/AS .05
151 Pedro Guerrero/AS .05
152 Ryne Sandberg/AS .35
153 Benito Santiago/AS .05
154 Rick Reuschel/AS .05
155 Bo Jackson/AS .35
156 Wade Boggs/AS .35
157 Kirby Puckett/AS .30
158 Harold Baines/AS .05
159 Julio Franco/AS .05
160 Cal Ripken Jr./AS .45
161 Ruben Sierra/AS .05
162 Mark McGwire/AS .40
163 Terry Steinbach/AS .05
164 Dave Stewart/AS .05
165 Bert Blyleven .05
166 Wally Joyner/285 .05
167 Kirk McCaskill/254 .05
168 Devon White/223 .05
169 Brian Downing/294 .05
170 Lance Parrish/296 .05
171 Chuck Finley .05
172 Jim Abbott/317 .05
173 Chili Davis/181 .05
174 Johnny Ray/260 .05
175 Bryan Harvey/141 .05
176 Mark McGwire .75
177 Jose Canseco/18 .15
178 Mike Moore .05
179 Dave Parker/42 .05
180 Bob Welch/38 .05
181 Rickey Henderson/173 .05
182 Dennis Eckersley/115 .20
183 Carney Lansford/86 .05
184 Dave Henderson/69 .05
185 Dave Stewart/82 .05
186 Terry Steinbach/23 .05
187 Fred McGriff .05
188 Junior Felix/37 .05
189 Ernie Whitt/93 .05
190 Dave Smith/61 .05
191 Jimmy Key/34 .05

192 George Bell/100 .05
193 Kelly Gruber .05
194 Tony Fernandez/53 .05
195 John Cerutti/43 .05
196 Tom Henke/140 .05
197 Nelson Liriano/58 .05
198 Robin Yount .40
199 Paul Molitor/106 .25
200 Dan Plesac .05
201 Teddy Higuera/60 .05
202 Gary Sheffield/109 .15
203 B.J. Surhoff/113 .05
204 Rob Deer/49 .05
205 Chris Bosio/104 .05
206 Glenn Braggs/96 .05
207 Jim Gantner/78 .05
208 Greg Brock/75 .05
209 Joe Carter .05
210 Jerry Browne/25 .05
211 Cory Snyder/105 .05
212 Joey Belle/103 .10
213 Bud Black/116 .05
214 Greg Swindell/133 .05
215 Doug Jones .05
216 Tom Candiotti/125 .05
217 John Farrell/139 .05
218 Pete O'Brien/130 .05
219 Brook Jacoby/124 .05
220 Alvin Davis .05
221 Harold Reynolds/131 .05
222 Scott Bankhead .05
223 Jeffrey Leonard/168 .05
224 Jim Presley/110 .05
225 Ken Griffey Jr./40 .40
226 Greg Briley/36 .05
227 Darnell Coles/88 .05
228 Mike Schooler/56 .05
229 Scott Bradley/95 .05
230 Randy Johnson/120 .25
231 Cal Ripken Jr. .90
232 Jeff Ballard/73 .05
233 Randy Milligan/144 .05
234 Joe Orsulak/76 .05
235 Billy Ripken/20 .05
236 Mark Williamson/21 .05
237 Mickey Tettleton .05
238 Gregg Olson/44 .05
239 Craig Worthington/54 .05
240 Bob Milacki/5 .05
241 Phil Bradley/132 .05
242 Nolan Ryan .90
243 Julio Franco/126 .05
244 Ruben Sierra .05
245 Harold Baines/128 .05
246 Jeff Kunkel/91 .05
247 Pete Incaviglia/81 .05
248 Kevin Brown/52 .05
249 Cecil Espy/127 .05
250 Rafael Palmeiro/122 .20
251 Steve Buechele/83 .05
252 Jeff Russell/29 .05
253 Wade Boggs .60
254 Mike Greenwell/99 .05
255 Roger Clemens/16 .35
256 Marty Barrett/80 .05
257 Dwight Evans/99 .05
258 Mike Boddicker/72 .05
259 Ellis Burks .05
260 John Dopson/174 .05
261 Rob Murphy/143 .05
262 Lee Smith/121 .05
263 Nick Esasky/77 .05
264 Bo Jackson .10
265 George Brett/32 .35
266 Bret Saberhagen .05
267 Kevin Seitzer/97 .05
268 Tom Gordon/47 .05
269 Kurt Stillwell/28 .05
270 Steve Farr/135 .05
271 Jim Eisenreich/64 .05
272 Mark Gubicza/21 .05
273 Jeff Montgomery/142 .05
274 Danny Tartabull/50 .05
275 Lou Whitaker .05
276 Jack Morris/128 .05
277 Frank Tanana/59 .05
278 Chet Lemon/17 .05
279 Fred Lynn/65 .05
280 Mike Heath/67 .05
281 Alan Trammell .05
282 Mike Henneman/84 .05
283 Gary Pettis/56 .05
284 Jeff Robinson/87 .05
285 Dave Bergman/166 .05
286 Kirby Puckett .60
287 Kent Hrbek/45 .05
288 Gary Gaetti .05
289 Jeff Reardon/98 .05
290 Brian Harper/167 .05
291 Gene Larkin/89 .05
292 Dan Gladden/138 .05
293 Al Newman/39 .05
294 Randy Bush/169 .05
295 Greg Gagne/31 .05
296 Allan Anderson/170 .05
297 Bobby Thigpen .05
298 Ozzie Guillen/15 .05
299 Ivan Calderon/30 .05
300 Carlos Martinez/119 .05
301 Steve Lyons/71 .05
302 Ron Kittle/118 .05
303 Carlton Fisk .40
304 Melido Perez/33 .05
305 Dave Gallagher/55 .05
306 Dan Pasqua/117 .05
307 Scott Fletcher/111 .05
308 Don Mattingly .65
309 Dave Righetti/62 .05

310 Steve Sax .05
311 Alvaro Espinoza/94 .05
312 Roberto Kelly/102 .05
313 Mel Hall/27 .05
314 Jesse Barfield/22 .05
315 Chuck Cary/51 .05
316 Bob Geren/14 .05
317 Andy Hawkins/172 .05
318 Don Slaught/137 .05
319 Jim Abbott/4 (Future Star) .05
320 Greg Briley/7 (Future Star) .05
321 Bob Geren/1 (Future Star) .05
322 Tom Gordon/2 (Future Star) .05
323 Ken Griffey Jr./3 (Future Star) .30
324 Gregg Jefferies/8 (Future Star) .10
325 Carlos Martinez/9 (Future Star) .05
326 Gary Sheffield/12 (Future Star) .15
327 Jerome Walton/11 (Future Star) .05
328 Craig Worthington/6 (Future Star) .05

TV All-Stars

This 66-card boxed set was sold only through a television offer in limited markets. Consequently, production numbers are relatively low and single cards are seldom offered in the hobby market. Most of the game's top stars are included in the issue. Fronts feature a high-gloss surface. On the red-bordered backs there are several lines of biographical data plus each player's "Career Bests" in various statistical categories, set against a pastel background shield. Issue price was $22.90.

	NM/M
Complete Set (66):	45.00
Common Player:	.25
1 Mark McGwire	6.50
2 Julio Franco	.25
3 Ozzie Guillen	.25
4 Carney Lansford	.25
5 Bo Jackson	.75
6 Kirby Puckett	3.50
7 Ruben Sierra	.25
8 Carlton Fisk	3.00
9 Nolan Ryan	9.00
10 Rickey Henderson	3.00
11 Jose Canseco	1.50
12 Mark Davis	.25
13 Dennis Eckersley	2.25
14 Chuck Finley	.25
15 Bret Saberhagen	.25
16 Dave Stewart	.25
17 Don Mattingly	5.00
18 Steve Sax	.25
19 Cal Ripken, Jr.	9.00
20 Wade Boggs	3.50
21 George Bell	.25
22 Mike Greenwell	.25
23 Robin Yount	3.00
24 Mickey Tettleton	.25
25 Roger Clemens	5.00
26 Fred McGriff	.25
27 Jeff Ballard	.25
28 Dwight Evans	.25
29 Paul Molitor	3.00
30 Gregg Olson	.25
31 Dan Plesac	.25
32 Greg Swindell	.25
33 Cito Gaston, Tony LaRussa	.25
34 Will Clark	.75
35 Roberto Alomar	.75
36 Barry Larkin	.25
37 Ken Caminiti	.25
38 Eric Davis	.25
39 Tony Gwynn	3.50
40 Kevin Mitchell	.25
41 Craig Biggio	.25
42 Mike Scott	.25
43 Joe Carter	.25
44 Jack Clark	.25
45 Glenn Davis	.25
46 Orel Hershiser	.25
47 Jay Howell	.25
48 Bruce Hurst	.25
49 Dave Smith	.25
50 Pedro Guerrero	.25
51 Ryne Sandberg	3.50
52 Ozzie Smith	3.50
53 Howard Johnson	.25
54 Von Hayes	.25
55 Tim Raines	.25
56 Darryl Strawberry	.25
57 Mike LaValliere	.25
58 Dwight Gooden	.25
59 Bobby Bonilla	.25
60 Tim Burke	.25
61 Sid Fernandez	.25
62 Andres Galarraga	.25
63 Mark Grace	.25
64 Joe Magrane	.25
65 Mitch Williams	.25
66 Roger Craig, Don Zimmer	.25

TV Cardinals Team Set

Available only as a boxed set via a limited television offer, this team set includes cards of all players on the opening day roster plus the manager, selected coaches and many of the organization's top prospects. In many cases this is the first card of a player in major league uniform, and in some cases represents the only card which will ever be issued of the player as a major leaguer. Cards feature a high-gloss front surface. Backs have a red border and feature a "ghost image" of the photo on the front as a background to the statistical and biographical data. Because of the relatively limited production and the fact it was sold as a boxed set only, single cards are seldom available.

	NM/M
Complete Set (66):	20.00
Common Player:	.25
1 Whitey Herzog	.25
2 Steve Braun	.25
3 Rich Hacker	.25
4 Dave Ricketts	.25
5 Jim Riggleman	.25
6 Mike Roarke	.25
7 Cris Carpenter	.25
8 John Costello	.25
9 Danny Cox	.25
10 Ken Dayley	.25
11 Jose DeLeon	.25
12 Frank DiPino	.25
13 Ken Hill	.25
14 Howard Hilton	.25
15 Ricky Horton	.25
16 Joe Magrane	.25
17 Greg Mathews	.25
18 Bryn Smith	.25
19 Scott Terry	.25
20 Bob Tewksbury	.25
21 John Tudor	.25
22 Todd Worrell	.25
23 Tom Pagnozzi	.25
24 Todd Zeile	.50
25 Pedro Guerrero	.25
26 Tim Jones	.25
27 Jose Oquendo	.25
28 Terry Pendleton	.50
29 Ozzie Smith	15.00
30 Denny Walling	.25
31 Tom Brunansky	.25
32 Vince Coleman	.50
33 Dave Collins	.25
34 Willie McGee	.50
35 John Morris	.25
36 Milt Thompson	.25
37 Gibson Alba	.25
38 Scott Arnold	.25
39 Rod Brewer	.25
40 Greg Carmona	.25
41 Mark Clark	.25
42 Stan Clarke	.25
43 Paul Coleman	.25
44 Todd Crosby	.25
45 Brad DuVall	.25
46 John Ericks	.25
47 Bien Figueroa	.25
48 Terry Francona	.25
49 Ed Fulton	.25
50 Bernard Gilkey	1.00
51 Ernie Camacho	.25
52 Mike Hinkle	.25
53 Ray Lankford	1.00
54 Julian Martinez	.25
55 Jesus Mendez	.25
56 Mike Milchin	.25
57 Mauricio Nunez	.25
58 Omar Olivares	.25
59 Geronimo Pena	.25
60 Mike Perez	.25
61 Gaylen Pitts	.25
62 Mark Riggins	.25
63 Tim Sherrill	.25
64 Roy Silver	.25
65 Ray Stephens	.25
66 Craig Wilson	.25

TV Cubs Team Set

Sold only in boxed set form via a limited television offer, this 66-card issue includes all players on the team's 1990 opening day roster as well as the manager, selected coaches and some of the organization's top minor league prospects. For the latter group, this sets offers the first - and in many cases the only - card of the player in a major league uniform. The cards have a high-gloss front surface. Card backs feature a "ghost image" of the color photo used on the front as a background to the stats and biographical information. A red border completes the back design. Because the set was sold only in boxed form, and production was relatively low, single cards are seldom seen in the market.

	NM/M
Complete Set (66):	45.00
Common Player:	.35
1 Don Zimmer	.35
2 Joe Altobelli	.35
3 Chuck Cottier	.35
4 Jose Martinez	.35
5 Dick Pole	.35
6 Phil Roof	.35
7 Paul Assenmacher	.35
8 Mike Bielecki	.35
9 Mike Harkey	.35
10 Joe Kraemer	.35
11 Les Lancaster	.35
12 Greg Maddux	20.00
13 Jose Nunez	.35
14 Jeff Pico	.35
15 Rick Sutcliffe	.75
16 Dean Wilkins	.35
17 Mitch Williams	.35
18 Steve Wilson	.35
19 Damon Berryhill	.35
20 Joe Girardi	.35
21 Rick Wrona	.35
22 Shawon Dunston	.50
23 Mark Grace	5.00
24 Domingo Ramos	.35
25 Luis Salazar	.35
26 Ryne Sandberg	20.00
27 Greg Smith	.35
28 Curtis Wilkerson	.35
29 Dave Clark	.35
30 Doug Dascenzo	.35
31 Andre Dawson	7.50
32 Lloyd McClendon	.35
33 Dwight Smith	.35
34 Jerome Walton	.35
35 Marvell Wynne	.35
36 Alex Arias	.35
37 Bob Bafia	.35
38 Brad Bierley	.35
39 Shawn Boskie	.35
40 Danny Clay	.35
41 Rusty Crockett	.35
42 Earl Cunningham	.35
43 Len Damian	.35
44 Darrin Duffy	.35
45 Ty Griffin	.35
46 Brian Guinn	.35
47 Phil Hannon	.35
48 Phil Harrison	.35
49 Jeff Hearron	.35
50 Greg Kallevig	.35
51 Cedric Landrum	.35
52 Bill Long	.35
53 Derrick May	.35
54 Ray Mullino	.35
55 Erik Pappas	.35
56 Steve Parker	.35
57 Dave Pavlas	.35
58 Laddie Renfroe	.35
59 Jeff Small	.35
60 Doug Strange	.35
61 Gary Varsho	.35
62 Hector Villanueva	.35
63 Rick Wilkins	.35
64 Dana Williams	.35
65 Bill Wrona	.35
66 Fernando Zarranz	.35

TV Mets Team Set

This late-season issue, sold only as a boxed set via a television offer in limited areas, features all of the players on the 1990 opening day roster, plus the manager, selected coaches and many of the organization's top minor league prospects. For many of the prospects, this is the first, if not the only, card on which they appear in major league uniform. A highlight of the back design is a "ghost image" full-color reproduction of the front photo, used as a background to the statistical and biographical information. A red border dominates the remainder of the back design. Because it was sold only as a boxed set, and production was relatively limited, single cards are seldom available.

	NM/M
Complete Set (66):	10.00
Common Player:	.35
1 Dave Johnson	.35
2 Mike Cubbage	.35
3 Doc Edwards	.35
4 Bud Harrelson	.35
5 Greg Pavlick	.35
6 Mel Stottlemyre, Sr.	.35
7 Blaine Beatty	.35
8 David Cone	1.00
9 Ron Darling	.35
10 Sid Fernandez	.35
11 John Franco	.50
12 Dwight Gooden	.35
13 Jeff Innis	.35
14 Julio Machado	.35
15 Jeff Musselman	.35
16 Bob Ojeda	.35
17 Alejandro Pena	.35
18 Frank Viola	.35
19 Wally Whitehurst	.35
20 Barry Lyons	.35
21 Orlando Mercado	.35
22 Mackey Sasser	.35
23 Kevin Elster	.35
24 Gregg Jefferies	.50
25 Howard Johnson	.35
26 Dave Magadan	.35
27 Mike Marshall	.35
28 Tom O'Malley	.35
29 Tim Teufel	.35
30 Mark Carreon	.35
31 Kevin McReynolds	.35
32 Keith Miller	.35
33 Darryl Strawberry	.50
34 Lou Thornton	.35
35 Shawn Barton	.35
36 Tim Bogar	.35
37 Terry Bross	.35
38 Kevin Brown	.35
39 Mike DeButch	.35
40 Alex Diaz	.35
41 Chris Donnels	.35
42 Jeff Gardner	.35
43 Denny Gonzalez	.35
44 Kenny Graves	.35
45 Manny Hernandez	.35
46 Keith Hughes	.35
47 Todd Hundley	.50
48 Chris Jelic	.35
49 Dave Liddell	.35
50 Terry McDaniel	.35
51 Cesar Mejia	.35
52 Scott Nielsen	.35
53 Dale Plummer	.35
54 Darren Reed	.35
55 Gil Roca	.35
56 Jaime Roseboro	.35
57 Roger Samuels	.35

58	Zoilo Sanchez	.35
59	Pete Schourek	.35
60	Craig Shipley	.35
61	Ray Soff	.35
62	Steve Swisher	.35
63	Kelvin Torve	.35
64	Dave Trautwein	.35
65	Julio Valera	.35
66	Alan Zinter	.35

TV Red Sox Team Set

This 66-card set was available only via a television offer in certain limited areas. Production was relatively low and single cards are hard to find. Player selection includes all those on the team's opening day roster in 1990, plus the manager, selected coaches and the team's top minor league prospects. In many cases this represents the first, or even the only, appearance of these prospects on major league baseball cards. Fronts have a high-gloss surface. Card backs, bordered in red, feature a "ghost image" reproduction of the front photo as a background to the statistics and biographical data.

		NM/M
Complete Set (66):		40.00
Common Player:		.35
1	Joe Morgan	.35
2	Dick Berardino	.35
3	Al Bumbry	.35
4	Bill Fischer	.35
5	Richie Hebner	.35
6	Rac Slider	.35
7	Mike Boddicker	.35
8	Roger Clemens	25.00
9	John Dopson	.35
10	Wes Gardner	.35
11	Greg Harris	.35
12	Dana Kiecker	.35
13	Dennis Lamp	.35
14	Rob Murphy	.35
15	Jeff Reardon	.35
16	Mike Rochford	.35
17	Lee Smith	.50
18	Rich Gedman	.35
19	John Marzano	.35
20	Tony Pena	.35
21	Marty Barrett	.35
22	Wade Boggs	15.00
23	Bill Buckner	.50
24	Danny Heep	.35
25	Jody Reed	.35
26	Luis Rivera	.35
27	Billy Jo Robidoux	.35
28	Ellis Burks	.35
29	Dwight Evans	.35
30	Mike Greenwell	.35
31	Randy Kutcher	.35
32	Carlos Quintana	.35
33	Kevin Romine	.35
34	Ed Nottle	.35
35	Mark Meleski	.35
36	Steve Bast	.35
37	Greg Blosser	.35
38	Tom Bolton	.35
39	Scott Cooper	.35
40	Zach Crouch	.35
41	Steve Curry	.35
42	Mike Dalton	.35
43	John Flaherty	.35
44	Angel Gonzalez	.35
45	Eric Hetzel	.35
46	Daryl Irvine	.35
47	Joe Johnson	.35
48	Rick Lancellotti	.35
49	John Leister	.35
50	Derek Livernois	.35
51	Josias Manzanillo	.35
52	Kevin Morton	.35
53	Julius McDougal	.35
54	Tim Naehring	.35
55	Jim Pankovits	.35
56	Mickey Pina	.35
57	Phil Plantier	.35
58	Jerry Reed	.35
59	Larry Shikles	.35
60	Tito Stewart	.35
61	Jeff Stone	.35
62	John Trautwein	.35
63	Gary Tremblay	.35
64	Mo Vaughn	2.50
65	Scott Wade	.35
66	Eric Wedge	.35

TV Yankees Team Set

• DON MATTINGLY •

The first - and in many cases the only - baseball card appearance of top minor league prospects occurs in this special 66-card boxed set which was sold only via a special television offer in limited markets. The set also includes all players on the team's opening day roster, plus the manager and selected coaches. Card fronts have a high-gloss surface. On back, framed by a red border, the design features a "ghost image" of the color front photo, used as a background to the statistical and biographical information. Because the cards were sold only as a complete set, single cards are seldom available.

		NM/M
Complete Set (66):		60.00
Common Player:		.35
1	Bucky Dent	.35
2	Mark Connor	.35
3	Billy Connors	.35
4	Mike Ferraro	.35
5	Joe Sparks	.35
6	Champ Summers	.35
7	Greg Cadaret	.35
8	Chuck Cary	.35
9	Lee Guetterman	.35
10	Andy Hawkins	.35
11	Dave LaPoint	.35
12	Tim Leary	.35
13	Lance McCullers	.35
14	Alan Mills	.35
15	Clay Parker	.35
16	Pascual Perez	.35
17	Eric Plunk	.35
18	Dave Righetti	.35
19	Jeff Robinson	.35
20	Rick Cerone	.35
21	Bob Geren	.35
22	Steve Balboni	.35
23	Mike Blowers	.35
24	Alvaro Espinoza	.35
25	Don Mattingly	40.00
26	Steve Sax	.35
27	Wayne Tolleson	.35
28	Randy Velarde	.35
29	Jesse Barfield	.35
30	Mel Hall	.35
31	Roberto Kelly	.35
32	Luis Polonia	.35
33	Deion Sanders	1.00
34	Dave Winfield	15.00
35	Steve Adkins	.35
36	Oscar Azocar	.35
37	Bob Brower	.35
38	Britt Burns	.35
39	Bob Davidson	.35
40	Brian Dorsett	.35
41	Dave Eiland	.35
42	John Fishel	.35
43	Andy Fox	.35
44	John Habyan	.35
45	Cullen Hartzog	.35
46	Sterling Hitchcock	.35
47	Brian Johnson	.35
48	Jimmy Jones	.35
49	Scott Kamieniecki	.35
50	Mark Leiter	.35
51	Jim Leyritz	.35
52	Jason Maas	.35
53	Kevin Maas	.35
54	Hensley Meulens	.35
55	Kevin Mmahat	.35
56	Rich Monteleone	.35
57	Vince Phillips	.35
58	Carlos Rodriguez	.35
59	Dave Sax	.35
60	Willie Smith	.35
61	Van Snider	.35
62	Andy Stankiewicz	.35
63	Wade Taylor	.35
64	Ricky Torres	.35
65	Jim Walewander	.35
66	Bernie Williams	4.00

1989 Major League Debut

MIKE BLOWERS

This 150-card set chronicles the debut date of all 1989 Major League rookies. Two checklist cards are also included in this boxed set, listing the players in order of debut date, though the cards are numbered alphabetically. The card fronts resemble the 1990 Topps cards in style. A debut banner appears in an upper corner. The flip sides are horizontal and are printed in black on yellow stock, providing an overview of the player's first game. The set is packaged in a special collectors box and was only available through hobby dealers.

		NM/M
Complete Set (150):		10.00
Common Player:		.05
1	Jim Abbott	.05
2	Beau Allred	.05
3	Wilson Alvarez	.05
4	Kent Anderson	.05
5	Eric Anthony	.05
6	Kevin Appier	.05
7	Larry Arndt	.05
8	John Barfield	.05
9	Billy Bates	.05
10	Kevin Batiste	.05
11	Blaine Beatty	.05
12	Stan Belinda	.05
13	Juan Bell	.05
14	Joey Belle	.25
15	Andy Benes	.05
16	Mike Benjamin	.05
17	Geronimo Berroa	.05
18	Mike Blowers	.05
19	Brian Brady	.05
20	Francisco Cabrera	.05
21	George Canale	.05
22	Jose Cano	.05
23	Steve Carter	.05
24	Pat Combs	.05
25	Scott Coolbaugh	.05
26	Steve Cummings	.05
27	Pete Dalena	.05
28	Jeff Datz	.05
29	Bobby Davidson	.05
30	Drew Denson	.05
31	Gary DiSarcina	.05
32	Brian DuBois	.05
33	Mike Dyer	.05
34	Wayne Edwards	.05
35	Junior Felix	.05
36	Mike Fetters	.05
37	Steve Finley	.05
38	Darren Fletcher	.05
39	LaVel Freeman	.05
40	Steve Frey	.05
41	Mark Gardner	.05
42	Joe Girardi	.05
43	Juan Gonzalez	.50
44	Goose Gozzo	.05
45	Tommy Greene	.05
46	Ken Griffey Jr.	3.00
47	Jason Grimsley	.05
48	Marquis Grissom	.05
49	Mark Guthrie	.05
50	Chip Hale	.05
51	John Hardy	.05
52	Gene Harris	.05
53	Mike Hartley	.05
54	Scott Hemond	.05
55	Xavier Hernandez	.05
56	Eric Hetzel	.05
57	Greg Hibbard	.05
58	Mark Higgins	.05
59	Glenallen Hill	.05
60	Chris Hoiles	.05
61	Shawn Holman	.05
62	Dann Howitt	.05
63	Mike Huff	.05
64	Terry Jorgenson	.05
65	Dave Justice	.25
66	Jeff King	.05
67	Matt Kinzer	.05
68	Joe Kraemer	.05
69	Marcus Lawton	.05
70	Derek Lilliquist	.05
71	Scott Little	.05
72	Greg Litton	.05
73	Rick Lueken	.05
74	Julio Machado	.05
75	Tom Magrann	.05
76	Kelly Mann	.05
77	Randy McCament	.05
78	Ben McDonald	.05
79	Chuck McElroy	.05
80	Jeff McKnight	.05
81	Kent Mercker	.05
82	Matt Merullo	.05
83	Hensley Meulens	.05
84	Kevin Mmahat	.05
85	Mike Munoz	.05
86	Dan Murphy	.05
87	Jaime Navarro	.05
88	Randy Nosek	.05
89	John Olerud	.15
90	Steve Olin	.05
91	Joe Oliver	.05
92	Francisco Oliveras	.05
93	Greg Olson	.05
94	John Orton	.05
95	Dean Palmer	.05
96	Ramon Pena	.05
97	Jeff Peterek	.05
98	Marty Pevey	.05
99	Rusty Richards	.05
100	Jeff Richardson	.05
101	Rob Richie	.05
102	Kevin Ritz	.05
103	Rosario Rodriguez	.05
104	Mike Roesler	.05
105	Kenny Rogers	.05
106	Bobby Rose	.05
107	Alex Sanchez	.05
108	Deion Sanders	.25
109	Jeff Schaefer	.05
110	Jeff Schulz	.05
111	Mike Schwabe	.05
112	Dick Scott	.05
113	Scott Scudder	.05
114	Rudy Seanez	.05
115	Joe Skalski	.05
116	Dwight Smith	.05
117	Greg Smith	.05
118	Mike Smith	.05
119	Paul Sorrento	.05
120	Sammy Sosa	3.00
121	Billy Spiers	.05
122	Mike Stanton	.05
123	Phil Stephenson	.05
124	Doug Strange	.05
125	Russ Swan	.05
126	Kevin Tapani	.05
127	Stu Tate	.05
128	Greg Vaughn	.05
129	Robin Ventura	.15
130	Randy Veres	.05
131	Jose Vizcaino	.05
132	Omar Vizquel	.05
133	Larry Walker	.25
134	Jerome Walton	.05
135	Gary Wayne	.05
136	Lenny Webster	.05
137	Mickey Weston	.05
138	Jeff Wetherby	.05
139	John Wetteland	.05
140	Ed Whited	.05
141	Wally Whitehurst	.05
142	Kevin Wickander	.05
143	Dean Wilkins	.05
144	Dana Williams	.05
145	Paul Wilmet	.05
146	Craig Wilson	.05
147	Matt Winters	.05
148	Eric Yelding	.05
149	Clint Zavaras	.05
150	Todd Zeile	.05
----	Checklist (1 of 2)	.05
----	Checklist (2 of 2)	.05

Pre-Production Sample Sheet

To preview its 40th anniversary set, Topps distributed this 7-1/2" x 10-1/2" uncut sheet. Fronts are identical to the issued versions of each player's card while backs are printed in blue with a large anniversary logo, the player's name, a copyright line and "1991 PRE-PRODUCTION / SAMPLE."

		NM/M
Uncut Sheet:		15.00
Complete Set (9):		15.00
Common Player:		1.00
(1)	Wade Boggs	3.00
(2)	Jose Canseco	2.00
(3)	Roger Clemens	6.00
(4)	Rickey Henderson	2.50
(5)	Bo Jackson	1.50
(6)	Kirt Manwaring	1.00
(7)	Willie Randolph	1.00
(8)	Benny Santiago	1.00
(9)	Walt Weiss	1.00

1991 Topps

Topps celebrated its 40th anniversary in 1991 with the biggest promotional campaign in baseball card history. More than 300,000 vintage Topps cards (or certificates redeemable for valuable older cards) produced from 1952 to 1990 were randomly inserted in packs. Also a grand prize winner received a complete set from each year, and others received a single set from 1952-1990. The 1991 Topps card fronts feature the "Topps 40 Years of Baseball" logo in the upper-left corner. Colored borders frame the player photos. All players of the same team have cards with the same frame/border colors. Both action and posed shots appear in full-color on the card fronts. The flip sides are printed horizontally and feature complete statistics. Record Breakers and other special cards were once again included in the set. The cards measure 2-1/2" x 3-1/2". Many cards can be found with variations in the sheet-letter (A-F) designations in the copyright line on back.

		NM/M
Unopened Factory Set, Retail (792):		30.00
Unopened Factory Set, Hobby (792):		25.00
Complete Set (792):		20.00
Common Player:		.05
Wax Pack (15):		.50
Wax Box (36):		12.50
Cello Pack (34):		1.00
Cello Box (24):		15.00
Rack Pack (45):		1.00
Rack Box (24):		15.00
Vending Box (500):		7.50
1	Nolan Ryan	.75
2	George Brett (Record Breaker)	.25
3	Carlton Fisk (Record Breaker)	.20
4	Kevin Maas (Record Breaker)	.05
5	Cal Ripken, Jr. (Record Breaker)	.40
6	Nolan Ryan (Record Breaker)	.40
7	Ryne Sandberg (Record Breaker)	.30
8	Bobby Thigpen (Record Breaker)	.05
9	Darrin Fletcher RC	.05
10	Gregg Olson	.05
11	Roberto Kelly	.05
12	Paul Assenmacher	.05
13	Mariano Duncan	.05
14	Dennis Lamp	.05
15	Von Hayes	.05
16	Mike Heath	.05
17	Jeff Brantley	.05
18	Nelson Liriano	.05
19	Jeff Robinson	.05
20	Pedro Guerrero	.05
21	Joe M. Morgan	.05
22	Storm Davis	.05
23	Jim Gantner	.05
24	Dave Martinez	.05
25	Tim Belcher	.05
26	Luis Sojo	.05
27	Bobby Witt	.05
28	Alvaro Espinoza	.05
29	Bob Walk	.05
30	Gregg Jefferies	.05
31	Colby Ward RC	.05
32	Mike Simms RC	.05
33	Barry Jones	.05
34	Atlee Hammaker	.05
35	Greg Maddux	.50
36	Donnie Hill	.05
37	Tom Bolton	.05
38	Scott Bradley	.05
39	Jim Neidlinger RC	.05
40	Kevin Mitchell	.05
41	Ken Dayley	.05
42a	Chris Hoiles RC (White inner photo frame.)	6.00
42b	Chris Hoiles RC (Charcoal inner photo frame.)	.10
43	Roger McDowell	.05
44	Mike Felder	.05
45	Chris Sabo	.05
46	Tim Drummond	.05
47	Brook Jacoby	.05
48	Dennis Boyd	.05
49a	Pat Borders (40 stolen bases in Kinston 1986)	.20
49b	Pat Borders (0 stolen bases in Kinston 1986)	.10
50	Bob Welch	.05
51	Art Howe	.05
52	Francisco Oliveras RC	.05
53	Mike Sharperson	.05
54	Gary Mielke	.05
55	Jeffrey Leonard	.05
56	Jeff Parrett	.05
57	Jack Howell	.05
58	Mel Stottlemyre	.05
59	Eric Yelding	.05
60	Frank Viola	.05
61	Stan Javier	.05
62	Lee Guetterman	.05
63	Milt Thompson	.05
64	Tom Herr	.05
65	Bruce Hurst	.05
66	Terry Kennedy	.05
67	Rick Honeycutt	.05
68	Gary Sheffield	.25
69	Steve Wilson	.05
70	Ellis Burks	.05
71	Jim Acker	.05
72	Junior Ortiz	.05
73	Craig Worthington	.05
74	Shane Andrews RC (#1 Draft Pick)	.10
75	Jack Morris	.05
76	Jerry Browne	.05
77	Drew Hall	.05
78	Geno Petralli	.05
79	Frank Thomas	.35
80a	Fernando Valenzuela (No diamond after 104 ER in 1990.)	.25
80b	Fernando Valenzuela (Diamond after 104 ER in 1990.)	.05
81	Cito Gaston	.05
82	Tom Glavine	.20
83	Daryl Boston	.05
84	Bob McClure	.05
85	Jesse Barfield	.05
86	Les Lancaster	.05
87	Tracy Jones	.05
88	Bob Tewksbury	.05
89	Darren Daulton	.05
90	Danny Tartabull	.05
91	Greg Colbrunn RC (Future Star)	.05
92	Danny Jackson	.05
93	Ivan Calderon	.05
94	John Dopson	.05
95	Paul Molitor	.35
96	Trevor Wilson	.05
97a	Brady Anderson (3H, 2RBI in Sept. scoreboard)	.05
97b	Brady Anderson (14H, 3 RBI in Sept. scoreboard)	.05
98	Sergio Valdez	.05
99	Chris Gwynn	.05
100a	Don Mattingly (10 hits 1990)	.50
100b	Don Mattingly (101 hits in 1990)	.50
101	Rob Ducey	.05
102	Gene Larkin	.05
103	Tim Costo RC (#1 Draft Pick)	.05
104	Don Robinson	.05
105	Kevin McReynolds	.05
106	Ed Nunez	.05
107	Luis Polonia	.05
108	Matt Young	.05
109	Greg Riddoch	.05
110	Tom Henke	.05
111	Andres Thomas	.05
112	Frank DiPino	.05
113	Carl Everett RC (#1 Draft Pick)	.50
114	Lance Dickson RC (Future Star)	.05
115	Hubie Brooks	.05
116	Mark Davis	.05
117	Dion James	.05
118	Tom Edens RC	.05
119	Carl Nichols RC	.05
120	Joe Carter	.05
121	Eric King	.05
122	Paul O'Neill	.05
123	Greg Harris	.05
124	Randy Bush	.05
125	Steve Bedrosian	.05
126	Bernard Gilkey RC	.10
127	Joe Price	.05
128	Travis Fryman	.05
129	Mark Eichhorn	.05
130	Ozzie Smith	.50

#	Player	Price
131a	Checklist 1 (Phil Bradley #727.)	.05
131b	Checklist 1 (Phil Bradley #717.)	.05
132	Jamie Quirk	.05
133	Greg Briley	.05
134	Kevin Elster	.05
135	Jerome Walton	.05
136	Dave Schmidt	.05
137	Randy Ready	.05
138	Jamie Moyer	.05
139	Jeff Treadway	.05
140	Fred McGriff	.05
141	Nick Leyva	.05
142	Curtis Wilkerson	.05
143	John Smiley	.05
144	Dave Henderson	.05
145	Lou Whitaker	.05
146	Dan Plesac	.05
147	Carlos Baerga	.05
148	Rey Palacios	.05
149	Al Osuna RC	.05
150	Cal Ripken, Jr.	.75
151	Tom Browning	.05
152	Mickey Hatcher	.05
153	Bryan Harvey	.05
154	Jay Buhner	.05
155a	Dwight Evans (Diamond after 162 G 1982.)	.10
155b	Dwight Evans (No diamond after 162 G 1982.)	.05
156	Carlos Martinez	.05
157	John Smoltz	.05
158	Jose Uribe	.05
159	Joe Boever	.05
160	Vince Coleman	.05
161	Tim Leary	.05
162	Ozzie Canseco RC	.10
163	Dave Johnson	.05
164	Edgar Diaz	.05
165	Sandy Alomar	.05
166	Harold Baines	.05
167a	Randy Tomlin RC ("Harriburg" 1989-90.)	.05
167b	Randy Tomlin RC ("Harrisburg" 1989-90.)	.05
168	John Olerud	.05
169	Luis Aquino	.05
170	Carlton Fisk	.35
171	Tony LaRussa	.05
172	Pete Incaviglia	.05
173	Jason Grimsley	.05
174	Ken Caminiti	.05
175	Jack Armstrong	.05
176	John Orton RC	.05
177	Reggie Harris RC	.05
178	Dave Valle	.05
179	Pete Harnisch	.05
180	Tony Gwynn	.50
181	Duane Ward	.05
182	Junior Noboa	.05
183	Clay Parker	.05
184	Gary Green	.05
185	Joe Magrane	.05
186	Rod Booker	.05
187	Greg Cadaret	.05
188	Damon Berryhill	.05
189	Daryl Irvine RC	.05
190	Matt Williams	.05
191	Willie Blair RC	.05
192	Rob Deer	.05
193	Felix Fermin	.05
194	Xavier Hernandez RC	.05
195	Wally Joyner	.05
196	Jim Vatcher RC	.05
197	Chris Nabholz RC	.05
198	R.J. Reynolds	.05
199	Mike Hartley RC	.05
200	Darryl Strawberry	.05
201	Tom Kelly	.05
202	Jim Leyritz RC	.20
203	Gene Harris	.05
204	Herm Winningham	.05
205	Mike Perez RC	.05
206	Carlos Quintana	.05
207	Gary Wayne	.05
208	Willie Wilson	.05
209	Ken Howell	.05
210	Lance Parrish	.05
211	Brian Barnes RC (Future Star)	.05
212	Steve Finley	.05
213	Frank Wills	.05
214	Joe Girardi	.05
215	Dave Smith	.05
216	Greg Gagne	.05
217	Chris Bosio	.05
218	Rick Parker RC	.05
219	Jack McDowell	.05
220	Tim Wallach	.05
221	Don Slaught	.05
222	Brian McRae RC	.10
223	Allan Anderson	.05
224	Juan Gonzalez	.20
225	Randy Johnson	.35
226	Alfredo Griffin	.05
227	Steve Avery	.05
228	Rex Hudler	.05
229	Rance Mulliniks	.05
230	Sid Fernandez	.05
231	Doug Rader	.05
232	Jose DeJesus	.05
233	Al Leiter	.05
234	Scott Erickson RC	.10
235	Dave Parker	.05
236a	Frank Tanana (No diamond after 269 SO 1975.)	.10
236b	Frank Tanana (Diamond after 269 SO 1975.)	.05
237	Rick Cerone	.05
238	Mike Dunne	.05
239	Darren Lewis RC	.05
240	Mike Scott	.05
241	Dave Clark	.05
242	Mike LaCoss	.05
243	Lance Johnson	.05
244	Mike Jeffcoat	.05
245	Kal Daniels	.05
246	Kevin Wickander	.05
247	Jody Reed	.05
248	Tom Gordon	.05
249	Bob Melvin	.05
250	Dennis Eckersley	.30
251	Mark Lemke	.05
252	Mel Rojas RC	.05
253	Garry Templeton	.05
254	Shawn Boskie RC	.05
255	Brian Downing	.05
256	Greg Hibbard	.05
257	Tom O'Malley	.05
258	Chris Hammond RC	.05
259	Hensley Meulens	.05
260	Harold Reynolds	.05
261	Bud Harrelson	.05
262	Tim Jones	.05
263	Checklist 2	.05
264	Dave Hollins RC	.05
265	Mark Gubicza	.05
266	Carmen Castillo	.05
267	Mark Knudson	.05
268	Tom Brookens	.05
269	Joe Hesketh	.05
270a	Mark McGwire (1987 SLG .618)	.75
270b	Mark McGwire (1987 SLG 618)	.75
271	Omar Olivares RC	.05
272	Jeff King	.05
273	Johnny Ray	.05
274	Ken Williams	.05
275	Alan Trammell	.05
276	Bill Swift	.05
277	Scott Coolbaugh	.05
278	Alex Fernandez RC (#1 Draft Pick)	.10
279a	Jose Gonzalez (Photo of Billy Bean, left-handed batter.)	.75
279b	Jose Gonzalez (Correct photo, right-handed batter.)	.05
280	Bret Saberhagen	.05
281	Larry Sheets	.05
282	Don Carman	.05
283	Marquis Grissom	.05
284	Bill Spiers	.05
285	Jim Abbott	.05
286	Ken Oberkfell	.05
287	Mark Grant	.05
288	Derrick May RC	.05
289	Tim Birtsas	.05
290	Steve Sax	.05
291	John Wathan	.05
292	Bud Black	.05
293	Jay Bell	.05
294	Mike Moore	.05
295	Rafael Palmeiro	.30
296	Mark Williamson	.05
297	Manny Lee	.05
298	Omar Vizquel	.05
299	Scott Radinsky RC	.05
300	Kirby Puckett	.50
301	Steve Farr	.05
302	Tim Teufel	.05
303	Mike Boddicker	.05
304	Kevin Reimer RC	.05
305	Mike Scioscia	.05
306a	Lonnie Smith (136 G 1990)	.10
306b	Lonnie Smith (135 G 1990)	.05
307	Andy Benes	.05
308	Tom Pagnozzi	.05
309	Norm Charlton	.05
310	Gary Carter	.35
311	Jeff Pico	.05
312	Charlie Hayes	.05
313	Ron Robinson	.05
314	Gary Pettis	.05
315	Roberto Alomar	.15
316	Gene Nelson	.05
317	Mike Fitzgerald	.05
318	Rick Aguilera	.05
319	Jeff McKnight RC	.05
320	Tony Fernandez	.05
321	Bob Rodgers	.05
322	Terry Shumpert RC	.05
323	Cory Snyder	.05
324a	Ron Kittle ("6 Home Runs" in career summary)	.10
324b	Ron Kittle ("7 Home Runs" in career summary)	.05
325	Brett Butler	.05
326	Ken Patterson	.05
327	Ron Hassey	.05
328	Walt Terrell	.05
329	Dave Justice	.05
330	Dwight Gooden	.05
331	Eric Anthony	.05
332	Kenny Rogers	.05
333	Chipper Jones RC (#1 Draft Pick)	6.00
334	Todd Benzinger	.05
335	Mitch Williams	.05
336	Matt Nokes	.05
337a	Keith Comstock (Mariners logo.)	.05
337b	Keith Comstock (Cubs logo.)	1.50
338	Luis Rivera	.05
339	Larry Walker	.05
340	Ramon Martinez	.05
341	John Moses	.05
342	Mickey Morandini RC	.10
343	Jose Oquendo	.05
344	Jeff Russell	.05
345	Len Dykstra	.05
346	Jesse Orosco	.05
347	Greg Vaughn	.05
348	Todd Stottlemyre	.05
349	Dave Gallagher	.05
350	Glenn Davis	.05
351	Joe Torre	.05
352	Frank White	.05
353	Tony Castillo	.05
354	Sid Bream	.05
355	Chili Davis	.05
356	Mike Marshall	.05
357	Jack Savage	.05
358	Mark Parent	.05
359	Chuck Cary	.05
360	Tim Raines	.05
361	Scott Garrelts	.05
362	Hector Villanueva	.05
363	Rick Mahler	.05
364	Dan Pasqua	.05
365	Mike Schooler	.05
366a	Checklist 3 (Carl Nichols #19.)	.05
366b	Checklist 3 (Carl Nichols #119.)	.05
367	Dave Walsh RC	.05
368	Felix Jose	.05
369	Steve Searcy	.05
370	Kelly Gruber	.05
371	Jeff Montgomery	.05
372	Spike Owen	.05
373	Darrin Jackson	.05
374	Larry Casian RC	.05
375	Tony Pena	.05
376	Mike Harkey	.05
377	Rene Gonzales	.05
378a	Wilson Alvarez RC (No 1989 Port Charlotte stats.)	.50
378b	Wilson Alvarez RC (1989 Port Charlotte stats)	.20
379	Randy Velarde	.05
380	Willie McGee	.05
381	Jim Leyland	.05
382	Mackey Sasser	.05
383	Pete Smith	.05
384	Gerald Perry	.05
385	Mickey Tettleton	.05
386	Cecil Fielder/AS	.05
387	Julio Franco/AS	.05
388	Kelly Gruber/AS	.05
389	Alan Trammell/AS	.05
390	Jose Canseco/AS	.15
391	Rickey Henderson/AS	.20
392	Ken Griffey Jr./AS	.35
393	Carlton Fisk/AS	.20
394	Bob Welch/AS	.05
395	Chuck Finley/AS	.05
396	Bobby Thigpen/AS	.05
397	Eddie Murray/AS	.20
398	Ryne Sandberg/AS	.30
399	Matt Williams/AS	.05
400	Barry Larkin/AS	.05
401	Barry Bonds/AS	.40
402	Darryl Strawberry/AS	.05
403	Bobby Bonilla/AS	.05
404	Mike Scoscia/AS	.05
405	Doug Drabek/AS	.05
406	Frank Viola/AS	.05
407	John Franco/AS	.05
408	Ernie Riles	.05
409	Mike Stanley	.05
410	Dave Righetti	.05
411	Lance Blankenship	.05
412	Dave Bergman	.05
413	Terry Mulholland	.05
414	Sammy Sosa	.60
415	Rick Sutcliffe	.05
416	Randy Milligan	.05
417	Bill Krueger	.05
418	Nick Esasky	.05
419	Jeff Reed	.05
420	Bobby Thigpen	.05
421	Alex Cole	.05
422	Rick Rueschel	.05
423	Rafael Ramirez	.05
424	Calvin Schiraldi	.05
425	Andy Van Slyke	.05
426	Joe Grahe RC	.05
427	Rick Dempsey	.05
428	John Barfield RC	.05
429	Stump Merrill	.05
430	Gary Gaetti	.05
431	Paul Gibson	.05
432	Delino DeShields	.05
433	Pat Tabler	.05
434	Julio Machado RC	.05
435	Kevin Maas	.05
436	Scott Bankhead	.05
437	Doug Dascenzo	.05
438	Vicente Palacios	.05
439	Dickie Thon	.05
440	George Bell	.05
441	Zane Smith	.05
442	Charlie O'Brien	.05
443	Jeff Innis	.05
444	Glenn Braggs	.05
445	Greg Swindell	.05
446	Craig Grebeck RC	.05
447	John Burkett	.05
448	Craig Lefferts	.05
449	Juan Berenguer	.05
450	Wade Boggs	.50
451	Neal Heaton	.05
452	Bill Schroeder	.05
453	Lenny Harris	.05
454a	Kevin Appier (No 1990 Omaha stats.)	.15
454b	Kevin Appier (1990 Omaha stats)	.05
455	Walt Weiss	.05
456	Charlie Leibrandt	.05
457	Todd Hundley	.05
458	Brian Holman	.05
459	Tom Trebelhorn	.05
460	Dave Steib	.05
461a	Robin Ventura (Gray inner photo frame at left.)	.15
461b	Robin Ventura (Red inner photo frame at left.)	.05
462	Steve Frey	.05
463	Dwight Smith	.05
464	Steve Buechele	.05
465	Ken Griffey	.05
466	Charles Nagy RC	.05
467	Dennis Cook	.05
468	Tim Hulett	.05
469	Chet Lemon	.05
470	Howard Johnson	.05
471	Mike Lieberthal RC (#1 Draft Pick)	.50
472	Kirt Manwaring	.05
473	Curt Young	.05
474	Phil Plantier RC	.10
475	Teddy Higuera	.05
476	Glenn Wilson	.05
477	Mike Fetters	.05
478	Kurt Stillwell	.05
479	Bob Patterson	.05
480	Dave Magadan	.05
481	Eddie Whitson	.05
482	Tino Martinez	.05
483	Mike Aldrete	.05
484	Dave LaPoint	.05
485	Terry Pendleton	.05
486	Tommy Greene RC	.05
487	Rafael Belliard	.05
488	Jeff Manto RC	.05
489	Bobby Valentine	.05
490	Kirk Gibson	.05
491	Kurt Miller RC (#1 Draft Pick)	.05
492	Ernie Whitt	.05
493	Jose Rijo	.05
494	Chris James	.05
495	Charlie Hough	.05
496	Marty Barrett	.05
497	Ben McDonald	.05
498	Mark Salas	.05
499	Melido Perez	.05
500	Will Clark	.05
501	Mike Bielecki	.05
502	Carney Lansford	.05
503	Roy Smith	.05
504	Julio Valera RC	.05
505	Chuck Finley	.05
506	Darnell Coles	.05
507	Steve Jeltz	.05
508	Mike York RC	.05
509	Glenallen Hill	.05
510	John Franco	.05
511	Steve Balboni	.05
512	Jose Mesa	.05
513	Jerald Clark	.05
514	Mike Stanton	.05
515	Alvin Davis	.05
516	Karl Rhodes RC	.05
517	Joe Oliver	.05
518	Cris Carpenter	.05
519	Sparky Anderson	.10
520	Mark Grace	.05
521	Joe Orsulak	.05
522	Stan Belinda	.05
523	Rodney McCray RC	.05
524	Darrel Akerfelds	.05
525	Willie Randolph	.05
526a	Moises Alou (37 R 1990 Pirates)	.20
526b	Moises Alou (0 R 1990 Pirates)	.15
527a	Checklist 4 (Kevin McReynolds #719)	.05
527b	Checklist 4 (Kevin McReynolds #105)	.05
528	Denny Martinez	.05
529	Mark Newfield RC (#1 Draft Pick)	.05
530	Roger Clemens	.60
531	Dave Rhode RC	.05
532	Kirk McCaskill	.05
533	Oddibe McDowell	.05
534	Mike Jackson	.05
535	Ruben Sierra	.05
536	Mike Witt	.05
537	Jose Lind	.05
538	Bip Roberts	.05
539	Scott Terry	.05
540	George Brett	.60
541	Domingo Ramos	.05
542	Rob Murphy	.05
543	Junior Felix	.05
544	Alejandro Pena	.05
545	Dale Murphy	.15
546	Jeff Ballard	.05
547	Mike Pagliarulo	.05
548	Jaime Navarro	.05
549	John McNamara	.05
550	Eric Davis	.05
551	Bob Kipper	.05
552	Jeff Hamilton	.05
553	Joe Klink RC	.05
554	Brian Harper	.05
555	Turner Ward RC	.05
556	Gary Ward	.05
557	Wally Whitehurst	.05
558	Otis Nixon	.05
559	Adam Peterson	.05
560	Greg Smith RC	.05
561	Tim McIntosh RC (Future Star)	.05
562	Jeff Kunkel	.05
563	Brent Knackert RC	.05
564	Dante Bichette	.05
565	Craig Biggio	.05
566	Craig Wilson RC	.05
567	Dwayne Henry	.05
568	Ron Karkovice	.05
569	Curt Schilling	.05
570	Barry Bonds	.75
571	Pat Combs	.05
572	Dave Anderson	.05
573	Rich Rodriguez RC	.05
574	John Marzano	.05
575	Robin Yount	.35
576	Jeff Kaiser RC	.05
577	Bill Doran	.05
578	Dave West	.05
579	Roger Craig	.05
580	Dave Stewart	.05
581	Luis Quinones	.05
582	Marty Clary	.05
583	Tony Phillips	.05
584	Kevin Brown	.05
585	Pete O'Brien	.05
586	Fred Lynn	.05
587	Jose Offerman RC	.05
588a	Mark Whiten RC (Hand inside left border.)	.05
588b	Mark Whiten RC (Hand over left border.)	.20
589	Scott Ruskin RC	.05
590	Eddie Murray	.35
591	Ken Hill	.05
592	B.J. Surhoff	.05
593a	Mike Walker RC (No 1990 Canton-Akron stats.)	.15
593b	Mike Walker RC (1990 Canton-Akron stats)	.05
594	Rich Garces RC (Future Star)	.05
595	Bill Landrum	.05
596	Ronnie Walden RC (#1 Draft Pick)	.05
597	Jerry Don Gleaton	.05
598	Sam Horn	.05
599a	Greg Myers (No 1990 Syracuse stats.)	.10
599b	Greg Myers (1990 Syracuse stats)	.05
600	Bo Jackson	.10
601	Bob Ojeda	.05
602	Casey Candaele	.05
603a	Wes Chamberlain RC (Photo of Louie Meadows, no bat.)	.75
603b	Wes Chamberlain RC (Correct photo, holding bat.)	.05
604	Billy Hatcher	.05
605	Jeff Reardon	.05
606	Jim Gott	.05
607	Edgar Martinez	.05
608	Todd Burns	.05
609	Jeff Torborg	.05
610	Andres Galarraga	.05
611	Dave Eiland	.05
612	Steve Lyons	.05
613	Eric Show	.05
614	Luis Salazar	.05
615	Bert Blyleven	.05
616	Todd Zeile	.05
617	Bill Wegman	.05
618	Sil Campusano	.05
619	David Wells	.05
620	Ozzie Guillen	.05
621	Ted Power	.05
622	Jack Daugherty	.05
623	Jeff Blauser	.05
624	Tom Candiotti	.05
625	Terry Steinbach	.05
626	Gerald Young	.05
627	Tim Layana RC	.05
628	Greg Litton	.05
629	Wes Gardner	.05
630	Dave Winfield	.35
631	Mike Morgan	.05
632	Lloyd Moseby	.05
633	Kevin Tapani	.05
634	Henry Cotto	.05
635	Andy Hawkins	.05
636	Geronimo Pena RC	.05
637	Bruce Ruffin	.05
638	Mike Macfarlane	.05
639	Frank Robinson	.05
640	Andre Dawson	.20
641	Mike Henneman	.05
642	Hal Morris	.05
643	Jim Presley	.05
644	Chuck Crim	.05
645	Juan Samuel	.05
646	Andujar Cedeno RC	.05
647	Mark Portugal	.05
648	Lee Stevens RC	.05
649	Bill Sampen RC	.05
650	Jack Clark	.05
651	Alan Mills RC	.05
652	Kevin Romine	.05
653	Anthony Telford RC	.05
654	Paul Sorrento RC	.05
655	Erik Hanson	.05
656a	Checklist 5 (Vincente Palacios #348.)	.05
656b	Checklist 5 (Palacios #433.)	.05
656c	Checklist 5 (Palacios #438.)	.05
657	Mike Kingery	.05
658	Scott Aldred RC	.05
659	Oscar Azocar RC	.05
660	Lee Smith	.05
661	Steve Lake	.05
662	Rob Dibble	.05
663	Greg Brock	.05
664	John Farrell	.05
665	Mike LaValliere	.05
666	Danny Darwin	.05
667	Kent Anderson	.05
668	Bill Long	.05
669	Lou Pinella	.05
670	Rickey Henderson	.35
671	Andy McGaffigan	.05
672	Shane Mack	.05
673	Greg Olson RC	.05
674a	Kevin Gross (No diamond after 89 BB 1988.)	.10
674b	Kevin Gross (Diamond after 89 BB 1988.)	.05
675	Tom Brunansky	.05
676	Scott Chiamparino RC	.05
677	Billy Ripken	.05
678	Mark Davidson	.05
679	Bill Bathe RC	.05
680	David Cone	.05
681	Jeff Schaefer RC	.05
682	Ray Lankford RC	.15
683	Derek Lilliquist	.05
684	Milt Cuyler RC	.05
685a	Doug Drabek (White inner photo frame)	6.00
685b	Doug Drabek (Charcoal inner photo frame)	.05
686	Mike Gallego	.05
687a	John Cerutti (4.46 ERA 1990)	.05
687b	John Cerutti (4.76 ERA 1990)	.05
688	Rosario Rodriguez RC	.05
689	John Kruk	.05
690	Orel Hershiser	.05
691	Mike Blowers	.05
692a	Efrain Valdez RC (No text below stats.)	.15
692b	Efrain Valdez RC (Two lines of text below stats.)	.05
693	Francisco Cabrera	.05
694	Randy Veres	.05
695	Kevin Seitzer	.05
696	Steve Olin	.05
697	Shawn Abner	.05
698	Mark Guthrie	.05
699	Jim Lefebvre	.05
700	Jose Canseco	.25
701	Pascual Perez	.05
702	Tim Naehring RC	.05
703	Juan Agosto	.05
704	Devon White	.05
705	Robby Thompson	.05
706a	Brad Arnsberg (68.2 IP Rangers 1990)	.05
706b	Brad Arnsberg (62.2 IP Rangers 1990)	.05
707	Jim Eisenreich	.05
708	John Mitchell RC	.05
709	Matt Sinatro	.05
710	Kent Hrbek	.05
711	Jose DeLeon	.05
712	Ricky Jordan	.05
713	Scott Scudder	.05
714	Marvell Wynne	.05
715	Tim Burke	.05
716	Bob Geren	.05
717	Phil Bradley	.05
718	Steve Crawford	.05
719	Keith Miller	.05
720	Cecil Fielder	.05
721	Mark Lee RC	.05
722	Wally Backman	.05
723	Candy Maldonado	.05
724	David Segui RC	.10
725	Ron Gant	.05
726	Phil Stephenson	.05
727	Mookie Wilson	.05
728	Scott Sanderson	.05
729	Don Zimmer	.05
730	Barry Larkin	.05
731	Jeff Gray RC	.05
732	Franklin Stubbs	.05
733	Kelly Downs	.05
734	John Russell	.05
735	Ron Darling	.05
736	Dick Schofield	.05
737	Tim Crews	.05
738	Mel Hall	.05
739	Russ Swan RC	.05
740	Ryne Sandberg	.50
741	Jimmy Key	.05
742	Bryn Smith	.05
743	Nelson Santovenia	.05
744	Doug Jones	.05
745	John Shelby	.05
746	Tony Fossas	.05
747	Al Newman	.05
748		
749	Greg Harris	.05

750	Bobby Bonilla	.05
751	Wayne Edwards RC	.05
752	Kevin Bass	.05
753	Paul Marak RC	.05
754	Bill Pecota	.05
755	Mark Langston	.05
756	Jeff Huson	.05
757	Mark Gardner	.05
758	Mike Devereaux	.05
759	Bobby Cox	.05
760	Benny Santiago	.05
761	Larry Andersen	.05
762	Mitch Webster	.05
763	Dana Kiecker RC	.05
764	Mark Carreon	.05
765	Shawon Dunston	.05
766	Jeff Robinson	.05
767	Dan Wilson RC (#1 Draft Pick)	.10
768	Donn Pall	.05
769	Tim Sherrill RC	.05
770	Jay Howell	.05
771	Gary Redus	.05
772	Kent Mercker RC	.05
773	Tom Foley	.05
774	Dennis Rasmussen	.05
775	Julio Franco	.05
776	Brent Mayne RC	.05
777	John Candelaria	.05
778	Danny Gladden	.05
779	Carmelo Martinez	.05
780a	Randy Myers (Career losses 15.)	.10
780b	Randy Myers (Career losses 19.)	
781	Darryl Hamilton	.05
782	Jim Deshaies	.05
783	Joel Skinner	.05
784	Willie Fraser	.05
785	Scott Fletcher	.05
786	Eric Plunk	.05
787	Checklist 6	.05
788	Bob Milacki	.05
789	Tom Lasorda	.05
790	Ken Griffey Jr.	.60
791	Mike Benjamin RC	.05
792	Mike Greenwell	.05

Tiffany

Topps ended its annual run of special collectors' edition boxed sets in 1991, producing the glossy sets inconsiderably more limited quantity than in previous years. Cards are identical to the regular 1991 Topps set except for the use of white cardboard stock and a high-gloss front finish.

	NM/M
Unopened Set (792):	135.00
Complete Set (792):	85.00
Common Player:	.10

Desert Shield

As a special treat for U.S. armed services personnel serving in the Persian Gulf prior to and during the war with Iraq, Topps produced a special edition featuring a gold-foil overprint honoring the military effort. Enough cards were produced to equal approximately 6,800 sets. While some cards actually reached the troops in the Middle East, many were short-stopped by military supply personnel stateside and sold into the hobby. Many of the cards sent to Saudi Arabia never returned to the U.S., however, making the supply of available cards somewhat scarce. The checklist cards in the set were not overprinted. At least two types of counterfeit overprint have been seen on genuine Topps cards in an attempt to cash in on the scarcity of these war "veterans."

	NM/M
Complete Set (792):	1,200
Common Player:	1.00
Wax Pack:	60.00

Traded

"Team USA" players are featured in the 1991 Topps Traded set. The cards feature the same style as the regular 1991 issue, including the 40th anniversary logo. The set includes 132 cards and showcases rookies and traded players along with "Team USA." The cards are numbered with a "T" designation in alphabetical order. Wax-pack versions have a gray cardboard stock (unlike the box-set's white stock). Each of the wax-pack cards can be found with one or two asterisks preceding the copyright line on back.

	NM/M
Unopened Retail or Hobby Set (132):	12.00
Complete Set (132):	10.00
Common Player:	.05
Wax Pack (7):	.65
Wax Box (36):	15.00
1	Juan Agosto	.05
2	Roberto Alomar	.15
3	Wally Backman	.05
4	Jeff Bagwell RC	3.00
5	Skeeter Barnes RC	.05
6	Steve Bedrosian	.05
7	Derek Bell RC	.05
8	George Bell	.05
9	Rafael Belliard	.05
10	Dante Bichette	.05
11	Bud Black	.05
12	Mike Boddicker	.05
13	Sid Bream	.05
14	Hubie Brooks	.05
15	Brett Butler	.05
16	Ivan Calderon	.05
17	John Candelaria	.05
18	Tom Candiotti	.05
19	Gary Carter	.50
20	Joe Carter	.05
21	Rick Cerone	.05
22	Jack Clark	.05
23	Vince Coleman	.05
24	Scott Coolbaugh	.05
25	Danny Cox	.05
26	Danny Darwin	.05
27	Chili Davis	.05
28	Glenn Davis	.05
29	Steve Decker RC	.05
30	Rob Deer	.05
31	Rich DeLucia RC	.05
32	John Dettmer RC (USA)	.05
33	Brian Downing	.05
34	Darren Dreifort RC (USA)	.25
35	Kirk Dressendorfer	.05
36	Jim Essian	.05
37	Dwight Evans	.05
38	Steve Farr	.05
39	Jeff Fassero RC	.05
40	Junior Felix	.05
41	Tony Fernandez	.05
42	Steve Finley	.05
43	Jim Fregosi	.05
44	Gary Gaetti	.05
45	Jason Giambi RC (USA)	4.00
46	Kirk Gibson	.05
47	Leo Gomez RC	.05
48	Luis Gonzalez RC	1.00
49	Jeff Granger RC (USA)	.10
50	Todd Greene RC (USA)	.15
51	Jeffrey Hammonds RC (USA)	.15
52	Mike Hargrove	.05
53	Pete Harnisch	.05
54	Rick Helling RC (USA)	.10
55	Glenallen Hill	.05
56	Charlie Hough	.05
57	Pete Incaviglia	.05
58	Bo Jackson	.05
59	Danny Jackson	.05
60	Reggie Jefferson RC	.05
61	Charles Johnson RC (USA)	.15
62	Jeff Johnson RC	.05
63	Todd Johnson RC (USA)	.05
64	Barry Jones	.05
65	Chris Jones	.05
66	Scott Kamieniecki	.05
67	Pat Kelly RC	.05
68	Darryl Kile RC	.05
69	Chuck Knoblauch RC	.05
70	Bill Krueger	.05

71	Scott Leius RC	.05
72	Donnie Leshnock RC (USA)	.05
73	Mark Lewis	.05
74	Candy Maldonado	.05
75	Jason McDonald RC (USA)	.05
76	Willie McGee	.05
77	Fred McGriff	.05
78	Billy McMillon RC (USA)	.05
79	Hal McRae	.05
80	Dan Melendez RC (USA)	.05
81	Orlando Merced RC	.05
82	Jack Morris	.05
83	Phil Nevin RC (USA)	.50
84	Otis Nixon	.05
85	Johnny Oates	.05
86	Bob Ojeda	.05
87	Mike Pagliarulo	.05
88	Dean Palmer RC	.05
89	Dave Parker	.05
90	Terry Pendleton	.05
91	Tony Phillips RC (USA)	.10
92	Doug Piatt RC	.05
93	Ron Polk (U.S.A.)	.05
94	Tim Raines	.05
95	Willie Randolph	.05
96	Dave Righetti	.05
97	Ernie Riles	.05
98	Chris Roberts RC (USA)	.05
99	Jeff Robinson (Angels)	.05
100	Jeff Robinson (Orioles)	.05
101	Ivan Rodriguez RC	3.00
102	Steve Rodriguez RC (USA)	.05
103	Tom Runnells	.05
104	Scott Sanderson	.05
105	Bob Scanlan RC	.05
106	Pete Schourek RC	.10
107	Gary Scott RC	.05
108	Paul Shuey RC (USA)	.10
109	Doug Simons RC	.05
110	Dave Smith	.05
111	Cory Snyder	.05
112	Luis Sojo	.05
113	Kennie Steenstra RC (USA)	.05
114	Darryl Strawberry	.05
115	Franklin Stubbs	.05
116	Todd Taylor RC (USA)	.05
117	Wade Taylor RC	.05
118	Garry Templeton	.05
119	Mickey Tettleton	.05
120	Tim Teufel	.05
121	Mike Timlin	.05
122	David Tuttle RC (USA)	.05
123	Mo Vaughn RC	.25
124	Jeff Ware RC (USA)	.05
125	Devon White	.05
126	Mark Whiten	.05
127	Mitch Williams	.05
128	Craig Wilson RC (USA)	.05
129	Willie Wilson	.05
130	Chris Wimmer RC (USA)	.05
131	Ivan Zweig RC (USA)	.05
132	Checklist	.05

Traded Tiffany

The final year of production for Topps "Tiffany" parallel boxed sets saw production levels slashed for the 132-card Traded version. Value of the sets has risen dramatically with the hobby's perception of the set's scarcity and the development of key rookies such as Bagwell, Giambi and I-Rod. Like the regular Traded set, cards are numbered in alphabetical order with a "T" suffix.

	NM/M
Unopened Set (132):	165.00
Complete Set (132):	90.00
Common Player:	.25
Stars and Rookies:	4X

Traded Brooks Robinson Bronze

This 1/4-size metal replica of Robinson's first-ever Topps card was issued to dealers who purchased cases of 1991 Topps Traded sets. Each detail of the 1957 Topps Robinson card is reproduced on the 1-1/4" x 1-3/4" bronze metal mini-card, right down to the stats.

71	Scott Leius RC	.05

Box Panel Cards

Styled like the standard 1991 Topps cards, this 16-card set honors milestones of the featured players. The cards were found on the bottom of wax pack boxes. The cards are designated in alphabetical order by (A-P) and are not numbered.

		NM/M
Complete Set (16):		6.00
Common Player:		.15
A	Bert Blyleven	.15
B	George Brett	1.25
C	Brett Butler	.15
D	Andre Dawson	.50
E	Dwight Evans	.15
F	Carlton Fisk	.75
G	Alfredo Griffin	.15
H	Rickey Henderson	.75
I	Willie McGee	.15
J	Dale Murphy	.50
K	Eddie Murray	.75
L	Dave Parker	.15
M	Jeff Reardon	.15
N	Nolan Ryan	2.25
O	Juan Samuel	.15
P	Robin Yount	.75

All-Star Glossy Set of 22

Continuing the same basic format used since 1984, these glossy-front rack-pack inserts honor the players, manager and honorary captains of the previous year's All-Star Game. Fronts have a league logo in the lower-left corner, a 1990 All-Star banner above the photo and a Topps 40th anniversary logo superimposed over the photo. Backs have a shield and star design and the legend "1990 All-Star Commemorative Set" above the player's name, position and card number. Backs are printed in red and blue.

		NM/M
Complete Set (22):		3.00
Common Player:		.05
1	Tony LaRussa	.05
2	Mark McGwire	.85
3	Steve Sax	.05
4	Wade Boggs	.50
5	Cal Ripken, Jr.	1.00
6	Rickey Henderson	.40
7	Ken Griffey Jr.	.75
8	Jose Canseco	.30
9	Sandy Alomar, Jr.	.15
10	Bob Welch	.05
11	Al Lopez	.05
12	Roger Craig	.05
13	Will Clark	.50
14	Ryne Sandberg	.50
15	Chris Sabo	.05
16	Ozzie Smith	.50
17	Kevin Mitchell	.05
18	Len Dykstra	.05
19	Andre Dawson	.15
20	Mike Scoscia	.05
21	Jack Armstrong	.05
22	Juan Marichal	.05

		NM/M
328	Brooks Robinson	15.00

Glossy Rookies

Similar in format to previous years' glossy rookies sets, this 33-card issue was available one per pack in 100-card jumbo cello packs. Card fronts have a colored "1990 Rookies" banner above the player photo, with the player's name in red in a yellow bar beneath. The Topps 40th anniversary logo appears in one of the upper corners of the photo. Backs are printed in red and blue and feature a "1990 Rookies Commemorative Set" shield logo. The player's name, position, team and card number are printed beneath. Cards are numbered alphabetically.

		NM/M
Complete Set (33):		2.00
Common Player:		.10
1	Sandy Alomar, Jr.	.10
2	Kevin Appier	.10
3	Steve Avery	.10
4	Carlos Baerga	.10
5	John Burkett	.10
6	Alex Cole	.10
7	Pat Combs	.10
8	Delino DeShields	.10
9	Travis Fryman	.10
10	Marquis Grissom	.10
11	Mike Harkey	.10
12	Glenallen Hill	.10
13	Jeff Huson	.10
14	Felix Jose	.10
15	Dave Justice	.25
16	Jim Leyritz	.10
17	Kevin Maas	.10
18	Ben McDonald	.10
19	Kent Mercker	.10
20	Hal Morris	.10
21	Chris Nabholz	.10
22	Tim Naehring	.10
23	Jose Offerman	.10
24	John Olerud	.25
25	Scott Radinsky	.10
26	Scott Ruskin	.10
27	Kevin Tapani	.10
28	Frank Thomas	1.50
29	Randy Tomlin	.10
30	Greg Vaughn	.10
31	Robin Ventura	.25
32	Larry Walker	.10
33	Todd Zeile	.10

East Coast National Reprints

Produced in Topps' 40th anniversary year, this four-card set was issued at the 1991 East Coast National card show, the first card show in which Topps had ever participated. A total of 40,000 sets were reportedly issued in the now-standard 2-1/2" x 3-1/2" format. Fronts reproduce first Topps cards of four baseball greats while backs, printed in blue, carry a reprint notice, ad for the card show and Topps copyright.

		NM/M
Complete Set (4):		7.50
Common Card:		1.50
(1)	Mickey Mantle/1952	5.00
(2)	Hank Aaron/1954	3.00
(3)	Frank Robinson/1957	1.50
(4)	Stan Musial/1958	1.50

Gallery of Champions

Topps final issue of metallic mini-cards continued the theme of honoring the previous year's winners of major awards. The 1/4-size (1-1/4" x 1-3/4") ingots were issued in complete boxed sets of aluminum, bronze and silver in special display cases. To promote quantity sales, Topps offered a special pewter version of the Rickey Henderson ingot.

		NM/M
Complete Aluminum Set (12):		22.50
Complete Bronze Set (12):		45.00
Complete Silver Set (12):		180.00
(1a)	Sandy Alomar Jr./Aluminum	1.00
(1b)	Sandy Alomar Jr./Bronze	2.50
(1s)	Sandy Alomar Jr./Silver	6.00
(2a)	Barry Bonds/Aluminum	10.00
(2b)	Barry Bonds/Bronze	15.00
(2s)	Barry Bonds/Silver	65.00
(3a)	George Brett/Aluminum	7.50
(3b)	George Brett/Bronze	10.00
(3s)	George Brett/Silver	50.00
(4a)	Doug Drabek/Aluminum	1.00
(4b)	Doug Drabek/Bronze	2.50
(4s)	Doug Drabek/Silver	6.00
(5a)	Cecil Fielder/Aluminum	1.00
(5b)	Cecil Fielder/Bronze	2.50
(5s)	Cecil Fielder/Silver	6.00
(6a)	John Franco/Aluminum	1.00
(6b)	John Franco/Bronze	2.50
(6s)	John Franco/Silver	6.00
(7a)	Rickey Henderson/Aluminum	3.00
(7b)	Rickey Henderson/Bronze	6.00
(7s)	Rickey Henderson/Silver	35.00
(7p)	Rickey Henderson/Pewter	15.00
(8a)	Dave Justice/Aluminum	1.25
(8b)	Dave Justice/Bronze	3.00
(8s)	Dave Justice/Silver	9.00
(9a)	Willie McGee/Aluminum	1.00
(9b)	Willie McGee/Bronze	2.50
(9s)	Willie McGee/Silver	6.00
(10a)	Ryne Sandberg/Aluminum	1.00
(10b)	Ryne Sandberg/Bronze	7.50
(10s)	Ryne Sandberg/Silver	40.00
(11a)	Bobby Thigpen/Aluminum	1.00
(11b)	Bobby Thigpen/Bronze	2.50
(11s)	Bobby Thigpen/Silver	6.00
(12a)	Bob Welch/Aluminum	1.00
(12b)	Bob Welch/Bronze	2.50
(12s)	Bob Welch/Silver	6.00

Golden Spikes Award

Each year the United States Baseball Federation honors the outstanding amateur player with the Golden Spikes Award. This card was handed out at the Nov. 20, 1991 awards banquet honoring Arizona State star Mike Kelly. Production was reported as 600 cards.

	NM/M
Mike Kelly	85.00

Joe Garagiola

Virtually identical to the personal business card which Topps produced for long-time NBC announcer and former major leaguer Joe Garagiola in 1976, this 1991 version makes mention of the Today Show on both front and back. The front is in the format of a 1973 Topps card and has a color portrait. The back resembles the 1976 Topps card, is in black-and-white and provides contact information.

		NM/M
1	Joe Garagiola	8.00

Micro

		NM/M
Complete Set (792):		9.00
Common Player:		.05
Stars/Rookies:		1-1.5X

Babe Ruth

This 11-card set by Topps was released in honor of the NBC movie about Babe Ruth. The cards were released on a limited basis. The card fronts feature full-color photos from the movie, while the flip sides are printed horizontally and describe the front photo. The cards are numbered on the back.

		NM/M
Complete Set (11):		12.50
Common Player:		1.00
1	Sunday Oct. 6, NBC	1.00
2	Stephen Lang as Babe Ruth	1.00
3	Bruce Weitz as Miller Huggins	1.00
4	Lisa Zane as Claire Ruth	1.00
5	Donald Moffat as Jacob Ruppert	1.00
6	Neil McDonough as Lou Gehrig	1.00
7	Pete Rose as Ty Cobb	5.00
8	Baseball Consultant (Rod Carew)	2.50
9	Miller Huggins, Babe Ruth	1.00
10	Ruth In Action	1.00
11	Babe Calls His Shot	1.00

Superstar Stand-Ups

Another of Topps' efforts over the years to market candy containers with a baseball player theme, the 1991 Superstar Stand-Ups were a test issue. Sold in a color-printed paper envelope, Stand-Ups are a hard plastic container filled with candy tablets. In bright see-through colors, the containers measure 2-1/16" x 2-9/16" and are vaguely shaped like a head and

shoulders. A paper label attached to the front of the plastic has a player portrait with his team in a banner above and his name in a strip at bottom. Backs have a baseball design on the label with the Topps 40th anniversary logo at top. The player's name, team and position are in color bars at the bottom, with the item number at left. At center are the player's height, weight, birth date, batting and throwing preference and the year and number of his Topps rookie card. Clear (non-colored) plastic containers are also known for each player, though their relative scarcity to the colored pieces is currently undetermined.

		NM/M
Complete Set (36):		45.00
Common Player:		1.00
Wax Pack (1):		1.50
Wax Box (36):		30.00
1	Jim Abbott	1.00
2	Sandy Alomar	1.00
3	Wade Boggs	2.50
4	Barry Bonds	5.00
5	Bobby Bonilla	1.00
6	George Brett	3.00
7	Jose Canseco	1.50
8	Will Clark	1.00
9	Roger Clemens	3.00
10	Eric Davis	1.00
11	Andre Dawson	1.50
12	Len Dykstra	1.00
13	Cecil Fielder	1.00
14	Carlton Fisk	2.00
15	Dwight Gooden	1.00
16	Mark Grace	1.00
17	Ken Griffey Jr.	3.50
18	Tony Gwynn	2.50
19	Rickey Henderson	2.00
20	Bo Jackson	1.50
21	Dave Justice	1.00
22	Kevin Maas	1.00
23	Ramon Martinez	1.00
24	Don Mattingly	3.00
25	Ben McDonald	1.00
26	Mark McGwire	4.00
27	Kevin Mitchell	1.00
28	Cal Ripken, Jr.	5.00
29	Nolan Ryan	5.00
30	Ryne Sandberg	2.50
31	Ozzie Smith	2.50
32	Dave Stewart	1.00
33	Darryl Strawberry	1.00
34	Frank Viola	1.00
35	Matt Williams	1.00
36	Robin Yount	2.00

"1953" Topps Archives Promos

This nine-card set was issued to promote Topps' 1953 Archives set. Besides seven of the cards being reprinted from the '53 set, the promo set included two of the "new" 1953-style cards which were included in the Archives issue - cards of Hank Aaron and Eleanor Engle, the first woman to sign a minor league contract in modern times. Card fronts are identical to the issued Archives cards, while the backs are white with red Archives logo and "Pre-production Sample" notation.

		NM/M
Complete Set (9):		75.00
Common Player:		7.50
(1)	Hank Aaron	12.00
(2)	Roy Campanella	7.50
(3)	Eleanor Engle	7.50
(4)	Bob Feller	7.50
(5)	Whitey Ford	7.50
(6)	Mickey Mantle	20.00
(7)	Willie Mays	12.00
(8)	Jackie Robinson	12.00
(9)	Satchell Paige	10.00

"1953" Topps Archives

Billed as "The Ultimate 1953 Set," this issue reproduced 273 of the original 274-card 1953 Topps set.

(Card #174, Billy Loes, was not reproduced due to lack of permission from the former Dodgers pitcher, though cards with #174 are known with a Loes back and another player on the front.) The Archives issue downsized the cards from their original 2-5/8" x 3-3/4" size to the now-standard 2-1/2" x 3-1/2" format. More than 50 cards of players who were not included in the 1953 Topps set were created as part of the Archives issue. Because Topps chose to use black-and-white photos and colorized backgrounds for most of the "extended" cards, rather than paintings as on the originals, collector interest in the Archives issue was diminished. Only 18,000 cases were reportedly produced.

		NM/M
Complete Set (337):		45.00
Common Player:		.10
Wax Pack (12):		1.50
Wax Box (36):		35.00
1	Jackie Robinson	7.50
2	Luke Easter	.10
3	George Crowe	.10
4	Ben Wade	.10
5	Joe Dobson	.10
6	Sam Jones	.10
7	Bob Borkowski	.10
8	Clem Koshorek	.10
9	Joe Collins	.10
10	Smoky Burgess	.10
11	Sal Yvars	.10
12	Howie Judson	.10
13	Conrado Marrero	.10
14	Clem Labine	.10
15	Bobo Newsom	.10
16	Peanuts Lowrey	.10
17	Billy Hitchcock	.10
18	Ted Lepcio	.10
19	Mel Parnell	.10
20	Hank Thompson	.10
21	Billy Johnson	.10
22	Howie Fox	.10
23	Toby Atwell	.10
24	Ferris Fain	.10
25	Ray Boone	.10
26	Dale Mitchell	.10
27	Roy Campanella	1.50
28	Eddie Pellagrini	.10
29	Hal Jeffcoat	.10
30	Willard Nixon	.10
31	Ewell Blackwell	.10
32	Clyde Vollmer	.10
33	Bob Kennedy	.10
34	George Shuba	.10
35	Irv Noren	.10
36	Johnny Groth	.10
37	Eddie Mathews	1.00
38	Jim Hearn	.10
39	Eddie Miksis	.10
40	John Lipon	.10
41	Enos Slaughter	.50
42	Gus Zernial	.10
43	Gil McDougald	.30
44	Ellis Kinder	.10
45	Grady Hatton	.10
46	Johnny Klippstein	.10
47	Bubba Church	.10
48	Bob Del Greco	.10
49	Faye Throneberry	.10
50	Chuck Dressen	.10
51	Frank Campos	.10
52	Ted Gray	.10
53	Sherman Lollar	.10
54	Bob Feller	1.00
55	Maurice McDermott	.10
56	Gerald Staley	.10
57	Carl Scheib	.10
58	George Metkovich	.10
59	Karl Drews	.10
60	Cloyd Boyer	.10
61	Early Wynn	.50
62	Monte Irvin	.50
63	Gus Niarhos	.10
64	Dave Philley	.10
65	Earl Harrist	.10
66	Orestes Minoso	.25
67	Roy Sievers	.10
68	Del Rice	.10
69	Dick Brodowski	.10

70	Ed Yuhas	.10
71	Tony Bartirome	.10
72	Fred Hutchinson	.10
73	Eddie Robinson	.10
74	Joe Rossi	.10
75	Mike Garcia	.10
76	Pee Wee Reese	1.00
77	John Mize	.75
78	Al Schoendienst	.50
79	Johnny Wyrostek	.10
80	Jim Hegan	.10
81	Joe Black	.10
82	Mickey Mantle	12.50
83	Howie Pollet	.10
84	Bob Hooper	.10
85	Bobby Morgan	.10
86	Billy Martin	.35
87	Ed Lopat	.20
88	Willie Jones	.10
89	Chuck Stobbs	.10
90	Hank Edwards	.10
91	Ebba St. Claire	.10
92	Paul Minner	.10
93	Hal Rice	.10
94	William Kennedy	.10
95	Willard Marshall	.10
96	Virgil Trucks	.10
97	Don Kolloway	.10
98	Cal Abrams	.10
99	Dave Madison	.10
100	Bill Miller	.10
101	Ted Wilks	.10
102	Connie Ryan	.10
103	Joe Astroth	.10
104	Yogi Berra	1.50
105	Joe Nuxhall	.10
106	John Antonelli	.10
107	Danny O'Connell	.10
108	Bob Porterfield	.10
109	Alvin Dark	.10
110	Herman Wehmeier	.10
111	Hank Sauer	.10
112	Ned Garver	.10
113	Jerry Priddy	.10
114	Phil Rizzuto	1.00
115	George Spencer	.10
116	Frank Smith	.10
117	Sid Gordon	.10
118	Gus Bell	.10
119	John Sain	.25
120	Davey Williams	.10
121	Walt Dropo	.10
122	Elmer Valo	.10
123	Tommy Byrne	.10
124	Sibby Sisti	.10
125	Dick Williams	.20
126	Bill Connelly	.10
127	Clint Courtney	.10
128	Wilmer Mizell	.10
129	Keith Thomas	.10
130	Turk Lown	.10
131	Harry Byrd	.10
132	Tom Morgan	.10
133	Gil Coan	.10
134	Rube Walker	.10
135	Al Rosen	.25
136	Ken Heintzelman	.10
137	John Rutherford	.10
138	George Kell	.50
139	Sammy White	.10
140	Tommy Glaviano	.10
141	Allie Reynolds	.25
142	Vic Wertz	.10
143	Billy Pierce	.20
144	Bob Schultz	.10
145	Harry Dorish	.10
146	Granville Hamner	.10
147	Warren Spahn	1.00
148	Mickey Grasso	.10
149	Dom DiMaggio	.25
150	Harry Simpson	.10
151	Hoyt Wilhelm	.50
152	Bob Adams	.10
153	Andy Seminick	.10
154	Dick Groat	.20
155	Dutch Leonard	.10
156	Jim Rivera	.10
157	Bob Addis	.10
158	John Logan	.10
159	Wayne Terwilliger	.10
160	Bob Young	.10
161	Vern Bickford	.10
162	Ted Kluszewski	.35
163	Fred Hatfield	.10
164	Frank Shea	.10
165	Billy Hoeft	.10
166	Bill Hunter	.10
167	Art Schult	.10
168	Willard Schmidt	.10
169	Dizzy Trout	.10
170	Bill Werle	.10
171	Bill Glynn	.10
172	Rip Repulski	.10
173	Preston Ward	.10
174	Ron Kline	.10
175	Don Hoak	.10
176	Jim Dyck	.10
177	Jim Waugh	.10
178	Gene Hermanski	.10
179	Virgil Stallcup	.10
180	Al Zarilla	.10
181	Bob Hofman	.10
182	Stu Miller	.10
183	Hal Brown	.10
184	Jim Pendleton	.10
185	Charlie Bishop	.10
186	Jim Fridley	.10
187	Richie Ashburn	.50
188	Andy Carey	.10

189	Ray Jablonski	.10
190	Dixie Walker	.10
191	Ralph Kiner	.50
192	Wally Westlake	.10
193	Mike Clark	.10
194	Eddie Kazak	.10
195	Ed McGhee	.10
196	Bob Keegan	.10
197	Del Crandall	.10
198	Forrest Main	.10
199	Marion Fricano	.10
200	Gordon Goldsberry	.10
201	Paul La Palme	.10
202	Carl Sawatski	.10
203	Cliff Fannin	.10
204	Dick Bokelmann	.10
205	Vern Benson	.10
206	Ed Bailey	.10
207	Whitey Ford	1.00
208	Jim Wilson	.10
209	Jim Greengrass	.10
210	Bob Cerv	.10
211	J.W. Porter	.10
212	Jack Dittmer	.10
213	Ray Scarborough	.10
214	Bill Bruton	.10
215	Gene Conley	.10
216	Jim Hughes	.10
217	Murray Wall	.10
218	Les Fusselman	.10
219	Pete Runnels	.10
220	Satchell Paige	4.00
221	Bob Milliken	.10
222	Vic Janowicz	.10
223	John O'Brien	.10
224	Lou Sleater	.10
225	Bobby Shantz	.20
226	Ed Erautt	.10
227	Morris Martin	.10
228	Hal Newhouser	.10
229	Rocky Krshnich	.10
230	Johnny Lindell	.10
231	Solly Hemus	.10
232	Dick Kokos	.10
233	Al Aber	.10
234	Ray Murray	.10
235	John Hetki	.10
236	Harry Perkowski	.10
237	Clarence Podbielan	.10
238	Cal Hogue	.10
239	Jim Delsing	.10
240	Freddie Marsh	.10
241	Al Sima	.10
242	Charlie Silvera	.10
243	Carlos Bernier	.10
244	Willie Mays	7.50
245	Bill Norman	.10
246	Roy Face	.10
247	Mike Sandlock	.10
248	Gene Stephens	.10
249	Ed O'Brien	.10
250	Bob Wilson	.10
251	Sid Hudson	.10
252	Henry Foiles	.10
253	Preacher Roe	.10
254	Dixie Howell	.10
255	Les Peden	.10
256	Bob Boyd	.10
257	Bob Oldis	.10
258	Jim Gilliam	.35
259	Roy McMillan	.10
260	Sam Calderone	.10
261	Bob Oldis	.10
262	John Podres	.35
263	Gene Woodling	.35
264	Jackie Jensen	.35
265	Bob Cain	.10
266	Duane Pillette	.10
267	Vern Stephens	.10
268	Bill Antonello	.10
269	Harvey Haddix	.10
270	John Riddle	.10
271	Ken Raffensberger	.10
272	Don Lund	.10
273	Willie Miranda	.10
274	Joe Coleman	.10
275	Milt Bolling	.10
276	Jimmie Dykes	.10
277	Ralph Houk	.35
278	Frank Thomas	.10
279	Bob Lemon	.50
280	Joe Adcock	.25
281	Jimmy Piersall	.10
282	Mickey Vernon	.10
283	Robin Roberts	.50
284	Rogers Hornsby	.50
285	Hank Bauer	.10
286	Hoot Evers	.10
287	Whitey Lockman	.10
288	Ralph Branca	.25
289	Wally Post	.10
290	Phil Cavarretta	.10
291	Gil Hodges	.25
292	Roy Smalley	.10
293	Bob Friend	.10
294	Dusty Rhodes	.10
295	Eddie Stanky	.10
296	Harvey Kuenn	.25
297	Marty Marion	.10
298	Sal Maglie	.10
299	Lou Boudreau	.50
300	Carl Furillo	.25
301	Bobo Holloman	.10
302	Steve O'Neill	.10
303	Carl Erskine	.25
304	Leo Durocher	.25
305	Lew Burdette	.10
306	Richie Ashburn	.50
307	Hoyt Wilhelm	.50

313	Bucky Harris	.50
314	Joe Garagiola	.50
315	Johnny Pesky	.10
316	Fred Haney	.10
317	Hank Aaron	7.50
318	Curt Simmons	.10
319	Ted Williams	7.50
320	Don Newcombe	.35
321	Charlie Grimm	.10
322	Paul Richards	.10
323	Wes Westrum	.10
324	Vern Law	.10
325	Casey Stengel	1.00
326	Hall of Fame Inductees (Dizzy Dean, Al Simmons)	1.00
327	Duke Snider	1.00
328	Bill Rigney	.10
329	Al Lopez	.50
330	Bobby Thomson	.35
331	Nellie Fox	.50
332	Eleanor Engle	.10
333	Larry Doby	.50
334	Billy Goodman	.10
335	Checklist 1-140	.10
336	Checklist 141-280	.10
337	Checklist 281-337	.10

1990 Major League Debut

This 171-card set features the players who made their Major League debut in 1990. The cards are styled like the 1991 Topps cards and are numbered in alphabetical order. The card backs are printed horizontally and feature information about the player's debut and statistics. The issue was sold only as a boxed set through hobby channels.

		NM/M
Complete Set (171):		5.00
Common Player:		.05
1	Paul Abbott	.05
2	Steve Adkins	.05
3	Scott Aldred	.05
4	Gerald Alexander	.05
5	Moises Alou	.25
6	Steve Avery	.05
7	Oscar Azocar	.05
8	Carlos Baerga	.05
9	Kevin Baez	.05
10	Jeff Baldwin	.05
11	Brian Barnes	.05
12	Kevin Bearse	.05
13	Kevin Belcher	.05
14	Mike Bell	.05
15	Sean Berry	.05
16	Joe Bitker	.05
17	Willie Blair	.05
18	Brian Bohanon	.05
19	Mike Bordick	.05
20	Shawn Boskie	.05
21	Rod Brewer	.05
22	Kevin Brown	.05
23	Dave Burba	.05
24	Jim Campbell	.05
25	Ozzie Canseco	.05
26	Chuck Carr	.05
27	Larry Casian	.05
28	Andujar Cedeno	.05
29	Wes Chamberlain	.05
30	Scott Chiamparino	.05
31	Steve Chitren	.05
32	Pete Coachman	.05
33	Alex Cole	.10
34	Jeff Conine	.05
35	Scott Cooper	.05
36	Milt Cuyler	.05
37	Steve Decker	.05
38	Rich DeLucia	.05
39	Delino DeShields	.05
40	Mark Dewey	.05
41	Carlos Diaz	.05
42	Lance Dickson	.05
43	Narciso Elvira	.05
44	Luis Encarnacion	.05
45	Scott Erickson	.05
46	Paul Faries	.05
47	Howard Farmer	.05
48	Alex Fernandez	.05
49	Travis Fryman	.05
50	Rich Garces	.05
51	Carlos Garcia	.05
52	Mike Gardiner	.05
53	Bernard Gilkey	.05
54	Tom Gilles	.05

#	Player	Price
55	Jerry Goff	.05
56	Leo Gomez	.05
57	Luis Gonzalez	.75
58	Joe Grahe	.05
59	Craig Grebeck	.05
60	Kip Gross	.05
61	Eric Gunderson	.05
62	Chris Hammond	.05
63	Dave Hansen	.05
64	Reggie Harris	.05
65	Bill Haselman	.05
66	Randy Hennis	.05
67	Carlos Hernandez	.05
68	Howard Hilton	.05
69	Dave Hollins	.05
70	Darren Holmes	.05
71	John Hoover	.05
72	Steve Howard	.05
73	Thomas Howard	.05
74	Todd Hundley	.05
75	Daryl Irvine	.05
76	Chris Jelic	.05
77	Dana Kiecker	.05
78	Brent Knackert	.05
79	Jimmy Kremers	.05
80	Jerry Kutzler	.05
81	Ray Lankford	.05
82	Tim Layana	.05
83	Terry Lee	.05
84	Mark Leiter	.05
85	Scott Leius	.05
86	Mark Leonard	.05
87	Darren Lewis	.05
88	Scott Lewis	.05
89	Jim Leyritz	.05
90	Dave Liddell	.05
91	Luis Lopez	.05
92	Kevin Maas	.05
93	Bob MacDonald	.05
94	Carlos Maldonado	.05
95	Chuck Malone	.05
96	Ramon Manon	.05
97	Jeff Manto	.05
98	Paul Marak	.05
99	Tino Martinez	.05
100	Derrick May	.05
101	Brent Mayne	.05
102	Paul McClellan	.05
103	Rodney McCray	.05
104	Tim McIntosh	.05
105	Brian McRae	.05
106	Jose Melendez	.05
107	Orlando Merced	.05
108	Alan Mills	.05
109	Gino Minutelli	.05
110	Mickey Morandini	.05
111	Pedro Munoz	.05
112	Chris Nabholz	.05
113	Tim Naehring	.05
114	Charles Nagy	.05
115	Jim Neidlinger	.05
116	Rafael Novoa	.05
117	Jose Offerman	.05
118	Omar Olivares	.05
119	Javier Ortiz	.05
120	Al Osuna	.05
121	Rick Parker	.05
122	Dave Pavlas	.05
123	Geronimo Pena	.05
124	Mike Perez	.05
125	Phil Plantier	.05
126	Jim Poole	.05
127	Tom Quinlan	.05
128	Scott Radinsky	.05
129	Darren Reed	.05
130	Karl Rhodes	.05
131	Jeff Richardson	.05
132	Rich Rodriguez	.05
133	Dave Rohde	.05
134	Mel Rojas	.05
135	Vic Rosario	.05
136	Rich Rowland	.05
137	Scott Ruskin	.05
138	Bill Sampen	.05
139	Andres Santana	.05
140	David Segui	.05
141	Jeff Shaw	.05
142	Tim Sherrill	.05
143	Terry Shumpert	.05
144	Mike Simms	.05
145	Daryl Smith	.05
146	Luis Sojo	.05
147	Steve Springer	.05
148	Ray Stephens	.05
149	Lee Stevens	.05
150	Mel Stottlemyre, Jr.	.05
151	Glenn Sutko	.05
152	Anthony Telford	.05
153	Frank Thomas	3.00
154	Randy Tomlin	.05
155	Brian Traxler	.05
156	Efrain Valdez	.05
157	Rafael Valdez	.05
158	Julio Valera	.05
159	Jim Vatcher	.05
160	Hector Villanueva	.05
161	Hector Wagner	.05
162	Dave Walsh	.05
163	Steve Wapnick	.05
164	Colby Ward	.05
165	Turner Ward	.05
166	Terry Wells	.05
167	Mark Whiten	.05
168	Mike York	.05
169	Cliff Young	.05
170	Checklist	.05
171	Checklist	.05

1992 Topps Pre-Production

To preview its 1992 card set for dealers, Topps distributed a nine-card sheet in the basic format of its 1992 issue. The 8" x 10" sheets are often found cut into standard 2-1/2" x 3-1/2" singles. Card numbers on the backs of these promo cards do not correspond to the same cards in the regular set, and the stats for 1991 are not included. The preview cards have an orange oval on back, with the words, "1992 Pre-Production Sample."

		NM/M
Uncut Sheet:		6.00
Complete Set (9):		6.00
Common Player:		1.00
3	Shawon Dunston	1.00
16	Mike Heath	1.00
18	Todd Frowirth	1.00
20	Bip Roberts	1.00
131	Rob Dibble	1.00
174	Otis Nixon	1.00
273	Dennis Martinez	1.00
325	Brett Butler	1.00
798	Tom Lasorda	1.00

1992 Topps

This 792-card set features white stock much like the 1991 issue. The card fronts feature full-color action and posed photos with a gray inner frame and the player name and position at bottom. Backs feature biographical information, statistics and stadium photos on player cards where space is available. All-Star cards and #1 Draft Pick cards are once again included. Topps brought back four-player rookie cards in 1992. Nine Top Prospect cards of this nature can be found within the set. "Match the Stats" game cards were inserted into packs of 1992 Topps cards. Special bonus cards were given away to winners of this insert game. This was the first Topps regular-issue baseball card set since 1951 which was sold without bubblegum.

		NM/M
Unopened Fact. Set (802):		30.00
Complete Set (792):		20.00
Common Player:		.05
Golds:		4X
Wax Pack (14):		.50
Wax Box (36):		12.50
Cello Pack (34):		1.00
Cello Box (24):		16.00
Vending Box (500):		6.00
1	Nolan Ryan	.75
2	Rickey Henderson (Record Breaker)	.20
3	Jeff Reardon (Record Breaker)	.05
4	Nolan Ryan (Record Breaker)	.40
5	Dave Winfield (Record Breaker)	.20
6	Brien Taylor RC (Draft Pick)	.05

#	Player	Price
7	Jim Olander RC	.05
8	Bryan Hickerson RC	.05
9	John Farrell (Draft Pick)	.05
10	Wade Boggs	.45
11	Jack McDowell	.05
12	Luis Gonzalez	.05
13	Mike Scioscia	.05
14	Wes Chamberlain	.05
15	Denny Martinez	.05
16	Jeff Montgomery	.05
17	Randy Milligan	.05
18	Greg Cadaret	.05
19	Jamie Quirk	.05
20	Bip Roberts	.05
21	Buck Rodgers	.05
22	Bill Wegman	.05
23	Chuck Knoblauch	.05
24	Randy Myers	.05
25	Ron Gant	.05
26	Mike Bielecki	.05
27	Juan Gonzalez	.20
28	Mike Schooler	.05
29	Mickey Tettleton	.05
30	John Kruk	.05
31	Bryn Smith	.05
32	Chris Nabholz	.05
33	Carlos Baerga	.05
34	Jeff Juden	.05
35	Dave Righetti	.05
36	Scott Ruffcorn RC (Draft Pick)	.05
37	Luis Polonia	.05
38	Tom Candiotti	.05
39	Greg Olson	.05
40	Cal Ripken, Jr.	.75
41	Craig Lefferts	.05
42	Mike Macfarlane	.05
43	Jose Lind	.05
44	Rick Aguilera	.05
45	Gary Carter	.35
46	Steve Farr	.05
47	Rex Hudler	.05
48	Scott Scudder	.05
49	Damon Berryhill	.05
50	Ken Griffey Jr.	.55
51	Tom Runnells	.05
52	Juan Bell	.05
53	Tommy Gregg	.05
54	David Wells	.05
55	Rafael Palmeiro	.30
56	Charlie O'Brien	.05
57	Donn Pall	.05
58	Top Prospects-Catchers (Brad Ausmus RC, Jim Campanis RC, Dave Nilsson RC, Doug Robbins RC)	.15
59	Mo Vaughn	.05
60	Tony Fernandez	.05
61	Paul O'Neill	.05
62	Gene Nelson	.05
63	Randy Ready	.05
64	Bob Kipper	.05
65	Willie McGee	.05
66	Scott Stahoviak RC (Draft Pick)	.05
67	Luis Salazar	.05
68	Marvin Freeman	.05
69	Kenny Lofton	.05
70	Gary Gaetti	.05
71	Erik Hanson	.05
72	Eddie Zosky RC	.05
73	Brian Barnes	.05
74	Scott Leius	.05
75	Bret Saberhagen	.05
76	Mike Gallego	.05
77	Jack Armstrong	.05
78	Ivan Rodriguez	.35
79	Jesse Orosco	.05
80	Dave Justice	.05
81	Ced Landrum RC	.05
82	Doug Simons RC	.05
83	Tommy Greene	.05
84	Leo Gomez	.05
85	Jose DeLeon	.05
86	Steve Finley	.05
87	Bob MacDonald RC	.05
88	Darrin Jackson	.05
89	Neal Heaton	.05
90	Robin Yount	.35
91	Jeff Reed	.05
92	Lenny Harris	.05
93	Reggie Jefferson	.05
94	Sammy Sosa	.45
95	Scott Bailes	.05
96	Tom McKinnon RC (Draft Pick)	.05
97	Luis Rivera	.05
98	Mike Harkey	.05
99	Jeff Treadway	.05
100	Jose Canseco	.25
101	Omar Vizquel	.05
102	Scott Kamieniecki RC	.05
103	Ricky Jordan	.05
104	Jeff Ballard	.05
105	Felix Jose	.05
106	Mike Boddicker	.05
107	Dan Pasqua	.05
108	Mike Timlin RC	.10
109	Roger Craig	.05
110	Ryne Sandberg	.45
111	Mark Carreon	.05
112	Oscar Azocar	.05
113	Mike Greenwell	.05
114	Mark Portugal	.05
115	Terry Pendleton	.05
116	Willie Randolph	.05
117	Scott Terry	.05
118	Chili Davis	.05
119	Mark Gardner	.05
120	Alan Trammell	.05
121	Derek Bell	.05
122	Gary Varsho	.05
123	Bob Ojeda	.05
124	Shawn Livsey RC (Draft Pick)	.05
125	Chris Hoiles	.05
126	Top Prospects-1st Baseman (Rico Brogna, John Jaha, Ryan Klesko, Dave Staton)	.05
127	Carlos Quintana	.05
128	Kurt Stillwell	.05
129	Melido Perez	.05
130	Alvin Davis	.30
131	Checklist 1	.05
132	Eric Show	.05
133	Rance Mulliniks	.05
134	Darryl Kile	.05
135	Von Hayes	.05
136	Bill Doran	.05
137	Jeff Robinson	.05
138	Monty Fariss	.05
139	Jeff Innis	.05
140	Mark Grace	.05
141	Jim Leyland	.05
142	Todd Van Poppel	.05
143	Paul Gibson	.05
144	Bill Swift	.05
145	Danny Tartabull	.05
146	Al Newman	.05
147	Cris Carpenter	.05
148	Anthony Young RC	.05
149	Brian Bohanon RC	.05
150	Roger Clemens	.50
151	Jeff Hamilton	.05
152	Charlie Leibrandt	.05
153	Ron Karkovice	.05
154	Hensley Meulens	.05
155	Scott Bankhead	.05
156	Manny Ramirez RC (Draft Pick)	3.00
157	Keith Miller	.05
158	Todd Frohwirth	.05
159	Darrin Fletcher	.05
160	Bobby Bonilla	.05
161	Casey Candaele	.05
162	Paul Faries RC	.05
163	Dana Kiecker	.05
164	Shane Mack	.05
165	Mark Langston	.05
166	Geronimo Pena	.05
167	Andy Allanson	.05
168	Dwight Smith	.05
169	Chuck Crim	.05
170	Alex Cole	.05
171	Bill Plummer	.05
172	Juan Berenguer	.05
173	Brian Downing	.05
174	Steve Frey	.05
175	Orel Hershiser	.05
176	Ramon Garcia RC	.05
177	Danny Gladden	.05
178	Jim Acker	.05
179	Top Prospects-2nd Baseman (Cesar Bernhardt RC, Bobby DeJardin RC, Armando Moreno RC, Andy Stankiewicz RC)	.05
180	Kevin Mitchell	.05
181	Hector Villanueva	.05
182	Jeff Reardon	.05
183	Brent Mayne	.05
184	Jimmy Jones	.05
185	Benny Santiago	.05
186	Cliff Floyd RC (Draft Pick)	.50
187	Ernie Riles	.05
188	Jose Guzman	.05
189	Junior Felix	.05
190	Glenn Davis	.05
191	Charlie Hough	.05
192	Dave Fleming RC	.05
193	Omar Oliveras RC	.05
194	Eric Karros	.05
195	David Cone	.05
196	Frank Castillo RC	.05
197	Glenn Braggs	.05
198	Scott Aldred	.05
199	Jeff Blauser	.05
200	Len Dykstra	.05
201	Buck Showalter	.05
202	Rick Honeycutt	.05
203	Greg Myers	.05
204	Trevor Wilson	.05
205	Jay Howell	.05
206	Luis Sojo	.05
207	Jack Clark	.05
208	Julio Machado	.05
209	Lloyd McClendon	.05
210	Ozzie Guillen	.05
211	Jeremy Hernandez RC	.05
212	Randy Velarde	.05
213	Les Lancaster	.05
214	Andy Mota RC	.05
215	Rich Gossage	.05
216	Brent Gates RC (Draft Pick)	.05
217	Brian Harper	.05
218	Mike Flanagan	.05
219	Jerry Browne	.05
220	Jose Rijo	.05
221	Skeeter Barnes	.05
222	Jaime Navarro	.05
223	Mel Hall	.05
224	Brett Barberie RC	.05
225	Roberto Alomar	.15
226	Pete Smith	.05
227	Daryl Boston	.05
228	Eddie Whitson	.05
229	Shawn Boskie	.05
230	Dick Schofield	.05
231	Brian Drahman RC	.05
232	John Smiley	.05
233	Mitch Webster	.05
234	Terry Steinbach	.05
235	Jack Morris	.05
236	Bill Pecota	.05
237	Jose Hernandez RC	.05
238	Greg Litton	.05
239	Brian Holman	.05
240	Andres Galarraga	.05
241	Gerald Young	.05
242	Mike Mussina	.30
243	Alvaro Espinoza	.05
244	Darren Daulton	.05
245	John Smoltz	.05
246	Jason Pruitt RC (Draft Pick)	.05
247	Chuck Finley	.05
248	Jim Gantner	.05
249	Tony Fossas	.05
250	Ken Griffey	.05
251	Kevin Elster	.05
252	Dennis Rasmussen	.05
253	Terry Kennedy	.05
254	Ryan Bowen RC	.05
255	Robin Ventura	.05
256	Mike Aldrete	.05
257	Jeff Russell	.05
258	Jim Lindeman	.05
259	Ron Darling	.05
260	Devon White	.05
261	Tom Lasorda	.05
262	Terry Lee RC	.05
263	Bob Patterson	.05
264	Checklist 2	.05
265	Teddy Higuera	.05
266	Roberto Kelly	.05
267	Steve Bedrosian	.05
268	Brady Anderson	.05
269	Ruben Amaro RC	.05
270	Tony Gwynn	.45
271	Tracy Jones	.05
272	Jerry Don Gleaton	.05
273	Craig Grebeck	.05
274	Bob Scanlan RC	.05
275	Todd Zeile	.05
276	Shawn Green RC (Draft Pick)	1.50
277	Scott Chiamparino	.05
278	Darryl Hamilton	.05
279	Jim Clancy	.05
280	Carlos Martinez	.05
281	Kevin Appier	.05
282	John Wehner RC	.05
283	Reggie Sanders	.05
284	Gene Larkin	.05
285	Bob Welch	.05
286	Gilberto Reyes RC	.05
287	Pete Schourek	.05
288	Andujar Cedeno	.05
289	Mike Morgan	.05
290	Bo Jackson	.10
291	Phil Garner	.05
292	Ray Lankford	.05
293	Mike Henneman	.05
294	Dave Valle	.05
295	Alonzo Powell RC	.05
296	Tom Brunansky	.05
297	Kevin Brown	.05
298	Kelly Gruber	.05
299	Charles Nagy	.05
300	Don Mattingly	.50
301	Kirk McCaskill	.05
302	Joey Cora	.05
303	Dan Plesac	.05
304	Joe Oliver	.05
305	Tom Glavine	.25
306	Al Shirley RC (Draft Pick)	.05
307	Bruce Ruffin	.05
308	Craig Shipley RC	.05
309	Dave Martinez	.05
310	Jose Mesa	.05
311	Henry Cotto	.05
312	Mike LaValliere	.05
313	Kevin Tapani	.05
314	Jeff Huson	.05
315	Juan Samuel	.05
316	Curt Schilling	.25
317	Mike Bordick RC	.05
318	Steve Howe	.05
319	Tony Phillips	.05
320	George Bell	.05
321	Lou Pinella	.05
322	Tim Burke	.05
323	Milt Thompson	.05
324	Danny Darwin	.05
325	Joe Orsulak	.05
326	Eric King	.05
327	Jay Buhner	.05
328	Joel Johnston RC	.05
329	Franklin Stubbs	.05
330	Will Clark	.05
331	Steve Lake	.05
332	Chris Jones RC	.05
333	Pat Tabler	.05
334	Kevin Gross	.05
335	Dave Henderson	.05
336	Greg Anthony RC (Draft Pick)	.05
337	Alejandro Pena	.05
338	Shawn Abner	.05
339	Tom Browning	.05
340	Otis Nixon	.15
341	Bob Geren	.05
342	Tim Spehr RC	.05
343	Jon Vander Wal RC	.20
344	Jack Daugherty	.05
345	Zane Smith	.05
346	Rheal Cormier RC	.05
347	Kent Hrbek	.05
348	Rick Wilkins RC	.10
349	Steve Lyons	.05
350	Gregg Olson	.05
351	Greg Riddoch	.05
352	Ed Nunez	.05
353	Braulio Castillo RC	.05
354	Dave Bergman	.05
355	Warren Newson RC	.05
356	Luis Quinones	.05
357	Mike Witt	.05
358	Ted Wood RC	.05
359	Mike Moore	.05
360	Lance Parrish	.05
361	Barry Jones	.05
362	Javier Ortiz RC	.05
363	John Candelaria	.05
364	Glenallen Hill	.05
365	Duane Ward	.05
366	Checklist 3	.05
367	Rafael Belliard	.05
368	Bill Krueger	.05
369	Steve Whitaker RC (Draft Pick)	.05
370	Shawon Dunston	.05
371	Dante Bichette	.05
372	Kip Gross RC	.05
373	Don Robinson	.05
374	Bernie Williams	.05
375	Bert Blyleven	.05
376	Chris Donnels RC	.05
377	Bob Zupcic RC	.05
378	Joel Skinner	.05
379	Steve Chitren	.05
380	Barry Bonds	.75
381	Sparky Anderson	.10
382	Sid Fernandez	.05
383	Dave Hollins	.05
384	Mark Lee	.05
385	Tim Wallach	.05
386	Will Clark/AS	.05
387	Ryne Sandberg/AS	.20
388	Howard Johnson/AS	.05
389	Barry Larkin/AS	.05
390	Barry Bonds/AS	.40
391	Ron Gant/AS	.05
392	Bobby Bonilla/AS	.05
393	Craig Biggio/AS	.05
394	Denny Martinez/AS	.05
395	Tom Glavine/AS	.05
396	Lee Smith/AS	.05
397	Cecil Fielder/AS	.05
398	Julio Franco/AS	.05
399	Wade Boggs/AS	.20
400	Cal Ripken, Jr./AS	.40
401	Jose Canseco/AS	.15
402	Joe Carter/AS	.05
403	Ruben Sierra/AS	.05
404	Matt Nokes/AS	.05
405	Roger Clemens/AS	.25
406	Jim Abbott/AS	.05
407	Bryan Harvey/AS	.05
408	Bob Milacki	.05
409	Geno Petralli	.05
410	Dave Stewart	.05
411	Mike Jackson	.05
412	Luis Aquino	.05
413	Tim Teufel	.05
414	Jeff Ware (Draft Pick)	.05
415	Jim Deshaies	.05
416	Ellis Burks	.05
417	Allan Anderson	.05
418	Alfredo Griffin	.05
419	Wally Whitehurst	.05
420	Sandy Alomar	.05
421	Juan Agosto	.05
422	Sam Horn	.05
423	Jeff Fassero	.05
424	Paul McClellan RC	.05
425	Cecil Fielder	.05
426	Tim Raines	.05
427	Eddie Taubensee RC	.05
428	Dennis Boyd	.05
429	Tony LaRussa	.05
430	Steve Sax	.05
431	Tom Gordon	.05
432	Billy Hatcher	.05
433	Cal Eldred	.05
434	Wally Backman	.05
435	Mark Eichhorn	.05
436	Mookie Wilson	.05
437	Scott Servais RC	.10
438	Mike Maddux	.05
439	Chico Walker RC	.05
440	Doug Drabek	.05
441	Rob Deer	.05
442	Dave West	.05
443	Spike Owen	.05
444	Tyrone Hill RC (Draft Pick)	.05
445	Matt Williams	.05
446	Mark Lewis	.05
447	David Segui	.05
448	Tom Pagnozzi	.05
449	Jeff Johnson RC	.05
450	Mark McGwire	.65
451	Tom Henke	.05
452	Wilson Alvarez	.05
453	Gary Redus	.05
454	Darren Holmes	.05
455	Pete O'Brien	.05
456	Pat Combs	.05
457	Hubie Brooks	.05
458	Frank Tanana	.05

459	Tom Kelly	.05
460	Andre Dawson	.25
461	Doug Jones	.05
462	Rich Rodriguez	.05
463	Mike Simms RC	.05
464	Mike Jeffcoat	.05
465	Barry Larkin	.05
466	Stan Belinda	.05
467	Lonnie Smith	.05
468	Gary Harris	.05
469	Jim Eisenreich	.05
470	Pedro Guerrero	.05
471	Jose DeJesus	.05
472	Rich Rowland RC	.05
473	Top Prospects-3rd Baseman (Frank Bolick RC, Craig Paquette RC, Tom Redington RC, Paul Russo RC)	.05
474	Mike Rossiter RC (Draft Pick)	.05
475	Robby Thompson	.05
476	Randy Bush	.05
477	Greg Hibbard	.05
478	Dale Sveum	.05
479	Chito Martinez RC	.05
480	Scott Sanderson	.05
481	Tino Martinez	.05
482	Jimmy Key	.05
483	Terry Shumpert	.05
484	Mike Hartley	.05
485	Chris Sabo	.05
486	Bob Walk	.05
487	John Cerutti	.05
488	Scott Cooper RC	.05
489	Bobby Cox	.05
490	Julio Franco	.05
491	Jeff Brantley	.05
492	Mike Devereaux	.05
493	Jose Offerman	.05
494	Gary Thurman	.05
495	Carney Lansford	.05
496	Joe Grahe	.05
497	Andy Ashby RC	.10
498	Gerald Perry	.05
499	Dave Otto	.05
500	Vince Coleman	.05
501	Rob Mallicoat RC	.05
502	Greg Briley	.05
503	Pascual Perez	.05
504	Aaron Sele RC (Draft Pick)	.25
505	Bobby Thigpen	.05
506	Todd Benzinger	.05
507	Candy Maldonado	.05
508	Bill Gullickson	.05
509	Doug Dascenzo	.05
510	Frank Viola	.05
511	Kenny Rogers	.05
512	Mike Heath	.05
513	Kevin Bass	.05
514	Kim Batiste RC	.05
515	Delino DeShields	.05
516	Ed Sprague RC	.05
517	Jim Gott	.05
518	Jose Melendez RC	.05
519	Hal McRae	.05
520	Jeff Bagwell	.35
521	Joe Hesketh	.05
522	Milt Cuyler	.05
523	Shawn Hillegas	.05
524	Don Slaught	.05
525	Randy Johnson	.35
526	Doug Piatt RC	.05
527	Checklist 4	.05
528	Steve Foster RC	.05
529	Joe Girardi	.05
530	Jim Abbott	.05
531	Larry Walker	.05
532	Mike Huff	.05
533	Mackey Sasser	.05
534	Benji Gil RC (Draft Pick)	.05
535	Dave Stieb	.05
536	Willie Wilson	.05
537	Mark Leiter RC	.05
538	Jose Uribe	.05
539	Thomas Howard	.05
540	Ben McDonald	.05
541	Jose Tolentino RC	.05
542	Keith Mitchell RC	.05
543	Jerome Walton	.05
544	Cliff Brantley RC	.05
545	Andy Van Slyke	.05
546	Paul Sorrento	.05
547	Herm Winningham	.05
548	Mark Guthrie	.05
549	Joe Torre	.05
550	Darryl Strawberry	.05
551	Top Prospects-Shortstops (Manny Alexander, Alex Arias, Wil Cordero, Chipper Jones)	.25
552	Dave Gallagher	.05
553	Edgar Martinez	.05
554	Donald Harris	.05
555	Frank Thomas	.35
556	Storm Davis	.05
557	Dickie Thon	.05
558	Scott Garrelts	.05
559	Steve Olin	.05
560	Rickey Henderson	.35
561	Jose Vizcaino	.05
562	Wade Taylor RC	.05
563	Pat Borders	.05
564	Jimmy Gonzalez RC (Draft Pick)	.05
565	Lee Smith	.05
566	Bill Sampen	.05
567	Dean Palmer	.05
568	Bryan Harvey	.05
569	Tony Pena	.05
570	Lou Whitaker	.05
571	Randy Tomlin	.05
572	Greg Vaughn	.05
573	Kelly Downs	.05
574	Steve Avery	.05
575	Kirby Puckett	.45
576	Heathcliff Slocumb RC	.05
577	Kevin Seitzer	.05
578	Lee Guetterman	.05
579	Johnny Oates	.05
580	Greg Maddux	.45
581	Stan Javier	.05
582	Vicente Palacios	.05
583	Mel Rojas	.05
584	Wayne Rosenthal RC	.05
585	Lenny Webster RC	.05
586	Rod Nichols	.05
587	Mickey Morandini	.05
588	Russ Swan	.05
589	Mariano Duncan	.05
590	Howard Johnson	.05
591	Top Prospects-Outfielders (Jacob Brumfield RC, Jeromy Burnitz RC, Alan Cockrell RC, D.J. Dozier RC)	.25
592	Denny Neagle RC	.10
593	Steve Decker	.05
594	Brian Barber RC (Draft Pick)	.05
595	Bruce Hurst	.05
596	Kent Mercker	.05
597	Mike Magnante RC	.05
598	Jody Reed	.05
599	Steve Searcy	.05
600	Paul Molitor	.05
601	Dave Smith	.05
602	Mike Fetters	.05
603	Luis Mercedes RC	.05
604	Chris Gwynn	.05
605	Scott Erickson	.05
606	Brook Jacoby	.05
607	Todd Stottlemyre	.05
608	Scott Bradley	.05
609	Mike Hargrove	.05
610	Eric Davis	.05
611	Brian Hunter RC	.05
612	Pat Kelly	.05
613	Pedro Munoz RC	.05
614	Al Osuna	.05
615	Matt Merullo	.05
616	Larry Andersen	.05
617	Junior Ortiz	.05
618	Top Prospects-Outfielders (Cesar Hernandez RC, Steve Hosey RC, Dan Peltier RC, Jeff McNeely RC)	.10
619	Danny Jackson	.05
620	George Brett	.50
621	Dan Gakeler RC	.05
622	Steve Buechele	.05
623	Bob Tewksbury	.05
624	Shawn Estes RC (Draft Pick)	.25
625	Kevin McReynolds	.05
626	Chris Haney RC	.05
627	Mike Sharperson	.05
628	Mark Williamson	.05
629	Wally Joyner	.05
630	Carlton Fisk	.05
631	Armando Reynoso RC	.05
632	Felix Fermin	.05
633	Mitch Williams	.05
634	Manuel Lee	.05
635	Harold Baines	.05
636	Greg Harris	.05
637	Orlando Merced	.05
638	Chris Bosio	.05
639	Wayne Housie RC	.05
640	Xavier Hernandez	.05
641	David Howard RC	.05
642	Tim Crews	.05
643	Rick Cerone	.05
644	Terry Leach	.05
645	Deion Sanders	.10
646	Craig Wilson	.05
647	Marquis Grissom	.05
648	Scott Fletcher	.05
649	Norm Charlton	.05
650	Jesse Barfield	.05
651	Joe Slusarski RC	.05
652	Bobby Rose	.05
653	Dennis Lamp	.05
654	Allen Watson RC (Draft Pick)	.05
655	Brett Butler	.05
656	Top Prospects-Outfielders (Rudy Pemberton RC, Henry Rodriguez RC, Lee Tinsley RC, Gerald Williams RC)	.10
657	Dave Johnson	.05
658	Checklist 5	.05
659	Brian McRae	.05
660	Fred McGriff	.05
661	Bill Landrum	.05
662	Juan Guzman	.05
663	Greg Gagne	.05
664	Ken Hill	.05
665	Dave Haas RC	.05
666	Tom Foley	.05
667	Roberto Hernandez RC	.10
668	Dwayne Henry	.05
669	Jim Fregosi	.05
670	Harold Reynolds	.05
671	Mark Whiten	.05
672	Eric Plunk	.05
673	Todd Hundley	.05
674	Mo Sanford RC	.05
675	Bobby Witt	.05
676	Top Prospects-Pitchers (Pat Mahomes RC, Sam Militello RC, Roger Salkeld, Turk Wendell RC)	.15
677	John Marzano	.05
678	Joe Klink	.05
679	Pete Incaviglia	.05
680	Dale Murphy	.15
681	Rene Gonzales	.05
682	Andy Benes	.05
683	Jim Poole RC	.05
684	Trever Miller RC (Draft Pick)	.10
685	Scott Livingstone RC	.05
686	Rich DeLucia	.05
687	Harvey Pulliam RC	.05
688	Tim Belcher	.05
689	Mark Lemke	.05
690	John Franco	.05
691	Walt Weiss	.05
692	Scott Ruskin	.05
693	Jeff King	.05
694	Mike Gardiner RC	.05
695	Gary Sheffield	.30
696	Joe Boever	.05
697	Mike Felder	.05
698	John Habyan	.05
699	Cito Gaston	.05
700	Ruben Sierra	.05
701	Scott Radinsky	.05
702	Lee Stevens	.05
703	Mark Wohlers RC	.05
704	Curt Young	.05
705	Dwight Evans	.05
706	Rob Murphy	.05
707	Gregg Jefferies	.05
708	Tom Bolton	.05
709	Chris James	.05
710	Kevin Maas	.05
711	Ricky Bones RC	.05
712	Curt Wilkerson	.05
713	Roger McDowell	.05
714	Calvin Reese RC (Draft Pick)	.10
715	Craig Biggio	.05
716	Kirk Dressendorfer RC	.05
717	Ken Dayley	.05
718	B.J. Surhoff	.05
719	Terry Mulholland	.05
720	Kirk Gibson	.05
721	Mike Pagliarulo	.05
722	Walt Terrell	.05
723	Jose Oquendo	.05
724	Kevin Morton RC	.05
725	Dwight Gooden	.05
726	Kirt Manwaring	.05
727	Chuck McElroy	.05
728	Dave Burba RC	.05
729	Art Howe	.05
730	Ramon Martinez	.05
731	Donnie Hill	.05
732	Nelson Santovenia	.05
733	Bob Melvin	.05
734	Scott Hatteberg RC (Draft Pick)	.10
735	Greg Swindell	.05
736	Lance Johnson	.05
737	Kevin Reimer	.05
738	Dennis Eckersley	.35
739	Rob Ducey	.05
740	Ken Caminiti	.05
741	Mark Gubicza	.05
742	Billy Spiers	.05
743	Darren Lewis	.05
744	Chris Hammond	.05
745	Dave Magadan	.05
746	Bernard Gilkey	.05
747	Willie Banks RC	.05
748	Matt Nokes	.05
749	Jerald Clark	.05
750	Travis Fryman	.05
751	Steve Wilson	.05
752	Billy Ripken	.05
753	Paul Assenmacher	.05
754	Charlie Hayes	.05
755	Alex Fernandez	.05
756	Gary Pettis	.05
757	Rob Dibble	.05
758	Tim Naehring	.05
759	Jeff Torborg	.05
760	Ozzie Smith	.45
761	Mike Fitzgerald	.05
762	John Burkett	.05
763	Kyle Abbott	.05
764	Tyler Green RC (Draft Pick)	.05
765	Pete Harnisch	.05
766	Mark Davis	.05
767	Kal Daniels	.05
768	Jim Thome	.35
769	Jack Howell	.05
770	Sid Bream	.05
771	Arthur Rhodes RC	.10
772	Garry Templeton	.05
773	Hal Morris	.05
774	Bud Black	.05
775	Ivan Calderon	.05
776	Doug Henry RC	.05
777	John Olerud	.05
778	Tim Leary	.05
779	Jay Bell	.05
780	Eddie Murray	.35
781	Paul Abbott RC	.05
782	Phil Plantier	.05
783	Joe Magrane	.20
784	Ken Patterson	.05
785	Albert Belle	.05
786	Royce Clayton	.05
787	Checklist 6	.05
788	Mike Stanton	.05
789	Bobby Valentine	.05
790	Joe Carter	.05
791	Danny Cox	.05
792	Dave Winfield	.35

Gold Promo Sheet

Similar in form and function to the nine-card promo sheet issued for the regular 1992 Topps set, this 8" x 11" sheet previewed the Topps Gold cards for dealers. Fronts are identical to the regular-issue '92 Topps cards. Backs differ in that actual 1991 stats are not printed, and there is a diamond over the stat box which reads, "1992 Pre-Production Sample." Card numbers on the gold preview cards correspond to the regular Topps cards. Single cards in the standard 2-1/2" x 3-1/2" size are frequently offered cut from these sheets.

		NM/M
	Complete Set (Sheet):	8.00
	Complete Set (9):	8.00
	Common Player:	1.00
1	Nolan Ryan	4.00
15	Dennis Martinez	1.00
20	Bip Roberts	1.00
40	Cal Ripken, Jr.	4.00
261	Tom Lasorda	1.00
370	Shawon Dunston	1.00
516	Mike Heath	1.00
655	Brett Butler	1.00
757	Rob Dibble	1.00

Gold

Topps Gold cards share a checklist and format with the regular-issue 1992 Topps baseball issue except the color bars with the player's name and team printed beneath the photo have been replaced with gold foil. On back the light blue Topps logo printed beneath the stats has been replaced with a gold "ToppsGold" logo. Topps Gold cards were random inserts in all forms of packs. Additionally, factory sets of Gold cards were sold which included an autographed card of Yankees #1 draft pick Brien Taylor, and which had the checklist cards replaced with player cards. Several errors connected with the gold name/team strips are noted; no corrected versions were issued.

	NM/M
Unopened Fact. Set (793):	75.00
Complete Set (792):	35.00
Common Player:	.20

86	Steve Finley (Incorrect name, Mark Davidson, on gold strip.)	.20
131	Terry Mathews	.20
264	Rod Beck	1.00
288	Andujar Cedeno (Incorrect team, Yankees, listed on gold strip.)	.60
366	Tony Perezchica	.20
465	Barry Larkin (Incorrect team, Astros, listed on gold strip.)	2.50
527	Terry McDaniel	.20
532	Mike Huff (Incorrect team, Red Sox, listed on gold strip.)	.20
658	John Ramos	.20
787	Brian Williams	.20
793	Brien Taylor (Autographed edition of 12,000; factory sets only.)	7.50

Gold Winners

A second gold-foil enhanced parallel version of the regular 1992 Topps issue was the Gold Winner cards awarded as prizes in a scratch-off contest found in each pack. Winner cards are identical to the Topps Gold cards except for the addition of a gold-foil "Winner" and star added above the team name. Due to a flaw in the design of the scratch-off game cards, it was easy to win every time and the Winner cards had to be produced in quantities far greater than originally planned, making them rather common. Six checklist cards from the regular issue were replaced with player cards in the Winners edition. Cards were sent to winners in 10-card cello packs.

		NM/M
	Complete Set (792):	30.00
	Common Player:	.10
	Cello Pack (10):	.75
131	Terry Mathews	.15
264	Rod Beck	.25
366	Tony Perezchica	.15
465a	Barry Larkin (Team name incorrect, Astros.)	2.00
465b	Barry Larkin (Team name correct, Reds.)	.75
527	Terry McDaniel	.15
658	John Ramos	.15
787	Brian Williams	.15

Traded

Members of the United States baseball team are featured in this 132-card boxed set released by Topps. The cards are styled after the regular 1992 Topps cards and are numbered alphabetically. Several United States baseball players featured in this set were also featured in the 1991 Topps Traded set.

		NM/M
	Complete Set (132):	50.00
	Common Player:	.05
	Golds:	2-4X
1	Willie Adams RC (USA)	.05
2	Jeff Alkire (USA)	.05
3	Felipe Alou	.05
4	Moises Alou	.10
5	Ruben Amaro RC	.05
6	Jack Armstrong	.05
7	Scott Bankhead	.05
8	Tim Belcher	.05
9	George Bell	.05
10	Freddie Benavides RC	.05
11	Todd Benzinger	.05
12	Joe Boever	.05
13	Ricky Bones	.05
14	Bobby Bonilla	.05
15	Hubie Brooks	.05
16	Jerry Browne	.05
17	Jim Bullinger	.05
18	Dave Burba	.05
19	Kevin Campbell RC	.05
20	Tom Candiotti	.05
21	Mark Carreon	.05
22	Gary Carter	.75
23	Archi Cianfrocco	.05
24	Phil Clark	.05
25	Chad Curtis RC	.50
26	Eric Davis	.05
27	Tim Davis (USA)	.05
28	Gary DiSarcina	.05
29	Darren Dreifort (USA)	.05
30	Mariano Duncan	.05
31	Mike Fitzgerald	.05
32	John Flaherty	.05
33	Darrin Fletcher	.05
34	Scott Fletcher	.05
35	Ron Fraser (USA)	.05
36	Andres Galarraga	.05
37	Dave Gallagher	.05
38	Mike Gallego	.05
39	Nomar Garciaparra RC (USA)	30.00
40	Jason Giambi (USA)	1.00
41	Danny Gladden	.05
42	Rene Gonzales	.05
43	Jeff Granger (USA)	.05
44	Rick Greene (USA)	.05
45	Jeffrey Hammonds (USA)	.05
46	Charlie Hayes	.05
47	Von Hayes	.05
48	Rick Helling RC (USA)	.05
49	Butch Henry RC	.05
50	Carlos Hernandez RC	.05
51	Ken Hill	.05
52	Butch Hobson	.05
53	Vince Horsman RC	.05
54	Pete Incaviglia	.05
55	Gregg Jefferies	.05
56	Charles Johnson (USA)	.05
57	Doug Jones	.05
58	Brian Jordan RC	2.00
59	Wally Joyner	.05
60	Daron Kirkreit RC (USA)	.20
61	Bill Krueger	.05
62	Gene Lamont	.05
63	Jim Lefebvre	.05
64	Danny Leon RC	.05
65	Pat Listach	.05
66	Kenny Lofton	.05
67	Dave Martinez	.05
68	Derrick May	.05
69	Kirk McCaskill	.05
70	Chad McConnell RC (USA)	.05
71	Kevin McReynolds	.05
72	Rusty Meacham RC	.05
73	Keith Miller	.05
74	Kevin Mitchell	.05
75	Jason Moler RC (USA)	.05
76	Mike Morgan	.05
77	Jack Morris	.05
78	Calvin Murray RC (USA)	.05
79	Eddie Murray	.75
80	Randy Myers	.05
81	Denny Neagle RC	.05
82	Phil Nevin (USA)	.10
83	Dave Nilsson	.05
84	Junior Ortiz	.05
85	Donovan Osborne	.05
86	Bill Pecota	.05
87	Melido Perez	.05
88	Mike Perez RC	.05
89	Hipolito Pena RC	.05
90	Willie Randolph	.05
91	Darren Reed RC	.05
92	Bip Roberts	.05
93	Chris Roberts (USA)	.05
94	Steve Rodriguez (USA)	.05
95	Bruce Ruffin	.05
96	Scott Ruskin	.05
97	Bret Saberhagen	.05
98	Rey Sanchez RC	.05
99	Steve Sax	.05
100	Curt Schilling	.25
101	Dick Schofield	.05
102	Gary Scott	.05
103	Kevin Seitzer	.05
104	Frank Seminara RC	.05
105	Gary Sheffield	.35
106	John Smiley	.05
107	Cory Snyder	.05
108	Paul Sorrento	.05
109	Sammy Sosa	1.50
110	Matt Stairs RC	.05
111	Andy Stankiewicz	.05
112	Kurt Stillwell	.05
113	Rick Sutcliffe	.05
114	Bill Swift	.05
115	Jeff Tackett RC	.05
116	Danny Tartabull	.05
117	Eddie Taubensee RC	.05
118	Dickie Thon	.05
119	Michael Tucker RC (USA)	.25

120	Scooter Tucker RC	.05
121	Marc Valdes RC (USA)	.05
122	Julio Valera RC	.05
123	Jason Varitek RC (USA)	15.00
124	Ron Villone RC (USA)	.05
125	Frank Viola	.05
126	B.J. Wallace RC (USA)	.05
127	Dan Walters RC	.05
128	Craig Wilson (USA)	.05
129	Chris Wimmer (USA)	.05
130	Dave Winfield	.75
131	Herm Winningham	.05
132	Checklist	.05

Traded Gold

A reported 6,000 sets of 1992 Topps Traded were produced in a gold edition, with gold-foil strips on front bearing the player and team names. The cards are in all other respects identical to the regular boxed Traded issue.

	NM/M
Complete Unopened Set (132):	75.00
Complete Set (132):	65.00
Common Player:	.25
Stars/Rookies:	4X

Golden Spikes Award

At a Nov. 17, 1992 awards ceremony, Phil Nevin was presented with the U.S. Baseball Federation's Golden Spikes Award, emblematic of his selection as the outstanding amatuer player in the nation. Topps created and handed out at the affair a reported 600 of these cards.

	NM/M
Phil Nevin	45.00

Kids

In a market which had increasingly become the province of adult collectors, Topps in 1992 offered an issue unashamedly aimed at the youngster. Called "Topps Kids," the 132-card set features bright colors, garish graphics and the game's top stars. Sold at 35 cents per pack (with bubble gum), the issue was even priced for the young collector. Unfortunately, the concept was a flop and was not re-

peated in subsequent years. Card fronts feature player photos, sometimes with the player's head on a cartoon body, against a background of wild designs or cartoon ballpark action. Player names at bottom were rendered in superhero comic-book style. Backs feature a few 1991 and career stats, and/or a cartoon or two about the player or baseball trivia.

		NM/M
Complete Set (132):		7.50
Common Player:		.05
Wax Pack (7):		.40
Wax Box (36):		6.00
1	Ryne Sandberg	.45
2	Andre Dawson	.25
3	George Bell	.05
4	Mark Grace	.05
5	Shawon Dunston	.05
6	Tim Wallach	.05
7	Ivan Calderon	.05
8	Marquis Grissom	.05
9	Delino DeShields	.05
10	Denny Martinez	.05
11	Dwight Gooden	.05
12	Howard Johnson	.05
13	John Franco	.05
14	Gregg Jefferies	.05
15	Kevin McReynolds	.05
16	David Cone	.05
17	Len Dykstra	.05
18	John Kruk	.05
19	Von Hayes	.05
20	Mitch Williams	.05
21	Barry Bonds	.75
22	Bobby Bonilla	.05
23	Andy Van Slyke	.05
24	Doug Drabek	.05
25	Ozzie Smith	.45
26	Pedro Guerrero	.05
27	Todd Zeile	.05
28	Lee Smith	.05
29	Felix Jose	.05
30	Jose DeLeon	.05
31	David Justice	.05
32	Ron Gant	.05
33	Terry Pendleton	.05
34	Tom Glavine	.25
35	Otis Nixon	.05
36	Steve Avery	.05
37	Barry Larkin	.05
38	Eric Davis	.05
39	Chris Sabo	.05
40	Rob Dibble	.05
41	Paul O'Neill	.05
42	Jose Rijo	.05
43	Craig Biggio	.05
44	Jeff Bagwell	.35
45	Ken Caminiti	.05
46	Steve Finley	.05
47	Darryl Strawberry	.05
48	Ramon Martinez	.05
49	Brett Butler	.05
50	Eddie Murray	.35
51	Kal Daniels	.05
52	Orel Hershiser	.05
53	Tony Gwynn	.45
54	Benny Santiago	.05
55	Fred McGriff	.05
56	Bip Roberts	.05
57	Tony Fernandez	.05
58	Will Clark	.05
59	Kevin Mitchell	.05
60	Matt Williams	.05
61	Willie McGee	.05
62	Dave Righetti	.05
63	Cal Ripken, Jr.	.75
64	Ben McDonald	.05
65	Glenn Davis	.05
66	Gregg Olson	.05
67	Roger Clemens	.50
68	Wade Boggs	.45
69	Mike Greenwell	.05
70	Ellis Burks	.05
71	Sandy Alomar	.05
72	Greg Swindell	.05
73	Albert Belle	.05
74	Mark Whiten	.05
75	Alan Trammell	.05
76	Cecil Fielder	.05
77	Lou Whitaker	.05
78	Travis Fryman	.05
79	Tony Phillips	.05
80	Robin Yount	.35
81	Paul Molitor	.05
82	B.J. Surhoff	.05
83	Greg Vaughn	.05
84	Don Mattingly	.50
85	Steve Sax	.05
86	Kevin Maas	.05
87	Mel Hall	.05
88	Roberto Kelly	.05
89	Joe Carter	.05
90	Roberto Alomar	.15
91	Dave Stieb	.05
92	Kelly Gruber	.05
93	Tom Henke	.05
94	Chuck Finley	.05
95	Wally Joyner	.05
96	Dave Winfield	.35
97	Jim Abbott	.05
98	Mark Langston	.05
99	Frank Thomas	.35

100	Ozzie Guillen	.05
101	Bobby Thigpen	.05
102	Robin Ventura	.05
103	Bo Jackson	.10
104	Tim Raines	.05
105	George Brett	.50
106	Danny Tartabull	.05
107	Bret Saberhagen	.05
108	Brian McRae	.05
109	Kirby Puckett	.45
110	Scott Erickson	.05
111	Kent Hrbek	.05
112	Chuck Knoblauch	.05
113	Chili Davis	.05
114	Rick Aguilera	.05
115	Jose Canseco	.25
116	Dave Henderson	.05
117	Dave Stewart	.05
118	Rickey Henderson	.35
119	Dennis Eckersley	.30
120	Harold Baines	.05
121	Mark McGwire	.60
122	Ken Griffey Jr.	.60
123	Harold Reynolds	.05
124	Erik Hanson	.05
125	Edgar Martinez	.05
126	Randy Johnson	.35
127	Nolan Ryan	.75
128	Ruben Sierra	.05
129	Julio Franco	.05
130	Rafael Palmeiro	.30
131	Juan Gonzalez	.20
132	Checklist	.05

Micro

Topps returned for a second year with a micro parallel of its regular-issue baseball set, in a format about 40% the size of the standard cards. Sold only in complete-set form, the 1" x 1-3/8" cards also included a dozen gold-enhanced star cards. Stars and rookies among the micros are valued at a percentage of the corresponding regular card.

		NM/M
Complete Set (804):		9.00
Common Player:		.05
Stars/Rookies: 50-100 Percent		
1	Nolan Ryan	
	(Record Breaker)	2.00
2	Rickey Henderson	
	(Record Breaker)	.65
10	Wade Boggs	.75
50	Ken Griffey Jr.	1.00
100	Jose Canseco	.60
270	Tony Gwynn	.75
300	Don Mattingly	.90
380	Barry Bonds	2.00
397	Cecil Fielder/AS	.50
403	Ruben Sierra/AS	.50
460	Andre Dawson	.55
725	Dwight Gooden	.50

Triple Header Photo Balls

Picture a slightly oversize ping pong ball painted like a baseball with the heads and facsimile autographs of three different players on it and you've got the idea behind the Triple Headers test issue. Very limited in distribution, the team balls were sold in a small box with a package of candy.

		NM/M
Complete Set (26):		100.00
Common Ball:		3.50
(1)	California Angels	
	(Chuck Finley, Dave Winfield,	
	Wally Joyner)	4.00

(2)	Houston Astros (Jeff Bagwell, Craig Biggio, Ken Caminiti)	4.50
(3)	Oakland Athletics (Dave Henderson, Jose Canseco, Rickey Henderson)	4.50
(4)	Toronto Blue Jays (Roberto Alomar, Kelly Gruber, Joe Carter)	4.00
(5)	Atlanta Braves (Ron Gant, Tom Glavine, Dave Justice)	4.00
(6)	Milwaukee Brewers (Greg Vaughn, Paul Molitor, Robin Yount)	4.50
(7)	St. Louis Cardinals (Todd Zeile, Pedro Guerrero, Ozzie Smith)	4.50
(8)	Chicago Cubs (Ryne Sandberg, George Bell, Mark Grace)	4.50
(9)	Los Angeles Dodgers (Ramon Martinez, Eddie Murray, Darryl Strawberry)	4.50
(10)	Montreal Expos (Delino DeShields, Dennis Martinez, Ivan Calderon)	3.50
(11)	San Francisco Giants (Will Clark, Kevin Mitchell, Matt Williams)	3.50
(12)	Cleveland Indians (Sandy Alomar Jr., Alex Cole, Mark Lewis)	3.50
(13)	Seattle Mariners (Ken Griffey Jr., Harold Reynolds, Ken Griffey Sr.)	10.00
(14)	New York Mets (Vince Coleman, Dwight Gooden, Howard Johnson)	3.50
(15)	Baltimore Orioles (Ben McDonald, Cal Ripken Jr., Gregg Olson)	12.50
(16)	San Diego Padres (Benito Santiago, Fred McGriff, Tony Gwynn)	5.00
(17)	Philadelphia Phillies (Len Dykstra, John Kruk, Dale Murphy)	3.50
(18)	Pittsburgh Pirates (Andy Van Slyke, Barry Bonds, Bobby Bonilla)	12.50
(19)	Cincinnati Reds (Chris Sabo, Eric Davis, Barry Larkin)	3.50
(20)	Boston Red Sox (Wade Boggs, Mike Greenwell, Roger Clemens)	6.00
(21)	Kansas City Royals (George Brett, Danny Tartabull, Bret Saberhagen)	6.00
(22)	Texas Rangers (Julio Franco, Nolan Ryan, Juan Gonzalez)	12.50
(23)	Minnesota Twins (Scott Erickson, Kirby Puckett, Kent Hrbek)	5.00
(24)	Detroit Tigers (Cecil Fielder, Tony Phillips, Alan Trammell)	3.50
(25)	Chicago White Sox (Carlton Fisk, Robin Ventura, Frank Thomas)	5.00
(26)	New York Yankees (Don Mattingly, Steve Sax, Willie Randolph)	6.00

1991 Major League Debut

This 194-card set highlights the debut date of 1991 Major League rookies. Two checklist cards are also included in this boxed set. The card fronts resemble the 1992 Topps cards. A debut banner appears in the lower-right corner of the card front. The set is packaged in an attractive collector

box and the cards are numbered alphabetically. This set was available only through hobby dealers.

		NM/M
Complete Set (194):		12.50
Common Player:		.05
1	Kyle Abbott	.05
2	Dana Allison	.05
3	Rich Amaral	.05
4	Ruben Amaro	.05
5	Andy Ashby	.05
6	Jim Austin	.05
7	Jeff Bagwell	4.00
8	Jeff Banister	.05
9	Willie Banks	.05
10	Bret Barberie	.05
11	Kim Batiste	.05
12	Chris Beasley	.05
13	Rod Beck	.05
14	Derek Bell	.05
15	Esteban Beltre	.05
16	Freddie Benavides	.05
17	Rickey Bones	.05
18	Denis Boucher	.05
19	Ryan Bowen	.05
20	Cliff Brantley	.05
21	John Briscoe	.05
22	Scott Brosius	.05
23	Terry Bross	.05
24	Jarvis Brown	.05
25	Scott Bullett	.05
26	Kevin Campbell	.05
27	Amalio Carreno	.05
28	Matias Carrillo	.05
29	Jeff Carter	.05
30	Vinny Castilla	.05
31	Braulio Castillo	.05
32	Frank Castillo	.05
33	Darrin Chapin	.05
34	Mike Christopher	.05
35	Mark Clark	.05
36	Royce Clayton	.05
37	Stu Cole	.05
38	Gary Cooper	.05
39	Archie Corbin	.05
40	Rheal Cormier	.05
41	Chris Cron	.05
42	Mike Dalton	.05
43	Mark Davis	.05
44	Francisco de la Rosa	.05
45	Chris Donnels	.05
46	Brian Drahman	.05
47	Tom Drees	.05
48	Kirk Dressendorfer	.05
49	Bruce Egloff	.05
50	Cal Eldred	.05
51	Jose Escobar	.05
52	Tony Eusebio	.05
53	Hector Fajardo	.05
54	Monty Farriss	.05
55	Jeff Fassero	.05
56	Dave Fleming	.05
57	Kevin Flora	.05
58	Steve Foster	.05
59	Dan Gakeler	.05
60	Ramon Garcia	.05
61	Chris Gardner	.05
62	Jeff Gardner	.05
63	Chris George	.05
64	Ray Giannelli	.05
65	Tom Goodwin	.05
66	Mark Grater	.05
67	Johnny Guzman	.05
68	Juan Guzman	.05
69	Dave Haas	.05
70	Chris Haney	.05
71	Shawn Hare	.05
72	Donald Harris	.05
73	Doug Henry	.05
74	Pat Hentgen	.05
75	Gil Heredia	.05
76	Jeremy Hernandez	.05
77	Jose Hernandez	.05
78	Roberto Hernandez	.05
79	Bryan Hickerson	.05
80	Milt Hill	.05
81	Vince Horsman	.05
82	Wayne Housie	.05
83	Chris Howard	.05
84	David Howard	.05
85	Mike Humphreys	.05
86	Brian Hunter	.05
87	Jim Hunter	.05
88	Mike Ignasiak	.05
89	Reggie Jefferson	.05
90	Jeff Johnson	.05
91	Joel Johnson	.05
92	Calvin Jones	.05
93	Chris Jones	.05
94	Stacy Jones	.05
95	Jeff Juden	.05
96	Scott Kamieniecki	.05
97	Eric Karros	.05
98	Pat Kelly	.05
99	John Kiely	.05
100	Darryl Kile	.05
101	Wayne Kirby	.05
102	Garland Kiser	.05
103	Chuck Knoblauch	.05
104	Randy Knorr	.05
105	Tom Kramer	.05
106	Ced Landrum	.05
107	Patrick Lennon	.05
108	Jim Lewis	.05
109	Mark Lewis	.05
110	Doug Lindsey	.05
111	Scott Livingstone	.05

112	Kenny Lofton	.10
113	Ever Magallanes	.05
114	Mike Magnante	.05
115	Barry Manuel	.05
116	Josias Manzanillo	.05
117	Chito Martinez	.05
118	Terry Mathews	.05
119	Rob Mauer	.05
120	Tim Mauser	.05
121	Terry McDaniel	.05
122	Rusty Meacham	.05
123	Luis Mercedes	.05
124	Paul Miller	.05
125	Keith Mitchell	.05
126	Bobby Moore	.05
127	Kevin Morton	.05
128	Andy Mota	.05
129	Jose Mota	.05
130	Mike Mussina	2.00
131	Jeff Mutis	.05
132	Denny Neagle	.05
133	Warren Newson	.05
134	Jim Olander	.05
135	Erik Pappas	.05
136	Jorge Pedre	.05
137	Yorkis Perez	.05
138	Mark Petkovsek	.05
139	Doug Piatt	.05
140	Jeff Plympton	.05
141	Harvey Pulliam	.05
142	John Ramos	.05
143	Mike Remlinger	.05
144	Laddie Renfroe	.05
145	Armando Reynoso	.05
146	Arthur Rhodes	.05
147	Pat Rice	.05
148	Nikco Riesgo	.05
149	Carlos Rodriguez	.05
150	Ivan Rodriguez	3.00
151	Wayne Rosenthal	.05
152	Rico Rossy	.05
153	Stan Royer	.05
154	Rey Sanchez	.05
155	Reggie Sanders	.05
156	Mo Sanford	.05
157	Bob Scanlan	.05
158	Pete Schourek	.05
159	Gary Scott	.05
160	Tim Scott	.05
161	Tony Scruggs	.05
162	Scott Servais	.05
163	Doug Simons	.05
164	Heathcliff Slocumb	.05
165	Joe Slusarski	.05
166	Tim Spehr	.05
167	Ed Sprague	.05
168	Jeff Tackett	.05
169	Eddie Taubensee	.05
170	Wade Taylor	.05
171	Jim Thome	2.50
172	Mike Timlin	.05
173	Jose Tolentino	.05
174	John Vander Wal	.05
175	Todd Van Poppel	.05
176	Mo Vaughn	.50
177	Dave Wainhouse	.05
178	Don Wakamatsu	.05
179	Bruce Walton	.05
180	Kevin Ward	.05
181	Dave Weathers	.05
182	Eric Wedge	.05
183	John Wehner	.05
184	Rick Wilkins	.05
185	Bernie Williams	.50
186	Brian Williams	.05
187	Ron Witmeyer	.05
188	Mark Wohlers	.05
189	Ted Wood	.05
190	Anthony Young	.05
191	Eddie Zosky	.05
192	Bob Zupcic	.05
193	Checklist	.05
194	Checklist	.05

Pre-Production

Specially marked 1992 Topps factory sets included this nine-card preview of the coming year's issue. The preview cards are identical to the regular-issue versions except the backs have a gray oval over the stats box with the notation, "1993 Pre-Production Sample."

	NM/M
Complete Set (9):	7.50
Common Player:	.35

1	Robin Yount	.75
2	Barry Bonds	3.00
11	Eric Karros	.50
32	Don Mattingly	1.00
100	Mark McGwire	2.00
150	Frank Thomas	.75
179	Ken Griffey Jr.	1.50
230	Carlton Fisk	.75
250	Chuck Knoblauch	.50

Pre-Production Sheet

Originally produced as an 8" x 11" nine-card sheet, these pre-production sample cards are rarely found as singles. Cards are in the same basic format as the regular-issue 1993 Topps cards. Backs differ in that all cards are numbered "000" with all zeroes for 1992 stats and bogus career highlights. A large gray circle over the stats box reads "1993 Pre-Production Sample For General Look Only."

		NM/M
Uncut Sheet:		6.00
Complete Set (9):		6.00
Common Player:		.50
(1)	Roberto Alomar	.60
(2)	Bobby Bonilla	.50
(3)	Gary Carter	1.00
(4)	Andre Dawson	.75
(5)	Dave Fleming	.50
(6)	Ken Griffey Jr.	3.00
(7)	Pete Incaviglia	.50
(8)	Spike Owen	.50
(9)	Larry Walker	.50

1993 Topps

Topps issued in a two-series format in 1993. Series I includes cards #1-396; Series II comprises #397-825. The card fronts feature full-color photos enclosed by a white border. The player's name and team appear at the bottom. The backs feature an additional player photo and biographical information at the top. The bottom box includes statistics and player information. The cards are numbered in red in a yellow flag on the back. The factory set includes the regular 825 cards plus 10 gold parallels, three Black Gold inserts and nine 1994 preview cards.

	NM/M
Unopened Fact. Set (847):	40.00
Complete Set (825):	30.00
Common Player:	.05
Golds:	3X
Series 1 Wax Pack (15):	1.00
Series 1 Wax Box (36):	25.00
Series 2 Wax Pack (15):	.75
Series 2 Wax Box (36):	15.00
Series 1 Jumbo Pack (41):	2.00
Series 1 Jumbo Box (24):	30.00
Series 2 Jumbo Pack (41):	1.50
Series 2 Jumbo Box (24):	20.00

1	Robin Yount	.50
2	Barry Bonds	1.00
3	Ryne Sandberg	.60
4	Roger Clemens	.65
5	Tony Gwynn	.60
6	Jeff Tackett RC	.05
7	Pete Incaviglia	.05
8	Mark Wohlers	.05
9	Kent Hrbek	.05
10	Will Clark	.05
11	Eric Karros	.05
12	Lee Smith	.05
13	Esteban Beltre	.05
14	Greg Briley	.05
15	Marquis Grissom	.05
16	Dan Plesac	.05
17	Dave Hollins	.05
18	Terry Steinbach	.05
19	Ed Nunez	.05
20	Tim Salmon	.05
21	Luis Salazar	.05
22	Jim Eisenreich	.05
23	Todd Stottlemyre	.05
24	Tim Naehring	.05
25	John Franco	.05
26	Skeeter Barnes	.05
27	Carlos Garcia RC	.05
28	Joe Orsulak	.05
29	Dwayne Henry	.05
30	Fred McGriff	.05
31	Derek Lilliquist	.05
32	Don Mattingly	.65
33	B.J. Wallace (1992 Draft Pick)	.05
34	Juan Gonzalez	.25
35	John Smoltz	.05
36	Scott Servais	.05
37	Lenny Webster	.05
38	Chris James	.05
39	Roger McDowell	.05
40	Ozzie Smith	.60
41	Alex Fernandez	.05
42	Spike Owen	.05
43	Ruben Amaro	.05
44	Kevin Seitzer	.05
45	Dave Fleming	.05
46	Eric Fox RC	.05
47	Bob Scanlan	.05
48	Bert Blyleven	.05
49	Brian McRae	.05
50	Roberto Alomar	.20
51	Mo Vaughn	.05
52	Bobby Bonilla	.05
53	Frank Tanana	.05
54	Mike LaValliere	.05
55	Mark McLemore	.05
56	Chad Mottola RC (1992 Draft Pick)	.10
57	Norm Charlton	.05
58	Jose Melendez	.05
59	Carlos Martinez	.05
60	Roberto Kelly	.05
61	Gene Larkin	.05
62	Rafael Belliard	.05
63	Al Osuna	.05
64	Scott Chiamparino	.05
65	Brett Butler	.05
66	John Burkett	.05
67	Felix Jose	.05
68	Omar Vizquel	.05
69	John Vander Wal	.05
70	Roberto Hernandez	.05
71	Ricky Bones	.05
72	Jeff Grotewold RC	.05
73	Mike Moore	.05
74	Steve Buechele	.05
75	Juan Guzman	.05
76	Kevin Appier	.05
77	Junior Felix	.05
78	Greg Harris	.05
79	Dick Schofield	.05
80	Cecil Fielder	.05
81	Lloyd McClendon	.05
82	David Segui	.05
83	Reggie Sanders	.05
84	Kurt Stillwell	.05
85	Sandy Alomar	.05
86	John Habyan	.05
87	Kevin Reimer	.05
88	Mike Stanton	.05
89	Eric Anthony	.05
90	Scott Erickson	.05
91	Craig Colbert	.05
92	Tom Pagnozzi	.05
93	Pedro Astacio RC	.10
94	Lance Johnson	.05
95	Larry Walker	.05
96	Russ Swan	.05
97	Scott Fletcher	.05
98	Derek Jeter RC (1992 Draft Pick)	10.00
99	Mike Williams RC	.05
100	Mark McGwire	.85
101	Jim Bullinger RC	.05
102	Brian Hunter	.05
103	Jody Reed	.05
104	Mike Butcher RC	.05
105	Gregg Jefferies	.05
106	Howard Johnson	.05
107	John Kiely RC	.05
108	Jose Lind	.05
109	Sam Horn	.05
110	Barry Larkin	.05
111	Bruce Hurst	.05
112	Brian Barnes	.05
113	Thomas Howard	.05
114	Mel Hall	.05
115	Robby Thompson	.05
116	Mark Lemke	.05
117	Eddie Taubensee	.05
118	David Hulse	.05
119	Pedro Munoz	.05
120	Ramon Martinez	.05
121	Todd Worrell	.05
122	Joey Cora	.05
123	Moises Alou	.05
124	Franklin Stubbs	.05
125	Pete O'Brien	.05
126	Bob Ayrault RC	.05
127	Carney Lansford	.05
128	Kal Daniels	.05
129	Joe Grahe	.05
130	Jeff Montgomery	.05
131	Dave Winfield	.50
132	Preston Wilson RC (1992 Draft Pick)	.75
133	Steve Wilson	.05
134	Lee Guetterman	.05
135	Mickey Tettleton	.05
136	Jeff King	.05
137	Alan Mills	.05
138	Joe Oliver	.05
139	Gary Gaetti	.05
140	Gary Sheffield	.30
141	Dennis Cook	.05
142	Charlie Hayes	.05
143	Jeff Huson	.05
144	Kent Mercker	.05
145	Eric Young RC	.10
146	Scott Leius	.05
147	Bryan Hickerson	.05
148	Steve Finley	.05
149	Rheal Cormier	.05
150	Frank Thomas	.50
151	Archi Cianfrocco RC	.05
152	Rich DeLucia	.05
153	Greg Vaughn	.05
154	Wes Chamberlain	.05
155	Dennis Eckersley	.40
156	Sammy Sosa	.60
157	Gary DiSarcina	.05
158	Kevin Koslofski RC	.05
159	Doug Linton RC	.05
160	Lou Whitaker	.05
161	Chad McDonnell (1992 Draft Pick)	.05
162	Joe Hesketh	.05
163	Tim Wakefield RC	.10
164	Leo Gomez	.05
165	Jose Rijo	.05
166	Tim Scott RC	.05
167	Steve Olin	.05
168	Kevin Maas	.05
169	Kenny Rogers	.05
170	Dave Justice	.05
171	Doug Jones	.05
172	Jeff Reboulet RC	.05
173	Andres Galarraga	.05
174	Randy Velarde	.05
175	Kirk McCaskill	.05
176	Darren Lewis	.05
177	Lenny Harris	.05
178	Jeff Fassero	.05
179	Ken Griffey Jr.	.75
180	Darren Daulton	.05
181	John Jaha	.05
182	Ron Darling	.05
183	Greg Maddux	.60
184	Damion Easley RC	.10
185	Jack Morris	.05
186	Mike Magnante	.05
187	John Dopson	.05
188	Sid Fernandez	.05
189	Tony Phillips	.05
190	Doug Drabek	.05
191	Sean Lowe RC (1992 Draft Pick)	.05
192	Bob Milacki	.05
193	Steve Foster RC	.05
194	Jerald Clark	.05
195	Pete Harnisch	.05
196	Pat Kelly	.05
197	Jeff Frye	.05
198	Alejandro Pena	.05
199	Junior Ortiz	.05
200	Kirby Puckett	.60
201	Jose Uribe	.05
202	Mike Scioscia	.05
203	Bernard Gilkey	.05
204	Dan Pasqua	.05
205	Gary Carter	.50
206	Henry Cotto	.05
207	Paul Molitor	.50
208	Mike Hartley	.05
209	Jeff Parrett	.05
210	Mark Langston	.05
211	Doug Dascenzo	.05
212	Rick Reed	.05
213	Candy Maldonado	.05
214	Danny Darwin	.05
215	Pat Howell RC	.05
216	Mark Leiter	.05
217	Kevin Mitchell	.05
218	Ben McDonald	.05
219	Bip Roberts	.05
220	Benny Santiago	.05
221	Carlos Baerga	.05
222	Bernie Williams	.05
223	Roger Pavlik RC	.05
224	Sid Bream	.05
225	Matt Williams	.05
226	Willie Banks	.05
227	Jeff Bagwell	.50
228	Tom Goodwin	.05
229	Mike Perez	.05
230	Carlton Fisk	.50
231	John Wetteland	.05
232	Tino Martinez	.05
233	Rick Greene RC (1992 Draft Pick)	.05
234	Tim McIntosh	.05
235	Mitch Williams	.05
236	Kevin Campbell RC	.05
237	Jose Vizcaino	.05
238	Chris Donnels	.05
239	Mike Boddicker	.05
240	John Olerud	.05
241	Mike Gardiner	.05
242	Charlie O'Brien	.05
243	Rob Deer	.05
244	Denny Neagle	.05
245	Chris Sabo	.05
246	Gregg Olson	.05
247	Frank Seminara	.05
248	Scott Scudder	.05
249	Tim Burke	.05
250	Chuck Knoblauch	.05
251	Mike Bielecki	.05
252	Xavier Hernandez	.05
253	Jose Guzman	.05
254	Cory Snyder	.05
255	Orel Hershiser	.05
256	Wil Cordero	.05
257	Luis Alicea	.05
258	Mike Schooler	.05
259	Craig Grebeck	.05
260	Duane Ward	.05
261	Bill Wegman	.05
262	Mickey Morandini	.05
263	Vince Horsman RC	.05
264	Paul Sorrento	.05
265	Andre Dawson	.25
266	Rene Gonzales	.05
267	Keith Miller	.05
268	Derek Bell	.05
269	Todd Steverson RC (1992 Draft Pick)	.05
270	Frank Viola	.05
271	Wally Whitehurst	.05
272	Kurt Knudsen RC	.05
273	Dan Walters RC	.05
274	Rick Sutcliffe	.05
275	Andy Van Slyke	.05
276	Paul O'Neill	.05
277	Mark Whiten	.05
278	Chris Nabholz	.05
279	Todd Burns	.05
280	Tom Glavine	.25
281	Butch Henry RC	.05
282	Shane Mack	.05
283	Mike Jackson	.05
284	Henry Rodriguez	.05
285	Bob Tewksbury	.05
286	Ron Karkovice	.05
287	Mike Gallego	.05
288	Dave Cochrane	.05
289	Jesse Orosco	.05
290	Dave Stewart	.05
291	Tommy Greene	.05
292	Rey Sanchez	.05
293	Rob Ducey	.05
294	Brent Mayne	.05
295	Dave Stieb	.05
296	Luis Rivera	.05
297	Jeff Innis	.05
298	Scott Livingstone	.05
299	Bob Patterson	.05
300	Cal Ripken, Jr.	1.00
301	Cesar Hernandez	.05
302	Randy Myers	.05
303	Brook Jacoby	.05
304	Melido Perez	.05
305	Rafael Palmeiro	.40
306	Damon Berryhill	.05
307	Dan Serafini RC (1992 Draft Pick)	.05
308	Darryl Kile	.05
309	J.T. Bruett RC	.05
310	Dave Righetti	.05
311	Jay Howell	.05
312	Geronimo Pena	.05
313	Greg Hibbard	.05
314	Mark Gardner	.05
315	Edgar Martinez	.05
316	Dave Nilsson	.05
317	Kyle Abbott	.05
318	Willie Wilson	.05
319	Paul Assenmacher	.05
320	Tim Fortugno RC	.05
321	Rusty Meacham	.05
322	Pat Borders	.05
323	Mike Greenwell	.05
324	Willie Randolph	.05
325	Bill Gullickson	.05
326	Gary Varsho	.05
327	Tim Hulett	.05
328	Scott Ruskin	.05
329	Mike Maddux	.05
330	Danny Tartabull	.05
331	Kenny Lofton	.05
332	Geno Petralli	.05
333	Otis Nixon	.05
334	Jason Kendall RC (1992 Draft Pick)	.50
335	Mark Portugal	.05
336	Mike Pagliarulo	.05
337	Kirt Manwaring	.05
338	Bob Ojeda	.05
339	Mark Clark RC	.05
340	John Kruk	.05
341	Mel Rojas	.05
342	Erik Hanson	.05
343	Doug Henry	.05
344	Jack McDowell	.05
345	Harold Baines	.05
346	Chuck McElroy	.05
347	Luis Sojo	.05
348	Andy Stankiewicz	.05
349	Hipolito Pichardo RC	.05
350	Joe Carter	.05
351	Ellis Burks	.05
352	Rich Schourek	.05
353	Buddy Groom RC	.05
354	Jay Bell	.05
355	Brady Anderson	.05
356	Freddie Benavides	.05
357	Phil Stephenson	.05
358	Kevin Wickander	.05
359	Mike Stanley	.05
360	Ivan Rodriguez	.40
361	Scott Bankhead	.05
362	Luis Gonzalez	.05
363	John Smiley	.05
364	Trevor Wilson	.05
365	Tom Candiotti	.05
366	Craig Wilson	.05
367	Steve Sax	.05
368	Delino Deshields	.05
369	Jaime Navarro	.05
370	Dave Valle	.05
371	Mariano Duncan	.05
372	Rod Nichols	.05
373	Mike Morgan	.05
374	Julio Valera	.05
375	Wally Joyner	.05
376	Tom Henke	.05
377	Herm Winningham	.05
378	Orlando Merced	.05
379	Mike Munoz	.05
380	Todd Hundley	.05
381	Mike Flanagan	.05
382	Tim Belcher	.05
383	Jerry Browne	.05
384	Mike Benjamin	.05
385	Jim Leyritz	.05
386	Ray Lankford	.05
387	Devon White	.05
388	Jeremy Hernandez	.05
389	Brian Harper	.05
390	Wade Boggs	.60
391	Derrick May	.05
392	Travis Fryman	.05
393	Ron Gant	.05
394	Checklist 1-132	.05
395	Checklist 133-264	.05
396	Checklist 265-396	.05
397	George Brett	.65
398	Bobby Witt	.05
399	Daryl Boston	.05
400	Bo Jackson	.10
401	Fred McGriff, Frank Thomas/AS	.20
402	Ryne Sandberg, Carlos Baerga/AS	.30
403	Gary Sheffield, Edgar Martinez/AS	.05
404	Barry Larkin, Travis Fryman/AS	.05
405	Andy Van Slyke, Ken Griffey Jr./AS	.40
406	Larry Walker, Kirby Puckett/AS	.20
407	Barry Bonds, Joe Carter/AS	.50
408	Darren Daulton, Brian Harper/AS	.05
409	Greg Maddux, Roger Clemens/AS	.25
410	Tom Glavine, Dave Fleming/AS	.05
411	Lee Smith, Dennis Eckersley/AS	.15
412	Jamie McAndrew RC	.05
413	Pete Smith	.05
414	Juan Guerrero	.05
415	Todd Frohwirth	.05
416	Randy Tomlin	.05
417	B.J. Surhoff	.05
418	Jim Gott	.05
419	Mark Thompson RC (1992 Draft Pick)	.05
420	Ken Tapani	.05
421	Curt Schilling	.25
422	J.T. Snow RC	.40
423	Top Prospects 1B (Ryan Klesko, Ivan Cruz, Bubba Smith, Larry Sutton)	.05
424	John Valentin	.05
425	Joe Girardi	.05
426	Nigel Wilson RC	.05
427	Bob MacDonald	.05
428	Todd Zeile	.05
429	Milt Cuyler	.05
430	Eddie Murray	.50
431	Rich Amaral	.05
432	Pete Young	.05
433	Rockies Future Stars (Roger Bailey, Tom Schmidt)	.05
434	Jack Armstrong (1992 Draft Pick)	.50
435	Willie McGee	.05
436	Greg Harris	.05
437	Chris Hammond	.05
438	Ritchie Moody RC (1992 Draft Pick)	.05
439	Bryan Harvey	.05
440	Ruben Sierra	.05
441	Marlins Future Stars (Don Lemon, Todd Pridy)	.05
442	Kevin McReynolds	.05
443	Terry Leach	.05
444	David Nied	.05
445	Dale Murphy	.15
446	Luis Mercedes	.05
447	Keith Shepherd RC	.05
448	Ken Caminiti	.05
449	James Austin	.05
450	Darryl Strawberry	.05
451	Top Prospects 2B (Ramon Caraballo, Jon Shave, Brent Gates, Quinton McCracken RC)	.10
452	Bob Wickman	.05
453	Victor Cole	.05
454	John Johnstone RC	.05
455	Chili Davis	.05
456	Scott Taylor	.05
457	Tracy Woodson	.05
458	David Wells	.05
459	Derek Wallace RC (1992 Draft Pick)	.05
460	Randy Johnson	.50
461	Steve Reed RC	.05
462	Felix Fermin	.05
463	Scott Aldred	.05
464	Greg Colbrunn	.05
465	Tony Fernandez	.05
466	Mike Felder	.05
467	Lee Stevens	.05
468	Matt Whiteside	.05
469	Dave Hansen	.05
470	Rob Dibble	.05
471	Dave Gallagher	.05
472	Chris Gwynn	.05
473	Dave Henderson	.05
474	Ozzie Guillen	.05
475	Jeff Reardon	.05
476	Rockies Future Stars (Mark Voisard, Will Scalzitti)	.05
477	Jimmy Jones	.05
478	Greg Cadaret	.05
479	Todd Pratt	.05
480	Pat Listach	.05
481	Ryan Luzinski RC (1992 Draft Pick)	.05
482	Darren Reed	.05
483	Brian Griffiths RC	.05
484	John Wehner	.05
485	Glenn Davis	.05
486	Eric Wedge RC	.05
487	Jesse Hollins	.05
488	Manuel Lee	.05
489	Scott Fredrickson RC	.05
490	Omar Olivares	.05
491	Shawn Hare	.05
492	Tom Lampkin	.05
493	Jeff Nelson	.05
494	Top Prospects 3B (Kevin Young, Adell Davenport, Eduardo Perez, Lou Lucca)	.05
495	Ken Hill	.05
496	Reggie Jefferson	.05
497	Marlins Future Stars (Matt Petersen, Willie Brown)	.05
498	Bud Black	.05
499	Chuck Crim	.05
500	Jose Canseco	.30
501	Major League Managers (Johnny Oates, Bobby Cox)	.05
502	Major League Managers (Butch Hobson, Jim Lefebvre)	.05
503	Major League Managers (Buck Rodgers, Tony Perez)	.05
504	Major League Managers (Gene Lamont, Don Baylor)	.10
505	Major League Managers (Mike Hargrove, Rene Lachemann)	.05
506	Major League Managers (Sparky Anderson, Art Howe)	.10
507	Major League Managers (Hal McRae, Tommy Lasorda)	.05
508	Major League Manager (Phil Garner, Felipe Alou)	.05
509	Major League Managers (Tom Kelly, Jeff Torborg)	.05
510	Major League Managers (Buck Showalter, Jim Fregosi)	.05
511	Major League Managers (Tony LaRussa, Jim Leyland)	.10
512	Major League Managers (Lou Piniella, Joe Torre)	.10
513	Major League Managers (Toby Harrah, Jim Riggleman)	.05
514	Major League Managers (Cito Gaston, Dusty Baker)	.05
515	Greg Swindell	.05
516	Alex Arias	.05
517	Bill Pecota	.05
518	Benji Grigsby RC (1992 Draft Pick)	.05
519	David Howard	.05
520	Charlie Hough	.05
521	Kevin Flora	.05
522	Shane Reynolds	.05
523	Doug Bochtler RC	.05
524	Chris Hoiles	.05
525	Scott Sanderson	.05
526	Mike Sharperson	.05
527	Mike Fetters	.05
528	Paul Quantrill	.05

#	Player	Price
529	Top Propsects SS (Dave Silvestri, Chipper Jones, Benji Gil, Jeff Patzke)	.25
530	Sterling Hitchcock	.05
531	Joe Millette	.05
532	Tom Brunansky	.05
533	Frank Castillo	.05
534	Randy Knorr	.05
535	Jose Oquendo	.05
536	Dave Haas	.05
537	Rockies Future Stars (Jason Hutchins, Ryan Turner)	.05
538	Jimmy Baron (1992 Draft Pick)	.05
539	Kerry Woodson	.05
540	Ivan Calderon	.05
541	Denis Boucher	.05
542	Royce Clayton	.05
543	Reggie Williams	.05
544	Steve Decker	.05
545	Dean Palmer	.05
546	Hal Morris	.05
547	Ryan Thompson RC	.05
548	Lance Blankenship	.05
549	Hensley Meulens	.05
550	Scott Radinsky	.05
551	Eric Young RC	.10
552	Jeff Blauser	.05
553	Andujar Cedeno	.05
554	Arthur Rhodes	.05
555	Terry Mulholland	.05
556	Darryl Hamilton	.05
557	Pedro Martinez	.50
558	Marlins Future Stars (Ryan Whitman, Mark Skeels)	.05
559	Jamie Arnold RC (1992 Draft Pick)	.05
560	Zane Smith	.05
561	Matt Nokes	.05
562	Bob Zupcic	.05
563	Shawn Boskie	.05
564	Mike Timlin	.05
565	Jerald Clark	.05
566	Rod Brewer	.05
567	Mark Carreon	.05
568	Andy Benes	.05
569	Shawn Barton	.05
570	Tim Wallach	.05
571	Dave Mlicki	.05
572	Trevor Hoffman	.05
573	John Patterson	.05
574	DeShawn Warren (1992 Draft Pick)	.05
575	Monty Fariss	.05
576	Top Prospects OF (Darrell Sherman, Damon Buford, Cliff Floyd, Michael Moore)	.05
577	Tim Costo	.05
578	Dave Magadan	.05
579	Rockies Future Stars (Neil Garret, Jason Bates)	.05
580	Walt Weiss	.05
581	Chris Haney	.05
582	Shawn Abner	.05
583	Marvin Freeman	.05
584	Casey Candaele	.05
585	Ricky Jordan	.05
586	Jeff Tabaka	.05
587	Manny Alexander	.05
588	Mike Trombley	.05
589	Carlos Hernandez	.05
590	Cal Eldred	.05
591	Alex Cole	.05
592	Phil Plantier	.05
593	Brett Merriman	.05
594	Jerry Nielsen	.05
595	Shawon Dunston	.05
596	Jimmy Key	.05
597	Gerald Perry	.05
598	Rico Brogna	.05
599	Marlins Future Stars (Clemente Nunez, Dan Robinson)	.05
600	Bret Saberhagen	.05
601	Craig Shipley	.05
602	Henry Mercedes	.05
603	Jim Thome	.40
604	Rod Beck	.05
605	Chuck Finley	.05
606	J. Owens	.05
607	Dan Smith	.05
608	Bill Doran	.05
609	Lance Parrish	.05
610	Denny Martinez	.05
611	Tom Gordon	.05
612	Byron Mathews (1992 Draft Pick)	.05
613	Joel Adamson	.05
614	Brian Williams	.05
615	Steve Avery	.05
616	Top Prospects OF (Matt Mieske, Tracy Sanders, Midre Cummings, Ryan Freeburg)	.05
617	Craig Lefferts	.05
618	Tony Pena	.05
619	Billy Spiers	.05
620	Todd Benzinger	.05
621	Rockies Future Stars (Mike Kotarski, Greg Boyd)	.05
622	Ben Rivera	.05
623	Al Martin RC	.05
624	Sam Militello	.05
625	Rick Aguilera	.05
626	Danny Gladden	.05
627	Andres Berumen	.05
628	Kelly Gruber	.05
629	Cris Carpenter	.05
630	Mark Grace	.05
631	Jeff Brantley	.05
632	Chris Widger (1992 Draft Pick)	.05
633	Russian Angels (Rodolf Razjigaev, Evgenyi Puchkov, Ilya Bogatyrev)	.10
634	Mo Sanford	.05
635	Albert Belle	.05
636	Tim Teufel	.05
637	Greg Myers	.05
638	Brian Bohanon	.05
639	Mike Bordick	.05
640	Dwight Gooden	.05
641	Marlins Future Stars (Pat Leahy, Gavin Baugh)	.05
642	Milt Hill	.05
643	Luis Aquino	.05
644	Dante Bichette	.05
645	Bobby Thigpen	.05
646	Rich Scheid	.05
647	Brian Sackinsky (1992 Draft Pick)	.05
648	Ryan Hawblitzel	.05
649	Tom Marsh	.05
650	Terry Pendleton	.05
651	Rafael Bournigal RC	.05
652	Dave West	.05
653	Steve Hosey	.05
654	Gerald Williams	.05
655	Scott Cooper	.05
656	Gary Scott	.05
657	Mike Harkey	.05
658	Top Prospects OF (Jeromy Burnitz, Melvin Nieves, Rich Becker, Shon Walker)	.05
659	Ed Sprague	.05
660	Alan Trammell	.05
661	Rockies Future Stars (Garvin Alston, Mike Case)	.05
662	Donovan Osborne	.05
663	Jeff Gardner	.05
664	Calvin Jones	.05
665	Darrin Fletcher	.05
666	Glenallen Hill	.05
667	Jim Rosenbohm (1992 Draft Pick)	.05
668	Scott Lewis	.05
669	Kip Yaughn	.05
670	Julio Franco	.05
671	Dave Martinez	.05
672	Kevin Bass	.05
673	Todd Van Poppel	.05
674	Mark Gubicza	.05
675	Tim Raines	.05
676	Rudy Seanez	.05
677	Charlie Leibrandt	.05
678	Randy Milligan	.05
679	Kim Batiste	.05
680	Craig Biggio	.05
681	Darren Holmes	.05
682	John Candelaria	.05
683	Marlins Future Stars (Jerry Stafford, Eddie Christian)	.05
684	Pat Mahomes	.05
685	Bob Walk	.05
686	Russ Springer	.05
687	Tony Sheffield (1992 Draft Picks)	.05
688	Dwight Smith	.05
689	Eddie Zosky	.05
690	Bien Figueroa	.05
691	Jim Tatum	.05
692	Chad Kreuter	.05
693	Rich Rodriguez	.05
694	Shane Turner	.05
695	Kent Bottenfield	.05
696	Jose Mesa	.05
697	Darrell Whitmore RC	.05
698	Ted Wood	.05
699	Chad Curtis	.05
700	Nolan Ryan	1.00
701	Top Prospects C (Mike Piazza, Carlos Delgado, Brook Fordyce, Donnie Leshnock)	.85
702	Tim Pugh RC	.05
703	Jeff Kent	.05
704	Rockies Future Stars (Jon Goodrich, Danny Figueroa)	.05
705	Bob Welch	.05
706	Sherard Clinkscales (1992 Draft Pick)	.05
707	Donn Pall	.05
708	Greg Olson	.05
709	Jeff Juden	.05
710	Mike Mussina	.30
711	Scott Chiamparino	.05
712	Stan Javier	.05
713	John Doherty	.05
714	Kevin Gross	.05
715	Greg Gagne	.05
716	Steve Cooke	.05
717	Steve Farr	.05
718	Jay Buhner	.05
719	Butch Henry	.05
720	David Cone	.05
721	Rick Wilkins	.05
722	Chuck Carr	.05
723	Kenny Felder RC (1992 Draft Pick)	.05
724	Guillermo Velasquez	.05
725	Billy Hatcher	.05
726	Marlins Future Stars (Mike Veneziale, Ken Kendrena)	.05
727	Jonathan Hurst	.05
728	Steve Frey	.05
729	Mark Leonard	.05
730	Charles Nagy	.05
731	Donald Harris	.05
732	Travis Buckley	.05
733	Tom Browning	.05
734	Anthony Young	.05
735	Steve Shifflett	.05
736	Jeff Russell	.05
737	Wilson Alvarez	.05
738	Lance Painter	.05
739	Dave Weathers	.05
740	Len Dykstra	.05
741	Mike Devereaux	.05
742	Top Prospects SP (Rene Arocha, Alan Embree, Tim Crabtree RC, Brien Taylor)	.05
743	Dave Landaker (1992 Draft Pick)	.05
744	Chris George	.05
745	Eric Davis	.05
746	Rockies Future Stars (Mark Strittmatter RC, LaMarr Rogers)	.05
747	Carl Willis	.05
748	Stan Belinda	.05
749	Scott Kamieniecki	.05
750	Rickey Henderson	.50
751	Eric Hillman	.05
752	Pat Hentgen	.05
753	Jim Corsi	.05
754	Brian Jordan	.05
755	Bill Swift	.05
756	Mike Henneman	.05
757	Harold Reynolds	.05
758	Sean Berry	.05
759	Charlie Hayes	.05
760	Luis Polonia	.05
761	Darrin Jackson	.05
762	Mark Lewis	.05
763	Rob Maurer	.05
764	Willie Greene	.05
765	Vince Coleman	.05
766	Todd Revenig	.05
767	Rich Ireland (1992 Draft Pick)	.05
768	Mike MacFarlane	.05
769	Francisco Cabrera	.05
770	Robin Ventura	.05
771	Kevin Ritz	.05
772	Chito Martinez	.05
773	Cliff Brantley	.05
774	Curtis Leskanic	.05
775	Chris Bosio	.05
776	Jose Offerman	.05
777	Mark Guthrie	.05
778	Don Slaught	.05
779	Rich Monteleone	.05
780	Jim Abbott	.05
781	Jack Clark	.05
782	Marlins Future Stars (Rafael Mendoza, Dan Roman)	.05
783	Heathcliff Slocumb	.05
784	Jeff Branson	.05
785	Kevin Brown	.05
786	Top Prospects RP (Mike Christopher, Ken Ryan, Aaron Taylor, Gus Gandarillas)	.05
787	Mike Matthews (1992 Draft Pick)	.05
788	Mackey Sasser	.05
789	Jeff Conine	.05
790	George Bell	.05
791	Pat Rapp	.05
792	Joe Boever	.05
793	Jim Poole	.05
794	Andy Ashby	.05
795	Deion Sanders	.10
796	Scott Brosius	.05
797	Brad Pennington (Coming Attraction)	.05
798	Greg Blosser (Coming Attraction)	.05
799	Jim Edmonds RC (Coming Attraction)	1.00
800	Shawn Jeter (Coming Attraction)	.05
801	Jesse Levis (Coming Attraction)	.05
802	Phil Clark (Coming Attraction)	.05
803	Ed Pierce (Coming Attraction)	.05
804	Jose Valentin RC (Coming Attraction)	.05
805	Terry Jorgensen (Coming Attraction)	.05
806	Mark Hutton (Coming Attraction)	.05
807	Troy Neel (Coming Attraction)	.05
808	Bret Boone (Coming Attraction)	.05
809	Chris Colon (Coming Attraction)	.05
810	Domingo Martinez RC (Coming Attraction)	.05
811	Javier Lopez (Coming Attraction)	.05
812	Matt Walbeck (Coming Attraction)	.05
813	Dan Wilson (Coming Attraction)	.05
814	Scooter Tucker (Coming Attraction)	.05
815	Billy Ashley RC (Coming Attraction)	.05
816	Tim Laker RC (Coming Attraction)	.05
817	Bobby Jones (Coming Attraction)	.05
818	Brad Brink (Coming Attraction)	.05
819	William Pennyfeather (Coming Attraction)	.05
820	Stan Royer (Coming Attraction)	.05
821	Doug Brocail (Coming Attraction)	.05
822	Kevin Rogers (Coming Attraction)	.05
823	Checklist 397-528	.05
824	Checklist 541-691	.05
825	Checklist 692-825	.05

Gold

Expanding on the concept begun in 1992, Topps issued a "gold" version of each of its regular 1993 cards as a package insert. One Gold card was found in each wax pack; three per rack-pack and five per jumbo cello pack. Ten Gold cards were included in each factory set. Identical in format to the regular-issue 1993 Topps cards, the Gold version replaces the black or white Topps logo on front with a "ToppsGold" logo in gold-foil. The color bars and angled strips beneath the player photo which carry the player and team ID on regular cards are replaced with a gold-foil version on the insert cards. Backs are identical to the regular cards. The six checklist cards in the regular issue were replaced in the Gold version with cards of players who do not appear in the 1993 Topps set.

		NM/M
Complete Set (825):		40.00
Common Player:		.15
394	Bernardo Brito	.25
395	Jim McNamara	.25
396	Rich Sauveur	.25
823	Keith Brown	.25
824	Russ McGinnis	.25
825	Mike Walker	.25

Black Gold

Randomly inserted in regular 1993 Topps packs, as well as 10 per factory set, Black Gold cards are found in both single-player versions and "Winner" cards. The single-player cards feature an action photo set against a black background and highlighted at top and bottom with gold foil. Backs have another player photo at left, again on a black background. A career summary is printed in a blue box at right. A "Topps Black Gold" logo appears at top-left, and the player's name is printed in gold foil in an art deco device at top-right. The Winner cards picture tiny versions of the Black Gold player cards for which they could be redeemed by mail. Some, perhaps all, of the mail-in cards can also be found on which the miniature card pictures on front do not correspond to the players named on back. In addition, with each mail-in redemption set, a non-redeemable version of the Winner card was also sent.

		NM/M
Complete Set (44)		7.50
Common Player:		.10
Winner A (1-11):		1.00
Winner B (12-22):		1.00
Winner C (23-33):		1.00
Winner D (34-44):		1.00
Winner AB (1-22):		3.00
Winner CD (23-44):		3.00
Winner ABCD (1-44):		5.00
1	Barry Bonds	1.50
2	Will Clark	.10
3	Darren Daulton	.10
4	Andre Dawson	.25
5	Delino DeShields	.10
6	Tom Glavine	.20
7	Marquis Grissom	.10
8	Tony Gwynn	.75
9	Eric Karros	.10
10	Ray Lankford	.10
11	Barry Larkin	.10
12	Greg Maddux	.75
13	Fred McGriff	.10
14	Joe Oliver	.10
15	Terry Pendleton	.10
16	Bip Roberts	.10
17	Ryne Sandberg	.75
18	Gary Sheffield	.40
19	Lee Smith	.10
20	Ozzie Smith	.75
21	Andy Van Slyke	.10
22	Larry Walker	.10
23	Roberto Alomar	.20
24	Brady Anderson	.10
25	Carlos Baerga	.10
26	Joe Carter	.10
27	Roger Clemens	.85
28	Mike Devereaux	.10
29	Dennis Eckersley	.60
30	Cecil Fielder	.10
31	Travis Fryman	.10
32	Juan Gonzalez	.35
33	Ken Griffey Jr.	1.00
34	Brian Harper	.10
35	Pat Listach	.10
36	Kenny Lofton	.10
37	Edgar Martinez	.10
38	Jack McDowell	.10
39	Mark McGwire	1.00
40	Kirby Puckett	.75
41	Mickey Tettleton	.10
42	Frank Thomas	.65
43	Robin Ventura	.10
44	Dave Winfield	.65

Colorado Rockies Inaugural Year

To mark the team's inaugural year in the Major Leagues, Topps produced a special run of 10,000 of its 1993 factory sets in which each card was embossed with a special gold seal incorporating the Rockies logo. Sets sold for $100 at the team's normal souvenir outlets. The factory sets were sealed with a sticker featuring the inaugural year logo.

	NM/M
Complete Set (825):	80.00
Common Player:	.50

Florida Marlins Inaugural Year

To commemorate the team's inaugural year in the Major Leagues, Topps produced a special edition of 6,000 of its 1993 factory sets in which every card was embossed with a special gold seal incorporating the Marlins logo. The sets were sold for $100 at the team's normal souvenir outlets. Factory sets are sealed with a sticker incorporating the inaugural year logo.

	NM/M
Complete Set (825):	100.00
Common Player:	.50

Traded

The 1993 Topps Traded baseball set features many players in their new uniforms as a result of trades, free agent signings and rookie call-ups. The set also features 35 expansion players from the Colorado Rockies and Florida Marlins, as well as 22 Team USA members exclusive to Topps. The 132-card set is packed in a color deluxe printed box.

		NM/M
Complete Set (132):		20.00
Common Player:		.05
1	Barry Bonds	2.00
2	Rich Renteria	.05
3	Aaron Sele	.05
4	Carlton Loewer RC (USA)	.10
5	Erik Pappas	.05
6	Greg McMichael RC	.05
7	Freddie Benavides	.05
8	Kirk Gibson	.05
9	Tony Fernandez	.05
10	Jay Gainer RC (USA)	.05
11	Orestes Destrade	.05
12	A.J. Hinch RC (USA)	.40
13	Bobby Munoz	.05
14	Tom Henke	.05
15	Rob Butler	.05
16	Gary Wayne	.05
17	David McCarty	.05
18	Walt Weiss	.05
19	Todd Helton RC (USA)	15.00
20	Mark Whiten	.05
21	Ricky Gutierrez	.05
22	Dustin Hermanson RC (USA)	.40
23	Sherman Obando RC	.05
24	Mike Piazza	2.00
25	Jeff Russell	.05
26	Jason Bere	.05
27	Jack Voight RC	.05
28	Chris Bosio	.05
29	Phil Hiatt	.05
30	Matt Beaumont RC (USA)	.05
31	Andres Galarraga	.05
32	Greg Swindell	.05
33	Vinny Castilla	.05
34	Pat Clougherty RC (USA)	.05
35	Greg Briley	.05
36	Dallas Green, Davey Johnson	.05
37	Tyler Green	.05
38	Craig Paquette	.05
39	Danny Sheaffer	.05

#	Player	Price
40	Jim Converse	.05
41	Terry Harvey	.05
42	Phil Plantier	.05
43	Doug Saunders RC	.05
44	Benny Santiago	.05
45	Dante Powell RC (USA)	.10
46	Jeff Parrett	.05
47	Wade Boggs	.85
48	Paul Molitor	.75
49	Turk Wendell	.05
50	David Wells	.05
51	Gary Sheffield	.35
52	Kevin Young	.05
53	Nelson Liriano	.05
54	Greg Maddux	.85
55	Derek Bell	.05
56	Matt Turner RC	.05
57	Charlie Nelson RC (USA)	.05
58	Mike Hampton	.05
59	Troy O'Leary RC	.10
60	Benji Gil	.05
61	Mitch Lyden RC	.05
62	J.T. Snow	.05
63	Damon Buford	.05
64	Gene Harris	.05
65	Randy Myers	.05
66	Felix Jose	.05
67	Todd Dunn RC (USA)	.05
68	Jimmy Key	.05
69	Pedro Castellano	.05
70	Mark Merila RC (USA)	.05
71	Rich Rodriguez	.05
72	Matt Mieske	.05
73	Pete Incaviglia	.05
74	Carl Everett '	.05
75	Jim Abbott	.05
76	Luis Aquino	.05
77	Rene Arocha RC	.05
78	Jon Shave RC	.05
79	Todd Walker RC (USA)	1.00
80	Jack Armstrong	.05
81	Jeff Richardson	.05
82	Blas Minor	.05
83	Dave Winfield	.75
84	Paul O'Neill	.05
85	Steve Reich RC (USA)	.10
86	Chris Hammond	.05
87	Hilly Hathaway RC	.05
88	Fred McGriff	.05
89	Dave Telgheder RC	.05
90	Richie Lewis RC	.05
91	Brent Gates	.05
92	Andre Dawson	.15
93	Andy Barkett RC (USA)	.05
94	Doug Drabek	.05
95	Joe Klink	.05
96	Willie Blair	.05
97	Danny Graves RC (USA)	.05
98	Pat Meares	.05
99	Mike Lansing	.05
100	Marcos Armas RC	.05
101	Darren Grass RC (USA)	.05
102	Chris Jones	.05
103	Ken Ryan RC	.05
104	Ellis Burks	.05
105	Bobby Kelly	.05
106	Dave Magadan	.05
107	Paul Wilson RC (USA)	.25
108	Rob Natal	.05
109	Paul Wagner	.05
110	Jeromy Burnitz	.05
111	Monty Fariss	.05
112	Kevin Mitchell	.05
113	Scott Pose RC	.05
114	Dave Stewart	.05
115	Russ Johnson RC (USA)	.10
116	Armando Reynoso	.05
117	Geronimo Berroa	.05
118	Woody Williams RC	.15
119	Tim Bogar RC	.05
120	Bob Scafa RC (USA)	.05
121	Henry Cotto	.05
122	Gregg Jefferies	.05
123	Norm Charlton	.05
124	Bret Wagner RC (USA)	.05
125	David Cone	.05
126	Daryl Boston	.05
127	Tim Wallach	.05
128	Mike Martin RC (USA)	.05
129	John Cummings RC	.05
130	Ryan Bowen	.05
131	John Powell RC (USA)	.05
132	Checklist	.05

Full Shot Super

Just as rivals Upper Deck and Donruss did, Topps issued a set of 21 oversized cards (3-1/2"x5") that was available in retail outlets in packages that contained one of the large cards and two packs of regular issue Topps cards from the same year. The Topps Full Shot cards feature many of the top players in the game, and unlike the Upper Deck oversized cards, the Topps cards were not enlarged versions of existing cards but rather photos and a design that appeared only in this format.

	NM/M
Complete Set (21):	65.00
Common Player:	2.00
1 Frank Thomas	4.00
2 Ken Griffey Jr.	8.00
3 Barry Bonds	9.00
4 Juan Gonzalez	2.50
5 Roberto Alomar	2.50
6 Mike Piazza	6.50
7 Tony Gwynn	4.50
8 Jeff Bagwell	3.50
9 Tim Salmon	2.00
10 John Olerud	2.00
11 Cal Ripken, Jr.	9.00
12 David McCarty	2.00
13 Darren Daulton	2.00
14 Carlos Baerga	2.00
15 Roger Clemens	5.00
16 John Kruk	2.00
17 Barry Larkin	2.00
18 Gary Sheffield	2.00
19 Tom Glavine	2.50
20 Andres Galarraga	2.00
21 Fred McGriff	2.00

Golden Spikes Award

Darren Dreifort was the 1993 recipient of the U.S. Baseball Federation's Golden Spikes Award, emblematic of his selection as the outstanding amateur player in the nation. Topps created and handed out at the awards ceremony this special card.

	NM/M
Darren Dreifort	125.00

Magazine Jumbo Rookies

The final four issues of Topps' Magazine in 1993 substituted a 5-1/2" x 8" enlargement of a player's Topps rookie card in place of four of the standard-size inserts found previously. The jumbo rookie cards are identical, front and back, to the original rookie cards but carry a reprint notice on front. In an attempt to increase sales to subscribers and at the newsstands, the stars pictured autographed 100 of their cards to be randomly bound into the magazine and given away in prize drawings.
NM/M

		NM/M
Complete Set (4):		7.50
Common Player:		1.00
(1)	Dennis Eckersley (1976 Topps)	1.00
(2)	Dave Winfield (1974 Topps)	1.00
(3)	George Brett (1975 Topps)	2.00
(4)	Jerry Koosman, Nolan Ryan (1968 Topps)	4.00

Micro

Topps returned for a final year with a micro parallel of its regular-issue baseball set, in a format about 40 percent the size of the standard cards. Sold only in complete-set form, the 1"x1-3/8' cards also included a dozen prismatic- foil bordered star cards. Stars and rookies among the micros are valued at a percentage of the corresponding regular card.

	NM/M
Complete Set (837):	11.00
Common Player:	.05
Stars/Rookies:	1-1.5X
1 Robin Yount	.75
20 Tim Salmon	.50
32 Don Mattingly	1.25
50 Roberto Alomar	.60
150 Frank Thomas	.75
155 Dennis Eckersley	.65
179 Ken Griffey Jr.	1.50
200 Kirby Puckett	1.00
397 George Brett	1.25
426 Nigel Wilson	.50
444 David Nied	.50
700 Nolan Ryan	2.00

Preview

Two different versions of this nine-card set exist. A cellowrapped version, designated (a) in the checklist, was given away to dealers and the hobby press. A second version, designated (b), was included in 1993 Topps factory sets. It is currently unknown which version, if either, will become more valuable due to demand and perceived scarcity. Both versions are similar to the regular-issue '94 Topps cards, except for the sample notation on back.

	NM/M
Complete Set (a)(9):	10.00
Complete Set (b)(9):	10.00
Common Player (a):	.30
Common Player (b):	.30
2a Barry Bonds (Vertical format.)	4.00
2b Barry Bonds (Horizontal)	4.00
6a Jeff Tackett (Full bat label visible.)	.30
6b Jeff Tackett (Partial bat label.)	.30
34a Juan Gonzalez (Green triangle behind "Juan.")	.75
34b Juan Gonzalez (Brown triangle.)	.75
225a Matt Williams (Green triangle behind "Matt.")	.30
225b Matt Williams (Blue triangle.)	.30
294a Carlos Quintana (Team/position yellow.)	.30
294b Carlos Quintana (Team/position black.)	.30
331a Ken Lofton (Team/position white.)	.30
331b Ken Lofton (Team/position black.)	.30
390a Wade Boggs (Team/position yellow.)	2.00
390b Wade Boggs (Team/position black.)	2.00
397a George Brett (Vertical format.)	3.00
397b George Brett (Horizontal)	3.00
700a Nolan Ryan (Vertical format.)	4.00
700b Nolan Ryan (Horizontal)	4.00

1994 Topps

Once again released in two 396-card series, Topps' basic issue for 1994 offers a standard mix of regular player cards, Future Stars, multi-player rookie cards and double-header All-Star cards. On most cards the player photo on front is framed in a home-plate shaped design. The player's name appears in script beneath the photo and a team color-coded strip at bottom carries the team name and position designation. On back is a player photo, a red box at top with biographical details and a marbled panel which carries the stats and a career highlight. Cards are UV coated on each side. Inserts include a gold-foil enhanced parallel card in every pack, plus random Black Gold cards. Factory hobby sets include the 792 base cards plus 10 gold parallels, three Black Gold inserts and three Finest pre-production cards. Factory retails sets have the 792 base cards, 10 Gold, three Black Gold, 10 1995 Topps pre-production cards and three Superstar Sampler cards.

	NM/M
Unopened Retail Set (818):	60.00
Unopened Hobby Set (808):	50.00
Complete Set (792):	35.00
Common Player:	.05
Golds:	2X
Series 1 or 2 Pack (12):	.50
Series 1 or 2 Wax Box (36):	15.00
1 Mike Piazza (All-Star Rookie)	.85
2 Bernie Williams	.05
3 Kevin Rogers	.05
4 Paul Carey (Future Star)	.05
5 Ozzie Guillen	.05
6 Derrick May	.05
7 Jose Mesa	.05
8 Todd Hundley	.05
9 Chris Haney	.05
10 John Olerud	.05
11 Andujar Cedeno	.05
12 John Smiley	.05
13 Phil Plantier	.05
14 Willie Banks	.05
15 Jay Bell	.05
16 Doug Henry	.05
17 Lance Blankenship	.05
18 Greg Harris	.05
19 Scott Livingstone	.05
20 Bryan Harvey	.05
21 Wil Cordero (All-Star Rookie)	.05
22 Roger Pavlik	.05
23 Mark Lemke	.05
24 Jeff Nelson	.05
25 Todd Zeile	.05
26 Billy Hatcher	.05
27 Joe Magrane	.05
28 Tony Longmire (Future Star)	.05
29 Omar Daal	.05
30 Kirt Manwaring	.05
31 Melido Perez	.05
32 Tim Hulett	.05
33 Jeff Schwarz	.05
34 Nolan Ryan	1.00
35 Jose Guzman	.05
36 Felix Fermin	.05
37 Jeff Innis	.05
38 Brent Mayne	.05
39 Huck Flener RC	.05
40 Jeff Bagwell	.50
41 Kevin Wickander	.05
42 Ricky Gutierrez	.05
43 Pat Mahomes	.05
44 Jeff King	.05
45 Cal Eldred	.05
46 Craig Paquette	.05
47 Richie Lewis	.05
48 Tony Phillips	.05
49 Armando Reynoso	.05
50 Moises Alou	.05
51 Manuel Lee	.05
52 Otis Nixon	.05
53 Billy Ashley (Future Star)	.05
54 Mark Whiten	.05
55 Jeff Russell	.05
56 Chad Curtis	.05
57 Kevin Stocker	.05
58 Mike Jackson	.05
59 Matt Nokes	.05
60 Chris Bosio	.05
61 Damon Buford	.05
62 Tim Belcher	.05
63 Glenallen Hill	.05
64 Bill Wertz	.05
65 Eddie Murray	.50
66 Tom Gordon	.05
67 Alex Gonzalez (Future Star)	.05
68 Eddie Taubensee	.05
69 Jacob Brumfield	.05
70 Andy Benes	.05
71 Rich Becker (Future Star)	.05
72 Steve Cooke (All-Star Rookie)	.05
73 Billy Spiers	.05
74 Scott Brosius	.05
75 Alan Trammell	.05
76 Luis Aquino	.05
77 Jerald Clark	.05
78 Mel Rojas	.05
79 OF Prospects (Billy Masse, Stanton Cameron, Tim Clark, Craig McClure)	.05
80 Jose Canseco	.30
81 Greg McMichael (All-Star Rookie)	.05
82 Brian Turang	.05
83 Tom Urban	.05
84 Garret Anderson (Future Star)	.05
85 Tony Pena	.05
86 Ricky Jordan	.05
87 Jim Gott	.05
88 Pat Kelly	.05
89 Bud Black	.05
90 Robin Ventura	.05
91 Rick Sutcliffe	.05
92 Jose Bautista	.05
93 Bob Ojeda	.05
94 Phil Hiatt	.05
95 Tim Pugh	.05
96 Randy Knorr	.05
97 Todd Jones (Future Star)	.05
98 Ryan Thompson	.05
99 Tim Mauser	.05
100 Kirby Puckett	.60
101 Mark Dewey	.05
102 B.J. Surhoff	.05
103 Sterling Hitchcock	.05
104 Alex Arias	.05
105 David Wells	.05
106 Daryl Boston	.05
107 Mike Stanton	.05
108 Gary Redus	.05
109a Delino DeShields (Red "Expos, 2B.")	2.00
109b Delino DeShields (Yellow "Expos, 2B.")	.05
110 Lee Smith	.05
111 Greg Litton	.05
112 Frank Rodriguez (Future Star)	.05
113 Russ Springer	.05
114 Mitch Williams	.05
115 Eric Karros	.05
116 Jeff Brantley	.05
117 Jack Voight	.05
118 Jason Bere	.05
119 Kevin Roberson	.05
120 Jimmy Key	.05
121 Reggie Jefferson	.05
122 Jeromy Burnitz	.05
123 Billy Brewer (Future Star)	.05
124 Willie Canate	.05
125 Greg Swindell	.05
126 Hal Morris	.05
127 Brad Ausmus	.05
128 George Tsamis	.05
129 Denny Neagle	.05
130 Pat Listach	.05
131 Steve Karsay	.05
132 Bret Barberie	.05
133 Mark Leiter	.05
134 Greg Colbrunn	.05
135 David Nied	.05
136 Dean Palmer	.05
137 Steve Avery	.05
138 Bill Haselman	.05
139 Tripp Cromer (Future Star)	.05
140 Frank Viola	.05
141 Rene Gonzales	.05
142 Curt Schilling	.25
143 Tim Wallach	.05
144 Bobby Munoz	.05
145 Brady Anderson	.05
146 Rod Beck	.05
147 Mike LaValliere	.05
148 Greg Hibbard	.05
149 Kenny Lofton	.05
150 Dwight Gooden	.05
151 Greg Gagne	.05
152 Ray McDavid (Future Star)	.05
153 Chris Donnels	.05
154 Dan Wilson	.05
155 Todd Stottlemyre	.05
156 David McCarty	.05
157 Paul Wagner	.05
158 SS Prospects (Orlando Miller, Brandon Wilson, Derek Jeter, Mike Neal)	1.00
159 Mike Fetters	.05
160 Scott Lydy	.05
161 Darrell Whitmore	.05
162 Bob MacDonald	.05
163 Vinny Castilla	.05
164 Denis Boucher	.05
165 Ivan Rodriguez	.40
166 Ron Gant	.05
167 Tim Davis	.05
168 Steve Dixon	.05
169 Scott Fletcher	.05
170 Terry Mulholland	.05
171 Greg Myers	.05
172 Brett Butler	.05
173 Bob Wickman	.05
174 Dave Martinez	.05
175 Fernando Valenzuela	.05
176 Craig Grebeck	.05
177 Shawn Boskie	.05
178 Albie Lopez	.05
179 Butch Huskey (Future Star)	.05
180 George Brett	.65
181 Juan Guzman	.05
182 Eric Anthony	.05
183 Bob Dibble	.05
184 Craig Shipley	.05
185 Kevin Tapani	.05
186 Marcus Moore	.05
187 Graeme Lloyd	.05
188 Mike Bordick	.05
189 Chris Hammond	.05
190 Cecil Fielder	.05
191 Curtis Leskanic	.05
192 Lou Frazier	.05
193 Steve Dreyer	.05
194 Javier Lopez (Future Star)	.05
195 Edgar Martinez	.05
196 Allen Watson	.05
197 John Flaherty	.05
198 Kurt Stillwell	.05
199 Danny Jackson	.05
200 Cal Ripken, Jr.	1.00
201 Mike Bell (Draft Pick)	.05
202 Alan Benes RC (Draft Pick)	.10
203 Matt Farner RC (Draft Pick)	.05
204 Jeff Granger RC (Draft Pick)	.05
205 Brooks Kieschnick RC (Draft Pick)	.05
206 Jeremy Lee (Draft Pick)	.05
207 Charles Peterson RC (Draft Pick)	.05
208 Andy Rice (Draft Pick)	.05
209 Billy Wagner RC (Draft Pick)	.25
210 Kelly Wunsch (Draft Pick)	.05
211 Tom Candiotti	.05
212 Domingo Jean (Draft Pick)	.05
213 John Burkett	.05
214 George Bell	.05
215 Dan Plesac	.05
216 Manny Ramirez (Future Star)	.60
217 Mike Maddux	.05
218 Kevin McReynolds	.05
219 Pat Borders	.05
220 Doug Drabek	.05
221 Larry Luebbers	.05
222 Trevor Hoffman	.05
223 Pat Meares	.05
224 Danny Miceli (Future Star)	.05
225 Greg Vaughn	.05
226 Scott Hemond	.05
227 Pat Rapp	.05
228 Kirk Gibson	.05
229 Lance Painter	.05
230 Larry Walker	.05
231 Benji Gil (Future Star)	.05
232 Mark Wohlers	.05
233 Rich Amaral	.05
234 Erik Pappas	.05
235 Scott Cooper	.05
236 Mike Butcher	.05
237 OF Prospects (Curtis Pride RC, Shawn Green, Mark Sweeney, Eddie Davis)	.35
238 Kim Batiste	.05
239 Paul Assenmacher	.05
240 Will Clark	.05
241 Jose Offerman	.05
242 Todd Frohwirth	.05
243 Tim Raines	.05
244 Rick Wilkins	.05
245 Bret Saberhagen	.05
246 Thomas Howard	.05
247 Stan Belinda	.05
248 Rickey Henderson	.50
249 Brian Williams	.05

No.	Player	Price
250	Barry Larkin	.05
251	Jose Valentin (Future Star)	.05
252	Lenny Webster	.05
253	Blas Minor	.05
254	Tim Teufel	.05
255	Bobby Witt	.05
256	Walt Weiss	.05
257	Chad Kreuter	.05
258	Roberto Mejia	.05
259	Cliff Floyd (Future Star)	.05
260	Julio Franco	.05
261	Rafael Belliard	.05
262	Marc Newfield	.05
263	Gerald Perry	.05
264	Ken Ryan	.05
265	Chili Davis	.05
266	Dave West	.05
267	Royce Clayton	.05
268	Pedro Martinez	.50
269	Mark Hutton	.05
270	Frank Thomas	.50
271	Brad Pennington	.05
272	Mike Harkey	.05
273	Sandy Alomar	.05
274	Dave Gallagher	.05
275	Wally Joyner	.05
276	Ricky Trlicek	.05
277	Al Osuna	.05
278	Calvin Reese (Future Star)	.05
279	Kevin Higgins	.05
280	Rick Aguilera	.05
281	Orlando Merced	.05
282	Mike Mohler	.05
283	John Jaha	.05
284	Robb Nen	.05
285	Travis Fryman	.05
286	Mark Thompson (Future Star)	.05
287	Mike Lansing (All-Star Rookie)	.05
288	Craig Lefferts	.05
289	Damon Berryhill	.05
290	Randy Johnson	.50
291	Jeff Reed	.05
292	Danny Darwin	.05
293	J.T. Snow (All-Star Rookie)	.05
294	Tyler Green	.05
295	Chris Hoiles	.05
296	Roger McDowell	.05
297	Spike Owen	.05
298	Salomon Torres (Future Star)	.05
299	Wilson Alvarez	.05
300	Ryne Sandberg	.60
301	Derek Lilliquist	.05
302	Howard Johnson	.05
303	Greg Cadaret	.05
304	Pat Hentgen	.05
305	Craig Biggio	.05
306	Scott Service	.05
307	Melvin Nieves	.05
308	Mike Trombley	.05
309	Carlos Garcia (All-Star Rookie)	.05
310	Robin Yount	.50
311	Marcos Armas	.05
312	Rich Rodriguez	.05
313	Justin Thompson (Future Star)	.05
314	Danny Sheaffer	.05
315	Ken Hill	.05
316	P Propsects (Chad Ogea RC, Duff Brumley RC, Terrell Wade RC, Chris Michalak RC)	.10
317	Cris Carpenter	.05
318	Jeff Blauser	.05
319	Ted Power	.05
320	Ozzie Smith	.60
321	John Dopson	.05
322	Chris Turner	.05
323	Pete Incaviglia	.05
324	Alan Mills	.05
325	Jody Reed	.05
326	Rich Monteleone	.05
327	Mark Carreon	.05
328	Donn Pall	.05
329	Matt Walbeck (Future Star)	.05
330	Charles Nagy	.05
331	Jeff McKnight	.05
332	Jose Lind	.05
333	Mike Timlin	.05
334	Doug Jones	.05
335	Kevin Mitchell	.05
336	Luis Lopez	.05
337	Shane Mack	.05
338	Randy Tomlin	.05
339	Matt Mieske	.05
340	Mark McGwire	.85
341	Nigel Wilson (Future Star)	.05
342	Danny Gladden	.05
343	Mo Sanford	.05
344	Sean Berry	.05
345	Kevin Brown	.05
346	Greg Olson	.05
347	Dave Magadan	.05
348	Rene Arocha	.05
349	Carlos Quintana	.05
350	Jim Abbott	.05
351	Gary DiSarcina	.05
352	Ben Rivera	.05
353	Carlos Hernandez	.05
354	Darren Lewis	.05
355	Harold Reynolds	.05
356	Scott Ruffcorn (Future Star)	.05
357	Mark Gubicza	.05
358	Paul Sorrento	.05
359	Anthony Young	.05
360	Mark Grace	.05
361	Rob Butler	.05
362	Kevin Bass	.05
363	Eric Helfand (Future Star)	.05
364	Derek Bell	.05
365	Scott Erickson	.05
366	Al Martin	.05
367	Ricky Bones	.05
368	Jeff Branson	.05
369	3B Prospects (Luis Ortiz, David Bell, Jason Giambi, George Arias RC)	.30
370a	Benny Santiago	.05
370b	Mark McLemore (Originally checklisted as #379.)	.05
371	John Doherty	.05
372	Joe Girardi	.05
373	Tim Scott	.05
374	Marvin Freeman	.05
375	Deion Sanders	.10
376	Roger Salkeld	.05
377	Bernard Gilkey	.05
378	Tony Fossas	.05
380	Darren Daulton	.05
381	Chuck Finley	.05
382	Mitch Webster	.05
383	Gerald Williams	.05
384	Frank Thomas, Fred McGriff/AS	.30
385	Roberto Alomar, Robby Thompson/AS	.05
386	Wade Boggs, Matt Williams/AS	.35
387	Cal Ripken, Jr., Jeff Blauser/AS	.50
388	Ken Griffey Jr., Len Dykstra/AS	.40
389	Juan Gonzalez, Dave Justice/AS	.10
390	Albert Belle, Barry Bonds/AS	.45
391	Mike Stanley, Mike Piazza/AS	.45
392	Jack McDowell, Greg Maddux/AS	.45
393	Jimmy Key, Tom Glavine/AS	.05
394	Jeff Montgomery, Randy Myers/AS	.05
395	Checklist 1	.05
396	Checklist 2	.05
397	Tim Salmon (All-Star Rookie)	.10
398	Todd Benzinger	.05
399	Frank Castillo	.05
400	Ken Griffey Jr.	.75
401	John Kruk	.05
402	Dave Telgheder	.05
403	Gary Gaetti	.05
404	Jim Edmonds	.05
405	Don Slaught	.05
406	Jose Oquendo	.05
407	Bruce Ruffin	.05
408	Phil Clark	.05
409	Joe Klink	.05
410	Lou Whitaker	.05
411	Kevin Seitzer	.05
412	Darrin Fletcher	.05
413	Kenny Rogers	.05
414	Bill Pecota	.05
415	Dave Fleming	.05
416	Luis Alicea	.05
417	Paul Quantrill	.05
418	Damion Easley	.05
419	Wes Chamberlain	.05
420	Harold Baines	.05
421	Scott Radinsky	.05
422	Rey Sanchez	.05
423	Junior Ortiz	.05
424	Jeff Kent	.05
425	Brian McRae	.05
426	Ed Sprague	.05
427	Tom Edens	.05
428	Willie Greene	.05
429	Bryan Hickerson	.05
430	Dave Winfield	.50
431	Pedro Astacio	.05
432	Mike Gallego	.05
433	Dave Burba	.05
434	Bob Walk	.05
435	Darryl Hamilton	.05
436	Vince Horsman	.05
437	Bob Natal	.05
438	Mike Henneman	.05
439	Willie Blair	.05
440	Denny Martinez	.05
441	Dan Peltier	.05
442	Tony Tarasco	.05
443	John Cummings	.05
444	Geronimo Pena	.05
445	Aaron Sele	.05
446	Stan Javier	.05
447	Mike Williams	.05
448	1B Prospects (Greg Pirkl, Roberto Petagine, D.J. Boston, Shawn Wooten)	.05
449	Jim Poole	.05
450	Carlos Baerga	.05
451	Bob Scanlan	.05
452	Lance Johnson	.05
453	Eric Hillman	.05
454	Keith Miller	.05
455	Dave Stewart	.05
456	Pete Harnisch	.05
457	Roberto Kelly	.05
458	Tim Worrell	.05
459	Pedro Munoz	.05
460	Orel Hershiser	.05
461	Randy Velarde	.05
462	Trevor Wilson	.05
463	Jerry Goff	.05
464	Bill Wegman	.05
465	Dennis Eckersley	.40
466	Jeff Conine (All-Star Rookie)	.05
467	Joe Boever	.05
468	Dante Bichette	.05
469	Jeff Shaw	.05
470	Rafael Palmeiro	.40
471	Phil Leftwich RC	.05
472	Jay Buhner	.05
473	Bob Tewksbury	.05
474	Tim Naehring	.05
475	Tom Glavine	.25
476	Dave Hollins	.05
477	Arthur Rhodes	.05
478	Joey Cora	.05
479	Mike Morgan	.05
480	Albert Belle	.05
481	John Franco	.05
482	Hipolito Pichardo	.05
483	Duane Ward	.05
484	Luis Gonzalez	.05
485	Joe Oliver	.05
486	Wally Whitehurst	.05
487	Mike Benjamin	.05
488	Eric Davis	.05
489	Scott Kamieniecki	.05
490	Kent Hrbek	.05
491	John Hope RC	.05
492	Jesse Orosco	.05
493	Troy Neel	.05
494	Ryan Bowen	.05
495	Mickey Tettleton	.05
496	Chris Jones	.05
497	John Wetteland	.05
498	David Hulse	.05
499	Greg Maddux	.60
500	Bo Jackson	.10
501	Donovan Osborne	.05
502	Mike Greenwell	.05
503	Steve Frey	.05
504	Jim Eisenreich	.05
505	Robby Thompson	.05
506	Leo Gomez	.05
507	Dave Staton	.05
508	Wayne Kirby (All-Star Rookie)	.05
509	Tim Bogar	.05
510	David Cone	.05
511	Devon White	.05
512	Xavier Hernandez	.05
513	Tim Costo	.05
514	Gene Harris	.05
515	Jack McDowell	.05
516	Kevin Gross	.05
517	Scott Leius	.05
518	Lloyd McClendon	.05
519	Alex Diaz RC	.05
520	Wade Boggs	.60
521	Bob Welch	.05
522	Henry Cotto	.05
523	Mike Moore	.05
524	Tim Laker	.05
525	Andres Galarraga	.05
526	Jamie Moyer	.05
527	2B Prospects (Norberto Martin, Ruben Santana, Jason Hardtke, Chris Sexton)	.05
528	Sid Bream	.05
529	Erik Hanson	.05
530	Ray Lankford	.05
531	Rob Deer	.05
532	Rod Correia	.05
533	Roger Mason	.05
534	Mike Devereaux	.05
535	Jeff Montgomery	.05
536	Dwight Smith	.05
537	Jeremy Hernandez	.05
538	Ellis Burks	.05
539	Bobby Jones	.05
540	Paul Molitor	.50
541	Jeff Juden	.05
542	Chris Sabo	.05
543	Larry Casian	.05
544	Jeff Gardner	.05
545	Ramon Martinez	.05
546	Paul O'Neill	.05
547	Steve Hosey	.05
548	Dave Nilsson	.05
549	Ron Darling	.05
550	Matt Williams	.05
551	Jack Armstrong	.05
552	Bill Krueger	.05
553	Freddie Benavides	.05
554	Jeff Fassero	.05
555	Chuck Knoblauch	.05
556	Guillermo Velasquez	.05
557	Joel Johnston	.05
558	Tom Lampkin	.05
559	Todd Van Poppel	.05
560	Gary Sheffield	.30
561	Skeeter Barnes	.05
562	Darren Holmes	.05
563	John Vander Wal	.05
564	Mike Ignasiak	.05
565	Fred McGriff	.05
566	Luis Polonia	.05
567	Mike Perez	.05
568	John Valentin	.05
569	Mike Felder	.05
570	Tommy Greene	.05
571	David Segui	.05
572	Roberto Hernandez	.05
573	Steve Wilson	.05
574	Willie McGee	.05
575	Randy Myers	.05
576	Darrin Jackson	.05
577	Eric Plunk	.05
578	Mike MacFarlane	.05
579	Doug Brocail	.05
580	Steve Finley	.05
581	John Roper	.05
582	Danny Cox	.05
583	Chip Hale	.05
584	Scott Bullett	.05
585	Kevin Reimer	.05
586	Brent Gates	.05
587	Matt Turner	.05
588	Rich Rowland	.05
589	Kent Bottenfield	.05
590	Marquis Grissom	.05
591	Doug Strange	.05
592	Jay Howell	.05
593	Omar Vizquel	.05
594	Rheal Cormier	.05
595	Andre Dawson	.25
596	Hilly Hathaway	.05
597	Todd Pratt	.05
598	Mike Mussina	.30
599	Alex Fernandez	.05
600	Don Mattingly	.65
601	Frank Thomas (Measures of Greatness)	.25
602	Ryne Sandberg (Measures of Greatness)	.30
603	Wade Boggs (Measures of Greatness)	.30
604	Cal Ripken, Jr. (Measures of Greatness)	.50
605	Barry Bonds (Measures of Greatness)	.50
606	Ken Griffey Jr. (Measures of Greatness)	.40
607	Kirby Puckett (Measures of Greatness)	.35
608	Darren Daulton (Measures of Greatness)	.05
609	Paul Molitor (Measures of Greatness)	.25
610	Terry Steinbach	.05
611	Todd Worrell	.05
612	Jim Thome	.40
613	Chuck McElroy	.05
614	John Habyan	.05
615	Sid Fernandez	.05
616	OF Prospects (Eddie Zambrano, Glenn Murray, Chad Mottola, Jermaine Allensworth RC)	.05
617	Steve Bedrosian	.05
618	Rob Ducey	.05
619	Tom Browning	.05
620	Tony Gwynn	.60
621	Carl Willis	.05
622	Kevin Young	.05
623	Rafael Novoa	.05
624	Jerry Browne	.05
625	Charlie Hough	.05
626	Chris Gomez	.05
627	Steve Reed	.05
628	Kirk Rueter	.05
629	Matt Whiteside	.05
630	Dave Justice	.05
631	Brad Holman	.05
632	Brian Jordan	.05
633	Scott Bankhead	.05
634	Torey Lovullo	.05
635	Len Dykstra	.05
636	Ben McDonald	.05
637	Steve Howe	.05
638	Jose Vizcaino	.05
639	Bill Swift	.05
640	Darryl Strawberry	.05
641	Steve Farr	.05
642	Tom Kramer	.05
643	Joe Orsulak	.05
644	Tom Henke	.05
645	Joe Carter	.05
646	Ken Caminiti	.05
647	Reggie Sanders	.05
648	Andy Ashby	.05
649	Derek Parks	.05
650	Andy Van Slyke	.05
651	Juan Bell	.05
652	Roger Smithberg	.05
653	Chuck Carr	.05
654	Bill Gullickson	.05
655	Charlie Hayes	.05
656	Chris Nabholz	.05
657	Karl Rhodes	.05
658	Pete Smith	.05
659	Bret Boone	.05
660	Gregg Jefferies	.05
661	Bob Zupcic	.05
662	Steve Sax	.05
663	Mariano Duncan	.05
664	Jeff Tackett	.05
665	Mark Langston	.05
666	Steve Buechele	.05
667	Candy Maldonado	.05
668	Woody Williams	.05
669	Tim Wakefield	.05
670	Danny Tartabull	.05
671	Charlie O'Brien	.05
672	Felix Jose	.05
673	Bobby Ayala	.05
674	Scott Servais	.05
675	Roberto Alomar	.15
676	Pedro Martinez	.05
677	Eddie Guardado	.05
678	Mark Lewis	.05
679	Jaime Navarro	.05
680	Ruben Sierra	.05
681	Rick Renteria	.05
682	Storm Davis	.05
683	Cory Snyder	.05
684	Ron Karkovice	.05
685	Juan Gonzalez	.25
686	C Prospects (Chris Howard, Carlos Delgado, Jason Kendall, Paul Bako)	.40
687	John Smoltz	.05
688	Brian Dorsett	.05
689	Omar Olivares	.05
690	Mo Vaughn	.05
691	Joe Grahe	.05
692	Mickey Morandini	.05
693	Tino Martinez	.05
694	Brian Barnes	.05
695	Mike Stanley	.05
696	Mark Clark	.05
697	Dave Hansen	.05
698	Willie Wilson	.05
699	Pete Schourek	.05
700	Barry Bonds	1.00
701	Kevin Appier	.05
702	Tony Fernandez	.05
703	Darryl Kile	.05
704	Archi Cianfrocco	.05
705	Jose Rijo	.05
706	Brian Harper	.05
707	Zane Smith	.05
708	Dave Henderson	.05
709	Angel Miranda	.05
710	Orestes Destrade	.05
711	Greg Gohr	.05
712	Eric Young	.05
713	P Prospects (Todd Williams, Ron Watson, Kirk Bullinger, Mike Welch)	.05
714	Tim Spehr	.05
715	Hank Aaron (20th Anniversary #715)	.50
716	Nate Minchey	.05
717	Mike Blowers	.05
718	Kent Mercker	.05
719	Tom Pagnozzi	.05
720	Roger Clemens	.65
721	Eduardo Perez	.05
722	Milt Thompson	.05
723	Gregg Olson	.05
724	Kirk McCaskill	.05
725	Sammy Sosa	.60
726	Alvaro Espinoza	.05
727	Henry Rodriguez	.05
728	Jim Leyritz	.05
729	Steve Scarsone	.05
730	Bobby Bonilla	.05
731	Chris Gwynn	.05
732	Al Leiter	.05
733	Bip Roberts	.05
734	Mark Portugal	.05
735	Terry Pendleton	.05
736	Dave Valle	.05
737	Paul Kilgus	.05
738	Greg Harris	.05
739	Jon Ratliff RC (Draft Pick)	.05
740	Kirk Presley RC (Draft Pick)	.05
741	Josue Estrada RC (Draft Pick)	.05
742	Wayne Gomes RC (Draft Pick)	.10
743	Pat Watkins RC (Draft Pick)	.05
744	Jamey Wright RC (Draft Pick)	.05
745	Jay Powell RC (Draft Pick)	.05
746	Ryan McGuire RC (Draft Pick)	.05
747	Marc Barcelo RC (Draft Pick)	.05
748	Sloan Smith RC (Draft Pick)	.05
749	John Wasdin RC (Draft Pick)	.05
750	Marc Valdes (Draft Pick)	.05
751	Dan Ehler RC (Draft Pick)	.05
752	Andre King RC (Draft Pick)	.05
753	Greg Keagle RC (Draft Pick)	.05
754	Jason Myers RC (Draft Pick)	.05
755	Dax Winslett RC (Draft Pick)	.05
756	Casey Whitten RC (Draft Pick)	.05
757	Tony Fuduric RC (Draft Pick)	.05
758	Greg Norton RC (Draft Pick)	.05
759	Jeff D'Amico RC (Draft Pick)	.05
760	Ryan Hancock RC (Draft Pick)	.05
761	David Cooper RC (Draft Pick)	.05
762	Kevin Orie RC (Draft Pick)	.05
763	John O'Donoghue, Mike Oquist (Coming Attractions)	.05
764	Cory Bailey, Scott Hatteberg (Coming Attractions)	.05
765	Mark Holzemer, Paul Swingle (Coming Attractions)	.05
766	James Baldwin, Rod Bolton (Coming Attractions)	.05
767	Jerry DiPoto RC, Julian Tavarez RC (Coming Attractions)	.10
768	Danny Bautista, Sean Bergman (Coming Attractions)	.05
769	Bob Hamelin, Joe Vitiello (Coming Attractions)	.05
770	Mark Kiefer, Troy O'Leary (Coming Attractions)	.05
771	Denny Hocking, Oscar Munoz (Coming Attractions)	.05
772	Russ Davis, Brien Taylor (Coming Attractions)	.05
773	Kurt Abbott, Miguel Jimenez (Coming Attractions)	.05
774	Kevin King, Eric Plantenberg (Coming Attractions)	.05
775	Jon Shave, Desi Wilson (Coming Attractions)	.05
776	Domingo Cedeno, Paul Spoljaric (Coming Attractions)	.05
777	Chipper Jones, Ryan Klesko (Coming Attractions)	.75
778	Steve Trachsel, Turk Wendell (Coming Attractions)	.05
779	Johnny Ruffin, Jerry Spradlin (Coming Attractions)	.05
780	Jason Bates, John Burke (Coming Attractions)	.05
781	Carl Everett, Dave Weathers (Coming Attractions)	.05
782	Gary Mota, James Mouton (Coming Attractions)	.05
783	Raul Mondesi, Ben Van Ryn (Coming Attractions)	.05
784	Gabe White, Rondell White (Coming Attractions)	.05
785	Brook Fordyce, Bill Pulsipher (Coming Attractions)	.05
786	Kevin Foster, Gene Schall (Coming Attractions)	.05
787	Rich Aude, Midre Cummings (Coming Attractions)	.05
788	Brian Barber, Richard Batchelor (Coming Attractions)	.05
789	Brian Johnson RC, Scott Sanders (Coming Attractions)	.05
790	Rikkert Faneyte, J.R. Phillips (Coming Attractions)	.05
791	Checklist 3	.05
792	Checklist 4	.05

Gold

This premium parallel set was issued as inserts in virtually all forms of Topps packaging. Identical in all other ways to the regular Topps cards, the Gold version replaces the white or black Topps logo on front with a gold-foil "Topps Gold" logo, and prints either the player name or card title in gold foil. The four checklist cards from the regular issue are replaced with cards of players not found in the regular Topps set.

	NM/M
Complete Set (792):	50.00
Common Player:	.15

Black Gold

Black Gold inserts returned for 1994 randomly included in all types of Topps packaging. Single cards, as well as cards redeemable by mail for 11, 22 or 44 Black Gold cards, were produced. The basic single-player card features an action photo, the background of which has been almost completely blacked out. At top is the team name in black letters against a gold prismatic foil background. The player name at bottom is in the same gold foil. On back, bordered in white, is a background which fades from black at top to gray at the bottom and is gridded with white lines. At left is another player action photo. The Topps Black Gold logo and player name appear in gold foil; the latter printed on a simulated wooden board "hanging" from the top of the card. A second hanging plank has player stats and rankings from the 1993 season. The multi-card redemption cards come in two versions. The type found in packs has all 11, 22 or 44 of the cards pictured on front in miniature and redemption details printed on back. A second version, returned with the single cards won, has on back a checklist and non-redemption notice. Stated odds of winning Black Gold cards were one in 72 packs for single cards; one in 180 packs for 11-card winners and one in 720 packs (one per foil-pack case) for a 22-card winner.

	NM/M
Complete Set (44):	10.00
Complete Series 1 (22):	6.00
Complete Series 2 (22):	4.00
Common Player:	.10
1 Roberto Alomar	.20
2 Carlos Baerga	.10
3 Albert Belle	.10
4 Joe Carter	.10
5 Cecil Fielder	.10
6 Travis Fryman	.10
7 Juan Gonzalez	.25
8 Ken Griffey Jr.	.75
9 Chris Hoiles	.10
10 Randy Johnson	.45
11 Kenny Lofton	.10
12 Jack McDowell	.10
13 Paul Molitor	.45
14 Jeff Montgomery	.10
15 John Olerud	.10
16 Rafael Palmeiro	.60
17 Kirby Puckett	.60
18 Cal Ripken, Jr.	1.50
19 Tim Salmon	.10
20 Mike Stanley	.10
21 Frank Thomas	.50
22 Robin Ventura	.10
23 Jeff Bagwell	.45
24 Jay Bell	.10
25 Craig Biggio	.10
26 Jeff Blauser	.10
27 Barry Bonds	1.50
28 Darren Daulton	.10
29 Len Dykstra	.10
30 Andres Galarraga	.10
31 Ron Gant	.10
32 Tom Glavine	.10
33 Mark Grace	.10
34 Marquis Grissom	.10
35 Gregg Jefferies	.10
36 Dave Justice	.10
37 John Kruk	.10
38 Greg Maddux	.60
39 Fred McGriff	.10
40 Randy Myers	.10
41 Mike Piazza	1.00
42 Sammy Sosa	.60
43 Robby Thompson	.10
44 Matt Williams	.10
--- Winner A	.50
--- Winner B	.50
--- Winner C	.50
--- Winner D	.50
--- Winner A/B	.60
--- Winner C/D	.60
--- Winner A/B/C/D	.75

Traded

Topps Traded features top prospects and rookies as well as traded veterans. Also included in the boxed set is an eight-card Topps Finest subset of six MVPs and two Rookie of the Year cards. Regular cards have the same design as the previously released '94 Topps set. "Anatomy of a Trade" is a two-card subset that includes Roberto Kelly/Deion Sanders and

Pedro Martinez/Delino DeShields on a split, puzzle-like front. There is also a Prospect card, showcasing a top prospect from AAA, AA and A, as well as a top-rated draft pick. In addition, there are 12 Draft Pick cards included in the Traded set. Finally, two cards pay tribute to Ryne Sandberg, one in a Phillies uniform, one with the Cubs.

	NM/M
Complete Set (140):	25.00
Common Player:	.05
1 Paul Wilson (Draft Pick)	.05
2 Bill Taylor	.05
3 Dan Wilson	.05
4 Mark Smith	.05
5 Toby Borland	.05
6 Dave Clark	.05
7 Denny Martinez	.05
8 Dave Gallagher	.05
9 Josias Manzanillo	.05
10 Brian Anderson	.05
11 Damon Berryhill	.05
12 Alex Cole	.05
13 Jacob Shumate (Draft Pick)	.05
14 Oddibe McDowell	.05
15 Willie Banks	.05
16 Jerry Browne	.05
17 Donnie Elliott	.05
18 Ellis Burks	.05
19 Chuck McElroy	.05
20 Luis Polonia	.05
21 Brian Harper	.05
22 Mark Portugal	.05
23 Dave Henderson	.05
24 Mark Acre	.05
25 Julio Franco	.05
26 Darren Hall	.05
27 Eric Anthony	.05
28 Sid Fernandez	.05
29 Rusty Greer RC	.25
30 Riccardo Ingram	.05
31 Gabe White	.05
32 Tim Belcher	.05
33 Terrence Long RC (Draft Pick)	.50
34 Mark Dalesandro RC	.05
35 Mike Kelly	.05
36 Jack Morris	.05
37 Jeff Brantley	.05
38 Larry Barnes RC (Draft Pick)	.05
39 Brian Hunter	.05
40 Otis Nixon	.05
41 Bret Wagner (Draft Pick)	.05
42 Anatomy of a Trade (Pedro Martinez, Delino DeShields)	.25
43 Heathcliff Slocumb	.05
44 Ben Grieve RC (Draft Pick)	.25
45 John Hudek	.05
46 Shawon Dunston	.05
47 Greg Colbrunn	.05
48 Joey Hamilton	.05
49 Marvin Freeman	.05
50 Terry Mulholland	.05
51 Keith Mitchell	.05
52 Dwight Smith	.05
53 Shawn Boskie	.05
54 Kevin Witt RC (Draft Pick)	.05
55 Ron Gant	.05
56 1994 Prospects (Trenidad Hubbard, Jason Schmidt RC, Larry Sutton, Stephen Larkin RC)	3.00
57 Jody Reed	.05
58 Rick Helling	.05
59 John Powell (Draft Pick)	.05
60 Eddie Murray	.60
61 Joe Hall	.05
62 Jorge Fabregas	.05
63 Mike Mordecai	.05
64 Ed Vosberg	.05
65 Rickey Henderson	.60
66 Tim Grieve (Draft Pick)	.05
67 Jon Lieber	.05
68 Chris Howard	.05
69 Matt Walbeck	.05
70 Chan Ho Park	.05
71 Bryan Eversgerd	.05
72 John Dettmer	.05
73 Erik Hanson	.05
74 Mike Thurman (Draft Pick)	.05

75 Bobby Ayala	.05
76 Rafael Palmeiro	.50
77 Bret Boone	.05
78 Paul Shuey (Future Star)	.05
79 Kevin Foster	.05
80 Dave Magadan	.05
81 Bip Roberts	.05
82 Howard Johnson	.05
83 Xavier Hernandez	.05
84 Ross Powell	.05
85 Doug Million RC (Draft Pick)	.05
86 Geronimo Berroa	.05
87 Mark Farris RC (Draft Pick)	.05
88 Butch Henry	.05
89 Junior Felix	.05
90 Bo Jackson	.25
91 Hector Carrasco	.05
92 Charlie O'Brien	.05
93 Omar Vizquel	.05
94 David Segui	.05
95 Dustin Hermanson (Draft Pick)	.05
96 Gar Finnvold	.05
97 Dave Stevens	.05
98 Corey Pointer (Draft Pick)	.05
99 Felix Fermin	.05
100 Lee Smith	.05
101 Reid Ryan (Draft Pick)	.15
102 Bobby Munoz	.05
103 Anatomy of a Trade (Deion Sanders, Roberto Kelly)	.05
104 Turner Ward	.05
105 William Van Landingham	.05
106 Vince Coleman	.05
107 Stan Javier	.05
108 Darrin Jackson	.05
109 C.J. Nitkowski (Draft Pick)	.05
110 Anthony Young	.05
111 Kurt Miller	.05
112 Paul Konerko RC (Draft Pick)	15.00
113 Walt Weiss	.05
114 Daryl Boston	.05
115 Will Clark	.05
116 Matt Smith RC (Draft Pick)	.05
117 Mark Leiter	.05
118 Gregg Olson	.05
119 Tony Pena	.05
120 Jose Vizcaino	.05
121 Rick White	.05
122 Rich Rowland	.05
123 Jeff Reboulet	.05
124 Greg Hibbard	.05
125 Chris Sabo	.05
126 Doug Jones	.05
127 Tony Fernandez	.05
128 Carlos Reyes	.05
129 Kevin Brown (Draft Pick)	.05
130 Commemorative (Ryne Sandberg)	1.00
131 Commemorative (Ryne Sandberg)	1.00
132 Checklist 1-132	.05

Traded Finest Inserts

Eight Finest cards were included in the 1994 Topps Traded set. Cards picture the player on a blue and gold background. Either Rookie of the Year or MVP is printed across the bottom opposite the player's name, indicating the player's candidacy for such an award in 1994. Backs offer a portrait photo, stats through the All-Star break and comments on the player's season to that point.

	NM/M
Complete Set (8):	6.00
Common Player:	.25
1 Greg Maddux	1.50
2 Mike Piazza	2.00
3 Matt Williams	.25
4 Raul Mondesi	.25
5 Ken Griffey Jr.	2.00
6 Kenny Lofton	.25
7 Frank Thomas	1.25
8 Manny Ramirez	1.00

Bilingual

Produced in a limited edition said to be 5,000 sets, this issue is a close parallel to the regular 1994

Topps baseball card issue. Each card is virtually identical to the regular Topps card except that backs are printed in English and Spanish. The set was test marketed in areas with a high percentage of Hispanic population and was also sold through Topps' Stadium Club. The bilingual edition was sold only in factory set form. A special feature of the set was the inclusion of 10 "Topps Leyendas/Legends" cards of former Latin stars.

	NM/M
Factory Set (792+10):	225.00
Common Player:	.50
1 Felipe Alou	3.00
2 Ruben Amaro	1.00
3 Luis Aparicio	7.50
4 Rod Carew	7.50
5 Chico Carrasquel	1.50
6 Orlando Cepeda	7.50
7 Juan Marichal	7.50
8 Minnie Minoso	6.00
9 Cookie Rojas	1.00
10 Luis Tiant	2.00

"1954" Archives

Marketed as "The Ultimate 1954 Series," the Archives set was a virtual reproduction of the popular 1954 Topps issue. Of the 250 cards in the original set, 248 were included in the Archives release. Ted Williams, who was on cards #1 and 250 in the '54 set, was contractually prohibited by Upper Deck from appearing in the Archives issue. Eight "1954 Prospect" cards featuring future Hall of Famers and star players were appended to the reproduction cards to create a 256-card Archives issue. Cards were sold in 12-card packs, with one Gold card in each pack. There were 1,954 personally autographed cards of Henry Aaron inserted at random, along with cards that could be redeemed for genuine 1954 Topps cards and complete sets of Gold Archives cards. The Archives cards were produced in the now-standard 2-1/2" x 3-1/2" size, instead of the original 1954 dimensions of 2-5/8" x 3-3/4". That format allowed the Archives cards to have a white border at top which the originals lack. While the card backs identify the Archives issue, they do not specify a 1994 production date anywhere.

	NM/M
Complete Set (256):	90.00
Common Player:	.25
Wax Pack (12):	4.00
Wax Box (24):	65.00
2 Gus Zernial	.25
3 Monte Irvin	.75
4 Hank Sauer	.25
5 Ed Lopat	.25
6 Pete Runnels	.25
7 Ted Kluszewski	.60

8 Bobby Young	.25
9 Harvey Haddix	.25
10 Jackie Robinson	4.50
11 Paul Smith	.25
12 Del Crandall	.25
13 Billy Martin	.60
14 Preacher Roe	.40
15 Al Rosen	.25
16 Vic Janowicz	.25
17 Phil Rizzuto	1.00
18 Walt Dropo	.25
19 Johnny Lipon	.25
20 Warren Spahn	.75
21 Bobby Shantz	.25
22 Jim Greengrass	.25
23 Luke Easter	.25
24 Granny Hamner	.25
25 Harvey Kuenn	.25
26 Ray Jablonski	.25
27 Ferris Fain	.25
28 Paul Minner	.25
29 Jim Hegan	.25
30 Eddie Mathews	.75
31 Johnny Klippstein	.25
32 Duke Snider	1.50
33 Johnny Schmitz	.25
34 Jim Rivera	.25
35 Junior Gilliam	.40
36 Hoyt Wilhelm	.75
37 Whitey Ford	1.25
38 Eddie Stanky	.25
39 Sherman Lollar	.25
40 Mel Parnell	.25
41 Willie Jones	.25
42 Don Mueller	.25
43 Dick Groat	.25
44 Ned Garver	.25
45 Richie Ashburn	.75
46 Ken Raffensberger	.25
47 Ellis Kinder	.25
48 Billy Hunter	.25
49 Ray Murray	.25
50 Yogi Berra	1.50
51 Johnny Lindell	.25
52 Vic Power	.25
53 Jack Dittmer	.25
54 Vern Stephens	.25
55 Phil Cavarretta	.25
56 Willie Miranda	.40
57 Luis Aloma	.25
58 Bob Wilson	.25
59 Gene Conley	.25
60 Frank Baumholtz	.25
61 Bob Cain	.25
62 Eddie Robinson	.40
63 Johnny Pesky	.25
64 Hank Thompson	.25
65 Bob Swift	.25
66 Ted Lepcio	.25
67 Jim Willis	.25
68 Sam Calderone	.25
69 Bud Podbielan	.25
70 Larry Doby	.75
71 Frank Smith	.25
72 Preston Ward	.25
73 Wayne Terwilliger	.25
74 Bill Taylor	.25
75 Fred Haney	.25
76 Bob Scheffing	.25
77 Ray Boone	.25
78 Ted Kazanski	.25
79 Andy Pafko	.25
80 Jackie Jensen	.25
81 Dave Hoskins	.25
82 Milt Bolling	.25
83 Joe Collins	.40
84 Dick Cole	.25
85 Bob Turley	.75
86 Billy Herman	.25
87 Roy Face	.25
88 Matt Batts	.25
89 Howie Pollet	.25
90 Willie Mays	4.50
91 Bob Oldis	.25
92 Wally Westlake	.25
93 Sid Hudson	.25
94 Ernie Banks	4.50
95 Hal Rice	.25
96 Charlie Silvera	.40
97 Jerry Lane	.25
98 Joe Black	.25
99 Bob Hofman	.25
100 Bob Keegan	.25
101 Gene Woodling	.40
102 Gil Hodges	1.25
103 Jim Lemon	.25
104 Mike Sandlock	.25
105 Andy Carey	.40
106 Dick Kokos	.25
107 Duane Pillette	.25
108 Thornton Kipper	.25
109 Bill Bruton	.25
110 Harry Dorish	.25
111 Jim Delsing	.25
112 Bill Renna	.25
113 Bob Boyd	.25
114 Dean Stone	.25
115 "Rip" Repulski	.25
116 Steve Bilko	.25
117 Solly Hemus	.25
118 Carl Scheib	.25
119 Johnny Antonelli	.25
120 Roy McMillan	.25
121 Clem Labine	.25
122 Johnny Logan	.25
123 Bobby Adams	.25
124 Marion Fricano	.25
125 Harry Perkowski	.25

126 Ben Wade	.25
127 Steve O'Neill	.25
128 Hank Aaron	7.50
129 Forrest Jacobs	.25
130 Hank Bauer	.75
131 Reno Bertoia	.25
132 Tom Lasorda	3.00
133 Del Baker	.25
134 Cal Hogue	.25
135 Joe Presko	.25
136 Connie Ryan	.25
137 Wally Moon	.25
138 Bob Borkowski	.25
139 Ed & Johnny O'Brien	.60
140 Tom Wright	.25
141 Joe Jay	.25
142 Tom Poholsky	.25
143 Rollie Hemsley	.25
144 Bill Werle	.25
145 Elmer Valo	.25
146 Don Johnson	.25
147 John Riddle	.25
148 Bob Trice	.25
149 Jim Robertson	.25
150 Dick Kryhoski	.25
151 Alex Grammas	.25
152 Mike Blyzka	.25
153 Rube Walker	.25
154 Mike Fornieles	.25
155 Bob Kennedy	.25
156 Joe Coleman	.25
157 Don Lenhardt	.25
158 Peanuts Lowrey	.25
159 Dave Philley	.25
160 Red Kress	.25
161 John Hetki	.25
162 Herman Wehmeier	.25
163 Frank House	.25
164 Stu Miller	.25
165 Jim Pendleton	.25
166 Johnny Podres	.40
167 Don Lund	.25
168 Morrie Martin	.25
169 Jim Hughes	.25
170 Dusty Rhodes	.25
171 Leo Kiely	.25
172 Hal Brown	.25
173 Jack Harshman	.25
174 Tom Qualters	.25
175 Frank Leja	.40
176 Bob Keely	.25
177 Bob Milliken	.25
178 Bill Glynn	.25
179 Gair Allie	.25
180 Wes Westrum	.25
181 Mel Roach	.25
182 Chuck Harmon	.25
183 Earle Combs	.25
184 Ed Bailey	.25
185 Chuck Stobbs	.25
186 Karl Olson	.25
187 Heinie Manush	.25
188 Dave Jolly	.25
189 Bob Ross	.25
190 Ray Herbert	.25
191 Dick Schofield	.25
192 Cot Deal	.25
193 Johnny Hopp	.25
194 Bill Sarni	.25
195 Bill Consolo	.25
196 Stan Jok	.25
197 Schoolboy Rowe	.25
198 Carl Sawatski	.25
199 Rocky Nelson	.25
200 Larry Jansen	.25
201 Al Kaline	4.50
202 Bob Purkey	.25
203 Harry Brecheen	.25
204 Angel Scull	.25
205 Johnny Sain	.40
206 Ray Crone	.25
207 Tom Oliver	.25
208 Grady Hatton	.25
209 Charlie Thompson	.25
210 Bob Buhl	.25
211 Don Hoak	.25
212 Mickey Micelotta	.25
213 John Fitzpatrick	.25
214 Arnold Portocarrero	.25
215 Ed McGhee	.25
216 Al Sima	.25
217 Paul Schreiber	.25
218 Fred Marsh	.25
219 Charlie Kress	.25
220 Ruben Gomez	.25
221 Dick Brodowski	.25
222 Bill Wilson	.25
223 Joe Haynes	.25
224 Dick Weik	.25
225 Don Liddle	.25
226 Jehosie Heard	.25
227 Buster Mills	.25
228 Gene Hermanski	.25
229 Bob Talbot	.25
230 Bob Kuzava	.40
231 Roy Smalley	.25
232 Lou Limmer	.25
233 Augie Galan	.25
234 Jerry Lynch	.25
235 Vern Law	.25
236 Paul Penson	.25
237 Mike Ryba	.25
238 Al Aber	.25
239 Bill Skowron	.25
240 Sam Mele	.25
241 Bob Miller	.25
242 Curt Roberts	.25
243 Ray Blades	.25

244	Leroy Wheat	.25
245	Roy Sievers	.25
246	Howie Fox	.25
247	Eddie Mayo	.25
248	Al Smith	.25
249	Wilmer Mizell	.25
251	Roberto Clemente	7.50
252	Bob Grim	.40
253	Elston Howard	.75
254	Harmon Killebrew	1.25
255	Camilo Pascual	.25
256	Herb Score	.25
257	Bill Virdon	.25
258	Don Zimmer	.50

"1954" Archives Gold

WILLIE MAYS
outfield NEW YORK GIANTS

Issued as a premium insert at the rate of one per foil pack, gold versions of each of the cards in the 1954 Archives set differ from the regular cards only in that the team logo at top and player facsimile autograph on bottom are printed in gold foil. Redemption cards for complete Archives gold sets were also randomly inserted into Archives packs.

	NM/M
Complete Set (256):	150.00
Common Player:	.45
128 Hank Aaron/Auto.	125.00

1995 Topps Pre-Production

The "Baker's Dozen" version of Topps' 1994 factory baseball card set includes a 10-card pre-production sample of the company's 1995 issue. The sample features nine regular-issue cards and one of them in its Spectralite foil-printed version, as used on the Cyberstats insert cards. Cards are virtually identical to the regular '95 Topps except the backs have a "PP" prefix to the card number and "PRE-PRODUCTION SAMPLE" instead of 1994 season stats.

		NM/M
Complete Set (9):		6.00
Complete Set, Cyberstats (9):		20.00
1	Larry Walker	.50
1	Larry Walker (Spectralite)	1.50
2	Mike Piazza	2.50
2	Mike Piazza (Spectralite)	7.50
3	Greg Vaughn	.50
3	Greg Vaughn (Spectralite)	1.50
4	Sandy Alomar Jr.	.50
4	Sandy Alomar Jr. (Spectralite)	1.50
5	Travis Fryman	.50
5	Travis Fryman (Spectralite)	1.50
6	Ken Griffey Jr.	2.50
6	Ken Griffey Jr. (Spectralite)	7.50
7	Mike Devereaux	.50
7	Mike Devereaux (Spectralite)	1.50
8	Roberto Hernandez	.50
8	Roberto Hernandez (Spectralite)	1.50
9	Alex Fernandez	.50
9	Alex Fernandez (Spectralite)	1.50

1995 Topps

P–CHICAGO WHITE SOX

Topps 1995 baseball arrived offering Cyberstats, which projected full-season statistics for the strike shortened year, as well as League Leaders and Stadium Club First Day Issue pre-production inserts. Series 1 comprises 396 cards, including subsets of Draft Picks, Star Tracks, a Babe Ruth commemorative card and the Topps All-Stars, featuring two players per card at each position. Regular cards have a ragged white border around the player photo, with his name in gold foil under the picture. Series 2 concluded the Cyberstats inserts and added 264 cards to the regular set. Subsets in Series 2 include a continuation of the Draft Picks as well as two-player On Deck cards and four-player Prospects cards, arranged by position. Besides the 660 base cards, hobby-version factory sets include 10 Stadium Club 1st Day previews and seven Cyberstat Season in Review cards. Two versions of the retail factory sets were made. One has 660 regular cards, 20 Cyberstats parallels and four League Leader inserts. The other has the base set of 660 plus 10 Opening Day cards and seven Cyberstat Season in Review.

		NM/M
Unopened Hobby Set (677):		100.00
Unopened Retail Set (684):		75.00
Unopened Retail Set (677):		85.00
Complete Set (660):		45.00
Common Player:		.05
Series 1 or 2 Pack (15):		1.25
Series 1 or 2 Wax Box (36):		25.00
1	Frank Thomas	.75
2	Mickey Morandini	.05
3a	Babe Ruth (100th Birthday, no gold "Topps" logo)	2.00
3b	Babe Ruth (100th Birthday, gold "Topps" logo)	2.00
4	Scott Cooper	.05
5	David Cone	.05
6	Jacob Shumate (Draft Pick)	.05
7	Trevor Hoffman	.05
8	Shane Mack	.05
9	Delino DeShields	.05
10	Matt Williams	.05
11	Sammy Sosa	1.00
12	Gary DiSarcina	.05
13	Kenny Rogers	.05
14	Jose Vizcaino	.05
15	Lou Whitaker	.05
16	Ron Darling	.05
17	Dave Nilsson	.05
18	Chris Hammond	.05
19	Sid Bream	.05
20	Denny Martinez	.05
21	Orlando Merced	.05
22	John Wetteland	.05
23	Mike Devereaux	.05
24	Rene Arocha	.05
25	Jay Buhner	.05
26	Darren Holmes	.05
27	Hal Morris	.05
28	Brian Buchanan RC (Draft Pick)	.10
29	Keith Miller	.05
30	Paul Molitor	.75
31	Dave West	.05
32	Tony Tarasco	.05
33	Scott Sanders	.05
34	Eddie Zambrano	.05
35	Ricky Bones	.05
36	John Valentin	.05
37	Kevin Tapani	.05
38	Tim Wallach	.05
39	Darren Lewis	.05
40	Travis Fryman	.05
41	Mark Leiter	.05
42	Jose Bautista	.05
43	Pete Smith	.05
44	Bret Barberie	.05
45	Dennis Eckersley	.65

46	Ken Hill	.05
47	Chad Ogea (Star Track)	.05
48	Pete Harnisch	.05
49	James Baldwin (Future Star)	.05
50	Mike Mussina	.45
51	Al Martin	.05
52	Mark Thompson (Star Track)	.05
53	Matt Smith (Draft Pick)	.05
54	Joey Hamilton (All-Star Rookie)	.05
55	Edgar Martinez	.05
56	John Smiley	.05
57	Rey Sanchez	.05
58	Mike Timlin	.05
59	Ricky Bottalico (Star Track)	.05
60	Jim Abbott	.05
61	Mike Kelly	.05
62	Brian Jordan	.05
63	Ken Ryan	.05
64	Matt Mieske	.05
65	Rick Aguilera	.05
66	Ismael Valdes	.05
67	Royce Clayton	.05
68	Junior Felix	.05
69	Harold Reynolds	.05
70	Juan Gonzalez	.35
71	Kelly Stinnett	.05
72	Carlos Reyes	.05
73	Dave Weathers	.05
74	Mel Rojas	.05
75	Doug Drabek	.05
76	Charles Nagy	.05
77	Tim Raines	.05
78	Midre Cummings	.05
79	1B Prospects (Gene Schall, Scott Talanoa RC, Harold Williams RC, Ray Brown RC)	.05
80	Rafael Palmeiro	.65
81	Charlie Hayes	.05
82	Ray Lankford	.05
83	Tim Davis	.05
84	C.J. Nitkowski RC (Draft Pick)	.05
85	Andy Ashby	.05
86	Gerald Williams	.05
87	Terry Shumpert	.05
88	Heathcliff Slocumb	.05
89	Domingo Cedeno	.05
90	Mark Grace	.05
91	Brad Woodall RC (Star Track)	.10
92	Gar Finnvold	.05
93	Jaime Navarro	.05
94	Carlos Hernandez	.05
95	Mark Langston	.05
96	Chuck Carr	.05
97	Mike Gardiner	.05
98	David McCarty	.05
99	Cris Carpenter	.05
100	Barry Bonds	2.00
101	David Segui	.05
102	Scott Brosius	.05
103	Mariano Duncan	.05
104	Kenny Lofton	.05
105	Ken Caminiti	.05
106	Darrin Jackson	.05
107	Jim Poole	.05
108	Wil Cordero	.05
109	Danny Miceli	.05
110	Walt Weiss	.05
111	Tom Pagnozzi	.05
112	Terrence Long (Draft Pick)	.05
113	Bret Boone	.05
114	Daryl Boston	.05
115	Wally Joyner	.05
116	Rob Butler	.05
117	Rafael Belliard	.05
118	Luis Lopez	.05
119	Tony Fossas	.05
120	Len Dykstra	.05
121	Mike Morgan	.05
122	Denny Hocking	.05
123	Kevin Gross	.05
124	Todd Benzinger	.05
125	John Doherty	.05
126	Eduardo Perez	.05
127	Dan Smith	.05
128	Joe Orsulak	.05
129	Brent Gates	.05
130	Jeff Conine	.05
131	Doug Henry	.05
132	Paul Sorrento	.05
133	Mike Hampton	.05
134	Tim Spehr	.05
135	Julio Franco	.05
136	Mike Dyer	.05
137	Chris Sabo	.05
138	Rheal Cormier	.05
139	Paul Konerko (Draft Pick)	.25
140	Dante Bichette	.05
141	Chuck McElroy	.05
142	Mike Stanley	.05
143	Bob Hamelin (All-Star Rookie)	.05
144	Tommy Greene	.05
145	John Smoltz	.05
146	Ed Sprague	.05
147	Ray McDavid (Star Track)	.05
148	Otis Nixon	.05
149	Turk Wendell	.05
150	Chris James	.05
151	Derek Parks	.05
152	Jose Offerman	.05
153	Tony Clark (Future Star)	.05

154	Chad Curtis	.05
155	Mark Portugal	.05
156	Bill Pulsipher (Future Star)	.05
157	Troy Neel	.05
158	Dave Winfield	.75
159	Bill Wegman	.05
160	Benny Santiago	.05
161	Jose Mesa	.05
162	Luis Gonzalez	.05
163	Alex Fernandez	.05
164	Freddie Benavides	.05
165	Ben McDonald	.05
166	Blas Minor	.05
167	Bret Wagner (Draft Pick)	.05
168	Mac Suzuki (Future Star)	.05
169	Roberto Mejia	.05
170	Wade Boggs	1.00
171	Calvin Reese (Future Star)	.05
173	Hipolito Pichardo	.05
174	Kim Batiste	.05
175	Darren Hall	.05
176	Tom Glavine	.25
177	Phil Plantier	.05
178	Chris Howard	.05
179	Karl Rhodes	.05
	LaTroy Hawkins (Future Star)	.05
180	Raul Mondesi (All-Star Rookie)	.05
181	Jeff Reed	.05
182	Milt Cuyler	.05
183	Jim Edmonds	.05
184	Hector Fajardo	.05
185	Jeff Kent	.05
186	Wilson Alvarez	.05
187	Geronimo Berroa	.05
188	Billy Spiers	.05
189	Derek Lilliquist	.05
190	Craig Biggio	.05
191	Roberto Hernandez	.05
192	Bob Natal	.05
193	Bobby Ayala	.05
194	Travis Miller RC (Draft Pick)	.10
195	Bob Tewksbury	.05
196	Rondell White	.05
197	Steve Cooke	.05
198	Jeff Branson	.05
199	Derek Jeter (Future Star)	2.00
200	Tim Salmon	.05
201	Steve Frey	.05
202	Kent Mercker	.05
203	Randy Johnson	.75
204	Todd Worrell	.05
205	Mo Vaughn	.05
206	Howard Johnson	.05
207	John Wasdin (Future Star)	.05
208	Eddie Williams	.05
209	Tim Belcher	.05
210	Jeff Montgomery	.05
211	Kirt Manwaring	.05
212	Ben Grieve (Draft Pick)	.05
213	Pat Hentgen	.05
214	Shawon Dunston	.05
215	Mike Greenwell	.05
216	Alex Diaz	.05
217	Pat Mahomes	.05
218	Dave Hanson	.05
219	Kevin Rogers	.05
220	Cecil Fielder	.05
221	Andrew Lorraine (Star Track)	.05
222	Jack Armstrong	.05
223	Todd Hundley	.05
224	Mark Acre	.05
225	Darrell Whitmore	.05
226	Randy Milligan	.05
227	Wayne Kirby	.05
228	Darryl Kile	.05
229	Bob Zupcic	.05
230	Jay Bell	.05
231	Dustin Hermanson (Draft Pick)	.05
232	Harold Baines	.05
233	Alan Benes (Future Star)	.05
234	Felix Fermin	.05
235	Ellis Burks	.05
236	Jeff Brantley	.05
237	OF Prospects (Brian Hunter, Jose Malave, Shane Pullen, Karim Garcia RC)	.40
238	Matt Nokes	.05
239	Ben Rivera	.05
240	Joe Carter	.05
241	Jeff Granger (Star Track)	.05
242	Terry Pendleton	.05
243	Melvin Nieves	.05
244	Frank Rodriguez (Future Star)	.05
245	Darryl Hamilton	.05
246	Brooks Kieschnick (Future Star)	.05
247	Todd Hollandsworth (Future Star)	.05
248	Joe Rosselli (Future Star)	.05
249	Bill Gullickson	.05
250	Chuck Knoblauch	.05
251	Kurt Miller (Star Track)	.05
252	Bobby Jones	.05
253	Lance Blankenship	.05
254	Matt Whiteside	.05
255	Darrin Fletcher	.05
256	Eric Plunk	.05
257	Shane Reynolds	.05
258	Norberto Martin	.05
259	Mike Thurman (Draft Pick)	.05
260	Andy Van Slyke	.05
261	Dwight Smith	.05

262	Allen Watson	.05
263	Dan Wilson	.05
264	Brent Mayne	.05
265	Bip Roberts	.05
266	Sterling Hitchcock	.05
267	Alex Gonzalez (Star Track)	.05
268	Greg Harris	.05
269	Ricky Jordan	.05
270	Johnny Ruffin	.05
271	Mike Stanton	.05
272	Rich Rowland	.05
273	Steve Trachsel	.05
274	Pedro Munoz	.05
275	Ramon Martinez	.05
276	Dave Henderson	.05
277	Chris Gomez (All-Star Rookie)	.05
278	Joe Grahe	.05
279	Rusty Greer	.05
280	John Franco	.05
281	Mike Bordick	.05
282	Jeff D'Amico (Future Star)	.05
283	Dave Magadan	.05
284	Tony Pena	.05
285	Greg Swindell	.05
286	Doug Million (Draft Pick)	.05
287	Gabe White (Star Track)	.05
288	Trey Beamon (Future Star)	.05
289	Arthur Rhodes	.05
290	Juan Guzman	.05
291	Jose Oquendo	.05
292	Willie Blair	.05
293	Eddie Taubensee	.05
294	Steve Howe	.05
295	Greg Maddux	1.00
296	Mike MacFarlane	.05
297	Curt Schilling	.25
298	Phil Clark	.05
299	Woody Williams	.05
300	Jose Canseco	.40
301	Aaron Sele	.05
302	Carl Willis	.05
303	Steve Buechele	.05
304	Dave Burba	.05
305	Orel Hershiser	.05
306	Damion Easley	.05
307	Mike Henneman	.05
308	Josias Manzanillo	.05
309	Kevin Seitzer	.05
310	Ruben Sierra	.05
311	Bryan Harvey	.05
312	Jim Thome	.45
313	Ramon Castro RC (Draft Pick)	.05
314	Lance Johnson	.05
315	Marquis Grissom	.05
316	SP Prospects (Terrell Wade, Juan Acevedo, Matt Arrandale, Eddie Priest RC)	.05
317	Paul Wagner	.05
318	Jamie Moyer	.05
319	Todd Zeile	.05
320	Chris Bosio	.05
321	Steve Reed	.05
322	Erik Hanson	.05
323	Luis Polonia	.05
324	Ryan Klesko	.05
325	Kevin Appier	.05
326	Jim Eisenreich	.05
327	Randy Knorr	.05
328	Craig Shipley	.05
329	Tim Naehring	.05
330	Randy Myers	.05
331	Alex Cole	.05
332	Jim Gott	.05
333	Mike Jackson	.05
334	John Flaherty	.05
335	Chili Davis	.05
336	Benji Gil (Star Track)	.05
337a	Jason Jacome (No Diamond Vision logo on back photo.)	.25
337b	Jason Jacome (Diamond Vision logo on back photo.)	.05
338	Stan Javier	.05
339	Mike Fetters	.05
340	Rick Renteria	.05
341	Kevin Witt (Draft Pick)	.05
342	Scott Servais	.05
343	Craig Grebeck	.05
344	Kirk Rueter	.05
345	Don Slaught	.05
346	Armando Benitez RC (Star Track)	.15
347	Ozzie Smith	1.00
348	Mike Blowers	.05
349	Armando Reynoso	.05
350	Barry Larkin	.05
351	Mike Williams	.05
352	Scott Kamieniecki	.05
353	Gary Gaetti	.05
354	Todd Stottlemyre	.05
355	Fred McGriff	.05
356	Tim Mauser	.05
357	Chris Gwynn	.05
358	Frank Castillo	.05
359	Jeff Reboulet	.05
360	Roger Clemens	1.00
361	Mark Carreon	.05
362	Chad Kreuter	.05
363	Mark Farris (Draft Pick)	.05
364	Bob Welch	.05
365	Dean Palmer	.05
366	Jeromy Burnitz	.05
367	B.J. Surhoff	.05
368	Mike Butcher	.05

369	RP Prospects (Brad Clontz, Steve Phoenix, Scott Gentile, Bucky Buckles)	.05
370	Eddie Murray	.75
371	Orlando Miller (Star Track)	.05
372	Ron Karkovice	.05
373	Richie Lewis	.05
374	Lenny Webster	.05
375	Jeff Tackett	.05
376	Tom Urbani	.05
377	Tino Martinez	.05
378	Mark Dewey	.05
379	Charlie O'Brien	.05
380	Terry Mulholland	.05
381	Thomas Howard	.05
382	Chris Haney	.05
383	Billy Hatcher	.05
384	Jeff Bagwell, Frank Thomas/AS	.45
385	Bret Boone, Carlos Baerga/AS	.05
386	Matt Williams, Wade Boggs/AS	.30
387	Wil Cordero, Cal Ripken Jr./AS	1.00
388	Barry Bonds, Ken Griffey Jr./AS	1.00
389	Tony Gwynn, Albert Belle/AS	.50
390	Dante Bichette, Kirby Puckett/AS	.50
391	Mike Piazza, Mike Stanley/AS	.75
392	Greg Maddux, David Cone/AS	.50
393	Danny Jackson, Jimmy Key/AS	.05
394	John Franco, Lee Smith/AS	.05
395	Checklist 1-198	.05
396	Checklist 199-396	.05
397	Ken Griffey Jr.	1.25
398	Rick Heiserman RC (Draft Pick)	.05
399	Don Mattingly	1.00
400	Henry Rodriguez	.05
401	Lenny Harris	.05
402	Ryan Thompson	.05
403	Darren Oliver	.05
404	Omar Vizquel	.05
405	Jeff Bagwell	.75
406	Doug Webb RC (Draft Pick)	.05
407	Todd Van Poppel	.05
408	Leo Gomez	.05
409	Mark Whiten	.05
410	Pedro Martinez	.05
411	Reggie Sanders	.05
412	Kevin Foster	.05
413	Danny Tartabull	.05
414	Jeff Blauser	.05
415	Mike Magnante	.05
416	Tom Candiotti	.05
417	Rod Beck	.05
418	Jody Reed	.05
419	Vince Coleman	.05
420	Danny Jackson	.05
421	Ryan Nye RC (Draft Pick)	.05
422	Larry Walker	.05
423	Russ Johnson (Draft Pick)	.05
424	Pat Borders	.05
425	Lee Smith	.05
426	Paul O'Neill	.05
427	Devon White	.05
428	Jim Bullinger	.05
429	SP Prospects (Greg Hansell, Brian Sackinsky, Carey Paige, Rob Welch)	.05
430	Steve Avery	.05
431	Tony Gwynn	1.00
432	Pat Meares	.05
433	Bill Swift	.05
434	David Wells	.05
435	John Briscoe	.05
436	Roger Pavlik	.05
437	Jayson Peterson RC (Draft Pick)	.05
438	Roberto Alomar	.15
439	Billy Brewer	.05
440	Gary Sheffield	.40
441	Lou Frazier	.05
442	Terry Steinbach	.05
443	Jay Payton RC (Draft Pick)	.25
444	Jason Bere	.05
445	Denny Neagle	.05
446	Andres Galarraga	.05
447	Hector Carrasco	.05
448	Bill Risley	.05
449	Andy Benes	.05
450	Jim Leyritz	.05
451	Jose Oliva	.05
452	Greg Vaughn	.05
453	Rich Monteleone	.05
454	Tony Eusebio	.05
455	Chuck Finley	.05
456	Kevin Brown	.05
457	Joe Boever	.05
458	Bobby Munoz	.05
459	Bret Saberhagen	.05
460	Kurt Abbott	.05
461	Bobby Witt	.05
462	Cliff Floyd	.05
463	Mark Clark	.05
464	Andujar Cedeno	.05
465	Marvin Freeman	.05
466	Mike Piazza	1.25
467	Willie Greene	.05
468	Pat Kelly	.05

#	Player	Price
469	Carlos Delgado	.40
470	Willie Banks	.05
471	Matt Walbeck	.05
472	Mark McGwire	1.50
473	McKay Christensen (Draft Pick)	.05
474	Alan Trammell	.05
475	Tom Gordon	.05
476	Greg Colbrunn	.05
477	Darren Daulton	.05
478	Albie Lopez	.05
479	Robin Ventura	.05
480	C Prospects (Eddie Perez RC, Jason Kendall, Einar Diaz RC, Bret Hemphill)	.20
481	Bryan Eversgerd	.05
482	Dave Fleming	.05
483	Scott Livingstone	.05
484	Pete Schourek	.05
485	Bernie Williams	.05
486	Mark Lemke	.05
487	Eric Karros	.05
488	Scott Ruffcorn	.05
489	Billy Ashley	.05
490	Rico Brogna	.05
491	John Burkett	.05
492	Cade Gaspar RC (Draft Pick)	.05
493	Jorge Fabregas	.05
494	Greg Gagne	.05
495	Doug Jones	.05
496	Troy O'Leary	.05
497	Pat Rapp	.05
498	Butch Henry	.05
499	John Olerud	.05
500	John Hudek	.05
501	Jeff King	.05
502	Bobby Bonilla	.05
503	Albert Belle	.05
504	Rick Wilkins	.05
505	John Jaha	.05
506	Nigel Wilson	.05
507	Sid Fernandez	.05
508	Deion Sanders	.05
509	Gil Heredia	.05
510	Scott Elarton RC (Draft Pick)	.10
511	Melido Perez	.05
512	Greg McMichael	.05
513	Rusty Meacham	.05
514	Shawn Green	.35
515	Carlos Garcia	.05
516	Dave Stevens	.05
517	Eric Young	.05
518	Omar Daal	.05
519	Kirk Gibson	.05
520	Spike Owen	.05
521	Jacob Cruz RC (Draft Pick)	.05
522	Sandy Alomar	.05
523	Steve Bedrosian	.05
524	Ricky Gutierrez	.05
525	Dave Veres	.05
526	Gregg Jefferies	.05
527	Jose Valentin	.05
528	Robb Nen	.05
529	Jose Rijo	.05
530	Sean Berry	.05
531	Mike Gallego	.05
532	Roberto Kelly	.05
533	Kevin Stocker	.05
534	Kirby Puckett	1.00
535	Chipper Jones	1.00
536	Russ Davis	.05
537	Jon Lieber	.05
538	Trey Moore RC (Draft Pick)	.05
539	Joe Girardi	.05
540	2B Prospects (Quilvio Veras, Arquimedez Pozo, Miguel Cairo, Jason Camilli)	.05
541	Tony Phillips	.05
542	Brian Anderson	.05
543	Ivan Rodriguez	.65
544	Jeff Cirillo	.05
545	Joey Cora	.05
546	Chris Hoiles	.05
547	Bernard Gilkey	.05
548	Mike Lansing	.05
549	Jimmy Key	.05
550	Mark Wohlers	.05
551	Chris Clemons RC (Draft Pick)	.05
552	Vinny Castilla	.05
553	Mark Guthrie	.05
554	Mike Lieberthal	.05
555	Tommy Davis RC (Draft Pick)	.05
556	Robby Thompson	.05
557	Danny Bautista	.05
558	Will Clark	.05
559	Rickey Henderson	.75
560	Todd Jones	.05
561	Jack McDowell	.05
562	Carlos Rodriguez	.05
563	Mark Eichhorn	.05
564	Jeff Nelson	.05
565	Eric Anthony	.05
566	Randy Velarde	.05
567	Javy Lopez	.05
568	Kevin Mitchell	.05
569	Steve Karsay	.05
570	Brian Meadows RC (Draft Pick)	.10
571	SS Prospects (Rey Ordonez RC, Mike Metcalfe, Ray Holbert, Kevin Orie)	.40
572	John Kruk	.05
573	Scott Leius	.05
574	John Patterson	.05
575	Kevin Brown	.05
576	Mike Moore	.05
577	Manny Ramirez	.75
578	Jose Lind	.05
579	Derrick May	.05
580	Cal Eldred	.05
581	3B Prospects (David Bell, Joel Chelmis, Lino Diaz, Aaron Boone RC)	.15
582	J.T. Snow	.05
583	Luis Sojo	.05
584	Moises Alou	.05
585	Dave Clark	.05
586	Dave Hollins	.05
587	Nomar Garciaparra (Draft Pick)	2.00
588	Cal Ripken Jr.	2.00
589	Pedro Astacio	.05
590	J.R. Phillips	.05
591	Jeff Frye	.05
592	Bo Jackson	.10
593	Steve Ontiveros	.05
594	David Nied	.05
595	Brad Ausmus	.05
596	Carlos Baerga	.05
597	James Mouton	.05
598	Ozzie Guillen	.05
599	OF Prospects (Ozzie Timmons, Curtis Goodwin, Johnny Damon, Jeff Abbott RC)	.25
600	Yorkis Perez	.05
601	Rich Rodriguez	.05
602	Mark McLemore	.05
603	Jeff Fassero	.05
604	John Roper	.05
605	Mark Johnson RC (Draft Pick)	.10
606	Wes Chamberlain	.05
607	Felix Jose	.05
608	Tony Longmire	.05
609	Duane Ward	.05
610	Brett Butler	.05
611	William Van Landingham	.05
612	Mickey Tettleton	.05
613	Brady Anderson	.05
614	Reggie Jefferson	.05
615	Mike Kingery	.05
616	Derek Bell	.05
617	Scott Erickson	.05
618	Bob Wickman	.05
619	Phil Leftwich	.05
620	Dave Justice	.05
621	Paul Wilson (Draft Pick)	.05
622	Pedro Martinez	.75
623	Terry Mathews	.05
624	Brian McRae	.05
625	Bruce Ruffin	.05
626	Steve Finley	.05
627	Ron Gant	.05
628	Rafael Bournigal	.05
629	Darryl Strawberry	.05
630	Luis Alicea	.05
631	Mark Smith, Scott Klingenbeck (On Deck)	.05
632	Cory Bailey, Scott Hatteberg (On Deck)	.05
633	Todd Greene, Troy Percival (On Deck)	.05
634	Rod Bolton, Olmedo Saenz (On Deck)	.05
635	Herb Perry, Steve Kline (On Deck)	.05
636	Sean Bergman, Shannon Penn (On Deck)	.05
637	Joe Vitiello, Joe Randa (On Deck)	.05
638	Jose Mercedes, Duane Singleton (On Deck)	.05
639	Marty Cordova, Marc Barcelo (On Deck)	.05
640	Ruben Rivera, Andy Pettitte (On Deck)	.05
641	Willie Adams, Scott Spiezio (On Deck)	.05
642	Eddie Diaz, Desi Relaford (On Deck)	.05
643	Jon Shave, Terrell Lowery (On Deck)	.05
644	Paul Spoljaric, Angel Martinez (On Deck)	.05
645	Damon Hollins, Tony Graffanino (On Deck)	.05
646	Darron Cox, Doug Glanville (On Deck)	.05
647	Tim Belk, Pat Watkins (On Deck)	.05
648	Rod Pedraza, Phil Schneider (On Deck)	.05
649	Marc Valdes, Vic Darensbourg (On Deck)	.05
650	Rick Huisman, Roberto Petagine (On Deck)	.05
651	Ron Coomer, Roger Cedeno (On Deck)	.05
652	Carlos Perez RC, Shane Andrews (On Deck)	.10
653	Jason Isringhausen, Chris Roberts (On Deck)	.05
654	Kevin Jordan, Wayne Gomes (On Deck)	.05
655	Esteban Loaiza, Steve Pegues (On Deck)	.05
656	John Frascatore, Terry Bradshaw (On Deck)	.05
657	Bryce Florie, Andres Berumen (On Deck)	.05
658	Keith Williams, Dan Carlson (On Deck)	.05
659	Checklist	.05
660	Checklist	.05

Cyberstats

Inserted into all types of Topps packaging at the rate of about one per 15 cards, this special series attempted to "complete" the statistics from the strike-shortened 1994 baseball season for nearly 400 players. Topps used computer modeling to predict how each player would have ended the season. Fronts of the cards are the same as found in the regular Topps set, except they have been printed on metallic foil. Backs have a black background.

#	Player	NM/M
	Complete Set (396):	25.00
	Common Player:	.10
1	Frank Thomas	.75
2	Mickey Morandini	.10
3	Todd Worrell	.10
4	David Cone	.10
5	Trevor Hoffman	.10
6	Shane Mack	.10
7	Delino DeShields	.10
8	Matt Williams	.10
9	Sammy Sosa	1.00
10	Gary DiSarcina	.10
11	Kenny Rogers	.10
12	Jose Vizcaino	.10
13	Lou Whitaker	.10
14	Ron Darling	.10
15	Dave Nilsson	.10
16	Dennis Martinez	.10
17	Orlando Merced	.10
18	John Wetteland	.10
19	Mike Devereaux	.10
20	Rene Arocha	.10
21	Jay Buhner	.10
22	Hal Morris	.10
23	Paul Molitor	.75
24	Dave West	.10
25	Scott Sanders	.10
26	Eddie Zambrano	.10
27	Ricky Bones	.10
28	John Valentin	.10
29	Kevin Tapani	.10
30	Tim Wallach	.10
31	Darren Lewis	.10
32	Travis Fryman	.10
33	Bret Barberie	.10
34	Dennis Eckersley	.65
35	Ken Hill	.10
36	Pete Harnisch	.10
37	Mike Mussina	.50
38	Dave Winfield	.75
39	Joey Hamilton	.10
40	Edgar Martinez	.10
41	John Smiley	.10
42	Jim Abbott	.10
43	Mike Kelly	.10
44	Brian Jordan	.10
45	Ken Ryan	.10
46	Matt Mieske	.10
47	Rick Aguilera	.10
48	Ismael Valdes	.10
49	Royce Clayton	.10
50	Juan Gonzalez	.35
51	Mel Rojas	.10
52	Doug Drabek	.10
53	Charles Nagy	.10
54	Tim Raines	.10
55	Midre Cummings	.10
56	Rafael Palmeiro	.65
57	Charlie Hayes	.10
58	Ray Lankford	.10
59	Tim Davis	.10
60	Andy Ashby	.10
61	Mark Grace	.10
62	Mark Langston	.10
63	Chuck Carr	.10
64	Barry Bonds	2.00
65	David Segui	.10
66	Mariano Duncan	.10
67	Kenny Lofton	.10
68	Ken Caminiti	.10
69	Darrin Jackson	.10
70	Wil Cordero	.10
71	Walt Weiss	.10
72	Tom Pagnozzi	.10
73	Bret Boone	.10
74	Wally Joyner	.10
75	Luis Lopez	.10
76	Len Dykstra	.10
77	Pedro Munoz	.10
78	Kevin Gross	.10
79	Eduardo Perez	.10
80	Brent Gates	.10
81	Jeff Conine	.10
82	Paul Sorrento	.10
83	Julio Franco	.10
84	Chris Sabo	.10
85	Dante Bichette	.10
86	Mike Stanley	.10
87	Bob Hamelin	.10
88	Tommy Greene	.10
89	Jeff Brantley	.10
90	Ed Sprague	.10
91	Otis Nixon	.10
92	Chad Curtis	.10
93	Chuck McElroy	.10
94	Troy Neel	.10
95	Benito Santiago	.10
96	Jose Mesa	.10
97	Luis Gonzalez	.10
98	Alex Fernandez	.10
99	Ben McDonald	.10
100	Wade Boggs	1.00
101	Tom Glavine	.35
102	Phil Plantier	.10
103	Raul Mondesi	.10
104	Jim Edmonds	.10
105	Jeff Kent	.10
106	Wilson Alvarez	.10
107	Geronimo Berroa	.10
108	Craig Biggio	.10
109	Roberto Hernandez	.10
110	Bobby Ayala	.10
111	Bob Tewksbury	.10
112	Rondell White	.10
113	Steve Cooke	.10
114	Tim Salmon	.10
115	Kent Mercker	.10
116	Randy Johnson	.75
117	Mo Vaughn	.10
118	Eddie Williams	.10
119	Jeff Montgomery	.10
120	Kirt Manwaring	.10
121	Pat Hentgen	.10
122	Shawon Dunston	.10
123	Tim Belcher	.10
124	Cecil Fielder	.10
125	Todd Hundley	.10
126	Mark Acre	.10
127	Darrell Whitmore	.10
128	Darryl Kile	.10
129	Jay Bell	.10
130	Harold Baines	.10
131	Felix Fermin	.10
132	Ellis Burks	.10
133	Joe Carter	.10
134	Terry Pendleton	.10
135	Junior Felix	.10
136	Bill Gullickson	.10
137	Melvin Nieves	.10
138	Chuck Knoblauch	.10
139	Bobby Jones	.10
140	Darrin Fletcher	.10
141	Andy Van Slyke	.10
142	Allen Watson	.10
143	Dan Wilson	.10
144	Bip Roberts	.10
145	Sterling Hitchcock	.10
146	Johnny Ruffin	.10
147	Steve Trachsel	.10
148	Ramon Martinez	.10
149	Dave Henderson	.10
150	Chris Gomez	.10
151	Rusty Greer	.10
152	John Franco	.10
153	Mike Bordick	.10
154	Dave Magadan	.10
155	Greg Swindell	.10
156	Arthur Rhodes	.10
157	Juan Guzman	.10
158	Greg Maddux	1.00
159	Mike Macfarlane	.10
160	Curt Schilling	.35
161	Jose Canseco	.40
162	Aaron Sele	.10
163	Steve Buechele	.10
164	Orel Hershiser	.10
165	Mike Henneman	.10
166	Kevin Seitzer	.10
167	Ruben Sierra	.10
168	Alex Cole	.10
169	Jim Thome	.65
170	Lance Johnson	.10
171	Marquis Grissom	.10
172	Jamie Moyer	.10
173	Todd Zeile	.10
174	Chris Bosio	.10
175	Steve Howe	.10
176	Luis Polonia	.10
177	Ryan Klesko	.10
178	Kevin Appier	.10
179	Tim Naehring	.10
180	Randy Myers	.10
181	Mike Jackson	.10
182	Chili Davis	.10
183	Jason Jacome	.10
184	Stan Javier	.10
185	Scott Servais	.10
186	Kirk Rueter	.10
187	Don Slaught	.10
188	Ozzie Smith	1.00
189	Barry Larkin	.10
190	Gary Gaetti	.10
191	Fred McGriff	.10
192	Roger Clemens	1.00
193	Dean Palmer	.10
194	Jeromy Burnitz	.10
195	Scott Kamieniecki	.10
196	Eddie Murray	.75
197	Ron Karkovice	.10
198	Tino Martinez	.10
199	Ken Griffey Jr.	1.25
200	Don Mattingly	1.00
201	Henry Rodriguez	.10
202	Lenny Harris	.10
203	Ryan Thompson	.10
204	Darren Oliver	.10
205	Omar Vizquel	.10
206	Jeff Bagwell	.75
207	Todd Van Poppel	.10
208	Leo Gomez	.10
209	Mark Whiten	.10
210	Pedro Martinez	.10
211	Reggie Sanders	.10
212	Kevin Foster	.10
213	Danny Tartabull	.10
214	Jeff Blauser	.10
215	Mike Magnante	.10
216	Tom Candiotti	.10
217	Rod Beck	.10
218	Jody Reed	.10
219	Vince Coleman	.10
220	Danny Jackson	.10
221	Larry Walker	.10
222	Pat Borders	.10
223	Lee Smith	.10
224	Paul O'Neill	.10
225	Devon White	.10
226	Jim Bullinger	.10
227	Steve Avery	.10
228	Tony Gwynn	1.00
229	Pat Meares	.10
230	Bill Swift	.10
231	David Wells	.10
232	John Briscoe	.10
233	Roger Pavlik	.10
234	Roberto Alomar	.30
235	Billy Brewer	.10
236	Gary Sheffield	.40
237	Lou Frazier	.10
238	Terry Steinbach	.10
239	Omar Daal	.10
240	Jason Bere	.10
241	Denny Neagle	.10
242	Danny Bautista	.10
243	Hector Carrasco	.10
244	Bill Risley	.10
245	Andy Benes	.10
246	Jim Leyritz	.10
247	Jose Oliva	.10
248	Greg Vaughn	.10
249	Rich Monteleone	.10
250	Tony Eusebio	.10
251	Chuck Finley	.10
252	Joe Boever	.10
253	Bobby Munoz	.10
254	Bret Saberhagen	.10
255	Kurt Abbott	.10
256	Bobby Witt	.10
257	Cliff Floyd	.10
258	Mark Clark	.10
259	Andujar Cedeno	.10
260	Marvin Freeman	.10
261	Mike Piazza	1.25
262	Pat Kelly	.10
263	Carlos Delgado	.45
264	Willie Banks	.10
265	Matt Walbeck	.10
266	Mark McGwire	1.50
267	Alan Trammell	.10
268	Tom Gordon	.10
269	Greg Colbrunn	.10
270	Darren Daulton	.10
271	Albie Lopez	.10
272	Robin Ventura	.10
273	Bryan Eversgerd	.10
274	Dave Fleming	.10
275	Scott Livingstone	.10
276	Pete Schourek	.10
277	Bernie Williams	.10
278	Mark Lemke	.10
279	Eric Karros	.10
280	Billy Ashley	.10
281	Rico Brogna	.10
282	John Burkett	.10
283	Jorge Fabregas	.10
284	Greg Gagne	.10
285	Doug Jones	.10
286	Troy O'Leary	.10
287	Pat Rapp	.10
288	Butch Henry	.10
289	John Olerud	.10
290	John Hudek	.10
291	Jeff King	.10
292	Bobby Bonilla	.10
293	Albert Belle	.10
294	Rick Wilkins	.10
295	John Jaha	.10
296	Sid Fernandez	.10
297	Deion Sanders	.10
298	Gil Heredia	.10
299	Melido Perez	.10
300	Greg McMichael	.10
301	Rusty Meacham	.10
302	Shawn Green	.35
303	Carlos Garcia	.10
304	Dave Stevens	.10
305	Eric Young	.10
306	Kirk Gibson	.10
307	Spike Owen	.10
308	Sandy Alomar	.10
309	Ricky Gutierrez	.10
310	Dave Veres	.10
311	Gregg Jefferies	.10
312	Jose Valentin	.10
313	Robb Nen	.10
314	Jose Rijo	.10
315	Sean Berry	.10
316	Mike Gallego	.10
317	Roberto Kelly	.10
318	Kevin Stocker	.10
319	Kirby Puckett	1.00
320	Jon Lieber	.10
321	Joe Girardi	.10
322	Tony Phillips	.10
323	Brian Anderson	.10
324	Ivan Rodriguez	.65
325	Jeff Cirillo	.10
326	Joey Cora	.10
327	Chris Hoiles	.10
328	Bernard Gilkey	.10
329	Mike Lansing	.10
330	Jimmy Key	.10
331	Vinny Castilla	.10
332	Mark Guthrie	.10
333	Mike Lieberthal	.10
334	Will Clark	.10
335	Rickey Henderson	.75
336	Todd Jones	.10
337	Jack McDowell	.10
338	Carlos Rodriguez	.10
339	Mark Eichhorn	.10
340	Jeff Nelson	.10
341	Eric Anthony	.10
342	Randy Velarde	.10
343	Javier Lopez	.10
344	Kevin Mitchell	.10
345	Steve Bedrosian	.10
346	John Kruk	.10
347	Scott Leius	.10
348	John Patterson	.10
349	Kevin Brown	.10
350	Mike Moore	.10
351	Manny Ramirez	.75
352	Jose Lind	.10
353	Derrick May	.10
354	Cal Eldred	.10
355	J.T. Snow	.10
356	Luis Sojo	.10
357	Moises Alou	.10
358	Dave Clark	.10
359	Dave Hollins	.10
360	Cal Ripken Jr.	2.00
361	Pedro Astacio	.10
362	Tony Longmire	.10
363	Jeff Frye	.10
364	Bo Jackson	.20
365	Steve Ontiveros	.10
366	David Nied	.10
367	Brad Ausmus	.10
368	Carlos Baerga	.10
369	James Mouton	.10
370	Ozzie Guillen	.10
371	Yorkis Perez	.10
372	Rich Rodriguez	.10
373	Mark McLemore	.10
374	Jeff Fassero	.10
375	John Roper	.10
376	Wes Chamberlain	.10
377	Felix Jose	.10
378	Brett Butler	.10
379	William Van Landingham	.10
380	Mickey Tettleton	.10
381	Brady Anderson	.10
382	Reggie Jefferson	.10
383	Mike Kingery	.10
384	Derek Bell	.10
385	Scott Erickson	.10
386	Bob Wickman	.10
387	Phil Leftwich	.10
388	Dave Justice	.10
389	Pedro Martinez	.75
390	Terry Mathews	.10
391	Brian McRae	.10
392	Bruce Ruffin	.10
393	Steve Finley	.10
394	Rafael Bournigal	.10
395	Darryl Strawberry	.10
396	Luis Alicea	.10

Cyberstat Season in Review

This special edition of Cyberstat cards was available only in Topps factory sets. Carrying forward the idea of computerized projections to complete the strike-shortened 1994 season, the Season in Review cards speculate on career milestones and the playoffs that never happened. The Season in Review cards have player action photos printed on a foil background resembling the U.S. flag. Names are in gold foil. Backs have a black background and a recap of the computer simulation.

		NM/M
Complete Set (7):		10.00
Common Player:		1.00
1	Barry Bonds (61 Home Runs)	6.00
2	Jose Canseco (AL West One-Game Playoff)	2.00
3	Juan Gonzalez (AL Divisional Playoffs)	1.50
4	Fred McGriff (NL Divisional Playoffs)	1.00
5	Carlos Baerga (ALCS MVP)	1.00
6	Ryan Klesko (NLCS MVP)	1.00
7	Kenny Lofton (World Series MVP)	1.00

League Leaders

League Leaders is a 50-card insert sold in one of every six retail packs only of both Series I and II. The set includes the top five players in each league across 10 statistical categories. Cards featured the statistical category running up the right side, with the player's name across the bottom. Photo backgrounds have been darkened and posterized to make the player action stand out. Backs have the player's stat rankings within his division and league, and a bar graph at bottom gives his performance in that statistical category for the previous five seasons.

		NM/M
Complete Set (50):		20.00
Common Player:		.15
1	Albert Belle	.15
2	Kevin Mitchell	.15
3	Wade Boggs	1.50
4	Tony Gwynn	1.50
5	Moises Alou	.15
6	Andres Galarraga	.15
7	Matt Williams	.15
8	Barry Bonds	4.00
9	Frank Thomas	.75
10	Jose Canseco	.15
11	Jeff Bagwell	.75
12	Kirby Puckett	1.50
13	Julio Franco	.15
14	Albert Belle	.15
15	Fred McGriff	.15
16	Kenny Lofton	.15
17	Otis Nixon	.15
18	Brady Anderson	.15
19	Deion Sanders	.15
20	Chuck Carr	.15
21	Pat Hentgen	.15
22	Andy Benes	.15
23	Roger Clemens	1.75
24	Greg Maddux	1.50
25	Pedro Martinez	.75
26	Paul O'Neill	.15
27	Jeff Bagwell	.75
28	Frank Thomas	.75
29	Hal Morris	.15
30	Kenny Lofton	.15
31	Ken Griffey Jr.	2.00
32	Jeff Bagwell	.75
33	Albert Belle	.15
34	Fred McGriff	.15
35	Cecil Fielder	.15
36	Matt Williams	.15
37	Joe Carter	.15
38	Dante Bichette	.15
39	Frank Thomas	.75
40	Mike Piazza	2.00
41	Craig Biggio	.15
42	Vince Coleman	.15
43	Marquis Grissom	.15
44	Chuck Knoblauch	.15
45	Darren Lewis	.15
46	Randy Johnson	.75
47	Jose Rijo	.15
48	Chuck Finley	.15
49	Bret Saberhagen	.15
50	Kevin Appier	.15

Total Bases Finest

Printed in Topps Finest technology, including a peel-off plastic protector coating on the front, these cards honor the 1994 statistical leaders in total bases. The cards have a silver waffle-texture background on front as a background to the color action photo. At bottom is a team logo and team-color bar with the player's name. Backs feature a portrait photo and the player's total base stats. These inserts are found in Series II Topps packs at an average rate of one per 36 packs (one box).

		NM/M
Complete Set (15):		12.00
Common Player:		.50
1	Jeff Bagwell	1.25
2	Albert Belle	.50
3	Ken Griffey Jr.	2.00
4	Frank Thomas	1.25
5	Matt Williams	.50
6	Dante Bichette	.50
7	Barry Bonds	2.50
8	Moises Alou	.50
9	Andres Galarraga	.50
10	Kenny Lofton	.50
11	Rafael Palmeiro	.50
12	Tony Gwynn	1.50
13	Kirby Puckett	1.50
14	Jose Canseco	.50
15	Jeff Conine	.50

Traded and Rookies

Traded players, free agents signed by new teams and all the up-and-coming rookies are the meat of the 1995 Topps Traded and Rookies set, sold for the first time exclusively in foil-pack form. Maintaining the same format used in Series 1 and 2 Topps, the updates also reused the Future Star, Draft Pick and Star Track subsets, along with four-player Prospects cards. New subsets included Rookie of the Year Candidates, All-Stars, On Deck and "At the Break," 10 cards chronicling star players' performances through the first half of the 1995 season. A double-thick, foil-printed version of the "At the Break" cards called "Power Boosters" were the only inserts in the Traded/Rookies set.

		NM/M
Complete Set (165):		30.00
Common Player:		.05
Pack (11):		2.50
Wax Box (36):		60.00
1	Frank Thomas (At The Break)	.50
2	Ken Griffey Jr. (At The Break)	.65
3	Barry Bonds (At The Break)	1.00
4	Albert Belle (At The Break)	.05
5	Cal Ripken Jr. (At The Break)	1.00
6	Mike Piazza (At The Break)	.75
7	Tony Gwynn (At The Break)	.60
8	Jeff Bagwell (At The Break)	.45
9	Mo Vaughn (At The Break)	.05
10	Matt Williams (At The Break)	.05
11	Ray Durham	.05
12	Juan LeBron (Photo Carlos Beltran.) RC (Draft Pick)	5.00
13	Shawn Green (Rookie of the Year Candidate)	.50
14	Kevin Gross	.05
15	Jon Nunnally RC	.05
16	Brian Maxcy RC	.05
17	Mark Kiefer	.05
18	Carlos Beltran RC (Draft Pick)(Photo actually Juan Beltran).	15.00
19	Mike Mimbs RC	.05
20	Larry Walker	.05
21	Chad Curtis	.05
22	Jeff Barry	.05
23	Joe Oliver	.05
24	Tomas Perez RC	.05
25	Michael Barrett RC (Draft Pick)	1.50
26	Brian McRae	.05
27	Derek Bell	.05
28	Ray Durham (Rookie of the Year Candidate)	.05
29	Todd Williams	.05
30	Ryan Jaroncyk RC (Draft Pick)	.05
31	Todd Steverson	.05
32	Mike Devereaux	.05
33	Rheal Cormier	.05
34	Benny Santiago	.05
35	Bobby Higginson RC	.50
36	Jack McDowell	.05
37	Mike Macfarlane	.05
38	Tony McKnight RC (Draft Pick)	.05
39	Brian Hunter (Rookie of the Year Candidate)	.05
40	Hideo Nomo RC (Star Track)	2.00
41	Brett Butler	.05
42	Donovan Osborne	.05
43	Scott Karl	.05
44	Tony Phillips	.05
45	Marty Cordova (Rookie of the Year Candidate)	.20
46	Dave Mlicki	.05
47	Bronson Arroyo RC (Draft Pick)	4.00
48	John Burkett	.05
49	J.D. Smart RC (Draft Pick)	.05
50	Mickey Tettleton	.05
51	Todd Stottlemyre	.05
52	Mike Perez	.05
53	Terry Mulholland	.05
54	Edgardo Alfonzo	.05
55	Zane Smith	.05
56	Jacob Brumfield	.05
57	Andujar Cedeno	.05
58	Jose Parra	.05
59	Manny Alexander	.05
60	Tony Tarasco	.05
61	Orel Hershiser	.05
62	Tim Scott	.05
63	Felix Rodriguez RC	.05
64	Ken Hill	.05
65	Marquis Grissom	.05
66	Lee Smith	.05
67	Jason Bates (Rookie of the Year Candidate)	.05
68	Felipe Lira	.05
69	Alex Hernandez RC (Draft Pick)	.10
70	Tony Fernandez	.05
71	Scott Radinsky	.05
72	Jose Canseco	.05
73	Mark Grudzielanek RC	.50
74	Ben Davis RC (Draft Pick)	.25
75	Jim Abbott	.05
76	Roger Bailey	.05
77	Gregg Jefferies	.05
78	Erik Hanson	.05
79	Brad Radke RC	1.50
80	Jaime Navarro	.05
81	John Wetteland	.05
82	Chad Fonville RC	.05
83	John Mabry	.05
84	Glenallen Hill	.05
85	Ken Caminiti	.05
86	Tom Goodwin	.05
87	Darren Bragg	.05
88	1995 Prospects (Pitchers) (Pat Ahearne RC, Gary Rath RC, Larry Wimberly RC, Robbie Bell RC)	.10
89	Jeff Russell	.05
90	Dave Gallagher	.05
91	Steve Finley	.05
92	Vaughn Eshelman	.05
93	Kevin Jarvis	.05
94	Mark Gubicza	.05
95	Tim Wakefield	.05
96	Bob Tewksbury	.05
97	Sid Roberson RC	.05
98	Tom Henke	.05
99	Michael Tucker (Future Star)	.05
100	Jason Bates	.05
101	Otis Nixon	.05
102	Mark Whiten	.05
103	Dilson Torres	.05
104	Melvin Bunch	.05
105	Terry Pendleton	.05
106	Corey Jenkins RC	.05
107	On Deck (Glenn Dishman RC, Rob Grable RC)	.05
108	Reggie Taylor RC (Draft Pick)	.05
109	Curtis Goodwin (Rookie of the Year Candidate)	.05
110	David Cone	.05
111	Antonio Osuna	.05
112	Paul Shuey	.05
113	Doug Jones	.05
114	Mark McLemore	.05
115	Kevin Ritz	.05
116	John Kruk	.05
117	Trevor Wilson	.05
118	Jerald Clark	.05
119	Julian Tavarez	.05
120	Tim Pugh	.05
121	Todd Zeile	.05
122	1995 Prospects (Fielders) (Mark Sweeney RC, George Arias, Richie Sexson RC, Brian Schneider RC)	4.00
123	Bobby Witt	.05
124	Hideo Nomo (Rookie of the Year Candidate)	1.00
125	Joey Cora	.05
126	Jim Scharrer RC (Draft Pick)	.05
127	Paul Quantrill	.05
128	Chipper Jones (Rookie of the Year Candidate)	.75
129	Kenny James RC (Draft Pick)	.05
130	On Deck (Lyle Mouton, Mariano Rivera)	.15
131	Tyler Green (Rookie of the Year Candidate)	.05
132	Brad Clontz	.05
133	Jon Nunnally (Rookie of the Year Candidate)	.05
134	Dave Magadan	.05
135	Al Leiter	.05
136	Bret Barberie	.05
137	Bill Swift	.05
138	Scott Cooper	.05
139	Roberto Kelly	.05
140	Charlie Hayes	.05
141	Pete Harnisch	.05
142	Rich Amaral	.05
143	Rudy Seanez	.05
144	Pat Listach	.05
145	Quilvio Veras (Rookie of the Year Candidate)	.05
146	Jose Olmeda RC (Draft Pick)	.05
147	Roberto Petagine	.05
148	Kevin Brown	.05
149	Phil Plantier	.05
150	Carlos Perez RC (Rookie of the Year Candidate)	.05
151	Pat Borders	.05
152	Tyler Green	.05
153	Stan Belinda	.05
154	Dave Stewart	.05
155	Andre Dawson	.25
156	Frank Thomas, Fred McGriff/AS	.30
157	Carlos Baerga, Craig Biggio/AS	.05
158	Wade Boggs, Matt Williams/AS	.35
159	Cal Ripken Jr., Ozzie Smith/AS	.75
160	Ken Griffey Jr., Tony Gwynn/AS	.40
161	Albert Belle, Barry Bonds/AS	.75
162	Kirby Puckett, Len Dykstra/AS	.35
163	Ivan Rodriguez, Mike Piazza/AS	.40
164	Randy Johnson, Hideo Nomo/AS	.25
165	Checklist	.05

Traded and Rookies Power Boosters

Virtually identical to the first 10 cards of the 1995 Topps Traded and Rookies issue, the "At the Break" subset is the only insert found in Traded packs. Cards are printed on double-thick cardboard stock on metallized foil. The chase cards are found at an average rate of one per 36 packs.

		NM/M
Complete Set (10):		20.00
Common Player:		.75
1	Frank Thomas	1.50
2	Ken Griffey Jr.	3.00
3	Barry Bonds	5.00
4	Albert Belle	.75
5	Cal Ripken Jr.	5.00
6	Mike Piazza	3.00
7	Tony Gwynn	2.50
8	Jeff Bagwell	1.50
9	Mo Vaughn	.75
10	Matt Williams	.75

Those cards are designated with an "N" suffix in parentheses. The old larger format of the vintage cards has been reduced to the standard 2-1/2" x 3-1/2" format for the Archives versions. Cards are UV coated on each side. Each card carries its original or an "extended" card number in the normal location, plus a tiny Archives series card number at the bottom in the fine print. The numbers on cards #97-109 do not coincide with those listed on the checklist card. The only chase cards in the issue were autographed versions of Sandy Koufax's 1956 Archives card. Cards #111-165 are short-printed in relation to cards #1-110.

	NM/M
Complete Set (165):	75.00
Wax Pack (10):	5.00
Wax Box (24):	110.00

Opening Day

This 10-card set featuring top performers on the belated opening day of the 1995 season was available exclusively in retail factory sets. Card fronts feature color action photos printed on textured foil in a U.S. flag-like design. A large colorful Opening Day logo appears in an upper corner while the player's key stats from that game appear in a foil box at lower-right. Backs have a portrait photo along with complete details and a stats line of the opening day performance.

		NM/M
Complete Set (10):		7.50
Common Player:		.75
1	Kevin Appier	.75
2	Dante Bichette	.75
3	Ken Griffey Jr.	3.50
4	Todd Hundley	.75
5	John Jaha	.75
6	Fred McGriff	.75
7	Raul Mondesi	.75
8	Manny Ramirez	2.50
9	Danny Tartabull	.75
10	Devon White	.75

Archives Brooklyn Dodgers

In a departure from its program of complete set reissues, Topps' Archives baseball series for 1995 was a tribute to the 40th anniversary of the Brooklyn Dodgers' 1955 World's Series victory over the archrival Yankees. Besides reprinting all of the Dodgers' cards from the 1952-56 Topps sets and the 1955 Bowman issue, the Archives release included some 30 "cards that never were," done in the styles of the 1952-55 Topps issues.

1	Andy Pafko (52T)	.25
2	Wayne Terwilliger (52T)	.10
3	Billy Loes (52T)	.25
4	Gil Hodges (52T)	.50
5	Duke Snider (52T)	.75
6	Jim Russell (52T)	.10
7	Chris Van Cuyk (52T)	.10
8	Preacher Roe (52T)	.10
9	Johnny Schmitz (52T)	.10
10	Bud Podbielan (52T)	.10
11	Phil Haugstad (52T)	.10
12	Clyde King (52T)	.10
13	Billy Cox (52T)	.10
14	Rocky Bridges (52T)	.10
15	Carl Erskine (52T)	.10
16	Erv Palica (52T)	.10
17	Ralph Branca (52T)	.10
18	Jackie Robinson (52T)	2.00
19	Roy Campanella (52T)	.75
20	Rube Walker (52T)	.10
21	Johnny Rutherford (52T)	.10
22	Joe Black (52T)	.25
23	George Shuba (52T)	.10
24	Pee Wee Reese (52T)	.75
25	Clem Labine (52T)	.10
26	Bobby Morgan (52T)	.10
27	Cookie Lavagetto (52T)	.10
28	Chuck Dressen (52T)	.10
29	Ben Wade (52T)	.10
30	Rocky Nelson (52T)	.10
31	Billy Herman (52T)	.10
32	Jake Pitler (52T)	.10
33	Dick Williams (52T)	.10
34	Cal Abrams (52N)	.25
35	Carl Furillo (52N)	.25
36	Don Newcombe (52N)	.25
37	Jackie Robinson (53T)	2.00
38	Ben Wade (53T)	.10
39	Clem Labine (53T)	.10
40	Roy Campanella (53T)	.75
41	George Shuba (53T)	.10
42	Chuck Dressen (53T)	.10
43	Pee Wee Reese (53T)	.75
44	Joe Black (53T)	.25
45	Bobby Morgan (53T)	.10
46	Dick Williams (53T)	.10
47	Rube Walker (53T)	.10
48	Johnny Rutherford (53T)	.10
49	Billy Loes (53T)	.15
50	Don Hoak (53T)	.10
51	Jim Hughes (53T)	.10
52	Bob Milliken (53T)	.10
53	Preacher Roe (53T)	.10
54	Dixie Howell (53T)	.10
55	Junior Gilliam (53T)	.10
56	Johnny Podres (53T)	.10
57	Bill Antonello (53T)	.10
58	Ralph Branca (53N)	.25
59	Gil Hodges (53N)	.60
60	Carl Furillo (53N)	.45
61	Carl Erskine (53N)	.25
62	Don Newcombe (53N)	.25
63	Duke Snider (53N)	.75
64	Billy Cox (53N)	.25
65	Russ Meyer (53N)	.25
66	Jackie Robinson (54T)	2.00
67	Preacher Roe (54T)	.10
68	Duke Snider (54T)	.75
69	Junior Gilliam (54T)	.10
70	Billy Herman (54T)	.10
71	Joe Black (54T)	.15
72	Gil Hodges (54T)	.50
73	Clem Labine (54T)	.10
74	Ben Wade (54T)	.10
75	Tommy Lasorda (54T)	1.00
76	Rube Walker (54T)	.10
77	Johnny Podres (54T)	.10
78	Jim Hughes (54T)	.10
79	Bob Milliken (54T)	.10
80	Charlie Thompson (54T)	.10
81	Don Hoak (54T)	.10
82	Roberto Clemente (54N)	1.00
83	Don Zimmer (54N)	.25
84	Roy Campanella (54N)	1.00
85	Billy Cox (54N)	.45
86	Carl Erskine (54N)	.45
87	Carl Furillo (54N)	.45
88	Don Newcombe (54N)	.45
89	Pee Wee Reese (54N)	1.00
90	George Shuba (54N)	.10

91	Junior Gilliam (55T)	.10
92	Billy Herman (55T)	.10
93	Johnny Podres (55T)	.10
94	Don Hoak (55T)	.10
95	Jackie Robinson (55T)	2.00
96	Jim Hughes (55T)	.10
97	Bob Borkowski (55N)	.10
98	Sandy Amoros (55T)	.10
99	Karl Spooner (55T)	.10
100	Don Zimmer (55T)	.10
101	Rube Walker (55T)	.10
102	Bob Milliken (55T)	.10
103	Sandy Koufax (55T)	2.00
104	Joe Black (55T)	.20
105	Clem Labine (55T)	.10
106	Gil Hodges (55T)	.50
107	Ed Roebuck (55T)	.10
108	Bert Hamric (55T)	.10
109	Duke Snider (55T)	.75
110	Walter Alston (55N)	.25
111	Roger Craig (55N)	.75
112	Don Drysdale (55N)	3.00
113	Dixie Howell (55N)	.50
114	Frank Kellert (55N)	.50
115	Tommy Lasorda (55N)	2.50
116	Chuck Templeton (55N)	.50
117	World Series Game 3, Dodgers Stay Alive (Jackie Robinson (55N))	1.00
118	World Series Game 4, Series Knotted (Gil Hodges (55N))	1.00
119	World Series Game 5, Dodgers Lead (Duke Snider (55N))	1.00
120	World Series Game 7, Dodgers Reign (Johnny Podres (55N))	1.00
121	Don Hoak (55B)	.35
122	Roy Campanella (55B)	2.00
123	Pee Wee Reese (55B)	2.00
124	Bob Darnell (55B)	.50
125	Don Zimmer (55B)	.50
126	George Shuba (55B)	.50
127	Johnny Podres (55B)	.50
128	Junior Gilliam (55B)	.65
129	Don Newcombe (55B)	.65
130	Jim Hughes (55B)	.50
131	Gil Hodges (55B)	2.00
132	Carl Furillo (55B)	1.00
133	Carl Erskine (55B)	.50
134	Erv Palica (55B)	.50
135	Russ Meyer (55B)	.50
136	Billy Loes (55B)	.50
137	Walt Moryn (55B)	.50
138	Chico Fernandez (55B)	.50
139	Charley Neal (55B)	.50
140	Ken Lehman (55B)	.50
141	Walter Alston (55B)	1.00
142	Jackie Robinson (56T)	6.00
143	Sandy Amoros (56T)	.50
144	Ed Roebuck (56T)	.50
145	Roger Craig (56T)	.50
146	Sandy Koufax (56T)	5.00
146a	Sandy Koufax (56T, autographed)	650.00
147	Karl Spooner (56T)	.50
148	Don Zimmer (56T)	.50
149	Roy Campanella (56T)	3.00
150	Gil Hodges (56T)	2.50
151	Duke Snider (56T)	4.50
152	Team photo (56T)	5.00
153	Johnny Podres (56T)	.50
154	Don Bessent (56T)	.50
155	Carl Furillo (56T)	.75
156	Randy Jackson (56T)	.50
157	Carl Erskine (56T)	.50
158	Don Newcombe (56T)	.65
159	Pee Wee Reese (56T)	2.50
160	Billy Loes (56T)	.50
161	Junior Gilliam (56T)	.65
162	Clem Labine (56T)	.50
163	Charley Neal (56T)	.50
164	Rube Walker (56T)	.50
165	Checklist	.05

1995 Topps DIII

Describing its cards as featuring "infinite depth perspectives" with game-action photos, Topps entered the 3-D card market with its Dimension III product. Utilizing "super thick laminated construction" to provide the illusion of depth, the cards feature borderless action photos on front. Backs are conventionally printed with a color portrait photo and several sets of stats that go beyond the usual to the provide a more in-depth look at the player's performance.

	NM/M
Complete Set (59):	10.00
Common Player:	.15
Retail Pack (3):	.50
Retail Wax Box (24):	9.00
Hobby Pack (5):	.65
Hobby Wax Box (24):	12.50
1	Dave Justice	.15
2	Cal Ripken Jr.	2.50
3	Ruben Sierra	.15
4	Roberto Alomar	.25
5	Dennis Martinez	.15
6	Todd Zeile	.15
7	Albert Belle	.15
8	Chuck Knoblauch	.15
9	Roger Clemens	1.25
10	Cal Eldred	.15
11	Dennis Eckersley	.75
12	Andy Benes	.15
13	Moises Alou	.15
14	Andres Galarraga	.15
15	Jim Thome	.65
16	Tim Salmon	.15
17	Carlos Garcia	.15
18	Scott Leius	.15
19	Jeff Montgomery	.15
20	Brian Anderson	.15
21	Will Clark	.15
22	Bobby Bonilla	.15
23	Mike Stanley	.15
24	Barry Bonds	2.50
25	Jeff Conine	.15
26	Paul O'Neill	.15
27	Mike Piazza	1.50
28	Tom Glavine	.35
29	Jim Edmonds	.15
30	Lou Whitaker	.15
31	Jeff Frye	.15
32	Ivan Rodriguez	.75
33	Bret Boone	.15
34	Mike Greenwell	.15
35	Mark Grace	.15
36	Darren Lewis	.15
37	Don Mattingly	1.25
38	Jose Rijo	.15
39	Robin Ventura	.15
40	Bob Hamelin	.15
41	Tim Wallach	.15
42	Tony Gwynn	1.00
43	Ken Griffey Jr.	1.50
44	Doug Drabek	.15
45	Rafael Palmeiro	.75
46	Dean Palmer	.15
47	Bip Roberts	.15
48	Barry Larkin	.15
49	Dave Nilsson	.15
50	Wil Cordero	.15
51	Travis Fryman	.15
52	Chuck Carr	.15
53	Rey Sanchez	.15
54	Walt Weiss	.15
55	Joe Carter	.15
56	Len Dykstra	.15
57	Orlando Merced	.15
58	Ozzie Smith	1.00
59	Chris Gomez	.15

DIII Zone

A barrage of baseballs in the background, behind a player action photo, are featured on the front of this DIII chase set. Backs have a blazing baseball across the top and a description and stats of the pictured player's hot streaks of the previous season — those times when athletes are said to be "in the zone." The inserts are found on average of one per six packs.

	NM/M
Complete Set (6):	4.00
Common Player:	.50
1	Frank Thomas	1.00
2	Kirby Puckett	1.50
3	Jeff Bagwell	1.00
4	Fred McGriff	.50
5	Raul Mondesi	.50
6	Kenny Lofton	.50

1995 Topps Embossed

Taking the embossed sports-card idea which Action Packed developed years earlier to a new level, Topps Embossed baseball features the tactile image on both sides of the card. Fronts have a lightly textured border while the central player photo is deeply embossed. The player name is embossed in gold-foil letters at bottom. Backs have another embossed player photo and various levels of embossing around the borders and boxes which contain stats and trivia.

	NM/M
Complete Set (140):	7.50
Common Player:	.10
Embossed Golds:	2X
Wax Pack (6+1):	1.50
Wax Box (24):	22.50
1	Kenny Lofton	.10
2	Gary Sheffield	.35
3	Hal Morris	.10
4	Cliff Floyd	.10
5	Pat Hentgen	.10
6	Tony Gwynn	.75
7	Jose Valentin	.10
8	Jason Bere	.10
9	Jeff Kent	.10
10	John Valentin	.10
11	Brian Anderson	.10
12	Deion Sanders	.10
13	Ryan Thompson	.10
14	Ruben Sierra	.10
15	Jay Bell	.10
16	Chuck Carr	.10
17	Brent Gates	.10
18	Bret Boone	.10
19	Paul Molitor	.60
20	Chili Davis	.10
21	Ryan Klesko	.10
22	Will Clark	.10
23	Greg Vaughn	.10
24	Moises Alou	.10
25	Ray Lankford	.10
26	Jose Rijo	.10
27	Bobby Jones	.10
28	Rick Wilkins	.10
29	Cal Eldred	.10
30	Juan Gonzalez	.30
31	Royce Clayton	.10
32	Bryan Harvey	.10
33	Dave Nilsson	.10
34	Chris Hoiles	.10
35	David Nied	.10
36	Javy Lopez	.10
37	Tim Wallach	.10
38	Bobby Bonilla	.10
39	Danny Tartabull	.10
40	Andy Benes	.10
41	Dean Palmer	.10
42	Chris Gomez	.10
43	Kevin Appier	.10
44	Brady Anderson	.10
45	Alex Fernandez	.10
46	Roberto Kelly	.10
47	Dave Hollins	.10
48	Chuck Finley	.10
49	Wade Boggs	.75
50	Travis Fryman	.10
51	Ken Griffey Jr.	1.00
52	John Olerud	.10
53	Delino DeShields	.10
54	Ivan Rodriguez	.50
55	Tommy Greene	.10
56	Tom Pagnozzi	.10
57	Bip Roberts	.10
58	Luis Gonzalez	.10
59	Rey Sanchez	.10
60	Ken Ryan	.10
61	Darren Daulton	.10
62	Rick Aguilera	.10
63	Wally Joyner	.10
64	Mike Greenwell	.10
65	Jay Buhner	.10
66	Craig Biggio	.10
67	Charles Nagy	.10
68	Devon White	.10
69	Randy Johnson	.60
70	Shawon Dunston	.10
71	Kirby Puckett	.75
72	Paul O'Neill	.10
73	Tino Martinez	.10
74	Carlos Garcia	.10
75	Ozzie Smith	.75
76	Cecil Fielder	.10
77	Mike Stanley	.10
78	Lance Johnson	.10
79	Tony Phillips	.10
80	Bobby Munoz	.10
81	Kevin Tapani	.10
82	William Van Landingham	.10
83	Dante Bichette	.10
84	Tom Candiotti	.10
85	Wil Cordero	.10
86	Jeff Conine	.10
87	Joey Hamilton	.10
88	Mark Whiten	.10
89	Jeff Montgomery	.10
90	Andres Galarraga	.10
91	Roberto Alomar	.20
92	Orlando Merced	.10
93	Mike Mussina	.35
94	Pedro Martinez	.60
95	Carlos Baerga	.10
96	Steve Trachsel	.10
97	Lou Whitaker	.10
98	David Cone	.10
99	Chuck Knoblauch	.10
100	Frank Thomas	.60
101	Dave Justice	.10
102	Raul Mondesi	.10
103	Rickey Henderson	.60
104	Doug Drabek	.10
105	Sandy Alomar	.10
106	Roger Clemens	.85
107	Mark McGwire	.20
108	Tim Salmon	.10
109	Greg Maddux	.75
110	Mike Piazza	1.00
111	Tom Glavine	.30
112	Walt Weiss	.10
113	Cal Ripken Jr.	1.50
114	Eddie Murray	.60
115	Don Mattingly	.85
116	Ozzie Guillen	.10
117	Bob Hamelin	.10
118	Jeff Bagwell	.60
119	Eric Karros	.10
120	Barry Bonds	1.50
121	Mickey Tettleton	.10
122	Mark Langston	.10
123	Robin Ventura	.10
124	Bret Saberhagen	.10
125	Albert Belle	.10
126	Rafael Palmeiro	.50
127	Fred McGriff	.10
128	Jimmy Key	.10
129	Barry Larkin	.10
130	Tim Raines	.10
131	Len Dykstra	.10
132	Todd Zeile	.10
133	Joe Carter	.10
134	Matt Williams	.10
135	Terry Steinbach	.10
136	Manny Ramirez	.60
137	John Wetteland	.10
138	Rod Beck	.10
139	Mo Vaughn	.10
140	Darren Lewis	.10

Embossed Golden Idols

The only insert in the Topps Embossed baseball set was a parallel set of the 140 cards rendered in gold tones on front and inserted at the rate of one per pack. Backs are identical to the regular version.

	NM/M
Complete Set (140):	25.00
Common Player:	.25

Legends of the '60s

Twelve of the true superstars of the 1960s are featured on one of their best Topps card designs in this collection of 6-oz. bronze metal cards. In 2-1/2" x 3-1/2" size, the ingots' fronts reproduce one of the player's 1960s Topps cards. Backs have been modified to present entire career stats. The set was sold in a mail-order subscription plan and included a custom wood box to house the collection.

	NM/M
Complete Set (12):	100.00
Common Player:	7.50

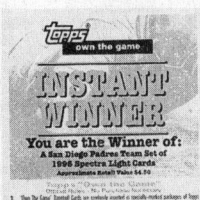

(1)	Hank Aaron/1965	10.00
(2)	Roberto Clemente/1965	10.00
(3)	Don Drysdale/1965	7.50
(4)	Bob Gibson/1964	7.50
(5)	Harmon Killebrew/1968	7.50
(6)	Juan Marichal/1966	7.50
(7)	Willie Mays/1964	10.00
(8)	Willie McCovey/1961	7.50
(9)	Brooks Robinson/1969	7.50
(10)	Frank Robinson/1962	7.50
(11)	Billy Williams/1967	7.50
(12)	Carl Yastrzemski/1966	7.50

Own the Game Instant Winner

Randomly packaged at a rate between 1:60 and 1:120, depending on type of packaging, Instant Winner cards were available in 1995 Topps baseball. The grand prize was a $40,000 "Baseball Passport" good for games, flights, hotels, etc., for 60 days during the 1996 season. Other prizes included personalized Topps baseball cards picturing the winner and Topps Spectra Light cards in team sets, league sets or a complete set. Prize cards had to be redeemed by Jan. 31, 1996.

Ted Williams Tunnel Opening Commemorative

This card was produced as the header for a 13-card set distributed at a luncheon in conjunction with Dec. 15, 1995 opening day ceremonies for the Ted Williams Tunnel, connecting South Boston with the city's airport, running beneath Boston Harbor. Just 3,000 sets were reported produced. This card is in the style of Topps' regular 1996 baseball card set and features gold-foil highlights on front. A career summary is on back. The card was later offered free with a $75 purchase from Topps Stadium Club. (See also 1995 Choice Marketing Ted Williams Tunnel Opening Day Set.)

	NM/M
9	Ted Williams	35.00

"1952" Gold Mickey Mantle

This down-sized (2-1/2" x 3-1/2") version of Topps' first Mickey Mantle card was produced with embossed 22K gold-foil design on front and back and individually serial numbered within an edition of 50,000.

	NM/M
311	Mickey Mantle	10.00

Pre-Production

This set of promo cards was reportedly included in some 1995 Topps factory Hobby sets as an un-advertised insert. Cards are in the format of the forthcoming 1996 issue but do not have 1995 stats or career updates, and are numbered with a "PP" prefix.

	NM/M
Complete Set (9):	25.00
Common Player:	2.00
PP1	Cal Ripken Jr.	10.00
PP2	Thomas Howard	2.00
PP3	Rafael Bournigal	2.00
PP4	Ron Gant	2.00
PP5	Chipper Jones	7.50
PP6	Frank Thomas	6.00
PP7	Barry Bonds	10.00
PP8	Fred McGriff	2.00
PP9	Hideo Nomo	6.00

1996 Topps

At 440 cards, the basic Topps set for 1996 was the smallest regular-issue from the company since it adopted the 2-1/2" x 3-1/2" format in 1957. Honoring the late Mickey Mantle on card No. 7, Topps announced it would hereafter retire that card number. Subsets in the 220-card Series 1 are Star Power, Commemoratives, Draft Picks, Tribute, AAA Stars and Future Stars. Series 2 subsets repeat Star Power and Draft Picks and add Prospects, Now Appearing and Rookie All-Stars. Three different factory sets were available with each including the 440-card base set and various inserts. The "Cereal Box" set, so named because of the resemblance of its four component boxes to single-serving cereal boxes, has four of the Mantle inserts. The Retail and Hobby sets each include seven randomly packed chase cards, a plastic-cased #7 Mantle card labeled "Last Day Production" and a Mantle Foundation card. In addition the Retail version has one of the 19 Mantle reprints.

	NM/M
Unopened Hobby Set (449):	40.00
Unopened Retail Set (450):	40.00
Unopened Cereal Box Set (444):	35.00
Complete Set (440):	25.00
Common Player:	.05
Wax Pack (12):	1.50
Wax Box (36):	35.00
Cello Pack (17):	2.50
Cello Box (24):	40.00
Vending Box (500):	12.50
1	Tony Gwynn (Star Power) .50
2	Mike Piazza (Star Power) .75
3	Greg Maddux (Star Power) .50
4	Jeff Bagwell (Star Power) .40
5	Larry Walker (Star Power) .05
6	Barry Larkin (Star Power) .05
7	Mickey Mantle (Commemorative) 4.00
8	Tom Glavine (Star Power) .05
9	Craig Biggio (Star Power) .05
10	Barry Bonds (Star Power) 1.00
11	Heathcliff Slocumb (Star Power) .05
12	Matt Williams (Star Power) .05
13	Todd Helton (Draft Pick) .75
14	Mark Redman (Draft Pick) .05
15	Michael Barrett (Draft Pick) .05
16	Ben Davis (Draft Pick) .05
17	Juan LeBron (Draft Pick) .05
18	Tony McKnight (Draft Pick) .05
19	Ryan Jaroncyk (Draft Pick) .05
20	Corey Jenkins (Draft Pick) .05
21	Jim Scharrer (Draft Pick) .05
22	Mark Bellhorn RC (Draft Pick) .10
23	Jarrod Washburn RC (Draft Pick) .50
24	Geoff Jenkins RC (Draft Pick) 1.00
25	Sean Casey RC (Draft Pick) 3.00
26	Brett Tomko RC (Draft Pick) .10
27	Tony Fernandez .05
28	Rich Becker .05
29	Andujar Cedeno .05
30	Paul Molitor .75
31	Brent Gates .05
32	Glenallen Hill .05
33	Mike MacFarlane .05
34	Manny Alexander .05
35	Todd Zeile .05
36	Joe Girardi .05
37	Tony Tarasco .05
38	Tim Belcher .05
39	Tom Goodwin .05
40	Orel Hershiser .05
41	Tripp Cromer .05
42	Sean Bergman .05
43	Troy Percival .05
44	Kevin Stocker .05
45	Albert Belle .05
46	Tony Eusebio .05
47	Sid Roberson .05
48	Todd Hollandsworth .05
49	Mark Wohlers .05
50	Kirby Puckett 1.00
51	Darren Holmes .05
52	Ron Karkovice .05
53	Al Martin .05
54	Pat Rapp .05
55	Mark Grace .05
56	Greg Gagne .05
57	Stan Javier .05
58	Scott Sanders .05
59	J.T. Snow .05
60	David Justice .05
61	Royce Clayton .05
62	Kevin Foster .05
63	Tim Naehring .05
64	Orlando Miller .05
65	Mike Mussina .35
66	Jim Eisenreich .05
67	Felix Fermin .05
68	Bernie Williams .05
69	Robb Nen .05
70	Ron Gant .05
71	Felipe Lira .05
72	Jacob Brumfield .05
73	John Mabry .05
74	Mark Carreon .05
75	Carlos Baerga .05
76	Jim Dougherty .05
77	Ryan Thompson .05
78	Scott Leius .05
79	Roger Pavlik .05
80	Gary Sheffield .45

81	Julian Tavarez .05
82	Andy Ashby .05
83	Mark Lemke .05
84	Omar Vizquel .05
85	Darren Daulton .05
86	Mike Lansing .05
87	Rusty Greer .05
88	Dave Stevens .05
89	Jose Offerman .05
90	Tom Henke .05
91	Troy O'Leary .05
92	Michael Tucker .05
93	Marvin Freeman .05
94	Alex Diaz .05
95	John Wetteland .05
96	Cal Ripken Jr. (Tribute Card) 1.00
97	Mike Mimbs .05
98	Bobby Higginson .05
99	Edgardo Alfonzo .05
100	Frank Thomas .75
101	Steve Gibralter, Bob Abreu (AAA Stars) .05
102	Brian Givens, T.J. Mathews (AAA Stars) .05
103	Chris Pritchett, Trenidad Hubbard (AAA Stars) .05
104	Eric Owens, Butch Huskey (AAA Stars) .05
105	Doug Drabek .05
106	Tomas Perez .05
107	Mark Leiter .05
108	Joe Oliver .05
109	Tony Castillo .05
110	Checklist .05
111	Kevin Seitzer .05
112	Pete Schourek .05
113	Sean Berry .05
114	Todd Stottlemyre .05
115	Joe Carter .05
116	Jeff King .05
117	Dan Wilson .05
118	Kurt Abbott .05
119	Lyle Mouton .05
120	Jose Rijo .05
121	Curtis Goodwin .05
122	Jose Valentin RC .05
123	Ellis Burks .05
124	David Cone .05
125	Eddie Murray .75
126	Brian Jordan .05
127	Darrin Fletcher .05
128	Curt Schilling .25
129	Ozzie Guillen .05
130	Kenny Rogers .05
131	Tom Pagnozzi .05
132	Garret Anderson .05
133	Bobby Jones .05
134	Chris Gomez .05
135	Mike Stanley .05
136	Hideo Nomo .35
137	Jon Nunnally .05
138	Tim Wakefield .05
139	Steve Finley .05
140	Ivan Rodriguez .65
141	Quilvio Veras .05
142	Mike Fetters .05
143	Mike Greenwell .05
144	Bill Pulsipher .05
145	Mark McGwire 1.50
146	Frank Castillo .05
147	Greg Vaughn .05
148	Pat Hentgen .05
149	Walt Weiss .05
150	Randy Johnson .75
151	David Segui .05
152	Benji Gil .05
153	Tom Candiotti .05
154	Geronimo Berroa .05
155	John Franco .05
156	Jay Bell .05
157	Mark Gubicza .05
158	Hal Morris .05
159	Wilson Alvarez .05
160	Derek Bell .05
161	Ricky Bottalico .05
162	Bret Boone .05
163	Brad Radke .05
164	John Valentin .05
165	Steve Avery .05
166	Mark McLemore .05
167	Danny Jackson .05
168	Tino Martinez .05
169	Shane Reynolds .05
170	Terry Pendleton .05
171	Jim Edmonds .05
172	Esteban Loaiza .05
173	Ray Durham .05
174	Carlos Perez .05
175	Raul Mondesi .05
176	Steve Ontiveros .05
177	Chipper Jones 1.00
178	Otis Nixon .05
179	John Burkett .05
180	Gregg Jefferies .05
181	Denny Martinez .05
182	Ken Caminiti .05
183	Doug Jones .05
184	Brian McRae .05
185	Don Mattingly 1.00
186	Mel Rojas .05
187	Marty Cordova .05
188	Vinny Castilla .05
189	John Smoltz .05
190	Travis Fryman .05
191	Chris Hoiles .05
192	Chuck Finley .05

193	Ryan Klesko .05
194	Alex Fernandez .05
195	Dante Bichette .05
196	Eric Karros .05
197	Roger Clemens 1.00
198	Randy Myers .05
199	Tony Phillips .05
200	Cal Ripken Jr. 2.00
201	Rod Beck .05
202	Chad Curtis .05
203	Jack McDowell .05
204	Gary Gaetti .05
205	Ken Griffey Jr. 1.25
206	Ramon Martinez .05
207	Jeff Kent .05
208	Brad Ausmus .05
209	Devon White .05
210	Jason Giambi (Future Star) .45
211	Nomar Garciaparra (Future Star) 1.00
212	Billy Wagner (Future Star) .05
213	Todd Greene (Future Star) .05
214	Paul Wilson (Future Star) .05
215	Johnny Damon (Future Star) .25
216	Alan Benes (Future Star) .05
217	Karim Garcia (Future Star) .10
218	Dustin Hermanson (Future Star) .05
219	Derek Jeter (Future Star) 2.00
220	Checklist .05
221	Kirby Puckett (Star Power) .50
222	Cal Ripken Jr. (Star Power) 1.00
223	Albert Belle (Star Power) .40
224	Randy Johnson (Star Power) .40
225	Wade Boggs (Star Power) .50
226	Carlos Baerga (Star Power) .05
227	Ivan Rodriguez (Star Power) .30
228	Mike Mussina (Star Power) .25
229	Frank Thomas (Star Power) .40
230	Ken Griffey Jr. (Star Power) .75
231	Jose Mesa (Star Power) .05
232	Matt Morris RC (Draft Pick) 1.00
233	Craig Wilson RC (Draft Pick) .50
234	Alvie Shepherd RC (Draft Pick) .05
235	Randy Winn RC (Draft Pick) .05
236	David Yocum RC (Draft Pick) .05
237	Jason Brester RC (Draft Pick) .05
238	Shane Monahan RC (Draft Pick) .05
239	Brian McNichol RC (Draft Pick) .05
240	Reggie Taylor (Draft Pick) .05
241	Garrett Long (Draft Pick) .05
242	Jonathan Johnson RC (Draft Pick) .05
243	Jeff Liefer RC (Draft Pick) .05
244	Brian Powell RC (Draft Pick) .05
245	Brian Buchanan (Draft Pick) .05
246	Mike Piazza 1.25
247	Edgar Martinez .05
248	Chuck Knoblauch .05
249	Andres Galarraga .05
250	Tony Gwynn 1.00
251	Lee Smith .05
252	Sammy Sosa 1.00
253	Jim Thome .45
254	Frank Rodriguez .05
255	Charlie Hayes .05
256	Bernard Gilkey .05
257	John Smiley .05
258	Brady Anderson .05
259	Rico Brogna .05
260	Kirt Manwaring .05
261	Len Dykstra .05
262	Tom Glavine .25
263	Vince Coleman .05
264	John Olerud .05
265	Orlando Merced .05
266	Kent Mercker .05
267	Terry Steinbach .05
268	Brian Hunter .05
269	Jeff Fassero .05
270	Jay Buhner .05
271	Jeff Brantley .05
272	Tim Raines .05
273	Jimmy Key .05
274	Mo Vaughn .05
275	Andre Dawson .25
276	Jose Mesa .05
277	Brett Butler .05
278	Luis Gonzalez .05
279	Steve Sparks .05
280	Chili Davis .05
281	Carl Everett .05
282	Jeff Cirillo .05
283	Thomas Howard .05
284	Paul O'Neill .05
285	Pat Meares .05
286	Mickey Tettleton .05
287	Rey Sanchez .05
288	Bip Roberts .05

289	Roberto Alomar .15
290	Ruben Sierra .05
291	John Flaherty .05
292	Bret Saberhagen .05
293	Barry Larkin .05
294	Sandy Alomar .05
295	Ed Sprague .05
296	Gary DiSarcina .05
297	Marquis Grissom .05
298	John Frascatore .05
299	Will Clark .05
300	Barry Bonds 2.00
301	Ozzie Smith 1.00
302	Dave Nilsson .05
303	Pedro Martinez .75
304	Joey Cora .05
305	Rick Aguilera .05
306	Craig Biggio .05
307	Jose Vizcaino .05
308	Jeff Montgomery .05
309	Moises Alou .05
310	Robin Ventura .05
311	David Wells .05
312	Delino DeShields .05
313	Trevor Hoffman .05
314	Andy Benes .05
315	Deion Sanders .05
316	Jim Bullinger .05
317	John Jaha .05
318	Greg Maddux 1.00
319	Tim Salmon .05
320	Ben McDonald .05
321	Sandy Martinez RC .05
322	Dan Miceli .05
323	Wade Boggs 1.00
324	Ismael Valdes .05
325	Juan Gonzalez .35
326	Charles Nagy .05
327	Ray Lankford .05
328	Mark Portugal .05
329	Bobby Bonilla .05
330	Reggie Sanders .05
331	Jamie Brewington .05
332	Aaron Sele .05
333	Pete Harnisch .05
334	Cliff Floyd .05
335	Cal Eldred .05
336	Jason Bates (Now Appearing) .05
337	Tony Clark (Now Appearing) .05
338	Jose Herrera (Now Appearing) .05
339	Alex Ochoa (Now Appearing) .05
340	Mark Loretta (Now Appearing) .05
341	Donne Wall RC (Now Appearing) .05
342	Jason Kendall (Now Appearing) .05
343	Shannon Stewart (Now Appearing) .05
344	Brooks Kieschnick (Now Appearing) .05
345	Chris Snopek (Now Appearing) .05
346	Ruben Rivera (Now Appearing) .05
347	Jeff Suppan (Now Appearing) .05
348	Phil Nevin (Now Appearing) .05
349	John Wasdin (Now Appearing) .05
350	Jay Payton (Now Appearing) .05
351	Tim Crabtree (Now Appearing) .05
352	Rick Krivda (Now Appearing) .05
353	Bob Wolcott (Now Appearing) .05
354	Jimmy Haynes (Now Appearing) .05
355	Herb Perry (Now Appearing) .05
356	Ryne Sandberg 1.00
357	Harold Baines .05
358	Chad Ogea .05
359	Lee Tinsley .05
360	Matt Williams .05
361	Randy Velarde .05
362	Jose Canseco .40
363	Larry Walker .05
364	Kevin Appier .05
365	Darryl Hamilton .05
366	Jose Lima .05
367	Javy Lopez .05
368	Dennis Eckersley .65
369	Jason Isringhausen .05
370	Mickey Morandini .05
371	Scott Cooper .05
372	Jim Abbott .05
373	Paul Sorrento .05
374	Chris Hammond .05
375	Lance Johnson .05
376	Kevin Brown .05
377	Luis Alicea .05
378	Andy Pettitte .25
379	Dean Palmer .05
380	Jeff Bagwell .75
381	Jaime Navarro .05
382	Rondell White .05
383	Erik Hanson .05
384	Pedro Munoz .05
385	Heathcliff Slocumb .05
386	Wally Joyner .05
387	Bob Tewksbury .05

388	David Bell .05
389	Fred McGriff .05
390	Mike Henneman .05
391	Robby Thompson .05
392	Norm Charlton .05
393	Cecil Fielder .05
394	Benito Santiago .05
395	Rafael Palmeiro .65
396	Ricky Bones .05
397	Rickey Henderson .75
398	C.J. Nitkowski .05
399	Shawon Dunston .05
400	Manny Ramirez .75
401	Bill Swift .05
402	Chad Fonville .05
403	Joey Hamilton .05
404	Alex Gonzalez .05
405	Roberto Hernandez .05
406	Jeff Blauser .05
407	LaTroy Hawkins .05
408	Greg Colbrunn .05
409	Todd Hundley .05
410	Glenn Dishman .05
411	Joe Vitiello .05
412	Todd Worrell .05
413	Wil Cordero .05
414	Ken Hill .05
415	Carlos Garcia .05
416	Bryan Rekar .05
417	Shawn Green (Topps Rookie All-Star) .40
418	Tyler Green .05
419	Mike Blowers .05
420	Kenny Lofton .05
421	Denny Neagle .05
422	Jeff Conine .05
423	Mark Langston .05
424	Steve Cox, Jesse Ibarra RC, Derrek Lee, Ron Wright RC (Prospects) .05
425	Jim Bonnici RC, Billy Owens, Richie Sexson, Daryle Ward RC (Prospects) .10
426	Kevin Jordan, Bobby Morris RC, Desi Relaford, Adam Riggs RC (Prospects) .10
427	Tim Harkrider, Rey Ordonez, Neifi Perez, Enrique Wilson (Prospects) .05
428	Bartolo Colon, Doug Million, Rafael Orellano, Ray Ricken RC (Prospects) .05
429	Jeff D'Amico, Marty Janzen RC, Gary Rath, Clint Sodowsky (Prospects) .05
430	Matt Drews, Rich Hunter RC, Matt Ruebel RC, Bret Wagner (Prospects) .05
431	Jaime Bluma, Dave Coggin RC, Steve Montgomery, Brandon Reed (Prospects) .05
432	Mike Figga, Raul Ibanez RC, Paul Konerko, Julio Mosquera (Prospects) .25
433	Brian Barber, Marc Kroon, Marc Valdes, Don Wengert (Prospects) .05
434	George Arias, Chris Haas RC, Scott Rolen, Scott Spiezio (Prospects) .50
435	Brian Banks RC, Vladimir Guerrero, Andruw Jones, Billy McMillon (Prospects) .50
436	Roger Cedeno, Derrick Gibson, Ben Grieve, Shane Spencer RC (Prospects) .50
437	Anton French, Demond Smith, Darond Stovall RC, Keith Williams (Prospects) .05
438	Michael Coleman RC, Jacob Cruz, Richard Hidalgo, Charles Peterson (Prospects) .10
439	Trey Beamon, Yamil Benitez, Jermaine Dye, Angel Echeverria (Prospects) .05
440	Checklist .05

Classic Confrontations

Head-to-head stats among baseball's top pitchers and hitters are featured in this insert set. The cards were seeded one per pack in the special 50-cent packs sold exclusively at Wal-Mart during the T206 Honus Wagner card giveaway promotion. Fronts have player action poses against a granite background and are highlighted in gold foil. Backs have a portrait photo and stats.

	NM/M
Complete Set (15):	3.50
Common Player:	.06
1	Ken Griffey Jr. .65
2	Cal Ripken Jr. 1.00
3	Edgar Martinez .45
4	Kirby Puckett .45
5	Frank Thomas .35
6	Barry Bonds 1.00
7	Reggie Sanders .05
8	Andres Galarraga .05
9	Tony Gwynn .45
10	Mike Piazza .65
11	Randy Johnson .35
12	Mike Mussina .25
13	Roger Clemens .50
14	Tom Glavine .25
15	Greg Maddux .45

Mickey Mantle Commemorative Last Day

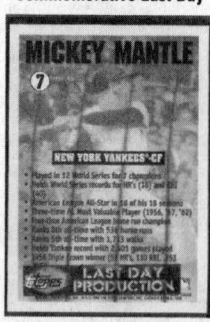

To mark the last day on which Topps would produce a #7 baseball card, the Mantle card from its 1996 set was issued in this sealed plastic case with a gold-foil logo on back.

	NM/M
7	Mickey Mantle 5.00

Mickey Mantle Reprints

One of Mickey Mantle's regular-issue Bowman or Topps cards from each year 1951-1969 was reproduced in 2-1/2" x 3-1/2" format as a Series 1 insert. Each card carries a gold-foil commemorative seal in one corner of the front. The reprints are found one per six retail packs and, in hobby, once per nine packs. The 1965-69 reprints were somewhat shortprinted (four 1965-69 cards for each five 1951-1964) and are 20 percent scarcer.

	NM/M
Complete Set (19):	90.00
Common Mantle:	5.00
Common SP Mantle (15-19):	8.00
1	1951 Bowman #253 15.00
2	1952 Topps #311 15.00
3	1953 Topps #82 5.00
4	1954 Bowman #65 5.00
5	1955 Bowman #202 5.00
6	1956 Topps #135 5.00
7	1957 Topps #95 5.00
8	1958 Topps #150 5.00
9	1959 Topps #10 5.00
10	1960 Topps #350 5.00
11	1961 Topps #300 5.00
12	1962 Topps #200 5.00
13	1963 Topps #200 5.00
14	1964 Topps #50 5.00

15	1965 Topps #350	8.00
16	1966 Topps #50	8.00
17	1967 Topps #150	8.00
18	1968 Topps #280	8.00
19	1969 Topps #500	8.00

Mickey Mantle Finest Reprints

Nineteen of Mickey Mantle's regular-issue Bowman and Topps cards from 1951-1969 were printed in Finest technology for this Series 2 insert set. Each card's chrome front is protected with a peel-off plastic layer. Average insertion rate for the Mantle Finest reprints is one per 18 packs. The 1965-69 reprints were printed in a ratio of four for every five 1951-64 reprints, making them 20 percent scarcer. Unmarked Refractor versions of each card were inserted at an average rate of 1:144 packs.

		NM/M
Complete Set (19):		90.00
Common Card (1-14):		6.00
Common Shortprint (15-19):		8.00
Refractors:		3X
Inserted 1:144		
1	1951 Bowman #253	15.00
2	1952 Topps #311	15.00
3	1953 Topps #82	6.00
4	1954 Bowman #65	6.00
5	1955 Bowman #202	6.00
6	1956 Topps #135	6.00
7	1957 Topps #95	6.00
8	1958 Topps #150	6.00
9	1959 Topps #10	6.00
10	1960 Topps #350	6.00
11	1961 Topps #300	6.00
12	1962 Topps #200	6.00
13	1963 Topps #200	6.00
14	1964 Topps #50	6.00
15	1965 Topps #350	8.00
16	1966 Topps #50	8.00
17	1967 Topps #150	8.00
18	1968 Topps #280	8.00
19	1969 Topps #500	8.00

Mickey Mantle Case Inserts

Inserted one per case of Series 2 Topps, these special versions of the 19 Mickey Mantle reprint cards come sealed in a soft plastic holder. The plastic sleeve has a gold-foil stamp at bottom-back which reads "FACTORY TOPPS SEAL 1996." Like the other Mantle reprints, the 1965-69 cards are somewhat scarcer due to short-printing.

		NM/M
Complete Set (19):		375.00
Common Mantle:		20.00
Common SP Mantle (15-19):		30.00
1	1951 Bowman #253	60.00
2	1952 Topps #311	60.00
3	1953 Topps #82	30.00
4	1954 Bowman #65	20.00
5	1955 Bowman #202	20.00
6	1956 Topps #135	20.00
7	1957 Topps #95	20.00
8	1958 Topps #150	20.00
9	1959 Topps #10	20.00
10	1960 Topps #350	20.00
11	1961 Topps #300	20.00
12	1962 Topps #200	20.00
13	1963 Topps #200	20.00
14	1964 Topps #50	20.00
15	1965 Topps #350	30.00
16	1966 Topps #50	30.00
17	1967 Topps #150	30.00
18	1968 Topps #280	30.00
19	1969 Topps #500	30.00

Mickey Mantle Redemption

Each of the 19 Mantle reprint cards, minus the commemorative gold-foil stamp on front, was also issued in a sweepstakes set. Seeded one per 108 packs, these cards could be sent in for a chance to win the authentic Mantle card pictured on front. Between one and 10 genuine Mantles were awarded for each of the 19 years. Cards entered in the sweepstakes were not returned when the contest ended Oct. 15, 1996. The sweepstakes cards are a Series 2 exclusive insert.

		NM/M
Complete Set (19):		200.00
Common Mantle:		10.00
Inserted 1:108 Series 2 Retail		
1	1951 Bowman #253	35.00
2	1952 Topps #311	35.00
3	1953 Topps #82	15.00
4	1954 Bowman #65	10.00
5	1955 Bowman #202	10.00
6	1956 Topps #135	10.00
7	1957 Topps #95	10.00
8	1958 Topps #150	10.00
9	1959 Topps #10	10.00
10	1960 Topps #350	10.00
11	1961 Topps #300	10.00
12	1962 Topps #200	10.00
13	1963 Topps #200	10.00
14	1964 Topps #50	10.00
15	1965 Topps #350	10.00
16	1966 Topps #50	10.00
17	1967 Topps #150	10.00
18	1968 Topps #280	10.00
19	1969 Topps #500	10.00

Mickey Mantle Commemorative Card Sheet

In conjunction with its program of reprinting most of the Mick's Topps and Bowman cards of the 1950s-1960s, Topps created this limited edition (numbered to 10,000) framed sheet depicting 20 cards surrounding an enlarged portrait from his famed 1952 Topps card. The sheet is embossed with a gold-foil #7 seal and was sold with a certificate of authenticity from Topps' president. The framed sheet measures about 19-1/2" x 25".

	NM/M
Framed Sheet:	80.00

Mickey Mantle Foundation

This black-and-white card was an insert exclusive to specially marked 1996 Topps factory sets. In standard 2-1/2" x 3-1/2" format, the card offers on its back information about the foundation and its work in health care and organ donation causes.

	NM/M
Mickey Mantle	4.00

Masters of the Game

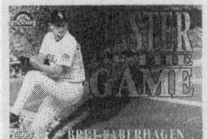

Appearing at a one per 18 pack rate, these inserts are exclusive to Series 1 hobby packs.

		NM/M
Complete Set (20):		20.00
Common Player:		.35
1	Dennis Eckersley	.75
2	Denny Martinez	.35
3	Eddie Murray	1.00
4	Paul Molitor	1.00
5	Ozzie Smith	1.50
6	Rickey Henderson	1.00
7	Tim Raines	.35
8	Lee Smith	.35
9	Cal Ripken Jr.	4.00
10	Chili Davis	.35
11	Wade Boggs	1.50
12	Tony Gwynn	1.50
13	Don Mattingly	2.00
14	Bret Saberhagen	.35
15	Kirby Puckett	1.50
16	Joe Carter	.35
17	Roger Clemens	2.00
18	Barry Bonds	4.00
19	Greg Maddux	1.50
20	Frank Thomas	

Mystery Finest

Each Mystery Finest insert has an opaque black film over the card front, concealing the identity of the player until removed. The inserts are seeded at the rate of one per 36 packs.

		NM/M
Complete Set (21):		25.00
Common Player:		.50
Refractors:		1.5X
M1	Hideo Nomo	1.00
M2	Greg Maddux	2.00
M3	Randy Johnson	1.50
M4	Chipper Jones	2.00
M5	Marty Cordova	.50
M6	Garret Anderson	.50
M7	Cal Ripken Jr.	4.00
M8	Kirby Puckett	2.00
M9	Tony Gwynn	2.00
M10	Manny Ramirez	1.50
M11	Jim Edmonds	.50
M12	Mike Piazza	2.50
M13	Barry Bonds	4.00
M14	Raul Mondesi	.50
M15	Sammy Sosa	2.00
M16	Ken Griffey Jr.	2.50
M17	Albert Belle	.50
M18	Dante Bichette	.50
M19	Mo Vaughn	.50
M20	Jeff Bagwell	1.50
M21	Frank Thomas	1.50

5-Star Mystery Finest

The 5-Star Mystery Finest inserts have an opaque black film over the card front, like the regular Mystery Finest, but has the words "5-Star" in large letters across the background. They are inserted at the average rate of one per 36 packs.

		NM/M
Complete Set (5):		12.50
Common Player:		2.00
Refractors:		2X
M22	Hideo Nomo	2.00
M23	Cal Ripken Jr.	5.00
M24	Mike Piazza	3.00
M25	Ken Griffey Jr.	3.00
M26	Frank Thomas	2.50

Power Boosters

This insert set is printed in Topps' "Power Matrix" technology, replacing two regular cards when found on the average of once per 36 packs. The Power Boosters reproduce the Star Power and Draft Picks subsets on a double-thick card.

		NM/M
Complete Set (26):		30.00
Common Player:		1.00
1	Tony Gwynn (Star Power)	2.00
2	Mike Piazza (Star Power)	3.00
3	Greg Maddux (Star Power)	2.00
4	Jeff Bagwell (Star Power)	1.50
5	Larry Walker (Star Power)	1.00
6	Barry Larkin (Star Power)	1.00
7	Tom Glavine (Star Power)	1.25
8	Craig Biggio (Star Power)	1.00
9	Barry Bonds (Star Power)	4.00
10	Heathcliff Slocumb (Star Power)	1.00
11	Matt Williams (Star Power)	1.00
12	Todd Helton (Draft Pick)	4.00
13	Mark Redman (Draft Pick)	1.00
14	Michael Barrett (Draft Pick)	1.00
15	Ben Davis (Draft Pick)	1.00
16	Juan LeBron (Draft Pick)	1.00
17	Tony McKnight (Draft Pick)	1.00
18	Ryan Jaroncyk (Draft Pick)	1.00
19	Corey Jenkins (Draft Pick)	1.00
20	Jim Scharrer (Draft Pick)	1.00
21	Mark Bellhorn (Draft Pick)	1.00
22	Jarrod Washburn (Draft Pick)	1.00
23	Geoff Jenkins (Draft Pick)	1.00
24	Sean Casey (Draft Pick)	2.00
25	Brett Tomko (Draft Pick)	1.00

Profiles-AL

Ten cards from this insert issue can be found in each of Topps Series 1 and 2. Analyzing an up-and-coming star, the cards are found every 12th pack, on average.

		NM/M
Complete Set (20):		8.00
Common Player:		.25
1	Roberto Alomar	.30
2	Carlos Baerga	.25
3	Albert Belle	.25
4	Cecil Fielder	.25
5	Ken Griffey Jr.	1.00
6	Randy Johnson	.60
7	Paul O'Neill	.25
8	Cal Ripken Jr.	1.50
9	Frank Thomas	.60
10	Mo Vaughn	.25
11	Jay Buhner	.25
12	Marty Cordova	.25
13	Jim Edmonds	.25
14	Juan Gonzalez	.35
15	Kenny Lofton	.25
16	Edgar Martinez	.25
17	Don Mattingly	.75
18	Mark McGwire	1.25
19	Rafael Palmeiro	.50
20	Tim Salmon	.25

Profiles-NL

Projected future stars of the National League are featured in this insert set. Ten players each are found in Series 1 and 2 packs at the rate of one per 12, on average.

		NM/M
Complete Set (20):		7.00
Common Player:		.25
1	Jeff Bagwell	.60
2	Derek Bell	.25
3	Barry Bonds	1.50
4	Greg Maddux	.75
5	Fred McGriff	.25
6	Raul Mondesi	.25
7	Mike Piazza	1.00
8	Reggie Sanders	.25
9	Sammy Sosa	.75
10	Larry Walker	.25
11	Dante Bichette	.25
12	Andres Galarraga	.25
13	Ron Gant	.25
14	Tom Glavine	.35
15	Chipper Jones	.75
16	David Justice	.25
17	Barry Larkin	.25
18	Hideo Nomo	.40
19	Gary Sheffield	.40
20	Matt Williams	.25

Road Warriors

These inserts feature top hitters and were only found in Series 2 packs sold at Wal-Mart stores. Cards have an RW prefix to their number. Fronts have action photos and gold foil highlights. Backs feature a portrait photo and hitting stats from the player's favorite out-of-town ballparks.

		NM/M
Complete Set (20):		9.00
Common Player:		.25
1	Derek Bell	.25
2	Albert Belle	.25
3	Craig Biggio	.25
4	Barry Bonds	2.50
5	Jay Buhner	.25
6	Jim Edmonds	.25
7	Gary Gaetti	.25
8	Ron Gant	.25
9	Edgar Martinez	.25
10	Tino Martinez	.25
11	Mark McGwire	1.50
12	Mike Piazza	1.25
13	Manny Ramirez	1.00
14	Tim Salmon	.25
15	Reggie Sanders	.25
16	Frank Thomas	1.00
17	John Valentin	.25
18	Mo Vaughn	.25
19	Robin Ventura	.25
20	Matt Williams	.25

Wrecking Crew

Printed on foilboard stock, cards of 15 players known for their hitting prowess are featured in this insert set. Found only in Series 2 hobby packs, the inserts are a one per 72 packs find, on average. Cards are numbered with a "WC" prefix.

		NM/M
Complete Set (15):		20.00
Common Player:		.50
1	Jeff Bagwell	1.50
2	Albert Belle	.50
3	Barry Bonds	5.00
4	Jose Canseco	.75
5	Joe Carter	.50
6	Cecil Fielder	.50
7	Ron Gant	.50
8	Juan Gonzalez	.75
9	Ken Griffey Jr.	3.00
10	Fred McGriff	.50
11	Mark McGwire	4.00
12	Mike Piazza	3.00
13	Frank Thomas	1.50
14	Mo Vaughn	.50
15	Matt Williams	.50

Team Topps

Some of baseball's most popular players and their teammates are featured on specially marked cards sold in blister packed team sets along with a jumbo "Big Topps" version of the team superstar's card. The team sets were a Wal-Mart exclusive, selling for around $5. Most of the Team Topps cards are identical to the regular-issue versions except for the addition of a gold-foil Team Topps logo on card front. Several cards in this special issue have had their regular and Star Power backs transposed.

		NM/M
Complete Set (84):		25.00
Common Player:		.10
Orioles Team Set (19):		8.00
Cal Ripken, Jr. Big Topps:		4.00
34	Manny Alexander	.10
65	Mike Mussina (Star Power front, regular back.)	.50
96	Cal Ripken Jr. (2,131)	1.25
121	Curtis Goodwin	.10
183	Doug Jones	.10
191	Chris Hoiles	.10
200	Cal Ripken Jr.	2.50
222	Cal Ripken Jr. (Star Power)	1.25
228	Mike Mussina (Regular-front, Star Power back.)	.50
234	Alvie Shepherd (Draft Pick)	.10
258	Brady Anderson	.10
320	Ben McDonald	.10
329	Bobby Bonilla	.10
352	Rick Krivda (Now Appearing)	.10
354	Jimmy Haynes (Now Appearing)	.10
357	Harold Baines	.10
376	Kevin Brown	.10
395	Rafael Palmeiro	.65
Cubs Team Set (16):		5.00
Ryne Sandberg Big Topps:		3.00
35	Todd Zeile	.10
55	Mark Grace	.10

62	Kevin Foster	.10
146	Frank Castillo	.10
184	Brian McRae	.10
198	Randy Myers	.10
239	Brian McNichol (Draft Pick)	.10
252	Sammy Sosa	1.00
278	Luis Gonzalez	.10
287	Rey Sanchez	.10
316	Jim Bullinger	.10
344	Brooks Kieshnick (Now Appearing)	.10
356	Ryne Sandberg	1.00
381	Jaime Navarro	.10
399	Shawon Dunston	.10

White Sox Team Set (15): 5.00
Frank Thomas Big Topps: 2.50

52	Ron Karkovice	.10
100	Frank Thomas	.75
119	Lyle Mouton	.10
129	Ozzie Guillen	.10
159	Wilson Alvarez	.10
173	Ray Durham (All-Star Rookie)	.10
194	Alex Fernandez	.10
229	Frank Thomas (Star Power)	.40
243	Jeff Liefer (Draft Pick)	.10
272	Tim Raines	.10
310	Robin Ventura	.10
345	Chris Snopek (Now Appearing)	.10
375	Lance Johnson	.10
405	Roberto Hernandez	.10

Yankees Team Set (19): 8.00
Derek Jeter Big Topps: 4.00

7	Mickey Mantle	3.00
27	Tony Fernandez	.10
68	Bernie Williams	.10
95	John Wetteland	.10
124	David Cone	.10
135	Mike Stanley	.10
185	Don Mattingly	1.25
203	Jack McDowell	.10
219	Derek Jeter (Future Star)	2.50
225	Wade Boggs (Star Power)	.50
245	Brian Buchanan (Draft Pick)	.10
273	Jimmy Key	.10
284	Paul O'Neill	.10
290	Ruben Sierra	.10
323	Wade Boggs	1.00
346	Ruben Rivera (Now Appearing)	.10
361	Randy Velarde	.10
378	Andy Pettitte	.35

Rangers Team Set (15): 5.00
Juan Gonzalez Big Topps: 2.00

79	Roger Pavlik	.10
87	Rusty Greer	.10
130	Kenny Rogers	.10
140	Ivan Rodriguez	.65
152	Benji Gil	.10
166	Mark McLemore	.10
178	Otis Nixon	.10
227	Ivan Rodriguez (Star Power)	.35
242	Jonathan Johnson (Draft Pick)	.10
286	Mickey Tettleton	.10
299	Will Clark	.10
325	Juan Gonzalez	.35
387	Bob Tewksbury	.10
379	Dean Palmer	.10

American League Champion Cleveland Indians

Sold in a blister pack at Wal-Mart stores, this team set features specially overprinted versions of the Indians' regular '96 Topps cards, along with a super-size "Big Topps" card of Albert Belle. Each card carries a color logo recognizing the Tribe's A.L. Championship season of 1995. Sets sold for around $5.

Complete Set (21): 4.00
Common Player: .10
Albert Belle Big Topps: 2.00

25	Sean Casey	1.50
40	Orel Hershiser	.10
45	Albert Belle	.10
75	Carlos Baerga	.10
81	Julian Tavarez	.10
84	Omar Vizquel	.10
125	Eddie Murray	.75
181	Denny Martinez	.10
223	Albert Belle (Star Power)	.10
226	Carlos Baerga (Star Power)	.10
231	Jose Mesa (Star Power)	.10
253	Jim Thome	.65
276	Jose Mesa	.10
294	Sandy Alomar	.10
326	Charles Nagy	.10
355	Herb Perry	.10
358	Chad Ogea	.10
373	Paul Sorrento	.10
400	Manny Ramirez	.75
414	Ken Hill	.10
420	Kenny Lofton	.10

A.L. West Champion Seattle Mariners

These specially marked versions of Topps regular '96 cards were sold for around $5 in a blister pack with a Ken Griffey, Jr. "Big Topps" card. The team sets were a Wal-Mart exclusive. Each of the Mariners' cards is overprinted with a color A.L. West Champions logo. Cards are otherwise identical to the regular issue.

Complete Set (18): 3.50
Common Player: .10
Ken Griffey, Jr. Big Topps: 3.50

38	Tim Belcher	.10
67	Felix Fermin	.10
94	Alex Diaz	.10
117	Dan Wilson	.10
150	Randy Johnson	.75
168	Tino Martinez	.10
205	Ken Griffey Jr.	1.50
224	Randy Johnson (Star Power)	.40
230	Ken Griffey Jr. (Star Power)	.75
238	Shane Monahan (Draft Pick)	.10
247	Edgar Martinez	.10
263	Vince Coleman	.10
270	Jay Buhner	.10
304	Joey Cora	.10
314	Andy Benes	.10
353	Bob Wolcott (Now Appearing)	.10
392	Norm Charlton	.10
419	Mike Blowers	.10

Dodger Stadium 35th Anniversary L.A. Dodgers

Celebrating 35 seasons of play in Chavez Ravine, this team set was issued in a blister pack with a jumbo Hideo Nomo "Big Topps" card. Selling for about $5, the team set was a Wal-Mart exclusive. Otherwise identical to the regular '96 Topps cards, these are overprinted with a colorful 35 Seasons logo. The backs of the two Mike Piazza cards in the set were switched. His regular card has the Star Power back (#2) while his Star Power card (#246) has the regular-issue back.

Complete Set (16): 5.00
Common Player: .10
Hideo Nomo Big Topps: 2.00

2	Mike Piazza (Star Power back)	2.50
48	Todd Hollandsworth	.10
89	Jose Offerman	.10
136	Hideo Nomo (All-Star Rookie)	1.00
153	Tom Candiotti	.10
175	Raul Mondesi	.10
196	Eric Karros	.10
206	Ramon Martinez	.10
217	Karim Garcia (Future Star)	.25
236	David Yocum (Draft Pick)	.10
246	Mike Piazza (Star Power front)	2.50
277	Brett Butler	.10
312	Delino DeShields	.10
324	Ismael Valdes	.10
402	Chad Fonville	.10
412	Todd Worrell	.10

World Champions Atlanta Braves

These specially marked versions of Topps regular 1996 cards feature a color World Champions logo overprinted on the front of each card. They were sold as a team set along with a 3-1/2" x 5" "Big Topps" card at Wal-Mart stores for around $5.

Complete Set (17): 4.00
Common Player: .10
Greg Maddux Big Topps: 3.00

3	Greg Maddux (Star Power)	.50
8	Tom Glavine (Star Power)	.15
12	Jim Scharrer (Draft Pick)	.10
49	Mark Wohlers	.10
60	David Justice	.10
83	Mark Lemke	.10
165	Steve Avery	.10
177	Chipper Jones (All-Star Rookie)	2.00
189	John Smoltz	.10
193	Ryan Klesko	.10
262	Tom Glavine	.30
266	Kent Mercker	.10
297	Marquis Grissom	.10
318	Greg Maddux	1.00
367	Javy Lopez	.10
389	Fred McGriff	.10
406	Jeff Blauser	.10

Big Topps

These double-size (3-1/2" x 5") cards are found exclusively in team-set blister packs prepared by Treat Entertainments for sale at Wal-Mart stores. Suggested retail price was just under $5. The Big Topps cards feature the fronts of the players' regular 1996 Topps card set against a marbled green background. Backs are in black-and-white with copyright data and licensors' logos. The unnumbered cards are checklisted here alphabetically.

Complete Set (9): 20.00
Common Player: 2.00

(1)	Albert Belle	2.00
(2)	Juan Gonzalez	2.00
(3)	Ken Griffey Jr.	3.50
(4)	Derek Jeter	4.00
(5)	Greg Maddux	3.00
(6)	Hideo Nomo	2.00
(7)	Cal Ripken Jr.	4.00
(8)	Ryne Sandberg	3.00
(9)	Frank Thomas	2.00

1996 Topps Chrome Promo Sheet

This promotional sheet was issued to promote the first annual issue of Topps Chrome baseball cards. The 8" x 5" sheet reproduces three of the card fronts from the forthcoming set in Topps' "Brilliant Chromium" technology. Back of the sheet is conventionally printed and advertises the set and its chase cards.

Sheet: 5.00

1996 Topps Chrome

In conjunction with baseball's postseason, Topps introduced the premiere edition of Chrome Baseball. The set has 165 of the elite players from 1996 Topps Series 1 and 2. Card #7 is a Mickey Mantle tribute card. There are two insert sets: Masters of the Game and Wrecking Crew, and scarcer Refractor versions for each.

Complete Set (165): 40.00
Common Player: .10
Refractors: 3X
Pack (4): 2.00
Wax Box (24): 30.00

1	Tony Gwynn (Star Power)	1.00
2	Mike Piazza (Star Power)	1.25
3	Greg Maddux (Star Power)	1.00
4	Jeff Bagwell (Star Power)	.75
5	Larry Walker (Star Power)	.10
6	Barry Larkin (Star Power)	.10
7	Mickey Mantle (Commemorative)	9.00
8	Tom Glavine (Star Power)	.10
9	Craig Biggio (Star Power)	.10
10	Barry Bonds (Star Power)	2.00
11	Heathcliff Slocumb (Star Power)	.10
12	Matt Williams (Star Power)	.10
13	Todd Helton (Draft Pick)	2.00
14	Paul Molitor	1.50
15	Glenallen Hill	.10
16	Troy Percival	.10
17	Albert Belle	.10
18	Mark Wohlers	.10
19	Kirby Puckett	2.00
20	Mark Grace	.10
21	J.T. Snow	.10
22	David Justice	.10
23	Mike Mussina	.75
24	Bernie Williams	.10
25	Ron Gant	.10
26	Carlos Baerga	.10
27	Gary Sheffield	.65
28	Cal Ripken Jr. (Tribute Card)	2.00
29	Frank Thomas	1.50
30	Kevin Seitzer	.10
31	Joe Carter	.10
32	Jeff King	.10
33	David Cone	.10
34	Eddie Murray	1.50
35	Brian Jordan	.10
36	Garret Anderson	.10
37	Hideo Nomo	.75
38	Steve Finley	.10
39	Ivan Rodriguez	1.25
41	Mark McGwire	3.00
42	Greg Vaughn	.10
43	Randy Johnson	1.50
44	David Segui	.10
45	Derek Bell	.10
46	John Valentin	.10
47	Steve Avery	.10
48	Tino Martinez	.10
49	Shane Reynolds	.10
50	Jim Edmonds	.10
51	Raul Mondesi	.10
52	Chipper Jones	2.00
53	Gregg Jefferies	.10
54	Ken Caminiti	.10
55	Brian McRae	.10
56	Don Mattingly	2.25
57	Marty Cordova	.10
58	Vinny Castilla	.10
59	John Smoltz	.10
60	Travis Fryman	.10
61	Ryan Klesko	.10
62	Alex Fernandez	.10
63	Dante Bichette	.10
64	Eric Karros	.10
65	Roger Clemens	2.25
66	Randy Myers	.10
67	Cal Ripken Jr.	4.00
68	Rod Beck	.10
69	Jack McDowell	.10
70	Ken Griffey Jr.	2.50
71	Ramon Martinez	.10
72	Jason Giambi (Future Star)	.75
73	Nomar Garciaparra (Future Star)	2.00
74	Billy Wagner (Future Star)	.10
75	Todd Greene (Future Star)	.10
76	Paul Wilson (Future Star)	.10
77	Johnny Damon (Future Star)	.35
78	Alan Benes (Future Star)	.10
79	Karim Garcia (Future Star)	.25
80	Derek Jeter (Future Star)	4.00
81	Kirby Puckett (Star Power)	1.00
82	Cal Ripken Jr. (Star Power)	2.00
83	Albert Belle (Star Power)	.10
84	Randy Johnson (Star Power)	.40
85	Wade Boggs (Star Power)	1.00
86	Carlos Baerga (Star Power)	.10
87	Ivan Rodriguez (Star Power)	.35
88	Mike Mussina (Star Power)	.30
89	Frank Thomas (Star Power)	.75
90	Ken Griffey Jr. (Star Power)	1.25
91	Jose Mesa (Star Power)	.10
92	Matt Morris RC (Draft Pick)	1.00
93	Mike Piazza	2.50
94	Edgar Martinez	.10
95	Chuck Knoblauch	.10
96	Andres Galarraga	.10
97	Tony Gwynn	2.00
98	Lee Smith	.10
99	Sammy Sosa	2.00
100	Jim Thome	1.25
101	Bernard Gilkey	.10
102	Brady Anderson	.10
103	Rico Brogna	.10
104	Lenny Dykstra	.10
105	Tom Glavine	.35
106	John Olerud	.10
107	Terry Steinbach	.10
108	Brian Hunter	.10
109	Jay Buhner	.10
110	Mo Vaughn	.10
111	Jose Mesa	.10
112	Brett Butler	.10
113	Chili Davis	.10
114	Paul O'Neill	.10
115	Roberto Alomar	.35
116	Barry Larkin	.10
117	Marquis Grissom	.10
118	Will Clark	.10
119	Barry Bonds	4.00
120	Ozzie Smith	2.00
121	Pedro Martinez	1.50
122	Craig Biggio	.10
123	Moises Alou	.10
124	Robin Ventura	.10
125	Greg Maddux	2.00
126	Tim Salmon	.10
127	Wade Boggs	2.00
128	Ismael Valdes	.10
129	Juan Gonzalez	.75
130	Ray Lankford	.10
131	Bobby Bonilla	.10
132	Reggie Sanders	.10
133	Alex Ochoa (Now Appearing)	.10
134	Mark Loretta (Now Appearing)	.10
135	Jason Kendall (Now Appearing)	.10
136	Brooks Kieschnick (Now Appearing)	.10
137	Chris Snopek (Now Appearing)	.10
138	Ruben Rivera (Now Appearing)	.10
139	Jeff Suppan (Now Appearing)	.10
140	John Wasdin (Now Appearing)	.10
141	Jay Payton (Now Appearing)	.10
142	Rick Krivda (Now Appearing)	.10
143	Jimmy Haynes (Now Appearing)	.10
144	Ryne Sandberg	2.00
145	Matt Williams	.10
146	Jose Canseco	.65
147	Larry Walker	.10
148	Kevin Appier	.10
149	Javy Lopez	.10
150	Dennis Eckersley	1.25
151	Jason Isringhausen	.10
152	Dean Palmer	.10
153	Jeff Bagwell	1.50
154	Rondell White	.10
155	Wally Joyner	.10
156	Fred McGriff	.10
157	Cecil Fielder	.10
158	Rafael Palmeiro	1.25
159	Rickey Henderson	1.50
160	Shawon Dunston	.10
161	Manny Ramirez	1.50
162	Alex Gonzalez	.10
163	Shawn Green	.45
164	Kenny Lofton	.10
165	Jeff Conine	.10

Masters of the Game

These 1996 Topps Chrome inserts were seeded one per every 12 packs. Each of the cards is also reprinted in a Refractor version; these cards are seeded one per every 36 packs.

Complete Set (20): 35.00
Common Player: 1.00
Refractors: 1.5X

1	Dennis Eckersley	2.00
2	Denny Martinez	1.00
3	Eddie Murray	2.50
4	Paul Molitor	2.50
5	Ozzie Smith	3.50
6	Rickey Henderson	1.00
7	Tim Raines	1.00
8	Lee Smith	1.00
9	Cal Ripken Jr.	6.00
10	Chili Davis	1.00
11	Wade Boggs	3.50
12	Tony Gwynn	3.50
13	Don Mattingly	1.00
14	Bret Saberhagen	1.00
15	Kirby Puckett	3.50
16	Joe Carter	1.00
17	Roger Clemens	4.00
18	Barry Bonds	6.00
19	Greg Maddux	3.50
20	Frank Thomas	2.50

Wrecking Crew

Wrecking Crew insert cards were inserted one per every 24 packs of 1996 Topps Chrome Baseball. Refractor versions were also made for these cards; they are seeded one per every 72 packs. Cards are numbered with a "WC" prefix.

Complete Set (15): 25.00

Common Player:		1.00
Refractors:		1.5X
1	Jeff Bagwell	2.50
2	Albert Belle	1.00
3	Barry Bonds	5.00
4	Jose Canseco	1.50
5	Joe Carter	1.00
6	Cecil Fielder	1.00
7	Ron Gant	1.00
8	Juan Gonzalez	1.25
9	Ken Griffey Jr.	3.50
10	Fred McGriff	1.00
11	Mark McGwire	4.00
12	Mike Piazza	4.00
13	Frank Thomas	2.50
14	Mo Vaughn	1.00
15	Matt Williams	1.00

1996 Topps Gallery

MARQUIS GRISSOM

This 180-card set is printed on 24-point stock utilizing metallic inks and a high-definition printing process. Then a high-gloss film is applied to each card, followed by foil stamping. The regular set is broken down into five subsets - The Classics, The Modernists, The Futurists, The Masters and New Editions. Each theme has a different design. Gallery also has four insert sets. Player's Private Issue cards are a parallel set to the main issue; these cards are seeded one per every 12 packs. The backs are sequentially numbered from 0-999, with the first 100 cards sent to the players; the rest are inserted into packs. The backs are UV coated on the photo only, to allow for autographing. The other insert sets are Expressionists, Photo Gallery and a Mickey Mantle Masterpiece card.

		NM/M
Complete Set (180):		20.00
Common Player:		.10
Private Issue:		8X
Pack (8):		1.50
Wax Box (24):		27.50
1	Tom Glavine	.35
2	Carlos Baerga	.10
3	Dante Bichette	.10
4	Mark Langston	.10
5	Ray Lankford	.10
6	Moises Alou	.10
7	Marquis Grissom	.10
8	Ramon Martinez	.10
8p	Ramon Martinez (Unmarked promo, "Pitcher" spelled out under photo on back.)	2.50
9	Steve Finley	.10
10	Todd Hundley	.10
11	Brady Anderson	.10
12	John Valentin	.10
13	Heathcliff Slocumb	.10
14	Ruben Sierra	.10
15	Jeff Conine	.10
16	Jay Buhner	.10
16p	Jay Buhner (Unmarked promo; height, weight and "Bats" on same line.)	2.50
17	Sammy Sosa	1.00
18	Doug Drabek	.10
19	Jose Mesa	.10
20	Jeff King	.10
21	Mickey Tettleton	.10
22	Jeff Montgomery	.10
23	Alex Fernandez	.10
24	Greg Vaughn	.10
25	Chuck Finley	.10
26	Terry Steinbach	.10
27	Rod Beck	.10
28	Jack McDowell	.10
29	Mark Wohlers	.10
30	Lenny Dykstra	.10
31	Bernie Williams	.10
32	Travis Fryman	.10
33	Jose Canseco	.45
34	Ken Caminiti	.10
35	Devon White	.10
36	Bobby Bonilla	.10
37	Paul Sorrento	.10
38	Ryne Sandberg	1.00
39	Derek Bell	.10
40	Bobby Jones	.10

41	J.T. Snow	.10
42	Denny Neagle	.10
43	Tim Wakefield	.10
44	Andres Galarraga	.10
45	David Segui	.10
46	Lee Smith	.10
47	Mel Rojas	.10
48	John Franco	.10
49	Pete Schourek	.10
50	John Wetteland	.10
51	Paul Molitor	.75
52	Ivan Rodriguez	.65
53	Chris Hoiles	.10
54	Mike Greenwell	.10
55	Orel Hershiser	.10
56	Brian McRae	.10
57	Geronimo Berroa	.10
58	Craig Biggio	.10
59	David Justice	.10
59p	David Justice (Unmarked promo; height,weight and "Bats" on same line.)	2.50
60	Lance Johnson	.10
61	Andy Ashby	.10
62	Randy Myers	.10
63	Gregg Jefferies	.10
64	Kevin Appier	.10
65	Rick Aguilera	.10
66	Shane Reynolds	.10
67	John Smoltz	.10
68	Ron Gant	.10
69	Eric Karros	.10
70	Jim Thome	.65
71	Terry Pendleton	.10
72	Kenny Rogers	.10
73	Robin Ventura	.10
74	Dave Nilsson	.10
75	Brian Jordan	.10
76	Glenallen Hill	.10
77	Greg Colbrunn	.10
78	Roberto Alomar	.25
79	Rickey Henderson	.75
80	Carlos Garcia	.10
81	Dean Palmer	.10
82	Mike Stanley	.10
83	Hal Morris	.10
84	Wade Boggs	1.00
85	Chad Curtis	.10
86	Roberto Hernandez	.10
87	John Olerud	.10
88	Frank Castillo	.10
89	Rafael Palmeiro	.65
90	Trevor Hoffman	.10
91	Marty Cordova	.10
92	Hideo Nomo	.10
93	Johnny Damon	.30
94	Bill Pulsipher	.10
95	Garret Anderson	.10
96	Ray Durham	.10
97	Ricky Bottalico	.10
98	Carlos Perez	.10
99	Troy Percival	.10
100	Chipper Jones	1.00
101	Esteban Loaiza	.10
102	Mark Loretta	.10
103	Jon Nunnally	.10
104	Andy Pettitte	.35
105	Lyle Mouton	.10
106	Jason Isringhausen	.10
107	Brian Hunter	.10
108	Quilvio Veras	.10
109	Jim Edmonds	.10
110	Ryan Klesko	.10
111	Pedro Martinez	.75
112	Joey Hamilton	.10
113	Vinny Castilla	.10
114	Alex Gonzalez	.10
115	Raul Mondesi	.10
116	Rondell White	.10
117	Dan Miceli	.10
118	Tom Goodwin	.10
119	Bret Boone	.10
120	Shawn Green	.35
121	Jeff Cirillo	.10
122	Rico Brogna	.10
123	Chris Gomez	.10
124	Ismael Valdes	.10
125	Javy Lopez	.10
126	Manny Ramirez	.75
127	Paul Wilson	.10
128	Billy Wagner	.10
129	Eric Owens	.10
130	Todd Greene	.10
131	Karim Garcia	.10
132	Jimmy Haynes	.10
133	Michael Tucker	.10
134	John Wasdin	.10
135	Brooks Kieschnick	.10
136	Alex Ochoa	.10
137	Ariel Prieto	.10
138	Tony Clark	.10
139	Mark Loretta	.10
140	Rey Ordonez	.10
141	Chris Snopek	.10
142	Roger Cedeno	.10
143	Derek Jeter	2.00
144	Jeff Suppan	.10
145	Greg Maddux	1.00
146	Ken Griffey Jr.	1.25
147	Tony Gwynn	1.00
148	Darren Daulton	.10
149	Will Clark	.10
150	Mo Vaughn	.10
151	Reggie Sanders	.10
152	Kirby Puckett	1.00
153	Paul O'Neill	.10
154	Tim Salmon	.10
155	Mark McGwire	1.50

156	Barry Bonds	2.00
157	Albert Belle	.10
158	Edgar Martinez	.10
159	Mike Mussina	.35
160	Cecil Fielder	.10
161	Kenny Lofton	.10
162	Randy Johnson	.75
163	Juan Gonzalez	.35
164	Jeff Bagwell	.10
165	Joe Carter	.10
166	Mike Piazza	1.25
167	Eddie Murray	.75
168	Cal Ripken Jr.	2.00
169	Barry Larkin	.10
170	Chuck Knoblauch	.10
171	Chili Davis	.10
172	Fred McGriff	.10
173	Matt Williams	.10
174	Roger Clemens	1.00
175	Frank Thomas	.75
176	Dennis Eckersley	.10
177	Gary Sheffield	.40
178	David Cone	.10
179	Larry Walker	.10
180	Mark Grace	.10

Players Private Issue

ARIEL PRIETO

The first 999 examples of each of the base cards in the Gallery issue are designated on the front with a gold-foil stamp as "Players Private Issue." The first 100 of those cards were given to the depicted player, the others are randomly packed. Besides the logo on front, the PPI cards are identified on back with an individual serial number.

		NM/M
Complete Set (180):		200.00
Common Player:		1.00
Stars:		8X

Expressionists

MARK McGWIRE

These 1996 Topps Gallery inserts feature 20 team leaders printed on triple foil-stamped and texture-embossed cards. Cards are seeded one per every 24 packs.

		NM/M
Complete Set (20):		20.00
Common Player:		.35
1	Mike Piazza	3.00
2	J.T. Snow	.35
3	Ken Griffey Jr.	3.00
4	Kirby Puckett	2.00
5	Carlos Baerga	.35
6	Chipper Jones	2.00
7	Hideo Nomo	.75
8	Mark McGwire	4.00
9	Gary Sheffield	.75
10	Randy Johnson	1.25
11	Ray Lankford	.35
12	Sammy Sosa	2.00
13	Denny Martinez	.35
14	Jose Canseco	.75
15	Tony Gwynn	2.00
16	Edgar Martinez	.35
17	Reggie Sanders	.35
18	Andres Galarraga	.35
19	Albert Belle	.35
20	Barry Larkin	.35

Masterpiece

Topps continues its tribute to Mickey Mantle with this 1996 Topps

Masterpiece

Gallery insert card. The card, seeded one per every 48 packs, has three photos of Mantle on the front, with his comprehensive career statistics on the back.

		NM/M
MP1	Mickey Mantle	6.00

Photo Gallery

Photo Gallery is a collection of 15 cards featuring photography of baseball's biggest stars and greatest moments from the last season. The text on the card includes details of the card's front and back photos. The cards are seeded one per every 30 packs. Cards are numbered with a "PG" prefix.

		NM/M
Complete Set (15):		20.00
Common Player:		.75
1	Eddie Murray	2.00
2	Randy Johnson	2.00
3	Cal Ripken Jr.	5.00
4	Bret Boone	.75
5	Frank Thomas	2.00
6	Jeff Conine	.75
7	Johnny Damon	.85
8	Roger Clemens	3.00
9	Albert Belle	.75
10	Ken Griffey Jr.	4.00
11	Kirby Puckett	2.50
12	David Justice	.75
13	Bobby Bonilla	.75
14	Larry Walker, Andres Galarraga, Vinny Castilla, Dante Bichette	1.00
15	Mark Wohlers, Javier Lopez	.75

Derek Jeter Panel

The method of issue for this triple-size (about 7-1/2" x 3-1/2") panel is uncertain. It has been reported that the piece was inserted into some 1995 Topps Hobby factory sets as an unadvertised bonus. The front has an action sequence showing the Yankees shortstop turning a double play. On back is personal data, minor and major league stats, a repeat of the center photo and a few sentences about the budding superstar.

		NM/M
	Derek Jeter	7.50

Landmark Medallions

Milestones of the 1995 season are recalled in this set of limited edition (2,000) medallions. Each of the 2-1/2" x 3-1/2" pieces features a Topps Finest technology card bonded to a 1/8" thick, 4-oz. burnished bronze ingot, then clear-coated. Backs have career stats and a description of the milestone minted into the bronze. The issue was sold only as complete sets through Topps Stadium Club; issue price was $100.

	NM/M
Complete Set (4):	75.00

LANDMARK
GREG MADDUX

Common Player:		10.00
1	Greg Maddux (4th straight Cy Young)	20.00
2	Albert Belle (First 50 HR/50 2B season)	10.00
3	Cal Ripken, Jr. (2,131 consecutive games)	35.00
4	Eddie Murray (3,000 hits)	15.00

1996 Topps Laser

Topps' 1996 Laser Baseball was the first set to use laser-cut technology on every card, creating surgically-precise latticework across the entire card. Every card in the 128-card regular issue set features one of four designs laser-cut into 20-point stock. One card from each of the four different designs is found in each four-card pack. Three different laser-cut insert sets were also produced: Bright Spots, Power Cuts and Stadium Stars. Cards 1-8 from each insert set were in Series 1 packs; cards 9-16 were seeded in Series 2 packs. A slightly oversize (1-5/8" x 3-5/8") checklist card in each pack helped protect the delicate die-cut details from damage.

		NM/M
Complete Set (128):		27.50
Common Player:		.10
Series 1 or 2 Pack (4):		1.50
Series 1 or 2 Wax Box (24):		22.50
1	Moises Alou	.10
2	Derek Bell	.10
3	Joe Carter	.10
4	Jeff Conine	.10
5	Darren Daulton	.10
6	Jim Edmonds	.10
7	Ron Gant	.10
8	Juan Gonzalez	.50
9	Brian Jordan	.10
10	Ryan Klesko	.10
11	Paul Molitor	1.00
12	Tony Phillips	.10
13	Manny Ramirez	1.00
14	Sammy Sosa	1.50
15	Devon White	.10
16	Bernie Williams	.10
17	Garret Anderson	.10
18	Jay Bell	.10
19	Craig Biggio	.10
20	Bobby Bonilla	.10
21	Ken Caminiti	.10
22	Shawon Dunston	.10
23	Mark Grace	.10
23p	Mark Grace (Unmarked promo, plain, rather than brushed, gold foil.)	2.00
24	Gregg Jefferies	.10
25	Jeff King	.10
26	Javy Lopez	.10
27	Edgar Martinez	.10
28	Dean Palmer	.10
29	J.T. Snow	.10
30	Mike Stanley	.10
30p	Mike Stanley (Unmarked promo; plain, rather than brushed, gold foil.)	1.00
31	Terry Steinbach	.10
32	Robin Ventura	.10
33	Roberto Alomar	.20

34	Jeff Bagwell	1.00
35	Dante Bichette	.10
36	Wade Boggs	1.50
37	Barry Bonds	3.00
38	Jose Canseco	.50
39	Vinny Castilla	.10
40	Will Clark	.10
41	Marty Cordova	.10
42	Ken Griffey Jr.	2.00
43	Tony Gwynn	1.50
44	Rickey Henderson	1.00
45	Chipper Jones	1.50
46	Mark McGwire	2.50
47	Brian McRae	.10
48	Ryne Sandberg	1.50
49	Andy Ashby	.10
50	Alan Benes	.10
51	Andy Benes	.10
52	Roger Clemens	1.75
53	Doug Drabek	.10
54	Dennis Eckersley	.75
55	Tom Glavine	.35
56	Randy Johnson	1.00
57	Mark Langston	.10
58	Denny Martinez	.10
59	Jack McDowell	.10
60	Hideo Nomo	.50
61	Shane Reynolds	.10
62	John Smoltz	.10
63	Paul Wilson	.10
64	Mark Wohlers	.10
65	Shawn Green	.35
66	Marquis Grissom	.10
67	Dave Hollins	.10
68	Todd Hundley	.10
69	David Justice	.10
70	Eric Karros	.10
71	Ray Lankford	.10
72	Fred McGriff	.10
73	Hal Morris	.10
74	Eddie Murray	1.00
75	Paul O'Neill	.10
76	Rey Ordonez	.10
77	Reggie Sanders	.10
78	Gary Sheffield	.45
79	Jim Thome	.75
80	Rondell White	.10
81	Travis Fryman	.10
82	Derek Jeter	3.00
83	Chuck Knoblauch	.10
84	Barry Larkin	.10
85	Tino Martinez	.10
86	Raul Mondesi	.10
87	John Olerud	.10
88	Rafael Palmeiro	.75
89	Mike Piazza	2.00
90	Cal Ripken Jr.	3.00
91	Ivan Rodriguez	.75
92	Frank Thomas	1.00
93	John Valentin	.10
94	Mo Vaughn	.10
95	Quilvio Veras	.10
96	Matt Williams	.10
97	Brady Anderson	.10
98	Carlos Baerga	.10
99	Albert Belle	.10
100	Jay Buhner	.10
101	Johnny Damon	.35
102	Chili Davis	.10
103	Ray Durham	.10
104	Lenny Dykstra	.10
105	Cecil Fielder	.10
106	Andres Galarraga	.10
107	Brian Hunter	.10
108	Kenny Lofton	.10
109	Kirby Puckett	1.50
110	Tim Salmon	.10
111	Greg Vaughn	.10
112	Larry Walker	.10
113	Rick Aguilera	.10
114	Kevin Appier	.10
115	Kevin Brown	.10
116	David Cone	.10
117	Alex Fernandez	.10
118	Chuck Finley	.10
119	Joey Hamilton	.10
120	Jason Isringhausen	.10
121	Greg Maddux	1.50
122	Pedro Martinez	1.00
123	Jose Mesa	.10
124	Jeff Montgomery	.10
125	Mike Mussina	.50
126	Randy Myers	.10
127	Kenny Rogers	.10
128	Ismael Valdes	.10
	Series 1 Checklist	.05
	Series 2 Checklist	.05

Bright Spots

Top young stars are featured on these insert cards, which use etched silver and gold diffraction foil. The cards are seeded one per 20 packs. Numbers 1-8 are in Series 1 packs; cards 9-16 are in Series 2 packs.

		NM/M
Complete Set (16):		17.50
Common Player:		.50
1	Brian Hunter	.50
2	Derek Jeter	4.50
3	Jason Kendall	.50
4	Brooks Kieschnick	.50
5	Rey Ordonez	.50
6	Jason Schmidt	.50
7	Chris Snopek	.50

8	Bob Wolcott	.50
9	Alan Benes	.50
10	Marty Cordova	.50
11	Jimmy Haynes	.50
12	Todd Hollandsworth	.50
13	Derek Jeter	4.50
14	Chipper Jones	3.00
15	Hideo Nomo	1.00
16	Paul Wilson	.50

Power Cuts

This insert set spotlights 16 of the game's top power hitters on etched foil and gold diffraction foil cards. These cards were seeded one per 40 packs; numbers 1-8 were in Series 1 packs; cards 9-16 were in Series 2 packs.

		NM/M
Complete Set (16):		20.00
Common Player:		.75
1	Albert Belle	.75
2	Jay Buhner	.75
3	Fred McGriff	.75
4	Mike Piazza	3.00
5	Tim Salmon	.75
6	Frank Thomas	2.00
7	Mo Vaughn	.75
8	Matt Williams	.75
9	Jeff Bagwell	2.00
10	Barry Bonds	5.00
11	Jose Canseco	1.00
12	Cecil Fielder	.75
13	Juan Gonzalez	1.00
14	Ken Griffey Jr.	3.00
15	Sammy Sosa	2.50
16	Larry Walker	.75

Stadium Stars

These 1996 Topps Laser cards are the most difficult to find; they are seeded one per every 60 packs. The 16 cards feature a laser-sculpted cover that folds back to reveal striated silver and gold etched diffraction foil on each card front. Cards 1-8 were in Series I packs; numbers 9-16 were Series II inserts.

		NM/M
Complete Set (16):		45.00
Common Player:		1.50
1	Carlos Baerga	1.50
2	Barry Bonds	10.00
3	Andres Galarraga	1.50
4	Ken Griffey Jr.	7.50
5	Barry Larkin	1.50
6	Raul Mondesi	1.50
7	Kirby Puckett	5.00
8	Cal Ripken Jr.	10.00
9	Will Clark	1.50
10	Roger Clemens	6.00
11	Tony Gwynn	5.00
12	Randy Johnson	4.00
13	Kenny Lofton	1.50
14	Edgar Martinez	1.50
15	Ryne Sandberg	5.00
16	Frank Thomas	4.00

League Leaders Finest Bronze

Specially designed Topps Finest cards are bedded to a slab of bronze and clear-coated in this set honoring major award winners from the 1995 season. A "League Leaders" logo at top has the player's award inscribed. Backs of the 2-3/4" x 3-3/4" ingots are silk-screened with season and career stats. The issue was sold only in complete sets (2,000 limit) through Topps Stadium Club for $80.

		NM/M
Complete Set (6):		75.00
Common Player:		10.00
(1)	Mo Vaughn (A.L. MVP)	10.00
(2)	Barry Larkin (N.L. MVP)	10.00
(3)	Randy Johnson (A.L. CY)	15.00
(4)	Greg Maddux (N.L. CY)	30.00
(5)	Marty Cordova (A.L. ROY)	10.00
(6)	Hideo Nomo (N.L. ROY)	15.00

Legends of the '50s

A dozen of the greatest players of the 1950s ever to grace a Topps card are featured in this set of bronze replicas. Each player's card is reproduced in a 4-oz. bronze version in 2-1/2" x 3-1/2" format. The card fronts are faithfully reproduced on each ingot, while the backs have been modified to present the player's lifetime stats. The ingots were sold through Topps' Stadium Club for about $45 apiece through a monthly subscription plan. The complete set was housed in a special wooden display case. The ingots are checklisted here alphabetically, with the year of Topps card reproduced noted parenthetically.

		NM/M
Complete Set (12):		275.00
Common Player:		20.00
(1)	Ernie Banks/1954	20.00
(2)	Yogi Berra/1952	20.00
(3)	Roy Campanella/1952	20.00
(4)	Whitey Ford/1953	20.00
(5)	Mickey Mantle/1952	35.00
(6)	Eddie Mathews/1952	20.00
(7)	Willie Mays/1953	25.00
(8)	Stan Musial/1959	20.00
(9)	Jackie Robinson/1952	20.00
(10)	Duke Snider/1955	20.00
(11)	Warren Spahn/1952	20.00
(12)	Ted Williams/1954 (#250)	30.00

"1952" Gold Willie Mays

This reproduction of Topps' 1952 card #261 is embossed and covered in 22-karat gold foil. Each full-size replica card is serially numbered within an edition of 50,000.

		NM/M
261	Willie Mays	12.00

"1954" Ted Williams Gold

This reproduction of Topps' 1954 card #1, Ted Williams, is embossed and covered in 22-karat gold foil. Each full-size replica card is serially numbered within an edition of 50,000.

		NM/M
1	Ted Williams	12.00

"1959" Stan Musial Gold

Topps' first regular-issue card of Stan Musial was reproduced in a full-size (2-1/2" x 3-1/2") 22-karat gold foil edition sold through Topps' Stadium Club. Each of the gold replicas bears a unique serial number. Issue price of the card was about $30.

		NM/M
150	Stan Musial	10.00

1997 Topps

Topps' 1997 set includes the first-ever player cards of the expansion Diamondbacks and Devil Rays; 16 Mickey Mantle reprints; a special Jackie Robinson tribute card; 27 Willie Mays Topps and Bowman reprints; randomly-inserted Willie Mays autographed reprint cards; and Inter-League Finest and Finest Refractors cards. The base set has 275 cards in Series 1 and 220 cards in Series 2. Each card front has a glossy coating on the photo and a spot matte finish on the border, with gold-foil graphics. Card backs have informative text, complete player stats and biographies, and a second photo. Mantle reprints, seeded one per 12 packs, feature the 16 remaining Mantle cards which were not reprinted in 1996, stamped with a gold foil logo, and numbered from #21 to #36. Willie Mays has 27 of his cards reprinted and seeded one per eight packs. Each card also has a gold foil stamp. As a special hobby-exclusive bonus, 1,000 Mays reprints were autographed and randomly inserted in packs. Five other insert sets were made: All-Stars, Inter-League Finest and Inter-League Finest Refractors, Sweet Strokes and Hobby Masters. Two factory sets, comprising the 495 base cards and either seven or eight random inserts were produced and currently enjoy a significant premium over hand-collated sets.

		NM/M
Unopened Fact. Set (504):		110.00
Unopened Fact. Set (503):		145.00
Complete Set (495):		65.00
Common Player:		.05
Ser. 1 or 2 Pack (11):		1.00
Ser. 1 or 2 Wax Box (36):		20.00
Ser. 1 or 2 Vending Box (500):		12.00
1	Barry Bonds	2.00
2	Tom Pagnozzi	.05
3	Terrell Wade	.05
4	Jose Valentin	.05
5	Mark Clark	.05
6	Brady Anderson	.05
7	Wade Boggs	1.00
8	Scott Stahoviak	.05
9	Andres Galarraga	.05
10	Steve Avery	.05
11	Rusty Greer	.05
12	Derek Jeter	2.00
13	Ricky Bottalico	.05
14	Andy Ashby	.05
15	Paul Shuey	.05
16	F.P. Santangelo	.05
17	Royce Clayton	.05
18	Mike Mohler	.05
19	Mike Piazza	1.50
20	Jaime Navarro	.05
21	Billy Wagner	.05
22	Mike Timlin	.05
23	Garret Anderson	.05
24	Ben McDonald	.05
25	Mel Rojas	.05
26	John Burkett	.05
27	Jeff King	.05
28	Reggie Jefferson	.05
29	Kevin Appier	.05
30	Paul Molitor	.75
31	Felipe Lira	.05
32	Kevin Tapani	.05
33	Mark Portugal	.05
34	Carlos Garcia	.05
35	Joey Cora	.05
36	David Segui	.05
37	Mark Grace	.05
38	Erik Hanson	.05
39	Jeff D'Amico	.05
40	Jay Buhner	.05
41	B.J. Surhoff	.05
42	Jackie Robinson	1.50
43	Roger Pavlik	.05
44	Hal Morris	.05
45	Mariano Duncan	.05
46	Harold Baines	.05
47	Jorge Fabregas	.05
48	Jose Herrera	.05
49	Jeff Cirillo	.05
50	Tom Glavine	.25
51	Pedro Astacio	.05
52	Mark Gardner	.05
53	Arthur Rhodes	.05
54	Troy O'Leary	.05
55	Bip Roberts	.05
56	Mike Lieberthal	.05
57	Shane Andrews	.05
58	Scott Karl	.05
59	Gary DiSarcina	.05
60	Andy Pettitte	.25
61a	Kevin Elster	.05
61b	Mike Fetters (Should be #84.)	.05
62	Mark McGwire	1.75
63	Dan Wilson	.05
64	Mickey Morandini	.05
65	Chuck Knoblauch	.05
66	Tim Wakefield	.05
67	Raul Mondesi	.05
68	Todd Jones	.05
69	Albert Belle	.05
70	Trevor Hoffman	.05
71	Eric Young	.05
72	Robert Perez	.05
73	Butch Huskey	.05
74	Brian McRae	.05
75	Jim Edmonds	.05
76	Mike Henneman	.05
77	Frank Rodriguez	.05
78	Danny Tartabull	.05
79	Robby Nen	.05
80	Reggie Sanders	.05
81	Ron Karkovice	.05
82	Benny Santiago	.05
83	Mike Lansing	.05
85	Craig Biggio	.05
86	Mike Bordick	.05
87	Ray Lankford	.05
88	Charles Nagy	.05
89	Paul Wilson	.05
90	John Wetteland	.05
91	Tom Candiotti	.05
92	Carlos Delgado	.45
93	Derek Bell	.05
94	Mark Lemke	.05
95	Edgar Martinez	.05
96	Rickey Henderson	.75
97	Greg Myers	.05
98	Jim Leyritz	.05
99	Mark Johnson	.05
100	Dwight Gooden (Season Highlights)	.05
101	Al Leiter (Season Highlights)	.05
102a	John Mabry (Season Highlights)(Last line on back ends "... Mabry."))	.05
102b	John Mabry (Season Highlights) (Last line on back ends "...walked.")	.05
103	Alex Ochoa (Season Highlights)	.05
104	Mike Piazza (Season Highlights)	.75
105	Jim Thome	.65
106	Ricky Otero	.05
107	Jamey Wright	.05
108	Frank Thomas	.75
109	Jody Reed	.05
110	Orel Hershiser	.05
111	Terry Steinbach	.05
112	Mark Loretta	.05
113	Turk Wendell	.05
114	Marvin Benard	.05
115	Kevin Brown	.05
116	Robert Person	.05
117	Joey Hamilton	.05
118	Francisco Cordova	.05
119	John Smiley	.05
120	Travis Fryman	.05
121	Jimmy Key	.05
122	Tom Goodwin	.05
123	Mike Greenwell	.05
124	Juan Gonzalez	.35
125	Pete Harnisch	.05
126	Roger Cedeno	.05
127	Ron Gant	.05
128	Mark Langston	.05
129	Tim Crabtree	.05
130	Greg Maddux	1.00
131	William Van Landingham	.05
132	Wally Joyner	.05
133	Randy Myers	.05
134	John Valentin	.05
135	Bret Boone	.05
136	Bruce Ruffin	.05
137	Chris Snopek	.05
138	Paul Molitor	.75
139	Mark McLemore	.05
140	Rafael Palmeiro	.65
141	Herb Perry	.05
142	Luis Gonzalez	.05
143	Doug Drabek	.05
144	Ken Ryan	.05
145	Todd Hundley	.05
146	Ellis Burks	.05
147	Ozzie Guillen	.05
148	Rich Becker	.05
149	Sterling Hitchcock	.05
150	Bernie Williams	.05
151	Mike Stanley	.05
152	Roberto Alomar	.25
153	Jose Mesa	.05
154	Steve Trachsel	.05
155	Alex Gonzalez	.05
156	Troy Percival	.05
157	John Smoltz	.05
158	Pedro Martinez	.75
159	Jeff Conine	.05
160	Bernard Gilkey	.05
161	Jim Eisenreich	.05
162	Mickey Tettleton	.05
163	Justin Thompson	.05
164	Jose Offerman	.05
165	Tony Phillips	.05
166	Ismael Valdes	.05
167	Ryne Sandberg	1.00
168	Matt Mieske	.05
169	Geronimo Berroa	.05
170	Otis Nixon	.05
171	John Mabry	.05
172	Shawon Dunston	.05
173	Omar Vizquel	.05
174	Chris Holles	.05
175	Doc Gooden	.05
176	Wilson Alvarez	.05
177	Todd Hollandsworth	.05
178	Roger Salkeld	.05
179	Rey Sanchez	.05
180	Rey Ordonez	.05
181	Denny Martinez	.05
182	Ramon Martinez	.05
183	Dave Nilsson	.05
184	Marquis Grissom	.05
185	Randy Velarde	.05
186	Ron Coomer	.05
187	Tino Martinez	.05
188	Jeff Brantley	.05
189	Steve Finley	.05
190	Andy Benes	.05
191	Terry Adams	.05
192	Mike Blowers	.05
193	Russ Davis	.05
194	Darryl Hamilton	.05
195	Jason Kendall	.05
196	Johnny Damon	.25
197	Dave Martinez	.05
198	Mike Macfarlane	.05
199	Norm Charlton	.05
200	Doug Million, Damian Moss, Bobby Rodgers (Prospect)	.05
201	Geoff Jenkins, Raul Ibanez, Mike Cameron (Prospect)	.05
202	Sean Casey, Jim Bonnici, Dmitri Young (Prospect)	.15
203	Jed Hansen, Homer Bush, Felipe Crespo (Prospect)	.05
204	Kevin Orie, Gabe Alvarez, Aaron Boone (Prospect)	.05
205	Ben Davis, Kevin Brown, Bobby Estalella (Prospect)	.05
206	Billy McMillon, Bubba Trammell RC, Dante Powell (Prospect)	.25
207	Jarrod Washburn, Marc Wilkins RC, Glendon Rusch (Prospect)	.05
208	Brian Hunter	.05
209	Jason Giambi	.45
210	Henry Rodriguez	.05
211	Edgar Renteria	.05
212	Edgardo Alfonzo	.05
213	Fernando Vina	.05
214	Shawn Green	.40
215	Ray Durham	.05
216	Joe Randa	.05
217	Armando Reynoso	.05
218	Eric Davis	.05
219	Bob Tewksbury	.05
220	Jacob Cruz	.05
221	Glenallen Hill	.05
222	Gary Gaetti	.05
223	Donne Wall	.05
224	Brad Clontz	.05
225	Marty Janzen	.05
226	Todd Worrell	.05
227	John Franco	.05
228	David Wells	.05
229	Gregg Jefferies	.05
230	Tim Naehring	.05
231	Thomas Howard	.05
232	Roberto Hernandez	.05
233	Kevin Ritz	.05
234	Julian Tavarez	.05
235	Ken Hill	.05
236	Greg Gagne	.05
237	Bobby Chouinard	.05
238	Joe Carter	.05
239	Jermaine Dye	.05
240	Antonio Osuna	.05
241	Julio Franco	.05
242	Mike Grace	.05
243	Aaron Sele	.05
244	David Justice	.05
245	Sandy Alomar	.05
246	Jose Canseco	.45
247	Paul O'Neill	.05
248	Sean Berry	.05
249	Nick Bierbrodt RC, Kevin Sweeney RC (Diamond Backs)	.05
250	Larry Rodriguez RC, Vladimir Nunez RC (Diamond Backs)	.10
251	Ron Hartman, David Hayman (Diamond Backs)	.05
252	Alex Sanchez, Matt Quataro (Devil Rays)	.05
253	Ronni Seberino, Pablo Ortega RC (Devil Rays)	.05
254	Rex Hudler	.05
255	Orlando Miller	.05
256	Mariano Rivera	.10
257	Brad Radke	.05
258	Bobby Higginson	.05
259	Jay Bell	.05
260	Mark Grudzielanek	.05
261	Lance Johnson	.05
262	Ken Caminiti	.05
263	J.T. Snow	.05
264	Gary Sheffield	.45
265	Darrin Fletcher	.05
266	Eric Owens	.05
267	Luis Castillo	.05
268	Scott Rolen	.65
269	Todd Noel RC, John Oliver (Draft Pick)	.05
270	Robert Stratton RC, Corey Lee RC (Draft Pick)	.05
271	Gil Meche RC, Matt Halloran RC (Draft Pick)	.50
272	Eric Milton RC, Dermal Brown (Draft Pick)	.25
273	Josh Garrett RC, Chris Reitsma RC (Draft Pick)	.10
274	A.J. Zapp RC, Jason Marquis RC (Draft Pick)	.50
275	Checklist	.05
276a	Checklist	.05
276b	Chipper Jones (Should be #277.)	1.00
278	Orlando Merced	.05
279	Ariel Prieto	.05
280	Al Leiter	.05
281	Pat Meares	.05
282	Darryl Strawberry	.05
283	Jamie Moyer	.05
284	Scott Servais	.05
285	Delino DeShields	.05
286	Danny Graves	.05
287	Gerald Williams	.05
288	Todd Greene	.05
289	Rico Brogna	.05
290	Derrick Gibson	.05
291	Joe Girardi	.05
292	Darren Lewis	.05
293	Nomar Garciaparra	1.00
294	Greg Colbrunn	.05
295	Jeff Bagwell	.75
296	Brent Gates	.05
297	Jose Vizcaino	.05
298	Alex Ochoa	.05
299	Sid Fernandez	.05
300	Ken Griffey Jr.	1.50
301	Chris Gomez	.05
302	Wendell Magee	.05
303	Darren Oliver	.05
304	Mel Nieves	.05
305	Sammy Sosa	1.00
306	George Arias	.05
307	Jack McDowell	.05
308	Stan Javier	.05
309	Kimera Bartee	.05
310	James Baldwin	.05
311	Rocky Coppinger	.05
312	Keith Lockhart	.05
313	C.J. Nitkowski	.05
314	Allen Watson	.05
315	Darryl Kile	.05
316	Amaury Telemaco	.05
317	Jason Isringhausen	.05
318	Manny Ramirez	.75
319	Terry Pendleton	.05
320	Tim Salmon	.05
321	Eric Karros	.05
322	Mark Whiten	.05
323	Rick Krivda	.05
324	Brett Butler	.05
325	Randy Johnson	.75
326	Eddie Taubensee	.05
327	Mark Leiter	.05
328	Kevin Gross	.05
329	Ernie Young	.05
330	Pat Hentgen	.05
331	Rondell White	.05
332	Bobby Witt	.05
333	Eddie Murray	.75
334	Tim Raines	.05
335	Jeff Fassero	.05
336	Chuck Finley	.05
337	Willie Adams	.05
338	Chan Ho Park	.05
339	Jay Powell	.05
340	Ivan Rodriguez	.65
341	Jermaine Allensworth	.05
342	Jay Payton	.05
343	T.J. Mathews	.05
344	Tony Batista	.05
345	Ed Sprague	.05
346	Jeff Kent	.05
347	Scott Erickson	.05
348	Jeff Suppan	.05

349 Pete Schourek .05
350 Kenny Lofton .05
351 Alan Benes .05
352 Fred McGriff .05
353 Charlie O'Brien .05
354 Darren Bragg .05
355 Alex Fernandez .05
356 Al Martin .05
357 Bob Wells .05
358 Chad Mottola .05
359 Devon White .05
360 David Cone .05
361 Bobby Jones .05
362 Scott Sanders .05
363 Karim Garcia .15
364 Kirt Manwaring .05
365 Chili Davis .05
366 Mike Hampton .05
367 Chad Ogea .05
368 Curt Schilling .25
369 Phil Nevin .05
370 Roger Clemens 1.25
371 Willie Greene .05
372 Kenny Rogers .05
373 Jose Rijo .05
374 Bobby Bonilla .05
375 Mike Mussina .35
376 Curtis Pride .05
377 Todd Walker .05
378 Jason Bere .05
379 Heathcliff Slocumb .05
380 Dante Bichette .05
381 Carlos Baerga .05
382 Livan Hernandez .05
383 Jason Schmidt .05
384 Kevin Stocker .05
385 Matt Williams .05
386 Bartolo Colon .05
387 Will Clark .05
388 Dennis Eckersley .65
389 Brooks Kieschnick .05
390 Ryan Klesko .05
391 Mark Carreon .05
392 Tim Worrell .05
393 Dean Palmer .05
394 Wil Cordero .05
395 Javy Lopez .05
396 Rich Aurilia .05
397 Greg Vaughn .05
398 Vinny Castilla .05
399 Jeff Montgomery .05
400 Cal Ripken Jr. 2.00
401 Walt Weiss .05
402 Brad Ausmus .05
403 Ruben Rivera .05
404 Mark Wohlers .05
405 Rick Aguilera .05
406 Tony Clark .05
407 Lyle Mouton .05
408 Bill Pulsipher .05
409 Jose Rosado .05
410 Tony Gwynn 1.00
411 Cecil Abbott .05
412 John Flaherty .05
413 Lenny Dykstra .05
414 Ugueth Urbina .05
415 Brian Jordan .05
416 Bob Abreu .05
417 Craig Paquette .05
418 Sandy Martinez .05
419 Jeff Blauser .05
420 Barry Larkin .05
421 Kevin Seitzer .05
422 Tim Belcher .05
423 Paul Sorrento .05
424 Cal Eldred .05
425 Robin Ventura .05
426 John Olerud .05
427 Bob Wolcott .05
428 Matt Lawton .05
429 Rod Beck .05
430 Shane Reynolds .05
431 Mike James .05
432 Steve Wojciechowski .05
433 Vladimir Guerrero .75
434 Dustin Hermanson .05
435 Marty Cordova .05
436 Marc Newfield .05
437 Todd Stottlemyre .05
438 Jeffrey Hammonds .05
439 Dave Stevens .05
440 Hideo Nomo .35
441 Mark Thompson .05
442 Mark Lewis .05
443 Quinton McCracken .05
444 Cliff Floyd .05
445 Denny Neagle .05
446 John Jaha .05
447 Mike Sweeney .05
448 John Wasdin .05
449 Chad Curtis .05
450 Mo Vaughn .05
451 Donovan Osborne .05
452 Ruben Sierra .05
453 Michael Tucker .05
454 Kurt Abbott .05
455 Andruw Jones .75
456 Shannon Stewart .05
457 Scott Brosius .05
458 Juan Guzman .05
459 Ron Villone .05
460 Moises Alou .05
461 Larry Walker .05
462 Eddie Murray (Season Highlights) .40
463 Paul Molitor (Season Highlights) .40

464 Hideo Nomo (Season Highlights) .20
465 Barry Bonds (Season Highlights) 1.00
466 Todd Hundley (Season Highlights) .05
467 Rheal Cormier .05
468 Jason Conti RC .05
469 Rod Barajas RC .05
470 Jared Sandberg, Cedric Bowers RC .05
471 Paul Wilders, Chie Gunner RC .05
472 Mike Decelle, Marcus McCain RC .05
473 Todd Zeile .05
474 Neifi Perez .05
475 Jeromy Burnitz .05
476 Trey Beamon .05
477 John Patterson, Braden Looper (Draft Picks) .15
478 Danny Peoples RC, Jake Westbrook RC (Draft Picks) .25
479 Eric Chavez RC, Adam Eaton (Draft Picks) .75
480 Joe Lawrence RC, Pete Tucci (Draft Picks) .05
481 Kris Benson, Billy Koch RC (Draft Picks) .25
482 John Nicholson, Andy Prater (Draft Picks) .25
483 Mark Kotsay RC, Mark Johnson (Draft Picks) .25
484 Armando Benitez .05
485 Mike Matheny .05
486 Jeff Reed .05
487 Mark Bellhorn, Russ Johnson, Enrique Wilson (Prospects) .05
488 Ben Grieve, Richard Hidalgo, Scott Morgan RC (Prospects) .05
489 Paul Konerko, Derrek Lee, Ron Wright (Prospects) .50
490 Wes Helms, Bill Mueller RC, Brad Seitzer (Prospects) .50
491 Jeff Abbott, Shane Monahan, Edgard Velazquez (Prospects) .05
492 Jimmy Anderson RC, Ron Blazier, Gerald Witasick Jr. (Prospects) .05
493 Darin Blood, Heath Murray, Carl Pavano (Prospects) .05
494 Mark Redman, Mike Villano RC, Nelson Figueroa (Prospects) .05
495 Checklist .05
496 Checklist .05

All-Stars

Topps' 1997 All-Stars insert cards, printed on a dazzling rainbow foilboard, feature the top players from each position. There are 22 cards, 11 from each league, which showcase the top three players from each position as voted by Topps' sports department. On the front of each card is a photo of a "first team" all-star player; the back has a different photo of that player, who appears alongside the "second team" and "third team" selections. These cards are seeded one per every 18 1997 Topps Series I packs. Cards are numbered with an "AS" prefix.

NM/M
Complete Set (22): 12.00
Common Player: .25
1 Ivan Rodriguez .75
2 Todd Hundley .25
3 Frank Thomas 1.00
4 Andres Galarraga .25
5 Chuck Knoblauch .25
6 Eric Young .25
7 Jim Thome .75
8 Chipper Jones 1.50
9 Cal Ripken Jr. 3.00
10 Barry Larkin .25
11 Albert Belle .25
12 Barry Bonds 3.00
13 Ken Griffey Jr. 2.00
14 Ellis Burks .25
15 Juan Gonzalez .60
16 Gary Sheffield .50
17 Andy Pettitte .35
18 Tom Glavine .35
19 Pat Hentgen .25
20 John Smoltz .25
21 Roberto Hernandez .25
22 Mark Wohlers .25

Inter-League Match Ups

The double-sided Inter-League Finest and Inter-League Finest Refractors (seeded one in 36 and one in 216 Topps Series 1 packs respectively) feature top individual matchups from inter-league rivalries. One player from each major league team is represented, for a total of 28 players on 14 different cards. Each card is covered with a Finest clear protector. Cards are numbered with an "ILM" prefix.

NM/M
Complete Set (14): 16.00
Common Card: .50
Refractors: 1.5X
1 Mark McGwire, Barry Bonds 3.00
2 Tim Salmon, Mike Piazza 2.00
3 Ken Griffey Jr., Dante Bichette 2.00
4 Juan Gonzalez, Tony Gwynn 1.50
5 Frank Thomas, Sammy Sosa 1.50
6 Albert Belle, Barry Larkin .50
7 Johnny Damon, Brian Jordan .75
8 Paul Molitor, Jeff King 1.00
9 John Jaha, Jeff Bagwell 1.00
10 Bernie Williams, Todd Hundley .50
11 Joe Carter, Henry Rodriguez .50
12 Cal Ripken Jr., Gregg Jefferies 3.00
13 Mo Vaughn, Chipper Jones 1.50
14 Travis Fryman, Gary Sheffield .75

Awesome Impact

This flashy insert exclusive to Series 2 retail packaging features young players who have quickly made their mark in the big leagues. Fronts have player action photos against a background of silver prismatic geometric shapes. Backs are horizontal with a player portrait photo, recent stats and a few words about the player's current and projected impact. Stated odds of finding this insert are one per 18 packs. Cards are numbered with an "AI" prefix.

NM/M
Complete Set (20): 20.00
Common Player: .40
1 Jaime Bluma .40
2 Tony Clark .40
3 Jermaine Dye .40
4 Nomar Garciaparra 4.50
5 Vladimir Guerrero 3.00
6 Todd Hollandsworth .40
7 Derek Jeter 6.00
8 Andruw Jones 3.00
9 Chipper Jones 4.50
10 Jason Kendall .40
11 Brooks Kieschnick .40
12 Alex Ochoa .40
13 Rey Ordonez .40
14 Neifi Perez .40
15 Edgar Renteria .40
16 Mariano Rivera .40
17 Ruben Rivera .40
18 Scott Rolen 2.25
19 Billy Wagner .40
20 Todd Walker .40

Hobby Masters

These 20 cards lead the way as dealers' top selections. The cards, printed on 28-point diffraction foilboard, replace two regular cards in every 36th pack of 1997 Topps Series 1 product. Cards are numbered with a "HM" prefix.

NM/M
Complete Set (20): 30.00
Common Player: .75
1 Ken Griffey Jr. 3.00
2 Cal Ripken Jr. 4.50
3 Greg Maddux 2.25
4 Albert Belle .75
5 Tony Gwynn 2.25
6 Jeff Bagwell 1.50
7 Randy Johnson 1.50
8 Raul Mondesi .75
9 Juan Gonzalez 1.00
10 Kenny Lofton .75
11 Frank Thomas 1.50
12 Mike Piazza 3.00
13 Chipper Jones 2.25
14 Brady Anderson .75
15 Ken Caminiti .75
16 Barry Bonds 4.50
17 Mo Vaughn .75
18 Derek Jeter 4.50
19 Sammy Sosa 2.25
20 Andres Galarraga .75

Mickey Mantle Reprints

All 16 remaining Mickey Mantle cards that were not reprinted in 1996 Topps Baseball are found in this insert, seeded every 12 packs of Series I Topps. The set starts off with No. 21 and runs through No. 36 since the '96 reprints were numbered 1-20.

NM/M
Complete Set (16): 60.00

Derek Jeter Autograph

An authentically autographed card honoring Derek Jeter as Rookie of the Year was a random insert found on average of one per 576 packs of Topps Series 2.

NM/M
Derek Jeter 130.00

The Sporting News
AMERICAN LEAGUE ALL-STAR
MICKEY MANTLE
OUTFIELD

Common Card: 5.00
Inserted 1:12 Series 1
21 1953 Bowman #44 5.00
22 1953 Bowman #59 5.00
23 1957 Topps #407 5.00
24 1958 Topps #418 5.00
25 1958 Topps #487 5.00
26 1959 Topps #461 5.00
27 1959 Topps #564 5.00
28 1960 Topps #160 5.00
29 1960 Topps #563 5.00
30 1961 Topps #406 5.00
31 1961 Topps #475 5.00
32 1961 Topps #578 5.00
33 1962 Topps #18 5.00
34 1962 Topps #318 5.00
35 1962 Topps #471 5.00
36 1964 Topps #331 5.00

Mickey Mantle Finest

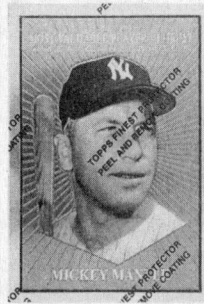

The Mickey Mantle reprint inserts found in Series 1 were re-issued in Series 2 in Finest technology, found on average of every 24 packs. Refractor versions of each Finest reprint were inserted at a 1:216 rate.

NM/M
Complete Set (16): 70.00
Common Card: 5.00
Inserted 1:24 Series 2
Refractor: 4X
Inserted 1:216
21 1953 Bowman #44 5.00
22 1953 Bowman #59 7.50
23 1957 Topps #407 5.00
24 1958 Topps #418 5.00
25 1958 Topps #487 5.00
26 1959 Topps #461 5.00
27 1959 Topps #564 5.00
28 1960 Topps #160 5.00
29 1960 Topps #563 5.00
30 1961 Topps #406 5.00
31 1961 Topps #475 5.00
32 1961 Topps #578 5.00
33 1962 Topps #18 5.00
34 1962 Topps #318 5.00
35 1962 Topps #471 5.00
36 1964 Topps #331 5.00

Mickey Mantle Case Inserts

WORLD SERIES BATTING FOES
MICKEY MANTLE - HANK AARON

Inserted one per case of Series 1 Topps, these reprints of 16 Mickey Mantle special cards of the 1950s-1960s come sealed in a soft plastic holder. The plastic sleeve has a gold-foil stamp at bottom-back which reads "FACTORY TOPPS SEAL 1997."

NM/M
Complete Set (16): 160.00
Common Card: 12.50
21 1953 Bowman #44 12.50
22 1953 Bowman #59 18.00
23 1957 Topps #407 12.50
24 1958 Topps #418 12.50
25 1958 Topps #487 12.50
26 1959 Topps #461 12.50
27 1959 Topps #564 12.50
28 1960 Topps #160 12.50
29 1960 Topps #563 12.50
30 1961 Topps #406 12.50
31 1961 Topps #475 12.50
32 1961 Topps #578 12.50
33 1962 Topps #18 12.50
34 1962 Topps #318 12.50
35 1962 Topps #471 12.50
36 1964 Topps #331 12.50

Willie Mays Reprints

GIANTS
WILLIE MAYS outfield

There are 27 different Willie Mays cards reprinted in Series 1 and seeded every eight packs. The inserts form a collection of Topps and Bowman cards from throughout Mays' career and each is highlighted by a special commemorative gold foil stamp. Many of the Mays reprints can also be found in an autographed edition, bearing a special "Certified Autograph Issue" gold-foil logo.

NM/M
Complete Set (27): 50.00
Common Card: 3.00
Autographed Card: 120.00
1 1951 Bowman #305 6.00
2 1952 Topps #261 4.00
3 1953 Topps #244 3.00
4 1954 Bowman #89 3.00
5 1954 Topps #90 3.00
6 1955 Bowman #184 3.00
7 1955 Topps #194 3.00
8 1956 Topps #130 3.00
9 1957 Topps #10 3.00
10 1958 Topps #5 3.00
11 1959 Topps #50 3.00
12 1960 Topps #200 3.00
13 1960 Topps #564 3.00
14 1961 Topps #150 3.00
15 1961 Topps #579 3.00
16 1962 Topps #300 3.00
17 1963 Topps #300 3.00
18 1964 Topps #150 3.00
19 1965 Topps #250 3.00
20 1966 Topps #1 3.00
21 1967 Topps #200 3.00
22 1968 Topps #50 3.00
23 1969 Topps #190 3.00
24 1970 Topps #600 3.00
25 1971 Topps #600 3.00
26 1972 Topps #49 3.00
27 1973 Topps #305 3.00

Willie Mays Reprint Autographs

According to Topps, only 19 of the 27 different Willie Mays cards reprinted in Series 1 exist in authentically autographed form, bearing a special "Certified Autograph Issue" gold-foil logo.

NM/M
Common Card: 120.00
1 1951 Bowman #305 150.00
2 1952 Topps #261 120.00
3 1953 Topps #244 120.00
6 1955 Bowman #184 120.00
7 1955 Topps #194 120.00
9 1957 Topps #10 120.00
10 1958 Topps #5 120.00
12 1960 Topps #200 120.00
13 1960 Topps #564 120.00
14 1961 Topps #150 120.00
15 1961 Topps #579 120.00
17 1963 Topps #300 120.00
18 1964 Topps #150 120.00
19 1965 Topps #250 120.00
20 1966 Topps #1 120.00

23	1969 Topps #190	120.00
24	1970 Topps #600	120.00
26	1972 Topps #49	120.00
27	1973 Topps #305	120.00

Willie Mays Finest

Series 2 offered collectors a chance to find Finest technology versions of each of the 27 commemorative reprint Topps and Bowman cards from throughout Mays' career. The Finest reprints are found one in every 30 packs, on average, with Refractor versions seeded 1:180.

		NM/M
Complete Set (27):		60.00
Common Card:		3.00
Refractor:		3X
Inserted 1:180		
1	1951 Bowman #305	6.00
2	1952 Topps #261	4.00
3	1953 Topps #244	3.00
4	1954 Bowman #89	3.00
5	1954 Topps #90	3.00
6	1955 Bowman #184	3.00
7	1955 Topps #194	3.00
8	1956 Topps #130	3.00
9	1957 Topps #10	3.00
10	1958 Topps #5	3.00
11	1959 Topps #50	3.00
12	1960 Topps #200	3.00
13	1960 Topps #564	3.00
14	1961 Topps #150	3.00
15	1961 Topps #579	3.00
16	1962 Topps #300	3.00
17	1963 Topps #300	3.00
18	1964 Topps #150	3.00
19	1965 Topps #250	3.00
20	1966 Topps #1	3.00
21	1967 Topps #200	3.00
22	1968 Topps #50	3.00
23	1969 Topps #190	3.00
24	1970 Topps #600	3.00
25	1971 Topps #600	3.00
26	1972 Topps #49	3.00
27	1973 Topps #305	3.00

Willie Mays Commemorative Super

This oversize (4-1/4" x 5-3/4") version of card #2 (1952 Topps) in the Willie Mays Commemorative Reprint series was available exclusively in a special retail packaging of 10 1997 Topps Series 1 foil packs. Like the regular-size reprints, it has a gold-foil commemorative stamp on front.

		NM/M
2	Willie Mays (1952 Topps)	5.00

Season's Best

Season's Best features 25 players on prismatic illusion foilboard, and can be found every six packs. The set has the top five players from five statistical categories: home runs, RBIs, batting average, steals, and wins. Season's Best can be found in packs of Topps Series II, and later reprinted on chromium stock as part of Topps Chrome.

		NM/M
Complete Set (25):		12.00
Common Player:		.25
1	Tony Gwynn	1.50
2	Frank Thomas	1.25
3	Ellis Burks	.25
4	Paul Molitor	1.25
5	Chuck Knoblauch	.25
6	Mark McGwire	3.00
7	Brady Anderson	.25
8	Ken Griffey Jr.	2.00
9	Albert Belle	.25
10	Andres Galarraga	.25
11	Andres Galarraga	.25
12	Albert Belle	.25
13	Juan Gonzalez	.75
14	Mo Vaughn	.25
15	Rafael Palmeiro	1.00
16	John Smoltz	.25
17	Andy Pettitte	.50
18	Pat Hentgen	.25
19	Mike Mussina	.50
20	Andy Benes	.25
21	Kenny Lofton	.25
22	Tom Goodwin	.25
23	Otis Nixon	.25
24	Eric Young	.25
25	Lance Johnson	.25

Series 2 Supers

At 3-3/4" x 5-1/4", these premium cards are nearly identical to the regular-issue versions except for size. Also, whereas the regular cards have a front format which combines a high-gloss central area with a matte finish near the borders, the supers have just one finish on the front which is a semi-gloss. The supers also have different card numbers on back. One of the supers was included in each boxed lot of 15 Series II foil packs sold at large retail outlets with a price tag of about $15.

		NM/M
Complete Set (3):		10.00
1	Chipper Jones	3.00
2	Ken Griffey Jr.	4.00
3	Cal Ripken Jr.	5.00

Sweet Strokes

These retail-exclusive Sweet Strokes insert cards consist of 15 Power Matrix foil cards of the top hitters in the game. These players have the swings to produce game winning-hits. The cards were seeded one per every 12 1997 Topps Series I retail packs. Cards are numbered with a "SS" prefix.

		NM/M
Complete Set (15):		15.00

Number Crunchers

Common Player:		.35
1	Roberto Alomar	.35
2	Jeff Bagwell	1.25
3	Albert Belle	.35
4	Barry Bonds	3.00
5	Mark Grace	.35
6	Ken Griffey Jr.	2.00
7	Tony Gwynn	1.50
8	Chipper Jones	1.50
9	Edgar Martinez	.35
10	Mark McGwire	2.50
11	Rafael Palmeiro	1.00
12	Mike Piazza	2.00
13	Gary Sheffield	.75
14	Frank Thomas	1.25
15	Mo Vaughn	.35

Team Timber

Team Timber was a 16-card insert that was exclusive to retail packs and inserted one per 36. The set displays the game's top sluggers on laminated litho wood cards. Cards are numbered with a "TT" prefix.

		NM/M
Complete Set (16):		24.00
Common Player:		.50
1	Ken Griffey Jr.	3.00
2	Ken Caminiti	.50
3	Bernie Williams	.50
4	Jeff Bagwell	1.50
5	Frank Thomas	1.50
6	Andres Galarraga	.50
7	Barry Bonds	5.00
8	Rafael Palmeiro	1.25
9	Brady Anderson	.50
10	Juan Gonzalez	.75
11	Mo Vaughn	.50
12	Mark McGwire	4.00
13	Gary Sheffield	.90
14	Albert Belle	.50
15	Chipper Jones	2.50
16	Mike Piazza	3.00

1997 Topps Chrome

Chrome Baseball reprinted the top 165 cards from Topps Series I and II baseball on a chromium, metallized stock. Chrome sold in four-card packs and included three insert sets: Diamond Duos, which was created exclusively for this product, Season's Best and Topps All-Stars, which were both reprinted from Topps products. Refractor versions of each card were found every 12 packs.

		NM/M
Complete Set (165):		35.00
Common Player:		.10
Refractors:		2X
Pack (4):		1.50
Wax Box (24):		25.00
1	Barry Bonds	3.00
2	Jose Valentin	.10
3	Brady Anderson	.10
4	Wade Boggs	1.50
5	Andres Galarraga	.10
6	Rusty Greer	.10
7	Derek Jeter	3.00
8	Ricky Bottalico	.10
9	Mike Piazza	2.00
10	Garret Anderson	.10
11	Jeff King	.10
12	Kevin Appier	.10
13	Mark Grace	.10
14	Jeff D'Amico	.10
15	Jay Buhner	.10
16	Hal Morris	.10
17	Harold Baines	.10
18	Jeff Cirillo	.10
19	Tom Glavine	.35
20	Andy Pettitte	.35
21	Mark McGwire	2.50
22	Chuck Knoblauch	.10
23	Raul Mondesi	.10
24	Albert Belle	.10
25	Trevor Hoffman	.10
26	Eric Young	.10
27	Brian McRae	.10
28	Jim Edmonds	.10
29	Robb Nen	.10
30	Reggie Sanders	.10
31	Mike Lansing	.10
32	Craig Biggio	.10
33	Ray Lankford	.10
34	Charles Nagy	.10
35	Paul Wilson	.10
36	John Wetteland	.10
37	Derek Bell	.10
38	Edgar Martinez	.10
39	Rickey Henderson	1.00
40	Jim Thome	.75
41	Frank Thomas	1.00
42	Jackie Robinson (Tribute)	2.00
43	Terry Steinbach	.10
44	Kevin Brown	.10
45	Joey Hamilton	.10
46	Travis Fryman	.10
47	Juan Gonzalez	.50
48	Ron Gant	.10
49	Greg Maddux	1.50
50	Wally Joyner	.10
51	John Valentin	.10
52	Bret Boone	.10
53	Paul Molitor	1.00
54	Rafael Palmeiro	.75
55	Todd Hundley	.10
56	Ellis Burks	.10
57	Bernie Williams	.10
58	Roberto Alomar	.25
59	Jose Mesa	.10
60	Troy Percival	.10
61	John Smoltz	.10
62	Jeff Conine	.10
63	Bernard Gilkey	.10
64	Mickey Tettleton	.10
65	Justin Thompson	.10
66	Tony Phillips	.10
67	Ryne Sandberg	1.50
68	Geronimo Berroa	.10
69	Todd Hollandsworth	.10
70	Rey Ordonez	.10
71	Marquis Grissom	.10
72	Tino Martinez	.10
73	Steve Finley	.10
74	Andy Benes	.10
75	Jason Kendall	.10
76	Johnny Damon	.35
77	Jason Giambi	.50
78	Henry Rodriguez	.10
79	Edgar Renteria	.10
80	Ray Durham	.10
81	Gregg Jefferies	.10
82	Roberto Hernandez	.10
83	Joe Carter	.10
84	Jermaine Dye	.10
85	Julio Franco	.10
86	David Justice	.10
87	Jose Canseco	.50
88	Paul O'Neill	.10
89	Mariano Rivera	.15
90	Bobby Higginson	.10
91	Mark Grudzielanek	.10
92	Lance Johnson	.10
93	Ken Caminiti	.10
94	Gary Sheffield	.50
95	Luis Castillo	.10
96	Scott Rolen	.75
97	Chipper Jones	1.50
98	Darryl Strawberry	.10
99	Nomar Garciaparra	1.50
100	Jeff Bagwell	1.00
101	Ken Griffey Jr.	2.00
102	Sammy Sosa	1.50
103	Jack McDowell	.10
104	James Baldwin	.10
105	Rocky Coppinger	.10
106	Manny Ramirez	1.00
107	Tim Salmon	.10
108	Eric Karros	.10
109	Brett Butler	.10
110	Randy Johnson	1.00
111	Pat Hentgen	.10
112	Rondell White	.10
113	Eddie Murray	1.00
114	Ivan Rodriguez	.75
115	Jermaine Allensworth	.10
116	Ed Sprague	.10
117	Kenny Lofton	.50
118	Alan Benes	.10
119	Fred McGriff	.25
120	Alex Fernandez	.10
121	Al Martin	.10
122	Devon White	.10
123	David Cone	.10
124	Karim Garcia	.25
125	Chili Davis	.10
126	Roger Clemens	1.75
127	Bobby Bonilla	.10
128	Mike Mussina	.50
129	Todd Walker	.10
130	Dante Bichette	.10
131	Carlos Baerga	.10
132	Matt Williams	.10
133	Will Clark	.10
134	Dennis Eckersley	.75
135	Ryan Klesko	.10
136	Dean Palmer	.10
137	Javy Lopez	.10
138	Greg Vaughn	.10
139	Vinny Castilla	.10
140	Cal Ripken Jr.	3.00
141	Ruben Rivera	.10
142	Mark Wohlers	.10
143	Tony Clark	.10
144	Jose Rosado	.10
145	Tony Gwynn	1.50
146	Cecil Fielder	.10
147	Brian Jordan	.10
148	Bob Abreu	.10
149	Barry Larkin	.10
150	Robin Ventura	.10
151	John Olerud	.10
152	Rod Beck	.10
153	Vladimir Guerrero	1.00
154	Marty Cordova	.10
155	Todd Stottlemyre	.10
156	Hideo Nomo	.50
157	Denny Neagle	.10
158	John Jaha	.10
159	Mo Vaughn	.10
160	Andruw Jones	1.00
161	Moises Alou	.10
162	Larry Walker	.10
163	Eddie Murray (Season Highlights)	.75
164	Paul Molitor (Season Highlights)	.75
165	Checklist	.10

All-Stars

Topps Chrome All-Stars display the same 22 cards found in Topps Series I, however these are reprinted on a Chrome stock. Regular versions are seeded every 24 packs, while Refractor versions arrive every 72 packs. Cards are numbered with an "AS" prefix.

		NM/M
Complete Set (22):		25.00
Common Player:		.75
Refractors:		1.5X
1	Ivan Rodriguez	1.50
2	Todd Hundley	.75
3	Frank Thomas	2.00
4	Andres Galarraga	.75
5	Chuck Knoblauch	.75
6	Eric Young	.75
7	Jim Thome	1.50
8	Chipper Jones	3.00
9	Cal Ripken Jr.	6.00
10	Barry Larkin	.75
11	Albert Belle	.75
12	Barry Bonds	6.00
13	Ken Griffey Jr.	4.00
14	Ellis Burks	.75
15	Juan Gonzalez	1.00
16	Gary Sheffield	1.25
17	Andy Pettitte	1.00
18	Tom Glavine	1.00
19	Pat Hentgen	.75
20	John Smoltz	.75
21	Roberto Hernandez	.75
22	Mark Wohlers	.75

Diamond Duos

Diamond Duos is the only one of the three insert sets in Chrome Baseball that was developed exclusively for this product. The set has 10 cards featuring two superstar teammates on double-sided chromium cards. Diamond Duos are found every 36 packs, while Refractor versions are found every 108 packs. Cards are numbered with a "DD" prefix.

		NM/M
Complete Set (10):		17.50
Common Player:		.50
Refractors:		1.5X
1	Chipper Jones, Andruw Jones	2.00

Diamond Duos

2	Derek Jeter, Bernie Williams	4.00
3	Ken Griffey Jr., Jay Buhner	2.50
4	Kenny Lofton, Manny Ramirez	1.50
5	Jeff Bagwell, Craig Biggio	1.50
6	Juan Gonzalez, Ivan Rodriguez	1.25
7	Cal Ripken Jr., Brady Anderson	4.00
8	Mike Piazza, Hideo Nomo	2.50
9	Andres Galarraga, Dante Bichette	.50
10	Frank Thomas, Albert Belle	1.50

Season's Best

Season's Best includes the 25 players found in Topps Series II, but in a chromium version. The top five players from five statistical categories, including Leading Looters, Bleacher Reachers and Kings of Swing. Regular versions are seeded every 18 packs, with Refractors every 54 packs.

		NM/M
Complete Set (25):		17.50
Common Player:		.50
Refractors:		1.5X
1	Tony Gwynn	2.00
2	Frank Thomas	1.50
3	Ellis Burks	.50
4	Paul Molitor	1.50
5	Chuck Knoblauch	.50
6	Mark McGwire	4.00
7	Brady Anderson	.50
8	Ken Griffey Jr.	3.00
9	Albert Belle	.50
10	Andres Galarraga	.50
11	Andres Galarraga	.50
12	Albert Belle	.50
13	Juan Gonzalez	.75
14	Mo Vaughn	.50
15	Rafael Palmeiro	1.25
16	John Smoltz	.50
17	Andy Pettitte	.75
18	Pat Hentgen	.75
19	Mike Mussina	.75
20	Andy Benes	.50
21	Kenny Lofton	.50
22	Tom Goodwin	.50
23	Otis Nixon	.50
24	Eric Young	.50
25	Lance Johnson	.50

Jumbos

These large-format (3-3/4" x 5-1/4") Topps Chrome cards were produced for sale in special retail packaging offering one jumbo card and five packs of Topps Chrome for about $15. The jumbos are identical in design to the regular-issue Chrome cards of the same players. Because they were offered in a windowed retail package, it was easy for collectors to pick the card they wanted.

		NM/M
Complete Set (6):		10.00
Common Player:		.75
9	Mike Piazza	

94	Gary Sheffield	.75
97	Chipper Jones	1.50
101	Ken Griffey Jr.	2.00
102	Sammy Sosa	1.50
140	Cal Ripken Jr.	3.00

1997 Topps Gallery Pre-Production

In its second year Topps Gallery was produced in a greatly improved combination of card stock, graphic highlights and inserts. To reintroduce the hobby to the issue, Topps distributed these promotional samples to dealers and the press. Except for the "PP" prefix to the card number on front, the samples are virtually identical to the issued versions.

		NM/M
Complete Set (4):		25.00
Common Player:		3.00
1	Andruw Jones	5.00
2	Derek Jeter	9.00
3	Mike Piazza	10.00
4	Craig Biggio	3.00

1997 Topps Gallery

The second year of Gallery features 180 cards printed on extra-thick 24-point stock. Card fronts feature a player photo surrounded by an embossed foil "frame" to give each card the look of a piece of artwork. Backs contain career stats and biographical information on each player. Inserts include Peter Max Serigraphs, Signature Series Serigraphs, Player's Private Issue (parallel set), Photo Gallery and Gallery of Heroes. Cards were sold exclusively in hobby shops in eight-card packs for $4 each.

		NM/M
Complete Set (180):		20.00
Common Player:		.10
Pack (8):		1.50
Wax Box (24):		25.00
1	Paul Molitor	.75
2	Devon White	.10
3	Andres Galarraga	.10
4	Cal Ripken Jr.	3.00
5	Tony Gwynn	1.50
6	Mike Stanley	.10
7	Orel Hershiser	.10
8	Jose Canseco	.50
9	Chili Davis	.10
10	Harold Baines	.10
11	Rickey Henderson	.75
12	Darryl Strawberry	.10
13	Todd Worrell	.10
14	Cecil Fielder	.10
15	Gary Gaetti	.10
16	Bobby Bonilla	.10
17	Will Clark	.10
18	Kevin Brown	.10
19	Tom Glavine	.35
20	Wade Boggs	1.50
21	Edgar Martinez	.10
22	Lance Johnson	.10
23	Gregg Jefferies	.10
24	Bip Roberts	.10
25	Tony Phillips	.10
26	Greg Maddux	1.50
27	Mickey Tettleton	.10
28	Terry Steinbach	.10
29	Ryne Sandberg	1.50
30	Wally Joyner	.10
31	Joe Carter	.10
32	Ellis Burks	.10
33	Fred McGriff	.10
34	Barry Larkin	.10
35	John Franco	.10
36	Rafael Palmeiro	.65
37	Mark McGwire	2.50
38	Ken Caminiti	.10
39	David Cone	.10
40	Julio Franco	.10
41	Roger Clemens	1.75
42	Barry Bonds	3.00
43	Dennis Eckersley	.65
44	Eddie Murray	.75
45	Paul O'Neill	.10
46	Craig Biggio	.10
47	Roberto Alomar	.20
48	Mark Grace	.10
49	Matt Williams	.10
50	Jay Buhner	.10
51	John Smoltz	.10
52	Randy Johnson	.75
53	Ramon Martinez	.10
54	Curt Schilling	.35
55	Gary Sheffield	.50
56	Jack McDowell	.10
57	Brady Anderson	.10
58	Dante Bichette	.10
59	Ron Gant	.10
60	Alex Fernandez	.10
61	Moises Alou	.10
62	Travis Fryman	.10
63	Dean Palmer	.10
64	Todd Hundley	.10
65	Jeff Brantley	.10
66	Bernard Gilkey	.10
67	Geronimo Berroa	.10
68	John Wetteland	.10
69	Robin Ventura	.10
70	Ray Lankford	.10
71	Kevin Appier	.10
72	Larry Walker	.10
73	Juan Gonzalez	.40
74	Jeff King	.10
75	Greg Vaughn	.10
76	Steve Finley	.10
77	Brian McRae	.10
78	Paul Sorrento	.10
79	Ken Griffey Jr.	2.00
80	Omar Vizquel	.10
81	Jose Mesa	.10
82	Albert Belle	.10
83	Glenallen Hill	.10
84	Sammy Sosa	1.50
85	Andy Benes	.10
86	David Justice	.10
87	Marquis Grissom	.10
88	John Olerud	.10
89	Tino Martinez	.10
90	Frank Thomas	.75
91	Raul Mondesi	.10
92	Steve Trachsel	.10
93	Jim Edmonds	.10
94	Rusty Greer	.10
95	Joey Hamilton	.10
96	Ismael Valdes	.10
97	Dave Nilsson	.10
98	John Jaha	.10
99	Alex Gonzalez	.10
100	Javy Lopez	.10
101	Ryan Klesko	.10
102	Tim Salmon	.10
103	Bernie Williams	.10
104	Roberto Hernandez	.10
105	Chuck Knoblauch	.10
106	Mike Lansing	.10
107	Vinny Castilla	.10
108	Reggie Sanders	.10
109	Mo Vaughn	.10
110	Rondell White	.10
111	Ivan Rodriguez	.65
112	Mike Mussina	.40
113	Carlos Baerga	.10
114	Jeff Conine	.10
115	Jim Thome	.65
116	Manny Ramirez	.75
117	Kenny Lofton	.10
118	Wilson Alvarez	.10
119	Eric Karros	.10
120	Robb Nen	.10
121	Mark Wohlers	.10
122	Ed Sprague	.10
123	Pat Hentgen	.10
124	Juan Guzman	.10
125	Derek Bell	.10
126	Jeff Bagwell	.75
127	Eric Young	.10
128	John Valentin	.10
129	Al Martin (Photo actually Javy Lopez.)	
130	Trevor Hoffman	.10
131	Henry Rodriguez	.10
132	Pedro Martinez	.75
133	Mike Piazza	2.00
134	Brian Jordan	.10
135	Jose Valentin	.10
136	Jeff Cirillo	.10
137	Chipper Jones	1.50
138	Ricky Bottalico	.10
139	Hideo Nomo	.40
140	Troy Percival	.10
141	Rey Ordonez	.10
142	Edgar Renteria	.10
143	Luis Castillo	.10
144	Vladimir Guerrero	.75
145	Jeff D'Amico	.10
146	Andruw Jones	.75
147	Darin Erstad	.25
148	Bob Abreu	.10
149	Carlos Delgado	.45
150	Jamey Wright	.10
151	Nomar Garciaparra	1.50
152	Jason Kendall	.10
153	Jermaine Allensworth	.10
154	Scott Rolen	.65
155	Rocky Coppinger	.10
156	Paul Wilson	.10
157	Garret Anderson	.10
158	Mariano Rivera	.15
159	Ruben Rivera	.10
160	Andy Pettitte	.35
161	Derek Jeter	3.00
162	Neifi Perez	.10
163	Ray Durham	.10
164	James Baldwin	.10
165	Marty Cordova	.10
166	Tony Clark	.10
167	Michael Tucker	.10
168	Mike Sweeney	.10
169	Johnny Damon	.25
170	Jermaine Dye	.10
171	Alex Ochoa	.10
172	Jason Isringhausen	.10
173	Mark Grudzielanek	.10
174	Jose Rosado	.10
175	Todd Hollandsworth	.10
176	Alan Benes	.10
177	Jason Giambi	.45
178	Billy Wagner	.10
179	Justin Thompson	.10
180	Todd Walker	.10

Players Private Issue

A parallel version of the Gallery issue called Players Private Issue was produced as a 1:12 pack insert. The PPI cards differ from the regular version in the use of a "PPI-" prefix to the card number on front and the application of a small silver PPI seal in a lower corner. On back, the line "One of 250 Issued" has been added.

	NM/M
Common Player:	1.00
Stars:	5X

Gallery of Heroes

This 10-card die-cut insert features a design resembling stained glass. Cards were inserted 1:36 packs. Cards are numbered with a "GH" prefix.

		NM/M
Complete Set (10):		30.00
Common Player:		1.50
1	Derek Jeter	6.00
2	Chipper Jones	3.00
3	Frank Thomas	2.50
4	Ken Griffey Jr.	4.00
5	Cal Ripken Jr.	6.00
6	Mark McGwire	4.00
7	Mike Piazza	4.00
8	Jeff Bagwell	2.50
9	Tony Gwynn	3.00
10	Mo Vaughn	1.50

Peter Max

Noted artist Peter Max has painted renditions of 10 superstar players and offered his commentary about those players on the backs. Cards were inserted 1:24 packs. In addition, Max-autographed cards signed and numbered from an edition of 40 are inserted 1:1,200 packs.

		NM/M
Complete Set (10):		60.00
Common Player:		3.00
Peter Max Autographed:		100.00
1	Derek Jeter	10.00
2	Albert Belle	3.00
3	Ken Caminiti	3.00
4	Chipper Jones	6.00
5	Ken Griffey Jr.	7.50
6	Frank Thomas	5.00
7	Cal Ripken Jr.	10.00
8	Mark McGwire	9.00
9	Barry Bonds	6.00
10	Mike Piazza	7.50

Photo Gallery

This 21-card set features full-bleed, high-gloss action photos of some of the game's top stars. Cards were inserted 1:24 packs. They are numbered with a "PG" prefix.

		NM/M
Complete Set (16):		15.00
Common Player:		.50
1	World Series	.50
2	Paul Molitor	1.00
3	Eddie Murray	1.00
4	Ken Griffey Jr.	2.50
5	Chipper Jones	1.50
6	Derek Jeter	3.50
7	Frank Thomas	2.00
8	Mark McGwire	3.00
9	Kenny Lofton	.50
10	Gary Sheffield	.65
11	Mike Piazza	2.50
12	Vinny Castilla	.50
13	Andres Galarraga	.50
14	Andy Pettitte	.50
15	Robin Ventura	.50
16	Barry Larkin	.50

Screenplays

Twenty of the game's top stars were featured in this multi-part collectible. The packaging is a 5-1/8" diameter lithographed steel can. The can was shrink-wrapped at the factory with a round checklist disc covering the color player photo on top of the can. The top has a woodgrain border around the photo and a gold facsimile autograph. The back of the topper disc has a career summary of the player. Inside the tin is a 2-1/2" x 3-1/2" plastic motion card with several seconds of game action shown as the angle of view changes. The card is covered by a peel-off protective layer on front and back. Foam pieces in the package allow both the can and card to be displayed upright. Issue price was about $10 per can. The unnumbered cans are checklisted here alphabetically. Values shown are for can/card combinations.

		NM/M
Complete Set (20):		25.00
Common Player:		1.00
Pack (1):		2.50
Wax Box (21):		30.00
(1)	Jeff Bagwell	2.00
(2)	Albert Belle	1.00
(3)	Barry Bonds	5.00
(4)	Andres Galarraga	1.00
(5)	Nomar Garciaparra	2.50
(6)	Juan Gonzalez	1.25
(7)	Ken Griffey Jr.	3.00
(8)	Tony Gwynn	2.50
(9)	Derek Jeter	5.00
(10)	Randy Johnson	
(11)	Andruw Jones	2.00
(12)	Chipper Jones	2.50
(13)	Kenny Lofton	1.00
(14)	Mark McGwire	4.00
(15)	Paul Molitor	1.00
(16)	Hideo Nomo	1.25
(17)	Cal Ripken Jr.	5.00
(18)	Sammy Sosa	2.50
(19)	Frank Thomas	2.00
(20)	Jim Thome	1.50

Screenplays Inserts

		NM/M
Complete Set (6):		35.00
Common Player:		2.00
1	Larry Walker	2.00
2	Cal Ripken Jr.	12.50
3	Chipper Jones	6.00
4	Frank Thomas	5.00
5	Mike Piazza	7.50
6	Ken Griffey Jr.	7.50

1997 Topps Stars Promos

These promo cards introduced Topps' new line of premium cards. They are in the same basic format as the regular issue, but are marked "PRE-PRODUCTION / SAMPLE" in the stats box on back.

		NM/M
Complete Set (3):		5.00
Common Player:		1.00
PP1	Larry Walker	1.00
PP2	Roger Clemens	3.00
PP3	Frank Thomas	2.00

1997 Topps Stars

The premiere version of this product was sold only to hobby shops that were members of the Topps Home Team Advantage program. Each of the 125 regular cards in the set is printed on 20-point stock. Card fronts feature spot UV coating with a textured star pattern running down one side of the card. Inserts include the parallel Always Mint set, as well as '97 All-Stars, Future All-Stars, All-Star memories, and Autographed Rookie Reprints. Cards were sold in seven-card packs for $3 each.

		NM/M
Complete Set (125):		30.00
Common Player:		.10
Always Mint Stars, RC's:		8X
Pack (7):		3.00
Wax Box (24):		65.00
1	Larry Walker	.10
2	Tino Martinez	.10
3	Cal Ripken Jr.	3.00
4	Ken Griffey Jr.	2.00
5	Chipper Jones	1.50
6	David Justice	.10
7	Mike Piazza	2.00
8	Jeff Bagwell	1.00
9	Ron Gant	.10
10	Sammy Sosa	2.00
11	Tony Gwynn	1.50
12	Carlos Baerga	.10
13	Frank Thomas	1.00
14	Moises Alou	.10
15	Barry Larkin	.10
16	Ivan Rodriguez	.75
17	Greg Maddux	1.50
18	Jim Edmonds	.10
19	Jose Canseco	.50
20	Rafael Palmeiro	.75
21	Paul Molitor	1.00
22	Kevin Appier	.10
23	Raul Mondesi	.10
24	Lance Johnson	.10
25	Edgar Martinez	.10
26	Andres Galarraga	.10
27	Mo Vaughn	.10
28	Ken Caminiti	.10
29	Cecil Fielder	.10
30	Harold Baines	.10
31	Roberto Alomar	.25
32	Shawn Estes	.10
33	Tom Glavine	.35
34	Dennis Eckersley	.75
35	Manny Ramirez	1.00
36	John Olerud	.10
37	Juan Gonzalez	.50
38	Chuck Knoblauch	.10
39	Albert Belle	.10
40	Vinny Castilla	.10
41	John Smoltz	.10
42	Barry Bonds	3.00
43	Randy Johnson	1.00
44	Brady Anderson	.10
45	Jeff Blauser	.10
46	Craig Biggio	.10
47	Jeff Conine	.10
48	Marquis Grissom	.10
49	Mark Grace	.10
50	Roger Clemens	1.75
51	Mark McGwire	2.50
52	Fred McGriff	.50
53	Gary Sheffield	.50
54	Bobby Jones	.10
55	Eric Young	.10
56	Robin Ventura	.10
57	Wade Boggs	1.50
58	Joe Carter	.10
59	Ryne Sandberg	1.50
60	Matt Williams	.10
61	Todd Hundley	.10
62	Dante Bichette	.10
63	Chili Davis	.10
64	Kenny Lofton	.10
65	Jay Buhner	.10
66	Will Clark	.10
67	Travis Fryman	.10
68	Pat Hentgen	.10
69	Ellis Burks	.10
70	Mike Mussina	.40
71	Hideo Nomo	.50
72	Sandy Alomar	.10
73	Bobby Bonilla	.10
74	Rickey Henderson	1.00
75	David Cone	.10
76	Terry Steinbach	.10
77	Pedro Martinez	1.00
78	Jim Thome	.75
79	Rod Beck	.10
80	Randy Myers	.10
81	Charles Nagy	.10
82	Mark Wohlers	.10
83	Paul O'Neill	.10
84	Curt Schilling	.35
85	Joey Cora	.10
86	John Franco	.10
87	Kevin Brown	.10
88	Benito Santiago	.10
89	Ray Lankford	.10
90	Bernie Williams	.10
91	Jason Dickson	.10
92	Jeff Cirillo	.10
93	Nomar Garciaparra	2.00
94	Mariano Rivera	.15
95	Javy Lopez	.10
96	Tony Womack RC	.25
97	Jose Rosado	.10
98	Denny Neagle	.10
99	Darryl Kile	.10
100	Justin Thompson	.10
101	Juan Encarnacion	.10
102	Brad Fullmer	.10
103	Kris Benson RC	.75
104	Todd Helton	1.00
105	Paul Konerko	.10
106	Travis Lee RC	1.00
107	Todd Greene	.10
108	Mark Kotsay RC	.50
109	Carl Pavano	.10
110	Kerry Wood RC	4.00
111	Jason Romano RC	.10
112	Geoff Goetz RC	.10
113	Scott Hodges RC	.10
114	Aaron Akin RC	.10
115	Vernon Wells RC	6.00
116	Chris Stowe RC	.10
117	Brett Caradonna RC	.10
118	Adam Kennedy RC	1.00
119	Jayson Werth RC	.10
120	Glenn Davis RC	.10
121	Troy Cameron RC	.10
122	J.J. Davis RC	.10
123	Jason Dellaero RC	.10
124	Jason Standridge RC	.10
125	Lance Berkman RC	2.00

Always Mint

This set parallels the regular Topps Stars issue and was inserted at the announced rate of one card per 12 packs. Identical in design to the regular version, the Always

Mint cards have metallic foil background on the player portion of the front photos. Backs of the Always Mint parallels have a shiny metallic silver background.

	NM/M
Complete Set (125):	250.00
Common Player:	.50
Stars/Rookies:	8X

All-Star Memories

This 10-card insert features stars who have had memorable performances in previous All-Star Games. Cards feature a laser-cut cascade of stars on a foilboard stock. Backs have another photo and a description of the All-Star memory. The cards were inserted 1:24 packs. Cards are numbered with an "ASM" prefix.

		NM/M
Complete Set (10):		20.00
Common Player:		1.00
1	Cal Ripken Jr.	6.00
2	Jeff Conine	1.00
3	Mike Piazza	4.00
4	Randy Johnson	2.00
5	Ken Griffey Jr.	4.00
6	Fred McGriff	1.00
7	Moises Alou	1.00
8	Hideo Nomo	1.25
9	Larry Walker	1.00
10	Sandy Alomar	1.00

Future All-Stars

This 15-card set showcases the top candidates to make their All-Star Game debut in 1998. Cards feature a prismatic rainbow foil background and were inserted 1:12 packs. Cards are numbered with a "FAS" prefix.

		NM/M
Complete Set (15):		17.50
Common Player:		.75
1	Derek Jeter	4.00
2	Andruw Jones	2.50
3	Vladimir Guerrero	3.00
4	Scott Rolen	2.50
5	Jose Guillen	.75
6	Jose Cruz, Jr.	.75
7	Darin Erstad	2.50
8	Tony Clark	1.00
9	Scott Spiezio	.75

10	Kevin Orie	.75
11	Calvin Reese	.75
12	Billy Wagner	.75
13	Matt Morris	.75
14	Jeremi Gonzalez	.75
15	Hideki Irabu	.75

Rookie Reprints

Fifteen Topps rookie cards of Hall of Famers were reprinted as a one-per-six-packs insert. Regardless of original size, all reprints are 2-1/2" x 3-1/2" with a reprint notice on back.

		NM/M
Complete Set (15):		25.00
Common Player:		2.00
(1)	Luis Aparicio	2.00
(2)	Richie Ashburn	2.00
(3)	Jim Bunning	2.00
(4)	Bob Feller	2.00
(5)	Rollie Fingers	2.00
(6)	Monte Irvin	2.00
(7)	Al Kaline	3.00
(8)	Ralph Kiner	2.00
(9)	Eddie Mathews	3.00
(10)	Hal Newhouser	2.00
(11)	Gaylord Perry	2.00
(12)	Robin Roberts	2.00
(13)	Brooks Robinson	3.00
(14)	Enos Slaughter	2.00
(15)	Earl Weaver	2.00

Autographed Rookie Reprints

Fourteen different Hall of Famers autographed reprinted versions of their Topps rookie cards as a one-per-30-pack insert. Each card features a special certified stamp. Richie Ashburn was to have been card #2, but he died before he could autograph them.

		NM/M
Common Player:		15.00
(1)	Luis Aparicio	20.00
(3)	Jim Bunning	30.00
(4)	Bob Feller	35.00
(5)	Rollie Fingers	15.00
(6)	Monte Irvin	15.00
(7)	Al Kaline	30.00
(8)	Ralph Kiner	25.00
(9)	Eddie Mathews	75.00
(10)	Hal Newhouser	40.00
(11)	Gaylord Perry	15.00
(12)	Robin Roberts	30.00
(13)	Brooks Robinson	40.00
(14)	Enos Slaughter	30.00
(15)	Earl Weaver	20.00

1997 All-Stars

This 20-card insert honors participants of the 1997 All-Star Game in Cleveland. Cards were inserted 1:24 packs. Fronts are printed on prismatic foil with hundreds of stars in the background. On back is another photo and his All-Star Game 1997 and career stats. Cards are numbered with an "AS" prefix.

		NM/M
Complete Set (20):		60.00
Common Player:		1.50
1	Greg Maddux	6.00

2	Randy Johnson	4.50
3	Tino Martinez	1.50
4	Jeff Bagwell	4.50
5	Ivan Rodriguez	3.50
6	Mike Piazza	7.50
7	Cal Ripken Jr.	12.00
8	Ken Caminiti	1.50
9	Tony Gwynn	6.00
10	Edgar Martinez	1.50
11	Craig Biggio	1.50
12	Roberto Alomar	2.00
13	Larry Walker	1.50
14	Brady Anderson	1.50
15	Barry Bonds	12.00
16	Ken Griffey Jr.	7.50
17	Ray Lankford	1.50
18	Paul O'Neill	1.50
19	Jeff Blauser	1.50
20	Sandy Alomar	1.50

Dodger Rookie of the Year Collection

Available only through Topps Stadium Club and at Dodger Stadium, this set of special cards honors the five consecutive (1992-96) N.L. Rookies of the Year - all L.A. Dodgers - as well as the first-ever Rookie of the Year, Jackie Robinson. The cards feature reproductions of the players' rookie cards printed on front in metallic foil and with an N.L. Rookie of the Year logo and year banner. Backs are virtually identical to the regular-issue cards, but include a reprint line in the fine print. Raul Mondesi's card is a different version of the '94 Topps Coming Attractions subset card which he shared with Ben Van Ryn. Production was reported at 4,000 sets.

			NM/M
Complete Set (6):			35.00
Common Player:			3.00
1	Jackie Robinson		
	(1952 Topps)		20.00
2	Mike Piazza		
	(1992 Bowman)		10.00
3	Eric Karros (1993 Topps)		3.00
4	Raul Mondesi		
	(1994 Topps)		3.00
5	Hideo Nomo		
	(1995 Topps Traded)		7.50
6	Todd Hollandsworth		
	(1996 Topps)		3.00

"Pro Shooters" Photo Marbles

This limited distribution test issue was another attempt to market marbles with baseball player photos. The hard plastic 1" diameter marbles have a black composite band around the circumference. On one side is a player portrait, on the other is a team logo at center with the player name in a strip below and a number "... of 60" in a strip above. The Topps name does not appear. They were sold two per pack.

		NM/M
Complete Set (60):		1,000
Common Player:		10.00
1	Roberto Alomar	15.00
2	Brady Anderson	10.00
3	Carlos Baerga	10.00
4	Jeff Bagwell	30.00
5	Albert Belle	10.00
6	Dante Bichette	10.00
7	Craig Biggio	10.00
8	Wade Boggs	40.00
9	Barry Bonds	60.00
10	Jay Buhner	10.00
11	Ken Caminiti	10.00
12	Jose Canseco	15.00
13	Roger Clemens	42.50
14	David Cone	10.00
15	Cecil Fielder	10.00
16	Travis Fryman	10.00
17	Andres Galarraga	10.00
18	Ron Gant	10.00
19	Bernard Gilkey	10.00
20	Tom Glavine	12.50
21	Juan Gonzalez	15.00
22	Mark Grace	10.00
23	Ken Griffey Jr.	45.00
24	Tony Gwynn	40.00
25	Todd Hundley	10.00
26	John Jaha	10.00
27	Derek Jeter	60.00
28	Lance Johnson	10.00
29	Randy Johnson	30.00
30	Andruw Jones	30.00
31	Chipper Jones	40.00
32	Brian Jordan	10.00
33	Jason Kendall	10.00
34	Chuck Knoblauch	10.00
35	Ray Lankford	10.00
36	Barry Larkin	10.00
37	Kenny Lofton	10.00
38	Greg Maddux	40.00
39	Edgar Martinez	10.00
40	Fred McGriff	10.00
41	Mark McGwire	50.00
42	Paul Molitor	30.00
43	Raul Mondesi	30.00
44	Eddie Murray	30.00
45	Mike Mussina	15.00
46	Hideo Nomo	15.00
47	Rafael Palmeiro	25.00
48	Andy Pettitte	15.00
49	Mike Piazza	45.00
50	Cal Ripken Jr.	60.00
51	Ivan Rodriguez	25.00
52	Tim Salmon	10.00
53	Ryne Sandberg	40.00
54	Gary Sheffield	15.00
55	John Smoltz	10.00
56	Sammy Sosa	40.00
57	Frank Thomas	30.00
58	Mo Vaughn	10.00
59	Bernie Williams	10.00
60	Matt Williams	10.00
1 of 2	Checklist Card 1-30	30.00
2 of 2	Checklist Card 31-60	30.00

22k Gold

These 22-karat gold-foil cards were created for direct sale by Topps. They reproduce, front and back, Griffey's and Ripken's regular-issue 1997 Topps cards, and feature a 1997-style card of Irabu, who did not appear on a regular Topps card that year. The 2-1/2" x 3-1/2" cards are individually serial numbered and were sold in a protective display holder. Initially priced at $30 apiece, they were discounted in a later offer to $19.95.

		NM/M
Complete Set (3):		60.00
Common Player:		20.00
300	Ken Griffey Jr.	15.00
400	Cal Ripken Jr.	20.00
----	Hideki Irabu	15.00

1998 Topps Pre-Production

To give potential customers a feel for its 1998 baseball cards, Topps issued this series of pre-production samples. Cards are identical in format to the issued versions except they are numbered with a "PP" prefix and the 1997 stats line reads "PRE-PRODUCTION SAMPLE."

	NM/M
Complete Set (6):	4.00
Common Player:	.25

PP1	Carlos Baerga	.25
PP2	Jeff Bagwell	.75
PP3	Marquis Grissom	.25
PP4	Derek Jeter	1.50
PP5	Randy Johnson	.75
PP6	Mike Piazza	1.00

1998 Topps

Topps issued two series in 1998, a total of 503 base cards; 282 in Series 1 and 221 in Series 2. Cards feature a gold border instead of the traditional white of past years. The product features Roberto Clemente inserts and a tribute card No. 21 in the base set. Series 1 subsets Series Highlights, Expansion Team Prospects, Interleague Highlights, Season Highlights, Prospects and Draft Picks. Subsets in Series II included: Expansion Teams, InterLeague Preview, Season Highlights, Prospects and Draft Picks. Every card in the set is paralleled in a Minted in Cooperstown insert that was stamped onsite at the Baseball Hall of Fame in Cooperstown. Inserts in Series 1 include: Roberto Clemente Reprints, Clemente Finest, Clemente Tribute, Memorabililia Madness, Etch a Sketch, Mystery Finest, Flashback and Baby Boomers. Inserts in Series 2 included: Clemente Reprints, Clemente Finest, 1998 Rookie Class, Mystery Finest, Milestones, Focal Points, and Clout 9. A factory set includes the 503 base cards, eight randomly selected inserts and one Clemente card sealed in a gold-foil stamped soft plastic case.

		NM/M
Unopened Fact. Set (511):		85.00
Complete Set (503):		40.00
Common Player:		.05
Minted:		6X
Inserted 1:8		
Series 1 or 2 Pack (11):		1.00
Series 1 or 2 Wax Box (36):		25.00
1	Tony Gwynn	1.00
2	Larry Walker	.05
3	Billy Wagner	.05
4	Denny Neagle	.05
5	Vladimir Guerrero	.75
6	Kevin Brown	.05
8	Mariano Rivera	.10
9	Tony Clark	.05
10	Deion Sanders	.05
11	Francisco Cordova	.05
12	Matt Williams	.05
13	Carlos Baerga	.05
14	Mo Vaughn	.05
15	Bobby Witt	.05
16	Matt Stairs	.05
17	Chan Ho Park	.05
18	Mike Bordick	.05
19	Michael Tucker	.05
20	Frank Thomas	.75
21	Roberto Clemente	1.50
22	Dmitri Young	.05
23	Steve Trachsel	.05
24	Jeff Kent	.05
25	Scott Rolen	.50
26	John Thomson	.05

27	Joe Vitiello	.05
28	Eddie Guardado	.05
29	Charlie Hayes	.05
30	Juan Gonzalez	.40
31	Garret Anderson	.05
32	John Jaha	.05
33	Omar Vizquel	.05
34	Brian Hunter	.05
35	Jeff Bagwell	.75
36	Mark Lemke	.05
37	Doug Glanville	.05
38	Dan Wilson	.05
39	Steve Cooke	.05
40	Chili Davis	.05
41	Mike Cameron	.05
42	F.P. Santangelo	.05
43	Brad Ausmus	.05
44	Gary DiSarcina	.05
45	Pat Hentgen	.05
46	Wilton Guerrero	.05
47	Devon White	.05
48	Danny Patterson	.05
49	Pat Meares	.05
50	Rafael Palmeiro	.65
51	Mark Gardner	.05
52	Jeff Blauser	.05
53	Dave Hollins	.05
54	Carlos Garcia	.05
55	Ben McDonald	.05
56	John Mabry	.05
57	Trevor Hoffman	.05
58	Tony Fernandez	.05
59	Rich Loiselle	.05
60	Mark Leiter	.05
61	Pat Kelly	.05
62	John Flaherty	.05
63	Roger Bailey	.05
64	Tom Gordon	.05
65	Ryan Klesko	.05
66	Darryl Hamilton	.05
67	Jim Eisenreich	.05
68	Butch Huskey	.05
69	Mark Grudzielanek	.05
70	Marquis Grissom	.05
71	Mark McLemore	.05
72	Gary Gaetti	.05
73	Greg Gagne	.05
74	Lyle Mouton	.05
75	Jim Edmonds	.05
76	Shawn Green	.25
77	Greg Vaughn	.05
78	Terry Adams	.05
79	Kevin Polcovich **RC**	.05
80	Troy O'Leary	.05
81	Jeff Shaw	.05
82	Rich Becker	.05
83	David Wells	.05
84	Steve Karsay	.05
85	Charles Nagy	.05
86	B.J. Surhoff	.05
87	Jamey Wright	.05
88	James Baldwin	.05
89	Edgardo Alfonzo	.05
90	Jay Buhner	.05
91	Brady Anderson	.05
92	Scott Servais	.05
93	Edgar Renteria	.05
94	Mike Lieberthal	.05
95	Rick Aguilera	.05
96	Walt Weiss	.05
97	Deivi Cruz	.05
98	Kurt Abbott	.05
99	Henry Rodriguez	.05
100	Mike Piazza	1.25
101	Bill Taylor	.05
102	Todd Zeile	.05
103	Rey Ordonez	.05
104	Willie Greene	.05
105	Tony Womack	.05
106	Mike Sweeney	.05
107	Jeffrey Hammonds	.05
108	Kevin Orie	.05
109	Alex Gonzalez	.05
110	Jose Canseco	.50
111	Paul Sorrento	.05
112	Joey Hamilton	.05
113	Brad Radke	.05
114	Steve Avery	.05
115	Esteban Loaiza	.05
116	Stan Javier	.05
117	Chris Gomez	.05
118	Royce Clayton	.05
119	Orlando Merced	.05
120	Kevin Appier	.05
121	Mel Nieves	.05
122	Joe Girardi	.05
123	Rico Brogna	.05
124	Kent Mercker	.05
125	Manny Ramirez	.75
126	Jeromy Burnitz	.05
127	Kevin Foster	.05
128	Matt Morris	.05
129	Jason Dickson	.05
130	Tom Glavine	.25
131	Wally Joyner	.05
132	Rick Reed	.05
133	Todd Jones	.05
134	Dave Martinez	.05
135	Sandy Alomar	.05
136	Mike Lansing	.05
137	Sean Berry	.05
138	Doug Jones	.05
139	Todd Stottlemyre	.05
140	Jay Bell	.05
141	Jaime Navarro	.05
142	Chris Hoiles	.05
143	Joey Cora	.05
144	Scott Spiezio	.05

#	Player	Price
145	Joe Carter	.05
146	Jose Guillen	.05
147	Damion Easley	.05
148	Lee Stevens	.05
149	Alex Fernandez	.05
150	Randy Johnson	.75
151	J.T. Snow	.05
152	Chuck Finley	.05
153	Bernard Gilkey	.05
154	David Segui	.05
155	Dante Bichette	.05
156	Kevin Stocker	.05
157	Carl Everett	.05
158	Jose Valentin	.05
159	Pokey Reese	.05
160	Derek Jeter	2.00
161	Roger Pavlik	.05
162	Mark Wohlers	.05
163	Ricky Bottalico	.05
164	Ozzie Guillen	.05
165	Mike Mussina	.50
166	Gary Sheffield	.50
167	Hideo Nomo	.40
168	Mark Grace	.05
169	Aaron Sele	.05
170	Darryl Kile	.05
171	Shawn Estes	.05
172	Vinny Castilla	.05
173	Ron Coomer	.05
174	Jose Rosado	.05
175	Kenny Lofton	.05
176	Jason Giambi	.50
177	Hal Morris	.05
178	Darren Bragg	.05
179	Orel Hershiser	.05
180	Ray Lankford	.05
181	Hideki Irabu	.05
182	Kevin Young	.05
183	Javy Lopez	.05
184	Jeff Montgomery	.05
185	Mike Holtz	.05
186	George Williams	.05
187	Cal Eldred	.05
188	Tom Candiotti	.05
189	Glenallen Hill	.05
190	Brian Giles	.05
191	Dave Mlicki	.05
192	Garrett Stephenson	.05
193	Jeff Frye	.05
194	Joe Oliver	.05
195	Bob Hamelin	.05
196	Luis Sojo	.05
197	LaTroy Hawkins	.05
198	Kevin Elster	.05
199	Jeff Reed	.05
200	Dennis Eckersley	.65
201	Bill Mueller	.05
202	Russ Davis	.05
203	Armando Benitez	.05
204	Quilvio Veras	.05
205	Tim Naehring	.05
206	Quinton McCracken	.05
207	Raul Casanova	.05
208	Matt Lawton	.05
209	Luis Alicea	.05
210	Luis Gonzalez	.05
211	Allen Watson	.05
212	Gerald Williams	.05
213	David Bell	.05
214	Todd Hollandsworth	.05
215	Wade Boggs	1.00
216	Jose Mesa	.05
217	Jamie Moyer	.05
218	Darren Daulton	.05
219	Mickey Morandini	.05
220	Rusty Greer	.05
221	Jim Bullinger	.05
222	Jose Offerman	.05
223	Matt Karchner	.05
224	Woody Williams	.05
225	Mark Loretta	.05
226	Mike Hampton	.05
227	Willie Adams	.05
228	Scott Hatteberg	.05
229	Rich Amaral	.05
230	Terry Steinbach	.05
231	Glendon Rusch	.05
232	Bret Boone	.05
233	Robert Person	.05
234	Jose Hernandez	.05
235	Doug Drabek	.05
236	Jason McDonald	.05
237	Chris Widger	.05
238	Tom Martin RC	.05
239	Dave Burba	.05
240	Pete Rose II	.05
241	Bobby Ayala	.05
242	Tim Wakefield	.05
243	Dennis Springer	.05
244	Tim Belcher	.05
245	Jon Garland, Geoff Goetz (Draft Pick)	.05
246	Glenn Davis, Lance Berkman (Draft Pick)	.05
247	Vernon Wells, Aaron Akin (Draft Pick)	.10
248	Adam Kennedy, Jason Romano (Draft Pick)	.10
249	Jason Dellaero, Troy Cameron (Draft Pick)	.05
250	Alex Sanchez, Jared Sandberg RC (Expansion Team Prospects)	.10
251	Pablo Ortega, Jim Manias (Expansion Team Prospects)	.05

#	Player	Price
252	Jason Conti, Mike Stoner RC (Expansion Team Prospects)	.10
253	John Patterson, Larry Rodriguez (Expansion Team Prospects)	.05
254	Adrian Beltre, Ryan Minor RC, Aaron Boone (Prospect)	.15
255	Ben Grieve, Brian Buchanan, Dermal Brown (Prospect)	.05
256	Carl Pavano, Kerry Wood, Gil Meche (Prospect)	.15
257	David Ortiz, Daryle Ward, Richie Sexson (Prospect)	.50
258	Randy Winn, Juan Encarnacion, Andrew Vessel (Prospect)	.10
259	Kris Benson, Travis Smith, Courtney Duncan (Prospect)	.05
260	Chad Hermansen, Brent Butler, Warren Morris RC (Prospect)	.10
261	Ben Davis, Elieser Marrero, Ramon Hernandez (Prospect)	.05
262	Eric Chavez, Russell Branyan, Russ Johnson (Prospect)	.20
263	Todd Dunwoody, John Barnes, Ryan Jackson RC (Prospect)	.10
264	Matt Clement, Roy Halladay, Brian Fuentes RC (Prospect)	.05
265	Randy Johnson (Season Highlight)	.15
266	Kevin Brown (Season Highlight)	.05
267	Ricardo Rincon, Francisco Cordova (Season Highlight)	.05
268	Nomar Garciaparra (Season Highlight)	.50
269	Tino Martinez (Season Highlight)	.05
270	Chuck Knoblauch (Interleague)	.05
271	Pedro Martinez (Interleague)	.40
272	Denny Neagle (Interleague)	.05
273	Juan Gonzalez (Interleague)	.20
274	Andres Galarraga (Interleague)	.05
275	Checklist	.05
276	Checklist	.05
277	Moises Alou (World Series)	.05
278	Sandy Alomar (World Series)	.05
279	Gary Sheffield (World Series)	.05
280	Matt Williams (World Series)	.05
281	Livan Hernandez (World Series)	.05
282	Chad Ogea (World Series)	.05
283	Marlins Win (World Series)	.05
284	Tino Martinez	.05
285	Roberto Alomar	.20
286	Jeff King	.05
287	Brian Jordan	.05
288	Darin Erstad	.15
289	Ken Caminiti	.05
290	Jim Thome	.60
291	Paul Molitor	.75
292	Ivan Rodriguez	.65
293	Bernie Williams	.05
294	Todd Hundley	.05
295	Andres Galarraga	.05
296	Greg Maddux	1.00
297	Edgar Martinez	.05
298	Ron Gant	.05
299	Derek Bell	.05
300	Roger Clemens	1.00
301	Rondell White	.05
302	Barry Larkin	.05
303	Robin Ventura	.05
304	Jason Kendall	.05
305	Chipper Jones	1.00
306	John Franco	.05
307	Sammy Sosa	1.00
308	Troy Percival	.05
309	Chuck Knoblauch	.05
310	Ellis Burks	.05
311	Al Martin	.05
312	Tim Salmon	.05
313	Moises Alou	.05
314	Lance Johnson	.05
315	Justin Thompson	.05
316	Will Clark	.05
317	Barry Bonds	2.00
318	Craig Biggio	.05
319	John Smoltz	.05
320	Cal Ripken Jr.	2.00
321	Ken Griffey Jr.	1.25
322	Paul O'Neill	.05
323	Todd Helton	.65
324	John Olerud	.05
325	Mark McGwire	1.50
326	Jose Cruz Jr.	.05
327	Jeff Cirillo	.05
328	Dean Palmer	.05
329	John Wetteland	.05
330	Steve Finley	.05
331	Albert Belle	.05
332	Curt Schilling	.25
333	Raul Mondesi	.05

#	Player	Price
334	Andruw Jones	.75
335	Nomar Garciaparra	1.00
336	David Justice	.05
337	Andy Pettitte	.25
338	Pedro Martinez	.75
339	Travis Miller	.05
340	Chris Stynes	.05
341	Gregg Jefferies	.05
342	Jeff Fassero	.05
343	Craig Counsell	.05
344	Wilson Alvarez	.05
345	Bip Roberts	.05
346	Kelvim Escobar	.05
347	Mark Bellhorn	.05
348	Cory Lidle RC	.05
349	Fred McGriff	.05
350	Chuck Carr	.05
351	Bob Abreu	.05
352	Juan Guzman	.05
353	Fernando Vina	.05
354	Andy Benes	.05
355	Dave Nilsson	.05
356	Bobby Bonilla	.05
357	Ismael Valdes	.05
358	Carlos Perez	.05
359	Kirk Rueter	.05
360	Bartolo Colon	.05
361	Mel Rojas	.05
362	Johnny Damon	.25
363	Geronimo Berroa	.05
364	Reggie Sanders	.05
365	Jermaine Allensworth	.05
366	Orlando Cabrera	.05
367	Jorge Fabregas	.05
368	Scott Stahoviak	.05
369	Ken Cloude	.05
370	Donovan Osborne	.05
371	Roger Cedeno	.05
372	Neifi Perez	.05
373	Chris Holt	.05
374	Cecil Fielder	.05
375	Marty Cordova	.05
376	Tom Goodwin	.05
377	Jeff Suppan	.05
378	Jeff Brantley	.05
379	Mark Langston	.05
380	Shane Reynolds	.05
381	Mike Fetters	.05
382	Todd Greene	.05
383	Ray Durham	.05
384	Carlos Delgado	.30
385	Jeff D'Amico	.05
386	Brian McRae	.05
387	Alan Benes	.05
388	Heathcliff Slocumb	.05
389	Eric Young	.05
390	Travis Fryman	.05
391	David Cone	.05
392	Otis Nixon	.05
393	Jeremi Gonzalez	.05
394	Jeff Juden	.05
395	Jose Vizcaino	.05
396	Ugueth Urbina	.05
397	Ramon Martinez	.05
398	Robb Nen	.05
399	Harold Baines	.05
400	Delino DeShields	.05
401	John Burkett	.05
402	Sterling Hitchcock	.05
403	Mark Clark	.05
404	Terrell Wade	.05
405	Scott Brosius	.05
406	Chad Curtis	.05
407	Brian Johnson	.05
408	Roberto Kelly	.05
409	Dave Dellucci RC	.15
410	Michael Tucker	.05
411	Mark Kotsay	.05
412	Mark Lewis	.05
413	Ryan McGuire	.05
414	Shawon Dunston	.05
415	Brad Rigby	.05
416	Scott Erickson	.05
417	Bobby Jones	.05
418	Darren Oliver	.05
419	John Smiley	.05
420	T.J. Mathews	.05
421	Dustin Hermanson	.05
422	Mike Timlin	.05
423	Willie Blair	.05
424	Manny Alexander	.05
425	Bob Tewksbury	.05
426	Pete Schourek	.05
427	Reggie Jefferson	.05
428	Ed Sprague	.05
429	Jeff Conine	.05
430	Roberto Hernandez	.05
431	Tom Pagnozzi	.05
432	Jaret Wright	.05
433	Livan Hernandez	.05
434	Andy Ashby	.05
435	Todd Dunn	.05
436	Bobby Higginson	.05
437	Rod Beck	.05
438	Jim Leyritz	.05
439	Matt Williams	.05
440	Brett Tomko	.05
441	Joe Randa	.05
442	Chris Carpenter	.05
443	Dennis Reyes	.05
444	Al Leiter	.05
445	Jason Schmidt	.05
446	Ken Hill	.05
447	Shannon Stewart	.05
448	Enrique Wilson	.05
449	Fernando Tatis	.05
450	Jimmy Key	.05
451	Darrin Fletcher	.05
452	John Valentin	.05
453	Kevin Tapani	.05
454	Eric Karros	.05
455	Jay Bell	.05

#	Player	Price
456	Walt Weiss	.05
457	Devon White	.05
458	Carl Pavano	.05
459	John Flaherty	.05
460	Mike Lansing	.05
461	Richard Hidalgo	.05
462	Quinton McCracken	.05
463	Karim Garcia	.15
464	Miguel Cairo	.05
465	Edwin Diaz	.05
466	Bobby Smith	.05
467	Yamil Benitez	.05
468	Rich Butler RC	.05
469	Ben Ford RC	.05
470	Bubba Trammell	.05
471	Brent Brede	.05
472	Brooks Kieschnick	.05
473	Carlos Castillo	.05
474	Brad Radke (Season Highlight)	.05
475	Roger Clemens (Season Highlight)	.50
476	Curt Schilling (Season Highlight)	.05
477	John Olerud (Season Highlight)	.05
478	Mark McGwire (Season Highlight)	.75
479	Mike Piazza, Ken Griffey Jr. (Interleague)	.75
480	Jeff Bagwell, Frank Thomas (Interleague)	.50
481	Chipper Jones, Nomar Garciaparra (Interleague)	.75
482	Larry Walker, Juan Gonzalez (Interleague)	.30
483	Gary Sheffield, Tino Martinez (Interleague)	.05
484	Derrick Gibson, Michael Coleman, Norm Hutchins (Prospect)	.05
485	Braden Looper, Cliff Politte, Brian Rose (Prospect)	.05
486	Eric Milton, Jason Marquis, Corey Lee (Prospect)	.05
487	A.J. Hinch, Mark Osborne, Robert Fick RC (Prospect)	.10
488	Aramis Ramirez, Alex Gonzalez, Sean Casey (Prospect)	.15
489	Donnie Bridges RC, Tim Drew RC (Draft Pick)	.10
490	Ntema Ndungidi RC, Darnell McDonald RC (Draft Pick)	.10
491	Ryan Anderson RC, Mark Mangum (Draft Pick)	.25
492	J.J. Davis, Troy Glaus RC (Draft Pick)	2.00
493	Jayson Werth, Dan Reichert RC (Draft Pick)	.15
494	John Curtice RC, Mike Cuddyer RC (Draft Pick)	.25
495	Jack Cust RC, Jason Standridge (Draft Pick)	1.00
496	Brian Anderson (Expansion Team Prospect)	.05
497	Tony Saunders (Expansion Team Prospect)	.05
498	Vladimir Nunez, Jhensy Sandoval RC (Expansion Team Prospect)	.05
499	Brad Penny, Nick Bierbrodt (Expansion Team Prospect)	.05
500	Dustin Carr RC, Luis Cruz RC (Expansion Team Prospect)	.05
501	Marcus McCain RC, Cedrick Bowers RC (Expansion Team Prospect)	.05
502	Checklist	.05
503	Checklist	.05
504	Alex Rodriguez	1.50

Minted in Cooperstown

As part of an effort to promote interest in the various major sports' halls of fame, Topps produced this parallel version of its Series 1 baseball set. A special embossing machine was set up at the National Base-ball Hall of Fame in Cooperstown to apply a bronze-foil "MINTED IN COOPERSTOWN" logo to cards. Twenty-card sheets of the logoed cards were sold on the premises and single cards were inserted into foil packs.

	NM/M
Common Card:	.50
Stars/Rookies:	6X

Arizona Diamondbacks Inaugural Season

To mark the team's inaugural year in the Major Leagues, Topps produced a special run of 5,000 factory sets in which each card was embossed with a special gold seal incorporating the D-Backs logo. Sets were sold only at the team's normal souvenir outlets.

	NM/M
Complete Set (503):	80.00
Common Player:	.50
Stars/Rookies:	6X

Tampa Bay Devil Rays Inaugural Season

To mark the team's inaugural year in the Major Leagues, Topps produced a special run of 5,000 factory sets in which each card was embossed with a special gold seal incorporating the D-Rays logo. Sets were sold only at the team's normal souvenir outlets.

	NM/M
Complete Set (503):	100.00
Common Player:	.50
Stars/Rookies:	6X

Baby Boomers

This 15-card retail exclusive insert was seeded one per 36 packs of Series 1. It featured some of the top young players in the game and was numbered with a "BB" prefix.

		NM/M
Complete Set (15):		15.00
Common Player:		.75
Inserted 1:36 Retail		
1	Derek Jeter	6.00
2	Scott Rolen	1.00
3	Nomar Garciaparra	3.50
4	Jose Cruz Jr.	.75
5	Darin Erstad	.85
6	Todd Helton	1.50
7	Tony Clark	.75
8	Jose Guillen	.75
9	Andruw Jones	1.00
10	Vladimir Guerrero	1.50
11	Mark Kotsay	.75
12	Todd Greene	.75
13	Andy Pettitte	.85
14	Justin Thompson	.75
15	Alan Benes	.75

Roberto Clemente Reprints

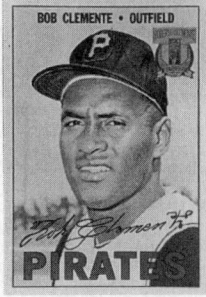

Nineteen different Topps Clemente cards were reprinted with a gold foil stamp and included 1998 Topps. Odd numbers were included in Series I, while even numbers were inserted into Series II, both at a rate of one per 18 packs. The insert was created to honor the memory of the 25th anniversary of Clemente's death.

		NM/M
Complete Set (19):		50.00
Common Card:		2.50
Inserted 1:18		
1	1955	4.00
2	1956	2.50
3	1957	2.50
4	1958	2.50
5	1959	2.50
6	1960	2.50
7	1961	2.50
8	1962	2.50
9	1963	2.50
10	1964	2.50
11	1965	2.50
12	1966	2.50
13	1967	2.50
14	1968	2.50
15	1969	2.50
16	1970	2.50
17	1971	2.50
18	1972	2.50
19	1973	2.50

Roberto Clemente Finest

Clemente Finest inserts were included in both Series I and II at a rate of one per 72 packs. There were a total of 19 different, with odd numbers in Series I and even numbers in Series II. The insert helped honor the memory of the 25th anniversary of his death.

		NM/M
Complete Set (19):		60.00
Common Card:		4.00
Inserted 1:72		
Refractors:		2X
Inserted 1:288		
1	1955	6.00
2	1956	4.00
3	1957	4.00
4	1958	4.00
5	1959	4.00
6	1960	4.00
7	1961	4.00
8	1962	4.00
9	1963	4.00
10	1964	4.00
11	1965	4.00
12	1966	4.00
13	1967	4.00
14	1968	4.00
15	1969	4.00
16	1970	4.00
17	1971	4.00
18	1972	4.00
19	1973	4.00

#	Player	Price
12	Todd Greene	.75
13	Andy Pettitte	.85
14	Justin Thompson	.75
15	Alan Benes	.75

Roberto Clemente "Tin" Reprints

Each of the 19 basic Clemente reprint cards can also be found in a factory-sealed, gold-foil stamped soft plastic case. These were inserted in special retail-only tin boxes and one per factory set of 1998 Topps.

		NM/M
Complete Set (19):		60.00
Common Card:		4.00
1	1955	8.00
2	1956	4.00
3	1957	4.00
4	1958	4.00
5	1959	4.00
6	1960	4.00
7	1961	4.00
8	1962	4.00
9	1963	4.00
10	1964	4.00
11	1965	4.00
12	1966	4.00
13	1967	4.00
14	1968	4.00
15	1969	4.00
16	1970	4.00
17	1971	4.00
18	1972	4.00
19	1973	4.00

Roberto Clemente Commemorative Tins

This series of commemorative tin card "packs" reproduces in an enlarged (about 3" x 4-5/8" x 3/4") format the front and back of four of Roberto Clemente's Topps cards. Each tin, originally retailing for about $5, contains a plastic-sealed Clemente reprint card.

	NM/M
Complete Set (4):	10.00
Roberto Clemente/1955	3.50
Roberto Clemente/1956	2.50
Roberto Clemente/1965	2.50
Roberto Clemente/1971	2.50

Roberto Clemente Tribute

Five Clemente Tribute cards were produced for Series I and inserted in one per 12 packs. The set features some classic photos of Clemente and honor his memory in the 25th anniversary of his death. Clemente Tribute cards are numbered with a "RC" prefix.

	NM/M
Complete Set (5):	3.00
Common Clemente:	.75
Inserted 1:12	
1-5 Roberto Clemente	.75

Clout 9

Clout 9 captured nine players known for their statistical supremacy. Cards were numbered with a "C" prefix and inserted one per 72 packs of Series 2.

	NM/M
Complete Set (9):	17.50
Common Player:	1.00
Inserted 1:72	

		NM/M
1	Edgar Martinez	1.00
2	Mike Piazza	5.00
3	Frank Thomas	2.00
4	Craig Biggio	1.00
5	Vinny Castilla	1.00
6	Jeff Blauser	1.00
7	Barry Bonds	7.50
8	Ken Griffey Jr.	5.00
9	Larry Walker	1.00

Etch-A-Sketch

Etch-a-Sketch featured nine different players depicted by nationally acclaimed artist George Vlosich III. Known as "The Etch-a-Sketch Kid," Vlosich created each one of these Series I inserts, which were inserted at a rate of one per 36 packs. Cards are numbered with an "ES" prefix.

		NM/M
Complete Set (9):		20.00
Common Player:		1.00
Inserted 1:36		
1	Albert Belle	1.00
2	Barry Bonds	6.00
3	Ken Griffey Jr.	4.00
4	Greg Maddux	4.00
5	Hideo Nomo	1.50
6	Mike Piazza	4.00
7	Cal Ripken Jr.	6.00
8	Frank Thomas	2.00
9	Mo Vaughn	1.00

Flashback

This double-sided insert offers "then and now" photos of 10 top major leaguers. One side pictures the player circa 1998, while the other side shows him at the beginning of his major league career. Flashback inserts were seeded one per 72 packs and numbered with a "FB" prefix.

		NM/M
Complete Set (10):		22.50
Common Player:		1.00
Inserted 1:72		
1	Barry Bonds	7.50
2	Ken Griffey Jr.	5.00
3	Paul Molitor	2.00
4	Randy Johnson	2.00
5	Cal Ripken Jr.	7.50
6	Tony Gwynn	3.00
7	Kenny Lofton	1.00
8	Gary Sheffield	1.50
9	Deion Sanders	1.50
10	Brady Anderson	1.00

Focal Point

This hobby exclusive insert focuses on the skills that have made the players great. Focal Point

inserts were available in Series 2 packs, seeded one per 36, and are numbered with a "FP" prefix.

		NM/M
Complete Set (15):		25.00
Common Player:		.75
Inserted 1:36		
1	Juan Gonzalez	.85
2	Nomar Garciaparra	2.50
3	Jose Cruz Jr.	.75
4	Cal Ripken Jr.	5.00
5	Ken Griffey Jr.	3.50
6	Ivan Rodriguez	1.00
7	Larry Walker	.75
8	Barry Bonds	5.00
9	Roger Clemens	3.00
10	Frank Thomas	1.50
11	Chuck Knoblauch	.75
12	Mike Piazza	3.50
13	Greg Maddux	2.50
14	Vladimir Guerrero	1.50
15	Andruw Jones	1.50

Hallbound

Hall Bound features players who were considered locks to be inducted into the Hall of Fame when their career was over. This insert was exclusive to Series 1 hobby packs and seeded one per 36. Cards are numbered with a "HB" prefix.

		NM/M
Complete Set (15):		45.00
Common Player:		1.50
1	Paul Molitor	2.50
2	Tony Gwynn	3.50
3	Wade Boggs	3.50
4	Roger Clemens	4.00
5	Dennis Eckersley	2.00
6	Cal Ripken Jr.	7.50
7	Greg Maddux	3.50
8	Rickey Henderson	2.50
9	Ken Griffey Jr.	5.00
10	Frank Thomas	2.50
11	Mark McGwire	6.00
12	Barry Bonds	7.50
13	Mike Piazza	5.00
14	Juan Gonzalez	1.50
15	Randy Johnson	2.50

Inter-League Mystery Finest

Five of the 1997 season's most intriguing inter-league matchups are showcased with four cards each in Inter-League Mystery Finest. Regular versions of this Se-

ries 1 insert are seeded one per 36 packs, while Refractor versions are seeded one per 144 packs. Cards are numbered with an "ILM" prefix.

		NM/M
Complete Set (20):		35.00
Common Player:		.75
Inserted 1:36		
Refractors:		1.5X
Inserted 1:144		
1	Chipper Jones	3.00
2	Cal Ripken Jr.	6.50
3	Greg Maddux	3.00
4	Rafael Palmeiro	1.50
5	Todd Hundley	.75
6	Derek Jeter	6.50
7	John Olerud	.75
8	Tino Martinez	.75
9	Larry Walker	.75
10	Ken Griffey Jr.	4.00
11	Andres Galarraga	.75
12	Randy Johnson	2.00
13	Mike Piazza	4.00
14	Jim Edmonds	.75
15	Eric Karros	.75
16	Tim Salmon	.75
17	Sammy Sosa	3.00
18	Frank Thomas	2.00
19	Mark Grace	.75
20	Albert Belle	.75

Milestones

Milestones features 10 records that could be broken during the 1998 season and the players who have the best shot at breaking them. This retail exclusive insert is seeded one per 36 packs and is numbered with a "MS" prefix.

		NM/M
Complete Set (10):		17.50
Common Player:		.75
MS1	Barry Bonds	5.00
MS2	Roger Clemens	2.50
MS3	Dennis Eckersley	1.00
MS4	Juan Gonzalez	.75
MS5	Ken Griffey Jr.	3.00
MS6	Tony Gwynn	2.00
MS7	Greg Maddux	2.00
MS8	Mark McGwire	4.00
MS9	Cal Ripken Jr.	5.00
MS10	Frank Thomas	1.25

Mystery Finest

This 20-card insert set features top players on bordered and borderless designs, with Refractor versions of each. Exclusive to Series 2 packs, bordered cards are seeded 1:36 packs, borderless are seeded 1:72 packs, bordered Refractors are 1:108 and borderless Refractors are seeded 1:288 packs. Mystery Finest inserts are numbered with a "M" prefix.

		NM/M
Complete Set (20):		25.00
Common Player:		.50
Inserted 1:36		
Borderless 1:72:		1.5X
Bordered Refractors 1:108:		1.5X
Borderless Refractors 1:288:		2X
1	Nomar Garciaparra	1.50
2	Chipper Jones	1.50
3	Scott Rolen	.75
4	Albert Belle	.50
5	Mo Vaughn	.50
6	Jose Cruz Jr.	.50
7	Mark McGwire	3.00
8	Derek Jeter	3.50
9	Tony Gwynn	1.50
10	Frank Thomas	1.00

		NM/M
11	Tino Martinez	.50
12	Greg Maddux	1.50
13	Juan Gonzalez	.75
14	Larry Walker	.50
15	Mike Piazza	2.50
16	Cal Ripken Jr.	3.50
17	Jeff Bagwell	1.00
18	Andruw Jones	1.00
19	Barry Bonds	3.50
20	Ken Griffey Jr.	2.50

Rookie Class

Rookie Class features 10 young stars from 1998 and was exclusive to Series II packs. The cards were inserted one per 12 packs and numbered with a "R" prefix.

		NM/M
Complete Set (10):		4.00
Common Player:		.25
Inserted 1:12		
1	Travis Lee	.50
2	Richard Hidalgo	.25
3	Todd Helton	2.00
4	Paul Konerko	.75
5	Mark Kotsay	.25
6	Derrek Lee	1.50
7	Eli Marrero	.25
8	Fernando Tatis	.25
9	Juan Encarnacion	.25
10	Ben Grieve	.25

1998 Topps Chrome

All 502 1998 Topps cards were reprinted in chromium versions for Topps Chrome. Chrome was released in two series; Series 1 containing 282 cards and Series 2 including 220 cards. Four-card packs had a suggested retail price of $3. Card fronts include a Topps Chrome logo. The issue offers a sampling of the inserts from Topps, along with Refractor versions of every card and insert. Series 1 inserts included: Flashbacks, Baby Boomers and Hallbound. Series 2 inserts included: Milestones, '98 Rookie Class and Clout 9.

		NM/M
Complete Set (502):		100.00
Common Player:		.10
Refractors:		5X
Inserted 1:12		
Foil Pack (4):		1.50
Foil Box (24):		25.00
1	Tony Gwynn	2.00
2	Larry Walker	.10
3	Billy Wagner	.10
4	Denny Neagle	.10
5	Vladimir Guerrero	1.50
6	Kevin Brown	.10
7	Mariano Rivera	.10
8	Tony Clark	.10
9	Deion Sanders	.10
10	Francisco Cordova	.10
11	Matt Williams	.10
12	Carlos Baerga	.10
13	Mo Vaughn	.10
14	Bobby Witt	.10
15	Matt Stairs	.10
16	Chan Ho Park	.10
17	Mike Bordick	.10
18	Mike Bordick	.10
19	Michael Tucker	.10

20	Frank Thomas	1.50
21	Roberto Clemente (Tribute)	2.50
22	Dmitri Young	.10
23	Steve Trachsel	.10
24	Jeff Kent	.10
25	Scott Rolen	.75
26	John Thomson	.10
27	Joe Vitiello	.10
28	Eddie Guardado	.10
29	Charlie Hayes	.10
30	Juan Gonzalez	.75
31	Garret Anderson	.10
32	John Jaha	.10
33	Omar Vizquel	.10
34	Brian Hunter	.10
35	Jeff Bagwell	1.50
36	Mark Lemke	.10
37	Doug Glanville	.10
38	Dan Wilson	.10
39	Steve Cooke	.10
40	Chili Davis	.10
41	Mike Cameron	.10
42	F.P. Santangelo	.10
43	Brad Ausmus	.10
44	Gary DiSarcina	.10
45	Pat Hentgen	.10
46	Wilton Guerrero	.10
47	Devon White	.10
48	Danny Patterson	.10
49	Pat Meares	.10
50	Rafael Palmeiro	1.00
51	Mark Gardner	.10
52	Jeff Blauser	.10
53	Dave Hollins	.10
54	Carlos Garcia	.10
55	Ben McDonald	.10
56	John Mabry	.10
57	Trevor Hoffman	.10
58	Tony Fernandez	.10
59	Rich Loiselle	.10
60	Mark Leiter	.10
61	Pat Kelly	.10
62	John Flaherty	.10
63	Roger Bailey	.10
64	Tom Gordon	.10
65	Ryan Klesko	.10
66	Darryl Hamilton	.10
67	Jim Eisenreich	.10
68	Butch Huskey	.10
69	Mark Grudzielanek	.10
70	Marquis Grissom	.10
71	Mark McLemore	.10
72	Gary Gaetti	.10
73	Greg Gagne	.10
74	Lyle Mouton	.10
75	Jim Edmonds	.10
76	Shawn Green	.35
77	Terry Vaughn	.10
78	Terry Adams	.10
79	Kevin Polcovich RC	.10
80	Troy O'Leary	.10
81	Jeff Shaw	.10
82	Rich Becker	.10
83	David Wells	.10
84	Steve Karsay	.10
85	Charles Nagy	.10
86	B.J. Surhoff	.10
87	Jamey Wright	.10
88	James Baldwin	.10
89	Edgardo Alfonzo	.10
90	Jay Buhner	.10
91	Brady Anderson	.10
92	Scott Servais	.10
93	Edgar Renteria	.10
94	Mike Lieberthal	.10
95	Rick Aguilera	.10
96	Walt Weiss	.10
97	Deivi Cruz	.10
98	Kurt Abbott	.10
99	Henry Rodriguez	.10
100	Mike Piazza	2.25
101	Bill Taylor	.10
102	Todd Zeile	.10
103	Rey Ordonez	.10
104	Willie Greene	.10
105	Tony Womack	.10
106	Mike Sweeney	.10
107	Jeffrey Hammonds	.10
108	Kevin Orie	.10
109	Alex Gonzalez	.10
110	Jose Canseco	.60
111	Paul Sorrento	.10
112	Joey Hamilton	.10
113	Brad Radke	.10
114	Steve Avery	.10
115	Esteban Loaiza	.10
116	Stan Javier	.10
117	Chris Gomez	.10
118	Royce Clayton	.10
119	Orlando Merced	.10
120	Kevin Appier	.10
121	Mel Nieves	.10
122	Joe Girardi	.10
123	Rico Brogna	.10
124	Kent Mercker	.10
125	Manny Ramirez	1.50
126	Jeromy Burnitz	.10
127	Kevin Foster	.10
128	Matt Morris	.10
129	Jason Dickson	.10
130	Tom Glavine	.35
131	Wally Joyner	.10
132	Rick Reed	.10
133	Todd Jones	.10
134	Dave Martinez	.10
135	Sandy Alomar	.10
136	Mike Lansing	.10

#	Player	Price
137	Sean Berry	.10
138	Doug Jones	.10
139	Todd Stottlemyre	.10
140	Jay Bell	.10
141	Jaime Navarro	.10
142	Chris Hoiles	.10
143	Joey Cora	.10
144	Scott Spiezio	.10
145	Joe Carter	.10
146	Jose Guillen	.10
147	Damion Easley	.10
148	Lee Stevens	.10
149	Alex Fernandez	.10
150	Randy Johnson	1.50
151	J.T. Snow	.10
152	Chuck Finley	.10
153	Bernard Gilkey	.10
154	David Segui	.10
155	Dante Bichette	.10
156	Kevin Stocker	.10
157	Carl Everett	.10
158	Jose Valentin	.10
159	Pokey Reese	.10
160	Derek Jeter	3.00
161	Roger Pavlik	.10
162	Mark Wohlers	.10
163	Ricky Bottalico	.10
164	Ozzie Guillen	.10
165	Mike Mussina	.60
166	Gary Sheffield	.50
167	Hideo Nomo	.75
168	Mark Grace	.10
169	Aaron Sele	.10
170	Darryl Kile	.10
171	Shawn Estes	.10
172	Vinny Castilla	.10
173	Ron Coomer	.10
174	Jose Rosado	.10
175	Kenny Lofton	.10
176	Jason Giambi	.65
177	Hal Morris	.10
178	Darren Bragg	.10
179	Orel Hershiser	.10
180	Ray Lankford	.10
181	Hideki Irabu	.10
182	Kevin Young	.10
183	Javy Lopez	.10
184	Jeff Montgomery	.10
185	Mike Holtz	.10
186	George Williams	.10
187	Cal Eldred	.10
188	Tom Candiotti	.10
189	Glenallen Hill	.10
190	Brian Giles	.10
191	Dave Mlicki	.10
192	Garrett Stephenson	.10
193	Jeff Frye	.10
194	Joe Oliver	.10
195	Bob Hamelin	.10
196	Luis Sojo	.10
197	LaTroy Hawkins	.10
198	Kevin Elster	.10
199	Jeff Reed	.10
200	Dennis Eckersley	1.00
201	Bill Mueller	.10
202	Russ Davis	.10
203	Armando Benitez	.10
204	Quilvio Veras	.10
205	Tim Naehring	.10
206	Quinton McCracken	.10
207	Raul Casanova	.10
208	Matt Lawton	.10
209	Luis Alicea	.10
210	Luis Gonzalez	.10
211	Allen Watson	.10
212	Gerald Williams	.10
213	David Bell	.10
214	Todd Hollandsworth	.10
215	Wade Boggs	2.00
216	Jose Mesa	.10
217	Jamie Moyer	.10
218	Darren Daulton	.10
219	Mickey Morandini	.10
220	Rusty Greer	.10
221	Jim Bullinger	.10
222	Jose Offerman	.10
223	Matt Karchner	.10
224	Woody Williams	.10
225	Mark Loretta	.10
226	Mike Hampton	.10
227	Willie Adams	.10
228	Scott Hatteberg	.10
229	Rich Amaral	.10
230	Terry Steinbach	.10
231	Glendon Rusch	.10
232	Bret Boone	.10
233	Robert Person	.10
234	Jose Hernandez	.10
235	Doug Drabek	.10
236	Jason McDonald	.10
237	Chris Widger	.10
238	Tom Martin RC	.10
239	Dave Burba	.10
240	Pete Rose	.10
241	Bobby Ayala	.10
242	Tim Wakefield	.10
243	Dennis Springer	.10
244	Tim Belcher	.10
245	Jon Garland, Geoff Goetz (Draft Pick)	.25
246	Glenn Davis, Lance Berkman (Draft Pick)	.25
247	Vernon Wells, Aaron Akin (Draft Pick)	.15
248	Adam Kennedy, Jason Romano (Draft Pick)	.25

#	Player	Price
249	Jason Dellaero, Troy Cameron (Draft Pick)	.10
250	Alex Sanchez, Jared Sandberg RC (Expansion)	.25
251	Pablo Ortega, James Manias RC (Expansion)	.10
252	Jason Conti, Mike Stoner RC (Expansion)	.10
253	John Patterson, Larry Rodriguez (Expansion)	.10
254	Adrian Beltre, Ryan Minor RC, Aaron Boone (Prospect)	.25
255	Ben Grieve, Brian Buchanan, Dermal Brown (Prospect)	.10
256	Carl Pavano, Kerry Wood, Gil Meche (Prospect)	.75
257	David Ortiz, Daryle Ward, Richie Sexson (Prospect)	.65
258	Randy Winn, Juan Encarnacion, Andrew Vessel (Prospect)	.10
259	Kris Benson, Travis Smith, Courtney Duncan (Prospect)	.15
260	Chad Hermansen, Brent Butler, Warren Morris RC (Prospect)	.15
261	Ben Davis, Elieser Marrero, Ramon Hernandez (Prospect)	.10
262	Eric Chavez, Russell Branyan, Russ Johnson (Prospect)	.25
263	Todd Dunwoody, John Barnes, Ryan Jackson RC (Prospect)	.15
264	Matt Clement, Roy Halladay, Brian Fuentes (Prospect)	.20
265	Randy Johnson (Season Highlight)	.50
266	Kevin Brown (Season Highlight)	.10
267	Francisco Cordova, Ricardo Rincon (Season Highlight)	.10
268	Nomar Garciaparra (Season Highlight)	.75
269	Tino Martinez (Season Highlight)	.10
270	Chuck Knoblauch (Inter-League)	.10
271	Pedro Martinez (Inter-League)	.40
272	Denny Neagle (Inter-League)	.10
273	Juan Gonzalez (Inter-League)	.20
274	Andres Galarraga (Inter-League)	.10
275	Checklist	.10
276	Checklist	.10
277	Moises Alou (World Series)	.10
278	Sandy Alomar (World Series)	.10
279	Gary Sheffield (World Series)	.10
280	Matt Williams (World Series)	.10
281	Livan Hernandez (World Series)	.10
282	Chad Ogea (World Series)	.10
283	Marlins Win (World Series)	.10
284	Tino Martinez	.10
285	Roberto Alomar	.35
286	Jeff King	.10
287	Brian Jordan	.10
288	Darin Erstad	.30
289	Ken Caminiti	.10
290	Jim Thome	.90
291	Paul Molitor	1.50
292	Ivan Rodriguez	1.00
293	Bernie Williams	.10
294	Todd Hundley	.10
295	Andres Galarraga	.10
296	Greg Maddux	2.00
297	Edgar Martinez	.10
298	Ron Gant	.10
299	Derek Bell	.10
300	Roger Clemens	2.00
301	Rondell White	.10
302	Barry Larkin	.10
303	Robin Ventura	.10
304	Jason Kendall	.10
305	Chipper Jones	2.00
306	John Franco	.10
307	Sammy Sosa	2.00
308	Troy Percival	.10
309	Chuck Knoblauch	.10
310	Ellis Burks	.10
311	Al Martin	.10
312	Tim Salmon	.10
313	Moises Alou	.10
314	Lance Johnson	.10
315	Justin Thompson	.10
316	Will Clark	.10
317	Barry Bonds	3.00
318	Craig Biggio	.10
319	John Smoltz	.10
320	Cal Ripken Jr.	3.00
321	Ken Griffey Jr.	2.25
322	Paul O'Neill	.10
323	Todd Helton	1.50

#	Player	Price
324	John Olerud	.10
325	Mark McGwire	2.50
326	Jose Cruz Jr.	.10
327	Jeff Cirillo	.10
328	Dean Palmer	.10
329	John Wetteland	.10
330	Steve Finley	.10
331	Albert Belle	.10
332	Curt Schilling	.35
333	Raul Mondesi	.10
334	Andruw Jones	1.50
335	Nomar Garciaparra	2.00
336	David Justice	.10
337	Andy Pettitte	.30
338	Pedro Martinez	1.50
339	Travis Miller	.10
340	Chris Stynes	.10
341	Gregg Jefferies	.10
342	Jeff Fassero	.10
343	Craig Counsell	.10
344	Wilson Alvarez	.10
345	Bip Roberts	.10
346	Kelvim Escobar	.10
347	Mark Bellhorn	.10
348	Cory Lidle	.10
349	Fred McGriff	.10
350	Chuck Carr	.10
351	Bob Abreu	.10
352	Juan Guzman	.10
353	Fernando Vina	.10
354	Andy Benes	.10
355	Dave Nilsson	.10
356	Bobby Bonilla	.10
357	Ismael Valdes	.10
358	Carlos Perez	.10
359	Kirk Rueter	.10
360	Bartolo Colon	.10
361	Mel Rojas	.10
362	Johnny Damon	.35
363	Geronimo Berroa	.10
364	Reggie Sanders	.10
365	Jermaine Allensworth	.10
366	Orlando Cabrera	.10
367	Jorge Fabregas	.10
368	Scott Stahoviak	.10
369	Ken Cloude	.10
370	Donovan Osborne	.10
371	Roger Cedeno	.10
372	Neifi Perez	.10
373	Chris Holt	.10
374	Cecil Fielder	.10
375	Marty Cordova	.10
376	Tom Goodwin	.10
377	Jeff Suppan	.10
378	Jeff Brantley	.10
379	Mark Langston	.10
380	Shane Reynolds	.10
381	Mike Fetters	.10
382	Todd Greene	.10
383	Ray Durham	.10
384	Carlos Delgado	.35
385	Jeff D'Amico	.10
386	Brian McRae	.10
387	Alan Benes	.10
388	Heathcliff Slocumb	.10
389	Eric Young	.10
390	Travis Fryman	.10
391	David Cone	.10
392	Otis Nixon	.10
393	Jeremi Gonzalez	.10
394	Jeff Juden	.10
395	Jose Vizcaino	.10
396	Ugueth Urbina	.10
397	Ramon Martinez	.10
398	Robb Nen	.10
399	Harold Baines	.10
400	Delino DeShields	.10
401	John Burkett	.10
402	Sterling Hitchcock	.10
403	Mark Clark	.10
404	Terrell Wade	.10
405	Scott Brosius	.10
406	Chad Curtis	.10
407	Brian Johnson	.10
408	Roberto Kelly	.10
409	Dave Dellucci RC	.25
410	Michael Tucker	.10
411	Mark Kotsay	.10
412	Mark Lewis	.10
413	Ryan McGuire	.10
414	Shawon Dunston	.10
415	Brad Rigby	.10
416	Scott Erickson	.10
417	Bobby Jones	.10
418	Darren Oliver	.10
419	John Smiley	.10
420	T.J. Mathews	.10
421	Dustin Hermanson	.10
422	Mike Timlin	.10
423	Willie Blair	.10
424	Manny Alexander	.10
425	Bob Tewksbury	.10
426	Pete Schourek	.10
427	Reggie Jefferson	.10
428	Ed Sprague	.10
429	Jeff Conine	.10
430	Roberto Hernandez	.10
431	Tom Pagnozzi	.10
432	Jaret Wright	.10
433	Livan Hernandez	.10
434	Andy Ashby	.10
435	Todd Dunn	.10
436	Bobby Higginson	.10
437	Rod Beck	.10
438	Jim Leyritz	.10
439	Matt Williams	.10
440	Brett Tomko	.10
441	Joe Randa	.10

#	Player	Price
442	Chris Carpenter	.10
443	Dennis Reyes	.10
444	Al Leiter	.10
445	Jason Schmidt	.10
446	Ken Hill	.10
447	Shannon Stewart	.10
448	Enrique Wilson	.10
449	Fernando Tatis	.10
450	Jimmy Key	.10
451	Darrin Fletcher	.10
452	John Valentin	.10
453	Kevin Tapani	.10
454	Eric Karros	.10
455	Jay Bell	.10
456	Walt Weiss	.10
457	Devon White	.10
458	Carl Pavano	.10
459	Mike Lansing	.10
460	John Flaherty	.10
461	Richard Hidalgo	.10
462	Quinton McCracken	.10
463	Karim Garcia	.20
464	Miguel Cairo	.10
465	Edwin Diaz	.10
466	Bobby Smith	.10
467	Yamil Benitez	.10
468	Rich Butler RC	.10
469	Ben Ford RC	.10
470	Bubba Trammell	.10
471	Brent Brede	.10
472	Brooks Kieschnick	.10
473	Carlos Castillo	.10
474	Brad Radke (Season Highlight)	.10
475	Roger Clemens (Season Highlight)	1.00
476	Curt Schilling (Season Highlight)	.15
477	John Olerud (Season Highlight)	.10
478	Mark McGwire (Season Highlight)	1.25
479	Mike Piazza, Ken Griffey Jr. (Interleague)	1.25
480	Jeff Bagwell, Frank Thomas (Interleague)	1.00
481	Chipper Jones, Nomar Garciaparra (Interleague)	1.00
482	Larry Walker, Juan Gonzalez (Interleague)	.20
483	Gary Sheffield, Tino Martinez (Interleague)	.10
484	Derrick Gibson, Michael Coleman, Norm Hutchins (Prospect)	.10
485	Braden Looper, Cliff Politte, Brian Rose (Prospect)	.15
486	Eric Milton, Jason Marquis, Corey Lee (Prospect)	.25
487	A.J. Hinch, Mark Osborne, Robert Fick RC (Prospect)	.25
488	Aramis Ramirez, Alex Gonzalez, Sean Casey (Prospect)	.25
489	Donnie Bridges RC, Tim Drew RC (Draft Pick)	.20
490	Ntema Ndungidi RC, Darnell McDonald RC (Draft Pick)	.10
491	Ryan Anderson RC, Mark Mangum (Draft Pick)	.50
492	J.J. Davis, Troy Glaus RC (Draft Pick)	.50
493	Jayson Werth, Dan Reichert (Draft Pick)	.10
494	John Curtice RC, Mike Cuddyer RC (Draft Pick)	.50
495	Jack Cust RC, Jason Standridge (Draft Pick)	4.00
496	Brian Anderson (Expansion Team Prospect)	.10
497	Tony Saunders (Expansion Team Prospect)	.10
498	Vladimir Nunez, Jhensy Sandoval RC (Expansion Team Prospect)	.10
499	Brad Penny, Nick Bierbrodt (Expansion Team Prospect)	.10
500	Dustin Carr RC, Luis Cruz RC (Expansion Team Prospect)	.10
501	Marcus McCain RC, Cedrick Bowers RC (Expansion Team Prospect)	.10
502	Checklist	.10
503	Checklist	.10
504	Alex Rodriguez	2.50

Refractors

Each card in the regular Topps Series 1 and Series 2 Chrome issue could also be found in a refractor version seeded approximately one per 12 packs. Refractor versions are so designated above the card number on back.

	NM/M
Common Player:	.50
Stars/Rookies:	5X

Baby Boomers

This 15-card insert featured players with less than three years of experience. Cards were inserted one per 24 packs, with Refractor versions found every 72 packs of Series I. Cards were numbered with a "BB" prefix.

		NM/M
Complete Set (15):		16.00
Common Player:		.75
Inserted 1:24		
Refractors:		1.5X
Inserted 1:72		
1	Derek Jeter	6.00
2	Scott Rolen	.90
3	Nomar Garciaparra	3.50
4	Jose Cruz Jr.	.75
5	Darin Erstad	.90
6	Todd Helton	1.50
7	Tony Clark	.75
8	Jose Guillen	.75
9	Andruw Jones	1.50
10	Vladimir Guerrero	1.50
11	Mark Kotsay	.75
12	Todd Greene	.75
13	Andy Pettitte	.90
14	Justin Thompson	.75
15	Alan Benes	.75

Clout 9

This nine-card insert included players for their statistical supremacy. Clout 9 cards were found in Series II packs at a rate of one per 24 packs, with Refractor versions every 72 packs. Cards are numbered with a "C" prefix.

		NM/M
Complete Set (9):		15.00
Common Player:		.75
Inserted 1:24		
Refractors:		1.5X
Inserted 1:72		
1	Edgar Martinez	.75
2	Mike Piazza	3.50
3	Frank Thomas	1.50
4	Craig Biggio	.75
5	Vinny Castilla	.75
6	Jeff Blauser	.75
7	Barry Bonds	6.00
8	Ken Griffey Jr.	3.50
9	Larry Walker	.75

Flashback

This 10-card double-sided insert features top players as they looked in 1998 on one side, and how they looked when they first appeared in the majors on the other side. Flashback inserts were seeded one per 24 packs of Series I, with Refractors every 72 packs. This insert was numbered with a "FB" prefix.

		NM/M
Complete Set (10):		16.00
Common Player:		.75
Inserted 1:24		
Refractors:		1.5X
Inserted 1:72		

1	Barry Bonds	6.00
2	Ken Griffey Jr.	3.50
3	Paul Molitor	1.50
4	Randy Johnson	1.50
5	Cal Ripken Jr.	6.00
6	Tony Gwynn	2.50
7	Kenny Lofton	.75
8	Gary Sheffield	.85
9	Deion Sanders	.75
10	Brady Anderson	.75

Hallbound

Hallbound highlighted 15 players destined for the Hall of Fame on die-cut cards. Inserted at a rate of one per 24 packs of Series I, with Refractors every 72 packs, these were numbered with a "HB" prefix.

		NM/M
Complete Set (15):		35.00
Common Player:		1.50
Inserted 1:24		
Refractors:		1.5X
Inserted 1:72		
1	Paul Molitor	2.00
2	Tony Gwynn	2.50
3	Wade Boggs	2.50
4	Roger Clemens	3.00
5	Dennis Eckersley	1.50
6	Cal Ripken Jr.	6.00
7	Greg Maddux	2.50
8	Rickey Henderson	2.00
9	Ken Griffey Jr.	3.50
10	Frank Thomas	4.00
11	Mark McGwire	4.50
12	Barry Bonds	6.00
13	Mike Piazza	3.50
14	Juan Gonzalez	1.50
15	Randy Johnson	2.00

Milestones

Ten superstars who were within reach of major records for the 1998 season are featured in Milestones. This Series II insert was seeded one per 24 packs, with Refractor versions seeded one per 72 packs. Milestones were numbered with a "MS" prefix.

		NM/M
Complete Set (10):		25.00
Common Player:		1.00
Inserted 1:24		
Refractors:		1.5X
Inserted 1:72		
1	Barry Bonds	6.00
2	Roger Clemens	3.00
3	Dennis Eckersley	1.00
4	Juan Gonzalez	1.00
5	Ken Griffey Jr.	3.50
6	Tony Gwynn	2.50
7	Greg Maddux	2.50
8	Mark McGwire	4.50
9	Cal Ripken Jr.	6.00
10	Frank Thomas	1.50

Rookie Class

This insert featured 10 players with less than one year of major league experience. Inserted in Series II packs at a rate of one per 12 packs, with Refractors every 24 packs, '98 Rookie Class inserts were numbered with an "R" prefix.

	NM/M
Complete Set (10):	10.00

		NM/M
Common Player:		.75
Inserted 1:12		
Refractors:		1.5X
Inserted 1:24		
1	Travis Lee	1.00
2	Richard Hidalgo	.75
3	Todd Helton	4.50
4	Paul Konerko	1.50
5	Mark Kotsay	.75
6	Derek Lee	3.00
7	Eli Marrero	.75
8	Fernando Tatis	.75
9	Juan Encarnacion	.75
10	Ben Grieve	.75

Super Chrome

This 36-card oversized set featured some of the top players from Chrome on 4-1/8" x 5-3/4" cards. The product sold in three-card packs and featured the same photography as Topps and Topps Chrome before it, but added a Super Chrome logo. Refractor versions of each card were also available, inserted one per 12 packs.

		NM/M
Complete Set (36):		20.00
Common Player:		.25
Refractors:		1.5X
Inserted 1:12		
Pack (3):		2.50
Wax Box (12):		25.00
1	Tony Gwynn	1.00
2	Larry Walker	.25
3	Vladimir Guerrero	.75
4	Mo Vaughn	.75
5	Frank Thomas	.75
6	Barry Larkin	.25
7	Scott Rolen	.65
8	Juan Gonzalez	.75
9	Jeff Bagwell	.75
10	Ryan Klesko	.25
11	Mike Piazza	1.50
12	Randy Johnson	.75
13	Derek Jeter	3.00
14	Gary Sheffield	.50
15	Hideo Nomo	.50
16	Tino Martinez	.25
17	Ivan Rodriguez	.65
18	Bernie Williams	.25
19	Greg Maddux	1.00
20	Roger Clemens	1.25
21	Roberto Clemente	2.00
22	Chipper Jones	1.00
23	Sammy Sosa	1.00
24	Tony Clark	.25
25	Barry Bonds	3.00
26	Craig Biggio	.25
27	Cal Ripken Jr.	3.00
28	Ken Griffey Jr.	1.50
29	Todd Helton	.65
30	Mark McGwire	2.00
31	Jose Cruz	.25
32	Albert Belle	.25
33	Andruw Jones	.75
34	Nomar Garciaparra	1.00
35	Andy Pettitte	.45
36	Alex Rodriguez	2.00

1998 Topps Gallery Pre-Production Samples

To introduce its premium Gallery line for 1998, Topps issued this set of pre-production samples

showcasing several of the different technologies to be found in the issue. The samples are virtually identical to the issued versions except for the use of a "PP" prefix to the card number.

		NM/M
Complete Set (5):		7.50
Common Player:		1.50
PP1	Andruw Jones (Portraits)	1.50
PP2	Juan Gonzalez (Permanent Collection)	1.00
PP3	Barry Bonds (Expressionists)	3.00
PP4	Derek Jeter (Exhibitions)	3.00
PP5	Nomar Garciaparra (Impressions)	2.00

1998 Topps Gallery

Gallery returned in 1998 with a 150-card set broken up into five different subsets - Exhibitions, Impressions, Expressionists, Portraits and Permanent Collection. The set was paralleled twice - first in a Player's Private Issue set and, second in Gallery Proofs. Gallery cards were made to look like works of art instead of simply a photo of the player on cardboard, and were sold in six-card packs. Inserts in this single-series product include: Photo Gallery, Gallery of Heroes and Awards Gallery.

		NM/M
Complete Set (150):		15.00
Common Player:		.10
Pack (6):		1.50
Wax Box (24):		25.00
1	Andruw Jones	1.00
2	Fred McGriff	.10
3	Wade Boggs	1.50
4	Pedro Martinez	1.00
5	Matt Williams	.10
6	Wilson Alvarez	.10
7	Henry Rodriguez	.10
8	Jay Bell	.10
9	Marquis Grissom	.10
10	Darryl Kile	.10
11	Chuck Knoblauch	.10
12	Kenny Lofton	.10
13	Quinton McCracken	.10
14	Andres Galarraga	.10
15	Brian Jordan	.10
16	Mike Lansing	.10
17	Travis Fryman	.10
18	Tony Saunders	.10
19	Moises Alou	.10
20	Travis Lee	.10
21	Garret Anderson	.10
22	Ken Caminiti	.10
23	Pedro Astacio	.10
24	Ellis Burks	.10
25	Albert Belle	.10
26	Alan Benes	.10
27	Jay Buhner	.10
28	Derek Bell	.10
29	Jeromy Burnitz	.10
30	Kevin Appier	.10
31	Jeff Cirillo	.10
32	Bernard Gilkey	.10
33	David Cone	.10
34	Jason Dickson	.10
35	Jose Cruz Jr.	.10
36	Marty Cordova	.10
37	Ray Durham	.10
38	Jaret Wright	.10
39	Billy Wagner	.10
40	Roger Clemens	1.75
41	Juan Gonzalez	.50
42	Jeremi Gonzalez	.10
43	Mark Grudzielanek	.10
44	Tom Glavine	.35
45	Barry Larkin	.10
46	Lance Johnson	.10
47	Bobby Higginson	.10
48	Mike Mussina	.50
49	Al Martin	.10
50	Mark McGwire	2.50
51	Todd Hundley	.10
52	Ray Lankford	.10
53	Jason Kendall	.10
54	Javy Lopez	.10
55	Ben Grieve	.10

56	Randy Johnson	1.00
57	Jeff King	.10
58	Mark Grace	.10
59	Rusty Greer	.10
60	Greg Maddux	1.50
61	Jeff Kent	.10
62	Rey Ordonez	.10
63	Hideo Nomo	.50
64	Charles Nagy	.10
65	Rondell White	.10
66	Todd Helton	.75
67	Jim Thome	.75
68	Denny Neagle	.10
69	Ivan Rodriguez	.75
70	Vladimir Guerrero	1.00
71	Jorge Posada	.10
72	J.T. Snow Jr.	.10
73	Reggie Sanders	.10
74	Scott Rolen	.75
75	Robin Ventura	.10
76	Mariano Rivera	.15
77	Cal Ripken Jr.	3.00
78	Justin Thompson	.10
79	Mike Piazza	2.00
80	Kevin Brown	.10
81	Sandy Alomar	.10
82	Craig Biggio	.10
83	Vinny Castilla	.10
84	Eric Young	.10
85	Bernie Williams	.10
86	Brady Anderson	.10
87	Bobby Bonilla	.10
88	Tony Clark	.10
89	Dan Wilson	.10
90	John Wetteland	.10
91	Barry Bonds	3.00
92	Chan Ho Park	.10
93	Carlos Delgado	.35
94	David Justice	.10
95	Chipper Jones	1.50
96	Shawn Estes	.10
97	Jason Giambi	.60
98	Ron Gant	.10
99	John Olerud	.10
100	Frank Thomas	1.00
101	Jose Guillen	.10
102	Brad Radke	.10
103	Troy Percival	.10
104	John Smoltz	.10
105	Edgardo Alfonzo	.10
106	Dante Bichette	.10
107	Larry Walker	.10
108	John Valentin	.10
109	Roberto Alomar	.30
110	Mike Cameron	.10
111	Eric Davis	.10
112	Johnny Damon	.35
113	Darin Erstad	.30
114	Omar Vizquel	.10
115	Derek Jeter	3.00
116	Tony Womack	.10
117	Edgar Renteria	.10
118	Raul Mondesi	.10
119	Tony Gwynn	1.50
120	Ken Griffey Jr.	2.00
121	Jim Edmonds	.10
122	Brian Hunter	.10
123	Neifi Perez	.10
124	Dean Palmer	.10
125	Alex Rodriguez	2.50
126	Tim Salmon	.10
127	Curt Schilling	.35
128	Kevin Orie	.10
129	Andy Pettitte	.30
130	Gary Sheffield	.50
131	Jose Rosado	.10
132	Manny Ramirez	1.00
133	Rafael Palmeiro	.75
134	Sammy Sosa	1.50
135	Jeff Bagwell	1.00
136	Delino DeShields	.10
137	Ryan Klesko	.10
138	Mo Vaughn	.10
139	Steve Finley	.10
140	Nomar Garciaparra	1.50
141	Paul Molitor	1.00
142	Pat Hentgen	.10
143	Eric Karros	.10
144	Bobby Jones	.10
145	Tino Martinez	.10
146	Matt Morris	.10
147	Livan Hernandez	.10
148	Edgar Martinez	.10
149	Paul O'Neill	.10
150	Checklist	.10

Player's Private Issue

Player's Private Issue inserts parallel the 150-card base set with a distinct design and embossing. The average insertion rate is one per 12 packs.

	NM/M
Common Player:	1.00
Stars/Rookies:	4X
Production 250 Sets	

Player's Private Issue Auction Cards

These special auction points cards were seeded one per pack of Gallery. Fronts are identical to the much scarcer PPI cards. Backs, however, differ greatly. Where regular PPI cards have a player photo, serial number, etc., these auction points cards have details of the procedure by which points could be accumulated and used to bid for original photos and printing plates. The redemption period ended Oct. 16, 1998.

	NM/M
Complete Set (150):	60.00
Common Player:	.25
Stars/Rookies:	1.5X

Gallery Proofs

This hobby-only parallel set included all 150 cards in the base set. Gallery Proofs were sequentially numbered to 125 sets.

	NM/M
Common Player:	1.50
Stars/Rookies:	4X
Production 125 Sets	

Awards Gallery

Awards Gallery featured 10 players who earned the highest honors in the game on a horizontal design. Fronts featured a shot of the player and the award he won on silver foilboard. These were inserted every 24 packs and numbered with an "AG" prefix.

		NM/M
Complete Set (10):		18.00
Common Player:		1.00
Inserted 1:24		
1	Ken Griffey Jr.	4.00
2	Larry Walker	1.00
3	Roger Clemens	2.50
4	Pedro Martinez	1.50
5	Nomar Garciaparra	2.00
6	Scott Rolen	1.00
7	Frank Thomas	1.50
8	Tony Gwynn	2.00
9	Mark McGwire	5.00
10	Livan Hernandez	1.00

Gallery of Heroes

Gallery of Heroes is a 15-card insert printed on colored, die-cut plastic that resembles a stained glass window. Cards were inserted one per 24 packs and numbered with a "GH" prefix. More is less in the case in the jumbo (3-1/4" x 4-1/2") version of the

cards which were inserted one per hobby box. Cards are numbered with a "GH" prefix.

		NM/M
Complete Set (15):		80.00
Common Player:		1.25
Inserted 1:24		
Jumbo Version (1:24): 75 Percent		
1	Ken Griffey Jr.	8.00
2	Derek Jeter	15.00
3	Barry Bonds	15.00
4	Alex Rodriguez	12.00
5	Frank Thomas	4.00
6	Nomar Garciaparra	6.00
7	Mark McGwire	12.00
8	Mike Piazza	8.00
9	Cal Ripken Jr.	15.00
10	Jose Cruz Jr.	1.25
11	Jeff Bagwell	4.00
12	Chipper Jones	6.00
13	Juan Gonzalez	2.00
14	Hideo Nomo	2.00
15	Greg Maddux	6.00

Photo Gallery

This 10-card insert captured unique shots of players on a silver foilboard design. Photo Gallery inserts were seeded one per 24 packs and numbered with a "PG" prefix.

		NM/M
Complete Set (10):		25.00
Common Player:		1.00
Inserted 1:24		
1	Alex Rodriguez	3.00
2	Frank Thomas	2.00
3	Derek Jeter	4.00
4	Cal Ripken Jr.	4.00
5	Ken Griffey Jr.	2.50
6	Mike Piazza	2.50
7	Nomar Garciaparra	2.25
8	Tim Salmon	1.00
9	Jeff Bagwell	2.00
10	Barry Bonds	4.00

Printing Plates

The aluminum press plates used to print the Gallery cards were issued as random pack inserts. Each card's front and back can be found in four different color variations. Because of the unique nature of each plate, assignment of catalog values is not feasible.

	NM/M
Common Player, Front:	50.00
Common Player, Back:	35.00

Gold Label Class 1 (Fielding, Follow-Thru)

Topps debuted its Gold Label brand with 100 cards printed on 30-point "spectral-reflective" stock

with gold foil stamping and two shots of the player on each card front. Cards arrived in Gold Label, Black Label and Red Label versions, each with varying levels of scarcity. The rarity of the cards was determined by the photo and foil stamping on the cards. In the foreground of each card front, the photograph is the same, but in the background one of three shots is featured. Class 1, fielding, are considered base cards; Class 2, running (inserted 1:4 packs) and Class 3, hitting (inserted 1:8 packs) are seeded levels. For pitching the levels are: Class 1, set position (base); Class 2, throwing (inserted 1:4 packs) and Class 3, follow-through (inserted 1:8 packs). Black Label cards are scarcer, while Red Label cards are scarcer yet. In addition, 1 of 1 cards exist for each Class and version. Class 1 cards have matte gold-foil graphic highlights on front. Black Label Class 1 cards were inserted one per eight packs. Red Label Class 1 cards are a 1:99 insert and are serially numbered to 100.

		NM/M
Complete Set (100):		12.00
Gold Label Common Player:		.10
Black Label Common Player:		.35
Black Label Stars/RC's:		4X
Red Label Common Player:		1.50
Red Label Stars/RC's:		12X
Pack (5):		2.00
Wax Box (24):		40.00
1	Kevin Brown	.10
2	Greg Maddux	1.25
3	Albert Belle	.10
4	Andres Galarraga	.10
5	Craig Biggio	.10
6	Matt Williams	.10
7	Derek Jeter	3.00
8	Randy Johnson	1.00
9	Jay Bell	.10
10	Jim Thome	.75
11	Roberto Alomar	.30
12	Tom Glavine	.35
13	Reggie Sanders	.10
14	Tony Gwynn	1.25
15	Mark McGwire	2.00
16	Jeromy Burnitz	.10
17	Andruw Jones	1.00
18	Jay Buhner	.10
19	Robin Ventura	.10
20	Jeff Bagwell	1.00
21	Roger Clemens	1.25
22	Masato Yoshii RC	.25
23	Travis Fryman	.10
24	Rafael Palmeiro	.75
25	Alex Rodriguez	2.00
26	Sandy Alomar	.10
27	Chipper Jones	1.25
28	Rusty Greer	.10
29	Cal Ripken Jr.	3.00
30	Tony Clark	.10
31	Derek Bell	.10
32	Fred McGriff	.10
33	Paul O'Neill	.10
34	Moises Alou	.10
35	Henry Rodriguez	.10
36	Steve Finley	.10
37	Marquis Grissom	.10
38	Jason Giambi	.60
39	Javy Lopez	.10
40	Damion Easley	.10
41	Mariano Rivera	.15
42	Mo Vaughn	.40
43	Mike Mussina	.40
44	Jason Kendall	.10
45	Pedro Martinez	1.00
46	Frank Thomas	1.00
47	Jim Edmonds	.10
48	Hideki Irabu	.10
49	Eric Karros	.10
50	Juan Gonzalez	.50
51	Ellis Burks	.10
52	Dean Palmer	.10
53	Scott Rolen	.60
54	Raul Mondesi	.10
55	Quinton McCracken	.10
56	John Olerud	.10
57	Ken Caminiti	.10
58	Brian Jordan	.10
59	Wade Boggs	1.25
60	Mike Piazza	1.50
61	Darin Erstad	.30
62	Curt Schilling	.35
63	David Justice	.10
64	Kenny Lofton	.10
65	Barry Bonds	3.00
66	Ray Lankford	.10
67	Brian Hunter	.10
68	Chuck Knoblauch	.10
69	Vinny Castilla	.10
70	Vladimir Guerrero	1.00
71	Tim Salmon	.10
72	Larry Walker	.10
73	Paul Molitor	1.00
74	Barry Larkin	.10

75	Edgar Martinez	.10
76	Bernie Williams	.10
77	Dante Bichette	.10
78	Nomar Garciaparra	1.25
79	Ben Grieve	.10
80	Ivan Rodriguez	.75
81	Todd Helton	.75
82	Ryan Klesko	.10
83	Sammy Sosa	1.25
84	Travis Lee	.10
85	Jose Cruz	.10
86	Mark Kotsay	.10
87	Richard Hidalgo	.10
88	Rondell White	.10
89	Greg Vaughn	.10
90	Gary Sheffield	.50
91	Paul Konerko	.25
92	Mark Grace	.10
93	Kevin Millwood RC	1.00
94	Manny Ramirez	1.00
95	Tino Martinez	.10
96	Brad Fullmer	.10
97	Todd Walker	.10
98	Carlos Delgado	.45
99	Kerry Wood	.60
100	Ken Griffey Jr.	1.50

Gold Label Class 2 (Running, Set Position)

Class 2 Gold Label and parallels feature background photos on front of position players running and pitchers in the set position. Class 2 cards have sparkling silver-foil graphic highlights on front and were inserted one per two packs. Black Label Class 2 cards were inserted one per 16 packs. Red Label Class 2 cards are a 1:198 insert and are serially numbered to 50.

	NM/M
Complete Set (100):	50.00
Gold Label Common Player:	.35
Gold Label Stars/RC's:	2X
Black Label Common Player:	1.00
Black Label Stars/RC's:	4X
Red Label Common Player:	4.00
Red Label Stars/RC's:	25X

Gold Label Class 3 (Hitting, Throwing)

Class 3 Gold Label and parallels feature background photos on front of position players hitting and pitchers throwing. Class 3 cards have sparkling gold-foil graphic highlights on front and were inserted one per four packs. Black Label Class 3 cards were inserted one per 32 packs. Red Label Class 2 cards are a 1:396 insert and are serially numbered to 25.

	NM/M
Complete Set (100):	120.00
Common Player:	.75
Black Label Stars/RC's:	2.5X
Black Label Common Player:	2.00
Black Label Stars/RC's:	6X
Red Label Common Player:	6.00
Red Label Stars/RC's:	35X

Gold Label 1 of 1

Each of the Classes and color versions of Topps Gold Label cards was paralleled in a 1 of 1 insert which was to be found on average of one per 1,085 packs. Each player, thus, can be found on nine different 1 of 1 cards in the issue.

Gold Label Home Run Race

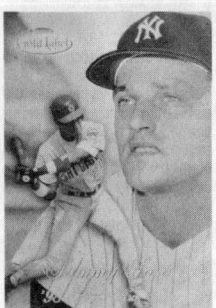

Home Run Race of '98 was a four-card insert set. Each of the current players' cards features a background photo of Roger Maris, while the fourth card features two shots of Maris. Gold, Black and Red Label versions are identified by the different foil-stamp logos. Gold cards were inserted 1:12 packs, Black Label cards were inserted 1:48 packs and Red Label cards were sequentially numbered to 61 and inserted 1:4,055 packs. The Home Run Race inserts are exclusive to Topps Home Team Advantage boxes.

	NM/M
Complete Set (4):	7.50
Common Player:	2.00
Black Label:	2X
Red Label:	4X
HR1 Roger Maris	3.00
HR2 Mark McGwire	3.00
HR3 Ken Griffey Jr.	2.50
HR4 Sammy Sosa	2.00

Opening Day

Topps Opening Day was a retail exclusive product comprising 165 cards, with 110 from Series 1 and 55 from Series 2. The cards from Series 2 were available in this product prior to the regular-issue cards being released. Opening Day cards feature a silver border vs. the gold border in the regular set, and include a silver-foil Opening Day stamp.

	NM/M
Complete Set (165):	10.00
Common Player:	.05
Wax Pack (7):	.65
Wax Box (22):	10.00

1	Tony Gwynn	.65
2	Larry Walker	.05
3	Billy Wagner	.05
4	Denny Neagle	.05
5	Vladimir Guerrero	.50
6	Kevin Brown	.05
7	Mariano Rivera	.15
8	Tony Clark	.05
9	Deion Sanders	.05
10	Matt Williams	.05
11	Carlos Baerga	.05
12	Mo Vaughn	.05
13	Chan Ho Park	.05
14	Frank Thomas	.50
15	John Jaha	.05
16	Steve Trachsel	.05
17	Jeff Kent	.05
18	Scott Rolen	.40
19	Juan Gonzalez	.25
20	Garret Anderson	.05
21	Roberto Clemente	1.00
22	Omar Vizquel	.05
23	Brian Hunter	.05
24	Jeff Bagwell	.50
25	Chili Davis	.05
26	Mike Cameron	.05
27	Pat Hentgen	.05
28	Wilton Guerrero	.05
29	Devon White	.05
30	Rafael Palmeiro	.40
31	Jeff Blauser	.05
32	Dave Hollins	.05
33	Trevor Hoffman	.05
34	Ryan Klesko	.05
35	Butch Huskey	.05
36	Mark Grudzielanek	.05
37	Marquis Grissom	.05
38	Jim Edmonds	.05
39	Greg Vaughn	.05
40	David Wells	.05
41	Charles Nagy	.05
42	B.J. Surhoff	.05
43	Edgardo Alfonzo	.05
44	Jay Buhner	.05
45	Brady Anderson	.05
46	Edgar Renteria	.05
47	Rick Aguilera	.05
48	Henry Rodriguez	.05
49	Mike Piazza	.75
50	Todd Zeile	.05
51	Rey Ordonez	.05
52	Tony Womack	.05
53	Mike Sweeney	.05
54	Jeffrey Hammonds	.05
55	Kevin Orie	.05
56	Alex Gonzalez	.05
57	Jose Canseco	.35
58	Joey Hamilton	.05
59	Brad Radke	.05
60	Kevin Appier	.05
61	Manny Ramirez	.50
62	Jeromy Burnitz	.05
63	Matt Morris	.05
64	Jason Dickson	.05
65	Tom Glavine	.25
66	Wally Joyner	.05
67	Todd Jones	.05
68	Sandy Alomar	.05
69	Mike Lansing	.05
70	Todd Stottlemyre	.05
71	Jay Bell	.05
72	Joey Cora	.05
73	Scott Spiezio	.05
74	Joe Carter	.05
75	Jose Guillen	.05
76	Damion Easley	.05
77	Alex Fernandez	.05
78	Randy Johnson	.50
79	J.T. Snow	.05
80	Bernard Gilkey	.05
81	David Segui	.05
82	Dante Bichette	.05
83	Derek Jeter	1.50
84	Mark Wohlers	.05
85	Ricky Bottalico	.05
86	Mike Mussina	.35
87	Gary Sheffield	.05
88	Hideo Nomo	.25
89	Mark Grace	.05
90	Darryl Kile	.05
91	Shawn Estes	.05
92	Vinny Castilla	.05
93	Jose Rosado	.05
94	Kenny Lofton	.05
95	Jason Giambi	.35
96	Ray Lankford	.05
97	Hideki Irabu	.05
98	Javy Lopez	.05
99	Jeff Montgomery	.05
100	Dennis Eckersley	.40
101	Armando Benitez	.05
102	Tim Naehring	.05
103	Luis Gonzalez	.05
104	Todd Hollandsworth	.05
105	Wade Boggs	.65
106	Mickey Morandini	.05
107	Rusty Greer	.05
108	Terry Steinbach	.05
109	Pete Rose II	.05
110	Checklist	.05
111	Tino Martinez	.05
112	Roberto Alomar	.20
113	Jeff King	.05
114	Brian Jordan	.05
115	Darin Erstad	.25
116	Ken Caminiti	.05
117	Jim Thome	.60
118	Paul Molitor	.50

119	Ivan Rodriguez	.40
120	Bernie Williams	.05
121	Todd Hundley	.05
122	Andres Galarraga	.05
123	Greg Maddux	.65
124	Edgar Martinez	.05
125	Ron Gant	.05
126	Derek Bell	.05
127	Roger Clemens	.70
128	Rondell White	.05
129	Barry Larkin	.05
130	Robin Ventura	.05
131	Jason Kendall	.05
132	Chipper Jones	.75
133	John Franco	.05
134	Sammy Sosa	.65
135	Chuck Knoblauch	.05
136	Ellis Burks	.05
137	Al Martin	.05
138	Tim Salmon	.05
139	Moises Alou	.05
140	Lance Johnson	.05
141	Justin Thompson	.05
142	Will Clark	.05
143	Barry Bonds	1.50
144	Craig Biggio	.05
145	John Smoltz	.05
146	Cal Ripken Jr.	1.50
147	Ken Griffey Jr.	.75
148	Paul O'Neill	.05
149	Todd Helton	.40
150	John Olerud	.05
151	Mark McGwire	1.00
152	Jose Cruz Jr.	.05
153	Jeff Cirillo	.05
154	Dean Palmer	.05
155	John Wetteland	.05
156	Eric Karros	.05
157	Steve Finley	.05
158	Albert Belle	.05
159	Curt Schilling	.25
160	Raul Mondesi	.05
161	Andruw Jones	.50
162	Nomar Garciaparra	.65
163	David Justice	.05
164	Andy Pettitte	.20
165	Pedro Martinez	.50

SportzCubz Prototypes

This rare "Product Prototype" (says so right on the back) was designed to allow collectors to get creative in making 3-D structures featuring their favorite ballplayers. About 3" square, the plastic pieces have slots and tabs which would allow them to be connected in a variety of ways. Fronts have action photos on a large team logo. Backs have a portrait photo, personal data, recent stats, a career highlight or two and essential licensing data. The product was never rolled out for public consumption and it is unknown to what extent the prototypes were produced or have found their way into collectors' hands. Therefore, no pricing is provided.

Complete Set (25):

1998 Topps Stars Pre-Production

These promotional cards introduced the new Stars brand from Topps to dealers and the hobby press. The cards are virtually identical to the regularly-issued version except for the numbering on back, which has a "PP" prefix and serial numbers "000/000."

	NM/M
Complete Set (6):	5.00
Common Player:	.50
PP1 Mike Piazza	3.00
PP2 Darin Erstad	.60
PP3 Vinny Castilla	.50
PP4 Craig Biggio	.50
PP5 Ivan Rodriguez	.75
PP6 Pedro Martinez	1.00

1998 Topps Stars

Topps Stars adopted an all-sequential numbering format in 1998 with a 150-card set. Every card was numbered to 9,799, red (9,799), silver (4,399), gold (2,299) and

gold rainbow format (99) with different color foil to distinguish the groups. Players were each judged in five categories: arm strength, hit for average, power, defense and speed. Inserts in the product include: Galaxy, Luminaries, Supernovas, Rookie Reprints and Rookie Reprint Autographs. All regular-issue cards and inserts were individually numbered except the Rookie Reprints.

	NM/M
Complete Set, Red or Bronze (150):	24.00
Common Player, Red or Bronze:	.10
Production 9,799 sets each.	
Pack (6):	1.25
Wax Box (24):	25.00
1 Greg Maddux	1.50
2 Darryl Kile	.10
3 Rod Beck	.10
4 Ellis Burks	.10
5 Gary Sheffield	.40
6 David Ortiz	.10
7 Marquis Grissom	.10
8 Tony Womack	.10
9 Mike Mussina	.60
10 Bernie Williams	.10
11 Andy Benes	.10
12 Rusty Greer	.10
13 Carlos Delgado	.35
14 Jim Edmonds	.10
15 Raul Mondesi	.10
16 Andres Galarraga	.10
17 Wade Boggs	1.50
18 Paul O'Neill	.10
19 Edgar Renteria	.10
20 Tony Clark	.10
21 Vladimir Guerrero	1.00
22 Moises Alou	.10
23 Bernard Gilkey	.10
24 Lance Johnson	.10
25 Ben Grieve	.10
26 Sandy Alomar	.10
27 Ray Durham	.10
28 Shawn Estes	.10
29 David Segui	.10
30 Javy Lopez	.10
31 Steve Finley	.10
32 Rey Ordonez	.10
33 Derek Jeter	3.00
34 Henry Rodriguez	.10
35 Mo Vaughn	.10
36 Richard Hidalgo	.10
37 Omar Vizquel	.10
38 Johnny Damon	.35
39 Brian Hunter	.10
40 Matt Williams	.10
41 Chuck Finley	.10
42 Jeromy Burnitz	.10
43 Livan Hernandez	.10
44 Delino DeShields	.10
45 Charles Nagy	.10
46 Scott Rolen	.75
47 Neifi Perez	.10
48 John Wetteland	.10
49 Eric Milton	.10
50 Mike Piazza	2.00
51 Cal Ripken Jr.	3.00
52 Mariano Rivera	.25
53 Butch Huskey	.10
54 Quinton McCracken	.10
55 Jose Cruz Jr.	.10
56 Brian Jordan	.10
57 Hideo Nomo	.50
58 Masato Yoshii	.10
59 Cliff Floyd	.10
60 Jose Guillen	.10
61 Jeff Shaw	.10
62 Edgar Martinez	.10
63 Rondell White	.10
64 Hal Morris	.10
65 Barry Larkin	.10
66 Eric Young	.10
67 Ray Lankford	.10
68 Derek Bell	.10
69 Charles Johnson	.10
70 Robin Ventura	.10
71 Chuck Knoblauch	.10
72 Kevin Brown	.10
73 Jose Valentin	.10
74 Jay Buhner	.10
75 Tony Gwynn	1.50
76 Andy Pettitte	.30

77	Edgardo Alfonzo	.10
78	Kerry Wood	.40
79	Darin Erstad	.30
80	Paul Konerko	.15
81	Jason Kendall	.10
82	Tino Martinez	.10
83	Brad Radke	.10
84	Jeff King	.10
85	Travis Lee	.10
86	Jeff Kent	.10
87	Trevor Hoffman	.10
88	David Cone	.10
89	Jose Canseco	.40
90	Juan Gonzalez	.50
91	Todd Hundley	.10
92	John Valentin	.10
93	Sammy Sosa	1.50
94	Jason Giambi	.40
95	Chipper Jones	1.50
96	Jeff Blauser	.10
97	Brad Fullmer	.10
98	Derrek Lee	.60
99	Denny Neagle	.10
100	Ken Griffey Jr.	2.00
101	David Justice	.10
102	Tim Salmon	.10
103	J.T. Snow	.10
104	Fred McGriff	.10
105	Brady Anderson	.10
106	Larry Walker	.10
107	Jeff Cirillo	.10
108	Andruw Jones	1.00
109	Manny Ramirez	1.00
110	Justin Thompson	.10
111	Vinny Castilla	.10
112	Chan Ho Park	.10
113	Mark Grudzielanek	.10
114	Mark Grace	.10
115	Ken Caminiti	.10
116	Ryan Klesko	.10
117	Rafael Palmeiro	.75
118	Pat Hentgen	.10
119	Eric Karros	.10
120	Randy Johnson	1.00
121	Roberto Alomar	.25
122	John Olerud	.10
123	Paul Molitor	1.00
124	Dean Palmer	.10
125	Nomar Garciaparra	1.50
126	Curt Schilling	.30
127	Jay Bell	.10
128	Craig Biggio	.10
129	Marty Cordova	.10
130	Ivan Rodriguez	.75
131	Todd Helton	.75
132	Jim Thome	.65
133	Albert Belle	.10
134	Mike Lansing	.10
135	Mark McGwire	2.50
136	Roger Clemens	1.75
137	Tom Glavine	.30
138	Ron Gant	.10
139	Alex Rodriguez	2.50
140	Jeff Bagwell	1.00
141	John Smoltz	.10
142	Kenny Lofton	.10
143	Dante Bichette	.10
144	Pedro Martinez	1.00
145	Barry Bonds	3.00
146	Travis Fryman	.10
147	Bobby Jones	.10
148	Bobby Higginson	.10
149	Reggie Sanders	.10
150	Frank Thomas	1.00
	Checklist	.05

Silver

	NM/M
Common Silver:	.50
Silver Stars:	1.5X
Production 4,399 Sets	

Gold

	NM/M
Common Gold:	1.00
Gold Stars:	2X
Production 2,299 Sets	

Gold Rainbow

Each card in Topps Stars was available in a Gold Rainbow version. This was the most limited of the five parallels and was numbered to 99. Cards featured gold prismatic foil on the front and were seeded every 46 packs.

	NM/M
Common Gold Rainbow:	4.00
Gold Rainbow Stars:	8X
Production 99 Sets	

Galaxy

Galaxy featured 10 players who possess all five skills featured in Topps Stars Baseball. Four versions were available and sequentially numbered, including: Bronze (numbered to 100, inserted 1:682 packs), Silver (numbered to 75, inserted 1:910), Gold (numbered to 50, inserted 1:1,364) and Gold Rainbow (numbered to 5, inserted 1:13,643).

	NM/M
Complete Set (10):	150.00
Common Player:	7.50
Production 100 Sets	
Silvers:	1.5X
Production 75 Sets	
Golds:	2X
Production 50 Sets	
Gold Rainbows: Values Undetermined	
Production Five Sets	
G1 Barry Bonds	40.00
G2 Jeff Bagwell	15.00
G3 Nomar Garciaparra	20.00
G4 Chipper Jones	20.00
G5 Ken Griffey Jr.	25.00
G6 Sammy Sosa	20.00
G7 Larry Walker	7.50
G8 Alex Rodriguez	35.00
G9 Craig Biggio	7.50
G10 Raul Mondesi	7.50

Luminaries

Luminaries feature three top players in each "tool" group. The 15-card insert has four parallel sequentially numbered versions inserted as follows: bronze (numbered to 100, inserted 1:455), silver (numbered to 75, inserted 1:606), gold (numbered to 50, inserted 1:910) and gold rainbow (numbered to 5, inserted 1:9,095).

	NM/M
Complete Set (15):	140.00
Common Player:	4.00
Production 100 Sets	
Silver (75 Sets):	1.5X
Gold (50 Sets):	1.5X
Gold Rainbow (Five Sets):	
Values Undetermined	
L1 Ken Griffey Jr.	15.00
L2 Mark McGwire	20.00
L3 Juan Gonzalez	5.00
L4 Tony Gwynn	12.50
L5 Frank Thomas	10.00
L6 Mike Piazza	15.00
L7 Chuck Knoblauch	4.00
L8 Kenny Lofton	4.00
L9 Barry Bonds	25.00
L10 Matt Williams	4.00
L11 Raul Mondesi	4.00
L12 Ivan Rodriguez	7.50
L13 Alex Rodriguez	20.00
L14 Nomar Garciaparra	12.50
L15 Ken Caminiti	4.00

Supernovas

Supernovas was a 10-card insert in Topps Stars and included rookies and prospects who either have all five tools focused on in the product, or excel dramatically in one of the five. Four sequentially numbered levels were available, with insert rates as follows: bronze (numbered to 100, inserted 1:682), silver (numbered to 75, inserted 1:910), gold (numbered to 50, inserted 1:1,364) and gold rainbow (numbered to 5, inserted 1:13,643).

	NM/M
Complete Set (10):	35.00
Common Player:	2.00
Production 100 Sets	
Silver:	1.5X
Production 75 Sets	
Gold:	1.5X
Production 50 Sets	
Gold Rainbow: Values Undetermined	
Production Five Sets	
S1 Ben Grieve	2.00
S2 Travis Lee	4.00
S3 Todd Helton	10.00
S4 Adrian Beltre	2.50
S5 Derrek Lee	6.00
S6 David Ortiz	6.00
S7 Brad Fullmer	2.00
S8 Mark Kotsay	2.00
S9 Paul Konerko	2.50
S10 Kerry Wood	6.00

Rookie Reprints

Topps reprinted the rookie cards of five Hall of Famers in Rookie Reprints. The cards are inserted one per 24 packs and have UV coating.

	NM/M
Complete Set (5):	7.00
Common Player:	1.50
1968 Johnny Bench	1.50
1953 Whitey Ford	1.50
1965 Joe Morgan	1.50
1973 Mike Schmidt	2.50
1960 Carl Yastrzemski	2.00

Rookie Reprints Autographs

Autographed versions of all five Rookie Reprint inserts were available and seeded one per 273 packs. Each card arrive with a Topps "Certified Autograph Issue" stamp to ensure its authenticity.

	NM/M
Complete Set (5):	175.00
Common Player:	25.00
1968 Johnny Bench	75.00
1953 Whitey Ford	50.00
1965 Joe Morgan	25.00
1973 Mike Schmidt	90.00
1960 Carl Yastrzemski	90.00

1998 Topps Stars 'N Steel

Stars 'N Steel was a 44-card set printed on four-colored textured film laminate bonded to a sheet of 25-gauge metal. Regular cards featured a silver colored border while gold versions were also available and seeded one per 12 packs. Stars 'N Steel was available only to Home Team Advantage members and was packaged in three-card packs that arrived in a sturdy, tri-fold stand-up display unit. A second parallel version was

CHIPPER JONES

also available featuring gold holographic technology and was seeded one per 40 packs.

	NM/M
Complete Set (44):	40.00
Common Player:	.25
Golds:	2X
Holographics:	7X
Pack (3):	3.50
Wax Box (12):	30.00
1 Roberto Alomar	.50
2 Jeff Bagwell	1.25
3 Albert Belle	.25
4 Dante Bichette	.25
5 Barry Bonds	4.00
6 Jay Buhner	.25
7 Ken Caminiti	.25
8 Vinny Castilla	.25
9 Roger Clemens	2.25
10 Jose Cruz Jr.	.25
11 Andruw Jones	.25
12 Nomar Garciaparra	2.00
13 Juan Gonzalez	.65
14 Mark Grace	.25
15 Ken Griffey Jr.	2.50
16 Tony Gwynn	2.00
17 Todd Hundley	.25
18 Derek Jeter	4.00
19 Randy Johnson	1.25
20 Andruw Jones	1.25
21 Chipper Jones	2.00
22 David Justice	.25
23 Ray Lankford	.25
24 Barry Larkin	.25
25 Kenny Lofton	.25
26 Greg Maddux	2.00
27 Edgar Martinez	.25
28 Tino Martinez	.25
29 Mark McGwire	3.00
30 Paul Molitor	1.25
31 Rafael Palmeiro	1.00
32 Mike Piazza	2.50
33 Manny Ramirez	1.25
34 Cal Ripken Jr.	4.00
35 Ivan Rodriguez	1.00
36 Scott Rolen	.75
37 Tim Salmon	.25
38 Gary Sheffield	.50
39 Sammy Sosa	2.00
40 Frank Thomas	1.25
41 Jim Thome	1.00
42 Mo Vaughn	.25
43 Larry Walker	.25
44 Bernie Williams	.25

1998 Topps TEK Pre-Production

MARK McGWIRE

Each of three players' Tek cards can also be found in two versions marked diagonally across the card number on back "Pre-production." The gold-foil version is much scarcer than the silver.

	NM/M
Complete Set, Silver (3):	10.00
Complete Set, Gold (3):	45.00
23 Mark McGwire/Silver	6.00
23 Mark McGwire/Gold	30.00
45 Roger Clemens/Silver	5.00
45 Roger Clemens/Gold	20.00
? Raul Mondesi/Silver	.50
? Raul Mondesi/Gold	2.50

1998 Topps TEK

  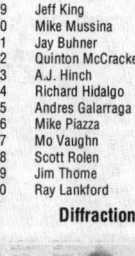

SALMON

A myriad of collecting methods was created with this innovative product which features 90 different players each printed on an acetate stock with 90 different background patterns. A parallel series utilizing Diffraction technology was inserted at the rate of one per six packs. Each of the 8,100 different cards was created in the same quantity, so there is no differentiation in value among patterns.

	NM/M
Complete Set (90):	75.00
Common Player:	.25
Pack (4):	4.00
Wax Box (20):	80.00
1 Ben Grieve	.25
2 Kerry Wood	1.50
3 Barry Bonds	8.00
4 John Olerud	.25
5 Ivan Rodriguez	2.00
6 Frank Thomas	2.50
7 Bernie Williams	.25
8 Dante Bichette	.25
9 Alex Rodriguez	6.00
10 Tom Glavine	.50
11 Eric Karros	.25
12 Craig Biggio	.25
13 Mark McGwire	6.00
14 Derek Jeter	8.00
15 Nomar Garciaparra	4.00
16 Brady Anderson	.25
17 Vladimir Guerrero	2.50
18 David Justice	.25
19 Chipper Jones	4.00
20 Jim Edmonds	.25
21 Roger Clemens	4.50
22 Mark Kotsay	.25
23 Tony Gwynn	4.00
24 Todd Walker	.25
25 Tino Martinez	.25
26 Andruw Jones	2.50
27 Sandy Alomar	.25
28 Sammy Sosa	4.00
29 Gary Sheffield	1.50
30 Ken Griffey Jr.	5.00
31 Aramis Ramirez	.25
32 Curt Schilling	.50
33 Robin Ventura	.25
34 Darin Erstad	1.25
35 Todd Dunwoody	.25
36 Paul O'Neill	.25
37 Vinny Castilla	.25
38 Randy Johnson	2.50
39 Rafael Palmeiro	2.00
40 Pedro Martinez	2.50
41 Derek Bell	.25
42 Carlos Delgado	.50
43 Matt Williams	.25
44 Kenny Lofton	.25
45 Edgar Renteria	.25
46 Albert Belle	.25
47 Jeromy Burnitz	.25
48 Adrian Beltre	.40
49 Greg Maddux	4.00
50 Cal Ripken Jr.	8.00
51 Jason Kendall	.25
52 Ellis Burks	.25
53 Paul Molitor	2.50
54 Moises Alou	.25
55 Raul Mondesi	.25
56 Barry Larkin	.25
57 Tony Clark	.25
58 Travis Lee	.25
59 Juan Gonzalez	1.25
60 Troy Glaus RC	3.00
61 Jose Cruz Jr.	.25
62 Paul Konerko	.40
63 Edgar Martinez	.25
64 Javy Lopez	.25
65 Manny Ramirez	2.50
66 Roberto Alomar	.25
67 Ken Caminiti	.25
68 Todd Helton	1.50
69 Chuck Knoblauch	.25
70 Kevin Brown	.25
71 Tim Salmon	.25
72 Orlando Hernandez RC	1.00
73 Jeff Bagwell	2.50
74 Brian Jordan	.25
75 Derek Lee	1.50
76 Brad Fullmer	.25

78 Mark Grace	.25
79 Jeff King	.25
80 Mike Mussina	1.50
81 Jay Buhner	.25
82 Quinton McCracken	.25
83 A.J. Hinch	.25
84 Richard Hidalgo	.25
85 Andres Galarraga	.25
86 Mike Piazza	5.00
87 Mo Vaughn	.25
88 Scott Rolen	1.50
89 Jim Thome	2.00
90 Ray Lankford	.25

Diffraction

ERIC KARROS

Not only can each of the 90 cards in Topps TEK be found in 90 different background patterns, but each can be found in a parallel edition printed with diffraction foil. The parallels are inserted on an average of one per six packs. Like the regular issue TEKs, all patterns are produced equally and there is no value differentiation among them.

	NM/M
Complete Set (90):	400.00
Common Player:	4.00
Stars/RC's:	4X

1999 Topps Pre-Production

To give potential customers a feel for its 1999 baseball cards, Topps issued this series of pre-production samples. Cards are identical in format to the issued versions except they are numbered with a "PP" prefix and the 1998 stats line reads "PRE-PRODUCTION SAMPLE."

	NM/M
Complete Set (6):	7.00
Common Player:	.50
PP1 Roger Clemens	2.00
PP2 Sammy Sosa	2.00
PP3 Derek Jeter	2.50
PP4 Walt Weiss	.50
PP5 Darin Erstad	.75
PP6 Jason Kendall	.50

1999 Topps

Released in two series, the 462-card set includes two home run record subsets, featuring McGwire and Sosa. McGwire's subset card #220 has 70 different versions,

commemorating each of his home runs, including where it was hit, the pitcher, date and estimated distance. Sosa's subset card #461 has 66 different versions. Other subsets include World Series Highlights, Prospects, Draft Picks and Season Highlights. Each pack contains 11 cards with an SRP of $1.29. MVPs are the only parallel. They feature a special Topps MVP logo; 100 cards of each player exist. If the player on the card was named a weekly Topps MVP, collectors won a special set of redemption cards.

	NM/M
Unop. Hobby Set (462):	40.00
Unop. Retail Set (463):	50.00
Complete Set (462):	35.00
Common Player:	.05
MVP Stars/Rookies:	20X
Ser. 1 or 2 Hobby Pack (11):	1.25
Ser. 1 or 2 Hobby Box (36):	40.00
Ser. 1 or 2 Retail Pack (8):	1.00
Ser. 1 or 2 Retail Box (22):	20.00
Ser. 1 or 2 Jumbo Pack (40):	3.50
Ser. 1 or 2 Jumbo Box (12):	30.00
1 Roger Clemens	1.00
2 Andres Galarraga	.05
3 Scott Brosius	.05
4 John Flaherty	.05
5 Jim Leyritz	.05
6 Ray Durham	.05
7 Joe Vizcaino	.05
8 Will Clark	.05
9 David Wells	.05
10 Jose Guillen	.05
11 Scott Hatteberg	.05
12 Edgardo Alfonzo	.05
13 Mike Bordick	.05
14 Manny Ramirez	.75
15 Greg Maddux	1.00
16 David Segui	.05
17 Darryl Strawberry	.05
18 Brad Radke	.05
19 Kerry Wood	.40
20 Matt Anderson	.05
21 Derrek Lee	.60
22 Mickey Morandini	.05
23 Paul Konerko	.15
24 Travis Lee	.05
25 Ken Hill	.05
26 Kenny Rogers	.05
27 Paul Sorrento	.05
28 Quivio Veras	.05
29 Todd Walker	.05
30 Ryan Jackson	.05
31 John Olerud	.05
32 Doug Glanville	.05
33 Nolan Ryan	2.00
34 Ray Lankford	.05
35 Mark Loretta	.05
36 Jason Dickson	.05
37 Sean Bergman	.05
38 Quinton McCracken	.05
39 Bartolo Colon	.05
40 Brady Anderson	.05
41 Chris Stynes	.05
42 Jorge Posada	.05
43 Justin Thompson	.05
44 Johnny Damon	.30
45 Armando Benitez	.05
46 Brant Brown	.05
47 Charlie Hayes	.05
48 Darren Dreifort	.05
49 Juan Gonzalez	.40
50 Chuck Knoblauch	.05
51 Todd Helton (Rookie All-Star)	.75
52 Rick Reed	.05
53 Chris Gomez	.05
54 Gary Sheffield	.45
55 Rod Beck	.05
56 Rey Sanchez	.05
57 Garret Anderson	.05
58 Jimmy Haynes	.05
59 Steve Woodard	.05
60 Rondell White	.05
61 Vladimir Guerrero	.75
62 Eric Karros	.05
63 Russ Davis	.05
64 Mo Vaughn	.05
65 Sammy Sosa	1.00
66 Troy Percival	.05
67 Kenny Lofton	.05
68 Bill Taylor	.05
69 Mark McGwire	1.50
70 Roger Cedeno	.05
71 Javy Lopez	.05
72 Damion Easley	.05
73 Andy Pettitte	.25
74 Tony Gwynn	1.00
75 Ricardo Rincon	.05
76 F.P. Santangelo	.05
77 Jay Bell	.05
78 Scott Servais	.05
79 Jose Canseco	.40
80 Roberto Hernandez	.05
81 Todd Dunwoody	.05
82 John Wetteland	.05
83 Mike Caruso (Rookie All-Star)	.05
84 Derek Jeter	2.00
85 Aaron Sele	.05
86 Jose Lima	

#	Player	Price
88	Ryan Christenson	.05
89	Jeff Cirillo	.05
90	Jose Hernandez	.05
91	Mark Kotsay (Rookie All-Star)	.05
92	Darren Bragg	.05
93	Albert Belle	.05
94	Matt Lawton	.05
95	Pedro Martinez	.75
96	Greg Vaughn	.05
97	Neifi Perez	.05
98	Gerald Williams	.05
99	Derek Bell	.05
100	Ken Griffey Jr.	1.25
101	David Cone	.05
102	Brian Johnson	.05
103	Dean Palmer	.05
104	Javier Valentin	.05
105	Trevor Hoffman	.05
106	Butch Huskey	.05
107	Dave Martinez	.05
108	Billy Wagner	.05
109	Shawn Green	.30
110	Ben Grieve (Rookie All-Star)	.05
111	Tom Goodwin	.05
112	Jaret Wright	.05
113	Aramis Ramirez	.05
114	Dmitri Young	.05
115	Hideki Irabu	.05
116	Roberto Kelly	.05
117	Jeff Fassero	.05
118	Mark Clark	.05
119	Jason McDonald	.05
120	Matt Williams	.05
121	Dave Burba	.05
122	Bret Saberhagen	.05
123	Deivi Cruz	.05
124	Chad Curtis	.05
125	Scott Rolen	.65
126	Lee Stevens	.05
127	J.T. Snow Jr.	.05
128	Rusty Greer	.05
129	Brian Meadows	.05
130	Jim Edmonds	.05
131	Ron Gant	.05
132	A.J. Hinch (Rookie All-Star)	.05
133	Shannon Stewart	.05
134	Brad Fullmer	.05
135	Cal Ripken	.05
136	Matt Walbeck	.05
137	Carl Everett	.05
138	Walt Weiss	.05
139	Fred McGriff	.05
140	Darin Erstad	.25
141	Dave Nilsson	.05
142	Eric Young	.05
143	Dan Wilson	.05
144	Jeff Reed	.05
145	Brett Tomko	.05
146	Terry Steinbach	.05
147	Seth Greisinger	.05
148	Pat Meares	.05
149	Livan Hernandez	.05
150	Jeff Bagwell	.75
151	Bob Wickman	.05
152	Omar Vizquel	.05
153	Eric Davis	.05
154	Larry Sutton	.05
155	Magglio Ordonez (Rookie All-Star)	.40
156	Eric Milton	.05
157	Darren Lewis	.05
158	Rick Aguilera	.05
159	Mike Lieberthal	.05
160	Robb Nen	.05
161	Brian Giles	.05
162	Jeff Brantley	.05
163	Gary DiSarcina	.05
164	John Valentin	.05
165	David Dellucci	.05
166	Chan Ho Park	.05
167	Masato Yoshii	.05
168	Jason Schmidt	.05
169	LaTroy Hawkins	.05
170	Bret Boone	.05
171	Jerry DiPoto	.05
172	Mariano Rivera	.10
173	Mike Cameron	.05
174	Scott Erickson	.05
175	Charles Johnson	.05
176	Bobby Jones	.05
177	Francisco Cordova	.05
178	Todd Jones	.05
179	Jeff Montgomery	.05
180	Mike Mussina	.40
181	Bob Abreu	.05
182	Ismael Valdes	.05
183	Andy Fox	.05
184	Woody Williams	.05
185	Denny Neagle	.05
186	Jose Valentin	.05
187	Darrin Fletcher	.05
188	Gabe Alvarez	.05
189	Eddie Taubensee	.05
190	Edgar Martinez	.05
191	Jason Kendall	.05
192	Darryl Kile	.05
193	Jeff King	.05
194	Rey Ordonez	.05
195	Andruw Jones	.75
196	Tony Fernandez	.05
197	Jamey Wright	.05
198	B.J. Surhoff	.05
199	Vinny Castilla	.05
200	David Wells (Season Highlight)	.05
201	Mark McGwire (Season Highlight)	.75
202	Sammy Sosa (Season Highlight)	.50
203	Roger Clemens (Season Highlight)	.50
204	Kerry Wood (Season Highlight)	.15
205	Lance Berkman, Mike Frank, Gabe Kapler (Prospects)	.15
206	Alex Escobar RC, Ricky Ledee, Mike Stoner (Prospects)	.25
207	Peter Bergeron RC, Jeremy Giambi, George Lombard (Prospects)	.30
208	Michael Barrett, Ben Davis, Robert Fick (Prospects)	.05
209	Pat Cline, Ramon Hernandez, Jayson Werth (Prospects)	.05
210	Bruce Chen, Chris Enochs, Ryan Anderson (Prospects)	.05
211	Mike Lincoln, Octavio Dotel, Brad Penny (Prospects)	.05
212	Chuck Abbott, Brent Butler, Danny Klassen (Prospects)	.05
213	Chris Jones, Jeff Urban RC (Draft Pick)	.05
214	Arturo McDowell RC, Tony Torcato RC (Draft Pick)	.25
215	Josh McKinley RC, Jason Tyner RC (Draft Pick)	.25
216	Matt Burch RC, Seth Etherton RC (Draft Pick)	.25
217	Mamon Tucker RC, Rick Elder RC (Draft Pick)	.10
218	J.M. Gold RC, Ryan Mills RC (Draft Pick)	.10
219	Adam Brown RC, Choo Freeman RC (Draft Pick)	.25
220	Home Run Record #1 (M. McGwire)	20.00
220	HR Record #2-60 (M. McGwire)	6.00
220	HR Record #61-62 (M. McGwire)	10.00
220	HR Record #63-69 (M. McGwire)	15.00
220	HR Record #70 (Mark McGwire)	40.00
221	Larry Walker (League Leader)	.05
222	Bernie Williams (League Leader)	.05
223	Mark McGwire (League Leader)	.75
224	Ken Griffey Jr. (League Leader)	.65
225	Sammy Sosa (League Leader)	.50
226	Juan Gonzalez (League Leader)	.20
227	Dante Bichette (League Leader)	.05
228	Alex Rodriguez (League Leader)	.75
229	Sammy Sosa (League Leader)	.50
230	Derek Jeter (League Leader)	1.00
231	Greg Maddux (League Leader)	.50
232	Roger Clemens (League Leader)	.50
233	Ricky Ledee (World Series)	.05
234	Chuck Knoblauch (World Series)	.05
235	Bernie Williams (World Series)	.05
236	Tino Martinez (World Series)	.05
237	Orlando Hernandez (World Series)	.05
238	Scott Brosius (World Series)	.05
239	Andy Pettitte (World Series)	.05
240	Mariano Rivera (World Series)	.05
241	Checklist	.05
242	Checklist	.05
243	Tom Glavine	.25
244	Andy Benes	.05
245	Sandy Alomar	.05
246	Wilton Guerrero	.05
247	Alex Gonzalez	.05
248	Roberto Alomar	.30
249	Ruben Rivera	.05
250	Eric Chavez	.15
251	Ellis Burks	.05
252	Richie Sexson	.05
253	Steve Finley	.05
254	Dwight Gooden	.05
255	Dustin Hermanson	.05
256	Kirk Rueter	.05
257	Steve Trachsel	.05
258	Gregg Jefferies	.05
259	Matt Stairs	.05
260	Shane Reynolds	.05
261	Gregg Olson	.05
262	Kevin Tapani	.05
263	Matt Morris	.05
264	Carl Pavano	.05
265	Nomar Garciaparra	1.00
266	Kevin Young	.05
267	Rick Helling	.05
268	Mark Leiter	.05
269	Brian McRae	.05
270	Cal Ripken Jr.	2.00
271	Jeff Abbott	.05
272	Tony Batista	.05
273	Bill Simas	.05
274	Brian Hunter	.05
275	John Franco	.05
276	Devon White	.05
277	Rickey Henderson	.75
278	Chuck Finley	.05
279	Mike Blowers	.05
280	Mark Grace	.05
281	Randy Winn	.05
282	Bobby Bonilla	.05
283	David Justice	.05
284	Shane Monahan	.05
285	Kevin Brown	.05
286	Todd Zeile	.05
287	Al Martin	.05
288	Troy O'Leary	.05
289	Darryl Hamilton	.05
290	Tino Martinez	.05
291	David Ortiz	.45
292	Tony Clark	.05
293	Ryan Minor	.05
294	Reggie Sanders	.05
295	Wally Joyner	.05
296	Cliff Floyd	.05
297	Shawn Estes	.05
298	Pat Hentgen	.05
299	Scott Elarton	.05
300	Alex Rodriguez	1.50
301	Ozzie Guillen	.05
302	Manny Martinez	.05
303	Ryan McGuire	.05
304	Brad Ausmus	.05
305	Alex Gonzalez	.05
306	Brian Jordan	.05
307	John Jaha	.05
308	Mark Grudzielanek	.05
309	Juan Guzman	.05
310	Tony Womack	.05
311	Dennis Reyes	.05
312	Marty Cordova	.05
313	Ramiro Mendoza	.05
314	Robin Ventura	.05
315	Rafael Palmeiro	.60
316	Ramon Martinez	.05
317	John Mabry	.05
318	Dave Hollins	.05
319	Tom Candiotti	.05
320	Al Leiter	.05
321	Rico Brogna	.05
322	Jimmy Key	.05
323	Bernard Gilkey	.05
324	Jason Giambi	.45
325	Craig Biggio	.05
326	Troy Glaus	.65
327	Delino DeShields	.05
328	Fernando Vina	.05
329	John Smoltz	.05
330	Jeff Kent	.05
331	Roy Halladay	.05
332	Andy Ashby	.05
333	Tim Wakefield	.05
334	Tim Belcher	.05
335	Bernie Williams	.05
336	Desi Relaford	.05
337	John Burkett	.05
338	Mike Hampton	.05
339	Royce Clayton	.05
340	Mike Piazza	1.25
341	Jeremi Gonzalez	.05
342	Mike Lansing	.05
343	Jamie Moyer	.05
344	Ron Coomer	.05
345	Barry Larkin	.05
346	Fernando Tatis	.05
347	Chili Davis	.05
348	Bobby Higginson	.05
349	Hal Morris	.05
350	Larry Walker	.05
351	Carlos Guillen	.05
352	Miguel Tejada	.05
353	Travis Fryman	.05
354	Jarrod Washburn	.05
355	Chipper Jones	1.00
356	Todd Stottlemyre	.05
357	Henry Rodriguez	.05
358	Eli Marrero	.05
359	Alan Benes	.05
360	Tim Salmon	.05
361	Luis Gonzalez	.05
362	Scott Spiezio	.05
363	Chris Carpenter	.05
364	Bobby Howry	.05
365	Raul Mondesi	.05
366	Ugueth Urbina	.05
367	Tom Evans	.05
368	Kerry Ligtenberg RC	.15
369	Adrian Beltre	.15
370	Ryan Klesko	.05
371	Wilson Alvarez	.05
372	John Thomson	.05
373	Tony Saunders	.05
374	Mike Stanley	.05
375	Ken Caminiti	.05
376	Jay Buhner	.05
377	Bill Mueller	.05
378	Jeff Blauser	.05
379	Edgar Renteria	.05
380	Jim Thome	.60
381	Joey Hamilton	.05
382	Calvin Pickering	.05
383	Marquis Grissom	.05
384	Omar Daal	.05
385	Curt Schilling	.25
386	Jose Cruz Jr.	.05
387	Chris Widger	.05
388	Pete Harnisch	.05
389	Charles Nagy	.05
390	Tom Gordon	.05
391	Bobby Smith	.05
392	Derrick Gibson	.05
393	Jeff Conine	.05
394	Carlos Perez	.05
395	Barry Bonds	2.00
396	Mark McLemore	.05
397	Juan Encarnacion	.05
398	Wade Boggs	1.00
399	Ivan Rodriguez	.65
400	Moises Alou	.05
401	Jeromy Burnitz	.05
402	Sean Casey	.10
403	Jose Offerman	.05
404	Joe Fontenot	.05
405	Kevin Millwood	.05
406	Lance Johnson	.05
407	Richard Hidalgo	.05
408	Mike Jackson	.05
409	Brian Anderson	.05
410	Jeff Shaw	.05
411	Preston Wilson	.05
412	Todd Hundley	.05
413	Jim Parque	.05
414	Justin Baughman	.05
415	Dante Bichette	.05
416	Paul O'Neill	.05
417	Miguel Cairo	.05
418	Randy Johnson	.75
419	Jesus Sanchez	.05
420	Carlos Delgado	.30
421	Ricky Ledee	.05
422	Orlando Hernandez	.05
423	Frank Thomas	.75
424	Pokey Reese	.05
425	Carlos Lee, Mike Lowell, Kit Pellow RC (Prospect)	.25
426	Michael Cuddyer, Mark DeRosa, Jerry Hairston Jr. (Prospect)	.05
427	Marlon Anderson, Ron Belliard, Orlando Cabrera (Prospect)	.10
428	Micah Bowie RC, Phil Norton RC, Randy Wolf (Prospect)	.10
429	Jack Cressend, Jason Rakers, John Rocker (Prospect)	.10
430	Ruben Mateo, Scott Morgan, Mike Zywica RC (Prospect)	.10
431	Jason LaRue, Matt LeCroy RC, Mitch Meluskey (Prospect)	.10
432	Gabe Kapler, Armando Rios, Fernando Seguignol (Prospect)	.10
433	Adam Kennedy, Mickey Lopez RC, Jackie Rexrode (Prospect)	.10
434	Jose Fernandez RC, Jeff Liefer, Chris Truby (Prospect)	.10
435	Corey Koskie, Doug Mientkiewicz, Damon Minor (Prospect)	.10
436	Roosevelt Brown RC, Dernell Stenson, Vernon Wells (Prospect)	.10
437	A.J. Burnett RC, John Nicholson, Billy Koch (Prospect)	.25
438	Matt Belisle RC, Matt Roney RC (Draft Pick)	.05
439	Austin Kearns RC, Chris George RC (Draft Pick)	.25
440	Nate Bump RC, Nate Cornejo RC (Draft Pick)	.40
441	Brad Lidge RC, Mike Nannini RC (Draft Pick)	.25
442	Matt Holiday RC, Jeff Winchester RC (Draft Pick)	.25
443	Adam Everett RC, Chip Ambres RC (Draft Pick)	.05
444	Pat Burrell RC, Eric Valent RC (Draft Pick)	1.50
445	Roger Clemens (Strikeout Kings)	.50
446	Kerry Wood (Strikeout Kings)	.15
447	Curt Schilling (Strikeout Kings)	.05
448	Randy Johnson (Strikeout Kings)	.40
449	Pedro Martinez (Strikeout Kings)	.40
450	Jeff Bagwell, Andres Galarraga, Mark McGwire (All-Topps)	.50
451	John Olerud, Jim Thome, Tino Martinez (All-Topps)	.30
452	Alex Rodriguez, Nomar Garciaparra, Derek Jeter (All-Topps)	.60
453	Vinny Castilla, Chipper Jones, Scott Rolen (All-Topps)	.40
454	Sammy Sosa, Ken Griffey Jr., Juan Gonzalez (All-Topps)	.50
455	Barry Bonds, Manny Ramirez, Larry Walker (All-Topps)	.60
456	Frank Thomas, Tim Salmon, David Justice (All-Topps)	.30
457	Travis Lee, Todd Helton, Ben Grieve (All-Topps)	.30
458	Vladimir Guerrero, Greg Vaughn, Bernie Williams (All-Topps)	.25
459	Mike Piazza, Ivan Rodriguez, Jason Kendall (All-Topps)	.50
460	Roger Clemens, Kerry Wood, Greg Maddux (All-Topps)	.45
461	Home Run Parade #1 (Sammy Sosa)	10.00
461	HR Parade #2-60 (Sammy Sosa)	4.00
461	HR Parade #61-62 (Sammy Sosa)	10.00
461	HR Parade #63-65 (Sammy Sosa)	6.00
461	HR Parade #66 (Sammy Sosa)	20.00
462	Checklist	.05
463	Checklist	.05

All-Matrix

This 30-card set features holo-foil card fronts and features the top stars in the game. Each card is numbered with a "AM" prefix on card backs and are seeded 1:18 packs.

		NM/M
Complete Set (30):		45.00
Common Player:		.75
Inserted 1:18		
AM1	Mark McGwire	6.00
AM2	Sammy Sosa	3.50
AM3	Ken Griffey Jr.	4.50
AM4	Greg Vaughn	.75
AM5	Albert Belle	.75
AM6	Vinny Castilla	.75
AM7	Jose Canseco	1.25
AM8	Juan Gonzalez	1.25
AM9	Manny Ramirez	2.50
AM10	Andres Galarraga	.75
AM11	Rafael Palmeiro	2.00
AM12	Alex Rodriguez	6.00
AM13	Mo Vaughn	.75
AM14	Eric Chavez	1.25
AM15	Gabe Kapler	.75
AM16	Calvin Pickering	.75
AM17	Ruben Mateo	.75
AM18	Roy Halladay	1.25
AM19	Jeremy Giambi	.75
AM20	Alex Gonzalez	.75
AM21	Ron Belliard	.75
AM22	Marlon Anderson	.75
AM23	Carlos Lee	.75
AM24	Kerry Wood	1.25
AM25	Roger Clemens	3.50
AM26	Curt Schilling	1.25
AM27	Kevin Brown	.75
AM28	Randy Johnson	2.50
AM29	Pedro Martinez	2.50
AM30	Orlando Hernandez	.75

MVP Promotion

Each of the 198 regular-issue players' cards in Series 1 and cards #243-444 in Series 2 were issued in a parallel version of 100 each for use in an MVP of the Week sweepstakes. Overprinted with a large gold-foil seal on front, the MVP cards have contest rules on back. The MVP cards were inserted at ratios of between 1:142 (HTA) and 1:515 (Hobby) packs. Cards of players who won MVP of the Week during the 1999 season could be redeemed for a special set of MVP cards prior to the Dec. 31, 1999 deadline. Winning players' cards are checklisted here according to their regular-issue card number. Because they were not returned when redeemed, they are in shorter supply than non-winning cards, though market value is not significantly affected.

	NM/M
Common Player:	3.00
Stars/Rookies:	20X

MVP Redemption

Person redeeming winning MVP contest cards prior to Dec. 31, 1999, received this set of 25 cards corresponding to the weekly winners. Cards have an MVP prefix.

		NM/M
Complete Set (25):		30.00
Common Player:		.50
1	Raul Mondesi	.50
2	Tim Salmon	.50
3	Fernando Tatis	.50
4	Larry Walker	.50
5	Fred McGriff	.50
6	Nomar Garciaparra	3.00
7	Rafael Palmeiro	1.50
8	Randy Johnson	.50
9	Mike Lieberthal	.50
10	B.J. Surhoff	.50
11	Todd Helton	2.00
12	Tino Martinez	.50
13	Scott Rolen	1.50
14	Mike Piazza	4.00
15	David Cone	.50
16	Tony Clark	.50
17	Roberto Alomar	.60
18	Miguel Tejada	.75
19	Alex Rodriguez	5.00
20	J.T. Snow	.50
21	Ray Lankford	.50
22	Mo Vaughn	.50
23	Paul O'Neill	.50
24	Chipper Jones	3.00
25	Mark McGwire	5.00

All-Topps Mystery Finest

This 33-card set features a black opaque covering that collectors peel off to reveal the player. Each card is numbered with a "M" prefix and inserted 1:36 packs. A parallel Refractor version is also randomly seeded and inserted 1:144 packs.

		NM/M
Complete Set (33):		100.00
Common Player:		1.00
Inserted 1:36		
Refractors:		1.5X
Inserted 1:144		
M1	Jeff Bagwell	4.25
M2	Andres Galarraga	1.00
M3	Mark McGwire	9.00
M4	John Olerud	1.00
M5	Jim Thome	2.50
M6	Tino Martinez	1.00
M7	Alex Rodriguez	9.00
M8	Nomar Garciaparra	6.00
M9	Derek Jeter	12.50
M10	Vinny Castilla	1.00
M11	Chipper Jones	5.00
M12	Scott Rolen	3.00
M13	Sammy Sosa	5.00
M14	Ken Griffey Jr.	7.50
M15	Juan Gonzalez	2.00

M16	Barry Bonds	12.50
M17	Manny Ramirez	4.50
M18	Larry Walker	1.00
M19	Frank Thomas	4.50
M20	Tim Salmon	1.00
M21	David Justice	1.00
M22	Travis Lee	1.50
M23	Todd Helton	4.50
M24	Ben Grieve	1.00
M25	Vladimir Guerrero	4.50
M26	Greg Vaughn	1.00
M27	Bernie Williams	1.00
M28	Mike Piazza	7.50
M29	Ivan Rodriguez	3.50
M30	Jason Kendall	1.00
M31	Roger Clemens	6.00
M32	Kerry Wood	2.00
M33	Greg Maddux	5.00

Autographs

Autographs were inserted exclusively in hobby packs in both Topps series 1 and 2. Each series had eight cards with each one carrying the Topps Certified Autograph Issue stamp. Series 1 Autographs were seeded 1:532 packs while Series 2 were found 1:501 packs.

		NM/M
Common Player:		8.00
Series 1 Inserted 1:532 H		
Series 2 Inserted 1:501 H		
A1	Roger Clemens	100.00
A2	Chipper Jones	50.00
A3	Scott Rolen	25.00
A4	Alex Rodriguez	100.00
A5	Andres Galarraga	8.00
A6	Rondell White	8.00
A7	Ben Grieve	8.00
A8	Troy Glaus	20.00
A9	Moises Alou	15.00
A10	Barry Bonds	180.00
A11	Vladimir Guerrero	35.00
A12	Andruw Jones	10.00
A13	Darin Erstad	12.00
A14	Shawn Green	16.00
A15	Eric Chavez	15.00
A16	Pat Burrell	30.00

Hall of Fame

Found exclusively in hobby packs, Hall of Fame Collection is a 10-card set featured on cards that silhouette their images against their respective Hall of Fame plaques. These were seeded 1:12 packs.

		NM/M
Complete Set (10):		8.00
Common Player:		.50
Inserted 1:12 H		
HOF1	Mike Schmidt	1.50
HOF2	Brooks Robinson	.75
HOF3	Stan Musial	1.50
HOF4	Willie McCovey	.50
HOF5	Eddie Mathews	.75
HOF6	Reggie Jackson	1.50
HOF7	Ernie Banks	1.00
HOF8	Whitey Ford	.75
HOF9	Bob Feller	.50
HOF10	Yogi Berra	1.00

Lords of the Diamond

Inserted in every 18 packs this 15-card set features the top players in the game including Barry Bonds

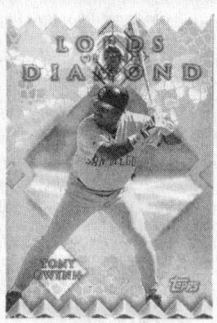

and Ken Griffey Jr. Card fronts include a holographic look with die-cutting across the top of the card on a silver background.

		NM/M
Complete Set (15):		13.00
Common Player:		.25
Inserted 1:18		
LD1	Ken Griffey Jr.	1.25
LD2	Chipper Jones	1.00
LD3	Sammy Sosa	1.00
LD4	Frank Thomas	.75
LD5	Mark McGwire	1.50
LD6	Jeff Bagwell	.75
LD7	Alex Rodriguez	1.50
LD8	Juan Gonzalez	.40
LD9	Barry Bonds	2.00
LD10	Nomar Garciaparra	1.00
LD11	Darin Erstad	.35
LD12	Tony Gwynn	1.00
LD13	Andres Galarraga	.25
LD14	Mike Piazza	1.25
LD15	Greg Maddux	1.00

New Breed

The next generation of stars are featured in this 15-card set that showcases the young talent on a silver foil card. These are seeded 1:18 packs.

		NM/M
Complete Set (15):		9.00
Common Player:		.25
Inserted 1:18		
NB1	Darin Erstad	.50
NB2	Brad Fullmer	.25
NB3	Kerry Wood	.50
NB4	Nomar Garciaparra	1.50
NB5	Travis Lee	.35
NB6	Scott Rolen	.75
NB7	Todd Helton	.75
NB8	Vladimir Guerrero	1.00
NB9	Derek Jeter	3.00
NB10	Alex Rodriguez	2.00
NB11	Ben Grieve	.25
NB12	Andruw Jones	.75
NB13	Paul Konerko	.40
NB14	Aramis Ramirez	.25
NB15	Adrian Beltre	.35

Picture Perfect

This 10-card set features a full bleed photo of baseball's biggest stars, including Derek Jeter and Ken Griffey Jr. These are found one per eight packs.

		NM/M
Complete Set (10):		5.00
Common Player:		.25
Inserted 1:8		
P1	Ken Griffey Jr.	.75
P2	Kerry Wood	.30
P3	Pedro Martinez	.45
P4	Mark McGwire	.90
P5	Greg Maddux	.60
P6	Sammy Sosa	.60
P7	Greg Vaughn	.25
P8	Juan Gonzalez	.30
P9	Jeff Bagwell	.45
P10	Derek Jeter	1.50

Power Brokers

This 20-card set features baseball's biggest superstars including McGwire, Sosa and Chipper Jones. The cards are die-cut at the top and printed on Finest technology. Power Brokers are inserted in every 36 packs. A Refractor parallel version also exists, which are seeded 1:144 packs.

		NM/M
Complete Set (20):		20.00
Common Player:		.25
Inserted 1:36		
Refractors:		1.5X
Inserted 1:144		
PB1	Mark McGwire	3.00
PB2	Andres Galarraga	.25
PB3	Ken Griffey Jr.	2.00
PB4	Sammy Sosa	1.50
PB5	Juan Gonzalez	.50
PB6	Alex Rodriguez	3.00
PB7	Frank Thomas	1.50
PB8	Jeff Bagwell	1.00
PB9	Vinny Castilla	.25
PB10	Mike Piazza	2.00
PB11	Greg Vaughn	.25
PB12	Barry Bonds	4.00
PB13	Mo Vaughn	.25
PB14	Jim Thome	.65
PB15	Larry Walker	.25
PB16	Chipper Jones	1.50
PB17	Nomar Garciaparra	1.50
PB18	Manny Ramirez	1.00
PB19	Roger Clemens	1.75
PB20	Kerry Wood	.65

Record Numbers

This 10-card set highlights achievements from the game's current stars, including Nomar Garciaparra's 30 game hitting streak, the longest by a rookie in major league history. These inserts are randomly seeded 1:8 packs, each card is numbered on the back with a "RN" prefix.

		NM/M
Complete Set (10):		8.00
Common Player:		.50
Inserted 1:8		
RN1	Mark McGwire	1.50
RN2	Mike Piazza	1.00
RN3	Curt Schilling	.75
RN4	Ken Griffey Jr.	1.50
RN5	Sammy Sosa	.75
RN6	Nomar Garciaparra	.75
RN7	Kerry Wood	.50
RN8	Roger Clemens	1.50
RN9	Cal Ripken Jr.	2.00
RN10	Mark McGwire	1.50

Record Numbers Gold

This is a parallel of the Record Numbers insert set, each card features the appropriate sequential numbering based on the featured players' highlighted record. Each card is numbered with a "RN" prefix on the back.

		NM/M
Common Player:		8.00
RN1	Mark McGwire/70	40.00
RN2	Mike Piazza/362	15.00
RN3	Curt Schilling/319	8.00
RN4	Ken Griffey Jr./350	20.00
RN5	Sammy Sosa/20	20.00
RN6	Nomar Garciaparra/30	20.00
RN7	Kerry Wood/20	15.00
RN8	Roger Clemens/20	20.00
RN9	Cal Ripken Jr./2,632	15.00
RN10	Mark McGwire/162	20.00

Nolan Ryan Reprints

Topps reprinted all 27 of Nolan Ryan's basic Topps cards, with 14 odd numbers appearing in Series 1 and the remaining 13 even cards inserted into Series 2 packs. Each card is stamped with a gold Topps commemorative stamp on the front for identification. Reprints were seeded in every 18 packs. Ryan also autographed a number of the reprints for both series. Series 1 Ryan autographs are seeded 1:4,260, with Series 2 autographs found 1:5,007 packs. Ryan autographs were inserted exclusively in hobby packs.

		NM/M
Complete Set (27):		40.00
Common Ryan:		3.00
Inserted 1:18		
Nolan Ryan Autograph:		150.00
1	Nolan Ryan/1968	7.50
2	Nolan Ryan/1969	4.50
3	Nolan Ryan/1970	3.00
4	Nolan Ryan/1971	3.00
5	Nolan Ryan/1972	3.00
6	Nolan Ryan/1973	3.00
7	Nolan Ryan/1974	3.00
8	Nolan Ryan/1975	3.00
9	Nolan Ryan/1976	3.00
10	Nolan Ryan/1977	3.00
11	Nolan Ryan/1978	3.00
12	Nolan Ryan/1979	3.00
13	Nolan Ryan/1980	3.00
14	Nolan Ryan/1981	3.00
15	Nolan Ryan/1982	3.00
16	Nolan Ryan/1983	3.00
17	Nolan Ryan/1984	3.00
18	Nolan Ryan/1985	3.00
19	Nolan Ryan/1986	3.00
20	Nolan Ryan/1987	3.00
21	Nolan Ryan/1988	3.00
22	Nolan Ryan/1989	3.00
23	Nolan Ryan/1990	3.00
24	Nolan Ryan/1991	3.00
25	Nolan Ryan/1992	3.00
26	Nolan Ryan/1993	3.00
27	Nolan Ryan/1994	3.00

Nolan Ryan Reprint Autographs

Topps reprinted all 27 of Nolan Ryan's basic Topps cards, with 14 odd numbers appearing in Series 1 and the remaining 13 even cards inserted into Series 2 packs. Each card is stamped with a gold Topps commemorative stamp on the front for identification. Ryan-autographed reprints, found exclu-

sively in hobby packs, are seeded 1:4,260 in Series 1, with Series 2 autographs found 1:5,007 packs.

		NM/M
Common Card:		150.00
1	Nolan Ryan/1968	200.00
2	Nolan Ryan/1969	150.00
3	Nolan Ryan/1970	150.00
4	Nolan Ryan/1971	150.00
5	Nolan Ryan/1972	150.00
6	Nolan Ryan/1973	150.00
7	Nolan Ryan/1974	150.00
8	Nolan Ryan/1975	150.00
9	Nolan Ryan/1976	150.00
10	Nolan Ryan/1977	150.00
11	Nolan Ryan/1978	150.00
12	Nolan Ryan/1979	150.00
13	Nolan Ryan/1980	150.00
14	Nolan Ryan/1981	150.00
15	Nolan Ryan/1982	150.00
16	Nolan Ryan/1983	150.00
17	Nolan Ryan/1984	150.00
18	Nolan Ryan/1985	150.00
19	Nolan Ryan/1986	150.00
20	Nolan Ryan/1987	150.00
21	Nolan Ryan/1988	150.00
22	Nolan Ryan/1989	150.00
23	Nolan Ryan/1990	150.00
24	Nolan Ryan/1991	150.00
25	Nolan Ryan/1992	150.00
26	Nolan Ryan/1993	150.00
27	Nolan Ryan/1994	150.00

Nolan Ryan Finest Reprints

This 27-card set reprinted all 27 of Ryan's basic Topps cards. Odd numbers were distributed in Series 1 packs, with even numbers distributed in Series 2 packs. These are seeded 1:72 packs in both series 1 and 2 packs. A Refractor parallel version is inserted 1:288 packs.

		NM/M
Complete Set (27):		125.00
Common Card:		5.00
Inserted 1:72		
Refractors:		2X
Inserted 1:288		
1	1968	12.50
2	1969	7.50
3	1970	5.00
4	1971	5.00
5	1972	5.00
6	1973	5.00
7	1974	5.00
8	1975	5.00
9	1976	5.00
10	1977	5.00
11	1978	5.00
12	1979	5.00
13	1980	5.00
14	1981	5.00
15	1982	5.00
16	1983	5.00
17	1984	5.00
18	1985	5.00
19	1986	5.00
20	1987	5.00
21	1988	5.00
22	1989	5.00
23	1990	5.00
24	1991	5.00
25	1992	5.00
26	1992	5.00
27	1992	5.00

Traded and Rookies

Identical in design to the base 1999 Topps cards the 121-card set includes players involved in pre and mid-season transactions as well as top prospects and 1999 Draft Picks. Released in a boxed set, each set also includes one autographed card from the 75 rookie/draft pick cards in the set.

		NM/M
Unopened Set (122):		40.00
Complete Set, No Autograph		
(121):		15.00
Common Player:		.10
1	Seth Etherton	.10
2	Mark Harriger RC	.10
3	Matt Wise RC	.25
4	Carlos Hernandez RC	.15
5	Julio Lugo RC	.25
6	Mike Nannini	.10
7	Justin Bowles RC	.10
8	Mark Mulder RC	.75
9	Roberto Vaz RC	.10
10	Felipe Lopez RC	.75
11	Matt Belisle	.10
12	Micah Bowie	.10
13	Ruben Quevedo RC	.10
14	Jose Garcia RC	.10
15	David Kelton RC	.25
16	Phillip Norton	.10
17	Corey Patterson RC	.75
18	Ron Walker RC	.10
19	Paul Hoover RC	.10
20	Ryan Rupe RC	.15
21	J.D. Closser RC	.10
22	Rob Ryan RC	.10
23	Steve Colyer RC	.10
24	Bubba Crosby RC	.50
25	Luke Prokopec RC	.10
26	Matt Blank RC	.10
27	Josh McKinley	.10
28	Nate Bump	.10
29	Giuseppe Chiaramonte RC	.10
30	Arturo McDowell	.10
31	Tony Torcato	.10
32	Dave Roberts	.10
33	C.C. Sabathia RC	2.00
34	Sean Spencer RC	.10
35	Chip Ambres	.10
36	A.J. Burnett	.15
37	Mo Bruce RC	.10
38	Jason Tyner	.10
39	Mamon Tucker	.10
40	Sean Burroughs RC	.25
41	Kevin Eberwein RC	.10
42	Junior Herndon RC	.10
43	Bryan Wolff RC	.10
44	Pat Burrell	.50
45	Eric Valent	.10
46	Carlos Pena RC	1.00
47	Mike Zywica	.10
48	Adam Everett	.10
49	Juan Pena RC	.50
50	Adam Dunn RC	3.00
51	Austin Kearns	.75
52	Jacobo Sequea RC	.10
53	Choo Freeman	.10
54	Jeff Winchester	.10
55	Matt Burch	.10
56	Chris George	.10
57	Scott Mullen RC	.10
58	Kit Pellow	.10
59	Mark Quinn RC	.15
60	Nate Cornejo	.10
61	Ryan Mills RC	.25
62	Kevin Beirne RC	.10
63	Kip Wells RC	.50
64	Juan Rivera RC	.25
65	Alfonso Soriano RC	4.00
66	Josh Hamilton RC	8.00
67	Josh Girdley RC	.10
68	Kyle Snyder RC	.15
69	Mike Paradis RC	.10
70	Jason Jennings RC	.25
71	David Walling RC	.10
72	Omar Ortiz RC	.10
73	Jay Gehrke RC	.10
74	Casey Burns RC	.10
75	Carl Crawford RC	2.00
76	Reggie Sanders	.10
77	Will Clark	.10
78	David Wells	.10
79	Paul Konerko	.20
80	Armando Benitez	.10
81	Brant Brown	.10

#	Player	Price
82	Mo Vaughn	.10
83	Jose Canseco	.25
84	Albert Belle	.10
85	Dean Palmer	.10
86	Greg Vaughn	.10
87	Mark Clark	.10
88	Pat Meares	.10
89	Eric Davis	.10
90	Brian Giles	.10
91	Jeff Brantley	.10
92	Bret Boone	.10
93	Ron Gant	.10
94	Mike Cameron	.10
95	Charles Johnson	.10
96	Denny Neagle	.10
97	Brian Hunter	.10
98	Jose Hernandez	.10
99	Rick Aguilera	.10
100	Tony Batista	.10
101	Roger Cedeno	.10
102	Creighton Gubanich	.10
103	Tim Belcher	.10
104	Bruce Aven	.10
105	Brian Daubach RC	.25
106	Ed Sprague	.10
107	Michael Tucker	.10
108	Homer Bush	.10
109	Armando Reynoso	.10
110	Brook Fordyce	.10
111	Matt Mantei	.10
112	Jose Guillen	.10
113	Kenny Rogers	.10
114	Livan Hernandez	.10
115	Butch Huskey	.10
116	David Segui	.10
117	Darryl Hamilton	.10
118	Jim Leyritz	.10
119	Randy Velarde	.10
120	Bill Taylor	.10
121	Kevin Appier	.10

Traded and Rookies Autographs

These autographs have identical photos and design from the Traded and Rookies set. Seeded one per boxed set, each card has a "Topps Certified Autograph Issue" stamp ensuring its authenticity. Cards of the first 75 rookies/draft picks included in the 121-card boxed set can be found in this autographed version.

		NM/M
	Common Player:	3.00
	Inserted 1:Set	
1	Seth Etherton	3.00
2	Mark Harriger	3.00
3	Matt Wise	5.00
4	Carlos Hernandez	5.00
5	Julio Lugo	10.00
6	Mike Nannini	3.00
7	Justin Bowles	3.00
8	Mark Mulder	15.00
9	Roberto Vaz	3.00
10	Felipe Lopez	15.00
11	Matt Belisle	3.00
12	Micah Bowie	5.00
13	Ruben Quevedo	5.00
14	Jose Garcia	5.00
15	David Kelton	5.00
16	Phillip Norton	3.00
17	Corey Patterson	15.00
18	Ron Walker	3.00
19	Paul Hoover	3.00
20	Ryan Rupe	5.00
21	J.D. Closser	5.00
22	Rob Ryan	3.00
23	Steve Colyer	5.00
24	Bubba Crosby	10.00
25	Luke Prokopec	3.00
26	Matt Blank	3.00
27	Josh McKinley	5.00
28	Nate Bump	5.00
29	Giuseppe Chiaramonte	3.00
30	Arturo McDowell	3.00
31	Tony Torcato	5.00
32	Dave Roberts	10.00
33	C.C. Sabathia	100.00
34	Sean Spencer	3.00
35	Chip Ambres	5.00
36	A.J. Burnett	25.00
37	Mo Bruce	3.00
38	Jason Tyner	3.00
39	Mamon Tucker	3.00
40	Sean Burroughs	5.00
41	Kevin Eberwein	3.00
42	Junior Herndon	3.00
43	Bryan Wolff	3.00
44	Pat Burrell	25.00
45	Eric Valent	5.00
46	Carlos Pena	30.00
47	Mike Zywica	3.00
48	Adam Everett	10.00
49	Juan Pena	5.00
50	Adam Dunn	80.00
51	Austin Kearns	15.00
52	Jacobo Sequea	3.00
53	Choo Freeman	5.00
54	Jeff Winchester	3.00
55	Matt Burch	3.00
56	Chris George	4.00
57	Scott Mullen	3.00
58	Kit Pellow	3.00
59	Mark Quinn	3.00
60	Nate Cornejo	5.00
61	Ryan Mills	3.00
62	Kevin Beirne	4.00
63	Kip Wells	5.00
64	Juan Rivera	8.00
65	Alfonso Soriano	60.00
66	Josh Hamilton	200.00
67	Josh Girdley	3.00
68	Kyle Snyder	5.00
69	Mike Paradis	3.00
70	Jason Jennings	10.00
71	David Walling	3.00
72	Omar Ortiz	3.00
73	Jay Gehrke	5.00
74	Casey Burns	3.00
75	Carl Crawford	60.00

Supers

These oversize (3-1/2" x 5") versions of Topps cards were issued one per box in hobby and Home Team Advantage boxes. Eight cards were issued in each of Series 1 and 2. Other than their size and the card numbers on back, the supers are identical to the regular versions.

		NM/M
	Complete Set (16):	17.50
	Common Player:	.50
1	Roger Clemens	1.25
2	Greg Maddux	1.25
3	Kerry Wood	.75
4	Juan Gonzalez	.75
5	Sammy Sosa	1.25
6	Mark McGwire	2.50
7	Ken Griffey Jr.	2.00
8	Ben Grieve	.50
1	Nomar Garciaparra	1.25
2	Cal Ripken Jr.	3.00
3	Alex Rodriguez	2.00
4	Mike Piazza	1.50
5	Larry Walker	.50
6	Chipper Jones	1.25
7	Barry Bonds	3.00
8	Frank Thomas	1.00

Action Flats

"Dynamic action poses . . . painstakingly capturing one of their signature plays" are featured in this issue of plastic player figures. The figures are about 3" tall by 2-1/2" wide and stand on a plastic base. In the manner of early 20th Century tin soldiers, there is little depth to the figures. Each handpainted figure is sold in a plastic-windowed box which includes a special foil-stamped version of the player's 1999 Topps card inside. Each figure was also produced in a short-printed "away" jersey version, with 10 of the players seeded at the rate of one per 12 figures, Sosa at a 1:24 rate and McGwire at a 1:36 rate. Suggested retail price at issue was $2.99. Values shown are for un-opened packages.

		NM/M
	Complete Set, "Home" (12):	6.00
	Complete Set, "Away" (12):	12.00
	Common Player, "Home":	.50
	Common Player, "Away":	.75
1	Chipper Jones	.50
2	Greg Maddux	.50
3	Mark McGwire	1.00
4	Sammy Sosa	.50
5	Kerry Wood	.50
6	Barry Bonds	1.50
7	Alex Rodriguez	1.00
8	Ken Griffey Jr.	.75
9	Cal Ripken Jr.	1.50
10	Juan Gonzalez	.50
11	Nomar Garciaparra	.50
12	Derek Jeter	1.50
1	Chipper Jones	.75
2	Greg Maddux	.75
3	Mark McGwire	1.50
4	Sammy Sosa	.75
5	Kerry Wood	.75
6	Barry Bonds	2.00
7	Alex Rodriguez	1.50
8	Ken Griffey Jr.	1.00
9	Cal Ripken Jr.	2.00
10	Juan Gonzalez	.75
11	Nomar Garciaparra	.75
12	Derek Jeter	2.00

1999 Topps Chrome

The 462-card base set is a chromium parallel version of Topps baseball. Included are the Mark McGwire #220 and Sammy Sosa #461 home run subset cards, which commemorate each of their home runs. Each pack contains four cards with a S.R.P. of $3.00 per pack.

		NM/M
	Complete Set (461):	75.00
	Common Player:	.15
	Refractors:	4X
	Inserted 1:12	
	Ser. 1 or 2 Pack (4):	1.50
	Ser. 1 or 2 Box (24):	30.00
1	Roger Clemens	1.75
2	Andres Galarraga	.15
3	Scott Brosius	.15
4	John Flaherty	.15
5	Jim Leyritz	.15
6	Ray Durham	.15
7	Joe Vizcaino	.15
8	Will Clark	.15
9	David Wells	.15
10	Jose Guillen	.15
11	Scott Hatteberg	.15
12	Edgardo Alfonzo	.15
13	Mike Bordick	.15
14	Manny Ramirez	1.00
15	Greg Maddux	1.50
16	David Segui	.15
17	Darryl Strawberry	.15
18	Brad Radke	.15
19	Kerry Wood	.40
20	Matt Anderson	.15
21	Derek Lee	.60
22	Mickey Morandini	.15
23	Paul Konerko	.30
24	Travis Lee	.15
25	Ken Hill	.15
26	Kenny Rogers	.15
27	Paul Sorrento	.15
28	Quilvio Veras	.15
29	Todd Walker	.15
30	Ryan Jackson	.15
31	John Olerud	.15
32	Doug Glanville	.15
33	Nolan Ryan	3.00
34	Ray Lankford	.15
35	Mark Loretta	.15
36	Jason Dickson	.15
37	Sean Bergman	.15
38	Quinton McCracken	.15
39	Bartolo Colon	.15
40	Brady Anderson	.15
41	Chris Stynes	.15
42	Jorge Posada	.15
43	Justin Thompson	.15
44	Johnny Damon	.40
45	Armando Benitez	.15
46	Brant Brown	.15
47	Charlie Hayes	.15
48	Darren Dreifort	.15
49	Juan Gonzalez	.50
50	Chuck Knoblauch	.15
51	Todd Helton (Rookie All-Star)	1.00
52	Rick Reed	.15
53	Chris Gomez	.15
55	Gary Sheffield	.50
56	Rod Beck	.15
57	Rey Sanchez	.15
58	Garret Anderson	.15
59	Jimmy Haynes	.15
60	Steve Woodard	.15
61	Rondell White	.15
62	Vladimir Guerrero	1.00
63	Eric Karros	.15
64	Russ Davis	.15
65	Mo Vaughn	.15
66	Sammy Sosa	1.50
67	Troy Percival	.15
68	Kenny Lofton	.15
69	Bill Taylor	.15
70	Mark McGwire	2.50
71	Roger Cedeno	.15
72	Javy Lopez	.15
73	Damion Easley	.15
74	Andy Pettitte	.35
75	Tony Gwynn	1.50
76	Ricardo Rincon	.15
77	F.P. Santangelo	.15
78	Jay Bell	.15
79	Scott Servais	.15
80	Jose Canseco	.50
81	Roberto Hernandez	.15
82	Todd Dunwoody	.15
83	John Wetteland	.15
84	Mike Caruso (Rookie All-Star)	.15
85	Derek Jeter	3.00
86	Aaron Sele	.15
87	Jose Lima	.15
88	Ryan Christenson	.15
89	Jeff Cirillo	.15
90	Jose Hernandez	.15
91	Mark Kotsay (Rookie All-Star)	.15
92	Darren Bragg	.15
93	Albert Belle	.15
94	Matt Lawton	.15
95	Pedro Martinez	1.00
96	Greg Vaughn	.15
97	Neifi Perez	.15
98	Gerald Williams	.15
99	Derek Bell	.15
100	Ken Griffey Jr.	2.00
101	David Cone	.15
102	Brian Johnson	.15
103	Dean Palmer	.15
104	Javier Valentin	.15
105	Trevor Hoffman	.15
106	Butch Huskey	.15
107	Dave Martinez	.15
108	Billy Wagner	.15
109	Shawn Green	.35
110	Ben Grieve (Rookie All-Star)	.15
111	Tom Goodwin	.15
112	Jaret Wright	.15
113	Aramis Ramirez	.15
114	Dmitri Young	.15
115	Hideki Irabu	.15
116	Roberto Kelly	.15
117	Jeff Fassero	.15
118	Mark Clark	.15
119	Jason McDonald	.15
120	Matt Williams	.15
121	Dave Burba	.15
122	Bret Saberhagen	.15
123	Deivi Cruz	.15
124	Chad Curtis	.15
125	Scott Rolen	.75
126	Lee Stevens	.15
127	J.T. Snow Jr.	.15
128	Rusty Greer	.15
129	Brian Meadows	.15
130	Jim Edmonds	.15
131	Ron Gant	.15
132	A.J. Hinch (Rookie All-Star)	.15
133	Shannon Stewart	.15
134	Brad Fullmer	.15
135	Cal Eldred	.15
136	Matt Walbeck	.15
137	Carl Everett	.15
138	Walt Weiss	.15
139	Fred McGriff	.15
140	Darin Erstad	.40
141	Dave Nilsson	.15
142	Eric Young	.15
143	Dan Wilson	.15
144	Jeff Reed	.15
145	Brett Tomko	.15
146	Terry Steinbach	.15
147	Seth Greisinger	.15
148	Pat Meares	.15
149	Livan Hernandez	.15
150	Jeff Bagwell	1.00
151	Bob Wickman	.15
152	Omar Vizquel	.15
153	Eric Davis	.15
154	Larry Sutton	.15
155	Magglio Ordonez (Rookie All-Star)	.45
156	Eric Milton	.15
157	Darren Lewis	.15
158	Rick Aguilera	.15
159	Mike Lieberthal	.15
160	Robb Nen	.15
161	Brian Giles	.15
162	Jeff Brantley	.15
163	Gary DiSarcina	.15
164	John Valentin	.15
165	David Dellucci	.15
166	Chan Ho Park	.15
167	Masato Yoshii	.15
168	Jason Schmidt	.15
169	LaTroy Hawkins	.15
170	Bret Boone	.15
171	Jerry DiPoto	.15
172	Mariano Rivera	.25
173	Mike Cameron	.15
174	Scott Erickson	.15
175	Charles Johnson	.15
176	Bobby Jones	.15
177	Francisco Cordova	.15
178	Todd Jones	.15
179	Jeff Montgomery	.15
180	Mike Mussina	.50
181	Bob Abreu	.15
182	Ismael Valdes	.15
183	Andy Fox	.15
184	Woody Williams	.15
185	Denny Neagle	.15
186	Jose Valentin	.15
187	Darrin Fletcher	.15
188	Gabe Alvarez	.15
189	Eddie Taubensee	.15
190	Edgar Martinez	.15
191	Jason Kendall	.15
192	Darryl Kile	.15
193	Jeff King	.15
194	Rey Ordonez	.15
195	Andruw Jones	1.00
196	Tony Fernandez	.15
197	Jamey Wright	.15
198	B.J. Surhoff	.15
199	Vinny Castilla	.15
200	David Wells (Season Highlight)	.15
201	Mark McGwire (Season Highlight)	1.25
202	Sammy Sosa (Season Highlight)	.75
203	Roger Clemens (Season Highlight)	.85
204	Kerry Wood (Season Highlight)	.20
205	Lance Berkman, Mike Frank, Gabe Kapler (Prospects)	.15
206	Alex Escobar RC, Ricky Ledee, Mike Stoner (Prospects)	.50
207	Peter Bergeron RC, Jeremy Giambi, George Lombard (Prospects)	.50
208	Michael Barrett, Ben Davis, Robert Fick (Prospects)	.15
209	Pat Cline, Ramon Hernandez, Jayson Werth (Prospects)	.20
210	Bruce Chen, Chris Enochs, Ryan Anderson (Prospects)	.15
211	Mike Lincoln, Octavio Dotel, Brad Penny (Prospects)	.15
212	Chuck Abbott, Brent Butler, Danny Klassen (Prospects)	.15
213	Chris Jones, Jeff Urban RC (Draft Pick)	.15
214	Arturo McDowell RC, Tony Torcato RC (Draft Pick)	.25
215	Josh McKinley RC, Jason Tyner RC (Draft Pick)	.30
216	Matt Burch RC, Seth Etherton RC (Draft Pick)	.15
217	Mamon Tucker RC, Rick Elder RC (Draft Pick)	.20
218	J.M. Gold RC, Ryan Mills RC (Draft Pick)	.15
219	Adam Brown RC, Choo Freeman RC (Draft Pick)	.20
220	Mark McGwire HR #1 (Record Breaker)	15.00
220	Mark McGwire HR #2-60	10.00
220	McGwire HR #61-62	15.00
220	McGwire HR #63-69	12.50
220	McGwire HR #70	40.00
221	Larry Walker (League Leader)	.15
222	Bernie Williams (League Leader)	.15
223	Mark McGwire (League Leader)	1.25
224	Ken Griffey Jr. (League Leader)	1.00
225	Sammy Sosa (League Leader)	.75
226	Juan Gonzalez (League Leader)	.35
227	Dante Bichette (League Leader)	.15
228	Alex Rodriguez (League Leader)	1.25
229	Sammy Sosa (League Leader)	.75
230	Derek Jeter (League Leader)	1.50
231	Greg Maddux (League Leader)	.75
232	Roger Clemens (League Leader)	.75
233	Ricky Ledee (World Series)	.15
234	Chuck Knoblauch (World Series)	.15
235	Bernie Williams (World Series)	.15
236	Tino Martinez (World Series)	.15
237	Orlando Hernandez (World Series)	.15
238	Scott Brosius (World Series)	.15
239	Andy Pettitte (World Series)	.15
240	Mariano Rivera (World Series)	.15
241	Checklist	.15
242	Checklist	.15
243	Tom Glavine	.35
244	Andy Benes	.15
245	Sandy Alomar	.15
246	Wilton Guerrero	.15
247	Alex Gonzalez	.15
248	Roberto Alomar	.30
249	Ruben Rivera	.15
250	Eric Chavez	.15
251	Ellis Burks	.15
252	Richie Sexson	.15
253	Steve Finley	.15
254	Dwight Gooden	.15
255	Dustin Hermanson	.15
256	Kirk Rueter	.15
257	Steve Trachsel	.15
258	Gregg Jefferies	.15
259	Matt Stairs	.15
260	Shane Reynolds	.15
261	Gregg Olson	.15
262	Kevin Tapani	.15
263	Matt Morris	.15
264	Carl Pavano	.15
265	Nomar Garciaparra	1.50
266	Kevin Young	.15
267	Rick Helling	.15
268	Matt Franco	.15
269	Brian McRae	.15
270	Cal Ripken Jr.	3.00
271	Jeff Abbott	.15
272	Tony Batista	.15
273	Bill Simas	.15
274	Brian Hunter	.15
275	John Franco	.15
276	Devon White	.15
277	Rickey Henderson	1.00
278	Chuck Finley	.15
279	Mike Blowers	.15
280	Mark Grace	.15
281	Randy Winn	.15
282	Bobby Bonilla	.15
283	David Justice	.15
284	Shane Monahan	.15
285	Kevin Brown	.15
286	Todd Zeile	.15
287	Al Martin	.15
288	Troy O'Leary	.15
289	Darryl Hamilton	.15
290	Tino Martinez	.15
291	David Ortiz	.50
292	Tony Clark	.15
293	Ryan Minor	.15
294	Reggie Sanders	.15
295	Wally Joyner	.15
296	Cliff Floyd	.15
297	Shawn Estes	.15
298	Pat Hentgen	.15
299	Scott Elarton	.15
300	Alex Rodriguez	2.50
301	Ozzie Guillen	.15
302	Hideo Nomo	.15
303	Ryan McGuire	.15
304	Brad Ausmus	.15
305	Alex Gonzalez	.15
306	Brian Jordan	.15
307	John Jaha	.15
308	Mark Grudzielanek	.15
309	Juan Guzman	.15
310	Tony Womack	.15
311	Dennis Reyes	.15
312	Marty Cordova	.15
313	Ramiro Mendoza	.15
314	Robin Ventura	.15
315	Rafael Palmeiro	.65
316	Ramon Martinez	.15
317	Pedro Astacio	.15
318	Dave Hollins	.15
319	Tom Candiotti	.15
320	Al Leiter	.15
321	Rico Brogna	.15
322	Reggie Jefferson	.15
323	Bernard Gilkey	.15
324	Jason Giambi	.40
325	Craig Biggio	.15
326	Troy Glaus	.75
327	Delino DeShields	.15
328	Fernando Vina	.15
329	John Smoltz	.15
330	Jeff Kent	.15
331	Roy Halladay	.15
332	Andy Ashby	.15
333	Tim Wakefield	.15
334	Roger Clemens	1.75
335	Bernie Williams	.15
336	Desi Relaford	.15
337	John Burkett	.15
338	Mike Hampton	.15
339	Royce Clayton	.15
340	Mike Piazza	2.00
341	Jeremi Gonzalez	.15
342	Mike Lansing	.15
343	Jamie Moyer	.15
344	Ron Coomer	.15
345	Barry Larkin	.15
346	Fernando Tatis	.15
347	Chili Davis	.15
348	Bobby Higginson	.15

349	Hal Morris	.15
350	Larry Walker	.15
351	Carlos Guillen	.15
352	Miguel Tejada	.30
353	Travis Fryman	.15
354	Jarrod Washburn	.15
355	Chipper Jones	1.50
356	Todd Stottlemyre	.15
357	Henry Rodriguez	.15
358	Eli Marrero	.15
359	Alan Benes	.15
360	Tim Salmon	.15
361	Luis Gonzalez	.15
362	Scott Spiezio	.15
363	Chris Carpenter	.15
364	Bobby Howry	.15
365	Raul Mondesi	.15
366	Ugueth Urbina	.15
367	Tom Evans	.15
368	Kerry Ligtenberg RC	.40
369	Adrian Beltre	.35
370	Ryan Klesko	.15
371	Wilson Alvarez	.15
372	John Thomson	.15
373	Tony Saunders	.15
374	Mike Stanley	.15
375	Ken Caminiti	.15
376	Jay Buhner	.15
377	Bill Mueller	.15
378	Jeff Blauser	.15
379	Edgar Renteria	.15
380	Jim Thome	.60
381	Joey Hamilton	.15
382	Calvin Pickering	.15
383	Marquis Grissom	.15
384	Omar Daal	.15
385	Curt Schilling	.35
386	Jose Cruz Jr.	.15
387	Chris Widger	.15
388	Pete Harnisch	.15
389	Charles Nagy	.15
390	Tom Gordon	.15
391	Bobby Smith	.15
392	Derrick Gibson	.15
393	Jeff Conine	.15
394	Carlos Perez	.15
395	Barry Bonds	3.00
396	Mark McLemore	.15
397	Juan Encarnacion	.15
398	Wade Boggs	1.50
399	Ivan Rodriguez	.75
400	Moises Alou	.15
401	Jeromy Burnitz	.15
402	Sean Casey	.25
403	Jose Offerman	.15
404	Joe Fontenot	.15
405	Kevin Millwood	.15
406	Lance Johnson	.15
407	Richard Hidalgo	.15
408	Mike Jackson	.15
409	Brian Anderson	.15
410	Jeff Shaw	.15
411	Preston Wilson	.15
412	Todd Hundley	.15
413	Jim Parque	.15
414	Justin Baughman	.15
415	Dante Bichette	.15
416	Paul O'Neill	.15
417	Miguel Cairo	.15
418	Randy Johnson	1.00
419	Jesus Sanchez	.15
420	Carlos Delgado	.35
421	Ricky Ledee	.15
422	Orlando Hernandez	.15
423	Frank Thomas	1.00
424	Pokey Reese	.15
425	Carlos Lee, Mike Lowell, Kit Pellow RC (Prospect)	.40
426	Michael Cuddyer, Mark DeRosa, Jerry Hairston Jr. RC (Prospect)	.60
427	Marlon Anderson, Ron Belliard, Orlando Cabrera (Prospect)	.45
428	Micah Bowie RC, Phil Norton RC, Randy Wolf (Prospect)	.35
429	Jack Cressend, Jason Rakers, John Rocker (Prospect)	.25
430	Ruben Mateo, Scott Morgan, Mike Zywica RC (Prospect)	.25
431	Jason LaRue, Matt LeCroy RC, Mitch Meluskey RC (Prospect)	.25
432	Gabe Kapler, Armando Rios RC, Fernando Seguignol (Prospect)	.25
433	Adam Kennedy, Mickey Lopez RC, Jackie Rexrode (Prospect)	.25
434	Jose Fernandez RC, Jeff Liefer, Chris Truby (Prospect)	.25
435	Corey Koskie, Doug Mientkiewicz RC, Damon Minor (Prospect)	.60
436	Roosevelt Brown RC, Dernell Stenson, Vernon Wells (Prospect)	.25
437	A.J. Burnett RC, John Nicholson, Billy Koch (Prospect)	.75

438	Matt Belisle RC, Matt Roney RC (Draft Pick)	.30
439	Austin Kearns RC, Chris George RC (Draft Pick)	3.00
440	Nate Bump RC, Nate Cornejo RC (Draft Pick)	.40
441	Brad Lidge RC, Mike Nannini RC (Draft Pick)	.60
442	Matt Holliday RC, Jeff Winchester RC (Draft Pick)	8.00
443	Adam Everett RC, Chip Ambres RC (Draft Pick)	.30
444	Pat Burrell RC, Eric Valent RC (Draft Pick)	3.00
445	Roger Clemens (Strikeout Kings)	.85
446	Kerry Wood (Strikeout Kings)	.20
447	Curt Schilling (Strikeout Kings)	.15
448	Randy Johnson (Strikeout Kings)	.50
449	Pedro Martinez (Strikeout Kings)	.50
450	Jeff Bagwell, Andres Galarraga, Mark McGwire (All-Topps)	1.25
451	John Olerud, Jim Thome, Tino Martinez (All-Topps)	.40
452	Alex Rodriguez, Nomar Garciaparra, Derek Jeter (All-Topps)	1.50
453	Vinny Castilla, Chipper Jones, Scott Rolen (All-Topps)	.75
454	Sammy Sosa, Ken Griffey Jr., Juan Gonzalez (All-Topps)	1.00
455	Barry Bonds, Manny Ramirez, Larry Walker (All-Topps)	1.50
456	Frank Thomas, Tim Salmon, David Justice (All-Topps)	.60
457	Travis Lee, Todd Helton, Ben Grieve (All-Topps)	.50
458	Vladimir Guerrero, Greg Vaughn, Bernie Williams (All-Topps)	.50
459	Mike Piazza, Ivan Rodriguez, Jason Kendall (All-Topps)	1.00
460	Roger Clemens, Kerry Wood, Greg Maddux (All-Topps)	1.00
461	Sammy Sosa #1 (Home Run Parade)	10.00
461	Sammy Sosa HR #2-60	6.00
461	S. Sosa HR #61-62	10.00
461	S. Sosa HR #63-65	7.50
461	S. Sosa HR #66	20.00
---	Checklist 1-100	.15
---	Checklist - inserts	.15

All-Etch

Inserted in Series 2 packs, All-Etch has three different styles of inserts. '99 Rookie Rush features rookies who have the best shot of winning '99 Rookie of the Year. Club 40 features 13 players who hit 40 homers or more in 1998, and Club K features seven pitchers known for their strikeout abilities. Each is inserted 1:6 packs, while Refractor versions are seeded 1:24 packs.

		NM/M
Complete Set (30):		15.00
Common Player:		.35
Inserted 1:6		
Refractors:		1.5X
Inserted 1:24		
1	Mark McGwire	3.00
2	Sammy Sosa	1.50
3	Ken Griffey Jr.	2.00
4	Greg Vaughn	.25
5	Albert Belle	.25
6	Vinny Castilla	.25
7	Jose Canseco	.50
8	Juan Gonzalez	.50
9	Manny Ramirez	1.00
10	Andres Galarraga	.25
11	Rafael Palmeiro	.75

12	Alex Rodriguez	3.00
13	Mo Vaughn	.25
14	Eric Chavez	.40
15	Gabe Kapler	.25
16	Calvin Pickering	.25
17	Ruben Mateo	.25
18	Roy Halladay	.40
19	Jeremy Giambi	.25
20	Alex Gonzalez	.25
21	Ron Belliard	.25
22	Marlon Anderson	.25
23	Carlos Lee	.25
24	Kerry Wood	.50
25	Roger Clemens	1.50
26	Curt Schilling	.50
27	Kevin Brown	.25
28	Randy Johnson	1.00
29	Pedro Martinez	1.00
30	Orlando Hernandez	.25

Early Road to the Hall

This insert set spotlights players with less than 10 years in the Majors but who are gunning towards their respective spots in Cooperstown. The cards feature chromium technology, with an insert rate of 1:12 packs. A Refractor parallel edition, numbered to 100 each, was a 1:944 hobby-only insert.

		NM/M
Complete Set (10):		12.00
Common Player:		.50
Inserted 1:12		
Refractors (#'d to 100):		6X
ER1	Nomar Garciaparra	1.50
ER2	Derek Jeter	3.00
ER3	Alex Rodriguez	2.50
ER4	Juan Gonzalez	.50
ER5	Ken Griffey Jr.	2.00
ER6	Chipper Jones	1.50
ER7	Vladimir Guerrero	1.00
ER8	Jeff Bagwell	1.00
ER9	Ivan Rodriguez	.75
ER10	Frank Thomas	1.00

Fortune 15

Fortune 15 showcases baseball's best players and hot rookies. They are inserted in Series 2 packs at a rate of 1:12. A Refractor version also exists found exclusively in hobby packs at a rate of 1:627 packs. Refractors are sequentially numbered to 100.

		NM/M
Complete Set (15):		17.50
Common Player:		.50
Inserted 1:12		
Refractors (#'d to 100):		4X
1	Alex Rodriguez	2.25
2	Nomar Garciaparra	1.25
3	Derek Jeter	3.00
4	Troy Glaus	.75
5	Ken Griffey Jr.	1.50
6	Vladimir Guerrero	1.00
7	Kerry Wood	.65
8	Eric Chavez	.65
9	Greg Maddux	1.25
10	Mike Piazza	1.50
11	Sammy Sosa	1.25
12	Mark McGwire	2.25
13	Ben Grieve	.50
14	Chipper Jones	1.25
15	Manny Ramirez	1.00

Home Run Heroes

These cards were part of an unannounced multi-manufacturer (Fleer, Upper Deck, Topps, Pacific) insert program exclusive to Wal-Mart. Each company produced cards of Mark McGwire and Sammy Sosa, along with two other premier sluggers. Each company's cards share a "Power Elite" logo at top and a "Home Run Heroes" logo vertically at right.

		NM/M
Complete Set (4):		5.00
Common Player:		1.00
9	Mark McGwire	2.00
10	Sammy Sosa	1.50
11	Alex Rodriguez	2.00
12	Vladimir Guerrero	1.00

Lords of the Diamond

Parallel to the Topps version, this insert set features die-cutting across the card top and is seeded 1:8 in Series 1 packs. Refractor versions can be found 1:24 packs.

		NM/M
Complete Set (15):		20.00
Common Player:		.40
Inserted 1:8		
Refractors:		2X
Inserted 1:24		
LD1	Ken Griffey Jr.	2.00
LD2	Chipper Jones	1.50
LD3	Sammy Sosa	1.50
LD4	Frank Thomas	1.25
LD5	Mark McGwire	2.50
LD6	Jeff Bagwell	1.25
LD7	Alex Rodriguez	2.25
LD8	Juan Gonzalez	.65
LD9	Barry Bonds	3.00
LD10	Nomar Garciaparra	1.50
LD11	Darin Erstad	.50
LD12	Tony Gwynn	1.50
LD13	Andres Galarraga	.40
LD14	Mike Piazza	2.00
LD15	Greg Maddux	1.50

New Breed

A parallel version utilizing chromium technology, this insert set features the top young stars in the game and is seeded 1:24 packs. A Refractor version also exists, found 1:72 packs.

		NM/M
Complete Set (15):		30.00
Common Player:		.50
Inserted 1:24		
Refractors:		1.5X
Inserted 1:72		
NB1	Darin Erstad	.75
NB2	Brad Fullmer	.50
NB3	Kerry Wood	.75
NB4	Nomar Garciaparra	5.00
NB5	Travis Lee	.65
NB6	Scott Rolen	2.00
NB7	Todd Helton	3.00
NB8	Vladimir Guerrero	3.00
NB9	Derek Jeter	7.50
NB10	Alex Rodriguez	6.00
NB11	Ben Grieve	.50
NB12	Andruw Jones	3.00
NB13	Paul Konerko	.75
NB14	Aramis Ramirez	.50
NB15	Adrian Beltre	.75

Record Numbers

This insert set salutes nine record-setters who have earned a mark of distinction, including Cal Ripken Jr. for his record setting consecutive game streak. Inserted randomly in Series 2 packs at a rate of 1:36 packs. Refractor parallel versions are seeded 1:144 packs.

		NM/M
Complete Set (10):		20.00
Common Player:		.50
Inserted 1:36		
Refractors:		1.5X
Inserted 1:144		
1	Mark McGwire	3.00
2	Craig Biggio	.50
3	Barry Bonds	4.00
4	Ken Griffey Jr.	2.50
5	Sammy Sosa	2.00
6	Alex Rodriguez	3.00
7	Kerry Wood	1.00
8	Roger Clemens	2.00
9	Cal Ripken Jr.	4.00
10	Mark McGwire	3.00

Traded and Rookies

Actually issued in 2000, this parallel of the Topps Traded set utilizing Chromium technology was issued only in complete set form.

		NM/M
Complete Set (121):		40.00
Common Player:		.15
1	Seth Etherton	.15
2	Mark Harriger RC	.25
3	Matt Wise RC	.50
4	Carlos Hernandez RC	.50
5	Julio Lugo RC	1.00
6	Mike Nannini	.15
7	Justin Bowles RC	.25
8	Mark Mulder RC	1.00
9	Roberto Vaz RC	.15
10	Felipe Lopez RC	1.50
11	Matt Belisle	.15
12	Micah Bowie	.15
13	Ruben Quevedo RC	.25
14	Jose Garcia RC	.15
15	David Kelton RC	.50
16	Phillip Norton	.15

17	Corey Patterson RC	1.00
18	Ron Walker RC	.15
19	Paul Hoover RC	.25
20	Ryan Rupe RC	.25
21	J.D. Closser RC	.15
22	Rob Ryan RC	.15
23	Steve Colyer RC	.15
24	Bubba Crosby RC	.50
25	Luke Prokopec RC	.15
26	Matt Blank RC	.15
27	Josh McKinley	.15
28	Nate Bump	.15
29	Giuseppe Chiaramonte RC	.15
30	Arturo McDowell	.15
31	Tony Torcato	.15
32	Dave Roberts	.15
33	C.C. Sabathia RC	6.00
34	Sean Spencer RC	.15
35	Chip Ambres	.15
36	A.J. Burnett	.50
37	Mo Bruce RC	.15
38	Jason Tyner	.15
39	Mamon Tucker	.15
40	Sean Burroughs RC	.50
41	Kevin Eberwein RC	.15
42	Junior Herndon RC	.25
43	Bryan Wolff RC	.15
44	Pat Burrell	1.00
45	Eric Valent	.15
46	Carlos Pena RC	3.00
47	Mike Zywica	.15
48	Adam Everett	.15
49	Juan Pena RC	.50
50	Adam Dunn RC	10.00
51	Austin Kearns	1.00
52	Jacobo Sequea RC	.15
53	Choo Freeman	.50
54	Jeff Winchester	.15
55	Matt Burch	.15
56	Chris George	.25
57	Scott Mullen RC	.15
58	Kit Pellow	.15
59	Mark Quinn RC	.50
60	Nate Cornejo	.15
61	Ryan Mills RC	.15
62	Kevin Beirne RC	.15
63	Kip Wells RC	.50
64	Juan Rivera RC	1.00
65	Alfonso Soriano RC	6.00
66	Josh Hamilton RC	18.00
67	Josh Girdley RC	.15
68	Kyle Snyder RC	.15
69	Mike Paradis RC	.25
70	Jason Jennings RC	.25
71	David Walling RC	.15
72	Omar Ortiz RC	.15
73	Jay Gehrke RC	.15
74	Casey Burns RC	.15
75	Carl Crawford RC	8.00
76	Reggie Sanders	.15
77	Will Clark	.15
78	David Wells	.15
79	Paul Konerko	.25
80	Armando Benitez	.15
81	Brant Brown	.15
82	Mo Vaughn	.25
83	Jose Canseco	.50
84	Albert Belle	.15
85	Dean Palmer	.15
86	Greg Vaughn	.15
87	Mark Clark	.15
88	Pat Meares	.15
89	Eric Davis	.15
90	Brian Giles	.15
91	Jeff Brantley	.15
92	Bret Boone	.15
93	Ron Gant	.15
94	Mike Cameron	.15
95	Charles Johnson	.15
96	Denny Neagle	.15
97	Brian Hunter	.15
98	Jose Hernandez	.15
99	Rick Aguilera	.15
100	Tony Batista	.15
101	Roger Cedeno	.15
102	Creighton Gubanich	.15
103	Tim Belcher	.15
104	Bruce Aven	.15
105	Brian Daubach RC	.50
106	Ed Sprague	.15
107	Michael Tucker	.15
108	Homer Bush	.15
109	Armando Reynoso	.15
110	Brook Fordyce	.15
111	Matt Mantei	.15
112	Jose Guillen	.15
113	Kenny Rogers	.15
114	Livan Hernandez	.15
115	Butch Huskey	.15
116	David Segui	.15
117	Darryl Hamilton	.15
118	Jim Leyritz	.15
119	Randy Velarde	.15
120	Bill Taylor	.15
121	Kevin Appier	.15

Super Chrome

Using identical photos from Topps Chrome Baseball, Topps supersized 36 players to 4-1/8" x 5-3/4" card size. The cards are done on standard chromium technology. Each pack contains three oversized cards and sells for S.R.P. of $4.99. There also is a Refractor parallel set, which are seeded 1:12 packs.

		NM/M
Complete Set (36):		45.00
Common Player:		.50
Refractors:		2X
Inserted 1:12		
Pack (3):		4.50
Wax Box (12):		48.00
1	Roger Clemens	2.25
2	Andres Galarraga	.50
3	Manny Ramirez	1.50
4	Greg Maddux	2.00
5	Kerry Wood	.75
6	Travis Lee	.75
7	Nolan Ryan	4.50
8	Juan Gonzalez	.75
9	Vladimir Guerrero	1.50
10	Sammy Sosa	2.00
11	Mark McGwire	3.00
12	Javy Lopez	.50
13	Tony Gwynn	2.00
14	Derek Jeter	4.50
15	Albert Belle	.50
16	Pedro Martinez	1.50
17	Greg Vaughn	.50
18	Ken Griffey Jr.	2.50
19	Ben Grieve	.50
20	Vinny Castilla	.50
21	Moises Alou	.50
22	Barry Bonds	4.50
23	Nomar Garciaparra	2.00
24	Chipper Jones	2.00
25	Mike Piazza	2.50
26	Alex Rodriguez	3.00
27	Ivan Rodriguez	1.25
28	Frank Thomas	1.50
29	Larry Walker	.50
30	Troy Glaus	1.00
31	David Wells (Season Highlight)	.50
32	Roger Clemens (Season Highlight)	1.00
33	Kerry Wood (Season Highlight)	.50
34	Mark McGwire (Home Run Record)	3.00
35	Sammy Sosa (Home Run Parade)	2.00
36	World Series	.50

1999 Topps Gallery Pre-Production

Topps debuted its 1999 Gallery set with this trio of sample cards. Format is virtually identical to issued cards except for the use of a "PP" prefix to the card numbers on back.

		NM/M
Complete Set (3):		5.00
Common Player:		2.00
PP1	Scott Rolen	2.00
PP2	Andres Galarraga (Masters)	2.00
PP3	Brad Fullmer (Artisans)	2.00

1999 Topps Gallery

This 150-card base set features a white textured border surrounding the player image with the player's name, team name and Topps Gallery logo stamped in gold foil. The first 100 cards in the set portray veteran players while the next 50 cards are short-printed in three subsets: Masters, Artisans

TODD HELTON

and Apprentices. Card backs have a monthly batting or pitching record from the '98 season, a player photo and vital information.

		NM/M
Complete Set (150):		60.00
Common Player (1-100):		.10
Common Player (101-150):		.25
Player's Private Issue:		5X
PPI SP's:		3X
Production 250 Sets		
Pack (6):		3.00
Wax Box (24):		45.00
1	Mark McGwire	1.50
2	Jim Thome	.35
3	Bernie Williams	.10
4	Larry Walker	.10
5	Juan Gonzalez	.30
6	Ken Griffey Jr.	1.00
7	Raul Mondesi	.10
8	Sammy Sosa	.75
9	Greg Maddux	.75
10	Jeff Bagwell	.60
11	Vladimir Guerrero	.60
12	Scott Rolen	.25
13	Nomar Garciaparra	.75
14	Mike Piazza	1.00
15	Travis Lee	.15
16	Carlos Delgado	.35
17	Darin Erstad	.25
18	David Justice	.10
19	Cal Ripken Jr.	2.00
20	Derek Jeter	2.00
21	Tony Clark	.10
22	Barry Larkin	.10
23	Greg Vaughn	.10
24	Jeff Kent	.10
25	Wade Boggs	.75
26	Andres Galarraga	.10
27	Ken Caminiti	.10
28	Jason Kendall	.10
29	Todd Helton	.60
30	Chuck Knoblauch	.10
31	Roger Clemens	.85
32	Jeromy Burnitz	.10
33	Javy Lopez	.10
34	Roberto Alomar	.25
35	Eric Karros	.10
36	Ben Grieve	.10
37	Eric Davis	.10
38	Rondell White	.10
39	Dmitri Young	.10
40	Ivan Rodriguez	.50
41	Paul O'Neill	.10
42	Jeff Cirillo	.10
43	Kerry Wood	.30
44	Albert Belle	.10
45	Frank Thomas	.60
46	Manny Ramirez	.60
47	Tom Glavine	.25
48	Mo Vaughn	.10
49	Jose Cruz Jr.	.10
50	Sandy Alomar	.10
51	Edgar Martinez	.10
52	John Olerud	.10
53	Todd Walker	.10
54	Tim Salmon	.10
55	Derek Bell	.10
56	Matt Williams	.10
57	Alex Rodriguez	1.50
58	Rusty Greer	.10
59	Vinny Castilla	.10
60	Jason Giambi	.30
61	Mark Grace	.10
62	Jose Canseco	.40
63	Gary Sheffield	.40
64	Brad Fullmer	.10
65	Trevor Hoffman	.10
66	Mark Kotsay	.10
67	Mike Mussina	.25
68	Johnny Damon	.30
69	Tino Martinez	.10
70	Curt Schilling	.25
71	Jay Buhner	.10
72	Kenny Lofton	.10
73	Randy Johnson	.60
74	Kevin Brown	.10
75	Brian Jordan	.10
76	Craig Biggio	.10
77	Barry Bonds	2.00
78	Tony Gwynn	.75
79	Jim Edmonds	.10
80	Shawn Green	.35
81	Todd Hundley	.10
82	Cliff Floyd	.10
83	Jose Guillen	.10
84	Dante Bichette	.10

		NM/M
85	Moises Alou	.10
86	Chipper Jones	.75
87	Ray Lankford	.10
88	Fred McGriff	.10
89	Rod Beck	.10
90	Dean Palmer	.10
91	Pedro Martinez	.60
92	Andruw Jones	.60
93	Robin Ventura	.10
94	Ugueth Urbina	.10
95	Orlando Hernandez	.10
96	Sean Casey	.15
97	Denny Neagle	.10
98	Troy Glaus	.60
99	John Smoltz	.10
100	Al Leiter	.10
101	Ken Griffey Jr.	1.50
102	Frank Thomas	.75
103	Mark McGwire	2.00
104	Sammy Sosa	1.00
105	Chipper Jones	1.00
106	Alex Rodriguez	2.00
107	Nomar Garciaparra	.40
108	Juan Gonzalez	.40
109	Derek Jeter	3.00
110	Mike Piazza	1.50
111	Barry Bonds	3.00
112	Tony Gwynn	1.00
113	Cal Ripken Jr.	3.00
114	Greg Maddux	1.00
115	Roger Clemens	1.25
116	Brad Fullmer	.25
117	Kerry Wood	.50
118	Ben Grieve	.25
119	Todd Helton	.65
120	Kevin Millwood	.25
121	Sean Casey	.35
122	Vladimir Guerrero	.75
123	Travis Lee	.25
124	Troy Glaus	.65
125	Bartolo Colon	.25
126	Andruw Jones	.75
127	Scott Rolen	.25
128	Alfonso Soriano RC	4.00
129	Nick Johnson RC	1.00
130	Matt Belisle RC	.25
131	Jorge Toca RC	.25
132	Masao Kida RC	.25
133	Carlos Pena RC	1.50
134	Adrian Beltre	.40
135	Eric Chavez	.40
136	Carlos Beltran	.65
137	Alex Gonzalez	.25
138	Ryan Anderson	.25
139	Ruben Mateo	.25
140	Bruce Chen	.25
141	Pat Burrell RC	3.00
142	Michael Barrett	.25
143	Carlos Lee	.25
144	Mark Mulder RC	1.00
145	Choo Freeman RC	.50
146	Gabe Kapler	.25
147	Juan Encarnacion	.25
148	Jeremy Giambi	.25
149	Jason Tyner RC	.35
150	George Lombard	.25
		.10
Checklist Folder 1 (1:3 Packs)		.10
Checklist Folder 2 (1:3)		.10
Checklist Folder 3 (1:3)		.10
Checklist Folder 4 (1:12)		.25
Checklist Folder 5 (1:240)		1.50
Checklist Folder 6 (1:640)		3.00

Player's Private Issue

ANDRES GALARRAGA

This parallel to the 150 regular cards in 1999 Gallery is limited to 250 serially numbered cards of each. Stated odds of insertion were one per 17 packs.

	NM/M
Common Player:	1.00
Stars:	5X
SP's:	3X
Production 250 Sets	

Autograph Cards

Three of baseball's top young third basemen are featured in this autographed set. The insertion odds are 1:209.

	NM/M
Common Player:	10.00

ADRIAN BELTRE

Inserted 1:209

		NM/M
GA1	Troy Glaus	15.00
GA2	Adrian Beltre	10.00
GA3	Eric Chavez	10.00

Awards Gallery

KERRY WOOD
NL ROOKIE OF THE YEAR

This 10-card set features players who have earned the highest honors in baseball. Each insert commemorates the player's award by stamping his achievement on the bottom of the card front. Card fronts have silver borders surrounding the player's image. These are seeded 1:12 and card numbers have a "AG" prefix.

		NM/M
Complete Set (10):		12.50
Common Player:		.50
Inserted 1:12		
AG1	Kerry Wood	.75
AG2	Ben Grieve	.50
AG3	Roger Clemens	2.50
AG4	Tom Glavine	.75
AG5	Juan Gonzalez	.75
AG6	Sammy Sosa	3.00
AG7	Ken Griffey Jr.	3.00
AG8	Mark McGwire	4.00
AG9	Bernie Williams	.50
AG10	Larry Walker	.50

Exhibitions

ALEX RODRIGUEZ

This 20-card set is done on textured 24-point stock and features baseball's top stars. Exhibitions are seeded 1:48 packs.

		NM/M
Complete Set (20):		75.00
Common Player:		2.00
Inserted 1:48		
E1	Sammy Sosa	4.50
E2	Mark McGwire	7.50
E3	Greg Maddux	4.50
E4	Roger Clemens	5.00
E5	Ben Grieve	2.00
E6	Kerry Wood	2.25
E7	Ken Griffey Jr.	6.00
E8	Tony Gwynn	4.50
E9	Cal Ripken Jr.	10.00
E10	Frank Thomas	4.00
E11	Jeff Bagwell	4.00
E12	Derek Jeter	10.00
E13	Alex Rodriguez	7.50
E14	Nomar Garciaparra	4.50
E15	Manny Ramirez	4.00
E16	Vladimir Guerrero	4.00
E17	Darin Erstad	2.25
E18	Scott Rolen	3.00
E19	Mike Piazza	6.00
E20	Andres Galarraga	2.00

Gallery of Heroes

KEN GRIFFEY Jr.

This 10-card set is done on card stock that simulates medieval stained glass. Gallery of Heroes are found 1:24 packs.

		NM/M
Complete Set (10):		30.00
Common Player:		.75
Inserted 1:24		
GH1	Mark McGwire	6.00
GH2	Sammy Sosa	3.50
GH3	Ken Griffey Jr.	4.50
GH4	Mike Piazza	4.50
GH5	Derek Jeter	7.50
GH6	Nomar Garciaparra	4.50
GH7	Kerry Wood	1.50
GH8	Ben Grieve	.75
GH9	Chipper Jones	3.50
GH10	Alex Rodriguez	6.00

Heritage

JUAN GONZALEZ
outfielder — TEXAS RANGERS

Nineteen contemporary legends and Hall-of-Famer Hank Aaron are artistically depicted using the 1953 Topps design as a template. For a chance to bid on the original art used in the development of this insert set, collectors were able to enter the Topps Gallery Auction. Collectors could accumulate auction points found in Topps Gallery packs. Heritages are seeded 1:12 packs. A parallel called Heritage Proofs are also randomly inserted 1:48 packs and have a chrome styrene insert.

		NM/M
Complete Set (20):		100.00
Common Player:		2.50
Inserted 1:12		
Heritage Proofs:		1.5X
Inserted 1:48		
TH1	Hank Aaron	10.00
TH2	Ben Grieve	2.50
TH3	Nomar Garciaparra	7.50
TH4	Roger Clemens	8.50
TH5	Travis Lee	2.50
TH6	Tony Gwynn	7.50
TH7	Alex Rodriguez	12.50
TH8	Ken Griffey Jr.	10.00
TH9	Derek Jeter	15.00
TH10	Sammy Sosa	7.50
TH11	Scott Rolen	2.50
TH12	Chipper Jones	7.50
TH13	Cal Ripken Jr.	15.00
TH14	Kerry Wood	3.00
TH15	Barry Bonds	15.00
TH16	Juan Gonzalez	3.00
TH17	Mike Piazza	10.00
TH18	Greg Maddux	7.50
TH19	Frank Thomas	6.00
TH20	Mark McGwire	12.50

Heritage Proofs

Heritage Proofs are a parallel to the 1953-style inserts. Printed on chrome styrene, the proofs have a silver metallic background on front and notation on bottom-back, "1953

ALEX RODRIGUEZ
SEATTLE MARINERS

TOPPS HERITAGE PROOF." The proof versions are found on average of one per 48 packs.

		NM/M
Complete Set (20):		175.00
Common Player:		3.00
TH1	Hank Aaron	15.00
TH2	Ben Grieve	3.00
TH3	Nomar Garciaparra	10.00
TH4	Roger Clemens	11.50
TH5	Travis Lee	3.00
TH6	Tony Gwynn	10.00
TH7	Alex Rodriguez	15.00
TH8	Ken Griffey Jr.	12.50
TH9	Derek Jeter	20.00
TH10	Sammy Sosa	12.50
TH11	Scott Rolen	5.00
TH12	Chipper Jones	10.00
TH13	Cal Ripken Jr.	20.00
TH14	Kerry Wood	4.00
TH15	Barry Bonds	20.00
TH16	Juan Gonzalez	7.50
TH17	Mike Piazza	12.50
TH18	Greg Maddux	10.00
TH19	Frank Thomas	7.50
TH20	Mark McGwire	15.00

Heritage Lithographs

ROGER CLEMENS
NEW YORK YANKEES

Eight of the paintings used to create the Heritage inserts for 1999 Topps Gallery were reproduced as enlarged limited-edition offset lithographs. The paintings of Bill Purdom and James Fiorentino were reproduced in an 18" x 25" serially-numbered, artist-signed edition of 600 pieces each. The lithos were offered through Bill Goff Inc / Good Sports at $60 each unframed.

		NM/M
Complete Set (8):		480.00
Single Player:		60.00
(1)	Roger Clemens	60.00
(2)	Nomar Garciaparra	60.00
(3)	Ken Griffey Jr.	60.00
(4)	Derek Jeter	60.00
(5)	Mark McGwire	60.00
(6)	Mike Piazza	60.00
(7)	Cal Ripken Jr.	60.00
(8)	Sammy Sosa	60.00

Heritage Super Promos

Actually issued as a Topps handout at the 2000 National Sports Collectors Convention Corporate Block Party, this set depicts eight of the 1953 Topps-style cards which had been created for the Gallery Heritage insert series in 1999. The super-size (3-3/4" x 5-1/8") promos are printed on thin, glossy stock. Fronts have card-style artwork by Bill Goff or Bill Purdom. Backs are in black-and-white with player information and advertising by the artists, along with MLB and MLBPA licensor logos. The un-numbered cards are checklisted here alphabetically.

		NM/M
Complete Set (8):		40.00
Common Player:		4.00
(1)	Roger Clemens	4.50

(2)	Nomar Garciaparra	4.00
(3)	Ken Griffey Jr.	5.00
(4)	Derek Jeter	7.50
(5)	Mark McGwire	6.00
(6)	Mike Piazza	5.00
(7)	Cal Ripken Jr.	7.50
(8)	Sammy Sosa	4.00

Press Plates

The aluminum press plates used to print the Gallery cards were inserted at a rate of one per 985 packs. Each card's front and back can be found in four different color variations. Because of the unique nature of each plate, assignment of catalog values is not feasible.

	NM/M
Common Player:	25.00

1999 Topps Gold Label Pre-Production

This trio of pre-production samples previews Topps' 1999 version of its high-end Gold Label brand. Cards are nearly identical in format to the issued version except for the "PP" prefix to card numbers on back.

		NM/M
Complete Set (3):		3.00
Common Player:		1.00
PP1	Tom Glavine	1.00
PP2	Tino Martinez	1.00
PP3	Jim Thome	2.00

1999 Topps Gold Label Class 1

Pedro Martinez

This set consists of 100 cards on 35-point spectral-reflective rainbow stock with gold foil stamping. All cards are available in three versions each with the same foreground photo, but with different background photos that vary by category: Class 1 (fielding), Class 2 (running, 1:2), Class 3 (hitting, 1:4). In addition each variation has a different version of the player's team logo in the background. Variations for pitchers are Class 1, set position; Class 2, wind-up, and Class 3, throwing. Black Label par-

---

allels were inserted at the rate of between 1:8 and 1:12, depending on packaging. Red Label parallels, serially numbered to 100 each were inserted at rates from 1:118 to 1:148. A One to One parallel version also exists and is limited to one numbered card for each variation and color (Gold, Black and Red), for a total of 900 cards inserted about one per 1,500 packs.

		NM/M
Complete Set (100):		30.00
Common Gold Label:		.10
Common Black Label:		.50
Black Label Stars:		3X
Common Red Label:		2.00
Red Label Stars:		12X
Pack (5):		3.00
Wax Box (24):		50.00
1	Mike Piazza	2.00
2	Andres Galarraga	.10
3	Mark Grace	.10
4	Tony Clark	.10
5	Jim Thome	.60
6	Tony Gwynn	1.50
7	Kelly Dransfeldt RC	.15
8	Eric Chavez	.25
9	Brian Jordan	.10
10	Todd Hundley	.10
11	Rondell White	.10
12	Dmitri Young	.10
13	Jeff Kent	.10
14	Derek Bell	.10
15	Todd Helton	.75
16	Chipper Jones	1.50
17	Albert Belle	.10
18	Barry Larkin	.10
19	Dante Bichette	.10
20	Gary Sheffield	.50
21	Cliff Floyd	.10
22	Derek Jeter	3.00
23	Jason Giambi	.50
24	Ray Lankford	.10
25	Alex Rodriguez	2.50
26	Ruben Mateo	.10
27	Wade Boggs	1.50
28	Carlos Delgado	.45
29	Tim Salmon	.10
30	Alfonso Soriano RC	5.00
31	Javy Lopez	.10
32	Jason Kendall	.10
33	Nick Johnson RC	1.00
34	A.J. Burnett RC	1.00
35	Troy Glaus	.75
36	Pat Burrell RC	3.00
37	Jeff Cirillo	.10
38	David Justice	.10
39	Ivan Rodriguez	.75
40	Bernie Williams	.10
41	Jay Buhner	.10
42	Mo Vaughn	.10
43	Randy Johnson	1.00
44	Pedro Martinez	1.00
45	Larry Walker	.10
46	Todd Walker	.10
47	Roberto Alomar	.25
48	Kevin Brown	.10
49	Mike Mussina	.40
50	Tom Glavine	.25
51	Curt Schilling	.25
52	Ken Caminiti	.10
53	Brad Fullmer	.10
54	Bobby Seay RC	.10
55	Orlando Hernandez	.10
56	Sean Casey	.10
57	Al Leiter	.10
58	Sandy Alomar	.10
59	Mark Kotsay	.10
60	Matt Williams	.10
61	Raul Mondesi	.10
62	Joe Crede RC	5.00
63	Jim Edmonds	.10
64	Jose Cruz Jr.	.10
65	Juan Gonzalez	.50
66	Sammy Sosa	1.50
67	Cal Ripken Jr.	3.00
68	Vinny Castilla	.10
69	Craig Biggio	.10
70	Mark McGwire	2.50
71	Greg Vaughn	.10
72	Greg Maddux	1.50
73	Paul O'Neill	.10
74	Scott Rolen	.65
75	Ben Grieve	.10
76	Vladimir Guerrero	1.00
77	John Olerud	.10
78	Eric Karros	.10
79	Jeromy Burnitz	.10
80	Jeff Bagwell	1.00
81	Kenny Lofton	.10
82	Manny Ramirez	1.00
83	Andruw Jones	1.00
84	Travis Lee	.15
85	Darin Erstad	.25
86	Nomar Garciaparra	1.50
87	Frank Thomas	1.00
88	Moises Alou	.10
89	Tino Martinez	.10
90	Carlos Pena RC	1.50
91	Shawn Green	.40
92	Rusty Greer	.10
93	Matt Belisle RC	.25
94	Adrian Beltre	.25
95	Roger Clemens	1.75

96	John Smoltz	.10
97	Mark Mulder RC	1.00
98	Kerry Wood	.50
99	Barry Bonds	3.00
100	Ken Griffey Jr.	2.00
	Checklist folder	.05

Class 2

Joe Crede

Background photos for Class 2 Gold Label and color parallels show position players running and pitchers in their windup. Class 2 Gold Label cards are inserted at the rate of one in two Home Team Advantage packs, and one in four retail packs. Black Label versions are inserted 1:16 HTA and 1:24 R. Red Labels, numbered to 50 each, are found in HTA at a 1:237 rate, and in retail at 1:296.

	NM/M
Complete Set (100):	75.00
Common Gold Label:	.25
Gold Label Stars:	1.5X
Common Black Label:	2.00
Black Label Stars:	4X
Common Red Label:	6.00
Red Label Stars:	15X

Class 3

Pat Burrell

Background photos for Class 3 Gold Label and color parallels show position players hitting and pitchers pitching. Class 3 Gold Label cards are inserted at the rate of one in four Home Team Advantage packs, and one in eight retail packs. Black Label versions are inserted 1:32 HTA and 1:48 R. Red Labels, numbered to 25 each, are found in HTA at a 1:473 rate, and in retail at 1:591.

	NM/M
Complete Set (100):	125.00
Common Gold Label:	.50
Gold Label Stars: 2	
Common Black Label:	3.00
Black Label Stars:	6X
Common Red Label:	12.00
Red Label Stars:	35X

One to One

Nomar Garciaparra

Depending on type of packaging, these rare parallels are found at the rate of only one per approximately 1,200-1,600 packs. Each of the three Classes in Gold, Red and Black versions can be found as a One to One insert, for a total of nine "unique" cards for each player in the base set and three in the Race to Aaron insert series. Backs of the One to One cards are printed in silver foil with a "1/1" foil serial number.

	NM/M
Common Player, Base Set:	50.00
Common Player, Race to Aaron:	150.00

Race to Aaron

Vladimir Guerrero
Race to Aaron

This 10-card set features the best current players who are chasing Hank Aaron's career home run and career RBI records. Each player is pictured in the foreground with Aaron silhouetted in the background on the card front. These are seeded 1:12 packs. Two parallel versions also exist: Black and Red. Blacks have black foil stamping and are seeded 1:48 packs. Reds have red foil stamping and are limited to 44 sequentially numbered sets.

		NM/M
Complete Set (10):		20.00
Common Player:		1.00
Blacks:		2X
Reds:		12X
1	Mark McGwire	4.50
2	Ken Griffey Jr.	3.00
3	Alex Rodriguez	4.50
4	Vladimir Guerrero	1.50
5	Albert Belle	1.00
6	Nomar Garciaparra	2.50
7	Ken Griffey Jr.	3.00
8	Alex Rodriguez	4.50
9	Juan Gonzalez	1.00
10	Barry Bonds	7.50

Name Mismatches

David Justice

Because of faulty alignment when the gold-foil logo and player name were applied to card fronts, some Gold Label cards are found with the wrong name on front. Because each of these error cards is rare or possibly unique, and the demand is dependent on the combination of photo and name, it is not possible to assign values.

1999 Topps Opening Day

This retail exclusive product is comprised of 165 cards. Base cards have a silver border, and the Opening Day logo stamped with silver foil. Packs are pre-priced at $.99, each pack has seven cards. Hank Aaron autographs are randomly seeded and are stamped with the Topps "Certi-

---

Sandy Alomar

fied Autograph Issue" stamp. The insertion rate for the autograph is 1:29,642 packs.

		NM/M
Complete Set (165):		20.00
Common Player:		.10
Hank Aaron Autograph:		150.00
Pack (7):		1.50
Wax Box (24):		20.00
1	Hank Aaron	3.00
2a	Roger Clemens	1.25
2b	Andres Galarraga (Should be #3.)	.10
4	Scott Brosius	.10
5	Ray Durham	.10
6	Will Clark	.10
7	David Wells	.10
8	Jose Guillen	.10
9	Edgardo Alfonzo	.10
10	Manny Ramirez	.75
11	Greg Maddux	1.00
12	David Segui	.10
13	Darryl Strawberry	.10
14	Brad Radke	.10
15	Kerry Wood	.35
16	Paul Konerko	.30
17	Travis Lee	.25
18	Kenny Rogers	.10
19	Todd Walker	.10
20	John Olerud	.10
21	Nolan Ryan	2.00
22	Ray Lankford	.10
23	Bartolo Colon	.10
24	Brady Anderson	.10
25	Jorge Posada	.10
26	Justin Thompson	.10
27	Juan Gonzalez	.40
28	Chuck Knoblauch	.10
29	Todd Helton	.65
30	Gary Sheffield	.40
31	Rod Beck	.10
32	Garret Anderson	.10
33	Rondell White	.10
34	Vladimir Guerrero	.75
35	Eric Karros	.10
36	Mo Vaughn	.10
37	Sammy Sosa	1.00
38	Kenny Lofton	.10
39	Mark McGwire	2.00
40	Javy Lopez	.10
41	Damion Easley	.10
42	Andy Pettitte	.30
43	Tony Gwynn	1.00
44	Jay Bell	.10
45	Jose Canseco	.45
46	John Wetteland	.10
47	Mike Caruso	.10
48	Derek Jeter	3.00
49	Aaron Sele	.10
50	Jeff Cirillo	.10
51	Mark Kotsay	.10
52	Albert Belle	.10
53	Matt Lawton	.10
54	Pedro Martinez	.75
55	Greg Vaughn	.10
56	Neifi Perez	.10
57	Derek Bell	.10
58	Ken Griffey Jr.	1.50
59	David Cone	.10
60	Dean Palmer	.10
61	Trevor Hoffman	.10
62	Billy Wagner	.10
63	Shawn Green	.25
64	Ben Grieve	.10
65	Tom Goodwin	.10
66	Jaret Wright	.10
67	Dmitri Young	.10
68	Hideki Irabu	.10
69	Jeff Fassero	.10
70	Matt Williams	.10
71	Bret Saberhagen	.10
72	Chad Curtis	.10
73	Scott Rolen	.60
74	J.T. Snow Jr.	.10
75	Rusty Greer	.10
76	Jim Edmonds	.10
77	Ron Gant	.10
78	A.J. Hinch	.10
79	Shannon Stewart	.10
80	Brad Fullmer	.10
81	Walt Weiss	.10
82	Fred McGriff	.10
83	Darin Erstad	.25
84	Eric Young	.10
85	Livan Hernandez	.10
86	Jeff Bagwell	.75
87	Omar Vizquel	.10

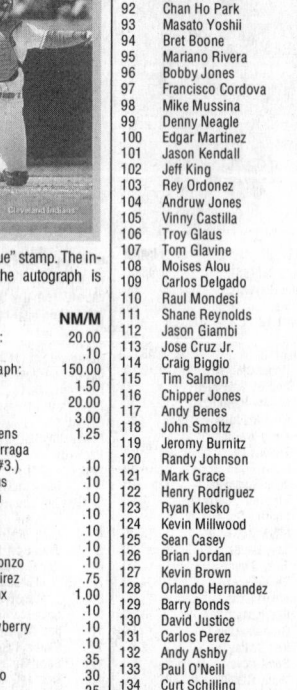

Sandy Alomar

88	Eric Davis	.10
89	Magglio Ordonez	.25
90	John Valentin	.10
91	Dave Dellucci	.10
92	Chan Ho Park	.10
93	Masato Yoshii	.10
94	Bret Boone	.10
95	Mariano Rivera	.20
96	Bobby Jones	.10
97	Francisco Cordova	.10
98	Mike Mussina	.40
99	Denny Neagle	.10
100	Edgar Martinez	.10
101	Jason Kendall	.10
102	Jeff King	.10
103	Rey Ordonez	.10
104	Andruw Jones	.75
105	Vinny Castilla	.10
106	Troy Glaus	.65
107	Tom Glavine	.40
108	Moises Alou	.10
109	Carlos Delgado	.40
110	Raul Mondesi	.10
111	Shane Reynolds	.10
112	Jason Giambi	.60
113	Jose Cruz Jr.	.10
114	Craig Biggio	.10
115	Tim Salmon	.10
116	Chipper Jones	1.00
117	Andy Benes	.10
118	John Smoltz	.10
119	Jeromy Burnitz	.10
120	Randy Johnson	.75
121	Mark Grace	.10
122	Henry Rodriguez	.10
123	Ryan Klesko	.10
124	Kevin Millwood	.10
125	Sean Casey	.20
126	Brian Jordan	.10
127	Kevin Brown	.10
128	Orlando Hernandez	.10
129	Barry Bonds	3.00
130	David Justice	.10
131	Carlos Perez	.10
132	Andy Ashby	.10
133	Paul O'Neill	.10
134	Curt Schilling	.40
135	Alex Rodriguez	2.00
136	Cliff Floyd	.10
137	Rafael Palmeiro	.60
138	Nomar Garciaparra	1.00
139	Mike Piazza	1.50
140	Roberto Alomar	.30
141	Todd Hundley	.10
142	Jeff Kent	.10
143	Barry Larkin	.10
144	Cal Ripken Jr.	3.00
145	Jay Buhner	.10
146	Kevin Young	.10
147	Ivan Rodriguez	.65
148	Al Leiter	.10
149	Sandy Alomar	.10
150	Bernie Williams	.10
151	Ellis Burks	.10
152	Wally Joyner	.10
153	Bobby Higginson	.10
154	Tony Clark	.10
155	Larry Walker	.10
156	Frank Thomas	.75
157	Tino Martinez	.10
158	Jim Thome	.60
159	Dante Bichette	.10
160	David Wells (Season Highlights)	.10
161	Roger Clemens (Season Highlights)	.50
162	Kerry Wood (Season Highlights)	.15
163	Mark McGwire (HR Record #70)	4.00
164	Sammy Sosa (HR Record #66)	1.50
165	Checklist	.10

1999 Topps Stars Pre-Production

Five-card cello packs of pre-production samples were distributed to introduce Topps' new concept for its Stars brand. The samples follow the format of the issued versions except for the use of a "PP" prefix to the card number on back.

	NM/M
Complete Set (5):	5.00
Common Player:	.75

PP1	Paul O'Neill (Base card.)	.75
PP2	Vinny Castilla (One-star.)	.75
PP3	Darin Erstad (Two-star.)	1.00
PP4	Kerry Wood (Three-star.)	1.50
PP5	Chipper Jones (Four-star.)	3.00

1999 Topps Stars

Topps Stars consists of 180 cards on 20-point stock with foil stamping and metallic inks. The set is comprised of 150 base cards and 30 subset cards: Luminaries and Supernovas. Packs contain six cards; three base cards, two One-Star and one Two-Star card on the average.

		NM/M
Complete Set (180):		20.00
Common Player:		.05
Pack (6):		1.50
Wax Box (24):		25.00
1	Ken Griffey Jr.	.75
2	Chipper Jones	.50
3	Mike Piazza	.75
4	Nomar Garciaparra	.50
5	Derek Jeter	1.50
6	Frank Thomas	.40
7	Ben Grieve	.05
8	Mark McGwire	1.00
9	Sammy Sosa	.50
10	Alex Rodriguez	1.00
11	Troy Glaus	.35
12	Eric Chavez	.25
13	Kerry Wood	.30
14	Barry Bonds	1.50
15	Vladimir Guerrero	.40
16	Albert Belle	.05
17	Juan Gonzalez	.20
18	Roger Clemens	.60
19	Ruben Mateo	.05
20	Cal Ripken Jr.	1.50
21	Darin Erstad	.25
22	Jeff Bagwell	.40
23	Roy Halladay	.10
24	Todd Helton	.35
25	Michael Barrett	.05
26	Manny Ramirez	.40
27	Fernando Seguignol	.05
28	Pat Burrell RC	2.00
29	Andruw Jones	.40
30	Randy Johnson	.40
31	Jose Canseco	.05
32	Brad Fullmer	.05
33	Alex Escobar RC	.25
34	Alfonso Soriano RC	3.00
35	Larry Walker	.05
36	Matt Clement	.05
37	Mo Vaughn	.05
38	Bruce Chen	.05
39	Travis Lee	.20
40	Adrian Beltre	.10
41	Alex Gonzalez	.05
42	Jason Tyner RC	.10
43	George Lombard	.05
44	Scott Rolen	.25
45	Mark Mulder RC	.50
46	Gabe Kapler	.05
47	Choo Freeman RC	.10
48	Tony Gwynn	.50
49	A.J. Burnett RC	.10
50	Matt Belisle RC	.10
51	Greg Maddux	.50
52	John Smoltz	.05
53	Mark Grace	.05
54	Wade Boggs	.05
55	Bernie Williams	.05
56	Pedro Martinez	.05
57	Barry Larkin	.05
58	Orlando Hernandez	.05
59	Jason Kendall	.05
60	Mark Kotsay	.05
61	Jim Thome	.35
62	Gary Sheffield	.30
63	Preston Wilson	.05
64	Rafael Palmeiro	.35
65	David Wells	.05
66	Shawn Green	.30
67	Tom Glavine	.25
68	Jeromy Burnitz	.05
69	Kevin Brown	.05
70	Rondell White	.05
71	Roberto Alomar	.25
72	Cliff Floyd	.05
73	Craig Biggio	.05
74	Greg Vaughn	.05
75	Ivan Rodriguez	.35

76	Vinny Castilla	.05
77	Todd Walker	.05
78	Paul Konerko	.15
79	Andy Brown RC	.05
80	Todd Hundley	.05
81	Dmitri Young	.05
82	Tony Clark	.05
83	Nick Johnson RC	.50
84	Mike Caruso	.05
85	David Ortiz	.35
86	Matt Williams	.05
87	Raul Mondesi	.05
88	Kenny Lofton	.05
89	Miguel Tejada	.10
90	Dante Bichette	.05
91	Jorge Posada	.05
92	Carlos Beltran	.25
93	Carlos Delgado	.30
94	Javy Lopez	.05
95	Aramis Ramirez	.05
96	Neifi Perez	.05
97	Marlon Anderson	.05
98	David Cone	.05
99	Moises Alou	.05
100	John Olerud	.05
101	Tim Salmon	.05
102	Jason Giambi	.30
103	Sandy Alomar	.05
104	Curt Schilling	.25
105	Andres Galarraga	.05
106	Rusty Greer	.05
107	Bobby Seay RC	.05
108	Eric Young	.05
109	Brian Jordan	.05
110	Eric Davis	.05
111	Will Clark	.05
112	Andy Ashby	.05
113	Edgardo Alfonzo	.05
114	Paul O'Neill	.05
115	Denny Neagle	.05
116	Eric Karros	.05
117	Ken Caminiti	.05
118	Garret Anderson	.05
119	Todd Stottlemyre	.05
120	David Justice	.05
121	Francisco Cordova	.05
122	Robin Ventura	.05
123	Mike Mussina	.25
124	Hideki Irabu	.05
125	Justin Thompson	.05
126	Mariano Rivera	.15
127	Delino DeShields	.05
128	Steve Finley	.05
129	Jose Cruz Jr.	.05
130	Ray Lankford	.05
131	Jim Edmonds	.05
132	Charles Johnson	.05
133	Al Leiter	.05
134	Jose Offerman	.05
135	Eric Milton	.05
136	Dean Palmer	.05
137	Johnny Damon	.25
138	Andy Pettitte	.20
139	Ray Durham	.05
140	Ugueth Urbina	.05
141	Marquis Grissom	.05
142	Ryan Klesko	.05
143	Brady Anderson	.05
144	Bobby Higginson	.05
145	Chuck Knoblauch	.05
146	Rickey Henderson	.40
147	Kevin Millwood	.05
148	Fred McGriff	.05
149	Damion Easley	.05
150	Tino Martinez	.05
151	Greg Maddux (Luminaries)	.30
152	Scott Rolen (Luminaries)	.20
153	Pat Burrell (Luminaries)	.75
154	Roger Clemens (Luminaries)	.35
155	Albert Belle (Luminaries)	.05
156	Troy Glaus (Luminaries)	.25
157	Cal Ripken Jr. (Luminaries)	.75
158	Alfonso Soriano (Luminaries)	.75
159	Manny Ramirez (Luminaries)	.25
160	Eric Chavez (Luminaries)	.10
161	Kerry Wood (Luminaries)	.20
162	Tony Gwynn (Luminaries)	.30
163	Barry Bonds (Luminaries)	.75
164	Ruben Mateo (Luminaries)	.05
165	Todd Helton (Luminaries)	.20
166	Darin Erstad (Luminaries)	.05
167	Jeff Bagwell (Luminaries)	.25
168	Juan Gonzalez (Luminaries)	.15
169	Mo Vaughn (Luminaries)	.05
170	Vladimir Guerrero (Luminaries)	.25
171	Nomar Garciaparra (Supernovas)	.35
172	Derek Jeter (Supernovas)	.75
173	Alex Rodriguez (Supernovas)	.50
174	Ben Grieve (Supernovas)	.05
175	Mike Piazza (Supernovas)	.40
176	Chipper Jones (Supernovas)	.50
177	Frank Thomas (Supernovas)	.25
178	Ken Griffey Jr. (Supernovas)	.40
179	Sammy Sosa (Supernovas)	.35

180	Mark McGwire (Supernovas)	.50
	Checklist 1 (1-45)	.05
	Checklist 2 (46-136)	.05
	Checklist 3 (137-150, inserts)	.05

Foil

MIGUEL TEJADA

Metallic foil in the background and a serial number on back from within a specific edition identifies this parallel. Stated odds of insertion were one in 15 packs for parallels of the 180 base cards, numbered to 299 each. One-Star foil parallels are numbered to 249 and inserted 1:33. The Two-Star Foils are numbered to 199 each and found on average of one per 82 packs. With insertion odds of 1:410, the Three-Star Foil parallels are numbered within an edition of 99. At the top of the scarcity scale, the Foil Four-Star parallels are sequentially numbered to 49 and are a one per 650-pack find.

	NM/M
Complete Base Set (180):	90.00
Common Foil Player:	.15
Foil Stars:	3X

One-Star

★ ALEX RODRIGUEZ

One-Star inserts include card numbers 1-100 from the base set and have silver foil stamping with one star on the bottom left portion of the card front. These are seeded two per pack. A foil One-Star parallel also is randomly seeded and sequentially numbered to 249 sets. These are a 1:33 pack insert.

		NM/M
Complete Set (100):		25.00
Common Player:		.10
Foils (249 Each):		2X
1	Ken Griffey Jr.	1.25
2	Chipper Jones	1.00
3	Mike Piazza	1.25
4	Nomar Garciaparra	1.00
5	Derek Jeter	2.00
6	Frank Thomas	.75
7	Ben Grieve	.10
8	Mark McGwire	1.50
9	Sammy Sosa	1.00
10	Alex Rodriguez	1.50
11	Troy Glaus	.65
12	Eric Chavez	.25
13	Kerry Wood	.35
14	Barry Bonds	2.00
15	Vladimir Guerrero	.75
16	Albert Belle	.10
17	Juan Gonzalez	.40
18	Roger Clemens	1.00
19	Ruben Mateo	.10
20	Cal Ripken Jr.	2.00
21	Darin Erstad	.30
22	Jeff Bagwell	.75
23	Roy Halladay	.20
24	Todd Helton	.65
25	Michael Barrett	.10
26	Manny Ramirez	.75
27	Fernando Seguignol	.10
28	Pat Burrell	1.00

29	Andruw Jones	.75
30	Randy Johnson	.75
31	Jose Canseco	.40
32	Brad Fullmer	.10
33	Alex Escobar	.25
34	Alfonso Soriano	1.00
35	Larry Walker	.10
36	Matt Clement	.25
37	Mo Vaughn	.10
38	Bruce Chen	.10
39	Travis Lee	.15
40	Adrian Beltre	.20
41	Alex Gonzalez	.10
42	Jason Tyner	.10
43	George Lombard	.10
44	Scott Rolen	.50
45	Mark Mulder	.50
46	Gabe Kapler	.10
47	Choo Freeman	.10
48	Tony Gwynn	1.00
49	A.J. Burnett	.15
50	Matt Belisle	.10
51	Greg Maddux	1.00
52	John Smoltz	.10
53	Mark Grace	.10
54	Wade Boggs	1.00
55	Bernie Williams	.10
56	Pedro Martinez	.75
57	Barry Larkin	.10
58	Orlando Hernandez	.10
59	Jason Kendall	.10
60	Mark Kotsay	.10
61	Jim Thome	.45
62	Gary Sheffield	.40
63	Preston Wilson	.10
64	Rafael Palmeiro	.60
65	David Wells	.10
66	Shawn Green	.30
67	Tom Glavine	.30
68	Jeromy Burnitz	.10
69	Kevin Brown	.10
70	Rondell White	.10
71	Roberto Alomar	.25
72	Cliff Floyd	.10
73	Craig Biggio	.10
74	Greg Vaughn	.10
75	Ivan Rodriguez	.60
76	Vinny Castilla	.10
77	Todd Walker	.10
78	Paul Konerko	.20
79	Andy Brown	.10
80	Todd Hundley	.10
81	Dmitri Young	.10
82	Tony Clark	.10
83	Nick Johnson	.50
84	Mike Caruso	.10
85	David Ortiz	.40
86	Matt Williams	.10
87	Raul Mondesi	.10
88	Kenny Lofton	.10
89	Miguel Tejada	.10
90	Dante Bichette	.10
91	Jorge Posada	.10
92	Carlos Beltran	.20
93	Carlos Delgado	.25
94	Javy Lopez	.10
95	Aramis Ramirez	.10
96	Neifi Perez	.10
97	Marlon Anderson	.10
98	David Cone	.10
99	Moises Alou	.10
100	John Olerud	.10

Two-Star

Two-Stars are inserted one per pack and feature light gold metallic inks and foil stamping. Two-Stars include card numbers 1-50 from the base set. A Two-Star foil parallel is also randomly seeded and limited to 199 sequentially numbered sets.

		NM/M
Complete Set (50):		50.00
Common Player:		.25
Foils:		3X
1	Ken Griffey Jr.	4.00
2	Chipper Jones	1.50
3	Mike Piazza	2.00
4	Nomar Garciaparra	1.50
5	Derek Jeter	3.00
6	Frank Thomas	1.00
7	Ben Grieve	.25
8	Mark McGwire	2.50
9	Sammy Sosa	1.50
10	Alex Rodriguez	2.50
11	Troy Glaus	.75

12	Eric Chavez	.30
13	Kerry Wood	.40
14	Barry Bonds	3.00
15	Vladimir Guerrero	1.00
16	Albert Belle	.25
17	Juan Gonzalez	.50
18	Roger Clemens	1.75
19	Ruben Mateo	.25
20	Cal Ripken Jr.	3.00
21	Darin Erstad	.75
22	Jeff Bagwell	1.00
23	Roy Halladay	.40
24	Todd Helton	.75
25	Michael Barrett	.25
26	Manny Ramirez	1.00
27	Fernando Seguignol	.25
28	Pat Burrell	1.50
29	Andruw Jones	1.00
30	Randy Johnson	1.00
31	Jose Canseco	.50
32	Brad Fullmer	.25
33	Alex Escobar	.25
34	Alfonso Soriano	1.00
35	Larry Walker	.25
36	Matt Clement	.30
37	Mo Vaughn	.25
38	Bruce Chen	.25
39	Travis Lee	.30
40	Adrian Beltre	.30
41	Alex Gonzalez	.25
42	Jason Tyner	.25
43	George Lombard	.25
44	Scott Rolen	.65
45	Mark Mulder	.45
46	Gabe Kapler	.25
47	Choo Freeman	.25
48	Tony Gwynn	1.50
49	A.J. Burnett	.30
50	Matt Belisle	.25

Three-Star

Three-Star inserts are a partial parallel from the base set including cards 1-20. Inserted 1:5 packs, these cards feature refractive silver foil stamping along with gold metallic inks. A Three-Star parallel also is randomly inserted featuring gold stamping and limited to 99 serial numbered sets, inserted one per 410 packs.

		NM/M
Complete Set (20):		30.00
Common Player:		.50
Foils:		4X
1	Ken Griffey Jr.	2.50
2	Chipper Jones	2.00
3	Mike Piazza	2.50
4	Nomar Garciaparra	2.00
5	Derek Jeter	4.00
6	Frank Thomas	1.50
7	Ben Grieve	.50
8	Mark McGwire	3.00
9	Sammy Sosa	2.00
10	Alex Rodriguez	3.00
11	Troy Glaus	1.25
12	Eric Chavez	.60
13	Kerry Wood	.75
14	Barry Bonds	4.00
15	Vladimir Guerrero	1.50
16	Albert Belle	.50
17	Juan Gonzalez	.75
18	Roger Clemens	2.25
19	Ruben Mateo	.50
20	Cal Ripken Jr.	4.00

Four-Star

Four-Star inserts include cards numbered 1-10 from the base set and are seeded 1:10 packs. The cards feature dark metallic inks and refractive foil stamping on front. A Four-Star parallel is also randomly seeded and has gold metallic inks. Sequentially numbered to 49, it is inserted at the rate of one per 650 packs.

		NM/M
Complete Set (10):		30.00
Common Player:		1.00
Foils:		2X
1	Ken Griffey Jr.	4.00
2	Chipper Jones	3.00
3	Mike Piazza	4.00
4	Nomar Garciaparra	3.00
5	Derek Jeter	6.00

6	Frank Thomas	2.50
7	Ben Grieve	1.00
8	Mark McGwire	5.00
9	Sammy Sosa	3.00
10	Alex Rodriguez	5.00

Bright Futures

This 10-card set features top prospects with a brilliant future ahead of them. Each card features foil stamping and is sequentially numbered to 1,999. Cards have a "BF" prefix to the number. A metallized foil parallel version is also randomly seeded (1:2,702) and limited to 30 numbered sets.

		NM/M
Complete Set (10):		20.00
Common Player:		1.50
Production 1,999 Sets		
Foil (30 Each):		8X
1	Troy Glaus	3.00
2	Eric Chavez	2.00
3	Adrian Beltre	2.00
4	Michael Barrett	1.50
5	Fernando Seguignol	1.50
6	Alex Gonzalez	1.50
7	Matt Clement	1.50
8	Pat Burrell	6.00
9	Ruben Mateo	1.50
10	Alfonso Soriano	6.00

Galaxy

Mark McGwire

This 10-card set highlights the top players in baseball with foil stamping and limited to 1,999 numbered sets, inserted at the rate of one per 41 packs. Each card is numbered on the back with a "G" prefix. A Galaxy foil parallel version is randomly seeded (1:2,702) and sequentially numbered to 30 sets.

		NM/M
Complete Set (10):		25.00
Common Player:		1.00
Production 1,999 Sets		
Foil (30 Each):		8X
1	Mark McGwire	5.00
2	Roger Clemens	3.00
3	Nomar Garciaparra	4.00
4	Alex Rodriguez	5.00
5	Kerry Wood	1.50
6	Ben Grieve	1.00
7	Derek Jeter	6.00
8	Vladimir Guerrero	2.50
9	Ken Griffey Jr.	4.00
10	Sammy Sosa	3.00

Rookie Reprints

Topps reprinted five Hall of Famers' rookie cards. The rookie reprints are inserted 1:65 packs and limited to 2,500 numbered sets.

		NM/M
Complete Set (5):		10.00
Common Player:		2.00
Production 2,500 Sets		
1	Frank Robinson	2.00
2	Ernie Banks	3.00

bob gibson

Robert Gibson

ST. LOUIS CARDINALS
PITCHER

3	Yogi Berra	3.00
4	Bob Gibson	2.00
5	Tom Seaver	2.00

Rookie Reprints Autographs

These foil stamped inserts feature the "Topps Certified Autograph Issue" stamp and are inserted 1:406 packs. The Ernie Banks autograph is inserted 1:812 packs.

		NM/M
Complete Set (5):		150.00
Common Player:		20.00
Inserted 1:406		
Banks Inserted 1:812		
1	Frank Robinson	25.00
2	Ernie Banks	70.00
3	Yogi Berra	35.00
4	Bob Gibson	20.00
5	Tom Seaver	65.00

1999 Topps Stars 'N Steel

Using Serilusion technology, each borderless card features a four-colored textured film laminate bonded to a sheet of strong 25-gauge metal. Each pack contains three cards, packaged in a stand-up tri-fold display unit, at an S.R.P. of $9.99. There are two parallels to the 44-card set, Gold and Domed Holographics. Golds are seeded 1:12 packs, Holographics are found every 24 packs.

		NM/M
Complete Set (44):		65.00
Common Player:		1.50
Gold:		4X
Inserted 1:12		
Holographic Dome:		6X
Inserted 1:24		
Pack (3):		4.00
Wax Box (12):		40.00
1	Kerry Wood	1.00
2	Ben Grieve	.50
3	Chipper Jones	3.00
4	Alex Rodriguez	5.00
5	Mo Vaughn	.50
6	Bernie Williams	.50
7	Juan Gonzalez	1.00
8	Vinny Castilla	.50
9	Tony Gwynn	3.00
10	Manny Ramirez	2.00
11	Raul Mondesi	.50
12	Roger Clemens	3.50
13	Darin Erstad	.50
14	Barry Bonds	6.00
15	Cal Ripken Jr.	6.00
16	Barry Larkin	.50
17	Scott Rolen	1.00
18	Albert Belle	.50
19	Craig Biggio	.50
20	Tony Clark	.50
21	Mark McGwire	5.00

22	Andres Galarraga	.50
23	Kenny Lofton	.50
24	Pedro Martinez	2.00
25	Paul O'Neill	.50
26	Ken Griffey Jr.	4.00
27	Travis Lee	75.00
28	Tim Salmon	.50
29	Frank Thomas	2.00
30	Larry Walker	.50
31	Moises Alou	.50
32	Vladimir Guerrero	2.00
33	Ivan Rodriguez	1.50
34	Derek Jeter	6.00
35	Greg Vaughn	.50
36	Gary Sheffield	1.00
37	Carlos Delgado	1.00
38	Greg Maddux	3.00
39	Sammy Sosa	3.00
40	Mike Piazza	4.00
41	Nomar Garciaparra	3.00
42	Dante Bichette	.50
43	Jeff Bagwell	2.00
44	Jim Thome	1.50

'N Steel Gold Domed Holographics

NOMAR GARCIAPARRA

This parallel edition was inserted at a rate of one per box. Cards are basically the same as the regular-issue, except for the use of holographic foil highlights on front and the presence of a thick plastic dome which covers the front.

		NM/M
Complete Set (44):		600.00
Common Player:		6.00
Stars:		8X

1999 Topps TEK Pre-Production

The second edition of Topps TEK was introduced with this trio of star cards. The preview cards are virtually identical in format to the issued version, except for the use of "PP" prefixes to card numbers on back.

		NM/M
Complete Set (3):		5.00
Common Player:		1.00
PP1A	Derek Jeter	4.00
PP2A	Moises Alou	1.00
PP3A	Tony Clark	1.00

1999 Topps TEK

Pat Burrell

Topps TEK baseball contains 45 players, with all cards printed on a transparent, 27-point stock. Each player is featured in two different versions (A & B), which are noted on the card back. The versions are differentiated by type of player uniform (home is version A and away uniforms are version B). Each version also has 30 different baseball focused background patterns; as a result every player in the 45-card set has 60 total cards. There also is a Gold parallel set that has a gold design and all versions are paralleled. Each gold card is numbered to 10, with an insertion rate of 1:15 packs.

		NM/M
Complete Set (45):		30.00
Common Player:		.25
Common Gold		
(10 Each Variation):		2.00
Gold Stars:		10X
Pack (4):		3.00
Wax Box (20):		45.00
1	Ben Grieve	.25
2	Andres Galarraga	.25
3	Travis Lee	.35
4	Larry Walker	.25
5	Ken Griffey Jr.	2.50
6	Sammy Sosa	2.00
7	Mark McGwire	3.00
8	Roberto Alomar	.40
9	Wade Boggs	2.00
10	Troy Glaus	.75
11	Craig Biggio	.25
12	Kerry Wood	.50
13	Vladimir Guerrero	1.00
14	Albert Belle	.25
15	Mike Piazza	2.50
16	Chipper Jones	2.00
17	Randy Johnson	1.00
18	Adrian Beltre	.45
19	Barry Bonds	4.00
20	Jim Thome	.65
21	Greg Vaughn	.25
22	Scott Rolen	.65
23	Ivan Rodriguez	.75
24	Derek Jeter	4.00
25	Cal Ripken Jr.	4.00
26	Mark Grace	.25
27	Bernie Williams	.25
28	Darin Erstad	.75
29	Eric Chavez	.35
30	Tom Glavine	.50
31	Jeff Bagwell	1.00
32	Manny Ramirez	1.00
33	Tino Martinez	.25
34	Todd Helton	.75
35	Jason Kendall	.25
36	Pat Burrell RC	2.50
37	Tony Gwynn	2.00
38	Nomar Garciaparra	2.00
39	Frank Thomas	1.00
40	Orlando Hernandez	.25
41	Juan Gonzalez	.50
42	Alex Rodriguez	3.00
43	Greg Maddux	2.00
44	Mo Vaughn	.25
45	Roger Clemens	2.25
	Version A Checklist Folder (Orange)	.05
	Version B Checklist Folder (Green)	.05

Gold

Travis Lee

Each of the two player versions on each of the 30 background patterns was paralleled in a gold insert version. Cards share the same front and back designs and photos but feature gold graphics. Each card is serially numbered within an edition of just 10. Insertion rate is one per 15 packs.

		NM/M
Common Gold:		2.00
Gold Stars:		10X

Fantastek Phenoms

This 10-card set highlights top young prospects on a transparent plastic stock with silver and

FANTASTEK PHENOMS

Eric Chavez

blue highlighting. These are inserted 1:18 packs.

		NM/M
Complete Set (10):		15.00
Common Player:		.75
Inserted 1:18		
F1	Eric Chavez	1.50
F2	Troy Glaus	4.00
F3	Pat Burrell	4.00
F4	Alex Gonzalez	.75
F5	Carlos Lee	1.00
F6	Ruben Mateo	.75
F7	Carlos Beltran	2.00
F8	Adrian Beltre	1.50
F9	Bruce Chen	.75
F10	Ryan Anderson	.75

Teknicians

Mark McGwire

This 10-card set focuses on baseball's top stars on a clear, plastic stock utilizing metallic blue, silver and red inks. These are inserted 1:18 packs.

		NM/M
Complete Set (10):		24.00
Common Player:		1.00
Inserted 1:18		
T1	Ken Griffey Jr.	3.00
T2	Mark McGwire	4.00
T3	Kerry Wood	1.00
T4	Ben Grieve	1.00
T5	Sammy Sosa	2.50
T6	Derek Jeter	6.00
T7	Alex Rodriguez	4.00
T8	Roger Clemens	2.50
T9	Nomar Garciaparra	2.50
T10	Vladimir Guerrero	1.50

2000 Topps Pre-Production

Though carrying a "PP" prefix as previous years' pre-production samples, this three-card issue was not distributed until July-August at the National and SportsFest conventions. The three-card cello packs contain cards which differ from the regular issued versions only in their numbers and the fact that they have white borders, rather than the pewter borders found on regular-issue cards.

		NM/M
Complete Set (3):		5.00
Common Player:		2.00
PP1	Brady Anderson	2.00
PP2	Jason Kendall	2.00
PP3	Ryan Klesko	2.00

2000 Topps

Released in two series the card fronts have a silver border with the Topps logo, player name and position stamped with gold foil. Card backs have complete year-by-year statistics along with a small photo in the upper right portion and the player's vital information. Subsets within the first series 239-card set include Draft Picks, Prospects, Magic Moments, Season Highlights and 20th Century's Best. The Topps MVP promotion is a parallel

JEFF BAGWELL

of 200 of the base cards, excluding subsets, with a special Topps MVP logo. 100 cards of each player was produced and if the featured player is named MVP for a week, collectors win a prize.

		NM/M
Complete Set (478):		50.00
Complete Series I Set (239):		25.00
Complete Series II Set (239):		25.00
Common Player:		.10
MVP Stars:		20-40X
Yng Stars & RC's:		10-20X
Production 100 Sets		
5 Versions for 236-240, 475-479		
Pack (11):		1.00
Wax Box (36):		30.00
1	Mark McGwire	1.00
2	Tony Gwynn	.75
3	Wade Boggs	.75
4	Cal Ripken Jr.	1.50
5	Matt Williams	.10
6	Jay Buhner	.10
7	Jeff Conine	.10
8	Todd Greene	.10
9	Mike Lieberthal	.10
10	Steve Avery	.10
11	Bret Saberhagen	.10
12	Magglio Ordonez	.20
13	Brad Radke	.10
14	Derek Jeter	1.50
15	Javy Lopez	.10
16	Russ David	.10
17	Armando Benitez	.10
18	B.J. Surhoff	.10
19	Darryl Kile	.10
20	Mark Lewis	.10
21	Mike Williams	.10
22	Mark McLemore	.10
23	Sterling Hitchcock	.10
24	Darin Erstad	.20
25	Ricky Gutierrez	.10
26	John Jaha	.10
27	Homer Bush	.10
28	Darrin Fletcher	.10
29	Mark Grace	.10
30	Fred McGriff	.10
31	Omar Daal	.10
32	Eric Karros	.10
33	Orlando Cabrera	.15
34	J.T. Snow Jr.	.10
35	Luis Castillo	.10
36	Rey Ordonez	.10
37	Bob Abreu	.20
38	Warren Morris	.10
39	Juan Gonzalez	.20
40	Mike Lansing	.10
41	Chili Davis	.10
42	Dean Palmer	.10
43	Hank Aaron	1.00
44	Jeff Bagwell	.60
45	Jose Valentin	.10
46	Shannon Stewart	.10
47	Kent Bottenfield	.10
48	Jeff Shaw	.10
49	Sammy Sosa	.75
50	Randy Johnson	.60
51	Benny Agbayani	.10
52	Dante Bichette	.10
53	Pete Harnisch	.10
54	Frank Thomas	.60
55	Jorge Posada	.10
56	Todd Walker	.10
57	Juan Encarnacion	.15
58	Mike Sweeney	.10
59	Pedro Martinez	.60
60	Lee Stevens	.10
61	Brian Giles	.10
62	Chad Ogea	.10
63	Ivan Rodriguez	.50
64	Roger Cedeno	.10
65	David Justice	.10
66	Steve Trachsel	.10
67	Eli Marrero	.10
68	Dave Nilsson	.10
69	Ken Caminiti	.10
70	Tim Raines	.10
71	Brian Jordan	.10
72	Jeff Blauser	.10
73	Bernard Gilkey	.10
74	John Flaherty	.10
75	Brent Mayne	.10
76	Jose Vidro	.10
77	Jeff Fassero	.10
78	Bruce Aven	.10
79	John Olerud	.10
80	Pokey Reese	.10

82	Woody Williams	.10
83	Ed Sprague	.10
84	Joe Girardi	.10
85	Barry Larkin	.10
86	Mike Caruso	.10
87	Bobby Higginson	.10
88	Roberto Kelly	.10
89	Edgar Martinez	.10
90	Mark Kotsay	.10
91	Paul Sorrento	.10
92	Eric Young	.10
93	Carlos Delgado	.40
94	Troy Glaus	.50
95	Ben Grieve	.10
96	Jose Lima	.10
97	Garret Anderson	.10
98	Luis Gonzalez	.10
99	Carl Pavano	.10
100	Alex Rodriguez	1.25
101	Preston Wilson	.10
102	Ron Gant	.10
103	Harold Baines	.10
104	Rickey Henderson	.60
105	Gary Sheffield	.40
106	Mickey Morandini	.10
107	Jim Edmonds	.10
108	Kris Benson	.10
109	Adrian Beltre	.20
110	Alex Fernandez	.10
111	Dan Wilson	.10
112	Mark Clark	.10
113	Greg Vaughn	.10
114	Neifi Perez	.10
115	Paul O'Neill	.10
116	Jermaine Dye	.10
117	Todd Jones	.10
118	Terry Steinbach	.10
119	Greg Norton	.10
120	Curt Schilling	.25
121	Todd Zeile	.10
122	Edgardo Alfonzo	.10
123	Ryan McGuire	.10
124	Stan Javier	.10
125	John Smoltz	.10
126	Bob Wickman	.10
127	Richard Hidalgo	.10
128	Chuck Finley	.10
129	Billy Wagner	.10
130	Todd Hundley	.10
131	Dwight Gooden	.10
132	Russ Ortiz	.10
133	Mike Lowell	.10
134	Reggie Sanders	.10
135	John Valentin	.10
136	Brad Ausmus	.10
137	Chad Kreuter	.10
138	David Cone	.10
139	Brook Fordyce	.10
140	Roberto Alomar	.25
141	Charles Nagy	.10
142	Brian Hunter	.10
143	Mike Mussina	.30
144	Robin Ventura	.10
145	Kevin Brown	.10
146	Pat Hentgen	.10
147	Ryan Klesko	.10
148	Derek Bell	.10
149	Andy Sheets	.10
150	Larry Walker	.10
151	Scott Williamson	.10
152	Jose Offerman	.10
153	Doug Mientkiewicz	.10
154	John Snyder RC	.10
155	Sandy Alomar	.10
156	Joe Nathan	.10
157	Lance Johnson	.10
158	Odalis Perez	.10
159	Hideo Nomo	.25
160	Steve Finley	.10
161	Dave Martinez	.10
162	Matt Walbeck	.10
163	Bill Spiers	.10
164	Fernando Tatis	.10
165	Kenny Lofton	.10
166	Paul Byrd	.10
167	Aaron Sele	.10
168	Eddie Taubensee	.10
169	Reggie Jefferson	.10
170	Roger Clemens	.85
171	Francisco Cordova	.10
172	Mike Bordick	.10
173	Wally Joyner	.10
174	Marvin Benard	.10
175	Jason Kendall	.10
176	Mike Stanley	.10
177	Chad Allen	.10
178	Carlos Beltran	.25
179	Deivi Cruz	.10
180	Chipper Jones	.75
181	Vladimir Guerrero	.60
182	Dave Burba	.10
183	Tom Goodwin	.10
184	Brian Daubach	.10
185	Jay Bell	.10
186	Roy Halladay	.25
187	Miguel Tejada	.25
188	Armando Rios	.10
189	Fernando Vina	.10
190	Eric Davis	.10
191	Henry Rodriguez	.10
192	Joe McEwing	.10
193	Jeff Kent	.10
194	Mike Jackson	.10
195	Mike Morgan	.10
196	Jeff Montgomery	.10
197	Jeff Zimmerman	.10
198	Tony Fernandez	.10
199	Jason Giambi	.40

No.	Player	NM/M
200	Jose Canseco	.40
201	Alex Gonzalez	.10
202	Jack Cust, Mike Colangelo, Dee Brown	.10
203	Felipe Lopez, Alfonso Soriano, Pablo Ozuna	.75
204	Erubiel Durazo, Pat Burrell, Nick Johnson	.25
205	John Sneed RC, Kip Wells, Matt Blank	.10
206	Josh Kalinowski RC, Michael Tejera RC, Chris Mears	.10
207	Roosevelt Brown, Corey Patterson, Lance Berkman	.25
208	Kit Pellow, Kevin Barker, Russ Branyan	.10
209	B.J. Garbe RC, Larry Bigbie RC	.25
210	Eric Munson, Bobby Bradley RC	.25
211	Josh Girdley, Kyle Snyder	.10
212	Chance Caple RC, Jason Jennings	.25
213	Ryan Christiansen RC, Brett Myers RC	.75
214	Jason Stumm RC, Rob Purvis RC	.25
215	David Walling, Mike Paradis	.10
216	Omar Ortiz, Jay Gehrke	.10
217	David Cone (Season Highlights)	.10
218	Jose Jimenez (Season Highlights)	.10
219	Chris Singleton (Season Highlights)	.10
220	Fernando Tatis (Season Highlights)	.10
221	Todd Helton (Season Highlights)	.20
222	Kevin Millwood (Post-Season Highlights)	.15
223	Todd Pratt (Post-Season Highlights)	.10
224	Orlando Hernandez (Post-Season Highlights)	.20
225	(Post-Season Highlights)	.10
226	(Post-Season Highlights)	.10
227	Bernie Williams (Post-Season Highlights)	.25
228	Mariano Rivera (Post-Season Highlights)	.20
229	Tony Gwynn (20th Century's Best)	.50
230	Wade Boggs (20th Century's Best)	.25
231	Tim Raines (20th Century's Best)	.10
232	Mark McGwire (20th Century's Best)	2.00
233	Rickey Henderson (20th Century's Best)	.25
234	Rickey Henderson (20th Century's Best)	.25
235	Roger Clemens (20th Century's Best)	1.50
236	Mark McGwire (Magic Moments)	2.00
237	Hank Aaron (Magic Moments)	2.00
238	Cal Ripken Jr. (Magic Moments)	3.00
239	Wade Boggs (Magic Moments)	.75
240	Tony Gwynn (Magic Moments)	1.00
	Series 1 checklist (1-201)	.05
	Series 1 checklist (202-240, inserts)	.05
241	Tom Glavine	.25
242	David Wells	.10
243	Kevin Appier	.10
244	Troy Percival	.10
245	Ray Lankford	.10
246	Marquis Grissom	.10
247	Randy Winn	.10
248	Miguel Batista	.10
249	Darren Dreifort	.10
250	Barry Bonds	1.50
251	Harold Baines	.10
252	Cliff Floyd	.10
253	Freddy Garcia	.10
254	Kenny Rogers	.10
255	Ben Davis	.10
256	Charles Johnson	.10
257	John Burkett	.10
258	Desi Relaford	.10
259	Al Martin	.10
260	Andy Pettitte	.20
261	Carlos Lee	.10
262	Matt Lawton	.10
263	Andy Fox	.10
264	Chan Ho Park	.10
265	Billy Koch	.10
266	Dave Roberts	.10
267	Carl Everett	.10
268	Orel Hershiser	.10
269	Trot Nixon	.10
270	Rusty Greer	.10
271	Will Clark	.10
272	Quilvio Veras	.10
273	Rico Brogna	.10
274	Devon White	.10
275	Tim Hudson	.25
276	Mike Hampton	.10
277	Miguel Cairo	.10
278	Darren Oliver	.10
279	Jeff Cirillo	.10
280	Al Leiter	.10
281	Brant Brown	.10
282	Carlos Febles	.10
283	Pedro Astacio	.10
284	Juan Guzman	.10
285	Orlando Hernandez	.20
286	Paul Konerko	.15
287	Tony Clark	.10
288	Aaron Boone	.10
289	Ismael Valdes	.10
290	Moises Alou	.10
291	Kevin Tapani	.10
292	John Franco	.10
293	Todd Zeile	.10
294	Jason Schmidt	.15
295	Johnny Damon	.25
296	Scott Brosius	.10
297	Travis Fryman	.10
298	Jose Vizcaino	.10
299	Eric Chavez	.20
300	Mike Piazza	1.00
301	Matt Clement	.10
302	Cristian Guzman	.10
303	Darryl Strawberry	.10
304	Jeff Abbott	.10
305	Brett Tomko	.10
306	Mike Lansing	.10
307	Eric Owens	.10
308	Livan Hernandez	.10
309	Rondell White	.10
310	Todd Stottlemyre	.10
311	Chris Carpenter	.10
312	Ken Hill	.10
313	Mark Loretta	.10
314	John Rocker	.10
315	Richie Sexson	.25
316	Ruben Mateo	.10
317	Joe Randa	.10
318	Mike Sirotka	.10
319	Jose Rosado	.10
320	Matt Mantei	.10
321	Kevin Millwood	.10
322	Gary DiSarcina	.10
323	Dustin Hermanson	.10
324	Mike Stanton	.10
325	Kirk Rueter	.10
326	Damian Miller	.10
327	Doug Glanville	.10
328	Scott Rolen	.50
329	Ray Durham	.10
330	Butch Huskey	.10
331	Mariano Rivera	.20
332	Darren Lewis	.10
333	Ramiro Mendoza	.10
334	Mark Grudzielanek	.10
335	Mike Cameron	.10
336	Kelvim Escobar	.10
337	Bret Boone	.10
338	Mo Vaughn	.10
339	Craig Biggio	.10
340	Michael Barrett	.10
341	Marlon Anderson	.10
342	Bobby Jones	.10
343	John Halama	.10
344	Todd Ritchie	.10
345	Chuck Knoblauch	.10
346	Rick Reed	.10
347	Kelly Stinnett	.10
348	Tim Salmon	.10
349	A.J. Hinch	.10
350	Jose Cruz Jr.	.10
351	Roberto Hernandez	.10
352	Edgar Renteria	.10
353	Jose Hernandez	.10
354	Brad Fullmer	.10
355	Trevor Hoffman	.10
356	Troy O'Leary	.10
357	Justin Thompson	.10
358	Kevin Young	.10
359	Hideki Irabu	.10
360	Jim Thome	.50
361	Todd Dunwoody	.10
362	Octavio Dotel	.10
363	Omar Vizquel	.10
364	Raul Mondesi	.10
365	Shane Reynolds	.10
366	Bartolo Colon	.10
367	Chris Widger	.10
368	Gabe Kapler	.10
369	Bill Simas	.10
370	Tino Martinez	.10
371	John Thomson	.10
372	Delino DeShields	.10
373	Carlos Perez	.10
374	Eddie Perez	.10
375	Jeromy Burnitz	.10
376	Jimmy Haynes	.10
377	Travis Lee	.10
378	Darryl Hamilton	.10
379	Jamie Moyer	.10
380	Alex Gonzalez	.10
381	John Wetteland	.10
382	Vinny Castilla	.10
383	Jeff Suppan	.10
384	Chad Curtis	.10
385	Robb Nen	.10
386	Wilson Alvarez	.10
387	Andres Galarraga	.25
388	Mike Remlinger	.10
389	Geoff Jenkins	.10
390	Matt Stairs	.10
391	Bill Mueller	.10
392	Mike Lowell	.10
393	Andy Ashby	.10
394	Ruben Rivera	.10
395	Todd Helton	.50
396	Bernie Williams	.10
397	Royce Clayton	.10
398	Manny Ramirez	.60
399	Kerry Wood	.25
400	Ken Griffey Jr.	.75
401	Enrique Wilson	.10
402	Joey Hamilton	.10
403	Shawn Estes	.10
404	Ugueth Urbina	.10
405	Albert Belle	.10
406	Rick Helling	.10
407	Steve Parris	.10
408	Eric Milton	.10
409	Dave Mlicki	.10
410	Shawn Green	.25
411	Jaret Wright	.10
412	Tony Womack	.10
413	Vernon Wells	.15
414	Ron Belliard	.10
415	Ellis Burks	.10
416	Scott Erickson	.10
417	Rafael Palmeiro	.35
418	Damion Easley	.10
419	Jamey Wright	.10
420	Corey Koskie	.10
421	Bobby Howry	.10
422	Ricky Ledee	.10
423	Dmitri Young	.10
424	Sidney Ponson	.10
425	Greg Maddux	.75
426	Jose Guillen	.10
427	Jon Lieber	.10
428	Andy Benes	.10
429	Randy Velarde	.10
430	Sean Casey	.20
431	Torii Hunter	.10
432	Ryan Rupe	.10
433	David Segui	.10
434	Rich Aurilia	.10
435	Nomar Garciaparra	.75
436	Denny Neagle	.10
437	Ron Coomer	.10
438	Chris Singleton	.10
439	Tony Batista	.10
440	Andruw Jones	.60
441	Adam Piatt, Aubrey Huff, Sean Burroughs (Prospects)	.40
442	Rafael Furcal, Jason Dallero, Travis Dawkins (Prospects)	.10
443	Wilton Veras, Joe Crede, Mike Lamb RC (Prospects)	.10
444	Julio Zuleta RC, Dernell Stenson, Jorge Toca (Prospects)	.20
445	Tim Raines Jr., Gary Mathews Jr., Garry Maddox Jr. RC (Prospects)	.20
446	Matt Riley, Mark Mulder, C.C. Sabathia (Prospects)	.25
447	Scott Downs RC, Chris George, Matt Belisle (Prospects)	.10
448	Doug Mirabelli, Ben Petrick, Jayson Werth (Prospects)	.10
449	Josh Hamilton, Corey Myers RC (Draft Picks)	.50
450	Ben Christensen RC, Brett Myers (Draft Picks)	.20
451	Barry Zito RC, Ben Sheets RC (Draft Picks)	2.00
452	Ty Howington RC, Kurt Ainsworth RC (Draft Picks)	.25
453	Rick Asadoorian RC, Vince Faison RC (Draft Picks)	.25
454	Keith Reed RC, Jeff Heaverlo RC (Draft Picks)	.20
455	Mike MacDougal RC, Jay Gehrke (Draft Picks)	.25
456	Mark McGwire (Season Highlights)	.75
457	Cal Ripken Jr. (Season Highlights)	1.00
458	Wade Boggs (Season Highlights)	.25
459	Tony Gwynn (Season Highlights)	.50
460	Jesse Orosco (Season Highlights)	.10
461	Nomar Garciaparra, Larry Walker (League Leaders)	.50
462	Mark McGwire, Ken Griffey Jr. (League Leaders)	.50
463	Mark McGwire, Manny Ramirez (League Leaders)	.50
464	Randy Johnson, Pedro Martinez (League Leaders)	.25
465	Randy Johnson, Pedro Martinez (League Leaders)	.25
466	Luis Gonzalez, Derek Jeter (League Leaders)	.50
467	Manny Ramirez, Larry Walker (League Leaders)	.50
468	Tony Gwynn (20th Century's Best)	.50
469	Mark McGwire (20th Century's Best)	2.00
470	Frank Thomas (20th Century's Best)	.50
471	Harold Baines (20th Century's Best)	.10
472	Roger Clemens (20th Century's Best)	.75
473	John Franco (20th Century's Best)	.10
474	John Franco (20th Century's Best)	.10
475	Ken Griffey Jr. (Magic Moments)	1.50
476	Barry Bonds (Magic Moments)	2.00
477	Sammy Sosa (Magic Moments)	1.25
478	Derek Jeter (Magic Moments)	2.50
479	Alex Rodriguez (Magic Moments)	2.00

Hank Aaron Reprints

This 23-card set reprints all of Aaron's 23-regular issued Topps cards and are seeded 1:18 packs.

		NM/M
	Complete Set (23):	60.00
	Common Aaron:	3.00
	Inserted 1:18	
	Autographed:	300.00
	"Limited Edition" 4,000 Sets:	1X
1	Hank Aaron/1954	8.00
2	Hank Aaron/1955	3.00
3	Hank Aaron/1956	3.00
4	Hank Aaron/1957	3.00
5	Hank Aaron/1958	3.00
6	Hank Aaron/1959	3.00
7	Hank Aaron/1960	3.00
8	Hank Aaron/1961	3.00
9	Hank Aaron/1962	3.00
10	Hank Aaron/1963	3.00
11	Hank Aaron/1964	3.00
12	Hank Aaron/1965	3.00
13	Hank Aaron/1966	3.00
14	Hank Aaron/1967	3.00
15	Hank Aaron/1968	3.00
16	Hank Aaron/1969	3.00
17	Hank Aaron/1970	3.00
18	Hank Aaron/1971	3.00
19	Hank Aaron/1972	3.00
20	Hank Aaron/1973	3.00
21	Hank Aaron/1974	3.00
22	Hank Aaron/1975	3.00
23	Hank Aaron/1976	3.00

Hank Aaron Chrome Reprints

This 23-card set reprints Aaron's regular issued Topps cards utilizing Chromium technology. Each card has a commemorative logo and are seeded 1:72 packs. A Refractor parallel version is also randomly inserted 1:288 packs and have Refractor printed underneath the number on the card back.

	NM/M
Complete Set (23):	90.00
Common Aaron:	5.00
Inserted 1:72	
Refractors:	3X
Inserted 1:288	

1	Hank Aaron/1954	10.00
2	Hank Aaron/1955	5.00
3	Hank Aaron/1956	5.00
4	Hank Aaron/1957	5.00
5	Hank Aaron/1958	5.00
6	Hank Aaron/1959	5.00
7	Hank Aaron/1960	5.00
8	Hank Aaron/1961	5.00
9	Hank Aaron/1962	5.00
10	Hank Aaron/1963	5.00
11	Hank Aaron/1964	5.00
12	Hank Aaron/1965	5.00
13	Hank Aaron/1966	5.00
14	Hank Aaron/1967	5.00
15	Hank Aaron/1968	5.00
16	Hank Aaron/1969	5.00
17	Hank Aaron/1970	5.00
18	Hank Aaron/1971	5.00
19	Hank Aaron/1972	5.00
20	Hank Aaron/1973	5.00
21	Hank Aaron/1974	5.00
22	Hank Aaron/1975	5.00
23	Hank Aaron/1976	5.00

All-Star Rookie Team

		NM/M
	Complete Set (10):	10.00
	Common Player:	.25
	Inserted 1:36	
	"Limited Edition" 4,000 Sets:	1X
1	Mark McGwire	3.00
2	Chuck Knoblauch	.25
3	Chipper Jones	2.00
4	Cal Ripken Jr.	4.00
5	Manny Ramirez	.75
6	Jose Canseco	.75
7	Ken Griffey Jr.	2.00
8	Mike Piazza	2.00
9	Dwight Gooden	.25
10	Billy Wagner	.25

All-Topps Team

This insert set spotlights 10 National League (Series 1) and 10 A.L. (Series 2) players who are deemed the best at their respective position. On front, a Hall of Fame style plaque design features gold-foil highlights. Backs offer stat comparisons to contemporary players and Hall of Fame greats at their position. These were seeded 1:12 packs. Cards are numbered with an "AT" prefix.

		NM/M
	Complete Set (20):	15.00
	Common Player:	.25
	Inserted 1:12	
	"Limited Edition" 4,000 Sets:	1X
1	Greg Maddux	1.50
2	Mike Piazza	1.50
3	Mark McGwire	2.50
4	Craig Biggio	.40
5	Chipper Jones	1.50
6	Barry Larkin	.40
7	Barry Bonds	2.50
8	Andruw Jones	.75
9	Sammy Sosa	1.50
10	Larry Walker	.50
11	Pedro Martinez	1.00
12	Ivan Rodriguez	.50
13	Rafael Palmeiro	.50
14	Roberto Alomar	.50
15	Cal Ripken Jr.	3.00
16	Derek Jeter	3.00
17	Albert Belle	.25
18	Ken Griffey Jr.	1.50
19	Manny Ramirez	.75
20	Jose Canseco	.50

Autographs

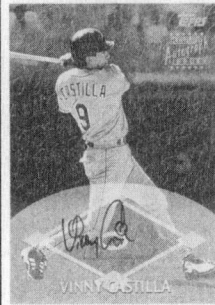

Inserted exclusively in Series 1 and 2 hobby packs, each card features the "Topps Certified Autograph Issue" stamp and is autographed on the card front.

		NM/M
	Common Player:	8.00
	Group A 1:7,589	
	Group B 1:4,553	
	Group C 1:518	
	Group D 1:911	
	Group E 1:1,138	
1	Alex Rodriguez (A)	100.00
2	Tony Gwynn (A)	50.00
3	Vinny Castilla (B)	15.00
4	Sean Casey (B)	15.00
5	Shawn Green (C)	25.00
6	Rey Ordonez (C)	8.00
7	Matt Lawton (C)	15.00
8	Tony Womack (C)	8.00
9	Gabe Kapler (D)	10.00
10	Pat Burrell (D)	20.00
11	Preston Wilson (D)	15.00
12	Troy Glaus (D)	30.00
13	Carlos Beltran (D)	40.00
14	Josh Girdley (E)	8.00
15	B.J. Garbe (E)	8.00
16	Derek Jeter (A)	125.00
17	Cal Ripken Jr. (A)	150.00
18	Ivan Rodriguez (B)	40.00
19	Rafael Palmeiro (B)	40.00
20	Vladimir Guerrero (E)	45.00
21	Raul Mondesi (C)	15.00
22	Scott Rolen (C)	40.00
23	Billy Wagner (C)	10.00
24	Fernando Tatis (D)	8.00
25	Ruben Mateo (D)	8.00
26	Carlos Febles (D)	8.00
27	Mike Sweeney (E)	10.00
28	Alex Gonzalez (D)	10.00
29	Miguel Tejada (D)	40.00
30	Josh Hamilton (E)	50.00

Century Best

		NM/M
	Common Player:	2.00
	Ser. 1 1:869 H	
	Ser. 2 1:362	
CB1	Tony Gwynn/339	8.00
CB2	Wade Boggs/578	4.00
CB3	Lance Johnson/117	2.00
CB4	Mark McGwire/522	20.00
CB5	Rickey Henderson/1,334	4.00
CB6	Rickey Henderson/2,103	4.00
CB7	Roger Clemens/247	12.00
CB8	Tony Gwynn/3,067	6.00
CB9	Mark McGwire/587	20.00
CB10	Frank Thomas/440	6.00
CB11	Harold Baines/1,583	2.00
CB12	Roger Clemens/3,316	8.00
CB13	John Franco/264	2.00
CB14	John Franco/416	2.00

Combos

		NM/M
	Complete Set (10):	15.00
	Common Card:	1.00
	Inserted 1:18	
	"Limited Edition" 4,000 Sets:	1X
1	Roberto Alomar, Manny Ramirez, Kenny Lofton, Jim Thome	1.00

Strikeout Kings
RANDY JOHNSON / PEDRO MARTINEZ

2	Tom Glavine, Greg Maddux, John Smoltz	1.50
3	Derek Jeter, Bernie Williams, Tino Martinez	3.00
4	Ivan Rodriguez, Mike Piazza	1.50
5	Nomar Garciaparra, Alex Rodriguez, Derek Jeter	3.00
6	Sammy Sosa, Mark McGwire	3.00
7	Pedro Martinez, Randy Johnson	1.00
8	Barry Bonds, Ken Griffey Jr.	2.50
9	Chipper Jones, Ivan Rodriguez	1.50
10	Cal Ripken Jr., Tony Gwynn, Wade Boggs	3.00

Hands of Gold

Hands of Gold

This seven-card insert set highlights players who have won at least five gold gloves. Each card is foil stamped and die-cut and is seeded 1:18 packs.

		NM/M
Complete Set (7):		5.00
Common Player:		.25
Inserted 1:18		
"Limited Edition" 4,000 Sets:		1X
1	Barry Bonds	2.50
2	Ivan Rodriguez	.75
3	Ken Griffey Jr.	1.50
4	Roberto Alomar	.75
5	Tony Gwynn	1.00
6	Omar Vizquel	.25
7	Greg Maddux	1.50

Mark McGwire 1985 Rookie Reprint

MARK McGWIRE FIRST BASE

This insert pays tribute to baseball's reigning single season home run record holder by reprinting his '85 Topps Rookie card. Card fronts have a commemorative gold stamp and is seeded 1:36 packs.

		NM/M
Complete Set (1):		6.00
	Mark McGwire	6.00

Own the Game

		NM/M
Complete Set (30):		15.00
Common Player:		.15
Inserted 1:12		

SCOTT WILLIAMSON

"Limited Edition" 4,000 Sets:		1X
1	Derek Jeter	2.00
2	B.J. Surhoff	.15
3	Luis Gonzalez	.25
4	Manny Ramirez	.50
5	Rafael Palmeiro	.40
6	Mark McGwire	1.50
7	Mark McGwire	1.50
8	Sammy Sosa	1.00
9	Ken Griffey Jr.	1.00
10	Larry Walker	.25
11	Nomar Garciaparra	1.50
12	Derek Jeter	2.00
13	Larry Walker	.25
14	Mark McGwire	1.50
15	Manny Ramirez	.50
16	Pedro Martinez	.75
17	Randy Johnson	.75
18	Kevin Millwood	.25
19	Pedro Martinez	.75
20	Randy Johnson	.75
21	Kevin Brown	.25
22	Chipper Jones	1.00
23	Ivan Rodriguez	.50
24	Mariano Rivera	.25
25	Scott Williamson	.15
26	Carlos Beltran	.25
27	Randy Johnson	.75
28	Pedro Martinez	.75
29	Sammy Sosa	1.00
30	Manny Ramirez	.75

Perennial All-Stars

PERENNIAL ALL-STARS

KEN GRIFFEY JR.

This 10-card set highlights 10 superstars who have consistently achieved All-Star recognition. Card fronts feature a silver holographic foil throughout, while card backs have the featured player's career All-Star statistics. These were seeded 1:18 packs. Cards are numbered with a "PA" prefix.

		NM/M
Complete Set (10):		10.00
Common Player:		.50
Inserted 1:18		
"Limited Edition" 4,000 Sets:		1X
1	Ken Griffey Jr.	1.00
2	Derek Jeter	2.00
3	Sammy Sosa	1.00
4	Cal Ripken Jr.	2.00
5	Mike Piazza	1.00
6	Nomar Garciaparra	1.50
7	Jeff Bagwell	.50
8	Barry Bonds	1.50
9	Alex Rodriguez	1.50
10	Mark McGwire	1.50

Power Players

This 20-card set highlights the top power hitters in the game and are printed on a holographic silver foil front. They are numbered with a "P" prefix and are seeded 1:8 packs.

		NM/M
Complete Set (20):		10.00
Common Player:		.25
Inserted 1:8		
"Limited Edition" 4,000 Sets:		1X
1	Juan Gonzalez	.50
2	Ken Griffey Jr.	1.00
3	Mark McGwire	1.50
4	Nomar Garciaparra	1.50
5	Barry Bonds	1.50
6	Mo Vaughn	.25

7	Larry Walker	.25
8	Alex Rodriguez	1.50
9	Jose Canseco	.25
10	Jeff Bagwell	.50
11	Manny Ramirez	.50
12	Albert Belle	.25
13	Frank Thomas	.50
14	Mike Piazza	1.00
15	Chipper Jones	1.00
16	Sammy Sosa	1.00
17	Vladimir Guerrero	.50
18	Scott Rolen	.50
19	Raul Mondesi	.25
20	Derek Jeter	2.00

Stadium Relics

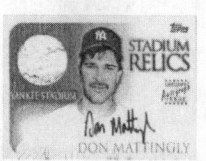

STADIUM RELICS
DON MATTINGLY

Inserted exclusively in Home-Team Advantage packs, this five-card set features historical baseball stadiums and the autograph of the players who made them sacred. Besides the player autograph, the cards also have a piece of base from the featured stadium embedded into each card. These were seeded 1:165 HTA packs and are numbered with a "SR" prefix.

		NM/M
Common Player:		40.00
Inserted 1:165 HTA		
1	Don Mattingly	150.00
2	Carl Yastrzemski	100.00
3	Ernie Banks	75.00
4	Johnny Bench	75.00
5	Willie Mays	150.00
6	Mike Schmidt	100.00
7	Lou Brock	50.00
8	Al Kaline	75.00
9	Paul Molitor	60.00
10	Eddie Matthews	75.00

Supers

ALEX RODRIGUEZ

Each box of Topps foil packs includes one upwrapped box-topper card in an oversize (3-1/2" x 5") format. Except for its size, the super version differs from the same players' issued cards only in the numbering on back which designates each card "x of 8."

		NM/M
Complete Set (16):		35.00
Common Player:		1.00
Inserted 1:box		
1	Mark McGwire	5.00
2	Hank Aaron	5.00
3	Derek Jeter	3.00
4	Sammy Sosa	3.00
5	Alex Rodriguez	3.00
6	Chipper Jones	4.00
7	Cal Ripken Jr.	4.00
8	Pedro Martinez	2.00
1	Barry Bonds	1.50
2	Orlando Hernandez	1.00

3	Mike Piazza	3.00
4	Manny Ramirez	1.50
5	Ken Griffey Jr.	4.00
6	Rafael Palmeiro	1.00
7	Greg Maddux	2.50
8	Nomar Garciaparra	3.00

21st Century Topps

ANDRUW JONES

Printed on a silver holographic foil front, this 10-card set highlights young players who are poised to thrive into the next millenium. These are seeded 1:18 packs are numbered on the card backs with a "C" prefix.

		NM/M
Complete Set (10):		5.00
Common Player:		.25
Inserted 1:18		
"Limited Edition" 4,000 Sets:		1X
1	Ben Grieve	.25
2	Alex Gonzalez	.25
3	Derek Jeter	2.00
4	Sean Casey	.25
5	Nomar Garciaparra	1.50
6	Alex Rodriguez	1.50
7	Scott Rolen	.50
8	Andruw Jones	.50
9	Vladimir Guerrero	.50
10	Todd Helton	.50

2000 Topps Traded and Rookies

BARRY ZITO

		NM/M
Complete Set (135):		25.00
Common Player:		.10
Unopened Set (136):		50.00
1	Mike MacDougal RC	.20
2	Andy Tracy RC	.20
3	Brandon Phillips RC	1.00
4	Brandon Inge RC	.75
5	Robbie Morrison RC	.25
6	Josh Pressley RC	.20
7	Todd Moser RC	.25
8	Rob Purvis RC	.25
9	Chance Caple RC	.25
10	Ben Sheets	.75
11	Russ Jacobson RC	.10
12	Brian Cole RC	.10
13	Brad Baker RC	.25
14	Alex Cintron RC	.40
15	Lyle Overbay RC	.75
16	Mike Edwards RC	.20
17	Sean McGowan RC	.25
18	Jose Molina RC	.25
19	Marcos Castillo RC	.20
20	Josue Espada RC	.20
21	Alex Gordon RC	.20
22	Rob Pugmire RC	.10
23	Jason Stumm RC	.25
24	Ty Howington RC	.40
25	Brett Myers RC	.50
26	Maicer Izturis RC	.10
27	John McDonald RC	.10
28	Wilfredo Rodriguez RC	.25
29	Carlos Zambrano RC	1.00
30	Alejandro Diaz RC	.20
31	Geraldo Guzman RC	.20
32	J.R. House RC	.50
33	Elvin Nina RC	.20
34	Juan Pierre RC	.50
35	Ben Johnson RC	.50
36	Jeff Bailey RC	.20
37	Miguel Olivo RC	.75
38	Francisco Rodriguez RC	2.00
39	Tony Pena Jr. RC	.20

40	Miguel Cabrera RC	10.00
41	Asdrubal Oropeza RC	.10
42	Junior Zamora RC	.10
43	Jovanny Cedeno RC	.25
44	John Sneed RC	.10
45	Josh Kalinowski RC	.10
46	Mike Young RC	2.00
47	Rico Washington RC	.10
48	Chad Durbin RC	.40
49	Junior Brignac RC	.25
50	Carlos Hernandez RC	.40
51	Cesar Izturis RC	.50
52	Oscar Salazar RC	.25
53	Pat Strange RC	.25
54	Rick Asadoorian RC	.15
55	Keith Reed RC	.25
56	Leo Estrella RC	.10
57	Wascar Serrano RC	.10
58	Richard Gomez RC	.25
59	Ramon Santiago RC	.25
60	Jovanny Sosa RC	.25
61	Aaron Rowand RC	.50
62	Junior Guerrero RC	.25
63	Luis Terrero RC	.25
64	Brian Sanches RC	.10
65	Scott Sobkowiak RC	.25
66	Gary Majewski RC	.10
67	Barry Zito	.75
68	Ryan Christianson RC	.40
69	Cristian Guerrero RC	.40
70	Tomas de la Rosa RC	.10
71	Andrew Beinbrink RC	.10
72	Ryan Knox RC	.10
73	Alex Graman RC	.20
74	Juan Guzman RC	.10
75	Ruben Salazar RC	.40
76	Luis Matos RC	.40
77	Tony Mota RC	.10
78	Doug Davis RC	.50
79	Ben Christensen RC	.25
80	Mike Lamb RC	.10
81	Adrian Gonzalez RC (Draft Picks)	4.00
82	Mike Stodolka RC (Draft Picks)	.25
83	Adam Johnson RC (Draft Picks)	.25
84	Matt Wheatland RC (Draft Picks)	.25
85	Corey Smith RC (Draft Picks)	.50
86	Rocco Baldelli RC (Draft Picks)	.50
87	Keith Bucktrot RC (Draft Picks)	.25
88	Adam Wainwright RC (Draft Picks)	2.00
89	Scott Thorman RC (Draft Picks)	.50
90	Tripper Johnson RC (Draft Picks)	.25
91	Jim Edmonds	.25
92	Masato Yoshii	.10
93	Adam Kennedy	.10
94	Darryl Kile	.10
95	Mark McLemore	.10
96	Ricky Gutierrez	.10
97	Juan Gonzalez	.40
98	Melvin Mora	.10
99	Dante Bichette	.10
100	Lee Stevens	.10
101	Roger Cedeno	.10
102	John Olerud	.25
103	Eric Young	.10
104	Mickey Morandini	.10
105	Travis Lee	.10
106	Greg Vaughn	.10
107	Todd Zeile	.10
108	Chuck Finley	.10
109	Ismael Valdes	.10
110	Ron Henika	.10
111	Pat Hentgen	.10
112	Ryan Klesko	.10
113	Derek Bell	.10
114	Hideo Nomo	.40
115	Aaron Sele	.10
116	Fernando Vina	.10
117	Wally Joyner	.10
118	Brian Hunter	.10
119	Joe Girardi	.10
120	Omar Daal	.10
121	Brook Fordyce	.10
122	Jose Valentin	.10
123	Curt Schilling	.40
124	B.J. Surhoff	.10
125	Henry Rodriguez	.10
126	Mike Bordick	.10
127	David Justice	.25
128	Charles Johnson	.10
129	Will Clark	.25
130	Dwight Gooden	.10
131	David Segui	.10
132	Denny Neagle	.10
133	Andy Ashby	.10
134	Bruce Chen	.10
135	Jason Bere	.10

Autographs

		NM/M
Common Player:		4.00
Inserted 1:Set		
1	Mike MacDougal	4.00
2	Andy Tracy	8.00
3	Brandon Phillips	50.00
4	Brandon Inge	15.00
5	Robbie Morrison	4.00
6	Josh Pressley	4.00
7	Todd Moser	4.00

ANDREW BEINBRINK

8	Rob Purvis	4.00
9	Chance Caple	4.00
10	Ben Sheets	15.00
11	Russ Jacobson	4.00
12	Brian Cole	4.00
13	Brad Baker	4.00
14	Alex Cintron	4.00
15	Lyle Overbay	10.00
16	Mike Edwards	4.00
17	Sean McGowan	4.00
18	Jose Molina	4.00
19	Marcos Castillo	4.00
20	Josue Espada	4.00
21	Alex Gordon	4.00
22	Rob Pugmire	4.00
23	Jason Stumm	4.00
24	Ty Howington	4.00
25	Brett Myers	10.00
26	Maicer Izturis	8.00
27	John McDonald	4.00
28	Wilfredo Rodriguez	4.00
29	Carlos Zambrano	15.00
30	Alejandro Diaz	4.00
31	Geraldo Guzman	4.00
32	J.R. House	8.00
33	Elvin Nina	4.00
34	Juan Pierre	15.00
35	Ben Johnson	10.00
36	Jeff Bailey	4.00
37	Miguel Olivo	10.00
38	Francisco Rodriguez	20.00
39	Tony Pena Jr.	4.00
40	Miguel Cabrera	450.00
41	Asdrubal Oropeza	4.00
42	Junior Zamora	4.00
43	Jovanny Cedeno	4.00
44	John Sneed	4.00
45	Josh Kalinowski	8.00
46	Mike Young	60.00
47	Rico Washington	4.00
48	Chad Durbin	4.00
49	Junior Brignac	4.00
50	Carlos Hernandez	4.00
51	Cesar Izturis	10.00
52	Oscar Salazar	4.00
53	Pat Strange	4.00
54	Rick Asadoorian	4.00
55	Keith Reed	4.00
56	Leo Estrella	4.00
57	Wascar Serrano	4.00
58	Richard Gomez	4.00
59	Ramon Santiago	4.00
60	Jovanny Sosa	4.00
61	Aaron Rowand	15.00
62	Junior Guerrero	4.00
63	Luis Terrero	10.00
64	Brian Sanches	4.00
65	Scott Sobkowiak	4.00
66	Gary Majewski	4.00
67	Barry Zito	25.00
68	Ryan Christianson	8.00
69	Cristian Guerrero	4.00
70	Tomas de la Rosa	4.00
71	Andrew Beinbrink	4.00
72	Ryan Knox	4.00
73	Alex Graman	4.00
74	Juan Guzman	4.00
75	Ruben Salazar	4.00
76	Luis Matos	8.00
77	Tony Mota	4.00
78	Doug Davis	8.00
79	Ben Christensen	4.00
80	Mike Lamb	10.00

2000 Topps Opening Day

PAUL BYRD

Essentially identical in design to 2000 Topps regular cards, Opening Day has a silver border with "2000 Opening Day" stamped in silver foil on the card front. The checklist is made up of cards from Series 1 and 2 from Topps base set with identical photos. The rookie reprint card of Hank Aaron was intended to carry card #110, but it does not appear, only the original '54 Topps card #128.

	NM/M
Complete Set (165):	30.00
Common Player:	.15
Pack (8):	1.00
Wax Box (36):	25.00

1	Mark McGwire	2.00
2	Tony Gwynn	1.00
3	Wade Boggs	.40
4	Cal Ripken Jr.	2.50
5	Matt Williams	.20
6	Jay Buhner	.15
7	Mike Lieberthal	.15
8	Magglio Ordonez	.25
9	Derek Jeter	2.00
10	Javy Lopez	.25
11	Armando Benitez	.15
12	Darin Erstad	.25
13	Mark Grace	.25
14	Eric Karros	.15
15	J.T. Snow Jr.	.15
16	Luis Castillo	.15
17	Rey Ordonez	.15
18	Bob Abreu	.15
19	Warren Morris	.15
20	Juan Gonzalez	.75
21	Dean Palmer	.15
22	Hank Aaron	2.00
23	Jeff Bagwell	.75
24	Sammy Sosa	1.50
25	Randy Johnson	.75
26	Dante Bichette	.15
27	Frank Thomas	.75
28	Pedro Martinez	.75
29	Brian Giles	.20
30	Ivan Rodriguez	.50
31	Roger Cedeno	.15
32	David Justice	.25
33	Ken Caminiti	.15
34	Brian Jordan	.15
35	John Olerud	.25
36	Pokey Reese	.15
37	Barry Larkin	.25
38	Edgar Martinez	.15
39	Carlos Delgado	.50
40	Troy Glaus	.40
41	Ben Grieve	.15
42	Jose Lima	.15
43	Luis Gonzalez	.25
44	Alex Rodriguez	2.00
45	Preston Wilson	.20
46	Rickey Henderson	.40
47	Gary Sheffield	.25
48	Jim Edmonds	.25
49	Greg Vaughn	.15
50	Neifi Perez	.15
51	Paul O'Neill	.15
52	Jermaine Dye	.15
53	Curt Schilling	.15
54	Edgardo Alfonzo	.15
55	John Smoltz	.20
56	Chuck Finley	.15
57	Billy Wagner	.15
58	David Cone	.25
59	Roberto Alomar	.50
60	Charles Nagy	.15
61	Mike Mussina	.50
62	Robin Ventura	.15
63	Kevin Brown	.15
64	Pat Hentgen	.15
65	Ryan Klesko	.15
66	Derek Bell	.15
67	Larry Walker	.25
68	Scott Williamson	.15
69	Jose Offerman	.15
70	Doug Mientkiewicz	.15
71	John Snyder	.15
72	Sandy Alomar	.15
73	Joe Nathan	.15
74	Steve Finley	.15
75	Dave Martinez	.15
76	Fernando Tatis	.15
77	Kenny Lofton	.20
78	Paul Byrd	.15
79	Aaron Sele	.15
80	Roger Clemens	1.50
81	Francisco Cordova	.15
82	Wally Joyner	.15
83	Jason Kendall	.25
84	Carlos Beltran	.25
85	Chipper Jones	1.50
86	Vladimir Guerrero	.75
87	Tom Goodwin	.15
88	Brian Daubach	.15
89	Jay Bell	.15
90	Roy Halladay	.25
91	Miguel Tejada	.40
92	Eric Davis	.15
93	Henry Rodriguez	.15
94	Joe McEwing	.15
95	Jeff Kent	.25
96	Jeff Zimmerman	.15
97	Tony Fernandez	.15
98	Jason Giambi	.75
99	Jose Canseco	.40
100	Alex Gonzalez	.15
101	Erubiel Durazo, Pat Burrell, Nick Johnson (Prospects)	.40
102	Corey Patterson, Roosevelt Brown, Lance Berkman (Prospects)	.25
103	Eric Munson, Bobby Bradley RC (Draft Picks)	.25
104	Josh Hamilton, Corey Myers RC (Draft Picks)	.25
105	Mark McGwire (Magic Moments)	2.00
106	Hank Aaron (Magic Moments)	2.00
107	Cal Ripken Jr. (Magic Moments)	2.50
108	Wade Boggs (Magic Moments)	.40
109	Tony Gwynn (Magic Moments)	1.00
(110)	Hank Aaron (Rookie Reprint)	2.00
111	Tom Glavine	.40
112	Mo Vaughn	.20
113	Tino Martinez	.25
114	Craig Biggio	.25
115	Tim Hudson	.25
116	John Wetteland	.15
117	Ellis Burks	.15
118	David Wells	.15
119	Rico Brogna	.15
120	Greg Maddux	1.50
121	Jeromy Burnitz	.15
122	Raul Mondesi	.25
123	Rondell White	.25
124	Barry Bonds	2.00
125	Orlando Hernandez	.25
126	Bartolo Colon	.15
127	Tim Salmon	.25
128	Kevin Young	.15
129	Troy O'Leary	.15
130	Jim Thome	.50
131	Ray Durham	.15
132	Tony Clark	.15
133	Mariano Rivera	.25
134	Omar Vizquel	.15
135	Ken Griffey Jr.	1.50
136	Shawn Green	.40
137	Cliff Floyd	.15
138	Al Leiter	.15
139	Mike Hampton	.15
140	Mike Piazza	1.50
141	Andy Pettitte	.25
142	Albert Belle	.20
143	Scott Rolen	.75
144	Rusty Greer	.15
145	Kevin Millwood	.25
146	Ivan Rodriguez	.75
147	Nomar Garciaparra	1.50
148	Denny Neagle	.15
149	Manny Ramirez	.75
150	Vinny Castilla	.15
151	Andruw Jones	.50
152	Johnny Damon	.15
153	Eric Milton	.15
154	Todd Helton	.50
155	Rafael Palmeiro	.50
156	Damion Easley	.15
157	Carlos Febles	.15
158	Paul Konerko	.25
159	Bernie Williams	.50
160	Ken Griffey Jr. (Magic Moments)	1.50
161	Barry Bonds (Magic Moments)	2.00
162	Sammy Sosa (Magic Moments)	2.00
163	Derek Jeter (Magic Moments)	2.00
164	Alex Rodriguez (Magic Moments)	2.00
165	Checklist (Magic Moments)	.15

Autographs

	NM/M
Common Player:	25.00

1	Edgardo Alfonzo	25.00
2	Wade Boggs	60.00
3	Robin Ventura	25.00
4	Josh Hamilton	50.00
5	Vernon Wells	30.00

2000 Topps Chrome

The base set consists of 478 cards utilizing Topps Chromium technology and features the same

photos and basic design as the 2000 Topps base set. Subsets include Prospects, Draft Picks, 20th Century's Best, Magic Moments and Post Season Highlights. A parallel Refractor version is also available 1:12 packs.

	NM/M
Complete Set (478):	100.00
Complete Series I Set (239):	50.00
Complete Series II Set (239):	50.00
Common Player:	.25
Pack (4):	1.50
Wax Box (24):	30.00

1	Mark McGwire	3.00
2	Tony Gwynn	1.50
3	Wade Boggs	.75
4	Cal Ripken Jr.	4.00
5	Matt Williams	.40
6	Jay Buhner	.40
7	Mike Lieberthal	.25
8	Jeff Conine	.25
9	Todd Greene	.25
10	Mike Lieberthal	.25
11	Steve Avery	.25
12	Bret Saberhagen	.25
13	Magglio Ordonez	.50
14	Brad Radke	.25
15	Derek Jeter	4.00
16	Javy Lopez	.50
17	Russ David	.25
18	Armando Benitez	.25
19	B.J. Surhoff	.25
20	Darryl Kile	.25
21	Mark Lewis	.25
22	Mike Williams	.25
23	Mark McLemore	.25
24	Sterling Hitchcock	.25
25	Darin Erstad	.50
26	Ricky Gutierrez	.25
27	John Jaha	.25
28	Homer Bush	.25
29	Darrin Fletcher	.25
30	Mark Grace	.75
31	Fred McGriff	.50
32	Omar Daal	.25
33	Eric Karros	.25
34	Orlando Cabrera	.40
35	J.T. Snow Jr.	.25
36	Luis Castillo	.25
37	Rey Ordonez	.25
38	Bob Abreu	.40
39	Warren Morris	.25
40	Juan Gonzalez	1.00
41	Mike Lansing	.25
42	Chili Davis	.25
43	Dean Palmer	.25
44	Hank Aaron	3.00
45	Jeff Bagwell	1.00
46	Jose Valentin	.25
47	Shannon Stewart	.25
48	Kent Bottenfield	.25
49	Jeff Shaw	.25
50	Sammy Sosa	2.00
51	Randy Johnson	1.50
52	Benny Agbayani	.25
53	Dante Bichette	.25
54	Pete Harnisch	.25
55	Frank Thomas	1.00
56	Jorge Posada	.75
57	Todd Walker	.25
58	Juan Encarnacion	.40
59	Mike Sweeney	.25
60	Pedro Martinez	1.50
61	Lee Stevens	.25
62	Brian Giles	.50
63	Chad Ogea	.25
64	Ivan Rodriguez	1.00
65	Roger Cedeno	.25
66	David Justice	.50
67	Steve Trachsel	.25
68	Eli Marrero	.25
69	Dave Nilsson	.25
70	Ken Caminiti	.25
71	Tim Raines	.25
72	Brian Jordan	.25
73	Jeff Blauser	.25
74	Bernard Gilkey	.25
75	John Flaherty	.25
76	Brent Mayne	.25
77	Jose Vidro	.25
78	Jeff Fassero	.25
79	Bruce Aven	.25
80	John Olerud	.50
81	Juan Guzman	.25
82	Woody Williams	.25
83	Ed Sprague	.25
84	Joe Girardi	.25
85	Barry Larkin	.50
86	Mike Caruso	.25
87	Bobby Higginson	.25
88	Roberto Kelly	.25
89	Edgar Martinez	.40
90	Mark Kotsay	.25
91	Paul Sorrento	.25
92	Eric Young	.25
93	Carlos Delgado	1.00
94	Troy Glaus	1.00
95	Ben Grieve	.25
96	Jose Lima	.25
97	Garret Anderson	.50
98	Luis Gonzalez	.50
99	Carl Pavano	.25
100	Alex Rodriguez	3.00
101	Preston Wilson	.40
102	Ron Gant	.40
103	Harold Baines	.25
104	Rickey Henderson	.50
105	Gary Sheffield	.75
106	Mickey Morandini	.25
107	Jim Edmonds	.50
108	Kris Benson	.25
109	Adrian Beltre	.25
110	Alex Fernandez	.25
111	Dan Wilson	.25
112	Mark Clark	.25
113	Greg Vaughn	.25
114	Neifi Perez	.25
115	Paul O'Neill	.50
116	Jermaine Dye	.25
117	Todd Jones	.25
118	Terry Steinbach	.25
119	Greg Norton	.25
120	Curt Schilling	.75
121	Todd Zeile	.25
122	Edgardo Alfonzo	.25
123	Ryan McGuire	.25
124	Stan Javier	.25
125	John Smoltz	.40
126	Bob Wickman	.25
127	Richard Hidalgo	.25
128	Chuck Finley	.25
129	Billy Wagner	.25
130	Todd Hundley	.25
131	Dwight Gooden	.40
132	Russ Ortiz	.25
133	Mike Lowell	.25
134	Reggie Sanders	.25
135	John Valentin	.25
136	Brad Ausmus	.25
137	Chad Kreuter	.25
138	David Cone	.40
139	Brook Fordyce	.25
140	Roberto Alomar	.75
141	Charles Nagy	.25
142	Brian Hunter	.25
143	Mike Mussina	.75
144	Robin Ventura	.40
145	Kevin Brown	.40
146	Pat Hentgen	.25
147	Ryan Klesko	.40
148	Derek Bell	.25
149	Andy Sheets	.25
150	Larry Walker	.50
151	Scott Williamson	.25
152	Jose Offerman	.25
153	Doug Mientkiewicz	.25
154	John Snyder RC	.40
155	Sandy Alomar	.25
156	Joe Nathan	.25
157	Lance Johnson	.25
158	Odalis Perez	.25
159	Hideo Nomo	.75
160	Steve Finley	.25
161	Dave Martinez	.25
162	Matt Walbeck	.25
163	Bill Spiers	.25
164	Fernando Tatis	.25
165	Kenny Lofton	.40
166	Paul Byrd	.25
167	Aaron Sele	.25
168	Eddie Taubensee	.25
169	Reggie Jefferson	.25
170	Roger Clemens	2.50
171	Francisco Cordova	.25
172	Mike Bordick	.25
173	Wally Joyner	.25
174	Marvin Benard	.25
175	Jason Kendall	.40
176	Mike Stanley	.25
177	Chad Allen	.25
178	Carlos Beltran	.50
179	Deivi Cruz	.25
180	Chipper Jones	2.00
181	Vladimir Guerrero	1.50
182	Dave Burba	.25
183	Tom Goodwin	.25
184	Brian Daubach	.25
185	Jay Bell	.25
186	Roy Halladay	.50
187	Miguel Tejada	.50
188	Armando Rios	.25
189	Fernando Vina	.25
190	Eric Davis	.40
191	Henry Rodriguez	.25
192	Joe McEwing	.25
193	Jeff Kent	.50
194	Mike Jackson	.25
195	Mike Morgan	.25
196	Jeff Montgomery	.25
197	Jeff Zimmerman	.25
198	Tony Fernandez	.25
199	Jason Giambi	1.00
200	Jose Canseco	.50
201	Alex Gonzalez	.25
202	Jack Cust, Mike Colangelo, Dee Brown	.50
203	Felipe Lopez, Alfonso Soriano, Pablo Ozuna	3.00
204	Erubiel Durazo, Pat Burrell, Nick Johnson	.75
205	John Sneed RC, Kip Wells, Matt Blank	.50
206	Josh Kalinowski RC, Michael Tejera RC, Chris Mears	.50
207	Roosevelt Brown, Corey Patterson, Lance Berkman	.50
208	Kit Pellow, Kevin Barker, Russ Branyan	.40
209	B.J. Garbe RC, Larry Bigbie RC	2.00
210	Eric Munson, Bobby Bradley RC	.75
211	Josh Girdley, Kyle Snyder	.50
212	Chance Caple RC, Jason Jennings	.50
213	Ryan Christiansen RC, Brett Myers RC	3.00
214	Jason Stumm RC, Rob Purvis RC	.50
215	David Walling, Mike Paradis	.40
216	Omar Ortiz, Jay Gehrke	.40
217	David Cone (Season Highlights)	.40
218	Jose Jimenez (Season Highlights)	.25
219	Chris Singleton (Season Highlights)	.25
220	Fernando Tatis (Season Highlights)	.25
221	Todd Helton (Season Highlights)	1.00
222	Kevin Millwood (Post-Season Highlights)	.50
223	Todd Pratt (Post-Season Highlights)	.25
224	Orlando Hernandez (Post-Season Highlights)	.25
225	Post-Season Highlights	.25
226	Post-Season Highlights	.25
227	Bernie Williams (Post-Season Highlights)	.75
228	Mariano Rivera (Post-Season Highlights)	.50
229	Tony Gwynn (20th Century's Best)	1.50
230	Wade Boggs (20th Century's Best)	.50
231	Tim Raines (20th Century's Best)	.25
232	Mark McGwire (20th Century's Best)	3.00
233	Rickey Henderson (20th Century's Best)	.75
234	Rickey Henderson (20th Century's Best)	.75
235	Roger Clemens (20th Century's Best)	.75
236	Mark McGwire (Magic Moments)	5.00
237	Hank Aaron (Magic Moments)	5.00
238	Cal Ripken Jr. (Magic Moments)	6.00
239	Wade Boggs (Magic Moments)	1.00
240	Tony Gwynn (Magic Moments)	3.00
	Series 1 checklist (1-201)	.05
	Series 1 checklist (202-240, inserts)	.05
241	Tom Glavine	.50
242	David Wells	.25
243	Kevin Appier	.25
244	Troy Percival	.25
245	Ray Lankford	.25
246	Marquis Grissom	.25
247	Randy Winn	.25
248	Miguel Batista	.25
249	Darren Dreifort	.25
250	Barry Bonds	3.00
251	Harold Baines	.25
252	Cliff Floyd	.25
253	Freddy Garcia	.40
254	Kenny Rogers	.25
255	Ben Davis	.25
256	Charles Johnson	.25
257	John Burkett	.25
258	Desi Relaford	.25
259	Al Martin	.25
260	Andy Pettitte	.50
261	Carlos Lee	.25
262	Matt Lawton	.25
263	Andy Fox	.25
264	Chan Ho Park	.25
265	Billy Koch	.25
266	Dave Roberts	.25
267	Carl Everett	.25
268	Orel Hershiser	.25
269	Trot Nixon	.25
270	Rusty Greer	.25
271	Will Clark	.75
272	Quilvio Veras	.25
273	Rico Brogna	.25
274	Devon White	.25
275	Tim Hudson	.50
276	Mike Hampton	.25
277	Miguel Cairo	.25
278	Darren Oliver	.25
279	Jeff Cirillo	.25
280	Al Leiter	.25
281	Brant Brown	.25
282	Carlos Febles	.25
283	Pedro Astacio	.25
284	Juan Guzman	.25
285	Orlando Hernandez	.25
286	Paul Konerko	.25
287	Tony Clark	.25
288	Aaron Boone	.50
289	Ismael Valdes	.25
290	Moises Alou	.50
291	Kevin Tapani	.25
292	John Franco	.25
293	Todd Zeile	.25
294	Jason Schmidt	.25
295	Johnny Damon	.40
296	Scott Brosius	.25
297	Travis Fryman	.40
298	Jose Vizcaino	.25
299	Eric Chavez	.50
300	Mike Piazza	2.00
301	Matt Clement	.25
302	Cristian Guzman	.25
303	Darryl Strawberry	.40
304	Jeff Abbott	.25
305	Brett Tomko	.25
306	Mike Lansing	.25
307	Eric Owens	.25
308	Livan Hernandez	.25
309	Rondell White	.25
310	Todd Stottlemyre	.25
311	Chris Carpenter	.25
312	Ken Hill	.25
313	Mark Loretta	.25
314	John Rocker	.25
315	Richie Sexson	.75
316	Ruben Mateo	.25
317	Ramon Martinez	.25
318	Mike Sirotka	.25
319	Jose Rosado	.25
320	Matt Mantei	.25
321	Kevin Millwood	.50
322	Gary DiSarcina	.25
323	Dustin Hermanson	.25
324	Mike Stanton	.25
325	Kirk Rueter	.25
326	Damian Miller	.25
327	Doug Glanville	.25
328	Scott Rolen	1.00
329	Ray Durham	.25
330	Butch Huskey	.25
331	Mariano Rivera	.50
332	Darren Lewis	.25
333	Ramiro Mendoza	.25
334	Mark Grudzielanek	.25
335	Mike Cameron	.25
336	Kelvim Escobar	.25
337	Bret Boone	.40
338	Mo Vaughn	.40
339	Craig Biggio	.25
340	Michael Barrett	.25
341	Marlon Anderson	.25
342	Bobby Jones	.25
343	John Halama	.25
344	Todd Ritchie	.25
345	Chuck Knoblauch	.25
346	Rick Reed	.25
347	Kelly Stinnett	.25
348	Tim Salmon	.50
349	A.J. Hinch	.25
350	Jose Cruz Jr.	.25
351	Roberto Hernandez	.25
352	Edgar Renteria	.25
353	Jose Hernandez	.25
354	Brad Fullmer	.25
355	Trevor Hoffman	.25
356	Troy O'Leary	.25
357	Justin Thompson	.25
358	Kevin Young	.25
359	Hideki Irabu	.25
360	Jim Thome	1.00
361	Todd Dunwoody	.25
362	Octavio Dotel	.25
363	Omar Vizquel	.40
364	Raul Mondesi	.40
365	Shane Reynolds	.25
366	Bartolo Colon	.25
367	Chris Widger	.25
368	Gabe Kapler	.25
369	Bill Simas	.25
370	Tino Martinez	.50
371	John Thomson	.25
372	Delino DeShields	.25
373	Carlos Perez	.25
374	Eddie Perez	.25
375	Jeromy Burnitz	.25
376	Jimmy Haynes	.25
377	Travis Lee	.25
378	Darryl Hamilton	.25
379	Jamie Moyer	.25
380	Alex Gonzalez	.25
381	John Wetteland	.25
382	Vinny Castilla	.40
383	Jeff Suppan	.25
384	Chad Curtis	.25
385	Robb Nen	.25
386	Wilson Alvarez	.25
387	Andres Galarraga	.50
388	Mike Remlinger	.25
389	Geoff Jenkins	.40
390	Matt Stairs	.25
391	Bill Mueller	.25
392	Mike Lowell	.25
393	Andy Ashby	.25
394	Ruben Rivera	.25
395	Todd Helton	1.00
396	Bernie Williams	.75

397	Royce Clayton	.25
398	Manny Ramirez	1.00
399	Kerry Wood	.75
400	Ken Griffey Jr.	2.00
401	Enrique Wilson	.25
402	Joey Hamilton	.25
403	Shawn Estes	.25
404	Ugueth Urbina	.25
405	Albert Belle	.30
406	Rick Helling	.25
407	Steve Parris	.25
408	Eric Milton	.25
409	Dave Mlicki	.25
410	Shawn Green	.50
411	Jaret Wright	.25
412	Tony Womack	.25
413	Vernon Wells	.50
414	Ron Belliard	.25
415	Ellis Burks	.25
416	Scott Erickson	.25
417	Rafael Palmeiro	.75
418	Damion Easley	.25
419	Jamey Wright	.25
420	Corey Koskie	.25
421	Bobby Howry	.25
422	Ricky Ledee	.25
423	Dmitri Young	.25
424	Sidney Ponson	.25
425	Greg Maddux	2.00
426	Jose Guillen	.25
427	Jon Lieber	.25
428	Andy Benes	.25
429	Randy Velarde	.25
430	Sean Casey	.40
431	Torii Hunter	.50
432	Ryan Rupe	.25
433	David Segui	.25
434	Rich Aurilia	.25
435	Nomar Garciaparra	3.00
436	Denny Neagle	.25
437	Ron Coomer	.25
438	Chris Singleton	.25
439	Tony Batista	.25
440	Andruw Jones	1.00
441	Adam Piatt, Aubrey Huff, Sean Burroughs (Prospects)	.50
442	Rafael Furcal, Jason Dallero, Travis Dawkins (Prospects)	.50
443	Wilton Veras, Joe Crede, Mike Lamb RC (Prospects)	.50
444	Julio Zuleta RC, Dernell Stenson, Jorge Toca (Prospects)	.25
445	Tim Raines Jr., Gary Mathews Jr., Garry Maddux Jr. RC (Prospects)	.50
446	Matt Riley, Mark Mulder, C.C. Sabathia (Prospects)	.25
447	Scott Downs RC, Chris George, Matt Belisle (Prospects)	.50
448	Doug Mirabelli, Ben Petrick, Jayson Werth (Prospects)	.75
449	Josh Hamilton, Corey Myers RC (Draft Picks)	1.50
450	Ben Christensen RC, Brett Myers (Draft Picks)	.50
451	Barry Zito RC, Ben Sheets RC (Draft Picks)	5.00
452	Ty Howington RC, Kurt Ainsworth RC (Draft Picks)	1.00
453	Rick Asadoorian RC, Vince Faison RC (Draft Picks)	.50
454	Keith Reed RC, Jeff Heaverlo RC (Draft Picks)	.50
455	Mike MacDougal RC, Jay Gehrke (Draft Picks)	.75
456	Mark McGwire (Season Highlights)	3.00
457	Cal Ripken Jr. (Season Highlights)	4.00
458	Wade Boggs (Season Highlights)	.75
459	Tony Gwynn (Season Highlights)	1.50
460	Jesse Orosco (Season Highlights)	.25
461	Nomar Garciaparra, Larry Walker (League Leaders)	1.50
462	Mark McGwire, Ken Griffey Jr. (League Leaders)	1.50
463	Mark McGwire, Manny Ramirez (League Leaders)	1.50
464	Randy Johnson, Pedro Martinez (League Leaders)	1.00
465	Randy Johnson, Pedro Martinez (League Leaders)	1.00
466	Luis Gonzalez, Derek Jeter (League Leaders)	1.50
467	Manny Ramirez, Larry Walker (League Leaders)	.75
468	Tony Gwynn (20th Century's Best)	1.50
469	Mark McGwire (20th Century's Best)	3.00

470	Frank Thomas (20th Century's Best)	.75
471	Harold Baines (20th Century's Best)	.25
472	Roger Clemens (20th Century's Best)	1.50
473	John Franco (20th Century's Best)	.25
474	John Franco (20th Century's Best)	.25
475	Ken Griffey Jr. (Magic Moments)	3.00
476	Barry Bonds (Magic Moments)	5.00
477	Sammy Sosa (Magic Moments)	4.00
478	Derek Jeter (Magic Moments)	6.00
479	Alex Rodriguez (Magic Moments)	5.00

Refractors

A parallel to the base set, Refractors have a reflective sheen to them when held up to light. They are seeded 1:12 packs and have "Refractor" written underneath the card number on the back.

Stars:		3-5X
Young Stars/RC's:		1-2X
Inserted 1:12		

All-Star Rookie Team

This 10-card set highlights players who lived up to the high expectations placed on them during their rookie season. These are seeded 1:16 packs and are numbered with an "RT" prefix on the card back. A Refractor parallel is also randomly inserted, seeded 1:80 packs. "Refractor" is printed under the card number on the back.

	NM/M
Complete Set (10):	10.00
Common Player:	.50
Inserted 1:16	
Refractors:	2-3X
Inserted 1:80	

1	Mark McGwire	3.00
2	Chuck Knoblauch	.50
3	Chipper Jones	2.00
4	Cal Ripken Jr.	4.00
5	Manny Ramirez	1.00
6	Jose Canseco	.75
7	Ken Griffey Jr.	2.00
8	Mike Piazza	2.00
9	Dwight Gooden	.50
10	Billy Wagner	.50

All-Topps Team

These feature top National League players and picks a top player for each position. They have a brown border utilizing Topps Chromium technology. Card backs have a small photo along with statistical comparisons made to current and former greats for their respective position. Backs are numbered with an "AT" prefix and are seeded 1:32 packs. A Refractor parallel is inserted 1:160 packs.

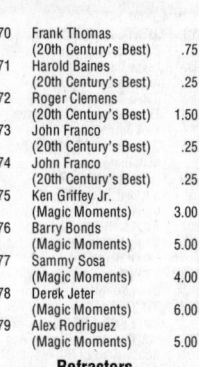

LARRY WALKER
All-Topps NL Team

	NM/M
Complete Set (20):	40.00
Complete Series I Set (10):	20.00
Complete Series II Set (10):	20.00
Common Player:	.50
Inserted 1:32	
Refractors:	2-3X
Inserted 1:160	

1	Greg Maddux	3.00
2	Mike Piazza	3.00
3	Mark McGwire	5.00
4	Craig Biggio	1.00
5	Chipper Jones	1.00
6	Barry Larkin	1.00
7	Barry Bonds	5.00
8	Andruw Jones	1.50
9	Sammy Sosa	3.00
10	Larry Walker	1.00
11	Pedro Martinez	2.00
12	Ivan Rodriguez	1.00
13	Rafael Palmeiro	1.00
14	Roberto Alomar	1.00
15	Cal Ripken Jr.	6.00
16	Derek Jeter	6.00
17	Albert Belle	.50
18	Ken Griffey Jr.	3.00
19	Manny Ramirez	1.50
20	Jose Canseco	1.00

Allegiance

Allegiance features 20 stars who have spent their entire career with one team. They are seeded 1:16 and are numbered with a "TA" prefix. There is also a hobby-exclusive Refractor parallel version, sequentially numbered to 100 and inserted 1:424 packs.

	NM/M
Complete Set (20):	30.00
Common Player:	.75
Inserted 1:16	
Refractors:	5X
Inserted 1:424	

1	Derek Jeter	6.00
2	Ivan Rodriguez	1.00
3	Alex Rodriguez	5.00
4	Cal Ripken Jr.	6.00
5	Mark Grace	1.00
6	Tony Gwynn	2.00
7	Juan Gonzalez	1.50
8	Frank Thomas	1.50
9	Manny Ramirez	1.50
10	Barry Larkin	.75
11	Bernie Williams	1.50
12	Raul Mondesi	.75
13	Vladimir Guerrero	1.50
14	Craig Biggio	.75
15	Nomar Garciaparra	4.00
16	Andruw Jones	1.50
17	Jim Thome	1.00
18	Scott Rolen	1.00
19	Chipper Jones	3.00
20	Ken Griffey Jr.	3.00

Combos

Ten player combinations linked by a common element are featured in this set. Combos are found 1:16 packs and are numbered with a "TC" prefix on the card back. A Refractor parallel is randomly seeded 1:80 packs and have "Refractor" printed under the card number on the back.

Strikeout Kings
RANDY JOHNSON • PEDRO MARTINEZ

	NM/M
Complete Set (10):	20.00
Common Player:	1.00
Inserted 1:16	
Refractors:	2-3X
Inserted 1:80	

1	Manny Ramirez, Kenny Lofton, Jim Thome, Roberto Alomar	1.00
2	Tom Glavine, Greg Maddux, John Smoltz	2.00
3	Derek Jeter, Bernie Williams, Tino Martinez	4.00
4	Ivan Rodriguez, Mike Piazza	2.00
5	Nomar Garciaparra, Alex Rodriguez, Derek Jeter	4.00
6	Sammy Sosa, Mark McGwire	4.00
7	Pedro Martinez, Randy Johnson	1.50
8	Barry Bonds, Ken Griffey Jr.	3.00
9	Chipper Jones, Ivan Rodriguez	2.00
10	Cal Ripken Jr., Tony Gwynn, Wade Boggs	4.00

Kings

This 10-card set spotlights hitters who have averaged 30 or more homeruns per season for their career. Kings are seeded 1:32 packs and are numbered with an "CK" prefix on the card back. A Refractor parallel is also randomly inserted and are serially numbered to the featured player's career homerun total.

	NM/M
Complete Set (10):	25.00
Common Player:	1.50
Inserted 1:32	

1	Mark McGwire	5.00
2	Sammy Sosa	3.00
3	Ken Griffey Jr.	3.00
4	Mike Piazza	3.00
5	Alex Rodriguez	5.00
6	Manny Ramirez	1.50
7	Barry Bonds	6.00
8	Nomar Garciaparra	4.00
9	Chipper Jones	3.00
10	Vladimir Guerrero	1.50

Mark McGwire 1985 Rookie Reprint

This insert is a chromium reprinted version of McGwire's 1985 Topps rookie card. Each card features a commemorative gold-foil stamp. The insertion rate is 1:32 packs. A hobby-exclusive Refractor version is also inserted, limited to 70 sequentially numbered sets and seeded 1:12,116 packs.

	NM/M
Complete Set (1):	5.00
Inserted 1:32	
Refractor:	50.00
Production 70 cards.	
Mark McGwire	5.00

Millennium Stars

New Millennium Stars

This 10-card set features stars who had less than three years major league experience in 2000. Millennium Stars are seeded 1:32 packs and are numbered with an "NMS" prefix. A Refractor parallel is randomly inserted in 1:160 packs and has "Refractor" printed under the card number on the back.

	NM/M
Complete Set (10):	10.00
Common Player:	.50
Inserted 1:32	
Refractors:	2-3X
Inserted 1:160	

1	Nomar Garciaparra	4.00
2	Vladimir Guerrero	1.50
3	Sean Casey	.75
4	Richie Sexson	1.00
5	Todd Helton	1.50
6	Carlos Beltran	.75
7	Kevin Millwood	.75
8	Ruben Mateo	.50
9	Pat Burrell	1.00
10	Alfonso Soriano	2.00

Own the Game

This 30-card set spotlights statistical stars and 1999 Major League Baseball award winners. These were seeded 1:11 packs and are numbered with an "OTG" prefix on the card back. A Refractor parallel is randomly inserted 1:55 packs and has "Refractor" written under the card number on the back.

	NM/M
Complete Set (30):	30.00
Common Player:	.25
Inserted 1:12	
Refractors:	2-3X
Inserted 1:55	

1	Derek Jeter	4.00
2	B.J. Surhoff	.25
3	Luis Gonzalez	.50
4	Manny Ramirez	1.00
5	Rafael Palmeiro	1.00
6	Mark McGwire	3.00
7	Mark McGwire	3.00
8	Sammy Sosa	2.00
9	Ken Griffey Jr.	2.00
10	Larry Walker	.50
11	Nomar Garciaparra	3.00
12	Derek Jeter	4.00
13	Larry Walker	.50
14	Mark McGwire	3.00
15	Manny Ramirez	1.00
16	Pedro Martinez	1.50
17	Randy Johnson	.50
18	Kevin Millwood	.50
19	Pedro Martinez	1.50
20	Randy Johnson	1.50
21	Kevin Brown	.50
22	Chipper Jones	2.00
23	Ivan Rodriguez	1.00
24	Mariano Rivera	.50
25	Scott Williamson	.25
26	Carlos Beltran	.50
27	Randy Johnson	1.50
28	Pedro Martinez	1.50
29	Sammy Sosa	2.00
30	Manny Ramirez	1.00

Power Players

POWER
DEREK JETER

Twenty of the leading power hitters are featured on a colorful design. They are seeded 1:8 packs and are numbered with a "P" prefix. A Refractor parallel is also randomly seeded 1:40 packs.

	NM/M
Complete Set (20):	25.00
Common Player:	.25
Inserted 1:8	
Refractors:	2-3X
Inserted 1:40	

1	Juan Gonzalez	1.00
2	Ken Griffey Jr.	2.00
3	Mark McGwire	3.00
4	Nomar Garciaparra	3.00
5	Barry Bonds	3.00
6	Mo Vaughn	.40
7	Larry Walker	.50
8	Alex Rodriguez	3.00
9	Jose Canseco	.75
10	Jeff Bagwell	1.00
11	Manny Ramirez	1.00
12	Albert Belle	.25
13	Frank Thomas	1.00
14	Mike Piazza	2.00
15	Chipper Jones	2.00
16	Sammy Sosa	2.00
17	Vladimir Guerrero	1.00
18	Scott Rolen	1.00
19	Raul Mondesi	.40
20	Derek Jeter	4.00

21st Century Topps

21st CENTURY TOPPS
TODD HELTON

This 10-card set focuses on the top young stars in baseball heading into the next century. These were seeded 1:16 packs and are numbered with a "C" prefix on the card back. A Refractor parallel version is also seeded 1:80 packs.

	NM/M
Complete Set (10):	10.00
Common Player:	.25
Inserted 1:16	
Refractors:	2-3X
Inserted 1:80	

1	Ben Grieve	.25
2	Alex Gonzalez	.25
3	Derek Jeter	4.00
4	Sean Casey	.50
5	Nomar Garciaparra	3.00
6	Alex Rodriguez	3.00
7	Scott Rolen	1.00
8	Andruw Jones	1.00
9	Vladimir Guerrero	1.00
10	Todd Helton	1.00

Chrome Traded and Rookies

	NM/M
Complete Set (135):	60.00
Common Player:	.25

1	Mike MacDougal RC	.50
2	Andy Tracy RC	.50
3	Brandon Phillips RC	3.00
4	Brandon Inge RC	.50
5	Robbie Morrison RC	.50
6	Josh Pressley RC	.50
7	Todd Moser RC	.50
8	Rob Purvis RC	.50
9	Chance Caple RC	.50
10	Ben Sheets	1.00
11	Russ Jacobson RC	.50
12	Brian Cole RC	.50

13	Brad Baker RC	.50
14	Alex Cintron RC	.50
15	Lyle Overbay RC	.75
16	Mike Edwards RC	.50
17	Sean McGowan RC	.50
18	Jose Molina RC	.50
19	Marcos Castillo RC	.50
20	Josue Espada RC	.50
21	Alex Gordon RC	.50
22	Rob Pugmire RC	.50
23	Jason Stumm RC	.50
24	Ty Howington RC	.50
25	Brett Myers RC	.50
26	Maicer Izturis RC	.50
27	John McDonald RC	.50
28	Wilfredo Rodriguez RC	.50
29	Carlos Zambrano RC	1.50
30	Alejandro Diaz RC	.50
31	Geraldo Guzman RC	.50
32	J.R. House RC	.50
33	Elvin Nina RC	.50
34	Juan Pierre RC	2.00
35	Ben Johnson RC	.50
36	Jeff Bailey RC	.50
37	Miguel Olivo RC	.50
38	Francisco Rodriguez RC	4.00
39	Tony Pena Jr. RC	.50
40	Miguel Cabrera RC	30.00
41	Asdrubal Oropeza RC	.50
42	Junior Zamora RC	.50
43	Jovanny Cedeno RC	.50
44	John Sneed RC	.50
45	Josh Kalinowski RC	.50
46	Mike Young RC	4.00
47	Rico Washington RC	.50
48	Chad Durbin RC	.50
49	Junior Brignac RC	.50
50	Carlos Hernandez RC	.50
51	Cesar Izturis RC	.50
52	Oscar Salazar RC	.50
53	Pat Strange RC	.50
54	Rick Asadoorian RC	.50
55	Keith Reed RC	.50
56	Leo Estrella RC	.50
57	Wascar Serrano RC	.50
58	Richard Gomez RC	.50
59	Ramon Santiago RC	.50
60	Jovanny Sosa RC	.50
61	Aaron Rowand RC	1.50
62	Junior Guerrero RC	.50
63	Luis Terrero RC	.50
64	Brian Sanches RC	.50
65	Scott Sobkowiak RC	.50
66	Gary Majewski RC	.50
67	Barry Zito	2.50
68	Ryan Christianson RC	.50
69	Cristian Guerrero RC	.50
70	Tomas de la Rosa RC	.50
71	Andrew Beinbrink RC	.50
72	Ryan Knox RC	.50
73	Alex Graman RC	.50
74	Juan Guzman RC	.50
75	Ruben Salazar RC	.50
76	Luis Matos RC	.50
77	Tony Mota RC	.50
78	Doug Davis RC	.50
79	Ben Christensen RC	.50
80	Mike Lamb	.50
81	Adrian Gonzalez RC (Draft Picks)	8.00
82	Mike Stodolka RC (Draft Picks)	.50
83	Adam Johnson RC (Draft Picks)	.50
84	Matt Wheatland RC (Draft Picks)	.50
85	Corey Smith RC (Draft Picks)	.50
86	Rocco Baldelli RC (Draft Picks)	2.00
87	Keith Bucktrot RC (Draft Picks)	.50
88	Adam Wainwright RC (Draft Picks)	6.00
89	Scott Thorman RC (Draft Picks)	1.00
90	Tripper Johnson RC (Draft Picks)	.50
91	Jim Edmonds	.50
92	Masato Yoshii	.25
93	Adam Kennedy	.25
94	Darryl Kile	.25
95	Mark McLemore	.25
96	Ricky Gutierrez	.25
97	Juan Gonzalez	.25
98	Melvin Mora	.25
98	Dante Bichette	.25
100	Lee Stevens	.25

101	Roger Cedeno	.25
102	John Olerud	.40
103	Eric Young	.25
104	Mickey Morandini	.25
105	Travis Lee	.25
106	Greg Vaughn	.25
107	Todd Zeile	.25
108	Chuck Finley	.25
109	Ismael Valdes	.25
110	Ron Henika	.25
111	Pat Hentgen	.25
112	Ryan Klesko	.40
113	Derek Bell	.25
114	Hideo Nomo	1.00
115	Aaron Sele	.25
116	Fernando Vina	.25
117	Wally Joyner	.25
118	Brian Hunter	.25
119	Joe Girardi	.25
120	Omar Daal	.25
121	Brook Fordyce	.25
122	Jose Valentin	.25
123	Curt Schilling	.50
124	B.J. Surhoff	.25
125	Henry Rodriguez	.25
126	Mike Bordick	.25
127	David Justice	.50
128	Charles Johnson	.25
129	Will Clark	.50
130	Dwight Gooden	.25
131	David Segui	.25
132	Denny Neagle	.25
133	Andy Ashby	.25
134	Bruce Chen	.25
135	Jason Bere	.25

FanFest Honus Wagner T206 Reprint

In conjunction with the forthcoming sale of the finest-known T206 Honus Wagner card in July 2000, Topps produced this reprint as a promotional device for the seller (Robert Edwards Auction) and principal venue (eBay). The card was distributed at the All-Star FanFest in Atlanta. Front of the 1-1/2" x 2-5/8" card reproduces the 1909 Wagner card. The black-and-white back details the history of the card and makes note of the upcoming sale.

	NM/M
Honus Wagner	5.00

2000 Topps Gallery

The base set consists of 150 cards. Cards 101-150 are broken down into two subsets Masters of the Game (20 cards) and Students of the Game (30 cards). The subset cards are found one per pack. Card fronts have a tan textured border around the player photo with the player name, team and Gallery logo stamped in gold foil. Card backs have a small photo, brief career note and the featured player's '99

statistics. Gallery was a hobby exclusive product. Five-card packs carried a $3 SRP.

	NM/M
Complete Set (150):	40.00
Common Player:	.15
Common (101-150):	.50
Inserted 1:1	
Pack (6):	2.00
Wax Box (24):	40.00
1 Nomar Garciaparra	1.50
2 Kevin Millwood	.25
3 Jay Bell	.15
4 Rusty Greer	.15
5 Bernie Williams	.50
6 Barry Larkin	.25
7 Carlos Beltran	.25
8 Damion Easley	.15
9 Magglio Ordonez	.25
10 Matt Williams	.20
11 Shannon Stewart	.15
12 Ray Lankford	.15
13 Vinny Castilla	.20
14 Miguel Tejada	.25
15 Craig Biggio	.25
16 Chipper Jones	1.00
17 Albert Belle	.20
18 Doug Glanville	.15
19 Brian Giles	.25
20 Shawn Green	.25
21 J.T. Snow Jr.	.15
22 Luis Gonzalez	.25
23 Carlos Delgado	.50
24 J.D. Drew	.25
25 Ivan Rodriguez	.50
26 Tino Martinez	.25
27 Erubiel Durazo	.20
28 Scott Rolen	.25
29 Gary Sheffield	.40
30 Manny Ramirez	.50
31 Luis Castillo	.15
32 Fernando Tatis	.15
33 Darin Erstad	.25
34 Tim Hudson	.25
35 Sammy Sosa	1.00
36 Jason Kendall	.25
37 Todd Walker	.15
38 Orlando Hernandez	.25
39 Pokey Reese	.15
40 Mike Piazza	1.00
41 B.J. Surhoff	.15
42 Tony Gwynn	.75
43 Kevin Brown	.25
44 Preston Wilson	.25
45 Kenny Lofton	.25
46 Rondell White	.20
47 Frank Thomas	.50
48 Neifi Perez	.15
49 Edgardo Alfonzo	.15
50 Ken Griffey Jr.	1.00
51 Barry Bonds	1.50
52 Brian Jordan	.15
53 Raul Mondesi	.25
54 Troy Glaus	.50
55 Curt Schilling	.40
56 Mike Mussina	.50
57 Brian Daubach	.15
58 Roger Clemens	1.00
59 Carlos Febles	.15
60 Todd Helton	.50
61 Mark Grace	.40
62 Randy Johnson	.75
63 Jeff Bagwell	.50
64 Tom Glavine	.25
65 Adrian Beltre	.20
66 Rafael Palmeiro	.50
67 Paul O'Neill	.25
68 Robin Ventura	.25
69 Ray Durham	.15
70 Mark McGwire	1.50
71 Greg Vaughn	.15
72 Javy Lopez	.25
73 Jeromy Burnitz	.15
74 Mike Lieberthal	.15
75 Cal Ripken Jr.	2.00
76 Juan Gonzalez	.50
77 Sean Casey	.25
78 Jermaine Dye	.15
79 John Olerud	.25
80 Jose Canseco	.40
81 Eric Karros	.20
82 Roberto Alomar	.40
83 Ben Grieve	.15
84 Greg Maddux	1.00
85 Pedro Martinez	.75
86 Tony Clark	.15
87 Richie Sexson	.25
88 Cliff Floyd	.15
89 Eric Chavez	.25
90 Andruw Jones	.50
91 Vladimir Guerrero	.50
92 Alex Gonzalez	.15
93 Jim Thome	.50
94 Bob Abreu	.25
95 Derek Jeter	2.00
96 Larry Walker	.25
97 John Smoltz	.25
98 Mo Vaughn	.20
99 Jason Giambi	.50
100 Alex Rodriguez	1.50
101 Mark McGwire (Masters of the Game)	2.50
102 Sammy Sosa (Masters of the Game)	1.50
103 Alex Rodriguez (Masters of the Game)	2.50

104	Derek Jeter (Masters of the Game)	3.00
105	Greg Maddux (Masters of the Game)	1.50
106	Jeff Bagwell (Masters of the Game)	.75
107	Nomar Garciaparra (Masters of the Game)	2.00
108	Mike Piazza (Masters of the Game)	1.50
109	Pedro Martinez (Masters of the Game)	1.00
110	Chipper Jones (Masters of the Game)	1.50
111	Randy Johnson (Masters of the Game)	1.00
112	Barry Bonds (Masters of the Game)	2.50
113	Ken Griffey Jr. (Masters of the Game)	1.50
114	Manny Ramirez (Masters of the Game)	.75
115	Ivan Rodriguez (Masters of the Game)	.75
116	Juan Gonzalez (Masters of the Game)	.75
117	Vladimir Guerrero (Masters of the Game)	.75
118	Tony Gwynn (Masters of the Game)	1.00
119	Larry Walker (Masters of the Game)	.50
120	Cal Ripken Jr. (Masters of the Game)	3.00
121	Josh Hamilton (Students of the Game)	.50
122	Corey Patterson (Students of the Game)	.50
123	Pat Burrell (Students of the Game)	.50
124	Nick Johnson (Students of the Game)	.50
125	Adam Piatt (Students of the Game)	.50
126	Rick Ankiel (Students of the Game)	.50
127	A.J. Burnett (Students of the Game)	.50
128	Ben Petrick (Students of the Game)	.50
129	Rafael Furcal (Students of the Game)	.75
130	Alfonso Soriano (Students of the Game)	2.00
131	Dee Brown (Students of the Game)	.50
132	Ruben Mateo (Students of the Game)	.50
133	Pablo Ozuna (Students of the Game)	.50
134	Sean Burroughs (Students of the Game)	.75
135	Mark Mulder (Students of the Game)	.75
136	Jason Jennings (Students of the Game)	.50
137	Eric Munson (Students of the Game)	.50
138	Vernon Wells (Students of the Game)	.50
139	Brett Myers RC (Students of the Game)	1.50
140	Ben Christensen RC (Students of the Game)	.50
141	Bobby Bradley RC (Students of the Game)	.50
142	Ruben Salazar RC (Students of the Game)	.50
143	Ryan Christianson RC (Students of the Game)	.50
144	Corey Myers RC (Students of the Game)	.50
145	Aaron Rowand RC (Students of the Game)	1.00
146	Julio Zuleta RC (Students of the Game)	.50
147	Kurt Ainsworth RC (Students of the Game)	1.00
148	Scott Downs RC (Students of the Game)	.50
149	Larry Bigbie RC (Students of the Game)	1.50
150	Chance Caple RC (Students of the Game)	.50

Players Private Issue

A parallel to the 150-card base set, Players Private Issue differ from the base cards with silver foil stamping on the card front and "Players Private Issue" stamped in silver foil across the card bottom. Card backs are serial numbered in an edition of 250 sets.

Stars (1-100):	4-8X
SPs (101-150):	2-4X
Production 250 Sets	

Autographs

This five-card set features top prospects. Each card is stamped with the Topps Certified Autograph Issue logo and the Topps Authentication sticker. Autographs are seeded 1:153 packs.

		NM/M
Common Player:		5.00
Inserted 1:153		
RA	Rick Ankiel	15.00
RM	Ruben Mateo	5.00
CP	Corey Patterson	15.00
BP	Ben Petrick	5.00
VW	Vernon Wells	20.00

Gallery Exhibits

This 30-card set traces the history of art from medieval to contemporary. Card fronts have gold foil stamping and the card backs are numbered with a "GE" prefix and are found 1:18 packs.

		NM/M
Complete Set (30):		50.00
Common Player:		.50
Inserted 1:18		
1	Mark McGwire	5.00
2	Jeff Bagwell	1.50
3	Mike Piazza	3.00
4	Alex Rodriguez	5.00
5	Nomar Garciaparra	4.00
6	Ivan Rodriguez	1.50
7	Chipper Jones	3.00
8	Cal Ripken Jr.	6.00
9	Tony Gwynn	2.00
10	Jose Canseco	1.00
11	Albert Belle	.50
12	Greg Maddux	3.00
13	Barry Bonds	5.00
14	Ken Griffey Jr.	3.00
15	Juan Gonzalez	1.50
16	Rickey Henderson	1.00
17	Craig Biggio	.75
18	Vladimir Guerrero	1.50
19	Rey Ordonez	.50
20	Roberto Alomar	1.00
21	Derek Jeter	6.00
22	Manny Ramirez	1.50
23	Shawn Green	1.00
24	Sammy Sosa	3.00
25	Larry Walker	1.00
26	Pedro Martinez	2.00
27	Randy Johnson	2.00
28	Pat Burrell	1.00
29	Josh Hamilton	1.50
30	Corey Patterson	1.00

Gallery of Heroes

This 10-card set is printed on an acetate stock that simulates stained glass. Gallery of Heroes are

found on the average of 1:24 packs and are numbered with a "GH" prefix on the card back.

		NM/M
Complete Set (10):		20.00
Common Player:		1.00
Inserted 1:24		
1	Alex Rodriguez	3.00
2	Chipper Jones	2.00
3	Pedro Martinez	1.50
4	Sammy Sosa	2.00
5	Mark McGwire	3.00
6	Nomar Garciaparra	3.00
7	Vladimir Guerrero	1.00
8	Ken Griffey Jr.	2.00
9	Mike Piazza	2.00
10	Derek Jeter	4.00

Press Plates

The aluminum press plates used to print the Gallery cards were inserted at a rate of one per 1,200 packs. Each card's front and back can be found in four different color variations. Because of the unique nature of each plate, assignment of catalog values in not feasible.

	NM/M
Common Player:	50.00

Proof Positive

This 10-card set features both positive and negative photography. Done on a horizontal format the inserts pair a current star with a top prospect at the same position. Printed on a clear polycarbonate stock they were inserted 1:48 packs and are numbered with a "P" prefix.

		NM/M
Complete Set (10):		40.00
Common Player:		3.00
Inserted 1:48		
1	Ken Griffey Jr., Ruben Mateo	4.00
2	Derek Jeter, Alfonso Soriano	6.00
3	Mark McGwire, Pat Burrell	6.00
4	Pedro Martinez, A.J. Burnett	3.00
5	Alex Rodriguez, Rafael Furcal	4.00
6	Sammy Sosa, Corey Patterson	4.00
7	Randy Johnson, Rick Ankiel	3.00
8	Chipper Jones, Adam Piatt	4.00
9	Nomar Garciaparra, Pablo Ozuna	6.00
10	Mike Piazza, Eric Munson	4.00

Topps Heritage

Twenty current players are artistically depicted using the 1954 Topps card design as a template. They are seeded 1:12 packs and are numbered on the card back with a "TGH" prefix. As an added bonus the original artwork used in the development of the set is available through the Topps Gallery Auction. Auction points cards are found in every pack of Gallery.

		NM/M
Complete Set (20):		100.00
Common Player:		2.00
Inserted 1:12		
Proofs:		1-2X
Inserted 1:27		
1	Mark McGwire	12.00
2	Sammy Sosa	8.00
3	Greg Maddux	8.00
4	Mike Piazza	8.00
5	Ivan Rodriguez	4.00
6	Manny Ramirez	4.00
7	Jeff Bagwell	4.00
8	Sean Casey	2.00
9	Orlando Hernandez	2.00
10	Randy Johnson	5.00
11	Pedro Martinez	5.00
12	Vladimir Guerrero	4.00
13	Shawn Green	2.50
14	Ken Griffey Jr.	8.00
15	Alex Rodriguez	12.00
16	Nomar Garciaparra	10.00
17	Derek Jeter	15.00
18	Tony Gwynn	5.00
19	Chipper Jones	8.00
20	Cal Ripken Jr.	15.00

Lithos

Eight cards from the Topps Gallery set were issued in the form of limited edition lithographs by Bill Goff Inc. Measuring 18" x 25", the lithographs were each produced in an edition of 600, with 60 artist's proofs. Issue price on the lithos was $80 for single-player pieces and $100 for the multi-player prints.

		NM/M
Complete Set (8):		675.00
Common Player:		80.00
(1)	Shawn Green	
	(1954 Topps Style)	80.00
(2)	Ken Griffey Jr.	
	(1954 Topps Style)	80.00
(3)	Chipper Jones	
	(1954 Topps Style)	80.00
(4)	Pedro Martinez	
	(1954 Topps Style)	80.00
(5)	Alex Rodriguez	
	(1954 Topps Style)	80.00
(6)	Ivan Rodriguez	
	(1954 Topps Style)	80.00
(7)	Three of a Kind	
	(Nomar Garciaparra,	
	Alex Rodriguez,	
	Derek Jeter)	100.00
(8)	Torre's Terrors (Paul O'Neill,	
	Derek Jeter, Bernie Williams,	
	Tino Martinez)	100.00

2000 Topps Gold Label Pre-Production

A Derek Jeter card in each of the three classes of Gold Label was produced as a promo and distributed in three-card cello packs.

		NM/M
Complete Set (3):		7.50
Common Card:		3.00
PP1	Derek Jeter/Btg	3.00
PP2	Derek Jeter/Fldg	3.00
PP3	Derek Jeter/Running	3.00

2000 Topps Gold Label Class 1

Each base card in the 100-card set has three different classes, each noted on the card back below

the featured player's team logo. Each base card is also printed on 35-point rainbow styrene stock with gold foil stamping. Besides the notation on the card back, Class 1's can also be identified by the action in the background photo. Hitters are hitting and pitchers are at the start of their wind-up. A Gold die-cut parallel is also randomly seeded and are serially numbered to 100.

		NM/M
Complete Set (100):		25.00
Common Player:		.25
Gold Parallel:		4-8X
Production 100 Sets		
Pack (3):		2.00
Wax Box (24):		30.00
1	Sammy Sosa	1.50
2	Greg Maddux	1.50
3	Dee Brown	.25
4	Rondell White	.40
5	Fernando Tatis	.25
6	Troy Glaus	.75
7	Nick Johnson	.40
8	Albert Belle	.30
9	Scott Rolen	.75
10	Rafael Palmeiro	.50
11	Tony Gwynn	1.00
12	Kevin Brown	.40
13	Roberto Alomar	.50
14	John Olerud	.40
15	Rick Ankiel	.25
16	Chipper Jones	1.50
17	Craig Biggio	.40
18	Mark Mulder	.40
19	Carlos Delgado	.75
20	Alex Gonzalez	.25
21	Gabe Kapler	.25
22	Derek Jeter	3.00
23	Carlos Beltran	.40
24	Todd Helton	.75
25	Mark McGwire	2.50
26	Ben Grieve	.25
27	Rafael Furcal	.40
28	Vernon Wells	.40
29	Greg Vaughn	.25
30	Vladimir Guerrero	.75
31	Mike Piazza	1.50
32	Roger Clemens	2.00
33	Barry Larkin	.40
34	Pedro Martinez	1.00
35	Matt Williams	.30
36	Mo Vaughn	.30
37	Tim Hudson	.40
38	Andruw Jones	.75
39	Vinny Castilla	.25
40	Frank Thomas	.75
41	Pokey Reese	.25
42	Corey Patterson	.40
43	Jeromy Burnitz	.25
44	Preston Wilson	.40
45	Juan Gonzalez	.75
46	Brian Giles	.40
47	Todd Walker	.25
48	Magglio Ordonez	.40
49	Alfonso Soriano	1.00
50	Ken Griffey Jr.	1.50
51	Michael Barrett	.25
52	Shawn Green	.50
53	Erubiel Durazo	.40
54	Adam Piatt	.25
55	Pat Burrell	.50
56	Mike Mussina	.50
57	Bernie Williams	.75
58	Sean Casey	.40
59	Randy Johnson	1.00
60	Jeff Bagwell	.75
61	Eric Chavez	.50
62	Josh Hamilton	.50
63	A.J. Burnett	.50
64	Jim Thome	.75
65	Raul Mondesi	.40
66	Jason Kendall	.40
67	Mike Lieberthal	.25
68	Robin Ventura	.40
69	Ivan Rodriguez	.50
70	Larry Walker	.50
71	Eric Munson	.25
72	Brian Jordan	.25
73	Edgardo Alfonzo	.25
74	Curt Schilling	.50
75	Nomar Garciaparra	2.00
76	Mark Grace	.50
77	Shannon Stewart	.25
78	J.D. Drew	.40
79	Jack Cust	.25
80	Cal Ripken Jr.	3.00
81	Bob Abreu	.40
82	Ruben Mateo	.25
83	Orlando Hernandez	.25
84	Kris Benson	.25
85	Barry Bonds	2.50
86	Manny Ramirez	.50
87	Jose Canseco	.50
88	Sean Burroughs	.25
89	Kevin Millwood	.40
90	Alex Rodriguez	2.50
91	Brett Myers RC	1.00
92	Rick Asadoorian RC	.40
93	Ben Christensen RC	.40
94	Bobby Bradley RC	.50
95	Corey Myers RC	.50
96	Brad Baisley RC	.50
97	Aaron McNeal RC	.50
98	Aaron Rowand RC	.75
99	Scott Downs RC	.40
100	Michael Tejera RC	.40

Class 2

Each base card in the 100-card set has three different classes, each noted on the card back below the featured player's team logo. Each base card is also printed on 35-point rainbow styrene stock with gold foil stamping. Besides the notation on the card back, Class 2's can also be identified by the action in the background photo. Hitters are fielding and pitchers are in a throwing motion. A Gold die-cut parallel is also randomly seeded and are serially numbered to 100.

Same prices as Class 1.
Gold Parallel: 4-8X

Class 3

Each base card in the 100-card set has three different classes, each noted on the card back below the featured player's team logo. Each base card is also printed on 35-point rainbow styrene stock with gold foil stamping. Besides the notation on the card back, Class 3's can also be identified by the action in the background photo. Hitters are running and pitchers are in their follow through. A Gold die-cut parallel is also randomly seeded and are serially numbered to 100.

Same prices as Class 1.
Gold Parallel: 4-8X
Production 100 Sets

Bullion

This 10-card set features three teammates superimposed over their team logo on a gold holo-foiled front with gold foil stamping. They are seeded 1:53 packs and are numbered on the card back with a "B" prefix.

		NM/M
Complete Set (10):		125.00
Common Player:		4.00
Inserted 1:53		

1	Jim Thome, Manny Ramirez, Roberto Alomar	6.00
2	Derek Jeter, Orlando Hernandez, Bernie Williams	15.00
3	Chipper Jones, Andruw Jones, Greg Maddux	12.00
4	Alex Rodriguez, Jay Buhner, John Olerud	20.00
5	Nomar Garciaparra, Pedro Martinez, Brian Daubach	15.00
6	Mark McGwire, J.D. Drew, Rick Ankiel	20.00
7	Sammy Sosa, Mark Grace, Kerry Wood	15.00
8	Ken Griffey Jr., Sean Casey, Barry Larkin	20.00
9	Mike Piazza, Edgardo Alfonzo, Robin Ventura	15.00
10	Randy Johnson, Matt Williams, Erubiel Durazo	6.00

End of the Rainbow

This 15-card set highlights some of baseball's top prospects on a silver holo foiled card front with gold foil stamping. Card backs are numbered with an "ER" prefix and are seeded 1:11 packs.

		NM/M
Complete Set (15):		8.00
Common Player:		.50
Inserted 1:11		
1	Pat Burrell	1.50
2	Corey Patterson	1.00
3	Josh Hamilton	1.50
4	Eric Munson	.50
5	Sean Burroughs	.75
6	Jack Cust	.50
7	Rafael Furcal	.75
8	Ruben Salazar	.50
9	Brett Myers	1.00
10	Wes Anderson	.50
11	Nick Johnson	1.00
12	Scott Downs	.50
13	Choo Freeman	.50
14	Brad Baisley	.50
15	A.J. Burnett	.75

Prospector's Dream

These inserts feature 10 players whose success was projected early in their careers. Card fronts feature gold holo foil with the player name,

Gold Label logo and insert name stamped in gold foil. Card backs are numbered with an "PD" prefix. They are inserted 1:26 packs.

		NM/M
Complete Set (10):		15.00
Common Player:		.50
Inserted 1:26		
1	Mark McGwire	3.00
2	Alex Rodriguez	3.00
3	Nomar Garciaparra	3.00
4	Pat Burrell	.75
5	Todd Helton	1.00
6	Derek Jeter	4.00
7	Adam Piatt	.50
8	Chipper Jones	2.00
9	Shawn Green	.75
10	Josh Hamilton	1.50

The Treasury

This 25-card set spotlights 15 veterans and 10 prospects on a silver holo foiled front with gold foil stamping. They have an insertion ratio of 1:21 packs and are numbered on the card back with an "T" prefix.

		NM/M
Complete Set (25):		40.00
Common Player:		.50
Inserted 1:21		
1	Ken Griffey Jr.	3.00
2	Derek Jeter	6.00
3	Chipper Jones	3.00
4	Manny Ramirez	1.50
5	Nomar Garciaparra	4.00
6	Sammy Sosa	3.00
7	Cal Ripken Jr.	6.00
8	Alex Rodriguez	5.00
9	Mike Piazza	3.00
10	Pedro Martinez	2.00
11	Vladimir Guerrero	1.50
12	Jeff Bagwell	1.50
13	Shawn Green	1.00
14	Greg Maddux	3.00
15	Mark McGwire	5.00
16	Josh Hamilton	1.50
17	Corey Patterson	1.00
18	Dee Brown	.50
19	Rafael Furcal	.50
20	Pat Burrell	1.00
21	Alfonso Soriano	3.00
22	Adam Piatt	.50
23	A.J. Burnett	.75
24	Mark Mulder	.75
25	Ruben Mateo	.50

Name Mismatches

Because of faulty alignment when the gold-foil logo and player name were applied to card fronts, some Gold Label cards are found with the wrong name on front. Because each of these error cards is rare or possibly unique, and the demand is dependent on the combination of photo and name, it is not possible to assign values.

2000 Topps HD

This super-premium product consists of 100 regular base cards comprised of 88 veterans and 12 rookies. The base cards feature hyper-color technology and printed

on a very thick 50-pt. card stock. Card backs have a small photo, career highlight and complete year-by-year statistics. A Platinum parallel to the base set is also randomly seeded and are sequentially numbered to 99 sets.

		NM/M
Complete Set (100):		30.00
Common Player:		.25
Platinums:		4-8X
Production 99 Sets		
Pack (4):		1.50
Wax Box (20):		30.00
1	Derek Jeter	3.00
2	Andruw Jones	.75
3	Ben Grieve	.25
4	Carlos Beltran	.40
5	Randy Johnson	1.00
6	Javy Lopez	.40
7	Gary Sheffield	.50
8	John Olerud	.40
9	Vinny Castilla	.25
10	Barry Larkin	.40
11	Tony Clark	.25
12	Roberto Alomar	.50
13	Brian Jordan	.25
14	Wade Boggs	.50
15	Carlos Febles	.25
16	Alfonso Soriano	1.50
17	A.J. Burnett	.25
18	Matt Williams	.25
19	Alex Gonzalez	.25
20	Larry Walker	.40
21	Jeff Bagwell	.75
22	Al Leiter	.25
23	Ken Griffey Jr.	1.50
24	Ruben Mateo	.25
25	Mark Grace	.50
26	Carlos Delgado	.75
27	Vladimir Guerrero	.75
28	Kenny Lofton	.50
29	Rusty Greer	.25
30	Pedro Martinez	1.00
31	Todd Helton	.75
32	Ray Lankford	.25
33	Jose Canseco	.50
34	Raul Mondesi	.40
35	Mo Vaughn	.40
36	Eric Chavez	.40
37	Manny Ramirez	.75
38	Jason Kendall	.40
39	Mike Mussina	.50
40	Dante Bichette	.25
41	Troy Glaus	.75
42	Rickey Henderson	.50
43	Pablo Ozuna	.25
44	Michael Barrett	.25
45	Tony Gwynn	1.00
46	John Smoltz	.40
47	Rafael Palmeiro	.50
48	Curt Schilling	.40
49	Todd Walker	.25
50	Greg Vaughn	.25
51	Orlando Hernandez	.25
52	Jim Thome	.75
53	Pat Burrell	.50
54	Tim Salmon	.40
55	Tom Glavine	.40
56	Travis Lee	.25
57	Gabe Kapler	.25
58	Greg Maddux	1.50
59	Scott Rolen	.50
60	Cal Ripken Jr.	3.00
61	Preston Wilson	.40
62	Ivan Rodriguez	.50
63	Johnny Damon	.40
64	Bernie Williams	.50
65	Barry Bonds	2.50
66	Sammy Sosa	1.50
67	Robin Ventura	.40
68	Tony Fernandez	.25
69	Jay Bell	.25
70	Mark McGwire	2.50
71	Jeromy Burnitz	.25
72	Chipper Jones	1.50
73	Josh Hamilton	.50
74	Darin Erstad	.40
75	Alex Rodriguez	2.50
76	Sean Casey	.40
77	Tino Martinez	.40
78	Juan Gonzalez	.75
79	Cliff Floyd	.25
80	Craig Biggio	.40
81	Shawn Green	.50
82	Adrian Beltre	.25
83	Mike Piazza	1.50
84	Nomar Garciaparra	2.00
85	Kevin Brown	.40
86	Roger Clemens	2.00
87	Frank Thomas	.75
88	Albert Belle	.25
89	Erubiel Durazo	.25
90	David Walling	.25
91	John Sneed RC	.50
92	Larry Bigbie RC	.50
93	B.J. Garbe RC	.50
94	Bobby Bradley RC	.75
95	Ryan Christiansen RC	.50
96	Jay Gerhke RC	.50
97	Jason Stumm RC	.50
98	Brett Myers RC	1.50
99	Chance Caple RC	.50
100	Corey Myers RC	.75

Autographs

This two-card set features Cal Ripken Jr. and Derek Jeter. Card fronts include the Topps "Certified Autograph Issue" logo stamp as well as the Topps 3M authentication sticker to verify its authenticity. The insert rate for Jeter is 1:859 and Ripken Jr. 1:4,386.

		NM/M
Jeter 1:859		
Ripken 1:4,386		
1	Derek Jeter	150.00
2	Cal Ripken Jr.	250.00

Ballpark Figures

This 10-card set features a baseball field designed die-cut. These are seeded 1:11 packs and are numbered with a "BF" prefix on the card back.

		NM/M
Complete Set (10):		15.00
Common Player:		.50
Inserted 1:11		
1	Mark McGwire	3.00
2	Ken Griffey Jr.	2.00
3	Nomar Garciaparra	3.00
4	Derek Jeter	4.00
5	Sammy Sosa	2.00
6	Mike Piazza	2.00
7	Juan Gonzalez	1.00
8	Larry Walker	.75
9	Ben Grieve	.50
10	Barry Bonds	3.00

Clearly Refined

This 10-card set focuses on baseball's top young stars heading into the 2000 season. They are printed on high definition card stock and are seeded 1:20 packs. These are numbered with a "CR" prefix on the card back.

		NM/M
Complete Set (10):		8.00
Common Player:		.50
Inserted 1:20		
1	Alfonso Soriano	3.00
2	Ruben Mateo	.50
3	Josh Hamilton	1.00
4	Chad Hermansen	.50
5	Ryan Anderson	.50

6	Nick Johnson	1.00
7	Octavio Dotel	.50
8	Peter Bergeron	.50
9	Adam Piatt	.50
10	Pat Burrell	2.00

Image

This 10-card insert set highlights those batters with the best eyes at the plate. These were seeded 1:44 packs and are numbered with a "HD" prefix on the card back.

		NM/M
Complete Set (10):		30.00
Common Player:		1.00
Inserted 1:44		
1	Sammy Sosa	3.00
2	Mark McGwire	5.00
3	Derek Jeter	6.00
4	Albert Belle	.40
5	Vladimir Guerrero	1.50
6	Ken Griffey Jr.	3.00
7	Mike Piazza	3.00
8	Alex Rodriguez	5.00
9	Barry Bonds	5.00
10	Nomar Garciaparra	4.00

On The Cutting Edge

This 10-card insert set is die-cut down the right hand side of the card highlighting the five-tool stars top five baseball attributes. These are inserted 1:22 packs and are numbered with a "CE" prefix on the card back.

		NM/M
Complete Set (10):		15.00
Common Player:		.50
Inserted 1:22		
1	Andruw Jones	1.00
2	Nomar Garciaparra	3.00
3	Barry Bonds	3.00
4	Larry Walker	.50
5	Vladimir Guerrero	1.00
6	Jeff Bagwell	1.00
7	Derek Jeter	4.00
8	Sammy Sosa	2.00
9	Alex Rodriguez	3.00
10	Ken Griffey Jr.	2.00

Opening Day 2K

As part of a multi-manufacturer promotion, Topps issued eight cards of an "Opening Day 2K" set. Packages containing some of the 32 cards in the issue were distributed by MLB teams early in the season. The cards were also available exclusively as inserts in Topps Opening Day packs sold at KMart stores early in the season. The Topps OD2K cards have gold-foil graphic highlights on front. Backs have portrait photos, stats and are numbered with an "OD" prefix.

		NM/M
Complete Set (8):		6.00
Common Player:		.50
1	Mark McGwire	2.00
2	Barry Bonds	.75
3	Ivan Rodriguez	.75
4	Sean Casey	.65
5	Derek Jeter	3.00
6	Vladimir Guerrero	1.00
7	Preston Wilson	.65
8	Ben Grieve	.50

2000 Topps Stars

The base set consists of 200 cards, including a 50-card Spotlights subset (151-200). Card fronts have a shadow image of the featured player in the background of the player photo. The Topps Stars logo, player name, team logo and position are stamped in silver foil.

		NM/M
Complete Set (200):		35.00
Common Player:		.10
Pack (6):		2.00
Box (24):		40.00
1	Vladimir Guerrero	.75
2	Eric Karros	.10
3	Omar Vizquel	.20
4	Ken Griffey Jr.	1.50
5	Preston Wilson	.20
6	Albert Belle	.20
7	Ryan Klesko	.10
8	Bob Abreu	.20
9	Warren Morris	.10
10	Rafael Palmeiro	.40
11	Nomar Garciaparra	2.00
12	Dante Bichette	.10
13	Jeff Cirillo	.10
14	Carlos Beltran	.25
15	Tony Clark	.10
16	Ray Durham	.10
17	Mark McGwire	2.00
18	Jim Thome	.50
19	Todd Walker	.10
20	Richie Sexson	.40
21	Adrian Beltre	.10
22	Jay Bell	.10
23	Craig Biggio	.25
24	Ben Grieve	.15
25	Greg Maddux	1.50
26	Fernando Tatis	.10
27	Jeromy Burnitz	.10
28	Vinny Castilla	.10
29	Mark Grace	.25
30	Derek Jeter	2.00
31	Larry Walker	.25
32	Ivan Rodriguez	.50
33	Curt Schilling	.40
34	Mike Lamb RC	.25
35	Kevin Brown	.20
36	Andruw Jones	.40
37	Chris Mears RC	.10
38	Bartolo Colon	.15
39	Edgardo Alfonzo	.15
40	Brady Anderson	.20
41	Andres Galarraga	.25
42	Scott Rolen	.50
43	Manny Ramirez	.75
44	Carlos Delgado	.50
45	David Cone	.10
46	Carl Everett	.10
47	Chipper Jones	1.50
48	Barry Bonds	2.00
49	Dean Palmer	.10
50	Frank Thomas	.75
51	Paul O'Neill	.25
52	Mo Vaughn	.20
53	Todd Helton	.75
54	Jason Giambi	1.00
55	Brian Jordan	.10
56	Luis Gonzalez	.25
57	Alex Rodriguez	2.00
58	J.D. Drew	.10
59	Javy Lopez	.20
60	Tony Gwynn	1.00
61	Jason Kendall	.20
62	Pedro Martinez	.75
63	Matt Williams	.20
64	Gary Sheffield	.40
65	Roberto Alomar	.50
66	Lyle Overbay RC	1.00
67	Jeff Bagwell	.75
68	Tim Hudson	.40
69	Sammy Sosa	1.50
70	Keith Reed RC	.10
71	Robin Ventura	.20
72	Cal Ripken Jr.	2.50
73	Alex Gonzalez	.10
74	Aaron McNeal RC	.10
75	Mike Lieberthal	.10
76	Brian Giles	.25
77	Kevin Millwood	.10
78	Troy O'Leary	.10
79	Raul Mondesi	.20
80	John Olerud	.20
81	David Justice	.25
82	Erubiel Durazo	.10

83	Shawn Green	.40
84	Tino Martinez	.20
85	Greg Vaughn	.15
86	Tom Glavine	.25
87	Jose Canseco	.40
88	Kenny Lofton	.25
89	Brian Daubach	.10
90	Mike Piazza	1.50
91	Randy Johnson	.75
92	Pokey Reese	.10
93	Troy Glaus	.50
94	Kerry Wood	.25
95	Sean Casey	.20
96	Magglio Ordonez	.40
97	Bernie Williams	.50
98	Juan Gonzalez	.75
99	Barry Larkin	.25
100	Orlando Hernandez	.20
101	Roger Clemens	1.50
102	Bob Gibson (Retired Stars)	.25
103	Gary Carter (Retired Stars)	.10
104	Willie Stargell (Retired Stars)	.10
105	Joe Morgan (Retired Stars)	.40
106	Brooks Robinson (Retired Stars)	.50
107	Ozzie Smith (Retired Stars)	.50
108	Carl Yastrzemski (Retired Stars)	.25
109	Al Kaline (Retired Stars)	.40
110	Frank Robinson (Retired Stars)	.50
111	Lance Berkman (Shining Prospects)	.10
112	Adam Piatt (Shining Prospects)	.10
113	Vernon Wells (Shining Prospects)	.10
114	Rafael Furcal (Shining Prospects)	.10
115	Rick Ankiel (Shining Prospects)	.25
116	Corey Patterson (Shining Prospects)	.25
117	Josh Hamilton (Shining Prospects)	1.00
118	Jack Cust (Shining Prospects)	.20
119	Josh Girdley (Shining Prospects)	.10
120	Pablo Ozuna (Shining Prospects)	.10
121	Sean Burroughs (Shining Prospects)	.25
122	Pat Burrell (Shining Prospects)	.25
123	Chad Hermansen (Shining Prospects)	.10
124	Ruben Mateo (Shining Prospects)	.10
125	Ben Petrick (Shining Prospects)	.10
126	Dee Brown (Shining Prospects)	.10
127	Eric Munson (Shining Prospects)	.10
128	Ruben Salazar (Shining Prospects)	.10
129	Kip Wells (Shining Prospects)	.10
130	Alfonso Soriano (Shining Prospects)	1.00
131	Mark Mulder (Shining Prospects)	.25
132	Roosevelt Brown (Shining Prospects)	.10
133	Nick Johnson (Shining Prospects)	.40
134	Kyle Snyder (Shining Prospects)	.10
135	David Walling (Shining Prospects)	.10
136	Geraldo Guzman RC	.25
137	John Sneed RC	.10
138	Ben Christensen RC	.40
139	Corey Myers RC	.25
140	Jose Ortiz RC	.75
141	Ryan Christianson RC	.25
142	Brett Myers RC	1.00
143	Bobby Bradley RC	.25
144	Rick Asadoorian RC	.25
145	Julio Zuleta RC	.40
146	Ty Howington RC	1.00
147	Josh Kalinowski RC	.40
148	B.J. Garbe RC	.50
149	Scott Downs RC	.40
150	Dan Wright RC	.25
151	Jeff Bagwell (Veterans)	.50
152	Vladimir Guerrero (Veterans)	.50
153	Mike Piazza (Veterans)	1.00
154	Juan Gonzalez (Veterans)	.40
155	Ivan Rodriguez (Veterans)	.40
156	Manny Ramirez (Veterans)	.40
157	Sammy Sosa (Veterans)	1.00
158	Chipper Jones (Veterans)	.75
159	Shawn Green (Veterans)	.20
160	Ken Griffey Jr. (Veterans)	.75
161	Cal Ripken Jr. (Veterans)	1.25
162	Nomar Garciaparra (Veterans)	1.00
163	Derek Jeter (Veterans)	1.00
164	Barry Bonds (Veterans)	1.00
165	Greg Maddux (Veterans)	.75

166	Mark McGwire (Veterans)	1.00
167	Roberto Alomar (Veterans)	.25
168	Alex Rodriguez (Veterans)	1.25
169	Randy Johnson (Veterans)	.40
170	Tony Gwynn (Veterans)	.50
171	Pedro Martinez (Veterans)	.40
172	Bob Gibson (Retired Stars)	.25
173	Gary Carter (Retired Stars)	.10
174	Willie Stargell (Retired Stars)	.25
175	Joe Morgan (Retired Stars)	.25
176	Brooks Robinson (Retired Stars)	.40
177	Ozzie Smith (Retired Stars)	.40
178	Carl Yastrzemski (Retired Stars)	.25
179	Al Kaline (Retired Stars)	.25
180	Frank Robinson (Retired Stars)	.40
181	Adam Piatt (Prospects)	.20
182	Alfonso Soriano (Prospects)	.75
183	Corey Patterson (Prospects)	.25
184	Vernon Wells (Prospects)	.40
185	Pat Burrell (Prospects)	.20
186	Mark Mulder (Prospects)	.25
187	Eric Munson (Prospects)	.10
188	Rafael Furcal (Prospects)	.15
189	Rick Ankiel (Prospects)	.25
190	Ruben Mateo (Prospects)	.10
191	Sean Burroughs (Prospects)	.20
192	Josh Hamilton (Prospects)	.10
193	Brett Myers	1.00
194	Ben Christensen	.20
195	Ty Howington	.25
196	Rick Asadoorian	.20
197	Josh Kalinowski	.20
198	Corey Myers	.25
199	Ryan Christianson	.25
200	John Sneed	.25

Blue

A parallel to the 200-card base set the player shadow has blue tint and the Topps Stars logo, player name, team logo and position are stamped in blue foil. Cards 1-150 are serially numbered on the card back to 299 and cards 151-200 are serially numbered to 99.

Stars (1-150):	3-5X
Production 299 Sets	
Stars (151-180):	4-8X
Rookies (181-200):	2-4X
Production 99 Sets	

All-Star Authority

This 14-card set features a gold and silver holo foiled front with gold etching. Card backs are numbered with an "AS" prefix. They are found on the average of 1:13 packs.

		NM/M
Complete Set (14):		25.00
Common Player:		1.00
Inserted 1:13		
1	Mark McGwire	3.00

2	Sammy Sosa	2.00
3	Ken Griffey Jr.	2.00
4	Cal Ripken Jr.	4.00
5	Tony Gwynn	1.50
6	Barry Bonds	4.00
7	Mike Piazza	2.00
8	Pedro Martinez	1.50
9	Chipper Jones	2.00
10	Manny Ramirez	1.00
11	Alex Rodriguez	3.00
12	Derek Jeter	4.00
13	Nomar Garciaparra	3.00
14	Roberto Alomar	1.00

Autographs

A combination of retired and current players make up this 13-card set. The set is broken down into two levels: A and B. Level A autographs are seeded 1:382 packs and Level B autographs are found in 1:1,636 packs. Each card features the Topps "Certified Autograph Issue" stamp and the Topps "Genuine Issue" sticker on the card back. Card backs are numbered with the featured player's initials.

		NM/M
Common Player:		10.00
Group A 1:382		
Group B 1:1,636		
RA	Rick Ankiel/A	15.00
GC	Gary Carter/B	60.00
RF	Rafael Furcal/A	15.00
BG	Bob Gibson/A	25.00
DJ	Derek Jeter/A	90.00
AK	Al Kaline/B	50.00
KM	Kevin Millwood/A	15.00
JM	Joe Morgan/A	40.00
BR	Brooks Robinson/B	40.00
FR	Frank Robinson/B	40.00
OS	Ozzie Smith/B	35.00
WS	Willie Stargell/B	50.00
CY	Carl Yastrzemski/B	65.00

Game Gear Bats

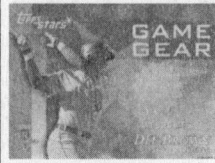

A piece of the featured player's game-used bat is embedded into the card front and are seeded 1:175 packs.

		NM/M
Common Player:		10.00
Group A 1:2,289		
Group B 1:1,153		
Group C 1:409		
1	Rafael Furcal/C	10.00
2	Sean Burroughs/B	10.00
3	Corey Patterson/B	10.00
4	Chipper Jones/B	40.00
5	Vernon Wells/C	15.00
6	Alfonso Soriano/B	25.00
7	Eric Munson/C	10.00
8	Ben Petrick/B	10.00
9	Dee Brown/C	10.00
10	Lance Berkman/C	15.00

Game Gear Jersey

A piece of the featured player's game-used jersey is embedded into the card front and are seeded 1:382 packs.

		NM/M
Common Player:		10.00
Inserted 1:382		
1	Kevin Millwood	10.00
2	Brad Penny	10.00
3	J.D. Drew	15.00

Progression

Each of the nine cards features three players on a horizontal format, progressing from past, present and future stars at each of the nine positions. They were seeded 1:13 packs and are numbered on the back with an "P" prefix.

	NM/M
Complete Set (9):	15.00
Common Player:	1.00
Inserted 1:13	
1 Bob Gibson, Pedro Martinez, Rick Ankiel	1.50
2 Gary Carter, Mike Piazza, Ben Petrick	2.00
3 Willie Stargell, Mark McGwire, Pat Burrell	3.00
4 Joe Morgan, Roberto Alomar, Ruben Salazar	1.00
5 Brooks Robinson, Chipper Jones, Sean Burroughs	2.00
6 Ozzie Smith, Derek Jeter, Rafael Furcal	3.00
7 Carl Yastrzemski, Barry Bonds, Josh Hamilton	
8 Al Kaline, Ken Griffey Jr., Ruben Mateo	2.00
9 Frank Robinson, Manny Ramirez, Corey Patterson	1.50

Walk of Fame

This 15-card set spotlights the top stars on a silver and gold holo foiled card front. Card backs feature comparative commentary with the all-time best at their respective positions and are numbered with an "WF" prefix. They are seeded 1:8 packs.

	NM/M
Complete Set (15):	15.00
Common Player:	.75
Inserted 1:8	
1 Cal Ripken Jr.	3.00
2 Ken Griffey Jr.	1.50
3 Mark McGwire	2.00
4 Sammy Sosa	1.50
5 Alex Rodriguez	2.00
6 Derek Jeter	2.50
7 Nomar Garciaparra	2.00
8 Chipper Jones	1.50
9 Manny Ramirez	1.00
10 Mike Piazza	1.50
11 Vladimir Guerrero	1.00
12 Barry Bonds	3.00
13 Tony Gwynn	1.00
14 Roberto Alomar	.75
15 Pedro Martinez	1.00

Subway Series Parade Promos

During the October 30 World Series victory parade in New York, Topps randomly distributed a pair of special cards promoting its forthcoming Subway Series boxed set. Besides regular versions of each card, a foil version was also produced in a hand-numbered edition of 1,000 each, with 500 given to Topps employees. Cards have group photos of the team's celebrating on front, with the title in a

black band on top, along with a team logo and the subway station number. Backs are in blue and orange on white and have a team logo printed beneath a short post-season summary. At bottom are ads for Topps' Subway Series commemorative set and information on a sweepstakes for 2001 Yankees or Mets tickets.

	NM/M
N.L. Champs	3.00
N.L. Champs (Foil)	6.00
Yankees Win Subway Series	5.00
Yankees Win Subway Series (Foil)	10.00

Subway Series Parade Promos - Mets Win

To cover themselves in the event the Mets had won the 2000 Subway Series against the Yankees, Topps printed up a "Mets Win" card for distribution as a promo for its Subway Series set. When the Yankees won, the Mets Win card was not released. Early in 2002, a quantity (50) of these cards surfaced, reportedly having been given to a Topps employee in 2000. The Mets Win cards are nearly identical to the issued Yankees version, with an on-field celebration group hug on front and information about the Series on back, along with information about the Subway Series card set and other Topps products.

	NM/M
Mets Win Subway Series	90.00

Subway Series

Rick Reed
2000 New York City Subway Series

	NM/M
Complete Fact. Set (101):	70.00
Complete Set (100):	20.00
Common Player:	.20
1 Mike Piazza	3.00
2 Jay Payton	.20
3 Edgardo Alfonzo	.40
4 Todd Pratt	.20
5 Todd Zeile	.20
6 Mike Bordick	.20
7 Robin Ventura	.40
8 Benny Agbayani	.20
9 Timo Perez	.50
10 Kurt Abbott	.20
11 Matt Franco	.20
12 Bubba Trammell	.20
13 Darryl Hamilton	.20
14 Lenny Harris	.20
15 Joe McEwing	.20
16 Mike Hampton	.40
17 Al Leiter	.40
18 Rick Reed	.20
19 Bobby Jones	.20
20 Glendon Rusch	.20
21 Armando Benitez	.20
22 John Franco	.20
23 Rick White	.20
24 Dennis Cook	.20
25 Turk Wendell	.20
26 Bobby Valentine	.20
27 Derek Jeter	4.00
28 Chuck Knoblauch	.40
29 Tino Martinez	.30
30 Jorge Posada	.40
31 Luis Sojo	.20
32 Scott Brosius	.20
33 Chris Turner	.20
34 Bernie Williams	.75
35 David Justice	.75
36 Paul O'Neill	.40
37 Glenallen Hill	.20
38 Jose Vizcaino	.20
39 Luis Polonia	.20
40 Clay Bellinger	.20
41 Orlando Hernandez	.40
42 Roger Clemens	1.50
43 Andy Pettitte	.50
44 Denny Neagle	.40
45 Dwight Gooden	.30

46 David Cone	.20
47 Mariano Rivera	.50
48 Jeff Nelson	.20
49 Mike Stanton	.20
50 Jason Grimsley	.20
51 Jose Canseco	.75
52 Joe Torre	.50
53 Edgardo Alfonzo	.40
54 Darryl Hamilton	.20
55 John Franco	.20
56 Benny Agbayani	.20
57 Bobby Jones	.20
58 New York Mets	.20
59 Bobby Valentine	.20
60 Mike Piazza	3.00
61 Armando Benitez	.20
62 Mike Piazza	3.00
63 Mike Piazza	3.00
64 Todd Zeile	.20
65 Timo Perez	.50
66 Timo Perez	.50
67 Mike Hampton	.40
68 Andy Pettitte	.50
69 Tino Martinez	.30
70 Joe Torre	.50
71 New York Yankees	.40
72 Orlando Hernandez	.40
73 Bernie Williams	.75
74 Andy Pettitte	.50
75 Mariano Rivera	.50
76 New York Yankees	.40
77 Roger Clemens	1.50
78 Derek Jeter	4.00
79 David Justice	.75
80 Mariano Rivera	.50
81 Tino Martinez	.30
82 New York Yankees	.40
83 Jorge Posada	.40
84 Chuck Knoblauch	.40
85 Jose Vizcaino	.20
86 Roger Clemens	1.50
87 Mike Piazza	3.00
88 Clay Bellinger	.20
89 Robin Ventura	.40
90 Benny Agbayani	.20
91 Orlando Hernandez	.40
92 Derek Jeter	4.00
93 Mike Piazza	3.00
94 Mariano Rivera	.50
95 Derek Jeter	3.00
96 Luis Sojo	.20
97 New York Yankees	.40
98 Mike Hampton	.40
99 David Justice	.75
100 Derek Jeter	4.00

Series Fan Fare

Mike Piazza
Catcher

	NM/M
Common Player:	25.00
Inserted 1:Set	
1 Timo Perez	35.00
2 Edgardo Alfonzo	40.00
3 Mike Piazza	120.00
4 Robin Ventura	35.00
5 Todd Zeile	25.00
6 Benny Agbayani	25.00
7 Jay Payton	25.00
8 Mike Bordick	25.00
9 Matt Franco	25.00
10 Mike Hampton	40.00
11 Al Leiter	40.00
12 Rick Reed	25.00
13 Bobby Jones	25.00
14 Glendon Rusch	25.00
15 Darryl Hamilton	25.00
16 Turk Wendell	25.00
17 John Franco	25.00
18 Armando Benitez	25.00
19 Chuck Knoblauch	35.00
20 Derek Jeter	200.00
21 David Justice	40.00
22 Bernie Williams	50.00
23 Jorge Posada	40.00
24 Paul O'Neill	50.00
25 Tino Martinez	35.00
26 Luis Sojo	25.00
27 Scott Brosius	25.00
28 Jose Canseco	50.00
29 Orlando Hernandez	35.00
30 Roger Clemens	100.00
31 Andy Pettitte	40.00
32 Denny Neagle	25.00
33 David Cone	25.00
34 Jeff Nelson	25.00
35 Mike Stanton	25.00
36 Mariano Rivera	60.00

2000 Topps TEK

Forty-five players make up this set including 5 rookies (41-45). Each card is printed on a transparent, polycarbonate stock with patterns 1-15 featuring silver foil metalization. All 45 players are featured on 20 different player focused background patterns. Card backs

have two numbers, the first is the player's card number within the set and the second is the pattern number. Patterns 16-20 have color variations and have an insertion rate of 1:10 packs. Each pack contains 4 TEK cards with an SRP of $5.

	NM/M
Complete Set (45):	25.00
Common Player:	.40
Common Rookie (41-45):	.75
2,000 serial numbered rookies.	
Pack (4):	2.00
Box (20):	30.00
1 Mike Piazza	1.50
2 Chipper Jones	1.50
3 Juan Gonzalez	.75
4 Ivan Rodriguez	.50
5 Cal Ripken Jr.	3.00
6 A.J. Burnett	.40
7 Jim Thome	.50
8 Mo Vaughn	.40
9 Andruw Jones	.75
10 Mark McGwire	2.00
11 Jose Canseco	.50
12 Shawn Green	.50
13 Barry Bonds	3.00
14 Bernie Williams	.50
15 Manny Ramirez	.75
16 Greg Maddux	1.50
17 Carlos Beltran	.40
18 Pedro Martinez	1.00
19 Jeff Bagwell	.75
20 Sammy Sosa	2.00
21 J.D. Drew	.40
22 Randy Johnson	1.00
23 Larry Walker	.40
24 Frank Thomas	1.50
25 Orlando Hernandez	.40
26 Scott Rolen	.75
27 Tony Gwynn	1.00
28 Rick Ankiel	.50
29 Roberto Alomar	.75
30 Ken Griffey Jr.	1.50
31 Vladimir Guerrero	1.00
32 Derek Jeter	3.00
33 Nomar Garciaparra	2.00
34 Alex Rodriguez	2.50
35 Sean Casey	.40
36 Adam Piatt (Prospects)	.40
37 Corey Patterson (Prospects)	.40
38 Josh Hamilton (Prospects)	.50
39 Pat Burrell (Prospects)	.50
40 Eric Munson (Prospects)	.40
41 Ruben Salazar RC (Rookies)	.75
42 John Sneed RC (Rookies)	.75
43 Josh Girdley RC (Rookies)	.75
44 Brett Myers RC (Rookies)	4.00
45 Rick Asadoorian RC (Rookies)	.75

Color

Color variations make up patterns 16-20 of the base set and instead of metallic silver foil have a different color background. They are seeded on the average of 1:10 packs.

	NM/M
Patterns 16-20:	1-2X

Gold

This parallel to the base set has a rounded top corner and rounded bottom corner with a gold background. Each pattern is serially numbered on the card back in an edition of 10 sets.

Stars:	8-15X
Rookies:	4-8X
Production 10 Sets	

ArchiTEKs

Printed on a clear, polycarbonate card stock the TEK logo, and player name are stamped in gold foil. Card backs are numbered with an "A" prefix. They are found on the average of 1:5 packs.

	NM/M
Complete Set (18):	20.00
Common Player:	.50
Inserted 1:5	
1 Nomar Garciaparra	2.00
2 Derek Jeter	3.00
3 Chipper Jones	1.50
4 Vladimir Guerrero	1.00
5 Mark McGwire	2.50
6 Ken Griffey Jr.	1.50
7 Mike Piazza	1.50
8 Jeff Bagwell	1.00
9 Larry Walker	.50
10 Manny Ramirez	1.00
11 Alex Rodriguez	2.00
12 Sammy Sosa	2.00
13 Shawn Green	.50
14 Juan Gonzalez	.75
15 Barry Bonds	3.00
16 Pedro Martinez	1.00
17 Cal Ripken Jr.	3.00
18 Ivan Rodriguez	.75

DramaTEK Performers

Printed on a clear, polycarbonate stock, the insert name and TEK logo are stamped in blue foil. Card backs are numbered with a "DP" prefix and are seeded 1:10 packs.

	NM/M
Complete Set (9):	15.00
Common Player:	1.50
Inserted 1:10	
1 Mark McGwire	3.00
2 Sammy Sosa	2.50
3 Ken Griffey Jr.	2.00

4 Nomar Garciaparra	3.00
5 Chipper Jones	2.00
6 Mike Piazza	3.00
7 Alex Rodriguez	3.00
8 Derek Jeter	3.00
9 Vladimir Guerrero	1.50

TEKtonics

This nine-card set features baseball's top hitters on a die-cut design on a clear, polycarbonate stock. Card backs are numbered with a "TT" prefix and are inserted 1:30 packs.

	NM/M
Complete Set (9):	35.00
Common Player:	4.00
Inserted 1:30	
1 Derek Jeter	6.00
2 Mark McGwire	6.00
3 Ken Griffey Jr.	4.00
4 Mike Piazza	6.00
5 Alex Rodriguez	6.00
6 Chipper Jones	4.00
7 Nomar Garciaparra	6.00
8 Sammy Sosa	5.00
9 Cal Ripken Jr.	8.00

2001 Topps Promo Cards

Johnny Bench
GOLDEN ANNIVERSARY GREAT

Since a 50th anniversary only comes around once, Topps made a big deal in promoting its 2001 baseball card issue with an oversize promo pack. Each gold-foil finfold pack contains eight 9" x 12-1/2" glossy promo cards. Fronts reproduce various cards from the base set, subsets and inserts while backs provide further photos and details.

	NM/M
Complete Set (8):	25.00
Common Player:	3.00
(1) Hank Aaron (1954 Topps)	7.50
(2) Johnny Bench (Golden Anniversary Great)	4.00
(3) Mark McGwire (Base card.)	5.00
(4) Nolan Ryan (King of Kings)	15.00
(5) Mike Schmidt (Golden Greats)	4.00
(6) Bob Gibson, Pedro Martinez (Topps Combos)	3.00
(7) Checklist	.50
(8) Header	.50

2001 Topps

	NM/M
Complete Set (790):	70.00
Complete Ser. 1 Set (405):	30.00
Complete Ser. 2 Set (385):	40.00
Common Player:	.10
Complete Factory Set, Blue (795):	75.00
Complete Factory Set, Gold (795):	75.00
Ser. 1 Pack (10):	1.50
Ser. 1 Box (36):	45.00
Ser. 2 Pack (10):	1.50
Ser. 2 Box (36):	45.00
1 Cal Ripken Jr.	1.50
2 Chipper Jones	.10
3 Roger Cedeno	.10
4 Garret Anderson	.10
5 Robin Ventura	.10

No.	Player	Value
6	Daryle Ward	.10
7	Not Issued	.10
8	Ron Gant	.20
9	Phil Nevin	.10
10	Jermaine Dye	.10
11	Chris Singleton	.10
12	Mike Stanton	.10
13	Brian Hunter	.10
14	Mike Redmond	.10
15	Jim Thome	.25
16	Brian Jordan	.10
17	Joe Girardi	.10
18	Steve Woodard	.10
19	Dustin Hermanson	.10
20	Shawn Green	.30
21	Todd Stottlemyre	.10
22	Dan Wilson	.10
23	Todd Pratt	.10
24	Derek Lowe	.10
25	Juan Gonzalez	.40
26	Clay Bellinger	.10
27	Jeff Fassero	.10
28	Pat Meares	.10
29	Eddie Taubensee	.10
30	Paul O'Neill	.25
31	Jeffrey Hammonds	.10
32	Pokey Reese	.10
33	Mike Mussina	.30
34	Rico Brogna	.10
35	Jay Buhner	.10
36	Steve Cox	.10
37	Quilvio Veras	.10
38	Marquis Grissom	.10
39	Shigetoshi Hasegawa	.10
40	Shane Reynolds	.10
41	Adam Piatt	.10
42	Luis Polonia	.10
43	Brook Fordyce	.10
44	Preston Wilson	.10
45	Ellis Burks	.10
46	Armando Rios	.10
47	Chuck Finley	.10
48	Dan Plesac	.10
49	Shannon Stewart	.10
50	Mark McGwire	1.00
51	Mark Loretta	.10
52	Gerald Williams	.10
53	Eric Young	.10
54	Peter Bergeron	.10
55	Dave Hansen	.10
56	Arthur Rhodes	.10
57	Bobby Jones	.10
58	Matt Clement	.10
59	Mike Benjamin	.10
60	Pedro Martinez	.50
61	Jose Canseco	.40
62	Matt Anderson	.10
63	Torii Hunter	.10
64	Carlos Lee	.10
65	David Cone	.10
66	Ray Sanchez	.10
67	Eric Chavez	.20
68	Rick Helling	.10
69	Manny Alexander	.10
70	John Franco	.10
71	Mike Bordick	.10
72	Andres Galarraga	.25
73	Jose Cruz Jr.	.10
74	Mike Matheny	.10
75	Randy Johnson	.50
76	Richie Sexson	.10
77	Vladimir Nunez	.10
78	Harold Baines	.10
79	Aaron Boone	.10
80	Darin Erstad	.40
81	Alex Gonzalez	.10
82	Gil Heredia	.10
83	Shane Andrews	.10
84	Todd Hundley	.10
85	Bill Mueller	.10
86	Mark McLemore	.10
87	Scott Spiezio	.10
88	Kevin McGlinchy	.10
89	Bubba Trammell	.10
90	Manny Ramirez	.50
91	Mike Lamb	.10
92	Scott Karl	.10
93	Brian Buchanan	.10
94	Chris Turner	.10
95	Mike Sweeney	.10
96	John Wetteland	.10
97	Rob Bell	.10
98	Pat Rapp	.10
99	John Burkett	.10
100	Derek Jeter	1.50
101	J.D. Drew	.25
102	Jose Offerman	.10
103	Rick Reed	.10
104	Will Clark	.30
105	Rickey Henderson	.25
106	Dave Berg	.10
107	Kirk Rueter	.10
108	Lee Stevens	.10
109	Jay Bell	.10
110	Fred McGriff	.20
111	Julio Zuleta	.10
112	Brian Anderson	.10
113	Orlando Cabrera	.10
114	Alex Fernandez	.10
115	Derek Bell	.10
116	Eric Owens	.10
117	Brian Bohannon	.10
118	Dennys Reyes	.10
119	Mike Stanley	.10
120	Jorge Posada	.20
121	Rich Becker	.10
122	Paul Konerko	.10
123	Mike Remlinger	.10
124	Travis Lee	.10
125	Ken Caminiti	.10
126	Kevin Barker	.10
127	Paul Quantrill	.10
128	Ozzie Guillen	.10
129	Kevin Tapani	.10
130	Mark Johnson	.10
131	Randy Wolf	.10
132	Michael Tucker	.10
133	Darren Lewis	.10
134	Joe Randa	.10
135	Jeff Cirillo	.10
136	David Ortiz	.10
137	Herb Perry	.10
138	Jeff Nelson	.10
139	Chris Stynes	.10
140	Johnny Damon	.10
141	Desi Relaford	.10
142	Jason Schmidt	.10
143	Charles Johnson	.10
144	Pat Burrell	.40
145	Gary Sheffield	.25
146	Tom Glavine	.25
147	Jason Isringhausen	.10
148	Chris Carpenter	.10
149	Jeff Suppan	.10
150	Ivan Rodriguez	.50
151	Luis Sojo	.10
152	Ron Villone	.10
153	Mike Sirotka	.10
154	Chuck Knoblauch	.20
155	Jason Kendall	.10
156	Dennis Cook	.10
157	Bobby Estalella	.10
158	Jose Guillen	.10
159	Thomas Howard	.10
160	Carlos Delgado	.50
161	Benji Gil	.10
162	Tim Bogar	.10
163	Kevin Elster	.10
164	Scott Downs	.10
165	Andy Benes	.10
166	Adrian Beltre	.10
167	David Bell	.10
168	Turk Wendell	.10
169	Pete Harnisch	.10
170	Roger Clemens	.75
171	Scott Williamson	.10
172	Kevin Jordan	.10
173	Brad Penny	.10
174	John Flaherty	.10
175	Troy Glaus	.50
176	Kevin Appier	.10
177	Walt Weiss	.10
178	Tyler Houston	.10
179	Michael Barrett	.10
180	Mike Hampton	.10
181	Francisco Cordova	.10
182	Mike Jackson	.10
183	David Segui	.10
184	Carlos Febles	.10
185	Roy Halladay	.10
186	Seth Etherton	.10
187	Charlie Hayes	.10
188	Fernando Tatis	.10
189	Steve Trachsel	.10
190	Livan Hernandez	.10
191	Joe Oliver	.10
192	Stan Javier	.10
193	B.J. Surhoff	.10
194	Rob Ducey	.10
195	Barry Larkin	.25
196	Danny Patterson	.10
197	Bobby Howry	.10
198	Dmitri Young	.10
199	Brian Hunter	.10
200	Alex Rodriguez	1.00
201	Hideo Nomo	.25
202	Luis Alicea	.10
203	Warren Morris	.10
204	Antonio Alfonseca	.10
205	Edgardo Alfonzo	.20
206	Mark Grudzielanek	.10
207	Fernando Vina	.10
208	Willie Greene	.10
209	Homer Bush	.10
210	Jason Giambi	.30
211	Mike Morgan	.10
212	Steve Karsay	.10
213	Matt Lawton	.10
214	Wendell Magee Jr.	.10
215	Rusty Greer	.10
216	Keith Lockhart	.10
217	Billy Koch	.10
218	Todd Hollandsworth	.10
219	Raul Ibanez	.10
220	Tony Gwynn	.75
221	Carl Everett	.20
222	Hector Carrasco	.10
223	Jose Valentin	.10
224	Deivi Cruz	.10
225	Bret Boone	.10
226	Kurt Abbott	.10
227	Melvin Mora	.10
228	Danny Graves	.10
229	Jose Jimenez	.10
230	James Baldwin	.10
231	C.J. Nitkowski	.10
232	Jeff Zimmerman	.10
233	Mike Lowell	.10
234	Hideki Irabu	.10
235	Greg Vaughn	.20
236	Omar Daal	.10
237	Darren Dreifort	.10
238	Gil Meche	.10
239	Damian Jackson	.10
240	Frank Thomas	.75
241	Travis Miller	.10
242	Jeff Frye	.10
243	Dave Magadan	.10
244	Luis Castillo	.10
245	Bartolo Colon	.10
246	Steve Kline	.10
247	Shawon Dunston	.10
248	Rick Aguilera	.10
249	Omar Olivares	.10
250	Craig Biggio	.20
251	Scott Schoeneweis	.10
252	Dave Veres	.10
253	Ramon Martinez	.10
254	Jose Vidro	.10
255	Todd Helton	.50
256	Greg Norton	.10
257	Jacque Jones	.10
258	Jason Grimsley	.10
259	Dan Reichert	.10
260	Robb Nen	.10
261	Mark Clark	.10
262	Scott Hatteberg	.10
263	Doug Brocail	.10
264	Mark Johnson	.10
265	Eric Davis	.20
266	Terry Shumpert	.10
267	Kevin Millar	.10
268	Ismael Valdes	.10
269	Richard Hidalgo	.20
270	Randy Velarde	.10
271	Bengie Molina	.10
272	Tony Womack	.10
273	Enrique Wilson	.10
274	Jeff Brantley	.10
275	Rick Ankiel	.25
276	Terry Mulholland	.10
277	Ron Belliard	.10
278	Terrence Long	.10
279	Alberto Castillo	.10
280	Royce Clayton	.10
281	Joe McEwing	.10
282	Jason McDonald	.10
283	Ricky Bottalico	.10
284	Keith Foulke	.10
285	Brad Radke	.10
286	Gabe Kapler	.10
287	Pedro Astacio	.10
288	Armando Reynoso	.10
289	Darryl Kile	.10
290	Reggie Sanders	.10
291	Esteban Yan	.10
292	Joe Nathan	.10
293	Jay Payton	.10
294	Francisco Cordero	.10
295	Gregg Jefferies	.10
296	LaTroy Hawkins	.10
297	Jeff Tam	.10
298	Jacob Cruz	.10
299	Chris Holt	.10
300	Vladimir Guerrero	.75
301	Marvin Benard	.10
302	Matt Franco	.10
303	Mike Williams	.10
304	Sean Bergman	.10
305	Juan Encarnacion	.10
306	Russ Davis	.10
307	Hanley Frias	.10
308	Ramon Hernandez	.10
309	Matt Walbeck	.10
310	Bill Spiers	.10
311	Bob Wickman	.10
312	Sandy Alomar	.10
313	Eddie Guardado	.10
314	Shane Halter	.10
315	Geoff Jenkins	.20
316	Gerald Witasick	.10
317	Damian Miller	.10
318	Darrin Fletcher	.10
319	Rafael Furcal	.25
320	Mark Grace	.25
321	Mark Mulder	.10
322	Joe Torre (Managers)	.10
323	Bobby Cox (Managers)	.10
324	Mike Scioscia (Managers)	.10
325	Mike Hargrove (Managers)	.10
326	Jimy Williams (Managers)	.10
327	Jerry Manuel (Managers)	.10
328	Buck Showalter (Managers)	.10
329	Charlie Manuel (Managers)	.10
330	Don Baylor (Managers)	.10
331	Phil Garner (Managers)	.10
332	Jack McKeon (Managers)	.10
333	Tony Muser (Managers)	.10
334	Buddy Bell (Managers)	.10
335	Tom Kelly (Managers)	.10
336	John Boles (Managers)	.10
337	Art Howe (Managers)	.10
338	Larry Dierker (Managers)	.10
339	Lou Piniella (Managers)	.10
340	Davey Johnson (Managers)	.10
341	Larry Rothschild (Managers)	.10
342	Davey Lopes (Managers)	.10
343	Johnny Oates (Managers)	.10
344	Felipe Alou (Managers)	.10
345	Jim Fregosi (Managers)	.10
346	Bobby Valentine (Managers)	.10
347	Terry Francona (Managers)	.10
348	Gene Lamont (Managers)	.10
349	Tony LaRussa (Managers)	.10
350	Bruce Bochy (Managers)	.10
351	Dusty Baker (Managers)	.10
352	Adrian Gonzalez, Adam Johnson (Draft Picks)	.75
353	Matt Wheatland, Brian Digby (Draft Picks)	.40
354	Tripper Johnson, Scott Thorman (Draft Picks)	.10
355	Phil Dumatrait, Adam Wainwright (Draft Picks)	.50
356	Scott Heard, David Parrish RC (Draft Picks)	.10
357	Rocco Baldelli, Mark Folsom RC (Draft Picks)	.40
358	Dominic Rich RC, Aaron Herr (Draft Picks)	.40
359	Mike Stodolka, Sean Burnett (Draft Picks)	.25
360	Derek Thompson, Corey Smith (Draft Picks)	.40
361	Danny Borrell RC, Jason Bourgeois RC (Draft Picks)	.50
362	Chin-Feng Chen, Corey Patterson, Josh Hamilton (Prospects)	.25
363	Ryan Anderson, Barry Zito, C.C. Sabathia (Prospects)	.50
364	Scott Sobkowiak, David Walling, Ben Sheets (Prospects)	.50
365	Ty Howington, Josh Kalinowski, Josh Girdley (Prospects)	.10
366	Hee Seop Choi RC, Aaron McNeal, Jason Hart (Prospects)	1.00
367	Bobby Bradley, Kurt Ainsworth, Chin-Hui Tsao (Prospects)	.40
368	Mike Glendenning, Kenny Kelly, Juan Silvestri RC (Prospects)	.25
369	J.R. House, Ramon Castro, Ben Davis (Prospects)	.25
370	Chance Caple, Rafael Soriano RC, Pasqual Coco (Prospects)	.50
371	Travis Hafner RC, Eric Munson, Bucky Jacobsen (Prospects)	1.50
372	Jason Conti, Chris Wakeland, Brian Cole (Prospects)	.20
373	Scott Seabol, Aubrey Huff, Joe Crede (Prospects)	.40
374	Adam Everett, Jose Ortiz, Keith Ginter (Prospects)	.25
375	Carlos Hernandez, Geraldo Guzman, Adam Eaton (Prospects)	.25
376	Bobby Kielty, Milton Bradley, Juan Rivera (Prospects)	.25
377	Mark McGwire (Golden Moments)	.75
378	Don Larsen (Golden Moments)	.20
379	Bobby Thomson (Golden Moments)	.10
380	Bill Mazeroski (Golden Moments)	.20
381	Reggie Jackson (Golden Moments)	.40
382	Kirk Gibson (Golden Moments)	.10
383	Roger Maris (Golden Moments)	.10
384	Cal Ripken Jr. (Golden Moments)	.75
385	Hank Aaron (Golden Moments)	.75
386	Joe Carter (Golden Moments)	.10
387	Cal Ripken Jr. (Season Highlights)	.75
388	Randy Johnson (Season Highlights)	.30
389	Ken Griffey Jr. (Season Highlights)	.50
390	Troy Glaus (Season Highlights)	.30
391	Kazuhiro Sasaki (Season Highlights)	.40
392	Sammy Sosa, Troy Glaus (League Leaders)	.50
393	Todd Helton, Edgar Martinez (League Leaders)	.25
394	Nomar Garciaparra, Todd Helton (League Leaders)	.50
395	Barry Bonds, Jason Giambi (League Leaders)	.40
396	Todd Helton, Manny Ramirez (League Leaders)	.25
397	Todd Helton, Darin Erstad (League Leaders)	.25
398	Kevin Brown, Pedro Martinez (League Leaders)	.25
399	Randy Johnson, Pedro Martinez (League Leaders)	.25
400	Will Clark (Playoff Highlights)	.20
401	NY Mets Divisional Highlight	.10
402	NY Yankees Divisional Highlight	.10
403	Seattle Mariners Divisional Highlight	.10
404	Mike Hampton (Playoff Highlights)	.10
405	NY Yankees ALCS Highlight	.75
406	World Series Highlight	1.00
407	Jeff Bagwell	.50
408	Brant Brown	.10
409	Brad Fullmer	.10
410	Dean Palmer	.10
411	Gregg Zaun	.10
412	Jose Vizcaino	.10
413	Jeff Abbott	.10
414	Travis Fryman	.15
415	Mike Cameron	.10
416	Matt Mantei	.10
417	Alan Benes	.10
418	Mickey Morandini	.10
419	Troy Percival	.10
420	Eddie Perez	.10
421	Vernon Wells	.10
422	Ricky Gutierrez	.10
423	Carlos Hernandez	.10
424	Chan Ho Park	.15
425	Armando Benitez	.10
426	Sidney Ponson	.10
427	Adrian Brown	.10
428	Ruben Mateo	.20
429	Alex Ochoa	.10
430	Jose Rosado	.10
431	Masato Yoshii	.10
432	Corey Koskie	.10
433	Andy Pettitte	.20
434	Brian Daubach	.10
435	Sterling Hitchcock	.10
436	Timo Perez	.10
437	Shawn Estes	.10
438	Tony Armas Jr.	.10
439	Danny Bautista	.10
440	Randy Winn	.10
441	Wilson Alvarez	.10
442	Rondell White	.15
443	Jeromy Burnitz	.10
444	Kelvim Escobar	.10
445	Paul Bako	.10
446	Javier Vazquez	.10
447	Eric Gagne	.10
448	Kenny Lofton	.20
449	Mark Kotsay	.10
450	Jamie Moyer	.10
451	Delino DeShields	.10
452	Rey Ordonez	.10
453	Russ Ortiz	.10
454	Dave Burba	.10
455	Eric Karros	.15
456	Felix Martinez	.10
457	Tony Batista	.10
458	Bobby Higginson	.10
459	Jeff D'Amico	.10
460	Shane Spencer	.10
461	Brent Mayne	.10
462	Glendon Rusch	.10
463	Chris Gomez	.10
464	Jeff Shaw	.10
465	Damon Buford	.10
466	Mike DiFelice	.10
467	Jimmy Haynes	.10
468	Billy Wagner	.10
469	A.J. Hinch	.10
470	Gary DiSarcina	.10
471	Tom Lampkin	.10
472	Adam Eaton	.10
473	Brian Giles	.15
474	John Thomson	.10
475	Cal Eldred	.10
476	Ramiro Mendoza	.10
477	Scott Sullivan	.10
478	Scott Rolen	.25
479	Todd Ritchie	.10
480	Pablo Ozuna	.10
481	Carl Pavano	.10
482	Matt Morris	.10
483	Matt Stairs	.10
484	Tim Belcher	.10
485	Lance Berkman	.15
486	Brian Meadows	.10
487	Bobby Abreu	.10
488	John Vander Wal	.10
489	Donnie Sadler	.10
490	Damion Easley	.10
491	David Justice	.25
492	Ray Durham	.10
493	Todd Zeile	.10
494	Desi Relaford	.10
495	Cliff Floyd	.10
496	Scott Downs	.10
497	Barry Bonds	1.00
498	Jeff D'Amico	.10
499	Octavio Dotel	.10
500	Kent Mercker	.10
501	Craig Grebeck	.10
502	Roberto Hernandez	.10
503	Matt Williams	.15
504	Bruce Aven	.10
505	Brett Tomko	.10
506	Kris Benson	.10
507	Neifi Perez	.10
508	Alfonso Soriano	.50
509	Keith Osik	.10
510	Matt Franco	.10
511	Steve Finley	.10
512	Olmedo Saenz	.10
513	Esteban Loaiza	.10
514	Adam Kennedy	.10
515	Scott Elarton	.10
516	Moises Alou	.15
517	Bryan Rekar	.10
518	Darryl Hamilton	.10
519	Osvaldo Fernandez	.10
520	Kip Wells	.10
521	Bernie Williams	.40
522	Mike Darr	.10
523	Marlon Anderson	.10
524	Derrek Lee	.10
525	Ugueth Urbina	.10
526	Vinny Castilla	.10
527	David Wells	.10
528	Jason Marquis	.10
529	Orlando Palmeiro	.10
530	Carlos Perez	.10
531	J.T. Snow Jr.	.10
532	Al Leiter	.15
533	Jimmy Anderson	.10
534	Brett Laxton	.10
535	Butch Huskey	.10
536	Orlando Hernandez	.20
537	Magglio Ordonez	.15
538	Willie Blair	.10
539	Kevin Sefcik	.10
540	Chad Curtis	.10
541	John Halama	.10
542	Andy Fox	.10
543	Juan Guzman	.10
544	Frank Menechino	.10
545	Raul Mondesi	.15
546	Tim Salmon	.15
547	Ryan Rupe	.10
548	Jeff Reed	.10
549	Mike Mordecai	.10
550	Jeff Kent	.15
551	Wiki Gonzalez	.10
552	Kenny Rogers	.10
553	Kevin Young	.10
554	Brian Johnson	.10
555	Tom Goodwin	.10
556	Tony Clark	.10
557	Mac Suzuki	.10
558	Brian Moehler	.10
559	Jim Parque	.10
560	Mariano Rivera	.20
561	Trot Nixon	.10
562	Mike Mussina	.30
563	Nelson Figueroa	.10
564	Alex Gonzalez	.10
565	Benny Agbayani	.10
566	Ed Sprague	.10
567	Scott Erickson	.10
568	Abraham Nunez	.10
569	Jerry DiPoto	.10
570	Sean Casey	.10
571	Wilton Veras	.10
572	Joe Mays	.10
573	Bill Simas	.10
574	Doug Glanville	.10
575	Scott Sauerbeck	.10
576	Ben Davis	.10
577	Jesus Sanchez	.10
578	Ricardo Rincon	.10
579	John Olerud	.15
580	Curt Schilling	.15
581	Alex Cora	.10
582	Pat Hentgen	.10
583	Javy Lopez	.15
584	Ben Grieve	.15
585	Frank Castillo	.10
586	Kevin Stocker	.10
587	Mark Sweeney	.10
588	Ray Lankford	.10
589	Turner Ward	.10
590	Felipe Crespo	.10
591	Omar Vizquel	.15
592	Mike Lieberthal	.10
593	Ken Griffey Jr.	1.00
594	Troy O'Leary	.10
595	Dave Mlicki (Front photo actually Brian Moehler.)	
596	Manny Ramirez	.50
597	Mike Lansing	.10
598	Rich Aurilia	.10
599	Russ Branyan	.10
600	Russ Johnson	.10
601	Gregg Colbrunn	.10
602	Andruw Jones	.40
603	Henry Blanco	.10
604	Jarrod Washburn	.10
605	Tony Eusebio	.10
606	Aaron Sele	.10
607	Charles Nagy	.10
608	Ryan Klesko	.10
609	Dante Bichette	.10
610	Bill Haselman	.10
611	Jerry Spradlin	.10
612	Alex Rodriguez	1.00
613	Jose Silva	.10
614	Darren Oliver	.10
615	Pat Mahomes	.10
616	Roberto Alomar	.40
617	Edgar Renteria	.10

618	Jon Lieber	.10
619	John Rocker	.10
620	Miguel Tejada	.15
621	Mo Vaughn	.15
622	Jose Lima	.10
623	Kerry Wood	.15
624	Mike Timlin	.10
625	Wil Cordero	.10
626	Albert Belle	.15
627	Bobby Jones	.10
628	Doug Mirabelli	.10
629	Jason Tyner	.10
630	Andy Ashby	.10
631	Jose Hernandez	.10
632	Devon White	.10
633	Ruben Rivera	.10
634	Steve Parris	.10
635	David McCarty	.10
636	Jose Canseco	.25
637	Todd Walker	.10
638	Stan Spencer	.10
639	Wayne Gomes	.10
640	Freddy Garcia	.10
641	Jeremy Giambi	.10
642	Luis Lopez	.10
643	John Smoltz	.10
644	Kelly Stinnett	.10
645	Kevin Brown	.10
646	Wilton Guerrero	.10
647	Al Martin	.10
648	Woody Williams	.10
649	Brian Rose	.10
650	Rafael Palmeiro	.30
651	Pete Schourek	.10
652	Kevin Jarvis	.10
653	Mark Redman	.10
654	Ricky Ledee	.10
655	Larry Walker	.20
656	Paul Byrd	.10
657	Jason Bere	.10
658	Rick White	.10
659	Calvin Murray	.10
660	Greg Maddux	1.00
661	Ron Gant	.10
662	Eli Marrero	.10
663	Graeme Lloyd	.10
664	Trevor Hoffman	.10
665	Nomar Garciaparra	1.00
666	Glenallen Hill	.10
667	Matt LeCroy	.10
668	Justin Thompson	.10
669	Brady Anderson	.10
670	Miguel Batista	.10
671	Erubiel Durazo	.10
672	Kevin Millwood	.10
673	Mitch Meluskey	.10
674	Luis Gonzalez	.15
675	Edgar Martinez	.10
676	Robert Person	.10
677	Benito Santiago	.10
678	Todd Jones	.10
679	Tino Martinez	.15
680	Carlos Beltran	.10
681	Gabe White	.10
682	Bret Saberhagen	.10
683	Jeff Conine	.10
684	Jaret Wright	.10
685	Bernard Gilkey	.10
686	Garrett Stephenson	.10
687	Jamey Wright	.10
688	Sammy Sosa	1.00
689	John Jaha	.10
690	Ramon Martinez	.10
691	Robert Fick	.10
692	Eric Milton	.10
693	Denny Neagle	.10
694	Ron Coomer	.10
695	John Valentin	.10
696	Placido Polanco	.10
697	Tim Hudson	.15
698	Marty Cordova	.10
699	Chad Kreuter	.10
700	Frank Catalanotto	.10
701	Tim Wakefield	.10
702	Jim Edmonds	.15
703	Michael Tucker	.10
704	Cristian Guzman	.10
705	Joey Hamilton	.10
706	Mike Piazza	1.00
707	Dave Martinez	.10
708	Mike Hampton	.15
709	Bobby Bonilla	.10
710	Juan Pierre	.10
711	John Parrish	.10
712	Kory DeHaan	.10
713	Brian Tollberg	.10
714	Chris Truby	.10
715	Emil Brown	.10
716	Ryan Dempster	.10
717	Rich Garces	.10
718	Mike Myers	.10
719	Luis Ordaz	.10
720	Kazuhiro Sasaki	.10
721	Mark Quinn	.10
722	Ramon Ortiz	.10
723	Kerry Ligtenberg	.10
724	Rolando Arrojo	.10
725	Tsuyoshi Shinjo **RC**	1.00
726	Ichiro Suzuki **RC**	15.00
727	Roy Oswalt, Pat Strange, Jon Rauch (Prospects)	.25
728	Phil Wilson **RC**, Jake Peavy **RC**, Darwin Cubillan **RC** (Prospects)	.75
729	Steve Smyth **RC**, Mike Bynum, Nathan Haynes (Prospects)	.40

730	Michael Cuddyer, Joe Lawrence, Choo Freeman (Prospects)	.10
731	Carlos Pena, Larry Barnes, Dewayne Wise (Prospects)	.10
732	Gookie Dawkins, Erick Almonte **RC**, Felipe Lopez (Prospects)	.40
733	Alex Escobar, Eric Valent, Brad Wilkerson (Prospects)	.10
734	Toby Hall, Rod Barajas, Jeff Goldbach **RC** (Prospects)	.10
735	Jason Romano, Marcus Giles, Pablo Ozuna (Prospects)	.10
736	Dee Brown, Jack Cust, Vernon Wells (Prospects)	.10
737	David Espinosa, Luis Montanez **RC** (Draft Picks)	.40
738	Anthony Pluta, Justin Wayne **RC** (Draft Picks)	.50
739	Josh Axelson **RC**, Carmen Cali **RC** (Draft Picks)	.50
740	Shaun Boyd **RC**, Chris Morris **RC** (Draft Picks)	.50
741	Tommy Arko **RC**, Dan Moylan **RC** (Draft Picks)	.50
742	Luis Cotto **RC**, Luis Escobar (Draft Picks)	.40
743	Brandon Mims **RC**, Blake Williams **RC** (Draft Picks)	.40
744	Chris Russ **RC**, Bryan Edwards (Draft Picks)	.40
745	Joe Torres, Ben Diggins (Draft Picks)	.10
746	Mark Dalesandro, Edwin Encarnacion **RC** (Draft Picks)	.50
747	Brian Bass **RC**, Odannis Ayala **RC** (Draft Picks)	.40
748	Jason Kaanoi **RC**, Michael Mathews **RC** (Draft Picks)	.10
749	Stuart McFarland **RC**, Adam Sterrett **RC** (Draft Picks)	.40
750	David Krynzel, Grady Sizemore (Draft Picks)	.50
751	Keith Bucktrot, Dane Sardinha (Draft Picks)	.10
752	Anaheim Angels	.10
753	Arizona Diamondbacks	.10
754	Atlanta Braves	.10
755	Baltimore Orioles	.10
756	Boston Red Sox	.10
757	Chicago Cubs	.10
758	Chicago White Sox	.10
759	Cincinnati Reds	.10
760	Cleveland Indians	.10
761	Colorado Rockies	.10
762	Detroit Tigers	.10
763	Florida Marlins	.10
764	Houston Astros	.10
765	Kansas City Royals	.10
766	Los Angeles Dodgers	.10
767	Milwaukee Brewers	.10
768	Minnesota Twins	.10
769	Montreal Expos	.10
770	New York Mets	.10
771	New York Yankees	.75
772	Oakland Athletics	.10
773	Philadelphia Phillies	.10
774	Pittsburgh Pirates	.10
775	San Diego Padres	.10
776	San Francisco Giants	.10
777	Seattle Mariners	.10
778	St. Louis Cardinals	.10
779	Tampa Bay Devil Rays	.10
780	Texas Rangers	.10
781	Toronto Blue Jays	.10
782	Bucky Dent (Golden Moments)	.10
783	Jackie Robinson (Golden Moments)	1.00
784	Roberto Clemente (Golden Moments)	1.00
785	Nolan Ryan (Golden Moments)	1.50
786	Kerry Wood (Golden Moments)	.10
787	Rickey Henderson (Golden Moments)	.20
788	Lou Brock (Golden Moments)	.10
789	David Wells (Golden Moments)	.10
790	Andruw Jones (Golden Moments)	.25
791	Carlton Fisk (Golden Moments)	.10

Gold

Stars: 8-15X

Prospects and RC's: 3-6X
Inserted 1:17

Home Team Advantage

Cards which bear a bright, embossed gold-foil "Topps Home Team Advantage" seal in a lower corner originated in the Topps factory set. Individual cards may command a small premium from single-player specialist collectors.

Common Player:
Star: +25 Percent

A Look Ahead

		NM/M
	Complete Set (10):	15.00
	Common Player:	.50
	Inserted 1:25	
1	Vladimir Guerrero	1.50
2	Derek Jeter	4.00
3	Todd Helton	1.00
4	Alex Rodriguez	3.00
5	Ken Griffey Jr.	2.00
6	Nomar Garciaparra	3.00
7	Chipper Jones	2.00
8	Ivan Rodriguez	1.00
9	Pedro Martinez	1.50
10	Rick Ankiel	.50

A Tradition Continued

		NM/M
	Complete Set (30):	50.00
	Common Player:	.50
	Inserted 1:17	
1	Chipper Jones	3.00
2	Cal Ripken Jr.	6.00
3	Mike Piazza	3.00
4	Ken Griffey Jr.	3.00
5	Randy Johnson	1.50
6	Derek Jeter	5.00

7	Scott Rolen	1.50
8	Nomar Garciaparra	4.00
9	Roberto Alomar	1.00
10	Greg Maddux	3.00
11	Ivan Rodriguez	1.50
12	Jeff Bagwell	1.50
13	Ivan Rodriguez	1.50
14	Pedro Martinez	2.00
15	Sammy Sosa	4.00
16	Jim Edmonds	1.00
17	Mo Vaughn	.50
18	Barry Bonds	5.00
19	Larry Walker	.75
20	Mark McGwire	4.00
21	Vladimir Guerrero	2.00
22	Andruw Jones	1.50
23	Todd Helton	1.50
24	Kevin Brown	.75
25	Tony Gwynn	2.00
26	Manny Ramirez	1.50
27	Roger Clemens	4.00
28	Frank Thomas	1.50
29	Shawn Green	.75
30	Jim Thome	1.50

Autographs

	NM/M
Common Player:	
Group A 1:22,866	
Group B 1:3,054	
Group C 1:1,431	
Group D 1:18,339	
Group E 1:13,737	
Group F 1:11,015	
Group G 1:625	
HA	Hank Aaron	275.00
DA	Dick Allen	25.00
RA	Rick Ankiel	20.00
RB	Rocco Baldelli	15.00
EB	Ernie Banks	100.00
YB	Yogi Berra	80.00
LB	Lou Brock	50.00
PB	Pat Burrell	15.00
RC	Rod Carew	50.00
MC	Mike Cuellar	15.00
WF	Whitey Ford	40.00
RF	Rafael Furcal	25.00
BG	Bob Gibson	40.00
AG	Adrian Gonzalez	40.00
SH	Scott Heard	15.00
WH	Willie Hernandez	10.00
AJ	Adam Johnson	10.00
CJ	Chipper Jones	80.00
SK	Sandy Koufax	600.00
ML	Mike Lamb	10.00
VL	Vernon Law	15.00
JM	Jason Marquis	10.00
WM	Willie Mays	250.00
MO	Magglio Ordonez	20.00
AP	Andy Pafko	30.00
BR	Brooks Robinson	80.00
JR	Joe Rudi	15.00
MS	Mike Schmidt	100.00
MS	Mike Stodolka	15.00
RS	Ron Swoboda	30.00
GT	Garry Templeton	10.00
JV	Jose Vidro	10.00
MW	Matt Wheatland	10.00
TZ	Todd Zeile	10.00

Autographs Series 2

		NM/M
	Common Player:	10.00
DA	Denny Abreu	10.00
TA	Tony Alvarez	10.00
RB	Rocco Baldelli	15.00
GB	George Bell	10.00
JB	Johnny Bench	75.00
BB	Barry Bonds	150.00

MB	Milton Bradley	15.00
GHB	George Brett	150.00
MAB	Mike Bynum	10.00
EB	Eric Byrnes	10.00
JC	Jorge Cantu	15.00
CC	Chris Clapinski	10.00
WD	Willie Davis	20.00
JDD	J.D. Drew	15.00
TDLR	Tomas de la Rosa	10.00
CD	Chad Durbin	10.00
CE	Carl Erskine	25.00
BE	Brian Esposito	15.00
WF	Whitey Ford	40.00
EF	Eddy Furniss	15.00
BG	Bob Gibson	40.00
MG	Mike Glendenning	15.00
AG	Adrian Gonzalez	30.00
NG	Nick Green	10.00
KG	Kevin Gregg	10.00
DG	Dick Groat	15.00
GG	Geraldo Guzman	10.00
YH	Yamid Haad	10.00
TH	Todd Helton	40.00
AH	Aaron Herr	15.00
KH	Ken Holtzman	20.00
RJ	Reggie Jackson	125.00
NJ	Neil Jenkins	15.00
AJ	Adam Johnson	10.00
TJ	Tripper Johnson	15.00
BK	Bobby Kielty	10.00
JL	John Lackey	20.00
ML	Matt Lawton	15.00
CL	Colby Lewis	15.00
MFL	Mike Lockwood	20.00
GM	Gary Matthews	15.00
LM	Luis Montanez	10.00
EM	Eric Munson	10.00
SM	Stan Musial	180.00
BO	Ben Oglivie	15.00
AO	Augie Ojeda	10.00
ER	Erasmo Ramirez	15.00
CR	Chris Richard	15.00
JR	Juan Rincon	10.00
LR	Luis Rivas	20.00
SR	Scott Rolen	25.00
NR	Nolan Ryan	200.00
JS	Juan Salas	10.00
TS	Tom Seaver	150.00
CS	Carlos Silva	12.00
GS	Grady Sizemore	40.00
CCS	Corey Smith	10.00
MS	Mike Stodolka	10.00
MS	Mike Sweeney	15.00
KT	Kent Tekulve	20.00
DT	Derek Thompson	10.00
ST	Scott Thorman	10.00
BT	Brian Tollberg	15.00
JW	Justin Wayne	20.00
MW	Michael Wenner	15.00
MJW	Matt Wheatland	15.00
WW	Wilbur Wood	20.00
CY	Carl Yastrzemski	80.00

Base Hit

		NM/M
	Common Player:	25.00
BH1	Mike Scioscia	35.00
BH2	Larry Dierker	25.00
BH3	Art Howe	25.00
BH4	Jim Fregosi	25.00
BH5	Bobby Cox	35.00
BH6	Davey Lopes	25.00
BH7	Tony LaRussa	30.00
BH8	Don Baylor	35.00
BH9	Larry Rothschild	25.00
BH10	Buck Showalter	30.00
BH11	Davey Johnson	30.00
BH12	Felipe Alou	30.00
BH13	Charlie Manuel	25.00
BH14	Lou Piniella	30.00
BH15	John Boles	25.00
BH16	Bobby Valentine	30.00
BH17	Mike Hargrove	25.00
BH18	Bruce Bochy	25.00
BH19	Terry Francona	25.00
BH20	Gene Lamont	25.00
BH21	Johnny Oates	25.00
BH22	Jimy Williams	25.00
BH23	Jack McKeon	25.00
BH24	Buddy Bell	25.00
BH25	Tony Muser	25.00
BH26	Phil Garner	25.00
BH27	Tom Kelly	25.00
BH28	Jerry Manuel	25.00

Before There Was Topps

		NM/M
	Complete Set (10):	20.00
	Common Player:	1.50
	Inserted 1:25	
BT1	Lou Gehrig	4.00
BT2	Babe Ruth	5.00
BT3	Cy Young	2.00
BT4	Walter Johnson	2.00
BT5	Ty Cobb	4.00
BT6	Tris Speaker	1.50
BT7	Honus Wagner	2.00

Lou Gehrig

BT8	Christy Mathewson	1.50
BT9	Grover Alexander	1.50
BT0	Joe DiMaggio	4.00

Combos

		NM/M
	Complete Set (20):	25.00
	Common Player:	1.50
	Inserted 1:12	
1	Yogi Berra, Whitey Ford, Reggie Jackson, Don Mattingly, Derek Jeter	3.00
2	Brooks Robinson, Cal Ripken Jr.	3.00
3	Barry Bonds, Willie Mays	3.00
4	Bob Gibson, Pedro Martinez	1.50
5	Ivan Rodriguez, Johnny Bench	2.00
6	Ernie Banks, Alex Rodriguez	2.50
7	Joe Morgan, Ken Griffey Jr., Barry Larkin, Johnny Bench	2.50
8	Vladimir Guerrero, Roberto Clemente	2.50
9	Ted Williams, Carl Yastrzemski, Nomar Garciaparra	3.00
10	Joe Torre, Casey Stengel	1.50
11	Kevin Brown, Sandy Koufax, Don Drysdale	3.00
12	Mark McGwire, Sammy Sosa, Roger Maris, Babe Ruth	3.00
13	Ted Williams, Carl Yastrzemski, Nomar Garciaparra	3.00
14	Greg Maddux, Roger Clemens, Cy Young	2.00
15	Tony Gwynn, Ted Williams	3.00
16	Cal Ripken Jr., Lou Gehrig	4.00
17	Sandy Koufax, Randy Johnson, Warren Spahn, Steve Carlton	3.00
18	Mike Piazza, Josh Gibson	2.00
19	Barry Bonds, Willie Mays	3.00
20	Jackie Robinson, Larry Doby	2.50

Future Archives Gold Bordered Reprints

		NM/M
	Complete Set (20):	60.00
	Common Player:	2.00

Inserted five per factory set.

1	Barry Bonds/1987	6.00
2	Chipper Jones/1991	8.00
3	Cal Ripken Jr./1982	12.00
4	Shawn Green/1992	4.00
5	Frank Thomas/1990	5.00
6	Derek Jeter/1993	9.00
7	Geoff Jenkins/1996	2.00
8	Jim Edmonds/1993	2.00
9	Bernie Williams/1990	2.00
10	Sammy Sosa/1990	4.00
11	Rickey Henderson/1980	6.00
12	Tony Gwynn/1983	6.00
13	Randy Johnson/1989	3.00
14	Juan Gonzalez/1990	3.00
15	Gary Sheffield/1989	2.00
16	Manny Ramirez/1992	3.00
17	Pokey Reese/1992	2.00
18	Preston Wilson/1993	2.00
19	Jay Payton/1995	2.00
20	Rafael Palmeiro/1987	3.00

Golden Anniversary

		NM/M
Complete Set (50):		60.00
Common Player:		.50
Inserted 1:10		
1	Hank Aaron	3.00
2	Ernie Banks	1.50
3	Mike Schmidt	3.00
4	Willie Mays	4.00
5	Johnny Bench	1.50
6	Tom Seaver	1.00
7	Frank Robinson	1.00
8	Sandy Koufax	3.00
9	Bob Gibson	1.00
10	Ted Williams	4.00
11	Cal Ripken Jr.	5.00
12	Tony Gwynn	1.50
13	Mark McGwire	3.00
14	Ken Griffey Jr.	2.00
15	Greg Maddux	2.00
16	Roger Clemens	3.00
17	Barry Bonds	2.00
18	Rickey Henderson	.75
19	Mike Piazza	2.00
20	Jose Canseco	1.00
21	Derek Jeter	4.00
22	Nomar Garciaparra	3.00
23	Alex Rodriguez	3.00
24	Sammy Sosa	2.50
25	Ivan Rodriguez	1.00
26	Vladimir Guerrero	1.50
27	Chipper Jones	2.00
28	Jeff Bagwell	1.00
29	Pedro Martinez	1.50
30	Randy Johnson	1.50
31	Pat Burrell	1.00
32	Josh Hamilton	1.00
33	Nick Johnson	.50
34	Corey Patterson	.50
35	Eric Munson	.50
36	Sean Burroughs	.50
37	Alfonso Soriano	1.50
38	Chin-Feng Chen	.50
39	Barry Zito	.75
40	Adrian Gonzalez	.50
41	Mark McGwire	3.00
42	Nomar Garciaparra	3.00
43	Todd Helton	1.00
44	Matt Williams	.50
45	Troy Glaus	.75
46	Geoff Jenkins	.50
47	Frank Thomas	1.00
48	Mo Vaughn	.50
49	Barry Larkin	.75
50	J.D. Drew	.50

Hit Parade

		NM/M
Complete Set (6):		
Common Player:		25.00
1:2,600 Retail		
HP1	Reggie Jackson	40.00
HP2	Dave Winfield	25.00
HP3	Eddie Murray	25.00

HP4	Rickey Henderson	25.00
HP5	Robin Yount	25.00
HP6	Carl Yastrzemski	65.00

King of Kings

		NM/M
Common Card:		25.00
Inserted 1:2,056		
1	Hank Aaron	75.00
2	Nolan Ryan	75.00
3	Rickey Henderson	30.00
5	Bob Gibson	25.00
6	Nolan Ryan	75.00

King of Kings Golden Edition

		NM/M
Production 50 cards.		
KKGE	Hank Aaron, Nolan Ryan, Rickey Henderson	250.00

Noteworthy

		NM/M
Complete Set (50):		40.00
Common Player:		.50
Inserted 1:8		
TN1	Mark McGwire	2.00
TN2	Derek Jeter	2.50
TN3	Sammy Sosa	2.00
TN4	Todd Helton	1.00
TN5	Alex Rodriguez	2.00
TN6	Chipper Jones	1.50
TN7	Barry Bonds	3.00
TN8	Ken Griffey Jr.	1.50
TN9	Nomar Garciaparra	2.00
TN10	Frank Thomas	1.00
TN11	Randy Johnson	1.00
TN12	Cal Ripken Jr.	3.00
TN13	Mike Piazza	1.50
TN14	Ivan Rodriguez	1.00
TN15	Jeff Bagwell	1.00
TN16	Vladimir Guerrero	1.00
TN17	Greg Maddux	1.50
TN18	Tony Gwynn	1.00
TN19	Larry Walker	.50
TN20	Juan Gonzalez	.75
TN21	Scott Rolen	1.00
TN22	Jason Giambi	1.00
TN23	Jeff Kent	.50
TN24	Pat Burrell	.75
TN25	Pedro Martinez	1.00
TN26	Willie Mays	2.00
TN27	Whitey Ford	.75
TN28	Jackie Robinson	2.00
TN29	Ted Williams	2.50
TN30	Babe Ruth	3.00
TN31	Warren Spahn	1.00
TN32	Nolan Ryan	3.00
TN33	Yogi Berra	1.00
TN34	Mike Schmidt	2.00
TN35	Steve Carlton	.75
TN36	Brooks Robinson	1.00
TN37	Bob Gibson	1.00
TN38	Reggie Jackson	1.00
TN39	Johnny Bench	1.50
TN40	Ernie Banks	1.00
TN41	Eddie Mathews	1.00
TN42	Don Mattingly	2.50
TN43	Duke Snider	.75
TN44	Hank Aaron	2.00
TN45	Roberto Clemente	2.00
TN46	Harmon Killebrew	1.00
TN47	Frank Robinson	1.00
TN48	Stan Musial	2.00
TN49	Lou Brock	.50
TN50	Joe Morgan	.50

Originals

		NM/M
Common Player:		10.00
Series 1 1:1,172		
Series 2 1:1,023		
1	Roberto Clemente/1955	80.00
2	Carl Yastrzemski/1960	30.00
3	Mike Schmidt/1974	30.00
4	Wade Boggs/1983	10.00
5	Chipper Jones/1991	15.00
6	Willie Mays	40.00
7	Lou Brock	15.00
8	Dave Parker	10.00
9	Barry Bonds	40.00
10	Alex Rodriguez	25.00

The Shot Heard Round The World Autograph

	NM/M
B. Thomson/R. Branca	
Ralph Branca, Bobby Thomson	40.00

Through the Years

		NM/M
Complete Set (50):		100.00
Common Player:		1.50
Inserted 1:8		
1	Yogi Berra	2.00
2	Roy Campanella	2.00
3	Willie Mays	5.00
4	Andy Pafko	1.50
5	Jackie Robinson	4.00
6	Stan Musial	2.00
7	Duke Snider	2.00
8	Warren Spahn	2.50
9	Ted Williams	6.00
10	Eddie Mathews	2.00
11	Willie McCovey	2.00
12	Frank Robinson	2.00
13	Ernie Banks	3.00
14	Hank Aaron	5.00
15	Sandy Koufax	4.00
16	Bob Gibson	2.00
17	Harmon Killebrew	2.00
18	Whitey Ford	2.00
19	Roberto Clemente	5.00
20	Juan Marichal	1.50
21	Johnny Bench	2.00
22	Willie Stargell	1.50
23	Joe Morgan	1.50
24	Carl Yastrzemski	2.00
25	Reggie Jackson	2.00
26	Tom Seaver	2.00
27	Steve Carlton	1.50
28	Jim Palmer	1.50
29	Rod Carew	1.50
30	George Brett	2.00
31	Roger Clemens	4.00

32	Don Mattingly	5.00
33	Ryne Sandberg	3.00
34	Mike Schmidt	4.00
35	Cal Ripken Jr.	6.00
36	Tony Gwynn	3.00
37	Ozzie Smith	3.00
38	Wade Boggs	1.50
39	Nolan Ryan	6.00
40	Robin Yount	2.00
41	Mark McGwire	4.00
42	Ken Griffey Jr.	5.00
43	Sammy Sosa	4.00
44	Alex Rodriguez	4.00
45	Barry Bonds	4.00
46	Mike Piazza	3.00
47	Chipper Jones	3.00
48	Greg Maddux	3.00
49	Nomar Garciaparra	4.00
50	Derek Jeter	5.00

Two of a Kind

		NM/M
Inserted 1:30,167		
TK	Bo Jackson, Deion Sanders	75.00

What Could've Been

		NM/M
Complete Set (10):		15.00
Common Player:		1.00
Inserted 1:25		
WCB1	Josh Gibson	3.00
WCB2	Leroy "Satchel" Paige	3.00
WCB3	Walter "Buck" Leonard	2.00
WCB4	James "Cool Papa" Bell	2.00
WCB5	Andrew "Rube" Foster	2.00
WCB6	Martin Dihigo	1.00
WCB7	William "Judy" Johnson	1.50
WCB8	Mule Suttles	1.00
WCB9	Ray Dandridge	1.00
WCB10	John Henry "Pop" Lloyd	2.00

2001 Topps Opening Day

		NM/M
Complete Set (165):		35.00
Common Player:		.15
Pack (7):		1.00
Box (24):		20.00
1	Cal Ripken Jr.	2.50
2	Chipper Jones	1.50
3	Garret Anderson	.40
4	Robin Ventura	.20
5	Jermaine Dye	.15
6	Jim Thome	.75
7	Brian Jordan	.15
8	Shawn Green	.40
9	Juan Gonzalez	.75
10	Paul O'Neill	.25
11	Pokey Reese	.15
12	Mike Mussina	.40
13	Jay Buhner	.15
14	Shane Reynolds	.15
15	Adam Piatt	.15
16	Preston Wilson	.15
17	Ellis Burks	.15
18	Chuck Finley	.15
19	Shannon Stewart	.15
20	Mark McGwire	2.00
21	Mark Loretta	.15
22	Bobby Jones	.15
23	Matt Clement	.15
24	Pedro J. Martinez	1.00
25	Carlos Lee	.15
26	John Franco	.15
27	Andres Galarraga	.25
28	Jose Cruz Jr.	.15
29	Randy Johnson	.75
30	Richie Sexson	.40
31	Darin Erstad	.30
32	Manny Ramirez	.75
33	Mike Sweeney	.15
34	John Wetteland	.15
35	Derek Jeter	2.50
36	J.D. Drew	.15
37	Rick Reed	.15
38	Jay Bell	.15
39	Fred McGriff	.25
40	Orlando Cabrera	.15
41	Eric Owens	.15
42	Jorge Posada	.40
43	Jeff Cirillo	.15
44	Johnny Damon	.25
45	Charles Johnson	.15
46	Pat Burrell	.40
47	Gary Sheffield	.40
48	Tom Glavine	.30
49	Ivan Rodriguez	.75
50	Chuck Knoblauch	.15

51	Jason Kendall	.15
52	Carlos Delgado	.60
53	Roger Clemens	1.50
54	Brad Penny	.15
55	Troy Glaus	.75
56	Mike Hampton	.15
57	Carlos Febles	.15
58	Seth Etherton	.15
59	Fernando Tatis	.15
60	Livan Hernandez	.15
61	Barry Larkin	.30
62	Alex Rodriguez	2.00
63	Warren Morris	.15
64	Antonio Alfonseca	.15
65	Edgardo Alfonzo	.15
66	Fernando Vina	.15
67	Jason Giambi	.75
68	Matt Lawton	.15
69	Rusty Greer	.15
70	Tony Gwynn	1.00
71	Carl Everett	.15
72	Bret Boone	.25
73	James Baldwin	.15
74	Greg Vaughn	.15
75	Darren Dreifort	.15
76	Frank Thomas	1.00
77	Luis Castillo	.15
78	Bartolo Colon	.15
79	Craig Biggio	.25
80	Jose Vidro	.15
81	Todd Helton	.75
82	Jacque Jones	.15
83	Robb Nen	.15
84	Richard Hidalgo	.15
85	Tony Womack	.15
86	Rick Ankiel	.15
87	Terrence Long	.15
88	Brad Radke	.15
89	Gabe Kapler	.15
90	Pedro Astacio	.15
91	Darryl Kile	.15
92	Jay Payton	.15
93	Vladimir Guerrero	1.00
94	Juan Encarnacion	.15
95	Ramon Hernandez	.15
96	Sandy Alomar	.15
97	Geoff Jenkins	.25
98	Rafael Furcal	.25
99	Mark Grace	.25
100	Mark Mulder	.25
101	Jim Edmonds	.40
102	Tim Salmon	.25
103	Jeff Bagwell	.75
104	Jose Canseco	.40
105	Ben Grieve	.15
106	Ryan Klesko	.25
107	Javy Lopez	.25
108	Greg Maddux	1.50
109	Andruw Jones	.50
110	Jeromy Burnitz	.15
111	Ray Lankford	.15
112	Sammy Sosa	1.50
113	Raul Mondesi	.25
114	Mike Piazza	1.50
115	Todd Zeile	.15
116	Eric Karros	.15
117	Barry Bonds	2.50
118	J.T. Snow	.15
119	Jeff Kent	.15
120	David Justice	.25
121	Matt Williams	.25
122	Brian Giles	.25
123	Edgar Martinez	.15
124	Ken Griffey Jr.	1.50
125	Al Leiter	.25
126	Kevin Brown	.25
127	John Olerud	.25
128	Roberto Alomar	.50
129	Rafael Palmeiro	.40
130	Steve Finley	.15
131	Tim Hudson	.40
132	Scott Rolen	.75
133	Nomar Garciaparra	1.50
134	Mo Vaughn	.25
135	Larry Walker	.30
136	Albert Belle	.25
137	Ray Durham	.15
138	Andy Pettitte	.40
139	Mariano Rivera	.25
140	Bernie Williams	.25
141	David Wells	.15
142	Magglio Ordonez	.40
143	Kevin Millwood	.15
144	Cliff Floyd	.15
145	Rich Aurilia	.15
146	Eric Chavez	.25
147	Scott Elarton	.15
148	Tony Armas Jr.	.15
149	Mark Redman	.15
150	Javier Vazquez	.15
151	Adrian Gonzalez, Adam Johnson	.25
152	Mike Stodolka, Sean Burnett	.15
153	David Walling, Ben Sheets	.50
154	Chin-Feng Chen, Corey Patterson	
155	Josh Hamilton	.25
	Mark McGwire	
	(Golden Moments)	1.00
156	Bobby Thomson	
	(Golden Moments)	
157	Bill Mazeroski	
	(Golden Moments)	
158	Cal Ripken Jr.	
	(Golden Moments)	1.00
159	Hank Aaron	
	(Golden Moments)	1.00

160	Bucky Dent	
	(Golden Moments)	.15
161	Jackie Robinson	
	(Golden Moments)	1.00
162	Roberto Clemente	
	(Golden Moments)	1.00
163	Nolan Ryan	
	(Golden Moments)	1.00
164	Kerry Wood	
	(Golden Moments)	.25
165	Checklist	.15

Autographs

		NM/M
Common Autograph:		20.00
TH	Todd Helton	40.00
CJ	Chipper Jones	100.00
MO	Magglio Ordonez	25.00
CP	Corey Patterson	20.00

Team Logo Stickers

	NM/M
Complete Set (30):	6.00
Sticker:	.25
Each team represented.	

2001 Topps American Pie

		NM/M
Complete Set (150):		30.00
Common Player:		.20
Pack (5):		3.00
Box (24):		50.00
1	Al Kaline	.40
2	Al Oliver	.20
3	Andre Dawson	.20
4	Bert Blyleven	.20
5	Bill Buckner	.20
6	Bill Mazeroski	.20
7	Bob Gibson	.50
8	Bill Freeman	.20
9	Bobby Grich	.20
10	Bobby Murcer	.20
11	Bobby Richardson	.20
12	Boog Powell	.20
13	Brooks Robinson	.50
14	Carl Yastrzemski	.75
15	Carlton Fisk	.40
16	Clete Boyer	.20
17	Curt Flood	.20
18	Dale Murphy	.30
19	Tony Conigliaro	.20
20	Dave Parker	.20
21	Dave Winfield	.50
22	Dick Allen	.20
23	Dick Groat	.20
24	Don Drysdale	.50
25	Don Sutton	.20
26	Dwight Evans	.20
27	Eddie Mathews	.75
28	Elston Howard	.20
29	Frank Howard	.20
30	Frank Robinson	.50
31	Fred Lynn	.20
32	Gary Carter	.20
33	Gaylord Perry	.20
34	Norm Cash	.20
35	George Brett	1.50
36	George Foster	.20
37	Goose Gossage	.20
38	Graig Nettles	.20
39	Greg Luzinski	.20
40	Harmon Killebrew	.75
41	Jack Clark	.20
42	Jack Morris	.20
43	Jim Wynn	.20
44	Jim Kaat	.20
45	Jim Palmer	.20
46	Joe Pepitone	.20
47	Joe Rudi	.20
48	Johnny Bench	1.00
49	Juan Marichal	.40
50	Keith Hernandez	.20
51	Bucky Dent	.20
52	Lou Brock	.40
53	Ron Cey	.20
54	Luis Aparicio	.20
55	Luis Tiant	.20
56	Mark Fidrych	.20
57	Maury Wills	.20
58	Mickey Lolich	.20
59	Mickey Rivers	.20
60	Mike Schmidt	1.00
61	Moose Skowron	.20
62	Nolan Ryan	3.00
63	Orlando Cepeda	.20
64	Ozzie Smith	.75
65	Phil Niekro	.20
66	Reggie Jackson	.75

68 Reggie Smith .20
69 Rico Carty .20
70 Roberto Clemente 2.00
71 Robin Yount .75
72 Roger Maris 1.50
73 Rollie Fingers .20
74 Ron Guidry .20
75 Ron Santo .20
76 Ron Swoboda .20
77 Sal Bando .20
78 Sam McDowell .20
79 Steve Carlton .40
80 Thurman Munson 1.00
81 Tim McCarver .20
82 Tom Seaver .75
83 Mike Cuellar .20
84 Tony Kubek .20
85 Tommy John .20
86 Tony Perez .20
87 Tug McGraw .20
88 Vida Blue .20
89 Warren Spahn .75
90 Whitey Ford .50
91 Willie Mays 2.00
92 Willie McCovey .20
93 Willie Stargell .20
94 Yogi Berra 1.00
95 Stan Musial 1.00
96 Jim Piersall .20
97 Duke Snider .50
98 Bruce Sutter .30
99 Dave Concepcion .20
100 Darrell Evans .20
101 Dennis Eckersley .40
102 Hoyt Wilhelm .20
103 Minnie Minoso .20
104 Don Newcombe .20
105 Richie Ashburn .20
106 Alan Trammell .20
107 Jim "Catfish" Hunter .20
108 Lou Whitaker .20
109 Johnny Podres .20
110 Denny Martinez .20
111 Willie Horton .20
112 Dean Chance .20
113 Fergie Jenkins .20
114 Cecil Cooper .20
115 Rick Reuschel .20
116 Space Race (Events) .20
117 Man On The Moon (Events) .50
118 Woodstock (Events) .50
119 Peace Movement/Flower Power (Events) .20
120 N.Y. Worlds Fair (Events) .20
121 Vietnam War (Events) .20
122 Vietnam Cease Fire (Events) .20
123 Kennedy Elected President (Events) .50
124 Kennedy Assassination (Events) .20
125 Malcom X (Events) .20
126 Nixon Elected President (Events) .20
127 Watergate (Events) .20
128 Nixon Resigns (Events) .20
129 Cuban Missile Crisis (Events) .20
130 Astrodome (Events) .20
131 Secretariat (Events) .20
132 Lyndon Johnson Signs Civil Rights Bill (Events) .20
133 Atomic Bomb Test Ban Treaty (Events) .20
134 Bi Centennial (Events) .20
135 String Bikini (Events) .20
136 Birth Control Pill (Events) .20
137 Studio 54 (Events) .20
138 Motown (Events) .20
139 Microsoft Started (Events) .20
140 Internet Developed (Events) .20
141 John F. Kennedy (Personalities) 1.50
142 Marilyn Monroe (Personalities) 1.50
143 Elvis Presley (Personalities) 1.50
144 Jimi Hendrix (Personalities) 1.00
145 Arthur Ashe (Personalities) .20
146 Richard Nixon (Personalities) .20
147 James Dean (Personalities) .20
148 Janis Joplin (Personalities) .50
149 Frank Sinatra (Personalities) 1.00
150 Malcom X (Personalities) .50

Autoproofs Baseball Legends

No pricing due to scarcity.
Production 25 Sets

Decade Leaders

NM/M
Complete Set (10): 15.00
Common Player: 1.00
Inserted 1:12
DL1 Willie Stargell 1.50
DL2 Harmon Killebrew 1.50
DL3 Johnny Bench 2.00
DL4 Hank Aaron 3.00

DL5 Rod Carew 1.00
DL6 Roberto Clemente 3.00
DL7 Nolan Ryan 4.00
DL8 Bob Gibson 1.50
DL9 Jim Palmer 1.00
DL10 Juan Marichal 1.00

Entertainment Stars

NM/M
Production 500 Sets
1 Lou Ferrigno (Incredible Hulk) 50.00
2 Adam West (Batman) 60.00
3 Danny Bonaduce (Partridge Family) 30.00

Legends Autographs

NM/M
Common Player: 10.00
Inserted 1:211
TT1R Willie Mays 100.00
TT14R Johnny Bench 60.00
TT48R Bobby Richardson 20.00
TT8R Carl Yastrzemski 50.00
TT13R Warren Spahn 25.00
TT15R Reggie Jackson 50.00
TT18R Bob Gibson 20.00
TT25R Luis Tiant 10.00
TT29R Moose Skowron 10.00
TT31R Clete Boyer 10.00
TT33R Vida Blue 15.00
TT35R Joe Pepitone 10.00
TT37R Tug McGraw 15.00
TT47R Frank Howard 10.00
TT49R Tony Kubek 40.00
TT50R Mickey Lolich 10.00

Profiles In Courage

NM/M
Complete Set (20): 25.00
Common Player: 1.00
Inserted 1:8
PIC1 Roger Maris 2.00
PIC2 Lou Brock 1.00
PIC3 Brooks Robinson 1.50
PIC4 Carl Yastrzemski 1.50
PIC5 Mike Schmidt 2.50
PIC6 Hank Aaron 3.00
PIC7 Tom Seaver 1.50
PIC8 Willie Mays 3.00
PIC9 Graig Nettles 1.00
PIC10 Frank Robinson 1.50
PIC11 Rollie Fingers 1.00
PIC12 Tony Perez 1.00
PIC13 George Brett 1.50
PIC14 Robin Yount 1.50
PIC15 Nolan Ryan 4.00
PIC16 Warren Spahn 1.50
PIC17 Johnny Bench 2.00

PIC18 Vida Blue 1.00
PIC19 Roberto Clemente 3.00
PIC20 Thurman Munson 2.00

Rookie Reprint Relics

NM/M
Common Player: 10.00
Inserted 1:116
JB Johnny Bench 20.00
GB George Brett 40.00
SC Steve Carlton 15.00
GC Gary Carter 10.00
AD Andre Dawson 10.00
DE Dennis Eckersley 10.00
MF Mark Fidrych 10.00
BG Bobby Grich 10.00
RJ Reggie Jackson 15.00
JK Jim Kaat 10.00
TMC Tim McCarver 10.00
TM Thurman Munson 35.00
BM Bobby Murcer 10.00
AO Al Oliver 10.00
BP Boog Powell 10.00
OS Ozzie Smith 20.00
DS Don Sutton 10.00
DW Dave Winfield 10.00
RY Robin Yount 20.00

Timeless Classics Relics

NM/M
Common Player: 8.00
Inserted 1:80
Sam McDowell 8.00
Frank Howard 8.00
Dick Groat 8.00
Roger Maris 50.00
Orlando Cepeda 10.00
Willie Mays 40.00
Carl Yastrzemski 30.00
Roberto Clemente 60.00
Harmon Killebrew 20.00
Brooks Robinson 20.00
Tony Conigliaro 15.00
Frank Robinson 15.00
Hank Aaron 40.00
Willie McCovey 15.00
Rico Carty 8.00
Johnny Bench 20.00
Willie Stargell 15.00
Steve Carlton 15.00
Norm Cash 8.00
Reggie Jackson 15.00
Mike Schmidt 30.00
Mickey Rivers 8.00
Tom Seaver 20.00
George Brett 40.00
George Foster 8.00
Graig Nettles 8.00
Nolan Ryan 40.00
Dave Parker 10.00
Dick Allen 8.00
Fred Lynn 8.00
Keith Hernandez 8.00
Dave Winfield 15.00

Woodstock Relics

NM/M
Common Player: 8.00
Inserted 1:138
GB George Brett 40.00
BB Bill Buckner 8.00
OC Orlando Cepeda 10.00
DE Dwight Evans 8.00
CF Carlton Fisk 15.00
BF Bill Freehan 8.00
DG Dick Groat 8.00
RJ Reggie Jackson 15.00
TK Ted Kluszewski 8.00
FL Fred Lynn 8.00
WM Willie Mays 45.00
SM Stan Musial 40.00
TP Tony Perez 8.00
JP Jimmy Piersall 8.00
BR Brooks Robinson 15.00
FR Frank Robinson 15.00
JR Joe Rudi 8.00
DS Duke Snider 15.00
WS Willie Stargell 15.00
MW Maury Wills 8.00
DW Dave Winfield 15.00
WS Woodstock 15.00
JW Jim Wynn 8.00
CY Carl Yastrzemski 30.00
RY Robin Yount 20.00

2001 Topps Archives

NM/M
Complete Set (450): 150.00
Complete Series 1 (225): 75.00

Complete Series 2 (225): 75.00
Common Player: .40
Pack (8): 4.50
Box (20): 80.00
1 Johnny Antonelli .40
2 Yogi Berra 2.50
3 Dom DiMaggio .40
4 Carl Erskine .40
5 Joe Garagiola .50
6 Monte Irvin .40
7 Vernon Law .40
8 Eddie Mathews 2.00
9 Willie Mays 5.00
10 Gil McDougald .40
11 Andy Pafko .40
12 Phil Rizzuto .75
13 Preacher Roe .40
14 Hank Sauer .50
15 Bobby Shantz .40
16 Enos Slaughter .50
17 Warren Spahn 2.00
18 Mickey Vernon .40
19 Early Wynn .40
20 Whitey Ford 1.00
21 Johnny Podres .40
22 Ernie Banks 2.00
23 Moose Skowron .40
24 Harmon Killebrew 2.00
25 Ted Williams 6.00
26 Jimmy Piersall .40
27 Frank Thomas .40
28 Bill Mazeroski .50
29 Bobby Richardson .40
30 Frank Robinson 1.50
31 Stan Musial 3.00
32 Johnny Callison .40
33 Bob Gibson 2.00
34 Frank Howard .50
35 Willie McCovey .40
36 Carl Yastrzemski 2.00
37 Jim Maloney .40
38 Ron Santo .40
39 Lou Brock .75
40 Tim McCarver .50
41 Joe Pepitone .40
42 Boog Powell .50
43 Bill Freehan .40
44 Dick Allen .40
45 Willie Horton .40
46 Mickey Lolich .40
47 Wilbur Wood .40
48 Bert Campaneris .40
49 Rod Carew 1.50
50 Tug McGraw .40
51 Tony Perez .75
52 Luis Tiant .40
53 Bobby Murcer .40
54 Don Sutton .75
55 Ken Holtzman .40
56 Reggie Smith .40
57 Hal McRae .40
58 Roy White .40
59 Reggie Jackson 3.00
60 Graig Nettles .40
61 Joe Rudi .40
62 Vida Blue .50
63 Darrell Evans .40
64 David Concepcion .40
65 Bobby Grich .40
66 Greg Luzinski .40
67 Cecil Cooper .40
68 George Hendrick .40
69 Dwight Evans .40
70 Gary Matthews .40
71 Mike Schmidt 3.00
72 Dave Parker .40
73 Dave Winfield 1.00
74 Gary Carter .40
75 Dennis Eckersley .75
76 Kent Tekulve .40
77 Andre Dawson .75
78 Denny Martinez .40
79 Bruce Sutter .75
80 Jack Morris .40
81 Ozzie Smith 1.50
82 Lee Smith .40
83 Don Mattingly 4.00
84 Joe Carter .40
85 Kirby Puckett 3.00
86 Joe Adcock .40
87 Gus Bell .40
88 Roy Campanella 2.00
89 Jackie Jensen .40
90 Johnny Mize .75
91 Allie Reynolds .40
92 Al Rosen .40
93 Hal Newhouser .40
94 Harvey Kuenn .40

95 Nellie Fox .75
96 Elston Howard .40
97 Sal Maglie .40
98 Roger Maris 3.00
99 Norm Cash .40
100 Thurman Munson 2.50
101 Roy Campanella 1.50
102 Joe Garagiola .75
103 Dom DiMaggio .40
104 Johnny Mize .50
105 Allie Reynolds .40
106 Preacher Roe .40
107 Hal Newhouser .40
108 Monte Irvin .40
109 Carl Erskine .40
110 Enos Slaughter .40
111 Gil McDougald .40
112 Andy Pafko .40
113 Sal Maglie .40
114 Johnny Antonelli .40
115 Phil Rizzuto .50
116 Yogi Berra 1.50
117 Early Wynn .40
118 Mickey Vernon .40
119 Gus Bell .40
120 Ted Williams 4.00
121 Frank Thomas .40
122 Bobby Richardson .40
123 Whitey Ford 1.00
124 Vernon Law .40
125 Jimmy Piersall .40
126 Moose Skowron .40
127 Joe Adcock .40
128 Johnny Podres .40
129 Ernie Banks 1.50
130 Jim Maloney .40
131 Johnny Callison .40
132 Eddie Mathews 1.50
133 Joe Pepitone .40
134 Warren Spahn 1.50
135 Bill Mazeroski .40
136 Norm Cash .40
137 Bob Gibson 1.00
138 Harmon Killebrew 1.50
139 Frank Robinson 1.00
140 Ron Santo .40
141 Hank Sauer .40
142 Bobby Shantz .40
143 Nellie Fox .50
144 Elston Howard .40
145 Jackie Jensen .40
146 Al Rosen .40
147 Dick Allen .40
148 Bill Freehan .40
149 Boog Powell .40
150 Lou Brock .75
151 Rod Carew .75
152 Wilbur Wood .40
153 Thurman Munson 1.50
154 Ken Holtzman .40
155 Willie Horton .40
156 Mickey Lolich .40
157 Tim McCarver .40
158 Willie McCovey .40
159 Roy White .40
160 Bobby Murcer .40
161 Joe Rudi .40
162 Reggie Smith .40
163 Luis Tiant .40
164 Bert Campaneris .40
165 Frank Howard .40
166 Harvey Kuenn .40
167 Greg Luzinski .40
168 Tug McGraw .40
169 Willie Mays 3.00
170 Roger Maris 2.00
171 Vida Blue .40
172 Bobby Grich .40
173 Reggie Jackson 2.00
174 Hal McRae .40
175 Carl Yastrzemski 1.00
176 David Concepcion .40
177 Cecil Cooper .40
178 George Hendrick .40
179 Gary Matthews .40
180 Stan Musial 2.00
181 Graig Nettles .40
182 Don Sutton .50
183 Kent Tekulve .40
184 Bruce Sutter .75
185 Darrell Evans .40
186 Mike Schmidt 2.00
187 Dave Parker .40
188 Dwight Evans .40
189 Gary Carter .40
190 Jack Morris .40
191 Tony Perez .50
192 Dave Winfield .75
193 Andre Dawson .50
194 Lee Smith .40
195 Ozzie Smith 1.00
196 Denny Martinez .40
197 Don Mattingly 2.50
198 Joe Carter .40
199 Dennis Eckersley .75
200 Kirby Puckett 2.00
201 Walter Alston .75
202 Casey Stengel .75
203 Sparky Anderson .40
204 Tommy Lasorda .75
205 Whitey Herzog .40
206 Harmon Killebrew, Frank Howard, Reggie Jackson (League Leader) .40
207 Hank Aaron, Early Wynn, Ron Santo, Willie McCovey (League Leader) 2.50

208 Frank Robinson, Harmon Killebrew, Boog Powell (League Leader) 1.50
209 Tony Oliva, Frank Robinson, Frank Howard (League Leader) .75
210 Hank Aaron, Willie McCovey, Willie Mays, Orlando Cepeda (League Leader) 2.50
211 Hank Aaron, Frank Robinson, Willie Mays, Ernie Banks (League Leaders) 2.50
212 Carl Yastrzemski, Harmon Killebrew, Frank Howard (League Leaders) 1.50
213 Ernie Banks (Highlight) 1.50
214 Hank Aaron (Highlight) 2.50
215 Willie Mays (Highlight) 2.50
216 Al Kaline (Highlight) .75
217 Stan Musial (Highlight) 2.00
218 Duke Snider (Highlight) .75
219 Frank Robinson, Hank Bauer, Frank Robinson (Highlight) .50
220 Willie Mays, Stan Musial (Highlight) 1.50
221 Whitey Ford (World Series Highlight) .75
222 Jerry Koosman (World Series Highlight) .40
223 Bob Gibson (World Series Highlight) .75
224 Gil Hodges (World Series Highlight) .40
225 Reggie Jackson (World Series Highlight) 1.50
226 Hank Bauer .40
227 Ralph Branca .40
228 Joe Garagiola .75
229 Bob Feller 2.00
230 Dick Groat .40
231 George Kell .40
232 Bob Boone .40
233 Minnie Minoso .40
234 Billy Pierce .40
235 Robin Roberts .50
236 Johnny Sain .40
237 Red Schoendienst .40
238 Curt Simmons .40
239 Duke Snider 2.00
240 Bobby Thomson .40
241 Hoyt Wilhelm .40
242 Elroy Face .40
243 Ralph Kiner .75
244 Hank Aaron 4.00
245 Al Kaline 2.00
246 Don Larsen 1.50
247 Tug McGraw .40
248 Don Newcombe .75
249 Herb Score .40
250 Clete Boyer .40
251 Lindy McDaniel .40
252 Brooks Robinson 2.50
253 Orlando Cepeda .60
254 Larry Bowa .40
255 Mike Cuellar .40
256 Jim Perry .40
257 Dave Parker .40
258 Maury Wills .40
259 Willie Davis .40
260 Juan Marichal .60
261 Jim Bouton .40
262 Dean Chance .40
263 Sam McDowell .40
264 Whitey Ford 3.00
265 Bob Uecker 2.00
266 Willie Stargell 2.00
267 Rico Carty .40
268 Tommy John .40
269 Phil Niekro .60
270 Paul Blair .40
271 Steve Carlton 3.00
272 Jim Lonborg .40
273 Tony Perez .60
274 Ron Swoboda .40
275 Fergie Jenkins .75
276 Jim Palmer 1.50
277 Sal Bando .40
278 Tom Seaver 4.00
279 Johnny Bench 4.00
280 Nolan Ryan 6.00
281 Rollie Fingers .50
282 Sparky Lyle .40
283 Al Oliver .40
284 Bob Watson .40
285 Bill Buckner .40
286 Bert Blyleven .40
287 George Foster .40
288 Al Hrabosky .40
289 Cecil Cooper .40
290 Carlton Fisk 1.00
291 Mickey Rivers .40
292 Goose Gossage .40
293 Rick Reuschel .40
294 Bucky Dent .40
295 Frank Tanana .40
296 George Brett 4.00
297 Keith Hernandez .40
298 Fred Lynn .40
299 Robin Yount 3.00
300 Ron Guidry .40
301 Jack Clark .40
302 Mark Fidrych .40
303 Dale Murphy 1.50
304 Willie Hernandez .40
305 Lou Whitaker .40

(continued checklist)

306 Kirk Gibson .75
307 Wade Boggs 3.00
308 Ryne Sandberg 4.00
309 Orel Hershiser .40
310 Jimmy Key .40
311 Richie Ashburn .40
312 Smoky Burgess .40
313 Gil Hodges 1.50
314 Ted Kluszewski .40
315 Pee Wee Reese 1.00
316 Jackie Robinson 4.00
317 Harvey Haddix .40
318 Satchel Paige 3.00
319 Roberto Clemente 5.00
320 Carl Furillo .40
321 Don Drysdale 2.00
322 Curt Flood .40
323 Bob Allison .40
324 Tony Conigliaro .40
325 Dan Quisenberry .40
326 Ralph Branca .40
327 Bob Feller 1.00
328 Satchel Paige 3.00
329 George Kell .40
330 Pee Wee Reese 1.00
331 Bobby Thomson .40
332 Carl Furillo .40
333 Hank Bauer .40
334 Herb Score .40
335 Richie Ashburn .40
336 Billy Pierce .40
337 Duke Snider 2.00
338 Harvey Haddix .40
339 Robin Roberts .40
340 Dick Groat .40
341 Curt Simmons .40
342 Bob Uecker 1.00
343 Smoky Burgess .40
344 Jim Bouton .40
345 Elroy Face .40
346 Don Drysdale 1.00
347 Bob Allison .40
348 Clete Boyer .40
349 Dean Chance .40
350 Tony Conigliaro .40
351 Curt Flood .40
352 Hoyt Wilhelm .40
353 Ron Swoboda .40
354 Roberto Clemente 3.00
355 Tug McGraw .40
356 Orlando Cepeda .40
357 Joe Garagiola .40
358 Juan Marichal .50
359 Sam McDowell .40
360 Johnny Sain .40
361 Ted Kluszewski .40
362 Al Kaline 2.00
363 Lindy McDaniel .40
364 Don Newcombe .40
365 Jim Perry .40
366 Hank Aaron 4.00
367 Don Larsen 1.00
368 Mike Cuellar .40
369 Willie Davis .40
370 Ralph Kiner .50
371 Minnie Minoso .40
372 Larry Bowa .40
373 Brooks Robinson 1.00
374 Bob Boone .40
375 Jim Lonborg .40
376 Paul Blair .40
377 Rico Carty .40
378 Sal Bando .40
379 Mark Fidrych .40

NM/M
380 Al Hrabosky .40
381 Willie Stargell 1.00
382 Johnny Bench 2.50
383 Dave Parker .40
384 Sparky Lyle .40
385 Fergie Jenkins .50
386 Jim Palmer 1.00
387 Whitey Ford 2.00
388 Tony Perez .40
389 Mickey Rivers .40
390 Bob Watson .40
391 Rollie Fingers .40
392 George Foster .40
393 Al Oliver .40
394 Tom Seaver 3.00
395 Maury Wills .40
396 Steve Carlton 1.00
397 Cecil Cooper .40
398 Bill Buckner .40
399 Phil Niekro .40
400 Red Schoendienst .40
401 Ron Guidry .40
402 Willie Hernandez .40
403 Tommy John .40
404 Gil Hodges .40
405 Bucky Dent .40
406 Keith Hernandez .40
407 Dan Quisenberry .40
408 Fred Lynn .40
409 Rick Reuschel .40
410 Jackie Robinson 3.00
411 Goose Gossage .40
412 Bert Blyleven .40
413 Jack Clark .40
414 Carlton Fisk .50
415 Dale Murphy .75
416 Frank Tanana .40
417 George Brett 3.00
418 Robin Yount 2.50
419 Kirk Gibson .50
420 Lou Whitaker .40
421 Ryne Sandberg 2.50
422 Jimmy Key .40
423 Nolan Ryan 5.00
424 Wade Boggs .75
425 Orel Hershiser .40
426 Billy Martin (Managers) .40
427 Ralph Houk (Managers) .40
428 Chuck Tanner (Managers) .40
429 Earl Weaver (Managers) .40
430 Leo Durocher (Managers) .40
431 Tony Conigliaro, Norm Cash, Willie Horton (League Leaders) .40
432 Ernie Banks, Hank Aaron, Eddie Mathews, Clete Boyer (League Leaders) 1.50
433 Norm Cash, Frank Howard, Al Kaline, Jimmy Piersall (League Leaders) .40
434 Goose Gossage, Rollie Fingers (League Leaders) .40
435 Nolan Ryan, Tom Seaver (League Leaders) .40
436 Reggie Jackson, Willie Stargell (League Leaders) .75
437 Johnny Bench, Dick Allen (League Leaders) .75
438 Roger Maris (Decade Highlights) 3.00
439 Carl Yastrzemski (Decade Highlights) 2.00
440 Nolan Ryan (Decade Highlights) 4.00
441 Cincinnati Reds (Decade Highlights) .75
442 Tony Perez (Decade Highlights) .40
443 Steve Carlton (Decade Highlights) .75
444 Wade Boggs (Decade Highlights) .75
445 Andre Dawson (Decade Highlights) .40
446 Whitey Ford (World Series Highlights) 1.50
447 Hank Aaron (World Series Highlights) 4.00
448 Bob Gibson (World Series Highlights) .75
449 Roberto Clemente (World Series Highlights) 4.00
450 Orioles/Jackie Robinson (World Series Highlights) 1.50

Autographs

Common Player: 10.00
Inserted 1:Box
TAA1 Johnny Antonelli 15.00
TAA2 Hank Bauer 20.00
TAA3 Yogi Berra/50 350.00
TAA4 Ralph Branca 20.00
TAA5 Dom DiMaggio 40.00
TAA6 Joe Garagiola 50.00
TAA7 Carl Erskine 30.00
TAA8 Bob Feller 30.00
TAA9 Dick Groat 50.00
TAA10 Monte Irvin 20.00
TAA11 George Kell 20.00
TAA12 Vernon Law 15.00
TAA13 Bob Boone 10.00
TAA16 Willie Mays/50 500.00
TAA17 Gil McDougald 20.00
TAA18 Minnie Minoso 30.00
TAA19 Andy Pafko 30.00
TAA20 Billy Pierce 10.00
TAA21 Phil Rizzuto/200 120.00
TAA22 Robin Roberts 20.00
TAA23 Preacher Roe 20.00
TAA24 Johnny Sain 25.00
TAA25 Hank Sauer 25.00
TAA26 Red Schoendienst 25.00
TAA27 Bobby Shantz 10.00
TAA28 Curt Simmons 10.00
TAA29 Enos Slaughter 30.00
TAA30 Duke Snider 80.00
TAA31 Warren Spahn 125.00
TAA32 Bobby Thomson 25.00
TAA33 Mickey Vernon 15.00
TAA34 Hoyt Wilhelm 40.00
TAA35 Jim Wynn 15.00
TAA36 Elroy Face 10.00
TAA37 Gaylord Perry 40.00
TAA38 Ralph Kiner 50.00
TAA39 Johnny Podres 20.00
TAA40 Hank Aaron/50 1,400
TAA41 Ernie Banks/50 450.00
TAA42 Al Kaline 150.00
TAA43 Moose Skowron 15.00
TAA44 Don Larsen 200.00
TAA45 Harmon Killebrew 150.00
TAA46 Tug McGraw 35.00
TAA48 Don Newcombe 20.00
TAA49 Jimmy Piersall 20.00
TAA50 Herb Score 20.00
TAA51 Frank Thomas 10.00
TAA52 Clete Boyer 20.00
TAA53 Bill Mazeroski 75.00
TAA54 Lindy McDaniel 15.00
TAA55 Bobby Richardson 15.00
TAA56 Brooks Robinson/SP 200.00
TAA57 Frank Robinson 85.00
TAA58 Orlando Cepeda 80.00
TAA59 Stan Musial/50 300.00
TAA60 Larry Bowa 30.00
TAA61 Johnny Callison 15.00
TAA62 Mike Cuellar 15.00
TAA63 Bob Gibson/SP/50 200.00
TAA64 Jim Perry 15.00
TAA65 Frank Howard 20.00
TAA66 David Palmer 15.00
TAA67 Willie McCovey 100.00
TAA68 Maury Wills 15.00
TAA69 Carl Yastrzemski 220.00
TAA70 Willie Davis 10.00
TAA71 Jim Maloney 15.00
TAA73 Ron Santo 35.00
TAA74 Jim Bouton 30.00
TAA75 Lou Brock/50 200.00
TAA76 Dean Chance 15.00
TAA77 Tim McCarver/200 60.00
TAA78 Sam McDowell 20.00
TAA79 Joe Pepitone 20.00
TAA80 Whitey Ford 140.00
TAA81 Boog Powell 25.00
TAA82 Bill Freehan 10.00
TAA83 Dick Allen 40.00
TAA85 Rico Carty 10.00
TAA86 Willie Horton 10.00
TAA87 Willie Horton 10.00
TAA88 Tommy John 15.00
TAA89 Mickey Lolich 10.00
TAA90 Phil Niekro 30.00
TAA91 Wilbur Wood 10.00
TAA92 Paul Blair 10.00
TAA93 Bert Campaneris 10.00
TAA94 Steve Carlton 40.00
TAA96 Jim Lonborg 10.00
TAA97 Luis Aparicio 40.00
TAA98 Tony Perez 40.00
TAA99 Joe Morgan/200 65.00
TAA100 Ron Swoboda 30.00
TAA101 Luis Tiant 15.00
TAA102 Fergie Jenkins 35.00
TAA103 Bobby Murcer 10.00
TAA104 Jim Palmer 80.00
TAA106 Sal Bando 10.00
TAA107 Ken Holtzman 50.00
TAA108 Tom Seaver/200 225.00
TAA110 Johnny Bench 225.00
TAA111 Hal McRae 10.00
TAA112 Nolan Ryan 500.00
TAA113 Roy White 10.00
TAA114 Rollie Fingers 30.00
TAA115 Reggie Jackson/50 225.00
TAA116 Sparky Lyle 15.00
TAA117 Graig Nettles 20.00
TAA118 Al Oliver 10.00
TAA119 Joe Rudi 15.00
TAA120 Bob Watson 10.00
TAA121 Vida Blue 10.00
TAA122 Bill Buckner 10.00
TAA123 Darrell Evans 10.00
TAA124 Bert Blyleven 25.00
TAA125 David Concepcion 20.00
TAA126 George Foster 15.00
TAA127 Bobby Grich 10.00
TAA128 Al Hrabosky 10.00
TAA129 Greg Luzinski 25.00
TAA130 Cecil Cooper 15.00
TAA131 Ron Cey 10.00
TAA132 Carlton Fisk 100.00
TAA133 George Hendrick 10.00
TAA134 Mickey Rivers 10.00
TAA135 Dwight Evans 25.00
TAA136 Goose Gossage 10.00
TAA137 Gary Matthews 10.00
TAA138 Rick Reuschel 10.00
TAA139 Mike Schmidt/SP/50 320.00
TAA140 Bucky Dent 25.00
TAA141 Jim Kaat 25.00
TAA142 Frank Tanana 10.00
TAA143 Dave Winfield/200 100.00
TAA144 George Brett/SP/50 320.00
TAA145 Gary Carter/200 65.00
TAA146 Keith Hernandez 40.00
TAA147 Fred Lynn 20.00
TAA148 Robin Yount/SP/200 150.00
TAA149 Dennis Eckersley/SP/200 120.00
TAA150 Ron Guidry 50.00
TAA151 Kent Tekulve 10.00
TAA152 Jack Clark 10.00
TAA153 Andre Dawson/SP/200 65.00
TAA154 Mark Fidrych 25.00
TAA155 Denny Martinez/SP/200 40.00
TAA156 Dale Murphy 50.00
TAA157 Bruce Sutter 10.00
TAA158 Willie Hernandez 10.00
TAA159 Willie Hernandez 10.00
TAA160 Lou Whitaker 20.00
TAA161 Kirk Gibson 40.00
TAA163 Lee Smith 25.00
TAA164 Wade Boggs 100.00
TAA165 Ryne Sandberg/SP/200 175.00
TAA166 Don Mattingly 150.00
TAA167 Joe Carter/SP/200 50.00
TAA168 Orel Hershiser 50.00
TAA169 Kirby Puckett 160.00
TAA170 Jimmy Key 50.00

Baseball Bucks

NM/M
Valid to 3/02 for Topps merchandise:
TB1 Willie Mays ($1/15,000) 2.00
TB2 Roberto Clemente ($5/1,000) 4.00
TB3 Jackie Robinson ($10/500) 10.00

Game-Used Bat

NM/M
Common Player: 15.00
1 Johnny Bench 30.00
2 George Brett 50.00
3 Fred Lynn 15.00
4 Reggie Jackson 25.00
5 Mike Schmidt 50.00
6 Willie Stargell 20.00

Game-Used Bat Autograph

NM/M
Common Player: 120.00
Production 25 Sets
1 Johnny Bench 150.00
2 George Brett 200.00
3 Fred Lynn 75.00

Topps Final Autoproof

NM/M
Common Player: 30.00
Carlton Fisk 65.00
Wade Boggs 40.00
Willie Mays 150.00
Willie McCovey 50.00
Jim Palmer 50.00
Robin Roberts 50.00
Duke Snider 50.00
Warren Spahn 60.00
Hoyt Wilhelm 50.00
Carl Yastrzemski 100.00

2001 Topps Archives Reserve

NM/M
Complete Set (100): 90.00
Common Player: .75

Hobby Pack (5): 8.00
Hobby Box (10 + Auto. Ball): 125.00
1 Joe Adcock .75
2 Brooks Robinson 3.00
3 Luis Aparicio .75
4 Richie Ashburn .75
5 Hank Bauer .75
6 Johnny Bench 4.00
7 Wade Boggs 2.00
8 Moose Skowron .75
9 George Brett 5.00
10 Lou Brock 2.00
11 Roy Campanella 4.00
12 Willie Hernandez .75
13 Steve Carlton 2.00
14 Gary Carter .75
15 Hoyt Wilhelm .75
16 Orlando Cepeda .75
17 Roberto Clemente 8.00
18 Dale Murphy 1.50
19 Dave Concepcion .75
20 Dom DiMaggio .75
21 Larry Doby .75
22 Don Drysdale 4.00
23 Dennis Eckersley .75
24 Bob Feller 2.00
25 Rollie Fingers .75
26 Carlton Fisk 2.00
27 Nellie Fox 1.50
28 Mickey Rivers .75
29 Tommy John .75
30 Johnny Sain .75
31 Keith Hernandez .75
32 Gil Hodges .75
33 Elston Howard 3.00
34 Frank Howard .75
35 Bob Gibson 5.00
36 Fergie Jenkins .75
37 Jackie Jensen .75
38 Al Kaline 3.00
39 Harmon Killebrew 5.00
40 Ralph Kiner .75
41 Dick Groat .75
42 Don Larsen .75
43 Ralph Branca .75
44 Mickey Lolich .75
45 Juan Marichal 3.00
46 Roger Maris 6.00
47 Bobby Thomson .75
48 Eddie Mathews 4.00
49 Don Mattingly 8.00
50 Willie McCovey 2.00
51 Gil McDougald .75
52 Tug McGraw .75
53 Billy Pierce .75
54 Minnie Minoso .75
55 Johnny Mize 2.00
56 Elroy Face .75
57 Joe Morgan 1.50
58 Thurman Munson 5.00
59 Stan Musial 5.00
60 Phil Niekro .75
61 Paul Blair .75
62 Andy Pafko .75
63 Satchel Paige 5.00
64 Tony Perez .75
65 Sal Bando .75
66 Jimmy Piersall .75
67 Kirby Puckett 5.00
68 Phil Rizzuto 3.00
69 Robin Roberts .75
70 Jackie Robinson 8.00
71 Ryne Sandberg 3.00
72 Mike Schmidt 4.00
73 Red Schoendienst .75
74 Herb Score .75
75 Enos Slaughter .75
76 Ozzie Smith 3.00
77 Warren Spahn 2.00
78 Don Sutton .75
79 Luis Tiant .75
80 Ted Kluszewski .75
81 Whitey Ford 3.00
82 Maury Wills .75
83 Dave Winfield 2.00
84 Early Wynn .75
85 Carl Yastrzemski 3.00
86 Robin Yount 4.00
87 Bob Allison .75
88 Clete Boyer .75
89 Reggie Jackson 3.00
90 Yogi Berra 5.00
91 Willie Mays 8.00
92 Jim Palmer 2.00
93 Pee Wee Reese 2.00
94 Frank Robinson 2.00
95 Boog Powell .75
96 Willie Stargell 2.00
97 Nolan Ryan 10.00
98 Tom Seaver 4.00
99 Duke Snider 3.00
100 Bill Mazeroski .75

Autographs

NM/M
Common Autograph: 10.00
Inserted 1:10
1 Willie Mays 175.00
2 Whitey Ford 60.00
3 Nolan Ryan 180.00
4 Carl Yastrzemski 90.00
5 Frank Robinson 40.00
6 Tom Seaver 85.00
7 Warren Spahn 80.00
8 Johnny Bench 100.00
9 Reggie Jackson 85.00
10 Bob Gibson 40.00
11 Bob Feller 20.00

1969 ROOKIE STARS — NOLAN RYAN • P

12 Gil McDougald 15.00
13 Luis Tiant 15.00
14 Minnie Minoso 15.00
15 Herb Score 15.00
16 Moose Skowron 20.00
17 Maury Wills 15.00
18 Clete Boyer 20.00
19 Don Larsen 20.00
23 Tug McGraw 30.00
25 Robin Roberts 20.00
26 Frank Howard 20.00
28 Mickey Lolich 15.00
29 Tommy John 15.00
32 Dick Groat 20.00
33 Elroy Face 15.00
34 Paul Blair 10.00

Autographed Baseball

NM/M
Common Autograph: 20.00
Inserted 1:Box
1 Johnny Bench/100 80.00
2 Paul Blair/1,000 20.00
3 Clete Boyer/1,000 20.00
4 Ralph Branca/400 30.00
5 Elroy Face/1,000 25.00
6 Bob Feller/1,000 30.00
7 Whitey Ford/1,000 70.00
8 Bob Gibson/1,000 40.00
9 Dick Groat/1,000 30.00
10 Frank Howard/1,000 25.00
11 Reggie Jackson/100 80.00
12 Don Larsen/100 40.00
13 Mickey Lolich/500 20.00
14 Willie Mays/100 160.00
15 Gil McDougald/500 30.00
16 Tug McGraw/1,000 30.00
17 Minnie Minoso/1,000 30.00
18 Andy Pafko/500 30.00
19 Joe Pepitone/1,000 25.00
20 Robin Roberts/1,000 40.00
21 Frank Robinson/100 50.00
22 Nolan Ryan/100 150.00
23 Herb Score/500 20.00
24 Tom Seaver/100 80.00
25 Moose Skowron/1,000 30.00
26 Warren Spahn/100 80.00
27 Bobby Thomson/400 30.00
28 Luis Tiant/500 25.00
29 Carl Yastrzemski/100 120.00
30 Maury Wills/1,000 25.00

Bat Relics

NM/M
Common Player: 8.00
Overall Relic Odds 1:10
21 Al Kaline 20.00
22 Carl Yastrzemski 25.00
23 Carlton Fisk 15.00
24 Dale Murphy 8.00
25 Dave Winfield 15.00
26 Dick Groat 8.00
27 Dom DiMaggio 15.00

#	Player	Price
28	Don Mattingly	25.00
29	Gary Carter	8.00
30	George Kell	15.00
31	Harmon Killebrew	20.00
32	Jackie Jensen	15.00
33	Jackie Robinson	75.00
34	Jimmy Piersall	10.00
35	Joe Adcock	8.00
36	Joe Carter	8.00
37	Johnny Mize	10.00
38	Kirk Gibson	8.00
39	Mickey Vernon	8.00
40	Mike Schmidt	40.00
41	Ryne Sandberg	40.00
42	Ozzie Smith	25.00
43	Ted Kluszewski	10.00
44	Wade Boggs	15.00
45	Willie Mays	60.00
46	Duke Snider	20.00
47	Harvey Kuenn	8.00
48	Robin Yount	20.00
49	Red Schoendienst	8.00
50	Elston Howard	10.00
51	Bob Allison	8.00

Jersey Relics

FRANK HOWARD

#	Player	NM/M
	Common Player:	8.00
	Overall Relic Odds 1:10	
1	Brooks Robinson	15.00
2	Tony Conigliaro	15.00
3	Frank Howard	8.00
4	Don Sutton	10.00
5	Ferguson Jenkins	8.00
6	Frank Robinson	15.00
7	Don Mattingly	40.00
8	Willie Stargell	20.00
9	Moose Skowron	15.00
10	Fred Lynn	8.00
11	George Brett	40.00
12	Nolan Ryan	50.00
13	Orlando Cepeda	8.00
14	Reggie Jackson	20.00
15	Steve Carlton	15.00
16	Tom Seaver	20.00
17	Thurman Munson	25.00
18	Yogi Berra	20.00
19	Willie McCovey	10.00
20	Robin Yount	20.00

2001 Topps Chicago Cubs Reprints

BILLY WILLIAMS

This series of reprints of popular Cubs players' cards was part of Topps' 50th Anniversary celebration in 2001. Each card was printed in a serially-numbered edition of 30,000 and given to fans at special promotional dates. About 200 of each player's card were autographed and randomly distributed.

		NM/M
	Complete Set (10):	75.00
	Common Player:	5.00
1952	Andy Pafko	7.50
1952	Andy Pafko/Auto.	25.00
1958	Ernie Banks	20.00
1958	Ernie Banks/Auto.	75.00
1961	Ron Santo	7.50
1961	Ron Santo/Auto.	45.00
1971	Fergie Jenkins	7.50
1971	Fergie Jenkins/Auto.	45.00
1972	Billy Williams	7.50
1972	Billy Williams/Auto.	45.00
1979	Bruce Sutter	7.50
1979	Bruce Sutter/Auto.	45.00
1984	Ryne Sandberg	20.00
1984	Ryne Sandberg/Auto.	75.00
1985	Rick Sutcliffe	5.00
1985	Rick Sutcliffe/Auto.	25.00
1988	Andre Dawson	6.00
1988	Andre Dawson/Auto.	45.00
1998	Sammy Sosa	20.00
1998	Sammy Sosa/Auto.	75.00

2001 Topps Chrome

Juan GONZALEZ

#	Player	NM/M
	Complete Set (660):	225.00
	Complete Series 1 (330):	100.00
	Complete Series 2 (330):	125.00
	Common Player:	.25
	Series 1 Pack (4):	2.00
	Series 1 Box (24):	40.00
	Series 2 Pack (4):	6.00
	Series 2 Box (24):	120.00
1	Cal Ripken Jr.	3.00
2	Chipper Jones	1.00
3	Roger Cedeno	.25
4	Garret Anderson	.25
5	Robin Ventura	.25
6	Daryle Ward	.25
7	Phil Nevin	.25
8	Jermaine Dye	.25
9	Chris Singleton	.25
10	Mike Redmond	.25
11	Jim Thome	1.00
12	Brian Jordan	.25
13	Dustin Hermanson	.25
14	Shawn Green	.75
15	Todd Stottlemyre	.25
16	Dan Wilson	.25
17	Derek Lowe	.25
18	Juan Gonzalez	.50
19	Pat Meares	.25
20	Paul O'Neill	.50
21	Jeffrey Hammonds	.25
22	Pokey Reese	.25
23	Mike Mussina	.75
24	Rico Brogna	.25
25	Jay Buhner	.25
26	Steve Cox	.25
27	Quilvio Veras	.25
28	Marquis Grissom	.25
29	Shigetoshi Hasegawa	.25
30	Shane Reynolds	.25
31	Adam Piatt	.25
32	Preston Wilson	.25
33	Ellis Burks	.25
34	Armando Rios	.25
35	Chuck Finley	.25
36	Shannon Stewart	.25
37	Mark McGwire	2.50
38	Gerald Williams	.25
39	Eric Young	.25
40	Peter Bergeron	.25
41	Arthur Rhodes	.25
42	Bobby Jones	.25
43	Matt Clement	.25
44	Pedro Martinez	1.00
45	Jose Canseco	.50
46	Matt Anderson	.25
47	Torii Hunter	.50
48	Carlos Lee	.50
49	Eric Chavez	.25
50	Rick Helling	.25
51	John Franco	.25
52	Mike Bordick	.25
53	Andres Galarraga	.25
54	Jose Cruz Jr.	.25
55	Mike Matheny	.25
56	Randy Johnson	1.00
57	Richie Sexson	.25
58	Vladimir Nunez	.25
59	Aaron Boone	.25
60	Darin Erstad	.25
61	Alex Gonzalez	.25
62	Gil Heredia	.25
63	Shane Andrews	.25
64	Todd Hundley	.25
65	Bill Mueller	.25
66	Mark McLemore	.25
67	Scott Spiezio	.25
68	Kevin McGlinchy	.25
69	Manny Ramirez	1.00
70	Mike Lamb	.25
71	Brian Buchanan	.25
72	Mike Sweeney	.25
73	John Wetteland	.25
74	Rob Bell	.25
75	John Burkett	.25
76	Derek Jeter	3.00
77	J.D. Drew	.40
78	Jose Offerman	.25
79	Rick Reed	.25
80	Will Clark	.50
81	Rickey Henderson	.75
82	Kirk Rueter	.25
83	Lee Stevens	.25
84	Jay Bell	.25
85	Fred McGriff	.40
86	Julio Zuleta	.25
87	Brian Anderson	.25
89	Orlando Cabrera	.25
90	Alex Fernandez	.25
91	Derek Bell	.25
92	Eric Owens	.25
93	Dennys Reyes	.25
94	Mike Stanley	.25
95	Jorge Posada	.75
96	Paul Konerko	.50
97	Mike Remlinger	.25
98	Travis Lee	.25
99	Ken Caminiti	.25
100	Kevin Barker	.25
101	Ozzie Guillen	.25
102	Randy Wolf	.25
103	Michael Tucker	.25
104	Darren Lewis	.25
105	Joe Randa	.25
106	Jeff Cirillo	.25
107	David Ortiz	1.00
108	Herb Perry	.25
109	Jeff Nelson	.25
110	Chris Stynes	.25
111	Johnny Damon	1.00
112	Jason Schmidt	.25
113	Charles Johnson	.25
114	Pat Burrell	.50
115	Gary Sheffield	.75
116	Tom Glavine	.50
117	Jason Isringhausen	.25
118	Chris Carpenter	.50
119	Jeff Suppan	.25
120	Ivan Rodriguez	.75
121	Luis Sojo	.25
122	Ron Villone	.25
123	Mike Sirotka	.25
124	Chuck Knoblauch	.25
125	Jason Kendall	.25
126	Bobby Estalella	.25
127	Jose Guillen	.25
128	Carlos Delgado	.50
129	Benji Gil	.25
130	Einar Diaz	.25
131	Andy Benes	.25
132	Adrian Beltre	.50
133	Roger Clemens	3.00
134	Scott Williamson	.25
135	Brad Penny	.25
136	Troy Glaus	.40
137	Kevin Appier	.25
138	Walt Weiss	.25
139	Michael Barrett	.25
140	Mike Hampton	.25
141	Francisco Cordova	.25
142	David Segui	.25
143	Carlos Febles	.25
144	Roy Halladay	.50
145	Seth Etherton	.25
146	Fernando Tatis	.25
147	Livan Hernandez	.25
148	B.J. Surhoff	.25
149	Barry Larkin	.50
150	Bobby Howry	.25
151	Dmitri Young	.25
152	Brian Hunter	.25
153	Alex Rodriguez	3.00
154	Hideo Nomo	.50
155	Warren Morris	.25
156	Antonio Alfonseca	.25
157	Edgardo Alfonzo	.25
158	Mark Grudzielanek	.25
159	Fernando Vina	.25
160	Homer Bush	.25
161	Jason Giambi	.75
162	Steve Karsay	.25
163	Matt Lawton	.25
164	Rusty Greer	.25
165	Billy Koch	.25
166	Todd Hollandsworth	.25
167	Raul Ibanez	.25
168	Tony Gwynn	1.00
169	Carl Everett	.25
170	Hector Carrasco	.25
171	Jose Valentin	.25
172	Deivi Cruz	.25
173	Bret Boone	.25
174	Melvin Mora	.25
175	Danny Graves	.25
176	Jose Jimenez	.25
177	James Baldwin	.25
178	C.J. Nitkowski	.25
179	Jeff Zimmerman	.25
180	Mike Lowell	.25
181	Hideki Irabu	.25
182	Greg Vaughn	.25
183	Omar Daal	.25
184	Darren Dreifort	.25
185	Gil Meche	.25
186	Damian Jackson	.25
187	Frank Thomas	1.00
188	Luis Castillo	.25
189	Bartolo Colon	.25
190	Craig Biggio	.50
191	Scott Schoeneweis	.25
192	Dave Veres	.25
193	Ramon Martinez	.25
194	Jose Vidro	.25
195	Todd Helton	.75
196	Greg Norton	.25
197	Jacque Jones	.25
198	Jason Grimsley	.25
199	Dan Reichert	.25
200	Robb Nen	.25
201	Scott Hatteberg	.25
202	Terry Shumpert	.25
203	Kevin Millar	.25
204	Ismael Valdes	.25
205	Richard Hidalgo	.25
206	Randy Velarde	.25
207	Bengie Molina	.25
208	Tony Womack	.25
209	Enrique Wilson	.25
210	Jeff Brantley	.25
211	Rick Ankiel	.50
212	Terry Mulholland	.25
213	Ron Belliard	.25
214	Terrence Long	.25
215	Alberto Castillo	.25
216	Royce Clayton	.25
217	Joe McEwing	.25
218	Jason McDonald	.25
219	Ricky Bottalico	.25
220	Keith Foulke	.25
221	Brad Radke	.25
222	Gabe Kapler	.25
223	Pedro Astacio	.25
224	Armando Reynoso	.25
225	Darryl Kile	.25
226	Reggie Sanders	.25
227	Esteban Yan	.25
228	Joe Nathan	.25
229	Jay Payton	.25
230	Francisco Cordero	.25
231	Gregg Jefferies	.25
232	LaTroy Hawkins	.25
233	Jacob Cruz	.25
234	Chris Holt	.25
235	Vladimir Guerrero	1.00
236	Marvin Benard	.25
237	Alex Ramirez	.25
238	Mike Williams	.25
239	Sean Bergman	.25
240	Juan Encarnacion	.25
241	Russ Davis	.25
242	Ramon Hernandez	.25
243	Sandy Alomar	.25
244	Eddie Guardado	.25
245	Shane Halter	.25
246	Geoff Jenkins	.25
247	Brian Meadows	.25
248	Damian Miller	.25
249	Darrin Fletcher	.25
250	Rafael Furcal	.50
251	Mark Grace	.50
252	Mark Mulder	.25
253	Joe Torre (Managers)	.75
254	Bobby Cox (Managers)	.25
255	Mike Scioscia (Managers)	.25
256	Mike Hargrove (Managers)	.25
257	Jimy Williams (Managers)	.25
258	Jerry Manuel (Managers)	.25
259	Charlie Manuel (Managers)	.25
260	Don Baylor (Managers)	.25
261	Phil Garner (Managers)	.25
262	Tony Muser (Managers)	.25
263	Buddy Bell (Managers)	.25
264	Tom Kelly (Managers)	.25
265	John Boles (Managers)	.25
266	Art Howe (Managers)	.25
267	Larry Dierker (Managers)	.25
268	Lou Piniella (Managers)	.25
269	Larry Rothschild (Managers)	.25
270	Davey Lopes (Managers)	.25
271	Johnny Oates (Managers)	.25
272	Felipe Alou (Managers)	.25
273	Bobby Valentine (Managers)	.25
274	Tony LaRussa (Managers)	.25
275	Bruce Bochy (Managers)	.25
276	Dusty Baker (Managers)	.25
277	Adrian Gonzalez, Adam Johnson (Draft Picks and Prospects)	1.00
278	Matt Wheatland, Brian Digby (Draft Picks and Prospects)	.25
279	Tripper Johnson, Scott Thorman (Draft Picks and Prospects)	.75
280	Phil Dumatrait, Adam Wainwright (Draft Picks and Prospects)	1.00
281	Scott Heard, David Parrish RC (Draft Picks and Prospects)	.75
282	Rocco Baldelli, Mark Folsom RC (Draft Picks and Prospects)	1.00
283	Dominic Rich RC, Aaron Herr (Draft Picks and Prospects)	.75
284	Mike Stodolka, Sean Burnett (Draft Picks and Prospects)	.75
285	Derek Thompson, Corey Smith (Draft Picks and Prospects)	.75
286	Danny Borrell RC, Jason Bourgeois RC (Draft Picks and Prospects)	.75
287	Chin-Feng Chen, Corey Patterson, Josh Hamilton (Draft Picks and Prospects)	.75
288	Ryan Anderson, Barry Zito, C.C. Sabathia (Draft Picks and Prospects)	.75
289	Scott Sobkowiak, David Walling, Ben Sheets (Draft Picks and Prospects)	.75
290	Ty Howington, Josh Kalinowski, Josh Girdley (Draft Picks and Prospects)	.50
291	Hee Seop Choi RC, Aaron McNeal, Jason Hart (Draft Picks and Prospects)	.50
292	Bobby Bradley, Kurt Ainsworth, Chin-Hui Tsao (Draft Picks and Prospects)	.75
293	Mike Glendenning, Kenny Kelly, Juan Silvestri (Draft Picks and Prospects)	.50
294	J.R. House, Ramon Castro, Ben Davis (Draft Picks and Prospects)	.50
295	Chance Caple, Rafael Soriano RC, Pascual Coco (Draft Picks and Prospects)	1.00
296	Travis Hafner RC, Eric Munson, Bucky Jacobsen (Draft Picks and Prospects)	.50
297	Jason Conti, Chris Wakeland, Brian Cole (Draft Picks and Prospects)	.75
298	Scott Seabol, Aubrey Huff, Joe Crede (Draft Picks and Prospects)	.50
299	Adam Everett, Jose Ortiz, Keith Ginter (Draft Picks and Prospects)	.50
300	Carlos Hernandez, Geraldo Guzman, Adam Eaton (Draft Picks and Prospects)	.75
301	Bobby Kielty, Milton Bradley, Juan Rivera (Draft Picks and Prospects)	.50
302	Mark McGwire (Golden Moments)	2.00
303	Don Larsen (Golden Moments)	.75
304	Bobby Thomson (Golden Moments)	.25
305	Bill Mazeroski (Golden Moments)	.25
306	Reggie Jackson (Golden Moments)	1.00
307	Kirk Gibson (Golden Moments)	.25
308	Roger Maris (Golden Moments)	1.50
309	Cal Ripken Jr. (Golden Moments)	3.00
310	Hank Aaron (Golden Moments)	3.00
311	Joe Carter (Golden Moments)	.25
312	Cal Ripken Jr. (Season Highlights)	3.00
313	Randy Johnson (Season Highlights)	1.00
314	Ken Griffey Jr. (Season Highlights)	2.00
315	Troy Glaus (Season Highlights)	.25
316	Kazuhiro Sasaki (Season Highlights)	.25
317	Sammy Sosa, Troy Glaus (League Leaders)	1.00
318	Todd Helton, Edgar Martinez (League Leaders)	.50
319	Todd Helton, Nomar Garciaparra (League Leaders)	1.00
320	Barry Bonds, Jason Giambi (League Leaders)	1.50
321	Todd Helton, Manny Ramirez (League Leaders)	.50
322	Todd Helton, Darin Erstad (League Leaders)	.50
323	Kevin Brown, Pedro Martinez (League Leaders)	.50
324	Randy Johnson, Pedro Martinez (League Leaders)	.50
325	Will Clark (Post Season Highlights)	.40
326	New York Mets (Post Season Highlights)	.25
327	New York Yankees (Post Season Highlights)	1.00
328	Seattle Mariners (Post Season Highlights)	.25
329	Mike Hampton (Post Season Highlights)	.25
330	New York Yankees (Post Season Highlights)	1.00
331	World Series (Post Season Highlights)	1.50
332	Jeff Bagwell	1.00
333	Andy Pettitte	.75
334	Tony Armas Jr.	.25
335	Jeromy Burnitz	.25
336	Javier Vazquez	.25
337	Eric Karros	.25
338	Brian Giles	.25
339	Scott Rolen	1.00
340	David Justice	.25
341	Ray Durham	.25
342	Todd Zeile	.25
343	Cliff Floyd	.25
344	Barry Bonds	3.00
345	Matt Williams	.40
346	Steve Finley	.25
347	Scott Elarton	.25
348	Bernie Williams	.50
349	David Wells	.25
350	J.T. Snow	.25
351	Al Leiter	.25
352	Magglio Ordonez	.50
353	Raul Mondesi	.25
354	Tim Salmon	.40
355	Jeff Kent	.40
356	Mariano Rivera	.50
357	John Olerud	.25
358	Javy Lopez	.25
359	Ben Grieve	.25
360	Ray Lankford	.25
361	Ken Griffey Jr.	2.00
362	Rich Aurilia	.25
363	Andruw Jones	.50
364	Ryan Klesko	.50
365	Roberto Alomar	.50
366	Miguel Tejada	.50
367	Mo Vaughn	.25
368	Albert Belle	.50
369	Jose Canseco	.50
370	Kevin Brown	.25
371	Rafael Palmeiro	.50
372	Mark Redman	.25
373	Larry Walker	.50
374	Greg Maddux	2.00
375	Nomar Garciaparra	.75
376	Kevin Millwood	.25
377	Edgar Martinez	.25
378	Sammy Sosa	.75
379	Tim Hudson	.50
380	Jim Edmonds	.25
381	Mike Piazza	1.50
382	Brant Brown	.25
383	Brad Fullmer	.25
384	Alan Benes	.25
385	Mickey Morandini	.25
386	Troy Percival	.25
387	Eddie Perez	.25
388	Vernon Wells	.50
389	Ricky Gutierrez	.25
390	Rondell White	.25
391	Kevin Escobar	.25
392	Tony Batista	.25
393	Jimmy Haynes	.25
394	Billy Wagner	.25
395	A.J. Hinch	.25
396	Matt Morris	.25
397	Lance Berkman	.75
398	Jeff D'Amico	.25
399	Octavio Dotel	.25
400	Olmedo Saenz	.25
401	Esteban Loaiza	.25
402	Adam Kennedy	.25
403	Moises Alou	.25
404	Orlando Palmeiro	.25
405	Kevin Young	.25
406	Tom Goodwin	.25
407	Mac Suzuki	.25
408	Pat Hentgen	.25
409	Kevin Stocker	.25
410	Mark Sweeney	.25
411	Tony Eusebio	.25
412	Edgar Renteria	.25
413	John Rocker	.25
414	Jose Lima	.25
415	Kerry Wood	.50
416	Mike Timlin	.25
417	Jose Hernandez	.25
418	Jeremy Giambi	.25
419	Luis Lopez	.25
420	Mitch Meluskey	.25
421	Garrett Stephenson	.25
422	Jamey Wright	.25
423	John Jaha	.25
424	Placido Polanco	.25
425	Marty Cordova	.25
426	Joey Hamilton	.25
427	Travis Fryman	.25
428	Mike Cameron	.25
429	Matt Mantei	.25
430	Chan Ho Park	.25
431	Shawn Estes	.25
432	Danny Bautista	.25
433	Wilson Alvarez	.25
434	Kenny Lofton	.25
435	Russ Ortiz	.25
436	Dave Burba	.25
437	Felix Martinez	.25
438	Jeff Shaw	.25
439	Mike Difelice	.25
440	Roberto Hernandez	.25
441	Bryan Rekar	.25
442	Ugueth Urbina	.25
443	Vinny Castilla	.25
444	Carlos Perez	.25
445	Juan Guzman	.25
446	Ryan Rupe	.25
447	Mike Mordecai	.25
448	Ricardo Rincon	.25
449	Curt Schilling	.25
450	Alex Cora	.25
451	Turner Ward	.25
452	Omar Vizquel	.25
453	Russ Branyan	.25
454	Russ Johnson	.25
455	Gregg Colbrunn	.25
456	Charles Nagy	.25
457	Wil Cordero	.25
458	Jason Tyner	.25
459	Devon White	.25
460	Kelly Stinnett	.25
461	Wilton Guerrero	.25
462	Jason Bere	.25
463	Calvin Murray	.25
464	Miguel Batista	.25
465	Erubiel Durazo	.25
466	Luis Gonzalez	.25

467	Jaret Wright	.25	585	Frank Castillo	.25
468	Chad Kreuter	.25	586	Manny Ramirez	1.00
469	Armando Benitez	.25	587	Alex Rodriguez	3.00
470	Sidney Ponson	.25	588	Andy Ashby	.25
471	Adrian Brown	.25	589	Felipe Crespo	.25
472	Sterling Hitchcock	.25	590	Bobby Bonilla	.25
473	Timoniel Perez	.25	591	Denny Neagle	.25
474	Jamie Moyer	.25	592	Dave Martinez	.25
475	Delino DeShields	.25	593	Mike Hampton	.25
476	Glendon Rusch	.25	594	Gary DiSarcina	.25
477	Chris Gomez	.25	595	Tsuyoshi Shinjo RC	.75
478	Adam Eaton	.25	596	Albert Pujols RC	80.00
479	Pablo Ozuna	.25	597	Roy Oswalt, Pat Strange, Jon Rauch (Prospects)	.75
480	Bob Abreu	.50	598	Phil Wilson RC, Jake Peavy RC, Darwin Cubillan RC (Prospects)	8.00
481	Kris Benson	.25	599	Nathan Haynes, Steve Smyth RC, Mike Bynum (Prospects)	.75
482	Keith Osik	.25	600	Joe Lawrence, Choo Freeman, Michael Cuddyer (Prospects)	.50
483	Darryl Hamilton	.25	601	Larry Barnes, Dewayne Wise, Carlos Pena (Prospects)	.25
484	Marlon Anderson	.25	602	Felipe Lopez, Gookie Dawkins, Erick Almonte RC (Prospects)	1.00
485	Jimmy Anderson	.25	603	Brad Wilkerson, Alex Escobar, Eric Valent (Prospects)	.75
486	John Halama	.25	604	Jeff Goldbach RC, Toby Hall, Rod Barajas (Prospects)	.25
487	Nelson Figueroa	.25	605	Marcus Giles, Pablo Ozuna, Jason Romano (Prospects)	.25
488	Alex Gonzalez	.25	606	Vernon Wells, Jack Cust, Dee Brown (Prospects)	.25
489	Benny Agbayani	.25	607	Luis Montanez RC, David Espinosa (Draft Picks)	1.00
490	Ed Sprague	.25	608	John Lackey, Justin Wayne RC (Draft Picks)	1.00
491	Scott Erickson	.25	609	Josh Axelson RC, Carmen Cali RC (Draft Picks)	1.00
492	Doug Glanville	.25	610	Shaun Boyd RC, Chris Morris RC (Draft Picks)	1.00
493	Jesus Sanchez	.25	611	Dan Moylan RC, Tommy Arko RC (Draft Picks)	1.00
494	Mike Lieberthal	.25	612	Luis Cotto RC, Luis Escobar (Draft Picks)	1.00
495	Aaron Sele	.25	613	Blake Williams RC, Brandon Mims RC (Draft Picks)	1.00
496	Pat Mahomes	.25	614	Chris Russ RC, Bryan Edwards (Draft Picks)	1.00
497	Ruben Rivera	.25	615	Joe Torres, Ben Diggins (Draft Picks)	.25
498	Wayne Gomes	.25	616	Mark Dalesandro, Edwin Encarnacion RC (Draft Picks)	2.00
499	Freddy Garcia	.25	617	Brian Bass RC, Odannis Ayala RC (Draft Picks)	.50
500	Al Martin	.25	618	Jason Kaanoi RC, Michael Mathews RC (Draft Picks)	.50
501	Woody Williams	.25	619	Stuart McFarland RC, Adam Sterrett RC (Draft Picks)	1.00
502	Paul Byrd	.25	620	David Krynzel, Grady Sizemore (Draft Picks)	1.00
503	Rick White	.25	621	Keith Bucktrot, Dane Sardinha (Draft Picks)	.25
504	Trevor Hoffman	.25	622	Anaheim Angels	.25
505	Brady Anderson	.25	623	Arizona Diamondbacks	.25
506	Robert Person	.25	624	Atlanta Braves	.25
507	Jeff Conine	.25	625	Baltimore Orioles	.25
508	Chris Truby	.25	626	Boston Red Sox	.25
509	Emil Brown	.25	627	Chicago Cubs	.25
510	Ryan Dempster	.25	628	Chicago White Sox	.25
511	Ruben Mateo	.25	629	Cincinnati Reds	.25
512	Alex Ochoa	.25	630	Cleveland Indians	.25
513	Jose Rosado	.25	631	Colorado Rockies	.25
514	Masato Yoshii	.25	632	Detroit Tigers	.25
515	Brian Daubach	.25	633	Florida Marlins	.25
516	Jeff D'Amico	.25	634	Houston Astros	.25
517	Brent Mayne	.25	635	Kansas City Royals	.25
518	John Thomson	.25	636	Los Angeles Dodgers	.25
519	Todd Ritchie	.25	637	Milwaukee Brewers	.25
520	John Vander Wal	.25	638	Minnesota Twins	.25
521	Neifi Perez	.25	639	Montreal Expos	.25
522	Chad Curtis	.25	640	New York Mets	.25
523	Kenny Rogers	.25	641	New York Yankees	1.50
524	Trot Nixon	.25	642	Oakland Athletics	.25
525	Sean Casey	.25	643	Philadelphia Phillies	.25
526	Wilton Veras	.25	644	Pittsburgh Pirates	.25
527	Troy O'Leary	.25	645	San Diego Padres	.25
528	Dante Bichette	.25	646	San Francisco Giants	.25
529	Jose Silva	.25	647	Seattle Mariners	.25
530	Darren Oliver	.25	648	St. Louis Cardinals	.25
531	Steve Parris	.25	649	Tampa Bay Devil Rays	.25
532	David McCarty	.25	650	Texas Rangers	.25
533	Todd Walker	.25	651	Toronto Blue Jays	.25
534	Brian Rose	.25	652	Bucky Dent (Golden Moments)	.25
535	Pete Schourek	.25	653	Jackie Robinson (Golden Moments)	1.50
536	Ricky Ledee	.25	654	Roberto Clemente (Golden Moments)	1.50
537	Justin Thompson	.25	655	Nolan Ryan (Golden Moments)	2.50
538	Benito Santiago	.25	656	Kerry Wood (Golden Moments)	.50
539	Carlos Beltran	.75	657	Rickey Henderson (Golden Moments)	.75
540	Gabe White	.25	658	Lou Brock (Golden Moments)	.50
541	Bret Saberhagen	.25	659	David Wells (Golden Moments)	.25
542	Ramon Martinez	.25	660	Andruw Jones (Golden Moments)	.40
543	John Valentin	.25	661	Carlton Fisk (Golden Moments)	.25
544	Frank Catalanotto	.25			
545	Tim Wakefield	.25			
546	Michael Tucker	.25			
547	Juan Pierre	.25			
548	Rich Garces	.25			
549	Luis Ordaz	.25			
550	Jerry Spradlin	.25			
551	Corey Koskie	.25			
552	Cal Eldred	.25			
553	Alfonso Soriano	1.00			
554	Kip Wells	.25			
555	Orlando Hernandez	.25			
556	Bill Simas	.25			
557	Jim Parque	.25			
558	Joe Mays	.25			
559	Tim Belcher	.25			
560	Shane Spencer	.25			
561	Glenallen Hill	.25			
562	Matt LeCroy	.25			
563	Tino Martinez	.25			
564	Eric Milton	.25			
565	Ron Coomer	.25			
566	Cristian Guzman	.25			
567	Kazuhiro Sasaki	.25			
568	Mark Quinn	.25			
569	Eric Gagne	.25			
570	Kerry Ligtenberg	.25			
571	Rolando Arrojo	.25			
572	Jon Lieber	.25			
573	Jose Vizcaino	.25			
574	Jeff Abbott	.25			
575	Carlos Hernandez	.25			
576	Scott Sullivan	.25			
577	Matt Stairs	.25			
578	Tom Lampkin	.25			
579	Donnie Sadler	.25			
580	Desi Relaford	.25			
581	Scott Downs	.75			
582	Mike Mussina	.75			
583	Ramon Ortiz	.25			
584	Mike Myers	.25			

Retrofractors

Stars: 3-5X
Inserted 1:12

Before There Was Topps

Joe DiMaggio

NM/M
Complete Set (10): 40.00
Common Player: 3.00
Inserted 1:20
Refractors: 2-4X
Inserted 1:200
BT1 Lou Gehrig 8.00
BT2 Babe Ruth 10.00
BT3 Cy Young 5.00
BT4 Walter Johnson 3.00
BT5 Ty Cobb 3.00
BT6 Rogers Hornsby 3.00
BT7 Honus Wagner 4.00
BT8 Christy Mathewson 3.00
BT9 Grover Alexander 3.00
BT10 Joe DiMaggio 8.00

Combos

MOUND MARKSMEN — BOB GIBSON, PEDRO MARTINEZ

NM/M
Complete Set (20): 80.00
Common Card: 2.00
Inserted 1:12
Refractors: 2-4X
Inserted 1:120
1 Derek Jeter, Yogi Berra, Whitey Ford, Don Mattingly, Reggie Jackson 6.00
2 Chipper Jones, Mike Schmidt 6.00
3 Brooks Robinson, Cal Ripken Jr. 8.00
4 Bob Gibson, Pedro Martinez 3.00
5 Ivan Rodriguez, Johnny Bench 4.00
6 Ernie Banks, Alex Rodriguez 5.00
7 Joe Morgan, Ken Griffey Jr., Barry Larkin 5.00
8 Vladimir Guerrero, Roberto Clemente 6.00
9 Ken Griffey Jr., Hank Aaron 6.00
10 Casey Stengel, Joe Torre 2.00
TC11 Kevin Brown, Sandy Koufax, Don Drysdale 5.00
TC12 Mark McGwire, Sammy Sosa, Roger Marris, Babe Ruth 8.00
TC13 Ted Williams, Carl Yastrzemski, Nomar Garciaparra 8.00
TC14 Greg Maddux, Roger Clemens, Cy Young 5.00
TC15 Tony Gwynn, Ted Williams, Ernie Banks 6.00
TC16 Cal Ripken Jr., Lou Gehrig 10.00
TC17 Sandy Koufax, Randy Johnson, Warren Spahn, Steve Carlton 4.00
TC18 Mike Piazza, Josh Gibson 5.00
TC19 Barry Bonds, Willie Mays 8.00
TC20 Jackie Robinson, Larry Doby 5.00

Golden Anniversary

HANK AARON

NM/M
Complete Set (50): 120.00
Common Player: 1.00
Inserted 1:10
Refractors: 2-4X
Inserted 1:100
1 Hank Aaron 6.00
2 Ernie Banks 3.00
3 Mike Schmidt 5.00
4 Willie Mays 6.00
5 Johnny Bench 4.00
6 Tom Seaver 3.00
7 Frank Robinson 2.00
8 Sandy Koufax 5.00
9 Bob Gibson 3.00
10 Ted Williams 8.00
11 Cal Ripken Jr. 8.00
12 Tony Gwynn 3.00
13 Mark McGwire 6.00
14 Ken Griffey Jr. 4.00
15 Greg Maddux 4.00
16 Roger Clemens 6.00
17 Barry Bonds 8.00
18 Rickey Henderson 1.50
19 Mike Piazza 4.00
20 Jose Canseco 2.00
21 Derek Jeter 6.00
22 Nomar Garciaparra 5.00
23 Alex Rodriguez 5.00
24 Sammy Sosa 5.00
25 Ivan Rodriguez 2.00
26 Vladimir Guerrero 3.00
27 Chipper Jones 4.00
28 Jeff Bagwell 2.00
29 Pedro Martinez 3.00
30 Randy Johnson 3.00
31 Pat Burrell 1.50
32 Josh Hamilton 1.00
33 Ryan Anderson 1.00
34 Corey Patterson 1.50
35 Eric Munson 1.00
36 Sean Burroughs 1.00
37 C.C. Sabathia 1.00
38 Chin-Feng Chen 1.00
39 Barry Zito 1.50
40 Adrian Gonzalez 1.00
41 Mark McGwire 6.00
42 Nomar Garciaparra 5.00
43 Todd Helton 2.00
44 Matt Williams 1.00
45 Troy Glaus 1.50
46 Geoff Jenkins 1.00
47 Frank Thomas 2.00
48 Mo Vaughn 1.00
49 Barry Larkin 1.50
50 J.D. Drew 1.00

King of Kings

NM/M
Common Player: 25.00
Inserted 1:5,175 H
Inserted 1:5,209 R
KKR1 Hank Aaron 100.00
KKR2 Nolan Ryan 100.00
KKR3 Rickey Henderson 40.00
KKR5 Bob Gibson 25.00
KKR6 Nolan Ryan 100.00

King of Kings Golden Edition

Inserted 1:59,220 H

Past To Present

NM/M
Complete Set (10): 20.00
Common Player: 1.50
Inserted 1:18
Refractors: 1.5-3X
Inserted 1:180
1 Phil Rizzuto, Derek Jeter 6.00
2 Warren Spahn, Greg Maddux 4.00
3 Yogi Berra, Jorge Posada 3.00
4 Willie Mays, Barry Bonds 6.00
5 Red Schoendienst, Fernando Vina 1.50
6 Duke Snider, Shawn Green 2.00
7 Bob Feller, Bartolo Colon 1.50

PAST to PRESENT — BARRY BONDS, WILLIE MAYS

8 Johnny Mize, Tino Martinez 1.50
9 Larry Doby, Manny Ramirez 2.00
10 Eddie Mathews, Chipper Jones 3.00

Through The Years

WARREN SPAHN — PITCHER, MILWAUKEE BRAVES

NM/M
Complete Set (50): 200.00
Common Player: 2.00
Inserted 1:10
Refractors: 2-4X
Inserted 1:100
1 Yogi Berra 4.00
2 Roy Campanella 4.00
3 Willie Mays 8.00
4 Andy Pafko 2.00
5 Jackie Robinson 8.00
6 Stan Musial 8.00
7 Duke Snider 4.00
8 Warren Spahn 4.00
9 Ted Williams 10.00
10 Eddie Matthews 4.00
11 Willie McCovey 4.00
12 Frank Robinson 2.00
13 Ernie Banks 5.00
14 Hank Aaron 8.00
15 Sandy Koufax 6.00
16 Bob Gibson 4.00
17 Harmon Killebrew 3.00
18 Whitey Ford 4.00
19 Roberto Clemente 8.00
20 Juan Marichal 2.00
21 Johnny Bench 4.00
22 Willie Stargell 3.00
23 Joe Morgan 2.00
24 Carl Yastrzemski 5.00
25 Reggie Jackson 4.00
26 Tom Seaver 4.00
27 Steve Carlton 3.00
28 Jim Palmer 4.00
29 Rod Carew 3.00
30 George Brett 8.00
31 Roger Clemens 8.00
32 Don Mattingly 8.00
33 Ryne Sandberg 6.00
34 Mike Schmidt 8.00
35 Cal Ripken Jr. 10.00
36 Tony Gwynn 4.00
37 Ozzie Smith 5.00
38 Wade Boggs 3.00
39 Nolan Ryan 10.00
40 Robin Yount 4.00
41 Mark McGwire 8.00
42 Ken Griffey Jr. 5.00
43 Sammy Sosa 6.00
44 Alex Rodriguez 8.00
45 Barry Bonds 8.00
46 Mike Piazza 5.00
47 Chipper Jones 5.00
48 Greg Maddux 5.00
49 Nomar Garciaparra 6.00
50 Derek Jeter 8.00

Topps Originals

NM/M
Common Player: 15.00
Inserted 1:1,783 H
Inserted 1:1,788 R
Refractors 10 sets produced.
1 Roberto Clemente 180.00
2 Carl Yastrzemski 60.00
3 Mike Schmidt 75.00
4 Wade Boggs 20.00
5 Chipper Jones 40.00
6 Lou Brock 20.00
7 Dave Parker 15.00

ALEX RODRIGUEZ

9 Barry Bonds 80.00
10 Alex Rodriguez 50.00

What Could've Been

LEROY "SATCHEL" PAIGE

NM/M
Complete Set (10): 25.00
Common Player: 2.00
Inserted 1:30
Refractors: 2-4X
Inserted 1:300
WCB1 Josh Gibson 6.00
WCB2 Satchel Paige 6.00
WCB3 Buck Leonard 4.00
WCB4 James "Cool Pap Bell 4.00
WCB5 Andrew "Rube" Foster 3.00
WCB6 Martin Dihigo 2.00
WCB7 William "Judy" Johnson 3.00
WCB8 Mule Suttles 2.00
WCB9 Ray Dandridge 2.00
WCB10 John Henry Lloyd 2.00

2001 Topps & Topps Chrome Traded & Rookies

Bud SMITH — Cardinals 51

NM/M
Complete Topps Set (265): 140.00
Common Player: .10
Chrome Cards: 2-3X
Pack (8 + 2 Chrome): 8.00
Box (24): 175.00
T1 Sandy Alomar Jr. .10
T2 Kevin Appier .10
T3 Brad Ausmus .10
T4 Derek Bell .10
T5 Bret Boone .15
T6 Rico Brogna .10
T7 Ellis Burks .10
T8 Ken Caminiti .10
T9 Roger Cedeno .10
T10 Royce Clayton .10
T11 Enrique Wilson .10
T12 Rheal Cormier .10
T13 Eric Davis .10
T14 Shawon Dunston .10
T15 Andres Galarraga .10
T16 Tom Gordon .10
T17 Mark Grace .50
T18 Jeffrey Hammonds .10
T19 Dustin Hermanson .10
T20 Quinton McCracken .10
T21 Todd Hundley .10
T22 Charles Johnson .10
T23 Marquis Grissom .10
T24 Jose Mesa .10
T25 Terry Mulholland .10
T26 John Rocker .10
T27 Jeff Frye .10
T28 Reggie Sanders .10
T29 David Segui .10

T30	Mike Sirotka	.10
T31	Fernando Tatis	.10
T32	Steve Trachsel	.10
T33	Ismael Valdes	.10
T34	Randy Velarde	.10
T35	Brian Boehringer	.10
T36	Mike Bordick	.10
T37	Ken Bottenfield	.10
T38	Pat Rapp	.10
T39	Jeff Nelson	.10
T40	Ricky Bottalico	.10
T41	Deion Sanders	.25
T42	Hideo Nomo	.25
T43	Bill Mueller	.10
T44	Roberto Kelly	.10
T45	Chris Holt	.10
T46	Mike Jackson	.10
T47	Devon White	.10
T48	Gerald Williams	.10
T49	Eddie Taubensee	.10
T50	Brian Hunter	.10
T51	Nelson Cruz	.10
T52	Jeff Fassero	.10
T53	Bubba Trammell	.10
T54	Bo Porter	.10
T55	Greg Norton	.10
T56	Benito Santiago	.10
T57	Ruben Rivera	.10
T58	Dee Brown	.10
T59	Jose Canseco	.50
T60	Chris Michalak	.10
T61	Tim Worrell	.10
T62	Matt Clement	.10
T63	Bill Pulsipher	.10
T64	Troy Brohawn	.10
T65	Mark Kotsay	.10
T66	Jose Lima	.10
T67	Shea Hillenbrand	.25
T68	Ted Lilly	.10
T69	Jermaine Dye	.10
T70	Jerry Hairston Jr.	.10
T71	John Mabry	.10
T72	Kurt Abbott	.10
T73	Eric Owens	.10
T74	Jeff Brantley	.10
T75	Vinny Castilla	.10
T76	Ron Villone	.10
T77	Ricky Henderson	.40
T78	Jason Grimsley	.10
T79	Christian Parker RC	.10
T80	Donnie Wall	.10
T81	Alex Arias	.10
T82	Willis Roberts	.10
T83	Ryan Minor	.10
T84	Jason LaRue	.10
T85	Ruben Sierra	.10
T86	Johnny Damon	.75
T87	Juan Gonzalez	.40
T88	Mac Suzuki	.10
T89	Tony Batista	.10
T90	Jay Witasick	.10
T91	Brent Abernathy	.10
T92	Paul LoDuca	.10
T93	Wes Helms	.10
T94	Milton Bradley	.10
T95	Matt LeCroy	.10
T96	A.J. Hinch	.10
T97	Bud Smith RC	.10
T98	Adam Dunn	.50
T99	Albert Pujols, Ichiro Suzuki	15.00
T100	Carlton Fisk	.25
T101	Tim Raines	.25
T102	Juan Marichal	.25
T103	Dave Winfield	.50
T104	Reggie Jackson	1.00
T105	Cal Ripken Jr.	3.00
T106	Ozzie Smith	1.00
T107	Tom Seaver	1.00
T108	Lou Piniella	.25
T109	Dwight Gooden	.25
T110	Bret Saberhagen	.25
T111	Gary Carter	.25
T112	Jack Clark	.25
T113	Rickey Henderson	.75
T114	Barry Bonds	3.00
T115	Bobby Bonilla	.25
T116	Jose Canseco	.50
T117	Will Clark	.50
T118	Andres Galarraga	.25
T119	Bo Jackson	.50
T120	Wally Joyner	.25
T121	Ellis Burks	.25
T122	David Cone	.25
T123	Greg Maddux	1.00
T124	Willie Randolph	.25
T125	Dennis Eckersley	.25
T126	Matt Williams	.40
T127	Joe Morgan	.50
T128	Fred McGriff	.40
T129	Roberto Alomar	.50
T130	Lee Smith	.25
T131	David Wells	.25
T132	Ken Griffey Jr.	2.00
T133	Deion Sanders	.50
T134	Nolan Ryan	2.00
T135	David Justice	.25
T136	Joe Carter	.25
T137	Jack Morris	.25
T138	Mike Piazza	1.50
T139	Barry Bonds	2.00
T140	Terrence Long	.10
T141	Ben Grieve	.10
T142	Richie Sexson	.25
T143	Sean Burroughs	.10
T144	Alfonso Soriano	.50
T145	Bob Boone	.10
T146	Larry Bowa	.10

T147	Bob Brenly	.10
T148	Buck Martinez	.10
T149	Lloyd McClendon	.10
T150	Jim Tracy	.10
T151	Jared Abruzzo RC	.50
T152	Kurt Ainsworth	.10
T153	Willie Bloomquist	.10
T154	Ben Broussard	.10
T155	Bobby Bradley	.10
T156	Mike Bynum	.10
T157	Ken Harvey	.10
T158	Ryan Christianson	.10
T159	Ryan Kohlmeier	.10
T160	Joe Crede	.50
T161	Jack Cust	.10
T162	Ben Diggins	.10
T163	Phil Dumatrait	.10
T164	Alex Escobar	.10
T165	Miguel Olivo	.10
T166	Chris George	.10
T167	Marcus Giles	.10
T168	Keith Ginter	.10
T169	Josh Girdley	.10
T170	Tony Alvarez	.10
T171	Scott Seabol	.10
T172	Josh Hamilton	.50
T173	Jason Hart	.10
T174	Israel Alcantara	.10
T175	Jake Peavy	2.50
T176	Stubby Clapp RC	.40
T177	D'Angelo Jimenez	.10
T178	Nick Johnson	.10
T179	Ben Johnson	.10
T180	Larry Bigbie	.10
T181	Allen Levrault	.10
T182	Felipe Lopez	.10
T183	Sean Burnett	.10
T184	Nick Neugebauer	.10
T185	Austin Kearns	.25
T186	Corey Patterson	.25
T187	Carlos Pena	.10
T188	Ricardo Rodriguez RC	.50
T189	Juan Rivera	.10
T190	Grant Roberts	.10
T191	Adam Pettyjohn RC	.25
T192	Jared Sandberg	.10
T193	Xavier Nady	.10
T194	Dane Sardinha	.10
T195	Shawn Sonnier	.10
T196	Rafael Soriano	.25
T197	Brian Specht RC	.25
T198	Aaron Myette	.10
T199	Juan Uribe RC	.40
T200	Jayson Werth	.10
T201	Brad Wilkerson	.10
T202	Horacio Estrada	.10
T203	Joel Pineiro	.10
T204	Matt LeCroy	.10
T205	Michael Coleman	.10
T206	Ben Sheets	.40
T207	Eric Byrnes	.10
T208	Sean Burroughs	.10
T209	Ken Harvey	.10
T210	Travis Hafner	1.50
T211	Erick Almonte	.10
T212	Jason Belcher RC	.50
T213	Wilson Betemit RC	.75
T214	Hank Blalock RC	1.50
T215	Danny Borrell	.10
T216	John Buck RC	.50
T217	Freddie Bynum RC	.50
T218	Noel Devarez RC	.25
T219	Juan Diaz RC	.25
T220	Felix Diaz RC	.25
T221	Josh Fogg RC	.50
T222	Matt Ford RC	.25
T223	Scott Heard	.10
T224	Ben Hendrickson RC	.25
T225	Cody Ross RC	.50
T226	Adrian Hernandez RC	.40
T227	Alfredo Amezaga RC	.50
T228	Bob Keppel RC	.25
T229	Ryan Madson RC	.75
T230	Octavio Martinez RC	.25
T231	Hee Seop Choi	.40
T232	Thomas Mitchell	.10
T233	Luis Montanez	.10
T234	Andy Morales RC	.40
T235	Justin Morneau RC	10.00
T236	Greg "Toe" Nash RC	.25
T237	Valentino Pasucci RC	.25
T238	Roy Smith RC	.40
T239	Antonio Perez RC	.40
T240	Chad Petty RC	.50
T241	Steve Smyth	.10
T242	Jose Reyes RC	10.00
T243	Eric Reynolds RC	.40
T244	Dominic Rich	.10
T245	Jason Richardson RC	.25
T246	Ed Rogers RC	.40
T247	Albert Pujols RC	50.00
T248	Esix Snead RC	.25
T249	Luis Torres RC	.25
T250	Matt White RC	.40
T251	Blake Williams	.10
T252	Chris Russ	.10
T253	Joe Kennedy RC	.25
T254	Jeff Randazzo RC	.25
T255	Beau Hale RC	.25
256	Brad Hennessey RC	.25
257	Jake Gautreau RC	.25
258	Jeff Mathis RC	.50
259	Aaron Heilman RC	.50
260	Bronson Sardinha RC	.50
261	Irvin Guzman RC	3.00
262	Gabe Gross RC	.50
263	J.D. Martin RC	.40
264	Chris Smith RC	.25
265	Kenny Baugh RC	.40

Autographs

GOLDEN ANNIVERSARY TRADED STAR

NM/M

Common Autograph:		15.00
JD	Johnny Damon	30.00
MM	Mike Mussina	25.00

Legends Autographs

NM/M

Common Player:		
TT51	Ralph Branca	15.00
TTF47	Frank Howard	25.00
TTF50	Mickey Lolich	15.00
TT37	Tug McGraw	15.00
TT48F	Bobby Richardson	20.00
TT36F	Enos Slaughter	25.00
TT13	Warren Spahn	40.00
TT43	Bobby Thomson	20.00

Relics

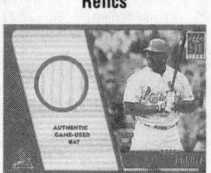

NM/M

Common Player:		4.00
Inserted 1:29		
SA	Sandy Alomar Jr.	4.00
DB	Derek Bell	4.00
BB	Bobby Bonilla	4.00
BB	Bret Boone	4.00
RB	Rico Brogna	4.00
KC	Ken Caminiti	4.00
JC	Jose Canseco	8.00
ROC	Roger Cedeno	4.00
RSC	Royce Clayton	4.00
JD	Johnny Damon	10.00
ED	Eric Davis	4.00
JD	Jermaine Dye	4.00
AG	Andres Galarraga	4.00
RG	Ron Gant	4.00
JG	Juan Gonzalez	6.00
MG	Mark Grace	8.00
MG	Marquis Grissom	4.00
JH	Jeffrey Hammonds	4.00
MH	Mike Hampton	4.00
DH	Dustin Hermanson	4.00
TH	Todd Hundley	4.00
CJ	Charles Johnson	4.00
FM	Fred McGriff	5.00
BM	Bill Mueller	4.00
DN	Denny Neagle	4.00
HR	Hideo Nomo	25.00
NP	Neifi Perez	4.00
TR	Tim Raines	4.00
RS	Ruben Sierra	4.00
MS	Matt Stairs	4.00
KS	Kelly Stinnett	4.00
FT	Fernando Tatis	4.00
DW	David Wells	4.00
GW	Gerald Williams	4.00
EW	Enrique Wilson	4.00

Dual-Traded Relics

NM/M

Common Player:		4.00
DB	Derek Bell	4.00
MG	Mark Grace	10.00

BG	Ben Grieve	4.00
DH	Dustin Hermanson	4.00
MR	Manny Ramirez	15.00

Farewell Dual Relic

NM/M

Inserted 1:4,693		
RG	Cal Ripken, Tony Gwynn	80.00

Hall of Fame Relics

NM/M

Complete Set (1):		
PW	Kirby Puckett, Dave Winfield	40.00

Rookie Relics

NM/M

Common Player:		4.00
Inserted 1:91		
AP	Albert Pujols	150.00
TS	Tsuyoshi Shinjo	4.00
AB	Angel Berroa	6.00
BO	Bill Ortega	4.00
HC	Humberto Cota	4.00
JL	Jason Lane	4.00
JS	Jamal Strong	4.00
JV	Jose Valverde	4.00
JY	Jason Young	4.00
NC	Nate Cornejo	4.00
NN	Nick Neugebauer	4.00
PF	Pedro Feliz	4.00
RS	Richard Stahl	4.00
SB	Sean Burroughs	4.00
SS	Jae Weong Seo	4.00
WB	Wilson Betemit	8.00
WR	Wilken Ruan	4.00

Who Would Have Thought

NM/M

Complete Set (20):		15.00
Common Player:		.75
Inserted 1:8		
WWH1	Nolan Ryan	3.00
WWH2	Ozzie Smith	1.50
WWH3	Tom Seaver	1.50
WWH4	Steve Carlton	.75
WWH5	Reggie Jackson	1.50
WWH6	Frank Robinson	1.00
WWH7	Keith Hernandez	.75
WWH8	Andre Dawson	.75
WWH9	Lou Brock	.75
WWH10	Dennis Eckersley	.75
WWH11	Dave Winfield	1.00
WWH12	Rod Carew	1.00
WWH13	Willie Randolph	.75
WWH14	Doc Gooden	.75
WWH15	Carlton Fisk	1.00
WWH16	Dale Murphy	.75
WWH17	Paul Molitor	1.00
WWH18	Gary Carter	.75
WWH19	Wade Boggs	1.00
WWH20	Willie Mays	3.00

2001 Topps eTopps

Operating along the lines of a stock exchange, with collectors able to buy and sell the cards without ever taking physical possession, eTopps was launched in October and had about 10 "Initial Player Offerings" (new cards) issued per week to a total of 75. Issue price and quantity available were announced at the time of release. If a card was

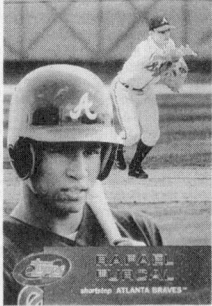

not sold out during its five-day order period, the unsold cards were destroyed. Fronts have portrait and action photos, player identification and an eTopps logo, printed on refractive metalic foil. Backs, labeled, "Inaugural Edition," have a portrait photo, personal data and stats, along with 2000 highlights and a projection for the 2001 season. A circular holographic seal at top-right has a serial number. Each card is issued in a thick plastic holder that is sealed with an eTopps holographic sticker. Cards are skip-numbered between 1-150, as it was originally intended that 150 cards would be issued the first year. Shown in parentheses for each player are the initial offering price and the quantity reported issued by Topps. Values shown are for cards in a virtual portfolio, rather than "in hand." Taking physical possession of a card from an eTopps portfolio requires payment of a delivery fee of $7.

	NM/M	
Complete Set (75):		1,350
Common Player:		1.50
1	Nomar Garciaparra ($9.50 / 1,315)	10.00
2	Chipper Jones ($9.50 / 674)	90.00
3	Jeff Bagwell ($6.50 / 485)	35.00
4	Randy Johnson ($6.50 / 1,499)	20.00
7	Adam Dunn ($6.50 / 4,197)	5.00
8	J.D. Drew ($6.50 / 767)	10.00
9	Larry Walker ($6.50 / 420)	25.00
10	Edgardo Alfonzo ($6.50 / 338)	65.00
11	Lance Berkman ($6.50 / 595)	35.00
12	Tony Gwynn ($6.50 / 828)	30.00
13	Andruw Jones ($6.50 / 908)	22.50
15	Troy Glaus ($6.50 / 862)	10.00
17	Sammy Sosa ($9.50 / 2,487)	5.00
21	Darin Erstad ($3.50 / 664)	10.00
22	Barry Bonds ($9.50 / 1,567)	95.00
27	Derek Jeter ($9.50 / 1,041)	50.00
29	Curt Schilling ($6.50 / 2,125)	5.00
30	Roberto Alomar ($6.50 / 448)	20.00
31	Luis Gonzalez ($6.50 / 1,104)	3.00
32	Jimmy Rollins ($3.50 / 1,307)	5.00
34	Joe Crede ($3.50 / 1,050)	10.00
39	Sean Casey ($6.50 / 537)	30.00
46	Alex Rodriguez ($9.50 / 2,212)	35.00
47	Tom Glavine ($6.50 / 437)	35.00
	Jose Ortiz ($3.50 / 738)	5.00
51	Cal Ripken Jr. ($6.50 / 2,201)	30.00
52	Bobby Abreu ($3.50 / 677)	27.50
55	Alex Escobar ($3.50 / 931)	4.00
56	Ivan Rodriguez ($6.50 / 698)	15.00
59	Jeff Kent ($6.50 / 452)	20.00
62	Rick Ankiel ($6.50 / 752)	6.00
65	Craig Biggio ($6.50 / 410)	40.00
66	Carlos Delgado ($6.50 / 398)	40.00

68	Greg Maddux ($6.50 / 1,031)	15.00
69	Kerry Wood ($3.50 / 1,056)	9.00
71	Todd Helton ($6.50 / 978)	20.00
72	Mariano Rivera ($6.50 / 824)	20.00
73	Jason Kendall ($3.50 / 672)	10.00
75	Scott Rolen ($6.50 / 498)	40.00
76	Kazuhiro Sasaki ($6.50 / 5,000)	2.00
77	Roy Oswalt ($6.50 / 915)	20.00
78	C.C. Sabathia ($6.50 / 1,974)	3.00
83	Brian Giles ($6.50 / 400)	25.00
87	Rafael Furcal ($3.50 / 646)	9.00
88	Mike Mussina ($6.50 / 793)	12.50
89	Gary Sheffield ($6.50 / 359)	50.00
92	Mark McGwire ($9.50 / 2,908)	10.00
94	Tsuyoshi Shinjo ($3.50 / 3,000)	1.50
99	Jose Vidro ($3.50 / 443)	25.00
100	Ichiro Suzuki ($6.50 / 10,000)	12.50
105	Manny Ramirez ($6.50 / 1,074)	15.00
109	Juan Gonzalez ($6.50 / 558)	9.00
112	Ken Griffey Jr. ($9.50 / 2,398)	12.00
114	Tim Hudson ($6.50 / 663)	17.50
115	Nick Johnson ($6.50 / 1,217)	5.00
118	Jason Giambi ($9.50 / 897)	10.00
122	Rafael Palmeiro ($6.50 / 464)	20.00
124	Vladimir Guerrero ($6.50 / 854)	30.00
125	Vernon Wells ($6.50 / 349)	80.00
127	Roger Clemens ($9.50 / 1,462)	30.00
128	Frank Thomas ($6.50 / 834)	15.00
129	Carlos Beltran ($3.50 / 489)	50.00
130	Pat Burrell ($6.50 / 1,253)	15.00
131	Pedro Martinez ($9.50 / 1,038)	15.00
132	Mike Piazza ($9.50 / 1,379)	10.00
135	Luis Montanez ($3.50 / 5,000)	1.50
140	Sean Burroughs ($3.50 / 5,000)	1.50
141	Barry Zito ($6.50 / 843)	22.50
142	Bobby Bradley ($3.50 / 5,000)	1.50
143	Albert Pujols ($6.50 / 5,000)	45.00
143a	Albert Pujols (32 autographed pieces sold by Topps 6/05 at $199 each.)	1,500
144	Ben Sheets ($3.50 / 1,713)	5.00
145	Alfonso Soriano ($3.50 / 1,699)	15.00
146	Josh Hamilton ($6.50 / 5,000)	5.00
147	Eric Munson ($3.50 / 5,000)	1.50
150	Mark Mulder ($3.50 / 4,335)	2.00

2001 Topps Fusion

	NM/M	
Complete Set (250):		100.00
Common Player:		.25
Pack (5):		2.50
Box (24):		50.00
1-3	Albert Belle	.25
4	Nick Bierbrodt	.25
5-8	Alex Rodriguez	2.50
9	Eric Munson	.25
10	Barry Bonds	3.00

11	Andruw Jones		.75
12	Antonio Alfonseca		.25
13	Andres Galarraga		.40
14	Joe Crede		.25
15	Barry Larkin		.40
16-17	Barry Bonds		3.00
18	Andruw Jones		.75
19	C.C. Sabathia		.25
20	Bobby Higginson		.25
21	Barry Larkin		.40
22	Ben Grieve		.25
23	Barry Bonds		3.00
24	Corey Patterson		.25
25	Carlos Delgado		.75
26	Bernie Williams		.50
27	Brian Giles		.40
28	Barry Larkin		.40
29	Gookie Dawkins		.25
30	Chipper Jones		1.50
31	Brian Giles		.40
32	Carlos Delgado		.75
33	Ben Grieve		.25
34	Geoff Goetz		.25
35	Cristian Guzman		.25
36	Cal Ripken Jr.		3.00
37	Chipper Jones		1.50
38	Bernie Williams		.50
39	Pablo Ozuna		.25
40	Dante Bichette		.25
41	Carlos Delgado		.75
42	Craig Biggio		.25
43	Cal Ripken Jr.		3.00
44	Tim Redding		.25
45	Darin Erstad		.50
46	Chipper Jones		1.50
47	Darin Erstad		.50
48	Carlos Delgado		.75
49	Josh Hamilton		.50
50	Derek Jeter		3.00
51	Darin Erstad		.50
52	Dean Palmer		.25
53	Chipper Jones		1.50
54	Chin-Feng Chen		.25
55	Edgar Martinez		.25
56	Derek Jeter		3.00
57	Derek Jeter		3.00
58	Craig Biggio		.25
59	Keith Ginter		.25
60	Edgardo Alfonzo		.25
61	Edgar Martinez		.25
62	Edgardo Alfonzo		.25
63	David Justice		.50
64	Roy Oswalt		.25
65	Eric Karros		.25
66	Edgardo Alfonzo		.25
67	Frank Thomas		1.00
68	Dean Palmer		.25
69	Alfonso Soriano		1.00
70	Fernando Vina		.25
71	Frank Thomas		1.00
72	Garret Anderson		.40
73	Derek Jeter		3.00
74	Bobby Bradley		.25
75	Frank Thomas		1.00
76	Gary Sheffield		.25
77	Geoff Jenkins		.25
78	Edgar Martinez		.25
79	Nick Johnson		.25
80	Fred McGriff		.40
81	Geoff Jenkins		.25
82	Greg Maddux		1.50
83	Edgardo Alfonzo		.25
84	Hee Seop Choi **RC**		2.00
85	Garret Anderson		.25
86	Greg Maddux		1.50
87	Ivan Rodriguez		.75
88	Eric Karros		.25
89	Scott Seabol		.25
90-91	Ivan Rodriguez		.75
92	J.D. Drew		.25
93	Frank Thomas		1.00
94	Ryan Anderson		.25
95-96	Jason Giambi		.75
97	Jason Kendall		.25
98	Gary Sheffield		.50
99	Milton Bradley		.25
100-101	Jason Kendall		.25
102	Jeff Bagwell		.75
103	Greg Maddux		1.50
104	Sean Burroughs		.25
105	Jay Bell		.25
106	Jeff Bagwell		.75
107	Jeffrey Hammonds		.25
108	Ivan Rodriguez		.75
109	Ben Petrick		.25
110	Jeff Bagwell		.75
111	Jeff Cirillo		.25
112	Jermaine Dye		.25
113	J.T. Snow Jr.		.25
114	Ben Davis		.25
115	Jeff Cirillo		.25
116	Jeff Kent		.25
117	Jeromy Burnitz		.25
118	Jay Bell		.25
119	Jason Hart		.25
120	Jeff Kent		.25
121	Jermaine Dye		.25
122	John Olerud		.25
123	Jeff Bagwell		.75
124	Jeff Segar **RC**		.50
125-126	Jeromy Burnitz		.25
127	Johnny Damon		.25
128	Jim Edmonds		.40
129	Tim Christman **RC**		.50
130	Jim Thome		.75
131	Jim Edmonds		.25
132	Jorge Posada		.50
133	Jim Thome		.75

134	Danny Borrell **RC**		.50
135	Johnny Damon		.25
136	Jim Thome		.75
137	Jose Vidro		.25
138	Ken Griffey Jr.		1.50
139	Sean Burnett		.25
140	Larry Walker		.40
141	Jose Vidro		.25
142	Ken Griffey Jr.		1.50
143	Larry Walker		.40
144	Robert Keppell **RC**		1.00
145	Luis Castillo		.25
146	Ken Griffey Jr.		1.50
147	Kevin Brown		.40
148	Manny Ramirez		.75
149	David Parrish **RC**		.50
150	Manny Ramirez		.75
151	Kevin Brown		.40
152	Luis Castillo		.25
153	Mark Grace		.40
154	Mike Jacobs **RC**		.50
155	Mark Grace		.50
156	Larry Walker		.40
157	Magglio Ordonez		.40
158	Mark McGwire		2.00
159	Adam Johnson		.25
160	Mark McGwire		2.00
161	Magglio Ordonez		.50
162	Mark McGwire		2.00
163	Matt Williams		.40
164	Oscar Ramirez **RC**		.50
165	Mike Piazza		1.50
166	Manny Ramirez		1.50
167	Mike Piazza		1.50
168	Mike Mussina		.50
169	Odannis Ayala **RC**		.25
170	Mike Sweeney		.25
171	Mark McGwire		.25
172	Nomar Garciaparra		2.50
173	Mike Piazza		1.50
174	J.R. House		.25
175	Neifi Perez		.25
176	Mike Piazza		1.50
177	Pedro Martinez		1.00
178	Mo Vaughn		.25
179	Shawn Fagan **RC**		.50
180	Nomar Garciaparra		2.50
181	Mo Vaughn		.25
182	Rafael Palmeiro		.25
183	Nomar Garciaparra		2.50
184	Chris Bass **RC**		.75
185	Raul Mondesi		.25
186	Nomar Garciaparra		2.50
187	Randy Johnson		1.00
188	Omar Vizquel		.25
189	Erick Almonte **RC**		1.00
190	Ray Durham		.25
191	Pedro Martinez		1.00
192	Robb Nen		.25
193	Pedro Martinez		1.00
194	Luis Montanez **RC**		1.00
195	Ray Lankford		.25
196	Rafael Palmeiro		.50
197	Roberto Alomar		.75
198	Rafael Palmeiro		.50
199	Chad Petty **RC**		.25
200	Richard Hidalgo		.25
201	Randy Johnson		1.00
202	Robin Ventura		.25
203	Randy Johnson		1.00
204	Derek Thompson		.25
205	Sammy Sosa		2.00
206	Roberto Alomar		.75
207	Sammy Sosa		2.00
208	Raul Mondesi		.25
209	Scott Heard		.25
210	Scott Rolen		.25
211	Sammy Sosa		2.00
212	Scott Rolen		.75
213	Roberto Alomar		.75
214	Dominic Rich **RC**		.50
215	Sean Casey		.25
216	Scott Rolen		.75
217	Sean Casey		.25
218	Robin Ventura		.25
219	William Smith **RC**		.50
220	Tim Salmon		.40
221	Sean Casey		.25
222	Shannon Stewart		.25
223	Sammy Sosa		2.00
224	Joel Pieniero **RC**		.50
225	Tino Martinez		.25
226	Shawn Green		.40
227	Shawn Green		.40
228	Scott Rolen		.50
229	Greg Morrison **RC**		.50
230	Tony Gwynn		1.00
231	Todd Helton		.75
232	Steve Finley		.25
233	Scott Williamson		.25
234	Talmadge Nunnari		.25
235	Tony Womack		.25
236	Tony Batista		.25
237	Tim Salmon		.40
238	Shawn Green		.40
239	Carlos Villalobos **RC**		.50
240-241	Troy Glaus		.50
242	Todd Helton		.75
243	Tim Salmon		.40
244	Marco Scutaro **RC**		.75
245	Troy O'Leary		.25
246-248	Vladimir Guerrero		1.00
249	Horacio Estrada		.25
250	Vladimir Guerrero		1.00

Autographs

	NM/M
Common Player:	5.00
Inserted 1:23	

1	Rafael Furcal	15.00
2	Mike Lamb	5.00
3	Jason Marquis	5.00
4	Milton Bradley	8.00
5	Barry Zito	15.00
6	Derek Lee	20.00
7	Corey Patterson	10.00
8	Josh Hamilton	30.00
9	Sean Burroughs	5.00
10	Jason Hart	5.00
11	Luis Montanez	5.00
12	Robert Keppell	5.00
13	Blake Williams	5.00
14	Phil Wilson	5.00
15	Jake Peavy	250.00
16	Alex Rodriguez	100.00
17	Ivan Rodriguez	20.00
18	Don Larsen	20.00
19	Todd Helton	20.00
20	Carlos Delgado	15.00
21	Geoff Jenkins	10.00
22	Willie Stargell	60.00
23	Frank Robinson	30.00
24	Warren Spahn	40.00
25	Harmon Killebrew	30.00
26-30	Chipper Jones	40.00
31	Rocco Baldelli	10.00
32	Keith Ginter	5.00
33	J.R. House	5.00
34	Alex Cabrera	10.00
35	Tony Alvarez	5.00
36	Pablo Ozuna	5.00
37	Juan Salas	5.00

Feature

	NM/M
Common Player:	4.00
Inserted 1:51	

1	Ivan Rodriguez	8.00
2	Rickey Henderson	15.00
3	John Smoltz	5.00
4	Tom Glavine	5.00
5	Willie Stargell	10.00
6	Frank Thomas	8.00
7	Carlos Delgado	8.00
8	Todd Helton	8.00
9	Adrian Gonzalez	8.00
10	Pat Burrell	8.00
11	Jose Vidro	4.00
12	Roberto Alomar	8.00
13	Chipper Jones	15.00
14	Robin Ventura	8.00
15	J.D. Drew	5.00
16	Matt Lawton	4.00
17	Josh Hamilton	10.00
18	Chin-Feng Chen	25.00
19	Rafael Furcal	8.00
20	Miguel Tejada	8.00
21	Josh Beckett	10.00
22	Ryan Anderson	4.00

Double Feature

	NM/M
Common Duo:	10.00

1	Ivan Rodriguez, Rickey Henderson	40.00
2	John Smoltz, Tom Glavine	15.00
3	Willie Stargell, Frank Thomas	20.00
4	Carlos Delgado, Todd Helton	15.00
5	Adrian Gonzalez, Pat Burrell	15.00
6	Jose Vidro, Roberto Alomar	15.00
7	Chipper Jones, Robin Ventura	20.00
8	J.D. Drew, Matt Lawton	10.00
9	Josh Hamilton, Chin-Feng Chen	25.00
10	Rafael Furcal, Miguel Tejada	15.00
11	Josh Beckett, Ryan Anderson	15.00

2001 Topps Gallery

	NM/M
Complete Set (152):	100.00
Common Player:	.15
Common Rookie:	1.50
Inserted 1:3.5	
Common Prospect:	.50
Inserted 1:2.5	
Common Retired:	1.00
Inserted 1:5	
Pack (6):	5.00
Box (24):	100.00

ICHIRO SUZUKI
SeattleMariners

Set price includes one Suzuki rookie.

1	Darin Erstad	.40
2	Chipper Jones	1.50
3	Nomar Garciaparra	.75
4	Fernando Vina	.15
5	Bartolo Colon	.25
6	Bobby Higginson	.15
7	Antonio Alfonseca	.15
8	Mike Sweeney	.15
9	Kevin Brown	.25
10	Jose Vidro	.15
11	Derek Jeter	3.00
12	Jason Giambi	.50
13	Pat Burrell	.50
14	Jeff Kent	.25
15	Alex Rodriguez	2.50
16	Rafael Palmeiro	.50
17	Garret Anderson	.40
18	Brad Fullmer	.15
19	Doug Glanville	.15
20	Mark Quinn	.15
21	Mo Vaughn	.25
22	Andruw Jones	.50
23	Pedro Martinez	1.00
24	Ken Griffey Jr.	1.50
25	Roberto Alomar	.50
26	Dean Palmer	.15
27	Jeff Bagwell	.50
28	Jermaine Dye	.15
29	Chan Ho Park	.15
30	Vladimir Guerrero	1.00
31	Bernie Williams	.50
32	Ben Grieve	.15
33	Jason Kendall	.15
34	Barry Bonds	3.00
35	Jim Edmonds	.40
36	Ivan Rodriguez	.50
37	Javy Lopez	.25
38	J.T. Snow	.15
39	Erubiel Durazo	.15
40	Terrence Long	.15
41	Tim Salmon	.25
42	Greg Maddux	1.50
43	Sammy Sosa	1.00
44	Sean Casey	.25
45	Jeff Cirillo	.15
46	Juan Gonzalez	.40
47	Richard Hidalgo	.25
48	Shawn Green	.25
49	Jeromy Burnitz	.15
50	Willie Mays	15.00
51	David Justice	.25
52	Tim Hudson	.40
53	Brian Giles	.25
54	Robb Nen	.15
55	Fernando Tatis	.15
56	Tony Batista	.15
57	Pokey Reese	.15
58	Ray Durham	.15
59	Greg Vaughn	.15
60	Kazuhiro Sasaki	.15
61	Troy Glaus	.40
62	Rafael Furcal	.40
63	Magglio Ordonez	.40
64	Jim Thome	.75
65	Todd Helton	.75
66	Preston Wilson	.15
67	Moises Alou	.25
68	Gary Sheffield	.25
69	Geoff Jenkins	.15
70	Mike Piazza	1.50
71	Jorge Posada	.50
72	Bobby Abreu	.40
73	Phil Nevin	.15
74	John Olerud	.15
75	Mark McGwire	1.50
76	Jose Cruz Jr.	.15
77	David Segui	.15
78	Neifi Perez	.15
79	Omar Vizquel	.25
80	Rick Ankiel	.50
81	Randy Johnson	1.00
82	Albert Belle	.15
83	Frank Thomas	.75
84	Manny Ramirez	.75
85	Larry Walker	.25
86	Luis Castillo	.15
87	Johnny Damon	.50
88	Adrian Beltre	.25
89	Cristian Guzman	.15
90	Jay Payton	.15
91	Miguel Tejada	.40
92	Scott Rolen	.75
93	Ryan Klesko	.40
94	Edgar Martinez	.25
95	Fred McGriff	.25
96	Carlos Delgado	.50
97	Barry Zito	.40

98	Mike Lieberthal	.15
99	Trevor Hoffman	.15
100	Gabe Kapler	.15
101	Edgardo Alfonzo	.15
102	Corey Patterson	.50
103	Alfonso Soriano	1.00
104	Keith Ginter	.50
105	Keith Reed	.50
106	Nick Johnson	.50
107	Carlos Pena	.50
108	Vernon Wells	.50
109	Roy Oswalt	.50
110	Alex Escobar	.50
111	Adam Everett	.50
112	Jimmy Rollins	1.00
113	Marcus Giles	.50
114	Jack Cust	.50
115	Chin-Feng Chen	1.00
116	Pablo Ozuna	.50
117	Ben Sheets	.50
118	Adrian Gonzalez	.50
119	Ben Davis	.50
120	Eric Valent	.50
121	Scott Heard	.50
122	David Parrish **RC**	1.50
123	Sean Burnett	.50
124	Derek Thompson	.50
125	Tim Christman **RC**	1.50
126	Mike Jacobs **RC**	1.00
127	Luis Montanez **RC**	1.50
128	Chris Bass **RC**	1.50
129	William Smith **RC**	1.50
130	Justin Wayne **RC**	2.00
131	Shawn Fagan **RC**	1.50
132	Chad Petty **RC**	1.50
133	J.R. House	.50
134	Joel Pineiro	.50
135	Albert Pujols **RC**	40.00
136	Carmen Cali **RC**	1.50
137	Steve Smyth **RC**	1.50
138	John Lackey	.50
139	Bob Keppel **RC**	1.50
140	Dominic Rich **RC**	1.50
141	Josh Hamilton	1.00
142	Nolan Ryan	5.00
143	Tom Seaver	1.50
145	Reggie Jackson	1.50
146	Johnny Bench	1.50
147	Brooks Robinson	1.50
148	Carl Yastrzemski	1.50
149	Al Kaline	1.00
150	Bob Feller	1.00
151a	Ichiro Suzuki/ English	20.00
151b	Ichiro Suzuki/ Japanese **RC**	20.00

Autographs

	NM/M
Common Autograph:	15.00
Inserted 1:232	

RA	Rick Ankiel	30.00
BB	Barry Bonds	150.00
PB	Pat Burrell	20.00
AG	Adrian Gonzalez	25.00
AR	Alex Rodriguez	120.00
IR	Ivan Rodriguez	50.00

Baseball Bucks

	NM/M

1:102 insert; used in Gallery Auction:

$5	Johnny Bench	1.50

Heritage

	NM/M
Complete Set (10):	30.00
Common Player:	2.00
Inserted 1:8	

1	Todd Helton	3.00
2	Greg Maddux	4.00
3	Pedro Martinez	4.00
4	Orlando Cepeda	2.00
5	Willie McCovey	2.00
6	Ken Griffey Jr.	3.00
7	Alex Rodriguez	6.00

DEREK JETER

8	Derek Jeter	8.00
9	Mark McGwire	5.00
10	Vladimir Guerrero	3.00

Heritage Relic

GREG MADDUX

	NM/M
Common Player:	10.00
Inserted 1:133	

Orlando Cepeda	10.00
Greg Maddux	25.00
Pedro Martinez	20.00
Willie McCovey	

Heritage Autographed Relic

	NM/M

Production 25 Sets

Orlando Cepeda	75.00
Willie McCovey	100.00

Star Gallery

	NM/M
Complete Set (10):	15.00
Common Player:	1.00
Inserted 1:8	

1	Vladimir Guerrero	1.00
2	Alex Rodriguez	2.50
3	Derek Jeter	3.00
4	Nomar Garciaparra	2.50
5	Ken Griffey Jr.	1.50
6	Mark McGwire	2.00
7	Chipper Jones	1.50
8	Sammy Sosa	2.00
9	Barry Bonds	3.00
10	Mike Piazza	1.50

Originals Relics

	NM/M
Common Player:	8.00
Inserted 1:133	

RA	Roberto Alomar	10.00
JD	Jermaine Dye	8.00
DE	Darin Erstad	8.00
JG	Jason Giambi	10.00
AG	Adrian Gonzalez	8.00
SG	Shawn Green	10.00
AJ	Andruw Jones	10.00
JK	Jason Kendall	8.00
JFK	Jeff Kent	8.00

RP	Rafael Palmeiro	10.00
PR	Pokey Reese	8.00
SS	Sammy Sosa	20.00
RV	Robin Ventura	8.00
BW	Bernie Williams	10.00
PW	Preston Wilson	8.00

Press Plates

The aluminum press plates used to print the Gallery cards were inserted at a rate of one per 1,200 packs. Each card's front and back can be found in four different color variations. Because of the unique nature of each plate, assignment of catalog values in not feasible.

	NM/M
Common Player:	50.00

Team Topps Legends Autographs

		NM/M
Common Autograph:		10.00
Inserted 1:286		
23R	Gil McDougald	10.00
27F	Andy Pafko	20.00
10R	Frank Robinson	20.00
28F	Herb Score	10.00
25R	Luis Tiant	10.00

2001 Topps Gold Label

		NM/M
Complete Set (115):		80.00
Common Player:		.25
Common Rookie:		4.00
Production 999		
Golds:		2-3X
Production 999		
Gold Rookies:		2-3X
Production 99		
Pack (5):		3.00
Box (24):		50.00
1	Adrian Beltre	.40
2	Danny Borrell RC	4.00
3	Albert Belle	.25
4	Alex Cabrera	.25
5	Alex Rodriguez	2.50
6	Andruw Jones	.50
7	Antonio Alfonseca	.25
8	Barry Bonds	3.00
9	Barry Larkin	.50
10	Ben Grieve	.25
11	Ben Molina	.25
12	Bernie Williams	.50
13	Bobby Abreu	.40
14	Bobby Higginson	.25

15	Brad Fullmer	.25
16	Brian Giles	.40
17	Cal Ripken Jr.	3.00
18	Carlos Delgado	.50
19	Chad Petty RC	4.00
20	Charles Johnson	.25
21	Chipper Jones	1.50
22	Cristian Guzman	.25
23	Darin Erstad	.40
24	David Justice	.40
25	David Segui	.25
26	Derek Jeter	2.50
27	Edgar Martinez	.40
28	Edgardo Alfonzo	.25
29	Fernando Tatis	.25
30	Eric Karros	.25
31	Eric Munson	.25
32	Eric Young	.25
33	Frank Thomas	.75
34	Fernando Vina	.25
35	Garret Anderson	.50
36	Gary Sheffield	.50
37	Geoff Jenkins	.40
38	Greg Maddux	2.00
39	Ivan Rodriguez	.50
40	J.D. Drew	.40
41	J.R. House	.25
42	J.T. Snow Jr.	.25
43	Jason Giambi	.50
44	Jason Kendall	.40
45	Jay Payton	.25
46	Jeff Bagwell	.50
47	Jeff Cirillo	.25
48	Jeff Kent	.40
49	Chan Ho Park	.25
50	Jermaine Dye	.25
51	Jeromy Burnitz	.25
52	Jim Edmonds	.50
53	Jim Thome	.75
54	John Olerud	.50
55	Johnny Damon	.40
56	Jorge Posada	.50
57	Jose Cruz Jr.	.25
58	Jose Vidro	.25
59	Josh Hamilton	.50
60	Juan Gonzalez	.50
61	Steve Smyth RC	4.00
62	Justin Wayne RC	4.00
63	Kazuhiro Sasaki	.25
64	Ken Griffey Jr.	2.00
65	Kevin Brown	.40
66	Kevin Young	.25
67	Larry Walker	.40
68	Luis Castillo	.25
69	Steve Finley	.25
70	Magglio Ordonez	.50
71	Manny Ramirez	.75
72	Mark McGwire	2.00
73	Mark Quinn	.25
74	Miguel Tejada	.25
75	Mike Piazza	1.50
76	Mike Sweeney	.25
77	Mo Vaughn	.25
78	Moises Alou	.40
79	Nomar Garciaparra	.75
80	Pat Burrell	.50
81	Paul Konerko	.40
82	Pedro Martinez	1.00
83	Phil Nevin	.25
84	Preston Wilson	.25
85	Rafael Furcal	.40
86	Todd Zeile	.25
87	Randy Johnson	1.00
88	Travis Lee	.25
89	Carl Everett	.25
90	Quilvio Veras	.25
91	Rick Ankiel	.50
92	Rick Brosseau RC	4.00
93	Robert Keppell RC	4.00
94	Roberto Alomar	.50
95	Ryan Klesko	.40
96	Sammy Sosa	1.00
97	Scott Heard	4.00
98	Scott Rolen	.75
99	Sean Casey	.25
100	Shawn Green	.40
101	Terrence Long	.25
102	Tim Salmon	.40
103	Todd Helton	.75
104	Tom Glavine	.50
105	Tony Batista	.25
106	Travis Baptist RC	4.00
107	Troy Glaus	.50
108	Victor Hall RC	4.00
109	Vladimir Guerrero	1.00
110	Tim Hudson	.40
111	Brian Roberts RC	2.00
112	Virgil Chevalier RC	4.00
113	Fernando Rodney RC	4.00
114	Paul Phillips RC	4.00
115	Cesar Bolivar RC	4.00

Class 2

Stars:		1-2X
Inserted 1:4		
Rookies:		1-1.5X
Production 699		
Golds:		2-3X

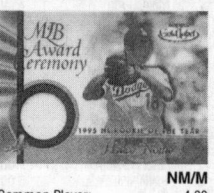

Production 699	
Gold Rookies:	2-3X
Production 69	

Class 3

Stars:		2-3X
Inserted 1:12		
Rookies:		1-2X
Production 299		
Golds:		3-5X
Production 299		
Gold Rookies:		2-4X
Production 29		

Masterpiece

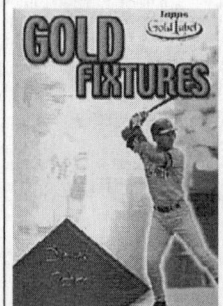

A 1-of-1 "masterpiece" card was created for each card in each of the three Classes of Topps Gold Label. Because of scarcity and widely varying demand, catalog values cannot be given.

	NM/M
Common Player:	50.00

Gold Fixtures

		NM/M
Complete Set (10):		150.00
Common Player:		8.00
Inserted 1:374		
1	Alex Rodriguez	20.00
2	Mark McGwire	20.00
3	Derek Jeter	25.00
4	Nomar Garciaparra	20.00
5	Chipper Jones	15.00
6	Sammy Sosa	20.00
7	Ken Griffey Jr.	15.00
8	Carlos Delgado	8.00
9	Frank Thomas	10.00
10	Barry Bonds	25.00

MLB Awards Ceremony

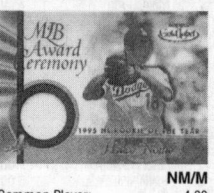

			NM/M
Common Player:			4.00
Inserted 1:24			
SA	Sandy Alomar/Bat		4.00
JB	Jeff Bagwell/Bat		8.00
AB	Albert Belle/Bat		4.00
CB	Carlos Beltran/Bat		4.00
DB	Dante Bichette		4.00
BB	Barry Bonds/Jsy		25.00
BB	Barry Bonds/Bat		25.00
SB	Scott Brosius/Bat		4.00
JC	Jose Canseco/Jsy		6.00
JC	Jose Canseco/Bat		6.00
WC	Will Clark/Bat		6.00
RC	Roger Clemens/Jsy		20.00
MC	Marty Cordova/Bat		4.00
RF	Rafael Furcal/Bat		6.00
AG	Andres Galarraga/Bat		4.00
NG	Nomar Garciaparra/Jsy		20.00
NG	Nomar Garciaparra/Bat		20.00
JG	Jason Giambi/Bat		8.00
TG	Troy Glaus/Bat		8.00
TG	Tom Glavine/Jsy		6.00
JG	Juan Gonzalez/Jsy		8.00
JG	Juan Gonzalez/Bat		8.00
DG	Dwight Gooden/Jsy		4.00
BG	Ben Grieve/Jsy		4.00
KG	Ken Griffey Jr./Jsy		15.00
KG	Ken Griffey Jr./Bat		15.00
TG	Tony Gwynn/Bat		10.00
TH	Todd Helton/Bat		8.00
RH	Rickey Henderson/Jsy		10.00
TH	Todd Hollandsworth/Bat		4.00
DJ	Derek Jeter/Bat		25.00
RJ	Randy Johnson/Jsy		10.00
CJ	Chipper Jones/Jsy		10.00
DJ	David Justice/Jsy		5.00
JK	Jeff Kent/Bat		4.00
CK	Chuck Knoblauch/Bat		4.00
BL	Barry Larkin/Bat		8.00
GM	Greg Maddux/Jsy		15.00
EM	Edgar Martinez/Bat		4.00
PM	Pedro Martinez/Jsy		10.00
FM	Fred McGriff/Bat		5.00
MM	Mark McGwire/Bat		60.00
MM	Mark McGwire/Jsy		60.00
RM	Raul Mondesi/Bat		4.00
HN	Hideo Nomo/Jsy		25.00
JO	John Olerud/Bat		4.00
PO	Paul O'Neill/Bat		5.00
MP	Mike Piazza/Bat		12.00
CR	Cal Ripken Jr./Jsy		35.00
AR	Alex Rodriguez/Bat		15.00
IR	Ivan Rodriguez/Bat		15.00
SR	Scott Rolen/Jsy		8.00
TS	Tim Salmon/Jsy		4.00
KS	Kazuhiro Sasaki/Jsy		5.00
GS	Gary Sheffield/Bat		4.00
JS	John Smoltz/Jsy		4.00
SS	Sammy Sosa/Bat		15.00
SS	Sammy Sosa/Jsy		15.00
DS	Darryl Strawberry/Jsy		4.00
DS	Darryl Strawberry/Bat		4.00
FT	Frank Thomas/Bat		8.00
FT	Frank Thomas/Bat		8.00
MV	Mo Vaughn/Jsy		4.00
MV	Mo Vaughn/Bat		4.00
LW	Larry Walker/Bat		5.00
LW	Larry Walker/Jsy		5.00
JW	John Wetteland/Jsy		4.00
BW	Bernie Williams/Bat		8.00
MW	Matt Williams/Bat		5.00

2001 Topps HD

		NM/M
Complete Set (120):		50.00
Common Player:		.25
Common (101-120):		1.00
Inserted 1:6		
Pack (4):		2.50
Box (20):		40.00
1	Derek Jeter	4.00
2	Magglio Ordonez	.50
3	Eric Munson	.25
4	Jermaine Dye	.25
5	Larry Walker	.40
6	Pokey Reese	.25
7	Pedro Martinez	1.00
8	Rafael Palmeiro	.75
9	Jason Kendall	.40
10	Mike Lieberthal	.25
11	Ryan Klesko	.40
12	Cal Ripken Jr.	3.00
13	Mike Piazza	1.50
14	Adam Sterrett RC	.75
15	John Olerud	.40
16	Manny Ramirez	.75
17	Chad Petty RC	.75
18	Vladimir Guerrero	1.00
19	Kevin Brown	.40
20	Luis Cotto RC	.50
21	Josh Hamilton	.75
22	Mark Grace	.50
23	Mark McGwire	2.50
24	Jeromy Burnitz	.25
25	Andruw Jones	.50
26	Raul Mondesi	.40
27	Stuart McFarland RC	.75
28	Craig Biggio	.40
29	Troy Glaus	.50
30	Carlos Delgado	.50
31	Rafael Furcal	.40
32	J.D. Drew	.25
33	Corey Patterson	.50
34	Gary Sheffield	.50
35	Jeff Kent	.40
36	Alex Rodriguez	2.50
37	Edgardo Alfonzo	.25
38	Jeff Segar RC	.50
39	Bobby Abreu	.40
40	Brian Giles	.40
41	Jason Smith RC	.40
42	Mo Vaughn	.50
43	Pat Burrell	.50
44	Barry Larkin	.50
45	Carlos Beltran	.50
46	Eric Mosley RC	.40
47	Alfonso Soriano	1.00
48	Tim Salmon	.40
49	Jason Giambi	.50
50	Greg Maddux	1.50
51	Randy Johnson	1.00
52	Jose Vidro	.25
53	Edgar Martinez	.40
54	Albert Belle	.40
55	Ivan Rodriguez	.75
56	Sean Casey	.25
57	Jorge Posada	.50
58	Preston Wilson	.25
59	Paul Konerko	.40
60	Todd Helton	.75
61	Dominic Rich RC	.50
62	Tony Gwynn	1.00
63	Bernie Williams	.75
64	Anthony Brewer RC	.50
65	Shawn Green	.50
66	Jeff Bagwell	.50
67	Jose Cruz Jr.	.25
68	Darin Erstad	.40
69	Jim Edmonds	.50
70	Frank Thomas	.75
71	Ryan Anderson	.50
72	Scott Rolen	.75
73	Jeff Cirillo	.25
74	Chris Bass RC	.50
75	William Smith RC	.50
76	Trot Nixon	.25
77	Bobby Bradley	.25
78	Odannis Ayala RC	.50
79	Jim Thome	.75
80	Sammy Sosa	1.00
81	Geoff Jenkins	.40
82	Ben Grieve	.25
83	Andres Galarraga	.40
84	Rick Ankiel	.50
85	Barry Bonds	3.00
86	Alex Gonzalez	.25
87	Sean Burroughs	.25
88	Nomar Garciaparra	1.50
89	Ken Griffey Jr.	1.50
90	Tim Hudson	.50
91	Chipper Jones	1.50
92	Matt Williams	.40
93	Roberto Alomar	.75
94	Adrian Gonzalez	.50
95	Juan Gonzalez	.50
96	Brian Bass RC	.50
97	Rick Brosseau RC	.50
98	Mariano Rivera	.75
99	James Baldwin	.25
100	Dean Palmer	.25
101	Pedro Martinez	2.00
102	Randy Johnson	2.00
103	Greg Maddux	4.00
104	Sammy Sosa	2.50
105	Mark McGwire	5.00
106	Ivan Rodriguez	1.50
107	Mike Piazza	3.00
108	Chipper Jones	3.00
109	Vladimir Guerrero	2.00
110	Alex Rodriguez	5.00
111	Ken Griffey Jr.	3.00
112	Cal Ripken Jr.	6.00
113	Derek Jeter	6.00
114	Barry Bonds	6.00
115	Nomar Garciaparra	2.00
116	Jeff Bagwell	1.50
117	Todd Helton	1.00
118	Darin Erstad	1.00
119	Shawn Green	1.00
120	Roberto Alomar	1.00

Platinum

Stars (1-100):	4-8X

Stars (101-120):	2-4X
Production 199 Sets	

Autographed Cards

	NM/M
Common Player:	10.00
Inserted 1:431	
1	Todd Horton	25.00
2	Rick Ankiel	20.00
3	Mark Quinn	10.00
4	Adrian Gonzalez	15.00

Game Defined

	NM/M
Complete Set (10):	25.00
Common Player:	1.50
Inserted 1:24	
Platinum:	1.5-2X
Inserted 1:72	
1	Ken Griffey Jr.	3.00
2	Derek Jeter	5.00
3	Sammy Sosa	3.00
4	Mark McGwire	4.00
5	Todd Helton	1.50
6	Mike Piazza	3.00
7	Chipper Jones	2.50
8	Vladimir Guerrero	1.50
9	Alex Rodriguez	3.00
10	Nomar Garciaparra	3.00

Game-Worn Jersey

	NM/M
Common Card:	5.00
Inserted 1:108	
Cards 5-8 are redemptions.	
1	Grant Roberts	5.00
2	Vernon Wells	10.00
3	Travis Dawkins	5.00
4	Ramon Ortiz	5.00
5	Steve Finley	5.00
6	Ramon Hernandez	5.00
7	Jay Payton	8.00
8	Jeromy Burnitz	5.00

Images of Excellence

	NM/M
Complete Set (10):	15.00
Common Player:	1.00
Inserted 1:8	
Platinum:	1.5-2X
Inserted 1:24	
1	Willie Mays	2.50
2	Reggie Jackson	1.00
3	Ernie Banks	1.50
4	Hank Aaron	2.50
5	Ted Williams	2.50
6	Mike Schmidt	2.00
7	Tom Seaver	1.00
8	Johnny Bench	1.50
9	George Brett	2.50
10	Nolan Ryan	3.00

20-20

	NM/M
Complete Set (10):	15.00
Common Player:	.50
Inserted 1:12	
Platinum:	1.5-2X

Inserted 1:36

1	Barry Bonds	4.00
2	Chipper Jones	2.00
3	Ken Griffey Jr.	2.00
4	Alex Rodriguez	3.00
5	Ivan Rodriguez	1.00
6	Sammy Sosa	2.50
7	Roberto Alomar	.75
8	Larry Walker	.50
9	Shawn Green	.75
10	Jeff Bagwell	1.00

2001 Topps Heritage Pre-Production

ROGER CLEMENS

To introduce its retro-look 2001 Heritage baseball set, Topps issued a cello-packaged, three-card promo set. The cards are in the same format as the regular-issue Heritage series, except that all the stats on back are zeroes and all the cards are numbered with a "PP" prefix.

		NM/M
Complete Set (3):		6.00
Common Player:		2.00
PP1	Kevin Brown	2.00
PP2	Andres Galarraga	2.00
PP3	Roger Clemens	4.00

2001 Topps Heritage

MANNY RAMIREZ

		NM/M
Complete Set (407):		275.00
Complete Master Set (487):		320.00
Common Player:		.50
Common SP (311-407):		2.50
Inserted 1:2		
Pack (8):		13.00
Box (24):		275.00
1	Kris Benson	.50
2	Brian Jordan	.50
3	Fernando Vina	.50
4	Mike Sweeney	.50
5	Rafael Palmeiro	2.00
6	Paul O'Neill	1.00
7	Todd Helton	2.50
8	Ramiro Mendoza	.50
9	Kevin Millwood	1.00
10	Chuck Knoblauch	.50
11	Derek Jeter	10.00
12	Alex Rodriguez	8.00
13	Geoff Jenkins	.75
14	David Justice	1.00
15	David Cone	.50
16	Andres Galarraga	1.00
17	Garret Anderson	1.00
18	Roger Cedeno	.50
19	Randy Velarde	.50
20	Carlos Delgado	2.00
21	Quilvio Veras	.50
22	Jose Vidro	.50
23	Corey Patterson	.75
24	Jorge Posada	1.00
25	Eddie Perez	.50
26	Jack Cust	.50
27	Sean Burroughs	.75
28	Randy Wolf	.50
29	Mike Lamb	.50
30	Rafael Furcal	.75
31	Barry Bonds	8.00
32	Tim Hudson	.75
33	Tom Glavine	1.50
34	Javy Lopez	.75
35	Aubrey Huff	.50
36	Wally Joyner	.50
37	Magglio Ordonez	1.00
38	Matt Lawton	.50
39	Mariano Rivera	1.00
40	Andy Ashby	.50
41	Mark Buehrle	3.00
42	Esteban Loaiza	.50
43	Mark Redman	.50
44	Mark Quinn	.50
45	Tino Martinez	.75
46	Joe Mays	.50
47	Walt Weiss	.50
48	Roger Clemens	6.00
49	Greg Maddux	5.00
50	Richard Hidalgo	.75
51	Orlando Hernandez	.75
52	Chipper Jones	5.00
53	Ben Grieve	.50
54	Jimmy Haynes	.50
55	Ken Caminiti	.50
56	Tim Salmon	1.00
57	Andy Pettitte	1.00
58	Darin Erstad	1.00
59	Marquis Grissom	.50
60	Raul Mondesi	.75
61	Bengie Molina	.50
62	Miguel Tejada	1.00
63	Jose Cruz Jr.	.50
64	Billy Koch	.50
65	Troy Glaus	2.00
66	Cliff Floyd	.50
67	Tony Batista	.50
68	Jeff Bagwell	2.50
69	Billy Wagner	.50
70	Eric Chavez	.75
71	Troy Percival	.50
72	Andruw Jones	2.50
73	Shane Reynolds	.50
74	Barry Zito	2.50
75	Roy Halladay	1.00
76	David Wells	.50
77	Jason Giambi	1.50
78	Scott Elarton	.50
79	Moises Alou	.75
80	Adam Piatt	.50
81	Wilton Veras	.50
82	Darryl Kile	.50
83	Johnny Damon	.50
84	Tony Armas Jr.	.50
85	Ellis Burks	.50
86	Jamey Wright	.50
87	Jose Vizcaino	.50
88	Bartolo Colon	.50
89	Carmen Cali RC	.50
90	Kevin Brown	.75
91	Josh Hamilton	.75
92	Jay Buhner	.50
93	Scott Pratt RC	.50
94	Alex Cora	.50
95	Luis Montanez RC	1.00
96	Dmitri Young	.50
97	J.T. Snow Jr.	.50
98	Damion Easley	.50
99	Greg Norton	.50
100	Matt Wheatland	.50
101	Chin-Feng Chen	.50
102	Tony Womack	.50
103	Adam Kennedy	.50
104	J.D. Drew	.50
105	Carlos Febles	.50
106	Jim Thome	1.00
107	Danny Graves	.50
108	Dave Mlicki	.50
109	Ron Coomer	.50
110	James Baldwin	.50
111	Shaun Boyd RC	.75
112	Brian Bohannon	.50
113	Jacque Jones	.50
114	Alfonso Soriano	1.50
115	Tony Clark	.50
116	Terrence Long	.50
117	Todd Hundley	.50
118	Kazuhiro Sasaki	.50
119	Brian Sellier RC	.50
120	John Olerud	.75
121	Javier Vazquez	.50
122	Sean Burnett	.50
123	Matt LeCroy	.50
124	Erubiel Durazo	.50
125	Juan Encarnacion	.50
126	Pablo Ozuna	.50
127	Russ Ortiz	.50
128	David Segui	.50
129	Mark McGwire	3.00
130	Mark Grace	1.00
131	Fred McGriff	.75
132	Carl Pavano	.50
133	Derek Thompson	.50
134	Shawn Green	.75
135	B.J. Surhoff	.50
136	Michael Tucker	.50
137	Jason Isringhausen	.50
138	Eric Milton	.50
139	Mike Stodolka	.50
140	Milton Bradley	.50
141	Curt Schilling	.75
142	Sandy Alomar	.50
143	Brent Mayne	.50
144	Todd Jones	.50
145	Charles Johnson	.50
146	Dean Palmer	.50
147	Masato Yoshii	.50
148	Edgar Renteria	.50
149	Joe Randa	.50
150	Adam Johnson	.50
151	Greg Vaughn	.50
152	Adrian Beltre	.75
153	Glenallen Hill	.50
154	David Parrish RC	.50
155	Neifi Perez	.50
156	Pete Harnisch	.50
157	Paul Konerko	.50
158	Dennys Reyes	.50
159	Jose Lima	.50
160	Eddie Taubensee	.50
161	Miguel Cairo	.50
162	Jeff Kent	.75
163	Dustin Hermanson	.50
164	Alex Gonzalez	.50
165	Hideo Nomo	.75
166	Sammy Sosa	2.00
167	C.J. Nitkowski	.50
168	Cal Eldred	.50
169	Jeff Abbott	.50
170	Jim Edmonds	.75
171	Mark Mulder	.75
172	Dominic Rich RC	.50
173	Ray Lankford	.50
174	Danny Borrell RC	.75
175	Rick Aguilera	.50
176	Shannon Stewart	.50
177	Steve Finley	.50
178	Jim Parque	.50
179	Kevin Appier	.50
180	Adrian Gonzalez	.75
181	Tom Goodwin	.50
182	Kevin Tapani	.50
183	Fernando Tatis	.50
184	Mark Grudzielanek	.50
185	Ryan Anderson	.50
186	Jeffrey Hammonds	.50
187	Corey Koskie	.50
188	Brad Fullmer	.50
189	Rey Sanchez	.50
190	Michael Barrett	.50
191	Rickey Henderson	1.00
192	Jermaine Dye	.50
193	Scott Brosius	.50
194	Matt Anderson	.50
195	Brian Buchanan	.50
196	Derrek Lee	.50
197	Larry Walker	.75
198	David Krynzel	.50
199	Vinny Castilla	.50
200	Ken Griffey Jr.	2.00
201	Matt Stairs	.50
202	Ty Howington	.50
203	Andy Benes	.50
204	Luis Gonzalez	.75
205	Brian Moehler	.50
206	Harold Baines	.50
207	Pedro Astacio	.50
208	Cristian Guzman	.50
209	Kip Wells	.50
210	Frank Thomas	1.00
211	Jose Rosado	.50
212	Vernon Wells	.50
213	Bobby Higginson	.50
214	Juan Gonzalez	1.00
215	Omar Vizquel	.75
216	Bernie Williams	1.00
217	Aaron Sele	.50
218	Shawn Estes	.50
219	Roberto Alomar	1.00
220	Rick Ankiel	.50
221	Josh Kalinowski	.50
222	David Bell	.50
223	Keith Foulke	.50
224	Craig Biggio	.75
225	Shawn Fagan RC	.50
226	Scott Williamson	.50
227	Ron Belliard	.50
228	Chris Singleton	.50
229	Alex Serrano	.50
230	Deivi Cruz	.50
231	Eric Munson	.50
232	Luis Castillo	.50
233	Edgar Martinez	.50
234	Jeff Shaw	.50
235	Jeromy Burnitz	.50
236	Richie Sexson	.75
237	Will Clark	1.00
238	Ron Villone	.50
239	Kerry Wood	1.00
240	Rich Aurilia	.50
241	Mo Vaughn	.50
242	Travis Fryman	.50
243	Manny Ramirez	1.00
244	Chris Stynes	.50
245	Ray Durham	.50
246	Juan Uribe RC	.50
247	Juan Guzman	.50
248	Lee Stevens	.50
249	Devon White	.50
250	Kyle Lohse RC	1.50
251	Bryan Wolff	.50
252	Rick Brousseau RC	.50
253	Eric Young	.50
254	Freddy Garcia	.50
255	Jay Bell	.50
256	Steve Cox	.50
257	Torii Hunter	.50
258	Jose Canseco	.75
259	Brad Ausmus	.50
260	Jeff Cirillo	.50
261	Brad Penny	.50
262	Antonio Alfonseca	.50
263	Russ Branyan	.50
264	Scott Heard	.50
265	John Lackey	.50
266	Justin Wayne RC	1.00
267	Brad Radke	.50
268	Todd Stottlemyre	.50
269	Mark Loretta	.50
270	Matt Williams	.50
271	Kenny Lofton	.50
272	Jeff D'Amico	.50
273	Jamie Moyer	.50
274	Darren Dreifort	.50
275	Denny Neagle	.50
276	Orlando Cabrera	.50
277	Chuck Finley	.50
278	Miguel Batista	.50
279	Carlos Beltran	.50
280	Eric Karros	.50
281	Mark Kotsay	.50
282	Ryan Dempster	.50
283	Barry Larkin	.75
284	Jeff Suppan	.50
285	Gary Sheffield	.75
286	Jose Valentin	.50
287	Robb Nen	.50
288	Chan Ho Park	.50
289	John Halama	.50
290	Steve Smyth RC	.50
291	Gerald Williams	.50
292	Preston Wilson	.50
293	Victor Hall RC	.75
294	Ben Sheets	.50
295	Eric Davis	.50
296	Kirk Rueter	.50
297	Chad Petty RC	.75
298	Kevin Millar	.50
299	Marvin Benard	.50
300	Vladimir Guerrero	1.00
301	Livan Hernandez	.50
302	Travis Baptist RC	.75
303	Bill Mueller	.50
304	Mike Cameron	.50
305	Randy Johnson	1.50
306	Alan Mahaffey RC	.50
307	Timo Perez (No facsimile autograph.)	.50
308	Pokey Reese	.50
309	Ryan Rupe	.50
310	Carlos Lee	.50
311	Doug Glanville	2.50
312	Jay Payton	2.50
313	Troy O'Leary	2.50
314	Francisco Cordero	2.50
315	Rusty Greer	2.50
316	Cal Ripken Jr.	25.00
317	Ricky Ledee	2.50
318	Brian Daubach	2.50
319	Robin Ventura	2.50
320	Todd Zeile	2.50
321	Francisco Cordova	2.50
322	Henry Rodriguez	2.50
323	Pat Meares	2.50
324	Glendon Rusch	2.50
325	Keith Osik	2.50
326	Robert Keppell RC	3.00
327	Bobby Jones	2.50
328	Alex Ramirez	2.50
329	Robert Person	2.50
330	Ruben Mateo	2.50
331	Rob Bell	2.50
332	Carl Everett	2.50
333	Jason Schmidt	2.50
334	Scott Rolen	5.00
335	Jimmy Anderson	2.50
336	Bret Boone	2.50
337	Delino DeShields	2.50
338	Trevor Hoffman	2.50
339	Bob Abreu	3.00
340	Mike Williams	2.50
341	Mike Hampton	2.50
342	John Wetteland	2.50
343	Scott Erickson	2.50
344	Enrique Wilson	2.50
345	Tim Wakefield	2.50
346	Mike Lowell	3.00
347	Todd Pratt	2.50
348	Brook Fordyce	2.50
349	Benny Agbayani	2.50
350	Gabe Kapler	2.50
351	Sean Casey	2.50
352	Darren Oliver	2.50
353	Todd Ritchie	2.50
354	Kenny Rogers	2.50
355	Jason Kendall	2.50
356	John Vander Wal	2.50
357	Ramon Martinez	2.50
358	Edgardo Alfonzo	2.50
359	Phil Nevin	2.50
360	Albert Belle	2.50
361	Ruben Rivera	2.50
362	Pedro Martinez	10.00
363	Derek Lowe	2.50
364	Pat Burrell	2.50
365	Mike Mussina	5.00
366	Brady Anderson	2.50
367	Darren Lewis	2.50
368	Sidney Ponson	2.50
369	Adam Eaton	2.50
370	Eric Owens	2.50
371	Aaron Boone	2.50
372	Matt Clement	2.50
373	Derek Bell	2.50
374	Trot Nixon	2.50
375	Travis Lee	2.50
376	Mike Benjamin	2.50
377	Jeff Zimmerman	2.50
378	Mike Lieberthal	2.50
379	Rick Reed	2.50
380	Nomar Garciaparra	5.00
381	Omar Daal	2.50
382	Ryan Klesko	2.50
383	Rey Ordonez	2.50
384	Kevin Young	2.50
385	Rick Helling	2.50
386	Brian Giles	3.00
387	Tony Gwynn	8.00
388	Ed Sprague	2.50
389	J.R. House	2.50
390	Scott Hatteberg	2.50
391	John Valentin	2.50
392	Melvin Mora	2.50
393	Royce Clayton	2.50
394	Jeff Fassero	2.50
395	Manny Alexander	2.50
396	John Franco	2.50
397	Luis Alicea	2.50
398	Ivan Rodriguez	5.00
399	Kevin Jordan	2.50
400	Jose Offerman	2.50
401	Jeff Conine	2.50
402	Seth Etherton	2.50
403	Mike Bordick	2.50
404	Al Leiter	3.00
405	Mike Piazza	10.00
406	Armando Benitez	2.50
407	Warren Morris	2.50

Chrome

DAVID WELLS

		NM/M
Common Player:		3.00
Production 552 Sets		
1	Cal Ripken Jr.	40.00
2	Jim Thome	8.00
3	Derek Jeter	40.00
4	Andres Galarraga	4.00
5	Carlos Delgado	8.00
6	Roberto Alomar	8.00
7	Tom Glavine	10.00
8	Gary Sheffield	8.00
9	Mo Vaughn	3.00
10	Preston Wilson	3.00
11	Mike Mussina	8.00
12	Greg Maddux	30.00
13	Ivan Rodriguez	10.00
14	Al Leiter	3.00
15	Seth Etherton	3.00
16	Edgardo Alfonzo	3.00
17	Richie Sexson	3.00
18	Andruw Jones	10.00
19	Bartolo Colon	3.00
20	Darin Erstad	5.00
21	Kevin Brown	4.00
22	Mike Sweeney	3.00
23	Mike Piazza	30.00
24	Rafael Palmeiro	8.00
25	Terrence Long	3.00
26	Kazuhiro Sasaki	3.00
27	John Olerud	5.00
28	Mark McGwire	30.00
29	Fred McGriff	5.00
30	Todd Helton	10.00
31	Curt Schilling	10.00
32	Alex Rodriguez	30.00
33	Jeff Kent	5.00
34	Pat Burrell	8.00
35	Jim Edmonds	5.00
36	Mark Mulder	5.00
37	Troy Glaus	8.00
38	Jay Payton	5.00
39	Jermaine Dye	5.00
40	Larry Walker	5.00
41	Ken Griffey Jr.	30.00
42	Jeff Bagwell	10.00
43	Rick Ankiel	5.00
44	Mark Redman	3.00
45	Edgar Martinez	5.00
46	Mike Hampton	4.00
47	Manny Ramirez	10.00
48	Ray Durham	5.00
49	Rafael Furcal	5.00
50	Sean Casey	4.00
51	Jose Canseco	5.00
52	Barry Bonds	40.00
53	Tim Hudson	8.00
54	Barry Zito	5.00
55	Chuck Finley	5.00
56	Magglio Ordonez	5.00
57	David Wells	5.00
58	Jason Giambi	8.00
59	Tony Gwynn	15.00
60	Vladimir Guerrero	15.00
61	Randy Johnson	15.00
62	Bernie Williams	8.00
63	Craig Biggio	5.00
64	Jason Kendall	5.00
65	Pedro Martinez	15.00
66	Mark Quinn	3.00
67	Frank Thomas	15.00
68	Nomar Garciaparra	15.00
69	Brian Giles	5.00
70	Shawn Green	5.00
71	Roger Clemens	25.00
72	Sammy Sosa	15.00
73	Juan Gonzalez	8.00
74	Orlando Hernandez	4.00
75	Chipper Jones	20.00
76	Josh Hamilton	10.00
77	Adam Johnson	3.00
78	Shaun Boyd	3.00
79	Alfonso Soriano	15.00
80	Derek Thompson	3.00
81	Adrian Gonzalez	8.00
82	Ryan Anderson	3.00
83	Corey Patterson	5.00
84	J.R. House	3.00
85	Sean Burroughs	3.00
86	Scott Heard	3.00
87	John Lackey	8.00
88	Ben Sheets	8.00
89	Wilson Betemit	3.00
90	Robert Keppell	3.00
91	Luis Montanez	3.00
92	Sean Burnett	3.00
93	Justin Wayne	5.00
94	Eric Munson	3.00
95	Steve Smyth	3.00
96	Rick Brousseau	3.00
97	Carmen Cali	3.00
98	Brian Sellier	3.00
99	David Parrish	3.00
100	Danny Borrell	3.00
101	Chad Petty	3.00
102	Dominic Rich	3.00
103	Shawn Fagan	3.00
104	Alex Serrano	3.00
105	Juan Uribe	3.00
106	Travis Baptist	3.00
107	Alan Mahaffey	3.00
108	Kyle Lohse	5.00
109	Victor Hall	3.00
110	Scott Pratt	3.00

Classic Renditions

Classic Renditions
Nomar Garciaparra
Boston Red Sox

		NM/M
Complete Set (10):		15.00
Common Player:		1.00
Inserted 1:5		
1	Mark McGwire	2.50
2	Nomar Garciaparra	2.00
3	Barry Bonds	3.00
4	Sammy Sosa	1.50
5	Chipper Jones	1.50
6	Pat Burrell	1.00
7	Frank Thomas	1.00
8	Manny Ramirez	1.00
9	Derek Jeter	3.00
10	Ken Griffey Jr.	2.00

Classic Renditions Autographs

Classic Renditions
Chipper Jones • Atlanta Braves

		NM/M
Production 25 Sets		
BB	Barry Bonds	500.00
CJ	Chipper Jones	350.00
NG	Nomar Garciaparra	150.00

Clubhouse Collection Autographs

		NM/M
Common Player:		
MM	Minnie Monoso/25	120.00
RS	Red Schoendienst/25	150.00

Clubhouse Collection Game-Used

		NM/M
Common Player:		25.00
MM	Minnie Monoso	25.00
RS	Red Schoendienst	30.00
DS	Duke Snider	40.00
EM	Eddie Mathews	40.00
CJ	Chipper Jones	40.00
RA	Richie Ashburn	30.00
FT	Frank Thomas	40.00
FV	Fernando Vina	25.00

CLUBHOUSE COLLECTION

CHIPPER JONES

SG	Shawn Green	30.00
WM	Willie Mays	150.00
BB	Barry Bonds	80.00
SR	Scott Rolen	40.00

Clubhouse Collection Dual Game-Used

		NM/M
Common Card:		75.00
Production 52 Sets		
MMFT	Minnie Monoso, Frank Thomas	100.00
RSFV	Red Schoendienst, Fernando Vina	75.00
DSSG	Duke Snider, Shawn Green	150.00
RAPB	Richie Ashburn, Scott Rolen	100.00
EMCJ	Eddie Mathews, Chipper Jones	125.00
WMBB	Willie Mays, Barry Bonds	250.00

Grandstand Glory

		NM/M
Common Player:		20.00
Inserted 1:211		
PR	Phil Rizzuto	30.00
YB	Yogi Berra	30.00
RA	Richie Ashburn	20.00
RR	Robin Roberts	20.00
WM	Willie Mays	60.00
NF	Nellie Fox	20.00
JR	Jackie Robinson	50.00

New Age Performers

		NM/M
Complete Set (15):		20.00
Common Player:		1.00
Inserted 1:8		
1	Mike Piazza	1.50
2	Sammy Sosa	2.00
3	Alex Rodriguez	2.50
4	Barry Bonds	3.00
5	Ken Griffey Jr.	1.50
6	Chipper Jones	1.50
7	Randy Johnson	1.00
8	Derek Jeter	3.00
9	Nomar Garciaparra	2.00
10	Mark McGwire	2.50
11	Jeff Bagwell	1.00
12	Pedro Martinez	1.00
13	Todd Helton	1.00
14	Vladimir Guerrero	1.00
15	Greg Maddux	2.00

Real One Autographs

BARRY BONDS

		NM/M
Common Player:		30.00
Current MLB Players		
200 Blue-Inked Produced		
Red Ink:		1-1.5X
52 Red-Inked Produced		
Prices listed for Blue sigs.		
RH	Richard Hidalgo	30.00
TL	Terrence Long	30.00
CD	Carlos Delgado	60.00
CJ	Chipper Jones	160.00
TG	Tom Glavine	100.00
GJ	Geoff Jenkins	40.00
JM	Joe Mays	30.00
FV	Fernando Vina	30.00
CP	Corey Patterson	40.00
JV	Jose Vidro	30.00
BB	Barry Bonds	275.00
AR	Alex Rodriguez	250.00
AH	Aubrey Huff	40.00
SPB	Sean Burroughs	30.00
RW	Randy Wolf	30.00
KB	Kris Benson	30.00
ML	Mike Lamb	30.00
TH	Todd Helton	80.00
MQ	Mark Quinn	30.00
MS	Mike Sweeney	30.00
ML	Matt Lawton	35.00
MO	Magglio Ordonez	40.00
MB	Mark Buehrle	50.00
MR	Mark Redman	30.00
CF	Cliff Floyd	30.00
NG	Nomar Garciaparra	150.00

1952 MLB Players

MV	Mickey Vernon	40.00
HB	Hank Bauer	80.00
DD	Dom DiMaggio	100.00
LD	Larry Doby	100.00
JG	Joe Garagiola	80.00
DG	Dick Groat	70.00
MI	Monte Irvin	80.00
VL	Vernon Law	60.00
EM	Eddie Matthews	200.00
WM	Willie Mays	250.00
GM	Gil McDougald	60.00
MM	Minnie Monoso	85.00
AP	Andy Pafko	60.00
PFR	Phil Rizzuto	125.00
PR	Preacher Roe	100.00
JS	Johnny Sain	75.00
HS	Hank Sauer	75.00
RS	Red Schoendienst	80.00
BS	Bobby Shantz	50.00
CS	Curt Simmons	50.00
ES	Enos Slaughter	100.00
DS	Duke Snider	200.00
WS	Warren Spahn	125.00
BT	Bobby Thomson	90.00
HW	Hoyt Wilhelm	90.00
RR	Robin Roberts	80.00

Then and Now

Then and Now

Pee Wee Reese — Brooklyn Dodgers®
Nomar Garciaparra — Boston Red Sox®

		NM/M
Complete Set (10):		15.00
Common Player:		1.50
Inserted 1:8		
1	Yogi Berra, Mike Piazza	1.50
2	Duke Snider, Sammy Sosa	2.00
3	Willie Mays, Ken Griffey Jr.	2.00
4	Phil Rizzuto, Derek Jeter	3.00
5	Pee Wee Reese, Nomar Garciaparra	2.00
6	Jackie Robinson, Alex Rodriguez	2.50

7	Johnny Mize, Mark McGwire	2.50
8	Bob Feller, Pedro Martinez	1.50
9	Robin Roberts, Greg Maddux	2.00
10	Warren Spahn, Randy Johnson	1.50

Time Capsule

		NM/M
Common Player:		20.00
Inserted 1:369		
WM	Willie Mays	75.00
TW	Ted Williams	85.00
DN	Don Newcombe	20.00
WF	Whitey Ford	30.00
WMTW	Ted Williams, Willie Mays/52	200.00

2001 Topps Reserve

JASON GIAMBI

		NM/M
Complete Set (151):		
Common Player:		.40
Common SP (101-150):		4.00
Production 1,500		
Sealed Hobby Box (10):		125.00
1	Darin Erstad	.40
2	Moises Alou	.50
3	Tony Batista	.40
4	Andruw Jones	.50
5	Edgar Renteria	.40
6	Eric Young	.40
7	Steve Finley	.40
8	Adrian Beltre	.40
9	Vladimir Guerrero	1.00
10	Barry Bonds	3.00
11	Juan Gonzalez	.50
12	Jay Buhner	.40
13	Luis Castillo	.40
14	Cal Ripken Jr.	3.00
15	Bob Abreu	.40
16	Ivan Rodriguez	.75
17	Nomar Garciaparra	.75
18	Todd Helton	.75
19	Bobby Higginson	.40
20	Jorge Posada	.50
21	Tim Salmon	.50
22	Jason Giambi	.75
23	José Cruz Jr.	.40
24	Chipper Jones	1.50
25	Jim Edmonds	.40
26	Gerald Williams	.40
27	Randy Johnson	1.00
28	Gary Sheffield	.50
29	Jeff Kent	.40
30	Jim Thome	.75
31	John Olerud	.40
32	Cliff Floyd	.40
33	Mike Lowell	.40
34	Phil Nevin	.40
35	Scott Rolen	.75
36	Alex Rodriguez	2.50
37	Ken Griffey Jr.	2.00
38	Neifi Perez	.40
39	Christian Guzman	.40
40	Mariano Rivera	.50
41	Troy Glaus	.50
42	Johnny Damon	.50
43	Rafael Furcal	.50
44	Jeromy Burnitz	.40
45	Mark McGwire	2.00
46	Fred McGriff	.40
47	Matt Williams	.40
48	Kevin Brown	.40
49	J.T. Snow	.40
50	Kenny Lofton	.40
51	Al Martin	.40
52	Antonio Alfonseca	.40
53	Edgardo Alfonzo	.40
54	Ryan Klesko	.40
55	Pat Burrell	.50
56	Rafael Palmeiro	.50
57	Sean Casey	.40
58	Jeff Cirillo	.40
59	Ray Durham	.40
60	Derek Jeter	3.00

61	Jeff Bagwell	.50
62	Carlos Delgado	.50
63	Tom Glavine	.50
64	Richie Sexson	.50
65	J.D. Drew	.40
66	Ben Grieve	.40
67	Mark Grace	.50
68	Shawn Green	.40
69	Robb Nen	.40
70	Omar Vizquel	.40
71	Edgar Martinez	.40
72	Preston Wilson	.40
73	Mike Piazza	1.50
74	Tony Gwynn	1.00
75	Jason Kendall	.40
76	Manny Ramirez	.75
77	Pokey Reese	.40
78	Mike Sweeney	.40
79	Magglio Ordonez	.50
80	Bernie Williams	.50
81	Richard Hidalgo	.40
82	Brad Fullmer	.40
83	Greg Maddux	2.00
84	Geoff Jenkins	.40
85	Sammy Sosa	1.00
86	Luis Gonzalez	.40
87	Eric Karros	.40
88	Jose Vidro	.40
89	Rich Aurilia	.40
90	Roberto Alomar	.50
91	Mike Cameron	.40
92	Mike Mussina	.50
93	Albert Belle	.40
94	Mike Lieberthal	.40
95	Brian Giles	.40
96	Pedro Martinez	1.00
97	Barry Larkin	.50
98	Jermaine Dye	.40
99	Frank Thomas	.75
100	David Justice	.50
101	Gary Johnson RC	4.00
102	Matt Ford RC	4.00
103	Albert Pujols RC	120.00
104	Brad Cresse	4.00
105	Valentino Pascucci RC	4.00
106	Bob Keppel RC	4.00
107	Luis Torres RC	4.00
108	Tony Blanco RC	4.00
109	Ronnie Corona RC	4.00
110	Phil Wilson RC	4.00
111	John Buck RC	6.00
112	Jim Journell RC	4.00
113	Victor Hall RC	4.00
114	Jeff Andra RC	4.00
115	Greg Nash RC	4.00
116	Travis Hafner RC	10.00
117	Casey Fossum RC	4.00
118	Miguel Olivo	4.00
119	Elpidio Guzman RC	4.00
120	Jason Belcher RC	4.00
121	Esix Snead RC	4.00
122	Joe Thurston RC	4.00
123	Rafael Soriano RC	6.00
124	Ed Rogers RC	4.00
125	Omar Beltre RC	4.00
126	Brett Gray RC	4.00
127	Devi Mendez RC	4.00
128	Freddie Bynum RC	4.00
129	David Krynzel RC	4.00
130	Blake Williams RC	4.00
131	Reggie Abercrombie RC	4.00
132	Miguel Villilo RC	4.00
133	Ryan Madson RC	4.00
134	Matt Thompson RC	4.00
135	Mark Burnett RC	4.00
136	Andy Beal RC	4.00
137	Ryan Ludwick RC	15.00
138	Roberto Miniel RC	4.00
139	Steve Smyth RC	4.00
140	Ben Washborn RC	4.00
141	Marvin Seale RC	4.00
142	Reggie Griggs RC	4.00
143	Seung Song RC	4.00
144	Chad Petty RC	4.00
145	Noel Devarez RC	4.00
146	Matt Butler RC	4.00
147	Brett Evert RC	4.00
148	Cesar Izturis RC	4.00
149	Troy Farnsworth RC	4.00
150	Brian Schmitt RC	4.00
151	Ichiro Suzuki RC	30.00

Game-Used Bat

		NM/M
Common Player:		4.00
Inserted 1:Box		
JB	Jeff Bagwell	8.00
BB	Barry Bonds	25.00
CD	Carlos Delgado	4.00
JE	Jim Edmonds	4.00
DE	Darin Erstad	4.00
RF	Rafael Furcal	4.00
NG	Nomar Garciaparra	8.00
VG	Vladimir Guerrero	10.00
TG	Tony Gwynn	10.00
CJ	Chipper Jones	10.00
MP	Mike Piazza	15.00
AR	Alex Rodriguez	15.00
IR	Ivan Rodriguez	8.00
BW	Bernie Williams	8.00

Game-Worn Uniform

		NM/M
Common Player:		4.00
Inserted 1:Box		
RA	Roberto Alomar	8.00
BB	Barry Bonds	25.00
CD	Carlos Delgado	4.00

AUTHENTIC GAME-WORN UNIFORMS
CARLOS DELGADO

JE	Jim Edmonds	4.00
NG	Nomar Garciaparra	4.00
JG	Juan Gonzalez	4.00
SG	Shawn Green	4.00
VG	Vladimir Guerrero	8.00
TG	Tony Gwynn	10.00
TH	Todd Helton	8.00
RJ	Randy Johnson	8.00
CJ	Chipper Jones	10.00
DJ	David Justice	4.00
GM	Greg Maddux	15.00
PM	Pedro Martinez	8.00
RP	Rafael Palmeiro	4.00
AR	Alex Rodriguez	15.00
IR	Ivan Rodriguez	8.00
SR	Scott Rolen	8.00
FT	Frank Thomas	8.00

Rookie Autographed Baseballs

		NM/M
Common Player:		10.00
Inserted 1:Box w/holder.		
	Reggie Abercrombie	10.00
	Jeff Andra	10.00
	Andy Beal	10.00
	Jason Belcher	10.00
	Omar Beltre	10.00
	Tony Blanco	15.00
	John Buck	15.00
	Mark Burnett	10.00
	Freddie Bynum	10.00
	Ronnie Corona	10.00
	Noel Devarez	10.00
	Matt Ford	10.00
	Casey Fossum	10.00
	Brett Gray	10.00
	Reggie Griggs	10.00
	Elpidio Guzman	10.00
	Travis Hafner	30.00
	Victor Hall	10.00
	Gary Johnson	10.00
	Jim Journell	10.00
	Bob Keppel	10.00
	David Krynzel	10.00
	Ryan Ludwick	40.00
	Ryan Madson	15.00
	Deivi Mendez	10.00
	Roberto Miniel	10.00
	Greg Nash	10.00
	Miguel Olivo	10.00
	Valentino Pascucci	10.00
	Chad Petty	10.00
	Albert Pujols	675.00
	Ed Rogers	10.00
	Marvin Seale	10.00
	Steve Smyth	10.00
	Esix Snead	10.00
	Seung Song	10.00
	Rafael Soriano	15.00
	Matt Thompson	10.00
	Joe Thurston	10.00
	Luis Torres	10.00
	Miguel Villilo	10.00
	Ben Washburn	10.00
	Blake Williams	10.00
	Phil Wilson	10.00

Rookie Graded Autograph

VICTOR HALL

		NM/M
Common Rookie:		10.00
Inserted 1:Box		
Prices for PSA 8		
PSA 9s:		1.5X
	Reggie Abercrombie	10.00
	Jeff Andra	10.00
	Andy Beal	10.00
	Jason Belcher	10.00
	Omar Beltre	10.00
	Tony Blanco	10.00
	John Buck	10.00
	Mark Burnett	10.00
	Freddie Bynum	10.00
	Ronnie Corona	10.00
	Noel Devarez	10.00
	Matt Ford	10.00
	Casey Fossum	10.00
	Brett Gray	10.00
	Reggie Griggs	10.00
	Elpidio Guzman	10.00
	Travis Hafner	40.00
	Victor Hall	10.00
	Gary Johnson	10.00
	Jim Journell	10.00
	Bob Keppel	10.00
	David Krynzel	10.00
	Ryan Ludwick	30.00
	Ryan Madson	15.00
	Deivi Mendez	10.00
	Roberto Miniel	10.00
	Greg Nash	10.00
	Miguel Olivo	10.00
	Valentino Pascucci	10.00
	Chad Petty	10.00
	Albert Pujols	600.00
	Ed Rogers	10.00
	Marvin Seale	10.00
	Steve Smyth	10.00
	Esix Snead	10.00
	Seung Song	10.00
	Rafael Soriano	15.00
	Matt Thompson	10.00
	Joe Thurston	15.00
	Luis Torres	15.00
	Miguel Villilo	10.00
	Ben Washburn	10.00
	Blake Williams	10.00
	Phil Wilson	10.00

2001 Topps Stars

ALBERT PUJOLS

		NM/M
Complete Set (200):		90.00
Common Player:		.15
Pack (6):		5.00
Box (24):		100.00
1	Darin Erstad	.25
2	Luis Gonzalez	.25
3	Rafael Furcal	.40
4	Dante Bichette	.15
5	Sammy Sosa	.75
6	Ken Griffey Jr.	1.50
7	Jim Thome	.50
8	Bobby Higginson	.15
9	Cliff Floyd	.15
10	Lance Berkman	.50
11	Eric Karros	.15
12	Jeromy Burnitz	.15
13	Jose Vidro	.15
14	Benny Agbayani	.15
15	Jorge Posada	.50
16	Ramon Hernandez	.15
17	Jason Kendall	.25
18	Jeff Kent	.25
19	John Olerud	.40
20	Al Martin	.15
21	Gerald Williams	.15
22	Gabe Kapler	.25
23	Carlos Delgado	.50
24	Mariano Rivera	.50
25	Javy Lopez	.25
26	Paul Konerko	.25
27	Daryle Ward	.15
28	Mike Lieberthal	.15
29	Tom Goodwin	.15
30	Garret Anderson	.40
31	Steve Finley	.15
32	Brian Jordan	.15
33	Nomar Garciaparra	.50
34	Ray Durham	.25
35	Sean Casey	.25
36	Kenny Lofton	.25
37	Dean Palmer	.15
38	Jeff Bagwell	.50
39	Mike Sweeney	.15
40	Adrian Beltre	.40
41	Richie Sexson	.25
42	Vladimir Guerrero	.50

#	Player	Price
43	Derek Jeter	2.00
44	Miguel Tejada	.40
45	Doug Glanville	.15
46	Brian Giles	.25
47	Marvin Benard	.15
48	Edgar Martinez	.25
49	Edgar Renteria	.15
50	Fred McGriff	.25
51	Ivan Rodriguez	.50
52	Brad Fullmer	.15
53	Antonio Alfonseca	.15
54	Tom Glavine	.50
55	Warren Morris	.15
56	Johnny Damon	.15
57	Dmitri Young	.15
58	Mo Vaughn	.15
59	Randy Johnson	.75
60	Greg Maddux	1.00
61	Carl Everett	.15
62	Magglio Ordonez	.40
63	Pokey Reese	.15
64	Todd Helton	.50
65	Preston Wilson	.15
66	Richard Hidalgo	.15
67	Jermaine Dye	.25
68	Gary Sheffield	.25
69	Geoff Jenkins	.25
70	Edgardo Alfonzo	.25
71	Paul O'Neill	.25
72	Terrence Long	.15
73	Bob Abreu	.40
74	Kevin Young	.15
75	J.T. Snow	.15
76	Alex Rodriguez	1.50
77	Jim Edmonds	.25
78	Mark McGwire	1.50
79	Tony Batista	.15
80	Darrin Fletcher	.15
81	Robb Nen	.15
82	Jose Offerman	.15
83	Travis Fryman	.25
84	Joe Randa	.15
85	Omar Vizquel	.25
86	Tim Salmon	.25
87	Andruw Jones	.40
88	Albert Belle	.15
89	Manny Ramirez	.50
90	Frank Thomas	.50
91	Barry Larkin	.40
92	Neifi Perez	.15
93	Luis Castillo	.15
94	Moises Alou	.25
95	Mark Quinn	.25
96	Kevin Brown	.25
97	Cristian Guzman	.15
98	Mike Piazza	1.00
99	Bernie Williams	.40
100	Jason Giambi	.50
101	Scott Rolen	.75
102	Phil Nevin	.15
103	Rich Aurilia	.15
104	Mike Cameron	.15
105	Fernando Vina	.15
106	Greg Vaughn	.15
107	Jose Cruz	.15
108	Raul Mondesi	.15
109	Ben Molina	.15
110	Pedro Martinez	.75
111	Todd Hollandsworth	.15
112	Jacque Jones	.15
113	Rickey Henderson	.25
114	Troy Glaus	.50
115	Chipper Jones	1.00
116	Delino DeShields	.15
117	Eric Young	.15
118	Jose Valentin	.15
119	Roberto Alomar	.40
120	Jeff Cirillo	.15
121	Mike Lowell	.25
122	Julio Lugo	.15
123	Shawn Green	.25
124	Marquis Grissom	.15
125	Matt Lawton	.15
126	Jay Payton	.15
127	David Justice	.25
128	Eric Chavez	.25
129	Pat Burrell	.50
130	Ryan Klesko	.25
131	Barry Bonds	2.00
132	Jay Buhner	.15
133	J.D. Drew	.25
134	Rafael Palmeiro	.50
135	Shannon Stewart	.15
136	Juan Gonzalez	.40
137	Tony Womack	.15
138	Carlos Lee	.25
139	Derrek Lee	.50
140	Ben Grieve	.15
141	Ron Belliard	.15
142	Stan Musial	1.50
143	Ernie Banks	1.00
144	Jim Palmer	.50
145	Tony Perez	.25
146	Duke Snider	.50
147	Rod Carew	.40
148	Warren Spahn	.75
149	Yogi Berra	.75
150	Juan Marichal	.50
151	Eric Munson	.15
152	Carlos Pena	.25
153	Joe Crede	.15
154	Ryan Anderson	.15
155	Milton Bradley	.15
156	Sean Burroughs	.15
157	Corey Patterson	.25
158	C.C. Sabathia	.40
159	Ben Petrick	.15
160	Aubrey Huff	.15

#	Player	Price
161	Gookie Dawkins	.15
162	Ben Sheets	.25
163	Pablo Ozuna	.15
164	Eric Valent	.15
165	Rod Barajas	.15
166	Chin-Feng Chen	.40
167	Josh Hamilton	.50
168	Keith Ginter	.15
169	Vernon Wells	.25
170	Dernell Stenson	.15
171	Alfonso Soriano	.75
172	Jason Marquis	.15
173	Nick Johnson	.15
174	Adam Everett	.15
175	Jimmy Rollins	.50
176	Ben Diggins	.25
177	John Lackey	.25
178	Scott Heard	.15
179	Brian Hitchcox RC	.50
180	Odanis Ayala RC	.50
181	Scott Pratt RC	.50
182	Greg Runser RC	.50
183	Chris Russ RC	.50
184	Derek Thompson	.50
185	Jason Jones RC	.50
186	Dominic Rich RC	.50
187	Chad Petty RC	.50
188	Steve Smyth RC	.50
189	Bryan Hebson RC	.50
190	Danny Borrell RC	.50
191	Bob Keppel RC	.50
192	Justin Wayne RC	1.00
193	Reggie Abercrombie RC	1.00
194	Travis Baptist RC	.50
195	Shawn Fagan RC	.50
196	Jose Reyes RC	8.00
197	Chris Bass RC	.50
198	Albert Pujols RC	40.00
199	Luis Cotto RC	.50
200	Jake Peavy RC	5.00

Game Gear Bats Autographs
Inserted 1:12,240
No pricing due to scarcity.

Game Gear Jerseys

		NM/M
	Common Player:	4.00
	Inserted 1:61	
EA	Edgardo Alfonzo	4.00
RA	Roberto Alomar	8.00
BB	Barry Bonds	25.00
LC	Luis Castillo	4.00
TG	Tony Gwynn	10.00
TH	Todd Helton	8.00
AJ	Andruw Jones	8.00
CJ	Chipper Jones	10.00
EM	Edgar Martinez	5.00
MO	Magglio Ordonez	5.00
MP	Mike Piazza	15.00
SS	Sammy Sosa	25.00
SHS	Shannon Stewart	4.00
FT	Frank Thomas	8.00
JV	Jose Vidro	4.00

Game Gear Jerseys Autographs

BARRY BONDS Outfielder

Inserted 1:19,288
No pricing due to scarcity.

Progression

		NM/M
	Complete Set (9):	10.00
	Common Player:	1.00
	Inserted 1:8	
P1	Ernie Banks, Alex Rodriguez, Felipe Lopez	3.00
P2	Yogi Berra, Ivan Rodriguez, Ramon Hernandez	2.00
P3	Tony Perez, Carlos Delgado, Eric Munson	1.00
P4	Rod Carew, Roberto Alomar, Jose Ortiz	1.00
P5	Stan Musial, Darin Erstad, Alex Escobar	2.00
P6	Jim Palmer, Kevin Brown, Kurt Ainsworth	1.00
P7	Duke Snider, Jim Edmonds, Vernon Wells	1.00
P8	Warren Spahn, Randy Johnson, Ryan Anderson	1.50
P9	Juan Marichal, Bartolo Colon, Bobby Bradley	1.00

Players Choice Award Nominees

		NM/M
	Complete Set (10):	15.00
	Common Player:	1.50

Game Gear

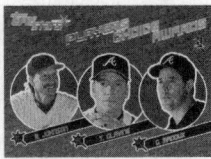

		Price
MC	Michael Cuddyer	5.00
BD	Ben Davis	5.00
JDD	J.D. Drew	5.00
ED	Erubiel Durazo	5.00
JE	Juan Encarnacion	5.00
RF	Rafael Furcal	8.00
AK	Adam Kennedy	5.00
GL	George Lombard	5.00
TL	Terrence Long	5.00
FL	Felipe Lopez	5.00
GM	Gary Mathews	5.00
CP	Corey Patterson	5.00
NP	Neifi Perez	5.00
AP	Adam Piatt	5.00
SR	Scott Rolen	15.00
FS	Fernando Seguignol	5.00
RS	Richie Sexson	10.00

Elimination
Stars: 5-10X
Production 100 Sets
Redemp. deadline 10/19/01.

Gold

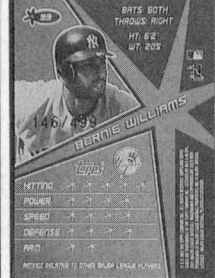

Stars: 2-5X
Production 499 Sets

Onyx
Stars: 6-12X
Rookies: 4-6X
Production 99 Sets

Autographs

		NM/M
	Common Player:	15.00
	Inserted 1:353	
EB	Ernie Banks	50.00
YB	Yogi Berra	40.00
RC	Rod Carew	30.00
CD	Carlos Delgado	15.00
TH	Todd Helton	30.00
JM	Juan Marichal	25.00
EM	Eric Munson	10.00
SM	Stan Musial	80.00
JP	Jim Palmer	25.00
TP	Tony Perez	15.00
IR	Ivan Rodriguez	25.00
DS	Duke Snider	35.00
WS	Warren Spahn	40.00

Game Gear Bats

		NM/M
	Common Player:	5.00
	Inserted 1:187	
AB	Adrian Beltre	5.00
LB	Lance Berkman	6.00
SB	Sean Burroughs	5.00

Topps Stars Game Gear

		Price
	Inserted 1:12	
1	Barry Bonds, Carlos Delgado, Todd Helton	4.00
2	Gary Sheffield, Eric Davis, Turk Wendell	1.50
3	Alex Rodriguez, Carlos Delgado, Frank Thomas	3.00
4	David Wells, Pedro Martinez, Andy Pettitte	2.00
5	Mark Quinn, Terrence Long, Kazuhiro Sasaki	1.50
6	Jay Buhner, Frank Thomas, Bobby Higginson	1.50
7	Barry Bonds, Todd Helton, Jeff Kent	4.00
8	Tom Glavine, Randy Johnson, Greg Maddux	2.50
9	Rick Ankiel, Rafael Furcal, Jay Payton	1.50
10	Moises Alou, Andres Galarraga, Jeff D'Amico	1.50

Player Choice Awards Relics

		NM/M
	Common Player:	10.00
	Inserted 1:1,530	
1	Carlos Delgado	15.00
2	Eric Davis	10.00
3	Carlos Delgado	15.00
4	Pedro Martinez	25.00
5	Terrence Long	10.00
6	Frank Thomas	20.00
7	Todd Helton	15.00
8	Randy Johnson	25.00
9	Rafael Furcal	15.00
10	Andres Galarraga	10.00

2001 Topps Tribute

OAKLAND ATHLETICS
FINGERS 34

		NM/M
	Complete Set (90):	200.00
	Common Player:	2.00
	Pack (3):	75.00
	Box (6):	425.00
1	Pee Wee Reese	2.00
2	Babe Ruth	15.00
3	Ralph Kiner	2.00
4	Brooks Robinson	5.00
5	Don Sutton	2.00
6	Carl Yastrzemski	8.00
7	Roger Maris	10.00
8	Andre Dawson	2.00
9	Luis Aparicio	2.00
10	Wade Boggs	4.00
11	Johnny Bench	8.00
12	Ernie Banks	6.00
13	Thurman Munson	5.00
14	Harmon Killebrew	5.00
15	Ted Kluszewski	2.00
16	Bob Feller	3.00
17	Mike Schmidt	10.00
18	Warren Spahn	4.00
19	Jim Palmer	3.00
20	Don Mattingly	12.00
21	Willie Mays	10.00
22	Gil Hodges	2.00
23	Juan Marichal	3.00
24	Robin Yount	4.00
25	Nolan Ryan	12.00
26	Dave Winfield	4.00
27	Hank Greenberg	4.00
28	Honus Wagner	8.00
29	Nolan Ryan	12.00
30	Phil Niekro	2.00
31	Robin Roberts	2.00
32	Casey Stengel	3.00
33	Willie McCovey	2.00
34	Roy Campanella	4.00
35	Rollie Fingers	2.00
36	Tom Seaver	5.00
37	Jackie Robinson	10.00
38	Hank Aaron	10.00
39	Bob Gibson	4.00
40	Carlton Fisk	4.00
41	Hank Aaron	10.00
42	George Brett	10.00
43	Orlando Cepeda	2.00
44	Red Schoendienst	2.00
45	Don Drysdale	4.00
46	Mel Ott	4.00
47	Casey Stengel	3.00
48	Al Kaline	4.00
49	Reggie Jackson	5.00
50	Tony Perez	2.00
51	Ozzie Smith	6.00
52	Billy Martin	4.00
53	Bill Dickey	2.00
54	Catfish Hunter	2.00
55	Duke Snider	4.00
56	Dale Murphy	2.00
57	Bobby Doerr	2.00
58	Earl Averill	2.00
59	Carlton Fisk	4.00
60	Tom Lasorda	2.00
61	Lou Gehrig	12.00
62	Enos Slaughter	2.00
63	Jim Bunning	2.00
64	Rollie Fingers	2.00
65	Frank Robinson	4.00
66	Earl Weaver	2.00
67	Eddie Mathews	5.00
68	Kirby Puckett	5.00
69	Phil Rizzuto	4.00
70	Lou Brock	4.00
71	Walt Alston	2.00
72	Bill Pierce	2.00
73	Joe Morgan	4.00
74	Roberto Clemente	12.00
75	Whitey Ford	4.00
76	Richie Ashburn	2.00
77	Elston Howard	2.00
78	Gary Carter	2.00
79	Carl Hubbell	2.00
80	Yogi Berra	6.00
81	Ken Boyer	2.00
82	Nolan Ryan	12.00
83	Bill Mazeroski	2.00
84	Dizzy Dean	4.00
85	Nellie Fox	2.00
86	Stan Musial	10.00
87	Steve Carlton	4.00
88	Willie Stargell	4.00
89	Hal Newhouser	2.00
90	Frank Robinson	4.00

Franchise Figures

		NM/M
	Inserted 1:34	
AL	Walt Alston, Tommy Lasorda	50.00
AFF	Luis Aparicio, Nellie Fox, Carlton Fisk	125.00
BPKR	Johnny Bench, Tony Perez, Ted Kluszewski, Frank Robinson, Joe Morgan	150.00
CD	Gary Carter, Andre Dawson	40.00
HDB	Bill Dickey, Elston Howard, Yogi Berra	150.00
FY	Carlton Fisk, Carl Yastrzemski	150.00
HSS	Gil Hodges, Casey Stengel, Tom Seaver	150.00
JM	Reggie Jackson, Billy Martin	125.00
KG	Al Kaline, Hank Greenberg	150.00
MMC	Willie Mays, Willie McCovey, Orlando Cepeda	200.00
MCS	Bill Mazeroski, Roberto Clemente, Willie Stargell	185.00
MM	Thurman Munson, Don Mattingly	200.00
MMA	Dale Murphy, Ed Mathews, Hank Aaron	185.00
PK	Kirby Puckett, Harmon Killebrew	100.00
RSC	Pee Wee Reese, Duke Snider, Roy Campanella	160.00
RR	Brooks Robinson, Frank Robinson	75.00
RG	Babe Ruth, Lou Gehrig	500.00
SAC	Mike Schmidt, Richie Ashburn, Steve Carlton	125.00
SBSM	Ozzie Smith, Lou Brock, Red Schoendienst, Stan Musial	125.00

Game-Used Bat Relics

Lou Gehrig

		NM/M
	Common Player:	20.00
	Inserted 1:2	
HA	Hank Aaron	50.00
LA	Luis Aparicio	20.00
RA	Richie Ashburn	25.00
KB	Ken Boyer	20.00
GB	George Brett	40.00
LB	Lou Brock	20.00
RC	Roy Campanella	30.00
RCL	Roberto Clemente	80.00
CF	Carlton Fisk	25.00
LG	Lou Gehrig	160.00
HG	Hank Greenberg	50.00
GH	Gil Hodges	25.00
RJ	Reggie Jackson	30.00
AK	Al Kaline	30.00
HK	Harmon Killebrew	30.00
RM	Roger Maris	50.00
BM	Billy Martin	20.00
DM	Don Mattingly	50.00
WM	Willie McCovey	25.00
TM	Thurman Munson	35.00
PWR	Pee Wee Reese	20.00
BRO	Brooks Robinson	30.00
FRR	Frank Robinson	30.00
BR	Babe Ruth	200.00
OS	Ozzie Smith	35.00
CS	Casey Stengel	20.00
HW	Honus Wagner	200.00
CY	Carl Yastrzemski	40.00

Game-Worn Patch And Number Relics

MATHEWS 41

		NM/M
	Common Player:	60.00
	Inserted 1:61	
WA	Walt Alston	60.00
JB	Johnny Bench	180.00
YB	Yogi Berra	150.00
WB	Wade Boggs	80.00
LB	Lou Brock	60.00
BD	Bill Dickey	150.00
BDO	Bobby Doerr	100.00
HK	Harmon Killebrew	250.00
TL	Tom Lasorda	80.00
JM	Juan Marichal	75.00
EM	Eddie Mathews	150.00
KB	Kirby Puckett	250.00
NR	Nolan Ryan	300.00
MS	Mike Schmidt	250.00
RS	Red Schoendienst	80.00
DW	Dave Winfield	80.00
CY	Carl Yastrzemski	200.00
RY	Robin Yount	100.00

Retired Game-Worn Relics

Bill Dickey

		NM/M
	Common Player:	20.00
	Inserted 1:2	
WA	Walt Alston	20.00
EB	Ernie Banks	30.00
EBA	Ernie Banks	30.00
JB	Johnny Bench	30.00
YB	Yogi Berra	30.00
WB	Wade Boggs	20.00
GB	George Brett	50.00
LB	Lou Brock	25.00
SC	Steve Carlton	25.00
DD	Dizzy Dean	40.00
BD	Bill Dickey	25.00
BDO	Bobby Doerr	25.00
NF	Nellie Fox	20.00
HK	Harmon Killebrew	30.00
TL	Tom Lasorda	20.00
JMG	Juan Marichal	30.00

EM	Eddie Mathews	30.00
DM	Don Mattingly	50.00
WMF	Willie Mays	75.00
WMW	Willie Mays	75.00
SM	Stan Musial	75.00
JP	Jim Palmer	20.00
KP	Kirby Puckett	30.00
FR	Frank Robinson	25.00
NRA	Nolan Ryan	80.00
NRH	Nolan Ryan	80.00
NRR	Nolan Ryan	80.00
MSB	Mike Schmidt	50.00
MSW	Mike Schmidt	50.00
RS	Red Schoendienst	20.00
WST	Willie Stargell	20.00
CS	Casey Stengel	20.00
DW	Dave Winfield	20.00
CY	Carl Yastrzemski/White	40.00
CYA	Carl Yastrzemski/Gray	40.00
RY	Robin Yount	30.00

Frank Robinson Dual Relic
NM/M
Inserted 1:860
FR-RO Frank Robinson ... 90.00

Nolan Ryan Tri-Relic

NM/M
Randomly inserted.
NR Nolan Ryan ... 475.00

Casey Stengel Dual Relic

NM/M
Inserted 1:860
CS Casey Stengel ... 100.00

Vintage Buy-Back Cards
No pricing due to scarcity.

2001 Topps/Post Collector's Series

FIRST BASE
MARK McGWIRE

Baseball cards returned to boxes of Post cereals in 2001 with a special edition of Topps cards. The baseball cards were issued two per cello pack along with an introductory "pass" to the cereal company's web site for kids. The top card in each pack was visible through a window cut in the specially marked cereal boxes. The 2-1/2" x 3-1/2" cards have game-action photos which are borderless at the top and sides. At bottom are color strips with the player's position and name. A team logo in the lower-left corner of the photo and the Topps 50th anniversary logo is at upper-left. Backs have a portrait photo, facsimile autograph, biographical data, recent stats and various league, and sponsor logos.

NM/M
Complete Set (18): ... 10.00

Common Player:		.25
1	Alex Rodriguez	1.50
2	Barry Bonds	2.00
3	Bernie Williams	.35
4	Frank Thomas	.75
5	Greg Maddux	1.00
6	Mark McGwire	1.50
7	Manny Ramirez	.75
8	Orlando Hernandez	.25
9	Pedro Martinez	.60
10	Gary Sheffield	.45
11	Jermaine Dye	.25
12	Mike Piazza	1.50
13	Barry Larkin	.25
14	Brad Radke	.25
15	Ivan Rodriguez	.60
16	Moises Alou	.25
17	Tony Gwynn	1.00
18	Todd Helton	.75

2001 Topps/Post 500 Home Run Club

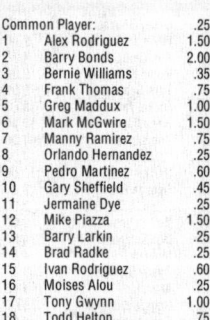

WILLIE McCOVEY
INDUCTED IN 1986
521 CAREER HOME RUNS

Baseball cards returned to boxes of Post cereals in 2001 with a special edition of Topps cards. The baseball cards were issued two per cello pack. The top card in each pack was visible through a window cut in the specially marked cereal boxes. The 2-1/2" x 3-1/2" cards have player photos in a white diamond on a wood-look background. Player name is in a red strip below. At center-left is a Hall of Fame logo, with a 500 Home Run Club logo opposite. The Topps 50th anniversary logo is at upper-left. Backs have complete major league stats, biographical data and various league and sponsor logos.

NM/M
Complete Set (8): ... 7.50

Common Player:		1.00
1	Babe Ruth	2.00
2	Ernie Banks	1.50
3	Jimmie Foxx	1.00
4	Willie McCovey	1.00
5	Frank Robinson	1.00
6	Harmon Killebrew	1.00
7	Mike Schmidt	1.50
8	Reggie Jackson	1.50

2002 Topps Promos

SAMMY SOSA

Topps previewed the format of its 2002 base set with a three-card promo issue.

NM/M
Complete Set (3): ... 6.00
Common Player: ... 2.00
P1 Sammy Sosa ... 3.00
P2 Jason Giambi ... 2.00
P3 Curt Schilling ... 2.00

2002 Topps

TODD HELTON

NM/M
Complete Set (718): ... 70.00
Complete Factory Set (723): ... 80.00
Complete Series 1 (365): ... 35.00
Complete Series 2 (354): ... 35.00
Common Player: ... .10
Pack (10): ... 1.50
Box (36): ... 40.00
1 Pedro Martinez ... .50

2	Mike Stanton	.10
3	Brad Penny	.10
4	Mike Matheny	.10
5	Johnny Damon	.20
6	Bret Boone	.20
7	Not Issued (Retired)	.10
8	Chris Truby	.10
9	B.J. Surhoff	.10
10	Mike Hampton	.10
11	Juan Pierre	.10
12	Mark Buehrle	.10
13	Bob Abreu	.20
14	David Cone	.10
15	Aaron Sele	.10
16	Fernando Tatis	.10
17	Bobby Jones	.10
18	Rick Helling	.10
19	Dmitri Young	.10
20	Mike Mussina	.40
21	Mike Sweeney	.10
22	Cristian Guzman	.10
23	Ryan Kohlmeier	.10
24	Adam Kennedy	.10
25	Larry Walker	.25
26	Eric Davis	.10
27	Jason Tyner	.10
28	Eric Young	.10
29	Jason Marquis	.10
30	Luis Gonzalez	.20
31	Kevin Tapani	.10
32	Orlando Cabrera	.10
33	Marty Cordova	.10
34	Brad Ausmus	.10
35	Livan Hernandez	.10
36	Alex Gonzalez	.10
37	Edgar Renteria	.20
38	Bengie Molina	.10
39	Frank Menechino	.10
40	Rafael Palmeiro	.40
41	Brad Fullmer	.10
42	Julio Zuleta	.10
43	Darren Dreifort	.10
44	Trot Nixon	.10
45	Trevor Hoffman	.10
46	Vladimir Nunez	.10
47	Mark Kotsay	.10
48	Kenny Rogers	.10
49	Ben Petrick	.10
50	Jeff Bagwell	.40
51	Juan Encarnacion	.10
52	Ramiro Mendoza	.10
53	Brian Meadows	.10
54	Chad Curtis	.10
55	Aramis Ramirez	.25
56	Mark McLemore	.10
57	Dante Bichette	.10
58	Scott Schoeneweis	.10
59	Jose Cruz Jr.	.10
60	Roger Clemens	1.00
61	Jose Guillen	.10
62	Darren Oliver	.10
63	Chris Reitsma	.10
64	Jeff Abbott	.10
65	Robin Ventura	.10
66	Denny Neagle	.10
67	Al Martin	.10
68	Benito Santiago	.10
69	Roy Oswalt	.20
70	Juan Gonzalez	.40
71	Garret Anderson	.25
72	Bobby Bonilla	.10
73	Danny Bautista	.10
74	J.T. Snow Jr.	.10
75	Derek Jeter	1.50
76	John Olerud	.10
77	Kevin Appier	.10
78	Phil Nevin	.20
79	Sean Casey	.20
80	Troy Glaus	.40
81	Joe Randa	.10
82	Jose Valentin	.10
83	Ricky Bottalico	.10
84	Todd Zeile	.10
85	Barry Larkin	.10
86	Bob Wickman	.10
87	Jeff Shaw	.10
88	Greg Vaughn	.10
89	Fernando Vina	.10
90	Mark Mulder	.25
91	Paul Bako	.10
92	Aaron Boone	.10
93	Esteban Loaiza	.10
94	Richie Sexson	.40
95	Alfonso Soriano	.50
96	Tony Womack	.10
97	Paul Shuey	.10
98	Melvin Mora	.10
99	Tony Gwynn	.50

100	Vladimir Guerrero	.50
101	Keith Osik	.10
102	Randy Velarde	.10
103	Scott Williamson	.10
104	Daryle Ward	.10
105	Doug Mientkiewicz	.10
106	Stan Javier	.10
107	Russ Ortiz	.10
108	Wade Miller	.10
109	Luke Prokopec	.10
110	Andruw Jones	.40
111	Ron Coomer	.10
112	Dan Wilson	.10
113	Luis Castillo	.10
114	Derek Bell	.10
115	Gary Sheffield	.20
116	Ruben Rivera	.10
117	Paul O'Neill	.20
118	Craig Paquette	.10
119	Chris Michalak	.10
120	Brad Radke	.10
121	Jorge Fabregas	.10
122	Randy Winn	.10
123	Tom Goodwin	.10
124	Jaret Wright	.10
125	Manny Ramirez	.40
126	Al Leiter	.20
127	Ben Davis	.10
128	Frank Catalanotto	.10
129	Jose Cabrera	.10
130	Magglio Ordonez	.20
131	Jose Macias	.10
132	Ted Lilly	.10
133	Chris Holt	.10
134	Eric Milton	.10
135	Shannon Stewart	.10
136	Omar Olivares	.10
137	David Segui	.10
138	Jeff Nelson	.10
139	Matt Williams	.25
140	Ellis Burks	.10
141	Jason Bere	.10
142	Jimmy Haynes	.10
143	Ramon Hernandez	.10
144	Craig Counsell (Front photo actually Greg Colbrunn)	.10
145	John Smoltz	.10
146	Homer Bush	.10
147	Quilvio Veras	.10
148	Esteban Yan	.10
149	Ramon Ortiz	.10
150	Carlos Delgado	.30
151	Lee Stevens	.10
152	Wil Cordero	.10
153	Mike Bordick	.10
154	John Flaherty	.10
155	Omar Daal	.10
156	Todd Ritchie	.10
157	Carl Everett	.10
158	Scott Sullivan	.10
159	Deivi Cruz	.10
160a	Albert Pujols (Back photo is Placido Polanco) (In cap.)	1.00
160b	Albert Pujols (Back photo corrected)(No cap.)	10.00
161	Royce Clayton	.10
162	Jeff Suppan	.10
163	C.C. Sabathia	.10
164	Jimmy Rollins	.25
165	Rickey Henderson	.25
166	Rey Ordonez	.10
167	Shawn Estes	.10
168	Reggie Sanders	.10
169	Jon Lieber	.10
170	Armando Benitez	.10
171	Mike Remlinger	.10
172	Billy Wagner	.10
173	Troy Percival	.10
174	Devon White	.10
175	Ivan Rodriguez	.40
176	Dustin Hermanson	.10
177	Brian Anderson	.10
178	Graeme Lloyd	.10
179	Russ Branyan	.10
180	Bobby Higginson	.10
181	Alex Gonzalez	.10
182	John Franco	.10
183	Sidney Ponson	.10
184	Jose Mesa	.10
185	Todd Hollandsworth	.10
186	Kevin Young	.10
187	Tim Wakefield	.10
188	Craig Biggio	.20
189	Jason Isringhausen	.10
190	Mark Quinn	.10
191	Glendon Rusch	.10
192	Damian Miller	.10
193	Sandy Alomar	.10
194	Scott Brosius	.10
195	Dave Martinez	.10
196	Danny Graves	.10
197	Shea Hillenbrand	.10
198	Jimmy Anderson	.10
199	Travis Lee	.10
200	Randy Johnson	.50
201	Carlos Beltran	.25
202	Jerry Hairston Jr.	.10
203	Jesus Sanchez	.10
204	Eddie Taubensee	.10
205	David Wells	.10
206	Russ Davis	.10
207	Michael Barrett	.10
208	Marquis Grissom	.10
209	Byung-Hyun Kim	.10
210	Hideo Nomo	.25
211	Ryan Rupe	.10
212	Ricky Gutierrez	.10

213	Darryl Kile	.10
214	Rico Brogna	.10
215	Terrence Long	.10
216	Mike Jackson	.10
217	Jamey Wright	.10
218	Adrian Beltre	.20
219	Benny Agbayani	.10
220	Chuck Knoblauch	.10
221	Randy Wolf	.10
222	Andy Ashby	.10
223	Corey Koskie	.10
224	Roger Cedeno	.10
225	Ichiro Suzuki	1.00
226	Keith Foulke	.10
227	Ryan Minor	.10
228	Shawon Dunston	.10
229	Alex Cora	.10
230	Jeromy Burnitz	.10
231	Mark Grace	.25
232	Aubrey Huff	.10
233	Jeffrey Hammonds	.10
234	Olmedo Saenz	.10
235	Brian Jordan	.10
236	Jeremy Giambi	.10
237	Joe Girardi	.10
238	Eric Gagne	.25
239	Masato Yoshii	.10
240	Greg Maddux	.75
241	Bryan Rekar	.10
242	Ray Durham	.10
243	Torii Hunter	.20
244	Derek Lee	.10
245	Jim Edmonds	.25
246	Einar Diaz	.10
247	Brian Bohanon	.10
248	Ron Belliard	.10
249	Mike Lowell	.20
250	Sammy Sosa	1.00
251	Richard Hidalgo	.10
252	Bartolo Colon	.10
253	Jorge Posada	.25
254	LaTroy Hawkins	.10
255	Paul LoDuca	.10
256	Carlos Febles	.10
257	Nelson Cruz	.10
258	Edgardo Alfonzo	.10
259	Joey Hamilton	.10
260	Cliff Floyd	.10
261	Wes Helms	.10
262	Jay Bell	.10
263	Mike Cameron	.10
264	Paul Konerko	.10
265	Jeff Kent	.20
266	Robert Fick	.10
267	Allen Levrault	.10
268	Placido Polanco	.10
269	Marlon Anderson	.10
270	Mariano Rivera	.20
271	Chan Ho Park	.10
272	Jose Vizcaino	.10
273	Jeff D'Amico	.10
274	Mark Gardner	.10
275	Travis Fryman	.10
276	Darren Lewis	.10
277	Bruce Bochy	.10
278	Jerry Manuel	.10
279	Bob Brenly	.10
280	Don Baylor	.10
281	Davey Lopes	.10
282	Jerry Narron	.10
283	Tony Muser	.10
284	Hal McRae	.10
285	Bobby Cox	.10
286	Larry Dierker	.10
287	Phil Garner	.10
288	Jimy Williams	.10
289	Bobby Valentine	.10
290	Dusty Baker	.10
291	Lloyd McLendon	.10
292	Mike Scioscia	.10
293	Buck Martinez	.10
294	Larry Bowa	.10
295	Tony LaRussa	.10
296	Jeff Torborg	.10
297	Tom Kelly	.10
298	Mike Hargrove	.10
299	Art Howe	.10
300	Lou Pinella	.10
301	Charlie Manuel	.10
302	Buddy Bell	.10
303	Tony Perez	.10
304	Bob Boone	.10
305	Joe Torre	.25
306	Jim Tracy	.10
307	Jason Lane	.10
308	Chris George	.10
309	Hank Blalock	.25
310	Joe Borchard	.10
311	Marlon Byrd	.10
312	Raymond Cabrera RC	.10
313	Freddy Sanchez RC	.40
314	Scott Wiggins RC	.40
315	Jason Maule RC	.30
316	Dionys Cesar RC	.40
317	Boof Bonser RC	.10
318	Juan Tolentino RC	.40
319	Earl Snyder RC	.10
320	Travis Wade RC	.25
321	Napoleon Calzado RC	.10
322	Eric Glaser RC	.40
323	Craig Kuzmic RC	.10
324	Nic Jackson RC	.50
325	Mike Rivera RC	.10
326	Jason Bay RC	1.00
327	Chris Smith	.10
328	Jake Gautreau	.10
329	Gabe Gross	.10
330	Kenny Baugh	.10

331	J.D. Martin	.10
332	Barry Bonds	1.00
333	Rickey Henderson	.25
334	Bud Smith	.10
335	Rickey Henderson	.25
336	Barry Bonds	1.00
337	Ichiro Suzuki, Jason Giambi, Roberto Alomar	.50
338	Alex Rodriguez, Ichiro Suzuki, Bret Boone	.50
339	Alex Rodriguez, Jim Thome, Rafael Palmeiro	.40
340	Bret Boone, Juan Gonzalez, Alex Rodriguez	.40
341	Freddy Garcia, Mike Mussina, Joe Mays	.15
342	Hideo Nomo, Mike Mussina, Roger Clemens	.40
343	Larry Walker, Todd Helton, Moises Alou	.25
344	Sammy Sosa, Todd Helton, Barry Bonds	.40
345	Barry Bonds, Sammy Sosa, Luis Gonzalez	.40
346	Sammy Sosa, Todd Helton, Luis Gonzalez	.40
347	Curt Schilling, Randy Johnson, John Burkett	.20
348	Randy Johnson, Curt Schilling, Chan Ho Park	.20
349	Seattle Mariners	.25
350	Oakland A's	.10
351	New York Yankees	.50
352	Cleveland Indians	.10
353	Arizona Diamondbacks	.10
354	Atlanta Braves	.10
355	St. Louis Cardinals	.10
356	Houston Astros	.10
357	D'backs vs. Rockies	.10
358	Mets vs. Pirates	.10
359	Braves vs. Phillies	.10
360	D'backs vs. Phillies	.10
361	Yankees vs. White Sox	.10
362	Cubs vs. Reds	.10
363	Angels vs. Mariners	.10
364	Astros vs. Giants	.10
365	Barry Bonds Race to 70 #1	10.00
365	Barry Bonds HR #2-69	8.00
365	Barry Bonds HR #70	15.00
365	Barry Bonds HR #71	10.00
365	Barry Bonds HR #72	10.00
365	Barry Bonds HR #73	50.00
366	Pat Meares	.10
367	Mike Lieberthal	.10
368	Scott Erickson	.10
369	Ron Gant	.10
370	Moises Alou	.25
371	Chad Kreuter	.10
372	Willis Roberts	.10
373	Toby Hall	.10
374	Miguel Batista	.10
375	John Burkett	.10
376	Cory Lidle	.10
377	Nick Neugebauer	.10
378	Jay Payton	.10
379	Steve Karsay	.10
380	Eric Chavez	.20
381	Kelly Stinnett	.10
382	Jarrod Washburn	.10
383	C.J. Nitkowski	.10
384	Jeff Conine	.10
385	Fred McGriff	.10
386	Marvin Benard	.10
387	Dave Burba	.10
388	Dennis Cook	.10
389	Rick Reed	.10
390	Tom Glavine	.25
391	Rondell White	.15
392	Matt Morris	.10
393	Pat Rapp	.10
394	Robert Person	.10
395	Omar Vizquel	.15
396	Jeff Cirillo	.10
397	Dave Mlicki	.10
398	Jose Ortiz	.10
399	Ryan Dempster	.10
400	Curt Schilling	.25
401	Peter Bergeron	.10
402	Kyle Lohse	.10
403	Craig Wilson	.10
404	David Justice	.20
405	Darin Erstad	.20
406	Jose Mercedes	.10
407	Carl Pavano	.10
408	Albie Lopez	.10
409	Alex Ochoa	.10
410	Chipper Jones	.50
411	Tyler Houston	.10
412	Dean Palmer	.10
413	Damian Jackson	.10
414	Josh Towers	.10
415	Rafael Furcal	.20
416	Ken Caminiti	.10
417	Herb Perry	.10
418	Mike Sirotka	.10
419	Mark Wohlers	.10
420	Nomar Garciaparra	1.00
421	Felipe Lopez	.10
422	Joe McEwing	.10
423	Jacque Jones	.10
424	Julio Franco	.10
425	Frank Thomas	.40
426	So Taguchi RC	.50
427	Kazuhisa Ishii RC	.40
428	D'Angelo Jimenez	.10

Base Checklist

#	Player	$	#	Player	$	#	Player	$
429	Chris Stynes	.10	547	Bubba Trammell	.10	665	San Francisco Giants	.10
430	Kerry Wood	.50	548	Scott Elarton	.10	666	Seattle Mariners	.10
431	Chris Singleton	.10	549	Mike Darr	.10	667	St. Louis Cardinals	.10
432	Erubiel Durazo	.10	550	Ken Griffey Jr.	1.00	668	Tampa Bay Devil Rays	.10
433	Matt Lawton	.10	551	Ugueth Urbina	.10	669	Texas Rangers	.10
434	Bill Mueller	.10	552	Todd Jones	.10	670	Toronto Blue Jays	.10
435	Jose Canseco	.25	553	Delino DeShields	.10	671	Juan Cruz	.25
436	Ben Grieve	.10	554	Adam Piatt	.10	672	Kevin Cash RC	.50
437	Terry Mulholland	.10	555	Jason Kendall	.10	673	Jimmy Gobble RC	.75
438	David Bell	.10	556	Hector Ortiz	.10	674	Mike Hill RC	.40
439	A.J. Pierzynski	.10	557	Turk Wendell	.10	675	Taylor Buchholz RC	.40
440	Adam Dunn	.40	558	Rob Bell	.10	676	Bill Hall	.10
441	Jon Garland	.10	559	Sun-Woo Kim	.10	677	Brett Roneberg RC	.40
442	Jeff Fassero	.10	560	Raul Mondesi	.10	678	Royce Huffman RC	.40
443	Julio Lugo	.10	561	Brent Abernathy	.10	679	Chris Tritle RC	.40
444	Carlos Guillen	.10	562	Seth Etherton	.10	680	Nate Espy RC	.40
445	Orlando Hernandez	.20	563	Shawn Wooten	.10	681	Nick Alvarez RC	.50
446	Mark Loretta	.10	564	Jay Buhner	.10	682	Jason Botts RC	.40
447	Scott Spiezio	.10	565	Andres Galarraga	.10	683	Ryan Gripp RC	.50
448	Kevin Millwood	.20	566	Shane Reynolds	.10	684	Dan Phillips RC	.50
449	Jamie Moyer	.10	567	Rod Beck	.10	685	Pablo Arias RC	.50
450	Todd Helton	.40	568	Dee Brown	.10	686	John Rodriguez RC	.40
451	Todd Walker	.10	569	Pedro Feliz	.10	687	Rich Harden RC	1.00
452	Jose Lima	.10	570	Ryan Klesko	.10	688	Neal Frendling RC	.50
453	Brook Fordyce	.10	571	John Vander Wal	.10	689	Rich Thompson RC	.40
454	Aaron Rowand	.10	572	Nick Bierbrodt	.10	690	Greg Montalbano RC	.40
455	Barry Zito	.20	573	Joe Nathan	.10	691	Leonard Dinardo RC	.40
456	Eric Owens	.10	574	James Baldwin	.10	692	Ryan Raburn RC	.40
457	Charles Nagy	.10	575	J.D. Drew	.20	693	Josh Barfield	.25
458	Raul Ibanez	.10	576	Greg Colbrunn	.10	694	David Bacani RC	.40
459	Joe Mays	.10	577	Doug Glanville	.10	695	Dan Johnson RC	.50
460	Jim Thome	.50	578	Rey Sanchez	.10	696	Mike Mussina (Gold Glove Award Winners)	.25
461	Adam Eaton	.10	579	Todd Van Poppel	.10	697	Ivan Rodriguez (Gold Glove Award Winners)	.25
462	Felix Martinez	.10	580	Rich Aurilia	.10	698	Doug Mientkiewicz (Gold Glove Award Winners)	.10
463	Vernon Wells	.10	581	Chuck Finley	.10	699	Roberto Alomar (Gold Glove Award Winners)	.25
464	Donnie Sadler	.10	582	Abraham Nunez	.10	700	Eric Chavez (Gold Glove Award Winners)	.15
465	Tony Clark	.10	583	Kenny Lofton	.20	701	Omar Vizquel (Gold Glove Award Winners)	.10
466	Jose Hernandez	.10	584	Brian Daubach	.10	702	Mike Cameron (Gold Glove Award Winners)	.10
467	Ramon Martinez	.10	585	Miguel Tejada	.25	703	Torii Hunter (Gold Glove Award Winners)	.10
468	Rusty Greer	.10	586	Nate Cornejo	.10	704	Ichiro Suzuki (Gold Glove Award Winners)	.50
469	Rod Barajas	.10	587	Kazuhiro Sasaki	.15	705	Greg Maddux (Gold Glove Award Winners)	.50
470	Lance Berkman	.25	588	Chris Richard	.10	706	Brad Ausmus (Gold Glove Award Winners)	.10
471	Brady Anderson	.10	589	Armando Reynoso	.10	707	Todd Helton (Gold Glove Award Winners)	.25
472	Pedro Astacio	.10	590	Tim Hudson	.20	708	Fernando Vina (Gold Glove Award Winners)	.10
473	Shane Halter	.10	591	Neifi Perez	.10	709	Scott Rolen (Gold Glove Award Winners)	.40
474	Bret Prinz	.10	592	Steve Cox	.10	710	Orlando Cabrera (Gold Glove Award Winners)	.15
475	Edgar Martinez	.20	593	Henry Blanco	.10	711	Andruw Jones (Gold Glove Award Winners)	.15
476	Steve Trachsel	.10	594	Ricky Ledee	.10	712	Jim Edmonds (Gold Glove Award Winners)	.15
477	Gary Matthews Jr.	.10	595	Tim Salmon	.20	713	Larry Walker (Gold Glove Award Winners)	.15
478	Ismael Valdes	.10	596	Luis Rivas	.10	714	Roger Clemens (Cy Young Award Winners)	.50
479	Juan Uribe	.10	597	Jeff Zimmerman	.10	715	Randy Johnson (Cy Young Award Winners)	.25
480	Shawn Green	.20	598	Matt Stairs	.10	716	Ichiro Suzuki (MVP Award Winners)	.50
481	Kirk Rueter	.10	599	Preston Wilson	.10	717	Barry Bonds (MVP Award Winners)	.75
482	Damion Easley	.10	600	Mark McGwire	1.50	718	Ichiro Suzuki (ROY Award Winners)	.50
483	Chris Carpenter	.10	601	Timo Perez	.10	719	Albert Pujols (ROY Award Winners)	.50
484	Kris Benson	.10	602	Matt Anderson	.10			
485	Antonio Alfonseca	.10	603	Todd Hundley	.10		**Gold**	
486	Kyle Farnsworth	.10	604	Rick Ankiel	.25		NM/M	
487	Brandon Lyon	.10	605	Tsuyoshi Shinjo	.10		Complete Set (659):	700.00
488	Hideki Irabu	.10	606	Woody Williams	.10		Stars:	5-10X
489	David Ortiz	.25	607	Jason LaRue	.10		Production 2,002 Sets	
490	Mike Piazza	1.00	608	Carlos Lee	.10			
491	Derek Lowe	.10	609	Russ Johnson	.10		**2002 Topps Limited**	
492	Chris Gomez	.10	610	Scott Rolen	.50		NM/M	
493	Mark Johnson	.10	611	Brent Mayne	.10		Complete Set (790):	165.00
494	John Rocker	.10	612	Darrin Fletcher	.10		Includes all 73 B. Bonds #365 HR cards.	
495	Eric Karros	.10	613	Ray Lankford	.10			
496	Bill Haselman	.10	614	Troy O'Leary	.10		**Aces**	
497	Dave Veres	.10	615	Javier Lopez	.20		NM/M	
498	Gil Heredia	.10	616	Randy Velarde	.10		Common Player:	10.00
499	Tomokazu Ohka	.10	617	Vinny Castilla	.10		Inserted 1:1,180	
500	Barry Bonds	1.50	618	Milton Bradley	.10	MH	Mike Hampton	.10
501	David Dellucci	.10	619	Ruben Mateo	.10	RJ	Randy Johnson	20.00
502	Ed Sprague	.10	620	Jason Giambi	.40	GM	Greg Maddux	30.00
503	Tom Gordon	.10	621	Andy Benes	.10			
504	Javier Vazquez	.10	622	Tony Eusebio	.10			
505	Ben Sheets	.25	623	Andy Pettitte	.20			
506	Wilton Guerrero	.10	624	Jose Offerman	.10			
507	John Halama	.10	625	Mo Vaughn	.20			
508	Mark Redman	.10	626	Steve Sparks	.10			
509	Jack Wilson	.10	627	Mike Matthews	.10			
510	Bernie Williams	.40	628	Robb Nen	.10			
511	Miguel Cairo	.10	629	Kip Wells	.10			
512	Denny Hocking	.10	630	Kevin Brown	.20			
513	Tony Batista	.10	631	Arthur Rhodes	.10			
514	Mark Grudzielanek	.10	632	Gabe Kapler	.10			
515	Jose Vidro	.10	633	Jermaine Dye	.10			
516	Sterling Hitchcock	.10	634	Josh Beckett	.25			
517	Billy Koch	.10	635	Pokey Reese	.10			
518	Matt Clement	.10	636	Benji Gil	.10			
519	Bruce Chen	.10	637	Marcus Giles	.10			
520	Roberto Alomar	.40	638	Julian Tavarez	.10			
521	Orlando Palmeiro	.10	639	Jason Schmidt	.25			
522	Steve Finley	.10	640	Alex Rodriguez	1.25			
523	Danny Patterson	.10	641	Anaheim Angels	.10			
524	Terry Adams	.10	642	Arizona Diamondbacks	.10			
525	Tino Martinez	.10	643	Atlanta Braves	.10			
526	Tony Armas Jr.	.10	644	Baltimore Orioles	.10			
527	Geoff Jenkins	.20	645	Boston Red Sox	.10			
528	Chris Michalak	.10	646	Chicago Cubs	.10			
529	Corey Patterson	.20	647	Chicago White Sox	.10			
530	Brian Giles	.20	648	Cincinnati Reds	.10			
531	Jose Jimenez	.10	649	Cleveland Indians	.10			
532	Joe Kennedy	.10	650	Colorado Rockies	.10			
533	Armando Rios	.10	651	Detroit Tigers	.10			
534	Osvaldo Fernandez	.10	652	Florida Marlins	.10			
535	Ruben Sierra	.10	653	Houston Astros	.10			
536	Octavio Dotel	.10	654	Kansas City Royals	.10			
537	Luis Sojo	.10	655	Los Angeles Dodgers	.10			
538	Brent Butler	.10	656	Milwaukee Brewers	.10			
539	Pablo Ozuna	.10	657	Minnesota Twins	.10			
540	Freddy Garcia	.10	658	Montreal Expos	.10			
541	Chad Durbin	.10	659	New York Mets	.10			
542	Orlando Merced	.10	660	New York Yankees	.10			
543	Michael Tucker	.10	661	Oakland Athletics	.10			
544	Roberto Hernandez	.10	662	Philadelphia Phillies	.10			
545	Pat Burrell	.25	663	Pittsburgh Pirates	.10			
546	A.J. Burnett	.10	664	San Diego Padres	.10			

PM Pedro Martinez 20.00
MM Mark Mulder 10.00

All-World Team

NM/M
Complete Set (25): 25.00
Common Player: .50
Inserted 1:12

		$
AW-1	Ichiro Suzuki	3.00
AW-2	Barry Bonds	4.00
AW-3	Pedro Martinez	1.50
AW-4	Juan Gonzalez	1.00
AW-5	Larry Walker	.50
AW-6	Sammy Sosa	3.00
AW-7	Mariano Rivera	.75
AW-8	Vladimir Guerrero	1.50
AW-9	Alex Rodriguez	3.00
AW-10	Albert Pujols	3.00
AW-11	Luis Gonzalez	.50
AW-12	Ken Griffey Jr.	2.50
AW-13	Kazuhiro Sasaki	.50
AW-14	Bob Abreu	.50
AW-15	Todd Helton	1.00
AW-16	Nomar Garciaparra	2.50
AW-17	Miguel Tejada	.75
AW-18	Roger Clemens	3.00
AW-19	Mike Piazza	2.50
AW-20	Carlos Delgado	1.00
AW-21	Derek Jeter	4.00
AW-22	Hideo Nomo	.75
AW-23	Randy Johnson	1.50
AW-24	Ivan Rodriguez	1.00
AW-25	Chan Ho Park	.50

Autographs

NM/M
Common Player: 5.00

		$
TA1	Carlos Delgado	30.00
TA2	Ivan Rodriguez	40.00
TA3	Miguel Tejada	20.00
TA4	Geoff Jenkins	10.00
TA5	Johnny Damon	40.00
TA6	Tim Hudson	25.00
TA7	Terrence Long	10.00
TA8	Gabe Kapler	10.00
TA9	Magglio Ordonez	20.00
TA10	Barry Bonds	150.00
TA11	Pat Burrell	20.00
TA12	Mike Mussina	40.00
TA13	Eric Valent	5.00
TA14	Xavier Nady	10.00
TA15	Cristian Guerrero	5.00
TA16	Ben Sheets	15.00
TA17	Corey Patterson	10.00
TA18	Carlos Pena	5.00
TA19	Alex Rodriguez	80.00

Series 2

		$
TA-AB	Adrian Beltre	15.00
TA-JD	Jermaine Dye	15.00
TA-AE	Alex Escobar	8.00
TA-CF	Cliff Floyd	15.00
TA-RF	Rafael Furcal	15.00
TA-BG	Brian Giles	10.00
TA-KG	Keith Ginter	8.00
TA-TG	Troy Glaus	30.00
TA-BGR	Ben Grieve	8.00
TA-CG	Cristian Guzman	15.00
TA-JH	Josh Hamilton	40.00
TA-NJ	Nick Johnson	5.00
TA-RK	Ryan Klesko	10.00
TA-JO	Jose Ortiz	10.00
TA-RO	Roy Oswalt	15.00
TA-RP	Rafael Palmeiro	50.00
TA-AR	Alex Rodriguez	80.00
TA-JR	Jimmy Rollins	25.00
TA-RS	Richie Sexson	15.00
TA-MS	Mike Sweeney	15.00
TA-JW	Justin Wayne	10.00
TA-BW	Brad Wilkerson	10.00

Battery Mates Relic

NM/M
Inserted 1:4,401
ML Greg Maddux, Javy Lopez 30.00
LP Al Leiter, Mike Piazza 30.00

Coaches Collection Relics

NM/M
Common Card: 8.00
Inserted 1:236 Retail

		$
AH	Art Howe	8.00
AT	Alan Trammell	15.00
BM	Bruce Bochy	8.00
BM	Buck Martinez	8.00
BV	Bobby Valentine	15.00
BW	Billy Williams	15.00
BBE	Buddy Bell	15.00
BBR	Bob Brenly	15.00
DB	Dusty Baker	20.00
DL	Davey Lopes	15.00
DBA	Don Baylor	15.00
EH	Elrod Hendricks	8.00
EM	Eddie Murray	40.00
FW	Frank White	15.00
HM	Hal McRae	8.00
JT	Joe Torre	10.00
KG	Ken Griffey Sr.	8.00
LB	Larry Bowa	15.00
LP	Lance Parrish	15.00
MH	Mike Hargrove	15.00
MS	Mike Scioscia	15.00
MW	Mookie Wilson	10.00
PG	Phil Garner	10.00
PM	Paul Molitor	40.00
TP	Tony Perez	10.00
WR	Willie Randolph	15.00

Draft Picks

NM/M
Complete Set (10): 40.00
1-5 in Green Factory Sets
6-10 in Holiday Factory Sets

		$
1	Scott Moore	6.00
2	Val Majewski	6.00
3	Brian Slocum	4.00
4	Chris Gruler	6.00
5	Mark Schramek	4.00
6	Joe Saunders	6.00
7	Jeff Francis	8.00
8	Royce Ring	6.00
9	Greg Miller	8.00
10	Brandon Weeden	4.00

Dueces Are Wild

NM/M
Common Card: 15.00
Inserted 1:1,962
JG Randy Johnson, Luis Gonzalez 30.00
BK Barry Bonds, Jeff Kent 40.00
TA Jim Thome, Roberto Alomar 30.00
WH Larry Walker, Todd Helton 25.00
BG Bret Boone, Freddy Garcia 15.00

East Meets West

NM/M
Complete Set (8): 6.00
Common Player: 1.00
Inserted 1:24
EW-HN Hideo Nomo, Masanori Murakami 2.00
EW-HI Hideki Irabu, Masanori Murakami 1.00
EW-SH Shigetoshi Hasegawa, Masanori Murakami 1.00
EW-MY Masato Yoshii, Masanori Murakami 1.00
EW-TS Tsuyoshi Shinjo, Masanori Murakami 1.00
EW-KS Kazuhiro Sasaki, Masanori Murakami 1.00
EW-MS Mac Suzuki, Masanori Murakami 1.00
EW-TO Tomo Ohka, Masanori Murakami 1.00

East Meets West Relics

NM/M
Common Player: 15.00
Inserted 1:3,419
HN Hideo Nomo 40.00
KS Kazuhiro Sasaki 15.00
TS Tsuyoshi Shinjo 15.00

Ebbets Field Seat Relics

NM/M
Inserted 1:9,116

		$
JB	Joe Black	125.00
RC	Roy Campanella	250.00
BC	Billy Cox	125.00
CF	Carl Furillo	125.00
GH	Gil Hodges	250.00
AP	Andy Pafko	125.00
PWR	Pee Wee Reese	250.00
JR	Jackie Robinson	250.00
DS	Duke Snider	200.00

Dual Ebbets/Yankee Seat Relic
Complete Set (1):

Dual Ebbets/Yankee Autographed Seat Relic
Complete Set (1):

Ebbets Field/Yankee Stadium Seat Dual Relic
Complete Set (1):

Hall of Fame Vintage BuyBacks AutoProofs

NM/M
Common Autograph: 15.00

		$
BR16	Brooks Robinson 82 KM/200	50.00
EW10	Earl Weaver 87/100	15.00
FJ33	Fergie Jenkins 84/100	15.00
GP26	Gaylord Perry 82/100	15.00
GP29	Gaylord Perry 83/100	15.00
GP30	Gaylord Perry 83 SV/200	15.00
OC1	Orlando Cepeda 82 KM/200	15.00
RF15	Rollie Fingers 81/300	15.00
RF16	Rollie Fingers 81 LL/100	15.00
RF18	Rollie Fingers 82/100	15.00
RF19	Rollie Fingers 82 IA/200	15.00
RF21	Rollie Fingers 82 KM/300	15.00
RF22	Rollie Fingers 83/200	15.00
RF24	Rollie Fingers 84/200	15.00
RF27	Rollie Fingers 85/300	15.00
RF28	Rollie Fingers 86/100	15.00
SC5	Steve Carlton 84 LL/100	25.00
SC6	Steve Carlton 85/200	25.00
SC8	Steve Carlton 87/200	25.00

Heart of the Order Relic

NM/M
Inserted 1:4,247
KBA Jeff Kent, Barry Bonds, Rich Aurilia 75.00
TGA Jim Thome, Juan Gonzalez, Roberto Alomar 50.00
ARB Bob Abreu, Scott Rolen, Pat Burrell 50.00
OWM Paul O'Neill, Bernie Williams, Tino Martinez 50.00

Hit and Run Relic

NM/M
Inserted 1:4,241
JD Johnny Damon 10.00
DE Darin Erstad 10.00
RF Rafael Furcal 10.00

Hobby Masters

NM/M
Complete Set (20): 40.00
Common Player: 1.00
Inserted 1:25

		$
1	Mark McGwire	5.00
2	Derek Jeter	5.00
3	Chipper Jones	2.00
4	Roger Clemens	4.00
5	Vladimir Guerrero	2.00
6	Ichiro Suzuki	3.00
7	Todd Helton	1.50
8	Alex Rodriguez	4.00
9	Albert Pujols	4.00
10	Sammy Sosa	3.00
11	Ken Griffey Jr.	3.00
12	Randy Johnson	2.00
13	Nomar Garciaparra	3.00
14	Ivan Rodriguez	1.50
15	Manny Ramirez	1.50
16	Barry Bonds	5.00
17	Mike Piazza	3.00
18	Pedro Martinez	1.50
19	Jeff Bagwell	1.50
20	Luis Gonzalez	1.00

Jack of All Trades

NM/M
Inserted 1:1,350
RO Roberto Alomar/Bat 20.00
BB Barry Bonds/Jsy 35.00
AJ Andruw Jones/Jsy 10.00
IR Ivan Rodriguez/Jsy 15.00
BW Bernie Williams/Jsy 15.00

Kings of the Clubhouse

NM/M
Common Player: 10.00
Inserted 1:1,449 Ser. 2
TG Tom Glavine/Jsy 15.00
TH Todd Helton/Jsy 15.00
RJ Randy Johnson/Jsy 20.00
EM Edgar Martinez/Jsy 10.00
PO Paul O'Neill/Bat 20.00

Like Father Like Son Relic

NM/M
Common Duo:
Inserted 1:1,304 Retail
AL Roberto Alomar, Sandy Alomar, Sandy Alomar Jr. 40.00
BE Dale Berra, Yogi Berra 50.00
BON Bobby Bonds, Barry Bonds 80.00
BOO Bob Boone, Bret Boone, Aaron Boone 40.00
CR Jose Cruz, Jose Cruz Jr. 40.00

Own The Game

NM/M
Complete Set (30): 25.00
Common Player: .50
Inserted 1:12

		$
OG1	Moises Alou	.75
OG2	Roberto Alomar	.75
OG3	Luis Gonzalez	.50
OG4	Bret Boone	.75
OG5	Barry Bonds	4.00
OG6	Jim Thome	1.50
OG7	Jimmy Rollins	.75
OG8	Cristian Guzman	.50
OG9	Lance Berkman	.75
OG10	Mike Sweeney	.50
OG11	Rich Aurilia	.50
OG12	Ichiro Suzuki	2.50
OG13	Luis Gonzalez	.50
OG14	Ichiro Suzuki	2.50
OG15	Jimmy Rollins	.75
OG16	Roger Cedeno	.50

OG17	Barry Bonds	4.00
OG18	Jim Thome	1.50
OG19	Curt Schilling	1.00
OG20	Roger Clemens	3.00
OG21	Curt Schilling	1.00
OG22	Brad Radke	.50
OG23	Greg Maddux	2.00
OG24	Mark Mulder	.75
OG25	Jeff Shaw	.50
OG26	Mariano Rivera	.75
OG27	Randy Johnson	1.50
OG28	Pedro Martinez	1.50
OG29	John Burkett	.50
OG30	Tim Hudson	.75

Pine Tar Series

NM/M

Common Player: 15.00
Inserted 1:4,420

BB	Barry Bonds	60.00
LG	Luis Gonzalez	20.00
TG	Tony Gwynn	40.00
TH	Todd Helton	25.00
AP	Albert Pujols	40.00

Series 2
Inserted 1:1,043
Trademark Series: 1.5-2X
Inserted 1:2,087 Ser. 2
Prime Cuts Barrel: 2-4X
Inserted 1:7,824 Ser. 2

WB	Wilson Betemit	15.00
SB	Sean Burroughs	15.00
JC	Joe Crede	20.00
AD	Adam Dunn	30.00
AE	Alex Escobar	15.00
MG	Marcus Giles	15.00
AG	Alexis Gomez	15.00
TH	Toby Hall	15.00
JH	Josh Hamilton	20.00
NJ	Nick Johnson	15.00
XN	Xavier Nady	15.00
CP	Corey Patterson	20.00
CPE	Carlos Pena	15.00
AR	Aaron Rowand	25.00
RS	Ruben Salazar	15.00

Prime Cuts Autograph Series

No Pricing

Prime Cuts Pine Tar Series

NM/M

Common Player: 15.00
Inserted 1:4,420

BB	Barry Bonds	60.00
LG	Luis Gonzalez	20.00
TG	Tony Gwynn	40.00
TH	Todd Helton	25.00
AP	Albert Pujols	40.00

Series 2
Inserted 1:1,043
Trademark Series: 1.5-2X
Inserted 1:2,087 Ser. 2
Prime Cuts Barrel: 2-4X
Inserted 1:7,824 Ser. 2

WB	Wilson Betemit	15.00
SB	Sean Burroughs	15.00
JC	Joe Crede	20.00
AD	Adam Dunn	30.00
AE	Alex Escobar	15.00
MG	Marcus Giles	15.00
AG	Alexis Gomez	15.00
TH	Toby Hall	15.00
JH	Josh Hamilton	20.00
NJ	Nick Johnson	15.00
XN	Xavier Nady	15.00
CP	Corey Patterson	20.00
CPE	Carlos Pena	15.00
AR	Aaron Rowand	25.00
RS	Ruben Salazar	15.00

Ring Masters

NM/M

Complete Set (10): 15.00
Common Player: .50
Inserted 1:25

1	Derek Jeter	4.00
2	Mark McGwire	2.00
3	Mariano Rivera	1.00
4	Gary Sheffield	.75
5	Al Leiter	.50
6	Chipper Jones	1.50
7	Roger Clemens	2.00
8	Greg Maddux	2.00
9	Roberto Alomar	1.00
10	Paul O'Neill	.50

Team Topps Legends Autographs

NM/M

Common Player: 25.00

TT6R	Whitey Ford	60.00
TT8R	Bob Gibson	40.00
TT47R	Frank Howard	25.00
TT46F	Robin Roberts	25.00
TT13F	Warren Spahn	40.00

Series 2

Three of a Kind

NM/M

Common Card:
Inserted 1:2,039

SPA	Tsuyoshi Shinjo, Mike Piazza, Edgardo Alfonzo	50.00
LOC	Carlos Lee, Magglio Ordonez, Jose Canseco	50.00
FBJ	Rafael Furcal, Wilson Betemit, Andruw Jones	40.00
PSW	Jorge Posada, Alfonso Soriano, Bernie Williams	50.00
BDB	A.J. Burnett, Ryan Dempster, Josh Beckett	40.00

Trademark Series

Common Player:

Turn Two Relic

NM/M

Inserted 1:4,401

TW	Alan Trammell, Lou Whitaker	40.00
VA	Omar Vizquel, Roberto Alomar	40.00

Yankee Stadium Seat Relics

NM/M

Inserted 1:579

HB	Hank Bauer	100.00
YB	Yogi Berra	250.00
JC	Joe Collins	100.00
BM	Billy Martin	250.00
GM	Gil McDougald	100.00
JM	Johnny Mize	100.00
AR	Allie Reynolds	100.00
PR	Phil Rizzuto	250.00
GW	Gene Woodling	100.00

2 Bagger Relic

NM/M

Inserted 1:3,733

TG	Tony Gwynn	30.00
TH	Todd Helton	20.00
SR	Scott Rolen	20.00

1952 Player Autographs

NM/M

Inserted 1:7,524

HBA	Hank Bauer	75.00
YBA	Yogi Berra	100.00
PRA	Preacher Roe	70.00

1952 Reprint Autographs

NM/M

Common Autograph: 25.00
Inserted 1:10,268

JBA	Joe Black	90.00
CEA	Carl Erskine	50.00
GMA	Gil McDougal	40.00
APA	Andy Pafko	60.00
PRA	Phil Rizzuto	80.00
DSA	Duke Snider	100.00

1952 World Series Highlights

1952 WORLD SERIES HIGHLIGHTS
REYNOLDS RELIEVES LOPAT IN GAME 2

NM/M

Complete Set (7): 10.00
Common Player: 2.00
Inserted 1:25

52WS-1	Dodgers' Game 1 Starting Line Up	3.00
52WS-2	Dodgers Celebrate Game 3 Win!	2.00
52WS-3	Carl Erskine Wins Game 5	2.00

Series 2

52WS-2	Game 2	2.00
52WS-4	Game 4	2.00
52WS-6	Game 6	2.00
52WS-7	Game 7	2.00

1952 World Series Tribute

BILLY COX
Billy Cox

NM/M

Complete Set (19): 50.00

	Common Player:	3.00

Inserted 1:25

1	Roy Campanella	4.00
2	Duke Snider	4.00
3	Carl Erskine	3.00
4	Andy Pafko	3.00
5	Johnny Mize	3.00
6	Billy Martin	4.00
7	Phil Rizzuto	4.00
8	Gil McDougal	3.00
9	Allie Reynolds	3.00
10	Jackie Robinson	4.00

Series 2

11	Preacher Roe	3.00
12	Gil Hodges	3.00
13	Billy Cox	3.00
14	Yogi Berra	4.00
15	Gene Woodling	3.00
16	Jerry Sain	3.00
17	Ralph Houk	3.00
18	Joe Collins	3.00
19	Hank Bauer	3.00

2002 Topps American Pie Spirit of America

NM/M

Complete Set (150): 30.00
Common Player: .25
Pack (7): 5.00
Box (24): 100.00

1	Warren Spahn	.75
2	Reggie Jackson	.75
3	Bill Mazeroski	.25
4	Carl Yastrzemski	.75
5	Whitey Ford	.75
6	Ralph Houk	.25
7	Rod Carew	.50
8	Kirk Gibson	.25
9	Bobby Thomson	.25
10	Don Newcombe	.25
11	Gaylord Perry	.25
12	Bruce Sutter	.40
13	Bob Gibson	.50
14	Brooks Robinson	1.00
15	Steve Carlton	.50
16	Robin Yount	1.00
17	Ernie Banks	.75
18	Lou Brock	.25
19	Al Kaline	.75
20	Carlton Fisk	.75
21	Frank Robinson	.75
22	Bobby Bonds	.25
23	Andre Dawson	.25
24	Rich "Goose" Gossage	.25
25	Fred Lynn	.25
26	Keith Hernandez	.25
27	Rollie Fingers	.25
28	Juan Marichal	.25
29	Maury Wills	.25
30	Dave Winfield	.50
31	Frank Howard	.25
32	Tony Gwynn	1.00
33	Jim Palmer	.50
34	Mike Schmidt	1.50
35	Bo Jackson	.75
36	Ferguson Jenkins	.25
37	Bobby Richardson	.25
38	Harmon Killebrew	.75
39	Monte Irvin	.25
40	Jim Abbott	.50
41	Wade Boggs	.75
42	Jackie Robinson	2.00
43	Ralph Branca	.25
44	Minnie Minoso	.25
45	Tug McGraw	.25
46	Willie Mays	2.00
47	Nolan Ryan	3.00
48	Duke Snider	1.00
49	Tom Seaver	1.00
50	Casey Stengel	.50
51	D-Day	.75
52	Gulf War	.25
53	Vietnam War	.25
54	Korean War	.25
55	Secret Service	.25
56	Crayons	.25
57	Hoover Dam	.25
58	Penicillin	.25
59	Polio Vaccine	.25
60	Empire State Building	.25
61	Television	.25
62	Free Speech	.25
63	Voyager Mission	.25
64	Space Shuttle	.25
65	Ellis Island	.25
66	Statue of Liberty	.25
67	Battle of the Bulge	.25
68	Battle of Midway	.25
69	Iwo Jima	.25
70	Panama Canal	.25
71	Spirit of St. Louis/ Lindbergh	.25
72	Civil Rights/We Shall Overcome	.25
73	Space Race	.25
74	Alaska Pipeline	.25
75	Teddy Bear	.25
76	Sea Biscuit	.25
77	Bazooka Joe	.25
78	Mt. Rushmore	.25
79	Yellowstone Park	.25
80	Niagara Falls	.25
81	Grand Canyon	.25
82	Hoola Hoop	.25
83	George Patton	.50
84	Audie Murphy	.25
85	Amelia Earhart	.25
86	Glen Miller	.25
87	Rick Monday	.25
88	Buzz Aldrin	.25
89	Rosa Parks	.25
90	Edward R. Murrow	.25
91	Susan B. Anthony	.25
92	Bobby Kennedy	.25
93	Gloria Steinem	.25
94	Hank Greenberg	.75
95	Jimmy Doolittle	.25
96	Thurgood Marshall	.25
97	Ernest Hemingway	.75
98	Henry Ford	.25
99	Wright Brothers	.25
100	Thomas Edison	.75
101	Albert Einstein	.75
102	Will Rogers	.25
103	George Gershwin	.25
104	Irving Berlin	.25
105	Frank Lloyd Wright	.25
106	Howard Hughes	.25
107	George M. Cohan	.25
108	Jack Kerouac	.25
109	Harry Houdini	.25
110	Helen Keller	.25
111	John McCain	.25
112	Andrew Carnegie	.25
113	Sandra Day O'Connor	.25
114	Brooklyn Bridge	.25
115	Douglas MacArthur	.25
116	Elvis Presley	1.00
117	George Burns	.25
118	Judy Garland	.50
119	Buddy Holly	.25
120	Don McLean	.25
121	Marilyn Monroe	1.00
122	Humphrey Bogart	.50
123	Gary Cooper	.25
124	The Andrews Sisters	.25
125	Jim Thorpe	1.00
126	Joe Louis	.75
127	Jesse Owens	.50
128	Kate Smith	.25
129	W.C. Fields	.25
130	Bette Davis	.25
131	Jayne Mansfield	.25
132	Teddy Roosevelt	.25
133	Franklin D. Roosevelt	.75
134	Harry Truman	.25
135	Dwight Eisenhower	.50
136	George H.W. Bush	.50
137	George W. Bush	.50
138	John F. Kennedy	1.00
139	Lyndon B. Johnson	.25
140	William Taft	.25
141	Horace Harding	.25
142	Woodrow Wilson	.25
143	Richard Nixon	.25
144	Bill Clinton	.25
145	Jimmy Carter	.25
146	Herbert Hoover	.25
147	Gerald Ford	.25
148	Ronald Reagan	.25
149	Calvin Coolidge	.25
150	William McKinley	.25

2002 Topps American Pie American Sluggers

AMERICAN SLUGGERS
Kirk Gibson

NM/M

Complete Set (25): 25.00
Common Player: .50
Inserted 1:1
Each card issued in blue, gold, silver and red; no value differential.

AD	Andre Dawson	.50
AK	Al Kaline	1.00
BR	Brooks Robinson	1.00
CC	Cecil Cooper	.50
CF	Carlton Fisk	1.00
CY	Carl Yastrzemski	2.00
DS	Duke Snider	1.00
DW	Dave Winfield	1.00
EM	Eddie Mathews	1.00
FH	Frank Howard	.50
FL	Fred Lynn	.50
FR	Frank Robinson	1.00
GB	George Brett	3.00
GF	George Foster	.50
HK	Harmon Killebrew	1.00
JC	Jack Clark	.50
JCC	Joe Carter	.50
KG	Kirk Gibson	.50
MI	Monte Irvin	.25
MS	Mike Schmidt	3.00
RC	Rod Carew	1.00
RJ	Reggie Jackson	2.50
RS	Ryne Sandberg	2.00
TK	Ted Kluszewski	1.00
WM	Willie Mays	4.00

American Pie Through the Years Relics

NM/M

Common Player: 8.00
Inserted 1:11

JA	Jim Abbott	15.00
DA	Dick Allen	8.00
JB	Johnny Bench	20.00
WB	Wade Boggs	10.00
BB	Bill Buckner	8.00
JC	Jack Clark	8.00
AD	Andre Dawson	10.00
KT	Jim Kaat	10.00
EM	Eddie Mathews	15.00
DM	Don Mattingly	40.00
WM	Willie Mays	40.00
MM	Minnie Minoso	15.00
RM	Rick Monday	10.00
JM	Joe Morgan	10.00
TM	Thurman Munson	30.00
AL	Al Oliver	8.00
DP	Dave Parker	10.00
GP	Gaylord Perry	10.00
FR	Frank Robinson	15.00
JR	Joe Rudi	10.00
NR	Nolan Ryan	40.00
TS	Tom Seaver	20.00
WS	Willie Stargell	15.00
DS	Darryl Strawberry	15.00
DW	Dave Winfield	12.00
CY	Carl Yastrzemski	20.00

2002 Topps Archives

NM/M

Complete Set (200): 70.00
Common Player: .40
Pack (8): 3.00
Box (20): 50.00

1	Willie Mays	3.00
2	Dale Murphy	.40
3	Dave Winfield	.75
4	Roger Maris	2.00
5	Ron Cey	.40
6	Lee Smith	.40
7	Len Dykstra	.40
8	Ray Fosse	.40
9	Warren Spahn	1.00
10	Herb Score	.40
11	Jim Wynn	.40
12	Sam McDowell	.40
13	Fred Lynn	.40
14	Yogi Berra	1.50
15	Ron Santo	.40
16	Alvin Dark	.40
17	Bill Buckner	.40
18	Rollie Fingers	.60
19	Tony Gwynn	1.50
20	Red Schoendienst	.40
21	Gaylord Perry	.40
22	Jose Cruz	.40
23	Dennis Martinez	.40
24	Dave McNally	.40
25	Norm Cash	.40
26	Ted Kluszewski	.40
27	Rick Reuschel	.40
28	Bruce Sutter	.75
29	Don Larsen	.40
30	Claudell Washington	.40
31	Luis Aparicio	.40
32	Clete Boyer	.40
33	Rich "Goose" Gossage	.40
34	Ray Knight	.40
35	Roy Campanella	1.50
36	Tug McGraw	.40
37	Bob Lemon	.40
38	Willie Stargell	1.00
39	Roberto Clemente	3.00
40	Jim Fregosi	.40
41	Reggie Smith	.40
42	Dave Parker	.40
43	Darrell Evans	.40
44	Ryne Sandberg	2.00
45	Manny Mota	.40
46	Dennis Eckersley	.60
47	Nellie Fox	.40
48	Gil Hodges	.40
49	Reggie Jackson	1.50
50	Bobby Shantz	.40
51	Cecil Cooper	.40
52	Jim Kaat	.40
53	George Hendrick	.40
54	Johnny Podres	.40
55	Bob Gibson	1.00
56	Vern Law	.40
57	Joe Adcock	.40
58	Jack Clark	.40
59	Bill Mazeroski	.40
60	Carl Yastrzemski	1.50
61	Bobby Murcer	.40
62	Davey Johnson	.40
63	Jim Palmer	.75
64	Roy Face	.40
65	Dean Chance	.40
66	Bill "Moose" Skowron	.40
67	Dwight Evans	.40
68	Kirk Gibson	.40
69	Sal Bando	.40
70	Mike Schmidt	2.00
71	Bo Jackson	.40
72	Chris Chambliss	.40
73	Fergie Jenkins	.75
74	Brooks Robinson	1.50
75	Bobby Richardson	.40
76	Duke Snider	1.50
77	Allie Reynolds	.40
78	Harmon Killebrew	1.50
79	Steve Carlton	1.00
80	Bert Blyleven	.40
81	Phil Niekro	.40
82	Lew Burdette	.40
83	Hoyt Wilhelm	.40
84	Curt Flood	.40
85	Guillermo Hernandez	.40
86	Robin Yount	1.50
87	Robin Roberts	.40
88	Whitey Ford	1.00
89	Tony Oliva	.75
90	Don Newcombe	.40
91	Al Oliver	.40
92	Mike Cuellar	.40
93	Mike Scott	.40
94	Dick Allen	.40
95	Jimmy Piersall	.40
96	Bill Freehan	.40
97	Willie Horton	.40
98	Bob Friend	.40
99	Ken Holtzman	.40
100	Rico Carty	.40
101	Gil McDougald	.40
102	Lee May	.40
103	Joe Pepitone	.40
104	Gene Tenace	.40
105	Gary Carter	.40
106	Tim McCarver	.40
107	Ernie Banks	1.50
108	George Foster	.40
109	Lou Brock	1.00
110	Dick Groat	.40
111	Graig Nettles	.40
112	Boog Powell	.40
113	Joe Carter	.40
114	Juan Marichal	.75
115	Larry Doby	.40
116	Fernando Valenzuela	.40
117	Luis Tiant	.40
118	Early Wynn	.40
119	Bill Madlock	.40
120	Eddie Mathews	1.50
121	George Brett	3.00
122	Al Kaline	1.50
123	Frank Howard	.40
124	Mickey Lolich	.40
125	Kirby Puckett	3.00
126	Bob Cerv	.40
127	Will Clark	.40
128	Vida Blue	.40
129	Kevin Mitchell	.40
130	Bucky Dent	.40
131	Tom Seaver	2.00
132	Jerry Koosman	.40
133	Orlando Cepeda	.40
134	Nolan Ryan	4.00
135	Tony Kubek	.40
136	Don Drysdale	1.00
137	Paul Blair	.40
138	Elston Howard	.40
139	Joe Rudi	.40
140	Tommie Agee	.40
141	Richie Ashburn	.40
142	Jim Bunning	.40
143	Hank Sauer	.40
144	Greg Luzinski	.40
145	Ron Guidry	.40

146	Rod Carew	1.00
147	Andre Dawson	.75
148	Keith Hernandez	.40
149	Carlton Fisk	1.00
150	Cleon Jones	.40
151	Don Mattingly	3.00
152	Vada Pinson	.40
153	Ozzie Smith	1.50
154	Dave Concepcion	.40
155	Al Rosen	.40
156	Tommy John	.40
157	Bob Ojeda	.40
158	Frank Robinson	1.50
159	Darryl Strawberry	.40
160	Bobby Bonds	.40
161	Bert Campaneris	.40
162	Jim "Catfish" Hunter	.40
163	Bud Harrelson	.40
164	Dwight Gooden	.40
165	Wade Boggs	1.00
166	Joe Morgan	1.00
167	Ron Swoboda	.40
168	Hank Aaron	4.00
169	Steve Garvey	.40
170	Mickey Rivers	.40
171	Johnny Bench	3.00
172	Ralph Terry	.40
173	Billy Pierce	.40
174	Thurman Munson	2.50
175	Don Sutton	.40
176	Sparky Anderson	.40
177	Gil Hodges	.40
178	Davey Johnson	.40
179	Frank Robinson	1.50
180	Red Schoendienst	.40
181	Roger Maris	2.00
182	Willie Mays	3.00
183	Luis Aparicio	.40
184	Nellie Fox	.40
185	Ernie Banks	1.50
186	Orlando Cepeda	.75
187	Whitey Ford	1.00
188	Bob Gibson	1.00
189	Bill Mazeroski	.40
190	Hank Aaron	3.00
191	League Leaders (Elston Howard, Harmon Killebrew, Carl Yastrzemski)	.75
192	League Leaders (Orlando Cepeda, Jackie Robinson, Willie Mays)	2.00
193	League Leaders (Hank Aaron, Roberto Clemente, Dick Allen)	2.00
194	League Leaders (Tom Seaver, Phil Niekro, Fergie Jenkins, Juan Marichal)	1.00
195	League Leaders (Jim Palmer, Jim Hunter, Dennis Eckersley)	.65
196	Hank Aaron	3.00
197	Brooks Robinson	1.50
198	Tom Seaver	1.50
199	Jim Palmer	.75
200	Lou Brock	1.00

Autographs

		NM/M
Common Autograph:		10.00
Inserted 1:22		
HA	Hank Aaron	300.00
DA	Dick Allen	25.00
SB	Sal Bando	20.00
EB	Ernie Banks	125.00
BB	Bobby Bonds	25.00
BG	George Brett	250.00
JBU	Jim Bunning	40.00
LB	Lew Burdette	20.00
BC	Bert Campaneris	10.00
GC	Gary Carter	50.00
RCE	Ron Cey	15.00
CC	Chris Chambliss	15.00
JCR	Jose Cruz	15.00
AD	Alvin Dark	25.00
BD	Bucky Dent	20.00
LD	Len Dykstra	20.00
DEV	Darrell Evans	15.00
GF	George Foster	15.00
JF	Jim Fregosi	10.00
SG	Steve Garvey	15.00
DG	Dwight Gooden	25.00
DGR	Dick Groat	15.00
BH	Bud Harrelson	15.00
WH	Willie Hernandez	10.00
KH	Keith Hernandez	40.00
BJ	Bo Jackson	80.00
FJ	Fergie Jenkins	20.00
TJ	Tommy John	15.00
JK	Jim Kaat	20.00
AK	Al Kaline	125.00
HK	Harmon Killebrew	110.00
JKO	Jerry Koosman	65.00
GL	Greg Luzinski	20.00
FL	Fred Lynn	20.00
DM	Dave McNally	20.00

KM	Kevin Mitchell	20.00
DN	Don Newcombe	15.00
TO	Tony Oliva	30.00
JP	Jim Palmer	50.00
DP	Dave Parker	20.00
GP	Gaylord Perry	20.00
BP	Billy Pierce	10.00
JPI	Jimmy Piersall	15.00
JPO	Johnny Podres	15.00
BPO	Boog Powell	25.00
KP	Kirby Puckett	150.00
MR	Mickey Rivers	10.00
BRO	Brooks Robinson	80.00
JR	Joe Rudi	15.00
RS	Ron Santo	30.00
MS	Mike Schmidt	150.00
LS	Lee Smith	20.00
RSM	Reggie Smith	15.00
BS	Bruce Sutter	35.00
RT	Ralph Terry	25.00
HW	Hoyt Wilhelm	20.00
DW	Dave Winfield	85.00
RY	Robin Yount	100.00

AutoProofs

		NM/M
Quantity produced listed		
1	Gary Carter/80	40.00
2	Jose Cruz/95	25.00
4	Bo Jackson/300	50.00
5	Kevin Mitchell/65	25.00
6	Kirby Puckett/80	80.00
7	Mike Schmidt/147	90.00
8	Ozzie Smith/105	75.00
9	Darryl Strawberry/181	40.00
11	Robin Yount/39	100.00

Game-Used Bat

		NM/M
Common Player:		
Group A 1:106		
Group B 1:282		
JB	Johnny Bench	20.00
GB	George Brett	40.00
GC	Gary Carter	10.00
JC	Joe Carter	10.00
NC	Norm Cash	10.00
AD	Andre Dawson	8.00
DE	Dwight Evans	8.00
BF	Bill Freehan	8.00
WH	Willie Horton	10.00
RJ	Reggie Jackson	15.00
DM	Don Mattingly	50.00
RM	Roger Maris	50.00
JM	Joe Morgan	10.00
DP	Dave Parker	10.00
BR	Brooks Robinson	20.00
RS	Ron Santo	20.00
WS	Willie Stargell	15.00
CY	Carl Yastrzemski	40.00
RY	Robin Yount	20.00

Game-Worn Uniform

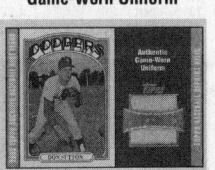

		NM/M
Common Player:		8.00
Inserted 1:28		
SA	Sparky Anderson	10.00
WB	Wade Boggs	15.00
BB	Bobby Bonds	8.00
GB	George Brett	30.00
OC	Orlando Cepeda	10.00
WC	Will Clark	20.00
DC	Dave Concepcion	8.00
DE	Dennis Eckersley	10.00
SG	Steve Garvey	10.00
FL	Fred Lynn	8.00
DM	Dale Murphy	20.00
PN	Phil Niekro	10.00
GP	Gaylord Perry	10.00
KP	Kirby Puckett	20.00
FR	Frank Robinson	15.00
NR	Nolan Ryan	40.00
RS	Ryne Sandberg	30.00
OS	Ozzie Smith	10.00
DS	Don Sutton	10.00
DW	Dave Winfield	20.00

Stadium Seat

		NM/M
Common Player:		8.00
RA	Richie Ashburn	15.00
SA	Sparky Anderson	10.00
EB	Ernie Banks	25.00
YB	Yogi Berra	20.00
JB	Jim Bunning	10.00
RC	Rod Carew	20.00
JC	Joe Carter	10.00
NF	Nellie Fox	15.00
RG	Ron Guidry	10.00
TK	Ted Kluszewski	15.00
BL	Bob Lemon	10.00
ML	Mickey Lolich	10.00
EM	Eddie Mathews	20.00
SM	Sam McDowell	8.00
JP	Jim Palmer	15.00
DP	Dave Parker	10.00
HS	Herb Score	10.00

2002 Topps Archives Reserve

		NM/M
Complete Set (100):		100.00
Common Player:		.75
Box (10 Packs + Auto. Baseball):		125.00
1	Lee Smith	.75
2	Gaylord Perry	.75
3	Al Oliver	.75
4	Rich "Goose" Gossage	.75
5	Bill Madlock	.75
6	Rod Carew	1.50
7	Fred Lynn	.75
8	Frank Robinson	2.00
9	Al Kaline	2.50
10	Len Dykstra	.75
11	Carlton Fisk	1.50
12	Nellie Fox	1.00
13	Reggie Jackson	3.00
14	Bob Gibson	2.00
15	Bill Buckner	.75
16	Harmon Killebrew	2.00
17	Gary Carter	1.50
18	Dave Winfield	1.50
19	Ozzie Smith	2.50
20	Dwight Evans	.75
21	Dave Concepcion	.75
22	Joe Morgan	1.00
23	Clete Boyer	.75
24	Will Clark	1.50
25	Lee May	.75
26	Kevin Mitchell	.75
27	Roger Maris	3.00
28	Mickey Lolich	.75
29	Luis Aparicio	.75
30	George Foster	.75
31	Don Mattingly	6.00
32	Fernando Valenzuela	.75
33	Bobby Bonds	.75
34	Jim Palmer	1.50
35	Dennis Eckersley	1.00
36	Kirby Puckett	3.00
37	Jose Cruz	.75
38	Richie Ashburn	.75
39	Whitey Ford	2.00
40	Robin Roberts	.75
41	Don Newcombe	.75
42	Roy Campanella	2.50
43	Dennis Martinez	.75
44	Larry Doby	1.00
45	Steve Garvey	.75
46	Thurman Munson	3.00
47	Dale Murphy	1.50
48	Bill "Moose" Skowron	.75
49	Tom Seaver	3.00
50	Orlando Cepeda	.75
51	Graig Nettles	.75
52	Willie Stargell	1.50
53	Yogi Berra	2.50
54	Steve Carlton	1.50
55	Don Sutton	.75
56	Brooks Robinson	1.50
57	Vida Blue	.75
58	Rollie Fingers	1.00
59	Jim Bunning	.75
60	Nolan Ryan	8.00
61	Hank Aaron	6.00
62	Fergie Jenkins	1.00
63	Andre Dawson	1.00
64	Ernie Banks	2.50
65	Early Wynn	.75
66	Duke Snider	1.50
67	Red Schoendienst	.75
68	Don Drysdale	1.50
69	Jim "Catfish" Hunter	1.00
70	George Brett	6.00
71	Elston Howard	.75
72	Wade Boggs	1.50
73	Keith Hernandez	.75
74	Billy Pierce	.75
75	Ted Kluszewski	.75
76	Carl Yastrzemski	4.00
77	Bert Blyleven	.75
78	Tony Oliva	.75
79	Joe Carter	.75
80	Johnny Bench	3.00
81	Tony Gwynn	3.00
82	Mike Schmidt	4.00
83	Phil Niekro	.75
84	Juan Marichal	.75
85	Eddie Mathews	2.50
86	Boog Powell	.75
87	Dwight Gooden	.75
88	Darryl Strawberry	.75
89	Roberto Clemente	6.00
90	Ryne Sandberg	5.00
91	Jack Clark	.75
92	Willie Mays	6.00
93	Ron Guidry	.75
94	Kirk Gibson	.75
95	Lou Brock	1.00
96	Robin Yount	2.50
97	Bill Mazeroski	.75
98	Dave Parker	.75
99	Hoyt Wilhelm	.75
100	Warren Spahn	1.50

Autographed Baseballs

		NM/M
Common Auto. Ball:		15.00
Inserted 1:Box		
	Luis Aparicio/1,600	25.00
	Ernie Banks/50	75.00
	Yogi Berra/100	85.00
	Lou Brock/400	40.00
	Jim Bunning/500	35.00
	Gary Carter/500	40.00
	Rich Gossage/500	20.00
	Fergie Jenkins/1,000	15.00
	Al Kaline/250	75.00
	Harmon Killebrew/250	60.00
	Joe Morgan/250	40.00
	Graig Nettles/1,600	15.00
	Jim Palmer/400	25.00
	Gaylord Perry/500	15.00
	Brooks Robinson/500	40.00
	Mike Schmidt/500	125.00
	Duke Snider/100	65.00
	Dave Winfield/1650	30.00
	Robin Yount/250	90.00

Best Years Autographs

		NM/M
Common Autograph:		12.00
Inserted 1:15 Hobby		
LA	Luis Aparicio	15.00
EB	Ernie Banks	70.00
YB	Yogi Berra	60.00
LB	Lou Brock	25.00
GC	Gary Carter	20.00
FJ	Fergie Jenkins	12.00
AK	Al Kaline	40.00
HK	Harmon Killebrew	40.00
WM	Willie Mays	120.00
JM	Joe Morgan	25.00
GN	Graig Nettles	12.00
GP	Gaylord Perry	15.00
BR	Brooks Robinson	25.00
MS	Mike Schmidt	125.00
LS	Lee Smith	12.00
DS	Duke Snider	60.00
RY	Robin Yount	80.00

Best Years Game-Used Bat

		NM/M
Common Player:		10.00
Inserted 1:22		
HAB	Hank Aaron	40.00
GBB	George Brett	25.00
OC	Orlando Cepeda	10.00
CF	Carlton Fisk	10.00
RM	Roger Maris	70.00
EMB	Eddie Mathews	20.00
DMB	Don Mattingly	30.00
TM	Thurman Munson	30.00
DW	Dave Winfield	10.00
CYB	Carl Yastrzemski	25.00

Best Years Game-Worn Uni.

		NM/M
Common Player:		10.00
Inserted 1:7 Hobby		
EB	Ernie Banks	25.00
JBU	Johnny Bench	15.00
WBJ	Wade Boggs	10.00
GCJ	Gary Carter	12.00
WC	Will Clark	15.00
NF	Nellie Fox	15.00
TG	Tony Gwynn	15.00
JM	Juan Marichal	12.00
WM	Willie Mays	35.00
KPJ	Kirby Puckett	15.00
BR	Brooks Robinson	12.00
NR	Nolan Ryan	30.00
RSJ	Red Schoendienst	10.00
WS	Willie Stargell	15.00
RYU	Robin Yount	12.00

Team Topps Legends Autographs

		NM/M
Common Player:		
	Rich "Goose" Gossage	10.00
	Graig Nettles	10.00
	Jim Palmer	15.00
	Gaylord Perry	15.00

2002 Topps Chrome

		NM/M
Complete Set (685):		200.00
Common Player:		.25
Pack (4):		2.00
Box (24):		40.00
1	Pedro Martinez	1.00
2	Mike Stanton	.25
3	Brad Penny	.25
4	Mike Matheny	.25
5	Johnny Damon	.25
6	Bret Boone	.25
7	Retired # not issued	
8	Chris Truby	.25
9	B.J. Surhoff	.25
10	Mike Hampton	.25
11	Juan Pierre	.25
12	Mark Buehrle	.25
13	Bob Abreu	.50
14	David Cone	.25
15	Aaron Sele	.25
16	Fernando Tatis	.25
17	Bobby Jones	.25
18	Rick Helling	.25
19	Dmitri Young	.25
20	Mike Mussina	.50
21	Mike Sweeney	.25
22	Cristian Guzman	.25
23	Ryan Kohlmeier	.25
24	Adam Kennedy	.25
25	Larry Walker	.50
26	Eric Davis	.25
27	Jason Tyner	.25
28	Eric Young	.25
29	Jason Marquis	.25
30	Luis Gonzalez	.25
31	Kevin Tapani	.25
32	Orlando Cabrera	.40
33	Marty Cordova	.25
34	Brad Ausmus	.25
35	Livan Hernandez	.25
36	Alex Gonzalez	.25
37	Edgar Renteria	.50
38	Bengie Molina	.25
39	Frank Menechino	.25
40	Rafael Palmeiro	1.00
41	Brad Fullmer	.25
42	Julio Zuleta	.25
43	Darren Dreifort	.25
44	Trot Nixon	.50
45	Trevor Hoffman	.25
46	Vladimir Nunez	.25
47	Mark Kotsay	.25
48	Kenny Rogers	.25
49	Ben Petrick	.25
50	Jeff Bagwell	.50
51	Juan Encarnacion	.25
52	Ramiro Mendoza	.25
53	Brian Meadows	.25
54	Chad Curtis	.25
55	Aramis Ramirez	.50
56	Mark McLemore	.25
57	Dante Bichette	.25
58	Scott Schoeneweis	.25
59	Jose Cruz	.25
60	Roger Clemens	3.00
61	Jose Guillen	.25
62	Darren Oliver	.25
63	Chris Reitsma	.25
64	Jeff Abbott	.25
65	Robin Ventura	.50
66	Denny Neagle	.25
67	Al Martin	.25
68	Benito Santiago	.25
69	Roy Oswalt	.50
70	Juan Gonzalez	.50
71	Garret Anderson	.40
72	Bobby Bonilla	.25
73	Danny Bautista	.25
74	J.T. Snow	.25
75	Derek Jeter	4.00
76	John Olerud	.40
77	Kevin Appier	.25
78	Phil Nevin	.25
79	Sean Casey	.40
80	Troy Glaus	.50
81	Joe Randa	.25
82	Jose Valentin	.25
83	Ricky Bottalico	.25
84	Todd Zeile	.25
85	Barry Larkin	.50
86	Bob Wickman	.25
87	Jeff Shaw	.25
88	Greg Vaughn	.25
89	Fernando Vina	.25
90	Mark Mulder	.40
91	Paul Bako	.25
92	Aaron Boone	.25
93	Esteban Loaiza	.25
94	Richie Sexson	.25
95	Alfonso Soriano	1.00
96	Tony Womack	.25
97	Paul Shuey	.25
98	Melvin Mora	.25
99	Tony Gwynn	1.50
100	Vladimir Guerrero	1.50
101	Keith Osik	.25
102	Randy Velarde	.25
103	Scott Williamson	.25
104	Daryle Ward	.25
105	Doug Mientkiewicz	.25
106	Stan Javier	.25
107	Russ Ortiz	.25
108	Wade Miller	.25
109	Luke Prokopec	.25
110	Andruw Jones	.50
111	Ron Coomer	.25
112	Dan Wilson	.25
113	Luis Castillo	.25
114	Derek Bell	.25
115	Gary Sheffield	.50
116	Ruben Rivera	.25
117	Paul O'Neill	.25
118	Craig Paquette	.25
119	Kelvim Escobar	.25
120	Brad Radke	.25
121	Jorge Fabregas	.25
122	Randy Winn	.25
123	Tom Goodwin	.25
124	Jaret Wright	.25
125	Bonds-Race to 73	40.00
126	Al Leiter	.25
127	Ben Davis	.25
128	Frank Catalanotto	.25
129	Jose Cabrera	.25
130	Magglio Ordonez	.50
131	Jose Macias	.25
132	Ted Lilly	.25
133	Chris Holt	.25
134	Eric Milton	.25
135	Shannon Stewart	.25
136	Omar Olivares	.25
137	David Segui	.25
138	Jeff Nelson	.25
139	Matt Williams	.50
140	Ellis Burks	.25
141	Jason Bere	.25
142	Jimmy Haynes	.25
143	Ramon Hernandez	.25
144	Craig Counsell	.25
145	John Smoltz	.50
146	Homer Bush	.25
147	Quilvio Veras	.25
148	Esteban Yan	.25
149	Ramon Ortiz	.25
150	Carlos Delgado	.50

No.	Player	Price		No.	Player	Price		No.	Player	Price		No.	Player	Price		No.	Player	Price
151	Lee Stevens	.25		269	Marlon Anderson	.25		421	Felipe Lopez	.25		539	Pablo Ozuna	.25		657	Minnesota Twins	.25
152	Wil Cordero	.25		270	Mariano Rivera	.50		422	Joe McEwing	.25		540	Freddy Garcia	.25		658	Montreal Expos	.25
153	Mike Bordick	.25		271	Chan Ho Park	.25		423	Jacque Jones	.25		541	Chad Durbin	.25		659	New York Mets	.25
154	John Flaherty	.25		272	Jose Vizcaino	.25		424	Julio Franco	.25		542	Orlando Merced	.25		660	New York Yankees	1.00
155	Omar Daal	.25		273	Jeff D'Amico	.25		425	Frank Thomas	1.00		543	Michael Tucker	.25		661	Oakland Athletics	.25
156	Todd Ritchie	.25		274	Mark Gardner	.25		426	Kent Bottenfield	.25		544	Roberto Hernandez	.25		662	Philadelphia Phillies	.25
157	Carl Everett	.25		275	Travis Fryman	.25		427	Mac Suzuki	.25		545	Pat Burrell	.50		663	Pittsburgh Pirates	.25
158	Scott Sullivan	.25		276	Darren Lewis	.25		428	D'Angelo Jimenez	.25		546	A.J. Burnett	.25		664	San Diego Padres	.25
159	Deivi Cruz	.25		277	Bruce Bochy	.25		429	Chris Stynes	.25		547	Bubba Trammell	.25		665	San Francisco Giants	.25
160	Albert Pujols	3.00		278	Jerry Manuel	.25		430	Kerry Wood	.50		548	Scott Elarton	.25		666	Seattle Mariners	.25
161	Royce Clayton	.25		279	Bob Brenly	.25		431	Chris Singleton	.25		549	Mike Darr	.25		667	St. Louis Cardinals	.25
162	Jeff Suppan	.25		280	Don Baylor	.25		432	Erubiel Durazo	.25		550	Ken Griffey Jr.	2.50		668	Tampa Bay Devil Rays	.25
163	C.C. Sabathia	.50		281	Davey Lopes	.25		433	Matt Lawton	.25		551	Ugueth Urbina	.25		669	Texas Rangers	.25
164	Jimmy Rollins	.75		282	Jerry Narron	.25		434	Bill Mueller	.25		552	Todd Jones	.25		670	Toronto Blue Jays	.25
165	Rickey Henderson	.50		283	Tony Muser	.25		435	Jose Canseco	.50		553	Delino DeShields	.25		671	Juan Cruz	.25
166	Rey Ordonez	.25		284	Hal McRae	.25		436	Ben Grieve	.25		554	Adam Piatt	.25		672	Kevin Cash RC	.50
167	Shawn Estes	.25		285	Bobby Cox	.25		437	Terry Mulholland	.25		555	Jason Kendall	.25		673	Jimmy Gobble RC	.50
168	Reggie Sanders	.25		286	Larry Dierker	.25		438	David Bell	.25		556	Hector Ortiz	.25		674	Mike Hill RC	.50
169	Jon Lieber	.25		287	Phil Garner	.25		439	A.J. Pierzynski	.25		557	Turk Wendell	.25		675	Taylor Buchholz RC	.75
170	Armando Benitez	.25		288	Jimmy Williams	.25		440	Adam Dunn	1.00		558	Rob Bell	.25		676	Bill Hall	.75
171	Mike Remlinger	.25		289	Bobby Valentine	.25		441	Jon Garland	.25		559	Sun-Woo Kim	.25		677	Brett Roneberg RC	.75
172	Billy Wagner	.25		290	Dusty Baker	.25		442	Jeff Fassero	.25		560	Raul Mondesi	.50		678	Royce Huffman RC	.75
173	Troy Percival	.25		291	Lloyd McLendon	.25		443	Julio Lugo	.25		561	Brent Abernathy	.25		679	Chris Tritle RC	.50
174	Devon White	.25		292	Mike Scioscia	.25		444	Carlos Guillen	.40		562	Seth Etherton	.25		680	Nate Espy RC	.50
175	Ivan Rodriguez	.50		293	Buck Martinez	.25		445	Orlando Hernandez	.25		563	Shawn Wooten	.25		681	Nick Alvarez RC	.50
176	Dustin Hermanson	.25		294	Larry Bowa	.25		446	Mark Loretta	.25		564	Jay Buhner	.25		682	Jason Botts RC	.50
177	Brian Anderson	.25		295	Tony LaRussa	.25		447	Scott Spiezio	.25		565	Andres Galarraga	.25		683	Ryan Gripp RC	.75
178	Graeme Lloyd	.25		296	Jeff Torborg	.25		448	Kevin Millwood	.50		566	Shane Reynolds	.25		684	Dan Phillips RC	.50
179	Russell Branyan	.25		297	Tom Kelly	.25		449	Jamie Moyer	.25		567	Rod Beck	.25		685	Pablo Arias RC	.75
180	Bobby Higginson	.25		298	Mike Hargrove	.25		450	Todd Helton	1.00		568	Dee Brown	.25		686	John Rodriguez RC	.75
181	Alex Gonzalez	.25		299	Art Howe	.25		451	Todd Walker	.25		569	Pedro Feliz	.25		687	Rich Harden RC	4.00
182	John Franco	.25		300	Lou Piniella	.25		452	Jose Lima	.25		570	Ryan Klesko	.25		688	Neal Frendling RC	1.00
183	Sidney Ponson	.25		301	Charlie Manuel	.25		453	Brook Fordyce	.25		571	John Vander Wal	.25		689	Rich Thompson RC	.50
184	Jose Mesa	.25		302	Buddy Bell	.25		454	Aaron Rowand	.25		572	Nick Bierbrodt	.25		690	Greg Montalbano RC	1.00
185	Todd Hollandsworth	.25		303	Tony Perez	.25		455	Barry Zito	.50		573	Joe Nathan	.25		691	Leonard Dinardo RC	.75
186	Kevin Young	.25		304	Bob Boone	.25		456	Eric Owens	.25		574	James Baldwin	.25		692	Ryan Raburn RC	.75
187	Tim Wakefield	.25		305	Joe Torre	.25		457	Charles Nagy	.25		575	J.D. Drew	.40		693	Josh Barfield	.50
188	Craig Biggio	.50		306	Jim Tracy	.25		458	Raul Ibanez	.25		576	Greg Colbrunn	.25		694	David Bacani RC	.75
189	Jason Isringhausen	.25		307	Jason Lane	.25		459	Joe Mays	.25		577	Doug Glanville	.25		695	Dan Johnson RC	.50
190	Mark Quinn	.25		308	Chris George	.25		460	Jim Thome	1.00		578	Rey Sanchez	.25		696	Mike Mussina	.50
191	Glendon Rusch	.25		309	Hank Blalock	.50		461	Adam Eaton	.25		579	Todd Van Poppel	.25		697	Ivan Rodriguez	.50
192	Damian Miller	.25		310	Joe Borchard	.25		462	Felix Martinez	.25		580	Rich Aurilia	.25		698	Doug Mientkiewicz	.25
193	Sandy Alomar	.25		311	Marlon Byrd	.25		463	Vernon Wells	.25		581	Chuck Finley	.25		699	Roberto Alomar	.50
194	Scott Brosius	.25		312	Raymond Cabrera RC	.50		464	Donnie Sadler	.25		582	Abraham Nunez	.25		700	Eric Chavez	.25
195	Dave Martinez	.25		313	Freddy Sanchez RC	2.00		465	Tony Clark	.25		583	Kenny Lofton	.25		701	Omar Vizquel	.25
196	Danny Graves	.25		314	Scott Wiggins RC	.50		466	Jose Hernandez	.25		584	Brian Daubach	.25		702	Mike Cameron	.25
197	Shea Hillenbrand	.25		315	Jason Maule RC	.50		467	Ramon Martinez	.25		585	Miguel Tejada	.75		703	Torii Hunter	.50
198	Jimmy Anderson	.25		316	Dionys Cesar RC	.50		468	Rusty Greer	.25		586	Nate Cornejo	.25		704	Ichiro Suzuki	1.50
199	Travis Lee	.25		317	Boof Bonser	.25		469	Rod Barajas	.25		587	Kazuhiro Sasaki	.50		705	Greg Maddux	1.00
200	Randy Johnson	1.50		318	Juan Tolentino RC	.50		470	Lance Berkman	.75		588	Chris Richard	.25		706	Brad Ausmus	.25
201	Carlos Beltran	.50		319	Earl Snyder RC	.50		471	Brady Anderson	.25		589	Armando Reynoso	.25		707	Todd Helton	.75
202	Jerry Hairston Jr.	.25		320	Travis Wade RC	.50		472	Pedro Astacio	.25		590	Tim Hudson	.75		708	Fernando Vina	.25
203	Jesus Sanchez	.25		321	Napoleon Calzado RC	.50		473	Shane Halter	.25		591	Neifi Perez	.25		709	Scott Rolen	.75
204	Eddie Taubensee	.25		322	Eric Glaser RC	.50		474	Bret Prinz	.25		592	Steve Cox	.25		710	Orlando Cabrera	.25
205	David Wells	.25		323	Craig Kuzmic RC	.50		475	Edgar Martinez	.50		593	Henry Blanco	.25		711	Andruw Jones	.50
206	Russ Davis	.25		324	Nic Jackson RC	.50		476	Steve Trachsel	.25		594	Ricky Ledee	.25		712	Jim Edmonds	.25
207	Michael Barrett	.25		325	Mike Rivera	.25		477	Gary Matthews Jr.	.25		595	Tim Salmon	.25		713	Larry Walker	.25
208	Marquis Grissom	.25		326	Jason Bay RC	6.00		478	Ismael Valdes	.25		596	Luis Rivas	.25		714	Roger Clemens	1.50
209	Byung-Hyun Kim	.25		327	Chris Smith	.25		479	Juan Uribe	.25		597	Jeff Zimmerman	.25		715	Randy Johnson	.75
210	Hideo Nomo	.40		328	Jake Gautreau	.25		480	Shawn Green	.40		598	Matt Stairs	.25		716	Ichiro Suzuki	1.50
211	Ryan Rupe	.25		329	Gabe Gross	.25		481	Kirk Rueter	.25		599	Preston Wilson	.25		717	Barry Bonds	2.00
212	Ricky Gutierrez	.25		330	Kenny Baugh	.25		482	Damion Easley	.25		600	Mark McGwire	4.00		718	Ichiro Suzuki	1.50
213	Darryl Kile	.25		331	J.D. Martin	.25		483	Chris Carpenter	.40		601	Timo Perez	.25		719	Albert Pujols	1.50
214	Rico Brogna	.25		366	Pat Meares	.25		484	Kris Benson	.25		602	Matt Anderson	.25				
215	Terrence Long	.25		367	Mike Lieberthal	.25		485	Antonio Alfonseca	.25		603	Todd Hundley	.25				
216	Mike Jackson	.25		368	Scott Erickson	.25		486	Kyle Farnsworth	.25		604	Rick Ankiel	.25				
217	Jamey Wright	.25		369	Ron Gant	.25		487	Brandon Lyon	.25		605	Tsuyoshi Shinjo	.25				
218	Adrian Beltre	.50		370	Moises Alou	.50		488	Hideki Irabu	.25		606	Woody Williams	.25				
219	Benny Agbayani	.25		371	Chad Kreuter	.25		489	David Ortiz	.75		607	Jason LaRue	.25				
220	Chuck Knoblauch	.25		372	Willis Roberts	.25		490	Mike Piazza	2.50		608	Carlos Lee	.50				
221	Randy Wolf	.25		373	Toby Hall	.25		491	Derek Lowe	.25		609	Russ Johnson	.25				
222	Andy Ashby	.25		374	Miguel Batista	.25		492	Chris Gomez	.25		610	Scott Rolen	1.00				
223	Corey Koskie	.25		375	John Burkett	.25		493	Mark Johnson	.25		611	Brent Mayne	.25				
224	Roger Cedeno	.25		376	Cory Lidle	.25		494	John Rocker	.25		612	Darrin Fletcher	.25				
225	Ichiro Suzuki	3.00		377	Nick Neugebauer	.25		495	Eric Karros	.25		613	Ray Lankford	.25				
226	Keith Foulke	.25		378	Jay Payton	.25		496	Bill Haselman	.25		614	Troy O'Leary	.25				
227	Ryan Minor	.25		379	Steve Karsay	.25		497	Dave Veres	.25		615	Javier Lopez	.25				
228	Shawon Dunston	.25		380	Eric Chavez	.50		498	Gil Heredia	.25		616	Randy Velarde	.25				
229	Alex Cora	.25		381	Kelly Stinnett	.25		499	Tomokazu Ohka	.25		617	Vinny Castilla	.25				
230	Jeromy Burnitz	.25		382	Jarrod Washburn	.25		500	Barry Bonds	4.00		618	Milton Bradley	.25				
231	Mark Grace	.50		383	C.J. Nitkowski	.25		501	David Dellucci	.25		619	Ruben Mateo	.25				
232	Aubrey Huff	.25		384	Jeff Conine	.25		502	Ed Sprague	.25		620	Jason Giambi	1.00				
233	Jeffrey Hammonds	.25		385	Fred McGriff	.50		503	Tom Gordon	.25		621	Andy Benes	.25				
234	Olmedo Saenz	.25		386	Marvin Benard	.25		504	Javier Vazquez	.25		622	Joe Mauer RC	15.00				
235	Brian Jordan	.25		387	Dave Burba	.25		505	Ben Sheets	.50		623	Andy Pettitte	.75				
236	Jeremy Giambi	.25		388	Dennis Cook	.25		506	Wilton Guerrero	.25		624	Jose Offerman	.25				
237	Joe Girardi	.25		389	Rick Reed	.25		507	John Halama	.25		625	Mo Vaughn	.40				
238	Eric Gagne	.25		390	Tom Glavine	.75		508	Mark Redman	.25		626	Steve Sparks	.25				
239	Masato Yoshii	.25		391	Rondell White	.25		509	Jack Wilson	.25		627	Mike Matthews	.25				
240	Greg Maddux	2.00		392	Matt Morris	.50		510	Bernie Williams	.50		628	Robb Nen	.25				
241	Bryan Rekar	.25		393	Pat Rapp	.25		511	Miguel Cairo	.25		629	Kip Wells	.25				
242	Ray Durham	.25		394	Robert Person	.25		512	Denny Hocking	.25		630	Kevin Brown	.25				
243	Torii Hunter	.50		395	Omar Vizquel	.40		513	Tony Batista	.25		631	Arthur Rhodes	.25				
244	Derek Lee	.50		396	Jeff Cirillo	.25		514	Mark Grudzielanek	.25		632	Gabe Kapler	.25				
245	Jim Edmonds	.40		397	Dave Mlicki	.25		515	Jose Vidro	.25		633	Jermaine Dye	.25				
246	Einar Diaz	.25		398	Jose Ortiz	.25		516	Sterling Hitchcock	.25		634	Josh Beckett	.75				
247	Brian Bohanon	.25		399	Ryan Dempster	.25		517	Billy Koch	.25		635	Pokey Reese	.25				
248	Ron Belliard	.25		400	Curt Schilling	.75		518	Matt Clement	.25		636	Benji Gil	.25				
249	Mike Lowell	.50		401	Peter Bergeron	.25		519	Bruce Chen	.25		637	Marcus Giles	.25				
250	Sammy Sosa	.75		402	Kyle Lohse	.25		520	Roberto Alomar	1.00		638	Julian Tavarez	.25				
251	Richard Hidalgo	.25		403	Craig Wilson	.25		521	Orlando Palmeiro	.25		639	Jason Schmidt	.25				
252	Bartolo Colon	.25		404	David Justice	.75		522	Steve Finley	.25		640	Alex Rodriguez	3.00				
253	Jorge Posada	.50		405	Darin Erstad	.50		523	Danny Patterson	.25		641	Anaheim Angels	.25				
254	LaTroy Hawkins	.25		406	Jose Mercedes	.25		524	Terry Adams	.25		642	Arizona Diamondbacks	.25				
255	Paul LoDuca	.25		407	Carl Pavano	.25		525	Tino Martinez	.50		643	Atlanta Braves	.25				
256	Carlos Febles	.25		408	Albie Lopez	.25		526	Tony Armas Jr.	.25		644	Baltimore Orioles	.25				
257	Nelson Cruz	.25		409	Alex Ochoa	.25		527	Geoff Jenkins	.25		645	Boston Red Sox	.25				
258	Edgardo Alfonzo	.25		410	Chipper Jones	1.50		528	Chris Michalak	.25		646	Chicago Cubs	.25				
259	Joey Hamilton	.25		411	Tyler Houston	.25		529	Corey Patterson	.50		647	Chicago White Sox	.25				
260	Cliff Floyd	.25		412	Dean Palmer	.25		530	Brian Giles	.40		648	Cincinnati Reds	.25				
261	Wes Helms	.25		413	Damian Jackson	.25		531	Jose Jimenez	.25		649	Cleveland Indians	.25				
262	Jay Bell	.25		414	Josh Towers	.25		532	Joe Kennedy	.25		650	Colorado Rockies	.25				
263	Mike Cameron	.25		415	Rafael Furcal	.50		533	Armando Rios	.25		651	Detroit Tigers	.25				
264	Paul Konerko	.40		416	Mike Morgan	.25		534	Osvaldo Fernandez	.25		652	Florida Marlins	.25				
265	Jeff Kent	.50		417	Herb Perry	.25		535	Ruben Sierra	.25		653	Houston Astros	.25				
266	Robert Fick	.25		418	Mike Sirotka	.25		536	Octavio Dotel	.25		654	Kansas City Royals	.25				
267	Allen Levrault	.25		419	Mark Wohlers	.25		537	Luis Sojo	.25		655	Los Angeles Dodgers	.25				
268	Placido Polanco	.25		420	Nomar Garciaparra	.75		538	Brent Butler	.25		656	Milwaukee Brewers	.25				

Black Refractor

Stars: 5-10X
Production 50 Sets

Gold Refractor

Stars: 2-4X
Inserted 1:4

Aces

		NM/M
	Common Player:	10.00
KB	Kevin Brown	10.00
TH	Tim Hudson	10.00
AL	Al Leiter	10.00
CS	Curt Schilling	15.00
BZ	Barry Zito	10.00

Batterymates

		NM/M
Inserted 1:349		
GL	Tom Glavine, Javy Lopez	20.00
HP	Mike Hampton, Ben Petrick	10.00

Deuces Are Wild

		NM/M
Common Card:		
Inserted 1:428		
CA	Andruw Jones, Chipper Jones	40.00
BT	Bernie Williams, Tino Martinez	25.00
RC	Ryan Dempster, Cliff Floyd	10.00

Jack of All Trades

		NM/M
Common Player:		10.00
CJ	Chipper Jones	20.00
MO	Magglio Ordonez	10.00
AR	Alex Rodriguez	25.00

Kings of the Clubhouse

		NM/M
Common Player:		15.00
JB	Jeff Bagwell	15.00
TG	Tony Gwynn	20.00
AR	Alex Rodriguez	25.00

Like Father, Like Son Relics

		NM/M
Inserted 1:790		
WI	Preston Wilson, Mookie Wilson	10.00

Three of a Kind

		NM/M
Common Card		
AIR	Alex Rodriguez, Ivan Rodriguez, Rafael Palmeiro	50.00
BEJ	Bret Boone, Edgar Martinez, John Olerud	25.00
JCL	Jeff Bagwell, Craig Biggio, Lance Berkman	40.00

Top Of The Order

		NM/M
Common Player:		8.00
Inserted 1:106		
BA	Benny Agbayani/Jsy	8.00
PB	Peter Bergeron/Jsy	8.00
CB	Craig Biggio/Jsy	15.00
JD	Johnny Damon/Bat	10.00
RF	Rafael Furcal/Bat	10.00
RH	Rickey Henderson/Bat	20.00
JK	Jason Kendall/Bat	10.00
CK	Chuck Knoblauch/Bat	8.00
PL	Paul LoDuca/Bat	10.00
KL	Kenny Lofton/Jsy	10.00
JP	Juan Pierre/Bat	10.00
SS	Shannon Stewart/Jsy	10.00

1952 Player Reprints

		NM/M
Complete Set (19):		50.00
Common Card:		3.00
Inserted 1:8		
Refractors:		2X
Inserted 1:24		
52R-1	Roy Campanella	4.00
52R-2	Duke Snider	4.00
52R-3	Carl Erskine	3.00
52R-4	Andy Pafko	3.00
52R-5	Johnny Mize	3.00
52R-6	Billy Martin	4.00
52R-7	Phil Rizzuto	4.00
52R-8	Gil McDougald	3.00
52R-9	Allie Reynolds	3.00
52R-10	Jackie Robinson	3.00
52R-11	Preacher Roe	3.00
52R-12	Gil Hodges	3.00
52R-13	Billy Cox	3.00
52R-14	Yogi Berra	4.00
52R-15	Gene Woodling	3.00
52R-16	Johnny Sain	3.00
52R-17	Ralph Houk	3.00
52R-18	Joe Collins	3.00
52R-19	Hank Bauer	3.00

2002 Topps eTopps

ERIC HINSKE
TORONTO BLUE JAYS

Topps continued its on-line card program with a second annual eTopps edition in 2002. Initial Player Offerings were again made for only one week with allocations having to be made for some cards in high demand. After the IPO, cards could be bought and sold within portfolios, or physically delivered (for a fee) for more traditional venues. The 2-1/2" x 3-1/2" cards are printed on metallic foil with vertical portrait and action photos on front. Horizontal backs have another portrait photo, a 2001 recap and 2002 "prospectus," and a few biographical bits and stats. The listings here include the initial offering price and the number of cards sold during the open ordering period. Values shown are for cards in a virtual portfolio, rather than "in hand." Taking physical possession of a card from an eTopps portfolio costs about $7.

		NM/M
Complete Set (107):		185.00
Common Player:		1.50
1	Ichiro Suzuki ($9.50 / 9,477)	2.00
2	Jason Giambi ($9.50 / 5,142)	1.50
3	Roberto Alomar ($6.50 / 2,711)	1.50
4	Bret Boone ($4 / 2,000)	6.00
5	Frank Catalanotto ($6.50 / 2,000)	6.00
6	Alex Rodriguez ($9.50 / 6,393)	3.00
7	Jim Thome ($6.50 / 2,927)	2.00
8	Toby Hall ($6.50 / 2,000)	1.50
9	Troy Glaus ($6.50 / 4,323)	1.50
10	Derek Jeter ($9.50 / 8,000)	4.00
11	Alfonso Soriano ($6.50 / 5,000)	1.50
12	Eric Chavez ($6.50 / 4,334)	1.50
13	Preston Wilson ($4 / 2,000)	1.50
14	Bernie Williams ($6.50 / 4,436)	1.50
15	Larry Walker ($6.50 / 2,546)	1.50
16	Todd Helton ($9.50 / 3,430)	1.50
17	Moises Alou ($6.50 / 2,856)	1.50
18	Lance Berkman ($6.50 / 5,000)	1.50
19	Chipper Jones ($6.50 / 4,734)	1.50
20	Andruw Jones ($6.50 / 4,849)	1.50
21	Barry Bonds ($9.50 / 6,658)	7.50
22	Sammy Sosa ($9.50 / 8,000)	1.50
23	Luis Gonzalez ($6.50 / 2,671)	1.50
24	Shawn Green ($6.50 / 4,438)	1.50
25	Jeff Bagwell ($9.50 / 3,359)	1.50
26	Albert Pujols ($6.50 / 5,531)	4.00
27	Rafael Palmeiro ($6.50 / 2,700)	1.50
28	Jimmy Rollins ($4 / 5,000)	1.50
29	Vladimir Guerrero ($6.50 / 6,000)	1.50
30	Jeff Kent ($6.50 / 3,000)	1.50
31	Ken Griffey Jr. ($9.50 / 4,569)	2.00
32	Magglio Ordonez ($6.50 / 4,000)	1.50
33	Mike Piazza ($9.50 / 4,202)	1.50
34	Pedro Martinez ($9.50 / 6,000)	1.50

35	Mark Mulder ($6.50 / 4,000)	1.50
36	Roger Clemens ($9.50 / 4,567)	2.50
37	Freddy Garcia ($6.50 / 4,986)	1.50
38	Tim Hudson ($6.50 / 2,000)	1.50
39	Mike Mussina ($6.50 / 3,708)	1.50
40	Joe Mays ($4 / 3,000)	1.50
41	Barry Zito ($6.50 / 3,590)	1.50
42	Jermaine Dye ($6.50 / 2,693)	1.50
43	Mariano Rivera ($6.50 / 3,709)	1.50
44	Randy Johnson ($9.50 / 6,211)	1.50
45	Curt Schilling ($6.50 / 5,190)	1.50
46	Greg Maddux ($9.50 / 4,008)	1.50
47	Javier Vazquez ($6.50 / 3,000)	1.50
48	Kerry Wood ($6.50 / 3,346)	1.50
49	Wilson Betemit ($6.50 / 2,377)	1.50
50	Adam Dunn ($6.50 / 6,000)	1.50
51	Josh Beckett ($6.50 / 5,000)	2.00
52	Paul LoDuca ($4 / 3,998)	1.50
53	Ben Sheets ($4 / 3,842)	1.50
54	Eric Valent ($4 / 5,000)	1.50
55	Brian Giles ($6.50 / 2,000)	1.50
56	Mo Vaughn ($6.50 / 2,772)	1.50
57	C.C. Sabathia ($6.50 / 2,525)	1.50
58	Nick Johnson ($6.50 / 5,000)	1.50
59	Miguel Tejada ($6.50 / 4,000)	1.50
60	Carlos Delgado ($6.50 / 3,604)	1.50
61	Tsuyoshi Shinjo ($4 / 3,000)	1.50
62	Juan Gonzalez ($6.50 / 2,361)	1.50
63	Mike Sweeney ($6.50 / 3,175)	1.50
64	Ivan Rodriguez ($9.50 / 3,000)	1.50
65	Bud Smith ($4.00 / 3,000)	2.00
66	Brandon Duckworth ($6.50 / 2,000)	4.00
67	Xavier Nady ($4 / 4,000)	1.50
68	D'Angelo Jimenez ($6.50 / 1,725)	1.50
69	Roy Oswalt ($6.50 / 3,523)	1.50
70	J.D. Drew ($9.50 / 3,195)	1.50
71	Cliff Floyd ($6.50 / 3,575)	1.50
72	Kevin Brown ($6.50 / 3,000)	1.50
73	Gary Sheffield ($6.50 / 2,593)	2.00
74	Aramis Ramirez ($6.50 / 3,000)	1.50
75	Nomar Garciaparra ($9.50 / 5,090)	1.50
76	Phil Nevin ($6.50 / 2,348)	1.50
77	Juan Cruz ($4 / 4,000)	1.50
78	Hideo Nomo ($6.50 / 2,857)	1.50
79	Chris George ($4 / 3,000)	1.50
80	Matt Morris ($4 / 3,000)	1.50
81	Corey Patterson ($6.50 / 4,000)	1.50
82	Joel Pineiro ($6.50 / 4,776)	1.50
83	Mark Buehrle ($4 / 3,000)	4.00
84	Shannon Stewart ($4 / 1,992)	1.50
85	Kazuhiro Sasaki ($6.50 / 4,000)	1.50
86	Carlos Pena ($4 / 4,000)	1.50
87	Brad Penny ($6.50 / 3,000)	1.50
88	Rich Aurilia ($6.50 / 2,795)	2.00
89	Wade Miller ($4 / 4,000)	1.50
90	Tim Raines Jr. ($4 / 5,000)	1.50
91	Kazuhisa Ishii ($6.50 / 6,000)	1.50
92	Hank Blalock ($6.50 / 5,000)	3.00
93	So Taguchi ($4 /5,000)	1.50
94	Mark Prior ($9.50 / 5,000)	9.00
95	Rickey Henderson ($9.50 / 4,013)	3.50
96	Austin Kearns ($6.50 / 6,000)	1.50
97	Tom Glavine ($9.50 / 3,000)	1.50
98	Manny Ramirez ($6.50 / 4,905)	1.50

99	Shea Hillenbrand ($6.50 / 4,000)	1.50
100	Junior Spivey ($6.50 / 5,000)	1.50
101	Derek Lowe ($6.50 / 4,911)	1.50
102	Torii Hunter ($6.50 / 4,000)	1.50
103	Juan Rivera ($6.50 / 4,000)	1.50
104	Eric Hinske ($6.50 / 5,000)	1.50
105	Bobby Hill ($6.50 / 5,000)	1.50
106	Rafael Soriano ($6.50 / 4,000)	1.50
107	Jim Edmonds ($6.50 / 3,851)	2.00

2002 Topps eTopps Classics

PITTSBURGH PIRATES

Topps expanded its eTopps line-up in 2002 with the issue of 20 cards of former greats. Like regular eTopps cards, they could only be ordered during a one-week Initial Player Offering period. Cards were issued in a quantity of 4,000 each at $12.50. Fronts have a color or colorized action photo, backs have a picture of one of that player's Topps cards, along with career notes, stats, etc. Values shown are latest auction prices realized on the date cited and represent cards in a virtual portfolio rather than "in hand". The cost to physically move a card from an eTopps portfolio into one's possession is about $7.

		NM/M
Complete Set (20):		90.00
Common Player:		3.50
1	Babe Ruth	15.00
2	Tom Seaver	3.50
3	Honus Wagner	4.00
4	Warren Spahn	3.50
5	Frank Robinson	3.50
6	Whitey Ford	3.50
7	Bob Gibson	3.50
8	Reggie Jackson	5.00
9	Joe Morgan	3.50
10	Harmon Killebrew	3.50
11	Eddie Mathews	3.50
12	Willie Mays	9.00
12a	Willie Mays (2004 autographed edition of 100)	135.00
13	Brooks Robinson	3.50
14	Ty Cobb	5.00
15	Carl Yastrzemski	4.00
16	Jackie Robinson	7.00
17	Mike Schmidt	4.50
18	Nolan Ryan	9.00
19	Duke Snider	3.50
20	Stan Musial	4.50

2002 Topps eTopps Events

GREEN BLASTS
4 HOME RUNS

Special events during the 2002 season were commemorated by Topps with the issue of special eTopps cards. Like the regular-issue eTopps, the cards were only available directly from Topps on-line. Five thousand of each card were issued with an initial order

price of $8 each. Only the baseball related Events cards are listed here. Values shown are for cards in a virtual portfolio. Taking physical possession of a card from an eTopps portfolio costs about $7 apiece.

		NM/M
1	Mike Cameron (Four HR)(5,000)	1.00
2	Shawn Green (Four HR, 19 TB)(5,000)	1.00
3	Oakland A's (20 Straight Wins)(5,000)	1.00
5	Greg Maddux (15+ Wins, 15 Years)(3,851)	1.50

2002 Topps Gallery

		NM/M
Complete Set (200):		60.00
Common Player:		.25
Common (151-200):		.75
Inserted 1:1		
Pack (6):		1.50
Box (24):		30.00
1	Jason Giambi	.50
2	Mark Grace	.40
3	Bret Boone	.40
4	Antonio Alfonseca	.25
5	Kevin Brown	.40
6	Cristian Guzman	.25
7	Magglio Ordonez	.40
8	Luis Gonzalez	.40
9	Jorge Posada	.40
10	Roberto Alomar	.50
11	Mike Sweeney	.25
12	Jeff Kent	.40
13	Matt Morris	.25
14	Alfonso Soriano	.75
15	Adam Dunn	.50
16	Neifi Perez	.25
17	Todd Walker	.25
18	J.D. Drew	.40
19	Eric Chavez	.40
20	Alex Rodriguez	1.50
21	Ray Lankford	.25
22	Roger Cedeno	.25
23	Chipper Jones	.75
24	Jose Canseco	.50
25	Mike Piazza	1.50
26	Freddy Garcia	.25
27	Todd Helton	.50
28	Tino Martinez	.40
29	Kazuhiro Sasaki	.25
30	Curt Schilling	.50
31	Mark Buehrle	.25
32	John Olerud	.40
33	Brad Radke	.25
34	Steve Sparks	.25
35	Jason Tyner	.25
36	Jeff Shaw	.25
37	Mariano Rivera	.40
38	Russ Ortiz	.25
39	Richard Hidalgo	.25
40	Barry Bonds	2.00
41	John Burkett	.25
42	Tim Hudson	.40
43	Mike Hampton	.25
44	Orlando Cabrera	.25
45	Barry Zito	.40
46	C.C. Sabathia	.25
47	Chan Ho Park	.25
48	Tom Glavine	.40
49	Aramis Ramirez	.40
50	Lance Berkman	.40
51	Al Leiter	.25
52	Phil Nevin	.25
53	Javier Vazquez	.25
54	Troy Glaus	.40
55	Tsuyoshi Shinjo	.25
56	Albert Pujols	1.50
57	John Smoltz	.40
58	Derek Jeter	2.00
59	Robb Nen	.25
60	Jason Kendall	.25
61	Eric Gagne	.50
62	Vladimir Guerrero	.75
63	Corey Patterson	.40
64	Rickey Henderson	.50
65	Jack Wilson	.25
66	Jason LaRue	.25
67	Sammy Sosa	1.50
68	Ken Griffey Jr.	1.00
69	Randy Johnson	.75
70	Nomar Garciaparra	1.50
71	Ivan Rodriguez	.75
72	J.T. Snow	.25
73	Darryl Kile	.25

74	Andruw Jones	.50
75	Brian Giles	.40
76	Pedro Martinez	.75
77	Jeff Bagwell	.50
78	Rafael Palmeiro	.50
79	Ryan Dempster	.25
80	Jeff Cirillo	.25
81	Geoff Jenkins	.40
82	Brandon Duckworth	.25
83	Roger Clemens	1.50
84	Fred McGriff	.40
85	Hideo Nomo	.50
86	Larry Walker	.40
87	Sean Casey	.40
88	Trevor Hoffman	.25
89	Robert Fick	.25
90	Armando Benitez	.25
91	Jeromy Burnitz	.25
92	Bernie Williams	.50
93	Carlos Delgado	.50
94	Troy Percival	.25
95	Nate Cornejo	.25
96	Derrek Lee	.40
97	Jose Ortiz	.25
98	Brian Jordan	.25
99	Jose Cruz	.25
100	Ichiro Suzuki	1.50
101	Jose Mesa	.25
102	Tim Salmon	.40
103	Bud Smith	.25
104	Paul LoDuca	.25
105	Juan Pierre	.25
106	Ben Grieve	.25
107	Russell Branyan	.25
108	Bobby Abreu	.25
109	Moises Alou	.40
110	Richie Sexson	.50
111	Jerry Hairston Jr.	.25
112	Marlon Anderson	.25
113	Juan Gonzalez	.50
114	Craig Biggio	.40
115	Carlos Beltran	.25
116	Eric Milton	.25
117	Cliff Floyd	.25
118	Rich Aurilia	.25
119	Adrian Beltre	.40
120	Jason Bere	.25
121	Darin Erstad	.40
122	Ben Sheets	.25
123	Johnny Damon	.40
124	Jimmy Rollins	.40
125	Shawn Green	.40
126	Greg Maddux	1.00
127	Mark Mulder	.25
128	Bartolo Colon	.25
129	Shannon Stewart	.25
130	Ramon Ortiz	.25
131	Kerry Wood	.75
132	Ryan Klesko	.25
133	Preston Wilson	.25
134	Roy Oswalt	.40
135	Rafael Furcal	.25
136	Eric Karros	.25
137	Nick Neugebauer	.25
138	Doug Mientkiewicz	.25
139	Paul Konerko	.40
140	Bobby Higginson	.25
141	Garret Anderson	.40
142	Wes Helms	.25
143	Brent Abernathy	.25
144	Scott Rolen	.75
145	Dmitri Young	.25
146	Jim Thome	.75
147	Raul Mondesi	.40
148	Pat Burrell	.40
149	Gary Sheffield	.40
150	Miguel Tejada	.40
151	Brandon Inge	.75
152	Carlos Pena	.75
153	Jason Lane	.75
154	Nathan Haynes	.75
155	Hank Blalock	1.50
156	Juan Cruz	.75
157	Morgan Ensberg	.75
158	Sean Burroughs	.75
159	Ed Rogers	.75
160	Nick Johnson	.75
161	Orlando Hudson	.75
162	Anastacio Martinez RC	.75
163	Jeremy Affeldt	.75
164	Brandon Claussen	.75
165	Deivis Santos	.75
166	Mike Rivera	.75
167	Carlos Silva	.75
168	Valentino Pascucci	.75
169	Xavier Nady	.75
170	David Espinosa	.75
171	Dan Phillips RC	.75
172	Tony Fontana RC	.75
173	Juan Silvestre	.75
174	Henry Pichardo RC	.75
175	Pablo Arias RC	.75
176	Brett Roneberg RC	.75
177	Chad Qualls RC	.75
178	Greg Sain RC	.75
179	Rene Reyes RC	.75
180	So Taguchi	1.00
181	Dan Johnson RC	1.00
182	Justin Backsmeyer RC	.75
183	Juan Gonzalez	.75
184	Jason Ellison RC	.75
185	Kazuhisa Ishii RC	1.00
186	Joe Mauer RC	10.00
187	James Shanks RC	.75
188	Kevin Cash RC	.75
189	J.J. Trujillo RC	.75
190	Jorge Padilla RC	1.00
191	Nolan Ryan	4.00

192	George Brett	3.00
193	Ryne Sandberg	2.00
194	Robin Yount	1.50
195	Tom Seaver	1.00
196	Mike Schmidt	1.00
197	Frank Robinson	1.00
198	Harmon Killebrew	1.00
199	Kirby Puckett	2.00
200	Don Mattingly	4.00

Autographs

		NM/M
Common Player:		8.00
Inserted 1:192		
LB	Lance Berkman	35.00
BBO	Bret Boone	20.00
JD	J.D. Drew	25.00
LG	Luis Gonzalez	20.00
SG	Shawn Green	25.00
JL	Jason Lane	8.00
MO	Magglio Ordonez	20.00
JP	Jorge Posada	40.00
JS	Juan Silvestre	8.00

Baseball Bucks

		NM/M
Used for gallery original art auctions:		
$5	Nolan Ryan	2.50

Originals Relics

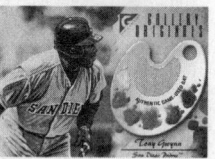

		NM/M
Common Player:		8.00
Inserted 1:169		
BBO	Bret Boone	8.00
JC	Jose Canseco	10.00
CD	Carlos Delgado	8.00
JG	Juan Gonzalez	10.00
LG	Luis Gonzalez	8.00
TG	Tony Gwynn	15.00
TH	Todd Helton	12.00
AJ	Andruw Jones	8.00
CJ	Chipper Jones	10.00
TM	Tino Martinez	10.00
MP	Mike Piazza	20.00
AP	Albert Pujols	35.00
AR	Alex Rodriguez	15.00
AS	Alfonso Soriano	10.00
BW	Bernie Williams	10.00

Heritage

AL KALINE
DETROIT TIGERS

		NM/M
Complete Set (25):		100.00
Common Player:		2.00
Inserted 1:12		
RA	Roberto Alomar	4.00
BBO	Bret Boone	2.00
RC	Roger Clemens	8.00
JG	Jason Giambi	3.00
LG	Luis Gonzalez	2.00
SG	Shawn Green	3.00
KG	Ken Griffey Jr.	6.00
TG	Tony Gwynn	4.00
RJ	Reggie Jackson	4.00
CJ	Chipper Jones	4.00
AK	Al Kaline	4.00
GM	Greg Maddux	5.00
PM	Pedro Martinez	4.00
MM	Mark McGwire	10.00
SM	Stan Musial	5.00
MP	Mike Piazza	4.00
BR	Brooks Robinson	4.00
AR	Alex Rodriguez	8.00
NR	Nolan Ryan	10.00
MS	Mike Schmidt	6.00
TS	Tom Seaver	4.00
TSH	Tsuyoshi Shinjo	2.00
SS	Sammy Sosa	8.00

CY	Carl Yastrzemski	5.00
RY	Robin Yount	5.00

Heritage Autographs
NM/M
Inserted 1:240

BBO	Bret Boone	20.00
LG	Luis Gonzalez	25.00
SG	Shawn Green	25.00

Heritage Relics
NM/M
Common Player: 8.00
Inserted 1:85

BBO	Bret Boone	8.00
LG	Luis Gonzalez	15.00
TG	Tony Gwynn	15.00
CJ	Chipper Jones	10.00
GM	Greg Maddux	15.00
PM	Pedro Martinez	15.00
MP	Mike Piazza	15.00
AR	Alex Rodriguez	15.00
TS	Tsuyoshi Shinjo	8.00

Press Plates

The aluminum press plates used to print the Gallery cards were inserted at a rate of one per 1,200 packs. Each card's front and back can be found in four different color variations. Because of the unique nature of each plate, assignment of catalog values in not feasible.

NM/M
Common Player: 50.00

Team Topps Legends Autographs
NM/M
Inserted 1:1,019

Luis Aparicio	15.00
Jim Bunning	20.00
Fergie Jenkins	15.00
Carl Yastrzemski	65.00

2002 Topps Gold Label

NM/M
Complete Set (200): 60.00
Common Player: .25
Pack (4): 3.00
Box (18): 40.00

1	Alex Rodriguez	1.50
2	Derek Jeter	2.00
3	Luis Gonzalez	.40
4	Troy Glaus	.40
5	Albert Pujols	1.50
6	Lance Berkman	.40
7	J.D. Drew	.40
8	Chipper Jones	.75
9	Miguel Tejada	.40
10	Randy Johnson	.75
11	Mike Cameron	.25
12	Brian Giles	.40
13	Roger Cedeno	.25
14	Kerry Wood	.75
15	Ken Griffey Jr.	1.00
16	Carlos Lee	.25
17	Todd Helton	.50
18	Gary Sheffield	.40
19	Richie Sexson	.40
20	Vladimir Guerrero	.75
21	Bobby Higginson	.25
22	Roger Clemens	1.50
23	Barry Zito	.40
24	Juan Pierre	.25
25	Pedro Martinez	.75
26	Sean Casey	.40
27	David Segui	.25
28	Jose Garcia	.25
29	Curt Schilling	.50
30	Bernie Williams	.40
31	Ben Grieve	.25
32	Hideo Nomo	.40
33	Aramis Ramirez	.40
34	Cristian Guzman	.25
35	Rich Aurilia	.25
36	Greg Maddux	1.00
37	Eric Chavez	.40
38	Shawn Green	.40
39	Luis Rivas	.25
40	Magglio Ordonez	.40
41	Jose Vidro	.25
42	Mariano Rivera	.40
43	Chris Tritle RC	.50
44	C.C. Sabathia	.25
45	Larry Walker	.40
46	Raul Mondesi	.25
47	Kevin Brown	.40
48	Jeff Bagwell	.50
49	Earl Snyder RC	.50
50	Jason Giambi	.50
51	Ichiro Suzuki	1.50
52	Andruw Jones	.50
53	Ivan Rodriguez	.50
54	Jim Edmonds	.40
55	Preston Wilson	.25
56	Greg Vaughn	.25
57	Jon Lieber	.25
58	Justin Sherrod RC	.50
59	Marcus Giles	.25
60	Roberto Alomar	.40
61	Pat Burrell	.40
62	Doug Mientkiewicz	.25
63	Mark Mulder	.40
64	Mike Hampton	.25
65	Adam Dunn	.50
66	Moises Alou	.40
67	Jose Cruz Jr.	.25
68	Derek Bell	.25
69	Sammy Sosa	1.50
70	Joe Mays	.25
71	Phil Nevin	.25
72	Edgardo Alfonzo	.25
73	Barry Bonds	2.00
74	Edgar Martinez	.40
75	Juan Encarnacion	.25
76	Jason Tyner	.25
77	Edgar Renteria	.40
78	Bret Boone	.40
79	Scott Rolen	.75
80	Nomar Garciaparra	1.50
81	Frank Thomas	.50
82	Roy Oswalt	.40
83	Tsuyoshi Shinjo	.25
84	Ben Sheets	.40
85	Hank Blalock	.40
86	Carlos Delgado	.50
87	Tim Hudson	.40
88	Alfonso Soriano	.75
89	Michael Hill RC	.50
90	Jim Thome	.75
91	Craig Biggio	.40
92	Ryan Klesko	.25
93	Geoff Jenkins	.40
94	Matt Morris	.40
95	Jorge Posada	.40
96	Cliff Floyd	.25
97	Jimmy Rollins	.40
98	Mike Sweeney	.25
99	Frank Catalanotto	.25
100	Mike Piazza	1.25
101	Mark Quinn	.25
102	Torii Hunter	.40
103	Lee Stevens	.25
104	Byung-Hyug Kim	.25
105	Freddy Sanchez RC	.50
106	David Cone	.25
107	Jerry Hairston Jr.	.25
108	Kyle Farnsworth	.25
109	Rafael Furcal	.25
110	Bartolo Colon	.25
111	Juan Rivera	.25
112	Kevin Young	.25
113	Chris Narveson RC	1.00
114	Richard Hidalgo	.25
115	Andy Pettitte	.40
116	Darin Erstad	.40
117	Corey Koskie	.25
118	Rickey Henderson	.50
119	Derrek Lee	.40
120	Sean Burroughs	.25
121	Paul Konerko	.25
122	Ross Peeples RC	.50
123	Terrence Long	.25
124	John Smoltz	.40
125	Brandon Duckworth	.25
126	Luis Maza	.25
127	Morgan Ensberg	.25
128	Eric Valent	.25
129	Shannon Stewart	.25
130	D'Angelo Jimenez	.25
131	Jeff Cirillo	.25
132	Jack Cust	.25
133	Dmitri Young	.25
134	Darryl Kile	.25
135	Reggie Sanders	.25
136	Marlon Byrd	.25
137	Napoleon Calzado RC	.50
138	Javy Lopez	.40
139	Orlando Cabrera	.25
140	Mike Mussina	.40
141	Josh Beckett	.25
142	Kazuhiro Sasaki	.25
143	Jermaine Dye	.25
144	Carlos Beltran	.40
145	Trevor Hoffman	.25
146	Kazuhisa Ishii RC	2.00
147	Alex Gonzalez	.25
148	Marty Cordova	.25
149	Kevin Deaton RC	.50
150	Toby Hall	.25
151	Rafael Palmeiro	.50
152	John Olerud	.40
153	David Eckstein	.25
154	Doug Glanville	.25
155	Johnny Damon	.40
156	Javier Vazquez	.25
157	Jason Bay RC	2.00
158	Robb Nen	.25
159	Rafael Soriano	.25
160	Placido Polanco	.25
161	Garret Anderson	.40
162	Aaron Boone	.25
163	Mike Lieberthal	.25
164	Joe Mauer RC	15.00
165	Matt Lawton	.25
166	Juan Tolentino RC	.50
167	Alex Gonzalez	.25
168	Steve Finley	.25
169	Troy Percival	.25
170	Bud Smith	.25
171	Freddie Garcia	.25
172	Ray Lankford	.25
173	Tim Redding	.25
174	Ryan Dempster	.25
175	Travis Lee	.25
176	Jeff Kent	.40
177	Ramon Hernandez	.25
178	Carl Everett	.25
179	Tom Glavine	.40
180	Juan Gonzalez	.50
181	Nick Johnson	.25
182	Mike Lowell	.40
183	Al Leiter	.25
184	Jason Maule RC	.50
185	Wilson Betemit	.25
186	Tino Martinez	.25
187	Jason Standridge	.25
188	Mike Peeples RC	.50
189	Jason Kendall	.40
190	Fred McGriff	.40
191	John Rodriguez RC	.50
192	Brett Roneberg RC	.50
193	Marlyn Tisdale RC	.50
194	J.T. Snow	.25
195	Craig Kuzmic RC	.75
196	Cory Lidle	.25
197	Alex Cintron	.25
198	Fernando Vina	.25
199	Austin Kearns	.50
200	Paul LoDuca	.25

Class One Gold

315/500 — JUAN TOLENTINO

Stars: 2-4X
Production 500 Sets

Class Two Platinum

1697/250 — JUAN ENCARNACION

Stars: 4-8X
Production 250 Sets

Class Three Titanium
Stars: 6-10X
Production 100 Sets

Platinum Memorabilia
Platinum: .75-1.5X
Titanium Memorabilia: 1-2X

All-Star MVP Winners
NM/M
Common Player: 8.00

RA	Roberto Alomar	10.00
SA	Sandy Alomar	8.00
BLB	Bobby Bonds	8.00
DC	Dave Concepcion	8.00
SG2	Steve Garvey	10.00
KG	Ken Griffey Sr.	8.00
BM1	Bill Madlock	8.00
FM	Fred McGriff	10.00
DP3	Dave Parker	8.00
TP	Tony Perez	10.00
MP	Mike Piazza	15.00
KP2	Kirby Puckett	15.00
TR	Tim Raines	8.00

Batting Average
NM/M
Common Player: 8.00

WB	Wade Boggs	15.00

Cy Young Winners
NM/M
Common Player: 8.00

RWC	Roger Clemens	15.00
DE	Dennis Eckersley	8.00
RJ	Randy Johnson	12.00
BS	Bret Saberhagen	8.00
JS	John Smoltz	8.00

Home Run Champions
NM/M
Common Player: 8.00

BB2	Barry Bonds	20.00
GF	George Foster	8.00
TK2	Ted Kluszewski	15.00
KM2	Kevin Mitchell	8.00
DM2	Dale Murphy	40.00
AR	Alex Rodriguez	15.00
DS1	Darryl Strawberry	10.00

League Championship MVP Winners
NM/M
Common Player: 8.00

GB2	George Brett	40.00
WC	Will Clark	15.00
CC	Craig Counsell	8.00
RH	Rickey Henderson	15.00
JL	Javier Lopez	8.00
AEP	Andy Pettitte	12.00
KP1	Kirby Puckett	15.00
FW	Frank White	8.00
BFW	Bernie Williams	10.00

MLB Moments in Time

NM/M
Common Player: 8.00

BLB	Barry Bonds	20.00
BB1	Bret Boone	8.00
BB2	Bret Boone	8.00
CD	Carlos Delgado	8.00
TG	Tony Gwynn	15.00
TH	Toby Hall	8.00
CL	Carlos Lee	8.00
JL	Javy Lopez	8.00
MO	Magglio Ordonez	10.00
RP1	Rafael Palmeiro	10.00
RP2	Rafael Palmeiro	10.00
AR	Alex Rodriguez	15.00

MVP Winners
NM/M
Common Player: 8.00

EB	Ernie Banks	20.00
DB	Don Baylor	8.00
YB	Yogi Berra	15.00
BB1	Barry Bonds	20.00
GB1	George Brett	40.00
SG1	Steve Garvey	8.00
KHG	Kirk Gibson	8.00
KH	Keith Hernandez	10.00
RJ1	Reggie Jackson	15.00
DM	Don Mattingly	40.00
KM1	Kevin Mitchell	8.00
JM	Joe Morgan	8.00
DM1	Dale Murphy	40.00
DP1	Dave Parker	8.00
BR	Brooks Robinson	15.00
FR	Frank Robinson	12.00
RS	Ryne Sandberg	40.00
HS	Hank Sauer	8.00
WS	Willie Stargell	15.00
JT	Joe Torre	10.00
MW	Maury Wills	8.00
CY1	Carl Yastrzemski	30.00
RY	Robin Yount	20.00

RBI Leaders
NM/M
Common Player: 8.00

BRB	Bret Boone	8.00
BRB2	Bret Boone	8.00
GC	Gary Carter	8.00
GL	Greg Luzinski	8.00

EM1	Eddie Murray	12.00
AO	Al Oliver	8.00
DP2	Dave Parker	8.00
DW	Dave Winfield	12.00

Rookie of the Year Winners
NM/M
Common Player: 8.00

DA	Dick Allen	15.00
AB	Al Bumbry	8.00
RC1	Rod Carew	15.00
CF	Carlton Fisk	15.00
MH	Mike Hargrove	8.00
DJ	Dave Justice	10.00
EM2	Eddie Murray	12.00
LP	Lou Piniella	10.00
AP	Albert Pujols	20.00
DS2	Darryl Strawberry	15.00
FV	Fernando Valenzuela	8.00
BW	Billy Williams	10.00

World Series MVP Winners

NM/M
Common Player: 8.00

JB	Johnny Bench	15.00
RCC	Ron Cey	8.00
RJ2	Reggie Jackson	15.00
PM	Paul Molitor	15.00
MR	Mariano Rivera	10.00

2002 Topps Heritage

KERRY WOOD — pitcher CHICAGO CUBS

NM/M
Complete Set (440): 325.00
Common Player: .25
Common (364-446): 3.00
Inserted 1:2
Pack (8): 4.00
Box (24): 90.00

1	Ichiro Suzuki/SP	10.00
2	Darin Erstad	.50
3	Rod Beck	.25
4	Doug Mientkiewicz	.25
5	Mike Sweeney	.25
6	Roger Clemens	2.50
7	Jason Tyner	.25
8	Alex Gonzalez	.25
9	Eric Young	.25
10	Randy Johnson	1.50
10	Randy Johnson/SP	6.00
11	Aaron Sele	.25
12	Tony Clark	.25
13	C.C. Sabathia	.25
14	Melvin Mora	.25
15	Tim Hudson	.50
16	Ben Petrick	.25
17	Tom Glavine	.75
18	Jason Lane	.25
19	Larry Walker	.50
20	Mark Mulder	.25
21	Steve Finley	.25
22	Bengie Molina	.25
23	Rob Bell	.25
24	Nathan Haynes	.25
25	Rafael Furcal	.50
25	Rafael Furcal/SP	3.00
26	Mike Mussina	1.00
27	Paul LoDuca	.25
28	Torii Hunter	.50
29	Carlos Lee	.25
30	Jimmy Rollins	.50
31	Arthur Rhodes	.25
32	Ivan Rodriguez	1.00
33	Wes Helms	.25
34	Cliff Floyd	.25
35	Julian Tavarez	.25
36	Mark McGwire	4.00
37	Chipper Jones/SP	6.00
38	Denny Neagle	.25
39	Odalis Perez	.25
40	Antonio Alfonseca	.25
41	Edgar Renteria	.25
42	Troy Glaus	.75
43	Scott Brosius	.25
44	Abraham Nunez	.25
45	Jamey Wright	.25
46	Bobby Bonilla	.25
47	Ismael Valdes	.25
48	Chris Reitsma	.25
49	Neifi Perez	.25
50	Juan Cruz	.25
51	Kevin Brown	.50
52	Ben Grieve	.25
53	Alex Rodriguez/SP	10.00
54	Charles Nagy	.25
55	Reggie Sanders	.25
56	Nelson Figueroa	.25
57	Felipe Lopez	.25
58	Bill Ortega	.25
59	Mac Suzuki	.25
60	Johnny Estrada	.25
61	Bob Wickman	.25
62	Doug Glanville	.25
63	Jeff Cirillo	.50
63	Jeff Cirillo/SP	3.00
64	Corey Patterson	.50
65	Aaron Myette	.25
66	Magglio Ordonez	.50
67	Ellis Burks	.25
68	Miguel Tejada	.50
69	John Olerud	.25
69	John Olerud/SP	4.00
70	Greg Vaughn	.25
71	Andy Pettitte	.75
72	Mike Matheny	.25
73	Brandon Duckworth	.25
74	Scott Schoeneweis	.25
75	Mike Lowell	.50
76	Einar Diaz	.25
77	Tino Martinez	.50
78	Matt Williams	.25
79	Jason Young RC	1.00
80	Nate Cornejo	.25
81	Andres Galarraga	.40
82	Bernie Williams/SP	6.00
83	Ryan Klesko	.25
84	Dan Wilson	.25
85	Henry Pichardo RC	.25
86	Ray Durham	.25
87	Omar Daal	.25
88	Derrek Lee	.25
89	Al Leiter	.50
90	Darrin Fletcher	.25
91	Josh Beckett	.75
92	Johnny Damon	.25
92	Johnny Damon/SP	5.00
93	Abraham Nunez	.25
94	Ricky Ledee	.25
95	Richie Sexson	.75
96	Adam Kennedy	.25
97	Raul Mondesi	.25
98	John Burkett	.25
99	Ben Sheets	.50
99	Ben Sheets/SP	4.00
100	Preston Wilson	.25
100	Preston Wilson/SP	3.00
101	Boof Bonser	.25
102	Shigetoshi Hasegawa	.25
103	Carlos Febles	.25
104	Jorge Posada/SP	5.00
105	Michael Tucker	.25
106	Roberto Hernandez	.25
107	Juan Rodriguez RC	.75
108	Danny Graves	.25
109	Rich Aurilia	.25
110	Jon Lieber	.25
111	Tim Hummel RC	.50
112	J.T. Snow	.25
113	Kris Benson	.25
114	Derek Jeter	4.00
115	John Franco	.25
116	Matt Stairs	.25
117	Ben Davis	.25
118	Darryl Kile	.25
119	Mike Peeples RC	.50
120	Kevin Tapani	.25
121	Armando Benitez	.25
122	Damian Miller	.25
123	Jose Jimenez	.25
124	Pedro Astacio	.25
125	Marlyn Tisdale RC	.50
126	Deivi Cruz	.25
127	Paul O'Neill	.75
128	Jermaine Dye	.25
129	Marcus Giles	.25
130	Mark Loretta	.25
131	Garret Anderson	.50
132	Todd Ritchie	.25
133	Joe Crede	.25
134	Kevin Millwood	.50
135	Shane Reynolds	.25
136	Mark Grace	.75
137	Shannon Stewart	.25
138	Nick Neugebauer	.25
139	Nic Jackson RC	.75
140	Robb Nen	.25
141	Dmitri Young	.25
142	Kevin Appier	.25
143	Jack Cust	.25
144	Andres Torres	.25
145	Frank Thomas	1.00
146	Jason Kendall	.25
147	Greg Maddux	2.00
148	David Justice	.50
149	Hideo Nomo	.25
150	Bret Boone	.50
151	Wade Miller	.25
152	Jeff Kent	.50
153	Scott Williamson	.25
154	Julio Lugo	.25
155	Bobby Higginson	.25
156	Geoff Jenkins	.25
157	Darren Dreifort	.25
158	Freddy Sanchez RC	1.00
159	Bud Smith	.25
160	Phil Nevin	.25

No.	Player	Price
161	Cesar Izturis	.25
162	Sean Casey	.50
163	Jose Ortiz	.25
164	Brent Abernathy	.25
165	Kevin Young	.25
166	Daryle Ward	.25
167	Trevor Hoffman	.25
168	Rondell White	.25
169	Kip Wells	.25
170	John Vander Wal	.25
171	Jose Lima	.25
172	Wilton Guerrero	.25
173	Aaron Dean	.25
174	Rick Helling	.25
175	Juan Pierre	.25
176	Jay Bell	.25
177	Craig House	.25
178	David Bell	.25
179	Pat Burrell	.50
180	Eric Gagne	.75
181	Adam Pettyjohn	.25
182	Ugueth Urbina	.25
183	Peter Bergeron	.25
184	Adrian Gonzalez	.25
184	Adrian Gonzalez/SP	4.00
185	Damion Easley	.25
186	Gookie Dawkins	.25
187	Matt Lawton	.25
188	Frank Catalanotto	.25
189	David Wells	.25
190	Roger Cedeno	.25
191	Brian Giles	.50
192	Julio Zuleta	.25
193	Timo Perez	.25
194	Billy Wagner	.25
195	Craig Counsell	.25
196	Brent Miadich	.25
197	Gary Sheffield	.75
198	Richard Hidalgo	.50
199	Juan Uribe	.25
200	Curt Schilling	1.00
201	Javy Lopez	.50
202	Jimmy Haynes	.25
203	Jim Edmonds	.75
204	Pokey Reese	.25
204	Pokey Reese/SP	3.00
205	Matt Clement	.25
206	Dean Palmer	.25
207	Nick Johnson	.25
208	Nate Espy RC	.75
209	Pedro Feliz	.25
210	Aaron Rowand	.25
211	Masato Yoshii	.25
212	Jose Cruz	.25
213	Paul Byrd	.25
214	Mark Phillips RC	1.00
215	Benny Agbayani	.25
216	Frank Menechino	.25
217	John Flaherty	.25
218	Brian Boehringer	.25
219	Todd Hollandsworth	.25
220	Sammy Sosa/SP	8.00
221	Steve Sparks	.25
222	Homer Bush	.25
223	Mike Hampton	.50
224	Bobby Abreu	.50
225	Barry Larkin	.75
226	Ryan Rupe	.25
227	Bubba Trammell	.25
228	Todd Zeile	.25
229	Jeff Shaw	.25
230	Alex Ochoa	.25
231	Orlando Cabrera	.25
232	Jeremy Giambi	.25
233	Tomo Ohka	.25
234	Luis Castillo	.25
235	Chris Holt	.25
236	Shawn Green	.50
237	Sidney Ponson	.25
238	Lee Stevens	.25
239	Hank Blalock	.50
240	Randy Winn	.25
241	Pedro Martinez	1.50
242	Vinny Castilla	.25
243	Steve Karsay	.25
244	Barry Bonds/SP	15.00
245	Jason Bere	.25
246	Scott Rolen	1.50
246	Scott Rolen/SP	6.00
247	Ryan Kohlmeier	.25
248	Kerry Wood	1.50
249	Aramis Ramirez	.50
250	Lance Berkman	.75
251	Omar Vizquel	.25
252	Juan Encarnacion	.25
253	David Segui	.25
254	Brian Anderson	.25
255	Jay Payton	.25
256	Mark Grudzielanek	.25
257	Jimmy Anderson	.25
258	Eric Valent	.25
259	Chad Durbin	.25
260	Alex Gonzalez	.25
261	Scott Dunn	.25
262	Scott Elarton	.25
263	Tom Gordon	.25
264	Moises Alou	.50
265	Mark Buehrle	.25
266	Jerry Hairston Jr.	.25
267	Luke Prokopec	.25
268	Graeme Lloyd	.25
269	Bret Prinz	.25
270	Chris Carpenter	.25
271	Ryan Minor	.25
272	Jeff D'Amico	.25
273	Raul Ibanez	.25
274	Joe Mays	.25
275	Livan Hernandez	.25
276	Chris Carpenter	.25
277	Ryan Minor	.25
278	Jeff D'Amico	.25
279	Raul Ibanez	.25
280	Joe Mays	.25
281	Livan Hernandez	.25

No.	Player	Price
282	Robin Ventura	.40
283	Gabe Kapler	.40
284	Tony Batista	.25
285	Ramon Hernandez	.25
286	Craig Paquette	.25
287	Mark Kotsay	.25
288	Mike Lieberthal	.25
289	Joe Borchard	.25
290	Cristian Guzman	.25
291	Craig Biggio	.50
292	Joaquin Benoit	.25
293	Ken Caminiti	.25
294	Sean Burroughs	.25
295	Eric Karros	.25
296	Eric Chavez	.50
297	LaTroy Hawkins	.25
298	Alfonso Soriano	1.00
299	John Smoltz	.25
300	Adam Dunn	1.00
301	Ryan Dempster	.25
302	Travis Hafner	.50
303	Russell Branyan	.25
304	Dustin Hermanson	.25
305	Jim Thome	1.50
306	Carlos Beltran	.75
307	Jason Botts RC	.25
308	David Cone	.25
309	Ivanon Coffie	.25
310	Brian Jordan	.25
311	Todd Walker	.25
312	Jeromy Burnitz	.25
313	Tony Armas	.25
314	Jeff Conine	.25
315	Todd Jones	.25
316	Roy Oswalt	.50
317	Aubrey Huff	.25
318	Josh Fogg	.25
319	Jose Vidro	.25
320	Jace Brewer	.25
321	Mike Redmond	.25
322	Noochie Varner RC	1.00
323	Russ Ortiz	.25
324	Edgardo Alfonzo	.25
325	Ruben Sierra	.25
326	Calvin Murray	.25
327	Marlon Anderson	.25
328	Albie Lopez	.25
329	Chris Gomez	.25
330	Fernando Tatis	.25
331	Stubby Clapp	.25
332	Rickey Henderson	.75
333	Brad Radke	.25
334	Brent Mayne	.25
335	Cory Lidle	.25
336	Edgar Martinez	.50
337	Aaron Boone	.25
338	Jay Witasick	.25
339	Benito Santiago	.25
340	Jose Mercedes	.25
341	Fernando Vina	.25
342	A.J. Pierzynski	.25
343	Jeff Bagwell	1.00
344	Brian Bohanon	.25
345	Adrian Beltre	.50
346	Troy Percival	.25
347	Napoleon Calzado RC	.75
348	Ruben Rivera	.25
349	Rafael Soriano	.25
350	Damian Jackson	.25
351	Joe Randa	.25
352	Chan Ho Park	.25
353	Dante Bichette	.25
354	Bartolo Colon	.25
355	Jason Bay RC	5.00
356	Shea Hillenbrand	.25
357	Matt Morris	.50
358	Brad Penny	.25
359	Mark Quinn	.25
360	Marquis Grissom	.25
361	Henry Blanco	.25
362	Billy Koch	.25
363	Mike Cameron	.25
364	Albert Pujols	10.00
365	Paul Konerko	.50
366	Eric Milton	.25
367	Nick Bierbrodt	.25
368	Rafael Palmeiro	5.00
369	Jorge Padilla RC	.25
370	Jason Giambi	4.00
371	Mike Piazza	10.00
372	Alex Cora	.25
373	Todd Helton	6.00
374	Juan Gonzalez	6.00
375	Mariano Rivera	6.00
376	Jason LaRue	.25
377	Tony Gwynn	6.00
378	Wilson Betemit	3.00
379	J.J. Trujillo RC	3.00
380	Brad Ausmus	3.00
381	Chris George	3.00
382	Jose Canseco	5.00
383	Ramon Ortiz	3.00
384	John Rocker	3.00
385	Rey Ordonez	3.00
386	Ken Griffey Jr.	10.00
387	Juan Pena	3.00
388	Michael Barrett	3.00
389	J.D. Drew	4.00
390	Corey Koskie	3.00
391	Vernon Wells	3.00
392	Juan Tolentino RC	3.00
393	Luis Gonzalez	4.00
394	Terrance Long	3.00
395	Travis Lee	3.00
396	Earl Snyder RC	3.00
397	Nomar Garciaparra	10.00
398	Jason Schmidt	3.00
399	David Espinosa	3.00

No.	Player	Price
400	Steve Green	3.00
401	Jack Wilson	3.00
402	Chris Tritle RC	3.00
403	Angel Berroa	3.00
404	Josh Towers	3.00
405	Andruw Jones	4.00
406	Brent Butler	3.00
407	Craig Kuzmic RC	3.00
408	Derek Bell	3.00
409	Eric Glaser RC	3.00
410	Joel Pineiro	3.00
411	Alexis Gomez	3.00
412	Mike Rivera	3.00
413	Shawn Estes	3.00
414	Milton Bradley	3.00
415	Carl Everett	3.00
416	Kazuhiro Sasaki	3.00
417	Tony Fontana RC	3.00
418	Josh Pearce	3.00
419	Gary Matthews Jr.	3.00
420	Raymond Cabrera RC	3.00
421	Joe Kennedy	3.00
422	Jason Maule RC	3.00
423	Casey Fossum	3.00
424	Christian Parker	3.00
425	Laynce Nix RC	5.00
426	Byung-Hyun Kim	3.00
427	Freddy Garcia	3.00
428	Herbert Perry	3.00
429	Jason Marquis	3.00
430	Sandy Alomar Jr.	3.00
431	Roberto Alomar	5.00
432	Tsuyoshi Shinjo	3.00
433	Tim Wakefield	3.00
434	Robert Fick	3.00
435	Vladimir Guerrero	6.00
436	Jose Mesa	3.00
437	Scott Spiezio	3.00
438	Jose Hernandez	3.00
439	Jose Acevedo	3.00
440	Brian West RC	3.00
441	Barry Zito	4.00
442	Luis Maza	3.00
443	Marlon Byrd	4.00
444	A.J. Burnett	3.00
445	Dee Brown	3.00
446	Carlos Delgado	5.00

Chrome

Stars (1-100): 6-10X
RC's: 3-6X
Production 553 Sets

Classic Renditions

	NM/M
Complete Set (10):	10.00
Common Player:	.50
Inserted 1:12	
CR-1 Kerry Wood	2.00
CR-2 Brian Giles	1.00
CR-3 Roger Cedeno	.50
CR-4 Jason Giambi	1.50
CR-5 Albert Pujols	4.00
CR-6 Mark Buehrle	.50
CR-7 Cristian Guzman	.50
CR-8 Jimmy Rollins	.50
CR-9 Jim Thome	2.00
CR-10 Shawn Green	1.00

Classic Renditions Autographs

Production 25 Sets

Clubhouse Collection

	NM/M
Common Player:	15.00
Jersey 1:332	
Bat 1:498	
RA Rich Aurilia/Bat	15.00
YB Yogi Berra/Jsy	40.00
BB Barry Bonds/Bat	60.00
AD Alvin Dark/Bat	25.00
NG Nomar Garciaparra/Bat	50.00
GK George Kell/Jsy	25.00
GM Greg Maddux/Jsy	30.00
EM Eddie Mathews/Jsy	35.00
WM Willie Mays/Bat	75.00
CP Corey Patterson/Bat	20.00
JP Jorge Posada/Bat	25.00
HS Hank Sauer/Bat	20.00

Clubhouse Collection Auto. Relics

No Pricing
Production 25 Sets

Clubhouse Collection Dual Relics

	NM/M
Production 53 Sets	
SM Eddie Mathews, Greg Maddux	150.00
BP Yogi Berra, Jorge Posada	125.00
SP Hank Sauer, Corey Patterson	75.00
KR George Kell, Nomar Garciaparra	100.00
DA Alvin Dark, Rich Aurilia	100.00
MB Willie Mays, Barry Bonds	200.00

Grandstand Glory Stadium Seat

	NM/M
Common Player:	10.00
Inserted 1:133	
RC Roy Campanella	25.00
BF Bob Feller	20.00
WF Whitey Ford	20.00
TK Ted Kluszewski	20.00
BM Billy Martin	25.00
HN Hal Newhouser	15.00
SP Satchel Paige	40.00
BP Billy Pierce	10.00
HS Hank Sauer	15.00
BS Bobby Shantz	15.00
WS Warren Spahn	20.00
EW Early Wynn	15.00

New Age Performers

	NM/M
Complete Set (15):	30.00
Common Player:	1.00
Inserted 1:15	
NA-1 Luis Gonzalez	1.00
NA-2 Mark McGwire	5.00
NA-3 Barry Bonds	5.00
NA-4 Ken Griffey Jr.	3.00
NA-5 Ichiro Suzuki	3.00
NA-6 Sammy Sosa	3.00
NA-7 Andruw Jones	1.00
NA-8 Derek Jeter	5.00
NA-9 Todd Helton	1.50
NA-10 Alex Rodriguez	4.00
NA-11 Jason Giambi	1.50
NA-12 Bret Boone	1.00
NA-13 Roberto Alomar	1.50
NA-14 Albert Pujols	4.00
NA-15 Vladimir Guerrero	1.50

Real One Autographs

	NM/M
Common Autograph:	20.00
Inserted 1:180	
Red Ink:	.75-1.5X
Production 53	
YB Yogi Berra	100.00
JB Joe Black	50.00
RB Ray Boone	60.00
AC Andy Carey	40.00
RCL Roger Clemens	125.00
AD Alvin Dark	60.00
DD Dom DiMaggio	80.00
JE Jim Edmonds	60.00
RF Roy Face	60.00
BF Bob Feller	80.00
WF Whitey Ford	80.00
CG Brian Giles	25.00
CG Cristian Guzman	20.00
MI Monte Irvin	60.00
GK George Kell	60.00
WM Willie Mays	200.00
GM Gil McDougald	75.00
OM Orestes Minoso	60.00
JP John Podres	60.00
PR Phil Rizzuto	80.00
ARO Alex Rodriguez	140.00
PRO Preacher Roe	60.00
AR Al Rosen	75.00
ASC Al Schoendienst	50.00
BS Bobby Shantz	50.00
ES Enos Slaughter	80.00
WS Warren Spahn	100.00
HW Hoyt Wilhelm	60.00

Real One Autographs Red Ink

Red Ink: .75-1.5X
Production 53 Sets

Team Topps Legends Autographs

	NM/M
Inserted 1:613	
Vida Blue	20.00
Frank Howard	30.00
Mickey Lolich	25.00
Frank Robinson	40.00
Bobby Thomson	30.00

Then and Now

	NM/M
Complete Set (10):	15.00
Common Player:	1.00
Inserted 1:15	
TN-1 Ed Mathews, Barry Bonds	4.00
TN-2 Al Rosen, Alex Rodriguez	4.00
TN-3 Carl Furillo, Larry Walker	1.00
TN-4 Mickey Vernon, Ichiro Suzuki	3.00
TN-5 Roy Campanella, Sammy Sosa	3.00
TN-6 Al Rosen, Bret Boone	1.00
TN-7 Warren Spahn, Randy Johnson	2.00
TN-8 Ed Lopat, Freddy Garcia	1.00
TN-9 Robin Roberts, Randy Johnson	2.00
TN-10 Billy Pierce, Hideo Nomo	1.50

2002 Topps Opening Day

	NM/M
Complete Set (165):	40.00
Common Player:	.10
Pack (7):	1.00
Box (36):	30.00

No.	Player	Price
1	Roy Oswalt	.25
2	Derek Jeter	2.00
3	Dmitri Young	.10
4	Ramon Hernandez	.10
5	Albert Pujols	1.50
6	Sean Casey	.25
7	Joe Randa	.10
8	Craig Counsell	.10
9	John Olerud	.25
10	Troy Glaus	.40
11	Adam Kennedy	.10
12	Carlos Delgado	.40
13	Bobby Abreu	.20
14	J.T. Snow Jr.	.10
15	Ivan Rodriguez	.50
16	Mike Lowell	.25
17	Juan Pierre	.10
18	Magglio Ordonez	.30
19	Greg Maddux	1.00
20	Jorge Posada	.25
21	Johnny Damon	.20
22	Mike Hampton	.10
23	Paul LoDuca	.10
24	Terrence Long	.10
25	Jeff Bagwell	.50
26	Shannon Stewart	.10
27	Brad Radke	.10
28	Brian Jordan	.10
29	Lee Stevens	.10
30	Cliff Floyd	.10
31	Roger Clemens	1.00
32	Mike Matheny	.10
33	Alfonso Soriano	.50
34	Randy Johnson	.75
35	Mike Sweeney	.10
36	Jose Cruz Jr.	.20
37	Fernando Tatis	.10
38	Eric Young	.10
39	Ruben Rivera	.10
40	Mike Mussina	.50
41	Alex Gonzalez	.10
42	Edgardo Alfonzo	.10
43	Torii Hunter	.25
44	Richie Sexson	.25
45	Bret Boone	.20
46	John Smoltz	.20
47	Bengie Molina	.10
48	Trot Nixon	.10
49	Mike Cameron	.10
50	Mariano Rivera	.25
51	Ichiro Suzuki	1.50
52	Cristian Guzman	.10
53	Andruw Jones	.40
54	Jerry Hairston Jr.	.10
55	Brad Fullmer	.10
56	Luis Gonzalez	.25
57	Placido Polanco	.10
58	Jason Tyner	.10
59	Dan Wilson	.10
60	Jim Edmonds	.25
61	Larry Walker	.25
62	Edgar Renteria	.25
63	Orlando Cabrera	.10
64	Sammy Sosa	1.50
65	Derrek Lee	.20
66	C.C. Sabathia	.20
67	Aaron Boone	.10
68	Royce Clayton	.10
69	Darryl Kile	.10
70	Vladimir Guerrero	.75
71	Bud Smith	.10
72	Adrian Beltre	.20
73	Barry Bonds	15.00
74	Ben Petrick	.10
75	Derek Bell	.10
76	Jeff Kent	.20
77	Ricky Gutierrez	.10
78	Rafael Palmeiro	.50
79	Doug Mientkiewicz	.10
80	Fernando Vina	.10
81	Mark Mulder	.20
82	Carlos Beltran	.25
83	Juan Encarnacion	.10
84	Jimmy Rollins	.20
85	Pedro J. Martinez	.25
86	Aramis Ramirez	.25
87	Reggie Sanders	.10
88	Gary Sheffield	.25
89	Bartolo Colon	.10
90	Jose Macias	.10
91	Bobby Higginson	.10
92	Craig Biggio	.20
93	Al Leiter	.20
94	Juan Gonzalez	.50
95	Jose Valentin	.10
96	Jon Lieber	.10
97	Alex Gonzalez	.10
98	Jose Mesa	.10
99	Sandy Alomar	.10
100	Barry Bonds	2.00
101	Todd Walker	.10
102	Kevin Young	.10
103	Ken Griffey Jr.	1.00
104	Mark McGwire	2.00
105	Jason Giambi	.50
106	Todd Helton	.50
107	Mike Piazza	1.00
108	Nomar Garciaparra	1.50
109	Bernie Williams	.40
110	Shawn Wooten	.10
111	Eric Chavez	.20
112	Curt Schilling	.40
113	Roberto Alomar	.50
114	Chipper Jones	.75
115	Edgar Martinez	.20
116	Shawn Green	.20
117	Ben Grieve	.10
118	Jermaine Dye	.10
119	Steve Finley	.10
120	Adam Dunn	.25
121	Preston Wilson	.10
122	Lance Berkman	.25
123	Ben Sheets	.25
124	Ryan Klesko	.10
125	Brian Giles	.10
126	Marcus Giles	.10
127	Craig Wilson	.10
128	Miguel Tejada	.25
129	Andres Galarraga	.10
130	Alex Rodriguez	1.50
131	David Justice	.25
132	Barry Zito	.25
133	Scott Rolen	.75
134	Brent Abernathy	.10
135	Raul Mondesi	.20
136	Josh Towers	.10
137	Rafael Furcal	.10
138	Gabe Kapler	.10
139	Fred McGriff	.25
140	Jeff Conine	.10
141	Mike Lieberthal	.10
142	Frank Thomas	.50
143	Jason Kendall	.10
144	Toby Hall	.10
145	Pat Burrell	.30
146	J.D. Drew	.25
147	Javier Lopez	.25
148	Carlos Lee	.10
149	Doug Glanville	.10
150	Ruben Sierra	.10

151	Julio Franco	.10
152	Tim Hudson	.20
153	Rich Aurilia	.10
154	Geoff Jenkins	.10
155	Tsuyoshi Shinjo	.10
156	Moises Alou	.20
157	Jim Thome	.75
158	Steve Cox	.10
159	Kevin Brown	.20
160	Barry Bonds	.50
161	Rickey Henderson	.20
162	Bud Smith	.10
163	Rickey Henderson	.20
164	Barry Bonds	.50
165	Checklist	.10

Autographs
NM/M
	Common Auto.:	10.00
GJ	Geoff Jenkins	15.00
NJ	Nick Johnson	10.00
BS	Ben Sheets	25.00

2002 Topps Pristine

SAMMY SOSA
CHICAGO CUBS

NM/M
Complete Set (210):
Common Player: .75
Common Uncommon RC: 3.00
Production 1,999
Common Rare RC: 5.00
Production 799
Pack (8): 30.00
Box (5): 125.00

1	Alex Rodriguez	5.00
2	Carlos Delgado	1.50
3	Jimmy Rollins	.75
4	Jason Kendall	.75
5	John Olerud	1.00
6	Albert Pujols	5.00
7	Curt Schilling	2.00
8	Gary Sheffield	1.00
9	Johnny Damon	1.00
10	Ichiro Suzuki	4.00
11	Pat Burrell	1.00
12	Garret Anderson	1.00
13	Andruw Jones	1.50
14	Kerry Wood	2.00
15	Kenny Lofton	1.00
16	Adam Dunn	1.50
17	Juan Pierre	.75
18	Josh Beckett	1.00
19	Roy Oswalt	1.00
20	Derek Jeter	6.00
21	Jose Vidro	1.00
22	Richie Sexson	1.50
23	Mike Sweeney	.75
24	Jeff Kent	1.00
25	Jason Giambi	1.50
26	Bret Boone	1.00
27	J.D. Drew	1.00
28	Shannon Stewart	.75
29	Miguel Tejada	1.00
30	Barry Bonds	6.00
31	Randy Johnson	2.00
32	Pedro J. Martinez	2.00
33	Magglio Ordonez	1.00
34	Todd Helton	1.00
35	Craig Biggio	1.00
36	Shawn Green	1.00
37	Vladimir Guerrero	2.00
38	Mo Vaughn	1.00
39	Alfonso Soriano	2.00
40	Barry Zito	1.00
41	Aramis Ramirez	1.00
42	Ryan Klesko	1.00
43	Ruben Sierra	.75
44	Tino Martinez	.75
45	Toby Hall	.75
46	Ivan Rodriguez	1.50
47	Raul Mondesi	.75
48	Carlos Pena	.75
49	Darin Erstad	1.00
50	Sammy Sosa	4.00
51	Bartolo Colon	1.00
52	Robert Fick	.75
53	Cliff Floyd	.75
54	Brian Jordan	.75
55	Torii Hunter	1.00
56	Roberto Alomar	1.00
57	Roger Clemens	4.00
58	Mark Mulder	1.00
59	Brian Giles	.75
60	Mike Piazza	4.00
61	Rich Aurilia	.75
62	Freddy Garcia	.75
63	Jim Edmonds	1.50
64	Eric Hinske	.75
65	Jeremy Giambi	.75
66	Javier Vazquez	.75
67	Cristian Guzman	.75
68	Paul LoDuca	.75
69	Bobby Abreu	1.00
70	Nomar Garciaparra	4.00
71	Troy Glaus	1.00
72	Chipper Jones	2.00
73	Scott Rolen	2.00
74	Lance Berkman	1.00
75	C.C. Sabathia	.75
76	Bernie Williams	1.00
77	Rafael Palmeiro	1.50
78	Phil Nevin	.75
79	Kazuhiro Sasaki	.75
80	Eric Chavez	1.00
81	Jorge Posada	1.00
82	Edgardo Alfonzo	.75
83	Geoff Jenkins	1.00
84	Preston Wilson	.75
85	Jim Thome	2.00
86	Frank Thomas	1.50
87	Jeff Bagwell	1.50
88	Greg Maddux	3.00
89	Mark Prior	3.00
90	Larry Walker	1.00
91	Luis Gonzalez	1.00
92	Tim Hudson	1.00
93	Tsuyoshi Shinjo	.75
94	Juan Gonzalez	1.50
95	Shea Hillenbrand	.75
96	Paul Konerko	.75
97	Tom Glavine	1.50
98	Marty Cordova	.75
99	Moises Alou	1.00
100	Ken Griffey Jr.	4.00
101	Hank Blalock	1.50
102	Matt Morris	1.00
103	Robb Nen	.75
104	Mike Cameron	.75
105	Mark Buehrle	.75
106	Sean Burroughs	.75
107	Orlando Cabrera	.75
108	Jeromy Burnitz	.75
109	Juan Uribe	.75
110	Eric Milton	.75
111	Carlos Lee	.75
112	Jose Mesa	.75
113	Morgan Ensberg	.75
114	Mike Rivera	.75
115	Juan Cruz	.75
116	Mike Lieberthal	.75
117	Armando Benitez	.75
118	Vinny Castilla	.75
119	Russ Ortiz	.75
120	Mike Lowell	1.00
121	Corey Patterson	1.00
122	Mike Mussina	1.50
123	Rafael Furcal	.75
124	Mark Grace	1.50
125	Ben Sheets	1.00
126	John Smoltz	1.00
127	Fred McGriff	1.00
128	Nick Johnson	.75
129	J.T. Snow	.75
130	Jeff Cirillo	.75
131	Trevor Hoffman	.75
132	Kevin Brown	1.00
133	Mariano Rivera	1.50
134	Marlon Anderson	.75
135	Al Leiter	.75
136	Doug Mientkiewicz	.75
137	Eric Karros	.75
138	Bobby Higginson	.75
139	Sean Casey	1.00
140	Troy Percival	.75
141	Willie Mays	5.00
142	Carl Yastrzemski	3.00
143	Stan Musial	4.00
144	Harmon Killebrew	3.00
145	Mike Schmidt	3.00
146	Duke Snider	2.00
147	Brooks Robinson	3.00
148	Frank Robinson	2.00
149	Nolan Ryan	8.00
150	Reggie Jackson	3.00
151	Joe Mauer/C RC	5.00
152	Joe Mauer/U RC	40.00
153	Joe Mauer/R RC	50.00
154	Colt Griffin/C	5.00
155	Colt Griffin/U	5.00
156	Colt Griffin/R	5.00
157	Jason Simontacchi/C RC	1.50
158	Jason Simontacchi/U RC	3.00
159	Jason Simontacchi/R RC	5.00
160	Casey Kotchman/C	5.00
161	Casey Kotchman/U	8.00
162	Casey Kotchman/R	15.00
163	Greg Sain/C RC	1.50
164	Greg Sain/U RC	3.00
165	Greg Sain/R RC	5.00
166	David Wright/C	30.00
167	David Wright/U	40.00
168	David Wright/R	50.00
169	Scott Hairston/C	4.00
170	Scott Hairston/U	6.00
171	Scott Hairston/R	10.00
172	Rolando Viera/C RC	1.50
173	Rolando Viera/U RC	3.00
174	Rolando Viera/R RC	5.00
175	Tyrell Godwin/C	1.50
176	Tyrell Godwin/U	3.00
177	Tyrell Godwin/R	5.00
178	Jesus Cota/C RC	1.50
179	Jesus Cota/U RC	3.00
180	Jesus Cota/R RC	5.00
181	Dan Johnson/C RC	3.00
182	Dan Johnson/U RC	5.00
183	Dan Johnson/R RC	8.00
184	Mario Ramos/C	1.50
185	Mario Ramos/U	3.00
186	Mario Ramos/R	5.00
187	Jason Dubois/C RC	2.00
188	Jason Dubois/U RC	3.00
189	Jason Dubois/R RC	5.00
190	Jonny Gomes/C RC	6.00
191	Jonny Gomes/U RC	12.00
192	Jonny Gomes/R RC	20.00
193	Chris Snelling/C RC	2.00
194	Chris Snelling/U RC	4.00
195	Chris Snelling/R RC	6.00
196	Hansel Izquierdo/C RC	2.00
197	Hansel Izquierdo/U RC	4.00
198	Hansel Izquierdo/R RC	6.00
199	So Taguchi/C RC	3.00
200	So Taguchi/U RC	5.00
201	So Taguchi/R RC	8.00
202	Kazuhisa Ishii/C RC	3.00
203	Kazuhisa Ishii/U RC	5.00
204	Kazuhisa Ishii/R RC	8.00
205	Jorge Padilla/C RC	1.50
206	Jorge Padilla/U RC	3.00
207	Jorge Padilla/R RC	5.00
208	Earl Snyder/C RC	2.00
209	Earl Snyder/U RC	4.00
210	Earl Snyder/R RC	6.00

Refractors

JAVIER VAZQUEZ
MONTREAL EXPOS

Stars (1-150):		2-4X
Production 149		
Common Rookies:		.75-1.5X
Production 1,999		
Uncommon Rookies:		1-2X
Production 799		
Rare Rookies:		2-3X
Production 149		
Gold Refractors (1-150):		3-5X
Gold Common RC's:		4-8X
Gold Uncommon RC's:		2-4X
Gold Rare RC's:		1-2X

Production 70 Sets
All Refractors are uncirculated.

Fall Memories

FALL MEMORIES
LUIS GONZALEZ
ARIZONA DIAMONDBACKS

NM/M
Common Player: 5.00
Varying quantities produced.
JB	Johnny Bench	15.00
BB	Barry Bonds	30.00
GB	George Brett	25.00
TG	Tom Glavine	8.00
LG	Luis Gonzalez	8.00
MG	Mark Grace	12.00
SG	Shawn Green	6.00
TH	Todd Helton	8.00
RJ	Reggie Jackson	15.00
AJ	Andruw Jones	8.00
CP	Chipper Jones	10.00
TM	Tino Martinez	8.00
WM	Willie Mays	40.00
EM	Eddie Murray	15.00
JP	Jorge Posada	8.00
KP	Kirby Puckett	15.00
CS	Curt Schilling	8.00
GS	Gary Sheffield	8.00
AS	Alfonso Soriano	10.00
BW	Bernie Williams	8.00

In The Gap

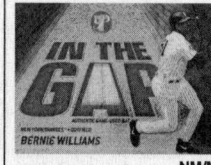

IN THE GAP
BERNIE WILLIAMS

NM/M
Common Player: 5.00
Varying quantities produced.
RA	Roberto Alomar	10.00
LB	Lance Berkman	8.00
WBE	Wilson Betemit	8.00
WB	Wade Boggs	8.00

BBO	Barry Bonds	25.00
EC	Eric Chavez	8.00
CD	Carlos Delgado	6.00
AD	Adam Dunn	10.00
JE	Jim Edmonds	6.00
DE	Darin Erstad	5.00
NG	Nomar Garciaparra	15.00
TG	Tony Gwynn	15.00
TH	Todd Helton	8.00
RH	Rickey Henderson	10.00
AJ	Andruw Jones	10.00
JK	Jeff Kent	5.00
RK	Ryan Klesko	8.00
PL	Paul LoDuca	10.00
RP	Rafael Palmeiro	10.00
MP	Mike Piazza	15.00
AP	Albert Pujols	15.00
ARA	Aramis Ramirez	8.00
AR	Alex Rodriguez	15.00
IR	Ivan Rodriguez	8.00
TS	Tsuyoshi Shinjo	5.00
AS	Alfonso Soriano	10.00
LW	Larry Walker	5.00
BW	Bernie Williams	15.00
PW	Preston Wilson	5.00

Patches
No Pricing
Production 25 Sets

Personal Endorsements
NM/M
Common Autograph: 8.00
Inserted 1:Box
RA	Roberto Alomar	30.00
KB	Kenny Baugh	8.00
LB	Lance Berkman	30.00
BB	Barry Bonds	180.00
DB	Dewon Brazelton	15.00
JD	Johnny Damon	30.00
GF	Gavin Floyd	25.00
CG	Cristian Guzman	10.00
IG	Irvin Guzman	10.00
OH	Orlando Hudson	10.00
KI	Kazuhisa Ishii	30.00
CK	Casey Kotchman	20.00
JL	Jason Lane	8.00
CW	Corwin Malone	8.00
NN	Nick Neugebauer	8.00
AP	Albert Pujols	200.00
JR	Jimmy Rollins	25.00
BS	Ben Sheets	20.00
JS	Juan Silvestre	8.00
ST	So Taguchi	15.00
MT	Marcus Thames	8.00

Popular Demand

POPULAR DEMAND
Jeff Bagwell Houston Astros

NM/M
Common Player: 5.00
Varying quantities produced.
RA	Roberto Alomar	10.00
JB	Jeff Bagwell	10.00
WB	Wade Boggs	8.00
BBO	Barry Bonds	25.00
BB	Bret Boone	5.00
CD	Carlos Delgado	5.00
AD	Adam Dunn	8.00
NG	Nomar Garciaparra	15.00
SG	Shawn Green	5.00
TG	Tony Gwynn	12.00
TH	Todd Helton	8.00
CJ	Chipper Jones	12.00
DM	Don Mattingly	35.00
MP	Mike Piazza	15.00
AP	Albert Pujols	20.00
AR	Alex Rodriguez	15.00
IR	Ivan Rodriguez	8.00
CS	Curt Schilling	8.00
FT	Frank Thomas	10.00
LW	Larry Walker	5.00

Portions

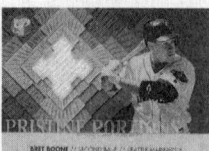

PRISTINE PORTIONS
BRET BOONE / SECOND BASE / QUATRO MARKERS

NM/M
Common Player: 5.00
Varying quantities produced.
RA	Roberto Alomar	10.00
JB	Jeff Bagwell	10.00
LB	Lance Berkman	8.00
CB	Craig Biggio	8.00
BBO	Barry Bonds	20.00
BB	Bret Boone	5.00
CD	Carlos Delgado	5.00
RD	Ryan Dempster	5.00
AD	Adam Dunn	8.00
CF	Cliff Floyd	5.00
RF	Rafael Furcal	5.00

NG	Nomar Garciaparra	15.00
CG	Cristian Guzman	5.00
TH	Todd Helton	8.00
NJ	Nick Johnson	5.00
LD	Paul LoDuca	5.00
GM	Greg Maddux	10.00
EM	Edgar Martinez	10.00
MM	Mike Mussina	10.00
MO	Magglio Ordonez	5.00
RP	Rafael Palmeiro	8.00
MP	Mike Piazza	15.00
JP	Jorge Posada	8.00
AP	Albert Pujols	15.00
AR	Alex Rodriguez	15.00
IR	Ivan Rodriguez	8.00
NR	Nolan Ryan	30.00
KS	Kazuhiro Sasaki	5.00

2002 Topps Reserve

KEARNS

NM/M
Complete Set (150): 120.00
Common Player: .25
Common (136-150): 4.00
Production 999
Silver parallel (1-135): 4-8X
Silver (136-150): .75-1.5X
Production 150
Box:10 Packs & 1 Auto.
Helmet: 100.00

1	Alex Rodriguez	2.50
2	Tsuyoshi Shinjo	.50
3	Craig Biggio	.40
4	Troy Glaus	.50
5	Mike Rivera	.25
6	Curt Schilling	.50
7	Garret Anderson	.50
8	Ben Sheets	.50
9	Todd Helton	.75
10	Paul Konerko	.50
11	Sammy Sosa	2.00
12	Bud Smith	.25
13	Jeff Bagwell	.75
14	Albert Pujols	2.00
15	Jose Vidro	.25
16	Carlos Delgado	.25
17	Torii Hunter	.50
18	Jerry Hairston Jr.	.25
19	Troy Percival	.25
20	Vladimir Guerrero	1.00
21	Geoff Jenkins	.40
22	Carlos Pena	.25
23	Juan Gonzalez	.75
24	Raul Mondesi	.25
25	Jimmy Rollins	.50
26	Mariano Rivera	.50
27	Jorge Posada	.50
28	Magglio Ordonez	.50
29	Roberto Alomar	.50
30	Randy Johnson	1.00
31	Xavier Nady	.25
32	Terrence Long	.25
33	Chipper Jones	1.00
34	Rich Aurilia	.25
35	Aramis Ramirez	.50
36	Jim Thome	1.00
37	Bret Boone	.50
38	Angel Berroa	.25
39	Jeff Conine	.25
40	Cliff Floyd	.25
41	Pedro J. Martinez	1.00
42	J.D. Drew	.50
43	Kazuhiro Sasaki	.25
44	Jon Rauch	.25
45	Orlando Hudson	.25
46	Scott Rolen	.50
47	Rafael Furcal	.25
48	Brad Penny	.25
49	Miguel Tejada	.50
50	Orlando Cabrera	.25
51	Bobby Abreu	.50
52	Darin Erstad	.50
53	Edgar Martinez	.40
54	Ben Grieve	.25
55	Shawn Green	.50
56	Ivan Rodriguez	.75
57	Josh Beckett	.50
58	Ray Durham	.25
59	Jason Hart	.25
60	Nathan Haynes	.25
61	Jason Giambi	.75
62	Eric Chavez	.40
63	Matt Morris	.40
64	Lance Berkman	.50
65	Jeff Kent	.50
66	Andruw Jones	.50
67	Brian Giles	.50
68	Morgan Ensberg	.25
69	Pat Burrell	.50
70	Ken Griffey Jr.	2.00
71	Carlos Beltran	.50
72	Ichiro Suzuki	2.00
73	Larry Walker	.50
74	J.J. Putz RC	.50
75	Mike Piazza	2.00
76	Rafael Palmeiro	.75
77	Mark Prior	2.00
78	Toby Hall	.25
79	Pokey Reese	.25
80	Mike Mussina	.50
81	Omar Vizquel	.25
82	Shannon Stewart	.25
83	Jeromy Burnitz	.25
84	Bernie Williams	.50
85	C.C. Sabathia	.25
86	Mike Hampton	.25
87	Kevin Brown	.50
88	Juan Cruz	.25
89	Jeff Weaver	.25
90	Jason Lane	.25
91	Adam Dunn	.75
92	Jose Cruz Jr.	.25
93	Marlon Anderson	.25
94	Jeff Cirillo	.25
95	Mark Buehrle	.25
96	Austin Kearns	.50
97	Tim Hudson	.25
98	Brian Jordan	.25
99	Phil Nevin	.25
100	Barry Bonds	3.00
101	Derek Jeter	3.00
102	Javier Vazquez	.40
103	Jason Kendall	.40
104	Jim Edmonds	.50
105	Kenny Kelly	.25
106	Juan Pena	.25
107	Mark Grace	.50
108	Roger Clemens	2.00
109	Barry Zito	.25
110	Greg Vaughn	.25
111	Greg Maddux	1.50
112	Richie Sexson	.25
113	Jermaine Dye	.25
114	Kerry Wood	1.00
115	Matt Lawton	.25
116	Sean Casey	.50
117	Gary Sheffield	.50
118	Preston Wilson	.25
119	Cristian Guzman	.25
120	Mike Sweeney ✓	.25
121	Neifi Perez	.25
122	Paul LoDuca	.25
123	Luis Gonzalez	.25
124	Ryan Klesko	.25
125	Alfonso Soriano	1.00
126	Bobby Higginson	.25
127	Juan Pierre	.25
128	Moises Alou	.25
129	Roy Oswalt	.50
130	Nomar Garciaparra	2.00
131	Fred McGriff	.40
132	Edgardo Alfonzo	.40
133	Johnny Damon	.40
134	Dewon Brazelton	.25
135	Mark Mulder	.50
136	So Taguchi RC	5.00
137	Mario Ramos	4.00
138	Dan Johnson RC	5.00
139	Hansel Izquierdo RC	5.00
140	Kazuhisa Ishii RC	5.00
141	Jon Switzer	.25
142	Chris Tritle RC	6.00
143	Chris Snelling RC	5.00
144	Chone Figgins RC	8.00
145	Dan Phillips RC	4.00
146	John Rodriguez RC	4.00
147	Colt Griffin	8.00
148	Jonny Gomes RC	10.00
149	Josh Barfield	5.00
150	Joe Mauer RC	35.00

Silver
Stars (1-135):	4-8X
SP's (136-150):	.75-1.5X

Autographed Mini-Helmets

NM/M
Common Helmet: 20.00
Gold Ink Autographs: No Pricing
Production 25
Roberto Alomar	40.00
Moises Alou	25.00
Lance Berkman	40.00
Bret Boone	20.00
Eric Chavez	30.00
Adam Dunn	40.00
Cliff Floyd	20.00
Troy Glaus	40.00
Luis Gonzalez	30.00

Todd Helton	50.00	
Magglio Ordonez	25.00	
Rafael Palmeiro	40.00	
Albert Pujols	220.00	
Alex Rodriguez	125.00	
Scott Rolen	35.00	
Jimmy Rollins	40.00	
Alfonso Soriano	50.00	
Barry Zito	30.00	

Game-Used Baseball
NM/M
Inserted 1:1,761
I	Ichiro Suzuki	65.00

Game-Used Bat

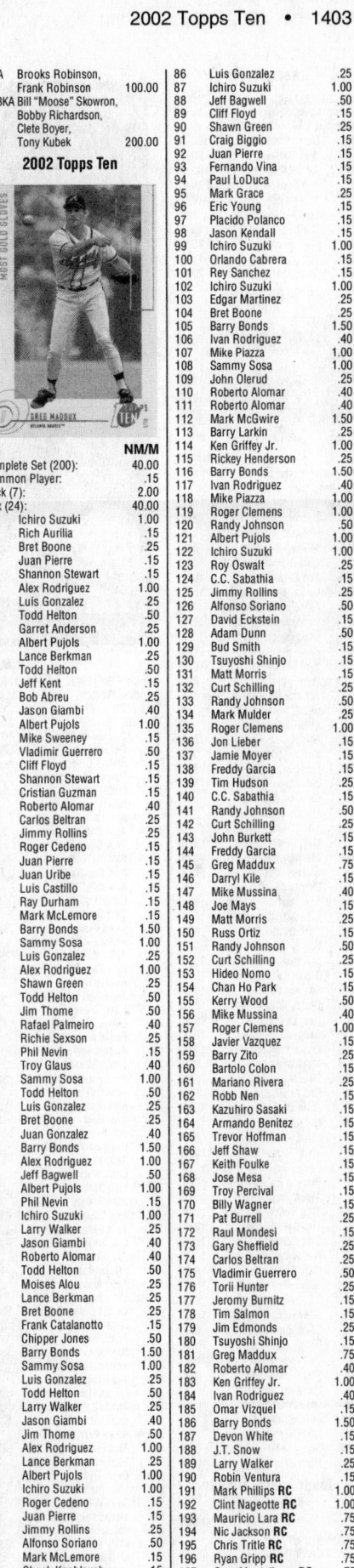

NM/M
Common Player: 5.00
Inserted 1:12
RA	Roberto Alomar	10.00
JB	Jeff Bagwell	10.00
BB	Barry Bonds	20.00
CD	Carlos Delgado	8.00
JG	Juan Gonzalez	8.00
LG	Luis Gonzalez	5.00
TG	Tony Gwynn	12.00
RH	Rickey Henderson	10.00
CJ	Chipper Jones	10.00
AJ	Andruw Jones	8.00
TM	Tino Martinez	8.00
RP	Rafael Palmeiro	8.00
MB	Mike Piazza	15.00
AP	Albert Pujols	15.00
AR	Alex Rodriguez	12.00
IR	Ivan Rodriguez	8.00
TS	Tsuyoshi Shinjo	5.00
AS	Alfonso Soriano	10.00
FT	Frank Thomas	8.00
BW	Bernie Williams	8.00

Game-Worn Patch
No Pricing
Production 25 Sets

Game-Worn Uniform
NM/M
Common Player: 5.00
Inserted 1:5
BB	Barry Bonds	20.00
BBO	Bret Boone	5.00
DE	Darin Erstad	5.00
NG	Nomar Garciaparra	15.00
LG	Luis Gonzalez	5.00
TG	Tony Gwynn	10.00
TH	Todd Helton	8.00
RJ	Randy Johnson	10.00
AJ	Andruw Jones	6.00
CJ	Chipper Jones	10.00
GM	Greg Maddux	12.00
PM	Pedro Martinez	10.00
MM	Mark Mulder	5.00
MO	Magglio Ordonez	5.00
RP	Rafael Palmeiro	8.00
MP	Mike Piazza	12.00
AP	Albert Pujols	15.00
AR	Alex Rodriguez	12.00
IR	Ivan Rodriguez	8.00
SR	Scott Rolen	10.00
KS	Kazuhiro Sasaki	5.00
CS	Curt Schilling	8.00
FT	Frank Thomas	8.00
KW	Kerry Wood	10.00

2002 Topps Super Teams
NM/M
Complete Set: 40.00
Common Player: .25

Pack (7):		3.50
Box (20):		60.00
1	Leo Durocher	.25
2	Whitey Lockman	.25
3	Alvin Dark	.25
4	Monte Irvin	.50
5	Willie Mays	2.50
6	Wes Westrum	.25
7	Johnny Antonelli	.25
8	Sal Maglie	.25
9	Dusty Rhodes	.25
10	Davey Williams	.25
11	Hoyt Wilhelm	.25
12	Don Mueller	.25
13	Dusty Rhodes	.25
14	Willie Mays, Monte Irvin, Dusty Rhodes	.75
15	Walt Alston	.25
16	Gil Hodges	.75
17	Jim Gilliam	.25
18	Pee Wee Reese	.50
19	Jackie Robinson	2.00
20	Duke Snider	1.00
21	Carl Furillo	.25
22	Roy Campanella	1.00
23	Don Newcombe	.25
24	Don Hoak	.25
25	Johnny Podres	.25
26	Clem Labine	.25
27	Johnny Podres	.25
28	Pee Wee Reese, Jackie Robinson, Duke Snider	1.00
29	Fred Haney	.25
30	Joe Adcock	.25
31	Frank Torre	.25
32	Red Schoendienst	.25
33	Johnny Logan	.25
34	Eddie Mathews	1.00
35	Hank Aaron	3.00
36	Andy Pafko	.25
37	Wes Covington	.25
38	Lew Burdette	.25
39	Warren Spahn	1.00
40	Del Crandall	.25
41	Lew Burdette	.25
42	Warren Spahn, Eddie Mathews, Hank Aaron	1.50
43	Danny Murtaugh	.25
44	Dick Stuart	.25
45	Bill Mazeroski	.25
46	Dick Groat	.25
47	Don Hoak	.25
48	Gino Cimoli	.25
49	Bill Virdon	.25
50	Roberto Clemente	2.50
51	Smoky Burgess	.25
52	Bob Friend	.25
53	Vernon Law	.25
54	Roy Face	.25
55	Bill Mazeroski	.25
56		
57	Roberto Clemente, Bill Mazeroski, Dick Groat	1.00
58	Ralph Houk	1.00
59	Bill "Moose" Skowron	.50
60	Bobby Richardson	.25
61	Tony Kubek	.25
62	Clete Boyer	.25
63	Yogi Berra	1.50
64	Bob Cerv	.25
65	Roger Maris	1.50
66	Elston Howard	.25
67	Whitey Ford	1.00
68	Ralph Terry	.25
69	Johnny Blanchard	.25
70	Whitey Ford	1.00
71	Yogi Berra, Roger Maris, Elston Howard, Bill "Moose" Skowron	1.00
72	Red Schoendienst	.25
73	Orlando Cepeda	.40
74	Julian Javier	.25
75	Dal Maxvill	.25
76	Mike Shannon	.25
77	Lou Brock	.75
78	Roger Maris	1.50
79	Curt Flood	.25
80	Tim McCarver	.25
81	Steve Carlton	.75
82	Bob Gibson	1.00
83	Nelson Briles	.25
84	Bobby Tolan	.25
85	Bob Gibson	1.00
86	Bob Gibson, Steve Carlton, Orlando Cepeda, Lou Brock	.50
87	Gil Hodges	.25
88	Ed Kranepool	.25
89	Buddy Harrelson	.25
90	Wayne Garrett	.25
91	Cleon Jones	.25
92	Tommie Agee	.25
93	Ron Swoboda	.25
94	Al Weis	.25
95	Jerry Grote	.25
96	Tom Seaver	1.00
97	Jerry Koosman	.25
98	Tug McGraw	.25
99	Nolan Ryan	3.00
100	Donn Clendenon	.25
101	Tom Seaver, Jerry Koosman, Tug McGraw, Nolan Ryan	1.00
102	Earl Weaver	.25
103	Boog Powell	.25
104	Davey Johnson	.25
105	Mark Belanger	.25
106	Brooks Robinson	1.00
107	Don Buford	.25
108	Paul Blair	.25

109	Frank Robinson	1.00
110	Dick Hall	.25
111	Jim Palmer	.75
112	Mike Cuellar	.25
113	Dave McNally	.25
114	Andy Etchebarren	.25
115	Brooks Robinson	1.00
116	Dick Hall, Jim Palmer, Mike Cuellar, Dave McNally	.40
117	Alvin Dark	.25
118	Gene Tenace	.25
119	Dick Green	.25
120	Bert Campaneris	.25
121	Sal Bando	.25
122	Reggie Jackson	.25
123	Joe Rudi	.25
124	Claudell Washington	.25
125	Ray Fosse	.25
126	Vida Blue	.40
127	Rollie Fingers	.25
128	Jim "Catfish" Hunter	.50
129	Ken Holtzman	.25
130	Rollie Fingers	.25
131	Jim "Catfish" Hunter, Sal Bando, Reggie Jackson, Rollie Fingers	.50
132	Davey Johnson	.25
133	Keith Hernandez	.25
134	Wally Backman	.25
135	Rafael Santana	.25
136	Ray Knight	.25
137	Len Dykstra	.25
138	Darryl Strawberry	.25
139	Kevin Mitchell	.25
140	Dwight Gooden	.25
141	Bob Ojeda	.25
142	Sid Fernandez	.25
143	Ron Darling	.25
144	Gary Carter	.25
145	Ray Knight	.25
146	Darryl Strawberry, Dwight Gooden, Keith Hernandez	.25

Retrofractor
Cards (1-146): 2-4X
#'d to year team won World Series.

Autographs
NM/M
Common Autograph: 10.00
Inserted 1:19
YB	Yogi Berra	60.00
VB	Vida Blue	15.00
CB	Clete Boyer	15.00
SC	Steve Carlton	25.00
MI	Monte Irvin	15.00
RJ	Reggie Jackson	50.00
TK	Tony Kubek	30.00
TM	Tug McGraw	15.00
AP	Andy Pafko	20.00
JP	Jim Palmer	25.00
JPO	Johnny Podres	15.00
BR	Bobby Richardson	15.00
BRO	Brooks Robinson	30.00
NR	Nolan Ryan	150.00
TS	Tom Seaver	15.00
MS	Bill "Moose" Skowron	20.00
WS	Warren Spahn	40.00
HW	Hoyt Wilhelm	15.00

A View To a Thrill Seat Relics
NM/M
Common Player: 10.00
Inserted 1:30
HA	Hank Aaron	20.00
YB	Yogi Berra	20.00
LB	Lew Burdette	10.00
RC	Roberto Clemente	50.00
WF	Whitey Ford	15.00
BG	Bob Gibson	15.00
RMB	Roger Maris/Cardinals	20.00
RMY	Roger Maris/Yankees	40.00
EM	Eddie Matfiews	15.00
WM	Willie Mays	30.00
BM	Bill Mazeroski	10.00
JP	Jim Palmer	15.00
BP	Boog Powell	10.00
BR	Brooks Robinson	15.00
FR	Frank Robinson	15.00
RS	Red Schoendienst	15.00
DS	Duke Snider	15.00
WS	Warren Spahn	15.00

A View To A Thrill Auto. Relics

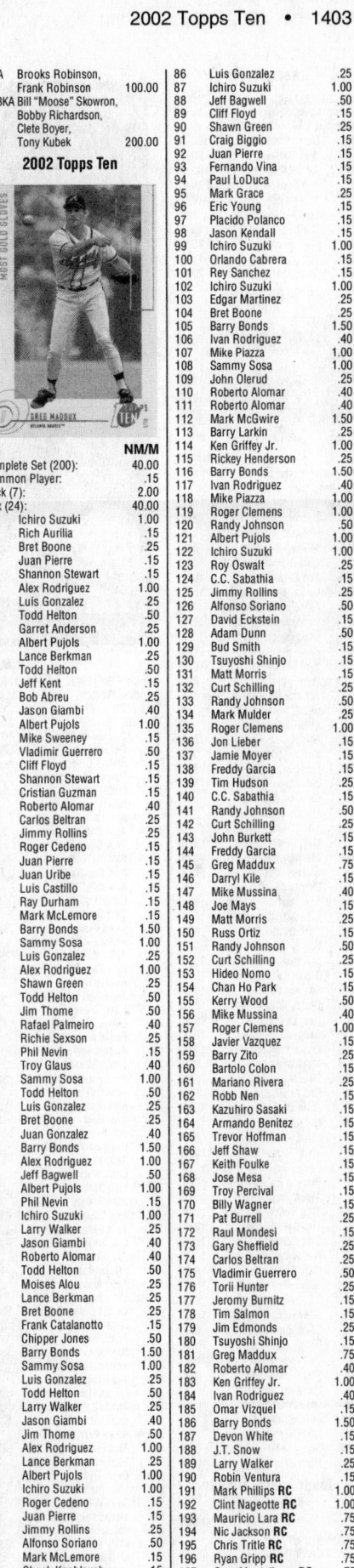

NM/M
Complete Set (5): 10.00
Common Card: 2.00
Inserted 1:10
BG	Lou Brock, Bob Gibson	2.00
FB	Whitey Ford, Yogi Berra	4.00
MI	Willie Mays, Monte Irvin	4.00
RR	Brooks Robinson, Frank Robinson	3.00
SRBK	Bill "Moose" Skowron, Bobby Richardson, Clete Boyer, Tony Kubek	2.00

Super Teammates Autographs
NM/M
Production 50 Sets
BGA	Lou Brock, Bob Gibson	100.00
FBA	Whitey Ford, Yogi Berra	150.00
MIA	Willie Mays, Monte Irvin	180.00

WFA	Whitey Ford/61	100.00
BGA	Bob Gibson/67	60.00
WMA	Willie Mays/54	150.00
DSA	Duke Snider/55	80.00
WSA	Warren Spahn/57	60.00

Classic Combos
NM/M
Common Card: 40.00
Inserted 1:865
AJ	Tommie Agee, Cleon Jones	40.00
JR	Reggie Jackson, Joe Rudi	40.00
RR	Brooks Robinson, Frank Robinson	50.00
SK	Tom Seaver, Jerry Koosman	50.00
SRBK	Bill "Moose" Skowron, Bobby Richardson, Clete Boyer, Tony Kubek	80.00

Relics
NM/M
Common Player: 10.00
TA	Tommie Agee/Bat	20.00
SBB	Sal Bando/Bat	10.00
SBJ	Sal Bando/Jsy	10.00
MB	Mark Belanger/Bat	10.00
PB	Paul Blair/Bat	10.00
CB	Clete Boyer/Bat	10.00
LB	Lew Burdette/Jsy	15.00
SB	Smoky Burgess/Bat	10.00
BC	Bert Campaneris/Jsy	15.00
GC	Gary Carter/Jacket	20.00
GCB	Gary Carter/Bat	15.00
GCJ	Gary Carter/Jsy	15.00
OC	Orlando Cepeda/Bat	15.00
BCE	Bob Cerv/Bat	15.00
GCI	Gino Cimoli/Bat	10.00
DC	Del Crandel/Bat	10.00
MC	Mike Cuellar/Jsy	10.00
RD	Ron Darling/Jsy	10.00
LD	Len Dykstra/Bat	15.00
RF	Ray Fosse/Bat	10.00
BF	Bob Friend/Jsy	10.00
WG	Wayne Garrett/Bat	10.00
DG	Dwight Gooden/Jsy	15.00
DH	Don Hoak/Bat	10.00
RH	Ralph Houk/Jsy	10.00
RJ	Reggie Jackson/Bat	35.00
DJ	Davey Johnson/Bat	10.00
CJ	Cleon Jones/Bat	20.00
RK	Ray Knight/Bat	10.00
JK	Jerry Koosman/Jsy	15.00
EK	Ed Kranepool/Jsy	15.00
TK	Tony Kubek/Bat	25.00
TM	Tug McGraw/Jsy	10.00
DM	Dave McNally/Jsy	10.00
KM	Kevin Mitchell/Bat	10.00
AP	Andy Pafko/Bat	10.00
BR	Bobby Richardson/Bat	25.00
BRO	Brooks Robinson/Bat	25.00
FR	Frank Robinson/Bat	20.00
JR	Joe Rudi/Bat	10.00
NR	Nolan Ryan/Bat	75.00
RS	Red Schoendienst/Bat	10.00
TS	Tom Seaver/Bat	20.00
MS	"Moose" Skowron/Bat	10.00
DS	Darryl Strawberry/Bat	20.00
CW	Claudell Washington/Bat	10.00

Super Teammates

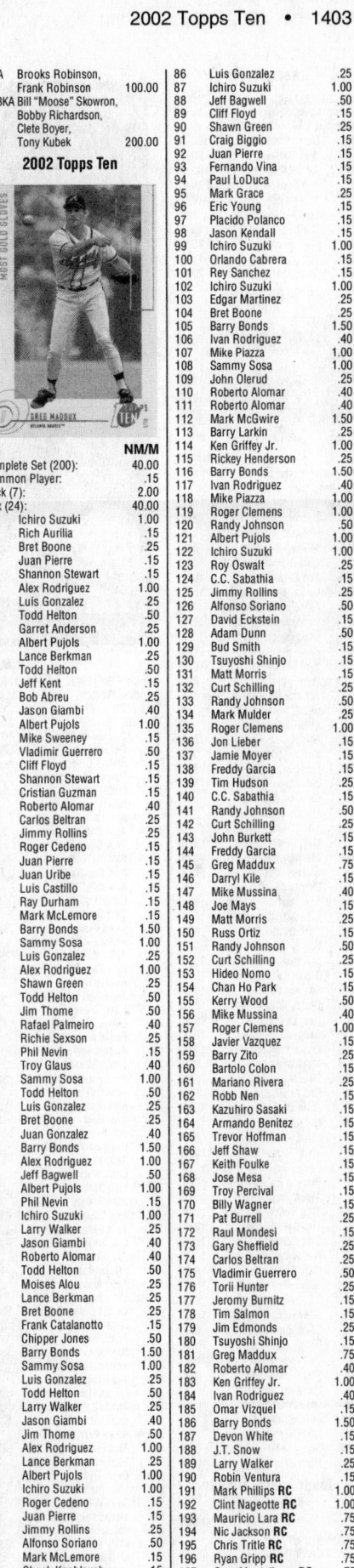

NM/M
Complete Set (5): 10.00
Common Card: 2.00
Inserted 1:10
BG	Lou Brock, Bob Gibson	2.00
FB	Whitey Ford, Yogi Berra	4.00
MI	Willie Mays, Monte Irvin	4.00
RR	Brooks Robinson, Frank Robinson	3.00
SRBK	Bill "Moose" Skowron, Bobby Richardson, Clete Boyer, Tony Kubek	2.00

RRA	Brooks Robinson, Frank Robinson	100.00
SRBKA	Bill "Moose" Skowron, Bobby Richardson, Clete Boyer, Tony Kubek	200.00

2002 Topps Ten

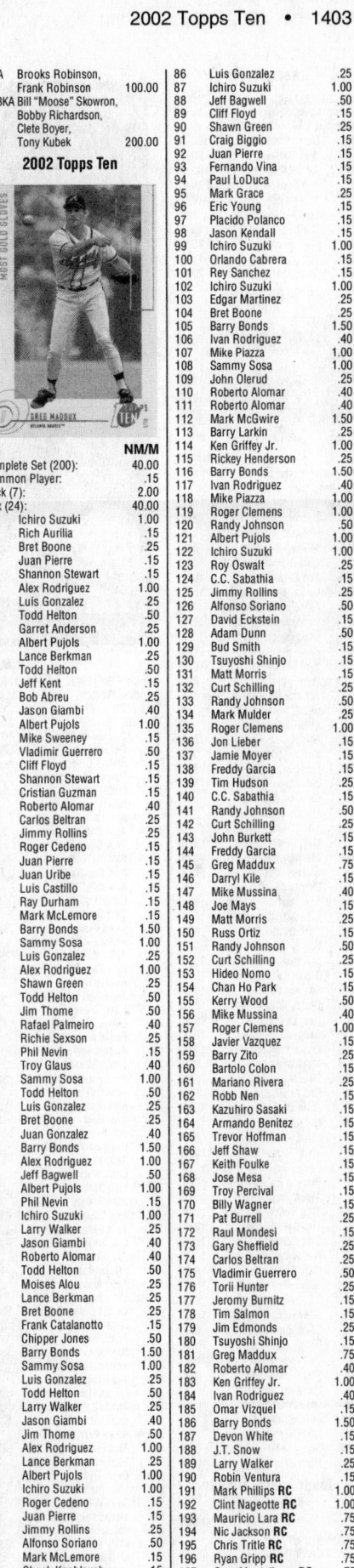

NM/M
Complete Set (200): 40.00
Common Player: .15
Pack (7): 2.00
Box (24): 40.00
1	Ichiro Suzuki	1.00
2	Rich Aurilia	.15
3	Bret Boone	.25
4	Juan Pierre	.15
5	Shannon Stewart	.15
6	Alex Rodriguez	1.00
7	Luis Gonzalez	.25
8	Todd Helton	.50
9	Garret Anderson	.25
10	Albert Pujols	1.00
11	Lance Berkman	.25
12	Todd Helton	.50
13	Jeff Kent	.15
14	Bob Abreu	.25
15	Jason Giambi	.40
16	Albert Pujols	1.00
17	Mike Sweeney	.15
18	Vladimir Guerrero	.50
19	Cliff Floyd	.15
20	Shannon Stewart	.15
21	Cristian Guzman	.15
22	Roberto Alomar	.40
23	Carlos Beltran	.25
24	Jimmy Rollins	.25
25	Roger Cedeno	.15
26	Juan Pierre	.15
27	Juan Uribe	.15
28	Luis Castillo	.15
29	Ray Durham	.15
30	Mark McLemore	.15
31	Barry Bonds	1.50
32	Sammy Sosa	1.00
33	Luis Gonzalez	.25
34	Alex Rodriguez	1.00
35	Shawn Green	.25
36	Todd Helton	.50
37	Jim Thome	.50
38	Rafael Palmeiro	.40
39	Richie Sexson	.25
40	Phil Nevin	.15
41	Troy Glaus	.40
42	Sammy Sosa	1.00
43	Todd Helton	.50
44	Luis Gonzalez	.25
45	Bret Boone	.25
46	Juan Gonzalez	.25
47	Barry Bonds	1.50
48	Alex Rodriguez	1.00
49	Jeff Bagwell	.50
50	Albert Pujols	1.00
51	Phil Nevin	.15
52	Ichiro Suzuki	1.00
53	Larry Walker	.25
54	Jason Giambi	.40
55	Roberto Alomar	.40
56	Todd Helton	.50
57	Moises Alou	.25
58	Lance Berkman	.25
59	Bret Boone	.25
60	Frank Catalanotto	.15
61	Chipper Jones	.50
62	Barry Bonds	1.50
63	Sammy Sosa	1.00
64	Luis Gonzalez	.25
65	Todd Helton	.50
66	Larry Walker	.25
67	Jason Giambi	.40
68	Jim Thome	.50
69	Alex Rodriguez	1.00
70	Lance Berkman	.25
71	Albert Pujols	1.00
72	Ichiro Suzuki	1.00
73	Roger Cedeno	.15
74	Juan Pierre	.15
75	Jimmy Rollins	.25
76	Alfonso Soriano	.50
77	Mark McLemore	.15
78	Chuck Knoblauch	.15
79	Vladimir Guerrero	.50
80	Bob Abreu	.25
81	Mike Cameron	.15
82	Sammy Sosa	1.00
83	Alex Rodriguez	1.00
84	Todd Helton	.50
85	Barry Bonds	1.50

86	Luis Gonzalez	.25
87	Ichiro Suzuki	1.00
88	Jeff Bagwell	.50
89	Cliff Floyd	.15
90	Shawn Green	.25
91	Craig Biggio	.25
92	Juan Pierre	.15
93	Fernando Vina	.15
94	Paul LoDuca	.15
95	Mark Grace	.25
96	Eric Young	.15
97	Placido Polanco	.15
98	Jason Kendall	.15
99	Ichiro Suzuki	1.00
100	Orlando Cabrera	.15
101	Rey Sanchez	.15
102	Ichiro Suzuki	1.00
103	Edgar Martinez	.25
104	Bret Boone	.25
105	Barry Bonds	1.50
106	Ivan Rodriguez	.40
107	Mike Piazza	1.00
108	Sammy Sosa	1.00
109	John Olerud	.25
110	Roberto Alomar	.40
111	Roberto Alomar	.40
112	Mark McGwire	1.50
113	Barry Larkin	.25
114	Ken Griffey Jr.	1.00
115	Rickey Henderson	.25
116	Barry Bonds	1.50
117	Ivan Rodriguez	.40
118	Mike Piazza	1.00
119	Roger Clemens	1.00
120	Randy Johnson	.50
121	Albert Pujols	1.00
122	Ichiro Suzuki	1.00
123	Roy Oswalt	.25
124	C.C. Sabathia	.15
125	Jimmy Rollins	.25
126	Alfonso Soriano	.50
127	David Eckstein	.15
128	Adam Dunn	.50
129	Bud Smith	.15
130	Tsuyoshi Shinjo	.15
131	Matt Morris	.15
132	Curt Schilling	.25
133	Randy Johnson	.50
134	Mark Mulder	.25
135	Roger Clemens	1.00
136	Jon Lieber	.15
137	Jamie Moyer	.15
138	Freddy Garcia	.15
139	Tim Hudson	.25
140	C.C. Sabathia	.15
141	Randy Johnson	.50
142	Curt Schilling	.25
143	John Burkett	.15
144	Freddy Garcia	.15
145	Greg Maddux	.75
146	Darryl Kile	.15
147	Mike Mussina	.40
148	Joe Mays	.15
149	Matt Morris	.25
150	Russ Ortiz	.15
151	Randy Johnson	.50
152	Curt Schilling	.25
153	Hideo Nomo	.15
154	Chan Ho Park	.15
155	Kerry Wood	.25
156	Mike Mussina	.40
157	Roger Clemens	1.00
158	Javier Vazquez	.15
159	Barry Zito	.25
160	Bartolo Colon	.25
161	Mariano Rivera	.25
162	Robb Nen	.15
163	Kazuhiro Sasaki	.15
164	Armando Benitez	.15
165	Trevor Hoffman	.15
166	Jeff Shaw	.15
167	Keith Foulke	.15
168	Jose Mesa	.15
169	Troy Percival	.15
170	Billy Wagner	.15
171	Pat Burrell	.25
172	Raul Mondesi	.15
173	Gary Sheffield	.25
174	Carlos Beltran	.25
175	Vladimir Guerrero	.50
176	Torii Hunter	.25
177	Jeromy Burnitz	.15
178	Tim Salmon	.15
179	Jim Edmonds	.15
180	Tsuyoshi Shinjo	.15
181	Greg Maddux	.75
182	Roberto Alomar	.40
183	Ken Griffey Jr.	1.00
184	Ivan Rodriguez	.25
185	Omar Vizquel	.15
186	Barry Bonds	1.50
187	Devon White	.15
188	J.T. Snow	.15
189	Larry Walker	.25
190	Robin Ventura	.15
191	Mark Phillips RC	1.00
192	Clint Nageotte RC	1.00
193	Mauricio Lara RC	.75
194	Nic Jackson RC	.75
195	Chris Tritle RC	.75
196	Ryan Gripp RC	.75
197	Greg Montalbano RC	.75
198	Noochie Varner RC	.75
199	Nick Alvarez RC	.75
200	Craig Kuzmic RC	.75

Die-Cut
Stars (1-200): 2-4X
Inserted 1:4

Autographs

		NM/M
	Common Autograph:	10.00
	Inserted 1:67	
BB	Barry Bonds	180.00
BBO	Bret Boone	20.00
RCL	Roger Clemens	100.00
JE	Jim Edmonds	25.00
CF	Cliff Floyd	10.00
LG	Luis Gonzalez	15.00
CG	Cristian Guzman	10.00
RO	Roy Oswalt	15.00
JR	Jimmy Rollins	15.00
BZ	Barry Zito	20.00

Relics

		NM/M
	Common Player:	8.00
	Bat Relic 1:27	
	Jersey Relic 1:26	
BA	Bob Abreu/Bat	12.00
RA	Roberto Alomar/Bat	15.00
MA	Moises Alou/Bat	8.00
GA	Garret Anderson/Bat	10.00
JBA	Jeff Bagwell/Jsy	15.00
CB	Carlos Beltran/Bat	10.00
AB	Armando Benitez/Jsy	8.00
LB	Lance Berkman/Bat	15.00
CBI	Craig Biggio/Jsy	15.00
BB	Barry Bonds/Jsy	25.00
BBO	Bret Boone/Bat	10.00
JBU	John Burkett/Jsy	8.00
JB	Jeromy Burnitz/Jsy	8.00
MC	Mike Cameron/Bat	10.00
LC	Luis Castillo/Bat	8.00
RC	Roger Cedeno/Bat	8.00
BC	Bartolo Colon/Jsy	8.00
RD	Ray Durham/Bat	8.00
JE	Jim Edmonds/Bat	15.00
CF	Cliff Floyd/Bat	8.00
FG	Freddy Garcia/Jsy	8.00
JGO	Juan Gonzalez/Bat	10.00
LG	Luis Gonzalez/Bat	10.00
MG	Mark Grace/Bat	20.00
SG	Shawn Green/Bat	10.00
CG	Cristian Guzman/Bat	8.00
TH	Todd Helton/Bat	15.00
THO	Trevor Hoffman/Jsy	10.00
THU	Torii Hunter/Bat	15.00
RJ	Randy Johnson/Jsy	20.00
CJ	Chipper Jones/Bat	20.00
JK	Jason Kendall/Jsy	10.00
JKE	Jeff Kent/Jsy	10.00
CK	Chuck Knoblauch/Bat	10.00
PL	Paul LoDuca/Bat	10.00
GM	Greg Maddux/Jsy	20.00
EM	Edgar Martinez/Jsy	10.00
MM	Mark McLemore/Bat	8.00
PM	Raul Mondesi/Bat	8.00
PN	Phil Nevin/Bat	8.00
JO	John Olerud/Jsy	10.00
RP	Rafael Palmeiro/Jsy	12.00
CP	Chan Ho Park/Jsy	8.00
MP	Mike Piazza/Jsy	20.00
JP	Juan Pierre/Jsy	10.00
PP	Placido Polanco/Bat	10.00
AP	Albert Pujols/Bat	25.00
AR	Alex Rodriguez/Jsy	15.00
TS	Tim Salmon/Bat	10.00
CS	Curt Schilling/Jsy	15.00
RS	Richie Sexson/Bat	10.00
GS	Gary Sheffield/Jsy	10.00
TSH	Tsuyoshi Shinjo/Bat	10.00
JS	J.T. Snow/Bat	10.00
AS	Alfonso Soriano/Bat	15.00
SS	Shannon Stewart/Bat	8.00
MS	Mike Sweeney/Bat	15.00
JT	Jim Thome/Bat	20.00
RV	Robin Ventura/Bat	8.00
FV	Fernando Vina/Bat	10.00
OV	Omar Vizquel/Bat	10.00
BW	Billy Wagner/Bat	10.00
LW	Larry Walker/Bat	10.00
DW	Devon White/Bat	8.00
BZ	Barry Zito/Jsy	10.00

Team Topps Legends Autographs

		NM/M
	Common Player:	
	Carl Yastrzemski	65.00

2002 Topps Total Pre-Production

		NM/M
	Complete Set (3):	6.00
	Common Player:	2.00
PP1	Barry Bonds	2.00

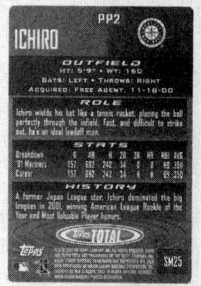

PP2	Ichiro	2.00
PP3	Hank Blalock	2.00

2002 Topps Total

		NM/M
	Complete Set (990):	125.00
	Common Player:	.10
	Pack (10):	1.00
	Box (36):	30.00
1	Joe Mauer RC	10.00
2	Derek Jeter	2.00
3	Shawn Green	.25
4	Vladimir Guerrero	.50
5	Mike Piazza	1.50
6	Brandon Duckworth	.10
7	Aramis Ramirez	.10
8	Josh Barfield	1.00
9	Troy Glaus	.40
10	Sammy Sosa	1.00
11	Rod Barajas	.10
12	Tsuyoshi Shinjo	.25
13	Larry Bigbie	.10
14	Tino Martinez	.10
15	Craig Biggio	.25
16	Anastacio Martinez RC	.40
17	John McDonald	.10
18	Kyle Kane RC	.30
19	Aubrey Huff	.10
20	Juan Cruz	.10
21	Doug Creek	.10
22	Luther Hackman	.10
23	Rafael Furcal	.10
24	Andres Torres	.10
25	Jason Giambi	.50
26	Jose Paniagua	.10
27	Jose Offerman	.10
28	Alex Arias	.10
29	J.M. Gold	.10
30	Jeff Bagwell	.50
31	Brent Cookson RC	.20
32	Kelly Wunsch	.10
33	Larry Walker	.25
34	Luis Gonzalez	.25
35	John Franco	.10
36	Roy Oswalt	.25
37	Tom Glavine	.25
38	C.C. Sabathia	.10
39	Jay Gibbons	.10
40	Wilson Betemit	.10
41	Tony Armas	.10
42	Mo Vaughn	.10
43	Gerard Oakes RC	.40
44	Dmitri Young	.10
45	Tim Salmon	.10
46	Barry Zito	.25
47	Adrian Gonzalez	.10
48	Joe Davenport	.10
49	Adrian Hernandez	.10
50	Randy Johnson	.50
51	Benito Baez	.10
52	Adam Pettyjohn	.10
53	Alex Escobar	.10
54	Stevenson Agosto RC	.25
55	Omar Daal	.10
56	Mike Buddie	.10
57	Dave Williams	.10
58	Marquis Grissom	.10
59	Pat Burrell	.25
60	Mark Prior	2.00
61	Mike Bynum	.10
62	Mike Hill RC	.25
63	Brandon Backe RC	.25
64	Dan Wilson	.10
65	Nick Johnson	.10
66	Jason Grimsley	.10
67	Russ Johnson	.10
68	Todd Walker	.10
69	Kyle Farnsworth	.10

70	Ben Broussard	.10
71	Garrett Guzman RC	.50
72	Terry Mulholland	.10
73	Tyler Houston	.10
74	Jace Brewer	.10
75	Chris Baker RC	.25
76	Frank Catalanotto	.10
77	Mike Redmond	.10
78	Matt Wise	.10
79	Fernando Vina	.10
80	Kevin Brown	.10
81	Grant Balfour	.10
82	Clint Nageotte RC	.75
83	Jeff Tam	.10
84	Steve Trachsel	.10
85	Tomokazu Ohka	.10
86	Keith McDonald	.10
87	Jose Ortiz	.10
88	Rusty Greer	.10
89	Jeff Suppan	.10
90	Moises Alou	.10
91	Juan Encarnacion	.10
92	Tyler Yates RC	.40
93	Scott Strickland	.10
94	Brent Butler	.10
95	Jon Rauch	.10
96	Brian Mallette RC	.25
97	Joe Randa	.10
98	Cesar Crespo	.10
99	Felix Rodriguez	.10
100	Chipper Jones	.75
101	Victor Martinez	.10
102	Danny Graves	.10
103	Brandon Berger RC	.10
104	Carlos Garcia	.10
105	Alfonso Soriano	.75
106	Allan Simpson RC	.25
107	Brad Thomas	.10
108	Devon White	.10
109	Scott Chiasson	.10
110	Cliff Floyd	.10
111	Scott Williamson	.10
112	Julio Zuleta	.10
113	Terry Adams	.10
114	Zach Day	.10
115	Ben Grieve	.10
116	Mark Ellis	.10
117	Bobby Jenks RC	.75
118	LaTroy Hawkins	.10
119	Tim Raines Jr.	.10
120	Juan Uribe	.10
121	Bob Scanlan	.10
122	Brad Nelson RC	.50
123	Adam Johnson	.10
124	Raul Casanova	.10
125	Jeff D'Amico	.10
126	Aaron Cook RC	.50
127	Alan Benes	.10
128	Mark Little	.10
129	Randy Wolf	.10
130	Phil Nevin	.10
131	Guillermo Mota	.10
132	Nick Neugebauer	.10
133	Pedro Borbon	.10
134	Doug Mientkiewicz	.10
135	Edgardo Alfonzo	.10
136	Dustan Mohr	.10
137	Dan Reichert	.10
138	Dewon Brazelton	.10
139	Orlando Cabrera	.10
140	Todd Hollandsworth	.10
141	Darren Dreifort	.10
142	Jose Valentin	.10
143	Josh Kalinowski	.10
144	Randy Keisler	.10
145	Bret Boone	.10
146	Roosevelt Brown	.10
147	Brent Abernathy	.10
148	Jorge Julio	.10
149	Alex Gonzalez	.10
150	Juan Pierre	.10
151	Roger Cedeno	.10
152	Javier Vazquez	.10
153	Armando Benitez	.10
154	Dave Burba	.10
155	Brad Penny	.10
156	Ryan Jensen	.10
157	Jeromy Burnitz	.10
158	Matt Childers RC	.40
159	Wilmy Caceres	.10
160	Roger Clemens	.10
161	Michael Tejera	.10
162	Jason Christiansen	.10
163	Pokey Reese	.10
164	Ivanon Coffie	.10
165	Joaquin Benoit	.10
166	Mike Matheny	.10
167	Eric Cammack	.10
168	Alex Graman	.10
169	Brook Fordyce	.10
170	Mike Lieberthal	.10
171	Giovanni Carrara	.10
172	Antonio Perez	.10
173	Fernando Tatis	.10
174	Jason Bay RC	2.00
175	Jason Botts RC	.50
176	Danys Baez	.10
177	Shea Hillenbrand	.10
178	Jack Cust	.10
179	Clay Bellinger	.10
180	Roberto Alomar	.10
181	Graeme Lloyd	.10
182	Clint Weibl RC	.40
183	Royce Clayton	.10
184	Ben Davis	.10
185	Brian Adams	.25
186	Jack Wilson	.10
187	David Coggin	.10

188	Derrick Turnbow	.10
189	Vladimir Nunez	.10
190	Mariano Rivera	.10
191	Wilson Guzman	.10
192	Michael Barrett	.10
193	Corey Patterson	.10
194	Luis Sojo	.10
195	Scott Elarton	.10
196	Charles Thomas	.25
197	Ricky Bottalico	.10
198	Wilfredo Rodriguez	.10
199	Ricardo Rincon	.10
200	John Smoltz	.10
201	Travis Miller	.10
202	Ben Weber	.10
203	T.J. Tucker	.10
204	Terry Shumpert	.10
205	Bernie Williams	.10
206	Russ Ortiz	.10
207	Nate Rolison	.10
208	Jose Cruz Jr.	.10
209	Bill Ortega	.10
210	Carl Everett	.10
211	Luis Lopez	.10
212	Brian Wolfe RC	.25
213	Doug Davis	.10
214	Troy Mattes	.10
215	Al Leiter	.10
216	Joe Mays	.10
217	Bobby Smith	.10
218	J.J. Trujillo RC	.25
219	Hideo Nomo	.25
220	Jimmy Rollins	.25
221	Bobby Seay	.10
222	Mike Thurman	.10
223	Bartolo Colon	.10
224	Jesus Sanchez	.10
225	Ray Durham	.10
226	Juan Diaz	.10
227	Lee Stevens	.10
228	Ben Howard RC	.75
229	James Moulton	.10
230	Paul Quantrill	.10
231	Randy Knorr	.10
232	Abraham Nunez	.10
233	Mike Fetters	.10
234	Mario Encarnacion	.10
235	Jeremy Fikac	.10
236	Travis Lee	.10
237	Bob File	.10
238	Pete Harnisch	.10
239	Randy Galvez RC	.25
240	Geoff Goetz	.10
241	Gary Glover	.10
242	Troy Percival	.10
243	Lenny Dinardo RC	.40
244	Jonny Gomes RC	1.00
245	Jesus Medrano RC	.25
246	Rey Ordonez	.10
247	Juan Gonzalez	.50
248	Jose Guillen	.10
249	Franklin German RC	.25
250	Mike Mussina	.40
251	Ugueth Urbina	.10
252	Melvin Mora	.10
253	Gerald Williams	.10
254	Jared Sandberg	.10
255	Darrin Fletcher	.10
256	A.J. Pierzynski	.10
257	Lenny Harris	.10
258	Blaine Neal	.10
259	Denny Neagle	.10
260	Jason Hart	.10
261	Henry Mateo	.10
262	Rheal Cormier	.10
263	Luis Terrero	.10
264	Shigetoshi Hasegawa	.10
265	Bill Haselman	.10
266	Scott Hatteberg	.10
267	Adam Hyzdu	.10
268	Mike Williams	.10
269	Marlon Anderson	.10
270	Bruce Chen	.10
271	Eli Marrero	.10
272	Jimmy Haynes	.10
273	Bronson Arroyo	.10
274	Kevin Jordan	.10
275	Rick Helling	.10
276	Mark Loretta	.10
277	Dustin Hermanson	.10
278	Pablo Ozuna	.10
279	Syketo Anderson RC	.25
280	Jermaine Dye	.10
281	Will Smith	.10
282	Brian Daubach	.10
283	Eric Hinske	.10
284	Joe Jiannetti RC	.40
285	Chan Ho Park	.10
286	Curtis Legendre RC	.25
287	Jeff Reboulet	.10
288	Scott Rolen	.50
289	Chris Richard	.10
290	Eric Chavez	.10
291	Scot Shields	.10
292	Donnie Sadler	.10
293	Dave Veres	.10
294	Craig Counsell	.10
295	Armando Reynoso	.10
296	Kyle Lohse	.10
297	Arthur Rhodes	.10
298	Sidney Ponson	.10
299	Trevor Hoffman	.10
300	Kerry Wood	.25
301	Danny Bautista	.10
302	Scott Sauerbeck	.10
303	Johnny Estrada	.10
304	Mike Timlin	.10
305	Orlando Hernandez	.25

306	Tony Clark	.10
307	Tomas Perez	.10
308	Marcus Giles	.10
309	Mike Bordick	.10
310	Jorge Posada	.25
311	Jason Conti	.10
312	Kevin Millar	.10
313	Paul Shuey	.10
314	Jake Mauer RC	.75
315	Luke Hudson	.10
316	Angel Berroa	.10
317	Fred Bastardo RC	.25
318	Shawn Estes	.10
319	Andy Ashby	.10
320	Ryan Klesko	.10
321	Kevin Appier	.10
322	Juan Pena	.10
323	Alex Herrera	.10
324	Robb Nen	.10
325	Orlando Hudson	.10
326	Lyle Overbay	.10
327	Ben Sheets	.25
328	Mike DiFelice	.10
329	Pablo Arias RC	.25
330	Mike Sweeney	.10
331	Rick Ankiel	.25
332	Tomas De La Rosa	.10
333	Kazuhisa Ishii RC	.50
334	Jose Reyes	.10
335	Jeremy Giambi	.10
336	Jose Mesa	.10
337	Ralph Roberts RC	.25
338	Jose Nunez	.10
339	Curt Schilling	.40
340	Sean Casey	.20
341	Bob Wells	.10
342	Carlos Beltran	.10
343	Alexis Gomez	.10
344	Brandon Claussen	.25
345	Buddy Groom	.10
346	Mark Phillips RC	.50
347	Francisco Cordova	.10
348	Joe Oliver	.10
349	Danny Patterson	.10
350	Joel Pineiro	.10
351	J.R. House	.10
352	Benny Agbayani	.10
353	Jose Vidro	.10
354	Reed Johnson RC	.25
355	Mike Lowell	.10
356	Scott Schoeneweis	.10
357	Brian Jordan	.10
358	Steve Finley	.10
359	Randy Choate	.10
360	Jose Lima	.10
361	Miguel Olivo	.10
362	Kenny Rogers	.10
363	David Justice	.20
364	Brandon Knight	.10
365	Joe Kennedy	.10
366	Eric Valent	.10
367	Nelson Cruz	.10
368	Brian Giles	.25
369	Charles Gibson Jr.	.10
370	Juan Pena	.10
371	Mark Redman	.10
372	Billy Koch	.10
373	Ted Lilly	.10
374	Craig Paquette	.10
375	Kevin Jarvis	.10
376	Scott Erickson	.10
377	Josh Paul	.10
378	Darwin Cubillan	.10
379	Nelson Figueroa	.10
380	Darin Erstad	.20
381	Jeremy Hill RC	.10
382	Elvin Nina	.10
383	David Wells	.25
384	Jay Caligiuri RC	.40
385	Freddy Garcia	.10
386	Damian Miller	.10
387	Bobby Higginson	.10
388	Alejandro Giron RC	.25
389	Ivan Rodriguez	.40
390	Ed Rogers	.10
391	Andy Benes	.10
392	Matt Blank	.10
393	Ryan Vogelsong	.10
394	Kelly Ramos RC	.25
395	Eric Karros	.10
396	Bobby Jones	.10
397	Omar Vizquel	.25
398	Matt Perisho	.10
399	Delino DeShields	.10
400	Carlos Hernandez	.10
401	Derrek Lee	.10
402	Kirk Rueter	.10
403	David Wright RC	20.00
404	Paul LoDuca	.10
405	Brian Schneider	.10
406	Milton Bradley	.10
407	Daryle Ward	.10
408	Cody Ransom	.10
409	Fernando Rodney	.10
410	John Suomi RC	.20
411	Joe Girardi	.10
412	Demetrius Heath RC	.25
413	John Foster RC	.25
414	Doug Glanville	.10
415	Ryan Kohlmeier	.10
416	Mike Matthews	.10
417	Craig Wilson	.10
418	Jay Witasick	.10
419	Jay Payton	.10
420	Andruw Jones	.40
421	Benji Gil	.10
422	Jeff Liefer	.10
423	Kevin Young	.10

424	Richie Sexson	.25
425	Cory Lidle	.10
426	Shane Halter	.10
427	Jesse Foppert	.40
428	Jose Molina	.10
429	Nick Alvarez RC	.40
430	Brian L. Hunter	.10
431	Clifford Bartosh RC	.25
432	Junior Spivey	.10
433	Eric Good RC	.25
434	Chin-Feng Chen	.10
435	T.J. Mathews	.10
436	Rich Rodriguez	.10
437	Bobby Abreu	.20
438	Joe McEwing	.10
439	Michael Tucker	.10
440	Preston Wilson	.10
441	Mike MacDougal	.10
442	Shannon Stewart	.10
443	Bob Howry	.10
444	Mike Benjamin	.10
445	Erik Hiljus	.10
446	Ryan Gripp RC	.25
447	Jose Vizcaino	.10
448	Shawn Wooten	.10
449	Steve Kent RC	.25
450	Ramiro Mendoza	.10
451	Jake Westbrook	.10
452	Joe Lawrence	.10
453	Jae Weong Seo	.10
454	Ryan Fry RC	.20
455	Darren Lewis	.10
456	Brad Wilkerson	.10
457	Gustavo Chacin RC	.25
458	Adrian Brown	.10
459	Mike Cameron	.10
460	Bud Smith	.10
461	Derrick Lewis	.10
462	Derek Lowe	.10
463	Matt Williams	.10
464	Jason Jennings	.10
465	Albie Lopez	.10
466	Felipe Lopez	.10
467	Luke Allen	.10
468	Brian Anderson	.10
469	Matt Riley	.10
470	Ryan Dempster	.10
471	Matt Ginter	.10
472	David Ortiz	.10
473	Cole Barthel	.10
474	Damian Jackson	.10
475	Andy Van Hekken	.10
476	Doug Brocail	.10
477	Denny Hocking	.10
478	Sean Douglass	.10
479	Eric Owens	.10
480	Ryan Ludwick	.10
481	Todd Pratt	.10
482	Aaron Sele	.10
483	Edgar Renteria	.10
484	Raymond Cabrera RC	.25
485	Brandon Lyon	.10
486	Chase Utley	.75
487	Robert Fick	.10
488	Wilfredo Cordero	.10
489	Octavio Dotel	.10
490	Paul Abbott	.10
491	Jason Kendall	.10
492	Jarrod Washburn	.10
493	Dane Sardinha	.10
494	Jung Bong	.10
495	J.D. Drew	.10
496	Jason Schmidt	.10
497	Mike Magnante	.10
498	Jorge Padilla RC	.50
499	Eric Gagne	.10
500	Todd Helton	.50
501	Jeff Weaver	.10
502	Alex Sanchez	.10
503	Ken Griffey Jr.	.10
504	Abraham Nunez	.10
505	Reggie Sanders	.10
506	Casey Kotchman	2.00
507	Jim Mann	.10
508	Matt LeCroy	.10
509	Frank Castillo	.10
510	Geoff Jenkins	.10
511	Jayson Durocher RC	.20
512	Ellis Burks	.10
513	Aaron Fultz	.10
514	Hiram Bocachica	.10
515	Nate Espy RC	.25
516	Placido Polanco	.10
517	Kerry Ligtenberg	.10
518	Doug Nickle	.10
519	Ramon Ortiz	.10
520	Greg Swindell	.10
521	J.J. Davis	.10
522	Sandy Alomar	.10
523	Chris Carpenter	.10
524	Vance Wilson	.10
525	Nomar Garciaparra	1.00
526	Jim Mecir	.10
527	Taylor Buchholz RC	.25
528	Brent Mayne	.10
529	John Rodriguez RC	.25
530	David Segui	.10
531	Nate Cornejo	.10
532	Gil Heredia	.10
533	Esteban Loaiza	.10
534	Pat Mahomes	.10
535	Matt Morris	.20
536	Todd Stottlemyre	.10
537	Brian Lesher	.10
538	Arturo McDowell	.10
539	Felix Diaz	.10
540	Mark Mulder	.10
541	Kevin Frederick RC	.25

#	Player	Price
542	Andy Fox	.10
543	Dionys Cesar RC	.10
544	Justin Miller	.10
545	Keith Osik	.10
546	Shane Reynolds	.10
547	Mike Myers	.10
548	Raul Chavez RC	.25
549	Joe Nathan	.10
550	Ryan Anderson	.10
551	Jason Marquis	.10
552	Marty Cordova	.10
553	Kevin Tapani	.10
554	Jimmy Anderson	.10
555	Pedro Martinez	.50
556	Rocky Biddle	.10
557	Alex Ochoa	.10
558	D'Angelo Jimenez	.10
559	Wilkin Ruan	.10
560	Terrence Long	.10
561	Mark Lukasiewicz	.10
562	Jose Santiago	.10
563	Brad Fullmer	.10
564	Corky Miller	.10
565	Matt White	.10
566	Mark Grace	.30
567	Raul Ibanez	.10
568	Josh Towers	.10
569	Juan Gonzalez	.40
570	Brian Buchanan	.10
571	Ken Harvey	.10
572	Jeffrey Hammonds	.10
573	Wade Miller	.10
574	Elpidio Guzman	.10
575	Kevin Olsen	.10
576	Austin Kearns	.40
577	Tim Kalita RC	.40
578	David Dellucci	.10
579	Alex Gonzalez	.10
580	Joe Orloski RC	.20
581	Gary Matthews Jr.	.10
582	Ryan Mills	.10
583	Erick Almonte	.10
584	Jeremy Affeldt	.10
585	Chris Trible RC	1.00
586	Michael Cuddyer	.10
587	Kris Foster	.10
588	Russell Branyan	.10
589	Darren Oliver	.10
590	Freddie Money RC	.25
591	Carlos Lee	.10
592	Tim Wakefield	.10
593	Bubba Trammell	.10
594	John Koronka RC	3.00
595	Geoff Blum	.10
596	Darryl Kile	.10
597	Neifi Perez	.10
598	Torii Hunter	.10
599	Luis Castillo	.10
600	Mark Buehrle	.10
601	Jeff Zimmerman	.10
602	Mike DeJean	.10
603	Julio Lugo	.10
604	Chad Hermansen	.10
605	Keith Foulke	.10
606	Lance Davis	.10
607	Jeff Austin RC	.25
608	Brandon Inge	.10
609	Orlando Merced	.10
610	Johnny Damon	.10
611	Doug Henry	.10
612	Adam Kennedy	.10
613	Wiki Gonzalez	.10
614	Brian West RC	.25
615	Andy Pettitte	.25
616	Chone Figgins RC	1.00
617	Matt Lawton	.10
618	Paul Rigdon	.10
619	Keith Lockhart	.10
620	Tim Redding	.10
621	John Parrish	.10
622	Chad Hutchinson	.10
623	Todd Greene	.10
624	David Eckstein	.10
625	Greg Montalbano RC	1.00
626	Joe Beimel	.10
627	Adrian Beltre	.20
628	Charles Nagy	.10
629	Cristian Guzman	.10
630	Toby Hall	.10
631	Jose Hernandez	.10
632	Jose Macias	.10
633	Jaret Wright	.10
634	Steve Parris	.10
635	Gene Kingsdale	.10
636	Tim Worrell	.10
637	Billy Martin	.10
638	Jovanny Cedeno	.10
639	Curt Leskanic	.10
640	Tim Hudson	.20
641	Juan Castro	.10
642	Rafael Soriano	.10
643	Juan Rincon	.10
644	Mark DeRosa	.10
645	Carlos Pena	.25
646	Robin Ventura	.20
647	Odalis Perez	.10
648	Damion Easley	.10
649	Benito Santiago	.10
650	Alex Rodriguez	1.50
651	Aaron Rowand	.10
652	Alex Cora	.10
653	Bobby Kielty	.10
654	Jose Rodriguez	.10
655	Herbert Perry	.10
656	Jeff Urban	.10
657	Paul Bako	.10
658	Shane Spencer	.10
659	Pat Hentgen	.10
660	Jeff Kent	.20
661	Mark McLemore	.10
662	Chuck Knoblauch	.10
663	Blake Stein	.10
664	Brett Roneberg RC	.25
665	Josh Phelps	.10
666	Byung-Hyun Kim	.10
667	Dave Martinez	.10
668	Mike Maroth	.10
669	Shawn Chacon	.10
670	Billy Wagner	.10
671	Luis Alicea	.10
672	Sterling Hitchcock	.10
673	Adam Piatt	.10
674	Ryan Franklin	.10
675	Luke Prokopec	.10
676	Alfredo Amezega	.10
677	Gookie Dawkins	.10
678	Eric Byrnes	.10
679	Barry Larkin	.25
680	Albert Pujols	1.00
681	Edwards Guzman	.10
682	Jason Bere	.10
683	Adam Everett	.10
684	Greg Colbrunn	.10
685	Brandon Puffer RC	.40
686	Mark Kotsay	.10
687	Willie Bloomquist	.10
688	Hank Blalock	.25
689	Travis Hafner	.10
690	Lance Berkman	.40
691	Joe Crede	.10
692	Chuck Finley	.10
693	John Grabow	.10
694	Randy Winn	.10
695	Mike James	.10
696	Kris Benson	.10
697	Bret Prinz	.10
698	Jeff Williams	.10
699	Eric Munson	.10
700	Mike Hampton	.10
701	Ramon E. Martinez	.10
702	Hansel Izquierdo RC	.25
703	Nathan Haynes	.10
704	Eddie Taubensee	.10
705	Esteban German	.10
706	Ross Gload	.10
707	Matthew Merricks RC	.20
708	Chris Piersoll RC	.25
709	Seth Greisinger	.10
710	Ichiro Suzuki	1.00
711	Cesar Izturis	.10
712	Brad Cresse	.10
713	Carl Pavano	.10
714	Steve Sparks	.10
715	Dennis Tankersley	.10
716	Kelvim Escobar	.10
717	Jason LaRue	.10
718	Corey Koskie	.10
719	Vinny Castilla	.10
720	Tim Drew	.10
721	Chin-Hui Tsao	.10
722	Paul Byrd	.10
723	Alex Cintron	.10
724	Orlando Palmeiro	.10
725	Ramon Hernandez	.10
726	Mark Johnson	.10
727	B.J. Ryan	.10
728	Wendell Magee	.10
729	Michael Coleman	.10
730	Mario Ramos	.50
731	Mike Stanton	.10
732	Dee Brown	.10
733	Brad Ausmus	.10
734	Napoleon Calzado RC	.25
735	Woody Williams	.10
736	Paxton Crawford	.10
737	Jason Karnuth	.10
738	Michael Restovich	.10
739	Ramon Castro	.10
740	Maggio Ordonez	.25
741	Tom Gordon	.10
742	Mark Grudzielanek	.10
743	Jamie Moyer	.10
744	Marlyn Tisdale RC	.20
745	Steve Kline	.10
746	Adam Eaton	.10
747	Eric Glaser RC	.25
748	Sean DePaula	.10
749	Greg Norton	.10
750	Steve Reed	.10
751	Ricardo Aramboles	.10
752	Matt Mantei	.10
753	Gene Stechschulte	.10
754	Chuck McElroy	.10
755	Barry Bonds	1.50
756	Matt Anderson	.10
757	Yorvit Torrealba	.10
758	Jason Standridge	.10
759	Desi Relaford	.10
760	Jolbert Cabrera	.10
761	Chris George	.10
762	Erubiel Durazo	.10
763	Paul Konerko	.25
764	Tike Redman	.10
765	Chad Ricketts RC	.20
766	Roberto Hernandez	.10
767	Mark Lewis	.10
768	Livan Hernandez	.10
769	Carlos Brackley RC	.25
770	Kazuhiro Sasaki	.10
771	Bill Hall	.10
772	Nelson Castro RC	.25
773	Eric Milton	.10
774	Tom Davey	.10
775	Todd Ritchie	.10
776	Seth Etherton	.10
777	Chris Singleton	.10
778	Robert Averette RC	.20
779	Robert Person	.10
780	Fred McGriff	.25
781	Richard Hidalgo	.10
782	Kris Wilson	.10
783	John Rocker	.10
784	Justin Kaye	.10
785	Glendon Rusch	.10
786	Greg Vaughn	.10
787	Mike Lamb	.10
788	Greg Myers	.10
789	Nate Field RC	.25
790	Jim Edmonds	.25
791	Olmedo Saenz	.10
792	Jason Johnson	.10
793	Mike Lincoln	.10
794	Todd Coffey	.10
795	Jesus Sanchez	.10
796	Aaron Myette	.10
797	Tony Womack	.10
798	Chad Kreuter	.10
799	Brady Clark	.10
800	Adam Dunn	.50
801	Jacque Jones	.10
802	Kevin Millwood	.10
803	Mike Rivera	.10
804	Jim Thome	.40
805	Jeff Conine	.10
806	Elmer Dessens	.10
807	Randy Velarde	.10
808	Carlos Delgado	.30
809	Steve Karsay	.10
810	Casey Fossum	.10
811	J.C. Romero	.10
812	Chris Truby	.10
813	Tony Graffanino	.10
814	Wascar Serrano	.10
815	Delvin James	.10
816	Pedro Feliz	.10
817	Damian Rolls	.10
818	Scott Linebrink	.10
819	Rafael Palmeiro	.40
820	Javy Lopez	.10
821	Larry Barnes	.10
822	Brian Lawrence	.10
823	Scotty Layfield RC	.25
824	Jeff Cirillo	.10
825	Willis Roberts	.10
826	Rich Harden RC	2.00
827	Chris Snelling RC	1.00
828	Gary Sheffield	.25
829	Jeff Heaverlo	.10
830	Matt Clement	.10
831	Rich Garces	.10
832	Rondell White	.10
833	Henry Pichardo RC	.25
834	Aaron Boone	.10
835	Ruben Sierra	.10
836	Deivis Santos	.10
837	Tony Batista	.10
838	Rob Bell	.10
839	Frank Thomas	.50
840	Jose Silva	.10
841	Dan Johnson RC	.50
842	Steve Cox	.10
843	Jose Acevedo	.10
844	Jay Bell	.10
845	Mike Sirotka	.10
846	Garret Anderson	.10
847	James Shanks RC	.25
848	Trot Nixon	.10
849	Keith Ginter	.10
850	Tim Spooneybarger	.10
851	Matt Stairs	.10
852	Chris Stynes	.10
853	Marvin Bernard	.10
854	Raul Mondesi	.20
855	Jeremy Owens	.10
856	Jon Garland	.10
857	Mitch Meluskey	.10
858	Chad Durbin	.10
859	John Burkett	.10
860	Jon Switzer	.10
861	Peter Bergeron	.10
862	Jesus Colome	.10
863	Todd Hundley	.10
864	Ben Petrick	.10
865	So Taguchi RC	.75
866	Ryan Drese	.10
867	Mike Trombley	.10
868	Rick Reed	.10
869	Mark Teixeira	.20
870	Corey Thurman RC	.10
871	Brian Roberts	.10
872	Mike Timlin	.10
873	Chris Reitsma	.10
874	Jeff Fassero	.10
875	Carlos Valderrama	.10
876	John Lackey	.10
877	Travis Fryman	.10
878	Ismael Valdes	.10
879	Rick White	.10
880	Edgar Martinez	.10
881	Dean Palmer	.10
882	Matt Allegra RC	.10
883	Greg Sain RC	.25
884	Carlos Silva	.10
885	Jose Valverde RC	.25
886	Dernell Stenson	.10
887	Todd Van Poppel	.10
888	Wes Anderson	.10
889	Bill Mueller	.10
890	Morgan Ensberg	.10
891	Marcus Thames	.10
892	Adam Walker RC	.10
893	John Halama	.10
894	Frank Menechino	.10
895	Greg Maddux	1.00
896	Gary Bennett	.10
897	Mauricio Lara RC	.25
898	Mike Young	.10
899	Travis Phelps	.10
900	Rich Aurilia	.10
901	Henry Blanco	.10
902	Carlos Febles	.10
903	Scott MacRae	.10
904	Lou Merloni	.10
905	Dicky Gonzalez	.10
906	Jeff DaVanon	.10
907	A.J. Burnett	.10
908	Einar Diaz	.10
909	Julio Franco	.10
910	John Olerud	.25
911	Mark Hamilton RC	.25
912	David Riske	.10
913	Jason Tyner	.10
914	Britt Reames	.10
915	Vernon Wells	.10
916	Eddie Perez	.10
917	Edwin Almonte RC	.25
918	Enrique Wilson	.10
919	Chris Gomez	.10
920	Jayson Werth	.10
921	Jeff Nelson	.10
922	Freddy Sanchez RC	.75
923	John Vander Wal	.10
924	Chad Qualls RC	.25
925	Gabe White	.10
926	Chad Harville	.10
927	Ricky Gutierrez	.10
928	Carlos Guillen	.10
929	B.J. Surhoff	.10
930	Chris Woodard	.10
931	Ricardo Rodriguez	.10
932	Jimmy Gobble RC	1.00
933	Jon Lieber	.10
934	Craig Kuzmic RC	.25
935	Eric Young	.10
936	Gregg Zaun	.10
937	Miguel Batista	.10
938	Danny Wright	.10
939	Todd Zeile	.10
940	Chad Zerbe	.10
941	Jason Young RC	.50
942	Ronnie Belliard	.10
943	John Ennis RC	.10
944	John Flaherty	.10
945	Jerry Hairston Jr.	.10
946	Al Levine	.10
947	Antonio Alfonseca	.10
948	Brian Moehler	.10
949	Calvin Murray	.10
950	Nick Bierbrodt	.10
951	Sun-Woo Kim	.10
952	Noochie Varner RC	.50
953	Luis Rivas	.10
954	Donnie Bridges	.10
955	Ramon Vazquez	.10
956	Luis Garcia	.10
957	Mark Quinn	.10
958	Armando Rios	.10
959	Chad Fox	.10
960	Hee Seop Choi	.10
961	Turk Wendell	.10
962	Adam Roller RC	.20
963	Grant Roberts	.10
964	Ben Molina	.10
965	Juan Rivera	.10
966	Matt Kinney	.10
967	Rod Beck	.10
968	Xavier Nady	.10
969	Masato Yoshii	.10
970	Miguel Tejada	.25
971	Danny Kolb	.10
972	Mike Remlinger	.10
973	Ray Lankford	.10
974	Ryan Minor	.10
975	J.T. Snow	.10
976	Brad Radke	.10
977	Jason Lane	.10
978	Jamey Wright	.10
979	Tom Goodwin	.10
980	Erik Bedard	.10
981	Gabe Kapler	.10
982	Brian Reith	.10
983	Nic Jackson RC	.50
984	Kurt Ainsworth	.10
985	Jason Isringhausen	.10
986	Willie Harris	.10
987	David Cone	.10
988	Bob Wickman	.10
989	Wes Helms	.10
990	Josh Beckett	.25

Award Winners

JORGE POSADA

	NM/M
Complete Set (30):	25.00
Common Player:	.50
Inserted 1:6	
AW1 Ichiro Suzuki	2.00
AW2 Albert Pujols	2.00
AW3 Barry Bonds	3.00
AW4 Ichiro Suzuki	2.00
AW5 Randy Johnson	1.00
AW6 Roger Clemens	2.00
AW7 Jason Giambi	.75
AW8 Bret Boone	.50
AW9 Troy Glaus	.75
AW10 Alex Rodriguez	2.50
AW11 Juan Gonzalez	.75
AW12 Ichiro Suzuki	.75
AW13 Jorge Posada	.75
AW14 Edgar Martinez	.75
AW15 Todd Helton	.75
AW16 Jeff Kent	.50
AW17 Albert Pujols	2.00
AW18 Rich Aurilia	.50
AW19 Barry Bonds	3.00
AW20 Luis Gonzalez	.50
AW21 Sammy Sosa	.50
AW22 Mike Piazza	2.00
AW23 Mike Hampton	.50
AW24 Ruben Sierra	.50
AW25 Matt Morris	.50
AW26 Curt Schilling	.75
AW27 Alex Rodriguez	2.50
AW28 Barry Bonds	3.00
AW29 Jim Thome	1.00
AW30 Barry Bonds	3.00

Total Production

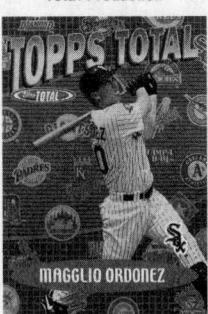

MAGGLIO ORDONEZ

	NM/M
Complete Set (10):	15.00
Common Player:	.75
Inserted 1:12	
TP1 Alex Rodriguez	3.00
TP2 Barry Bonds	3.00
TP3 Ichiro Suzuki	2.00
TP4 Edgar Martinez	.75
TP5 Jason Giambi	1.00
TP6 Todd Helton	1.00
TP7 Nomar Garciaparra	2.50
TP8 Vladimir Guerrero	1.00
TP9 Sammy Sosa	2.00
TP10 Chipper Jones	2.00

Total Topps

	NM/M
Complete Set (50):	35.00
Common Player:	.50
Inserted 1:3	
TT1 Roberto Alomar	.75
TT2 Moises Alou	.50
TT3 Jeff Bagwell	1.00
TT4 Lance Berkman	.75
TT5 Barry Bonds	2.00
TT6 Bret Boone	.50
TT7 Kevin Brown	.50
TT8 Eric Chavez	.50
TT9 Roger Clemens	1.50
TT10 Carlos Delgado	.50
TT11 Cliff Floyd	.50
TT12 Nomar Garciaparra	2.50
TT13 Jason Giambi	1.00
TT14 Brian Giles	.75
TT15 Troy Glaus	.75
TT16 Tom Glavine	.50
TT17 Luis Gonzalez	.50
TT18 Juan Gonzalez	.75
TT19 Shawn Green	.50
TT20 Ken Griffey Jr.	2.50
TT21 Vladimir Guerrero	1.00
TT22 Jorge Posada	.75
TT23 Todd Helton	.75
TT24 Tim Hudson	.50
TT25 Derek Jeter	4.00
TT26 Randy Johnson	1.00
TT27 Andruw Jones	.75
TT28 Chipper Jones	2.00
TT29 Jeff Kent	.50
TT30 Greg Maddux	2.00
TT31 Edgar Martinez	.50
TT32 Pedro Martinez	1.00
TT33 Maggilo Ordonez	.50
TT34 Rafael Palmeiro	.50
TT35 Mike Piazza	2.00
TT36 Albert Pujols	2.00
TT37 Aramis Ramirez	.50
TT38 Mariano Rivera	.50
TT39 Alex Rodriguez	3.00
TT40 Ivan Rodriguez	.75
TT41 Curt Schilling	.50
TT42 Gary Sheffield	.50
TT43 Sammy Sosa	2.00
TT44 Ichiro Suzuki	4.00
TT45 Miguel Tejada	.50
TT46 Frank Thomas	1.00
TT47 Jim Thome	.75
TT48 Larry Walker	.50
TT49 Bernie Williams	.50
TT50 Kerry Wood	.50

2002 Topps Traded & Rookies

SHAWN RIGGANS

	NM/M
Complete Set (275):	125.00
Common Player:	.15
Common SP (1-110):	.50
Chrome Cards:	2-4X
2:Pack	
Pack (10):	3.00
Box (24):	60.00
T1 Jeff Weaver	.50
T2 Jay Powell	.50
T3 Alex Gonzalez	.50
T4 Jason Isringhausen	.50
T5 Darren Oliver	.50
T6 Hector Ortiz	.50
T7 Chuck Knoblauch	.50
T8 Brian L. Hunter	.50
T9 Dustan Mohr	.50
T10 Eric Hinske	.50
T11 Roger Cedeno	.50
T12 Eddie Perez	.50
T13 Jeromy Burnitz	.50
T14 Bartolo Colon	.50
T15 Rick Helling	.50
T16 Dan Plesac	.50
T17 Scott Strickland	.50
T18 Antonio Alfonseca	.50
T19 Ricky Gutierrez	.50
T20 John Valentin	.50
T21 Raul Mondesi	.50
T22 Ben Davis	.50
T23 Nelson Figueroa	.50
T24 Earl Snyder	.50
T25 Robin Ventura	.50
T26 Jimmy Haynes	.50
T27 Kenny Kelly	.50
T28 Morgan Ensberg	.50
T29 Reggie Sanders	.50
T30 Shigetoshi Hasegawa	.50
T31 Allen Levrault	.50
T32 Russell Branyan	.50
T33 Jose Guillen	.50
T34 Jose Paniagua	.50
T35 Kent Mercker	.50
T36 Jesse Orosco	.50
T37 Gregg Zaun	.50
T38 Reggie Taylor	.50
T39 Andres Galarraga	.50
T40 Chris Truby	.50
T41 Bruce Chen	.50
T42 Darren Lewis	.50
T43 Ryan Kohlmeier	.50
T44 John McDonald	.50
T45 Omar Daal	.50
T46 Matt Clement	.50
T47 Glendon Rusch	.50
T48 Chan Ho Park	.50
T49 Benny Agbayani	.50
T50 Juan Gonzalez	1.50
T51 Carlos Baerga	.50
T52 Tim Raines	.50
T53 Kevin Appier	.50
T54 Marty Cordova	.50
T55 Jeff D'Amico	.50
T56 Dmitri Young	.50
T57 Roosevelt Brown	.50
T58 Dustin Hermanson	.50
T59 Jose Rijo	.50
T60 Todd Ritchie	.50
T61 Lee Stevens	.50
T62 Shane Heams	.50
T63 Eric Young	.50
T64 Chuck Finley	.50
T65 Dicky Gonzalez	.50
T66 Jose Macias	.50
T67 Gabe Kapler	.50
T68 Sandy Alomar Jr.	.50
T69 Henry Blanco	.50
T70 Julian Tavarez	.50
T71 Paul Bako	.50
T72 Dave Burba	.50
T73 Brian Jordan	.50
T74 Rickey Henderson	1.00
T75 Kevin Mench	.50
T76 Hideo Nomo	1.00
T77 Mark Sweeney	.50
T78 Brad Fullmer	.50
T79 Carl Everett	.50
T80 David Wells	.50

T81	Aaron Sele	.50
T82	Todd Hollandsworth	.50
T83	Vicente Padilla	.50
T84	Chris Latham	.50
T85	Corky Miller	.50
T86	Josh Fogg	.50
T87	Calvin Murray	.50
T88	Craig Paquette	.50
T89	Jay Payton	.50
T90	Carlos Pena	.50
T91	Juan Encarnacion	.50
T92	Rey Sanchez	.50
T93	Ryan Dempster	.50
T94	Mario Encarnacion	.50
T95	Jorge Julio	.50
T96	John Mabry	.50
T97	Todd Zeile	.50
T98	Johnny Damon	.50
T99	Deivi Cruz	.50
T100	Gary Sheffield	.50
T101	Ted Lilly	.50
T102	Todd Van Poppel	.50
T103	Shawn Estes	.50
T104	Cesar Izturis	.50
T105	Ron Coomer	.50
T106	Grady Little	.50
T107	Jimy Williams	.50
T108	Tony Pena	.50
T109	Frank Robinson	.50
T110	Ron Gardenhire	.50
T111	Dennis Tankersley	.15
T112	Alejandro Cadena RC	.25
T113	Justin Reid RC	.25
T114	Nate Field RC	.25
T115	Rene Reyes RC	.25
T116	Nelson Castro RC	.25
T117	Miguel Olivo	.15
T118	David Espinosa	.25
T119	Chris Bootcheck RC	.40
T120	Rob Henkel RC	.25
T121	Steve Bechler RC	.25
T122	Mark Outlaw RC	.25
T123	Henry Pichardo RC	.25
T124	Michael Floyd RC	.25
T125	Richard Lane RC	.25
T126	Peter Zamora RC	.25
T127	Javier Colina RC	.25
T128	Greg Sain RC	.25
T129	Ronnie Merrill RC	.25
T130	Gavin Floyd	1.50
T131	Josh Bonifay RC	.25
T132	Tommy Marx RC	.25
T133	Gary Cates Jr. RC	.25
T134	Neal Cotts	.25
T135	Angel Berroa	.25
T136	Elio Serrano RC	.25
T137	J.J. Putz RC	.25
T138	Ruben Gotay RC	.25
T139	Eddie Rogers RC	.25
T140	Wily Mo Pena	.25
T141	Tyler Yates RC	.25
T142	Colin Young RC	.25
T143	Chance Caple	.15
T144	Ben Howard RC	.25
T145	Ryan Bukvich RC	.25
T146	Clifford Bartosh RC	.25
T147	Brandon Claussen	.25
T148	Cristian Guerrero	.15
T149	Derrick Lewis	.15
T150	Eric Miller RC	.25
T151	Justin Huber RC	.75
T152	Adrian Gonzalez	.15
T153	Brian West RC	.25
T154	Chris Baker RC	.25
T155	Drew Henson	.75
T156	Scott Hairston	.75
T157	Jason Simontacchi RC	.75
T158	Jason Arnold	.40
T159	Brandon Phillips	.15
T160	Adam Roller RC	.25
T161	Scotty Layfield RC	.25
T162	Freddie Money RC	.25
T163	Noochie Varner RC	.50
T164	Terrance Hill RC	.25
T165	Jeremy Hill RC	.25
T166	Carlos Cabrera RC	.25
T167	Jose Morban RC	.25
T168	Kevin Frederick RC	.25
T169	Mark Teixeira	.75
T170	Brian Rogers RC	.15
T171	Anastacio Martinez RC	.25
T172	Bobby Jenks RC	.75
T173	David Gil RC	.25
T174	Andres Torres	.15
T175	James Barrett RC	.15
T176	Jimmy Journell RC	.15
T177	Brett Kay RC	.25
T178	Jason Young RC	.25
T179	Mark Hamilton RC	.25
T180	Jose Bautista RC	.50
T181	Blake McGinley RC	.25
T182	Ryan Mottl RC	.25
T183	Jeff Austin RC	.25
T184	Xavier Nady	.25
T185	Kyle Kane RC	.25
T186	Travis Foley	.15
T187	Nathan Kaup RC	.25
T188	Eric Cyr RC	.25
T189	Josh Cisneros RC	.25
T190	Brad Nelson RC	.25
T191	Clint Weibl RC	.25
T192	Ron Calloway RC	.15
T193	Jung Bong	.15
T194	Rolando Viera RC	.25
T195	Jason Bulger RC	.25
T196	Chone Figgins RC	.75
T197	Jimmy Alvarez RC	.25
T198	Joel Crump RC	.25

T199	Ryan Doumit RC	1.00
T200	Demetrius Heath RC	.25
T201	John Ennis RC	.25
T202	Doug Sessions RC	.25
T203	Clinton Hosford RC	.25
T204	Chris Narveson RC	.40
T205	Ross Peeples RC	.25
T206	Alexander Requena RC	.25
T207	Matt Erickson RC	.25
T208	Brian Forystek RC	.25
T209	Dewon Brazelton	.15
T210	Nathan Haynes	.15
T211	Jack Cust	.15
T212	Jesse Foppert	.75
T213	Jesus Cota RC	.25
T214	Juan Gonzalez	.15
T215	Tim Kalita RC	.25
T216	Manny Delcarmen RC	.50
T217	Jim Kavourias RC	.25
T218	C.J. Wilson RC	.25
T219	Edwin Yan RC	.25
T220	Andy Van Hekken	.15
T221	Michael Cuddyer	.25
T222	Jeff Verplancke RC	.25
T223	Mike Wilson RC	.25
T224	Corwin Malone	.15
T225	Chris Snelling RC	.50
T226	Joe Rogers RC	.25
T227	Jason Bay	.50
T228	Ezequiel Astacio RC	.25
T229	Joey Hammond RC	.25
T230	Chris Duffy RC	.25
T231	Mark Prior	.25
T232	Hansel Izquierdo RC	.25
T233	Franklyn German RC	.25
T234	Alexis Gomez	.15
T235	Jorge Padilla RC	.25
T236	Ryan Snare RC	.25
T237	Deivis Santos	.15
T238	Taggert Bozied RC	.25
T239	Mike Peeples RC	.25
T240	Ronald Acuna RC	.25
T241	Koyie Hill	.25
T242	Garrett Guzman RC	.25
T243	Ryan Church RC	1.00
T244	Tony Fontana RC	.25
T245	Keto Anderson RC	.25
T246	Brad Bouras RC	.25
T247	Jason Dubois RC	.50
T248	Angel Guzman RC	.25
T249	Joel Hanrahan RC	.25
T250	Joe Jiannetti RC	.25
T251	Sean Pierce RC	.25
T252	Jake Mauer RC	.25
T253	Marshall McDougall RC	.50
T254	Edwin Almonte RC	.25
T255	Shawn Riggans RC	.25
T256	Steven Shell	.15
T257	Kevin Hooper RC	.40
T258	Michael Frick RC	.25
T259	Travis Chapman RC	.40
T260	Tim Hummel RC	.25
T261	Adam Morrissey RC	.25
T262	Dontrelle Willis RC	1.00
T263	Justin Sherrod RC	.25
T264	Gerald Smiley RC	.25
T265	Tony Miller RC	.25
T266	Nolan Ryan	1.50
T267	Reggie Jackson	.75
T268	Steve Garvey	.15
T269	Wade Boggs	.25
T270	Sammy Sosa	1.00
T271	Curt Schilling	.25
T272	Mark Grace	.25
T273	Jason Giambi	.50
T274	Ken Griffey Jr.	.75
T275	Roberto Alomar	.40

Gold

MARK PRIOR

Gold Stars:	2-4X
Production 2,002 Sets	
Chrome Refractors:	3-5X
Inserted 1:12	

Farewell Relics

NM/M

Randomly inserted.

JC	Jose Canseco	10.00

Hall of Fame Relics

NM/M

Randomly inserted.

HOF-OS	Ozzie Smith	25.00

Signature Moves Autographs

NM/M

Common Autograph:		8.00
Inserted 1:91		

RA	Roberto Alomar	30.00
MA	Moises Alou	15.00
TBL	Tony Blanco	8.00
BB	Boof Bonser	8.00
AC	Antoine Cameron	10.00
BC	Brandon Claussen	15.00
MC	Matt Cooper	8.00
JD	Johnny Damon	30.00
JDA	Jeff DaVanon	8.00
VD	Victor Diaz	12.00
RH	Ryan Hannaman	8.00
KI	Kazuhisa Ishii	25.00
JP	Juan Pena	8.00
JS	Juan Silvestre	8.00
CS	Chris Smith	8.00
DT	Dennis Tankersley	8.00
MT	Marcus Thames	8.00
CU	Chase Utley	200.00
JW	Justin Wayne	8.00

Team Topps Legends Autographs

NM/M

Common Autograph:		10.00
Inserted 1:1,097		
	Johnny Bench	40.00
	Vida Blue	10.00
	Clete Boyer	12.00
	Whitey Ford	30.00
	Bob Gibson	25.00
	Joe Pepitone	10.00
	Bobby Richardson	10.00
	Bill "Moose" Skowron	10.00
	Enos Slaughter	18.00
	Carl Yastrzemski	60.00

Tools of the Trade Relics

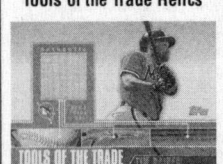

TOOLS OF THE TRADE

NM/M

Common Player:		5.00
Bat Relics 1:34		
Jersey Relics 1:426		
RAB	Roberto Alomar/Bat	8.00
MA	Moises Alou/Bat	5.00
DB	David Bell/Bat	5.00
JBU	Jeromy Burnitz/Bat	5.00
JC	Jose Canseco/Bat	10.00
VC	Vinny Castilla/Bat	5.00
JCI	Jeff Cirillo/Bat	5.00
TC	Tony Clark/Bat	5.00
JDB	Johnny Damon/Bat	5.00
CE	Carl Everett/Bat	5.00
BF	Brad Fullmer/Bat	5.00
AG	Andres Galarraga/Bat	6.00
JG	Juan Gonzalez/Jsy	6.00
RHB	Rickey Henderson/Bat	10.00
BJ	Brian Jordan/Bat	5.00
DJ	David Justice/Bat	5.00
CK	Chuck Knoblauch/Bat	5.00
MLB	Matt Lawton/Bat	5.00
KL	Kenny Lofton/Bat	5.00
TM	Tino Martinez/Bat	6.00
CP	Carlos Pena/Bat	6.00
JP	Josh Phelps/Jsy	6.00
TR	Tim Raines/Bat	5.00
RS	Reggie Sanders/Bat	5.00
GS	Gary Sheffield/Bat	5.00
TS	Tsuyoshi Shinjo/Bat	5.00
RSI	Ruben Sierra/Bat	5.00
MT	Michael Tucker/Bat	5.00
MV	Mo Vaughn/Jsy	6.00
MVB	Mo Vaughn/Bat	6.00
RV	Robin Ventura/Bat	6.00
RW	Rondell White/Bat	5.00
EY	Eric Young/Bat	5.00

Topps of the Trade Dual Relics

NM/M

Common Card:		6.00
Inserted 1:539		
MA	Moises Alou	10.00
HN	Hideo Nomo	35.00
CP	Chan Ho Park	8.00

2002 Topps Tribute

NM/M

Complete Set (90):		120.00
Common Player:		1.50
Pack (5):		35.00
Box (6):		150.00
1	Hank Aaron	6.00
2	Rogers Hornsby	2.50
3	Bobby Thomson	1.50
4	Eddie Collins	1.50
5	Joe Carter	1.50
6	Jim Palmer	1.50
7	Willie Mays	6.00
8	Willie Stargell	2.50
9	Vida Blue	1.50
10	Whitey Ford	3.00
11	Bob Gibson	3.00

NEW YORK

12	Nellie Fox	2.00
13	Napoleon Lajoie	2.00
14	Frankie Frisch	1.50
15	Nolan Ryan	10.00
16	Brooks Robinson	2.50
17	Kirby Puckett	5.00
18	Fergie Jenkins	1.50
19	Edd Roush	1.50
20	Honus Wagner	6.00
21	Richie Ashburn	1.50
22	Bob Feller	1.50
23	Joe Morgan	1.50
24	Orlando Cepeda	1.50
25	Steve Garvey	1.50
26	Hank Greenberg	1.50
27	Stan Musial	5.00
28	Sam Crawford	1.50
29	Jim Rice	1.50
30	Hack Wilson	2.50
31	Lou Brock	1.50
32	Mickey Vernon	1.50
33	Chuck Klein	1.50
34	Joe Jackson	6.00
35	Duke Snider	3.00
36	Ryne Sandberg	5.00
37	Johnny Bench	5.00
38	Sam Rice	1.50
39	Lou Gehrig	8.00
40	Robin Yount	3.00
41	Don Sutton	1.50
42	Jim Bottomley	1.50
43	Billy Herman	1.50
44	Zach Wheat	1.50
45	Juan Marichal	1.50
46	Bert Blyleven	1.50
47	Jackie Robinson	6.00
48	Gil Hodges	1.50
49	Mike Schmidt	6.00
50	Dale Murphy	1.50
51	Phil Rizzuto	1.50
52	Ty Cobb	6.00
53	Andre Dawson	1.50
54	Fred Lindstrom	1.50
55	Roy Campanella	3.00
56	Don Larsen	2.00
57	Harry Heilmann	1.50
58	Jim "Catfish" Hunter	1.50
59	Frank Robinson	2.00
60	Bill Mazeroski	1.50
61	Roger Maris	6.00
62	Dave Winfield	2.50
63	Warren Spahn	2.50
64	Babe Ruth	10.00
65	Ernie Banks	4.00
66	Wade Boggs	2.00
67	Carl Yastrzemski	3.00
68	Ron Santo	1.50
69	Dennis Martinez	1.50
70	Yogi Berra	4.00
71	Paul Waner	1.50
72	George Brett	6.00
73	Eddie Mathews	3.00
74	Bill Dickey	1.50
75	Carlton Fisk	2.00
76	Thurman Munson	5.00
77	Reggie Jackson	4.00
78	Phil Niekro	1.50
79	Luis Aparicio	1.50
80	Steve Carlton	1.50
81	Tris Speaker	1.50
82	Johnny Mize	1.50
83	Tom Seaver	4.00
84	Heinie Manush	1.50
85	Tommy John	1.50
86	Joe Cronin	1.50
87	Don Mattingly	8.00
88	Kirk Gibson	1.50
89	Bo Jackson	3.00
90	Mel Ott	1.50

First Impressions

HONUS WAGNER

3000

Cards #'d 51-86:		3-5X
Cards #'d 26-50:		4-8X
#'d to last two digits of Rk year		
Lasting Impressions		
Cards #'d 51-96:		3-5X
Cards #'d 26-50:		4-8X
#'d to last two digits of final season.		
Production under 25 not priced.		

Marks of Excellence

NM/M

Inserted 1:61

LB	Lou Brock	50.00
SC	Steve Carlton	50.00
DL	Don Larsen	50.00
SM	Stan Musial	100.00
MS	Mike Schmidt	85.00
WS	Warren Spahn	85.00

Marks of Excellence Relics

NM/M

Inserted 1:61

FJ	Fergie Jenkins	40.00
DM	Don Mattingly	120.00
JP	Jim Palmer	40.00
BR	Brooks Robinson	75.00
DS	Duke Snider	60.00
RY	Robin Yount	70.00

Matching Marks Dual

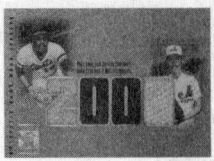

NM/M

Common Card:		10.00
Inserted 1:11		
SBA	Ron Santo, Ernie Banks	25.00
YK	Carl Yastrzemski, Chuck Klein	65.00
WY	Dave Winfield, Carl Yastrzemski	25.00
WYO	Dave Winfield, Robin Yount	20.00
SM	Duke Snider, Willie Mays	85.00
RJ	Frank Robinson, Reggie Jackson	50.00
GH	Steve Garvey, Gil Hodges	20.00
AR	Hank Aaron, Babe Ruth	300.00
GA	Hank Greenberg, Richie Ashburn	80.00
PJ	Jim Palmer, Tommy John	20.00
NS	Phil Niekro, Tom Seaver	15.00
SR	Willie Stargell, Jim Rice	15.00
BF	Johnny Bench, Carlton Fisk	50.00
RS	Nolan Ryan, Tom Seaver	125.00
JS	Fergie Jenkins, Tom Seaver	35.00
YP	Robin Yount, Kirby Puckett	60.00
SB	Tris Speaker, George Brett	100.00
BM	Vida Blue, Dennis Martinez	10.00
BB	Wade Boggs, George Brett	40.00
MA	Willie Mays, Hank Aaron	200.00
BS	Bert Blyleven, Don Sutton	15.00

Memorable Materials

75

NM/M

Common Player:		10.00
Season parallel:		1.5-3X
#'d to last two digits yr event occurred		
Jsy Number para.#'d 40-75:		1.5-3X
Under 40 not priced.		
Numbered to jersey #.		
HA	Hank Aaron	40.00
GB	George Brett	35.00
RC	Roy Campanella	30.00
JC	Joe Carter	10.00
CF	Carlton Fisk	20.00
KG	Kirk Gibson	15.00
BJ	Bo Jackson	25.00
RJ	Reggie Jackson	20.00
CK	Chuck Klein	20.00
RM	Roger Maris	75.00
DM	Don Mattingly	40.00
BM	Bill Mazeroski	15.00
JM	Joe Morgan	15.00
TM	Thurman Munson	50.00

KP	Kirby Puckett	30.00
PR	Phil Rizzuto	25.00
JR	Jackie Robinson	50.00
NR	Nolan Ryan	50.00
BT	Bobby Thomson	15.00
HW	Hack Wilson	40.00
CY	Carl Yastrzemski	30.00

Milestone Materials

M

NM/M

Common Player:		10.00
Inserted 1:4		
Season parallel #'d 51-95:		1.5-3X
#'d to last two digits milestone season.		
Jersey number par.#'d 51-95: 1.5-3X		
Numbered to jersey number.		
Under 50 not priced yet.		
LA	Luis Aparicio	15.00
EB	Ernie Banks	30.00
JB	Johnny Bench	20.00
YB	Yogi Berra	25.00
WB	Wade Boggs	15.00
JBO	Jim Bottomley	20.00
OC	Orlando Cepeda	15.00
TC	Ty Cobb	150.00
EC	Eddie Collins	30.00
SC	Sam Crawford	25.00
JC	Joe Cronin	20.00
AD	Andre Dawson	15.00
BD	Bill Dickey	15.00
BF	Bob Feller	15.00
WF	Whitey Ford	25.00
NF	Nellie Fox	30.00
FF	Frankie Frisch	25.00
LG	Lou Gehrig	150.00
BG	Bob Gibson	15.00
HH	Harry Heilmann	20.00
BH	Billy Herman	10.00
RH	Rogers Hornsby	50.00
CH	Jim "Catfish" Hunter	12.00
RJ	Reggie Jackson	20.00
NL	Napoleon Lajoie	60.00
FL	Fred Lindstrom	15.00
HM	Heinie Manush	20.00
JMA	Juan Marichal	15.00
EM	Eddie Mathews	20.00
WH	Willie Mays	45.00
JM	Johnny Mize	15.00
DM	Dale Murphy	20.00
MO	Mel Ott	40.00
JP	Jim Palmer	15.00
SR	Sam Rice	20.00
BRO	Brooks Robinson	20.00
FR	Frank Robinson	25.00
ER	Edd Roush	25.00
BR	Babe Ruth	160.00
NR	Nolan Ryan	50.00
RS	Ryne Sandberg	30.00
TS	Tom Seaver	15.00
DS	Duke Snider	20.00
TSP	Tris Speaker	65.00
WS	Willie Stargell	15.00
MV	Mickey Vernon	15.00
HW	Honus Wagner	140.00
PW	Paul Waner	30.00
ZW	Zach Wheat	40.00
RY	Robin Yount	25.00

Pasttime Patches

NM/M

Inserted 1:92

JB	Johnny Bench	125.00
WB	Wade Boggs	90.00
GB	George Brett	200.00
BD	Bill Dickey	100.00
EM	Eddie Mathews	125.00
DM	Don Mattingly	160.00
JP	Jim Palmer	75.00
KP	Kirby Puckett	125.00
NRA	Nolan Ryan	200.00
NRR	Nolan Ryan	200.00
DW	Dave Winfield	100.00
CY	Carl Yastrzemski	180.00
RY	Robin Yount	100.00

Signature Cuts

SIGNATURE CUTS

NM/M

Reported production two each.
Inserted 1:9936

SC-TC	Ty Cobb (4/04 Auction)	4,725

"The Catch" Dual

NM/M

Inserted 1:1,023

MW	Willie Mays, Vic Wertz	250.00
MW	Willie Mays, Vic Wertz/54	300.00

2002 Topps206

SCHMIDT, PHILADELPHIA

	NM/M
Complete Set (456):	150.00
Common Player:	.20
Common (141-155, 271-285):	1.00
Inserted 1:2	
Series I Pack (8):	6.00
Series I Box (20):	100.00
Series II Pack (8):	4.00
Series II Box (20):	60.00
Series III Pack (8):	6.00
Series III Box (20):	100.00

#	Player	Price
1	Vladimir Guerrero	.75
2	Sammy Sosa	1.50
3	Garret Anderson	.40
4	Rafael Palmeiro	.50
5	Juan Gonzalez	.50
6	John Smoltz	.40
7	Mark Mulder	.40
8	Jon Lieber	.20
9	Greg Maddux	1.00
10	Moises Alou	.40
11	Joe Randa	.20
12	Bobby Abreu	.40
13	Ryan Kohlmeier	.20
14	Kerry Wood	.75
15	Craig Biggio	.40
16	Curt Schilling	.50
17	Brian Jordan	.20
18	Edgardo Alfonzo	.20
19	Darren Dreifort	.20
20	Todd Helton	.50
21	Ramon Ortiz	.20
22	Ichiro Suzuki	1.50
23	Jimmy Rollins	.50
24	Darin Erstad	.40
25	Shawn Green	.40
26	Tino Martinez	.30
27	Bret Boone	.40
28	Alfonso Soriano	.75
29	Chan Ho Park	.40
30	Roger Clemens	1.50
31	Cliff Floyd	.20
32	Johnny Damon	.40
33	Frank Thomas	.50
34	Barry Bonds	2.00
35	Luis Gonzalez	.40
36	Carlos Lee	.20
37	Roberto Alomar	.50
38	Carlos Delgado	.50
39	Nomar Garciaparra	1.50
40	Jason Kendall	.20
41	Scott Rolen	.75
42	Tom Glavine	.40
43	Ryan Klesko	.20
44	Brian Giles	.40
45	Bud Smith	.20
46	Charles Nagy	.20
47	Tony Gwynn	.75
48	C.C. Sabathia	.20
49	Manny Ramirez	.75
50	Jerry Hairston Jr.	.20
51	Jeromy Burnitz	.20
52	David Justice	.40
53	Bartolo Colon	.20
54	Andres Galarraga	.30
55	Jeff Weaver	.20
56	Terrance Long	.20
57	Tsuyoshi Shinjo	.20
58	Barry Zito	.40
59	Mariano Rivera	.40
60	John Olerud	.20
61	Randy Johnson	.75
62	Kenny Lofton	.40
63	Jermaine Dye	.20
64	Troy Glaus	.50
65	Larry Walker	.40
66	Hideo Nomo	.50
67	Mike Mussina	.50
68	Paul LoDuca	.20
69	Magglio Ordonez	.40
70	Paul O'Neill	.40
71	Sean Casey	.20
72	Lance Berkman	.40
73	Adam Dunn	.40
74	Aramis Ramirez	.20
75	Rafael Furcal	.40
76	Gary Sheffield	.40
77	Todd Hollandsworth	.20
78	Chipper Jones	1.00
79	Bernie Williams	.50
80	Richard Hidalgo	.25
81	Eric Chavez	.40
82	Mike Piazza	1.50
83	J.D. Drew	.40
84	Ken Griffey Jr.	1.00
85	Joe Kennedy	.20
86	Joel Pineiro	.20
87	Josh Towers	.20
88	Andruw Jones	.50
89	Carlos Beltran	.40
90	Mike Cameron	.40
91	Albert Pujols	1.50
92	Alex Rodriguez	1.50
93	Omar Vizquel	.30
94	Juan Encarnacion	.20
95	Jeff Bagwell	.50
96	Jose Canseco	.40
97	Ben Sheets	.40
98	Mark Grace	.40
99	Mike Sweeney	.20
100	Mark McGwire	2.00
101	Ivan Rodriguez	.75
102	Rich Aurilia	.20
103	Cristian Guzman	.20
104	Roy Oswalt	.40
105	Tim Hudson	.40
106	Brent Abernathy	.20
107	Mike Hampton	.20
108	Miguel Tejada	.40
109	Bobby Higginson	.20
110	Edgar Martinez	.40
111	Jorge Posada	.40
112	Jason Giambi	.50
113	Pedro Astacio	.20
114	Kazuhiro Sasaki	.20
115	Preston Wilson	.20
116	Jason Bere	.20
117	Mark Quinn	.20
118	Pokey Reese	.20
119	Derek Jeter	2.00
120	Shannon Stewart	.20
121	Jeff Kent	.40
122	Jeremy Giambi	.20
123	Pat Burrell	.40
124	Jim Edmonds	.40
125	Mark Buehrle	.40
126	Kevin Brown	.40
127	Raul Mondesi	.40
128	Pedro Martinez	.75
129	Jim Thome	.75
130	Russ Ortiz	.20
131	Brandon Duckworth	.20
132	Ryan Jamison RC	.50
133	Brandon Inge	.20
134	Felipe Lopez	.20
135	Jason Lane	.20
136	Forrest Johnson RC	.50
137	Greg Nash	.20
138	Covelli Crisp	.20
139	Nick Neugebauer	.20
140	Dustan Mohr	.20
141	Freddy Sanchez RC	1.00
142	Justin Backsmeyer RC	1.00
143	Jorge Julio	1.00
144	Ryan Mottl RC	1.00
145	Chris Tritle RC	1.00
146	Noochie Varner RC	1.00
147	Brian Rogers	1.00
148	Michael Hill RC	1.00
149	Luis Pineda	1.00
150	Rich Thompson RC	1.00
151	Bill Hall	1.00
152	Jose Dominguez RC	1.50
153	Justin Woodrow RC	1.00
154	Nic Jackson RC	1.00
155	Laynce Nix RC	2.00
156	Hank Aaron	3.00
157	Ernie Banks	1.50
158	Johnny Bench	1.50
159	George Brett	4.00
160	Carlton Fisk	.50
161	Bob Gibson	.75
162	Reggie Jackson	1.00
163	Don Mattingly	4.00
164	Kirby Puckett	1.50
165	Frank Robinson	1.50
166	Nolan Ryan	5.00
167	Tom Seaver	1.00
168	Mike Schmidt	2.00
169	Dave Winfield	.50
170	Carl Yastrzemski	1.00
171	Frank Chance	.75
172	Ty Cobb	3.00
173	Sam Crawford	1.00
174	Johnny Evers	.75
175	John McGraw	1.00
176	Eddie Plank	.50
177	Tris Speaker	1.00
178	Joe Tinker	.50
179	Honus Wagner	5.00
180	Cy Young	2.50
181	Javier Vazquez	.20
182	Mark Mulder	.40
183	Roger Clemens	1.50
184	Kazuhisa Ishii RC	.75
185	Roberto Alomar	.50
186	Lance Berkman	.40
187	Adam Dunn	.50
188	Aramis Ramirez	.40
189	Chuck Knoblauch	.20
190	Nomar Garciaparra	1.50
191	Brad Penny	.20
192	Gary Sheffield	.40
193	Alfonso Soriano	.75
194	Andruw Jones	.50
195	Randy Johnson	.75
196	Corey Patterson	.40
197	Milton Bradley	.20
198	Johnny Damon	.40
199	Paul LoDuca	.20
200	Albert Pujols	1.50
201	Scott Rolen	.75
202	J.D. Drew	.40
203	Vladimir Guerrero	.75
204	Jason Giambi	.50
205	Moises Alou	.40
206	Magglio Ordonez	.40
207	Carlos Febles	.20
208	So Taguchi RC	.75
209	Rafael Palmeiro	.50
210	David Wells	.50
211	Orlando Cabrera	.20
212	Sammy Sosa	1.50
213	Armando Benitez	.20
214	Wes Helms	.20
215	Mariano Rivera	.40
216	Jimmy Rollins	.50
217	Matt Lawton	.20
218	Shawn Green	.40
219	Bernie Williams	.50
220	Bret Boone	.40
221	Alex Rodriguez	2.00
222	Roger Cedeno	.20
223	Marty Cordova	.20
224	Fred McGriff	.40
225	Chipper Jones	.75
226	Kerry Wood	.75
227	Larry Walker	.40
228	Robin Ventura	.40
229	Robert Fick	.20
230	Tino Martinez	.40
231	Ben Petrick	.20
232	Neifi Perez	.20
233	Pedro Martinez	.75
234	Brian Jordan	.20
235	Freddy Garcia	.20
236	Derek Jeter	2.00
237	Ben Grieve	.20
238	Barry Bonds	2.00
239	Luis Gonzalez	.40
240	Shane Halter	.20
241	Brian Giles	.40
242	Bud Smith	.20
243	Richie Sexson	.40
244	Barry Zito	.40
245	Eric Milton	.20
246	Ivan Rodriguez	.50
247	Toby Hall	.20
248	Mike Piazza	1.50
249	Ruben Sierra	.20
250	Tsuyoshi Shinjo	.20
251	Jermaine Dye	.20
252	Roy Oswalt	.40
253	Todd Helton	.50
254	Adrian Beltre	.40
255	Doug Mientkiewicz	.20
256	Ichiro Suzuki	1.50
257	C.C. Sabathia	.20
258	Paul Konerko	.20
259	Ken Griffey Jr.	1.00
260	Jeromy Burnitz	.20
261	Hank Blalock	.50
262	Mark Prior	1.50
263	Josh Beckett	.50
264	Carlos Pena	.20
265	Sean Burroughs	.20
266	Austin Kearns	.40
267	Chin-Hui Tsao	.20
268	Dewon Brazelton	.20
269	J.D. Martin	.20
270	Marlon Byrd	.20
271	Joe Mauer RC	10.00
272	Jason Botts RC	1.00
273	Mauricio Lara RC	1.00
274	Jonny Gomes RC	2.00
275	Gavin Floyd	1.50
276	Alexander Requena RC	1.00
277	Jimmy Gobble RC	1.00
278	Chris Duffy RC	1.00
279	Colt Griffin	1.00
280	Ryan Church RC	1.50
281	Beltran Perez	1.00
282	Clint Nageotte RC	1.50
283	Justin Schuda RC	1.00
284	Scott Hairston	1.50
285	Mario Ramos	1.00
286	Tom Seaver	2.00
287	Hank Aaron	3.00
288	Mike Schmidt	3.00
289	Robin Yount	1.50
290	Joe Morgan	1.00
291	Frank Robinson	1.00
292	Reggie Jackson	2.00
293	Nolan Ryan	4.00
294	Dave Winfield	1.00
295	Willie Mays	3.00
296	Brooks Robinson	1.50
297	Mark McGwire	3.00
298	Honus Wagner	3.00
299	Sherry Magee	1.00
300	Frank Chance	1.00
301	Larry Doyle	1.00
302	John McGraw	2.00
303	Jimmy Collins	1.00
304	Buck Herzog	.50
305	Sam Crawford	1.00
306	Cy Young	2.50
307	Honus Wagner	3.00
308	Alex Rodriguez	1.50
308	Alex Rodriguez/ SP Blue Jsy	4.00
309	Vernon Wells	.20
310	Barry Bonds	2.00
310	Barry Bonds/ SP Cream Jsy	6.00
311	Vicente Padilla	.20
312	Alfonso Soriano	.75
312	A.Soriano/ SP No Wristband	1.50
313	Mike Piazza	1.50
314	Jacque Jones	.20
315	Shawn Green/SP	1.50
316	Paul Byrd	.20
317	Lance Berkman	.40
318	Larry Walker	.40
319	Ken Griffey Jr./SP	3.00
320	Shea Hillenbrand	.20
321	Jay Gibbons	.20
322	Andruw Jones	.50
323	Luis Gonzalez/SP	1.50
324	Garret Anderson	.40
325	Roy Halladay	.40
326	Randy Winn	.20
327	Matt Morris	.40
328	Robb Nen	.20
329	Trevor Hoffman	.20
330	Kip Wells	.20
331	Orlando Hernandez	.30
332	Rey Ordonez	.20
333	Torii Hunter	.40
334	Geoff Jenkins	.40
335	Eric Karros	.40
336	Mike Lowell	.40
337	Nick Johnson	.20
338	Randall Simon	.20
339	Ellis Burks	.20
340	Sammy Sosa	1.50
340	Sammy Sosa/ SP Blue Jsy	4.00
341	Pedro J. Martinez	.75
342	Junior Spivey	.20
343	Vinny Castilla	.20
344	Randy Johnson/SP	2.00
345	Chipper Jones/SP	1.50
346	Orlando Hudson	.20
347	Albert Pujols/SP	5.00
348	Rondell White	.20
349	Vladimir Guerrero	.75
350	Mark Prior	1.00
350	Mark Prior/ SP Red Background	3.00
351	Eric Gagne	.50
352	Todd Zeile	.20
353	Manny Ramirez/SP	2.00
354	Kevin Millwood	.40
355	Troy Percival	.20
356	Jason Giambi	.50
356	Jason Giambi/ SP White Jsy	1.50
357	Bartolo Colon	.20
358	Jeremy Giambi	.20
359	Jose Cruz Jr.	.20
360	Ichiro Suzuki	1.50
360	Ichiro/SP Blue Warm-Up	3.00
361	Eddie Guardado	.20
362	Ivan Rodriguez	.50
363	Carl Crawford	.20
364	Jason Simontacchi RC	.50
365	Kenny Lofton	.40
366	Raul Mondesi	.20
367	A.J. Pierzynski	.20
368	Ugueth Urbina	.20
369	Rodrigo Lopez	.20
370	Nomar Garciaparra	1.50
370	N. Garciaparra/SP 1 Bat	3.00
371	Craig Counsell	.20
372	Barry Larkin	.40
373	Carlos Pena	.20
374	Luis Castillo	.20
375	Raul Ibanez	.20
376	Kazuhisa Ishii/SP	1.50

Series 2

#	Player	Price
377	Derek Lowe	.20
378	Curt Schilling	.50
379	Jim Thome	.75
380	Derek Jeter	2.00
380	D. Jeter/SP Blue background	5.00

Series 3

#	Player	Price
381	Pat Burrell	.50
382	Jamie Moyer	.20
383	Eric Hinske	.20
384	Scott Rolen	.75
385	Miguel Tejada/SP	1.50
386	Andy Pettitte	.40
387	Mike Lieberthal	.20
388	Al Leiter	.40
389	Todd Helton/SP	2.00
390	Adam Dunn	.50
390	Adam Dunn/SP with bat	2.00
391	Cliff Floyd	.20
392	Tim Salmon	.40
393	Joe Torre	.50
394	Bobby Cox	.20
395	Tony LaRussa	.20
396	Art Howe	.20
397	Bob Brenly	.20
398	Ron Gardenhire	.20
399	Mike Cuddyer	.20
400	Joe Mauer	2.50
401	Mark Teixeira	.50
402	Hee Seop Choi	.20
403	Angel Berroa	.20
404	Jesse Foppert	.20
405	Bobby Crosby	.50
406	Jose Reyes	.50
407	Casey Kotchman	.25
408	Aaron Heilman	.20
409	Adrian Gonzalez	.20
410	Delwyn Young RC	.75
411	Brett Myers	.20
412	Justin Huber RC	.50
413	Drew Henson	.20
414	Taggert Bozied RC	.50
415	Dontrelle Willis RC	2.00
416	Rocco Baldelli	.50
417	Jason Stokes RC	2.50
418	Brandon Phillips	.20
419	Jake Blalock/SP RC	1.00
420	Micah Schilling/SP RC	.20
421	Denard Span/SP RC	2.00
422	James Loney/SP RC	4.00
423	Wes Bankston/SP RC	1.50
424	Jeremy Hermida/SP RC	2.00
425	Curtis Granderson/SP RC	8.00
426	Jason Pridie/SP RC	1.00
427	Larry Broadway/SP RC	1.00
428	Khalil Greene/SP RC	1.00
429	Joey Votto/SP RC	20.00
430	B.J. Upton/SP RC	3.00
431	Sergio Santos/SP RC	2.00
432	Brian Dopirak/SP RC	2.00
433	Ozzie Smith/SP	2.00
434	Wade Boggs/SP	1.00
435	Yogi Berra/SP	3.00
436	Al Kaline/SP	2.00
437	Robin Roberts/SP	1.00
438	Roberto Clemente/SP	8.00
439	Gary Carter/SP	1.00
440	Fergie Jenkins/SP	1.00
441	Orlando Cepeda/SP	1.00
442	Rod Carew/SP	1.50
443	Harmon Killebrew/SP	2.50
444	Duke Snider/SP	2.00
445	Stan Musial/SP	5.00
446	Hank Greenberg/SP	1.00
447	Lou Brock/SP	1.00
448	Jim Palmer/SP	.50
449	John McGraw	.75
450	Mordecai Brown	.50
451	Christy Mathewson	1.00
452	Sam Crawford	.50
453	Bill O'Hara	.50
454	Joe Tinker	.50
455	Napoleon Lajoie	.75
456	Honus Wagner	3.00

T206 Mini Parallel

MONDESI, TORONTO

Polar Bear:	2-3X
Tolstoi Black:	2-5X
Average 4:Box	
Tolstoi Red:	4-8X
Average 2:Box	
Cycle:	6-12X
Average 1:Box	
Series 2	
Polar Bear:	2-3X
Piedmont Black:	3-5X
Piedmont Red:	4-8X
Carolina Brights:	6-12X
Series 3	
Polar Bear:	2-3X
Sweet Caporal Red:	3-5X
Sweet Caporal Blue or Black:	4-6X
Uzit:	6-12X
Bazooka Backs:	No Pricing
Production 30	
Drum Backs:	No Pricing
Production 20	
Lenox Variations:	No Pricing
Production 10	
American Beauty Variation:	No Pricing
Production 5	

Autographs

	NM/M
Common Player:	8.00
Inserted 1:41	
BB	Barry Bonds 200.00
RC	Roger Clemens 120.00
JE	Jim Edmonds 30.00
BG	Brian Giles 10.00
CG	Cristian Guzman 10.00
BI	Brandon Inge 10.00
RJ	Ryan Jamison 8.00
FJ	Forrest Johnson 8.00
JJ	Jorge Julio 10.00
FL	Felipe Lopez 10.00
GN	Greg Nash 8.00
MO	Magglio Ordonez 20.00
AR	Alex Rodriguez 100.00
JR	Jimmy Rollins 25.00
BZ	Barry Zito 15.00

Autographs Series 2

	NM/M
Common Player:	8.00
Inserted 1:55	
MA	Moises Alou 30.00
LB	Lance Berkman 35.00
HB	Hank Blalock 20.00
DB	Dewon Brazelton 8.00
MB	Marlon Byrd 10.00
EC	Eric Chavez 15.00
JD	Johnny Damon 25.00
GF	Gavin Floyd 20.00
LG	Luis Gonzalez 15.00
KI	Kazuhisa Ishii 15.00
JDM	J.D. Martin 8.00
JM	Joe Mauer 75.00
MP	Mark Prior 20.00
AP	Albert Pujols 150.00
SR	Scott Rolen 20.00
RS	Richie Sexson 15.00
BS	Ben Sheets 20.00
BSM	Bud Smith 10.00
ST	So Taguchi 20.00
CT	Chris Tritle 10.00

Autographs Series 3

	NM/M
Common Autograph:	8.00
MB	Milton Bradley 10.00
JC	Jose Cruz Jr. 15.00
DE	David Eckstein 8.00
DH	Drew Henson 15.00
ML	Mike Lamb 8.00
MT	Marcus Thames 8.00
JV	Jose Vidro 10.00

Relics

	NM/M
Common Player:	5.00
Overall Relics 1:11	
RA	Roberto Alomar/Jsy 10.00
JB	Jeff Bagwell/Jsy 10.00
CB	Craig Biggio/Jsy 8.00
BB	Barry Bonds/Jsy 25.00
BBO	Bret Boone/Jsy 8.00
MC	Mike Cameron/Jsy 5.00
JC	Jose Canseco/Bat 10.00
CD	Carlos Delgado/Jsy 8.00
JED	Jim Edmonds/Jsy 10.00
CF	Cliff Floyd/Jsy 5.00
JGI	Jason Giambi/Jsy 8.00
JG	Jeremy Giambi/Jsy 5.00
TG	Tom Glavine/Jsy 8.00
SG	Shawn Green/Jsy 8.00
TGW	Tony Gwynn/Jsy 15.00
TH	Todd Helton/Jsy 10.00
RJ	Randy Johnson/Jsy 15.00
AJ	Andruw Jones/Jsy 8.00
CJ	Chipper Jones/Jsy 10.00
CL	Carlos Lee/Jsy 5.00
KL	Kenny Lofton/Jsy 5.00
GM	Greg Maddux/Jsy 15.00
EM	Edgar Martinez/Jsy 10.00
TM	Tino Martinez/Jsy 5.00
JO	John Olerud/Jsy 5.00
PO	Paul O'Neill/Jsy 8.00
MO	Magglio Ordonez/Jsy 6.00
CP	Chan Ho Park/Bat 5.00
MP	Mike Piazza/Jsy 15.00
AP	Albert Pujols/Bat 25.00
IR	Ivan Rodriguez/Jsy 10.00
AS	Alfonso Soriano/Bat 8.00
SS	Shannon Stewart/Bat 8.00
FT	Frank Thomas/Jsy 10.00
JT	Jim Thome/Jsy 20.00
LW	Larry Walker/Jsy 5.00
JW	Jeff Weaver/Jsy 5.00
BW	Bernie Williams/Jsy 8.00
BZ	Barry Zito/Jsy 8.00

Relics Series 2

	NM/M
Common Player:	5.00
Jerseys 1:18	
Bats 1:40	
RA	Roberto Alomar/Bat 10.00
JB	Jeff Bagwell/Jsy 8.00
BB	Barry Bonds/Jsy 20.00

BBO	Bret Boone/Jsy	6.00
KB	Kevin Brown/Jsy	6.00
AB	A.J. Burnett/Jsy	5.00
SB	Sean Burroughs/Bat	8.00
EC	Eric Chavez/Bat	8.00
TC	Ty Cobb/Bat	420.00
JC	Jimmy Collins/Bat	45.00
SCR	Sam Crawford/Bat	50.00
JD	Johnny Damon/Bat	12.00
RD	Ryan Dempster/Jsy	5.00
BD	Brandon Duckworth/Jsy	5.00
AD	Adam Dunn/Bat	10.00
DE	Darin Erstad/Jsy	5.00
JEV	Johnny Evers/Bat	50.00
CF	Cliff Floyd/Jsy	5.00
TGL	Tom Glavine/Jsy	8.00
JG	Juan Gonzalez/Bat	5.00
MG	Mark Grace/Bat	10.00
SG	Shawn Green/Jsy	6.00
CG	Cristian Guzman/Jsy	5.00
TG	Tony Gwynn/Jsy	15.00
TH	Toby Hall/Jsy	5.00
JH	Josh Hamilton/Jsy	10.00
THE	Todd Helton/Jsy	5.00
RH	Rickey Henderson/Bat	15.00
BH	Buck Herzog/Bat	30.00
JJ	Jason Jennings/Jsy	5.00
RJ	Randy Johnson/Jsy	10.00
AJ	Andruw Jones/Jsy	5.00
CJO	Chipper Jones/Jsy	10.00
JK	Jeff Kent/Jsy	5.00
BL	Barry Larkin/Jsy	5.00
TL	Travis Lee/Bat	5.00
GM	Greg Maddux/Jsy	12.00
EM	Edgar Martinez/Bat	5.00
TM	Tino Martinez/Bat	10.00
JM	Joe Mays/Jsy	5.00
JMC	John McGraw/Bat	60.00
FM	Fred McGriff/Bat	8.00
JO	John Olerud/Jsy	5.00
RP	Rafael Palmeiro/Jsy	5.00
BP	Brad Penny/Jsy	5.00
MP	Mike Piazza/Jsy	15.00
AP	Albert Pujols/Jsy	15.00
ARA	Aramis Ramirez/Bat	5.00
AR	Alex Rodriguez/Bat	20.00
IR	Ivan Rodriguez/Bat	5.00
CS	Curt Schilling/Bat	15.00
GS	Gary Sheffield/Bat	8.00
TS	Tsuyoshi Shinjo/Bat	5.00
AS	Alfonso Soriano/Bat	8.00
MT	Miguel Tejada/Bat	8.00
FT	Frank Thomas/Jsy	15.00
JTH	Jim Thome/Bat	15.00
JT	Joe Tinker/Bat	40.00
MV	Mo Vaughn/Bat	8.00
RV	Robin Ventura/Bat	5.00
HWA	Honus Wagner/Bat	400.00
LW	Larry Walker/Jsy	5.00
BW	Bernie Williams/Jsy	5.00
MW	Matt Williams/Jsy	5.00
PW	Preston Wilson/Jsy	5.00

Relics Series 3
NM/M

	Common Player:	5.00
RA	Roberto Alomar/Bat	8.00
JB	Jeff Bagwell/Bat	8.00
WB	Wilson Betemit/Bat	5.00
PB	Pat Burrell/Bat	10.00
EC	Eric Chavez/Jsy	8.00
AD	Adam Dunn/Bat	10.00
JE	Jim Edmonds/Jsy	8.00
NG	Nomar Garciaparra/Bat	20.00
LG	Luis Gonzalez/Jsy	5.00
TG	Tony Gwynn/Jsy	10.00
TH	Todd Helton/Jsy	8.00
RH	Rickey Henderson/Bat	15.00
NJ	Nick Johnson/Bat	5.00
RJ	Randy Johnson/Jsy	10.00
AJ	Andruw Jones/Jsy	5.00
CJ	Chipper Jones/Jsy	10.00
PM	Pedro Martinez/Jsy	12.00
DM	Doug Mientkiewicz/Jsy	6.00
RP	Rafael Palmeiro/Jsy	8.00
CP	Corey Patterson/Bat	5.00
MP	Mike Piazza/Jsy	15.00
AP	Albert Pujols/Bat	20.00
AR	Alex Rodriguez/Bat	15.00
IR	Ivan Rodriguez/Bat	8.00
SR	Scott Rolen/Bat	10.00
CS	Curt Schilling/Bat	8.00
GS	Gary Sheffield/Bat	8.00
TS	Tsuyoshi Shinjo/Bat	5.00
AS	Alfonso Soriano/Bat	10.00
MTE	Miguel Tejada/Jsy	8.00
FT	Frank Thomas/Jsy	15.00
JT	Jim Thome/Jsy	10.00
MV	Mo Vaughn/Jsy	5.00
BW	Bernie Williams/Jsy	5.00
BZ	Barry Zito/Jsy	6.00

Reprint Relics
NM/M

	Common Player:	75.00
SC	Sam Crawford	90.00
JE	Johnny Evers	90.00
JM	John McGraw	75.00
TS	Tris Speaker	140.00
HW	Honus Wagner	400.00

Team Topps Legends Autographs
NM/M
Inserted 1:7,093

Nolan Ryan	400.00

Team Topps Legends Autographs Series 2
NM/M
Inserted 1:260

Ralph Branca	25.00
Andy Pafko	20.00
Joe Pepitone	10.00
Tom Seaver	60.00
Warren Spahn	25.00
Luis Tiant	10.00

Team 206
NM/M

	Complete Set (20):	10.00
	Common Player:	.25
	Inserted 1:Pack	
1	Barry Bonds	2.00
2	Ivan Rodriguez	.50
3	Luis Gonzalez	.25
4	Jason Giambi	.50
5	Pedro Martinez	.75
6	Larry Walker	.25
7	Bobby Abreu	.40
8	Derek Jeter	2.00
9	Bret Boone	.40
10	Mike Piazza	1.00
11	Alex Rodriguez	1.50
12	Roger Clemens	1.50
13	Albert Pujols	1.50
14	Randy Johnson	.75
15	Sammy Sosa	1.50
16	Cristian Guzman	.25
17	Shawn Green	.40
18	Curt Schilling	.50
19	Ichiro Suzuki	1.00
20	Chipper Jones	.75

Team 206 Series 2
NM/M

	Complete Set (25):	10.00
	Common Player:	.25
	Inserted 1:1	
1	Alex Rodriguez	1.50
2	Sammy Sosa	1.50
3	Jason Giambi	.50
4	Nomar Garciaparra	1.25
5	Ichiro Suzuki	1.00
6	Chipper Jones	.75
7	Derek Jeter	2.00
8	Barry Bonds	2.00
9	Mike Piazza	1.50
10	Randy Johnson	.75
11	Shawn Green	.25
12	Todd Helton	.50
13	Luis Gonzalez	.25
14	Albert Pujols	1.50
15	Curt Schilling	.50
16	Scott Rolen	.75
17	Ivan Rodriguez	.50
18	Roberto Alomar	.50
19	Cristian Guzman	.25
20	Bret Boone	.25
21	Barry Zito	.40
22	Larry Walker	.25
23	Eric Chavez	.25
24	Roger Clemens	1.50
25	Pedro Martinez	.75

Team 206 Series 3
NM/M

	Complete Set (30):	10.00
	Common Player:	.25
	Inserted 1:1	
1	Ichiro Suzuki	1.00
2	Kazuhisa Ishii	.25
3	Alex Rodriguez	1.50
4	Mark Prior	1.00
5	Derek Jeter	2.00
6	Sammy Sosa	1.50
7	Nomar Garciaparra	1.00
8	Mike Piazza	1.00
9	Jason Giambi	.50
10	Vladimir Guerrero	.75
11	Curt Schilling	.50
12	Jim Thome	.75
13	Adam Dunn	.50
14	Albert Pujols	1.50
15	Pat Burrell	.50
16	Chipper Jones	.75
17	Randy Johnson	.75
18	Todd Helton	.50
19	Luis Gonzalez	.25
20	Alfonso Soriano	.75
21	Shawn Green	.40
22	Pedro J. Martinez	.75
23	Lance Berkman	.40
24	Ivan Rodriguez	.50
25	Larry Walker	.25
26	Andruw Jones	.25
27	Ken Griffey Jr.	1.00
28	Eric Hinske	.25
29	Mike Sweeney	.25
30	Miguel Tejada	.50

2002 Topps 1982 California Angels Reprints

Commemorating the 20th anniversary of the A.L. West Championship Angels, Fox Sport Net issued this reprint set of the team's stars. Fronts are identical to the originals. Backs also closely reproduce the 1982 versions, but have a shaded box at the right end with a card number and updated copy-

right information. Fifteen thousand sets, cello-wrapped with a sponsor's header card, were given to fans attending an Anaheim game.

NM/M

	Complete Set (10):	10.00
	Common Player:	.50
1	Don Baylor	1.00
2	Rod Carew	2.00
3	Doug DeCinces	.50
4	Brian Downing	.50
5	Reggie Jackson	5.00
6	Fred Lynn	1.00
7	Geoff Zahn	.50
8	Bob Boone	1.00
9	Bob Grich	.75
--	Header Card	.05

2002 Topps Chicago Cubs Reprints

For a second year the Cubs contracted with Topps to provide a series of reprint cards for use as give-aways at special games throughout the season. Each reprint features a Wrigley Field logo on front and is sequentially numbered to 20,000 in a strip of gold foil on back. Each card was distributed in a cello wrapper with the date of the promotion and names of the sponsor(s).

NM/M

	Complete Set (11):	35.00
	Common Player:	2.50
1954	Ernie Banks	12.50
1961	Don Cardwell	2.50
1961	Billy Williams	5.00
1962	Ken Hubbs	3.50
1969	Ken Holtzman	2.50
1972	Milt Pappas	2.50
1979	Dave Kingman	3.00
1980	Bill Buckner	3.00
1984	Lee Smith	3.00
1998	Kerry Wood	4.00
2002	Sammy Sosa	5.00

2002 Topps Milwaukee Brewers Reprints

Topps cards of former Brewers favorites were reprinted and distributed one per month at selected home games. The cards are nearly identical to the originals ex-

cept for a sponsor's (St. Michael Hospital) logo on front and a reprint notice on back.

NM/M

	Complete Set (6):	25.00
	Common Player:	4.00
(1)	Don Money/1978	4.00
(2)	Cecil Cooper/1979	4.00
(3)	Ben Oglivie/1980	4.00
(4)	Gorman Thomas/1981	4.00
(5)	Robin Yount/1982	7.50
(6)	Paul Molitor/1992	7.50

2002 Topps/Post Collector's Series

For a second consecutive year in 2002, Post cereals packaged a special edition of Topps cards. The baseball cards were issued two per cello pack. The 2-1/2" x 3-1/2" cards have game-action photos with the background printed in a matte finish. The player portion of the photo and the surrounding team-color coded graphics at the sides and bottom have spot gloss. At bottom-right are the player's position and name. A team logo in the lower-left corner and the Topps logo is at upper-left. Backs have a portrait photo, biographical data, 2001 monthly stats and various league and sponsor logos. An album to house the collection was available by mail for $8.95 and two proofs of purchase.

NM/M

	Complete Set (30):	10.00
	Common Player:	.25
	Album:	9.00
1	Alex Rodriguez	1.50
2	Pedro Martinez	.50
3	Bernie Williams	.35
4	Mike Piazza	1.00
5	Jim Edmonds	.25
6	Rich Aurilia	.25
7	Sammy Sosa	1.25
8	Sean Casey	.25
9	Ichiro	2.00
10	Jason Giambi	.40
11	Todd Helton	.50
12	Chipper Jones	1.00
13	Frank Thomas	.65
14	Scott Rolen	.35
15	Carlos Delgado	.35
16	Jeff Bagwell	.65
17	Jim Thome	.25
18	Shawn Green	.35
19	Luis Gonzales	.50
20	Vladimir Guerrero	.65
21	Troy Glaus	.50
22	Ryan Klesko	.25
23	Jeromy Burnitz	.25
24	Bobby Higginson	.25
25	Jason Kendall	.25
26	Cliff Floyd	.25
27	Greg Vaughn	.25
28	Brad Radke	.25
29	Mike Sweeney	.25
30	Jeff Conine	.25

2003 Topps

NM/M

Complete Set (720):	70.00

Sealed Factory Set (725):		70.00
Complete Series 1 Set (366):		35.00
Complete Series 2 Set (355):		35.00
Common Player:		.10
Series 1 & 2 Pack (10):		1.50
Series 1 & 2 Box (36):		35.00
Series 2 Jumbo Box:		45.00
White Topps "throw-back" logo.		
Series 1 (1:8852): Value Undetermined		
Series 2 (1:4487): Value Undetermined		
1a	Alex Rodriguez (Red Topps)	1.00
2	Dan Wilson	.10
3	Jimmy Rollins	.25
4	Jermaine Dye	.10
5	Steve Karsay	.10
6	Timoniel Perez	.10
7	Jose Vidro	.10
8	Eddie Guardado	.10
10a	Mark Prior (Red Topps)	.50
11a	Curt Schilling (Red Topps)	.40
12	Dennis Cook	.10
13	Andruw Jones	.40
14	David Segui	.10
15	Trot Nixon	.10
16	Antonio Alfonseca	.10
17	Magglio Ordonez	.20
18	Jason LaRue	.10
19	Danys Baez	.10
20a	Todd Helton (Red Topps)	.40
21	Denny Neagle	.10
22	Dave Mlicki	.10
23	Roberto Hernandez	.10
24	Odalis Perez	.10
25	Nick Neugebauer	.10
26	David Ortiz	.10
27	Andres Galarraga	.15
28	Edgardo Alfonzo	.10
29	Chad Bradford	.10
30a	Jason Giambi (Red Topps)	.40
31	Brian Giles	.25
32	Deivi Cruz	.10
33	Robb Nen	.10
34	Jeff Nelson	.10
35	Edgar Renteria	.10
36	Aubrey Huff	.10
37	Brandon Duckworth	.10
38	Juan Gonzalez	.40
39	Sidney Ponson	.10
40	Eric Hinske	.10
41	Kevin Appier	.10
42	Danny Bautista	.10
43	Javier Lopez	.10
44	Jeff Conine	.10
45	Carlos Baerga	.10
46	Ugueth Urbina	.10
47	Mark Buehrle	.10
48	Aaron Boone	.10
49	Chuck Finley	.10
50a	Sammy Sosa (Red Topps)	1.00
51	Jose Jimenez	.10
52	Chris Truby	.10
53	Luis Castillo	.10
54	Orlando Merced	.10
55	Brian Jordan	.10
56	Eric Young	.10
57	Bobby Kielty	.10
58	Luis Rivas	.10
59	Brad Wilkerson	.10
60	Roberto Alomar	.40
61a	Roger Clemens (Red Topps)	1.00
62	Scott Hatteberg	.10
63	Andy Ashby	.10
64	Mike Williams	.10
65	Ron Gant	.10
66	Benito Santiago	.10
67	Bret Boone	.10
68	Matt Morris	.10
69	Troy Glaus	.40
70	Austin Kearns	.25
71	Jim Thome	.40
72	Rickey Henderson	.40
73a	Luis Gonzalez (Red Topps)	.20
74	Brad Fullmer	.10
75	Benny Agbayani	.10
76	Randy Wolf	.10
77a	Miguel Tejada (Red Topps)	.25
78	Jimmy Anderson	.10
79	Ramon Martinez	.10
80a	Ivan Rodriguez (Red Topps)	.40
81	John Flaherty	.10
82	Shannon Stewart	.10
83	Orlando Arrojo	.10
84	Rafael Furcal	.10
85	Kenny Rogers	.10
86	Bud Smith	.10
87	Mo Vaughn	.15
88	Jose Cruz Jr.	.10
89	Mike Matheny	.10
90a	Alfonso Soriano (Red Topps)	.50
91	Orlando Cabrera	.10
92	Jeffrey Hammonds	.10
93	Hideo Nomo	.25
94	Carlos Febles	.10
95	Billy Wagner	.10
96	Alex Gonzalez	.10
97	Todd Zeile	.10
98	Omar Vizquel	.20
99	Jose Rijo	.10
100a	Ichiro Suzuki (Red Topps)	1.00
101	Steve Cox	.10
102	Hideki Irabu	.10
103	Roy Halladay	.10
104	David Eckstein	.10
105	Greg Maddux	.75
106	Chris Richard	.10
107	Travis Driskill	.10
108	Fred McGriff	.15
109	Frank Thomas	.50
110	Shawn Green	.20
111	Ruben Quevedo	.10
112	Jacque Jones	.10
113	Tomokazu Ohka	.10
114	Joe McEwing	.10
115	Ramiro Mendoza	.10
116	Mark Mulder	.20
117	Mike Lieberthal	.10
118	Jack Wilson	.10
119	Randall Simon	.10
120	Bernie Williams	.40
121	Marvin Benard	.10
122	Jamie Moyer	.10
123	Andy Benes	.10
124	Tino Martinez	.10
125	Esteban Yan	.10
126	Gabe Kapler	.10
127	Jason Isringhausen	.10
128	Chris Carpenter	.10
129	Mike Cameron	.10
130a	Gary Sheffield (Red Topps)	.25
131	Geronimo Gil	.10
132	Brian Daubach	.10
133	Corey Patterson	.10
134	Aaron Rowand	.10
135	Chris Reitsma	.10
136	Bob Wickman	.10
137	Paul Shuey	.10
138	Jason Jennings	.10
139	Brandon Inge	.10
140	Larry Walker	.20
141	Ramon Santiago	.10
142	Hansel Izquierdo	.10
143	Jose Vizcaino	.10
144	Mark Quinn	.10
145	Michael Tucker	.10
146	Darren Dreifort	.10
147	Mark Loretta	.10
148	Corey Koskie	.10
149	Tony Armas Jr.	.10
150a	Kazuhisa Ishii (Red Topps)	.10
151	Al Leiter	.10
152	Steve Trachsel	.10
153	Mike Stanton	.10
154	David Justice	.15
155	Marlon Anderson	.10
156	Jason Kendall	.10
157	Brian Lawrence	.10
158	J.T. Snow Jr.	.10
159	Edgar Martinez	.10
160a	Pat Burrell (Red Topps)	.25
161	Kerry Robinson	.10
162	Greg Vaughn	.10
163	Carl Everett	.10
164	Vernon Wells	.10
165	Jose Mesa	.10
166	Troy Percival	.10
167	Erubiel Durazo	.10
168	Jason Marquis	.10
169	Jerry Hairston Jr.	.10
170a	Vladimir Guerrero (Red Topps)	.50
171	Byung-Hyun Kim	.10
172	Marcus Giles	.10
173	Johnny Damon	.10
174	Jon Lieber	.10
175	Ray Durham	.10
176	Sean Casey	.10
177a	Adam Dunn (Red Topps)	.40
178	Juan Pierre	.10
179	Damion Easley	.10
180a	Barry Zito (Red Topps)	.25
181	Abraham Nunez	.10
182	Pokey Reese	.10
183	Jeff Kent	.20
184	Russ Ortiz	.10
185	Ruben Sierra	.10
186	Brent Abernathy	.10
187	Ismael Valdes	.10
188	Darrin Fletcher	.10
189	Craig Counsell	.10
190	David Wells	.10
191	Ramon Hernandez	.10
192	Adam Kennedy	.10
193	Tony Womack	.10
194	Wes Helms	.10
195	Tony Batista	.10
196	Rolando Arrojo	.10
197	Matt Clement	.10
198	Sandy Alomar	.10
199	Scott Sullivan	.10
200a	Albert Pujols (Red Topps)	1.00
201	Kirk Rueter	.10
202	Phil Nevin	.10
203	Kip Wells	.10
204	Ron Coomer	.10
205	Jeromy Burnitz	.10
206	Kyle Lohse	.10
207	Paul Bako	.10
208	Paul LoDuca	.10
209	Carlos Beltran	.10
210	Roy Oswalt	.25
211	Mike Lowell	.10
212	Robert Fick	.10
213	Todd Jones	.10
214	C.C. Sabathia	.10
215	Danny Graves	.10

No.	Player	Price
216	Todd Hundley	.10
217	Tim Wakefield	.10
218	Dustin Hermanson	.10
219	Kevin Millwood	.10
220	Jorge Posada	.25
221	Bobby Jones	.10
222	Carlos Guillen	.10
223	Fernando Vina	.10
224	Ryan Rupe	.10
225	Kelvim Escobar	.10
226	Ramon Ortiz	.10
227	Junior Spivey	.10
228	Juan Cruz	.10
229	Melvin Mora	.10
230a	Lance Berkman (Red Topps)	.25
231	Brent Butler	.10
232	Matt Anderson	.10
233	Derrek Lee	.10
234	Matt Lawton	.10
235	Chuck Knoblauch	.10
236	Eric Gagne	.10
237	Alex Sanchez	.10
238	Denny Hocking	.10
239	Rick Reed	.10
240	Rey Ordonez	.10
241	Orlando Hernandez	.10
242	Robert Person	.10
243	Sean Burroughs	.10
244	Jeff Cirillo	.10
245	Mike Lamb	.10
246	Jose Valentin	.10
247	Ellis Burks	.10
248	Shawn Chacon	.10
249	Josh Beckett	.10
250a	Nomar Garciaparra (Red Topps)	1.00
251	Craig Biggio	.20
252	Joe Randa	.10
253	Mark Grudzielanek	.10
254	Glendon Rusch	.10
255	Michael Barrett	.10
256	Tyler Houston	.10
257	Ryan Dempster	.10
258	Wade Miller	.10
259	Adrian Beltre	.20
260	Vicente Padilla	.10
261	Kazuhiro Sasaki	.10
262	Mike Scioscia	.10
263	Bobby Cox	.10
264	Mike Hargrove	.10
265	Grady Little	.10
266	Alex Gonzalez	.10
267	Jerry Manuel	.10
268	Bob Boone	.10
269	Joel Skinner	.10
270	Clint Hurdle	.10
271	Luis Pujols	.10
272	Bob Brenly	.10
273	Jeff Torborg	.10
274	Jimy Williams	.10
275	Tony Pena	.10
276	Jim Tracy	.10
277	Jerry Royster	.10
278	Ron Gardenhire	.10
279	Frank Robinson	.10
280	Bobby Valentine	.10
281	Joe Torre	.10
282	Art Howe	.10
283	Larry Bowa	.10
284	Lloyd McClendon	.10
285	Bruce Bochy	.10
286	Dusty Baker	.10
287	Lou Piniella	.10
288	Tony LaRussa	.10
289	Hal McRae	.10
290	Jerry Narron	.10
291	Carlos Tosca	.10
292	Chris Duncan RC	1.00
293	Franklin Gutierrez RC	1.00
294	Adam LaRoche	.10
295	Manuel Ramirez RC	.10
296	Il Kim RC	.10
297	Wayne Lydon RC	.20
298	Daryl Clark RC	.25
299	Sean Pierce	.10
300a	Andy Marte RC (Red Topps)	.50
301	Matt Peterson RC	.25
302	Gonzalo Lopez RC	.25
303	Bernie Castro RC	.25
304	Cliff Lee	.10
305	Jason Perry RC	.40
306	Jaime Bubela RC	.10
307	Alexis Rios RC	.10
308	Brendan Harris RC	.40
309	Ramon Martinez	.10
310	Terry Tiffee RC	.40
311	Kevin Youkilis RC	1.00
312	Ruddy Lugo RC	.10
313	C.J. Wilson	.10
314	Mike McNutt RC	.10
315	Jeff Clark RC	.10
316	Mark Malaska RC	.10
317	Doug Waechter RC	.25
318	Derell McCall RC	.10
319	Scott Tyler	.10
320	Craig Brazell RC	.10
321a	Walter Young (Red Topps)	.10
322a	Marlon Byrd, Jorge Padilla (Red Topps)	.10
323	Chris Snelling, Shin-Soo Choo	.10
324a	Hank Blalock, Mark Teixeira (Red Topps)	.10
325	Josh Hamilton, Carl Crawford	.40
326	Orlando Hudson, Josh Phelps	.10
327	Jack Cust, Rene Reyes	.10
328	Angel Berroa, Alexis Gomez	.10
329	Michael Cuddyer, Michael Restovich	.10
330	Juan Rivera, Marcus Thames	.10
331	Brandon Puffer, Jung Bong	.10
332	Mike Cameron	.10
333	Shawn Green	.25
334	Team Shot	.10
335	Jason Giambi	.25
336	Derek Lowe	.10
337	Manny Ramirez, Mike Sweeney, Bernie Williams	.25
338	Alfonso Soriano, Alex Rodriguez, Derek Jeter	.50
339	Alex Rodriguez, Jim Thome, Rafael Palmeiro	.40
340	Magglio Ordonez, Alex Rodriguez, Miguel Tejada	.40
341	Pedro Martinez, Derek Lowe, Barry Zito	.10
342	Pedro Martinez, Roger Clemens, Mike Mussina	.10
343	Larry Walker, Vladimir Guerrero, Todd Helton	.25
344	Sammy Sosa, Albert Pujols, Shawn Green	.40
345	Sammy Sosa, Lance Berkman, Shawn Green	.40
346	Lance Berkman, Albert Pujols, Pat Burrell	.25
347	Randy Johnson, Greg Maddux, Tom Glavine	.25
348	Randy Johnson, Curt Schilling, Kerry Wood	.25
349	AL Divison Series	.20
350	AL & NL Divison Series	.20
351	AL & NL Divison Series	.20
352	NL Divison Series	.20
353	AL Championship Series	.20
354	Postseason Highlight	.10
355	NL Championship Series	.10
356	Jason Giambi	.25
357	Alfonso Soriano	.50
358	Alex Rodriguez	.75
359	Eric Chavez	.10
360	Torii Hunter	.10
361	Bernie Williams	.20
362	Garret Anderson	.10
363	Jorge Posada	.20
364	Derek Lowe	.10
365	Barry Zito	.20
366	Manny Ramirez	.25
367	Mike Scioscia	.10
368a	Francisco Rodriguez (Red Topps)	.10
369	Andres Galarraga	.10
370a	Chipper Jones (Red Topps)	.50
371	Chris Singleton	.10
372	Cliff Floyd	.10
373	Bobby Hill	.10
374	Antonio Osuna	.10
375	Barry Larkin	.25
376	Charles Nagy	.10
377	Denny Stark	.10
378	Dean Palmer	.10
379	Eric Owens	.10
380a	Randy Johnson (Red Topps)	.50
381	Jeff Suppan	.10
382	Eric Karros	.10
383	Luis Vizcaino	.10
384	Johan Santana	.10
385	Javier Vazquez	.10
386	John Thomson	.10
387a	Nick Johnson (Red Topps)	.10
388	Mark Ellis	.10
389	Doug Glanville	.10
390a	Ken Griffey Jr. (Red Topps)	.75
391	Bubba Trammell	.10
392	Livan Hernandez	.10
393	Desi Relaford	.10
394	Eli Marrero	.10
395	Jared Sandberg	.10
396a	Barry Bonds (Red Topps)	1.50
397	Esteban Loaiza	.10
398	Aaron Sele	.10
399	Geoff Blum	.10
400a	Derek Jeter (Red Topps)	1.50
401	Eric Byrnes	.10
402	Mike Timlin	.10
403	Mark Kotsay	.10
404	Rich Aurilia	.10
405	Joel Pineiro	.10
406	Chuck Finley	.10
407	Bengie Molina	.10
408	Steve Finley	.10
409	Julio Franco	.10
410	Marty Cordova	.10
411	Shea Hillenbrand	.10
412	Mark Bellhorn	.10
413	Jon Garland	.10
414	Reggie Taylor	.10
415	Milton Bradley	.10
416	Carlos Pena	.10
417	Andy Fox	.10
418	Brad Ausmus	.10
419	Brent Mayne	.10
420	Paul Quantrill	.10
421a	Carlos Delgado (Red Topps)	.20
422	Kevin Mench	.10
423	Joe Kennedy	.10
424	Mike Crudale	.10
425	Mark McLemore	.10
426	Bill Mueller	.10
427	Robert Mackowiak	.10
428	Ricky Ledee	.10
429	Ted Lilly	.10
430	Sterling Hitchcock	.10
431	Scott Strickland	.10
432	Damion Easley	.10
433a	Torii Hunter (Red Topps)	.25
434	Brad Radke	.10
435	Geoff Jenkins	.10
436	Paul Byrd	.10
437	Morgan Ensberg	.10
438	Mike Maroth	.10
439	Mike Hampton	.10
440	Adam Hyzdu	.10
441	Vance Wilson	.10
442	Todd Ritchie	.10
443	Flash Gordon	.10
444	John Burkett	.10
445	Rodrigo Lopez	.10
446	Tim Spooneybarger	.10
447	Quinton McCracken	.10
448	Tim Salmon	.20
449	Jarrod Washburn	.10
450a	Pedro Martinez (Red Topps)	.50
451	Dustan Mohr	.10
452	Julio Lugo	.10
453	Scott Stewart	.10
454	Armando Benitez	.10
455	Raul Mondesi	.20
456	Robin Ventura	.10
457	Bobby Abreu	.20
458	Josh Fogg	.10
459	Ryan Klesko	.20
460	Tsuyoshi Shinjo	.10
461a	Jim Edmonds (Red Topps)	.25
462	Cliff Politte	.10
463	Chan Ho Park	.10
464	John Mabry	.10
465	Woody Williams	.10
466	Jason Michaels	.10
467	Scott Schoeneweis	.10
468	Brian Anderson	.10
469	Brett Tomko	.10
470	Scott Erickson	.10
471	Tony Clark	.10
472	Danny Wright	.10
473	Jason Schmidt	.10
474	Scott Williamson	.10
475	Einar Diaz	.10
476	Jay Payton	.10
477	Juan Acevedo	.10
478	Ben Grieve	.10
479	Raul Ibanez	.10
480	Richie Sexson	.25
481	Rick Reed	.10
482	Pedro Astacio	.10
483	Adam Piatt	.10
484	Bud Smith	.10
485	Tomas Perez	.10
486	Adam Eaton	.10
487	Rafael Palmeiro	.25
488	Jason Tyner	.10
489a	Scott Rolen (Red Topps)	.50
490	Randy Winn	.10
491	Ryan Jensen	.10
492	Trevor Hoffman	.10
493	Craig Wilson	.10
494	Jeremy Giambi	.10
495	Daryle Ward	.10
496	Shane Spencer	.10
497	Andy Pettitte	.25
498	John Franco	.10
499	Masato Yoshii	.10
500a	Mike Piazza (Red Topps)	1.00
501	Cristian Guzman	.10
502	Jose Hernandez	.10
503	Octavio Dotel	.10
504	Brad Penny	.10
505	Jose Ortiz	.10
506	Ryan Dempster	.10
507	Joe Crede	.10
508	Chad Hermansen	.10
509	Gary Matthews Jr.	.10
510	Matt Franco	.10
511	Ben Weber	.10
512	Dave Berg	.10
513	Michael Young	.10
514	Frank Catalanotto	.10
515a	Darin Erstad (Red Topps)	.25
516	Matt Williams	.10
517	B.J. Surhoff	.10
518	Kerry Ligtenberg	.10
519	Mike Bordick	.10
520	Arthur Rhodes	.10
521	Joe Girardi	.10
522	D'Angelo Jimenez	.10
523	Paul Konerko	.10
524	Jose Macias	.10
525	Joe Mays	.10
526	Marquis Grissom	.10
527	Neifi Perez	.10
528	Preston Wilson	.10
529	Jeff Weaver	.10
530a	Eric Chavez (Red Topps)	.25
531	Placido Polanco	.10
532	Ray Lankford	.10
533	James Baldwin	.10
534	Toby Hall	.10
535	Brendan Donnelly	.10
536	Benji Gil	.10
537	Damian Moss	.10
538	Jorge Julio	.10
539	Matt Clement	.10
540	Brian Moehler	.10
541	Lee Stevens	.10
542	Jimmy Haynes	.10
543	Kevin Millar	.10
544	Dave Roberts	.10
545	J.C. Romero	.10
546	Bartolo Colon	.10
547	Roger Cedeno	.10
548	Mariano Rivera	.20
549	Billy Koch	.10
550a	Manny Ramirez (Red Topps)	.50
551	Travis Lee	.10
552	Oliver Perez	.10
553	Tim Worrell	.10
554	Rafael Soriano	.10
555	Damian Miller	.10
556	John Smoltz	.10
557	Willis Roberts	.10
558a	Tim Hudson (Red Topps)	.25
559	Moises Alou	.20
560	Gary Glover	.10
561	Corky Miller	.10
562	Ben Broussard	.10
563	Gabe Kapler	.10
564	Chris Woodward	.10
565	Paul Wilson	.10
566	Todd Hollandsworth	.10
567	So Taguchi	.10
568	John Olerud	.20
569	Reggie Sanders	.10
570	Jake Peavy	.10
571	Kris Benson	.10
572	Todd Pratt	.10
573	Ray Durham	.10
574	David Wells	.10
575	Chris Widger	.10
576	Shawn Wooten	.10
577	Tom Glavine	.25
578	Antonio Alfonseca	.10
579	Keith Foulke	.10
580	Shawn Estes	.10
581	Travis Fryman	.10
582	Dmitri Young	.10
583	A.J. Burnett	.10
584	Richard Hidalgo	.10
585a	Mike Sweeney (Red Topps)	.10
586	Alex Cora	.10
587	Matt Stairs	.10
588	Doug Mientkiewicz	.10
589	Fernando Tatis	.10
590	David Weathers	.10
591	Cory Lidle	.10
592	Dan Plesac	.10
593a	Jeff Bagwell (Red Topps)	.50
594	Steve Sparks	.10
595	Sandy Alomar Jr.	.10
596	John Lackey	.10
597	Rick Helling	.10
598	Mark DeRosa	.10
599	Carlos Lee	.10
600a	Garret Anderson (Red Topps)	.20
601	Vinny Castilla	.10
602	Ryan Drese	.10
603	LaTroy Hawkins	.10
604	David Bell	.10
605	Freddy Garcia	.10
606	Miguel Cairo	.10
607	Scott Spiezio	.10
608	Mike Remlinger	.10
609	Tony Graffanino	.10
610	Russell Branyan	.10
611	Chris Magruder	.10
612	Jose Contreras RC	.75
613	Carl Pavano	.10
614	Kevin Brown	.10
615	Tyler Houston	.10
616	A.J. Pierzynski	.10
617	Tony Fiore	.10
618	Peter Bergeron	.10
619	Rondell White	.10
620	Brett Myers	.10
621	Kevin Young	.10
622	Kenny Lofton	.10
623	Ben Davis	.10
624	J.D. Drew	.10
625	Chris Gomez	.10
626	Karim Garcia	.10
627	Ricky Gutierrez	.10
628	Mark Redman	.10
629	Juan Encarnacion	.10
630	Anaheim Angels	.25
631	Arizona Diamondbacks	.10
632	Atlanta Braves	.10
633	Baltimore Orioles	.10
634	Boston Red Sox	.25
635	Chicago Cubs	.10
636	Chicago White Sox	.10
637	Cincinnati Reds	.10
638	Cleveland Indians	.10
639	Colorado Rockies	.10
640	Detroit Tigers	.10
641	Florida Marlins	.10
642	Houston Astros	.10
643	Kansas City Royals	.10
644	Los Angeles Dodgers	.10
645	Milwaukee Brewers	.10
646	Minnesota Twins	.10
647	Montreal Expos	.10
648	New York Mets	.10
649	New York Yankees	.50
650	Oakland Athletics	.10
651	Philadelphia Phillies	.10
652	Pittsburgh Pirates	.10
653	San Diego Padres	.10
654	San Francisco Giants	.10
655	Seattle Mariners	.10
656	St. Louis Cardinals	.10
657	Tampa Bay Devil Rays	.10
658	Texas Rangers	.10
659	Toronto Blue Jays	.10
660	Bryan Bullington RC	.40
661	Jeremy Guthrie	.10
662	Joey Gomes	.25
663	Evel Bastida-Martinez RC	.40
664	Brian Wright RC	.10
665	B.J. Upton	.10
666	Jeff Francis	.10
667	Drew Meyer	.10
668	Jeremy Hermida	.10
669	Khalil Greene	.75
670	Darrell Rasner	.10
671	Cole Hamels	.50
672	James Loney	.10
673	Sergio Santos	.10
674	Jason Pridie	.10
675	Brandon Phillips, Victor Martinez	.10
676	Hee Seop Choi, Nic Jackson	.10
677	Dontrelle Willis, Jason Stokes	.10
678	Chad Tracy, Lyle Overbay	.10
679	Joe Borchard, Corwin Malone	.10
680	Joe Mauer, Justin Morneau	.25
681	Drew Henson, Brandon Claussen	.10
682	Chase Utley, Gavin Floyd	.25
683	Taggert Bozied, Xavier Nady	.25
684	Aaron Heilman, Jose Reyes	.25
685	Kenny Rogers	.10
686	Bengie Molina	.10
687	John Olerud	.10
688	Bret Boone	.10
689	Eric Chavez	.15
690	Alex Rodriguez	.75
691	Darin Erstad	.15
692	Ichiro Suzuki	.50
693	Torii Hunter	.15
694	Greg Maddux	.50
695	Brad Ausmus	.10
696	Todd Helton	.20
697	Fernando Vina	.10
698	Scott Rolen	.25
699	Edgar Renteria	.10
700	Andruw Jones	.20
701	Larry Walker	.10
702	Jim Edmonds	.10
703	Barry Zito	.10
704	Randy Johnson	.40
705	Miguel Tejada	.15
706	Barry Bonds	.75
707	Eric Hinske	.10
708	Jason Jennings	.10
709	Todd Helton	.20
710	Jeff Kent	.10
711	Edgar Renteria	.10
712	Scott Rolen	.25
713	Barry Bonds	.75
714	Sammy Sosa	.50
715	Vladimir Guerrero	.40
716	Mike Piazza	.75
717	Curt Schilling	.20
718	Randy Johnson	.40
719	Bobby Cox	.10
720	World Series Card	.10
721	World Series Card	.10

Black
Stars: 10-20X
Production 52 Sets

Gold

Stars: 3-6X
Production 2,003 Sets

Autographs

		NM/M
Common Autograph:		8.00
HB	Hank Blalock	20.00
MB	Mark Buehrle	20.00
EC	Eric Chavez	25.00
DE	Darin Erstad	15.00
OH	Orlando Hudson	10.00
AK	Austin Kearns	15.00
JL	Jason Lane	10.00
PL	Paul LoDuca	12.00
JDM	J.D. Martin	8.00
JM	Joe Mauer	40.00
EM	Eric Milton	10.00
NN	Nick Neugebauer	8.00
MP	Mark Prior	40.00
SR	Scott Rolen	50.00
BS	Ben Sheets	15.00
MTE	Mark Teixeira	20.00
MTH	Marcus Thames	8.00

Autographs Series 2

		NM/M
Common Autograph:		8.00
JB	Josh Beckett	30.00
LB	Lance Berkman	40.00
CE	Clint Everts	8.00
CF	Cliff Floyd	20.00
BH	Brad Hawpe	8.00
EH	Eric Hinske	10.00
TH	Torii Hunter	20.00
AK	Austin Kearns	15.00
PK	Paul Konerko	20.00
PL	Paul LoDuca	15.00
MO	Magglio Ordonez	20.00
JPH	Josh Phelps	10.00
AP	Albert Pujols	120.00
MT	Miguel Tejada	30.00
BU	B.J. Upton	25.00
JV	Jose Vidro	10.00
DW	Dontrelle Willis	25.00
BZ	Barry Zito	30.00

All-Stars

		NM/M
Complete Set (20):		20.00
Common Player:		.50
Inserted 1:15		
TAS1	Alfonso Soriano	1.50
TAS2	Barry Bonds	4.00
TAS3	Ichiro Suzuki	2.00
TAS4	Alex Rodriguez	3.00
TAS5	Miguel Tejada	.75
TAS6	Nomar Garciaparra	2.50
TAS7	Jason Giambi	1.00
TAS8	Manny Ramirez	1.00
TAS9	Derek Jeter	4.00
TAS10	Garret Anderson	.50
TAS11	Barry Zito	.50
TAS12	Sammy Sosa	2.00
TAS13	Adam Dunn	.50
TAS14	Vladimir Guerrero	1.50
TAS15	Mike Piazza	2.50
TAS16	Shawn Green	.50
TAS17	Luis Gonzalez	.50
TAS18	Todd Helton	.75
TAS19	Torii Hunter	.75
TAS20	Curt Schilling	.75

Topps Blue Backs

		NM/M
Complete Set (40):		50.00
Common Player:		.75
Inserted 1:12		
BB1	Albert Pujols	2.00
BB2	Barry Bonds	5.00
BB3	Ichiro Suzuki	3.00
BB4	Sammy Sosa	2.50
BB5	Kazuhisa Ishii	.75
BB6	Alex Rodriguez	4.00
BB7	Derek Jeter	5.00
BB8	Vladimir Guerrero	2.00
BB9	Ken Griffey Jr.	2.50
BB10	Jason Giambi	2.50
BB11	Todd Helton	1.00
BB12	Mike Piazza	3.00
BB13	Nomar Garciaparra	3.00
BB14	Chipper Jones	2.50
BB15	Ivan Rodriguez	1.00
BB16	Luis Gonzalez	.75
BB17	Pat Burrell	1.00
BB18	Mark Prior	1.50
BB19	Adam Dunn	1.00
BB20	Jeff Bagwell	1.50
BB21	Austin Kearns	1.00
BB22	Alfonso Soriano	2.00
BB23	Jim Thome	1.50
BB24	Bernie Williams	1.00
BB25	Pedro J. Martinez	2.00
BB26	Lance Berkman	1.00
BB27	Randy Johnson	2.00
BB28	Rafael Palmeiro	1.00

BB29	Richie Sexson	.75
BB30	Troy Glaus	1.50
BB31	Shawn Green	.75
BB32	Larry Walker	.75
BB33	Eric Hinske	.75
BB34	Andruw Jones	1.50
BB35	Carlos Delgado	1.00
BB36	Curt Schilling	1.50
BB37	Greg Maddux	2.50
BB38	Jimmy Rollins	.75
BB39	Eric Chavez	1.00
BB40	Scott Rolen	1.00

Draft Picks

Complete Set (10): 30.00
1-5 issued in retail sets.
6-10 issued in holiday sets.

1	Brandon Wood	10.00
2	Ryan Wagner	3.00
3	Sean Rodriguez	3.00
4	Chris Lubanski	4.00
5	Chad Billingsley	6.00
6	Javi Herrera	3.00
7	Brian McFall	3.00
8	Nicholas Markakis	6.00
9	Adam Miller	3.00
10	Daric Barton	4.00

Flashback

NM/M
Complete Set (14): 50.00
Common Player: 2.00
HTA exclusive.

GB	George Brett	6.00
LD	Lenny Dykstra	3.00
HK	Harmon Killebrew	6.00
BM	Bill Madlock	2.00
EM	Eddie Mathews	4.00
DM	Dale Murphy	5.00
JP	Jim Palmer	3.00
MP	Mike Piazza	6.00
RR	Robin Roberts	3.00
AR	Al Rosen	4.00
NR	Nolan Ryan	10.00
TS	Tom Seaver	5.00
WS	Warren Spahn	4.00
CY	Carl Yastrzemski	6.00

2003 Topps Futures Game

Flashback photos of alumni of the All-Star Futures Game are featured on this set of cards given away at the 2003 event July 13 in connection with All-Star Weekend in Chicago. The design follows the basic Topps format for 2003 and includes a special Futures Game logo.

NM/M
Complete Set (6): 5.00
Common Player: .50

1	Alfonso Soriano	2.00
2	Pat Burrell	1.00
3	Adam Dunn	1.00
4	Barry Zito	.75
5	Mark Buehrle	.50
6	Rafael Furcal	.75

Hit Parade

NM/M
Complete Set (30): 30.00
Common Player: .50
Inserted 1:15

HP1	Barry Bonds	4.00
HP2	Sammy Sosa	2.50
HP3	Rafael Palmeiro	1.00

HP4	Fred McGriff	.75
HP5	Ken Griffey Jr.	2.50
HP6	Juan Gonzalez	1.00
HP7	Andres Galarraga	.50
HP8	Jeff Bagwell	1.50
HP9	Frank Thomas	1.50
HP10	Matt Williams	.50
HP11	Barry Bonds	4.00
HP12	Rafael Palmeiro	1.00
HP13	Fred McGriff	.75
HP14	Andres Galarraga	.50
HP15	Ken Griffey Jr.	2.50
HP16	Sammy Sosa	2.50
HP17	Jeff Bagwell	1.50
HP18	Juan Gonzalez	1.00
HP19	Frank Thomas	1.50
HP20	Matt Williams	.50
HP21	Rickey Henderson	1.00
HP22	Rafael Palmeiro	1.00
HP23	Roberto Alomar	1.00
HP24	Barry Bonds	4.00
HP25	Mark Grace	1.00
HP26	Fred McGriff	.75
HP27	Julio Franco	.50
HP28	Craig Biggio	.50
HP29	Andres Galarraga	.50
HP30	Barry Larkin	.50

Hobby Masters

Complete Set (20): 40.00
Common Player: 1.00
Inserted 1:18

HM1	Ichiro Suzuki	4.00
HM2	Kazuhisa Ishii	1.00
HM3	Derek Jeter	6.00
HM4	Barry Bonds	5.00
HM5	Sammy Sosa	3.00
HM6	Alex Rodriguez	5.00
HM7	Mike Piazza	4.00
HM8	Chipper Jones	3.00
HM9	Vladimir Guerrero	2.00
HM10	Nomar Garciaparra	4.00
HM11	Todd Helton	1.00
HM12	Jason Giambi	3.00
HM13	Ken Griffey Jr.	3.00
HM14	Albert Pujols	2.00
HM15	Ivan Rodriguez	1.00
HM16	Mark Prior	3.00
HM17	Adam Dunn	1.50
HM18	Randy Johnson	2.00
HM19	Pedro J. Martinez	2.00
HM20	Alfonso Soriano	3.00

Own The Game

Complete Set (30): 30.00
Common Player: .50
Inserted 1:12

OG1	Ichiro Suzuki	3.00
OG2	Barry Bonds	4.00
OG3	Todd Helton	.75
OG4	Larry Walker	.75
OG5	Mike Sweeney	.50
OG6	Sammy Sosa	2.50
OG7	Lance Berkman	.75
OG8	Alex Rodriguez	2.50
OG9	Jim Thome	1.25
OG10	Shawn Green	.75
OG11	Troy Glaus	1.00
OG12	Richie Sexson	.50
OG13	Paul Konerko	.50
OG14	Jason Giambi	2.50
OG15	Chipper Jones	2.50
OG16	Torii Hunter	.50
OG17	Albert Pujols	1.50
OG18	Jose Vidro	.50
OG19	Alfonso Soriano	2.00

OG20	Luis Castillo	.50
OG21	Mike Lowell	.50
OG22	Garret Anderson	.50
OG23	Jimmy Rollins	.50
OG24	Curt Schilling	1.00
OG25	Kazuhisa Ishii	.50
OG26	Randy Johnson	1.50
OG27	Tom Glavine	.75
OG28	Roger Clemens	2.50
OG29	Pedro J. Martinez	1.50
OG30	Derek Lowe	.50

Prime Cuts Autograph

NM/M
Production 50 Sets

EC	Eric Chavez	100.00
LB	Lance Berkman	120.00
AJ	Andruw Jones	100.00
CJ	Chipper Jones	150.00
MO	Magglio Ordonez	100.00
MT	Miguel Tejada	120.00

Prime Cuts Pine Tar Series

NM/M
Pine Tar Series
Production 200 Sets
Trademark Series: 1-1.5X
Production 100 Sets
Prime Cuts Series: 1.5-2X
Production 50 Sets

RA	Roberto Alomar	20.00
LB	Lance Berkman	15.00
EC	Eric Chavez	20.00
AD	Adam Dunn	25.00
DE	Darin Erstad	15.00
NG	Nomar Garciaparra	40.00
JG	Juan Gonzalez	15.00
TH	Todd Helton	25.00
AJ	Andruw Jones	20.00
CJ	Chipper Jones	30.00
RP	Rafael Palmeiro	20.00
MP	Mike Piazza	30.00
AP	Albert Pujols	40.00
AR	Alex Rodriguez	25.00
IR	Ivan Rodriguez	25.00
SR	Scott Rolen	25.00
AS	Alfonso Soriano	25.00
MT	Miguel Tejada	15.00
FT	Frank Thomas	30.00
MV	Mo Vaughn	10.00
BW	Bernie Williams	25.00

Prime Cuts Pine Tar Series 2

NM/M
Pine Tar Series:
Production 200

RA	Roberto Alomar	20.00
LB	Lance Berkman	15.00
HB	Hank Blalock	25.00
BBO	Barry Bonds	40.00
EC	Eric Chavez	15.00
CD	Carlos Delgado	10.00
AD	Adam Dunn	25.00
NG	Nomar Garciaparra	30.00
LG	Luis Gonzalez	8.00
TG	Tony Gwynn	20.00
RH	Rickey Henderson	25.00
RJ	Randy Johnson	25.00
EM	Edgar Martinez	20.00
TM	Tino Martinez	15.00
MO	Magglio Ordonez	10.00
RP	Rafael Palmeiro	15.00
JP	Jorge Posada	15.00
AP	Albert Pujols	40.00
MP	Mark Prior	20.00
AR	Alex Rodriguez	25.00
AS	Alfonso Soriano	20.00

Trademark Series: 1-1.5X
Production 100
Prime Cuts: 1.5-2.5X
Production 50

Record Breakers

LUIS CASTILLO

94 XBHs in 2001
Houston Astros' Extra Base Hits Season Leader
Lance Berkman

NM/M
Complete Set (50): 40.00
Common Player: .50
Inserted 1:6

JB	Jeff Bagwell	1.50
LBE	Lance Berkman	1.00
BB	Barry Bonds	5.00
GB	George Brett	2.50
LB	Lou Brock	.50
RCA	Rod Carew	.50
LC	Luis Castillo	.50
RC	Roger Clemens	2.50
CD	Carlos Delgado	.50
CF	Cliff Floyd	.50
GF	George Foster	.50

AG	Andres Galarraga	.50
JG	Jason Giambi	2.50
BG	Bob Gibson	1.00
TG	Troy Glaus	.50
JGO	Juan Gonzalez	1.00
LGO	Luis Gonzalez	.50
SG	Shawn Green	.75
HG	Hank Greenberg	.50
KG	Ken Griffey Jr.	3.00
VG	Vladimir Guerrero	1.50
RG	Ron Guidry	.50
TH	Todd Helton	1.00
RH	Rickey Henderson	.75
FJ	Fergie Jenkins	.50
RJ	Randy Johnson	1.50
CJ	Chipper Jones	3.00
HK	Harmon Killebrew	.50
CK	Chuck Klein	.50
JM	Juan Marichal	.50
PM	Pedro J. Martinez	1.50
EM	Eddie Mathews	.50
DM	Don Mattingly	4.00
FM	Fred McGriff	.50
JO	John Olerud	.50
RP	Rafael Palmeiro	1.00
MP	Mike Piazza	3.00
FR	Frank Robinson	1.00
AR	Alex Rodriguez	4.00
NR	Nolan Ryan	6.00
MSC	Mike Schmidt	3.00
CS	Curt Schilling	1.00
TS	Tom Seaver	1.00
RS	Richie Sexson	.50
GS	Gary Sheffield	.50
SS	Sammy Sosa	3.00
MS	Mike Sweeney	.50
HW	Hack Wilson	.50
PW	Preston Wilson	.50
RY	Robin Yount	1.00

Record Breakers Series 2

NM/M
Complete Set (50): 40.00
Common Player: .50
Inserted 1:6

RA	Roberto Alomar	1.00
GA	Garret Anderson	.75
LA	Luis Aparicio	.50
JB	Jeff Bagwell	1.50
LB	Lance Berkman	1.00
CB	Craig Biggio	.75
WB	Wade Boggs	.75
BB	Barry Bonds	5.00
GB	George Brett	2.50
LBR	Lou Brock	.75
JD	Johnny Damon	.50
CD	Carlos Delgado	.50
LD	Lenny Dykstra	.50
DE	Darin Erstad	.50
BF	Bob Feller	.75
GF	George Foster	.50
NG	Nomar Garciaparra	3.00
LG	Luis Gonzalez	.50
DG	Dwight Gooden	.50
SG	Shawn Green	.75
KG	Ken Griffey Jr.	2.50
VG	Vladimir Guerrero	1.50
TG	Tony Gwynn	1.50
TH	Todd Helton	1.00
RH	Rickey Henderson	1.00
RJ	Randy Johnson	1.50
JK	Jeff Kent	.50
TK	Ted Kluszewski	.50
GM	Greg Maddux	2.50
JM	Juan Marichal	.50
EM	Edgar Martinez	.50
WM	Willie Mays	4.00
JME	Jose Mesa	.50
PM	Paul Molitor	1.00
JP	Jim Palmer	.75
TR	Tim Raines	.50
MR	Manny Ramirez	1.50
JR	Jim Rice	.50
FR	Frank Robinson	1.00
AR	Alex Rodriguez	4.00
TS	Tom Seaver	2.00
RS	Richie Sexson	.75
JS	John Smoltz	.50
SS	Sammy Sosa	2.50
WS	Willie Stargell	1.00
IS	Ichiro Suzuki	2.50
FT	Frank Thomas	1.50
JT	Jim Thome	1.50
LW	Larry Walker	.50
RY	Robin Yount	2.00

Record Breakers Autographs

NM/M
Common Autograph:

CF	Cliff Floyd	20.00
LG	Luis Gonzalez	30.00
FJ	Fergie Jenkins	25.00
CJ	Chipper Jones	75.00
HK	Harmon Killebrew	60.00
RP	Rafael Palmeiro	60.00
MS	Mike Schmidt	100.00
RS	Richie Sexson	30.00
MSW	Mike Sweeney	30.00
RY	Robin Yount	75.00

Record Breakers Autographs Series 2

NM/M
Common Autograph: 25.00
Inserted 1:2,436

LA	Luis Aparicio	40.00
LB	Lance Berkman	40.00

LBR	Lou Brock	40.00
GF	George Foster	25.00
JM	Juan Marichal	40.00
DM	Don Mattingly	125.00
WM	Willie Mays	150.00

Record Breakers Relics

AUTHENTIC GAME-USED BAT
51 2Bs in 1962 Cincinnati Reds' Doubles Season Leader
Frank Robinson

NM/M
Common Player: 6.00

JB	Jeff Bagwell/Jsy	8.00
LB	Lance Berkman/Bat	10.00
GB	George Brett/Bat	25.00
LC	Luis Castillo/Bat	6.00
CD	Carlos Delgado/Jsy	8.00
LGO	Luis Gonzalez/Jsy	8.00
SG	Shawn Green/Jsy	8.00
HG	Hank Greenberg/Bat	30.00
TH	Todd Helton/Jsy	10.00
RH	Rickey Henderson/Bat	15.00
CJ	Chipper Jones/Jsy	12.00
PM	Pedro Martinez/Jsy	15.00
DM	Don Mattingly/Bat	35.00
MP	Mike Piazza/Bat	15.00
FR	Frank Robinson/Bat	12.00
AR	Alex Rodriguez/Jsy	15.00
NR	Nolan Ryan/Jsy	35.00
MS	Mike Sweeney/Bat	8.00
HW	Hack Wilson/Bat	50.00
RY	Robin Yount/Jsy	15.00

Record Breaker Relics Series 2

NM/M
Common Player: 5.00

WB	Wade Boggs/Bat	10.00
GB	George Brett/Bat	25.00
CD	Carlos Delgado/Jsy	6.00
DE	Darin Erstad/Jsy	5.00
LG	Luis Gonzalez/Jsy	5.00
TH	Todd Helton/Jsy	8.00
RH	Rogers Hornsby/Bat	35.00
TK	Ted Kluszewski/Bat	15.00
EM	Edgar Martinez/Bat	12.00
JR	Jim Rice/Jsy	8.00
FR	Frank Robinson/Bat	12.00
AR	Alex Rodriguez/Jsy	15.00
NRA	Nolan Ryan/Jsy	30.00
RS	Richie Sexson/Jsy	8.00
FT	Frank Thomas/Bat	10.00
RY	Robin Yount	12.00

Red Backs

FOUL BALL
RAFAEL PALMEIRO
FOUL BALL

NM/M
Complete Set (40): 50.00
Common Player: .50
Inserted 1:12

TRB1	Nomar Garciaparra	3.00
TRB2	Ichiro Suzuki	2.50
TRB3	Alex Rodriguez	4.00
TRB4	Sammy Sosa	2.50
TRB5	Barry Bonds	5.00
TRB6	Vladimir Guerrero	1.50
TRB7	Derek Jeter	5.00
TRB8	Miguel Tejada	1.00
TRB9	Alfonso Soriano	2.00
TRB10	Manny Ramirez	1.50
TRB11	Adam Dunn	1.00
TRB12	Jason Giambi	2.50
TRB13	Mike Piazza	2.50
TRB14	Scott Rolen	1.50
TRB15	Shawn Green	.75
TRB16	Randy Johnson	2.00
TRB17	Todd Helton	1.00
TRB18	Garret Anderson	1.00
TRB19	Curt Schilling	1.00
TRB20	Albert Pujols	2.00
TRB21	Chipper Jones	2.00
TRB22	Luis Gonzalez	.50

TRB23	Mark Prior	1.50
TRB24	Jim Thome	1.50
TRB25	Ivan Rodriguez	1.00
TRB26	Torii Hunter	1.00
TRB27	Lance Berkman	1.00
TRB28	Troy Glaus	1.50
TRB29	Andruw Jones	1.00
TRB30	Barry Zito	.75
TRB31	Jeff Bagwell	1.50
TRB32	Magglio Ordonez	.75
TRB33	Pat Burrell	1.50
TRB34	Mike Sweeney	1.00
TRB35	Rafael Palmeiro	1.00
TRB36	Larry Walker	.50
TRB37	Carlos Delgado	.50
TRB38	Brian Giles	.50
TRB39	Pedro J. Martinez	.50
TRB40	Greg Maddux	2.50

Nolan Ryan No-Hitters

NM/M
Complete Set (7): 45.00
Common Ryan (1-7): 8.00
RB-NR1-7 Nolan Ryan 8.00

Topps Nolan Ryan Record Breakers Autographs

NM/M
Inserted 1:1,894
HTA Exclusive

NR	Nolan Ryan	200.00
NRA	Nolan Ryan	200.00
NRR	Nolan Ryan	200.00

Stadium Seat Relics

NM/M
Common Player: 15.00
Inserted 1:37 Series 2 HTA

JB	Johnny Bench	30.00
DC	Dave Concepcion	20.00
AD	Adam Dunn	20.00
KG	Ken Griffey Jr.	25.00
AK	Austin Kearns	20.00
BL	Barry Larkin	25.00
JM	Joe Morgan	15.00
PO	Paul O'Neill	15.00
TP	Tony Perez	20.00
TS	Tom Seaver	25.00

Team Topps Legends Autographs

TOPPS LEGENDS
WILLIE MAYS
SAN FRANCISCO GIANTS

NM/M
Common Player:

	Vida Blue	20.00
	Bob Feller	25.00
	Willie Mays	125.00
	Gil McDougald	12.00
	Robin Roberts	25.00
	Bobby Thomson	20.00
	Luis Tiant	8.00
	Carl Yastrzemski	50.00

Team Topps Legends Autographs Series 2

Common Player:

Topps Turn Back The Clock Autographs

NM/M
Common Player:

LD	Lenny Dykstra	15.00
BM	Bill Madlock	10.00
DM	Dale Murphy	40.00
JP	Jim Palmer	20.00

2003 Topps All-Time Fan Favorites

1st BASE — CECIL COOPER — BREWERS

		NM/M
Complete Set (150):		30.00
Common Player:		.25
Pack (6):		4.00
Box (24):		75.00
1	Willie Mays	3.00
2	Whitey Ford	1.00
3	Stan Musial	2.50
4	Paul Blair	.25
5	Harold Reynolds	.25
6	Bob Friend	.25
7	Rod Carew	.75
8	Kirk Gibson	.25
9	Graig Nettles	.25
10	Ozzie Smith	1.00
11	Tony Perez	.25
12	Tim Wallach	.25
13	Bert Campaneris	.25
14	Cory Snyder	.25
15	Dave Parker	.25
16	Darrell Evans	.25
17	Joe Pepitone	.25
18	Don Sutton	.25
19	Dale Murphy	1.00
20	George Brett	2.50
21	Carlton Fisk	.50
22	Bob Watson	.25
23	Wally Joyner	.25
24	Paul Molitor	1.00
25	Keith Hernandez	.25
26	Jerry Koosman	.25
27	George Bell	.25
28	Boog Powell	.25
29	Bruce Sutter	.75
30	Ernie Banks	1.50
31	Steve Lyons	.25
32	Earl Weaver	.25
33	Dave Stieb	.25
34	Alan Trammell	.25
35	Bret Saberhagen	.25
36	J.R. Richard	.25
37	Mickey Rivers	.25
38	Juan Marichal	.75
39	Gaylord Perry	.75
40	Don Mattingly	3.00
41	Bobby Grich	.25
42	Steve Sax	.25
43	Sparky Anderson	.25
44	Luis Aparicio	.25
45	Fergie Jenkins	.50
46	Jim Palmer	.75
47	Howard Johnson	.25
48	Dwight Evans	.25
49	Bill Buckner	.25
50	Cal Ripken Jr.	4.00
51	Jose Cruz	.25
52	Tony Oliva	.25
53	Bobby Richardson	.25
54	Luis Tiant	.25
55	Warren Spahn	1.00
56	Phil Rizzuto	1.00
57	Eric Davis	.25
58	Vida Blue	.25
59	Steve Balboni	.25
60	Mike Schmidt	2.50
61	Ken Griffey Sr.	.25
62	Jim Abbott	.25
63	Whitey Herzog	.25
64	Rich "Goose" Gossage	.25
65	Tony Armas	.25
66	Bill "Moose" Skowron	.25
67	Don Newcombe	.25
68	Bill Madlock	.25
69	Lance Parrish	.25
70	Reggie Jackson	1.50
71	Willie Wilson	.25
72	Terry Pendleton	.25
73	Jimmy Piersall	.25
74	George Foster	.25
75	Bob Horner	.25
76	Chris Sabo	.25
77	Fred Lynn	.25
78	Jim Rice	.25
79	Maury Wills	.25
80	Yogi Berra	1.50
81	Johnny Sain	.25
82	Tom Lasorda	.50
83	Bill Mazeroski	.25
84	John Kruk	.25
85	Bob Feller	.75
86	Frank Robinson	.75
87	Red Schoendienst	.25
88	Gary Carter	.50
89	Andre Dawson	.50
90	Tim McCarver	.25
91	Robin Yount	1.00
92	Phil Niekro	.25
93	Joe Morgan	.25
94	Darren Daulton	.25
95	Bobby Thomson	.25
96	Alvin Davis	.25
97	Robin Roberts	.25
98	Kirby Puckett	1.50
99	Jack Clark	.25
100	Hank Aaron	3.00
101	Orlando Cepeda	.50
102	Vern Law	.25
103	Cecil Cooper	.25
104	Don Larsen	.50
105	Mario Mendoza	.25
106	Tony Gwynn	1.50
107	Ernie Harwell	.25
108a	Monte Irvin (No facsimile autograph.)	.75
108b	Monte Irvin (W/facsimile autograph.)	1.50
109	Tommy John	.25

110	Rollie Fingers	.75
111	Johnny Podres	.25
112	Jeff Reardon	.25
113	Buddy Bell	.25
114	Dwight Gooden	.50
115	Garry Templeton	.25
116	Johnny Bench	2.00
117	Joe Rudi	.25
118	Ron Guidry	.50
119	Vince Coleman	.25
120	Al Kaline	2.00
121	Carl Yastrzemski	1.50
122	Hank Bauer	.25
123	Mark Fidrych	.25
124	Paul O'Neill	.50
125	Ron Cey	.25
126	Willie McGee	.25
127	Harmon Killebrew	1.50
128	Dave Concepcion	.25
129	Harold Baines	.25
130	Lou Brock	.50
131	Lee Smith	.25
132	Willie McCovey	.75
133	Steve Garvey	.25
134	Kent Tekulve	.25
135	Tom Seaver	1.50
136	Bo Jackson	1.00
137	Walt Weiss	.25
138	Brook Jacoby	.25
139	Dennis Eckersley	.50
140	Duke Snider	1.00
141	Lenny Dykstra	.25
142	Greg Luzinski	.25
143	Jim Bunning	.25
144	Jose Canseco	.75
145	Ron Santo	.25
146	Bert Blyleven	.25
147	Wade Boggs	.75
148	Brooks Robinson	1.00
149	Ray Knight	.25
150	Nolan Ryan	4.00

Refractors

Cards (1-150): 3-6X
Production 299 Sets

Autographs

		NM/M
Common Autograph:		8.00
SP's Production 50		
HA	Hank Aaron/SP	300.00
JA	Jim Abbott	10.00
SA	Sparky Anderson/SP	30.00
LA	Luis Aparicio	10.00
TA	Tony Armas	10.00
HBA	Harold Baines	15.00
SB	Steve Balboni	8.00
EB	Ernie Banks/SP	120.00
HB	Hank Bauer/SP	35.00
BBE	Buddy Bell	15.00
GB	George Bell	15.00
JBE	Johnny Bench/SP	100.00
YB	Yogi Berra/SP	100.00
BBI	Buddy Biancalana	8.00
PB	Paul Blair	10.00
VB	Vida Blue	15.00
BB	Bert Blyleven	15.00
WB	Wade Boggs/SP	75.00
GBR	George Brett/SP	250.00
LB	Lou Brock/SP	60.00
BBU	Bill Buckner	10.00
JB	Jim Bunning/SP	75.00
BC	Bert Campaneris	10.00
JOS	Jose Canseco/SP	60.00
RCA	Rod Carew/SP	75.00
GC	Gary Carter/SP	40.00
JCA	Joe Carter/SP	35.00
OC	Orlando Cepeda/SP	60.00

RCE	Ron Cey	10.00
JC	Jack Clark	15.00
VC	Vince Coleman	10.00
DC	Dave Concepcion/SP	35.00
CC	Cecil Cooper	10.00
JCR	Jose Cruz	10.00
RDA	Ron Darling	10.00
DD	Darren Daulton	15.00
AD	Alvin Davis	8.00
ED	Eric Davis	15.00
ADA	Andre Dawson/SP	50.00
DDE	Doug DeCinces	15.00
RD	Rob Dibble	15.00
LDU	Leon Durham	10.00
LD	Lenny Dykstra	10.00
DEV	Dennis Eckersley/SP	60.00
DE	Darrell Evans	10.00
DEV	Dwight Evans/SP	40.00
BF	Bob Feller	40.00
MF	Mark Fidrych	10.00
RF	Rollie Fingers/SP	40.00
CF	Carlton Fisk/SP	60.00
WF	Whitey Ford/SP	100.00
GF	George Foster	10.00
BFR	Bob Friend	10.00
SG	Steve Garvey	20.00
KGI	Kirk Gibson/SP	75.00
GG	Dwight Gooden/SP	30.00
RG	Rich "Goose" Gossage/SP	30.00
BGR	Bobby Grich	10.00
KG	Ken Griffey Sr./SP	30.00
RGU	Ron Guidry	15.00
TG	Tony Gwynn/SP	100.00
EH	Ernie Harwell	40.00
KH	Keith Hernandez/SP	60.00
WHE	Willie Hernandez	10.00
TH	Tom Herr	10.00
WH	Whitey Herzog	20.00
BH	Bob Horner	8.00
MI	Monte Irvin	40.00
BJ	Bo Jackson/SP	100.00
RJ	Reggie Jackson/SP	100.00
BJA	Brook Jacoby	8.00
FJ	Fergie Jenkins	15.00
TJ	Tommy John	15.00
HJ	Howard Johnson	10.00
WJ	Wally Joyner	10.00
AK	Al Kaline/SP	75.00
HK	Harmon Killebrew/SP	80.00
RK	Ralph Kiner/SP	65.00
RKI	Ron Kittle	10.00
RY	Ray Knight	10.00
JK	Jerry Koosman	20.00
JKR	John Kruk/SP	60.00
CL	Carney Lansford	15.00
DL	Don Larsen	15.00
TL	Tom Lasorda/SP	40.00
VL	Vern Law	15.00
BL	Bill Lee	10.00
CLE	Chet Lemon	10.00
GL	Greg Luzinski	15.00
FL	Fred Lynn/SP	20.00
SL	Steve Lyons	15.00
BMA	Bill Madlock	15.00
JMA	Juan Marichal/SP	75.00
DON	Don Mattingly/SP	100.00
WM	Willie Mays/SP	150.00
BMZ	Bill Mazeroski/SP	50.00
TM	Tim McCarver/SP	40.00
WMC	Willie McCovey/SP	60.00
MCG	Willie McGee/SP	60.00
TMC	Tug McGraw	20.00
MM	Mario Mendoza	10.00
KM	Kevin Mitchell	10.00
PM	Paul Molitor/SP	60.00
JMO	John Montefusco	10.00
JM	Joe Morgan/SP	30.00
DM	Dale Murphy/SP	60.00
SM	Stan Musial/SP	120.00
GN	Graig Nettles	15.00
DN	Don Newcombe/SP	40.00
PN	Phil Niekro/SP	40.00
AO	Al Oliver	10.00
PO	Paul O'Neill/SP	75.00
MP	Mike Pagliarulo	10.00
JP	Jim Palmer/SP	60.00
DP	Dave Parker/SP	40.00
LP	Lance Parrish	10.00
TP	Terry Pendleton	15.00
JPE	Joe Pepitone	10.00
TPE	Tony Perez/SP	65.00
GP	Gaylord Perry	10.00
BP	Boog Powell	15.00
KP	Kirby Puckett/SP	65.00
JRE	Jeff Reardon	10.00
HR	Harold Reynolds/SP	40.00
JRI	Jim Rice/SP	45.00
JR	J.R. Richard	10.00
CR	Cal Ripken Jr./SP	225.00
MR	Mickey Rivers	10.00
PR	Phil Rizzuto/SP	75.00
RR	Robin Roberts	25.00
BRO	Brooks Robinson/SP	100.00
FR	Frank Robinson/SP	75.00
JRU	Joe Rudi	10.00
NR	Nolan Ryan/SP	200.00
BSA	Bret Saberhagen/SP	40.00
CS	Chris Sabo	8.00
RSA	Ron Santo	25.00
SS	Steve Sax	15.00
MS	Mike Schmidt/SP	125.00
RS	Red Schoendienst	15.00
TSE	Tom Seaver/SP	75.00
KS	Kevin Seitzer	10.00
BS	Bill "Moose" Skowron	15.00
LS	Lee Smith	10.00
OS	Ozzie Smith/SP	100.00

DSN	Duke Snider/SP	60.00
CN	Cory Snyder	15.00
WS	Warren Spahn	40.00
CSP	Chris Speier	10.00
DS	Dave Stieb	15.00
BSU	Bruce Sutter	35.00
DSU	Don Sutton/SP	40.00
KT	Kent Tekulve	10.00
GT	Garry Templeton	10.00
BT	Bobby Thomson/SP	25.00
LT	Luis Tiant/SP	40.00
AT	Alan Trammell	20.00
TW	Tim Wallach	10.00
BW	Bob Watson	10.00
EW	Earl Weaver	10.00
WW	Walt Weiss	8.00
MW	Maury Wills	10.00
WWI	Willie Wilson/SP	25.00
CY	Carl Yastrzemski/SP	150.00
SY	Steve Yeager	10.00
RYO	Robin Yount/SP	100.00

Best Seat Relics

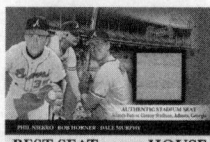

		NM/M
Common Card:		20.00
BS1	Jim Palmer, Frank Robinson, Brooks Robinson	25.00
BS2	Wally Joyner, Rod Carew, Bobby Grich	20.00
BS3	Phil Garner, Willie Stargell, Dave Parker, Kent Tekulve	15.00
BS4	Rollie Fingers, Robin Yount, Paul Molitor	25.00
BS5	Phil Niekro, Dale Murphy, Bob Horner	20.00

Relics

		NM/M
Common Player:		5.00
HBA	Harold Baines/Bat	8.00
GBR	George Brett/Jsy	25.00
JOS	Jose Canseco/Bat	8.00
RCA	Rod Carew/Bat	10.00
GC	Gary Carter/Bat	5.00
NC	Norm Cash/Jsy	25.00
VC	Vince Coleman/Bat	5.00
JCR	Jose Cruz/Bat	5.00
RDA	Ron Darling/Jsy	5.00
ADA	Andre Dawson/Bat	8.00
LD	Lenny Dykstra/Bat	5.00
DEC	Dennis Eckersley/Jsy	8.00
CF	Curt Flood/Bat	5.00
GF	George Foster/Bat	5.00
BFR	Bob Friend/Jsy	5.00
SG	Steve Garvey/Bat	5.00
KGI	Kirk Gibson/Bat	5.00
KH	Keith Hernandez/Bat	8.00
WHE	Willie Hernandez/Bat	5.00
BH	Bob Horner/Bat	5.00
BJ	Bo Jackson/Bat	20.00
WJ	Wally Joyner/Bat	5.00
GL	Greg Luzinski/Bat	5.00
FL	Fred Lynn/Bat	5.00
DON	Don Mattingly/Bat	30.00
MCG	Willie McGee/Bat	5.00
TMC	Tug McGraw/Jsy	8.00
KM	Kevin Mitchell/Bat	5.00
JM	Joe Morgan/Bat	10.00
DM	Dale Murphy/Bat	10.00
PO	Paul O'Neill/Bat	8.00
DP	Dave Parker/Bat	5.00
LP	Lance Parrish/Bat	5.00
KP	Kirby Puckett/Bat	20.00
HR	Harold Reynolds/Bat	5.00
JRI	Jim Rice/Bat	8.00
BR	Bobby Richardson/Bat	10.00
JRU	Joe Rudi/Bat	5.00
CS	Chris Sabo/Bat	5.00
MS	Mike Schmidt/Bat	20.00
WS	Willie Stargell/Bat	5.00
AT	Alan Trammell/Bat	10.00
MW	Maury Wills/Bat	5.00

Team Topps Leg. Auto.

		NM/M
Common Autograph:		10.00
	Paul Blair	10.00
	Lou Brock	30.00
	Jim Bunning	15.00
	Gary Carter	30.00
	Rich "Goose" Gossage	15.00
	Al Kaline	50.00
	Willie Mays	120.00
	Joe Morgan	30.00
	Stan Musial	75.00
	Graig Nettles	15.00
	Johnny Sain	15.00
	Mike Schmidt	75.00

2003 Topps Bazooka

		NM/M
Complete Set (280):		40.00
Common Player:		.15
Pack (8):		2.00
Box (24):		40.00
Card #7 has 31 variations.		

1	Luis Castillo	.15
2	Randy Winn	.15
3	Orlando Hudson	.15
4	Fernando Vina	.15
5	Pat Burrell	.15
6	Brad Wilkerson	.15
7	Bazooka Joe	.25
8	Javy Lopez	.25
9	Juan Pierre	.15
10	Hideo Nomo	.40
11	Barry Larkin	.25
12	Alfonso Soriano	.75
13	Rodrigo Lopez	.15
14	Mark Ellis	.15
15	Tim Salmon	.25
16	Garret Anderson	.25
17	Aaron Boone	.15
18	Jason Kendall	.15
19	Hee Seop Choi	.15
20	Jorge Posada	.40
21	Sammy Sosa	1.50
22	Mark Prior	.75
23	Mark Teixeira	.40
24	Manny Ramirez	.50
25	Jim Thome	.75
26	A.J. Pierzynski	.15
27	Scott Rolen	.75
28	Austin Kearns	.15
29	Bret Boone	.15
30	Ken Griffey Jr.	1.00
31	Greg Maddux	1.00
32	Derek Lowe	.15
33	David Wells	.15
34	A.J. Burnett	.15
35	Randall Simon	.15
36	Nick Johnson	.15
37	Junior Spivey	.15
38	Eric Gagne	.40
39	Darin Erstad	.25
40	Marty Cordova	.15
41	Brett Myers	.15
42	Mo Vaughn	.25
43	Randy Wolf	.15
44	Vicente Padilla	.15
45	Elmer Dessens	.15
46	Jason Simontacchi	.15
47	John Mabry	.15
48	Torii Hunter	.25
49	Lyle Overbay	.15
50	Kirk Saarloos	.15
51	Bernie Williams	.50
52	Wade Miller	.15
53	Bobby Abreu	.25
54	Wilson Betemit	.15
55	Edwin Almonte	.15
56	Jarrod Washburn	.15
57	Drew Henson	.25
58	Tony Batista	.15
59	Juan Rivera	.15
60	Larry Walker	.25
61	Brandon Phillips	.15
62	Franklyn German	.15
63	Victor Martinez	.25
64	Moises Alou	.25
65	Nomar Garciaparra	1.00
66	Willie Harris	.15
67	Sean Casey	.25
68	Omar Vizquel	.25
69	Robert Fick	.15
70	Curt Schilling	.50
71	Adam Kennedy	.15
72	Scott Hairston	.15
73	Jimmy Journell	.15
74	Rafael Furcal	.25
75	Barry Zito	.25
76	Ed Rogers	.15
77	Cliff Floyd	.15
78	Matt Clement	.15
79	Mike Lowell	.25
80	Randy Johnson	.75
81	Craig Biggio	.25
82	Carlos Beltran	.25
83	Paul LoDuca	.15
84	Jose Vidro	.15
85	Gary Sheffield	.40
86	Jacque Jones	.15
87	Corey Hart	.15
88	Roberto Alomar	.40
89	Robin Ventura	.25
90	Pedro Martinez	.75
91	Scott Hatteberg	.15
92	Marlon Byrd	.15
93	Pokey Reese	.15
94	Sean Burroughs	.15
95	Magglio Ordonez	.25
96	Tsuyoshi Shinjo	.15
97	John Olerud	.15
98	Edgar Renteria	.25

99	Ben Grieve	.15
100	Mariano Rivera	.25
101	Ivan Rodriguez	.50
102	Josh Phelps	.15
103	Nobuaki Yoshida RC	.40
104	Roy Halladay	.15
105	Mark Buehrle	.15
106	Chan Ho Park	.15
107	Joe Kennedy	.15
108	Shin-Soo Choo	.15
109	Ryan Jensen	.15
110	Todd Helton	.50
111	Chris Duncan RC	1.00
112	Taggert Bozied	.15
113	Sean Burnett	.15
114	Mike Lieberthal	.15
115	Josh Beckett	.40
116	Andy Pettitte	.40
117	Jose Reyes	.25
118	Bartolo Colon	.15
119	Justin Morneau	.25
120	Lance Berkman	.25
121	Mike Wodnicki RC	.40
122	Craig Brazell RC	.50
123	Troy Glaus	.40
124	John Smoltz	.15
125	Mike Sweeney	.15
126	Jay Gibbons	.15
127	Kerry Wood	.75
128	Ellis Burks	.15
129	Carlos Pena	.15
130	Shawn Green	.25
131	Jason Stokes	.15
132	Raul Ibanez	.15
133	Francisco Rodriguez	.25
134	Adrian Beltre	.25
135	Richie Sexson	.40
136	Paul Byrd	.15
137	Bobby Kielty	.15
138	Dewon Brazelton	.15
139	Jeremy Griffiths	.15
140	Vladimir Guerrero	.75
141	Jake Peavy	.15
142	Bryan Bullington RC	1.00
143	Orlando Cabrera	.15
144	Scott Erickson	.15
145	Doug Mientkiewicz	.15
146	Derrek Lee	.25
147	Daryl Clark RC	.40
148	Trevor Hoffman	.15
149	Gabe Gross	.15
150	Roger Clemens	1.50
151	Khalil Greene	1.00
152	Cory Doyne RC	.40
153	Brandon Roberson RC	.40
154	Josh Fogg	.15
155	Eric Chavez	.25
156	Kris Benson	.15
157	Billy Koch	.15
158	Jermaine Dye	.25
159	Kip Bouknight RC	.40
160	Brian Giles	.25
161	Justin Huber	.15
162	Mike Restovich	.15
163	Brandon Webb RC	1.00
164	Odalis Perez	.15
165	Phil Nevin	.15
166	Dontrelle Willis	.15
167	Aaron Heilman	.15
168	Dustin Moseley RC	.40
169	Rylan Reed RC	.40
170	Miguel Tejada	.40
171	Nic Jackson	.15
172	Anthony Webster RC	.40
173	Jorge Julio	.15
174	Kevin Millwood	.25
175	Brian Jordan	.15
176	Terry Tiffee RC	.40
177	Dallas McPherson	.15
178	Freddy Garcia	.15
179	Jamie Moyer	.15
180	Rafael Palmeiro	.50
181	Mike O'Keefe RC	.40
182	Kevin Youkilis RC	1.00
183	Kip Wells	.15
184	Joe Mauer	.25
185	Edgar Martinez	.25
186	Jaime Bubela RC	.40
187	Jose Hernandez	.15
188	Josh Hamilton	.25
189	Matt Diaz RC	.40
190	Chipper Jones	.75
191	Kevin Mench	.15
192	Joey Gomes	.15
193	Shannon Stewart	.15
194	Damian Miller	.15
195	Mike Piazza	1.00
196	Damian Moss	.15
197	Mike Fontenot	.15
198	Shea Hillenbrand	.15
199	Evel Bastida-Martinez RC	.40
200	Jason Giambi	.40
201	Aron Weston RC	.40
202	Frank Thomas	.50
203	Carlos Lee	.15
204	C.C. Sabathia	.15
205	Jim Edmonds	.40
206	Jemel Spearman RC	.40
207	Jason Jennings	.15
208	Jeremy Bonderman	1.00
209	Preston Wilson	.15
210	Eric Hinske	.15
211	Will Smith	.15
212	Matthew Hagen RC	.40
213	Joe Randa	.15
214	James Loney	.25
215	Carlos Delgado	.25
216	Kris Kroski RC	.50

#	Player	Price
217	Cristian Guzman	.15
218	Tomokazu Ohka	.15
219	Al Leiter	.15
220	Adam Dunn	.50
221	Raul Mondesi	.25
222	Donald Hood RC	.40
223	Mark Mulder	.25
224	Mike Williams	.15
225	Ryan Klesko	.25
226	Rich Aurilia	.15
227	Chris Snelling	.15
228	Gary Schneidmiller RC	.40
229	Ichiro Suzuki	1.50
230	Luis Gonzalez	.25
231	Rocco Baldelli	.15
232	Callix Crabbe RC	.40
233	Adrian Gonzalez	.15
234	Corey Koskie	.15
235	Tom Glavine	.40
236	Kevin Beavers RC	.15
237	Frank Catalanotto	.15
238	Kevin Cash	.15
239	Nick Trzesniak RC	.50
240	Paul Konerko	.25
241	Jose Cruz Jr.	.15
242	Hank Blalock	.50
243	J.D. Drew	.25
244	Kazuhiro Sasaki	.15
245	Jeff Bagwell	.50
246	Jason Schmidt	.25
247	Xavier Nady	.15
248	Aramis Ramirez	.40
249	Jimmy Rollins	.20
250	Alex Rodriguez	1.50
251	Terrence Long	.15
252	Derek Jeter	2.00
253	Edgardo Alfonzo	.15
254	Toby Hall	.15
255	Kazuhisa Ishii	.15
256	Brad Nelson	.15
257	Kevin Brown	.15
258	Roy Oswalt	.25
259	Mike Cameron	.15
260	Juan Gonzalez	.40
261	Dmitri Young	.15
262	Jose Jimenez	.15
263	Wily Mo Pena	.25
264	Joe Borchard	.15
265	Mike Mussina	.50
266	Fred McGriff	.25
267	Johnny Damon	.25
268	Joel Pineiro	.15
269	Andruw Jones	.25
270	Tim Hudson	.25
271	Chad Tracy	.15
272	Brad Fullmer	.15
273	Boof Bonser	.15
274	Clint Nageotte	.15
275	Jeff Kent	.25
276	Tino Martinez	.15
277	Matt Morris	.15
278	Jonny Gomes	.15
279	Benito Santiago	.15
280	Albert Pujols	1.50

Mini

DMITRI YOUNG 1B

Stars:	1-30X
Inserted 1:1	

Silver

ROBERTO ALOMAR 2B

Stars:	1-30X
Inserted 1:1	

Blasts

		NM/M
Common Player:		4.00
Refractors:		3-4X
Production 25 Sets		
RA	Roberto Alomar	6.00
LB	Lance Berkman	6.00
WB	Wilson Betemit	4.00
JD	Johnny Damon	6.00
CD	Carlos Delgado	5.00
JDD	J.D. Drew	8.00
DE	Darin Erstad	4.00
AG	Andres Galarraga	4.00
LG	Luis Gonzalez	4.00
SG	Shawn Green	6.00
TG	Tony Gwynn	8.00
RH	Rickey Henderson	10.00
DH	Drew Henson	4.00
NJ	Nick Johnson	4.00
CJ	Chipper Jones	10.00
RK	Ryan Klesko	4.00
PL	Paul LoDuca	4.00
EM	Edgar Martinez	8.00
TM	Tino Martinez	8.00
RM	Raul Mondesi	4.00
RP	Rafael Palmeiro	6.00
MP	Mike Piazza	12.00
JP	Jorge Posada	8.00
ANR	Aramis Ramirez	4.00
MR	Manny Ramirez	8.00
AR	Alex Rodriguez	12.00
IR	Ivan Rodriguez	8.00
GS	Gary Sheffield	6.00
TS	Tsuyoshi Shinjo	4.00
AS	Alfonso Soriano	10.00
MS	Mike Sweeney	4.00
RV	Robin Ventura	4.00
BW	Bernie Williams	10.00

Comics

SAMMY SOSA 3 YRS WITH 60-PLUS HRS

		NM/M
Complete Set (12):		4.00
Common Player:		.30
Inserted 1:4		
	Roger Clemens	.40
	Nomar Garciaparra	.60
	Jason Giambi	.40
	Derek Jeter	.75
	Randy Johnson	.30
	Chipper Jones	.40
	Mike Piazza	.50
	Albert Pujols	.30
	Alex Rodriguez	.60
	Alfonso Soriano	.40
	Sammy Sosa	.40
	Ichiro Suzuki	.50

Piece of Americana

CURT SCHILLING

		NM/M
Common Player:		5.00
Refractors:		3-4X
Production 25 Sets		
JB	Jeff Bagwell	10.00
CB	Craig Biggio	5.00
BB	Bret Boone	5.00
DB	Dewon Brazelton	5.00
CD	Carlos Delgado	5.00
AD	Adam Dunn	10.00
JE	Jim Edmonds	6.00
RF	Rafael Furcal	5.00
NG	Nomar Garciaparra	15.00
SG	Shawn Green	5.00
CG	Cristian Guzman	5.00
TG	Tony Gwynn	10.00
THA	Toby Hall	5.00
TH	Todd Helton	5.00
AH	Aubrey Huff	5.00
AJ	Andruw Jones	5.00
CJ	Chipper Jones	10.00
JK	Jeff Kent	5.00
AL	Al Leiter	5.00
PL	Paul LoDuca	6.00
MM	Mike Mussina	6.00
MO	Magglio Ordonez	6.00
RP	Rafael Palmeiro	6.00
MP	Mike Piazza	12.00
PA	Albert Pujols	10.00
IR	Ivan Rodriguez	5.00
CS	Curt Schilling	8.00
FT	Frank Thomas	6.00
LW	Larry Walker	5.00
PW	Preston Wilson	5.00

Stand-Ups

JIM THOME PHILADELPHIA PHILLIES • FIRST BASE

		NM/M
Complete Set (25):		20.00
Common Player:		.40
Inserted 1:8		
1	Albert Pujols	2.50
2	Alfonso Soriano	1.00
3	Ichiro Suzuki	2.00
4	Sammy Sosa	2.00
5	Randy Johnson	1.00
6	Torii Hunter	.50
7	Vladimir Guerrero	1.00
8	Nomar Garciaparra	2.00
9	Alex Rodriguez	3.00
10	Troy Glaus	.50
11	Greg Maddux	1.50
12	Derek Jeter	3.00
13	Lance Berkman	.40
14	Larry Walker	.40
15	Adam Dunn	.50
16	Shawn Green	.50
17	Curt Schilling	.75
18	Todd Helton	.75
19	Pedro Martinez	1.00
20	Pat Burrell	.50
21	Miguel Tejada	.50
22	Manny Ramirez	1.00
23	Mike Piazza	1.50
24	Chipper Jones	1.00
25	Jason Giambi	1.00

4-On-1 Stickers

		NM/M
Complete Set (55):		10.00
Common Sticker:		.20
Inserted 1:4		
1	Mark Prior, Roy Oswalt, Jarrod Washburn, Barry Zito	.30
2	Troy Glaus, Shea Hillenbrand, Eric Chavez, Eric Hinske	.30
3	Orlando Hudson, Alfonso Soriano, Roberto Alomar, Jose Vidro	.40
4	Nomar Garciaparra, Derek Jeter, Miguel Tejada, Alex Rodriguez	.75
5	Jason Giambi, Jim Thome, Todd Helton, Rafael Palmeiro	.40
6	Mike Williams, Trevor Hoffman, Billy Koch, John Smoltz	.20
7	Jorge Posada, Mike Piazza, A.J. Pierzynski, Ivan Rodriguez	.50
8	Vladimir Guerrero, Jim Edmonds, Manny Ramirez, Brad Wilkerson	.40
9	Shawn Green, Sammy Sosa, Torii Hunter, Larry Walker	.40
10	Bernie Williams, Ken Griffey Jr., Ichiro Suzuki, Adam Dunn	.50
11	John Olerud, Mike Lieberthal, Terrence Long, Drew Henson	.20
12	Edgar Martinez, Bret Boone, Mo Vaughn, Robert Fisk	.20
13	Randy Johnson, Roger Clemens, Pedro Martinez, Greg Maddux	.40
14	Curt Schilling, Tim Hudson, Tom Glavine, Kerry Wood	.20
15	Paul Konerko, Mike Sweeney, Cristian Guzman, Scott Rolen	.20
16	Josh Phelps, Brandon Phillips, Hee Seop Choi, Hank Blalock	.20
17	Benito Santiago, Barry Larkin, Gary Sheffield, Carlos Delgado	.20
18	Juan Rivera, Jose Reyes, Sean Burroughs, Carlos Pena	.20
19	Tony Batista, Tim Salmon, Jeff Bagwell, Raul Ibanez	.25
20	Edgardo Alfonzo, Nic Jackson, Luis Castillo, Damian Miller	.20
21	David Wells, Ryan Klesko, Phil Nevin, Jeff Kent	.20
22	Derek Lowe, Vicente Padilla, Kevin Millwood, Joel Pineiro	.20
23	Fernando Vina, Darin Erstad, Jimmy Rollins, Doug Mientkiewicz	.20
24	Joe Mauer, Justin Huber, Jason Stokes, Chad Tracy	.20
25	Austin Kearns, Junior Spivey, Brett Myers, Victor Martinez	.25
26	Khalil Greene, Gabe Gross, Kevin Cash, James Loney	.20
27	Albert Pujols, Mark Buehrle, Chipper Jones, Lance Berkman	.40
28	Adam Kennedy, Craig Biggio, Johnny Damon, Randy Winn	.20
29	Brian Giles, J.D. Drew, Marlon Byrd, Joe Borchard	.20
30	Al Leiter, Mike Mussina, Bartolo Colon, Freddy Garcia	.20
31	Jason Kendall, Richie Sexson, Mike Lowell, Paul LoDuca	.20
32	Pat Burrell, Garret Anderson, Cliff Floyd, Andruw Jones	.25
33	Xavier Nady, Bobby Abreu, Taggert Bozied, Adrian Beltre	.20
34	Rocco Baldelli, Dontrelle Willis, Chris Snelling, Mark Teixeira	.20
35	Willie Harris, Nick Johnson, Jason Jennings, Kazuhisa Ishii	.20
36	Mark Mulder, Sean Burnett, Paul Byrd, Josh Beckett	.20
37	Corey Koskie, Aramis Ramirez, Tino Martinez, Moises Alou	.20
38	Jose Cruz Jr., Roy Halliday, Dewon Brazelton, Jonny Gomes	.20
39	Odalis Perez, Kevin Brown, Matt Clement, Randy Wolf	.20
40	Eric Gagne, Jose Jimenez, Franklyn German, Edwin Almonte	.20
41	Luis Gonzalez, Shannon Stewart, Brian Jordan, Juan Gonzalez	.25
42	Toby Hall, Joe Kennedy, Javier Lopez, Damian Moss	.20
43	Magglio Ordonez, Carlos Lee, Randall Simon, Dmitri Young	.20
44	Sean Casey, Aaron Boone, Jacque Jones, Michael Restovich	.20
45	Adrian Gonzalez, Corey Hart, Fred McGriff, Frank Thomas	.25
46	C.C. Sabathia, Omar Vizquel, Andy Pettitte, Robin Ventura	.20
47	Jason Schmidt, Ellis Burks, Joe Randa, Tsuyoshi Shinjo	.20
48	Mike Cameron, Pokey Reese, Jermaine Dye, Preston Wilson	.20
49	Chan Ho Park, Kazuhiro Sasaki, Tomokazu Ohka, Hideo Nomo	.20
50	Jason Simontacchi, Kip Wells, Matt Morris, Rodrigo Lopez	.20
51	Dallas McPherson, Josh Hamilton, Jeremy Bonderman, Aaron Heilman	.25
52	Nobuaki Yoshida, Chris Duncan, Craig Brazell, Bryan Bullington	.20
53	Daryl Clark, Brandon Webb, Dustin Moseley, Mike O'Keefe	.20
54	Kevin Youkilis, Jaime Bubela, Matt Diaz, Joey Gomes	.20
55	Kris Kroski, Donald Hood, Gary Schneidmiller, Callix Crabbe	.20

2003 Topps Chicago Cubs Reprints

BOBBY HILL • 2B

For a third year the Cubs contracted with Topps to provide a series of reprint cards for use as giveaways at special games throughout the season. Each reprint features a Wrigley Field logo on front and is sequentially numbered to 20,000 in a strip of gold foil on back. Each card was distributed in a cello wrapper with the date of the promotion and names of the sponsor(s).

		NM/M
Complete Set (6):		10.00
Common Player:		2.00
(1)	Glenn Beckert	2.00
(2)	Hee Seop Choi	2.00
(3)	Bobby Hill	2.00
(4)	Bill Madlock	2.00
(5)	Ron Santo	4.00
(6)	Steve Stone	2.00

2003 Topps Chrome

ADAM DUNN CF

		NM/M
Complete Set (440):		160.00
Common Player:		.25
Series 1 & 2 Hobby Pack (4):		2.50
Hobby Box (24):		50.00
1	Alex Rodriguez	3.00
2	Eddie Guardado	.25
3	Curt Schilling	1.00
4	Andruw Jones	.50
5	Magglio Ordonez	.75
6	Todd Helton	.75
7	Odalis Perez	.25
8	Edgardo Alfonzo	.25
9	Eric Hinske	.25
10	Danny Bautista	.25
11	Sammy Sosa	1.50
12	Roberto Alomar	.75
13	Roger Clemens	2.00
14	Austin Kearns	.50
15	Luis Gonzalez	.50
16	Mo Vaughn	.50
17	Alfonso Soriano	1.50
18	Orlando Cabrera	.25
19	Hideo Nomo	.75
20	Omar Vizquel	.25
21	Greg Maddux	2.50
22	Fred McGriff	.50
23	Frank Thomas	1.00
24	Shawn Green	.75
25	Jacque Jones	.25
26	Bernie Williams	.75
27	Corey Patterson	.75
28	Cesar Izturis	.25
29	Larry Walker	.75
30	Darren Dreifort	.25
31	Al Leiter	.25
32	Jason Marquis	.25
33	Sean Casey	.25
34	Craig Counsell	.25
35	Albert Pujols	3.00

#	Player	Price
36	Kyle Lohse	.25
37	Paul LoDuca	.25
38	Roy Oswalt	.50
39	Danny Graves	.25
40	Kevin Millwood	.25
41	Lance Berkman	.75
42	Denny Hocking	.25
43	Jose Valentin	.25
44	Josh Beckett	.75
45	Nomar Garciaparra	.75
46	Craig Biggio	.50
47	Omar Daal	.25
48	Jimmy Rollins	.50
49	Jermaine Dye	.50
50	Edgar Renteria	.50
51	Brandon Duckworth	.25
52	Luis Castillo	.25
53	Andy Ashby	.25
54	Mike Williams	.25
55	Benito Santiago	.25
56	Bret Boone	.25
57	Randy Wolf	.25
58	Ivan Rodriguez	.75
59	Shannon Stewart	.25
60	Jose Cruz Jr.	.25
61	Billy Wagner	.25
62	Alex Gonzalez	.25
63	Ichiro Suzuki	2.50
64	Joe McEwing	.25
65	Mark Mulder	.50
66	Mike Cameron	.25
67	Corey Koskie	.25
68	Marlon Anderson	.25
69	Jason Kendall	.25
70	J.T. Snow Jr.	.25
71	Edgar Martinez	.50
72	Vernon Wells	.25
73	Vladimir Guerrero	1.25
74	Adam Dunn	1.00
75	Barry Zito	.50
76	Jeff Kent	.50
77	Russ Ortiz	.25
78	Phil Nevin	.25
79	Carlos Beltran	1.00
80	Mike Lowell	.50
81	Bob Wickman	.25
82	Junior Spivey	.25
83	Melvin Mora	.25
84	Derrek Lee	.50
85	Chuck Knoblauch	.25
86	Eric Gagne	.75
87	Orlando Hernandez	.50
88	Robert Person	.25
89	Elmer Dessens	.25
90	Wade Miller	.25
91	Adrian Beltre	.50
92	Kazuhiro Sasaki	.25
93	Timoniel Perez	.25
94	Jose Vidro	.25
95	Geronimo Gil	.25
96	Trot Nixon	.25
97	Denny Neagle	.25
98	Roberto Hernandez	.25
99	David Ortiz	1.50
100	Robb Nen	.25
101	Sidney Ponson	.25
102	Kevin Appier	.25
103	Javier Lopez	.50
104	Jeff Conine	.25
105	Mark Buehrle	.25
106	Jason Simontacchi	.25
107	Jose Jimenez	.25
108	Brian Jordan	.25
109	Brad Wilkerson	.25
110	Scott Hatteberg	.25
111	Matt Morris	.50
112	Miguel Tejada	.50
113	Rafael Furcal	.50
114	Steve Cox	.25
115	Roy Halladay	.25
116	David Eckstein	.25
117	Tomokazu Ohka	.25
118	Jack Wilson	.25
119	Randall Simon	.25
120	Jamie Moyer	.25
121	Andy Benes	.25
122	Tino Martinez	.25
123	Esteban Yan	.25
124	Jason Isringhausen	.25
125	Chris Carpenter	.25
126	Aaron Rowand	.25
127	Brandon Inge	.25
128	Jose Vizcaino	.25
129	Jose Mesa	.25
130	Troy Percival	.25
131	Jon Lieber	.25
132	Brian Giles	.50
133	Aaron Boone	.25
134	Bobby Higginson	.25
135	Luis Rivas	.25
136	Troy Glaus	.75
137	Jim Thome	1.00
138	Ramon Martinez	.25
139	Jay Gibbons	.25
140	Mike Lieberthal	.25
141	Juan Uribe	.25
142	Gary Sheffield	.75
143	Ramon Santiago	.25
144	Ben Sheets	.50
145	Tony Armas Jr.	.25
146	Kazuhisa Ishii	.25
147	Erubiel Durazo	.25
148	Jerry Hairston Jr.	.25
149	Byung-Hyun Kim	.25
150	Marcus Giles	.25
151	Johnny Damon	.75
152	Terrence Long	.25
153	Juan Pierre	.25

#	Player	Price
154	Aramis Ramirez	.75
155	Brent Abernathy	.25
156	Ismael Valdes	.25
157	Mike Mussina	1.00
158	Ramon Hernandez	.25
159	Adam Kennedy	.25
160	Tony Womack	.25
161	Tony Batista	.25
162	Kip Wells	.25
163	Jeromy Burnitz	.25
164	Todd Hundley	.25
165	Tim Wakefield	.25
166	Derek Lowe	.25
167	Jorge Posada	.75
168	Ramon Ortiz	.25
169	Brent Butler	.25
170	Shane Halter	.25
171	Matt Lawton	.25
172	Alex Sanchez	.25
173	Eric Milton	.25
174	Vicente Padilla	.25
175	Steve Karsay	.25
176	Mark Prior	.50
177	Kerry Wood	.50
178	Jason LaRue	.25
179	Danys Baez	.25
180	Nick Neugebauer	.25
181	Andres Galarraga	.25
182	Jason Giambi	.75
183	Aubrey Huff	.25
184	Juan Gonzalez	.50
185	Ugueth Urbina	.25
186	Rickey Henderson	.75
187	Brad Fullmer	.25
188	Todd Zeile	.25
189	Jason Jennings	.25
190	Vladimir Nunez	.25
191	David Justice	.50
192	Brian Lawrence	.25
193	Pat Burrell	.50
194	Pokey Reese	.25
195	Robert Fick	.25
196	C.C. Sabathia	.25
197	Fernando Vina	.25
198	Sean Burroughs	.25
199	Ellis Burks	.25
200	Joe Randa	.25
201	Chris Duncan RC	3.00
202	Franklin Gutierrez RC	1.00
203	Adam LaRoche RC	1.00
204	Manuel Ramirez RC	1.00
205	Il Kim RC	1.00
206	Daryl Clark RC	1.00
207	Sean Pierce	.25
208	Andy Marte RC	1.00
209	Bernie Castro RC	1.00
210	Jason Perry RC	1.00
211	Jaime Bubela RC	1.00
212	Alexis Rios	1.00
213	Brendan Harris RC	1.00
214	Ramon A. Martinez RC	1.00
215	Terry Tiffee RC	1.00
216	Kevin Youkilis RC	4.00
217	Derell McCall RC	1.00
218	Scott Tyler	1.00
219	Craig Brazell RC	1.00
220	Walter Young	1.00
221	Francisco Rodriguez	.40
222	Chipper Jones	2.00
223	Chris Singleton	.25
224	Cliff Floyd	.25
225	Bobby Hill	.25
226	Antonio Osuna	.25
227	Barry Larkin	.50
228	Dean Palmer	.25
229	Eric Owens	.25
230	Randy Johnson	1.00
231	Jeff Suppan	.25
232	Eric Karros	.25
233	Johan Santana	.25
234	Javier Vazquez	.25
235	John Thomson	.25
236	Nick Johnson	.25
237	Mark Ellis	.25
238	Doug Glanville	.25
239	Ken Griffey Jr.	2.50
240	Bubba Trammell	.25
241	Livan Hernandez	.25
242	Desi Relaford	.25
243	Eli Marrero	.25
244	Jared Sandberg	.25
245	Barry Bonds	3.00
246	Aaron Sele	.25
247	Derek Jeter	3.00
248	Eric Byrnes	.25
249	Rich Aurilia	.25
250	Joel Pineiro	.25
251	Chuck Finley	.25
252	Bengie Molina	.25
253	Steve Finley	.25
254	Marty Cordova	.25
255	Shea Hillenbrand	.25
256	Milton Bradley	.25
257	Carlos Pena	.25
258	Brad Ausmus	.25
259	Carlos Delgado	.75
260	Kevin Mench	.25
261	Joe Kennedy	.25
262	Mark McLemore	.25
263	Bill Mueller	.25
264	Ricky Ledee	.25
265	Ted Lilly	.25
266	Sterling Hitchcock	.25
267	Scott Strickland	.25
268	Damion Easley	.25
269	Torii Hunter	.50
270	Brad Radke	.25
271	Geoff Jenkins	.25

#	Player	Price
272	Paul Byrd	.25
273	Morgan Ensberg	.25
274	Mike Hampton	.25
275	Flash Gordon	.25
276	John Burkett	.25
277	Rodrigo Lopez	.25
278	Tim Spooneybarger	.25
279	Quinton McCracken	.25
280	Tim Salmon	.50
281	Jarrod Washburn	.25
282	Pedro J. Martinez	1.00
283	Julio Lugo	.25
284	Armando Benitez	.25
285	Raul Mondesi	.50
286	Robin Ventura	.25
287	Bobby Abreu	.50
288	Josh Fogg	.25
289	Ryan Klesko	.50
290	Tsuyoshi Shinjo	.25
291	Jim Edmonds	.75
292	Chan Ho Park	.25
293	John Mabry	.25
294	Woody Williams	.25
295	Scott Schoeneweis	.25
296	Brian Anderson	.25
297	Brett Tomko	.25
298	Scott Erickson	.25
299	Tony Clark	.25
300	Danny Wright	.25
301	Jason Schmidt	.75
302	Scott Williamson	.25
303	Einar Diaz	.25
304	Jay Payton	.25
305	Juan Acevedo	.25
306	Ben Grieve	.25
307	Raul Ibanez	.25
308	Richie Sexson	.75
309	Rick Reed	.25
310	Pedro Astacio	.25
311	Bud Smith	.25
312	Tomas Perez	.25
313	Adam Eaton	.25
314	Rafael Palmeiro	.75
315	Jason Tyner	.25
316	Scott Rolen	1.00
317	Randy Winn	.25
318	Ryan Jensen	.25
319	Trevor Hoffman	.25
320	Craig Wilson	.25
321	Jeremy Giambi	.25
322	Andy Pettitte	.50
323	John Franco	.25
324	Felipe Lopez	.25
325	Mike Piazza	1.50
326	Cristian Guzman	.25
327	Jose Hernandez	.25
328	Octavio Dotel	.25
329	Brad Penny	.25
330	Charles Johnson	.25
331	Ryan Dempster	.25
332	Joe Crede	.25
333	Chad Hermansen	.25
334	Gary Matthews Jr.	.25
335	Frank Catalanotto	.25
336	Darin Erstad	.50
337	Matt Williams	.25
338	B.J. Surhoff	.25
339	Kerry Ligtenberg	.25
340	Mike Bordick	.25
341	Joe Girardi	.25
342	D'Angelo Jimenez	.25
343	Paul Konerko	.25
344	Joe Mays	.25
345	Marquis Grissom	.25
346	Neifi Perez	.25
347	Preston Wilson	.25
348	Jeff Weaver	.25
349	Eric Chavez	.50
350	Placido Polanco	.25
351	Ray Lankford	.25
352	James Baldwin	.25
353	Toby Hall	.25
354	Benji Gil	.25
355	Damian Moss	.25
356	Jorge Julio	.25
357	Matt Clement	.25
358	Lee Stevens	.25
359	Dave Roberts	.25
360	J.C. Romero	.25
361	Bartolo Colon	.25
362	Roger Cedeno	.25
363	Mariano Rivera	.50
364	Billy Koch	.25
365	Manny Ramirez	1.50
366	Travis Lee	.25
367	Oliver Perez	.25
368	Rafael Soriano	.25
369	Damian Miller	.25
370	John Smoltz	.50
371	Willis Roberts	.25
372	Tim Hudson	.50
373	Moises Alou	.50
374	Corky Miller	.25
375	Ben Broussard	.25
376	Gabe Kapler	.25
377	Chris Woodward	.25
378	Todd Hollandsworth	.25
379	So Taguchi	.25
380	John Olerud	.50
381	Reggie Sanders	.25
382	Jake Peavy	.25
383	Kris Benson	.25
384	Ray Durham	.25
385	David Wells	.25
386	Tom Glavine	.75
387	Antonio Alfonseca	.25
388	Keith Foulke	.25
389	Shawn Estes	.25

#	Player	Price
390	Mark Grace	.50
391	Dmitri Young	.25
392	A.J. Burnett	.25
393	Richard Hidalgo	.25
394	Mike Sweeney	.25
395	Doug Mientkiewicz	.25
396	Cory Lidle	.25
397	Jeff Bagwell	1.00
398	Steve Sparks	.25
399	Sandy Alomar Jr.	.25
400	John Lackey	.25
401	Rick Helling	.25
402	Carlos Lee	.25
403	Garret Anderson	.50
404	Vinny Castilla	.25
405	David Bell	.25
406	Freddy Garcia	.25
407	Scott Spiezio	.25
408	Russell Branyan	.25
409	Jose Contreras RC	3.00
410	Kevin Brown	.50
411	Tyler Houston	.25
412	A.J. Pierzynski	.25
413	Peter Bergeron	.25
414	Brett Myers	.25
415	Kenny Lofton	.25
416	Ben Davis	.25
417	J.D. Drew	.50
418	Ricky Gutierrez	.25
419	Mark Redman	.25
420	Juan Encarnacion	.25
421	Bryan Bullington RC	1.00
422	Jeremy Guthrie	.50
423	Joey Gomes	.50
424	Evel Bastida-Martinez RC	1.00
425	Brian Wright RC	1.00
426	B.J. Upton	.25
427	Jeff Francis	.25
428	Jeremy Hermida	.25
429	Khalil Greene	1.00
430	Darrell Rasner	.25
431	Brandon Phillips, Victor Martinez	.75
432	Hee Seop Choi, Nic Jackson	.75
433	Dontrelle Willis, Jason Stokes	.75
434	Chad Tracy, Lyle Overbay	.25
435	Joe Borchard, Corwin Malone	.25
436	Joe Mauer, Justin Morneau	1.00
437	Drew Henson, Brandon Claussen	.25
438	Chase Utley, Gavin Floyd	.50
439	Taggert Bozied, Xavier Nady	.25
440	Aaron Heilman, Jose Reyes	1.50

Refractors

Stars: 1-2X
Production 699 Sets
Gold Refractors: 1.5-3X
Production 449 Sets
Black Refractors: 3-5X
Production 199 Sets

Uncirculated X-Fractors

Stars: 5-10X
Inserted 1:Hobby Box
Production 50 Sets

Blue Backs Relics

		NM/M
Common Player:		6.00
Bat Relics Inserted 1:236		
RA	Roberto Alomar/Bat	10.00

JBA	Jeff Bagwell/Jsy	10.00
JB	Josh Beckett/Jsy	10.00
LB	Lance Berkman/Bat	8.00
EC	Eric Chavez/Jsy	6.00
AD	Adam Dunn/Jsy	15.00
NG	Nomar Garciaparra/Jsy	15.00
SG	Shawn Green/Jsy	6.00
NJ	Nick Johnson/Bat	8.00
PK	Paul Konerko/Jsy	8.00
MO	Magglio Ordonez/Jsy	8.00
MP	Mike Piazza/Jsy	15.00
AP	Albert Pujols/Jsy	15.00
AR	Alex Rodriguez/Bat	15.00
JR	Jimmy Rollins/Jsy	6.00
TS	Tsuyoshi Shinjo/Bat	8.00
AS	Alfonso Soriano/Jsy	10.00
FT	Frank Thomas/Jsy	8.00
BW	Bernie Williams/Bat	10.00
KW	Kerry Wood/Jsy	8.00

Record Breakers Relics

		NM/M
Common Player:		5.00
JB	Jeff Bagwell	8.00
BB	Barry Bonds	20.00
BB2	Barry Bonds	20.00
BB3	Barry Bonds	20.00
JC	Jose Canseco	10.00
RC	Rod Carew	8.00
RC2	Rod Carew	8.00
DLE	Dennis Eckersley	8.00
DE	Darin Erstad	5.00
LG	Luis Gonzalez	5.00
RH	Rickey Henderson	15.00
RJ	Randy Johnson	8.00
DM	Don Mattingly	30.00
PM	Paul Molitor	15.00
MR	Manny Ramirez	15.00
HR	Harold Reynolds	5.00
AR	Alex Rodriguez	15.00
TS	Tom Seaver	20.00
JS	John Smoltz	8.00
SS	Sammy Sosa	15.00

Record Breakers Relics Series 2

		NM/M
Common Player:		5.00
JB	Jeff Bagwell	8.00
BB	Barry Bonds	20.00
BB2	Barry Bonds	20.00
BB3	Barry Bonds	20.00
JC	Jose Canseco	10.00
RC	Rod Carew	8.00
RC2	Rod Carew	8.00
DLE	Dennis Eckersley	8.00
DE	Darin Erstad	5.00
LG	Luis Gonzalez	5.00
RH	Rickey Henderson	15.00
RJ	Randy Johnson	8.00
DM	Don Mattingly	30.00
PM	Paul Molitor	15.00
MR	Manny Ramirez	15.00
HR	Harold Reynolds	5.00
AR	Alex Rodriguez	15.00
TS	Tom Seaver	20.00
JS	John Smoltz	8.00
SS	Sammy Sosa	15.00

Red Backs Relics

		NM/M
Common Player:		5.00
Inserted 1:49		
RA	Roberto Alomar	8.00
GA	Garret Anderson	8.00
JB	Jeff Bagwell	8.00
PB	Pat Burrell	5.00
AD	Adam Dunn	8.00

NG	Nomar Garciaparra	12.00
TH	Todd Helton	8.00
TKH	Torii Hunter	8.00
RJ	Randy Johnson	8.00
AJ	Andruw Jones	8.00
CJ	Chipper Jones	10.00
PM	Pedro J. Martinez	10.00
MP	Mike Piazza	10.00
AP	Albert Pujols	15.00
MR	Manny Ramirez	10.00
AR	Alex Rodriguez	10.00
SR	Scott Rolen	8.00
CS	Curt Schilling	8.00
AS	Alfonso Soriano	10.00
MS	Mike Sweeney	5.00

2003 Topps eTopps

Topps continued its on-line card program with a third annual eTopps edition in 2003. Initial Player Offerings were again made for only one week with allocations having to made for some cards in high demand. The number of each card actually sold in shown parenthetically. After the IPO, cards could be bought and sold within portfolios, or physically delivered (for a fee) for more traditional venues. The 2-1/2" x 3-1/2" cards are printed on metallic foil with vertical portrait and action photos on front. Horizontal backs have another portrait photo, a 2002 recap and 2003 "prospectus," and a few biographical bits and stats. The listings here include the initial offering price and the number of cards sold during the open ordering period. Values shown are for cards in a virtual portfolio, rather than "in hand." Taking physical possession of a card from an eTopps portfolio costs about $6 apiece.

		NM/M
Complete Set (122):		275.00
Common Player:		1.50
1	Troy Glaus ($6.50 / 1,454)	1.50
2	Manny Ramirez ($6.50 / 1,970)	1.50
3	Magglio Ordonez ($6.50 / 1,007)	3.00
4	Jim Thome ($6.50 / 3,393)	1.50
5	Torii Hunter ($6.50 / 2,027)	1.50
6	Jason Giambi ($9.50 / 2,065)	1.50
7	Tim Hudson ($6.50 / 1,690)	1.50
8	Ichiro ($6.50 / 3,465)	2.50
9	Aubrey Huff ($6.50 / 3,234)	1.50
10	Alex Rodriguez ($9.50 / 2,847)	4.00
11	Francisco Rodriguez ($6.50 / 3,627)	1.50
12	Joe Borchard ($4 / 3,000)	1.50
13	Mark Teixeira ($9.50 / 5,000)	5.00
14	Marlon Byrd ($6.50 / 1,822)	1.50
15	Carlos Delgado ($6.50 / 2,500)	1.50
16	Tom Glavine ($6.50 / 2,407)	1.50
17	Curt Schilling ($6.50 / 1,333)	1.50
18	Mark Prior ($9.50 / 4,000)	1.50
19	Ken Griffey Jr. ($6.50 / 1,238)	4.00
20	Todd Helton ($6.50 / 2,315)	1.50
21	Jeff Bagwell ($6.50 / 1,678)	1.75
22	Shawn Green ($6.50 / 1,162)	1.50
23	Vladimir Guerrero ($9.50 / 2,523)	1.75
24	Roberto Alomar ($6.50 / 1,394)	1.50
25	Brian Giles ($6.50 / 1,500)	2.00
26	Barry Bonds ($9.50 / 4,000)	9.00
27	Albert Pujols ($9.50 / 3,000)	5.00
28	Nomar Garciaparra ($9.50 / 2,177)	1.50
29	Alfonso Soriano ($9.50 / 3,500)	1.50
30	Barry Zito ($6.50 / 2,500)	2.00
31	Edgar Martinez ($6.50 / 2,732)	3.00
32	Ivan Rodriguez ($6.50 / 1,436)	1.50
33	Greg Maddux ($6.50 / 2,004)	2.00
34	Sammy Sosa ($9.50 / 1,425)	2.00
35	Austin Kearns ($6.50 / 3,000)	1.50
36	Craig Biggio ($6.50 / 1,317)	1.75
37	Mike Piazza ($6.50 / 1,355)	2.25
38	Andruw Jones ($6.50 / 1,589)	2.75
39	Jeff Kent ($6.50 / 1,685)	1.50
40	Roy Oswalt ($6.50 / 2,108)	2.75
41	Miguel Tejada ($6.50 / 2,630)	1.75
42	Derek Jeter ($9.50 / 3,054)	3.75
43	Pedro Martinez ($9.50 / 1,754)	1.50
44	Jarrod Washburn ($6.50 / 1,196)	2.00
45	Randy Johnson ($9.50 / 1,117)	5.25
46	Bernie Williams ($6.50 / 1,750)	1.50
47	Chipper Jones ($6.50 / 1,443)	1.75
48	Gary Sheffield ($6.50 / 1,500)	1.75
49	Larry Walker ($6.50 / 1,001)	3.50
50	Lance Berkman ($6.50 / 1,107)	2.50
51	Garret Anderson ($6.50 / 2,647)	1.50
52	Jason Schmidt ($6.50 / 1,840)	3.25
53	Rodrigo Lopez ($4 / 1,500)	2.50
54	Oliver Perez ($4 / 1,996)	3.00
55	Derek Lowe ($6.50 / 1,434)	1.50
56	Vicente Padilla ($6.50 / 995)	3.50
57	Paul Konerko ($6.50 / 1,151)	3.00
58	Bartolo Colon ($6.50 / 2,028)	1.50
59	Omar Vizquel ($4.00 / 3,413)	2.00
60	Adam Dunn ($6.50 / 1,812)	1.50
61	Carlos Pena ($4 / 1,402)	1.50
62	Richie Sexson ($6.50 / 1,380)	2.25
63	Paul Byrd ($4 / 2,000)	1.50
64	Eric Gagne ($6.50 / 2,929)	1.50
65	Brad Radke ($4 / 827)	4.50
66	A.J. Burnett ($6.50 / 1,009)	11.50
67	Brandon Phillips ($4 / 4,000)	1.50
68	Mike Hampton ($6.50 / 763)	9.00
69	Tim Salmon ($6.50 / 1,548)	1.50
70	Roger Clemens ($9.50 / 3,000)	2.75
71	Jake Peavy ($4 / 2,500)	3.75
72	Pat Burrell ($6.50 / 1,168)	2.75
73	Ben Sheets ($4 / 1,500)	8.00
74	Fred McGriff ($6.50 / 1,323)	1.75
75	John Smoltz ($6.50 / 3,161)	5.00
76	Josh Phelps ($6.50 / 2,500)	1.50
77	John Olerud ($6.50 / 1,620)	3.00
78	Eric Chavez ($4 / 2,054)	1.50
79	Jeff Weaver ($4 / 1,877)	1.50
80	Scott Rolen ($6.50 / 2,000)	2.00
81	Carl Crawford ($6.50 / 1,518)	3.00
82	Rafael Palmeiro ($6.50 / 1,500)	1.50
83	Roy Halladay ($6.50 / 2,500)	2.50
84	Josh Beckett ($6.50 / 1,130)	4.50
85	Jorge Posada ($6.50 / 2,171)	1.50
86	Mark Mulder ($6.50 / 2,000)	1.50
87	Eric Milton ($4 / 1,758)	1.50
88	Angel Berroa ($6.50 / 1,614)	1.50
89	Jason Lane ($4 / 1,952)	1.50

90	Kerry Wood	
	($6.50 / 2,000)	1.50
91	Brad Wilkerson	
	($4 / 2,944)	1.50
92	Orlando Hudson	
	($4 / 2,500)	2.50
93	Mike Mussina	
	($6.50 / 2,000)	1.50
94	Hee Seop Choi	
	($6.50 / 3,000)	1.50
95	Chris Snelling	
	($6.50 / 2,879)	1.50
96	Tomo Ohka ($4 / 1,975)	1.50
97	Andy Pettitte ($4 / 2,367)	1.50
98	Drew Henson	
	($4 / 3,000)	1.50
99	Chin-Feng Chen	
	($4 / 2,500)	1.50
100	Jason Jennings	
	($6.50 / 1,761)	1.50
101	Hideki Matsui	
	($9 / 8,000)	2.00
102	Jose Contreras	
	($9.50 / 6,000)	1.50
103	Rocco Baldelli	
	($6.50 / 5,000)	2.25
104	Jeremy Bonderman	
	($6.50 / 3,000)	3.50
105	Jesse Foppert	
	($6.50 / 3,500)	5.00
106	Randy Wolf	
	($6.50 / 1,874)	1.50
107	Kevin Millwood	
	($6.50 / 3,000)	1.50
108	Eric Byrnes	
	($6.50 / 2,500)	1.50
109	Edgar Renteria	
	($6.50 / 2,015)	1.50
110	Jose Reyes	
	($6.50 / 5,000)	4.00
111	Dontrelle Willis	
	($6.50 / 5,000)	3.00
112	Mike Lowell	
	($6.50 / 2,500)	1.50
113	Jerome Williams	
	($6.50 / 3,000)	3.00
114	Esteban Loaiza	
	($6.50 / 2,364)	1.50
115	Gil Meche	
	($6.50 / 2,000)	1.75
116	Ty Wigginton	
	($4 / 2,000)	1.50
118	Brett Myers	
	($6.50 / 2,115)	1.50
119	Miguel Cabrera	
	($6.50 / 2,610)	13.50
120	Brandon Webb	
	($6.50 / 3,000)	1.50
121	Aaron Heilman	
	($6.50 / 1,229)	2.00
122	Rich Harden	
	($6.50 / 5,000)	2.75
123	Morgan Ensberg	
	($6.50 / 1,329)	2.75

2003 Topps eTopps All-Star Most Valuable Player

This card was offered for $5 in the weeks after the All-Star Game, with production set at 4,000.

		NM/M
1	All-Star MVP	
	(Garret Anderson)	1.50

2003 Topps eTopps All-Star Top Vote Getters

This card was offered for $5 in the weeks preceding the All-Star Game, with no limit set on production. The players appearing on the card were announced after the voting.

		NM/M
1	Ichiro Suzuki,	
	Albert Pujols/3,938	4.00

2003 Topps eTopps Classics

Topps continued its eTopps Classics line-up in 2003 with 20 cards of former greats. Numbering and format were contiguous with the 2002 issue. Like regular eTopps cards, Classics could only be ordered during a one-week Initial Player Offering period. Cards were issued in a

quantity of up to 4,000 each at $12.50. The number of cards actually sold is shown parenthetically. Fronts have a color or colorized action photo, backs have a picture of one of that player's Topps cards, along with career notes, stats, etc. Values shown are for cards in a virtual portfolio, rather than "in hand." Taking physical possession of a card from an eTopps portfolio costs about $6 apiece.

		NM/M
Complete Set (20):		210.00
Common Player:		9.00
21	Gary Carter/908	9.00
22	Eddie Murray/930	12.00
23	Luis Aparicio/778	17.50
24	Lou Brock/1,135	9.00
25	George Brett/1,128	17.50
26	Bob Feller/962	10.00
27	Carlton Fisk/890	10.00
28	Willie McCovey/915	11.00
29	Willie Stargell/843	14.00
30	Roberto Clemente/	
	1,664	20.00
31	Lou Gehrig/3,049	9.00
32	Johnny Bench/1,144	20.00
33	Walter Johnson/888	11.00
34	Christy Mathewson/868	10.00
35	Rogers Hornsby/826	12.00
36	Lefty Grove/885	9.50
37	Josh Gibson/1,133	9.00
38	Mel Ott/917	9.00
39	Nap Lajoie/886	9.00
40	Yogi Berra/1,281	9.00

2003 Topps eTopps Events

Highlights of the 2003 season were commemorated by Topps with the issue of special eTopps cards. Like the regular-issue eTopps, the cards were only available directly from Topps on-line. Up to 5,000 of each card were possible with an initial order price of $8 each. Only the baseball related Events cards are listed here, along with the number of cards actually sold during the one-week ordering window. Values shown represent cards in a virtual portfolio rather than "in hand." To physically take possession of a card in a portfolio costs about $7 apiece.

		NM/M
ES9	Rafael Palmeiro/1,633	
	(Joins 500-HR Club)	2.00
ES10	Roger Clemens/3,418	
	(Records 300 W''s &	
	4000 K's)	5.00
ES11	Barry Bonds/2,649	
	(Establishes 500-500	
	Club)	6.00
ES13	Carlos Delgado/630	
	(Smashes 4 Home Runs)	8.00

2003 Topps eTopps FanFest Promos

Attendees visiting Topps' booth at the All-Star FanFest could obtain a pair of eTopps promo cards. Fronts are identical to the is-

sued versions except for the appearance of an All-Star Game logo. Backs have an offer of $5 off an initial eTopps order.

		NM/M
	Luis Aparicio (Classic)	2.00
	Mark Buehrle	2.00

2003 Topps Gallery

		NM/M
Complete Set (200):		60.00
Common Player:		.25
SP's Inserted 1:20		
Pack (5):		2.50
Box (20):		45.00
1	Jason Giambi	.50
1	Jason Giambi/SP	
	Drk Blue Jsy	2.00
2	Miguel Tejada	.50
3	Mike Lieberthal	.25
4	Jason Kendall	.40
5	Robb Nen	.25
6	Freddy Garcia	.25
7	Scott Rolen	.75
8	David Wells	.25
9	Rafael Palmeiro	.75
10	Garret Anderson	.50
11	Curt Schilling	.75
12	Greg Maddux	1.00
13	Rodrigo Lopez	.25
14	Nomar Garciaparra	1.50
14	N.Garciaparra/SP	
	Navy Elbow Pad	3.00
15	Kerry Wood	.75
16	Frank Thomas	.75
17	Ken Griffey Jr.	1.00
18	Jim Thome	.75
19	Todd Helton	.75
20	Lance Berkman	.50
21	Robert Fick	.25
22	Kevin Brown	.40
23	Richie Sexson	.50
24	Eddie Guardado	.25
25	Vladimir Guerrero	1.00
26	Mike Piazza	1.50
27	Bernie Williams	.50
28	Eric Chavez	.40
29	Jimmy Rollins	.25
30	Ichiro Suzuki	1.50
30	Ichiro Suzuki/SP	
	Black Long Shirt	3.00
31	J.D. Drew	.40
32	Nick Johnson	.25
33	Shannon Stewart	.25
34	Tim Salmon	.40
35	Andruw Jones	.75
36	Jay Gibbons	.25
37	Johnny Damon	.50
38	Fred McGriff	.40
39	Carlos Lee	.25
40	Adam Dunn	.75
40	Adam Dunn/SP	
	Red Sleeves & Helmet	1.50
41	Jason Jennings	.25
42	Mike Lowell	.40
43	Mike Sweeney	.25
44	Shawn Green	.50
45	Doug Mientkiewicz	.25
46	Bartolo Colon	.40
47	Edgardo Alfonzo	.25
48	Roger Clemens	2.00
49	Randy Wolf	.25
50	Alex Rodriguez	2.00
50	Alex Rodriguez/SP	
	Red Undershirt	4.00
51	Vernon Wells	.40
52	Kenny Lofton	.40
53	Mariano Rivera	.50
54	Brian Jordan	.25
55	Roberto Alomar	.40
56	Carlos Pena	.25
57	Moises Alou	.40
58	John Smoltz	.50
59	Adam Kennedy	.25
60	Randy Johnson	1.00
61	Mark Buehrle	.25
62	C.C. Sabathia	.40
63	Craig Biggio	.40
64	Eric Karros	.25
65	Jose Vidro	.25
66	Tim Hudson	.40
67	Trevor Hoffman	.25
68	Bret Boone	.25
69	Carl Crawford	.75
70	Derek Jeter	2.50
71	Troy Percival	.25
72	Gary Sheffield	.25

73	Rickey Henderson	.50
74	Paul Konerko	.50
75	Larry Walker	.40
76	Pat Burrell	.50
77	Brian Giles	.40
78	Jeff Kent	.40
79	Kazuhiro Sasaki	.25
80	Chipper Jones	1.00
81	Darin Erstad	.40
82	Sean Casey	.40
83	Luis Gonzalez	.40
84	Roy Oswalt	.40
85	Dustan Mohr	.25
86	Al Leiter	.25
87	Mike Mussina	.50
88	Vicente Padilla	.25
89	Rich Aurilia	.25
90	Albert Pujols	2.00
91	John Olerud	.40
92	Ivan Rodriguez	.75
93	Eric Hinske	.25
94	Phil Nevin	.25
95	Barry Zito	.50
96	Armando Benitez	.25
97	Torii Hunter	.50
98	Paul LoDuca	.25
99	Preston Wilson	.40
100	Sammy Sosa	1.50
100	Sammy Sosa/SP	
	No Shin Guard	4.00
101	Jarrod Washburn	.25
102	Steve Finley	.25
103	Cliff Floyd	.25
104	Mark Prior	1.00
105	Austin Kearns	.50
106	Jeff Bagwell	.75
107	A.J. Pierzynski	.25
108	Pedro J. Martinez	1.00
109	Orlando Cabrera	.25
110	Raul Mondesi	.25
111	Russ Ortiz	.25
112	Ruben Sierra	.25
113	Tino Martinez	.25
114	Manny Ramirez	.75
115	Troy Glaus	.50
116	Magglio Ordonez	.50
117	Omar Vizquel	.40
118	Carlos Beltran	.40
119	Jose Hernandez	.25
120	Javier Vazquez	.25
121	Jorge Posada	.50
122	Aramis Ramirez	.25
123	Jason Schmidt	.40
124	Jamie Moyer	.25
125	Jim Edmonds	.50
126	Aubrey Huff	.25
127	Carlos Delgado	.50
128	Junior Spivey	.25
129	Tom Glavine	.50
130	Marty Cordova	.25
131	Derek Lowe	.25
132	Ellis Burks	.25
133	Barry Bonds	2.50
134	Josh Beckett	.25
135	Raul Ibanez	.25
136	Kazuhisa Ishii	.25
137	Geoff Jenkins	.25
138	Eric Milton	.25
139	Mo Vaughn	.25
140	Mark Mulder	.40
141	Bobby Abreu	.40
142	Ryan Klesko	.40
143	Tsuyoshi Shinjo	.25
144	Jose Mesa	.25
145	Shea Hillenbrand	.25
146	Edgar Renteria	.25
147	Juan Gonzalez	.50
148	Edgar Martinez	.25
149	Matt Morris	.25
150	Alfonso Soriano	1.00
150	Alfonso Soriano/SP	
	No Elbow Pad	2.50
151	Bryan Bullington RC	1.00
151	Bryan Bullington/SP	
	Red Background RC	3.00
152	Andy Marte RC	1.00
152	Andy Marte/SP	
	No Necklace RC	2.00
153	Brendan Harris RC	1.00
154	Juan Camacho RC	1.00
155	Byron Gettis RC	1.00
156	Daryl Clark RC	1.00
157	J.D. Durbin RC	1.00
158	Craig Brazell RC	1.00
158	Craig Brazell/SP	
	Black Jsy RC	2.00
159	Jason Kubel RC	2.00
160	Brandon Roberson RC	1.00
161	Jose Contreras RC	2.00
162	Hanley Ramirez RC	10.00
163	Jaime Bubela RC	1.00
164	Chris Duncan RC	1.50
165	Tyler Johnson RC	1.00
166	Adam LaRoche	.25
167	Walter Young	.25
168	Ryan Kibler	.25
169	Tommy Whiteman RC	.25
170	Trey Hodges	.25
171	Francisco Rodriguez	.25
172	Jason Arnold	.25
173	Brett Myers	.25
174	Rocco Baldelli	.50
175	Adrian Gonzalez	.25
176	Dontrelle Willis	1.00
177	Kris Honel	.25
178	Marlon Byrd	.25
179	Aaron Heilman	.25
180	Casey Kotchman	.25

181	Miguel Cabrera	.25
182	Hee Seop Choi	.50
183	Drew Henson	.25
184	Jose Reyes	.50
185	Michael Cuddyer	.25
186	Brandon Phillips	.25
187	Victor Martinez	.25
188	Joe Mauer	.40
189	Hank Blalock	.75
190	Mark Teixeira	.25
191	Willie Mays	2.00
192	George Brett	2.00
193	Tony Gwynn	1.00
194	Carl Yastrzemski	1.00
195	Nolan Ryan	3.00
196	Reggie Jackson	.75
197	Mike Schmidt	1.50
198	Cal Ripken Jr.	3.00
199	Don Mattingly	2.00
200	Tom Seaver	.75

Rainbow Refractors

Stars (1-200):	2-3X
Inserted 1:1	
Rookies (151-165):	1X
Inserted 1:1	

Currency Collection

		NM/M
Common Player:		4.00
Inserted 1:Box		
BA	Bobby Abreu	6.00
HC	Hee Seop Choi	6.00
BC	Bartolo Colon	4.00
LG	Luis Gonzalez	4.00
VG	Vladimir Guerrero	12.00
KI	Kazuhisa Ishii	4.00
AJ	Andruw Jones	8.00
RL	Rodrigo Lopez	6.00
PM	Pedro J. Martinez	10.00
RM	Raul Mondesi	4.00
MO	Magglio Ordonez	8.00
VP	Vicente Padilla	6.00
RP	Rafael Palmeiro	8.00
AP	Albert Pujols	20.00
MR	Manny Ramirez	8.00
ER	Edgar Renteria	6.00
JR	Jose Reyes	8.00
MRI	Mariano Rivera	10.00
FR	Francisco Rodriguez	4.00
KS	Kazuhiro Sasaki	4.00
AS	Alfonso Soriano	8.00
SS	Sammy Sosa	15.00
IS	Ichiro Suzuki	15.00
OV	Omar Vizquel	10.00
LW	Larry Walker	5.00

Heritage

		NM/M
Complete Set (25):		75.00
Common Player:		1.50
Inserted 1:10		
WB	Wade Boggs	1.50
GB	George Brett	8.00
JC	Jose Canseco	1.50
RC	Roger Clemens	6.00
AD	Adam Dunn	2.00
NG	Nomar Garciaparra	2.00
TG	Tom Glavine	1.50
SG	Shawn Green	1.50
TGW	Tony Gwynn	3.00
RH	Rickey Henderson	2.00
DJ	Derek Jeter	8.00
RJ	Randy Johnson	3.00
HK	Harmon Killebrew	4.00
KR	Jerry Koosman,	
	Nolan Ryan	10.00
WM	Willie Mays	8.00
HN	Hideo Nomo	2.00
KP	Kirby Puckett	3.00
IR	Ivan Rodriguez	2.00
DS	Duke Snider	2.00
AS	Alfonso Soriano	3.00
IS	Ichiro Suzuki	5.00
MT	Miguel Tejada	1.50
JT	Jim Thome	2.00
BW	Bernie Williams	2.00
CY	Carl Yastrzemski	3.00

Heritage Relics

		NM/M
Common Player:		5.00
WB	Wade Boggs	5.00
GB	George Brett	20.00
JC	Jose Canseco	8.00
RC	Roger Clemens	15.00
SG	Shawn Green	5.00
TG	Tony Gwynn	10.00
RH	Rickey Henderson	10.00
HK	Harmon Killebrew	25.00
HN	Hideo Nomo	15.00
KP	Kirby Puckett	15.00

Heritage Autographed Relics

		NM/M
Inserted 1:3,260		
WB	Wade Boggs	70.00
KP	Kirby Puckett/25	80.00

Originals Relics

		NM/M
Common Player:		5.00
RA	Roberto Alomar	6.00
MA	Moises Alou	5.00
LB	Lance Berkman	5.00
BB	Bret Boone	5.00
AD	Adam Dunn	6.00
NG	Nomar Garciaparra	12.00
LG	Luis Gonzalez	5.00
SG	Shawn Green	5.00
TG	Tony Gwynn	8.00
TH	Todd Helton	8.00
RH	Rickey Henderson	8.00
DH	Drew Henson	5.00
THU	Torii Hunter	8.00
AJ	Andruw Jones	6.00
CJ	Chipper Jones	8.00
JM	Joe Mauer	10.00
MO	Magglio Ordonez	5.00
RP	Rafael Palmeiro	5.00
MP	Mike Piazza	10.00
AP	Albert Pujols	15.00
MR	Manny Ramirez	8.00
AR	Alex Rodriguez	10.00
IR	Ivan Rodriguez	6.00
GS	Gary Sheffield	6.00
AS	Alfonso Soriano	8.00
MT	Miguel Tejada	5.00
FT	Frank Thomas	8.00
JT	Jim Thome	8.00
BW	Bernie Williams	5.00
CY	Carl Yastrzemski	20.00

2003 Topps Gallery HOF Edition

	NM/M
Complete Set (74):	35.00
Common Player:	.40
SP Variations:	2-4X
Inserted 1:1	
Pack (5):	4.00
Box (20):	70.00

No.	Player	Price
1	Willie Mays	2.00
2	Al Kaline	1.50
3	Hank Aaron	2.00
4	Carl Yastrzemski	1.00
5	Luis Aparicio	.40
6	Sam Crawford	.40
7	Tom Lasorda	.40
8	John McGraw	.40
9	Edd Roush	.40
10	Reggie Jackson	1.00
11	Jim "Catfish" Hunter	.40
12	Roberto Clemente	2.00
13	Ralph Kiner	.40
14	Frankie Frisch	.40
15	Nolan Ryan	4.00
16	Brooks Robinson	1.00
17	Phil Niekro	.40
18	Joe Cronin	.40
19	Joe Tinker	.40
20	Johnny Bench	1.50
21	Harry Heilmann	.40
22	Ernie Harwell	.40
23	Warren Spahn	1.00
24	George Kelly	.40
25	Phil Rizzuto	.40
26	Robin Roberts	.40
27	Ozzie Smith	1.00
28	Jim Palmer	.40
29	Duke Snider	1.00
30	Bob Feller	.40
31	Buck Leonard	.40
32	Kirby Puckett	1.00
33	Monte Irvin	.40
34	Chuck Klein	.40
35	Willie Stargell	.75
36	Juan Marichal	.40
37	Lou Brock	.40
38	Bucky Harris	.40
39	Bobby Doerr	.40
40	Lee MacPhail	.40
41	Heinie Manush	.40
42	George Brett	1.50
43	Harmon Killebrew	1.50
44	Whitey Ford	1.00
45	Eddie Mathews	1.50
46	Gaylord Perry	.40
47	Red Schoendienst	.40
48	Earl Weaver	.40
49	Joe Morgan	.40
50	Mike Schmidt	2.00
51	Willie McCovey	.40
52	Stan Musial	2.00
53	Don Sutton	.40
54	Hank Greenberg	.40
55	Robin Yount	1.00
56	Tom Seaver	1.00
57	Tony Perez	.40
58	George Sisler	.40
59	Jim Bottomley	.40
60	Yogi Berra	1.50
61	Fred Lindstrom	.40
62	Napoleon Lajoie	.40
63	Frank Robinson	1.00
64	Carlton Fisk	.40
65	Orlando Cepeda	.40
66	Fergie Jenkins	.40
67	Ernie Banks	1.50
68	Bill Mazeroski	.40
69	Jim Bunning	.40
70	Rollie Fingers	.40
71	Jimmie Foxx	1.50
72	Rod Carew	.40
73	Sparky Anderson	.40
74	George Kell	.40

Refractors

Cards (1-74):	2-4X
Inserted 1:1	
SP Refractors:	4-8X
Inserted 1:Box	

Accent Mark Autograph

	NM/M
Common Player:	.40
Refractors:	1-2X
Production 25 Sets	
YB Yogi Berra	65.00
BD Bobby Doerr	40.00
LM Lee MacPhail	40.00

Red Schoendienst

		NM/M
RR	Robin Roberts	40.00
RS	Red Schoendienst	30.00
WS	Warren Spahn	30.00

ARTifact Relics

Hoyt Wilhelm

		NM/M
Common Player:		8.00
Refractors:		1.5-3X
Production 25 Sets		
HA	Hank Aaron/Bat	25.00
SA	Sparky Anderson/Jsy	8.00
LA	Luis Aparicio/Bat	15.00
EB	Ernie Banks/Jsy	30.00
JBE	Johnny Bench/Bat	12.00
JB	Jim Bottomley/Bat	15.00
GB	George Brett/Jsy	25.00
RCA	Rod Carew/Jsy	15.00
OC	Orlando Cepeda/Bat	8.00
TC	Ty Cobb/Bat	80.00
EC	Eddie Collins/Bat	12.00
SC	Sam Crawford/Bat	20.00
BD	Bobby Doerr/Jsy	15.00
CF	Carlton Fisk/Bat	8.00
FF	Frankie Frisch/Bat	15.00
LG	Lou Gehrig/Bat	125.00
HG	Hank Greenberg/Bat	25.00
BH	Bucky Harris/Bat	12.00
HH	Harry Heilmann/Bat	20.00
RJ	Reggie Jackson/Bat	12.00
AK	Al Kaline/Bat	15.00
GK	George Kelly/Bat	20.00
HK	Harmon Killebrew/Jsy	25.00
CK	Chuck Klein/Bat	15.00
TLA	Tom Lasorda/Jsy	15.00
HM	Heinie Manush/Bat	15.00
EM	Eddie Mathews/Bat	30.00
WM	Willie Mays/Jsy	45.00
WMC	Willie McCovey/Bat	8.00
JM	Joe Morgan/Bat	20.00
SM	Stan Musial/Bat	25.00
PN	Phil Niekro/Jsy	6.00
JP	Jim Palmer/Jsy	20.00
TP	Tony Perez/Bat	8.00
GP	Gaylord Perry/Jsy	8.00
KP	Kirby Puckett/Bat	12.00
BRO	Brooks Robinson/Bat	12.00
FR	Frank Robinson/Bat	20.00
JR	Jackie Robinson/Bat	35.00
ER	Edd Roush/Bat	20.00
BR	Babe Ruth/Bat	140.00
NR	Nolan Ryan/Bat	40.00
MS	Mike Schmidt/Bat	25.00
TS	Tom Seaver/Bat	25.00
GS	George Sisler/Bat	12.00
OS	Ozzie Smith/Bat	15.00
DS	Duke Snider/Bat	12.00
WS	Willie Stargell/Bat	10.00
DSU	Don Sutton/Bat	8.00
JT	Joe Tinker/Bat	20.00
HW	Honus Wagner/Bat	140.00
PW	Paul Waner/Bat	20.00
HWI	Hoyt Wilhelm/Jsy	8.00
CY	Carl Yastrzemski/Bat	20.00
RY	Robin Yount/Bat	15.00

ARTifact Auto. Relics

		NM/M
Common Player:		30.00
Refractors:		1-1.5X
Production 25 Sets		
OC	Orlando Cepeda	30.00
BD	Bobby Doerr	45.00
AK	Al Kaline	75.00
HK	Harmon Killebrew	75.00
JM	Joe Morgan	50.00
JP	Jim Palmer	50.00
BRO	Brooks Robinson	60.00
MS	Mike Schmidt	225.00
RS	Red Schoendienst	30.00

DS	Duke Snider	50.00
RY	Robin Yount	125.00

Currency Connection

		NM/M
Common Player:		12.00
1:Box		
EB	Ernie Banks	20.00
OC	Orlando Cepeda	15.00
TC	Ty Cobb	40.00
BF	Bob Feller	25.00
LG	Lou Gehrig	35.00
HG	Hank Greenberg	20.00
WM	Willie Mays	20.00
WMA	Willie Mays	20.00
WMC	Willie McCovey	12.00
SM	Stan Musial	30.00
JR	Jackie Robinson	25.00
BR	Babe Ruth	60.00

Patch Relics

		NM/M
Common Player:		40.00
Production 25 Sets		
GB	George Brett	125.00
CH	Jim "Catfish" Hunter	40.00
FJ	Fergie Jenkins	40.00
HK	Harmon Killebrew	80.00
TL	Tom Lasorda	40.00
EM	Eddie Matthews	80.00
WM	Willie McCovey	40.00
JP	Jim Palmer	40.00
NR	Nolan Ryan	125.00
MS	Mike Schmidt	125.00
OS	Ozzie Smith	75.00
CY	Carl Yastrzemski	80.00
RY	Robin Yount	85.00

Team Topps Legends Autos.

	NM/M
Common Player:	
Vern Law	20.00
Johnny Sain	30.00

2003 Topps Heritage

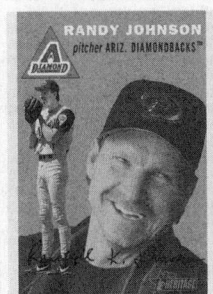

	NM/M
Complete Set (430):	350.00
Common Player:	.40
Common High # SP (364-430):	5.00
Pack (8):	5.00
Box (24):	100.00

No.	Player	Price
1	Alex Rodriguez	3.00
1	Alex Rodriguez/Black/SP	10.00
2	Jose Cruz Jr.	.40
3	Ichiro Suzuki/SP	10.00
4	Rich Aurilia	.40
5	Trevor Hoffman	.40
6	Brian Giles	.75
6	Brian Giles/Old Logo/SP	5.00
7	Albert Pujols	2.00
7	Albert Pujols/Black/SP	10.00
8	Vicente Padilla	.40
9	Bobby Crosby	.40
10	Derek Jeter	4.00
10	Derek Jeter/Old Logo/SP	15.00
11	Pat Burrell	.50
11	Pat Burrell/Old Logo/SP	5.00
12	Armando Benitez	.40
13	Javier Vazquez	.40
14	Justin Morneau	.75
15	Doug Mientkiewicz	.40
16	Kevin Brown	.40
17	Alexis Gomez	.40
18	Lance Berkman	.75
18	Lance Berkman/Black/SP	5.00
19	Adrian Gonzalez	.50

Main set (continued)

No.	Player	Price
20	Todd Helton	.75
20	Todd Helton/Black/SP	6.00
21	Carlos Pena	.40
22	Matt Lawton	.40
23	Elmer Dessens	.40
24	Hee Seop Choi	.40
25	Chris Duncan/SP RC	6.00
26	Ugueth Urbina	.40
27	Rodrigo Lopez	.40
27	Rodrigo Lopez/Old Logo/SP	4.00
28	Damian Moss	.40
29	Steve Finley	.40
30	Sammy Sosa	1.50
30	Sammy Sosa/Old Logo/SP	6.00
31	Kevin Cash	.40
32	Kenny Rogers	.40
33	Ben Grieve	.40
34	Jason Simontacchi	.40
35	Shin-Soo Choo	.40
36	Freddy Garcia	.40
37	Jesse Foppert	.40
38	Tony LaRussa	.40
39	Mark Kotsay	.40
40	Barry Zito	.75
41	Josh Fogg	.40
42	Marlon Byrd	.40
43	Marcus Thames	.40
44	Al Leiter	.50
45	Michael Barrett	.40
46	Jake Peavy	.75
47	Dustan Mohr	.40
48	Alex Sanchez	.40
49	Chin-Feng Chen	.40
50	Kazuhisa Ishii	.40
50	Kazuhisa Ishii/Black/SP	5.00
51	Carlos Beltran	.75
52	Franklin Gutierrez RC	1.50
53	Miguel Cabrera	1.00
54	Roger Clemens	2.50
55	Juan Cruz	.40
56	Jason Young	.40
57	Alex Herrera	.40
58	Aaron Boone	.40
59	Mark Buehrle	.50
60	Larry Walker	.75
61	Morgan Ensberg	.40
62	Barry Larkin	.75
63	Joe Borchard	.40
64	Jason Dubois	.40
65	Juan Acevedo	.40
66	Jay Gibbons	.40
67	Vinny Castilla	.40
68	Jeff Mathis	.40
69	Curt Schilling	1.00
70	Garret Anderson	.50
71	Josh Phelps	.40
72	Chan Ho Park	.40
73	Edgar Renteria	.50
74	Kazuhiro Sasaki	.40
75	Lloyd McClendon	.40
76	Jon Lieber	.40
77	Rolando Viera	.40
78	Jeff Conine	.40
79	Kevin Millwood	.40
80	Randy Johnson	1.50
80	Randy Johnson/Black/SP	8.00
81	Troy Percival	.40
82	Cliff Floyd	.40
83	Tony Graffanino	.40
84	Austin Kearns	.50
85	Manuel Ramirez/SP RC	4.00
86	Jim Tracy	.40
87	Rondell White	.40
88	Trot Nixon	.40
89	Carlos Lee	.50
90	Mike Lowell	.50
91	Raul Ibanez	.40
92	Ricardo Rodriguez	.40
93	Ben Sheets	.50
94	Jason Perry/SP RC	4.00
95	Mark Teixeira	.75
96	Brad Fullmer	.40
97	Casey Kotchman	.40
98	Craig Counsell	.40
99	Jason Marquis	.40
100	Nomar Garciaparra	2.00
100	Nomar Garciaparra/Old Logo/SP	5.00
101	Ed Rogers	.40
102	Wilson Betemit	.40
103	Wayne Lydon RC	1.00
104	Jack Cust	.40
105	Derek Lee	.75
106	Jim Kavourias	.40
107	Joe Randa	.40
108	Taylor Buchholz	.40
109	Gabe Kapler	.40
110	Preston Wilson	.40
111	Craig Biggio	.50
112	Paul LoDuca	.40
113	Eddie Guardado	.40
114	Andres Galarraga	.40
115	Edgardo Alfonzo	.40
116	Robin Ventura	.40
117	Jeremy Giambi	.40
118	Ray Durham	.40
119	Mariano Rivera	.50
120	Jimmy Rollins	.40
121	Dennis Tankersley	.40
122	Jason Schmidt	.50
123	Bret Boone	.40
124	Josh Hamilton	.75
125	Scott Rolen	.75
126	Steve Cox	.40
127	Larry Bowa	.40
128	Adam LaRoche/SP	5.00
129	Ryan Klesko	.40
130	Tim Hudson	.50
131	Brandon Claussen	.40
132	Craig Brazell/SP RC	4.00
133	Grady Little	.40
134	Jarrod Washburn	.40
135	Lyle Overbay	.40
136	John Burkett	.40
137	Daryl Clark RC	.75
138	Kirk Rueter	.40
139	Joe Mauer, Jake Mauer	1.00
139	Joe Mauer, Jake Mauer/Black/SP	6.00
140	Troy Glaus	.75
141	Trey Hodges/SP	4.00
142	Dallas McPherson	.40
143	Art Howe	.40
144	Jesus Cota	.40
145	J.R. House	.40
146	Reggie Sanders	.40
147	Clint Nageotte	.40
148	Jim Edmonds	.50
149	Carl Crawford	.50
150	Mike Piazza	2.00
150	Mike Piazza/Black/SP	10.00
151	Seung Jun Song	.40
152	Roberto Hernandez	.40
153	Marquis Grissom	.40
154	Billy Wagner	.40
155	Josh Beckett	.50
156	Randall Simon	.40
156	Randall Simon/Old Logo/SP	4.00
157	Ben Broussard	.40
158	Russell Branyan	.40
159	Frank Thomas	1.00
160	Alex Escobar	.40
161	Mark Bellhorn	.40
162	Melvin Mora	.40
163	Andruw Jones	.75
164	Danny Bautista	.40
165	Ramon Ortiz	.40
166	Wily Mo Pena	.50
167	Jose Jimenez	.40
168	Mark Redman	.40
169	Angel Berroa	.40
170	Andy Marte/SP RC	4.00
171	Juan Gonzalez	.75
172	Fernando Vina	.40
173	Joel Pineiro	.40
174	Boof Bonser	.40
175	Bernie Castro/SP RC	4.00
176	Bobby Cox	.40
177	Jeff Kent	.50
178	Oliver Perez	.40
179	Chase Utley	1.00
180	Mark Mulder	.50
181	Bobby Abreu	.50
182	Ramiro Mendoza	.40
183	Aaron Heilman	.40
184	A.J. Pierzynski	.40
185	Eric Gagne	.75
186	Kirk Saarloos	.40
187	Ron Gardenhire	.40
188	Dmitri Young	.40
189	Todd Zeile	.40
190	Jim Thome	1.00
190	Jim Thome/Old Logo/SP	8.00
191	Cliff Lee	.50
192	Matt Morris	.40
193	Robert Fick	.40
194	C.C. Sabathia	.40
195	Alexis Rios	.40
196	D'Angelo Jimenez	.40
197	Edgar Martinez	.50
198	Robb Nen	.40
199	Taggert Bozied	.40
200	Vladimir Guerrero/SP	8.00
201	Walter Young/SP	4.00
202	Brendan Harris RC	1.00
203	Mike Hargrove	.40
204	Vernon Wells	.50
205	Hank Blalock	.75
206	Mike Cameron	.40
207	Tony Batista	.40
208	Matt Williams	.40
209	Tony Womack	.40
210	Ramon A. Martinez RC	.40
211	Aaron Sele	.40
212	Mark Grace	.75
213	Joe Crede	.75
214	Ryan Dempster	.40
215	Omar Vizquel	.40
216	Juan Pierre	.40
217	Denny Bautista	.40
218	Chuck Knoblauch	.40
219	Eric Karros	.40
220	Victor Diaz	.40
221	Jacque Jones	.40
222	Jose Vidro	.40
223	Joe McEwing	.40
224	Nick Johnson	.40
225	Eric Chavez	.50
226	Jose Mesa	.40
227	Aramis Ramirez	.75
228	John Lackey	.40
229	David Bell	.40
230	John Olerud	.50
231	Tino Martinez	.40
232	Randy Winn	.40
233	Todd Hollandsworth	.40
234	Ruddy Lugo RC	.75
235	Carlos Delgado	.75
236	Chris Narveson	.40
237	Tim Salmon	.75
238	Orlando Palmeiro	.40
239	Jeff Clark/SP RC	4.00
240	Byung-Hyun Kim	.40
241	Mike Remlinger	.40
242	Johnny Damon	1.00
243	Corey Patterson	.50
244	Paul Konerko	.75
245	Danny Graves	.40
246	Ellis Burks	.40
247	Gavin Floyd	.40
248	Jaime Bubela RC	.75
249	Sean Burroughs	.40
250	Alex Rodriguez/SP	10.00
251	Gabe Gross	.40
252	Rafael Palmeiro	.75
253	Dewon Brazelton	.40
254	Jimmy Journell	.40
255	Rafael Soriano	.40
256	Jerome Williams	.40
257	Xavier Nady	.40
258	Mike Williams	.40
259	Randy Wolf	.40
260	Miguel Tejada	.75
260	Miguel Tejada/Black/SP	5.00
261	Juan Rivera	.40
262	Rey Ordonez	.40
263	Bartolo Colon	.40
264	Eric Milton	.40
265	Jeffrey Hammonds	.40
266	Odalis Perez	.40
267	Mike Sweeney	.40
268	Richard Hidalgo	.40
269	Alex Gonzalez	.40
270	Aaron Cook	.40
271	Earl Snyder	.40
272	Todd Walker	.40
273	Aaron Rowand	.40
274	Matt Clement	.40
275	Anastacio Martinez	.40
276	Mike Bordick	.40
277	John Smoltz	.50
278	Scott Hairston	.40
279	David Eckstein	.40
280	Shannon Stewart	.40
281	Carl Everett	.40
282	Aubrey Huff	.40
283	Mike Mussina	.75
284	Ruben Sierra	.40
285	Russ Ortiz	.40
286	Brian Lawrence	.40
287	Kip Wells	.40
288	Placido Polanco	.40
289	Ted Lilly	.40
290	Andy Pettitte	.40
291	John Buck	.40
292	Orlando Cabrera	.40
293	Cristian Guzman	.40
294	Ruben Quevedo	.40
295	Cesar Izturis	.40
296	Ryan Ludwick	.40
297	Roy Oswalt	.75
298	Jason Stokes	.40
299	Mike Hampton	.40
300	Pedro Martinez	1.50
301	Nic Jackson	.40
302	Magglio Ordonez	.50
302	Magglio Ordonez/Old Logo/SP	5.00
303	Manny Ramirez	1.00
304	Jorge Julio	.40
305	Javy Lopez	.50
306	Roy Halladay	.50
307	Kevin Mench	.40
308	Jason Isringhausen	.40
309	Carlos Guillen	.40
310	Tsuyoshi Shinjo	.40
311	Phil Nevin	.40
312	Pokey Reese	.40
313	Jorge Padilla	.40
314	Jermaine Dye	.40
315	David Wells	.40
316	Mo Vaughn	.40
317	Bernie Williams	.75
318	Michael Restovich	.40
319	Jose Hernandez	.40
320	Richie Sexson	.75
321	Daryle Ward	.40
322	Luis Castillo	.40
323	Rene Reyes	.40
324	Victor Martinez	.40
325	Adam Dunn	.75
325	Adam Dunn/Old Logo/SP	6.00
326	Corwin Malone	.40
327	Kerry Wood	.50
328	Rickey Henderson	.75
329	Marty Cordova	.40
330	Greg Maddux	2.00
331	Miguel Batista	.40
332	Chris Bootcheck	.40
333	Carlos Baerga	.40
334	Antonio Alfonseca	.40
335	Shane Halter	.40
336	Juan Encarnacion	.40
337	Flash Gordon	.40
338	Hideo Nomo	.40
339	Torii Hunter	.75
340	Alfonso Soriano	1.00
340	Alfonso Soriano/Black/SP	6.00
341	Roberto Alomar	.75
342	David Justice	.40
343	Mike Lieberthal	.40
344	Jeff Weaver	.40
345	Timoniel Perez	.40
346	Travis Lee	.40
347	Sean Casey	.40
348	Willie Harris	.40
349	Derek Lowe	.40
350	Tom Glavine	.75
351	Eric Hinske	.40
352	Rocco Baldelli	.40
353	J.D. Drew	.60

354	Jamie Moyer	.40
355	Todd Linden	.40
356	Benito Santiago	.40
357	Brad Baker	.40
358	Alex Gonzalez	.40
359	Brandon Duckworth	.40
360	John Rheinecker	.40
361	Orlando Hernandez	.40
362	Pedro Astacio	.40
363	Brad Wilkerson	.40
364	David Ortiz	8.00
365	Geoff Jenkins	4.00
366	Brian Jordan	4.00
367	Paul Byrd	4.00
368	Jason Lane	4.00
369	Jeff Bagwell	6.00
370	Bobby Higginson	4.00
371	Juan Uribe	4.00
372	Lee Stevens	4.00
373	Jimmy Haynes	4.00
374	Jose Valentin	4.00
375	Ken Griffey Jr.	10.00
376	Shea Hillenbrand	4.00
377	Gary Matthews Jr.	4.00
378	Gary Sheffield	5.00
379	Rick Helling	4.00
380	Junior Spivey	4.00
381	Francisco Rodriguez	4.00
382	Chipper Jones	6.00
383	Orlando Hudson	4.00
384	Ivan Rodriguez	6.00
385	Chris Snelling	4.00
386	Kenny Lofton	4.00
387	Eric Cyr	4.00
388	Jason Kendall	4.00
389	Marlon Anderson	4.00
390	Billy Koch	4.00
391	Shelly Duncan	4.00
392	Jose Reyes	6.00
393	Fernando Tatis	4.00
394	Michael Cuddyer	4.00
395	Mark Prior	6.00
396	Dontrelle Willis	4.00
397	Jay Payton	4.00
398	Brandon Phillips	4.00
399	Dustin Moseley RC	4.00
400	Jason Giambi	5.00
401	John Mabry	4.00
402	Ron Gant	4.00
403	J.T. Snow	4.00
404	Jeff Cirillo	4.00
405	Darin Erstad	4.00
406	Luis Gonzalez	4.00
407	Marcus Giles	4.00
408	Brian Daubach	4.00
409	Moises Alou	4.00
410	Raul Mondesi	4.00
411	Adrian Beltre	4.00
412	A.J. Burnett	4.00
413	Jason Jennings	4.00
414	Edwin Almonte	4.00
415	Fred McGriff	4.00
416	Tim Raines Jr.	4.00
417	Rafael Furcal	4.00
418	Erubiel Durazo	4.00
419	Drew Henson	4.00
420	Kevin Appier	4.00
421	Chad Tracy	4.00
422	Adam Wainwright	4.00
423	Choo Freeman	4.00
424	Sandy Alomar Jr.	4.00
425	Corey Koskie	4.00
426	Jeromy Burnitz	4.00
427	Jorge Posada	6.00
428	Jason Arnold	4.00
429	Brett Myers	4.00
430	Shawn Green	5.00

Chrome

		NM/M
Common Player:		1.00
Production 1,954 Sets		
Refractors:		1.5-2X
Production 554 Sets		
THC1	Alex Rodriguez	8.00
THC2	Ichiro Suzuki	8.00
THC3	Brian Giles	1.50
THC4	Albert Pujols	4.00
THC5	Derek Jeter	10.00
THC6	Pat Burrell	1.00
THC7	Lance Berkman	2.00
THC8	Todd Helton	2.00
THC9	Chris Duncan	20.00
THC10	Rodrigo Lopez	1.00
THC11	Sammy Sosa	5.00
THC12	Barry Zito	2.00
THC13	Marlon Byrd	1.00
THC14	Al Leiter	1.00

THC15	Kazuhisa Ishii	1.50
THC16	Franklin Gutierrez	1.00
THC17	Roger Clemens	5.00
THC18	Mark Buehrle	1.00
THC19	Larry Walker	1.50
THC20	Curt Schilling	2.50
THC21	Garret Anderson	1.50
THC22	Randy Johnson	3.00
THC23	Cliff Floyd	1.00
THC24	Austin Kearns	2.00
THC25	Manuel Ramirez	1.00
THC26	Raul Ibanez	1.00
THC27	Jason Perry	1.00
THC28	Mark Teixeira	2.00
THC29	Nomar Garciaparra	6.00
THC30	Wayne Lydon	1.00
THC31	Preston Wilson	1.00
THC32	Paul LoDuca	1.00
THC33	Edgardo Alfonzo	1.00
THC34	Jeremy Giambi	1.00
THC35	Mariano Rivera	1.50
THC36	Jimmy Rollins	2.00
THC37	Bret Boone	1.00
THC38	Scott Rolen	2.00
THC39	Adam LaRoche	1.00
THC40	Tim Hudson	1.50
THC41	Craig Brazell	1.00
THC42	Daryl Clark	1.00
THC43	Joe Mauer, Jake Mauer	3.00
THC44	Troy Glaus	2.50
THC45	Sean Pierce	1.00
THC46	Carl Crawford	2.00
THC47	Mike Piazza	6.00
THC48	Josh Beckett	1.00
THC49	Randall Simon	1.00
THC50	Frank Thomas	2.50
THC51	Andruw Jones	2.00
THC52	Andy Marte	4.00
THC53	Bernie Castro	1.00
THC54	Jim Thome	3.00
THC55	Alexis Rios	1.00
THC56	Vladimir Guerrero	4.00
THC57	Walter Young	1.00
THC58	Hank Blalock	1.50
THC59	Ramon A. Martinez	1.00
THC60	Jacque Jones	1.00
THC61	Nick Johnson	1.00
THC62	Ruddy Lugo	1.00
THC63	Carlos Delgado	1.50
THC64	Jeff Clark	1.00
THC65	Johnny Damon	1.00
THC66	Jaime Bubela	1.00
THC67	Alex Rodriguez	8.00
THC68	Rafael Palmeiro	2.00
THC69	Miguel Tejada	2.00
THC70	Bartolo Colon	1.00
THC71	Mike Sweeney	1.00
THC72	John Smoltz	1.00
THC73	Shannon Stewart	1.00
THC74	Mike Mussina	2.00
THC75	Roy Oswalt	1.50
THC76	Pedro Martinez	4.00
THC77	Magglio Ordonez	2.00
THC78	Manny Ramirez	3.00
THC79	David Wells	1.00
THC80	Richie Sexson	1.50
THC81	Adam Dunn	2.50
THC82	Greg Maddux	5.00
THC83	Alfonso Soriano	5.00
THC84	Roberto Alomar	2.00
THC85	Derek Lowe	1.00
THC86	Tom Glavine	2.00
THC87	Jeff Bagwell	6.00
THC88	Ken Griffey Jr.	6.00
THC89	Shea Hillenbrand	1.00
THC90	Gary Sheffield	1.50
THC91	Chipper Jones	5.00
THC92	Orlando Hudson	1.00
THC93	Jose Cruz Jr.	1.00
THC94	Mark Prior	2.50
THC95	Jason Giambi	5.00
THC96	Luis Gonzalez	1.50
THC97	Drew Henson	1.50
THC98	Cristian Guzman	1.00
THC99	Shawn Green	1.50
THC100	Jose Vidro	1.00

Clubhouse Collection Autographed

No Pricing
Production 25 Sets

Clubhouse Collection Relics

		NM/M
Common Player:		10.00
EB	Ernie Banks	25.00
AD	Adam Dunn	15.00
JG	Jim Gilliam	12.00
SG	Shawn Green	10.00
CJ	Chipper Jones	15.00
AK	Al Kaline	25.00
EM	Eddie Mathews	20.00
WM	Willie Mays	40.00
AP	Albert Pujols	25.00
AR	Alex Rodriguez	15.00
DS	Duke Snider	15.00
KW	Kerry Wood	10.00

Clubhouse Collection Dual Relics

		NM/M
Production 54 Sets		
SG	Duke Snider, Shawn Green	80.00
BW	Ernie Banks, Kerry Wood	80.00
MJ	Eddie Mathews, Chipper Jones	100.00

Flashbacks

		NM/M
Complete Set (10):		12.00
Common Player:		.75
Inserted 1:12		
F1	Willie Mays	3.00
F2	Yogi Berra	2.00
F3	Ted Kluszewski	.75
F4	Stan Musial	3.00
F5	Hank Aaron	2.00
F6	Duke Snider	1.50
F7	Richie Ashburn	.75
F8	Robin Roberts	.75
F9	Mickey Vernon	.75
F10	Don Larsen	.75

Flashbacks Autographs

Production 25:

Grandstand Glory

		NM/M
Common Player:		10.00
RA	Richie Ashburn	15.00
EB	Ernie Banks	20.00
YB	Yogi Berra	20.00
DG	Dick Groat	12.00
AK	Al Kaline	15.00
TK	Ted Kluszewski	12.00
EM	Eddie Mathews	15.00
WM	Willie Mays	35.00
AP.	Andy Pafko	10.00
PR	Phil Rizzuto	15.00
HS	Hank Sauer	10.00
DS	Duke Snider	15.00
WS	Warren Spahn	15.00

New Age Performers

		NM/M
Complete Set (15):		20.00
Common Player:		.75
Inserted 1:15		
NA1	Mike Piazza	3.00
NA2	Ichiro Suzuki	3.00
NA3	Derek Jeter	4.00
NA4	Alex Rodriguez	3.00
NA5	Sammy Sosa	2.00
NA6	Jason Giambi	2.00
NA7	Vladimir Guerrero	1.50
NA8	Albert Pujols	1.50
NA9	Todd Helton	.75
NA10	Nomar Garciaparra	2.50
NA11	Randy Johnson	1.50
NA12	Jim Thome	1.00
NA13	Andruw Jones	.75
NA14	Miguel Tejada	.75
NA15	Alfonso Soriano	1.50

Real One Autographs

		NM/M
Common Autograph:		15.00
Inserted 1:188		
Special Editions (Red Ink):		1.5-2X
Production 54		
HA	Hank Aaron	300.00
EB	Ernie Banks	150.00
MB	Matt Batts	25.00
HB	Hank Bauer	40.00
LB	Lance Berkman	50.00
YB	Yogi Berra	80.00
MBL	Mike Blyzka	25.00
JC	Jose Cruz Jr.	15.00
RF	Roy Face	40.00
WF	Whitey Ford	60.00
DG	Dick Groat	40.00
GH	Gene Hermanski	25.00
CH	Cal Hogue	25.00
MI	Monte Irvin	50.00
LJ	Larry Jansen	30.00
AK	Al Kaline	80.00
CK	Charlie Kress	25.00
DK	Dick Kryhoski	25.00
TL	Tom Lasorda	70.00
VL	Vern Law	30.00
DL	Don Lenhardt	25.00
DLU	Don Lund	25.00
EM	Eddie Mayo	25.00
WM	Willie Mays	200.00
MM	Mickey Micelotta	25.00
RM	Ray Murray	25.00
AP	Andy Pafko	60.00
PP	Paul Penson	30.00
JPO	Johnny Podres	40.00
JP	Joe Presko	25.00
PR	Phil Rizzuto	50.00
PRO	Preacher Roe	50.00
JR	Jimmy Rollins	25.00
BR	Bob Ross	25.00
JS	Johnny Sain	40.00
MS	Mike Sandlock	25.00
CS	Carl Scheib	25.00
BSH	Bobby Shantz	40.00
BS	Bill "Moose" Skowron	40.00
DS	Duke Snider	80.00
BT	Bob Talbot	25.00
JV	Jose Vidro	15.00
BWE	Bill Werle	25.00
LW	Leroy Wheat	25.00
JW	Jim Willis	25.00

Real One Special Edition Autographs

		NM/M
Production 54 Sets		
RO-MB	Matt Batts	50.00
RO-HB	Hank Bauer	75.00
RO-MBL	Mike Blyzka	40.00
RO-RF	Roy Face	60.00
RO-WF	Whitey Ford	120.00
RO-DG	Dick Groat	60.00
RO-MI	Monte Irvin	80.00
RO-LJ	Larry Jansen	35.00
RO-CK	Charlie Kress	60.00
RO-TL	Tom Lasorda	65.00
RO-VL	Vern Law	40.00
RO-DL	Don Lenhardt	75.00
RO-EM	Eddie Mayo	45.00
RO-MM	Mickey Micelotta	40.00
RO-RM	Ray Murray	45.00
RO-PP	Paul Penson	70.00
RO-JPO	Johnny Podres	70.00
RO-JP	Joe Presko	50.00
RO-PR	Phil Rizzuto	75.00
RO-PRO	Preacher Roe	80.00
RO-BR	Bob Ross	40.00
RO-JS	Johnny Sain	65.00
RO-MS	Mike Sandlock	50.00
RO-CS	Carl Scheib	35.00
RO-BSH	Bobby Shantz	60.00
RO-BS	Bill "Moose" Skowron	80.00
RO-BT	Bob Talbot	50.00
RO-BWE	Bill Werle	50.00
RO-LW	Leroy Wheat	50.00
RO-JW	Jim Willis	60.00

Team Legends Autographs

		NM/M
Common Autograph:		35.00
	Luis Aparicio	35.00
	Jim Bunning	35.00
	Al Kaline	70.00
	Don Larsen	40.00
	Duke Snider	35.00

Then and Now

		NM/M
Complete Set (10):		12.00
Common Card:		.75
Inserted 1:15		
TN1	Ted Kluszewski, Alex Rodriguez	3.00
TN2	Ted Kluszewski, Alex Rodriguez	3.00
TN3	Robin Roberts, Randy Johnson	1.00
TN4	Don Mueller, Alfonso Soriano	1.50
TN5	Stan Musial, Garret Anderson	2.00
TN6	Minnie Minoso, Johnny Damon	.75
TN7	Robin Roberts, Randy Johnson	1.00
TN8	Duke Snider, Alex Rodriguez	3.00
TN9	Robin Roberts, Randy Johnson	1.00
TN10	Johnny Antonelli, Pedro Martinez	1.00

2003 Topps Opening Day

		NM/M
Complete Set (165):		30.00
Common Player:		.10
Pack (6):		1.00
Box (36):		30.00
1	Alex Rodriguez	1.00
2	Jarrod Washburn	.10
3	Kevin Brown	.10
4	Chipper Jones	.75
5	Ken Griffey Jr.	.75
6	Shea Hillenbrand	.10
7	Moises Alou	.10
8	Carlos Lee	.10
9	Marty Cordova	.10
10	Derek Jeter	1.50
11	Dmitri Young	.10
12	Barry Bonds	1.50
13	Jeff Bagwell	.40
14	Paul Byrd	.10
15	Carlos Delgado	.20
16	Richie Sexson	.10
17	Torii Hunter	.20
18	Bartolo Colon	.10
19	Robin Ventura	.10
20	Mike Piazza	1.00
21	Tim Hudson	.20
22	Brett Myers	.10
23	Ryan Klesko	.10
24	Tsuyoshi Shinjo	.10
25	Cliff Floyd	.10
26	Scott Rolen	.50
27	Randy Winn	.10
28	Rafael Palmeiro	.25
29	Carlos Pena	.10
30	Randy Johnson	.50
31	Jimmy Rollins	.20
32	Jermaine Dye	.10
33	Jose Vidro	.10
34	Jorge Julio	.10
35	Mark Prior	.50
36	Curt Schilling	.40
37	A.J. Pierzynski	.10
38	Andruw Jones	.25
39	Kerry Wood	.40
40	Todd Helton	.40
41	Magglio Ordonez	.20
42	Darin Erstad	.20
43	Barry Larkin	.20
44	Edgardo Alfonzo	.10
45	Jason Giambi	.25
46	Eric Chavez	.20
47	Brian Giles	.20
48	Raul Ibanez	.20
49	Edgar Renteria	.20
50	Sammy Sosa	.75
51	Bobby Hill	.10
52	A.J. Burnett	.10
53	Juan Gonzalez	.25
54	Eric Hinske	.10
55	Roberto Alomar	.25
56	Javier Lopez	.10
57	Mark Buehrle	.10
58	Garret Anderson	.10
59	Mike Hampton	.10
60	Rich Aurilia	.10
61	Brian Jordan	.10
62	Brad Wilkerson	.10
63	Geoff Jenkins	.10
64	Brad Radke	.10
65	Roger Clemens	1.00
66	Scott Hatteberg	.10
67	Mike Williams	.10
68	Steve Finley	.10
69	Benito Santiago	.10
70	John Smoltz	.20
71	Bret Boone	.10
72	Matt Morris	.10
73	Manny Ramirez	.50
74	Troy Glaus	.25
75	Austin Kearns	.25

76	Jim Thome	.50
77	Luis Gonzalez	.20
78	Freddy Garcia	.20
79	Randy Wolf	.10
80	Miguel Tejada	.25
81	Paul Konerko	.20
82	Ivan Rodriguez	.25
83	Shannon Stewart	.10
84	Rafael Furcal	.10
85	Cristian Guzman	.10
86	Mo Vaughn	.10
87	Jose Cruz Jr.	.10
88	Alfonso Soriano	.50
89	Orlando Cabrera	.10
90	Ichiro Suzuki	1.00
91	Omar Vizquel	.20
92	Hideo Nomo	.25
93	Roy Halladay	.10
94	Mike Sweeney	.10
95	Greg Maddux	.75
96	David Eckstein	.10
97	Jay Gibbons	.10
98	Andy Pettitte	.25
99	Frank Thomas	.40
100	Shawn Green	.25
101	Jacque Jones	.10
102	Pedro J. Martinez	.50
103	Mark Mulder	.20
104	Rodrigo Lopez	.10
105	Bernie Williams	.20
106	Aaron Boone	.10
107	Mike Lieberthal	.10
108	Jim Edmonds	.25
109	Tino Martinez	.20
110	Gary Sheffield	.25
111	Mike Cameron	.10
112	Jason Jennings	.10
113	Larry Walker	.20
114	Corey Koskie	.10
115	Kazuhisa Ishii	.10
116	Jose Hernandez	.10
117	Al Leiter	.10
118	David Justice	.10
119	Jason Kendall	.10
120	Edgar Martinez	.20
121	Pat Burrell	.20
122	Vladimir Guerrero	.50
123	Juan Rivera	.10
124	Byung-Hyun Kim	.10
125	Adam Dunn	.40
126	Tim Salmon	.10
127	Terrence Long	.10
128	Johnny Damon	.25
129	Aramis Ramirez	.25
130	Barry Zito	.20
131	Mike Lowell	.20
132	Adam Kennedy	.10
133	J.D. Drew	.10
134	Tony Batista	.10
135	Albert Pujols	1.50
136	Doug Mientkiewicz	.10
137	Phil Nevin	.10
138	Paul LoDuca	.10
139	Roy Oswalt	.20
140	Jeff Kent	.20
141	Robert Fick	.10
142	Aubrey Huff	.10
143	C.C. Sabathia	.10
144	Tim Wakefield	.10
145	Derek Lowe	.10
146	Kevin Millwood	.10
147	Jorge Posada	.25
148	Fernando Vina	.10
149	Junior Spivey	.10
150	Lance Berkman	.25
151	Eric Gagne	.25
152	Mariano Rivera	.25
153	Alex Sanchez	.10
154	Ellis Burks	.10
155	Josh Beckett	.10
156	Nomar Garciaparra	1.00
157	Craig Biggio	.20
158	Adrian Beltre	.25
159	Vicente Padilla	.10
160	Mike Cameron HL	.10
161	Shawn Green HL	.10
162	A's Team Shot HL	.10
163	Jason Giambi HL	.10
164	Derek Lowe HL	.10
165	Checklist	.10

Stickers

	NM/M
Stars:	.5-1.5X
Inserted 1:1	

2003 Topps Pristine

	NM/M
Complete Set (190):	

Common Player:	1.00		
Common Rookie:	1.00		
Common Uncommon RC:	2.50		
Production 1,499			
Common Rare RC:	5.00		
Production 499			
Pack (8):	30.00		
Box (5):	140.00		

#	Player	Price
1	Pedro J. Martinez	2.50
2	Derek Jeter	6.00
3	Alex Rodriguez	6.00
4	Miguel Tejada	1.50
5	Nomar Garciaparra	2.50
6	Austin Kearns	1.50
7	Jose Vidro	1.00
8	Bret Boone	1.00
9	Scott Rolen	2.00
10	Mike Sweeney	1.00
11	Jason Schmidt	1.00
12	Alfonso Soriano	2.50
13	Tim Hudson	1.50
14	A.J. Pierzynski	1.00
15	Lance Berkman	2.00
16	Frank Thomas	2.00
17	Gary Sheffield	1.50
18	Jarrod Washburn	1.00
19	Hideo Nomo	1.50
20	Barry Zito	1.50
21	Kevin Millwood	1.50
22	Matt Morris	1.00
23	Carl Crawford	1.00
24	Carlos Delgado	2.00
25	Mike Piazza	3.00
26	Brad Radke	1.00
27	Richie Sexson	1.50
28	Kevin Brown	1.00
29	Carlos Beltran	2.00
30	Curt Schilling	2.00
31	Chipper Jones	3.00
32	Paul Konerko	1.50
33	Larry Walker	1.50
34	Jeff Bagwell	2.00
35	Jason Giambi	1.50
36	Mark Mulder	1.50
37	Vicente Padilla	1.00
38	Kris Benson	1.00
39	Bernie Williams	1.50
40	Jim Thome	2.00
41	Roger Clemens	5.00
42	Roberto Alomar	1.50
43	Torii Hunter	1.50
44	Bobby Abreu	1.50
45	Jeff Kent	1.00
46	Roy Oswalt	1.50
47	Bartolo Colon	1.00
48	Greg Maddux	4.00
49	Tom Glavine	1.50
50	Sammy Sosa	3.00
51	Ichiro Suzuki	4.00
52	Mark Prior	1.50
53	Manny Ramirez	2.00
54	Andruw Jones	1.50
55	Randy Johnson	3.00
56	Garret Anderson	1.00
57	Roy Halladay	1.00
58	Rafael Palmeiro	2.00
59	Rocco Baldelli	1.50
60	Albert Pujols	6.00
61	Edgar Renteria	1.00
62	John Olerud	1.00
63	Rich Aurilia	1.00
64	Ryan Klesko	1.00
65	Brian Giles	1.50
66	Eric Chavez	1.50
67	Jorge Posada	1.50
68	Cliff Floyd	1.00
69	Vladimir Guerrero	2.00
70	Cristian Guzman	1.00
71	Raul Ibanez	1.00
72	Paul LoDuca	1.00
73	A.J. Burnett	1.00
74	Ken Griffey Jr.	4.00
75	Mark Buehrle	1.50
76	Moises Alou	1.00
77	Adam Dunn	2.00
78	Tony Batista	1.00
79	Troy Glaus	1.50
80	Luis Gonzalez	1.00
81	Shea Hillenbrand	1.00
82	Kerry Wood	1.00
83	Magglio Ordonez	1.00
84	Omar Vizquel	1.00
85	Bobby Higginson	1.00
86	Mike Lowell	1.00
87	Runelvys Hernandez	1.00
88	Shawn Green	1.00
89	Erubiel Durazo	1.00
90	Pat Burrell	1.50
91	Todd Helton	2.00
92	Jim Edmonds	1.50
93	Aubrey Huff	1.00
94	Eric Hinske	1.00
95	Barry Bonds	6.00
96	Willie Mays	5.00
97	Bo Jackson	2.00
98	Carl Yastrzemski	5.00
99	Don Mattingly	5.00
100	Gary Carter	1.50
101	Jose Contreras/C RC	2.00
102	Jose Contreras/U RC	4.00
103	Jose Contreras/R RC	8.00
104	Dan Haren/C	3.00
105	Dan Haren/U	6.00
106	Dan Haren/R	10.00
107	Michel Hernandez/C RC	1.00
108	Michel Hernandez/U RC	2.50
109	Michel Hernandez/R RC	5.00
110	Bobby Basham/C RC	1.00
111	Bobby Basham/U RC	2.50
112	Bobby Basham/R RC	5.00
113	Bryan Bullington/U RC	1.50
114	Bryan Bullington/U RC	2.50
115	Bryan Bullington/R RC	5.00
116	Bernie Castro/C RC	1.00
117	Bernie Castro/U RC	2.50
118	Bernie Castro/R RC	5.00
119	Chien-Ming Wang/C RC	8.00
120	Chien-Ming Wang/U RC	12.00
121	Chien-Ming Wang/R RC	20.00
122	Eric Crozier/C RC	1.00
123	Eric Crozier/U RC	2.50
124	Eric Crozier/R RC	5.00
125	Michael Garciaparra/C	1.00
126	Michael Garciaparra/U	2.50
127	Michael Garciaparra/R	5.00
128	Joey Gomes/C	1.00
129	Joey Gomes/U	2.50
130	Joey Gomes/R	5.00
131	Wilfredo Ledezma/C RC	1.00
132	Wilfredo Ledezma/U RC	2.50
133	Wilfredo Ledezma/R RC	5.00
134	Branden Florence/C RC	1.00
135	Branden Florence/U RC	2.50
136	Branden Florence/R RC	5.00
137	Jeremy Bonderman/C	1.00
138	Jeremy Bonderman/U	3.00
139	Jeremy Bonderman/R	5.00
140	Travis Ishikawa/C RC	1.00
141	Travis Ishikawa/U RC	2.50
142	Travis Ishikawa/R RC	5.00
143	Ben Francisco/C RC	1.00
144	Ben Francisco/U RC	2.50
145	Ben Francisco/R RC	5.00
146	Jason Kubel/C RC	3.00
147	Jason Kubel/U RC	5.00
148	Jason Kubel/R RC	8.00
149	Tyler Martin/C RC	1.00
150	Tyler Martin/U RC	2.50
151	Tyler Martin/R RC	5.00
152	Jason Perry/C	1.50
153	Jason Perry/U	3.00
154	Jason Perry/R	5.00
155	Ryan Shealy/C RC	1.50
156	Ryan Shealy/U RC	3.00
157	Ryan Shealy/R RC	5.00
158	Hanley Ramirez/C RC	12.00
159	Hanley Ramirez/U RC	15.00
160	Hanley Ramirez/R RC	25.00
161	Rajai Davis/C RC	2.00
162	Rajai Davis/U RC	4.00
163	Rajai Davis/R RC	6.00
164	Gary Schneidmiller/C RC	1.00
165	Gary Schneidmiller/U RC	2.50
166	Gary Schneidmiller/R RC	5.00
167	Haj Turay/C RC	1.00
168	Haj Turay/U RC	2.50
169	Haj Turay/R RC	5.00
170	Kevin Youkilis/C RC	4.00
171	Kevin Youkilis/U RC	8.00
172	Kevin Youkilis/R RC	15.00
173	Shane Bazzell/C RC	1.00
174	Shane Bazzell/U RC	2.50
175	Shane Bazzell/R RC	5.00
176	Elizardo Ramirez/C RC	1.50
177	Elizardo Ramirez/U RC	3.00
178	Elizardo Ramirez/R RC	5.00
179	Robinson Cano/C RC	20.00
180	Robinson Cano/U RC	25.00
181	Robinson Cano/R RC	40.00
182	Nook Logan/C RC	1.00
183	Nook Logan/U RC	2.50
184	Nook Logan/R RC	5.00
185	Dustin McGowan/C RC	2.00
186	Dustin McGowan/U RC	3.00
187	Dustin McGowan/R RC	5.00
188	Ryan Howard/C	25.00
189	Ryan Howard/U	30.00
190	Ryan Howard/R	50.00

Plates

No pricing due to scarcity.
Four plates per player.

Refractors

Veterans (1-100):		4-6X
Production 99		
Common RC's:		.75-1.5X
Production 1,599		
Uncommon RC's:		1-2X
Production 499		
Rare RC's:		1.5-3X
Production 99		
Veteran Gold Refrac.(1-100):		4-8X
Rookie Golds (101-190):		2-4X
Production 69 Sets		

Bomb Squad

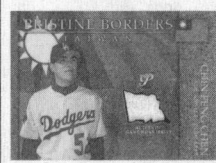

Common Duo:		6.00
Inserted 1:12		
Refractors:		No Pricing
Production 25 Sets		
CD	Eric Chavez, Erubiel Durazo	6.00
VG	Robin Ventura, Jason Giambi	10.00
WG	Matt Williams, Mark Grace	8.00
RM	Scott Rolen, Tino Martinez	10.00
BM	Adrian Beltre, Fred McGriff	6.00
GS	Troy Glaus, Scott Spiezio	8.00
KM	Corey Koskie, Doug Mientkiewicz	6.00
BT	David Bell, Jim Thome	10.00
BK	Sean Burroughs, Ryan Klesko	6.00
AS	Edgardo Alfonzo, J.T. Snow	6.00
TP	Mark Teixeira, Rafael Palmeiro	10.00

Borders

		NM/M
Common Player:		4.00
Inserted 1:9		
Refractors:		No Pricing
Production 25 Sets		
CC	Chin-Feng Chen	40.00
VG	Vladimir Guerrero	8.00
CG	Cristian Guzman	4.00
KI	Kazuhisa Ishii	4.00
AJ	Andruw Jones	6.00
PM	Pedro J. Martinez	8.00
MO	Magglio Ordonez	4.00
AP	Albert Pujols	15.00
MR	Manny Ramirez	6.00
IR	Ivan Rodriguez	6.00
TS	Tsuyoshi Shinjo	4.00
AS	Alfonso Soriano	8.00
SS	Sammy Sosa	10.00
MT	Miguel Tejada	4.00
BW	Bernie Williams	6.00

Corners

		NM/M
Common Duo:		6.00
Inserted 1:12		
Refractors:		No Pricing
Production 25 Sets		

Factor

		NM/M
Common Player:		4.00
Refractors:		No Pricing
Production 25 Sets		
MO1	Moises Alou	4.00
MO2	Moises Alou	4.00
GA1	Garret Anderson	5.00
GA2	Garret Anderson	5.00
JRB	Jeff Bagwell	6.00
JB	Johnny Bench	10.00
LB1	Lance Berkman	5.00
LB2	Lance Berkman	5.00
HB	Hank Blalock	5.00
BB	Barry Bonds	15.00
GB1	George Brett	12.00
GB2	George Brett	12.00
GC	Gary Carter	5.00
EC1	Eric Chavez	4.00
EC2	Eric Chavez	4.00
CC	Carl Crawford	4.00
AD	Adam Dunn	6.00
DE1	Darin Erstad	4.00
DE2	Darin Erstad	4.00
CF	Cliff Floyd	4.00
NG1	Nomar Garciaparra	10.00
NG2	Nomar Garciaparra	10.00
JG	Jason Giambi	6.00
TG1	Troy Glaus	5.00
TG2	Troy Glaus	5.00
JAG	Juan Gonzalez	5.00
LG	Luis Gonzalez	4.00
SG	Shawn Green	5.00
VG1	Vladimir Guerrero	8.00
VG2	Vladimir Guerrero	8.00
TH	Todd Helton	5.00
RH	Rickey Henderson	10.00
AJ	Andruw Jones	5.00
CJ	Chipper Jones	8.00
JK	Jeff Kent	4.00
MO	Magglio Ordonez	4.00
RP	Rafael Palmeiro	5.00
MP	Mike Piazza	10.00
AP1	Albert Pujols	15.00
AP2	Albert Pujols	15.00
MR	Manny Ramirez	5.00
AR1	Alex Rodriguez	10.00
AR2	Alex Rodriguez	10.00
TS	Tim Salmon	4.00
MS1	Mike Schmidt	12.00
MS2	Mike Schmidt	12.00
GS	Gary Sheffield	5.00
AS	Alfonso Soriano	5.00
SS1	Sammy Sosa	10.00
SS2	Sammy Sosa	10.00
MT	Miguel Tejada	4.00
JT	Jim Thome	10.00

Top Mini

		NM/M
Common Player:		1.00
RB	Rocco Baldelli	1.50
BWB	Bobby Basham	1.00
JB	Jeremy Bonderman	4.00
BB	Barry Bonds	6.00
BPB	Bryan Bullington	3.00
RJC	Robinson Cano	20.00
BC	Bernie Castro	1.00
EC	Eric Chavez	1.00
RC	Roger Clemens	5.00
JC	Jose Contreras	2.00
ELC	Eric Crozier	1.00
RD	Rajai Davis	1.00
NG	Nomar Garciaparra	5.00
JG	Jason Giambi	2.00
BG	Brian Giles	1.50
VG	Vladimir Guerrero	3.00
DH	Dan Haren	4.00
MH	Michel Hernandez	1.00
RH	Ryan Howard	60.00
DJ	Derek Jeter	6.00
AK	Austin Kearns	2.00
JK	Jeff Kent	1.50
JJK	Jason Kubel	4.00
WL	Wilfredo Ledezma	1.00
NL	Nook Logan	1.00
TM	Tyler Martin	1.00
DM	Dustin McGowan	3.00
MO	Magglio Ordonez	1.00
MJP	Mike Piazza	4.00
MP	Mark Prior	6.00
ER	Elizardo Ramirez	1.00
AR	Alex Rodriguez	6.00
RS	Ryan Shealy	3.00
AS	Alfonso Soriano	3.00
SS	Sammy Sosa	4.00
IS	Ichiro Suzuki	3.00
MT	Miguel Tejada	1.50
JT	Jim Thome	2.00
CW	Chien-Ming Wang	40.00
KY	Kevin Youkilis	6.00

Mini Autograph

		NM/M
Production 100		
RC	Roger Clemens	125.00

Personal Endorsements

		NM/M
Common Autograph:		6.00
Golds:		No Pricing
Production 25 Sets		
AB	Andrew Brown	6.00

RYC	Ryan Church	10.00
DE	David Eckstein	10.00
LF	Lew Ford	10.00
JG	Jay Gibbons	10.00
RJH	Rich Harden	25.00
KH	Ken Harvey	6.00
PK	Paul Konerko	20.00
ML	Mike Lowell	10.00
VM	Victor Martinez	20.00
BM	Brett Myers	10.00
JP	Josh Phelps	8.00
SR	Scott Rolen	25.00
FS	Felix Sanchez	6.00
KS	Kelly Shoppach	15.00
MS	Mike Sweeney	10.00
FV	Fernando Vina	6.00

Primary Elements

		NM/M
Many not priced due to scarcity.		
Production 50 Sets		
Refractors:		No Pricing
Production 10		
BRB	Bret Boone	15.00
NG	Nomar Garciaparra	35.00
LG	Luis Gonzalez	10.00
SG	Shawn Green	10.00
TH	Todd Helton	20.00
TKH	Torii Hunter	20.00
KI	Kazuhisa Ishii	10.00
AJ	Andruw Jones	15.00
CJ	Chipper Jones	20.00
PM	Pedro J. Martinez	20.00
MO	Magglio Ordonez	10.00
RP	Rafael Palmeiro	15.00
MP	Mike Piazza	25.00
AR	Alex Rodriguez	50.00
MT	Miguel Tejada	15.00
BZ	Barry Zito	15.00

Solo Bonds

		NM/M
Common Bonds:		20.00
Refractors:		No Pricing
Production 25		
GG	Barry Bonds	20.00
HR	Barry Bonds	20.00
BB	Barry Bonds	20.00
MVP	Barry Bonds	20.00

Double Bonds

		NM/M
Common Duo:		25.00
Refractors:		No Pricing
Production 25		
BJ	Barry Bonds, Randy Johnson	50.00
BT	Miguel Tejada, Barry Bonds	25.00
BM	Willie Mays, Barry Bonds	75.00
BR	Alex Rodriguez, Barry Bonds	35.00

2003 Topps Retired Signature Edition

		NM/M
Complete Set (110):		100.00
Common Player:		.50
Pack (5):		30.00
Box (5):		120.00
1	Willie Mays	4.00
2	Tony Perez	1.00
3	Tom Seaver	2.00
4	Johnny Bench	4.00
5	Rod Carew	1.50
6	Red Schoendienst	.50
7	Phil Rizzuto	1.00
8	Ozzie Smith	2.50
9	Maury Wills	.50
10	Hank Aaron	4.00
11	Jim Palmer	1.00
12	Jose Cruz	.50
13	Dave Parker	.50
14	Don Sutton	.75
15	Brooks Robinson	2.00
16	Bo Jackson	1.50
17	Andre Dawson	.75
18	Fergie Jenkins	.75
19	George Foster	.50
20	George Brett	5.00
21	Jerry Koosman	.50
22	John Kruk	.50
23	Kent Tekulve	.50
24	Lee Smith	.50
25	Nolan Ryan	5.00
26	Paul O'Neill	.50
27	Rich "Goose" Gossage	.50

28	Ron Santo	.50
29	Tom Lasorda	.75
30	Tony Gwynn	2.00
31	Vida Blue	.50
32	Whitey Herzog	.50
33	Willie McGee	.50
34	Bill Mazeroski	.50
35	Al Kaline	3.00
36	Bobby Richardson	.50
37	Carlton Fisk	1.00
38	Darrell Evans	.50
39	Dave Concepcion	.50
40	Cal Ripken Jr.	5.00
41	Dwight Evans	.50
42	Earl Weaver	.50
43	Fred Lynn	.50
44	Greg Luzinski	.50
45	Duke Snider	1.50
46	Hank Bauer	.50
47	Jim Rice	.50
48	Johnny Sain	.50
49	Lenny Dykstra	.50
50	Mike Schmidt	4.00
51	Orlando Cepeda	1.00
52	Ralph Kiner	.75
53	Robin Roberts	.50
54	Ron Guidry	.50
55	Steve Garvey	.50
56	Tony Oliva	.75
57	Whitey Ford	1.00
58	Willie McCovey	1.00
59	Phil Niekro	.50
60	Stan Musial	3.00
61	Rollie Fingers	.50
62	Robin Yount	2.00
63	Alan Trammell	.50
64	Bill Buckner	.50
65	Bob Feller	1.00
66	Bruce Sutter	.75
67	Dale Murphy	1.00
68	Dennis Eckersley	1.00
69	Don Newcombe	.50
70	Don Mattingly	5.00
71	Dwight Gooden	.50
72	Frank Robinson	1.50
73	Gary Carter	.50
74	Graig Nettles	.50
75	Harmon Killebrew	2.00
76	Jim Bunning	.50
77	Joe Morgan	1.00
78	Joe Rudi	.50
79	Jose Canseco	1.00
80	Ernie Banks	3.00
81	Luis Aparicio	.50
82	Luis Tiant	.50
83	Mark Fidrych	.50
84	Kirk Gibson	.50
85	Lou Brock	1.00
86	Juan Marichal	1.00
87	Monte Irvin	.50
88	Paul Molitor	1.00
89	Tommy John	.50
90	Warren Spahn	1.50
91	Wade Boggs	1.50
92	Reggie Jackson	2.00
93	Kirby Puckett	3.00
94	Boog Powell	.50
95	Carl Yastrzemski	2.00
96	Bobby Thomson	.50
97	Bill "Moose" Skowron	.50
98	Bill Madlock	.50
99	Sparky Anderson	.50
100	Yogi Berra	2.00
101	Bobby Doerr	.50
102	Gaylord Perry	.50
103	George Kell	.50
104	Harold Reynolds	.50
105	Joe Carter	.50
106	Johnny Podres	.50
107	Ron Cey	.50
108	Tim McCarver	.50
109	Tug McGraw	.50
110	Don Larsen	1.00

Black

Cards (1-110):		2-4X
Production 99 Sets		

Autographs

		NM/M
Common Autograph:		10.00
Inserted 1:1		
Refractors:		1-2.5X
Production 25 Sets		
HA	Hank Aaron/30	300.00
JA	Jim Abbott	20.00
SA	Sparky Anderson	20.00

2003 Topps Retired Signature Edition

Code	Player	Price
LA	Luis Aparicio	12.00
HB	Harold Baines	10.00
EB	Ernie Banks/24	175.00
HBA	Hank Bauer	20.00
JBE	Johnny Bench	65.00
YB	Yogi Berra/25	150.00
VB	Vida Blue	15.00
BB	Bert Blyleven	10.00
WB	Wade Boggs/77	125.00
GB	George Brett/25	180.00
LB	Lou Brock/76	120.00
BBU	Bill Buckner	10.00
JB	Jim Bunning/76	100.00
JCA	Jose Canseco	40.00
RCA	Rod Carew	60.00
GC	Gary Carter/77	100.00
JC	Joe Carter	25.00
OC	Orlando Cepeda/75	180.00
RCE	Ron Cey	10.00
JCR	Jose Cruz	10.00
AD	Andre Dawson	20.00
BD	Bobby Doerr	10.00
LD	Lenny Dykstra	20.00
DEC	Dennis Eckersley	65.00
DE	Darrell Evans	10.00
DEV	Dwight Evans/78	80.00
BF	Bob Feller	20.00
MF	Mark Fidrych	20.00
RF	Rollie Fingers	25.00
CF	Carlton Fisk	65.00
WF	Whitey Ford	65.00
GF	George Foster	10.00
SG	Steve Garvey	15.00
KG	Kirk Gibson	40.00
DG	Dwight Gooden	30.00
RG	Rich "Goose" Gossage	15.00
BGR	Bobby Grich	10.00
KGR	Ken Griffey Sr.	25.00
RGU	Ron Guidry	15.00
TG	Tony Gwynn/25	165.00
WH	Whitey Herzog	15.00
BH	Bob Horner	10.00
MI	Monte Irvin	60.00
BJ	Bo Jackson	75.00
RJ	Reggie Jackson	100.00
FJ	Fergie Jenkins	20.00
TJ	Tommy John	25.00
AK	Al Kaline	75.00
GK	George Kell	30.00
HK	Harmon Killebrew/76	150.00
RK	Ralph Kiner	125.00
JK	Jerry Koosman	25.00
JKR	John Kruk	35.00
DL	Don Larsen	15.00
TL	Tommy Lasorda/76	100.00
GL	Greg Luzinski	15.00
FL	Fred Lynn	20.00
BM	Bill Madlock	10.00
JMA	Juan Marichal	35.00
DON	Don Mattingly/81	175.00
BMA	Bill Mazeroski	15.00
TM	Tim McCarver	25.00
WMC	Willie McCovey	50.00
WMG	Willie McGee	25.00
TMC	Tug McGraw	50.00
PM	Paul Molitor	75.00
JM	Joe Morgan	35.00
DM	Dale Murphy	40.00
SM	Stan Musial/28	185.00
PN	Phil Niekro	15.00
GN	Graig Nettles	10.00
DN	Don Newcombe	15.00
TO	Tony Oliva	25.00
PO	Paul O'Neill	50.00
JP	Jim Palmer	50.00
DP	Dave Parker	20.00
LP	Lance Parrish	10.00
TP	Terry Pendleton	10.00
TP	Tony Perez	40.00
GP	Gaylord Perry	10.00
JPI	Jimmy Piersall	10.00
JPO	Johnny Podres	10.00
BP	Boog Powell	10.00
HR	Harold Reynolds	20.00
JR	Jim Rice	30.00
BR	Bobby Richardson	15.00
CR	Cal Ripken Jr./25	340.00
PR	Phil Rizzuto/70	140.00
RR	Robin Roberts	25.00
BRO	Brooks Robinson/75	140.00
FR	Frank Robinson	60.00
JRU	Joe Rudi	10.00
NR	Nolan Ryan/77	200.00
BSA	Bret Saberhagen	25.00
RSA	Ron Santo	50.00
MS	Mike Schmidt/83	200.00
RS	Red Schoendienst/83	100.00
TS	Tom Seaver	65.00
BS	Bill "Moose" Skowron	10.00
LS	Lee Smith	15.00
OS	Ozzie Smith	65.00
DSN	Duke Snider/75	100.00
WS	Warren Spahn	50.00
DS	Dave Stieb	15.00
BSU	Bruce Sutter	35.00
DSU	Don Sutton	20.00
KT	Kent Tekulve	10.00
BT	Bobby Thomson	10.00
LT	Luis Tiant	10.00
AT	Alan Trammell	20.00
BW	Bob Watson	10.00
EW	Earl Weaver	12.00
MW	Maury Wills	15.00
CY	Carl Yastrzemski	80.00
RY	Robin Yount/25	150.00

2003 Topps Total

Chien-Ming WANG

	NM/M
Complete Set (990):	125.00
Common Player:	.10
Pack (10):	1.00
Box (36):	25.00

#	Player	Price
1	Brent Abernathy	.10
2	Bobby Hill	.10
3	Victor Martinez	.10
4	Chip Ambres	.10
5	Matt Anderson	.10
6	Ricardo Aramboles	.10
7	Carlos Pena	.10
8	Aaron Guiel	.10
9	Luke Allen	.10
10	Francisco Rodriguez	.20
11	Jason Marquis	.10
12	Edwin Almonte	.10
13	Grant Balfour	.10
14	Adam Piatt	.10
15	Andy Phillips	.10
16	Adrian Beltre	.10
17	Brandon Backe	.10
18	Dave Berg	.10
19	Brett Myers	.10
20	Brian Meadows	.10
21	Chin-Feng Chen	.25
22	Blake Williams	.10
23	Josh Bard	.10
24	Josh Beckett	.10
25	Kip Bouknight RC	.20
26	Matt Childers	.10
27	Adam Everett	.10
28	Mike Bordick	.10
29	Antonio Alfonseca	.10
30	Doug Creek	.10
31	J.D. Drew	.20
32	Milton Bradley	.10
33	David Wells	.10
34	Vance Wilson	.10
35	Jeff Fassero	.10
36	Sandy Alomar	.10
37	Ryan Vogelsong	.10
38	Roger Clemens	1.25
39	Juan Gonzalez	.40
40	Dustin Hermanson	.10
41	Andy Ashby	.10
42	Adam Hyzdu	.10
43	Ben Broussard	.10
44	Ryan Klesko	.10
45	Chris Buglovsky	.10
46	Bud Smith	.10
47	Aaron Boone	.10
48	Cliff Floyd	.10
49	Alex Cora	.10
50	Curt Schilling	.40
51	Michael Cuddyer	.10
52	Mike Venafro	.10
53	Carlos Gullien	.10
54	Angel Berroa	.10
55	Eli Marrero	.10
56	A.J. Burnett	.10
57	Oliver Perez	.10
58	Matt Morris	.25
59	Valerio De Los Santos	.10
60	Austin Kearns	.50
61	Darren Dreifort	.10
62	Jason Standridge	.10
63	Carlos Silva	.10
64	Moises Alou	.20
65	Jason Anderson	.10
66	Russell Branyan	.10
67	B.J. Ryan	.10
68	Cory Aldridge	.10
69	Ellis Burks	.10
70	Troy Glaus	.50
71	Kelly Wunsch	.10
72	Brad Wilkerson	.10
73	Jayson Durocher	.10
74	Tony Fiore	.10
75	Brian Giles	.10
76	Billy Wagner	.10
77	Neifi Perez	.10
78	Jose Valverde	.10
79	Brent Butler	.10
80	Mario Ramos	.10
81	Kerry Robinson	.10
82	Brent Mayne	.10
83	Sean Casey	.10
84	Danys Baez	.10
85	Chase Utley	.25
86	Jared Sandberg	.10
87	Terrence Long	.10
88	Kevin Walker	.10
89	Royce Clayton	.10
90	Shea Hillenbrand	.10
91	Brad Lidge	.10
92	Shawn Chacon	.10
93	Kevin Frederick	.10
94	Chris Snelling	.10
95	Omar Vizquel	.20
96	Joe Borchard	.10
97	Matt Belisle	.10
98	Steve Smyth	.10
99	Raul Mondesi	.20
100	Chipper Jones	1.00
101	Victor Alvarez	.10
102	J.M. Gold	.10
103	Willis Roberts	.10
104	Eddie Guardado	.10
105	Brad Voyles	.10
106	Bronson Arroyo	.10
107	Juan Castro	.10
108	Dan Pleasac	.10
109	Ramon Castro	.10
110	Tim Salmon	.25
111	Damion Easley	.10
112	J.D. Closser	.10
113	Mark Buehrle	.10
114	Steve Karsay	.10
115	Cristian Guerrero	.10
116	Brad Ausmus	.10
117	Cristian Guzman	.10
118	Dan Wilson	.10
119	Jake Westbrook	.10
120	Manny Ramirez	.50
121	Jason Giambi	.75
122	Bob Wickman	.10
123	Aaron Cook	.10
124	Alfredo Amezaga	.10
125	Corey Thurman	.10
126	Brandon Puffer	.10
127	Hee Seop Choi	.25
128	Javier Vazquez	.10
129	Carlos Valderrama	.10
130	Jerome Williams	.10
131	Wilson Betemit	.10
132	Bruce Chen	.10
133	Esteban Yan	.10
134	Brandon Berger	.10
135	Bill Hall	.10
136	LaTroy Hawkins	.10
137	Nate Cornejo	.10
138	Jim Mecir	.10
139	Joe Crede	.10
140	Andres Galarraga	.10
141	Dave Williams	.10
142	Joey Eischen	.10
143	Mike Timlin	.10
144	Jose Cruz Jr.	.10
145	Wes Helms	.10
146	Brian Roberts	.10
147	Bret Prinz	.10
148	Brian Hunter	.10
149	Chad Hermansen	.10
150	Andruw Jones	.40
151	Kurt Ainsworth	.10
152	Clifford Bartosh	.10
153	Kyle Lohse	.10
154	Brian Jordan	.10
155	Coco Crisp	.10
156	Tomas Perez	.10
157	Keith Foulke	.10
158	Chris Carpenter	.10
159	Mike Remlinger	.10
160	Dewon Brazelton	.10
161	Brook Fordyce	.10
162	Rusty Greer	.10
163	Scott Downs	.10
164	Jason Dubois	.10
165	David Coggin	.10
166	Jose Hernandez	.10
167	Carlos Hernandez	.10
168	Matt Williams	.10
169	Rheal Cormier	.10
170	Duaner Sanchez	.10
171	Craig Counsell	.10
172	Edgar Martinez	.20
173	Zack Greinke	.10
174	Pedro Feliz	.10
175	Randy Choate	.10
176	Jon Garland	.10
177	Keith Ginter	.10
178	Carlos Febles	.10
179	Gregor Blanco RC	.10
180	Jack Cust	.10
181	Koyie Hill	.10
182	Ricky Gutierrez	.10
183	Ben Grieve	.10
184	Livan Hernandez	.10
185	Jason Isringhausen	.10
186	Gookie Dawkins	.10
187	Roberto Alomar	.40
188	Eric Junge	.10
189	Carlos Beltran	.10
190	Denny Hocking	.10
191	Jason Schmidt	.10
192	Cory Lidle	.10
193	Robert Mackowiak	.10
194	Charlton Jimerson RC	.10
195	Darin Erstad	.25
196	Jason Davis	.10
197	Luis Castillo	.10
198	Juan Encarnacion	.10
199	Jeffrey Hammonds	.10
200	Nomar Garciaparra	1.50
201	Ryan Christianson	.10
202	Willie Banks	.10
203	Damian Moss	.10
204	Chris Richard	.10
205	Todd Hundley	.10
206	Paul Bako	.10
207	Adam Kennedy	.10
208	Scott Hatteberg	.10
209	Andy Pratt	.10
210	Ken Griffey Jr.	1.00
211	Chris George	.10
212	Lance Niekro	.10
213	Greg Colbrunn	.10
214	Herbert Perry	.10
215	Cody Ransom	.10
216	Craig Biggio	.25
217	Miguel Batista	.10
218	Alex Escobar	.10
219	Willie Harris	.10
220	Scott Strickland	.10
221	Felix Rodriguez	.10
222	Torii Hunter	.25
223	Tyler Houston	.10
224	Darrell May	.10
225	Benito Santiago	.10
226	Ryan Dempster	.10
227	Andy Fox	.10
228	Jung Bong	.10
229	Jose Macias	.10
230	Shannon Stewart	.10
231	Buddy Groom	.10
232	Eric Valent	.10
233	Scott Schoeneweis	.10
234	Corey Hart	.10
235	Brett Tomko	.10
236	Shane Bazzell RC	.20
237	Tim Hummel	.10
238	Al Reyes	.10
239	Daryle Ward	.10
240	Ismael Valdes	.10
241	Brian Fuentes	.10
242	Cesar Izturis	.10
243	Mark Bellhorn	.10
244	Geoff Jenkins	.10
245	Derek Jeter	2.00
246	Anderson Machado	.10
247	Dave Roberts	.10
248	Jaime Cerda	.10
249	Woody Williams	.10
250	Vernon Wells	.20
251	Jon Lieber	.10
252	Franklyn German	.10
253	David Segui	.10
254	Freddy Garcia	.10
255	James Baldwin	.10
256	Tony Alvarez	.10
257	Walter Young	.10
258	Alex Herrera	.10
259	Robert Fick	.10
260	Rob Bell	.10
261	Ross Gload	.10
262	Dee Brown	.10
263	Mike Bacsik	.10
264	Corey Patterson	.10
265	Marvin Bernard	.10
266	Eddie Rogers	.10
267	Elio Serrano	.10
268	D'Angelo Jimenez	.10
269	Adam Johnson	.10
270	Gregg Zaun	.10
271	Nick Johnson	.10
272	Geoff Goetz	.10
273	Ryan Drese	.10
274	Eric DuBose	.10
275	Barry Zito	.25
276	Mike Crudale	.10
277	Paul Byrd	.10
278	Eric Gagne	.10
279	Aramis Ramirez	.10
280	Ray Durham	.10
281	Tony Graffanino	.10
282	Jeremy Guthrie	.10
283	Erik Bedard	.10
284	Vince Faison	.10
285	Bobby Kielty	.10
286	Francis Beltran	.10
287	Alexis Gomez	.10
288	Vladimir Guerrero	.75
289	Kevin Appier	.10
290	Gil Meche	.10
291	Marquis Grissom	.10
292	John Burkett	.10
293	Vinny Castilla	.10
294	Tyler Walker	.10
295	Shane Halter	.10
296	Geronimo Gil	.10
297	Eric Hinske	.10
298	Adam Dunn	.50
299	Mike Kinkade	.10
300	Mark Prior	.50
301	Corey Koskie	.10
302	David Dellucci	.10
303	Todd Helton	.40
304	Greg Miller	.10
305	Delvin James	.10
306	Humberto Cota	.10
307	Aaron Harang	.10
308	Jeremy Hill	.10
309	Billy Koch	.10
310	Brandon Claussen	.10
311	Matt Ginter	.10
312	Jason Lane	.10
313	Ben Weber	.10
314	Alan Benes	.10
315	Oscar Henriquez	.10
316	Danny Graves	.10
317	Jason Johnson	.10
318	Jason Grimsley	.10
319	Steve Kline	.10
320	Johnny Damon	.25
321	Jay Gibbons	.10
322	J.J. Putz	.10
323	Stephen Randolph RC	.10
324	Bobby Higginson	.10
325	Kazuhisa Ishii	.10
326	Carlos Lee	.10
327	J.R. House	.10
328	Mark Loretta	.10
329	Mike Matheny	.10
330	Ben Diggins	.10
331	Seth Etherton	.10
332	Eli Whiteside RC	.20
333	Juan Rivera	.10
334	Jeff Conine	.10
335	John McDonald	.10
336	Erik Hiljus	.10
337	David Eckstein	.10
338	Jeff Bagwell	.50
339	Matt Holliday	.25
340	Jeff Liefer	.10
341	Greg Myers	.10
342	Scott Sauerbeck	.10
343	Omar Infante	.10
344	Ryan Langerhans	.10
345	Abraham Nunez	.10
346	Mike MacDougal	.10
347	Travis Phelps	.10
348	Dan Reichert	.10
349	Alex Rodriguez	1.50
350	Bobby Seay	.10
351	Ichiro Suzuki	1.00
352	Brandon Inge	.10
353	Jack Wilson	.10
354	John Ennis	.10
355	Jamal Strong	.10
356	Jason Jennings	.10
357	Jeff Kent	.20
358	Scott Chiasson	.10
359	Jeremy Griffiths	.10
360	Paul Konerko	.10
361	Jeff Austin	.10
362	Todd Van Poppel	.10
363	Sun-Woo Kim	.10
364	Jerry Hairston	.10
365	Tony Torcato	.10
366	Arthur Rhodes	.10
367	Jose Jimenez	.10
368	Matt LeCroy	.10
369	Curtis Lesanic	.10
370	Ramon Vasquez	.10
371	Joe Randa	.10
372	John Franco	.10
373	Charles Johnson	.10
374	Craig Wilson	.10
375	Michael Young	.10
376	Mark Ellis	.10
377	Joe Mauer	.25
378	Checklist	.10
379	Jason Kendall	.10
380	Checklist	.10
381	Alex Gonzalez	.10
382	Flash Gordon	.10
383	John Buck	.10
384	Shigetoshi Hasegawa	.10
385	Scott Stewart	.10
386	Luke Hudson	.10
387	Todd Jones	.10
388	Fred McGriff	.25
389	Mike Sweeney	.10
390	Marlon Anderson	.10
391	Terry Adams	.10
392	Mark DeRosa	.10
393	Doug Mientkiewicz	.10
394	Miguel Cairo	.10
395	Jamie Moyer	.10
396	Josh Towers	.10
397	Matt Clement	.10
398	Bengie Molina	.10
399	Marcus Thames	.10
400	Nick Bierbrodt	.10
401	Tim Kalita	.10
402	Corwin Malone	.10
403	Jesse Orosco	.10
404	Brandon Phillips RC	.10
405	Eric Cyr	.10
406	Jason Michaels	.10
407	Julio Lugo	.10
408	Gabe Kapler	.10
409	Mark Mulder	.25
410	Adam Eaton	.10
411	Ken Harvey	.10
412	Jolbert Cabrera	.10
413	Eric Milton	.10
414	Josh Hall RC	.20
415	Bob File	.10
416	Brett Evert	.10
417	Ron Chiavacci	.10
418	Jorge De La Rosa	.10
419	Quinton McCracken	.10
420	Luther Hackman	.10
421	Gary Knotts	.10
422	Kevin Brown	.20
423	Jeff Cirillo	.10
424	Damaso Marte	.10
425	Chan Ho Park	.10
426	Nathan Haynes	.10
427	Matt Lawton	.10
428	Mike Stanton	.10
429	Bernie Williams	.40
430	Kevin Jarvis	.10
431	Joe McEwing	.10
432	Mark Kotsay	.10
433	Juan Cruz	.10
434	Russ Ortiz	.10
435	Jeff Nelson	.10
436	Alan Embree	.10
437	Miguel Tejada	.25
438	Kirk Saarloos	.10
439	Cliff Lee	.10
440	Ryan Ludwick	.10
441	Derrek Lee	.10
442	Bobby Abreu	.20
443	Dustan Mohr	.10
444	Nook Logan RC	.25
445	Seth McClung	.10
446	Miguel Olivo	.10
447	Henry Blanco	.10
448	Seung Jun Song	.10
449	Kris Wilson	.10
450	Xavier Nady	.10
451	Corky Miller	.10
452	Jim Thome	.50
453	George Lombard	.10
454	Rey Ordonez	.10
455	Deivis Santos	.10
456	Mike Myers	.10
457	Edgar Renteria	.10
458	Braden Looper	.10
459	Guillermo Mota	.10
460	Scott Rolen	.50
461	Lance Berkman	.10
462	Jeff Heaverlo	.10
463	Ramon Hernandez	.10
464	Jason Simontacchi	.10
465	So Taguchi	.10
466	Dave Veres	.10
467	Shane Loux	.10
468	Rodrigo Lopez	.10
469	Bubba Trammell	.10
470	Scott Sullivan	.10
471	Mike Mussina	.40
472	Ramon Ortiz	.10
473	Lyle Overbay	.10
474	Mike Lowell	.10
475	Greg Vaughn	.10
476	Larry Bigbie	.10
477	Rey Sanchez	.10
478	Magglio Ordonez	.25
479	Rondell White	.10
480	Jay Witasick	.10
481	Jimmy Rollins	.25
482	Mike Maroth	.10
483	Mark Quinn	.10
484	Nick Neugebauer	.10
485	Victor Zambrano	.10
486	Travis Lee	.10
487	Bobby Bradley	.10
488	Marcus Giles	.10
489	Steve Trachsel	.10
490	Derek Lowe	.10
491	Hideo Nomo	.25
492	Brad Hawpe	.10
493	Jesus Medrano	.10
494	Rick Ankiel	.25
495	Pasqual Coco	.10
496	Michael Barrett	.10
497	Joe Beimel	.10
498	Marty Cordova	.10
499	Aaron Sele	.10
500	Sammy Sosa	1.00
501	Ivan Rodriguez	.40
502	Keith Osik	.10
503	Hank Blalock	.25
504	Craig Monroe	.10
505	Junior Spivey	.10
506	Edgardo Alfonzo	.10
507	Alex Graman	.10
508	J.J. Davis	.10
509	Roger Cedeno	.10
510	Joe Roa	.10
511	Wily Mo Pena	.10
512	Eric Munson	.10
513	Arnie Munoz RC	.10
514	Miguel Asencio	.10
515	Andy Pettitte	.25
516	Jim Edmonds	.25
517	Jeff DaVanon	.10
518	Aaron Myette	.10
519	C.C. Sabathia	.10
520	Gerardo Garcia	.10
521	Brian Schneider	.10
522	Wes Obermueller	.10
523	John Mabry	.10
524	Casey Fossum	.10
525	Toby Hall	.10
526	Denny Neagle	.10
527	Willie Bloomquist	.10
528	A.J. Pierzynski	.10
529	Bartolo Colon	.10
530	Chad Harville	.10
531	Blaine Neal	.10
532	Luis Terrero Jr.	.10
533	Reggie Taylor	.10
534	Melvin Mora	.10
535	Tino Martinez	.10
536	Peter Bergeron	.10
537	Jorge Padilla	.10
538	Oscar Villarreal RC	.20
539	David Weathers	.10
540	Mike Lamb	.10
541	Greg Norton	.10
542	Michael Tucker	.10
543	Ben Kozlowski	.10
544	Alex Sanchez	.10
545	Trey Lunsford	.10
546	Abraham Nunez	.10
547	Mike Lincoln	.10
548	Orlando Hernandez	.10
549	Kevin Mench	.10
550	Garret Anderson	.25
551	Kyle Farnsworth	.10
552	Kevin Olsen	.10
553	Joel Pineiro	.10
554	Jose Mesa	.10
555	Jorge Julio	.10
556	Jorge Posada	.40
557	Jose Ortiz	.10
558	Mike Tonis	.10
559	Gabe White	.10
560	Rafael Furcal	.10
561	Matt Franco	.10
562	Trey Hodges	.10
563	Esteban German	.10

No.	Player	Price
564	Josh Fogg	.10
565	Fernando Tatis	.10
566	Alex Cintron	.10
567	Grant Roberts	.10
568	Gene Stechschulte	.10
569	Rafael Palmeiro	.25
570	Mike Hampton	.10
571	Ben Davis	.10
572	Dean Palmer	.10
573	Jerrod Riggan	.10
574	Nate Frese	.10
575	Josh Phelps	.10
576	Freddie Bynum	.10
577	Morgan Ensberg	.10
578	Juan Rincon	.10
579	Kazuhiro Sasaki	.10
580	Yorvit Torrealba	.10
581	Tim Wakefield	.10
582	Sterling Hitchcock	.10
583	Craig Paquette	.10
584	Kevin Millwood	.25
585	Damian Rolls	.10
586	Brad Baisley	.10
587	Kyle Snyder	.10
588	Paul Quantrill	.10
589	Trot Nixon	.10
590	J.T. Snow	.10
591	Kevin Young	.10
592	Tomokazu Ohka	.10
593	Brian Boehringer	.10
594	Danny Patterson	.10
595	Jeff Tam	.10
596	Anastacio Martinez	.10
597	Rod Barajas	.10
598	Octavio Dotel	.10
599	Jason Tyner	.10
600	Gary Sheffield	.40
601	Ruben Quevedo	.10
602	Jay Payton	.10
603	Mo Vaughn	.10
604	Pat Burrell	.40
605	Fernando Vina	.10
606	Wes Anderson	.10
607	Alex Gonzalez	.10
608	Ted Lilly	.10
609	Nick Punto	.10
610	Ryan Madson	.10
611	Odalis Perez	.10
612	Chris Woodward	.10
613	John Olerud	.25
614	Brad Cresse	.10
615	Chad Zerbe	.10
616	Brad Penny	.10
617	Barry Larkin	.40
618	Brandon Duckworth	.10
619	Brad Radke	.10
620	Giovanni Carrara	.10
621	Juan Pierre	.10
622	Rick Reed	.10
623	Omar Daal	.10
624	Jose Hernandez	.10
625	Greg Maddux	1.00
626	Henry Mateo	.10
627	Kip Wells	.10
628	Kevin Cash	.10
629	Mark Redman	.10
630	Luis Gonzalez	.25
631	Jason Conti	.10
632	Ricardo Rincon	.10
633	Mike Bynum	.10
634	Mike Redmond	.10
635	Chance Capel	.10
636	Chris Widger	.10
637	Michael Restovich	.10
638	Mark Grudzielanek	.10
639	Brandon Larson	.10
640	Luis De Los Santos	.10
641	Javy Lopez	.20
642	Rene Reyes	.10
643	Orlando Merced	.10
644	Jason Phillips	.10
645	Luis Ugueto	.10
646	Ron Calloway	.10
647	Josh Paul	.10
648	Todd Greene	.10
649	Joe Girardi	.10
650	Todd Ritchie	.10
651	Lou Merloni	.10
652	Shawn Wooten	.10
653	David Riske	.10
654	Luis Rivas	.10
655	Roy Halladay	.10
656	Travis Driskill	.10
657	Ricky Ledee	.10
658	Tony Perez	.10
659	Fernando Rodney	.10
660	Trevor Hoffman	.10
661	Pat Hentgen	.10
662	Bret Boone	.10
663	Ryan Jensen	.10
664	Ricardo Rodriguez	.10
665	Jeremy Lambert	.10
666	Troy Percival	.10
667	Jon Rauch	.10
668	Mariano Rivera	.25
669	Jason LaRue	.10
670	J.C. Romero	.10
671	Cody Ross	.10
672	Eric Byrnes	.10
673	Paul LoDuca	.10
674	Brad Fullmer	.10
675	Cliff Politte	.10
676	Justin Miller	.10
677	Nic Jackson	.10
678	Kris Benson	.10
679	Carl Sadler	.10
680	Joe Nathan	.10
681	Julio Santana	.10
682	Wade Miller	.10
683	Josh Pearce	.10
684	Tony Armas	.10
685	Al Leiter	.10
686	Raul Ibanez	.10
687	Danny Bautista	.10
688	Travis Hafner	.10
689	Rylan Reed RC	.20
690	Pedro J. Martinez	.75
691	Ramon Santiago	.10
692	Felipe Lopez	.10
693	David Ross	.10
694	Chone Figgins	.10
695	Antonio Osuna	.10
696	Jay Powell	.10
697	Roy Smith	.10
698	Alexis Rios	.10
699	Tanyon Sturtze	.10
700	Turk Wendell	.10
701	Richard Hidalgo	.10
702	Joe Mays	.10
703	Jorge Sosa	.10
704	Eric Karros	.10
705	Steve Finley	.10
706	Sean Smith	.10
707	Jeremy Giambi	.10
708	Scott Hodges	.10
709	Vicente Padilla	.10
710	Bert Snow	.10
711	Aaron Rowand	.10
712	Dennis Tankersley	.10
713	Rick Bauer	.10
714	Tim Olson RC	.25
715	Jeff Urban	.10
716	Steve Sparks	.10
717	Glendon Rusch	.10
718	Ricky Stone	.10
719	Benji Gil	.10
720	Pete Walker	.10
721	Tim Worrell	.10
722	Michael Tejera	.10
723	David Kelton	.10
724	Britt Reames	.10
725	John Stephens	.10
726	Mark McLemore	.10
727	Jeff Zimmerman	.10
728	Checklist	.10
729	Andres Torres	.10
730	Checklist	.10
731	Johan Santana	.10
732	Dane Sardinha	.10
733	Rodrigo Rosario	.10
734	Frank Thomas	.50
735	Tom Glavine	.25
736	Doug Mirabelli	.10
737	Juan Uribe	.10
738	Ryan Anderson	.10
739	Sean Burroughs	.10
740	Eric Chavez	.25
741	Enrique Wilson	.10
742	Elmer Dessens	.10
743	Marlon Byrd	.10
744	Brendan Donnelly	.10
745	Gary Bennett	.10
746	Roy Oswalt	.25
747	Andy Van Hekken	.10
748	Jesus Colome	.10
749	Erick Almonte	.10
750	Frank Catalanotto	.10
751	Matt Herges	.10
752	Carlos Delgado	.40
753	Ryan Franklin	.10
754	Wilken Ruan	.10
755	Kelvim Escobar	.10
756	Tim Drew	.10
757	Jarrod Washburn	.10
758	Runelvys Hernandez	.10
759	Cory Vance	.10
760	Doug Glanville	.10
761	Ryan Rupe	.10
762	Jermaine Dye	.10
763	Mike Cameron	.10
764	Scott Erickson	.10
765	Richie Sexson	.25
766	Jose Vidro	.10
767	Brian West	.10
768	Shawn Estes	.10
769	Brian Tallet	.10
770	Larry Walker	.25
771	Josh Hamilton	.25
772	Orlando Hudson	.10
773	Justin Morneau	.20
774	Ryan Bukvich	.10
775	Mike Gonzalez	.10
776	Tsuyoshi Shinjo	.10
777	Matt Mantei	.10
778	Jimmy Journell	.10
779	Brian Lawrence	.10
780	Mike Lieberthal	.10
781	Scott Mullen	.10
782	Zach Day	.10
783	John Thomson	.10
784	Ben Sheets	.10
785	Damon Minor	.10
786	Jose Valentin	.10
787	Armando Benitez	.10
788	Jamie Walker	.10
789	Preston Wilson	.10
790	Josh Wilson	.10
791	Phil Nevin	.10
792	Roberto Hernandez	.10
793	Mike Williams	.10
794	Jake Peavy	.10
795	Paul Shuey	.10
796	Chad Bradford	.10
797	Bobby Jenks	.10
798	Sean Douglass	.10
799	Damian Miller	.10
800	Mark Wohlers	.10
801	Ty Wigginton	.10
802	Alfonso Soriano	1.00
803	Randy Johnson	.75
804	Placido Polanco	.10
805	Drew Henson	.10
806	Tony Womack	.10
807	Pokey Reese	.10
808	Albert Pujols	.75
809	Shane Reynolds	.10
810	Mike Rivera	.10
811	John Lackey	.10
812	Brian Wright RC	.20
813	Eric Good	.10
814	Dernell Stenson	.10
815	Kirk Rueter	.10
816	Todd Zeile	.10
817	Brad Thomas	.10
818	Shawn Sedlacek	.10
819	Garrett Stephenson	.10
820	Mark Teixeira	.25
821	Tim Hudson	.10
822	Mike Koplove	.10
823	Chris Reitsma	.10
824	Rafael Soriano	.10
825	Ugueth Urbina	.10
826	Matt White	.10
827	Colin Young	.10
828	Pat Strange	.10
829	Juan Pena	.10
830	Joe Thurston	.10
831	Shawn Green	.25
832	Pedro Astacio	.10
833	Danny Wright	.10
834	Weston O'Brien RC	.20
835	Luis Lopez	.10
836	Randall Simon	.10
837	Jaret Wright	.10
838	Jayson Werth	.10
839	Endy Chavez	.10
840	Checklist	.10
841	Chad Paronto	.10
842	Randy Winn	.10
843	Sidney Ponson	.10
844	Robin Ventura	.10
845	Rich Aurilia	.10
846	Joaquin Benoit	.10
847	Barry Bonds	2.00
848	Carl Crawford	.10
849	Jeromy Burnitz	.10
850	Orlando Cabrera	.10
851	Luis Vizcaino	.10
852	Randy Wolf	.10
853	Benny Agbayani	.10
854	Jeremy Affeldt	.10
855	Einar Diaz	.10
856	Carl Everett	.10
857	Wiki Gonzalez	.10
858	Steve Belcher	.10
859	Travis Harper	.10
860	Mike Piazza	1.25
861	Will Ohman	.10
862	Eric Young	.10
863	Jason Grabowski	.10
864	Rett Johnson RC	.20
865	Aubrey Huff	.10
866	John Smoltz	.10
867	Mickey Callaway	.10
868	Joe Kennedy	.10
869	Tim Redding	.10
870	Colby Lewis	.10
871	Salomon Torres	.10
872	Marco Scutaro	.10
873	Tony Batista	.10
874	Dmitri Young	.10
875	Scott Williamson	.10
876	Scott Spezio	.10
877	John Webb	.10
878	Jose Acevedo	.10
879	Kevin Orie	.10
880	Jacque Jones	.10
881	Ben Francisco RC	.75
882	Bobby Basham RC	.25
883	Corey Shafer RC	.20
884	J.D. Durbin RC	.20
885	Chien-Ming Wang RC	1.50
886	Adam Stern	.10
887	Wayne Lydon RC	.20
888	Derell McCall RC	.20
889	Jon Nelson RC	.20
890	Willie Eyre RC	.20
891	Ramon A. Martinez RC	.20
892	Adrian Myers RC	.20
893	Jamie Athas RC	.20
894	Ismael Castro RC	.20
895	David Martinez	.10
896	Terry Tiffee RC	.20
897	Nathan Panther RC	.25
898	Kyle Roat RC	.20
899	Kason Gabbard RC	.75
900	Hanley Ramirez RC	5.00
901	Bryan Grace RC	.20
902	B.J. Barns RC	.50
903	Greg Bruso RC	.15
904	Mike Neu RC	.15
905	Dustin Yount RC	.50
906	Shane Victorino RC	.20
907	Brian Burgamy RC	.20
908	Beau Kemp RC	.20
909	Jen Cabreja RC	.20
910	Dexter Cooper RC	.20
911	Chris Colton RC	.20
912	David Cash RC	.20
913	Bernie Castro RC	.20
914	Luis Hodge RC	.20
915	Jeff Clark RC	.20
916	Jason Kubel RC	1.00
917	T.J. Bohn RC	.20
918	Luke Steidlmayer RC	.20
919	Natthew Petterson	.10
920	Darrell Rasner	.10
921	Scott Tyler	.10
922	Gary Schneidmiller RC	.20
923	Kerry Wood	.20
924	Ryan Cameron RC	.20
925	Wilfredo Rodriguez	.20
926	Rajai Davis RC	.20
927	Evel Bastida-Martinez RC	.20
928	Chris Duncan RC	1.00
929	David Pember RC	.20
930	Branden Florence RC	.20
931	Eric Eckenstahler	.20
932	Hong-Chih Kuo RC	1.00
933	Il Kim RC	.20
934	Michael Garciaparra	.50
935	Tommy Whiteman RC	.20
936	Gary Harris RC	.20
937	Derry Hammond	.20
938	Joey Gomes	.20
939	Donald Hood RC	.20
940	Clay Hensley RC	.50
941	David Pahucki RC	.20
942	Wilton Reynolds RC	.20
943	Michael Hinckley RC	.20
944	Josh Willingham RC	.50
945	Pete LaForest RC	.20
946	Pete Smart	.20
947	Jay Stizman	.10
948	Mark Malaska RC	.20
949	Mike Gallo RC	.20
950	Tyler Martin RC	.20
951	Shane Victorino	.10
952	Ryan Howard	25.00
953	Daryl Clark RC	.20
954	Dayton Buller	.20
955	Carlos Zambrano	.20
956	Chris Booker	.20
957	Brandon Watson RC	.20
958	Matt DeMarco RC	.20
959	Doug Waechter RC	.75
960	Callix Crabbe RC	.20
961	Jairo Garcia RC	.20
962	Jason Perry RC	.20
963	Eric Riggs RC	.20
964	Travis Ishikawa RC	.40
965	Jorge Piedra RC	.20
966	Manuel Ramirez RC	.20
967	Tyler Johnson RC	.20
968	Jaime Bubela RC	.20
969	Haj Turay RC	.20
970	Tyson Graham RC	.20
971	David DeJesus RC	.50
972	Franklin Gutierrez RC	.50
973	Craig Brazell RC	.50
974	Keith Stamler RC	.20
975	Jemel Spearman RC	.20
976	Kade Johnson RC	.10
977	Nick Trzesniak RC	.20
978	Bill Simon RC	.20
979	Matthew Hagen RC	.20
980	Kris Kroski RC	.20
981	Prentice Redman RC	.50
982	Kevin Randel RC	.20
983	Thomari Stori-Harden	.10
984	Brian Shackelford RC	.20
985	Mike Adams RC	.20
986	Brian McCann RC	5.00
987	Mike McNutt RC	.20
988	Aron Weston RC	.20
989	Dustin Moseley RC	.20
990	Bryan Bullington RC	.50

(Award Winners insert)

		NM/M
Complete Set (30):		20.00
Common Player:		.50
Inserted 1:12		
AW1	Barry Zito	.75
AW2	Randy Johnson	1.50
AW3	Miguel Tejada	.75
AW4	Barry Bonds	3.00
AW5	Sammy Sosa	2.00
AW6	Barry Bonds	3.00
AW7	Mike Piazza	2.50
AW8	Todd Helton	.75
AW9	Jeff Kent	.50
AW10	Edgar Renteria	.50
AW11	Scott Rolen	.75
AW12	Vladimir Guerrero	1.00
AW13	Mike Hampton	.50
AW14	Jason Giambi	1.50
AW15	Alfonso Soriano	1.50
AW16	Alex Rodriguez	3.00
AW17	Eric Chavez	.50
AW18	Jorge Posada	.50
AW19	Bernie Williams	.75
AW20	Maggio Ordonez	.50
AW21	Garret Anderson	.50
AW22	Manny Ramirez	1.00
AW23	Jason Jennings	.50
AW24	Eric Hinske	.50
AW25	Billy Koch	.50
AW26	John Smoltz	.50
AW27	Alex Rodriguez	3.00
AW28	Barry Bonds	3.00
AW29	Tony LaRussa	.50
AW30	Mike Scioscia	.50

Total Production

		NM/M
Complete Set (10):		10.00
Common Player:		.40
Inserted 1:18		
TP1	Barry Bonds	2.50
TP2	Manny Ramirez	.75
TP3	Albert Pujols	1.00
TP4	Jason Giambi	1.00
TP5	Maggio Ordonez	.40
TP6	Mike Piazza	1.50
TP7	Todd Helton	.75
TP8	Miguel Tejada	.50
TP9	Sammy Sosa	1.50
TP10	Alex Rodriguez	2.50

Total Signatures

		NM/M
Common Autograph:		
Inserted 1:176		
MB	Marlon Byrd	10.00
EM	Eli Marrero	8.00
BP	Brandon Phillips	10.00
MT	Marcus Thames	8.00
TT	Tony Torcato	8.00

Silver

Stars (1-990): 1-2X
Inserted 1:1

Award Winners

Total Topps

		NM/M
Complete Set (50):		25.00
Common Player:		.25
Inserted 1:7		
TT1	Ichiro Suzuki	1.50
TT2	Alex Rodriguez	2.50
TT3	Barry Bonds	2.50
TT4	Jason Giambi	1.00
TT5	Troy Glaus	.75
TT6	Greg Maddux	1.50
TT7	Albert Pujols	1.50
TT8	Randy Johnson	1.00
TT9	Chipper Jones	1.50
TT10	Maggio Ordonez	.25
TT11	Jim Thome	.75
TT12	Jeff Kent	.50
TT13	Curt Schilling	.50
TT14	Alfonso Soriano	1.00
TT15	Rafael Palmeiro	.50
TT16	Carlos Delgado	.50
TT17	Torii Hunter	.50
TT18	Pat Burrell	.50
TT19	Adam Dunn	.75
TT20	Roberto Alomar	.50
TT21	Eric Chavez	.40
TT22	Derek Jeter	3.00
TT23	Nomar Garciaparra	2.00
TT24	Lance Berkman	.40
TT25	Jim Edmonds	.40
TT26	Todd Helton	.75
TT27	Sammy Sosa	1.50
TT28	Phil Nevin	.25
TT29	Andruw Jones	.40
TT30	Barry Zito	.50
TT31	Richie Sexson	.40
TT32	Ken Griffey Jr.	1.50
TT33	Gary Sheffield	.40
TT34	Shawn Green	.40
TT35	Mike Sweeney	.25
TT36	Mike Lowell	.25
TT37	Larry Walker	.40
TT38	Manny Ramirez	.75
TT39	Miguel Tejada	.40
TT40	Mike Piazza	2.00
TT41	Scott Rolen	.75
TT42	Brian Giles	.40
TT43	Garret Anderson	.40
TT44	Vladimir Guerrero	.75
TT45	Bartolo Colon	.25
TT46	Jorge Posada	.40
TT47	Ivan Rodriguez	.50
TT48	Ryan Klesko	.25
TT49	Jose Vidro	.25
TT50	Pedro J. Martinez	.75

2003 Topps Traded & Rookies

		NM/M
Complete Set (275):		50.00
Common Player:		.15
Pack (8 + 2 Chrome):		2.00
Box (24):		40.00
Chrome Cards:		2-4X
T1	Juan Pierre	.15
T2	Mark Grudzielanek	.15
T3	Tanyon Sturtze	.15
T4	Greg Vaughn	.15
T5	Greg Myers	.15
T6	Randall Simon	.15
T7	Todd Hundley	.15
T8	Marlon Anderson	.15
T9	Jeff Reboulet	.15
T10	Alex Sanchez	.15
T11	Mike Rivera	.15
T12	Todd Walker	.15
T13	Ray King	.15
T14	Shawn Estes	.15
T15	Gary Mathews Jr.	.15
T16	Jaret Wright	.15
T17	Edgardo Alfonzo	.15
T18	Omar Daal	.15
T19	Ryan Rupe	.15
T20	Tony Clark	.15
T21	Damon Minor	.15
T22	Mike Stanton	.15
T23	Ramon Martinez	.15
T24	Armando Rios	.15
T25	Johnny Estrada	.15
T26	Joe Girardi	.15
T27	Ivan Rodriguez	.75
T28	Robert Fick	.15
T29	Rick White	.15
T30	Robert Person	.15
T31	Alan Benes	.15
T32	Chris Carpenter	.40
T33	Chris Widger	.15
T34	Travis Hafner	.40
T35	Mike Venafro	.15
T36	Jon Lieber	.15
T37	Orlando Hernandez	.15
T38	Aaron Myette	.15
T39	Paul Bako	.15
T40	Erubiel Durazo	.15
T41	Mark Guthrie	.15
T42	Steve Avery	.15
T43	Damian Jackson	.15
T44	Rey Ordonez	.15
T45	John Flaherty	.15
T46	Byung-Hyun Kim	.15
T47	Tom Goodwin	.15
T48	Elmer Dessens	.15
T49	Al Martin	.15
T50	Gene Kingsale	.15
T51	Lenny Harris	.15

T52	David Ortiz	.75
T53	John Rocker	.15
T54	Mike DiFelice	.15
T55	Nick Bierbrodt	.15
T56	Todd Zeile	.15
T57	Roberto Hernandez	.15
T58	Albie Lopez	.15
T59	Roberto Alomar	.50
T60	Russ Ortiz	.15
T61	Brian Daubach	.15
T62	Carl Everett	.15
T63	Jeromy Burnitz	.15
T64	Mark Bellhorn	.15
T65	Ruben Sierra	.15
T66	Mike Fetters	.15
T67	Armando Benitez	.15
T68	Deivi Cruz	.15
T69	Jose Cruz Jr.	.15
T70	Jeremy Fikac	.15
T71	Jeff Kent	.25
T72	Andres Galarraga	.25
T73	Rickey Henderson	.50
T74	Royce Clayton	.15
T75	Troy O'Leary	.15
T76	Ron Coomer	.15
T77	Greg Colbrunn	.15
T78	Wes Helms	.15
T79	Kevin Millwood	.25
T80	Damion Easley	.15
T81	Bobby Kielty	.15
T82	Keith Osik	.15
T83	Ramiro Mendoza	.15
T84	Shea Hillenbrand	.15
T85	Shannon Stewart	.15
T86	Eddie Perez	.15
T87	Ugueth Urbina	.15
T88	Orlando Palmeiro	.15
T89	Graeme Lloyd	.15
T90	John Vander Wal	.15
T91	Gary Bennett	.15
T92	Shane Reynolds	.15
T93	Steve Parris	.15
T94	Julio Lugo	.15
T95	John Halama	.15
T96	Carlos Baerga	.15
T97	Jim Parque	.15
T98	Mike Williams	.15
T99	Fred McGriff	.25
T100	Kenny Rogers	.15
T101	Matt Herges	.15
T102	Jay Bell	.15
T103	Esteban Yan	.15
T104	Eric Owens	.15
T105	Aaron Fultz	.15
T106	Rey Sanchez	.15
T107	Jim Thome	.75
T108	Aaron Boone	.25
T109	Raul Mondesi	.25
T110	Kenny Lofton	.25
T111	Jose Guillen	.15
T112	Aramis Ramirez	.40
T113	Sidney Ponson	.15
T114	Scott Williamson	.15
T115	Robin Ventura	.25
T116	Dusty Baker	.15
T117	Felipe Alou	.15
T118	Buck Showalter	.15
T119	Jack McKeon	.15
T120	Art Howe	.15
T121	Bobby Crosby	.40
T122	Adrian Gonzalez	.25
T123	Kevin Cash	.15
T124	Shin-Soo Choo	.15
T125	Chin-Feng Chen	.25
T126	Miguel Cabrera	.75
T127	Jason Young	.15
T128	Alex Herrera	.15
T129	Jason Dubois	.15
T130	Jeff Mathis	.15
T131	Casey Kotchman	.25
T132	Ed Rogers	.15
T133	Wilson Betemit	.15
T134	Jim Kavourias	.15
T135	Taylor Buchholz	.15
T136	Adam LaRoche	.15
T137	Dallas McPherson	.40
T138	Jesus Cota	.15
T139	Clint Nageotte	.15
T140	Boof Bonser	.15
T141	Walter Young	.15
T142	Joe Crede	.25
T143	Denny Bautista	.15
T144	Victor Diaz	.15
T145	Chris Narveson	.15
T146	Gabe Gross	.15
T147	Jimmy Journell	.15
T148	Rafael Soriano	.15
T149	Jerome Williams	.15
T150	Aaron Cook	.15
T151	Anastacio Martinez	.15
T152	Scott Hairston	.15
T153	John Buck	.15
T154	Ryan Ludwick	.15
T155	Chris Bootcheck	.15
T156	John Rheinecker	.15
T157	Jason Lane	.15
T158	Shelley Duncan	.15
T159	Adam Wainwright	.15
T160	Jason Arnold	.15
T161	Jonny Gomes	.15
T162	James Loney	.50
T163	Mike Fontenot	.15
T164	Khalil Greene	.25
T165	Sean Burnett	.15
T166	David Martinez	.15
T167	Felix Pie **RC**	2.00
T168	Joe Valentine **RC**	.50
T169	Brandon Webb **RC**	2.00

T170	Matt Diaz **RC**	.25
T171	Lew Ford **RC**	.75
T172	Jeremy Griffiths	.25
T173	Matt Hensley **RC**	.50
T174	Charlie Manning **RC**	.25
T175	Elizardo Ramirez **RC**	.75
T176	Greg Aquino **RC**	.25
T177	Felix Sanchez **RC**	.50
T178	Kelly Shoppach **RC**	.75
T179	Bubba Nelson **RC**	.50
T180	Mike O'Keefe **RC**	.25
T181	Hanley Ramirez **RC**	8.00
T182	Todd Wellemeyer **RC**	.75
T183	Dustin Moseley **RC**	.25
T184	Eric Crozier **RC**	.50
T185	Ryan Shealy **RC**	.75
T186	Jeremy Bonderman	.75
T187	Thomari Story-Harden **RC**	.40
T188	Dusty Brown **RC**	.50
T189	Rob Hammock **RC**	.40
T190	Jorge Piedra **RC**	.25
T191	Chris De La Cruz **RC**	.25
T192	Eli Whiteside **RC**	.25
T193	Jason Kubel **RC**	1.50
T194	Jon Schuerholz **RC**	.25
T195	Stephen Randolph **RC**	.25
T196	Andy Sisco	.75
T197	Sean Smith	.15
T198	Jon-Mark Sprowl **RC**	.75
T199	Matt Kata **RC**	.40
T200	Robinson Cano **RC**	10.00
T201	Nook Logan **RC**	.25
T202	Ben Francisco **RC**	1.00
T203	Arnie Munoz **RC**	.25
T204	Eric Chavez	.15
T205	Eric Riggs **RC**	.25
T206	Beau Kemp **RC**	.25
T207	Travis Wong **RC**	.50
T208	Dustin Yount **RC**	.50
T209	Brian McCann	6.00
T210	Wilton Reynolds **RC**	.25
T211	Matt Bruback **RC**	.50
T212	Andrew Brown **RC**	.25
T213	Edgar Gonzalez **RC**	.25
T214	Eider Torres **RC**	.25
T215	Aquilino Lopez **RC**	.25
T216	Bobby Basham **RC**	.50
T217	Tim Olson **RC**	.50
T218	Nathan Panther **RC**	.50
T219	Bryan Grace **RC**	.25
T220	Dusty Gomon **RC**	.25
T221	Wilfredo Ledezma **RC**	.25
T222	Josh Willingham **RC**	.75
T223	David Cash **RC**	.25
T224	Oscar Villarreal **RC**	.25
T225	Jeff Duncan **RC**	.50
T226	Kade Johnson **RC**	.25
T227	Luke Steidlmayer **RC**	.25
T228	Brandon Watson **RC**	.50
T229	Jose Morales **RC**	.25
T230	Mike Gallo **RC**	.25
T231	Tyler Adamcyzk **RC**	.50
T232	Adam Stern	.15
T233	Brennan King **RC**	.25
T234	Dan Haren	1.00
T235	Michel Hernandez **RC**	.25
T236	Ben Fritz	.15
T237	Clay Hensley **RC**	.50
T238	Tyler Johnson **RC**	.25
T239	Pete LaForest **RC**	.25
T240	Tyler Martin **RC**	.25
T241	J.D. Durbin **RC**	.50
T242	Shane Victorino **RC**	1.50
T243	Rajai Davis **RC**	1.00
T244	Ismael Castro **RC**	.25
T245	Chien-Ming Wang **RC**	1.00
T246	Travis Ishikawa **RC**	.40
T247	Corey Shafer **RC**	.50
T248	Gary Schneidmiller **RC**	.25
T249	David Pember **RC**	.25
T250	Keith Stamler **RC**	.25
T251	Tyson Graham **RC**	.25
T252	Ryan Cameron **RC**	.25
T253	Eric Eckenstahler **RC**	.25
T254	Matthew Peterson **RC**	.25
T255	Dustin McGowan **RC**	.50
T256	Prentice Redman **RC**	.40
T257	Haj Turay **RC**	.25
T258	Carlos Guzman **RC**	.40
T259	Matt DeMarco **RC**	.25
T260	Derek Michaelis **RC**	.25
T261	Brian Burgamy **RC**	.25
T262	Jay Sitzman **RC**	.25
T263	Chris Fallon **RC**	.25
T264	Mike Adams **RC**	.25
T265	Clint Barmes **RC**	.75
T266	Eric Reed **RC**	.50
T267	Willie Eyre **RC**	.25
T268	Carlos Duran **RC**	.40
T269	Nick Trzesniak **RC**	.25
T270	Ferdin Tejeda **RC**	.50
T271	Michael Garciaparra	.25
T272	Michael Hinckley **RC**	.75
T273	Branden Florence **RC**	.25
T274	Trent Oeltjen **RC**	.40
T275	Mike Neu **RC**	.25

Chrome Refractor

Stars:	4-8X
Rookies:	2-4X
Inserted 1:12	

Gold

Stars:	5-10X
Rookies:	1-2.5X
Production 2003 Sets	

Future Phenoms

		NM/M
Common Player:		4.00
RB	Rocco Baldelli	6.00
WB	Wilson Betemit	4.00
HB	Hank Blalock	6.00
WPB	Willie Bloomquist	15.00
MB	Marlon Byrd	4.00
CC	Chin-Feng Chen	20.00
CDC	Carl Crawford	6.00
TH	Travis Hafner	4.00
TAH	Trey Hodges	4.00
JM	Justin Morneau	10.00
BP	Brandon Phillips	4.00
MR	Michael Restovich	6.00
CS	Chris Snelling	4.00
MT	Mark Teixeira	8.00
JT	Joe Thurston	4.00

Hall of Fame

		NM/M
Common Player:		8.00
GC	Gary Carter	8.00
EM	Eddie Murray	15.00

Hall of Fame Dual

		NM/M
Complete Set (1):		
CM	Gary Carter,	
	Eddie Murray	25.00

Signature Moves

		NM/M
Common Player:		8.00
EA	Erick Almonte	8.00
DB	David Bell	10.00
JB	Joe Borchard	8.00
BC	Bartolo Colon	12.00
JC	Jose Cruz Jr.	8.00
JJC	Jack Cust	10.00
RF	Robert Fick	8.00
CF	Cliff Floyd	15.00
JF	Jesse Foppert	10.00
JG	Joey Gomes	8.00
KG	Khalil Greene	25.00
JL	James Loney	25.00
VM	Victor Martinez	20.00
FP	Felix Pie	60.00
ER	Elizardo Ramirez	12.00
JR	Jose Reyes	40.00
JS	Jason Stokes	15.00
MT	Mark Teixeira	25.00
BU	B.J. Upton	25.00
WY	Walter Young	10.00

Tools of the Trade

		NM/M
Common Player:		4.00
EA	Edgardo Alfonzo	4.00
DB	David Bell	4.00
JC	Jose Cruz Jr.	4.00
ED	Erubiel Durazo	4.00
RD	Ray Durham	4.00
RF	Robert Fick	4.00
CF	Cliff Floyd	4.00
AG	Andres Galarraga	5.00
JG	Jeremy Giambi	4.00
TG	Tom Glavine	6.00
EK	Eric Karros	5.00
JK	Jeff Kent	5.00
KL	Kenny Lofton	10.00
FL	Felipe Lopez	6.00
FM	Fred McGriff	5.00

KM	Kevin Millar	5.00
RO	Rey Ordonez	4.00
JP	Juan Pierre	5.00
SH	Tsuyoshi Shinjo	4.00
SS	Shane Spencer	4.00
JT	Jim Thome	10.00
BT	Bubba Trammell	4.00
RW	Rondell White	4.00
PW	Preston Wilson	4.00
TZ	Todd Zeile	6.00

Tools of the Trade Dual

		NM/M
Common Player:		10.00
KM	Kevin Millwood	10.00
IR	Ivan Rodriguez	15.00
JT	Jim Thome	15.00

2003 Topps Tribute

		NM/M
Common Player:		4.00

		NM/M
Complete Set (110):		300.00
Common Player:		1.00
Common Auto. (101-110):		10.00
Pack (5):		35.00
Box (6):		160.00
1	Jim Thome	2.50
2	Edgardo Alfonzo	2.50
3	Edgar Martinez	1.50
4	Scott Rolen	2.50
5	Eric Hinske	1.00
6	Mark Mulder	1.50
7	Jason Giambi	2.50
8	Bernie Williams	2.00
9	Cliff Floyd	1.00
10	Ichiro Suzuki	5.00
11	Pat Burrell	1.50
12	Garret Anderson	1.50
13	Gary Sheffield	1.50
14	Johnny Damon	3.00
15	Kerry Wood	1.50
16	Bartolo Colon	1.00
17	Adam Dunn	2.00
18	Omar Vizquel	1.50
19	Todd Helton	2.00
20	Nomar Garciaparra	4.00
21	A.J. Burnett	1.00
22	Craig Biggio	1.50
23	Carlos Beltran	2.50
24	Kazuhisa Ishii	1.00
25	Vladimir Guerrero	2.50
26	Roberto Alomar	2.00
27	Roger Clemens	6.00
28	Tim Hudson	2.00
29	Brian Giles	1.50
30	Barry Bonds	8.00
31	Jim Edmonds	1.50
32	Rafael Palmeiro	1.50
33	Francisco Rodriguez	1.00
34	Andruw Jones	2.00
35	Shea Hillenbrand	1.00
36	Moises Alou	1.50
37	Luis Gonzalez	1.00
38	Darin Erstad	1.00
39	John Smoltz	1.50
40	Derek Jeter	8.00
41	Aubrey Huff	1.00
42	Eric Chavez	1.50
43	Doug Mientkiewicz	1.00
44	Lance Berkman	2.00
45	Josh Beckett	1.50
46	Austin Kearns	1.50
47	Frank Thomas	2.50
48	Pedro J. Martinez	3.00
49	Tim Salmon	1.50
50	Alex Rodriguez	8.00
51	Ryan Klesko	1.00
52	Tom Glavine	1.50
53	Shawn Green	1.50
54	Jeff Kent	1.50
55	Carlos Pena	1.50
56	Paul Konerko	1.50
57	Troy Glaus	2.00
58	Manny Ramirez	2.00
59	Jason Jennings	1.00
60	Randy Johnson	3.00
61	Ivan Rodriguez	2.00
62	Roy Oswalt	1.50
63	Kevin Brown	1.50
64	Jose Vidro	1.00
65	Jorge Posada	1.50
66	Mike Piazza	5.00
67	Bret Boone	2.00
68	Carlos Delgado	2.00
69	Jimmy Rollins	1.50
70	Alfonso Soriano	3.00
71	Greg Maddux	5.00
72	Mark Prior	2.00
73	Jeff Bagwell	2.50

74	Richie Sexson	2.00
75	Sammy Sosa	4.00
76	Curt Schilling	2.00
77	Mike Sweeney	1.00
78	Torii Hunter	1.50
79	Larry Walker	1.50
80	Miguel Tejada	1.50
81	Rich Aurilia	1.00
82	Bobby Abreu	1.50
83	Phil Nevin	1.00
84	Rodrigo Lopez	1.00
85	Chipper Jones	3.00
86	Ken Griffey Jr.	5.00
87	Mike Lowell	1.00
88	Magglio Ordonez	1.50
89	Barry Zito	1.50
90	Albert Pujols	8.00
91	Corey Shafer **RC**	2.00
92	Dan Haren	5.00
93	Jeremy Bonderman	6.00
94	Branden Florence **RC**	2.00
95	Evel Bastida-Martinez **RC**	2.00
96	Brian Wright **RC**	2.00
97	Elizardo Ramirez **RC**	2.00
98	Michael Garciaparra **RC**	2.00
99	Clay Hensley **RC**	3.00
100	Bobby Basham **RC**	2.00
101	Jose Contreras	15.00
102	Bryan Bullington **RC**	15.00
103	Joey Gomes	10.00
104	Craig Brazell **RC**	10.00
105	Andy Marte **RC**	10.00
106	Hanley Ramirez **RC**	100.00
107	Ryan Shealy **RC**	10.00
108	Daryl Clark **RC**	10.00
109	Tyler Johnson **RC**	15.00
110	Ben Francisco **RC**	20.00

Gold Proof

Cards (1-100):	No Pricing
Production 25	
Autos. (101-110) are 1 of 1.	

Red Proof

Stars (1-100):	2-4X
Production 225	
Autos. (101-110):	1-2.5X
Production 50	

Matching Marks Dual Relics

		NM/M
Common Duo:		10.00
Premiere Proofs:		1.5X
Production 50		
PH	Rafael Palmeiro, Rickey Henderson	15.00
GR	Nomar Garciaparra, Alex Rodriguez	25.00
AP	Roberto Alomar, Rafael Palmeiro	15.00
MP	Fred McGriff, Rafael Palmeiro	10.00
HR	Rickey Henderson, Manny Ramirez	15.00
RP	Manny Ramirez, Mike Piazza	20.00
BG	Jeff Bagwell, Juan Gonzalez	10.00
BP	Barry Bonds, Rafael Palmeiro	35.00
SB	Sammy Sosa, Jeff Bagwell	20.00
SG	Alfonso Soriano, Vladimir Guerrero	20.00
MG	Fred McGriff, Juan Gonzalez	10.00
PA	Rafael Palmeiro, Roberto Alomar	15.00

Memorable Materials

		NM/M
Common Player:		8.00
Premiere Proofs:		1.5X
Production 50		
BB	Barry Bonds	30.00
JG	Jason Giambi	8.00
JG2	Jason Giambi	8.00
TG	Troy Glaus	8.00
LG	Luis Gonzalez	8.00
SG	Shawn Green	8.00
VG	Vladimir Guerrero	10.00
RH	Rickey Henderson	8.00
TH	Torii Hunter	8.00
AJ	Andruw Jones	8.00
GM	Greg Maddux	15.00
AP	Albert Pujols	20.00
CR	Cal Ripken Jr.	45.00
AR	Alex Rodriguez	15.00
AS	Alfonso Soriano	10.00
SS	Sammy Sosa	15.00
SS2	Sammy Sosa	15.00
MT	Miguel Tejada	8.00
KW	Kerry Wood	8.00

Milestone Materials

		NM/M
Common Player:		8.00
Premiere Proofs:		1.5X
Production 50		
RA	Roberto Alomar	10.00
JB1-2	Jeff Bagwell	10.00
BB1-5	Barry Bonds	25.00
NG	Nomar Garciaparra	20.00
JG1-2	Juan Gonzalez	10.00
VG	Vladimir Guerrero	10.00
TH	Todd Helton	10.00
RH1-5	Rickey Henderson	10.00
CJ	Chipper Jones	12.00
FM1-3	Fred McGriff	8.00
RP1-4	Rafael Palmeiro	10.00
MP1-2	Mike Piazza	15.00
MR1-2	Manny Ramirez	10.00
AR	Alex Rodriguez	15.00
SS1-3	Sammy Sosa	15.00
FT	Frank Thomas	12.00

Modern Marks Autographs

		NM/M
Common Autograph:		10.00
Premiere Proofs:		1.5X
Production 50		
LB	Lance Berkman	20.00
RC	Roger Clemens	120.00
CF	Cliff Floyd	10.00
EH	Eric Hinske	10.00
TH	Torii Hunter	15.00
PK	Paul Konerko	15.00
PL	Paul LoDuca	15.00
MO	Magglio Ordonez	15.00

Perennial All-Stars Relics

		NM/M
Common Player:		8.00
Premiere Proofs:		1.5X
Production 50		
RA	Roberto Alomar	10.00
CB	Craig Biggio	8.00
BB	Barry Bonds	25.00
RC	Roger Clemens	20.00
RH	Rickey Henderson	15.00
CJ	Chipper Jones	10.00
GM	Greg Maddux	15.00
EM	Edgar Martinez	15.00
EM	Pedro J. Martinez	15.00
MM	Mike Mussina	15.00
MP	Mike Piazza	20.00
MR	Manny Ramirez	15.00
AR	Alex Rodriguez	15.00
IR	Ivan Rodriguez	8.00
BS	Benito Santiago	8.00
CS	Curt Schilling	8.00
GS	Gary Sheffield	8.00
JS	John Smoltz	20.00
SS	Sammy Sosa	20.00
FT	Frank Thomas	8.00
LW	Larry Walker	8.00
BW	Bernie Williams	10.00

Performance Tribute Doubles

		NM/M
Common Duo:		10.00
Premiere Proofs:		1.5X
Production 50		
ZJ	Barry Zito, Randy Johnson	15.00

Contemporary Collection

SA	Alfonso Soriano, Roberto Alomar	15.00
RR	Cal Ripken Jr., Alex Rodriguez	60.00
RT	Alex Rodriguez, Miguel Tejada	15.00
GG	Luis Gonzalez, Troy Glaus	10.00
PW	Albert Pujols, Kerry Wood	25.00
RG	Alex Rodriguez, Nomar Garciaparra	30.00
BJ	Barry Bonds, Chipper Jones	25.00
SG	Sammy Sosa, Juan Gonzalez	15.00
PS	Mike Piazza, Benito Santiago	15.00
PR	Mike Piazza, Ivan Rodriguez	15.00
MM	Pedro J. Martinez, Greg Maddux	15.00
CM	Roger Clemens, Greg Maddux	35.00
JP	Chipper Jones, Mike Piazza	20.00

Performance Tribute Triples

		NM/M
Common Trio:		20.00
Premiere Proofs:		1.5X
Production 50		
SMP	Sammy Sosa, Rafael Palmeiro, Fred McGriff	25.00
CMJ	Roger Clemens, Greg Maddux, Randy Johnson	30.00
RHP	Manny Ramirez, Mike Piazza, Rickey Henderson	30.00
STB	Sammy Sosa, Frank Thomas, Jeff Bagwell	20.00
BMP	Barry Bonds, Fred McGriff, Rafael Palmeiro	30.00

Solo Bonds

		NM/M
Premiere Proof:		1.5X
Production 50		
SB	Barry Bonds	25.00

Double Bonds

		NM/M
Premiere Proof:		1.5X
Production 50		
BT-DB	Barry Bonds	40.00

Triple Bonds

		NM/M
Premiere Proof:		1.5X
Production 50		
TB	Barry Bonds	60.00

Team Tribute Doubles

		NM/M
Common Duo:		10.00
Premiere Proofs:		1.5X
Production 50		
MS	Greg Maddux, John Smoltz	35.00
IN	Kazuhisa Ishii, Hideo Nomo	25.00
WH	Larry Walker, Todd Helton	10.00
BB	Craig Biggio, Jeff Bagwell	15.00
RP	Alex Rodriguez, Rafael Palmeiro	15.00
GR	Nomar Garciaparra, Manny Ramirez	20.00

Team Tribute Triples

		NM/M
Common Trio:		15.00
Premiere Proofs:		1.5X
Production 50		
JSJ	Andruw Jones, Gary Sheffield, Chipper Jones	30.00

GRM	Nomar Garciaparra, Manny Ramirez, Pedro J. Martinez	40.00
ASP	Moises Alou, Sammy Sosa, Corey Patterson	30.00
TOK	Frank Thomas, Magglio Ordonez, Paul Konerko	20.00
BBB	Craig Biggio, Lance Berkman, Jeff Bagwell	20.00
MHM	Joe Mauer, Torii Hunter, Doug Mientkiewicz	25.00
SGV	Alfonso Soriano, Jason Giambi, Robin Ventura	25.00
CTM	Eric Chavez, Miguel Tejada, Mark Mulder	15.00
HZM	Tim Hudson, Barry Zito, Mark Mulder	25.00
TBB	Jim Thome, Marlon Byrd, Pat Burrell	20.00
MOB	Edgar Martinez, John Olerud, Bret Boone	20.00
PER	Albert Pujols, Jim Edmonds, Scott Rolen	40.00
RGP	Alex Rodriguez, Juan Gonzalez, Rafael Palmeiro	25.00
RBT	Alex Rodriguez, Hank Blalock, Mark Teixeira	25.00

Tribute to the Stars

		NM/M
Common Player:		10.00
Premiere Proofs:		1.5X
Production 50		
RA	Roberto Alomar	15.00
GA	Garret Anderson	15.00
LB	Lance Berkman	10.00
BB	Barry Bonds	50.00
PB	Pat Burrell	15.00
EC	Eric Chavez	15.00
AD	Adam Dunn	15.00
NG	Nomar Garciaparra	40.00
TG	Troy Glaus	15.00
VG	Vladimir Guerrero	15.00
TH	Todd Helton	15.00
RH	Rickey Henderson	15.00
THU	Torii Hunter	10.00
AJ	Andruw Jones	10.00
CJ	Chipper Jones	15.00
GM	Greg Maddux	20.00
RP	Rafael Palmeiro	10.00
MP	Mike Piazza	20.00
AP	Albert Pujols	40.00
AR	Alex Rodriguez	30.00
AS	Alfonso Soriano	15.00
SS	Sammy Sosa	25.00
FT	Frank Thomas	15.00
JT	Jim Thome	15.00
LW	Larry Walker	10.00

Tribute to the Stars Patchworks

		NM/M
Common Player:		25.00
Production 50 Sets		
JB	Jeff Bagwell	35.00
BB	Barry Bonds	80.00
NG	Nomar Garciaparra	50.00
LG	Luis Gonzalez	25.00
SG	Shawn Green	25.00
TH	Todd Helton	35.00
THU	Torii Hunter	25.00
RJ	Randy Johnson	40.00
CJ	Chipper Jones	35.00
GM	Greg Maddux	50.00
PM	Pedro J. Martinez	40.00
RP	Rafael Palmeiro	30.00
AP	Albert Pujols	80.00
MR	Manny Ramirez	35.00
AR	Alex Rodriguez	50.00
AR2	Alex Rodriguez	50.00
CS	Curt Schilling	25.00
SS	Sammy Sosa	40.00
FT	Frank Thomas	35.00
KW	Kerry Wood	30.00

40/40 Club

		NM/M
Premiere Proof:		1.5X
Production 50		
CBR	Jose Canseco, Barry Bonds, Alex Rodriguez	85.00

600 HR Club Relic

		NM/M
Premiere Proofs:		1.5X

Production 50		
Gold:		No Pricing
Production One Set		
HA-600	Hank Aaron	35.00
BB-600	Barry Bonds	30.00
WM-600	Willie Mays	45.00
BR-600	Babe Ruth	125.00

600 HR Club Double Relic

		NM/M
Premiere Proofs:		1.5X
Production 50		
BA-600	Barry Bonds, Hank Aaron	80.00
BA-600	Barry Bonds, Willie Mays	80.00
BA-600	Barry Bonds, Babe Ruth	200.00

600 HR Club Quad Relic

		NM/M
Premiere Proof:		1X
Production 25		
BA-600	Hank Aaron, Babe Ruth, Willie Mays, Barry Bonds	625.00

2003 Topps Tribute All-Star Edition

		NM/M
Complete Set (50):		50.00
Common Player:		1.00
Pack (5):		40.00
Box (6):		200.00
1	Willie Mays	8.00
2	Don Mattingly	1.00
3	Hoyt Wilhelm	1.00
4	Hank Aaron	8.00
5	Hank Greenberg	1.00
6	Johnny Bench	5.00
7	Duke Snider	3.00
8	Carl Yastrzemski	3.00
9	Jim Palmer	1.00
10	Roberto Clemente	8.00
11	Mike Schmidt	1.00
12	Joe Cronin	1.00
13	Lou Brock	1.00
14	Orlando Cepeda	1.00
15	Bill Mazeroski	1.00
16	Whitey Ford	3.00
17	Rod Carew	1.00
18	Joe Morgan	1.00
19	Luis Aparicio	1.00
20	Nolan Ryan	10.00
21	Bobby Doerr	1.00
22	Dale Murphy	2.00
23	Bob Feller	1.00
24	Paul Molitor	1.00
25	Tom Seaver	3.00
26	Ozzie Smith	3.00
27	Stan Musial	6.00
28	Willie McCovey	1.00
29	Gary Carter	1.00
30	Reggie Jackson	3.00
31	Gaylord Perry	1.00
32	George Brett	8.00
33	Rocky Colavito	1.00
34	Wade Boggs	2.00
35	Cal Ripken Jr.	8.00
36	Carlton Fisk	1.00
37	Al Kaline	3.00
38	Kirby Puckett	4.00
39	Phil Rizzuto	2.00
40	Willie Stargell	1.00
41	Harmon Killebrew	3.00
42	Red Schoendienst	1.00
43	Tony Gwynn	3.00
44	Ralph Kiner	1.00
45	Yogi Berra	4.00
46	Jim "Catfish" Hunter	1.00
47	Frank Robinson	2.00
48	Ernie Banks	4.00
49	Warren Spahn	2.00
50	Brooks Robinson	3.00

Premier Proof

Cards (1-50):		4-8X
Numbered to last two digits of 1st.		
All-Star Year.		

All-Star Signing

		NM/M
Common Autograph:		40.00
Premier Proofs:		1.5-2X
Production 25 Sets		
LB	Lou Brock	50.00
GC	Gary Carter	40.00
OC	Orlando Cepeda	40.00
AD	Andre Dawson	40.00
TG	Tony Gwynn	80.00

AK	Al Kaline	75.00
DMA	Don Mattingly	125.00
DM	Dale Murphy	75.00
JP	Jim Palmer	40.00
MS	Mike Schmidt	100.00
DSN	Duke Snider	45.00

Memorable Match-up Relic

		NM/M
Common Card:		50.00
Production 150 Sets		
Premier Proofs:		1.5-2X
Production 25 Sets		
YB	Carl Yastrzemski, Johnny Bench	70.00
BS	George Brett, Mike Schmidt	120.00
MJ	Willie Mays, Reggie Jackson	65.00
BF	Johnny Bench, Carlton Fisk	50.00
CM	Gary Carter, Don Mattingly	85.00
KA	Harmon Killebrew, Hank Aaron	125.00
BG	Wade Boggs, Tony Gwynn	60.00
PG	Kirby Puckett, Tony Gwynn	60.00
YBR	Carl Yastrzemski, Lou Brock	60.00

Perennial Patch Relics

		NM/M
Common Player:		40.00
Production 30 Sets		
WB	Wade Boggs	75.00
GB	George Brett	220.00
GC	Gary Carter	40.00
TG	Tony Gwynn	125.00
HK	Harmon Killebrew	90.00
WM	Willie McCovey	40.00
JM	Joe Morgan	40.00
DMU	Dale Murphy	120.00
CR	Cal Ripken Jr.	225.00
NR	Nolan Ryan/Rangers	200.00
NRA	Nolan Ryan/Astros	200.00
MS	Mike Schmidt	200.00
OS	Ozzie Smith	120.00
WS	Willie Stargell	75.00
CY	Carl Yastrzemski	190.00

Tribute Relics

		NM/M
Common Player:		10.00
Inserted 1:1		
HA	Hank Aaron	35.00
LA	Luis Aparicio	10.00
EB	Ernie Banks	20.00
JBE	Johnny Bench	20.00
YB	Yogi Berra	40.00
WB	Wade Boggs	15.00
GB	George Brett	20.00
LB	Lou Brock/bat	30.00
LBU	Lou Brock/Jersey	40.00
RCA	Roy Campanella	20.00
ROD	Rod Carew	15.00
GC	Gary Carter	10.00
OC	Orlando Cepeda	12.00
RC	Roberto Clemente	60.00
TC	Ty Cobb	100.00
JCR	Joe Cronin	15.00
AD	Andre Dawson	10.00
DD	Dizzy Dean	40.00
BD	Bobby Doerr	10.00
BF	Bob Feller	15.00
CF	Carlton Fisk	15.00
WF	Whitey Ford	30.00
JF	Jimmie Foxx	40.00
LG	Lou Gehrig	125.00
HG	Hank Greenberg	40.00
TG	Tony Gwynn	20.00
RH	Rogers Hornsby	40.00
CH	Jim "Catfish" Hunter	10.00
RJ	Reggie Jackson	15.00
AK	Al Kaline	25.00
HK	Harmon Killebrew	20.00
NL	Napoleon Lajoie	60.00
EM	Eddie Mathews	15.00
DMA	Don Mattingly	30.00
WM	Willie Mays	40.00
BM	Bill Mazeroski	20.00
WMC	Willie McCovey	18.00
JMI	Johnny Mize	30.00
PM	Paul Molitor	15.00
JMO	Joe Morgan	10.00
TM	Thurman Munson	30.00
DM	Dale Murphy	50.00
SM	Stan Musial	40.00
DN	Don Newcombe	10.00

MO	Mel Ott	30.00
JP	Jim Palmer	10.00
KP	Kirby Puckett	20.00
CRB	Cal Ripken Jr.	40.00
PR	Phil Rizzuto	15.00
BRO	Brooks Robinson	15.00
FR	Frank Robinson	10.00
JR	Jackie Robinson	40.00
BR	Babe Ruth	140.00
NR	Nolan Ryan/Rangers	40.00
NRA	Nolan Ryan/Astros	40.00
MS	Mike Schmidt	20.00
RS	Red Schoendienst	15.00
TSE	Tom Seaver	25.00
OS	Ozzie Smith	15.00
DSN	Duke Snider	20.00
TS	Tris Speaker	75.00
WST	Willie Stargell	20.00
HW	Honus Wagner	125.00
WHI	Hoyt Wilhelm	10.00
CY	Carl Yastrzemski	30.00

1st Class Cuts

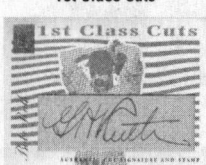

		NM/M
Production One Set		
FC-TC	Ty Cobb (3/03 Auction)	7,600
FC-JR	Jackie Robinson (3/03 Auction)	3,500
FC-BR	Babe Ruth (6/04 Auction)	7,300

2003 Topps Tribute World Series

		NM/M
Complete Set (150):		150.00
Common Player:		1.00
Pack (5):		50.00
Box (6):		260.00
1	Willie Mays	8.00
2	Gary Carter	1.50
3	Yogi Berra	4.00
4	Dennis Eckersley	1.50
5	Willie McCovey	1.00
6	Willie Stargell	2.00
7	Mike Schmidt	8.00
8	Robin Yount	4.00
9	Bucky Harris	1.00
10	Carl Yastrzemski	4.00
11	Lenny Dykstra	1.00
12	Boog Powell	1.00
13	Bill Lee	1.00
14	Lou Brock	1.50
15	Bob Friend	1.00
16	Hank Greenberg	1.50
17	Maury Wills	1.00
18	Tommy Lasorda	1.00
19	Bill "Moose" Skowron	1.00
20	Frank Robinson	2.00
21	Rollie Fingers	1.00
22	Doug DeCinces	1.00
23	Eric Davis	1.00
24	Johnny Podres	1.00
25	Darrell Evans	1.00
26	Ron Cey	1.00
27	Ray Knight	1.00
28	Don Larsen	1.00
29	Harold Baines	1.00
30	Brooks Robinson	4.00
31	Wade Boggs	2.00
32	Joe Morgan	1.00
33	Kirk Gibson	1.00
34	Tommy John	1.00
35	Monte Irvin	1.00
36	Rich "Goose" Gossage	1.00
37	Tug McGraw	1.00
38	Walt Weiss	1.00
39	Bill Madlock	1.00
40	Juan Marichal	2.00
41	Willie McGee	1.00
42	Joe Cronin	1.00
43	Paul Blair	1.00
44	Norm Cash	1.00
45	Ken Griffey Sr.	1.00
46	Bret Saberhagen	1.00
47	Don Sutton	1.00
48	Kirby Puckett	4.00
49	Keith Hernandez	1.00
50	George Brett	8.00
51	Bobby Richardson	1.00

52	Jose Canseco	2.00
53	Greg Luzinski	1.00
54	Bill Mazeroski	1.00
55	Red Schoendienst	1.00
56	Graig Nettles	1.00
57	Jerry Koosman	1.00
58	Tony Perez	1.00
59	Jim Rice	1.00
60	Duke Snider	4.00
61	David Justice	1.00
62	Johnny Sain	1.00
63	Chuck Klein	1.00
64	Sparky Anderson	1.00
65	Alan Trammell	2.00
66	Willie Wilson	1.00
67	Hoyt Wilhelm	1.00
68	Joe Pepitone	1.00
69	Darren Daulton	1.00
70	Tom Seaver	4.00
71	Jim "Catfish" Hunter	1.00
72	Tim McCarver	1.00
73	Dave Parker	1.00
74	Earl Weaver	1.00
75	Ted Kluszewski	1.00
76	John Kruk	1.00
77	Dwight Evans	1.00
78	Ron Darling	1.00
79	Tony Oliva	1.00
80	Johnny Bench	5.00
81	Sam Crawford	1.00
82	Steve Yeager	1.00
83	Paul Molitor	2.00
84	Bert Campaneris	1.00
85	Mickey Rivers	1.00
86	Vince Coleman	1.00
87	Kent Tekulve	1.00
88	Dwight Gooden	1.00
89	Whitey Herzog	1.00
90	Whitey Ford	4.00
91	Warren Spahn	3.00
92	Fred Lynn	1.00
93	Joe Tinker	1.00
94	Bill Buckner	1.00
95	Bob Feller	2.00
96	Hank Bauer	1.00
97	Joe Rudi	1.00
98	Steve Sax	1.00
99	Bruce Sutter	1.50
100	Nolan Ryan	10.00
101	Bobby Thomson	1.00
102	Bob Watson	1.00
103	Vida Blue	1.00
104	Robin Roberts	1.00
105	Orlando Cepeda	2.00
106	Jim Bottomley	1.00
107	Heinie Manush	1.00
108	Jim Gilliam	1.00
109	Dave Concepcion	1.00
110	Al Kaline	5.00
111	Howard Johnson	1.00
112	Phil Rizzuto	2.00
113	Steve Garvey	1.00
114	George Foster	1.00
115	Carlton Fisk	2.00
116	Don Newcombe	1.00
117	Lance Parrish	1.00
118	Reggie Jackson	4.00
119	Luis Aparicio	1.00
120	Jim Palmer	1.50
121	Ron Guidry	1.50
122	Frankie Frisch	1.00
123	Chet Lemon	1.00
124	Cecil Cooper	1.00
125	Harmon Killebrew	4.00
126	Luis Tiant	1.00
127	John McGraw	1.00
128	Paul O'Neill	1.00
129	Jack Clark	1.00
130	Stan Musial	6.00
131	Mike Schmidt	4.00
132	Kirby Puckett	4.00
133	Carlton Fisk	1.50
134	Bill Mazeroski	1.00
135	Johnny Podres	1.00
136	Robin Yount	1.50
137	David Justice	1.00
138	Bobby Thomson	1.00
139	Joe Carter	1.00
140	Reggie Jackson	1.50
141	Kirk Gibson	1.50
142	Whitey Ford	1.50
143	Don Larsen	1.50
144	Duke Snider	1.50
145	Carl Yastrzemski	1.50
146	Johnny Bench	2.00
147	Lou Brock	1.00
148	Ted Kluszewski	1.00
149	Jim Palmer	1.00
150	Willie Mays	5.00

Gold

Golds (1-150): 4-8X
Production 100 Sets

Relic

NM/M
Common Player: 10.00
Production 425 unless noted.
Golds: No Pricing
Production 25

HA	Hank Aaron/50	60.00
HB	Hank Bauer/50	30.00
JBE	Johnny Bench/50	25.00
YB	Yogi Berra	20.00
WB	Wade Boggs/50	15.00
JB	Jim Bottomley/50	30.00
GB	George Brett	25.00
LB	Lou Brock	10.00
JC	Jose Canseco	15.00
NC	Norm Cash/50	25.00
OC	Orlando Cepeda/50	30.00
RC	Roberto Clemente/50	120.00
TC	Ty Cobb	120.00
SC	Sam Crawford/50	50.00
CF	Carlton Fisk	40.00
JF	Jimmie Foxx/50	80.00
FF	Frankie Frisch	15.00
LG	Lou Gehrig/50	185.00
HG	Hank Greenberg/50	60.00
TG	Tony Gwynn	20.00
BH	Bucky Harris	10.00
RH	Rogers Hornsby	35.00
CH	Jim "Catfish" Hunter	15.00
RJ	Reggie Jackson	15.00
HK	Harmon Killebrew	25.00
CK	Chuck Klein	10.00
TK	Ted Kluszewski	10.00
HM	Heinie Manush/50	35.00
JM	Juan Marichal	15.00
RM	Roger Maris/50	75.00
BMA	Billy Martin	15.00
WM	Willie Mays	50.00
BM	Bill Mazeroski	15.00
WMC	Willie McCovey	10.00
TM	Thurman Munson	30.00
SM	Stan Musial	30.00
KP	Kirby Puckett	20.00
CR	Cal Ripken Jr.	35.00
FR	Frank Robinson	15.00
JR	Jackie Robinson	40.00
ER	Edd Roush/50	40.00
BR	Babe Ruth	140.00
MS	Mike Schmidt	25.00
RS	Red Schoendienst	10.00
TS	Tom Seaver	15.00
OS	Ozzie Smith	20.00
TSP	Tris Speaker/50	90.00
WS	Willie Stargell/50	30.00
BT	Bobby Thomson	15.00
JT	Joe Tinker	30.00
HW	Honus Wagner/50	150.00
CY	Carl Yastrzemski	30.00
RY	Robin Yount	20.00

Autographed Relic

NM/M
Inserted 1:55
Golds: No Pricing
Production 25 Sets

LB	Lou Brock	40.00
JC	Jose Canseco	40.00
CF	Carlton Fisk	120.00
HK	Harmon Killebrew	75.00
WM	Willie Mays	275.00
BM	Bill Mazeroski	60.00
MS	Mike Schmidt	100.00
BT	Bobby Thomson	40.00

Cut Signature Relic
No pricing due to scarcity.
Production One Set

Fan Fare Relic

NM/M
Common Player: 10.00
Inserted 1:Box

HB	Hank Bauer	10.00
YB	Yogi Berra	20.00
WF	Whitey Ford	15.00
DJ	David Justice	10.00
DL	Don Larsen	15.00
BM	Billy Martin	15.00
DN	Don Newcombe	10.00
PO	Paul O'Neill	15.00
JP	Johnny Podres	15.00
PR	Phil Rizzuto	15.00
MS	Bill "Moose" Skowron	10.00
DS	Duke Snider	15.00

Memorab. Match-Up Relic

NM/M
Common Player: 10.00
Varying quantities produced.

GF	Hank Greenberg, Frankie Frisch/34	90.00
GK	Hank Greenberg, Chuck Klein/35	90.00
PR	Phil Rizzuto, Willie Mays/51	150.00
FS	Whitey Ford, Duke Snider/53	75.00
AS	Luis Aparicio, Duke Snider/59	35.00
MF	Bill Mazeroski, Whitey Ford/60	50.00
KB	Al Kaline, Lou Brock/68	75.00
RS	Frank Robinson, Tom Seaver/69	40.00
RBE	Brooks Robinson, Johnny Bench/70	55.00
AM	Sparky Anderson, Billy Martin/76	25.00
SP	Willie Stargell, Jim Palmer/79	40.00
SB	Mike Schmidt, George Brett/80	50.00
SY	Ozzie Smith, Robin Yount/82	50.00
SRI	Mike Schmidt, Cal Ripken Jr./83	120.00
TG	Alan Trammell, Tony Gwynn/84	50.00
WB	Mookie Wilson, Bill Buckner/86	40.00
EG	Dennis Eckersley, Kirk Gibson/88	35.00

Pastime Patches Relics
No pricing due to scarcity.
Production 15 Sets

Series Signatures
NM/M
Common Autograph: 25.00
Golds: No Pricing
Production 25

SA	Sparky Anderson	25.00
JC	Joe Carter	25.00
WF	Whitey Ford	60.00
SG	Steve Garvey	25.00
KG	Kirk Gibson	30.00
DJ	David Justice	40.00
AK	Al Kaline	50.00
DN	Don Newcombe	40.00
JP	Jim Palmer	30.00
BR	Brooks Robinson	75.00
MS	Bill "Moose" Skowron	25.00
AT	Alan Trammell	25.00
EW	Earl Weaver	25.00
MW	Maury Wills	25.00
MWI	Mookie Wilson	30.00

Team Tribute Relic
NM/M
Common Card: 15.00
Production 275 unless noted.

YLK	Carl Yastrzemski, Fred Lynn, Carlton Fisk	50.00
OSD	Paul O'Neill, Chris Sabo, Eric Davis	25.00
FPG	George Foster, Tony Perez, Ken Griffey Jr.	25.00
CPM	Dave Concepcion, Tony Perez, Joe Morgan	50.00
KCA	Al Kaline, Norm Cash	40.00
TA	Alan Trammell, Sparky Anderson	15.00
GT	Kirk Gibson, Alan Trammell	25.00
SB	Bret Saberhagen, George Brett	40.00
CYG	Ron Cey, Steve Yeager, Steve Garvey	30.00
YM	Robin Yount, Paul Molitor	35.00
SRK	Tom Seaver, Nolan Ryan, Jerry Koosman	50.00
HCD	Keith Hernandez, Gary Carter, Lenny Dykstra	30.00

GB	Lou Gehrig, Babe Ruth/25	500.00
EC	Dennis Eckersley, Jose Canseco	25.00
HJ	Jim "Catfish" Hunter, Reggie Jackson	30.00
SPM	Willie Stargell, Dave Parker, Bill Madlock	30.00
CM	Orlando Cepeda, Juan Marichal	30.00
MM	Willie Mays, Willie McCovey	50.00
SMC	Ozzie Smith, Willie McGee, Vince Coleman	40.00

Tribute Singles
NM/M
Common Player: 8.00
Premiere Proofs: 1.5X
Production 50

TG	Troy Glaus	8.00
MR	Mariano Rivera	10.00

Tribute Doubles
NM/M
Common Duo: 10.00
Premiere Proofs: 1.5X
Production 50

PP	Jorge Posada, Andy Pettitte	15.00
WO	Bernie Williams, Paul O'Neill	15.00
LP	John Lackey, Troy Percival	10.00
SJ	Curt Schilling, Randy Johnson	15.00
BG	Barry Bonds, Troy Glaus	35.00
WG	Bernie Williams, Luis Gonzalez	10.00
PC	Mike Piazza, Roger Clemens	35.00

Tribute Triples

NM/M
Common Trio: 15.00
Premiere Proofs: 1.5X
Production 50

LGP	John Lackey, Troy Glaus, Troy Percival	15.00
EGS	Darin Erstad, Troy Glaus, Tim Salmon	15.00

2003 Topps 205

NM/M
Complete Set (335): 150.00
Common Player: .20
SP's inserted 1:5
25 variations in base set and minis
Mini-Cards(316-335):
Exclusive Mini Cards
Price for minis (316-335) are Polar Bear
Series 1 or 2 Pack (8): 4.00
Series 1 or 2 Box (20): 65.00

1	Barry Bonds	2.50
1	Barry Bonds/Variation	3.00
2	Bret Boone	.40
3	Albert Pujols	2.00
3	Albert Pujols/Variation	2.00
4	Carl Crawford	.20
5	Bartolo Colon	.20
6	Cliff Floyd	.20
7	John Olerud	.40
8	Jason Giambi	.50
8	Jason Giambi/Variation	.75
9	Edgardo Alfonzo	.20
10	Ivan Rodriguez	.50
11	Jim Edmonds	.50
12	Mike Piazza	1.50
12	Mike Piazza/Variation	2.00
13	Greg Maddux	1.50
14	Jose Vidro	.20
15	Vladimir Guerrero	.75
15	Vladimir Guerrero/Variation	1.00
16	Bernie Williams	.50
17	Roger Clemens	
18	Miguel Tejada	.50
18	Miguel Tejada/Variation	.75
19	Carlos Delgado	.50
19	Alfonso Soriano	.75
20	Alfonso Soriano/Variation	.75
21	Bobby Cox	.20
22	Mike Scioscia	.20
23	John Smoltz	.40
24	Luis Gonzalez	.40
25	Shawn Green	.40
26	Raul Ibanez	.20
27	Andruw Jones	.50
28	Josh Beckett	.50
29	Derek Lowe	.40
30	Todd Helton	.75
31	Barry Larkin	.40
32	Jason Jennings	.20
33	Darin Erstad	.40
34	Magglio Ordonez	.40
35	Mike Sweeney	.20
36	Kazuhisa Ishii	.20
37	Ron Gardenhire	.20
38	Tim Hudson	.40
39	Tim Salmon	.50
40	Pat Burrell	.40
41	Pat Burrell/Variation	.50
41	Manny Ramirez	.75
42	Nick Johnson	.20
43	Tom Glavine	.50
44	Mark Mulder	.40
45	Brian Jordan	.20
46	Rafael Palmeiro	.50
47	Vernon Wells	.40
48	Bob Brenly	.20
49	C.C. Sabathia	.20
50	Alex Rodriguez	2.50
50	Alex Rodriguez/Variation	2.50
51	Sammy Sosa	1.50
51	Sammy Sosa/Variation	2.00
52	Paul Konerko	.20
53	Craig Biggio	.40
54	Moises Alou	.20
55	Johnny Damon	.50
56	Torii Hunter	.40
57	Omar Vizquel	.20
58	Orlando Hernandez	.20
59	Barry Zito	.40
60	Lance Berkman	.50
61	Carlos Beltran	.40
62	Edgar Renteria	.40
63	Ben Sheets	.40
64	Doug Mientkiewicz	.20
65	Troy Glaus	.50
66	Preston Wilson	.20
67	Kerry Wood	.75
68	Frank Thomas	.75
69	Jimmy Rollins	.20
70	Brian Giles	.40
71	Bobby Higginson	.20
72	Larry Walker	.40
73	Randy Johnson	1.00
74	Tony LaRussa	.20
75	Derek Jeter	3.00
75	Derek Jeter/Variation	3.00
76	Bobby Abreu	.40
77	Adam Dunn	.75
77	Adam Dunn/Variation	.75
78	Ryan Klesko	.20
79	Francisco Rodriguez	.20
80	Scott Rolen	.50
81	Roberto Alomar	.50
82	Joe Torre	.50
83	Jim Thome	.50
84	Kevin Millwood	.40
85	J.T. Snow	.20
86	Trevor Hoffman	.20
87	Jay Gibbons	.20
88	Mark Prior	1.00
88	Mark Prior/Variation	1.50
89	Rich Aurilia	.20
90	Chipper Jones	1.00
91	Richie Sexson	.20
92	Gary Sheffield	.50
93	Pedro J. Martinez	1.00
94	Rodrigo Lopez	.20
95	Al Leiter	.20
96	Jorge Posada	.50
97	Luis Castillo	.20
98	Aubrey Huff	.20
99	A.J. Pierzynski	.20
100	Ichiro Suzuki	2.00
100	Ichiro Suzuki/Variation	2.00
101	Eric Chavez	.40
102	Brett Myers	.20
103	Jason Kendall	.20
104	Jeff Kent	.50
105	Eric Hinske	.20
106	Jacque Jones	.20
107	Phil Nevin	.20
108	Roy Oswalt	.40
109	Curt Schilling	.75
110	Nomar Garciaparra	2.00
110	Nomar Garciaparra/Variation	2.00
111	Garret Anderson	.40
112	Eric Gagne	.50
113	Javier Vazquez	.40
114	Jeff Bagwell	.75
115	Mike Lowell	.20
116	Carlos Pena	.20
117	Ken Griffey Jr.	1.50
118	Tony Batista	.20
119	Edgar Martinez	.50
120	Austin Kearns	.50
121	Jason Stokes	.20
122	Jose Reyes	.50
123	Rocco Baldelli	.40
124	Joe Borchard	.20
125	Joe Mauer	.50
126	Gavin Floyd	.20
127	Mark Teixeira	.50
128	Jeremy Guthrie	.20
129	B.J. Upton	.40
130	Khalil Greene	.40
131	Hanley Ramirez RC	5.00
132	Andy Marte RC	1.00
133	J.D. Durbin RC	1.00
134	Jason Kubel RC	1.00
135	Craig Brazell RC	.75
136	Bryan Bullington RC	1.00
137	Jose Contreras RC	1.00
138	Brian Burgamy RC	.75
139	Evel Bastida-Martinez RC	.50
140	Joey Gomes	1.00
141	Ismael Castro RC	.75
142	Travis Wong RC	.75
143	Michael Garciaparra	.50
144	Arnaldo Munoz RC	.50
145	Louis Sockalexis	2.00
146	Dick Hoblitzell	1.00
147	George "Peaches" Graham	.50
148	Hal Chase	.50
149	John McGraw	1.00
150	Bobby Wallace	.50
151	Dave Shean	.20
152	Dick Hoblitzell/SP	3.00
153	Hal Chase	.50
154	George Wiltse	.20
155	George Brett	2.00
156	Willie Mays	3.00
157	Honus Wagner/SP	4.00
158	Nolan Ryan	3.00
159	Reggie Jackson	1.00
160	Mike Schmidt	1.50
161	Josh Barfield	.20
162	Grady Sizemore	.20
163	Justin Morneau	.40
164	Laynce Nix	.20
165	Zack Greinke	.20
166	Victor Martinez	.50
167	Jeff Mathis	.20
168	Casey Kotchman	.20
169	Gabe Gross	.20
170	Edwin Jackson RC	1.50
171	Delmon Young/SP RC	4.00
172	Eric Duncan/SP	2.00
173	Brian Snyder/SP	1.50
174	Chris Lubanski/SP RC	4.00
175	Ryan Harvey/SP RC	4.00
176	Nicholas Markakis/SP RC	5.00
177	Chad Billingsley/SP RC	2.00
178	Elizardo Ramirez	.50
179	Ben Francisco	.20
180	Franklin Gutierrez/SP	4.00
181	Aaron Hill/SP	2.00
182	Kevin Correia	.50
183	Kelly Shoppach RC	.75
184	Felix Pie/SP RC	4.00
185	Adam Loewen/SP RC	4.00
186	Danny Garcia	.20
187	Rickie Weeks/SP RC	5.00
188	Robby Hammock/SP RC	1.00
189	Ryan Wagner/SP RC	1.00
190	Matt Kata/SP	1.00
191	Bo Hart/SP RC	1.00
192	Brandon Webb/SP RC	4.00
193	Bengie Molina	.20
194	Junior Spivey	.20
195	Gary Sheffield	.20
196	Jason Johnson	.20
197	David Ortiz	.75
198	Roberto Alomar	.50
199	Wily Mo Pena	.20
200	Sammy Sosa	2.00
201	Jay Payton	.20
202	Dmitri Young	.20
203	Derek Lee	.40
204	Jeff Bagwell	.75
204	Jeff Bagwell/Variation	.75
205	Runelvys Hernandez	.20
206	Kevin Brown	.40
207	Wes Helms	.20
208	Eddie Guardado	.20
209	Orlando Cabrera	.20
210	Alfonso Soriano	.75
211	Ty Wigginton	.20
212	Rich Harden	.40
212	Rich Harden/Variation	.40
213	Mike Lieberthal	.20
214	Brian Giles	.40
215	Jason Schmidt	.40
216	Jamie Moyer	.20
217	Matt Morris	.20
218	Victor Zambrano	.20
219	Roy Halladay	.50
220	Mike Hampton	.20
221	Kevin Millar	.20
222	Hideo Nomo	.50
223	Milton Bradley	.20
224	Jose Guillen	.20
225	Derek Jeter	3.00
226	Rondell White	.20
227	Hank Blalock	.50
228	Hank Blalock/Variation	.50
228	Shigetoshi Hasegawa	.20
229	Mike Mussina	.50
230	Cristian Guzman	.20
231	Todd Helton	.75
231	Todd Helton/Variation	.75
232	Kenny Lofton	.40
233	Carl Everett	.20
234	Shea Hillenbrand	.20
235	Brad Fullmer	.20
236	Bernie Williams	.50
237	Vicente Padilla	.20
238	Tim Worrell	.20
239	Juan Gonzalez	.40
240	Ichiro Suzuki	2.00
241	Aaron Boone	.20
242	Shannon Stewart	.20
243	Barry Zito	.40
243	Barry Zito/Variation	.40
244	Reggie Sanders	.20
245	Scott Podsednik	.40
246	Miguel Cabrera	.75
247	Angel Berroa	.20
248	Carlos Zambrano	.40
249	Marlon Byrd	.20
250	Mark Prior	1.00
251	Esteban Loaiza	.20
252	David Eckstein	.20
253	Alex Cintron	.20
254	Melvin Mora	.20
255	Russ Ortiz	.20
256	Carlos Lee	.20
257	Tino Martinez	.20
258	Randy Wolf	.20
259	Jason Phillips	.20
260	Vladimir Guerrero	1.00
261	Brad Wilkerson	.20
262	Ivan Rodriguez	.75
263	Matt Lawton	.20
264	Adam Dunn	.50
265	Joe Borowski	.20
266	Jody Gerut	.20
267	Alex Rodriguez	2.50
268	Brendan Donnelly	.20
269	Randy Johnson	1.00
269	Randy Johnson/Variation	1.00
270	Nomar Garciaparra	2.50
271	Javy Lopez	.50
272	Travis Hafner	.20
273	Juan Pierre	.20
274	Morgan Ensberg	.20
275	Albert Pujols	2.00
276	Jason LaRue	.20
277	Paul LoDuca	.20
278	Andy Pettitte	.50
279	Mike Piazza	1.50
280	Jim Thome	1.00
280	Jim Thome/Variation	1.00
281	Marquis Grissom	.20
282	Woody Williams	.20
283	Curt Schilling	.75
283	Curt Schilling/Variation	.75
284	Chipper Jones	1.00
284	Chipper Jones/Variation	1.00
285	Deivi Cruz	.20
286	Johnny Damon	.50
287	Chin-Hui Tsao	.20
288	Alex Gonzalez	.20
289	Billy Wagner	.20
290	Jason Giambi	.50
291	Keith Foulke	.20
292	Jerome Williams	.20
293	Livan Hernandez	.20
294	Aaron Guiel	.20
295	Randall Simon	.20
296	Byung-Hyun Kim	.20
297	Jorge Julio	.20
298	Miguel Batista	.20
299	Rafael Furcal	.20
300	Dontrelle Willis/SP	1.00
300	Dontrelle Willis/Variation	1.00
301	Alex Sanchez	.20
302	Shawn Chacon	.20
303	Matt Clement	.20
304	Luis Matos	.20
305	Steve Finley	.20
306	Marcus Giles	.20
307	David Wells	.20
308	Jeromy Burnitz	.20
309	Mike MacDougal	.20
310	Mariano Rivera	.40
311	Adrian Beltre	.20
312	Mark Loretta	.20
313	Ugueth Urbina	.20
314	Bill Mueller	.20
315	Johan Santana	.50
316	Willie Mays	2.00
317	Delmon Young	4.00
318	Rickie Weeks	4.00
319	Ryan Wagner	.50
320	Brandon Webb	.75
321	Chris Lubanski	1.00
322	Ryan Harvey	1.00
323	Nicholas Markakis	1.00
324	Chad Billingsley	1.00
325	Aaron Hill	.40
326	Brian Snyder	.40
327	Eric Duncan	.40
328	Sammy Sosa	1.50
329	Alfonso Soriano	.50
330	Ichiro Suzuki	2.00
331	Alex Rodriguez	2.00
332	Nomar Garciaparra	2.00
333	Albert Pujols	2.00
334	Jim Thome	1.00
335	Dontrelle Willis	.50

Mini Parallel

Polar Bear:	1-2X
Sovereign:	1-2X
Sovereign Green:	2-3X
American Beauty:	1-2X
Amer. Beauty Purple:	3-5X
Cycle:	1-2X
Cycle Purple:	3-5X
Drum:	2-4X
Honest:	1-2X
Honest Purple:	3-5X
Piedmont:	1-2X
Piedmont Purple:	3-5X
Sweet Caporal:	1-2X

GLAUS ANAHEIM AMER.

AL	Al Leiter/Jsy	4.00
KL	Kenny Lofton/Jsy	4.00
DL	Derek Lowe/Jsy	4.00
GM	Greg Maddux/Jsy	15.00
PM	Pedro Martinez/Jsy	10.00
MO	Magglio Ordonez/Jsy	4.00
RO	Roy Oswalt/Jsy	4.00
RP	Rafael Palmeiro/Jsy	6.00
TP	Troy Percival/Jsy	4.00
MP	Mike Piazza/Bat	10.00
AP	Albert Pujols/Jsy	20.00
MR	Manny Ramirez/Bat	8.00
AR	Alex Rodriguez/Jsy	10.00
SR	Scott Rolen/Bat .	15.00
CS	Curt Schilling/Jsy	6.00
JS	John Smoltz/Jsy	8.00
AS	Alfonso Soriano/Jsy	10.00
MS	Mike Sweeney/Bat	4.00
JT	Jim Thome/Bat	12.00
MV	Mo Vaughn/Jsy	4.00
BW	Bernie Williams/Bat	10.00
BZ	Barry Zito/Jsy	4.00

Series 2

Sweet Caporal Purple: 3-5X
Bazooka: No Pricing
Production Five Sets
Brooklyn: 1.5-4X
Brooklyn: Varies for common, rare & Unc.

T-205 Autographs

		NM/M
Common Autograph:	12.00
LB	Lance Berkman	25.00
MB	Marlon Byrd	10.00
CF	Cliff Floyd	15.00
TH	Torii Hunter	15.00
PL	Paul LoDuca	15.00
MO	Magglio Ordonez	20.00
JR	Jose Reyes	30.00
SR	Scott Rolen	40.00
MS	Mike Sweeney	20.00

Series 2

HA	Hank Aaron/50	280.00
LC	Luis Castillo	10.00
ED	Eric Duncan	20.00
RH	Rich Harden	25.00
FP	Felix Pie	40.00
RWA	Ryan Wagner	15.00
JW	Jerome Williams	20.00
DW	Dontrelle Willis	25.00

T-205 Relics

		NM/M
Common Player:	4.00
RA	Roberto Alomar/Bat	6.00
GA	Garret Anderson/Jsy	5.00
JB	Jeff Bagwell/Jsy	6.00
LB	Lance Berkman/Bat	8.00
BB	Barry Bonds	25.00
AB	A.J. Burnett/Jsy	4.00
LC	Luis Castillo/Jsy	4.00
EC	Eric Chavez/Bat	5.00
JD	Johnny Damon/Bat	4.00
AD	Adam Dunn/Bat	8.00
RF	Rafael Furcal/Bat	6.00
EG	Eric Gagne/Jsy	8.00
NG	Nomar Garciaparra/Jsy	15.00
BG	Brian Giles/Bat	6.00
LG	Luis Gonzalez/Jsy	4.00
TH	Todd Helton/Jsy	10.00
KI	Kazuhisa Ishii/Jsy	6.00
JJ	Jason Jennings/Jsy	4.00
NJ	Nick Johnson/Bat	4.00
RJ	Randy Johnson/Jsy	8.00
JK	Jeff Kent/Bat	4.00

AL	Al Leiter/Jsy	4.00
KL	Kenny Lofton/Jsy	4.00
DL	Derek Lowe/Jsy	4.00
GM	Greg Maddux/Jsy	15.00
PM	Pedro Martinez/Jsy	10.00
MO	Magglio Ordonez/Jsy	4.00
RO	Roy Oswalt/Jsy	4.00
RP	Rafael Palmeiro/Jsy	6.00
TP	Troy Percival/Jsy	4.00
MP	Mike Piazza/Bat	10.00
AP	Albert Pujols/Jsy	20.00
MR	Manny Ramirez/Bat	8.00
AR	Alex Rodriguez/Jsy	10.00
SR	Scott Rolen/Bat .	15.00
CS	Curt Schilling/Jsy	6.00
JS	John Smoltz/Jsy	8.00
AS	Alfonso Soriano/Jsy	10.00
MS	Mike Sweeney/Bat	4.00
JT	Jim Thome/Bat	12.00
MV	Mo Vaughn/Jsy	4.00
BW	Bernie Williams/Bat	10.00
BZ	Barry Zito/Jsy	4.00

Series 2

RA	Roberto Alomar	6.00
JB	Jeff Bagwell	8.00
RBB	Rocco Baldelli/Bat	8.00
RB	Rocco Baldelli/Jsy	8.00
CB	Craig Biggio	4.00
HB	Hank Blalock	6.00
WB	Wade Boggs	15.00
BB	Bret Boone	10.00
GB	George Brett	25.00
KB	Kevin Brown	4.00
SB	Sean Burroughs	4.00
MC	Mike Cameron	4.00
JC	Jose Canseco	8.00
GC	Gary Carter	8.00
RC	Roger Clemens	15.00
CD	Carlos Delgado	6.00
BD	Brandon Duckworth	4.00
JE	Jim Edmonds	6.00
DE	Darin Erstad	4.00
RF	Rafael Furcal	4.00
NG	Nomar Garciaparra	10.00
JG	Jason Giambi	6.00
JGI	Jeremy Giambi	4.00
BG	Brian Giles	4.00
TG	Troy Glaus	6.00
JGO	Juan Gonzalez	6.00
LG	Luis Gonzalez	4.00
MG	Mark Grace	10.00
MGR	Marquis Grissom	4.00
VG	Vladimir Guerrero	8.00
CG	Cristian Guzman	4.00
RH	Rickey Henderson	8.00
RJ	Randy Johnson	8.00
AJ	Andruw Jones	6.00
CJB	Chipper Jones	12.00
KL	Kenny Lofton	4.00
GM	Greg Maddux	10.00
EM	Edgar Martinez	4.00
PM	Pedro J. Martinez	8.00
TM	Tino Martinez	6.00
FM	Fred McGriff	4.00
MM	Mark Mulder	4.00
EMU	Eddie Murray	25.00
JO	John Olerud	4.00
PO	Paul O'Neill	4.00
RP	Rafael Palmeiro	6.00
CP	Corey Patterson	10.00
BP	Brad Penny	4.00
MP	Mike Piazza	10.00
JP	Jorge Posada	15.00
APB	Albert Pujols/bat	20.00
AP	Albert Pujols/jersey	20.00
ARA	Aramis Ramirez	4.00
FR	Frank Robinson	15.00
AR	Alex Rodriguez	10.00
IR	Ivan Rodriguez	8.00
SR	Scott Rolen	6.00
NR	Nolan Ryan	40.00
CS	Curt Schilling	6.00
MS	Mike Schmidt	25.00
GS	Gary Sheffield	6.00
TS	Tsuyoshi Shinjo	4.00
AS	Alfonso Soriano	6.00
SS	Sammy Sosa	15.00
SST	Shannon Stewart	4.00
MT	Mark Teixeira	6.00
MTE	Miguel Tejada	8.00
FT	Frank Thomas	8.00
RV	Robin Ventura	4.00
LW	Larry Walker	6.00
VW	Vernon Wells	8.00
BW	Bernie Williams	8.00
DW	Dontrelle Willis	6.00

Team Topps Legends Autographs

		NM/M
Common Player:	
	Stan Musial	65.00
	Jim Palmer	20.00
	Gaylord Perry	10.00
	Robin Yount	75.00

Triple Folder

		NM/M
Complete Set (100):	60.00
Common Card:	.25
Inserted 1:1	
Series 1 Brooklyn Variation:	4-8X
Inserted 1:72	
Series 2 Brooklyn Variation:	2-4X
Inserted 1:29	
TF1	Barry Bonds, Jason LaRue	1.50
TF2	Alfonso Soriano, Derek Jeter	1.50
TF3	Alex Rodriguez, Miguel Tejada	1.50
TF4	Nomar Garciaparra, Derek Jeter	2.00
TF5	Omar Vizquel, Alex Rodriguez	1.50
TF6	Paul Konerko, Omar Vizquel	.25
TF7	Paul Konerko, Magglio Ordonez	.25
TF8	Doug Mientkiewicz, Darin Erstad	.25
TF9	Jason Kendall, Jimmy Rollins	.25
TF10	Shawn Green, Roberto Alomar	.25
TF11	Derek Jeter, Roberto Alomar	1.50
TF12	Bobby Abreu, Luis Castillo	.25
TF13	Randy Johnson, Curt Schilling	.75
TF14	Mike Piazza, Kerry Wood	1.00
TF15	Roger Clemens, Jorge Posada	1.00
TF16	Ichiro Suzuki, Ryan Klesko	1.00
TF17	Alfonso Soriano, Chipper Jones	1.00
TF18	Barry Bonds, Nick Johnson	1.50
TF19	Chipper Jones, Andruw Jones	.75
TF20	Bobby Abreu, Paul Konerko	.25
TF21	Rafael Palmeiro, Alex Rodriguez	1.50
TF22	Eric Hinske, Carlos Delgado	.25
TF23	Nomar Garciaparra, Jay Gibbons	1.00
TF24	Mike Piazza, Luis Gonzalez	1.00
TF25	J.T. Snow, Vladimir Guerrero	.50
TF26	Jason Giambi, Bernie Williams	.75
TF27	Miguel Tejada, Richie Sexson	.25
TF28	Doug Mientkiewicz, Jimmy Rollins	.25
TF29	Eric Chavez, Derek Jeter	2.00
TF30	Alfonso Soriano, Bret Boone	1.00
TF31	Chipper Jones, Mike Piazza	1.00
TF32	Ichiro Suzuki, Bret Boone	1.00
TF33	Bobby Abreu, Mike Piazza	1.00
TF34	Jimmy Rollins, Pat Burrell	.25
TF35	Ichiro Suzuki, Miguel Tejada	1.00
TF36	Jason LaRue, Barry Bonds	1.50
TF37	Derek Jeter, Alfonso Soriano	1.50
TF38	Miguel Tejada, Alex Rodriguez	1.50
TF39	Derek Jeter, Nomar Garciaparra	2.00
TF40	Alex Rodriguez, Omar Vizquel	1.50
TF41	Curt Schilling, Randy Johnson	.75
TF42	Jorge Posada, Roger Clemens	1.50
TF43	Ryan Klesko, Ichiro Suzuki	1.00
TF44	Nick Johnson, Barry Bonds	1.50
TF45	Alex Rodriguez, Rafael Palmeiro	1.50
TF46	Vladimir Guerrero, J.T. Snow	.50
TF47	Derek Jeter, Eric Chavez	2.00
TF48	Bret Boone, Ichiro Suzuki	1.00
TF49	Mike Piazza, Bobby Abreu	1.00
TF50	Miguel Tejada, Ichiro Suzuki	1.00
TF51	Juan Pierre, Jim Thome	.50
TF52	Kevin Millwood, Jim Thome	.50
TF53	Hank Blalock, Jorge Posada	.25
TF54	Deivi Cruz, Hank Blalock	.25
TF55	Rafael Furcal, Ty Wigginton	.25
TF56	Jim Thome, Nomar Garciaparra	1.50
TF57	Craig Biggio, Jason Giambi	.75
TF58	Aaron Boone, Jason Giambi	.75
TF59	Jason Giambi, Bernie Williams	.75

TF60	Cristian Guzman, Jody Gerut	.25
TF61	Todd Helton, Jose Reyes	.50
TF62	Derek Jeter, Hank Blalock	2.00
TF63	Mike Piazza, Jimmy Rollins	1.00
TF64	Bernie Williams, Derek Jeter	2.00
TF65	Andruw Jones, Rafael Furcal	.50
TF66	Mike Piazza, Andruw Jones	1.00
TF67	Mike Piazza, Cliff Floyd	1.00
TF68	Jason Kendall, Albert Pujols	1.50
TF69	Nomar Garciaparra, Manny Ramirez	1.50
TF70	Jorge Posada, Alex Rodriguez	1.50
TF71	Derek Jeter, Alex Rodriguez	2.00
TF72	Mike Sweeney, Alex Rodriguez	1.50
TF73	Marquis Grissom, Ivan Rodriguez	.50
TF74	Jason Phillips, Gary Sheffield	.40
TF75	Chipper Jones, Gary Sheffield	1.00
TF76	Junior Spivey, Gary Sheffield	.40
TF77	Al Leiter, Ichiro Suzuki	1.00
TF78	Jose Vidro, Jim Thome	.75
TF79	Jimmy Rollins, Paul LoDuca	.25
TF80	Alex Rodriguez, Rafael Palmeiro	1.50
TF81	Albert Pujols, Jim Edmonds	1.50
TF82	Eric Chavez, Mike Sweeney	.25
TF83	Cristian Guzman, Jimmy Rollins	.25
TF84	Alfonso Soriano, Bernie Williams	.50
TF85	Ichiro Suzuki, Derek Jeter	2.00
TF86	Jimmy Rollins, Derek Lee	.25
TF87	Shawn Green, Paul LoDuca	.25
TF88	Carlos Delgado, Jorge Posada	.50
TF89	Dmitri Young, C.C. Sabathia	.25
TF90	Dontrelle Willis, Shawn Chacon	.25
TF91	Edgar Martinez, Alex Rodriguez	1.50
TF92	Edgar Martinez, Carlos Delgado	.50
TF93	Edgar Martinez, Esteban Loaiza	.25
TF94	Roy Halladay, C.C. Sabathia	.25
TF95	Ichiro Suzuki, Albert Pujols	1.50
TF96	Ichiro Suzuki, Shigetoshi Hasegawa	1.00
TF97	Geoff Jenkins, Aaron Boone	.25
TF98	Nomar Garciaparra, Alfonso Soriano	1.50
TF99	Jorge Posada, Alfonso Soriano	.75
TF100	Vernon Wells, Garret Anderson	.25

Triple Folder Autographs

		NM/M
Inserted 1:355	
RH	Rich Harden	40.00
RW	Ryan Wagner	40.00
JW	Jerome Williams	35.00
DW	Dontrelle Willis	40.00

World Series Lineup

Inserted 1:27,440
No Pricing

2004 Topps Pre-Production

Jason GIAMBI
FIRST BASE

		NM/M
Complete Set (3):	4.00
Common Player:	1.00
PP1	Jason Giambi	3.00
PP2	Curt Schilling	1.50
PP3	Jimmy Rollins	1.00

2004 Topps

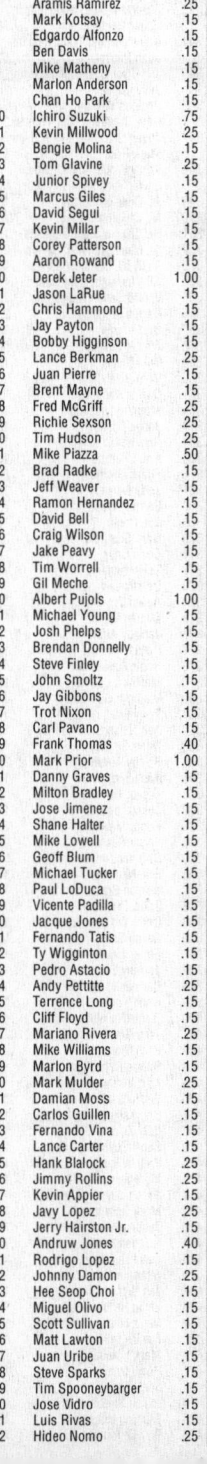

BRAVES

Javy LOPEZ
CATCHER

		NM/M
Complete Set (732):	60.00
Complete Team Factory Set (737):	75.00
Complete Factory Set (742):	75.00
Common Player:	.15
Pack (10):	2.00
Box (36):	55.00
Jumbo Box (12):	65.00
1	Jim Thome	.40
2	Aramis Ramirez	.25
3	Mark Kotsay	.15
4	Edgardo Alfonzo	.15
5	Ben Davis	.15
6	Mike Matheny	.15
7	Marlon Anderson	.15
8	Chan Ho Park	.15
9	Ichiro Suzuki	.75
10	Kevin Millwood	.25
11	Bengie Molina	.15
12	Tom Glavine	.25
13	Junior Spivey	.15
14	Marcus Giles	.15
15	David Segui	.15
16	Kevin Millar	.15
17	Corey Patterson	.15
18	Aaron Rowand	.15
19	Derek Jeter	1.00
20	Jason LaRue	.15
21	Chris Hammond	.15
22	Jay Payton	.15
23	Bobby Higginson	.15
24	Lance Berkman	.25
25	Juan Pierre	.15
26	Brent Mayne	.15
27	Fred McGriff	.25
28	Richie Sexson	.25
29	Tim Hudson	.25
30	Mike Piazza	.50
31	Brad Radke	.15
32	Jeff Weaver	.15
33	Ramon Hernandez	.15
34	David Bell	.15
35	Craig Wilson	.15
36	Jake Peavy	.15
37	Tim Worrell	.15
38	Gil Meche	.15
39	Albert Pujols	1.00
40	Michael Young	.15
41	Josh Phelps	.15
42	Brendan Donnelly	.15
43	Steve Finley	.15
44	John Smoltz	.25
45	Jay Gibbons	.15
46	Trot Nixon	.15
47	Carl Pavano	.15
48	Frank Thomas	.40
49	Mark Prior	1.00
50	Danny Graves	.15
51	Milton Bradley	.15
52	Jose Jimenez	.15
53	Shane Halter	.15
54	Mike Lowell	.15
55	Geoff Blum	.15
56	Michael Tucker	.15
57	Paul LoDuca	.15
58	Vicente Padilla	.15
59	Jacque Jones	.15
60	Fernando Tatis	.15
61	Ty Wigginton	.15
62	Pedro Astacio	.15
63	Andy Pettitte	.25
64	Terrence Long	.15
65	Cliff Floyd	.15
66	Mariano Rivera	.25
67	Mike Williams	.15
68	Marlon Byrd	.15
69	Mark Mulder	.25
70	Damian Moss	.15
71	Carlos Guillen	.15
72	Fernando Vina	.15
73	Lance Carter	.15
74	Hank Blalock	.25
75	Jimmy Rollins	.25
76	Kevin Appier	.15
77	Javy Lopez	.25
78	Jerry Hairston Jr.	.15
79	Andruw Jones	.40
80	Rodrigo Lopez	.15
81	Johnny Damon	.25
82	Hee Seop Choi	.15
83	Miguel Olivo	.15
84	Scott Sullivan	.15
85	Matt Lawton	.15
86	Juan Uribe	.15
87	Steve Sparks	.15
88	Tim Spooneybarger	.15
89	Jose Vidro	.15
90	Luis Rivas	.15
91	Hideo Nomo	.25

93	Javier Vazquez	.15
94	Al Leiter	.15
95	Darren Dreifort	.15
96	Mike DeJean	.15
97	Zach Day	.15
98	Jorge Posada	.25
99	John Halama	.15
100	Alex Rodriguez	1.00
101	Orlando Palmeiro	.15
102	Dave Berg	.15
103	Brad Fullmer	.15
104	Mike Hampton	.15
105	Willis Roberts	.15
106	Ramiro Mendoza	.15
107	Juan Cruz	.15
108	Esteban Loaiza	.15
109	Aaron Boone	.15
110	Todd Helton	.40
111	Braden Looper	.15
112	Octavio Dotel	.15
113	Mike MacDougal	.15
114	Cesar Izturis	.15
115	Johan Santana	.15
116	José Contreras	.25
117	Placido Polanco	.15
118	Kenny Lofton	.15
119	Adam Eaton	.15
120	Vernon Wells	.25
121	Ben Grieve	.15
122	Randy Winn	.15
123	Ismael Valdes	.15
124	Eric Owens	.15
125	Curt Schilling	.25
126	Russ Ortiz	.15
127	Mark Buehrle	.15
128	Danys Baez	.15
129	Dmitri Young	.15
130	Kazuhisa Ishii	.15
131	A.J. Pierzynski	.15
132	Michael Barrett	.15
133	Joe McEwing	.15
134	Robin Ventura	.15
135	Tom Wilson	.15
136	Carlos Zambrano	.15
137	Brett Tomko	.15
138	Jeff Nelson	.15
139	Jarrod Washburn	.15
140	Greg Maddux	.75
141	Craig Counsell	.15
142	Reggie Taylor	.15
143	Omar Vizquel	.25
144	Alex Gonzalez	.15
145	Billy Wagner	.15
146	Brian Jordan	.15
147	Wes Helms	.15
148	Kyle Lohse	.15
149	Timoniel Perez	.15
150	Jason Giambi	.50
151	Erubiel Durazo	.15
152	Mike Lieberthal	.15
153	Jason Kendall	.15
154	Xavier Nady	.15
155	Kirk Rueter	.15
156	Mike Cameron	.15
157	Miguel Cairo	.15
158	Woody Williams	.15
159	Toby Hall	.15
160	Bernie Williams	.25
161	Darin Erstad	.25
162	Matt Mantei	.15
163	Geronimo Gil	.15
164	Bill Mueller	.15
165	Damian Miller	.15
166	Tony Graffanino	.15
167	Sean Casey	.15
168	Brandon Phillips	.15
169	Mike Remlinger	.15
170	Adam Dunn	.25
171	Carlos Lee	.15
172	Juan Encarnacion	.15
173	Angel Berroa	.15
174	Desi Relaford	.15
175	Paul Quantrill	.15
176	Ben Sheets	.15
177	Eddie Guardado	.15
178	Rocky Biddle	.15
179	Mike Stanton	.15
180	Eric Chavez	.25
181	Jason Michaels	.15
182	Terry Adams	.15
183	Kip Wells	.15
184	Brian Lawrence	.15
185	Bret Boone	.25
186	Tino Martinez	.15
187	Aubrey Huff	.15
188	Kevin Mench	.15
189	Tim Salmon	.25
190	Carlos Delgado	.40
191	John Lackey	.15
192	Oscar Villarreal	.15
193	Sidney Ponson	.15
194	Derek Lowe	.15
195	Mark Grudzielanek	.15
196	Flash Gordon	.15
197	Matt Clement	.15
198	Scott Williamson	.15
199	Brandon Inge	.15
200	Nomar Garciaparra	1.00
201	Antonio Osuna	.15
202	Jose Mesa	.15
203	Randall Simon	.15
204	Jack Wilson	.15
205	Ray Durham	.15
206	Freddy Garcia	.15
207	J.D. Drew	.15
208	Einar Diaz	.15
209	Roy Halladay	.25
210	David Eckstein	.15

#	Player	Price
211	Jason Marquis	.15
212	Jorge Julio	.15
213	Tim Wakefield	.15
214	Moises Alou	.25
215	Bartolo Colon	.25
216	Jimmy Haynes	.15
217	Preston Wilson	.15
218	Luis Castillo	.15
219	Richard Hidalgo	.15
220	Manny Ramirez	.40
221	Mike Mussina	.40
222	Randy Wolf	.15
223	Kris Benson	.15
224	Ryan Klesko	.25
225	Rich Aurilia	.15
226	Kelvim Escobar	.15
227	Francisco Cordero	.15
228	Kazuhiro Sasaki	.15
229	Danny Bautista	.15
230	Rafael Furcal	.15
231	Travis Driskill	.15
232	Kyle Farnsworth	.15
233	Jose Valentin	.15
234	Felipe Lopez	.15
235	C.C. Sabathia	.15
236	Brad Penny	.15
237	Brad Ausmus	.15
238	Raul Ibanez	.15
239	Adrian Beltre	.15
240	Rocco Baldelli	.25
241	Orlando Hudson	.15
242	Dave Roberts	.15
243	Doug Mientkiewicz	.15
244	Brad Wilkerson	.15
245	Scott Strickland	.15
246	Sterling Hitchcock	.15
247	Chad Bradford	.15
248	Gary Bennett	.15
249	Jose Cruz Jr.	.15
250	Jeff Kent	.25
251	Josh Beckett	.25
252	Ramon Ortiz	.15
253	Miguel Batista	.15
254	Jung Bong	.15
255	Deivi Cruz	.15
256	Alex Gonzalez	.15
257	Shawn Chacon	.15
258	Runelvys Hernandez	.15
259	Joe Mays	.15
260	Eric Gagne	.15
261	Dustan Mohr	.15
262	Tomokazu Ohka	.15
263	Eric Byrnes	.15
264	Frank Catalanotto	.15
265	Cristian Guzman	.15
266	Orlando Cabrera	.15
267	Mike Scioscia	.15
268	Bob Brenly	.15
269	Bobby Cox	.15
270	Mike Hargrove	.15
271	Grady Little	.15
272	Dusty Baker	.15
273	Jerry Manuel	.15
274	Bob Boone	.15
275	Eric Wedge	.15
276	Clint Hurdle	.15
277	Alan Trammell	.15
278	Jack McKeon	.15
279	Jimy Williams	.15
280	Tony Pena	.15
281	Jim Tracy	.15
282	Ned Yost	.15
283	Ron Gardenhire	.15
284	Frank Robinson	.25
285	Art Howe	.15
286	Joe Torre	.25
287	Ken Macha	.15
288	Larry Bowa	.15
289	Lloyd McClendon	.15
290	Bruce Bochy	.15
291	Felipe Alou	.15
292	Bob Melvin	.15
293	Tony LaRussa	.15
294	Lou Piniella	.15
295	Buck Showalter	.15
296	Carlos Tosca	.15
297	Anthony Acevedo RC	.15
298	Anthony Lerew RC	.75
299	Blake Hawksworth RC	.50
300	Brayan Pena RC	.50
301	Casey Myers RC	.50
302	Craig Ansman RC	.50
303	David Murphy	.40
304	David Crouthers	.20
305	Dioner Navarro RC	.40
306	Donald Levinski	.40
307	Jesse Roman RC	.40
308	Sung Ki Jung RC	.25
309	Jon Knott RC	.40
310	Josh Labandeira RC	.25
311	Kenny Perez RC	.40
312	Khalid Ballouli RC	.25
313	Kyle Davies RC	.40
314	Marcus McBeth RC	.40
315	Matt Creighton RC	.40
316	Chris O'Riordan RC	.50
317	Mike Gosling	.15
318	Nic Ungs RC	.40
319	Omar Falcon RC	.40
320	Rodney Choy Foo RC	.50
321	Tim Frend RC	.50
322	Todd Self RC	.50
323	Tydus Meadows RC	.40
324	Yadier Molina RC	.50
325	Zachary Duke RC	2.00
326	Zach Miner RC	1.00
327	Bernie Castro, Khalil Greene	.15
328	Ryan Madson, Elizardo Ramirez	.15
329	Rich Harden, Bobby Crosby	.15
330	Zack Greinke, Jimmy Gobble	.15
331	Bobby Jenks, Casey Kotchman	.15
332	Sammy Sosa	.50
333	Kevin Millwood	.25
334	Rafael Palmeiro	.25
335	Roger Clemens	.75
336	Eric Gagne	.15
337	Bill Mueller, Manny Ramirez, Derek Jeter	.50
338	Vernon Wells, Ichiro Suzuki, Michael Young	.40
339	Alex Rodriguez, Frank Thomas, Carlos Delgado	.50
340	Carlos Delgado, Alex Rodriguez, Bret Boone	.15
341	Pedro Martinez, Tim Hudson, Esteban Loaiza	.25
342	Esteban Loaiza, Pedro Martinez, Roy Halladay	.25
343	Albert Pujols, Todd Helton, Edgar Renteria	.50
344	Albert Pujols, Todd Helton, Juan Pierre	.50
345	Jim Thome, Richie Sexson, Javy Lopez	.25
346	Preston Wilson, Gary Sheffield, Jim Thome	.25
347	Jason Schmidt, Kevin Brown, Mark Prior	.50
348	Kerry Wood, Mark Prior, Javier Vazquez	.50
349	AL Division Series	.15
350	NL Division Series	.15
351	NL Championship Series	.15
352	AL Championship Series	.25
353	AL & NL Division Series	.15
354	AL Championship Series	.15
355	World Series Highlights	.15
356	Carlos Delgado	.15
357	Bret Boone	.15
358	Alex Rodriguez	.50
359	Bill Mueller	.15
360	Vernon Wells	.15
361	Garret Anderson	.15
362	Magglio Ordonez	.15
363	Jorge Posada	.15
364	Roy Halladay	.15
365	Andy Pettitte	.15
366	Frank Thomas	.25
367	Jody Gerut	.15
368	Sammy Sosa	.75
369	Joe Crede	.15
370	Gary Sheffield	.25
371	Coco Crisp	.15
372	Torii Hunter	.15
373	Derek Lee	.15
374	Adam Everett	.15
375	Miguel Tejada	.25
376	Jeremy Affeldt	.15
377	Robin Ventura	.15
378	Scott Podsednik	.40
379	Matthew LeCroy	.15
380	Vladimir Guerrero	.40
381	Tony Clark	.15
382	Jeff Nelson	.15
383	Chris Singleton	.15
384	Bobby Abreu	.15
385	Josh Fogg	.15
386	Trevor Hoffman	.15
387	Jesse Foppert	.15
388	Edgar Martinez	.25
389	Edgar Renteria	.25
390	Chipper Jones	.25
391	Eric Munson	.15
392	Dewon Brazelton	.15
393	John Thomson	.15
394	Chris Woodward	.15
395	Aaron Sele	.15
396	Elmer Dessens	.15
397	Johnny Estrada	.15
398	Damian Moss	.15
399	Gabe Kapler	.15
400	Dontrelle Willis	.40
401	Troy Glaus	.25
402	Raul Mondesi	.20
403	Shane Reynolds	.15
404	Kurt Ainsworth	.15
405	Pedro J. Martinez	.50
406	Eric Karros	.15
407	Billy Koch	.15
408	Scott Schoeneweis	.15
409	Paul Wilson	.15
410	Mike Sweeney	.25
411	Jason Bay	.15
412	Mark Redman	.15
413	Jason Jennings	.15
414	Rondell White	.15
415	Todd Hundley	.15
416	Shannon Stewart	.15
417	Jae Weong Seo	.15
418	Livan Hernandez	.15
419	Mark Ellis	.15
420	Pat Burrell	.25
421	Mark Loretta	.15
422	Robb Nen	.15
423	Joel Pineiro	.15
424	Jason Simontacchi	.15
425	Sterling Hitchcock	.15
426	Rey Ordonez	.15
427	Greg Myers	.15
428	Shane Spencer	.15
429	Carlos Baerga	.15
430	Garret Anderson	.25
431	Horacio Ramirez	.15
432	Brian Roberts	.15
433	Damian Jackson	.15
434	Doug Glanville	.15
435	Brian Daubach	.15
436	Alex Escobar	.15
437	Alex Sanchez	.15
438	Jeff Bagwell	.40
439	Darrell May	.15
440	Shawn Green	.25
441	Geoff Jenkins	.25
442	Endy Chavez	.15
443	Nick Johnson	.15
444	Jose Guillen	.15
445	Tomas Perez	.15
446	Phil Nevin	.15
447	Jason Schmidt	.25
448	Julio Mateo	.15
449	So Taguchi	.15
450	Randy Johnson	.50
451	Paul Byrd	.15
452	Chone Figgins	.15
453	Larry Bigbie	.15
454	Scott Williamson	.15
455	Ramon Martinez	.15
456	Roberto Alomar	.25
457	Ryan Dempster	.15
458	Ryan Ludwick	.15
459	Ramon Santiago	.15
460	Jeff Conine	.15
461	Brad Lidge	.15
462	Ken Harvey	.15
463	Guillermo Mota	.15
464	Rick Reed	.15
465	Joey Eischen	.15
466	Wade Miller	.15
467	Steve Karsay	.15
468	Chase Utley	.25
469	Matt Stairs	.15
470	Yorvit Torrealba	.15
471	Joe Kennedy	.15
472	Reed Johnson	.15
473	Victor Zambrano	.15
474	Jeff DaVanon	.15
475	Luis Gonzalez	.25
476	Rod Barajas	.15
477	Ray King	.15
478	Jack Cust	.15
479	Omar Daal	.15
480	Todd Walker	.15
481	Shawn Estes	.15
482	Chris Reitsma	.15
483	Jake Westbrook	.15
484	Jeremy Bonderman	.25
485	A.J. Burnett	.25
486	Roy Oswalt	.25
487	Kevin Brown	.25
488	Eric Milton	.15
489	Claudio Vargas	.15
490	Roger Cedeno	.15
491	David Wells	.15
492	Scott Hatteberg	.15
493	Ricky Ledee	.15
494	Eric Young	.15
495	Armando Benitez	.15
496	Dan Haren	.15
497	Carl Crawford	.25
498	Laynce Nix	.15
499	Eric Hinske	.15
500	Ivan Rodriguez	.40
501	Scot Shields	.15
502	Brandon Webb	.15
503	Mark DeRosa	.15
504	Jhonny Peralta	.15
505	Adam Kennedy	.15
506	Tony Batista	.15
507	Jeff Suppan	.15
508	Kenny Lofton	.25
509	Scott Sullivan	.15
510	Ken Griffey Jr.	.60
511	Billy Traber	.15
512	Larry Walker	.25
513	Mike Maroth	.15
514	Todd Hollandsworth	.15
515	Kirk Saarloos	.15
516	Carlos Beltran	.25
517	Andy Ashby	.15
518	Jose Macias	.15
519	Karim Garcia	.15
520	Jose Reyes	.40
521	Brandon Duckworth	.15
522	Brian Giles	.15
523	J.T. Snow Jr.	.15
524	Jamie Moyer	.15
525	Jason Isringhausen	.15
526	Julio Lugo	.15
527	Mark Teixeira	.25
528	Cory Lidle	.15
529	Lyle Overbay	.15
530	Troy Percival	.15
531	Robby Hammock	.15
532	Robert Fick	.15
533	Jason Johnson	.15
534	Brandon Lyon	.15
535	Antonio Alfonseca	.15
536	Tom Goodwin	.15
537	Paul Konerko	.15
538	D'Angelo Jimenez	.15
539	Ben Broussard	.15
540	Magglio Ordonez	.25
541	Ellis Burks	.15
542	Carlos Pena	.15
543	Chad Fox	.15
544	Jeriome Robertson	.15
545	Travis Hafner	.15
546	Joe Randa	.15
547	Wil Cordero	.15
548	Brady Clark	.15
549	Ruben Sierra	.15
550	Barry Zito	.25
551	Brett Myers	.15
552	Oliver Perez	.15
553	Trey Hodges	.15
554	Benito Santiago	.15
555	David Ross	.15
556	Ramon Vazquez	.15
557	Joe Nathan	.15
558	Dan Wilson	.15
559	Garrett Stephenson	.15
560	Jim Edmonds	.25
561	Shawn Wooten	.15
562	Matt Kata	.15
563	Vinny Castilla	.15
564	Marty Cordova	.15
565	Aramis Ramirez	.15
566	Carl Everett	.15
567	Ryan Freel	.15
568	Jason Davis	.15
569	Mark Bellhorn	.15
570	Craig Monroe	.15
571	Ugueth Urbina	.15
572	Tim Redding	.15
573	Kevin Appier	.15
574	Jeromy Burnitz	.15
575	Miguel Cabrera	.40
576	Orlando Hernandez	.15
577	Casey Blake	.15
578	Aaron Boone	.15
579	Jermaine Dye	.15
580	Jerome Williams	.15
581	John Olerud	.15
582	Scott Rolen	.40
583	Bobby Kielty	.15
584	Travis Lee	.15
585	Jeff Cirillo	.15
586	Scott Spiezio	.15
587	Stephen Randolph	.15
588	Melvin Mora	.15
589	Mike Timlin	.15
590	Kerry Wood	.50
591	Tony Womack	.15
592	Jody Gerut	.15
593	Franklyn German	.15
594	Morgan Ensberg	.15
595	Odalis Perez	.15
596	Michael Cuddyer	.15
597	Jon Lieber	.15
598	Mike Williams	.15
599	Jose Hernandez	.15
600	Alfonso Soriano	.50
601	Marquis Grissom	.15
602	Matt Morris	.25
603	Damian Rolls	.15
604	Juan Gonzalez	.25
605	Aquilino Lopez	.15
606	Jose Valverde	.15
607	Scott Sauerbeck	.15
608	Joe Borowski	.15
609	Josh Bard	.15
610	Austin Kearns	.25
611	Chin-Hui Tsao	.15
612	Wilfredo Ledezma	.15
613	Aaron Guiel	.15
614	LaTroy Hawkins	.15
615	Tony Armas Jr.	.15
616	Steve Trachsel	.15
617	Ted Lilly	.15
618	Todd Pratt	.15
619	Sean Burroughs	.15
620	Rafael Palmeiro	.40
621	Jeremi Gonzalez	.15
622	Quinton McCracken	.15
623	David Ortiz	.25
624	Randall Simon	.15
625	Wily Mo Pena	.15
626	Nate Cornejo	.15
627	Brian Anderson	.15
628	Corey Koskie	.15
629	Keith Foulke	.15
630	Rheal Cormier	.15
631	Sidney Ponson	.15
632	Gary Matthews Jr.	.15
633	Herbert Perry	.15
634	Shea Hillenbrand	.15
635	Craig Biggio	.25
636	Barry Larkin	.25
637	Orlando Merced	.15
638	Anaheim Angels	.15
639	Arizona Diamondbacks	.15
640	Atlanta Braves	.15
641	Baltimore Orioles	.15
642	Boston Red Sox	.25
643	Chicago Cubs	.40
644	Chicago White Sox	.15
645	Cincinnati Reds	.15
646	Cleveland Indians	.15
647	Colorado Rockies	.15
648	Detroit Tigers	.15
649	Florida Marlins	.15
650	Houston Astros	.15
651	Kansas City Royals	.15
652	Los Angeles Dodgers	.15
653	Milwaukee Brewers	.15
654	Minnesota Twins	.15
655	Montreal Expos	.15
656	New York Mets	.15
657	New York Yankees	.50
658	Oakland Athletics	.15
659	Philadelphia Phillies	.15
660	Pittsburgh Pirates	.15
661	San Diego Padres	.15
662	San Francisco Giants	.15
663	Seattle Mariners	.15
664	St. Louis Cardinals	.15
665	Tampa Bay Devil Rays	.15
666	Texas Rangers	.15
667	Toronto Blue Jays	.15
668	Kyle Sleeth	.15
669	Bradley Sullivan	.15
670	Carlos Quentin	.50
671	Conor Jackson	1.00
672	Jeffrey Allison	.15
673	Matthew Moses	.25
674	Tim Stauffer	.15
675	Estee Harris RC	.25
676	David Aardsma	.15
677	Omar Quintanilla	.25
678	Aaron Hill	.15
679	Tony Richie	.15
680	Lastings Milledge	3.00
681	Brad Snyder	.25
682	Jason Hirsh	.50
683	Logan Kensing RC	.40
684	Chris Lubanski	.15
685	Ryan Harvey	.15
686	Ryan Wagner	.15
687	Rickie Weeks	.50
688	Jeremy Guthrie, Grady Sizemore	.25
689	Edwin Jackson, Greg Miller	.15
690	Neal Cotts, Jeremy Reed	.15
691	Nicholas Markakis, Adam Loewen	.15
692	Delmon Young, B.J. Upton	.75
693	Nomar Garciaparra, Alfonso Soriano	.50
694	Ichiro Suzuki, Albert Pujols	.50
695	Jim Thome, Mike Schmidt	.40
696	Mike Mussina	.25
697	Bengie Molina	.15
698	John Olerud	.15
699	Bret Boone	.25
700	Eric Chavez	.25
701	Alex Rodriguez	.75
702	Mike Cameron	.15
703	Ichiro Suzuki	.75
704	Torii Hunter	.15
705	Mike Hampton	.15
706	Mike Matheny	.15
707	Derek Lee	.15
708	Luis Castillo	.15
709	Scott Rolen	.40
710	Edgar Renteria	.25
711	Andruw Jones	.25
712	Jose Cruz Jr.	.15
713	Jim Edmonds	.25
714	Roy Halladay	.25
715	Eric Gagne	.25
716	Alex Rodriguez	.75
717	Angel Berroa	.15
718	Dontrelle Willis	.25
719	Todd Helton	.25
720	Marcus Giles	.15
721	Edgar Renteria	.25
722	Scott Rolen	.25
723	Albert Pujols	.75
724	Gary Sheffield	.25
725	Javy Lopez	.25
726	Eric Gagne	.25
727	Randy Wolf	.15
728	Bobby Cox	.15
729	Scott Podsednik	.40
730	World Series Game 4	.15
731	World Series Game 5	.15
732	World Series Game 6	.15
733	World Series MVP	.25

Black

Black (1-733):	15-30X
Production 53 Sets	

Gold

Stars (1-733):	5-10X
Production 2,004 Sets	

1st Edition

	NM/M
Stars:	3-5X
HTA Exclusive	
1st Edition Pack (10):	3.00
1st Edition Box (20):	55.00

2004 Topps Team Factory Sets

	NM/M
Complete Astros Set (737):	75.00
Complete Cubs Set (737):	75.00
Complete Red Sox Set (737):	75.00

Complete Yankees Set (737):	75.00
1	Brooks Conrad	1.00
2	Hector Giminez	1.00
3	Kevin Davidson	1.00
4	Chris Burke	3.00
5	John Buck	1.00
1	Bobby Brownlie	2.00
2	Felix Pie	3.00
3	Jon Connolly	1.00
4	David Kelton	1.00
5	Ricky Nolasco	2.00
1	David Murphy	1.00
2	Kevin Youkilis	3.00
3	Juan Cedeno	1.00
4	Matt Murton	1.00
5	Kenny Perez	1.00
1	Rudy Guillen	1.00
2	David Parrish	2.00
3	Brad Halsey	1.00
4	Hector Made	1.00
5	Robinson Cano	6.00

All-Stars

	NM/M
Complete Set (20):	20.00
Common Player:	.50
Inserted 1:16	
TAS1	Jason Giambi	1.50
TAS2	Ichiro Suzuki	2.50
TAS3	Alex Rodriguez	3.00
TAS4	Albert Pujols	3.00
TAS5	Alfonso Soriano	1.50
TAS6	Nomar Garciaparra	2.50
TAS7	Andruw Jones	1.00
TAS8	Carlos Delgado	.75
TAS9	Gary Sheffield	.75
TAS10	Jorge Posada	.75
TAS11	Magglio Ordonez	.75
TAS12	Kerry Wood	1.50
TAS13	Garret Anderson	.50
TAS14	Bret Boone	.50
TAS15	Hank Blalock	.50
TAS16	Mike Lowell	.50
TAS17	Todd Helton	1.00
TAS18	Vernon Wells	.50
TAS19	Roger Clemens	3.00
TAS20	Scott Rolen	1.50

All-Star Patch Relics

No Pricing	
Inserted 1:7,698	

All-Star Stitches

	NM/M
Common Player:	5.00
Inserted 1:137	
GA	Garret Anderson	6.00
HB	Hank Blalock	6.00
AB	Aaron Boone	5.00
BD	Brendan Donnelly	5.00
CE	Carl Everett	5.00
KF	Keith Foulke	5.00
RF	Rafael Furcal	8.00
EGA	Eric Gagne	8.00
NG	Nomar Garciaparra	15.00
TG	Troy Glaus	8.00
EG	Eddie Guardado	5.00
SH	Shigetoshi Hasegawa	5.00
TH	Todd Helton	8.00
RH	Ramon Hernandez	5.00
AJ	Andruw Jones	5.00
EL	Esteban Loaiza	5.00
PL	Paul LoDuca	5.00
JL	Javy Lopez	8.00
ML	Mike Lowell	5.00
EM	Edgar Martinez	5.00
MMO	Melvin Mora	5.00
JM	Jamie Moyer	5.00
MM	Mark Mulder	6.00
RO	Russ Ortiz	5.00
JP	Jorge Posada	8.00
ER	Edgar Renteria	5.00

AR	Alex Rodriguez	15.00
SR	Scott Rolen	10.00
JS	Jason Schmidt	6.00
JV	Jose Vidro	5.00
BW	Billy Wagner	5.00
VW	Vernon Wells	6.00
RWH	Rondell White	5.00
WW	Woody Williams	6.00
PW	Preston Wilson	5.00
RW	Randy Wolf	5.00
KW	Kerry Wood	8.00

American Treasures Cut Signatures

No Pricing
Inserted 1:658,152

American Treasures Dual

Complete Set (1):

American Treasures Presidential Signatures

No Pricing
Production One Set

Autographs

		NM/M
Common Player:		
JB	Josh Beckett	50.00
HB	Hank Blalock	20.00
CF	Cliff Floyd	8.00
JG	Jay Gibbons	15.00
KG	Khalil Greene	10.00
EH	Eric Hinske	10.00
TH	Torii Hunter	25.00
AK	Austin Kearns	25.00
PK	Paul Konerko	15.00
PL	Paul LoDuca	10.00
ML	Mike Lowell	8.00
VM	Victor Martinez	20.00
MO	Magglio Ordonez	15.00
JP	Josh Phelps	8.00
MP	Mark Prior	40.00
ER	Elizardo Ramirez	8.00
BS	Benito Santiago	15.00
MS	Mike Sweeney	20.00
MT	Mark Teixeira	25.00
BU	B.J. Upton	20.00
JV	Jose Vidro	8.00
Series 2		
GA	Garret Anderson	35.00
LB	Lance Berkman	35.00
AB	Aaron Boone	35.00
BB	Bobby Brownlie	30.00
MC	Miguel Cabrera	40.00
ZG	Zack Greinke	40.00
AH	Aubrey Huff	20.00
DM	Dustin McGowan	15.00
SP	Scott Podsednik	25.00
JP	Jorge Posada	40.00
IR	Ivan Rodriguez	45.00
SR	Scott Rolen	30.00
DW	Dontrelle Willis	30.00

Derby Digs

		NM/M
Common Player:		8.00
Inserted 1:585		
GA	Garret Anderson	8.00
BB	Bret Boone	8.00
CD	Carlos Delgado	8.00
JE	Jim Edmonds	8.00
JG	Jason Giambi	15.00
AP	Albert Pujols	25.00
RS	Richie Sexson	8.00

Draft Pick Bonus

		NM/M
Complete Set (15):		50.00
Complete Holiday Set (10):		30.00
Complete Retail Set (5):		20.00
1	Josh Johnson	4.00
2	Donny Lucy	4.00
3	Greg Golson	6.00
4	K.C. Herren	4.00
5	Jeff Marquez	4.00
6	Mark Rogers	8.00
7	Eric Hurley	4.00
8	Gio Gonzalez	6.00
9	Thomas Diamond	6.00
10	Matt Bush	8.00
11	Kyle Waldrop	4.00
12	Neil Walker	6.00
13	Mike Ferris	4.00
14	Ray Liotta	4.00
15	Phillip Hughes	15.00

Fall Classic Covers

		NM/M
Complete Set (99):		125.00
Common Card:		2.00
Inserted 1:12		
FC1903	1903 World Series	2.00
FC1905	1905 World Series	2.00
FC1906	1906 World Series	2.00
FC1907	1907 World Series	2.00
FC1908	1908 World Series	2.00
FC1909	1909 World Series	2.00

FC1910	1910 World Series	2.00
FC1911	1911 World Series	2.00
FC1912	1912 World Series	2.00
FC1913	1913 World Series	2.00
FC1914	1914 World Series	2.00
FC1915	1915 World Series	2.00
FC1916	1916 World Series	2.00
FC1917	1917 World Series	2.00
FC1918	1918 World Series	2.00
FC1919	1919 World Series	2.00
FC1920	1920 World Series	2.00
FC1921	1921 World Series	2.00
FC1922	1922 World Series	2.00
FC1923	1923 World Series	2.00
FC1924	1924 World Series	2.00
FC1925	1925 World Series	2.00
FC1926	1926 World Series	2.00
FC1927	1927 World Series	2.00
FC1928	1928 World Series	2.00
FC1929	1929 World Series	2.00
FC1930	1930 World Series	2.00
FC1931	1931 World Series	2.00
FC1932	1932 World Series	2.00
FC1933	1933 World Series	2.00
FC1934	1934 World Series	2.00
FC1935	1935 World Series	2.00
FC1936	1936 World Series	2.00
FC1937	1937 World Series	2.00
FC1938	1938 World Series	2.00
FC1939	1939 World Series	2.00
FC1940	1940 World Series	2.00
FC1941	1941 World Series	2.00
FC1942	1942 World Series	2.00
FC1943	1943 World Series	2.00
FC1944	1944 World Series	2.00
FC1945	1945 World Series	2.00
FC1946	1946 World Series	2.00
FC1947	1947 World Series	2.00
FC1948	1948 World Series	2.00
FC1949	1949 World Series	2.00
FC1950	1950 World Series	2.00
FC1951	1951 World Series	2.00
FC1952	1952 World Series	2.00
FC1953	1953 World Series	2.00
FC1954	1954 World Series	2.00
FC1955	1955 World Series	2.00
FC1956	1956 World Series	2.00
FC1957	1957 World Series	2.00
FC1958	1958 World Series	2.00
FC1959	1959 World Series	2.00
FC1960	1960 World Series	2.00
FC1961	1961 World Series	2.00
FC1962	1962 World Series	2.00
FC1963	1963 World Series	2.00
FC1964	1964 World Series	2.00
FC1965	1965 World Series	2.00
FC1966	1966 World Series	2.00
FC1967	1967 World Series	2.00
FC1968	1968 World Series	2.00
FC1969	1969 World Series	2.00
FC1970	1970 World Series	2.00
FC1971	1971 World Series	2.00
FC1972	1972 World Series	2.00
FC1973	1973 World Series	2.00
FC1974	1974 World Series	2.00
FC1975	1975 World Series	2.00
FC1976	1976 World Series	2.00
FC1977	1977 World Series	2.00
FC1978	1978 World Series	2.00
FC1979	1979 World Series	2.00
FC1980	1980 World Series	2.00
FC1981	1981 World Series	2.00
FC1982	1982 World Series	2.00
FC1983	1983 World Series	2.00
FC1984	1984 World Series	2.00
FC1985	1985 World Series	2.00
FC1986	1986 World Series	2.00
FC1987	1987 World Series	2.00
FC1988	1988 World Series	2.00
FC1989	1989 World Series	2.00
FC1990	1990 World Series	2.00
FC1991	1991 World Series	2.00
FC1992	1992 World Series	2.00
FC1993	1993 World Series	2.00
FC1995	1995 World Series	2.00
FC1996	1996 World Series	2.00
FC1997	1997 World Series	2.00
FC1998	1998 World Series	2.00
FC1999	1999 World Series	2.00
FC2000	2000 World Series	2.00
FC2001	2001 World Series	2.00
FC2002	2002 World Series	2.00
FC2003	2003 World Series	2.00

Hit Parade

	NM/M
Complete Set (30):	20.00
Common Player:	.50

Rafael Palmeiro

Inserted 1:7		
HP1	Sammy Sosa	3.00
HP2	Rafael Palmeiro	1.00
HP3	Fred McGriff	.50
HP4	Ken Griffey Jr.	2.00
HP5	Juan Gonzalez	1.00
HP6	Frank Thomas	1.00
HP7	Andres Galarraga	1.00
HP8	Jim Thome	1.50
HP9	Jeff Bagwell	1.00
HP10	Mike Piazza	2.00
HP11	Rafael Palmeiro	1.00
HP12	Sammy Sosa	3.00
HP13	Fred McGriff	.50
HP14	Andres Galarraga	1.00
HP15	Juan Gonzalez	1.00
HP16	Frank Thomas	1.00
HP17	Jeff Bagwell	1.00
HP18	Ken Griffey Jr.	2.00
HP19	Ruben Sierra	.50
HP20	Ellis Burks	.50
HP21	Rafael Palmeiro	1.00
HP22	Roberto Alomar	.75
HP23	Julio Franco	.50
HP24	Andres Galarraga	.50
HP25	Fred McGriff	.50
HP26	Craig Biggio	.75
HP27	Barry Larkin	.75
HP28	Edgar Martinez	.50
HP29	Ellis Burks	.50
HP30	Sammy Sosa	3.00

Hobby Masters

ALFONSO SORIANO

		NM/M
Complete Set (20):		40.00
Common Player:		.75
Inserted 1:12		
HM1	Albert Pujols	3.00
HM2	Mark Prior	4.00
HM3	Alex Rodriguez	4.00
HM4	Nomar Garciaparra	3.00
HM5	Barry Bonds	4.00
HM6	Sammy Sosa	3.00
HM7	Alfonso Soriano	2.00
HM8	Ichiro Suzuki	2.50
HM9	Derek Jeter	4.00
HM10	Jim Thome	1.50
HM11	Jason Giambi	1.50
HM12	Mike Piazza	2.50
HM13	Barry Zito	1.00
HM14	Randy Johnson	2.00
HM15	Adam Dunn	1.00
HM16	Vladimir Guerrero	2.00
HM17	Gary Sheffield	.75
HM18	Carlos Delgado	1.00
HM19	Chipper Jones	2.50
HM20	Dontrelle Willis	1.00

Own the Game

GARRET ANDERSON

		NM/M
Complete Set (30):		25.00
Common Player:		.50
Inserted 1:18		
OG1	Jim Thome	1.50
OG2	Albert Pujols	3.00
OG3	Alex Rodriguez	3.00
OG4	Barry Bonds	4.00
OG5	Ichiro Suzuki	2.00
OG6	Derek Jeter	3.00
OG7	Nomar Garciaparra	3.00
OG8	Alfonso Soriano	1.50
OG9	Gary Sheffield	.75
OG10	Jason Giambi	1.00
OG11	Todd Helton	1.00
OG12	Garret Anderson	.50
OG13	Carlos Delgado	1.00
OG14	Manny Ramirez	1.00
OG15	Richie Sexson	.75
OG16	Vernon Wells	.50
OG17	Preston Wilson	.50
OG18	Frank Thomas	1.00
OG19	Shawn Green	.75
OG20	Rafael Furcal	.50
OG21	Juan Pierre	.50
OG22	Javy Lopez	.50
OG23	Edgar Renteria	.50
OG24	Mark Prior	3.00
OG25	Pedro J. Martinez	1.50
OG26	Kerry Wood	1.00
OG27	Curt Schilling	.75
OG28	Roy Halladay	.50
OG29	Eric Gagne	.50
OG30	Brandon Webb	.50

Presidential Pastime

		NM/M
Complete Set (42):		100.00
Common President:		3.00
Inserted 1:6		
PP1	George Washington	8.00
PP2	John Adams	4.00
PP3	Thomas Jefferson	4.00
PP4	James Madison	4.00
PP5	James Monroe	4.00
PP6	John Quincy Adams	4.00
PP7	Andrew Jackson	4.00
PP8	Martin Van Buren	3.00
PP9	William H. Harrison	4.00
PP10	John Tyler	4.00
PP11	James K. Polk	3.00
PP12	Zachary Taylor	3.00
PP13	Millard Fillmore	3.00
PP14	Franklin Pierce	3.00
PP15	James Buchanan	3.00
PP16	Abraham Lincoln	6.00
PP17	Andrew Johnson	3.00
PP18	Ulysses S. Grant	4.00
PP19	Rutherford B. Hayes	3.00
PP20	James Garfield	3.00
PP21	Chester A. Arthur	3.00
PP22	Grover Cleveland	3.00
PP23	Benjamin Harrison	3.00
PP24	William McKinley	3.00
PP25	Theodore Roosevelt	4.00
PP26	William H. Taft	4.00
PP27	Woodrow Wilson	4.00
PP28	Warren Harding	4.00
PP29	Calvin Coolidge	4.00
PP30	Herbert Hoover	3.00
PP31	Franklin D. Roosevelt	4.00
PP32	Harry S. Truman	4.00
PP33	Dwight D. Eisenhower	4.00
PP34	John F. Kennedy	6.00
PP35	Lyndon B. Johnson	3.00
PP36	Richard Nixon	3.00
PP37	Gerald Ford	3.00
PP38	Jimmy Carter	3.00
PP39	Ronald Reagan	4.00
PP40	George H.W. Bush	3.00
PP41	Bill Clinton	3.00
PP42	George W. Bush	3.00

Presidential First Pitch Relics

		NM/M
Common Player:		15.00
Inserted 1:592		
GHB	George H.W. Bush	25.00
GB	George W. Bush	25.00
BC	Bill Clinton	40.00
CC	Calvin Coolidge	15.00
DE	Dwight D. Eisenhower	15.00
GF	Gerald Ford	30.00
WH	Warren Harding	30.00
HH	Herbert Hoover	30.00
LJ	Lyndon B. Johnson	30.00
JK	John F. Kennedy	50.00
RN	Richard Nixon	30.00
RR	Ronald Reagan	30.00
FR	Franklin D. Roosevelt	40.00
WT	William H. Taft	30.00
HT	Harry S. Truman	30.00
WW	Woodrow Wilson	25.00

Series Seats Relics

	NM/M
Common Player:	10.00

		NM/M
Inserted 1:316		
LA	Luis Aparicio	15.00
BF	Bob Feller	12.00
RJ	Reggie Jackson	20.00
AK	Al Kaline	20.00
HK	Harmon Killebrew	25.00
WM	Willie Mays	25.00
BM	Bill Mazeroski	20.00
PM	Paul Molitor	20.00
JP	Jim Palmer	15.00
LP	Lou Piniella	10.00
BP	Boog Powell	10.00
BR	Brooks Robinson	15.00
FR	Frank Robinson	15.00
WS	Warren Spahn	15.00
RY	Robin Yount	20.00

Series Stitches Relics

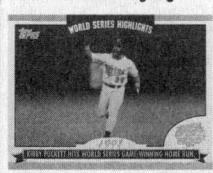

		NM/M
Common Player:		10.00
JBE	Josh Beckett	10.00
JB	Johnny Bench	25.00
GB	George Brett	30.00
JCA	Jose Canseco	15.00
GC	Gary Carter	12.00
JC	Joe Carter	10.00
RC	Roger Clemens	15.00
LD	Lenny Dykstra	10.00
SG	Steve Garvey	15.00
KG	Kirk Gibson	10.00
DG	Dwight Gooden	15.00
RJA	Reggie Jackson	20.00
RJ	Randy Johnson	15.00
CJ	Chipper Jones	15.00
DJ	David Justice	15.00
HK	Harmon Killebrew	30.00
WM	Willie Mays	50.00
PO	Paul O'Neill	10.00
KP	Kirby Puckett	25.00
FR	Frank Robinson	20.00
MS	Mike Schmidt	30.00
TS	Tom Seaver	15.00
AS	Alfonso Soriano	15.00
RY	Robin Yount	20.00

Team Topps Legends Autographs

		NM/M
Inserted 1:766		
SG	Steve Garvey	15.00
BP	Boog Powell	10.00

World Series Highlights

		NM/M
Complete Set (30):		35.00
Common Player:		1.00
Inserted 1:18		
LB	Lou Brock	1.00
CF	Carlton Fisk	1.50
KG	Kirk Gibson	1.00
RJ	Reggie Jackson	2.00
DL	Don Larsen	1.00
MM	Willie Mays	4.00
BM	Bill Mazeroski	1.00
SM	Stan Musial	3.00
JP	Jim Palmer	1.00
KP	Kirby Puckett	2.00
BR	Brooks Robinson	2.00
MS	Mike Schmidt	4.00
TS	Tom Seaver	2.00
CY	Carl Yastrzemski	2.00
RY	Robin Yount	2.00
Series 2		
DB	Dusty Baker	1.00
JB	Johnny Bench	2.50
JCA	Jose Canseco	1.50
JC	Joe Carter	1.00
WF	Whitey Ford	2.00
LG	Luis Gonzalez	1.00
AJ	Andruw Jones	1.50
DJ	David Justice	1.00
AK	Al Kaline	2.00
WM	Willie McCovey	1.00
JP	Johnny Podres	1.00
FR	Frank Robinson	1.50
OS	Ozzie Smith	2.00
DS	Duke Snider	1.50
BT	Bobby Thomson	1.00

World Series Highlights Autographs

		NM/M
Common Player:		
LB	Lou Brock	30.00
CF	Carlton Fisk	50.00
KG	Kirk Gibson	30.00

DL	Don Larsen	25.00
BM	Bill Mazeroski	30.00
JP	Jim Palmer	25.00
BR	Brooks Robinson	40.00
MS	Mike Schmidt	65.00
RY	Robin Yount	50.00
Series 2		
DB	Dusty Baker	20.00
JB	Johnny Bench	50.00
WF	Whitey Ford	35.00
RJ	Reggie Jackson	40.00
DJ	David Justice	30.00
AK	Al Kaline	40.00
SM	Stan Musial	75.00
JP	Johnny Podres	15.00
DS	Duke Snider	35.00
BT	Bobby Thomson	20.00

2004 Topps All-Time Fan Favorites

Gary Carter

	NM/M
Complete Set (150):	35.00
Common Player:	.25
Pack (6):	4.00
Box (24):	80.00

1	Willie Mays	2.50
2	Bob Gibson	.75
3	Dave Steib	.25
4	Tim McCarver	.25
5	Reggie Jackson	.75
6	John Candelaria	.25
7	Lenny Dykstra	.25
8	Tony Oliva	.50
9	Frank Viola	.25
10	Don Mattingly	2.50
11	Garry Maddox	.25
12	Randy Jones	.25
13	Joe Carter	.25
14	Orlando Cepeda	.50
15	Bob Sheppard	.25
16	Bobby Grich	.25
17	George Scott	.25
18	Mickey Rivers	.25
19	Ron Santo	.25
20	Mike Schmidt	2.00
21	Luis Aparicio	.25
22	Cesar Geronimo	.25
23	Jack Morris	.25
24	Jeffrey Loria	.25
25	George Brett	2.00
26	Paul O'Neill	.25
27	Reggie Smith	.25
28	Robin Yount	1.00
29	Andre Dawson	.50
30	Whitey Ford	.75
31	Ralph Kiner	.50
32	Will Clark	.50
33	Keith Hernandez	.25
34	Tony Fernandez	.25
35	Willie McGee	.25
36	Harmon Killebrew	.75
37	Dave Kingman	.25
38	Kirk Gibson	.25
39	Terry Steinbach	.25
40	Frank Robinson	.75
41	Chet Lemon	.25
42	Mike Cuellar	.25
43	Darrell Evans	.25
44	Don Kessinger	.25
45	Dave Concepcion	.25
46	Sparky Anderson	.25
47	Bret Saberhagen	.25
48	Brett Butler	.25
49	Kent Hrbek	.25
50	Hank Aaron	2.50
51	Rudolph Giuliani	.25
52	Clete Boyer	.25
53	Mookie Wilson	.25
54	Dave Stewart	.25
55	Gary Matthews	.25
56	Roy Face	.25
57	Vida Blue	.25
58	Jimmy Key	.25
59	Al Hrabosky	.25
60	Al Kaline	.75
61	Mike Scott	.25
62	Jack McDowell	.25
63	Reggie Jackson	.75
64	Earl Weaver	.25
65	Ernie Harwell	.25
66	David Justice	.25
67	Wilbur Wood	.25
68	Mike Boddicker	.25
69	Don Zimmer	.25
70	Jim Palmer	.50
71	Doug DeCinces	.25
72	Ryne Sandberg	1.00
73	Don Newcombe	.25

#	Player	Price
74	Denny Martinez	.25
75	Carl Yastrzemski	1.50
76	Bake McBride	.25
77	Andy Van Slyke	.25
78	Bruce Sutter	.50
79	Bobby Valentine	.25
80	Johnny Bench	1.50
81	Orel Hershiser	.25
82	Danny Tartabull	.25
83	Lou Whitaker	.25
84	Alan Trammell	.50
85	Sam McDowell	.25
86	Ray Knight	.25
87	Fernando Valenzuela	.25
88	Ben Oglivie	.25
89	Billy Beane	.25
90	Yogi Berra	1.00
91	Jose Canseco	.50
92	Bobby Bonilla	.25
93	Darren Daulton	.25
94	Harold Reynolds	.25
95	Lou Brock	.50
96	Pete Incaviglia	.25
97	Eric Gregg	.25
98	Devon White	.25
99	Kelly Gruber	.25
100	Nolan Ryan	3.00
101	Carlton Fisk	.50
102	George Foster	.25
103	Dennis Eckersley	.25
104	Rick Sutcliffe	.25
105	Cal Ripken Jr.	3.00
106	Norm Cash	.25
107	Charlie Hough	.25
108	Paul Molitor	.75
109	Maury Wills	.25
110	Tom Seaver	1.00
111	Brooks Robinson	1.00
112	Jim Rice	.25
113	Dwight Gooden	.25
114	Harold Baines	.25
115	Tim Raines	.25
116	Roy Smalley	.25
117	Richie Allen	.25
118	Ron Swoboda	.25
119	Ron Guidry	.25
120	Duke Snider	.75
121	Ferguson Jenkins	.50
122	Mark Fidrych	.25
123	Buddy Bell	.25
124	Bo Jackson	.50
125	Stan Musial	1.50
126	Jesse Barfield	.25
127	Tony Gwynn	1.00
128	Phil Garner	.25
129	Dale Murphy	.75
130	Wade Boggs	.50
131	Sid Fernandez	.25
132	Monte Irvin	.25
133	Peter Ueberroth	.25
134	Gary Gaetti	.25
135	Gorman Thomas	.25
136	Davey Lopes	.25
137	Sy Berger	.25
138	Buck O'Neil	.25
139	Herb Score	.25
140	Rod Carew	.75
141	Joe Buck	.25
142	Willie Horton	.25
143	Hal McRae	.25
144	Rollie Fingers	.25
145	Tom Brunansky	.25
146	Fay Vincent	.25
147	Gary Carter	.50
148	Bobby Richardson	.25
149	Steve Garvey	.25
150	Don Larsen	.50

Refractor

Cards (1-150): 3-6X
Production 299 Sets

Autographs

		NM/M
	Common Autograph:	10.00
	Inserted 2:Box	
	SP's Noted	
HA	Hank Aaron/50	350.00
RA	Richie Allen	15.00
SA	Sparky Anderson/100	20.00
LA	Luis Aparicio/100	40.00
HB	Harold Baines/100	20.00
JB	Jesse Barfield	10.00
BB	Billy Beane/100	25.00
BBE	Buddy Bell	20.00
JBE	Johnny Bench/100	150.00
SB	Sy Berger	50.00
YB	Yogi Berra/50	90.00

	Player	Price
VB	Vida Blue	15.00
MB	Mike Boddicker	15.00
WB	Wade Boggs/50	100.00
BMB	Bobby Bonilla	20.00
GB	George Brett/50	100.00
LB	Lou Brock/100	60.00
TB	Tom Brunansky	25.00
JB	Joe Buck/100	30.00
JCA	Jose Canseco/100	65.00
RC	Rod Carew/100	60.00
GC	Gary Carter/50	60.00
JC	Joe Carter/100	45.00
OC	Orlando Cepeda/100	65.00
DC	Dave Concepcion/100	40.00
DD	Darren Daulton	15.00
AD	Andre Dawson/100	40.00
LD	Lenny Dykstra/100	20.00
DEC	Dennis Eckersley/100	40.00
DE	Darrell Evans	10.00
SF	Sid Fernandez/100	40.00
TF	Tony Fernandez	15.00
MF	Mark Fidrych/100	40.00
RF	Rollie Fingers/100	40.00
WF	Whitey Ford/100	100.00
GF	George Foster	10.00
SG	Steve Garvey/100	30.00
CG	Cesar Geronimo/100	65.00
BG	Bob Gibson/100	90.00
DG	Dwight Gooden/50	60.00
EG	Eric Gregg	15.00
BGR	Bobby Grich	10.00
RG	Ron Guidry/100	50.00
TG	Tony Gwynn/50	100.00
EH	Ernie Harwell	25.00
KH	Keith Hernandez/50	25.00
OH	Orel Hershiser	30.00
WH	Willie Horton	15.00
CH	Charlie Hough	15.00
AH	Al Hrabosky	15.00
PI	Pete Incaviglia	20.00
MI	Monte Irvin/100	25.00
BJ	Bo Jackson/50	100.00
RJ2	Reggie Jackson	80.00
FJ	Ferguson Jenkins	15.00
RJ	Randy Jones	10.00
DJ	David Justice	25.00
AK	Al Kaline/100	100.00
DKE	Don Kessinger	15.00
JK	Jimmy Key/100	45.00
HK	Harmon Killebrew/100	85.00
RK	Ralph Kiner	40.00
DK	Dave Kingman	40.00
RKN	Ray Knight/100	40.00
DLA	Don Larsen	15.00
CL	Chet Lemon	15.00
DL	Davey Lopes	10.00
GM	Gary Mathews	10.00
DON	Don Mattingly/50	125.00
WM	Willie Mays/50	225.00
TM	Tim McCarver	40.00
JM	Jack McDowell	15.00
SM	Sam McDowell/100	15.00
WMC	Willie McGee/100	50.00
PM	Paul Molitor/50	85.00
JMO	Jack Morris	10.00
DM	Dale Murphy/50	75.00
SM	Stan Musial/100	100.00
BO	Buck O'Neil	30.00
PO	Paul O'Neill/50	60.00
BO	Ben Oglivie	15.00
TO	Tony Oliva	30.00
JP	Jim Palmer/50	100.00
TR	Tim Raines	25.00
HR	Harold Reynolds/100	30.00
JR	Jim Rice/100	30.00
BR	Bobby Richardson	15.00
CR	Cal Ripken Jr./50	200.00
MR	Mickey Rivers	15.00
BRO	Brooks Robinson/50	100.00
FR	Frank Robinson/100	80.00
NR	Nolan Ryan	175.00
RYN	Ryne Sandberg/100	45.00
RS	Ron Santo	30.00
MS	Mike Schmidt/100	120.00
GS	George Scott	15.00
MSC	Mike Scott	10.00
TSE	Tom Seaver/50	100.00
DSN	Duke Snider/100	75.00
DS	Dave Stewart	15.00
DST	Dave Stieb	25.00
RSU	Rick Sutcliffe/100	40.00
BSU	Bruce Sutter	35.00
RSW	Ron Swoboda	15.00
AT	Alan Trammell/100	60.00
PU	Peter Ueberroth/100	60.00
BV	Bobby Valentine/100	50.00
AV	Andy Van Slyke/100	65.00

	Player	Price
FVI	Fay Vincent/100	50.00
EW	Earl Weaver	15.00
MW	Maury Wills	15.00
MWI	Mookie Wilson	10.00
WW	Wilbur Wood	15.00
CY	Carl Yastrzemski/50	100.00
RY	Robin Yount/50	100.00
DZ	Don Zimmer	30.00

Best Seat In The House

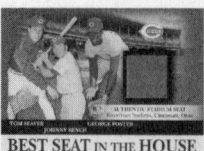

BEST SEAT IN THE HOUSE

		NM/M
	Common Card:	15.00
BS1	Tom Seaver, Johnny Bench, George Foster	15.00
BS2	Frank Robinson, Jim Palmer, Brooks Robinson	15.00
BS3	Dave Parker, Bill Madlock, Bill Mazeroski	15.00
BS4	Kent Hrbek, Rod Carew, Harmon Killebrew	30.00

Relics

FRANK ROBINSON

		NM/M
	Common Player:	5.00
WB	Wade Boggs	10.00
GB	George Brett	15.00
LB	Lou Brock	10.00
JC	Jose Canseco/Jsy	8.00
JCB	Jose Canseco/Bat	8.00
GC	Gary Carter	8.00
DE	Dennis Eckersley	5.00
CF	Carlton Fisk	10.00
GF	George Foster	5.00
KG	Kirk Gibson	5.00
KH	Keith Hernandez	8.00
RJ	Reggie Jackson	10.00
DJ	David Justice	5.00
HK	Harmon Killebrew	20.00
WM	Willie Mays	30.00
JM	Joe Morgan	5.00
GN	Graig Nettles	8.00
JP	Jim Palmer	8.00
DP	Dave Parker	5.00
KP	Kirby Puckett	10.00
HR	Harold Reynolds	5.00
JR	Jim Rice	5.00
BR	Brooks Robinson	12.00
FRB	Frank Robinson/Bat	8.00
FR	Frank Robinson/Jsy	8.00
NR	Nolan Ryan	25.00
BS	Bret Saberhagen	5.00
MS	Mike Schmidt	15.00
SS	Darryl Strawberry	8.00
EW	Earl Weaver	8.00
MW	Maury Wills	5.00
CY	Carl Yastrzemski	20.00

2004 Topps Bazooka

BARTOLO COLON

		NM/M
	Complete Set (300):	40.00
	Common Player:	.15
	Variations (30): Same Price	
	Pack (8):	2.00
	Box (24):	40.00
1	Bobby Abreu	.25
2	Jesse Foppert	.15
3	Shea Hillenbrand	.15
4	Jose Lima	.15

#	Player	Price
5	Manny Ramirez	.50
6	Denny Neagle	.15
7	Frank Thomas	.50
8	A.J. Burnett	.15
9	Carl Everett	.15
10	Scott Podsednik	.25
11	Travis Lee	.15
12	Mike Mussina	.40
13	Runelvys Hernandez	.15
14	Shannon Stewart	.15
15	Miguel Cabrera	.40
16	Edgardo Alfonzo	.15
17	Victor Zambrano	.15
18	Rafael Furcal	.15
19	Eric Hinske	.15
20	Paul LoDuca	.15
21	Phil Nevin	.15
22	Aramis Ramirez	.15
23	Jim Thome	.75
24	Jeromy Burnitz	.15
25	Mark Prior	1.50
26	Ramon Hernandez	.15
27	Cliff Lee	.15
28	Greg Myers	.15
29	Robert Fick	.15
30	Mike Sweeney	.15
31	Carlos Zambrano	.15
32	Roberto Alomar	.40
33	Orlando Cabrera	.25
34	Orlando Hudson	.15
35	Nomar Garciaparra	1.50
36	Esteban Loaiza	.15
37	Laynce Nix	.15
38	Joe Randa	.15
39	Juan Uribe	.15
40	Pat Burrell	.40
41	Steve Finley	.15
42	Livan Hernandez	.15
43	Al Leiter	.15
44	Brett Myers	.15
45	Jody Gerut	.15
46	Mark Teixeira	.40
47	Barry Zito	.40
48	Moises Alou	.25
49	Mike Cameron	.15
50	Albert Pujols	1.50
51	Tim Hudson	.25
52	Kenny Lofton	.25
53	Trot Nixon	.15
54	Tim Redding	.15
55	Marlon Byrd	.15
56	Javier Vazquez	.25
57	Sean Burroughs	.15
58	Cliff Floyd	.15
59	Juan Rivera	.15
60	Mike Lieberthal	.15
61	Xavier Nady	.15
62	Brad Radke	.15
63	Miguel Tejada	.40
64	Ichiro Suzuki	1.00
65	Garret Anderson	.25
66	Sean Casey	.15
67	Jason Giambi	.75
68	Aubrey Huff	.25
69	Javy Lopez	.25
70	Hideo Nomo	.25
71	Mark Redman	.15
72	Jose Vidro	.15
73	Rich Aurilia	.15
74	Luis Castillo	.15
75	Jay Gibbons	.15
76	Torii Hunter	.25
77	Derek Lowe	.15
78	Wes Obermueller	.15
79	Edgar Renteria	.15
80	Jeff Bagwell	.50
81	Fernando Vina	.15
82	Frank Catalanotto	.15
83	Marcus Giles	.15
84	Raul Ibanez	.15
85	Mike Lowell	.25
86	Tomokazu Ohka	.15
87	Jose Reyes	.25
88	Omar Vizquel	.25
89	Shawn Chacon	.15
90	Rocco Baldelli	.25
91	Brian Giles	.25
92	Kazuhisa Ishii	.15
93	Greg Maddux	1.00
94	John Olerud	.25
95	Eric Chavez	.25
96	Doug Waechter	.15
97	Tony Batista	.25
98	Jeriome Robertson	.15
99	Troy Glaus	.25
100	Eric Gagne	.25
101	Pedro J. Martinez	.75
102	Magglio Ordonez	.15
103	Alex Rodriguez	2.00
104	Jason Bay	.15
105	Larry Walker	.25
106	Matt Clement	.15
107	Tom Glavine	.25
108	Geoff Jenkins	.25
109	Victor Martinez	.25
110	David Ortiz	.15
111	Ivan Rodriguez	.25
112	Jarrod Washburn	.15
113	Josh Beckett	.25
114	Bartolo Colon	.25
115	Juan Gonzalez	.40
116	Derek Jeter	2.00
117	Edgar Martinez	.25
118	Ramon Ortiz	.15
119	Scott Rolen	.75
120	Brandon Webb	.15
121	Carlos Beltran	.25
122	Jose Contreras	.25

#	Player	Price
123	Luis Gonzalez	.25
124	Jason Johnson	.15
125	Luis Matos	.15
126	Russ Ortiz	.15
127	Damian Rolls	.15
128	David Wells	.15
129	Adrian Beltre	.15
130	Shawn Green	.15
131	Nate Cornejo	.15
132	Nick Johnson	.15
133	Joe Mays	.15
134	Roy Oswalt	.25
135	C.C. Sabathia	.25
136	Vernon Wells	.25
137	Kris Benson	.15
138	Carl Crawford	.25
139	Ken Griffey Jr.	1.00
140	Randy Johnson	.75
141	Fred McGriff	.25
142	Vicente Padilla	.15
143	Tim Salmon	.25
144	Kip Wells	.15
145	Lance Berkman	.25
146	Jose Cruz Jr.	.15
147	Marquis Grissom	.15
148	Jacque Jones	.15
149	Gil Meche	.15
150	Vladimir Guerrero	.75
151	Reggie Sanders	.15
152	Ty Wigginton	.15
153	Angel Berroa	.15
154	Johnny Damon	.25
155	Rafael Palmeiro	.50
156	Chipper Jones	.75
157	Kevin Millar	.15
158	Corey Patterson	.15
159	Johan Santana	.15
160	Bernie Williams	.40
161	Craig Biggio	.25
162	Carlos Delgado	.50
163	Aaron Guiel	.15
164	Wade Miller	.15
165	Andruw Jones	.50
166	Jay Payton	.15
167	Benito Santiago	.15
168	Woody Williams	.15
169	Casey Blake	.15
170	Adam Dunn	.40
171	Jose Guillen	.15
172	Brian Jordan	.15
173	Kevin Millwood	.25
174	Carlos Pena	.15
175	Curt Schilling	.50
176	Jerome Williams	.15
177	Hank Blalock	.25
178	Erubiel Durazo	.15
179	Cristian Guzman	.15
180	Austin Kearns	.40
181	Raul Mondesi	.15
182	Andy Pettitte	.25
183	Jason Schmidt	.25
184	Jeremy Bonderman	.25
185	Dontrelle Willis	.25
186	Ray Durham	.15
187	Jerry Hairston Jr.	.15
188	Jason Kendall	.15
189	Melvin Mora	.15
190	Jeff Kent	.25
191	Jae Weong Seo	.15
192	Jack Wilson	.15
193	Cesar Izturis	.15
194	Jermaine Dye	.15
195	Roy Halladay	.25
196	Jason Phillips	.15
197	Matt Morris	.25
198	Mike Piazza	1.00
199	Richie Sexson	.40
200	Alfonso Soriano	.75
201	Mark Mulder	.25
202	David Eckstein	.15
203	Mike Hampton	.15
204	Ryan Klesko	.25
205	Damian Moss	.15
206	Juan Pierre	.15
207	Ben Sheets	.25
208	Randy Winn	.15
209	Bret Boone	.25
210	Jim Edmonds	.25
211	Rich Harden	.15
212	Paul Konerko	.15
213	Jamie Moyer	.15
214	A.J. Pierzynski	.15
215	Gary Sheffield	.25
216	Randy Wolf	.15
217	Kevin Brown	.25
218	Morgan Ensberg	.15
219	Bo Hart	.15
220	Bill Mueller	.15
221	Corey Koskie	.15
222	Joel Pineiro	.15
223	Preston Wilson	.15
224	Aaron Boone	.15
225	Kerry Wood	.50
226	Darin Erstad	.25
227	Wes Helms	.15
228	Brian Lawrence	.15
229	Mark Buehrle	.15
230	Sammy Sosa	1.25
231	Sidney Ponson	.15
232	Dmitri Young	.15
233	Ellis Burks	.15
234	Kelvim Escobar	.15
235	Todd Helton	.50
236	Matt Lawton	.15
237	Eric Munson	.15
238	Jorge Posada	.50
239	Junior Spivey	.15
240	Michael Young	.25

#	Player	Price
241	Ramon Nivar	.15
242	Edwin Jackson	.15
243	Felix Pie	.15
244	Ryan Wagner	.15
245	Grady Sizemore	.25
246	Bobby Jenks	.15
247	Chad Billingsley	.15
248	Casey Kotchman	.15
249	Bobby Crosby	.15
250	Khalil Greene	.15
251	Danny Garcia	.15
252	Nicholas Markakis	.15
253	Bernie Castro	.15
254	Aaron Hill	.15
255	Josh Barfield	.15
256	Ryan Wagner	.15
257	Ryan Harvey	.15
258	Jimmy Gobble	.15
259	Ryan Madson	.15
260	Zack Greinke	.15
261	Rene Reyes	.15
262	Eric Duncan	.15
263	Chris Lubanski	.15
264	Jeff Mathis	.15
265	Rickie Weeks	.25
266	Justin Morneau	.25
267	Brian Snyder	.15
268	Neal Cotts	.15
269	Joe Borchard	.15
270	Larry Bigbie	.15
271	Marcus McBeth RC	.40
272	Tydus Meadows RC	.40
273	Zach Miner RC	.50
274	Anthony Lerew RC	.40
275	Yadier Molina RC	.40
276	Jon Knott RC	.40
277	Matthew Moses RC	.40
278	Sung Jung RC	.40
279	Mike Gosling	.15
280	David Murphy RC	.40
281	Tim Frend RC	.40
282	Casey Myers RC	.40
283	Brayan Pena RC	.40
284	Omar Falcon RC	.40
285	Blake Hawksworth RC	.40
286	Jesse Roman RC	.40
287	Kyle Davies RC	.40
288	Matt Creighton RC	.40
289	Rodney Choy Foo RC	.40
290	Kyle Sleeth	.15
291	Carlos Quentin	.50
292	Khalid Ballouli RC	.40
293	Tim Stauffer	.15
294	Craig Ansman RC	.40
295	Dioner Navarro RC	.40
296	Josh Labandeira RC	.40
297	Jeff Allison	.15
298	Anthony Acevedo RC	.40
299	Brad Sullivan	.15
300	Conor Jackson	.50

Red

Cards (1-300): 1-2X
Inserted 1:1

Mini

Stars (1-300): 1-2X
Inserted 1:1

Adventures

BAZOOKA ADVENTURES — CHIPPER JONES

		NM/M
	Common Player:	4.00
EA	Edgardo Alfonzo	4.00
JB	Jeff Bagwell	8.00
LB	Lance Berkman	6.00
CB	Craig Biggio	4.00
KB	Kevin Brown	4.00
PB	Pat Burrell	6.00
MB	Marlon Byrd	4.00
SC	Sean Casey	4.00
LC	Luis Castillo	4.00
EC	Eric Chavez	5.00
AD1	Adam Dunn	6.00
AD2	Adam Dunn	6.00
CE	Carl Everett	4.00
CF	Cliff Floyd	4.00
NG	Nomar Garciaparra	10.00
JG	Jason Giambi	4.00
JDG	Jeremy Giambi	4.00
TEG	Troy Glaus	5.00
TG	Tom Glavine	5.00
LG	Luis Gonzalez	4.00
SG	Shawn Green	5.00
BG	Ben Grieve	4.00
VG	Vladimir Guerrero	8.00
CG	Cristian Guzman	4.00
TH	Toby Hall	4.00
TAH1	Tim Hudson	4.00

TAH2	Tim Hudson	4.00
GJ	Geoff Jenkins	4.00
RJ	Randy Johnson	8.00
AJ	Andruw Jones	6.00
CJ	Chipper Jones	8.00
JK	Jason Kendall	4.00
PK	Paul Konerko	4.00
PL	Paul LoDuca	4.00
ML	Mike Lowell	4.00
GM	Greg Maddux	8.00
KM	Kevin Millwood	6.00
MM	Mark Mulder	5.00
MCM	Mike Mussina	6.00
HN	Hideo Nomo	8.00
JO	John Olerud	4.00
RP1	Rafael Palmeiro	6.00
RP2	Rafael Palmeiro	6.00
BP	Brad Penny	4.00
MP1	Mike Piazza	10.00
MP2	Mike Piazza	10.00
AP	Albert Pujols	15.00
MR	Manny Ramirez	6.00
AR1	Alex Rodriguez	10.00
AR2	Alex Rodriguez	10.00
TJS	Tim Salmon	5.00
CS	Curt Schilling	8.00
AS	Alfonso Soriano	6.00
MT	Miguel Tejada	4.00
JT	Jim Thome	8.00
LW	Larry Walker	4.00
JW	Jarrod Washburn	4.00
BW	Bernie Williams	6.00
DW	Dontrelle Willis	6.00
PW	Preston Wilson	4.00
KW	Kerry Wood	6.00
BZ	Barry Zito	6.00

Blasts

		NM/M
	Common Player:	4.00
RA	Roberto Alomar	6.00
MA	Moises Alou	4.00
RSA	Rich Aurilia	4.00
JB	Jeff Bagwell	8.00
RB	Rocco Baldelli	8.00
TB	Tony Batista	4.00
CIB	Carlos Beltran	4.00
LB	Lance Berkman	5.00
CB	Craig Biggio	4.00
HB	Hank Blalock	6.00
BB	Bret Boone	5.00
JNB	Jeromy Burnitz	4.00
SB	Sean Burroughs	4.00
CC	Carl Crawford	4.00
AD	Adam Dunn	6.00
CE	Carl Everett	4.00
BF	Brad Fullmer	4.00
RF	Rafael Furcal	4.00
AJG	Andres Galarraga	4.00
NG	Nomar Garciaparra	12.00
JG	Jason Giambi	8.00
TG	Troy Glaus	5.00
AG	Juan Gonzalez	4.00
JAG	Juan Gonzalez	6.00
LG	Luis Gonzalez	4.00
SG	Shawn Green	6.00
MG	Marquis Grissom	4.00
VG	Vladimir Guerrero	8.00
CG	Cristian Guzman	4.00
NH	Nathan Haynes	4.00
TKH	Todd Helton	6.00
AH	Aubrey Huff	4.00
TH	Torii Hunter	5.00
CJ	Chipper Jones	8.00
PK	Paul Konerko	4.00
ML	Matt Lawton	4.00
CL	Carlos Lee	4.00
PL	Paul LoDuca	4.00
EM	Edgar Martinez	4.00
TM	Tino Martinez	6.00
FM	Fred McGriff	5.00
DM	John Mientkiewicz	4.00
JO	John Olerud	4.00
MO	Magglio Ordonez	4.00
RP	Rafael Palmeiro	8.00
CP	Corey Patterson	4.00
MP	Mike Piazza	10.00
JP	Jorge Posada	6.00
AP	Albert Pujols	15.00
ANR	Aramis Ramirez	4.00
MR	Manny Ramirez	6.00
JR	Juan Rivera	4.00
AR	Alex Rodriguez	10.00
IR	Ivan Rodriguez	6.00
SR	Scott Rolen	8.00
TJS	Tim Salmon	5.00
GS	Gary Sheffield	6.00
RS	Ruben Sierra	4.00
AS	Alfonso Soriano	8.00
SS	Shannon Stewart	4.00
ST	So Taguchi	5.00
MCT	Mark Teixeira	5.00
MT	Miguel Tejada	5.00
FT	Frank Thomas	8.00
MAT	Michael Tucker	4.00
MV	Mo Vaughn	4.00
OV	Omar Vizquel	4.00

Comics

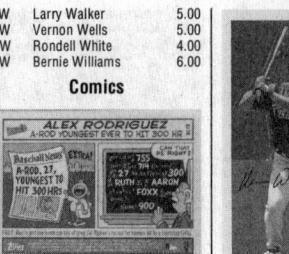

		NM/M
	Complete Set (24):	6.00
	Common Player:	.25
	Inserted 1:4	
BC1	Garret Anderson	.25
BC2	Jeff Bagwell	.50
BC3	Hank Blalock	.25
BC4	Roy Halladay	.25
BC5	Dontrelle Willis	.25
BC6	Roger Clemens	.75
BC7	Carlos Delgado	.40
BC8	Rafael Furcal	.25
BC9	Eric Gagne	.25
BC10	Nomar Garciaparra	.75
BC11	Derek Jeter	.75
BC12	Esteban Loaiza	.25
BC13	Kevin Millwood	.25
BC14	Bill Mueller	.25
BC15	Rafael Palmeiro	.40
BC16	Albert Pujols	.75
BC17	Jose Reyes	.25
BC18	Alex Rodriguez	.75
BC19	Alfonso Soriano	.40
BC20	Sammy Sosa	.50
BC21	Ichiro Suzuki	.50
BC22	Frank Thomas	.40
BC23	Brad Wilkerson	.25
BC24	Houston Astros	.25

One-Liners

		NM/M
	Common Player:	5.00
DA	Dick Allen	8.00
JB	Johnny Bench	10.00
BB	Bert Blyleven	5.00
WB1	Wade Boggs	6.00
WB2	Wade Boggs	6.00
GB	George Brett	20.00
BC	Bert Campaneris	5.00
RC	Rod Carew	8.00
GC	Gary Carter	5.00
JCA	Joe Carter	5.00
OC	Orlando Cepeda	5.00
RD	Ron Darling	5.00
AD	Andre Dawson	8.00
DE	Dennis Eckersley	10.00
KG1	Kirk Gibson	5.00
KG2	Kirk Gibson	5.00
DW	Dwight Gooden	5.00
KH	Keith Hernandez	5.00
RJ	Reggie Jackson	10.00
DJ1	David Justice	8.00
DJ2	David Justice	8.00
HK	Harmon Killebrew	20.00
JK	Jerry Koosman	5.00
BM	Bill Madlock	5.00
WM	Willie Mays	30.00
WMC	Willie McGee	8.00
TM	Tug McGraw	5.00
JM	Joe Morgan	8.00
DM	Dale Murphy	15.00
EM	Eddie Murray	10.00
PN	Phil Niekro	5.00
DP	Dave Parker	5.00
GP	Gaylord Perry	5.00
KP1	Kirby Puckett	10.00
KP2	Kirby Puckett	10.00
FR	Frank Robinson	10.00
NR	Nolan Ryan	15.00
BS	Bret Saberhagen	5.00
RSA	Ron Santo	10.00
MS	Mike Schmidt	15.00
RS	Red Schoendienst	5.00
TS	Tom Seaver	8.00
WS	Willie Stargell	8.00
CY	Carl Yastrzemski	15.00
RY	Robin Yount	10.00

Stand-Ups

		NM/M
	Complete Set (25):	20.00
	Common Player:	.50
	Inserted 1:8	
1	Jose Reyes	.50
2	Jim Thome	1.00
3	Roy Halladay	.50
4	Jason Giambi	1.00
5	Dontrelle Willis	.50
6	Mike Piazza	1.50
7	Chipper Jones	1.00
8	Mark Prior	2.00

LW	Larry Walker	5.00
VW	Vernon Wells	5.00
RW	Rondell White	4.00
BW	Bernie Williams	6.00

		NM/M
9	Todd Helton	.75
10	Miguel Cabrera	.75
11	Derek Jeter	3.00
12	Nomar Garciaparra	2.00
13	Alex Rodriguez	3.00
14	Miguel Tejada	.50
15	Carlos Delgado	.75
16	Pedro J. Martinez	1.00
17	Sammy Sosa	2.00
18	Ichiro Suzuki	1.50
19	Vladimir Guerrero	1.00
20	Alfonso Soriano	1.00
21	Eric Chavez	.50
22	Albert Pujols	2.50
23	Ivan Rodriguez	.75
24	Vernon Wells	.50
25	Eric Gagne	.50

Tattoos

		NM/M
	Complete Set (55):	8.00
	Common Player:	.15
	Inserted 1:4	
JB	Jeff Bagwell	.25
BAZ	Bazooka Logo	.15
LB	Lance Berkman	.15
CB	Craig Biggio	.15
KB	Kevin Brown	.15
PB	Pat Burrell	.15
MB	Marlon Byrd	.15
SC	Sean Casey	.15
LC	Luis Castillo	.15
EC	Eric Chavez	.15
AD	Adam Dunn	.15
CF	Cliff Floyd	.15
NG	Nomar Garciaparra	.75
JG	Jason Giambi	.40
TFG	Troy Glaus	.25
TG	Tom Glavine	.15
LG	Luis Gonzalez	.15
SG	Shawn Green	.15
VG	Vladimir Guerrero	.40
CG	Cristian Guzman	.15
TH	Toby Hall	.15
TAH	Tim Hudson	.15
GJ	Geoff Jenkins	.15
RJ	Randy Johnson	.40
AJ	Andruw Jones	.25
CJ	Chipper Jones	.40
JK	Jason Kendall	.15
PK	Paul Konerko	.15
PL	Paul LoDuca	.15
ML	Mike Lowell	.15
GM	Greg Maddux	.25
KM	Kevin Millwood	.15
MM	Mark Mulder	.15
MCM	Mike Mussina	.25
HN	Hideo Nomo	.15
JO	John Olerud	.15
RP	Rafael Palmeiro	.25
BP	Brad Penny	.15
MP	Mike Piazza	.50
AP	Albert Pujols	.75
MR	Manny Ramirez	.25
AR	Alex Rodriguez	1.00
TJS	Tim Salmon	.15
CS	Curt Schilling	.25
AS	Alfonso Soriano	.40
MT	Miguel Tejada	.25
JT	Jim Thome	.25
TOP	Topps Logo	.15
LW	Larry Walker	.15
JW	Jarrod Washburn	.15
BW	Bernie Williams	.25
DW	Dontrelle Willis	.15
PW	Preston Wilson	.15
KW	Kerry Wood	.25
BZ	Barry Zito	.25

4-on-1 Stickers

		NM/M
	Complete Set (40):	8.00
	Common Player:	.20
	Inserted 1:4	
1	Rich Harden, Dontrelle Willis, Jerome Williams, Brandon Webb	.20
2	Eric Duncan, Derek Jeter, Alfonso Soriano, Jason Giambi	.75
3	Grady Sizemore, Rocco Baldelli, Ichiro Suzuki, Vladimir Guerrero	.50
4	Roy Halladay, Pedro J. Martinez, Curt Schilling, Brett Myers	.40
5	Alex Rodriguez, Angel Berroa, Jose Reyes, Khalil Greene	.75
6	Kerry Wood, Adam Dunn, Jeff Kent, Scott Rolen	.40
7	Miguel Cabrera, Scott Podsednik, Bo Hart, Mark Teixeira	.20
8	Rickie Weeks, Josh Barfield, Albert Pujols, Vernon Wells	.50
9	Torii Hunter, Garret Anderson, Bobby Abreu, Ken Griffey Jr.	.40
10	Jay Gibbons, Chipper Jones, Mike Piazza, Mike Sweeney	.50
11	David Ortiz, Nick Johnson, Carlos Delgado, Frank Thomas	.40
12	Todd Helton, Jose Vidro, Mike Lowell, Miguel Tejada	.20
13	Randy Wolf, Mark Mulder, Johan Santana, Randy Johnson	.40
14	Bret Boone, Aubrey Huff, Eric Chavez, Javy Lopez	.20
15	Jason Schmidt, Roy Oswalt, Joel Pineiro, Mark Prior	.20
16	Kevin Millwood, Andy Pettitte, Matt Morris, Tim Hudson	.20
17	Javier Vazquez, Esteban Loaiza, Orlando Cabrera, Roberto Alomar	.20
18	Al Leiter, David Wells, Mike Hampton, Jarrod Washburn	.20
19	Paul LoDuca, Mike Lieberthal, Brian Giles, Andruw Jones	.20
20	Magglio Ordonez, Corey Patterson, Aaron Boone, Jeff Bagwell	.40
21	Troy Glaus, Edgar Martinez, Manny Ramirez, Raul Ibanez	.30
22	Sammy Sosa, Barry Zito, Bartolo Colon, Austin Kearns	.20
23	Jim Edmonds, Gary Sheffield, Preston Wilson, Shawn Green	.20
24	Bernie Williams, Juan Pierre, Josh Beckett, Mike Mussina	.20
25	Ramon Hernandez, Jason Kendall, Jason Phillips, A.J. Pierzynski	.20
26	Pat Burrell, Laynce Nix, Mike Cameron, Cliff Floyd	.20
27	Eric Gagne, Carl Crawford, Jose Guillen, Steve Finley	.20
28	Ellis Burks, Livan Hernandez, Derek Lowe, Kazuhisa Ishii	.20
29	Jorge Posada, Jeff Mathis, Victor Martinez, Ivan Rodriguez	.20
30	Jim Thome, Marcus Giles, Nomar Garciaparra, Hank Blalock	.50
31	Edgar Renteria, Bobby Crosby, Neal Cotts, Russ Ortiz	.20
32	Zack Greinke, Cristian Guzman, Cesar Izturis, Kevin Brown	.20
33	Bobby Jenks, Ramon Nivar, Richie Sexson, Ryan Klesko	.20
34	Omar Vizquel, Carlos Pena, Rafael Furcal, Gil Meche	.20
35	Kenny Lofton, Tim Salmon, Marquis Grissom, Craig Biggio	.20
36	Kyle Davies, Anthony Lerew, Brayan Pena, Sung Jung	.20
37	Rodney Choy Foo, Craig Ansman, David Murphy, Matthew Moses	.20
38	Carlos Quentin, Dioner Navarro, Marcus McBeth, Josh Labandeira	.20
39	Kyle Sleeth, Conor Jackson, Brad Sullivan, Jeff Allison	.20
40	Yadier Molina, Jon Knott, Blake Hawksworth, Tim Stauffer	.20

2004 Topps Chicago Cubs Reprints

For a fourth year the Cubs contracted with Topps to provide a series of reprint cards for use as give-aways at special games throughout the season. Each re-print features a Wrigley Field logo on front and is sequentially num-bered to 20,000 in a strip of gold foil on back. Each card was distrib-uted in a cello wrapper with the date of the promotion and names of the sponsor(s).

		NM/M
	Complete Set (2):	5.00
	Common Player:	2.00
(1)	Shawon Dunston	2.00
(2)	Mark Prior	2.00

2004 Topps Chrome

		NM/M
	Complete Set (466):	
	Common Player:	.25
	Common Rookie Auto.	
	(221-246):	10.00
	Inserted 1:21	
	Series 1 Pack (4):	3.50
	Series 1 Box (20):	50.00
	Series 2 Pack (4):	3.50
	Series 2 Box (20):	50.00
1	Jim Thome	1.00
2	Reggie Sanders	.25
3	Mark Kotsay	.25
4	Edgardo Alfonzo	.25
5	Tim Wakefield	.25
6	Moises Alou	.50
7	Jorge Julio	.25
8	Bartolo Colon	.50
9	Chan Ho Park	.25
10	Ichiro Suzuki	3.00
11	Kevin Millwood	.40
12	Preston Wilson	.40
13	Tom Glavine	.75
14	Junior Spivey	.25
15	Marcus Giles	.40
16	David Segui	.25
17	Kevin Millar	.25
18	Corey Patterson	.40
19	Aaron Rowand	.25
20	Derek Jeter	4.00
21	Luis Castillo	.25
22	Manny Ramirez	1.50
23	Jay Payton	.25
24	Bobby Higginson	.25
25	Lance Berkman	.75
26	Juan Pierre	.25
27	Mike Mussina	1.00
28	Fred McGriff	.50
29	Richie Sexson	.75
30	Tim Hudson	.50
31	Mike Piazza	2.00
32	Brad Radke	.25
33	Jeff Weaver	.25
34	Ramon Hernandez	.25
35	David Bell	.25
36	Randy Wolf	.25
37	Jake Peavy	.50
38	Tim Worrell	.25
39	Gil Meche	.25
40	Albert Pujols	4.00
41	Michael Young	.25
42	Josh Phelps	.25
43	Brendan Donnelly	.25
44	Steve Finley	.25

45	John Smoltz	.50
46	Jay Gibbons	.25
47	Trot Nixon	.25
48	Carl Pavano	.25
49	Frank Thomas	1.00
50	Mark Prior	1.00
51	Danny Graves	.25
52	Milton Bradley	.25
53	Kris Benson	.25
54	Ryan Klesko	.25
55	Mike Lowell	.25
56	Geoff Blum	.25
57	Michael Tucker	.25
58	Paul LoDuca	.25
59	Vicente Padilla	.25
60	Jacque Jones	.25
61	Fernando Tatis	.25
62	Ty Wigginton	.25
63	Rich Aurilia	.25
64	Andy Pettitte	.75
65	Terrence Long	.25
66	Cliff Floyd	.25
67	Mariano Rivera	.75
68	Kelvim Escobar	.25
69	Marlon Byrd	.25
70	Mark Mulder	.50
71	Francisco Cordero	.25
72	Carlos Guillen	.25
73	Fernando Vina	.25
74	Lance Carter	.25
75	Hank Blalock	.75
76	Jimmy Rollins	.50
77	Francisco Rodriguez	.50
78	Javy Lopez	.50
79	Jerry Hairston Jr.	.25
80	Andruw Jones	.75
81	Rodrigo Lopez	.25
82	Johnny Damon	1.00
83	Hee Seop Choi	.25
84	Kazuhiro Sasaki	.25
85	Danny Bautista	.25
86	Matt Lawton	.25
87	Juan Uribe	.25
88	Rafael Furcal	.25
89	Kyle Farnsworth	.25
90	Jose Vidro	.25
91	Luis Rivas	.25
92	Hideo Nomo	.75
93	Javier Vazquez	.50
94	Al Leiter	.40
95	Jose Valentin	.25
96	Alex Cintron	.25
97	Zach Day	.25
98	Jorge Posada	.75
99	C.C. Sabathia	.25
100	Alex Rodriguez	3.00
101	Brad Penny	.25
102	Brad Ausmus	.25
103	Raul Ibanez	.25
104	Mike Hampton	.25
105	Adrian Beltre	.50
106	Ramiro Mendoza	.25
107	Rocco Baldelli	.75
108	Esteban Loaiza	.25
109	Russell Branyan	.25
110	Todd Helton	1.00
111	Braden Looper	.25
112	Octavio Dotel	.25
113	Mike MacDougal	.25
114	Cesar Izturis	.25
115	Johan Santana	1.00
116	Jose Contreras	.25
117	Placido Polanco	.25
118	Jason Phillips	.25
119	Orlando Hudson	.25
120	Vernon Wells	.25
121	Ben Grieve	.25
122	Dave Roberts	.25
123	Ismael Valdes	.25
124	Eric Owens	.25
125	Curt Schilling	1.00
126	Russ Ortiz	.25
127	Mark Buehrle	.50
128	Doug Mientkiewicz	.25
129	Dmitri Young	.25
130	Kazuhisa Ishii	.25
131	A.J. Pierzynski	.25
132	Brad Wilkerson	.25
133	Joe McEwing	.25
134	Alex Cora	.25
135	Jose Cruz Jr.	.25
136	Carlos Zambrano	.50
137	Jeff Kent	.50
138	Shigetoshi Hasegawa	.25
139	Jarrod Washburn	.25
140	Greg Maddux	2.00
141	Josh Beckett	.75
142	Miguel Batista	.25
143	Omar Vizquel	.40
144	Alex Gonzalez	.25
145	Billy Wagner	.25
146	Brian Jordan	.25
147	Wes Helms	.25
148	Deivi Cruz	.25
149	Alex Gonzalez	.25
150	Jason Giambi	1.00
151	Erubiel Durazo	.25
152	Mike Lieberthal	.25
153	Jason Kendall	.25
154	Xavier Nady	.25
155	Kirk Rueter	.25
156	Mike Cameron	.25
157	Miguel Cairo	.25
158	Woody Williams	.25
159	Toby Hall	.25
160	Bernie Williams	.75
161	Darin Erstad	.50
162	Matt Mantei	.25

#	Player	Price
163	Shawn Chacon	.25
164	Bill Mueller	.25
165	Damian Miller	.25
166	Tony Graffanino	.25
167	Sean Casey	.25
168	Brandon Phillips	.25
169	Runelvys Hernandez	.25
170	Adam Dunn	.75
171	Carlos Lee	.50
172	Juan Encarnacion	.25
173	Angel Berroa	.25
174	Desi Relaford	.25
175	Joe Mays	.25
176	Ben Sheets	.50
177	Eddie Guardado	.25
178	Rocky Biddle	.25
179	Eric Gagne	.50
180	Eric Chavez	.50
181	Jason Michaels	.25
182	Dustan Mohr	.25
183	Kip Wells	.25
184	Brian Lawrence	.25
185	Bret Boone	.25
186	Tino Martinez	.40
187	Aubrey Huff	.25
188	Kevin Mench	.25
189	Tim Salmon	.50
190	Carlos Delgado	1.00
191	John Lackey	.25
192	Eric Byrnes	.25
193	Luis Matos	.25
194	Derek Lowe	.50
195	Mark Grudzielanek	.25
196	Flash Gordon	.25
197	Matt Clement	.25
198	Byung-Hyun Kim	.25
199	Brandon Inge	.25
200	Nomar Garciaparra	1.50
201	Frank Catalanotto	.25
202	Cristian Guzman	.25
203	Bo Hart	.25
204	Jack Wilson	.25
205	Ray Durham	.25
206	Freddy Garcia	.25
207	J.D. Drew	.50
208	Orlando Cabrera	.25
209	Roy Halladay	.50
210	David Eckstein	.25
211	Omar Falcon RC	2.00
212	Todd Self RC	2.00
213	David Murphy	2.00
214	Dioner Navarro RC	2.00
215	Marcus McBeth RC	2.00
216	Chris O'Riordan RC	2.00
217	Rodney Choy Foo RC	2.00
218	Tim Frend RC	2.00
219	Yadier Molina RC	8.00
220	Zachary Duke RC	3.00
221	Anthony Lerew/ Auto. RC	10.00
222	Blake Hawksworth/ Auto. RC	10.00
223	Brayan Pena/Auto. RC	10.00
224	Craig Ansman/Auto. RC	10.00
225	Jon Knott/Auto. RC	10.00
226	Josh Labandeira/ Auto. RC	10.00
227	Khalid Ballouli/Auto. RC	10.00
228	Kyle Davies/Auto. RC	10.00
229	M. Creighton/Auto. RC	10.00
230	Mike Gosling/Auto.	10.00
231	Nic Ungs/Auto. RC	10.00
232	Zach Miner/Auto. RC	10.00
233	Donald Levinski/Auto.	10.00
234	Bradley Sullivan	15.00
235	Carlos Quentin	40.00
236	Conor Jackson	10.00
237	Estee Harris RC	15.00
238	Jeffrey Allison	10.00
239	Kyle Sleeth	10.00
240	Matthew Moses	15.00
241	Tim Stauffer	15.00
242	Brad Snyder	10.00
243	Jason Hirsh	15.00
244	Lastings Milledge	20.00
245	Logan Kensing RC	10.00
246	Kory Casto	10.00
247	David Aardsma	1.50
248	Omar Quintanilla	2.00
249	Ervin Santana RC	4.00
250	Merkin Valdez RC	2.00
251	Vito Chiaravalloti RC	2.00
252	Travis Blackley RC	2.00
253	Chris Shelton RC	2.00
254	Rudy Guillen RC	2.00
255	Bobby Brownlie RC	2.00
256	Paul Maholm RC	2.00
257	Roger Clemens	3.00
258	Laynce Nix	.25
259	Eric Hinske	.25
260	Ivan Rodriguez	1.00
261	Brandon Webb	.50
262	Jhonny Peralta	.25
263	Adam Kennedy	.25
264	Tony Batista	.25
265	Jeff Suppan	.25
266	Kenny Lofton	.50
267	Scott Sullivan	.25
268	Ken Griffey Jr.	2.00
269	Billy Traber	.25
270	Larry Walker	.50
271	Todd Hollandsworth	.25
272	Carlos Beltran	1.00
273	Carl Crawford	.50
274	Karim Garcia	.25
275	Jose Reyes	.75
276	Brandon Duckworth	.25
277	Brian Giles	.50
278	J.T. Snow Jr.	.25
279	Jamie Moyer	.25
280	Julio Lugo	.25
281	Mark Teixeira	.75
282	Cory Lidle	.25
283	Lyle Overbay	.50
284	Troy Percival	.25
285	Robby Hammock	.25
286	Jason Johnson	.25
287	Brandon Lyon	.25
288	Antonio Alfonseca	.25
289	Tom Goodwin	.25
290	Paul Konerko	.50
291	D'Angelo Jimenez	.25
292	Ben Broussard	.25
293	Magglio Ordonez	.50
294	Carlos Pena	.25
295	Chad Fox	.25
296	Jeriome Robertson	.25
297	Travis Hafner	.50
298	Joe Randa	.25
299	Brady Clark	.25
300	Barry Zito	.75
301	Ruben Sierra	.25
302	Brett Myers	.25
303	Oliver Perez	.25
304	Benito Santiago	.25
305	David Ross	.25
306	Joe Nathan	.25
307	Jim Edmonds	.50
308	Matt Kata	.25
309	Vinny Castilla	.25
310	Marty Cordova	.25
311	Aramis Ramirez	.50
312	Carl Everett	.25
313	Ryan Freel	.25
314	Mark Bellhorn	.25
315	Ugueth Urbina	.25
316	Tim Redding	.25
317	Jeromy Burnitz	.25
318	Miguel Cabrera	1.00
319	Orlando Hernandez	.25
320	Casey Blake	.25
321	Aaron Boone	.25
322	Jermaine Dye	.25
323	Jerome Williams	.25
324	John Olerud	.25
325	Scott Rolen	1.00
326	Bobby Kielty	.25
327	Travis Lee	.25
328	Jeff Cirillo	.25
329	Scott Spiezio	.25
330	Melvin Mora	.25
331	Mike Timlin	.25
332	Kerry Wood	.50
333	Tony Womack	.25
334	Jody Gerut	.25
335	Morgan Ensberg	.25
336	Odalis Perez	.25
337	Michael Cuddyer	.25
338	Jose Hernandez	.25
339	LaTroy Hawkins	.25
340	Marquis Grissom	.25
341	Matt Morris	.50
342	Juan Gonzalez	.75
343	Jose Valverde	.25
344	Joe Borowski	.25
345	Josh Bard	.25
346	Austin Kearns	.50
347	Chin-Hui Tsao	.25
348	Wilfredo Ledezma	.25
349	Aaron Guiel	.25
350	Alfonso Soriano	1.00
351	Ted Lilly	.25
352	Sean Burroughs	.25
353	Rafael Palmeiro	.75
354	Quinton McCracken	.25
355	David Ortiz	1.00
356	Randall Simon	.25
357	Wily Mo Pena	.25
358	Brian Anderson	.25
359	Corey Koskie	.25
360	Keith Foulke	.25
361	Sidney Ponson	.25
362	Gary Matthews Jr.	.25
363	Herbert Perry	.25
364	Shea Hillenbrand	.25
365	Craig Biggio	.50
366	Barry Larkin	.50
367	Orlando Merced	.25
368	Sammy Sosa	1.50
369	Joe Crede	.50
370	Gary Sheffield	.75
371	Coco Crisp	.50
372	Torii Hunter	.50
373	Derrek Lee	.50
374	Adam Everett	.25
375	Miguel Tejada	.50
376	Jeremy Affeldt	.25
377	Robin Ventura	.25
378	Scott Podsednik	.75
379	Matthew LeCroy	.25
380	Vladimir Guerrero	1.50
381	Steve Karsay	.25
382	Jeff Nelson	.25
383	Chase Utley	.75
384	Bobby Abreu	.50
385	Josh Fogg	.25
386	Trevor Hoffman	.25
387	Matt Stairs	.25
388	Edgar Martinez	.50
389	Edgar Renteria	.25
390	Chipper Jones	1.50
391	Eric Munson	.25
392	Dewon Brazelton	.25
393	John Thomson	.25
394	Chris Woodward	.25
395	Joe Kennedy	.25
396	Reed Johnson	.25
397	Johnny Estrada	.25
398	Damian Moss	.25
399	Victor Zambrano	.25
400	Dontrelle Willis	.50
401	Troy Glaus	.75
402	Raul Mondesi	.25
403	Jeff DaVanon	.25
404	Kurt Ainsworth	.25
405	Pedro J. Martinez	1.50
406	Eric Karros	.25
407	Billy Koch	.25
408	Luis Gonzalez	.50
409	Jack Cust	.25
410	Mike Sweeney	.25
411	Jason Bay	.75
412	Mark Redman	.25
413	Jason Jennings	.25
414	Rondell White	.25
415	Todd Hundley	.25
416	Shannon Stewart	.25
417	Jae Weong Seo	.25
418	Livan Hernandez	.25
419	Mark Ellis	.25
420	Pat Burrell	.50
421	Mark Loretta	.25
422	Robb Nen	.25
423	Joel Pineiro	.25
424	Todd Walker	.25
425	Jeremy Bonderman	.50
426	A.J. Burnett	.25
427	Greg Myers	.25
428	Roy Oswalt	.50
429	Carlos Baerga	.25
430	Garret Anderson	.50
431	Horacio Ramirez	.25
432	Brian Roberts	.25
433	Kevin Brown	.50
434	Eric Milton	.25
435	Brian Daubach	.25
436	Alex Escobar	.25
437	Alex Sanchez	.25
438	Jeff Bagwell	1.00
439	Claudio Vargas	.25
440	Shawn Green	.50
441	Geoff Jenkins	.25
442	David Wells	.25
443	Nick Johnson	.25
444	Jose Guillen	.25
445	Scott Hatteberg	.25
446	Phil Nevin	.25
447	Jason Schmidt	.50
448	Ricky Ledee	.25
449	So Taguchi	.25
450	Randy Johnson	.75
451	Eric Young	.25
452	Chone Figgins	.25
453	Larry Bigbie	.25
454	Scott Williamson	.25
455	Ramon Martinez	.25
456	Roberto Alomar	.50
457	Ryan Dempster	.25
458	Ryan Ludwick	.25
459	Ramon Santiago	.25
460	Jeff Conine	.25
461	Brad Lidge	.25
462	Ken Harvey	.25
463	Guillermo Mota	.25
464	Rick Reed	.25
465	Armando Benitez	.25
466	Wade Miller	.25

Refractors

Item	Price
Cards (1-220, 247-466):	1-2X
Inserted 1:4	
Rookie Auto. (221-246):	1.5-2X
Production 100	
Gold Refractor (1-220):	1-2X
Inserted 1:5	
Rookie Gold Refractor (221-246):	2-3X
Production 50	
Black Refractor (1-220):	2-4X
Inserted 1:10	
Rookie Black Refractor:	No Pricing
Production 25	

Fashionably Great

		NM/M
	Common Player:	5.00
	Inserted 1:Box	
JB	Jeff Bagwell	10.00
CB	Craig Biggio	5.00
HB	Hank Blalock	8.00
JBO	Joe Borchard	5.00
KB	Kevin Brown	5.00
EC	Eric Chavez	6.00
CD	Carlos Delgado	6.00
AD	Adam Dunn	5.00
FG	Freddy Garcia	5.00
CF	Cliff Floyd	5.00
NG	Nomar Garciaparra	10.00
TH	Trevor Hoffman	5.00
TH	Tim Hudson	5.00
AJ	Andruw Jones	6.00
CJ	Chipper Jones	8.00
DL	Derek Lowe	4.00
PM	Pedro J. Martinez	8.00
FM	Fred McGriff	8.00
MM	Mark Mulder	6.00
BM	Brett Myers	6.00
JO	John Olerud	6.00
RP	Rafael Palmeiro	8.00
WP	Wily Mo Pena	5.00
MP	Mike Piazza	10.00
AP	Albert Pujols	15.00
MR	Manny Ramirez	8.00
JR	Juan Rivera	5.00
AR	Alex Rodriguez	12.00
IR	Ivan Rodriguez	8.00
CS	Curt Schilling	6.00
JS	John Smoltz	6.00
SS	Sammy Sosa	12.00
MS	Mike Sweeney	5.00
FT	Frank Thomas	10.00
JV	Jose Vidro	5.00
BW	Billy Wagner	6.00
VW	Vernon Wells	5.00

Handle With Care

No pricing due to scarcity.
Production Five Sets

Presidential First Pitch Relics

		NM/M
	Common President:	10.00
	Inserted 1:15	
GHB	George H.W. Bush	20.00
GB	George W. Bush	25.00
BC	Bill Clinton	20.00
CC	Calvin Coolidge	20.00
DE	Dwight D. Eisenhower	20.00
GF	Gerald Ford	30.00
WH	Warren Harding	15.00
HH	Herbert Hoover	25.00
LJ	Lyndon B. Johnson	30.00
RN	Richard Nixon	25.00
RR	Ronald Reagan	30.00
FR	Franklin D. Roosevelt	30.00
WT	William H. Taft	25.00
HT	Harry S. Truman	25.00
WW	Woodrow Wilson	10.00

Presidential Pastime Refractors

		NM/M
	Common President:	3.00
	X-fractors:	3-5X
	Inserted 1:400	
PP1	George Washington	10.00
PP2	John Adams	3.00
PP3	Thomas Jefferson	6.00
PP4	James Madison	4.00
PP5	James Monroe	4.00
PP6	John Quincy Adams	4.00
PP7	Andrew Jackson	3.00
PP8	Martin Van Buren	3.00
PP9	William H. Harrison	3.00
PP10	John Tyler	3.00
PP11	James K. Polk	3.00
PP12	Zachary Taylor	3.00
PP13	Millard Fillmore	3.00
PP14	Franklin Pierce	3.00
PP15	James Buchanan	3.00
PP16	Abraham Lincoln	8.00
PP17	Andrew Johnson	3.00
PP18	Ulysses S. Grant	5.00
PP19	Rutherford B. Hayes	3.00
PP20	James Garfield	3.00
PP21	Chester A. Arthur	3.00
PP22	Grover Cleveland	3.00
PP23	Benjamin Harrison	3.00
PP24	William McKinley	3.00
PP25	Theodore Roosevelt	5.00
PP26	William H. Taft	3.00
PP27	Woodrow Wilson	3.00
PP28	Warren Harding	3.00
PP29	Calvin Coolidge	3.00
PP30	Herbert Hoover	3.00
PP31	Franklin D. Roosevelt	5.00
PP32	Harry S. Truman	3.00
PP33	Dwight D. Eisenhower	3.00
PP34	John F. Kennedy	8.00
PP35	Lyndon B. Johnson	3.00
PP36	Richard Nixon	4.00
PP37	Gerald Ford	3.00
PP38	Jimmy Carter	3.00
PP39	Ronald Reagan	3.00
PP40	George H.W. Bush	3.00
PP41	Bill Clinton	3.00
PP42	George W. Bush	3.00

Town Heroes

		NM/M
	Common Player:	5.00
LB	Lance Berkman	5.00
EC	Eric Chavez	5.00
NG	Nomar Garciaparra	12.00
JG	Jason Giambi	8.00
RH	Rich Harden	5.00
TH	Tim Hudson	5.00
CJ	Chipper Jones	8.00
MM	Mark Mulder	5.00
HN	Hideo Nomo	5.00
RP	Rafael Palmeiro	8.00

CHROME-TOWN HEROES
KERRY WOOD — CHICAGO CUBS — PITCHER

MP	Mark Prior	8.00
AP	Albert Pujols	15.00
MR	Manny Ramirez	8.00
JR	Jose Reyes	5.00
AR	Alex Rodriguez	10.00
SS	Sammy Sosa	10.00
SST	Shannon Stewart	5.00
MT	Miguel Tejada	5.00
FT	Frank Thomas	8.00
KW	Kerry Wood	10.00
BZ	Barry Zito	6.00

2004 Topps Clubhouse Collection Relics

		NM/M
	Common Player:	4.00
	Two Relics Per Pack	
	Pack (2):	18.00
	Box (10):	140.00
HA	Hank Aaron/113	50.00
BA	Bobby Abreu	6.00
RA	Roberto Alomar	6.00
EA	Edgardo Alfonzo/286	4.00
TA	Tony Armas Jr.	4.00
JB	Jeff Bagwell	8.00
RB	Rocco Baldelli	6.00
TB	Tony Batista	4.00
HB	Hank Bauer	10.00
JPB	Josh Beckett/195	6.00
JBE	Johnny Bench	10.00
AB	Armando Benitez	4.00
LB	Lance Berkman	4.00
YB	Yogi Berra	10.00
HBL	Hank Blalock	6.00
WB	Wade Boggs/250	8.00
BB	Bret Boone	6.00
GB	George Brett	12.00
KB	Kevin Brown	4.00
JBU	Jeromy Burnitz	4.00
PB	Pat Burrell	6.00
MB	Marlon Byrd	4.00
MC	Miguel Cabrera	8.00
GC	Gary Carter/221	8.00
JCA	Joe Carter/259	6.00
RLC	Roger Cedeno	4.00
OC	Orlando Cepeda	6.00
RCE	Roy Cey	6.00
EC	Eric Chavez	6.00
CFC	Chin-Feng Chen	6.00
JC	Jeff Cirillo	4.00
WC	Will Clark	8.00
RC	Roberto Clemente	75.00
DC	Dave Concepcion	4.00
CCR	Carl Crawford	4.00
CD	Carlos Delgado/200	6.00
AD	Adam Dunn	8.00
DE	Dennis Eckersley	10.00
CE	Carl Everett	4.00
SF	Steve Finley	4.00
CFL	Cliff Floyd	4.00
WF	Whitey Ford/296	15.00
BF	Brad Fullmer/200	4.00
JF	Jonathan Fulton	6.00
RF	Rafael Furcal	4.00
EG	Eric Gagne	8.00
NG	Nomar Garciaparra	12.00
JG	Jason Giambi	8.00
TGL	Troy Glaus	6.00
TG	Tom Glavine	8.00
AG	Adrian Gonzalez	4.00
LG	Luis Gonzalez	4.00
JGO	Juan Gonzalez	8.00
MG	Mark Grace	8.00
SG	Shawn Green	4.00
KG	Ken Griffey Jr./200	15.00
MDG	Marquis Grissom	4.00
VG	Vladimir Guerrero	8.00
CG	Cristian Guzman	4.00
TGW	Tony Gwynn	10.00
MH	Mickey Hall	4.00
EH	Estee Harris/206	4.00
THE	Todd Helton	8.00
RHE	Rickey Henderson	10.00
RH	Ramon Hernandez	4.00
OH	Orel Hershiser	8.00
JH	James Houser/182	4.00
OHU	Orlando Hudson	4.00
TH	Tim Hudson	6.00
THU	Torii Hunter	6.00
KI	Kazuhisa Ishii	4.00
RJ	Reggie Jackson	10.00
DJ	Derek Jeter	20.00
AJ	Andruw Jones	6.00
CJ	Chipper Jones	8.00
AK	Al Kaline	8.00
JKE	Jeff Kent/200	6.00
PK	Paul Konerko	6.00
BL	Barry Larkin/200	10.00
AL	Al Leiter	4.00
SL	Steve Lerud	4.00
EL	Esteban Loaiza	4.00
PL	Paul LoDuca	4.00
JL	Javy Lopez	6.00
DL	Derek Lowe/200	4.00
CL	Chris Lubanski/209	8.00
GM	Greg Maddux	15.00
EMA	Edgar Martinez/200	6.00
PM	Pedro Martinez/200	10.00
TM	Tino Martinez	4.00
EM	Eddie Mathews/174	25.00
WM	Willie Mays	60.00
FM	Fred McGriff	6.00
KM	Kevin Millwood	4.00
MM	Mark Mulder	4.00
EMU	Eddie Murray	12.00
BM	Brett Myers	4.00
HN	Hideo Nomo/207	8.00
JO	John Olerud	8.00
MO	Magglio Ordonez	4.00
RP	Rafael Palmeiro/200	10.00
CP	Chan Ho Park	4.00
DP	Dave Parker/292	10.00
CPA	Corey Patterson/267	8.00
WP	Wily Mo Pena	4.00
TPE	Troy Percival	4.00
TP	Tony Perez	10.00
MP	Mike Piazza	10.00
JP	Jorge Posada/264	8.00
AP	Albert Pujols	15.00
ARA	Aramis Ramirez	8.00
MR	Manny Ramirez/207	8.00
JRE	Jose Reyes	6.00
CR	Cal Ripken Jr.	20.00
MRI	Mariano Rivera/239	8.00
FR	Frank Robinson	8.00
JR	Jackie Robinson/262	50.00
AR	Alex Rodriguez	10.00
IR	Ivan Rodriguez	10.00
SR	Scott Rolen	10.00
JRO	Jimmy Rollins	6.00
NR	Nolan Ryan	20.00
CS	C.C. Sabathia	4.00
TS	Tim Salmon	6.00
RSA	Ryne Sandberg	15.00
JS	Jay Sborz	6.00
CSC	Curt Schilling	8.00
MS	Mike Schmidt	15.00
RS	Richie Sexson/200	6.00
GS	Gary Sheffield	6.00
RSI	Ruben Sierra	6.00
OS	Ozzie Smith	15.00
JSM	John Smoltz	6.00
DS	Duke Snider	15.00
AS	Alfonso Soriano	6.00
SS	Sammy Sosa	12.00
WS	Willie Stargell/200	10.00
CST	Casey Stengel/217	8.00
MSW	Mike Sweeney	4.00
MTE	Miguel Tejada	6.00
MT	Mark Teixeira	6.00
FT	Frank Thomas	8.00
JT	Jim Thome	8.00
FV	Fernando Valenzuela	6.00
JVI	Jose Vidro	4.00
BWA	Billy Wagner	6.00
LW	Larry Walker	4.00
VW	Vernon Wells/200	4.00
BW	Bernie Williams	6.00
PW	Preston Wilson	4.00
JV	Javier Vazquez	4.00
CY	Carl Yastrzemski	15.00
RY	Robin Yount	12.00
BZ	Barry Zito/230	6.00

Black

Black:	2-3X
Production 25 Sets	

Copper

Copper:	.75-1.5X
Production 99 Sets	

Red

Red:	No Pricing
Production One Set	

All-Star Appeal Ball

No Pricing
Production 10 Sets

All-Star Appeal Ball Auto.

		NM/M
	Production 30 Sets	
GA	Garret Anderson	30.00
HB	Hank Blalock	35.00
JP	Jorge Posada	50.00

All-Star Appeal Base

	NM/M
Common Player:	5.00
Production 65 Sets	
On Deck Circle:	1X
Production 90 Sets	
GA	Garret Anderson	8.00
HB	Hank Blalock	8.00
BB	Bret Boone	5.00
CD	Carlos Delgado	6.00
JE	Jim Edmonds	8.00
RF	Rafael Furcal	6.00
NG	Nomar Garciaparra	15.00
JG	Jason Giambi	8.00
TG	Troy Glaus	6.00
LG	Luis Gonzalez	6.00
TH	Todd Helton	8.00
AJ	Andruw Jones	6.00
JL	Javy Lopez	8.00
ML	Mike Lowell	8.00
EM	Edgar Martinez	8.00
MO	Magglio Ordonez	6.00
JP	Jorge Posada	8.00
AP	Albert Pujols	25.00
ER	Edgar Renteria	8.00
AR	Alex Rodriguez	15.00
SR	Scott Rolen	10.00
RS	Richie Sexson	6.00
GS	Gary Sheffield	8.00
AS	Alfonso Soriano	10.00
VW	Vernon Wells	6.00
PW	Preston Wilson	5.00

All_Star Appeal Base Auto.

		NM/M
Production 50 Sets		
GA	Garret Anderson	25.00
JP	Jorge Posada	35.00
GS	Gary Sheffield	25.00

All-Star Appeal On Deck Circle

		NM/M
Common Player:		5.00
Production 90 Sets		
GA	Garret Anderson	8.00
HB	Hank Blalock	8.00
AB	Aaron Boone	5.00
BB	Bret Boone	5.00
LC	Luis Castillo	5.00
CD	Carlos Delgado	6.00
JE	Jim Edmonds	8.00
CE	Carl Everett	5.00
RF	Rafael Furcal	6.00
NG	Nomar Garciaparra	15.00
JG	Jason Giambi	6.00
TG	Troy Glaus	6.00
LG	Luis Gonzalez	6.00
TH	Todd Helton	8.00
AJ	Andruw Jones	6.00
PL	Paul LoDuca	5.00
JL	Javy Lopez	8.00
ML	Mike Lowell	8.00
EM	Edgar Martinez	8.00
MM	Melvin Mora	5.00
MO	Magglio Ordonez	6.00
JP	Jorge Posada	8.00
AP	Albert Pujols	20.00
ER	Edgar Renteria	8.00
AR	Alex Rodriguez	15.00
SR	Scott Rolen	10.00
RS	Richie Sexson	6.00
GS	Gary Sheffield	8.00
AS	Alfonso Soriano	10.00
JV	Jose Vidro	5.00
VW	Vernon Wells	6.00
RW	Rondell White	5.00
PW	Preston Wilson	5.00

All-Star Appeal On Deck Auto.

		NM/M
Quantity produced listed		
GA	Garret Anderson/320	15.00
HB	Hank Blalock/920	15.00
JP	Jorge Posada/420	30.00
GS	Gary Sheffield/170	25.00

Legends Relics

		NM/M
Common Player:		5.00
BR1	Babe Ruth/60	175.00
BR2	Babe Ruth/171	150.00
BR3	Babe Ruth/45	200.00
EB1	Ernie Banks/143	15.00
EB2	Ernie Banks/47	20.00
EB6	Ernie Banks/71	15.00

LG1	Lou Gehrig/49	125.00
LG2	Lou Gehrig/184	100.00
LG3	Lou Gehrig/52	125.00
TC3	Ty Cobb/47	120.00
WM1	Willie Mays/52	70.00
WM2	Willie Mays/141	60.00

Double Play Relics

		NM/M
Production 75 Sets		
CLE	Omar Vizquel, Brandon Phillips, Travis Hafner	10.00
NYM	Ty Wigginton, Jose Reyes, Mike Piazza	25.00
NYY	Derek Jeter, Alex Rodriguez, Jason Giambi	50.00
PHI	Jimmy Rollins, David Bell, Jim Thome	20.00
SDP	Khalil Greene, Sean Burroughs, Phil Nevin	10.00

Frozen Ropes Relics

		NM/M
Common Player:		5.00
Production 50 Sets		
BA	Bobby Abreu	8.00
JB	Jeff Bagwell	10.00
RB	Rocco Baldelli	8.00
JBE	Johnny Bench	20.00
LB	Lance Berkman	5.00
CB	Craig Biggio	6.00
HB	Hank Blalock	10.00
WB	Wade Boggs	8.00
GC	Gary Carter	8.00
EC	Eric Chavez	8.00
ADA	Andre Dawson	8.00
AD	Adam Dunn	10.00
CE	Carl Everett	5.00
RF	Rafael Furcal	5.00
JG	Jason Giambi	8.00
LG	Luis Gonzalez	5.00
SG	Shawn Green	5.00
VG	Vladimir Guerrero	15.00
TH	Todd Helton	10.00
AH	Aubrey Huff	5.00
CJ	Chipper Jones	15.00
PK	Paul Konerko	5.00
EM	Edgar Martinez	8.00
DM	Don Mattingly	40.00
DMU	Dale Murphy	12.00
MO	Magglio Ordonez	5.00
RP	Rafael Palmeiro	10.00
MP	Mike Piazza	15.00
KP	Kirby Puckett	15.00
AP	Albert Pujols	25.00
MR	Manny Ramirez	10.00
JR	Jose Reyes	8.00
BR	Brooks Robinson	15.00
AR	Alex Rodriguez	15.00
IR	Ivan Rodriguez	10.00
RS	Ryne Sandberg	40.00
MS	Mike Schmidt	40.00
GS	Gary Sheffield	6.00
OS	Ozzie Smith	25.00
DS	Duke Snider	15.00
AS	Alfonso Soriano	10.00
SS	Sammy Sosa	15.00
MT	Miguel Tejada	8.00
JT	Jim Thome	8.00
BW	Bernie Williams	8.00
PW	Preston Wilson	5.00
CY	Carl Yastrzemski	20.00

Heart of the Line-Up Relics

		NM/M
Production 100 unless noted.		
ARI	Steve Finley, Richie Sexson, Luis Gonzalez	15.00
CHC	Sammy Sosa, Moises Alou, Aramis Ramirez	35.00
CHW	Magglio Ordonez, Frank Thomas, Carlos Lee/78	20.00
CIN	Ken Griffey Jr., Austin Kearns, Adam Dunn	20.00
COL	Todd Helton, Larry Walker, Preston Wilson	15.00
NYY	Alex Rodriguez, Jason Giambi, Gary Sheffield	35.00
PHI	Jim Thome, Pat Burrell, Bobby Abreu	20.00
SEA	Edgar Martinez, Bret Boone, John Olerud	15.00
STL	Albert Pujols, Jim Edmonds, Scott Rolen	40.00

TEX	Alfonso Soriano, Mark Teixeira, Hank Blalock	20.00
TOR	Vernon Wells, Carlos Delgado, Eric Hinske	10.00

Patch Place Relics

No Pricing
Production 25 or less.

Power Pieces Relics

		NM/M
Quantity produced listed.		
CD	Carlos Delgado/25	8.00
THU	Torii Hunter/48	5.00
AJ	Andruw Jones/25	10.00
PM	Pedro Martinez/45	10.00
WM	Willie Mays/24	85.00
BM	Brett Myers/39	5.00
BP	Brad Penny/31	5.00
MP	Mike Piazza/31	40.00
NR	Nolan Ryan/34	50.00
CS	Curt Schilling/38	5.00
BZ	Barry Zito/75	6.00

2004 Topps Cracker Jack

	NM/M
Complete Set with SP's (250):	160.00
Common Player:	.25
Common SP:	2.00
SP's inserted 1:3	
Pack (8):	3.00
Box (24):	60.00
1	Jose Reyes/SP	2.00
2	Edgar Renteria	.25
3	Albert Pujols	2.00
3	Albert Pujols/SP/Swinging	6.00
4	Garret Anderson	.50
5	Bobby Abreu	.40
6	Andruw Jones	.75
7	Jeff Kent	.40
8	Magglio Ordonez	.50
9	Kris Benson	.25
10	Luis Gonzalez	.50
11	Corey Patterson	.50
12	Connie Mack	.25
13	Vernon Wells/SP	2.00
14	Jim Edmonds	.50
15	Bret Boone	.50
16	Travis Lee	.25
17	Alex Rodriguez/SP	6.00
No #	Alex Rodriguez	2.00
18	Erubiel Durazo	.25
19	Brett Myers	.25
20	Scott Rolen/SP	3.00
21	Paul LoDuca	.25
22	Geoff Jenkins	.50
23	Charles Comiskey	.25
24	Cliff Floyd	.25
25	Jim Thome	.75
25	Jim Thome/SP/Fldg	3.00
26	Russ Ortiz	.25
27	Bill Mueller	.25
28	Kenny Lofton	.40
29	Jay Gibbons	.40
30	Ken Griffey Jr.	1.50
31	Jeff Bagwell	.75
32	Jose Lima	.25
33	Brad Radke	.25
34	Ramon Hernandez	.25
35	Brian Giles/SP	2.00
36	Jeremy Bonderman	.25
37	Jerome Williams	.25
38	Rafael Palmeiro	.50
39	Scott Podsednik	.75
40	Rafael Furcal	.40
41	Roy Oswalt	.40
42	Orlando Hudson	.25
43	Todd Helton	.75
44	Kerry Wood	1.00
45	Tom Glavine	.40
46	David Eckstein	.25
47	Trot Nixon	.25
48	Preston Wilson	.25
49	Eric Gagne/SP	3.00
50	Ichiro Suzuki/SP	6.00
51	Juan Gonzalez	.75
52	Torii Hunter	.50
53	Bartolo Colon	.40
54	Dick Hoblitzell	.25
55	Al Leiter	.25
56	Johnny Damon	.40
57	Larry Walker	.40
58	Brian Jordan	.25
59	Richie Sexson/SP	3.00
60	Orlando Cabrera	.25

61	Jason Phillips	.25
62	Phil Nevin	.25
63	John Olerud	.40
64	Miguel Tejada	.50
65	Nap Lajoie	.50
66	C.C. Sabathia	.25
67	Ty Wigginton	.25
68	Troy Glaus	.25
69	Mike Piazza	1.50
70	Craig Biggio	.40
71	Cristian Guzman	.25
72	Dmitri Young	.25
73	Roger Clemens	2.00
74	Runelvys Hernandez	.25
75	Nomar Garciaparra	2.00
76	Mark Mulder	.40
77	Derek Lowe	.40
78	Paul Konerko	.25
79	Sammy Sosa/SP	5.00
80	Vladimir Guerrero	1.00
81	Xavier Nady	.25
82	Joel Pineiro	.25
83	Chipper Jones	1.50
84	Manny Ramirez	.75
85	Burt Shotton	.25
86	Raul Ibanez/SP	2.00
87	Eric Chavez	.25
88	Frank Catalanotto	.25
89	Dontrelle Willis	.50
90	Roy Halladay	.50
91	Jermaine Dye	.25
92	Jason Kendall	.25
93	Jacque Jones	.25
94	Gary Sheffield	.50
95	Gary Sheffield/SP/Yankees	3.00
96	Mike Lieberthal	.25
97	Adam Dunn	.50
98	Carl Crawford	.25
99	Reggie Sanders	.25
100	Mark Prior/SP	6.00
101	Luis Matos	.25
102	Barry Zito	.50
103	Randy Johnson	1.00
104	Kevin Brown	.50
105	Pat Burrell	.50
106	Steve Finley	.25
107	Moises Alou	.25
108	David Ortiz/SP	3.00
109	Austin Kearns/SP	2.00
110	Carlos Beltran	.50
111	Shawn Green	.40
112	Javier Vazquez	.50
113	Hideo Nomo	.50
114	Kazuhisa Ishii	.25
115	Corey Koskie	.25
116	Kevin Millwood	.25
117	Randy Wolf	.40
118	Darin Erstad	.25
119	Fernando Vina	.25
120	Pedro J. Martinez	1.00
121	Melvin Mora	.25
122	Carl Everett	.25
123	Matt Morris	.40
124	Greg Maddux	1.50
125	Jason Schmidt	.25
126	Mark Teixeira/SP	3.00
127	Randy Winn	.25
128	Rich Aurilia	.25
129	Vicente Padilla	.25
130	Tim Hudson	.50
131	Marlon Byrd	.25
132	Jae Weong Seo	.25
133	Branch Rickey	.25
134	A.J. Pierzynski	.25
135	Ryan Klesko	.40
136	Eric Hinske	.25
137	Mike Cameron	.25
138	Roberto Alomar	.50
139	Jarrod Washburn	.25
140	Curt Schilling	.75
140	Curt Schilling/SP/Red Sox	3.00
141	Omar Vizquel	.25
142	Mike Sweeney	.25
143	Wade Miller	.25
144	Jose Vidro	.25
145	Rich Harden/SP	2.00
146	Eric Munson	.25
147	Lance Berkman	.50
148	Mark Buehrle	.25
149	Carlos Delgado	.75
150	Sean Burroughs	.25
151	Kevin Millar	.25
152	Frank Thomas	.75
153	Adrian Beltre	.25
154	Shannon Stewart	.25
155	Johan Santana	.25
156	Edgardo Alfonzo	.25
157	Jose Cruz Jr.	.25
158	Sidney Ponson	.25
159	Edgar Martinez	.50
160	Jamie Moyer	.25
161	Tony Batista	.25
162	Wes Helms	.25
163	Brandon Webb/SP	2.00
164	Gil Meche	.25
165	Marcus Giles/SP	2.00
166	Angel Berroa/SP	2.00
167	Rocco Baldelli/SP	3.00
168	Michael Young	.25
169	Esteban Loaiza	.25
170	Casey Blake	.25
171	Jody Gerut	.25
172	Bo Hart/SP	2.00
173	Kelvim Escobar	.25
174	Aaron Guiel	.25
175	Javy Lopez/SP	3.00

176	Aubrey Huff	.25
177	Hank Blalock	.25
178	Edwin Jackson	.25
178	Edwin Jackson/SP/#104	2.00
179	Delmon Young/SP	3.00
180	Bobby Jenks	.25
181	Felix Pie	.25
181	Felix Pie/SP/#80	2.00
182	Jeremy Reed/SP	2.00
183	Aaron Hill	.25
184	Casey Kotchman/SP	2.00
185	Grady Sizemore	.50
186	Joe Mauer/SP	3.00
187	Ryan Harvey	.25
188	Neal Cotts	.25
189	Victor Martinez	.25
190	Rene Reyes	.25
191	Eric Duncan	.25
192	B.J. Upton/SP	3.00
193	Khalil Greene/SP	2.00
194	Bobby Crosby	.25
195	Rickie Weeks/SP	3.00
196	Zack Greinke/SP	2.00
197	Laynce Nix	.25
198	Vito Chiaravalloti/SP RC	2.00
199	Estee Harris RC	.25
200	Jon Knott/SP RC	.25
201	Dioner Navarro RC	.75
201	Dioner Navarro/SP/#236	2.00
202	Craig Ansman/SP RC	.50
203	Travis Blackley/SP	1.00
204	Yadier Molina RC	.50
205	Rodney Choy Foo RC	.50
206	Kyle Sleeth/SP	5.00
207	Jeff Allison	1.00
208	Josh Labandeira/SP RC	.50
209	Lastings Milledge/SP	8.00
210	Rudy Guillen/SP RC	.50
211	Blake Hawksworth/SP RC	3.00
212	David Aardsma	.50
213	Shawn Hill RC	.50
214	Erick Aybar/SP RC	3.00
215	Ervin Santana	1.00
216	Tim Stauffer/SP	1.00
217	Merkin Valdez RC	1.00
218	Jack McKeon	.25
219	Derrek Lee	.50
220	Josh Beckett/SP	.25
221	Luis Castillo	.25
222	Mike Lowell	.50
223	Juan Pierre	.40
224	Ivan Rodriguez	.50
224	Ivan Rodriguez/SP/Tigers	3.00
225	A.J. Burnett	.25
226	Miguel Cabrera/SP	4.00
227	Jeffrey Loria	.25
228	Joe Torre	.50
229	Jason Giambi	.75
229	Jason Giambi/SP/Fldg	3.00
230	Aaron Boone	.25
231	Jose Contreras	.25
232	Derek Jeter/SP	6.00
233	Nick Johnson	.25
234	Mike Mussina	.75
235	Andy Pettitte	.50
236	Jorge Posada/SP	3.00
237	Alfonso Soriano	.75
238	Bernie Williams	.50

Mini

Mini:	1-2X
Mini SP:	1X
Inserted 1:Pack	
Mini SPs Inserted 1:20	
SP's are same as in base set.	

Mini Autograph

		NM/M
Common Autograph:		8.00
Inserted 1:258		
95	Gary Sheffield/50	40.00
112	Javier Vazquez	15.00
163	Brandon Webb	15.00
165	Marcus Giles	12.00
221	Luis Castillo	8.00
226	Miguel Cabrera	35.00

Mini Blue

Mini Blue:	3-6X
Mini Blue SP:	1-2X
Inserted 1:10	
Mini Blue SP's Inserted 1:60	
SP's are same as in base set.	

Mini White

No Pricing
Production One Set

Sticker

Stickers:	1X
SP Stickers:	.5X

Secret Surprise Signatures

		NM/M
Common Autograph:		8.00
CF	Cliff Floyd	15.00
BG	Brian Giles	15.00
AH	Aubrey Huff	15.00
ML	Mike Lamb	8.00
DM	Dustin McGowan	20.00
FP	Felix Pie	20.00
SP	Scott Podsednik	20.00
SR	Scott Rolen	30.00
MV	Merkin Valdez	15.00
JW	Jerome Williams	20.00
DW	Dontrelle Willis	30.00

Take Me Out to/Ballgame Relics

		NM/M
Common Player:		5.00
BA	Bobby Abreu	5.00
MA	Moises Alou	6.00
GA	Garret Anderson	8.00
JB	Jeff Bagwell	8.00
RB	Rocco Baldelli	8.00
LB	Lance Berkman	5.00
AB	Angel Berroa	5.00
CB	Craig Biggio	8.00
HB	Hank Blalock	6.00
BB1	Bret Boone/Bat	5.00
BB2	Bret Boone/Jsy	5.00
PB	Pat Burrell	6.00
MC	Miguel Cabrera	6.00
EC	Eric Chavez	5.00
AD	Adam Dunn	6.00
JE	Jim Edmonds	5.00
RF	Rafael Furcal	6.00
NG	Nomar Garciaparra/Bat	10.00
NG	Nomar Garciaparra/Jsy	10.00
JG	Jason Giambi	8.00
MG	Marcus Giles	5.00
TG	Troy Glaus	5.00
LG	Luis Gonzalez	5.00
SG	Shawn Green/Bat	5.00
SG	Shawn Green/Jsy	5.00
TH	Todd Helton	8.00
TKH	Torii Hunter	5.00
CJ	Chipper Jones	8.00
PL	Paul LoDuca	5.00
JL	Javy Lopez/Bat	5.00
JL	Javy Lopez/Jsy	5.00
MP	Mike Piazza	10.00
AP	Albert Pujols/Bat	15.00
AP	Albert Pujols/Jsy	15.00
MR	Manny Ramirez	8.00
JR	Jose Reyes	6.00
AR	Alex Rodriguez/Bat/Yankees	15.00
AR	Alex Rodriguez/Jsy	15.00
IR	Ivan Rodriguez	8.00
JRO	Jimmy Rollins	5.00
AS	Alfonso Soriano/Bat	8.00
AS	Alfonso Soriano/Jsy	8.00
SS	Sammy Sosa/Bat	10.00
SS	Sammy Sosa/Jsy	10.00
MS	Mike Sweeney	5.00
MT	Mark Teixeira	6.00
MT	Miguel Tejada	5.00
JT	Jim Thome	8.00
LW	Larry Walker	5.00
VW	Vernon Wells	5.00
KW	Kerry Wood	8.00
MY	Michael Young	5.00

1,2,3 Strikes You're Out Relics

		NM/M
Common Player:		4.00
JB	Josh Beckett	8.00
KB	Kevin Brown	6.00
EG	Eric Gagne	8.00
RH	Rich Harden	4.00
RJ	Randy Johnson	8.00
DL	Derek Lowe	6.00
PM	Pedro J. Martinez	6.00
KM	Kevin Millwood	4.00
MM	Mark Mulder	6.00
MM	Mike Mussina	15.00
BM	Brett Myers	4.00
HN	Hideo Nomo	8.00
CS	C.C. Sabathia	4.00
CS	Curt Schilling	15.00
JS	John Smoltz	6.00
BW	Billy Wagner	4.00
KW	Kerry Wood	10.00
BZ	Barry Zito	6.00

2004 Topps eTopps

Topps continued its on-line card program for a fourth year in 2004. Individual Player Offerings ($4.50-7.50 per card) were again made for one week, with alloca-

76	Bill Mueller (1,977)	1.75
78	Randy Johnson (2,725)	1.50
79	Carlos Beltran (2,500)	1.50
80	Pedro Martinez (1,726)	1.50
81	Lew Ford (1,932)	1.50
82	Javier Vazquez (1,936)	1.50
83	Kevin Brown (2,635)	1.50
84	Johnny Estrada (1,590)	1.50
85	Ken Griffey Jr. (2,396)	2.75
87	Jorge Posada (2,176)	1.50
89	Bobby Crosby (3,498)	2.50
90	Sammy Sosa (3,248)	1.50
91	Shingo Takatsu (1,678)	1.50
92	Akinori Otsuka (1,544)	1.50
93	Michael Young (2,004)	3.25
94	Aaron Miles (1,608)	1.50
95	Miguel Tejada (1,548)	1.50
96	Chad Tracy (2,534)	2.50
99	Todd Helton (1,998)	1.50
100	Alex Rodriguez (5,000)	2.50
101	Bartolo Colon (1,973)	1.50
102	Philadelphia Phillies (2,500)	1.50
103	Seattle Mariners (2,500)	1.50
104	Atlanta Braves (2,500)	1.50
105	Chicago White Sox (2,458)	1.50
106	Pittsburgh Pirates (2,500)	1.50
107	St. Louis Cardinals (2,500)	1.75
108	Houston Astros (2,500)	1.50
109	Toronto Blue Jays (2,500)	1.50
110	Arizona Diamondbacks (1,818)	8.00
111	New York Mets (2,570)	1.50
112	Minnesota Twins (2,500)	1.50
113	Baltimore Orioles (2,750)	1.50
114	Cleveland Indians (2,219)	1.50
115	Boston Red Sox (3,750)	5.25
116	Tampa Bay Devil Rays (2,191)	1.50
117	Chicago Cubs (3,750)	1.50
118	Texas Rangers (2,500)	1.50
119	Cincinnati Reds (2,500)	1.50
120	Anaheim Angels (2,500)	1.50
121	Colorado Rockies (2,500)	1.50
122	K.C. Royals (2,120)	1.50
123	Florida Marlins (2,500)	1.50
124	Oakland A's (2,375)	1.50
125	L.A. Dodgers (2,155)	1.50
126	Milwaukee Brewers (2,500)	1.50
127	S.F. Giants (2,500)	1.50
128	Montreal Expos (2,500)	1.50
129	San Diego Padres (2,500)	1.50
130	New York Yankees (3,750)	1.50
131	Detroit Tigers (2,750)	1.50
132	Matt Holliday (2,425)	2.00
133	Zack Greinke (3,750)	3.00

2004 Topps eTopps Classics

Topps continued its eTopps Classics line-up in 2004 with 20 cards of former greats. Numbering and format were contiguous with earlier issues. Like regular eTopps cards, Classics could only be ordered during a one-week Initial Player Offering period. Cards were issued in a quantity of 1,200 each at $9.50. The number of cards actually sold is shown parenthetically. Fronts have a color or colorized action photo, backs have a picture of one of that player's Topps cards, along with career notes, stats, etc. Values shown are for cards in a virtual portfolio, rather than "in hand." Taking physical possession of a card from an eTopps portfolio costs about $6 apiece.

		NM/M
Complete Set (20):		175.00
Common Player:		8.00
41	Orlando Cepeda (806)	10.00
42	Wade Boggs (908)	10.00
43	Al Kaline (962)	9.00
44	Jim Palmer (768)	20.00
45	Ozzie Smith (1,161)	8.00
46	Rod Carew (908)	8.00
47	Paul Molitor (850)	8.00
48	Hank Aaron (1,250)	25.00
49	Robin Yount (1,002)	8.00
50	Hank Greenberg (769)	15.00
51	Robin Roberts (807)	10.00
52	Casey Stengel (898)	8.00
53	Cy Young (1,200)	9.00
54	Thurman Munson (1,250)	9.00
55	Roy Campanella (984)	8.00
56	Satchel Paige (1,222)	8.00
57	Tris Speaker (795)	11.00
58	Jimmie Foxx (952)	9.00
59	Dizzy Dean (967)	8.00
60	"Cool Papa" Bell (988)	8.00

2004 Topps eTopps Econ

A four-card set honoring local athletes was issued in conjunction with the 25th National Sports Collectors Convention and the 2nd Topps Econ in Cleveland in late July. Only one baseball player was included. Persons purchasing VIP admission packs at the show received a version of the card without the eTopps authenticity sticker on back.

		NM/M
1	Bob Lemon ($5.25 / 978)	3.25
1	Bob Lemon (Unstickered show version.)	2.00

2004 Topps eTopps Events Series

Values shown are for cards in a virtual portfolio rather than "in hand." Each card originally sold for $4.50. Quantity actually issued is shown parenthetically.

		NM/M
Complete Set (12):		25.00
Common Card:		1.50
1	Alex Rodriguez, Curt Schilling (1,500)	2.50
2	Albert Pujols, Carlos Beltran (1,298)	2.00
3	Hideki Matsui, Mariano Rivera (1,294)	2.00
4	Carlos Beltran (1,427)	1.50
5	Jeff Kent, David Ortiz (1,126)	1.50
6	Jim Edmonds (983)	6.00
7	Derek Lowe, Johnny Damon (2,116)	1.50
8	Scott Rolen, Albert Pujols (1,119)	3.00
9	Mark Bellhorn, Curt Schilling (1,173)	1.50
10	Pedro Martinez (1,250)	1.50
11	Derek Lowe (2,565)	2.00
12	Manny Ramirez (1,500)	2.00

2004 Topps Heritage

	NM/M
Complete Set (475):	400.00
Common Player:	.40
Common SP (398-475):	4.00
Variations & SP's Inserted 1:2	
Pack (8):	5.00
Box (24):	100.00
1	Jim Thome	1.50
1	Jim Thome/SP/Hitting	8.00
2	Nomar Garciaparra/SP	10.00
3	Aramis Ramirez	.50
4	Rafael Palmeiro/SP	6.00
5	Danny Graves	.40
6	Casey Blake	.40
7	Juan Uribe	.40
8	Dmitri Young	.40
8	Dmitri Young/SP/Old Logo	4.00
9	Billy Wagner	.40
10	Jason Giambi	.75
10	Jason Giambi/SP/Batting Stance	6.00
11	Carlos Beltran	1.00
12	Chad Hermansen	.40
13	B.J. Upton	.75
14	Dustan Mohr	.40
15	Endy Chavez	.40
16	Cliff Floyd	.40
17	Bernie Williams	.75
18	Eric Chavez	.75
19	Chase Utley	.75
20	Randy Johnson	1.50
21	Vernon Wells	.50
22	Juan Gonzalez	.75
23	Joe Kennedy	.40
24	Bengie Molina	.40
25	Carlos Lee	.40
26	Horacio Ramirez	.40
27	Anthony Acevedo RC	1.00
28	Sammy Sosa/SP	10.00
29	Jon Garland	.40
30	Adam Dunn	1.00
30	Adam Dunn/SP/Hitting	6.00
31	Aaron Rowand	.40
32	Jody Gerut	.40
33	Chin-Hui Tsao	.40
34	Alex Sanchez	.40
35	A.J. Burnett	.40
36	Brad Ausmus	.40
37	Blake Hawksworth RC	1.50
38	Francisco Rodriguez	.40
39	Alex Cintron	.40
40	Chipper Jones	1.50
40	Chipper Jones/SP/Fdng	6.00
41	Deivi Cruz	.40
42	Bill Mueller	.40
43	Joe Borowski	.40
44	Jimmy Haynes	.40
45	Mark Loretta	.40
46	Jerome Williams	.40
47	Gary Sheffield/SP	6.00
48	Richard Hidalgo	.40
49	Jason Kendall	.40
49	Jason Kendall/SP/Old Logo	4.00
50	Ichiro Suzuki/SP	8.00
51	Jim Edmonds	.75
52	Frank Catalanotto	.40
53	Jose Contreras	.40
54	Mo Vaughn	.40
55	Brendan Donnelly	.40
56	Luis Gonzalez	.40
57	Robert Fick	.40
58	Laynce Nix	.40
59	Johnny Damon	.75
60	Magglio Ordonez	.50
60	Magglio Ordonez/SP/Hitting	6.00
61	Matt Clement	.40
62	Ryan Ludwick	.40
63	Luis Castillo	.40
64	David Crouthers	.40
65	Dave Berg	.40
66	Kyle Davies RC	3.00
67	Tim Salmon	.50
68	Marcus Giles	.40
69	Marty Cordova	.40
70	Todd Helton	1.00
70	Todd Helton/SP/Purple Jsy	6.00
71	Jeff Kent	.50
72	Michael Tucker	.40
73	Cesar Izturis	.40
74	Paul Quantrill	.40
75	Conor Jackson	3.00
76	Placido Polanco	.40
77	Adam Eaton	.40
78	Ramon Hernandez	.40
79	Edgardo Alfonzo	.40
80	Dioner Navarro RC	1.00
81	Woody Williams	.40
82	Rey Ordonez	.40
83	Randy Winn	.40
84	Casey Myers RC	1.00
85	Rodney Choy Foo RC	2.00
85	Rodney Choy Foo/SP/Old Logo	6.00
86	Ray Durham	.40
87	Sean Burroughs	.40
88	Tim Frend RC	3.00
89	Shigetoshi Hasegawa	.40
90	Jeff Allison	.40
91	Orlando Hudson	.40
92	Matt Creighton/SP RC	6.00
93	Tim Worrell	.40
94	Kris Benson	.40

95	Mike Lieberthal	.40
96	David Wells	.40
97	Jason Phillips	.40
98	Bobby Cox	.40
99	Johan Santana	.75
100	Alex Rodriguez	3.00
100	Alex Rodriguez/SP/Throwing	10.00
101	John Vander Wal	.40
102	Orlando Cabrera	.50
103	Hideo Nomo	.75
104	Todd Walker	.40
105	Jason Johnson	.40
106	Matt Mantei	.40
107	Jarrod Washburn	.40
108	Preston Wilson	.40
109	Carl Pavano	.40
110	Geoff Blum	.40
111	Eric Gagne	.50
112	Geoff Jenkins	.40
113	Joe Torre	.50
114	Jon Knott RC	1.50
115	Hank Blalock	.75
116	John Olerud	.40
117	Pat Burrell	.75
117	Pat Burrell/Old Logo	5.00
118	Aaron Boone	.40
119	Zach Day	.40
120	Frank Thomas	1.00
120	Frank Thomas/Old Logo	6.00
121	Kyle Farnsworth	.40
122	Derek Lowe	.50
123	Zach Miner/SP RC	6.00
124	Matt Moses/SP	8.00
125	Jesse Roman RC	1.50
126	Josh Phelps	.40
127	Nic Ungs RC	1.50
128	Dan Haren	.40
129	Kirk Rueter	.40
130	Jack McKeon	.40
131	Keith Foulke	.40
132	Garrett Stephenson	.40
133	Wes Helms	.40
134	Raul Ibanez	.50
135	Morgan Ensberg	.40
136	Jay Payton	.40
137	Billy Koch	.40
138	Mark Grudzielanek	.40
139	Rodrigo Lopez	.40
140	Corey Patterson	.40
141	Troy Percival	.40
142	Shea Hillenbrand	.40
143	Brad Fullmer	.40
144	Ricky Nolasco	2.00
145	Mark Teixeira	.75
146	Tydus Meadows RC	1.50
147	Toby Hall	.40
148	Orlando Palmeiro	.40
149	Khalid Ballouli RC	1.50
150	Grady Little	.40
151	David Eckstein	.40
152	Kenny Perez RC	1.50
153	Ben Grieve	.40
154	Ismael Valdes	.40
155	Bret Boone	.50
156	Jesse Foppert	.40
157	Vicente Padilla	.40
158	Bobby Abreu	.75
159	Scott Hatteberg	.40
160	Carlos Quentin	5.00
161	Anthony Lerew RC	1.50
162	Lance Carter	.40
163	Robb Nen	.40
164	Zach Duke/SP RC	5.00
165	Xavier Nady	.40
166	Kip Wells	.40
167	Kevin Millwood	.40
168	Jon Lieber	.40
169	Jose Reyes	.50
170	Eric Byrnes	.40
171	Paul Konerko	.40
172	Chris Lubanski	.40
173	Jae Weong Seo	.40
174	Corey Koskie	.40
175	Tim Stauffer	.40
176	John Lackey	.40
177	Danny Bautista	.40
178	Shane Reynolds	.40
179	Jorge Julio	.40
180	Manny Ramirez	1.00
180	Manny Ramirez/SP/Old Logo	6.00
181	Alex Gonzalez	.40
182	Moises Alou	.75
182	Moises Alou/SP/Old Logo	6.00
183	Mark Buehrle	.40
184	Carlos Guillen	.40
185	Nate Cornejo	.40
186	Billy Traber	.40
187	Jason Jennings	.40
188	Eric Munson	.40
189	Braden Looper	.40
190	Juan Encarnacion	.40
191	Dusty Baker	.40
192	Travis Lee	.40
193	Miguel Cairo	.40
194	Rich Aurilia/SP	5.00
195	Flash Gordon	.40
196	Freddy Garcia	.40
197	Brian Lawrence	.40
198	Jorge Posada/SP	8.00
199	Javier Vazquez	.40
200	Albert Pujols	3.00
200	Albert Pujols/SP/Old Logo	12.00
201	Victor Zambrano	.40
202	Eli Marrero	.40

203	Joel Pineiro	.40
204	Rondell White	.40
205	Craig Ansman RC	2.00
206	Michael Young	.40
207	Carlos Baerga	.40
208	Andruw Jones	1.00
209	Jerry Hairston Jr.	.40
210	Shawn Green/SP	6.00
211	Ron Gardenhire	.40
212	Darin Erstad	.40
213	Brandon Webb	.50
213	Brandon Webb/SP/Glove In Air	6.00
214	Greg Maddux	2.00
215	Reed Johnson	.40
216	John Thomson	.40
217	Tino Martinez	.40
218	Mike Cameron	.40
219	Edgar Martinez	.40
220	Eric Young	.40
221	Reggie Sanders	.40
222	Randy Wolf	.40
223	Erubiel Durazo	.40
224	Mike Mussina	.75
225	Tom Glavine	.75
226	Troy Glaus	.75
227	Oscar Villarreal	.40
228	David Segui	.40
229	Jeff Suppan	.40
230	Kenny Lofton	.50
231	Esteban Loaiza	.40
232	Felipe Lopez	.40
233	Matt Lawton	.40
234	Mark Bellhorn	.40
235	Wilfredo Ledezma	.40
236	Todd Hollandsworth	.40
237	Octavio Dotel	.40
238	Darren Dreifort	.40
239	Paul LoDuca	.40
240	Richie Sexson	.75
241	Doug Mientkiewicz	.40
242	Luis Rivas	.40
243	Claudio Vargas	.40
244	Mark Ellis	.40
245	Brett Myers	.40
246	Jake Peavy	.50
247	Marquis Grissom	.40
248	Armando Benitez	.40
249	Ryan Franklin	.40
250	Alfonso Soriano	1.50
250	Alfonso Soriano/SP/Fldg	6.00
251	Tim Hudson	.40
252	Shannon Stewart	.40
253	A.J. Pierzynski	.40
254	Runelvys Hernandez	.40
255	Roy Oswalt	.40
256	Shawn Chacon	.40
257	Tony Graffanino	.40
258	Tim Wakefield	.40
259	Damian Miller	.40
260	Joe Crede	.40
261	Jason LaRue	.40
262	Jose Jimenez	.40
263	Juan Pierre	.40
264	Wade Miller	.40
265	Odalis Perez	.40
266	Eddie Guardado	.40
267	Rocky Biddle	.40
268	Jeff Nelson	.40
269	Terrence Long	.40
270	Ramon Ortiz	.40
271	Raul Mondesi	.50
272	Ugueth Urbina	.40
273	Jeromy Burnitz	.40
274	Brad Radke	.40
275	Jose Vidro	.40
276	Bobby Jenks	.40
277	Ty Wigginton	.40
278	Jose Guillen	.40
279	Delmon Young	.75
280	Brian Giles	.50
281	Jason Schmidt	.40
282	Nicholas Markakis	.40
283	Felipe Alou	.40
284	Carl Crawford	.40
285	Neifi Perez	.40
286	Miguel Tejada	.75
287	Victor Martinez	.40
288	Adam Kennedy	.40
289	Kerry Ligtenberg	.40
290	Scott Williamson	.40
291	Tony Womack	.40
292	Travis Hafner	.40
293	Bobby Crosby	.40
294	Chad Billingsley	.40
295	Russ Ortiz	.40
296	John Burkett	.40
297	Carlos Zambrano	.40
298	Randall Simon	.40
299	Juan Castro	.40
300	Mike Lowell	.40
301	Fred McGriff	.50
302	Glendon Rusch	.40
303	Sung Ki Jung RC	.40
304	Rocco Baldelli	.75
305	Fernando Vina	.40
306	Gil Meche	.40
307	Jose Cruz Jr.	.40
308	Bernie Castro	.40
309	Scott Spiezio	.40
310	Paul Byrd	.40
311	Jay Gibbons	.40
311	Jay Gibbons/SP/Old Logo	6.00
312	Trot Nixon	.40
313	Chris O'Riordan RC	1.50
314	Julio Lugo	.40
315	Ben Davis	.40

tions having to be made for some cards in high demand. The number of each card actually sold is shown parenthetically. After the IPO, cards could be bought and sold within portfolios, or physically delivered (for a fee) for more traditional venues. The 2-1/2" x 3-1/2" cards' fronts have an action photo at top and a strip of fading portrait photos below. Backs repeat the portrait photo, have a 2003 recap and 2004 "prospectus," and a few biographical bits and stats. New for 2004 was a subset of team cards picturing several stars. A total of 119 cards was issued, skip-numbered between 1-133. Values shown are for cards in a virtual portfolio, rather than "in hand." Taking physical possession of a card from an eTopps portfolio costs about $6 apiece.

		NM/M
Complete Set (119):		175.00
Common Player:		1.50
1	Andy Pettitte (1,991)	1.50
2	Jason Giambi (1,565)	1.50
3	Kevin Youkilis (2,171)	1.75
4	Casey Blake (1,420)	1.50
5	Ryan Ludwick (1,321)	1.50
6	Craig Wilson (1,544)	1.50
7	Curt Schilling (2,216)	1.50
8	Mark Prior (3,750)	1.50
9	Casey Kotchman (2,006)	1.75
10	Scott Podsednik (2,500)	1.75
11	Carlos Guillen (1,541)	1.50
12	Clint Nageotte (1,526)	1.50
13	Melvin Mora (1,432)	1.50
14	Ivan Rodriguez (2,104)	1.75
15	Travis Hafner (2,500)	3.00
16	Mike Piazza (2,500)	1.50
17	Brian Giles (1,267)	2.00
18	Derek Jeter (2,708)	5.75
19	Edwin Jackson (3,655)	1.50
20	Chipper Jones (2,158)	1.50
21	Jody Gerut (1,436)	1.50
22	Carlos Lee (1,562)	2.00
23	Jason Schmidt (1,659)	1.75
25	Ichiro (2,228)	1.75
27	Corey Patterson (2,500)	1.50
30	Kerry Wood (1,824)	1.50
31	Jim Thome (1,908)	1.50
32	Hideki Matsui (2,500)	2.00
33	Rocco Baldelli (2,500)	1.50
34	Jose Reyes (1,739)	1.50
35	Dontrelle Willis (3,750)	1.50
36	Miguel Cabrera (3,750)	2.00
37	Brandon Webb (2,072)	1.50
38	Rich Harden (1,823)	2.75
40	Vladimir Guerrero (1,913)	1.50
41	Hank Blalock (3,303)	1.50
42	Kazuo Matsui (5,000)	1.50
43	Joe Mauer (4,888)	3.00
44	Keith Foulke (1,896)	1.50
45	Josh Beckett (3,178)	1.50
46	Jamie Moyer (1,573)	1.50
47	Victor Martinez (2,500)	2.25
49	Derrek Lee (1,920)	1.50
51	Roger Clemens (3,750)	2.25
52	David Ortiz (1,655)	2.25
53	Jason Bay (2,336)	4.75
54	Erubiel Durazo (1,577)	1.50
55	Gary Sheffield (1,639)	1.50
56	Jeff Kent (2,036)	1.50
57	Ken Harvey (1,621)	1.50
58	Jason Varitek (2,698)	1.50
59	Jeromy Burnitz (2,148)	1.50
60	Nomar Garciaparra (2,074)	1.50
61	Javy Lopez (3,204)	1.50
62	Eric Gagne (2,279)	1.50
63	Khalil Greene (3,456)	3.00
64	Carlos Zambrano (3,492)	1.50
65	Lyle Overbay (2,789)	1.50
68	Laynce Nix (1,760)	1.50
69	Manny Ramirez (1,909)	1.75
70	Alfonso Soriano (1,820)	1.50
71	Mike Lieberthal (1,479)	1.50
72	Juan Pierre (2,500)	1.50
73	Frank Thomas (1,835)	1.50
74	Sean Casey (1,851)	1.50
75	Albert Pujols (3,750)	4.25

316	Mike Williams	.40
317	Trevor Hoffman	.40
318	Andy Pettitte	.75
319	Orlando Hernandez	.40
320	Juan Rivera	.40
321	Elizardo Ramirez	.40
322	Junior Spivey	.40
323	Tony Batista	.40
324	Mike Remlinger	.40
325	Alex Gonzalez	.40
326	Aaron Hill	.40
327	Steve Finley	.40
328	Vinny Castilla	.40
329	Eric Duncan	.40
330	Mike Gosling	.40
331	Eric Hinske	.40
332	Scott Rolen	1.50
333	Benito Santiago	.40
334	Jimmy Gobble	.40
335	Bobby Higginson	.40
336	Kelvim Escobar	.40
337	Mike DeJean	.40
338	Sidney Ponson	.40
339	Todd Self RC	1.50
340	Jeff Cirillo	.40
341	Jimmy Rollins	.50
342	Barry Zito	.75
342	Barry Zito/SP/Green Jsy	6.00
343	Felix Pie	.40
344	Matt Morris	.40
345	Kazuhiro Sasaki	.40
346	Jack Wilson	.40
347	Nick Johnson	.40
348	Wil Cordero	.40
349	Ryan Madson	.40
350	Torii Hunter	.75
351	Andy Ashby	.40
352	Aubrey Huff	.40
353	Brad Lidge	.40
354	Derrek Lee	.40
355	Yadier Molina RC	4.00
356	Paul Wilson	.40
357	Omar Vizquel	.50
358	Rene Reyes	.40
359	Marlon Anderson	.40
360	Bobby Kielty	.40
361	Ryan Wagner	.40
361	Ryan Wagner/	
	SP/Old Logo	5.00
362	Justin Morneau	.50
363	Shane Spencer	.40
364	David Bell	.40
365	Matt Stairs	.40
366	Joe Borchard	.40
367	Mark Redman	.40
368	Dave Roberts	.40
369	Desi Relaford	.40
370	Rich Harden	.40
371	Fernando Tatis	.40
372	Eric Karros	.40
373	Eric Milton	.40
374	Mike Sweeney	.40
375	Brian Daubach	.40
376	Brian Snyder	.40
377	Chris Reitsma	.40
378	Kyle Lohse	.40
379	Livan Hernandez	.40
380	Robin Ventura	.40
381	Jacque Jones	.40
382	Danny Kolb	.40
383	Casey Kotchman	.40
384	Cristian Guzman	.40
385	Josh Beckett	1.00
386	Khalil Greene	.40
387	Greg Myers	.40
388	Francisco Cordero	.40
389	Donald Levinski	.40
390	Roy Halladay	.75
391	J.D. Drew	.40
392	Jamie Moyer	.40
393	Ken Macha	.40
394	Jeff DaVanon	.40
395	Matt Kata	.40
396	Jack Cust	.40
397	Mike Timlin	.40
398	Zack Greinke	4.00
399	Byung-Hyun Kim	4.00
400	Kazuhisa Ishii	4.00
401	Brayan Pena RC	4.00
402	Garret Anderson	6.00
403	Kyle Sleeth	4.00
404	Javy Lopez	4.00
405	Damian Moss	4.00
406	David Ortiz	4.00
407	Pedro J. Martinez	8.00
408	Hee Seop Choi	4.00
409	Carl Everett	4.00
410	Dontrelle Willis	5.00
411	Ryan Harvey	4.00
412	Russell Branyan	4.00
413	Milton Bradley	4.00
414	Marcus McBeth RC	4.00
415	Carlos Pena	4.00
416	Ivan Rodriguez	6.00
417	Craig Biggio	5.00
418	Angel Berroa	4.00
419	Brian Jordan	4.00
420	Scott Podsednik	4.00
421	Omar Falcon RC	4.00
422	Joe Mays	4.00
423	Brad Wilkerson	4.00
424	Al Leiter	4.00
425	Derek Jeter	15.00
426	Mark Mulder	4.00
427	Marlon Byrd	4.00
428	David Murphy	4.00
429	Phil Nevin	4.00
430	J.T. Snow Jr.	4.00

431	Brad Sullivan	4.00
432	Bo Hart	4.00
433	Josh Labandeira RC	4.00
434	Chan Ho Park	4.00
435	Carlos Delgado	6.00
436	Curt Schilling	6.00
437	John Smoltz	5.00
438	Luis Matos	4.00
439	Mark Prior	5.00
440	Roberto Alomar	6.00
441	Coco Crisp	4.00
442	Austin Kearns	4.00
443	Larry Walker	5.00
444	Neal Cotts	4.00
445	Jeff Bagwell	6.00
446	Adrian Beltre	4.00
447	Grady Sizemore	6.00
448	Keith Ginter	4.00
449	Vladimir Guerrero	8.00
450	Lyle Overbay	4.00
451	Rafael Furcal	4.00
452	Melvin Mora	4.00
453	Kerry Wood	4.00
454	Jose Valentin	4.00
455	Ken Griffey Jr.	8.00
456	Brandon Phillips	4.00
457	Miguel Cabrera	8.00
458	Edwin Jackson	4.00
459	Eric Owens	4.00
460	Miguel Batista	4.00
461	Mike Hampton	4.00
462	Kevin Millar	4.00
463	Bartolo Colon	4.00
464	Sean Casey	4.00
465	C.C. Sabathia	5.00
466	Rickie Weeks	4.00
467	Brad Penny	4.00
468	Mike MacDougal	4.00
469	Kevin Brown	4.00
470	Lance Berkman	5.00
471	Ben Sheets	4.00
472	Mariano Rivera	5.00
473	Mike Piazza	8.00
474	Ryan Klesko	4.00
475	Edgar Renteria	4.00

Chrome

		NM/M
Complete Set (110):		
Common Player:		1.00
Production 1,955 Sets		
Refractor:		1.5-2X
Production 555 Sets		
Black Refractor:		2-4X
Production 55 Sets		
THC1	Sammy Sosa	8.00
THC2	Nomar Garciaparra	8.00
THC3	Ichiro Suzuki	6.00
THC4	Rafael Palmeiro	3.00
THC5	Carlos Delgado	2.50
THC6	Troy Glaus	2.00
THC7	Jay Gibbons	1.50
THC8	Frank Thomas	3.00
THC9	Pat Burrell	2.00
THC10	Albert Pujols	8.00
THC11	Brandon Webb	1.50
THC12	Chipper Jones	4.00
THC13	Magglio Ordonez	2.00
THC14	Adam Dunn	2.00
THC15	Todd Helton	2.50
THC16	Jason Giambi	3.00
THC17	Alfonso Soriano	3.00
THC18	Barry Zito	2.00
THC19	Jim Thome	3.00
THC20	Alex Rodriguez	8.00
THC21	Hee Seop Choi	1.00
THC22	Pedro J. Martinez	3.00
THC23	Kerry Wood	3.00
THC24	Bartolo Colon	1.50
THC25	Austin Kearns	2.00
THC26	Ken Griffey Jr.	5.00
THC27	Coco Crisp	1.00
THC28	Larry Walker	1.50
THC29	Ivan Rodriguez	2.50
THC30	Dontrelle Willis	2.00
THC31	Miguel Cabrera	2.50
THC32	Jeff Bagwell	2.50
THC33	Lance Berkman	1.50
THC34	Shawn Green	1.50
THC35	Kevin Brown	1.50
THC36	Vladimir Guerrero	3.00
THC37	Mike Piazza	5.00
THC38	Derek Jeter	10.00
THC39	John Smoltz	1.50
THC40	Mark Prior	8.00
THC41	Gary Sheffield	2.00
THC42	Curt Schilling	2.00
THC43	Randy Johnson	3.00
THC44	Luis Gonzalez	1.50
THC45	Andruw Jones	2.50
THC46	Greg Maddux	5.00
THC47	Tony Batista	1.00
THC48	Esteban Loaiza	1.00
THC49	Chin-Hui Tsao	1.00
THC50	Mike Lowell	1.50
THC51	Jeff Kent	1.50
THC52	Richie Sexson	2.00
THC53	Torii Hunter	2.00

THC54	Jose Vidro	1.00
THC55	Jose Reyes	3.00
THC56	Jimmy Rollins	1.00
THC57	Bret Boone	1.50
THC58	Rocco Baldelli	2.00
THC59	Hank Blalock	2.00
THC60	Rickie Weeks	2.00
THC61	Rodney Choy Foo	1.00
THC62	Zach Miner	3.00
THC63	Brayan Pena	1.00
THC64	David Murphy	1.00
THC65	Matt Creighton	1.00
THC66	Kyle Sleeth	1.00
THC67	Matthew Moses	1.00
THC68	Josh Labandeira	1.00
THC69	Grady Sizemore	1.00
THC70	Edwin Jackson	1.00
THC71	Marcus McBeth	1.00
THC72	Bradley Sullivan	1.00
THC73	Zachary Duke	3.00
THC74	Omar Falcon	1.00
THC75	Conor Jackson	2.00
THC76	Carlos Quentin	4.00
THC77	Craig Ansman	1.00
THC78	Mike Gosling	1.00
THC79	Kyle Davies	1.00
THC80	Anthony Lerew	1.00
THC81	Sung Jung	1.00
THC82	David Crouthers	1.00
THC83	Kenny Perez	1.00
THC84	Jeffrey Allison	1.00
THC85	Nic Ungs	1.00
THC86	Donald Levinski	1.00
THC87	Anthony Acevedo	1.00
THC88	Todd Self	1.00
THC89	Tim Frend	1.00
THC90	Tydus Meadows	1.00
THC91	Khalid Ballouli	1.00
THC92	Dioner Navarro	1.00
THC93	Casey Myers	1.00
THC94	Jon Knott	1.00
THC95	Tim Stauffer	1.00
THC96	Ricky Nolasco	4.00
THC97	Blake Hawksworth	1.00
THC98	Jesse Roman	1.00
THC99	Yadier Molina	1.00
THC100	Chris O'Riordan	1.00
THC101	Cliff Floyd	1.00
THC102	Nick Johnson	1.00
THC103	Edgar Martinez	1.50
THC104	Brett Myers	1.00
THC105	Francisco Rodriguez	1.00
THC106	Scott Rolen	3.00
THC107	Mark Teixeira	2.00
THC108	Miguel Tejada	2.00
THC109	Vernon Wells	1.50
THC110	Jerome Williams	1.00

Clubhouse Collection

		NM/M
Common Player:		5.00
BA	Bobby Abreu	6.00
RB	Rocco Baldelli	12.00
LB	Lance Berkman	6.00
YB	Yogi Berra	35.00
HB	Hank Blalock	8.00
BB	Bret Boone	6.00
KB	Kevin Brown	6.00
EC	Eric Chavez	5.00
RC	Roger Clemens	15.00
JD	Johnny Damon	10.00
AD	Adam Dunn	6.00
RF	Rafael Furcal	6.00
EG	Eric Gagne	8.00
NG	Nomar Garciaparra	15.00
JG	Jason Giambi	8.00
MG	Marcus Giles	6.00
TG	Troy Glaus	6.00
LG	Luis Gonzalez	6.00
SG	Shawn Green	6.00
TH	Tim Hudson	6.00
THU	Torii Hunter	8.00
KI	Kazuhisa Ishii	6.00
RJ	Randy Johnson	10.00
AJ	Andruw Jones	6.00
CJ	Chipper Jones	8.00
AK	Al Kaline	25.00
HK	Harmon Killebrew	30.00
PL	Paul LoDuca	5.00
JL	Javy Lopez	6.00
GM	Greg Maddux	20.00
PM	Pedro J. Martinez	10.00
WM	Willie Mays	100.00
FM	Fred McGriff	6.00
MM	Mark Mulder	5.00
SM	Stan Musial	20.00
BM	Brett Myers	5.00
AP	Albert Pujols	15.00
MR	Manny Ramirez	8.00
JRE	Jose Reyes	8.00
AR	Alex Rodriguez	10.00
IR	Ivan Rodriguez	6.00
SRB	Scott Rolen/bat	8.00
SR	Scott Rolen/jsy	8.00
JR	Jimmy Rollins	5.00
CS	C.C. Sabathia	5.00
GS	Gary Sheffield	8.00

JS	John Smoltz	8.00
DS	Duke Snider	30.00
AS	Alfonso Soriano	10.00
SS	Sammy Sosa	15.00
MS	Mike Sweeney	5.00
MTE	Mark Teixeira	6.00
MT	Miguel Tejada/jsy	6.00
MTB	Miguel Tejada/bat	8.00
JT	Jim Thome	10.00
VW	Vernon Wells	6.00
KW	Kerry Wood	10.00
BZ	Barry Zito	6.00

Clubhouse Collection Autograph

F6	Stan Musial	3.00
F7	Harmon Killebrew	2.00
F8	Herb Score	.50
F9	Whitey Ford	1.00
F10	Robin Roberts	.50

	NM/M
Inserted 15,186	
Production 25 Sets	
WM Willie Mays	400.00

Clubhouse Collection - Dual

		NM/M
Production 55 Sets		
BC	Yogi Berra,	
	Roger Clemens	160.00
GS	Shawn Green,	
	Duke Snider	150.00

Doubleheader

	NM/M
Complete Set (30):	50.00
Common Player:	.75
Inserted 1:Box	
1 Alex Rodriguez	5.00
2 Nomar Garciaparra	4.00
3 Ichiro Suzuki	4.00
4 Albert Pujols	4.00
5 Sammy Sosa	4.00
6 Derek Jeter	6.00
7 Jim Thome	2.00
8 Adam Dunn	1.00
9 Jason Giambi	2.00
10 Ivan Rodriguez	1.50
11 Todd Helton	1.50
12 Luis Gonzalez	.75
13 Jeff Bagwell	1.50
14 Lance Berkman	1.00
15 Alfonso Soriano	2.00
16 Dontrelle Willis	1.50
17 Mark Prior	4.00
18 Vladimir Guerrero	2.00
19 Mike Piazza	3.00
20 Roger Clemens	4.00
21 Randy Johnson	2.00
22 Curt Schilling	1.50
23 Gary Sheffield	1.00
24 Pedro J. Martinez	2.00
25 Carlos Delgado	1.50
26 Jimmy Rollins	.75
27 Andruw Jones	1.50
28 Chipper Jones	3.00
29 Rocco Baldelli	1.50
30 Hank Blalock	1.00

Flashbacks

	NM/M
Complete Set (10):	8.00
Common Player:	.50
Inserted 1:12	
F1 Duke Snider	.50
F2 Johnny Podres	.50
F3 Don Newcombe	.50
F4 Al Kaline	1.50
F5 Willie Mays	4.00

Flashbacks Autograph

Inserted 1:30,373

Grandstand Glory

		NM/M
Common Player:		20.00
YB	Yogi Berra	20.00
AK	Al Kaline	30.00
HK	Harmon Killebrew	30.00
SM	Stan Musial	35.00
WS	Warren Spahn	35.00

New Age Performers

		NM/M
Complete Set (15):		15.00
Common Player:		.75
Inserted 1:5		
NAP1	Jason Giambi	1.50
NAP2	Ichiro Suzuki	2.50
NAP3	Alex Rodriguez	3.00
NAP4	Alfonso Soriano	1.50
NAP5	Albert Pujols	3.00
NAP6	Nomar Garciaparra	3.00
NAP7	Mark Prior	3.00
NAP8	Derek Jeter	4.00
NAP9	Sammy Sosa	2.50
NAP10	Carlos Delgado	1.00
NAP11	Jim Thome	1.50
NAP12	Todd Helton	1.00
NAP13	Gary Sheffield	.75
NAP14	Vladimir Guerrero	1.50
NAP15	Josh Beckett	1.00

Real One Autograph

		NM/M
Common Autograph:		30.00
Inserted 1:230		
Red Autograph:		1.5-2X
Production 55		
GA	Gair Allie	50.00
EB	Ernie Banks	100.00
YB	Yogi Berra	100.00
BB	Bob Borkowski	40.00
BC	Billy Consolo	55.00
CF	Cliff Floyd	30.00
BG	Bill Glynn	45.00
JG	Johnny Gray	45.00
AH	Aubrey Huff	30.00
AK	Al Kaline	100.00
HK	Harmon Killebrew	90.00
TK	Thornton Kipper	45.00
BK	Bob Kline	45.00
SK	Steve Kraly	60.00
LL	Lou Limmer	60.00
ML	Mike Lowell	40.00
WM	Willie Mays	185.00
SM	Stan Musial	140.00
DN	Don Newcombe	65.00
MO	Magglio Ordonez	35.00
JP	Jim Pearce	45.00
HP	Harry Perkowski	50.00
DP	Duane Pillette	40.00
JPO	Johnny Podres	45.00
SR	Scott Rolen	45.00
FS	Frank Smith	45.00
DS	Duke Snider	85.00
VT	"Jake" Thies	45.00
HV	Harold Valentine	45.00
DW	Dontrelle Willis	50.00
BW	Bill Wilson	40.00
TW	Tom Wright	45.00

Team Topps Legends

		NM/M
Inserted 1:505		
	Davey Johnson	12.00
	Joe Rudi	15.00

Then And Now

	NM/M
Complete Set (6):	8.00
Common Player:	.75
Inserted 1:15	
TN1 Willie Mays, Jim Thome	4.00
TN2 Al Kaline, Albert Pujols	4.00
TN3 Duke Snider,	
Carlos Delgado	1.50
TN4 Robin Roberts,	
Roy Halladay	1.50
TN5 Don Newcombe,	
Johan Santana	1.50
TN6 Herb Score, Kerry Wood	1.50

2004 Topps National Trading Card Day

As part of its participation in NTCD on April 3, Topps issued a 12-card foil pack with four baseball player cards, two football and three each basketball and hockey, plus a header. Only the baseball players are listed here. Fronts have action photos, gold-foil highlights and a NTCD logo. Backs have recent stats, a photo portrait and biographical data.

		NM/M
Unopened Pack:		3.00
Common Player:		.25
1	Rocco Baldelli	.35
2	Mark Prior	.50
3	Dontrelle Willis	.25
4	Jason Giambi	.25

2004 Topps Opening Day

		NM/M
Complete Set (165):		25.00
Common Player:		.10
Pack (6):		.25
Box (36):		30.00
1	Jim Thome	.50
2	Edgardo Alfonzo	.10
3	Marlon Anderson	.10
4	Ichiro Suzuki	1.00
5	Frank Thomas	.40
6	Tom Glavine	.25
7	Bo Hart	.10
8	Marcus Giles	.10
9	Kevin Millar	.10
10	Derek Jeter	1.50
11	Corey Patterson	.10
12	Jay Payton	.10
13	Lance Berkman	.20
14	Juan Pierre	.10
15	Mike Piazza	.75
16	Richie Sexson	.40
17	Tim Hudson	.25

No.	Player	Price
18	Fred McGriff	.20
19	Brad Radke	.10
20	John Smoltz	.20
21	Jay Gibbons	.10
22	Michael Young	.10
23	Steve Finley	.10
24	Ramon Hernandez	.10
25	Albert Pujols	1.25
26	Trot Nixon	.10
27	Kevin Millwood	.25
28	Mark Prior	1.00
29	Mike Lowell	.20
30	Paul LoDuca	.10
31	Jacque Jones	.10
32	Ty Wigginton	.10
33	Cliff Floyd	.10
34	Marlon Byrd	.10
35	Mark Mulder	.20
36	Johnny Damon	.20
37	Jimmy Rollins	.25
38	Javy Lopez	.25
39	Andruw Jones	.40
40	Hank Blalock	.25
41	Hee Seop Choi	.10
42	Jose Vidro	.10
43	Hideo Nomo	.25
44	Javier Vazquez	.10
45	Jorge Posada	.25
46	Al Leiter	.10
47	Orlando Cabrera	.10
48	Mike Hampton	.10
49	Esteban Loaiza	.10
50	Todd Helton	.40
51	Jose Contreras	.20
52	Jason L. Phillips	.10
53	Vernon Wells	.20
54	Randy Winn	.10
55	Curt Schilling	.40
56	Mark Buehrle	.10
57	Dmitri Young	.10
58	Kazuhisa Ishii	.10
59	A.J. Pierzynski	.10
60	Greg Maddux	.75
61	Jarrod Washburn	.10
62	Omar Vizquel	.10
63	Alex Gonzalez	.10
64	Sean Casey	.10
65	Eric Chavez	.20
66	Mike Lieberthal	.10
67	Jason Kendall	.10
68	Mike Cameron	.10
69	Woody Williams	.10
70	Nomar Garciaparra	1.00
71	Bernie Williams	.20
72	Darin Erstad	.20
73	Bill Mueller	.10
74	Damian Miller	.10
75	Jason Giambi	.50
76	Adam Dunn	.25
77	Carlos Lee	.10
78	Angel Berroa	.10
79	Erubiel Durazo	.10
80	Bret Boone	.20
81	Aubrey Huff	.20
82	Carlos Delgado	.40
83	Toby Hall	.10
84	Roy Halladay	.25
85	Preston Wilson	.10
86	Bartolo Colon	.20
87	Moises Alou	.20
88	Luis Castillo	.10
89	Manny Ramirez	.40
90	Garret Anderson	.25
91	Ryan Klesko	.20
92	Rich Aurilia	.10
93	Rafael Furcal	.20
94	Rocco Baldelli	.40
95	Eric Gagne	.20
96	Jeff Kent	.20
97	Josh Beckett	.40
98	Alex Gonzalez	.10
99	Jose Cruz Jr.	.10
100	Alex Rodriguez	1.25
101	Troy Glaus	.25
102	Carlos Beltran	.20
103	Luis Gonzalez	.20
104	A.J. Burnett	.10
105	Gary Sheffield	.25
106	Benito Santiago	.10
107	Tony Batista	.10
108	David Ortiz	.20
109	Shannon Stewart	.10
110	Jim Edmonds	.20
111	Kenny Lofton	.20
112	Paul Konerko	.10
113	Rafael Palmeiro	.40
114	Pat Burrell	.25
115	Barry Zito	.25
116	Edgar Martinez	.20
117	Austin Kearns	.20
118	Geoff Jenkins	.20
119	Mike Mussina	.25
120	Alfonso Soriano	.50
121	Shea Hillenbrand	.10
122	Ivan Rodriguez	.40
123	Kerry Wood	.40
124	Scott Rolen	.25
125	Jeff Bagwell	.40
126	Roberto Alomar	.25
127	Carl Crawford	.10
128	Mike Sweeney	.10
129	Melvin Mora	.20
130	Larry Walker	.20
131	Matt Morris	.10
132	Shawn Green	.20
133	Scott Podsednik	.10
134	Phil Nevin	.10
135	Dontrelle Willis	.25
136	Torii Hunter	.25
137	Carl Everett	.10
138	Pedro J. Martinez	.50
139	Roy Oswalt	.25
140	Vladimir Guerrero	.50
141	Chipper Jones	.75
142	Jose Reyes	.25
143	Sammy Sosa	1.00
144	Nick Johnson	.10
145	Miguel Tejada	.25
146	Bobby Abreu	.20
147	Magglio Ordonez	.25
148	Sean Burroughs	.10
149	Jody Gerut	.10
150	Jermaine Dye	.10
151	Craig Biggio	.25
152	Randy Johnson	.50
153	Jeff Conine	.10
154	Edgar Renteria	.20
155	Mark Teixeira	.25
156	Eric Hinske	.10
157	Kevin Brown	.20
158	Ken Griffey Jr.	.75
159	Brandon Webb	.10
160	Brian Giles	.20
161	Jason Schmidt	.20
162	Aramis Ramirez	.10
163	Aaron Boone	.10
164	Miguel Cabrera	.40
165	Checklist	.10

Autograph

NM/M

Common Autograph: 10.00
Inserted 1:629

Code	Player	Price
JD	Jeff Duncan	20.00
RH	Rich Harden	20.00
AT	Andres Torres	10.00
RW	Ryan Wagner	25.00
DW	Dontrelle Willis	30.00

2004 Topps Originals Signature Edition

WILLIE MAYS

NM/M

Common Autograph: 10.00
Pack (4): 45.00
Box (6): 220.00
Second number reflects quantity produced.

Code	Player	Price
JA1	Jim Abbott 88 TR/339	20.00
SA5	Sparky Anderson 83 MG/67	15.00
SA6	Sparky Anderson 84 MG/97	15.00
SA7	Sparky Anderson 85 MG/73	15.00
LA9	Luis Aparicio 69/49	20.00
LA12	Luis Aparicio 72/15	25.00
HB2	Harold Baines 82/31	30.00
HB3	Harold Baines 83/19	30.00
HB5	Harold Baines 85/97	15.00
HB6	Harold Baines 86/93	15.00
HB7	Harold Baines 87/115	15.00
JB2	Jesse Barfield 83/45	15.00
JB4	Jesse Barfield 85/60	15.00
JB5	Jesse Barfield 86/37	15.00
JB6	Jesse Barfield 87/180	10.00
KB2	Kevin Bass 84/71	10.00
KB3	Kevin Bass 85/30	10.00
KB4	Kevin Bass 86/44	10.00
KB5	Kevin Bass 87/74	10.00
KB6	Kevin Bass 90 TR/35	10.00
BB5	Buddy Bell 79/135	15.00
BB8	Buddy Bell 82/34	15.00
BB9	Buddy Bell 83/83	15.00
BB10	Buddy Bell 84/22	15.00
BB15	Buddy Bell 88/36	15.00
GB2	George Bell 84/67	15.00
GB3	George Bell 85/32	15.00
GB4	George Bell 86/46	15.00
GB5	George Bell 87/204	10.00
JBE2	Johnny Bench 79/14	125.00
JBE5	Johnny Bench 82/16	125.00
YB10	Yogi Berra 85/92 MG/22	100.00
VB7	Vida Blue 79/21	20.00
VB7	Vida Blue 81/227	15.00
VB8	Vida Blue 82/53	15.00
BBL4	Bert Blyleven 79/45	25.00
BBL6	Bert Blyleven 81/29	25.00
BBL8	Bert Blyleven 83/41	20.00
BBL10	Bert Blyleven 85/40	20.00
BBL11	Bert Blyleven 86/62	20.00
BBL12	Bert Blyleven 87/54	25.00
MB2	Mike Boddicker 84/59	15.00
MB3	Mike Boddicker 85/139	10.00
MB4	Mike Boddicker 86/66	10.00
MB5	Mike Boddicker 87/88	10.00
WB2	Wade Boggs 84/20	75.00
WB3	Wade Boggs 85/25	75.00
WB5	Wade Boggs 87/45	60.00
LB4	Lou Brock 70/20	50.00
LB13	Lou Brock 79/27	50.00
TB2	Tom Brunansky 83/27	15.00
TB3	Tom Brunansky 84/62	15.00
TB5	Tom Brunansky 86/28	15.00
TB6	Tom Brunansky 87/193	10.00
BU8	Bill Buckner 81/39	20.00
BU9	Bill Buckner 82/38	20.00
BU10	Bill Buckner 83/47	15.00
BU11	Bill Buckner 84/31	20.00
BU12	Bill Buckner 84 TR/24	20.00
BU13	Bill Buckner 85/80	15.00
BU14	Bill Buckner 86/63	15.00
BC5	Bert Campaneris 79/10	7.00
BC7	Bert Campaneris 84/28	15.00
JC2	John Candelaria 79/77	20.00
JC4	John Candelaria 81/19	30.00
JC5	John Candelaria 82/42	25.00
JC6	John Candelaria 83/77	20.00
JC8	John Candelaria 85/61	20.00
JC9	John Candelaria 86/36	20.00
JCA2	Jose Canseco 87/99	60.00
RC4	Rod Carew 79/29	60.00
RC6	Rod Carew 81/21	75.00
RC7	Rod Carew 82/18	75.00
GC3	Gary Carter 79/21	40.00
GC4	Gary Carter 80/24	40.00
GC5	Gary Carter 81/22	40.00
JCR2	Joe Carter 86/24	50.00
JCR3	Joe Carter 87/23	50.00
RCE3	Ron Cey 79/55	15.00
RCE6	Ron Cey 82/34	15.00
RCE7	Ron Cey 83/42	15.00
RCE8	Ron Cey 83 TR/68	15.00
RCE11	Ron Cey 86/43	15.00
VC2	Vince Coleman 87/299	15.00
VC3	Vince Coleman 88/34	20.00
VC4	Vince Coleman 91 TR/23	25.00
DC6	Dave Concepcion 80/21	40.00
DC8	Dave Concepcion 82/43	30.00
DC9	Dave Concepcion 83/19	30.00
DC10	Dave Concepcion 84/24	40.00
DC11	Dave Concepcion 85/41	30.00
DC12	Dave Concepcion 86/69	25.00
JCU8	Jose Cruz Sr. 82/28	15.00
JCU9	Jose Cruz Sr. 83/102	10.00
JCU10	Jose Cruz Sr. 84/67	10.00
JCU11	Jose Cruz Sr. 85/68	15.00
JCU12	Jose Cruz Sr. 86/31	15.00
RD3	Ron Darling 87/224	15.00
DD2	Darren Daulton 87/269	10.00
DD4	Darren Daulton 92/32	15.00
DD5	Darren Daulton 94/17	20.00
DD6	Darren Daulton 96/22	20.00
ED3	Eric Davis 87/336	15.00
AD3	Andre Dawson 80/27	25.00
AD4	Andre Dawson 81/37	25.00
AD5	Andre Dawson 82/55	20.00
AD6	Andre Dawson 83/47	20.00
AD7	Andre Dawson 84/25	25.00
AD8	Andre Dawson 85/22	25.00
AD9	Andre Dawson 86/22	20.00
DDE2	Doug DeCinces 79/38	20.00
DDE3	Doug DeCinces 80/24	20.00
DDE4	Doug DeCinces 81/24	20.00
DDE5	Doug DeCinces 82/42	20.00
DDE6	Doug DeCinces 83/75	15.00
DDE7	Doug DeCinces 84/19	20.00
DDE8	Doug DeCinces 85/54	15.00
DDE9	Doug DeCinces 86/74	15.00
BD6	Bucky Dent 82/49	20.00
BD7	Bucky Dent 83/92	15.00
BD8	Bucky Dent 84/63	15.00
RDI2	Rob Dibble 90/31	25.00
RDI3	Rob Dibble 91/62	20.00
RDI4	Rob Dibble 92/56	20.00
RDI6	Rob Dibble 93/47	15.00
RDI7	Rob Dibble 94/37	15.00
LD2	Leon Durham 82/51	10.00
LD3	Leon Durham 83/52	10.00
LD4	Leon Durham 84/151	10.00
LD7	Leon Durham 87/87	10.00
LDY2	Lenny Dykstra 87/200	15.00
LDY3	Lenny Dykstra 88/30	25.00
LDY4	Lenny Dykstra 89/17	30.00
DE3	Dennis Eckersley 79/44	40.00
DE4	Dennis Eckersley 80/40	40.00
DEV5	Darrell Evans 79/19	20.00
DEV7	Darrell Evans 81/15	20.00
DEV8	Darrell Evans 82/25	20.00
DEV9	Darrell Evans 83/63	15.00
DEV10	Darrell Evans 84/81	10.00
DEV11	Darrell Evans 85/48	15.00
DEV12	Darrell Evans 86/82	10.00
SF2	Sid Fernandez 86/18	30.00
SF3	Sid Fernandez 87/211	15.00
SF4	Sid Fernandez 87/191	10.00
TF2	Tony Fernandez 86/41	15.00
TF3	Tony Fernandez 87/228	10.00
MF3	Mark Fidrych 81/32	30.00
MF4	Mark Fidrych 80/16	40.00
CF2	Cecil Fielder 87/208	30.00
CF3	Cecil Fielder 88/26	50.00
CF4	Cecil Fielder 89/16	50.00
RF3	Rollie Fingers 79/52	20.00
RF4	Rollie Fingers 80/15	40.00
RF5	Rollie Fingers 81/18	40.00
CFI3	Carlton Fisk 79/24	60.00
CFI4	Carlton Fisk 80/32	50.00
CFI6	Carlton Fisk 82/30	50.00
GF6	George Foster 79/20	20.00
GF10	George Foster 83/39	15.00
GF11	George Foster 84/112	10.00
GF12	George Foster 85/76	10.00
GF13	George Foster 86/64	10.00
SG4	Steve Garvey 79/26	30.00
SG7	Steve Garvey 82/122	15.00
SG9	Steve Garvey 84/32	20.00
SG10	Steve Garvey 85/129	15.00
CG3	Cesar Geronimo 79/28	15.00
CG5	Cesar Geronimo 81/21	15.00
CG6	Cesar Geronimo 82/52	10.00
CG7	Cesar Geronimo 83/67	10.00
CG8	Cesar Geronimo 84/70	10.00
KGI2	Kirk Gibson 82/35	20.00
KGI3	Kirk Gibson 83/35	20.00
KGI5	Kirk Gibson 85/44	20.00
KGI6	Kirk Gibson 86/44	20.00
KGI7	Kirk Gibson 87/65	20.00
DG3	Dwight Gooden 87/52	30.00
RG7	Rich "Goose" Gossage 81/21	20.00
RG8	Rich "Goose" Gossage 82/30	
RG9	Rich "Goose" Gossage 83/34	20.00
RG10	Rich "Goose" Gossage 84/90	15.00
RG12	Rich "Goose" Gossage 86/30	15.00
BG2	Bobby Grich 79/29	20.00
BG3	Bobby Grich 80/70	15.00
BG5	Bobby Grich 82/45	15.00
BG6	Bobby Grich 83/85	10.00
BG7	Bobby Grich 84/57	15.00
BG8	Bobby Grich 85/36	15.00
KG5	Ken Griffey Sr. 80/15	30.00
KG7	Ken Griffey Sr. 82/18	30.00
KG8	Ken Griffey Sr. 83/70	15.00
KG9	Ken Griffey Sr. 84/52	15.00
KG10	Ken Griffey Sr. 85/32	20.00
KG11	Ken Griffey Sr.	
KGU2	Kelly Gruber 88/77	10.00
KGU3	Kelly Gruber 89/44	10.00
KGU4	Kelly Gruber 90/86	10.00
KGU5	Kelly Gruber 91/52	10.00
KGU6	Kelly Gruber 92/55	10.00
KGU7	Kelly Gruber 93/26	10.00
RGU4	Ron Guidry 80/22	40.00
RGU5	Ron Guidry 81/104	20.00
RGU6	Ron Guidry 82/53	40.00
RGU7	Ron Guidry 83/46	40.00
RGU8	Ron Guidry 84/40	40.00
RGU9	Ron Guidry 85/50	40.00
TG2	Tony Gwynn 84/95	60.00
KH3	Keith Hernandez 80/38	50.00
KH4	Keith Hernandez 81/19	50.00
KH5	Keith Hernandez 82/156	20.00
KH6	Keith Hernandez 83/17	50.00
TH2	Tom Herr 81/22	15.00
TH3	Tom Herr 82/42	15.00
TH4	Tom Herr 83/80	15.00
TH5	Tom Herr 84/30	15.00
TH6	Tom Herr 85/17	15.00
TH7	Tom Herr 86/28	15.00
TH8	Tom Herr 87/134	10.00
OH2	Orel Hershiser 86/23	20.00
OH3	Orel Hershiser 87/218	20.00
WH4	Whitey Herzog 83 MG/63	10.00
WH5	Whitey Herzog 84 MG/85	10.00
WH6	Whitey Herzog 85 MG/75	10.00
WH7	Whitey Herzog 86 MG/66	10.00
WH8	Whitey Herzog 87 MG/117	10.00
WH9	Whitey Herzog 88 MG/35	15.00
BH5	Bob Horner 83/69	15.00
BH6	Bob Horner 84/63	15.00
BH8	Bob Horner 86/118	15.00
BH9	Bob Horner 87/38	15.00
CH2	Charlie Hough 83/19	20.00
CH3	Charlie Hough 84/50	10.00
CH4	Charlie Hough 85/57	10.00
CH5	Charlie Hough 86/66	10.00
CH6	Charlie Hough 87/46	10.00
CH7	Charlie Hough 91 TR/70	10.00
CH8	Charlie Hough 92/25	15.00
CH9	Charlie Hough 92/15	
AH6	Al Hrabosky 78/20	20.00
AH7	Al Hrabosky 79/40	15.00
AH8	Al Hrabosky 80/61	10.00
AH9	Al Hrabosky 81/38	15.00
AH11	Al Hrabosky 89 Sr./20	15.00
BJ2	Bo Jackson 87/100	60.00
RJ8	Reggie Jackson 84/73	75.00
RJ11	Reggie Jackson 85/17	75.00
RJ12	Reggie Jackson 86/17	75.00
BJA2	Brook Jacoby 86/133	10.00
BJA3	Brook Jacoby 87/191	10.00
FJ8	Fergie Jenkins 78/17	30.00
FJ10	Fergie Jenkins 80/37	30.00
FJ11	Fergie Jenkins 81/32	30.00
FJ12	Fergie Jenkins 82/65	20.00
FJ14	Fergie Jenkins 84/42	30.00
WJ2	Wally Joyner 87/335	15.00
DJ3	David Justice 93/32	20.00
AK10	Al Kaline 67/18	120.00
AK16	Al Kaline 73/25	100.00
JK2	Jimmy Key 86/21	10.00
JK3	Jimmy Key 87/263	10.00
JK5	Jimmy Key 92/37	10.00
DK4	Dave Kingman 81/25	30.00
DK6	Dave Kingman 83/32	20.00
DK7	Dave Kingman 86/25	30.00
RK2	Ron Kittle 85/86	10.00
RK3	Ron Kittle 86/55	10.00
RK4	Ron Kittle 87/201	10.00
RKN5	Ray Knight 82/122	15.00
RKN6	Ray Knight 83/36	20.00
RKN7	Ray Knight 84/26	20.00
RKN8	Ray Knight 85/68	15.00
RKN9	Ray Knight 86/80	15.00
RKN10	Ray Knight 87 TR/90	15.00
JKR2	John Kruk 87/214	15.00
JKR3	John Kruk 92/22	35.00
CL3	Carney Lansford 81/184	10.00
CL5	Carney Lansford 83/40	15.00
CL6	Carney Lansford 85/35	15.00
CL7	Carney Lansford 86/76	10.00
CLE3	Chet Lemon 79/24	20.00
CLE6	Chet Lemon 82/23	20.00
CLE7	Chet Lemon 83/35	15.00
CLE8	Chet Lemon 84/42	15.00
CLE9	Chet Lemon 85/32	15.00
CLE10	Chet Lemon 86/136	15.00
CLE11	Chet Lemon 87/27	20.00
JL2	Jim Leyritz 91/38	10.00
JL3	Jim Leyritz 93/49	10.00
JL4	Jim Leyritz 94/16	20.00
JL6	Jim Leyritz 97/62	10.00
JL7	Jim Leyritz 98/20	20.00
JL8	Jim Leyritz 99/124	10.00
JL9	Jim Leyritz 00/40	10.00
DL4	Davey Lopes 79/71	10.00
DL5	Davey Lopes 80/19	15.00
DL7	Davey Lopes 82/23	15.00
DL8	Davey Lopes 83/65	10.00
DL10	Davey Lopes 85/24	15.00
DL11	Davey Lopes 86/40	10.00
DL12	Davey Lopes 01 MG/67	10.00
DL13	Davey Lopes 02 MG/19	15.00
GL7	Greg Luzinski 80/21	30.00
GL9	Greg Luzinski 82/34	20.00
GL10	Greg Luzinski 83/75	10.00
GL11	Greg Luzinski 84/85	15.00
GL12	Greg Luzinski 85/32	15.00
BM7	Bill Madlock 82/26	15.00
BM8	Bill Madlock 83/55	15.00
BM9	Bill Madlock 84/69	15.00
BM10	Bill Madlock 85/60	15.00
BM11	Bill Madlock 86/63	15.00
BM12	Bill Madlock 87/42	15.00
GM3	Gary Matthews Sr. 83/20	15.00
GM4	Gary Matthews Sr. 84/43	10.00
GM5	Gary Matthews Sr. 85/39	10.00
GM6	Gary Matthews Sr. 86/38	10.00
GM7	Gary Matthews Sr. 87/82	10.00
GM8	Gary Matthews Sr. 88/30	10.00
DM3	Don Mattingly 87/84	100.00
WM9	Willie Mays 72/25	300.00
TM5	Tim McCarver 79/22	20.00
JM2	Jack McDowell 89/36	20.00
JM3	Jack McDowell 90 TR/61	15.00
JM4	Jack McDowell 91/33	20.00
JM5	Jack McDowell 92/38	10.00
JM6	Jack McDowell 93/27	20.00
JM9	Jack McDowell 96/15	25.00
JM10	Jack McDowell 97/27	20.00
WMC2	Willie McGee 84/66	25.00
WMC3	Willie McGee 85/44	25.00
WMC4	Willie McGee 86/24	40.00
WMC5	Willie McGee 87/117	25.00
PM1	Paul Molitor 79/15	60.00
PM2	Paul Molitor 80/26	50.00
PM4	Paul Molitor 82/32	50.00
JMO9	Joe Morgan 81/32	30.00
JMO10	Joe Morgan 82/18	40.00
JMO11	Joe Morgan 83/49	25.00
JMO13	Joe Morgan 84/73	15.00
JMO14	Joe Morgan 85/40	25.00
DMU2	Dale Murphy 82/51	40.00
DMU3	Dale Murphy 84/29	40.00
DMU8	Dale Murphy 86/25	50.00
DMU9	Dale Murphy 87/91	25.00
SM5	Stan Musial 62/16	150.00
AO6	Al Oliver 79/42	15.00
AO8	Al Oliver 81/54	15.00
AO9	Al Oliver 82/55	15.00
AO10	Al Oliver 83/50	15.00
AO11	Al Oliver 84/51	15.00
AO12	Al Oliver 85/46	15.00
AO13	Al Oliver 86/44	15.00
PO2	Paul O'Neill 89/24	50.00
PO3	Paul O'Neill 90/18	50.00
PO4	Paul O'Neill 91/24	50.00
PO5	Paul O'Neill 97/33	40.00
JP3	Jim Palmer 81/23	30.00
JP4	Jim Palmer 82/23	30.00
JP5	Jim Palmer 87/191	25.00
DP6	Dave Parker 82/73	30.00
DP7	Dave Parker 83/30	30.00
DP9	Dave Parker 85/45	25.00
DP10	Dave Parker 86/29	30.00
BP9	Boog Powell 73/17	30.00
BP11	Boog Powell 75/19	40.00
TR2	Tim Raines 82/43	20.00
TR3	Tim Raines 83/26	25.00
TR5	Tim Raines 85/43	20.00
TR6	Tim Raines 86/21	20.00
TR7	Tim Raines 87/211	15.00
HR2	Harold Reynolds 87/255	10.00
JR7	Jim Rice 81/123	20.00
JR8	Jim Rice 82/24	35.00
JR9	Jim Rice 83/71	25.00
CR4	Cal Ripken Jr. 86/74	120.00
MR2	Mickey Rivers 79/35	15.00
MR5	Mickey Rivers 82/49	15.00
MR6	Mickey Rivers 83/79	15.00
MR7	Mickey Rivers 84/91	10.00
MR8	Mickey Rivers 85/34	15.00
BR11	Brooks Robinson 74/20	75.00
BR13	Brooks Robinson 76/17	75.00
JRU9	Joe Rudi 79/24	15.00
JRU10	Joe Rudi 80/45	15.00
JRU11	Joe Rudi 82/26	15.00
JRU12	Joe Rudi 83/75	15.00
NR5	Nolan Ryan 83/23	200.00
NR6	Nolan Ryan 84/20	200.00
NR8	Nolan Ryan 86/20	200.00
BS2	Bret Saberhagen 86/23	25.00
BS3	Bret Saberhagen 87/230	15.00
RS2	Ryne Sandberg 84/37	100.00
RS5	Ryne Sandberg 87/32	100.00
SS2	Steve Sax 83/34	15.00
SS4	Steve Sax 85/33	15.00
SS5	Steve Sax 86/45	15.00
SS6	Steve Sax 87/215	10.00
MS2	Mike Schmidt 80/100	60.00
MSC3	Mike Scott 82/32	15.00
MSC4	Mike Scott 83/55	15.00
MSC5	Mike Scott 84/28	15.00
MSC6	Mike Scott 86/73	10.00
MSC7	Mike Scott 87/36	15.00
MSC8	Mike Scott 88/21	15.00
TS2	Tom Seaver 79/14	85.00
TS4	Tom Seaver 81/16	100.00
TS5	Tom Seaver 82/25	100.00
KS2	Kevin Seitzer 88/88	10.00
KS3	Kevin Seitzer 89/39	10.00
KS4	Kevin Seitzer 90/18	15.00
KS5	Kevin Seitzer 91/39	10.00
KS6	Kevin Seitzer 92/49	10.00
KS9	Kevin Seitzer 93/38	10.00
KS10	Kevin Seitzer 94/22	15.00
KS13	Kevin Seitzer 97/22	15.00
LS5	Lee Smith 86/29	25.00
LS6	Lee Smith 87/237	15.00
LS7	Lee Smith 88/27	25.00
OS2	Ozzie Smith 81/28	60.00
OS3	Ozzie Smith 82/27	60.00
OS5	Ozzie Smith 84/19	75.00
OS6	Ozzie Smith 85/16	75.00
RM8	Reggie Smith 79/15	25.00
RM9	Reggie Smith 80/16	25.00
RM10	Reggie Smith 81/14	25.00
RM11	Reggie Smith 82/32	15.00
RM12	Reggie Smith 83/48	15.00
DS8	Duke Snider 64/18	150.00
CS2	Cory Snyder 87/291	10.00
CS3	Cory Snyder 91/39	15.00
DSW2	Dave Stewart 83/41	15.00
DSW3	Dave Stewart 84/60	15.00
DSW4	Dave Stewart 85/23	15.00
DSW5	Dave Stewart 86/53	15.00
DSW6	Dave Stewart 87/171	10.00
DSE2	Dave Stieb 81/21	35.00
DSE3	Dave Stieb 82/34	30.00
DSE4	Dave Stieb 83/70	25.00
DSE5	Dave Stieb 84/20	35.00
DSE6	Dave Stieb 85/45	25.00
DSE7	Dave Stieb 86/69	25.00
DSE8	Dave Stieb 87/75	25.00
DSR2	Darryl Strawberry 85/32	25.00
DSR3	Darryl Strawberry 86/24	25.00
DSR4	Darryl Strawberry 87/183	20.00
DSR5	Darryl Strawberry 87 AS/110	20.00
RU3	Rick Sutcliffe 82/53	20.00
RU4	Rick Sutcliffe 83/43	20.00
RU5	Rick Sutcliffe 84/33	20.00
RU6	Rick Sutcliffe 85/82	20.00
RU8	Rick Sutcliffe 87/19	20.00
BSU6	Bruce Sutter 82/111	20.00
BSU7	Bruce Sutter 83/45	25.00
BSU8	Bruce Sutter 84/24	30.00
BSU9	Bruce Sutter 85/19	35.00
BSU10	Bruce Sutter 86/78	25.00
BSU11	Bruce Sutter 87/36	25.00
KT5	Kent Tekulve 81/17	20.00
KT6	Kent Tekulve 82/36	15.00
KT7	Kent Tekulve 84/71	15.00
KT8	Kent Tekulve 84/71	15.00
KT9	Kent Tekulve 85/41	15.00
KT10	Kent Tekulve 86/57	15.00
KT11	Kent Tekulve 87/34	15.00
KT12	Kent Tekulve 88/20	20.00
LT2	Luis Tiant 68/16	40.00
LT11	Luis Tiant 79/22	30.00
LT12	Luis Tiant 80/23	30.00
LT13	Luis Tiant 81/20	30.00
LT14	Luis Tiant 82/51	15.00
LT15	Luis Tiant 83/58	15.00
AT2	Alan Trammell 80/17	30.00
AT3	Alan Trammell 81/26	30.00
AT4	Alan Trammell 83/21	30.00
AT5	Alan Trammell 84/57	30.00
AT7	Alan Trammell 85/39	30.00
AT8	Alan Trammell 86/23	30.00
AT9	Alan Trammell 87/15	30.00
AV2	Andy Van Slyke 85/35	35.00
AV3	Andy Van Slyke 86/37	30.00
AV4	Andy Van Slyke 87/178	25.00
AV5	Andy Van Slyke 87 TR/130	25.00
FV3	Frank Viola 85/23	15.00
FV4	Frank Viola 86/99	15.00
FV5	Frank Viola 87/209	15.00
TW2	Tim Wallach 83/49	15.00
TW4	Tim Wallach 85/46	15.00

TW5	Tim Wallach 86/44	15.00
TW6	Tim Wallach 87/197	10.00
BW3	Bob Watson 79/77	10.00
BW6	Bob Watson 82/23	20.00
BW7	Bob Watson 83/93	10.00
BW8	Bob Watson 84/64	10.00
BW9	Bob Watson 85/68	10.00
EW4	Earl Weaver 78 MG/52	15.00
EW5	Earl Weaver 83 MG/38	20.00
EW7	Earl Weaver 86 MG/107	15.00
EW8	Earl Weaver 87 MG/175	10.00
WW2	Walt Weiss 89/34	10.00
WW3	Walt Weiss 91/30	10.00
WW4	Walt Weiss 92/71	10.00
WW7	Walt Weiss 97/49	10.00
WW10	Walt Weiss 99/40	10.00
WW11	Walt Weiss 01/51	10.00
MW2	Mookie Wilson 82/20	20.00
MW3	Mookie Wilson 83/41	15.00
MW5	Mookie Wilson 85/51	15.00
MW6	Mookie Wilson 86/47	15.00
MW7	Mookie Wilson 87/67	15.00
CY4	Carl Yastrzemski 80/60	100.00
CY5	Carl Yastrzemski 81/35	120.00
SY5	Steve Yeager 79/23	25.00
SY9	Steve Yeager 83/80	10.00
SY12	Steve Yeager 86/47	15.00
SY13	Steve Yeager 86 TR/100	10.00
RY5	Robin Yount 80/18	100.00
RY6	Robin Yount 81/23	100.00
RY9	Robin Yount 84/15	125.00
RY11	Robin Yount 86/21	100.00

2004 Topps Pristine

	NM/M
Complete Set (190):	
Common Player:	1.00
Common Rookie:	1.50
Common Uncommon RC:	3.00
Production 999	
Common Rare RC:	6.00
Production 499	
Pack (8):	35.00
Box (5):	140.00

1	Jim Thome	2.00
2	Ryan Klesko	1.00
3	Ichiro Suzuki	4.00
4	Rocco Baldelli	1.00
5	Vernon Wells	1.00
6	Javier Vazquez	1.00
7	Billy Wagner	1.00
8	Jose Reyes	1.00
9	Lance Berkman	1.00
10	Alex Rodriguez	6.00
11	Pat Burrell	1.00
12	Mark Mulder	1.00
13	Mike Piazza	3.00
14	Miguel Cabrera	2.00
15	Larry Walker	1.00
16	Carlos Lee	1.00
17	Mark Prior	2.00
18	Pedro J. Martinez	2.00
19	Melvin Mora	1.00
20	Sammy Sosa	4.00
21	Bartolo Colon	1.00
22	Luis Gonzalez	1.00
23	Marcus Giles	1.00
24	Ken Griffey Jr.	3.00
25	Ivan Rodriguez	1.50
26	Carlos Beltran	1.50
27	Geoff Jenkins	1.00
28	Nick Johnson	1.00
29	Gary Sheffield	1.50
30	Alfonso Soriano	2.00
31	Scott Rolen	2.00
32	Garret Anderson	1.00
33	Richie Sexson	1.00
34	Curt Schilling	1.50
35	Greg Maddux	3.00
36	Adam Dunn	1.50
37	Preston Wilson	1.00
38	Josh Beckett	1.50
39	Roy Oswalt	1.00
40	Derek Jeter	6.00
41	Jason Kendall	1.00
42	Bret Boone	1.00
43	Torii Hunter	1.00
44	Roy Halladay	1.00
45	Edgar Renteria	1.00
46	Troy Glaus	1.00
47	Chipper Jones	2.00
48	Manny Ramirez	1.50
49	C.C. Sabathia	1.00
50	Albert Pujols	5.00
51	Randy Wolf	1.00
52	Eric Chavez	1.00

53	Kevin Brown	1.00
54	Cliff Floyd	1.00
55	Jeff Bagwell	1.50
56	Frank Thomas	1.50
57	David Ortiz	1.50
58	Rafael Palmeiro	1.50
59	Randy Johnson	2.00
60	Vladimir Guerrero	2.00
61	Carlos Delgado	1.00
62	Hank Blalock	1.50
63	Jim Edmonds	1.00
64	Jason Schmidt	1.00
65	Mike Lieberthal	1.00
66	Tim Hudson	1.00
67	Jorge Posada	1.00
68	Jose Vidro	1.00
69	Eric Gagne	1.00
70	Roger Clemens	5.00
71	Mike Lowell	1.00
72	Dontrelle Willis	1.00
73	Austin Kearns	1.00
74	Kerry Wood	2.00
75	Miguel Tejada	1.50
76	Bobby Abreu	1.00
77	Edgar Martinez	1.00
78	Joe Mauer	1.00
79	Mike Sweeney	1.00
80	Jason Giambi	1.00
81	Mark Teixeira	1.50
82	Aubrey Huff	1.00
83	Brian Giles	1.00
84	Barry Zito	1.00
85	Mike Mussina	1.50
86	Brandon Webb	1.00
87	Andruw Jones	1.50
88	Javy Lopez	1.00
89	Bill Mueller	1.00
90	Scott Podsednik	1.00
91	Moises Alou	1.00
92	Esteban Loaiza	1.00
93	Magglio Ordonez	1.00
94	Jeff Kent	1.00
95	Todd Helton	1.50
96	Juan Pierre	1.00
97	Jody Gerut	1.00
98	Angel Berroa	1.00
99	Shawn Green	1.00
100	Nomar Garciaparra	3.00
101	David Aardsma/C	1.50
102	David Aardsma/U	4.00
103	David Aardsma/R	8.00
104	Erick Aybar/C RC	5.00
105	Erick Aybar/U RC	10.00
106	Erick Aybar/R RC	15.00
107	Chad Bentz/C RC	1.50
108	Chad Bentz/U RC	3.00
109	Chad Bentz/R RC	6.00
110	Travis Blackley/C	1.50
111	Travis Blackley/U RC	3.00
112	Travis Blackley/R RC	6.00
113	Bobby Brownlie/C RC	2.00
114	Bobby Brownlie/U RC	3.00
115	Bobby Brownlie/R RC	6.00
116	Alberto Callaspo/C RC	3.00
117	Alberto Callaspo/U RC	5.00
118	Alberto Callaspo/R RC	8.00
119	Kazuo Matsui/C RC	4.00
120	Kazuo Matsui/U RC	5.00
121	Kazuo Matsui/R RC	8.00
122	Jesse Crain/C	2.00
123	Jesse Crain/U	3.00
124	Jesse Crain/R	5.00
125	Howie Kendrick/C RC	8.00
126	Howie Kendrick/U RC	10.00
127	Howie Kendrick/R RC	15.00
128	Blake Hawksworth/C RC	1.50
129	Blake Hawksworth/U RC	3.00
130	Blake Hawksworth/R RC	6.00
131	Conor Jackson/C	2.00
132	Conor Jackson/U	5.00
133	Conor Jackson/R	8.00
134	Paul Maholm/C RC	1.50
135	Paul Maholm/U RC	3.00
136	Paul Maholm/R RC	6.00
137	Lastings Milledge/C	3.00
138	Lastings Milledge/U	5.00
139	Lastings Milledge/R	8.00
140	Matt Moses/C	2.00
141	Matt Moses/U	3.00
142	Matt Moses/R	5.00
143	David Murphy/C	1.50
144	David Murphy/U	3.00
145	David Murphy/R	6.00
146	Dioner Navarro/C RC	3.00
147	Dioner Navarro/U RC	3.00
148	Dioner Navarro/R RC	6.00
149	Dustin Nippert/C RC	1.50
150	Dustin Nippert/U RC	3.00
151	Dustin Nippert/R RC	6.00
152	Vito Chiaravalloti/C RC	2.00
153	Vito Chiaravalloti/U RC	3.00
154	Vito Chiaravalloti/R RC	6.00
155	Akinori Otsuka/C RC	2.00
156	Akinori Otsuka/U RC	3.00
157	Akinori Otsuka/R RC	5.00
158	Casey Daigle/C RC	1.50
159	Casey Daigle/U RC	3.00
160	Casey Daigle/R RC	6.00
161	Carlos Quentin/C	5.00
162	Carlos Quentin/U	10.00
163	Carlos Quentin	15.00
164	Omar Quintanilla/C	2.00
165	Omar Quintanilla/U	3.00
166	Omar Quintanilla/R	5.00
167	Chris Saenz/C RC	1.50
168	Chris Saenz/U RC	3.00
169	Chris Saenz/R RC	6.00
170	Ervin Santana/C RC	3.00

171	Ervin Santana/U RC	5.00
172	Ervin Santana/R RC	10.00
173	Chris Shelton/C RC	3.00
174	Chris Shelton/U RC	3.00
175	Chris Shelton/R RC	5.00
176	Kyle Sleeth/C	1.50
177	Kyle Sleeth/U	3.00
178	Kyle Sleeth/R	6.00
179	Brad Snyder/U	2.00
180	Brad Snyder/U	3.00
181	Brad Snyder/R	5.00
182	Tim Stauffer/C	2.00
183	Tim Stauffer/U	3.00
184	Tim Stauffer/R	5.00
185	Shingo Takatsu/C RC	2.00
186	Shingo Takatsu/U RC	4.00
187	Shingo Takatsu/R RC	6.00
188	Merkin Valdez/C RC	1.50
189	Merkin Valdez/U RC	3.00
190	Merkin Valdez/R RC	6.00

Refractors

Veterans (1-100):		4-8X
Production 49		
Common RC's:		.75-1.5X
Production 999		
UnCommon RC's:		1-2X
Production 399		
Rare RC's:		1.5-3X
Production 49		

Gold Refractors

Veterans (1-100):		4-8X
Common RC's:		4-8X
Uncommon RC's:		3-5X
Rare RC's:		1.5-3X
Production 41 Sets		

Fantasy Favorite Relics

	NM/M
Common Player:	4.00
Refractor:	2-4X
Production 25 Sets	

MA	Moises Alou	6.00
JB	Jeff Bagwell	8.00
RB	Rocco Baldelli	6.00
AB	Angel Berroa	4.00
BB	Bret Boone	4.00
JD	Johnny Damon	8.00
CD	Carlos Delgado	8.00
RF	Rafael Furcal	4.00
RFJ	Rafael Furcal	4.00
EG	Eric Gagne	10.00
NG	Nomar Garciaparra	10.00
SG	Shawn Green	4.00
MG	Mark Grudzielanek	4.00
VG	Vladimir Guerrero	8.00
THE	Todd Helton	8.00
TH	Tim Hudson	6.00
DJ	Derek Jeter	20.00
AJ	Andruw Jones	6.00
CJ	Chipper Jones	8.00
CK	Corey Koskie	4.00
KL	Kenny Lofton	4.00
PM	Pedro J. Martinez	8.00
MPI	Mike Piazza	10.00
MP	Mark Prior	8.00
AP	Albert Pujols	15.00
AR	Alex Rodriguez	12.00
JR	Jimmy Rollins	4.00
MT	Mark Teixeira	4.00
FT	Frank Thomas	8.00
JT	Jim Thome	10.00
JV	Jose Vidro	4.00
LW	Larry Walker	4.00
BW	Brandon Webb	4.00
PW	Preston Wilson	4.00
KW	Kerry Wood	8.00

Going, Going, Gone! Relics

	NM/M
Common Player:	4.00
Refractor:	2-4X
Production 25 Sets	

LB	Lance Berkman	4.00
BB	Bret Boone	4.00
AD	Adam Dunn	8.00

JG	Juan Gonzalez	6.00
LG	Luis Gonzalez	4.00
VG	Vladimir Guerrero	8.00
LG	Luis Gonzalez	4.00
TH	Todd Helton	8.00
CJ	Chipper Jones	8.00
JJ	Jacque Jones	4.00
JK	Jeff Kent	4.00
RK	Ryan Klesko	4.00
MO	Magglio Ordonez	4.00
DO	David Ortiz	10.00
MP	Mike Piazza	10.00
AP	Albert Pujols	15.00
MR	Manny Ramirez	8.00
AR	Alex Rodriguez	12.00
SR	Scott Rolen	8.00
AS	Alfonso Soriano	8.00
SS	Sammy Sosa	10.00
FT	Frank Thomas	8.00
JT	Jim Thome	10.00
VW	Vernon Wells	4.00

Key Acquisitions Relics

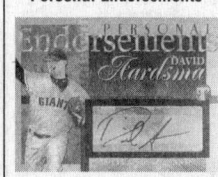

	NM/M
Common Player:	4.00
Inserted 1:8	
Refractors:	2-4X
Production 25 Sets	

HC	Hee Seop Choi	4.00
JG	Juan Gonzalez	6.00
VG	Vladimir Guerrero	8.00
JL	Javy Lopez	4.00
AR	Alex Rodriguez	12.00
IR	Ivan Rodriguez	8.00
GS	Gary Sheffield	6.00
AS	Alfonso Soriano	8.00

Mini

	NM/M
Common Player:	2.00
Inserted 1:5	

DA	David Aardsma	5.00
EA	Erick Aybar	4.00
VC	Vito Chiaravalloti	3.00
NG	Nomar Garciaparra	4.00
JG	Jason Giambi	2.00
VG	Vladimir Guerrero	4.00
BH	Blake Hawksworth	4.00
CJA	Conor Jackson	4.00
DJ	Derek Jeter	6.00
CJ	Chipper Jones	3.00
HK	Howie Kendrick	10.00
KM	Kazuo Matsui	3.00
LM	Lastings Milledge	6.00
MM	Matt Moses	4.00
DM	David Murphy	3.00
DN	Dioner Navarro	10.00
AO	Akinori Otsuka	3.00
MPI	Mike Piazza	3.00
MP	Mark Prior	3.00
AP	Albert Pujols	6.00
AR	Alex Rodriguez	4.00
KS	Kyle Sleeth	4.00
SS	Sammy Sosa	4.00
TS	Tim Stauffer	3.00
IS	Ichiro Suzuki	5.00
ST	Shingo Takatsu	3.00
JT	Jim Thome	3.00
MV	Merkin Valdez	3.00
DW	Dontrelle Willis	3.00
KW	Kerry Wood	4.00

Mini Relics

	NM/M
Common Player:	5.00
Inserted 1:51	

JB	Jeff Bagwell	20.00
EG	Eric Gagne	15.00
NG	Nomar Garciaparra	12.00
CJ	Chipper Jones	12.00
PM	Pedro J. Martinez	12.00
MPI	Mike Piazza	12.00
MP	Mark Prior	12.00
AP	Albert Pujols	25.00
PW	Preston Wilson	5.00
KW	Kerry Wood	10.00

Patch Place Relics

	NM/M
Common Player:	10.00

	Refractor:	No Pricing
	Production 10 Sets	
JB	Jeff Bagwell	20.00
RB	Rocco Baldelli	12.00
JBE	Josh Beckett	15.00
BB	Bret Boone	10.00
LC	Luis Castillo	10.00
CC	Chin-Feng Chen	40.00
CD	Carlos Delgado	10.00
AD	Adam Dunn	15.00
RF	Rafael Furcal	10.00
EG	Eric Gagne	15.00
NG	Nomar Garciaparra	40.00
LG	Luis Gonzalez	10.00
SG	Shawn Green	10.00
THE	Todd Helton	15.00
TH	Tim Hudson	10.00
RJ	Randy Johnson	20.00
AJ	Andruw Jones	10.00
CJ	Chipper Jones	15.00
AK	Austin Kearns	10.00
PL	Paul LoDuca	10.00
ML	Mike Lowell	10.00
PM	Pedro J. Martinez	20.00
MPI	Mike Piazza	35.00
MP	Mark Prior	20.00
AP	Albert Pujols	40.00
JR	Jose Reyes	15.00
JS	John Smoltz	15.00
SS	Sammy Sosa	10.00
FT	Frank Thomas	20.00
DW	Dontrelle Willis	10.00
PW	Preston Wilson	10.00
KW	Kerry Wood	20.00
BZ	Barry Zito	15.00

Personal Endorsements

	NM/M
Common Autograph:	6.00
Golds:	1.5-3X
Production 25 Sets	

DA	David Aardsma	15.00
GA	Garret Anderson	10.00
LB	Lance Berkman	20.00
HB	Hank Blalock	20.00
MC	Miguel Cabrera	30.00
VC	Vito Chiaravalloti	10.00
BC	Bobby Crosby	25.00
JF	Jennie Finch	120.00
MG	Marcus Giles	10.00
VG	Vladimir Guerrero	50.00
EH	Estee Harris	10.00
AH	Aubrey Huff	8.00
CJ	Conor Jackson	20.00
CL	Chris Lubanski	10.00
JM	Joe Mauer	35.00
WM	Willie Mays	200.00
DM	Dustin McGowan	6.00
BM	Brett Myers	10.00
SP	Scott Podsednik	10.00
JP	Jorge Posada	40.00
AR	Alex Rodriguez	150.00
IR	Ivan Rodriguez	40.00
ES	Ervin Santana	10.00
GS	Gary Sheffield	40.00
GS	Grady Sizemore	25.00
JV	Javier Vazquez	15.00
BW	Brandon Webb	8.00
DY	Delmon Young	15.00

Two of a Kind Autograph

Production 13

1, 2, 3 Triple Relics

	NM/M
Inserted 1:171	
Refractor:	1.5-2X
Production 25 Sets	

NYY	Kenny Lofton, Derek Jeter, Alex Rodriguez	50.00
CHC	Mark Grudzielanek, Alex Gonzalez, Sammy Sosa	40.00
BOS	Johnny Damon, Bill Mueller, Nomar Garciaparra	40.00

2004 Topps Retired Signature Edition

	NM/M
Complete Set (110):	125.00
Common Player:	1.00
Pack (5):	35.00
Box (5):	140.00

1	Willie Mays	6.00
2	Tony Gwynn	3.00
3	Dale Murphy	2.00
4	Lenny Dykstra	1.00
5	Johnny Bench	4.00
6	Bill Buckner	1.00
7	Ferguson Jenkins	1.50
8	George Brett	6.00
9	Ralph Kiner	2.00
10	Ernie Banks	4.00
11	Hal McRae	1.00
12	Lou Brock	2.00
13	Keith Hernandez	1.00
14	Jose Canseco	2.00
15	Whitey Ford	2.50
16	Dave Kingman	1.00
17	Tim Raines	1.00
18	Paul O'Neill	1.50
19	Lou Whitaker	1.00
20	Mike Schmidt	5.00
21	Wally Joyner	1.00
22	Kirk Gibson	1.00
23	Ryne Sandberg	5.00
24	Luis Tiant	1.00
25	Al Kaline	4.00
26	Brooks Robinson	3.00
27	Don Zimmer	1.00
28	Nolan Ryan	6.00
29	Maury Wills	1.00
30	Stan Musial	4.00
31	Garry Maddox	1.00
32	Tom Brunansky	1.00
33	Don Mattingly	5.00
34	Earl Weaver	1.00
35	Bobby Grich	1.00
36	Orlando Cepeda	1.50
37	Alan Trammell	1.50
38	Al Hrabosky	1.00
39	Davey Lopes	1.00
40	Rod Carew	2.00
41	Robin Yount	4.00
42	Dwight Gooden	1.00
43	Andre Dawson	1.50
44	Hank Aaron	6.00
45	Norm Cash	1.00
46	Reggie Jackson	2.50
47	Jim Rice	1.00
48	Carlton Fisk	2.00
49	Dave Parker	1.00
50	Cal Ripken Jr.	6.00
51	Roy Face	1.00
52	Bob Gibson	2.50
53	Jimmy Key	1.00
54	Al Oliver	1.00
55	Don Larsen	1.50
56	Tom Seaver	3.00
57	Tony Armas	1.00
58	Dave Stieb	1.00
59	Will Clark	2.00
60	Duke Snider	2.50
61	Cesar Geronimo	1.00
62	Ron Kittle	1.00
63	Ron Santo	2.00
64	Mickey Rivers	1.00
65	Jimmy Piersall	1.00
66	Ron Swoboda	1.00
67	Kent Hrbek	1.00
68	Dennis Eckersley	1.50
69	Greg Luzinski	1.00
70	Harmon Killebrew	1.50
71	Ron Guidry	1.50
72	Steve Garvey	2.00
73	Andy Van Slyke	1.00
74	Rich "Goose" Gossage	1.00
75	Ozzie Smith	3.00
76	Richie Allen	1.00
77	Vida Blue	1.00
78	Tony Oliva	1.00
79	Darryl Strawberry	2.00
80	Frank Robinson	2.00
81	Bruce Sutter	1.50
82	Dave Concepcion	1.00
83	Darrell Evans	1.00
84	Jack Morris	2.00
85	Bo Jackson	2.00
86	Orel Hershiser	1.00
87	Rob Dibble	1.00
88	Wade Boggs	3.00
89	Fernando Valenzuela	1.00
90	Jim Palmer	2.00
91	George Foster	1.00
92	Mike Scott	1.00
93	Paul Molitor	2.50
94	Gary Carter	2.00
95	Bobby Richardson	1.00
96	Rollie Fingers	1.00
97	Tim McCarver	1.00
98	John Candelaria	1.00
99	Dave Winfield	3.00
100	Yogi Berra	2.00
101	Bill Madlock	1.00
102	Jack McDowell	1.00
103	Luis Aparicio	2.00
104	Graig Nettles	1.00
105	Dave Stewart	1.00
106	Darren Daulton	1.00
107	Gary Gaetti	1.00
108	Tony Fernandez	1.00
109	Buddy Bell	1.00
110	Carl Yastrzemski	4.00

Black

Black (1-110):	4-6X
Production 99 Sets	

Chrome Autographs

		NM/M
	Common Autograph:	10.00
	Inserted 1:1	
	Refractor:	2-4X
	SP Refractor:	.75-2X
	Production 25 Sets	
HA	Hank Aaron/SP/50	320.00
TA	Tony Armas	10.00
EB	Ernie Banks/SP/50	180.00
BBE	Buddy Bell	12.00
JB	Johnny Bench/SP/75	80.00
YB	Yogi Berra/SP/75	80.00
VB	Vida Blue	10.00
WB	Wade Boggs	40.00
TB	Tom Brunansky	10.00
BB	Bill Buckner	12.00
JC	John Candelaria	20.00
JCA	Jose Canseco	35.00
RC	Rod Carew	35.00
GC	Gary Carter	20.00
OC	Orlando Cepeda	15.00
DD	Darren Daulton	10.00
BD	Bucky Dent	10.00
RD	Rob Dibble	12.00
DEC	Dennis Eckersley	30.00
DE	Darrell Evans	10.00
RF	Roy Face	15.00
TF	Tony Fernandez	10.00
WF	Whitey Ford/SP/75	90.00
RF	Rollie Fingers	15.00
CF	Carlton Fisk	40.00
GF	George Foster	12.00
CG	Cesar Geronimo	25.00
BG	Bob Gibson/SP/75	75.00
KG	Kirk Gibson	10.00
DG	Dwight Gooden/SP/75	40.00
GG	Rich "Goose" Gossage	15.00
BGR	Bobby Grich	10.00
TG	Tony Gwynn/SP/75	75.00
OH	Orel Hershiser	25.00
AH	Al Hrabosky	10.00
FJ	Ferguson Jenkins	15.00
WJ	Wally Joyner	10.00
JK	Jimmy Key	10.00
RK	Ralph Kiner	50.00
RKI	Ron Kittle	10.00
DL	Davey Lopes	10.00
GL	Greg Luzinski	15.00
BM	Bill Madlock	10.00
DM	Don Mattingly/SP/75	100.00
JM	Jack McDowell	10.00
PM	Paul Molitor	50.00
DM	Dale Murphy	25.00
SM	Stan Musial/SP/50	160.00
GN	Graig Nettles	12.00
TO	Tony Oliva	20.00
AO	Al Oliver	12.00
PO	Paul O'Neill	40.00
DP	Dave Parker	20.00
JP	Jimmy Piersall	15.00
BR	Bobby Richardson	15.00
CR	Cal Ripken Jr./SP/25	275.00
BRO	Brooks Robinson/SP/75	90.00
FR	Frank Robinson	30.00
NR	Nolan Ryan/SP/25	300.00
RSA	Ryne Sandberg	75.00
RS	Ron Santo	20.00
MS	Mike Schmidt/SP/75	150.00
TS	Tom Seaver/SP/75	75.00
OS	Ozzie Smith/SP/75	100.00
DSN	Duke Snider/SP/50	90.00
DST	Dave Stieb	12.00
DS	Darryl Strawberry	30.00
BS	Bruce Sutter	25.00
RS	Ron Swoboda	10.00
LT	Luis Tiant	10.00
AT	Alan Trammell	20.00
EW	Earl Weaver	10.00
MW	Maury Wills	10.00
CY	Carl Yastrzemski/SP/25	180.00
RY	Robin Yount/SP/50	125.00
DZ	Don Zimmer	20.00

Chrome Co-Signers

No Pricing
Production 25 Sets

2004 Topps Total

	NM/M
Complete Set (880):	100.00
Common Player:	.10
Pack (10):	1.00
Box (36):	30.00

#	Player	Price
1	Kevin Brown	.25
2	Mike Mordecai	.10
3	Seung Jun Song	.10
4	Mike Maroth	.10
5	Mike Lieberthal	.10
6	Billy Koch	.10
7	Mike Stanton	.10
8	Brad Penny	.10
9	Brooks Kieschnick	.10
10	Carlos Delgado	.40
11	Brady Clark	.10
12	Ramon Martinez	.10
13	Dan Wilson	.10
14	Guillermo Mota	.10
15	Trevor Hoffman	.10
16	Tony Batista	.10
17	Rusty Greer	.10
18	David Weathers	.10
19	Horacio Ramirez	.10
20	Aubrey Huff	.10
21	Casey Blake	.10
22	Ryan Bukvich	.10
23	Garrett Atkins	.10
24	Jose Contreras	.10
25	Chipper Jones	.75
26	Neifi Perez	.10
27	Scott Linebrink	.10
28	Matt Kinney	.10
29	Michael Restovich	.10
30	Scott Rolen	.75
31	John Franco	.10
32	Toby Hall	.10
33	Wily Mo Pena	.10
34	Dennis Tankersley	.10
35	Robb Nen	.10
36	Jose Valverde	.10
37	Chin-Feng Chen	.10
38	Gary Knotts	.10
39	Scott Elarton	.10
40	Bret Boone	.25
41	Josh Phelps	.10
42	Jason Larue	.10
43	Tim Redding	.10
44	Greg Myers	.10
45	Darin Erstad	.25
46	Kip Wells	.10
47	Matt Ford	.10
48	Jerome Williams	.10
49	Brian Meadows	.10
50	Albert Pujols	1.50
51	Kirk Saarloos	.10
52	Scott Eyre	.10
53	John Flaherty	.10
54	Rafael Soriano	.10
55	Shea Hillenbrand	.10
56	Kyle Farnsworth	.10
57	Nate Cornejo	.10
58	Kerry Robinson	.10
59	Yan Vogelsong	.10
60	Ryan Klesko	.20
61	Luke Hudson	.10
62	Justin Morneau	.20
63	Frank Catalanotto	.10
64	Derrick Turnbow	.10
65	Marcus Giles	.10
66	Mark Mulder	.25
67	Matt Anderson	.10
68	Mike Matheny	.10
69	Brian Lawrence	.10
70	Bobby Abreu	.10
71	Damian Moss	.10
72	Richard Hidalgo	.10
73	Mark Kotsay	.10
74	Mike Cameron	.10
75	Troy Glaus	.10
76	Matt Holliday	.25
77	Byung-Hyun Kim	.10
78	Aaron Sele	.10
79	Danny Graves	.10
80	Barry Zito	.40
81	Matt LeCroy	.10
82	Jason Isringhausen	.10
83	Colby Lewis	.10
84	Franklyn German	.10
85	Luis Matos	.10
86	Mike Timlin	.10
87	Miguel Batista	.10
88	John McDonald	.10
89	Joey Eischen	.10
90	Mike Mussina	.50
91	Jack Wilson	.20
92	Aaron Cook	.10
93	John Parrish	.10
94	Jose Valentin	.10
95	Johnny Damon	.20
96	Pat Burrell	.25
97	Brendan Donnelly	.10
98	Lance Carter	.10
99	Omar Daal	.10
100	Ichiro Suzuki	1.00
101	Robin Ventura	.10
102	Brian Shouse	.10
103	Kevin Jarvis	.10
104	Jason Young	.10
105	Moises Alou	.25
106	Wes Obermueller	.10
107	David Segui	.10
108	Mike MacDougal	.10
109	John Buck	.10
110	Gary Sheffield	.25
111	Yorvit Torrealba	.10
112	Matt Kata	.10
113	David Bell	.10
114	Juan Gonzalez	.40
115	Kelvim Escobar	.10
116	Ruben Sierra	.10
117	Todd Wellemeyer	.10
118	Jamie Walker	.10
119	Will Cunnane	.10
120	Cliff Floyd	.10
121	Aramis Ramirez	.40
122	Damaso Marte	.10
123	Juan Castro	.10
124	Chris Woodward	.10
125	Andruw Jones	.50
126	Ben Weber	.10
127	Dee Brown	.10
128	Steve Reed	.10
129	Gabe Kapler	.10
130	Miguel Cabrera	.75
131	Billy McMillon	.10
132	Julio Mateo	.10
133	Preston Wilson	.10
134	Tony Clark	.10
135	Carlos Lee	.20
136	Carlos Baerga	.10
137	Mike Crudale	.10
138	David Ross	.10
139	Josh Fogg	.10
140	Dmitri Young	.10
141	Cliff Lee	.10
142	Mike Lowell	.25
143	Jason Lane	.10
144	Pedro Feliz	.10
145	Ken Griffey Jr.	1.00
146	Dustin Hermanson	.10
147	Scott Hodges	.10
148	Aquilino Lopez	.10
149	Wes Helms	.10
150	Jason Giambi	.50
151	Erasmo Ramirez	.10
152	Sean Burroughs	.10
153	J.T. Snow	.10
154	Eddie Guardado	.10
155	C.C. Sabathia	.10
156	Kyle Lohse	.10
157	Roberto Hernandez	.10
158	Jason Simontacchi	.10
159	Tim Spooneybarger	.10
160	Alfonso Soriano	.50
161	Mike Gonzalez	.10
162	Alex Cora	.10
163	Kevin Gryboski	.10
164	Steve Cox	.10
165	Luis Castillo	.10
166	Odalis Perez	.10
167	Alex Sanchez	.10
168	Robert Mackowiak	.10
169	Francisco Rodriguez	.10
170	Roy Oswalt	.25
171	Omar Infante	.10
172	Ryan Jensen	.10
173	Ben Broussard	.10
174	Mark Hendrickson	.10
175	Manny Ramirez	.50
176	Rob Bell	.10
177	Adam Everett	.10
178	Chris George	.10
179	Ricky Gutierrez	.10
180	Eric Gagne	.40
181	Scott Schoeneweis	.10
182	Kris Benson	.10
183	Amaury Telemaco	.10
184	John Riedling	.10
185	Juan Pierre	.10
186	Ramon Ortiz	.10
187	Luis Rivas	.10
188	Larry Bigbie	.10
189	Robby Hammock	.10
190	Geoff Jenkins	.20
191	Chad Cordero	.10
192	Mark Ellis	.10
193	Mark Loretta	.10
194	Ryan Drese	.10
195	Lance Berkman	.10
196	Kevin Appier	.10
197	Enrique Calero (Kiko)	.10
198	Mickey Callaway	.10
199	Chase Utley	.25
200	Nomar Garciaparra	1.00
201	Kevin Cash	.10
202	Ramiro Mendoza	.10
203	Shane Reynolds	.10
204	Chris Spurling	.10
205	Aaron Guiel	.10
206	Mark Derosa	.10
207	Adam Kennedy	.10
208	Andy Pettitte	.25
209	Rafael Palmeiro	.50
210	Luis Gonzalez	.25
211	Ryan Franklin	.10
212	Bob Wickman	.10
213	Ron Calloway	.10
214	Jae Weong Seo	.10
215	Kazuhisa Ishii	.10
216	Sterling Hitchcock	.10
217	Jimmy Gobble	.10
218	Chad Moeller	.10
219	Jake Peavy	.10
220	John Smoltz	.25
221	Erick Almonte	.10
222	David Wells	.10
223	Brad Lidge	.10
224	Carlos Zambrano	.25
225	Kerry Wood	.75
226	Alex Cintron	.10
227	Javier Lopez	.25
228	Jeremy Griffiths	.10
229	Jon Garland	.10
230	Curt Schilling	.50
231	Alex Gonzalez	.10
232	Jay Gibbons	.10
233	Damian Jackson	.10
234	Jerome Robertson	.10
235	Johan Santana	.10
236	Jose Guillen	.10
237	Jeff Connie	.10
238	Matt Roney	.10
239	Desi Relaford	.10
240	Frank Thomas	.50
241	Danny Patterson	.10
242	Kevin Mench	.10
243	Mike Redmond	.10
244	Jeff Suppan	.10
245	Carl Everett	.10
246	Jack Cressend	.10
247	Matt Mantei	.10
248	Enrique Wilson	.10
249	Craig Counsell	.10
250	Mark Prior	1.50
251	Jared Sandberg	.10
252	Scott Strickland	.10
253	Lew Ford	.10
254	Hee Seop Choi	.10
255	Jason Phillips	.10
256	Jason Jennings	.10
257	Todd Pratt	.10
258	Matt Herges	.10
259	Kerry Ligtenberg	.10
260	Austin Kearns	.25
261	Jay Witasick	.10
262	Tony Armas Jr.	.10
263	Tom Martin	.10
264	Oliver Perez	.10
265	Jorge Posada	.40
266	Joe Beimel	.10
267	Ben Hendrickson	.10
268	Reggie Sanders	.10
269	Julio Lugo	.10
270	Josh Beckett	.40
271	Kyle Snyder	.10
272	Felipe Lopez	.10
273	Kevin Millar	.10
274	Travis Hafner	.20
275	Magglio Ordonez	.10
276	Marlon Byrd	.10
277	Scott Spiezio	.10
278	Mark Corey	.10
279	Tim Salmon	.25
280	Alex Gonzalez	.10
281	Marquis Grissom	.20
282	Miguel Olivo	.10
283	Orlando Hudson	.10
284	Rondell White	.10
285	Jermaine Dye	.10
286	Paul Shuey	.10
287	Brandon Inge	.10
288	B.J. Surhoff	.10
289	Edgar Gonzalez	.10
290	Angel Berroa	.10
291	Claudio Vargas	.10
292	Cesar Izturis	.10
293	Brandon Phillips	.10
294	Jeff Duncan	.10
295	Randy Wolf	.10
296	Barry Larkin	.25
297	Felix Rodriguez	.10
298	Robb Quinlan	.10
299	Brian Jordan	.10
300	Dontrelle Willis	.25
301	Doug Davis	.10
302	Ricky Stone	.10
303	Travis Harper	.10
304	Jaret Wright	.10
305	Edgardo Alfonzo	.10
306	Quinton McCracken	.10
307	Jason Bay	.10
308	Joe Randa	.10
309	Steve Sparks	.10
310	Roy Halladay	.25
311	Antonio Alfonseca	.10
312	Michael Cuddyer	.10
313	John Patterson	.10
314	Chris Widger	.10
315	Shigetoshi Hasegawa	.10
316	Tim Wakefield	.10
317	Scott Hatteberg	.10
318	Mike Remlinger	.10
319	Jose Vizcaino	.10
320	Rocco Baldelli	.25
321	David Riske	.10
322	Steve Karsay	.10
323	Peter Bergeron	.10
324	Jeff Weaver	.10
325	Larry Walker	.25
326	Jack Cust	.10
327	Bo Hart	.10
328	Rod Beck	.10
329	Jose Acevedo	.10
330	Hank Blalock	.40
331	Flash Gordon	.10
332	Brian Fuentes	.10
333	Tomas Perez	.10
334	Lenny Harris	.10
335	Matt Morris	.25
336	Jeremi Gonzalez	.10
337	David Eckstein	.10
338	Aaron Rowand	.10
339	Rick Bauer	.10
340	Jim Edmonds	.25
341	Joe Borowski	.10
342	Eric Dubose	.10
343	D'Angelo Jimenez	.10
344	Tomokazu Ohka	.10
345	Victor Zambrano	.10
346	Joe McEwing	.10
347	Jorge Sosa	.10
348	Keith Ginter	.10
349	A.J. Pierzynski	.10
350	Mike Sweeney	.25
351	Shawn Chacon	.10
352	Matt Clement	.25
353	Vance Wilson	.10
354	Benito Santiago	.10
355	Eric Hinske	.10
356	Vladimir Guerrero	.75
357	Kenny Rogers	.10
358	Aaron Boone	.10
359	Jay Powell	.10
360	Phil Nevin	.10
361	Willie Harris	.10
362	Ty Wigginton	.10
363	Chad Fox	.10
364	Junior Spivey	.10
365	Brandon Webb	.10
366	Brett Myers	.10
367	Alexis Gomez	.10
368	Dave Roberts	.10
369	LaTroy Hawkins	.10
370	Kevin Millwood	.25
371	Brian Schneider	.10
372	Blaine Neal	.10
373	Jeromy Burnitz	.10
374	Ted Lilly	.10
375	Shawn Green	.25
376	Carlos Pena	.10
377	Gil Meche	.10
378	Jeff Bagwell	.50
379	Alex Escobar	.10
380	Erubiel Durazo	.10
381	Cristian Guzman	.10
382	Rocky Biddle	.10
383	Craig Wilson	.25
384	Rey Sanchez	.10
385	Russ Ortiz	.10
386	Freddy Garcia	.10
387	Luis Vizcaino	.10
388	David Ortiz	.40
389	Jose Molina	.10
390	Edgar Martinez	.25
391	Nate Bump	.10
392	Brent Mayne	.10
393	Ray King	.10
394	Paul Wilson	.10
395	Melvin Mora	.10
396	Morgan Ensberg	.10
397	Ramon Hernandez	.10
398	Juan Rincon	.10
399	Ron Mahay	.10
400	Jeff Kent	.25
401	Cal Eldred	.10
402	Mike Difelice	.10
403	Valerio De Los Santos	.10
404	Steve Finley	.10
405	Trot Nixon	.10
406	Kevin Walker	.10
407	John Vander Wal	.10
408	Ray Durham	.10
409	Aaron Heilman	.10
410	Edgar Renteria	.25
411	Mike Hampton	.10
412	Kirk Rueter	.10
413	Jim Mecir	.10
414	Brian Roberts	.10
415	Paul Konerko	.25
416	Reed Johnson	.10
417	Roger Clemens	1.50
418	Coco Crisp	.10
419	Carlos Hernandez	.10
420	Scott Podsednik	.40
421	Miguel Cairo	.10
422	Abraham Nunez	.10
423	Endy Chavez	.10
424	Eric Munson	.10
425	Torii Hunter	.25
426	Ben Howard	.10
427	Chris Gomez	.10
428	Francisco Cordero	.10
429	Jeffrey Hammonds	.10
430	Shannon Stewart	.10
431	Einar Diaz	.10
432	Eric Byrnes	.10
433	Marty Cordova	.10
434	Matt Ginter	.10
435	Victor Martinez	.10
436	Geronimo Gil	.10
437	Grant Balfour	.10
438	Ramon Vazquez	.10
439	Jose Cruz	.10
440	Orlando Cabrera	.10
441	Joe Kennedy	.10
442	Scott Williamson	.10
443	Troy Percival	.10
444	Derrek Lee	.25
445	Runelvys Hernandez	.10
446	Mark Grudzielanek	.10
447	Trey Hodges	.10
448	Jimmy Haynes	.10
449	Eric Milton	.10
450	Todd Helton	.50
451	Gregg Zaun	.10
452	Woody Williams	.10
453	Todd Walker	.10
454	Gary Matthews	.10
455	Fernando Vina	.10
456	Omar Vizquel	.10
457	Roberto Alomar	.40
458	Bill Hall	.10
459	Juan Rivera	.10
460	Tom Glavine	.40
461	Ramon Castro	.10
462	Cory Vance	.10
463	Dan Miceli	.10
464	Lyle Overbay	.10
465	Craig Biggio	.25
466	Ricky Ledee	.10
467	Michael Barrett	.10
468	Jason Anderson	.10
469	Matt Stairs	.10
470	Jarrod Washburn	.10
471	Todd Hundley	.10
472	Grant Roberts	.10
473	Randy Winn	.10
474	Pat Hentgen	.10
475	Jose Vidro	.10
476	Tony Torcato	.10
477	Jeremy Affeldt	.10
478	Carlos Guillen	.10
479	Paul Quantrill	.10
480	Rafael Furcal	.10
481	Adam Melhuse	.10
482	Jerry Hairston	.10
483	Adam Bernero	.10
484	Terrence Long	.10
485	Paul Lo Duca	.10
486	Corey Koskie	.10
487	John Lackey	.10
488	Chad Zerbe	.10
489	Vinny Castilla	.10
490	Corey Patterson	.20
491	John Olerud	.20
492	Josh Bard	.10
493	Darren Dreifort	.10
494	Jason Standridge	.10
495	Ben Sheets	.25
496	Jose Castillo	.10
497	Jay Payton	.10
498	Rob Bowen	.10
499	Bobby Higginson	.10
500	Alex Rodriguez	1.50
501	Octavio Dotel	.10
502	Rheal Cormier	.10
503	Felix Heredia	.10
504	Dan Wright	.10
505	Michael Young	.10
506	Wilfredo Ledezma	.10
507	Sun-Woo Kim	.10
508	Michael Tejera	.10
509	Herbert Perry	.10
510	Esteban Loaiza	.10
511	Alan Embree	.10
512	Ben Davis	.10
513	Greg Colbrunn	.10
514	Josh Hall	.10
515	Raul Ibanez	.10
516	Jayson Werth	.10
517	Corky Miller	.10
518	Jason Marquis	.10
519	Roger Cedeno	.10
520	Adam Dunn	.50
521	Paul Byrd	.10
522	Sandy Alomar	.10
523	Salomon Torres	.10
524	John Halama	.10
525	Mike Piazza	1.00
526	Buddy Groom	.10
527	Adrian Beltre	.25
528	Chad Harville	.10
529	Javier Vazquez	.20
530	Jody Gerut	.10
531	Elmer Dessens	.10
532	B.J. Ryan	.10
533	Chad Durbin	.10
534	Doug Mirabelli	.10
535	Bernie Williams	.40
536	Jeff Davanon	.10
537	Dave Berg	.10
538	Geoff Blum	.10
539	John Thomson	.10
540	Jeremy Bonderman	.10
541	Jeff Zimmerman	.10
542	Derek Lowe	.10
543	Scot Shields	.10
544	Michael Tucker	.10
545	Tim Hudson	.40
546	Ryan Ludwick	.10
547	Rick Reed	.10
548	Placido Polanco	.10
549	Tony Graffanino	.10
550	Garret Anderson	.40
551	Timoniel Perez	.10
552	Jesus Colome	.10
553	R.A. Dickey	.10
554	Tim Worrell	.10
555	Jason Kendall	.10
556	Tom Goodwin	.10
557	Joaquin Benoit	.10
558	Stephen Randolph	.10
559	Miguel Tejada	.40
560	A.J. Burnett	.10
561	Ben Diggins	.10
562	Juan Cruz	.10
563	Zach Day	.10
564	Antonio Perez	.10
565	Jason Schmidt	.25
566	Armando Benitez	.10
567	Denny Neagle	.10
568	Eric Eckenstahler	.10
569	Chan Ho Park	.10
570	Carlos Beltran	.40
571	Brett Tomko	.10
572	Henry Mateo	.10
573	Ken Harvey	.10
574	Matt Lawton	.10
575	Mariano Rivera	.25
576	Darrell May	.10
577	Jamie Moyer	.10
578	Paul Bako	.10
579	Cory Lidle	.10
580	Jacque Jones	.10
581	Jolbert Cabrera	.10
582	Jason Grimsley	.10
583	Danny Kolb	.10
584	Billy Wagner	.10
585	Rich Aurilia	.10
586	Vicente Padilla	.10
587	Oscar Villarreal	.10
588	Rene Reyes	.10
589	Jon Lieber	.10
590	Nick Johnson	.10
591	Bobby Crosby	.10
592	Steve Trachsel	.10
593	Brian Boehringer	.10

No	Player	Price
594	Juan Uribe	.10
595	Bartolo Colon	.20
596	Bobby Hill	.10
597	Andy Van Hekken	.10
598	Carl Pavano	.10
599	Kurt Ainsworth	.10
600	Derek Jeter	2.00
601	Doug Mientkiewicz	.10
602	Orlando Pameiro	.10
603	J.C. Romero	.10
604	Scott Sullivan	.10
605	Brad Radke	.10
606	Fernando Rodney	.10
607	Jim Brower	.10
608	Josh Towers	.10
609	Brad Fullmer	.10
610	Jose Reyes	.25
611	Ryan Wagner	.10
612	Joe Mays	.10
613	Jung Bong	.10
614	Curtis Leskanic	.10
615	Al Leiter	.10
616	Wade Miller	.10
617	Keith Foulke	.10
618	Casey Fossum	.10
619	Craig Monroe	.10
620	Hideo Nomo	.25
621	Bob File	.10
622	Steve Kline	.10
623	Bobby Kielty	.10
624	Dewon Brazelton	.10
625	Eric Chavez	.25
626	Chris Carpenter	.10
627	Trever Miller	.10
628	Jason Davis	.10
629	Jose Jimenez	.10
630	Vernon Wells	.10
631	Kenny Lofton	.25
632	Chad Bradford	.10
633	Brad Wilkerson	.10
634	Pokey Reese	.10
635	Richie Sexson	.40
636	Chin-Hui Tsao	.10
637	Eli Marrero	.10
638	Chris Reitsma	.10
639	Daryle Ward	.10
640	Mark Teixeira	.25
641	Corwin Malone	.10
642	Adam Eaton	.10
643	Jimmy Rollins	.25
644	Brian Anderson	.10
645	Bill Mueller	.10
646	Jake Westbrook	.10
647	Bengie Molina	.10
648	Jorge Julio	.10
649	Billy Traber	.10
650	Randy Johnson	.75
651	Javy Lopez	.25
652	Doug Glanville	.10
653	Jeff Cirillo	.10
654	Tino Martinez	.10
655	Mark Buehrle	.10
656	Jason Michaels	.10
657	Damian Rolls	.10
658	Rosman Garcia	.10
659	Scott Hairston	.10
660	Carl Crawford	.10
661	Livan Hernandez	.10
662	Danny Bautista	.10
663	Brad Ausmus	.10
664	Juan Acevedo	.10
665	Sean Casey	.10
666	Pedro Martinez	.75
667	Milton Bradley	.10
668	Braden Looper	.10
669	Paul Abbott	.10
670	Joel Pinero	.10
671	Luis Terrero	.10
672	Rodrigo Lopez	.10
673	Joe Crede	.10
674	Mike Koplove	.10
675	Brian Giles	.25
676	Jeff Nelson	.10
677	Russell Branyan	.10
678	Mike DeJean	.10
679	Brian Daubach	.10
680	Ellis Burks	.10
681	Ryan Dempster	.10
682	Cliff Politte	.10
683	Brian Reith	.10
684	Scott Stewart	.10
685	Allan Simpson	.10
686	Shawn Estes	.10
687	Jason Johnson	.10
688	Wil Cordero	.10
689	Kelly Stinnett	.10
690	Jose Lima	.10
691	Gary Bennett	.10
692	T.J. Tucker	.10
693	Shane Spencer	.10
694	Chris Hammond	.10
695	Chris Singleton	.10
696	Xavier Nady	.10
697	Cody Ransom	.10
698	Ron Villone	.10
699	Brook Fordyce	.10
700	Sammy Sosa	1.50
701	Terry Adams	.10
702	Ricardo Rincon	.10
703	Tike Redman	.10
704	Chris Stynes	.10
705	Mark Redman	.10
706	Juan Encarnacion	.10
707	Jhonny Peralta	.10
708	Denny Hocking	.10
709	Ivan Rodriguez	.50
710	Jose Hernandez	.10
711	Brandon Duckworth	.10
712	Dave Burba	.10
713	Joe Nathan	.10
714	Dan Smith	.10
715	Karim Garcia	.10
716	Arthur Rhodes	.10
717	Shawn Wooten	.10
718	Ramon Santiago	.10
719	Luis Ugueto	.10
720	Danys Baez	.10
721	Alfredo Amezaga	.10
722	Sidney Ponson	.10
723	Joe Mauer	.50
724	Jesse Foppert	.10
725	Todd Greene	.10
726	Dan Haren	.10
727	Brandon Larson	.10
728	Bobby Jenks	.10
729	Grady Sizemore	.25
730	Ben Grieve	.10
731	Khalil Greene	.10
732	Chad Gaudin	.10
733	Johnny Estrada	.10
734	Joe Valentine	.10
735	Tim Raines	.10
736	Brandon Claussen	.10
737	Sam Marsonek	.10
738	Delmon Young	.25
739	David Dellucci	.10
740	Sergio Mitre	.10
741	Nick Neugebauer	.10
742	Laynce Nix	.10
743	Joe Thurston	.10
744	Ryan Langerhans	.10
745	Pete LaForest	.10
746	Arnie Munoz	.10
747	Rickie Weeks	.25
748	Neal Cotts	.10
749	Jonny Gomes	.10
750	Jim Thome	.75
751	Jon Rauch	.10
752	Edwin Jackson	.10
753	Ryan Madson	.10
754	Chad Tracy	.10
755	Eddie Perez	.10
756	Joe Borchard	.10
757	Jeremy Guthrie	.10
758	Jose Mesa	.10
759	Doug Waechter	.10
760	J.D. Drew	.25
761	Adam LaRoche	.10
762	Rich Harden	.10
763	Justin Speier	.10
764	Todd Zeile	.10
765	Turk Wendell	.10
766	Mark Bellhorn	.10
767	Mike Jackson	.10
768	Chone Figgins	.10
769	Mike Neu	.10
770	Greg Maddux	.10
771	Frank Brooks	.10
772	Alec Zumwalt RC	.25
773	Glendon Rusch	.10
774	Dustan Mohr	.10
775	Shane Halter	.10
776	Tom Wilson	.10
777	So Taguchi	.10
778	Eric Karros	.10
779	Ramon Nivar	.10
780	Marlon Anderson	.10
781	Brayan Pena	.10
782	Chris O'Riordan	.10
783	Dioner Navarro RC	.50
784	Alberto Callaspo RC	.50
785	Hector Gimenez RC	.25
786	Yadier Molina RC	3.00
787	Kevin Richardson	.25
788	Brian Pilkington	.10
789	Adam Greenberg	.50
790	Ervin Santana RC	1.50
791	Brent Colamarino	.75
792	Ben Himes	.10
793	Todd Self RC	.25
794	Brad Vericker	.25
795	Donald Kelly RC	.25
796	Brock Jacobsen	.25
797	Brock Peterson	.25
798	Carlos Sosa	.50
799	Chad Chop	.10
800	Matt Moses	1.00
801	Chris Aguila RC	.25
802	David Murphy	.50
803	Don Sutton RC	1.00
804	Jereme Milons	.10
805	Jon Coutlangus	.10
806	Greg Thissen	.10
807	Jose Capellan RC	1.00
808	Chad Santos RC	.10
809	Wardell Starling RC	.10
810	Kevin Kouzmanoff	2.00
811	David Davidson	.40
812	Michael Mooney	.10
813	Rodney Choy Foo	.10
814	Reid Gorecki	.10
815	Rudy Guillen RC	1.00
816	Harvey Garcia	.10
817	Warner Madrigal RC	.50
818	Kenny Perez	.10
819	Joaquin Arias RC	.25
820	Benji Dequin	.10
821	Lastings Milledge	2.00
822	Blake Hawksworth RC	.50
823	Estee Harris RC	.10
824	Bobby Brownlie RC	.75
825	Wanell Severino RC	.10
826	Bobby Madritsch	.10
827	Travis Hanson	.40
828	Brandon Medders RC	.25
829	Kevin Howard RC	.50
830	Brian Steffek	.10
831	Terry Jones	.10
832	Anthony Acevedo	.40
833	Kory Casto	.10
834	Brooks Conrad	.40
835	Juan Gutierrez RC	.50
836	Charlie Zink RC	.40
837	David Aardsma	.40
838	Carl Loadenthal	.10
839	Donald Levinski	.10
840	Dustin Nippert RC	.75
841	Calvin Hayes	.10
842	Felix Hernandez RC	4.00
843	Tyler Davidson	.50
844	George Sherrill RC	.10
845	Craig Ansman RC	.10
846	Jeffrey Allison	.10
847	Tommy Murphy RC	.10
848	Jerome Gamble RC	.10
849	Jesse English RC	.10
850	Alex Romero RC	.10
851	Joel Zumaya RC	.50
852	Carlos Quentin	1.00
853	Jose Valdez	.25
854	J.J. Furmaniak RC	.50
855	Juan Cedeno RC	.10
856	Kyle Sleeth	.50
857	Josh Labandeira RC	.25
858	Lee Gwaltney	.10
859	Lincoln Holdzkom RC	.25
860	Ivan Ochoa	.10
861	Luke Anderson	.10
862	Conor Jackson	.50
863	Matt Capps RC	.10
864	Merkin Valdez RC	.75
865	Paul Bacot	.50
866	Erick Aybar RC	1.00
867	Scott Proctor RC	.50
868	Tim Stauffer	.10
869	Matt Creighton RC	.10
870	Zach Miner RC	.50
871	Danny Gonzalez RC	.10
872	Tom Farmer	.10
873	John Santor	.10
874	Logan Kensing RC	.25
875	Vito Chiaravalloti RC	.50
876	Checklist	.10
877	Checklist	.10
878	Checklist	.10
879	Checklist	.10
880	Checklist	.10

Total Production

NM/M

Complete Set (10): 10.00
Common Player: .50
Inserted 1:18

No	Player	Price
TP1	Alex Rodriguez	3.00
TP2	Albert Pujols	3.00
TP3	Sammy Sosa	2.50
TP4	Carlos Delgado	.50
TP5	Gary Sheffield	.50
TP6	Manny Ramirez	1.00
TP7	Jim Thome	1.00
TP8	Todd Helton	.75
TP9	Garret Anderson	.50
TP10	Nomar Garciaparra	2.00

Silver

Stars: 2-3X
Inserted 1:1

Press Plates

No Pricing
Production one for each color.

Autograph

TOTAL SIGNATURES

NM/M

Inserted 1:414 — 8.00

	Player	Price
GB	Grant Balfour	8.00
LB	Larry Bigbie	10.00
BC	Brandon Claussen	8.00
TH	Toby Hall	8.00
JJ	Jimmy Journell	8.00

Total Award Winners

NM/M

Complete Set (30): 20.00
Common Player: .50
Inserted 1:7

No	Player	Price
AW1	Roy Halladay	.50
AW2	Eric Gagne	.50
AW3	Alex Rodriguez	3.00
AW4	Albert Pujols	3.00
AW5	Alex Rodriguez	3.00
AW6	Jorge Posada	.50
AW7	Javy Lopez	.50
AW8	Carlos Delgado	.50
AW9	Todd Helton	.75
AW10	Bret Boone	.50
AW11	Jose Vidro	.50
AW12	Bill Mueller	.50
AW13	Mike Lowell	.50
AW14	Alex Rodriguez	3.00
AW15	Edgar Renteria	.50
AW16	Garret Anderson	.50
AW17	Albert Pujols	3.00
AW18	Manny Ramirez	1.00
AW19	Vernon Wells	.50
AW20	Gary Sheffield	.50
AW21	Edgar Martinez	.50
AW22	Mike Hampton	.50
AW23	Angel Berroa	.50
AW24	Dontrelle Willis	.50
AW25	Keith Foulke	.50
AW26	Eric Gagne	.50
AW27	Alex Rodriguez	3.00
AW28	Albert Pujols	3.00
AW29	Tony Pena	.50
AW30	Jack McKeon	.50

Total Topps

TOTALTOPPS

NM/M

Complete Set (50): 25.00
Common Player: .50
Inserted 1:7

No	Player	Price
TT1	Derek Jeter	3.00
TT2	Jose Reyes	.50
TT3	Miguel Tejada	.50
TT4	Larry Walker	.50
TT5	Frank Thomas	.75
TT6	Carlos Delgado	.50
TT7	Vernon Wells	.50
TT8	Jeff Bagwell	.75
TT9	Jason Giambi	.75
TT10	Mike Lowell	.50
TT11	Shannon Stewart	.50
TT12	Mike Piazza	1.50
TT13	Todd Helton	.75
TT14	Austin Kearns	.50
TT15	Jim Edmonds	.50
TT16	Jose Vidro	.50
TT17	Andruw Jones	.50
TT18	Gary Sheffield	.50
TT19	Eric Chavez	.50
TT20	Magglio Ordonez	.50
TT21	Geoff Jenkins	.50
TT22	Ken Griffey Jr.	1.50
TT23	Jeff Kent	.50
TT24	Jorge Posada	.50
TT25	Albert Pujols	2.00
TT26	Javy Lopez	.50
TT27	Alfonso Soriano	1.00
TT28	Brian Giles	.50
TT29	Mike Sweeney	.50
TT30	Miguel Cabrera	1.00
TT31	Luis Gonzalez	.50
TT32	Scott Rolen	1.00
TT33	Jim Thome	1.00
TT34	Garret Anderson	.75
TT35	Vladimir Guerrero	1.00
TT36	Shawn Green	.50
TT37	Hank Blalock	.75
TT38	Marcus Giles	.50
TT39	Torii Hunter	.50
TT40	Sammy Sosa	2.00
TT41	Nomar Garciaparra	2.00
TT42	Bobby Abreu	.50
TT43	Richie Sexson	.75
TT44	Manny Ramirez	.75
TT45	Troy Glaus	.75
TT46	Preston Wilson	.50
TT47	Ivan Rodriguez	.75
TT48	Ichiro Suzuki	1.50
TT49	Chipper Jones	1.00
TT50	Alex Rodriguez	3.00

2004 Topps Traded & Rookies

NM/M

Complete Set (220): 50.00
Common Player: .10
Chrome cards: 2-4X
Pack (10): 4.00
Box (24): 85.00

No	Player	Price
T1	Pokey Reese	.10
T2	Tony Womack	.10
T3	Michael Barrett	.10
T4	Juan Uribe	.10
T5	J.D. Drew	.25
T6	Marlon Anderson	.10
T7	Carlos Guillen	.10
T8	Royce Clayton	.10
T9	Fernando Vina	.10
T10	Milton Bradley	.10
T11	Eddie Perez	.10
T12	Ben Grieve	.10
T13	Brian Jordan	.10
T14	Tony Graffanino	.10
T15	Billy Wagner	.10
T16	Terrence Long	.10
T17	Casey Fossum	.10
T18	Denny Hocking	.10
T19	Reggie Sanders	.10
T20	Javy Lopez	.25
T21	Jay Payton	.10
T22	Cliff Politte	.10
T23	Eddie Guardado	.10
T24	Andy Pettitte	.50
T25	Richie Sexson	.40
T26	Ronnie Belliard	.10
T27	Michael Tucker	.10
T28	Brad Fullmer	.10
T29	Orlando Palmeiro	.10
T30	Bartolo Colon	.10
T31	Larry Walker	.40
T32	Mark Kotsay	.10
T33	Jason Marquis	.10
T34	Dustan Mohr	.10
T35	Javier Vazquez	.10
T36	Nomar Garciaparra	1.50
T37	Tino Martinez	.25
T38	Hee Seop Choi	.10
T39	Damian Miller	.10
T40	Jose Lima	.10
T41	Todd Zeile	.10
T42	Raul Ibanez	.10
T43	Danys Baez	.10
T44	Tony Clark	.10
T45	Greg Maddux	1.00
T46	Craig Counsell	.10
T47	Orlando Cabrera	.25
T48	Jose Cruz Jr.	.10
T49	Kris Benson	.10
T50	Alex Rodriguez	2.00
T51	Steve Finley	.10
T52	Ramon Hernandez	.10
T53	Esteban Loaiza	.10
T54	Ugueth Urbina	.10
T55	Jeff Weaver	.10
T56	Flash Gordon	.10
T57	Jose Contreras	.10
T58	Paul LoDuca	.10
T59	Junior Spivey	.10
T60	Curt Schilling	1.00
T61	Brad Penny	.10
T62	Braden Looper	.10
T63	Miguel Cairo	.10
T64	Juan Encarnacion	.10
T65	Miguel Batista	.10
T66	Terry Francona	.10
T67	Lee Mazzilli	.10
T68	Al Pedrique	.10
T69	Ozzie Guillen	.10
T70	Phil Garner	.10
T71	Matt Bush RC	.50
T72	Homer Bailey RC	1.00
T73	Greg Golson RC	.50
T74	Kyle Waldrop RC	.50
T75	Richie Robnett RC	.50
T76	Jay Rainville RC	.50
T77	Bill Bray RC	.50
T78	Phillip Hughes RC	8.00
T79	Scott Elbert RC	.50
T80	Josh Fields RC	.50
T81	Justin Orenduff RC	.50
T82	Dan Putnam RC	.50
T83	Chris Nelson RC	.50
T84	Blake DeWitt RC	1.00
T85	J.P. Howell RC	.50
T86	Huston Street RC	1.00
T87	Kurt Suzuki RC	1.50
T88	Erick San Pedro RC	.50
T89	Matt Tuiasosopo RC	.50
T90	Matt Macri RC	.50
T91	Chad Tracy	.20
T92	Scott Hairston	.20
T93	Jonny Gomes	.20
T94	Chin-Feng Chen	.20
T95	Chien-Ming Wang	.50
T96	Dustin McGowan	.20
T97	Chris Burke	.20
T98	Denny Bautista	.20
T99	Preston Larrison	.20
T100	Kevin Youkilis	.40
T101	John Maine	.20
T102	Guillermo Quiroz	.20
T103	David Krynzel	.20
T104	David Kelton	.20
T105	Edwin Encarnacion	.20
T106	Chad Gaudin	.20
T107	Sergio Mitre	.20
T108	Laynce Nix	.20
T109	David Parrish	.20
T110	Brandon Claussen	.20
T111	Frank Francisco RC	.25
T112	Brian Dallimore RC	.25
T113	Jim Crowell RC	.25
T114	Andres Blanco RC	.25
T115	Eduardo Villacis RC	.50
T116	Kazuhito Tadano RC	.25
T117	Aaron Baldiris RC	.25
T118	Justin Germano RC	.25
T119	Joey Gathright RC	.50
T120	Franklyn Gracesqui RC	.25
T121	Chin-Lung Hu RC	.50
T122	Scott Olsen RC	1.00
T123	Tyler Davidson	.50
T124	Fausto Carmona RC	1.00
T125	Tim Hutting RC	.50
T126	Ryan Meaux RC	.25
T127	Jon Connolly RC	.25
T128	Hector Made RC	.75
T129	Jamie Brown RC	.25
T130	Paul McAnulty RC	.50
T131	Chris Saenz RC	.25
T132	Marland Williams RC	.25
T133	Mike Huggins RC	.25
T134	Jesse Crain	.50
T135	Chad Bentz RC	.25
T136	Kazuo Matsui RC	.75
T137	Paul Maholm RC	.75
T138	Brock Jacobsen RC	.25
T139	Casey Daigle RC	.25
T140	Nyjer Morgan RC	.50
T141	Tom Mastny RC	.25
T142	Kody Kirkland RC	.50
T143	Jose Capellan RC	.50
T144	Felix Hernandez RC	5.00
T145	Shawn Hill RC	.25
T146	Danny Gonzalez RC	.25
T147	Scott Dohmann RC	.50
T148	Tommy Murphy RC	.50
T149	Akinori Otsuka RC	.25
T150	Miguel Perez RC	.50
T151	Mike Rouse	.25
T152	Ramon Ramirez RC	.50
T153	Luke Hughes RC	.25
T154	Howie Kendrick RC	2.00
T155	Ryan Budde	.25
T156	Charlie Zink RC	.25
T157	Warner Madrigal RC	.50
T158	Jason Szuminski RC	.25
T159	Chad Chop RC	.25
T160	Shingo Takatsu RC	.50
T161	Matt Lemanczyk RC	.50
T162	Wardell Starling RC	.50
T163	Nick Gorneault RC	.50
T164	Scott Proctor RC	.50
T165	Brooks Conrad RC	.50
T166	Hector Gimenez RC	.50
T167	Kevin Howard RC	.50
T168	Vince Perkins RC	.25
T169	Brock Peterson RC	.25
T170	Chris Shelton RC	.50
T171	Erick Aybar RC	1.00
T172	Paul Bacot RC	.25
T173	Matt Capps RC	.50
T174	Kory Casto RC	.25
T175	Juan Cedeno RC	.25
T176	Vito Chiaravalloti RC	.50
T177	Alec Zumwalt RC	.50
T178	J.J. Furmaniak RC	.50
T179	Lee Gwaltney RC	.50
T180	Donald Kelly RC	.25
T181	Benji Dequin RC	.25
T182	Brant Colamarino RC	.75
T183	Juan Gutierrez RC	.50
T184	Carl Loadenthal RC	.50
T185	Ricky Nolasco RC	1.50
T186	Jeff Salazar RC	.50
T187	Rob Tejeda RC	.50
T188	Alex Romero RC	.25

T189	Yoann Torrealba RC	.25
T190	Carlos Sosa RC	.25
T191	Tim Bittner RC	.50
T192	Chris Aguila RC	.25
T193	Jason Frasor RC	.25
T194	Reid Gorecki RC	.50
T195	Dustin Nippert RC	.25
T196	Javier Guzman RC	.25
T197	Harvey Garcia RC	.25
T198	Ivan Ochoa RC	.25
T199	Dave Wallace RC	.25
T200	Joel Zumaya RC	1.00
T201	Casey Kopitzke RC	.25
T202	Lincoln Holdzkom RC	.25
T203	Chad Santos RC	.25
T204	Brian Pilkington RC	.25
T205	Terry Jones RC	.25
T206	Jerome Gamble RC	.25
T207	Brad Eldred RC	.50
T208	David Pauley RC	.50
T209	Kevin Davidson RC	.25
T210	Damaso Espino RC	.25
T211	Tom Farmer RC	.50
T212	Michael Mooney RC	.25
T213	James Tomlin RC	.25
T214	Greg Thissen RC	.25
T215	Calvin Hayes RC	.25
T216	Fernando Cortez RC	.25
T217	Sergio Silva RC	.25
T218	Jon DeVries RC	.25
T219	Don Sutton RC	1.00
T220	Leo Nunez RC	.25
T221	Barry Bonds HTA Redemption	5.00

Gold
Stars: 5-10X
Rookies: 2-3X
Production 2,004 Sets

Blue Refractor
No Pricing
Production One Set

Chrome Refractor
Stars: 4-8X
Rookies: 2-4X
Inserted 1:12

X-Fractor
No Pricing
Production 20 Sets

Printing Plates
No pricing due to scarcity.

Dual Transactions Relic
NM/M
Common Player:
Inserted 1:562

RP	Rafael Palmeiro	15.00
AR	Alex Rodriguez	25.00
CS	Curt Schilling	15.00

Future Phenoms
NM/M
Common Player: 5.00

KC	Kevin Cash	5.00
BC	Bobby Crosby	10.00
ED	Eric Duncan	5.00
AG	Adrian Gonzalez	8.00
NG	Nick Green	5.00
JH	J.J. Hardy	5.00
EJ	Edwin Jackson	5.00
MM	Mark Malaska	5.00
VM	Victor Martinez	8.00
KM	Kazuo Matsui	5.00
LM	Lastings Milledge	15.00
JM	Justin Morneau	10.00
DN	Dioner Navarro	8.00
RN	Ramon Nivar	5.00
BU	B.J. Upton	12.00
JW	Jayson Werth	10.00
DY	Delmon Young	10.00

Hall of Fame Relic
NM/M
Common Player:

DE	Dennis Eckersley	10.00
PM	Paul Molitor	15.00

Hall of Fame Dual Relic
NM/M
Inserted 1:3,388

ME	Paul Molitor, Dennis Eckersley	30.00

Signature Cuts
No Pricing
Production One Set

Signature Moves
NM/M
Common Autograph: 10.00

MB	Milton Bradley	15.00
MK	Mark Kotsay	10.00
EM	Eli Marrero	10.00
MN	Mike Neu	10.00
AR	Alex Rodriguez	160.00
JV	Javier Vazquez	10.00
FV	Fernando Vina	10.00
AW	Adam Wainwright	35.00

Transactions Relics
NM/M
Common Player: 5.00
Inserted 1:106

RA	Roberto Alomar	8.00
JB	Jeromy Burnitz	5.00

HC	Hee Seop Choi	5.00
RC	Roger Clemens	15.00
CE	Carl Everett	5.00
JG	Juan Gonzalez	8.00
VG	Vladimir Guerrero	10.00
BJ	Brian Jordan	5.00
KL	Kenny Lofton	5.00
JL	Javy Lopez	5.00
RP	Rafael Palmeiro	8.00
AP	Andy Pettitte	8.00
AR	Alex Rodriguez	25.00
IR	Ivan Rodriguez	10.00
RS	Reggie Sanders	5.00
RLS	Richie Sexson	8.00
GS	Gary Sheffield	10.00
MT	Miguel Tejada	8.00
RW	Rondell White	5.00

2004 Topps Tribute HOF

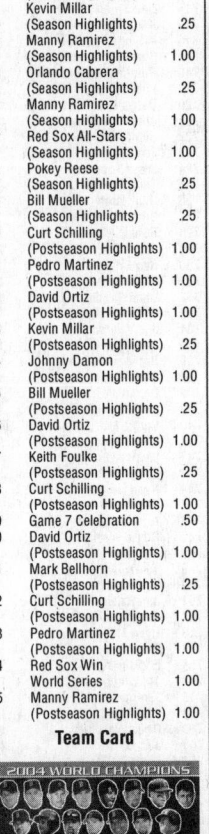

	NM/M
Complete Set (80):	120.00
Common Player:	2.00
Pack (5):	50.00
Box (6):	260.00
1 Willie Mays	8.00
2 Richie Ashburn	2.00
3 Babe Ruth	10.00
4 Lou Gehrig	8.00
5 Carl Yastrzemski	5.00
6 Fergie Jenkins	2.00
7 Cool Papa Bell	3.00
8 Johnny Bench	4.00
9 Satchel Paige	4.00
10 Ty Cobb	6.00
11 Robin Roberts	2.00
12 Eddie Mathews	3.00
13 Tom Seaver	3.00
14 Kirby Puckett	3.00
15 Stan Musial	5.00
16 Ralph Kiner	2.00
17 Reggie Jackson	3.00
18 Walter Johnson	4.00
19 Phil Niekro	2.00
20 Mike Schmidt	6.00
21 Brooks Robinson	3.00
22 Jimmie Foxx	4.00
23 Nellie Fox	2.00
24 Joe Morgan	2.00
25 Cy Young	4.00
26 Hank Greenberg	3.00
27 Josh Gibson	3.00
28 Robin Yount	3.00
29 Hoyt Wilhelm	2.00
30 Yogi Berra	4.00
31 Rollie Fingers	2.00
32 Gaylord Perry	2.00
33 Ozzie Smith	4.00
34 Jim Palmer	3.00
35 Harmon Killebrew	4.00
36 Bob Feller	3.00
37 Chuck Klein	2.00
38 Mordecai Brown	2.00
39 Napoleon Lajoie	3.00
40 Al Kaline	3.00
41 Paul Molitor	3.00
42 Jackie Robinson	5.00
43 Mel Ott	3.00
44 Hank Aaron	6.00
45 Rod Carew	2.00
46 Rogers Hornsby	3.00
47 Bob Gibson	2.00
48 Juan Marichal	2.00
49 Bill Mazeroski	2.00
50 Roberto Clemente	8.00
51 Willie McCovey	2.00
52 Red Schoendienst	2.00
53 Nolan Ryan	8.00
54 Dennis Eckersley	2.00
55 Monte Irvin	2.00
56 George Kell	2.00
57 Gary Carter	2.00
58 Tony Perez	2.00
59 Carlton Fisk	2.00
60 Duke Snider	4.00
61 Bobby Doerr	2.00
62 John McGraw	2.00
63 George Sisler	2.00
64 Orlando Cepeda	2.00
65 Earl Weaver	2.00
66 Roy Campanella	3.00
67 Tris Speaker	3.00
68 Sparky Anderson	2.00
69 Willie Stargell	2.00
70 Honus Wagner	3.00
71 Lou Brock	2.00
72 Whitey Ford	3.00
73 George Brett	8.00
74 Luis Aparicio	2.00
75 Ernie Banks	4.00
76 Jim Bunning	2.00
77 Warren Spahn	3.00
78 Jim "Catfish" Hunter	2.00
79 Pee Wee Reese	2.00
80 Frank Robinson	2.00

Gold
Gold Print Run 61-99: 2-3X
Gold p/r 36-60: 2-4X
#'d to last 2 digits of HOF induction yr

Cooperstown Classmates Dual Cut Sig.
No Pricing
Production One Set

Cooperstown Classmates Dual Relic
	NM/M
Common Duo:	20.00
Gold:	.75-1.5X
Production 25	
ME	Paul Molitor, Dennis Eckersley/75	35.00
KK	Chuck Klein, Al Kaline/75	35.00
RB	Nolan Ryan, George Brett/50	60.00
MP	Joe Morgan, Jim Palmer/75	20.00
SK	Duke Snider, Al Kaline/50	60.00
PC	Gaylord Perry, Rod Carew/50	30.00
BY	Johnny Bench, Carl Yastrzemski/75	50.00
CR	Orlando Cepeda, Nolan Ryan/75	60.00
MR	Juan Marichal, Brooks Robinson/50	35.00

Cooperstown Cut Signatures

NM/M
No Pricing
Production One Set

JF	Jimmie Foxx (10/05 Auction)	1,940
MO	Mel Ott (8/05 Auction)	2,025

Cut Signatures
No Pricing
Production One Set

Dual Cut Signatures
No Pricing
Production One Set

Hall of Fame Patches Relics
	NM/M
Common Player:	20.00
Gold:	.75-1.5X

Production 1-25
No pricing for production 15 or less.

GB	George Brett/50	40.00
RC	Rod Carew/100	25.00
DE	Dennis Eckersley/50	25.00
RJ	Reggie Jackson/50	25.00
FR	Frank Robinson/39	35.00
NR	Nolan Ryan/100	50.00
MS	Mike Schmidt/100	40.00
MS2	Mike Schmidt/100	40.00
RY	Robin Yount/35	40.00

Tribute Relics

NM/M
Common Player: 10.00
Golds: 1-30X
Production 25 Sets

HA	Hank Aaron/Bat	5.00
JB	Johnny Bench/Jsy/250	15.00
JB2	Johnny Bench/Bat	5.00
GB	George Brett/Jsy	15.00
GBB	George Brett/Bat	15.00
LBB	Lou Brock/Bat	5.00
GC	Gary Carter/Jsy/200	15.00
GCU	Gary Carter/Jsy	10.00
OC	Orlando Cepeda/Bat/100	20.00
RC	Roberto Clemente/Bat	50.00
TC	Ty Cobb/Jsy/20	275.00
TCB	Ty Cobb/Bat	75.00
CF	Carlton Fisk/Wall/300	20.00
WF	Whitey Ford/Jsy/50	60.00
JF	Jimmie Foxx/Bat/25	100.00
LG	Lou Gehrig/Bat/52	300.00
BG	Bob Gibson/Jsy	15.00
HG	Hank Greenberg/Bat	20.00
RH	Rogers Hornsby/Bat	40.00
RJ	Reggie Jackson/Jsy/110	15.00
RJB	Reggie Jackson/Bat/200	10.00
AK	Al Kaline/Jsy/125	20.00
AKB	Al Kaline/Bat	15.00
HK	Harmon Killebrew/Bat/135	30.00
CK	Chuck Klein/Bat/107	20.00
JMA	Juan Marichal/Jsy/125	10.00
WM1	Willie Mays/Glv/110	150.00
WM2	Willie Mays/Bat	30.00
WM3	Willie Mays/Jsy	30.00
WM4	Willie Mays/Jsy	30.00
WM5	Willie Mays/Jsy	30.00
PM	Paul Molitor/Jsy	10.00
PMB	Paul Molitor/Bat	10.00
JM	Joe Morgan/Jsy	10.00
SM	Stan Musial/Jsy	20.00
MO	Mel Ott/Bat/25	100.00
JP	Jim Palmer/Jsy	10.00
JP2	Jim Palmer/Jsy	10.00
KP	Kirby Puckett/Jsy/175	15.00
KPB	Kirby Puckett/Bat	10.00
BRO	Brooks Robinson/Bat	10.00
FR	Frank Robinson/Jsy	10.00
FRA	Frank Robinson/Jsy	10.00
FRB	Frank Robinson/Bat	10.00
JR	Jackie Robinson/Bat	25.00
BR	Babe Ruth/Bat/163	150.00
NR	Nolan Ryan/Jsy	25.00
NRA	Nolan Ryan/Jsy/425	25.00
NRJ	Nolan Ryan/Jsy	25.00
MS	Mike Schmidt/Jsy/50	30.00
MSB	Mike Schmidt/Bat	15.00
TS	Tom Seaver/Jsy	10.00
GS	George Sisler/Bat/455	25.00
OS	Ozzie Smith/Bat	15.00
DS	Duke Snider/Bat	10.00
TSP	Tris Speaker/Bat/85	120.00
HW	Honus Wagner/Bat/118	120.00
EW	Earl Weaver/Jsy/25	20.00
CY	Carl Yastrzemski/Wall/300	30.00
CYU	Carl Yastrzemski/Jsy	15.00
RY	Robin Yount/Jsy/50	25.00

Tribute Relic Autographs
	NM/M
Common Player:	40.00
Gold:	No Pricing

Production Five Sets

AKB	Al Kaline/95	60.00
BRO	Brooks Robinson/95	50.00
NRJ	Nolan Ryan/95	140.00
EW	Earl Weaver/55	40.00
CYU	Carl Yastrzemski/95	85.00

2004 Topps World Champions Boston Red Sox

	NM/M
Complete Boxed Set (56):	25.00
Common Player:	.25
1 Bronson Arroyo	.25
2 Alan Embree	.25
3 Keith Foulke	.25
4 Curt Leskanic	.25
5 Derek Lowe	.50
6 Pedro Martinez	2.00
7 Ramiro Mendoza	.25
8 Mike Myers	.25
9 Curt Schilling	2.00
10 Mike Timlin	.25
11 Tim Wakefield	.25
12 Scott Williamson	.25
13 Doug Mirabelli	.25
14 Mark Bellhorn	.25
15 Orlando Cabrera	.50
16 Ricky Gutierrez	.25
17 Doug Mientkiewicz	.25
18 Kevin Millar	.50
19 Bill Mueller	.25
20 Pokey Reese	.25
21 Kevin Youkilis	.25
22 Johnny Damon	1.50
23 Gabe Kapler	.25
24 David McCarty	.25
25 Trot Nixon	.25
26 Manny Ramirez	2.00
27 Dave Roberts	.25
28 Ellis Burks	.25
29 David Ortiz	2.00
30 Terry Francona	.25
31 Red Sox Team Card	.50
32 Curt Schilling (Season Highlights)	1.00
33 Kevin Millar (Season Highlights)	.25
34 Manny Ramirez (Season Highlights)	1.00
35 Orlando Cabrera (Season Highlights)	.25
36 Manny Ramirez (Season Highlights)	1.00
37 Red Sox All-Stars (Season Highlights)	1.00
38 Pokey Reese (Season Highlights)	.25
39 Bill Mueller (Season Highlights)	.25
40 Curt Schilling (Postseason Highlights)	1.00
41 Pedro Martinez (Postseason Highlights)	1.00
42 David Ortiz (Postseason Highlights)	1.00
43 Kevin Millar (Postseason Highlights)	.25
44 Johnny Damon (Postseason Highlights)	1.00
45 Bill Mueller (Postseason Highlights)	.25
46 David Ortiz (Postseason Highlights)	1.00
47 Keith Foulke (Postseason Highlights)	1.00
48 Curt Schilling (Postseason Highlights)	1.00
49 Game 7 Celebration (Postseason Highlights)	.50
50 David Ortiz (Postseason Highlights)	1.00
51 Mark Bellhorn (Postseason Highlights)	.25
52 Curt Schilling (Postseason Highlights)	1.00
53 Pedro Martinez (Postseason Highlights)	1.00
54 Red Sox Win World Series	1.00
55 Manny Ramirez (Postseason Highlights)	1.00

Team Card

NM/M
Inserted 1:Set

Red Sox Team Card	1.00

2004 Topps/Poland Spring N.Y. Yankees

This cello-wrapped stadium give-away set was sponsored by the team's bottled water concessionaire. Fronts have poses or action photos with team and sponsor logos in opposite corners. Backs have a close-up repeat of part of the front photo, along with personal data, lifetime stats and logos.

	NM/M
Complete Set (5):	10.00
Common Player:	2.00
1 Goose Gossage	2.00
2 Ron Guidry	2.00
3 Don Mattingly	6.00
4 Don Larsen	2.00
-- Sponsor's Card	.05

2005 Topps

	NM/M
Complete Set (732):	75.00
Factory Holiday Set (742):	80.00
Factory Hobby Set (737):	80.00
Common Player:	.10
Pack (10):	2.00
Box (36):	60.00
1 Alex Rodriguez	1.50
2 Placido Polanco	.10
3 Torii Hunter	.25
4 Lyle Overbay	.10
5 Johnny Damon	.40
6 Johnny Estrada	.10
7 Francisco Rodriguez	.10
8 Jason LaRue	.10
10 Sammy Sosa	1.00
11 Randy Wolf	.10
12 Jason Bay	.25
13 Tom Glavine	.25
14 Michael Tucker	.10
15 Brian Giles	.20
16 Dan Wilson	.10
17 Jim Edmonds	.40
18 Danys Baez	.10
19 Roy Halladay	.50
20 Hank Blalock	.20
21 Darin Erstad	.20
22 Robby Hammock	.10
23 Mike Hampton	.10
24 Mark Bellhorn	.10
25 Jim Thome	.50
26 Scott Schoeneweis	.10
27 Jody Gerut	.10
28 Vinny Castilla	.10
29 Luis Castillo	.10
30 Ivan Rodriguez	.50
31 Craig Biggio	.20
32 Joe Randa	.10
33 Dave Roberts	.10
34 Scott Podsednik	.10
35 Cliff Floyd	.10
36 Livan Hernandez	.10
37 Eric Byrnes	.10
38 Ricky Ledee	.10
39 Jack Wilson	.10
40 Gary Sheffield	.40
41 Chan Ho Park	.10
42 Carl Crawford	.25
43 Miguel Batista	.10
44 David Bell	.10
45 Jeff DaVanon	.10
46 Brandon Webb	.25
47 Bronson Arroyo	.10
48 Melvin Mora	.10
49 David Ortiz	.50
50 Andruw Jones	.40
51 Chone Figgins	.10
52 Danny Graves	.10
53 Preston Wilson	.10
54 Jeremy Bonderman	.10
55 Chad Fox	.10
56 Dan Miceli	.10
57 Jimmy Gobble	.10
58 Darren Dreifort	.10
59 Matt LeCroy	.10
60 Jose Vidro	.10
61 Al Leiter	.10
62 Javier Vazquez	.10
63 Erubiel Durazo	.10
64 Doug Glanville	.10
65 Scot Shields	.10
66 Edgardo Alfonzo	.10
67 Ryan Franklin	.10
68 Francisco Cordero	.10
69 Brett Myers	.10
70 Curt Schilling	.50
71 Matt Kata	.10
72 Mark DeRosa	.10
73 Rodrigo Lopez	.10
74 Tim Wakefield	.10
75 Frank Thomas	.50
76 Jimmy Rollins	.25
77 Barry Zito	.25
78 Hideo Nomo	.25
79 Brad Wilkerson	.10
80 Adam Dunn	.50
81 Billy Traber	.10
82 Fernando Vina	.10
83 Nate Robertson	.10
84 Brad Ausmus	.10
85 Mike Sweeney	.10
86 Kip Wells	.10
87 Doug Mientkiewicz	.10
88 Zach Day	.10
89 Tony Clark	.10
90 Bret Boone	.10
91 Mark Loretta	.10
92 Jerome Williams	.10
93 Randy Winn	.10
94 Marlon Anderson	.10
95 Aubrey Huff	.10
96 Kevin Mench	.10
97 Frank Catalanotto	.10
98 Flash Gordon	.10
99 Scott Hatteberg	.10
100 Albert Pujols	1.50
101 Jose Molina, Bengie Molina	.10
102 Oscar Villarreal	.10
103 Jay Gibbons	.10

#	Player	Price
104	Byung-Hyun Kim	.10
105	Joe Borowski	.10
106	Mark Grudzielanek	.10
107	Mark Buehrle	.10
108	Paul Wilson	.10
109	Ronnie Belliard	.10
110	Larry Walker	.40
111	Tim Redding	.10
112	Hee Seop Choi	.10
113	Darrell May	.10
114	Jose Hernandez	.10
115	Ben Sheets	.25
116	Johan Santana	.40
117	Billy Wagner	.20
118	Mariano Rivera	.25
119	Steve Trachsel	.10
120	Akinori Otsuka	.10
121	Bobby Kielty	.10
122	Felix Rodriguez	.10
123	Raul Ibanez	.10
124	Mike Matheny	.10
125	Vernon Wells	.10
126	Jason Isringhausen	.10
127	Jose Guillen	.10
128	Danny Bautista	.10
129	Marcus Giles	.10
130	Javy Lopez	.25
131	Kevin Millar	.10
132	Kyle Farnsworth	.10
133	Carl Pavano	.10
134	D'Angelo Jimenez	.10
135	Casey Blake	.10
136	Matt Holliday	.25
137	Bobby Higginson	.10
138	Ramon Castro	.10
139	Alex Gonzalez	.10
140	Jeff Kent	.20
141	Aaron Guiel	.10
142	Shawn Green	.25
143	Bill Hall	.10
144	Shannon Stewart	.10
145	Juan Rivera	.10
146	Ty Wigginton	.10
147	Mike Mussina	.50
148	Eric Chavez	.25
149	Randall Simon	.10
150	Vladimir Guerrero	.75
151	Alex Cintron	.10
152	Horacio Ramirez	.10
153	Sidney Ponson	.10
154	Trot Nixon	.10
155	Greg Maddux	1.00
156	Esteban Loaiza	.10
157	Ryan Freel	.10
158	Matt Lawton	.10
159	Shawn Chacon	.10
160	Josh Beckett	.25
161	Ken Harvey	.10
162	Juan Cruz	.10
163	Juan Encarnacion	.10
164	Wes Helms	.10
165	Brad Radke	.10
166	Claudio Vargas	.10
167	Mike Cameron	.10
168	Jose Contreras	.10
169	Bobby Crosby	.10
170	Mike Lieberthal	.10
171	Robert Mackowiak	.10
172	Sean Burroughs	.10
173	J.T. Snow Jr.	.10
174	Paul Konerko	.10
175	Luis Gonzalez	.10
176	John Lackey	.10
177	Antonio Alfonseca	.10
178	Brian Roberts	.10
179	Bill Mueller	.10
180	Carlos Lee	.10
181	Corey Patterson	.25
182	Sean Casey	.25
183	Cliff Lee	.10
184	Jason Jennings	.10
185	Dmitri Young	.10
186	Brad Penny	.10
187	Andy Pettitte	.25
188	Juan Gonzalez	.25
189	Paul LoDuca	.10
190	Jason Phillips	.10
191	Rocky Biddle	.10
192	Lew Ford	.10
193	Mark Mulder	.25
194	Bobby Abreu	.25
195	Jason Kendall	.10
196	Terrence Long	.10
197	A.J. Pierzynski	.10
198	Eddie Guardado	.10
199	So Taguchi	.10
200	Jason Giambi	.25
201	Tony Batista	.10
202	Kyle Lohse	.10
203	Trevor Hoffman	.25
204	Tike Redman	.10
205	Neifi Perez	.10
206	Gil Meche	.10
207	Chris Carpenter	.10
208	Josh Phelps	.10
209	Eric Young	.10
210	Doug Waechter	.10
211	Jarrod Washburn	.10
212	Chad Tracy	.10
213	John Smoltz	.25
214	Jorge Julio	.10
215	Alex Gonzalez	.10
216	Shingo Takatsu	.10
217	Jose Acevedo	.10
218	Jason Davis	.10
219	Shawn Estes	.10
220	Lance Berkman	.25
221	Carlos Guillen	.10

#	Player	Price
222	Jeremy Affeldt	.10
223	Cesar Izturis	.10
224	Scott Sullivan	.10
225	Kazuo Matsui	.25
226	Josh Fogg	.10
227	Jason Schmidt	.25
228	Jason Marquis	.10
229	Scott Spiezio	.10
230	Miguel Tejada	.40
231	Bartolo Colon	.10
232	Jose Valverde	.10
233	Derrek Lee	.25
234	Scott Williamson	.10
235	Joe Crede	.10
236	Cory Lidle	.10
237	Mike MacDougal	.10
238	Eric Gagne	.25
239	Alex Sanchez	.10
240	Miguel Cabrera	.75
241	Luis Rivas	.10
242	Adam Everett	.10
243	Jason Johnson	.10
244	Travis Hafner	.25
245	Jose Valentin	.10
246	Stephen Randolph	.10
247	Rafael Furcal	.25
248	Adam Kennedy	.10
249	Luis Matos	.10
250	Mark Prior	.75
251	Angel Berroa	.10
252	Phil Nevin	.10
253	Oliver Perez	.10
254	Orlando Hudson	.10
255	Victor Zambrano	.10
256	Khalil Greene	.25
257	Tim Worrell	.10
258	Carlos Zambrano	.25
259	Elmer Dessens	.10
260	Gerald Laird	.10
261	Jose Cruz Jr.	.10
262	Michael Barrett	.10
263	Michael Young (Uncorrected error - Photo is Rod Barajas.)	.10
264	Toby Hall	.10
265	Woody Williams	.10
266	Rich Harden	.10
267	Mike Sciscia	.10
268	Al Pedrique	.10
269	Bobby Cox	.10
270	Lee Mazzilli	.10
271	Terry Francona	.10
272	Dusty Baker	.10
273	Ozzie Guillen	.10
274	Dave Miley	.10
275	Eric Wedge	.10
276	Clint Hurdle	.10
277	Alan Trammell	.10
278	Jack McKeon	.10
279	Phil Garner	.10
280	Tony Pena	.10
281	Jim Tracy	.10
282	Ned Yost	.10
283	Ron Gardenhire	.10
284	Frank Robinson	.25
285	Art Howe	.10
286	Joe Torre	.25
287	Ken Macha	.10
288	Larry Bowa	.10
289	Lloyd McClendon	.10
290	Bruce Bochy	.10
291	Felipe Alou	.10
292	Bob Melvin	.10
293	Tony LaRussa	.10
294	Lou Piniella	.10
295	Buck Showalter	.10
296	Carlos Tosca	.10
297	Steven Doetsch RC	.10
298	Melky Cabrera RC	.50
299	Luis Ramirez RC	.10
300	Chris Seddon RC	.10
301	Nate Schierholtz	.50
302	Ian Kinsler RC	2.00
303	Brandon Moss RC	.50
304	Chadd Blasko RC	.10
305	Jeremy West RC	.50
306	Sean Marshall RC	.50
307	Matt DeSalvo RC	.50
308	Ryan Sweeney RC	.50
309	Matt Lindstrom RC	.50
310	Ryan Goleski RC	.50
311	Brett Harper RC	.25
312	Chris Roberson RC	.10
313	Andre Ethier RC	1.50
314	Chris Denorfia RC	.10
315	Ian Bladergroen RC	.75
316	Darren Fenster RC	.10
317	Kevin West RC	.10
318	Chaz Lytle RC	.50
319	James Jurries RC	.10
320	Matt Rogelstad RC	.10
321	Wade Robinson RC	.10
322	Jake Dittler RC	.10
323	Edgar Huerta RC	.10
324	Kole Strayhorn RC	.10
325	Jose Vaquedano RC	.10
326	Elvys Quezada RC	.10
327	John Maine, Val Majewski	.10
328	Rickie Weeks, J.J. Hardy	.10
329	Gabe Gross, Guillermo Quiroz	.10
330	David Wright, Craig Brazell RC	1.50
331	Dallas McPherson, Jeff Mathis	.10
332	Randy Johnson	.10
333	Randy Johnson	.10
334	Ichiro Suzuki	.10

#	Player	Price
335	Ken Griffey Jr.	.10
336	Greg Maddux	.10
337	Ichiro Suzuki, Melvin Mora, Vladimir Guerrero	.10
338	Ichiro Suzuki, Michael Young, Vladimir Guerrero	.10
339	Manny Ramirez, Paul Konerko, David Ortiz	.10
340	Miguel Tejada, David Ortiz, Manny Ramirez	.10
341	Johan Santana, Curt Schilling, Jake Westbrook	.10
342	Johan Santana, Pedro J. Martinez, Curt Schilling	.10
343	Todd Helton, Mark Loretta, Adrian Beltre	.10
344	Juan Pierre, Mark Loretta, Jack Wilson	.10
345	Adrian Beltre, Adam Dunn, Albert Pujols	.10
346	Vinny Castilla, Scott Rolen, Albert Pujols	.10
347	Jake Peavy, Randy Johnson, Ben Sheets	.10
348	Randy Johnson, Ben Sheets, Jason Schmidt	.10
349	Postseason Highlight	.10
350	Postseason Highlight	.10
351	Postseason Highlight	.10
352	Postseason Highlight	.10
353	Postseason Highlight	.10
354	Postseason Highlight	.10
355	Postseason Highlight	.10
356	Paul Konerko	.10
357	Alfonso Soriano	.10
358	Miguel Tejada	.10
359	Melvin Mora	.10
360	Vladimir Guerrero	.10
361	Ichiro Suzuki	.10
362	Manny Ramirez	.25
363	Ivan Rodriguez	.10
364	Johan Santana	.10
365	Paul Konerko	.10
366	David Ortiz	.10
367	Bobby Crosby	.10
368	Sox Celebration WS4	1.50
369	Garret Anderson	.25
370	Randy Johnson	.75
371	Charles Thomas	.10
372	Rafael Palmeiro	.40
373	Kevin Youkilis	.10
374	Freddy Garcia	.10
375	Magglio Ordonez	.10
376	Aaron Harang	.10
377	Grady Sizemore	.25
378	Chin-Hui Tsao	.10
379	Eric Munson	.10
380	Juan Pierre	.10
381	Brad Lidge	.10
382	Brian Anderson	.10
383	Alex Cora	.10
384	Brady Clark	.10
385	Todd Helton	.40
386	Chad Cordero	.10
387	Kris Benson	.10
388	Brad Halsey	.10
389	Jermaine Dye	.10
390	Manny Ramirez	.50
391	Daryle Ward	.10
392	Adam Eaton	.10
393	Brett Tomko	.10
394	Bucky Jacobsen	.10
395	Dontrelle Willis	.40
396	B.J. Upton	.25
397	Rocco Baldelli	.10
398	Ted Lilly	.10
399	Ryan Drese	.10
400	Ichiro Suzuki	1.25
401	Brendan Donnelly	.10
402	Brandon Lyon	.10
403	Nick Green	.10
404	Jerry Hairston Jr.	.10
405	Mike Lowell	.10
406	Kerry Wood	.50
407	Carl Everett	.10
408	Hideki Matsui	1.25
409	Omar Vizquel	.25
410	Joe Kennedy	.10
411	Carlos Pena	.10
412	Armando Benitez	.10
413	Carlos Beltran	.50
414	Kevin Appier	.10
415	Jeff Weaver	.10
416	Chad Moeller	.10
417	Joe Mays	.10
418	Terrmel Sledge	.10
419	Richard Hidalgo	.10
420	Kenny Lofton	.10
421	Justin Duchscherer	.10
422	Eric Milton	.10
423	Jose Mesa	.10
424	Ramon Hernandez	.10
425	Jose Reyes	.25
426	Joel Pineiro	.10
427	Matt Morris	.10
428	John Halama	.10
429	Gary Matthews Jr.	.10
430	Ryan Madson	.10
431	Mark Kotsay	.10
432	Carlos Delgado	.10
433	Casey Kotchman	.10
434	Gary Aquino	.10
435	Eli Marrero	.10
436	David Newhan	.10
437	Larry Walker	.10
438	LaTroy Hawkins	.10
439	Jose Contreras	.10

#	Player	Price
440	Ken Griffey Jr.	1.00
441	C.C. Sabathia	.10
442	Brandon Inge	.10
443	Peter Munro	.10
444	John Buck	.10
445	Hee Seop Choi	.10
446	Chris Capuano	.10
447	Jesse Crain	.10
448	Geoff Jenkins	.10
449	Brian Schneider	.10
450	Mike Piazza	1.00
451	Jorge Posada	.40
452	Nick Swisher	.10
453	Kevin Millwood	.25
454	Mike Gonzalez	.10
455	Jake Peavy	.25
456	Dustin Hermanson	.10
457	Jeremy Reed	.10
458	Julian Tavarez	.10
459	Geoff Blum	.10
460	Alfonso Soriano	.50
461	Alexis Rios	.10
462	David Eckstein	.10
463	Shea Hillenbrand	.10
464	Russ Ortiz	.10
465	Kurt Ainsworth	.10
466	Orlando Cabrera	.10
467	Carlos Silva	.10
468	Ross Gload	.10
469	Josh Phelps	.10
470	Marquis Grissom	.10
471	Mike Maroth	.10
472	Guillermo Mota	.10
473	Chris Burke	.10
474	David DeJesus	.10
475	Jose Lima	.10
476	Cristian Guzman	.10
477	Nick Johnson	.10
478	Victor Zambrano	.10
479	Rod Barajas	.10
480	Damian Miller	.10
481	Chase Utley	.25
482	Todd Pratt	.10
483	Sean Burnett	.10
484	David Wells	.10
485	Dustan Mohr	.10
486	Bobby Madritsch	.10
487	Ray King	.10
488	Reed Johnson	.10
489	R.A. Dickey	.10
490	Scott Kazmir	.25
491	Tony Womack	.10
492	Tomas Perez	.10
493	Esteban Loaiza	.10
494	Tomokazu Ohka	.10
495	Mike Lamb	.10
496	Ramon Ortiz	.10
497	Richie Sexson	.40
498	J.D. Drew	.25
499	David Segui	.10
500	Barry Bonds	2.00
501	Aramis Ramirez	.25
502	Wily Mo Pena	.10
503	Jeromy Burnitz	.10
504	Craig Monroe	.10
505	Nomar Garciaparra	1.00
506	Brandon Backe	.10
507	Marcus Thames	.10
508	Derek Lowe	.10
509	Doug Davis	.10
510	Joe Mauer	.25
511	Endy Chavez	.10
512	Bernie Williams	.25
513	Mark Redman	.10
514	Jason Michaels	.10
515	Craig Wilson	.10
516	Ryan Klesko	.10
517	Ray Durham	.10
518	Jose Lopez	.10
519	Jeff Suppan	.10
520	Julio Lugo	.10
521	Mike Wood	.10
522	David Bush	.10
523	Juan Rincon	.10
524	Paul Quantrill	.10
525	Marlon Byrd	.10
526	Roy Oswalt	.25
527	Rondell White	.10
528	Troy Glaus	.25
529	Scott Hairston	.10
530	Chipper Jones	.75
531	Daniel Cabrera	.10
532	Doug Mientkiewicz	.10
533	Glendon Rusch	.10
534	Jon Garland	.10
535	Austin Kearns	.10
536	Jake Westbrook	.10
537	Aaron Miles	.10
538	Omar Infante	.10
539	Paul LoDuca	.10
540	Morgan Ensberg	.10
541	Tony Graffanino	.10
542	Milton Bradley	.25
543	Keith Ginter	.10
544	Justin Morneau	.40
545	Tony Armas Jr.	.10
546	Mike Stanton	.10
547	Kevin Brown	.10
548	Marco Scutaro	.10
549	Tim Hudson	.25
550	Pat Burrell	.25
551	Ty Wigginton	.10
552	Jeff Cirillo	.10
553	Jim Brower	.10
554	Jamie Moyer	.10
555	Larry Walker	.10
556	Dewon Brazelton	.10
557	Brian Jordan	.10

#	Player	Price
558	Josh Towers	.10
559	Shigetoshi Hasegawa	.10
560	Octavio Dotel	.10
561	Travis Lee	.10
562	Michael Cuddyer	.10
563	Junior Spivey	.10
564	Zack Greinke	.25
565	Roger Clemens	1.50
566	Chris Shelton	.10
567	Ugueth Urbina	.10
568	Rafael Betancourt	.10
569	Willie Harris	.10
570	Todd Hollandsworth	.10
571	Keith Foulke	.10
572	Larry Bigbie	.10
573	Paul Byrd	.10
574	Troy Percival	.10
575	Pedro Martinez	.75
576	Matt Clement	.10
577	Ryan Wagner	.10
578	Jeff Francis	.10
579	Jeff Conine	.10
580	Wade Miller	.10
581	Matt Stairs	.10
582	Gavin Floyd	.10
583	Kazuhisa Ishii	.10
584	Victor Santos	.10
585	Jacque Jones	.10
586	Sunny Kim	.10
587	Dan Kolb	.10
588	Cory Lidle	.10
589	Jose Castillo	.10
590	Alex Gonzalez	.10
591	Kirk Rueter	.10
592	Jolbert Cabrera	.10
593	Erik Bedard	.10
594	Ben Grieve	.10
595	Ricky Ledee	.10
596	Mark Hendrickson	.10
597	Laynce Nix	.10
598	Jason Frasor	.10
599	Kevin Gregg	.10
600	Derek Jeter	1.50
601	Luis Terrero	.10
602	Jaret Wright	.10
603	Edwin Jackson	.10
604	Dave Roberts	.10
605	Moises Alou	.25
606	Aaron Rowand	.10
607	Kazuhito Tadano	.10
608	Luis Gonzalez	.10
609	A.J. Burnett	.25
610	Jeff Bagwell	.40
611	Brad Penny	.10
612	Craig Counsell	.10
613	Corey Koskie	.10
614	Mark Ellis	.10
615	Felix Rodriguez	.10
616	Jay Payton	.10
617	Hector Luna	.10
618	Miguel Olivo	.10
619	Rob Bell	.10
620	Scott Rolen	.50
621	Ricardo Rodriguez	.10
622	Eric Hinske	.10
623	Tim Salmon	.10
624	Adam LaRoche	.10
625	B.J. Ryan	.10
626	Roberto Alomar	.25
627	Steve Finley	.10
628	Joe Nathan	.10
629	Scott Linebrink	.10
630	Vicente Padilla	.10
631	Raul Mondesi	.10
632	Yadier Molina	.10
633	Tino Martinez	.10
634	Mark Teixeira	.25
635	Kelvim Escobar	.10
636	Pedro Felix	.10
637	Rich Aurilia	.10
638	Los Angeles Angels of Anaheim	.10
639	Arizona Diamondbacks	.10
640	Atlanta Braves	.10
641	Baltimore Orioles	.10
642	Boston Red Sox	.10
643	Chicago Cubs	.10
644	Chicago White Sox	.10
645	Cincinnati Reds	.10
646	Cleveland Indians	.10
647	Colorado Rockies	.10
648	Detroit Tigers	.10
649	Florida Marlins	.10
650	Houston Astros	.10
651	Kansas City Royals	.10
652	Los Angeles Dodgers	.10
653	Milwaukee Brewers	.10
654	Minnesota Twins	.10
655	Montreal Expos	.10
656	New York Mets	.10
657	New York Yankees	.10
658	Oakland Athletics	.10
659	Philadelphia Phillies	.10
660	Pittsburgh Pirates	.10
661	San Diego Padres	.10
662	San Francisco Giants	.10
663	Seattle Mariners	.10
664	St. Louis Cardinals	.10
665	Tampa Bay Devil Rays	.10
666	Texas Rangers	.10
667	Toronto Blue Jays	.10
668	Billy Butler RC	1.50
669	Wes Swackhamer RC	.10
670	Matt Campbell RC	.10
671	Ryan Webb RC	.50
672	Glen Perkins RC	.10
673	Michael Rogers RC	.10
674	Kevin Melillo RC	.25

#	Player	Price
675	Erik Cordier RC	.50
676	Landon Powell RC	.50
677	Justin Verlander RC	1.50
678	Eric Nielsen RC	.25
679	Alexander Smit RC	.25
680	Ryan Garko RC	.50
681	Bobby Livingston RC	.25
682	Jeff Niemann RC	.50
683	Wladimir Balentien RC	.50
684	Chip Cannon RC	.50
685	Yorman Bazardo RC	.50
686	Michael Bourn RC	.10
687	Andy LaRoche RC	2.00
688	Felix Hernandez, Justin Leone	.50
689	Ryan Howard, Cole Hamels	.75
690	Matt Cain, Merkin Valdez	.25
691	Andy Marte, Jeff Francoeur	.10
692	Chad Billingsley, Joel Guzman	.10
693	Jerry Hairston Jr., Scott Hairston	.10
694	Miguel Tejada, Lance Berkman	.25
695	Kenny Rogers	.10
696	Ivan Rodriguez	.25
697	Darin Erstad	.10
698	Bret Boone	.10
699	Eric Chavez	.10
700	Derek Jeter	1.00
701	Vernon Wells	.10
702	Ichiro Suzuki	.75
703	Torii Hunter	.10
704	Greg Maddux	.50
705	Mike Matheny	.10
706	Todd Helton	.25
707	Luis Castillo	.10
708	Scott Rolen	.40
709	Cesar Izturis	.10
710	Jim Edmonds	.25
711	Andruw Jones	.25
712	Steve Finley	.10
713	Johan Santana	.25
714	Roger Clemens	1.00
715	Vladimir Guerrero	.40
716	Barry Bonds	1.50
717	Bobby Crosby	.10
718	Jason Bay	.10
719	Albert Pujols	1.00
720	Mark Loretta	.10
721	Edgar Renteria	.10
722	Scott Rolen	.40
723	J.D. Drew	.10
724	Jim Edmonds	.25
725	Johnny Estrada	.10
726	Jason Schmidt	.10
727	Chris Carpenter	.10
728	Eric Gagne	.10
729	Jason Bay	.10
730	Bobby Cox	.10
731	Game 1	.50
732	Game 2	.50
733	Game 3	.50
734	Game 4	.50

Black

1st Edition: 20-50X
Production 54 Sets

Gold

Stars:	5-10X

Production 2,005 Sets

1st Edition

	NM/M
Stars:	3-5X
HTA Exclusive	
1st Edition Pack (10):	4.00
1st Edition Box (20):	65.00

All-Stars

	NM/M
Complete Set (15):	20.00
Common Player:	
Inserted 1:9	
TAS1 Todd Helton	.75
TAS2 Albert Pujols	3.00
TAS3 Vladimir Guerrero	1.00
TAS4 Ichiro Suzuki	2.00
TAS5 Randy Johnson	1.00
TAS6 Manny Ramirez	1.00
TAS7 Sammy Sosa	2.00
TAS8 Alfonso Soriano	1.00
TAS9 Jim Thome	1.00
TAS10 Barry Bonds	3.00

TAS11	Roger Clemens	3.00
TAS12	Mike Piazza	1.50
TAS13	Derek Jeter	3.00
TAS14	Alex Rodriguez	2.50
TAS15	Carlos Beltran	1.00

All-Star Patches
No Pricing
Production 25 Sets

All-Star Stitches Relics
NM/M

Common Player:		5.00
Inserted 1:96		
BA	Bobby Abreu	8.00
MA	Moises Alou	10.00
RB	Ronnie Belliard	5.00
CB	Carlos Beltran	10.00
LB	Lance Berkman	10.00
HB	Hank Blalock	10.00
MC	Miguel Cabrera	10.00
CC	Carl Crawford	5.00
JE	Johnny Estrada	8.00
EG	Eric Gagne	10.00
JG	Jason Giambi	10.00
TG	Tom Glavine	10.00
FG	Flash Gordon	5.00
VG	Vladimir Guerrero	10.00
KH	Ken Harvey	5.00
TH	Todd Helton	10.00
JK	Jeff Kent	8.00
DK	Danny Kolb	8.00
BL	Barry Larkin	10.00
MLA	Matt Lawton	5.00
TL	Ted Lilly	8.00
EL	Esteban Loaiza	5.00
PL	Paul LoDuca	5.00
MLO	Mark Loretta	8.00
ML	Mike Lowell	8.00
VM	Victor Martinez	10.00
MM	Mark Mulder	10.00
JN	Joe Nathan	8.00
DO	David Ortiz	20.00
CP	Carl Pavano	10.00
MP	Mike Piazza	12.00
AP	Albert Pujols	25.00
MR	Manny Ramirez	10.00
ER	Edgar Renteria	8.00
MRI	Mariano Rivera	10.00
FR	Francisco Rodriguez	10.00
IR	Ivan Rodriguez	10.00
SR	Scott Rolen	12.00
CS	C.C. Sabathia	8.00
BS	Ben Sheets	10.00
GS	Gary Sheffield	10.00
AS	Alfonso Soriano	10.00
SS	Sammy Sosa	15.00
MT	Miguel Tejada	10.00
JT	Jim Thome	12.00
JW	Jack Wilson	10.00
MY	Michael Young	15.00
CZ	Carlos Zambrano	10.00

Autographs
NM/M

Common Autograph:		
CB	Carlos Beltran	30.00
MC	Miguel Cabrera	40.00
JC	Jose Capellan	10.00
EC	Eric Chavez	20.00
DD	David DeJesus	10.00
ZG	Zack Greinke	30.00
CK	Casey Kotchman	10.00
JMA	John Maine	25.00
DM	Dallas McPherson	10.00
ARI	Alexis Rios	15.00
AR	Alex Rodriguez	200.00
CT	Chad Tracy	10.00
VW	Vernon Wells	20.00
DW	David Wright	75.00
Series 2		
JB	Jason Bay	25.00
CB	Carlos Beltran	30.00
MB	Milton Bradley	25.00
BB	Billy Butler	25.00
MC	Matt Campbell	10.00
EC	Eric Chavez	20.00
ECO	Erik Cordier	10.00
CC	Carl Crawford	15.00
EG	Eric Gagne	20.00
FH	Felix Hernandez	30.00
SK	Scott Kazmir	25.00
ML	Mark Loretta	15.00
GP	Glen Perkins	15.00
LP	Landon Powell	15.00
AR2	Alex Rodriguez/50	250.00
IR	Ivan Rodriguez	40.00
MR	Michael Rogers	10.00
JS	Johan Santana	40.00
TS	Terrmel Sledge	10.00
CW	Craig Wilson	10.00

Barry Bonds Home Run Highlights

Complete Set (330):
Common Bonds: 1.50

Inserted 1:4
BB1-330 Barry Bonds 1.50

Bonds MVP
NM/M
Production 25-500

BBI2	Barry Bonds/50	40.00
BBI3	Barry Bonds/100	30.00
BBI4	Barry Bonds/200	25.00
BBI5	Barry Bonds/300	20.00
BBI6	Barry Bonds/400	15.00
BBI7	Barry Bonds/500	15.00

Bonds MVP Autographs
No Pricing

Bonds MVP Relics
NM/M
Production 25-500

BBR3	Barry Bonds/100	50.00
BBR4	Barry Bonds/200	40.00
BBR5	Barry Bonds/300	40.00
BBR6	Barry Bonds/400	25.00
BBR7	Barry Bonds/500	25.00

Celebrity Threads Relics
NM/M

Common Player:		8.00
Inserted 1:562		
CC	Cesar Cedeno	8.00
CF	Cecil Fielder	15.00
RF	Rollie Fingers	12.00
GG	Rich "Goose" Gossage	10.00
HR	Harold Reynolds	8.00
MS	Mike Scott	8.00
OS	Ozzie Smith	25.00
DW	Dave Winfield	15.00

Dem Bums

RUSS MEYER

NM/M

Complete Set (21):		60.00
Common Player:		4.00
Inserted 1:12		
WA	Walter Alston	4.00
BB	Bob Borkowski	4.00
RC	Roy Campanella	6.00
RCR	Roger Craig	4.00
CF	Carl Furillo	4.00
JG	Jim Gilliam	4.00
DH	Don Hoak	4.00
JH	Jim Hughes	4.00
RM	Russ Meyer	4.00
JR	Jackie Robinson	8.00
ER	Ed Roebuck	4.00
GS	George Shuba	4.00
KS	Karl Spooner	4.00
CE	Carl Erskine	4.00
CL	Clem Labine	4.00
DN	Don Newcombe	4.00
DS	Duke Snider	6.00
DZ	Don Zimmer	4.00
JB	Joe Black	4.00
JP	Johnny Podres	4.00
RW	Rube Walker	4.00

Dem Bums Autographs
NM/M

Common Autograph:		30.00
CE	Carl Erskine	30.00
CL	Clem Labine	50.00
JP	Johnny Podres	30.00
DS	Duke Snider	50.00
DZ	Don Zimmer	50.00

Dem Bums Cuts
No Pricing
Production One Set

Derby Digs Relics
NM/M

Common Player:		15.00
Production 100 Sets		
LB	Lance Berkman	15.00
HB	Hank Blalock	20.00
DO	David Ortiz	35.00
SS	Sammy Sosa	40.00
MT	Miguel Tejada	15.00
JT	Jim Thome	25.00
Series 2		
Production 10 Sets		

Factory Set Team Bonus
NM/M

Complete Cubs Set (5):	15.00
Complete Yankees Set (5):	15.00
Complete Red Sox Set (5):	15.00
Complete Giants Set (5):	15.00
Complete Nationals Set (5):	15.00
Complete Tigers Set (5):	15.00

Issued in team themed factory sets.

Factory Set Draft Picks Bonus
NM/M

Complete Set (5):		50.00
One set per factory set.		
1	Beau Jones	4.00

2	Cliff Pennington	4.00
3	Chris Volstad	4.00
4	Ricky Romero	4.00
5	Jay Bruce	25.00

Factory Set First Year Draft Bonus
NM/M

Complete Set (10):		50.00
One set per Green Factory Set		
1	Nick Webber	3.00
2	Aaron Thompson	4.00
3	Matt Garza	8.00
4	Tyler Greene	4.00
5	Ryan Braun	15.00
6	C.J. Henry	4.00
7	Ryan Zimmerman	15.00
8	John Mayberry Jr.	4.00
9	Cesar Carrillo	3.00
10	Mark McCormick	4.00

Factory Set First Year Player Bonus
NM/M

Complete Set (5):		15.00
Issued in red factory sets		
1	Bill McCarthy	4.00
2	John Hudgins	4.00
3	Kyle Nichols	4.00
4	Thomas Pauly	4.00
5	Philip Humber	4.00

Grudge Match

NM/M

Complete Set (10):		
Common Duo:		1.00
Inserted 1:24		
GM1	Jorge Posada, Pedro J. Martinez	2.00
GM2	Mike Piazza, Roger Clemens	3.00
GM3	Mariano Rivera, Luis Gonzalez	1.00
GM4	Carlos Zambrano, Jim Edmonds	1.00
GM5	Aaron Boone, Tim Wakefield	1.00
GM6	Manny Ramirez, Roger Clemens	1.00
GM7	Michael Tucker, Eric Gagne	1.00
GM8	Ivan Rodriguez, J.T. Snow	1.00
GM9	Alex Rodriguez, Bronson Arroyo	1.00
GM10	Corky Miller, Sammy Sosa	2.50

Hit Parade

NM/M

Complete Set (30):		25.00
Common Player:		.50
Inserted 1:12		
HR1	Barry Bonds	4.00
HR2	Sammy Sosa	2.50
HR3	Rafael Palmeiro	1.00
HR4	Ken Griffey Jr.	2.00
HR5	Jeff Bagwell	1.00
HR6	Frank Thomas	1.00
HR7	Juan Gonzalez	.75
HR8	Jim Thome	1.00
HR9	Gary Sheffield	1.00
HR10	Manny Ramirez	1.50
RBI1	Barry Bonds	4.00
RBI2	Rafael Palmeiro	1.00
RBI3	Sammy Sosa	2.50
RBI4	Jeff Bagwell	1.00
RBI5	Ken Griffey Jr.	2.00
RBI6	Frank Thomas	1.00
RBI7	Juan Gonzalez	.75
RBI8	Gary Sheffield	1.00
RBI9	Ruben Sierra	.50
RBI10	Manny Ramirez	1.50
HIT1	Rafael Palmeiro	.50
HIT2	Barry Bonds	4.00
HIT3	Roberto Alomar	.75
HIT4	Craig Biggio	.50
HIT5	Julio Franco	.50
HIT6	Steve Finley	.50
HIT7	Jeff Bagwell	1.00
HIT8	B.J. Surhoff	.50
HIT9	Marquis Grissom	.50
HIT10	Sammy Sosa	2.50

Hobby Masters

NOMAR GARCIAPARRA CHICAGO CUBS

NM/M

Complete Set (20):		25.00
Common Player:		.75
Inserted 1:18		
HM1	Alex Rodriguez	4.00
HM2	Sammy Sosa	2.50
HM3	Ichiro Suzuki	3.00
HM4	Albert Pujols	4.00
HM5	Derek Jeter	4.00
HM6	Jim Thome	1.50
HM7	Vladimir Guerrero	1.50
HM8	Nomar Garciaparra	2.00
HM9	Mike Piazza	2.00
HM10	Jason Giambi	.75
HM11	Ivan Rodriguez	1.00
HM12	Alfonso Soriano	1.50
HM13	Dontrelle Willis	.75
HM14	Chipper Jones	1.50
HM15	Mark Prior	1.50
HM16	Todd Helton	1.00
HM17	Randy Johnson	1.00
HM18	Hank Blalock	1.00
HM19	Ken Griffey Jr.	2.00
HM20	Roger Clemens	3.00

Midsummer Covers Relics
No Pricing
Production 10 Sets
Series 2
Production 10 Sets

On-Deck Relics
NM/M

Inserted 1:1,493		
CB	Carlos Beltran	15.00
HB	Hank Blalock	12.00
TH	Todd Helton	12.00
AP	Albert Pujols	30.00
AR	Alex Rodriguez	25.00
IR	Ivan Rodriguez	15.00
SR	Scott Rolen	15.00
AS	Alfonso Soriano	15.00
SS	Sammy Sosa	25.00
JT	Jim Thome	15.00

Own The Game

DAVID ORTIZ

NM/M

Complete Set (30):		15.00
Common Player:		.50
Inserted 1:12		
OG1	Ichiro Suzuki	3.00
OG2	Todd Helton	1.00
OG3	Adrian Beltre	1.00
OG4	Albert Pujols	4.00
OG5	Adam Dunn	1.00
OG6	Jim Thome	1.50
OG7	Miguel Tejada	.75
OG8	David Ortiz	1.50
OG9	Manny Ramirez	1.50
OG10	Scott Rolen	1.00
OG11	Gary Sheffield	.75
OG12	Vladimir Guerrero	1.50
OG13	Jim Edmonds	.50
OG14	Ivan Rodriguez	1.00
OG15	Lance Berkman	.50
OG16	Michael Young	.50
OG17	Juan Pierre	.50
OG18	Craig Biggio	.50
OG19	Johnny Damon	.75
OG20	Jimmy Rollins	.50
OG21	Scott Podsednik	.50
OG22	Bobby Abreu	.50
OG23	Lyle Overbay	.50
OG24	Carl Crawford	.50
OG25	Mark Loretta	.50
OG26	Vinny Castilla	.50
OG27	Curt Schilling	1.00
OG28	Johan Santana	.75
OG29	Randy Johnson	1.50
OG30	Pedro J. Martinez	1.50

Power Brokers Cut Signatures
Complete Set (51):
Common Player:

2005 Topps National Convention

STAN MUSIAL

A latter-day attempt to recreate the "missing" four cards from its original high-number series, these cards were available only as a cello-wrapped set to purchasers of the VIP Attendee package at the 2005 National Sports Collectors Convention in Chicago. Cards are in the original 3-3/4" x 2-5/8" format.

NM/M

Complete Set (4):		20.00
Common Player:		3.00
175	Stan Musial	4.00
186	Whitey Ford	6.00
203	Bob Feller	5.00
209	Herb Score	3.00

Spokesman

Alex Rodriguez

NM/M

Complete Set (4):		10.00
Common Player:		3.00
Inserted 1:24		
ARI1-4	Alex Rodriguez	3.00

Spokesman Autographs
NM/M
Production 1-200

ARA3	Alex Rodriguez/100	200.00
ARA4	Alex Rodriguez/200	180.00

Spokesman Relics
NM/M
Production 1-800

ARR2	Alex Rodriguez/50	30.00
ARR3	Alex Rodriguez/300	20.00
ARR4	Alex Rodriguez/800	20.00

Spokesman Relic
NM/M

Inserted 1:5,627		
AR	Alex Rodriguez	50.00

Spokesman Relic Autographs
NM/M
13 Sets

Touch'em All Relics
Common Player:
Production 50 Sets
Series 2
Production 50 Sets

World Treasures
No Pricing
Production One Set

World Treasures - Dual
No Pricing
Production One Set

World Champion Red Sox Relics
NM/M

Common Player:		
OC	Orlando Cabrera	20.00
OC2	Orlando Cabrera	20.00
JD	Johnny Damon	25.00
JD2	Johnny Damon	25.00
DL	Derek Lowe	20.00
PM	Pedro Martinez	20.00
DMI	Doug Mientkiewicz	15.00
KM	Kevin Millar	15.00
BM	Bill Mueller	15.00
BM2	Bill Mueller	15.00
TN	Trot Nixon	20.00
DO	David Ortiz	20.00
DO2	David Ortiz	20.00
MR	Manny Ramirez	25.00
MR2	Manny Ramirez	25.00
MR3	Manny Ramirez	25.00
PR	Pokey Reese	15.00
DR	Dave Roberts	15.00
CS	Curt Schilling	25.00
KY	Kevin Youkilis	15.00

1955 World Series Cut Signatures
Complete Set (21):
Common Player:

1955 World Series Dual Cut Signatures
Complete Set (3):
Common Player:
Production One Set

2005 Topps 1955 Luis Aparicio

LUIS APARICIO

This original format (3-3/4" x 2-5/8") card was only available at the Chicago White Sox booth during the 2005 National Sports Collectors Convention in Chicago.

NM/M

NAT1	Luis Aparicio	7.50

2005 Topps All-Time Fan Favorites

LOU BROCK

NM/M

Complete Set (142):		40.00
Common Player:		.25
Pack (6):		5.00
Box (24):		110.00
1	Andy Van Slyke	.25
2	Bill Freehan	.25
3	Bo Jackson	.75
4	Mark Grace	.50
5	Chuck Knoblauch	.25
6	Candy Maldonado	.25
7	David Cone	.25
8	Don Mattingly	1.50
9	Darryl Strawberry	.25
10	Dick Williams	.25
11	Frank Robinson	.75
12	Glenn Hubbard	.25
13	Jim Abbott	.25
14	Jeff Brantley	.25
15	John Elway	2.00
16	Jim Leyland	.25
17	Jesse Orosco	.25
18	Joe Pepitone	.25
19	J.R. Richard	.25
20	Jerome Walton	.25
21	Kevin Maas	.25
22	Lou Brock	.50
23	Lou Whitaker	.25
24	Carl Erskine	.25
25	John Candelaria	.25
26	Mike Norris	.25
27	Nolan Ryan	2.00
28	Pedro Guerrero	.25
29	Roger Craig	.25
30	Ron Gant	.25
31	Sid Bream	.25
32	Sid Fernandez	.25
33	Tony LaRussa	.25
34	Tom Seaver	.75
35	Yogi Berra	.75
36	Andre Dawson	.25
37	Al Kaline	.75
38	Brett Butler	.25
39	Bob Gibson	.75
40	Bill Mazeroski	.25

41	Matty Alou	.25
42	Chet Lemon	.25
43	Cal Ripken Jr.	2.00
44	Dusty Baker	.25
45	Dwight Gooden	.25
46	Dave Winfield	.50
47	Ernie Banks	1.00
48	Gary Carter	.50
49	Howard Johnson	.25
50	Mike Schmidt	1.50
51	Matt Williams	.25
52	Ozzie Smith	1.00
53	Atlee Hammaker	.25
54	Cleon Jones	.25
55	Dave Johnson	.25
56	Denny McLain	.25
57	Don Zimmer	.25
58	Gregg Jefferies	.25
59	Jay Buhner	.25
60	Johnny Bench	.75
61	George Brett	1.50
62	Dale Murphy	.50
63	Bob Welch	.25
64	Paul O'Neill	.25
65	Mark Lemke	.25
66	Kevin McReynolds	.25
67	Jesus Alou	.25
68	Joe Pignatano	.25
69	Jim Lonborg	.25
70	Jerry Grote	.25
71	Joaquin Andujar	.25
72	Gary Gaetti	.25
73	Edgar Martinez	.25
74	Ron Darling	.25
75	Duke Snider	.75
76	Dave Magadan	.25
77	Doug Drabek	.25
78	Carl Yastrzemski	1.00
79	Mitch Williams	.25
80	Marvin Miller	.25
81	Michael Kay	.25
82	Lonnie Smith	.25
83	John Wetteland	.25
84	Johnny Podres	.25
85	Joe Morgan	.25
86	Juan Marichal	.50
87	Jeffrey Leonard	.25
88	Bob Feller	.50
89	Brooks Robinson	.75
90	Clem Labine	.25
91	Barry Lyons	.25
92	Harmon Killebrew	.75
93	Jim Frey	.25
94	John Kruk	.25
95	Ed Kranepool	.25
96	Jose Oquendo	.25
97	Johnny Pesky	.25
98	John Tudor	.25
99	Keith Hernandez	.25
100	Monte Irvin	.50
101	Marty Barrett	.25
102	Oscar Gamble	.25
103	Hank Bauer	.25
104	Ron Blomberg	.25
105	Rod Carew	.50
106	Rick Dempsey	.25
107	Walt Jocketty	.25
108	Tom Kelly	.25
109	Steve Carlton	.50
110	Rick Monday	.25
111	Rob Dibble	.25
112	Shawon Dunston	.25
113	Tony Gwynn	.75
114	Tom Niedenfuer	.25
115	Bob Bernier	.25
116	Anthony Young	.25
117	Reggie Jackson	.75
118	Steve Garvey	.25
119	Tim Raines	.25
120	Whitey Ford	.75
121	Rafael Santana	.25
122	Scott Brosius	.25
123	Stan Musial	1.50
124	Ron Santo	.50
125	Wade Boggs	.75
126	Jose Canseco	.50
127	Brady Anderson	.25
128	Vida Blue	.25
129	Charlie Hough	.25
130	Jim Kaat	.25
131	Zane Smith	.25
132	Bob Boone	.25
133	Travis Fryman	.25
134	Harold Baines	.25
135	Orlando Cepeda	.25
136	Mike Cuellar	.25
137	Tito Fuentes	.25
138	Daryl Boston	.25
139	Jim Leyritz	.25
140	Bill "Moose" Skowron	.25
141	Theo Epstein	.25
142	Barry Bonds	3.00

Refractor
Stars (1-142): 3-5X
Production 299 Sets

Gold Refractor
No Pricing
Production 25 Sets

Printing Plates
No Pricing
Production one set per color (4):

Autographs
NM/M
Common Autograph: 15.00

Rainbow: No Pricing
Production 10 Sets

JA	Jim Abbott	30.00
JAN	Joaquin Andujar	20.00
DB	Dusty Baker	25.00
MB	Marty Barrett	15.00
JBE	Dr. Jim Beckett/SP/90	100.00
JB	Johnny Bench/SP/40	125.00
YB	Yogi Berra/SP/90	125.00
RB	Ron Blomberg	15.00
JBR	Jeff Brantley	20.00
SB	Sid Bream	15.00
GB	George Brett/SP/40	250.00
SBR	Scott Brosius/SP/90	85.00
JBU	Jay Buhner	20.00
BB	Brett Butler	20.00
SC	Steve Carlton/SP/90	60.00
GC	Gary Carter	25.00
DC	David Cone	25.00
RCR	Roger Craig	25.00
RD	Rick Dempsey	15.00
DD	Doug Drabek	20.00
SD	Shawon Dunston	20.00
JE	John Elway/SP/40	250.00
BFE	Bob Feller	85.00
SF	Sid Fernandez	15.00
WF	Whitey Ford/SP/90	150.00
BF	Bill Freehan	20.00
GG	Gary Gaetti	15.00
OG	Oscar Gamble	15.00
RG	Ron Gant/SP/90	50.00
SG	Steve Garvey	50.00
BG	Bob Gibson/SP/90	100.00
DG	Dwight Gooden	40.00
JG	Jerry Grote	30.00
TG	Tony Gwynn/SP/90	125.00
AH	Atlee Hammaker	15.00
GH	Glenn Hubbard	20.00
MI	Monte Irvin	50.00
BJ	Bo Jackson	70.00
RJ	Reggie Jackson/SP/40	100.00
GJ	Gregg Jefferies	40.00
WJ	Walt Jocketty/SP/90	60.00
DJ	Dave Johnson	20.00
HJ	Howard Johnson	20.00
CJ	Cleon Jones	35.00
AK	Al Kaline	60.00
TK	Tom Kelly	25.00
HK	Harmon Killebrew	85.00
CK	Chuck Knoblauch	25.00
JK	John Kruk	30.00
CL	Clem Labine	40.00
TL	Tony LaRussa	30.00
MLE	Mark Lemke	15.00
CLE	Chet Lemon	15.00
JLE	Jim Leyland	20.00
JLO	Jim Lonborg	15.00
BL	Barry Lyons	15.00
KM	Kevin Maas	15.00
DMA	Dave Magadan	20.00
CM	Candy Maldonado	15.00
JMA	Juan Marichal/SP/40	140.00
EM	Edgar Martinez	30.00
DM	Don Mattingly	140.00
BM	Bill Mazeroski	75.00
DMC	Denny McLain	30.00
KMC	Kevin McReynolds	15.00
MM	Marvin Miller/SP/90	80.00
RM	Rick Monday	30.00
DMU	Dale Murphy	30.00
SM	Stan Musial/SP/40	150.00
TN	Tom Niedenfuer	15.00
MNO	Mike Norris	15.00
PO	Paul O'Neill	60.00
JO	Jesse Orosco	25.00
JOQ	Jose Oquendo	15.00
JPE	Joe Pepitone	25.00
JPY	Johnny Pesky	65.00
JP	Jim Pignatano	30.00
TR	Tim Raines	25.00
JR	J.R. Richard	15.00
CR	Cal Ripken Jr./SP/90	200.00
BR	Brooks Robinson/SP/90	125.00
FR	Frank Robinson	100.00
NR	Nolan Ryan/SP/40	200.00
RS	Rafael Santana	20.00
RSA	Ron Santo/SP/90	75.00
MS	Mike Schmidt/SP/40	160.00
LS	Lonnie Smith	15.00
DSN	Duke Snider/SP/40	60.00
DS	Darryl Strawberry	25.00
JT	John Tudor	35.00
AV	Andy Van Slyke	25.00
JW	Jerome Walton	15.00
BW	Bob Welch	30.00
JWE	John Wetteland	20.00
LW	Lou Whitaker/SP/90	60.00
DWI	Dick Williams/SP/90	75.00
MW	Matt Williams	25.00
MWI	Mitch Williams	25.00
DW	Dave Winfield/SP/90	125.00
CY	Carl Yastrzemski/SP/90	125.00
AY	Anthony Young	15.00
DZ	Don Zimmer/SP/40	50.00

Best Seat in House
NM/M
Production 125 unless noted.
Rainbow: No Pricing
Production 25 Sets

MFBJ	Don Mattingly, Whitey Ford, Yogi Berra, Reggie Jackson/50	50.00

RRRD	Brooks Robinson, Rick Dempsey, Frank Robinson, Cal Ripken Jr.	25.00
RR	Brooks Robinson, Cal Ripken Jr.	25.00
CR	Cal Ripken Jr., Frank Robinson	25.00
JD	Dave Johnson, Rick Dempsey	10.00
KMLW	Al Kaline, Lou Whitaker, Chet Lemon, Denny McLain	20.00

Fan Favorite Relics

NM/M
Inserted 1:Box
Rainbow: No Pricing
Production 25 Sets

WB	Wade Boggs	8.00
JCC	Jose Canseco/350	8.00
RC	Rod Carew/200	8.00
GC	Gary Carter/350	5.00
JC	Joe Carter/350	5.00
VC	Vince Coleman/200	5.00
ED	Eric Davis/350	5.00
AD	Andre Dawson/350	5.00
BD	Bucky Dent/200	5.00
LD	Lenny Dykstra/200	5.00
CF	Cecil Fielder/200	5.00
TG	Tony Gwynn/200	15.00
KH	Keith Hernandez/200	5.00
BJ	Bo Jackson/200	12.00
RJ	Reggie Jackson/350	10.00
WJ	Wally Joyner/200	5.00
WM	Willie McGee/350	5.00
DM	Dale Murphy/200	10.00
SM	Stan Musial/50	20.00
PO	Paul O'Neill/200	15.00
JR	Jim Rice/200	5.00
BR	Brooks Robinson/350	10.00
NR	Nolan Ryan/135	25.00
DS	Darryl Strawberry/350	5.00
BS	Bruce Sutter/350	7.50
MW	Mookie Wilson/135	5.00
CY	Carl Yastrzemski/50	25.00

League Leaders Tr-Signers
Production 50 Sets

Originals Relics
NM/M
Production 50 Sets
Actual vintage cards used.

WB	Wade Boggs/Bat	15.00
RC	Rod Carew/Bat	20.00
GC	Gary Carter/Bat	10.00
AD	Andre Dawson/Bat	10.00
TG	Tony Gwynn/Jsy	20.00
BJ	Bo Jackson/Jsy	25.00
RJ	Reggie Jackson/Bat	20.00
DM	Dale Murphy/Bat	15.00
JR	Jim Rice/Bat	15.00
NR	Nolan Ryan/Jsy	35.00

Ripken Commem. Balls

Rookie Dual Autograph
NM/M
Production 50 Sets

SC	Tom Seaver, Rod Carew	160.00

2005 Topps Bazooka

ALEX RODRIGUEZ — NEW YORK YANKEES®

NM/M
Complete Set (220): 35.00
Common Player: .15
Common (191-220): .25
Box (24): 50.00
Pack (8): 2.50

1	Eric Gagne	.40
2	Aramis Ramirez	.25
3	Hank Blalock	.50
4	Jason Kendall	.15
5	Jeromy Burnitz	.15
6	Jose Guillen	.15
7	Tom Glavine	.40
8	Adrian Beltre	.25
9	Jason Bay	.25
10	Mark Teixeira	.40
11	Moises Alou	.15
12	Ronnie Belliard	.15
13	Aaron Guiel	.15
14	Vladimir Guerrero	.75
15	Scott Podsednik	.15
16	Alfonso Soriano	.75
17	Craig Wilson	.15
18	Jose Reyes	.25
19	Mark Prior	.75
20	Preston Wilson	.15
21	Shawn Green	.25
22	Troy Glaus	.15
23	Dmitri Young	.15
24	Garret Anderson	.15
25	Kazuo Matsui	.25
26	Kerry Wood	.75
27	Michael Young	.15
28	Oliver Perez	.15
29	Bartolo Colon	.15
30	Richie Sexson	.40
31	Brad Penny	.15
32	Carlos Guillen	.15
33	Carlos Zambrano	.25
34	David Wright	.50
35	Al Leiter	.15
36	Jack Wilson	.15
37	Ryan Drese	.15
38	Darin Erstad	.15
39	Derrek Lee	.25
40	Ivan Rodriguez	.50
41	Kenny Rogers	.15
42	Mike Piazza	1.00
43	Phil Nevin	.15
44	Geoff Jenkins	.15
45	Jorge Posada	.40
46	Khalil Greene	.40
47	Randy Johnson	.75
48	Rondell White	.15
49	Sammy Sosa	1.25
50	Vernon Wells	.15
51	Ben Sheets	.40
52	Brian Giles	.15
53	Carlos Delgado	.40
54	Derek Jeter	2.00
55	Jeremy Bonderman	.15
56	Magglio Ordonez	.25
57	Chad Tracy	.15
58	Kevin Brown	.15
59	Luis Castillo	.15
60	Lyle Overbay	.15
61	Mark Buehrle	.15
62	Mark Loretta	.15
63	Orlando Hudson	.15
64	Adam Dunn	.25
65	Frank Thomas	.50
66	Jake Peavy	.25
67	Jason Giambi	.40
68	Joe Mauer	.25
69	Marcus Giles	.15
70	Mike Lowell	.25
71	Roy Halladay	.15
72	Aaron Rowand	.15
73	Alex Rodriguez	1.50
74	Brian Lawrence	.15
75	Gabe Gross	.15
76	Johnny Estrada	.15
77	Justin Morneau	.40
78	Miguel Cabrera	.75
79	Alex Rios	.15
80	Gary Sheffield	.40
81	Jason Schmidt	.15
82	Juan Pierre	.15
83	Paul Konerko	.15
84	Jermaine Dye	.15
85	Rafael Furcal	.15
86	Torii Hunter	.25
87	A.J. Pierzynski	.15
88	Carl Pavano	.15
89	Carlos Lee	.15
90	J.D. Drew	.25
91	Javier Vazquez	.25
92	Lew Ford	.15
93	Ted Lilly	.15
94	Austin Kearns	.15
95	Chipper Jones	.40
96	Erubiel Durazo	.15
97	Johan Santana	.25
98	Josh Beckett	.25
99	Mariano Rivera	.25
100	Mark Mulder	.25
101	Andruw Jones	.25
102	Barry Zito	.25
103	Bret Boone	.15
104	Paul LoDuca	.15
105	Shannon Stewart	.15
106	Wily Mo Pena	.25
107	Dontrelle Willis	.25
108	Eric Chavez	.25
109	Jamie Moyer	.15
110	Joe Nathan	.15
111	Sidney Ponson	.15
112	John Smoltz	.25
113	Ichiro Suzuki	1.50
114	Javy Lopez	.15
115	Victor Martinez	.25
116	Ken Griffey Jr.	1.00
117	Lance Berkman	.25
118	Scott Hatteberg	.15
119	Jim Edmonds	.25
120	Kazuhisa Ishii	.15
121	Miguel Tejada	.40
122	Roger Clemens	2.00
123	Ryan Freel	.15
124	Albert Pujols	2.00
125	Hideo Nomo	.25
126	Mark Kotsay	.15
127	Melvin Mora	.15
128	Roy Oswalt	.25
129	Sean Casey	.25
130	Casey Blake	.15
131	Edgar Renteria	.25
132	Jeff Kent	.25
133	Rafael Palmeiro	.50
134	Tim Hudson	.25
135	Tony Batista	.15
136	Andy Pettitte	.25
137	Brian Roberts	.15
138	Jose Vidro	.15
139	Omar Vizquel	.15
140	Rich Harden	.15
141	Scott Rolen	.75
142	Carlos Beltran	.50
143	Chris Carpenter	.15
144	Manny Ramirez	.75
145	Nick Johnson	.15
146	Pat Burrell	.25
147	C.C. Sabathia	.15
148	Johnny Damon	.50
149	Juan Rivera	.15
150	Ken Harvey	.15
151	Kevin Millwood	.15
152	Larry Walker	.50
153	Aubrey Huff	.15
154	Curt Schilling	.75
155	Jake Westbrook	.15
156	Randy Wolf	.15
157	Zach Day	.15
158	Zack Greinke	.15
159	Brad Wilkerson	.15
160	Carl Crawford	.15
161	Jim Thome	.75
162	Mike Sweeney	.15
163	Pedro J. Martinez	.75
164	Travis Hafner	.25
165	Bobby Abreu	.25
166	Cliff Floyd	.15
167	David DeJesus	.15
168	David Ortiz	.75
169	Rocco Baldelli	.50
170	Todd Helton	.50
171	Dallas McPherson	.25
172	Kevin Youkilis	.25
173	Val Majewski	.15
174	Grady Sizemore	.25
175	Joey Gathright	.15
176	Rickie Weeks	.25
177	Jason Kubel	.15
178	Robinson Cano	.25
179	Nick Swisher	.25
180	Ryan Howard	.50
181	Tim Stauffer	.15
182	Merkin Valdez	.15
183	B.J. Upton	.40
184	Scott Kazmir	.40
185	Chris Burke	.15
186	Felix Hernandez	.50
187	Freddy Guzman	.15
188	Josh Labandeira	.15
189	Willy Taveras	.15
190	Casey Kotchman	.15
191	Steven Doetsch RC	.25
192	Melky Cabrera RC	.25
193	Luis Ramirez RC	.25
194	Chris Seddon RC	.40
195	Chad Orvella RC	.50
196	Ian Kinsler RC	1.50
197	Brandon Moss RC	1.00
198	Chadd Blasko RC	.50
199	Jeremy West RC	.75
200	Sean Marshall RC	.50
201	Matt DeSalvo RC	.50
202	Ryan Sweeney RC	1.50
203	Matt Lindstrom RC	.25
204	Ryan Goleski RC	.40
205	Brett Harper RC	.25
206	Chris Roberson RC	.25
207	Andre Ethier RC	1.00
208	Chris Denorfia RC	.25
209	Darren Fenster RC	.25
210	Elvys Quezada RC	.25
211	Kevin West RC	.50
212	Chaz Lytle RC	.50
213	James Jurries RC	.25
214	Matt Rogelstad RC	.25
215	Wade Robinson RC	.25
216	Ian Bladergroen RC	.75
217	Jake Dittler RC	.25
218	Nate McLouth RC	.50
219	Kole Strayhorn RC	.25
220	Jose Vaquedano RC	.25

Gold Chunks

ARAMIS RAMIREZ — CHICAGO CUBS™

Golds: 1-2X
Inserted 1:1

Minis
Mini: 1-2x
Inserted 1:1

Blasts

BAZOOKA BLASTS — DERREK LEE — Chicago Cubs

NM/M
Common Bat: 4.00

RA	Roberto Alomar	6.00
RB	Ron Belliard	4.00
AB	Angel Berroa	4.00
CB	Craig Biggio	8.00
HB	Hank Blalock	4.00
JB	Jeromy Burnitz	4.00
SB	Sean Burroughs	4.00
MC	Miguel Cabrera	10.00
VC	Vinny Castilla	4.00
TC	Tony Clark	4.00
JC	Jeff Conine	4.00
JCJ	Jose Cruz Jr.	4.00
AD	Adam Dunn	6.00
ME	Morgan Ensberg	4.00
DE	Darin Erstad	4.00
CE	Carl Everett	4.00
CF	Chone Figgins	4.00
JF	Julio Franco	4.00
NG	Nomar Garciaparra	8.00
AGO	Adrian Gonzalez	4.00
AG	Alex Gonzalez	4.00
LG	Luis Gonzalez	4.00
VG	Vladimir Guerrero	8.00
CGU	Carlos Guillen	4.00
CG	Cristian Guzman	4.00
TH	Todd Helton	6.00
LH	Livan Hernandez	4.00
RH	Richard Hidalgo	4.00
JK	Jeff Kent	4.00
PK	Paul Konerko	4.00
DL	Derrek Lee	4.00
ML	Mike Lowell	6.00
PM	Pedro Martinez	6.00
TM	Tino Martinez	4.00
VM	Victor Martinez	4.00
KM	Kazuo Matsui	8.00
MO	Magglio Ordonez	4.00
DO	David Ortiz	10.00
ARA	Aramis Ramirez	6.00
MR	Manny Ramirez	6.00
AR	Alex Rodriguez	20.00
CS	Curt Schilling	6.00
GS	Gary Sheffield	4.00
RS	Ruben Sierra	4.00
MT	Miguel Tejada	6.00
BU	B.J. Upton	10.00
JV	Jose Valentin	4.00
JVI	Jose Vidro	4.00
LW	Larry Walker	6.00
JW	Jayson Werth	4.00
PW	Preston Wilson	4.00
DW	David Wright	10.00
MY	Michael Young	4.00

Comics
NM/M
Complete Set (24): 8.00
Common Player: .25
Inserted 1:4

1	Randy Johnson	.50
2	Gary Sheffield	.25
3	Ken Griffey Jr.	.75
4	Alex Rodriguez	.75
5	Vladimir Guerrero	.50
6	David Bell	.25
7	Carlos Pena	.25
8	Eric Gagne	.25
9	Jim Thome	.50
10	Cleveland Indians	.50
11	Greg Maddux	.50
12	Miguel Tejada	.50
13	Ichiro Suzuki	.75
14	Mariano Rivera	.50
15	Juan Pierre	.25
16	Carl Crawford	.50
17	Mike Mussina	.50
18	Vladimir Guerrero	.50
19	Oliver Perez	.25
20	Ichiro Suzuki	.75
21	Johan Santana	.25
22	Kevin Brown	.25
23	Mike Piazza	.50
24	Randy Johnson	.50

Fun Facts Relics

BAZOOKA FUN FACT — DARREN DAULTON

NM/M
Common Relic: 4.00

HB	Harold Baines	4.00
WB	Wade Boggs	6.00
GB	George Brett	12.00

JC	Jose Canseco	8.00
RC	Rod Carew	12.00
GC	Gary Carter	4.00
DD	Darren Daulton	4.00
DE	Darrell Evans	4.00
CF	Cecil Fielder	8.00
KG	Ken Griffey Sr.	4.00
WH	Willie Horton	4.00
WJ	Wally Joyner	4.00
DJ	David Justice	4.00
DJ2	David Justice	4.00
RK	Ron Kittle	4.00
JL	Jim Leyritz	4.00
DP	Dave Parker	4.00
HR	Harold Reynolds	4.00
MR	Mickey Rivers	4.00
MS	Mike Schmidt	10.00
OS	Ozzie Smith	20.00
CS	Cory Snyder	4.00
DS	Darryl Strawberry	4.00
WW	Walt Weiss	4.00

Moments Relics

		NM/M
	Common Relic:	6.00
MB	Matt Bush	8.00
RH	Ramon Hernandez	6.00
TL	Terrence Long	6.00
MM	Mark Mulder	6.00
MP	Mike Piazza	12.00
JP	Jorge Posada	8.00
AP	Albert Pujols	25.00
AR	Alex Rodriguez	12.00
IR	Ivan Rodriguez	8.00
KR	Kenny Rogers	6.00
AS	Alfonso Soriano	6.00
MT	Mark Teixeira	6.00
FT	Frank Thomas	6.00

Tatoos

		NM/M
	Common Player:	.25
	Inserted 1:4	
1	Alex Rodriguez	.50
2	Randy Johnson	.50
3	Jim Thome	.25
4	Pedro Martinez	.50
5	Roger Clemens	.50
6	Troy Glaus	.25
7	Todd Helton	.25
8	Albert Pujols	.50
9	Sammy Sosa	.50
10	David Wright	.50
11	Mike Piazza	.50
12	Gary Sheffield	.25
13	David Ortiz	.50
14	Hank Blalock	.25
15	Miguel Tejada	.25
16	Dontrelle Willis	.25
17	Ivan Rodriguez	.25
18	Nomar Garciaparra	.50
19	Alfonso Soriano	.25
20	Adrian Beltre	.25
21	Torii Hunter	.25
22	Brian Giles	.25
23	Chipper Jones	.25
24	Carlos Beltran	.25
25	Manny Ramirez	.50

4-on-1 Stickers

		NM/M
	Common Sticker:	.50
	Inserted 1:3 Hobby	
1	Alex Rodriguez, Hank Blalock, Scott Rolen, Mike Lowell	1.50
2	Jorge Posada, Ivan Rodriguez, Joe Mauer, Johnny Estrada	.75
3	Ichiro Suzuki, Carlos Beltran, Jim Edmonds, Brian Giles	1.50
4	Jim Thome, Mark Teixeira, Paul Konerko, Lyle Overbay	1.00
5	Jose Reyes, Mark Loretta, Jose Vidro, Luis Castillo	.50
6	Miguel Tejada, Derek Jeter, Michael Young, Edgar Renteria	2.00
7	Roy Oswalt, Rich Harden, Johan Santana, Mark Prior	1.00
8	Mariano Rivera, Eric Gagne, Joe Nathan, John Smoltz	.50
9	Larry Walker, Carl Crawford, Preston Wilson, Garret Anderson	.50

10	Wily Mo Pena, Mark Kotsay, Alex Rios, Geoff Jenkins .50
11	Victor Martinez, David Wright, Justin Morneau, Jason Bay .75
12	Carlos Lee, Andruw Jones, Ronnie Belliard, Eric Chavez .50
13	Vladimir Guerrero, Vernon Wells, Miguel Cabrera, Adrian Beltre 1.00
14	David Ortiz, Marcus Giles, Jeff Kent, Bobby Abreu .50
15	Juan Pierre, Torii Hunter, J.D. Drew, Austin Kearns .50
16	Bartolo Colon, Manny Ramirez, Ken Griffey Jr., Dontrelle Willis 1.50
17	Andy Pettitte, Tim Hudson, Curt Schilling, Randy Johnson 1.00
18	Jamie Moyer, Zach Day, Al Leiter, Oliver Perez .50
19	Kazuo Matsui, Roger Clemens, Khalil Greene, Javier Vazquez 2.00
20	Pedro Martinez, Rocco Baldelli, Mike Piazza, Melvin Mora 1.50
21	Hideo Nomo, Kazuhisa Ishii, Ken Harvey, Mike Sweeney .50
22	Casey Blake, Ryan Freel, Bret Boone, Javy Lopez .50
23	Craig Wilson, Shawn Green, Aramis Ramirez, Darin Erstad .50
24	Troy Glaus, Lance Berkman, Scott Podsednik, Adam Dunn .50
25	Albert Pujols, Gary Sheffield, Chipper Jones, Magglio Ordonez 2.00
26	Johnny Damon, Carlos Zambrano, Jason Schmidt, Ted Lilly 1.00
27	Sidney Ponson, Chris Carpenter, C.C. Sabathia, Kevin Millwood .50
28	Carl Pavano, Mark Mulder, Rafael Furcal, Jack Wilson .50
29	Jeremy Bonderman, Jake Westbrook, Zack Greinke, Tom Glavine .50
30	Omar Vizquel, Carlos Guillen, Roy Halladay, Ben Sheets .50
31	Kerry Wood, Kevin Brown, Moises Alou, Travis Hafner .75
32	Nick Johnson, Erubiel Durazo, Alfonso Soriano, Jason Giambi .50
33	Chad Tracy, Richie Sexson, Aubrey Huff, Brian Roberts .50
34	Todd Helton, Dmitri Young, Jeromy Burnitz, Jose Guillen .75
35	Juan Rivera, Shannon Stewart, Sammy Sosa, Cliff Floyd 1.00
36	Pat Burrell, Gabe Gross, Aaron Guiel, Paul LoDuca .50
37	A.J. Pierzynski, Orlando Hudson, David DeJesus, Brian Lawrence .50
38	Josh Beckett, Barry Zito, Mark Buehrle, Randy Wolf .50
39	Brad Penny, Jake Peavy, Rondell White, Brad Wilkerson .50
40	Ryan Drese, Kenny Rogers, Jermaine Dye, Lew Ford .50
41	Aaron Rowand, Jason Kendall, Tony Batista, Derrek Lee .50
42	Phil Nevin, Sean Casey, Rafael Palmeiro, Frank Thomas .75
43	Scott Hatteberg, Josh Labandeira, Jason Kubel, Nick Swisher .50
44	Freddy Guzman, Tim Stauffer, Merkin Valdez, Felix Hernandez .50
45	Willy Taveras, Grady Sizemore, Joey Gathright, Carlos Delgado .50
46	Scott Kazmir, Rickie Weeks, Dallas McPherson, Kevin Youkilis 1.00
47	Val Majewski, Casey Kotchman, Ryan Howard, Chris Burke .50
48	Robinson Cano, B.J. Upton, Jake Dittler, Ian Bladergroen 1.00
49	Brett Harper, James Jurries, Jeremy West, Matt Rogelstad 1.00

50	Darren Fenster, Nate Schierholtz, Brandon Moss, Ryan Sweeney 2.00
51	Chris Roberson, Steven Doetsch, Andre Ethier, Kevin West .50
52	Melky Cabrera, Ryan Goleski, Chris Denorfia, Chaz Lytle 1.00
53	Luis Ramirez, Matt DeSalvo, Sean Marshall, Jose Vaquedano .50
54	Chris Seddon, Chadd Blasko, Elvys Quezada, Wade Robinson .50
55	Nate McLouth, Matt Lindstrom, Kole Strayhorn, Ian Kinsler 2.50

2005 Topps Chicago White Sox World Series Commemorative

		NM/M
	Complete Boxed Set (56):	.25
	Common Card:	.25
1	Mark Buehrle	.50
2	A.J. Pierzynski	.50
3	Juan Uribe	.50
4	Tadahito Iguchi	.50
5	Paul Konerko	.75
6	Frank Thomas	2.50
7	Jermaine Dye	.50
8	Aaron Rowand	.50
9	Timo Perez	.50
10	Jose Contreras	.50
11	Carl Everett	.50
12	Pablo Ozuna	.50
13	Geoff Blum	.50
14	Cliff Politte	.50
15	Freddy Garcia	.50
16	Bobby Jenks	.50
17	Dustin Hermanson	.50
18	Neal Cotts	.50
19	Chris Widger	.50
20	Jon Garland	.50
21	Luis Vizcaino	.50
22	Damaso Marte	.50
23	Scott Podsednik	.75
24	Willie Harris	.50
25	Orlando Hernandez	.50
26	Joe Crede	.50
27	Ross Gload	.50
28	Brian Anderson	.50
29	Brandon McCarthy	.50
30	Ozzie Guillen	.50
31	Team Photo	.50
32	Buehrle Pitches 6+	.25
33	Sox Win 99 Games	.25
34	Buehrle Named Starter	.25
35	Podsednik Steals 59	.25
36	Konerko Tops 40 HRs	.25
37	Pierzynski Hits 2 of 5	.25
38	Chicago Socks Boston	.25
39	Sox Sweep Sox	.25
40	Pierzynski Safe	.25
41	Paul Hits Bunyanesque Homer	.25
42	It's a South Side Series	.25
43	Sox Starters Win Four (Buehrle)	.25
44	Sox Starters Win Four (Garland)	.25
45	Sox Starters Win Four (Garcia)	.25
46	Sox Starters Win Four (Contreras)	.25
47	World Series Game 1 (Crede, Jenks)	.25
48	World Series Game 2 (Konerko, Podsednik)	.25
49	World Series Game 3 (Blum)	.25
50	World Series Game 4 (Garcia, Uribe)	.25
51	World Series Game 4 (Garcia, Uribe)	.25
52	Astros Get Swept	.25
53	World Series Games 1, 4 (Podsednik, Dye, Iguchi)	.25
54	ALCS MVP (Konerko)	.25
55	World Series MVP (Dye)	.25
	Team Composite Box Topper (4-5/8" x 3-1/4")	4.00

2005 Topps Chrome

		NM/M
	Complete Set (472):	
	Common Player:	.25

	Common Rookie Auto. (221-252):		10.00
	Inserted 1:20		
	Series 1 Hobby Pack (4):		3.00
	Series 1 Hobby Box (20):		50.00
	Series 2 Hobby Pack (4):		5.00
	Series 2 Hobby Box (20):		90.00
1	Alex Rodriguez		2.50
2	Placido Polanco		.25
3	Torii Hunter		.50
4	Lyle Overbay		.25
5	Johnny Damon		.75
6	Johnny Estrada		.25
7	Rich Harden		.25
8	Francisco Rodriguez		.25
9	Jarrod Washburn		.25
10	Sammy Sosa		1.00
11	Randy Wolf		.25
12	Jason Bay		.50
13	Tom Glavine		.25
14	Michael Tucker		.25
15	Brian Giles		.25
16	Chad Tracy		.25
17	Jim Edmonds		.50
18	John Smoltz		.50
19	Roy Halladay		.50
20	Hank Blalock		.75
21	Darin Erstad		.50
22	Todd Walker		.50
23	Mike Hampton		.25
24	Mark Bellhorn		.25
25	Jim Thome		1.00
26	Shingo Takatsu		.25
27	Jody Gerut		.25
28	Vinny Castilla		.25
29	Luis Castillo		.25
30	Ivan Rodriguez		.75
31	Craig Biggio		.50
32	Joe Randa		.25
33	Adrian Beltre		.50
34	Scott Podsednik		.50
35	Cliff Floyd		.25
36	Livan Hernandez		.25
37	Eric Byrnes		.25
38	Jose Acevedo		.25
39	Jack Wilson		.25
40	Gary Sheffield		.75
41	Chan Ho Park		.25
42	Carl Crawford		.50
43	Shawn Estes		.25
44	David Bell		.25
45	Jeff DaVanon		.25
46	Brandon Webb		.25
47	Lance Berkman		.50
48	Melvin Mora		.25
49	David Ortiz		1.00
50	Andruw Jones		.50
51	Chone Figgins		.25
52	Danny Graves		.25
53	Preston Wilson		.25
54	Jeremy Bonderman		.25
55	Carlos Guillen		.25
56	Cesar Izturis		.25
57	Kazuo Matsui		.25
58	Jason Schmidt		.50
59	Jason Marquis		.25
60	Jose Vidro		.25
61	Al Leiter		.40
62	Javier Vazquez		.25
63	Erubiel Durazo		.25
64	Scott Spiezio		.25
65	Scot Shields		.25
66	Edgardo Alfonzo		.25
67	Miguel Tejada		.50
68	Francisco Cordero		.25
69	Brett Myers		.25
70	Curt Schilling		1.00
71	Matt Kata		.25
72	Bartolo Colon		.25
73	Rodrigo Lopez		.25
74	Tim Wakefield		.25
75	Frank Thomas		.75
76	Jimmy Rollins		.25
77	Barry Zito		.50
78	Hideo Nomo		.50
79	Brad Wilkerson		.25
80	Adam Dunn		.75
81	Derrek Lee		.25
82	Joe Crede		.25
83	Nate Robertson		.25
84	John Thomson		.25
85	Mike Sweeney		.25
86	Kip Wells		.25
87	Eric Gagne		.50
88	David Wells		.25
89	Alex Sanchez		.25
90	Bret Boone		.25
91	Mark Loretta		.25

92	Miguel Cabrera	1.00
93	Randy Winn	.25
94	Adam Everett	.25
95	Aubrey Huff	.25
96	Kevin Mench	.25
97	Frank Catalanotto	.25
98	Flash Gordon	.25
99	Scott Hatteberg	.25
100	Albert Pujols	3.00
101	Jose Molina	.25
102	Jason Johnson	.25
103	Jay Gibbons	.25
104	Byung-Hyun Kim	.25
105	Joe Borowski	.25
106	Mark Grudzielanek	.25
107	Mark Buehrle	.25
108	Paul Wilson	.25
109	Ronnie Belliard	.25
110	Reggie Sanders	.25
111	Tim Redding	.25
112	Brian Lawrence	.25
113	Travis Hafner	.40
114	Jose Hernandez	.25
115	Ben Sheets	.50
116	Johan Santana	.75
117	Billy Wagner	.40
118	Mariano Rivera	.50
119	Steve Trachsel	.25
120	Akinori Otsuka	.25
121	Jose Valentin	.25
122	Orlando Hernandez	.25
123	Raul Ibanez	.25
124	Mike Matheny	.25
125	Vernon Wells	.25
126	Jason Isringhausen	.25
127	Jose Guillen	.25
128	Danny Bautista	.25
129	Marcus Giles	.25
130	Javy Lopez	.40
131	Kevin Millar	.25
132	Kyle Farnsworth	.25
133	Carl Pavano	.25
134	Rafael Furcal	.25
135	Casey Blake	.25
136	Matt Holliday	.50
137	Bobby Higginson	.25
138	Adam Kennedy	.25
139	Alex Gonzalez	.25
140	Jeff Kent	.40
141	Aaron Guiel	.25
142	Shawn Green	.40
143	Bill Hall	.25
144	Shannon Stewart	.25
145	Juan Rivera	.25
146	Coco Crisp	.25
147	Mike Mussina	.50
148	Eric Chavez	.50
149	Jon Lieber	.25
150	Vladimir Guerrero	1.00
151	Alex Cintron	.25
152	Luis Matos	.25
153	Sidney Ponson	.25
154	Trot Nixon	.25
155	Greg Maddux	2.00
156	Edgar Renteria	.50
157	Ryan Freel	.25
158	Matt Lawton	.25
159	Mark Prior	1.00
160	Josh Beckett	.50
161	Ken Harvey	.25
162	Angel Berroa	.25
163	Juan Encarnacion	.25
164	Wes Helms	.25
165	Brad Radke	.25
166	Phil Nevin	.25
167	Mike Cameron	.25
168	Billy Koch	.25
169	Bobby Crosby	.50
170	Mike Lieberthal	.25
171	Robert Mackowiak	.25
172	Sean Burroughs	.25
173	J.T. Snow Jr.	.25
174	Paul Konerko	.40
175	Luis Gonzalez	.25
176	John Lackey	.25
177	Oliver Perez	.25
178	Brian Roberts	.25
179	Bill Mueller	.25
180	Carlos Lee	.25
181	Corey Patterson	.25
182	Sean Casey	.40
183	Cliff Lee	.40
184	Jason Jennings	.25
185	Dmitri Young	.25
186	Juan Uribe	.25
187	Andy Pettitte	.25
188	Juan Gonzalez	.25
189	Orlando Hudson	.25
190	Jason Phillips	.25
191	Braden Looper	.25
192	Lew Ford	.25
193	Mark Mulder	.40
194	Bobby Abreu	.25
195	Jason Kendall	.25
196	Khalil Greene	.50
197	A.J. Pierzynski	.25
198	Tim Worrell	.25
199	So Taguchi	.25
200	Jason Giambi	.25
201	Tony Batista	.25
202	Carlos Zambrano	.25
203	Trevor Hoffman	.25
204	Odalis Perez	.25
205	Jose Cruz Jr.	.25
206	Michael Barrett	.25
207	Chris Carpenter	.25
208	Michael Young	.25

209	Toby Hall	.25
210	Woody Williams	.25
211	Chris Denorfia RC	1.00
212	Darren Fenster RC	1.00
213	Elvys Quezada RC	2.00
214	Ian Kinsler RC	5.00
215	Matt Lindstrom RC	2.00
216	Ryan Goleski RC	2.00
217	Ryan Sweeney	3.00
218	Sean Marshall RC	1.00
219	Steven Doetsch RC	2.00
220	Wade Robinson RC	3.00
221	Andre Ethier	45.00
222	Brandon Moss RC	10.00
223	Chadd Blasko RC	10.00
224	Chris Roberson RC	10.00
225	Chris Seddon RC	10.00
226	Ian Bladergroen RC	10.00
227	Jake Dittler RC	10.00
228	Jose Vaquedano RC	10.00
229	Jeremy West RC	10.00
230	Kole Strayhorn RC	10.00
231	Kevin West RC	10.00
232	Luis Ramirez RC	10.00
233	Melky Cabrera RC	20.00
234	Nate Schierholtz RC	15.00
235	Billy Butler RC	40.00
236	Brandon Szymanski RC	10.00
237	Chad Orvella RC	10.00
238	Chip Cannon RC	10.00
239	Eric Nielsen RC	10.00
240	Erik Cordier RC	10.00
241	Glen Perkins RC	15.00
242	Justin Verlander RC	50.00
243	Kevin Melillo RC	10.00
244	Landon Powell RC	10.00
245	Matt Campbell RC	10.00
246	Michael Rogers RC	15.00
247	Nate McLouth RC	15.00
248	Scott Mathieson RC	10.00
249	Shane Costa RC	10.00
250	Tony Giarratano RC	10.00
251	Tyler Pelland RC	10.00
252	Wes Swackhamer RC	10.00
253	Garret Anderson	.50
254	Randy Johnson	1.00
255	Charles Thomas	.25
256	Rafael Palmeiro	.75
257	Kevin Youkilis	.25
258	Freddy Garcia	.25
259	Magglio Ordonez	.25
260	Aaron Harang	.25
261	Grady Sizemore	.50
262	Chin-Hui Tsao	.25
263	Eric Munson	.25
264	Juan Pierre	.25
265	Brad Lidge	.25
266	Brian Anderson	.25
267	Todd Helton	.75
268	Chad Cordero	.25
269	Kris Benson	.25
270	Brad Halsey	.25
271	Jermaine Dye	.25
272	Manny Ramirez	1.00
273	Adam Eaton	.25
274	Brett Tomko	.25
275	Bucky Jacobsen	.25
276	Dontrelle Willis	.50
277	B.J. Upton	.25
278	Rocco Baldelli	.25
279	Ryan Drese	.25
280	Ichiro Suzuki	2.50
281	Brandon Lyon	.25
282	Nick Green	.25
283	Jerry Hairston	.25
284	Mike Lowell	.25
285	Kerry Wood	1.00
286	Omar Vizquel	.25
287	Carlos Beltran	.25
288	Carlos Pena	.25
289	Jeff Weaver	.25
290	Chad Moeller	.25
291	Joe Mays	.25
292	Termel Sledge	.25
293	Richard Hidalgo	.25
294	Justin Duchscherer	.25
295	Eric Milton	.25
296	Ramon Hernandez	.25
297	Jose Reyes	.50
298	Joel Pineiro	.25
299	Matt Morris	.25
300	John Halama	.25
301	Gary Matthews	.25
302	Ryan Madson	.25
303	Mark Kotsay	.25
304	Carlos Delgado	.50
305	Casey Kotchman	.25
306	Greg Aquino	.25
307	LaTroy Hawkins	.25
308	Jose Contreras	.25
309	Ken Griffey Jr.	2.00
310	C.C. Sabathia	.25
311	Brandon Inge	.25
312	John Buck	.25
313	Hee Seop Choi	.25
314	Chris Capuano	.25
315	Jesse Crain	.25
316	Geoff Jenkins	.25
317	Mike Piazza	2.00
318	Jorge Posada	.50
319	Nick Swisher	.25
320	Kevin Millwood	.25
321	Mike Gonzalez	.25
322	Jake Peavy	.25
323	Dustin Hermanson	.25
324	Jeremy Reed	.25
325	Alfonso Soriano	1.00
326	Alexis Rios	.25

327	David Eckstein	.25
328	Shea Hillenbrand	.25
329	Russ Ortiz	.25
330	Kurt Ainsworth	.25
331	Orlando Cabrera	.25
332	Carlos Silva	.25
333	Ross Gload	.25
334	Josh Phelps	.25
335	Mike Maroth	.25
336	Guillermo Mota	.25
337	Chris Burke	.25
338	David DeJesus	.25
339	Jose Lima	.25
340	Cristian Guzman	.25
341	Nick Johnson	.25
342	Victor Zambrano	.25
343	Rod Barajas	.25
344	Damian Miller	.25
345	Chase Utley	.50
346	Sean Burnett	.25
347	David Wells	.25
348	Dustan Mohr	.25
349	Bobby Madritsch	.25
350	Reed Johnson	.25
351	R.A. Dickey	.25
352	Scott Kazmir	.25
353	Tony Womack	.25
354	Thomas Perez	.25
355	Esteban Loaiza	.25
356	Tomokazu Ohka	.25
357	Ramon Ortiz	.25
358	Richie Sexson	.50
359	J.D. Drew	.40
360	Barry Bonds	4.00
361	Aramis Ramirez	.50
362	Wily Mo Pena	.25
363	Jeromy Burnitz	.25
364	Nomar Garciaparra	2.00
365	Brandon Backe	.25
366	Derek Lowe	.25
367	Doug Davis	.25
368	Joe Mauer	.75
369	Endy Chavez	.25
370	Bernie Williams	.50
371	Jason Michaels	.25
372	Craig Wilson	.25
373	Ryan Klesko	.25
374	Ray Durham	.25
375	Jose Lopez	.25
376	Jeff Suppan	.25
377	David Bush	.25
378	Marlon Byrd	.25
379	Roy Oswalt	.40
380	Rondell White	.25
381	Troy Glaus	.50
382	Scott Hairston	.25
383	Chipper Jones	1.00
384	Daniel Cabrera	.25
385	Jon Garland	.25
386	Austin Kearns	.25
387	Jake Westbrook	.25
388	Aaron Miles	.25
389	Omar Infante	.25
390	Paul LoDuca	.25
391	Morgan Ensberg	.25
392	Tony Graffanino	.25
393	Milton Bradley	.25
394	Keith Ginter	.25
395	Justin Morneau	.75
396	Tony Armas Jr.	.25
397	Kevin Brown	.25
398	Marco Scutaro	.25
399	Tim Hudson	.50
400	Pat Burrell	.40
401	Jeff Cirillo	.25
402	Larry Walker	.50
403	Dewon Brazelton	.25
404	Shigetoshi Hasegawa	.25
405	Octavio Dotel	.25
406	Michael Cuddyer	.25
407	Junior Spivey	.25
408	Zack Greinke	.25
409	Roger Clemens	3.00
410	Chris Shelton	.25
411	Ugueth Urbina	.25
412	Rafael Betancourt	.25
413	Willie Harris	.25
414	Keith Foulke	.25
415	Larry Bigbie	.25
416	Paul Byrd	.25
417	Troy Percival	.25
418	Pedro J. Martinez	1.00
419	Matt Clement	.25
420	Ryan Wagner	.25
421	Jeff Francis	.25
422	Jeff Conine	.25
423	Wade Miller	.25
424	Gavin Floyd	.25
425	Kazuhisa Ishii	.25
426	Victor Santos	.25
427	Jacque Jones	.25
428	Hideki Matsui	2.00
429	Cory Lidle	.25
430	Jose Castillo	.25
431	Alex Gonzalez	.25
432	Kirk Rueter	.25
433	Jolbert Cabrera	.25
434	Erik Bedard	.25
435	Ricky Ledee	.25
436	Mark Hendrickson	.25
437	Laynce Nix	.25
438	Jason Frasor	.25
439	Kevin Gregg	.25
440	Derek Jeter	3.00
441	Jaret Wright	.25
442	Edwin Jackson	.25
443	Moises Alou	.50
444	Aaron Rowand	.25

445	Kazuhito Tadano	.25
446	Luis Gonzalez	.40
447	A.J. Burnett	.40
448	Jeff Bagwell	.50
449	Brad Penny	.25
450	Corey Koskie	.25
451	Mark Ellis	.25
452	Hector Luna	.25
453	Miguel Olivo	.25
454	Scott Rolen	1.00
455	Ricardo Rodriguez	.25
456	Eric Hinske	.25
457	Tim Salmon	.25
458	Adam LaRoche	.25
459	B.J. Ryan	.25
460	Steve Finley	.25
461	Joe Nathan	.25
462	Vicente Padilla	.25
463	Yadier Molina	.25
464	Tino Martinez	.25
465	Mark Teixeira	.50
466	Kelvim Escobar	.25
467	Pedro Feliz	.25
468	Ryan Garko RC	4.00
469	Bobby Livingston RC	.25
470	Yorman Bazardo RC	3.00
471	Michael Bourn	2.00
472	Andy LaRoche RC	10.00

Refractor

Refractor:		2-3X
Inserted 1:6		
Rookie Auto. (221-252):		1-1.5X
Production 500		

Black Refractor

Black Refractor:		3-5X
Production 225		
Rookie Auto. (221-252):		1.5-3X
Production 200		

Gold Refractor

No Pricing
Production One Set

X-Fractor

Cards (1-220):		5-10X
Rookie Auto. (221-234):		No Pricing
Production 25 Sets		

Printing Plates

No Pricing
Production one set per color.

A-Rod Throwbacks

		NM/M
Common A-Rod:		3.00
ARI1-4	Alex Rodriguez	3.00

Chrome The Game Relics

		NM/M
Common Player:		5.00
Inserted 1:Box		
JB	Jeff Bagwell	8.00
WB	Wade Boggs	6.00
TH	Torii Hunter	5.00
MPI	Mike Piazza	8.00
JP	Jorge Posada	6.00
MP	Mark Prior	8.00
AR	Alex Rodriguez	15.00
JS	John Smoltz	8.00
AS	Alfonso Soriano	5.00
SS	Sammy Sosa	10.00
MY	Michael Young	5.00

Chrome The Game Patch Relics

		NM/M
Common Player:		10.00
JB	Jeff Bagwell	15.00
JBE	Josh Beckett	10.00
LB	Lance Berkman	10.00
BB	Bret Boone	10.00
AD1	Adam Dunn	15.00
AD2	Adam Dunn	15.00
TG	Troy Glaus	10.00
TH	Todd Helton	10.00
KI	Kazuhisa Ishii	10.00
CJ	Chipper Jones	20.00
PL	Paul LoDuca	10.00
ML	Mike Lowell	10.00
PM	Pedro Martinez	20.00
HN	Hideo Nomo	20.00
MO	Magglio Ordonez	10.00
MPI	Mike Piazza	20.00
AP	Albert Pujols	25.00
AR	Alex Rodriguez	25.00
CS	C.C. Sabathia	10.00
SS	Sammy Sosa	20.00
MT	Mark Teixeira	15.00
FT	Frank Thomas	15.00
DW	Dontrelle Willis	10.00
KW	Kerry Wood	20.00

Dem Bums Autographs

		NM/M
Inserted 1:1,816		
CE	Carl Erskine	50.00
DS	Duke Snider	85.00

2005 Topps Cracker Jack

CHRIS CARPENTER
St. Louis - National League

		NM/M
Complete Set (240):		
Common Player:		.25
Common SP:		3.00
Inserted 1:3		
Pack (8):		4.00
Box (20):		70.00
1	David Wright/SP	8.00
2	Rafael Furcal	.25
3	Alex Rodriguez	1.50
3	Alex Rodriguez/SP/Fldg	5.00
4	Victor Martinez/SP	3.00
5	Ken Griffey Jr.	1.50
6	Bobby Crosby/SP	.25
7	Ivan Rodriguez	.50
8	Darin Erstad	.25
9	Javy Lopez	.25
10	Brian Giles	.25
11	Aaron Rowand/SP	3.00
12	Joe Torre	.25
13	Zack Greinke/SP	.25
14	Shannon Stewart	.25
15	Jack Wilson	.25
16	Jose Vidro	.25
17	Josh Beckett	.40
---	Josh Beckett (No number.)	4.00
18	Barry Zito	.40
19	Bret Boone	.25
20	Greg Maddux	1.00
21	Carl Crawford/SP	3.00
22	Mark Teixeira	.50
23	Jason Schmidt	.40
24	Kazuhisa Ishii	.25
25	Mike Piazza	1.00
26	Daniel Cabrera/SP	3.00

27	Mike Lieberthal	.25
28	Gil Meche	.25
29	Phil Nevin	.25
30	Adrian Beltre/SP	3.00
31	Chipper Jones/SP	4.00
32	Zach Day	.25
33	Ben Sheets	.40
34	Carlos Zambrano	.40
35	Melvin Mora	.25
36	Joe Mauer	.75
37	Ken Harvey	.25
38	Bernie Williams	.40
39	Mike Maroth	.25
40	Eric Chavez	.40
41	Matt Lawton/SP	3.00
42	Ray Durham	.25
43	Vernon Wells	.25
44	Mike Lowell	.25
45	Jim Thome	.50
46	Joel Pineiro	.25
47	Lance Berkman	.40
48	Ryan Klesko	.25
49	Adam Dunn	.50
50	Vladimir Guerrero	.75
51	Eric Gagne/SP	4.00
52	Richie Sexson	.40
53	Javier Vazquez	.25
54	Roy Oswalt	.40
55	Carlos Delgado	.50
56	John Buck/SP	3.00
57	Kenny Rogers	.25
58	Sidney Ponson	.25
59	Vicente Padilla	.25
60	Mark Prior/SP	.75
60	Mark Prior/SP/Portrait	4.00
61	A.J. Pierzynski	.25
62	Aubrey Huff	.25
63	Shea Hillenbrand	.25
64	Carlos Guillen	.25
65	Lyle Overbay	.25
66	Al Leiter	.25
67	Eric Hinske	.25
68	Laynce Nix	.25
69	Scott Hairston	.25
70	Roger Clemens	2.00
71	Cesar Izturis/SP	3.00
72	Shawn Green	.25
73	Marcus Giles	.25
74	Rafael Palmeiro	.50
75	Melky Cabrera/SP	3.00
76	Gary Sheffield/SP	4.00
76	Juan Pierre	.25
77	Pat Burrell	.40
78	Sean Burroughs	.25
79	Frank Thomas	.50
80	Andruw Jones	.40
81	C.C. Sabathia	.25
82	Jeff Bagwell	.50
83	Tom Glavine	.40
84	Craig Wilson/SP	3.00
85	Johan Santana	.75
85	Johan Santana/SP/Portrait	4.00
86	Raul Ibanez	.25
87	Sean Casey	.25
88	Bucky Jacobsen	.25
89	B.J. Upton	.40
90	Bobby Abreu	.40
91	Geoff Jenkins	.25
92	Troy Glaus	.40
93	Dontrelle Willis	.40
94	Jose Lima	.25
95	Rocco Baldelli	.25
96	Aramis Ramirez	.40
97	Paul LoDuca	.25
98	Torii Hunter	.40
99	Jay Payton	.25
100	Carlos Beltran	.50
101	Jaret Wright	.25
102	Jason Bay	.40
103	Cliff Floyd	.25
104	Mike Sweeney	.25
105	Sammy Sosa	1.50
106	Khalil Greene/SP	4.00
107	David DeJesus	.25
108	Jermaine Dye	.25
109	Miguel Cabrera	.75
110	Miguel Tejada/SP	5.00
111	Johnny Estrada/SP	3.00
112	Ronnie Belliard/SP	3.00
113	Austin Kearns	.25
114	Erubiel Durazo	.25
115	Preston Wilson	.25
116	Hideo Nomo	.40
117	Dmitri Young	.25
118	Jon Lieber	.25
119	Derrek Lee	.40
120	Todd Helton	.50
121	Omar Vizquel	.25
122	Wily Mo Pena	.25
123	J.D. Drew	.40
124	Matt Holliday	.25
125	Ichiro Suzuki	1.50
126	Mark Buehrle/SP	3.00
127	Eric Munson	.25
128	Jeff Kent	.25
129	Kerry Wood	.75
130	Mariano Rivera	.50
131	Nick Johnson	.25
132	Randy Winn	.25
133	Phil Garner	.25
134	Jose Reyes	.50
135	Michael Young/SP	3.00
135	Ian Kinsler/SP	6.00
136	Jose Contreras	.25
137	Oliver Perez	.25
138	Roy Halladay	.40
139	Kevin Millwood	.25

140	Jorge Posada	.40
141	Mike Cameron	.25
142	Edgardo Alfonzo	.25
143	Chris Shelton	.25
144	Luis Castillo	.25
145	Alfonso Soriano	.75
146	Ryan Drese/SP	3.00
147	Mark Mulder	.40
148	Jason Giambi	.25
149	Travis Hafner	.25
150	Randy Johnson	.75
151	Paul Konerko/SP	3.00
152	Mike Mussina	.50
153	Brad Wilkerson	.25
154	Tim Hudson	.40
155	Garret Anderson	.40
156	Chase Utley/SP	3.00
157	Jamie Moyer	.25
158	Scott Kazmir	.40
159	Brett Myers	.25
160	Kazuo Matsui	.25
161	Orlando Hudson	.25
162	Luis Gonzalez	.25
163	Kevin Youkilis	.25
164	Jason Kendall/SP	.25
165	Landon Powell/SP	3.00
166	Hank Blalock	.50
167	Mark Loretta/SP	3.00
168	Miguel Cairo	.25
169	Corey Patterson	.40
170	Carlos Zambrano	.25
171	Magglio Ordonez	.25
172	J.T. Snow	.25
173	Randy Wolf	.25
174	Rich Harden	.40
175	Bartolo Colon	.25
176	Derek Jeter	2.00
177	Casey Kotchman/SP	3.00
178	Val Majewski	.25
179	Grady Sizemore	.50
180	Rickie Weeks	.25
181	Robinson Cano	.75
182	Nick Swisher/SP	3.00
183	Ryan Howard	1.50
184	John Van Benschoten	.25
185	Delmon Young	.50
186	Aaron Hill	.25
187	Chris Burke/SP	3.00
188	Merkin Valdez	.25
189	Jeremy Reed	.25
190	Conor Jackson	.25
191	Joey Gathright/SP	3.00
192	Gavin Floyd	.25
193	Joe Blanton	.25
194	Jason Kubel	.25
195	Jeff Francis	.25
196	Angel Guzman/SP	3.00
197	Dallas McPherson	.25
198	Melky Cabrera RC	1.00
199	Jake Dittler	.25
200	Elvys Quezada RC	.50
201	Ian Kinsler/SP RC	5.00
202	Nate McLouth RC	1.00
203	Chris Seddon RC	.75
204	Chad Orvella RC	.50
205	Ian Bladergroen RC	.25
206	James Jurries/SP RC	3.00
207	Landon Powell RC	.75
208	Eric Nielsen RC	.50
209	Chris Roberson RC	.50
210	Andre Ethier	2.00
211	Chris Denorfia/SP RC	3.00
212	Darren Fenster RC	.50
213	Jeremy West RC	.50
214	Sean Marshall RC	.50
215	Ryan Sweeney	.50
216	Steven Doetsch/SP RC	3.00
217	Kevin Melillo RC	.50
218	Chip Cannon RC	1.00
219	Tony LaRussa	.25
220	Chris Carpenter	.25
221	Edgar Renteria/SP/Red Sox	3.00
221	Edgar Renteria/SP Cardinals	3.00
222	Albert Pujols	2.00
223	Jim Edmonds	.40
224	Jason Marquis	.25
225	Scott Rolen/SP	4.00
226	Larry Walker/SP	4.00
227	Matt Morris	.25
228	Mike Matheny	.25
228	Mike Matheny/SP Cardinals	3.00
229	Jeromy Burnitz	.25
230	Terry Francona	.25
231	Johnny Damon/SP	4.00
232	Keith Foulke	.25
233	Trot Nixon	.25
234	Manny Ramirez	.75
235	David Ortiz/SP	4.00
236	Pedro Martinez/SP/Mets	4.00
236	Pedro J. Martinez/SP/Red Sox	4.00
237	Curt Schilling	.75
238	Kevin Millar	.25
239	Bill Mueller	.25
240	Mark Bellhorn	.25
240	Josh Beckett/SP	3.00

Mini Blue

Stars:		8-15X
SP's:		4-6X
Production 50 Sets		

Mini Grey

No Pricing
Production 25 Sets

Mini Red

Stars:		1-2X
Inserted 1:1		
SP's:		.75-1.5X
Inserted 1:20		

Mini Stickers

Stars:		1-2X
Inserted 1:1		
SP's:		.75-1.5X
Inserted 1:20		

Mini White

No Pricing
Production One Set

Autographs

		NM/M
Production 50 Sets		
Bonds Production 25		
GA	Garret Anderson/50	30.00
CB	Carlos Beltran/50	80.00
EC	Eric Chavez/50	30.00
CC	Carl Crawford/50	40.00
EG	Eric Gagne	40.00
AR	Alex Rodriguez	250.00
CS	C.C. Sabathia/50	50.00
JS	Johan Santana	60.00
CW	Craig Wilson/50	25.00
DW	David Wright/50	150.00

Secret Surprise Autographs

		NM/M
Common Auto.:		8.00
GA	Garret Anderson	15.00
EC	Eric Chavez	15.00
CC	Carl Crawford	10.00
EG	Eric Gagne	20.00
AG	Angel Guzman	8.00
SK	Scott Kazmir	25.00
MK	Mark Kotsay/100	15.00
ML	Mark Loretta/100	15.00
DM	Dallas McPherson/100	15.00
KM	Kevin Millar	15.00
MM	Melvin Mora	15.00
CN	Chris Nelson	10.00
RR	Richie Robnett	10.00
AR	Alex Rodriguez/100	250.00
CS	C.C. Sabathia	20.00
JS	Johan Santana	50.00
CT	Curtis Thigpen	15.00
CW	Craig Wilson	10.00
DW	David Wright	50.00

Take Me Out To/Ballgame Relics

		NM/M
Inserted 1:16		
JB	Jeff Bagwell	6.00
RB	Ronnie Belliard	4.00
CB	Carlos Beltran	8.00
AB	Adrian Beltre	6.00
LB1	Lance Berkman	8.00
LB2	Lance Berkman	4.00
AB1	Angel Berroa	4.00
AB2	Angel Berroa	4.00
CBI	Craig Biggio	6.00
HB1	Hank Blalock	8.00
HB2	Hank Blalock	8.00
HB3	Hank Blalock	8.00
SB	Sean Burroughs	4.00
MC	Miguel Cabrera	8.00
VC	Vinny Castilla	4.00
EC1	Eric Chavez	6.00
EC2	Eric Chavez	6.00
BC	Bobby Cox	4.00
CC	Coco Crisp	4.00
BCR	Bobby Crosby	4.00
AD	Adam Dunn	8.00
JE1	Jim Edmonds	4.00
JE2	Jim Edmonds	4.00
DE	Darin Erstad	4.00
JE	Johnny Estrada	4.00
RF	Rafael Furcal	4.00
JG	Jody Gerut	4.00
JGI	Jay Gibbons	4.00
MG	Marcus Giles	4.00
TG	Troy Glaus	6.00
LG	Luis Gonzalez	4.00
NG	Nick Green	4.00
SG	Shawn Green	4.00
VG	Vladimir Guerrero	10.00
JGU	Jose Guillen	6.00
CG	Cristian Guzman	4.00
TH	Todd Helton	8.00
THU	Torii Hunter	6.00
JJ	Jacque Jones	4.00
JK	Jason Kendall	4.00
BK	Bobby Kielty	4.00
RK	Ryan Klesko	4.00
PK	Paul Konerko	4.00
MK	Mark Kotsay	4.00
AL	Adam LaRoche	6.00

VM Victor Martinez 6.00
KME Kevin Mench 4.00
DM Doug Mientkiewicz 4.00
KM Kevin Millar 10.00
MM Melvin Mora 6.00
PN Phil Nevin 4.00
LN Laynce Nix 4.00
MO Magglio Ordonez 4.00
DO David Ortiz 10.00
RP Rafael Palmeiro 8.00
CP Corey Patterson 6.00
MP Mike Piazza 12.00
JP1 Jorge Posada 8.00
JP2 Jorge Posada 8.00
AP Albert Pujols 20.00
MR Manny Ramirez 10.00
JR Jeremy Reed 8.00
MRE Mike Restovich 4.00
AR Alex Rodriguez 15.00
ARA Aramis Ramirez 6.00
IR1 Ivan Rodriguez 8.00
IR2 Ivan Rodriguez 8.00
RS Reggie Sanders 4.00
BS Benito Santiago 4.00
GS Gary Sheffield 8.00
AS Alfonso Soriano 8.00
MT1 Mark Teixeira 8.00
MT2 Mark Teixeira 8.00
MT3 Mark Teixeira 8.00
MTE1 Miguel Tejada 8.00
MTE2 Miguel Tejada 8.00
CT Charles Thomas 4.00
JT Jim Thome 8.00
JTO Joe Torre 10.00
OV Omar Vizquel 6.00
BW Bernie Williams 8.00
DW Dontrelle Willis 6.00
MY Michael Young 6.00

1,2,3 Strikes You're Out Relics

Inserted 1:204

NM/M
JB Josh Beckett 8.00
RD Ryan Drese 5.00
RO Russ Ortiz 5.00
BR Brad Radke 5.00
CS Curt Schilling 15.00
JW Jaret Wright 8.00

2005 Topps eTopps Alex Rodriguez Promos

NM/M
Complete Set (3): 12.00
Common Card: 4.00
1 of 100: 2X
1 of 50: 3X
AR1 Alex Rodriguez (Follow-through.) 4.00
AR2 Alex Rodriguez/Throwing 4.00
AR3 Alex Rodriguez/Btg 4.00

2005 Topps eTopps

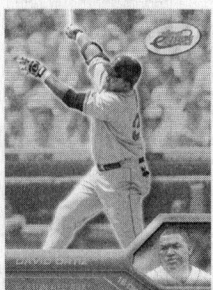

Topps continued its on-line card program for a fifth year in 2005. Initial Player Offerings (about $5-7 per card) were again made for one week, with allocations having to be made for some cards in high demand. The number of each card actually sold is shown parenthetically. After the IPO, cards could be bought and sold within portfolios, or physically delivered for a fee. The 2-1/2" x 3-1/2" cards' fronts have an action photo at top and a portrait photo below. Backs repeat the portrait photo, have a 2004 recap and 2005 "prospectus," and a few biographical bits and stats. A total of 111 cards was issued, skip-numbered between 1-220. Values shown are for cards in a virtual portfolio, rather than "in hand."

NM/M
Complete Set (111): 325.00
Common Player: 1.50
1 Los Angeles Angels of Anaheim (1,018) 1.50
2 Arizona Diamondbacks (1,000) 1.50
3 Atlanta Braves (1,275) 2.00
4 Baltimore Orioles (1,189) 1.50
5 Boston Red Sox (2,538) 1.50
6 Chicago Cubs (1,300) 1.50
7 Chicago White Sox (1,199) 2.75
8 Cincinnati Reds (770) 1.50
9 Cleveland Indians (974) 1.50
10 Colorado Rockies (736) 1.50
11 Detroit Tigers (832) 1.50
12 Florida Marlins (863) 1.50
13 Houston Astros (1,227) 2.00
14 Kansas City Royals (807) 1.50
15 Los Angeles Dodgers (1,000) 1.50
16 Milwaukee Brewers (728) 1.50
17 Minnesota Twins (888) 1.50
18 New York Mets (1,300) 1.50
19 New York Yankees (2,600) 1.75
20 Oakland Athletics (739) 1.75
21 Philadelphia Phillies (890) 1.50
22 Pittsburgh Pirates (776) 2.00
23 San Diego Padres (818) 1.50
24 San Francisco Giants (1,051) 2.50
25 Seattle Mariners (800) 1.50
26 St. Louis Cardinals (1,300) 2.00
27 Tampa Bay Devil Rays (688) 1.75
28 Texas Rangers (705) 1.50
29 Toronto Blue Jays (701) 1.50
30 Washington Nationals (1,300) 2.00
31 Adrian Beltre (1,298) 1.75
33 Albert Pujols (2,600) 5.50
34 Alex Rodriguez (2,259) 4.00
35 Alexis Rios (1,158) 1.50
36 Alfonso Soriano (793) 5.50
40 Carlos Beltran (1,630) 1.75
41 Carl Crawford (820) 3.00
43 Carlos Guillen (920) 2.00
44 Chipper Jones (927) 4.00
45 Carl Pavano (826) 2.50
46 Curt Schilling (1,288) 1.50
47 Derek Jeter (2,000) 3.50
48 David Ortiz (981) 3.50
49 David Wright (2,956) 8.00
50 David Wells (851) 5.00
51 Eric Gagne (688) 1.50
53 Gary Sheffield (857) 3.25
54 Hank Blalock (814) 3.75
55 Hideki Matsui (1,200) 4.00
56 Ichiro Suzuki (2,223) 2.00
57 Ivan Rodriguez (773) 4.00
61 Johan Santana (2,600) 7.25
63 Jim Thome (750) 6.50
64 Ken Griffey Jr. (1,200) 3.50
67 Kerry Wood (756) 4.25
68 Livan Hernandez (1,200) 1.50
69 Miguel Cabrera (1,200) 4.00
71 Mark Prior (1,337) 1.75
72 Mike Piazza (1,057) 2.50
73 Manny Ramirez (1,200) 2.00
74 Miguel Tejada (944) 2.75
75 Mark Teixeira (1,037) 4.00
77 Pedro Martinez (1,163) 1.75
80 Roger Clemens (1,667) 3.00
82 Randy Johnson (2,196) 1.50
86 Sammy Sosa (1,200) 1.50
89 Todd Helton (785) 3.50
91 Vladimir Guerrero (1,036) 2.50
95 Dallas McPherson (2,350) 2.25
Andy Marte (2,000) 5.25
115 Grady Sizemore (1,200) 4.00
133 David DeJesus (680) 9.00
142 J.J. Hardy (1,523) 2.50
149 Justin Morneau (1,664) 3.75
152 Chien-Ming Wang (1,200) 4.00
153 Dioner Navarro (939) 3.25
165 Gavin Floyd (1,485) 2.00
165 David Aardsma (889) 2.00
172 B.J. Upton (1,910) 3.00
175 Scott Kazmir (1,760) 4.25
175 Adrian Gonzalez (938) 8.00
181 Brendan Harris (977) 2.00
185 Tim Hudson (859) 2.25
186 Mark Mulder (860) 2.50
188 Jeff Bagwell (823) 2.75
189 Troy Glaus (824) 3.75
191 Jim Edmonds (874) 4.00
193 Johnny Damon (1,415) 2.00
195 Billy Wagner (939) 2.25
196 Dmitri Young (778) 2.75
198 David Eckstein (874) 5.00
199 Tadahito Iguchi (1,200) 2.50
200 Jason Bartlett (913) 2.50
201 Joe Blanton (1,097) 2.75
203 Huston Street (1,200) 7.75
204 Clint Barmes (2,000) 3.25
207 Brian Roberts (1,200) 1.75
208 John Garland (1,200) 2.25
209 Robinson Cano (1,200) 11.00
210 Zach Duke (2,000) 6.75
211a Rickie Weeks (1,675) 4.50
211b Brad Eldred (849) 5.00
212a Jeff Francoeur (2,000) 9.50
212b Felix Hernandez (2,000) 12.75
213 Jonathan Papelbon (1,500) 9.00
214 Conor Jackson (1,278) 3.25
215 Dan Johnson (1,000) 3.25
216 Prince Fielder (2,000) 15.00
217 Jeremy Hermida (1,400) 4.00
219 Melky Cabrera (1,000) 3.50
220 Ryan Howard (2,000) 6.00

2005 Topps eTopps Classics

Topps continued its eTopps Classics line-up in 2005 with five cards of former greats. Numbering and format were contiguous with earlier issues. Like regular eTopps cards, Classics could only be ordered during a one-week Initial Player Offering period. Cards were issued in a quantity of up to 2,000 each at $9.50. The number of cards actually sold is shown parenthetically. Fronts have a color photo, backs have a picture of one of that player's Topps cards, along with career notes, stats, etc. Values shown are for cards in a virtual portfolio, rather than "in hand."

NM/M
Complete Set (5): 45.00
Common Player: 6.00
61 Roger Maris (2,000) 9.00
62 Ryne Sandberg (1,000) 9.00
63 Don Mattingly (1,000) 15.00
64 Ernie Banks (1,657) 6.00
65 Mark Fidrych (976) 6.00

2005 Topps eTopps Classic Events

Great moments of late 20th Century baseball history are captured in this series. Each card has a front photo depicting the event, with a write-up on back. Cards were issued in quantities of up to nearly 1,200 each (actual number issued is shown parenthetically) at an issue price of $9.50. Values shown are for cards in "virtual portfolios" rather than "in hand."

NM/M
Complete Set (20): 145.00
Common Player: 4.00
1 Bobby Thomson (819) 5.00
2 Don Larsen (713) 4.50
3 Bill Mazeroski (731) 7.00
4 Bucky Dent (713) 5.50
5 George Brett (1,000) 6.75
6 Dwight Gooden (555) 11.50
7 Bob Gibson (728) 7.25
8 1989 World Series (1,000) 4.00
9 Kirk Gibson (714) 10.00
10 Reggie Jackson (979) 10.00
11 Carlton Fisk (861) 5.00
12 Mookie Wilson (577) 9.00
13 Yogi Berra (1,000) 4.00
14 Cal Ripken Jr. (1,000) 16.00
15 Denny McLain (576) 12.50
16 Josh Gibson (728) 5.75
17 Barry Bonds (1,000) 16.50
18 Joe Carter (557) 7.75
19 Nolan Ryan (1,000) 7.75
20 Rickey Henderson (748) 8.50

2005 Topps eTopps Events Series

Values shown are for cards in a virtual portfolio rather than "in hand." Each card originally sold for $4.50. Quantity actually issued is shown parenthetically.

NM/M
Complete Set (21): 50.00
Common Card: 1.50
1 NL Transactions (862) 1.50
2 AL Transactions (977) 1.50
3 Opening Day (Hideki Matsui, Randy Johnson) (1,000) 1.50
4 David Ortiz (1,000) 3.00
5 Lucky #7 (David Wright (1,000)) 2.50
6 Alex Rodriguez (1,000) 5.50
7 Derrek Lee (1,000) 1.75
8 Alex Rodriguez (1,000) 6.50
9 Nationals Win 10 (Nick Johnson, Livan Hernandez (678)) 3.50
10 Bob Abreu (800) 2.00
11 Miguel Tejada (642) 2.00
12 Rafael Palmeiro (1,000) 1.50
13 Greg Maddux (1,000) 2.00
14 Houston Astros (Andy Pettitte, Roger Clemens (650)) 2.75
15 Tony LaRussa (550) 4.00
16 Jeremy Hermida (760) 2.50
17 Houston Marathon (Chris Burke, Roger Clemens (1,000)) 1.75
18 Complete Series (Jose Contreras, Mark Buehrle (840)) 1.50
19 Houston Astros (579) 3.00
20 Chicago White Sox (1,000) 2.50
21 Jermaine Dye (746)

2005 Topps Gallery

NM/M
Complete Set (195): 175.00
Common Player: .25
Common SP (151-195): 1.00
Inserted 1:1
Variations 1:40
Pack (5): 6.00
Box (20): 100.00
1 Alex Rodriguez 2.50
1 Alex Rodriguez/ SP/Black Bat Glove 8.00
2 Eric Chavez .50
3 Mike Piazza 1.50
4 Bret Boone .25
5 Albert Pujols 3.00
6 Vernon Wells .25
7 Andruw Jones .50
8 Miguel Tejada .50
9 Johnny Damon .75
10 Nomar Garciaparra 2.00
11 Pat Burrell .40
12 Bartolo Colon .25
13 Johnny Estrada .25
14 Luis Gonzalez .40
15 Jay Gibbons .25
16 Curt Schilling 1.00
17 Aramis Ramirez .50
18 Frank Thomas .75
19 Adam Dunn .75
21 Sammy Sosa 2.00
22 Matt Lawton .25
23 Preston Wilson .25
24 Carlos Pena .25
25 Josh Beckett .75
26 Carlos Beltran .75
27 Juan Gonzalez .50
28 Adrian Beltre .50
29 Lyle Overbay .25
30 Justin Morneau .50
31 Derek Jeter 3.00
32 Barry Zito .25
33 Bobby Abreu .40
34 Jason Bay .25
35 Jose Reyes .50
36 Nick Johnson .25
37 Lew Ford .25
38 Scott Podsednik .25
39 Rocco Baldelli .40
40 Eric Hinske .25
40 Ichiro Suzuki 2.50
40 Ichiro Suzuki/ SP/Writing On Wall 8.00
41 Larry Walker .50
42 Mark Teixeira .50
43 Khalil Greene .25
44 Edgardo Alfonzo .25
45 Javier Vazquez .25
46 Cliff Floyd .25
47 Geoff Jenkins .25
48 Ken Griffey Jr. 2.00
49 Vinny Castilla .25
50 Mark Prior 1.00
51 Jose Guillen .25
52 J.D. Drew .50
53 Rafael Palmeiro .75
54 Kevin Youkilis .25
55 Derrek Lee .50
56 Freddy Garcia .25
57 Wily Mo Pena .25
58 C.C. Sabathia .25
59 Craig Biggio .40
60 Ivan Rodriguez .75
61 Angel Berroa .25
62 Ben Sheets .25
63 Johan Santana .75
64 Al Leiter .40
65 Bernie Williams .50
66 Bobby Crosby .50
67 Jack Wilson .25
68 A.J. Pierzynski .25
69 Jimmy Rollins .25
70 Jason Giambi .50
71 Tom Glavine .50
72 Kevin Brown .50
73 B.J. Upton .50
74 Edgar Renteria .25
75 Alfonso Soriano 1.00
76 Mike Lieberthal .25
77 Kazuo Matsui .25
78 Phil Nevin .25
79 Shawn Green .25
80 Miguel Cabrera 1.00
81 Todd Helton .75
82 Magglio Ordonez .40
83 Manny Ramirez 1.00
84 Bill Mueller .25
85 Troy Glaus .50
86 Richie Sexson .50
87 Javy Lopez .40
88 David Ortiz 1.00
89 Greg Maddux 1.50
90 Vladimir Guerrero 1.00
91 Jeromy Burnitz .25
92 Jeff Kent .40
93 Travis Hafner .40
94 Mark Buehrle .25
95 Paul LoDuca .25
96 Roy Oswalt .40
97 Torii Hunter .25
98 Gary Sheffield .75
99 Erubiel Durazo .25
100 Jim Thome 1.00
100 Jim Thome/ SP/Kid's Shirt Is Red 6.00
101 Ken Harvey .25
102 Shannon Stewart .25
103 Dmitri Young .25
104 Kevin Millar .25
105 Kerry Wood 1.00
106 Paul Konerko .25
107 Ronnie Belliard .40
108 Mike Lowell .40
109 Hee Seop Choi .25
110 Joe Mauer .50
111 David Wright 1.00
112 Jorge Posada .50
113 Tim Hudson .50
114 Brian Giles .25
115 Jason Schmidt .25
116 Aubrey Huff .75
117 Hank Blalock .25
118 Jim Edmonds .50
119 Raul Ibanez .25
120 Carlos Delgado .50
121 Craig Wilson .40
122 Ryan Klesko .25
123 Mark Mulder .25
124 Jose Vidro .25
125 Mike Sweeney .25
126 Lance Berkman .50
127 Juan Pierre .25
128 Austin Kearns .25
129 Moises Alou .25
130 Garret Anderson .50
131 Pedro J. Martinez 1.00
132 Melvin Mora .25
133 Marcus Giles .25
134 Corey Patterson .50
135 Carlos Lee .50
136 Sean Casey .40
137 Jody Gerut .25
138 Jose Valentin .25
139 Aaron Miles .25
140 Randy Johnson 1.00
141 Carlos Guillen .25
142 Dontrelle Willis .50
143 Jeff Bagwell .75
144 Jason Kendall .25
145 Mark Loretta .25
146 Scott Rolen 1.00
147 Carl Crawford .25
148 Michael Young .25
149 Jermaine Dye .25
150 Chipper Jones 1.00
151 Melky Cabrera RC 3.00
152 Chris Seddon RC 3.00
153 Nate Schierholtz RC 3.00
154 Ian Kinsler RC 6.00
154 Ian Kinsler/ SP/Gold Background 12.00
155 Brandon Moss RC 3.00
155 Brandon Moss/ SP/Red Hat 8.00
156 Chadd Blasko RC 3.00
157 Jeremy West RC 3.00
157 Jeremy West/ SP/Navy Blue Jsy 3.00
158 Sean Marshall RC 3.00
159 Ryan Sweeney 2.00
160 Matt Lindstrom RC 2.00
161 Ryan Goleski RC 4.00
162 Brett Harper RC 3.00
163 Chris Roberson RC 3.00
164 Andre Ethier 8.00
165 Ian Bladergroen RC 3.00
165 Ian Bladergroen/ SP/Swinging 6.00
166 James Jurries RC 3.00
167 Billy Butler RC 5.00
167 Billy Butler/SP/ Black Jsy 10.00
168 Michael Rogers RC 3.00
168 Michael Rogers/SP/ Baseball In Hand 8.00
169 Tyler Clippard RC 2.00
170 Luis Ramirez RC 3.00
171 Casey Kotchman 2.00
172 Chris Burke 2.00
173 Dallas McPherson 2.00
175 Edwin Jackson 1.00
175 Felix Hernandez 4.00
177 Gavin Floyd 1.00
177 Guillermo Quiroz 1.00
178 Jason Kubel 1.00
179 Jeff Mathis 1.00
180 Rickie Weeks 1.00
181 Ryan Howard 3.00
182 Franklin Gutierrez 1.00
183 Jeremy Reed 1.00
184 Carlos Quentin 5.00
185 Jeff Francis 2.00
186 Nolan Ryan 6.00
187 Hank Aaron 8.00
187 Hank Aaron/SP/Red 755 15.00
188 Duke Snider 5.00
189 Mike Schmidt 5.00
190 Ernie Banks 4.00
191 Frank Robinson 3.00
192 Harmon Killebrew 4.00
193 Al Kaline 4.00
194 Rod Carew 3.00
195 Johnny Bench 4.00

Artist's Proof

Stars (1-150): 2-4X
SP's (151-195): 1-2X
Inserted 1:1

Murray Olderman Sketches

No Pricing
Production One Set

Printing Plates

No Pricing
Production one for each color.

Gallo's Gallery Sketches

NM/M
Complete Set (20): 50.00
Common Player: 1.50
Inserted 1:15
HA Hank Aaron 6.00
HB Hank Blalock 1.50
NG Nomar Garciaparra 4.00
VG Vladimir Guerrero 2.00
TH Todd Helton 1.50
DJ Derek Jeter 6.00

GALLO'S GALLERY

HANK BLALOCK • TEXAS RANGERS®

RJ	Randy Johnson	2.00
CJ	Chipper Jones	2.00
MPI	Mike Piazza	4.00
MP	Mark Prior	2.00
AP	Albert Pujols	6.00
AR	Alex Rodriguez	5.00
IR	Ivan Rodriguez	1.50
NR	Nolan Ryan	6.00
MS	Mike Schmidt	5.00
AS	Alfonso Soriano	2.00
SS	Sammy Sosa	4.00
IS	Ichiro Suzuki	4.00
MT	Miguel Tejada	1.50
JT	Jim Thome	2.00

Heritage Insert

JOHNNY BENCH Catcher — REDS

Complete Set (25):		65.00
Common Player:		2.00
Inserted 1:15		
EB	Ernie Banks	4.00
CB	Carlos Beltran	3.00
JB	Johnny Bench	4.00
HB	Hank Blalock	2.00
GB	George Brett	6.00
JC	Jose Canseco	2.00
BG	Bob Gibson	3.00
AK	Al Kaline	3.00
DM	Don Mattingly	6.00
RP	Rafael Palmeiro	3.00
JP	Jim Palmer	2.00
AP	Albert Pujols	8.00
BR	Brooks Robinson	3.00
FR	Frank Robinson	2.00
RR	Frank Robinson, Brooks Robinson	3.00
RJ	Alex Rodriguez, Derek Jeter	8.00
IR	Ivan Rodriguez	3.00
NR	Nolan Ryan	8.00
CS	Curt Schilling	3.00
MS	Mike Schmidt	5.00
TS	Jim Thome, Mike Schmidt	3.00
OS	Ozzie Smith	3.00
DSN	Duke Snider	3.00
DS	Darryl Strawberry	2.00
DW	Dontrelle Willis	2.00

Heritage Relics

		NM/M
Common Player:		5.00
Inserted 1:40		
GB	George Brett	12.00
JC	Jose Canseco	8.00
DM	Don Mattingly	15.00
AP	Albert Pujols	15.00
AR	Alex Rodriguez	15.00
IR	Ivan Rodriguez	8.00
NR	Nolan Ryan	20.00
OS	Ozzie Smith	8.00
DS	Darryl Strawberry	4.00
DW	Dontrelle Willis	5.00

Heritage Relic Autographs

		NM/M
Production 25 Sets		

DM	Don Mattingly	75.00
AR	Alex Rodriguez	300.00
NR	Nolan Ryan	150.00

Originals Relics

FRANK THOMAS CHICAGO WHITE SOX

		NM/M
Common Player:		4.00
Inserted 1:10		
JB	Jeff Bagwell	8.00
RB	Rocco Baldelli	4.00
JBE	Josh Beckett	4.00
LB	Lance Berkman	4.00
AB	Angel Berroa	4.00
HB	Hank Blalock	8.00
HBB	Hank Blalock	8.00
MC	Miguel Cabrera	8.00
JD	Johnny Damon	8.00
RD	Ryan Drese	8.00
JG	Jason Giambi	6.00
MG	Marcus Giles	8.00
VG	Vladimir Guerrero	8.00
RH	Rich Harden	4.00
TH	Todd Helton	8.00
CJ	Chipper Jones	8.00
JL	Javy Lopez	4.00
ML	Mike Lowell	4.00
PM	Pedro J. Martinez	8.00
KM	Kazuo Matsui	6.00
LN	Laynce Nix	4.00
DO	David Ortiz	8.00
MP	Mike Piazza	8.00
MPB	Mike Piazza	8.00
MPR	Mark Prior	8.00
AP	Albert Pujols	15.00
MR	Manny Ramirez	8.00
JR	Jose Reyes	6.00
AR	Alex Rodriguez	12.00
IR	Ivan Rodriguez	8.00
AS	Alfonso Soriano	8.00
SS	Sammy Sosa	10.00
MT	Mark Teixeira	4.00
MTE	Miguel Tejada	8.00
FT	Frank Thomas	8.00
BU	B.J. Upton	8.00
BW	Bernie Williams	6.00
DW	Dontrelle Willis	8.00
KW	Kerry Wood	8.00
MY	Michael Young	4.00

Penmanship Autographs

		NM/M
Common Autograph:		10.00
JB	Jason Bartlett	10.00
TB	Taylor Buchholz	10.00
EC	Eric Chavez	15.00
FH	Felix Hernandez	30.00
AH	Aubrey Huff	15.00
JJ	Justin Jones	15.00
DM	Dallas McPherson	25.00
AR	Alex Rodriguez	250.00
VW	Vernon Wells	10.00

2005 Topps Heritage

DALLAS McPHERSON

		NM/M
Complete Set (475):		400.00
Common Player:		.40
Common SP (398-475):		4.00
SP's & Variations Inserted 1:2		
Pack (8):		5.00
Box (24):		100.00
1	Will Harridge	.40
2	Warren Giles	.40
3	Alfonso Soriano	1.00
3	Alfonso Soriano/ SP/Running	5.00
4	Mark Mulder	.75
5	Todd Helton/SP	5.00
6	Jason Bay	.40
6	Jason Bay/SP/ 1956 Pirates Uniform	5.00
7	Ichiro Suzuki	2.50
7	Ichiro Suzuki/SP/ Squatting On-Deck	8.00
8	Jim Tracy	.40
9	Gavin Floyd	.40
10	John Smoltz	.75

11	Chicago Cubs	.50
12	Darin Erstad	.40
13	Chad Tracy	.40
14	Charles Thomas	.40
15	Miguel Tejada	.75
16	Andre Ethier	6.00
17	Jeff Francis	.40
18	Derrek Lee	.50
19	Juan Uribe	.40
20	Jim Edmonds/SP	5.00
21	Kenny Lofton	.40
22	Brad Ausmus	.40
23	Jon Garland	.40
24	Edwin Jackson	.40
25	Joe Mauer	.75
26	Wes Helms	.40
27	Brian Schneider	.40
28	Kazuo Matsui	.40
29	Tom Gordon	.40
30	Hideo Nomo/SP	4.00
31	Albert Pujols/SP	15.00
31	Albert Pujols/SP/ 1956 Cards Uniform	15.00
32	Carl Crawford	.40
33	Vladimir Guerrero/SP	6.00
34	Nick Green	.40
35	Jay Gibbons	.40
36	Kevin Youkilis	.40
37	Billy Wagner	.40
38	Terrence Long	.40
39	Kevin Mench	.40
40	Garret Anderson	.50
41	Reed Johnson	.40
42	Reggie Sanders	.40
43	Kirk Rueter	.40
44	Jay Payton	.40
45	Tike Redman	.40
46	Mike Lieberthal	.40
47	Damian Miller	.40
48	Zach Day	.40
49	Juan Rincon	.40
50	Jim Thome	1.00
50	Jim Thome/SP/Fldg	6.00
51	Jose Guillen	.40
52	Richie Sexson	.75
53	Juan Cruz	.40
54	Byung-Hyun Kim	.40
55	Carlos Zambrano	.50
56	Carlos Lee	.40
57	Adam Dunn	.40
58	David Riske	.40
59	Carlos Guillen	.40
60	Larry Bowa	.40
61	Barry Bonds	4.00
62	Chris Woodward	.40
63	Matt DeSalvo RC	2.50
64	Brian Stavisky RC	1.00
65	Scot Shields	.40
66	J.D. Drew	.50
67	Erik Bedard	.40
68	Scott Williamson	.40
69	Mark Prior	1.00
69	Mark Prior/SP/ 1956 Cubs Uniform	6.00
70	Ken Griffey Jr.	2.00
71	Kazuhito Tadano	.40
72	Philadelphia Phillies	.40
73	Jeremy Reed	.40
74	Ricardo Rodriguez	.40
75	Carlos Delgado	.50
76	Eric Milton	.40
77	Miguel Olivo	.40
78	Edgardo Alfonzo	.40
78	Edgardo Alfonzo/SP/ 1956 Giants Uniform	4.00
79	Kazuhisa Ishii/SP	4.00
80	Jason Giambi	.75
81	Cliff Floyd	.40
82	Torii Hunter	.50
82	Torii Hunter/SP/ 1956 Senators Uniform	4.00
83	Odalis Perez	.40
84	Scott Podsednik	.40
85	Cleveland Indians	.40
86	Jeff Suppan	.40
87	Ray Durham	.40
88	Tyler Clippard RC	1.00
89	Ryan Howard	2.00
90	Cincinnati Reds	.40
91	Bengie Molina	.40
92	Danny Bautista	.40
93	Eli Marrero	.40
94	Larry Bigbie	.40
95	Atlanta Braves	.40
96	Merkin Valdez	.40
97	Rocco Baldelli	.40
98	Woody Williams	.40
99	Jason Frasor	.40
100	Baltimore Orioles	.40
101	Ivan Rodriguez/SP	6.00
102	Joe Kennedy	.40
103	Mike Lowell	.50
104	Armando Benitez	.40
105	Craig Biggio	.50
106	David DeJesus	.40
107	Adrian Beltre	.75
108	Phil Nevin	.40
109	Cristian Guzman	.40
110	Jorge Posada/SP	6.00
111	Boston Red Sox	.75
112	Jeff Mathis	.40
113	Bartolo Colon	.40
114	Alex Cintron	.40
115	Russ Ortiz	.40
116	Doug Mientkiewicz	.40
117	Placido Polanco	.40
118	Magglio Ordonez	.40

118	Magglio Ordonez/SP/ 1956 White Sox Uni.	4.00
119	Chris Seddon RC	1.00
120	Bobby Abreu	.50
121	Pittsburgh Pirates	.40
122	Dallas McPherson	.75
123	Rodrigo Lopez	.40
124	Mark Bellhorn	.40
125	Nomar Garciaparra	2.00
125	Nomar Garciaparra/SP/ 1956 Cubs Uniform	8.00
126	Sean Casey	.40
127	Ronnie Belliard	.40
128	Tom Goodwin	.40
129	Preston Wilson	.40
130	Andruw Jones/SP	5.00
131	Roberto Alomar	.75
132	John Buck	.40
133	Jason LaRue	.40
134	St. Louis Cardinals	.50
135	Alex Rodriguez/SP	10.00
135	Alex Rodriguez/SP/Fldg	10.00
136	Nate Robertson	.40
137	Juan Pierre	.40
138	Morgan Ensberg	.40
139	Vinny Castilla	.40
140	Jake Dittler	1.00
141	Chan Ho Park	.40
142	Felix Hernandez	2.50
143	Jason Isringhausen	.40
144	Dustan Mohr	.40
145	Khalil Greene	.40
146	Minnesota Twins	.40
147	Vicente Padilla	.40
148	Oliver Perez	.40
149	Brian Giles	.40
150	Shawn Green	.40
151	Matt Lawton	.40
152	Casey Blake	.40
153	Frank Thomas	.75
154	Orlando Hernandez	.40
155	Eric Chavez	.50
155	Eric Chavez/SP/ 1956 Kansas City Uni.	4.00
156	Chase Utley	.75
157	John Olerud	.40
158	Adam Eaton	.40
159	Josh Fogg	.40
160	Michael Tucker	.40
161	Kevin Brown	.40
162	Bobby Crosby	.50
163	Jason Schmidt	.50
164	Shannon Stewart	.40
165	Tony Womack	.40
166	Los Angeles Dodgers	.40
167	Franklin Gutierrez	.40
168	Ted Lilly	.40
169	Mark Teixeira	.50
170	Matt Morris	.40
171	Bucky Jacobsen	.40
172	Steven Doetsch RC	1.00
173	Jeff Weaver	.40
174	Tony Graffanino	.40
175	Jeff Bagwell	.75
176	Carl Pavano	.50
177	Junior Spivey	.40
178	Carlos Silva	.40
179	Tim Redding	.40
180	Brett Myers	.40
181	Mike Mussina	.75
182	Richard Hidalgo	.40
183	Nick Johnson	.40
184	Lew Ford	.40
185	Barry Zito	.50
186	Jimmy Rollins	.50
187	Jack Wilson	.40
188	Chicago White Sox	.40
189	Guillermo Quiroz	.40
190	Mark Hendrickson	.40
191	Jeremy Bonderman	.40
192	Jason Jennings	.40
193	Paul LoDuca	.40
194	A.J. Burnett	.40
195	Ken Harvey	.40
196	Geoff Jenkins	.40
197	Joe Mays	.40
198	Jose Vidro	.40
199	David Wright	.75
200	Randy Johnson	1.00
201	Jeff DeVanon	.40
202	Paul Byrd	.40
203	David Ortiz	1.00
204	Kyle Farnsworth	.40
205	Keith Foulke	.40
206	Joe Crede	.40
207	Austin Kearns	.40
208	Jody Gerut	.40
209	Shawn Chacon	.40
210	Carlos Pena	.40
211	Luis Castillo	.40
212	Chris Denorfia RC	1.00
213	Detroit Tigers	.40
214	Aubrey Huff	.40
215	Brad Fullmer	.40
216	Frank Catalanotto	.40
217	Raul Ibanez	.40
218	Ryan Klesko	.40
219	Octavio Dotel	.40
220	Robert Mackowiak	.40
221	Scott Hatteberg	.40
222	Pat Burrell	.40
223	Bernie Williams	.50
224	Kris Benson	.40
225	Eric Gagne	.50
226	San Francisco Giants	.40
227	Roy Oswalt	.40
228	Josh Beckett	.50
229	Lee Mazzilli	.40

230	Rickie Weeks	.40
231	Troy Glaus	.50
232	Chone Figgins	.40
233	John Thomson	.40
234	Trot Nixon	.40
235	Brad Penny	.40
236	Oakland Athletics	.40
237	Miguel Batista	.40
238	Ryan Drese	.40
239	Aaron Miles	.40
240	Randy Wolf	.40
241	Brian Lawrence	.40
242	A.J. Pierzynski	.40
243	Jamie Moyer	.40
244	Chris Carpenter	.40
245	So Taguchi	.40
246	Rob Bell	.40
247	Francisco Cordero	.40
248	Tom Glavine	.50
249	Jermaine Dye	.40
250	Cliff Lee	.50
251	New York Yankees	.75
252	Vernon Wells	.40
253	R.A. Dickey	.40
254	Larry Walker	.50
255	Randy Winn	.40
256	Pedro Feliz	.40
257	Mark Loretta	.40
258	Tim Worrell	.40
259	Kip Wells	.40
260	Cesar Izturis/SP	4.00
261	Carlos Beltran	.75
261	Carlos Beltran/SP/Btg	6.00
262	Juan Encarnacion	.40
263	Luis Gonzalez	.40
264	Grady Sizemore	.75
265	Paul Wilson	.40
266	Mark Buehrle	.40
267	Todd Hollandsworth	.40
268	Orlando Cabrera	.50
269	Sidney Ponson	.40
270	Mike Hampton	.40
271	Luis Gonzalez	.50
272	Brendan Donnelly	.40
273	Chipper Jones	1.00
273	Chipper Jones/SP/ Blue Background	6.00
274	Brandon Webb	.40
275	Marty Cordova	.40
276	Greg Maddux	2.00
277	Jose Contreras	.40
278	Aaron Harang	.40
279	Coco Crisp	.40
280	Bobby Higginson	.40
281	Guillermo Mota	.40
282	Andy Pettitte	.50
283	Jeremy West RC	3.00
284	Craig Brazell	.40
285	Eric Hinske	.40
286	Hank Blalock	.75
286	Hank Blalock/SP/Fldg	6.00
287	B.J. Upton	.75
288	Jason Marquis	.40
289	Matt Herges	.40
290	Ramon Hernandez	.40
291	Marlon Byrd	.40
292	Ryan Sweeney/SP	8.00
293	Esteban Loaiza	.40
294	Al Leiter	.50
295	Alex Gonzalez	.40
296	Johan Santana	.75
296	Johan Santana/SP/ 1956 Senators Uniform	6.00
297	Milton Bradley	.40
298	Mike Sweeney	.40
299	Wade Miller	.40
300	Sammy Sosa	2.00
300	Sammy Sosa/SP/ Blue Jsy	8.00
301	Wily Mo Pena	.40
302	Tim Wakefield	.40
303	Rafael Palmeiro	.75
304	Rafael Furcal	.40
305	David Eckstein	.40
306	David Segui	.40
307	Kevin Millar	.40
308	Matt Clement	.40
309	Wade Robinson RC	1.00
310	Brad Radke	.40
311	Steve Finley	.40
312	Lance Berkman	.50
312	Lance Berkman/SP/Fldg	5.00
313	Joe Randa	.40
314	Miguel Cabrera	1.00
315	Billy Koch	.40
316	Alex Sanchez	.40
317	Chin-Hui Tsao	.40
318	Omar Vizquel	.40
319	Ryan Freel	.40
320	LaTroy Hawkins	.40
321	Aaron Rowand	.40
322	Paul Konerko	.40
323	Joe Borowski	.40
324	Jarrod Washburn	.40
325	Jaret Wright	.40
326	Johnny Damon	.75
327	Corey Patterson	.50
328	Travis Hafner	.40
329	Shingo Takatsu	.40
330	Dmitri Young	.40
331	Matt Holliday	.50
332	Jeff Kent	.75
333	Desi Relaford	.40
334	Jose Hernandez	.40
335	Lyle Overbay	.40
336	Jacque Jones	.40
337	Terrmel Sledge	.40
338	Victor Zambrano	.40

339	Gary Sheffield	.75
340	Brad Wilkerson	.40
341	Ian Kinsler RC	5.00
342	Jesse Crain	.40
343	Orlando Hudson	.40
344	Laynce Nix	.40
345	Jose Cruz Jr.	.40
346	Edgar Renteria	.50
347	Eddie Guardado	.40
348	Jerome Williams	.40
349	Trevor Hoffman	.40
350	Mike Piazza	1.50
351	Jason Kendall	.40
352	Kevin Millwood	.40
353	Tim Hudson	.50
353	Tim Hudson/SP/ 1956 Braves Uniform	5.00
354	Paul Quantrill	.40
355	Jon Lieber	.40
356	Braden Looper	.40
357	Chad Cordero	.40
358	Joe Nathan	.40
359	Doug Davis	.40
360	Ian Bladergroen RC	1.00
361	Val Majewski	.40
362	Francisco Rodriguez	.40
363	Kelvim Escobar	.40
364	Marcus Giles	.40
365	Darren Fenster RC	1.00
366	David Bell	.40
367	Shea Hillenbrand	.40
368	Manny Ramirez	1.00
369	Ben Broussard	.40
370	Luis Ramirez RC	1.00
371	Dustin Hermanson	.40
372	Akinori Otsuka	.40
373	Chadd Blasko RC	1.00
374	Delmon Young	.75
375	Michael Young	.40
376	Bret Boone	.40
377	Jake Peavy	.40
378	Matt Lindstrom RC	1.00
379	Sean Burroughs	.40
380	Rich Harden	.40
381	Chris Roberson RC	1.00
382	John Lackey	.40
383	Johnny Estrada	.40
384	Matt Rogelstad RC	1.00
385	Toby Hall	.40
386	Adam LaRoche	.40
387	Bill Hall	.40
388	Tim Salmon	.50
389	Curt Schilling	1.00
389	Curt Schilling/SP/ Looking In	6.00
390	Michael Barrett	.40
391	Jose Acevedo	.40
392	Nate Schierholtz	1.00
393	J.T. Snow Jr.	.40
394	Mark Redman	.40
395	Ryan Madson	.40
396	Kevin West RC	.40
397	Ramon Ortiz	.40
398	Derek Lowe	4.00
399	Kerry Wood	6.00
400	Derek Jeter	15.00
401	Livan Hernandez	4.00
402	Casey Kotchman	6.00
403	Chaz Lytle RC	6.00
404	Alexis Rios	5.00
405	Scott Spiezio	4.00
406	Craig Wilson	4.00
407	Felix Rodriguez	4.00
408	D'Angelo Jimenez	4.00
409	Rondell White	4.00
410	Shawn Estes	4.00
411	Troy Percival	4.00
412	Melvin Mora	4.00
413	Aramis Ramirez	6.00
414	Carl Everett	4.00
415	Elvys Quezada RC	6.00
416	Ben Sheets	5.00
417	Matt Stairs	4.00
418	Adam Everett	4.00
419	Jason Johnson	4.00
420	Billy Butler RC	10.00
421	Justin Morneau	6.00
422	Jose Reyes	6.00
423	Mariano Rivera	5.00
424	Jose Vaquedano RC	5.00
425	Gabe Gross	5.00
426	Scott Rolen	6.00
427	Ty Wigginton	4.00
428	James Jurries RC	6.00
429	Pedro J. Martinez	6.00
430	Mark Grudzielanek	4.00
431	Josh Phelps	4.00
432	Ryan Goleski RC	5.00
433	Mike Matheny	4.00
434	Bobby Kielty	4.00
435	Tony Batista	4.00
436	Corey Koskie	4.00
437	Brad Lidge	4.00
438	Dontrelle Willis	4.00
439	Angel Berroa	4.00
440	Jason Kubel	4.00
441	Roy Halladay	4.00
442	Brian Roberts	4.00
443	Bill Mueller	4.00
444	Adam Kennedy	4.00
445	Brandon Moss RC	4.00
446	Sean Burnett	4.00
447	Eric Byrnes	4.00
448	Matt Campbell RC	6.00
449	Ryan Webb RC	6.00
450	Jose Valentin	4.00
451	Jake Westbrook	4.00
452	Glen Perkins RC	6.00

453	Alex Gonzalez	4.00
454	Jeromy Burnitz	4.00
455	Zack Greinke	4.00
456	Sean Marshall RC	6.00
457	Erubiel Durazo	4.00
458	Michael Cuddyer	4.00
459	Hee Seop Choi	4.00
460	Melky Cabrera RC	10.00
461	Jerry Hairston Jr.	4.00
462	Moises Alou	4.00
463	Michael Rogers RC	6.00
464	Javy Lopez	4.00
465	Freddy Garcia	4.00
466	Brett Harper RC	5.00
467	Juan Gonzalez	5.00
468	Kevin Melillo RC	5.00
469	Todd Walker	4.00
470	C.C. Sabathia	4.00
471	Kole Strayhorn	4.00
472	Mark Kotsay	4.00
473	Javier Vazquez	4.00
474	Mike Cameron	4.00
475	Wes Swackhamer RC	4.00

Chrome Parallel

NM/M
Complete Set (110):
Common Player: 1.00
Production 1,956 Sets
Refractors: 1.5-2X
Production 556 Sets
Black Refractor: 3-5X
Production 56 Sets

THC1	Will Harridge	2.00
THC2	Warren Giles	2.00
THC3	Alex Rodriguez	10.00
THC4	Alfonso Soriano	5.00
THC5	Barry Bonds	12.00
THC6	Todd Helton	3.00
THC7	Kazuo Matsui	1.50
THC8	Garret Anderson	1.50
THC9	Mark Prior	5.00
THC10	Jim Thome	4.00
THC11	Jason Giambi	2.00
THC12	Ivan Rodriguez	4.00
THC13	Mike Lowell	1.00
THC14	Vladimir Guerrero	5.00
THC15	Adrian Beltre	2.00
THC16	Andruw Jones	4.00
THC17	Jose Vidro	1.00
THC18	Josh Beckett	1.50
THC19	Mike Sweeney	1.50
THC20	Sammy Sosa	6.00
THC21	Scott Rolen	5.00
THC22	Javy Lopez	1.50
THC23	Albert Pujols	12.00
THC24	Adam Dunn	3.00
THC25	Ken Griffey Jr.	6.00
THC26	Torii Hunter	1.50
THC27	Jorge Posada	2.00
THC28	Magglio Ordonez	1.50
THC29	Shawn Green	1.50
THC30	Frank Thomas	3.00
THC31	Barry Zito	1.50
THC32	David Ortiz	5.00
THC33	Pat Burrell	1.50
THC34	Luis Gonzalez	1.50
THC35	Chipper Jones	5.00
THC36	Hank Blalock	3.00
THC37	Rafael Palmeiro	3.00
THC38	Lance Berkman	3.00
THC39	Miguel Cabrera	5.00
THC40	Paul Konerko	4.00
THC41	Jeff Kent	1.50
THC42	Gary Sheffield	3.00
THC43	Mike Piazza	6.00
THC44	Bret Boone	1.00
THC45	Kerry Wood	3.00
THC46	Derek Jeter	12.00
THC47	Pedro J. Martinez	5.00
THC48	Jason Bay	2.00
THC49	Ichiro Suzuki	8.00
THC50	Miguel Tejada	3.00
THC51	Richie Sexson	2.00
THC52	Jeff Bagwell	5.00
THC53	Lew Ford	1.00
THC54	Randy Johnson	5.00
THC55	Carlos Beltran	3.00
THC56	Greg Maddux	6.00
THC57	Lyle Overbay	1.00
THC58	Michael Young	5.00
THC59	Curt Schilling	5.00
THC60	Jose Reyes	3.00
THC61	Dontrelle Willis	1.50
THC62	Nomar Garciaparra	6.00
THC63	Paul LoDuca	1.00
THC64	Larry Walker	2.00
THC65	Andre Ethier	8.00
THC66	Matt DeSalvo	2.00
THC67	Brian Stavisky	2.00
THC68	Tyler Clippard	2.00
THC69	Chris Seddon	1.00
THC70	Steven Doetsch	3.00
THC71	Chris Denorfia	1.00
THC72	Jeremy West	3.00
THC73	Ryan Sweeney	3.00
THC74	Ian Kinsler	10.00
THC75	Ian Bladergroen	4.00
THC76	Darren Fenster	4.00
THC77	Luis Ramirez	2.00
THC78	Chadd Blasko	2.00
THC79	Matt Lindstrom	2.00
THC80	Chris Roberson	3.00
THC81	Matt Rogelstad	3.00
THC82	Nate Schierholtz	4.00
THC83	Kevin West	4.00
THC84	Chaz Lytle	4.00
THC85	Elvys Quezada	4.00
THC86	Billy Butler	10.00
THC87	Jose Vaquedano	4.00
THC88	James Jurries	4.00
THC89	Ryan Goleski	4.00
THC90	Brandon Moss	4.00
THC91	Matt Campbell	4.00
THC92	Ryan Webb	4.00
THC93	Glen Perkins	5.00
THC94	Sean Marshall	4.00
THC95	Melky Cabrera	8.00
THC96	Michael Rogers	4.00
THC97	Brett Harper	4.00
THC98	Kevin Melillo	4.00
THC99	Kole Strayhorn	4.00
THC100	Wes Swackhamer	4.00
THC101	Rickie Weeks	2.00
THC102	Delmon Young	4.00
THC103	Kazuhito Tadano	1.00
THC104	Kazuhisa Ishii	1.00
THC105	David Wright	4.00
THC106	Eric Gagne	3.00
THC107	So Taguchi	1.00
THC108	B.J. Upton	5.00
THC109	Shingo Takatsu	1.00
THC110	Akinori Otsuka	1.00

Clubhouse Collection Relics

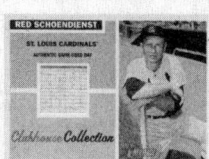

NM/M
Common Player: 5.00

LA	Luis Aparicio	8.00
EB	Ernie Banks	15.00
LB	Lance Berkman	5.00
MC	Miguel Cabrera	8.00
AK	Al Kaline	15.00
HK	Harmon Killebrew	15.00
AP	Albert Pujols	20.00
MR	Manny Ramirez	15.00
AR	Alex Rodriguez	15.00
RS	Red Schoendienst	8.00
GS	Gary Sheffield	8.00
AS	Alfonso Soriano	8.00
MT	Miguel Tejada	8.00
BW	Bernie Williams	5.00
DW	Dontrelle Willis	5.00

Clubhouse Collection Dual Relics

NM/M
Production 56 Sets

MP	Stan Musial, Albert Pujols	85.00
KR	Al Kaline, Ivan Rodriguez	65.00
BG	Ernie Banks, Nomar Garciaparra	85.00

Clubhouse Collection Relic Auto.

NM/M
Production 25 Sets

LA	Luis Aparicio	150.00
EB	Ernie Banks	200.00
BF	Bob Feller	175.00
AK	Al Kaline	175.00
DL	Don Larsen	175.00
SM	Stan Musial	200.00
FR	Frank Robinson	200.00
HS	Herb Score	150.00

Production 25 Sets

LA	Luis Aparicio	165.00
EB	Ernie Banks	200.00
AK	Al Kaline	200.00
HK	Harmon Killebrew	200.00
RS	Red Schoendienst	165.00

Flashbacks

caption: SEPTEMBER 30, 1956 HANK AARON WINS NL BATTING CROWN WITH .328 BATTING AVERAGE.

NM/M
Complete Set (15): 15.00

NM/M
Complete Set (10): 8.00
Common Player: .50
Inserted 1:12

HA	Hank Aaron	4.00
LA	Luis Aparicio	.50
EB	Ernie Banks	2.00
BF	Bob Feller	.50
AK	Al Kaline	1.50
DL	Don Larsen	.50
SM	Stan Musial	2.00
FR	Frank Robinson	1.00
HS	Herb Score	1.00
DS	Duke Snider	1.00

Flashbacks Autographs

NM/M
Common Player:
Production 25 Sets

LA	Luis Aparicio	125.00
EB	Ernie Banks	200.00
BF	Bob Feller	165.00
AK	Al Kaline	165.00
DL	Don Larsen	175.00
SM	Stan Musial	200.00
FR	Frank Robinson	200.00
HS	Herb Score	150.00

Flashbacks Relics

caption: SEPTEMBER 30, 1956 DUKE SNIDER'S 2 HOMERS LEAD DODGERS TO PENNANT ON LAST DAY OF SEASON. EBBETS FIELD, BROOKLYN, NEW YORK

NM/M
Common Player: 8.00
Inserted 1:96

HA	Hank Aaron	15.00
LA	Luis Aparicio	8.00
EB	Ernie Banks	15.00
BF	Bob Feller	10.00
AK	Al Kaline	15.00
DL	Don Larsen	8.00
SM	Stan Musial	15.00
FR	Frank Robinson	10.00
HS	Herb Score	8.00
DS	Duke Snider	10.00

Flashbacks Relic Autographs

caption: OCTOBER 8, 1956 DON LARSEN PITCHES A PERFECT GAME IN THE WORLD SERIES

NM/M
Production 25 Sets

LA	Luis Aparicio	150.00
EB	Ernie Banks	200.00
BF	Bob Feller	175.00
AK	Al Kaline	175.00
DL	Don Larsen	175.00
SM	Stan Musial	200.00
FR	Frank Robinson	200.00
HS	Herb Score	150.00

New Age Performers

caption: New Age Performers DEREK JETER shortstop NEW YORK YANKEES

NM/M
Complete Set (15): 15.00

Common Player: 1.00
Inserted 1:15

NAP1	Alfonso Soriano	1.50
NAP2	Alex Rodriguez	3.00
NAP3	Ichiro Suzuki	3.00
NAP4	Albert Pujols	4.00
NAP5	Vladimir Guerrero	1.50
NAP6	Jim Thome	1.50
NAP7	Derek Jeter	4.00
NAP8	Sammy Sosa	2.50
NAP9	Ivan Rodriguez	1.00
NAP10	Manny Ramirez	1.50
NAP11	Todd Helton	1.00
NAP12	David Ortiz	1.50
NAP13	Gary Sheffield	1.00
NAP14	Nomar Garciaparra	2.00
NAP15	Randy Johnson	1.50

Real One Autographs

NM/M
Production 200 Sets
Red Ink: 1.5-2X
Production 56 Sets

HA	Hank Aaron	275.00
JA	Joe Astroth	50.00
EB	Ernie Banks	125.00
YB	Yogi Berra	100.00
JB	Jim Brady	50.00
CD	Chuck Diering	50.00
BF	Bob Feller	70.00
JG	Jim Greengrass	50.00
MI	Monte Irvin	60.00
SJ	Spook Jacobs	50.00
FM	Fred Marsh	50.00
JM	Jake Martin	50.00
RM	Rudy Minarcin	50.00
PM	Paul Minner	50.00
BN	Bob Nelson	50.00
LP	Laurin Pepper	40.00
LPO	Leroy Powell	60.00
JSA	Jose Santiago	50.00
JS	Johnny Schmitz	50.00
DS	Duke Snider	85.00
AS	Art Swanson	50.00
BT	Bill Tremel	50.00
WW	Wally Westlake	50.00

Then and Now

caption: THEN NOW HANK AARON MILWAUKEE BRAVES ICHIRO SEATTLE MARINERS

NM/M
Complete Set (10): 8.00
Common Duo: .50
Inserted 1:15

TN1	Hank Aaron, Ichiro Suzuki	4.00
TN2	Don Newcombe, Curt Schilling	1.50
TN3	Robin Roberts, Livan Hernandez	1.50
TN4	Bob Friend, Livan Hernandez	.50
TN5	Herb Score, Randy Johnson	1.50
TN6	Whitey Ford, Jake Peavy	1.00
TN7	Jimmy Piersall, Lyle Overbay	.50
TN8	Clem Labine, Mariano Rivera	.75
TN9	Bill Bruton, Carl Crawford	.50
TN10	Eddie Yost, Bobby Abreu	.50

2005 Topps Opening Day

NM/M
Complete Set (165): 30.00
Common Player: .15
Pack (6): 1.00
Box (36): 30.00

1	Alex Rodriguez	1.50
2	Placido Polanco	.15
3	Torii Hunter	.25
4	Lyle Overbay	.15
5	Johnny Damon	.50
6	Mike Cameron	.15
7	Ichiro Suzuki	1.50
8	Francisco Rodriguez	.15
9	Bobby Crosby	.15
10	Sammy Sosa	1.25
11	Randy Wolf	.15
12	Jason Bay	.25
13	Mike Lieberthal	.15
14	Paul Konerko	.15
15	Brian Giles	.15
16	Luis Gonzalez	.25
17	Jim Edmonds	.40
18	Carlos Lee	.25
19	Corey Patterson	.40
20	Hank Blalock	.50
21	Sean Casey	.25
22	Dmitri Young	.25
23	Mark Mulder	.25
24	Bobby Abreu	.25
25	Jim Thome	.50
26	Jason Kendall	.15
27	Jason Giambi	.25
28	Vinny Castilla	.15
29	Tony Batista	.15
30	Ivan Rodriguez	.50
31	Craig Biggio	.25
32	Chris Carpenter	.15
33	Adrian Beltre	.40
34	Scott Podsednik	.15
35	Cliff Floyd	.15
36	Chad Tracy	.15
37	John Smoltz	.25
38	Shingo Takatsu	.15
39	Jack Wilson	.15
40	Gary Sheffield	.50
41	Lance Berkman	.25
42	Carl Crawford	.25
43	Carlos Guillen	.15
44	David Bell	.15
45	Kazuo Matsui	.25
46	Jason Schmidt	.25
47	Jason Marquis	.15
48	Melvin Mora	.15
49	David Ortiz	.50
50	Andruw Jones	.50
51	Miguel Tejada	.50
52	Bartolo Colon	.15
53	Derek Lee	.25
54	Eric Gagne	.25
55	Miguel Cabrera	.75
56	Travis Hafner	.15
57	Jose Valentin	.15
58	Mark Prior	.75
59	Phil Nevin	.15
60	Jose Vidro	.15
61	Khalil Greene	.25
62	Carlos Zambrano	.40
63	Erubiel Durazo	.15
64	Michael Young	.15
65	Woody Williams	.15
66	Edgardo Alfonzo	.15
67	Troy Glaus	.40
68	Garret Anderson	.25
69	Richie Sexson	.40
70	Curt Schilling	.75
71	Randy Johnson	.75
72	Chipper Jones	.75
73	J.D. Drew	.25
74	Russ Ortiz	.15
75	Frank Thomas	.50
76	Jimmy Rollins	.25
77	Barry Zito	.25
78	Rafael Palmeiro	.15
79	Brad Wilkerson	.15
80	Adam Dunn	.15
81	Doug Mientkiewicz	.15
82	Manny Ramirez	.75
83	Pedro J. Martinez	.75
84	Moises Alou	.25
85	Mike Sweeney	.15
86	Boston Red Sox WC	1.00
87	Matt Clement	.15
88	Nomar Garciaparra	1.00
89	Magglio Ordonez	.15
90	Bret Boone	.15
91	Mark Loretta	.15
92	Jose Contreras	.15
93	Randy Winn	.15
94	Austin Kearns	.15
95	Ken Griffey Jr.	1.25
96	Jake Westbrook	.15
97	Kazuhito Tadano	.15
98	C.C. Sabathia	.15
99	Todd Helton	.50
100	Albert Pujols	2.00
101	Jose Molina	.15
102	Aaron Miles	.15
103	Mike Lowell	.25
104	Paul LoDuca	.15
105	Juan Pierre	.15
106	Dontrelle Willis	.40
107	Jeff Bagwell	.40
108	Carlos Beltran	.50
109	Ronnie Belliard	.15
110	Roy Oswalt	.15
111	Zack Greinke	.15
112	Steve Finley	.15
113	Kazuhisa Ishii	.15
114	Justin Morneau	.40
115	Ben Sheets	.25
116	Johan Santana	.50
117	Billy Wagner	.15
118	Mariano Rivera	.25
119	Corey Koskie	.15
120	Akinori Otsuka	.15
121	Joe Mauer	.40
122	Jacque Jones	.15
123	Joe Nathan	.15
124	Nick Johnson	.15
125	Vernon Wells	.15
126	Mike Piazza	1.00
127	Jose Guillen	.15
128	Jose Reyes	.25
129	Marcus Giles	.15
130	Javy Lopez	.25
131	Kevin Millar	.15
132	Jorge Posada	.40
133	Carl Pavano	.15
134	Bernie Williams	.25
135	Kerry Wood	.75
136	Matt Holiday	.25
137	Kevin Brown	.15
138	Derek Jeter	2.00
139	Barry Bonds	2.00
140	Jeff Kent	.25
141	Mark Kotsay	.15
142	Shawn Green	.25
143	Tim Hudson	.25
144	Shannon Stewart	.15
145	Pat Burrell	.25
146	Gavin Floyd	.15
147	Mike Mussina	.50
148	Eric Chavez	.25
149	Jon Lieber	.15
150	Vladimir Guerrero	.75
151	Vicente Padilla	.15
152	Ryan Klesko	.15
153	Jake Peavy	.25
154	Scott Rolen	.75
155	Greg Maddux	1.00
156	Edgar Renteria	.25
157	Larry Walker	.25
158	Scott Kazmir	.25
159	B.J. Upton	.25
160	Mark Teixeira	.50
161	Ken Harvey	.15
162	Alfonso Soriano	.75
163	Carlos Delgado	.40
164	Alexis Rios	.15
165	Checklist	.15

Autographs

NM/M
Complete Set (6):
Common Player:

CC	Chad Cordero	10.00
FH	Felix Hernandez	25.00
AH	Aaron Hill	8.00
PM	Paul Maholm	8.00
OQ	Omar Quintanilla	15.00
AW	Anthony Whittington	8.00

MLB Game Worn Jersey Collection

NM/M
Target Retail Exclusive

37	Vladimir Guerrero	8.00
38	Albert Pujols	15.00
39	Torii Hunter	4.00
40	Alfonso Soriano	6.00
41	Bobby Abreu	6.00
42	Moises Alou	6.00
43	Sean Burroughs	4.00
44	Shannon Stewart	4.00
45	Troy Glaus	6.00
46	Fernando Vina	4.00
47	Dan Wilson	4.00
48	Paul Konerko	4.00
49	Jimmy Rollins	6.00
50	Livan Hernandez	4.00
51	Sean Casey	4.00
52	Paul LoDuca	4.00
53	Richie Sexson	6.00
54	Aubrey Huff	4.00

2005 Topps Pack Wars

caption: SEAN BURROUGHS 114 81 3B PACK WARS

NM/M
Complete Set (175): 40.00
Common Player: .25
Pack (7): 20.00
Box (7): 120.00

1	Alex Rodriguez	3.00
2	Eric Chavez	.40
3	Jimmy Rollins	.40
4	Jason Bay	.50
5	Nomar Garciaparra	2.00
6	Melvin Mora	.25
7	Bobby Abreu	.50
8	Bartolo Colon	.25
9	Orlando Cabrera	1.00
10	Albert Pujols	3.00
11	Barry Zito	.40
12	Vernon Wells	.40
13	J.D. Drew	.40
14	Darin Erstad	.25
15	Manny Ramirez	1.00
16	Derek Lee	.40
17	Juan Uribe	.25
18	Wily Mo Pena	.25
19	Jeromy Burnitz	.25
20	Dontrelle Willis	.25
21	Craig Biggio	.40
22	Cesar Izturis	.25
23	Geoff Jenkins	.25
24	Joe Mauer	.50
25	Derek Jeter	3.00
26	David Wright	1.00
27	Jose Vidro	.25
28	Bobby Crosby	.25
29	Khalil Greene	.25
30	Ichiro Suzuki	2.00
31	Reggie Sanders	.25
32	A.J. Pierzynski	.25
33	Corey Patterson	.25
34	Frank Thomas	.75
35	Craig Wilson	.25
36	Carl Crawford	.25
37	Michael Young	.25
38	Mark Kotsay	.25
39	Javier Vazquez	.25
40	Kazuo Matsui	.25
41	Lew Ford	.25
42	Corey Koskie	.25

43	Larry Walker	.50
44	Mike Lowell	.40
45	Todd Helton	.75
46	Travis Hafner	.25
47	Sean Casey	.25
48	Ken Griffey Jr.	1.50
49	Milton Bradley	.75
50	Ivan Rodriguez	.75
51	Carlos Lee	.25
52	Aramis Ramirez	.50
53	Curt Schilling	1.00
54	Russ Ortiz	.25
55	Randy Johnson	1.00
56	Preston Wilson	.25
57	Jay Gibbons	.25
58	Mike Lieberthal	.25
59	Johnny Damon	.75
60	Mark Prior	1.00
61	Freddy Garcia	.25
62	Casey Blake	.25
63	Chipper Jones	1.00
64	Carlos Guillen	.25
65	Juan Pierre	.25
66	Tom Glavine	.50
67	Alex Sanchez	.25
68	Tony Batista	.25
69	Paul LoDuca	.25
70	Hank Blalock	.75
71	Pedro Feliz	.25
72	Jim Edmonds	.25
73	Phil Nevin	.25
74	Rocco Baldelli	.25
75	Alfonso Soriano	1.00
76	David Bell	.25
77	Eric Hinske	.25
78	Jose Guillen	.25
79	Marcus Giles	.25
80	Rafael Palmeiro	.75
81	Jeff Bagwell	.75
82	Kerry Wood	1.00
83	Johan Santana	.75
84	Troy Glaus	.40
85	Andruw Jones	.50
86	Barry Bonds	3.00
87	Jermaine Dye	.25
88	Carlos Zambrano	.50
89	Aaron Rowand	.25
90	Garret Anderson	.40
91	Ryan Klesko	.25
92	Paul Konerko	.25
93	Jeff Kent	.40
94	Richie Sexson	.50
95	Lyle Overbay	.25
96	Torii Hunter	.40
97	Mike Cameron	.25
98	Eric Byrnes	.25
99	Jason Kendall	.25
100	Vladimir Guerrero	1.00
101	Johnny Estrada	.25
102	Mark Bellhorn	.25
103	Moises Alou	.40
104	Ronnie Belliard	.25
105	Adam Dunn	.25
106	Dmitri Young	.25
107	Luis Castillo	.25
108	Carlos Beltran	.75
109	Steve Finley	.25
110	Shannon Stewart	.25
111	Al Leiter	.25
112	Bernie Williams	.50
113	Roy Oswalt	.40
114	Sean Burroughs	.25
115	Randy Winn	.25
116	Tony Womack	.25
117	Jim Thome	1.00
118	Aubrey Huff	.25
119	Bret Boone	.25
120	Carlos Delgado	.40
121	Jason Schmidt	.50
122	Rafael Furcal	.25
123	Miguel Tejada	.75
124	Bill Mueller	.25
125	Pedro Martinez	1.00
126	Michael Barrett	.25
127	Jody Gerut	.25
128	Vinny Castilla	.25
129	Rondell White	.25
130	Magglio Ordonez	.25
131	Lance Berkman	.25
132	Alex Gonzalez	.25
133	Mike Sweeney	.25
134	Ben Sheets	.50
135	Jacque Jones	.25
136	Brad Wilkerson	.25
137	Cliff Floyd	.25
138	Kevin Brown	.25
139	Scott Hatteberg	.25
140	Gary Sheffield	.50
141	Justin Morneau	.50
142	Scott Podsednik	.25
143	Shawn Green	.40
144	David Ortiz	1.00
145	Josh Beckett	.50
146	Tim Hudson	.50
147	Matt Lawton	.25
148	Mark Buehrle	.25
149	Todd Walker	.25
150	Jason Giambi	.50
151	Brian Giles	.25
152	Erubiel Durazo	.25
153	Jack Wilson	.25
154	Jose Reyes	.50
155	Scott Rolen	1.00
156	Raul Ibanez	.25
157	Mark Teixeira	.50
158	Luis Gonzalez	.25
.159	Javy Lopez	.25
160	Greg Maddux	1.50

161	Kevin Millar	.25
162	Jose Valentin	.25
163	C.C. Sabathia	.25
164	Carlos Pena	.25
165	Miguel Cabrera	1.00
166	Adrian Beltre	.50
167	Sammy Sosa	2.00
168	Nick Johnson	.25
169	Jorge Posada	.25
170	Mike Piazza	1.50
171	Mark Mulder	.50
172	Mark Loretta	.25
173	Edgardo Alfonzo	.25
174	Edgar Renteria	.50
175	Pat Burrell	.25

Autographs

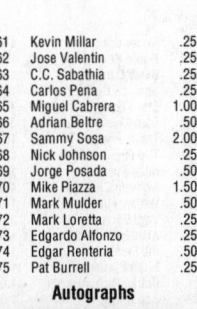

		NM/M
	Common Autograph:	15.00
CB	Carlos Beltran	30.00
HB	Hank Blalock	20.00
AB	Aaron Boone	20.00
MC	Miguel Cabrera	25.00
EC	Eric Chavez	15.00
JE	Johnny Estrada	10.00
ZG	Zack Greinke	20.00
VM	Victor Martinez	15.00
CS	C.C. Sabathia	15.00
VW	Vernon Wells	10.00
MY	Michael Young	15.00

Collector Chips

		NM/M
	Common Player:	8.00

Inserted 1:Box
Blue: No Pricing
Production 25 Sets
Red: No Pricing
Production 10 Sets

2	Ichiro Suzuki	30.00
3	Jim Thome	20.00
4	Albert Pujols	30.00
5	Vladimir Guerrero	15.00
6	Derek Jeter	30.00
7	Sammy Sosa	20.00
9	Ivan Rodriguez	10.00
11	Nomar Garciaparra	20.00
13	Ken Griffey Jr.	20.00
14	Todd Helton	10.00
15	Mike Piazza	20.00
16	Jorge Posada	10.00
17	Chipper Jones	10.00
18	Randy Johnson	15.00
19	Gary Sheffield	8.00
20	Mike Schmidt	25.00
21	Ernie Banks	20.00
22	Frank Robinson	20.00
23	Reggie Jackson	10.00
24	George Brett	25.00
25	Nolan Ryan	30.00

Cut Signatures

No Pricing

Relics

		NM/M
	Common Player:	8.00
RC	Roger Clemens	12.00
NG	Nomar Garciaparra	15.00
VG	Vladimir Guerrero	10.00
TH	Todd Helton	8.00
THB	Todd Helton	8.00
CJ	Chipper Jones	8.00
CJB	Chipper Jones	8.00
GM	Greg Maddux	10.00
PM	Pedro Martinez	8.00
RP	Rafael Palmeiro	8.00
MP	Albert Pujols	15.00
MR	Manny Ramirez	10.00
MRB	Manny Ramirez	10.00
AR	Alex Rodriguez	15.00
IR	Ivan Rodriguez	8.00
SR	Scott Rolen	10.00
GS	Gary Sheffield	8.00
AS	Alfonso Soriano	8.00
SS	Sammy Sosa	8.00
FT	Frank Thomas	8.00
JT	Jim Thome	8.00

Relic Autographs

		NM/M
	Common Autograph:	15.00

Production 200 Sets

CB	Carlos Beltran	40.00
HB	Hank Blalock	25.00
MC	Miguel Cabrera	30.00
EC	Eric Chavez	20.00
JE	Johnny Estrada	15.00
VM	Victor Martinez	15.00
MY	Michael Young	20.00

2005 Topps Pristine

		NM/M
	Common 1-100	.75
	Common Rookie (101-130):	1.00

Common (131-180): 3.00
Production 500
Common (181-205): 10.00
Production 100
Common (206-210):
Production 49
Pack (8): 30.00
Box (5): 125.00

1	Alex Rodriguez	3.00
2	Jake Peavy	.75
3	Bobby Crosby	.75
4	J.D. Drew	.75
5	Scott Rolen	1.50
6	Bobby Abreu	.75
7	Ken Griffey Jr.	2.50
8	Jeremy Bonderman	.75
9	Mike Sweeney	.75
10	Mark Prior	1.50
11	Tim Hudson	.75
12	Clint Barmes	.75
13	Jeff Bagwell	1.00
14	Andruw Jones	1.50
15	Carlos Delgado	.75
16	Rocco Baldelli	.75
17	Adam Dunn	1.50
18	Greg Maddux	2.00
19	Torii Hunter	.75
20	Miguel Tejada	1.50
21	Lyle Overbay	.75
22	Craig Wilson	.75
23	Scott Kazmir	.75
24	Alex Rios	.75
25	Ichiro Suzuki	3.00
26	Jorge Posada	1.00
27	Jose Reyes	.75
28	Hank Blalock	.75
29	Troy Glaus	.75
30	Todd Helton	1.50
31	Javy Lopez	.75
32	Barry Zito	1.00
33	Jimmy Rollins	.75
34	Mark Loretta	.75
35	Richie Sexson	.75
36	Nick Johnson	.75
37	Ivan Rodriguez	.75
38	Jeff Kent	.75
39	Jake Westbrook	.75
40	Carlos Beltran	1.00
41	Rich Harden	.75
42	Joe Mauer	1.00
43	Luis Gonzalez	.75
44	Frank Thomas	1.50
45	Michael Young	.75
46	Jason Schmidt	.75
47	Eric Chavez	.75
48	Vinny Castilla	.75
49	John Smoltz	1.00
50	Barry Bonds	4.00
51	Jim Edmonds	.75
52	Edgar Renteria	.75
53	Jose Vidro	.75
54	Chipper Jones	1.50
55	Curt Schilling	1.50
56	Victor Martinez	.75
57	Josh Beckett	.75
58	Derek Lee	1.50
59	Shawn Green	.75
60	Roger Clemens	4.00
61	Orlando Cabrera	.75
62	Mike Piazza	2.00
63	Gary Sheffield	.75
64	Carl Crawford	.75
65	Johan Santana	1.50
66	Oliver Perez	.75
67	Manny Ramirez	1.50
68	Paul Konerko	.75
69	Preston Wilson	.75
70	Sammy Sosa	2.00
71	Eric Gagne	.75
72	Geoff Jenkins	.75
73	Magglio Ordonez	.75
74	Kerry Wood	.75
75	Albert Pujols	4.00
76	Roy Halladay	1.00
77	Aubrey Huff	.75
78	Nomar Garciaparra	1.50
79	Brian Roberts	.75
80	Randy Johnson	1.50
81	Pat Burrell	.75
82	Brian Giles	.75
83	Mike Mussina	1.50
84	Mark Teixeira	1.50
85	Pedro Martinez	1.50
86	Jason Bay	.75
87	Mark Buehrle	.75
88	Rafael Furcal	.75
89	Juan Pierre	.75
90	Jim Thome	1.00

91	Ben Sheets	1.00
92	Alfonso Soriano	1.50
93	Adrian Beltre	.75
94	Miguel Cabrera	1.50
95	Derek Jeter	4.00
96	Vernon Wells	.75
97	Lance Berkman	1.00
98	Hideki Matsui	2.50
99	David Ortiz	1.50
100	Vladimir Guerrero	2.00
101	Justin Verlander RC	4.00
102	Billy Butler RC	2.00
103	Wladimir Balentien RC	1.50
104	Jeremy West RC	1.00
105	Philip Humber RC	2.00
106	Tyler Pelland RC	1.00
107	Andy LaRoche RC	2.00
108	Hernan Iribarren RC	1.00
109	Luke Scott RC	1.00
110	Landon Powell RC	1.00
111	Alexander Smit RC	1.00
112	Ryan Garko RC	1.00
113	Bear Bay RC	1.00
114	Ian Bladergroen RC	1.00
115	Manny Parra RC	2.00
116	Andy Sides RC	1.00
117	Travis Chick RC	1.00
118	Stefan Bailie RC	1.00
119	Chuck Tiffany RC	2.00
120	Buck Coats RC	1.00
121	Jeff Niemann RC	1.00
122	Jake Postlewait RC	1.00
123	Matt Campbell RC	1.00
124	Kevin Melillo RC	2.00
125	Mike Morse RC	1.00
126	Anthony Reyes RC	2.00
127	Casey McGehee RC	2.00
128	Cody Haerther RC	1.00
129	Brandon McCarthy RC	2.00
130	Glen Perkins RC	1.00
131	Moises Alou	3.00
132	Nomar Garciaparra	6.00
133	Scott Rolen	4.00
134	Miguel Tejada	4.00
135	Alex Rodriguez	10.00
136	Michael Young	3.00
137	Tim Hudson	5.00
138	Troy Glaus	3.00
139	Eric Chavez	3.00
140	David Ortiz	10.00
141	Andruw Jones	5.00
142	Richie Sexson	5.00
143	Jim Thome	5.00
144	Javy Lopez	3.00
145	Lance Berkman	3.00
146	Gary Sheffield	5.00
147	Dontrelle Willis	4.00
148	Curt Schilling	5.00
149	Jorge Posada	5.00
150	Vladimir Guerrero	8.00
151	Adam Dunn	5.00
152	Ryan Drese	3.00
153	Hank Blalock	3.00
154	Kerry Wood	5.00
155	Alfonso Soriano	5.00
156	Aramis Ramirez	5.00
157	Mark Mulder	4.00
158	Paul Konerko	4.00
159	Jim Edmonds	6.00
160	Roger Clemens	10.00
161	Mariano Rivera	6.00
162	Rafael Palmeiro	6.00
163	Mark Teixeira	6.00
164	Eric Gagne	3.00
165	Sammy Sosa	8.00
166	Brett Myers	3.00
167	Kazuhisa Ishii	3.00
168	Ken Harvey	3.00
169	Johnny Estrada	3.00
170	Todd Helton	5.00
171	Rich Harden	5.00
172	Johnny Damon	6.00
173	Manny Ramirez	8.00
174	Benito Santiago	3.00
175	Albert Pujols	15.00
176	Chipper Jones	.75
177	Miguel Cabrera	8.00
178	Jeff Bagwell	5.00
179	Ivan Rodriguez	5.00
180	Mike Piazza	8.00
181	Chip Cannon RC	6.00
182	Erik Cordier RC	10.00
183	Billy Butler RC	40.00
184	C.J. Smith RC	10.00
185	Alfonso Soriano	25.00
186	Bobby Livingston RC	15.00
187	Wladimir Balentien RC	15.00
188	Mike Morse RC	15.00
189	Wes Swackhamer RC	15.00
190	Justin Verlander RC	50.00
191	Jake Postlewait RC	15.00
192	Michael Rogers RC	20.00
193	Matt Campbell RC	15.00
194	Eric Nielsen RC	15.00
195	Gary Sheffield	20.00
196	Glen Perkins RC	10.00
197	Kevin Melillo RC	10.00
198	Chad Orvella RC	10.00
199	Jeff Niemann RC	25.00
200	Alex Rodriguez	180.00
201	Brian Stavisky RC	15.00
202	Brian Miller RC	15.00
203	Landon Powell RC	20.00
204	Philip Humber RC	20.00
205	Mariano Rivera	100.00
206	Curt Schilling	50.00
207	Nolan Ryan	150.00

Red

Red (1-130):	2-4X
Production 66	
Red (131-210):	No Pricing
Production Three Sets	

Uncirculated Bronze

Bronze (1-130):	1.5-3X
Production 375	
Bronze (131-180):	1-1.5X
Production 100	
Bronze (181-205):	No Pricing
Production 18	
Bronze (206-210):	No Pricing
Production 10	

Doubles Act Autographs

No Pricing
Production Five Sets

Fielder's Choice

No Pricing
Production Nine Sets

In The Name Patch

No Pricing
One card for each letter.

Personal Endorsements

		NM/M
Common		

Production 497 Sets
Uncirculated: No Pricing
Production Three Sets

MB	Milton Bradley	10.00
BB	Billy Butler	20.00
LC	Lance Cormier	8.00
SE	Scott Elbert	8.00
JF	Josh Fields	8.00
LH	Livan Hernandez	12.00
JPH	J.P. Howell	8.00
PH	Philip Humber	10.00
ZJ	Zach Jackson	8.00
BJ	Blake Johnson	8.00
BL	Bobby Livingston	8.00
CO	Chad Orvella	8.00
GP	Glen Perkins	15.00
LP	Landon Powell	8.00
MR	Mike Rodriguez	8.00
MRO	Mark Rogers	8.00
TS	Terrmel Sledge	8.00
CJS	C.J. Smith	8.00
JS	Jeremy Sowers	10.00
JV	Justin Verlander	20.00

Uncommon
Production 247 Sets

JB	Jason Bay	25.00
AB	Aaron Boone	10.00
MB	Matt Bush	15.00
BB	Billy Butler	20.00
CC	Chip Cannon	8.00
CE	Carl Erskine	10.00
HK	Harmon Killebrew	25.00
BL	Bobby Livingston	8.00
ML	Mark Loretta	8.00
DO	David Ortiz	40.00
CW	Craig Wilson	60.00
DW	David Wright	60.00
DZ	Don Zimmer	15.00

Rare
Production 97 Sets

GA	Garret Anderson	15.00
EB	Ernie Banks	50.00
SM	Stan Musial	50.00
MR	Mariano Rivera	100.00
TS	Tom Seaver	30.00
AS	Alfonso Soriano	25.00

Scarce
Production 22 Sets

Personal Pieces

		NM/M
Common		

Production 425
Uncirculated: No Pricing
Production Three Sets

JB	Jeff Bagwell	5.00
RB	Ronnie Belliard	3.00
AB	Adrian Beltre	3.00
LB	Lance Berkman	5.00
HB	Hank Blalock	5.00
EC	Eric Chavez	5.00
RC	Roger Clemens	12.00
BC	Bobby Crosby	5.00
JDD	J.D. Drew	5.00
AD	Adam Dunn	5.00
JE	Jim Edmonds	5.00
JES	Johnny Estrada	3.00
JG	Jason Giambi	5.00
JGI	Jay Gibbons	3.00
SG	Shawn Green	5.00
VG	Vladimir Guerrero	8.00
CG	Cristian Guzman	5.00
THA	Travis Hafner	5.00
TH	Todd Helton	5.00
THU	Tim Hudson	5.00
AJ	Andruw Jones	5.00
CJ	Chipper Jones	8.00

JL	Javy Lopez	3.00
ML	Mark Loretta	3.00
MLO	Mike Lowell	3.00
PM	Pedro Martinez	8.00
VM	Victor Martinez	3.00
KM	Kevin Millar	3.00
MM	Mark Mulder	5.00
BM	Brett Myers	3.00
LN	Laynce Nix	3.00
MP	Mike Piazza	8.00
MPR	Mark Prior	5.00
AP	Albert Pujols	15.00
BR	Brad Radke	3.00
MR	Manny Ramirez	8.00
ER	Edgar Renteria	3.00
MRI	Mariano Rivera	6.00
SR	Scott Rolen	6.00
CS	Curt Schilling	6.00
GS	Gary Sheffield	6.00
AS	Alfonso Soriano	5.00
MTE	Mark Teixeira	5.00
MT	Miguel Tejada	5.00
FT	Frank Thomas	8.00
JT	Jim Thome	5.00
BJU	B.J. Upton	3.00
BW	Bernie Williams	3.00
KW	Kerry Wood	5.00
BZ	Barry Zito	3.00

Uncommon
Production 200

CB	Carlos Beltran	5.00
AB	Adrian Beltre	3.00
MC	Miguel Cabrera	8.00
RC	Roger Clemens	12.00
JE	Jim Edmonds	5.00
EG	Eric Gagne	5.00
TG	Troy Glaus	3.00
TH	Torii Hunter	5.00
AJ	Andruw Jones	5.00
CJ	Chipper Jones	8.00
MM	Mark Mulder	5.00
MO	Magglio Ordonez	3.00
DO	David Ortiz	8.00
MP	Mike Piazza	8.00
JP	Jorge Posada	8.00
AP	Albert Pujols	15.00
MR	Manny Ramirez	8.00
MRI	Mariano Rivera	6.00
AR	Alex Rodriguez	15.00
IR	Ivan Rodriguez	5.00
SR	Scott Rolen	5.00
CS	Curt Schilling	6.00
AS	Alfonso Soriano	5.00
SS	Sammy Sosa	8.00
JT	Jim Thome	5.00

Rare

CB	Carlos Beltran	10.00
BB	Barry Bonds	40.00
RC	Roger Clemens	20.00
JD	Johnny Damon	12.00
EG	Eric Gagne	8.00
VG	Vladimir Guerrero	10.00
TH	Todd Helton	10.00
PM	Pedro Martinez	10.00
AP	Albert Pujols	25.00
AR	Alex Rodriguez	25.00

Scarce

Power Core

No Pricing
Production 3-10
Power Stick: No Pricing
Production One Set

Printing Plates

No Pricing
Production one set for each color.

Selective Swatch

No Pricing
Production One Set

2005 Topps Pristine Legends

		NM/M
Complete Set (140):		
Common Player:		1.00
Common SP (101-125):		2.00
Production 1,999		
Common SP (126-135):		3.00
Production 999		
Common SP (136-140):		4.00
Production 499		
Pack (8):		30.00
Box (5):		120.00

1	Vida Blue	1.00
2	Bert Blyleven	1.00
3	Joe Carter	1.00
4	Bill Buckner	1.00

#	Player	Price
5	Luis Aparicio	1.00
6	Ernie Banks	2.50
7	Wade Boggs	4.00
8	George Brett	4.00
9	Lou Brock	2.00
10	Rod Carew	2.00
11	Gary Carter	1.00
12	Andre Dawson	1.00
13	Dennis Eckersley	1.00
14	Rollie Fingers	1.00
15	Steve Garvey	1.00
16	Dwight Gooden	1.00
17	Rich "Goose" Gossage	1.00
18	Ron Guidry	1.00
19	Keith Hernandez	1.00
20	Charlie Hough	1.00
21	Bo Jackson	2.50
22	Monte Irvin	2.00
23	Reggie Jackson	2.00
24	Ferguson Jenkins	1.00
25	Ralph Kiner	1.00
26	Juan Marichal	1.00
27	Stan Musial	4.00
28	Tony Oliva	1.00
29	Jim Palmer	1.50
30	Dave Parker	1.00
31	Gaylord Perry	1.00
32	Jimmy Piersall	1.00
33	Johnny Podres	1.00
34	Brooks Robinson	2.00
35	Frank Robinson	2.00
36	Nolan Ryan	5.00
37	Tom Seaver	2.00
38	Ozzie Smith	3.00
39	Duke Snider	2.00
40	Bobby Thomson	1.00
41	Carl Yastrzemski	3.00
42	Maury Wills	1.00
43	Robin Yount	3.00
44	Matt Williams	1.00
45	Orel Hershiser	1.00
46	Tim McCarver	1.00
47	Don Newcombe	1.00
48	Paul O'Neill	1.00
49	Al Kaline	2.00
50	Harmon Killebrew	2.00
51	Dave Kingman	1.00
52	Ken Griffey	1.00
53	George Foster	1.00
54	Mark Fidrych	1.00
55	Orlando Cepeda	1.00
56	Don Larsen	1.00
57	Bill Madlock	1.00
58	Dale Murphy	1.50
59	Graig Nettles	1.00
60	Phil Niekro	1.00
61	Al Oliver	1.00
62	Harold Reynolds	1.00
63	Bobby Richardson	1.00
64	Mike Scott	1.00
65	Dave Stewart	1.00
66	Rick Sutcliffe	1.00
67	Bruce Sutter	1.50
68	Luis Tiant	1.00
69	Bob Watson	1.00
70	Walt Weiss	1.00
71	Don Zimmer	1.00
72	Tommy John	1.00
73	Ray Knight	1.00
74	Jack Morris	1.00
75	Mickey Rivers	1.00
76	Lee Smith	1.00
77	Darryl Strawberry	1.00
78	David Justice	1.00
79	Wally Joyner	1.00
80	Jimmy Key	1.00
81	John Kruk	1.00
82	Greg Luzinski	1.00
83	Mookie Wilson	1.00
84	Wilbur Wood	1.00
85	Tim Raines	1.00
86	Jim Rice	1.00
87	Tony Armas	1.00
88	Harold Baines	1.00
89	Bucky Dent	1.00
90	Darrell Evans	1.00
91	Cecil Fielder	1.00
92	Jose Cruz	1.00
93	Dave Concepcion	1.00
94	Ron Cey	1.00
95	Davey Lopes	1.00
96	Boog Powell	1.00
97	Buddy Bell	1.00
98	George Bell	1.00
99	Bert Campaneris	1.00
100	Chet Lemon	1.00
101	Bo Jackson	4.00
102	Will Clark	2.00
103	Cecil Fielder	2.00
104	Ron Cey	2.00
105	Tony Gwynn	5.00
106	Orel Hershiser	2.00
107	Jimmy Key	2.00
108	Paul Molitor	3.00
109	Pete Incaviglia	1.00
110	Wally Joyner	2.00
111	Dave Kingman	2.00
112	Ron Guidry	2.00
113	Ron Darling	2.00
114	Mookie Wilson	2.00
115	Reggie Jackson	2.00
116	Walt Weiss	2.00
117	Joe Carter	2.00
118	Cory Snyder	2.00
119	Dave Winfield	3.00
120	Terry Steinbach	2.00
121	Matt Williams	2.00
122	Ozzie Smith	5.00
123	Jack McDowell	2.00
124	Bob Horner	2.00
125	Don Kessinger	2.00
126	Minnie Minoso	3.00
127	Cecil Kaiser	3.00
128	Buck O'Neil	3.00
129	Monte Irvin	4.00
130	Jim Gilliam	3.00
131	Josh Gibson	4.00
132	Ernie Banks	6.00
133	Don Newcombe	3.00
134	Red Moore	3.00
135	Willie Pope	3.00
136	Gary Carter	4.00
137	Bo Jackson	6.00
138	George Brett	8.00
139	Joe Carter	4.00
140	Nolan Ryan	8.00

Refractor
Refractor (1-100):	1-1.5X
Production 549	
Refractor (101-125):	1.5-2X
Production 199	
Refractor (126-135):	1.5-2.5X
Production 99	
Refractor (136-140):	No Pricing
Production 25	

Refractors Gold Die-Cut
Gold (1-100):	3-4X
Gold (101-135):	1-2.5X
Gold (136-140):	1-1.5X
Production 65 Sets	

SuperFractor
No Pricing
Production One Set

Printing Plates
No Pricing
One set produced per color.

Celebrity Threads
NM/M
Inserted 1:18
Refractor: No Pricing
Production 25 Sets

MM	Marilyn Monroe	75.00
EP	Elvis Presley	65.00

Leading Indicators

TOTAL BASES LEADER – 1978 JIM RICE RED SOX

NM/M
Common Player: 4.00
Refractor: No Pricing
Production one or 25.

WB	Wade Boggs	10.00
RC	Rod Carew	8.00
AD	Andre Dawson	6.00
BF	Bob Feller	10.00
CF	Cecil Fielder	8.00
GF	George Foster	4.00
TG	Tony Gwynn	10.00
AK	Al Kaline	12.00
DK	Dave Kingman	6.00
RM	Roger Maris	35.00
DM	Don Mattingly	15.00
DBM	Dale Murphy	10.00
TO	Tony Oliva	6.00
PO	Paul O'Neill	10.00
DP	Dave Parker	4.00
GP	Gaylord Perry	4.00
TR	Tim Raines	4.00
TR2	Tim Raines	6.00
JR	Jim Rice	4.00
NR	Nolan Ryan	20.00
MS	Mike Scott	10.00
TS	Tom Seaver	10.00
DS	Darryl Strawberry	6.00
MW	Maury Wills	10.00
CY	Carl Yastrzemski	15.00

Personal Endorsements

NM/M
Common Autograph: 10.00
Gold: No Pricing
Production 25 Sets

JA	Jim Abbott	15.00
LA	Luis Aparicio	15.00
BB	Bert Blyleven	15.00
GB	George Brett	50.00
GC	Gary Carter	15.00
RD	Ron Darling	15.00
AD	Andre Dawson	15.00
DE	Dennis Eckersley	15.00
DWE	Darrell Evans	15.00
CF	Carlton Fisk	25.00
GF	George Foster	10.00
GG	Rich "Goose" Gossage	10.00
BG	Bobby Grich	10.00
KH	Keith Hernandez	12.00
BJ	Bo Jackson	60.00
RJ	Reggie Jackson	50.00
AK	Al Kaline	40.00
DL	Don Larsen	15.00
JM	Jack McDowell	10.00
SM	Stan Musial	50.00
GN	Graig Nettles	15.00
JO	Jesse Orosco	10.00
JP	Jim Palmer	15.00
JAP	Jimmy Piersall	15.00
CR	Cal Ripken Jr.	125.00
BR	Brooks Robinson	30.00
NR	Nolan Ryan	90.00
DS	Duke Snider	40.00
EW	Earl Weaver	15.00
CY	Carl Yastrzemski	50.00
RY	Robin Yount	50.00

Signature Marks

NM/M
No Pricing
Production One Set

RR	Sugar Ray Robinson (12/05 Auction)	1,000

Title Threads
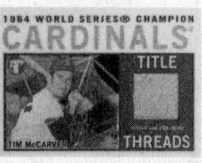

NM/M
Common Player: 4.00
Refractors: No Pricing
Production 25 Sets

WB	Wade Boggs	10.00
GC	Gary Carter	6.00
JC	Joe Carter	6.00
OC	Orlando Cepeda	8.00
BD	Bucky Dent	6.00
LD	Lenny Dykstra	6.00
RF	Rollie Fingers	6.00
GF	George Foster	4.00
CS	Cesar Geronimo	6.00
GG	Rich "Goose" Gossage	6.00
KG	Ken Griffey Sr.	6.00
OH	Orel Hershiser	8.00
WH	Willie Horton	10.00
MI	Monte Irvin	12.00
DJ	David Justice	6.00
JK	Jimmy Key	6.00
EK	Ed Kranepool	6.00
TM	Tim McCarver	6.00
GN	Graig Nettles	8.00
PO	Paul O'Neill	10.00
JP	Jim Palmer	8.00
DS	Darryl Strawberry	6.00
MW	Mookie Wilson	4.00

Valuable Performances

MOST VALUABLE PLAYER — KEITH HERNANDEZ MVP 1979 CARDINALS

NM/M
Common Player: 4.00
Refractor: No Pricing
Production one or 25.

YB	Yogi Berra	15.00
JC	Jose Canseco	10.00
AD	Andre Dawson	6.00
DE	Dennis Eckersley	8.00
CF	Cecil Fielder	8.00
SG	Steve Garvey	6.00
KH	Keith Hernandez	4.00
RJ	Reggie Jackson	10.00
HK	Harmon Killebrew	12.00
DBM	Don Mattingly	15.00
JM	Joe Morgan	6.00
DM	Dale Murphy	10.00
SM	Stan Musial	15.00
DP	Dave Parker	4.00
JR	Jim Rice	8.00
CR	Cal Ripken Jr.	25.00
FR	Frank Robinson	8.00
MS	Mike Schmidt	15.00
CY	Carl Yastrzemski	15.00
RY	Robin Yount	8.00

2005 Topps Retired Signature Edition

GIBSON

NM/M
Complete Set (110):	150.00
Common Player:	1.00
Pack (5):	30.00
Box (5):	125.00

#	Player	Price
1	Josh Gibson	1.00
2	Andre Dawson	1.00
3	Al Kaline	2.00
4	Andy Van Slyke	1.00
5	Brett Butler	1.00
6	Bob Gibson	1.50
7	Bo Jackson	2.00
8	Carlton Fisk	1.00
9	Chuck Knoblauch	1.00
10	Cal Ripken Jr.	6.00
11	Carl Yastrzemski	3.00
12	Tom Niedenfuer	1.00
13	Dennis Eckersley	1.00
14	Darryl Strawberry	1.00
15	Dwight Gooden	1.00
16	Davey Johnson	1.00
17	Don Mattingly	3.00
18	Dave Winfield	1.50
19	Don Zimmer	1.00
20	Ernie Banks	2.00
21	George Brett	3.00
22	Gary Carter	1.00
23	Gregg Jefferies	1.00
24	Harold Baines	1.00
25	Ryne Sandberg	2.00
26	Howard Johnson	1.00
27	Jim Abbott	1.00
28	Johnny Bench	2.00
29	Jay Buhner	1.00
30	Johnny Podres	1.00
31	Jose Canseco	1.50
32	Keith Hernandez	1.00
33	Lou Brock	1.00
34	Lou Whitaker	1.00
35	Mark Fidrych	1.00
36	Orlando Cepeda	1.00
37	Ozzie Smith	2.00
38	Paul O'Neill	1.00
39	Reggie Jackson	1.50
40	Sid Fernandez	1.00
41	Tony Gwynn	2.00
42	Tim Raines	1.00
43	Tom Seaver	1.50
44	Vida Blue	1.00
45	Brady Anderson	1.00
46	Bob Brenly	1.00
47	Bob Feller	1.00
48	Bill Mazeroski	1.00
49	Brooks Robinson	1.50
50	Harmon Killebrew	1.50
51	Bob Welch	1.00
52	Carl Erskine	1.00
53	Dale Murphy	1.00
54	Denny McClain	1.00
55	Dave Magadan	1.00
56	Duke Snider	1.50
57	Ed Kranepool	1.00
58	Frank Robinson	1.50
59	Jesus Alou	1.00
60	Joe Girardi	1.00
61	John Kruk	1.00
62	Jim Leyland	1.00
63	Juan Marichal	1.00
64	Johnny Pesky	1.00
65	Jesse Orosco	1.00
66	Ken Singleton	1.00
67	Matty Alou	1.00
68	Monte Irvin	1.00
69	Matt Williams	1.00
70	Pedro Guerrero	1.00
71	Ron Blomberg	1.00
72	Rod Carew	1.50
73	Rafael Santana	1.00
74	Ralph Kiner	1.00
75	Wade Boggs	1.50
76	Roger Craig	1.00
77	Robin Yount	2.00
78	Steve Carlton	1.00
79	Shawon Dunston	1.00
80	Steve Garvey	1.00
81	Stan Musial	3.00
82	Travis Fryman	1.00
83	Tito Fuentes	1.00
84	Mike Cuellar	1.00
85	Roberto Clemente	4.00
86	Whitey Ford	1.50
87	Yogi Berra	2.00
88	Atlee Hammaker	1.00
89	Bill Freehan	1.00
90	Brian Cashman	1.00
91	Bobby Richardson	1.00
92	Bob Boone	1.00
93	Charlie Hough	1.00
94	Glenn Hubbard	1.00
95	Grady Little	1.00
96	Jimmy Piersall	1.00
97	Jim Frey	1.00
98	Jerry Grote	1.00
99	Jim Leyritz	1.00
100	Nolan Ryan	5.00
101	Jim Kaat	1.00
102	Joe Pepitone	1.00
103	J.R. Richard	1.00
104	John Candelaria	1.00
105	Bill "Moose" Skowron	1.00
106	Rick Cerone	1.00
107	Ron Santo	1.00
108	Rick Dempsey	1.00
109	Roy White	1.00
110	Tippy Martinez	1.00

Black
Black (1-110):	4-6X
Production 54 Sets	

Gold

AL KALINE — Detroit Tigers

Gold (1-110):	2-4X
Production 500 Sets	

Holographic
No Pricing
Production One Set

Autographs

NM/M
Common Autograph: 10.00

JAA	Jim Abbott	20.00
JA	Jesus Alou	15.00
MA	Matty Alou	15.00
BA	Brady Anderson	15.00
HB	Harold Baines	15.00
EB	Ernie Banks	150.00
JB	Johnny Bench	200.00
YB	Yogi Berra	200.00
RB	Ron Blomberg	15.00
VB	Vida Blue	25.00
WB	Wade Boggs	50.00
BRB	Bob Boone	20.00
DLB	Daryl Boston	10.00
BEB	Bob Brenly	10.00
GB	George Brett	150.00
LB	Lou Brock	25.00
JCB	Jay Buhner	25.00
BB	Brett Butler	20.00
JRC	John Candelaria	15.00
JC	Jose Canseco	50.00
RCC	Rod Carew	30.00
SC	Steve Carlton	35.00
GC	Gary Carter	20.00
BC	Brian Cashman	85.00
OC	Orlando Cepeda	15.00
RC	Rick Cerone	15.00
RLC	Roger Craig	15.00
MC	Mike Cuellar	15.00
RD	Ron Darling	15.00
AD	Andre Dawson	25.00
RRD	Rick Dempsey	15.00
BD	Bob Dernier	20.00
SD	Shawon Dunston	35.00
CE	Carl Erskine	30.00
BF	Bob Feller	30.00
SF	Sid Fernandez	20.00
CF	Carlton Fisk	30.00
BAF	Bill Freehan	15.00
JF	Jim Frey	15.00
TDF	Travis Fryman	15.00
TF	Tito Fuentes	15.00
REG	Ron Gant	25.00
SG	Steve Garvey	20.00
BG	Bob Gibson	150.00
DG	Dwight Gooden	20.00
JG	Jerry Grote	20.00
PG	Pedro Guerrero	15.00
TG	Tony Gwynn	100.00
AH	Atlee Hammaker	10.00
TH	Toby Harrah	15.00
KH	Keith Hernandez	20.00
CH	Charlie Hough	15.00
GH	Glenn Hubbard	10.00
MI	Monte Irvin	50.00
BJ	Bo Jackson	100.00
RJ	Reggie Jackson	150.00
GJ	Gregg Jefferies	20.00
HJ	Howard Johnson	25.00
JLK	Jim Kaat	15.00
AK	Al Kaline	40.00
HK	Harmon Killebrew	100.00
RK	Ralph Kiner	35.00
EK	Ed Kranepool	15.00
JK	John Kruk	20.00
TL	Tony LaRussa	20.00
JL	Jim Leyland	15.00
JJL	Jim Leyritz	15.00
GL	Grady Little	15.00
JRL	Jim Lonborg	15.00
DJM	Dave Magadan	15.00
JM	Juan Marichal	25.00
TM	Tippy Martinez	10.00
DM	Don Mattingly	140.00
BM	Bill Mazeroski	45.00
DDM	Denny McLain	20.00
DBM	Dale Murphy	30.00
TN	Tom Niedenfuer	15.00
PO	Paul O'Neill	40.00
JO	Jesse Orosco	10.00
JP	Joe Pepitone	15.00
JMP	Johnny Pesky	25.00
JAP	Jimmy Piersall	15.00
JJP	Johnny Podres	50.00
TR	Tim Raines	25.00
JR	J.R. Richard	20.00
BCR	Bobby Richardson	20.00
CR	Cal Ripken Jr.	180.00
BR	Brooks Robinson	80.00
FR	Frank Robinson	60.00
NR	Nolan Ryan	250.00
RS	Ryne Sandberg	90.00
RFS	Rafael Santana	10.00
RES	Ron Santo	30.00
TS	Tom Seaver	50.00
MS	Bill "Moose" Skowron	15.00
OS	Ozzie Smith	125.00
ZS	Zane Smith	10.00
DS	Duke Snider	60.00
DES	Darryl Strawberry	50.00
BW	Bob Welch	15.00
LW	Lou Whitaker	35.00
RW	Roy White	15.00
MW	Matt Williams	30.00
DW	Dave Winfield	50.00
CY	Carl Yastrzemski	120.00
AY	Anthony Young	10.00
RY	Robin Yount	125.00
DZ	Don Zimmer	30.00

Co-Signers
NM/M
Some not priced.

BS	Wade Boggs, Ryne Sandberg/49	140.00
BF	Johnny Bench, Carlton Fisk/49	125.00
GF	Bob Gibson, Whitey Ford/49	100.00

2005 Topps Rookie Cup

FIRST YEAR

NM/M
Complete Set (160):	35.00
Common Player (1-150):	.15
Common Rookie Auto. (151-160):	8.00

Inserted 1:62

Pack (7):		4.00
Box (24):		75.00
1	Pat Corrales	.15
2	Ron Santo	.15
3	Joe Torre	.40
4	Boog Powell	.15
5	Tom Tresh	.15
6	Jonny Gomes	.15
7	Rico Carty	.15
8	Bert Campaneris	.15
9	Tony Oliva	.15
10	Ron Swoboda	.15
11	Tony Perez	.40
12	Joe Morgan	.40
13	Davey Johnson	.15
14	Cleon Jones	.15
15	Tom Seaver	.75
16	Rod Carew	.15
17	Rick Monday	.15
18	Johnny Bench	.75
19	Bobby Cox	.15
20	Jerry Koosman	.15
21	Al Oliver	.15
22	Lou Piniella	.25
23	Larry Bowa	.15
24	Chris Chambliss	.15
25	Bill Buckner	.15
26	Don Baylor	.15
27	Buddy Bell	.15
28	Carlton Fisk	.50
29	Gary Mathews	.15
30	Davey Lopes	.15
31	Bob Boone	.15
32	Bill Madlock	.15
33	Claudell Washington	.15
34	Jim Rice	.25
35	Gary Carter	.25
36	Willie Randolph	.15
37	Chet Lemon	.15
38	Andre Dawson	.25
39	Eddie Murray	.50
40	Paul Molitor	.50
41	Ozzie Smith	1.00
42	Jeffrey Leonard	.15
43	Lonnie Smith	.15
44	Mookie Wilson	.15
45	Tim Wallach	.15
46	Tim Raines	.25
47	Fernando Valenzuela	.15
48	Cal Ripken Jr.	2.00
49	Ryne Sandberg	1.00
50	Willie McGee	.15
51	Darryl Strawberry	.15
52	Julio Franco	.15
53	Brook Jacoby	.15
54	Dwight Gooden	.15
55	Roger McDowell	.15
56	Ozzie Guillen	.15
57	Vince Coleman	.15
58	Pete Incaviglia	.15
59	Wally Joyner	.15
60	Jose Canseco	.50
61	Cory Snyder	.15
62	Devon White	.15
63	Walt Weiss	.15
64	Mark Grace	.40
65	Ron Gant	.15
66	Chris Sabo	.15
67	Jay Buhner	.15
68	Gary Sheffield	.40
69	Gregg Jefferies	.15
70	Ken Griffey Jr.	1.50
71	Tom Gordon	.15
72	Jim Abbott	.15
73	David Justice	.25
74	Larry Walker	.15
75	Sandy Alomar	.15
76	Chuck Knoblauch	.15
77	Jeff Bagwell	.50
78	Luis Gonzalez	.25
79	Ivan Rodriguez	.50
80	Eric Karros	.15
81	Jeff Kent	.15
82	Kenny Lofton	.15
83	Moises Alou	.25
84	Reggie Sanders	.15
85	Jeff Conine	.15
86	J.T. Snow	.15
87	Tim Salmon	.25
88	Mike Piazza	1.00
89	Manny Ramirez	.75
90	Ryan Klesko	.15
91	Javy Lopez	.15
92	Chipper Jones	.75
93	Ray Durham	.15
94	Garret Anderson	.25
95	Shawn Green	.15
96	Hideo Nomo	.15
97	Jermaine Dye	.15
98	Tony Clark	.15
99	Joe Randa	.15
100	Derek Jeter	2.00
101	Jason Kendall	.15
102	Billy Wagner	.15
103	Andruw Jones	.50
104	Dmitri Young	.15
105	Scott Rolen	.50
106	Nomar Garciaparra	.75
107	Jose Cruz Jr.	.15
108	Scott Hatteberg	.15
109	Mark Kotsay	.15
110	Todd Helton	.50
111	Miguel Cairo	.15
112	Magglio Ordonez	.25
113	Kerry Wood	.25
114	Preston Wilson	.15
115	Alex Gonzalez	.15
116	Carlos Beltran	.50
117	Rafael Furcal	.25
118	Pat Burrell	.15
119	Adam Kennedy	.15
120	Terrence Long	.15
121	Jay Payton	.15
122	Bengie Molina	.15
123	Albert Pujols	2.00
124	Craig Wilson	.15
125	Alfonso Soriano	.50
126	Jimmy Rollins	.25
127	Adam Dunn	.50
128	Ichiro Suzuki	1.50
129	Roy Oswalt	.25
130	C.C. Sabathia	.15
131	Brad Wilkerson	.15
132	Nick Johnson	.15
133	Eric Hinske	.15
134	Austin Kearns	.25
135	Dontrelle Willis	.40
136	Mark Teixeira	.50
137	Rocco Baldelli	.25
138	Scott Podsednik	.25
139	Brandon Webb	.25
140	Jason Bay	.25
141	Adam LaRoche	.15
142	Khalil Greene	.25
143	Joe Mauer	.50
144	Matt Holliday	.25
145	Chad Tracy	.15
146	Garrett Atkins	.25
147	Tadahito Iguchi	1.00
148	Russ Adams	.15
149	Huston Street	.15
150	Dan Johnson	.15
151	J. Brent Cox RC	10.00
152	John Drennen RC	10.00
153	Ryan Tucker RC	10.00
154	Yunel Escobar RC	25.00
155	Jacob Marceaux RC	15.00
156	Mark Pawelek RC	15.00
157	Brandon Snyder RC	15.00
158	Wade Townsend RC	15.00
159	Troy Tulowitzki RC	15.00
160	Kevin Whelan RC	10.00

Blue

Blue (1-150):	3-6X
Blue (151-160):	1-2X
Production 50 Sets	

Gold

No Pricing
Production One Set

Green

Green (1-150):	2-4X
Production 199	
Green (151-160):	1-2X
Production 99	

Orange

Orange (1-150):	1.5-3X
Production 399	
Orange (151-160):	1X
Production 299	

Red

Red (1-150):	1-2X
Production 499	
Red (151-160):	1X
Production 399	

Silver

No Pricing
Production One Set

Yellow

Yellow (1-150):	2-3X
Production 299	
Yellow (151-160):	1X
Production 199	

Printing Plates

No Pricing
Production one set per color.

Autographs

NM/M

Common Autograph:		
Silver:		No Pricing
Production Five Sets		
Gold:		No Pricing
Production One Set		
JBA	Jason Bay	20.00
JB	Johnny Bench	65.00
AD	Andre Dawson	15.00
JD	Jermaine Dye	8.00
RF	Rafael Furcal	12.00
MG	Mark Grace	25.00
DRJ	Dan Johnson	8.00
DJ	Davey Johnson	8.00
AJ	Andruw Jones	40.00
CJ	Chipper Jones	40.00
DJ	David Justice	20.00
EK	Eric Karros	8.00
MK	Mark Kotsay	8.00
CK	Chuck Knoblauch	8.00
RM	Roger McDowell	10.00
PM	Paul Molitor	15.00
BP	Boog Powell	15.00
MR	Manny Ramirez	50.00
JR	Jim Rice	30.00
RSA	Ron Santo	25.00
TS	Tom Seaver	25.00
GS	Gary Sheffield	25.00
DS	Darryl Strawberry	25.00
RS	Ron Swoboda	10.00
JT	Joe Torre	25.00
BW	Brad Wilkerson	8.00
DW	Dontrelle Willis	20.00

Dual Autographs

NM/M
Inserted 1:118

GS	Mark Grace, Ron Santo	80.00
BW	Jason Bay, Dontrelle Willis	50.00
WD	Brad Wilkerson, Andre Dawson	50.00
CS	J. Brent Cox, Tom Seaver	40.00
RTW	Ryan Tucker, Dontrelle Willis	20.00
EF	Yunel Escobar, Rafael Furcal	25.00
MM	Jacob Marceaux, Roger McDowell	20.00
SP	Brandon Snyder, Boog Powell	25.00
TS	Wade Townsend, Tom Seaver	50.00
TW	Troy Tulowitzki, Walt Weiss	30.00
WM	Kevin Whelan, Roger McDowell	15.00

Reprints

NM/M

Complete Set (150):	60.00
Common Player:	1-2X Base Card
Reprints:	
2 Per Hobby Pack	
1 Per Retail Pack	
Chrome:	No Pricing
Production 25 Sets	
Refractor:	No Pricing
15 Sets	
Chrome Gold:	No Pricing
Production One Set	

1	Pat Corrales/66	.25
2	Ron Santo/61	.50
3	Joe Torre/62	.75
4	Boog Powell/63	.25
5	Tom Tresh/63	.25
6	Jonny Gomes/06	.25
7	Rico Carty/65	.25
8	Bert Campaneris/65	.25
9	Tony Oliva/65	.50
10	Ron Swoboda/66	.25
11	Tony Perez/66	.75
12	Joe Morgan/66	.75
13	Davey Johnson/67	.25
14	Cleon Jones/67	.25
15	Tom Seaver/68	1.00
16	Rod Carew/68	.75
17	Rick Monday/68	.25
18	Johnny Bench/69	1.50
19	Bobby Cox/69	.25
20	Jerry Koosman/69	.25
21	Al Oliver/70	.50
22	Lou Piniella/70	.40
23	Larry Bowa/71	.40
24	Chris Chambliss/72	.25
25	Bill Buckner/72	.25
26	Don Baylor/73	.25
27	Buddy Bell/73	.75
28	Carlton Fisk/73	.75
29	Gary Mathews/74	.25
30	Davey Lopes/74	.25
31	Bob Boone/74	.25
32	Bill Madlock/75	.25
33	Claudell Washington/75	.25
34	Jim Rice/76	.40
35	Gary Carter/76	.25
36	Willie Randolph/77	.25
37	Chet Lemon/77	.25
38	Andre Dawson/78	.40
39	Eddie Murray/78	.75
40	Paul Molitor/79	.75
41	Ozzie Smith/79	1.50
42	Jeffrey Leonard/80	.25
43	Lonnie Smith/81	.25
44	Mookie Wilson/82	.25
45	Tim Wallach/82	.25
46	Tim Raines/82	.40
47	Fernando Valenzuela/82	.25
48	Cal Ripken Jr./83	3.00
49	Ryne Sandberg/84	1.50
50	Willie McGee/83	.25
51	Darryl Strawberry/84	.25
52	Julio Franco/84	.25
53	Brook Jacoby/85	.25
54	Dwight Gooden/85	.25
55	Roger McDowell/86	.25
56	Ozzie Guillen/86	.25
57	Vince Coleman/86	.25
58	Pete Incaviglia/87	.25
59	Wally Joyner/87	.25
60	Jose Canseco/87	.75
61	Cory Snyder/87	.25
62	Devon White/89	.25
63	Walt Weiss/89	.25
64	Mark Grace/89	.50
65	Ron Gant/89	.25
66	Chris Sabo/89	.25
67	Jay Buhner/89	.25
68	Gary Sheffield/90	.25
69	Gregg Jefferies/90	.25
70	Ken Griffey Jr./90	2.00
71	Tom Gordon/90	.25
72	Jim Abbott/90	.25
73	David Justice/91	.40
74	Larry Walker/91	.40
75	Sandy Alomar Jr./91	.25
76	Chuck Knoblauch/92	.25
77	Jeff Bagwell/92	.50
78	Luis Gonzalez/92	.25
79	Ivan Rodriguez/92	.50
80	Eric Karros/93	.25
81	Jeff Kent/93	.25
82	Kenny Lofton/93	.25
83	Moises Alou/93	.25
84	Reggie Sanders/93	.25
85	Jeff Conine/94	.25
86	J.T. Snow/94	.25
87	Tim Salmon/94	.25
88	Mike Piazza/94	1.50
89	Manny Ramirez/95	.75
90	Ryan Klesko/95	.25
91	Javy Lopez/95	.25
92	Chipper Jones/96	1.00
93	Ray Durham/96	.25
94	Garret Anderson/96	.25
95	Shawn Green/96	.25
96	Hideo Nomo/96	.40
97	Jermaine Dye/97	.25
98	Tony Clark/97	.25
99	Joe Randa/97	.25
100	Derek Jeter/97	3.00
101	Jason Kendall/97	.25
102	Billy Wagner/97	.25
103	Andruw Jones/98	.75
104	Dmitri Young/98	.25
105	Scott Rolen/98	.25
106	Nomar Garciaparra/98	.75
107	Jose Cruz Jr./98	.25
108	Scott Hatteberg/98	.25
109	Mark Kotsay/99	.25
110	Todd Helton/99	.50
111	Miguel Cairo/99	.25
112	Magglio Ordonez/99	.25
113	Kerry Wood/99	.40
114	Preston Wilson/99	.25
115	Alex Gonzalez/00	.25
116	Carlos Beltran/00	.50
117	Rafael Furcal/01	.25
118	Pat Burrell/01	.25
119	Adam Kennedy/01	.25
120	Terrence Long/01	.25
121	Jay Payton/01	.25
122	Bengie Molina/01	.25
123	Albert Pujols/02	3.00
124	Craig Wilson/02	.25
125	Alfonso Soriano/02	.50
126	Jimmy Rollins/02	.50
127	Adam Dunn/02	.75
128	Ichiro Suzuki/02	2.00
129	Roy Oswalt/02	.40
130	C.C. Sabathia/02	.25
131	Brad Wilkerson/03	.25
132	Nick Johnson/03	.25
133	Eric Hinske/03	.25
134	Austin Kearns/03	.25
135	Dontrelle Willis/04	.75
136	Mark Teixeira/04	.75
137	Rocco Baldelli/04	.25
138	Scott Podsednik/04	.25
139	Brandon Webb/04	.25
140	Jason Bay/05	.25
141	Adam LaRoche/05	.25
142	Khalil Greene/05	.25
143	Joe Mauer/05	.50
144	Matt Holliday/05	.25
145	Chad Tracy/06	.25
146	Garrett Atkins/06	.25
147	Tadahito Iguchi/06	1.50
148	Russ Adams/06	.25
149	Huston Street/06	.25
150	Dan Johnson/06	.25

Original Relics

No Pricing
Production 1-10

2005 Topps Total

Barry Bonds

NM/M

Complete Set (770):		120.00
Common Player:		.15
Pack (10):		1.00
Box (36):		35.00
1	Rafael Furcal	.15
2	Tony Clark	.15
3	Hideki Matsui	1.25
4	Zach Day	.15
5	Garret Anderson	.40
6	B.J. Surhoff	.15
7	Trevor Hoffman	.15
8	Kenny Lofton	.15
9	Ross Gload	.15
10	Jorge Cantu	.15
11	Joel Pineiro	.15
12	Alex Cintron	.15
13	Mike Matheny	.15
14	Rod Barajas	.15
15	Ray Durham	.15
16	Danys Baez	.15
17	Brian Schneider	.15
18	Tike Redman	.15
19	Ricardo Rodriguez	.15
20	Mike Sweeney	.15
21	Greg Myers	.15
22	Chone Figgins	.15
23	Brian Lawrence	.15
24	Joe Nathan	.15
25	Placido Polanco	.15
26	Yadier Molina	.15
27	Gary Bennett	.15
28	Yorvit Torrealba	.15
29	Javier Valentin	.15
30	Jason Giambi	.25
31	Brandon Claussen	.15
32	Miguel Olivo	.15
33	Josh Bard	.15
34	Ramon Hernandez	.15
35	Geoff Jenkins	.15
36	Bobby Kielty	.15
37	Luis A. Gonzalez	.15
38	Benito Santiago	.15
39	Brandon Inge	.15
40	Mark Prior	.50
41	Mike Lieberthal	.15
42	Toby Hall	.15
43	Brad Ausmus	.15
44	Damian Miller	.15
45	Mark Kotsay	.15
46	John Buck	.15
47	Oliver Perez	.25
48	Matt Morris	.15
49	Raul Chavez	.15
50	Randy Johnson	.50
51	David Bush	.15
52	Jose Macias	.15
53	Paul Wilson	.15
54	Wilfredo Ledezma	.15
55	J.D. Drew	.25
56	Pedro Martinez	.50
57	Josh Towers	.15
58	Jamie Moyer	.15
59	Scott Elarton	.15
60	Ken Griffey Jr.	1.00
61	Steve Trachsel	.15
62	Bubba Crosby	.15
63	Michael Barrett	.15
64	Odalis Perez	.15
65	B.J. Upton	.25
66	Eric Bruntlett	.15
67	Carlos Zambrano	.15
68	Brandon League	.15
69	Carlos Silva	.15
70	Lyle Overbay	.25
71	Runelvys Hernandez	.15
72	Brad Penny	.15
73	Ty Wigginton	.15
74	Orlando Hudson	.15
75	Roy Oswalt	.15
76	Jason LaRue	.15
77	Ismael Valdez	.15
78	Calvin Pickering	.15
79	Bill Hall	.15
80	Carl Crawford	.25
81	Tomas Perez	.15
82	Joe Kennedy	.15
83	Chris Woodward	.15
84	Jason Lane	.15
85	Steve Finley	.15
86	Jeff Francis	.15
87	Felipe Lopez	.15
88	Chan Ho Park	.15
89	Joe Crede	.15
90	Jose Vidro	.15
91	Casey Kotchman	.25
92	Brandon Backe	.15
93	Mike Hampton	.15
94	Ryan Dempster	.15
95	Wily Mo Pena	.25
96	Matt Holliday	.25
97	A.J. Pierzynski	.15
98	Jason Jennings	.15
99	Eli Marrero	.15
100	Carlos Beltran	.40
101	Scott Kazmir	.25
102	Kenny Rogers	.15
103	Roy Halladay	.15
104	Alex Cora	.15
105	Richie Sexson	.15
106	Ben Sheets	.25
107	Bartolo Colon	.15
108	Eddie Perez	.15
109	Vicente Padilla	.15
110	Sammy Sosa	1.00
111	Mark Ellis	.15
112	Woody Williams	.15
113	Todd Greene	.15
114	Nook Logan	.15
115	Francisco Rodriguez	.15
116	Miguel Batista	.15
117	Livan Hernandez	.15
118	Chris Aguila	.15
119	Coco Crisp	.15
120	Jose Reyes	.25
121	Ricky Ledee	.15
122	Brad Radke	.15
123	Carlos Guillen	.15
124	Paul Bako	.15
125	Tom Glavine	.25
126	Chad Moeller	.15
127	Mark Buehrle	.15
128	Casey Blake	.15
129	Juan Rivera	.15
130	Preston Wilson	.15
131	Nate Robertson	.15
132	Julio Franco	.15
133	Derek Lowe	.15
134	Rob Bell	.15
135	Javy Lopez	.25
136	Javier Vazquez	.15
137	Desi Relaford	.15
138	Danny Graves	.15
139	Josh Fogg	.15
140	Bobby Crosby	.15
141	Ramon Castro	.15
142	Jerry Hairston Jr.	.15
143	Morgan Ensberg	.15
144	Brandon Webb	.25
145	Jack Wilson	.15
146	Bill Mueller	.15
147	Troy Glaus	.15
148	Armando Benitez	.15
149	Adam LaRoche	.15
150	Hank Blalock	.40
151	Ryan Franklin	.15
152	Kevin Millwood	.15
153	Jason Marquis	.15
154	Dewon Brazelton	.15
155	Al Leiter	.15
156	Garrett Atkins	.15
157	Todd Walker	.15
158	Kris Benson	.15
159	Eric Milton	.15
160	Bret Boone	.15
161	Matthew LeCroy	.15
162	Chris Widger	.15
163	Ruben Gotay	.15
164	Craig Monroe	.15
165	Travis Hafner	.25
166	Vance Wilson	.15
167	Jason Grabowski	.15
168	Tim Salmon	.25
169	Henry Blanco	.15
170	Josh Beckett	.25
171	Jake Westbrook	.15
172	Paul LoDuca	.15
173	Julio Lugo	.15
174	Juan Cruz	.15
175	Mark Mulder	.15
176	Juan Castro	.15
177	Damion Easley	.15
178	LaTroy Hawkins	.15
179	Jon Lieber	.15
180	Vernon Wells	.25
181	Jeff DaVanon	.15
182	Dustan Mohr	.15
183	Ryan Freel	.15
184	Doug Davis	.15
185	Sean Casey	.25
186	Robb Quinlan	.15
187	J.D. Closser	.15
188	Tim Wakefield	.15
189	Brian Jordan	.15
190	Adam Dunn	.40
191	Antonio Perez	.15
192	Brett Tomko	.15
193	John Flaherty	.15
194	Michael Cuddyer	.15
195	Ronnie Belliard	.15
196	Tony Womack	.15
197	Jason Johnson	.15
198	Victor Santos	.15
199	Dan Haren	.15
200	Derek Jeter	1.50
201	Brian Anderson	.15
202	Carlos Pena	.15
203	Jaret Wright	.15
204	Paul Byrd	.15
205	Shannon Stewart	.15
206	Chris Carpenter	.15
207	Matt Stairs	.15
208	Brad Hawpe	.15
209	Bobby Higginson	.15
210	Torii Hunter	.25
211	Shawn Green	.25
212	Todd Hollandsworth	.15
213	Scott Erickson	.15
214	C.C. Sabathia	.15
215	Mike Mussina	.40
216	Jason Kendall	.15
217	Todd Pratt	.15
218	Danny Kolb	.15
219	Tony Armas	.15
220	Edgar Renteria	.25
221	Dave Roberts	.15
222	Luis Rivas	.15
223	Adam Everett	.15
224	Jeff Cirillo	.15
225	Orlando Hernandez	.15
226	Ken Harvey	.15
227	Corey Patterson	.25
228	Humberto Cota	.15
229	A.J. Burnett	.25
230	Roger Clemens	1.50
231	Joe Randa	.15
232	David Dellucci	.15
233	Troy Percival	.15
234	Dustin Hermanson	.15
235	Eric Gagne	.15
236	Terry Tiffee	.15
237	Tony Graffanino	.15
238	Jayson Werth	.15
239	Michael Sweeney	.15
240	Chipper Jones	.75
241	Aramis Ramirez	.40
242	Frank Catalanotto	.15
243	Mike Maroth	.15
244	Kelvim Escobar	.15
245	Bobby Abreu	.25
246	Kyle Lohse	.15
247	Jason Isringhausen	.15
248	Jose Lima	.15
249	Adrian Gonzalez	.15

#	Player	Price
250	Alex Rodriguez	1.50
251	Ramon Ortiz	.15
252	Frank Menechino	.15
253	Keith Ginter	.15
254	Kip Wells	.15
255	Dmitri Young	.15
256	Craig Biggio	.25
257	Ramon E. Martinez	.15
258	Jason Bartlett	.15
259	Brad Lidge	.15
260	Brian Giles	.25
261	Luis Terrero	.15
262	Miguel Ojeda	.15
263	Rich Harden	.25
264	Jacque Jones	.15
265	Marcus Giles	.25
266	Carlos Zambrano	.25
267	Michael Tucker	.15
268	Wes Obermueller	.15
269	Peter Orr	.15
270	Jim Thome	.50
271	Omar Vizquel	.25
272	Jose Valentin	.15
273	Juan Uribe	.15
274	Doug Mirabelli	.15
275	Jeff Kent	.25
276	Brad Wilkerson	.15
277	Chris Burke	.25
278	Endy Chavez	.15
279	Richard Hidalgo	.15
280	John Smoltz	.25
281	Jarrod Washburn	.15
282	Larry Bigbie	.15
283	Edgardo Alfonzo	.15
284	Cliff Lee	.15
285	Carlos Lee	.25
286	Olmedo Saenz	.15
287	Tomokazu Ohka	.15
288	Ruben Sierra	.25
289	Nick Swisher	.15
290	Frank Thomas	.40
291	Aaron Cook	.15
292	Cody McKay	.15
293	Hee Seop Choi	.15
294	Carl Pavano	.25
295	Scott Rolen	.50
296	Matt Kata	.15
297	Terrence Long	.15
298	Jimmy Gobble	.15
299	Jason Repko	.15
300	Manny Ramirez	.50
301	Dan Wilson	.15
302	Jhonny Peralta	.15
303	John Mabry	.15
304	Adam Melhuse	.15
305	Kerry Wood	.25
306	Ryan Langerhans	.15
307	Antonio Alfonseca	.15
308	Marco Scutaro	.15
309	Jamey Carroll	.15
310	Lance Berkman	.25
311	Willie Harris	.15
312	Phil Nevin	.15
313	Gregg Zaun	.15
314	Michael Ryan	.15
315	Zack Greinke	.25
316	Ted Lilly	.15
317	David Eckstein	.15
318	Tony Torcato	.15
319	Robert Mackowiak	.15
320	Mark Teixeira	.40
321	Jason Phillips	.15
322	Jeremy Reed	.15
323	Bengie Molina	.15
324	Termel Sledge	.15
325	Justin Morneau	.40
326	Sandy Alomar Jr.	.15
327	Jon Garland	.25
328	Jay Payton	.15
329	Tino Martinez	.25
330	Jason Bay	.25
331	Jeff Conine	.15
332	Shawn Chacon	.15
333	Angel Berroa	.15
334	Reggie Sanders	.15
335	Kevin Brown	.15
336	Brady Clark	.15
337	Casey Fossum	.15
338	Raul Ibanez	.15
339	Derrek Lee	.40
340	Victor Martinez	.25
341	Kazuhisa Ishii	.15
342	Royce Clayton	.15
343	Trot Nixon	.15
344	Eric Young	.15
345	Aubrey Huff	.25
346	Brett Myers	.25
347	Joey Gathright	.15
348	Mark Grudzielanek	.15
349	Scott Spiezio	.15
350	Eric Chavez	.25
351	Einar Diaz	.15
352	Dallas McPherson	.15
353	John Thomson	.15
354	Neifi Perez	.15
355	Larry Walker	.25
356	Billy Wagner	.25
357	Mike Cameron	.15
358	Jimmy Rollins	.25
359	Kevin Mench	.15
360	Joe Mauer	.25
361	Jose Molina	.15
362	Joe Borchard	.15
363	Kevin Cash	.15
364	Jay Gibbons	.15
365	Khalil Greene	.25
366	Justin Leone	.15
367	Eddie Guardado	.15
368	Mike Lamb	.15
369	Matt Riley	.15
370	Luis Gonzalez	.25
371	Alfredo Amezaga	.15
372	J.J. Hardy	.15
373	Hector Luna	.15
374	Greg Aquino	.15
375	Jim Edmonds	.25
376	Joe Blanton	.15
377	Russell Branyan	.15
378	J.T. Snow	.15
379	Magglio Ordonez	.25
380	Rafael Palmeiro	.40
381	Andruw Jones	.25
382	David DeJesus	.15
383	Marquis Grissom	.15
384	Bobby Hill	.15
385	Kazuo Matsui	.15
386	Mark Loretta	.15
387	Chris Shelton	.15
388	Johnny Estrada	.15
389	Adam Hyzdu	.15
390	Nomar Garciaparra	1.00
391	Mark Teahen	.15
392	Chris Capuano	.15
393	Ben Broussard	.15
394	Daniel Cabrera	.15
395	Jeremy Bonderman	.25
396	Darin Erstad	.25
397	Alex S. Gonzalez	.15
398	Kevin Millar	.15
399	Freddy Garcia	.15
400	Alfonso Soriano	.50
401	Koyie Hill	.15
402	Omar Infante	.15
403	Alex Gonzalez	.15
404	Pat Burrell	.25
405	Wes Helms	.15
406	Junior Spivey	.15
407	Joe Mays	.15
408	Jason Stanford	.15
409	Gil Meche	.15
410	Tim Hudson	.25
411	Chase Utley	.25
412	Matt Clement	.15
413	Nick Green	.15
414	Jose Vizcaino	.15
415	Ryan Klesko	.15
416	Vinny Castilla	.15
417	Brian Roberts	.40
418	Geronimo Gil	.15
419	Gary Matthews	.15
420	Jeff Weaver	.15
421	Jerome Williams	.15
422	Andy Pettitte	.40
423	Randy Wolf	.15
424	D'Angelo Jimenez	.15
425	Moises Alou	.25
426	Eric Byrnes	.15
427	Mark Redman	.15
428	Jermaine Dye	.15
429	Cory Lidle	.15
430	Jason Schmidt	.15
431	Jason W. Smith	.15
432	Jose Castillo	.15
433	Pokey Reese	.15
434	Matt Lawton	.15
435	Jose Guillen	.15
436	Craig Counsell	.15
437	Jose Hernandez	.15
438	Braden Looper	.15
439	Scott Hatteberg	.15
440	Gary Sheffield	.40
441	Gabe Gross	.15
442	Chris Gomez	.15
443	Dontrelle Willis	.40
444	Jamey Wright	.15
445	Rocco Baldelli	.15
446	Bernie Williams	.25
447	Sean Burroughs	.15
448	Willie Bloomquist	.15
449	Luis Castillo	.15
450	Mike Piazza	1.00
451	Ryan Drese	.15
452	Pedro Feliz	.15
453	Horacio Ramirez	.15
454	Luis Matos	.15
455	Craig Wilson	.15
456	Russ Ortiz	.15
457	Xavier Nady	.15
458	Hideo Nomo	.25
459	Miguel Cairo	.15
460	Mike Lowell	.25
461	Corky Miller	.15
462	Bobby Madritsch	.15
463	Jose Contreras	.15
464	Johnny Damon	.75
465	Miguel Cabrera	.50
466	Eric Hinske	.15
467	Marlon Byrd	.15
468	Aaron Miles	.15
469	Ramon Vazquez	.15
470	Michael Young	.15
471	Alex Sanchez	.15
472	Shea Hillenbrand	.15
473	Jeff Bagwell	.40
474	Erik Bedard	.15
475	Jake Peavy	.40
476	Jody Gerut	.15
477	Randy Winn	.15
478	Kevin Youkilis	.15
479	Eric Dubose	.15
480	David Wright	.75
481	Wilson Valdez	.15
482	Cliff Floyd	.15
483	Jose Mesa	.15
484	Doug Mientkiewicz	.15
485	Jorge Posada	.40
486	Sidney Ponson	.15
487	David Krynzel	.15
488	Octavio Dotel	.15
489	Matt Treanor	.15
490	Johan Santana	.40
491	John Patterson	.15
492	So Taguchi	.15
493	Carl Everett	.15
494	Jason Dubois	.15
495	Albert Pujols	1.50
496	Kirk Rueter	.15
497	Geoff Blum	.15
498	Juan Encarnacion	.15
499	Mark Hendrickson	.15
500	Barry Bonds	2.00
501	Cesar Izturis	.15
502	David Wells	.15
503	Jorge Julio	.15
504	Cristian Guzman	.15
505	Juan Pierre	.15
506	Adam Eaton	.15
507	Nick Johnson	.25
508	Mike Redmond	.15
509	Daryle Ward	.15
510	Adrian Beltre	.25
511	Laynce Nix	.15
512	Reed Johnson	.15
513	Jeremy Affeldt	.15
514	R.A. Dickey	.15
515	Alex Rios	.15
516	Orlando Palmeiro	.15
517	Mark Belhorn	.15
518	Adam Kennedy	.15
519	Curtis Granderson	.15
520	Todd Helton	.40
521	Aaron Boone	.15
522	Milton Bradley	.25
523	Timoniel Perez	.15
524	Jeff Suppan	.15
525	Austin Kearns	.15
526	Charles Thomas	.15
527	Bronson Arroyo	.15
528	Roger Cedeno	.15
529	Russ Adams	.15
530	Barry Zito	.25
531	Bob Wickman	.15
532	Deivi Cruz	.15
533	Mariano Rivera	.40
534	J.J. Davis	.15
535	Greg Maddux	1.00
536	Ryan Vogelsong	.15
537	Josh Phelps	.15
538	Scott Hairston	.15
539	Vladimir Guerrero	.75
540	Ivan Rodriguez	.50
541	David Newhan	.15
542	David Bell	.15
543	Lew Ford	.15
544	Grady Sizemore	.25
545	David Ortiz	.75
546	Jose Cruz Jr.	.15
547	Aaron Rowand	.15
548	Marcus Thames	.15
549	Scott Podsednik	.25
550	Ichiro Suzuki	1.25
551	Eduardo Perez	.15
552	Chris Snyder	.15
553	Corey Koskie	.15
554	Miguel Tejada	.50
555	Orlando Cabrera	.15
556	Rondell White	.15
557	Wade Miller	.15
558	Rodrigo Lopez	.15
559	Chad Tracy	.15
560	Paul Konerko	.25
561	Wil Cordero	.15
562	John McDonald	.15
563	Jason Ellison	.15
564	Jason Michaels	.15
565	Melvin Mora	.25
566	Ryan Church	.15
567	Ryan Ludwick	.15
568	Erubiel Durazo	.15
569	Noah Lowry	.15
570	Curt Schilling	.50
571	Esteban Loaiza	.15
572	Freddy Sanchez	.15
573	Rich Aurilia	.15
574	Travis Lee	.15

#	Player	Price
575	Dennis Tankersley, Chris George	.15
576	Jason Christiansen, Kevin Correia	.15
577	Ryan Bukvich, Randy Williams	.15
578	Terry Agams, Gavin Floyd	.15
579	Seth Etherton, Dan Meyer	.15
580	Justin Lehr, Derrick Turnbow	.15
581	Mike Gosling, Brad Halsey	.15
582	Jim Mecir, Logan Kensing	.15
583	Brad Hennessey, Jeff Fassero	.15
584	Jason Grilli, John Adkins	.15
585	Jesse Crain, Juan Rincon	.15
586	Jaime Cerda, Nate Field	.15
587	Bartolome Fortunato, Jae Weong Seo	.15
588	Frank Brooks, Yhency Brazoban	.15
589	Jamie Walker, Ugueth Urbina	.15
590	Bret Prinz, Scott Proctor	.15
591	Bob Howry, Jason Davis	.15
592	Amaury Telemaco, Tim Worrell	.15
593	Jose Acevedo, Kent Mercker	.15
594	Chris Hammond, Scott Linebrink	.15
595	Fernando Nieve, John Franco	.15
596	Mike Lincoln, Randy Flores	.15
597	Joe Borowski, Kyle Farnsworth	.15
598	Jesus Colome, Lance Carter	.15
599	Abe Alvarez, Lenny DiNardo	.15
600	Chad Bradford, Kiko Calero	.15
601	David Aardsma, Jim Brower	.15
602	Geoff Geary, Ryan Madson	.15
603	Ben Howard, Nate Bump	.15
604	Chin-Hui Tsao, Jason Young	.15
605	Aaron Harang, Ryan Wagner	.15
606	Rick Bauer, Steve Kline	.15
607	Lance Cormier, Randy Choate	.15
608	Jon Leicester, Todd Wellemeyer	.15
609	Jason Frasor, Vinnie Chulk	.15
610	Brian Fuentes, Scott Dohmann	.15
611	Matt Ginter, Tyler Yates	.15
612	Cory Stewart, Salomon Torres	.15
613	Cal Eldred, Mike Myers	.15
614	Carlos Almanzar, Doug Brocail	.15
615	George Sherrill, J.J. Putz	.15
616	Bruce Chen, Matt Riley	.15
617	Ben Weber, David Weathers	.15
618	Dennys Reyes, Rudy Seanez	.15
619	Ricardo Rincon, Tim Harikkala	.15
620	D.J. Carrasco, Shawn Camp	.15
621	Allan Simpson, Javier Lopez	.15
622	Glendon Rusch, Mike Remlinger	.15
623	Kevin Gryboski, Roman Colon	.15
624	Chris Reitsma, Tom Martin	.15
625	Chad Qualls, Dan Wheeler	.15
626	Brooks Kieschnick, Matt Wise	.15
627	Justin Speier, Kerry Ligtenberg	.15
628	Francisco Cordero, Frank Francisco	.15
629	Matt Thornton, Rafael Soriano	.15
630	Mike Stanton, Steve Karsay	.15
631	Mike MacDougal, Scott Sullivan	.15
632	Brian Bruney, Oscar Villarreal	.15
633	Jeff Bennett, Mike Adams	.15
634	Dave Borkowski, Eddy Rodriguez	.15
635	David Riske, Rafael Betancourt	.15
636	Gary Glover, Jorge De La Rosa	.15
637	Justin Wayne, Matt Perisho	.15
638	Jeff Bajenaru, Luis Vizcaino	.15
639	Erasmo Ramirez, Ron Mahay	.15
640	John Grabow, Mike Gonzalez	.15
641	J.C. Romero, Matt Guerrier	.15
642	Brandon Duckworth, Tim Redding	.15
643	Franklin Nunez, Travis Harper	.15
644	Matt Herges, Tyler Walker	.15
645	Elmer Dessens, Wilson Alvarez	.15
646	Anastacio Martinez, Mark Malaska	.15
647	Gary Knotts, Roberto Novoa	.15
648	Jairo Garcia, Justin Duchscherer	.15
649	Aaron Rakers, Todd Williams	.15
650	Paul Quantrill, Tom Gordon	.15
651	Brandon Lyon, Shawn Estes	.15
652	Gustavo Chacin, Justin Miller	.15
653	John Lackey, Scot Shields	.15
654	Bobby Seay, Jorge Sosa	.15
655	Chad Cordero, Luis Ayala	.15
656	Julio Mateo, Ron Villone	.15
657	Byung-Hyun Kim, Matt Mantei	.15
658	Cliff Politte, Damaso Marte	.15
659	Joe Valentine, Luke Hudson	.15
660	John Riedling, Todd Jones	.15
661	Aaron Heilman, Heath Bell	.15

#	Player	Price
662	Akinori Otsuka, Blaine Neal	.15
663	Joe Horgan, Joey Eischen	.15
664	Grant Balfour, J.D. Durbin	.15
665	Alan Embree, Mike Timlin	.15
666	Keith Foulke	.15
667	Aaron Fultz, Rheal Cormier	.15
668	Kevin Gregg, Scott Dunn	.15
669	Franklyn German, Steve Coyler	
670	Scott Eyre, Wayne Franklin	.15
671	Brian Meadows, Mike Johnston	
672	Guillermo Mota, Tim Spooneybarger	.15
673	B.J. Ryan, Jason Grimsley	.15
674	Neal Cotts, Shingo Takatsu	.15
675	Felix Heredia, Mike DeJean	.15
676	Brian Shackelford, Josh Hancock	.15
677	Jon Rauch, T.J. Tucker	.15
678	Brian Shouse, Nick Regilio	.15
679	Julian Tavarez, Ray King	.15
680	Mike Wuertz, Stephen Randolph	.15
681	Gabe White, Jorge Vasquez	
682	Jose Valverde, Mike Koplove	
683	Arthur Rhodes, Scott Sauerbeck	.15
684	Felix Rodriguez, Tanyon Sturtze	.15
685	Duaner Sanchez, Giovanni Carrara	
686	Chad Harville, Mike Gallo	.15
687	Dave Williams, Sean Burnett	
688	Scott Atchison, Shigetoshi Hasegawa	
689	Claudio Vargas, Francis Beltran	.15
690	Brendan Donnelly, Esteban Yan	.15
691	Erwin Santana, Jeff Mathis	.15
692	Bill Bray, Clint Everts	.15
693	Jason Kubel, Trevor Plouffe	.15
694	Andy Marte, Jake Stevens	.15
695	Aaron Hill, Chad Gaudin	.15
696	Carlos Quentin, Jesus Cota	
697	Chris Young, Thomas Diamond	.15
698	Dan Johnson, Omar Quintanilla	.15
699	John Maine, Val Majewski	.15
700	James Houser, Jonny Gomes	
701	David Murphy, Hanley Ramirez	.25
702	Chris Lambert, Rick Ankiel	.25
703	Angel Guzman, Felix Pie	.15
704	Merkin Valdez, Nate Schierholtz	
705	Arnie Munoz, Gio Gonzalez	.15
706	Felix Hernandez, Travis Blackley	
707	Edwin Encarnacion, Tony Blanco	
708	Justin Germano, Tim Stauffer	
709	Jeremy Guthrie, Jeremy Sowers	
710	Jorge Cortes, Tom Gorzelanny	
711	Logan Kensing, Taylor Tankersley	.15
712	Neil Walker, Paul Maholm	.15
713	Carlos Hernandez, Willy Taveras	.50
714	Greg Golson, Ryan Howard	1.00
715	Blake DeWitt, Edwin Jackson	
716	Dan Putnam, Huston Street	
717	Mark Rogers, Rickie Weeks	.25
718	Phillip Hughes, Robinson Cano	.40
719	Jay Rainville, Kyle Waldrop	.15
720	Craig Brazell, Yusmeiro Petit	.15
721	Baltazar Lopez RC, Matt Brown RC	.25
722	Brett Price RC, Jerry Owens RC	.50
723	Dan Uggla RC, Kyle Nichols RC	5.00
724	Francisco Rosario RC, Jayce Tingler RC	
725	Eulogio de la Cruz RC, Tony Giarratano RC	.25
726	Matt Campbell RC, Shane Costa RC	.25
727	Bill McCarthy RC, Martin Prado RC	.25
728	Edinson Volquez RC, Ian Kinsler RC	5.00
729	Lorenzo Scott RC, Luis Ramirez RC	
730	Chris Seddon RC, Elliot Johnson RC	.75
731	Chris Dickerson RC, Thomas Pauly RC	.15

#	Player	Price
732	Jason Motte RC, Stuart Pomeranz RC	.25
733	Jose Vaquedano RC, Stefan Bailie RC	.25
734	D.J. Houlton RC, Wade Robinson RC	
735	Matt DeSalvo RC, Melky Cabrera RC	1.00
736	Brian Stavisky RC, Landon Powell RC	.25
737	Scott Mathieson RC, Scott Mitchinson RC	.50
738	Bear Bay RC, Sean Marshall RC	.50
739	Brandon McCarthy RC, Pedro Lopez RC	1.50
740	Alexander Smit RC, Jair Jurrjens RC	1.00
741	Matt Rogelstad RC, Ryan Feierabend RC	
742	Adam Boeve RC, Nate McLouth RC	.50
743	Kevin Melillo RC, Michael Rogers RC	.25
744	Heath Totten RC, Matthew Kemp RC	2.00
745	Trevor Hutchinson RC, Yorman Bazardo RC	.15
746	Jesse Gutierrez RC, Tyler Pelland RC	
747	Jeremy West RC, Willy Mota RC	
748	Ryan Garko RC, Ryan Goleski RC	
749	Bryan Triplett RC, Jared Gothreaux RC	.25
750	Glen Perkins RC, Kevin West RC	
751	Michael Esposito RC, Zachary Parker RC	.25
752	Brian Miller RC, Ryan Sweeney RC	
753	Buck Coats RC, Casey McGehee RC	1.00
754	Nate Cabrera RC, Zachary Cline RC	.15
755	Bobby Livingston RC, Mike Morse RC	
756	Brendan Ryan RC, Wes Swackhamer RC	
757	John Hudgins RC, Nick Masset RC	.25
758	George Kottaras RC, Peeter Ramos RC	
759	Elvys Quezada RC, T.J. Beam RC	.25
760	Dana Eveland RC, Travis Hinton RC	
761	Chris Vines RC, James Jurries RC	
762	Humberto Sanchez RC, Justin Verlander RC	2.00
763	Ian Bladergroen RC, Shawn Bowman RC	.50
764	J.B. Thurmond RC, Pat Misch RC	.25
765	Christian Colonel RC, Neil Wilson RC	.25
766	Checklist 1	.15
767	Checklist 2	.15
768	Checklist 3	.15
769	Checklist 4	.15
770	Checklist 5	.15

Silver

Stars:	1-30X
Inserted 1:1	

Press Plates

	NM/M
Common Card Front P. Plate:	25.00
Common Card Back P. Plate:	15.00
Stars not priced.	
Production one set per color (4):	

Award Winners

	NM/M
Complete Set (30):	15.00
Common Player:	.25
Inserted 1:10	
AW1 Barry Bonds	2.00
AW2 Vladimir Guerrero	.75
AW3 Roger Clemens	2.00
AW4 Johan Santana	.75
AW5 Jason Bay	.25
AW6 Bobby Crosby	.25
AW7 Eric Gagne	.40
AW8 Mariano Rivera	.50

AW9	Albert Pujols	2.00
AW10	Mark Teixeira	.50
AW11	Mark Loretta	.25
AW12	Alfonso Soriano	.75
AW13	Jack Wilson	.25
AW14	Miguel Tejada	.50
AW15	Adrian Beltre	.40
AW16	Melvin Mora	.25
AW17	Manny Ramirez	2.00
AW18	Jim Edmonds	.50
AW19	Bobby Abreu	.40
AW20	Manny Ramirez	.75
AW21	Gary Sheffield	.50
AW22	Vladimir Guerrero	.75
AW23	Johnny Estrada	.25
AW24	Victor Martinez	.25
AW25	Ivan Rodriguez	.50
AW26	Livan Hernandez	.25
AW27	David Ortiz	.75
AW28	Bobby Cox	.25
AW29	Buck Showalter	.25
AW30	Barry Bonds	2.00

Domination

NM/M

Complete Set (30): 15.00
Common Player: .25
Inserted 1:10

40	Mark Prior	.75
50	Randy Johnson	.75
56	Pedro Martinez	.75
60	Ken Griffey Jr.	1.00
100	Carlos Beltran	.50
110	Sammy Sosa	1.50
147	Troy Glaus	.50
150	Hank Blalock	.25
180	Vernon Wells	.25
190	Adam Dunn	.25
200	Derek Jeter	2.00
230	Roger Clemens	2.00
250	Alex Rodriguez	1.50
260	Brian Giles	.25
270	Jim Thome	.75
290	Frank Thomas	.50
300	Manny Ramirez	.75
345	Aubrey Huff	.25
350	Eric Chavez	.25
400	Alfonso Soriano	.75
465	Miguel Cabrera	.75
490	Johan Santana	.50
495	Albert Pujols	2.00
500	Barry Bonds	2.00
510	Adrian Beltre	.40
520	Todd Helton	.50
575	Vladimir Guerrero	.75
540	Ivan Rodriguez	.50
545	David Ortiz	.75
554	Miguel Tejada	.50

Domination Autograph

Production 10

Production

NM/M

Complete Set (10): 8.00
Common Player: .40
Inserted 1:15

AB	Adrian Beltre	.40
BB	Barry Bonds	2.00
VG	Vladimir Guerrero	.75
TH	Todd Helton	.50
AP	Albert Pujols	2.00
MR	Manny Ramirez	.75
AR	Alex Rodriguez	1.50
AS	Alfonso Soriano	.75
MT	Miguel Tejada	.50
JT	Jim Thome	.75

Signatures

NM/M

Common Autograph: 8.00

BB	Brian Bruney	8.00
RC	Robinson Cano	35.00
JG	Joey Gathright	10.00
ZG	Zack Greinke	20.00
BM	Brett Myers	12.00
TT	Terry Tiffee	15.00
DW	David Wright	50.00

Team Checklists

NM/M

Complete Set (30): 8.00
Common Player: .15

2	Miguel Tejada	.50
6	Frank Thomas	.50
8	Victor Martinez	.25
9	Todd Helton	.50
10	Ivan Rodriguez	.50

11	Miguel Cabrera	.50
12	Roger Clemens	1.00
13	Zack Greinke	.15
14	Vladimir Guerrero	.50
16	Ben Sheets	.25
17	Johan Santana	.25
18	Carlos Beltran	.50
19	Alex Rodriguez	1.00
20	Eric Chavez	.25
21	Jim Thome	.50
22	Jason Bay	.25
23	Brian Giles	.25
24	Barry Bonds	1.50
25	Ichiro Suzuki	1.00
26	Albert Pujols	1.00
27	Carl Crawford	.25
28	Alfonso Soriano	.50
29	Roy Halladay	.25
30	Jose Vidro	.15
7	Adam Dunn	.50
5	Kerry Wood	.50
1	Luis Gonzalez	.25
2	John Smoltz	.25
4	David Ortiz	.50
15	Eric Gagne	.25

Total Topps

NM/M

Complete Set (20): 12.00
Common Player: .25
Inserted 1:15

CB	Carlos Beltran	.50
AB	Adrian Beltre	.40
BB	Barry Bonds	2.00
EC	Eric Chavez	.25
RC	Roger Clemens	2.00
VG	Vladimir Guerrero	.75
TH	Todd Helton	.50
DJ	Derek Jeter	2.00
RJ	Randy Johnson	.75
GM	Greg Maddux	1.00
MP	Mike Piazza	1.00
AP	Albert Pujols	2.00
MR	Manny Ramirez	.75
AR	Alex Rodriguez	1.50
IR	Ivan Rodriguez	.50
JS	Johan Santana	.50
AS	Alfonso Soriano	.50
SS	Sammy Sosa	1.50
MT	Miguel Tejada	.50
JT	Jim Thome	.50

2005 Topps Total/Pepcid Phillies

This special version of Topps Total cards was an August 6 stadium giveaway on Phillies Alumni Night. Except for the numbering on the backs, most cards are identical to the regular Topps Total versions. A sponsor's card was included in the cello wrapped pack.

NM/M

Complete Set (22): 10.00
Common Player: .50

1	Jason Michaels	.50
2	Ryan Howard, Greg Golson	1.00
3	Tim Worrell, Pedro Liriano	.50
4	Geoff Geary, Ryan Madson	.50
5	Rheal Cormier, Aaron Fultz	.50
6	Kenny Lofton	.50
7	Pat Burrell	1.00
8	Bobby Abreu	.75
9	Chase Utley	.75
10	Jim Thome	1.00
11	Jimmy Rollins	1.00
12	Tomas Perez	.50
13	David Bell	.50
14	Todd Pratt	.50
15	Mike Lieberthal	.50
16	Billy Wagner	.50
17	Cory Lidle	.50
18	Brett Myers	.50
19	Vicente Padilla	.50
20	Randy Wolf	.50
21	Jon Lieber	.50
---	Pepcid Sponsor's Card	.50

2005 Topps Turkey Red

NM/M

Complete Set (315):
Common Player: .25
Common SP: .25
Inserted 1:4
Pack (8): 5.00
Box (24): 100.00

1	Barry Bonds/Gray Uni./SP	15.00
1	Barry Bonds	4.00
2	Michael Young	.25
3	Jim Edmonds	.50
4	Cliff Floyd	.25
5	Roger Clemens/Blue Sky/SP	12.00
5	Roger Clemens/Yellow Sky/SP	12.00
6	Hal Chase	.25
7	Shannon Stewart	.25
8	Fred Clarke	.25
9	Travis Hafner	.50
10	Sammy Sosa w/Name/SP	6.00
10	Sammy Sosa w/o Name/SP	6.00
11	Jermaine Dye	.25
12	Lyle Overbay	.25
13	Oliver Perez	.25
14	Red Dooin	.25
15	Kid Elberfeld	.25
16	Mike Piazza/Blue Uni./SP	6.00
16	Mike Piazza/Pinstripe	1.50
17	Bret Boone	.25
18	Hughie Jennings	.25
19	Jeff Francis	.25
20	Manny Ramirez/SP	6.00
21	Russ Ortiz	.25
22	Carlos Zambrano	.50
23	Luis Castillo	.25
24	David DeJesus	.25
25	Carlos Beltran/SP	5.00
26	Doug Davis	.25
27	Bobby Abreu	.50
28	Rich Harden/SP	4.00
29	Brian Giles	.25
30	Richie Sexson/SP	4.00
31	Nick Johnson	.25
32	Roy Halladay	.50
33	Andy Pettitte	.50
34	Miguel Cabrera	1.00
35	Jeff Kent	.25
36	Chone Figgins	.25
37	Carlos Lee	.50
38	Greg Maddux	2.00
39	Preston Wilson	.25
40	Chipper Jones	1.00
41	Coco Crisp	.25
42	Adam Dunn	.75
43	Miguel Tejada CL	.50
44	Gary Sheffield CL	.50
45	Javy Lopez CL	.50
46	Scott Rolen CL	.50
47	Todd Helton CL	.50
48	Roger Clemens CL	1.00
49	Jimmy Rollins CL	.40
50	Ichiro Suzuki CL	1.00
51	Cliff Floyd CL	.25
52	Johan Santana CL	.50
53	Mark Teixeira CL	.75
54	Chris Carpenter	.25
55	Roy Oswalt/SP	4.00
56	Casey Kotchman	.25
57	Torii Hunter	.25
58	Jose Reyes	.50
59	Wily Mo Pena/SP	4.00
60	Magglio Ordonez/SP	4.00
61	Aaron Miles	.25
62	Dallas McPherson	.25
63	Javy Lopez	.25
64	Luis Gonzalez	.25
65	David Ortiz	1.00
66	Jorge Posada	.50
67	Xavier Nady	.25
68	Larry Walker	.50
69	Mark Loretta	.25
70	Jim Thome/SP	5.00
71	Livan Hernandez	.25
72	Garrett Atkins	.25
73	Milton Bradley	.25
74	B.J. Upton	.25
75	Ichiro Suzuki w/Name/SP	8.00
75	Ichiro Suzuki w/o Name/SP	8.00
76	Aramis Ramirez	.25
77	Eric Milton	.25
78	Troy Glaus/SP	4.00
79	David Newhan	.25
80	Delmon Young	.25
81	Justin Morneau	.40
82	Ramon Ortiz	.25
83	Eric Chavez/Blue Sky	.25
83	Eric Chavez/Purple Sky/SP	4.00
84	Sean Burroughs	.25
85	Scott Rolen/SP	6.00
86	Rocco Baldelli	.25
87	Joe Mauer/SP	5.00
88	Tony Womack	.25
89	Ken Griffey Jr.	2.00
90	Alfonso Soriano/SP	6.00
91	Paul Konerko	.25
92	Guillermo Mota	.25
93	Lance Berkman	.50
94	Mark Buehrle	.25
95	Matt Clement	.25
96	Melvin Mora	.25
97	Khalil Greene	.25
98	David Wright	1.50
99	Jack Wilson	.25
100	Alex Rodriguez w/Bat/SP	10.00
100	Alex Rodriguez w/Glove/SP	10.00
101	Joe Nathan	.25
102	Adrian Beltre/Gray Uni./SP	4.00
102	Adrian Beltre/White Uni.	.25
103	Mike Sweeney	.25
104	Brad Lidge	.25
105	Shawn Green	.25
106	Miguel Tejada/SP	5.00
107	Derrek Lee	.75
108	Eric Hinske	.25
109	Eric Byrnes	.25
110	Hideki Matsui/SP	8.00
111	Tom Glavine	.50
112	Jimmy Rollins	.40
113	Ryan Drese	.25
114	Josh Beckett	.25
115	Curt Schilling/SP	6.00
116	Jeremy Bonderman	.25
117	Hideki Matsui	.25
118	Chase Utley	.50
119	Troy Percival	.25
120	Vladimir Guerrero w/Bat/SP	6.00
120	Vladimir Guerrero w/Glove/SP	6.00
121	Gary Sheffield	.50
122	Jeromy Burnitz	.25
123	Javier Vazquez	.25
124	Kevin Millar	.25
125	Randy Johnson/Blue Sky	1.00
125	Randy Johnson/Purple Sky/SP	5.00
126	Pat Burrell	.25
127	Jason Schmidt	.25
128	Jose Vidro	.25
129	Kip Wells	.25
130	Ivan Rodriguez w/Cap	.75
130	Ivan Rodriguez w/Helmet/SP	6.00
131	C.C. Sabathia	.25
132	Carlos Delgado/SP	4.00
133	Bartolo Colon	.25
134	Andruw Jones	.50
135	Kerry Wood	.50
136	Sidney Ponson	.25
137	Eric Gagne	.25
138	Rickie Weeks	.50
139	Mariano Rivera	.50
140	Bobby Crosby	.25
141	Jamie Moyer	.25
142	Corey Koskie	.25
143	John Smoltz	.50
144	Frank Thomas	.75
145	Cristian Guzman	.25
146	Paul LoDuca	.25
147	Geoff Jenkins	.25
148	Nick Swisher	.25
149	Jason Bay/SP	4.00
150	Albert Pujols/SP	10.00
151	Edwin Jackson	.25
152	Carl Crawford	.25
153	Mark Mulder	.50
154	Rafael Palmeiro	.75
155	Pedro Martinez/SP	6.00
156	Jake Westbrook	.25
157	Sean Casey	.25
158	Aaron Rowand	.25
159	J.D. Drew	.25
160	Johan Santana/Glove on Knee/SP	5.00
160	Johan Santana/Throwing/SP	5.00
161	Gavin Floyd	.25
162	Vernon Wells	.25
163	Aubrey Huff	.25
164	Jeff Bagwell	.50
165	David Wells	.25
166	Brad Penny	.25
167	Austin Kearns	.25
168	Mike Mussina	.50
169	Randy Wolf	.25
170	Tim Hudson/SP	4.00
171	Casey Blake	.25
172	Edgar Renteria	.50
173	Ben Sheets	.50
174	Kevin Brown	.25
175	Nomar Garciaparra/SP	8.00
176	Armando Benitez	.25
177	Jody Gerut	.25
178	Craig Biggio	.50
179	Omar Vizquel	.25
180	Jake Peavy	.50
181	Gustavo Chacin/SP	4.00
182	Johnny Damon	.75
183	Mike Lieberthal	.25
184	Felix Hernandez/SP	10.00
185	Zach Day/SP	4.00
186	Matt Cain	.25
187	Erubiel Durazo	.25
188	Zack Greinke	.25
189	Matt Morris	.25
190	Al Leiter	.25
191	Miguel Olivo	.25
192	Jose Capellan/SP	4.00
193	Adam Eaton	.25
194	Steven White/SP	4.00
195	Joe Randa	.25
196	Richard Hidalgo	.25
197	Orlando Cabrera	.25
198	Joel Guzman/SP	6.00
199	Garret Anderson	.50
200	Endy Chavez	.25
201	Andy Marte	.25
202	Jose Guillen	.25
203	Victor Martinez	.25
204	Johnny Estrada	.25
205	Damian Miller	.25
206	Ken Harvey	.25
207	Ronnie Belliard	.25
208	Chan Ho Park	.25
209	Laynce Nix	.25
210	Lew Ford	.25
211	Moises Alou	.50
212	Kris Benson	.25
213	Mike Gonzalez/SP	4.00
214	Chris Burke	.25
215	Juan Pierre	.25
216	Phil Nevin	.25
217	Jerry Hairston Jr.	.25
218	Jeremy Reed	.25
219	Scott Kazmir/SP	4.00
220	Mike Maroth	.25
221	Alex Rios	.25
222	Esteban Loaiza	.25
223	Terrmel Sledge	.25
224	Mark Prior/Blue Sky/SP	5.00
225	Mark Prior/Yellow Sky/SP	5.00
226	Hank Blalock	.50
227	Craig Wilson	.25
228	Cesar Izturis	.25
229	Dmitri Young	.25
230	Derek Jeter/Blue Sky/SP	15.00
230	Derek Jeter/Purple Sky/SP	15.00
231	Mark Kotsay	.25
232	Darin Erstad	.25
233	Brandon Backe/SP	4.00
234	Mike Lowell	.25
235	Scott Podsednik	.25
236	Michael Barrett	.25
237	Chad Tracy	.25
238	David Dellucci	.25
239	Brady Clark	.25
240	Jorge Cantu	.25
241	Wilfredo Ledezma	.25
242	Morgan Ensberg	.25
243	Omar Infante	.25
244	Corey Patterson	.25
245	Matt Holliday	.50
246	Vinny Castilla	.25
247	Jason Bartlett	.25
248	Noah Lowry	.25
249	Huston Street	.50
250	Russell Branyan	.25
251	Juan Uribe	.25
252	Larry Bigbie	.25
253	Grady Sizemore	.50
254	Pedro Feliz	.25
255	Brad Wilkerson	.25
256	Brandon Inge	.25
257	Dewon Brazelton	.25
258	Rodrigo Lopez	.25
259	Jacque Jones	.25
260	Jason Giambi	.50
261	Clint Barmes	.25
262	Willy Taveras	.25
263	Marcus Giles	.25
264	Joe Blanton	.25
265	John Thomson	.25
266	Steve Finley/SP	4.00
267	Kevin Millwood	.25
268	David Eckstein	.25
269	Barry Zito	.50
270	Todd Helton/Purple Sky/SP	5.00
270	Todd Helton/Yellow Sky/SP	5.00
271	Landon Powell RC	1.00
272	Justin Verlander RC	3.00
273	Wes Swackhamer RC	1.00
274	Wladimir Balentien RC	1.50
275	Philip Humber RC	1.00
276	Kevin Melillo RC	1.00
277	Billy Butler RC	5.00
278	Michael Rogers RC	1.00
279	Bobby Livingston RC	1.00
280	Glen Perkins RC	1.00
281	Michael Bourn RC	1.00
282	Tyler Pelland RC	1.00
283	Jeremy West RC	.25
284	Brandon McCarthy RC	2.00
285	Ian Kinsler RC	4.00
286	Chris Roberson RC	1.00
287	Melky Cabrera RC	1.00
288	Ryan Sweeney RC	1.00
289	Chip Cannon RC	1.50
290	Andy LaRoche RC	5.00
291	Chuck Tiffany RC	1.00
292	Ian Bladergroen RC	1.00
293	Bear Bay RC	1.00
294	Hernan Iribarren RC	1.00
295	Stuart Pomeranz RC	1.00
296	Luke Scott RC	1.00
297	Chuck James RC	2.00
298	Kennard Bibbs RC	1.00
299	Steve Bondurant RC	1.50
300	Tom Oldham RC	1.00
301	Nolan Ryan	3.00
302	Reggie Jackson	1.00
303	Tom Seaver	1.00
304	Al Kaline	1.50
305	Cal Ripken Jr.	4.00
306	Josh Gibson	1.50
307	Frank Robinson	1.00
308	Duke Snider	1.00
309	Wade Boggs	1.50
310	Tony Gwynn	2.00
311	Carl Yastrzemski	2.00
312	Ryne Sandberg	2.00
313	Gary Carter	1.00
314	Brooks Robinson	1.50
315	Ernie Banks	1.50

Red

Stars (1-315): 1-2X
SP's: .5-1X

White

Stars (1-315): 2-3X
SP's: 1-1.5X
Inserted 1:4

Black

Stars (1-315): 3-5X
SP's: 1.5-2X
Inserted 1:20

Gold

Stars (1-315): 5-10X
SP's: 3-5X
Production 50 Sets

Suede

No Pricing
Production One Set

Autographs

		NM/M
	Common Auto.:	10.00
	Cards are not serial numbered.	
MB	Matt Bush/17	20.00
CC	Carl Crawford/17	30.00
SE	Scott Elbert	20.00
JF	Josh Fields	15.00
EG	Eric Gagne/142	20.00
JG	Jody Gerut	10.00
JPH	J.P. Howell	15.00
ZJ	Zach Jackson	12.00
JJ	Jason Jaramillo	12.00
BJ	Blake Johnson	15.00
BM	Brett Myers/67	20.00
CN	Chris Nelson	10.00
DO	David Ortiz	50.00
ZP	Zachary Parker	12.00
DP	Dustin Pedroia	40.00
MR	Mariano Rivera/192	90.00
MRO	Mike Rodriguez	10.00
GS	Gary Sheffield	40.00
AS	Alfonso Soriano/142	40.00
JS	Jeremy Sowers	20.00

B-18 Blanket Boxloaders

		NM/M
	Common Blanket	8.00
	Barry Bonds	20.00
	Roger Clemens	20.00
	Todd Helton	8.00
	Derek Jeter	20.00
	Alex Rodriguez	15.00
	Curt Schilling	12.00
	Alfonso Soriano	8.00
	Ichiro Suzuki	15.00

Cabinet Boxloaders

		NM/M
	Inserted 1:Box	
BB	Barry Bonds	25.00
GB	George W. Bush	10.00
RJ	Randy Johnson	12.00
MP	Mike Piazza	12.00
AP	Albert Pujols	20.00
MR	Manny Ramirez	12.00
AR	Alex Rodriguez	20.00
SR	Scott Rolen	10.00
JS	Johan Santana	12.00
SS	Sammy Sosa	15.00
WT	William H. Taft	10.00
MT	Miguel Tejada	10.00
JT	Jim Thome	10.00
GW	George Washington	25.00

Cabinet Auto. Relics

	Production 5-450	
MB	Matt Bush/450	25.00
CC	Carl Crawford/450	20.00
JG	Jody Gerut/450	20.00
MK	Mark Kotsay/450	30.00
BM	Brett Myers/150	25.00
DO	David Ortiz/75	100.00
MR	Mariano Rivera/25	90.00
AR	Alex Rodriguez/25	400.00
GS	Gary Sheffield/25	100.00
AS	Alfonso Soriano/25	75.00

Relics

		NM/M
	Common Player:	4.00
JB	Jeff Bagwell	6.00
CB	Carlos Beltran	6.00
AB	Adrian Beltre	4.00
HB	Hank Blalock	4.00
BB	Barry Bonds	20.00
MC	Miguel Cabrera	8.00
RC	Roger Clemens	15.00
RC2	Roger Clemens	15.00
JD	Johnny Damon	4.00
JD2	Johnny Damon	10.00
VG	Vladimir Guerrero	8.00
TH	Todd Helton	4.00
CJ	Chipper Jones	8.00
ML	Mike Lowell	4.00
MM	Mark Mulder	4.00
MO	Maggio Ordonez	4.00
DO	David Ortiz	8.00
RP	Rafael Palmeiro	6.00
MP	Mike Piazza	6.00
MPR	Mark Prior	6.00
AP	Albert Pujols	15.00
MR	Manny Ramirez	8.00
AR	Alex Rodriguez	12.00
AR2	Alex Rodriguez	12.00
CS	Curt Schilling	8.00
GS	Gary Sheffield	6.00
AS	Alfonso Soriano	8.00
SS	Sammy Sosa	6.00
MTE	Mark Teixeira	6.00
MT	Miguel Tejada	6.00
JT	Jim Thome	6.00
LW	Larry Walker	4.00

2005 Topps Update

		NM/M
	Complete Set (330):	35.00
	Complete Factory Set (330):	40.00
	Common Player:	.10
	Pack (10):	2.00
	Box (36):	60.00
1	Sammy Sosa	1.00
2	Jeff Francoeur	.25
3	Tony Clark	.10
4	Michael Tucker	.10
5	Mike Matheny	.10
6	Eric Young	.10
7	Jose Valentin	.10
8	Matt Lawton	.10
9	Juan Rivera	.10
10	Shawn Green	.25
11	Aaron Boone	.10
12	Woody Williams	.10
13	Brad Wilkerson	.10
14	Anthony Reyes RC	1.50
15	Russ Adams	.10
16	Gustavo Chacin	.10
17	Mike Restovich	.10
18	Humberto Quintero	.10
19	Matt Ginter	.10
20	Scott Podsednik	.25
21	Byung-Hyun Kim	.10
22	Orlando Hernandez	.10
23	Mark Grudzielanek	.10
24	Jody Gerut	.10
25	Adrian Beltre	.25
26	Scott Schoeneweis	.10
27	Marlon Anderson	.10
28	Jason Vargas	.10
29	Claudio Vargas	.10
30	Jason Kendall	.10
31	Aaron Small	.10
32	Juan Cruz	.10
33	Placido Polanco	.10
34	Jorge Sosa	.10
35	John Olerud	.10
36	Ryan Langerhans	.10
37	Randy Winn	.10
38	Zachary Day	.25
39	Garrett Atkins	.10
40	Al Leiter	.10
41	Shawn Chacon	.10
42	Mark DeRosa	.10
43	Miguel Ojeda	.10
44	A.J. Pierzynski	.10
45	Carlos Lee	.10
46	LaTroy Hawkins	.10
47	Nick Green	.10
48	Shawn Estes	.10
49	Eli Marrero	.10
50	Jeff Kent	.25
51	Joe Randa	.10
52	Jose Hernandez	.10
53	Joe Blanton	.10
54	Huston Street	.25
55	Marlon Byrd	.10
56	Alex Sanchez	.10
57	Livan Hernandez	.10
58	Chris Young	.25
59	Brad Eldred	.25
60	Terrence Long	.10
61	Phil Nevin	.10
62	Kyle Farnsworth	.10
63	Jon Lieber	.10
64	Antonio Alfonseca	.10
65	Tony Graffanino	.10
66	Tadahito Iguchi RC	1.00
67	Brad Thompson	.10
68	Jose Vidro	.10
69	Jason Phillips	.10
70	Carl Pavano	.10
71	Pokey Reese	.10
72	Jerome Williams	.10
73	Kazuhisa Ishii	.10
74	Zach Day	.10
75	Edgar Renteria	.25
76	Mike Myers	.10
77	Jeff Cirillo	.10
78	Endy Chavez	.10
79	Jose Guillen	.10
80	Ugueth Urbina	.10
81	Vinny Castilla	.10
82	Javier Vazquez	.10
83	Willy Taveras	.10
84	Mark Mulder	.25
85	Mike Hargrove	.10
86	Buddy Bell	.10
87	Charlie Manuel	.10
88	Willie Randolph	.10
89	Bob Melvin	.10
90	Chris Lambert	.10
91	Homer Bailey	.20

92	Ervin Santana	.10
93	Bill Bray	.10
94	Thomas Diamond	.10
95	Trevor Plouffe	.10
96	James Houser	.10
97	Jake Stevens	.10
98	Anthony Whittington	.10
99	Phillip Hughes	.10
100	Greg Golson	.10
101	Paul Maholm	.10
102	Carlos Quentin	.10
103	Dan Johnson	.10
104	Mark Rogers	.10
105	Neil Walker	.10
106	Omar Quintanilla	.10
107	Blake DeWitt	.10
108	Taylor Tankersley	.10
109	David Murphy	.10
110	Felix Hernandez	.50
111	Craig Biggio	.10
112	Greg Maddux	.50
113	Bobby Abreu	.10
114	Alex Rodriguez	.75
115	Trevor Hoffman	.10
116	A.J. Pierzynski,	
	Tadahito Iguchi	.10
117	Reggie Sanders	.10
118	Bengie Molina,	
	Ervin Santana	.10
119	Chris Burke, Lance Berkman,	
	Adam LaRoche	.10
120	Garret Anderson	.25
121	A.J. Pierzynski	.10
122	Paul Konerko	.25
123	Joe Crede	.25
124	Mark Buehrle, Jon Garland	.10
125	Freddy Garcia,	
	Jose Contreras	.10
126	Reggie Sanders	.10
127	Roy Oswalt	.10
128	Roger Clemens	.75
129	Albert Pujols	.75
130	Roy Oswalt	.10
131	Joe Crede, Bobby Jenks	.10
132	Paul Konerko,	
	Scott Podsednik	.25
133	Geoff Blum	.10
134	White Sox Sweep	.10
135	Alex Rodriguez, David Ortiz,	
	Manny Ramirez	.50
136	Michael Young,	
	Alex Rodriguez,	
	Vladimir Guerrero	.25
137	David Ortiz, Mark Teixeira,	
	Manny Ramirez	.25
138	Bartolo Colon, Jon Garland,	
	Cliff Lee	.10
139	Kevin Millwood,	
	Johan Santana,	
	Mark Buehrle	.10
140	Johan Santana,	
	Randy Johnson,	
	John Lackey	.25
141	Andruw Jones, Derek Lee,	
	Albert Pujols	.50
142	Derek Lee, Albert Pujols,	
	Miguel Cabrera	.50
143	Andruw Jones, Albert Pujols,	
	Pat Burrell	.50
144	Dontrelle Willis,	
	Chris Carpenter,	
	Roy Oswalt	.10
145	Roger Clemens, Andy Pettitte,	
	Dontrelle Willis	.50
146	Jake Peavy, Chris Carpenter,	
	Pedro Martinez	.25
147	Mark Teixeira	.25
148	Brian Roberts	.10
149	Michael Young	.25
150	Alex Rodriguez	1.00
151	Johnny Damon	.25
152	Vladimir Guerrero	.25
153	Manny Ramirez	.25
154	David Ortiz	.25
155	Mariano Rivera	.25
156	Joe Nathan	.10
157	Albert Pujols	1.00
158	Jeff Kent	.10
159	Felipe Lopez	.10
160	Morgan Ensberg	.10
161	Miguel Cabrera	.25
162	Ken Griffey Jr.	.50
163	Andruw Jones	.25
164	Paul LoDuca	.10
165	Chad Cordero	.10
166	Ken Griffey Jr.	.50
167	Jason Giambi	.25
168	Willy Taveras	.10
169	Huston Street	.25
170	Chris Carpenter	.10
171	Bartolo Colon	.10
172	Bobby Cox	.10
173	Ozzie Guillen	.10
174	Andruw Jones	.25
175	Johnny Damon	.25
176	Alex Rodriguez	1.00
177	David Ortiz	.25
178	Manny Ramirez	.25
179	Miguel Tejada	.10
180	Vladimir Guerrero	.25
181	Mark Teixeira	.25
182	Ivan Rodriguez	.25
183	Brian Roberts	.10
184	Mark Buehrle	.10
185	Bobby Abreu	.10
186	Carlos Beltran	.25
187	Albert Pujols	1.00
188	Derek Lee	.25

189	Jim Edmonds	.25
190	Aramis Ramirez	.10
191	Mike Piazza	.50
192	Jeff Kent	.10
193	David Eckstein	.10
194	Chris Carpenter	.10
195	Bobby Abreu	.25
196	Ivan Rodriguez	.25
197	Carlos Lee	.10
198	David Ortiz	.25
199	Hee Seop Choi	.10
200	Andruw Jones	.25
201	Mark Teixeira	.25
202	Jason Bay	.10
203	Hanley Ramirez	.25
204	Shin-Soo Choo	.10
205	Justin Huber	.10
206	Nelson Cruz RC	4.00
207	Edwin Encarnacion	.10
208	Miguel Montero	.50
209	William Bergolla	.10
210	Luis Montanez	.10
211	Francisco Liriano	.50
212	Kevin Thompson	.10
213	B.J. Upton	.10
214	Conor Jackson	.10
215	Delmon Young	.25
216	Andy LaRoche	.50
217	Ryan Garko	.10
218	Josh Barfield	.10
219	Chris Young	.10
220	Justin Verlander	.25
221	Drew Anderson RC	.25
222	Luis Hernandez RC	.25
223	Jim Burt RC	.25
224	Mike Morse RC	.25
225	Elliot Johnson RC	.50
226	C.J. Smith RC	.25
227	Casey McGehee RC	1.00
228	Brian Miller RC	.15
229	Chris Vines RC	.40
230	D.J. Houlton RC	.25
231	Chuck Tiffany RC	.40
232	Humberto Sanchez RC	.75
233	Baltazar Lopez RC	.25
234	Russell Martin RC	1.00
235	Dana Eveland RC	.25
236	Johan Silva RC	.25
237	Adam Harben RC	.25
238	Brian Bannister RC	.25
239	Adam Boeve RC	.25
240	Tom Oldham RC	.25
241	Cody Haerther RC	.25
242	Dan Santin RC	.25
243	Daniel Haigwood RC	.25
244	Craig Tatum RC	.25
245	Martin Prado RC	1.50
246	Errol Simonitsch RC	.40
247	Lorenzo Scott RC	.25
248	Hayden Penn RC	.40
249	Heath Totten RC	.25
250	Nick Masset RC	.25
251	Pedro Lopez RC	.25
252	Benjamin Harrison	.15
253	Michael Spidale RC	.25
254	Jeremy Harts RC	.25
255	Danny Zell RC	.40
256	Kevin Collins RC	.15
257	Tony Arnerich RC	.15
258	Matt Albers RC	.50
259	Ricky Barrett RC	.25
260	Hernan Iribarren RC	.40
261	Sean Tracey RC	.25
262	Jerry Owens RC	.40
263	Steve Nelson RC	.25
264	Brandon McCarthy RC	.50
265	David Shepard RC	.25
266	Steve Bondurant RC	.25
267	Billy Sadler	.15
268	Ryan Feierabend RC	.25
269	Stuart Pomeranz RC	.40
270	Shaun Marcum RC	.50
271	Erik Schindewolf RC	.25
272	Stefan Bailie RC	.15
273	Mike Esposito RC	.25
274	Buck Coats RC	.40
275	Andy Sides RC	.25
276	Micah Schnurstein RC	.40
277	Jesse Gutierrez RC	.25
278	Jake Postlewait RC	.25
279	Willy Mota RC	.50
280	Ryan Speier RC	.25
281	Frank Mata RC	.25
282	Jair Jurrjens RC	1.50
283	Nick Touchstone RC	.25
284	Matthew Kemp RC	2.50
285	Vinny Rottino RC	.40
286	J.B. Thurmond RC	.40
287	Kelvin Pichardo RC	.25
288	Scott Mitchinson RC	.25
289	Darwinson Salazar RC	.25
290	George Kottaras RC	.40
291	Ken Durost RC	.40
292	Jonathan Sanchez RC	1.50
293	Brandon Moorhead RC	.25
294	Kennard Bibbs RC	.25
295	David Gassner RC	.25
296	Micah Furtado RC	.25
297	Ismael Ramirez RC	.25
298	Carlos Gonzalez RC	2.50
299	Brandon Sing RC	.50
300	Jason Motte RC	.25
301	Chuck James RC	1.00
302	Andy Santana RC	.25
303	Manny Parra RC	.75
304	Chris Young RC	1.00
305	Juan Senreiso RC	.25
306	Franklin Morales RC	1.00

307	Jared Gothreaux RC	.15
308	Jayce Tingler RC	.25
309	Matt Brown RC	.25
310	Frank Diaz RC	.40
311	Stephen Drew RC	2.00
312	Jered Weaver RC	3.00
313	Ryan Braun RC	3.00
314	John Mayberry Jr. RC	.75
315	Aaron Thompson RC	1.00
316	Cesar Carrillo RC	.50
317	Jacoby Ellsbury RC	4.00
318	Matt Garza RC	3.00
319	Cliff Pennington RC	.75
320	Colby Rasmus RC	2.00
321	Chris Volstad RC	1.00
322	Ricky Romero RC	1.50
323	Ryan Zimmerman RC	4.00
324	C.J. Henry RC	.75
325	Jay Bruce RC	6.00
326	Beau Jones RC	.50
327	Mark McCormick RC	.50
328	Eli Iorg RC	.50
329	Andrew McCutchen RC	2.50
330	Mike Costanzo RC	.50

Blue

No Pricing
Production One Set

Gold

Gold Rookies:		2-4X
Gold Stars:		4-8X
Production 2,005 Sets		

All-Star Patches

		NM/M
	Common Player:	15.00
BA	Bobby Abreu/65	15.00
MA	Moises Alou/65	20.00
JB	Jason Bay/50	20.00
CB	Carlos Beltran/60	25.00
MB	Mark Buehrle/60	20.00
MC	Miguel Cabrera/70	30.00
CC	Chris Carpenter/70	20.00
MCL	Matt Clement/70	15.00
BC	Bartolo Colon/65	15.00
CCO	Chad Cordero/65	15.00
JD	Johnny Damon/60	25.00
DE	David Eckstein/65	20.00
JE	Jim Edmonds/50	20.00
ME	Morgan Ensberg/60	15.00
JG	Jon Garland/70	20.00
LG	Luis Gonzalez/70	15.00
LH	Livan Hernandez/50	15.00
JI	Jason Isringhausen/65	15.00
AJ	Andruw Jones/70	25.00
JK	Jeff Kent/65	20.00
PK	Paul Konerko/70	20.00
CL	Carlos Lee/65	20.00
DL	Derrek Lee/65	20.00
BL	Brad Lidge/65	15.00
FL	Felipe Lopez/35	20.00
MM	Melvin Mora/30	20.00
JN	Joe Nathan/65	15.00
DO	David Ortiz/70	25.00
RO	Roy Oswalt/60	15.00
JP	Jake Peavy/60	20.00
MP	Mike Piazza/50	30.00
SP	Scott Podsednik/65	15.00
AP	Albert Pujols/35	50.00
ARA	Aramis Ramirez/60	20.00
MR	Manny Ramirez/65	25.00
MRI	Mariano Rivera/65	30.00
AR	Alex Rodriguez/50	30.00
KR	Kenny Rogers/50	15.00
JS	Johan Santana/60	30.00
GS	Gary Sheffield/50	20.00
JSM	John Smoltz/65	30.00
IS	Ichiro Suzuki/50	40.00
MTE	Mark Teixeira/60	20.00
MT	Miguel Tejada/60	20.00
BW	Billy Wagner/50	15.00
DW	Dontrelle Willis/60	20.00
MY	Michael Young/50	20.00

All-Star Stitches

		NM/M
	Common Player:	4.00
BA	Bobby Abreu/A	4.00
MA	Moises Alou/C	4.00
JB	Jason Bay/C	4.00
CB	Carlos Beltran/D	6.00
MB	Mark Buehrle/B	4.00
MC	Miguel Cabrera/E	8.00
CC	Chris Carpenter/A	4.00
LC	Luis Castillo/A	4.00
MCL	Matt Clement/B	4.00
BC	Bartolo Colon/B	4.00
CCO	Chad Cordero/B	4.00
JD	Johnny Damon/B	8.00
DE	David Eckstein/B	4.00
JE	Jim Edmonds/A	6.00
ME	Morgan Ensberg/B	4.00
JG	Jon Garland/E	4.00
LG	Luis Gonzalez/C	4.00
LH	Livan Hernandez/A	4.00
JI	Jason Isringhausen/F	4.00
AJ	Andruw Jones/C	6.00
JK	Jeff Kent/C	4.00
PK	Paul Konerko/A	4.00
CL	Carlos Lee/E	4.00
DL	Derrek Lee/F	6.00
BL	Brad Lidge/D	4.00
FL	Felipe Lopez/D	4.00
MM	Melvin Mora/B	4.00
JN	Joe Nathan/D	4.00
DO	David Ortiz/D	8.00
RO	Roy Oswalt/A	4.00

JP	Jake Peavy/D	4.00
MP	Mike Piazza/E	8.00
SP	Scott Podsednik/A	4.00
AP	Albert Pujols/E	20.00
ARA	Aramis Ramirez/E	4.00
MR	Manny Ramirez/E	8.00
MRI	Mariano Rivera/E	6.00
BR	Brian Roberts/C	4.00
AR	Alex Rodriguez/D	15.00
IR	Ivan Rodriguez/A	4.00
KR	Kenny Rogers/A	4.00
JS	Johan Santana/C	6.00
GS	Gary Sheffield/D	6.00
JSM	John Smoltz/D	6.00
IS	Ichiro Suzuki/A	20.00
MTE	Mark Teixeira/C	6.00
MT	Miguel Tejada/B	6.00
BW	Billy Wagner/C	4.00
DW	Dontrelle Willis/F	6.00
MY	Michael Young/A	4.00

Derby Digs Jersey

		NM/M
	Production 100 Sets	
BA	Bobby Abreu	25.00
JB	Jason Bay	15.00
AJ	Andruw Jones	25.00
CL	Carlos Lee	10.00
DO	David Ortiz	25.00
IR	Ivan Rodriguez	25.00
MT	Mark Teixeira	25.00

Hall of Fame Bat

		NM/M
	Complete Set (2):	
WB	Wade Boggs/A	10.00
RS	Ryne Sandberg/B	15.00

Hall of Fame Dual Bat

		NM/M
	Production 200 Sets	
BS	Wade Boggs,	
	Ryne Sandberg	25.00

Legendary Sacks

		NM/M
	Production 300 Sets	
JA	Jim Abbott	6.00
AD	Andre Dawson	6.00
MF	Mark Fidrych	4.00
RF	Rollie Fingers	6.00
BJ	Bo Jackson	8.00
HR	Harold Reynolds	4.00
OS	Ozzie Smith	8.00
LW	Lou Whitaker	4.00
DW	Dave Winfield	8.00

Midsummer Covers

		NM/M
	Production 150 Sets	
CB	Carlos Beltran	15.00
RC	Roger Clemens	25.00
VG	Vladimir Guerrero	25.00
DL	Derrek Lee	15.00
AP	Albert Pujols	40.00
BR	Brian Roberts	10.00
AR	Alex Rodriguez	30.00
IS	Ichiro Suzuki	50.00
MT	Miguel Tejada	15.00
DW	Dontrelle Willis	10.00

Printing Plates

No Pricing
Production one set per color.

Signature Moves

		NM/M
	Production 15-475 Sets	
	Red Foil:	No Pricing
	Production 25 Sets	
MA	Matt Albers/475	15.00
TC	Travis Chick/475	8.00
TG	Troy Glaus/275	20.00
TH	Tim Hudson/275	25.00
KI	Kazuhisa Ishii/275	15.00
GK	George Kottaras/475	15.00
BL	Bobby Livingston/475	10.00
MM	Mark Mulder/275	25.00
GP	Glen Perkins/275	15.00
JP	Jake Postlewait/275	10.00
HS	Humberto Sanchez	30.00
BS	Benito Santiago	20.00
RS	Richie Sexson/275	25.00
CJS	C.J. Smith/475	15.00
JV	Justin Verlander/275	35.00
TW	Tony Womack	15.00

Touch Em All Base

		NM/M
	Production 1,000 Sets	
VG	Vladimir Guerrero	10.00
DL	Derrek Lee	8.00
DO	David Ortiz	10.00
AP	Albert Pujols	20.00
MR	Manny Ramirez	10.00
AR	Alex Rodriguez	15.00
IR	Ivan Rodriguez	8.00
GS	Gary Sheffield	6.00
IS	Ichiro Suzuki	20.00
MT	Miguel Tejada	10.00

Washington Nationals Inaugural Lineup

		NM/M
	Inserted 1:10	
JN	Joe Nathan/D	4.00
DO	David Ortiz/B	8.00
RO	Roy Oswalt/A	4.00
	Ball Relics:	No Pricing
	Production Five Sets	

VC	Vinny Castilla	.50
JG	Jose Guillen	1.00
CG	Cristian Guzman	.50
LH	Livan Hernandez	.50
NJ	Nick Johnson	.50
BS	Brian Schneider	.50
TS	Terrmel Sledge	.50
JV	Jose Vidro	.50
BW	Brad Wilkerson	.50
TEAM	Team Photo	1.00

2005 Topps Chrome Update

NM/M
Complete Set (237):
Common Player: .25
Common Rookie (106-215): .50
Common Rk Auto. (221-237): 10.00
Pack (4): 4.00
Box (20): 70.00

UH1	Sammy Sosa	1.00
UH2	Jeff Francoeur	.50
UH3	Tony Clark	.25
UH4	Michael Tucker	.25
UH5	Mike Matheny	.25
UH6	Eric Young	.25
UH7	Jose Valentin	.25
UH8	Matt Lawton	.25
UH9	Juan Rivera	.25
UH10	Shawn Green	.50
UH11	Aaron Boone	.25
UH12	Woody Williams	.25
UH13	Brad Wilkerson	.25
UH14	Anthony Reyes RC	3.00
UH15	Gustavo Chacin	.25
UH16	Mike Restovich	.25
UH17	Humberto Quintero	.25
UH18	Matt Ginter	.25
UH19	Scott Podsednik	.50
UH20	Byung-Hyun Kim	.25
UH21	Orlando Hernandez	.25
UH22	Mark Grudzielanek	.25
UH23	Jody Gerut	.25
UH24	Adrian Beltre	.50
UH25	Scott Schoeneweis	.25
UH26	Marlon Anderson	.25
UH27	Jason Vargas	.25
UH28	Claudio Vargas	.25
UH29	Jason Kendall	.25
UH30	Aaron Small	.25
UH31	Juan Cruz	.25
UH32	Placido Polanco	.25
UH33	Jorge Sosa	.25
UH34	John Olerud	.25
UH35	Ryan Langerhans	.25
UH36	Randy Winn	.25
UH37	Zachary Duke	.50
UH38	Garrett Atkins	.25
UH39	Al Leiter	.25
UH40	Shawn Chacon	.25
UH41	Mark DeRosa	.25
UH42	Miguel Ojeda	.25
UH43	A.J. Pierzynski	.25
UH44	Carlos Lee	.25
UH45	LaTroy Hawkins	.25
UH46	Nick Green	.25
UH47	Shawn Estes	.25
UH48	Eli Marrero	.25
UH49	Jeff Kent	.25
UH50	Joe Randa	.25
UH51	Jose Hernandez	.25
UH52	Joe Blanton	.25
UH53	Huston Street	.25
UH54	Marlon Byrd	.25
UH55	Alex Sanchez	.25
UH56	Livan Hernandez	.25
UH57	Chris Young	.25
UH58	Brad Eldred	.25
UH59	Terrence Long	.25
UH60	Phil Nevin	.25
UH61	Kyle Farnsworth	.25
UH62	Jon Lieber	.25
UH63	Antonio Alfonseca	.25
UH64	Tony Graffanino	.25
UH65	Tadahito Iguchi	1.00
UH66	Brad Thompson	.25
UH67	Jose Vidro	.25
UH68	Jason Phillips	.25
UH69	Carl Pavano	.25
UH70	Pokey Reese	.25
UH71	Jerome Williams	.25
UH72	Kazuhisa Ishii	.25
UH73	Felix Hernandez	.25
UH74	Edgar Renteria	.50
UH75	Mike Myers	.25
UH76	Jeff Cirillo	.25
UH77	Endy Chavez	.25
UH78	Jose Guillen	.25
UH79	Ugueth Urbina	.25
UH80	Zach Day	.25
UH81	Javier Vazquez	.25
UH82	Willy Taveras	.25
UH83	Mark Mulder	.50
UH84	Vinny Castilla	.25
UH85	Russ Adams	.25
UH86	Homer Bailey	.25
UH87	Ervin Santana	.25
UH88	Bill Bray	.25
UH89	Thomas Diamond	.25
UH90	Trevor Plouffe	.25
UH91	James Houser	.25
UH92	Jake Stevens	.25
UH93	Anthony Whittington	.25
UH94	Phillip Hughes	.25
UH95	Greg Golson	.25
UH96	Paul Maholm	.25
UH97	Carlos Quentin	.25
UH98	Dan Johnson	.25
UH99	Mark Rogers	.25
UH100	Neil Walker	.25
UH101	Omar Quintanilla	.25
UH102	Blake DeWitt	.25
UH103	Taylor Tankersley	.25
UH104	David Murphy	.25
UH105	Chris Lambert	.25
UH106	Drew Anderson RC	.50
UH107	Luis Hernandez RC	.50
UH108	Jim Burt RC	.50
UH109	Mike Morse RC	.50
UH110	Elliot Johnson RC	1.00
UH111	C.J. Smith RC	.50
UH112	Casey McGehee RC	.50
UH113	Brian Miller RC	.50
UH114	Chris Vines RC	.50
UH115	D.J. Houlton RC	.50
UH116	Chuck Tiffany RC	2.00
UH117	Humberto Sanchez RC	2.00
UH118	Baltazar Lopez RC	.50
UH119	Russell Martin RC	2.00
UH120	Dana Eveland RC	.50
UH121	Johan Silva RC	.50
UH122	Adam Harben RC	.50
UH123	Brian Bannister RC	.75
UH124	Adam Boeve RC	.75
UH125	Tom Oldham RC	.75
UH126	Cody Haerther RC	.75
UH127	Dan Santin RC	.75
UH128	Daniel Haigwood RC	.50
UH129	Craig Tatum RC	.50
UH130	Martin Prado RC	1.50
UH131	Errol Simonitsch RC	.50
UH132	Lorenzo Scott RC	.75
UH133	Hayden Penn RC	.50
UH134	Heath Totten RC	.50
UH135	Nick Masset RC	.50
UH136	Pedro Lopez RC	.50
UH137	Benjamin Harrison RC	.50
UH138	Michael Spidale RC	.50
UH139	Jeremy Harts RC	.50
UH140	Danny Zell RC	.50
UH141	Kevin Collins RC	.50
UH142	Tony Arnerich RC	1.00
UH143	Matt Albers RC	1.00
UH144	Ricky Barrett RC	.50
UH145	Hernan Iribarren RC	.50
UH146	Sean Tracey RC	.50
UH147	Jerry Owens RC	1.00
UH148	Steve Nelson RC	.50
UH149	Brandon McCarthy RC	.75
UH150	David Shepard RC	.50
UH151	Steve Bondurant RC	.50
UH152	Billy Sadler RC	.50
UH153	Ryan Feierabend RC	.50
UH154	Stuart Pomeranz RC	.75
UH155	Shawn Marcum RC	1.00
UH156	Erik Schindelwolf RC	.50
UH157	Stefan Bailie RC	.50
UH158	Mike Esposito RC	.50
UH159	Buck Coats RC	.75
UH160	Andy Sides RC	.50
UH161	Micah Schnurstein RC	.50
UH162	Jesse Gutierrez RC	.50
UH163	Jake Postlewait RC	.50
UH164	Willy Mota RC	.50
UH165	Ryan Speier RC	.50
UH166	Frank Mata RC	.50
UH167	Jair Jurrjens RC	4.00
UH168	Nick Touchstone RC	.50
UH169	Matthew Kemp RC	6.00
UH170	Vinny Rottino RC	.50
UH171	J.B. Thurmond RC	.50
UH172	Kelvin Pichardo RC	.50
UH173	Scott Mitchinson RC	.50
UH174	Darwinson Salazar RC	.50
UH175	George Kottaras RC	.75
UH176	Ken Durost RC	.50
UH177	Jonathan Sanchez RC	3.00
UH178	Brandon Moorhead RC	.75
UH179	Kennard Bibbs RC	.50
UH180	David Gassner RC	.50
UH181	Micah Furtado RC	.50
UH182	Ismael Ramirez RC	.50
UH183	Carlos Gonzalez RC	5.00
UH184	Brandon Sing RC	.50
UH185	Jason Motte RC	.50
UH186	Chuck James RC	1.00
UH187	Andy Santana RC	.50
UH188	Manny Parra RC	1.00
UH189	Chris Young RC	2.00
UH190	Juan Senreiso RC	.50
UH191	Franklin Morales RC	.50
UH192	Jared Gothreaux RC	.50
UH193	Jayce Tingler RC	.50
UH194	Matt Brown RC	.50
UH195	Frank Diaz RC	1.50
UH196	Stephen Drew RC	4.00
UH197	Jered Weaver RC	5.00
UH198	Ryan Braun RC	25.00
UH199	John Mayberry Jr. RC	2.50
UH200	Aaron Thompson RC	2.00
UH201	Ben Copeland RC	2.00
UH202	Jacoby Ellsbury RC	15.00
UH203	Garrett Olson RC	3.00
UH204	Cliff Pennington RC	2.50
UH205	Colby Rasmus RC	10.00
UH206	Chris Volstad RC	3.00
UH207	Ricky Romero RC	5.00
UH208	Ryan Zimmerman RC	10.00
UH209	C.J. Henry RC	2.00
UH210	Nelson Cruz RC	5.00
UH211	Josh Wall RC	1.50
UH212	Nick Webber RC	.50
UH213	Paul Kelly RC	1.00
UH214	Kyle Winters RC	1.50
UH215	Mitch Boggs RC	.75
UH216	Craig Biggio	.50
UH217	Greg Maddux	1.00
UH218	Bobby Abreu	.25
UH219	Alex Rodriguez	2.00
UH220	Trevor Hoffman	.25
UH221	Trevor Bell RC	10.00
UH222	Jay Bruce RC	50.00
UH223	Travis Buck RC	10.00
UH224	Cesar Carrillo RC	15.00
UH225	Mike Costanzo RC	10.00
UH226	Brent Cox RC	10.00
UH227	Matt Garza RC	20.00
UH228	Josh Geer RC	10.00
UH229	Tyler Greene RC	10.00
UH230	Eli Iorg RC	10.00
UH231	Craig Italiano RC	10.00
UH232	Beau Jones RC	10.00
UH233	Mark McCormick RC	10.00
UH234	Andrew McCutchen RC	40.00
UH235	Micah Owings RC	15.00
UH236	Cesar Ramos RC	10.00
UH237	Chaz Roe RC	10.00

Refractor
Stars (1-105): 2-3X
Rookies (106-215): 1-2X
Inserted 1:5
Refractor Auto. (221-237): 1-1.5X
Production 500

Black Refractor
Black (1-105): 2-4X
Black (106-215): 2-3X
Production 250
Black Auto. (221-237): 1-2.5X
Production 200

Gold SuperFractor
No Pricing
Production One Set

Red X-Fractor
Red (1-105): 4-8X
Red (106-215): 6-12X
Production 65
Red Auto. (221-237): No Pricing
Production 25

Barry Bonds Home Run History

NM/M
Complete Set (15): 40.00
Common Bonds: 3.00
Inserted 1:12
Refractor: 1-2X
Inserted 1:71
Black Refractor: 2-3X
Production 200 Sets
Red X-Fractor: 4-6X
Production 25 Sets
Gold Super: No Pricing
Production One Set

BB1	Barry Bonds	3.00
BB25	Barry Bonds	3.00
BB50	Barry Bonds	3.00
BB75	Barry Bonds	3.00
BB100	Barry Bonds	3.00
BB125	Barry Bonds	3.00
BB150	Barry Bonds	3.00
BB175	Barry Bonds	3.00
BB200	Barry Bonds	3.00
BB225	Barry Bonds	3.00
BB250	Barry Bonds	3.00
BB300	Barry Bonds	3.00
BB325	Barry Bonds	3.00
BB350	Barry Bonds	3.00

Printing Plates
No Pricing
Production one set per color.

2005 Topps Washington Nationals Commemorative Set

NM/M
Complete Boxed Set (55): 20.00
Common Player: .50

1	Nationals Logo	.50
2	Jose Vidro	.75
3	Joe Horgan	.50
4	Danny Rueckel	.50
5	Wil Cordero	.50
6	Cristian Guzman	.75
7	Alex Escobar	.50
8	Tony Armas Jr.	.50
9	Zach Day	.50
10	Jamey Carroll	.50
11	Nick Johnson	.75
12	John Patterson	.50
13	Josh Karp	.50
14	Brendan Harris	.50
15	Gary Bennett	.50
16	Terrmel Sledge	.50
17	Tomo Ohka	.50
18	Chad Cordero	.50
19	Luis Ayala	.50
20	Tony Blanco	.50
21	Endy Chavez	.75
22	George Arias	.50
23	Chad Durbin	.50
24	Phil Hiatt	.50
25	Henry Mateo	.50
26	Livan Hernandez	.50
27	Larry Broadway	.60
28	T.J. Tucker	.50
29	J.J. Davis	.50
30	Brian Schneider	.50
31	Vinny Castilla	.50
32	Michael Hinckley	.50
33	Brandon Watson	.50
34	Claudio Vargas	.50
35	Ryan Church	.50
36	Jose Guillen	.65
37	Gary Majewski	.50
38	Jon Rauch	.50
39	Brad Wilkerson	.50
40	Francis Beltran	.50
41	Esteban Loaiza	.50
42	Carlos Baerga	.50
43	Sunny Kim	.50
44	Ian Desmond	.50
45	Jeffrey Hammonds	.50
46	Hector Carrasco	.50
47	Drew McMillan	.50
48	Jared Sandberg	.50
49	Frank Robinson	1.00
50	RFK Stadium	.50
51	Senators Become Twins in 1961	.50
52	Senators Move to Texas in 1972	.50
53	Nationals Top Orioles	.50
54	First Moves (Vinny Castilla, Jose Guillen)	.50
55	First Moves (Cristian Guzman, Esteban Loaiza)	.50

2005 Topps/Emerald Nuts S.F. Giants

The first 20,000 fans at the August 28 game at SBC Park received this foil-wrapped team set. High-gloss fronts are bordered in black with gold-foil highlights. Backs have a portrait photo, stats and career highlights. Cards are numbered with GTS prefix.

NM/M
Complete Set (31): 7.50
Common Player: .25

1	Barry Bonds	3.00
2	Armando Benitez	.25
3	Edgardo Alfonzo	.25
4	Kirk Rueter	.25
5	Ray Durham	.25
6	Michael Tucker	.25
7	Noah Lowry	.25
8	Jason Christiansen	.25
9	J.T. Snow	.35
10	Jason Schmidt	.35
11	Pedro Feliz	.25
12	Brett Tomko	.25
13	Jeff Fassero	.25
14	Mike Matheny	.25
15	Omar Vizquel	.25
16	Lance Niekro	.25
17	Scott Eyre	.25
18	Jesse Foppert	.25
19	Deivi Cruz	.25
20	Moises Alou	.35
21	Scott Munter	.25
22	Todd Linden	.25
23	Marquis Grissom	.25
24	Jason Ellison	.25
25	Tyler Walker	.25
26	LaTroy Hawkins	.25
27	Yorvit Torrealba	.25
28	Felipe Alou	.35
29	Coaches (Joe Lefebvre, Luis Pujols, Gene Glynn)	.25
30	Coaches (Dave Righetti, Ron Wotus, Mark Gardner)	.25
---	Checklist	.25

2005 Topps/Poland Spring Yankees Legends
Stadium giveaway July 30.

NM/M
Complete Set (5): 6.00
Common Player: 2.00

1	Paul O'Neill	2.00
2	Hank Bauer	2.00
3	Bill "Moose" Skowron	2.00
4	Graig Nettles	2.00
---	Sponsor's Card	.10

2006 Topps

NM/M
Complete Set (659): 60.00
Complete Hobby Set (664): 75.00
Complete Holiday Set (659): 75.00
Complete Cardinals Set (664): 75.00
Complete Cubs Set (664): 75.00
Complete Pirates Set (664): 75.00
Complete Red Sox Set (664): 75.00
Complete Yankees Set (664): 75.00
Common Player: .10
Series 1 & 2 hobby pack (10): 1.50
Series 1 & 2 hobby box (36): 40.00
Jumbo Pack (35): 4.00
Jumbo Box (12): 40.00

1	Alex Rodriguez	1.50
2	Jose Valentin	.10
3	Garrett Atkins	.25
4	Scott Hatteberg	.10
5	Carl Crawford	.25
6	Armando Benitez	.10
7	Mickey Mantle	5.00
8	Mike Morse	.10
9	Damian Miller	.10
10	Clint Barmes	.10
11	Michael Barrett	.10
12	Coco Crisp	.10
13	Tadahito Iguchi	.25
14	Chris Snyder	.10
15	Brian Roberts	.25
16	David Wright	1.00
17	Victor Santos	.10
18	Trevor Hoffman	.20
19	Jeremy Reed	.10
20	Bobby Abreu	.25
21	Lance Berkman	.25
22	Zach Day	.10
23	Jonny Gomes	.10
24	Jason Marquis	.10
25	Chipper Jones	.50
26	Scott Hairston	.10
27	Ryan Dempster	.10
28	Brandon Inge	.10
29	Aaron Harang	.20
30	Jon Garland	.10
31	Pokey Reese	.10
32	Mike MacDougal	.10
33	Mike Lieberthal	.10
34	Cesar Izturis	.10
35	Brad Wilkerson	.10
36	Jeff Suppan	.10
37	Adam Everett	.10
38	Bengie Molina	.10
39	Rickie Weeks	.25
40	Jorge Posada	.25
41	Rheal Cormier	.10
42	Reed Johnson	.10
43	Laynce Nix	.10
44	Carl Everett	.10
45	Greg Maddux	1.00
46	Jeff Francis	.10
47	Felipe Lopez	.10
48	Dan Johnson	.10
49	Humberto Cota	.10
50	Manny Ramirez	.50
51	Juan Uribe	.10
52	Jaret Wright	.10
53	Tomokazu Ohka	.10
54	Mike Matheny	.10
55	Joe Mauer	.25
56	Jarrod Washburn	.10
57	Randy Winn	.10
58	Pedro Feliz	.10
59	Kenny Rogers	.10
60	Rocco Baldelli	.10
61	Eric Hinske	.10
62	Damaso Marte	.10
63	Desi Relaford	.10
64	Juan Encarnacion	.10
65	Nomar Garciaparra	.50
66	Shawn Estes	.10
67	Brian Jordan	.10
68	Steve Kline	.10
69	Braden Looper	.10
70	Carlos Lee	.25
71	Tom Glavine	.25
72	Craig Biggio	.25
73	Steve Finley	.10
74	David Newhan	.10
75	Eric Gagne	.20
76	Tony Graffanino	.10
77	Dallas McPherson	.10
78	Nick Punto	.10
79	Mark Kotsay	.10
80	Kerry Wood	.25
81	Kyle Farnsworth	.10
82	Huston Street	.20
83	Endy Chavez	.10
84	So Taguchi	.10
85	Hank Blalock	.25
86	Brad Radke	.10
87	Chien-Ming Wang	.50
88	B.J. Surhoff	.10
89	Glendon Rusch	.10
90	Mark Buehrle	.25
91	Rafael Betancourt	.10
92	Lance Cormier	.10
93	Alex Gonzalez	.10
94	Matt Stairs	.10
95	Andy Pettitte	.25
96	Jesse Crain	.10
97	Kenny Lofton	.10
98	Geoff Blum	.10
99	Mark Redman	.10
100	Barry Bonds	1.50
101	Chad Orvella	.10
102	Xavier Nady	.10
103	Junior Spivey	.10
104	Bernie Williams	.25
105	Victor Martinez	.25
106	Nook Logan	.10
107	Mark Teahen	.10
108	Mike Lamb	.10
109	Jayson Werth	.10
110	Mariano Rivera	.25
111	Erubiel Durazo	.10
112	Ryan Vogelsong	.10
113	Bobby Madritsch	.10
114	Travis Lee	.10
115	Adam Dunn	.40
116	David Riske	.10
117	Troy Percival	.10
118	Chad Tracy	.20
119	Andy Marte	.10
120	Edgar Renteria	.20
121	Jason Giambi	.25
122	Justin Morneau	.40
123	J.T. Snow	.10
124	Danys Baez	.10
125	Carlos Delgado	.25
126	John Buck	.10
127	Shannon Stewart	.10
128	Mike Cameron	.10
129	Joe McEwing	.10
130	Richie Sexson	.10
131	Rod Barajas	.10
132	Russ Adams	.10
133	J.D. Closser	.10
134	Ramon Ortiz	.10
135	Josh Beckett	.50
136	Ryan Freel	.10
137	Victor Zambrano	.10
138	Ronnie Belliard	.10
139	Jason Michaels	.10
140	Brian Giles	.20
141	Randy Wolf	.10
142	Robinson Cano	.50
143	Joe Blanton	.10
144	Esteban Loaiza	.10
145	Troy Glaus	.25
146	Matt Clement	.10
147	Geoff Jenkins	.10
148	John Thomson	.10
149	A.J. Pierzynski	.25
150	Pedro Martinez	.50
151	Roger Clemens	1.50
152	Jack Wilson	.10
153	Ray King	.10
154	Ryan Church	.10
155	Paul LoDuca	.25
156	Dan Wheeler	.10

157	Carlos Zambrano	.25
158	Mike Timlin	.10
159	Brandon Claussen	.10
160	Travis Hafner	.25
161	Chris Shelton	.10
162	Rafael Furcal	.25
163	Flash Gordon	.10
164	Noah Lowry	.10
165	Larry Walker	.25
166	Dave Roberts	.10
167	Scott Schoeneweis	.10
168	Julian Tavarez	.10
169	Jhonny Peralta	.25
170	Vernon Wells	.25
171	Jorge Cantu	.10
172	Todd Greene	.10
173	Willy Taveras	.10
174	Corey Patterson	.10
175	Ivan Rodriguez	.40
176	Bobby Kielty	.10
177	Jose Reyes	.50
178	Barry Zito	.25
179	Deivi Cruz	.10
180	Mark Teixeira	.50
181	Chone Figgins	.25
182	Aaron Rowand	.25
183	Tim Wakefield	.10
184	Mike Maroth	.10
185	Johnny Damon	.50
186	Vicente Padilla	.10
187	Ryan Klesko	.10
188	Gary Matthews	.10
189	Jose Mesa	.10
190	Nick Johnson	.10
191	Freddy Tarcia	.10
192	Larry Bigbie	.10
193	Chris Ray	.10
194	Torii Hunter	.25
195	Mike Sweeney	.10
196	Brad Penny	.10
197	Jason Frasor	.10
198	Kevin Mench	.10
199	Adam Kennedy	.10
200	Albert Pujols	1.50
201	Jody Gerut	.10
202	Luis Gonzalez	.10
203	Zack Greinke	.25
204	Miguel Cairo	.10
205	Jimmy Rollins	.50
206	Edgardo Alfonzo	.10
207	Billy Wagner	.10
208	B.J. Ryan	.10
209	Orlando Hudson	.10
210	Preston Wilson	.10
211	Melvin Mora	.10
212	Bill Mueller	.10
213	Javy Lopez	.10
214	Wilson Betemit	.10
215	Garret Anderson	.10
216	Russell Branyan	.10
217	Jeff Weaver	.10
218	Doug Mientkiewicz	.10
219	Mark Ellis	.10
220	Jason Bay	.25
221	Adam LaRoche	.10
222	C.C. Sabathia	.25
223	Humberto Quintero	.10
224	Bartolo Colon	.20
225	Ichiro Suzuki	1.00
226	Brett Tomko	.10
227	Corey Koskie	.10
228	David Eckstein	.10
229	Cristian Guzman	.10
230	Jeff Kent	.25
231	Chris Capuano	.10
232	Rodrigo Lopez	.10
233	Jason Phillips	.10
234	Luis Rivas	.10
235	Cliff Floyd	.10
236	Gil Meche	.10
237	Adam Eaton	.10
238	Matt Morris	.10
239	Kyle Davies	.10
240	David Wells	.10
241	John Smoltz	.25
242	Felix Hernandez	.50
243	Kenny Rogers	.10
244	Mark Teixeira	.25
245	Orlando Hudson	.10
246	Derek Jeter	1.00
247	Eric Chavez	.20
248	Torii Hunter	.20
249	Vernon Wells	.20
250	Ichiro Suzuki	.50
251	Greg Maddux	.50
252	Mike Matheny	.10
253	Derrek Lee	.25
254	Luis Castillo	.10
255	Omar Vizquel	.10
256	Mike Lowell	.25
257	Andruw Jones	.25
258	Jim Edmonds	.20
259	Bobby Abreu	.25
260	Bartolo Colon	.10
261	Chris Carpenter	.25
262	Alex Rodriguez	1.00
263	Albert Pujols	1.00
264	Huston Street	.10
265	Ryan Howard	.50
266	Bob Melvin	.10
267	Bobby Cox	.10
268	Baltimore Orioles	.10
269	Boston Red Sox	.25
270	Chicago White Sox	.25
271	Dusty Baker	.10
272	Jerry Narron	.10
273	Cleveland Indians	.10
274	Clint Hurdle	.10

275	Detroit Tigers	.10
276	Jack McKeon	.10
277	Phil Garner	.10
278	Kansas City Royals	.10
279	Jim Tracy	.10
280	Angels	.10
281	Milwaukee Brewers	.10
282	Minnesota Twins	.10
283	Willie Randolph	.10
284	New York Yankees	.50
285	Oakland Athletics	.10
286	Charlie Manuel	.10
287	Pete Mackanin	.10
288	Bruce Bochy	.10
289	Felipe Alou	.10
290	Seattle Mariners	.10
291	Tony LaRussa	.10
292	Tampa Bay Devil Rays	.10
293	Texas Rangers	.10
294	Toronto Blue Jays	.10
295	Frank Robinson	.25
296	Anderson Hernandez **RC**	.10
297a	Alex Gordon (Complete card. Not officially issued.)	200.00
297b	Alex Gordon (Cut-out card.)	50.00
297c	Alex Gordon Blank Gold	50.00
298	Jason Botts **RC**	.25
299	Jeff Mathis **RC**	.10
300	Ryan Garko **RC**	.25
301	Charlton Jimerson **RC**	.25
302	Chris Denorfia **RC**	.25
303	Anthony Reyes **RC**	.25
304	Bryan Bullington **RC**	.25
305	Chuck James **RC**	.25
306	Danny Sandoval **RC**	.25
307	Walter Young **RC**	.25
308	Fausto Carmona **RC**	.25
309	Francisco Liriano **RC**	1.00
310	Hong-Chih Kuo **RC**	.75
311	Joe Saunders **RC**	.25
312	John Koronka **RC**	.25
313	Robert Andino **RC**	.25
314	Shaun Marcum **RC**	.25
315	Tom Gorzelanny **RC**	.25
316	Craig Breslow **RC**	.25
317	Chris Demaria **RC**	.25
318	Brayan Pena **RC**	.25
319	Rich Hill **RC**	.25
320	Rick Short **RC**	.25
321	C.J. Wilson **RC**	.25
322	Marshall McDougall **RC**	.25
323	Darrell Rasner **RC**	.25
324	Brandon Watson **RC**	.25
325	Paul McAnulty **RC**	.25
326	Derek Jeter, Alex Rodriguez	.50
327	Miguel Tejada, Melvin Mora	.25
328	Marcus Giles, Chipper Jones	.25
329	Manny Ramirez, David Ortiz	.25
330	Michael Barrett, Greg Maddux	.25
331	Matt Holliday	.50
332	Orlando Cabrera	.25
333	Ryan Langerhans	.10
334	Lew Ford	.10
335	Mark Prior	.25
336	Ted Lilly	.10
337	Michael Young	.25
338	Livan Hernandez	.10
339	Yadier Molina	.10
340	Eric Chavez	.10
341	Miguel Batista	.10
342	Bruce Chen	.10
343	Sean Casey	.10
344	Doug Davis	.10
345	Andruw Jones	.25
346	Hideki Matsui	1.00
347	Joe Randa	.10
348	Reggie Sanders	.10
349	Jason Jennings	.10
350	Joe Nathan	.10
351	Jose Lopez	.10
352	John Lackey	.10
353	Claudio Vargas	.10
354	Grady Sizemore	.50
355	Jonathan Papelbon **RC**	1.00
356	Luis Matos	.10
357	Orlando Hernandez	.10
358	Jamie Moyer	.10
359	Chase Utley	.50
360	Moises Alou	.25
361	Chad Cordero	.10
362	Brian McCann	.25
363	Jermaine Dye	.10
364	Ryan Madson	.10
365	Aramis Ramirez	.25
366	Matt Treanor	.10
367	Ray Durham	.10
368	Khalil Greene	.25
369	Mike Hampton	.10
370	Mike Mussina	.25
371	Brad Hawpe	.10
372	Marlon Byrd	.10
373	Woody Williams	.10
374	Victor Diaz	.10
375	Brady Clark	.10
376	Luis Gonzalez	.10
377	Raul Ibanez	.10
378	Tony Clark	.10
379	Shawn Chacon	.10
380	Marcus Giles	.10
381	Odalis Perez	.10
382	Steve Trachsel	.10
383	Russ Ortiz	.10

384	Toby Hall	.10
385	Bill Hall	.10
386	Luke Hudson	.10
387	Ken Griffey Jr.	1.00
388	Tim Hudson	.25
389	Brian Moehler	.10
390	Jake Peavy	.25
391	Casey Blake	.10
392	Sidney Ponson	.10
393	Brian Schneider	.10
394	J.J. Hardy	.10
395	Austin Kearns	.10
396	Pat Burrell	.25
397	Jason Vargas	.10
398	Ryan Howard	.75
399	Joe Crede	.10
400	Vladimir Guerrero	.50
401	Roy Halladay	.25
402	David Dellucci	.10
403	Brandon Webb	.25
404	Marlon Anderson	.10
405	Miguel Tejada	.25
406	Ryan Doumit	.10
407	Kevin Youkilis	.25
408	Jon Lieber	.10
409	Edwin Encarnacion	.25
410	Miguel Cabrera	.50
411	A.J. Burnett	.25
412	David Bell	.10
413	Gregg Zaun	.10
414	Lance Niekro	.10
415	Shawn Green	.10
416	Roberto Hernandez	.10
417	Jay Gibbons	.10
418	Johnny Estrada	.10
419	Omar Vizquel	.10
420	Gary Sheffield	.25
421	Brad Halsey	.10
422	Aaron Cook	.10
423	David Ortiz	.50
424	Tony Womack	.10
425	Joe Kennedy	.10
426	Dustin McGowan	.10
427	Carl Pavano	.10
428	Nick Green	.10
429	Francisco Cordero	.10
430	Octavio Dotel	.10
431	Julio Franco	.10
432	Brett Myers	.10
433	Casey Kotchman	.10
434	Frank Catalanotto	.10
435	Paul Konerko	.25
436	Keith Foulke	.10
437	Juan Rivera	.10
438	Todd Pratt	.10
439	Ben Broussard	.10
440	Scott Kazmir	.25
441	Rich Aurilia	.10
442	Craig Monroe	.10
443	Danny Kolb	.10
444	Curtis Granderson	.25
445	Jeff Francoeur	.25
446	Dustin Hermanson	.10
447	Jacque Jones	.10
448	Bobby Crosby	.10
449	Jason LaRue	.10
450	Derrek Lee	.40
451	Curt Schilling	.50
452	Jake Westbrook	.10
453	Daniel Cabrera	.10
454	Bobby Jenks	.10
455	Dontrelle Willis	.25
456	Brad Lidge	.10
457	Shea Hillenbrand	.10
458	Luis Castillo	.10
459	Mark Hendrickson	.10
460	Randy Johnson	.50
461	Placido Polanco	.10
462	Aaron Boone	.10
463	Todd Walker	.10
464	Nick Swisher	.25
465	Joel Pineiro	.10
466	Jay Payton	.10
467	Cliff Lee	.10
468	Johan Santana	.50
469	Josh Willingham **RC**	.25
470	Jeremy Bonderman	.10
471	Runelvys Hernandez	.10
472	Duaner Sanchez	.10
473	Jason Lane	.10
474	Trot Nixon	.10
475	Ramon Hernandez	.10
476	Mike Lowell	.25
477	Chan Ho Park	.10
478	Doug Waechter	.10
479	Carlos Silva	.10
480	Jose Contreras	.10
481	Vinny Castilla	.10
482	Chris Reitsma	.10
483	Jose Guillen	.10
484	Aaron Hill	.10
485	Kevin Millwood	.10
486	Wily Mo Pena	.10
487	Rich Harden	.10
488	Chris Carpenter	.25
489	Jason Bartlett	.10
490	Magglio Ordonez	.25
491	John Rodriguez	.10
492	Bob Wickman	.10
493	Eddie Guardado	.10
494	Kip Wells	.10
495	Adrian Beltre	.25
496	Jose Capellan **RC**	.10
497	Scott Podsednik	.10
498	Brad Thompson	.10
499	Aaron Heilman	.10
500	Derek Jeter	1.50
501	Emil Brown	.10

502	Morgan Ensberg	.20
503	Nate Bump	.10
504	Phil Nevin	.10
505	Jason Schmidt	.10
506	Michael Cuddyer	.10
507	John Patterson	.10
508	Dan Haren	.25
509	Freddy Sanchez	.10
510	J.D. Drew	.25
511	Dmitri Young	.10
512	Eric Milton	.10
513	Ervin Santana	.25
514	Mark Loretta	.10
515	Mark Grudzielanek	.10
516	Derrick Turnbow	.10
517	Danny Bautista	.10
518	Lyle Overbay	.10
519	Julio Lugo	.10
520	Carlos Beltran	.40
521	Jose Cruz Jr.	.10
522	Jason Isringhausen	.10
523	Bronson Arroyo	.10
524	Ben Sheets	.25
525	Zachary Duke	.10
526	Ryan Wagner	.10
527	Jose Vidro	.10
528	Doug Mirabelli	.10
529	Kris Benson	.10
530	Carlos Guillen	.25
531	Juan Pierre	.10
532	Scot Shields	.10
533	Scott Hatteberg	.10
534	Tim Stauffer	.10
535	Jim Edmonds	.25
536	Scott Eyre	.10
537	Ben Johnson **RC**	.10
538	Mark Mulder	.25
539	Juan Rincon	.10
540	Gustavo Chacin	.10
541	Oliver Perez	.10
542	Chris Young	.25
543	Edinson Volquez	.50
544	Mark Bellhorn	.10
545	Kelvim Escobar	.10
546	Andrew Sisco	.10
547	Derek Lowe	.25
548	Sean Burroughs	.10
549	Erik Bedard	.10
550	Alfonso Soriano	.40
551	Matt Murton	.10
552	Eric Byrnes	.10
553	Chris Duffy	.10
554	Kazuo Matsui	.10
555	Scott Rolen	.40
556	Robert Mackowiak	.10
557	Chris Burke	.10
558	Jeromy Burnitz	.10
559	Jerry Hairston Jr.	.10
560	Jim Thome	.40
561	Miguel Olivo	.10
562	Jose Castillo	.10
563	Brad Ausmus	.10
564	Yorvit Torrealba	.10
565	David DeJesus	.10
566	Paul Byrd	.10
567	Brandon Backe	.10
568	Aubrey Huff	.10
569	Mike Jacobs	.25
570	Todd Helton	.40
571	Angel Berroa	.10
572	Todd Jones	.10
573	Jeff Bagwell	.25
574	Darin Erstad	.10
575	Roy Oswalt	.25
576	Rondell White	.10
577	Alex Rios	.10
578	Wes Helms	.10
579	Javier Vazquez	.10
580	Frank Thomas	.40
581	Brian Fuentes	.10
582	Francisco Rodriguez	.10
583	Craig Counsell	.10
584	Jorge Sosa	.10
585	Mike Piazza	.50
586	Mike Scioscia	.10
587	Joe Torre	.25
588	Ken Macha	.10
589	John Gibbons	.10
590	Joe Maddon	.10
591	Eric Wedge	.10
592	Mike Hargrove	.10
593	Sam Perlozzo	.10
594	Buck Showalter	.10
595	Terry Francona	.10
596	Buddy Bell	.10
597	Jim Leyland	.10
598	Ron Gardenhire	.10
599	Ozzie Guillen	.10
600	Ned Yost	.10
601	Atlanta Braves	.10
602	Philadelphia Phillies	.10
603	New York Mets	.10
604	Washington Nationals	.10
605	Florida Marlins	.10
606	Houston Astros	.10
607	Chicago Cubs	.25
608	St. Louis Cardinals	.25
609	Pittsburgh Pirates	.10
610	Cincinnati Reds	.10
611	Colorado Rockies	.10
612	Los Angeles Dodgers	.10
613	San Francisco Giants	.10
614	San Diego Padres	.10
615	Arizona Diamondbacks	.10
616	Kenji Johjima **RC**	1.00
617	Ryan Zimmerman **RC**	2.00
618	Craig Hansen **RC**	.50
619	Joey Devine **RC**	.50

620	Hanley Ramirez **RC**	.50
621	Scott Olsen **RC**	.25
622	Jason Bergmann **RC**	.25
623	Geovany Soto **RC**	.75
624	J.J. Furmaniak **RC**	.25
625	Jeremy Accardo **RC**	.25
626	Mark Woodyard **RC**	.25
627	Matt Capps **RC**	.50
628	Tim Corcoran **RC**	.25
629	Ryan Jorgensen **RC**	.25
630	Ronny Paulino **RC**	.25
631	Dan Uggla **RC**	1.00
632	Ian Kinsler **RC**	.50
633	Josh Barfield **RC**	.25
634	Reggie Abercrombie **RC**	.25
635	Joel Zumaya **RC**	.50
636	Matt Cain **RC**	.50
637	Conor Jackson **RC**	.25
638	Bryan Anderson **RC**	.25
639	Prince Fielder **RC**	2.00
640	Jeremy Hermida **RC**	.25
641	Justin Verlander **RC**	1.00
642	Brian Bannister **RC**	.25
643	Willie Eyre **RC**	.25
644	Ricky Nolasco **RC**	.25
645	Paul Maholm **RC**	.25
646	Johnny Damon, Jason Giambi	.25
647	Rondell White, Lew Ford	.10
648	Orlando Hernandez, Orlando Hudson	.10
649	Adam Dunn, Ken Griffey Jr.	.25
650	Pat Burrell, Mike Lieberthal	.10
651	Jose Reyes, Kazuo Matsui	.10
652	Hank Blalock, Michael Young	.10
653	Prince Fielder, Rickie Weeks	.50
654	Travis Lee, Rocco Baldelli	.10
655	Derrick Lee, Aramis Ramirez	.25
656	Grady Sizemore, Aaron Boone	.25
657	Luis Gonzalez, Shawn Green, Koyie Hill	.10
658	Ivan Rodriguez, Carlos Guillen	.25
659	Alex Rodriguez, Gary Sheffield	.25
660	Ervin Santana, Francisco Rodriguez	.10

Black

Stars: 15-25X
Production 55 Sets
HTA Exclusive

2006 Topps eTopps Classics

Topps continued its eTopps Classics line-up in 2006 with cards of former greats. The format was the same as earlier issues. Like regular eTopps cards, Classics could only be ordered during a one-week Initial Player Offering period. Cards were issued in a quantity of up to 3,000 each at $9.50-12.50. The number of cards actually sold is shown parenthetically. Fronts have a color or colorized action photo, backs have a picture of one of that player's Topps cards, along with career notes, stats, etc. Values shown are for cards in a virtual portfolio, rather than "in hand." Taking physical possession of a card from an eTopps portfolio costs about $6 apiece.

Complete Set (xx):
Common Player:

Gold

Stars: 5-10X
Production 2,006 Sets

Platinum

No Pricing
Production One Set

Factory Set Rookie Bonus

		NM/M
1-5 issued in retail factory sets.
6-10 issued in hobby factory sets.

11-20 issued in holiday factory sets.

1	Nicholas Markakis	5.00
2	Kelly Shoppach	3.00
3	Jordan Tata	3.00
4	Ruddy Lugo	3.00
5	Josh Wilson	3.00
6	Fernando Nieve	3.00
7	Sendy Rleal	3.00
8	Jason Kubel	3.00
9	James Loney	5.00
10	Fabio Castro	3.00
11	Jonathan Broxton	3.00
12	Eliezer Alfonzo	3.00
13	Jason Hirsh	3.00
14	Rajai Davis	3.00
15	Henry Owens	5.00
16	Kevin Frandsen	3.00
17	Matt Garza	5.00
18	Chris Duncan	3.00
19	Chris Coste	3.00
20	Jeff Karstens	5.00

Factory Set Team Bonus

		NM/M

Issued in specified factory team sets.

BRS1	Jonathan Papelbon	10.00
BRS2	Manny Ramirez	5.00
BRS3	David Ortiz	5.00
BRS4	Josh Beckett	3.00
BRS5	Curt Schilling	4.00
CC1	Sean Marshall	3.00
CC2	Freddie Bynum	3.00
CC3	Derrek Lee	4.00
CC4	Juan Pierre	3.00
CC5	Carlos Zambrano	3.00
NYY1	Wilbert Nieves	3.00
NYY2	Alex Rodriguez	6.00
NYY3	Derek Jeter	8.00
NYY4	Mariano Rivera	5.00
NYY5	Randy Johnson	5.00
PP1	Matt Capps	3.00
PP2	Paul Maholm	3.00
PP3	Nate McLouth	3.00
PP4	John Van Benschoten	3.00
PP5	Jason Bay	4.00
SLC1	Adam Wainwright	4.00
SLC2	Skip Schumaker	3.00
SLC3	Albert Pujols	10.00
SLC4	Jim Edmonds	3.00
SLC5	Scott Rolen	5.00

Autographs

		NM/M
	Common Player:	
WB	Wade Boggs/250	50.00
JB	Jason Botts	10.00
MB	Milton Bradley	20.00
CB	Craig Breslow	10.00
FC	Fausto Carmona	15.00
BC	Brian Cashman/100	175.00
EC	Eric Chavez/200	60.00
LC	Lance Cormier	15.00
NC	Nelson Cruz	20.00
DD	Doug DeVore	8.00
TE	Theo Epstein/100	120.00
RG	Ryan Garko	20.00
AG	Alex Gordon	100.00
CG	Carlos Guillen	20.00
LH	Livan Hernandez	10.00
RH	Rich Hill	20.00
CJ	Chuck James	25.00
JJ	Josh Johnson	15.00
AL	Anthony Lerew	10.00
FL	Francisco Liriano	30.00
JM	Jeff Mathis	15.00
GN	Graig Nettles	25.00
SO	Scott Olsen	15.00
TO	Tim Olson	8.00
DO	David Ortiz/100	100.00
HR	Horacio Ramirez	10.00
DR	Darrell Rasner	10.00
ARE	Anthony Reyes	25.00
CR	Cal Ripken Jr./100	200.00
AR	Alex Rodriguez/100	450.00
RS	Ryne Sandberg/100	140.00
GS	Gary Sheffield/200	60.00
TS	Terrmel Sledge	15.00
BW	Brad Wilkerson	15.00
DW	Dave Winfield/100	150.00
MY	Michael Young	25.00

	Series 2	
GA	Garrett Atkins	20.00
CB	Clint Barmes	15.00
JB	Jose Bautista	15.00
BB	Barry Bonds/120	400.00
RC	Robinson Cano	50.00
GC	Gary Carter/250	40.00
BC	Brandon Claussen	10.00
DD	Doug Drabek/250	20.00
JF	Jeff Francis	20.00
DJ	Dan Johnson	15.00
AJ	Andruw Jones/50	50.00
SK	Scott Kazmir	25.00
DL	Derrek Lee/250	50.00
BM	Brandon McCarthy	15.00
CO	Chad Orvella	10.00
JP	Jonathan Papelbon	60.00
WP	Wily Mo Pena/250	30.00
BR	Brian Roberts/250	60.00
DSN	Duke Snider/250	60.00
DS	Darryl Strawberry/250	25.00
CV	Claudio Vargas	15.00
RZ	Ryan Zimmerman	40.00

Hit Parade

		NM/M
	Common Player:	.50
RB11	Barry Bonds	

		NM/M
	Common Team:	.50
WI	Chicago White Sox	2.00
MN	New York Mets	1.00
RR	Texas Rangers	1.00
BP	Milwaukee Brewers	.50
RC	Cincinnati Reds	1.00
PC	Philadelphia Phillies	1.00
OD	Baltimore Orioles	1.00
RD	Colorado Rockies	.50
DB	Los Angeles Dodgers	2.00
RT	Kansas City Royals	.50
MA	Seattle Mariners	1.00
AM	Houston Astros	1.00
PG	San Diego Padres	2.00
AY	Oakland Athletics	2.00
JT	Toronto Blue Jays	.50

Own the Game

		NM/M
	Complete Set (30):	20.00
	Common Player:	.50
	Inserted 1:12	
OG1	Derrek Lee	1.00
OG2	Michael Young	.75
OG3	Albert Pujols	3.00
OG4	Roger Clemens	3.00
OG5	Andy Pettitte	.75
OG6	Dontrelle Willis	.75
OG7	Michael Young	.75
OG8	Ichiro Suzuki	2.00
OG9	Derek Jeter	3.00
OG10	Andruw Jones	.75
OG11	Alex Rodriguez	3.00
OG12	David Ortiz	1.00
OG13	David Ortiz	1.00
OG14	Manny Ramirez	1.00
OG15	Mark Teixeira	1.00
OG16	Albert Pujols	3.00
OG17	Alex Rodriguez	3.00
OG18	Derek Jeter	3.00
OG19	Chad Cordero	.50
OG20	Francisco Rodriguez	.50
OG21	Mariano Rivera	.75
OG22	Chone Figgins	.50
OG23	Jose Reyes	.75
OG24	Scott Podsednik	.50
OG25	Jake Peavy	.75
OG26	Johan Santana	1.00
OG27	Pedro Martinez	1.00
OG28	Dontrelle Willis	.75
OG29	Chris Carpenter	.50
OG30	Bartolo Colon	.50

#	Player	Price
41	Ben Sheets	.40
42	Luis Castillo	.25
43	Carlos Delgado	.75
44	Cliff Floyd	.25
45	Danny Haren/SP	.50
46	Bobby Abreu	.25
47	Jeromy Burnitz	.25
48	Khalil Greene	.25
49	Moises Alou	.25
50	Alex Rodriguez/SP	5.00
51	Ervin Santana/SP	.50
52	Bartolo Colon/SP	.50
53	John Smoltz/SP	1.00
54	David Ortiz/SP	2.00
55	Hideki Matsui/SP	.50
56	Jermaine Dye/SP	.50
57	Victor Martinez/SP	.50
58	Willy Taveras/SP	.50
59	Brady Clark/SP	.50
60	Justin Morneau	.50
61	Xavier Nady	.25
62	Rich Harden	.25
63	Jack Wilson	.25
64	Brian Giles	.25
65	Jon Lieber/SP	.50
66	Dan Johnson	.25
67	Billy Wagner	.25
68	Rickie Weeks	.40
69	Chris Ray RC	.25
70	Chris Shelton	.25
71	Dmitri Young	.25
72	Ivan Rodriguez	.75
73	Jeremy Bonderman	.50
74	Justin Verlander RC	1.00
75	Randy Johnson	1.00
76	Magglio Ordonez	.50
77	Brandon Inge	.25
78	Placido Polanco	.25
79	Ryan Howard	1.00
80	Jason Bay	.50
81	Sean Casey	.25
82	Jeremy Hermida RC	.50
83	Mike Cameron	.25
84	Trevor Hoffman	.25
85	Mike Matheny/SP	.50
86	Steve Finley	.25
87	Adam Everett	.25
88	Jason Isringhausen	.25
89	Jonny Gomes	.25
90	Barry Zito	.25
91	Bobby Crosby	.25
92	Eric Chavez	.25
93	Frank Thomas	.75
94	Huston Street	.25
95	Jorge Posada	.50
96	Casey Kotchman	.25
97	Darin Erstad	.25
98	Chipper Jones	1.00
99	Jeff Francoeur	.50
100	Barry Bonds	3.00
101	Alfonso Soriano	1.00
102	Brandon Claussen	.25
103	Aaron Boone	.25
104	Roger Clemens	3.00
105	Andy Pettitte/SP	.75
106	Nick Johnson	.25
107	Tom Gordon	.25
108	Orlando Hernandez	.25
109	Francisco Rodriguez	.25
110	Orlando Cabrera	.25
111	Edgar Renteria	.25
112	Tim Hudson	.50
113	Coco Crisp	.25
114	Matt Clement	.25
115	Greg Maddux/SP	3.00
116	Paul Konerko	.50
117	Felipe Lopez	.25
118	Garrett Atkins	.50
119	Akinori Otsuka	.25
120	Craig Biggio	.50
121	Danys Baez	.25
122	Brad Penny	.25
123	Eric Gagne	.25
124	Lew Ford	.25
125	Mariano Rivera/SP	1.00
126	Carlos Beltran	.75
127	Pedro Martinez	1.00
128	Todd Helton	.75
129	Aaron Rowand	.25
130	Mike Lieberthal	.25
131	Oliver Perez	.25
132	Ryan Klesko	.25
133	Randy Winn	.25
134	Yuniesky Betancourt	.25
135	David Eckstein/SP	.50
136	Chad Orvella	.25
137	Toby Hall	.25
138	Hank Blalock	.50
139	B.J. Ryan	.25
140	Roy Halladay	.50
141	Livan Hernandez	.25
142	John Patterson	.25
143	Bengie Molina	.25
144	Brad Wilkerson	.25
145	Jorge Cantu/SP	.50
146	Mark Mulder	.50
147	Felix Hernandez	.50
148	Paul LoDuca	.25
149	Prince Fielder RC	4.00
150	Johnny Damon/SP	.50
151	Ryan Langerhans/SP	.50
152	Kris Benson/SP	.50
153	Curt Schilling/SP	2.00
154	Manny Ramirez/SP	2.00
155	Robinson Cano/SP	1.50
156	Derek Lee/SP	1.50
157	A.J. Pierzynski/SP	.50
158	Adam Dunn/SP	1.00

#	Player	Price
159	Cliff Lee/SP	.50
160	Grady Sizemore	.50
161	Jeff Francis	.50
162	Dontrelle Willis	.50
163	Brad Ausmus	.25
164	Preston Wilson	.25
165	Derek Lowe/SP	.50
166	Chris Capuano	.25
167	Joe Mauer	.50
168	Torii Hunter	.40
169	Chase Utley	.75
170	Zachary Duke	.25
171	Jason Schmidt	.25
172	Adrian Beltre	.25
173	Eddie Guardado	.25
174	Richie Sexson	.25
175	Miguel Cabrera/SP	2.00
176	Julio Lugo	.25
177	Francisco Cordero	.25
178	Kevin Millwood	.25
179	A.J. Burnett	.25
180	Jose Guillen	.25
181	Larry Bigbie	.25
182	Raul Ibanez	.25
183	Jake Peavy	.50
184	Pat Burrell	.50
185	Tom Glavine/SP	.75
186	J.J. Hardy	.25
187	Emil Brown	.25
188	Lance Berkman	.50
189	Marcus Giles	.25
190	Scott Podsednik	.25
191	Chone Figgins	.50
192	Melvin Mora	.25
193	Mark Loretta	.25
194	Carlos Zambrano	.50
195	Chien-Ming Wang	.75
196	Mark Prior	.50
197	Bobby Jenks	.25
198	Brian Fuentes	.25
199	Garret Anderson	.25
200	Ichiro Suzuki	2.00
201	Brian Roberts	.25
202	Jason Kendall	.25
203	Milton Bradley	.25
204	Jimmy Rollins	.75
205	Brett Myers/SP	.50
206	Joe Randa	.25
207	Mike Piazza	1.00
208	Matt Morris	.25
209	Omar Vizquel	.25
210	Jeremy Reed	.25
211	Chris Carpenter	.50
212	Jim Edmonds	.50
213	Scott Kazmir	.50
214	Travis Lee	.25
215	Michael Young/SP	.50
216	Rod Barajas	.25
217	Gustavo Chacin	.25
218	Lyle Overbay	.25
219	Troy Glaus	.50
220	Chad Cordero	.25
221	Jose Vidro	.25
222	Scott Rolen	.50
223	Carl Crawford	.50
224	Rocco Baldelli	.50
225	Mike Mussina	.50
226	Kelvim Escobar	.25
227	Corey Patterson	.25
228	Javy Lopez	.25
229	Jonathan Papelbon/ SP RC	5.00
230	Aramis Ramirez	.50
231	Tadahito Iguchi	.50
232	Morgan Ensberg	.25
233	Mark Grudzielanek	.25
234	Mike Sweeney	.25
235	Shawn Chacon/SP	.50
236	Nick Punto	.25
237	Geoff Jenkins	.25
238	Carlos Lee	.25
239	David DeJesus	.25
240	Brad Lidge	.25
241	Bob Wickman	.25
242	Jon Garland	.25
243	Kerry Wood	.50
244	Bronson Arroyo	.25
245	Matt Holliday/SP	.50
246	Josh Beckett	.75
247	Johan Santana	.75
248	Rafael Furcal	.50
249	Shannon Stewart	.25
250	Gary Sheffield	.50
251	Josh Barfield RC	.50
252	Kenji Johjima RC	.75
253	Ian Kinsler RC	1.50
254	Brian Anderson RC	.50
255	Matt Cain RC	1.00
256	Josh Willingham/SP RC	1.50
257	John Koronka RC	.50
258	Chris Duffy RC	.50
259	Brian McCann RC	2.00
260	Hanley Ramirez RC	3.00
261	Hong-Chih Kuo RC	.75
262	Francisco Liriano RC	2.00
263	Anderson Hernandez RC	.50
264	Ryan Zimmerman RC	4.00
265	Brian Bannister/SP RC	1.00
266	Nolan Ryan	2.00
267	Frank Robinson	.50
268	Roberto Clemente	3.00
269	Hank Greenberg	.50
270	Napoleon Lajoie	.25
271	Lloyd Waner	.25
272	Paul Waner	.25
273	Frankie Frisch	.25
274	Bill "Moose" Skowron	.25
275	Mickey Mantle	6.00

#	Player	Price
276	Brooks Robinson	1.00
277	Carl Yastrzemski	1.00
278	Johnny Pesky	.25
279	Stan Musial	1.50
280	Bill Mazeroski	.50
281	Harmon Killebrew	.75
282	Monte Irvin	.50
283	Bob Gibson	1.00
284	Ted Williams	2.00
285	Yogi Berra/SP	2.00
286	Ernie Banks	1.00
287	Bobby Doerr	.25
288	Josh Gibson	.50
289	Bob Feller	.25
290	Cal Ripken Jr.	3.00
291	Bobby Cox	.25
292	Terry Francona	.25
293	Dusty Baker	.25
294	Ozzie Guillen	.25
295	Jim Leyland	.50
296	Willie Randolph	.25
297	Joe Torre	.50
298	Felipe Alou	.25
299	Tony LaRussa	.25
300	Frank Robinson	.50
301	Mike Tyson	.25
302	Duke Paoa Kahanamoku	.25
303	Jennie Finch	2.00
304	Brandi Chastain	.25
305	Danica Patrick/SP	10.00
306	Wendy Guey	.25
307	Hulk Hogan	.25
308	Carl Lewis	.25
309	John Wooden	.25
310	Randy Couture	.25
311	Andy Irons	.25
312	Takeru Kobayashi	.25
313	Leon Spinks	.25
314	Jim Thorpe	1.00
315	Jerry Bailey/SP	.50
316	Adrian C. Anson	.25
317	John M. Ward	.25
318	Mike Kelly	.25
319	Cpt. Jack Glasscock	.25
320	Aaron Hill	.25
321	Derrick Turnbow	.25
322	Nicholas Markakis	.25
323	Brad Hawpe	.25
324	Kevin Mench	.25
325	John Lackey/SP	.50
326	Chester A. Arthur	.25
327	Ulysses S. Grant	.50
328	Abraham Lincoln	1.00
329	Grover Cleveland	.25
330	Benjamin Harrison	.25
331	Theodore Roosevelt	.50
332	Rutherford B. Hayes	.25
333	Chancellor Otto Von Bismarck	.25
334	Kaiser Wilhelm II	.25
335	Queen Victoria/SP	.50
336	Pope Leo XIII	.25
337	Thomas Edison	.50
338	Orville Wright	.50
339	Wilbur Wright	.50
340	Nathaniel Hawthorne	.25
341	Herman Melville	.25
342	Stonewall Jackson	.50
343	Robert E. Lee	.50
344	Andrew Carnegie	.25
345	John Rockefeller/SP	.25
346	Bob Fitzsimmons	.25
347	Billy the Kid	.25
348	Buffalo Bill	.50
349	Jesse James	.25
350	Statue of Liberty	.25

Mini

BRONSON ARROYO.
ALLEN & GINTER'S
BROOKLYN. NEW YORK

Mini:	2-4X
SP's:	1-2X
Mini SP's Inserted 1:13	
Mini (351-375):	No Pricing
#'s 351-375 Inserted In Rip Cards	
Allen & Ginter Back:	3-6X
Inserted 1:5	
A & G Back SP's:	2-3X
Inserted 1:65	
Bazooka Mini:	No Pricing
Production 25 Sets	
Black Mini:	5-10X
Inserted 1:10	
Black SP:	3-5X

Inserted 1:130	
Wood:	No Pricing
Production One Set	

Printing Plates

No Pricing
Production one set per color.

Relics

		NM/M
	Common Player:	4.00
CBA	Clint Barmes	4.00
CB	Carlos Beltran	10.00
BB	Barry Bonds	20.00
MB	Mark Buehrle	8.00
GWB	George W. Bush	300.00
MC	Miguel Cabrera	10.00
RC	Robinson Cano	20.00
JC	Jorge Cantu	6.00
EC	Eric Chavez	6.00
BC	Bobby Crosby	4.00
JD	Johnny Damon	12.00
CD	Carlos Delgado	8.00
ZD	Zachary Duke	8.00
JDY	Jermaine Dye	8.00
JF	Jeff Francoeur	15.00
JG	Jonny Gomes	6.00
VG	Vladimir Guerrero	10.00
TH	Travis Hafner	8.00
FH	Felix Hernandez	8.00
MH	Matt Holliday	8.00
RH	Ryan Howard	30.00
JFK	John F. Kennedy	375.00
PK	Paul Konerko	10.00
HCK	Hong-Chih Kuo	20.00
RL	Ryan Langerhans	8.00
MM	Mickey Mantle	125.00
PM	Pedro Martinez	10.00
VM	Victor Martinez	8.00
HM	Hideki Matsui	15.00
BM	Brandon McCarthy	4.00
DO	David Ortiz	15.00
RO	Roy Oswalt	6.00
JP	Jake Peavy	6.00
APE	Andy Pettitte	6.00
MPZ	Mike Piazza	10.00
MP	Mark Prior	10.00
AP	Albert Pujols	20.00
MR	Manny Ramirez	10.00
AR	Alex Rodriguez	20.00
JS	Johan Santana	10.00
CS	Curt Schilling	10.00
GS	Gary Sheffield	6.00
HS	Huston Street	6.00
NS	Nick Swisher	6.00
WT	Willy Taveras	6.00
MT	Miguel Tejada	10.00
FT	Frank Thomas	8.00
JT	Jim Thome	10.00
CU	Chase Utley	15.00
CMW	Chien-Ming Wang	50.00
DWI	Dontrelle Willis	8.00
DW	David Wright	15.00

Autographs

		NM/M
Cards are not serial numbered.		
JB	Jerry Bailey/200	80.00
JBA	Josh Barfield	10.00
CB	Clint Barmes	15.00
BB	Barry Bonds/25	500.00
MC	Miguel Cabrera/100	150.00
RC	Robinson Cano	80.00
BC	Brandi Chastain/200	15.00
EC	Eric Chavez	15.00
RA	Randy Couture	150.00
BF	Bob Feller	75.00
PF	Prince Fielder	80.00
JF	Jennie Finch/200	150.00
LF	Lew Ford	15.00
JG	Jonny Gomes	15.00
VG	Vladimir Guerrero/50	225.00
WG	Wendy Guey	30.00
TG	Tony Gwynn/50	250.00
TH	Travis Hafner	25.00
HH	Hulk Hogan/200	250.00
RH	Ryan Howard	150.00
AI	Andy Irons/200	40.00
KJ	Kenji Johjima/50	75.00
SK	Scott Kazmir	25.00
TK	Takeru Kobayashi/200	75.00
DL	Derek Lee	40.00
CL	Carl Lewis/200	120.00
FL	Francisco Liriano	30.00
VM	Victor Martinez	30.00
SM	Stan Musial/50	400.00
DP	Danica Patrick/100	500.00
WMP	Wily Mo Pena	20.00

#	Player	Price
CR	Cal Ripken Jr./50	300.00
AR	Alex Rodriguez/50	400.00
BJR	B.J. Ryan	15.00
NR	Nolan Ryan/50	375.00
ES	Ervin Santana	15.00
JS	Johan Santana/100	85.00
GS	Gary Sheffield/50	140.00
OS	Ozzie Smith/75	200.00
LS	Leon Spinks/200	75.00
HS	Huston Street	40.00
MT	Mike Tyson/200	275.00
CU	Chase Utley	80.00
BW	Billy Wagner	25.00
CMW	Chien-Ming Wang/100	200.00
DWI	Dontrelle Willis/100	40.00
JW	John Wooden/200	250.00
DW	David Wright	140.00
CY	Carl Yastrzemski/50	325.00
MY	Michael Young	35.00
RZ	Ryan Zimmerman	50.00

Dick Perez Sketches

		NM/M
Common Player		.25
Inserted 1:1		
Originals:		No Pricing
Production One Set		
ARI	Shawn Green	.25
ATL	Andruw Jones	.50
BAL	Miguel Tejada	.50
BOS	David Ortiz	1.00
CHC	Derek Lee	.50
CHW	Paul Konerko	.50
CIN	Ken Griffey Jr.	1.00
CLE	Travis Hafner	.50
COL	Todd Helton	.50
DET	Ivan Rodriguez	.50
FLA	Miguel Cabrera	.75
HOU	Lance Berkman	.25
KC	Mike Sweeney	.25
LAA	Vladimir Guerrero	.75
LAD	Rafael Furcal	.25
MIL	Carlos Lee	.25
MIN	Johan Santana	.50
NYM	David Wright	1.00
NYY	Alex Rodriguez	2.00
OAK	Huston Street	.25
PHI	Bobby Abreu	.50
PIT	Jason Bay	.50
SDP	Jake Peavy	.50
SEA	Ichiro Suzuki	1.50
SFG	Barry Bonds	2.00
STL	Albert Pujols	2.00
TAM	Aubrey Huff	.25
TEX	Mark Teixeira	.50
TOR	Vernon Wells	.25
WAS	Alfonso Soriano	.75

Postcards

		NM/M
Inserted 1:2 Hobby Boxes		
BB	Barry Bonds	4.00
JG	Josh Gibson	2.00
KG	Ken Griffey Jr.	3.00
VG	Vladimir Guerrero	2.00
DJ	Derek Jeter	4.00
MM	Mickey Mantle	10.00
DO	David Ortiz	2.00
AP	Albert Pujols	4.00
MR	Manny Ramirez	2.00
CR	Cal Ripken Jr.	6.00
AR	Alex Rodriguez	4.00
I	Ichiro Suzuki	3.00
MT	Miguel Tejada	1.50
TW	Ted Williams	4.00
DW	David Wright	3.00

Personalized Postcards

One Set Produced

Allen & Ginter N43

		NM/M
Inserted 1:2 Hobby Boxes		
1	Alex Rodriguez	4.00
2	Barry Bonds	4.00
3	Albert Pujols	4.00
4	Josh Gibson	2.00
5	Nolan Ryan	4.00
6	Ichiro Suzuki	3.00
7	Mickey Mantle	10.00
8	Ted Williams	4.00
9	David Wright	3.00
10	Ken Griffey Jr.	3.00
11	Mark Teixeira	1.50
12	Adrian C. Anson	2.00
13	Mike Tyson	3.00
14	Kenji Johjima	2.00
15	Ryan Zimmerman	2.00

Allen & Ginter N43 Autos

Production 10 Sets

Allen & Ginter N43 Relics

		NM/M
Production 50 Sets		
AP	Albert Pujols	100.00
JG	Josh Gibson	250.00

Rip Card

		NM/M
All prices for unripped cards.		
1-4: Production 10 Sets		
5-9: Production 15 Sets		
10-19: Production 25 Sets		
20-50: Production 99 Sets		
RIP20	Kenji Johjima	100.00
RIP21	Cap Anson	100.00
RIP22	Ryan Zimmerman	100.00
RIP23	Andruw Jones	100.00
RIP24	Barry Bonds	150.00
RIP25	Cal Ripken Jr.	150.00
RIP26	David Ortiz	100.00
RIP27	Hideki Matsui	150.00
RIP28	Ken Griffey Jr.	150.00
RIP29	Manny Ramirez	150.00
RIP30	Mickey Mantle	200.00
RIP31	Alex Rodriguez	150.00
RIP32	Miguel Cabrera	150.00
RIP33	Miguel Tejada	100.00
RIP34	Pedro Martinez	100.00
RIP35	Albert Pujols	150.00
RIP36	Alex Rodriguez	150.00
RIP37	Alex Rodriguez, Derek Jeter	150.00
RIP38	Barry Bonds	150.00
RIP39	Derek Jeter	180.00
RIP40	Ichiro Suzuki	150.00
RIP41	Ichiro Suzuki, Hideki Matsui	150.00
RIP42	Josh Gibson	150.00
RIP43	Mickey Mantle	200.00
RIP44	Jonathan Papelbon	150.00
RIP45	Mickey Mantle, Ted Williams	200.00
RIP46	Albert Pujols	150.00
RIP47	Roberto Clemente	150.00
RIP48	Roger Clemens	150.00
RIP49	Ted Williams	150.00
RIP50	Vladimir Guerrero	100.00

2006 Topps Bazooka

JOHNNY DAMON

		NM/M
Complete Set (220):		30.00
Common Player:		.10
Pack (8):		2.50
Box (24):		50.00
1	Josh Gibson	.50
2	Scott Podsednik	.10
3	Sammy Sosa	.75
4	Ivan Rodriguez	.40
5	Derek Jeter	1.50
6	Manny Ramirez	.50
7	Nook Logan	.10
8	Adam Dunn	.40
9	Travis Hafner	.25
10	Felix Hernandez	.40
11	Larry Bigbie	.10
12	Magglio Ordonez	.25
13	Josh Beckett	.25
14	Mike Sweeney	.10
15	Mickey Mantle	2.00
16	Grady Sizemore	.25
17	Brian Fuentes	.10
18	Wily Mo Pena	.10
19	Morgan Ensberg	.10
20	Tim Hudson	.25
21	Justin Verlander RC	.25
22	Jermaine Dye	.10

#	Player	Price
23	Miguel Cabrera	.50
24	Greg Maddux	1.00
25	Jason Giambi	.25
26	Ben Sheets	.25
27	Brad Radke	.10
28	Torii Hunter	.25
29	Mike Piazza	.75
30	Jason Kendall	.10
31	Pat Burrell	.25
32	Khalil Greene	.25
33	Brian Roberts	.25
34	C.C. Sabathia	.25
35	Mike Mussina	.40
36	Bob Wickman	.10
37	Dmitri Young	.10
38	Dontrelle Willis	.25
39	David DeJesus	.25
40	J.D. Drew	.25
41	Chad Tracy	.10
42	Joe Mauer	.25
43	Melvin Mora	.10
44	Carlos Zambrano	.25
45	Mariano Rivera	.25
46	Coco Crisp	.10
47	Derrek Lee	.50
48	Cliff Floyd	.10
49	Willy Taveras	.10
50	Albert Pujols	1.50
51	Aaron Boone	.10
52	Mark Mulder	.25
53	Brad Wilkerson	.10
54	Hank Blalock	.25
55	Hideki Matsui	1.00
56	Victor Martinez	.10
57	Jeremy Bonderman	.10
58	Felipe Lopez	.10
59	Paul LoDuca	.10
60	Derek Lowe	.10
61	Luis Gonzalez	.10
62	Paul Konerko	.25
63	Miguel Tejada	.40
64	Jeromy Burnitz	.10
65	Orlando Hernandez	.10
66	Curt Schilling	.50
67	Joe Nathan	.10
68	Jose Reyes	.25
69	David Wright	.75
70	Eric Chavez	.25
71	Rich Harden	.25
72	A.J. Pierzynski	.10
73	Trevor Hoffman	.10
74	Adrian Beltre	.10
75	Alex Rodriguez	1.50
76	Larry Walker	.25
77	Jorge Cantu	.10
78	Mark Teixeira	.40
79	Jeff Bagwell	.25
80	Jeff Francoeur	.25
81	Ichiro Suzuki	1.00
82	Jhonny Peralta	.10
83	Todd Helton	.25
84	Brad Penny	.10
85	Shawn Chacon	.10
86	Billy Wagner	.10
87	Jason Schmidt	.25
88	Austin Kearns	.10
89	Chris Carpenter	.10
90	Chipper Jones	.50
91	Shawn Green	.25
92	A.J. Burnett	.10
93	Joe Crede	.10
94	Mark Prior	.40
95	Andy Pettitte	.25
96	Edgar Renteria	.10
97	Roy Halladay	.25
98	Eric Milton	.10
99	Craig Biggio	.25
100	Barry Bonds	1.50
101	Troy Glaus	.10
102	Aaron Rowand	.10
103	Aramis Ramirez	.25
104	Nomar Garciaparra	.50
105	Randy Johnson	.50
106	David Ortiz	.50
107	Vinny Castilla	.10
108	Carl Crawford	.25
109	Zachary Duke	.10
110	Barry Zito	.25
111	Darin Erstad	.10
112	Chris Capuano	.10
113	Javy Lopez	.10
114	Lew Ford	.10
115	Robinson Cano	.25
116	Ronnie Belliard	.10
117	Placido Polanco	.10
118	Rickie Weeks	.25
119	Brad Lidge	.10
120	Andruw Jones	.40
121	Nick Swisher	.25
122	Bartolo Colon	.10
123	Juan Pierre	.10
124	Johan Santana	.50
125	Jorge Posada	.25
126	Jeff Francis	.10
127	Matt Holliday	.25
128	Carlos Delgado	.25
129	Zack Greinke	.10
130	Lyle Overbay	.10
131	Conor Jackson RC	.10
132	Mark Buehrle	.25
133	Chone Figgins	.10
134	Pedro Martinez	.25
135	Roger Clemens	1.50
136	Raul Ibanez	.10
137	Jim Edmonds	.25
138	Michael Young	.25
139	Preston Wilson	.10
140	Rafael Furcal	.10

#	Player	Price
141	Bobby Abreu	.25
142	Tadahito Iguchi	.25
143	B.J. Ryan	.10
144	Francisco Rodriguez	.10
145	J.T. Snow	.10
146	Aubrey Huff	.10
147	Mike Morse	.10
148	Jason Bay	.25
149	Roy Oswalt	.25
150	Carlos Beltran	.40
151	Carlos Lee	.25
152	Emil Brown	.10
153	Craig Monroe	.10
154	Kris Benson	.10
155	Gary Sheffield	.40
156	Jake Peavy	.25
157	David Eckstein	.10
158	Tom Glavine	.25
159	Jeff Kent	.25
160	Livan Hernandez	.10
161	Orlando Hudson	.10
162	Randy Winn	.10
163	Jimmy Rollins	.20
164	Luis Castillo	.10
165	Nick Johnson	.10
166	Johnny Damon	.50
167	Eric Gagne	.25
168	Geoff Jenkins	.10
169	Mike Cameron	.10
170	Marcus Giles	.10
171	Huston Street	.25
172	Moises Alou	.10
173	Scott Rolen	.50
174	Jose Vidro	.10
175	Alfonso Soriano	.40
176	Toby Hall	.10
177	Orlando Cabrera	.10
178	Brian Giles	.10
179	Erubiel Durazo	.10
180	Matt Morris	.10
181	Jack Wilson	.10
182	Brady Clark	.10
183	Shannon Stewart	.10
184	Kerry Wood	.25
185	Carl Pavano	.10
186	Chase Utley	.25
187	Omar Vizquel	.10
188	Vladimir Guerrero	.50
189	Richie Sexson	.25
190	John Smoltz	.25
191	Garret Anderson	.10
192	Jon Garland	.10
193	Julio Lugo	.10
194	Rocco Baldelli	.10
195	Jaret Wright	.10
196	Matt Clement	.10
197	Vernon Wells	.10
198	Sean Casey	.10
199	Lance Berkman	.25
200	Justin Morneau	.25
201	Shaun Marcum RC	.20
202	Chuck James RC	.20
203	Hong-Chih Kuo RC	.20
204	Darrell Rasner RC	.20
205	Anthony Reyes RC	.20
206	Francisco Liriano RC	.50
207	Joe Saunders RC	.20
208	Fausto Carmona RC	.20
209	Charlton Jimerson RC	.20
210	Bryan Bullington RC	.20
211	Tom Gorzelanny RC	.40
212	Anderson Hernandez RC	.20
213	Ryan Garko RC	.20
214	John Koronka RC	.20
215	Chris Denorfia RC	.20
216	Jeff Mathis RC	.20
217	Jose Bautista RC	.20
218	Danny Sandoval RC	.20
219	Robert Andino RC	.20
220	Justin Huber RC	.20

Gold

Stars: 1-2X
Inserted 1:1

Autographs

		NM/M
BM	Brandon McCarthy	10.00
KM	Kevin Millar	20.00
MM	Mike Morse	10.00
VZ	Victor Zambrano	10.00

Bazooka Basics

		NM/M
BA	Bobby Abreu	4.00
LB	Lance Berkman	6.00
CB	Craig Biggio	4.00
HB	Hank Blalock	4.00
SB	Sean Burroughs	4.00
MC	Miguel Cabrera	8.00
JD	Johnny Damon	8.00
CD	Carlos Delgado	4.00
EG	Eric Gagne	6.00
MG	Marcus Giles	4.00
MH	Matt Holliday	4.00
TH	Tim Hudson	4.00
HR	Hanley Ramirez	6.00
MR	Manny Ramirez	8.00
ER	Edgar Renteria	4.00
BR	Brian Roberts	4.00
AR	Alex Rodriguez	15.00
JR	Jimmy Rollins	4.00
AR	Aaron Rowand	4.00
TS	Terrmel Sledge	4.00
WT	Willy Taveras	4.00
FT	Frank Thomas	6.00
KT	Kevin Thompson	4.00
CU	Chase Utley	8.00
JV	Justin Verlander	6.00
RW	Rickie Weeks	4.00

Bazooka Blasts

		NM/M
BA	Bobby Abreu	4.00
MA	Moises Alou	4.00
JB	Jason Bay	8.00
CB	Carlos Beltran	6.00
HB	Hank Blalock	4.00
BB	Barry Bonds	20.00
CC	Coco Crisp	4.00
JD	Johnny Damon	8.00
JD	J.D. Drew	4.00
AD	Adam Dunn	6.00
CF	Cliff Floyd	4.00
TG	Troy Glaus	4.00
VG	Vladimir Guerrero	6.00
GJ	Geoff Jenkins	4.00
AJ	Andruw Jones	6.00
CJ	Chipper Jones	8.00
PK	Paul Konerko	6.00
DL	Derrek Lee	6.00
PL	Paul LoDuca	4.00
ML	Mark Loretta	4.00
MM	Mickey Mantle/100	175.00
VM	Victor Martinez	4.00
TN	Trot Nixon	4.00
DO	David Ortiz	8.00
CP	Corey Patterson	4.00
MP	Mike Piazza	8.00
AR	Aramis Ramirez	4.00
AR	Alex Rodriguez	15.00
GS	Gary Sheffield	6.00
SS	Sammy Sosa	8.00
MT	Miguel Tejada	8.00
JT	Jim Thome	6.00
PW	Preston Wilson	4.00
DW	David Wright	10.00

Bazooka Rewind

		NM/M
CB	Clint Barmes	4.00
WB	William Bergolla	4.00
LB	Lance Berkman	4.00
CBI	Craig Biggio	6.00
JB	Jason Botts	4.00
PB	Pat Burrell	4.00
RC	Robinson Cano	15.00
SC	Shin-Soo Choo	4.00
CC	Carl Crawford	6.00
NC	Nelson Cruz	6.00
JDA	Johnny Damon	8.00
JD	Jermaine Dye	4.00
CE	Carl Everett	4.00
RG	Ryan Garko	4.00
JG	Jon Garland	4.00
MG	Mark Grudzielanek	4.00
JG	Jose Guillen	4.00
CG	Cristian Guzman	4.00
JH	Justin Huber	4.00
MJ	Mike Jacobs	8.00
NJ	Nick Johnson	4.00
AJ	Andruw Jones	6.00
AK	Adam Kennedy	4.00
PK	Paul Konerko	6.00
AML	Adam LaRoche	4.00
CL	Carlos Lee	4.00
FL	Francisco Liriano	8.00
LM	Luis Montanez	4.00
MM	Miguel Montero	6.00
AP	A.J. Pierzynski	6.00
SP	Scott Podsednik	4.00
HR	Hanley Ramirez	6.00
MR	Manny Ramirez	8.00
ER	Edgar Renteria	4.00
BR	Brian Roberts	4.00
AR	Alex Rodriguez	15.00
JR	Jimmy Rollins	4.00
AR	Aaron Rowand	4.00
TS	Terrmel Sledge	4.00

Comics

	NM/M
Complete Set (24):	10.00
Common Player:	.25
Inserted 1:4	
1 Greg Maddux	1.00
2 Alex Rodriguez	1.00
3 Trevor Hoffman	.25
4 Rafael Palmeiro	.50
5 Roy Oswalt	.50
6 Bobby Abreu	.25
7 Miguel Tejada	.50
8 Vladimir Guerrero	.50
9 Mark Teixeira	.25
10 Zachary Duke	.25
11 Xavier Nady	.25
12 Alex Rodriguez	1.00
13 Jeremy Hermida	.25
14 Craig Biggio	.25
15 Manny Ramirez	.50
16 Texas Rangers	.25
17 Oakland A's	.25
18 Alex Rodriguez	1.00
19 Jason Giambi	.50
20 Aaron Small	.25
21 Jimmy Rollins	.25
22 Roger Clemens	1.00
23 White Sox/Mariners	.50
24 Andruw Jones	.50

Fortune

Stars: 1-2X
Inserted 1:1

Mickey Mantle Oversized Reprint

	NM/M
1952 Mickey Mantle	40.00
1953 Mickey Mantle	30.00
1956 Mickey Mantle	25.00
1957 Mickey Mantle	25.00
1958 Mickey Mantle	25.00
1959 Mickey Mantle	25.00
1960 Mickey Mantle	25.00
1961 Mickey Mantle	25.00
1962 Mickey Mantle	25.00
1963 Mickey Mantle	20.00
1964 Mickey Mantle	25.00
1965 Mickey Mantle	25.00
1966 Mickey Mantle	25.00
1967 Mickey Mantle	25.00
1968 Mickey Mantle	25.00
1969 Mickey Mantle	25.00

Stamps

	NM/M
Complete Set (30):	15.00
Common Player:	.50
Inserted 1:3 Hobby	
1 Bobby Abreu	.50
2 Lance Berkman	.50
3 Hank Blalock	.50
4 Barry Bonds	2.00
5 Mark Buehrle	.50
6 Miguel Cabrera	1.00
7 Jim Edmonds	.50
8 Morgan Ensberg	.50
9 Jeff Francoeur	.50
10 Roy Halladay	.50
11 Tim Hudson	.50
12 Derek Jeter	2.00
13 Andruw Jones	.75
14 Chipper Jones	.75
15 Derrek Lee	.75
16 Mickey Mantle	3.00
17 Victor Martinez	.50
18 Justin Morneau	.50
19 Manny Ramirez	1.00
20 Brian Roberts	.50
21 Alex Rodriguez	2.00
22 Ivan Rodriguez	.50
23 Johan Santana	.50
24 Alfonso Soriano	.50
25 Huston Street	.50

BW	Bernie Williams	6.00
DW	Dontrelle Willis	6.00
DW	Dontrelle Willis	6.00
CY	Chris Young	4.00

4-on-1 Stickers

	NM/M
1 Josh Gibson, Mickey Mantle, Alex Rodriguez, Barry Bonds	2.00
2 Jason Giambi, David Ortiz, Carlos Delgado, Jeff Bagwell	.75
3 Vernon Wells, Shannon Stewart, Carl Crawford, Torii Hunter	.50
4 Jason Kendall, Javy Lopez, Joe Mauer, Jorge Posada	.50
5 Roger Clemens, Andy Pettitte, Mike Mussina, Orlando Hernandez	1.00
6 Ivan Rodriguez, Rafael Palmeiro, Alfonso Soriano, Hank Blalock	.50
7 Pedro Martinez, Curt Schilling, Matt Clement, Derek Lowe	.75
8 J.D. Drew, Andruw Jones, Gary Sheffield, Vladimir Guerrero	.50
9 Tim Hudson, Greg Maddux, Tom Glavine, John Smoltz	.75
10 Justin Morneau, Albert Pujols, Mark Teixeira, Derrek Lee	1.00
11 B.J. Ryan, Bob Wickman, Mariano Rivera, Trevor Hoffman	.50
12 Mike Morse, Mike Cameron, Mike Piazza, Mike Sweeney	.75
13 Michael Young, Jimmy Rollins, David Eckstein, Orlando Cabrera	.50
14 A.J. Burnett, A.J. Pierzynski, C.C. Sabathia, J.T. Snow	.50
15 Hideki Matsui, Ichiro Suzuki, Tadahito Iguchi, Chase Utley	1.00
16 Barry Zito, Zachary Duke, Zack Greinke, Jeff Francis	.50
17 Mark Buehrle, Mark Mulder, Mark Prior, Marcus Giles	.75
18 Sammy Sosa, Manny Ramirez, Bobby Abreu, Wily Mo Pena	.75
19 Scott Podsednik, Preston Wilson, Juan Pierre, Carlos Beltran	.50
20 Francisco Rodriguez, Billy Wagner, Huston Street, Joe Nathan	.50
21 Melvin Mora, Morgan Ensberg, Scott Rolen, Eric Chavez	.50
22 Garret Anderson, Jim Edmonds, Johnny Damon, Moises Alou	.50
23 Derek Jeter, Edgar Renteria, Miguel Tejada, Julio Lugo	1.00
24 Felix Hernandez, Dontrelle Willis, Rich Harden, Brian Fuentes	.50
25 Bartolo Colon, Jason Schmidt, Jeremy Bonderman, Carlos Zambrano	.50
26 Randy Johnson, Johan Santana, Roy Halladay, Chris Carpenter	.75
27 Roy Oswalt, Shawn Chacon, Kris Benson, Josh Beckett	.50
28 Jose Reyes, Felipe Lopez, Rafael Furcal, Jhonny Peralta	.50
29 Justin Verlander, Kerry Wood, Livan Hernandez, Matt Morris	.50
30 Khalil Greene, Nomar Garciaparra, Omar Vizquel, Jack Wilson	.50
31 Pat Burrell, Rocco Baldelli, Shawn Green, Jason Bay	.50
32 Brad Lidge, Brad Penny, Brad Radke, Brian Roberts	.50
33 Jeff Francoeur, Willy Taveras, Rickie Weeks, Robinson Cano	.50
34 Geoff Jenkins, Lance Berkman, Larry Bigbie, Matt Holliday	.50
35 Paul LoDuca, Toby Hall, Victor Martinez, Carlos Lee	.50
36 Aramis Ramirez, Chipper Jones, David Wright, Troy Glaus	.75
37 Randy Winn, Brad Wilkerson, Craig Monroe, Aaron Rowand	.50
38 Aaron Boone, Adrian Beltre, Vinny Castilla, Chone Figgins	.50
39 Larry Walker, Cliff Floyd, Luis Gonzalez, Adam Dunn	.50
40 Ronnie Belliard, Jeff Kent, Jorge Cantu, Placido Polanco	.50
41 Craig Biggio, Jose Vidro, Luis Castillo, Orlando Hudson	.50
42 Grady Sizemore, Lew Ford, Nick Swisher, Brian Giles	.50
43 David DeJesus, Emil Brown, Coco Crisp, Jeromy Burnitz	.50
44 Eric Gagne, Eric Milton, Jake Peavy, Jaret Wright	.50
45 Aubrey Huff, Austin Kearns, Brady Clark, Nook Logan	.50
46 Ben Sheets, Carl Pavano, Chris Capuano, Jon Garland	.50
47 Darin Erstad, Dmitri Young, Erubiel Durazo, Travis Hafner	.50
48 Magglio Ordonez, Miguel Cabrera, Jermaine Dye, Conor Jackson	.50
49 Richie Sexson, Sean Casey, Chad Tracy, Lyle Overbay	.50
50 Nick Johnson, Paul Konerko, Raul Ibanez, Todd Helton	.50
51 Shaun Marcum, Chuck James, Hong-Chih Kuo, Darrell Rasner	.50
52 Anthony Reyes, Francisco Liriano, Joe Saunders, Fausto Carmona	.50
53 Charlton Jimerson, Bryan Bullington, Tom Gorzelanny; Anderson Hernandez	.50
54 Ryan Garko, John Koronka, Chris Denorfia, Jeff Mathis	.50
55 Jose Bautista, Danny Sandoval, Robert Andino, Alex Gordon	.50

2006 Topps Chrome

		NM/M
Complete Set (354):		
Common Player:		.25
Common Auto. (331-354):		10.00
Pack (4):		3.00
Box (24):		60.00
1	Alex Rodriguez	3.00
2	Garrett Atkins	.25
3	Carl Crawford	.50
4	Clint Barmes	.25
5	Tadahito Iguchi	.50
6	Brian Roberts	.50
7	Mickey Mantle	8.00
8	David Wright	2.00
9	Jeremy Reed	.25
10	Bobby Abreu	.50
11	Lance Berkman	.50
12	Jonny Gomes	.25
13	Jason Marquis	.25
14	Chipper Jones	1.00
15	Jon Garland	.25
16	Brad Wilkerson	.25
17	Rickie Weeks	.50
18	Jorge Posada	.50
19	Greg Maddux	2.00
20	Jeff Francis	.25
21	Felipe Lopez	.25
22	Dan Johnson	.25
23	Manny Ramirez	1.00
24	Joe Mauer	.75
25	Randy Winn	.25
26	Pedro Feliz	.25
27	Kenny Rogers	.25
28	Rocco Baldelli	.25
29	Nomar Garciaparra	.75
30	Carlos Lee	.50
31	Tom Glavine	.50
32	Craig Biggio	.50
33	Steve Finley	.25
34	Eric Gagne	.40
35	Dallas McPherson	.25
36	Mark Kotsay	.25
37	Kerry Wood	.50
38	Huston Street	.50
39	Hank Blalock	.50

#	Player	Price
40	Brad Radke	.25
41	Chien-Ming Wang	.75
42	Mark Buehrle	.40
43	Andy Pettitte	.50
44	Bernie Williams	.50
45	Victor Martinez	.50
46	Darin Erstad	.40
47	Gustavo Chacin	.25
48	Carlos Guillen	.50
49	Lyle Overbay	.25
50	Barry Bonds	3.00
51	Nook Logan	.25
52	Mark Teahen	.25
53	Mike Lamb	.25
54	Jayson Werth	.25
55	Mariano Rivera	.50
56	Julio Lugo	.25
57	Adam Dunn	.75
58	Troy Percival	.25
59	Chad Tracy	.25
60	Edgar Renteria	.50
61	Jason Giambi	.75
62	Justin Morneau	.75
63	Carlos Delgado	.50
64	John Buck	.25
65	Shannon Stewart	.25
66	Mike Cameron	.25
67	Richie Sexson	.50
68	Russ Adams	.25
69	Josh Beckett	.75
70	Ryan Freel	.25
71	Victor Zambrano	.25
72	Ronnie Belliard	.25
73	Brian Giles	.40
74	Randy Wolf	.25
75	Robinson Cano	.25
76	Joe Blanton	.25
77	Esteban Loaiza	.25
78	Troy Glaus	.50
79	Matt Clement	.25
80	Geoff Jenkins	.25
81	Roy Oswalt	.50
82	A.J. Pierzynski	.25
83	Pedro Martinez	1.00
84	Roger Clemens	3.00
85	Jack Wilson	.25
86	Mike Piazza	1.00
87	Paul LoDuca	.25
88	Jeff Bagwell	.50
89	Carlos Zambrano	.50
90	Brandon Claussen	.25
91	Travis Hafner	.50
92	Chris Shelton	.25
93	Rafael Furcal	.25
94	Frank Thomas	.75
95	Noah Lowry	.25
96	Jhonny Peralta	.25
97	Vernon Wells	.50
98	Jorge Cantu	.25
99	Willy Taveras	.25
100	Ivan Rodriguez	.50
101	Jose Reyes	.75
102	Barry Zito	.50
103	Mark Teixeira	.50
104	Chone Figgins	.50
105	Todd Helton	.50
106	Tim Wakefield	.25
107	Mike Maroth	.25
108	Johnny Damon	.25
109	David DeJesus	.25
110	Ryan Klesko	.25
111	Nick Johnson	.25
112	Freddy Garcia	.25
113	Torii Hunter	.50
114	Mike Sweeney	.25
115	Scott Rolen	.50
116	Jim Thome	.75
117	Adam Kennedy	.25
118	Albert Pujols	3.00
119	Kazuo Matsui	.25
120	Zack Greinke	.25
121	Jimmy Rollins	.25
122	Edgar Alfonzo	.25
123	Billy Wagner	.25
124	B.J. Ryan	.25
125	Orlando Hudson	.25
126	Preston Wilson	.25
127	Melvin Mora	.25
128	Alfonso Soriano	.75
129	Javy Lopez	.25
130	Wilson Betemit	.25
131	Garret Anderson	.25
132	Jason Bay	.50
133	Adam LaRoche	.25
134	C.C. Sabathia	.50
135	Bartolo Colon	.25
136	Ichiro Suzuki	2.00
137	Jim Edmonds	.50
138	David Eckstein	.25
139	Cristian Guzman	.25
140	Jeff Kent	.40
141	Chris Capuano	.25
142	Cliff Floyd	.25
143	Zachary Duke	.25
144	Matt Morris	.25
145	Jose Vidro	.25
146	David Wells	.25
147	John Smoltz	.50
148	Felix Hernandez	.50
149	Orlando Cabrera	.25
150	Mark Prior	.50
151	Ted Lilly	.25
152	Michael Young	.50
153	Livan Hernandez	.25
154	Yadier Molina	.25
155	Eric Chavez	.25
156	Miguel Batista	.25
157	Ben Sheets	.50
158	Oliver Perez	.25
159	Doug Davis	.25
160	Andruw Jones	.50
161	Hideki Matsui	1.50
162	Reggie Sanders	.25
163	Joe Nathan	.25
164	John Lackey	.50
165	Matt Murton	.25
166	Grady Sizemore	.75
167	Brad Thompson	.25
168	Kevin Millwood	.25
169	Orlando Hernandez	.25
170	Mark Mulder	.25
171	Chase Utley	.75
172	Moises Alou	.50
173	Wily Mo Pena	.25
174	Brian McCann	.50
175	Jermaine Dye	.40
176	Ryan Madson	.25
177	Aramis Ramirez	.50
178	Khalil Greene	.25
179	Mike Hampton	.25
180	Mike Mussina	.50
181	Rich Harden	.25
182	Woody Williams	.25
183	Chris Carpenter	.25
184	Brady Clark	.25
185	Luis Gonzalez	.25
186	Raul Ibanez	.25
187	Magglio Ordonez	.50
188	Adrian Beltre	.50
189	Marcus Giles	.25
190	Odalis Perez	.25
191	Derek Jeter	3.00
192	Jason Schmidt	.25
193	Toby Hall	.25
194	Danny Haren	.25
195	Tim Hudson	.50
196	Jake Peavy	.50
197	Casey Blake	.25
198	J.D. Drew	.50
199	Ervin Santana	.40
200	J.J. Hardy	.25
201	Austin Kearns	.25
202	Pat Burrell	.40
203	Jason Vargas	.25
204	Ryan Howard	1.50
205	Joe Crede	.25
206	Vladimir Guerrero	1.00
207	Roy Halladay	.50
208	David Dellucci	.25
209	Brandon Webb	.25
210	Ryan Church	.25
211	Miguel Tejada	.75
212	Mark Loretta	.25
213	Kevin Youkilis	.50
214	Jon Lieber	.25
215	Miguel Cabrera	1.00
216	A.J. Burnett	.50
217	David Bell	.25
218	Eric Byrnes	.50
219	Lance Niekro	.25
220	Shawn Green	.25
221	Ken Griffey Jr.	2.00
222	Johnny Estrada	.25
223	Omar Vizquel	.25
224	Gary Sheffield	.50
225	Brad Halsey	.25
226	Aaron Cook	.25
227	David Ortiz	1.00
228	Scott Kazmir	.50
229	Dustin McGowan	.50
230	Gregg Zaun	.25
231	Carlos Beltran	.75
232	Bob Wickman	.25
233	Brett Myers	.25
234	Casey Kotchman	.25
235	Jeff Francoeur	.50
236	Paul Konerko	.50
237	Juan Rivera	.25
238	Bobby Crosby	.25
239	Derrek Lee	.75
240	Curt Schilling	1.00
241	Jake Westbrook	.25
242	Dontrelle Willis	.50
243	Brad Lidge	.25
244	Randy Johnson	1.00
245	Nick Swisher	.50
246	Johan Santana	.75
247	Jeremy Bonderman	.25
248	Ramon Hernandez	.25
249	Mike Lowell	.25
250	Javier Vazquez	.25
251	Jose Contreras	.25
252	Aubrey Huff	.25
253	Kenny Rogers	.25
254	Mark Teixeira	.50
255	Orlando Hudson	.25
256	Derek Jeter	2.00
257	Eric Chavez	.25
258	Torii Hunter	.50
259	Vernon Wells	.50
260	Ichiro Suzuki	1.00
261	Greg Maddux	1.00
262	Mike Matheny	.25
263	Derrek Lee	.50
264	Luis Castillo	.25
265	Omar Vizquel	.25
266	Mike Lowell	.25
267	Andruw Jones	.50
268	Jim Edmonds	.50
269	Bobby Abreu	.50
270	Bartolo Colon	.25
271	Chris Carpenter	.25
272	Alex Rodriguez	2.00
273	Albert Pujols	2.00
274	Huston Street	.25
275	Ryan Howard	.75
276	Chris Denorfia RC	.50
277	John Van Benschoten RC	.50
278	Russell Martin RC	.50
279	Fausto Carmona RC	.75
280	Freddie Bynum RC	.50
281	Kelly Shoppach RC	.50
282	Chris Demaria RC	.50
283	Jordan Tata RC	.50
284	Ryan Zimmerman RC	4.00
285	Kenji Johjima RC	1.00
285	Kenji Johjima Auto RC	20.00
286	Ruddy Lugo RC	.50
287	Tommy Murphy RC	.50
288	Bobby Livingston RC	.50
289	Anderson Hernandez RC	.50
290	Brian Slocum RC	.50
291	Sendy Rleal RC	.50
292	Ryan Spilborghs RC	.50
293	Brandon Fahey RC	1.00
294	Jason Kubel RC	1.50
295	James Loney RC	1.50
296	Jeremy Accardo RC	.50
297	Fabio Castro RC	.50
298	Matt Capps RC	.75
299	Casey Janssen RC	1.00
300	Martin Prado RC	3.00
301	Ronny Paulino RC	.75
302	Josh Barfield RC	1.00
303	Joel Zumaya RC	1.00
304	Matt Cain RC	1.00
305	Conor Jackson RC	.50
306	Brian Anderson RC	.50
307	Prince Fielder RC	4.00
308	Jeremy Hermida RC	.75
309	Justin Verlander RC	4.00
310	Brian Bannister RC	.50
311	Josh Willingham RC	.50
312	John Rheinecker RC	.50
313	Nicholas Markakis RC	1.00
314	Jonathan Papelbon RC	2.00
315	Mike Jacobs RC	.75
316	Jose Capellan RC	.50
317	Michael Napoli RC	1.00
318	Ricky Nolasco RC	1.50
319	Ben Johnson RC	.50
320	Paul Maholm RC	.75
321	Drew Meyer RC	.50
322	Jeff Mathis RC	.50
323	Fernando Nieve RC	.50
324	John Koronka RC	.50
325	Wilbert Nieves RC	.50
326	Nate McLouth RC	1.00
327	Howie Kendrick RC	1.50
328	Sean Marshall RC	.75
329	Brandon Watson RC	.50
330	Skip Schumaker RC	.50
331	Ryan Garko/Auto. RC	10.00
332	Jason Bergmann/Auto. RC	10.00
333	Chuck James/Auto. RC	10.00
334	Adam Wainwright/Auto. RC	25.00
335	Daniel Ortmeier/Auto. RC	10.00
336	Francisco Liriano/Auto. RC	30.00
337	Craig Breslow/Auto. RC	10.00
338	Darrell Rasner/Auto. RC	10.00
339	Jason Botts/Auto. RC	10.00
340	Ian Kinsler/Auto. RC	30.00
341	Joey Devine/Auto. RC	10.00
342	Miguel Perez/Auto. RC	10.00
343	Scott Olsen/Auto. RC	10.00
344	Tyler Johnson/Auto. RC	10.00
345	Anthony Lerew/Auto. RC	10.00
346	Nelson Cruz/Auto. RC	30.00
347	Willie Eyre/Auto. RC	10.00
348	Josh Johnson/Auto. RC	15.00
349	Shawn Marcum/Auto. RC	15.00
350	Dustin Nippert/Auto. RC	10.00
351	Josh Wilson/Auto. RC	10.00
352	Hanley Ramirez/Auto. RC	30.00
353	Reggie Abercrombie/Auto. RC	10.00
354	Dan Uggla/Auto. RC	30.00

Refractors

Cards (1-330): 2-3X
Inserted 1:4
Rookie Auto. (331-354): 1-1.5X
Production 500

Black Refractors

Cards (1-330): 3-5X
Production 549
Rookie Auto. (331-354): 1.5-2X
Production 200

Blue Refractors

Cards (1-330): 2-4X
Inserted 1:8

Gold Super-Fractor

No Pricing
Production One Set

Red Refractors

Cards (1-330): 4-8X
Production 90
Rookie Auto. (331-354): No Pricing
Production 25

X-Fractor

Cards (1-330): 2-4X
Inserted 1:6 Retail

Printing Plates

No Pricing
Production one set per color.

Bonds Home Run History

		NM/M
Common Bonds:		2.00
Inserted 1:6		
Refractors:		2-4X
Black Refractor:		3-5X
Production 500 Sets		
Red Refractor:		10-20X
Production 25 Sets		
BBC375	Barry Bonds	2.00
BBC400	Barry Bonds	2.00
BBC425	Barry Bonds	2.00
BBC450	Barry Bonds	2.00
BBC475	Barry Bonds	2.00
BBC500	Barry Bonds	2.00
BBC525	Barry Bonds	2.00
BBC550	Barry Bonds	2.00
BBC575	Barry Bonds	2.00
BBC600	Barry Bonds	2.00
BBC625	Barry Bonds	2.00
BBC650	Barry Bonds	2.00
BBC675	Barry Bonds	2.00
BBC700	Barry Bonds	2.00

Mantle Home Run History

		NM/M
Common Mantle:		3.00
Inserted 1:6		
Refractor:		2-4X
Production 500 Sets		
Black Refractor:		3-5X
Production 200 Sets		
Red Refractor:		15-20X
Production 25 Sets		
MHRC1	Mickey Mantle	3.00
MHRC7	Mickey Mantle	3.00
MHRC10	Mickey Mantle	3.00
MHRC20	Mickey Mantle	3.00
MHRC30	Mickey Mantle	3.00
MHRC40	Mickey Mantle	3.00
MHRC40	Mickey Mantle	3.00
MHRC50	Mickey Mantle	3.00
MHRC60	Mickey Mantle	3.00
MHRC70	Mickey Mantle	3.00
MHRC80	Mickey Mantle	3.00
MHRC90	Mickey Mantle	3.00
MHRC100	Mickey Mantle	3.00
MHRC110	Mickey Mantle	3.00

Signers of the Constitution

		NM/M
Common Signer:		1.50
Inserted 1:7		
Refractors:		1-2X
Inserted 1:11		
AB	Abraham Baldwin	1.50
RB	Richard Bassett	1.50
GB	Gunning Bedford Jr.	1.50
JB	John Blair	1.50
WB	William Blount	1.50
DB	David Brearly	1.50
JBR	Jacob Broom	1.50
PB	Pierce Butler	1.50
DC	Daniel Carroll	1.50
GC	George Clymer	1.50
JD	Jonathan Dayton	1.50
JDI	John Dickinson	1.50
WF	William Few	1.50
TF	Thomas Fitzsimons	1.50
BF	Benjamin Franklin	4.00
NG	Nicholas Gilman	1.50
NGO	Nathaniel Gorham	1.50
AH	Alexander Hamilton	3.00
JI	Jared Ingersoll	1.50
DJ	Daniel of St. Thomas Jenifer	1.50
WJ	William Samuel Johnson	1.50
RK	Rufus King	1.50
JL	John Langdon	1.50
WL	William Livingston	1.50
JM	James Madison	2.00
JMC	James McHenry	1.50
TM	Thomas Mifflin	1.50
GM	Gouverneur Morris	1.50
RM	Robert Morris	1.50
WP	William Paterson	1.50
CCP	Charles Cotesworth Pinckney	1.50
CP	Charles Pinckney	1.50
GR	George Read	1.50
JR	John Rutledge	1.50
RS	Roger Sherman	1.50
RDS	Richard Dobbs Spaight	1.50
GW	George Washington	4.00
HW	Hugh Williamson	1.50
JW	James Wilson	1.50

Signers of Declaration/Independence

		NM/M
Common Signer:		1.50
Inserted 1:5		
Refractors:		1-2X
Inserted 1:9		
JA	John Adams	2.00
SA	Samuel Adams	1.50
JB	Josiah Bartlett	1.50
CB	Carter Braxton	1.50
CC	Charles Carroll	1.50
SC	Samuel Chase	1.50
AC	Abraham Clark	1.50
GC	George Clymer	1.50
WE	William Ellery	1.50
WF	William Floyd	1.50
BF	Benjamin Franklin	4.00
EG	Elbridge Gerry	1.50
BG	Button Gwinnett	1.50
LH	Lyman Hall	1.50
JH	John Hancock	3.00
BH	Benjamin Harrison	1.50
JHA	John Hart	1.50
JHE	Joseph Hewes	1.50
TH	Thomas Heyward Jr.	1.50
WH	William Hooper	1.50
SH	Stephen Hopkins	1.50
FH	Francis Hopkinson	1.50
SHU	Samuel Huntington	1.50
TJ	Thomas Jefferson	4.00
FL	Francis Lewis	1.50
FLL	Francis Lightfoot Lee	1.50
RHL	Richard Henry Lee	1.50
PL	Philip Livingston	1.50
TL	Thomas Lynch Jr.	1.50
TM	Thomas McKean	1.50
AM	Arthur Middleton	1.50
LM	Lewis Morris	1.50
RM	Robert Morris	1.50
JM	John Morton	1.50
TN	Thomas Nelson Jr.	1.50
WP	William Paca	1.50
RTP	Robert Treat Paine	1.50
JP	John Penn	1.50
GRE	George Read	1.50
CR	Caesar Rodney	1.50
GR	George Ross	1.50
BR	Benjamin Rush	1.50
ER	Edward Rutledge	1.50
RS	Roger Sherman	1.50
JS	James Smith	1.50
RST	Richard Stockton	1.50
TS	Thomas Stone	1.50
GT	George Taylor	1.50
MT	Matthew Thornton	1.50
GW	George Walton	1.50
WW	William Whipple	1.50
WWI	William Williams	1.50
JW	James Wilson	1.50
JWI	John Witherspoon	1.50
OW	Oliver Wolcott	1.50
GWY	George Wythe	1.50

2006 Topps Co-Signers

		NM/M
Complete Set (120):		
Common Player (1-100):		.25
Common Auto. (101-120):		10.00
Pack (6):		12.00
Box (12):		120.00
Note: Each parallel has three versions.		
1	Albert Pujols	3.00
2	Roger Clemens	3.00
3	Paul Konerko	.50
4	Jeff Francoeur	.50
5	Miguel Tejada	.75
6	Curt Schilling	1.00
7	Mickey Mantle	4.00
8	Miguel Cabrera	1.00
9	Derek Lee	1.00
10	Jeff Kent	.50
11	Gary Sheffield	.50
12	Rich Harden	.75
13	Scott Rolen	.75
14	David Wright	1.50
15	Troy Glaus	.50
16	Torii Hunter	.50
17	Nolan Ryan	2.00
18	Alfonso Soriano	.75
19	Hank Blalock	.50
20	Chase Utley	1.00
21	Ryan Howard	1.00
22	Robinson Cano	1.00
23	Derek Jeter	3.00
24	Huston Street	.50
25	Jason Giambi	.50
26	Rafael Furcal	.25
27	Rickie Weeks	.25
28	Ivan Rodriguez	.50
29	Travis Hafner	.50
30	Greg Maddux	2.00
31	Andruw Jones	.50
32	Andy Pettitte	.50
33	Scott Podsednik	.25
34	Francisco Rodriguez	.50
35	Josh Beckett	.75
36	Lance Berkman	.50
37	Roy Oswalt	.50
38	Pedro Martinez	1.00
39	Jimmy Rollins	.50
40	Johan Santana	.75
41	Randy Johnson	1.00
42	Mariano Rivera	.75
43	Nick Johnson	.25
44	Josh Gibson	.75
45	Shawn Green	.50
46	Adrian Beltre	.50
47	Johnny Damon	1.00
48	Joe Mauer	.75
49	Todd Helton	.50
50	Alex Rodriguez	2.50
51	Jake Peavy	.50
52	David Ortiz	1.00
53	Mark Buehrle	.50
54	Eric Gagne	.50
55	Hideki Matsui	1.50
56	Bobby Abreu	.50
57	Victor Martinez	.50
58	Brian Roberts	.50
59	Chipper Jones	1.00
60	Carlos Beltran	.75
61	Tim Hudson	.50
62	Carlos Lee	.50
63	Barry Zito	.50
64	Moises Alou	.50
65	Mark Teixeira	.50
66	Lyle Overbay	.25
67	Kerry Wood	.50
68	B.J. Ryan	.25
69	Jim Edmonds	.50
70	Carlos Delgado	.50
71	Magglio Ordonez	.50
72	Juan Pierre	.25
73	Manny Ramirez	1.00
74	Dontrelle Willis	.50
75	Ichiro Suzuki	2.00
76	Nomar Garciaparra	.50
77	Zachary Duke	.50
78	Chris Carpenter	.50
79	A.J. Burnett	.50
80	Scott Kazmir	.50
81	Carl Crawford	.50
82	Mark Prior	.50
83	Adam Dunn	.75
84	Justin Morneau	.50
85	Morgan Ensberg	.25
86	Pat Burrell	.25
87	Paul LoDuca	.25
88	Jason Bay	.50
89	Aubrey Huff	.25
90	Kevin Millwood	.25
91	Vernon Wells	.25
92	Javy Lopez	.25
93	Michael Young	.50
94	Felix Hernandez	.50
95	Ken Griffey Jr.	2.00
96	Bartolo Colon	.25
97	Billy Wagner	.25
98	Vladimir Guerrero	1.00
99	Jose Reyes	1.00
100	Barry Bonds	3.00
101	Anthony LeRew/Auto. RC	10.00
102	Ryan Zimmerman/440/Auto. RC	30.00
103	Craig Hansen/250/Auto. RC	10.00
104	Francisco Liriano/Auto. RC	25.00
105	Jason Botts/Auto. RC	10.00
106	Josh Johnson/Auto. RC	25.00
107	Hanley Ramirez/Auto. RC	30.00
108	Adam Wainwright/Auto. RC	30.00
109	Kenji Johjima/200/Auto. RC	25.00
110	Daniel Ortmeier/Auto. RC	10.00
111	Darrell Rasner/Auto. RC	10.00
112	Chuck James/Auto. RC	10.00
113	Nelson Cruz/Auto. RC	25.00
114	Hong-Chih Kuo/Auto. RC	20.00
115	Ryan Garko/Auto. RC	10.00
116	R. Abercrombie/Auto. RC	10.00
117	Ian Kinsler/Auto. RC	30.00

118	Joel Zumaya/Auto. **RC**	15.00
119	Willie Eyre/Auto. **RC**	10.00
120	Dan Uggla/Auto. **RC**	25.00

Bronze
Bronze (1-100):	2-3X
Production 150 Sets	

Blue
Blue (1-100):	2-3X
Production 125 Sets	

Gold
Gold (1-100):	2-3X
Production 115 Sets	

Hyper Silver - Bronze
Hyper Silver/Bronze (1-100):	2-3X
Production 75 Sets	

Hyper Silver - Blue
Hyper Silver/Blue:	No Pricing
Production 10 Sets	

Hyper Silver - Gold
Hyper Silver/Gold:	No Pricing
Production Five Sets	

Hyper Silver - Red
Hyper Silver/Red:	No Pricing
Production 25 Sets	

Silver - Bronze
Silver/Bronze (1-100):	2-3X
Production 125 Sets	

Silver - Blue
Silver/Blue (1-100):	2-3X
Production 75 Sets	

Silver - Gold
Silver/Gold (1-100):	3-4X
Production 50 Sets	

Silver - Red
Silver/Red (1-100):	2-3X
Production 100 Sets	

Dual Autographs
NM/M

Cards are not serial #'d.

CS2	David Wright, Alex Rodriguez/25	275.00
CS3	Victor Martinez, Kenji Johjima/25	75.00
CS4	Kenji Johjima, Felix Hernandez/18	200.00
CS5	David Ortiz, Manny Ramirez/25	150.00
CS6	Nolan Ryan, Roger Clemens/25	350.00
CS7	David Ortiz, Albert Pujols/25	350.00
CS8	Chipper Jones, Dale Murphy/25	100.00
CS11	Stan Musial, Albert Pujols/20	500.00
CS15	Prince Fielder, Ryan Zimmerman	50.00
CS16	Cal Ripken Jr., Ozzie Smith/25	275.00
CS18	Don Larsen, Yogi Berra/25	200.00
CS19	Mike Schmidt, Brooks Robinson/25	125.00
CS20	Ryan Zimmerman, Wade Boggs/25	50.00
CS22	Ryan Howard, Derrek Lee/75	80.00
CS23	Jeff Mathis, Chris Snyder	15.00
CS25	Ray Knight, Keith Hernandez/100	25.00
CS26	Mike Schmidt, Chase Utley/25	100.00
CS27	Billy Wagner, Paul LoDuca/50	70.00
CS28	Tony Gwynn, Wade Boggs/25	140.00
CS30	Dwight Gooden, Darryl Strawberry/50	40.00
CS31	Ryan Howard, Huston Street	40.00
CS32	Mariano Rivera, Huston Street/25	140.00
CS33	Prince Fielder, Ryan Howard/50	60.00
CS34	Robinson Cano, Chase Utley/75	60.00
CS36	David Justice, Chipper Jones/25	80.00
CS37	Jose Reyes, David Wright/50	200.00
CS38	Jeff Mathis, Ryan Garko	15.00
CS39	Brandon McCarthy, Pedro Lopez	15.00
CS40	David Justice, Dale Murphy/100	50.00
CS42	Joe Mauer, Francisco Liriano	40.00
CS44	Ryan Zimmerman, David Wright/100	100.00
CS45	Rick Rhoden, Dave Parker/100	10.00
CS46	Jonathan Papelbon, Craig Breslow	40.00
CS48	Dan Johnson, Prince Fielder/100	30.00
CS49	Victor Martinez, Ryan Garko	20.00
CS50	Ben Hendrickson, Anthony Reyes	15.00
CS51	Nelson Cruz, Prince Fielder/100	30.00
CS52	Jonathan Papelbon, Anthony Reyes	30.00
CS53	Ben Hendrickson, Rich Hill	20.00
CS54	Shin-Soo Choo, Kenji Johjima/25	85.00
CS55	Francisco Liriano, Johan Santana/100	100.00
CS56	Brandon McCarthy, Zachary Duke	15.00
CS57	Josh Johnson, Scott Olsen	15.00
CS58	Tommy John, Bob Welch	15.00
CS59	Roy White, Joe Pepitone	25.00
CS60	Cecil Fielder, Prince Fielder	60.00
CS62	Conor Jackson, Ryan Howard	50.00
CS63	Dontrelle Willis, Zachary Duke/50	25.00
CS64	Mariano Rivera, Billy Wagner/25	150.00
CS65	Hong-Chih Kuo, Shin-Soo Choo	30.00
CS66	Jim Leyritz, Cecil Fielder	50.00
CS67	Scott Kazmir, Francisco Liriano	40.00
CS68	Scott Kazmir, Roy Oswalt/50	50.00
CS69	Chuck James, Anthony LeRew	15.00
CS70	Cecil Fielder, Ryan Howard	60.00
CS71	Chien-Ming Wang, Hong-Chih Kuo/25	200.00
CS72	Shin-Soo Choo, Chien-Ming Wang/50	160.00
CS73	Nelson Cruz, Jason Botts	15.00
CS74	Francisco Liriano, Ervin Santana	30.00
CS75	Adam Wainwright, Anthony Reyes	30.00
CS76	Ervin Santana, Scott Kazmir	30.00
CS77	Robinson Cano, Gary Sheffield	50.00
CS78	David Wright, Miguel Cabrera/50	120.00
CS79	Dan Johnson, Conor Jackson	15.00
CS80	Frank Tanana, Mickey Tettleton	15.00
CS81	Andruw Jones, Chipper Jones	75.00
CS82	Morgan Ensberg, Roy Oswalt	25.00
CS83	Michael Young, Ozzie Smith	50.00
CS84	Grady Sizemore, Nick Swisher	40.00
CS85	Garrett Atkins, Clint Barmes	20.00

Dual Cut Signatures
No Pricing

Solo Sigs.
NM/M

Cards are not serial #'d.

CB	Clint Barmes	10.00
CBR	Craig Breslow	10.00
RC	Robinson Cano	50.00
GC	Gustavo Chacin	10.00
SSC	Shin-Soo Choo	15.00
JC	Jack Clark	10.00
AD	Andre Dawson	10.00
ZD	Zachary Duke	10.00
CF	Cecil Fielder	20.00
PF	Prince Fielder/250	40.00
RHI	Rich Hill	20.00
RH	Ryan Howard/100	100.00
DJ	Dan Johnson/250	10.00
CJ	Chipper Jones/25	80.00
AK	Al Kaline/100	50.00
SK	Scott Kazmir	20.00
DL	Don Larsen	20.00
DLE	Derrek Lee/50	40.00
VM	Victor Martinez/50	25.00
JM	Jeff Mathis	10.00
DM	Don Mattingly/50	120.00
JMA	Joe Mauer/75	30.00
CM	Craig Monroe	10.00
SO	Scott Olsen	15.00
DO	David Ortiz/25	60.00
JP	Jonathan Papelbon	60.00
ARE	Anthony Reyes	10.00
RR	Rick Rhoden	10.00
CR	Cal Ripken Jr./20	200.00
AR	Alex Rodriguez/20	125.00
NR	Nolan Ryan/20	125.00
ES	Ervin Santana/250	10.00
JS	Johan Santana/50	40.00
CS	Chris Snyder	8.00
DS	Darryl Strawberry	15.00
HS	Huston Street/250	25.00
DWI	Dontrelle Willis	15.00
DW	David Wright/75	80.00

2006 Topps Heritage

NM/M

Complete Set (485):	
Common Player:	.40
Common SP:	4.00
Pack (8):	4.00
Box (24):	75.00

1	David Ortiz/SP	8.00
2	Mike Piazza/SP	8.00
3	Daryle Ward	.40
4	Rafael Furcal	.75
5	Derek Lowe	.40
6	Eric Chavez	.50
7	Juan Uribe	.40
8	C.C. Sabathia	.75
9	Sean Casey	.40
10	Barry Bonds/SP	15.00
11	Gary Sheffield	.75
12	Ted Lilly	.50
13	Lew Ford	.40
14	Tom Gordon	.40
15	Curt Schilling	1.00
16	Jason Kendall	.40
17	Frank Catalanotto	.40
18	Pedro Martinez/SP	8.00
19	David Dellucci	.40
20	Andruw Jones	.75
20	Andruw Jones w/Seats/SP	6.00
21	Brad Halsey	.40
22	Vernon Wells	.75
23	Derek Jeter	4.00
23	Derek Jeter/Blue Letter/SP	15.00
24	Todd Helton	1.00
25	Randy Johnson/SP	8.00
26	Jay Gibbons	.40
27	Joe Mays	.40
28	Paul Konerko	.75
29	Lyle Overbay	.40
30	Jorge Posada	.75
31	Brandon Webb	.75
32	Marcus Giles	.40
33	J.T. Snow	.40
34	Todd Walker	.40
35	Wily Mo Pena/SP	5.00
36	Carlos Delgado	.75
37	David Wright	2.00
38	Shea Hillenbrand	.40
39	Daniel Cabrera	.40
40	Trevor Hoffman	.75
41	Matt Morris	.40
42	Mariano Rivera	1.00
43	Jeff Bagwell	1.00
44	J.D. Drew	.50
45	Carl Pavano	.40
46	Placido Polanco	.40
47	Adrian Beltre	.75
48	J.D. Closser	.40
49	Paul LoDuca	.40
50	Scott Rolen	.75
51	Bernie Williams	.75
52	Jose Guillen	.40
53	Aubrey Huff	.40
54	Greg Maddux	2.50
55	Derrek Lee/SP	8.00
56	Hideki Matsui	2.50
57	Jose Bautista	.40
58	Kyle Farnsworth	.40
59	Nate Robertson	.40
60	Sammy Sosa	1.00
61	Javier Vazquez	.40
62	Jeff Mathis **RC**	.40
63	Mark Buehrle	.75
64	Orlando Hernandez	.40
65	Brandon Claussen	.40
66	Miguel Batista	.40
67	Eddie Guardado	.40
68	Alex Gonzalez	.40
69	Kris Benson	.40
70	Bobby Abreu/SP	6.00
71	Vinny Castilla	.40
72	Ben Broussard	.40
73	Travis Hafner	.75
74	Dmitri Young	.40
75	Alex S. Gonzalez	.40
76	Jason Bay/SP	6.00
77	Charlton Jimerson	.40
78	Ryan Garko	.50
79	Lance Berkman	.75
80	Tim Hudson	.75
80	Tim Hudson/Blue Letter/SP	5.00
81	Guillermo Mota	.40
82	Chris Young	.75
83	Brad Lidge	.40
84	A.J. Pierzynski	.40
85	Maicer Izturis	.40
86	Vladimir Guerrero	1.50
87	J.J. Hardy	.40
88	Cesar Izturis	.40
89	Mark Ellis	.40
90	Chipper Jones	1.50
91	Chris Snelling/SP	4.00
92	Jose Reyes	1.00
93	Mike Lieberthal	.40
94	Octavio Dotel	.40
95	Alex Rodriguez/Fldg/SP	10.00
95	Alex Rodriguez W/Bat/SP	10.00
96	Brett Myers	.40
97	New York Yankees	1.00
98	Ryan Klesko	.40
99	Brian Jordan/SP	4.00
100	William Harridge, Warren Giles	.40
101	Adam Eaton	.40
102	Aaron Boone	.40
103	Alex Rios	.75
104	Andy Pettitte	.75
105	Barry Zito	.50
106	Bengie Molina/SP	4.00
107	Austin Kearns	.50
108	Adam Everett	.40
109	A.J. Burnett	.75
110	Mark Prior	.75
111	Russ Ortiz	.40
112	Adam Dunn	1.00
113	Byung-Hyun Kim	.40
114	Atlanta Braves	.50
115	Carlos Silva	.40
116	Chad Cordero	.40
117	Chone Figgins	.75
118	Chris Reitsma	.40
119	Coco Crisp	.40
120	David DeJesus	.40
121	Chris Snyder	.40
122	Brad Eldred	.40
123	Humberto Cota/SP	5.00
124	Erubiel Durazo	.40
125	Josh Beckett	1.00
126	Kenny Lofton	.40
127	Joe Nathan/SP	5.00
128	Bryan Bullington	.40
129	Jim Thome	1.00
130	Shawn Green	.75
131	LaTroy Hawkins	.40
132	Mark Kotsay	.40
133	Matt Lawton	.40
134	Luis Castillo	.40
135	Michael Barrett	.40
136	Preston Wilson	.40
137	Orlando Cabrera	.40
138	Chuck James **RC**	.40
139	Raul Ibanez	.40
140	Frank Thomas	1.00
141	Orlando Hudson	.40
142	Scott Kazmir	.75
143	Steve Finley	.40
144	Danny Sandoval **RC**	1.00
145	Javy Lopez	.40
146	Tony Giarratano	.40
147	Terrence Long	.40
148	Victor Martinez	.75
149	Toby Hall	.40
150	Fausto Carmona **RC**	.75
151	Tim Wakefield	.40
152	Troy Percival	.40
153	Chris Denorfia **RC**	.40
154	Junior Spivey	.40
155	Desi Relaford	.40
156	Francisco Liriano **RC**	.75
157	Corey Koskie	.40
158	Chris Carpenter	.75
159	Robert Andino **RC**	1.00
160	Cliff Floyd	.40
161	Pittsburgh Pirates	.40
162	Anderson Hernandez **RC**	.40
163	Mike Maroth	.40
164	Aaron Rowand	.75
165	Albert Pujols	4.00
165	Albert Pujols/Red Shirt/SP	15.00
166	David Bell	.40
167	Angel Berroa	.40
168	B.J. Ryan	.40
169	Bartolo Colon	.40
170	Hong-Chih Kuo	.75
171	Cincinnati Reds	.40
172	Bill Mueller	.40
173	John Koronka **RC**	.40
174	Billy Wagner	.40
175	Zack Greinke	.75
176	Rick Short **RC**	1.00
177	Yadier Molina	.40
178	Willy Taveras	.40
179	Wes Helms	.40
180	Wade Miller	.40
181	Luis Gonzalez	.40
182	Carlos Zambrano	.75
183	Chicago Cubs	.50
184	Victor Santos	.40
185	Tyler Walker	.40
186	Bobby Crosby	.40
187	Trot Nixon	.40
188	Nick Johnson	.40
189	Nick Swisher	.75
190	Brian Roberts	.40
191	Nomar Garciaparra	1.00
192	Oliver Perez	.40
193	Ramon Hernandez	.40
194	Randy Winn	.40
195	Ryan Church	.40
196	Ryan Wagner	.40
197	Todd Hollandsworth	.40
198	Detroit Tigers	.40
199	Tino Martinez	.75
200	Roger Clemens	3.00
200	Roger Clemens/Red Shirt/SP	12.00
201	Shawn Estes	.40
202	Justin Morneau	.75
203	Jeff Francis	.40
204	Oakland Athletics	.40
205	Jeff Francoeur	.75
206	C.J. Wilson	.40
207	Francisco Rodriguez	.40
208	Edgardo Alfonzo	.40
209	David Eckstein	.40
210	Cory Lidle	.40
211	Chase Utley	1.50
212	Rocco Baldelli	.40
212	Rocco Baldelli/Blue Letter/SP	5.00
213	So Taguchi	.40
214	Philadelphia Phillies	.40
215	Brad Hawpe	.40
216	Walter Young	.40
217	Tom Gorzelanny **RC**	.75
218	Shaun Marcum **RC**	.40
219	Ryan Howard	2.00
220	Damian Jackson	.40
221	Craig Counsell	.40
222	Damian Miller	.40
223	Derrick Turnbow	.40
224	Hank Blalock	.75
225	Brayan Pena	.40
226	Grady Sizemore	1.00
227	Ivan Rodriguez	1.00
228	Jason Isringhausen	.40
229	Brian Fuentes	.40
230	Jason Phillips	.40
231	Jason Schmidt	.50
232	Javier Valentin	.40
233	Jeff Kent	.75
234	John Buck	.40
235	Mike Matheny	.40
236	Jorge Cantu	.40
237	Jose Castillo	.40
238	Kenny Rogers	.40
239	Kerry Wood	.75
240	Kevin Mench	.40
241	Tim Stauffer	.40
242	Eric Milton	.40
243	St. Louis Cardinals	.75
244	Shawn Chacon	.40
245	Mike Jacobs **RC**	1.00
246	Ryan Dempster	.40
247	Todd Jones	.40
248	Tom Glavine	.75
249	Tony Graffanino	.40
250	Ichiro Suzuki	2.50
251	Baltimore Orioles	.50
252	Brad Radke	.40
253	Brad Wilkerson	.40
254	Carlos Lee	.75
255	Alex Gordon/Cut-Out	80.00
256	Gustavo Chacin	.40
257	Jermaine Dye	.75
258	Jose Mesa	.40
259	Julio Lugo	.40
260	Mark Redman	.40
261	Brandon Watson **RC**	.40
262	Pedro Feliz	.40
263	Esteban Loaiza	.40
264	Anthony Reyes	.40
265	Jose Contreras/SP	4.00
266	Tadahito Iguchi/SP	6.00
267	Mark Loretta/SP	4.00
268	Ray Durham/SP	4.00
269	Neifi Perez/SP	4.00
270	Washington Nationals	.40
271	Troy Glaus/SP	6.00
272	Matt Holliday/SP	8.00
273	Kevin Millwood/SP	4.00
274	Jon Lieber/SP	4.00
275	Cleveland Indians	.40
276	Jeremy Reed/SP	4.00
277	Garrett Atkins/SP	4.00
278	Geoff Jenkins/SP	4.00
279	Joey Gathright/SP	4.00
280	Ben Sheets/SP	4.00
281	Melvin Mora/SP	4.00
282	Jonathan Papelbon/SP **RC**	10.00
283	John Smoltz/SP	6.00
284	Jake Peavy/SP	6.00
285	Felix Hernandez/SP	6.00
286	Alfonso Soriano/SP	6.00
287	Bronson Arroyo/SP	4.00
288	Adam LaRoche/SP	6.00
289	Aramis Ramirez/SP	6.00
290	Brad Hennessey/SP	4.00
291	Conor Jackson/SP **RC**	4.00
292	Rod Barajas/SP	4.00
293	Chris Young/SP	4.00
294	Jeremy Bonderman/SP	4.00
295	Jack Wilson/SP	4.00
296	Jay Payton/SP	4.00
297	Danys Baez/SP	4.00
298	Jose Lima/SP	4.00
299	Luis A. Gonzalez/SP	4.00
300	Mike Sweeney/SP	4.00
301	Nelson Cruz/SP **RC**	4.00
302	Eric Gagne/SP	4.00
303	Juan Castro/SP	4.00
304	Joe Mauer/SP	5.00
305	Richie Sexson/SP	4.00
306	Roy Oswalt/SP	5.00
307	Rickie Weeks/SP	4.00
308	Pat Borders/SP	4.00
309	Mike Morse/SP	4.00
310	Matt Stairs/SP	4.00
311	Chad Tracy/SP	4.00
312	Matt Cain/SP **RC**	6.00
313	Mark Mulder/SP	4.00
314	Mark Grudzielanek/SP	4.00
315	Johnny Damon/SP	8.00
316	Casey Kotchman/SP	4.00
317	San Francisco Giants	.40
318	Chris Burke/SP	4.00
319	Carl Crawford/SP	5.00
320	Edgar Renteria/SP	4.00
321	Chan Ho Park/SP	4.00
322	Boston Red Sox	5.00
323	Robinson Cano/SP	8.00
324	Los Angeles Dodgers	.40
325	Miguel Tejada W/bat/SP	6.00
325	Miguel Tejada/Hand Up/SP	6.00
326	Jimmy Rollins/SP	6.00
327	Juan Pierre/SP	4.00
328	Dan Johnson/SP	4.00
329	Chicago White Sox	.40
330	Pat Burrell/SP	5.00
331	Ramon Ortiz/SP	4.00
332	Rondell White/SP	4.00
333	David Wells/SP	4.00
334	Michael Young/SP	5.00
335	Mike Mussina/SP	5.00
336	Moises Alou/SP	5.00
337	Scott Podsednik/SP	4.00
338	Rich Harden/SP	5.00
339	Mark Teahen/SP	4.00
340	Jacque Jones/SP	4.00
341	Jason Giambi/SP	5.00
342	Bill Hall/SP	4.00
343	Jon Garland/SP	4.00
344	Dontrelle Willis/SP	5.00
345	Danny Haren/SP	4.00
346	Brian Giles/SP	5.00
347	Brad Penny/SP	4.00
348	Brandon McCarthy/SP	4.00
349	Chien-Ming Wang/SP	5.00
350	Torii Hunter/Blue Letter/SP	5.00
350	Torii Hunter Red/Blue Letter/SP	5.00
351	Yhency Brazoban/SP	4.00
352	Rodrigo Lopez/SP	4.00
353	Paul McAnulty	.40
354	Francisco Cordero	.40
355	Brandon Inge	.40
356	Jason Lane	.40
357	Brian Schneider	.40
358	Dustin Hermanson	.40
359	Eric Hinske	.40
360	Jarrod Washburn	.40
361	Jayson Werth	.40
362	Craig Breslow **RC**	1.00
363	Jeff Weaver	.40
364	Jeromy Burnitz	.40
365	Jhonny Peralta	.40
366	Joe Crede	.40
367	Johan Santana	1.50
368	Jose Valentin	.40
369	Keith Foulke	.40
370	Larry Bigbie	.40
371	Manny Ramirez	1.50
372	Jim Edmonds	.75
373	Horacio Ramirez	.40
374	Garret Anderson	.75
375	Felipe Lopez	.40
376	Eric Byrnes	.40
377	Darin Erstad	.50
378	Carlos Zambrano	.75
379	Craig Biggio	.75
380	Darrell Rasner **RC**	.40
381	Dave Roberts	.40
382	Hanley Ramirez **RC**	1.50
383	Geoff Blum	.40
384	Joel Pineiro	.40
385	Kip Wells	.40
386	Kelvim Escobar	.40
387	John Patterson	.40
388	Jody Gerut	.40
389	Marshall McDougall	.40
390	Mike MacDougal	.40
391	Orlando Palmeiro	.40
392	Rich Aurilia	.40
393	Ronnie Belliard	.40
394	Rich Hill	.50
395	Scott Hatteberg	.40
396	Ryan Langerhans	.40
397	Richard Hidalgo	.40
398	Omar Vizquel	.40
399	Mike Lowell	.75
400	Astros' Aces/SP	8.00
401	Mike Cameron	.40
402	Matt Clement	.40
403	Miguel Cabrera	1.50
404	Milton Bradley	.40
405	Laynce Nix	.40
406	Robert Mackowiak	.40
407	White Sox Power Hitters	10.00
408	Mark Teixeira	1.00
409	Brady Clark	.40
410	Johnny Estrada	.40
411	Juan Encarnacion	.40
412	Morgan Ensberg	.40
413	Nook Logan	.40
414	Phil Nevin	.40
415	Reggie Sanders	.40
416	Roy Halladay	.75
417	Livan Hernandez	.40
418	Jose Vidro	.40
419	Shannon Stewart	.40
420	Brian Bruney	.40
421	Royce Clayton	.40
422	Chris Demaria **RC**	.75

423	Eduardo Perez	.40
424	Jeff Suppan	.40
425	Jaret Wright	.40
426	Joe Randa	.40
427	Bobby Kielty	.40
428	Jason Ellison	.40
429	Gregg Zaun	.40
430	Runelvys Hernandez	.40
431	Joe McEwing	.40
432	Jason LaRue	.40
433	Aaron Miles	.40
434	Adam Kennedy	.40
435	Ambiorix Burgos	.40
436	Armando Benitez	.40
437	Brad Ausmus	.40
438	Brandon Backe	.40
439	Brian Anderson RC	.40
440	Bruce Chen	.40
441	Carlos Guillen	.75
442	Casey Blake	.40
443	Chris Capuano	.40
444	Chris Duffy	.40
445	Chris Ray	.40
446	Clint Barmes	.40
447	Andrew Sisco	.40
448	Dallas McPherson	.40
449	Tanyon Sturtze	.40
450	Carlos Beltran	1.50
451	Jason Vargas	.40
452	Ervin Santana	.50
453	Jason Marquis	.40
454	Juan Rivera	.40
455	Jake Westbrook	.40
456	Jason Johnson	.40
457	Joe Blanton	.40
458	Kevin Millar	.40
459	John Thomson	.40
460	J.P. Howell	.40
461	Justin Verlander RC	1.00
462	Kelly Johnson	.40
463	Kyle Davies	.40
464	Lance Niekro	.40
465	Magglio Ordonez	.75
466	Melky Cabrera	.75
467	Nick Punto	.40
468	Paul Byrd	.40
469	Randy Wolf	.40
470	Ruben Gotay	.40
471	Ryan Madson	.40
472	Victor Diaz	.40
473	Xavier Nady	.40
474	Zachary Duke	.40
475	Huston Street	.75
475	Huston Street/ Blue Letter/SP	6.00
476	Brad Thompson	.40
477	Jonny Gomes	.40
478	B.J. Upton	.75
479	Jamey Carroll	.40
480	Mike Hampton	.40
481	Tony Clark	.40
482	Antonio Alfonseca	.40
483	Justin Duchscherer	.40
484	Mike Timlin	.40
485	Joe Saunders	.40

Chrome

		NM/M
Common Player:		2.00
Production 1,957 Sets		
Refractor:		1.5-2X
Production 557 Sets		
Black Refractor:		3-6X
Production 57 Sets		
1	Rafael Furcal	3.00
2	C.C. Sabathia	3.00
3	Sean Casey	2.00
4	Gary Sheffield	3.00
5	William Harridge, Warren Giles	2.00
6	Curt Schilling	3.00
7	Jay Gibbons	2.00
8	Paul Konerko	2.00
9	Lyle Overbay	2.00
10	Jorge Posada	3.00
11	Todd Walker	2.00
12	Carlos Delgado	3.00
13	David Wright	6.00
14	Matt Morris	2.00
15	Mariano Rivera	3.00
16	Jeff Bagwell	3.00
17	Carl Pavano	2.00
18	Adrian Beltre	3.00
19	Scott Rolen	2.00
20	Aubrey Huff	2.00
21	Hideki Matsui	6.00
22	Andruw Jones	3.00
23	Sammy Sosa	4.00
24	Mark Buehrle	3.00
25	Orlando Hernandez	2.00
26	Travis Hafner	3.00
27	Vladimir Guerrero	4.00
28	Chipper Jones	4.00
29	Jose Reyes	4.00
30	Roger Clemens	6.00
31	Aaron Boone	2.00
32	Andy Pettitte	3.00
33	David DeJesus	2.00
34	Shawn Green	2.00
35	Luis Castillo	2.00
36	Frank Thomas	3.00
37	Javy Lopez	2.00
38	Victor Martinez	3.00
39	Tim Wakefield	2.00
40	Cliff Floyd	2.00
41	Bartolo Colon	2.00
42	Billy Wagner	2.00
43	Dmitri Young	2.00
44	Mark Prior	2.00
45	Nick Johnson	2.00
46	Brian Roberts	3.00
47	Nomar Garciaparra	3.00
48	Jorge Cantu	2.00
49	Jeff Francoeur	3.00
50	Barry Bonds	8.00
51	Francisco Rodriguez	2.00
52	Rocco Baldelli	2.00
53	Ryan Howard	5.00
54	Hank Blalock	3.00
55	Ivan Rodriguez	3.00
56	Jason Schmidt	3.00
57	Jeff Kent	3.00
58	Jose Castillo	2.00
59	Kerry Wood	3.00
60	Chase Utley	4.00
61	Shawn Chacon	2.00
62	Tom Glavine	3.00
63	Ichiro Suzuki	6.00
64	Carlos Lee	3.00
65	Jeff Weaver	2.00
66	Jeromy Burnitz	2.00
67	Jhonny Peralta	2.00
68	Johan Santana	4.00
69	Keith Foulke	2.00
70	Manny Ramirez	4.00
71	Jim Edmonds	2.00
72	Garret Anderson	3.00
73	Felipe Lopez	2.00
74	Craig Biggio	3.00
75	Ryan Langerhans	2.00
76	Mike Cameron	2.00
77	Matt Clement	2.00
78	Miguel Cabrera	4.00
79	Mark Teixeira	3.00
80	Johnny Estrada	2.00
81	Nook Logan	2.00
82	Livan Hernandez	2.00
83	Roy Halladay	3.00
84	Jose Vidro	2.00
85	Shannon Stewart	2.00
86	Brian Bruney	2.00
87	Jaret Wright	2.00
88	Gregg Zaun	2.00
89	Jason LaRue	2.00
90	Adam Kennedy	2.00
91	Armando Benitez	2.00
92	Chris Ray	2.00
93	Clint Barmes	2.00
94	Ervin Santana	2.00
95	Justin Verlander	3.00
96	Magglio Ordonez	3.00
97	Todd Helton	3.00
98	Zachary Duke	2.00
99	Huston Street	3.00
100	Alex Rodriguez	8.00
101	Mike Hampton	2.00
102	Tony Clark	2.00
104	Barry Zito	2.00
105	Anderson Hernandez	2.00
106	B.J. Upton	3.00
107	Albert Pujols	10.00
108	Tim Hudson	3.00
109	Derek Jeter	10.00
110	Greg Maddux	6.00

Clubhouse Collection Relics

		NM/M
Common Player:		4.00
CB	Clint Barmes	4.00
BB	Barry Bonds	20.00
MC	Miguel Cabrera	8.00
RC	Robinson Cano	15.00
EC	Eric Chavez	4.00
SC	Shin-Soo Choo	4.00
CC	Carl Crawford	4.00
JD	Johnny Damon	6.00
JD2	Johnny Damon	6.00
AD	Adam Dunn	6.00
JE	Jim Edmonds	4.00
ME	Morgan Ensberg	4.00
JF	Jeff Francis	4.00
EG	Eric Gagne	4.00
KG	Khalil Greene	4.00
VG	Vladimir Guerrero	8.00
MH	Matt Holliday	8.00
TI	Tadahito Iguchi	8.00
CJ	Conor Jackson	4.00
AJ	Andruw Jones	6.00
AK	Al Kaline	20.00
DL	Derrek Lee	8.00
MM	Mickey Mantle	200.00
PM	Pedro Martinez	8.00
BM	Bill Mazeroski	30.00
MMU	Mark Mulder	4.00
SM	Stan Musial	35.00
DO	David Ortiz	10.00
JP	Jake Peavy	6.00
MP	Mike Piazza	8.00
AP	Albert Pujols	20.00
MR	Manny Ramirez	8.00
MR2	Manny Ramirez	8.00
BR	Brian Roberts	4.00
BR2	Brian Roberts	4.00
BRO	Brooks Robinson	30.00
FR	Frank Robinson	20.00
AR	Alex Rodriguez	20.00
AR2	Alex Rodriguez	20.00
JS	Johan Santana	6.00
CS	Curt Schilling	8.00
GS	Gary Sheffield	6.00
AS	Alfonso Soriano	6.00
MTE	Mark Teixeira	6.00
MT	Miguel Tejada	6.00
RW	Rickie Weeks	6.00
DWI	Dontrelle Willis	6.00
DW	David Wright	10.00

Clubhouse Collection Relic Auto.

		NM/M
Production 25 Sets		
CCA-3	Brooks Robinson	125.00
CCA-4	Al Kaline	200.00
CCA-5	Stan Musial	250.00

Clubhouse Collection Dual Relics

		NM/M
Production 57 Sets		
BR	Brooks Robinson, Brian Roberts	75.00
MR	Mickey Mantle, Alex Rodriguez	250.00
MP	Stan Musial, Albert Pujols	150.00

Clubhouse Collection Cut Sig. Relic

Production One Set

Flashbacks

		NM/M
Complete Set (10):		10.00
Common Player:		.50
Inserted 1:12		
EB	Ernie Banks	1.50
YB	Yogi Berra	1.50
WF	Whitey Ford	1.00
AK	Al Kaline	1.50
MM	Mickey Mantle	5.00
BM	Bill Mazeroski	.50
SM	Stan Musial	1.50
BRI	Bobby Richardson	.50
BR	Brooks Robinson	1.00
FR	Frank Robinson	1.00

Flashbacks Autographs

No Pricing
Production 25 Sets

Flashbacks Relics

		NM/M
EB	Ernie Banks	15.00
YB	Yogi Berra	20.00
WF	Whitey Ford	20.00
AK	Al Kaline	15.00
MM	Mickey Mantle	40.00
BM	Bill Mazeroski	10.00
SM	Stan Musial	50.00
BRI	Bobby Richardson	10.00
BR	Brooks Robinson	10.00
FR	Frank Robinson	10.00

Flashbacks Relic Autographs

No Pricing
Production 25 Sets

New Age Performers

		NM/M
Complete Set (15):		20.00
Common Player:		1.00
Inserted 1:15		
BB	Barry Bonds	4.00
MC	Miguel Cabrera	1.50
RC	Roger Clemens	4.00
VG	Vladimir Guerrero	1.50
CL	Carlos Lee	1.00
DL	Derrek Lee	1.50
PM	Pedro Martinez	1.50
DO	David Ortiz	1.50
GM	Mark Prior	1.00
AP	Albert Pujols	4.00
MR	Manny Ramirez	1.50
AR	Alex Rodriguez	4.00
GS	Gary Sheffield	1.00
I	Ichiro Suzuki	2.50
MT	Mark Teixeira	1.50

Real One Autographs

		NM/M
Production 200 Sets		
Red Ink:		1.5-2X
Production 57 Sets		
EB	Ernie Banks	120.00
YB	Yogi Berra	100.00
TB	Tommy Byrne	60.00
BC	Bob Chakales	50.00
JAC	Jack Collum	40.00
JCR	Jack Crimian	50.00
JD	Jack Dittmer	60.00
WF	Whitey Ford	100.00
DK	Don Kaiser	40.00
NK	Nellie King	50.00
LK	Lou Kretlow	50.00
PL	Paul LaPalme	50.00
JM	Joe Margoneri	60.00
WM	Windy McCall	40.00
JRM	John (Red) Murff	50.00
SM	Stan Musial	150.00
RN	Ron Negray	50.00
EOB	Eddie O'Brien	50.00
KO	Karl Olson	50.00
EO	Ernie Oravetz	50.00
MP	Mel Parnell	60.00
JP	Jim Pyburn	50.00
DR	Dusty Rhodes	50.00
FR	Frank Robinson	100.00
JSM	Jim Small	50.00
DS	Duke Snider	120.00
JSN	Jerry Snyder	60.00
CT	Charles Thompson	50.00
BW	Bob Wiesler	60.00

Real One Cut Signatures

Production One Set

Then and Now

		NM/M
Complete Set (10):		20.00
Common Duo:		1.00
Inserted 1:15		
TN1	Mickey Mantle, Alex Rodriguez	6.00
TN2	Ted Williams, Michael Young	3.00
TN3	Mickey Mantle, Jason Giambi	6.00
TN4	Luis Aparicio, Chone Figgins	1.00
TN5	Ted Williams, Alex Rodriguez	4.00
TN6	Stan Musial, Derrek Lee	2.00
TN7	Stan Musial, Derrek Lee	2.00
TN8	Red Schoendienst, Derrek Lee	1.50
TN9	Johnny Podres, Roger Clemens	4.00
TN10	Clem Labine, Chad Cordero	1.00

2006 Topps Opening Day

		NM/M
Complete Set (165):		25.00
Common Player:		.10
Pack (6):		1.00
Box (36):		30.00
1	Alex Rodriguez	1.50
2	Jhonny Peralta	.20
3	Garrett Atkins	.10
4	Vernon Wells	.25
5	Carl Crawford	.25
6	Josh Beckett	.25
7	Mickey Mantle	3.00
8	Willy Taveras	.10
9	Ivan Rodriguez	.40
10	Clint Barmes	.10
11	Jose Reyes	.25
12	Travis Hafner	.40
13	Tadahito Iguchi	.25
14	Barry Zito	.25
15	Brian Roberts	.25
16	David Wright	1.00
17	Mark Teixeira	.50
18	Roy Halladay	.25
19	Scott Rolen	.40
20	Bobby Abreu	.25
21	Lance Berkman	.25
23	Chone Figgins	.10
24	Aaron Rowand	.10
25	Chipper Jones	.50
26	Johnny Damon	.25
27	Matt Clement	.10
28	Nick Johnson	.10
29	Jon Garland	.10
30	Torii Hunter	.20
31	Mike Sweeney	.10
32	Mike Lieberthal	.10
33	Rafael Furcal	.20
34	Brad Wilkerson	.10
35	Brad Penny	.10
36	Jorge Cantu	.10
37	Paul Konerko	.25
38	Rickie Weeks	.25
39	Jorge Posada	.25
41	Albert Pujols	1.50
42	Zack Greinke	.10
43	Jimmy Rollins	.25
44	Mark Prior	.40
45	Greg Maddux	1.00
46	Jeff Francis	.10
47	Felipe Lopez	.10
48	Dan Johnson	.10
49	B.J. Ryan	.10
50	Manny Ramirez	.50
51	Melvin Mora	.20
52	Javy Lopez	.20
53	Garret Anderson	.20
54	Jason Bay	.25
55	Joe Mauer	.40
56	C.C. Sabathia	.10
57	Bartolo Colon	.10
58	Ichiro Suzuki	1.00
59	Andruw Jones	.50
60	Rocco Baldelli	.10
61	Jeff Kent	.20
62	Cliff Floyd	.10
63	John Smoltz	.20
64	Shawn Green	.20
65	Nomar Garciaparra	.50
66	Miguel Cabrera	.50
67	Vladimir Guerrero	.50
68	Gary Sheffield	.25
69	Jake Peavy	.25
70	Carlos Lee	.20
71	Tom Glavine	.25
72	Craig Biggio	.25
73	Steve Finley	.10
74	Adrian Beltre	.10
75	Eric Gagne	.10
76	Aubrey Huff	.10
77	Livan Hernandez	.10
78	Scott Podsednik	.10
79	Todd Helton	.40
80	Kerry Wood	.25
81	Randy Johnson	.50
82	Huston Street	.20
83	Pedro Martinez	.50
84	Roger Clemens	1.50
85	Hank Blalock	.20
86	Carlos Beltran	.40
87	Chien-Ming Wang	.25
88	Rich Harden	.25
89	Mike Mussina	.25
90	Mark Buehrle	.25
91	Michael Young	.20
92	Mark Mulder	.20
93	Khalil Greene	.25
94	Johan Santana	.50
95	Andy Pettitte	.25
96	Derek Jeter	1.50
97	Jack Wilson	.10
98	Ben Sheets	.25
99	Miguel Tejada	.40
100	Barry Bonds	1.50
101	Dontrelle Willis	.20
102	Curt Schilling	.50
103	Jose Contreras	.10
104	Jeremy Bonderman	.10
105	David Ortiz	.50
106	Lyle Overbay	.10
107	Robinson Cano	.50
108	Tim Hudson	.25
109	Paul LoDuca	.10
110	Mariano Rivera	.25
111	Derek Lee	.50
112	Morgan Ensberg	.20
113	Wily Mo Pena	.10
114	Roy Oswalt	.40
115	Adam Dunn	.40
116	Hideki Matsui	1.00
117	Pat Burrell	.25
118	Jason Schmidt	.20
119	Alfonso Soriano	.40
120	Aramis Ramirez	.25
121	Jason Giambi	.25
122	Orlando Hernandez	.20
123	Magglio Ordonez	.10
124	Troy Glaus	.25
125	Carlos Delgado	.25
126	Kevin Millwood	.10
127	Shannon Stewart	.10
128	Luis Castillo	.10
129	Jim Edmonds	.25
130	Richie Sexson	.25
131	Dmitri Young	.10
132	Russ Adams	.10
133	Nick Swisher	.10
134	Jermaine Dye	.10
135	Anderson Hernandez RC	.10
136	Justin Huber RC	.10
137	Jason Botts RC	.10
138	Jeff Mathis RC	.10
139	Ryan Garko RC	.10
140	Charlton Jimerson RC	.10
141	Chris Denorfia RC	.10
142	Anthony Reyes RC	.10
143	Bryan Bullington RC	.10
144	Chuck James RC	.10
145	Danny Sandoval RC	.25
146	Walter Young RC	.10
147	Fausto Carmona RC	.25
148	Francisco Liriano RC	.25
149	Hong-Chih Kuo RC	.10
150	Joe Saunders RC	.10
151	John Koronka RC	.10
152	Robert Andino RC	.10
153	Shaun Marcum RC	.10
154	Tom Gorzelanny RC	.10
155	Craig Breslow RC	.25
156	Chris Demaria RC	.50
157	Brayan Pena RC	.10
158	Rich Hill RC	.25
159	Rick Short RC	.10
160	Darrell Rasner RC	.10
161	C.J. Wilson RC	.10
162	Brandon Watson RC	.10
163	Paul McAnulty RC	.10
164	Marshall McDougall RC	.10
165	Checklist	.10

Red Foil

Red:		2-3X
Production 2,006 Sets		

Printing Plates

No Pricing
Production one set per color.

Autographs

		NM/M
BE	Brad Eldred	10.00
JE	Johnny Estrada	10.00
TH	Toby Hall	10.00
MK	Mark Kotsay	10.00
EM	Eli Marrero	10.00
VZ	Victor Zambrano	10.00

Opening Day Relics

		NM/M
Common Team:		25.00
WI	Chicago White Sox	40.00
MN	New York Mets	40.00
RR	Texas Rangers	30.00
BP	Milwaukee Brewers	25.00
RC	Cincinnati Reds	30.00
PC	Philadelphia Phillies	40.00
OD	Baltimore Orioles	25.00
RD	Colorado Rockies	25.00
DB	Los Angeles Dodgers	40.00
RT	Kansas City Royals	25.00
MA	Seattle Mariners	30.00
AM	Houston Astros	30.00
PG	San Diego Padres	40.00
AY	Oakland Athletics	40.00
JT	Toronto Blue Jays	30.00

SI For Kids

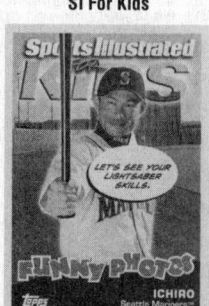

		NM/M
1	Vladimir Guerrero	.50
2	Marcus Giles	.15
3	Michael Young	.15
4	Derek Jeter	1.50
5	Barry Bonds	1.50
6	Ivan Rodriguez	.40
7	Miguel Cabrera	.50
8	Jim Edmonds	.15
9	Jack Wilson	.15
10	Khalil Greene	.15
11	Miguel Tejada	.25
12	Eric Chavez	.25
13	Shannon Stewart	.15
14	Julio Lugo	.15
15	Andruw Jones	.50
16	Nick Johnson, Randy Johnson	.50
17	Tadahito Iguchi, Ivan Rodriguez	.25
18	Roy Oswalt, Jose Reyes	.50
19	Manny Ramirez, Ronnie Belliard	.50
20	Todd Helton, Khalil Greene	.25
21	David Ortiz, Dontrelle Willis	.50

		NM/M
22	Ichiro Suzuki, Johnny Damon	.75
23	Craig Biggio, Jack Wilson	.15
24	Brian Roberts, Richie Sexson	.25
25	Chipper Jones, Marcus Giles	.50

2006 Topps Sterling

		NM/M
Common Player:		10.00
Production 250 Sets		
Box (Five Cards):		300.00
1-19	Barry Bonds	10.00
20-39	Mickey Mantle	25.00
40-43	Josh Gibson	30.00
44-53	Rickey Henderson	10.00
54-62	Ted Williams	15.00
63-67	Roberto Clemente	25.00
68-77	Nolan Ryan	20.00
78-96	Cal Ripken Jr.	20.00
97-101	Stan Musial	15.00
102-106	Reggie Jackson	15.00
107-111	Johnny Bench	15.00
112-121	George Brett	15.00
122-131	Don Mattingly	15.00
132-136	Roger Maris	20.00
137-146	Rod Carew	10.00
147-151	Yogi Berra	15.00
152-156	Mike Schmidt	15.00
157-175	Carl Yastrzemski	15.00
176-185	Tony Gwynn	15.00
186-190	Ryne Sandberg	15.00
191-200	Ozzie Smith	15.00

Framed Burgundy
Burgundy (1-200): 3-5X
Production 10 Sets

Framed Silver
No Pricing
Production One Set

Framed White
White (1-200): 1-1.5X
Production 50 Sets

Baseball Cut Signatures

		NM/M
SA	Sparky Anderson	40.00
LA	Luis Aparicio	40.00
LB	Lou Brock	50.00
RC	Rod Carew	50.00
SC	Steve Carlton	50.00
GC	Gary Carter	50.00
OC	Orlando Cepeda	35.00
DE	Dennis Eckersley	40.00
BF	Bob Feller	40.00
RF	Rollie Fingers	40.00
CF	Carlton Fisk	60.00
BG	Bob Gibson	50.00
MI	Monte Irvin	40.00
AK	Al Kaline	60.00
GK	George Kell	40.00
HK	Harmon Killebrew	70.00
RK	Ralph Kiner	50.00
JM	Juan Marichal	40.00
JMO	Joe Morgan	50.00
PN	Phil Niekro	40.00
JP	Jim Palmer	40.00
TP	Tony Perez	40.00
GP	Gaylord Perry	40.00
RR	Robin Roberts	40.00
BR	Brooks Robinson	60.00
FR	Frank Robinson	60.00
RS	Ryne Sandberg	80.00
MS	Mike Schmidt	75.00
RSH	Red Schoendienst	60.00
DS	Duke Snider	75.00
EW	Earl Weaver	30.00
RY	Robin Yount	70.00

Career Stats Relics
No Pricing
Production 10 Sets
Prime: No Pricing
Production One Set
Sterling Silver: No Pricing
Production One Set

Career Stats Relics Autographs
Production 10 Sets
Prime: No Pricing
Production One Set
Sterling Silver: No Pricing
Production One Set

Cut from the Same Cloth Signatures
Production 1-5

Cut Signatures

		NM/M
46	Elmer Valo	80.00
53	Carl Furillo	100.00
61	Hal Newhouser	60.00
64	Dick Sisler	65.00
65	Frank Shea	75.00
66	Monty Stratton	80.00
67	Lloyd Waner	150.00
68	Sal Maglie	70.00
69	Waite Hoyt	80.00
70	Warren Spahn	100.00
72	A.B. Chandler	60.00
73	Al Barlick	75.00
74	Bill Dickey	100.00
75	Bill Terry	80.00
76	Billy Herman	75.00
77	Bob Lemon	60.00
78	Buck Leonard	80.00
79	Charles Gehringer	100.00
81	Earl Averill	60.00
82	Hoyt Wilhelm	80.00
83	Jim "Catfish" Hunter	100.00
84	Joe Sewell	80.00
85	Judy Johnson	80.00
86	Carl Hubbell	85.00
87	Lou Boudreau	65.00
88	Luke Appling	80.00
89	Ray Dandridge	75.00
90	Rick Ferrell	60.00
91	Stan Coveleski	75.00
92	Willie Stargell	120.00

Five Relics
Production 10 Sets
Prime: No Pricing
Production 10 Sets
Sterling Silver: No Pricing
Production One Set

Five Relics Autographs
Production 10 Sets
Prime: No Pricing
Production 10 Sets
Sterling Silver: No Pricing
Production One Set

Josh Gibson Bat Barrel
Production One

Jumbo Jersey
Production 10 Sets
Prime: No Pricing
Production One Set
Patch: No Pricing
Production 10 Sets
Sterling Silver: No Pricing
Production One Set

Moments Relics

NM/M
Production 10 Sets
Prime: No Pricing
Production One Set

BB	Barry Bonds HR 1	75.00
BB	Barry Bonds HR 2	75.00
BB	Barry Bonds HR 3	75.00
BB	Barry Bonds HR 4	75.00
BB	Barry Bonds HR 5	75.00
BB	Barry Bonds HR 6	75.00
BB	Barry Bonds HR 7	75.00
BB	Barry Bonds HR 8	75.00
BB	Barry Bonds HR 9	75.00
BB	Barry Bonds HR 1	75.00
BB	Barry Bonds HR 2	75.00
BB	Barry Bonds HR 3	75.00
BB	Barry Bonds HR 4	75.00
BB	Barry Bonds HR 5	75.00
BB	Barry Bonds HR 6	75.00
BB	Barry Bonds HR 7	75.00
BB	Barry Bonds HR 8	75.00
BB	Barry Bonds HR 1	75.00
BB	Barry Bonds HR 2	75.00
BB	Barry Bonds HR 3	75.00
BB	Barry Bonds HR 4	75.00
BB	Barry Bonds HR 5	75.00
BB	Barry Bonds HR 6	75.00
BB	Barry Bonds HR 7	75.00
BB	Barry Bonds HR 8	75.00
BB	Barry Bonds	75.00
BB	Barry Bonds 1993	75.00
BB	Barry Bonds 1994	75.00
BB	Barry Bonds 1995	75.00
BB	Barry Bonds 1996	75.00
BB	Barry Bonds 1997	75.00
BB	Barry Bonds 1998	75.00
BB	Barry Bonds 1999	75.00
BB	Barry Bonds 1993	75.00
BB	Barry Bonds 2001	75.00
BB	Barry Bonds 2002	75.00
BB	Barry Bonds 2003	75.00
BB	Barry Bonds 2004	75.00
BB	Barry Bonds 1993	75.00
BB	Barry Bonds 1994	75.00
BB	Barry Bonds 1995	75.00
BB	Barry Bonds 1996	75.00
BB	Barry Bonds 1997	75.00
BB	Barry Bonds 1998	75.00
BB	Barry Bonds 2000	75.00
BB	Barry Bonds 2001	75.00
BB	Barry Bonds 2002	75.00
BB	Barry Bonds 2003	75.00
BB	Barry Bonds 2004	75.00
BB	Barry Bonds 2002	75.00
BB	Barry Bonds 2004	75.00
BB	Barry Bonds 1993	75.00
BB	Barry Bonds 1994	75.00
BB	Barry Bonds 1996	75.00
BB	Barry Bonds 1997	75.00
BB	Barry Bonds 2000	75.00
BB	Barry Bonds 2001	75.00
BB	Barry Bonds 2002	75.00
BB	Barry Bonds 2003	75.00
BB	Barry Bonds 2004	75.00
BB	Barry Bonds 1993	75.00
BB	Barry Bonds 1994	75.00
BB	Barry Bonds 1996	75.00
BB	Barry Bonds 2001	75.00
BB	Barry Bonds 2002	75.00
BB	Barry Bonds 2003	75.00
BB	Barry Bonds 2004	75.00
MM	Mickey Mantle WS HR 1	350.00
MM	Mickey Mantle WS HR 2	350.00
MM	Mickey Mantle WS HR 3	350.00
MM	Mickey Mantle WS HR 4	350.00
MM	Mickey Mantle WS HR 5	350.00
MM	Mickey Mantle WS HR 6	350.00
MM	Mickey Mantle WS HR 7	350.00
MM	Mickey Mantle WS HR 8	350.00
MM	Mickey Mantle WS HR 9	350.00
MM	Mickey Mantle WS HR 10	350.00
MM	Mickey Mantle WS HR 11	350.00
MM	Mickey Mantle WS HR 12	350.00
MM	Mickey Mantle WS HR 13	350.00
MM	Mickey Mantle WS HR 14	350.00
MM	Mickey Mantle WS HR 15	350.00
MM	Mickey Mantle WS HR 16	350.00
MM	Mickey Mantle WS HR 17	350.00
MM	Mickey Mantle WS HR 18	350.00
MM	Mickey Mantle 1952	350.00
MM	Mickey Mantle 1956	350.00
MM	Mickey Mantle 1957	350.00
MM	Mickey Mantle 1962	350.00
MM	Mickey Mantle 1953	350.00
MM	Mickey Mantle 1954	350.00
MM	Mickey Mantle 1955	350.00
MM	Mickey Mantle 1958	350.00
MM	Mickey Mantle 1959	350.00
MM	Mickey Mantle 1960	350.00
MM	Mickey Mantle 1961	350.00
MM	Mickey Mantle 1963	350.00
MM	Mickey Mantle 1965	350.00
MM	Mickey Mantle 1967	350.00
MM	Mickey Mantle 1968	350.00
MM	Mickey Mantle HR 1	350.00
MM	Mickey Mantle HR 7	350.00
MM	Mickey Mantle HR 10	350.00
MM	Mickey Mantle HR 2	350.00
MM	Mickey Mantle HR 3	350.00
MM	Mickey Mantle HR 4	350.00
MM	Mickey Mantle HR 5	350.00
MM	Mickey Mantle HR 8	350.00
MM	Mickey Mantle HR 9	350.00
MM	Mickey Mantle HR 11	350.00
MM	Mickey Mantle HR 12	350.00
MM	Mickey Mantle HR 13	350.00
MM	Mickey Mantle HR 14	350.00
MM	Mickey Mantle HR 15	350.00
MM	Mickey Mantle HR 16	350.00
MM	Mickey Mantle HR 17	350.00
MM	Mickey Mantle HR 19	350.00
MM	Mickey Mantle HR 20	350.00
MM	Mickey Mantle HR 25	350.00
MM	Mickey Mantle HR 21	350.00
MM	Mickey Mantle HR 22	350.00
MM	Mickey Mantle HR 23	350.00
MM	Mickey Mantle HR 24	350.00
MM	Mickey Mantle HR 26	350.00
MM	Mickey Mantle HR 27	350.00
MM	Mickey Mantle HR 28	350.00
MM	Mickey Mantle HR 29	350.00
MM	Mickey Mantle HR 30	350.00
MM	Mickey Mantle HR 31	350.00
MM	Mickey Mantle HR 32	350.00
MM	Mickey Mantle HR 33	350.00
MM	Mickey Mantle HR 34	350.00
MM	Mickey Mantle HR 35	350.00
MM	Mickey Mantle HR 36	350.00
MM	Mickey Mantle HR 37	350.00
MM	Mickey Mantle HR 38	350.00
MM	Mickey Mantle HR 39	350.00
MM	Mickey Mantle HR 40	350.00
MM	Mickey Mantle HR 50	350.00
MM	Mickey Mantle HR 60	350.00
MM	Mickey Mantle HR 41	350.00
MM	Mickey Mantle HR 42	350.00
MM	Mickey Mantle HR 43	350.00
MM	Mickey Mantle HR 44	350.00
MM	Mickey Mantle HR 45	350.00
MM	Mickey Mantle HR 46	350.00
MM	Mickey Mantle HR 47	350.00
MM	Mickey Mantle HR 48	350.00
MM	Mickey Mantle HR 49	350.00
MM	Mickey Mantle HR 51	350.00
MM	Mickey Mantle HR 52	350.00
MM	Mickey Mantle HR 53	350.00
MM	Mickey Mantle HR 54	350.00
MM	Mickey Mantle HR 55	350.00
MM	Mickey Mantle HR 56	350.00
MM	Mickey Mantle HR 57	350.00
MM	Mickey Mantle HR 58	350.00
MM	Mickey Mantle HR 59	350.00
MM	Mickey Mantle HR 75	350.00
MM	Mickey Mantle HR 61	350.00
MM	Mickey Mantle HR 62	350.00
MM	Mickey Mantle HR 63	350.00
MM	Mickey Mantle HR 64	350.00
MM	Mickey Mantle HR 65	350.00
MM	Mickey Mantle HR 67	350.00
MM	Mickey Mantle HR 68	350.00
MM	Mickey Mantle HR 69	350.00
MM	Mickey Mantle HR 70	350.00
MM	Mickey Mantle HR 71	350.00
MM	Mickey Mantle HR 72	350.00
MM	Mickey Mantle HR 73	350.00
MM	Mickey Mantle HR 74	350.00
MM	Mickey Mantle HR 76	350.00
MM	Mickey Mantle HR 77	350.00
MM	Mickey Mantle HR 78	350.00
MM	Mickey Mantle HR 80	350.00
MM	Mickey Mantle HR 90	350.00
MM	Mickey Mantle HR 81	350.00
MM	Mickey Mantle HR 82	350.00
MM	Mickey Mantle HR 83	350.00
MM	Mickey Mantle HR 84	350.00
MM	Mickey Mantle HR 85	350.00
MM	Mickey Mantle HR 86	350.00
MM	Mickey Mantle HR 87	350.00
MM	Mickey Mantle HR 88	350.00
MM	Mickey Mantle HR 89	350.00
MM	Mickey Mantle HR 91	350.00
MM	Mickey Mantle HR 92	350.00
MM	Mickey Mantle HR 93	350.00
MM	Mickey Mantle HR 94	350.00
MM	Mickey Mantle HR 95	350.00
MM	Mickey Mantle HR 96	350.00
MM	Mickey Mantle HR 97	350.00
MM	Mickey Mantle HR 98	350.00
MM	Mickey Mantle HR 99	350.00
MM	Mickey Mantle HR 100	350.00
JG	Josh Gibson	500.00
JG	Josh Gibson	500.00
JG	Josh Gibson	500.00
JG	Josh Gibson	500.00
JG	Josh Gibson	500.00
JG	Josh Gibson	500.00
JG	Josh Gibson	500.00
RH	Rickey Henderson 1980	60.00
RH	Rickey Henderson 1981	60.00
RH	Rickey Henderson 1982	60.00
RH	Rickey Henderson 1983	60.00
RH	Rickey Henderson 1990	60.00
RH	Rickey Henderson 1998	60.00
RH	Rickey Henderson 1989	60.00
RH	Rickey Henderson 1991	60.00
RH	Rickey Henderson 1985	60.00
RH	Rickey Henderson 1986	60.00
RH	Rickey Henderson 1987	60.00
RH	Rickey Henderson 1980	60.00
RH	Rickey Henderson 1983	60.00
RH	Rickey Henderson 1990	60.00
RH	Rickey Henderson 1982	60.00
RH	Rickey Henderson 1984	60.00
RH	Rickey Henderson 1991	60.00
RH	Rickey Henderson 1985	60.00
RH	Rickey Henderson 1987	60.00
RH	Rickey Henderson 1986	60.00
RH	Rickey Henderson 1988	60.00
RH	Rickey Henderson 1981	60.00
RH	Rickey Henderson 1989	60.00
RH	Rickey Henderson 1986	60.00
RH	Rickey Henderson 1985	60.00
RH	Rickey Henderson 1983	60.00
RH	Rickey Henderson 1998	60.00
RH	Rickey Henderson 1982	60.00
RH	Rickey Henderson 1989	60.00
RH	Rickey Henderson 1990	60.00
RH	Rickey Henderson 1981	60.00
RH	Rickey Henderson 1985	60.00
TW	Ted Williams 0.406	150.00
TW	Ted Williams 0.5	150.00
TW	Ted Williams 0.308	150.00
TW	Ted Williams 0.341	150.00
TW	Ted Williams 0.421	150.00
TW	Ted Williams 0.436	150.00
TW	Ted Williams 0.42	150.00
TW	Ted Williams 0.405	150.00
TW	Ted Williams 0.397	150.00
TW	Ted Williams 0.4	150.00
TW	Ted Williams 0.414	150.00
TW	Ted Williams 0.409	150.00
TW	Ted Williams 0.411	150.00
TW	Ted Williams 0.399	150.00
TW	Ted Williams 0.404	150.00
TW	Ted Williams HR 1	150.00
TW	Ted Williams HR 10	150.00
TW	Ted Williams HR 20	150.00
TW	Ted Williams HR 30	150.00
TW	Ted Williams HR 36	150.00
TW	Ted Williams HR 1	150.00
TW	Ted Williams HR 10	150.00
TW	Ted Williams HR 20	150.00
TW	Ted Williams HR 30	150.00
TW	Ted Williams HR 32	150.00
RC	Roberto Clemente HIT 1	200.00
RC	Roberto Clemente HIT 2	200.00
RC	Roberto Clemente HIT 3	200.00
RC	Roberto Clemente HIT 4	200.00
RC	Roberto Clemente HIT 5	200.00
RC	Roberto Clemente HIT 6	200.00
RC	Roberto Clemente HIT 7	200.00
RC	Roberto Clemente HIT 8	200.00
RC	Roberto Clemente HIT 9	200.00
RC	Roberto Clemente HIT 10	200.00
RC	Roberto Clemente HIT 11	200.00
RC	Roberto Clemente HIT 12	200.00
RC	Roberto Clemente HIT 21	200.00
RC	Roberto Clemente HIT 13	200.00
RC	Roberto Clemente HIT 14	200.00
RC	Roberto Clemente HIT 15	200.00
RC	Roberto Clemente HIT 16	200.00
RC	Roberto Clemente HIT 17	200.00
RC	Roberto Clemente HIT 18	200.00
RC	Roberto Clemente HIT 19	200.00
RC	Roberto Clemente HIT 20	200.00
RC	Roberto Clemente 1966	200.00
RC	Roberto Clemente 1971	200.00
RC	Roberto Clemente 1972	200.00
RC	Roberto Clemente 1961	200.00
RC	Roberto Clemente 1962	200.00
RC	Roberto Clemente 1963	200.00
RC	Roberto Clemente 1964	200.00
RC	Roberto Clemente 1965	200.00
RC	Roberto Clemente 1967	200.00
RC	Roberto Clemente 1968	200.00
RC	Roberto Clemente 1969	200.00
RC	Roberto Clemente 1970	200.00
NR	Nolan Ryan SO 1	100.00
NR	Nolan Ryan SO 50	100.00
NR	Nolan Ryan SO 100	100.00
NR	Nolan Ryan SO 200	100.00
NR	Nolan Ryan SO 10	100.00
NR	Nolan Ryan SO 20	100.00
NR	Nolan Ryan SO 30	100.00
NR	Nolan Ryan SO 40	100.00
NR	Nolan Ryan SO 60	100.00
NR	Nolan Ryan SO 70	100.00
NR	Nolan Ryan SO 80	100.00
NR	Nolan Ryan SO 90	100.00
NR	Nolan Ryan SO 125	100.00
NR	Nolan Ryan SO 150	100.00
NR	Nolan Ryan SO 175	100.00
NR	Nolan Ryan SO 300	100.00
NR	Nolan Ryan SO 350	100.00
NR	Nolan Ryan SO 380	100.00
NR	Nolan Ryan SO 382	100.00
NR	Nolan Ryan SO 383	100.00
NR	Nolan Ryan SO 250	100.00
NR	Nolan Ryan SO 275	100.00
NR	Nolan Ryan SO 310	100.00
NR	Nolan Ryan SO 320	100.00
NR	Nolan Ryan SO 330	100.00
NR	Nolan Ryan SO 340	100.00
NR	Nolan Ryan SO 360	100.00
NR	Nolan Ryan SO 370	100.00
NR	Nolan Ryan SO 375	100.00
NR	Nolan Ryan NO HIT 2	100.00
NR	Nolan Ryan NO HIT 3	100.00
NR	Nolan Ryan NO HIT 4	100.00
NR	Nolan Ryan NO HIT 5	100.00
NR	Nolan Ryan NO HIT 7	100.00
CR	Cal Ripken Jr. 1983	100.00
CR	Cal Ripken Jr. 1985	100.00
CR	Cal Ripken Jr. 1987	100.00
CR	Cal Ripken Jr. 1989	100.00
CR	Cal Ripken Jr. 1991	100.00
CR	Cal Ripken Jr. 1993	100.00
CR	Cal Ripken Jr. 1995	100.00
CR	Cal Ripken Jr. 1997	100.00
CR	Cal Ripken Jr. 1999	100.00
CR	Cal Ripken Jr. 2001	100.00
CR	Cal Ripken Jr. 1984	100.00
CR	Cal Ripken Jr. 1986	100.00
CR	Cal Ripken Jr. 1988	100.00
CR	Cal Ripken Jr. 1990	100.00
CR	Cal Ripken Jr. 1992	100.00
CR	Cal Ripken Jr. 1994	100.00
CR	Cal Ripken Jr. 1996	100.00
CR	Cal Ripken Jr. 1998	100.00
CR	Cal Ripken Jr. 2000	100.00
CR	Cal Ripken Jr. 1984	100.00
CR	Cal Ripken Jr. 1986	100.00
CR	Cal Ripken Jr. 1991	100.00
CR	Cal Ripken Jr. 1994	100.00
CR	Cal Ripken Jr. 1983	100.00
CR	Cal Ripken Jr. 1985	100.00
CR	Cal Ripken Jr. 1989	100.00
CR	Cal Ripken Jr. 1993	100.00
CR	Cal Ripken Jr. HIT 1	100.00
CR	Cal Ripken Jr. 1500	100.00
CR	Cal Ripken Jr. 2500	100.00
CR	Cal Ripken Jr. 2900	100.00
CR	Cal Ripken Jr. 3000	100.00
CR	Cal Ripken Jr. 3181	100.00
CR	Cal Ripken Jr. 100	100.00
CR	Cal Ripken Jr. 200	100.00
CR	Cal Ripken Jr. 300	100.00
CR	Cal Ripken Jr. 400	100.00
CR	Cal Ripken Jr. 500	100.00
CR	Cal Ripken Jr. 2100	100.00
CR	Cal Ripken Jr. 2200	100.00
CR	Cal Ripken Jr. 2300	100.00
CR	Cal Ripken Jr. 2400	100.00
CR	Cal Ripken Jr. 2600	100.00
CR	Cal Ripken Jr. 2700	100.00
CR	Cal Ripken Jr. 2800	100.00
CR	Cal Ripken Jr. HR 1	100.00
CR	Cal Ripken Jr. HR 100	100.00
CR	Cal Ripken Jr. HR 200	100.00
CR	Cal Ripken Jr. HR 300	100.00
CR	Cal Ripken Jr. HR 400	100.00
CR	Cal Ripken Jr. HR 431	100.00
CR	Cal Ripken Jr. HR 10	100.00
CR	Cal Ripken Jr. HR 25	100.00
CR	Cal Ripken Jr. HR 50	100.00
CR	Cal Ripken Jr. HR 75	100.00
CR	Cal Ripken Jr. HR 125	100.00
CR	Cal Ripken Jr. HR 150	100.00
CR	Cal Ripken Jr. HR 175	100.00
CR	Cal Ripken Jr. HR 225	100.00
CR	Cal Ripken Jr. HR 250	100.00
CR	Cal Ripken Jr. HR 275	100.00
CR	Cal Ripken Jr. HR 325	100.00
CR	Cal Ripken Jr. HR 350	100.00
CR	Cal Ripken Jr. HR 375	100.00
CR	Cal Ripken Jr. HR 425	100.00
CR	Cal Ripken Jr. GM 1	100.00
CR	Cal Ripken Jr. 500	100.00
CR	Cal Ripken Jr. 1000	100.00
CR	Cal Ripken Jr. 2000	100.00
CR	Cal Ripken Jr. 2130	100.00
CR	Cal Ripken Jr. 2131	100.00
CR	Cal Ripken Jr. 2632	100.00
CR	Cal Ripken Jr. 100	100.00
CR	Cal Ripken Jr. 200	100.00
CR	Cal Ripken Jr. 300	100.00
CR	Cal Ripken Jr. 400	100.00
CR	Cal Ripken Jr. 600	100.00
CR	Cal Ripken Jr. 700	100.00
CR	Cal Ripken Jr. 800	100.00
CR	Cal Ripken Jr. 900	100.00
CR	Cal Ripken Jr. 1250	100.00
CR	Cal Ripken Jr. 1500	100.00
CR	Cal Ripken Jr. 1750	100.00
CR	Cal Ripken Jr. 2500	100.00
CR	Cal Ripken Jr. 2600	100.00
SM	Stan Musial 1943	75.00
SM	Stan Musial 1946	75.00
SM	Stan Musial 1948	75.00
SM	Stan Musial 1950	75.00
SM	Stan Musial 1952	75.00
SM	Stan Musial 1942	75.00
SM	Stan Musial 1944	75.00
SM	Stan Musial 1947	75.00
SM	Stan Musial 1949	75.00
SM	Stan Musial 1951	75.00
SM	Stan Musial 1954	75.00
SM	Stan Musial 1956	75.00
SM	Stan Musial 1958	75.00
SM	Stan Musial 1960	75.00
SM	Stan Musial 1962	75.00
SM	Stan Musial 1953	75.00
SM	Stan Musial 1955	75.00
SM	Stan Musial 1957	75.00
SM	Stan Musial 1959	75.00
SM	Stan Musial 1961	75.00
RJ	Reggie Jackson HR 1	60.00
RJ	Reggie Jackson HR 100	60.00
RJ	Reggie Jackson HR 250	60.00
RJ	Reggie Jackson HR 300	60.00
RJ	Reggie Jackson HR 350	60.00
RJ	Reggie Jackson HR 400	60.00
RJ	Reggie Jackson HR 450	60.00
RJ	Reggie Jackson HR 550	60.00
RJ	Reggie Jackson HR 25	60.00
RJ	Reggie Jackson HR 50	60.00
RJ	Reggie Jackson HR 150	60.00
JB	Johnny Bench 1968	65.00
JB	Johnny Bench 1969	65.00
JB	Johnny Bench 1971	65.00
JB	Johnny Bench 1973	65.00
JB	Johnny Bench 1975	65.00
JB	Johnny Bench 1976	65.00
GB	George Brett HIT 1	60.00
GB	George Brett HIT 3	60.00
GB	George Brett HIT 5	60.00
GB	George Brett HIT 7	60.00
GB	George Brett HIT 10	60.00
GB	George Brett HIT 12	60.00
GB	George Brett HIT 15	60.00
GB	George Brett HIT 16	60.00
GB	George Brett HIT 17	60.00
GB	George Brett HIT 18	60.00
GB	George Brett HIT 2	60.00
GB	George Brett HIT 4	60.00
GB	George Brett HIT 6	60.00
GB	George Brett HIT 8	60.00
GB	George Brett HIT 9	60.00
GB	George Brett HIT 11	60.00
GB	George Brett HIT 13	60.00
GB	George Brett HIT 14	60.00
GB	George Brett 1976	60.00
GB	George Brett 1980	60.00
GB	George Brett 1990	60.00
GB	George Brett 1976	60.00
GB	George Brett 1977	60.00
GB	George Brett 1979	60.00
GB	George Brett 1981	60.00
GB	George Brett 1983	60.00
GB	George Brett 1985	60.00

Code	Player	Price
GB	George Brett 1988	60.00
GB	George Brett 1978	60.00
GB	George Brett 1980	60.00
GB	George Brett 1982	60.00
GB	George Brett 1984	60.00
GB	George Brett 1986	60.00
GB	George Brett 1980	60.00
GB	George Brett 1985	60.00
GB	George Brett 1988	60.00
RM	Roger Maris HR 1	125.00
RM	Roger Maris HR 2	125.00
RM	Roger Maris HR 5	125.00
RM	Roger Maris HR 9	125.00
RM	Roger Maris HR 10	125.00
RM	Roger Maris HR 15	125.00
RM	Roger Maris HR 3	125.00
RM	Roger Maris HR 4	125.00
RM	Roger Maris HR 6	125.00
RM	Roger Maris HR 7	125.00
RM	Roger Maris HR 8	125.00
RM	Roger Maris HR 11	125.00
RM	Roger Maris HR 12	125.00
RM	Roger Maris HR 13	125.00
RM	Roger Maris HR 14	125.00
RM	Roger Maris HR 20	125.00
RM	Roger Maris HR 25	125.00
RM	Roger Maris HR 30	125.00
RM	Roger Maris HR 16	125.00
RM	Roger Maris HR 17	125.00
RM	Roger Maris HR 18	125.00
RM	Roger Maris HR 19	125.00
RM	Roger Maris HR 21	125.00
RM	Roger Maris HR 22	125.00
RM	Roger Maris HR 23	125.00
RM	Roger Maris HR 24	125.00
RM	Roger Maris HR 26	125.00
RM	Roger Maris HR 27	125.00
RM	Roger Maris HR 28	125.00
RM	Roger Maris HR 29	125.00
YB	Yogi Berra 1951	75.00
YB	Yogi Berra 1951	75.00
YB	Yogi Berra 1954	75.00
YB	Yogi Berra 1955	75.00
MS	Mike Schmidt HR 1	50.00
MS	Mike Schmidt HR 2	50.00
MS	Mike Schmidt HR 3	50.00
MS	Mike Schmidt HR 4	50.00
CY	Carl Yastrzemski HR 1	60.00
CY	Carl Yastrzemski HR 5	60.00
CY	Carl Yastrzemski HR 10	60.00
CY	Carl Yastrzemski HR 15	60.00
CY	Carl Yastrzemski HR 2	60.00
CY	Carl Yastrzemski HR 3	60.00
CY	Carl Yastrzemski HR 4	60.00
CY	Carl Yastrzemski HR 6	60.00
CY	Carl Yastrzemski HR 7	60.00
CY	Carl Yastrzemski HR 8	60.00
CY	Carl Yastrzemski HR 9	60.00
CY	Carl Yastrzemski HR 11	60.00
CY	Carl Yastrzemski HR 12	60.00
CY	Carl Yastrzemski HR 13	60.00
CY	Carl Yastrzemski HR 14	60.00
CY	Carl Yastrzemski HR 20	60.00
CY	Carl Yastrzemski HR 25	60.00
CY	Carl Yastrzemski HR 30	60.00
CY	Carl Yastrzemski HR 16	60.00
CY	Carl Yastrzemski HR 17	60.00
CY	Carl Yastrzemski HR 18	60.00
CY	Carl Yastrzemski HR 19	60.00
CY	Carl Yastrzemski HR 21	60.00
CY	Carl Yastrzemski HR 22	60.00
CY	Carl Yastrzemski HR 23	60.00
CY	Carl Yastrzemski HR 24	60.00
CY	Carl Yastrzemski HR 26	60.00
CY	Carl Yastrzemski HR 28	60.00
CY	Carl Yastrzemski HR 29	60.00
CY	Carl Yastrzemski HR 35	60.00
CY	Carl Yastrzemski HR 40	60.00
CY	Carl Yastrzemski HR 44	60.00
CY	Carl Yastrzemski HR 31	60.00
CY	Carl Yastrzemski HR 32	60.00
CY	Carl Yastrzemski HR 33	60.00
CY	Carl Yastrzemski HR 34	60.00
CY	Carl Yastrzemski HR 36	60.00
CY	Carl Yastrzemski HR 37	60.00
CY	Carl Yastrzemski HR 38	60.00
CY	Carl Yastrzemski HR 39	60.00
CY	Carl Yastrzemski HR 41	60.00
CY	Carl Yastrzemski HR 42	60.00
CY	Carl Yastrzemski HR 43	60.00
CY	Carl Yastrzemski 1961	60.00
CY	Carl Yastrzemski 1964	60.00
CY	Carl Yastrzemski 1966	60.00
CY	Carl Yastrzemski 1967	60.00
CY	Carl Yastrzemski 1970	60.00
CY	Carl Yastrzemski 1972	60.00
CY	Carl Yastrzemski 1962	60.00
CY	Carl Yastrzemski 1963	60.00
CY	Carl Yastrzemski 1965	60.00
CY	Carl Yastrzemski 1968	60.00
CY	Carl Yastrzemski 1969	60.00
CY	Carl Yastrzemski 1971	60.00
CY	Carl Yastrzemski 1973	60.00
CY	Carl Yastrzemski 1975	60.00
CY	Carl Yastrzemski 1977	60.00
CY	Carl Yastrzemski 1980	60.00
CY	Carl Yastrzemski 1983	60.00
CY	Carl Yastrzemski 1974	60.00
CY	Carl Yastrzemski 1976	60.00
CY	Carl Yastrzemski 1978	60.00
CY	Carl Yastrzemski 1979	60.00
CY	Carl Yastrzemski 1981	60.00
CY	Carl Yastrzemski 1982	60.00
CY	Carl Yastrzemski 1963	60.00
CY	Carl Yastrzemski 1965	60.00
CY	Carl Yastrzemski 1966	60.00
CY	Carl Yastrzemski 1967	60.00

Code	Player	Price
CY	Carl Yastrzemski 1968	60.00
CY	Carl Yastrzemski 1969	60.00
CY	Carl Yastrzemski 1970	60.00
CY	Carl Yastrzemski 1971	60.00
CY	Carl Yastrzemski 1972	60.00
CY	Carl Yastrzemski 1973	60.00
CY	Carl Yastrzemski 1974	60.00
CY	Carl Yastrzemski 1975	60.00
CY	Carl Yastrzemski 1976	60.00
CY	Carl Yastrzemski 1977	60.00
CY	Carl Yastrzemski 1978	60.00
CY	Carl Yastrzemski 1979	60.00
CY	Carl Yastrzemski 1982	60.00
CY	Carl Yastrzemski 1983	60.00
TG	Tony Gwynn 1984	60.00
TG	Tony Gwynn 1987	60.00
TG	Tony Gwynn 1988	60.00
TG	Tony Gwynn 1989	60.00
TG	Tony Gwynn 1994	60.00
TG	Tony Gwynn 1995	60.00
TG	Tony Gwynn 1996	60.00
TG	Tony Gwynn 1997	60.00
RS	Ryne Sandberg 1984	70.00
RS	Ryne Sandberg 1988	70.00
RS	Ryne Sandberg 1990	70.00
RS	Ryne Sandberg 1992	70.00
RS	Ryne Sandberg 1983	70.00
RS	Ryne Sandberg 1985	70.00
RS	Ryne Sandberg 1987	70.00
RS	Ryne Sandberg 1989	70.00

Moments Relics Autographs

Code	Player	NM/M
	Production 10 Sets	
	Prime:	No Pricing
	Production One Set	
RH	Rickey Henderson 1980	125.00
RH	Rickey Henderson 1981	125.00
RH	Rickey Henderson 1982	125.00
RH	Rickey Henderson 1983	125.00
RH	Rickey Henderson 1984	125.00
RH	Rickey Henderson 1990	125.00
RH	Rickey Henderson 1998	125.00
RH	Rickey Henderson 1985	125.00
RH	Rickey Henderson 1986	125.00
RH	Rickey Henderson 1987	125.00
RH	Rickey Henderson 1980	125.00
RH	Rickey Henderson 1983	125.00
RH	Rickey Henderson 1990	125.00
RH	Rickey Henderson 1985	125.00
RH	Rickey Henderson 1987	125.00
RH	Rickey Henderson 1981	125.00
RH	Rickey Henderson 1990	125.00
RH	Rickey Henderson 1986	125.00
RH	Rickey Henderson 1983	125.00
RH	Rickey Henderson 1998	125.00
RH	Rickey Henderson 1990	125.00
NR	Nolan Ryan SO 1	300.00
NR	Nolan Ryan SO 50	300.00
NR	Nolan Ryan SO 100	300.00
NR	Nolan Ryan SO 200	300.00
NR	Nolan Ryan SO 300	300.00
NR	Nolan Ryan SO 350	300.00
NR	Nolan Ryan SO 380	300.00
NR	Nolan Ryan SO 382	300.00
NR	Nolan Ryan SO 383	300.00
NR	Nolan Ryan NO HIT 1	300.00
NR	Nolan Ryan NO HIT 2	300.00
NR	Nolan Ryan NO HIT 3	300.00
NR	Nolan Ryan NO HIT 4	300.00
NR	Nolan Ryan NO HIT 5	300.00
NR	Nolan Ryan NO HIT 6	300.00
NR	Nolan Ryan NO HIT 7	300.00
CR	Cal Ripken Jr. 1983	300.00
CR	Cal Ripken Jr. 1985	300.00
CR	Cal Ripken Jr. 1987	300.00
CR	Cal Ripken Jr. 1989	300.00
CR	Cal Ripken Jr. 1991	300.00
CR	Cal Ripken Jr. 1993	300.00
CR	Cal Ripken Jr. 1995	300.00
CR	Cal Ripken Jr. 1997	300.00
CR	Cal Ripken Jr. 2001	300.00
CR	Cal Ripken Jr. 1984	300.00
CR	Cal Ripken Jr. 1986	300.00
CR	Cal Ripken Jr. 1988	300.00
CR	Cal Ripken Jr. 1990	300.00
CR	Cal Ripken Jr. 1994	300.00
CR	Cal Ripken Jr. HIT 1	300.00
CR	Cal Ripken Jr. 1000	300.00
CR	Cal Ripken Jr. 1500	300.00
CR	Cal Ripken Jr. 2000	300.00
CR	Cal Ripken Jr. 2500	300.00
CR	Cal Ripken Jr. 3000	300.00
CR	Cal Ripken Jr. 3184	300.00
CR	Cal Ripken Jr. HR 100	300.00

Code	Player	Price
CR	Cal Ripken Jr. HR 200	300.00
CR	Cal Ripken Jr. HR 300	300.00
CR	Cal Ripken Jr. HR 400	300.00
CR	Cal Ripken Jr. HR 431	300.00
CR	Cal Ripken Jr. GM 1	300.00
CR	Cal Ripken Jr. 500	300.00
CR	Cal Ripken Jr. 1000	300.00
CR	Cal Ripken Jr. 2000	300.00
CR	Cal Ripken Jr. 2130	300.00
CR	Cal Ripken Jr. 2131	300.00
CR	Cal Ripken Jr. 2632	300.00
SM	Stan Musial 1941	150.00
SM	Stan Musial 1943	150.00
SM	Stan Musial 1946	150.00
SM	Stan Musial 1948	150.00
SM	Stan Musial 1950	150.00
SM	Stan Musial 1952	150.00
SM	Stan Musial 1954	150.00
SM	Stan Musial 1956	150.00
SM	Stan Musial 1958	150.00
SM	Stan Musial 1960	150.00
SM	Stan Musial 1962	150.00
SM	Stan Musial 1964	150.00
RJ	Reggie Jackson HR 1	150.00
RJ	Reggie Jackson HR 100	150.00
RJ	Reggie Jackson HR 200	150.00
RJ	Reggie Jackson HR 250	150.00
RJ	Reggie Jackson HR 300	150.00
RJ	Reggie Jackson HR 350	150.00
RJ	Reggie Jackson HR 400	150.00
RJ	Reggie Jackson HR 450	150.00
RJ	Reggie Jackson HR 500	150.00
RJ	Reggie Jackson HR 550	150.00
RJ	Reggie Jackson HR 563	150.00
RJ	Reggie Jackson WS HR 1	150.00
RJ	Reggie Jackson WS HR 2	150.00
RJ	Reggie Jackson WS HR 3	150.00
RJ	Reggie Jackson 500 HR	150.00
JB	Johnny Bench 1968	150.00
JB	Johnny Bench 1969	150.00
JB	Johnny Bench 1970	150.00
JB	Johnny Bench 1971	150.00
JB	Johnny Bench 1972	150.00
JB	Johnny Bench 1973	150.00
JB	Johnny Bench 1974	150.00
JB	Johnny Bench 1975	150.00
JB	Johnny Bench 1976	150.00
JB	Johnny Bench 1977	150.00
JB	Johnny Bench 1975	150.00
JB	Johnny Bench 1976	150.00
GB	George Brett HIT 1	150.00
GB	George Brett HIT 3	150.00
GB	George Brett HIT 5	150.00
GB	George Brett HIT 7	150.00
GB	George Brett HIT 10	150.00
GB	George Brett HIT 12	150.00
GB	George Brett HIT 15	150.00
GB	George Brett HIT 16	150.00
GB	George Brett HIT 17	150.00
GB	George Brett HIT 18	150.00
GB	George Brett 1976	150.00
GB	George Brett 1980	150.00
GB	George Brett 1990	150.00
GB	George Brett 1976	150.00
GB	George Brett 1977	150.00
GB	George Brett 1979	150.00
GB	George Brett 1981	150.00
GB	George Brett 1983	150.00
GB	George Brett 1985	150.00
GB	George Brett 1988	150.00
DM	Don Mattingly GS 1	140.00
DM	Don Mattingly GS 2	140.00
DM	Don Mattingly GS 3	140.00
DM	Don Mattingly GS 4	140.00
DM	Don Mattingly GS 5	140.00
DM	Don Mattingly GS 6	140.00
DM	Don Mattingly HR 1	140.00
DM	Don Mattingly HR 2	140.00
DM	Don Mattingly HR 3	140.00
DM	Don Mattingly HR 4	140.00
DM	Don Mattingly HR 5	140.00
DM	Don Mattingly HR 6	140.00
DM	Don Mattingly HR 7	140.00
DM	Don Mattingly HR 8	140.00
DM	Don Mattingly HR 9	140.00
DM	Don Mattingly 1985	140.00
DM	Don Mattingly 1986	140.00
DM	Don Mattingly 1987	140.00
DM	Don Mattingly 1988	140.00
DM	Don Mattingly 1989	140.00
DM	Don Mattingly 1991	140.00
DM	Don Mattingly 1992	140.00
DM	Don Mattingly 1993	140.00
DM	Don Mattingly 1994	140.00
DM	Don Mattingly 1984	140.00
DM	Don Mattingly 1985	140.00
DM	Don Mattingly 1986	140.00
DM	Don Mattingly 1987	140.00
DM	Don Mattingly 1988	140.00
DM	Don Mattingly 1989	140.00
DM	Don Mattingly HR 1	140.00
DM	Don Mattingly HR 2	140.00
DM	Don Mattingly HR 3	140.00
DM	Don Mattingly HR 4	140.00

Code	Player	Price
DM	Don Mattingly HR 5	140.00
DM	Don Mattingly HR 6	140.00
DM	Don Mattingly HR 7	140.00
DM	Don Mattingly HR 8	140.00
DM	Don Mattingly HR 9	140.00
RC	Rod Carew 1967	80.00
RC	Rod Carew 1968	80.00
RC	Rod Carew 1969	80.00
RC	Rod Carew 1970	80.00
RC	Rod Carew 1971	80.00
RC	Rod Carew 1972	80.00
RC	Rod Carew 1973	80.00
RC	Rod Carew 1974	80.00
RC	Rod Carew 1975	80.00
RC	Rod Carew 1976	80.00
RC	Rod Carew 1977	80.00
RC	Rod Carew 1978	80.00
RC	Rod Carew 1979	80.00
RC	Rod Carew 1980	80.00
RC	Rod Carew 1981	80.00
RC	Rod Carew 1982	80.00
RC	Rod Carew 1983	80.00
RC	Rod Carew SH 1	80.00
RC	Rod Carew SH 2	80.00
RC	Rod Carew SH 3	80.00
RC	Rod Carew SH 4	80.00
RC	Rod Carew SH 5	80.00
RC	Rod Carew SH 6	80.00
RC	Rod Carew SH 7	80.00
RC	Rod Carew 100	80.00
RC	Rod Carew 200	80.00
RC	Rod Carew 300	80.00
RC	Rod Carew 400	80.00
RC	Rod Carew 500	80.00
RC	Rod Carew 600	80.00
RC	Rod Carew 700	80.00
RC	Rod Carew 800	80.00
RC	Rod Carew 900	80.00
RC	Rod Carew 1969	80.00
RC	Rod Carew 1972	80.00
RC	Rod Carew 1973	80.00
RC	Rod Carew 1974	80.00
RC	Rod Carew 1975	80.00
RC	Rod Carew 1977	80.00
RC	Rod Carew 1978	80.00
YB	Yogi Berra 1947	160.00
YB	Yogi Berra 1949	160.00
YB	Yogi Berra 1950	160.00
YB	Yogi Berra 1951	160.00
YB	Yogi Berra 1952	160.00
YB	Yogi Berra 1953	160.00
YB	Yogi Berra 1956	160.00
YB	Yogi Berra 1958	160.00
YB	Yogi Berra 1961	160.00
YB	Yogi Berra 1962	160.00
YB	Yogi Berra 1948	160.00
YB	Yogi Berra 1949	160.00
YB	Yogi Berra 1950	160.00
YB	Yogi Berra 1951	160.00
YB	Yogi Berra 1952	160.00
YB	Yogi Berra 1953	160.00
YB	Yogi Berra 1954	160.00
YB	Yogi Berra 1955	160.00
YB	Yogi Berra 1956	160.00
YB	Yogi Berra 1957	160.00
YB	Yogi Berra 1958	160.00
YB	Yogi Berra 1959	160.00
YB	Yogi Berra 1960	160.00
YB	Yogi Berra 1961	160.00
YB	Yogi Berra 1962	160.00
MS	Mike Schmidt HR 1	140.00
MS	Mike Schmidt HR 2	140.00
MS	Mike Schmidt HR 3	140.00
MS	Mike Schmidt HR 4	140.00
MS	Mike Schmidt HIT 1	140.00
MS	Mike Schmidt HIT 2	140.00
MS	Mike Schmidt HIT 3	140.00
MS	Mike Schmidt HIT 4	140.00
MS	Mike Schmidt HIT 5	140.00
MS	Mike Schmidt HIT 6	140.00
MS	Mike Schmidt HIT 7	140.00
MS	Mike Schmidt HIT 8	140.00
MS	Mike Schmidt RUN 1	140.00
MS	Mike Schmidt RUN 2	140.00
MS	Mike Schmidt RUN 3	140.00
MS	Mike Schmidt RUN 4	140.00
MS	Mike Schmidt RUN 5	140.00
CY	Carl Yastrzemski HR 1	125.00
CY	Carl Yastrzemski HR 5	125.00
CY	Carl Yastrzemski HR 10	125.00
CY	Carl Yastrzemski HR 15	125.00
CY	Carl Yastrzemski HR 20	125.00
CY	Carl Yastrzemski HR 25	125.00
CY	Carl Yastrzemski HR 30	125.00
CY	Carl Yastrzemski HR 35	125.00
CY	Carl Yastrzemski HR 40	125.00
CY	Carl Yastrzemski HR 44	125.00
CY	Carl Yastrzemski 1961	125.00
CY	Carl Yastrzemski 1964	125.00
CY	Carl Yastrzemski 1966	125.00
CY	Carl Yastrzemski 1967	125.00
CY	Carl Yastrzemski 1970	125.00
CY	Carl Yastrzemski 1972	125.00
CY	Carl Yastrzemski 1973	125.00
CY	Carl Yastrzemski 1975	125.00
CY	Carl Yastrzemski 1977	125.00
CY	Carl Yastrzemski 1980	125.00
CY	Carl Yastrzemski 1983	125.00

Code	Player	Price
CY	Carl Yastrzemski 1963	125.00
CY	Carl Yastrzemski 1965	125.00
CY	Carl Yastrzemski 1966	125.00
CY	Carl Yastrzemski 1967	125.00
CY	Carl Yastrzemski 1968	125.00
CY	Carl Yastrzemski 1969	125.00
CY	Carl Yastrzemski 1970	125.00
CY	Carl Yastrzemski 1971	125.00
CY	Carl Yastrzemski 1972	125.00
CY	Carl Yastrzemski 1973	125.00
CY	Carl Yastrzemski 1974	125.00
CY	Carl Yastrzemski 1975	125.00
CY	Carl Yastrzemski 1976	125.00
CY	Carl Yastrzemski 1977	125.00
CY	Carl Yastrzemski 1978	125.00
CY	Carl Yastrzemski 1979	125.00
CY	Carl Yastrzemski 1983	125.00
TG	Tony Gwynn 1983	120.00
TG	Tony Gwynn 1984	120.00
TG	Tony Gwynn 1985	120.00
TG	Tony Gwynn 1986	120.00
TG	Tony Gwynn 1987	120.00
TG	Tony Gwynn 1988	120.00
TG	Tony Gwynn 1989	120.00
TG	Tony Gwynn 1990	120.00
TG	Tony Gwynn 1991	120.00
TG	Tony Gwynn 1992	120.00
TG	Tony Gwynn 1993	120.00
TG	Tony Gwynn 1994	120.00
TG	Tony Gwynn 1995	120.00
TG	Tony Gwynn 1996	120.00
TG	Tony Gwynn 1997	120.00
TG	Tony Gwynn 1998	120.00
TG	Tony Gwynn 1999	120.00
TG	Tony Gwynn 2000	120.00
TG	Tony Gwynn 2001	120.00
TG	Tony Gwynn 1984	120.00
TG	Tony Gwynn 1987	120.00
TG	Tony Gwynn 1988	120.00
\G	Tony Gwynn 1989	120.00
TG	Tony Gwynn 1990	120.00
TG	Tony Gwynn 1991	120.00
TG	Tony Gwynn 1992	120.00
TG	Tony Gwynn 1993	120.00
TG	Tony Gwynn 1994	120.00
TG	Tony Gwynn 1995	120.00
TG	Tony Gwynn 1996	120.00
TG	Tony Gwynn 1997	120.00
TG	Tony Gwynn 1984	120.00
TG	Tony Gwynn 1985	120.00
TG	Tony Gwynn 1986	120.00
TG	Tony Gwynn 1987	120.00
TG	Tony Gwynn 1989	120.00
TG	Tony Gwynn 1990	120.00
TG	Tony Gwynn 1991	120.00
TG	Tony Gwynn 1992	120.00
TG	Tony Gwynn 1993	120.00
TG	Tony Gwynn 1994	120.00
TG	Tony Gwynn 1995	120.00
TG	Tony Gwynn 1996	120.00
TG	Tony Gwynn 1997	120.00
TG	Tony Gwynn 1998	120.00
TG	Tony Gwynn 1999	120.00
TG	Tony Gwynn 1994	120.00
TG	Tony Gwynn 1995	120.00
RS	Ryne Sandberg 1984	150.00
RS	Ryne Sandberg 1988	150.00
RS	Ryne Sandberg 1989	150.00
RS	Ryne Sandberg 1990	150.00
RS	Ryne Sandberg 1991	150.00
RS	Ryne Sandberg 1992	150.00
RS	Ryne Sandberg 1983	150.00
RS	Ryne Sandberg 1985	150.00
RS	Ryne Sandberg 1986	150.00
RS	Ryne Sandberg 1987	150.00
RS	Ryne Sandberg 1988	150.00
RS	Ryne Sandberg 1989	150.00
RS	Ryne Sandberg 1990	150.00
RS	Ryne Sandberg 1991	150.00
OS	Ozzie Smith 1980	100.00
OS	Ozzie Smith 1981	100.00
OS	Ozzie Smith 1982	100.00
OS	Ozzie Smith 1983	100.00
OS	Ozzie Smith 1984	100.00
OS	Ozzie Smith 1985	100.00
OS	Ozzie Smith 1986	100.00
OS	Ozzie Smith 1987	100.00
OS	Ozzie Smith 1988	100.00
OS	Ozzie Smith 1989	100.00
OS	Ozzie Smith 1990	100.00
OS	Ozzie Smith 1991	100.00
OS	Ozzie Smith 1992	100.00
OS	Ozzie Smith 2B 1	100.00
OS	Ozzie Smith 2B 2	100.00
OS	Ozzie Smith 2B 3	100.00
OS	Ozzie Smith 2B 4	100.00
OS	Ozzie Smith 2B 5	100.00
OS	Ozzie Smith 2B 6	100.00
OS	Ozzie Smith 2B 7	100.00
OS	Ozzie Smith 2B 8	100.00
OS	Ozzie Smith 2B 9	100.00
OS	Ozzie Smith 2B 10	100.00
OS	Ozzie Smith 2B 11	100.00
OS	Ozzie Smith 2B 12	100.00
OS	Ozzie Smith 2B 13	100.00
OS	Ozzie Smith 2B 14	100.00
OS	Ozzie Smith 2B 15	100.00
OS	Ozzie Smith 2B 16	100.00
OS	Ozzie Smith 2B 17	100.00
OS	Ozzie Smith 2B 19	100.00
OS	Ozzie Smith 2B 20	100.00

Code	Player	Price
OS	Ozzie Smith 2B 22	100.00
OS	Ozzie Smith 2B 23	100.00
OS	Ozzie Smith 2B 24	100.00
OS	Ozzie Smith 2B 25	100.00
OS	Ozzie Smith 2B 26	100.00
OS	Ozzie Smith 2B 27	100.00
OS	Ozzie Smith 2B 28	100.00
OS	Ozzie Smith 2B 29	100.00
OS	Ozzie Smith 2B 30	100.00
OS	Ozzie Smith 2B 31	100.00
OS	Ozzie Smith 2B 32	100.00
OS	Ozzie Smith 2B 33	100.00
OS	Ozzie Smith 2B 34	100.00
OS	Ozzie Smith 2B 35	100.00
OS	Ozzie Smith 2B 36	100.00
OS	Ozzie Smith 2B 37	100.00
OS	Ozzie Smith 2B 38	100.00
OS	Ozzie Smith 2B 39	100.00
OS	Ozzie Smith 2B 40	100.00

Moments Relics Cut Signatures

Production 10 Sets	
Prime:	No Pricing
Production One Set	

Quad Relics

Production 10 Sets	
Prime:	No Pricing
Production 10 Sets	
Sterling Silver:	No Pricing
Production One Set	

Quad Relics Autographs

Production 10 Sets	
Prime:	No Pricing
Production 10 Sets	
Sterling Silver:	No Pricing
Production One Set	

Season Stats Relics

Production 10 Sets	
Prime:	No Pricing
Production One Set	
Sterling Silver:	No Pricing
Production One Set	

Season Stats Relics Autographs

Production 10 Sets	
Prime:	No Pricing
Production 10 Sets	
Sterling Silver:	No Pricing
Production One Set	

Six Relics

Production 10 Sets	
Prime:	No Pricing
Production 10 Sets	
Sterling Silver:	No Pricing
Production One Set	

Six Relics Autographs

Production 10 Sets	
Prime:	No Pricing
Production 10 Sets	
Sterling Silver:	No Pricing
Production One Set	

Triple Relics Autographs

Production 10 Sets	
Prime:	No Pricing
Production 10 Sets	
Sterling Silver:	No Pricing
Production One Set	

2006 Topps Triple Threads

#	Player	NM/M
	Complete Set (120):	
	Common (1-100):	.50
	Common (101-120):	10.00
	Production 225	
	Pack (6):	140.00
	Box (2):	250.00
1	Hideki Matsui	3.00
2	Josh Gibson	2.00
3	Roger Clemens	4.00
4	Paul Konerko	1.00
5	Brooks Robinson	1.00
6	Stan Musial	2.00
7	Dontrelle Willis	.50
8	Yogi Berra	1.50
9	John Smoltz	.75
10	Brian Roberts	.75
11	Gary Sheffield	.75
12	Wade Boggs	1.00
13	Alex Rodriguez	4.00
14	Ernie Banks	2.00
15	Ichiro Suzuki	3.00
16	Whitey Ford	1.00
17	Vladimir Guerrero	1.50
18	Tadahito Iguchi	.50
19	Robin Yount	1.50
20	Jason Schmidt	.50
21	Roberto Clemente	3.00
22	Andruw Jones	1.00
23	Don Mattingly	2.00
24	Joe Mauer	1.50
25	Barry Bonds	4.00
26	Johnny Damon	1.50
27	Chris Carpenter	.75
28	Garret Anderson	.50
29	Scott Rolen	1.50
30	Tim Hudson	.75
31	Dave Winfield	.75
32	Steve Carlton	.75
33	Miguel Tejada	1.00
34	Nolan Ryan	3.00

(Base set, continued)

#	Player	Price
35	Mark Buehrle	.75
36	Travis Hafner	.75
37	Rickie Weeks	.75
38	Sammy Sosa	1.50
39	Carlos Beltran	1.00
40	Todd Helton	1.00
41	Tom Seaver	1.00
42	Ted Williams	3.00
43	Alfonso Soriano	1.00
44	Reggie Jackson	1.00
45	Pedro Martinez	1.50
46	Randy Johnson	1.50
47	Ted Williams	3.00
48	Torii Hunter	1.50
49	Manny Ramirez	1.50
50	George Brett	3.00
51	Chipper Jones	1.50
52	Nomar Garciaparra	1.00
53	Richie Sexson	.75
54	David Ortiz	1.50
55	Derek Jeter	4.00
56	Mickey Mantle	8.00
57	Michael Young	.75
58	Aramis Ramirez	.75
59	Bartolo Colon	.50
60	Troy Glaus	.75
61	Carlos Delgado	.75
62	Mike Sweeney	.50
63	Jorge Cantu	.50
64	Mike Mussina	.75
65	Hank Blalock	.75
66	Frank Robinson	1.50
67	Carl Yastrzemski	2.00
68	Adam Dunn	1.00
69	Eric Chavez	.50
70	Curt Schilling	1.50
71	Jeff Francoeur	.75
72	C.C. Sabathia	.75
73	Roy Oswalt	.75
74	Carlos Lee	.75
75	Barry Zito	.75
76	Derek Lee	1.00
77	Greg Maddux	3.00
78	Ivan Rodriguez	.75
79	Jeff Kent	.75
80	Gary Carter	.75
81	Jose Reyes	1.00
82	Johan Santana	1.50
83	Magglio Ordonez	.75
84	Mark Prior	.75
85	Johnny Bench	2.00
86	Vernon Wells	.75
87	Mark Mulder	.50
88	Cal Ripken Jr.	6.00
89	Mark Teixeira	1.00
90	Miguel Cabrera	1.50
91	Duke Snider	1.00
92	Jason Giambi	.75
93	Albert Pujols	4.00
94	Carl Crawford	.75
95	Jim Edmonds	.50
96	Jose Contreras	.50
97	Victor Martinez	.75
98	Jeremy Bonderman	.50
99	Lance Berkman	.75
100	Rocco Baldelli	.50
101	Zach Duke/Auto Jsy	10.00
102	Felix Hernandez/ Auto. Jsy	40.00
103	Dan Johnson/Auto. Jsy	10.00
104	Brandon McCarthy/ Auto. Jsy	10.00
105	Huston Street/Auto. Jsy	15.00
106	Robinson Cano/ Auto. Jsy	50.00
107	Jason Bay/Auto. Jsy	20.00
108	Ryan Howard/Auto. Jsy	80.00
109	Ervin Santana/Auto. Jsy	15.00
110	Rich Harden/Auto. Jsy	15.00
111	Aaron Hill/Auto. Jsy	15.00
112	David Wright/Auto. Jsy	75.00
113	Rich Hill/Auto. Jsy RC	10.00
114	Nelson Cruz/ Auto. Jsy RC	30.00
115	Francisco Liriano/ Auto. Jsy RC	40.00
116	Hong-Chih Kuo/ Auto. Jsy RC	40.00
117	Ryan Garko/ Auto. Jsy RC	10.00
118	Craig Hansen/ Auto. Jsy RC	10.00
119	Shin-Soo Choo/ Auto. Jsy RC	30.00
120	Darrell Rasner/ Auto. Jsy RC	15.00

Sepia Tone
Sepia (1-100): 3-4X
Production 150
Sepia (101-120): 1X
Production 125

Emerald
Emerald (1-100): 4-6X
Production 99
Emerald (101-120): 1X
Production 75

Gold
Gold (1-100): 5-10X
Gold (101-120): 1-1.5X
Production 50 Sets

Sapphire
Sapphire (1-100): 8-15X
Sapphire (101-120): 1-2X
Production 25 Sets

Platinum
Platinum: No Pricing
Production One Set

Printing Plates
No Pricing
Production one set per color.

Heroes
NM/M
Inserted 1:Pack
Die-Cut: 2-3X
Production 50 Sets
Autograph: No Pricing
Production Three Sets

#	Player	Price
MM1	Mickey Mantle	8.00
MM2	Mickey Mantle	8.00
MM3	Mickey Mantle	8.00
MM4	Mickey Mantle	8.00
MM5	Mickey Mantle	8.00
MM6	Mickey Mantle	8.00
MM7	Mickey Mantle	8.00
MM8	Mickey Mantle	8.00
MM9	Mickey Mantle	8.00
MM10	Mickey Mantle	8.00
TW1	Ted Williams	5.00
TW2	Ted Williams	5.00
TW3	Ted Williams	5.00
TW4	Ted Williams	5.00
TW5	Ted Williams	5.00
TW1	Ted Williams	5.00
TW2	Ted Williams	5.00
TW3	Ted Williams	5.00
TW4	Ted Williams	5.00
TW5	Ted Williams	5.00
FR1	Frank Robinson	4.00
FR2	Frank Robinson	4.00
FR3	Frank Robinson	4.00
FR4	Frank Robinson	4.00
FR5	Frank Robinson	4.00
FR6	Frank Robinson	4.00
FR7	Frank Robinson	4.00
FR8	Frank Robinson	4.00
FR9	Frank Robinson	4.00
FR10	Frank Robinson	4.00
CY1	Carl Yastrzemski	4.00
CY2	Carl Yastrzemski	4.00
CY3	Carl Yastrzemski	4.00
CY4	Carl Yastrzemski	4.00
CY5	Carl Yastrzemski	4.00
CY6	Carl Yastrzemski	4.00
CY7	Carl Yastrzemski	4.00
CY8	Carl Yastrzemski	4.00
CY9	Carl Yastrzemski	4.00
CY10	Carl Yastrzemski	4.00

Heroes Co-Signer Autographs
No Pricing
Production Three Sets

Heroes Quad Signers
Production One Card

Heroes Cut Signatures
Production One Set

Triple Signed Hides
Production One Set

Triple Relic
NM/M
Production 18 Sets
Gold: No Pricing
Production Nine Sets
Platinum: No Pricing
Production Three Sets

#	Player	Price
1	Adam Dunn	30.00
2	Adam Dunn	30.00
3	Adrian Beltre	20.00
4	Adrian Beltre	20.00
5	Al Kaline	35.00
6	Al Kaline	35.00
7	Al Kaline	35.00
8	Albert Pujols	75.00
9	Albert Pujols	75.00
10	Albert Pujols	75.00
11	Albert Pujols	75.00
12	Alex Rodriguez	100.00
13	Alex Rodriguez	100.00
14	Alex Rodriguez	100.00
15	Alex Rodriguez	100.00
16	Alex Rodriguez	100.00
17	Alex Rodriguez	100.00
18	Alex Rodriguez	100.00
19	Alex Rodriguez	100.00
20	Alex Rodriguez	100.00
21	Alfonso Soriano	25.00
22	Alfonso Soriano	25.00
23	Andruw Jones	25.00
24	Andruw Jones	25.00
25	Andy Pettitte	30.00
26	Andy Pettitte	30.00
27	Aramis Ramirez	25.00
28	B.J. Upton	25.00
29	Barry Bonds	75.00
30	Barry Bonds	75.00
31	Barry Bonds	75.00
32	Barry Bonds	75.00
33	Barry Bonds	75.00
34	Barry Bonds	75.00
35	Barry Bonds	75.00
36	Barry Bonds	75.00
37	Barry Zito	20.00
38	Barry Zito	20.00
39	Ben Sheets	25.00
40	Bill Mazeroski	40.00
41	Bob Feller	30.00
42	Bobby Abreu	25.00
43	Bobby Cox	25.00
44	Bobby Doerr	20.00
45	Brad Lidge	20.00
46	Brian Giles	20.00
47	Brian Roberts	25.00
48	Cal Ripken Jr.	75.00
49	Cal Ripken Jr.	75.00
50	Cal Ripken Jr.	75.00
51	Carl Yastrzemski	50.00
52	Carl Yastrzemski	50.00
53	Carl Yastrzemski	50.00
54	Carlos Beltran	30.00
55	Carlos Beltran	30.00
56	Carlos Delgado	30.00
57	Carlton Fisk	40.00
58	Carlton Fisk	40.00
59	Carlton Fisk	40.00
60	Chipper Jones	50.00
61	Chipper Jones	50.00
62	Chipper Jones	50.00
63	Chris Carpenter	25.00
64	Craig Biggio	30.00
65	Craig Biggio	30.00
66	Curt Schilling	30.00
67	Curt Schilling	30.00
68	Curt Schilling	30.00
69	Curt Schilling	35.00
70	Dale Murphy	25.00
71	Darryl Strawberry	25.00
72	Darryl Strawberry	25.00
73	Dave Winfield	25.00
74	Dave Winfield	25.00
75	Dave Winfield	25.00
76	David Ortiz	35.00
77	David Ortiz	35.00
78	David Ortiz	35.00
79	Derrek Lee	35.00
80	Don Mattingly	40.00
81	Don Mattingly	40.00
82	Don Mattingly	40.00
83	Dontrelle Willis	20.00
84	Dontrelle Willis	20.00
85	Duke Snider	35.00
86	Dwight Gooden	25.00
87	Dwight Gooden	25.00
88	Eric Chavez	20.00
89	Ernie Banks	40.00
90	Ernie Banks	40.00
91	Ernie Banks	40.00
92	Frank Robinson	35.00
93	Frank Robinson	35.00
94	Frankie Frisch	30.00
95	Gary Carter	25.00
96	Gary Sheffield	25.00
97	Gary Sheffield	25.00
98	George Brett	50.00
99	George Brett	50.00
100	Greg Maddux	50.00
101	Hank Blalock	25.00
102	Hank Greenberg	75.00
103	Hank Greenberg	75.00
104	Hideki Matsui	80.00
105	Hideki Matsui	80.00
106	Hideki Matsui	80.00
107	Ichiro Suzuki	100.00
108	Ichiro Suzuki	100.00
109	Ichiro Suzuki	125.00
110	Ivan Rodriguez	25.00
111	Ivan Rodriguez	25.00
112	Ivan Rodriguez	25.00
113	Ivan Rodriguez	25.00
114	Jake Peavy	25.00
115	Javy Lopez	20.00
116	Jeff Bagwell	35.00
117	Jim Edmonds	25.00
118	Jim Thome	30.00
119	Joe Mauer	20.00
120	Joe Torre	25.00
121	Johan Santana	30.00
122	Johan Santana	30.00
123	Johnny Bench	40.00
124	Johnny Bench	40.00
125	Johnny Damon	30.00
126	Jon Garland	20.00
127	Jon Garland	20.00
128	Jorge Posada	30.00
129	Jorge Posada	30.00
130	Jose Canseco	25.00
131	Jose Reyes	25.00
132	Juan Marichal	25.00
133	Kerry Wood	25.00
134	Kerry Wood	25.00
135	Lance Berkman	30.00
136	Lance Berkman	30.00
137	Lloyd Waner	75.00
138	Lloyd Waner	75.00
139	Lou Brock	25.00
140	Manny Ramirez	30.00
141	Manny Ramirez	30.00
142	Mariano Rivera	40.00
143	Mariano Rivera	40.00
144	Mark Buehrle	20.00
145	Mark Mulder	20.00
146	Mark Mulder	20.00
147	Mark Prior	25.00
148	Mark Teixeira	30.00
149	Michael Young	25.00
150	Michael Young	25.00
151	Mickey Mantle	200.00
152	Mickey Mantle	200.00
153	Mickey Mantle	200.00
154	Mickey Mantle	200.00
155	Mickey Mantle	200.00
156	Miguel Cabrera	30.00
157	Miguel Tejada	25.00
158	Miguel Tejada	25.00
159	Miguel Tejada	25.00
160	Miguel Tejada	25.00
161	Mike Mussina	25.00
162	Mike Mussina	25.00
163	Mike Piazza	60.00
164	Mike Piazza	50.00
165	Mike Piazza	60.00
166	Mike Schmidt	40.00
167	Mike Schmidt	40.00
168	Mike Schmidt	40.00
169	Monte Irvin	30.00
170	Morgan Ensberg	20.00
171	Nolan Ryan	65.00
172	Nolan Ryan	65.00
173	Nolan Ryan	65.00
174	Nolan Ryan	65.00
175	Wade Boggs	40.00
176	Ozzie Smith	40.00
177	Ozzie Smith	40.00
178	Pat Burrell	25.00
179	Paul Konerko	20.00
180	Paul Konerko	20.00
181	Paul Konerko	20.00
182	Paul Molitor	30.00
183	Pedro Martinez	35.00
184	Pedro Martinez	35.00
185	Pedro Martinez	35.00
186	Randy Johnson	35.00
187	Randy Johnson	35.00
188	Reggie Jackson	40.00
189	Reggie Jackson	40.00
190	Rickey Henderson	40.00
191	Rickey Henderson	40.00
192	Rickey Henderson	40.00
193	Rickey Henderson	40.00
194	Rickie Weeks	20.00
195	Rickie Weeks	20.00
196	Roberto Clemente	125.00
197	Roberto Clemente	125.00
198	Robin Yount	40.00
199	Rod Carew	30.00
200	Roger Clemens	50.00
201	Roger Clemens	50.00
202	Roger Clemens	50.00
203	Roger Clemens	50.00
204	Roger Clemens	50.00
205	Roger Clemens	50.00
206	Roy Halladay	25.00
207	Roy Oswalt	25.00
208	Roy Oswalt	25.00
209	Ryne Sandberg	60.00
210	Ryne Sandberg	60.00
211	Sammy Sosa	50.00
212	Sammy Sosa	50.00
213	Sammy Sosa	50.00
214	Sammy Sosa	50.00
215	Sammy Sosa	50.00
216	Scott Rolen	25.00
217	Scott Rolen	25.00
218	Sean Burroughs	20.00
219	Stan Musial	50.00
220	Steve Carlton	25.00
221	Steve Carlton	25.00
222	Steve Carlton	25.00
223	Steve Garvey	20.00
224	Tadahito Iguchi	25.00
225	Ted Williams	120.00
226	Ted Williams	120.00
227	Tim Hudson	20.00
228	Tim Hudson	20.00
229	Todd Helton	25.00
230	Todd Helton	25.00
231	Todd Helton	25.00
232	Tom Seaver	40.00
233	Tony Gwynn	40.00
234	Tony Gwynn	40.00
235	Tony Gwynn	40.00
236	Torii Hunter	20.00
237	Torii Hunter	20.00
238	Travis Hafner	25.00
239	Vladimir Guerrero	40.00
240	Vladimir Guerrero	40.00
241	Willie Stargell	40.00
242	Willie Stargell	40.00
243	Willie Stargell	40.00
244	Willie Stargell	40.00
245	Willy Taveras	25.00

Triple Relic Combo
NM/M
Production 18 Sets
Gold: No Pricing
Production Nine Sets
Platinum: No Pricing
Production Three Sets

#	Players	Price
1	Albert Pujols, Alex Rodriguez, Barry Bonds	100.00
2	Alex Rodriguez, Barry Bonds, Albert Pujols	100.00
3	Albert Pujols, Alex Rodriguez, Manny Ramirez	100.00
4	Albert Pujols, Barry Bonds, Ted Williams	125.00
5	Alex Rodriguez, Barry Bonds, Chipper Jones	75.00
6	Alex Rodriguez, Roberto Clemente, Barry Bonds	125.00
7	Alex Rodriguez, Vladimir Guerrero, Ichiro Suzuki	80.00
8	Alex Rodriguez, Stan Musial, Ted Williams	120.00
9	Andruw Jones, Alfonso Soriano, Vladimir Guerrero, Mickey Mantle	160.00
10	Barry Bonds, Ichiro Suzuki, Roberto Clemente	150.00
11	Barry Bonds, Lloyd Waner, Roberto Clemente	160.00
12	Barry Bonds, Manny Ramirez, Andruw Jones	60.00
13	Barry Bonds, Manny Ramirez, Ted Williams	100.00
14	Barry Bonds, Roberto Clemente, Willie Stargell	125.00
15	Carl Yastrzemski, Paul Molitor	60.00
16	Don Mattingly, Paul Molitor, Manny Ramirez	40.00
17	Don Mattingly, Rod Carew, Tony Gwynn	70.00
18	Gary Sheffield, Vladimir Guerrero, Ivan Rodriguez	30.00
19	Hank Greenberg, Stan Musial, Ted Williams	125.00
20	Ichiro Suzuki, Chipper Jones, Barry Bonds	80.00
21	Ichiro Suzuki, Ted Williams, Roberto Clemente	150.00
22	Joe Morgan, Paul Molitor, Gary Carter	35.00
23	Manny Ramirez, Vladimir Guerrero, Roberto Clemente	90.00
24	Mike Piazza, Paul Molitor, Rickey Henderson	40.00
26	Paul Molitor, Andruw Jones, Robin Yount	40.00
27	Paul Molitor, Andruw Jones, Alfonso Soriano	35.00
28	Reggie Jackson, Vladimir Guerrero, Andruw Jones	35.00
29	Rickey Henderson, Wade Boggs	50.00
31	Stan Musial, Ted Williams, Tony Gwynn	70.00
32	Ted Williams, Ichiro Suzuki, Wade Boggs	140.00
33	Albert Pujols, Ted Williams, Mickey Mantle	250.00
34	Andruw Jones, George Brett, Chipper Jones	60.00
35	Greg Maddux, Nolan Ryan, Steve Carlton	60.00
36	Greg Maddux, Steve Carlton, Tom Seaver	50.00
37	Nolan Ryan, Steve Carlton, Tom Seaver	60.00
38	Nolan Ryan, Tom Seaver, Roger Clemens	60.00
39	Roger Clemens, Nolan Ryan, Tom Seaver	60.00
40	Barry Bonds, Rickey Henderson, Tony Gwynn	60.00
41	Cal Ripken Jr., Carl Yastrzemski, Paul Molitor	60.00
42	Cal Ripken Jr., George Brett, Roberto Clemente	150.00
43	Cal Ripken Jr., George Brett, Tony Gwynn	60.00
44	Cal Ripken Jr., Paul Molitor, Rickey Henderson	85.00
45	Cal Ripken Jr., Paul Molitor, Tony Gwynn	80.00
46	George Brett, Cal Ripken Jr., Rod Carew	80.00
47	George Brett, Cal Ripken Jr., Rod Carew	80.00
48	George Brett, Robin Yount, Rod Carew	60.00
49	George Brett, Tony Gwynn, Wade Boggs	60.00
50	George Brett, Tony Gwynn, Wade Boggs	60.00
51	Paul Molitor, Robin Yount, Wade Boggs	40.00
52	Paul Waner, Rickey Henderson, Stan Musial	60.00
53	Paul Waner, Rickey Henderson, Wade Boggs	50.00
54	Paul Waner, Rod Carew, Wade Boggs	50.00
55	Rickey Henderson, Stan Musial, Wade Boggs	50.00
56	Roberto Clemente, Robin Yount, Rod Carew	80.00
57	Roberto Clemente, Robin Yount, Rod Carew	90.00
58	Roberto Clemente, Robin Yount, Tony Gwynn	90.00
59	Rod Carew, Stan Musial, Tony Gwynn	90.00
60	Stan Musial, Tony Gwynn, Wade Boggs	30.00
61	Barry Bonds, Mickey Mantle, Frank Robinson	140.00
62	Barry Bonds, Mickey Mantle, Frank Robinson	160.00
63	Barry Bonds, Ted Williams, Mickey Mantle	160.00
64	Barry Bonds, Frank Robinson, Reggie Jackson	70.00
65	Barry Bonds, Frank Robinson, Harmon Killebrew	60.00
66	Frank Robinson, Barry Bonds, Mike Schmidt	60.00
67	Frank Robinson, Harmon Killebrew, Mickey Mantle	150.00
68	Josh Gibson, Barry Bonds, Mickey Mantle	200.00
69	Josh Gibson, Barry Bonds, Ted Williams	150.00
70	Mike Schmidt, Harmon Killebrew, Reggie Jackson	75.00
71	Dave Winfield, Vladimir Guerrero, Reggie Jackson	50.00
72	Rod Carew, Reggie Jackson, Vladimir Guerrero	30.00
73	Andruw Jones, Chipper Jones, Jeff Francoeur	30.00
74	Bobby Cox, Andruw Jones, Chipper Jones	50.00
75	Chipper Jones, Greg Maddux, Andruw Jones	50.00
76	Brian Roberts, Sammy Sosa, Miguel Tejada	40.00
77	Brooks Robinson, Cal Ripken Jr., Jim Palmer	65.00
78	Brooks Robinson, Jim Palmer, Frank Robinson	40.00
79	Cal Ripken Jr., Brooks Robinson, Miguel Tejada	50.00
80	Cal Ripken Jr., Frank Robinson, Sammy Sosa	80.00
81	Frank Robinson, Reggie Jackson, Brooks Robinson	75.00
82	Jim Palmer, Frank Robinson, Reggie Jackson	60.00
83	Jim Palmer, Reggie Jackson, Sammy Sosa	50.00
84	Jim Palmer, Sammy Sosa, Miguel Tejada	40.00
85	Miguel Tejada, Brian Roberts, Cal Ripken Jr.	80.00
86	Reggie Jackson, Frank Robinson, Sammy Sosa	50.00
87	Bobby Doerr, Carl Yastrzemski, Ted Williams	80.00
88	Carl Yastrzemski, David Ortiz, Manny Ramirez	50.00
89	Carl Yastrzemski, Ted Williams, David Ortiz	80.00
90	Carl Yastrzemski, Ted Williams, Manny Ramirez	80.00
91	Curt Schilling, David Ortiz, Johnny Damon	40.00
92	Curt Schilling, David Ortiz, Manny Ramirez	40.00
93	Curt Schilling, Manny Ramirez, Johnny Damon	40.00
94	David Ortiz, Johnny Damon, Manny Ramirez	50.00
95	Johnny Damon, Manny Ramirez, Ted Williams	60.00
96	Manny Ramirez, David Ortiz, Pedro Martinez	40.00
97	Manny Ramirez, Ted Williams, David Ortiz	60.00
98	Pedro Martinez, Roger Clemens, Manny Ramirez	50.00
99	Greg Maddux, Randy Johnson, Roger Clemens	50.00
100	Johan Santana, Pedro Martinez, Roger Clemens	60.00
101	Roger Clemens	50.00
102	Roger Clemens	50.00
103	Randy Johnson, Curt Schilling, Roger Clemens	75.00
104	Derrek Lee, Aramis Ramirez, Mark Prior	35.00
105	Derrek Lee, Ryne Sandberg, Sammy Sosa	65.00
106	Ernie Banks, Ryne Sandberg, Derrek Lee	60.00
107	Ernie Banks, Ryne Sandberg, Sammy Sosa	60.00
108	Greg Maddux, Ryne Sandberg, Ernie Banks	75.00
109	Mark Prior, Kerry Wood, Greg Maddux	50.00
110	Sammy Sosa, Ernie Banks, Derrek Lee	60.00
111	Frank Robinson, Joe Morgan, Johnny Bench	40.00
112	Johnny Bench, Frank Robinson, Tom Seaver	50.00
113	Johnny Bench, Tom Seaver, Joe Morgan	50.00

114 Jermaine Dye, Scott Podsednik, Tadahito Iguchi 40.00
115 Jim Thome, Paul Konerko, Tadahito Iguchi 60.00
116 Jon Garland, Scott Podsednik, Mark Buehrle 25.00
117 Jon Garland, Tadahito Iguchi, Mark Buehrle 30.00
118 Paul Konerko, Sammy Sosa, Carlton Fisk 40.00
119 Paul Konerko, Tadahito Iguchi, Jermaine Dye 40.00
120 Paul Konerko, Ivan Rodriguez, Hank Greenberg 60.00
121 Greg Maddux, Johan Santana, Roger Clemens 60.00
122 Juan Marichal, Nolan Ryan, Roger Clemens 80.00
123 Nolan Ryan, Randy Johnson, Whitey Ford 60.00
124 Cal Ripken Jr., Ozzie Smith, Mike Schmidt 60.00
125 Mike Schmidt, Cal Ripken Jr., Ozzie Smith 60.00
126 Al Kaline, Frank Robinson, Paul Waner 50.00
127 Al Kaline, Harmon Killebrew, Frank Robinson 75.00
128 Al Kaline, Mickey Mantle, Reggie Jackson 125.00
129 Al Kaline, Reggie Jackson, Stan Musial 60.00
130 Al Kaline, Robin Yount, Paul Waner 40.00
131 Barry Bonds, Chipper Jones, Manny Ramirez 65.00
132 Bob Feller, Juan Marichal, Nolan Ryan 60.00
133 Bob Feller, Whitey Ford, Steve Carlton 40.00
134 Bobby Doerr, Ted Williams, Wade Boggs 80.00
135 Brooks Robinson, Ozzie Smith, Ryne Sandberg 50.00
136 Carl Yastrzemski, George Brett, Paul Molitor 50.00
137 Carlton Fisk, Carl Yastrzemski, Wade Boggs 75.00
138 Joe Morgan, George Brett, Mike Schmidt 50.00
139 Yogi Berra, Carlton Fisk, Gary Carter 50.00
140 Andy Pettitte, Nolan Ryan, Brad Lidge 50.00
141 Andy Pettitte, Nolan Ryan, Randy Johnson 50.00
142 Andy Pettitte, Nolan Ryan, Roger Clemens 60.00
143 Andy Pettitte, Randy Johnson, Brad Lidge 30.00
144 Andy Pettitte, Roy Oswalt, Roger Clemens 50.00
145 Brad Lidge, Roy Oswalt, Andy Pettitte 35.00
146 Craig Biggio, Jeff Bagwell, Lance Berkman 40.00
147 Nolan Ryan, Roger Clemens, Randy Johnson 80.00
148 Roger Clemens, Brad Lidge, Andy Pettitte 50.00
149 Roger Clemens, Randy Johnson, Andy Pettitte 50.00
150 Ichiro Suzuki, Hideki Matsui 160.00
151 Ichiro Suzuki, Hideki Matsui, Kazuo Matsui 140.00
152 Ichiro Suzuki, Tadahito Iguchi, Hideki Matsui 150.00
153 Eric Gagne, Mike Piazza, Duke Snider 100.00
154 Gary Sheffield, Rickie Weeks, Paul Molitor 30.00
155 Paul Molitor, Gary Sheffield, Robin Yount 35.00
156 Robin Yount, Paul Molitor, Rickie Weeks 30.00
157 Harmon Killebrew, Rod Carew, Johan Santana 40.00
158 Harmon Killebrew, Torii Hunter, Rod Carew 40.00
159 Johan Santana, Joe Mauer, Torii Hunter 35.00
160 Paul Molitor, Rod Carew, Harmon Killebrew 40.00
161 Albert Pujols, Ichiro Suzuki, Barry Bonds 150.00
162 Alex Rodriguez, Barry Bonds, George Brett 150.00
163 Alex Rodriguez, Barry Bonds, Mickey Mantle 150.00
164 Alex Rodriguez, Ichiro Suzuki, Mickey Mantle 180.00
165 Alex Rodriguez, Reggie Jackson, Yogi Berra 50.00
166 Alex Rodriguez, Ted Williams, Mickey Mantle 200.00

167 Alex Rodriguez, Yogi Berra, Don Mattingly 60.00
168 Alex Rodriguez, Barry Bonds, Don Mattingly 70.00
169 Alex Rodriguez, Cal Ripken Jr., Miguel Tejada 60.00
170 Barry Bonds, Harmon Killebrew, Reggie Jackson 70.00
171 Barry Bonds, Roberto Clemente, Willie Stargell 120.00
172 Barry Bonds, Alex Rodriguez, Albert Pujols 100.00
173 Barry Bonds, Cal Ripken Jr., Mickey Mantle 200.00
174 Barry Bonds, Josh Gibson, Albert Pujols 120.00
175 Barry Bonds, Vladimir Guerrero, Ichiro Suzuki 75.00
176 Brooks Robinson, George Brett, Mike Schmidt 60.00
177 Cal Ripken Jr., Barry Bonds, Ichiro Suzuki 120.00
178 Cal Ripken Jr., Don Mattingly, George Brett 90.00
179 Cal Ripken Jr., George Brett, Don Mattingly 100.00
180 Cal Ripken Jr., Mike Schmidt, Don Mattingly 100.00
181 Cal Ripken Jr., Roger Clemens, Don Mattingly 125.00
182 Chipper Jones, Dale Murphy, Don Mattingly 75.00
183 Don Mattingly, Mickey Mantle, Reggie Jackson 150.00
184 George Brett, Johnny Bench, Mike Schmidt 80.00
185 George Brett, Johnny Bench, Mike Schmidt 180.00
186 Ichiro Suzuki, Barry Bonds, Mickey Mantle 180.00
187 Miguel Tejada, Ivan Rodriguez, Vladimir Guerrero 35.00
188 Ivan Rodriguez, Yogi Berra, Johnny Bench 50.00
189 Ivan Rodriguez, Yogi Berra, Johnny Bench 50.00
190 Johnny Bench, Mike Piazza, Yogi Berra 50.00
191 Mickey Mantle, Barry Bonds, Ted Williams 200.00
192 Mickey Mantle, Ichiro Suzuki, Roberto Clemente 200.00
193 Mickey Mantle, Roberto Clemente, Stan Musial 200.00
194 Mickey Mantle, Ted Williams, Roberto Clemente 220.00
195 Mickey Mantle, Vladimir Guerrero, Roberto Clemente 200.00
196 Miguel Tejada, Reggie Jackson, Rickey Henderson 40.00
197 Reggie Jackson, Alex Rodriguez, Yogi Berra 50.00
198 Roberto Clemente, Mickey Mantle, Barry Bonds 180.00
199 Buck O'Neil, Josh Gibson, Monte Irvin 100.00
200 Carlos Beltran, Carlos Delgado, David Wright 60.00
201 Carlos Beltran, Carlos Delgado, Jose Reyes 50.00
202 Carlos Beltran, David Wright, Pedro Martinez 60.00
203 Darryl Strawberry, Dwight Gooden, Gary Carter 30.00
204 David Wright, Carlos Beltran, Mike Piazza 60.00
205 David Wright, Mike Piazza, Jose Reyes 75.00
206 Jose Reyes, Kazuo Matsui, David Wright 40.00
207 Alex Rodriguez, Don Mattingly, Mickey Mantle 180.00
208 Alex Rodriguez, Hideki Matsui, Joe Torre 80.00
209 Alex Rodriguez, Hideki Matsui, Mickey Mantle 200.00
210 Don Mattingly, Mickey Mantle, Roger Clemens 200.00
211 Hideki Matsui, Gary Sheffield, Alex Rodriguez 50.00
212 Hideki Matsui, Gary Sheffield, Jorge Posada 50.00
213 Jorge Posada, Roger Clemens, Mike Mussina 75.00
214 Mickey Mantle, Whitey Ford, Yogi Berra 200.00

215 Mike Mussina, Whitey Ford, Roger Clemens 65.00
216 Roger Clemens, Mickey Mantle, Alex Rodriguez 200.00
217 Wade Boggs, Joe Torre, Alfonso Soriano 30.00
218 Barry Zito, Mark Mulder, Tim Hudson 25.00
219 Jose Canseco, Reggie Jackson, Rickey Henderson 40.00
220 Mark Mulder, Miguel Tejada, Tim Hudson 40.00
221 Bobby Abreu, Pat Burrell, Jim Thome 40.00
222 Curt Schilling, Mike Schmidt, Steve Carlton 50.00
223 Mike Schmidt, Pat Burrell, Scott Rolen 50.00
224 Barry Bonds, Roberto Clemente, Josh Gibson 150.00
225 Paul Waner, Roberto Clemente, Lloyd Waner 150.00
226 Willie Stargell, Bill Mazeroski, Roberto Clemente 140.00
227 Albert Pujols, Carlos Beltran, Dontrelle Willis 60.00
228 Albert Pujols, Dontrelle Willis, Ichiro Suzuki 90.00
229 Cal Ripken Jr., Albert Pujols, Orlando Cepeda 90.00
230 Cal Ripken Jr., Carlton Fisk, Tom Seaver 80.00
231 Cal Ripken Jr., Rod Carew, Carlton Fisk 75.00
232 Cal Ripken Jr., Rod Carew, Carlton Fisk 75.00
233 Jeff Bagwell, Albert Pujols, Mike Piazza 69.00
234 Mike Piazza, Jeff Bagwell, Scott Rolen 80.00
235 Rickey Henderson, Steve Garvey, Tony Gwynn 50.00
236 Adrian Beltre, Ichiro Suzuki, Alex Rodriguez 80.00
237 Ichiro Suzuki, Alex Rodriguez, Randy Johnson 90.00
238 Barry Bonds, Juan Marichal, Orlando Cepeda 75.00
239 Juan Marichal, Monte Irvin, Orlando Cepeda 40.00
240 Orlando Cepeda, Monte Irvin, Barry Bonds 60.00
241 Albert Pujols, Frankie Frisch, Stan Musial 120.00
242 Albert Pujols, Mark Mulder, Scott Rolen 65.00
243 Scott Rolen, Jim Edmonds, Albert Pujols 60.00
244 Stan Musial, Ozzie Smith, Albert Pujols 120.00
245 Alex Rodriguez, Ivan Rodriguez, Alfonso Soriano 50.00
246 Alex Rodriguez, Mark Teixeira, Alfonso Soriano 50.00
247 Alex Rodriguez, Nolan Ryan, Alfonso Soriano 50.00
248 Alfonso Soriano, Hank Blalock, Mark Teixeira 30.00
249 Alfonso Soriano, Hank Blalock, Michael Young 25.00
250 Mark Teixeira, Alfonso Soriano, Michael Young 30.00

Triple Relic Autograph

		NM/M
Production 18 Sets		
Gold:		No Pricing
Production Nine Sets		
Platinum:		No Pricing
Production Three Sets		
1	Albert Pujols	475.00
2	Albert Pujols	475.00
3	Albert Pujols	475.00
4	Alex Rodriguez	275.00
5	Alex Rodriguez	275.00
6	Alex Rodriguez	275.00
7	Derrek Lee	60.00
8	Barry Bonds	400.00
9	Ben Sheets	35.00
10	Ben Sheets	35.00
11	Brad Lidge	35.00
12	Brad Lidge	35.00
13	Cal Ripken Jr.	220.00
14	Cal Ripken Jr.	220.00
15	Cal Ripken Jr.	220.00
16	Carl Yastrzemski	100.00
17	Carl Yastrzemski	100.00
18	Carl Yastrzemski	100.00
19	Chase Utley	70.00
20	Chase Utley	70.00
21	Chien-Ming Wang	800.00
22	Chien-Ming Wang	400.00
23	Chien-Ming Wang	400.00
24	Chien-Ming Wang	400.00
25	Chris Carpenter	100.00
26	Chris Carpenter	100.00
27	Clint Barmes	25.00
28	Clint Barmes	25.00

Triple Relic Combos Autograph

		NM/M
Production 18 Sets		
Gold:		No Pricing
Production Nine Sets		
Platinum:		No Pricing
Production Three Sets		
1	Albert Pujols, Barry Bonds, Alex Rodriguez	1,000
2	Felix Hernandez, Alex Rodriguez, Shin-Soo Choo	150.00

29 Conor Jackson 40.00
30 Conor Jackson 40.00
31 David Ortiz 125.00
32 Don Mattingly 120.00
33 Don Mattingly 120.00
34 Don Mattingly 120.00
35 Duke Snider 75.00
36 Duke Snider 75.00
37 Ernie Banks 120.00
38 Frank Robinson 65.00
39 Frank Robinson 65.00
40 Frank Robinson 65.00
41 Garrett Atkins 35.00
42 Garrett Atkins 35.00
43 Derrek Lee 60.00
44 Derrek Lee 60.00
45 Derrek Lee 60.00
46 J.J. Hardy 40.00
47 J.J. Hardy 40.00
48 Jake Peavy 50.00
49 Jake Peavy 50.00
50 Jeff Francis 30.00
51 Jeff Francis 30.00
52 Joe Mauer 40.00
53 Joe Mauer 40.00
54 Joey Devine 25.00
55 Joey Devine 25.00
56 Johan Santana 75.00
57 Johan Santana 75.00
58 Johan Santana 75.00
59 Johan Santana 75.00
60 Johnny Bench 80.00
61 Johnny Bench 80.00
62 Johnny Bench 80.00
63 Johnny Damon 80.00
64 Jonny Gomes 40.00
65 Jonny Gomes 40.00
66 Jose Reyes 50.00
67 Jose Reyes 50.00
68 Justin Morneau 40.00
69 Justin Morneau 40.00
70 Lou Brock 60.00
71 Lou Brock 60.00
72 Lou Brock 60.00
73 Lou Brock 60.00
74 Manny Ramirez 100.00
75 Mariano Rivera 150.00
76 Mark Prior 50.00
77 Miguel Cabrera 70.00
78 Miguel Cabrera 70.00
79 Miguel Cabrera 70.00
80 Miguel Cabrera 70.00
81 Mike Schmidt 100.00
82 Mike Schmidt 100.00
83 Mike Schmidt 100.00
84 Morgan Ensberg 35.00
85 Morgan Ensberg 35.00
86 Nick Swisher 40.00
87 Nick Swisher 40.00
88 Nolan Ryan 150.00
89 Nolan Ryan 150.00
90 Nolan Ryan 150.00
91 Zach Duke 30.00
92 Zach Duke 30.00
93 Ozzie Smith 80.00
94 Ozzie Smith 80.00
95 Ozzie Smith 80.00
96 Pedro Martinez 125.00
97 Robin Yount 75.00
98 Robin Yount 75.00
99 Robin Yount 75.00
100 Rod Carew 50.00
101 Rod Carew 50.00
102 Rod Carew 50.00
103 Rod Carew 50.00
104 Roger Clemens 180.00
105 Roger Clemens 180.00
106 Ryan Langerhans 40.00
107 Ryan Langerhans 40.00
108 Ryne Sandberg 100.00
109 Ryne Sandberg 100.00
110 Ryne Sandberg 100.00
111 Scott Kazmir 40.00
112 Scott Kazmir 40.00
113 Stan Musial 100.00
114 Stan Musial 100.00
115 Stan Musial 100.00
116 Steve Carlton 40.00
117 Steve Carlton 40.00
118 Steve Carlton 40.00
119 Steve Garvey 40.00
120 Steve Garvey 40.00
121 Tony Gwynn 100.00
122 Tony Gwynn 100.00
123 Tony Gwynn 100.00
124 Travis Hafner 40.00
125 Travis Hafner 40.00
126 Victor Martinez 40.00
127 Victor Martinez 40.00
128 Wade Boggs 60.00
129 Wade Boggs 60.00
130 Wade Boggs 60.00

3 Nolan Ryan, Roger Clemens, Felix Hernandez 300.00
4 Johnny Damon, Alex Rodriguez, Robinson Cano 300.00
5 Manny Ramirez, Carl Yastrzemski, David Ortiz 250.00
6 Michael Young, Cal Ripken Jr., Ozzie Smith 300.00
7 Brian Roberts, Cal Ripken Jr., Frank Robinson 250.00
8 Stan Musial, Ozzie Smith, Lou Brock 180.00
9 Ozzie Smith, Stan Musial, Lou Brock 180.00
10 Tony Gwynn, Stan Musial, Rod Carew 180.00
11 Brooks Robinson, Cal Ripken Jr., Brian Roberts 200.00
12 Rod Carew, Robin Yount, Paul Molitor 120.00
13 Derrek Lee, Ryne Sandberg, Mark Prior 180.00
14 Chien-Ming Wang, Steve Carlton, Dontrelle Willis 275.00
15 Brad Lidge, Mariano Rivera, Huston Street 180.00
16 Morgan Ensberg, Wade Boggs, David Wright 120.00
17 Ben Sheets, Steve Carlton, Felix Hernandez 80.00
18 Victor Martinez, Johnny Bench, Joe Mauer 125.00
19 David Wright, Mike Schmidt, Aaron Hill 160.00
20 Chase Utley, Mike Schmidt, Ryan Howard 200.00
21 Felix Hernandez, Steve Carlton, Brandon McCarthy 75.00
22 David Wright, Miguel Cabrera, Jason Bay 140.00
23 Robinson Cano, Don Mattingly, Chien-Ming Wang 350.00
24 Justin Morneau, Don Mattingly, Travis Hafner 100.00
25 Steve Garvey, Don Mattingly, Dan Johnson 100.00
26 Travis Hafner, Miguel Cabrera, Jason Bay 100.00
27 Ben Sheets, Johan Santana, Jake Peavy 75.00
28 Ervin Santana, Johan Santana, Ben Sheets 70.00
29 Chris Carpenter, Johan Santana, Rich Harden 120.00
30 Zach Duke, Johan Santana, Brandon McCarthy 75.00

2006 Topps Turkey Red

	NM/M
Complete Set (316-630):	
Common Player:	.25
Common SP:	4.00
Inserted 1:4	
Pack (8):	4.00
Box (24):	75.00
316 Alex Rodriguez	3.00
316 Alex Rodriguez/Rangers/SP	8.00
316 Alex Rodriguez/M's/SP	8.00
317 Jeff Francoeur/SP	4.00
318 Shawn Green	.25
319 Daniel Cabrera	.25
320 Craig Biggio	.50
321 Jeremy Bonderman	.40
322 Mark Kotsay	.25
323 Cliff Floyd	.25
324 Jimmy Rollins	1.00
325 Magglio Ordonez	.50
325 Magglio Ordonez/W. Sox/SP	4.00
326 C.C. Sabathia	.75
327 Oliver Perez	.25
328 Orlando Hudson	.25
329 Chris Ray	.25
330 Manny Ramirez	1.00

331 Paul Konerko .50
332 Joe Mauer/SP 4.00
333 Jorge Posada .50
334 Mark Ellis .25
335 A.J. Burnett .50
336 Mike Sweeney .25
337 Shannon Stewart .25
338 Jake Peavy/SP 5.00
339 Carlos Delgado/Mets/SP 5.00
339 Carlos Delgado/B. Jays/SP 5.00
340 Brian Roberts .50
341 Dontrelle Willis .50
342 Aaron Rowand .50
343 Richie Sexson .50
343 Richie Sexson/Brewers/SP 4.00
344 Chris Carpenter .75
345 Carlos Zambrano .50
346 Nomar Garciaparra .75
347 Carlos Lee .50
348 Preston Wilson .25
348 Preston Wilson/Marlins/SP 4.00
349 Mariano Rivera .50
350 Ichiro Suzuki/SP 8.00
351 Mike Piazza 1.00
351 Mike Piazza/Mets/SP 4.00
352 Jason Schmidt .25
353 Jeff Weaver .25
354 Rocco Baldelli .25
355 Adam Dunn .75
356 Jeromy Burnitz .25
357 Chris Shelton/SP 4.00
358 Chone Figgins/SP 4.00
359 Javier Vazquez .25
360 Chipper Jones 1.00
361 Frank Thomas 1.00
362 Mark Loretta .25
363 Hideki Matsui 2.00
364 J.J. Hardy/SP 4.00
365 Todd Helton .75
366 Reggie Sanders .25
367 Jay Gibbons .25
368 Johnny Estrada .25
369 Grady Sizemore 1.00
370 Jim Thome .75
371 Ivan Rodriguez .75
372 Jason Bay .75
373 Carl Crawford .50
374 Adrian Beltre .50
375 Derrek Lee/SP 6.00
376 Miguel Olivo .25
377 Roy Oswalt .25
378 Coco Crisp .25
379 Moises Alou .50
380 Kevin Millwood .25
381 Mark Grudzielanek .25
382 Justin Morneau .75
383 Austin Kearns .40
384 Brad Penny .25
385 Troy Glaus .50
386 Cliff Lee .25
387 Armando Benitez .25
388 Clint Barmes .25
389 Orlando Cabrera .50
390 Jim Edmonds/SP 4.00
391 Jermaine Dye .50
392 Morgan Ensberg/SP 4.00
393 Paul LoDuca .25
394 Eric Chavez .25
395 Greg Maddux/SP 8.00
396 Jack Wilson .25
397 Omar Vizquel .25
398 Joe Nathan .25
399 Bobby Abreu .50
400 Barry Bonds/SP 8.00
401 Gary Sheffield .50
402 John Patterson .25
403 J.D. Drew .25
404 Bruce Chen .25
405 Johnny Damon 1.00
406 Aubrey Huff .25
407 Mark Mulder .25
408 Jamie Moyer .25
409 Carlos Guillen .50
410 Andruw Jones/SP 5.00
411 Jhonny Peralta/SP 4.00
412 Doug Davis .25
413 Aaron Miles .25
414 Jon Lieber .25
415 Aaron Hill .25
416 Josh Beckett/SP 5.00
417 Bobby Crosby .25
418 Noah Lowry/SP 4.00
419 Sidney Ponson .25
420 Luis Castillo .25
421 Brad Wilkerson .25
422 Felix Hernandez/SP 4.00
423 Vinny Castilla .25
424 Tom Glavine .50
425 Vladimir Guerrero 1.00
426 Javy Lopez .25
427 Ronnie Belliard .25
428 Dmitri Young .25
429 Johan Santana 1.00
430 David Ortiz/Red Sox/SP 5.00
430 David Ortiz/Twins/SP 5.00
431 Ben Sheets .50
432 Matt Holliday .75
433 Brian McCann .50
434 Joe Blanton .25
435 Sean Casey .25
436 Brad Lidge .25
437 Chad Tracy .25
438 Brett Myers .25
439 Matt Morris .25
440 Brian Giles .25

#	Player	Price
441	Zach Duke	.25
442	Jose Lopez	.25
443	Kris Benson	.25
444	Jose Reyes/SP	5.00
445	Travis Hafner	.75
446	Orlando Hernandez	.25
447	Edgar Renteria	.40
448	Scott Podsednik	.25
449	Nick Swisher/SP	4.00
450	Derek Jeter/SP	10.00
451	Scott Kazmir/SP	4.00
452	Hank Blalock	.50
453	Jake Westbrook	.25
454	Miguel Cabrera	1.00
454	Ken Griffey Jr.	2.00
455	Ken Griffey Jr./M's/SP	8.00
456	Rafael Furcal	.50
457	Lance Berkman	.50
458	Aramis Ramirez	.50
459	Xavier Nady	.25
459	Xavier Nady/Padres/SP	4.00
460	Randy Johnson	1.00
460	Randy Johnson/Astros/SP	6.00
461	Khalil Greene	.25
462	Bartolo Colon	.25
463	Mike Lowell	.50
464	David DeJesus	.25
465	Ryan Howard/SP	8.00
466	Tim Salmon	4.00
467	Mark Buehrle/SP	4.00
468	Curtis Granderson	.75
469	Kerry Wood	.25
470	Miguel Tejada	.75
471	Geoff Jenkins	.25
472	Jeremy Reed	.25
473	David Eckstein	.25
474	Lyle Overbay	.25
475	Michael Young	.50
476	Nick Johnson/Nats/SP	4.00
476	Nick Johnson/Yanks/SP	4.00
477	Carlos Beltran	1.00
478	Huston Street	.75
479	Brandon Webb	.75
480	Phil Nevin	.25
481	Ryan Madson/SP	4.00
482	Jason Giambi	.75
483	Angel Berroa	.25
484	Casey Blake	.25
485	Pat Burrell	.50
486	B.J. Ryan	.25
487	Torii Hunter	.50
488	Garret Anderson	.25
489	Chase Utley/SP	6.00
490	Matt Murton	.25
491	Rich Harden	.25
492	Garrett Atkins	.50
493	Tadahito Iguchi/SP	4.00
494	Jarrod Washburn	.25
495	Carl Everett	.25
496	Kameron Loe	.25
497	Jorge Cantu/SP	4.00
498	Chris Young	.50
499	Marcus Giles	.25
500	Albert Pujols	3.00
501	Alfonso Soriano/Nats/SP	5.00
501	Alfonso Soriano/Yanks/SP	5.00
502	Randy Winn	.25
503	Roy Halladay	.50
504	Victor Martinez	.50
505	Pedro Martinez	1.00
506	Rickie Weeks	.25
507	Dan Johnson	.25
508	Tim Hudson	.50
508	Tim Hudson/A's/SP	4.00
509	Mark Prior	.50
510	Melvin Mora	.25
511	Matt Clement	.25
512	Brandon Inge	.25
513	Mike Mussina	.75
514	Mike Cameron	.25
515	Barry Zito	.50
516	Luis Gonzalez	.25
517	Jose Castillo	.25
518	Andy Pettitte	.75
519	Wily Mo Pena	.25
520	Billy Wagner	.25
521	Ervin Santana/SP	4.00
522	Juan Pierre	.25
523	Dan Haren	.25
524	Adrian Gonzalez/SP	4.00
525	Robinson Cano	.75
526	Jeff Kent	.25
527	Cory Sullivan	.25
528	Joe Crede/SP	4.00
529	John Smoltz	.50
530	David Wright	2.00
531	Chad Cordero	.25
532	Scott Rolen/SP	5.00
533	Edwin Jackson	.25
534	Doug Mientkiewicz	.25
535	Mark Teixeira/SP	5.00
536	Kelvim Escobar	.25
537	Alex Rios	.50
538	Jose Vidro	.25
539	Alex Gonzalez	.25
540	Yadier Molina	.25
541	Ronny Cedeno/SP	4.00
542	Mark Hendrickson	.25
543	Russ Adams	.25
544	Chris Capuano	.25
545	Raul Ibanez	.25
546	Vicente Padilla	.25
547	Chris Duffy	.25
548	Bengie Molina	.25
549	Chien-Ming Wang	1.00
550	Curt Schilling	.50

#	Player	Price
551	Craig Wilson	.25
552	Mike Lieberthal	.25
553	Kazuo Matsui	.25
554	Jeff Francis	.25
555	Brady Clark	.25
556	Willy Taveras	.25
557	Mike Maroth	.25
558	Bernie Williams	.50
559	Edwin Encarnacion	.25
560	Vernon Wells	.25
561	Livan Hernandez/Nats	.25
561	Livan Hernandez/Giants/SP	4.00
562	Kenny Rogers	.25
563	Steve Finley	.25
564	Trot Nixon	.25
565	Jonny Gomes/SP	4.00
566	Brandon Phillips	.50
567	Shawn Chacon	.25
568	David Bush	.25
569	Jose Guillen	.25
570	Gustavo Chacin	.25
571	A. Rod Safe at the Plate CL	1.00
572	Pujols At Bat CL	1.00
573	Bonds On Deck CL	1.00
574	Breaking Up Two CL	1.00
575	Conference On The Mound CL	.25
576	Touch Em All CL	.25
577	Avoiding The Runner CL	.25
578	Bunting The Runner Over CL	.25
579	In The Hole CL	.50
580	Jeter Steals Third CL	1.00
581	Nolan Ryan	2.00
582	Cal Ripken Jr.	3.00
583	Carl Yastrzemski	1.00
584	Duke Snider	1.00
585	Tom Seaver	1.00
586	Mickey Mantle	5.00
587	Jim Palmer	.50
588	Gary Carter	.25
589	Stan Musial	1.50
590	Luis Aparicio	.25
591	Prince Fielder RC	4.00
592	Conor Jackson RC	.50
593	Jeremy Hermida RC	.50
594	Jeff Mathis RC	.50
595	Alay Soler RC	.50
596	Ryan Spilborghs RC	.50
597	Chuck James RC	.50
598	Josh Barfield RC	.50
599	Ian Kinsler RC	1.50
600	Val Majewski RC	.50
601	Brian Slocum RC	.50
602	Matthew Kemp RC	2.50
603	Nate McLouth RC	1.00
604	Sean Marshall RC	.50
605	Brian Bannister RC	.50
606	Ryan Zimmerman RC	4.00
607	Kendry Morales RC	2.50
608	Jonathan Papelbon RC	2.00
609	Matt Cain RC	2.00
610	Anderson Hernandez RC	.50
611	Jose Capellan RC	.50
612	Lastings Milledge RC	1.00
613	Francisco Liriano RC	2.00
614	Hanley Ramirez RC	2.00
615	Bryan Anderson RC	.50
616	Reggie Abercrombie RC	.50
617	Erick Aybar RC	1.00
618	James Loney RC	.75
619	Joel Zumaya RC	1.00
620	Travis Ishikawa RC	1.00
621	Jason Kubel RC	.50
622	Drew Meyer RC	.50
623	Kenji Johjima RC	1.00
624	Fausto Carmona RC	1.00
625	Nicholas Markakis RC	.50
626	John Rheinecker RC	.50
627	Melky Cabrera RC	1.00
628	Mike Pelfrey RC	4.00
629	Dan Uggla RC	1.50
630	Justin Verlander RC	4.00

Black

	Price
Stars (316-630):	3-5X
SP's:	1.5-2X
Inserted 1:20	

Gold

	Price
Stars (316-630):	5-10X
SP's:	3-5X
Inserted 1:60	

Red

	Price
Stars (316-630):	1-2X
SP's:	.5-1X

Suede

No Pricing
Production One Set

White

	Price
Stars (316-630):	2-3X
SP's:	1X
Inserted 1:4	

Autographs

		NM/M
Common Auto.:		8.00
Suede:		No Pricing
Production One Set		
GA	Garrett Atkins	8.00
JB	Josh Barfield	8.00
CB	Clint Barmes	10.00
MC	Miguel Cabrera	40.00
RC	Robinson Cano	60.00
JG	Jonny Gomes	25.00
RH	Ryan Howard	100.00
CJA	Conor Jackson	15.00
KJ	Kenji Johjima	30.00
DJ	Dan Johnson	15.00
CJ	Chipper Jones	60.00
DL	Derrek Lee	40.00
PL	Paul LoDuca	25.00
BM	Brian McCann	30.00
BMC	Brandon McCarthy/Exch.	10.00
MM	Mike Morse	10.00
RO	Roy Oswalt	25.00
AR	Alex Rodriguez	250.00
JS	Johan Santana/Exch.	65.00
HS	Huston Street/Exch.	25.00
NS	Nick Swisher/Exch.	20.00
CV	Claudio Vargas/Exch.	15.00
DW	David Wright	85.00

Autographs Black

		NM/M
Production 15 or 99		
GA	Garrett Atkins/99	15.00
JB	Josh Barfield/99	15.00
CB	Clint Barmes/99	15.00
CJA	Conor Jackson/99	15.00
DJ	Dan Johnson/99	15.00
BM	Brian McCann/99	40.00
BMC	Brandon McCarthy/99 Exch.	15.00
MM	Mike Morse/99	15.00
NS	Nick Swisher/99 Exch.	20.00
CV	Claudio Vargas/99 Exch.	15.00

Autographs Gold

		NM/M
Production 5 or 25		
JB	Josh Barfield/25	15.00
BM	Brian McCann/25	75.00
MM	Mike Morse/25	15.00
NS	Nick Swisher/25 Exch.	30.00

Autographs Red

		NM/M
Production 50 or 475		
GA	Garrett Atkins/475	10.00
JB	Josh Barfield/475	10.00
CB	Clint Barmes/475	12.00
MC	Miguel Cabrera/50	60.00
RC	Robinson Cano/50	100.00
JG	Jonny Gomes/50	20.00
RH	Ryan Howard/50	125.00
CJA	Conor Jackson/475	10.00
KJ	Kenji Johjima/50	30.00
DJ	Dan Johnson/475	10.00
CJ	Chipper Jones/50	100.00
DL	Derrek Lee/50	40.00
PL	Paul LoDuca/50	20.00
BM	Brian McCann/475	30.00
BMC	Brandon McCarthy/475 Exch.	10.00
MM	Mike Morse/475	10.00
RO	Roy Oswalt/50	30.00
AR	Alex Rodriguez/50	250.00
JS	Johan Santana/50	75.00
HS	Huston Street/50 Exch.	30.00
NS	Nick Swisher/475 Exch.	20.00
CV	Claudio Vargas/475 Exch.	8.00
DW	David Wright/50	100.00

Autographs White

		NM/M
Production 25 or 100		
GA	Garrett Atkins/200	10.00
JB	Josh Barfield/200	10.00
CB	Clint Barmes/200	10.00
CJA	Conor Jackson/200	10.00
DJ	Dan Johnson/200	10.00
BM	Brandon McCarthy/200 Exch.	10.00
BMC	Brandon McCarthy/200 Exch.	10.00
MM	Mike Morse/200	10.00
NS	Nick Swisher/200 Exch.	20.00
CV	Claudio Vargas/200 Exch.	10.00

B-18 Blankets

		NM/M
Inserted 1:2 Boxes		
Original B-18 Blanket:		No Pricing
Inserted 1:159 Boxes		
BB1	Barry Bonds/White	15.00
BB2	Barry Bonds/Red	15.00
VG1	Vladimir Guerrero/White	10.00

VG2	Vladimir Guerrero/Green	10.00
KJ1	Kenji Johjima/White	10.00
KJ2	Kenji Johjima/Green	10.00
DL1	Derrek Lee/White	10.00
DL2	Derrek Lee/Red	10.00
MM1	Mickey Mantle/White	25.00
MM2	Mickey Mantle/Blue	25.00
HM1	Hideki Matsui/White	10.00
HM2	Hideki Matsui/Blue	10.00
DO1	David Ortiz/White	10.00
DO2	David Ortiz/Orange	10.00
MR1	Manny Ramirez/White	10.00
MR2	Manny Ramirez/Orange	10.00
AR1	Alex Rodriguez/White	15.00
AR2	Alex Rodriguez/Blue	15.00
IS1	Ichiro Suzuki/White	10.00
IS2	Ichiro Suzuki/Green	10.00

Cabinet

		NM/M
Common Player:		
Inserted 1:2 Boxes		
Cabinet Original:		No Pricing
Inserted 1:4,340 Boxes		
Suede:		No Pricing
Inserted 1:634 Boxes		
JB	Josh Barfield	10.00
JBE	Josh Beckett	10.00
BB	Barry Bonds	25.00
JC	Jorge Cantu	10.00
CCA	Chris Carpenter	10.00
GC	Gary Carter	10.00
CC	Carl Crawford	10.00
JD	Johnny Damon	20.00
CD	Carlos Delgado	10.00
PF	Prince Fielder	20.00
JF	Jeff Francoeur	15.00
NG	Nomar Garciaparra	15.00
TG	Troy Glaus	10.00
JG	Jonny Gomes	10.00
KG	Ken Griffey Jr.	20.00
RH	Ryan Howard	20.00
DJ	Derek Jeter	30.00
NJ	Nick Johnson	10.00
RJ	Randy Johnson	20.00
AJ	Andruw Jones	15.00
DL	Derrek Lee	10.00
FL	Francisco Liriano	10.00
MM	Mickey Mantle	50.00
NM	Nicholas Markakis	10.00
PM	Pedro Martinez	15.00
HM	Hideki Matsui	15.00
DO	David Ortiz	20.00
JPA	Jonathan Papelbon	25.00
JP	Jake Peavy	10.00
MP	Mike Piazza	15.00
AP	Albert Pujols	30.00
AR	Alex Rodriguez	25.00
IR	Ivan Rodriguez	10.00
JR	Jimmy Rollins	10.00
NR	Nolan Ryan	25.00
JS	Johan Santana	15.00
DS	Duke Snider	20.00
AS	Alfonso Soriano	20.00
IS	Ichiro Suzuki	20.00
JT	Jim Thome	15.00
DW	David Wright	15.00
CY	Carl Yastrzemski	25.00

Cabinet Auto. Relics

No Pricing		
Inserted 1:86 Boxes		
Suede:		No Pricing
Production One Set		

Cabinet Auto. Relics Dual

No Pricing		
Inserted 1:1,368 Boxes		
Suede:		No Pricing
Production One Set		

Relics

		NM/M
Common Player:		4.00
Red:		1-1.5X
Production 150 Sets		
White:		1.5-2X
Production 99 Sets		
Black:		2-3X
Production 50 Sets		
Gold:		2-4X
Production 25 Sets		
Suede:		No Pricing
Production One Set		
CBA	Clint Barmes	4.00
CB	Carlos Beltran	8.00
LB	Lance Berkman	4.00
HB	Hank Blalock	4.00
MC	Miguel Cabrera	8.00
RC	Robinson Cano	15.00
CC	Chris Carpenter	8.00
EC	Eric Chavez	4.00
JC	Jose Contreras	6.00
JD	Johnny Damon	15.00
CD	Carlos Delgado	6.00
JE	Jim Edmonds	6.00
ME	Morgan Ensberg	4.00
JF	Jeff Francoeur	8.00
JG	Jon Garland	4.00
VG	Vladimir Guerrero	8.00
RHA	Roy Halladay	6.00
RIH	Rich Harden	4.00
JH	Jeremy Hermida	4.00
RH	Ryan Howard	25.00
TH	Torii Hunter	6.00
AJ	Andruw Jones	6.00
CJ	Chipper Jones	10.00

PK	Paul Konerko	8.00
DL	Derrek Lee	8.00
BL	Brad Lidge	6.00
PL	Paul LoDuca	4.00
PM	Pedro Martinez	10.00
HM	Hideki Matsui	15.00
JM	Joe Mauer	15.00
MM	Mike Mussina	10.00
DO	David Ortiz	15.00
RO	Roy Oswalt	6.00
APE	Andy Pettitte	8.00
MP	Mike Piazza	10.00
AP	Albert Pujols	20.00
MR	Manny Ramirez	8.00
JR	Jose Reyes	6.00
MRI	Mariano Rivera	8.00
BR	Brian Roberts	4.00
AR	Alex Rodriguez	15.00
JS	Johan Santana	10.00
IS	Ichiro Suzuki	25.00
MT	Mark Teixeira	8.00
BW	Bernie Williams	8.00
DWI	Dontrelle Willis	8.00
DW	David Wright	15.00

2006 Topps Updates & Highlights

		NM/M
Complete Factory Set (333):		40.00
Complete Set (330):		30.00
Common Player:		.10
UH1	Austin Kearns	.25
UH2	Adam Eaton	.10
UH3	Juan Encarnacion	.10
UH4	Jarrod Washburn	.10
UH5	Alex Gonzalez	.10
UH6	Toby Hall	.10
UH7	Preston Wilson	.10
UH8	Ramon Ortiz	.10
UH9	Jason Michaels	.10
UH10	Jeff Weaver	.10
UH11	Russell Branyan	.10
UH12	Brett Tomko	.10
UH13	Doug Mientkiewicz	.10
UH14	David Wells	.10
UH15	Corey Koskie	.10
UH16	Russ Ortiz	.10
UH17	Carlos Pena	.25
UH18	Mark Hendrickson	.10
UH19	Julian Tavarez	.10
UH20	Jeff Conine	.10
UH21	Dioner Navarro	.10
UH22	Bob Wickman	.10
UH23	Felipe Lopez	.10
UH24	Eddie Guardado	.10
UH25	David Dellucci	.10
UH26	Ryan Wagner	.10
UH27	Nick Green	.10
UH28	Gary Majewski	.10
UH29	Shea Hillenbrand	.10
UH30	Jae Weong Seo	.10
UH31	Royce Clayton	.10
UH32	David Riske	.10
UH33	Joey Gathright	.10
UH34	Robinson Tejeda	.10
UH35	Edwin Jackson	.10
UH36	Aubrey Huff	.10
UH37	Akinori Otsuka	.10
UH38	Juan Castro	.10
UH39	Zach Day	.10
UH40	Jeremy Accardo	.10
UH41	Shawn Green	.10
UH42	Kazuo Matsui	.10
UH43	J.J. Putz	.10
UH44	David Ross	.10
UH45	Scott Williamson	.10
UH46	Joe Borchard	.10
UH47	Elmer Dessens	.10
UH48	Odalis Perez	.10
UH49	Kelly Shoppach	.10
UH50	Brandon Phillips	.25
UH51	Guillermo Mota	.10
UH52	Alex Cintron	.10
UH53	Denny Bautista	.10
UH54	Josh Bard	.10
UH55	Julio Lugo	.10
UH56	Doug Mirabelli	.10
UH57	Kip Wells	.10
UH58	Adrian Gonzalez	.40
UH59	Shawn Chacon	.10
UH60	Marcus Thames	.10
UH61	Craig Wilson	.10
UH62	Cory Sullivan	.10
UH63	Ben Broussard	.10
UH64	Todd Walker	.10
UH65	Greg Maddux	1.00
UH66	Xavier Nady	.20
UH67	Oliver Perez	.10

UH68	Sean Casey	.10
UH69	Kyle Lohse	.10
UH70	Carlos Lee	.25
UH71	Rheal Cormier	.10
UH72	Ronnie Belliard	.10
UH73	Cory Lidle	.10
UH74	David Bell	.10
UH75	Wilson Betemit	.10
UH76	Danys Baez	.10
UH77	Mike Stanton	.10
UH78	Kevin Mench	.10
UH79	Sandy Alomar	.10
UH80	Cesar Izturis	.10
UH81	Jeremy Affeldt	.10
UH82	Matt Stairs	.10
UH83	Hector Luna	.10
UH84	Tony Graffanino	.10
UH85	J.P. Howell	.10
UH86	Bengie Molina	.10
UH87	Maicer Izturis	.10
UH88	Marco Scutaro	.10
UH89	Daryle Ward	.10
UH90	Sal Fasano	.10
UH91	Oscar Villarreal	.10
UH92	Gabe Gross	.10
UH93	Phil Nevin	.10
UH94	Damon Hollins	.10
UH95	Juan Cruz	.10
UH96	Marlon Anderson	.10
UH97	Jason Davis	.10
UH98	Ryan Shealy	.10
UH99	Francisco Cordero	.10
UH100	Bobby Abreu	.25
UH101	Roberto Hernandez	.10
UH102	Gary Bennett	.10
UH103	Aaron Sele	.10
UH104	Nook Logan	.10
UH105	Alfredo Amezaga	.10
UH106	Chris Woodward	.10
UH107	Kevin Jarvis	.10
UH108	B.J. Upton	.25
UH109	Alan Embree	.10
UH110	Milton Bradley	.20
UH111	Peter Orr	.10
UH112	Jeff Cirillo	.10
UH113	Corey Patterson	.10
UH114	Josh Paul	.10
UH115	Fernando Rodney	.10
UH116	Jerry Hairston	.10
UH117	Scott Proctor	.10
UH118	Ambiorix Burgos	.10
UH119	Jose Bautista	.10
UH120	Livan Hernandez	.10
UH121	John McDonald	.10
UH122	Ronny Cedeno	.10
UH123	Nate Robertson	.10
UH124	Jamey Carroll	.10
UH125	Alex Escobar	.10
UH126	Endy Chavez	.10
UH127	Jorge Julio	.10
UH128	Kenny Lofton	.10
UH129	Matt Diaz	.10
UH130	David Bush	.10
UH131	Jose Molina	.10
UH132	Mike MacDougal	.10
UH133	Benjamin Zobrist RC	.50
UH134	Shane Komine RC	.25
UH135	Casey Janssen RC	.50
UH136	Kevin Frandsen RC	.25
UH137	John Rheinecker RC	.25
UH138	Matthew Kemp RC	1.50
UH139	Scott Mathieson RC	.25
UH140	Jered Weaver RC	.75
UH141	Joel Guzman RC	.25
UH142	Anibal Sanchez RC	.25
UH143	Melky Cabrera RC	.50
UH144	Howie Kendrick RC	.50
UH145	Cole Hamels RC	1.00
UH146	Willy Aybar RC	.25
UH147	James Shields RC	.75
UH148	Kevin Thompson RC	.25
UH149	Jon Lester RC	1.50
UH150	Stephen Drew RC	.75
UH151	Andre Ethier RC	1.00
UH152	Jordan Tata RC	.50
UH153	Michael Napoli RC	.50
UH154	Kason Gabbard RC	.25
UH155	Lastings Milledge RC	.50
UH156	Erick Aybar RC	.50
UH157	Fausto Carmona RC	.50
UH158	Russell Martin RC	.75
UH159	David Pauley RC	.25
UH160	Andy Marte RC	.25
UH161	Carlos Quentin RC	.50
UH162	Franklin Gutierrez RC	.25
UH163	Taylor Buchholz RC	.25
UH164	Josh Johnson RC	.75
UH165	Chad Billingsley RC	.50
UH166	Kendry Morales RC	1.00
UH167	Adam Loewen RC	.25
UH168	Yusmeiro Petit RC	.25
UH169	Matt Albers RC	.25
UH170	John Maine RC	.50
UH171	Alex Rodriguez	1.00
UH172	Mike Piazza	.50
UH173	Cory Sullivan	.10
UH174	Anibal Sanchez	.25
UH175	Trevor Hoffman	.10
UH176	Barry Bonds	.75
UH177	Derek Jeter	1.00
UH178	Jose Reyes	.50
UH179	Manny Ramirez	.25
UH180	Vladimir Guerrero	.25
UH181	Mariano Rivera	.25
UH182	Postseason Highlights	.25
UH183	Postseason Highlights	.25
UH184	Postseason Highlights	.25
UH185	Postseason Highlights	.25

UH186	Postseason Highlights	.25	UH283	Ryan Howard	.75	
UH187	Postseason Highlights	.25	UH284	David Wright	.50	
UH188	Postseason Highlights	.25	UH285	Miguel Cabrera	.25	
UH189	Postseason Highlights	.25	UH286	David Ortiz	.25	
UH190	Postseason Highlights	.25	UH287	Jermaine Dye	.10	
UH191	Postseason Highlights	.25	UH288	Miguel Tejada	.25	
UH192	Postseason Highlights	.25	UH289	Lance Berkman	.25	
UH193	Postseason Highlights	.25	UH290	Troy Glaus	.10	
UH194	Postseason Highlights	.25	UH291	David Wright,		
UH195	Postseason Highlights	.25		Tom Glavine	.25	
UH196	Postseason Highlights	.25	UH292	Ryan Howard,		
UH197	Postseason Highlights	.25		Tom Gordon	.50	
UH198	Postseason Highlights	.25	UH293	Miguel Cabrera,		
UH199	Postseason Highlights	.25		Dontrelle Willis	.25	
UH200	Postseason Highlights	.25	UH294	Andruw Jones,		
UH201	Postseason Highlights	.25		John Smoltz	.25	
UH202	David Ortiz, Jermaine Dye,		UH295	Alfonso Soriano	.25	
	Travis Hafner	.25	UH296	Albert Pujols,		
UH203	Joe Mauer, Derek Jeter,			Chris Carpenter	.50	
	Robinson Cano	.50	UH297	Adam Dunn,		
UH204	David Ortiz, Justin Morneau,			Bronson Arroyo	.10	
	Raul Ibanez	.25	UH298	Lance Berkman,		
UH205	Carl Crawford,			Roy Oswalt	.25	
	Chone Figgins, Ichiro Suzuki		UH299	Chris Capuano,		
		.50		Prince Fielder	.25	
UH206	Johan Santana, Chien-		UH300	Freddy Sanchez,		
	Ming Wang, Jon Garland	.50		Jason Bay	.10	
UH207	Johan Santana,		UH301	Carlos Zambrano,		
	Roy Halladay, C.C. Sabathia			Juan Pierre	.10	
		.25	UH302	Adrian Gonzalez,		
UH208	Johan Santana,			Trevor Hoffman	.25	
	Jeremy Bonderman,		UH303	Derek Lowe,		
	John Lackey	.25		Rafael Furcal	.10	
UH209	Francisco Rodriguez,		UH304	Omar Vizquel,		
	Bobby Jenks, B.J. Ryan	.10		Jason Schmidt	.25	
UH210	Ryan Howard, Albert Pujols,		UH305	Brandon Webb,		
	Alfonso Soriano	1.00		Chad Tracy	.10	
UH211	Freddy Sanchez,		UH306	Matt Holliday,		
	Miguel Cabrera,			Garrett Atkins	.25	
	Albert Pujols	.50	UH307	Alex Rodriguez,		
UH212	Ryan Howard, Albert Pujols,			Chien-Ming Wang	.50	
	Lance Berkman	1.00	UH308	Curt Schilling,		
UH213	Jose Reyes, Juan Pierre,			David Ortiz	.25	
	Hanley Ramirez	.50	UH309	Roy Halladay,		
UH214	Derek Lowe, Brandon Webb,			Vernon Wells	.10	
	Carlos Zambrano	.25	UH310	Miguel Tejada,		
UH215	Roy Oswalt, Chris Carpenter,			Erik Bedard	.10	
	Brandon Webb	.25	UH311	Carl Crawford,		
UH216	Aaron Harang, Jake Peavy,			Scott Kazmir	.10	
	John Smoltz	.10	UH312	Jeremy Bonderman,		
UH217	Trevor Hoffman,			Magglio Ordonez	.10	
	Billy Wagner,		UH313	Justin Morneau,		
	Joe Borowski	.10		Johan Santana	.25	
UH218	Ichiro Suzuki	.50	UH314	Jon Garland,		
UH219	Derek Jeter	.75		Jermaine Dye	.10	
UH220	Alex Rodriguez	.75	UH315	Travis Hafner,		
UH221	David Ortiz	.50		C.C. Sabathia	.10	
UH222	Vladimir Guerrero	.25	UH316	Emil Brown,		
UH223	Ivan Rodriguez	.25		Mark Grudzielanek	.10	
UH224	Vernon Wells	.25	UH317	Frank Thomas, Barry Zito	.25	
UH225	Mark Loretta	.10	UH318	Jered Weaver,		
UH226	Kenny Rogers	.10		Vladimir Guerrero	.25	
UH227	Alfonso Soriano	.50	UH319	Michael Young,		
UH228	Carlos Beltran	.25		Gary Matthews	.25	
UH229	Albert Pujols	.75	UH320	Ichiro Suzuki, J.J. Putz	.50	
UH230	Jason Bay	.25	UH321	Derek Jeter,		
UH231	Edgar Renteria	.25		Robinson Cano	.50	
UH232	David Wright	.50	UH322	Mark Mulder,		
UH233	Chase Utley	.25		Chris Carpenter	.25	
UH234	Paul LoDuca	.10	UH323	Trevor Schmidt,		
UH235	Brad Penny	.10		Jason Schmidt	.10	
UH236	Derrick Turnbow	.10	UH324	David Wright,		
UH237	Mark Redman	.10		Paul LoDuca	.25	
UH238	Francisco Liriano	.25	UH325	Lance Berkman,		
UH239	A.J. Pierzynski	.10		Roy Oswalt	.25	
UH240	Grady Sizemore	.25	UH326	Derek Jeter, Jose Reyes	.50	
UH241	Jose Contreras	.25	UH327	David Wright, Cliff Floyd	.25	
UH242	Jermaine Dye	.25	UH328	Johan Santana,		
UH243	Jason Schmidt	.10		Francisco Liriano	.25	
UH244	Nomar Garciaparra	.25	UH329	Stephen Drew, J.D. Drew	.25	
UH245	Scott Kazmir	.25	UH330	Jeff Weaver	.25	
UH246	Johan Santana	.25				
UH247	Chris Capuano	.10				
UH248	Magglio Ordonez	.25				
UH249	Gary Matthews	.25				
UH250	Carlos Lee	.25				
UH251	David Eckstein	.10				
UH252	Michael Young	.10				
UH253	Matt Holliday	.25				
UH254	Lance Berkman	.25				
UH255	Scott Rolen	.25				
UH256	Bronson Arroyo	.10				
UH257	Barry Zito	.10				
UH258	Brian McCann	.25				
UH259	Jose Lopez	.10				
UH260	Chris Carpenter	.25				
UH261	Roy Halladay	.25				
UH262	Jim Thome	.25				
UH263	Dan Uggla	.25				
UH264	Mariano Rivera	.25				
UH265	Roy Oswalt	.25				
UH266	Tom Gordon	.10				
UH267	Troy Glaus	.25				
UH268	Bobby Jenks	.10				
UH269	Freddy Sanchez	.10				
UH270	Paul Konerko	.25				
UH271	Joe Mauer	.25				
UH272	B.J. Ryan	.10				
UH273	Ryan Howard	.75				
UH274	Brian Fuentes	.10				
UH275	Miguel Cabrera	.25				
UH276	Brandon Webb	.10				
UH277	Mark Buehrle	.10				
UH278	Trevor Hoffman	.10				
UH279	Jonathan Papelbon	.25				
UH280	Andruw Jones	.25				
UH281	Miguel Tejada	.25				
UH282	Carlos Zambrano	.25				

All-Star Stitches

			NM/M
Common Player:			4.00
Inserted 1:43			
Patch:			No Pricing
Production 10 Sets			
BA	Bronson Arroyo		8.00
JB	Jason Bay		15.00
CB	Carlos Beltran		10.00
LB	Lance Berkman		10.00
MB	Mark Buehrle		8.00
MC	Miguel Cabrera		10.00
RC	Robinson Cano		4.00
CFC	Chris Capuano		6.00
CC	Chris Carpenter		8.00
JC	Jose Contreras		6.00
JD	Jermaine Dye		6.00
DE	David Eckstein		15.00
BF	Brian Fuentes		4.00
TEG	Troy Glaus		6.00
TMG	Tom Glavine		4.00
TG	Tom Gordon		4.00
VG	Vladimir Guerrero		8.00
RH	Roy Halladay		6.00
TH	Trevor Hoffman		6.00
MH	Matt Holliday		6.00
RJH	Ryan Howard		25.00
BJ	Bobby Jenks		4.00
AJ	Andruw Jones		8.00
SK	Scott Kazmir		6.00
PK	Paul Konerko		8.00
CL	Carlos Lee		8.00
PL	Paul LoDuca		6.00
JL	Jose Lopez		4.00
ML	Mark Loretta		4.00
GM	Gary Matthews		6.00
JM	Joe Mauer		10.00
BM	Brian McCann		15.00
MO	Magglio Ordonez		6.00
DO	David Ortiz		15.00
RO	Roy Oswalt		6.00
JP	Jonathan Papelbon		20.00
BP	Brad Penny		4.00
AJP	A.J. Pierzynski		4.00
AP	Albert Pujols		25.00
MAR	Mark Redman		4.00
ER	Edgar Renteria		4.00
JR	Jose Reyes		15.00
MR	Mariano Rivera		8.00
AR	Alex Rodriguez		15.00
IR	Ivan Rodriguez		8.00
KR	Kenny Rogers		4.00
SR	Scott Rolen		8.00
BR	B.J. Ryan		4.00
FS	Freddy Sanchez		6.00
JS	Johan Santana		10.00
JDS	Jason Schmidt		6.00
GS	Grady Sizemore		10.00
AS	Alfonso Soriano		8.00
MT	Miguel Tejada		6.00
JT	Jim Thome		10.00
DT	Derrick Turnbow		4.00
DU	Dan Uggla		10.00
CU	Chase Utley		10.00
BW	Brandon Webb		8.00
VW	Vernon Wells		8.00
DW	David Wright		15.00
MY	Michael Young		6.00
CZ	Carlos Zambrano		8.00

All-Star Patches

No Pricing
Production 10 Sets

Barry Bonds HR History

		NMM
Common Bonds HR History:		1.00
Inserted 1:6		
Autographs:		No Pricing
Production Five Sets		
BB709-734	Barry Bonds	1.00

Black

Black:	15-25X
Production 55 Sets	

Gold

Gold:	5-10X
Production 2,006 Sets	

First Edition

1st Edition:	4-6X
Inserted 1:Hobby Box	

Platinum

Production One Set

All-Star Autographs

No Pricing
Production 25 Sets

Barry Bonds 715

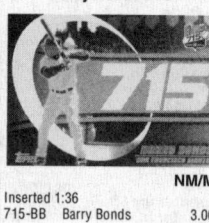

		NM/M
Inserted 1:36		
715-BB	Barry Bonds	3.00

Barry Bonds 715 Relic

		NM/M
Production 715		
	Barry Bonds	35.00

Chrome RC Box Topper

		NM/M
Production 599		
Inserted one per box.		
Refractors:		2-4X
Production 25 Sets		
1	Aaron Zobrist	3.00
2	Shane Komine	3.00
3	Casey Janssen	3.00
4	Kevin Frandsen	3.00
5	John Rheinecker	3.00
6	Matthew Kemp	10.00
7	Scott Mathieson	3.00
8	Jered Weaver	6.00
9	Joel Guzman	3.00
10	Anibal Sanchez	3.00
11	Melky Cabrera	3.00
12	Howie Kendrick	3.00
13	Cole Hamels	8.00
14	Willy Aybar	3.00
15	James Shields	5.00
16	Kevin Thompson	3.00
17	Jon Lester	20.00
18	Stephen Drew	6.00
19	Andre Ethier	8.00
20	Jordan Tata	3.00
21	Michael Napoli	6.00
22	Kason Gabbard	3.00
23	Lastings Milledge	5.00
24	Erick Aybar	3.00
25	Fausto Carmona	5.00
26	Russell Martin	5.00
27	David Pauley	3.00
28	Andy Marte	3.00
29	Carlos Quentin	5.00
30	Franklin Gutierrez	4.00
31	Taylor Buchholz	3.00
32	Josh Johnson	5.00
33	Chad Billingsley	6.00
34	Kendry Morales	8.00
35	Adam Loewen	3.00
36	Yusmeiro Petit	5.00
37	Matt Albers	3.00
38	John Maine	6.00
39	Josh Willingham	5.00
40	Taylor Tankersley	3.00
41	Pat Neshek	8.00
42	Francisco Rosario	3.00
43	Matt Smith	3.00
44	Jonathan Sanchez	5.00
45	Chris Demaria	3.00
46	Manuel Corpas	3.00
47	Kevin Reese	3.00
48	Brent Clevlen	3.00
49	Anderson Hernandez	3.00
50	Chris Roberson	3.00

Derby Digs Relics

		NM/M
Inserted 1:4,200		
JD	Jermaine Dye	25.00
TG	Troy Glaus	25.00

M. Mantle HR History

		NM/M
Common Mantle (102-201):		2.00
Inserted 1:4		

Mantle HR History Relics

		NM/M
Common Mantle:		140.00
Production Seven Sets		

Midsummer Covers

No Pricing
Production 10 Sets

Rookie Debut

		NM/M
Common Player:		1.00
Inserted 1:4		
RD1	Joel Zumaya	2.00
RD2	Ian Kinsler	2.00
RD3	Kenji Johjima	3.00
RD4	Josh Barfield	1.00
RD5	Nicholas Markakis	2.00
RD6	Dan Uggla	2.00
RD7	Eric Reed	1.00
RD8	Carlos Martinez	1.00
RD9	Angel Pagan	1.50
RD10	Jason Childers	1.00
RD11	Ruddy Lugo	1.00
RD12	James Loney	2.50
RD13	Fernando Nieve	1.00
RD14	Reggie Abercrombie	1.00
RD15	Boone Logan	1.00
RD16	Brian Bannister	1.00
RD17	Ricky Nolasco	1.50
RD18	Willie Eyre	1.00
RD19	Fabio Castro	1.00
RD20	Jordan Tata	1.00
RD21	Taylor Buchholz	1.50
RD22	Sean Marshall	1.00
RD23	John Rheinecker	1.00
RD24	Casey Janssen	1.00
RD25	Russell Martin	1.50
RD26	Yusmeiro Petit	1.50
RD27	Kendry Morales	1.50
RD28	Alay Soler	1.00
RD29	Jered Weaver	3.00
RD30	Matthew Kemp	2.00
RD31	Enrique Gonzalez	1.00
RD32	Lastings Milledge	2.00
RD33	James Shields	1.00
RD34	Kendry Morales	1.00
RD35	Zach Jackson	1.00
RD36	Zach Miner	1.00
RD37	Jon Lester	3.00
RD38	Chad Billingsley	2.00
RD39	Scott Thorman	1.00
RD40	Anibal Sanchez	2.00
RD41	Mike Thompson	1.00
RD42	T.J. Beam	1.00
RD43	Stephen Drew	3.00
RD44	Joe Saunders	1.00
RD45	Carlos Quentin	1.50

Rookie Debut Autographs

		NM/M
Common Autograph:		15.00
RA	Reggie Abercrombie	10.00
MA	Matt Albers	20.00
FC	Fausto Carmona	15.00
FF	Emiliano Fruto	15.00
IK	Ian Kinsler	20.00
JL	Jon Lester	40.00
BL	Bobby Livingston	15.00
AL	Adam Loewen	40.00
MN	Michael Napoli	30.00
RN	Ricky Nolasco	15.00
YP	Yusmeiro Petit	15.00
MP	Martin Prado	15.00
JS	Jeremy Sowers	15.00
ST	Scott Thorman	15.00

Signature Moves

		NM/M
Common Autograph:		
AH	Aubrey Huff	15.00
JL	Julio Lugo	15.00
BP	Brandon Phillips	20.00
BW	Brad Wilkerson	10.00
CW	Craig Wilson	10.00

Touch 'Em All Relics

		NM/M
Inserted 1:610		
CB	Carlos Beltran	20.00
RH	Ryan Howard	30.00
JM	Joe Mauer	15.00
DO	David Ortiz	20.00
AP	Albert Pujols	30.00
AR	Alex Rodriguez	25.00
IS	Ichiro Suzuki	25.00
MT	Miguel Tejada	10.00
DW	David Wright	25.00
MY	Michael Young	8.00

2006 Topps 1952 Edition

		NM/M
Complete Set (312):		
Common Player:		.25
Common SP (276-312):		5.00
Common 52 Logo Variation:		4.00
Inserted 1:5		
Pack (8):		4.50
Box (20):		80.00
1	Howie Kendrick RC	1.00
2	Enrique Gonzalez RC	.25
3	Chuck James RC	.25
4	Chris Britton RC	.50
5	David Pauley RC	.50
6	Angel Pagan RC	.25
7	Pat Neshek RC	.50
8	Walter Young RC	.25
9	Chris Denorfia RC	.25
10	Rafael Perez RC	.50
11	Ryan Spilborghs RC	.50
12	Jon Huber RC	.25
13	Jordan Tata RC	.25
14	Eric Reed RC	.25
15	Norris Hopper RC	.25
16	Scott Olsen RC	.25
17	Fernando Nieve RC	.25
18	Chris Booker RC	.25
19	Chad Billingsley RC	1.00
20	Carlos Villanueva RC	.25
21	Craig Hansen RC	.50
22	David Gassner RC	.25
23	Mike Pelfrey RC	3.00
24	Matt Smith RC	.50
25	Chris Roberson RC	.25
26	John Van Benschoten RC	.25
27	Kevin Frandsen RC	.50
28	Les Walrond RC	.50
29	James Shields RC	.75
30	Russell Martin RC	.50
31	Benjamin Zobrist RC	.25
32	John Rheinecker RC	.25
33	Francisco Rosario RC	.25
34	Santiago Ramirez RC	.25
35	Michael Napoli RC	.75
36	Tony Pena RC	.25
37	Jeff Karstens RC	.50
37	Jeff Karstens/	
38	52 Logo/SP RC	4.00
38	Phil Stockman RC	.25
39	Kurt Birkins RC	1.00
40	Dustin Pedroia RC	1.00
41	Buck Coats RC	.25
42	Jim Johnson RC	1.00
43	Angel Guzman RC	.25
44	Kelly Shoppach RC	.50
45	Josh Wilson RC	.25
46	Jack Hannahan RC	.25
47	Ricky Nolasco RC	.75
48	T.J. Bohn RC	.25
49	Joel Zumaya RC	.50
50	Philip Barzilla RC	.25
51	Justin Huber RC	.75
52	Willy Aybar RC	.25
52	Willy Aybar/	
	52 Logo/SP RC	4.00
53	Tony Gwynn Jr. RC	.50
54	Chris Barnwell RC	.50
55	Henry Owens RC	.75
56	Jeff Bajenaru RC	.50
57	Jonah Bayliss RC	.50
58	Joshua Sharpless RC	.50
59	Eliezer Alfonzo RC	.25
60	Bobby Livingston RC	.25
61	John Gall RC	.50
62	Ruddy Lugo RC	.25
63	Fabio Castro RC	.25
64	Casey Janssen RC	.75
65	Mike O'Connor RC	.50
66	Kendry Morales RC	1.00
67	James Hoey RC	.75
68	Dustin Moseley RC	.50
69	Peter Moylan RC	.50
70	Manny Delcarmen RC	.50
71	Rich Hill RC	.50
72	Boone Logan RC	.50
73	Cody Ross RC	.25
74	Fausto Carmona RC	.50
75	Ramon Ramirez RC	.50
76	Zach Miner RC	.50
77	Hanley Ramirez RC	1.00
78	Josh Johnson RC	.75
79	Taylor Buchholz RC	.25
80	Joe Nelson RC	.25
81	Hong-Chih Kuo RC	.50
82	Chris Mabeus RC	.25
83	Willie Eyre RC	.50
84	John Maine RC	.50
85	Yurendell DeCaster RC	.25
86	Mike Thompson RC	.50
87	Brian Wilson RC	.50
88	Matt Cain RC	.75
88	Matt Cain/52 Logo/	
	SP RC	8.00
89	Josh Rupe RC	.25
90	Tyler Johnson RC	.25
91	Jason Childers RC	.25
92	Wes Littleton RC	.25
93	Ty Taubenheim RC	.25
94	Saul Rivera RC	.25
95	Reggie Willits RC	1.00
96	Carlos Quentin RC	.50
97	Macay McBride RC	.25
98	Brandon Fahey RC	.25
99	Sean Marshall RC	.25

#	Player	Price
100	Sean Tracey RC	.25
101	Brian Slocum RC	.25
102	Choo Freeman RC	.25
103	Brent Clevlen RC	.25
104	Josh Willingham RC	.25
105	Chris Resop RC	.25
106	Chris Sampson RC	1.00
107	James Loney RC	.50
107	James Loney/ 52 Logo/SP RC	8.00
108	Matthew Kemp RC	1.00
109	Jason Kubel RC	.75
110	Brian Bannister RC	.50
111	Kevin Thompson RC	.25
112	Jeremy Brown RC	.25
113	Brian Sanches RC	.25
114	Nate McLouth RC	.50
115	Ben Johnson RC	.25
116	Jonathan Sanchez RC	.50
117	Mark Lowe RC	.25
118	Skip Schumaker RC	.50
119	Jason Hammel RC	.25
120	Drew Meyer RC	.25
121	Melvin Dorta RC	.25
122	Jeff Mathis RC	.25
123	Davis Romero RC	.25
124	Joey Devine RC	.50
125	Sendy Rleal RC	.50
126	Freddie Bynum RC	.25
127	Bryan Anderson RC	.25
128	Jeremy Sowers RC	.25
129	Ryan Shealy RC	.25
130	Reggie Abercrombie RC	.25
131	Matt Albers RC	.25
132	Lastings Milledge RC	.50
133	Robert Andino RC	.25
134	Chris Demaria RC	.50
135	Boof Bonser RC	.25
136	Alay Soler RC	.50
137	Wilbert Nieves RC	.25
138	Mike Rouse RC	.25
139	Carlos Ruiz RC	.25
140	Matt Capps RC	.25
141	Travis Ishikawa RC	.25
142	Josh Kinney RC	.50
143	Josh Rupe RC	.25
144	Shaun Marcum RC	.25
145	Jason Bergmann RC	.25
146	Tommy Murphy RC	.25
147	Martin Prado RC	.75
148	Val Majewski RC	.25
149	Ian Kinsler RC	.75
150	Joe Winkelsas RC	.25
151	Agustin Montero RC	.25
152	Joe Inglett RC	.50
153	Manuel Corpas RC	.50
154	Yusmeiro Petit RC	.25
155	Mark Woodyard RC	.25
156	Jeff Fulchino RC	.25
157	Stephen Andrade RC	.25
158	Tim Hamulack RC	.25
159	Colter Bean RC	.25
160	Anderson Hernandez RC	.25
161	Kevin Reese RC	.25
162	Jason Windsor RC	.25
163	Paul Maholm RC	.25
163	Paul Maholm/ 52 Logo/SP RC	4.00
164	Jeremy Accardo RC	.50
165	Joel Guzman RC	.25
166	Erick Aybar RC	.25
167	Scott Thorman RC	.25
168	Adam Loewen RC	.25
169	Carlos Marmol RC	.50
170	Bill Bray RC	.25
171	Edward Mujica RC	.50
172	Jeremy Hermida RC	.50
173	Taylor Tankersley RC	.25
174	Bobby Keppel RC	.25
175	Chris Young RC	.50
176	Josh Rabe RC	1.00
177	T.J. Beam RC	.25
178	Shane Komine RC	1.00
178	Shane Komine/ 52 Logo/SP	6.00
179	Scott Mathieson RC	.25
180	Josh Barfield RC	.25
181	Justin Knoedler RC	.25
182	Emiliano Fruto RC	.25
183	Adam Wainwright RC	1.50
184	Nick Masset RC	.25
185	Ryan Roberts RC	.25
186	Brandon Watson RC	.25
187	Chris Bootcheck RC	.25
188	Daniel Ortmeier RC	.25
189	Kevin Barry RC	.25
190	Cory Morris RC	.50
191	Kason Gabbard RC	.25
192	Tom Mastny RC	.25
193	David Aardsma RC	.25
194	Anthony Reyes RC	.25
195	Mike Jacobs RC	.50
196	Conor Jackson RC	.25
197	Kenji Johjima RC	.75
198	Jack Taschner RC	.25
199	Renyel Pinto RC	.25
200	Chad Santos RC	.25
201	Aaron Rakers RC	.25
202	Franklin Gutierrez RC	.25
203	Chris Coste RC	.25
204	Chris Iannetta RC	.50
205	Michael Vento RC	.25
206	Ryan O'Malley RC	.25
207	Jason Botts RC	.25
208	John Hattig Jr. RC	.25
209	Brandon Harper RC	.25
210	Ryan Theriot RC	1.00
211	Travis Hughes RC	.25
212	Paul Hoover RC	.25
213	Brayan Pena RC	.25
214	Craig Breslow RC	.75
215	Eude Brito RC	.25
216	Melky Cabrera RC	.50
216	Melky Cabrera/ 52 Logo/SP RC	4.00
217	Jonathan Broxton RC	.50
217	Jonathan Broxton/ 52 Logo/SP RC	5.00
218	Bryan Corey RC	.25
219	Ron Flores RC	.50
220	Andrew Brown RC	.25
221	Jaime Bubela RC	.25
222	Jason Bulger RC	.25
223	Alberto Callaspo RC	.75
224	Jose Capellan RC	.25
225	Cole Hamels RC	1.00
225	Cole Hamels/ 52 Logo/SP RC	6.00
226	Bernie Castro RC	.25
227	Shin-Soo Choo RC	1.00
228	Doug Clark RC	.25
229	Roy Corcoran RC	.50
230	Tim Corcoran RC	.75
231	Nelson Cruz RC	1.00
232	Rajai Davis RC	.25
233	Chris Duncan RC	.25
233	Chris Duncan/ 52 Logo/SP RC	5.00
234	Scott Dunn RC	.25
235	Mike Esposito RC	.25
236	Scott Feldman RC	.50
237	Luis Figueroa RC	.25
238	Bartolome Fortunato RC	.25
239	Alejandro Freire RC	.50
240	J.J. Furmaniak RC	.25
241	Nicholas Markakis RC	.50
242	Matt Garza RC	.75
243	Justin Germano RC	.25
244	Alexis Gomez RC	.25
245	Tom Gorzelanny RC	.25
246	Dan Uggla RC	.75
247	Jeremy Guthrie RC	.25
248	Stephen Drew RC	1.00
249	Brendan Harris RC	.25
250	Jeff Harris RC	.25
251	Corey Hart RC	.50
252	Chris Heintz RC	.25
253	Prince Fielder RC	2.00
254	Francisco Liriano RC	.50
255	Jason Hirsh RC	.25
256	J.R. House RC	.25
257	Zach Jackson RC	.25
258	Charlton Jimerson RC	.25
259	Greg Jones RC	.25
260	Mitch Jones RC	.25
261	Ryan Jorgensen RC	.25
262	Logan Kensing RC	.25
263	John Koronka RC	.25
264	Anthony Lerew RC	.25
265	Anibal Sanchez RC	.25
266	Juan Mateo RC	.50
267	Paul McAnulty RC	.25
268	Dustin McGowan RC	.50
269	Marty McLeary RC	.25
270	Ryan Zimmerman RC	2.00
271	Jason Nippert RC	.25
272	Eric O'Flaherty RC	.25
273	Ronny Paulino RC	.25
274	Tony Pena RC	.25
275	Hayden Penn RC	.50
276	Miguel Perez RC	5.00
277	Paul Phillips RC	5.00
278	Omar Quintanilla RC	5.00
279	Guillermo Quiroz RC	5.00
280	Darrell Rasner RC	5.00
281	Kenny Ray RC	5.00
282	Royce Ring RC	5.00
283	Brian Rogers RC	5.00
284	Ed Rogers RC	5.00
285	Danny Sandoval RC	5.00
286	Joe Saunders RC	5.00
287	Chris Schroder RC	5.00
288	Mike Smith RC	5.00
289	Travis Smith RC	5.00
290	Geovany Soto RC	8.00
291	Brian Sweeney RC	5.00
292	Jon Switzer RC	5.00
293	Joe Thurston RC	5.00
294	Jermaine Van Buren RC	5.00
295	Ryan Garko RC	5.00
296	Cla Meredith RC	5.00
297	Luke Scott RC	5.00
298	Andy Marte RC	5.00
299	Jered Weaver RC	10.00
300	Freddy Guzman RC	5.00
301	Jonathan Papelbon RC	10.00
302	John-Ford Griffin RC	5.00
303	Jon Lester RC	10.00
304	Shawn Hill RC	5.00
305	Brian Myrow RC	5.00
306	Anderson Garcia RC	5.00
307	Andre Ethier RC	8.00
308	Ben Hendrickson RC	5.00
309	Alejandro Machado RC	5.00
310	Justin Verlander RC	8.00
311	Mickey Mantle/Blue	40.00
311	Mickey Mantle/Black	15.00
311	Mickey Mantle/Green	15.00
311	Mickey Mantle/Orange	15.00
311	Mickey Mantle/Red	15.00
311	Mickey Mantle/Yellow	15.00
312	Steve Stemle RC	5.00

Chrome

		NM/M
Common Player:		1.50
Production 1,952 Sets		
Refractor:		2-3X
Production 552 Sets		
Gold Refractor:		4-6X
Production 52 Sets		
1	Howie Kendrick	2.00
2	David Pauley	1.50
3	Chris Denorfia	1.50
4	Jordan Tata	2.00
5	Fernando Nieve	1.50
6	Craig Hansen	2.00
7	Mickey Mantle	25.00
8	James Shields	3.00
9	Francisco Rosario	1.50
10	Jeff Karstens	3.00
11	Buck Coats	1.50
12	Josh Wilson	1.50
13	Joel Zumaya	2.00
14	Tony Gwynn Jr.	2.00
15	Jonah Bayliss	1.50
16	John Gall	1.50
17	Mike O'Connor	1.50
18	Peter Moylan	1.50
19	Cody Ross	1.50
20	Hanley Ramirez	4.00
21	Hong-Chih Kuo	3.00
22	Yurendell DeCaster	1.50
23	Sean Green	1.50
24	Ty Taubenheim	1.50
25	Macay McBride	1.50
26	Brian Slocum	1.50
27	Chris Resop	1.50
28	Jason Kubel	1.50
29	Brian Sanches	1.50
30	Mark Lowe	1.50
31	Melvin Dorta	1.50
32	Sendy Rleal	1.50
33	Ryan Shealy	1.50
34	Robert Andino	1.50
35	Wilbert Nieves	1.50
36	Travis Ishikawa	1.50
37	Jason Bergmann	1.50
38	Ian Kinsler	3.00
39	Manuel Corpas	1.50
40	Stephen Andrade	1.50
41	Kevin Reese	1.50
42	Joel Guzman	1.50
43	Carlos Marmol	3.00
44	Taylor Tankersley	1.50
45	T.J. Beam	1.50
46	Justin Knoedler	1.50
47	Ryan Roberts	1.50
48	Kevin Barry	1.50
49	David Aardsma	1.50
50	Kenji Johjima	3.00
51	Aaron Rakers	1.50
52	Michael Vento	1.50
53	Brandon Harper	1.50
54	Brayan Pena	1.50
55	Jonathan Broxton	2.00
56	Jaime Bubela	1.50
57	Cole Hamels	5.00
58	Roy Corcoran	1.50
59	Chris Duncan	4.00
60	Luis Figueroa	1.50
61	Kendry Morales	1.50
62	Tom Gorzelanny	1.50
63	Brendan Harris	1.50
64	Anibal Sanchez	1.50
65	Zach Jackson	1.50
66	Ryan Jorgensen	1.50
67	Josh Johnson	1.50
68	Marty McLeary	2.00
69	Ronny Paulino	1.50
70	Tyler Johnson	1.50
2	Reggie Abercrombie	1.50
72	Nick Markakis	5.00
73	J.J. Furmaniak	2.00
74	Prince Fielder	5.00
75	Enrique Gonzalez	1.50
76	Angel Pagan	1.50
77	Rafael Perez	2.00
78	Eric Reed	1.50
79	Chris Booker	1.50
80	David Gassner	1.50
81	John Van Benschoten	1.50
82	Russell Martin	5.00
83	Santiago Ramirez	1.50
84	Phil Stockman	1.50
85	Jim Johnson	1.50
86	Jack Hannahan	1.50
87	Philip Barzilla	1.50
88	Chris Barnwell	1.50
89	Joshua Sharpless	1.50
90	Chris Roberson	1.50

Debut Flashbacks

		NM/M
Common Player:		2.00
Chrome:		1.5-2X
Production 1,952 Sets		
Refractor:		2-3X
Production 552 Sets		
Gold Refractor:		4-6X
Production 52 Sets		
1	Dontrelle Willis	2.00
2	Carlos Beltran	3.00
3	Albert Pujols	8.00
4	Ichiro Suzuki	5.00
5	Mike Piazza	4.00
6	Nomar Garciaparra	3.00
7	Scott Rolen	3.00
8	Mariano Rivera	3.00
9	David Ortiz	4.00
10	Johnny Damon	4.00
11	Tom Glavine	3.00
12	David Wright	5.00
13	Greg Maddux	5.00
14	Manny Ramirez	4.00
15	Alex Rodriguez	6.00
16	Roger Clemens	6.00
17	Alfonso Soriano	3.00
18	Frank Thomas	3.00
19	Chipper Jones	4.00
20	Ivan Rodriguez	3.00

Dynamic Duos

DYNAMIC DUOS
ANDRE ETHIER   RUSSELL MARTIN

		NM/M
Common Duo:		1.00
Inserted 1:4		
1	Stephen Drew, Carlos Quentin	2.00
2	Jonathan Papelbon, Jon Lester	3.00
3	Joel Zumaya, Justin Verlander	4.00
4	Dan Uggla, Hanley Ramirez	1.50
5	Jonathan Broxton, Chad Billingsley	1.00
6	Francisco Liriano, Matt Garza	1.50
7	Lastings Milledge, John Maine	1.50
8	Chris Coste, Cole Hamels	2.00
9	Michael Napoli, Howie Kendrick	1.50
10	Joe Inglett, Andy Marte	1.00
11	Jeremy Hermida, Josh Willingham	1.00
12	Matthew Kemp, James Loney	1.50
13	Andre Ethier, Russell Martin	1.50
14	Melky Cabrera, Jeff Karstens	1.50
15	Ricky Nolasco, Scott Olsen, Josh Johnson, Anibal Sanchez	1.50

Autograph

BRIAN ANDERSON

	NM/M
Common Auto.:	8.00
Red Ink:	2-3X

Production 52 Sets

RA	Reggie Abercrombie	8.00
MA	Matt Albers	8.00
BA	Brian Anderson	8.00
EA	Erick Aybar	8.00
BPB	Brian Bannister	10.00
TJB	T.J. Bohn	8.00
BB	Boof Bonser	20.00
WB	Bill Bray	8.00
MC	Melky Cabrera	30.00
MTC	Matt Cain	25.00
FC	Fabio Castro	8.00
BC	Buck Coats	8.00
YD	Yurendell DeCaster	8.00
SD	Stephen Drew	25.00
KF	Kevin Frandsen	8.00
EF	Emiliano Fruto	8.00
MG	Matt Garza	20.00
EG	Enrique Gonzalez	8.00
FG	Franklin Gutierrez	10.00
AG	Angel Guzman	8.00
JG	Joel Guzman	8.00
CI	Chris Iannetta	10.00
CHJ	Chuck James	8.00
JWK	Jeff Karstens	20.00
MK	Matthew Kemp	25.00
HK	Howie Kendrick	30.00
JK	Josh Kinney	8.00
HCK	Hong-Chih Kuo	40.00
AL	Anthony Lerew	8.00
CM	Chris Mabeus	8.00
TM	Tom Mastny	15.00
SM	Scott Mathieson	8.00
JM	Jeff Mathis	8.00
KM	Kendry Morales	8.00
EM	Edward Mujica	8.00
MN	Michael Napoli	15.00
RO	Ryan O'Malley	8.00
AP	Angel Pagan	10.00
JP	Jonathan Papelbon	40.00
YP	Yusmeiro Petit	10.00
AS	Anibal Sanchez	8.00
JFS	Joe Saunders	15.00
JS	Joshua Sharpless	8.00
BS	Brian Slocum	8.00
DU	Dan Uggla	25.00
JVB	John Van Benschoten	8.00
JV	Justin Verlander	50.00
JW	Jered Weaver	40.00
RZ	Ryan Zimmerman	40.00
BZ	Benjamin Zobrist	10.00
JZ	Joel Zumaya	20.00

Ticket to Stardom Relics

No Pricing
Production 10 Sets

2007 Topps

	NM/M
Complete Set (661):	75.00
Common Player:	.10
Series 1 Hobby Pack (10):	3.00
Series 1 Hobby Box (36):	100.00
Series 1 Jumbo Pack (50):	15.00
Series 1 Jumbo Box (10):	140.00
Series 1 Rack Pack (22):	5.00
Series 1 Rack Box (24):	100.00
Series 2 Hobby Pack (10):	2.00
Series 2 Hobby Box (36):	60.00
Series 2 Jumbo Pack (50):	
Series 2 Jumbo Box (10):	90.00
Series 2 Rack Pack (22):	4.00
Series 2 Rack Box (24):	85.00
Series 1 Variations:	No Pricing
Inserted 1:3700 Wal-Mart	

#	Player	Price
1	John Lackey	.10
2	Nick Swisher	.25
3	Brad Lidge	.10
4	Bengie Molina	.10
5	Bobby Abreu	.25
6	Edgar Renteria	.25
7	Mickey Mantle	5.00
8	Preston Wilson	.10
9	Ryan Dempster	.10
10	C.C. Sabathia	.10
11	Julio Lugo	.10
12	J.D. Drew	.25
13	Miguel Batista	.10
14	Eliezer Alfonzo	.10
15	Andrew Miller RC	1.00
15	Andrew Miller/Posed RC	.10
16	Yuniesky Betancourt	.10
17	Saul Rivera	.10
18	Orlando Hernandez	.10
19	Alfredo Amezaga	.10
20	Delmon Young/ Face Right (RC)	.50
20	Delmon Young/ Face Left (RC)	.10
21	Javy Lopez	.10
22	Corey Patterson	.10
23	Josh Bard	.10
24	Tom Gordon	.10
25	Gary Matthews	.10
26	Jason Jennings	.10
27	Joey Gathright	.10
28	Brandon Inge	.10
29	Pat Neshek	.10
30	Bronson Arroyo	.10
31	Jay Payton	.10
32	Andy Pettitte	.25
33	Ervin Santana	.10
34	Paul Konerko	.25
35	Joel Zumaya	.25
36	Gregg Zaun	.10
37	Tony Gwynn	.50
38	Adam LaRoche	.10
39	Jim Edmonds	.25
40	Derek Jeter	15.00
41	Rich Hill	.25
42	Livan Hernandez	.10
43	Aubrey Huff	.10
44	Todd Greene	.10
45	Andre Ethier	.25
46	Jeremy Sowers	.10
47	Ben Broussard	.10
48	Darren Oliver	.10
49	Nook Logan	.10
50	Miguel Cabrera	.50
51	Carlos Lee	.25
52	Jose Castillo	.10
53	Mike Piazza	.75
54	Daniel Cabrera	.10
55	Cole Hamels	.40
56	Mark Loretta	.10
57	Brian Fuentes	.10
58	Todd Coffey	.10
59	Brent Clevlen	.10
60	John Smoltz	.25
61	Ross Gload	.10
62	Dan Wheeler	.10
63	Scott Proctor	.10
64	Bobby Kielty	.10
65	Dan Uggla	.25
66	Lyle Overbay	.10
67	Geoff Jenkins	.10
68	Michael Barrett	.10
69	Casey Fossum	.10
70	Ivan Rodriguez	.40
71	Jose Lopez	.10
72	Jake Westbrook	.10
73	Moises Alou	.25
74	Jose Valverde	.10
75	Jered Weaver	.25
76	Lastings Milledge	.25
77	Austin Kearns	.10
78	Adam Loewen	.10
79	Josh Barfield	.10
80	Johan Santana	.40
81	Ian Kinsler	.10
82	Ian Snell	.10
83	Mike Lowell	.10
84	Elizardo Ramirez	.10
85	Scott Rolen	.40
86	Shannon Stewart	.10
87	Alexis Gomez	.10
88	Jimmy Gobble	.10
89	Jamey Carroll	.10
90	Chipper Jones	.50
91	Carlos Silva	.10
92	Joe Crede	.25
93	Michael Napoli	.10
94	Willy Travis	.10
95	Rafael Furcal	.25
96	Phil Nevin	.10
97	David Bush	.10
98	Marcus Giles	.10
99	Joe Blanton	.10
100	Dontrelle Willis	.25
101	Scott Kazmir	.25
102	Jeff Kent	.25
103	Pedro Feliz	.10
104	Johnny Estrada	.10
105	Travis Hafner	.25
106	Ryan Garko	.10
107	Rafael Soriano	.10
108	Wes Helms	.10
109	Billy Wagner	.10
110	Aaron Rowand	.10
111	Felipe Lopez	.10
112	Jeff Conine	.10
113	Nicholas Markakis	.25
114	John Koronka	.10
115	B.J. Ryan	.10
116	Tim Wakefield	.10
117	David Ross	.10
118	Emil Brown	.10
119	Michael Cuddyer	.10
120	Jason Giambi	.40
121	Alex Cintron	.10
122	Luke Scott	.10
123	Chone Figgins	.10
124	Huston Street	.10
125	Carlos Delgado	.40
126	Daryle Ward	.10
127	Chris Duncan	.10
128	Damian Miller	.10
129	Aramis Ramirez	.25
130	Albert Pujols	1.50
131	Chris Snyder	.10
132	Ray Durham	.10
133	Franklin Gutierrez	.10
134	Mike Jacobs	.10
135	Troy Tulowitzki RC	.50
135	Troy Tulowitzki/ Throw (RC)	.10
136	Jon Rauch	.10
137	Jay Gibbons	.10
138	Adrian Gonzalez	.10
139	Randy Wolf	.10
140	Freddy Sanchez	.10
141	Rich Aurilia	.10
142	Trot Nixon	.10
143	Vicente Padilla	.10
144	Jack Wilson	.10

#	Player	Price
145	Jake Peavy	.25
146	Luke Hudson	.10
147	Javier Vazquez	.10
148	Scott Podsednik	.10
149	Ivan Rodriguez, Magglio Ordonez	.25
150	Todd Helton	.40
151	Kendry Morales	.25
152	Adam Everett	.10
153	Bob Wickman	.10
154	Bill Hall	.25
155	Jeremy Bonderman	.25
156	Ryan Theriot	.25
157	Rocco Baldelli	.25
158	Noah Lowry	.10
159	Jason Michaels	.10
160	Justin Verlander	.10
161	Eduardo Perez	.10
162	Chris Ray	.10
163	Dave Roberts	.10
164	Zachary Duke	.10
165	Mark Buehrle	.25
166	Hank Blalock	.25
167	Royce Clayton	.10
168	Mark Teahen	.10
169	Todd Jones	.10
170	Chien-Ming Wang	.50
171	Nick Punto	.10
172	Morgan Ensberg	.10
173	Robert Mackowiak	.10
174	Frank Catalanotto	.10
175	Matt Murton	.10
176	Alfonso Soriano, Carlos Beltran	.40
177	Francisco Cordero	.10
178	Jason Marquis	.10
179	Joe Nathan	.10
180	Roy Halladay	.25
181	Melvin Mora	.10
182	Ramon Ortiz	.10
183	Jose Valentin	.10
184	Gil Meche	.10
185	B.J. Upton	.25
186	Grady Sizemore	.40
187	Matt Cain	.25
188	Eric Byrnes	.10
189	Carl Crawford	.25
190	J.J. Putz	.10
191	Cla Meredith	.10
192	Matt Capps	.10
193	Rod Barajas	.10
194	Edwin Encarnacion	.10
195	James Loney	.10
196	Johnny Damon	.50
197	Freddy Garcia	.10
198	Mike Redmond	.10
199	Ryan Shealy	.10
200	Carlos Beltran	.40
201	Chuck James	.10
202	Mark Ellis	.10
203	Brad Ausmus	.10
204	Juan Rivera	.10
205	Cory Sullivan	.10
206	Ben Sheets	.25
207	Mark Mulder	.10
208	Carlos Quentin	.10
209	Jonathan Broxton	.10
210	Kazuo Matsui	.10
211	Armando Benitez	.10
212	Richie Sexson	.40
213	Josh Johnson	.10
214	Brian Schneider	.10
215	Craig Monroe	.10
216	Chris Duffy	.10
217	Chris Coste	.10
218	Clay Hensley	.10
219	Chris Gomez	.10
220	Hideki Matsui	.75
221	Robinson Tejeda	.10
222	Scott Hatteberg	.10
223	Jeff Francis	.10
224	Matt Thornton	.10
225	Robinson Cano	.40
226	New York Yankees	1.00
227	Oakland A's	.25
228	St. Louis Cardinals	.50
229	Minnesota Twins	.25
230	Barry Zito	.25
231	Baltimore Orioles	.25
232	Seattle Mariners	.25
233	Houston Astros	.25
234	Florida Marlins	.25
235	Reed Johnson	.10
236	Toronto Blue Jays	.25
237	Cincinnati Reds	.25
238	Philadelphia Phillies	.25
239	Anaheim Angels	.25
240	Chris Carpenter	.25
241	Atlanta Braves	.25
242	Washington Nationals	.25
243	Joe Torre	.50
244	Tampa Bay Devil Rays	.25
245	Chad Tracey	.10
246	Mike Hargrove	.10
247	Mike Scioscia	.10
248	Ron Gardenhire	.10
249	Tony LaRussa	.10
250	Anibal Sanchez	.25
251	Charlie Manuel	.10
252	John Gibbons	.10
253	Ken Macha	.10
254	Jerry Narron	.10
255	Brad Penny	.25
256	Bobby Cox	.25
257	Bob Melvin	.10
258	Mike Hargrove	.10
259	Phil Garner	.10
260	David Wright	1.00
261	Vinny Rottino (RC)	.25
262	Ryan Braun (RC)	2.50
263	Kevin Kouzmanoff (RC)	.50
264	David Murphy (RC)	.25
265	Jimmy Rollins	.25
266	Joe Maddon	.10
267	Grady Little	.10
268	Ryan Sweeney (RC)	.25
269	Fred Lewis (RC)	.25
270	Alfonso Soriano	.50
271	Delwyn Young (RC)	.25
271	Delwyn Young/Swing (RC)	.10
272	Jeff Salazar (RC)	.25
273	Miguel Montero (RC)	.25
274	Shawn Riggans (RC)	.25
275	Greg Maddux	1.00
276	Brian Stokes (RC)	.25
277	Philip Humber (RC)	.25
278	Scott Moore (RC)	.25
279	Adam Lind (RC)	.50
280	Curt Schilling	.50
281	Chris Narveson (RC)	.25
282	Oswaldo Navarro RC	.25
283	Drew Anderson (RC)	.25
284	Jerry Owens (RC)	.25
285	Randy Johnson	.50
286	Joaquin Arias (RC)	.25
287	Jose Garcia (RC)	.25
288	Shane Youman RC	.25
289	Brian Burres (RC)	.25
290	Matt Holliday	.50
291	Ryan Feierabend (RC)	.25
292	Josh Fields (RC)	.25
292	Josh Fields/Running (RC)	.25
293	Glen Perkins (RC)	.25
294	Mike Rabelo RC	.50
295	Jorge Posada	.25
296	Ubaldo Jimenez (RC)	.25
297	Brad Ausmus	.10
298	Eric Chavez	.25
299	Orlando Hudson	.10
300	Vladimir Guerrero	.50
301	Derek Jeter	1.00
302	Scott Rolen	.25
303	Mark Grudzielanek	.10
304	Kenny Rogers	.10
305	Frank Thomas	.25
306	Mike Cameron	.10
307	Torii Hunter	.25
308	Albert Pujols	1.00
309	Mark Teixeira	.25
310	Jonathan Papelbon	.50
311	Greg Maddux	.50
312	Carlos Beltran	.25
313	Ichiro Suzuki	.75
314	Andruw Jones	.25
315	Manny Ramirez	.25
316	Vernon Wells	.25
317	Omar Vizquel	.10
318	Ivan Rodriguez	.25
319	Brandon Webb	.25
320	Magglio Ordonez	.25
321	Johan Santana	.25
322	Ryan Howard	1.00
323	Justin Morneau	.25
324	Hanley Ramirez	.40
325	Joe Mauer	.25
326	Justin Verlander	.25
327	Derek Jeter, Bobby Abreu	.50
328	Carlos Delgado	.25
	David Wright	.50
329	Yadier Molina, Albert Pujols	
330	Ryan Howard	.50
331	Kelly Johnson	.10
332	Chris Young	.25
333	Mark Kotsay	.10
334	A.J. Burnett	.25
335	Brian McCann	.25
336	Woody Williams	.10
337	Jason Isringhausen	.10
338	Juan Pierre	.10
339	Jonny Gomes	.10
340	Roger Clemens	1.50
341	Akinori Iwamura RC	.75
342	Bengie Molina	.10
343	Shin-Soo Choo	.10
344	Kenji Johjima	.25
345	Joe Borowski	.10
346	Shawn Green	.10
347	Chicago Cubs	.10
348	Rodrigo Lopez	.10
349	Brian Giles	.25
350	Chase Utley	.50
351	Mark DeRosa	.10
352	Carl Pavano	.10
353	Kyle Lohse	.10
354	Chris Iannetta	.25
355	Oliver Perez	.10
356	Curtis Granderson	.25
357	Sean Casey	.10
358	Jason Tyner	.10
359	Jon Garland	.10
360	David Ortiz	.75
361	Adam Kennedy	.10
362	Chris Burke	.10
363	Bobby Crosby	.10
364	Conor Jackson	.25
365	Tim Hudson	.25
366	Rickie Weeks	.25
367	Cristian Guzman	.10
368	Mark Prior	.25
369	Benjamin Zobrist	.10
370	Troy Glaus	.25
371	Kenny Lofton	.10
372	Shane Victorino	.25
373	Cliff Lee	.10
374	Adrian Beltre	.25
375	Miguel Olivo	.10
376	Endy Chavez	.10
377	Zack Segovia (RC)	.25
378	Ramon Hernandez	.10
379	Chris Young	.25
380	Jason Schmidt	.25
381	Ronny Paulino	.10
382	Kevin Millwood	.10
383	Jon Lester	.25
384	Alex Gonzalez	.10
385	Brad Hawpe	.10
386	Placido Polanco	.10
387	Nate Robertson	.10
388	Torii Hunter	.25
389	Gavin Floyd	.10
390	Roy Oswalt	.40
391	Kelvim Escobar	.10
392	Craig Wilson	.10
393	Milton Bradley	.10
394	Aaron Hill	.10
395	Matt Diaz	.10
396	Chris Capuano	.10
397	Juan Encarnacion	.10
398	Jacque Jones	.10
399	James Shields	.10
400	Ichiro Suzuki	.75
401	Matthew Kemp	.25
402	Matt Morris	.10
403	Casey Blake	.10
404	Corey Hart	.25
405	Josh Willingham	.10
406	Ryan Madson	.10
407	Nick Johnson	.10
408	Kevin Millar	.10
409	Khalil Greene	.10
410	Tom Glavine	.25
411	Jason Bay	.25
412	Gerald Laird	.10
413	Coco Crisp	.10
414	Brandon Phillips	.10
415	Aaron Cook	.10
416	Mark Redman	.10
417	Mike Maroth	.10
418	Boof Bonser	.10
419	Jorge Cantu	.10
420	Jeff Weaver	.10
421	Melky Cabrera	.25
422	Francisco Rodriguez	.10
423	Mike Lamb	.10
424	Danny Haren	.25
425	Tomokazu Ohka	.10
426	Jeff Francoeur	.25
427	Randy Wolf	.10
428	So Taguchi	.10
429	Carlos Zambrano	.25
430	Justin Morneau	.50
431	Luis Gonzalez	.25
432	Takashi Saito	.25
433	Brandon Morrow RC	.75
434	Victor Martinez	.25
435	Felix Hernandez	.25
436	Ricky Nolasco	.10
437	Paul LoDuca	.10
438	Chad Cordero	.10
439	Miguel Tejada	.40
440	Mark Teixeira	.40
441	Pat Burrell	.25
442	Paul Maholm	.10
443	Mike Cameron	.10
444	Josh Beckett	.25
445	Pablo Ozuna	.10
446	Jaret Wright	.10
447	Angel Berroa	.10
448	Fernando Rodney	.10
449	Francisco Liriano	.25
450	Ken Griffey Jr.	1.00
451	Bobby Jenks	.10
452	Mike Mussina	.40
453	Howie Kendrick	.25
454	Milwaukee Brewers	.10
455	Dan Johnson	.10
456	Ted Lilly	.10
457	Mike Hampton	.10
458	J.J. Hardy	.25
459	Jeff Suppan	.10
460	Jose Reyes	1.00
461	Jae Weong Seo	.10
462	Edgar Gonzalez	.10
463	Russell Martin	.25
464	Omar Vizquel	.10
465	Jhonny Peralta	.25
466	Raul Ibanez	.10
467	Hanley Ramirez	.50
468	Kerry Wood	.10
469	Ryan Church	.10
470	Gary Sheffield	.25
471	David Wells	.10
472	David Dellucci	.10
473	Xavier Nady	.10
474	Michael Young	.25
475	Kevin Youkilis	.40
476	Aaron Harang	.10
477	Brian Lawrence	.10
478	Octavio Dotel	.10
479	Chris Shelton	.10
480	Matt Garza	.10
481	Jim Thome	.25
482	Jose Contreras	.10
483	Kris Benson	.10
484	John Maine	.10
485	Tadahito Iguchi	.10
486	Wandy Rodriguez	.10
487	Eric Chavez	.10
488	Vernon Wells	.25
489	Doug Davis	.10
490	Andruw Jones	.40
491	David Eckstein	.10
492	Michael Barrett	.10
493	Greg Norton	.10
494	Orlando Hudson	.10
495	Wilson Betemit	.10
496	Ryan Klesko	.10
497	Fausto Carmona	.10
498	Jarrod Washburn	.10
499	Aaron Boone	.10
500	Pedro Martinez	.50
501	Mike O'Connor	.10
502	Brian Roberts	.25
503	Jeff Cirillo	.10
504	Brett Myers	.25
505	Jose Bautista	.10
506	Akinori Otsuka	.10
507	Shea Hillenbrand	.10
508	Ryan Langerhans	.10
509	Josh Fogg	.10
510	Alex Rodriguez	1.50
511	Kenny Rogers	.10
512	Jason Kubel	.10
513	Jermaine Dye	.25
514	Mark Grudzielanek	.10
515	Josh Phelps	.10
516	Bartolo Colon	.25
517	Craig Biggio	.25
518	Esteban Loaiza	.10
519	Alex Rios	.25
520	Adam Dunn	.40
521	Derrick Turnbow	.10
522	Anthony Reyes	.10
523	Derrek Lee	.40
524	Ty Wigginton	.10
525	Jeremy Hermida	.10
526	Derek Lowe	.25
527	Randy Winn	.10
528	Paul Byrd	.10
529	Chris Snelling	.10
530	Brandon Webb	.25
531	Julio Franco	.10
532	Jose Vidro	.10
533	Erik Bedard	.25
534	Termel Sledge	.10
535	Jon Lieber	.10
536	Tom Gorzelanny	.10
537	Kip Wells	.10
538	Wily Mo Pena	.10
539	Chad Billingsley	.25
540	David DeJesus	.10
541	Omar Infante	.10
542	Rondell White	.10
543	Juan Uribe	.10
544	Miguel Cairo	.10
545	Orlando Cabrera	.25
546	Byung-Hyun Kim	.10
547	Jason Kendall	.10
548	Horacio Ramirez	.10
549	Trevor Hoffman	.25
550	Ronnie Belliard	.10
551	Chris Woodward	.10
552	Ramon Martinez	.10
553	Elizardo Ramirez	.10
554	Andy Marte	.10
555	John Patterson	.10
556	Scott Olsen	.10
557	Steve Trachsel	.10
558	Doug Mientkiewicz	.10
559	Randy Johnson	.50
560	Chan Ho Park	.10
561	Jamie Moyer	.10
562	Mike Gonzalez	.10
563	Nelson Cruz	.10
564	Alex Cora	.10
565	Ryan Freel	.10
566	Chris Stewart RC	.50
567	Carlos Guillen	.10
568	Jason Bartlett	.10
569	Mariano Rivera	.40
570	Norris Hopper	.10
571	Alex Escobar	.10
572	Gustavo Chacin	.10
573	Brandon McCarthy	.10
574	Seth McClung	.10
575	Yuniesky Betancourt	.10
576	Jason LaRue	.10
577	Dustin Pedroia	.25
578	Taylor Tankersley	.10
579	Garret Anderson	.10
580	Mike Sweeney	.10
581	Scott Thorman	.10
582	Joe Inglett	.10
583	Clint Barmes	.10
584	Willie Bloomquist	.10
585	Willy Aybar	.10
586	Brian Bannister	.10
587	Jose Guillen	.10
588	Brad Wilkerson	.10
589	Lance Berkman	.25
590	Toronto Blue Jays	.10
591	Florida Marlins	.10
592	Washington Nationals	.10
593	Los Angeles Angels	.10
594	Cleveland Indians	.10
595	Texas Rangers	.10
596	Detroit Tigers	.10
597	Arizona Diamondbacks	.10
598	Kansas City Royals	.10
599	Ryan Zimmerman	.40
600	Colorado Rockies	.10
601	Minnesota Twins	.10
602	Los Angeles Dodgers	.10
603	San Diego Padres	.10
604	Bruce Bochy	.10
605	Ron Washington	.10
606	Manny Acta	.10
607	Sam Perlozzo	.10
608	Terry Francona	.10
609	Jim Leyland	.10
610	Roy Halladay	1.00
611	Eric Wedge	.10
612	Ozzie Guillen	.10
613	Buddy Bell	.10
614	Bob Geren	.10
615	Lou Piniella	.10
616	Fredi Gonzalez	.10
617	Ned Yost	.10
618	Willie Randolph	.10
619	Bud Black	.10
620	Garrett Atkins	.10
621	Alexi Casilla RC	.25
622	Matt Chico (RC)	.25
623	Alejandro De Aza RC	.75
624	Jeremy Brown	.10
625	Josh Hamilton (RC)	1.00
626	Doug Slaten RC	.50
627	Andy Cannizaro RC	.50
628	Juan Salas (RC)	.50
629	Levale Speigner RC	.50
630	Daisuke Matsuzaka RC	4.00
631	Elijah Dukes RC	.50
632	Kevin Cameron RC	.50
633	Juan Perez RC	.50
634	Alex Gordon RC	1.00
635	Juan Lara RC	.50
636	Mike Rabelo RC	.50
637	Justin Hampson RC	.25
638	Cesar Jimenez RC	.25
639	Joe Smith RC	.50
640	Kei Igawa RC	.50
641	Hideki Okajima RC	.50
642	Sean Henn (RC)	.50
643	Jay Marshall RC	.50
644	Jared Burton RC	.50
645	Angel Sanchez RC	.50
646	Devern Hansack RC	.50
647	Juan Morillo (RC)	.25
648	Hector Gimenez (RC)	.25
649	Brian Barden RC	.50
650	Alex Rodriguez, Jason Giambi	1.00
651	Jason Michaels, Travis Hafner	.25
652	J. Johnson, Miguel Olivo	.10
653	Sean Casey, Placido Polanco	.10
654	Ivan Rodriguez, Fernando Rodney	.10
655	Dan Uggla, H. Ramirez	.25
656	Carlos Beltran, Jose Reyes	.50
657	Alex Rodriguez, Derek Jeter	1.00
658	Aaron Rowand, Jimmy Rollins	.25
659	Angel Berroa, Andres Blanco	.10
660	Yadier Molina	.10
661	Barry Bonds	2.00

Copper

Copper: 25-50X
Production 56 Sets

Gold

Gold: 8-15X
Production 2,007 Sets

Platinum

No Pricing
Production One Set

1st Edition

1st Edition: 5-10X
Hobby Exclusive 1:36

Red Back

Red Back (1-330): 1-2.5X
Inserted 2:Hobby, 10:HTA

Printing Plates

Production one set per color.

All-Stars

		NM/M
Complete Set (12):		15.00
Common Player:		1.00
Inserted 1:Rack Pack		
1	Alfonso Soriano	2.00
2	Paul Konerko	1.50
3	Carlos Beltran	2.00
4	Troy Glaus	1.00
5	Jason Bay	1.50
6	Vladimir Guerrero	2.50
7	Chase Utley	3.00
8	Michael Young	1.00
9	David Wright	3.00
10	Gary Matthews	1.00
11	Brad Penny	1.00
12	Roy Halladay	1.00

All-Star Rookies

		NM/M
Complete Set (10):		12.00
Common Player:		1.50
Inserted 1:Rack Pack		
1	Prince Fielder	2.00
2	Dan Uggla	1.50
3	Ryan Zimmerman	2.00
4	Hanley Ramirez	2.00
5	Melky Cabrera	1.50
6	Andre Ethier	1.50
7	Nicholas Markakis	1.50
8	Justin Verlander	2.00
9	Francisco Liriano	2.00
10	Russell Martin	1.50

A-Rod Road to 500

	NM/M
Series 1 A-Rod (1-25):	3.00
Series 2 A-Rod (201-225):	3.00

A-Rod Road to 500 Autographs

Production One Set

Distinguished Service

		NM/M
Complete Set (20):		25.00
Common Player:		2.00
Inserted 1:12 Hobby, 1:12 HTA		
1	Duke Snider	3.00
2	Yogi Berra	3.00
3	Bob Feller	2.00
4	Bobby Doerr	2.00
5	Monte Irvin	2.00
6	Dwight D. Eisenhower	2.00
7	George Marshall	2.00
8	Franklin D. Roosevelt	2.00
9	Harry S. Truman	2.00
10	Douglas MacArthur	2.00
11	Ralph Kiner	2.00
12	Hank Sauer	2.00
13	Elmer Valo	2.00
14	Bob Lemon	2.00
15	Hoyt Wilhelm	2.00
16	James Doolittle	2.00
17	Curtis Lemay	2.00
18	Omar Bradley	2.00
19	Chester Nimitz	2.00
20	Mark Clark	2.00
21	Joe DiMaggio	4.00
22	Warren Spahn	3.00
23	Stan Musial	3.00
24	Red Schoendienst	2.00
25	Ted Williams	4.00
26	Winston Churchill	2.00
27	Charles de Gaulle	2.00
28	George Bush	2.00
29	John F. Kennedy	3.00
30	Richard Bong	2.00

Distinguished Service Autograph

		NM/M
Inserted 1:20,000 Hobby		
BD	Bobby Doerr	50.00
BF	Bob Feller	60.00
DS	Duke Snider	75.00
MI	Monte Irvin	50.00
RK	Ralph Kiner	75.00

Distinguished Service Cut Signatures

Production One Set

Generation Now

		NM/M
All Ryan Howard's:		2.00
All Chase Utley's:		1.00
All C. Ming Wang's:		3.00
All Mike Napoli's:		.50
All Justin Morneau's:		1.00
All David Wright's:		2.00
All Jered Weaver's:		1.00
All Andre Ethier's:		1.00
All Delmon Young's:		1.00
All Russell Martin's:		.75
All Justin Verlander's:		1.00
All Hanley Ramirez's:		1.00
All Nick Markakis's:		1.00
All Nick Swisher's:		.75

Generation Now Autographs
Production One Set

Highlights Autographs
NM/M

Short prints are not serial #'d.

		NM/M
JH	John Hattig Jr.	8.00
AM	Andrew Miller	20.00
AS	Anibal Sanchez	10.00
MN	Michael Napoli	10.00
JL	James Loney	20.00
MH	Matt Holliday	35.00
TT	Troy Tulowitzki	25.00
HR	Hanley Ramirez	30.00
JF	Josh Fields	15.00
CQ	Carlos Quentin	15.00
MG	Matt Garza	10.00
JM	John Maine	25.00
MP	Mike Piazza/50	120.00
TH	Travis Hafner	20.00
KM	Kevin Mench	10.00
CU	Chase Utley	50.00
DW	David Wright	60.00
JM	Justin Morneau	25.00
JS	Johan Santana/250	60.00
MC	Miguel Cabrera/250	30.00
DY	Delmon Young	20.00
DWW	Dontrelle Willis	20.00
CW	Chien-Ming Wang/100	100.00
JS	John Smoltz/250	50.00
AS	Alfonso Soriano/100	80.00
DO	David Ortiz/100	80.00
RH	Ryan Howard/100	100.00
AR	Alex Rodriguez/25	250.00
EF	Emiliano Fruto	10.00
RZ	Ryan Zimmerman	25.00

Series 2

AB	Aaron Boone	10.00
AJ	Andruw Jones	15.00
AP	Albert Pujols	250.00
AR	Anthony Reyes	15.00
CG	Curtis Granderson	30.00
CW	Craig Wilson	15.00
DO	David Ortiz	60.00
DT	Derrick Turnbow	15.00
DU	Dan Uggla	20.00
DW	David Wright	50.00
DWW	Dontrelle Willis	20.00
EC	Endy Chavez	15.00
ES	Ervin Santana	15.00
JT	Jim Thome	40.00
JD	Johnny Damon	100.00
JG	Jon Garland	15.00
JV	Justin Verlander	50.00
JZ	Joel Zumaya	20.00
KE	Kelvim Escobar	10.00
KM	Kendry Morales	20.00
LM	Lastings Milledge	20.00
MC	Melky Cabrera	15.00
MTC	Matt Cain	20.00
PL	Paul LoDuca	20.00
RC	Robinson Cano	40.00
RH	Ryan Howard	100.00
RM	Russell Martin	20.00
RZ	Ryan Zimmerman	25.00
SC	Shawn Chacon	10.00
SP	Scott Podsednik	15.00
SR	Shawn Riggans	10.00
SSC	Shin-Soo Choo	25.00
ST	Steve Trachsel	15.00
TG	Tom Glavine	75.00
VG	Vladimir Guerrero	150.00

Highlights Relics

2006 HIGHLIGHTS
AUTHENTIC GAME-WORN PANTS
ALEX RODRIGUEZ

		NM/M
Common Player:		5.00
AP	Albert Pujols	25.00
AR	Alex Rodriguez	20.00
AS	Alfonso Soriano	15.00
BM	Brian McCann	15.00
CB	Carlos Beltran	10.00

CD	Carlos Delgado	8.00
CQ	Carlos Quentin	10.00
CB	Craig Biggio	10.00
CS	Curt Schilling	10.00
DO	David Ortiz	10.00
DW	Dontrelle Willis	8.00
ER	Edgar Renteria	5.00
FT	Frank Thomas	10.00
GS	Gary Sheffield	8.00
IS	Ichiro Suzuki	25.00
IR	Ivan Rodriguez	10.00
JB	Jason Bay	10.00
JPM	Joe Mauer	15.00
JAS	Johan Santana	20.00
JS	John Smoltz	10.00
JR	Jose Reyes	15.00
JM	Justin Morneau	15.00
MO	Magglio Ordonez	5.00
MAR	Manny Ramirez	10.00
MR	Mariano Rivera	15.00
MT	Miguel Tejada	8.00
PK	Paul Konerko	10.00
RC	Robinson Cano	15.00
RO	Roy Oswalt	8.00
RH	Ryan Howard	20.00
SK	Scott Kazmir	8.00
SR	Scott Rolen	10.00
TG	Tom Glavine	8.00
TG	Troy Glaus	5.00
VW	Vernon Wells	8.00

Series 2

AB	Adrian Beltre	5.00
AER	Alex Rodriguez	20.00
AJ	Andruw Jones	8.00
ALR	Anthony Reyes	5.00
AP	Albert Pujols	25.00
AR	Aramis Ramirez	8.00
AS	Alfonso Soriano	10.00
CJ	Chipper Jones	10.00
DE	David Eckstein	20.00
DO	David Ortiz	15.00
DW	David Wright	15.00
DWW	Dontrelle Willis	8.00
GA	Garrett Atkins	5.00
GS	Grady Sizemore	10.00
JD	Jermaine Dye	5.00
JDD	Johnny Damon	15.00
JT	Jim Thome	10.00
JV	Justin Verlander	20.00
LB	Lance Berkman	8.00
MC	Matt Cain	8.00
MCT	Mark Teixeira	8.00
MEC	Melky Cabrera	10.00
MR	Manny Ramirez	10.00
MT	Miguel Tejada	8.00
NS	Nick Swisher	8.00
PK	Paul Konerko	8.00
PM	Pedro Martinez	8.00
RC	Robinson Cano	15.00
RH	Roy Halladay	10.00
RJH	Ryan Howard	20.00
SK	Scott Kazmir	8.00
TG	Tom Glavine	10.00
VG	Vladimir Guerrero	8.00
VW	Vernon Wells	8.00

Hit Parade

HIT PARADE
LUIS GONZALEZ
HITS

		NM/M
Inserted 1:9		
1	Barry Bonds	2.00
2	Ken Griffey Jr.	1.50
3	Frank Thomas	1.00
4	Jim Thome	.75
5	Manny Ramirez	1.00
6	Alex Rodriguez	2.00
7	Gary Sheffield	.75
8	Mike Piazza	1.00
9	Carlos Delgado	.75
10	Chipper Jones	1.00
11	Barry Bonds	2.00
12	Ken Griffey Jr.	1.50
13	Frank Thomas	1.00
14	Manny Ramirez	1.00
15	Gary Sheffield	.75
16	Jeff Kent	.50
17	Alex Rodriguez	2.00
18	Luis Gonzalez	.50
19	Jim Thome	.75
20	Mike Piazza	1.00
21	Craig Biggio	.50
22	Barry Bonds	2.00
23	Julio Franco	.50
24	Steve Finley	.50
25	Omar Vizquel	.50
26	Ken Griffey Jr.	1.50
27	Gary Sheffield	.50
28	Luis Gonzalez	.50
29	Ivan Rodriguez	.75
30	Bernie Williams	.50

Hobby Masters

HOBBY MASTERS
ALBERT PUJOLS ST. LOUIS CARDINALS

		NM/M
Common Player:		.50
Inserted 1:6		
1	David Wright	3.00
2	Albert Pujols	4.00
3	David Ortiz	1.50
4	Ryan Howard	3.00
5	Alfonso Soriano	1.50
6	Delmon Young	1.50
7	Jered Weaver	1.50
8	Derek Jeter	4.00
9	Freddy Sanchez	.50
10	Alex Rodriguez	3.00
11	Johan Santana	1.50
12	Ichiro Suzuki	2.50
13	Andruw Jones	1.50
14	Vladimir Guerrero	1.50
15	Miguel Cabrera	1.50
16	Todd Helton	1.50
17	Manny Ramirez	1.50
18	Carlos Beltran	1.50
19	Justin Morneau	1.50
20	Francisco Liriano	1.00

Home Run Derby
NM/M

Production 999 Sets		
DO	David Ortiz	4.00
RH	Ryan Howard	8.00
JD	Jermaine Dye	2.00
AP	Albert Pujols	10.00
TH	Travis Hafner	2.00
AS	Alfonso Soriano	4.00
JT	Jim Thome	3.00
LB	Lance Berkman	2.00
FT	Frank Thomas	4.00
CB	Carlos Beltran	2.00
TG	Troy Glaus	2.00
AJ	Andruw Jones	2.00
JG	Jason Giambi	3.00
AD	Adam Dunn	3.00
PK	Paul Konerko	2.00
CD	Carlos Delgado	3.00
MR	Manny Ramirez	3.00
AR	Aramis Ramirez	3.00
AER	Alex Rodriguez	10.00
JB	Jason Bay	2.00
NS	Nick Swisher	3.00
BH	Bill Hall	2.00
JM	Justin Morneau	4.00
MH	Matt Holliday	4.00
RS	Richie Sexson	2.00
AL	Adam LaRoche	2.00
VG	Vladimir Guerrero	4.00
CU	Chase Utley	4.00
RI	Raul Ibanez	2.00
GA	Garrett Atkins	3.00
MT	Mark Teixeira	4.00
PB	Pat Burrell	2.00
VW	Vernon Wells	2.00
PF	Prince Fielder	10.00
TKH	Torii Hunter	3.00
CL	Carlos Lee	2.00
CM	Craig Monroe	2.00
KG	Ken Griffey Jr.	10.00
JC	Joe Crede	2.00
DU	Dan Uggla	2.00
GS	Grady Sizemore	4.00
MC	Miguel Cabrera	3.00
MOT	Miguel Tejada	3.00
DW	David Wright	8.00
DY	Delmon Young	4.00
MMT	Marcus Thames	2.00
JDD	Johnny Damon	4.00
JF	Jeff Francoeur	3.00
AB	Adrian Beltre	2.00
MP	Mike Piazza	4.00

In The Name
Production One Set

Josh Gibson HR History
NM/M

Common Gibson:		1.00
Inserted 1:9		

Mickey Mantle Home Run History

MICKEY MANTLE

		NM/M
Common Mantle HR History:		2.00
Inserted 1:9 Hobby		

Mickey Mantle Home Run History Relics
NM/M

Common Mantle:		150.00
Production Seven Sets		

Opening Day

April 2, 2007 OPENING DAY
Washington Nationals — Florida Marlins

		NM/M
Inserted 1:12		
1	New York Mets, St. Louis Cardinals	2.00
2	Atlanta Braves, Philadelphia Phillies	1.00
3	Florida Marlins, Washington Nationals	1.00
4	Tampa Bay Devil Rays, New York Yankees	2.00
5	Toronto Blue Jays, Detroit Tigers	1.00
6	Cleveland Indians, Chicago White Sox	1.00
7	Los Angeles Dodgers, Milwaukee Brewers	1.00
8	Chicago Cubs, Cincinnati Reds	1.00
9	Arizona Diamondbacks, Colorado Rockies	1.00
10	Boston Red Sox, Kansas City Royals	2.00
11	Oakland Athletics, Seattle Mariners	1.00
12	Baltimore Orioles, Minnesota Twins	1.00
13	Pittsburgh Pirates, Houston Astros	1.00
14	Texas Rangers, Anaheim Angels	1.00
15	San Diego Padres, San Francisco Giants	1.00

Own The Game

OWN the GAME
CARLOS BELTRAN
NEW YORK METS

		NM/M
Common Player:		.50
Inserted 1:6		
1	Ryan Howard	2.50
2	David Ortiz	1.00
3	Alfonso Soriano	1.00
4	Albert Pujols	3.00
5	Lance Berkman	.75
6	Jermaine Dye	.50
7	Travis Hafner	.75
8	Jim Thome	1.00
9	Carlos Beltran	1.00
10	Adam Dunn	.75
11	Ryan Howard	2.50
12	David Ortiz	1.00
13	Albert Pujols	3.00
14	Lance Berkman	.75
15	Justin Morneau	1.00
16	Andruw Jones	1.00
17	Jermaine Dye	.50
18	Travis Hafner	.75
19	Alex Rodriguez	3.00
20	David Wright	1.00
21	Johan Santana	1.00
22	Chris Carpenter	.75
23	Brandon Webb	.75
24	Roy Oswalt	.75
25	Josh Johnson	.75

Ted Williams 406
NM/M

Complete Set (18):		30.00
Common Williams:		2.50
Inserted 1:4 Target		

The Mickey Mantle Story
NM/M

Complete Set (30):		40.00
Common Mantle:		3.00

The Streak

THE STREAK
Joe DiMaggio

		NM/M
Common Joe DiMaggio (1-56):		1.50
Inserted 1:9		

The Streak Before The Streak

JOE DiMAGGIO
37

		NM/M
Common Joe DiMaggio (1-61):		1.50
Inserted 1:9		

Topps Stars

TOPPS STARS
TODD HELTON

		NM/M
Inserted 1:9		
1	Ryan Howard	1.50
2	Alfonso Soriano	1.00
3	Todd Helton	.75
4	Johan Santana	.75
5	David Wright	1.50
6	Albert Pujols	2.00
7	Daisuke Matsuzaka	3.00
8	Miguel Cabrera	1.00
9	David Ortiz	1.00
10	Alex Rodriguez	2.00
11	Vladimir Guerrero	1.00
12	Ichiro Suzuki	1.50
13	Derek Jeter	2.00
14	Lance Berkman	.50
15	Ryan Zimmerman	1.00

Trading Places

TRADING PLACES
ATLANTA BRAVES — SAN DIEGO PADRES
MARCUS GILES

		NM/M
Inserted 1:9		
1	Jeff Weaver	.50
2	Frank Thomas	1.00
3	Mike Piazza	1.00
4	Alfonso Soriano	1.00
5	Freddy Garcia	.50
6	Jason Marquis	.50
7	Ted Lilly	.50
8	Mark Loretta	.50
9	Marcus Giles	.50
10	Barry Zito	.50
11	Andy Pettitte	.75
12	J.D. Drew	.50
13	Gary Matthews	.50
14	Jay Payton	.50
15	Aubrey Huff	.50
16	Brian Bannister	.50

17	Jeff Conine	.50
18	Gary Sheffield	.75
19	Shea Hillenbrand	.50
20	Wes Helms	.50
21	Frank Catalanotto	.50
22	Adam LaRoche	.50
23	Mike Gonzalez	.50
24	Greg Maddux	1.50
25	Jason Schmidt	.50

Trading Places Autographs
NM/M

Common Auto:		10.00
AL	Adam LaRoche	10.00
BB	Brian Bannister	15.00
FC	Frank Catalanotto	10.00
FG	Freddy Garcia	10.00
GS	Gary Sheffield	40.00
JS	Jason Schmidt	15.00
MG	Mike Gonzalez	10.00
SH	Shea Hillenbrand	10.00
WH	Wes Helms	10.00

Trading Places Relics
NM/M

AP	Andy Pettitte	10.00
AS	Alfonso Soriano	10.00
BZ	Barry Zito	8.00
FT	Frank Thomas	10.00
GM	Greg Maddux	20.00
GS	Gary Sheffield	15.00
JW	Jeff Weaver	8.00
MG	Marcus Giles	5.00
ML	Mark Loretta	8.00
MP	Mike Piazza	20.00

Unlock the Mick

unlock the mick
MAJOR LEAGUE BASEBALL 2K7
EXCLUSIVE CHEATS ON BACK!

		NM/M
Complete Set (5):		
Common Mantle:		2.00
Inserted 1:18		
1-5	Mickey Mantle	2.00

Wal-Mart
NM/M

Complete Set (18):		40.00
Common Player:		1.50
Three per $9.99 Wal-Mart box.		
1	Frank Thomas	3.00
2	Mike Piazza	4.00
3	Ivan Rodriguez	2.00
4	David Ortiz	3.00
5	David Wright	4.00
6	Greg Maddux	4.00
7	Mickey Mantle	8.00
8	Jose Reyes	4.00
9	John Smoltz	1.50
10	Jim Edmonds	1.50
11	Ryan Howard	4.00
12	Miguel Cabrera	3.00
13	Carlos Delgado	2.00
14	Miguel Tejada	3.00
15	Ichiro Suzuki	4.00
16	Albert Pujols	5.00
17	Derek Jeter	5.00
18	Vladimir Guerrero	3.00

World Champion Relics
NM/M

Production 100 Sets		
Cards are not serial #'d.		
1	Jeff Weaver	60.00
2	Chris Duncan	60.00
3	Chris Carpenter	75.00
4	Yadier Molina	40.00
5	Albert Pujols	160.00
6	Jim Edmonds	65.00
7	Ronnie Belliard	50.00
8	So Taguchi	80.00
9	Juan Encarnacion	50.00
10	Scott Rolen	75.00
11	Anthony Reyes	60.00
12	Preston Wilson	50.00
13	Jeff Suppan	60.00
14	Adam Wainwright	120.00
15	David Eckstein	50.00

1952 Mickey Mantle Reprint Relic
Production 52

1953 Mickey Mantle Reprint Relic
Production 53

2007 Topps Allen & Ginter
NM/M

Complete Set (390):		
Common Player:		.25

PRINCE FIELDER.
ALLEN & GINTER'S
BROOKLYN 2007 NEW YORK

Mini Exclusives (351-390):No Pricing
Inserted in Rip Cards

Common SP:	2.00
Inserted 1:2	
Pack (8):	5.00
Box (24):	110.00

#	Player	Price
1	Ryan Howard	3.00
2	Mike Gonzalez	.25
3	Austin Kearns	.25
4	Josh Hamilton (RC)	1.00
5	Stephen Drew/SP	2.00
6	Matt Murton	.25
7	Mickey Mantle	5.00
8	Howie Kendrick	.25
9	Alexander Graham Bell	.25
10	Jason Bay	.50
11	Hank Blalock	.50
12	Johan Santana	.75
13	Eleanor Roosevelt	.25
14	Kei Igawa RC	.50
15	Jeff Francoeur	.50
16	Carl Crawford	.50
17	Jhonny Peralta	.25
18	Mariano Rivera	.25
19	Mario Andretti	.25
20	Vladimir Guerrero	.75
21	Adam Wainwright	.25
22	Huston Street	.25
23	Cael Sanderson	.25
24	Susan B. Anthony	.25
25	Jay Payton	.25
26	P.T. Barnum	.25
27	Scott Podsednik	.25
28	Willie Randolph	.25
29	Sean Casey	.25
30	Eiffel Tower	.25
31	Kenji Johjima	.25
32	Felix Hernandez	.25
33	Elijah Dukes RC	.50
34	Mark Grudzielanek	.25
35	J.D. Drew	.25
36	Kevin Kouzmanoff (RC)	.50
37	Jonathan Papelbon	.25
38	Bobby Crosby	.25
39	Brooklyn Bridge	.25
40	Adam Dunn	.50
41	Lyle Overbay	.25
42	Brian Fuentes	.25
43	Scott Rolen/SP	3.00
44	Matt Lindstrom (RC)	.50
45	Carlos Zambrano	.50
46	Cole Hamels	.50
47	Matthew Kemp	.25
48	Gary Matthews/SP	2.00
49	J.J. Putz	.25
50	Albert Pujols	2.00
51	Danny Haren	.25
52	Aaron Harang	.25
53	Ferris Wheel	.25
54	Juan Rivera	.25
55	Ken Griffey Jr.	1.50
56	Chien-Ming Wang	1.00
57	Sean Henn (RC)	.50
58	Mike Mussina/SP	3.00
59	Ian Snell	.25
60	Josh Barfield	.25
61	Justin Morneau	.75
62	Dwight D. Eisenhower	.25
63	Bengie Molina/SP	2.00
64	Brett Myers	.25
65	Andy Marte	.25
66	Bill Hall	.25
67	Ryan Shealy	.25
68	Joe Scott	.25
69	Mike Rabelo RC	.50
70	Jermaine Dye	.50
71	Andre Ethier	.25
72	Bruce Lee	1.50
73	Nick Punto	.25
74	Ervin Santana	.25
75	Troy Tulowitzki (RC)	1.50
76	Garret Anderson	.25
77	Ryan Freel	.25
78	Carlos Guillen	.50
79	John Smoltz	.75
80	Chase Utley	.75
81	Mike Sweeney	.25
82	Joe Frazier	1.00
83	Brad Lidge	.25
84	Casey Blake	.25
85	Ivan Rodriguez	.50
86	Roy Oswalt	.25
87	Akinori Iwamura RC	.75
88	Francisco Rodriguez	.25
89	John Lackey	.25
90	Miguel Cabrera	.75
91	Kevin Mench	.25
92	Victor Martinez	.50
93	Chad Tracy	.25
94	Charlie Manuel	.25
95	Hanley Ramirez	.75
96	Dontrelle Willis	.50
97	Doug Slaten RC	.50
98	Noah Lowry	.25
99	Shawn Green	.25
100	David Ortiz	1.00
101	Mark Reynolds RC	2.00
102	Preston Wilson	.25
103	Mohandas Gandhi	.25
104	Jeff Kent	.25
105	Lance Berkman	.50
106	C.C. Sabathia	.50
107	Jason Varitek/SP	3.00
108	Mark Twain	.25
109	Melvin Mora	.25
110	Michael Young/SP	2.00
111	Scott Hatteberg	.25
112	Erik Bedard	.50
113	Sitting Bull	.25
114	Homer Bailey (RC)	.50
115	Mark Teahen	.25
116	Ryan Braun (RC)	4.00
117	John Miles	.25
118	Coco Crisp	.25
119	Hunter Pence/SP (RC)	3.00
120	Delmon Young (RC)	1.00
121	Aramis Ramirez	.25
122	Magglio Ordonez	.25
123	Tadahito Iguchi	.25
124	Mark Selby	.25
125	Gil Meche	.25
126	Curt Schilling	.75
127	Brandon Phillips	.25
128	Milton Bradley	.25
129	Craig Monroe	.25
130	Jason Schmidt/SP	2.00
131	Nick Markakis	.50
132	Paul Konerko	.50
133	Carlos Gomez RC	1.50
134	Garrett Atkins	.25
135	Jered Weaver	.50
136	Edgar Renteria	.25
137	Jason Isringhausen/SP	2.00
138	Ray Durham	.25
139	Bob Baffert	.25
140	Nick Swisher	.25
141	Brian McCann	.50
142	Orlando Hudson	.25
143	Brian Bannister	.25
144	Manny Acta	.25
145	Jose Vidro	.25
146	Carlos Quentin	.25
147	Billy Butler (RC)	1.50
148	Kenny Rogers	.25
149	Tom Gordon	.25
150	Derek Jeter	2.00
151	Bob Wickman	.25
152	Carlos Lee/SP	2.00
153	Willy Taveras	.25
154	Paul LoDuca	.25
155	Ben Sheets	.25
156	Brian Roberts	.50
157	Freddy Adu	.25
158	Jason Kendall	.25
159	Michael Barrett/SP	2.00
160	Frank Thomas	.75
161	Manny Ramirez	.75
162	Stanley Kirsch	.25
163	Robinson Cano	.50
164	Phil Hughes (RC)	2.50
165	Joe Mauer	.50
166	Derrek Lee	.75
167	Jeff Weaver	.25
168	Joe Smith RC	.50
169	Louis Pasteur	.50
170	Gary Sheffield	.50
171	Luis Castillo	.25
172	Joe Torre	.50
173	Andy LaRoche (RC)	.50
174	Jamie Fischer	.25
175	Carlos Beltran	.50
176	Bronson Arroyo	.25
177	Rafael Furcal	.50
178	Juan Pierre/SP	2.00
179	Matt Cain	.50
180	Alfonso Soriano	.75
181	Joe Borowski	.25
182	Conor Jackson	.25
183	Groundhog Day	.25
184	Pat Burrell	.25
185	Troy Glaus	.25
186	Joel Zumaya	.25
187	Russell Martin	.50
188	Josh Willingham	.25
189	Jarrod Saltalamacchia (RC)	.50
190	Scott Kazmir	.50
191	Jeremy Hermida	.25
192	Tower Bridge	.25
193	Rich Hill/SP	2.00
194	Francisco Cordero/SP	.25
195	Mike Piazza	1.00
196	Brad Ausmus	.25
197	Greg Louganis	.25
198	Frank Catalanotto	.25
199	Alejandro De Aza RC	.50
200	David Wright	1.00
201	Freddy Sanchez	.25
202	Shea Hillenbrand	.25
203	Justin Verlander/SP	3.00
204	Alex Gordon RC	.50
205	Jimmy Rollins	.50
206	Mike Napoli	.25
207	Chris Burke	.25
208	Chipper Jones	.25
209	Randy Johnson	.75
210	Daisuke Matsuzaka RC	3.00
211	Orlando Cabrera	.25
212	B.J. Upton	.25
213	Lou Piniella	.25
214	Mike Cameron	.25
215	Luis Gonzalez	.25
216	Rickie Weeks	.25
217	Hideki Okajima RC	.50
218	Johnny Estrada	.25
219	Dan Uggla/SP	2.00
220	Ryan Zimmerman	.50
221	Tony Gwynn Jr.	.25
222	Rocco Baldelli/SP	2.00
223	Xavier Nady	.25
224	Josh Bard/SP	2.00
225	Raul Ibanez	.25
226	Chris Carpenter	.50
227	Matt DeSalvo (RC)	.25
228	Jack the Ripper	.25
229	Eric Chavez	.25
230	Jose Reyes	1.00
231	Glen Perkins (RC)	.50
232	Gregg Zaun	.25
233	Jim Thome	.75
234	Joe Crede	.25
235	Barry Zito	.25
236	Yoel Hernandez RC	1.00
237	Kelly Johnson	.25
238	Chris Young	.50
239	Fyodor Dostoevsky	.25
240	Miguel Tejada	.50
241	Doug Mientkiewicz	.25
242	Bobby Jenks	.25
243	Brad Hawpe/SP	2.00
244	Jay Marshall RC	.25
245	Brad Penny	.25
246	Johnny Damon	.75
247	Dave Roberts	.25
248	Ron Washington	.25
249	Mike Aponte	.25
250	Brandon Webb	.50
251	Andy Pettitte	.50
252	Bud Black	.25
253	Mike Cuddyer	.25
254	Chris Stewart RC	.25
255	Mark Teixeira	.75
256	Hideki Matsui	1.50
257	Curtis Granderson	.50
258	A.J. Pierzynski	.25
259	Tony LaRussa	.25
260	Andruw Jones	.75
261	Torii Hunter	.25
262	Mark Loretta	.25
263	Jim Edmonds/SP	2.00
264	Aaron Rowand	.25
265	Roy Halladay	.50
266	Freddy Garcia	.25
267	Reggie Sanders	.25
268	Washington Monument	.25
269	Franklin D. Roosevelt	.25
270	Alex Rodriguez	2.00
271	Wes Helms	.25
272	Mia Hamm	.50
273	Jorge Posada	.50
274	Tim Lincecum RC	6.00
275	Bobby Abreu	.25
276	Zachary Duke	.25
277	Carlos Delgado	.50
278	Julio Juarez	.25
279	Brandon Inge	.25
280	Todd Helton	.50
281	Marcus Giles	.25
282	Josh Johnson	.25
283	Chris Capuano	.25
284	B.J. Ryan	.25
285	Nick Johnson	.25
286	Khalil Greene	.25
287	Travis Hafner	.50
288	Ted Lilly	.25
289	Jim Leyland	.25
290	Prince Fielder	1.00
291	Trevor Hoffman	.25
292	Brian Giles	.25
293	Omar Vizquel	.25
294	Julio Lugo	.25
295	Jake Peavy	.50
296	Adrian Beltre	.25
297	Josh Beckett	.50
298	Harry S. Truman	.25
299	Mark Buehrle	.25
300	Ichiro Suzuki	1.50
301	Chris Duncan/SP	2.00
302	Augie Garrido/SP	.25
303	Tyler Clippard/SP (RC)	1.00
304	Ramon Hernandez	.25
305	Jeremy Bonderman	.50
306	Morgan Ensberg/SP	2.00
307	J.J. Hardy/SP	.25
308	Mark Zupan/SP	.25
309	Laila Ali/SP	4.00
310	Greg Maddux/SP	4.00
311	David Ross	.25
312	Chris Duffy	.25
313	Moises Alou	.25
314	Yadier Molina	.25
315	Corey Patterson	.25
316	Dan O'Brien/SP	2.00
317	Michael Bourn/SP (RC)	2.00
318	Jonny Gomes/SP	.25
319	Ken Jennings/SP	2.00
320	Barry Bonds/SP	5.00
321	Gary Hall Jr./SP	.25
322	Kerri Walsh/SP	2.00
323	Craig Biggio	.50
324	Ian Kinsler	.25
325	Grady Sizemore/SP	3.00
326	Alex Rios/SP	3.00
327	Ted Toles/SP	.25
328	Jason Jennings	.25
329	Vernon Wells/SP	.25
330	Bob Geren/SP	2.00
331	Dennis Rodman/SP	2.00
332	Tom Glavine	.50
333	Pedro Martinez	.75
334	Gustavo Molina/SP RC	3.00
335	Bartolo Colon/SP	.25
336	Misty May-Treanor/SP	2.00
337	Randy Winn	.25
338	Eric Byrnes	.25
339	Jason McElwain/SP	.25
340	Placido Polanco/SP	.25
341	Adrian Gonzalez	.50
342	Chad Coredo	.25
343	Jeff Francis	.25
344	Lastings Milledge	.25
345	Sammy Sosa	3.00
346	Jacque Jones	.25
347	Anibal Sanchez	.25
348	Roger Clemens/SP	4.00
349	Jesse Litsch/SP RC	.25
350	Adam LaRoche/SP	2.00

Mini

MARIANO RIVERA.
ALLEN & GINTER'S
BROOKLYN 2007 NEW YORK

Mini:	2-3X
Mini (351-390):	
#'s 351-390 Inserted in Rip Cards	
Allen & Ginter Back:	3-4X
Inserted 1:5	
Black Border:	4-6X
Inserted 1:10	
No Number:	10-20X
Production 50 Sets	
Bazooka Mini:	No Pricing
Production 25 Sets	
Wood:	No Pricing
Production One Set	

Printing Plates

Production one set per color.

Autographs

TOPPS CERTIFIED AUTOGRAPH
MARIO ANDRETTI
Topps
ALLEN & GINTER'S
BROOKLYN, NEW YORK 2007

NM/M
Short-prints are noted.
Red Ink: No Pricing
Production 10 Sets

		Price
CS	Cael Sanderson/200	100.00
MS	Mark Selby/200	50.00
SJF	Joe Frazier/120	250.00
DR	Dennis Rodman/200	125.00
MZ	Mark Zupan/200	50.00
FA	Freddy Adu/200	125.00
BB	Bob Baffert/200	120.00
TT	Ted Toles/200	100.00
KJ	Ken Jennings/200	120.00
GH	Gary Hall Jr./200	80.00
DO	Dan O'Brien/200	75.00
JF	Jamie Fischer/200	40.00
GL	Greg Louganis/200	50.00
MA	Mike Aponte/200	40.00
JJ	Julio Juarez/200	40.00
KW	Kerri Walsh/200	100.00
LA	Laila Ali/200	120.00
TS	Tommie Smith/200	120.00
MGA	Mario Andretti/200	150.00
AG	Augie Garrido/200	100.00
JMC	Jason McElwain/200	100.00
SG	Stanley Glenn/200	125.00
JMM	John Miles/200	125.00
JBS	Joe Scott/200	120.00
MH	Mia Hamm/200	220.00
MMT	Misty May-Treanor/200	100.00
BC	Brian Cashman/100	200.00
CMW	Chien-Ming Wang/200	250.00
AI	Akinori Iwamura	40.00
RH	Ryan Howard/100	125.00
HR	Hanley Ramirez	125.00
HK	Howie Kendrick	25.00
AR	Alex Rodriguez/225	300.00
DW	David Wright/200	120.00
RM	Russell Martin	40.00
AE	Andre Ethier	25.00
JT	Jim Thome/100	100.00
JM	Justin Morneau	40.00
ES	Ervin Santana	25.00
BH	Bill Hall	30.00
CH	Cole Hamels	75.00
MEI	Maicer Izturis	20.00
CG	Curtis Granderson	50.00
AG2	Adrian Gonzalez	25.00
TT	Troy Tulowitzki	30.00
JS	Johan Santana/100	150.00
JP	Jonathan Papelbon	50.00
MC	Miguel Cabrera/100	60.00
BPB	Brian Bannister	25.00
TH	Torii Hunter	30.00
RZ	Ryan Zimmerman	40.00
NM	Nicholas Markakis	25.00
JH	Jeremy Hermida	20.00
MN	Mike Napoli	25.00
NL	Nook Logan	20.00

Cut Signatures

Production One Set

Dick Perez Sketch Cards

RYAN HOWARD
AUTHENTIC DICK PEREZ SKETCH CARDS

NM/M

Complete Set (30):		15.00
Common Player:		.50
Inserted 1:1		
Dick Perez Originals:		No Pricing
Production One Set		
1	Brandon Webb	.50
2	Chipper Jones	1.00
3	Nick Markakis	.50
4	Daisuke Matsuzaka	2.00
5	Alfonso Soriano	.50
6	Jermaine Dye	.50
7	Adam Dunn	.50
8	Grady Sizemore	1.00
9	Troy Tulowitzki	.50
10	Gary Sheffield	.75
11	Hanley Ramirez	.75
12	Carlos Lee	.50
13	Mark Teahen	.50
14	Gary Matthews	.50
15	Andre Ethier	.50
16	Prince Fielder	1.50
17	Joe Mauer	.75
18	Jose Reyes	1.00
19	Derek Jeter	2.00
20	Nick Swisher	.50
21	Ryan Howard	1.50
22	Freddy Sanchez	.50
23	Greg Maddux	1.50
24	Raul Ibanez	.50
25	Barry Zito	.50
26	Jim Edmonds	.50
27	Delmon Young	.50
28	Michael Young	.50
29	Roy Halladay	.50
30	Ryan Zimmerman	.75

Mini Flags

UNITED KINGDOM
ALLEN & GINTER'S FLAGS
BROOKLYN, NEW YORK

NM/M

Common Card:		2.00
1	Angola	2.00
2	Argentina	2.00
3	Australia	2.00
4	Austria	2.00
5	Belgium	2.00
6	Brazil	2.00
7	Bulgaria	2.00
8	Canada	2.00
9	Chile	2.00
10	China	2.00
11	Colombia	2.00
12	Costa Rica	2.00
13	Denmark	2.00
14	Dominican Republic	2.00
15	Ecuador	2.00
16	Egypt	2.00
17	France	2.00
18	Germany	2.00
19	Greece	2.00
20	Greenland	2.00
21	Honduras	2.00
22	Iceland	2.00
23	India	2.00
24	Indonesia	2.00
25	Ireland	2.00
26	Israel	2.00
27	Italy	2.00
28	Ivory Coast	2.00
29	Jamaica	2.00
30	Japan	2.00
31	Kenya	2.00
32	Mexico	2.00
33	Morocco	2.00
34	Netherlands	2.00
35	Nigeria	2.00
36	Norway	2.00
37	Panama	2.00
38	Peru	2.00
39	Phillipines	2.00
40	Portugal	2.00
41	Puerto Rico	2.00
42	Russian Federation	2.00
43	Spain	2.00
44	Switzerland	2.00
45	Taiwan	2.00
46	Thailand	2.00
47	Turkey	2.00
48	United Arab Emirates	2.00
49	United Kingdom	2.00
50	United States	2.00

Mini Snakes

NM/M

Common Mini Snake:		25.00
1	Arizona Coral Snake	25.00
2	Copperhead	25.00
3	Black Mamba	25.00
4	King Cobra	25.00
5	Cottonmouth	25.00
		25.00

Mini Emperors

NM/M

Common Emperor:		5.00
1	Julius Caesar	5.00
2	Caesar Augustus	5.00
3	Tiberius	5.00
4	Caligula	5.00
5	Claudius	5.00
6	Nero	5.00
7	Titus	5.00
8	Hadrian	5.00
9	Marcus Aurelius	5.00
10	Septimus Severus	5.00

National Pride Box Loaders

UNITED STATES OF AMERICA

NM/M

Common Card:		5.00
Inserted 1:Box		
1	Kei Igawa, Daisuke Matsuzaka, Hideki Matsui, Ichiro Suzuki	8.00
2	Hideki Okajima, Akinori Iwamura, Kenji Johjima, Tadahito Iguchi	6.00
3	Bobby Abreu, Miguel Cabrera, Felix Hernandez, Johan Santana	6.00
4	Shin-Soo Choo, Chan Ho Park, Byung-Hyun Kim, Jae-Kuk Ryu	
5	Jason Bay, Russell Martin, Justin Morneau, Rich Harden	6.00
6	Hanley Ramirez, Manny Ramirez, Aramis Ramirez, Vladimir Guerrero	8.00

7 Jose Reyes, Pedro Martinez, David Ortiz, Albert Pujols 8.00
8 Carlos Beltran, Carlos Delgado, Ivan Rodriguez, Jorge Posada 6.00
9 Prince Fielder, Alex Rodriguez, Ryan Howard, David Wright 8.00
10 Brandon Webb, Justin Verlander, Greg Maddux, John Smoltz

N43 Box Loader
NM/M
Common Player: 4.00
Inserted 1:Box
AR Alex Rodriguez 8.00
RH Ryan Howard 6.00
DW David Wright 8.00
IS Ichiro Suzuki 6.00
AP Albert Pujols 6.00
DM Daisuke Matsuzaka 10.00
VG Vladimir Guerrero 4.00
BB Barry Bonds 8.00
PF Prince Fielder 6.00
RZ Ryan Zimmerman 4.00
DJ Ch Felicity's Diamond Jim 15.00
BL Bruce Lee 10.00
MA Mario Andretti 4.00
GL Greg Louganis 4.00
JF Joe Frazier 6.00

N43 Box Loader Autographs
Production 10 Sets

N43 Box Loader Relics
Production 25 Sets

Relics

Common Relic: 5.00
NM/M
KJ Ken Jennings/250 40.00
JF Jamie Fischer/250 30.00
TS Tommie Smith/250 50.00
KW Kerri Walsh/250 60.00
LA Laila Ali/250 50.00
JJ Julio Juarez/250 25.00
MH Mia Hamm/250 70.00
BL Bruce Lee/250 300.00
OO Dan O'Brien/250 20.00
SJF Joe Frazier/250 80.00
GH Gary Hall Jr./250 50.00
AL Adam LaRoche 8.00
AP Albert Pujols 30.00
AR Aramis Ramirez 8.00
CB Carlos Beltran 8.00
CC Carl Crawford 8.00
CK Casey Kotchman 5.00
EC Eric Chavez 8.00
EG Eric Gagne 8.00
HB Hank Blalock 5.00
HR Hanley Ramirez 8.00
JB Jason Bay 5.00
JG Jason Giambi 8.00
MC1 Miguel Cabrera 10.00
MC2 Miguel Cabrera 10.00
MG Marcus Giles 5.00
MMU Mark Mulder 5.00
MCM Mike Mussina 8.00
MP Mike Piazza 15.00
MR Manny Ramirez 10.00
MT Miguel Tejada 8.00
NS Nick Swisher 5.00
PF Prince Fielder 20.00
PK Paul Konerko 8.00
RC Robinson Cano 20.00
RH Rich Harden 5.00
RW Randy Winn 5.00
SD Stephen Drew 8.00
SP Scott Podsednik 5.00
SR1 Scott Rolen 8.00
SR2 Scott Rolen 8.00
TG Troy Glaus 5.00
VG Vladimir Guerrero 5.00
DAO David Ortiz/250 20.00
AER Alex Rodriguez/250 30.00
BB Barry Bonds/250 35.00
MM Mickey Mantle/250 150.00
BR Brian Roberts 8.00
BZ Barry Zito 5.00
CMS Curt Schilling 10.00
DW Dontrelle Willis 5.00
IR Ivan Rodriguez 8.00
PL Paul LoDuca 5.00

CLC Coco Crisp 8.00
CP Corey Patterson 5.00
CT Chad Tracy 5.00
DL Derrek Lee 8.00
RA Rich Aurilia 5.00
SS Sammy Sosa 10.00
TN Trot Nixon 5.00
BC Brian Cashman/250 35.00
AS Arthur Shorin/50 150.00
KO Keith Olbermann/100 150.00

Rip Cards
NM/M
Production 10-99 75.00
Prices are for unripped cards
Ripped cards 10-15 percen.
1 Grady Sizemore/90 125.00
2 Miguel Cabrera/75 125.00
3 Adam Dunn/95 125.00
4 Jose Reyes/99 150.00
5 Alfonso Soriano/99 125.00
6 Chase Utley/99 125.00
7 Frank Thomas/95 150.00
8 Andruw Jones/95 125.00
9 Nick Markakis/75 100.00
10 Felix Hernandez/99 125.00
11 Jered Weaver/99 125.00
12 Ivan Rodriguez/99 125.00
13 Joe Mauer/99 125.00
14 Derek Jeter/99 180.00
17 Miguel Tejada/95 100.00
18 Vladimir Guerrero/75 125.00
19 Greg Maddux/99 150.00
20 Michael Young/99 100.00
21 Barry Zito/99 125.00
22 Russell Martin/95 150.00
23 Daisuke Matsuzaka/99 180.00
24 Stephen Drew/95 100.00
25 Alex Rodriguez/99 150.00
26 J.D. Drew/99 100.00
27 Paul Konerko/99 100.00
28 Josh Hamilton/90 100.00
29 Mike Piazza/99 125.00
31 Carl Crawford/99 100.00
32 Adam LaRoche/99 100.00
33 Bill Hall/95 100.00
34 Scott Kazmir/99 100.00
35 Gary Matthews/99 100.00
36 Gary Sheffield/99 125.00
37 Francisco Rodriguez/95 100.00
38 Todd Helton/99 100.00
40 David Wright/99 150.00
42 Barry Bonds/99 180.00
43 Johan Santana/75 125.00
44 Albert Pujols/90 200.00
45 Carlos Lee/99 75.00
46 Cole Hamels/95 125.00
47 Prince Fielder/99 125.00
48 Hanley Ramirez/99 125.00
49 Ryan Zimmerman/90 125.00
50 Kei Igawa/75 100.00

2007 Topps Chrome

NM/M
Complete Set (363):
Common Player: .25
Common RC Auto. (331-363): 10.00
Pack (4): 3.00
Box (24): 60.00
1 Nick Swisher .50
2 Bobby Abreu .50
3 Edgar Renteria .50
4 Mickey Mantle 5.00
5 Preston Wilson .25
6 C.C. Sabathia .50
7 Julio Lugo .25
8 J.D. Drew .50
9 Jason Varitek .50
10 Orlando Hernandez .25
11 Corey Patterson .25
12 Josh Bard .25
13 Gary Matthews .25
14 Jason Jennings .25
15 Bronson Arroyo .25
16 Andy Pettitte .50
17 Ervin Santana .25
18 Paul Konerko .50
19 Adam LaRoche .50
20 Jim Edmonds .50
21 Derek Jeter 3.00
22 Aubrey Huff .25
23 Andre Ethier .50
24 Jeremy Sowers .25
25 Miguel Cabrera 1.00
26 Carlos Lee .50
27 Mike Piazza 1.00
28 Cole Hamels .75

29 Mark Loretta .25
30 John Smoltz .50
31 Dan Uggla .25
32 Lyle Overbay .25
33 Michael Barrett .25
34 Ivan Rodriguez .75
35 Jake Westbrook .25
36 Moises Alou .50
37 Jered Weaver .50
38 Lastings Milledge .50
39 Austin Kearns .25
40 Adam Loewen .25
41 Josh Barfield .25
42 Johan Santana 1.00
43 Ian Kinsler .50
44 Mike Lowell .50
45 Scott Rolen .75
46 Chipper Jones 1.00
47 Joe Crede .25
48 Rafael Furcal .50
49 David Bush .25
50 Marcus Giles .25
51 Joe Blanton .25
52 Dontrelle Willis .50
53 Scott Kazmir .50
54 Jeff Kent .50
55 Travis Hafner .50
56 Ryan Garko .25
57 Nicholas Markakis .50
58 Michael Cuddyer .25
59 Jason Giambi .50
60 Chone Figgins .50
61 Carlos Delgado .50
62 Aramis Ramirez .50
63 Albert Pujols 3.00
64 Gary Sheffield .75
65 Adrian Gonzalez .50
66 Prince Fielder 1.50
67 Freddy Sanchez .25
68 Jack Wilson .25
69 Jake Peavy .50
70 Javier Vazquez .25
71 Todd Helton .75
72 Bill Hall .25
73 Jeremy Bonderman .25
74 Rocco Baldelli .25
75 Noah Lowry .25
76 Justin Verlander .75
77 Mark Buehrle .25
78 Hank Blalock .25
79 Mark Teahen .25
80 Chien-Ming Wang 1.00
81 Roy Halladay .50
82 Melvin Mora .25
83 Grady Sizemore .75
84 Matt Cain .50
85 Carl Crawford .50
86 Johnny Damon .75
87 Freddy Garcia .25
88 Ryan Shealy .25
89 Carlos Beltran .25
90 Chuck James .25
91 Ben Sheets .50
92 Mark Mulder .25
93 Carlos Quentin .25
94 Richie Sexson .50
95 Brian Schneider .25
96 Hideki Matsui 2.00
97 Robinson Tejeda .25
98 Scott Hatteberg .25
99 Jeff Francis .25
100 Robinson Cano .50
101 Barry Zito .50
102 Reed Johnson .25
103 Chris Carpenter .50
104 Chad Tracy .25
105 Anibal Sanchez .25
106 Brad Penny .25
107 David Wright 2.00
108 Jimmy Rollins .75
109 Alfonso Soriano 1.00
110 Greg Maddux 1.00
111 Curt Schilling .75
112 Stephen Drew .25
113 Matt Holliday .50
114 Jorge Posada .50
115 Vladimir Guerrero 1.00
116 Frank Thomas .75
117 Jonathan Papelbon .50
118 Manny Ramirez 1.00
119 Magglio Ordonez .50
120 Joe Mauer .50
121 Ryan Howard 2.00
122 Chris Young .25
123 A.J. Burnett .25
124 Brian McCann .50
125 Juan Pierre .25
126 Jonny Gomes .25
127 Roger Clemens 2.50
128 Chad Billingsley .50
129 Kenji Johjima .25
130 Brian Giles .25
131 Chase Utley 1.00
132 Carl Pavano .25
133 Curtis Granderson .50
134 Sean Casey .25
135 Jon Garland .25
136 David Ortiz .75
137 Bobby Crosby .25
138 Conor Jackson .25
139 Tim Hudson .50
140 Rickie Weeks .25
141 Mark Prior .50
142 Benjamin Zobrist .25
143 Troy Glaus .25
144 Cliff Lee .25
145 Adrian Beltre .25
146 Endy Chavez .25

147 Ramon Hernandez .25
148 Chris Young .50
149 Jason Schmidt .25
150 Kevin Millwood .25
151 Placido Polanco .25
152 Torii Hunter .50
153 Roy Oswalt .50
154 Kelvim Escobar .25
155 Milton Bradley .25
156 Chris Capuano .25
157 Juan Encarnacion .25
158 Ichiro Suzuki 2.00
159 Matthew Kemp .50
160 Matt Morris .25
161 Casey Blake .25
162 Josh Willingham .25
163 Nick Johnson .25
164 Khalil Greene .25
165 Tom Glavine .75
166 Jason Bay .50
167 Brandon Phillips .50
168 Jorge Cantu .25
169 Jeff Weaver .25
170 Melky Cabrera .25
171 Danny Haren .50
172 Jeff Francoeur .50
173 Randy Wolf .25
174 Carlos Zambrano .50
175 Justin Morneau .75
176 Takashi Saito .25
177 Victor Martinez .50
178 Felix Hernandez .50
179 Paul LoDuca .25
180 Miguel Tejada .75
181 Mark Teixeira .75
182 Pat Burrell .25
183 Mike Cameron .25
184 Josh Beckett .50
185 Francisco Liriano .50
186 Ken Griffey Jr. 2.00
187 Mike Mussina .50
188 Howie Kendrick .25
189 Ted Lilly .25
190 Mike Hampton .25
191 Jeff Suppan .25
192 Jose Reyes 2.00
193 Russell Martin .50
194 Jhonny Peralta .25
195 Raul Ibanez .25
196 Hanley Ramirez 1.00
197 Kerry Wood .25
198 Gary Sheffield .50
199 David Dellucci .25
200 Xavier Nady .25
201 Michael Young .50
202 Kevin Youkilis .50
203 Aaron Harang .25
204 Mario Garza .50
205 Jim Thome .50
206 Jose Contreras .25
207 Tadahito Iguchi .25
208 Eric Chavez .25
209 Vernon Wells .50
210 Doug Davis .25
211 Andruw Jones .75
212 David Eckstein .25
213 J.J. Hardy .25
214 Orlando Hudson .25
215 Pedro Martinez 1.00
216 Brian Roberts .50
217 Brett Myers .25
218 Alex Rodriguez 3.00
219 Kenny Rogers .25
220 Jason Kubel .25
221 Jermaine Dye .50
222 Bartolo Colon .25
223 Craig Biggio .50
224 Alex Rios .50
225 Adam Dunn .75
226 Anthony Reyes .25
227 Derek Lee .50
228 Jeremy Hermida .25
229 Derek Lowe .25
230 Randy Winn .25
231 Brandon Webb .50
232 Jose Vidro .25
233 Erik Bedard .25
234 Jon Lieber .25
235 Wily Mo Pena .25
236 Kelly Johnson .25
237 David DeJesus .25
238 Andy Marte .25
239 Scott Olsen .25
240 Randy Johnson 1.00
241 Nelson Cruz .25
242 Carlos Guillen .50
243 Brandon McCarthy .25
244 Garret Anderson .25
245 Mike Sweeney .25
246 Brian Bannister .25
247 Jose Guillen .25
248 Brad Wilkerson .25
249 Lance Berkman .50
250 Ryan Zimmerman .50
251 Garrett Atkins .25
252 Johan Santana 1.00
253 Brandon Webb .50
254 Justin Verlander .75
255 Hanley Ramirez 1.00
256 Justin Morneau .75
257 Ryan Howard 2.00
258 Eric Chavez .25
259 Scott Rolen .75
260 Derek Jeter 3.00
261 Omar Vizquel .25
262 Mark Grudzielanek .25
263 Orlando Hudson .25
264 Mark Teixeira .50

265 Albert Pujols 3.00
266 Ivan Rodriguez .75
267 Brad Ausmus .25
268 Torii Hunter .50
269 Mike Cameron .25
270 Ichiro Suzuki 2.00
271 Carlos Beltran .75
272 Vernon Wells .50
273 Andruw Jones .50
274 Kenny Rogers .25
275 Greg Maddux 2.00
276 Danny Putnam (RC) 1.00
277 Chase Wright RC 1.00
278 Zach McClellan RC 1.00
279 Jamie Vermilyea RC 1.00
280 Felix Pie (RC) 1.50
281 Phil Hughes (RC) 6.00
282 Jon Knott (RC) 1.00
283 Micah Owings (RC) 1.00
284 Devern Hansack RC 1.00
285 Andy Cannizaro RC 1.00
286 Lee Gardner RC 1.00
287 Josh Hamilton (RC) 2.50
288 Angel Sanchez/Auto. RC 10.00
289 J.D. Durbin (RC) 1.00
290 Jamie Burke (RC) 1.00
291 Joseph Bisenius (RC) 1.00
292 Rick Vanden Hurk RC 1.50
293 Brian Barden RC 1.00
294 Levale Speigner RC 1.00
295 Kevin Cameron RC 1.00
296 Donald Kelly (RC) 1.00
297 Hideki Okajima RC 1.50
298 Andrew Miller RC 1.00
299 Delmon Young (RC) 1.00
300 Vinny Rottino (RC) 1.00
301 Philip Humber (RC) 1.00
302 Drew Anderson (RC) 1.00
303 Jerry Owens (RC) 1.00
304 Jose Garcia RC 1.00
305 Shane Youman RC 1.00
306 Ryan Feierabend (RC) 1.00
307 Mike Rabelo RC 1.00
308 Josh Fields (RC) 1.00
309 Jon Coutlangus (RC) 1.00
310 Travis Buck (RC) 1.00
311 Doug Slaten RC 1.00
312 Ryan Braun RC 4.00
313 Juan Salas (RC) 1.00
314 Matt Lindstrom RC 1.00
315 Cesar Jimenez RC 1.00
316 Jay Marshall RC 1.00
317 Jared Burton RC 1.00
318 Juan Perez RC 1.00
319 Elijah Dukes RC 1.50
320 Juan Lara RC 1.00
321 Justin Hampson (RC) 1.00
322 Kei Igawa RC 1.50
323 Zack Segovia (RC) 1.00
324 Alejandro De Aza RC 1.00
325 Brandon Morrow RC 2.00
326 Gustavo Molina RC 1.00
327 Joe Smith RC 1.00
328 Jose Flores RC 1.50
329 Jeff Baker (RC) 1.00
330 Daisuke Matsuzaka RC 4.00
331 Troy Tulowitzki/Auto. (RC) 25.00
332 John Danks/Auto. (RC) 15.00
333 Kevin Kouzmanoff/Auto. (RC) 15.00
334 David Murphy/Auto. (RC) 10.00
335 Ryan Sweeney/Auto. (RC) 10.00
336 Fred Lewis/Auto. (RC) 15.00
337 Delwyn Young/Auto. (RC) 10.00
338 Matt Chico/Auto. (RC) 10.00
339 Miguel Montero/Auto. (RC) 10.00
340 Shawn Riggans/Auto. (RC) 10.00
341 Brian Stokes/Auto. (RC) 10.00
342 Scott Moore/Auto. (RC) 10.00
343 Adam Lind/Auto. (RC) 15.00
344 Chris Narveson/Auto. (RC) 10.00
345 Alex Gordon/Auto. RC 20.00
346 Joaquin Arias/Auto. (RC) 10.00
347 Brian Burres/Auto. (RC) 10.00
348 Glen Perkins/Auto. (RC) 10.00
349 Ubaldo Jimenez/Auto. RC 50.00
350 Chris Stewart/Auto. RC 10.00
351 Beltran Perez/Auto. (RC) 10.00
352 Dennis Sarfate/Auto. (RC) 10.00
353 Carlos Maldonado/Auto. (RC) 10.00
354 Mitch Maier/Auto. RC 10.00
355 Kory Casto/Auto. (RC) 10.00
356 Juan Morillo/Auto. (RC) 10.00
357 Hector Gimenez/Auto. (RC) 10.00
358 Alexi Casilla/Auto. RC 15.00
359 Michael Bourn/Auto. (RC) 15.00
360 Sean Henn/Auto. (RC) 10.00
361 Tim Gradoville/Auto. RC 10.00
362 Akinori Iwamura/Auto. RC 20.00
363 Oswaldo Navarro/Auto. RC 10.00

Refractor
Refractor (1-330): 2-3X
Ref. RC Auto. (288, 331-363): 1-1.5X
Auto. Production 500

Red Refractor
Red Ref. (1-330): 4-8X
Production 99
Red Auto. (288, 331-363): 3-4X
Auto. Production 25

White Refractor
White Ref. (1-330): 3-4X
Production 660
White Auto. (288, 331-363): 1-1.5X
Auto. Production 200

Printing Plates
Production one set per color.

A-Rod Road to 500
NM/M
Complete Set (226-250): 40.00
Common A-Rod: 2.00

A-Rod Road to 500 Autographs
NM/M
Production One Set 40.00

Generation Now

NM/M
Common Player: .50
Refractor: 2-3X
Production 500 Sets
White Refractor: 3-4X
Production 200 Sets
Red Refractor: 3-5X
Production 99 Sets
GN201 Ryan Howard 2.00
GN203 Ryan Howard 2.00
GN204 Ryan Howard 2.00
GN205 Ryan Howard 2.00
GN208 Ryan Howard 2.00
GN209 Chase Utley 2.00
GN210 Chien-Ming Wang 3.00
GN211 Mike Napoli .50
GN213 Justin Morneau 2.00
GN214 Justin Morneau 2.00
GN215 Justin Morneau 2.00
GN216 Justin Morneau 2.00
GN217 Jered Weaver 1.00
GN218 Andre Ethier 1.00
GN219 Ryan Zimmerman 1.00
GN238 Ryan Zimmerman 1.00
GN264 Ryan Zimmerman 1.00
GN265 Delmon Young 1.00
GN269 Delmon Young 1.00
GN274 Delmon Young 1.00
GN278 Delmon Young 1.00
GN279 Russell Martin 1.00
GN280 Russell Martin 1.00
GN281 Russell Martin 1.00
GN282 Russell Martin 1.00
GN283 Justin Verlander 1.50
GN292 Justin Verlander 1.50
GN297 Justin Verlander 1.50
GN298 Justin Verlander 1.50
GN299 Hanley Ramirez 1.50
GN308 Hanley Ramirez 1.50
GN318 Hanley Ramirez 1.50
GN328 Hanley Ramirez 1.50
GN338 Hanley Ramirez 1.50
GN349 Hanley Ramirez 1.50
GN350 Nicholas Markakis 1.00
GN359 Nicholas Markakis 1.00
GN360 Nick Swisher .50
GN364 Nick Swisher .50
GN379 Nick Swisher .50
GN394 Nick Swisher .50

Mickey Mantle Home Run History

NM/M
Common Mantle: 2.00
Refractor: 2-3X
Production 500 Sets
White Refractor: 3-5X
Production 200 Sets
Red Refractor: 4-8X
Production 99 Sets

The Mickey Mantle Story
NM/M
Complete Set (30): 50.00
Common Mantle: 2.00
Refractor: 2-3X
Production 500 Sets
White Refractor: 3-4X
Production 200 Sets
Red Refractor: 3-6X

Production 99 Sets
1-30 Mickey Mantle   2.00

2007 Topps Co-Signers

MICKEY MANTLE

NM/M
Complete Set (122):
Common Player: .25
Common RC Auto.:   10.00
Pack (6):   10.00
Box (12):   100.00
1	Ryan Howard	2.00
2	Jered Weaver	.50
3	Brian McCann	.25
4	Garrett Atkins	.25
5	Travis Hafner	.50
6	Jason Schmidt	.25
7	Curtis Granderson	.25
8	Ben Sheets	.25
9	Chien-Ming Wang	1.50
10	Francisco Liriano	.50
11	Freddy Sanchez	.25
12	Roy Oswalt	.75
13	Jim Edmonds	.50
14	Matt Cain	.50
15	Jake Peavy	.75
16	Ryan Zimmerman	.75
17	Troy Glaus	.50
18	Kenji Johjima	.50
19	Curt Schilling	1.00
20	Alfonso Soriano	1.00
21	Adam Dunn	.75
22	Hanley Ramirez	.75
23	Mark Teahen	.25
24	Todd Helton	.75
25	Alex Rodriguez	3.00
26	Mike Mussina	.75
27	Jason Bay	.50
28	Carl Crawford	.50
29	Vernon Wells	.50
30	Rich Harden	.25
31	Justin Morneau	1.00
32	Andre Ethier	.25
33	Ramon Hernandez	.25
34	Erik Bedard	.50
35	Vladimir Guerrero	.50
36	Stephen Drew	.50
37	Felix Hernandez	.50
38	C.C. Sabathia	.50
39	Adrian Gonzalez	.50
40	Prince Fielder	1.00
41	Carlos Delgado	.75
42	Jimmy Rollins	.75
43	Raul Ibanez	.25
44	Jorge Cantu	.25
45	Michael Young	.25
46	Austin Kearns	.25
47	Ivan Rodriguez	.75
48	Chad Billingsley	.50
49	David Ortiz	1.00
50	David Wright	1.50
51	Justin Verlander	.75
52	Nicholas Markakis	.50
53	Miguel Cabrera	1.00
54	Lance Berkman	.50
55	Robinson Cano	.75
56	Jon Lieber	.25
57	Andruw Jones	.50
58	Danny Haren	.50
59	Grady Sizemore	.75
60	Gary Sheffield	.75
61	Paul LoDuca	.25
62	Cole Hamels	1.00
63	Richie Sexson	.25
64	David Eckstein	.25
65	Carlos Zambrano	.50
66	Scott Kazmir	.25
67	Anthony Reyes	.25
68	Mark Kotsay	.25
69	Miguel Tejada	.75

70	Pedro Martinez	1.00
71	Jack Wilson	.25
72	Joe Mauer	.75
73	Brian Giles	.25
74	Jonathan Papelbon	1.00
75	Albert Pujols	3.00
76	Nick Swisher	.25
77	Bill Hall	.50
78	Jose Contreras	.25
79	David DeJesus	.25
80	Bobby Abreu	.50
81	John Smoltz	.50
82	Chipper Jones	1.00
83	Mark Buehrle	.25
84	Josh Barfield	.25
85	Derrek Lee	.75
86	Jim Thome	.75
87	Kenny Rogers	.25
88	Jeremy Sowers	.25
89	Brandon Webb	.50
90	Roy Halladay	.50
91	Tadahito Iguchi	.50
92	Jeff Kent	.50
93	Johnny Damon	.50
94	Daisuke Matsuzaka RC	3.00
95	Mark Teixeira	.75
96a	Delmon Young **RC**	1.00
96b	Delmon Young/Auto.	15.00
97a	Jeff Baker **RC**	1.00
97b	Jeff Baker/Auto.	10.00
98a	Michael Bourn **(RC)**	1.00
98b	Michael Bourn/Auto.	10.00
99a	Ubaldo Jimenez **RC**	1.00
99b	Ubaldo Jimenez/Auto.	50.00
100a	Andrew Miller **(RC)**	1.50
100b	Andrew Miller/Auto.	15.00
101	Angel Sanchez/ Auto. **(RC)**	10.00
102	Troy Tulowitzki/ Auto. **(RC)**	25.00
103	Joaquin Arias/Auto. **RC**	10.00
104	Beltran Perez/Auto. **RC**	10.00
105	Josh Fields/Auto. **RC**	10.00
106	Hector Gimenez/ Auto. **RC**	10.00
107	Kevin Kouzmanoff/ Auto. **RC**	15.00
108	Miguel Montero/ Auto. **RC**	10.00
109	Philip Humber/Auto. **RC**	10.00
110	Jerry Owens/Auto. **RC**	10.00
111	Shawn Riggans/ Auto. **RC**	10.00
112	Brian Stokes/Auto. **RC**	10.00
113	Scott Moore/Auto. **RC**	10.00
114	David Murphy/ Auto. **(RC)**	10.00
115	Mitch Maier/Auto. **RC**	10.00
116	Adam Lind/Auto. **RC**	15.00
117	Adam Lind/Auto. **RC**	15.00
118	Dennis Sarfate/Auto. **RC**	10.00
119	Elijah Dukes/Auto. **(RC)**	10.00
120	Josh Hamilton/ Auto. **(RC)**	40.00
121	Alex Gordón/Auto. **RC**	20.00
122	Barry Bonds	3.00

Bronze
Bronze Non-Auto.:   2-3X
Bronze RC Auto.:   1X
Production 250 Sets

Blue
Blue Non-Auto.:   2-3X
Blue RC Auto.:   1X
Production 225 Sets

Gold
Gold Non-Auto.:   2-3X
Gold RC Auto.:   1X
Production 200 Sets

Red
Red Non-Auto.:   2-3X
Production 299 Sets
Red RC Auto.:   1X
Production 275 Sets

Silver-Red
Silver Red Non-Auto.:   2-3X
Silver Red RC Auto.:   1X
Production 175 Sets

Silver-Bronze
Silver Bronze Non-Auto.:   2-4X
Silver Bronze RC Auto.:   1-1.5X
Production 150 Sets

Silver-Blue
Silver Blue Non-Auto.:   2-4X
Silver Blue RC Auto.:   1-1.5X
Production 125 Sets

Silver-Gold
Silver Gold Non-Auto.:   2-4X
Silver Gold RC Auto.:   1-1.5X
Production 100 Sets

Hyper Silver-Red
Hyper Silver Red Non-Auto.: 2-4X
Hyper Silver Red RC Auto.: 1-1.5X
Production 75 Sets

Hyper Silver-Bronze
Hyper Silver Bronze Non-Auto.: 3-4X
Hyper Silver Bronze Auto.: 1-2X
Production 50 Sets

Hyper Silver Blue
No Pricing
Production 25 Sets

Hyper Silver Gold
No Pricing
Production Five Sets

Hyper Plaid Silver
No Pricing
Production One Set

Printing Plates
No Pricing
Production one set per color

A-Rod Road to 500
NM/M
Common A-Rod: 3.00
2:Box
Autograph: No Pricing
Production One Set

Cut Signatures Dual
Production One Set

Dual Autograph
NM/M
	Common Dual Auto.:	10.00
AH	Garrett Atkins, Matt Holliday	30.00
AI	Matt Albers, Chris Iannetta	10.00
AS	Matt Albers, Brian Slocum	10.00
BB	Brian Bannister, Floyd Bannister	20.00
BDE	Erik Bedard, Zachary Duke	20.00
BG	Jeremy Bonderman, Curtis Granderson	30.00
BS	Jeff Baker, Jeff Salazar	10.00
BV	Jeremy Bonderman, Justin Verlander	50.00
CC	Melky Cabrera, Robinson Cano	60.00
CJ	Chris Carpenter, Tyler Johnson	40.00
CK	Robinson Cano, Chuck Knoblauch	40.00
CM	Fabio Castro, Scott Mathieson	15.00
CW	Miguel Cabrera, Dontrelle Willis	30.00
CY	Alberto Callaspo, Chris Young	20.00
CZ	Alberto Callaspo, Benjamin Zobrist	15.00
GB	Garrett Atkins, Clint Barmes	15.00
GC	Curtis Granderson, Melky Cabrera	25.00
GM	Hector Gimenez, Miguel Montero	15.00
GS	Dwight Gooden, Darryl Strawberry	40.00
HH	Bill Hall, J.J. Hardy	30.00
HO	Ryan Howard, David Ortiz	100.00
IK	Chris Iannetta, Matthew Kemp	15.00
IM	Chris Iannetta, Miguel Montero	15.00
JJ	Andruw Jones, David Justice	50.00
JS	Ubaldo Jimenez, Dennis Sarfate	10.00
JY	Conor Jackson, Chris Young	25.00
KA	Howie Kendrick, Erick Aybar	25.00
KF	Kevin Kouzmanoff, Josh Fields	20.00
KG	Matthew Kemp, Franklin Gutierrez	15.00
KM	Josh Kinney, Tom Mastny	15.00
KMA	Jeff Karstens, Scott Mathieson	15.00
KZ	Austin Kearns, Ryan Zimmerman	25.00
LG	Adam LaRoche, Tom Gorzelanny	20.00
LK	Francisco Liriano, Jim Kaat	20.00
LL	Tony Larussa, Jim Leyland	50.00
LP	Francisco Liriano, Jonathan Papelbon	35.00
LV	Francisco Liriano, Justin Verlander	40.00
LY	Adam Lind, Delmon Young	20.00
MB	Nicholas Markakis, Brian Roberts	30.00
MC	Omar Minaya, Brian Cashman	60.00
MCA	Nicholas Markakis, Melky Cabrera	30.00
MG	Craig Monroe, Curtis Granderson	30.00
MH	John Maine, Philip Humber	30.00
MM	Lastings Milledge, John Maine	25.00
MMA	David Murphy, Mitch Maier	15.00

MP	Andrew Miller, Glen Perkins	30.00
MQ	Nicholas Markakis, Carlos Quentin	20.00
MS	Justin Morneau, Nick Swisher	30.00
MSL	Tom Mastny, Brian Slocum	10.00
MW	Lastings Milledge, David Wright	50.00
OB	Jerry Owens, Michael Bourn	15.00
PC	Angel Pagan, Buck Coats	15.00
PS	Yusmeiro Petit, Anibal Sanchez	15.00
PV	Jonathan Papelbon, Justin Verlander	50.00
SH	Jonathan Sanchez, Brad Hennessey	15.00
SM	Freddy Sanchez, Joe Mauer	30.00
SMA	Chris Stewart, Carlos Maldonado	15.00
SR	Brian Stokes, Shawn Riggans	15.00
VF	Justin Verlander, Mark Fidrych	50.00
VM	John Van Benschoten, Scott Mathieson	15.00
VP	Jason Varitek, Jorge Posada	80.00
WC	David Wright, Robinson Cano	80.00
WS	Dontrelle Willis, Anibal Sanchez	20.00
YL	Chris Young, Nook Logan	15.00
YU	Delmon Young, B.J. Upton	35.00
ZG	Benjamin Zobrist, Joel Guzman	15.00

Moon Shots Autographs
NM/M
	Common Auto.:	80.00
BA	Buzz Aldrin	200.00
WC	Walt Cunningham	80.00
WS	Wally Schirra	180.00
RC	Robert Crippen	80.00
CD	Charles Duke	80.00
AW	Alfred Worden	80.00
EM	Edgar Mitchell	80.00
FH	Fred Haise	100.00
RG	Richard Gordon	100.00
SC	Scott Carpenter	100.00

Moon Shots Autographs Dual
NM/M
	Common Dual Auto.:	100.00
AC	Garrett Atkins, Scott Carpenter	100.00
AD	Andre Dawson, Alfred Worden	140.00
DG	Jermaine Dye, Richard Gordon	100.00
HC	Ryan Howard, W. Cunningham	140.00
OS	David Ortiz, Wally Schirra	150.00
RA	Alex Rodriguez, Buzz Aldrin	375.00
SC	Alfonso Soriano, Robert Crippen	150.00
SH	Duke Snider, Fred Haise	160.00
WD	David Wright, Charles Duke	180.00
WM	Dave Winfield, Edgar Mitchell	125.00

Solo Sigs
NM/M
	Common Autograph:	10.00
AH	Aaron Hill	10.00
AL	Anthony Lerew	10.00
AS	Anibal Sanchez	10.00
BB	Boof Bonser	10.00
CB	Clint Barmes	10.00
CH	Cole Hamels	25.00
CJ	Chuck James	10.00
CQ	Carlos Quentin	15.00
DH	Dave Henderson	10.00
DU	Dan Uggla	15.00
ES	Ervin Santana	10.00
FL	Francisco Liriano	20.00
FS	Freddy Sanchez	15.00
GA	Garrett Atkins	10.00
HK	Howie Kendrick	15.00
HM	Hideki Matsui	250.00
HR	Hanley Ramirez	25.00
JM	Justin Morneau	15.00
JS	Jeremy Sowers	10.00
MC	Matt Cain	20.00
MH	Matt Holliday	30.00
NM	Nicholas Markakis	30.00
RC	Robinson Cano	30.00
RCE	Ronny Cedeno	10.00
RG	Ryan Garko	10.00
RH	Ryan Howard	60.00
RR	Rick Rhoden	10.00
VG	Vladimir Guerrero	50.00

Tri-Signers
NM/M
Inserted 1:288
| ANS | Joaquin Arias, Oswaldo Navarro, Angel Sanchez | 20.00 |

CPC	Melky Cabrera, Wily Mo Pena, Miguel Cabrera	40.00
HLC	Brad Hennessey, J. Sanchez, Matt Cain	40.00
JGK	Conor Jackson, Ryan Garko, Howie Kendrick	40.00
JHS	Chuck James, Cole Hamels, Jeremy Sowers	50.00
LNB	Francisco Liriano, Joe Nathan, Boof Bonser	50.00
MAR	Justin Morneau, Garrett Atkins, Brian Roberts	40.00
MLM	Justin Morneau, Francisco Liriano, Matt Garza	60.00
MLP	Justin Morneau, Francisco Liriano, Glen Perkins	50.00
MSG	Justin Morneau, Nick Swisher, Adrian Gonzalez	50.00
MYT	Andrew Miller, Delmon Young, Troy Tulowitzki	60.00
OPV	David Ortiz, Jonathan Papelbon, Jason Varitek	150.00
OWH	David Ortiz, David Wright, Ryan Howard	150.00
QJY	Carlos Quentin, Conor Jackson, Chris Young	40.00
RCC	Alex Rodriguez, Melky Cabrera, Robinson Cano	250.00
RWH	Alex Rodriguez, David Wright, Ryan Howard	250.00
SHH	Huston Street, Rich Harden, Danny Haren	50.00
TPW	Taylor Tankersley, Yusmeiro Petit, Dontrelle Willis	35.00
URW	Dan Uggla, Hanley Ramirez, Dontrelle Willis	50.00

Yankees Cut Signatures
Production One Set

2007 Topps Heritage

Adrian Gonzalez

1st BASE   SAN DIEGO PADRES

NM/M
Complete Set (495):   325.00
Common Player: .40
Common SP: 5.00
Inserted 1:2
Common Variation: 5.00
Inserted 1:6
Pack (8):   3.00
Box (24):   65.00
1	David Ortiz	1.50
2	Roger Clemens	3.00
2	Roger Clemens/ Yellow Team Name/SP	15.00
3	David Wells	.40
4	Ronny Paulino/SP	5.00
5	Derek Jeter/SP	15.00
6	Felix Hernandez	2.00
7	Todd Helton	1.00
8	David Eckstein	.40
8	David Eckstein/ Yellow Name/SP	5.00
9	Craig Wilson	.40
10	John Smoltz	.75
11	Robert Mackowiak	.40
11	Robert Mackowiak/ Yellow Team Name/SP	5.00
12	Scott Hatteberg	.40
13	Wilfredo Ledezma	5.00
13	Wilfredo Ledezma/ Yellow Team Name/SP	5.00
14	Bobby Abreu/SP	8.00
15	Austin Kearns	.40
16	Wilson Betemit	.40
17	Darren Oliver	.40
18	Josh Beckett	.40
19	San Francisco Giants	.40
20	Robinson Cano	1.00
20	Robinson Cano/ Yellow Team Name/SP	5.00
21	Matt Cain	1.00
22	Jason Kendall/SP	5.00
23	Mark Kotsay/SP	5.00
23	Mark Kotsay/ Yellow Name/SP	5.00
24	Yadier Molina/SP	.40
24	Yadier Molina/ Yellow Name/SP	5.00

25	Brad Penny	.40
26	Adrian Gonzalez	.75
27	Danny Haren	.40
28	Brian Giles	.50
29	Jose Lopez	.40
30	Ichiro Suzuki	2.50
30	Ichiro Suzuki/ Yellow Name/SP	10.00
31	Beltran Perez/SP **(RC)**	5.00
32	Brad Hawpe/SP	5.00
33	Jim Thome	1.50
33	Jim Thome/ Yellow Team Name/SP	8.00
34	Mark DeRosa	.40
35	Woody Williams	.40
35	Woody Williams/ Yellow Team Name/SP	5.00
36	Luis Gonzalez	.40
37	Billy Sadler **(RC)**	1.00
38	Dave Roberts	.40
39	Mitch Maier **(RC)**	1.00
40	Francisco Cordero/SP	5.00
41	Anthony Reyes/SP	8.00
42	Russell Martin	.40
43	Scott Proctor	.40
44	Washington Nationals	.40
45	Shane Victorino	.40
46	Joel Zumaya	.40
46	Joel Zumaya/ Yellow Name/SP	5.00
47	Delmon Young **(RC)**	1.00
48	Alex Rios	.40
49	Willy Taveras/SP	5.00
50	Mark Buehrle/SP	5.00
50	Mark Buehrle/ Yellow Team Name/SP	5.00
51	Livan Hernandez	.40
52	Jason Bay	1.00
52	Jason Bay/ Yellow Team Name/SP	5.00
53	Jose Valentin	.40
53	Jose Valentin/ Yellow Name/SP	5.00
54	Kevin Reese	.40
55	Felipe Lopez	.40
56	Ryan Sweeney **(RC)**	1.00
57	Kelvim Escobar	.40
57	Kelvim Escobar/ Yellow Name/SP	5.00
58	Nick Swisher/SP	5.00
58	Nick Swisher/ Yellow Team Name/SP	8.00
59	Kevin Millwood/SP	5.00
60	Preston Wilson	.40
60	Preston Wilson/ Yellow Name/SP	5.00
61	Mariano Rivera	.75
61	Mariano Rivera/ Yellow Name/SP	8.00
62	Josh Barfield	.40
63	Ryan Freel	.40
64	Tim Hudson	.75
65	Chris Narveson **(RC)**	1.00
65	Chris Narveson/ Yellow Name/SP	5.00
66	Matt Murton	.40
67	Melvin Mora/SP	5.00
68	Jason Jennings/SP	5.00
69	Emil Brown	.40
70	Magglio Ordonez	.40
70	Magglio Ordonez/ Yellow Name/SP	5.00
71	Los Angeles Dodgers	.40
72	Huston Street	.40
73	David Ross	.40
74	Juan Uribe	.40
75	Scott Podsednik	.40
76	Cole Hamels/SP	8.00
76	Cole Hamels/ Yellow Team Name/SP	8.00
77	Rafael Furcal/SP	5.00
77	Rafael Furcal/ Yellow Team Name/SP	5.00
78	Ryan Theriot	.40
78	Ryan Theriot/ Yellow Name/SP	5.00
79	Corey Patterson	.40
79	Corey Patterson/ Yellow Team Name/SP	5.00
80	Jered Weaver	.40
81	Stephen Drew	.75
81	Stephen Drew/ Yellow Team Name/SP	8.00
82	Adam Kennedy	.40
83	Tony Gwynn Jr.	.40
84	Erik Bedard	.40
85	Omar Vizquel/SP	5.00
85	Omar Vizquel/ Yellow Team Name/SP	5.00
86	Fred Lewis/SP **(RC)**	5.00
87	Brad Radke	.40
87	Shawn Chacon/ Yellow Name/SP	5.00
88	Frank Catalanotto	.40
89	Orlando Hudson	.40
90	Pat Burrell	.40
91	David DeJesus	.40
92	David Wright	2.50
92	David Wright/ Yellow Name/SP	10.00
93	Conor Jackson	.40
94	Xavier Nady/SP	5.00
95	Bill Hall/SP	8.00
96	Andre Ethier	.75
97	Jeff Suppan	.40
97	Jeff Suppan/ Yellow Name/SP	5.00
98	Ryan Zimmerman	

#	Player	Price
98	Ryan Zimmerman/ Yellow Name/SP	8.00
99	Yuniesky Betancourt	.40
100	Jose Contreras	.40
100	Jose Contreras/ Yellow Team Name/SP	5.00
101	Miguel Cairo	.40
101	Miguel Cairo/ Yellow Name/SP	5.00
102	Brian Roberts	.40
103	Carl Crawford/SP	8.00
104	Mike Lamb/SP	.40
105	Mark Ellis	.40
106	Scott Rolen	1.50
107	Garrett Atkins	.40
108	Hanley Ramirez	.75
108	Hanley Ramirez/ Yellow Team Name/SP	8.00
109	Trot Nixon	.40
110	Edgar Renteria	.40
111	Jeff Francis	.40
112	Marcus Thames/SP	5.00
113	Brian Burres/SP (RC)	5.00
114	Brian Schneider	.40
115	Jeremy Bonderman	.75
116	Ryan Madson	.40
117	Gerald Laird	.40
118	Roy Halladay	.75
119	Victor Martinez	.40
120	Greg Maddux	2.50
121	Jay Payton/SP	5.00
122	Jacque Jones/SP	.40
123	Juan Lara RC	1.00
124	Derrick Turnbow	.40
125	Adam Everett	.40
126	Michael Cuddyer	.40
127	Gil Meche	.40
128	Willy Aybar	.40
129	Jerry Owens RC	1.00
130	Manny Ramirez/SP	10.00
131	Howie Kendrick/SP	8.00
132	Byung-Hyun Kim	.40
133	Kevin Kouzmanoff (RC)	1.00
134	Philadelphia Phillies	.40
135	Joe Blanton	.40
136	Ray Durham	.40
137	Luke Hudson	.40
138	Eric Byrnes	.40
139	Ryan Braun/SP (RC)	10.00
140	Johnny Damon/SP	10.00
141	Ambiorix Burgos	.40
142	Hideki Matsui	.40
143	Josh Johnson	.40
144	Miguel Cabrera	.40
146	Delwyn Young (RC)	1.00
147	Chuck James	.40
148	Morgan Ensberg	.40
149	Jose Vidro/SP	5.00
150	Alex Rodriguez/SP	15.00
151	Carlos Maldonado (RC)	1.00
152	Jason Schmidt	.40
153	Alex Escobar	.40
154	Chris Gomez	.40
155	Endy Chavez	.40
156	Kris Benson	.40
157	Bronson Arroyo	.40
158	Cleveland Indians/SP	8.00
159	Chris Ray/SP	.40
160	Richie Sexson	.40
161	Huston Street	.40
162	Kevin Youkilis	.40
163	Armando Benitez	.40
164	Vinny Rottino (RC)	1.00
165	Garret Anderson	.40
166	Todd Greene	.40
167	Brian Stokes/SP (RC)	5.00
168	Albert Pujols/SP	15.00
169	Todd Coffey	.40
170	Jason Michaels	.40
171	David Dellucci	.40
172	Eric Milton	.40
173	Austin Kearns	.40
174	Kansas City Royals	.40
175	Andy Cannizaro RC	2.00
176	David Weathers/SP	5.00
177	Jermaine Dye/SP	5.00
178	Wily Mo Pena	.40
179	Chris Burke	.40
180	Jeff Weaver	.40
181	Juan Encarnacion	.40
182	Jeremy Hermida	.40
183	Tim Wakefield	.40
184	Rich Hill	.50
185	Aaron Hill/SP	5.00
186	Scot Shields/SP	5.00
187	Randy Johnson	.40
188	Dan Johnson	.40
189	Sean Marshall	.40
190	Marcus Giles	.40
191	Jonathan Broxton	.40
192	Mike Piazza	.40
193	Carlos Quentin	.40
194	Derek Lowe/SP	5.00
195	Russell Branyan/SP	5.00
196	Jason Marquis	.40
197	Khalil Greene	.40
198	Ryan Dempster	.40
199	Ronnie Belliard	.40
200	Josh Fogg	.40
201	Carlos Lee	.40
202	Chris Denorfia	.40
203	Kendry Morales/SP	5.00
204	Rafael Soriano/SP	.40
205	Brandon Phillips	.40
206	Andrew Miller RC	5.00
207	John Koronka	.40
208	Luis Castillo	.40
209	Angel Guzman	.40
210	Jim Edmonds	.40
211	Patrick Misch (RC)	1.00
212	Ty Wigginton/SP	.40
213	Brandon Inge/SP	5.00
214	Royce Clayton	.40
215	Ben Broussard	.40
216	St. Louis Cardinals	.40
217	Mark Mulder	.40
218	Kenji Johjima	.40
219	Joe Crede	.40
220	Danny Haren	.40
221	Josh Fields/SP (RC)	8.00
222	Pat Neshek/SP	10.00
223	Reed Johnson	.40
224	Mike Mussina	.40
225	Randy Winn	.40
226	Brian Rogers (RC)	.40
227	Juan Rivera	.40
228	Shawn Green	.40
229	Mike Napoli	.40
230	Chase Utley/SP	10.00
231	John Nelson/SP (RC)	.40
232	Casey Blake	.40
233	Lyle Overbay	.40
234	Adam LaRoche	.40
235	Jeff Weaver	.40
236	Johnny Estrada	.40
237	James Shields	.40
238	Jose Castillo	.40
239	Doug Davis/SP	5.00
240	Jason Giambi/SP	5.00
241	Mike Gonzalez	.40
242	Scott Downs	.40
243	Joe Inglett	.40
244	Matthew Kemp	.40
245	Ted Lilly	.40
246	New York Yankees	.40
247	Jamey Carroll	.40
248	Adam Wainwright/SP	8.00
249	Matt Thornton/SP	.40
250	Alfonso Soriano	.40
251	Tom Gordon	.40
252	Dennis Sarfate (RC)	.40
253	Zachary Duke	.40
254	Hank Blalock	.40
255	Johan Santana	.40
256	Chicago White Sox	.40
257	Aaron Cook/SP	5.00
258	Cliff Lee/SP	5.00
259	Miguel Tejada	.40
260	Mike Lowell	.40
261	Ian Snell	.40
262	Jason Tyner	.40
263	Troy Tulowitzki (RC)	1.00
264	Ervin Santana	.40
265	Jon Lester	.40
266	Andy Pettitte/SP	8.00
267	A.J. Pierzynski/SP	5.00
268	Rich Aurilia	.40
269	Phil Nevin	.40
270	Tom Glavine	.40
271	Chris Coste	.40
272	Moises Alou	.40
273	J.D. Drew	.40
274	Abraham Nunez	.40
275	Jorge Posada/SP	8.00
276	Jeff Conine/SP	5.00
277	Chad Cordero	.40
278	Nick Johnson	.40
279	Kevin Millar	.40
280	Mark Grudzielanek	.40
281	Chris Stewart RC	1.00
282	Nate Robertson	.40
283	Drew Anderson/SP	1.00
284	Doug Mientkiewicz/SP	5.00
285	Ken Griffey Jr./SP	10.00
286	Cory Sullivan	.40
287	Chris Carpenter	.40
288	Gary Matthews	.40
289	Justin Verlander	.40
	Jeff Weaver	.40
290	Vicente Padilla	.40
291	Chris Roberson	.40
292	Chris Young	.40
293	Ryan Garko/SP	5.00
294	Miguel Batista/SP	5.00
295	B.J. Upton	.40
296	Justin Verlander	.40
297	Benjamin Zobrist	.40
298	Ben Sheets	.40
299	Eric Chavez	.40
300	William Harridge, Warren Giles	.40
301	Placido Polanco	.40
302	Angel Sanchez/SP RC	5.00
303	Freddy Sanchez/SP	5.00
304	Magglio Ordonez, Carlos Guillen	.40
305	A.J. Burnett	.40
306	Juan Perez RC	1.00
307	Chris Britton	.40
308	Jon Garland	.40
309	Pedro Feliz	.40
310	Ryan Howard	.40
311	Aaron Harang/SP	5.00
312	Boston Red Sox/SP	5.00
313	Chad Billingsley	.40
314	Bobby Cox, Chipper Jones	.40
315	Johan Santana	.40
316	Juan Pierre	.40
317	Luke Scott	.40
318	Javier Valentin	.40
319	Mark Loretta	.40
320	Kenny Lofton/SP	5.00
321	Vladimir Guerrero/SP, Ivan Rodriguez/SP	8.00
322	Josh Willingham	.40
323	Lance Berkman	.40
324	Anibal Sanchez	.40
325	Maicer Izturis	.40
326	Brett Myers	.40
327	Chicago Cubs	.40
328	Francisco Liriano	.40
329	Craig Monroe/SP	5.00
330	Paul LoDuca/SP	5.00
331	Steve Trachsel	.40
332	Bernie Williams	.40
333	Carlos Guillen	.40
334	Johan Santana	.40
	Francisco Liriano	.40
335	David Bush	.40
336	Carlos Beltran	.40
337	Jason Isringhausen	.40
338	Todd Walker/SP	5.00
339	Jarrod Washburn/SP	5.00
340	Brandon Webb	.40
341	Pittsburgh Pirates	.40
342	Derrick Turnbow	.40
343	Chad Santos	.40
344	Brad Lidge	.40
345	Brad Ausmus	.40
346	Carlos Delgado	.40
347	Boone Logan/SP	5.00
348	Jimmy Rollins/SP	8.00
349	Orlando Hernandez	.40
350	Gary Sheffield	.40
351	Albert Pujols, Yadier Molina, Jim Edmonds, Chris Duncan	.40
352	Jake Peavy	.40
353	Jason Varitek	.40
354	Freddy Garcia	.40
355	Matt Diaz	.40
356	Bernie Castro/SP	5.00
357	Eric Stults/SP RC	.40
358	John Lackey	.40
359	Bobby Jenks	.40
360	Mark Teixeira	.40
361	Jonathan Papelbon	.40
362	Paul Konerko	.40
363	Erik Bedard	.40
364	Eliezer Alfonzo	.40
365	Fernando Rodney/SP	5.00
366	Chris Duncan/SP	8.00
367	Jose Diaz RC	1.00
368	Travis Hafner	.40
369	Matt Capps	.40
370	Ivan Rodriguez	.40
371	David Murphy (RC)	1.00
372	Carlos Zambrano	.40
373	Chris Iannetta	.40
374	Jose Mesa/SP	5.00
375	Michael Young/SP	8.00
376	Bill Bray	.40
377	Milwaukee Brewers	.40
378	Robert Mackowiak	.40
379	Barry Zito	.40
380	Clay Hensley	.40
381	J.J. Putz	.40
382	C.C. Sabathia	.40
383	Eduardo Perez/SP	5.00
384	Scott Moore/SP (RC)	8.00
385	Scott Olsen	.40
386	Ryan Howard, Chase Utley	.50
387	Aaron Rowand	.40
388	Mike Rouse	.40
389	Alexis Gomez	.40
390	Brian McCann	.40
391	Ryan Shealy	.40
392	Shane Youman/SP RC	8.00
393	Melky Cabrera/SP	8.00
394	Jeremy Sowers	.40
395	Casey Janssen	.40
396	Miguel Perez	.40
397	Detroit Tigers	.40
398	Reggie Abercrombie	.40
399	Ricky Nolasco	.40
400	Tadahito Iguchi	.40
401	Jose Reyes/SP	10.00
402	Juan Encarnacion/SP	5.00
403	Brandon Harper	.40
404	Torii Hunter	.40
405	Dan Uggla	.40
406	Orlando Cabrera	.40
407	Jose Capellan	.40
408	Baltimore Orioles	.40
409	Frank Thomas	.40
410	Francisco Rodriguez/SP	5.00
411	Ian Kinsler/SP	5.00
412	Billy Wagner	.40
413	Andy Marte	.40
414	Mike Jacobs	.40
415	Raul Ibanez	.40
416	Jhonny Peralta	.40
417	Chris Young	.40
418	Albert Pujols, Craig Monroe	.40
419	Scott Kazmir/SP	5.00
420	Norris Hopper/SP	8.00
421	Chris Capuano	.40
422	Troy Glaus	.40
423	Roy Oswalt	.40
424	Grady Sizemore	.40
425	Chone Figgins	.40
426	Chad Tracy	.40
427	Brian Fuentes	.40
428	Cincinnati Reds/SP	8.00
429	Ramon Hernandez/SP	5.00
430	Mike Cameron	.40
431	Dontrelle Willis	.40
432	Joshua Sharpless	.40
433	Adrian Beltre	.40
434	Curtis Granderson	.40
435	B.J. Ryan	.40
436	Ryan Howard, David Wright	.40
437	Vernon Wells/SP	8.00
438	Vladimir Guerrero/SP	8.00
439	Jake Westbrook	.40
440	Chipper Jones	.40
441	James Loney	.40
442	St. Louis Cardinals	.40
443	Oswaldo Navarro	.40
444	Joe Mauer	.40
445	Miguel Montero	.40
446	Franklin Gutierrez/SP	5.00
447	Mark Redman/SP	5.00
448	Mike Rabelo RC	1.00
449	Philip Humber	.40
450	Justin Morneau	.40
451	Hector Gimenez	.40
452	Matt Holliday	.50
453	Akinori Otsuka	.40
454	Prince Fielder	.40
455	Chien-Ming Wang/SP	10.00
456	Shawn Riggans/SP	8.00
457	John Maine	.40
458	Adam Lind (RC)	1.00
459	Ubaldo Jimenez	.40
460	Drew Anderson	.40
461	Cla Meredith	.40
462	Joaquin Arias	.40
463	Kenny Rogers	.40
464	Jose Garcia/SP	5.00
465	Pedro Martinez/SP	8.00
466	Jeff Salazar	.40
467	Glen Perkins (RC)	.40
468	Travis Ishikawa	.40
469	Joe Borowski	.40
470	Jeremy Brown	.40
471	Andre Ethier	.40
472	Taylor Tankersley	.40
473	Lastings Milledge/SP	8.00
474	Brian Sanchez/SP	8.00
475	Ozzie Guillen, Phil Garner	.40
476	Albert Pujols	.40
477	David Ortiz	.40
478	Chase Utley	.50
479	Mark Loretta	.40
480	David Wright	.40
481	Alex Rodriguez	.40
482	Edgar Renteria/SP	5.00
483	Derek Jeter/SP	15.00
484	Alfonso Soriano	.40
485	Vladimir Guerrero	.40
486	Carlos Beltran	.40
487	Vernon Wells	.40
488	Jason Bay	.40
489	Ichiro Suzuki	.40
490	Paul LoDuca	.40
491	Ivan Rodriguez/SP	8.00
492	Brad Penny/SP	5.00
493	Roy Halladay	.40
494	Brian Fuentes	.40
495	Kenny Rogers	.40

Chrome

Freddy Garcia

	NM/M
Common Player:	2.00
Production 1,958 Sets	
Refractors:	1.5-2X
Production 558 Sets	
Black Refractors:	3-6X
Production 58 Sets	
1 David Ortiz	6.00
2 John Smoltz	3.00
3 Brian Giles	2.00
4 Billy Sadler	4.00
5 Joel Zumaya	4.00
6 Felipe Lopez	3.00
7 Tim Hudson	3.00
8 David Ross	2.00
9 Adam Kennedy	2.00
10 David DeJesus	2.00
11 Jose Contreras	2.00
12 Trot Nixon	2.00
13 Roy Halladay	3.00
14 Gil Meche	2.00
15 Ray Durham	2.00
16 Delwyn Young	2.00
17 Endy Chavez	2.00
18 Vinny Rottino	3.00
19 Austin Kearns	2.00
20 Jeremy Hermida	3.00
21 Jonathan Broxton	3.00
22 Josh Fogg	2.00
23 Angel Guzman	2.00
24 Kenji Johjima	4.00
25 Juan Rivera	2.00
26 Johnny Estrada	2.00
27 Ted Lilly	2.00
28 Hank Blalock	3.00
29 Troy Tulowitzki	5.00
30 Moises Alou	3.00
32 Chris Stewart	2.00
33 Vicente Padilla	2.00
34 Eric Chavez	3.00
35 Jon Garland	2.00
36 Luke Scott	2.00
37 Brett Myers	5.00
38 David Bush	2.00
39 Brad Lidge	2.00
40 Jason Varitek	5.00
41 Paul Konerko	4.00
42 David Murphy	2.00
43 Clay Hensley	2.00
44 Alexis Gomez	2.00
46 Reggie Abercrombie	2.00
46 Jose Capellan	2.00
47 Jhonny Peralta	3.00
48 Chone Figgins	2.00
49 Curtis Granderson	3.00
50 Oswaldo Navarro	3.00
51 Matt Holliday	4.00
52 Cla Meredith	2.00
53 Jeremy Brown	3.00
54 Mark Loretta	2.00
55 Jason Bay	4.00
56 Roger Clemens	8.00
57 Robert Mackowiak	2.00
58 Robinson Cano	6.00
59 Jose Lopez	3.00
60 Dave Roberts	2.00
61 Delmon Young	6.00
62 Ryan Sweeney	2.00
63 Chris Narveson	2.00
64 Juan Uribe	2.00
65 Tony Gwynn Jr.	2.00
66 David Wright	8.00
67 Miguel Cairo	2.00
68 Edgar Renteria	2.00
69 Victor Martinez	3.00
70 Willy Aybar	2.00
71 Luke Hudson	2.00
72 Chuck James	2.00
73 Kris Benson	2.00
74 Garret Anderson	2.00
75 Tim Wakefield	2.00
76 Mike Piazza	6.00
77 Carlos Lee	4.00
78 Jim Edmonds	4.00
80 Joe Crede	4.00
81 Shawn Green	3.00
82 James Shields	4.00
84 Johan Santana	8.00
85 Ervin Santana	2.00
86 J.D. Drew	4.00
87 Nate Robertson	2.00
88 Chris Roberson	3.00
90 Pedro Feliz	2.00
91 Javier Valentin	2.00
93 Carlos Beltran	5.00
94 Brad Ausmus	2.00
95 Freddy Garcia	2.00
96 Erik Bedard	4.00
97 Carlos Zambrano	4.00
98 J.J. Putz	2.00
99 Brian McCann	4.00
100 Ricky Nolasco	2.00
102 Chris Young	4.00
103 Chad Tracy	2.00
104 B.J. Ryan	2.00
105 Joe Mauer	4.00
106 Akinori Otsuka	2.00
107 Joaquin Arias	2.00
108 Andre Ethier	2.00
109 David Wright	10.00
110 Ichiro Suzuki	8.00

A-Rod Road to 500

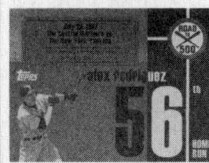

	NM/M
Common A-Rod:	3.00
Inserted 1:24	
Autograph:	No Pricing
Production 1 Set	
51-75 Alex Rodriguez	3.00

A-Rod Road to 500 Autograph

	NM/M
Common A-Rod:	3.00
Inserted 1:24	
Autograph:	No Pricing
Production 1 Set	
51-75 Alex Rodriguez	3.00

Clubhouse Collection

MOISES ALOU

	NM/M
Common Player:	2.00
SM Stan Musial	30.00
DS Duke Snider	20.00
FR Frank Robinson	20.00
BR Brooks Robinson	15.00
YB Yogi Berra	25.00
AK Al Kaline	20.00
AW Adam Wainwright	15.00
AJP Albert Pujols	20.00
AR Alex Rodriguez	20.00
ALR Anthony Reyes	10.00
BU B.J. Upton	8.00
BZ Barry Zito	8.00
BS Ben Sheets	10.00
BW Billy Wagner	8.00
BR Brian Roberts	10.00
CU Chase Utley	15.00
CJ Chipper Jones	15.00
CC Chris Carpenter	15.00
CD Chris Duncan	10.00
CJ Conor Jackson	10.00
DE David Eckstein	20.00
DO David Ortiz	15.00
DW David Wright	30.00
DY Delmon Young	10.00
DWW Dontrelle Willis	8.00
DM Doug Mientkiewicz	8.00
ER Edgar Renteria	8.00
EC Eric Chavez	8.00
ES Ervin Santana	8.00
FL Francisco Liriano	10.00
GS Gary Sheffield	10.00
HB Hank Blalock	8.00
IR Ivan Rodriguez	10.00
JS Jeff Suppan	8.00
JW Jeff Weaver	8.00
JR Jimmy Rollins	10.00
JD Johnny Damon	15.00
JRP Jorge Posada	10.00
JBR Jose Reyes	20.00
JV Jose Vidro	8.00
JP Juan Pierre	8.00
JM Justin Morneau	15.00
LB Lance Berkman	8.00
LG Luis Gonzalez	8.00
MO Magglio Ordonez	8.00
MR Manny Ramirez	10.00
MK Mark Kotsay	8.00
MT Mark Teixeira	8.00
MM Melvin Mora	8.00
MC Miguel Cabrera	10.00
MOT Miguel Tejada	8.00
MP Mike Piazza	15.00
MA Moises Alou	8.00
NS Nick Swisher	10.00
OV Omar Vizquel	8.00
PB Pat Burrell	10.00
PP Placido Polanco	8.00
RF Rafael Furcal	8.00
RS Richie Sexson	10.00
RB Ronnie Belliard	8.00
RH Ryan Howard	30.00
TH Todd Helton	10.00
TKH Torii Hunter	10.00
VM Victor Martinez	8.00
YM Yadier Molina	8.00

Clubhouse Collection Dual Relic

	NM/M
Production 58 Sets	
MP Stan Musial, Albert Pujols	180.00
KR Al Kaline, Ivan Rodriguez	80.00

Clubhouse Coll. Relic Autograph

Production 25 Sets

Felt Team Emblem

	NM/M
Inserted 1:Box	
Los Angeles Dodgers	3.00
Washington Senators	3.00
San Francisco Giants	3.00
Boston Red Sox	5.00
Cincinnati Redlegs	3.00
Pittsburgh Pirates	3.00
Milwaukee Braves	5.00
Chicago Cubs	5.00
Baltimore Orioles	3.00
New York Yankees	5.00
Cleveland Indians	3.00
St. Louis Cardinals	3.00
Kansas City Athletics	3.00
Detroit Tigers	3.00
Chicago White Sox	3.00
Philadelphia Phillies	3.00

Flashbacks

BALTIMORE WELCOMES BROOKS
BROOKS ROBINSON
APRIL 15, 1955

	NM/M
Common Player:	1.00

Inserted 1:12
SM	Stan Musial	2.00
AK	Al Kaline	2.00
BR	Brooks Robinson	2.00
RS	Red Schoendienst	1.00
LA	Luis Aparicio	1.00
WS	Warren Spahn	2.00
HS	Hank Sauer	1.00
LB	Lew Burdette	1.00
EY	Eddie Yost	1.00
JB	Jim Bunning	1.00

Flashback Autograph
No Pricing
Production 25 Sets

Flashbacks Relics
NM/M
	Common Player:	20.00
SM	Stan Musial	30.00
AK	Al Kaline	25.00
BR	Brooks Robinson	25.00
RS	Red Schoendienst	20.00
WS	Warren Spahn	25.00
LB	Lew Burdette	25.00
EY	Eddie Yost	20.00
JB	Jim Bunning	20.00

Flashbacks Relic Autograph
Production 25 Sets

Dual Flashbacks
Production 10 Sets

New Age Performers

NM/M
	Common Player:	1.00
Inserted 1:15
RH	Ryan Howard	3.00
AR	Alex Rodriguez	3.00
AS	Alfonso Soriano	2.00
DO	David Ortiz	2.00
TH	Trevor Hoffman	1.00
DJ	Derek Jeter	4.00
AAS	Anibal Sanchez	1.00
RC	Roger Clemens	3.00
JS	Johan Santana	2.00
AP	Albert Pujols	4.00
CJ	Chipper Jones	2.00
FT	Frank Thomas	2.00
IR	Ivan Rodriguez	1.50
IS	Ichiro Suzuki	3.00
CB	Craig Biggio	1.00

Real One Autographs
NM/M
Common Autograph:
Red Ink: 1.5-2X
Production 58 Sets
AK	Al Kaline	150.00
BH	Bob Henrich	60.00
BM	Bobby Morgan	60.00
BP	Buddy Pritchard	65.00
BR	Brooks Robinson	100.00
BT	Bill Taylor	50.00
BW	Bill Wight	50.00
CH	Chuck Harmon	50.00
CJD	Jim Derrington	40.00
CR	Charley Rabe	60.00
DM	Dave Melton	60.00
DS	Duke Snider	100.00
DW	David Wright	120.00
DWW	Dontrelle Willis	40.00
DY	Delmon Young	50.00
DZ	Don Zimmer	50.00
EM	Ed Mayer	40.00
GK	George Kell	75.00
HP	Harding Peterson	60.00
JC	Joe Caffie	60.00
JD	Joe Durham	70.00
JL	Joe Lonnett	50.00
JM	Justin Morneau	60.00
JP	Johnny Podres	60.00
LA	Luis Aparicio	60.00
LM	Lloyd Merritt	50.00
LS	Lou Sleater	50.00
MB	Milt Bolling	50.00
MEB	Mack Burk	50.00
OH	Orlando Hudson	40.00
PS	Paul Smith	60.00
RC	Ray Crone	60.00
RH	Ryan Howard	250.00
RS	Red Schoendienst	85.00
SP	Stan Palys	60.00
TT	Tim Thompson	50.00

Then and Now
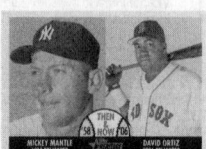
NM/M
Common Player: 1.00
Inserted 1:15
RH	Ryan Howard	3.00
DO	David Ortiz	2.00
JM	Joe Mauer	1.50
JR	Jose Reyes	2.00
JS	Johan Santana	2.00
AH	Aaron Harang	1.00
IS	Ichiro Suzuki	3.00
TH	Travis Hafner	1.50
FR	Francisco Rodriguez	1.00
CW	Chien-Ming Wang	2.00

1958 A.L. Home Run Champion

NM/M
Common Mantle: 3.00
Inserted 1:6
1-42 Mickey Mantle 3.00

1958 Cut Signatures
Production One Set

2007 Topps Moments & Milestones

NM/M
Complete Set (193):
Common Player: .50
Common RC (170-193): 5.00
Production 150 Sets
Pack (6): 7.00
Box (18): 100.00
1	Albert Pujols (37/5550)	4.00
2	Albert Pujols (130/19500)	4.00
3	Albert Pujols (194/29100)	4.00
4	Albert Pujols (112/16800)	4.00
5	Albert Pujols (47/7050)	4.00
6	Ichiro Suzuki (242/36300)	2.50
7	Ichiro Suzuki (34/5100)	2.50
8	Ichiro Suzuki (8/1200)	2.50
9	Ichiro Suzuki (56/8400)	2.50
10	Ichiro Suzuki (69/10350)	2.50
11	Ichiro Suzuki (8/1200)	2.50
12	Greg Maddux (20/3000)	3.00
13	Greg Maddux (199/29850)	3.00
14	Greg Maddux (20/3000)	3.00
15	Greg Maddux (197/29550)	3.00
16	Roger Clemens (24/3600)	3.00
17	Roger Clemens (10/1500)	5.00
18	Roger Clemens (238/35700)	3.00
19	Roger Clemens (20/3000)	3.00
20	Roger Clemens (256/38400)	3.00
21	Chipper Jones (45/6750)	1.50
22	Chipper Jones (110/16500)	1.50
23	Chipper Jones (181/27150)	1.50
24	Chipper Jones (116/17400)	1.50
25	Chipper Jones (41/6150)	1.50
26	Chipper Jones (25/3750)	1.50
27	Alex Rodriguez (47/7050)	4.00

28	Alex Rodriguez (118/17700)	4.00
29	Alex Rodriguez (181/27150)	4.00
30	Alex Rodriguez (124/18600)	4.00
31	Alex Rodriguez (30/4500)	4.00
32	Alex Rodriguez (17/2550)	8.00
33	Alex Rodriguez (48/7200)	4.00
34	Alex Rodriguez (130/19500)	4.00
35	Alex Rodriguez (194/29100)	4.00
36	Alex Rodriguez (124/18600)	4.00
37	Alex Rodriguez (29/4350)	6.00
38	Alex Rodriguez (21/3150)	6.00
39	Vladimir Guerrero (39/5850)	1.50
40	Vladimir Guerrero (126/18900)	1.50
41	Vladimir Guerrero (206/30900)	1.50
42	Vladimir Guerrero (124/18600)	1.50
43	Vladimir Guerrero (39/5850)	1.50
44	Vladimir Guerrero (13/1950)	1.50
45	Ken Griffey Jr. (56/8400)	3.00
46	Ken Griffey Jr. (147/22050)	3.00
47	Ken Griffey Jr. (185/27750)	3.00
48	Barry Zito (23/3450)	.75
49	Barry Zito (182/27300)	.75
50	Randy Johnson (18/2700)	1.50
51	Randy Johnson (294/44100)	1.50
52	Randy Johnson (6/900)	5.00
53	Randy Johnson (3/450)	20.00
54	Randy Johnson (17/2550)	1.50
55	Randy Johnson (364/54600)	1.50
56	Randy Johnson (12/1800)	1.50
57	Randy Johnson (2/300)	20.00
58	Prince Fielder (35/5250)	2.00
59	Prince Fielder (81/12150)	2.00
60	Dan Uggla (26/3900)	.50
61	Dan Uggla (27/4050)	.50
62	Dan Uggla (172/25800)	.50
63	Justin Verlander (17/2550)	3.00
64	Justin Verlander (124/18600)	1.50
65	Francisco Liriano (12/1800)	1.50
66	Francisco Liriano (144/21600)	1.50
67	Ryan Zimmerman (176/26400)	1.00
68	Ryan Zimmerman (110/16500)	1.00
69	Ryan Zimmerman (84/12600)	1.00
70	Hanley Ramirez (51/7650)	1.50
71	Hanley Ramirez (119/17850)	1.50
72	Hanley Ramirez (185/27750)	1.50
73	Russ Martin (65/9750)	1.00
74	Russ Martin (26/3900)	1.00
75	Mickey Mantle (173/25950)	5.00
76	Mickey Mantle (121/18150)	5.00
77	Mickey Mantle (146/21900)	5.00
78	Mickey Mantle (94/14100)	5.00
79	Mike Piazza (35/5250)	1.50
80	Mike Piazza (112/16800)	1.50
81	Derek Jeter (10/1500)	4.00
82	Derek Jeter (78/1700)	4.00
83	Derek Jeter (183/27450)	4.00
84	Dontrelle Willis (14/2100)	.75
85	Dontrelle Willis (142/21300)	.75
86	Dontrelle Willis (2/300)	2.00
87	Bobby Crosby (22/3300)	.50
88	Bobby Crosby (64/9600)	.50
89	Ryan Howard (22/3300)	3.00
90	Ryan Howard (63/9450)	3.00
91	Curt Schilling (21/3150)	1.50
92	Curt Schilling (203/30450)	1.50
93	Andruw Jones (52/7800)	1.50
94	Andruw Jones (128/19200)	1.50
95	Andruw Jones (11/1650)	1.50
96	Hideki Matsui (23/3450)	2.50
97	Hideki Matsui (116/17400)	2.50
98	Hideki Matsui (192/28800)	2.50
99	David Wright (27/4050)	2.50
100	David Wright (102/15300)	2.50

101	David Wright (42/6300)	2.50
102	David Wright (17/2550)	2.50
103	David Ortiz (75/11250)	2.00
104	David Wright (47/7050)	2.00
105	David Ortiz (11/1650)	2.00
106	Frank Thomas (38/5700)	1.50
107	Frank Thomas (101/15150)	1.50
108	Craig Biggio (40/6000)	1.00
109	Miguel Cabrera (33/4950)	2.00
110	Miguel Cabrera (116/17400)	2.00
111	Vernon Wells (12/1800)	1.00
112	Michael Young (24/3600)	1.00
113	Michael Young (40/6000)	1.00
114	Joe Mauer (144/21600)	1.50
115	Gary Sheffield (34/5100)	1.00
116	Jim Edmonds (42/6300)	1.00
117	Jorge Posada (19/2850)	1.00
118	Jorge Posada (23/3450)	1.00
119	Pat Burrell (32/4800)	.75
120	Adam Dunn (40/6000)	1.00
121	Johnny Damon (35/5250)	2.00
122	Scott Rolen (34/5100)	1.50
123	Paul Konerko (6/900)	3.00
124	Roy Halladay (22/3300)	1.50
125	Grady Sizemore (22/3300)	1.50
126	Grady Sizemore (37/5550)	1.50
127	John Smoltz (24/3600)	1.00
128	Jeff Kent (29/4350)	.75
129	Billy Wagner (38/5700)	.50
130	Mark Prior (18/2700)	.75
131	Eric Chavez (32/4800)	.75
132	Jimmy Rollins (41/6150)	1.50
133	Manny Ramirez (7/1050)	1.50
134	Manny Ramirez (45/6750)	1.50
135	Manny Ramirez (144/21600)	1.50
136	Derrek Lee (46/6900)	1.50
137	Derrek Lee (107/16050)	1.50
138	Tom Glavine (14/2100)	1.00
139	Tom Glavine (20/3000)	1.00
140	Jose Reyes (17/2550)	2.00
141	Pedro Martinez (15/2250)	1.50
142	Pedro Martinez (208/31200)	1.50
143	Mark Teixeira (43/6450)	1.00
144	Jake Peavy (13/1950)	1.00
145	Carlos Lee (32/4800)	.75
146	Josh Beckett (16/2400)	.75
147	Johan Santana (20/3000)	2.00
148	Todd Helton (33/4950)	1.50
149	Mariano Rivera (43/6450)	1.50
150	Travis Hafner (33/4950)	1.50
151	Jason Bay (24/3600)	1.00
152	Bobby Abreu (30/4500)	1.00
153	Mike Mussina (13/1950)	1.00
154	Miguel Tejada (34/5100)	1.00
155	Miguel Tejada (150/22500)	1.00
156	Robinson Cano (14/2100)	1.50
157	Robinson Cano (34/5100)	1.50
158	Ryan Zimmerman (23/3450)	1.00
159	Carlos Beltran (16/2400)	1.50
160	Carlos Beltran (17/2550)	1.50
161	Roger Clemens (18/2700)	3.00
162	Roger Clemens (218/32700)	3.00
163	Mickey Mantle (52/7800)	5.00
164	Mickey Mantle (130/19500)	5.00
165	Mickey Mantle (188/28200)	5.00
166	Mickey Mantle (132/19800)	5.00
167	Mickey Mantle (42/6300)	5.00
168	Mickey Mantle (97/14550)	5.00
169	Mickey Mantle (127/19050)	5.00
170	Daisuke Matsuzaka RC	30.00
171	Daisuke Matsuzaka RC	30.00
172	Daisuke Matsuzaka RC	30.00
173	Delmon Young (RC)	5.00
174	Delmon Young (RC)	5.00
175	Delmon Young (RC)	5.00
176	Andrew Miller RC	5.00
177	Andrew Miller RC	5.00
178	Andrew Miller RC	5.00
179	Troy Tulowitzki (RC)	8.00
180	Troy Tulowitzki (RC)	8.00
181	Troy Tulowitzki (RC)	8.00
182	Josh Fields (RC)	5.00
183	Josh Fields (RC)	5.00
184	Josh Fields (RC)	5.00
185	Jeff Baker (RC)	5.00
186	Jeff Baker (RC)	5.00
187	Jeff Baker (RC)	5.00
188	Philip Humber (RC)	5.00
189	Philip Humber (RC)	5.00
190	Philip Humber (RC)	5.00
191	Kevin Kouzmanoff (RC)	5.00
192	Kevin Kouzmanoff (RC)	5.00
193	Kevin Kouzmanoff (RC)	5.00

Black

Stars: 2-3X
Production 29 Sets

Red
No Pricing
Production One Set

Printing Plates
No Pricing
Production one set per color

A-Rod Road to 500

NM/M
Common A-Rod (101-125): 3.00
Inserted 2:Box

A-Rod Road to 500 Auto.
NM/M
Production One Set 3.00

Milestone Autographs
NM/M
Common Auto.: 10.00
Black: 1-1.5X
Production 40 Sets
Red: No Pricing
Production One Set
AJ	Andruw Jones/100	50.00
AR	Alex Rodriguez/100	180.00
BP	Brandon Phillips	15.00
BR	Brian Roberts	15.00
CJ	Conor Jackson	15.00
DO	David Ortiz	60.00
DW	David Wright	60.00
GA	Garrett Atkins	15.00
GS	Gary Sheffield/100	35.00
HS	Huston Street/200	20.00
JF	Jeff Francoeur	40.00
JG	Jason Giambi/100	50.00
JJG	Jonny Gomes	15.00
JL	Julio Lugo	15.00
JP	Jonathan Papelbon	40.00
JR	Jose Reyes/200	40.00
JS	Jeremy Sowers	10.00
KJ	Kenji Johjima	35.00
KM	Kendry Morales	15.00
LM	Lastings Milledge	15.00
MK	Matthew Kemp	15.00
MN	Mike Napoli	15.00
MP	Martin Prado	15.00
NS	Nick Swisher	15.00
RH	Ryan Howard/200	75.00
RP	Ronny Paulino	10.00
TH	Travis Hafner	15.00
VG	Vladimir Guerrero/100	50.00
WP	Wily Mo Pena/100	20.00

Rookie Autographs
NM/M
Common Auto.: 10.00
Black: 2-3X
Production 40 Sets
Red: No Pricing
Production One Set
AL	Adam Lind	10.00
AM	Andrew Miller	25.00
DM	David Murphy	10.00
HG	Hector Gimenez	10.00
JA	Joaquin Arias	10.00
KK	Kevin Kouzmanoff	15.00
MB	Michael Bourn	15.00
MM	Miguel Montero	15.00
SR	Shawn Riggans	10.00
TT	Troy Tulowitzki	20.00

2007 Topps Opening Day

NM/M
Complete Set (220): 35.00
Common Player: .15
Pack (6): 1.25
Box (36): 40.00
1	Bobby Abreu	.25
2	Mike Piazza	.75
3	Jake Westbrook	.15
4	Zachary Duke	.15
5	David Wright	1.00
6	Adrian Gonzalez	.25
7	Mickey Mantle	3.00
8	Bill Hall	.25
9	Robinson Cano	.25
10	Dontrelle Willis	.25
11	J.D. Drew	.25
12	Paul Konerko	.25
13	Austin Kearns	.15
14	Mike Lowell	.15
15	Magglio Ordonez	.15
16	Rafael Furcal	.25
17	Matt Cain	.25
18	Craig Monroe	.15
19	Matt Holliday	.25
20	Edgar Renteria	.25
21	Mark Buehrle	.15
22	Carlos Quentin	.15
23	C.C. Sabathia	.25
24	Nicholas Markakis	.25
25	Chipper Jones	.50
26	Jason Giambi	.40
27	Barry Zito	.25
28	Jake Peavy	.25
29	Hank Blalock	.25
30	Johnny Damon	.50
31	Chad Tracy	.15
32	Nick Swisher	.25
33	Willy Taveras	.15
34	Chuck James	.25
35	Carlos Delgado	.40
36	Livan Hernandez	.15
37	Freddy Garcia	.15
38	Bronson Arroyo	.15
39	Jack Wilson	.15
40	Dan Uggla	.25
41	Chris Carpenter	.50
42	Jorge Posada	.25
43	Joe Mauer	.40
44	Corey Patterson	.15
45	Chien-Ming Wang	.50
46	Derek Jeter	1.50
47	Carlos Beltran	.50
48	Jim Edmonds	.25
49	Jeremy Sowers	.25
50	Randy Johnson	.50
51	Jered Weaver	.25
52	Josh Barfield	.15
53	Scott Rolen	.40
54	Ryan Shealy	.15
55	Freddy Sanchez	.15
56	Javier Vazquez	.25
57	Jeremy Bonderman	.25
58	Miguel Cabrera	.50
59	Kazuo Matsui	.15
60	Curt Schilling	.50
61	Alfonso Soriano	.50
62	Orlando Hernandez	.15
63	Joe Blanton	.15
64	Aramis Ramirez	.25
65	Ben Sheets	.25
66	Jimmy Rollins	.25
67	Mark Loretta	.15
68	Cole Hamels	.25
69	Albert Pujols	1.50
70	Moises Alou	.25
71	Mark Teahen	.15
72	Roy Halladay	.25
73	Cory Sullivan	.15
74	Frank Thomas	.50
75	Ryan Howard	.25
76	Rocco Baldelli	.25
77	Manny Ramirez	.25
78	Ray Durham	.15
79	Gary Sheffield	.40
80	Jay Gibbons	.15
81	Todd Helton	.40
82	Gary Matthews	.15
83	Brandon Inge	.15
84	Jonathan Papelbon	.40
85	John Smoltz	.25
86	Chone Figgins	.15
87	Hideki Matsui	.75
88	Carlos Lee	.25
89	Jose Reyes	.75
90	Lyle Overbay	.15
91	Johan Santana	.50
92	Ian Kinsler	.25
93	Scott Kazmir	.25
94	Hanley Ramirez	.40
95	Greg Maddux	1.00
96	Johnny Estrada	.15
97	B.J. Upton	.25
98	Francisco Liriano	.25
99	Chase Utley	.50
100	Preston Wilson	.15
101	Marcus Giles	.15
102	Jeff Kent	.25
103	Grady Sizemore	.50
104	Ken Griffey Jr.	1.00
105	Garret Anderson	.15
106	Brian McCann	.25
107	Jon Garland	.15
108	Troy Glaus	.25
109	Brandon Webb	.25
110	Jason Schmidt	.25
111	Ramon Hernandez	.15
112	Justin Morneau	.50
113	Mike Cameron	.15

114	Andruw Jones	.40
115	Russell Martin	.15
116	Vernon Wells	.25
117	Orlando Hudson	.15
118	Derek Lowe	.15
119	Alex Rodriguez	1.50
120	Chad Billingsley	.15
121	Kenji Johjima	.15
122	Nick Johnson	.15
123	Danny Haren	.25
124	Mark Teixeira	.40
125	Jeff Francoeur	.25
126	Ted Lilly	.15
127	Jhonny Peralta	.15
128	Aaron Harang	.15
129	Ryan Zimmerman	.25
130	Jermaine Dye	.15
131	Orlando Cabrera	.25
132	Juan Pierre	.15
133	Brian Giles	.25
134	Jason Bay	.25
135	David Ortiz	.50
136	Chris Capuano	.15
137	Carlos Zambrano	.25
138	Luis Gonzalez	.15
139	Jeff Weaver	.15
140	Lance Berkman	.15
141	Raul Ibanez	.15
142	Jim Thome	.40
143	Jose Contreras	.15
144	David Eckstein	.15
145	Adam Dunn	.40
146	Alex Rios	.15
147	Garrett Atkins	.25
148	A.J. Burnett	.25
149	Jeremy Hermida	.15
150	Conor Jackson	.15
151	Adrian Beltre	.25
152	Torii Hunter	.25
153	Andrew Miller RC	.50
154	Ichiro Suzuki	1.00
155	Mark Redman	.15
156	Paul LoDuca	.15
157	Xavier Nady	.15
158	Stephen Drew	.25
159	Eric Chavez	.25
160	Pedro Martinez	.50
161	Derrek Lee	.40
162	David DeJesus	.15
163	Troy Tulowitzki (RC)	.25
164	Vinny Rottino (RC)	.25
165	Philip Humber (RC)	.25
166	Jerry Owens (RC)	.25
167	Ubaldo Jimenez (RC)	1.00
168	Michael Young	.25
169	Ryan Braun (RC)	.25
170	Kevin Kouzmanoff (RC)	.25
171	Oswaldo Navarro RC	.25
172	Miguel Montero (RC)	.25
173	Roy Oswalt	.25
174	Shane Youman RC	.25
175	Josh Fields (RC)	.25
176	Adam Lind (RC)	.25
177	Miguel Tejada	.40
178	Delwyn Young (RC)	.25
179	Scott Moore (RC)	.25
180	Fred Lewis (RC)	.25
181	Glen Perkins (RC)	.25
182	Vladimir Guerrero	.50
183	Drew Anderson (RC)	.25
184	Jeff Salazar (RC)	.25
185	Tom Gordon	.15
186	The Bird	.15
187	Justin Verlander	.40
188	Delmon Young (RC)	.50
189	Homer	.15
190	Wally the Green Monster	.15
191	Southpaw	.15
192	Dinger	.15
193	Carl Crawford	.15
194	Slider	.15
195	Gapper	.15
196	Paws	.15
197	Billy the Marlin	.15
198	Ivan Rodriguez	.15
199	Slugger	.15
200	Junction Jack	.15
201	Bernie the Brewer	.15
202	Travis Hafner	.40
203	Stomper	.15
204	Mr. Met	.15
205	The Moose	.15
206	Phillie Phanatic	.15
207	Prince Fielder	.50
208	Julio Lugo	.15
209	Pirate Parrot	.15
210	Joel Zumaya	.25
211	Swinging Friar	.15
212	Jay Payton	.15
213	Lou Seal	.15
214	Fredbird	.15
215	Screech	.15
216	TC Bear	.15
217	Andre Ethier	.15
218	Ervin Santana	.15
219	Melvin Mora	.15
220	Checklist	.15

Autographs

		NM/M
	Common Auto.:	10.00
EF	Emiliano Fruto	10.00
HK	Howie Kendrick	25.00
JT	Jordan Tata	25.00
JM	Juan Morillo	10.00
MC	Matt Cain	20.00
MK	Matthew Kemp	25.00
MN	Mike Napoli	15.00

OH	Orlando Hudson	15.00
RM	Robert Mackowiak	10.00
SS	Shannon Stewart	10.00

A-Rod Road to 500

	NM/M
Common A-Rod (76-100):	3.00

A-Rod Road to 500 Autograph
Production One Set

Diamond Stars

(image)

		NM/M
	Common Player:	.25
1	Ryan Howard	1.50
2	Alfonso Soriano	.75
3	Alex Rodriguez	1.50
4	David Ortiz	.75
5	Raul Ibanez	.25
6	Matt Holliday	.50
7	Delmon Young	.50
8	Derrick Turnbow	.25
9	Freddy Sanchez	.25
10	Troy Glaus	.50
11	A.J. Pierzynski	.25
12	Dontrelle Willis	.25
13	Justin Morneau	.75
14	Jose Reyes	1.00
15	Derek Jeter	1.50
16	Ivan Rodriguez	.25
17	Jay Payton	.25
18	Adrian Gonzalez	.25
19	David Eckstein	.25
20	Chipper Jones	.75
21	Aramis Ramirez	.50
22	David Wright	1.00
23	Mark Teixeira	.50
24	Stephen Drew	.50
25	Ichiro Suzuki	1.00

Movie Gallery

(image)

	NM/M
Alex Rodriguez	1.00

Puzzle

(image)

		NM/M
	Complete Puzzle:	10.00
	Common Player:	.25
1	Adam Dunn	.25
2	Adam Dunn	.25
3	Miguel Tejada	.25
4	Miguel Tejada	.25
5	Hanley Ramirez	.25
6	Hanley Ramirez	.25
7	Johan Santana	.50
8	Johan Santana	.50
9	Brandon Webb	.25
10	Brandon Webb	.25
11	David Wright	.75

12	David Wright	.75
13	Alex Rodriguez	.75
14	Alex Rodriguez	.75
15	Ryan Howard	.75
16	Ryan Howard	.75
17	Albert Pujols	1.00
18	Albert Pujols	1.00
19	Andruw Jones	.50
20	Andruw Jones	.50
21	Alfonso Soriano	.50
22	Alfonso Soriano	.50
23	Vladimir Guerrero	.50
24	Vladimir Guerrero	.50
25	David Ortiz	.50
26	David Ortiz	.50
27	Ichiro Suzuki	.75
28	Ichiro Suzuki	.75

2007 Topps Sterling

	NM/M
Common Mantle (1-24):	12.00
Common Bonds (25-48):	10.00
Common Ichiro (49-56):	8.00
Common Yastrzemski (57-64):	8.00
Common David Wright (65-76):	8.00
Common Clemente (77-81):	15.00
Common Johan Santana (82-89):	
Common Morneau (90-101):	6.00
Common R. Jackson (102-109):	6.00
Common Clemens (110-117):	8.00
Common T. Williams (118-122):	10.00
Common Berra (123-130):	8.00
Common Matsui (131-135):	8.00
Common R. Howard (136-143):	8.00
Common Gwynn (144-151):	8.00
Common Ortiz (152-159):	8.00
Common Seaver (160-167):	6.00
Common Pujols (168-175):	10.00
Common Musial (176-183):	8.00
Common Wang (184-191):	10.00
Common Sandberg (192-199):	8.00
Common Ryan (200-207):	15.00
Common Gibson (208-215):	6.00
Common Maris (216-220):	8.00
Common Ramirez (221-228):	8.00
Common Schmidt (229-236):	8.00
Common A-Rod (237-244):	10.00
Common Matsuzaka (245-249):	15.00
Common DiMaggio (250-254):	10.00

Production 250 Sets

1-24	Mickey Mantle	12.00
25-48	Barry Bonds	10.00
49-56	Ichiro Suzuki	8.00
57-64	Carl Yastrzemski	8.00
65-76	David Wright	8.00
77-81	Roberto Clemente	15.00
82-89	Johan Santana	8.00
90-101	Justin Morneau	6.00
102-109	Reggie Jackson	6.00
110-117	Roger Clemens	8.00
118-122	Ted Williams	10.00
123-130	Yogi Berra	8.00
131-135	Hideki Matsui	8.00
136-143	Ryan Howard	8.00
144-151	Tony Gwynn	8.00
152-159	David Ortiz	8.00
160-167	Tom Seaver	6.00
168-175	Albert Pujols	10.00
176-183	Stan Musial	8.00
184-191	Chien-Ming Wang	10.00
192-199	Ryne Sandberg	8.00
200-207	Nolan Ryan	15.00
208-215	Bob Gibson	6.00
216-220	Roger Maris	8.00
221-228	Manny Ramirez	8.00
229-236	Mike Schmidt	8.00
237-244	Alex Rodriguez	10.00
245-249	Daisuke Matsuzaka RC	15.00
250-254	Joe DiMaggio	10.00

Framed Burgundy

	NM/M
Burgundy:	3-4X

Production 14 Sets

Cherry Wood
Production One Set

Framed Gold

Gold:	4-5X

Production Nine Sets

Sterling Silver
Production One Set

White Suede

White Suede:	1-2X

Production 50 Sets

Bat Barrels
No Pricing
Production One Set

Career Stats Relics Autographs Quad

		NM/M

Production 10 Sets

1-5	Carl Yastrzemski	75.00
6-16	David Wright	120.00
17-22	Johan Santana	100.00
23-33	Justin Morneau	50.00
34-39	Reggie Jackson	60.00
40	Roger Clemens	100.00
41-48	Yogi Berra	120.00
50-56	Ryan Howard	100.00

57-62	Tony Gwynn	100.00
63-66	David Ortiz	100.00
67-73	Tom Seaver	80.00
74	Albert Pujols	300.00
75-80	Stan Musial	120.00
81-86	Chien-Ming Wang	200.00
87-92	Ryne Sandberg	120.00
93-98	Nolan Ryan	150.00
99-104	Bob Gibson	60.00
105-108	Manny Ramirez	75.00
109-113	Mike Schmidt	80.00
114-120	Alex Rodriguez	250.00

Career Stats Relics Auto. Triples

	NM/M

Production 10 Sets

1	Barry Bonds	250.00
2-7	Carl Yastrzemski	75.00
8-17	David Wright	100.00
18-24	Johan Santana	75.00
25-33	Justin Morneau	50.00
34	Justin Morneau	60.00
35-40	Reggie Jackson	60.00
41	Roger Clemens	100.00
42-48	Yogi Berra	100.00
49-54	Ryan Howard	100.00
55-61	Tony Gwynn	100.00
62-64	David Ortiz	80.00
65-70	Tom Seaver	80.00
71	Albert Pujols	250.00
72-77	Stan Musial	100.00
78-83	Chien-Ming Wang	200.00
84-89	Ryne Sandberg	100.00
90-95	Nolan Ryan	120.00
96-102	Bob Gibson	60.00
103-108	Manny Ramirez	60.00
109-113	Mike Schmidt	80.00
114-120	Alex Rodriguez	250.00

Career Stats Relics Five

	NM/M

Production 10 Sets

1-10	Mickey Mantle	180.00
11-21	Barry Bonds	50.00
22-25	Ichiro Suzuki	100.00
26	Carl Yastrzemski	50.00
27	David Wright	75.00
28-30	Roberto Clemente	140.00
31	Justin Morneau	25.00
32-34	Roger Clemens	40.00
35-37	Ted Williams	100.00
38	Yogi Berra	50.00
39	Hideki Matsui	75.00
40	Hideki Matsui	75.00
41	Ryan Howard	50.00
42	Tony Gwynn	40.00
43	David Ortiz	50.00
44	Tom Seaver	40.00
45-48	Albert Pujols	60.00
49	Chien-Ming Wang	50.00
50	Ryne Sandberg	40.00
51	Nolan Ryan	80.00
52	Bob Gibson	40.00
53	Roger Maris	40.00
54	Roger Maris	80.00
55	Manny Ramirez	40.00
56	Manny Ramirez	40.00
57	Mike Schmidt	60.00
58	Alex Rodriguez	100.00
59	Daisuke Matsuzaka	80.00
60	Joe DiMaggio	125.00

Career Stats Relics Quad

	NM/M

Production 10 Sets

1-10	Mickey Mantle	180.00
11	Mickey Mantle	50.00
12-21	Barry Bonds	50.00
22	Barry Bonds	100.00
23-25	Ichiro Suzuki	50.00
26	Ichiro Suzuki	50.00
27	Ichiro Suzuki	75.00
28	Carl Yastrzemski	140.00
29	David Wright	140.00
30	Roberto Clemente	140.00
31	Roberto Clemente	25.00
32	Johan Santana	40.00
33	Justin Morneau	40.00
34	Reggie Jackson	40.00
35	Roger Clemens	100.00
36	Roger Clemens	100.00
37	Ted Williams	100.00
38	Ted Williams	50.00
39	Hideki Matsui	75.00
40	Hideki Matsui	75.00
41	Ryan Howard	40.00
42	David Ortiz	40.00
43	David Ortiz	50.00
44	Tom Seaver	50.00
45-48	Albert Pujols	60.00
49	Stan Musial	50.00
50	Ryne Sandberg	75.00
51	Nolan Ryan	40.00
52	Bob Gibson	40.00
53	Roger Maris	80.00
54	Roger Maris	80.00
55	Manny Ramirez	75.00
56	Manny Ramirez	75.00
57	Mike Schmidt	80.00
58	Alex Rodriguez	100.00
59	Daisuke Matsuzaka	100.00
60	Joe DiMaggio	100.00

Career Stats Relics Six

	NM/M

Production 10 Sets

1-10	Mickey Mantle	180.00
11-20	Barry Bonds	50.00
21-24	Ichiro Suzuki	120.00
25	Carl Yastrzemski	60.00
26	David Wright	80.00
27-29	Roberto Clemente	160.00
30	Johan Santana	30.00
31	Justin Morneau	30.00
32	Reggie Jackson	50.00
33-35	Roger Clemens	50.00
36-39	Ted Williams	125.00
39	Yogi Berra	60.00
40	Hideki Matsui	80.00
41	Tony Gwynn	50.00
42	David Ortiz	60.00
43-45	Albert Pujols	60.00
46	Stan Musial	60.00
47	Chien-Ming Wang	80.00
48	Ryne Sandberg	60.00
49	Nolan Ryan	80.00
50	Bob Gibson	50.00
51-53	Roger Maris	80.00
54-56	Manny Ramirez	50.00
57	Mike Schmidt	75.00
58	Alex Rodriguez	100.00
59	Daisuke Matsuzaka	120.00
60	Joe DiMaggio	125.00

Career Stats Relics Triple

	NM/M

Production 10 Sets

1-11	Mickey Mantle	125.00
12-22	Barry Bonds	40.00
23-27	Ichiro Suzuki	100.00
28	Carl Yastrzemski	40.00
29	David Wright	50.00
30-31	Roberto Clemente	100.00
32	Justin Morneau	25.00
33	Reggie Jackson	30.00
34-36	Roger Clemens	40.00
37-38	Ted Williams	80.00
39	Yogi Berra	40.00
40-41	Hideki Matsui	60.00
42	Tony Gwynn	40.00
43-45	David Ortiz	50.00
46	Tom Seaver	40.00
47-49	Albert Pujols	40.00
50	Stan Musial	50.00
51	Ryne Sandberg	40.00
52	Nolan Ryan	60.00
53	Bob Gibson	30.00
54-56	Roger Maris	75.00
57-58	Mike Schmidt	65.00
59	Daisuke Matsuzaka	80.00
60-64	Joe DiMaggio	100.00

Cut Signatures
No Pricing
Production One Set

Jumbo Swatch

No Pricing	
Production 10 Sets	
Autographs:	No Pricing
Production 10 Sets	

Letter Patch
Production one per letter
Total print run listed

Moments Relics Autographs Eight
No Pricing
Production 10 Sets

Moments Relics Autographs Quad

		NM/M

Production 10 Sets

1	Barry Bonds	250.00
2-9	Carl Yastrzemski	75.00
10-20	David Wright	120.00
21	Johan Santana	100.00
22	Johan Santana	28.00
23-27	Johan Santana	100.00
28-38	Justin Morneau	50.00
39-46	Reggie Jackson	50.00
47-48	Roger Clemens	100.00
50-55	Yogi Berra	120.00
56-63	Ryan Howard	100.00
64-70	Tony Gwynn	100.00
71-74	David Ortiz	100.00
75-81	Tom Seaver	80.00
82	Albert Pujols	300.00
83-89	Stan Musial	120.00
90-97	Chien-Ming Wang	200.00
98-104	Ryne Sandberg	120.00
105-112	Nolan Ryan	150.00
113-120	Bob Gibson	60.00
121-128	Manny Ramirez	75.00
129-133	Mike Schmidt	80.00
134-140	Alex Rodriguez	250.00

Moments Relics Autographs Triple

		NM/M

Production 10 Sets

1	Barry Bonds	250.00
2-9	Carl Yastrzemski	75.00
10-20	David Wright	100.00
21-27	Johan Santana	75.00
28-38	Justin Morneau	50.00
39-45	Reggie Jackson	60.00
46-47	Roger Clemens	100.00
48-55	Yogi Berra	100.00
56-62	Ryan Howard	100.00
63-70	Tony Gwynn	100.00
71-72	David Ortiz	80.00

Moments Relics Eight

	NM/M

Production 10 Sets

1-2	Mickey Mantle	300.00
3-4	Barry Bonds	200.00
11-12	Hideki Matsui	150.00

Moments Relics Five

	NM/M

Production 10 Sets

1-15	Mickey Mantle	180.00
16-30	Barry Bonds	50.00
31	Ichiro Suzuki	100.00
32	Ichiro Suzuki	100.00
33	Ichiro Suzuki	100.00
34	Ichiro Suzuki	100.00
35	Carl Yastrzemski	50.00
36	David Wright	75.00
37-39	Roberto Clemente	140.00
40	Johan Santana	30.00
41	Justin Morneau	25.00
42-44	Roger Clemens	40.00
45-49	Ted Williams	100.00
50	Ryan Howard	50.00
51	David Ortiz	50.00
52	Tom Seaver	40.00
53-56	Albert Pujols	60.00
57	Stan Musial	50.00
58	Chien-Ming Wang	75.00
59	Nolan Ryan	80.00
60	Bob Gibson	50.00
61-63	Roger Maris	80.00
64-65	Manny Ramirez	50.00
66	Mike Schmidt	60.00
67	Alex Rodriguez	80.00
68-70	Daisuke Matsuzaka	80.00
71	Joe DiMaggio	125.00

Moments Relics Quad

	NM/M

Production 10 Sets

1-15	Mickey Mantle	180.00
16-17	Mickey Mantle	50.00
18-30	Barry Bonds	50.00
31-32	Barry Bonds	100.00
33-34	Ichiro Suzuki	100.00
35	Ichiro Suzuki	50.00
36	Ichiro Suzuki	75.00
37	Ichiro Suzuki	140.00
38	Carl Yastrzemski	50.00
39	David Wright	60.00
40-41	Roberto Clemente	125.00
42	Johan Santana	30.00
43	Justin Morneau	25.00
44-46	Roger Clemens	40.00
47-48	Ted Williams	100.00
50-51	Hideki Matsui	75.00
53-54	David Ortiz	50.00
55	Tom Seaver	40.00
56-58	Albert Pujols	50.00
59	Stan Musial	40.00
60	Bob Gibson	40.00
61-62	Roger Maris	50.00
63-64	Mike Schmidt	75.00
65-68	Daisuke Matsuzaka	80.00
69-71	Joe DiMaggio	125.00

Moments Relics Six

	NM/M

Production 10 Sets

1-15	Mickey Mantle	180.00
16-29	Barry Bonds	50.00
30-33	Ichiro Suzuki	100.00
34	David Wright	80.00
35-37	Roberto Clemente	160.00
38	Johan Santana	30.00
39	Justin Morneau	30.00
40	Reggie Jackson	50.00
41-45	Roger Clemens	50.00
46-48	Ted Williams	125.00
49-50	Hideki Matsui	80.00
51	Ron Howard	50.00
52-55	David Ortiz	60.00
56-60	Albert Pujols	50.00
61	Chien-Ming Wang	80.00
62	Ryne Sanberg	50.00
63	Nolan Ryan	50.00
64-66	Roger Maris	80.00
67	Mike Schmidt	75.00
68	Alex Rodriguez	100.00
69-70	Daisuke Matsuzaka	80.00
71	Joe DiMaggio	125.00

Moments Relics Triple

	NM/M

Production 10 Sets

1-17	Mickey Mantle	125.00
18-32	Barry Bonds	40.00
33-36	Ichiro Suzuki	100.00
37	David Wright	50.00
38-39	Roberto Clemente	100.00
40	Justin Morneau	25.00
41	Reggie Jackson	50.00
42-44	Roger Clemens	40.00
45-46	Ted Williams	50.00
47	Yogi Berra	50.00
48-49	Hideki Matsui	60.00

50	Tony Gwynn	40.00
51-54	David Ortiz	50.00
55	Tom Seaver	40.00
56-58	Albert Pujols	50.00
59	Stan Musial	50.00
60	Bob Gibson	30.00
61-62	Roger Maris	75.00
63	Mike Schmidt	65.00
64-67	Daisuke Matsuzaka	80.00
68-72	Joe DiMaggio	100.00

Stardom Relics Autographs Eight
No Pricing
Production 10 Sets

Stardom Relics Autographs Quad
NM/M
Production 10 Sets

1	Barry Bonds	250.00
2-8	Carl Yastrzemski	75.00
9-19	David Wright	120.00
20-27	Johan Santana	100.00
28-38	Justin Morneau	50.00
39-45	Reggie Jackson	60.00
46-47	Roger Clemens	100.00
48-54	Yogi Berra	120.00
56-63	Ryan Howard	100.00
64-70	Tony Gwynn	100.00
71-74	David Ortiz	100.00
75-81	Tom Seaver	80.00
82	Albert Pujols	300.00
83-89	Stan Musial	120.00
90-97	Chien-Ming Wang	200.00
98-104	Ryne Sandberg	120.00
105-111	Nolan Ryan	150.00
112-118	Bob Gibson	60.00
119-125	Manny Ramirez	75.00
126-132	Mike Schmidt	80.00
133-140	Alex Rodriguez	250.00

Stardom Relics Autographs Triple
NM/M

1	Barry Bonds	250.00
2-9	Carl Yastrzemski	75.00
10-20	David Wright	100.00
21-27	Johan Santana	75.00
28-38	Justin Morneau	50.00
39-46	Reggie Jackson	60.00
47-48	Roger Clemens	100.00
49-55	Yogi Berra	100.00
56-62	Ryan Howard	100.00
63-69	Tony Gwynn	100.00
70-72	David Ortiz	80.00
73	Tom Seaver	80.00
74	David Ortiz	80.00
75-79	Tom Seaver	80.00
80	Albert Pujols	250.00
81-88	Stan Musial	100.00
89-95	Chien-Ming Wang	200.00
96-103	Ryne Sandberg	100.00
104-111	Nolan Ryan	120.00
112-118	Bob Gibson	60.00
120-126	Manny Ramirez	60.00
127-133	Mike Schmidt	80.00
134-140	Alex Rodriguez	250.00

Stardom Relics Eight
NM/M
Production 10 Sets

1-2	Mickey Mantle	350.00
3-4	Barry Bonds	200.00
10-11	Hideki Matsui	125.00
14-15	David Ortiz	50.00

Stardom Relics Five
NM/M
Production 10 Sets

1-14	Mickey Mantle	180.00
15-29	Barry Bonds	50.00
30-33	Ichiro Suzuki	100.00
34	Carl Yastrzemski	50.00
35	David Wright	75.00
36-38	Roberto Clemente	140.00
39	Johan Santana	30.00
40	Justin Morneau	25.00
41	Reggie Jackson	40.00
42-44	Roger Clemens	50.00
45-47	Ted Williams	100.00
48	Yogi Berra	50.00
49-50	Hideki Matsui	75.00
51	Ryan Howard	50.00
52	Tony Gwynn	40.00
53	David Ortiz	50.00
54-57	Albert Pujols	60.00
58	Chien-Ming Wang	75.00
59	Nolan Ryan	80.00
60	Bob Gibson	40.00
61-63	Roger Maris	80.00
64-65	Manny Ramirez	40.00
66	Mike Schmidt	60.00
67	Alex Rodriguez	100.00
68-70	Daisuke Matsuzaka	80.00
71	Joe DiMaggio	100.00

Stardom Relics Quad
NM/M
Production 10 Sets

1-17	Mickey Mantle	180.00
18-32	Barry Bonds	50.00
33-37	Ichiro Suzuki	100.00
38	Carl Yastrzemski	50.00
39-40	Roberto Clemente	125.00
41	Johan Santana	30.00
42-44	Roger Clemens	50.00
45-46	Ted Williams	100.00
47	Yogi Berra	50.00
48-49	Hideki Matsui	75.00
50	Ryan Howard	50.00
51	Tony Gwynn	40.00
52-54	David Ortiz	50.00
55	Tom Seaver	40.00
56-58	Albert Pujols	50.00
59	Chien-Ming Wang	75.00
60	Ryne Sandberg	40.00
61	Bob Gibson	40.00
62-63	Roger Maris	80.00
64	Alex Rodriguez	60.00
65-68	Daisuke Matsuzaka	80.00
69-71	Joe DiMaggio	100.00

Stardom Relics Six
NM/M
Production 10 Sets

1-14	Mickey Mantle	180.00
15-28	Barry Bonds	50.00
29-32	Ichiro Suzuki	120.00
33	David Wright	80.00
34-36	Roberto Clemente	160.00
37	Johan Santana	30.00
38	Justin Morneau	30.00
39	Reggie Jackson	50.00
40-44	Roger Clemens	50.00
45-47	Ted Williams	125.00
48-49	Hideki Matsui	60.00
50	Ryan Howard	60.00
51-54	David Ortiz	60.00
55-59	Albert Pujols	60.00
60	Chien-Ming Wang	80.00
61	Ryne Sandberg	50.00
62	Nolan Ryan	80.00
63-65	Roger Maris	80.00
66	Mike Schmidt	75.00
67	Alex Rodriguez	100.00
68-69	Daisuke Matsuzaka	120.00
70	Joe DiMaggio	125.00

Stardom Relics Triple
NM/M
Production 10 Sets

1-17	Mickey Mantle	125.00
18-32	Barry Bonds	40.00
33-37	Ichiro Suzuki	100.00
38	Carl Yastrzemski	50.00
39	David Wright	50.00
40-41	Roberto Clemente	100.00
42	Justin Morneau	25.00
43-45	Roger Clemens	40.00
46-47	Ted Williams	80.00
48	Yogi Berra	50.00
49-50	Hideki Matsui	60.00
51-54	David Ortiz	50.00
55	Tom Seaver	40.00
56-58	Albert Pujols	50.00
59	Stan Musial	40.00
60	Nolan Ryan	60.00
61	Bob Gibson	30.00
62-63	Roger Maris	75.00
64-67	Daisuke Matsuzaka	80.00
68-72	Joe DiMaggio	100.00

2007 Topps Triple Threads

NM/M

Complete Set (189):		
Common Player (1-125):		1.00
Production 1,350		
Common Auto. (126-189):		10.00
Production 99		
Pack (6):		100.00
Box (2):		200.00
1	Alex Rodriguez	4.00
2	Barry Zito	1.00
3	Corey Patterson	1.00
4	Roberto Clemente	5.00
5	David Wright	3.00
6	Dontrelle Willis	1.00
7	Mickey Mantle	8.00
8	Adam Dunn	1.50
9	Richie Ashburn	2.00
10	Ryan Howard	3.00
11	Miguel Tejada	1.50
12	Ernie Banks	4.00
13	Ken Griffey Jr.	3.00
14	Johnny Bench	3.00
15	Ichiro Suzuki	3.00
16	Gil Meche	1.00
17	Kazuo Matsui	1.00
18	Matt Holliday	2.00
19	Juan Pierre	1.00
20	Yogi Berra	3.00
21	Bill Hall	1.00
22	Wade Boggs	2.00
23	Jason Bay	1.50
24	Troy Glaus	1.50
25	Paul Konerko	1.50
26	Rod Carew	2.00
27	Jay Gibbons	1.00
28	Frank Thomas	3.00
29	Joe Mauer	1.50
30	Carlos Beltran	2.00
31	Frank Robinson	3.00
32	Bobby Abreu	1.50
33	Roy Oswalt	1.50
34	Edgar Renteria	1.50
35	Magglio Ordonez	1.50
36	Mike Piazza	2.00
37	Trevor Hoffman	1.50
38	Eddie Mathews	3.00
39	Albert Pujols	4.00
40	Dennis Eckersley	1.00
41	Andruw Jones	2.00
42	Alfonso Soriano	2.00
43	Bob Feller	2.00
44	J.D. Drew	1.00
45	Jason Schmidt	1.00
46	Vladimir Guerrero	2.00
47	Reggie Jackson	3.00
48	Lance Berkman	1.50
49	Michael Young	1.00
50	Carlton Fisk	2.00
51	Brandon Webb	1.50
52	Adrian Beltre	1.00
53	Hideki Matsui	2.50
54	Bronson Arroyo	1.00
55	Tony Gwynn	3.00
56	Ray Durham	1.00
57	Garrett Atkins	1.50
58	Nolan Ryan	4.00
59	Daisuke Matsuzaka RC	15.00
60	Todd Helton	1.50
61	Carl Crawford	1.50
62	Jake Peavy	2.00
63	Rafael Furcal	1.00
64	Joe Morgan	2.00
65	Greg Maddux	3.00
66	Luis Aparicio	1.00
67	Derrek Lee	1.50
68	Johnny Damon	1.50
69	Mike Lowell	1.50
70	Roger Maris	3.00
71	Vernon Wells	1.50
72	Monte Irvin	2.00
73	Jermaine Dye	1.50
74	Miguel Cabrera	2.50
75	Barry Bonds	4.00
76	Stan Musial	3.00
77	Derek Lowe	1.00
78	Don Mattingly	4.00
79	Lyle Overbay	1.00
80	Chien-Ming Wang	3.00
81	Carlos Zambrano	1.50
82	Kei Igawa RC	2.00
83	Cole Hamels	1.50
84	Gary Sheffield	1.50
85	Nick Johnson	1.00
86	Brooks Robinson	3.00
87	Curt Schilling	1.50
88	Ryne Sandberg	3.00
89	Mike Cameron	1.00
90	Mike Schmidt	3.00
91	Chris Carpenter	1.50
92	Scott Rolen	1.50
93	Rocco Baldelli	1.00
94	C.C. Sabathia	1.50
95	Jeff Francis	1.00
96	Ozzie Smith	3.00
97	Aramis Ramirez	1.50
98	Aaron Harang	1.00
99	Duke Snider	3.00
100	David Ortiz	2.00
101	Raul Ibanez	1.00
102	Bruce Sutter	1.00
103	Gary Matthews	1.00
104	Chipper Jones	3.00
105	Craig Biggio	1.50
106	Roy Halladay	1.50
107	Hoyt Wilhelm	1.00
108	Manny Ramirez	1.00
109	Randy Johnson	2.00
110	Carl Yastrzemski	3.00
111	Mark Teixeira	1.00
112	Derek Jeter	4.00
113	Stephen Drew	1.00
114	Darryl Strawberry	1.00
115	Travis Hafner	1.00
116	Torii Hunter	1.50
117	Jim Edmonds	1.50
118	John Smoltz	1.50
119	Bo Jackson	3.00
120	Roger Clemens	3.00
121	Pedro Martinez	2.00
122	Rickey Henderson	2.00
123	Ivan Rodriguez	1.50
124	Robin Yount	2.00
125	Johan Santana	2.00
126a	Robinson Cano/Auto.	30.00
126b	Robinson Cano/Auto.	30.00
127a	Jose Reyes/Auto.	60.00
127b	Jose Reyes/Auto.	60.00
128a	Justin Morneau/Auto.	25.00
128b	Justin Morneau/Auto.	25.00
129a	Curtis Granderson/ Auto.	30.00
129b	Curtis Granderson/ Auto.	30.00
130a	Justin Verlander/Auto.	30.00
130b	Justin Verlander/Auto.	30.00
131	Prince Fielder/Auto.	30.00
132a	Ryan Zimmerman/Auto.	25.00
132b	Ryan Zimmerman/Auto.	25.00
133	Mike Napoli/Auto.	15.00
134	Melky Cabrera/Auto.	15.00
135	Jonathan Papelbon/ Auto.	40.00
136a	Nicholas Markakis/ Auto.	30.00
136b	Nicholas Markakis/ Auto.	30.00
137	B.J. Upton/Auto.	25.00
138a	Joel Zumaya/Auto.	15.00
138b	Joel Zumaya/Auto.	15.00
140	Nick Swisher/Auto.	15.00
141	Andre Ethier/Auto.	25.00
142a	Jered Weaver/Auto.	25.00
142b	Jered Weaver/Auto.	25.00
143	Matt Cain/Auto.	20.00
144	Lastings Milledge/Auto.	20.00
145	Brian McCann/Auto.	30.00
146	Shin-Soo Choo/Auto.	15.00
147a	Dan Uggla/Auto.	20.00
147b	Dan Uggla/Auto.	20.00
148	Hanley Ramirez/Auto.	40.00
149	Russell Martin/Auto.	30.00
150	Francisco Liriano/Auto.	25.00
151	Anthony Reyes/Auto.	10.00
152	Josh Barfield/Auto.	10.00
153	Anibal Sanchez/Auto.	10.00
154	Jeremy Hermida/Auto.	15.00
155	Kendry Morales/Auto.	10.00
156	Matthew Kemp/Auto.	30.00
157	Freddy Sanchez/Auto.	15.00
158	Howie Kendrick/Auto.	20.00
159	Scott Thorman/Auto.	10.00
160	Franklin Gutierrez/Auto.	15.00
161	Jason Bartlett/Auto.	10.00
162	Chris Duncan/Auto.	30.00
163	Maicer Izturis/Auto.	10.00
164	Jason Botts/Auto.	10.00
165	Tony Gwynn Jr./Auto.	30.00
166	Jorge Cantu/Auto.	10.00
167	Adam Jones/Auto.	30.00
168	Edinson Volquez/Auto.	40.00
169	Joey Gathright/Auto.	10.00
170	Carlos Marmol/Auto.	30.00
171	Benjamin Zobrist/Auto.	10.00
172	Josh Willingham/Auto.	10.00
173	Brad Thompson/Auto.	10.00
174a	Chris Ray/Auto.	15.00
174b	Ervin Santana/Auto.	20.00
175	Ronny Paulino/Auto.	10.00
176	Tyler Johnson/Auto.	15.00
177	J.J. Hardy/Auto.	20.00
178	Adrian Gonzalez/Auto.	20.00
179	Scott Kazmir/Auto.	20.00
180	Juan Morillo/Auto. (RC)	10.00
181a	Shawn Riggans/ Auto. (RC)	10.00
181b	Shawn Riggans/ Auto. (RC)	10.00
182	Brian Stokes/Auto. (RC)	10.00
183	Delmon Young/ Auto. (RC)	15.00
184a	Troy Tulowitzki/ Auto.	30.00
184b	Troy Tulowitzki/ Auto.	30.00
185	Adam Lind/Auto. (RC)	15.00
186	David Murphy/ Auto.	10.00
187a	Philip Humber/ Auto.	10.00
187b	Philip Humber/ Auto.	10.00
188a	Andrew Miller/Auto. RC	15.00
188b	Andrew Miller/Auto. RC	15.00
189a	Glen Perkins/Auto. (RC)	10.00
189b	Glen Perkins/Auto. (RC)	10.00

Sepia
Sepia (1-125):	1-2X
Production 559 Sets	
Autos. (126-189):	1X
Production 75 Sets	

Emerald
Emerald (1-125):	2-3X
Production 239 Sets	
Autos. (126-189):	1-1.5X
Production 50 Sets	

Gold
Gold (1-125):	3-4X
Production 99 Sets	
Autos. (126-189):	1-2X
Production 25 Sets	

Sapphire
Sapphire (1-125):	4-8X
Production 25 Sets	
Autos. (126-189):	No Pricing
Production 10 Sets	

Platinum
Production One Set

Printing Plates
Production one set per color

All-Star Triple Patches
No Pricing
Production Nine Sets
Platinum: No Pricing
Production One Set

Bat-Barrels
No Pricing

Logo Man
No Pricing
Production One Set

Relics
NM/M

Common Player:	20.00
Production 36 Sets	
Sepia:	1X
Production 27 Sets	
Emerald:	1-1.5X
Production 18 Sets	
Gold:	No Pricing
Production Nine Sets	
Sapphire:	No Pricing
Production Three Sets	
Platinum:	No Pricing
Production One Set	

1-3	Carl Yastrzemski	30.00
4-9	Roberto Clemente	100.00
10-15	Alex Rodriguez	50.00
16-18	Ryan Howard	40.00
19-21	David Wright	40.00
22-24	Chien-Ming Wang	100.00
25-27	Ichiro Suzuki	60.00
28-30	Hideki Matsui	80.00
31-33	Luis Aparicio	20.00
34-36	Joe DiMaggio	125.00
37-39	Ted Williams	100.00
40-48	Mickey Mantle	125.00
49-51	David Ortiz	30.00
52-54	Albert Pujols	50.00
55-57	Justin Morneau	20.00
58-63	Nolan Ryan	50.00
64-66	Manny Ramirez	20.00
67-69	Roger Maris	80.00
70-72	Daisuke Matsuzaka	50.00
73-75	Brian Cashman	25.00
76-78	Ernie Banks	40.00
79-81	Stan Musial	50.00
82-84	Duke Snider	30.00
85-87	Yogi Berra	50.00
88-90	Harmon Killebrew	40.00
91-93	Joe Mauer	25.00
94-96	Alfonso Soriano	25.00
97-102	Reggie Jackson	35.00
103-105	Vladimir Guerrero	30.00
106-108	Pedro Martinez	30.00
109-111	Roger Clemens	40.00
112-114	Randy Johnson	25.00
115-117	Don Mattingly	50.00
118-120	Bill Dickey	50.00
121a	Barry Bonds	100.00
121b	Bruce Sutter	20.00
122a	Barry Bonds	100.00
122b	Bruce Sutter	20.00
123a	Barry Bonds	100.00
123b	Bruce Sutter	20.00
124-126	John F. Kennedy	200.00
127-129	Johnny Bench	35.00
130-132	Mark Teixeira	25.00
133-135	Johan Santana	30.00
136-138	Alex Rodriguez	50.00
139-141	Brooks Robinson	30.00
142-144	Rickey Henderson	30.00
145-147	Ozzie Smith	50.00
148-150	Chipper Jones	30.00

Relics Autographs
NM/M

Production 18 Sets	
Gold:	No Pricing
Production Nine Sets	
Sapphire:	No Pricing
Production Three Sets	
Platinum:	No Pricing
Production One Set	

1-3	Alex Rodriguez	275.00
4-6	Chien-Ming Wang	200.00
7-9	David Ortiz	100.00
10-12	Manny Ramirez	75.00
13-15	Johnny Damon	75.00
16-18	Miguel Tejada	50.00
19-21	Carl Crawford	40.00
22-24	Johan Santana	60.00
25-27	Francisco Liriano	30.00
28-30	Bob Feller	50.00
31-33	Vladimir Guerrero	75.00
34-36	Ernie Banks	150.00
37-39	Yogi Berra	100.00
40-42	Nolan Ryan	150.00
43-45	Ozzie Smith	100.00
46-48	David Wright	100.00
49-51	Albert Pujols	350.00
52-54	Ryan Howard	120.00
55-57	Don Mattingly	100.00
58-60	Brooks Robinson	60.00
61-63	Robin Yount	75.00
64-66	Mike Schmidt	60.00
67-69	Carl Yastrzemski	100.00
70-72	Wade Boggs	50.00
73-75	Andre Dawson	50.00
76-78	Reggie Jackson	100.00
79-81	Miguel Cabrera	60.00
82-84	Tom Seaver	60.00
85-87	Ralph Kiner	65.00
88-90	Chipper Jones	100.00
91-93	Andruw Jones	30.00
94-96	Dontrelle Willis	30.00
97-99	Roger Maris	85.00
100-102	Johnny Bench	85.00
103-106	Joe Morgan	75.00
106-108	Ryne Sandberg	120.00
109-111	Dwight Gooden	40.00
112-114	Johnny Podres	50.00
115-117	Monte Irvin	50.00
118-120	Orlando Cepeda	50.00
121-123	Bo Jackson	140.00
124-126	Gary Sheffield	60.00
127-129	Tom Glavine	100.00
130-132	Tony LaRussa	40.00
133-135	Jim Leyland	50.00
136-138	Joe Torre	50.00
139-141	Gary Carter	75.00
142-144	Roy Oswalt	50.00
145-147	Carlos Delgado	50.00
148-150	Jason Varitek	75.00
151-153	Bobby Abreu	50.00
154-156	Juan Marichal	60.00
157-159	Frank Robinson	65.00
160-162	Jorge Posada	50.00
163-165	Luis Aparicio	50.00
166-168	Carlton Fisk	50.00
169-171	Dale Murphy	80.00
172-174	Mark Teixeira	60.00
175-177	Darryl Strawberry	50.00
178-180	Justin Morneau	50.00

Relics Combos Autographs
NM/M

Production 36 Sets	
Sepia:	1X
Production 27 Sets	
Emerald:	1-1.5X
Production 18 Sets	
Gold:	No Pricing
Production Nine Sets	
Sapphire:	No Pricing
Production Three Sets	
Platinum:	No Pricing
Production One Set	

1	Brooks Robinson, Robin Yount, Johnny Bench	125.00
2	Reggie Jackson, Joe Morgan, Ryne Sandberg	125.00
3	Tom Seaver, Bob Gibson, Nolan Ryan	180.00
4	Albert Pujols, Alex Rodriguez, Vladimir Guerrero	375.00
5	Tom Seaver, Roger Clemens, Dwight Gooden	160.00
6	Johan Santana, Tom Glavine, Roger Clemens	200.00
7	Alex Rodriguez, Chien-Ming Wang, Don Mattingly	300.00
8	Ryan Howard, Mike Schmidt, Bobby Abreu	150.00
9	Ryan Howard, David Ortiz, Albert Pujols	350.00
10	Alex Rodriguez, David Wright, Jose Reyes	300.00
11	Miguel Cabrera, Manny Ramirez, David Ortiz	125.00
12	Justin Verlander, Jered Weaver, Chien-Ming Wang	250.00
13	Ralph Kiner, Duke Snider, Yogi Berra	125.00
14	Ryan Howard, Alex Rodriguez, Andruw Jones	260.00
15	Adam Lind, Brian Stokes, David Murphy	30.00
16	Andrew Miller, Brian Stokes, Glen Perkins	50.00
17	Shawn Riggans, Troy Tulowitzki, Andrew Miller	80.00
18	Glen Perkins, Lastings Milledge, Troy Tulowitzki	50.00

Relics Combos
NM/M

Production 36 Sets	
Sepia:	1X
Production 27 Sets	
Emerald:	1-1.5X
Production 18 Sets	
Gold:	No Pricing
Production Nine Sets	
Sapphire:	No Pricing
Production Three Sets	
Platinum:	No Pricing
Production One Set	

1	Albert Pujols, Manny Ramirez, David Ortiz	40.00
2	Albert Pujols, Pedro Martinez, Vladimir Guerrero	40.00
3	Ivan Rodriguez, Carlos Delgado, Roberto Clemente	60.00
4	Roberto Clemente, Bernie Williams, Carlos Beltran	65.00
5	Jose Reyes, Alfonso Soriano, Miguel Tejada	30.00
6	Carl Crawford, Jose Reyes, Juan Pierre	25.00
7	Hideki Matsui, Ichiro Suzuki, So Taguchi	60.00
8	Miguel Cabrera, Johan Santana, Bobby Abreu	25.00
9	Alex Rodriguez, Mariano Rivera, Hideki Matsui	60.00
10	Reggie Jackson, Alex Rodriguez, Don Mattingly	50.00
11	Yogi Berra, Don Mattingly, Reggie Jackson	75.00
12	David Ortiz, Wade Boggs, Manny Ramirez	25.00

13 David Ortiz, Manny Ramirez, Pedro Martinez 30.00
14 Miguel Tejada, Eddie Murray, Brooks Robinson 30.00
15 Joe Mauer, Justin Morneau, Johan Santana 30.00
16 Harmon Killebrew, Joe Mauer, Justin Morneau 40.00
17 Justin Verlander, Ivan Rodriguez, Joel Zumaya 25.00
18 Barry Zito, Dennis Eckersley, Huston Street 20.00
19 Reggie Jackson, Rod Carew, Vladimir Guerrero 30.00
20 Vladimir Guerrero, Pedro Martinez, Moises Alou 30.00
21 Michael Young, Mark Teixeira, Alex Rodriguez 40.00
22 Edgar Martinez, Ichiro Suzuki, Alex Rodriguez 70.00
23 David Wright, Carlos Delgado, Jose Reyes 40.00
24 Jose Reyes, Pedro Martinez, David Wright 50.00
25 Jose Reyes, Carlos Beltran, David Wright 40.00
26 Ryan Howard, Chase Utley, Jimmy Rollins 50.00
27 Jeff Francoeur, Chipper Jones, Brian McCann 40.00
28 John Smoltz, Tom Glavine, Greg Maddux 40.00
29 Chipper Jones, Jeff Francoeur, Andruw Jones 40.00
30 Nolan Ryan, Pedro Martinez, Tom Seaver 50.00
31 Mike Schmidt, Jim Thome, Ryan Howard 40.00
32 Stan Musial, Albert Pujols, Ozzie Smith 60.00
33 Albert Pujols, David Eckstein, Jim Edmonds
34 Lance Berkman, Roy Oswalt, Craig Biggio 25.00
35 Roger Clemens, Roy Oswalt, Nolan Ryan 40.00
36 Frank Robinson, Joe Morgan, Johnny Bench 30.00
37 Paul Molitor, Prince Fielder, Robin Yount 40.00
38 Ernie Banks, Alfonso Soriano, Ryne Sandberg 50.00
39 Andre Ethier, Matthew Kemp, Jered Weaver 25.00
40 Chien-Ming Wang, Alex Rodriguez, Mariano Rivera 100.00
41 Albert Pujols, Ichiro Suzuki, Vladimir Guerrero 50.00
42 Albert Pujols, Alex Rodriguez, Ichiro Suzuki 75.00
43 Ryan Howard, Justin Morneau, Albert Pujols 50.00
44 Albert Pujols, Roberto Clemente, Ichiro Suzuki 100.00
45 Albert Pujols, Roberto Clemente, Mickey Mantle 150.00
46 Joe DiMaggio, Mickey Mantle, Alex Rodriguez 150.00
47 Ted Williams, Joe DiMaggio, Mickey Mantle 200.00
48 Roberto Clemente, Mickey Mantle, Reggie Jackson 125.00
49 Stan Musial, Roberto Clemente, Frank Robinson 100.00
50 Albert Pujols, Johnny Bench, Mickey Mantle 100.00
51 Carl Yastrzemski, Ted Williams, Mickey Mantle 140.00
52 Brandon Webb, Tom Seaver, Johan Santana 30.00
53 Roger Clemens, Dwight Gooden, Pedro Martinez 30.00
54 Johan Santana, Greg Maddux, Roger Clemens 35.00
55 Johan Santana, Pedro Martinez, Roger Clemens 30.00
56 Randy Johnson, Roger Clemens, Tom Glavine 30.00
57 Justin Verlander, Ryan Howard, Ichiro Suzuki 50.00
58 Dontrelle Willis, Carlos Beltran, Jason Bay 20.00
59 Albert Pujols, Scott Rolen, Ryan Howard 40.00
60 Roberto Clemente, Joe DiMaggio, Mickey Mantle 200.00
61 Stan Musial, Ernie Banks, Mickey Mantle 140.00

62 Mike Schmidt, Joe Morgan, Johnny Bench 35.00
63 George Brett, Robin Yount, Ozzie Smith 60.00
64 Albert Pujols, Ichiro Suzuki, Rod Carew 50.00
65 Alfonso Soriano, Mickey Mantle, Alex Rodriguez 100.00
66 Don Mattingly, Wade Boggs, Tony Gwynn 50.00
67 Rod Carew, Vladimir Guerrero, Garret Anderson 25.00
68 Tony Gwynn, Wade Boggs, George Brett 50.00
69 Vladimir Guerrero, Alfonso Soriano, Bobby Abreu 30.00
70 Darryl Strawberry, Carlos Beltran, Howard Johnson 30.00
71 Jim Thome, Manny Ramirez, Frank Thomas 30.00
72 Mickey Mantle, Mike Piazza, Mike Schmidt 120.00
73 Carl Yastrzemski, Alex Rodriguez, Dave Winfield 50.00
74 Johan Santana, Pedro Martinez, Roger Clemens 30.00
75 Greg Maddux, Nolan Ryan, Tom Seaver 60.00
76 Bob Gibson, Dwight Gooden, Greg Maddux 50.00
77 Roberto Clemente, Reggie Jackson, Manny Ramirez 75.00
78 Johnny Podres, Don Larsen, Lew Burdette 30.00
79 Ichiro Suzuki, Kenji Johjima, Tadahito Iguchi 70.00
80 Paul Molitor, Jimmy Rollins, Chase Utley 35.00
81 Gary Carter, Paul LoDuca, Mike Piazza 60.00
82 George Brett, Alex Rodriguez, David Wright 60.00
83 Hoyt Wilhelm, Phil Niekro, Tim Wakefield 35.00
84 Franklin D. Roosevelt, Harry S. Truman, Dwight D. Eisenhower 80.00
85 Ichiro Suzuki, Eric Chavez, Torii Hunter 50.00
86 Richard Nixon, Ronald Reagan, George W. Bush 100.00
87 John Smoltz, Carlos Delgado, Edgar Martinez 30.00
88 Manny Ramirez, Vladimir Guerrero, David Ortiz 30.00
89 Livan Hernandez, Orel Hershiser, Willie Stargell 20.00
90 David Ortiz, Ryan Howard, Albert Pujols 50.00
91 Chien-Ming Wang, Johan Santana, Jon Garland 80.00
92 Deion Sanders, Bo Jackson, Brian Jordan 60.00
93 Franklin D. Roosevelt, John F. Kennedy, Bill Clinton 125.00
94 Vladimir Guerrero, Ichiro Suzuki, Vernon Wells 50.00
95 Jim Thome, Jermaine Dye, Paul Konerko 25.00
96 A.J. Pierzynski, Kelvim Escobar, Josh Paul 20.00
97 Joe Carter, Rickey Henderson, Paul Molitor 50.00
98 Kirk Gibson, Dennis Eckersley 25.00
99 Luis Castillo, Moises Alou, Mark Prior 20.00
100 Mookie Wilson, Ray Knight, Bill Buckner 50.00

Relics Combos Double

NM/M

Production 36 Sets
Sepia: No Pricing
Production 27 Sets
Emerald: 1-1.5X
Production 18 Sets
Gold: No Pricing
Production Nine Sets
Sapphire: No Pricing
Production Three Sets
Platinum: No Pricing
Production One Set
1 Mickey Mantle, Joe DiMaggio 250.00
2 Alex Rodriguez, Chien-Ming Wang, Johnny Damon, Manny Ramirez, David Ortiz, Jason Varitek 100.00
3 David Wright, Carlos Beltran, Tom Glavine, Chipper Jones, Andruw Jones, John Smoltz 50.00

4 David Wright 50.00
5 Albert Pujols 70.00
6 Chien-Ming Wang 100.00
7 David Wright, Ryan Howard 60.00
8 Alex Rodriguez 70.00
9 Ryan Howard 60.00
10 Ichiro Suzuki 100.00
11 Albert Pujols, Pedro Martinez, David Ortiz, Vladimir Guerrero, Manny Ramirez, Alfonso Soriano 70.00
12 Ichiro Suzuki, So Taguchi, Hideki Matsui, Kazuo Matsui, Tadahito Iguchi, Kenji Johjima 140.00
13 Roberto Clemente, Ivan Rodriguez, Carlos Beltran, Bernie Williams, Carlos Delgado, Javy Lopez 125.00
14 Johan Santana, Miguel Cabrera, Bobby Abreu, Omar Vizquel, Ozzie Guillen, Luis Aparicio 50.00
15 Mickey Mantle, Joe DiMaggio, Ted Williams, Ernie Banks, Yogi Berra, Stan Musial 200.00
16 Mickey Mantle, Albert Pujols, Vladimir Guerrero, Ted Williams, Roberto Clemente, Joe DiMaggio 200.00
17 Mickey Mantle, Alex Rodriguez, Don Mattingly, Yogi Berra, Chien-Ming Wang, Reggie Jackson 200.00
18 Carl Yastrzemski, Manny Ramirez, David Ortiz, Pedro Martinez, Johnny Damon, Carlton Fisk 200.00
19 Justin Morneau, Torii Hunter, Joe Mauer, Johan Santana, Francisco Liriano, Harmon Killebrew 60.00
20 Justin Verlander, Joel Zumaya, Curtis Granderson, Magglio Ordonez, Ivan Rodriguez, Kenny Rogers 50.00
21 Nick Swisher, Huston Street, Reggie Jackson, Barry Zito, Jose Canseco, Dennis Eckersley 40.00
22 Vladimir Guerrero, Rod Carew, Jered Weaver, Reggie Jackson, Garret Anderson, Francisco Rodriguez 50.00
23 Vladimir Guerrero, Pedro Martinez, Moises Alou, Gary Carter, Andre Dawson, Randy Johnson 50.00
24 Nolan Ryan, Mark Teixeira, Michael Young, Alex Rodriguez, Ivan Rodriguez, Hank Blalock 65.00
25 Kenji Johjima, Ichiro Suzuki, Alex Rodriguez, Randy Johnson, Edgar Martinez, Richie Sexson 90.00
26 David Wright, Jose Reyes, Carlos Beltran, Pedro Martinez, Tom Glavine, Carlos Delgado 75.00
27 David Eckstein, Albert Pujols, Chris Carpenter, Stan Musial, Ozzie Smith, Jim Edmonds 75.00
28 Nolan Ryan, Andy Pettitte, Roger Clemens, Roy Oswalt, Lance Berkman, Craig Biggio 75.00
29 Ryan Howard, Chase Utley, Mike Schmidt, Jimmy Rollins, Richie Ashburn, Steve Carlton 100.00
30 Jeff Francoeur, Brian McCann, Chipper Jones, Andruw Jones, John Smoltz, Tim Hudson 70.00
31 Alfonso Soriano, Ernie Banks, Ryne Sandberg, Kerry Wood, Mark Prior, Andre Dawson 60.00
32 David Wright, Justin Morneau, Ryan Howard, Chien-Ming Wang, Chase Utley, Jose Reyes 75.00
33 David Ortiz 35.00
34 Roger Maris, Stan Musial, Roberto Clemente, Ernie Banks, Johnny Bench, Carl Yastrzemski 150.00
35 Albert Pujols, Jim Edmonds, Scott Rolen, Ivan Rodriguez, Kenny Rogers, Magglio Ordonez 50.00

36 Derrek Lee, Juan Pierre, Greg Maddux, Paul Konerko, Jermaine Dye, Jim Thome 60.00
37 David Wright, Paul LoDuca, Jose Reyes, Alex Rodriguez, Jason Giambi, Johnny Damon 75.00
38 Joe Mauer, Freddy Sanchez, Robinson Cano, Miguel Cabrera, Albert Pujols, Miguel Cabrera 75.00
39 Ryan Howard, David Ortiz, Albert Pujols, Alfonso Soriano, Lance Berkman, Jermaine Dye 75.00
40 Ryan Howard, Albert Pujols, David Ortiz, Lance Berkman, Justin Morneau, Andruw Jones 75.00
41 Johan Santana, Roy Oswalt, Chris Carpenter, Brandon Webb, Roy Halladay, C.C. Sabathia 50.00
42 Chien-Ming Wang, Johan Santana, Jon Garland, Randy Johnson, Kenny Rogers, Freddy Garcia 85.00
43 Johan Santana, Aaron Harang, Jake Peavy, John Smoltz, Carlos Zambrano, Jeremy Bonderman 50.00
44 Jeff Suppan, Roy Oswalt, Albert Pujols, Placido Polanco, Paul Konerko, David Ortiz 50.00
45 Orlando Cepeda, Monte Irvin, Bobby Thomson, Duke Snider, Johnny Podres, Don Zimmerman 50.00
46 Ryne Sandberg, Wade Boggs, Dennis Eckersley, Paul Molitor, Gary Carter, Eddie Murray 70.00
47 Jermaine Dye, Paul Konerko, A.J. Pierzynski, Craig Biggio, Lance Berkman, Morgan Ensberg 50.00
48 Roger Clemens, Randy Johnson, Greg Maddux, Curt Schilling, Pedro Martinez, John Smoltz 85.00
49 David Wright, Brooks Robinson, George Brett, Mike Schmidt, Alex Rodriguez, Eddie Murray 80.00
50 Alfonso Soriano, Bobby Abreu, Carlos Beltran, Vladimir Guerrero, Alex Rodriguez, Preston Wilson 70.00

Triple Signed Hide
Production One Set

2007 Topps Turkey Red

NM/M
Complete Set (186):
Common Player: .25
Common SP: 4.00
Inserted 1:4
Pack (8): 4.00
Box (24): 80.00
1 Ryan Howard 2.00
1 Ryan Howard/SP Ad Back 8.00
2 Dontrelle Willis .25
3 Matt Cain .50
4 John Maine .50
5 Cole Hamels .75
6 Corey Patterson .25
7 Mickey Mantle/SP 25.00
8 Johan Santana CL .75
9 Josh Beckett .75
10 Jimmy Rollins 1.00
11 Kenji Johjima .25
12 Orlando Hernandez .25
13 Jorge Posada CL .50
14 Ivan Rodriguez .75
15 Ichiro Suzuki 2.00
15 Ichiro Suzuki/SP Ad Back 6.00
16 Ken Griffey Jr. CL 1.50

17 Stephen Drew .25
18 B.J. Upton .50
19 Mickey Mantle 3.00
20 Alex Rodriguez 3.00
20 Alex Rodriguez/SP Ad Back 8.00
21 Adam Dunn .75
22 Adam Lind/SP (RC) 4.00
23 Adrian Gonzalez .50
24 Akinori Iwamura RC 2.00
25 Albert Pujols 3.00
25 Albert Pujols/SP Ad Back 8.00
26 Frank Thomas .50
27 Roy Halladay .50
28 Alejandro De Aza RC 1.00
29 Alex Gordon RC 1.00
30 Barry Bonds 3.00
31 Andrew Miller RC 1.00
32 Andruw Jones .75
33 Kurt Suzuki/SP (RC) 5.00
34 Mickey Mantle 3.00
35 Andy Pettitte .50
36 Tadahito Iguchi .25
37 Edgar Renteria .50
38 Tim Hudson .50
39 Micah Owings/SP .50
40 Chipper Jones 1.00
40 Chipper Jones/SP Ad Back 6.00
41 Barry Zito .50
42 Daisuke Matsuzaka CL 2.00
43 Jarrod Saltalamacchia/SP (RC) 4.00
44 Bill Hall .25
45 Billy Butler (RC) 1.00
46 Billy Wagner .25
47 Rich Harden/SP 4.00
48 Albert Pujols CL 1.00
49 Brandon Inge .25
50 Jason Giambi .50
51 Brandon Webb .75
52 Brandon Wood (RC) .50
53 Carl Crawford CL .50
54 Brian Giles .25
55 Josh Hamilton (RC) 2.00
56 Chase Utley 1.50
57 Chase Utley/SP Ad Back 6.00
58 Miguel Montero (RC) .50
59 Carl Crawford .50
60 Carlos Beltran 1.00
61 Mariano Rivera .50
62 Carlos Delgado .75
63 Carlos Lee/SP 5.00
64 Carlos Zambrano/SP 5.00
65 Miguel Tejada .50
66 Mike Cameron .25
67 Chase Utley/SP 8.00
68 Chase Wright RC 1.00
69 Chien-Ming Wang 1.00
70 Nick Swisher .50
71 David Wright 1.50
72 Mike Piazza/SP 5.00
73 Chris Carpenter .50
74 Mark Buehrle/SP 4.00
75 Tyler Clippard (RC) .50
76 Nicholas Markakis .50
77 Mickey Mantle 3.00
78 Curt Schilling 1.00
79 Curtis Granderson .75
80 Craig Biggio .50
81 Dallas Braden/SP RC 4.00
82 Dan Haren/SP 6.00
83 Dan Uggla .50
84 Danny Putnam (RC) .50
85 David DeJesus .25
86 David Eckstein .50
87 Tim Lincecum RC 6.00
88 Johnny Damon/SP 6.00
89 Justin Morneau 1.00
90 Delmon Young (RC) 1.00
91 Homer Bailey (RC) 1.00
92 Carlos Gomez RC 1.00
93 Josh Fields/SP (RC) 4.00
94 Derek Jeter 3.00
95 Derek Jeter/SP Ad Back 8.00
96 Derrek Lee .75
97 Donald Kelly (RC) .50
98 Doug Slaten RC .50
99 Dustin Moseley .25
100 Gary Sheffield .75
101 Orlando Hudson/SP 4.00
102 Elijah Dukes (RC) 1.00
103 Eric Byrnes/SP 4.00
104 Eric Chavez .50
105 Phil Hughes (RC) 1.00
105 Phil Hughes/SP Ad Back 4.00
106 Felix Hernandez/SP 5.00
106 Felix Hernandez/SP Ad Back 6.00
107 Mickey Mantle 3.00
108 Felix Pie (RC) .50
109 Derek Jeter CL 1.00
110 Daisuke Matsuzaka RC 5.00
110 Daisuke Matsuzaka/SP Ad Back 10.00
111 Francisco Rodriguez .50
112 Ramon Hernandez .25
113 Randy Johnson .50
114 Gary Matthews .25
115 Prince Fielder 1.00
116 Vladimir Guerrero CL .50
117 Mickey Mantle 3.00
118 Hideki Matsui 2.00
119 Hideki Okajima RC .50
120 Manny Ramirez 1.00
121 Hunter Pence/SP (RC) 5.00

122 Roy Oswalt .50
123 Josh Willingham/SP 4.00
124 Tom Gordon/SP .50
125 Michael Young .50
126 J.D. Drew .25
127 Ryan Zimmerman .50
128 James Shields/SP 4.00
129 Jack Wilson .25
130 David Ortiz 1.00
130 David Ortiz/SP Ad Back 6.00
131 Jose Reyes CL .50
132 Jamie Vermilyea RC .50
133 Jason Bay .50
134 Scott Kazmir/SP 4.00
135 Jason Isringhausen/SP 4.00
136 Jason Marquis/SP 4.00
137 Jason Schmidt .50
138 Shawn Green .25
139 Jeff Francoeur/SP 5.00
140 Alfonso Soriano 1.00
141 Kevin Kouzmanoff (RC) .50
142 Jered Weaver .50
143 Todd Helton/SP 5.00
144 Jermaine Dye .50
145 Jim Thome .75
146 Tom Glavine/SP 5.00
147 Joe Mauer .75
148 Joe Nathan .50
149 Joe Smith RC .50
150 Ken Griffey Jr. 2.00
150 Ken Griffey Jr./SP Ad Back 6.00
151 Grady Sizemore 1.00
152 Sammy Sosa/SP 5.00
153 Andy LaRoche (RC) 1.00
154 Travis Buck (RC) .50
155 Alex Rios .50
156 Travis Hafner .50
157 Jake Peavy .50
158 Jeff Kent .50
159 Johan Santana 1.00
159 Johan Santana/SP Ad Back 5.00
160 Ivan Rodriguez .75
161 Trevor Hoffman .50
162 Troy Glaus .50
163 Troy Tulowitzki (RC) 1.50
164 Jorge Posada .50
165 Kei Igawa/SP RC 4.00
166 Jose Reyes 1.00
167 Mickey Mantle 3.00
168 Chase Utley CL .50
169 Justin Verlander 1.00
170 Hanley Ramirez 1.00
171 Kelly Johnson/SP 4.00
172 Kelvin Jimenez RC .50
173 Roger Clemens 2.00
174 Khalil Greene/SP 5.00
175 Lance Berkman .50
176 Hanley Ramirez/CL .50
177 Kyle Kendrick RC .50
178 Magglio Ordonez .50
179 Marcus Giles/SP 4.00
180 Miguel Cabrera 1.00
180 Miguel Cabrera/SP Ad Back 5.00
181 Mark Teahen .25
182 Mark Teixeira/SP 5.00
183 Matt Chico/SP (RC) 4.00
184 Matt Holliday .75
185 Vladimir Guerrero 1.00
185 Vladimir Guerrero/SP Ad Back 5.00
186 Yovani Gallardo (RC) 1.00

Chrome

Chrome: 2-3X
Chrome SP's: 1X
Production 1,999 Sets

Chrome Refractors
Refractors: 3-4X
Refractor SP's: 1-2X
Production 999 Sets

Chrome Black Refractors
Refractors: 5-10X
Refractor SP's: 2-4X
Production 99 Sets

A-Rod Road to 500

Common A-Rod (301-325): Inserted 2:Box

A-Rod Road to 500 Autographs
Production One Set

Cabinet

		NM/M
Common Player:		3.00

Inserted 1:Box

JB	Jason Bay	5.00
LB	Lance Berkman	6.00
MC	Miguel Cabrera	6.00
CC	Chris Carpenter	8.00
SD	Stephen Drew	4.00
ED	Elijah Dukes	4.00
JD	Jermaine Dye	4.00
AD	Adam Dunn	4.00
PF	Prince Fielder	15.00
JF	Jeff Francoeur	10.00
AG	Alex Gordon	15.00
KG	Ken Griffey Jr.	15.00
VG	Vladimir Guerrero	8.00
FH	Felix Hernandez	5.00
RH	Ryan Howard	15.00
KI	Kei Igawa	4.00
AI	Akinori Iwamura	3.00
DJ	Derek Jeter	20.00
AJ	Andruw Jones	5.00
CL	Carlos Lee	4.00
MM	Mickey Mantle	25.00
NM	Nicholas Markakis	8.00
DM	Daisuke Matsuzaka	15.00
JM	Joe Mauer	8.00
JEM	Justin Morneau	5.00
HO	Hideki Okajima	5.00
DO	David Ortiz	15.00
MP	Mike Piazza	10.00
AP	Albert Pujols	20.00
HR	Hanley Ramirez	10.00
MR	Manny Ramirez	10.00
JR	Jose Reyes	15.00
AR	Alex Rodriguez	20.00
FR	Francisco Rodriguez	4.00
IR	Ivan Rodriguez	5.00
JS	Johan Santana	8.00
JDS	Jason Schmidt	3.00
GS	Grady Sizemore	10.00
AS	Alfonso Soriano	8.00
IS	Ichiro Suzuki	15.00
MT	Miguel Tejada	5.00
TT	Troy Tulowitzki	8.00
CU	Chase Utley	10.00
JV	Justin Verlander	5.00
CW	Chien-Ming Wang	6.00
BW	Brandon Webb	4.00
DW	David Wright	15.00
DY	Delmon Young	5.00
MY	Michael Young	5.00
RZ	Ryan Zimmerman	10.00
BZ	Barry Zito	3.00

Cabinet Dick Perez Autographs
NM/M
Production 25 Sets

JB	Jason Bay	30.00
LB	Lance Berkman	30.00
MC	Miguel Cabrera	30.00
CC	Chris Carpenter	30.00
SD	Stephen Drew	25.00
ED	Elijah Dukes	20.00
AD	Adam Dunn	25.00
JD	Jermaine Dye	30.00
PF	Prince Fielder	40.00
JF	Jeff Francoeur	30.00
AG	Alex Gordon	35.00
KG	Ken Griffey Jr.	50.00
VG	Vladimir Guerrero	30.00
FH	Felix Hernandez	30.00
RH	Ryan Howard	40.00
KI	Kei Igawa	25.00
AI	Akinori Iwamura	30.00
AJ	Andruw Jones	30.00
CL	Carlos Lee	30.00

MM	Mickey Mantle	100.00
NM	Nicholas Markakis	30.00
JM	Joe Mauer	30.00
JEM	Justin Morneau	30.00
HO	Hideki Okajima	30.00
DO	David Ortiz	50.00
MP	Mike Piazza	40.00
AP	Albert Pujols	80.00
HR	Hanley Ramirez	40.00
MR	Manny Ramirez	30.00
JR	Jose Reyes	40.00
AR	Alex Rodriguez	80.00
FR	Francisco Rodriguez	25.00
IR	Ivan Rodriguez	30.00
JS	Johan Santana	30.00
JDS	Jason Schmidt	25.00
GS	Grady Sizemore	40.00
AS	Alfonso Soriano	50.00
IS	Ichiro Suzuki	80.00
MT	Miguel Tejada	30.00
TT	Troy Tulowitzki	30.00
CU	Chase Utley	50.00
JV	Justin Verlander	30.00
CW	Chien-Ming Wang	50.00
BW	Brandon Webb	30.00
DW	David Wright	50.00
DY	Delmon Young	30.00
MY	Michael Young	30.00
RZ	Ryan Zimmerman	25.00
BZ	Barry Zito	30.00

Chromographs
NM/M

Common Autograph:		10.00
AG	Alex Gordon	40.00
AK	Austin Kearns	10.00
AR	Alex Rodriguez	250.00
BJ	Bobby Jenks	25.00
BW	Brad Wilkerson	10.00
CAH	Clay Hensley	10.00
CG	Curtis Granderson	75.00
CH	Cole Hamels	30.00
CJ	Chuck James	15.00
DE	Darin Erstad	10.00
DU	Dan Uggla	15.00
EC	Eric Chavez	10.00
FP	Felix Pie	20.00
GS	Gary Sheffield	40.00
HCK	Hong-Chih Kuo	20.00
HR	Hanley Ramirez	30.00
JB	Jason Bay	40.00
JD	Johnny Damon	15.00
JM	John Maine	20.00
JZ	Joel Zumaya	15.00
KE	Kelvim Escobar	10.00
LM	Lastings Milledge	20.00
MC	Melky Cabrera	30.00
MG	Mike Gonzalez	10.00
NM	Nicholas Markakis	25.00
NR	Nate Robertson	15.00
PL	Paul LoDuca	15.00
RC	Robinson Cano	40.00
RH	Ryan Howard	80.00
RJH	Rich Hill	10.00
RM	Robert Mackowiak	10.00
RNM	Russell Martin	25.00
SC	Sean Casey	25.00
SP	Scott Podsednik	10.00
SV	Shane Victorino	15.00
TG	Tony Gwynn Jr.	15.00
WN	Wilbert Nieves	10.00

Presidents
NM/M

Common President:		1.00

Inserted 1:12

1	George Washington	4.00
2	John Adams	2.00
3	Thomas Jefferson	3.00
4	James Madison	2.00
5	James Monroe	2.00
6	John Quincy Adams	2.00
7	Andrew Jackson	2.00
8	Martin Van Buren	1.00
9	William H. Harrison	1.00
10	John Tyler	1.00
11	James K. Polk	1.00
12	Zachary Taylor	1.00
13	Millard Fillmore	1.00
14	Franklin Pierce	1.00
15	James Buchanan	1.00
16	Abraham Lincoln	4.00
17	Andrew Johnson	1.00
18	Ulysses S. Grant	2.00
19	Rutherford B. Hayes	1.00
20	James Garfield	1.00
21	Chester A. Arthur	1.00
22	Grover Cleveland	1.00
23	Benjamin Harrison	1.00
24	Grover Cleveland	1.00
25	William McKinley	1.00
26	Theodore Roosevelt	3.00
27	William H. Taft	1.00
28	Woodrow Wilson	1.00
29	Warren G. Harding	1.00
30	Calvin Coolidge	1.00
31	Herbert Hoover	1.00
32	Franklin D. Roosevelt	3.00
33	Harry S. Truman	3.00
34	Dwight D. Eisenhower	3.00
35	John F. Kennedy	4.00
36	Lyndon B. Johnson	1.00
37	Richard Nixon	2.00
38	Gerald Ford	1.00
39	Jimmy Carter	2.00
40	Ronald Reagan	2.00
41	George H.W. Bush	2.00
42	Bill Clinton	2.00
43	George W. Bush	2.00

Relics

NM/M

Common Relic:		4.00
AB	Adrian Beltre	4.00
AD	Adam Dunn	6.00
AH	Aaron Harang	4.00
AJ1	Andruw Jones	6.00
AJ2	Andruw Jones	6.00
AM	Andrew Miller	8.00
ANB	Angel Berroa	4.00
AS	Alfonso Soriano	10.00
BB	Barry Bonds	30.00
BC	Bobby Crosby	4.00
BJR	B.J. Ryan	4.00
BR	Brian Roberts	6.00
BS	Brian Stokes	4.00
BT	Brad Thompson	4.00
BW	Brandon Webb	6.00
BZ	Benjamin Zobrist	6.00
CB1	Carlos Beltran	8.00
CB2	Carlos Beltran	8.00
CC	Coco Crisp	6.00
CD	Carlos Delgado	6.00
CH	Cole Hamels	10.00
CJ	Chipper Jones	10.00
CJC	Chris Carpenter	8.00
CL	Carlos Lee	6.00
CR	Chris Ray	4.00
CS	C.C. Sabathia	6.00
DN	Dioner Navarro	4.00
DO	David Ortiz	10.00
DR	Darrell Rasner	4.00
DU	Dan Uggla	6.00
DW	David Wright	15.00
DWA	Daryle Ward	4.00
DWW	Dontrelle Willis	6.00
DY	Delmon Young	6.00
ES	Ervin Santana	4.00
GP	Glen Perkins	4.00
HB	Hank Blalock	8.00
HR	Hanley Ramirez	8.00
IR	Ivan Rodriguez	8.00
IS	Ichiro Suzuki	20.00
JB	Josh Beckett	8.00
JC	Jorge Cantu	4.00
JD	Jermaine Dye	6.00
JE	Jim Edmonds	6.00
JF	Jeff Francoeur	8.00
JG	Jon Garland	4.00
JH	Josh Hamilton	10.00
JK	Jeff Kent	4.00
JM	Justin Morneau	8.00
JP	Josh Paul	4.00
JPM	Joe Mauer	8.00
JR	Jose Reyes	8.00
JRB	Jason Bay	6.00
JS	John Smoltz	8.00
JV2	Jason Varitek	10.00
JW	Jered Weaver	8.00
JZ	Joel Zumaya	6.00
KM	Kazuo Matsui	4.00
LB	Lance Berkman	6.00
LC	Luis Castillo	4.00
MC	Melky Cabrera	8.00
ME	Morgan Ensberg	4.00
MG	Marcus Giles	4.00
MJC	Miguel Cairo	4.00
MM	Mickey Mantle	125.00
MP	Mike Piazza	10.00
MR	Manny Ramirez	8.00
MT	Miguel Tejada	6.00
MY	Michael Young	6.00
NM	Nicholas Markakis	20.00
NP	Neifi Perez	4.00
NS	Nick Swisher	6.00
PM	Pedro Martinez	6.00
PP	Placido Polanco	6.00
RB1	Rocco Baldelli	4.00
RB2	Rocco Baldelli	4.00
RH	Ryan Howard	15.00
RJH	Rich Hill	6.00
RK	Ryan Klesco	4.00
RS	Reggie Sanders	4.00
RZ	Ryan Zimmerman	10.00
SR	Scott Rolen	8.00
SS	Sammy Sosa	8.00
ST	So Taguchi	4.00
TB	Travis Buck	4.00
TH	Travis Hafner	4.00
TI	Tadahito Iguchi	6.00
TJ	Tyler Johnson	8.00
VG	Vladimir Guerrero	8.00
VW	Vernon Wells	6.00

Silks
NM/M

Common Player:		15.00

Production 99 Sets

AD	Adam Dunn	15.00
AI	Akinori Iwamura	15.00
AIR	Alex Rios	15.00
AP	Albert Pujols	50.00
AR	Alex Rodriguez	50.00
AS	Alfonso Soriano	20.00
BB	Billy Butler	20.00
BLB	Barry Bonds	40.00
CH	Cole Hamels	25.00
CJ	Chipper Jones	25.00
CS	C.C. Sabathia	15.00

CY	Adrian Gonzalez	15.00
DH	Danny Haren	15.00
DJ	Derek Jeter	60.00
DM	Daisuke Matsuzaka	80.00
DO	David Ortiz	35.00
DU	Dan Uggla	15.00
DW	David Wright	30.00
DWW	Dontrelle Willis	20.00
EB	Erik Bedard	20.00
GS	Grady Sizemore	25.00
HP	Hunter Pence	30.00
HR	Hanley Ramirez	25.00
IS	Ichiro Suzuki	50.00
JAS	John Smoltz	20.00
JB	Josh Beckett	25.00
JBR	Jose Reyes	25.00
JD	Jermaine Dye	15.00
JH	J.J. Hardy	15.00
JL	John Lackey	15.00
JM	Justin Morneau	25.00
JP	Jake Peavy	20.00
JR	Jimmy Rollins	25.00
JRB	Jason Bay	15.00
JS	Johan Santana	25.00
JV	Justin Verlander	25.00
KG	Ken Griffey Jr.	40.00
MAR	Manny Ramirez	25.00
MH	Matt Holliday	25.00
MM	Mickey Mantle	80.00
MO	Magglio Ordonez	20.00
MR	Mark Reynolds	15.00
MT	Mark Teixeira	20.00
NS	Nick Swisher	20.00
PF	Prince Fielder	30.00
RH	Ryan Howard	40.00
RM	Russell Martin	20.00
RZ	Ryan Zimmerman	20.00
TH	Torii Hunter	20.00
VG	Vladimir Guerrero	15.00

2007 Topps Update

NM/M

Complete Set (330):		40.00
Common Player:		.10
Pack (10):		2.00
Box (36):		65.00
1	Tony Armas Jr.	.10
2	Shannon Stewart	.10
3	Jason Marquis	.10
4	Josh Wilson	.10
5	Steve Trachsel	.10
6	J.D. Drew	.25
7	Ronnie Belliard	.10
8	Trot Nixon	.10
9	Adam LaRoche	.25
10	Mark Loretta	.10
11	Matt Morris	.10
12	Marlon Anderson	.10
13	Jorge Julio	.10
14	Brady Clark	.10
15	David Wells	.10
16	Francisco Rosario	.10
17	Jason Ellison	.10
18	Adam Jones	.25
19	Russell Branyan	.10
20	Rob Bowen	.10
21	J.D. Durbin	.10
22	Jeff Salazar	.10
23	Tadahito Iguchi	.10
24	Brad Hennessey	.10
25	Mark Hendrickson	.10
26	Kameron Loe	.10
27	Yusmeiro Petit	.10
28	Olmedo Saenz	.10
29	Carlos Silva	.10
30	Kevin Frandsen	.10
31	Tony Pena	.10
32	Russ Ortiz	.10

33	Hong-Chih Kuo	.10
34	Paul McAnulty	.10
35	Hiram Bocachica	.10
36	Justin Germano	.10
37	Jason Simontacchi	.10
38	Jose Cruz	.10
39	Wilfredo Ledezma	.10
40	Chris Denorfia	.10
41	Ryan Langerhans	.10
42	Chris Snelling	.10
43	Ubaldo Jimenez	.10
44	Scott Spiezio	.10
45	Byung-Hyun Kim	.10
46	Brandon Lyon	.10
47	Scott Hairston	.10
48	Chad Durbin	.10
49	Sammy Sosa	.50
50	Jason Smith	.10
51	Zack Greinke	.10
52	Armando Benitez	.10
53	Randy Messenger	.10
54	Mark Teixeira	.50
55	Mike Maroth	.10
56	Jamie Burke	.10
57	Carlos Marmol	.10
58	David Weathers	.10
59	Ryan Doumit	.10
60	Michael Barrett	.10
61	Shawn Chacon	.10
62	Mike Fontenot	.10
63	Cesar Izturis	.10
64	Cliff Floyd	.10
65	Angel Pagan	.10
66	Aaron Miles	.10
67	Tony Graffanino	.10
68	Kevin Mench	.10
69	Claudio Vargas	.10
70	Jose Capellan	.10
71	A.J. Pierzynski	.10
72	Darin Erstad	.10
73	Boone Logan	.10
74	Luis Castillo	.10
75	Marcus Thames	.10
76	Neifi Perez	.10
77	Esteban German	.10
78	Tony Pena	.10
79	Adam Wainwright	.25
80	Reggie Sanders	.10
81	Kelly Shoppach	.10
82	Rafael Betancourt	.10
83	Tom Mastny	.10
84	Kyle Farnsworth	.10
85	Rick Ankiel	.25
86	Kevin Thompson	.10
87	Jeff Karstens	.10
88	Eric Hinske	.10
89	Doug Mirabelli	.10
90	Julian Tavarez	.10
91	Carlos Pena	.25
92	Brendan Harris	.10
93	Chris Sampson	.10
94	Al Reyes	.10
95	Dmitri Young	.10
96	Jason Bergmann	.10
97	Shawn Hill	.10
98	Greg Dobbs	.10
99	Carlos Ruiz	.10
100	Abraham Nunez	.10
100b	Jacoby Ellsbury (RC)	80.00
101	Jayson Werth	.10
102	Adam Eaton	.10
103	Antonio Alfonseca	.10
104	Jorge Sosa	.10
105	Ramon Castro	.10
106	Ruben Gotay	.10
107	Damion Easley	.10
108	David Newhan	.10
109	Jason Wood	.10
110	Reggie Abercrombie	.10
111	Kevin Gregg	.10
112	Henry Owens	.10
113	Willie Harris	.10
114	Peter Orr	.10
115	Casey Janssen	.10
116	Jason Frasor	.10
117	Jeremy Accardo	.10
118	John McDonald	.10
119	Matt Stairs	.10
120	Jason Phillips	.10
121	Justin Duchscherer	.10
122	Rich Harden	.10
123	Jack Cust	.10
124	Lenny DiNardo	.10
125	Joe Kennedy	.10
126	Chad Gaudin	.10
127	Marco Scutaro	.10
128	Brad Thompson	.10
129	Dustin Moseley	.10
130	Eric Gagne	.10
131	Marlon Byrd	.10
132	Scot Shields	.10
133	Victor Diaz	.10
134	Reggie Willits	.25
135	Jose Molina	.10
136	Ramon Vazquez	.10
137	Erick Aybar	.10
138	Sean Marshall	.10
139	Casey Kotchman	.25
140	Ryan Spilborghs	.10
141	Cameron Maybin RC	1.00
142	Jeremy Guthrie	.10
143	Jeff Baker	.10
144	Edwin Jackson	.10
145	Macay McBride	.10
146	Freddie Bynum	.10
147	Eric Patterson	.10
148	Dustin McGowan	.10
149	Homer Bailey (RC)	.75

150	Ryan Braun (RC)	3.00
151	Tony Abreu (RC)	.50
152	Tyler Clippard (RC)	.50
153	Mark Reynolds RC	1.00
154	Jesse Litsch RC	.50
155	Carlos Gomez RC	1.00
156	Matt DeSalvo (RC)	.50
157	Andy LaRoche (RC)	1.00
158	Tim Lincecum RC	5.00
159	Jarrod Saltalamacchia (RC)	.50
160	Hunter Pence (RC)	2.00
161	Brandon Wood (RC)	.50
162	Phil Hughes (RC)	3.00
163	Rocky Cherry RC	.50
164	Chase Wright RC	.50
165	Dallas Braden RC	.75
166	Felix Pie (RC)	.50
167	Zach McClellan RC	.50
168	Rick Vanden Hurk RC	.50
169	Micah Owings (RC)	.50
170	Jon Coutlangus (RC)	.25
171	Andrew Sonnanstine RC	.50
172	Yunel Escobar (RC)	.50
173	Kevin Slowey (RC)	.50
174	Curtis Thigpen (RC)	.25
175	Masumi Kuwata RC	.50
176	Kurt Suzuki (RC)	.25
177	Travis Buck (RC)	.25
178	Matt Lindstrom (RC)	.25
179	Jesus Flores RC	.50
180	Joakim Soria (RC)	.50
181	Nathan Haynes RC	.25
182	Matthew Brown RC	.25
183	Travis Metcalf RC	.25
184	Yovani Gallardo (RC)	1.00
185	Nate Schierholtz (RC)	.25
186	Kyle Kendrick RC	1.00
187	Kevin Melillo (RC)	.25
188	Ryan Rowland-Smith	.25
189	Lee Gronkiewicz RC	.50
190	Eulogio De La Cruz (RC)	.25
191	Brett Carroll RC	.50
192	Terry Evans RC	.50
193	Chase Headley (RC)	.50
194	Guillermo Rodriguez RC	.50
195	Marcus McBeth (RC)	.25
196	Brian Wolfe (RC)	.25
197	Troy Cate RC	.50
198	Mike Zagurski RC	.25
199	Yoel Hernandez	.25
200	Brad Salmon RC	.50
201	Alberto Arias RC	.50
202	Danny Putnam (RC)	.25
203	Jamie Vermilyea RC	.50
204	Kyle Lohse	.10
205	Sammy Sosa	.25
206	Tom Glavine	.25
207	Prince Fielder	.50
208	Mark Buehrle	.10
209	Troy Tulowitzki	.50
210	Daisuke Matsuzaka RC	3.00
211	Randy Johnson	.25
212	Justin Verlander	.25
213	Trevor Hoffman	.10
214	Alex Rodriguez	1.00
215	Ivan Rodriguez	.25
216	David Ortiz	.50
217	Placido Polanco	.10
218	Derek Jeter	1.00
219	Alex Rodriguez	1.00
220	Vladimir Guerrero	.25
221	Magglio Ordonez	.25
222	Ichiro Suzuki	.75
223	Russell Martin	.25
224	Prince Fielder	.50
225	Chase Utley	.50
226	Jose Reyes	.50
227	David Wright	.50
228	Carlos Beltran	.25
229	Barry Bonds	1.00
230	Ken Griffey Jr.	.75
231	Torii Hunter	.25
232	Jonathan Papelbon	.25
233	J.J. Putz	.10
234	Francisco Rodriguez	.25
235	C.C. Sabathia	.25
236	Johan Santana	.50
237	Justin Verlander	.25
238	Francisco Cordero	.10
239	Mike Lowell	.25
240	Cole Hamels	.25
241	Trevor Hoffman	.10
242	Manny Ramirez	.25
243	Jake Peavy	.25
244	Brad Penny	.10
245	Takashi Saito	.10
246	Ben Sheets	.10
247	Hideki Okajima	.25
248	Roy Oswalt	.25
249	Billy Wagner	.10
250	Carl Crawford	.25
251	Chris Young	.10
252	Brian McCann	.25
253	Derrek Lee	.25
254	Albert Pujols	1.00
255	Dmitri Young	.10
256	Orlando Hudson	.10
257	J.J. Hardy	.10
258	Miguel Cabrera	.50
259	Freddy Sanchez	.10
260	Matt Holliday	.25
261	Carlos Lee	.25
262	Aaron Rowand	.10
263	Alfonso Soriano	.25
264	Victor Martinez	.25
265	Jorge Posada	.25
266	Justin Morneau	.25

267	Brian Roberts	.25
268	Carlos Guillen	.10
269	Grady Sizemore	.50
270	Josh Beckett	.25
271	Danny Haren	.10
272	Bobby Jenks	.10
273	John Lackey	.10
274	Gil Meche	.10
275	Mike Fontenot, Khalil Greene	.10
276	Alex Rodriguez, Russell Martin	.50
277	Troy Tulowitzki, Jose Reyes	.50
278	Jorge Posada, Derek Jeter, Alex Rodriguez	1.00
279	Chase Utley, Ichiro Suzuki	.50
280	Carl Crawford, Carlos Guillen	.10
281	Cole Hamels, Russell Martin	.25
282	Jonathan Papelbon, Jorge Posada	.25
283	Carl Crawford, Victor Martinez	.25
284	Alfonso Soriano, J.J. Hardy	.25
285	Justin Morneau	.25
286	Prince Fielder	.50
287	Alex Rios	.25
288	Vladimir Guerrero	.50
289	Albert Pujols	1.00
290	Ryan Howard	.75
291	Magglio Ordonez	.25
292	Matt Holliday	.25
293	Wilson Betemit	.10
294	Todd Wellemeyer	.10
295	Scott Baker	.10
296	Edgar Gonzalez	.10
297	J.P. Howell	.10
298	Shaun Marcum	.10
299	Edinson Volquez	.50
300	Kason Gabbard	.10
301	Bob Howry	.10
302	J.A. Happ	.10
303	Scott Feldman	.10
304	D'Angelo Jimenez	.10
305	Orlando Palmeiro	.10
306	Paul Bako	.10
307	Kyle Davies	.10
308	Gabe Gross	.10
309	John Wasdin	.10
310	Jon Knott	.10
311	Josh Phelps	.10
312	Joba Chamberlain RC	2.00
312	Joba Chamberlain/ Reverse Negative	60.00
313	Octavio Dotel	.10
314	Craig Monroe	.10
315	Edward Mujica	.10
316	Brandon Watson	.10
317	Chris Schroder	.10
318	Scott Proctor	.10
319	Ty Wigginton	.10
320	Troy Percival	.10
321	Scott Linebrink	.10
322	David Murphy	.10
323	Jorge Cantu	.10
324	Dan Wheeler	.10
325	Jason Kendall	.10
326	Milton Bradley	.10
327	Justin Upton RC	3.00
328	Kenny Lofton	.10
329	Roger Clemens	1.00
330	Brian Burres	.10
SQ1	Poley Walnuts	40.00

1st Edition
1st Edition:
Hobby Exclusive 1:36   5-10X

Copper
Copper: 25-50X
Production 56 Sets

Gold

Gold: 8-15X
Production 2,007 Sets

Platinum
No Pricing
Production One Set

Red Back
Red Back (1-330):   1-2.5X
Inserted 2:Hobby, 10:HTA

Printing Plates
Production one set per color.

All-Star Stitches
NM/M
Common Player: 8.00
Inserted 1:45
Patch: No Pricing
Production 10 Sets

AIR	Alex Rios	10.00
AP	Albert Pujols	25.00
AR	Alex Rodriguez	25.00
ARR	Aaron Rowand	10.00
BF	Brian Fuentes	8.00
BJ	Bobby Jenks	10.00
BM	Brian McCann	15.00
BR	Brian Roberts	8.00
BS	Ben Sheets	10.00
BW	Brandon Webb	10.00
CB	Carlos Beltran	10.00
CC	Carl Crawford	10.00
CH	Cole Hamels	15.00
CL	Carlos Lee	10.00
CS	C.C. Sabathia	15.00
CU	Chase Utley	15.00
CY	Chris Young	8.00
DO	David Ortiz	15.00
DW	David Wright	20.00
DY	Dmitri Young	8.00
FR	Francisco Rodriguez	8.00
FC	Francisco Cordero	8.00
FS	Freddy Sanchez	10.00
GM	Gil Meche	8.00
GS	Grady Sizemore	15.00
HO	Hideki Okajima	20.00
IR	Ivan Rodriguez	10.00
IS	Ichiro Suzuki	30.00
JB	Josh Beckett	20.00
JEP	Jake Peavy	10.00
JH	J.J. Hardy	10.00
JL	John Lackey	10.00
JM	Justin Morneau	10.00
JP	J.J. Putz	8.00
JR	Jose Reyes	20.00
JRP	Jorge Posada	10.00
JRV	Jose Valverde	8.00
JS	Johan Santana	10.00
JV	Justin Verlander	10.00
MH	Matt Holliday	10.00
ML	Mike Lowell	10.00
MR	Manny Ramirez	15.00
OH	Orlando Hudson	8.00
PF	Prince Fielder	15.00
RH	Ryan Howard	20.00
RM	Russell Martin	15.00
RO	Roy Oswalt	10.00
TH	Torii Hunter	8.00
TS	Takashi Saito	15.00
TWH	Trevor Hoffman	8.00
VM	Victor Martinez	10.00

All-Star Dual Stitches
Production 25 Sets

All-Star Triple Stitches
Production 25 Sets

A-Rod Road to 500

NM/M
A-Rod (376-400):   3.00

A-Rod Road to 500 Autographs
Production One Set

Barry Bonds Home Run History

NM/M
Common Bonds (735-756):   3.00
Inserted 1:12

Barry Bonds Home Run King

NM/M
Inserted 1:36
HRK   Barry Bonds   5.00

Barry Bonds Home Run King Relic
NM/M
Production 756
HRK   Barry Bonds   50.00

Barry Bonds Home Run King Relic Auto
Production 20

Chrome
NM/M
Common Player: 5.00
Production 415 Sets

1	Homer Bailey	10.00
2	Ryan Braun	25.00
3	Tony Abreu	5.00
4	Tyler Clippard	8.00
5	Mark Reynolds	10.00
6	Jesse Litsch	5.00
7	Carlos Gomez	5.00
8	Matt DeSalvo	5.00
9	Andy LaRoche	8.00
10	Tim Lincecum	30.00
11	Jarrod Saltalamacchia	8.00
12	Hunter Pence	8.00
13	Brandon Wood	5.00
14	Phil Hughes	15.00
15	Rocky Cherry	5.00
16	Chase Wright	5.00
17	Dallas Braden	5.00
18	Felix Pie	5.00
19	Zach McClellan	5.00
20	Rick Vanden Hurk	5.00
21	Micah Owings	8.00
22	Jon Coutlangus	5.00
23	Andrew Sonnanstine	5.00
24	Yunel Escobar	5.00
25	Kevin Slowey	10.00
26	Curtis Thigpen	5.00
27	Masumi Kuwata	8.00
28	Kurt Suzuki	5.00
29	Travis Buck	5.00
30	Matt Lindstrom	5.00
31	Jesus Flores	5.00
32	Joakim Soria	5.00
33	Nathan Haynes	5.00
34	Matthew Brown	5.00
35	Travis Metcalf	5.00
36	Yovani Gallardo	8.00
37	Nate Schierholtz	5.00
38	Kyle Kendrick	6.00
39	Kevin Melillo	5.00
40	Cameron Maybin	15.00
41	Lee Gronkiewicz	5.00
42	Eulogio De La Cruz	5.00
43	Brett Carroll	5.00
44	Terry Evans	5.00
45	Chase Headley	5.00
46	Guillermo Rodriguez	5.00
47	Marcus McBeth	5.00
48	Brian Wolfe	5.00
49	Troy Cate	5.00
50	Justin Upton	30.00
51	Joba Chamberlain	10.00
52	Brad Salmon	5.00
53	Alberto Arias	5.00
54	Danny Putnam	5.00
55	Jamie Vermilyea	5.00

Generation Now

NM/M
All Ryan Zimmerman's: 1.00
All Justin Verlander's: 1.00
All Prince Fielder's: 2.00
All Ian Kinsler's: 1.00
All Kenji Johjima's: 1.00
All Jonathan Papelbon's: 1.00
All Jose Reyes': 2.00
All Curtis Granderson's: 1.00
All Josh Barfield's: .50

Generation Now Autographs
Production One Set

Highlights Autographs
NM/M
Some not priced due to scarcity.

DW	David Wright	60.00
RH	Ryan Howard	60.00
AR	Alex Rodriguez	200.00
JT	Jim Thome	40.00
AP	Albert Pujols	200.00
AJ	Andruw Jones	25.00
AG	Alex Gordon	15.00
GS	Gary Sheffield	30.00
JS	Jarrod Saltalamacchia	15.00
CJ	Conor Jackson	10.00
RC	Robinson Cano	30.00
PF	Prince Fielder	40.00
AE	Andre Ethier	20.00
JR	Jimmy Rollins	40.00
AL	Anthony Lerew	10.00
FC	Francisco Cordero	15.00
BB	Brian Bruney	10.00
AH	Aaron Heilman	10.00
CS	C.C. Sabathia	25.00
TT	Troy Tulowitzki	25.00
RB	Rod Barajas	10.00
RW	Ron Washington	10.00
AC	Asdrubal Cabrera	15.00
DE	Damion Easley	10.00
MC	Miguel Cairo	10.00

Mickey Mantle Home Run History

NM/M
Common Mantle HR History: 2.00
Inserted 1:9 Hobby

Mickey Mantle Home Run History Relics
NM/M
Common Mantle: 125.00
Production Seven Sets

Mickey Mantle Story

NM/M
Complete Set (15): 30.00
Common Mantle: 3.00
Inserted 1:18

1954 Mickey Mantle Reprint Relic
Production 54

Target
Common Mantle:
Target Exclusive

World Series Watch

NM/M
Inserted 1:36

1	New York Mets	1.00
2	Detroit Tigers	1.00
3	Boston Red Sox	5.00
4	Milwaukee Brewers	1.00
5	Cleveland Indians	1.00
6	Angels	1.00
7	San Diego Padres	1.00
8	Los Angeles Dodgers	1.00
9	Philadelphia Phillies	1.00
10	Chicago Cubs	1.00
11	St. Louis Cardinals	1.00
12	Arizona Diamondbacks	1.00
13	New York Yankees	1.00
14	Seattle Mariners	1.00
15	Atlanta Braves	1.00

2007 Topps 1952 Edition
NM/M
Complete Set (221):
Common RC: .25
Common Action Variation:
Inserted 1:6 Hobby
Common SP (208-221): 4.00
Inserted 1:6 Hobby
Hobby Pack (8): 5.00
Hobby Box (20): 90.00

1	Akinori Iwamura RC	.50
2	Angel Sanchez RC	.50
3	Luis Hernandez (RC)	.25
4	Joaquin Arias (RC)	.25
5	Troy Tulowitzki (RC)	2.00
5	Troy Tulowitzki/ Action/SP	5.00
6	Jesus Flores RC	.50
7	Mickey Mantle	3.00
8	Kory Casto (RC)	.25
9	Tony Abreu RC	.50
10	Kevin Kouzmanoff (RC)	.50
11	Travis Buck RC	.25
12	Kurt Suzuki (RC)	.25
13	Matt DeSalvo (RC)	.25
14	Jerry Owens (RC)	.25
15	Alex Gordon RC	1.00
16	Jeff Baker (RC)	.25
17	Ben Francisco (RC)	.25
18	Nate Schierholtz (RC)	.25
19	Nathan Haynes (RC)	.25
20	Ryan Braun RC	3.00
20	Ryan Braun/Action/SP	8.00
21	Brian Barden RC	.50
22	Sean Barker RC	.50
23	Alejandro De Aza RC	.50
24	Jamie Burke (RC)	.25
25	Michael Bourn (RC)	.25
26	Jeff Salazar (RC)	.25
27	Chase Headley (RC)	.25
28	Chris Basak RC	.50
29	Mike Fontenot (RC)	.25
30	Hunter Pence (RC)	1.00
30	Hunter Pence/Action/SP	8.00
31	Masumi Kuwata RC	.50
32	Ryan Rowland-Smith RC	.50
33	Tyler Clippard (RC)	.25
34	Matt Lindstrom (RC)	.25
35	Fred Lewis (RC)	.25
36	Brett Carroll RC	.50
37	Alexi Casilla RC	.50
38	Nick Gorneault (RC)	.25
39	Dennis Sarfate RC	.50
40	Felix Pie (RC)	.25
41	Miguel Montero (RC)	.25
42	Danny Putnam (RC)	.25
43	Shane Youman (RC)	.25
44	Andy LaRoche (RC)	1.00
45	Jarrod Saltalamacchia (RC)	.50
46	Kei Igawa RC	1.00
47	Don Kelly (RC)	.25
48	Fernando Cortez (RC)	.25
49	Travis Metcalf RC	.50
50	Daisuke Matsuzaka RC	1.00
50	Daisuke Matsuzaka/ Action/SP	8.00
51	Edwar Ramirez RC	.50
52	Ryan Sweeney (RC)	.50
53	Shawn Riggans (RC)	.25
54	Billy Sadler (RC)	.25
55	Billy Butler (RC)	.75
56	Andy Cavazos RC	.50
57	Sean Henn (RC)	.25
58	Brian Esposito (RC)	.25
59	Brandon Morrow RC	.50
60	Adam Lind (RC)	.50
61	Joe Smith RC	.50
62	Chris Stewart RC	.50
63	Eulogio De La Cruz (RC)	.25
64	Sean Gallagher (RC)	.25
65	Carlos Gomez RC	.50
66	Jailen Peguero RC	.50
67	Juan Perez RC	.50
68	Levale Speigner RC	.50
69	Jamie Vermilyea RC	.50
70	Delmon Young (RC)	.50
70	Delmon Young/Action/SP	3.00
71	Jo Jo Reyes (RC)	.25
72	Zack Segovia (RC)	.25
73	Andrew Sonnanstine RC	.50
74	Chase Wright RC	1.00
75	Josh Fields (RC)	.25
76	Jon Knott (RC)	.25
77	Guillermo Rodriguez RC	.50
78	Jon Coutlangus (RC)	.25
79	Kevin Cameron RC	.50
80	Mark Reynolds RC	.50
81	Brian Stokes (RC)	.25
82	Alberto Arias (RC)	.50
83	Yoel Hernandez RC	.50
84	David Murphy (RC)	.25
85	Josh Hamilton (RC)	1.00
86	Justin Hampson (RC)	.25
87	Doug Slaten RC	.50
88	Joseph Bisenius RC	.50
89	Troy Cate RC	.50
90	Homer Bailey (RC)	.75
91	Jacoby Ellsbury (RC)	3.00
92	Devern Hansack RC	.50
93	Zach McClellan (RC)	.25
94	Vinny Rottino (RC)	.25
95	Elijah Dukes RC	.50
96	Ryan Braun RC	.50
97	Lee Gardner (RC)	.25
98	Joakim Soria RC	.50
99	Jason Miller (RC)	.25
100	Hideki Okajima RC	.50
100	Hideki Okajima/Action/SP	4.00
101	John Danks (RC)	.50
102	Garrett Jones (RC)	.75
103	Jensen Lewis RC	.50
104	Clay Rapada RC	.50
105	Kyle Kendrick RC	.50
106	Eric Stults RC	.50
107	Jared Burton RC	.50
108	Julio DePaula RC	.50
109	Jesse Litsch RC	.50
110	Micah Owings RC	.50
111	Cory Doyne RC	.25
112	Jay Marshall RC	.25
113	Mike Schultz RC	.50
114	Juan Salas RC	.50
115	Matt Chico (RC)	.25
116	Brad Salmon RC	.50
117	Jeff Bailey RC	.50
118	Gustavo Molina RC	.50
119	Brian Burres RC	.50
120	Yovani Gallardo (RC)	2.00
121	Hector Gimenez (RC)	.25
122	Kelvin Jimenez RC	.50
123	Rick Vanden Hurk RC	.50
124	Billy Petrick RC	.25
125	Andrew Miller RC	.75
126	Rocky Cherry RC	.25
127	Jordan DeJong RC	.50
128	Eric Hull RC	.50
129	Kevin Mahar RC	.50
130	Tim Lincecum RC	.50
130	Tim Lincecum/Action/SP	15.00
131	Garrett Olson (RC)	.25
132	Neal Musser RC	.50
133	Mike Rabelo (RC)	.25
134	Dennis Dove (RC)	.25
135	J.D. Durbin (RC)	.25
136	Jose Garcia RC	.50
137	Marcus McBeth (RC)	.25
138	Curtis Thigpen (RC)	.25
139	Mike Zagurski RC	.50
140	Kevin Slowey (RC)	.25
141	Dewon Day RC	.50
142	Glen Perkins (RC)	.25
143	Brian Wolfe (RC)	.25
144	Dallas Braden (RC)	.50
145	J.A. Happ (RC)	.25
146	Lee Gronkiewicz RC	.50
147	Cesar Jimenez RC	.50
148	Mark McLemore (RC)	.25
149	Connor Robertson RC	.50
150	Phil Hughes (RC)	2.00
150	Phil Hughes/Action/SP	6.00
151	Matthew Brown RC	.50
152	Ryan Feierabend (RC)	.25
153	Brendan Ryan (RC)	.50
155	Terry Evans RC	.50
156	Eric Patterson (RC)	.25
157	Patrick Misch (RC)	.25
157	Darren Clarke RC	.50
158	Kevin Melillo (RC)	.25
159	Edwin Bellorin RC	.50
160	Ubaldo Jimenez (RC)	1.50
161	Ryan Budde RC	.50
162	Brian Buscher RC	.50
163	Juan Gutierrez RC	.50
164	Franklin Morales (RC)	.25
165	Carmen Pignatiello (RC)	.25
166	Jair Jurrjens (RC)	.25
167	Manny Acosta (RC)	.25
168	Ian Stewart (RC)	.25
169	Daniel Barone (RC)	.25
170	Justin Upton RC	3.00
170	Justin Upton/Action/SP	8.00
171	Tommy Watkins RC	.50
172	Ross Wolf RC	.50
173	Jack Cassel RC	.50
174	Asdrubal Cabrera RC	1.00
175	Mauro Zarate RC	.50
176	Aaron Laffey RC	.25
177	Marcus Gwyn RC	.50
178	Danny Richar RC	.50
179	Joel Hanrahan (RC)	.25
180	Cameron Maybin RC	1.00
181	John Lannan RC	.50
182	Shelley Duncan (RC)	.25
183	Brandon Wood (RC)	.50
184	Delwyn Young (RC)	.25
185	Manny Parra (RC)	.25
186	Ehren Wassermann RC	.50
187	Jose Reyes RC	.50
188	Jose Ascanio RC	.50
189	Alvin Colina RC	.50
190	Joba Chamberlain/ Action/SP	6.00
191	Yunel Escobar (RC)	.25
192	Carlos Maldonado (RC)	.25
193	Dan Meyer (RC)	.25
194	Scott Moore (RC)	.25
195	Romulo Sanchez RC	.50
196	Tom Shearn (RC)	.25
197	Craig Stansberry (RC)	.25
201	Joba Chamberlain RC	1.50
202	John Nelson/SP (RC)	5.00
203	Phil Dumatrait (RC)	.25
204	Brandon Moss (RC)	.25
205	Beltran Perez (RC)	.25
206	Drew Anderson (RC)	.50
207	Brett Campbell RC	.50
208	Andy Cannizaro/SP RC	8.00
209	Travis Chick/SP (RC)	5.00
210	Francisco Cruceta/ SP (RC)	4.00
211	Jose Diaz/SP (RC)	4.00
212	Jeff Fiorentino/SP (RC)	5.00
213	Tim Gradoville/SP RC	4.00
214	Kevin Hooper/SP RC	4.00
215	Philip Humber/SP (RC)	4.00
216	Juan Lara/SP RC	5.00
217	Mitch Maier/SP RC	4.00
218	Juan Morillo/SP (RC)	4.00
219	A.J. Murray/SP RC	5.00
220	Chris Narveson/SP (RC)	5.00
221	Oswaldo Navarro/SP RC	6.00

Black Back
Black Backs: 2-4X
Inserted 1:6 Hobby

A-Rod Road to 500
NM/M
A-Rod (476-500): 3.00

A-Rod Road to 500 Autograph
NM/M
Production One Set 3.00

Chrome

		NM/M
Common Player:		1.50

Production 1,952 Sets
Refractor: 2-3X
Production 552 Sets
Gold Refractor: 4-6X
Production 52 Sets

1	Akinori Iwamura	2.00
2	Angel Sanchez	1.50
3	Luis Hernandez	1.50
4	Troy Tulowitzki	5.00
5	Joaquin Arias	1.50
6	Jesus Flores	1.50
7	Brandon Wood	2.00
8	Kory Casto	1.50
9	Kevin Kouzmanoff	2.00
10	Tony Abreu	1.50
11	Travis Buck	1.50
12	Kurt Suzuki	1.50
13	Alejandro De Aza	1.50
14	Alex Gordon	6.00
15	Jerry Owens	1.50
16	Ryan Braun	8.00
17	Michael Bourn	1.50
18	Hunter Pence	6.00
19	Jeff Baker	1.50
20	Ben Francisco	1.50
21	Nate Schierholtz	1.50
22	Nathan Haynes	1.50
23	Andrew Miller	1.50
24	Sean Barker	1.50
25	Matt DeSalvo	1.50
26	Fred Lewis	1.50
27	Jamie Burke	1.50
28	Jeff Salazar	1.50
29	Chase Headley	2.00
30	Chris Basak	1.50
31	Mike Fontenot	1.50
32	Felix Pie	2.00
33	Masumi Kuwata	1.50
34	Daisuke Matsuzaka	5.00
35	Tim Lincecum	8.00
36	Jarrod Saltalamacchia	2.00
37	Tyler Clippard	2.00
38	Billy Butler	4.00
39	Matt Lindstrom	1.50
40	Brett Carroll	1.50
41	Alexi Casilla	1.50
42	Nick Gorneault	1.50
43	Matt Chico	1.50
44	Adam Lind	1.50
45	Miguel Montero	1.50
46	Danny Putnam	1.50
47	Delmon Young	2.00
48	Josh Fields	1.50
49	Carlos Gomez	2.00
50	Mark Reynolds	3.00
51	Shane Youman	2.00
52	Andy LaRoche	1.50
53	Kei Igawa	1.50
54	Don Kelly	1.50
55	Cameron Maybin	3.00
56	Travis Metcalf	1.50
57	Ubaldo Jimenez	1.50
58	Ryan Sweeney	1.50
59	Shawn Riggans	1.50
60	Jacoby Ellsbury	8.00
61	Andy Cavazos	1.50
62	Josh Hamilton	6.00
63	Homer Bailey	2.00
64	Sean Henn	1.50
65	Elijah Dukes	1.50
66	Brian Esposito	1.50
67	Brandon Morrow	1.50
68	Joe Smith	1.50
69	Chris Stewart	1.50
70	Eulogio De La Cruz	1.50
71	Sean Gallagher	1.50
72	Jailen Peguero	1.50
73	Juan Perez	1.50
74	Levale Speigner	1.50
75	Jamie Vermilyea	1.50
76	Hideki Okajima	2.00
77	Eric Patterson	1.50
78	Zack Segovia	1.50
79	Kyle Kendrick	1.50
80	Andrew Sonnanstine	1.50
81	Chase Wright	1.50
82	Jon Knott	1.50
83	Guillermo Rodriguez	1.50
84	Jon Coutlangus	1.50
85	Kevin Cameron	1.50
86	Brian Stokes	1.50
87	Alberto Arias	1.50
88	Delwyn Young	1.50
89	David Murphy	1.50
90	Micah Owings	1.50
91	Yovani Gallardo	4.00
92	Justin Hampson	1.50
93	Doug Slaten	1.50
94	Justin Upton	5.00
95	Joba Chamberlain	4.00

Dynamic Duos

		NM/M
Common Duo:		1.00

Inserted 1:4

1	Tim Lincecum, Nate Schierholtz	2.00
2	Joba Chamberlain, Phil Hughes	6.00
3	Ryan Braun, Yovani Gallardo	3.00
4	Kyle Kendrick, Michael Bourn	1.00
5	Delmon Young, Elijah Dukes	1.00
6	Hideki Okajima, Daisuke Matsuzaka	5.00
7	Justin Upton, Mark Reynolds	2.00
8	Eric Patterson, Felix Pie	1.00
9	Josh Hamilton, Homer Bailey	1.50
10	Ubaldo Jimenez, Troy Tulowitzki	2.00
11	Alex Gordon, Billy Butler	3.00
12	Delwyn Young, Andy LaRoche	2.00
13	Andrew Miller, Cameron Maybin	2.00
14	Joe Smith, Carlos Gomez	1.00
15	David Murphy, Jarrod Saltalamacchia	1.00

Debut Flashbacks

	NM/M
Complete Set (15):	10.00
Common Player:	.50

Inserted 1:6
Chrome: 2X
Production 1,952 Sets
Refractor: 3-4X
Production 552 Sets
Gold Refractor: 4-8X
Production 52 Sets

1	Vladimir Guerrero	1.50
2	Ken Griffey Jr.	3.00
3	Pedro Martinez	1.50
4	Carlos Delgado	.75
5	Gary Sheffield	1.00
6	Curt Schilling	1.00
7	Jorge Posada	.75
8	Miguel Tejada	.75
9	Trevor Hoffman	.50
10	Francisco Cordero	.50
11	Travis Hafner	.75
12	Paul LoDuca	.50
13	Jimmy Rollins	1.50
14	Magglio Ordonez	.75
15	Jim Edmonds	.50

Signatures

	NM/M
Common Auto.:	5.00
Red Ink:	1.5-2X

Production 52 Sets

AA	Alberto Arias	5.00
AC	Alexi Casilla	5.00
AG	Alex Gordon	15.00
AI	Akinori Iwamura	15.00
AL	Andy LaRoche	15.00
AM	Andrew Miller	10.00
AS	Angel Sanchez	5.00
ASL	Aaron Laffey	8.00
BB	Brian Barden	8.00
BC	Brett Carroll	8.00
BE	Brian Esposito	8.00
BF	Ben Francisco	8.00
BP	Ben Petrick	10.00
BPB	Brian Buscher	8.00
BS	Brian Stokes	8.00
BW	Brian Wolfe	8.00
CD	Cory Doyne	8.00
CM	Cameron Maybin	20.00
CS	Chris Stewart	10.00
CW	Chase Wright	10.00
DC	Darren Clarke	8.00
ER	Edwar Ramirez	15.00
FC	Francisco Cordero/SP	60.00
FL	Fred Lewis	15.00
FP	Felix Pie	15.00
GS	Gary Sheffield/SP	60.00
HO	Hideki Okajima	20.00
HP	Hunter Pence	50.00
JA	Joaquin Arias	10.00
JB	Jared Burton	20.00
JC	Jon Coutlangus	10.00
JCH	Joba Chamberlain	10.00
JH	Joel Hanrahan	10.00
JJR	Jo Jo Reyes	10.00
JL	Jensen Lewis	10.00
JM	Jason Miller	10.00
JRB	Joseph Bisenius	8.00
JSS	Jarrod Saltalamacchia	15.00
JU	Justin Upton	60.00
KK	Kevin Kouzmanoff	15.00
KS	Kurt Suzuki	15.00
LS	Levale Speigner	8.00
MB	Michael Bourn	15.00
MBB	Matthew Brown	8.00
ML	Matt Lindstrom	10.00
MM	Mark McLemore	8.00
NG	Nick Gorneault	15.00
NH	Nathan Haynes	8.00
PD	Phil Dumatrait	10.00
PH	Phil Hughes	60.00
PL	Paul LoDuca	15.00
RB	Ryan Braun	75.00
RC	Rocky Cherry	10.00
RDB	Ryan Budde	10.00
RZB	Ryan Braun	10.00
TB	Travis Buck	15.00
TC	Tyler Clippard	15.00
TL	Tim Lincecum	85.00
TM	Travis Metcalf	25.00
TPC	Troy Cate	8.00
YG	Yovani Gallardo	30.00
ZS	Zack Segovia	10.00

Signatures Combos

NM/M
Production 25 Sets

LO	Tim Lincecum, Hideki Okajima	125.00
ML	Andrew Miller, Matt Lindstrom	60.00
OI	Hideki Okajima, Akinori Iwamura	125.00
LB	Matt Lindstrom, Michael Bourn	40.00

Diamond Debut Tix Relics

Production 20 Sets

2008 Topps

	NM/M
Complete Set (660):	50.00
Common Player:	.10
Hobby Pack (10):	2.00
Hobby Box (36):	60.00

1	Alex Rodriguez	1.50
2	Barry Zito	.10
3	Jeff Suppan	.10
4	Rick Ankiel	.25
5	Scott Kazmir	.25
6	Felix Pie	.10
7	Mickey Mantle	4.00
8	Stephen Drew	.25
9	Randy Wolf	.10
10	Miguel Cabrera	.50
11	Yorvit Torrealba	.10
12	Jason Bartlett	.10
13	Kendry Morales	.10
14	Lenny DiNardo	.10
15	Magglio Ordonez, Ichiro Suzuki, Placido Polanco	.50
16	Kevin Gregg	.10
17	Cristian Guzman	.10
18	J.D. Durbin	.10
19	Robinson Tejada	.10
20	Daisuke Matsuzaka	1.00
21	Edwin Encarnacion	.10
22	Ron Washington	.10
23	Chin-Lung Hu (RC)	.25
24	Alex Rodriguez, Magglio Ordonez, Vladimir Guerrero	.50
25	Kazuo Matsui	.10
26	Manny Ramirez	.50
27	Bob Melvin	.10
28	Kyle Kendrick	.10
29	Anibal Sanchez	.10
30	Jimmy Rollins	.50
31	Ronny Paulino	.10
32	Howie Kendrick	.10
33	Joe Mauer	.25
34	Aaron Cook	.10
35	Cole Hamels	.25
36	Brendan Harris	.10
37	Jason Marquis	.10
38	Preston Wilson	.10
39	Yovani Gallardo	.25
40	Miguel Tejada	.25
41	Rich Aurilia	.10
42	Corey Hart	.25
43	Ryan Dempster	.10
44	Jonathan Broxton	.10
45	Dontrelle Willis	.10
46	Zack Greinke	.10
47	Orlando Cabrera	.25
48	Zachary Duke	.10
49	Orlando Hernandez	.10
50	Jake Peavy	.25
51	Erik Bedard	.25
52	Trevor Hoffman	.10
53	Hank Blalock	.10
54	Victor Martinez	.25
55	Chris Young	.10
56	Seth Smith (RC)	.25
57	Wladimir Balentien (RC)	.25
58	Matt Holliday, Ryan Howard, Miguel Cabrera	.50
59	Grady Sizemore	.50
60	Jose Reyes	.50
61	Alex Rodriguez, Carlos Pena, David Ortiz	.50
62	Rich Thompson (RC)	.25
63	Jason Michaels	.10
64	Mike Lowell	.10
65	Billy Wagner	.10
66	Brad Wilkerson	.10
67	Wes Helms	.10
68	Kevin Millar	.10
69	Bobby Cox	.10
70	Dan Uggla	.25
71	Jarrod Washburn	.10
72	Mike Piazza	.40
73	Mike Napoli	.10
74	Garrett Atkins	.25
75	Felix Hernandez	.25
76	Ivan Rodriguez	.25
77	Angel Guzman	.10
78	Radhames Liz RC	.10
79	Omar Vizquel	.10
80	Alex Rios	.25
81	Ray Durham	.10
82	So Taguchi	.10
83	Mark Reynolds	.10
84	Brian Fuentes	.10
85	Jason Bay	.25
86	Scott Podsednik	.10
87	Maicer Izturis	.10
88	Jack Cust	.10
89	Josh Willingham	.10
90	Vladimir Guerrero	.50
91	Marcus Giles	.10
92	Ross Detwiler RC	1.00
93	Kenny Lofton	.10
94	Bud Black	.10
95	John Lackey	.10
96	Sam Fuld RC	.50
97	Clint Sammons (RC)	.10
98	Ryan Howard, Chase Utley	.50
99	David Ortiz, Manny Ramirez	.25
100	Ryan Howard	.75
101	Ryan Braun	.50
102	Ross Ohlendorf RC	.50
103	Jonathan Albaladejo RC	.10
104	Kevin Youkilis	.25
105	Roger Clemens	1.00
106	Josh Bard	.10
107	Shawn Green	.10
108	B.J. Ryan	.10
109	Joe Nathan	.10
110	Justin Morneau	.40
111	Ubaldo Jimenez	.10
112	Jacque Jones	.10
113	Kevin Frandsen	.10
114	Mike Fontenot	.10
115	Johan Santana	.50
116	Chuck James	.10
117	Boof Bonser	.10
118	Marco Scutaro	.10
119	Jeremy Hermida	.10
120	Andruw Jones	.25
121	Mike Cameron	.10
122	Jason Varitek	.25
123	Terry Francona	.10
124	Bob Geren	.10
125	Tim Hudson	.25
126	Brandon Jones RC	.50
127	Steve Pearce RC	1.00
128	Kenny Lofton	.10
129	Kevin Hart (RC)	.25
130	Justin Upton	.50
131	Norris Hopper	.10
132	Ramon Vazquez	.10
133	Mike Bacsik	.10
134	Matt Stairs	.10
135	Brad Penny	.10
136	Robinson Cano	.40
137	Jamey Carroll	.10
138	Dan Wheeler	.10
139	Johnny Estrada	.10
140	Brandon Webb	.25
141	Ryan Klesko	.10
142	Chris Duncan	.10
143	Willie Harris	.10
144	Jerry Owens	.10
145	Magglio Ordonez	.25
146	Aaron Hill	.10
147	Marlon Anderson	.10
148	Gerald Laird	.10
149	Luke Hochevar RC	1.00
150	Alfonso Soriano	.40
151	Adam Loewen	.10
152	Bronson Arroyo	.10
153	Luis Mendoza (RC)	.50
154	David Ross	.10
155	Carlos Zambrano	.25
156	Brandon McCarthy	.10
157	Tim Redding	.10
158	Jose Bautista	.10
159	Luke Scott	.10
160	Ben Sheets	.25
161	Matt Garza	.10
162	Andy LaRoche	.10
163	Doug Davis	.10
164	Nate Schierholtz	.10
165	Tim Lincecum	.25
166	Andrew Sonnanstine	.10
167	Jason Hirsh	.10
168	Phil Hughes	.25
169	Adam Lind	.10
170	Scott Rolen	.25
171	John Maine	.10
172	Chris Ray	.10
173	Jamie Moyer	.10
174	Julian Tavarez	.10
175	Delmon Young	.10
176	Troy Patton (RC)	.25
177	Josh Anderson (RC)	.50
178	Dustin Pedroia	.25
179	Chris Young	.25
180	Jose Valverde	.10
181	Joe Borowski, Bobby Jenks, J.J. Putz	.25
182	Billy Buckner (RC)	.25
183	Paul Byrd	.10
184	Tadahito Iguchi	.10
185	Yunel Escobar	.10
186	Lastings Milledge	.10
187	Dustin McGowan	.10
188	Kei Igawa	.10
189	Esteban German	.10
190	Russell Martin	.25
191	Orlando Hudson	.10
192	Jim Edmonds	.10
193	J.J. Hardy	.10
194	Chad Billingsley	.10
195	Todd Helton	.25
196	Ross Gload	.10
197	Melky Cabrera	.10
198	Shannon Stewart	.10
199	Adrian Beltre	.10
200	Manny Ramirez	.40
201	Matt Capps	.10
202	Mike Lamb	.10
203	Jason Tyner	.10
204	Rafael Furcal	.10
205	Gil Meche	.10
206	Geoff Jenkins	.10
207	Jeff Kent	.10
208	David DeJesus	.10
209	Andy Phillips	.10
210	Mark Teahen	.10
211	Lyle Overbay	.10
212	Moises Alou	.10
213	Michael Barrett	.10
214	C.J. Wilson	.10
215	Bobby Jenks	.10
216	Ryan Garko	.10
217	Josh Beckett	.40
218	Clint Hurdle	.10
219	Kevin Kouzmanoff	.10
220	Roy Oswalt	.25
221	Ian Snell	.10
222	Mark Grudzielanek	.10
223	Odalis Perez	.10
224	Mark Buehrle	.10
225	Hunter Pence	.25
226	Kurt Suzuki	.10
227	Alfredo Amezaga	.10
228	Geoff Blum	.10
229	Dustin Pedroia	.25
230	Roy Halladay	.25
231	Casey Blake	.10
232	Clay Buchholz (RC)	.50
233	Jimmy Rollins	.25
234	Boston Red Sox	.25
234	Boston Red Sox w/Giuliani	15.00
235	Rich Harden	.10
236	Joe Koshansky (RC)	.25
237	Eric Wedge	.10
238	Shane Victorino	.10
239	Richie Sexson	.10
240	Jim Thome	.25
241	Ervin Santana	.10
242	Manny Acta	.10
243	Akinori Iwamura	.10
244	Adam Wainwright	.10
245	Danny Haren	.10
246	Jason Isringhausen	.10
247	Edgar Gonzalez	.10
248	Jose Contreras	.10
249	Chris Sampson	.10
250	Jonathan Papelbon	.25
251	Dan Johnson	.10
252	Dmitri Young	.10
253	Bronson Sardinha (RC)	.25
254	David Murphy	.10
255	Brandon Phillips	.10
256	Alex Rodriguez	1.00
257	Austin Kearns, Dmitri Young	.10
258	Manny Ramirez, Kevin Youkilis	.25
259	Emilio Bonifacio RC	.50
260	Chad Cordero	.10
261	Josh Barfield	.10
262	Brett Myers	.10
263	Nook Logan	.10
264	Byung-Hyun Kim	.10
265	Fredi Gonzalez	.10
266	Ryan Doumit	.10
267	Chris Burke	.10
268	Daric Barton (RC)	.25
269	James Loney	.25
270	C.C. Sabathia	.25
271	Chad Tracy	.10
272	Anthony Reyes	.10
273	Rafael Soriano	.10
274	Jermaine Dye	.10
275	C.C. Sabathia	.25
276	Brad Ausmus	.10
277	Aubrey Huff	.10
278	Xavier Nady	.10
279	Damion Easley	.10
280	Willie Randolph	.10
281	Carlos Ruiz	.10
282	Jon Lester	.25
283	Jorge Sosa	.10
284	Lance Broadway RC	.25
285	Tony LaRussa	.10
286	Jeff Clement (RC)	.25
287	Justin Morneau, Johan Santana, Joe Mauer	.25
288	Ivan Rodriguez, Justin Morneau, Justin Verlander	.25
289	Justin Ruggiano (RC)	.50
290	Edgar Renteria	.10
291	Eugenio Velez RC	.50
292	Mark Loretta	.10
293	Gavin Floyd	.10
294	Brian McCann	.25
295	Tim Wakefield	.10
296	Paul Konerko	.25
297	Jorge Posada	.25
298	Prince Fielder, Ryan Howard, Adam Dunn	.50
299	Cesar Izturis	.10
300	Chien-Ming Wang	.50
301	Chris Duffy	.10
302	Horacio Ramirez	.10
303	Jose Lopez	.10
304	Jose Vidro	.10
305	Carlos Delgado	.25
306	Scott Olsen	.10
307	Shawn Hill	.10
308	Felipe Lopez	.10
309	Ryan Church	.10
310	Kelvim Escobar	.10
311	Jeremy Guthrie	.10
312	Ramon Hernandez	.10
313	Kameron Loe	.10
314	Ian Kinsler	.10
315	David Weathers	.10
316	Scott Hatteberg	.10
317	Cliff Lee	.10
318	Ned Yost	.10
319	Joey Votto (RC)	1.00
320	Ichiro Suzuki	.10
321	J.R. Towles RC	1.00
322	Scott Kazmir, Johan Santana, Erik Bedard	.25
323	Jose Valverde, Francisco Cordero, Trevor Hoffman	.10
324	Jake Peavy	.25
325	Jim Leyland	.10
326	Matt Holliday, Chipper Jones, Hanley Ramirez	.25
327	Jake Peavy, Aaron Harang, John Smoltz	.25
328	Nyjer Morgan (RC)	.50
329	Lou Piniella	.10
330	Curtis Granderson	.25
331	Dave Roberts	.10
332	Grady Sizemore, Jhonny Peralta	.10
333	Jayson Nix (RC)	.25
334	Oliver Perez	.10
335	Eric Byrnes	.10
336	Jhonny Peralta	.25
337	Livan Hernandez	.10
338	Matt Diaz	.10
339	Troy Percival	.10
340	David Wright	.75
341	Daniel Cabrera	.10
342	Matt Belisle	.10
343	Kason Gabbard	.10
344	Mike Rabelo	.10
345	Carl Crawford	.25
346	Adam Everett	.10
347	Chris Capuano	.10
348	Craig Monroe	.10
349	Mike Mussina	.25
350	Mark Teixeira	.25
351	Bobby Crosby	.10
352	Miguel Batista	.10
353	Brendan Ryan	.10
354	Edwin Jackson	.10
355	Brian Roberts	.10
356	Manny Corpas	.10
357	Jeremy Accardo	.10
358	John Patterson	.10
359	Evan Meek RC	.50
360	David Ortiz	.50
361	Wesley Wright RC	.50
362	Fernando Hernandez RC	.50
363	Brian Barton RC	.50
364	Al Reyes	.10
365	Derrek Lee	.40
366	Jeff Weaver	.10
367	Khalil Greene	.10
368	Michael Bourn	.10
369	Luis Castillo	.10
370	Adam Dunn	.40
371	Rickie Weeks	.10
372	Matt Kemp	.25
373	Casey Kotchman	.10
374	Jason Jennings	.10
375	Fausto Carmona	.25
376	Willy Taveras	.10
377	Jake Westbrook	.10
378	Ozzie Guillen	.10
379	Hideki Okajima	.10
380	Grady Sizemore	.50
381	Jeff Francoeur	.40
382	Micah Owings	.10
383	Jered Weaver	.25
384	Carlos Quentin	.25
385	Troy Tulowitzki	.25
386	Julio Lugo	.10
387	Sean Marshall	.10
388	Jorge Cantu	.10
389	Callix Crabbe (RC)	.10
390	Troy Glaus	.25
391	Nick Markakis	.40
392	Joey Gathright	.10
393	Michael Cuddyer	.10
394	Mark Ellis	.10
395	Lance Berkman	.25
396	Randy Johnson	.40
397	Brian Wilson	.10
398	Kenji Johjima	.10
399	Jarrod Saltalamacchia	.10
400	Matt Holliday	.40
401	Scott Hairston	.10
402	Taylor Buchholz	.10
403	Nate Robertson	.10
404	Cecil Cooper	.10
405	Travis Hafner	.25
406	Takashi Saito	.10
407	Johnny Damon	.40
408	Edinson Volquez	.25
409	Jason Giambi	.25
410	Alex Gordon	.25
411	Jason Kubel	.10
412	Joel Zumaya	.10
413	Wandy Rodriguez	.10
414	Andrew Miller	.25
415	Derek Lowe	.25
416	Elijah Dukes	.25
417	Brian Bass	.25
418	Dioner Navarro	.25
419	Bengie Molina	.10
420	Nick Swisher	.25
421	Brandon Backe	.10

#	Player	Price
422	Erick Aybar	.10
423	Mike Scioscia	.10
424	Aaron Harang	.10
425	Hanley Ramirez	.50
426	Franklin Gutierrez	.10
427	Carlos Guillen	.25
428	Jair Jurrjens	.10
429	Billy Butler	.10
430	Ryan Braun	.50
431	Delwyn Young	.10
432	Jason Kendall	.10
433	Carlos Silva	.10
434	Ron Gardenhire	.10
435	Torii Hunter	.25
436	Joe Blanton	.10
437	Brandon Wood	.10
438	Jay Payton	.10
439	Josh Hamilton	.40
440	Pedro Martinez	.50
441	Miguel Olivo	.10
442	Luis Gonzalez	.10
443	Greg Dobbs	.10
444	Jack Wilson	.10
445	Hideki Matsui	.75
446	Randor Bierd RC	.50
447	Chipper Jones, Mark Teixeira	.40
448	Cameron Maybin	.10
449	Braden Looper	.10
450	Prince Fielder	.40
451	Brian Giles	.10
452	Kevin Slowey	.10
453	Josh Fogg	.10
454	Mike Hampton	.10
455	Derek Jeter	1.50
456	Chone Figgins	.25
457	Josh Fields	.10
458	Brad Hawpe	.10
459	Mike Sweeney	.10
460	Chase Utley	.50
461	Jacoby Ellsbury	.50
462	Freddy Sanchez	.10
463	John McLaren	.10
464	Rocco Baldelli	.10
465	Huston Street	.10
466	Miguel Cabrera, Ivan Rodriguez	.25
467	Nick Blackburn RC	.50
468	Gregor Blanco (RC)	.25
469	Brian Bocock RC	.50
470	Tom Gorzelanny	.10
471	Brian Schneider	.10
472	Shaun Marcum	.10
473	Joe Maddon	.10
474	Yuniesky Betancourt	.10
475	Adrian Gonzalez	.25
476	Johnny Cueto RC	1.00
477	Ben Broussard	.10
478	Geovany Soto	.25
479	Bobby Abreu	.25
480	Matt Cain	.25
481	Manny Parra	.10
482	Kazuo Fukumori RC	.50
483	Mike Jacobs	.10
484	Todd Jones	.10
485	J.J. Putz	.10
486	Javier Vazquez	.10
487	Corey Patterson	.10
488	Mike Gonzalez	.10
489	Joakim Soria	.10
490	Albert Pujols	1.50
491	Cliff Floyd	.10
492	Harvey Garcia (RC)	.25
493	Steve Holm RC	.50
494	Paul Maholm	.10
495	James Shields	.25
496	Brad Lidge	.10
497	Cla Meredith	.10
498	Matt Chico	.10
499	Milton Bradley	.10
500	Chipper Jones	.50
501	Elliot Johnson (RC)	.25
502	Alex Cora	.10
503	Jeremy Bonderman	.10
504	Conor Jackson	.25
505	B.J. Upton	.25
506	Jay Gibbons	.10
507	Mark DeRosa	.10
508	John Danks	.10
509	Alex Gonzalez	.10
510	Justin Verlander	.25
511	Jeff Francis	.10
512	Placido Polanco	.10
513	Rick Vanden Hurk	.10
514	Tony Pena	.10
515	A.J. Burnett	.10
516	Jason Schmidt	.10
517	Bill Hall	.10
518	Ian Stewart	.10
519	Travis Buck	.10
520	Vernon Wells	.10
521	Jayson Werth	.10
522	Nate McLouth	.10
523	Noah Lowry	.10
524	Raul Ibanez	.10
525	Gary Matthews	.10
526	Juan Encarnacion	.10
527	Marlon Byrd	.10
528	Paul LoDuca	.50
529	Masahide Kobayashi RC	.50
530	Ryan Zimmerman	.25
531	Hiroki Kuroda RC	1.00
532	Tim Lahey RC	.50
533	Kyle McClellan RC	.50
534	Matt Tupman RC	.50
535	Francisco Rodriguez	.10
536	Albert Pujols, Prince Fielder	.50
537	Scott Moore	.10
538	Alex Romero (RC)	.25
539	Clete Thomas RC	.50
540	John Smoltz	.40
541	Adam Jones	.10
542	Adam Kennedy	.10
543	Carlos Lee	.25
544	Chad Gaudin	.10
545	Chris Young	.10
546	Francisco Liriano	.10
547	Fred Lewis	.10
548	Garrett Olson	.10
549	Gregg Zaun	.10
550	Curt Schilling	.40
551	Erick Threets (RC)	.25
552	J.D. Drew	.25
553	Jo Jo Reyes	.10
554	Joe Borowski	.10
555	Josh Beckett	.40
556	John Gibbons	.10
557	John McDonald	.10
558	John Russell	.10
559	Jonny Gomes	.10
560	Aramis Ramirez	.40
561	Matt Tolbert RC	.50
562	Ronnie Belliard	.10
563	Ramon Troncoso RC	.50
564	Frank Catalanotto	.10
565	A.J. Pierzynski	.10
566	Kevin Millwood	.10
567	David Eckstein	.10
568	Jose Guillen	.10
569	Brad Hennessey	.10
570	Homer Bailey	.10
571	Eric Gagne	.10
572	Adam Eaton	.10
573	Tom Gordon	.10
574	Scott Baker	.10
575	Ty Wigginton	.10
576	David Bush	.10
577	John Buck	.10
578	Ricky Nolasco	.10
579	Jesse Litsch	.10
580	Ken Griffey Jr.	1.00
581	Kazuo Matsui	.10
582	Dusty Baker	.10
583	Nick Punto	.10
584	Ryan Theriot	.10
585	Brian Bannister	.10
586	Coco Crisp	.10
587	Chris Snyder	.10
588	Tony Gwynn	.10
589	Dave Trembley	.10
590	Mariano Rivera	.25
591	Rico Washington (RC)	.25
592	Matt Morris	.10
593	Randy Wells RC	.50
594	Mike Morse	.10
595	Francisco Cordero	.10
596	Joba Chamberlain	1.00
597	Kyle Davies	.10
598	Bruce Bochy	.10
599	Austin Kearns	.10
600	Tom Glavine	.25
601	Felipe Paulino RC	.50
602	Lyle Overbay, Vernon Wells	.10
603	Blake DeWitt (RC)	.25
604	Wily Mo Pena	.10
605	Andre Ethier	.10
606	Jason Bergmann	.10
607	Ryan Spilborghs	.10
608	Brian Burres	.10
609	Ted Lilly	.10
610	Carlos Beltran	.40
611	Garret Anderson	.10
612	Kelly Johnson	.10
613	Melvin Mora	.10
614	Rich Hill	.10
615	Pat Burrell	.10
616	Jon Garland	.10
617	Asdrubal Cabrera	.10
618	Pat Neshek	.10
619	Sergio Mitre	.10
620	Gary Sheffield	.40
621	Denard Span	.10
622	Jorge De La Rosa	.10
623	Trey Hillman	.10
624	Joe Torre	.10
625	Greg Maddux	1.00
626	Mike Redmond	.10
627	Mike Pelfrey	.10
628	Andy Pettitte	.25
629	Eric Chavez	.10
630	Chris Carpenter	.10
631	Joe Girardi	.10
632	Charlie Manuel	.10
633	Adam LaRoche	.10
634	Kenny Rogers	.10
635	Michael Young	.10
636	Rafael Betancourt	.10
637	Jose Castillo	.10
638	Juan Pierre	.10
639	Juan Uribe	.10
640	Carlos Pena	.25
641	Marcus Thames	.10
642	Mark Kotsay	.10
643	Matt Murton	.10
644	Reggie Willits	.10
645	Andy Marte	.10
646	Rajai Davis	.10
647	Randy Winn	.10
648	Ryan Freel	.10
649	Joe Crede	.10
650	Frank Thomas	.40
651	Martin Prado	.10
652	Rod Barajas	.10
653	Endy Chavez	.10
654	Willy Aybar	.10
655	Aaron Rowand	.10
656	Darin Erstad	.10
657	Jeff Keppinger	.10
658	Kerry Wood	.10
659	Vicente Padilla	.10
660	Yadier Molina	.10

Black

Black: 20-30X
Production 57 Sets

Gold

Gold: 5-10X
Production 2,008 Sets

Gold Foil

Gold Foil: 1-2X

Platinum

No Pricing
Production One Set

Printing Plates

No Pricing
Production one set per color.

Campaign 2008

		NM/M
	Common Candidate:	1.00
	Inserted 1:9	
JB	Joseph Biden	1.00
HC	Hillary Clinton	3.00
JE	John Edwards	2.00
RG	Rudy Giuliani	2.00
MH	Mike Huckabee	1.00
DK	Dennis Kucininch	1.00
JM	John McCain	3.00
BO	Barack Obama	6.00
RP	Ron Paul	1.00
BR	Bill Richardson	1.00
MR	Mitt Romney	1.00
FT	Fred Thompson	2.00

Campaign '08 Letter Patches

		NM/M
	Inserted 1:2,642	
HC	Hillary Clinton	50.00
BO	Barack Obama	150.00
JM	John McCain	60.00

Commemorative Patch Relics

		NM/M
	Production 499-539	
AIR	Alex Rios	15.00
AP	Albert Pujols	20.00
AR	Alex Rodriguez	25.00
BW	Brandon Webb	10.00
CC	Carl Crawford	8.00
CH	Cole Hamels	20.00
CMS	Curt Schilling	15.00
CS	C.C. Sabathia	15.00
CU	Chase Utley	20.00
DAO	David Ortiz	30.00
DO	David Ortiz	15.00
DP	Dustin Pedroia	25.00
DW	David Wright	25.00
GS	Grady Sizemore	15.00
HO	Hideki Okajima	20.00
IS	Ichiro Suzuki	30.00
JAV	Jason Varitek	20.00
JB	Josh Beckett	25.00
JCL	Julio Lugo	15.00
JDD	J.D. Drew	15.00
JE	Jacoby Ellsbury	40.00
JL	Jon Lester	25.00
JM	Justin Morneau	20.00
JP	Jake Peavy	15.00
JR	Jose Reyes	15.00
JRP	Jonathan Papelbon	25.00
JV	Justin Verlander	15.00
KY	Kevin Youkilis	20.00
MH	Matt Holliday	15.00
ML	Mike Lowell	25.00
MR	Manny Ramirez	20.00
MT	Mike Timlin	15.00
PF	Prince Fielder	20.00
RH	Ryan Howard	25.00
RM	Russell Martin	15.00

Historical Campaign Match-Ups

NM/M
Inserted 1:6

	Match-Up	Price
1792	George Washington, John Adams	2.00
1796	John Adams, Thomas Jefferson	1.00
1800	Thomas Jefferson, Aaron Burr	1.00
1804	Thomas Jefferson, Charles Pinckney	1.00
1808	James Madison, Charles Pinckney	.50
1812	James Madison, DeWitt Clinton	.50
1816	James Monroe, Rufus King	.50
1820	James Monroe, John Quincy Adams	.50
1824	John Quincy Adams, Andrew Jackson	.50
1828	Andrew Jackson, John Quincy Adams	.50
1832	Andrew Jackson, Henry Clay	.50
1836	Martin Van Buren, William Henry Harrison	.50
1840	William Henry Harrison, Martin Van Buren	.50
1844	James K. Polk, Henry Clay	.50
1848	Zachary Taylor, Lewis Cass	.50
1852	Franklin Pierce, Winfield Scott	.50
1856	James Buchanan, John C. Fremont	.50
1860	Abraham Lincoln, John C. Breckinridge	2.00
1864	Abraham Lincoln, George B. McClellan	2.00
1868	Ulysses S. Grant, Horatio Seymour	1.00
1872	Ulysses S. Grant, Horace Greeley	1.00
1876	Rutherford B. Hayes, Samuel J. Tilden	.50
1880	James Garfield, Winfield Scott Hancock	.50
1884	Grover Cleveland, James G. Blaine	.50
1888	Benjamin Harrison, Grover Cleveland	.50
1892	Grover Cleveland, Benjamin Harrison	.50
1896	William McKinley, William Jennings Bryan	.50
1900	William McKinley, William Jennings Bryan	.50
1904	Theodore Roosevelt, Alton B. Parker	.50
1908	William H. Taft, William Jennings Bryan	.50
1912	Woodrow Wilson, Theodore Roosevelt	.50
1916	Woodrow Wilson, Charles Evans Hughes	.50
1920	Warren G. Harding, James M. Cox	.50
1924	Calvin Coolidge, John W. Davis	.50
1928	Herbert Hoover, Al Smith	.50
1932	Franklin D. Roosevelt, Herbert Hoover	1.00
1936	Franklin D. Roosevelt, Alf Landon	1.00
1940	Franklin D. Roosevelt, Wendell Willkie	1.00
1944	Franklin D. Roosevelt, Thomas E. Dewey	1.00
1948	Harry S. Truman, Thomas E. Dewey	.50
1952	Dwight D. Eisenhower, Adlai Stevenson	.50
1956	Dwight D. Eisenhower, Adlai Stevenson	.50
1960	John F. Kennedy, Richard Nixon	2.00
1964	Lyndon B. Johnson, Barry Goldwater	.50
1968	Richard Nixon, Hubert H. Humphrey	.50
1972	Richard Nixon, George McGovern	.50
1976	Jimmy Carter, Gerald Ford	.50
1980	Ronald Reagan, Jimmy Carter	1.00
1984	Ronald Reagan, Walter Mondale	1.00
1988	George H.W. Bush, Michael Dukakis	.50
1992	Bill Clinton, George H.W. Bush	1.00
1996	Bill Clinton, Bob Dole	1.00
2000	George W. Bush, Al Gore	1.00
2004	George W. Bush, John Kerry	1.00
2008D	Hillary Clinton, Barack Obama	2.00

Historical Campaign Match-Ups Cut Signatures

Production One Set

Home Run Derby

		NM/M
	Common Player:	3.00
	Production 999 Sets	
1	Alex Rodriguez	15.00
2	Ryan Braun	8.00
3	Carlos Beltran	5.00
4	Alfonso Soriano	5.00
5	Prince Fielder	10.00
6	Carlos Lee	15.00
7	Albert Pujols	4.00
8	Chris Young	4.00
9	Justin Morneau	4.00
10	Ryan Howard	8.00
11	Dan Uggla	3.00
12	Pat Burrell	4.00
13	Adrian Gonzalez	4.00
14	Ken Griffey Jr.	10.00
15	Carlos Pena	4.00
16	Brandon Phillips	4.00
17	Jimmy Rollins	5.00
18	David Wright	8.00
19	Jim Thome	4.00
20	Adam Dunn	4.00
21	Chipper Jones	8.00
22	Hanley Ramirez	5.00
23	Brad Hawpe	3.00
24	Jermaine Dye	3.00
25	Matt Holliday	5.00
26	Magglio Ordonez	4.00
27	Aaron Rowand	3.00
28	Andruw Jones	3.00
29	Khalil Greene	3.00
30	David Ortiz	6.00
31	Frank Thomas	4.00
32	Victor Martinez	4.00
33	Russell Martin	4.00
34	Gary Sheffield	4.00
35	Vladimir Guerrero	4.00
36	Carlos Delgado	4.00
37	Travis Hafner	3.00
38	Alex Rios	3.00
39	Grady Sizemore	4.00
40	Miguel Cabrera	4.00
41	Ryan Zimmerman	4.00
42	Nick Markakis	4.00
43	Jason Bay	3.00
44	Delmon Young	3.00
45	Lance Berkman	4.00
46	Manny Ramirez	5.00
47	Jorge Posada	4.00
48	Derrek Lee	4.00
49	B.J. Upton	4.00
50	Chase Utley	5.00

In The Name Relics

No Pricing

Mickey Mantle Home Run History

NM/M
Common Mantle (502-536): 2.00
Inserted 1:9

Mickey Mantle 1956 Reprint Relic

		NM/M
	Production 56	
56MM	Mickey Mantle	100.00

New York Commemorative Patch Relics

		NM/M
	Common Patch:	20.00
	Production 100 Sets	
AR	Alex Rodriguez	75.00
JP	Jorge Posada	30.00
DJ	Derek Jeter	75.00
RC	Robinson Cano	30.00
JD	Johnny Damon	30.00
BA	Bobby Abreu	30.00
CMW	Chien-Ming Wang	50.00
MR	Mariano Rivera	40.00
PH	Phil Hughes	35.00
JC	Joba Chamberlain	50.00
MC	Melky Cabrera	25.00
JG	Jason Giambi	25.00
AP	Andy Pettitte	35.00
HM	Hideki Matsui	40.00
MM	Mike Mussina	40.00
DW	David Wright	40.00
JR	Jose Reyes	35.00
CD	Carlos Delgado	20.00
CB	Carlos Beltran	20.00
PM	Pedro Martinez	25.00
JM	John Maine	20.00
BW	Billy Wagner	20.00
MA	Moises Alou	20.00
RMC	Ryan Church	20.00
OP	Oliver Perez	20.00
BS	Brian Schneider	20.00
LC	Luis Castillo	20.00
EC	Endy Chavez	20.00
OH	Orlando Hernandez	20.00
MP	Mike Pelfrey	20.00

Own the Game

		NM/M
	Complete Set (25):	10.00
	Common Player:	.50
	Inserted 1:6	
1	Alex Rodriguez	2.00
2	Prince Fielder	1.00
3	Ryan Howard	.50
4	Carlos Pena	.50
5	Adam Dunn	.50
6	Matt Holliday	.75
7	David Ortiz	1.00
8	Jim Thome	.50
9	Lance Berkman	.50
10	Miguel Cabrera	.75
11	Alex Rodriguez	2.00
12	Magglio Ordonez	.50
13	Matt Holliday	.75
14	Ryan Howard	.50
15	Vladimir Guerrero	.75
16	Carlos Pena	.50
17	Mike Lowell	.50
18	Miguel Cabrera	.75
19	Prince Fielder	1.00
20	Carlos Lee	.50
21	Jake Peavy	.50
22	John Lackey	.50
23	Brandon Webb	.50
24	Brad Penny	.50
25	Fausto Carmona	.50

Red Hot Rookie Redemptions

		NM/M
1	Jay Bruce/Auto.	50.00
2	Justin Masterson	15.00
3	John Bowker	10.00
4	Kosuke Fukudome	30.00
5	Mike Aviles	15.00
6	Chris Davis	20.00
7	Chris Volstad	15.00
8	Jeff Samardzija	25.00
9	Brad Ziegler	15.00
10	Gio Gonzalez	8.00
11	Clayton Kershaw	12.00
12	Daniel Murphy	20.00
13	Chris Dickerson	15.00
14	Pablo Sandoval	15.00
15	Nick Evans	15.00
16	Clayton Richard	10.00

Silk

		NM/M
	Common Player:	10.00
	Production 50 Sets	
1	Alex Rodriguez	75.00
2	Scott Kazmir	15.00
3	Ivan Rodriguez	15.00
4	Joe Mauer	15.00
5	Ken Griffey Jr.	50.00
6	Nick Markakis	25.00
7	Mickey Mantle	100.00
8	Erik Bedard	15.00
9	Derrek Lee	20.00
10	Miguel Cabrera	15.00
11	Yovani Gallardo	15.00
12	Victor Martinez	15.00
13	Curtis Granderson	20.00
14	Chris Young	15.00
15	Jimmy Rollins	25.00
16	Dan Uggla	10.00
17	Felix Hernandez	15.00
18	Alex Rios	15.00
19	Jason Bay	15.00
20	Jose Reyes	25.00
21	Mike Lowell	15.00
22	Carl Crawford	15.00
23	Chipper Jones	40.00
24	Troy Glaus	15.00
25	Cole Hamels	20.00
26	Chris Young	15.00
27	Torii Hunter	15.00
28	Hideki Matsui	15.00
29	Freddy Sanchez	10.00
30	Josh Beckett	25.00
31	Mark Buehrle	10.00
32	Brian Bannister	10.00
33	Carlos Beltran	15.00
34	Dontrelle Willis	10.00
35	Vladimir Guerrero	25.00
36	Matt Holliday	20.00
37	Adam Dunn	20.00
38	Gary Matthews Jr.	15.00
39	Travis Hafner	15.00
40	Chase Utley	30.00
41	Vernon Wells	15.00
42	Lance Berkman	20.00

#	Player	Price
43	Jeff Francis	10.00
44	Curt Schilling	20.00
45	Alfonso Soriano	20.00
46	Jarrod Saltalamacchia	15.00
47	Hideki Okajima	10.00
48	Pedro Martinez	25.00
49	Jorge Posada	20.00
50	Justin Upton	20.00
51	Tom Gorzelanny	10.00
52	Carlos Delgado	15.00
53	Edgar Renteria	10.00
54	Chien-Ming Wang	30.00
55	C.C. Sabathia	20.00
56	B.J. Upton	20.00
57	Delmon Young	15.00
58	Tim Lincecum	25.00
59	Carlos Zambrano	20.00
60	Magglio Ordonez	15.00
61	Brandon Webb	20.00
62	Ben Sheets	15.00
63	Brad Penny	10.00
64	John Lackey	20.00
65	Hanley Ramirez	25.00
66	Gary Sheffield	20.00
67	Ubaldo Jimenez	10.00
68	Barry Zito	15.00
69	Daisuke Matsuzaka	60.00
70	Justin Morneau	20.00
71	Jacoby Ellsbury	75.00
72	John Smoltz	20.00
73	Chris Carpenter	15.00
74	Ryan Braun	35.00
75	Prince Fielder	25.00
76	Carlos Lee	20.00
77	Ryan Zimmerman	20.00
78	Troy Tulowitzki	20.00
79	Michael Young	15.00
80	Johan Santana	25.00
81	Hunter Pence	30.00
82	Adrian Gonzalez	15.00
83	Jake Peavy	20.00
84	Derek Jeter	75.00
85	Ichiro Suzuki	35.00
86	Miguel Tejada	20.00
87	Trevor Hoffman	10.00
88	Kevin Youkilis	20.00
89	David Wright	35.00
90	Albert Pujols	75.00
91	Todd Helton	20.00
92	Rich Harden	10.00
93	Fausto Carmona	10.00
94	Mark Teixeira	20.00
95	Justin Verlander	25.00
96	Tim Hudson	15.00
97	Jeff Francoeur	20.00
98	Manny Ramirez	25.00
99	David Ortiz	30.00
100	Ryan Howard	40.00

Stars

NM/M
Complete Set (25): 15.00
Common Player: .50
Inserted 1:6

#	Player	Price
1	Alex Rodriguez	2.00
2	Magglio Ordonez	.50
3	Justin Morneau	.50
4	Josh Beckett	.75
5	David Wright	1.00
6	Jimmy Rollins	.75
7	Ichiro Suzuki	1.00
8	Chipper Jones	1.00
9	Brandon Webb	.75
10	Ryan Howard	1.00
11	Derek Jeter	2.00
12	Vladimir Guerrero	.75
13	Manny Ramirez	.75
14	Jake Peavy	.50
15	David Ortiz	.75
16	Jose Reyes	.75
17	Miguel Cabrera	.75
18	Victor Martinez	.50
19	C.C. Sabathia	.50
20	Prince Fielder	.75
21	Alfonso Soriano	.75
22	Grady Sizemore	.75
23	Albert Pujols	2.00
24	Pedro Martinez	.75
25	Matt Holliday	.75

The Mickey Mantle Story

NM/M
Complete Set (20): 40.00
Complete Series 1 Set (10): 20.00

Complete Series 2 Set (10): 20.00
Common Mantle: 3.00
Inserted 1:18

The Presidential Stamp Collection

NM/M
Production 90 Sets

#	Player	Price
GW1	George Washington	50.00
GW2	George Washington	50.00
GW3	George Washington	50.00
GW4	George Washington	50.00
GW5	George Washington	50.00
GW6	George Washington	50.00
TJ1	Thomas Jefferson	60.00
TJ2	Thomas Jefferson	60.00
TJ3	Thomas Jefferson	60.00
TJ4	Thomas Jefferson	60.00
JM1	James Monroe	60.00
JQA1	John Quincy Adams	60.00
AJ1	Andrew Jackson	60.00
WHH1	William Henry Harrison	40.00
JT1	John Tyler	60.00
ZT1	Zachary Taylor	60.00
JB1	James Buchanan	50.00
AL1	Abraham Lincoln	60.00
AL2	Abraham Lincoln	60.00
AL3	Abraham Lincoln	60.00
JG1	James Garfield	50.00
BH1	Benjamin Harrison	50.00
TR1	Teddy Roosevelt	60.00
WW1	Woodrow Wilson	60.00
WGH1	Warren G. Harding	50.00
HH1	Herbert Hoover	40.00
FDR1	Franklin Delano Roosevelt	50.00
DDE1	Dwight D. Eisenhower	60.00
JFK1	John F. Kennedy	100.00
JFK2	John F. Kennedy	100.00

Series 2

#	Player	Price
GW7	George Washington	60.00
GW8	George Washington	60.00
GW9	George Washington	60.00
GW10	George Washington	60.00
GW11	George Washington	60.00
GW12	George Washington	60.00
GW13	George Washington	60.00
JM2	James Monroe	60.00
AL4	Abraham Lincoln	100.00
JG2	James Garfield	50.00
TR2	Theodore Roosevelt	60.00
TR3	Theodore Roosevelt	60.00
WW2	Woodrow Wilson	50.00
WGH2	Warren Harding	50.00
RBH1	Rutherford B. Hayes	60.00
RBH2	Rutherford B. Hayes	60.00
WM1	William McKinley	50.00
LBJ1	Lyndon B. Johnson	50.00
USG1	Ulysses S. Grant	60.00
USG2	Ulysses S. Grant	60.00
WHT1	William Taft	60.00
RN1	Richard Nixon	60.00
CAA1	Chester A. Arthur	50.00
AJO1	Andrew Johnson	60.00
HST1	Harry S. Truman	60.00
JMA1	James Madison	60.00
JKP1	James K. Polk	60.00
GC1	Grover Cleveland	60.00
MF1	Millard Fillmore	60.00
MVB1	Martin Van Buren	60.00
FP1	Franklin Pierce	60.00

Topps 50th Anniversary All-Rookie Team

NM/M
Complete Set (110): 75.00
Common Player: .50
#'s 56-110 in Series 2
Inserted 1:5

#	Player	Price
1	Darryl Strawberry	.50
2	Gary Sheffield	.75
3	Dwight Gooden	.50
4	Melky Cabrera	.75
5	Gary Carter	.50
6	Lou Piniella	.50
7	David Justice	.50
8	Andre Dawson	.50
9	Mark Ellis	.50
10	Dave Johnson	.50
11	Jermaine Dye	.50
12	Dan Johnson	.50
13	Alfonso Soriano	.75
14	Prince Fielder	1.50
15	Hanley Ramirez	1.00
16	Matt Holliday	.75
17	Justin Verlander	1.00
18	Mark Teixeira	.75
19	Julio Franco	.50
20	Ivan Rodriguez	.75
21	Jason Bay	.75
22	Brandon Webb	.75
23	Dontrelle Willis	.50
24	Brad Wilkerson	.50
25	Dan Uggla	.50
26	Ozzie Smith	1.00
27	Andruw Jones	.75
28	Garret Anderson	.50
29	Jimmy Rollins	1.00
30	Brian McCann	.50
31	Scott Podsednik	.50
32	Garrett Atkins	.50
33	Billy Wagner	.50
34	Chipper Jones	1.00
35	Roger McDowell	.50
36	Austin Kearns	.50
37	Boog Powell	.50
38	Ron Swoboda	.50
39	Roy Oswalt	.75
40	Mike Piazza	1.00
41	Albert Pujols	3.00
42	Ichiro Suzuki	2.00
43	C.C. Sabathia	.75
44	Todd Helton	.75
45	Scott Rolen	.75
46	Derek Jeter	3.00
47	Shawn Green	.50
48	Manny Ramirez	1.00
49	Tom Seaver	1.00
50	Kenny Lofton	.50
51	Francisco Liriano	.75
52	Ryan Zimmerman	.75
53	Jeff Francoeur	.75
54	Joe Mauer	.75
55	Magglio Ordonez	.75
56	Carlos Beltran	1.00
57	Andre Ethier	.50
58	Brian Bannister	.50
59	Chris Young	.75
60	Troy Tulowitzki	.75
61	Hideki Okajima	.75
62	Delmon Young	.50
63	Craig Wilson	.50
64	Hunter Pence	1.00
65	Tadahito Iguchi	.50
66	Mark Kotsay	.50
67	Nick Markakis	1.00
68	Russ Adams	.50
69	Russell Martin	1.00
70	James Loney	.75
71	Ryan Braun	1.50
72	Jonny Gomes	.50
73	Carlos Ruiz	.50
74	Willy Taveras	.50
75	Joe Torre	.50
76	Jeff Kent	.50
77	Huston Street	.50
78	Dustin Pedroia	1.00
79	Gustavo Chacin	.50
80	Adam Dunn	1.00
81	Pat Burrell	.75
82	Rocco Baldelli	.50
83	Chad Tracy	.50
84	Adam LaRoche	.50
85	Aaron Miles	.50
86	Khalil Greene	.50
87	Daniel Cabrera	.50
88	Mike Gonzalez	.50
89	Ty Wigginton	.50
90	Angel Berroa	.50
91	Moises Alou	.50
92	Miguel Olivo	.50
93	Nick Johnson	.50
94	Eric Hinske	.50
95	Ramon Santiago	.50
96	Jason Jennings	.50
97	Adam Kennedy	.50
98	Mike Lamb	.50
99	Rafael Furcal	.50
100	Jay Payton	.50
101	Bengie Molina	.50
102	Mark Redman	.50
103	Alex Gonzalez	.50
104	Ray Durham	.50
105	Miguel Cairo	.50
106	Kerry Wood	.75
107	Dmitri Young	.50
108	Jose Cruz	.50
109	Jose Guillen	.50
110	Scott Hatteberg	.50

Topps 50th Anniversary All-Rookie Team Autos.

Production 25 Sets
Series 2

Topps 50th Anniv. All-Rookie Team Relics

NM/M
Production 50 Sets

#	Player	Price
DS	Darryl Strawberry	20.00
AD	Andre Dawson	40.00
DW	Dontrelle Willis	10.00
MP	Mike Piazza	40.00
TS	Tom Seaver	40.00
OS	Ozzie Smith	40.00
IR	Ivan Rodriguez	25.00
DG	Dwight Gooden	15.00
GC	Gary Carter	20.00
AS	Alfonso Soriano	30.00
IS	Ichiro Suzuki	40.00
MH	Matt Holliday	25.00
JR	Jimmy Rollins	30.00
PF	Prince Fielder	40.00
DJ	David Justice	20.00
JV	Justin Verlander	40.00
AJ	Andruw Jones	20.00
CJ	Chipper Jones	30.00
RO	Roy Oswalt	20.00
BW	Brandon Webb	25.00

Series 2

#	Player	Price
BM	Brian McCann	15.00
HR	Hanley Ramirez	30.00
DU	Dan Uggla	10.00
GA	Garret Anderson	10.00
JB	Jason Bay	10.00
MT	Mark Teixeira	20.00
SP	Scott Podsednik	10.00
JM	Joe Mauer	25.00
AP	Albert Pujols	40.00
AD	Adam Dunn	15.00
CS	C.C. Sabathia	15.00
NJ	Nick Johnson	10.00
PB	Pat Burrell	15.00
TH	Todd Helton	10.00
MO	Magglio Ordonez	10.00
GS	Gary Sheffield	15.00
RB	Rocco Baldelli	10.00
AE	Andre Ethier	10.00
NM	Nick Markakis	20.00
FL	Francisco Liriano	15.00

Trading Card History

NM/M
Common Player: .50
Inserted 1:12
#26-50 HTA Exclusive
#51-75 Series 2

#	Player	Price
1	Jacoby Ellsbury	2.00
2	Joba Chamberlain	4.00
3	Daisuke Matsuzaka	3.00
4	Prince Fielder	1.00
5	Clay Buchholz	2.00
6	Alex Rodriguez	3.00
7	Mickey Mantle	4.00
8	Ryan Braun	2.00
9	Albert Pujols	3.00
10	Joe Mauer	1.50
11	Jose Reyes	1.50
12	Joey Votto	1.50
13	Johan Santana	1.00
14	Hunter Pence	1.00
15	Hideki Okajima	.50
16	Cameron Maybin	.50
17	Roger Clemens	1.00
18	Tim Lincecum	1.00
19	Mark Teixeira, Jeff Francoeur	.50
20	Justin Upton	1.00
21	Alfonso Soriano	1.00
22	Pedro Martinez	1.00
23	Chien-Ming Wang	1.50
24	Ichiro Suzuki	2.00
25	Grady Sizemore	1.00
26	Ryan Howard	2.00
27	David Wright	1.50
28	Chin-Lung Hu	.50
29	Justin Morneau	1.00
30	Ken Griffey Jr.	3.00
31	Chipper Jones	2.50
32	Justin Verlander	1.50
33	Manny Ramirez	1.50
34	Chase Utley	1.50
35	Ivan Rodriguez	.75
36	Josh Beckett	1.00
37	Tom Glavine	1.50
38	Vladimir Guerrero	1.50
39	Lance Berkman	1.00
40	Gary Sheffield	1.00
41	Luke Hochevar	.50
42	David Ortiz	1.50
43	Miguel Cabrera	1.50
44	Andruw Jones	.75
45	Hideki Matsui	2.50
46	C.C. Sabathia	.75
47	Magglio Ordonez	1.00
48	Pedro Martinez	1.50
49	Curtis Granderson	1.00
50	Derek Jeter	4.00
51	Victor Martinez	1.00
52	Hanley Ramirez	1.00
53	Jake Peavy	.75
54	Brandon Webb	.75
55	Matt Holliday	.75
56	Hiroki Kuroda	.50
57	Mike Lowell	.75
58	Carlos Lee	.75
59	Nick Markakis	.75
60	Carlos Beltran	.75
61	Francisco Rodriguez	.75
62	Troy Tulowitzki	.75
63	Russell Martin	.75
64	Justin Morneau	.75
65	Phil Hughes	.75
66	Torii Hunter	.75
67	Adam Dunn	.75
68	Raul Ibanez	.50
69	Robinson Cano	.75
70	Brad Hawpe	.50
71	Michael Young	.50
72	Jim Thome	.75
73	Chris Young	.75
74	Carlos Zambrano	.75
75	Felix Hernandez	1.00

World Champion Relics

NM/M
Production 100 Sets

#	Player	Price
1	Josh Beckett	60.00
2	Hideki Okajima	50.00
3	Curt Schilling	60.00
4	Jason Varitek	60.00
5	Mike Lowell	60.00
6	Jacoby Ellsbury	80.00
7	Dustin Pedroia	70.00
8	Jonathan Papelbon	60.00
9	Julio Lugo	30.00
10	Manny Ramirez	50.00
11	David Ortiz	60.00
12	Eric Gagne	40.00
13	Jon Lester	50.00
14	J.D. Drew	50.00
15	Kevin Youkilis	50.00

World Champion Autograph Relics

NM/M
Production 50 Sets

#	Player	Price
2	Hideki Okajima	150.00
3	Curt Schilling	150.00
4	Jason Varitek	150.00
5	Mike Lowell	150.00
6	Jacoby Ellsbury	300.00
7	Dustin Pedroia	200.00
9	Julio Lugo	100.00
10	Manny Ramirez	225.00

Year In Review

NM/M
Complete Set (120): 60.00
Common Player: .50
#'s 61-120 in Series 2
Inserted 1:6

#	Player	Price
1	Paul LoDuca	.50
2	Felix Hernandez	.75
3	Ian Snell	.50
4	Carlos Beltran	.50
5	Daisuke Matsuzaka	1.50
6	Jose Reyes	1.00
7	Alex Rodriguez	2.00
8	Scott Kazmir	.50
9	Adam Everett	.50
10	Josh Beckett, Josh Hamilton	.50
11	Craig Monroe	.50
12	Justin Morneau	.50
13	Roy Halladay	.75
14	Jeff Suppan	.50
15	Marco Scutaro	.50
16	Ivan Rodriguez	.75
17	Dmitri Young	.50
18	Mark Buehrle	.50
19	Alex Rodriguez	2.00
20	Joe Saunders	.50
21	Russell Martin	.50
22	Manny Ramirez	.75
23	Chase Utley	1.00
24	Travis Hafner	.50
25	Shawn Hill	.50
26	Daisuke Matsuzaka	1.50
27	Matt Belisle	.50
28	Troy Tulowitzki	.75
29	Andruw Jones	.50
30	Phil Hughes	.75
31	Derek Lee	.50
32	Ichiro Suzuki	1.50
33	Ichiro Suzuki	1.50
34	Julio Franco	.50
35	Chien-Ming Wang	.75
36	Hideki Matsui	1.00
37	Brad Penny	.50
38	Jack Wilson	.50
39	Francisco Cordero	.50
40	Omar Vizquel	.50
41	Tim Lincecum	.50
42	Bartolo Colon	.50
43	Fred Lewis	.50
44	Jeff Kent	.50
45	Randy Johnson	1.00
46	Rafael Furcal	.75
47	Delmon Young	.75
48	Andrew Miller	.75
49	David Ortiz, Mike Lowell	1.00
50	Justin Verlander	.75
51	C.C. Sabathia	.75
52	Felipe Lopez	.50
53	Oliver Perez	.50
54	John Smoltz	.75
55	Mark Reynolds	.50
56	Jeremy Accardo	.50
57	Todd Helton	.75
58	Adrian Beltre	.50
59	Carlos Delgado	.50
60	Chris Young	.50
61	Roy Halladay	.75
62	Kevin Youkilis	.50
63	Joe Blanton	.50
64	Chad Gaudin	.50
65	Derek Lowe	.50
66	C.C. Sabathia	.75
67	Luis Castillo	.50
68	Curt Schilling	.75
69	Pedro Feliz	.50
70	James Shields	.50
71	Masumi Kuwata	.50
72	Raul Ibanez	.50
73	Justin Verlander	.75
74	Tim Lincecum	.75
75	Hideki Matsui	1.00
76	Julio Franco	.50
77	Russell Branyan	.50
78	Chipper Jones	1.00
79	Chone Figgins	.50
80	Chris Young	.75
81	Sammy Sosa	.75
82	Miguel Tejada	.75
83	Wilfredo Ledezma	.75
84	Victor Martinez	.75
85	Dustin McGowan	.50
86	Mike Fontenot	.50
87	Mark Ellis	.50
88	Ryan Howard	1.50
89	Frank Thomas	.75
90	Aubrey Huff	.75
91	Jake Peavy	.75
92	Dan Haren	.75
93	Damian Miller	.50
94	Billy Butler	.75
95	Dmitri Young	.50
96	Chipper Jones	1.00
97	Justin Morneau	.75
98	Erik Bedard	.75
99	Scott Hatteberg	.50
100	Vladimir Guerrero	1.00
101	Ichiro Suzuki	1.00
102	Jose Reyes	1.00
103	Ryan Garko	.50
104	Jeff Francoeur	.75
105	Joe Mauer	.75
106	Manny Ramirez	1.00
107	Chase Utley	1.00
108	Magglio Ordonez	.75
109	Chris Young	.50
110	B.J. Upton	.75
111	Willie Harris	.50
112	Shelley Duncan	.50
113	Jon Lester	.75
114	Travis Buck	.50
115	Ryan Raburn	.50
116	Eric Byrnes	.50
117	Kenny Lofton	.50
118	Jason Isringhausen	.75
119	Todd Helton	.75
120	Carl Crawford	.75

2007 Highlight Relics

NM/M
Common Relic: 5.00

#	Player	Price
CB	Carlos Beltran	10.00
DO	David Ortiz	15.00
DW	David Wright	10.00
IR	Ivan Rodriguez	8.00
LB	Lance Berkman	8.00
MT	Miguel Tejada	8.00
TH	Todd Helton	8.00
JV	Justin Verlander	15.00
MH	Matt Holliday	8.00
AP	Albert Pujols	20.00
VG	Vladimir Guerrero	10.00
JR	Jose Reyes	10.00
PF	Prince Fielder	15.00
CC	Carl Crawford	5.00
MR	Manny Ramirez	8.00
IS	Ichiro Suzuki	20.00
EC	Eric Chavez	5.00
CM	Cameron Maybin	10.00
CS	Curt Schilling	8.00
DWW	Dontrelle Willis	5.00

Series 2

#	Player	Price
JT	Jim Thome	8.00
JB	Jeremy Bonderman	5.00
BP	Brandon Phillips	5.00
AG	Alex Gordon	10.00
RH	Ryan Howard	20.00
CU	Chase Utley	15.00
RZ	Ryan Zimmerman	8.00
DU	Dan Uggla	5.00

Code	Player	Price
HR	Hanley Ramirez	8.00
BU	B.J. Upton	8.00
DY	Delmon Young	5.00
VG	Vladimir Guerrero	8.00
RO	Roy Oswalt	5.00
PF	Prince Fielder	10.00
RB	Ryan Braun	15.00
AP	Albert Pujols	15.00
JR	Jose Reyes	10.00
DW	David Wright	10.00
IS	Ichiro Suzuki	15.00
AR	Aramis Ramirez	8.00
DL	Derrek Lee	8.00
BW	Brandon Webb	8.00
RF	Rafael Furcal	5.00
JL	James Loney	8.00
CMW	Chien-Ming Wang	20.00
ST	Scott Thorman	8.00
DO	David Ortiz	10.00
JP	Jake Peavy	8.00
CM	Cameron Maybin	8.00
CC	Carl Crawford	5.00

2007 Highlight Relic Autograph
Production 25 Sets

2007 Highlight Dual Relics
Production 25 Sets

2007 Highlight Autographs

Code	Player	NM/M
	Common Auto.:	10.00
AS	Alfonso Soriano	50.00
CMW	Chien-Ming Wang	125.00
GS	Gary Sheffield	40.00
JD	Johnny Damon	50.00
JP	Jake Peavy	30.00
JV	Jason Varitek	50.00
MR	Manny Ramirez	80.00
RJC	Robinson Cano	40.00
VG	Vladimir Guerrero	50.00
BP	Brad Penny	25.00
DH	Danny Haren	25.00
DW	David Wright	60.00
HR	Hanley Ramirez	60.00
JBR	Jose Reyes	60.00
JR	Jimmy Rollins	50.00
JTD	Jermaine Dye	20.00
MY	Michael Young	20.00
PF	Prince Fielder	50.00
CB	Clay Buchholz	80.00
CP	Carlos Pena	20.00
ED	Eulogio de la Cruz	15.00
ES	Ervin Santana	10.00
FC	Fausto Carmona	15.00
FS	Freddy Sanchez	15.00
JF	Josh Fields	15.00
JL	John Lackey	15.00
LC	Luis Castillo	15.00
MG	Matt Garza	15.00
NM	Nicholas Markakis	20.00
RM	Russell Martin	20.00
WN	Wilbert Nieves	15.00
YG	Yovani Gallardo	20.00
HK	Howie Kendrick	15.00
JB	John Buck	10.00
JM	Jose Molina	10.00
RC	Ramon Castro	10.00
RH	Rich Hill	20.00
CV	Carlos Villanueva	10.00
DM	Dustin Moseley	10.00
MB	Mike Bacsik	10.00
ME	Mark Ellis	10.00
RJM	Randy Messenger	10.00
SM	Scott Moore	10.00
TG	Tom Gorzelanny	15.00
UJ	Ubaldo Jimenez	10.00
AL	Adam Lind	15.00
JA	Josh Anderson	15.00
DB	Daric Barton	15.00
LB	Lance Broadway	10.00
SF	Sam Fuld	10.00
NJM	Nyjer Morgan	20.00
SS	Seth Smith	15.00

Series 2

Code	Player	Price
DW	David Wright	120.00
JM	Justin Morneau	25.00
JR	Jimmy Rollins	50.00
MT	Mark Teixeira	40.00
CMW	Chien-Ming Wang	75.00
DO	David Ortiz	75.00
CD	Carlos Delgado	20.00
VG	Vladimir Guerrero	75.00
JD	Johnny Damon	40.00
CF	Chone Figgins	15.00
KM	Kendry Morales	8.00
RN	Ricky Nolasco	10.00
TT	Taylor Tankersley	10.00
JW	Josh Willingham	15.00
JC	Joba Chamberlain	90.00
JKM	John Maine	15.00
MG	Matt Garza	15.00
BC	Bobby Crosby	10.00
SV	Shane Victorino	20.00
NM	Nick Markakis	20.00
FL	Francisco Liriano	15.00
RM	Russell Martin	20.00
MC	Melky Cabrera	15.00
RB	Ryan Braun	35.00
DE	Darin Erstad	15.00
JB	Jeremy Bonderman	15.00
JTD	Jermaine Dye	15.00
AH	Aaron Heilman	15.00
CC	Carl Crawford	15.00
JZ	Joel Zumaya	15.00
MMT	Marcus Thames	15.00
PJF	Pedro Feliciano	15.00

Code	Player	Price
CM	Craig Monroe	10.00
NR	Nate Robertson	10.00
EC	Eric Chavez	10.00
PF	Prince Fielder	30.00
RC	Robinson Cano	20.00
JAR	Jo Jo Reyes	15.00
DB	Dallas Braden	15.00
AK	Austin Kearns	8.00
CV	Claudio Vargas	10.00
HCK	Hong-Chih Kuo	20.00
JLC	Jorge Cantu	10.00
CW	Chase Wright	10.00
DY	Delwyn Young	8.00
RP	Ronny Paulino	8.00
ZG	Zack Greinke	20.00
JAB	Jason Bartlett	10.00
PH	Philip Humber	8.00
RR	Ryan Roberts	8.00
TG	Tom Gorzelanny	8.00
ES	Ervin Santana	10.00
FC	Fausto Carmona	10.00

50th Anniversary All-Rookie Team

	NM/M
Complete Set (110):	75.00
Common Player:	.50

#'s 56-110 in Series 2
Inserted 1:5

#	Player	Price
1	Darryl Strawberry	.50
2	Gary Sheffield	.75
3	Dwight Gooden	.50
4	Melky Cabrera	.75
5	Gary Carter	.50
6	Lou Piniella	.50
7	David Justice	.50
8	Andre Dawson	.75
9	Mark Ellis	.50
10	Dave Johnson	.50
11	Jermaine Dye	.50
12	Dan Johnson	.50
13	Alfonso Soriano	.50
14	Prince Fielder	1.50
15	Hanley Ramirez	1.00
16	Matt Holliday	.75
17	Justin Verlander	1.00
18	Mark Teixeira	.75
19	Julio Franco	.50
20	Ivan Rodriguez	.75
21	Jason Bay	.75
22	Brandon Webb	.75
23	Dontrelle Willis	.50
24	Brad Wilkerson	.50
25	Dan Uggla	.75
26	Ozzie Smith	1.00
27	Andruw Jones	.75
28	Garret Anderson	.50
29	Jimmy Rollins	1.00
30	Brian McCann	.75
31	Scott Podsednik	.50
32	Garrett Atkins	.50
33	Billy Wagner	.50
34	Chipper Jones	1.00
35	Roger McDowell	.50
36	Austin Kearns	.50
37	Boog Powell	.50
38	Ron Swoboda	.50
39	Roy Oswalt	.75
40	Mike Piazza	1.00
41	Albert Pujols	3.00
42	Ichiro Suzuki	2.00
43	C.C. Sabathia	.75
44	Todd Helton	.75
45	Scott Rolen	.75
46	Derek Jeter	3.00
47	Shawn Green	.50
48	Manny Ramirez	1.00
49	Tom Seaver	.50
50	Kenny Lofton	.50
51	Francisco Liriano	.75
52	Ryan Zimmerman	.75
53	Jeff Francoeur	.75
54	Joe Mauer	.75
55	Magglio Ordonez	.75
56	Carlos Beltran	1.00
57	Andre Ethier	.50
58	Brian Bannister	.50
59	Chris Young	.50
60	Troy Tulowitzki	.75
61	Hideki Okajima	.75
62	Delmon Young	.50
63	Craig Wilson	.50
64	Hunter Pence	1.00
65	Tadahito Iguchi	.50
66	Mark Kotsay	.50
67	Nick Markakis	1.00
68	Russ Adams	.50
69	Russell Martin	1.00
70	James Loney	.75
71	Ryan Braun	2.00
72	Jonny Gomes	.50
73	Carlos Ruiz	.50
74	Willy Taveras	.50
75	Joe Torre	1.00
76	Jeff Kent	.50
77	Huston Street	.50
78	Dustin Pedroia	1.00
79	Gustavo Chacin	.50
80	Adam Dunn	1.00
81	Pat Burrell	.75
82	Rocco Baldelli	.50
83	Chad Tracy	.50
84	Adam LaRoche	.50
85	Aaron Miles	.50
86	Khalil Greene	.50
87	Daniel Cabrera	.50
88	Mike Gonzalez	.50
89	Ty Wigginton	.50
90	Angel Berroa	.50
91	Moises Alou	.50
92	Miguel Olivo	.50
93	Nick Johnson	.50
94	Eric Hinske	.50
95	Ramon Santiago	.50
96	Jason Jennings	.50
97	Adam Kennedy	.50
98	Mike Lamb	.50
99	Rafael Furcal	.50
100	Jay Payton	.50
101	Bengie Molina	.50
102	Mark Redman	.50
103	Alex Gonzalez	.50
104	Ray Durham	.50
105	Miguel Cairo	.50
106	Kerry Wood	.75
107	Dmitri Young	.50
108	Jose Cruz	.50
109	Jose Guillen	.50
110	Scott Hatteberg	.50

50th Anniv. All-Rookie Team Relics

		NM/M
	Production 50 Sets	
DS	Darryl Strawberry	20.00
AD	Andre Dawson	40.00
DW	Dontrelle Willis	10.00
MP	Mike Piazza	40.00
TS	Tom Seaver	40.00
OS	Ozzie Smith	40.00
IR	Ivan Rodriguez	25.00
DG	Dwight Gooden	15.00
GC	Gary Carter	20.00
AS	Alfonso Soriano	30.00
IS	Ichiro Suzuki	50.00
MH	Matt Holliday	25.00
JR	Jimmy Rollins	35.00
PF	Prince Fielder	40.00
DJ	David Justice	20.00
JV	Justin Verlander	40.00
AJ	Andruw Jones	40.00
CJ	Chipper Jones	30.00
RO	Roy Oswalt	20.00
BW	Brandon Webb	25.00

Series 2

Code	Player	Price
BM	Brian McCann	15.00
HR	Hanley Ramirez	30.00
DU	Dan Uggla	10.00
GA	Garret Anderson	10.00
JB	Jason Bay	10.00
MT	Mark Teixeira	20.00
SP	Scott Podsednik	10.00
JM	Joe Mauer	25.00
AP	Albert Pujols	40.00
AD	Adam Dunn	15.00
CS	C.C. Sabathia	15.00
NJ	Nick Johnson	10.00
PB	Pat Burrell	15.00
TH	Todd Helton	15.00
MO	Magglio Ordonez	10.00
GS	Gary Sheffield	15.00
RB	Rocco Baldelli	10.00
AE	Andre Ethier	10.00
NM	Nick Markakis	20.00
FL	Francisco Liriano	15.00

50th Anniversary All-Rookie Team Autos
Production 25 Sets
Series 2

2008 Topps Allen & Ginter

	NM/M
Common Player (1-300):	.25
Common SP (301-350):	2.00
Inserted 1:2	
Mini Exclusives (351-400):	No Pricing
Rip Card Exclusive	
Pack (8):	5.00
Box (24):	110.00

#	Player	Price
1	Alex Rodriguez	2.00
2	Juan Pierre	.25
3	Benjamin Franklin	.50
4	Roy Halladay	.50
5	C.C. Sabathia	.50
6	Brian Barton RC	.50
7	Mickey Mantle	5.00
8	Brian Bass (RC)	.50
9	Ian Kinsler	.50
10	Manny Ramirez	.75
11	Michael Cuddyer	.25
12	Ian Snell	.25
13	Mike Lowell	.50
14	Adrian Gonzalez	.50
15	B.J. Upton	.50
16	Hiroki Kuroda RC	1.50
17	Kenji Johjima	.25
18	James Loney	.25
19	Albert Einstein	2.00
20	Vladimir Guerrero	.50
21	Miguel Tejada	.40
22	Chin-Lung Hu (RC)	1.00
23	A.J. Burnett	.25
24	Bobby Jenks	.25
25	Aramis Ramirez	.50
26	Corey Hart	.40
27	Brad Hawpe	.25
28	Adam LaRoche	.25
29	Empire State Building	.25
30	Miguel Cabrera	.75
31	Ryan Zimmerman	.40
32	Mark Ellis	.25
33	Nick Swisher	.25
34	Bill Hall	.25
35	Eric Byrnes	.25
36	Michael Young	.40
37	Pedro Martinez	.50
38	Andruw Jones	.25
39	J.R. Towles RC	1.00
40	Justin Upton	.40
41	Paul Konerko	.40
42	Luke Scott	.25
43	Rickie Weeks	.25
44	Adam Wainwright	.25
45	Justin Morneau	.50
46	Chris Young	.40
47	Chad Billingsley	.40
48	Kazuo Matsui	.25
49	Shane Victorino	.40
50	Albert Pujols	2.00
51	Brian McCann	.40
52	Carlos Delgado	.40
53	Chien-Ming Wang	.50
54	Takashi Saito	.25
55	Josh Beckett	.50
56	Nick Johnson	.25
57	Ben Sheets	.40
58	Johnny Damon	.50
59	Nicky Hayden	.25
60	Prince Fielder	.50
61	Adam Dunn	.50
62	Dustin Pedroia	.75
63	Jacoby Ellsbury	.75
64	Brad Penny	.25
65	Victor Martinez	.25
66	Joe Mauer	.40
67	Kevin Kouzmanoff	.25
68	Frank Thomas	.50
69	Stevie Williams	.25
70	Matt Holliday	.50
71	Fausto Carmona	.25
72	Clayton Kershaw RC	4.00
73	Tadahito Iguchi	.25
74	Khalil Greene	.25
75	Travis Hafner	.25
76	Jim Thome	.50
77	Joba Chamberlain	.50
78	Ivan Rodriguez	.40
79	Jose Guillen	.25
80	Hanley Ramirez	.75
81	Vernon Wells	.40
82	Jayson Nix (RC)	.25
83	Masahide Kobayashi RC	1.00
84	Bonnie Blair	.25
85	Curtis Granderson	.50
86	Kelvim Escobar	.25
87	Aaron Rowand	.25
88	Troy Glaus	.40
89	Billy Wagner	.25
90	Jose Reyes	.50
91	Scott Rolen	.40
92	Dan Jansen	.25
93	David Eckstein	.25
94	Tom Gorzelanny	.25
95	Garrett Atkins	.40
96	Carlos Zambrano	.25
97	Jeff Francis	.25
98	Kazuo Fukumori RC	1.00
99	John Bowker (RC)	1.00
100	David Wright	.50
101	Adrian Beltre	.40
102	Ray Durham	.25
103	Kerri Strug	.25
104	Orlando Hudson	.25
105	Jonathan Papelbon	.50
106	Brian Schneider	.25
107	Matt Biondi	.25
108	Alex Romero (RC)	1.00
109	Joey Chestnut	.25
110	Chase Utley	.75
111	Dan Uggla	.40
112	Akinori Iwamura	.25
113	Curt Schilling	.50
114	Trevor Hoffman	.25
115	Alex Rios	.40
116	Mariano Rivera	.50
117	Jeff Niemann (RC)	1.00
118	Geovany Soto	.50
119	Billy Mitchell	.25
120	Derek Jeter	2.00
121	Yovani Gallardo	.40
122	The Gateway Arch	.25
123	Josh Willingham	.25
124	Greg Maddux	1.50
125	John Lackey	.40
126	Chris Young	.25
127	Billy Butler	.25
128	Golden Gate Bridge	.25
129	Joey Votto (RC)	2.00
130	Tim Wakefield	.25
131	Todd Helton	.25
132	Gary Matthews Jr.	.25
133	Wild Bill Hickok	.25
134	Jason Varitek	.40
135	Robinson Cano	.25
136	Javier Vazquez	.25
137	Annie Oakley	.25
138	Andy Pettitte	.25
139	Greg Reynolds RC	1.50
140	Jimmy Rollins	.25
141	Jermaine Dye	.40
142	Eugenio Velez RC	1.50
143	J.J. Hardy	.25
144	Grand Canyon	.25
145	Bobby Abreu	.40
146	Scott Kazmir	.25
147	James Fennimore Cooper	.25
148	Mark Buehrle	.25
149	Freddy Sanchez	.25
150	Johan Santana	.50
151	Orlando Cabrera	.25
152	Lyle Overbay	.25
153	Clay Buchholz (RC)	3.00
154	Jesse Carlson RC	1.50
155	Troy Tulowitzki	.40
156	Delmon Young	.40
157	Ross Ohlendorf RC	2.00
158	Mary Shelley	.25
159	James Shields	.40
160	Alfonso Soriano	.50
161	Randy Winn	.25
162	Austin Kearns	.25
163	Jeremy Hermida	.25
164	Jorge Posada	.50
165	Justin Verlander	.50
166	Bram Stoker	.25
167	Marie Curie	.25
168	Melky Cabrera	.25
169	Howie Kendrick	.25
170	Jake Peavy	.50
171	J.D. Drew	.25
172	Pablo Picasso	.25
173	Rick Ankiel	.50
174	Jose Valverde	.25
175	Chipper Jones	.75
176	Claude Monet	.25
177	Evan Longoria RC	5.00
178	Jose Vidro	.25
179	Hideki Matsui	.75
180	Ryan Braun	.75
181	Moises Alou	.40
182	Nate McLouth	.25
183	Harriet Tubman	.25
184	Felix Hernandez	.50
185	Carlos Pena	.25
186	Jarrod Saltalamacchia	.25
187	Les Miles	.25
188	Kelly Johnson	.25
189	"Rampage" Jackson	1.00
190	Grady Sizemore	.50
191	Francisco Cordero	.25
192	Yunel Escobar	.25
193	Edwin Encarnacion	.25
194	Melvin Mora	.25
195	Russell Martin	.40
196	Edgar Renteria	.25
197	Bigfoot	.25
198	Steve Holm RC	1.00
199	Daric Barton (RC)	1.00
200	Tim Lincecum	.50
201	David Ortiz	.75
202	Jeff King	.25
203	Jhonny Peralta	.25
204	Julio Lugo	.25
205	J.J. Putz	.25
206	Jeff Francoeur	.25
207	Yuniesky Betancourt	.25
208	Bruce Jenner	.25
209	Clete Thomas RC	1.00
210	Carlos Lee	.50
211	Josh Hamilton	.75
212	Pyotr Ilyich Tchaikovsky	.25
213	Brendan Harris	.25
214	Dustin McGowan	.25
215	Aaron Harang	.25
216	Brett Myers	.25
217	Friedrich Nietzsche	.25
218	John Maine	.25
219	Charles Dickens	.25
220	Erik Bedard	.25
221	Tim Hudson	.25
222	Jeremy Bonderman	.25
223	Nyjer Morgan (RC)	1.00
224	Johnny Cueto RC	2.00
225	Roy Oswalt	.40
226	Rich Hill	.25
227	Frederick Douglass	.25
228	Derek Lowe	.25
229	Joe Blanton	.25
230	Carlos Beltran	.25
231	Huston Street	.25
232	Davy Crockett	.25
233	Pluto	.25
234	Jered Weaver	.25
235	Dan Haren	.25
236	Alex Gordon	.40
237	Zack Greinke	.25
238	Todd Clever	.25
239	Brian Bannister	.25
240	Magglio Ordonez	.40
241	Ryan Garko	.25
242	Takadzwa Ngwenya	.25
243	Gil Meche	.25
244	Mark Teahen	.25
245	Carlos Guillen	.25
246	Jeff Kent	.25
247	Lisa Leslie	.25
248	Lastings Milledge	.25
249	Serena Williams	.25
250	Ichiro Suzuki	1.00
251	Matt Cain	.25
252	Callix Crabbe (RC)	1.00
253	Nick Blackburn RC	1.00
254	Hunter Pence	.40
255	Cole Hamels	.50
256	Garret Anderson	.25
257	Luis Gonzalez	.25
258	Eric Chavez	.25
259	Francisco Rodriguez	.25
260	Mark Teixeira	.50
261	Bob Motley	.25
262	Mark Spitz	.25
263	Yadier Molina	.25
264	Adam Jones	.25
265	Brian Roberts	.25
266	Matt Kemp	.25
267	Andrew Miller	.25
268	Dean Karnazes	.25
269	Gary Sheffield	.40
270	Lance Berkman	.50
271	Paul LoDuca	.25
272	Matt Tolbert RC	1.00
273	Jay Bruce (RC)	5.00
274	John Smoltz	.50
275	Nick Markakis	.50
276	Oscar Wilde	.25
277	Dontrelle Willis	.25
278	Kevin Van Dam	.25
279	Jim Edmonds	.25
280	Brandon Webb	.50
281	Joe Nathan	.25
282	Jeanette Lee	.25
283	Andrew "William Ocean" Litz	.25
284	Daisuke Matsuzaka	1.00
285	Brandon Phillips	.25
286	Pat Burrell	.25
287	Chris Carpenter	.40
288	Pete Weber	.25
289	Derek Lee	.25
290	Ken Griffey Jr.	1.50
291	Rich Thompson (RC)	1.00
292	Elijah Dukes	.25
293	Pedro Feliz	.25
294	Torii Hunter	.50
295	Chone Figgins	.25
296	Hideki Okajima	.25
297	Max Scherzer RC	2.00
298	Greg Smith RC	1.00
299	Rafael Furcal	.40
300	Ryan Howard	.75
301	Felix Pie	2.00
302	Brad Lidge	2.00
303	Jason Bay	2.50
304	Victor Hugo	2.00
305	Randy Johnson	3.00
306	Carlos Gomez	2.00
307	Pat Neshek	2.00
308	Jed Lowrie (RC)	4.00
309	Ryan Church	2.00
310	Michael Bourn	2.00
311	B.J. Ryan	2.00
312	Brandon Wood	2.00
313	Harriet Beecher Stowe	2.00
314	Mike Cameron	2.00
315	Tom Glavine	3.00
316	Ervin Santana	3.00
317	Geoff Jenkins	2.00
318	Andre Ethier	2.00
319	Jason Giambi	2.00
320	Dmitri Young	2.00
321	Wily Mo Pena	2.00
322	Hank Blalock	2.00
323	James Bowie	2.00
324	Casey Kotchman	2.00
325	Stephen Drew	2.00
326	Adam Kennedy	2.00
327	A.J. Pierzynski	2.00
328	Richie Sexson	2.00
329	Jeff Clement (RC)	2.00
330	Luke Hochevar RC	1.00
331	Luis Castillo	2.00
332	Dave Roberts	2.00
333	Coco Crisp	2.00
334	Jo Jo Reyes	2.00
335	Phil Hughes	3.00
336	Allen Fisher	2.00
337	Jason Schmidt	2.00
338	Placido Polanco	2.00
339	Jack Cust	2.00
340	Carl Crawford	3.00
341	Ty Wigginton	2.00
342	Aubrey Huff	2.00
343	Bengie Molina	2.00
344	Matt Diaz	2.00
345	Francisco Liriano	2.00
346	Brandon Boggs (RC)	1.00
347	David DeJesus	2.00
348	Justin Masterson RC	1.50
349	Frank Morris	2.00
350	Kevin Youkilis	3.00

Mini

Mini:	2-3X
Mini (351-390):	No Pricing
#'s 351-390 Inserted in Rip Cards	
Allen & Ginter Back:	3-4X
Inserted 1:5	
Black Border:	4-6X
Inserted 1:10	
No Number:	10-20X
Production 50 Sets	
Bazooka Back:	No Pricing
Production 25 Sets	
Framed Cloth:	No Pricing
Production 10 Sets	
Wood:	No Pricing
Production One Set	

Ancient Icons

#	Icon	NM/M
	Common Icon:	5.00
1	Gilgamesh	5.00
2	Marduk	5.00
3	Beowulf	5.00
4	Poseidon	5.00
5	The Sphinx	5.00
6	Tutankhamen	5.00

7	Alexander the Great	5.00
8	Cleopatra	5.00
9	Sun Tzu	5.00
10	Quetzalcoatl	5.00
11	Isis	5.00
12	Hercules	5.00
13	King Arthur	5.00
14	Miyamoto Musashi	5.00
15	Genghis Khan	5.00
16	Zeus	5.00
17	Achilles	5.00
18	Confucius	5.00
19	Attila the Hun	5.00
20	Romulus & Remus	5.00

Autographs

NM/M
Common Auto.: 15.00
SP Autos. are noted

RH	Ryan Howard/90	100.00
DO	David Ortiz/90	100.00
MR	Manny Ramirez/90	100.00
MH	Matt Holliday/90	70.00
PF	Prince Fielder/90	80.00
JR	Jose Reyes/90	100.00
HP	Hunter Pence/90	75.00
DW	David Wright/240	140.00
BP	Brad Penny/240	35.00
HR	Hanley Ramirez/240	50.00
TLH	Travis Hafner/240	25.00
CC	Carl Crawford/240	30.00
TH	Torii Hunter/240	25.00
JC	Joba Chamberlain	120.00
NM	Nick Markakis	35.00
CG	Curtis Granderson	25.00
GJ	Geoff Jenkins	20.00
ALR	Alex Rios	20.00
MK	Matt Kemp	20.00
CB	Clay Buchholz	30.00
OH	Orlando Hudson	15.00
JF	Jeff Francis	15.00
FCC	Fausto Carmona	15.00
ES	Ervin Santana	15.00
FC	Francisco Cordero	15.00
JS	Jarrod Saltalamacchia	15.00
BPB	Brian Bannister	15.00
AE	Andre Ethier	15.00
IK	Ian Kinsler	20.00
JBF	Jeff Francoeur	25.00
MH	Marcus Henderson/Guitar Pick/100	200.00
BJ	Bruce Jenner/190	100.00
AF	Andrea Farina/190	40.00
AFI	Allen Fisher/190	35.00
AL	Andrew "WilliamOcean" Litz/190	40.00
BB	Bonnie Blair/190	75.00
BM	Bob Motley/190	60.00
BPM	Billy Mitchell/190	85.00
DJ	Dan Jansen/190	70.00
DK	Dean Karnazes/190	50.00
FM	Frank Morris/190	40.00
JJC	Joey Chestnut/190	75.00
JK	Jeff King/190	20.00
JL	Jeanette Lee/190	150.00
KS	Kerri Strug/190	75.00
KVD	Kevin Van Dam/190	60.00
LL	Lisa Leslie/190	75.00
LM	Les Miles/190	60.00
MB	Matt Biondi/190	50.00
MS	Mark Spitz/190	85.00
NH	Nicky Hayden/240	70.00
PW	Pete Weber/190	65.00
RJ	"Rampage" Jackson/190	140.00
SW	Serena Williams/190	140.00
TC	Todd Clever/190	75.00
SW	Stevie Williams/240	60.00
TN	Takudzwa Ngwenya/190	50.00
AM	Adriano Moraes/190	40.00
DB	Deep Blue/190	65.00

Baseball Icons

NM/M
Inserted 1:48

1	Cy Young	8.00
2	Walter Johnson	8.00
3	Jackie Robinson	8.00
4	Thurman Munson	8.00
5	Mel Ott	6.00
6	Honus Wagner	8.00
7	Pee Wee Reese	8.00
8	Tris Speaker	8.00
9	Christy Mathewson	6.00
10	Ty Cobb	8.00
11	Johnny Mize	8.00
12	Jimmie Foxx	8.00
13	Lou Gehrig	10.00
14	Roy Campanella	8.00
15	George Sisler	6.00
16	Rogers Hornsby	8.00
17	Babe Ruth	15.00

Cabinet Boxloaders

NM/M
Common Card: 4.00
Inserted 1:Box

BH1	Matt Holliday, Jamey Carroll, Michael Barrett, Brian Giles	4.00
BH2	Mike Lowell, Manny Ramirez, Jonathan Papelbon, Josh Beckett	4.00
BH3	Ryan Howard, Jimmy Rollins, Chase Utley, Cole Hamels	6.00
BH4	Alex Rodriguez, Frank Thomas, Jim Thome	6.00
BH5	Justin Verlander, Mark Buehrle, Clay Buchholz	4.00
HB1	General George Washington, General Nathanael Greene	4.00
HB2	General Horatio Gates, General John Burgoyne	4.00
HB3	General George Meade, General Robert E. Lee	4.00
HB4	Lt. Col. William B. Travis, Colonel James Bowie, Colonel Davy Crockett, General Antonio Lopez, de Santa Ana	4.00
HB5	General Dwight D. Eisenhower, Field Marshall Bernard Montgomery	4.00

Cabinet Boxloader Autograph

NM/M
Production 200

BF	Bigfoot	80.00

Cut Signatures

Production One Set

Dick Perez Originals

Production One Set

N43 Boxloaders

NM/M
Inserted 1:Box

RH	Ryan Howard	6.00
DO	David Ortiz	6.00
MR	Manny Ramirez	4.00
DW	David Wright	6.00
PF	Prince Fielder	6.00
JC	Joba Chamberlain	6.00
JR	Jose Reyes	5.00
HR	Hanley Ramirez	5.00
MH	Matt Holliday	4.00
CG	Curtis Granderson	4.00
CU	Chase Utley	5.00
RZ	Ryan Zimmerman	4.00
VG	Vladimir Guerrero	5.00
IS	Ichiro Suzuki	6.00
RB	Ryan Braun	6.00

N43 Boxloader Autographs

Production 15 Sets

N43 Boxloader Relics

No Pricing
Production 25 Sets

Relics

NM/M
Common Relic: 4.00

ER	Edgar Renteria	4.00
JD	J.D. Drew	5.00
PF	Prince Fielder	6.00
JV1	Jason Varitek	6.00
JG	Jay Gibbons	4.00
JDD	Johnny Damon	6.00
BR2	Brian Roberts	4.00
CC2	Carl Crawford	5.00
AD2	Adam Dunn	6.00
DY	Dmitri Young	4.00
RF	Rafael Furcal	6.00
BA	Bobby Abreu	6.00
IR2	Ivan Rodriguez	5.00
ALR	Alex Rios	5.00
VG	Vladimir Guerrero	8.00
WMP	Wily Mo Pena	4.00
JK	Jeff Kent	4.00
PL	Paul LoDuca	4.00
AK	Austin Kearns	4.00
DO1	David Ortiz	8.00
DW	David Wright	10.00
JTD	Jermaine Dye	4.00
IS	Ichiro Suzuki	15.00
BR1	Brian Roberts	5.00
HB	Hank Blalock	4.00
CK	Casey Kotchman	4.00
CS	Curt Schilling	6.00
AR	Aramis Ramirez	5.00
IR1	Ivan Rodriguez	6.00
SD	Stephen Drew	5.00
DO2	David Ortiz	8.00
AER	Alex Rodriguez	20.00
AP2	Albert Pujols	20.00
EC	Eric Chavez	4.00
CJ	Chipper Jones	10.00
JF	Jeff Francoeur	6.00
TG	Tom Glavine	6.00
AP1	Albert Pujols	20.00
VM	Victor Martinez	5.00
TH	Tim Hudson	4.00
ATK	Adam Kennedy	4.00
PK	Paul Konerko	5.00
AJP	A.J. Pierzynski	4.00
TLH	Todd Helton	6.00
AD1	Adam Dunn	6.00
CC1	Carl Crawford	5.00
MR	Manny Ramirez	8.00
JT	Jim Thome	6.00
RS	Richie Sexson	4.00
GA	Garret Anderson	4.00
JB	Jason Bay	6.00
RH	Ryan Howard	10.00
TPH	Travis Hafner	5.00
DM	Daisuke Matsuzaka	25.00
JV2	Jason Varitek	6.00
MH	Mike Hampton	4.00
MC	Melky Cabrera	4.00
DRY	Delwyn Young	4.00
MK	Matt Kemp	6.00
CZ	Carlos Zambrano	6.00
MT	Mark Teixeira	6.00
TSG	Tom Gorzelanny	4.00
MDC	Matt Capps	4.00
CAM	Carlos Marmol	4.00
JS	John Smoltz	6.00
BH	Brad Hawpe	4.00
BMM	Brian McCann	8.00
CG	Curtis Granderson	6.00
TT	Troy Tulowitzki	8.00
CU	Chase Utley	8.00
LB	Lance Berkman	6.00
RO	Roy Oswalt	6.00
MY	Michael Young	6.00
JJH	J.J. Hardy	5.00
JM	Joe Mauer	8.00
BC	Bobby Crosby	4.00
APB	Aaron Pryor/100	25.00
AW	Andre Ward/100	30.00
DG	Danny Green/100	30.00
EM	Edison Miranda/100	40.00
JFB	Jeff Fenech/100	25.00
JCJ	Joel Casamayor/100	25.00
KP	Kelly Pavlik/100	100.00
RM	Ray Mancini/75	75.00
SP	Samuel Peter/71	35.00
AM	Archie Moore/100	50.00
NH	Nicky Hayden/100	50.00
SW	Stevie Williams/250	20.00
BB	Bonnie Blair/250	20.00
DJ	Dan Jansen/250	20.00
KS	Kerri Strug/250	30.00
MB	Matt Biondi/250	20.00
TC	Todd Clever/250	25.00
TN	Takudzwa Ngwenya/250	15.00
LL	Lisa Leslie/250	30.00
SJW	Serena Williams/250	30.00
JC	Joey Chestnut/250	30.00
BM	Billy Mitchell/250	30.00
MS	Mark Spitz/250	30.00
FM	Frank Morris/250	20.00
AF	Andrea Farina/250	20.00
DK	Dean Karnazes/250	20.00
KVD	Kevin Van Dam/250	20.00
JL	Jeanette Lee/250	20.00
AL	Andrew "William Ocean" Litz/250	25.00
PW	Pete Weber/250	40.00
AFI	Allen Fisher/250	25.00
LM	Les Miles/250	20.00
RJ	"Rampage" Jackson/250	40.00
JKI	Jeff King/250	25.00
BJ	Bruce Jenner/250	25.00
BF	Bigfoot/250	60.00
ASM	Adriano Moraes/250	20.00

Rip Cards

NM/M
Prices for unripped cards.
Ripped cards 10 percent.

1	Erik Bedard/99	100.00
2	Jacoby Ellsbury/75	150.00
3	Chris Carpenter/99	100.00
4	Brandon Phillips/99	100.00
5	Daric Barton/99	100.00
6	Brian McCann/99	125.00
7	Dan Uggla/75	90.00
8	James Loney/99	80.00
9	James Shields/99	80.00
10	Curtis Granderson/75	100.00
11	Jason Bay/99	80.00
12	Alex Gordon/75	100.00
13	Alex Rios/99	80.00
14	Travis Hafner/99	80.00
15	Derek Jeter/25	250.00
16	Pedro Feliz/99	80.00
17	Thurman Munson/50	150.00
18	Grady Sizemore/75	120.00
19	Alex Rios/99	100.00
20	David Ortiz/50	150.00
21	Walter Johnson/28	200.00
22	Scott Rolen/99	100.00
23	John Smoltz/99	100.00
24	Mel Ott/28	200.00
25	Ryan Howard/50	180.00
26	Hiroki Kuroda/99	100.00
27	Johnny Damon/99	125.00
28	Jose Reyes/75	125.00
29	Felix Hernandez/99	100.00
30	John Lackey/99	80.00
31	Mark Teixeira/99	100.00
32	Jim Edmonds/99	100.00
33	Prince Fielder/50	150.00
34	Prince Fielder/50	150.00
35	Brian Bannister/99	80.00
36	Chipper Jones/50	150.00
37	Edgar Renteria/99	90.00
38	Roy Campanella/50	180.00
39	Troy Tulowitzki/99	90.00
40	Adam LaRoche/99	90.00
41	Phil Hughes/99	90.00
42	Pee Wee Reese/50	160.00
43	Adam Jones/99	90.00
44	Huston Street/99	90.00
45	Cliff Lee/99	100.00
46	Delmon Young/99	100.00
47	Joe Mauer/99	100.00
48	Johan Santana/28	150.00
49	Dmitri Young/99	80.00
50	Todd Helton/99	100.00
51	Carlos Beltran/99	140.00
52	J.J. Putz/99	100.00
53	Carlos Lee/99	100.00
54	Billy Butler/99	100.00
55	Miguel Cabrera/99	125.00
56	Derek Lee/99	100.00
57	Alfonso Soriano/75	100.00
58	Cole Hamels/99	100.00
59	Hanley Ramirez/75	120.00
60	Adrian Gonzalez/99	100.00
61	B.J. Upton/99	100.00
62	Tim Lincecum/75	150.00
63	Gary Matthews Jr./99	90.00
64	Justin Upton/75	140.00
65	Zack Greinke/99	100.00
66	Roy Oswalt/75	100.00
67	Jimmy Rollins/28	150.00
68	Miguel Tejada/99	100.00
69	Clay Buchholz/99	100.00
70	Andruw Jones/99	80.00
71	Chase Utley/75	100.00
72	Aaron Rowand/99	90.00
73	Johnny Mize/50	150.00
74	Jonathan Papelbon/75	125.00
75	Jarrod Saltalamacchia/99	90.00
76	Lance Berkman/50	100.00
77	Vernon Wells/99	90.00
78	Dontrelle Willis/99	90.00
79	Jim Thome/99	100.00
80	Torii Hunter/99	100.00
81	Russell Martin/75	100.00
82	Jake Peavy/99	100.00
83	Carlos Zambrano/99	100.00
84	Troy Glaus/99	100.00
85	Ryan Zimmerman/75	100.00
86	Evan Longoria/75	100.00
87	Yovani Gallardo/99	100.00
89	Josh Hamilton/75	100.00
90	Matt Holliday/75	125.00
91	Matt Cain/99	100.00
92	Francisco Cordero/99	80.00
93	Derek Lowe/99	100.00
94	Brandon Webb/75	100.00
95	Carlos Pena/99	100.00
97	Khalil Greene/99	90.00
99	C.C. Sabathia/75	100.00
100	Victor Martinez/99	100.00

U.S. State Cards

NM/M
Common Card: .25
Inserted 1:1

1	Alex Rios	.50
2	Curt Schilling	.50
3	Brian Bannister	.25
4	Torii Hunter	.50
5	Chase Utley	.75
6	Roy Halladay	.50
7	Brad Ausmus	.25
8	Ian Snell	.25
9	Lastings Milledge	.25
10	Nick Markakis	.50
11	Shane Victorino	.50
12	Jason Schmidt	.25
13	Curtis Granderson	.50
14	Scott Rolen	.50
15	Casey Blake	.25
16	Nate Robertson	.25
17	Brandon Webb	.50
18	Jonathan Papelbon	.50
19	Tim Stauffer	.25
20	Mark Teixeira	.50
21	Chris Capuano	.25
22	Jason Varitek	.50
23	Joe Mauer	.50
24	Dmitri Young	.25
25	Ryan Howard	.75
26	Taylor Tankersley	.25
27	Alex Gordon	.25
28	Barry Zito	.25
29	Chris Carpenter	.25
30	Derek Jeter	2.00
31	Cody Ross	.25
32	Alex Rodriguez	2.00
33	Ryan Zimmerman	.50
34	Travis Hafner	.25
35	Nick Swisher	.25
36	Matt Holliday	.50
37	Jacoby Ellsbury	.50
38	Ken Griffey Jr.	1.50
39	Paul Konerko	.50
40	Orlando Hudson	.25
41	Mark Ellis	.25
42	Todd Helton	.50
43	Adam Dunn	.50
44	Brandon Lyon	.25
45	David Wright	.75
46	Grady Sizemore	.50
47	Seth McClung	.25
48	Pat Neshek	.25
49	David Wright	.25
50	John Buck	.25

World's Greatest Victories

NM/M
Complete Set (20): 40.00
Common Card: 3.00

1	Kerri Strug	3.00
2	Mark Spitz	3.00
3	Jonas Salk	3.00
4	Man Walks on the Moon	3.00
5	Jon Lester	3.00
6	The Fall of the Berlin Wall	3.00
7	David and Goliath	3.00
8	Gary Carter and the '86 Mets	3.00
9	The Battle of Gettysburg	3.00
10	Deep Blue	3.00
11	The Allied Forces	3.00
12	Don Larsen	3.00
13	Truman Defeats Dewey	3.00
14	The American Revolution	3.00
15	2004 ALCS	3.00
16	The Battle of Thermopylae	3.00
17	Brown v. Board of Education	3.00
18	Team Orange	3.00
19	Bill Mazeroski	3.00
20	Cinderella	3.00

World Leaders

NM/M
Common World Leader: 2.50

1	Cristina Fernandez de Kirchner	2.50
2	Kevin Rudd	2.50
3	Guy Verhofstadt	2.50
4	Luiz Inacio Lula da Silva	2.50
5	Stephen Harper	2.50
6	Michelle Bachelet Jeria	2.50
7	Oscar Arias Sanchez	2.50
8	Mirek Topolanek	2.50
9	Anders Fogh Rasmussen	2.50
10	Leonel Fernandez Reyna	2.50
11	Mohamed Hosni Mubarak	2.50
12	Tarja Halonen	2.50
13	Nicolas Sarkozy	2.50
14	Yahya A.J.J. Jammeh	2.50
15	Angela Merkel	2.50
16	Konstandinos Karamanlis	2.50
17	Benedict XVI	2.50
18	Geir H. Haarde	2.50
19	Manmohan Singh	2.50
20	Susilo Bambang Yudhoyono	2.50
21	Bertie Ahern	2.50
22	Ehud Olmert	2.50
23	Bruce Golding	2.50
24	Yasuo Fukuda	2.50
25	Mwai Kibaki	2.50
26	Felipe de Jesus Calderon Hinojosa	2.50
27	Sanjaa Bayar	2.50
28	Armando Guebuza	2.50
29	Girija Prasad Koirala	2.50
30	Jan Peter Balkenende	2.50
31	Helen Clark	2.50
32	Jens Stoltenberg	2.50
33	Qaboos bin Said al-Said	2.50
34	Alan Garcia Perez	2.50
35	Gloria Macapagal-Arroyo	2.50
36	Donald Tusk	2.50
37	Vladimir Vladimirovich Putin	2.50
38	Robert Fico	2.50
39	Thabo Mbeki	2.50
40	Lee Myung-bak	2.50
41	Jose Luis Rodriguez Zapatero	2.50
42	Fredrik Reinfeldt	2.50
43	Pascal Couchepin	2.50
44	Jakaya Kikwete	2.50
45	Samak Sundaravavej	2.50
46	Tenzin Gyatso	2.50
47	Patrick Manning	2.50
48	Gordon Brown	2.50
49	George W. Bush	2.50
50	Nguyen Tan Dung	2.50

1 of 1 Relic Cards

Production One Set

2008 Topps Chrome

NM/M
Complete Set (239):
Common Player (1-220): .25
Common RC Auto. (221-239): 10.00

	Hobby Pack (4):	3.00
	Hobby Box (24):	65.00
1	Alex Rodriguez	3.00
2	Barry Zito	.50
3	Scott Kazmir	.50
4	Stephen Drew	.50
5	Miguel Cabrera	1.00
6	Daisuke Matsuzaka	1.00
7	Mickey Mantle	4.00
8	Jimmy Rollins	.75
9	Joe Mauer	.50
10	Cole Hamels	.50
11	Yovani Gallardo	.40
12	Miguel Tejada	.25
13	Dontrelle Willis	.25
14	Orlando Cabrera	.25
15	Jake Peavy	.50
16	Erik Bedard	.50
17	Victor Martinez	.50
18	Chris Young	.50
19	Jose Reyes	1.00
20	Mike Lowell	.40
22	Dan Uggla	.50
23	Garrett Atkins	.40
24	Felix Hernandez	.50
25	Ivan Rodriguez	.50
26	Alex Rios	.50
27	Jason Bay	.50
28	Vladimir Guerrero	1.00
29	John Lackey	.50
30	Ryan Howard	1.00
31	Kevin Youkilis	.50
32	Justin Morneau	.50
33	Johan Santana	.75
34	Jeremy Hermida	.25
35	Andruw Jones	.40
36	Mike Cameron	.25
38	Jason Varitek	.50
39	Tim Hudson	.50
40	Justin Upton	.50
41	Brad Penny	.50
42	Robinson Cano	.50
43	Brandon Webb	.50
44	Magglio Ordonez	.50
45	Aaron Hill	.25
47	Alfonso Soriano	.50
48	Carlos Zambrano	.50
49	Ben Sheets	.50
50	Tim Lincecum	.50
51	Phil Hughes	.50
52	Scott Rolen	.50
53	John Maine	.50
54	Delmon Young	.50
56	Tadahito Iguchi	.25
57	Yunel Escobar	.25
58	Russell Martin	.25
59	Orlando Hudson	.25
60	Jim Edmonds	.25
61	Todd Helton	.50
62	Melky Cabrera	.50
63	Adrian Beltre	.50
64	Manny Ramirez	1.00
65	Gil Meche	.25
66	David DeJesus	.25
67	Roy Oswalt	.50
68	Mark Buehrle	.50
69	Hunter Pence	.50
71	Dustin Pedroia	.40
72	Roy Halladay	.50
73	Rich Harden	.40
74	Jim Thome	.50
75	Akinori Iwamura	.25
76	Dan Haren	.50
77	Brandon Phillips	.50
78	Brett Myers	.25
80	James Loney	.40
81	C.C. Sabathia	.50
82	Jermaine Dye	.40
83	Carlos Ruiz	.25
84	Brian McCann	.50
85	Paul Konerko	.50
86	Jorge Posada	.50
87	Chien-Ming Wang	.50
88	Carlos Delgado	.50
89	Ichiro Suzuki	2.00
90	Elijah Dukes	.25
91	David Wright	1.00
92	Carl Crawford	.50
93	Mark Teixeira	.50
94	Bobby Crosby	.25
95	Brian Roberts	.40
96	David Ortiz	1.00
97	Derek Lee	.50
98	Adam Dunn	.50
99	Fausto Carmona	.50
100	Grady Sizemore	.75
101	Jeff Francoeur	.50
102	Jered Weaver	.50
103	Troy Tulowitzki	.50
104	Troy Glaus	.50
105	Nick Markakis	.50
106	Lance Berkman	.50
107	Randy Johnson	.75
108	Kenji Johjima	.25
109	Alex Gordon	.50
110	Derek Lowe	.40
111	Nick Swisher	.50
112	Aaron Harang	.40
113	Hanley Ramirez	1.00
114	Carlos Guillen	.50
115	Ryan Braun	1.00
116	Torii Hunter	.50
115	Joe Blanton	.25
116	Josh Hamilton	

117 Pedro Martinez .75
118 Hideki Matsui 1.00
119 Cameron Maybin .25
120 Prince Fielder .75
121 Derek Jeter 3.00
122 Chone Figgins .50
123 Chase Utley 1.00
124 Jacoby Ellsbury .75
125 Freddy Sanchez .25
126 Rocco Baldelli .25
127 Tom Gorzelanny .25
128 Adrian Gonzalez .50
129 Geovany Soto .50
130 Bobby Abreu .50
131 Albert Pujols 3.00
132 Chipper Jones 1.00
133 Jeremy Bonderman .25
134 B.J. Upton .50
135 Justin Verlander .50
136 Jeff Francis .25
137 A.J. Burnett .25
138 Travis Buck .25
139 Vernon Wells .50
140 Raul Ibanez .25
141 Ryan Zimmerman .50
142 John Smoltz .50
143 Carlos Lee .50
144 Chris Young .50
145 Francisco Liriano .50
146 Curt Schilling .50
147 Josh Beckett .75
148 Aramis Ramirez .25
149 Ronnie Belliard .25
150 Homer Bailey .50
151 Curtis Granderson .50
152 Ken Griffey Jr. 2.00
153 Kazuo Matsui .25
154 Brian Bannister .25
155 Joba Chamberlain 1.50
156 Tom Glavine .50
157 Carlos Beltran .75
158 Kelly Johnson .25
159 Rich Hill .25
160 Pat Burrell .50
161 Asdrubal Cabrera .25
162 Gary Sheffield .50
163 Greg Maddux 1.00
164 Eric Chavez .25
165 Chris Carpenter .50
166 Michael Young .50
167 Carlos Pena .50
168 Frank Thomas .75
169 Aaron Rowand .40
170 Yadier Molina .25
171 Luis Castillo .25
172 Ryan Theriot .25
173 Andre Ethier .25
174 Casey Kotchman .25
175 Rickie Weeks .40
176 Milton Bradley .25
177 Daniel Cabrera .25
178 Jo Jo Reyes .25
179 Livan Hernandez .25
180 Hideki Okajima .25
181 Matt Kemp .50
182 Jonny Gomes .25
183 Billy Butler .25
184 Adam LaRoche .25
185 Brad Hawpe .25
186 Paul Maholm .25
187 Placido Polanco .25
188 Noah Lowry .25
189 Gregg Zaun .25
190 Nate McLouth .25
191 Edinson Volquez .50
192 Jeff Niemann (RC) 1.00
193 Evan Longoria RC 8.00
194 Adam Jones .50
195 Eugenio Velez RC 1.00
196 Joey Votto (RC) 2.00
197 Nick Blackburn RC 1.00
198 Harvey Garcia (RC) 1.00
199 Hiroki Kuroda RC 2.00
200 Elliot Johnson (RC) 1.00
201 Luis Mendoza (RC) 1.00
202 Alex Romero (RC) 1.00
203 Gregor Blanco (RC) 1.00
204 Rico Washington (RC) 1.00
205 Brian Bocock RC 1.00
206 Evan Meek RC 1.00
207 Steve Holm RC 1.00
208 Matt Tupman RC 1.00
209 Fernando Hernandez RC 1.00
210 Randor Bierd RC 1.00
211 Blake DeWitt (RC) 2.00
212 Randy Wells RC 1.00
213 Wesley Wright RC 1.00
214 Clete Thomas RC 1.00
215 Kyle McClellan RC 1.00
216 Brian Bixler (RC) 1.00
217 Kazuo Fukumori RC 1.50
218 Burke Badenhop RC 1.00
219 Denard Span (RC) 1.50
220 Brian Bass (RC) 1.00
221 J.R. Towles/Auto. RC 15.00
222 Felipe Paulino/Auto. RC 10.00
223 Sam Fuld/Auto. RC 15.00
224 Kevin Hart/Auto. (RC) 10.00
225 Nyjer Morgan/
    Auto. (RC) 10.00
226 Daric Barton/
    Auto. (RC) 10.00
227 Armando Galarraga/
    Auto. RC 25.00
228 Chin-Lung Hu/
    Auto. RC 15.00
229 Clay Buchholz/
    Auto. (RC) 20.00

230 Rich Thompson/
    Auto. (RC) 10.00
231 Brian Barton/Auto. RC 15.00
232 Ross Ohlendorf/
    Auto. RC 15.00
233 Masahide Kobayashi/
    Auto. RC 10.00
234 Callix Crabbe/
    Auto. (RC) 10.00
235 Matt Tolbert/Auto. RC 15.00
236 Jayson Nix/Auto. (RC) 10.00
237 Johnny Cueto/Auto. RC 25.00
238 Evan Meek/Auto. RC 10.00
239 Randy Wells/Auto. RC 10.00

Refractor
Refractor (1-220): 2-3X
Inserted 1:3
Refractor Auto. (221-239): 1-1.25X
Autos. Production 500

Blue Refractor
Blue Autos. (221-239): 1-1.5X
Production 200 Sets

Copper Refractor

Copper Ref. (1-220): 3-4X
Production 599
Copper Autos. (221-239): 1.5-2X
Autos. Production 50

Red Refractor
Red Ref. (1-220): 10-20X
Red Autos. (221-239): 3-4X
Production 25 Sets

Superfractor
Production One Set

Printing Plates
Production one set per color.

All-Rookie Team

NM/M
Complete Set (23): 15.00
Common Player: .50
Inserted 1:9
1 Gary Sheffield .75
2 Ivan Rodriguez .50
3 Mike Piazza 1.00
4 Manny Ramirez 1.00
5 Chipper Jones 1.50
6 Derek Jeter 3.00
7 Andruw Jones .50
8 Alfonso Soriano 1.00
9 Jimmy Rollins 1.00
10 Albert Pujols 3.00
11 Ichiro Suzuki 2.00
12 Mark Teixeira .75
13 Matt Holliday .75
14 Joe Mauer .50
15 Prince Fielder .50
16 Hideki Okajima .50
17 Roy Oswalt .75
18 Hunter Pence .75
19 Nick Markakis .50
20 Ryan Zimmerman .50
21 Ryan Braun 1.50
22 C.C. Sabathia .50
23 Dustin Pedroia .50

Mickey Mantle HR History

NM/M
Common Mantle: 2.00
Inserted 1:12
Refractor: 2-3X
Production 400 Sets
Copper Refractor: 3-5X

Production 100 Sets
Red Refractor: No Pricing
Production 25 Sets

Target Continuity
Complete Set (30):
Common Player:
Target Exclusive

The Mickey Mantle Story

NM/M
Complete Set (10): 20.00
Common Mantle (46-55): 3.00
Inserted 1:20
Refractor: 2-3X
Production 400 Sets
Copper Refractor: 3-4X
Production 100 Sets
Red Refractor: No Pricing
Production 25 Sets

Topps Heritage Chrome

NM/M
Common Player (101-200): 3.00
Production 1,959 Sets
Refractor: 1-1.5X
Production 559 Sets
Black Refractor: 4-8X
Production 59 Sets
C101 Phil Hughes 4.00
C102 Hideki Okajima 3.00
C103 Chone Figgins 4.00
C104 Jose Vidro 3.00
C105 Johan Santana 8.00
C106 Paul Konerko 5.00
C107 Alfonso Soriano 8.00
C108 Kei Igawa 3.00
C109 Lastings Milledge 3.00
C110 Asdrubal Cabrera 3.00
C111 Brandon Jones 3.00
C112 Tom Gorzelanny 3.00
C113 Delmon Young 4.00
C114 Daric Barton 3.00
C115 David DeJesus 3.00
C116 Ryan Howard 8.00
C117 Tom Glavine 5.00
C118 Frank Thomas 5.00
C119 J.R. Towles 3.00
C120 Jeremy Bonderman 3.00
C121 Adrian Beltre 4.00
C122 Dan Haren 4.00
C123 Kazuo Matsui 3.00
C124 Joe Blanton 3.00
C125 Dan Uggla 4.00
C126 Stephen Drew 4.00
C127 Daniel Cabrera 3.00
C128 Jeff Clement 5.00
C129 Pedro Martinez 5.00
C130 Josh Anderson 3.00
C131 Orlando Hudson 3.00
C132 Jason Bay 4.00
C133 Eric Chavez 3.00
C134 Johnny Damon 5.00
C135 Lance Broadway 3.00
C136 Jake Peavy 5.00
C137 Carl Crawford 4.00
C138 Kenji Johjima 3.00
C139 Melky Cabrera 3.00
C140 Aaron Hill 3.00
C141 Carlos Lee 4.00
C142 Mark Buehrle 3.00
C143 Carlos Beltran 4.00
C144 Chin-Lung Hu 3.00
C145 C.C. Sabathia 4.00
C146 Dustin Pedroia 4.00
C147 Freddy Sanchez 3.00
C148 Kevin Youkilis 5.00
C149 Radhames Liz 3.00
C150 Jim Thome 5.00
C151 Greg Maddux 8.00
C152 Rich Hill 4.00
C153 Andy LaRoche 4.00
C154 Gil Meche 3.00
C155 Victor Martinez 4.00
C156 Mariano Rivera 5.00
C157 Kyle Kendrick 3.00
C158 Jarrod Saltalamacchia 3.00
C159 Tadahito Iguchi 3.00

C160 Eric Gagne 3.00
C161 Garrett Atkins 4.00
C162 Pat Burrell 4.00
C163 Akinori Iwamura 3.00
C164 Melvin Mora 3.00
C165 Joey Votto 5.00
C166 Brian Roberts 3.00
C167 Brett Myers 3.00
C168 Michael Young 3.00
C169 Adam Jones 5.00
C170 Carlos Zambrano 5.00
C171 Jeff Francoeur 5.00
C172 Brad Hawpe 4.00
C173 Andy Pettitte 4.00
C174 Ryan Garko 3.00
C175 Adrian Gonzalez 4.00
C176 Ted Lilly 3.00
C177 J.J. Hardy 3.00
C178 Jon Lester 3.00
C179 Carlos Pena 3.00
C180 Ross Detwiler 3.00
C181 Andruw Jones 3.00
C182 Gary Sheffield 4.00
C183 Dmitri Young 3.00
C184 Carlos Guillen 4.00
C185 Yovani Gallardo 4.00
C186 Alex Gordon 4.00
C187 Aaron Harang 3.00
C188 Travis Hafner 4.00
C189 Orlando Cabrera 4.00
C190 Bobby Abreu 4.00
C191 Randy Johnson 5.00
C192 Scott Kazmir 4.00
C193 Jason Varitek 4.00
C194 Mike Lowell 4.00
C195 A.J. Burnett 4.00
C196 Garret Anderson 3.00
C197 Chris Carpenter 4.00
C198 Jermaine Dye 4.00
C199 Luke Hochevar 5.00
C200 Steve Pearce 5.00

Trading Card History

NM/M
Common Player (1-50): .50
Inserted 1:4
1 Jacoby Ellsbury 1.00
2 Joba Chamberlain 2.00
3 Daisuke Matsuzaka 1.50
4 Prince Fielder 1.00
5 Alex Rodriguez 3.00
6 Mickey Mantle 4.00
7 Ryan Braun 1.50
8 Albert Pujols 3.00
9 Joe Mauer .50
10 Jose Reyes 1.50
11 Johan Santana 1.00
12 Hunter Pence .75
13 Hideki Okajima .50
14 Cameron Maybin .75
15 Tim Lincecum .75
16 Mark Teixeira,
   Jeff Francoeur .75
17 Justin Upton .75
18 Alfonso Soriano .75
19 Grady Sizemore 2.00
20 Ryan Howard 1.00
21 David Wright 1.00
22 Jimmy Rollins 1.00
23 Ken Griffey Jr. 2.00
24 Chipper Jones 1.00
25 Justin Verlander .75
26 Manny Ramirez .75
27 Chase Utley 1.00
28 Ivan Rodriguez .75
29 Josh Beckett .75
30 Vladimir Guerrero 1.00
31 Lance Berkman .75
32 Gary Sheffield .75
33 David Ortiz .75
34 Andruw Jones .50
35 Hideki Matsui 1.50
36 C.C. Sabathia .75
37 Magglio Ordonez .75
38 Pedro Martinez 1.00
39 Derek Jeter 3.00
40 Hanley Ramirez 1.00
41 Jake Peavy .50
42 Matt Holliday .75
43 Carlos Beltran .75
44 Troy Tulowitzki .75
45 Justin Morneau .75
46 Phil Hughes .75
47 Torii Hunter .75
48 Brad Hawpe .50

Wal-Mart Continuity
Complete Set (20):
Common Player:
Wal-Mart Exclusive

2008 Topps Co-Signers

NM/M
Common Player (1-100): .25
Common RC Auto. (99-112): 10.00
Pack (6): 10.00
Box (12): 100.00
1 Jacoby Ellsbury 1.00
2 Michael Young .50
3 Cameron Maybin .50
4 Dmitri Young .25
5 Grady Sizemore .75
6 Brandon Webb .75
7 Derrek Lee .75
8 Jeff Francis .25
9 Aaron Harang .25
10 John Smoltz .50
11 Nicholas Markakis .50
12 Tom Gorzelanny .25
13 Miguel Cabrera 1.00
14 Josh Beckett 1.00
15 Magglio Ordonez .50
16 Joe Mauer .50
17 Carl Crawford .50
18 Barry Zito .25
19 Brad Penny .25
20 C.C. Sabathia .50
21 Mark Buehrle .50
22 Carlos Lee .50
23 Chipper Jones 1.00
24 Chase Utley 1.00
25 David Ortiz 1.00
26 Justin Morneau .50
27 Erik Bedard .50
28 Greg Maddux 2.00
29 Joba Chamberlain 3.00
30 Vernon Wells .50
31 Orlando Hudson .25
32 Kevin Youkilis .50
33 Curtis Granderson .50
34 Chone Figgins .50
35 Jorge Posada .75
36 Ken Griffey Jr. 2.00
37 Tim Hudson .50
38 Nick Swisher .50
39 Carlos Beltran .75
40 Alex Gordon .50
41 Andre Ethier .25
42 Todd Helton .50
43 Miguel Tejada .50
44 Yadier Molina .50
45 Hanley Ramirez 1.00
46 Justin Verlander .50
47 Adam Dunn .50
48 Raul Ibanez .25
49 Scott Rolen .50
50 Alex Rodriguez 3.00
51 Garret Anderson .25
52 Andruw Jones .50
53 Matt Cain .50
54 Daisuke Matsuzaka 1.50
55 Ichiro Suzuki 2.00
56 Scott Kazmir .50
57 Jeff Kent .50
58 Aubrey Huff .25
59 Justin Upton .75
60 Prince Fielder 1.00
61 Alex Rios .50
62 Alfonso Soriano .75
63 Paul Konerko .50
64 Matt Holliday .75
65 Felix Hernandez .50
66 Ivan Rodriguez .50
67 John Maine .50
68 Roy Oswalt .75
69 Brian McCann .75
70 Albert Pujols 3.00
71 John Lackey .50
72 Travis Hafner .50
73 Gil Meche .25
74 Ben Sheets .50
75 Ryan Howard 1.00
76 Hideki Matsui 1.50
77 Mike Lowell .50
78 Danny Haren .50
79 Adrian Gonzalez .50
80 David Wright 1.50
81 Jason Bay .50
82 Carlos Zambrano .50
83 Johan Santana 1.00
84 David DeJesus .25
85 Ryan Zimmerman .50
86 Bobby Abreu .50

87 Richie Sexson .25
88 Eric Chavez .25
89 Derek Lowe .25
90 Jake Peavy .50
91 Joe Blanton .25
92 Jermaine Dye .25
93 Pedro Martinez .75
94 B.J. Upton .50
95 Vladimir Guerrero 1.00
96 Ross Ohlendorf RC 1.00
97 J.R. Towles RC 3.00
98 Jonathan Meloan RC 1.00
99 Chin-Lung Hu (RC) 2.00
99 Chin-Lung Hu/
   Auto. (RC) 25.00
100 Clay Buchholz (RC) 3.00
100 Clay Buchholz/
    Auto. (RC) 35.00
101 Willie Collazo/Auto. RC 15.00
102 David Davidson/
    Auto. RC 10.00
103 Joe Koshansky/
    Auto. (RC) 10.00
104 Sam Fuld/Auto. RC 10.00
105 Nyjer Morgan/
    Auto. (RC) 10.00
106 Clint Sammons/
    Auto. (RC) 10.00
107 Josh Anderson/
    Auto. (RC) 10.00
108 Bronson Sardinha/
    Auto. RC 15.00
109 Wladimir Balentien/
    Auto. (RC) 15.00
110 Kevin Hart/Auto. (RC) 10.00
111 Felipe Paulino/Auto. RC 10.00
112 Rob Johnson/
    Auto. (RC) 10.00

Gold
Gold (1-100): 2-3X
Autos. (99-112): 1-1.5X
Production 150 Sets

Green
Green (1-100): 2-3X
Autos. (99-112): 1X
Production 200 Sets

Blue
Blue (1-100): 2-3X
Non-Auto. Production 250
Autos. (99-112): 1X
Auto. Production 300

Bronze
Bronze (1-100): 2-3X
Non-Auto. Production 300
Autos. (99-112): 1X
Auto. Production 400

Red
Red (1-100): 2-3X
Non-Auto. Production 400
Autos. (99-112): 1X
Auto. Production 500

Hyper Plaid Silver
Production One Set

Hyper Plaid Bronze
Hyper-P Bronze (1-100): 3-4X
Autos. (99-112): 1-1.5X
Production 75 Sets

Hyper Plaid Blue
Hyper-P Blue (1-100): 3-5X
Autos. (99-112): 1.5X
Production 50 Sets

Hyper Plaid Gold
No Pricing
Production 10 Sets

Hyper Plaid Green
Hyper-P Green (1-100): 5-10X
Autos. (99-112): No Pricing
Production 25 Sets

Hyper Plaid Red
Hyper-P Red (1-100): 2-3X
Autos. (99-112): 1-1.5X
Production 100 Sets

Cowhide Dual Sigs.
Production One Set

Cut Signatures
No Pricing

Dual Autos.

NM/M
Common Dual Auto.: 15.00
CE Jack Cust, Mark Ellis 20.00
CC Robinson Cano,
   Asdrubal Cabrera 30.00
HC Felix Hernandez,
   Joba Chamberlain 100.00
SP Geovany Soto, Felix Pie 35.00

MM	Andrew Miller, Cameron Maybin	20.00
GS	Tom Gorzelanny, Freddy Sanchez	15.00
SG	Andrew Sonnanstine, Matt Garza	15.00
PS	Steve Pearce, Freddy Sanchez	15.00
BZ	Jason Bartlett, Benjamin Zobrist	15.00
BB	Daric Barton, Clay Buchholz	25.00
RO	Edwar Ramirez, Ross Ohlendorf	20.00
JA	Brandon Jones, Josh Anderson	15.00
OB	Garrett Olson, Brian Burres	15.00
DR	Chris Duncan, Brendan Ryan	30.00
FH	Jeff Francis, Jason Hirsh	15.00
MS	Carlos Marmol, Geovany Soto	50.00
PKS	Glen Perkins, Kevin Slowey	15.00
BA	Josh Banks, Jeremy Accardo	15.00
SC	Brian Schneider, Ramon Castro	20.00
FP	Sam Fuld, Felix Pie	25.00
RM	Alex Rios, Nicholas Markakis	30.00
FJ	Jeff Francis, Ubaldo Jimenez	15.00
BJ	Erik Bedard, Adam Jones	40.00
VC	Joey Votto, Daric Barton	25.00
LH	Andy LaRoche, Chin-Lung Hu	25.00
MD	Lastings Milledge, Elijah Dukes	20.00
SZ	Alex Smith, Ryan Zimmerman	20.00
MP	Joe Mason, Jonathan Papelbon	20.00
KC	Tim Kelly, Joba Chamberlain	60.00
HCA	Josue Herrera, Fausto Carmona	15.00
BM	Bill Buck, Cameron Maybin	20.00
JM	Dave Jennings, Nicholas Markakis	25.00
CG	Jerome Cochran, Curtis Granderson	20.00
OBA	Dan Ontiveros, Daric Barton	15.00
EH	Bob Engle, Felix Hernandez	20.00
LG	Don Lyle, Ryan Garko	15.00
DD	Juan Diaz, Julio Diaz	15.00
CB	Steve Cunningham, Shannon Briggs	25.00
CCC	Martin Castillo, Julio Cesar Chavez Jr.	30.00
PP	Samuel Peter, Aaron Pryor	35.00
MMJ	Juan Manuel Marquez, Chris John	15.00
PG	Daniel Ponce de Leon, Joan Guzman	15.00
MV	Rafael Marquez, Israel Vasquez	20.00
DB	Chad Dawson, Andre Berto	20.00
DG	Vic Darchinyan, Danny Green	15.00
CLC	Joel Casamayor, Jose Luis Castillo	20.00
KA	Roman Karmazin, Arthur Abraham	15.00
MB	Edison Miranda, O'Neil Bell	15.00
AC	Jorge Arce, Ivan Calderon	20.00
FC	Chone Figgins, Carl Crawford	25.00
PO	Jonathan Papelbon, Hideki Okajima	60.00
RR	Jimmy Rollins, Jose Reyes	50.00
FHO	Prince Fielder, Ryan Howard	50.00
WF	Dontrelle Willis, Mark Fidrych	20.00
RW	Jose Reyes, David Wright	100.00
SE	Arthur Shorin, Michael Eisner	70.00

Quad Cut Signatures
Production One Set

Quad-Signers
Common Quad:

Solo Sigs. Boxers
NM/M

	Common Boxer Auto.:	10.00
KP	Kelly Pavlik	60.00
EM	Edison Miranda	15.00
SB	Shannon Briggs	25.00
SP	Samuel Peter	20.00
JD	Juan Diaz	20.00
JUD	Julio Diaz	15.00
JC	Joel Casamayor	20.00

CJ	Chris John	15.00
SC	Steve Cunningham	15.00
OB	O'Neil Bell	10.00
DP	Daniel Ponce de Leon	15.00
JM	Juan Manuel Marquez	15.00
RM	Rafael Marquez	20.00
VD	Vic Darchinyan	10.00
JA	Jorge Arce	20.00
AA	Arthur Abraham	15.00
JG	Joan Guzman	15.00
JLC	Jose Luis Castillo	15.00
JCC	Julio Cesar Chavez Jr.	15.00
AB	Andre Berto	15.00
CD	Chad Dawson	15.00
AW	Andre Ward	15.00
AP	Aaron Pryor	30.00
RBBM	Ray Boom Boom Mancini	50.00
JF	Jeff Fenech	20.00
IC	Ivan Calderon	20.00
RK	Roman Karmazin	15.00
TA	Teddy Atlas	20.00
BS	Bert Sugar	20.00
FM	Fernando Montiel	20.00
IV	Israel Vasquez	25.00
MC	Martin Castillo	10.00
DAG	Danny Green	20.00

Tri-Signers
NM/M
Common Trio:
Some not priced.

PBG	Manny Parra, Ryan Braun, Yovani Gallardo	75.00

2008 Topps Heritage

NM/M

Complete Set (500):	275.00
Complete Hi Number Set (501-720):	125.00
Common Player:	.40
Common SP:	5.00
Inserted 1:3	
Common Black Back:	1.50
Common High # (501-720):	.40
Common High # SP:	5.00
Pack (8):	3.50
Box (24):	75.00
High Numbers Box (24):	60.00

1	Vladimir Guerrero	1.00
2	Placido Polanco	.40
2	Placido Polanco/ Black Back	1.50
3	Eric Byrnes	.40
3	Eric Byrnes/Black Back	1.50
4	Mark Teixeira	.75
5	Javier Vazquez	.40
5	Javier Vazquez/ Black Back	1.50
6	Jacoby Ellsbury	2.00
7	Joey Gathright	.40
7	Joey Gathright/ Black Back	1.50
8	Philadelphia Phillies	.75
8	Philadelphia Phillies/ Black Back	1.50
9	Andre Ethier	.40
9	Andre Ethier/Black Back	1.50
10	Alex Rodriguez	3.00
11	Luke Scott/SP	5.00
12	Curt Schilling	.40
12	Curt Schilling/Black Back	1.50
13	Billy Wagner	.40
13	Billy Wagner/Black Back	1.50
14	Gary Matthews Jr.	.40
14	Gary Matthews Jr./ Black Back	1.50
15	Sean Marshall	.50

16	Ichiro Suzuki	2.00
16	Ichiro Suzuki/Black Back	3.00
17	Jason Bay, Freddy Sanchez, Jack Wilson	.40
18	Dontrelle Willis	.40
18	Dontrelle Willis/ Black Back	1.50
19	Josh Willingham	.40
20	Jeff Kent	.50
21	Troy Tulowitzki	.75
21	Troy Tulowitzki/ Black Back	1.50
22	Brian Fuentes	.40
22	Brian Fuentes/Black Back	1.50
23	Robinson Cano	.75
23	Robinson Cano/ Black Back	1.50
24	Felix Hernandez	.75
24	Felix Hernandez/ Black Back	2.00
25	Edwin Encarnacion	.40
26	Fausto Carmona	.40
27	Greg Maddux	1.50
28	Ivan Rodriguez	.75
28	Ivan Rodriguez/ Black Back	1.50
29	Joe Nathan	.40
30	Paul Konerko	.75
31	Nook Logan	.40
32	Derek Lowe	.40
33	Jose Lopez	.40
34	Magglio Ordonez, Curtis Granderson	.50
34	Ordonez, Granderson/ Black Back	1.50
35	Adam LaRoche	.40
35	Adam LaRoche/ Black Back	1.50
36	Kenny Lofton	.40
37	Matt Capps	.40
38	Mark Reynolds	.40
39	Joe Mauer	.50
40	Tim Hudson	.40
40	Tim Hudson/Black Back	1.50
41	Kelvim Escobar	.40
41	Kelvim Escobar/ Black Back	1.50
42	Jason Jennings	.40
42	Jason Jennings/ Black Back	1.50
43	Victor Martinez	.75
44	Jason Kendall	.40
45	Chris Ray	.40
45	Chris Ray/Black Back	1.50
46	Jason Bergmann	.40
47	Jason Marquis	.40
48	Baltimore Orioles	.50
49	Bill Hall	.40
49	Bill Hall/Black Back	1.50
51	Ken Griffey Jr.	2.00
52	Chad Cordero	.40
52	Omar Vizquel	.40
52	Omar Vizquel/Black Back	1.50
53	Jim Edmonds	.50
54	Justin Upton	1.00
54	Justin Upton/Black Back	2.00
55	Josh Beckett	1.00
56	Jeff Francis	.40
57	Brad Lidge	.40
57	Brad Lidge/Black Back	1.50
58	Paul LoDuca	.40
58	Paul LoDuca/Black Back	1.50
59	John Patterson	.40
60	Andy Pettitte	.75
60	Andy Pettitte/Black Back	1.50
61	Brendan Harris	.40
61	Brendan Harris/ Black Back	1.50
62	Chris Young	.50
62	Chris Young/Black Back	1.50
63	Eric Chavez	.40
64	Francisco Rodriguez	.50
65	Jason Giambi	.50
65	Jason Giambi/Black Back	1.50
66	B.J. Ryan	.40
67	Rich Hill	.50
67	Rich Hill/Black Back	1.50
68	Derek Jeter	3.00
69	San Francisco Giants	.50
69	San Francisco Giants/ Black Back	1.50
70	Carlos Guillen	.50
71	Trevor Hoffman	.40
71	Trevor Hoffman/ Black Back	.40
72	Zachary Duke	.40
73	Dustin Pedroia	.75
74	Ryan Zimmerman, Dmitri Young	.50
75	Cole Hamels	.75
76	Carlos Delgado	.50
77	Jonathan Broxton	.40
78	Josh Hamilton	.50
78	Josh Hamilton/ Black Back	3.00
79	Mark Loretta	.40
79	Mark Loretta/Black Back	1.50
80	Grady Sizemore	1.00
81	Torii Hunter	.75
81	Torii Hunter/Black Back	1.50
82	Carlos Beltran	.50
82	Carlos Beltran/ Black Back	2.00
83	Jason Isringhausen	.40
83	Jason Isringhausen/ Black Back	1.50
84	Brad Penny	.40
84	Brad Penny/Black Back	1.50

85	Jayson Werth	.40
86	Alex Gordon	.75
87	David DeJesus	.40
88	Clay Buchholz (RC)	.75
89	Conor Jackson	.40
90	Hideki Matsui	.50
90	Hideki Matsui/Black Back	2.50
91	Matt Garza	.40
91	Matt Garza/Black Back	1.50
92	Phil Hughes	1.00
92	Phil Hughes/Black Back	2.50
93	Mike Piazza	.75
94	Chicago White Sox	.40
94	Chicago White Sox/ Black Back	1.50
95	Buddy Carlyle	.40
96	Mark DeRosa	.40
97	Brandon Webb	.40
98	Jon Garland	.40
98	Jon Garland/Black Back	1.50
99	Mariano Rivera	.75
100	Jack Cust	.40
101	Carlos Ruiz	.40
102	Moises Alou	.50
102	Moises Alou/Black Back	1.50
103	Bengie Molina	.40
104	Adam Jones	.40
105	Alfonso Soriano	1.00
106	Troy Glaus	.75
107	John Maine	.40
108	Pat Burrell	.50
109	David Eckstein	.40
110	Homer Bailey	.50
111	Cincinnati Reds	.40
112	Corey Hart	.50
113	Orlando Hernandez	.40
114	Orlando Cabrera	.50
115	Ryan Garko	.40
116	Wladimir Balentien	.40
116	Wladimir Balentien/ Black Back	1.50
117	Daric Barton	.50
117	Daric Barton/Black Back	1.50
118	Emilio Bonifacio RC	.75
119	Lance Broadway RC	.75
120	Jeff Clement	.40
121	David Davidson RC	.40
122	Ross Detwiler RC	.50
122	Ross Detwiler/Black Back	1.50
123	Sam Fuld RC	.50
124	Armando Galarraga RC	2.00
125	Harvey Garcia	.40
126	Daniel Giese	.40
126	Daniel Giese/Black Back	1.50
127	Alberto Gonzalez (RC)	.50
127	Alberto Gonzalez/ Black Back	1.50
128	Kevin Hart	.40
129	Luke Hochevar RC	1.00
129	Luke Hochevar/ Black Back	2.00
130	Chin-Lung Hu (RC)	.40
130	Chin-Lung Hu/Black Back	1.50
131	Brandon Jones RC	.75
132	Joe Koshansky	.40
133	Radhames Liz RC	.50
134	Donny Lucy	.40
135	Mitch Stetter RC	.50
135	Mitch Stetter/Black Back	1.50
136	Nyjer Morgan	.40
137	Ross Ohlendorf RC	.40
138	Steve Pearce RC	.50
139	Jeff Ridgway RC	.75
140	Bronson Sardinha	.40
141	Seth Smith	.40
142	Rich Thompson	.40
143	Erick Threets	.40
144	J.R. Towles RC	.50
145	Eugenio Velez RC	.50
146	Joey Votto	.40
147	Alfonso Soriano, Aramis Ramirez, Derek Lee	.50
148	Hunter Pence	.75
149	Barry Zito	.40
150	Albert Pujols	3.00
150	Albert Pujols/Black Back	5.00
151	Sammy Sosa	.50
152	Brian Bannister	.40
153	Reggie Willits	.40
155	Bobby Abreu	.75
155	Johnny Damon	.75
156	Johnny Damon/ Black Back	1.50
156	Brandon Webb, Jake Peavy	.50
157	Aramis Ramirez	.50
158	Mark Buehrle	.40
159	David Weathers	.40
160	Jack Wilson	.40
161	Josh Fogg	.40
162	Garrett Atkins	.40
163	Brad Ausmus	.40
164	Gil Meche	.40
165	Jeff Francoeur	.50
166	Grady Sizemore, Travis Hafner, Victor Martinez	.50
167	Juan Pierre	.50
168	Rafael Furcal	.40
169	J.J. Hardy	.50
170	Nicholas Markakis	.50
171	Delmon Young	.40
172	Oakland A's	.40
173	Ronny Paulino	.40
173	Ronny Paulino/ Black Back	1.50
174	Mike Cameron	.40

174	Mike Cameron/ Black Back	1.50
175	Jeff Weaver	.40
175	Jeff Weaver/Black Back	1.50
176	Preston Wilson	.40
176	Preston Wilson/ Black Back	1.50
177	Robinson Tejeda	.40
177	Robinson Tejeda/ Black Back	1.50
178	Adam Lind	.40
178	Adam Lind/Black Back	1.50
179	Austin Kearns	.40
180	Austin Kearns/Black Back	1.50
180	Jorge Posada	.75
180	Jorge Posada/Black Back	1.50
181	Tadahito Iguchi	.40
182	Matt Cain	.50
183	Yuniesky Betancourt	.40
184	Bronson Arroyo	.40
185	Brad Hawpe	.40
185	Brad Hawpe/Black Back	1.50
186	Rickie Weeks	.40
186	Rickie Weeks/Black Back	1.50
187	Carlos Silva	.40
187	Carlos Silva/Black Back	1.50
188	Adrian Gonzalez	.50
189	Kenji Johjima	.40
190	Chris Duncan	.40
191	James Shields	.50
192	Akinori Iwamura	.50
193	David Murphy	.40
194	Alex Rios	.75
195	Carlos Quentin	.40
195	Carlos Quentin/ Black Back	1.50
196	Jose Valverde	.40
196	Jose Valverde/Black Back	1.50
197	Derrek Lee	.75
197	Derrek Lee/Black Back	1.50
198	Jerry Owens	.40
198	Jerry Owens/Black Back	1.50
199	Russell Martin	.75
200	Yovani Gallardo	.75
201	Johan Santana	1.00
202	Nick Swisher	.50
203	So Taguchi	.40
204	Justin Morneau	.75
205	Milton Bradley	.40
206	Jake Westbrook	.40
207	Dave Roberts	.40
208	Billy Butler	.40
209	Lance Berkman	.75
210	J.J. Putz	.40
210	J.J. Putz/Black Back	1.50
211	Mike Sweeney	.40
211	Mike Sweeney/ Black Back	1.50
212	Andruw Jones, Chipper Jones	.50
213	Ricky Nolasco	.40
214	Andy LaRoche	.50
215	Ray Durham	.40
216	Francisco Cordero	.40
217	Jered Weaver	.40
218	Rafael Soriano	.40
219	Orlando Hudson	.40
220	Mike Lowell	.50
221	Chris Snyder	.40
222	Cesar Izturis	.40
223	St. Louis Cardinals	.50
224	David Wright	1.50
224	David Wright/Black Back	3.00
225	Pedro Martinez	1.00
225	Pedro Martinez/ Black Back	1.50
226	Rich Harden	.40
226	Rich Harden/Black Back	1.50
227	Shane Victorino	.40
227	Shane Victorino/ Black Back	1.50
228	Andrew Miller	.50
228	Andrew Miller/Black Back	.50
229	Chris Young	.50
230	Andruw Jones	.50
231	Kevin Gregg/SP	5.00
232	C.C. Sabathia	.75
233	Hanley Ramirez	1.00
234	Wandy Rodriguez	.40
235	Roy Oswalt	.75
236	Mark Grudzielanek	.40
237	Derek Jeter, Chien-Ming Wang, Robinson Cano	1.00
238	Todd Helton	.75
239	Zack Greinke	.40
240	Carlos Gomez	.40
241	Lastings Milledge	.40
242	Huston Street	.40
243	Danny Haren	.40
244	Carlos Pena	.75
245	Brad Wilkerson	.40
246	Roy Halladay	.40
247	Dmitri Young	.40
248	Boston Red Sox	1.00
249	Jonathan Papelbon	.75
250	Felix Pie	.40
251	Alex Gonzalez	.40
252	Bobby Crosby	.40
253	Justin Ruggiano RC	.75
254	Freddy Garcia	.40
255	Khalil Greene	.40
256	Rich Aurilia	.40
257	Jarrod Washburn	.40
258	B.J. Upton	.50
259	Michael Young	.40
260	Carlos Zambrano	.75
261	Livan Hernandez	.40

262	Derek Lowe, Brad Penny, Chad Billingsley	.40
262	Lowe, Penny, Billingsley/ Black Back	1.50
263	Melky Cabrera	.40
263	Melky Cabrera/ Black Back	1.50
264	Shannon Stewart	.40
264	Shannon Stewart/ Black Back	1.50
265	Aaron Rowand	.50
265	Aaron Rowand/ Black Back	1.50
266	Matt Morris	.40
266	Matt Morris/Black Back	1.50
267	Xavier Nady	.50
267	Xavier Nady/Black Back	1.50
268	Jim Thome	.75
269	Horacio Ramirez	.40
270	Prince Fielder	1.00
271	Andy Phillips	.40
272	Aaron Harang	.40
273	Josh Barfield	.40
274	Ubaldo Jimenez	.40
275	Anibal Sanchez	.40
276	Carlos Lee	.50
277	Mark Teahen	.40
278	Delwyn Young	.40
279	Kurt Suzuki	.40
280	Nate Schierholtz	.40
281	Raul Ibanez	.40
282	Jose Vidro	.40
283	Miguel Cabrera	1.00
283	Miguel Cabrera/ Black Back	2.00
284	Luis Gonzalez	.40
284	Luis Gonzalez/Black Back	1.50
285	Chad Billingsley	.40
285	Chad Billingsley/ Black Back	1.50
286	Tony Gwynn Jr.	.40
286	Tony Gwynn Jr./ Black Back	1.50
287	Matthew Kemp	.75
288	James Loney	.50
289	Brett Myers	.40
290	Nate McLouth	.40
291	Matt Chico	.40
291	Matt Chico, Jason Bergmann/ Black Back	.50
292	Chad Tracy	.40
293	Edgar Renteria	.40
294	Jay Payton	.40
295	Josh Johnson	.40
296	Josh Banks	.40
297	Bill Murphy	.40
298	Ben Sheets	.40
299	Jose Reyes	1.00
300	Chase Utley	1.00
301	Ronnie Belliard	.40
301	Ronnie Belliard/ Black Back	1.50
302	Wily Mo Pena	.40
303	Tim Lincecum	.75
304	Chicago Cubs	.75
305	John Lackey	.40
306	Stephen Drew	.75
307	Kelly Johnson	.40
308	Daisuke Matsuzaka	2.00
309	Craig Monroe	.40
310	Jerry Owens	.40
311	Jeff Suppan	.40
312	Tom Glavine	.75
313	Kei Igawa	.40
314	Mark Kotsay	.40
315	Jacque Jones/SP	5.00
316	Melvin Mora	.40
317	Matt Holliday, Hanley Ramirez	.75
318	Jarrod Saltalamacchia	.50
319	A.J. Burnett	.40
320	Casey Kotchman	.40
321	Randy Winn	.40
321	Randy Winn/Black Back	1.50
322	Richie Sexson	.40
322	Richie Sexson/ Black Back	1.50
323	Juan Encarnacion	.40
323	Juan Encarnacion/ Black Back	1.50
324	Rick Ankiel	.40
324	Rick Ankiel/Black Back	1.50
325	Dan Wheeler	.40
325	Dan Wheeler/Black Back	1.50
326	Brian Roberts	.40
327	David Ortiz	1.00
328	Garret Anderson	.40
329	Detroit Tigers	.50
330	Ty Wigginton	.40
330	Ty Wigginton/Black Back	1.50
331	Travis Hafner	.50
332	Howie Kendrick	.40
332	Howie Kendrick/ Black Back	1.50
333	Kevin Kouzmanoff	.40
333	Kevin Kouzmanoff/ Black Back	1.50
334	Matt Holliday	.50
334	Matt Holliday/Black Back	1.50
335	Brandon Phillips	.40
335	Brandon Phillips/ Black Back	1.50
336	Ian Kinsler	.40
336	Ian Kinsler/Black Back	2.00
337	Lyle Overbay	.40
337	Lyle Overbay/Black Back	1.50
338	Justin Verlander	.75

No.	Player	Price
338	Justin Verlander/ Black Back	2.00
339	Ian Snell	.50
340	Hank Blalock	.50
341	Vernon Wells	.50
342	Matt Chico	.40
343	Tim Wakefield	.40
344	Michael Bourn	.40
345	Chris Carpenter	.50
346	Josh Beckett, Daisuke Matsuzaka	1.00
347	Chuck James	.40
347	Chuck James/Black Back	1.50
348	Joba Chamberlain	3.00
349	Erik Bedard	.75
350	Jimmy Rollins	.75
350	Jimmy Rollins/ Black Back	1.50
351	Anthony Reyes	.40
352	Carl Crawford	.50
353	Jeremy Hermida	.40
354	Ervin Santana	.40
355	Edgar Gonzalez	.40
356	Yunel Escobar	.40
357	Yorvit Torrealba	.40
358	Hideki Okajima	.50
359	Paul Byrd	.40
360	Magglio Ordonez	.50
360	Magglio Ordonez/ Black Back	1.50
361	Joe Borowski	.40
362	Clint Sammons	.40
363	Chris Duffy	.40
364	Fred Lewis	.40
365	Adrian Beltre	.50
366	Alex Rodriguez	3.00
367	Troy Tulowitzki	.75
368	Prince Fielder	1.00
369	Clay Buchholz	.75
370	Justin Verlander	.75
370	Justin Verlander/ Black Back	1.50
371	Pedro Martinez	1.00
371	Pedro Martinez/ Black Back	1.50
372	Ryan Howard	1.00
372	Ryan Howard/Black Back	3.00
373	Ichiro Suzuki	2.00
374	Kenny Lofton	.40
375	Manny Ramirez	.75
376	Randy Johnson	1.00
377	Chris Capuano	.40
378	Johnny Estrada	.40
379	Franklin Morales	.40
380	Ryan Howard	1.00
381	Casey Blake/SP	5.00
382	Coco Crisp	.40
383	John Maine	.40
	Willie Randolph	.40
384	Jeremy Guthrie	.40
385	Geoff Jenkins	.40
386	Marlon Byrd	.40
387	Jeremy Bonderman	.50
388	Ryan Howard	1.00
389	Joe Girardi	.40
390	Ryan Braun	1.00
391	Ryan Zimmerman	.75
392	Dustin Pedroia, Kevin Youkilis, Mike Lowell	.75
393	Pittsburgh Pirates	.40
394	Ryan Spilborghs	.40
395	Eric Gagne	.40
396	Joe Blanton	.40
397	Washington Nationals	.40
398	Ryan Church	.40
399	Ted Lilly	.40
400	Manny Ramirez	.75
401	Chad Gaudin	.40
402	Dustin McGowan	.40
403	Scott Baker	.40
404	Franklin Gutierrez	.40
405	David Bush	.40
406	Aubrey Huff	.40
407	Jermaine Dye	.40
408	Chase Utley	.40
	Jimmy Rollins	.75
409	Jon Lester/SP	5.00
410	Aaron Cook	.40
411	Sergio Mitre	.40
412	Jason Bartlett	.40
413	Edwin Jackson	.40
414	J.D. Drew	.40
415	Freddy Sanchez	.40
415	Freddy Sanchez/ Black Back	1.50
416	Asdrubal Cabrera	.40
417	Nate Robertson	.40
418	Shaun Marcum	.40
419	Noah Lowry	.40
420	Atlanta Braves	.50
421	Jamie Moyer	.40
422	Michael Cuddyer	.40
423	Randy Wolf	.40
424	Juan Uribe	.40
425	Brian McCann	.50
426	Kyle Lohse/SP	5.00
427	Doug Davis/SP	5.00
428	Ian Snell, Tom Gorzelanny, Matt Capps/SP	5.00
429	Miguel Batista/SP	5.00
430	Chien-Ming Wang/SP	10.00
431	Jeff Salazar/SP	5.00
432	Yadier Molina/SP	5.00
433	Adam Wainwright/SP	5.00
434	Scott Kazmir/SP	5.00
435	Adam Dunn/SP	6.00
436	Ryan Freel/SP	5.00
437	Jhonny Peralta/SP	5.00
438	Kazuo Matsui/SP	5.00
439	Daniel Cabrera	.40
440	John Smoltz	.75
441	Emil Brown/SP	5.00
442	Gary Sheffield/SP	5.00
443	Jake Peavy/SP	8.00
444	Scott Rolen/SP	5.00
445	Kason Gabbard/SP	5.00
446	Aaron Hill/SP	5.00
447	Felipe Lopez/SP	5.00
448	Dan Uggla/SP	5.00
449	Willy Taveras/SP	5.00
450	Chipper Jones/SP	6.00
451	Josh Anderson/SP	5.00
452	Eric Byrnes, Chris Young, Justin Upton/SP	5.00
453	Braden Looper/SP	5.00
454	Brandon Inge/SP	5.00
455	Brian Giles/SP	5.00
456	Corey Patterson/SP	5.00
457	Los Angeles Dodgers/SP	5.00
458	Sean Casey/SP	5.00
459	Pedro Feliz/SP	5.00
460	Tom Gorzelanny	.40
461	Chone Figgins/SP	5.00
462	Kyle Kendrick/SP	5.00
463	Tony Pena/SP	5.00
464	Marcus Giles/SP	5.00
465	Augie Ojeda/SP	5.00
466	Micah Owings/SP	5.00
467	Ryan Theriot/SP	5.00
468	Shawn Green/SP	5.00
469	Frank Thomas/SP	6.00
470	Lenny DiNardo/SP	5.00
471	Jose Bautista/SP	5.00
472	Manny Corpas/SP	5.00
473	Kevin Millwood/SP	5.00
474	Kevin Youkilis/SP	5.00
475	Jose Contreras/SP	5.00
476	Cleveland Indians	.50
477	Julio Lugo/SP	5.00
478	Jason Bay	.75
479	Tony LaRussa/SP	5.00
480	Jim Leyland/SP	5.00
481	Derrek Lee/SP	6.00
482	Justin Morneau/SP	6.00
483	Orlando Hudson/SP	5.00
484	Brian Roberts/SP	5.00
485	Miguel Cabrera/SP	6.00
486	Mike Lowell/SP	5.00
487	J.J. Hardy/SP	5.00
488	Carlos Guillen/SP	5.00
489	Ken Griffey Jr./SP	8.00
490	Vladimir Guerrero/SP	6.00
491	Alfonso Soriano/SP	6.00
492	Ichiro Suzuki/SP	8.00
493	Matt Holliday/SP	6.00
494	Magglio Ordonez/SP	5.00
495	Brian McCann/SP	5.00
496	Victor Martinez/SP	5.00
497	Brad Penny/SP	5.00
498	Josh Beckett/SP	6.00
499	Cole Hamels/SP	6.00
500	Justin Verlander/SP	6.00
501	John Danks	.40
502	Jamey Wright	.40
503	Johnny Cueto RC	1.50
504	Todd Wellemeyer	.40
505	Chase Headley	.50
506	Takashi Saito	.40
507	Skip Schumaker	.40
508	Tampa Bay Rays	.50
509	Marcus Thames	.40
510	Joe Saunders	.40
511	Jair Jurrjens	.40
512	Ryan Sweeney	.40
513	Darin Erstad	.40
514	Brandon Backe	.40
514	Brandon Backe/ Black Back	1.50
515	Chris Volstad (RC)	1.00
516	Salomon Torres	.40
517	Brian Burres	.40
518	Brandon Boggs (RC)	1.00
519	Max Scherzer RC	3.00
520	Cliff Lee	.50
521	Angel Pagan	.40
522	Jason Kubel	.40
523	Jose Molina	.40
523	Jose Molina/Black Back	1.50
524	Hiroki Kuroda RC	1.50
525	Matt Harrison (RC)	.75
526	C.J. Wilson	.40
527	Robb Quinlan	.40
528	Darrell Rasner	.40
529	Frank Catalanotto	.40
529	Frank Catalanotto/ Black Back	1.50
530	Mike Mussina	.75
531	Ryan Doumit	.40
531	Ryan Doumit/Black Back	1.50
532	Willie Bloomquist	.40
532	Willie Bloomquist/ Black Back	1.50
533	Jonny Gomes	.40
534	Jesse Litsch	.40
535	Curtis Granderson	.75
536	A.J. Pierzynski	.40
537	Toronto Blue Jays	.50
538	Brian Buscher	.40
538	Brian Buscher/ Black Back	1.50
539	Kelly Shoppach	.40
539	Kelly Shoppach/ Black Back	1.50
540	Edinson Volquez	.50
541	Jon Rauch	.40
541	Jon Rauch/Black Back	1.50
542	Ramon Castro	.40
542	Ramon Castro/ Black Back	1.50
543	Greg Smith RC	.75
544	Sean Gallagher	.40
545	Justin Masterson RC	4.00
545	Justin Masterson/ Black Back	5.00
546	Milwaukee Brewers	.50
547	Jay Bruce (RC)	3.00
548	Glendon Rusch	.40
549	Jeremy Sowers	.40
549	Jeremy Sowers/ Black Back	1.50
550	Ryan Dempster	.40
551	Clete Thomas RC	1.00
552	Jose Castillo	.40
553	Brandon Lyon	.40
554	Vicente Padilla	.40
555	Jeff Keppinger	.40
556	Colorado Rockies	.40
557	Dallas Braden	.40
557	Dallas Braden/Black Back	1.50
558	Adam Kennedy	.40
559	Luis Mendoza (RC)	.75
560	Justin Duchscherer	.40
561	Mike Aviles RC	1.50
562	Jed Lowrie (RC)	1.00
563	Doug Mientkiewicz	.40
563	Doug Mientkiewicz/ Black Back	1.50
564	Chris Burke	.40
565	Dana Eveland	.40
566	Bryan LaHair RC	.75
567	Denard Span (RC)	1.00
568	Damion Easley	.40
569	Josh Fields	.40
570	Geovany Soto	1.00
571	Gerald Laird	.40
572	Bobby Jenks	.40
573	Andy Marte	.40
574	Mike Pelfrey	.40
575	Jerry Hairston	.40
576	Mike Lamb	.40
577	Ben Zobrist	.40
578	Carlos Gonzalez (RC)	1.00
579	Jose Guillen	.40
579	Jose Guillen/Black Back	1.50
580	Kosuke Fukudome RC	2.00
581	Gabe Kapler	.40
581	Gabe Kapler/Black Back	1.50
582	Florida Marlins	.40
583	Ramon Vazquez	.40
583	Ramon Vazquez/ Black Back	1.50
584	Wes Helms	.40
584	Wes Helms/Black Back	1.50
585	Minnesota Twins	.40
586	Cody Ross	.40
587	Mike Napoli	.40
588	Alexi Casilla	.40
589	Emmanuel Burriss RC	1.00
590	Brian Wilson	.40
591	Rod Barajas	.40
592	Mike Hampton	.40
592	Mike Hampton/ Black Back	1.50
593	Nick Blackburn RC	1.50
594	Joe Mather RC	1.50
595	Clayton Kershaw RC	2.50
595	Clayton Kershaw/ Black Back	3.00
596	Cliff Floyd	.40
596	Cliff Floyd/Black Back	1.50
597	Sidney Ponson	.40
597	Sidney Ponson/ Black Back	1.50
598	Brian Anderson	.40
599	Joe Inglett	.40
600	Miguel Tejada	.50
601	San Diego Padres	.40
602	Scott Hairston	.40
602	Scott Hairston/ Black Back	1.50
603	Joel Pineiro	.40
604	Fernando Tatis	.40
605	Greg Reynolds RC	1.00
606	Brian Moehler	.40
607	Kevin Millar	.40
607	Kevin Millar/Black Back	1.50
608	Ben Francisco	.40
609	Troy Percival	.40
610	Kerry Wood	.50
611	Max Ramirez RC	1.00
612	Jeff Baker	.40
613	Houston Astros	.40
614	Russell Branyan	.40
615	Todd Jones	.40
616	Brian Schneider	.40
617	Gregorio Petit RC	1.00
618	Matt Diaz	.40
619	Blake DeWitt (RC)	1.00
619	Blake DeWitt/Black Back	2.00
620	Cristian Guzman	.40
621	Jeff Samardzija RC	2.00
621	Jeff Samardzija/ Black Back	3.00
622	John Baker (RC)	.75
623	Eric Hinske	.40
624	Scott Olsen	.40
625	Greg Dobbs	.40
626	Carlos Marmol	.40
626	Carlos Marmol/ Black Back	1.50
627	Kansas City Royals	.40
628	Esteban German	.40
629	Dennis Sarfate	.40
630	Ryan Ludwick	.75
631	Mike Jacobs	.40
632	Tyler Yates	.40
633	Joel Hanrahan	.40
634	Manny Parra	.40
635	Maicer Izturis	.40
636	Juan Rivera	.40
637	Tim Redding	.40
638	Jose Arredondo RC	1.00
639	Mike Redmond	.40
639	Mike Redmond/ Black Back	1.50
640	Joe Crede	.40
641	Omar Infante	.40
642	Nick Punto	.40
643	Jeff Mathis	.40
644	Andy Sonnanstine	.40
645	Masahide Kobayashi RC	1.00
646	Marco Scutaro	.40
647	Matt Macri (RC)	.75
648	Ian Stewart/SP (RC)	.40
649	David Dellucci	.40
649	David Dellucci/ Black Back	1.50
650	Evan Longoria RC	6.00
651	Martin Prado	.40
651	Martin Prado/Black Back	1.50
652	Glen Perkins	.40
653	Alfredo Amezaga	.40
653	Alfredo Amezaga/ Black Back	1.50
654	Brett Gardner (RC)	2.00
655	Angel Berroa	.40
655	Angel Berroa/Black Back	1.50
656	Pablo Sandoval RC	.75
657	Jody Gerut	.40
658	Arizona Diamondbacks	.40
659	Ryan Freel	.40
659	Ryan Freel/Black Back	1.50
660	Dioner Navarro	.40
661	Endy Chavez	.40
661	Endy Chavez/Black Back	1.50
662	Jorge Campillo	.40
663	Mark Ellis	.40
664	John Buck	.40
665	Texas Rangers	.40
666	Jason Michaels	.40
667	Chris Dickerson RC	.50
668	Kevin Mench	.40
669	Aaron Miles	.40
670	Joakim Soria	.40
671	Chris Davis RC	.75
672	Taylor Teagarden RC	1.50
673	Taylor Teagarden/ Black Back	2.50
673	Willy Aybar	.40
674	Paul Maholm	.40
675	Mike Gonzalez	.40
676	Seattle Mariners	.40
677	Ryan Langerhans/SP	5.00
678	Alex Romero (RC)	.75
679	Erick Aybar	.40
680	George Sherrill	.40
681	John Bowker (RC)	.75
682	Zach Miner	.40
682	Zach Miner/Black Back	1.50
683	Jorge Cantu	.40
684	Jo Jo Reyes	.40
685	Ryan Raburn	.40
686	Gavin Floyd/SP	5.00
687	Kevin Slowey/SP	5.00
688	Gio Gonzalez/SP (RC)	5.00
689	Eric Patterson/SP	5.00
690	Jonathan Sanchez/SP	5.00
691	Oliver Perez/SP	5.00
692	John Lannan/SP	5.00
693	Ramon Hernandez/SP	5.00
694	Mike Fontenot/SP	5.00
695	Ross Gload/SP	5.00
696	Mark Sweeney/SP	5.00
697	Nick Hundley/SP (RC)	5.00
698	Kevin Correia/SP	5.00
699	Jeremy Reed/SP	5.00
700	Jonathan Sanchez/ SP R	5.00
701	Miguel Montero/SP	5.00
702	Gabe Gross/SP	5.00
703	Matt Stairs/SP	5.00
704	Kenny Rogers/SP	5.00
705	Mark Hendrickson/SP	5.00
706	Heath Bell/SP	5.00
707	Wilson Betemit/SP	5.00
708	Brandon Morrow/SP	5.00
709	Brendan Ryan/SP	5.00
710	Eric Hurley/SP (RC)	5.00
711	Anaheim Angels/SP	5.00
712	John Hannahan/SP	5.00
713	Seth McClung/SP	5.00
714	New York Mets/SP	5.00
715	Chris Perez/SP RC	6.00
716	Clayton Richard/SP (RC)	5.00
717	Jaime Garcia/SP RC	5.00
718	Matt Joyce/SP RC	5.00
719	Brad Ziegler/SP RC	5.00
720	Ivan Ochoa (RC)	.75

Advertising Panels

	NM/M
Common Panel:	3.00

Autographs

NM/M

Inserted 1:247

Red Ink:		1.5X

Production 59 Sets

MB	Mike Baxes	50.00
BB	Bob Blaylock	60.00
JB	Jim Bolger	50.00
TC	Tom Carroll	50.00

dustin pedroia

PC	Phil Clark	50.00
CE	Carl Erskine	60.00
RH	Russ Heman	50.00
RJ	Randy Jackson	50.00
TK	Ted Kazanski	50.00
CK	Chick King	50.00
KL	Ken Lehman	50.00
MM	Morrie Martin	60.00
BM	Bob Martyn	50.00
LM	Les Moss	60.00
JO	Johnny O'Brien	50.00
HP	Herb Plews	50.00
JP	J.W. Porter	60.00
TQ	Tom Qualters	50.00
BR	Bill Renna	50.00
BS	Bob Smith	50.00
BSP	Bob Speake	60.00
LT	Lee Tate	50.00
VV	Vito Valentinetti	40.00
GEZ	Gus Zernial	60.00
GZ	George Zuverink	60.00
MIM	Minnie Minoso	65.00
YB	Yogi Berra	120.00
LA	Luis Aparicio	80.00
WM	Bill Mazeroski	85.00
JC	Joba Chamberlain	150.00
FS	Freddy Sanchez	40.00
AR	Aramis Ramirez	40.00
SP	Scott Podsednik	40.00

High Series:

AJ	Al Jackson	35.00
AK	Al Kaline	75.00
BM	Brian McCann	25.00
BMS	Bill Skowron	40.00
BS	Barney Schultz	40.00
CE	Chuck Essegian	40.00
CG	Curtis Granderson	35.00
CK	Clayton Kershaw	40.00
DP	Dustin Pedroia	75.00
DR	Dusty Rhodes	40.00
DS	Duke Snider	60.00
FL	Fred Lewis	25.00
FR	Frank Robinson	50.00
GS	Geovany Soto	40.00
HL	Hector Lopez	40.00
JAB	Jay Bruce	40.00
JB	Jim Brosnan	40.00
JF	Jack Fisher	30.00
JH	Jay Hook	35.00
JK	Jim Kaat	40.00
MW	Maury Wills	30.00
OC	Orlando Cepeda	40.00
PG	Pumpsie Green	40.00
RC	Roger Craig	50.00
TD	Tommy Davis	60.00

Clubhouse Collection

NM/M

Common Player:		5.00
MIM	Minnie Minoso	40.00
YB	Yogi Berra	75.00
LA	Luis Aparicio	60.00
BG	Bob Gibson	40.00
WM	Bill Mazeroski	60.00
AD	Adam Dunn	5.00
AJ	Andruw Jones	5.00
AR	Aramis Ramirez	10.00
BA	Bobby Abreu	5.00
CC	Carl Crawford	8.00
CB	Carlos Beltran	5.00
CD	Carlos Delgado	5.00
CL	Carlos Lee	5.00
CAB	Craig Biggio	8.00
DL	Derrek Lee	8.00
DO	David Ortiz	15.00
DY	Dmitri Young	5.00
EC	Eric Chavez	5.00
FT	Frank Thomas	10.00
GA	Garret Anderson	5.00
HB	Hank Blalock	5.00
IR	Ivan Rodriguez	8.00
JE	Jim Edmonds	8.00
JS	John Smoltz	8.00
JD	Johnny Damon	10.00
JP	Jorge Posada	8.00
JV	Justin Verlander	10.00
LB	Lance Berkman	8.00
MC	Miguel Cabrera	10.00
MT	Mike Mussina	8.00
MM	Mike Mussina	8.00
PM	Pedro Martinez	8.00
RS	Richie Sexson	5.00
RO	Roy Oswalt	5.00
RH	Ryan Howard	15.00
RZ	Ryan Zimmerman	8.00
SG	Shawn Green	5.00
TH	Todd Helton	8.00
TKH	Torii Hunter	8.00

TLH	Travis Hafner	8.00

Hi Series:

BG	Bob Gibson	15.00
BM	Bill Mazeroski	20.00
BR	Brooks Robinson	20.00
RR	Robin Roberts	20.00
AJ	Andruw Jones	5.00
AR	Aramis Ramirez	8.00
CB	Carlos Beltran	8.00
CL	Cliff Lee	8.00
DL	Derrek Lee	8.00
DO	David Ortiz	10.00
DY	Dmitri Young	8.00
FT	Frank Thomas	8.00
MT	Miguel Tejada	5.00
PM	Pedro Martinez	8.00
RO	Roy Oswalt	6.00
RZ	Ryan Zimmerman	8.00
AG	Alex Gordon	8.00
AP	Albert Pujols	15.00
BD	Blake DeWitt	10.00
CG	Curtis Granderson	8.00
DH	Dan Haren	5.00
EB	Erik Bedard	5.00
JB	Jeremy Bonderman	5.00
JD	Jermaine Dye	5.00
JE	Johnny Estrada	5.00
JL	Julio Lugo	5.00
NF	Nellie Fox	25.00
RS	Darrell Rasner	5.00
SP	Steve Pearce	5.00
CL	Carlos Lee	5.00

Clubhouse Collection Dual Relics

NM/M

Production 59 Sets

MB	Bill Mazeroski, Jason Bay	125.00
BL	Ernie Banks, Derrek Lee	150.00
GE	Bob Gibson, Jim Edmonds	125.00
MH	Minnie Minoso, Travis Hafner	125.00
AK	Luis Aparicio, Paul Konerko	80.00

Hi Series:

CL	Orlando Cepeda, Fred Lewis	100.00
KG	Al Kaline, Curtis Granderson	125.00
RB	Frank Robinson, Jay Bruce	150.00
SK	Duke Snider, Clayton Kershaw	250.00
SR	Bill Skowron, Darrell Rasner	125.00

Clubhouse Collection Relic Auto.

NM/M

Production 25 Sets

BG	Bob Gibson	250.00
JC	Joba Chamberlain	180.00

High Series:

DS	Duke Snider	250.00

Chrome

billy wagner

PITCHER

NM/M

Common Player:		2.00
Production 1,959 Sets		
Refractor:		2X
Production 559 Sets		
Black Refractor:		4-6X
Production 59 Sets		

#'s 101-200 listed w/Topps Chrome

#'s 201-300 found in Hi #'s

1	Hunter Pence	4.00
2	Andre Ethier	2.00
3	Curt Schilling	4.00
4	Gary Matthews Jr.	2.00
5	Dontrelle Willis	2.00
6	Troy Tulowitzki	5.00
7	Robinson Cano	4.00
8	Felix Hernandez	5.00
9	Josh Hamilton	5.00
10	Justin Upton	5.00
11	Brad Penny	2.00
12	Hideki Matsui	4.00
13	J.J. Putz	2.00
14	Jorge Posada	3.00
15	Albert Pujols	8.00
16	Aaron Rowand	2.00
17	Ronnie Belliard	2.00
18	Rick Ankiel	3.00
19	Ian Kinsler	3.00

#	Player	Price
20	Justin Verlander	4.00
21	Lyle Overbay	2.00
22	Tim Hudson	3.00
23	Ryan Zimmerman	3.00
24	Ryan Braun	4.00
25	Jimmy Rollins	5.00
26	Kelvim Escobar	2.00
27	Adam LaRoche	2.00
28	Ivan Rodriguez	3.00
29	Billy Wagner	2.00
30	Ichiro Suzuki	8.00
31	Chris Young	2.00
32	Trevor Hoffman	2.00
33	Torii Hunter	2.00
34	Jason Isringhausen	2.00
35	Jose Valverde	2.00
36	Derrek Lee	4.00
37	Rich Harden	2.00
38	Andrew Miller	2.00
39	Miguel Cabrera	4.00
40	David Wright	8.00
41	Brandon Phillips	2.00
42	Magglio Ordonez	2.00
43	Eric Byrnes	2.00
44	John Smoltz	3.00
45	Brandon Webb	2.00
46	Barry Zito	2.00
47	Sammy Sosa	3.00
48	James Shields	3.00
49	Alex Rios	2.00
50	Matt Holliday	4.00
51	Chris Young	4.00
52	Roy Oswalt	3.00
53	Matthew Kemp	3.00
54	Tim Lincecum	4.00
55	Hanley Ramirez	4.00
56	Vladimir Guerrero	3.00
57	Mark Teixeira	3.00
58	Fausto Carmona	2.00
59	B.J. Ryan	2.00
60	Manny Ramirez	4.00
61	Carlos Delgado	3.00
62	Matt Cain	2.00
63	Brian Bannister	2.00
64	Russell Martin	3.00
65	Todd Helton	3.00
66	Roy Halladay	2.00
67	Lance Berkman	3.00
68	John Lackey	2.00
69	Daisuke Matsuzaka	5.00
70	Joe Mauer	4.00
71	Francisco Rodriguez	2.00
72	Derek Jeter	10.00
73	Homer Bailey	2.00
74	Jonathan Papelbon	3.00
75	Billy Butler	2.00
76	B.J. Upton	2.00
77	Ubaldo Jimenez	2.00
78	Erik Bedard	2.00
79	Jeff Kent	2.00
80	Ken Griffey Jr.	8.00
81	Josh Beckett	3.00
82	Jeff Francis	2.00
83	Grady Sizemore	4.00
84	John Maine	2.00
85	Cole Hamels	3.00
86	Nicholas Markakis	3.00
87	Ben Sheets	2.00
88	Jose Reyes	5.00
89	Vernon Wells	2.00
90	Justin Morneau	2.00
91	Brian McCann	2.00
92	Jacoby Ellsbury	5.00
93	Clay Buchholz	3.00
94	Prince Fielder	4.00
95	David Ortiz	4.00
96	Joba Chamberlain	5.00
97	Chien-Ming Wang	6.00
98	Chipper Jones	4.00
99	Chase Utley	4.00
100	Alex Rodriguez	8.00
201	Joe Saunders	2.00
202	Cliff Lee	3.00
203	Mike Mussina	3.00
204	Ryan Dempster	3.00
205	Edinson Volquez	2.00
206	Justin Duchscherer	2.00
207	Geovany Soto	4.00
208	Brian Wilson	2.00
209	Kerry Wood	3.00
210	Kosuke Fukudome	5.00
211	Cristian Guzman	2.00
212	Ryan Ludwick	4.00
213	Joe Crede	2.00
214	Dioner Navarro	2.00
215	Miguel Tejada	3.00
216	Joakim Soria	2.00
217	George Sherrill	3.00
218	John Danks	3.00
219	Jair Jurrjens	2.00
220	Evan Longoria	10.00
221	Hiroki Kuroda	3.00
222	Greg Smith	3.00
223	Dana Eveland	2.00
224	Ryan Sweeney	2.00
225	Mike Pelfrey	3.00
226	Nick Blackburn	2.00
227	Scott Olsen	2.00
228	Manny Parra	2.00
229	Tim Redding	2.00
230	Paul Maholm	2.00
231	Todd Wellemeyer	2.00
232	Jesse Litsch	2.00
233	Andrew Sonnanstine	2.00
234	Johnny Cueto	4.00
235	Vicente Padilla	2.00
236	Glen Perkins	2.00
237	Brian Burres	2.00

#	Player	Price
238	Jamey Wright	2.00
239	Chase Headley	3.00
240	Takashi Saito	2.00
241	Skip Schumaker	2.00
242	Curtis Granderson	4.00
243	A.J. Pierzynski	2.00
244	Jorge Cantu	2.00
245	Maicer Izturis	2.00
246	Kevin Mench	2.00
247	Jason Kubel	2.00
248	Rod Barajas	2.00
249	Jed Lowrie	5.00
250	Bobby Jenks	2.00
251	Jonny Gomes	2.00
252	Clete Thomas	3.00
253	Eric Hinske	2.00
254	Brett Gardner	4.00
255	Denard Span	4.00
256	Brian Anderson	2.00
257	Troy Percival	2.00
258	Darrell Rasner	2.00
259	Willy Aybar	2.00
260	John Bowker	2.00
261	Marco Scutaro	2.00
262	Adam Kennedy	2.00
263	Nick Punto	2.00
264	Mike Napoli	2.00
265	Carlos Gonzalez	4.00
266	Matt Macri	2.00
267	Marcus Thames	2.00
268	Benjamin Zobrist	2.00
269	Mark Ellis	2.00
270	Mike Aviles	2.00
271	Angel Pagan	2.00
272	Erick Aybar	2.00
273	Todd Jones	2.00
274	Brandon Boggs	3.00
275	Mike Jacobs	2.00
276	Mike Gonzalez	2.00
277	Mike Lamb	2.00
278	Robb Quinlan	2.00
279	Salomon Torres	2.00
280	Jose Castillo	2.00
281	Damion Easley	2.00
282	Jo Jo Reyes	3.00
283	Cody Ross	2.00
284	Alexi Casilla	2.00
285	Brandon Lyon	2.00
286	Greg Dobbs	2.00
287	Joel Pineiro	2.00
288	Chris Davis	5.00
289	Masahide Kobayashi	4.00
290	Darin Erstad	2.00
291	Matt Diaz	2.00
292	Brian Schneider	2.00
293	Gerald Laird	2.00
294	Ben Francisco	2.00
295	Brian Moehler	2.00
296	Aaron Miles	2.00
297	Max Scherzer	5.00
298	C.J. Wilson	2.00
300	Jay Bruce	8.00

Dick Perez

		NM/M
Common Card:		2.00

Wal-Mart Exclusive

#	Player	Price
1	Manny Ramirez	4.00
2	Cameron Maybin	2.00
3	Ryan Howard	4.00
4	David Ortiz	4.00
5	Tim Lincecum	5.00
6	David Wright	5.00
7	Mickey Mantle	10.00
8	Joba Chamberlain	6.00
9	Ichiro Suzuki	6.00
10	Prince Fielder	4.00

Dual Autographs

Production 25 Sets
High Series:

Flashbacks

		NM/M
Complete Set (10):		10.00
Common Player:		.50

Inserted 1:12

#	Player	Price
1	Minnie Minoso	.50
2	Luis Aparicio	.50
3	Ernie Banks	1.50
4	Bill Mazeroski	.50
5	Bob Gibson	1.50
6	Frank Robinson	1.50
7	Brooks Robinson	1.50
8	Mickey Mantle	3.00
9	Orlando Cepeda	.50
10	Eddie Mathews	1.50

Flashbacks Autographs

No Pricing
Production 25 Sets

Flashbacks Relics

		NM/M
Common Player:		
MIM	Minnie Minoso	20.00
LA	Luis Aparicio	15.00
EB	Ernie Banks	25.00
WM	Bill Mazeroski	20.00
BG	Bob Gibson	20.00
FR	Frank Robinson	20.00
BR	Brooks Robinson	20.00
MM	Mickey Mantle	50.00
OC	Orlando Cepeda	20.00
EM	Eddie Mathews	20.00

Flashbacks Dual Relics

No Pricing
Production 10 Sets

Flashbacks Stadium Relics

		NM/M
Common Player:		
MM	Minnie Minoso	15.00
LA	Luis Aparicio	15.00
EB	Ernie Banks	25.00
WM	Bill Mazeroski	20.00
BG	Bob Gibson	20.00

High Series:
Hi Series prod. 59 Sets

#		Price
DE	Dwight D. Eisenhower	60.00
MO	Motown	60.00
NK	Nikita Khrushchev	100.00

New Age Performers

		NM/M
Complete Set (15):		12.00
Common Player:		.50

Inserted 1:15

#	Player	Price
1	Magglio Ordonez	1.00
2	Ichiro Suzuki	2.00
3	Matt Holliday	1.00
4	Prince Fielder	1.00
5	David Wright	2.00
6	Jake Peavy	.75
7	Alex Rodriguez	3.00
8	John Lackey	.50
9	Vladimir Guerrero	1.00
10	Ryan Howard	1.00
11	Brandon Webb	.50
12	Manny Ramirez	1.00
13	Josh Beckett	1.00
14	Jimmy Rollins	1.00
15	David Ortiz	1.00

News Flashbacks

		NM/M
Complete Set (10):		10.00
Common Card:		1.00

Inserted 1:12

#		Price
1	Alaska becomes 49th State	1.00
2	The Day the Music Died	1.00
3	Castro becomes Prime Minister of Cuba	1.00
4	Dalai Lama flees to India	1.00
5	NASA 1st 7 Astronauts	1.00
6	Nixon and Khrushchev	1.00
7	Hawaii becomes 50th State	1.00
8	USSR's Luna 2	1.00
9	In Cold Blood murders committed	1.00
10	Antarctic Treaty	1.00

Rookie Performers

		NM/M
Complete Set (15):		25.00
Common Player:		1.00

Inserted 1:12 Hi Series

#	Player	Price
1	Clayton Kershaw	3.00
2	Mike Aviles	2.00
3	Armando Galarraga	2.00
4	Joey Votto	2.00
5	Kosuke Fukudome	3.00
6	Chris Davis	3.00
7	Jeff Samardzija	3.00
8	Carlos Gonzalez	2.00
9	Max Scherzer	2.50
10	Evan Longoria	4.00
11	Johnny Cueto	2.00
12	Hiroki Kuroda	2.00
13	John Bowker	2.00
14	Justin Masterson	4.00
15	Jay Bruce	6.00

Then & Now

		NM/M
Complete Set (10):		12.00
Common Duo:		1.00

Inserted 1:15

#	Players	Price
1	Alex Rodriguez, Eddie Mathews	3.00
2	Alex Rodriguez, Ernie Banks	3.00
3	Magglio Ordonez, Orlando Cepeda	1.00
4	Jose Reyes, Luis Aparicio	1.50
5	David Ortiz, Mickey Mantle	3.00
6	Erik Bedard, Johnny Podres	1.00
7	Josh Beckett, Early Wynn	1.00
8	Ichiro Suzuki, Minnie Minoso	2.00
9	David Ortiz, Frank Robinson	1.50
10	Jake Peavy, Don Drysdale	1.00

High Series:
Inserted 1:12

#	Players	Price
1	Ernie Banks, Jimmy Rollins	2.00
2	Nellie Fox, Alex Rodriguez	3.00
3	Larry Sherry, Mike Lowell	1.00
4	Willie McCovey, Ryan Braun	3.00
5	Bob Allison, Dustin Pedroia	2.50
6	Del Crandall, Russell Martin	1.50
7	Luis Aparicio, Orlando Cabrera	1.00
8	Early Wynn, Alex Rodriguez	3.00
9	Early Wynn, Jake Peavy	1.50
10	Sam Jones, C.C. Sabathia	2.00

T205 Mini

		NM/M
Complete Set (15):		
Common Player:		1.50

Target Exclusive

#	Player	Price
1	Albert Pujols	6.00
2	Clay Buchholz	1.50
3	Matt Holliday	2.00
4	Luke Hochevar	1.50
5	Alex Rodriguez	6.00
6	Joey Votto	2.00
7	Chin-Lung Hu	1.50
8	Ryan Braun	3.00
9	Joba Chamberlain	4.00
10	Ryan Howard	4.00
11	Ichiro Suzuki	5.00
12	Steve Pearce	1.50
13	Vladimir Guerrero	2.00
14	Wladimir Balentien	1.50
15	David Ortiz	3.00

1959 Cut Signatures

Production One Set

1959 Cut Signature Relics

Production One Set
Exclusive to Hi # packs

1959 Topps Originals

See 1959 Topps pricing.

2008 Flashbacks

		NM/M
Complete Set (10):		15.00
Common Player:		1.00

Inserted 1:12 Hi Series

#	Player	Price
1	Mark Teixeira	1.50
2	Tim Lincecum	2.50
3	Jon Lester	2.00
4	Ken Griffey Jr.	3.00
5	Kosuke Fukudome	3.00
6	Albert Pujols	4.00
7	Ichiro Suzuki	3.00
8	Felix Hernandez	1.50
9	Carlos Delgado	1.00
10	Josh Hamilton	3.00

2008 Topps Moments & Milestones

		NM/M
Common Player:		.50

Production 150 Sets

		Price
Pack (6):		5.00
Box (18):		80.00
1-2	Alex Rodriguez	3.00
3	Frank Thomas	3.00
4-7	Mickey Mantle	4.00
8	Greg Maddux	2.00
9	Troy Tulowitzki	1.00
10-11	Hunter Pence	1.00
12-14	Albert Pujols	3.00

#	Player	Price
13-14	Albert Pujols	3.00
16-17	David Ortiz	1.50
18-19	David Wright	2.00
20	Aaron Hill	.50
21	Eric Byrnes	.50
22	Dmitri Young	.50
23	Garret Anderson	.50
24-25	Jimmy Rollins	1.00
26	Joba Chamberlain	5.00
27	Magglio Ordonez	1.00
28-31	Ryan Howard	2.00
32	Trevor Hoffman	.50
33	Ken Griffey Jr.	2.00
34	Travis Hafner	.50
35	Joe Mauer	.75
36-37	Daisuke Matsuzaka	1.50
38-41	Curtis Granderson	1.50
42	Alex Gordon	1.00
43	Aramis Ramirez	1.00
44	Jonathan Papelbon	1.50
45	B.J. Upton	1.00
46	C.C. Sabathia	1.00
47	Carl Crawford	.75
48	Jason Bay	.75
49	Carlos Beltran	1.00
50	Carlos Guillen	.75
51	C.C. Sabathia	1.00
52	Gary Sheffield	1.00
53	Chris Young	.75
54	Dontrelle Willis	.50
55	Dustin Pedroia	1.00
56	Alfonso Soriano	1.00
57	Derek Jeter	3.00
58-61	Chase Utley	1.50
62-63	Ichiro Suzuki	2.50
64-65	Jorge Posada	1.00
66	Jose Reyes	2.00
67-68	Miguel Tejada	.75
69	Nick Swisher	1.00
70	Robinson Cano	1.00
71	Roy Halladay	.75
72	Ryan Zimmerman	1.00
73	Scott Rolen	.75
74	Tim Lincecum	1.00
75	Vernon Wells	.75
76-82	Roger Clemens	2.00
83	Michael Young	1.00
84	John Smoltz	1.00
85	Jim Thome	1.00
86-87	Johan Santana	1.50
88-89	Jack Cust	.50
90	Jake Peavy	1.00
91-92	Hanley Ramirez	1.50
93	Hideki Okajima	1.00
94	Grady Sizemore	1.00
95	Erik Bedard	1.00
96-97	Derek Lee	1.00
98-99	Delmon Young	1.00
100	Cole Hamels	1.00
101	Brad Hawpe	.50
102	Mike Lowell	1.00
103	Placido Polanco	.50
104	Nick Swisher	.50
105-106	Adrian Gonzalez	.75
107	Scott Kazmir	.50
108	Freddy Sanchez	.50
109	Jeremy Guthrie	.50
110	Chipper Jones	1.50
111	Chris Carpenter	.75
112	Andy Pettitte	1.00
113	Andruw Jones	.75
114	Bobby Abreu	.75
115-116	Eric Chavez	.50
117	Josh Hamilton	2.00
118-119	Manny Ramirez	1.00
120	Mariano Rivera	1.00
121	Kelly Johnson	.50
122	Jeff Kent	.75
123	Mark Teixeira	1.00
124-125	Matt Holliday	1.00
126	Huston Street	.50
127	Carlos Lee	.75
128	Brian Bannister	.50
129	Carlos Pena	1.00
130	Brian McCann	1.00
131	Prince Fielder	1.50
132	Randy Johnson	1.50
133	Russell Martin	1.00
134	Ryan Braun	1.50
135-136	Vladimir Guerrero	1.50
137	Tom Glavine	1.00
138-140	Miguel Cabrera	1.00
141-142	Pedro Martinez	1.00
143	Yovani Gallardo	.75
144	Brian Roberts	.50
150-153	Clay Buchholz (RC)	2.00
154-156	Billy Buckner	1.00
157-159	Jeff Clement	1.00
160-162	Radhames Liz	.50
163-165	Bronson Sardinha	.50
166-168	Seth Smith	.50
169-171	Chris Seddon	.50
172-174	Wladimir Balentien	1.00
175-177	Josh Banks	.50
178-180	Ross Detwiler	.50
181-183	Felipe Paulino	.50
184-186	Troy Patton	.50
187-189	Brandon Jones	1.00

Black

Black: 2-4X
Production 25 Sets

Blue

Blue: 3-5X
Production 10 Sets

Red

No Pricing
Production One Set

Printing Plates

No Pricing
Production one set per color.

Autographs

	NM/M
Common Auto.:	5.00
Black:	1-1.5X
Production 25 Sets	
Blue:	No Pricing
Production 10 Sets	
Red:	No Pricing
Production One Set	

#	Player	Price
CB	Clay Buchholz	30.00
JK	Joe Koshansky	8.00
NM	Nyjer Morgan	8.00
CH	Chin-Lung Hu	20.00
RT	Rich Thompson	8.00
SF	Sam Fuld	10.00
DB	Daric Barton	8.00
JA	Josh Anderson	8.00
JM	Jonathan Meloan	8.00
JT	J.R. Towles	15.00
SP	Steve Pearce	10.00
RO	Ross Ohlendorf	15.00
JR	Justin Ruggiano	8.00
LB	Lance Broadway	8.00
WB	Wladimir Balentien	8.00
AG	Armando Galarraga	20.00
FP	Felipe Paulino	8.00
JM	Jose Morales	8.00
RJ	Rob Johnson	8.00
BJ	Brandon Jones	10.00
BP	Brandon Phillips	20.00
MC	Melky Cabrera	8.00
MCA	Matt Cain	15.00
CR	Carlos Ruiz	8.00
BR	B.J. Ryan	10.00
TG	Tom Gorzelanny	8.00
AL	Adam Lind	8.00
RB	Ryan Braun	30.00
TJ	Todd Jones	8.00
BC	Bobby Crosby	8.00
FC	Fausto Carmona	15.00
FS	Freddy Sanchez	15.00
CP	Carlos Pena	15.00
JD	Jermaine Dye	8.00
CM	Cameron Maybin	15.00
JC	Jack Cust	10.00
RM	Russell Martin	15.00
AC	Asdrubal Cabrera	10.00
LM	Lastings Milledge	10.00
BH	Brad Hawpe	15.00
RC	Robinson Cano	20.00
RH	Rich Harden	8.00
CC	Carl Crawford	15.00
TH	Tim Hudson	15.00
DW	David Wright	50.00
AS	Alfonso Soriano	20.00
HR	Hanley Ramirez	20.00
JR	Jose Reyes	30.00
MH	Matt Holliday	20.00
JP	Jorge Posada	40.00
MIC	Miguel Cabrera	25.00
JH	Josh Hamilton	15.00

2008 Topps Opening Day

		NM/M
Complete Set (220):		30.00
Common Player:		.15
Pack (6):		1.00
Box (36):		30.00
1	Alex Rodriguez	1.50
2	Barry Zito	.25
3	Jeff Suppan	.15
4	Placido Polanco	.25
5	Scott Kazmir	.25
6	Ivan Rodriguez	.40
7	Mickey Mantle	2.00
8	Stephen Drew	.25
9	Ken Griffey Jr.	1.00
10	Miguel Cabrera	.50
11	Yorvit Torrealba	.15
12	Daisuke Matsuzaka	.75
13	Kyle Kendrick	.15
14	Jimmy Rollins	.50
15	Joe Mauer	.25
16	Cole Hamels	.25
17	Yovani Gallardo	.25
18	Miguel Tejada	.25
19	Corey Hart	.25
20	Nicholas Markakis	.25
21	Zack Greinke	.25

#	Player	Price
2	Orlando Cabrera	.25
3	Jake Peavy	.25
4	Erik Bedard	.25
5	Trevor Hoffman	.15
6	Derrek Lee	.40
7	Hank Blalock	.25
8	Victor Martinez	.25
9	Chris Young	.25
0	Jose Reyes	.50
1	Mike Lowell	.25
2	Curtis Granderson	.25
3	Dan Uggla	.25
4	Mike Piazza	.50
5	Garrett Atkins	.25
6	Felix Hernandez	.40
7	Alex Rios	.25
8	Mark Reynolds	.15
9	Jason Bay	.25
0	Josh Beckett	.40
1	Jack Cust	.15
2	Vladimir Guerrero	.50
3	Marcus Giles	.15
4	Kenny Lofton	.15
5	John Lackey	.15
6	Ryan Howard	1.00
7	Kevin Youkilis	.25
8	Gary Sheffield	.25
9	Justin Morneau	.25
0	Albert Pujols	1.00
1	Ubaldo Jimenez	.15
2	Johan Santana	.50
3	Chuck James	.15
4	Jeremy Hermida	.15
5	Andruw Jones	.25
6	Jason Varitek	.25
7	Tim Hudson	.25
8	Justin Upton	.50
9	Brad Penny	.25
0	Robinson Cano	.40
1	Johnny Estrada	.15
2	Brandon Webb	.25
3	Chris Duncan	.15
4	Aaron Hill	.15
5	Alfonso Soriano	.50
6	Carlos Zambrano	.25
7	Ben Sheets	.25
8	Andy LaRoche	.15
9	Tim Lincecum	.25
0	Phil Hughes	.25
1	Magglio Ordonez	.25
2	Scott Rolen	.25
3	John Maine	.15
4	Delmon Young	.25
5	Chase Utley	.50
6	Jose Valverde	.15
7	Tadahito Iguchi	.15
8	Checklist	
9	Russell Martin	.25
0	B.J. Upton	.25
1	Orlando Hudson	.15
2	Jim Edmonds	.15
3	J.J. Hardy	.15
4	Todd Helton	.40
5	Melky Cabrera	.15
6	Adrian Beltre	.25
7	Manny Ramirez	.25
8	Rafael Furcal	.25
9	Gil Meche	.15
0	Grady Sizemore	.50
1	Jeff Kent	.25
2	David DeJesus	.15
3	Lyle Overbay	.15
4	Moises Alou	.15
5	Frank Thomas	.50
6	Ryan Garko	.15
7	Kevin Kouzmanoff	.15
8	Roy Oswalt	.25
9	Mark Buehrle	.15
0	David Ortiz	.50
1	Hunter Pence	.25
2	David Wright	.75
3	Dustin Pedroia	.25
4	Roy Halladay	.25
5	Derek Jeter	1.50
6	Casey Blake	.15
7	Rich Harden	.15
8	Shane Victorino	.15
9	Richie Sexson	.25
0	Jim Thome	.40
1	Akinori Iwamura	.15
2	Danny Haren	.15
3	Jose Contreras	.15
4	Jonathan Papelbon	.25
5	Prince Fielder	.50
6	Dan Johnson	.15
7	Dmitri Young	.15
8	Brandon Phillips	.25
9	Brett Myers	.15
0	James Loney	.25
1	C.C. Sabathia	.25
2	Jermaine Dye	.15
3	Aubrey Huff	.15
4	Carlos Ruiz	.15
5	Hanley Ramirez	.50
6	Edgar Renteria	.15
7	Mark Loretta	.15
8	Brian McCann	.25
9	Paul Konerko	.25
0	Jorge Posada	.25
1	Chien-Ming Wang	.25
2	Jose Vidro	.15
3	Carlos Delgado	.25
4	Kelvim Escobar	.15
5	Pedro Martinez	.40
6	Jeremy Guthrie	.15
7	Ramon Hernandez	.15
8	Ian Kinsler	.25
9	Ichiro Suzuki	1.00

#	Player	Price
140	Garret Anderson	.15
141	Tom Gorzelanny	.15
142	Bobby Crosby	.15
143	Jeff Francoeur	.25
144	Josh Hamilton	.25
145	Mark Teixeira	.50
146	Fausto Carmona	.25
147	Alex Gordon	.40
148	Nick Swisher	.25
149	Justin Verlander	.50
150	Pat Burrell	.25
151	Chris Carpenter	.25
152	Matt Holliday	.50
153	Adam Dunn	.40
154	Curt Schilling	.25
155	Kelly Johnson	.15
156	Aaron Rowand	.25
157	Brian Roberts	.25
158	Bobby Abreu	.25
159	Carlos Beltran	.40
160	Lance Berkman	.25
161	Gary Matthews	.15
162	Jeff Francis	.15
163	Vernon Wells	.25
164	Dontrelle Willis	.15
165	Travis Hafner	.25
166	Brian Bannister	.15
167	Carlos Pena	.25
168	Raul Ibanez	.25
169	Aramis Ramirez	.25
170	Eric Byrnes	.25
171	Greg Maddux	1.00
172	John Smoltz	.25
173	Jarrod Saltalamacchia	.25
174	Hideki Okajima	.25
175	Javier Vazquez	.15
176	Aaron Harang	.25
177	Jhonny Peralta	.25
178	Carlos Lee	.25
179	Ryan Braun	1.00
180	Torii Hunter	.25
181	Hideki Matsui	1.00
182	Eric Chavez	.15
183	Freddy Sanchez	.15
184	Adrian Gonzalez	.25
185	Bengie Molina	.15
186	Kenji Johjima	.15
187	Carl Crawford	.25
188	Chipper Jones	.50
189	Chris Young	.25
190	Michael Young	.25
191	Troy Glaus	.25
192	Ryan Zimmerman	.50
193	Brian Giles	.15
194	Troy Tulowitzki	.25
195	Chin-Lung Hu (RC)	.50
196	Seth Smith (RC)	.25
197	Wladimir Balentien (RC)	.25
198	Rich Thompson (RC)	.25
199	Radhames Liz RC	.25
200	Ross Detwiler (RC)	.25
201	Sam Fuld RC	.25
202	Clint Sammons (RC)	.25
203	Ross Ohlendorf RC	.25
204	Jonathan Albaladejo RC	.25
205	Brandon Jones (RC)	.25
206	Steve Pearce RC	.75
207	Kevin Hart (RC)	.25
208	Luke Hochevar RC	.75
209	Troy Patton (RC)	.25
210	Josh Anderson (RC)	.25
211	Clay Buchholz (RC)	.50
212	Joe Koshansky (RC)	.25
213	Bronson Sardinha (RC)	.25
214	Emilio Bonifacio RC	.25
215	Daric Barton (RC)	.25
216	Lance Broadway RC	.25
217	Jeff Clement (RC)	.25
218	Joey Votto (RC)	.75
219	J.R. Towles RC	.50
220	Nyjer Morgan (RC)	.25

Gold

Gold: 2-3X

Autographs

NM/M

	Common Auto.:	
JB	Jeff Baker	15.00
KG	Kevin Gregg	15.00
AL	Anthony Lerew	15.00
NS	Nate Schierholtz	20.00
JCB	Jason Botts	15.00

Tattoos

NM/M

	Common Tattoo:	.25
PP	Phillie Phanatic	.25
WM	Wally the Green Monster	.25
MM	Mr. Met	.25
TM	The Moose	.25
LS	Lou Seal	.25
ST	Stomper	.25
BM	Billy the Marlin	.25
SL	Slider	.25
SF	Swinging Friar	.25
JJ	Junction Jack	.25
PIP	Pirate Parrot	.25
BB	Bernie Brewer	.25
FB	Fredbird	.25
TB	TC Bear	.25
PW	Paws	.25
NYY	New York Yankees	.25
NYM	N.Y. Mets	.25
BRS	Boston Red Sox	.25
SFG	San Francisco Giants	.25
CC	Chicago Cubs	.25
CL	Cleveland Indians	.25
CWS	Chicago White Sox	.25
LAA	L.A. Angels	.25
CR	Cincinnati Reds	.25
FM	Florida Marlins	.25
TBJ	Toronto Blue Jays	.25
AB	Atlanta Braves	.25
AD	Arizona Diamondbacks	.25
TDR	Tampa Bay Rays	.25
TR	Texas Rangers	.25

Flapper Cards

NM/M

	Common Player:	.50
AR	Alex Rodriguez	1.00
RH	Ryan Howard	.75
DW	David Wright	.75
DO	David Ortiz	.75
PF	Prince Fielder	.75
AP	Albert Pujols	1.00
IS	Ichiro Suzuki	.75
VG	Vladimir Guerrero	.50
DJ	Derek Jeter	1.00
JR	Jose Reyes	.75
KG	Ken Griffey Jr.	.75
GM	Greg Maddux	.75
MM	Mickey Mantle	1.00
MR	Manny Ramirez	.75
JB	Josh Beckett	.50
CJ	Chipper Jones	.50
RC	Roger Clemens	.75
DM	Daisuke Matsuzaka	.75

Puzzle

NM/M

Common Puzzle Card:	.50
Matt Holliday	.50
Vladimir Guerrero	.50
Jose Reyes	.50
Josh Beckett	.50
Albert Pujols	.50
Alex Rodriguez	.50
Jake Peavy	.50
David Ortiz	.50
Ryan Howard	.50
Ichiro	.50
Hanley Ramirez	.50
Grady Sizemore	.50
David Wright	.50
Alex Rios	.50

2008 Topps Triple Threads

NM/M

Common (1-145, 221-251): 1.00
Production 1,350
Common Jsy Auto. RC
(146-170): 10.00
Production 99
Team Initial Die-Cut Variation: 1X
Box (2): 160.00

#	Player	Price
1	David Wright	3.00
2	Nolan Ryan	5.00
3	Johnny Damon	1.50
4	Joe Mauer	1.50
5	Francisco Rodriguez	1.00
6	Carlos Beltran	1.00
7	Mickey Mantle	8.00
8	Brian Roberts	1.00
9	Lou Gehrig	5.00
10	Babe Ruth	6.00
11	Ryne Sandberg	3.00
12	Bob Gibson	2.00
13	Matt Kemp	1.50
14	Jered Weaver	1.50
15	Johnny Bench	2.00
16	Magglio Ordonez	1.00
17	Carl Yastrzemski	2.50
18	Derek Jeter	5.00
19	Gil Meche	1.00
20	Hanley Ramirez	2.00
21	Edgar Martinez	1.00
22	Steve Carlton	1.00
23	C.C. Sabathia	2.00
24	Chase Utley	2.00
25	Francisco Cordero	1.00
26	Mark Ellis	1.00
27	Jeff Kent	1.00
28	Brian Fuentes	1.00
29	Johan Santana	2.00
30	Ichiro Suzuki	3.00
31	Ken Griffey Jr.	4.00
32	Steve Garvey	1.00
33	Rafael Furcal	1.00
34	Chipper Jones	3.00
35	Roberto Clemente	5.00
36	Rich Harden	1.00
37	Cy Young	2.00
38	Albert Pujols	5.00
39	Dontrelle Willis	1.00
40	Mark Teixeira	1.50
41	Daisuke Matsuzaka	3.00
42	Harmon Killebrew	2.50
43	Darryl Strawberry	1.00
44	Eric Chavez	1.00
45	Don Larsen	1.50
46	Huston Street	1.00
47	Albert Belle	1.00
48	Prince Fielder	2.00
49	Garret Anderson	1.00
50	Matt Holliday	1.50
51	Travis Buck	1.00
52	Ben Sheets	1.00
53	George Brett	3.00
54	Dmitri Young	1.00
55	Phil Rizzuto	2.00
56	Jimmy Rollins	2.00
57	Manny Ramirez	3.00
58	Ozzie Smith	3.00
59	Dale Murphy	1.50
60	Bobby Crosby	1.00
61	Trevor Hoffman	1.00
62	Chien-Ming Wang	2.50
63	Jose Reyes	2.00
64	Vladimir Guerrero	2.00
65	Vida Blue	1.00
66	Rod Carew	1.50
67	Aaron Rowand	1.00
68	Hong-Chih Kuo	1.00
69	Mike Schmidt	3.00
70	Rogers Hornsby	1.50
71	Alex Rodriguez	5.00
72	Roger Maris	2.50
73	Travis Hafner	1.00
74	Tom Glavine	1.50
75	Pat Burrell	1.50
76	Pedro Martinez	2.00
77	Joba Chamberlain	3.00
78	Jason Varitek	1.50
79	Hideo Nomo	1.00
80	Frank Thomas	2.00
81	Rollie Fingers	1.00
82	Carl Crawford	1.50
83	Bobby Jenks	1.00
84	Victor Martinez	1.00
85	Ernie Banks	2.50
86	Josh Beckett	1.50
87	Jose Valverde	1.00
88	Reggie Jackson	1.50
89	Duke Snider	1.50
90	Mike Lowell	1.00
91	Dom DiMaggio	1.00
92	Torii Hunter	1.00
93	Alfonso Soriano	2.00
94	Justin Morneau	1.50
95	Carlos Delgado	1.00
96	Ty Cobb	4.00
97	Andruw Jones	1.00
98	Yogi Berra	2.00
99	Joe DiMaggio	4.00
100	Willie Randolph	1.00
101	Miguel Cabrera	2.00
102	Grady Sizemore	1.50
103	Michael Young	1.50
104	Wade Boggs	1.50
105	Rich "Goose" Gossage	1.00
106	Robin Roberts	1.00
107	Brooks Robinson	1.50
108	Jim Palmer	1.50
109	Jorge Posada	1.50
110	Keith Hernandez	1.00
111	Ivan Rodriguez	1.50
112	Carlos Lee	1.50
113	John Lackey	1.50
114	Alex Rios	1.50
115	Carlton Fisk	1.50
116	Gary Matthews	1.50
117	Bill Martin	1.00
118	Paul Molitor	2.00
119	Hideki Matsui	2.00
120	Al Kaline	2.00
121	Takashi Saito	1.00
122	Stan Musial	3.00
123	Ryan Howard	3.00
124	Whitey Ford	2.00
125	John Smoltz	1.50
126	Roy Oswalt	1.00
127	Jim Thome	1.50
128	Tony Gwynn	2.50
129	Dennis Eckersley	1.00
130	Ted Williams	5.00
131	Justin Verlander	1.50
132	David Ortiz	3.00
133	Tom Gordon	1.00
134	Tom Seaver	1.50
135	Red Schoendienst	1.00
136	Johnny Podres	1.00
137	Paul Konerko	1.50
138	Robin Yount	2.50
139	Todd Helton	1.50
140	Frank Robinson	2.00
141	J.J. Putz	1.00
142	Jackie Robinson	3.00
143	Brandon Webb	1.50
144	Eddie Murray	2.00
145	Freddy Sanchez	1.00
146	Josh Anderson (RC)	10.00
147	Daric Barton (RC)	10.00
148	Steve Pearce RC	15.00
149	Chin-Lung Hu (RC)	15.00
150	Clay Buchholz (RC)	25.00
151	J.R. Towles RC	15.00
152	Brandon Jones RC	10.00
153	Lance Broadway RC	10.00
154	Nyjer Morgan (RC)	10.00
155	Ross Ohlendorf RC	10.00
156	Chris Seddon (RC)	10.00
157	Jonathan Albaladejo RC	10.00
158	Seth Smith (RC)	10.00
159	Kevin Hart (RC)	15.00
160	Wladimir Balentien (RC)	15.00
161	Justin Ruggiano (RC)	10.00
162	Clint Sammons (RC)	15.00
163	Rich Thompson (RC)	15.00
164	David Davidson RC	10.00
165	Troy Patton (RC)	10.00
166	Joe Koshansky (RC)	15.00
167	Colt Morton RC	15.00
168	Armando Galarraga RC	25.00
169	Sam Fuld RC	15.00
170	Dustin Moseley	15.00
171	Tim Lincecum	75.00
172	Ryan Braun	60.00
173	Phil Hughes	40.00
174	Joba Chamberlain	25.00
175	Hunter Pence	20.00
176	Fausto Carmona	15.00
177	Ubaldo Jimenez	15.00
178	Cameron Maybin	20.00
179	Adam Jones	20.00
180	Brian Bannister	15.00
181	Jarrod Saltalamacchia	15.00
182	Alex Gordon	15.00
183	Russell Martin	15.00
184	John Maine	10.00
185	Hideki Okajima	15.00
186	Curtis Granderson	30.00
187	Delmon Young	15.00
188	Jo Jo Reyes	10.00
189	Yovani Gallardo	20.00
190	Ryan Zimmerman	20.00
191	Jeremy Guthrie	15.00
192	Dan Uggla	15.00
193	Andre Ethier	20.00
194	Chris Young	15.00
195	Elijah Dukes	15.00
196	Nick Markakis	25.00
197	Melky Cabrera	15.00
198	Cole Hamels	30.00
199	James Loney	15.00
200	Kevin Slowey	15.00
201	Carlos Marmol	15.00
202	Akinori Iwamura	15.00
203	Adrian Gonzalez	25.00
204	Brandon Phillips	20.00
205	J.J. Hardy	20.00
206	Tom Gorzelanny	10.00
207	Matt Cain	20.00
208	Matt Capps	10.00
209	Jeff Francis	15.00
210	Brian McCann	20.00
211	Matt Garza	15.00
212	Robinson Cano	30.00
213	Felix Hernandez	30.00
214	Yunel Escobar	15.00
215	Francisco Liriano	20.00
216	Rich Hill	10.00
217	Taylor Buchholz	10.00
218	Asdrubal Cabrera	15.00
219	Lastings Milledge	15.00
220	Honus Wagner	2.50
221	Walter Johnson	2.50
222	Thurman Munson	2.50
223	Roy Campanella	2.50
224	George Sisler	1.50
225	Pee Wee Reese	1.50
226	Johnny Mize	1.50
227	Jimmie Foxx	2.50
228	Tris Speaker	1.50
229	Christy Mathewson	1.50
230	Mel Ott	2.00
231	Ralph Kiner	1.00
232	Joey Votto (RC)	3.00
233	Hiroki Kuroda RC	1.50
234	John Bowker (RC)	1.50
235	Lance Berkman	1.50
236	Aaron Harang	1.50
237	B.J. Upton	1.50
238	Zack Greinke	1.00
239	Cal Ripken Jr.	6.00
240	Justin Upton	1.50
241	Roy Halladay	1.50
242	Orlando Hudson	1.50
243	Scott Kazmir	1.50
244	Matt Kemp	1.50
245	Mark Buehrle	1.50
246	Adam Dunn	1.50
247	Erik Bedard	1.50
248	Carlos Zambrano	1.50
249	Jeff Francoeur	1.50
250	Brad Penny	1.00
251	Brad Penny	1.00

Emerald

Emerald (1-145, 221-251): 1-1.5X
Production 240
Emerald Auto. (146-220): 1X
Auto. Production 50

Gold

Gold (1-145, 221-251): 2-3X
Production 99
Gold Auto. (146-220): 1-1.5X
Auto. Production 25

Sapphire

Sapphire: (1-145, 221-251): 4-8X
Production 25
Sapphire Auto. (146-220): No Pricing
Auto. Production 10

Sepia

Sepia (1-145, 221-251): .75-1X
Production 525
Sepia Auto. (146-220): 1X
Auto. Production 75

Printing Plates

Production one set per color.

Auto. RC Relic Pairs

NM/M

Common Duo: 20.00
Gold: 1-1.25X
Production 25 Sets
Sapphire: No Pricing
Production 10 Sets
Platinum: No Pricing
Production One Set

#	Players	Price
1	Steve Pearce, Nyjer Morgan	30.00
2	Cameron Maybin, Curtis Granderson	40.00
3	Melky Cabrera, Robinson Cano	40.00
4	Lastings Milledge, Elijah Dukes	20.00
5	Rich Hill, Sam Fuld	25.00
6	J.R. Towles, Jarrod Saltalamacchia	20.00
7	Clay Buchholz, Fausto Carmona	30.00
8	Ryan Braun, Ryan Zimmerman	50.00
9	Phil Hughes, Joba Chamberlain	80.00
10	Brandon Phillips, Homer Bailey	25.00

Auto. Relic Pairs

NM/M

Production 18 Sets
Gold: No Pricing
Production 9 Sets
Sapphire: No Pricing
Production 3 Sets
Platinum: No Pricing
Production One Set

#	Players	Price
1	Ryan Howard, David Wright	100.00
2	Manny Ramirez, David Ortiz	100.00
3	Frank Thomas, Jim Thome	80.00
4	Eddie Murray, Mike Schmidt	80.00
5	Paul Molitor, Prince Fielder	80.00
6	Jimmy Rollins, Ryan Howard	100.00
7	C.C. Sabathia, Johan Santana	80.00
8	Travis Hafner, Fausto Carmona	40.00
9	Robin Yount, Ozzie Smith	100.00
10	Whitey Ford, Yogi Berra	150.00

Auto. Relic Double Combos

Production 3 Sets

Presidential Cut Above

Production One Set

"Cut Above" Relics

Production One Set

Auto. Relics

NM/M

Production 18 Sets
Gold: No Pricing
Production 9 Sets
Sapphire: No Pricing
Production 3 Sets
Platinum: No Pricing
Production One Set

#	Player	Price
1-3	Prince Fielder	60.00
4-6	Vladimir Guerrero	75.00
7-9	Bob Gibson	50.00
10-12	Chien-Ming Wang	180.00
13-15	Johnny Podres	50.00
16-18	Frank Robinson	50.00
19-21	Robin Yount	60.00
22-24	David Ortiz	75.00
25-27	Chipper Jones	80.00
28-30	Cal Ripken Jr.	200.00
31-33	Carlton Fisk	50.00
34-36	Jason Varitek	50.00
37-39	Ernie Banks	80.00
40-42	Harmon Killebrew	75.00
43-45	Travis Hafner	40.00
46-48	Manny Ramirez	75.00
49-51	Tony Gwynn	75.00

#	Player	Price
52-54	Alfonso Soriano	50.00
55-57	Carl Yastrzemski	100.00
58-60	Jim Palmer	50.00
61-63	Jimmy Rollins	60.00
64-66	Frank Thomas	75.00
67-69	Brooks Robinson	75.00
70-72	Dom DiMaggio	50.00
73-75	George Kell	40.00
76-78	Wade Boggs	60.00
79-81	Johan Santana	60.00
82-84	Jose Reyes	80.00
85-87	Hanley Ramirez	50.00
88-90	Johnny Bench	75.00
91-93	Mike Lowell	50.00
94-96	Tom Seaver	60.00
97-99	John Smoltz	70.00
100-102	Ozzie Smith	75.00
103-105	Duke Snider	60.00
106-108	Steve Carlton	40.00
109-111	Jorge Posada	50.00
112-114	Andruw Jones	30.00
115-117	Reggie Jackson	75.00
118-120	C.C. Sabathia	50.00
121-123	Jim Thome	50.00
124-126	Mike Schmidt	75.00
127-129	Yogi Berra	100.00
130-132	Dontrelle Willis	35.00
133-135	Nolan Ryan	120.00
136-138	Rich "Goose" Gossage	40.00
139-141	Al Kaline	75.00
142-144	David Wright	100.00
145-147	Miguel Cabrera	50.00
148-150	Ryne Sandberg	100.00
151-153	Tom Glavine	70.00
154-156	Paul Molitor	50.00
157-159	Eddie Murray	60.00
160-162	Justin Verlander	40.00
163-165	Dale Murphy	60.00
166-168	Whitey Ford	75.00
169-171	Matt Holliday	40.00
172-174	Albert Pujols	250.00
175-177	Stan Musial	100.00
178-180	Ryan Howard	80.00
181-183	Johnny Cueto	30.00
184-186	Evan Longoria	180.00

Auto. Relic Combos

NM/M
Production 36 Sets
Emerald: No Pricing
Production 18 Sets
Gold: No Pricing
Production 9 Sets
Sepia: 1X
Production 27 Sets
Sapphire: No Pricing
Production 3 Sets
Platinum: No Pricing
Production One Set

#	Players	Price
1	Jose Reyes, Ozzie Smith, Hanley Ramirez	80.00
2	Albert Pujols, Manny Ramirez, Vladimir Guerrero	200.00
3	Keith Hernandez, Mike Schmidt, Dale Murphy	100.00
4	Frank Robinson, Carl Yastrzemski, Harmon Killebrew	180.00
5	Bob Gibson, Tom Seaver, Steve Carlton	90.00
6	Harmon Killebrew, Rod Carew, Brooks Robinson	150.00
7	David Wright, Ryan Howard, Albert Pujols	200.00
8	Prince Fielder, Eddie Murray, Ryan Howard	100.00
9	Nolan Ryan, George Brett, Robin Yount	180.00
10	Johnny Bench, Ivan Rodriguez, Carlton Fisk	80.00
11	Yogi Berra, Whitey Ford, Jorge Posada	150.00
12	Tony Gwynn, Dale Murphy, Darryl Strawberry	90.00
13	Mike Lowell, Manny Ramirez, David Ortiz	120.00
14	Joba Chamberlain, Jorge Posada, Chien-Ming Wang	160.00
15	Jeff Francis, Taylor Buchholz, Ubaldo Jimenez	25.00
16	Melky Cabrera, Ross Ohlendorf, Robinson Cano	40.00
17	Dan Uggla, Chris Seddon, Hanley Ramirez	
18	Alex Gordon, Evan Longoria, Ryan Zimmerman	60.00
19	Chris Young, Lastings Milledge, Melky Cabrera	25.00
20	Rich Hill, Johnny Cueto, Tom Gorzelanny	25.00
21	Dustin Moseley, Francisco Liriano, Felix Hernandez	35.00
22	Hanley Ramirez, James Loney, J.J. Hardy	40.00
23	Armando Galarraga, Fausto Carmona, Troy Patton	30.00

XXIV Relics

No Pricing
Production 18 Sets
Gold: No Pricing
Production 9 Sets
Sapphire: No Pricing
Production 3 Sets
Platinum: No Pricing
Production One Set

Jumbo Plus Relics

Production 3 Sets
Platinum: No Pricing
Production One Set

Letter Plus Relics

Production 3 Sets
Platinum: No Pricing
Production One Set

All-Star Patches

Production 9 Sets

All-Star Logo Man

1 of 1

Bat Barrels

Production One Set

Relics

NM/M
Production 36 Sets
Emerald: 1-1.2X
Production 18 Sets
Gold: No Pricing
Production 9 Sets
Sapphire: No Pricing
Production 3 Sets
Sepia: 1X
Production 27 Sets
Platinum: No Pricing
Production One Set

#	Player	Price
1-3	David Wright	30.00
4-6	Alex Rodriguez	40.00
7-9	Mickey Mantle	140.00
10-12	Duke Snider	25.00
13-15	Carlton Fisk	25.00
16-18	Ichiro Suzuki	50.00
19-21	Wade Boggs	25.00
22-24	Chien-Ming Wang	30.00
25-27	Alfonso Soriano	20.00
28-30	Ernie Banks	20.00
31-33	Jimmy Rollins	20.00
34-36	Bob Gibson	30.00
37-39	Brooks Robinson	30.00
40-42	Joe DiMaggio	80.00
43-45	Hideo Nomo	40.00
46-48	Ted Williams	75.00
49-51	David Ortiz	25.00
52-54	Frank Robinson	20.00
55-57	Tony Gwynn	25.00
58-60	Jose Reyes	25.00
61-63	Roger Maris	75.00
64-66	Mike Schmidt	30.00
67-69	Eddie Murray	20.00
70-72	Johnny Bench	20.00
73-75	Roberto Clemente	80.00
76-78	Steve Carlton	15.00
79-81	Grady Sizemore	25.00
82-84	Robin Yount	25.00
85-87	Hanley Ramirez	20.00
88-90	Al Kaline	25.00
91-93	Vladimir Guerrero	25.00
94-96	George Kell	25.00
97-99	Reggie Jackson	25.00
100-102	Tom Seaver	25.00
103-105	Johan Santana	20.00
106-108	Jason Varitek	20.00
109-111	Ryan Howard	25.00
112-114	Manny Ramirez	20.00
115-117	Miguel Cabrera	20.00
118-120	Jorge Posada	20.00
121-123	Nolan Ryan	40.00
124-126	Paul Molitor	15.00
127-129	Chipper Jones	20.00
130-132	Carl Yastrzemski	30.00
133-135	Whitey Ford	30.00
136-138	Yogi Berra	50.00
139-141	Albert Pujols	40.00
142-144	Jim Palmer	15.00
145-147	Harmon Killebrew	40.00
148-150	Ozzie Smith	25.00
151-153	Stan Musial	35.00
154-156	Ryne Sandberg	30.00
157-159	Matt Holliday	20.00
160-162	Carlos Beltran	15.00
163-165	Prince Fielder	20.00
166-168	Ivan Rodriguez	15.00
169-171	Victor Martinez	15.00
172-174	Justin Verlander	20.00
175-177	Reggie Jackson	25.00
178-180	Alfonso Soriano	15.00
181-183	Prince Fielder	20.00
184-186	Ichiro Suzuki	50.00
187-189	David Wright	30.00
190-192	Eddie Murray	20.00
193-195	Manny Ramirez	20.00
196-198	Mike Schmidt	30.00
199-201	Johnny Bench	25.00
202-204	Matt Holliday	20.00
205-207	Alex Rodriguez	40.00
208-210	Jose Reyes	25.00
211-213	Jimmy Rollins	20.00
214-216	David Ortiz	25.00
217-219	Robin Yount	25.00
220-222	Nolan Ryan	40.00
223-225	Ryan Howard	25.00
226	John F. Kennedy	200.00
227	Ty Cobb	150.00
228	Jimmie Foxx	75.00
229	Rogers Hornsby	75.00
230	George Sisler	75.00
231	Mel Ott	80.00
232	Jackie Robinson	120.00
233	Tris Speaker	80.00
234	Honus Wagner	250.00
235	Lou Gehrig	125.00
236	Pee Wee Reese	30.00
237	Roy Campanella	60.00
238	Johnny Mize	30.00
239	Thurman Munson	60.00
240	Babe Ruth	350.00

Relics Combos

NM/M
Production 36 Sets
Emerald: 1-1.25X
Production 18 Sets
Gold: No Pricing
Production 9 Sets
Sepia: 1-1.2X
Production 27 Sets
Sapphire: No Pricing
Production 3 Sets
Platinum: No Pricing
Production One Set

#	Players	Price
1	Alex Rodriguez, David Wright, Ryan Howard	50.00
2	Mickey Mantle, Ted Williams, Joe DiMaggio	180.00
3	Ted Williams, Carl Yastrzemski, Manny Ramirez	50.00
4	Magglio Ordonez, Ichiro Suzuki, Placido Polanco	35.00
5	Alex Rodriguez, Prince Fielder, Ryan Howard	40.00
6	Alex Rodriguez, Matt Holliday, Magglio Ordonez	30.00
7	Jose Reyes, Juan Pierre, Hanley Ramirez	30.00
8	Chien-Ming Wang, Alex Rodriguez, Mariano Rivera	40.00
9	Jake Peavy, Scott Kazmir, Johan Santana	25.00
10	Joe DiMaggio, Roberto Clemente, Mickey Mantle	180.00
11	Mark Buehrle, Justin Verlander, Clay Buchholz	20.00
12	Magglio Ordonez, Al Kaline, Curtis Granderson	35.00
13	Russell Martin, Andruw Jones, Rafael Furcal	20.00
14	Jason Varitek, Jorge Posada, Ivan Rodriguez	20.00
15	Yogi Berra, Mickey Mantle, Roger Maris	125.00
16	Gary Matthews, Vladimir Guerrero, Torii Hunter	15.00
17	Troy Tulowitzki, Matt Holliday, Todd Helton	25.00
18	Roberto Clemente, Carl Yastrzemski, Reggie Jackson	75.00
19	Ernie Banks, Alfonso Soriano, Ryne Sandberg	50.00
20	Mickey Mantle, Albert Pujols, Roberto Clemente	125.00
21	Lance Berkman, Carlos Lee, Hunter Pence	20.00
22	Alex Gordon, Ryan Braun, Ryan Zimmerman	30.00
23	Mickey Mantle, Alex Rodriguez, Ted Williams	150.00
24	Justin Morneau, Harmon Killebrew, Joe Mauer	40.00
25	Trevor Hoffman, Dennis Eckersley, Mariano Rivera	30.00
26	Jose Reyes, David Wright, John Maine	35.00
27	Daisuke Matsuzaka, Ichiro Suzuki, Hideki Matsui	85.00
28	Stan Musial, Albert Pujols, Rogers Hornsby	85.00
29	Vince DiMaggio, Joe DiMaggio, Dom DiMaggio	90.00
30	Mike Schmidt, George Brett, Steve Carlton	30.00
31	Nick Markakis, Brooks Robinson, Brian Roberts	35.00
32	Prince Fielder, Paul Molitor, Ryan Braun	30.00
33	Tim Lincecum, Joba Chamberlain, Brian Bannister	35.00
34	Prince Fielder, Ryan Howard, Andruw Jones	25.00
35	Alex Rodriguez, David Ortiz, Manny Ramirez	40.00
36	Jim Palmer, Pedro Martinez, Tom Seaver	35.00
37	Ichiro Suzuki, Todd Helton, Albert Pujols	40.00
38	Pedro Martinez, Roy Oswalt, Greg Maddux	30.00
39	Yogi Berra, Joe DiMaggio, Phil Rizzuto	125.00
40	Ernie Banks, Roberto Clemente, Carl Yastrzemski	60.00
41	Justin Morneau, Ryan Howard, Prince Fielder	30.00
42	Alex Gordon, George Brett, Brian Bannister	25.00
43	Ryan Howard, Albert Pujols, Manny Ramirez	40.00
44	Alex Rodriguez, Vladimir Guerrero, Prince Fielder	35.00
45	Randy Johnson, Nolan Ryan, Hideo Nomo	40.00
46	Rollie Fingers, Reggie Jackson, Vida Blue	25.00
47	Roberto Clemente, Ichiro Suzuki, Mickey Mantle	150.00
48	Brooks Robinson, Jim Palmer, Frank Robinson	30.00
49	Reggie Jackson, Steve Garvey, Willie Randolph	30.00
50	David Ortiz, Ted Williams, Manny Ramirez	50.00
51	Mickey Mantle, Alex Rodriguez, Joe DiMaggio	175.00
52	Duke Snider, Russell Martin, Steve Garvey	50.00
53	Ichiro Suzuki, Alfonso Soriano, Carlos Beltran	30.00
54	Chase Utley, Dan Uggla, Dustin Pedroia	35.00
55	Jose Reyes, Jimmy Rollins, Hanley Ramirez	30.00
56	Jimmy Rollins, Joe DiMaggio, Chase Utley	80.00
57	Johnny Bench, Ivan Rodriguez, Carlton Fisk	35.00
58	Pedro Martinez, Nolan Ryan, Johan Santana	40.00
59	Jose Reyes, Ozzie Smith, Jimmy Rollins	30.00
60	Jimmy Rollins, Jake Peavy, Ryan Braun	35.00
61	Alex Rodriguez, C.C. Sabathia, Dustin Pedroia	40.00
62	Delmon Young, Alex Rodriguez, Justin Upton	35.00
63	Alex Rodriguez, Frank Thomas, Jim Thome	40.00
64	Roger Maris, Mickey Mantle, Harmon Killebrew	125.00
65	Carlos Beltran, Chipper Jones, Jose Reyes	30.00
66	Jimmy Rollins, Matt Holliday, Prince Fielder	25.00
67	Alex Rodriguez, Magglio Ordonez, Vladimir Guerrero	30.00
68	Jake Peavy, Brandon Webb, Brad Penny	20.00
69	C.C. Sabathia, Josh Beckett, John Lackey	25.00
70	Ryan Braun, Troy Tulowitzki, Hunter Pence	25.00
71	Dustin Pedroia, Delmon Young, Brian Bannister	20.00
72	Victor Martinez, Grady Sizemore, Travis Hafner	25.00
73	Magglio Ordonez, Ichiro Suzuki, Vladimir Guerrero	35.00
74	Dan Uggla, Hanley Ramirez, Cameron Maybin	20.00
75	Ichiro Suzuki, Daisuke Matsuzaka, Akinori Iwamura	50.00
76	Jason Varitek, Alex Rodriguez, Chase Utley	25.00
77	Tris Speaker, Manny Ramirez, Travis Hafner	60.00
78	Eddie Mathews, Chipper Jones, Dale Murphy	50.00
79	Mike Schmidt, Ryan Howard, Richie Ashburn	50.00
80	Jimmy Rollins, Ryan Howard, Chase Utley	35.00
81	Matt Holliday, Carlos Beltran, Carlos Lee	20.00
82	Vladimir Guerrero, Magglio Ordonez, Ichiro Suzuki	30.00
83	Andruw Jones, Jeff Francoeur, Aaron Rowand, Carlos Beltran	20.00
84	Grady Sizemore, Ichiro Suzuki, Torii Hunter	35.00
85	Stan Musial, Carl Yastrzemski, Ted Williams	75.00
86	Alex Rodriguez	30.00
87	Chipper Jones, Brian McCann, Jeff Francoeur	35.00
88	Nolan Ryan	40.00
89	David Ortiz, Paul Molitor, Edgar Martinez	20.00
90	Alex Rodriguez, Albert Pujols, Manny Ramirez	40.00
91	Randy Johnson, Luis Gonzalez, Mariano Rivera	40.00
92	Rich "Goose" Gossage, George Brett, Billy Martin	40.00
93	Fausto Carmona, Joba Chamberlain, Grady Sizemore	30.00
94	Brian Giles, Matt Holliday, Michael Barrett	15.00
95	Franklin D. Roosevelt, Harry S. Truman, John F. Kennedy	75.00
96	George H.W. Bush, George W. Bush, Ronald Reagan	60.00
97	William Taft, Woodrow Wilson, Warren G. Harding	50.00
98	Johnny Damon, Chipper Jones, Matt Holliday	20.00
99	David Ortiz, Jose Reyes, Alfonso Soriano	25.00
100	Adrian Beltre, Albert Pujols, Placido Polanco	25.00
101	Joe DiMaggio, Mickey Mantle, Lou Gehrig	180.00
102	Ty Cobb, Babe Ruth, Honus Wagner	300.00
103	Roy Campanella, Thurman Munson, Johnny Bench	50.00
104	Pee Wee Reese, Jackie Robinson, Roy Campanella	120.00
105	Roberto Clemente, Ralph Kiner, Honus Wagner	175.00
106	Johnny Mize, Mel Ott, Rogers Hornsby	75.00
107	Reggie Jackson, Thurman Munson, Billy Martin	50.00
108	Jimmie Foxx, Lou Gehrig, Mel Ott	150.00
109	Roger Maris, Babe Ruth, Mickey Mantle	275.00
110	Honus Wagner, Ty Cobb, Tris Speaker	250.00
111	Jimmie Foxx, Ted Williams, Manny Ramirez	60.00

Relic Double Combos

NM/M
Production 36 Sets
Sepia: 1X
Production 27 Sets
Emerald: No Pricing
Production 18 Sets
Gold: No Pricing
Production 9 Sets
Sapphire: No Pricing
Production 3 Sets
Platinum: No Pricing
Production One Set

#	Players	Price
1	Joe DiMaggio, Mickey Mantle, Roger Maris, Roberto Clemente, Ted Williams, Tris Speaker	200.00
2	Ty Cobb, Rogers Hornsby, Joe DiMaggio, Ted Williams, Tony Gwynn, Ichiro Suzuki	200.00
3	Troy Tulowitzki, Chipper Jones, Kelly Johnson, Edgar Renteria	50.00
4	Albert Pujols, Bob Gibson, Rogers Hornsby, Stan Musial, Ozzie Smith, Red Schoendienst	100.00
5	Ryan Howard, Albert Pujols, Prince Fielder, Vladimir Guerrero, Alex Rodriguez, David Ortiz	65.00
6	Tom Seaver, Nolan Ryan, Steve Carlton, Dennis Eckersley, Jim Palmer, Whitey Ford	80.00
7	Jose Reyes, Hanley Ramirez, Jimmy Rollins, Carl Crawford, Brian Roberts, Ichiro Suzuki	50.00
8	Russell Martin, Brian McCann, Jorge Posada, Mike Piazza, Carlton Fisk, Yogi Berra	40.00
9	Joe DiMaggio, Mickey Mantle	180.00
10	Joe DiMaggio, Mickey Mantle, Roger Maris, Billy Martin, Phil Rizzuto, Whitey Ford	180.00
11	Frank Robinson, Carl Yastrzemski, Roberto Clemente, Mickey Mantle, Ted Williams, Harmon Killebrew	160.00
12	Roy Oswalt, Peter Munro, Kirk Saarloos, Brad Lidge, Octavio Dotel, Billy Wagner	30.00
13	Mickey Mantle, Joe DiMaggio, Ted Williams, David Wright, Ryan Howard, Alex Rodriguez	160.00
14	Alex Rodriguez, Hideki Matsui, Jorge Posada, Johnny Damon, Chien-Ming Wang, Joba Chamberlain	75.00
15	Akinori Iwamura, Hideki Matsui, Hideki Okajima, Kazuo Matsui, Ichiro Suzuki, Kenji Johjima	50.00
16	Russell Martin, Jason Bay, Erik Bedard, Rich Harden, Justin Morneau, Shawn Hill	30.00
17	Carlos Beltran, David Wright, Carlos Delgado, Jose Reyes, Pedro Martinez, John Maine	50.00
18	Travis Hafner, Victor Martinez, Grady Sizemore, C.C. Sabathia, Fausto Carmona, Bob Feller	40.00
19	Brooks Robinson, Jim Palmer, Eddie Murray, Brian Roberts, Nick Markakis, Melvin Mora	30.00
20	David Ortiz, Jason Varitek, Josh Beckett, Manny Ramirez, Mike Lowell, Hideki Okajima	75.00
21	Jose Vidro, Alex Rodriguez, Ichiro Suzuki, J.J. Putz, Edgar Martinez, Kenji Johjima	60.00
22	Alex Rodriguez, C.C. Sabathia, Dustin Pedroia, Jimmy Rollins, Jake Peavy, Ryan Braun	50.00
23	Mickey Mantle	200.00
24	Joe DiMaggio	100.00
25	Roberto Clemente	100.00
26	Carlos Lee, Roy Oswalt, Lance Berkman, Hunter Pence, Nolan Ryan, Kazuo Matsui	40.00
27	Jimmy Rollins, Mike Schmidt, Chase Utley, Cole Hamels, Robin Roberts, Ryan Howard	50.00
28	Johnny Podres, Whitey Ford, Brooks Robinson, Ernie Banks, Duke Snider, Bob Gibson	60.00
29	Ted Williams	80.00
30	Justin Morneau, Rod Carew, Francisco Liriano, Joe Mauer, Delmon Young, Harmon Killebrew	75.00
31	Justin Morneau, Ryan Howard, Albert Pujols, Prince Fielder, Carlos Delgado, Mark Teixeira	50.00
32	Magglio Ordonez, Al Kaline, Ivan Rodriguez, Curtis Granderson, Ty Cobb, Gary Sheffield	90.00
33	Carlton Fisk, Jim Thome, Jermaine Dye, Mark Buehrle, Paul Konerko, Luis Aparicio	40.00
34	Keith Hernandez, Dwight Gooden, Darryl Strawberry, David Wright, Pedro Martinez, Jose Reyes	40.00
35	Chipper Jones, John Smoltz, Brian McCann, Jeff Francoeur, Mark Teixeira, Tom Glavine	40.00
36	David Ortiz, Manny Ramirez, Jason Varitek, Alex Rodriguez, Jorge Posada, Johnny Damon	75.00
37	Roger Maris, Mickey Mantle	220.00
38	Ichiro Suzuki	60.00
39	Albert Pujols	80.00
40	Robin Yount, Paul Molitor, Rollie Fingers, Prince Fielder, Ryan Braun, Ben Sheets	50.00
41	Nolan Ryan, Alex Rodriguez, Ivan Rodriguez, Ian Kinsler, Michael Young, Hank Blalock	50.00

42 Vladimir Guerrero,
John Lackey, Jered Weaver,
Garret Anderson,
Torii Hunter,
Gary Matthews 35.00
43 Tim Lincecum, Rich Aurilia,
Barry Zito, Eric Chavez,
Mark Ellis,
Bobby Crosby 35.00
44 Russell Martin, Rafael Furcal,
Andruw Jones, Matt Kemp,
Jeff Kent,
Hong-Chih Kuo 40.00
45 David Wright, Carlos Beltran,
Jose Reyes, Ryan Howard,
Jimmy Rollins,
Chase Utley 50.00
46 Chien-Ming Wang 60.00
47 Ichiro Suzuki, Alex Rodriguez,
David Ortiz, Magglio Ordonez,
Ivan Rodriguez,
Vladimir Guerrero 50.00
48 Manny Ramirez, David Ortiz,
Mike Lowell, Travis Hafner,
Victor Martinez,
Grady Sizemore 50.00
49 Matt Holliday, Todd Helton,
Troy Tulowitzki,
Orlando Hudson,
Stephen Drew,
Chris Young 35.00
50 Manny Ramirez, David Ortiz,
Mike Lowell, Matt Holliday,
Todd Helton,
Troy Tulowitzki 50.00
51 Alex Rodriguez,
Mickey Mantle 75.00
52 Albert Pujols,
Vladimir Guerrero,
Manny Ramirez, David Ortiz,
Pedro Martinez,
Alfonso Soriano 50.00
53 Joe DiMaggio, Ty Cobb,
Babe Ruth, Lou Gehrig,
Ted Williams,
Mickey Mantle 500.00
54 George Sisler, Johnny Mize,
Rogers Hornsby,
Jimmie Foxx, Mel Ott,
Pee Wee Reese 160.00
55 Jackie Robinson,
Duke Snider,
Roy Campanella, Phil Rizzuto,
Mickey Mantle,
Yogi Berra 160.00

2008 Topps Update

NM/M
Complete Set (330): 40.00
Common Player: .15
Pack (6 Heritage + 2 Upd.): 3.00
Hobby Box (24): 60.00
1 Kosuke Fukudome RC 3.00
1 Kosuke Fukudome
Upside down image 40.00
2 Sean Casey .15
3 Freddie Bynum .15
4 Brent Lillibridge (RC) .25
5 Chipper Jones .75
6 Yamid Haad .15
7 Josh Anderson .15
8 Jeff Mathis .15
9 Shawn Riggans .15
10 Evan Longoria RC 5.00
10 Evan Longoria
upside down image 75.00
11 Matt Holliday .40
12 Trot Nixon .15
13 Geoff Blum .15
14 Bartolo Colon .15
15 Kevin Cash .15
16 Paul Janish (RC) .25
17 Russell Martin .25
18 Andy Phillips .15
19 Johnny Estrada .15
20 Justin Masterson RC 1.00
21 Darrell Rasner .15
22 Brian Moehler .15
23 Cristian Guzman .15
24 Tony Armas Jr. .15
25 Lance Berkman .40
26 Chris Iannetta .15
27 Reid Brignac .25
28 Miguel Tejada .25
29 Ryan Ludwick .25
30 Brendan Harris .15
31 Marco Scutaro .15
32 Cody Ross .15

33 Carlos Marmol .15
34 Nate McLouth .25
35 Hanley Ramirez .75
36 Xavier Nady .15
37 Connor Robertson .15
38 Carlos Villanueva .15
39 Jose Molina .15
40 Jon Rauch .15
41 Joe Mauer .40
42 Chip Ambres .15
43 Jason Bartlett .15
44 Ryan Sweeney .15
45 Eric Hurley (RC) .50
46 Kevin Youkilis .25
47 Dustin Pedroia .50
48 Grant Balfour .15
49 Ryan Ludwick .15
50 Matt Garza .15
51 Fernando Tatis .15
52 Derek Jeter 1.50
53 Justin Duchscherer .15
54 Matt Ginter .15
55 Cesar Izturis .15
56 Roy Halladay .15
57 Ramon Castro .15
58 Scott Kazmir .15
59 Cliff Lee .25
60 Jim Edmonds .25
61 Randy Wolf .15
62 Matt Albers .15
63 Eric Bruntlett .15
64 Joe Nathan .15
65 Alex Rodriguez 1.00
66 Robinson Cancel .15
67 Jamey Carroll .15
68 Jonathan Papelbon .40
69 Chad Moeller .15
70 George Sherrill .15
71 Mariano Rivera .25
72 Peter Orr .15
73 Jonathan Albaladejo .15
74 Corey Patterson .15
75 Matt Treanor .15
76 Francisco Rodriguez .15
77 Ervin Santana .15
78 Dallas Braden .15
79 Willie Harris .15
80 Erik Bedard .15
81 J.C. Romero .15
82 Joe Saunders .15
83 George Sherrill .15
84 Julian Tavarez .15
85 Chad Gaudin .15
86 David Aardsma .15
87 Ryan Langerhans .15
88 Dan Haren, Russ Martin .25
89 Joakim Soria .15
90 Dan Haren .25
91 Billy Buckner .15
92 Eric Hinske .15
93 Chris Coste .15
94 Edinson Volquez,
Russ Martin .25
95 Ichiro Suzuki 1.00
96 Vladimir Nunez .15
97 Sean Gallagher .15
98 Denny Bautista .15
99 Hanley Ramirez,
David Ortiz .50
100 Jay Bruce (RC) 3.00
100 Jay Bruce upside
down image 50.00
101 Dioner Navarro .15
102 Matt Murton .15
103 Chris Burke .15
104 Omar Infante .15
105 Daniel Giese (RC) .25
106 Carlos Guillen,
Josh Hamilton .25
107 Jason Varitek .15
108 Shin-Soo Choo .15
109 Alberto Callaspo .15
110 Jose Valverde .15
111 Brandon Boggs (RC) .25
112 Josh Hamilton, J.D. Drew .25
113 Justin Morneau .15
114 Billy Traber .15
115 Mike Lamb .15
116 Odalis Perez .15
117 Jed Lowrie (RC) .50
118 Justin Morneau,
David Ortiz .50
119 Ken Griffey Jr. 1.00
120 Angel Berroa .15
121 Jacque Jones .15
122 Dewayne Wise .15
123 Matt Joyce RC .75
124 Alex Rodriguez
     Evan Longoria 1.50
125 John Smoltz .40
126 Morgan Ensberg .15
127 Michael Young,
Derek Jeter 1.00
128 LaTroy Hawkins .15
129 Nick Adenhart (RC) .75
130 Mike Cameron .15
131 Manny Ramirez .75
132 Jorge De La Rosa .15
133 Tadahito Iguchi .15
134 Joey Devine .15
135 Jose Arredondo RC .50
136 Hanley Ramirez,
Albert Pujols 1.00
137 Evan Longoria 3.00
138 T.J. Beam .15
139 Jon Lieber .15
140 Dana Eveland .15
141 Michael Aubrey RC .75

142 Adrian Gonzalez,
Matt Holliday .25
143 Chipper Jones .50
144 Robinson Tejeda .15
145 Kip Wells .15
146 Carlos Gonzalez (RC) 1.00
147 Josh Banks (RC) .25
148 David Wright .75
149 Paul Hoover .15
150 Jon Lester .50
151 Darin Erstad .15
152 Steve Trachsel .15
153 Armando Galarraga RC 1.00
154 Grady Sizemore .50
155 Jay Bruce 1.00
156 Juan Rincon .15
157 Mark Hendrickson .15
158 Chad Durbin .15
159 Mike Aviles RC 1.00
160 Orlando Cabrera .25
161 Asdrubal Cabrera .15
162 Eric Stults .15
163 Miguel Cairo .15
164 Jason LaRue .15
165 Burke Badenhop RC .25
166 Ryan Braun .50
167 Justin Morneau .25
168 Benjamin Zobrist .15
169 Eulogio de la Cruz .15
170 Greg Smith (RC) .25
171 Brian Bixler (RC) .25
172 Evan Longoria 2.00
173 Randy Johnson .50
174 D.J. Carrasco .15
175 Luis Vizcaino .15
176 Brad Wilkerson .15
177 Emmanuel Burriss RC .25
178 Lance Berkman .25
179 Johnny Damon .25
180 Scott Rolen .25
181 Runelvys Hernandez .15
182 Sidney Ponson .15
183 Greg Reynolds RC .25
184 Chase Utley .50
185 Joey Votto .50
186 Wes Littleton .15
187 Rod Barajas .15
188 Ray Durham .15
189 Micah Hoffpauir RC .50
190 Manny Ramirez .50
191 Ian Kinsler .15
192 Craig Hansen .15
193 Jeremy Affeldt .15
194 Gary Bennett .15
195 Chris Carter (RC) .25
196 Dan Uggla .25
197 Michael Young .25
198 Andy LaRoche .15
199 Lance Cormier .15
200 Luke Scott .15
201 Travis Denker RC .50
202 Josh Hamilton .75
203 Joe Crede .15
204 Franquelis Osoria .15
205 Octavio Dotel .15
206 Russell Branyan .15
207 Alberto Gonzalez RC .50
208 Kerry Wood .15
209 Carlos Guillen .15
210 Joe Saunders .15
211 Brett Tomko .15
212 Guillermo Mota .15
213 German Duran RC .25
214 Carlos Zambrano .15
215 Josh Hamilton .50
216 Jason Bay .25
217 Willy Aybar .15
218 Salomon Torres .15
219 Damaso Marte .15
220 Geoff Jenkins .15
221 J.D. Drew .15
222 Dave Borkowski .15
223 Jeff Ridgway .15
224 Angel Pagan .15
225 Ryan Tucker (RC) .25
226 Brian McCann .25
227 Carlos Quentin .25
228 Joe Blanton .25
229 Adrian Gonzalez .25
230 Jason Jennings .15
231 Chris Davis RC .50
232 Geovany Soto .50
233 Grady Sizemore .50
234 Carl Pavano .15
235 Eddie Guardado .15
236 Chris Snelling .15
237 Manny Ramirez .50
238 Dan Uggla .25
239 Milton Bradley .15
240 Clayton Kershaw RC 1.00
241 Chase Utley .50
242 Raul Chavez .15
243 Joe Mather .15
244 Brandon Webb .25
245 Ryan Braun .75
246 Kelvin Jimenez .15
247 Scott Podsednik .15
248 Doug Mientkiewicz .15
249 Chris Volstad (RC) .50
250 Pedro Feliz .15
251 Mark Redman .15
252 Tony Clark .15
253 Josh Johnson .15
254 Jose Castillo .15
255 Brian Horwitz RC .25
256 Aramis Ramirez .15
257 Casey Blake .15
258 Arthur Rhodes .15

259 Aaron Boone .15
260 Emil Brown .15
261 Matt Macri (RC) .25
262 Brian Wilson .15
263 Eric Patterson .15
264 David Ortiz .75
265 Tony Abreu .15
266 Robert Mackowiak .15
267 Gregorio Petit RC .50
268 Alfonso Soriano .50
269 Robert Andino .15
270 Justin Duchscherer .15
271 Brad Thompson .15
272 Guillermo Quiroz .15
273 Chris Perez RC .50
274 Albert Pujols 1.00
275 Rich Harden .15
276 Corey Hart .25
277 John Rheinecker .15
278 So Taguchi .15
279 Alex Hinshaw RC .50
280 Max Scherzer RC 1.00
281 Chris Aguila .15
282 Carlos Marmol .15
283 Alex Cintron .15
284 Curtis Thigpen .15
285 Kosuke Fukudome 1.50
286 Aaron Cook .15
287 Chase Headley .25
288 Evan Longoria 2.00
289 Chris Gomez .15
290 Carlos Gomez .15
291 Jonathan Herrera RC .50
292 Ryan Dempster .15
293 Adam Dunn .40
294 Mark Teixeira .40
295 Aaron Miles .15
296 Gabe Gross .15
297 Cory Wade (RC) .25
298 Dan Haren .25
299 Jolbert Cabrera .15
300 C.C. Sabathia .50
301 Tony Pena .15
302 Brandon Moss .15
303 Taylor Teagarden RC .75
304 Brad Lidge .15
305 Ben Francisco .15
306 Casey Kotchman .15
307 Greg Norton .15
308 Shelley Duncan .15
309 John Bowker (RC) .50
310 Kyle Lohse .15
311 Oscar Salazar .15
312 Ivan Rodriguez .25
313 Tim Lincecum .50
314 Wilson Betemit .15
315 Sean Rodriguez (RC) .50
316 Ben Sheets .25
317 Brian Buscher .15
318 Kyle Farnsworth .15
319 Ruben Gotay .15
320 Heath Bell .15
321 Jeff Niemann (RC) .25
322 Edinson Volquez .50
323 Jorge Velandia .15
324 Ken Griffey Jr. 1.00
325 Clay Hensley .15
326 Kevin Mench .15
327 Hernan Iribarren (RC) .50
328 Billy Wagner .15
329 Jeremy Sowers .15
330 Johan Santana .50

Black

Black: 20-30X
Production 57 Sets

Gold

Gold: 5-10X
Production 2,008 Sets

Gold Foil

Gold Foil: 1-2X

Platinum

Production One Set

Rookie Box Loaders

NM/M
Inserted 1:Box 3.00
All cards are Refractors
1 Jay Bruce 10.00
2 Daniel Giese 5.00
3 Brandon Boggs 3.00
4 Jed Lowrie 8.00
5 Matt Joyce 6.00
6 Nick Adenhart 4.00
7 Jose Arredondo 3.00

8 Michael Aubry 4.00
9 Josh Banks 3.00
10 Armando Galarraga 8.00
11 Mike Aviles 3.00
12 Burke Badenhop 3.00
13 Reid Brignac 5.00
14 Emmanuel Burriss 3.00
15 Greg Reynolds 3.00
16 Chris Volstad 3.00
17 Brian Bixler 3.00
18 Chris Carter 3.00
19 Travis Denker 5.00
20 Alberto Gonzalez 3.00
21 Robinzon Diaz 3.00
22 Brett Gardner 3.00
23 Micah Hoffpauir 5.00
24 Hernan Iribarren 3.00
25 Greg Smith 3.00
26 German Duran 3.00
27 Kosuke Fukudome 10.00
28 Ryan Tucker 3.00
29 Paul Janish 3.00
30 Clayton Kershaw 8.00
31 Chris Davis 8.00
32 Joe Mather 3.00
33 Nick Hundley 5.00
34 Brian Horwitz 3.00
35 Carlos Gonzalez 6.00
36 Matt Macri 3.00
37 Gregorio Petit 3.00
38 Chris Perez 5.00
39 Alex Hinshaw 3.00
40 Max Scherzer 8.00
41 Jonathan Van Every 3.00
42 Jonathan Herrera 3.00
43 Cory Wade 4.00
44 Max Ramirez 5.00
45 John Bowker 3.00
46 Sean Rodriguez 3.00
47 Jeff Niemann 3.00
48 Taylor Teagarden 5.00
49 Mark Worrell 3.00
50 Evan Longoria 20.00
51 Chris Smith 4.00
52 Brent Lillibridge 3.00
53 Colt Morton 3.00
54 Eric Hurley 3.00
55 Justin Masterson 10.00

All-Star Stitches

NM/M
Common Player: 4.00
Inserted 1:44
Gold: 1-2X
Production 50 Sets
Platinum: No Pricing
Production One Set
AC Aaron Cook 4.00
AG Adrian Gonzalez 8.00
AP Albert Pujol 15.00
AR Aramis Ramirez 8.00
AER Alex Rodriguez 15.00
AS Alfonso Soriano 8.00
BL Brad Lidge 4.00
BM Brian McCann 8.00
BS Ben Sheets 6.00
WW Billy Wagner 4.00
BTW Brandon Webb 8.00
CG Cristian Guzman 8.00
CAG Carlos Guillen 4.00
CH Corey Hart 6.00
CJ Chipper Jones 10.00
CL Cliff Lee 8.00
CM Carlos Marmol 6.00
CQ Carlos Quentin 8.00
CU Chase Utley 10.00
CZ Carlos Zambrano 8.00
DH Dan Haren 6.00
DN Dioner Navarro 4.00
DO David Ortiz 10.00
DP Dustin Pedroia 10.00
DU Dan Uggla 8.00
DW David Wright 10.00
EL Evan Longoria 25.00
ES Ervin Santana 8.00
EV Edinson Volquez 8.00
FR Francisco Rodriguez 8.00
GPS Geovany Soto 15.00
GFS George Sherrill 4.00
GS Grady Sizemore 10.00
HR Hanley Ramirez 8.00
IK Ian Kinsler 8.00
IS Ichiro Suzuki 25.00
JC Joe Crede 6.00
JCD Justin Duchscherer 6.00
JD J.D. Drew 8.00
JH Josh Hamilton 20.00
JM Joe Mauer 8.00
JN Joe Nathan 6.00
JP Jonathan Papelbon 8.00
JES Joe Saunders 6.00
JS Joakim Soria 4.00
JV Jason Varitek 10.00
KF Kosuke Fukudome 20.00
KW Kerry Wood 6.00
KY Kevin Youkilis 10.00
LB Lance Berkman 8.00

MB Milton Bradley 6.00
MH Matt Holliday 8.00
MR Manny Ramirez 8.00
MSR Mariano Rivera 10.00
MT Miguel Tejada 6.00
MY Michael Young 6.00
NM Nate McLouth 8.00
RB Ryan Braun 10.00
RD Ryan Dempster 6.00
RH Roy Halladay 8.00
RL Ryan Ludwick 10.00
RM Russ Martin 8.00
SK Scott Kazmir 8.00
TL Tim Lincecum 15.00

All-Star Stitches Auto.

NM/M
Production 25 Sets
CJ Chipper Jones 160.00
DU Dan Uggla 40.00
TL Tim Lincecum 160.00
JH Josh Hamilton 150.00
DP Dustin Pedroia 125.00
JV Jason Varitek 90.00
RB Ryan Braun 75.00
EV Edinson Volquez 60.00
HR Hanley Ramirez 60.00
RM Russ Martin 100.00

All-Star Stitches Triple

NM/M
Production 25 Sets
RSS Francisco Rodriguez,
Ervin Santana,
Joe Saunders 40.00
HRI Josh Hamilton,
Manny Ramirez,
Ichiro Suzuki 50.00
RWJ Alex Rodriguez, David Wright,
Chipper Jones 75.00
HFB Matt Holliday,
Kosuke Fukudome,
Ryan Braun 50.00
PDO Dustin Pedroia, J.D. Drew,
David Ortiz 50.00
ZRD Carlos Zambrano,
Aramis Ramirez,
Ryan Dempster 75.00
PGB Albert Pujols,
Adrian Gonzalez,
Lance Berkman 50.00
WLW Kerry Wood, Brad Lidge,
Billy Wagner 40.00
MNM Russ Martin, Dioner Navarro,
Brian McCann 40.00
KBY Ian Kinsler, Milton Bradley,
Michael Young 50.00

All-Star Stitches Dual

NM/M
Production 25 Sets
HM Josh Hamilton,
Ryan Braun 40.00
RR Alex Rodriguez,
Manny Ramirez 50.00
FS Kosuke Fukudome,
Ichiro Suzuki 75.00
UU Chase Utley, Dan Uggla 40.00
LV Tim Lincecum,
Edinson Volquez 25.00
LS Cliff Lee, Ben Sheets 20.00
BP Lance Berkman,
Albert Pujols 50.00
RT Hanley Ramirez,
Miguel Tejada 25.00
RR Mariano Rivera,
Francisco Rodriguez 50.00

All-Star Jumbo Patches

No Pricing
Production 6 Sets

All-Star Jumbo Patches Auto.

Production 6 Sets

First Couples

NM/M
Common Couple: .75
Inserted 1:6
1 George Washington,
Martha Washington 2.50
2 John Adams,
Abigail Adams 1.50
3 Thomas Jefferson,
Martha Jefferson 1.50
4 James Madison,
Dolly Madison 1.00
5 James Monroe,
Elizabeth Kotright Monroe .75
6 John Quincy Adams,
Louisa Catherine Adams 1.00
7 Andrew Jackson,
Rachel Jackson 1.00
8 Martin Van Buren,
Hannah Van Buren .75

9	William Henry Harrison, Anna Harrison	.75
10	John Tyler, Julia Tyler	.75
11	James K. Polk, Sarah Polk	.75
12	Zachary Taylor, Margaret Taylor	.75
13	Millard Fillmore, Abigail Fillmore	.75
14	Franklin Pierce, Jane M. Pierce	.75
15	Abraham Lincoln, Mary Lincoln	2.50
16	Andrew Johnson, Eliza Johnson	1.50
17	Ulysses S. Grant, Julia Grant	1.50
18	Rutherford B. Hayes, Lucy Hayes	.75
19	James A. Garfield, Lucretia Garfield	.75
20	Chester A. Arthur, Elien Arthur	.75
21	Grover Cleveland, Frances Cleveland	.75
22	Benjamin Harrison, Caroline Harrison	.75
23	William McKinley, Ida McKinley	.75
24	Theodore Roosevelt, Edith Roosevelt	1.50
25	William H. Taft, Helen Taft	.75
26	Woodrow Wilson, Edith Wilson	.75
27	Warren G. Harding, Florence Harding	.75
28	Calvin Coolidge, Grace Coolidge	.75
29	Herbert Hoover, Lou Hoover	.75
30	Franklin D. Roosevelt, Eleanor Roosevelt	1.50
31	Harry S. Truman, Bess Truman	1.50
32	Dwight D. Eisenhower, Mamie Eisenhower	1.50
33	John F. Kennedy, Jacqueline Kennedy	3.00
34	Lyndon B. Johnson, Lady Bird Johnson	1.00
35	Richard M. Nixon, Pat Nixon	
36	Gerald R. Ford, Betty Ford	.75
37	Jimmy Carter, Rosalynn Carter	1.00
38	Ronald Reagan, Nancy Reagan	2.00
39	George H.W. Bush, Barbara Bush	2.00
40	Bill Clinton, Hillary Rodham Clinton	2.00
41	George W. Bush, Laura Bush	2.00

First Lady Cut Signatures
Production One Set

Presidential Stamp Collection

		NM/M
	Inserted 1:867	
AL4-6	Abraham Lincoln	50.00
AJWS1	Andrew Jackson, Winfield Scott	30.00
FDR1-5	Franklin D. Roosevelt	40.00
GW18-25	George Washington	40.00
GW26	George Washington (Inauguration)	50.00
JG3	James Garfield	25.00
JA1	John Adams	30.00
WW3	Woodrow Wilson	25.00

Silk

		NM/M
	Production 50 Sets	
101	Johan Santana	25.00
102	Cristian Guzman	8.00
103	Brendan Harris	8.00
104	Randy Wolf	10.00
105	Cliff Lee	20.00
106	Roy Halladay	20.00
107	Dustin Pedroia	25.00
108	Chris Iannetta	10.00
109	Kerry Wood	10.00
110	Jim Edmonds	15.00
111	Jon Rauch	8.00
112	Ryan Sweeney	10.00
113	Ryan Ludwick	20.00
114	George Sherrill	10.00
115	Matt Garza	15.00
116	Nate McLouth	20.00
117	Eric Hinske	10.00
118	Adrian Gonzalez	15.00
119	Carlos Marmol	10.00
120	Jose Valverde	10.00
121	Shane Victorino	20.00
122	Brad Wilkerson	10.00
123	Dana Eveland	10.00
124	Luke Scott	10.00
125	Mike Cameron	20.00
126	Ervin Santana	20.00
127	Ryan Dempster	15.00
128	Geoff Jenkins	10.00
129	Billy Wagner	10.00
130	Pedro Feliz	10.00
131	Stephen Drew	15.00
132	Mark Hendrickson	8.00
133	Orlando Hudson	10.00

134	Pat Burrell	20.00
135	Russell Martin	30.00
136	James Loney	15.00
137	Justin Masterson	50.00
138	Matt Kemp	20.00
139	Hiroki Kuroda	20.00
140	Joe Crede	10.00
141	Joakim Soria	10.00
142	Armando Galarraga	15.00
143	Jason Varitek	15.00
144	Aaron Cook	10.00
145	Orlando Cabrera	10.00
146	Ian Kinsler	20.00
147	Carlos Gomez	20.00
148	Mike Aviles	25.00
149	Carlos Guillen	15.00
150	Erik Bedard	15.00
151	J.D. Drew	15.00
152	Marco Scutaro	10.00
153	James Shields	20.00
154	Cesar Izturis	10.00
155	Akinori Iwamura	15.00
156	Aramis Ramirez	20.00
157	Joe Mauer	20.00
158	Brad Lidge	15.00
159	Milton Bradley	15.00
160	Jay Bruce	30.00
161	Andrew Miller	15.00
162	Mark Reynolds	10.00
163	Johnny Damon	20.00
164	Michael Bourn	10.00
165	Andre Ethier	15.00
166	Carlos Pena	20.00
167	Joe Nathan	20.00
168	Cody Ross	8.00
169	Joba Chamberlain	35.00
170	Clayton Kershaw	50.00
171	Francisco Rodriguez	15.00
172	Mark DeRosa	15.00
173	Ben Sheets	15.00
174	Brian Wilson	10.00
175	Emil Brown	10.00
176	Geovany Soto	25.00
177	Jason Giambi	10.00
178	Shaun Marcum	10.00
179	Edinson Volquez	20.00
180	Max Scherzer	20.00
181	Kelly Johnson	10.00
182	Mariano Rivera	25.00
183	Chris Perez	20.00
184	Jose Guillen	10.00
185	Kyle Lohse	10.00
186	Kosuke Fukudome	20.00
187	Takashi Saito	15.00
188	Mike Mussina	15.00
189	J.J. Putz	10.00
190	Evan Longoria	50.00
191	Jered Weaver	30.00
192	Grady Sizemore	30.00
193	Carlos Gonzalez	15.00
194	Brian McCann	15.00
195	Jonathan Papelbon	20.00
196	Dioner Navarro	10.00
197	Bobby Abreu	15.00
198	Carlos Quentin	15.00
199	Josh Hamilton	30.00
200	Dan Haren	15.00

Sketch Cards

		NM/M
	Inserted 1:214	
1	Adam Dunn	30.00
2	Adrian Gonzalez	30.00
3	Albert Pujols	100.00
4	Alex Gordon	40.00
5	Alex Rios	40.00
6	Alex Rodriguez	100.00
7	Alfonso Soriano	40.00
8	Aramis Ramirez	25.00
9	B.J. Upton	40.00
10	Ben Sheets	30.00
11	Bobby Jenks	20.00
12	Brandon Webb	30.00
13	Brian McCann	25.00
14	C.C. Sabathia	30.00
15	Carl Crawford	20.00
16	Carlos Beltran	40.00
17	Carlos Gomez	30.00
18	Carlos Lee	25.00
19	Carlos Quentin	40.00
20	Carlos Zambrano	35.00
21	Chase Utley	50.00
22	Chipper Jones	50.00
23	Chien-Ming Wang	60.00
24	Chris Young	30.00
25	Clayton Kershaw	25.00
26	Cliff Lee	30.00
27	Cole Hamels	40.00
28	Daisuke Matsuzaka	40.00
29	Dan Haren	30.00
30	Dan Uggla	25.00
31	David Ortiz	60.00
32	David Wright	75.00
33	Derek Jeter	100.00
34	Derrek Lee	30.00
35	Dustin Pedroia	40.00
36	Edinson Volquez	30.00
37	Ervin Santana	35.00
38	Felix Hernandez	50.00
39	Francisco Rodriguez	30.00
40	Geovany Soto	40.00
41	Grady Sizemore	60.00
42	Hanley Ramirez	30.00
43	Hunter Pence	30.00
44	Ichiro Suzuki	100.00
45	Jacoby Ellsbury	50.00
46	Jake Peavy	20.00
47	Jason Bay	25.00
48	Jay Bruce	50.00
49	Jeff Francoeur	25.00

52	Ryan Zimmerman	30.00
53	Jimmy Rollins	40.00
54	Joba Chamberlain	50.00
57	Johan Santana	40.00
58	John Smoltz	50.00
59	Johnny Cueto	40.00
60	Jonathan Papelbon	40.00
61	Jose Reyes	40.00
62	Jose Valverde	15.00
63	Josh Beckett	40.00
64	Josh Hamilton	75.00
65	Justin Morneau	30.00
67	Justin Verlander	40.00
68	Lance Berkman	35.00
69	Magglio Ordonez	25.00
70	Manny Ramirez	50.00
72	Mark Teixeira	40.00
73	Matt Garza	20.00
75	Matt Kemp	25.00
78	Miguel Cabrera	40.00
80	Nick Markakis	40.00
81	Pat Burrell	30.00
82	Pedro Martinez	25.00
83	Prince Fielder	50.00
85	Rick Ankiel	15.00
87	Roy Halladay	25.00
90	Ryan Braun	60.00
91	Ryan Howard	50.00
92	Scott Kazmir	25.00
93	Tim Hudson	30.00
94	Tim Lincecum	80.00
95	Torii Hunter	40.00
96	Troy Tulowitzki	25.00
97	Vernon Wells	20.00
99	Vladimir Guerrero	40.00

Take Me Out to the Ballgame

		NM/M
	Inserted 1:72	
1	100th Anniversary	2.00

The Mickey Mantle Story

		NM/M
	Common Mantle:	2.00
	Inserted 1:18	
66-75	Mickey Mantle	2.00

World Series Ring of Honor

		NM/M
	Common Player:	1.50
	Inserted 1:18	
	Gold:	No Pricing
	Production 25 Sets	
RK	Ray Knight	1.50
BS	Bruce Sutter	1.50
JP	Johnny Podres	2.00
LA	Luis Aparicio	1.50
MI	Monte Irvin	2.00
DC	David Cone	1.50
DJ	David Justice	1.50
ML	Mike Lowell	1.50
WF	Whitey Ford	3.00
DS	Duke Snider	3.00
OC	Orlando Cepeda	1.50

World Series Ring of Honor Autos.

		NM/M
	Inserted 1:2,569	
BS	Bruce Sutter	50.00
JP	Johnny Podres	35.00
LA	Luis Aparicio	35.00
MI	Monte Irvin	40.00
DC	David Cone	50.00
DJ	David Justice	40.00
ML	Mike Lowell	30.00
WF	Whitey Ford	60.00
DS	Duke Snider	60.00
OC	Orlando Cepeda	40.00

Year in Review

		NM/M
	Common Player:	.50
	Inserted 1:6	
121	Mark Teixeira	.75
122	Alex Gordon	.75
123	Jermaine Dye	.50
124	Vladimir Guerrero	.75
125	Alex Rodriguez	2.00
126	Tom Glavine	.75
127	Scott Rolen	.50
128	Billy Wagner	.75
129	Rick Ankiel	.75
130	Jack Cust	.50
131	Mike Mussina	.75
132	Magglio Ordonez	.75

133	Placido Polanco	.50
134	Russell Branyan	.50
135	David Price	3.00
136	Mike Cameron	.50
137	Brandon Webb	.75
138	Cameron Maybin	.75
139	Johan Santana	.75
140	Bobby Jenks	.50
141	Garret Anderson	.50
142	Jarrod Saltalamacchia	.50
143	Adrian Gonzalez	.75
144	Carlos Guillen	.50
145	Tom Shearn	.50
146	John Lackey	.50
147	Jayson Werth	.50
148	Aaron Harang	.50
149	Chien-Ming Wang	1.00
150	Scott Baker	.50
151	Clay Buchholz	.50
152	Tom Glavine	.75
153	Pedro Martinez	.75
154	Doug Davis	.50
155	Brandon Phillips	.75
156	Jason Varitek	1.00
157	Jim Thome	.75
158	Alex Rodriguez	2.00
159	Curtis Granderson	.75
160	Scott Kazmir	.75
161	Marlon Byrd	.50
162	David Ortiz	1.00
163	David Wells	.50
164	Johnny Damon	.75
165	Carlos Lee	.50
166	Jim Thome	.75
167	Frank Thomas	.75
168	Greg Maddux	1.50
169	Matt Holliday	.75
170	J.R. Towles	.50
171	Lance Berkman	.50
172	Melky Cabrera	.50
173	Vladimir Guerrero	.75
174	Nick Markakis	.75
175	Prince Fielder	1.00
176	Moises Alou	.50
177	Micah Owings	.50
178	Carlos Zambrano	.75

1957 Mickey Mantle Reprint Relic

		NM/M
	Production 57 Cards	
57	Mickey Mantle/bat	125.00

1986 N.Y. Mets Ring of Honor

		NM/M
	Common Player:	1.50
	Inserted 1:18	
	Gold:	No Pricing
	Production 25 Sets	
HJ	Howard Johnson	1.50
RD	Ron Darling	1.50
JO	Jesse Orosco	1.50
DJ	Davey Johnson	1.50
KM	Kevin Mitchell	1.50
DS	Darryl Strawberry	1.50
DG	Dwight Gooden	1.50
GC	Gary Carter	1.50
RK	Ray Knight	1.50
KH	Keith Hernandez	1.50

1986 N.Y. Mets Ring of Honor Autos.

		NM/M
	Inserted 1:2,849	
HJ	Howard Johnson	30.00
RD	Ron Darling	30.00
JO	Jesse Orosco	40.00
DJ	Davey Johnson	25.00
KM	Kevin Mitchell	30.00
DS	D.J. Strawberry	30.00
DG	Dwight Gooden	30.00
GC	Gary Carter	40.00
RK	Ray Knight	30.00
KH	Keith Hernandez	40.00

2008 Presidential Picks

		NM/M
	Production 100 Sets	
JM	John McCain	50.00
BO	Barack Obama	50.00

2008 Highlight Autographs

		NM/M
	Common Auto.:	8.00
	Some not priced due to scarcity.	
RB	Ryan Braun	100.00

CK	Clayton Kershaw	75.00
BP	Brandon Phillips	15.00
NM	Nick Markakis	25.00
JH	Josh Hamilton	80.00
MS	Max Scherzer	25.00
AC	Asdrubal Cabrera	15.00
BD	Blake DeWitt	30.00
MK	Masahide Kobayashi	15.00
DM	Dustin McGowan	15.00
CG	Carlos Gomez	20.00
ZG	Zack Greinke	25.00
BB	Billy Butler	20.00
JV	Joey Votto	40.00
EV	Edinson Volquez	20.00
AG	Armando Galarraga	20.00
BR	B.J. Ryan	10.00
JR	Jo Jo Reyes	8.00
BDB	Brian Barton	8.00
SH	Steve Holm	8.00
CR	Carlos Ruiz	10.00
SS	Seth Smith	8.00
JS	Jeff Salazar	8.00
MW	Mark Worrell	8.00

2009 World Baseball Classic

		NM/M
	Complete Set (25):	20.00
	Common Player:	.50
	Inserted 1:9	
1	Daisuke Matsuzaka	2.00
2	Alexei Ramirez	4.00
3	Derrek Lee	1.00
4	Akinori Iwamura	.50
5	Chase Utley	1.50
6	Jose Reyes	1.50
7	Jake Peavy	.50
8	Justin Huber	.50
9	Justin Morneau	1.00
10	Ichiro Suzuki	3.00
11	Adrian Gonzalez	1.00
12	Carlos Zambrano	1.00
13	Miguel Cabrera	1.00
14	Carlos Beltran	1.00
15	Albert Pujols	3.00
16	Paul Bell	.50
17	Frank Catalanotto	.50
18	Jason Varitek	.75
19	Andruw Jones	.50
20	Johan Santana	1.00
21	Carlos Lee	.50
22	David Ortiz	1.50
23	Francisco Rodriguez	.50
24	Chin-Lung Hu	.50
25	Kosuke Fukudome	1.00

2009 Topps

[Topps — Ryan Braun / Brewers card]

		NM/M
	Complete Set (660):	60.00
	Comp. Series 1 Set w/o SPs (330):	30.00
	Comp Series 2 Set w/o SPs (330):	30.00
	Common Player:	.15
	Common RC:	.50
	Hobby pack (10):	2.00
	Hobby Box (36):	60.00
1	Alex Rodriguez	.15
1	Babe Ruth/SP	30.00
2	Omar Vizquel	.15
2	Pee Wee Reese/SP	25.00
3	Andy Marte	.15
4	Chipper Jones, Albert Pujols, Matt Holliday	1.00
5	John Lackey	.25
6	Raul Ibanez	.15
7	Mickey Mantle	4.00
8	Terry Francona	.15
9	Dallas McPherson	.15
10	Dan Uggla	.25
11	Rogers Hornsby/SP	20.00
12	Fernando Tatis	.15
13	Andrew Carpenter RC	.50
13	Ryan Langerhans	.15
14	Jon Rauch	.15
15	Nate McLouth	.15
16	Evan Longoria	1.50

17	Bobby Cox	.15
18	George Sherrill	.15
19	Edgar Gonzalez	.15
20	Brad Lidge	.15
21	Jack Wilson	.15
22	Evan Longoria, David Price	2.00
23	Gerald Laird	.15
24	Frank Thomas	.50
25	Jon Lester	.40
26	Jason Giambi	.25
27	Jon Niese RC	.75
28	Mike Lowell	.25
29	Jerry Hairston	.15
30	Ken Griffey Jr.	1.00
30	Jackie Robinson/SP	30.00
31	Ian Stewart	.15
32	Daric Barton	.15
33	Jose Guillen	.15
34	Brandon Inge	.15
35	David Price RC	4.00
36	Kevin Slowey	.15
37	Erick Aybar	.15
38	Eric Wedge	.15
39	Nick Swisher	.15
40	Carl Crawford	.25
41	Mike Mussina	.40
42	Jeff Francoeur	.15
43	Joe Mauer, Dustin Pedroia, Milton Bradley	.40
44	Geoff Jenkins	.15
45	Barack Obama/SP	35.00
45	Aubrey Huff	.15
46	Brad Ziegler	.15
47	Jose Valverde	.15
48	Mike Napoli	.15
49	Kazuo Matsui	.15
50	David Ortiz	.75
51	Will Venable RC	.50
52	Marco Scutaro	.15
53	Jonathan Sanchez	.15
54	Dusty Baker	.15
55	J.J. Hardy	.15
56	Edwin Encarnacion	.15
57	Jo Jo Reyes	.15
58	Travis Snider RC	1.00
59	Eric Gagne	.15
60	Mariano Rivera	.50
60	Cy Young/SP	25.00
61	Lance Berkman, Carlos Lee	.40
62	Brian Barton	.15
63	Josh Outman RC	.50
64	Miguel Montero	.15
65	Mike Pelfrey	.15
66	Dustin Pedroia	.15
66	Ty Cobb/SP	25.00
67	Andruw Jones	.15
68	Kyle Lohse	.15
69	Rich Aurilia	.15
70	Jermaine Dye	.25
71	Mat Gamel RC	1.00
72	David Dellucci	.15
73	Shane Victorino	.40
74	Trey Hillman	.15
75	Rich Harden	.15
76	Marcus Thames	.15
77	Jed Lowrie	.15
78	Tim Lincecum	.15
79	David Eckstein	.15
80	Brian McCann	.40
81	Ryan Howard, Adam Dunn, Carlos Delgado	.50
82	Miguel Cairo	.15
83	Ryan Garko	.15
84	Rod Barajas	.15
85	Justin Verlander	.40
86	Kila Ka'aihue RC	.50
87	Brad Hawpe	.15
88	Fredi Gonzalez	.15
89	Jon Lester, Jason Bay	.40
90	Justin Morneau	.40
91	Cody Ross	.15
92	Luis Castillo	.15
93	James Parr RC	.50
94	Adam Lind	.15
95	Andrew Miller	.15
96	Dexter Fowler RC	.75
97	Willie Harris	.15
98	Akinori Iwamura	.15
99	Juan Castro	.15
100	David Wright	1.00
101	Nick Hundley	.15
102	Garrett Atkins	.15
103	Kyle Kendrick	.15
104	Brandon Moss	.15
105	Francisco Liriano	.40
106	Marlon Byrd	.15
107	Pedro Feliz	.15
108	Alcides Escobar RC	1.00
109	Tom Gorzelanny	.15
110	Hideki Matsui	.50
111	Troy Percival	.15
112	Hideki Okajima	.15
113	Chris Young	.25
114	Chris Dickerson	.15
115	Kevin Youkilis	.40
115	George Sisler/SP	25.00
116	Omar Infante	.15
117	Ron Gardenhire	.15
118	Josh Johnson	.15
119	Craig Counsell	.15
120	Mark Teixeira	.40
121	Greg Golson RC	.50
122	Joe Mather	.15
123	Casey Blake	.15
124	Reed Johnson	.15
125	Roy Oswalt	.25

#	Player	Price
126	Orlando Hudson	.15
127	Miguel Cabrera, Carlos Quentin, Alex Rodriguez	.75
128	Johnny Cueto	.15
129	Angel Berroa	.15
130	Vladimir Guerrero	.50
131	Joe Torre	.25
132	Juan Pierre	.15
133	Brandon Jones	.15
134	Evan Longoria	1.00
135	Carlos Delgado	.40
136	Tim Hudson	.25
137	Angel Salome RC	.50
138	Ubaldo Jimenez	.15
139	Matt Stairs	.15
140	Brandon Webb	.40
141	Mark Teahen	.15
142	Brad Penny	.15
143	Matt Joyce	.15
144	Matt Tuiasosopo RC	.50
145	Alex Gordon	.40
146	Glen Perkins	.15
147	Ryan Howard, David Wright, Adrian Gonzalez	.75
148	Ty Wigginton	.15
149	Juan Uribe	.15
150	Kosuke Fukudome	.25
151	Carl Pavano	.15
152	Cody Ransom	.15
153	Lastings Milledge	.15
154	A.J. Pierzynski	.15
155	Roy Halladay	.40
156	Carlos Pena	.15
157	Brandon Webb, Dan Haren	.25
158	Ray Durham	.15
159	Matt Antonelli RC	1.00
160	Evan Longoria	1.00
161	Brendan Harris	.15
162	Mike Cameron	.15
163	Ross Gload	.15
164	Bob Geren	.15
165	Matt Kemp	.40
166	Jeff Baker	.15
167	Aaron Harang	.15
168	Mark DeRosa	.15
169	Juan Miranda RC	.50
170	C.C. Sabathia	.15
170	C.C. Sabathia/SP	20.00
171	Jeff Bailey	.15
172	Yadier Molina	.15
173	Manny Delcarmen	.15
174	James Shields	.25
175	Jeff Samardzija	.15
176	Josh Hamilton, Justin Morneau, Miguel Cabrera	.75
177	Eric Hinske	.15
178	Frank Catalanotto	.15
179	Rafael Furcal	.15
180	Cliff Lee	.25
181	Jerry Manuel	.15
182	Daniel Murphy	.15
183	Jason Michaels	.15
184	Bobby Parnell RC	.75
185	Randy Johnson	.50
186	Ryan Madson	.15
187	John Garland	.15
188	Josh Bard	.15
189	Jay Payton	.15
190	Chien-Ming Wang	.50
191	Shane Victorino	.15
192	Collin Balester	.15
193	Zack Greinke	.25
194	Jeremy Guthrie	.15
195	Tim Lincecum	.75
195	Christy Mathewson/SP	20.00
196	Jason Motte RC	.50
197	Ronnie Belliard	.15
198	Conor Jackson	.25
199	Ramon Castro	.15
200	Chase Utley	.75
200	Jimmie Foxx/SP	20.00
201	Jarrod Saltalamacchia, Josh Hamilton	.75
202	Gaby Sanchez RC	.50
203	Jair Jurrjens	.15
204	Andrew Sonnanstine	.15
205	Miguel Tejada	.15
205	Honus Wagner/SP	20.00
206	Johan Santana, Tim Lincecum, Jake Peavy	.50
207	Joe Blanton	.15
208	James McDonald RC	.50
209	Alfredo Amezaga	.15
210	Geovany Soto	.50
210	Roy Campanella/SP	20.00
211	Ryan Rowland-Smith	.15
212	Denard Span	.15
213	Jeremy Sowers	.15
214	Scott Ebert RC	.50
215	Ian Kinsler	.40
216	Joe Saunders	.15
217	Albert Pujols	1.00
218	Emmanuel Burriss	.15
219	Shin-Soo Choo	.15
220	Jay Bruce	.75
221	Cliff Lee, Roy Halladay, Daisuke Matsuzaka	.50
222	Mark Sweeney	.15
223	Dave Roberts	.15
224	Max Scherzer	.25
225	Aaron Cook	.15
226	Neal Cotts	.15
227	Freddy Sandoval RC	.50
228	Scott Rolen	.25
229	Cesar Izturis	.15
230	Justin Upton	.40
231	Xavier Nady	.15
232	Gabe Kapler	.15
233	Erik Bedard	.15

#	Player	Price
234	John Russell	.15
235	Chad Billingsley	.40
236	Kelly Johnson	.25
237	Aaron Cunningham RC	.50
238	Jorge Cantu	.15
239	Brandon League	.15
240	Ryan Braun	.75
240	Mel Ott/SP	20.00
241	David Newhan	.15
242	Ricky Nolasco	.25
243	Chase Headley	.25
244	Sean Rodriguez	.15
245	Pat Burrell	.25
246	B.J. Upton, Carl Crawford, Evan Longoria	.75
247	Yuniesky Betancourt	.15
248	Scott Lewis RC	.50
249	Jack Hannahan	.15
250	Josh Hamilton	.75
251	Greg Smith	.15
252	Brandon Wood	.15
253	Edgar Renteria	.15
254	Cito Gaston	.15
255	Joe Crede	.15
256	Reggie Abercrombie	.15
257	George Kottaras RC	.50
258	Casey Kotchman	.15
259	Tim Lincecum, Dan Haren, Johan Santana	.50
260	Manny Ramirez	.75
261	Jose Bautista	.15
262	Mike Gonzalez	.15
263	Elijah Dukes	.15
264	David Bush	.15
265	Carlos Zambrano	.25
266	Todd Wellemeyer	.15
267	Michael Bowden RC	.75
268	Chris Burke	.15
269	Hunter Pence	.40
270	Grady Sizemore	.50
270	Tris Speaker/SP	20.00
271	Cliff Lee	.25
272	Chan Ho Park	.15
273	Brian Roberts	.25
274	Alex Hinshaw	.15
275	Alex Rios	.40
276	Geovany Soto	.50
277	Asdrubal Cabrera	.15
278	Philadelphia Phillies/SP	.50
279	Ryan Church	.15
280	Joe Saunders	.15
281	Tug Hulett	.15
282	Chris Lambert RC	.50
283	John Baker	.15
284	Luis Ayala	.15
285	Justin Duchscherer	.15
286	Odalis Perez	.15
287	Greg Maddux	1.00
287	Walter Johnson/SP	20.00
288	Guillermo Quiroz	.15
289	Josh Banks	.15
290	Albert Pujols	2.00
290	Lou Gehrig/SP	25.00
291	Chris Coste	.15
292	Francisco Cervelli RC	.75
293	Brian Bixler	.15
294	Brandon Boggs	.15
295	Derrek Lee	.40
296	Reid Brignac	.15
297	Bud Black	.15
298	Jonathan Van Every	.15
299	Cole Hamels	.40
300	Ichiro Suzuki	1.00
301	Clint Barmes	.15
302	Brian Giles	.25
303	Zach Duke	.15
304	Jason Kubel	.15
305	Ivan Rodriguez	.25
305	Thurman Munson/SP	25.00
306	Javier Vazquez	.15
307	A.J. Burnett, Ervin Santana, Roy Halladay	.40
308	Chris Duncan	.15
309	Humberto Sanchez RC	.50
310	Johan Santana	.75
311	Kelly Shoppach	.15
312	Ryan Sweeney	.15
313	Jamey Carroll	.15
314	Matt Treanor	.15
315	Hiroki Kuroda	.15
316	Brian Stokes	.15
317	Jarrod Saltalamacchia	.25
318	Manny Acta	.15
319	Brian Fuentes	.15
320	Miguel Cabrera	.50
320	Johnny Mize/SP	20.00
321	Scott Kazmir, David Price	1.50
322	John Buck	.15
323	Vicente Padilla	.15
324	Mark Reynolds	.15
325	Dustin McGowan	.15
326	Manny Ramirez	.50
327	Phil Coke RC	.50
328	Doug Mientkiewicz	.15
329	Gil Meche	.15
330	Daisuke Matsuzaka	.75
331	Luke Scott	.15
332	Chone Figgins	.25
333	Jeremy Sowers, Aaron Laffey	.15
334	Blake DeWitt	.15
335	Chris Young	.15
336	Jordan Schafer RC	.75
337	Bobby Jenks	.15
338	Daniel Cabrera	.15
339	Jim Leyland	.15
340	Joe Mauer	.40
340	Wade Boggs/SP	25.00
341	Willy Taveras	.15
342	Gerald Laird	.15
343	Ian Snell	.15

#	Player	Price
344	J.R. Towles	.15
345	Stephen Drew	.25
346	Mike Cameron	.25
347	Jason Bartlett	.15
348	Tony Pena	.15
349	Justin Masterson	.25
350	Dustin Pedroia	.75
350	Ryne Sandberg/SP	25.00
351	Chris Snyder	.15
352	Gregor Blanco	.15
353	Derek Jeter	2.00
353	Cal Ripken Jr./SP	25.00
354	Mike Aviles	.25
355	John Smoltz	.40
355	Jim Palmer/SP	20.00
356	Ervin Santana	.25
357	Huston Street	.15
358	Chad Tracy	.15
359	Jason Varitek	.25
360	Jorge Posada	.40
361	Alex Rios, Vernon Wells	.25
362	Luke Montz RC	.50
363	Jhonny Peralta	.25
364	Kevin Millwood	.15
365	Mark Buehrle	.25
366	Alexi Casilla	.15
367	Corey Patterson	.15
368	Trevor Hoffman	.25
369	Matt Harrison	.15
370	Victor Martinez	.25
371	Jeff Francis	.15
372	Rickie Weeks	.15
373	Joe Martinez RC	1.00
374	Kevin Kouzmanoff	.15
375	Carlos Quentin	.40
376	Rajai Davis	.15
377	Trevor Crowe RC	.75
378	Mark Hendrickson	.15
379	Howie Kendrick	.15
380	Aramis Ramirez	.40
381	Shairon Martis RC	1.00
382	Wily Mo Pena	.15
383	Everth Cabrera RC	.50
384	Bob Melvin	.15
385	Mike Jacobs	.15
386	Jonathan Papelbon	.40
387	Adam Everett	.15
388	Humberto Quintero	.15
389	Garrett Olson	.15
390	Joey Votto	.50
391	Dan Haren	.40
392	Brandon Phillips	.25
393	Alex Cintron	.15
394	Barry Zito	.25
395	Maggiio Ordonez	.25
396	Alex Cora	.15
397	Carlos Ruiz	.15
398	Cameron Maybin	.25
399	Wandy Rodriguez	.25
400	Alfonso Soriano	.50
400	Frank Robinson/SP	20.00
401	Tony LaRussa	.25
402	Nick Blackburn	.15
403	Trevor Cahill RC	1.00
404	Matt Capps	.15
405	Todd Helton	.40
406	Mark Ellis	.15
407	Dave Trembley	.15
408	Ronny Paulino	.15
409	Jesse Chavez RC	.50
410	Lou Piniella	.15
411	Troy Tulowitzki	.25
412	Taylor Teagarden	.15
413	Ruben Gotay	.15
414	Cha Sueng Baek	.15
415	Josh Beckett	.50
416	Bob Gibson/SP	25.00
416	Josh Whitesell RC	.75
417	Jason Marquis	.15
418	Andy Pettitte	.40
419	Braden Looper	.15
420	Scott Baker	.25
421	B.J. Ryan	.15
422	Hank Blalock	.25
423	Melvin Mora	.15
424	Jorge Campillo	.15
425	Curtis Granderson	.50
426	Pablo Sandoval	.15
427	Brian Duensing RC	.50
428	Jamie Moyer	.15
429	Mike Hampton	.15
430	Francisco Rodriguez	.15
431	Ramon Hernandez	.15
432	Wladimir Balentien	.15
433	Coco Crisp	.15
434	Carlos Guillen, Miguel Cabrera	.25
435	Carlos Lee	.50
436	Ryan Theriot	.40
437	Austin Kearns	.15
438	Mark Loretta	.15
439	Ryan Spilborghs	.15
440	Fausto Carmona	.15
441	Andrew Bailey RC	1.00
442	Cliff Pennington	.15
443	Gavin Floyd	.25
444	Jody Gerut	.15
445	Joe Nathan	.15
446	Matt Holliday	.40
447	Freddy Sanchez	.15
448	Jeff Clement	.15
449	Mark Grudzielanek	.15
450	Hanley Ramirez	.75
451	Ryan Perry RC	1.00
452	Orlando Cabrera	.15
453	Javier Valentin	.15
454	Carlos Silva	.15
455	Adam Jones	.40
456	Jason Kendall	.15
457	John Maine	.15
458	Jeremy Bonderman	.15
459	Brian Bannister	.15

#	Player	Price
460	Nick Markakis	.50
461	Mike Scioscia	.15
462	James Loney	.15
463	Brian Wilson	.15
464	Bobby Crosby	.15
465	Troy Glaus	.25
466	Wilson Betemit	.15
467	Chris Volstad	.25
468	Derek Lowe	.25
469	Michael Cuddyer	.15
470	Lance Berkman	.40
471	Kerry Wood	.25
472	Bill Hall	.15
473	Jered Weaver	.25
474	Franklin Gutierrez	.15
475	Chipper Jones	1.00
475	Mike Schmidt/SP	25.00
476	Edinson Volquez	.40
477	Juan Marichal/SP	25.00
477	Josh Willingham	.15
478	Jose Molina	.15
479	Brad Nelson RC	.50
480	Prince Fielder	.75
481	Matt Joyce	.15
482	Jason Jaramillo RC	.50
483	John Lannan	.15
484	Chris Carpenter	.50
485	Aaron Rowand	.15
486	J.J. Putz	.15
487	Travis Hafner	.15
488	Ozzie Guillen	.25
489	Matt Guerrier	.15
490	Joba Chamberlain	.75
490	Nolan Ryan/SP	25.00
491	Paul Bako	.15
492	Andre Ethier	.40
493	Ramiro Pena RC	.75
494	Gary Matthews	.15
495	Eric Chavez	.15
495	Brooks Robinson/SP	20.00
496	Charlie Manuel	.15
497	Clint Hurdle	.15
498	Kyle Davies	.15
499	Edwin Moreno RC	.50
500	Ryan Howard	1.00
501	Jeff Suppan	.15
502	Yovani Gallardo	.40
503	Carlos Gonzalez	.25
504	Ben Sheets	.25
505	Scott Olsen	.15
506	Paul Konerko	.25
507	Melky Cabrera	.25
508	Kenji Johjima	.15
509	Lou Montanez	.15
510	Ryan Ludwick	.40
511	Chad Qualls	.15
512	Steve Pearce	.15
513	Bronson Arroyo	.15
514	Nick Hundley	.15
515	Gary Sheffield	.40
515	Reggie Jackson/SP	25.00
516	Brian Anderson	.15
517	Kevin Frandsen	.15
518	Chris Perez	.15
519	Dioner Navarro	.15
520	Adrian Gonzalez	.15
520	Tony Gwynn/SP	25.00
521	Dana Eveland	.15
522	Gio Gonzalez	.15
523	Brandon Morrow	.15
524	Andy LaRoche	.15
525	Jimmy Rollins	.75
526	Bruce Bochy	.15
527	Jason Isringhausen	.15
528	Nick Swisher	.15
529	Fernando Rodney	.40
530	Felix Hernandez	.15
531	Frank Francisco	.15
532	Garret Anderson	.15
533	Darin Erstad	.15
534	Skip Schumaker	.15
535	Ryan Doumit	.15
536	Khalil Greene	.15
537	Anthony Reyes	.15
538	Carlos Guillen	.15
539	Mike Hinckley	.15
540	Russell Martin	.25
541	Jason Bay	.50
542	Chris Ray	.15
543	Travis Ishikawa	.15
544	Pat Neshek	.15
545	Matt Garza	.25
546	Matt Cain	.25
547	Jack Cust	.15
548	John Danks	.15
549	Randy Winn	.15
550	Carlos Beltran	.50
551	Tim Redding	.15
552	Eric Byrnes	.15
553	Jeff Karstens	.15
554	Adam LaRoche	.25
555	Joe Girardi	.15
556	Brendan Ryan	.15
557	Jayson Werth	.25
558	Edgar Renteria	.15
559	Esteban German	.15
560	Adrian Beltre	.25
561	Ryan Freel	.15
562	Cecil Cooper	.15
563	Francisco Cordero	.15
564	Jesus Flores	.15
565	Jose Lopez	.15
566	Dontrelle Willis	.15
567	Willy Aybar	.15
568	Greg Reynolds	.15
569	Ted Lilly	.15
570	David DeJesus	.15
571	David Price	.25
572	Michael Bourn	.15
573	Adam Wainwright	.15
574	Nate Schierholtz	.15
575	Clayton Kershaw	.15

#	Player	Price
576	Don Wakamatsu	.15
577	Jose Contreras	.15
578	Adam Kennedy	.15
579	Rocco Baldelli	.15
580	Scott Kazmir	.25
581	David Purcey	.15
582	Yunel Escobar	.15
583	Brett Anderson RC	.75
584	Ron Washington	.15
585	Pedro Martinez	.15
586	Nelson Cruz	.25
587	Adam Dunn	.50
588	Jorge De La Rosa	.15
589	Ricky Romero RC	.75
590	Johnny Damon	.50
591	Elvis Andrus RC	1.00
592	Fred Lewis	.15
593	Kenshin Kawakami RC	1.50
594	Milton Bradley	.15
595	Vernon Wells	.25
595	Robin Yount/SP	25.00
596	Radhames Liz	.15
597	Randy Wolf	.15
598	Micah Owings	.15
599	Placido Polanco	.25
600	Jake Peavy	.15
600	Greg Maddux/SP	25.00
601	Jimmy Rollins, Ryan Howard	1.00
602	Carlos Gomez	.15
603	Jose Reyes	.75
604	Gregg Zaun	.15
605	Rick Ankiel	.40
606	Nick Johnson	.15
607	Jarrod Washburn	.15
608	Cristian Guzman	.15
609	Juan Rivera	.15
610	Michael Young	.15
610	Paul Molitor/SP	25.00
611	Jeremy Hermida	.15
612	Joel Pineiro	.15
613	Kendry Morales	.15
614	David Murphy	.15
615	Robinson Cano	.40
616	Koji Uehara RC	1.50
617	Shaun Marcum	.15
618	Brandon Backe	.15
619	Chris Carter	.15
620	Ryan Zimmerman	.40
621	Oliver Perez	.15
622	Kurt Suzuki	.15
623	Aaron Hill	.15
624	Ben Francisco	.15
625	Jim Thome	.50
626	Scott Hairston	.15
627	Billy Butler	.15
628	Justin Upton, Chris Young	.40
629	Lyle Overbay	.15
630	A.J. Burnett	.15
631	Colby Rasmus RC	1.00
632	Brett Myers	.15
633	David Patton RC	.15
634	Chris Davis	.40
635	Joakim Soria	.15
636	Armando Galarraga	.25
637	Donald Veal RC	.15
638	Eugenio Velez	.15
639	Corey Hart	.40
640	B.J. Upton	.40
641	Jesse Litsch	.15
642	Ken Macha	.15
643	David Freese RC	1.50
644	Alfredo Aceves RC	.15
645	Paul Maholm	.15
646	Chris Iannetta	.15
647	Manny Parra	.15
648	J.D. Drew	.25
649	Luke Hochevar	.15
650	Cole Hamels	.75
650	Steve Carlton/SP	20.00
651	Jake Westbrook	.15
652	Doug Davis	.15
653	Nick Evans	.15
654	Brian Schneider	.15
655	Bengie Molina	.15
656	Delmon Young	.15
657	Aaron Heilman	.15
658	Rick Porcello RC	2.00
659	Torii Hunter	.40
660	Jacoby Ellsbury	.75
660	Carl Yastrzemski/SP	25.00

Black

Black:	20-30X
Black RC's:	6-10X
Production 58 Sets	

Gold

Gold:	4-6X
Gold RC's:	2-3X
Production 2,009 Sets	

Platinum

Production One Set

Printing Plates

Production one set per color.

American Legends Cut Signatures

Production One Set

Career Best Autographs

		NM/M
	Some not priced due to scarcity	
DO	David Ortiz	65.00
AP	Albert Pujols	200.00
AR	Aramis Ramirez	25.00
CB	Chad Billingsley	25.00
CC	Carl Crawford	20.00
CJ	Conor Jackson	20.00
CK	Clayton Kershaw	40.00
DU	Dan Uggla	15.00
EL	Evan Longoria	75.00
FH	Felix Hernandez	30.00
HR	Hanley Ramirez	40.00
JH	Josh Hamilton	40.00
JL	Jon Lester	35.00
NM	Nick Markakis	40.00
RB	Ryan Braun	50.00
RG	Ryan Garko	15.00
RM	Russell Martin	15.00
SK	Scott Kazmir	20.00
AG	Armando Galarraga	12.00
AI	Akinori Iwamura	15.00
CG	Curtis Granderson	20.00
CW	C.J. Wilson	5.00
DM	Dallas McPherson	5.00
DMM	Dustin McGowan	5.00
GA	Garrett Atkins	8.00
GS	Greg Smith	5.00
LH	Luke Hochevar	8.00
RP	Ronny Paulino	8.00
SR	Sean Rodriguez	8.00
SV	Shane Victorino	20.00
YG	Yovani Gallardo	15.00
ZG	Zack Greinke	25.00
PN	Pat Neshek	15.00
EK	Eddie Kunz	8.00
MG	Mat Gamel	20.00
SP	Steve Pearce	8.00
TS	Travis Snider	15.00

Series 2

CV	Chris Volstad	10.00
AS	Andrew Sonnanstine	10.00
CD	Chris Dickerson	10.00
RC	Robinson Cano	15.00
FL	Fred Lewis	10.00
GS	Greg Smith	8.00
AK	Austin Kearns	8.00
CG	Carlos Gomez	12.00
PF	Prince Fielder	25.00
JB	Jeff Baker	8.00
JL	Jon Lester	30.00
CK	Clayton Kershaw	20.00
BD	Blake DeWitt	15.00
JCH	Joba Chamberlain	35.00
FC	Fausto Carmona	10.00
AI	Akinori Iwamura	12.00
JN	Jeff Niemann	8.00
JH	Josh Hamilton	40.00
EL	Evan Longoria	100.00
FH	Felix Hernandez	20.00
CF	Chone Figgins	40.00
DP	David Price	40.00
LB	Lance Berkman	20.00
JS	Jeff Samardzija	20.00
DW	David Wright	70.00
JD	Johnny Damon	35.00

Career Best Relics

		NM/M
	Common Relic	4.00
JR	Jose Reyes	10.00
JE	Jacoby Ellsbury	10.00
AER	Alex Rodriguez	15.00
RH	Ryan Howard	10.00
JM	Justin Morneau	6.00
RG	Ryan Garko	6.00
BM	Brian McCann	6.00
JD	Jermaine Dye	6.00
AG	Alex Gordon	8.00
VM	Victor Martinez	6.00
DW	David Wright	10.00
DO	David Ortiz	8.00
AP	Albert Pujols	15.00
JB	Jeremy Bonderman	4.00
IS	Ichiro Suzuki	15.00
JA	Josh Anderson	4.00
CGG	Cristian Guzman	4.00

JH	Jeremy Hermida	4.00
SK	Scott Kazmir	6.00
FS	Freddy Sanchez	4.00
DM	Daisuke Matsuzaka	10.00
JC	Johnny Cueto	6.00
PF	Prince Fielder	8.00
CG	Curtis Granderson	6.00
CJ	Conor Jackson	6.00
AR	Aramis Ramirez	6.00
IK	Ian Kinsler	8.00
HO	Hideki Okajima	6.00
JP	Jonathan Papelbon	8.00
RB	Ryan Braun	10.00
MA	Mike Aviles	6.00
CM	Cameron Maybin	6.00

Series 2

GA	Garret Anderson	4.00
RBR	Ryan Braun	10.00
JB	Jay Bruce	10.00
MC	Miguel Cabrera	8.00
JC	Jorge Cantu	4.00
JCU	Johnny Cueto	4.00
RD	Ray Durham	4.00
PF	Prince Fielder	8.00
RF	Rafael Furcal	4.00
MO	Magglio Ordonez	4.00
AR	Alex Rodriguez	15.00
RBA	Rocco Baldelli	4.00
JBE	Josh Beckett	6.00
AB	Angel Berroa	4.00
CB	Carlos Beltran	6.00
EC	Eric Chavez	4.00
OD	Octavio Dotel	4.00
AE	Andre Ethier	4.00
CG	Curtis Granderson	8.00
CH	Cole Hamels	10.00
RH	Ryan Howard	12.00
CJ	Conor Jackson	4.00
MK	Matt Kemp	6.00
VM	Victor Martinez	4.00
ARA	Aramis Ramirez	4.00
JD	J.D. Drew	4.00
RC	Robinson Cano	8.00

Career Best Relic Autographs

		NM/M
Common Relic Auto.:		25.00

Production 50 Sets

AR	Alex Rodriguez	175.00
DP	Dustin Pedroia	90.00
DW	David Wright	75.00
JH	Josh Hamilton	50.00
JR	Jose Reyes	80.00
NM	Nick Markakis	50.00
PF	Prince Fielder	40.00
RB	Ryan Braun	60.00
HR	Hanley Ramirez	30.00
AR	Aramis Ramirez	25.00
CC	Carl Crawford	25.00

Series 2

AK	Austin Kearns	10.00
BD	Blake DeWitt	20.00
JC	Joba Chamberlain	40.00
FC	Fausto Carmona	12.00
AI	Akinori Iwamura	15.00
JH	Josh Hamilton	40.00
JL	Jon Lester	35.00
CC	Carl Crawford	20.00
FH	Felix Hernandez	25.00

Career Best Jumbo Patches

Production 20 Sets
Series 2
Series 2 Production 10 Sets

In the Name Letter Relics

Production One Set

K-Mart

		NM/M

K-Mart Exclusive

RV1	Chin-Lung Hu	1.00
RV2	Steve Pearce	1.00
RV3	Luke Hochevar	1.00
RV4	Joey Votto	2.00
RV5	Clay Buchholz	1.50
RV6	Emilio Bonifacio	1.00
RV7	Daric Barton	1.00
RV8	Eugenio Velez	1.00
RV9	J.R. Towles	1.00
RV10	Wladimir Balentien	1.00
RV11	Ross Detwiler	1.00
RV12	Troy Patton	1.00
RV13	Brandon Jones	1.00
RV14	Bill Buckner	1.00
RV15	Ross Ohlendorf	1.00

Legends Chrome Target Cereal

		NM/M

Exclusive in Target Cereal
Cards are Gold Refractors

GR1	Ted Williams	15.00
GR2	Bob Gibson	10.00
GR3	Babe Ruth	15.00
GR4	Roy Campanella	10.00
GR5	Ty Cobb	10.00
GR6	Cy Young	10.00
GR7	Mickey Mantle	20.00
GR8	Walter Johnson	10.00
GR9	Roberto Clemente	15.00
GR10	Jimmie Foxx	10.00

Legends Chrome Wal-Mart Cereal

		NM/M
Common Player:		8.00

	Wal-Mart Cereal Exclusive	
PR1	Ted Williams	15.00
PR2	Jackie Robinson	10.00
PR3	Babe Ruth	15.00
PR4	Honus Wagner	10.00
PR5	Lou Gehrig	15.00
PR6	Nolan Ryan	15.00
PR7	Mickey Mantle	20.00
PR8	Thurman Munson	12.00
PR9	Cal Ripken Jr.	15.00
PR10	George Sisler	8.00

Legends Commemorative Patch

		NM/M

Common Card:
Inserted 1:343 Hobby

LPR1	Babe Ruth	50.00
LPR2	Babe Ruth	50.00
LPR3	Lou Gehrig	35.00
LPR4	Lou Gehrig	35.00
LPR5	Jimmie Foxx	25.00
LPR6	Mel Ott	20.00
LPR7	Ted Williams	25.00
LPR8	Ted Williams	25.00
LPR9	Jackie Robinson	25.00
LPR10	Roy Campanella	25.00
LPR11	Mickey Mantle	50.00
LPR12	Mickey Mantle	50.00
LPR13	Ted Williams	25.00
LPR14	Roy Campanella	25.00
LPR15	Ted Williams	25.00
LPR16	Mickey Mantle	50.00
LPR17	Duke Snider	20.00
LPR18	Whitey Ford	25.00
LPR19	Jackie Robinson	25.00
LPR20	Mickey Mantle	50.00
LPR21	Don Larsen	20.00
LPR22	Ted Williams	30.00
LPR23	Ernie Banks	20.00
LPR24	Roberto Clemente	30.00
LPR25	Roberto Clemente	30.00
LPR26	Roberto Clemente	30.00
LPR27	Ernie Banks	25.00
LPR28	Mickey Mantle	50.00
LPR29	Roberto Clemente	30.00
LPR30	Nolan Ryan	25.00
LPR31	Tom Seaver	25.00
LPR32	Roberto Clemente	30.00
LPR33	Thurman Munson	30.00
LPR34	Carl Yastrzemski	25.00
LPR35	Nolan Ryan	25.00
LPR36	Bob Gibson	20.00
LPR37	Carl Yastrzemski	25.00
LPR38	Nolan Ryan	25.00
LPR39	Tom Seaver	25.00
LPR40	Reggie Jackson	20.00
LPR41	Reggie Jackson	20.00
LPR42	Thurman Munson	30.00
LPR43	Cal Ripken Jr.	40.00
LPR44	Mike Schmidt	25.00
LPR45	Cal Ripken Jr.	40.00
LPR46	Nolan Ryan	25.00
LPR47	Cal Ripken Jr.	40.00
LPR48	Nolan Ryan	25.00
LPR49	Cal Ripken Jr.	40.00
LPR50	Cal Ripken Jr.	40.00

Legends of the Game

		NM/M
Common Player:		1.00

Inserted 1:6
Gold: 2-4X
Production 99 Sets
Platinum: 8-12X
Production 25 Sets

1	Cy Young	2.00
2	Honus Wagner	2.00
3	Christy Mathewson	2.00
4	Ty Cobb	2.00
5	Walter Johnson	2.00
6	Tris Speaker	1.00
7	Babe Ruth	4.00
8	George Sisler	1.00
9	Rogers Hornsby	1.00
10	Jimmie Foxx	2.00
11	Lou Gehrig	3.00
12	Mel Ott	1.50
13	Jackie Robinson	2.00
14	Johnny Mize	1.00
15	Pee Wee Reese	1.00
16	Roy Campanella	2.00
17	Ted Williams	3.00
18	Roger Maris	2.00
19	Bob Gibson	1.50
20	Mickey Mantle	5.00
21	Roberto Clemente	3.00
22	Thurman Munson	3.00

23	Carl Yastrzemski	2.00
24	Nolan Ryan	2.00
25	Cal Ripken Jr.	5.00

Series 2

JM	Juan Marichal	1.50
SC	Steve Carlton	1.00
TG	Tony Gwynn	2.00
RJ	Reggie Jackson	2.00
BR	Brooks Robinson	2.00
FR	Frank Robinson	2.00
TG	Tom Glavine	1.50
MS	Mike Schmidt	2.50
GM	Greg Maddux	3.00
WB	Wade Boggs	1.50
JS	John Smoltz	1.00
RS	Ryne Sandberg	3.00
JP	Jim Palmer	2.00
RY	Robin Yount	2.50
PM	Paul Molitor	1.50
AR	Alex Rodriguez	4.00
MR	Mariano Rivera	5.00
AP	Albert Pujols	5.00
TH	Trevor Hoffman	1.00
VG	Vladimir Guerrero	1.50
RJ	Randy Johnson	1.50
MRA	Manny Ramirez	2.00
IS	Ichiro Suzuki	3.00

Legends of the Game Cut Signatures

Production One Set
Series 2

Legends of the Game Framed Stamps

		NM/M
Common Player:		20.00

Production 95 Sets

BR1-2	Babe Ruth	50.00
CM	Christy Mathewson	30.00
CY	Cy Young	30.00
GS	George Sisler	20.00
HW	Honus Wagner	40.00
JF	Jimmie Foxx	25.00
JR1-3	Jackie Robinson	35.00
LG1-3	Lou Gehrig	40.00
MM	Mickey Mantle	75.00
RC	Roberto Clemente	75.00
RH	Rogers Hornsby	25.00
TC	Ty Cobb	30.00
TS	Tris Speaker	35.00
WJ	Walter Johnson	30.00

Series 2
Series 2 Production 90

BR3-9	Babe Ruth	50.00
JR4-7	Jackie Robinson	25.00
MM2	Mickey Mantle	60.00

Legends of the Game Nickname Letter Patch

		NM/M
Common Card:		15.00

Each Letter #'d to 50
Total production listed.

BG	Bob Gibson/250	20.00
BO	Barack Obama/800	35.00
BR	Babe Ruth/350	40.00
CM	Christy Mathewson/300	20.00
CY	Carl Yastrzemski/150	20.00
CR	Cal Ripken Jr./350	40.00
CY	Cy Young/350	20.00
GS	George Sisler/400	15.00
HW	Honus Wagner/400	20.00
JB	Joseph Biden/650	15.00
JF	Jimmie Foxx/400	20.00
JM	Johnny Mize/450	15.00
JR	Jackie Robinson/300	25.00
LG	Lou Gehrig/450	20.00
MO	Michelle Obama/450	20.00
MM	Mickey Mantle/350	35.00
MM2	Mickey Mantle/650	35.00
MO	Mel Ott/300	20.00
NR	Nolan Ryan/700	40.00
PWR	Pee Wee Reese/300	20.00
RC	Roy Campanella/250	20.00
RC	Roberto Clemente/300	30.00
RH	Rogers Hornsby/250	20.00
RM	Roger Maris/700	20.00
TC	Ty Cobb/350	20.00
TM	Thurman Munson/350	25.00
TS	Tris Speaker/450	15.00
TW	Ted Williams/650	20.00

Legends of the Game Relics

No Pricing
Production 20 Sets

Mickey Mantle 1958 Reprint Relic

		NM/M

Production 58

MMR58	Mickey Mantle/ Jsy/58	150.00

Ring of Honor

		NM/M
Common Player:		.50

Inserted 1:6 hobby

1	David Justice	.50
2	Whitey Ford	.75
3	Orlando Cepeda	.75
4	Cole Hamels	.50
5	Darryl Strawberry	.50
6	Johnny Bench	1.00
7	David Ortiz	1.00
8	Derek Jeter	3.00
9	Dwight Gooden	.50
10	Brooks Robinson	.75
11	Ivan Rodriguez	.50
12	David Eckstein	.50
13	Derek Jeter	3.00
14	Paul Molitor	.75
15	Don Zimmer	.50
16	Jermaine Dye	.50
17	Gary Sheffield	.75
18	Bob Gibson	1.00
19	Pedro Martinez	.75
20	Manny Ramirez	1.00
21	Johnny Podres	.50
22	Johnny Podres	.50
23	Mariano Rivera	.75
24	Curt Schilling	.75
25	Lou Piniella	.50
26	Roberto Clemente	2.00
27	Kevin Mitchell	.50
28	Frank Robinson	1.00
29	Francisco Rodriguez	.50
30	Troy Glaus	.50
31	Tony LaRussa	.50
32	Mike Schmidt	1.00
33	Brad Lidge	.50
34	Randy Johnson	.75
35	Duke Snider	1.00
36	Rollie Fingers	.50
37	Luis Gonzalez	.50
38	Josh Beckett	.75
39	Gary Carter	.50
40	Bob Gibson	.75
41	Andy Pettitte	.75
42	Reggie Jackson	.75
43	Jim Leyland	.75
44	Mariano Rivera	.75
45	Albert Pujols	3.00
46	Don Larsen	.75
47	Roger Clemens	1.50
48	Tom Glavine	.50
49	Ryan Howard	1.00
50	Reggie Jackson	.75

Series 2

51	Carlos Ruiz	.50
52	Tyler Johnson	.50
53	Jason Varitek	.50
54	Darryl Strawberry	.50
55	Dusty Baker	.50
56	Dustin Pedroia	1.50
57	Jayson Werth	.75
58	Garret Anderson	.50
59	Dontrelle Willis	.50
60	David Justice	.50
61	Luis Aparicio	.50
62	John Smoltz	.50
63	Miguel Cabrera	1.00
64	Yadier Molina	.50
65	Jacoby Ellsbury	1.50
66	Mark Buehrle	.50
67	Johnny Damon	1.00
68	Brad Penny	.50
69	Joe Torre	.75
70	Chris Carpenter	.75
71	Bobby Cox	.50
72	Jonathan Papelbon	.75
73	Joe Girardi	.50
74	Aaron Rowand	.50

Ring of Honor Autographs

No Pricing
Inserted 1:4,000 Hobby
Series 2

TJ	Tyler Johnson	15.00
DB	Dusty Baker	25.00
JW	Jayson Werth	60.00
DJ	David Justice	25.00

Silk

		NM/M
Common Player:		10.00

Production 50 Sets

101-200 In Series 2

1	David Wright	40.00
2	Nate McLouth	20.00
3	Brandon Jones	10.00
4	Mike Mussina	20.00
5	Kevin Youkilis	20.00
6	Kyle Lohse	10.00
7	Rich Aurilia	10.00
8	Rich Harden	10.00
9	Chase Headley	15.00
10	Vladimir Guerrero	20.00
11	Denard Span	15.00
12	Andrew Miller	15.00
13	Justin Upton	20.00
14	Aaron Cook	10.00
15	Travis Snider	25.00
16	Scott Rolen	15.00
17	Chad Billingsley	15.00
18	Brandon Wood	10.00
19	Brad Lidge	10.00
20	Dexter Fowler	15.00
21	Ian Kinsler	20.00
22	Joe Crede	10.00
23	Jay Bruce	30.00
24	Frank Thomas	30.00
25	Roy Halladay	20.00
26	Justin Duchscherer	10.00
27	Carl Crawford	20.00
28	Jeff Francoeur	10.00
29	Mike Napoli	10.00
30	Ryan Braun	25.00
31	Yuniesky Betancourt	10.00
32	James Shields	10.00
33	Hunter Pence	15.00
34	Ian Stewart	10.00
35	David Price	30.00
36	Hideki Okajima	10.00
37	Brad Penny	10.00
38	Ivan Rodriguez	15.00
39	Chris Duncan	10.00
40	Johan Santana	20.00
41	Joe Saunders	10.00
42	Mark Reynolds	10.00
43	Tim Lincecum	50.00
44	Miguel Tejada	10.00
45	Geovany Soto	30.00
46	Mark DeRosa	10.00
47	Yadier Molina	30.00
48	Collin Balester	10.00
49	Zack Greinke	15.00
50	Manny Ramirez	25.00
51	Brian Giles	10.00
52	J.J. Hardy	15.00
53	Jarrod Saltalamacchia	10.00
54	Aubrey Huff	15.00
55	Carlos Zambrano	10.00
56	Ken Griffey Jr.	30.00
57	Daric Barton	10.00
58	Randy Johnson	20.00
59	John Garland	10.00
60	Daisuke Matsuzaka	30.00
61	Miguel Cabrera	20.00
62	Orlando Hudson	15.00
63	Johnny Cueto	15.00
64	Omar Vizquel	10.00
65	Derrek Lee	20.00
66	Brad Ziegler	15.00
67	Shane Victorino	15.00
68	Roy Oswalt	15.00
69	Cliff Lee	15.00
70	Ichiro Suzuki	35.00
71	Casey Blake	10.00
72	Kelly Shoppach	25.00
73	Ryan Sweeney	10.00
74	Carlos Pena	15.00
75	Carlos Delgado	15.00
76	Tim Hudson	15.00
77	Brandon Webb	10.00
78	Adam Lind	10.00
79	Akinori Iwamura	10.00
80	Mariano Rivera	15.00
81	Pat Burrell	10.00
82	Mark Teixeira	15.00
83	Matt Kemp	25.00
84	Jeff Samardzija	20.00
85	Kosuke Fukudome	10.00
86	Aaron Harang	10.00
87	Conor Jackson	10.00
88	Andrew Sonnanstine	10.00
89	Joe Blanton	10.00
90	C.C. Sabathia	15.00
91	Greg Maddux	40.00
92	Gabe Kapler	10.00
93	Garrett Atkins	10.00
94	Hideki Matsui	25.00
95	Chien-Ming Wang	15.00
96	Josh Johnson	10.00
97	Dustin McGowan	15.00
98	Gil Meche	10.00
99	Justin Morneau	10.00
100	Evan Longoria	35.00
101	Joe Mauer	20.00
102	Derek Jeter	100.00
103	Jorge Posada	20.00
104	Victor Martinez	10.00
105	Carlos Quentin	15.00
106	Jonathan Papelbon	20.00
107	Brandon Phillips	15.00
108	Alfonso Soriano	15.00
109	Carlos Lee	10.00
110	Joe Nathan	10.00
111	Jeremy Bonderman	10.00
112	Nick Markakis	20.00
113	Troy Glaus	15.00
114	Travis Hafner	15.00
115	Joba Chamberlain	25.00
116	Scott Olsen	10.00
117	Kenji Johjima	10.00

118	Carlos Guillen	15.00
119	Matt Cain	15.00
120	Clayton Kershaw	20.00
121	Yunel Escobar	10.00
122	Michael Young	15.00
123	Stephen Drew	15.00
124	Justin Masterson	20.00
125	Mike Aviles	15.00
126	Josh Beckett	20.00
127	Fausto Carmona	15.00
128	Gavin Floyd	10.00
129	Hanley Ramirez	25.00
130	Adam Jones	20.00
131	Jered Weaver	15.00
132	Edinson Volquez	15.00
133	Prince Fielder	20.00
134	Adrian Gonzalez	15.00
135	Jimmy Rollins	20.00
136	Felix Hernandez	20.00
137	Ryan Doumit	15.00
138	Russell Martin	15.00
139	Carlos Beltran	15.00
140	Nelson Cruz	15.00
141	Jeremy Hermida	10.00
142	Robinson Cano	20.00
143	Armando Galarraga	15.00
144	Luke Hochevar	15.00
145	Delmon Young	15.00
146	Chris Young	15.00
147	Dustin Pedroia	30.00
148	Ervin Santana	15.00
149	Jhonny Peralta	10.00
150	Alexi Casilla	10.00
151	Kevin Kouzmanoff	10.00
152	Aramis Ramirez	15.00
153	Joey Votto	20.00
154	Barry Zito	15.00
155	Cameron Maybin	15.00
156	Todd Helton	15.00
157	Curtis Granderson	25.00
158	Jamie Moyer	10.00
159	Wladimir Balentien	10.00
160	John Maine	10.00
161	Chris Carpenter	20.00
162	Andre Ethier	15.00
163	Yovani Gallardo	20.00
164	Nick Hundley	10.00
165	Brandon Morrow	10.00
166	Jason Bay	20.00
167	Randy Winn	10.00
168	Willy Aybar	10.00
169	David DeJesus	10.00
170	Scott Kazmir	15.00
171	Johnny Damon	20.00
172	Carlos Gomez	10.00
173	Jose Reyes	25.00
174	Rick Ankiel	15.00
175	Ryan Zimmerman	20.00
176	Jim Thome	15.00
177	Chris Davis	15.00
178	Paul Maholm	10.00
179	Manny Parra	10.00
180	Rickie Weeks	10.00
181	Dan Haren	15.00
182	Magglio Ordonez	10.00
183	Troy Tulowitzki	20.00
184	Freddy Sanchez	15.00
185	James Loney	15.00
186	Michael Cuddyer	10.00
187	Lance Berkman	15.00
188	Chipper Jones	25.00
189	Eric Chavez	15.00
190	Ryan Howard	30.00
191	Gary Sheffield	15.00
192	Eric Byrnes	10.00
193	Jayson Werth	20.00
194	Adrian Beltre	10.00
195	Fred Lewis	10.00
196	Vernon Wells	15.00
197	Jake Peavy	20.00
198	Joakim Soria	10.00
199	B.J. Upton	15.00
200	J.D. Drew	10.00

Target

		NM/M

Target Exclusive

1	Ted Williams	6.00
2	Bob Gibson	3.00
3	Babe Ruth	8.00
4	Honus Wagner	2.00
5	Lou Gehrig	5.00
6	Nolan Ryan	6.00
7	Mickey Mantle	8.00
8	Thurman Munson	4.00
9	Cal Ripken Jr.	8.00
10	George Sisler	1.50

Topps Town

		NM/M
	Common Player:	.25
	Gold:	1-2X
1	Alex Rodriguez	1.00
2	Roy Halladay	.25
3	Grady Sizemore	.50
4	Brandon Webb	.40
5	Evan Longoria	1.00
6	Johan Santana	.50
7	Hanley Ramirez	.50
8	Alex Gordon	.50
9	Ryan Howard	.75
10	Jake Peavy	.40
11	Nick Markakis	.25
12	Justin Morneau	.40
13	Albert Pujols	1.00
14	C.C. Sabathia	.50
15	Alfonso Soriano	.50
16	Ichiro Suzuki	.75
17	Francisco Rodriguez	.25
18	Miguel Cabrera	.25
19	Carlos Quentin	.25
20	Lance Berkman	.40
21	Chipper Jones	.50
22	Tim Lincecum	.50
23	Josh Hamilton	.50
24	Jay Bruce	.75
25	Daisuke Matsuzaka	.50

Series 2

26	Joe Mauer	.25
27	David Ortiz	.50
28	Jimmy Rollins	.50
29	Derek Jeter	1.00
30	Ryan Braun	.75
31	Vladimir Guerrero	.50
32	David Wright	.75
33	Carlos Lee	.25
34	Dustin Pedroia	.50
35	Prince Fielder	.50
36	Ian Kinsler	.50
37	Justin Upton	.25
38	Kosuke Fukudome	.25
39	Carlos Zambrano	.25
40	Nate McLouth	.25
41	Manny Ramirez	.50
42	Kevin Youkilis	.50
43	Curtis Granderson	.50
44	Todd Helton	.25
45	Alex Rios	.25
46	Roy Oswalt	.25
47	Carlos Beltran	.25
48	Mark Teixeira	.25
49	Daisuke Matsuzaka	.25
50	Chase Utley	.50

Turkey Red

		NM/M
	Complete Set (50):	40.00
	Common Player:	.50
	Inserted 1:4 Hobby	
1	Babe Ruth	5.00
2	Evan Longoria	3.00
3	Jimmie Foxx	1.50
4	Alex Rios	.50
5	Nick Markakis	1.00
6	Ian Kinsler	1.00
7	Andre Ethier	.50
8	Ryan Ludwick	.75
9	Tim Lincecum	1.50
10	Jackie Robinson	2.00
11	Bengie Molina	.50
12	Jermaine Dye	.50
13	Brian Giles	.50
14	Chase Utley	1.00
15	David Ortiz	1.00
16	Joe Mauer	.75
17	Conor Jackson	.50
18	Jose Lopez	.50
19	Brian McCann	1.00
20	George Sisler	1.00
21	Garret Anderson	.50
22	Cliff Lee	.50
23	Garrett Atkins	.50
24	Curtis Granderson	.75
25	Alex Rodriguez	2.50
26	Cristian Guzman	.50
27	Aubrey Huff	.50
28	Delmon Young	.75
29	Carlos Quentin	.75
30	Christy Mathewson	1.00
31	Justin Upton	1.00
32	Shane Victorino	1.00
33	Joey Votto	1.00
34	Kelly Johnson	.50
35	David Wright	2.00
36	Jacoby Ellsbury	.50
37	Kevin Kouzmanoff	.50
38	Hunter Pence	.75
39	Corey Hart	.75
40	Kosuke Fukudome	1.00
41	Cole Hamels	1.00
42	Geovany Soto	1.50
43	Torii Hunter	.50
44	Ervin Santana	.50
45	Miguel Cabrera	1.00
46	Josh Johnson	.50
47	Carlos Gomez	.50
48	Nate McLouth	.50
49	Ben Sheets	.50
50	Tris Speaker	1.00

Series 2

51	Josh Hamilton	1.50
52	Rich Harden	.50
53	Francisco Rodriguez	.50
54	Alex Gordon	.50
55	Manny Ramirez	.50
56	Carlos Zambrano	.50
57	Brandon Webb	.75
58	Alfonso Soriano	.50
59	Mel Ott	1.00
60	Carlos Lee	.75
61	Lou Gehrig	2.00
62	Adam Jones	.75
63	Josh Beckett	.75
64	Prince Fielder	1.00
65	Jimmy Rollins	.75
66	Justin Morneau	.75
67	Dan Uggla	.50
68	Lance Berkman	.75
69	Chipper Jones	1.50
70	Jon Lester	.75
71	Albert Pujols	3.00
72	Ryan Braun	1.50
73	Grady Sizemore	1.00
74	Carlos Beltran	.75
75	Hanley Ramirez	1.00
76	Jay Bruce	1.00
77	Derek Jeter	3.00
78	Matt Cain	.50
79	Roy Campanella	1.00
80	Rogers Hornsby	1.00
81	Ryan Zimmerman	1.00
82	Dustin Pedroia	1.50
83	B.J. Upton	.75
84	Jose Reyes	1.00
85	Johnny Mize	1.00
86	Magglio Ordonez	.50
87	Ty Cobb	2.00
88	Michael Young	.50
89	Todd Helton	1.00
90	Walter Johnson	1.00
91	Matt Kemp	.75
92	Adrian Gonzalez	.75
93	Pee Wee Reese	1.00
94	Ryan Doumit	.50
95	Ryan Howard	2.00
96	Ichiro Suzuki	2.00
97	Cy Young	1.00
98	Mark Teixeira	.75
99	Vladimir Guerrero	1.00
100	Honus Wagner	1.50

Wal-Mart

		NM/M
	Wal-Mart Exclusive	
1	Ted Williams	6.00
2	Bob Gibson	2.00
3	Babe Ruth	8.00
4	Roy Campanella	2.50
5	Ty Cobb	3.00
6	Cy Young	2.00
7	Mickey Mantle	10.00
8	Walter Johnson	2.50
9	Roberto Clemente	5.00
10	Jimmie Foxx	3.00

World Baseball Classic Rising Star Redempt.

		NM/M
	Common Redemption:	8.00
	Cards are Chrome	

World Champion Relics

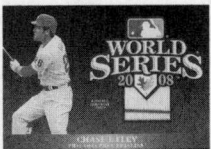

		NM/M
	Common Player:	25.00
	Production 100 Sets	
CH	Cole Hamels	50.00
CU	Chase Utley	40.00
JR	Jimmy Rollins	50.00
PB	Pat Burrell	25.00
RH	Ryan Howard	50.00

World Champion Autographs

		NM/M
	Inserted 1:20,000 Hobby	
CR	Carlos Ruiz	60.00
JW	Jayson Werth	75.00
SV	Shane Victorino	75.00

World Champion Relic Autographs

		NM/M
	Inserted 1:11,400 Hobby	
JR	Jimmy Rollins/50	120.00
RH	Ryan Howard/50	200.00

2009 Topps Allen & Ginter

		NM/M
	Complete Set (350):	75.00
	Common Player:	.25
	Common SP (301-350):	2.00
	Inserted 1:2	
	Mini Exclusives (351-400): No Pricing	
	Rip card exclusive.	
	Pack (8):	5.00
	Box (24):	100.00
1	Jay Bruce	.75
2	Zack Greinke	.50
3	Manny Parra	.25
4	Jorge Posada	.50
5	Luke Hochevar	.25
6	Adam Eaton	.25
7	John Smoltz	.50
8	Matt Cain	.25
9	Ryan Theriot	.40
10	Chone Figgins	.25
11	Jacoby Ellsbury	.75
12	Jermaine Dye	.40
13	Travis Hafner	.25
14	Troy Tulowitzki	.40
15	Alfred Nobel	.25
16	Josh Johnson	.40
17	Manny Ramirez	.50
18	Clyde Parris	.25
19	Mike Pelfrey	.25
20	Adam Jones	.50
21	Robinson Cano	.50
22	Mariano Rivera	.25
23	Kristin Armstrong	.25
24	Steve Wiebe	.25
25	Evan Longoria	1.50
26	Charles Goodyear	.25
27	Chien-Ming Wang	.25
28	Ervin Santana	.40
29	Jonathan Papelbon	.40
30	Ryan Howard	1.00
31	Nick Markakis	.25
32	Jeremy Bonderman	.25
33	Florence Nightingale	.25
34	Ryan Dempster	.25
35	Geovany Soto	.50
36	Joba Chamberlain	.50
37	Andre Ethier	.40
38	Troy Glaus	.25
39	Hanley Ramirez	.75
40	Jeremy Hermida	.25
41	Victor Martinez	.25
42	Mark Buehrle	.40
43	Koji Uehara RC	1.50
44	Freddy Sanchez	.25
45	Derrek Lee	.40
46	Brian Roberts	.40
47	J.J. Hardy	.40
48	Brigham Young	.25
49	Ubaldo Jimenez	.25
50	Pat Neshek	.25
51	Ryan Perry RC	1.50
52	Aaron Hill	.25
53	Clayton Kershaw	.75
54	Carlos Guillen	.25
55	Alex Rios	.40
56	Daniel Murphy RC	1.50
57	Frank Evans	.25
58	Brad Hawpe	.40
59	Mark Reynolds	.40
60	Matt Holliday	.50
61	Burke Kenny	.25
62	Dan Uggla	.40
63	Andrew Miller	.25
64	Jordan Zimmerman RC	1.50
65	Dexter Fowler RC	1.50
66	Alex Rodriguez	.75
67	Ian Kinsler	.75
68	Jamie Moyer	.25
69	James Loney	.40
70	Rick Ankiel	.40
71	Albert Pujols	2.00
72	Carlos Lee	.50
73	Vernon Wells	.40
74	Matt Tuiasosopo RC	.75
75	David Wright	1.00
76	Brandon Phillips	.40
77	Francisco Liriano	.40
78	Eric Byrnes	.25
79	Electron	.25
80	Joe Martinez RC	1.00
81	Willie Williams	.25
82	Justin Verlander	.50
83	Ludwig van Beethoven	.50
84	Justin Upton	.50
85	Jason Jaramillo RC	.75
86	Michael Cuddyer	.25
87	Aaron Cook	.25
88	Brad Penny	.25
89	Elvis Andrus RC	1.50
90	Bobby Crosby	.25
91	Alex Gordon	.25
92	Joe Mauer	.50
93	David DeJesus	.25
94	Paul Maholm	.25
95	David Patton RC	1.00
96	Geronimo	.25
97	Art Pennington	.25
98	Josh Whitesell RC	1.00
99	Chris Duncan	.25
100	Ichiro Suzuki	1.50
101	Andrew Bailey RC	1.00
102	Edinson Volquez	.40
103	Aaron Harang	.25
104	Jeff Francoeur	.25
105	Kurt Suzuki	.25
106	Mike Jacobs	.25
107	Bryan Berg	.25
108	Alamo	.25
109	Samuel Morse	.25
110	Kevin Youkilis	.25
111	Jason Giambi	.25
112	Millito Navarro	.25
113	Rafael Furcal	.40
114	Hideki Matsui	.25
115	Ryan Doumit	.25
116	Charles Darwin	.25
117	Blake DeWitt	.25
118	Scott Olsen	.25
119	Scott Lewis RC	.25
120	Edwin Moreno RC	.75
121	Ryan Church	.25
122	Dontrelle Willis	.25
123	Barry Zito	.25
124	Donald Veal RC	1.00
125	Randy Johnson	.75
126	Trevor Crowe RC	.25
127	J.D. Drew	.25
128	Red Moore	.25
129	Brian Giles	.25
130	Johnny Damon	.50
131	Rickie Weeks	.25
132	Anna Tunnicliffe	.25
133	Roy Halladay	.25
134	Jered Weaver	.25
135	Jeff Suppan	.25
136	Mickey Mantle	3.00
137	Mark Teixeira	.75
138	Garrett Atkins	.25
139	Daisuke Matsuzaka	.75
140	Loren Opstedahl	.25
141	Carlos Zambrano	.50
142	LaShawn Merritt	.25
143	Robbie Maddison	.25
144	Joakim Soria	.25
145	Todd Wellemeyer	.25
146	Rich Harden	.25
147	Coco Crisp	.25
148	Brad Lidge	.25
149	Chipper Jones	1.00
150	Prince Fielder	.75
151	Cole Hamels	.50
152	Phil Coke RC	1.00
153	C.C. Sabathia	.75
154	Corey Hart	.25
155	Yadier Molina	.25
156	Jayson Werth	.50
157	Jason Motte RC	.75
158	Sigmund Freud	.25
159	Denard Span	.40
160	Max Scherzer	.40
161	Justin Morneau	.50
162	Shane Victorino	.50
163	Matt Garza	.40
164	Erik Bedard	.40
165	Chase Utley	1.00
166	Gil Meche	.25
167	Jim Thome	.50
168	Adrian Gonzalez	.50
169	Kazuo Matsui	.25
170	Lance Berkman	.25
171	Brett Anderson RC	1.50
172	Jarrod Saltalamacchia	.25
173	Francisco Rodriguez	.25
174	John Lannan	.25
175	Alfonso Soriano	.50
176	Ramiro Pena RC	1.00
177	David Freese RC	2.00
178	Adam LaRoche	.25
179	Trevor Hoffman	.40
180	Russell Martin	.25
181	Aaron Rowand	.25
182	Jose Reyes	.75
183	Pedro Feliz	.25
184	Chris Young	.25
185	Dustin Pedroia	.75
186	Adrian Beltre	.25
187	Brett Myers	.25
188	Chris Davis	.25
189	Casey Kotchman	.25
190	B.J. Upton	.40
191	Hiroki Kuroda	.25
192	Ryan Zimmerman	.40
193	Khalil Greene	.25
194	Brandon Morrow	.25
195	Kevin Kouzmanoff	.25
196	Joey Votto	.40
197	Jhonny Peralta	.40
198	Raul Ibanez	.40
199	James McDonald RC	1.00
200	Carlos Quentin	.40
201	Travis Snider RC	.75
202	Conor Jackson	.25
203	Scott Kazmir	.40
204	Casey Blake	.25
205	Ryan Braun	1.00
206	Miguel Tejada	.40
207	Jack Cust	.25
208	Michael Young	.25
209	St. Patrick's Cathedral	.25
210	Johan Santana	.75
211	Kevin Millwood	.25
212	Mariel Zagunis	.25
213	Stephanie Brown Trafton	.25
214	Adam Dunn	.25
215	Jed Lowrie	.25
216	Derek Lowe	.25
217	Jorge Cantu	.25
218	Bobby Parnell RC	.25
219	Nate McLouth	.25
220	Suez Canal	.25
221	Brandon Webb	.25
222	Akinori Iwamura	.25
223	Scott Rolen	.40
224	Tim Lincecum	1.00
225	David Price RC	.75
226	Ricky Romero RC	.75
227	Nelson Cruz	.50
228	Will Simpson, Archie Bunker	.25
229	Mark Ellis	.25
230	Torii Hunter	.40
231	David Murphy	.25
232	Everth Cabrera RC	.75
233	John Lackey	.40
234	Wyatt Earp	.25
235	Roy Oswalt	.50
236	Edgar Renteria	.25
237	Walton Glenn Eller	.25
238	Vincent Van Gogh	.25
239	Chris Carpenter	.50
240	Hank Blalock	.25
241	Trevor Cahill RC	2.00
242	Mark Teahen	.25
243	Alexander Cartwright	.25
244	Carlos Beltran	.50
245	Todd Helton	.25
246	General Custer	.25
247	Jeff Clement	.25
248	Colby Rasmus RC	2.00
249	John Higby	.25
250	Grady Sizemore	.50
251	Carl Crawford	.40
252	Lastings Milledge	.25
253	Miguel Cabrera	.75
254	John Maine	.25
255	Aramis Ramirez	.25
256	Jose Lopez	.25
257	Heinrich Hertz	.25
258	Felix Hernandez	.50
259	Napoleon Bonaparte	.25
260	Louis Braille	.25
261	John Danks	.25
262	Magglio Ordonez	.40
263	Brian Duensing RC	1.00
264	Carlos Pena	.40
265	Paul Konerko	.25
266	Johnny Cueto	.25
267	Melvin Mora	.25
268	Andy Pettitte	.40
269	Brian McCann	.50
270	Josh Outman RC	.75
271	Jair Jurrjens	.40
272	Brad Nelson RC	.75
273	Jason Bay	.40
274	Josh Hamilton	.75
275	Vladimir Guerrero	.25
276	Michael Phelps	1.50
277	Kerry Wood	.40
278	Herb Simpson	.25
279	Jon Lester	.75
280	Shin-Soo Choo	.40
281	Jake Peavy	.50
282	Eric Chavez	.25
283	Mike Aviles	.25
284	Kenshin Kawakami RC	2.00
285	George Kottaras RC	.25
286	Matt Kemp	.50
287	James Shields	.25
288	Joe Saunders	.25
289	Milky Way	.25
290	Cat Osterman	.25
291	Josh Beckett	.50
292	Oliver Perez	.25
293	Ian Snell	.25
294	Tim Hudson	.25
295	Brett Gardner	.25
296	Bobby Abreu	.40
297	Kolan McConiughey	.25
298	Dan Haren	.40
299	Shairon Martis RC	1.00
300	David Ortiz	.75
301	Jonathan Sanchez/SP	2.00
302	Stephen Drew/SP	2.00
303	Rocco Baldelli/SP	2.00
304	Yunel Escobar/SP	2.00
305	Javier Vazquez/SP	2.00
306	Cliff Lee/SP	2.00
307	Hunter Pence/SP	2.00
308	Fausto Carmona/SP	2.00
309	Kosuke Fukudome/SP	2.00
310	Old Faithful/SP	2.00
311	Gavin Floyd/SP	2.00
312	A.J. Burnett/SP	2.00
313	Jeff Francis/SP	2.00
314	Chad Billingsley/SP	2.00
315	Andy LaRoche/SP	2.00
316	Rick Porcello/SP RC	5.00
317	John Baker/SP	2.00
318	Delmon Young/SP	2.00
319	Gary Sheffield/SP	2.00
320	B.J. Ryan/SP	2.00
321	Kelly Shoppach/SP	2.00
322	Chris Volstad/SP	2.00
323	Derek Jeter/SP	5.00
324	Wladimir Balentien/SP	2.00
325	Dioner Navarro/SP	2.00
326	Cameron Maybin/SP	2.00
327	Kenji Johjima/SP	2.00
328	Matt LaPorta/SP RC	4.00
329	Carlos Gomez/SP	2.00
330	Cristian Guzman/SP	2.00
331	Jeff Samardzija/SP	2.00
332	Curtis Granderson/SP	3.00
333	Nick Swisher/SP	2.00
334	Pat Burrell/SP	2.00
335	Justin Duchscherer/SP	2.00
336	Ryan Ludwick/SP	2.00
337	Billy Butler/SP	2.00
338	Jason Wong/SP	2.00
339	Jordan Schafer/SP RC	3.00
340	Richard Gatling/SP	2.00
341	Edgar Gonzalez/SP	2.00
342	Sitting Bull/SP	2.00
343	Doc Holliday/SP	2.00
344	Chris Young/SP	2.00
345	Carlos Delgado/SP	2.00
346	Dominique Wilkins/SP	3.00
347	Yovani Gallardo/SP	2.00
348	Justin Masterson/SP	2.00
349	Aubrey Huff/SP	2.00
350	Jimmy Rollins/SP	3.00

Autographs

		NM/M
	Common Auto.:	8.00
	SP's noted	
	Red Ink variations:	No Pricing
	Production 10 sets	
MC	Miguel Cabrera/49	100.00
DW	David Wright/49	180.00
JW	Jayson Werth/49	100.00
JR	Jose Reyes/49	100.00
JC	Joba Chamberlain/49	90.00
DO	David Ortiz/49	140.00
MH	Matt Holliday/49	80.00
RH	Ryan Howard/49	175.00
CJ	Conor Jackson	10.00
JF	Jeff Francoeur	10.00
JJ	Josh Johnson	10.00
CK	Clayton Kershaw	30.00
ES	Ervin Santana	10.00
AR	Alex Rios	12.00
HR	Hanley Ramirez	15.00
JP	Jonathan Papelbon	25.00
SO	Scott Olsen	8.00
JM	Justin Masterson	20.00
EL	Evan Longoria	65.00
TT	Troy Tulowitzki	15.00
MS	Max Scherzer	12.00
RB	Ryan Braun	35.00
JB	Jay Bruce	20.00
DS	Denard Span	15.00
CM	Cameron Maybin	15.00
AC	Alexi Casilla	10.00
RC	Ryan Church	15.00
JOC	Johnny Cueto	15.00
JCU	Jack Cust	15.00
BW	Blake DeWitt	12.00
RJH	Rich Hill	8.00
PH	Phil Hughes	15.00
MK	Matt Kemp	20.00
MLO	Mike Lowell	20.00
JRI	Juan Rivera	10.00
CG	Carlos Gomez	15.00
LM	LaShawn Merritt/239	20.00
AT	Anna Tunnicliffe/239	20.00
MZ	Mariel Zagunis/239	25.00
WE	Walton Glenn Eller/239	25.00
KA	Kristin Armstrong/239	25.00
SB	Stephanie Brown Trafton/239	20.00
DOW	Dominique Wilkins/239	25.00
MP1	Michael Phelps/8	600.00
MP2	Michael Phelps/8	600.00
MP3	Michael Phelps/8	600.00
MP4	Michael Phelps/8	600.00
MP5	Michael Phelps/8	600.00
MP6	Michael Phelps/8	600.00
MP7	Michael Phelps/8	600.00
MP8	Michael Phelps/8	600.00
FE	Frank Evans/239	35.00
AP	Art Pennington/239	40.00
RM	Red Moore/239	40.00
HS	Herb Simpson/239	40.00
CP	Clyde Parris/239	40.00
WW	Willie Williams/239	40.00
MN	Millito Navarro/239	70.00
BM	Billy the Marlin/239	40.00
HT	Hannah Teter/239	40.00
SD	Shani Davis/239	50.00
CO	Cat Osterman/239	50.00
RMA	Robbie Maddison/239	25.00
BC	Bob Crowley/239	25.00
RF	Richard Fosbury/239	30.00
SW	Steve Wiebe/239	30.00
WS	Will Simpson, Archie Bunker/239	25.00
MM	Mike Metzger/239	25.00
BBE	Bryan Berg/239	25.00
IK	Iris Kyle/239	20.00
BCA	Brian Cappelletto/239	25.00
LO	Loren Opstedahl/239	25.00
LC	Lynne Cox/239	25.00
BY	Brock Yates/239	25.00
JH	John Higby/239	25.00
BK	Burke Kenny/239	25.00
KM	Kolan McConiughey/239	25.00

YM	Yuto Miyazawa/239	60.00
MP	Michael Phelps	

Michael Phelps Box Loader Autographs

No Pricing

N43 Autographs

No Pricing
Production 15 Sets

N43 Auto Relics

No Pricing
Production 5 Sets

Relics

Common Relic:		4.00
YG	Yovani Gallardo	6.00
RH	Ryan Howard	8.00
IS	Ichiro Suzuki	10.00
MMO	Melvin Mora	4.00
VG	Vladimir Guerrero	6.00
CP	Corey Patterson	4.00
JD	Jermaine Dye	4.00
RZ	Ryan Zimmerman	4.00
MC	Mike Cameron	4.00
FL	Fred Lewis	4.00
BD	Blake DeWitt	4.00
RH2	Ryan Howard	8.00
PF	Prince Fielder	6.00
RB	Rocco Baldelli	4.00
RB2	Rocco Baldelli	4.00
CB	Carlos Beltran	6.00
HB	Hank Blalock	4.00
RC	Robinson Cano/195	10.00
EC	Eric Chavez/210	8.00
CC	Coco Crisp	4.00
EG	Eric Gagne	4.00
TH	Travis Hafner	4.00
JRH	Rich Harden	4.00
TLH	Todd Helton	6.00
THU	Tim Hudson	4.00
IS2	Ichiro Suzuki	10.00
CJ	Chipper Jones	6.00
CK	Casey Kotchman	4.00
HM	Hideki Matsui	10.00
DM	Daisuke Matsuzaka/110	15.00
MMU	Mark Mulder	4.00
DO	David Ortiz	8.00
RO	Roy Oswalt	4.00
AP	Albert Pujols/Bat	15.00
AP2	Albert Pujols/190/Hat	50.00
AP3	Albert Pujols/255/Jsy	20.00
HR	Hanley Ramirez/199	8.00
MR	Manny Ramirez	8.00
MR2	Manny Ramirez/190/Bat	12.00
AR	Alex Rios/90/bat	15.00
AER	Alex Rodriguez	15.00
SR	Scott Rolen	4.00
GS	Gary Sheffield	4.00
AS	Alfonso Soriano/191/Bat	10.00
NS	Nick Swisher/164/Bat	4.00
MTE	Miguel Tejada	4.00
JT	Jim Thome	6.00
CW	Chien-Ming Wang	10.00
DW	Dontrelle Willis	4.00
DAW	David Wright/Btg Glv	25.00
BZ	Barry Zito	4.00
CM	Cameron Maybin	4.00
AL	Adam LaRoche	4.00
MCA	Miguel Cabrera	6.00
DAW2	David Wright/Jsy	8.00
MO	Magglio Ordonez	4.00
KF	Kosuke Fukudome	6.00
CU	Chase Utley	8.00
RJB	Ryan Braun	6.00
TL	Tim Lincecum	10.00
EL	Evan Longoria	10.00
JR	Jimmy Rollins	4.00
GSI	Grady Sizemore	6.00
JB	Jay Bruce	6.00
MH	Matt Holliday	4.00
JU	Justin Upton	6.00
BU	B.J. Upton	4.00
CQ	Carlos Quentin	4.00
JM	Joe Mauer	6.00
JW	Jered Weaver	4.00
YE	Yunel Escobar	4.00
NM	Nate McLouth	4.00
RL	Ryan Ludwick	6.00
MT	Mark Teixeira	6.00
CS	C.C. Sabathia	6.00
VW	Vernon Wells	4.00
MM	Mickey Mantle/250/Pants	75.00
BTM	Billy the Marlin/250	15.00
LM	LaShawn Merritt/250	15.00
AT	Anna Tunnicliffe/250	10.00
MZ	Mariel Zagunis/250/Lame	20.00
WE	Walton Glenn Eller/250	10.00
KA	Kristin Armstrong/250	15.00
SB	Stephanie Brown Trafton/250	15.00
DOW	Dominique Wilkins/250	12.00
HT	Hannah Teter/250	15.00
SD	Shani Davis/250	15.00
CO	Cat Osterman/250	25.00
RMA	Robbie Maddison/250	10.00
BC	Bob Crowley/250	15.00
RF	Richard Fosbury/250	15.00
SW	Steve Wiebe/250	15.00
WS	Will Simpson, Archie Bunker/250	40.00
MME	Mike Metzger/250	15.00
BBE	Bryan Berg/250	15.00

IK	Iris Kyle/250	15.00
BCA	Brian Cappelletto/250	15.00
LO	Loren Opstedahl/250	20.00
LC	Lynne Cox/250	15.00
BY	Brock Yates/250	12.00
JHI	John Higby/250	15.00
BK	Burke Kenny/250	30.00
KM	Kolan McConiughey/250	15.00
MP	Michael Phelps/250	65.00
RD	Ryan Doumit	4.00

DNA Relics

No Pricing
Production One Set

N43 Relics

Production 25 Sets

AR	Alex Rodriguez	50.00
MR	Manny Ramirez	50.00
JH	Josh Hamilton	40.00
CU	Chase Utley	50.00
VG	Vladimir Guerrero	40.00
YD	Yu Darvish	100.00
JY	Jin Young Lee	20.00
YG	Yulieski Gourriel	40.00
NA	Norichika Aoki	50.00
FF	Fei Feng	25.00

Cut Signatures

No Pricing
Production One Set

National Pride

Common Player:		.50
	Inserted 1:1	
1	Ervin Santana	.50
2	Justin Upton	.75
3	Jason Bay	.50
4	Geovany Soto	.75
5	Ryan Dempster	.50
6	Johnny Cueto	.50
7	Chipper Jones	1.00
8	Fausto Carmona	.50
9	Carlos Guillen	.50
10	Jose Reyes	1.00
11	Hiroki Kuroda	.50
12	Prince Fielder	1.00
13	Justin Morneau	.75
14	Francisco Rodriguez	.50
15	Jorge Posada	.50
16	Jake Peavy	.50
17	Felix Hernandez	.75
18	Robinson Cano	.50
19	Erik Bedard	.50
20	Akinori Iwamura	.50
21	Scott Hairston	.50
22	David Wright	1.50
23	Chien-Ming Wang	.75
24	Chase Utley	1.00
25	Jonathan Sanchez	.50
26	Yunel Escobar	.50
27	John Lackey	.50
28	Melvin Mora	.50
29	Alfonso Soriano	.75
30	Jose Contreras	.75
31	Grady Sizemore	.75
32	Rich Harden	.50
33	Hanley Ramirez	1.00
34	Nick Markakis	.75
35	Manny Ramirez	1.00
36	Yovani Gallardo	.75
37	Johan Santana	.75
38	Mariano Rivera	.75
39	Shin-Soo Choo	.50
40	Hideki Matsui	.75
41	Raul Ibanez	.50
42	Edgar Renteria	.50
43	Jose Lopez	.50
44	Yuniesky Betancourt	.50
45	Evan Longoria	1.50
46	Carlos Ruiz	.50
47	Ryan Howard	1.00
48	Jorge Cantu	.50
49	Max Scherzer	.50
50	Jair Jurrjens	.50
51	Albert Pujols	2.00
52	Daisuke Matsuzaka	1.00
53	Vladimir Guerrero	.75
54	Carlos Zambrano	.50
55	Kosuke Fukudome	.50
56	Edinson Volquez	.50
57	Victor Martinez	.50
58	Derek Jeter	2.00
59	Miguel Cabrera	1.00
60	Stephen Drew	.50
61	Mark Teahen	.50
62	Ryan Braun	1.00
63	Carlos Beltran	.75
64	Francisco Liriano	.50
65	Carlos Delgado	.50
66	Joba Chamberlain	1.00
67	Adrian Gonzalez	.75
68	Ichiro Suzuki	1.50
69	Ryan Rowland-Smith	.50
70	Carlos Pena	.50
71	Josh Hamilton	.50
72	Edgar Gonzalez	.50
73	Carlos Lee	.50
74	Yadier Molina	.50
75	Alex Rodriguez	1.50

Dick Perez Originals

No Pricing
Production One Set

Highlight Sketches

Common Player:		1.00
	Inserted 1:6	

1	Aaron Boone	1.00
2	Ken Griffey Jr.	2.00
3	Randy Johnson	1.50
4	Carlos Zambrano	1.00
5	Josh Hamilton	1.50
6	Josh Beckett	1.50
7	Manny Ramirez	1.50
8	Derek Jeter	3.00
9	Frank Thomas	1.00
10	Jim Thome	1.00
11	Francisco Rodriguez	1.00
12	New York Yankees	1.50
13	David Wright	2.00
14	Ichiro Suzuki	2.00
15	Jon Lester	1.50
16	Alex Rodriguez	2.50
17	Chipper Jones	2.00
18	Derek Jeter	3.00
19	Albert Pujols	3.00
20	C.C. Sabathia	1.50
21	David Price	1.50
22	Ken Griffey Jr.	2.00
23	Brad Lidge	1.00
24	Mariano Rivera	1.50
25	Evan Longoria	2.00

N43

Common Card:		2.00
Inserted as a box topper.		
JU	Justin Upton	3.00
DM	Daisuke Matsuzaka	4.00
RH	Ryan Howard	4.00
DW	David Wright	4.00
TL	Tim Lincecum	4.00
AP	Albert Pujols	6.00
JH	Josh Hamilton	4.00
MR	Manny Ramirez	3.00
MC	Miguel Cabrera	3.00
GS	Grady Sizemore	3.00
CJ	Chipper Jones	4.00
EL	Evan Longoria	4.00
RHA	Roy Halladay	2.00
JB	Jay Bruce	3.00
AR	Alex Rodriguez	5.00

RIP Cards

Inserted 1:257
Prices for unripped cards.
Ripped cards 15% of listed price.
Production 5-99

1	Stephen Drew/25	100.00
2	Carlos Zambrano/25	100.00
3	Carlos Quentin/25	80.00
4	Paul Konerko/99	60.00
5	Bobby Abreu/25	80.00
6	Pat Neshek/99	60.00
7	Brian Giles/99	60.00
8	Jeff Francis/99	60.00
9	Jermaine Dye/50	80.00
10	Dan Uggla/25	80.00
11	Tim Hudson/50	75.00
12	Chris Young/50	75.00
13	Brad Penny/25	80.00
14	John Lackey/99	60.00
15	Todd Helton/25	100.00
16	Derek Lee/50	60.00
17	Cameron Maybin/99	60.00
18	Ryan Dempster/50	80.00
19	Yunel Escobar/99	60.00
20	Brian Roberts/25	100.00
21	Joakim Soria/50	80.00
22	Delmon Young/25	100.00
23	Miguel Tejada/50	80.00
24	Alex Gordon/25	100.00
25	Shane Victorino/99	60.00
26	Kerry Wood/25	80.00
27	Garrett Atkins/50	60.00
28	Fausto Carmona/99	60.00
29	Mike Jacobs/99	60.00
30	Kosuke Fukudome/25	100.00
31	Oliver Perez/99	60.00
32	James Loney/50	60.00
33	Rickie Weeks/99	60.00
34	Aubrey Huff/99	60.00
35	Chad Billingsley/50	80.00
36	Carlos Gomez/99	60.00
37	Mike Aviles/99	60.00
38	Joe Saunders/99	60.00
39	Derek Lowe/50	80.00
40	Travis Hafner/99	60.00
41	Andre Ethier/25	100.00
42	Brad Lidge/25	100.00
43	Kevin Kouzmanoff/50	80.00
44	Jose Lopez/25	100.00
45	Ryan Ludwick/50	80.00
46	Melvin Mora/99	60.00
47	Yadier Molina/99	60.00
48	Carlos Pena/99	60.00
49	Aramis Ramirez/50	80.00
50	Rocco Baldelli/50	80.00
51	Brandon Phillips/50	80.00
52	Jered Weaver/25	100.00
53	Eric Chavez/99	60.00
54	Torii Hunter/25	100.00
55	Akinori Iwamura/25	100.00
56	Mark Buehrle/50	80.00

Mini National Heroes

Common Card:		2.00
Inserted 1:12		
1	George Washington	4.00
2	Haile Selassie I	2.00
3	Toussaint L'Overture	2.00
4	Rigas Feraios	2.00
5	Yi Sun-sin	2.00
6	Guiseppe Garibaldi	2.00
7	Juan Santamaria	2.00
8	Tecun Uman	2.00

9	Jon Sigurosson	2.00
10	Mohandas Gandhi	2.00
11	Simon Bolivar	2.00
12	Alexander Nevsky	2.00
13	Lim Bo Seng	2.00
14	Sun Yat-sen	2.00
15	Tiradentes	2.00
16	Chiang Kai-Shek	2.00
17	William I	2.00
18	Severyn Nalyvaiko	2.00
19	Vasil Levski	2.00
20	Tadeusz Kosciuszko	2.00
21	Andranik Toros Ozanian	2.00
22	William Wallace	2.00
23	Oda Nobunaga	2.00
24	Milos Obilic	2.00
25	Niels Ebbeson	2.00
26	Jose Rizal	2.00
27	Alfonso Ugarte	2.00
28	Mustafa Ataturk	2.00
29	Nelson Mandela	2.00
30	El Cid	2.00
31	William Tell	2.00
32	Winston Churchill	2.00
33	Skanderbeg	2.00
34	General Jose de San Martin	2.00
35	Janos Damjanich	2.00
36	Joan of Arc	2.00
37	Abd al-Qadir	2.00
38	David Ben-Gurion	2.00
39	Benito Juarez	2.00
40	Marcus Garvey	2.00

Mini Worlds Biggest Hoaxes

Common Card:		2.00
Inserted 1:12		
1	Charles Ponzi	2.00
2	Alabama Changes Value of PI	2.00
3	The Runaway Bride	2.00
4	Idaho	2.00
5	The Turk	2.00
6	Enron	2.00
7	Anna Anderson	2.00
8	Ferdinand Waldo Demara	2.00
9	San Seriffe	2.00
10	D.B. Cooper	2.00
11	Wisconsin State Capitol Collapses	2.00
12	Victor Lustig	2.00
13	The War of the Worlds	2.00
14	George Parker	2.00
15	The Bathtub Hoax	2.00
16	The Cottingley Fairies	2.00
17	James Reavis	2.00
18	The Piltdown Man	2.00
19	The Cardiff Giant	2.00
20	Cold Fusion	2.00

Cabinet Box Loaders

Inserted 1:Hobby Box

1	Yurendell de Caster, Gene Kingsale	4.00
2	Frederich Cepeda, Yulieski Gourriel	4.00
3	David Wright, Brian Roberts	6.00
4	Norichika Aoki, Daisuke Matsuzaka	6.00
5	Hisashi Iwakuma, Ichiro Suzuki	6.00
6	Thomas Jefferson, John Hancock	4.00
7	George Washington, Alexander Hamilton	4.00
8	Harry S. Truman, Lester B. Pearson	4.00
9	Abraham Lincoln, Ulysses S. Grant	4.00
10	John F. Kennedy, Nikita Khrushchev	6.00

M. Phelps 1 of 1's Autos.

Production One Set

Code

Code:		3-5X base
Inserted 1:12 Hobby		

Mini

Mini (1-300):		1-2X
Mini SP (301-350):		1X basic SP
Mini SP's inserted 1:13		
Mini's 351-400 exclusive to Rip Cards		
Allen & Ginter Back:		2-3X
Inserted 1:5		
A & G Back SP's:		1.5X
A & G SP's inserted 1:65		
Bazooka Back:		No pricing
Production 25 Sets		
Black Border:		3-5X
Inserted 1:10		
Black SP:		2-3X basic SP
Inserted 1:130 Hobby		
Framed Cloth:		No Pricing
Production 10 Sets		
No Card Number:		10-20X
No # SP's:		2-4X
Production 50 Sets		
Wood: One set produced		

Mini Creatures

Common Card:		8.00
Inserted 1:48 Hobby		
1	Bigfoot	8.00
2	The Loch Ness Monster	8.00
3	Grendel	8.00

4	Unicorn	8.00
5	The Invisible Man	8.00
6	Kraken	8.00
7	Medusa	8.00
8	Sphinx	8.00
9	Minotaur	8.00
10	Dragon	8.00
11	Leviathan	8.00
12	Cyclops	8.00
13	Vampire	8.00
14	Griffin	8.00
15	Chupacabra	8.00
16	Cerberus	8.00
17	Hydra	8.00
18	Werewolf	8.00
19	Fairy	8.00
20	Yeti	8.00

Mini Creatures Autographs

No Pricing
Production 10

Printing Plates

No Pricing
Production one set per color.

Mini Creatures Relics

No Pricing
Production 10 Sets

Mini Extinct Creatures

Common Card:		
EA1	Velociraptor	20.00
EA2	Dodo	20.00
EA3	Xerces Blue	25.00
EA4	Labrador Duck	25.00
EA5	Eastern Elk	30.00

Mini Inventions of the Future

Common Card:		20.00
FI1	AeroMobile	20.00
FI2	Clock Defier	20.00
FI3	Protecto-Bubble	20.00
FI4	Here-to-There-o-matic	20.00
FI5	Mental Movies	20.00

2009 Topps American Heritage

	NM/M
Complete Set (150):	85.00
Common (1-125):	
Common SP (126-150):	4.00
Inserted 1:4	
Pack (8):	4.00
Box (24):	80.00

1	Mark Twain	.40
2	Harriet Beecher Stowe	.40
3	Washington Irving	.40
4	Edgar Allen Poe	.40
5	Nathaniel Hawthorne	.40
6	Emily Dickinson	.40
7	Walt Whitman	.40
8	Henry David Thoreau	.40
9	F. Scott Fitzgerald	.40
10	Ernest Hemingway	.40
11	Meriwether Lewis	.40
12	William Clark	.40
13	Robert Peary	.40
14	Daniel Boone	.40
15	Zebulon Pike	.40
16	Jebediah Strong Smith	.40
17	John Wesley Powell	.40
18	John Charles Fremont	.40
19	Amelia Earhart	.40
20	Christopher Columbus	.40
21	John Paul Jones	.40
22	Davy Crockett	.40
23	George Marshall	.40
24	Douglas MacArthur	.40
25	Winfield Scott	.40
26	William T. Sherman	.75
27	Chester Nimitz	.40
28	David Farragut	.40
29	Nathanael Greene	.40
30	George Meade	.40
31	Benjamin Franklin	.75
32	Alexander Hamilton	.40
33	Paul Revere	.40
34	Thomas Paine	.40
35	John Hancock	.75
36	Samuel Adams	.40
37	Crispus Attucks	.40
38	Patrick Henry	.40
39	Peyton Randolph	.40
40	Nathan Hale	.40
41	Thomas Edison	.75
42	Orville & Wilbur Wright	.40
43	George Washington Carver	.40
44	Alexander Graham Bell	.40
45	Samuel Morse	.40
46	Philo Farnsworth	.40
47	Stephanie Kwolek	.40
48	Robert Fulton	.40
49	Clarence Birdseye	.40
50	Elisha Otis	.40
51	Martin Luther King	1.00
52	Malcom X	.40
53	Harriet Tubman	.40
54	Frederick Douglass	.40
55	Barbara Rose Johns	.40
56	Susan B. Anthony	.40
57	Cesar Chavez	.40
58	W.E.B. DuBois	.40
59	Booker T. Washington	.40
60	Elizabeth Jennings Graham	.40

61	Thomas Eakins	.40
62	Ansel Adams	.40
63	Frederic Remington	.40
64	Georgia O'Keefe	.40
65	Jackson Pollack	.40
66	Norman Rockwell	.40
67	Andy Warhol	.40
68	Matthew Brady	.40
69	Thomas Nast	.40
70	Frederic Edwin Church	.40
71	Henry Clay	.40
72	John C. Calhoun	.40
73	Robert F. Kennedy	1.00
74	Daniel Webster	.40
75	John Jay	.40
76	Ron Livingston	.40
77	Charles Sumner	.40
78	Thurgood Marshall	.40
79	William Jennings Bryan	.40
80	Henry Cabot Lodge	.40
81	Wild Bill Cody	.40
82	P.T. Barnum	.40
83	George & Ira Gershwin	.40
84	Harry Houdini	.40
85	Buster Keaton	.40
86	Duke Ellington	.40
87	Joe Namath	1.00
88	Tony Pastor	.40
89	Will Rogers	.40
90	Clara Bow	.40
91	John D. Rockefeller	.40
92	Henry Ford	.40
93	John Paul Getty	.40
94	J.P. Morgan	.40
95	Samuel Colt	.40
96	William Randolph Hearst	.40
97	John Deere	.40
98	Estee Lauder	.40
99	Frank Woolworth	.40
100	Andrew Carnegie	.40
101	Landing at Plymouth Rock	.40
102	Boston Tea Party	.40
103	Signing of Declaration of Indep.	.40
104	Constitution is ratified	.40
105	Treaty of Paris	.40
106	G. Washington's Farewell Address	.40
107	Louisiana Purchase	.40
108	California Gold Rush	.40
109	Lincoln-Douglas Debates	.40
110	Emancipation Proclamation	.40
111	Treaty at Appomattox Courthouse	.40
112	Seward's Folly	.40
113	1st Trancontinental Railroad	.40
114	Treaty of Versailles	.40
115	Women get right to vote	.40
116	Mount Rushmore completed	.40
117	End of Prohibition	.40
118	V-E Day	.40
119	V-J Day	.40
120	Brown vs Board of Education	.40
121	Hawaii becomes 50th State	.40
122	First Televised Presidential Debate	.40
123	MLK "I have a dream" speech	.40
124	Man walks on moon	.40
125	Camp David Accords	.40
126	Barack Obama	5.00
127	Barack Obama	4.00
128	Barack Obama	5.00
129	Barack Obama	5.00
130	Barack Obama	5.00
131	Barack Obama	5.00
132	John McCain	4.00
133	John McCain	4.00
134	John McCain	4.00
135	John McCain	4.00
136	John McCain	4.00
137	John McCain	4.00
138	Barack Obama	5.00
139	Barack Obama	5.00
140	Barack Obama	5.00
141	John McCain	4.00
142	John McCain	4.00
143	John McCain	5.00
144	Joseph Biden, Sarah Palin	8.00
145	Barack Obama, John McCain	5.00
146	John McCain	5.00
147	Obama 2008 Election Night	5.00
148	Barack Obama	10.00
149	Joseph Biden	5.00
150	Michelle Obama	4.00

American History Cut Sigs.

Production One Set

American History Cut Relic

Production One Set

American History Dual Cut

Production One Set

American History Quad Cut

Production One Set

American Legends

NM/M

Common Legend: 5.00
Production 199 Sets

		NM/M
1	Walter Johnson	10.00
2	George Sisler	6.00
3	Ty Cobb	10.00
4	Thurman Munson	12.00
5	Christy Mathewson	8.00
6	Johnny Mize	8.00
7	Mickey Mantle	20.00
8	Babe Ruth	15.00
9	Rogers Hornsby	8.00
10	Pee Wee Reese	6.00
11	Lou Gehrig	15.00
12	Cy Young	10.00
13	Jimmie Foxx	8.00
14	Honus Wagner	12.00
15	Roy Campanella	12.00
16	Jackie Robinson	12.00
17	Mel Ott	6.00
18	Tris Speaker	5.00

American Legends Relics

NM/M
Production 25 Sets

JR	Jackie Robinson	50.00
BR	Babe Ruth	175.00
HW	Honus Wagner	180.00
RH	Rogers Hornsby	50.00

American Legends Cut Sigs

Production One Set

American Leg. Dual Relic

No Pricing
Production 20 Sets

Celebrities

NM/M
Common Celebrity: 1.50

1	Jackie Mason	1.50
2	B.B. King	3.00
3	Erik Estrada	1.50
4	Penn & Teller	3.00
5	Rip Torn	1.50
6	Jesse Ventura	2.00
7	Michael Phelps	4.00
8	David Cross	1.50
9	Keith Olbermann	1.50
10	Kerri Walsh, Misty May Treanor	4.00

Celebrity Autographs

NM/M
Some not priced.

JM	Jackie Mason/150	20.00
BBK	B.B. King/Redemp.	85.00
EE	Erik Estrada/150	25.00
JV	Jesse Ventura/150	30.00
KO	Keith Olbermann/100	20.00
PT	Penn & Teller/150	75.00

Celebrities Relic

NM/M
Common Card: 8.00

JM	Jackie Mason	8.00
BBK	B.B. King	25.00
EE	Erik Estrada	8.00
RT	Rip Torn	8.00
JV	Jesse Ventura	10.00
KO	Keith Olbermann	10.00
WM	Kerri Walsh, Misty May Treanor	25.00
PT	Penn & Teller	25.00

Chrome

NM/M
Complete Set (100): 100.00
Common Chrome: 2.00
Production 1,776 Sets
Refractors: 4-6X
Production 76 Sets

1	Mark Twain	4.00
2	Harriet Beecher Stowe	2.00
3	Washington Irving	2.00
4	Edgar Allen Poe	2.00
5	Nathaniel Hawthorne	2.00
6	Emily Dickinson	2.00
7	Walt Whitman	2.00
8	Henry David Thoreau	2.00
9	F. Scott Fitzgerald	2.00
10	Ernest Hemingway	4.00
11	Meriwether Lewis	2.00
12	William Clark	2.00
13	Robert Peary	2.00
14	Daniel Boone	4.00
15	Zebulon Pike	2.00
16	Jebediah Strong Smith	2.00
17	John Wesley Powell	2.00
18	John Charles Fremont	2.00
19	Amelia Earhart	2.00
20	Christopher Columbus	2.00
21	John Paul Jones	2.00
22	Davy Crockett	3.00
23	George Marshall	2.00
24	Douglas MacArthur	3.00
25	Winfield Scott	2.00
26	William T. Sherman	4.00
27	Chester Nimitz	2.00
28	David Farragut	3.00
29	Nathanael Greene	3.00
30	George Meade	3.00
31	Benjamin Franklin	5.00
32	Alexander Hamilton	4.00
33	Paul Revere	4.00
34	Thomas Paine	4.00
35	John Hancock	4.00
36	Samuel Adams	4.00
37	Crispus Attucks	2.00
38	Patrick Henry	2.00
39	Peyton Randolph	2.00
40	Nathan Hale	2.00
41	Thomas Edison	3.00
42	Orville & Wilbur Wright	2.00
43	George Washington Carver	
44	Alexander Graham Bell	2.00
45	Samuel Morse	2.00
46	Philo Farnsworth	2.00
47	Stephanie Kwolek	2.00
48	Robert Fulton	2.00
49	Clarence Birdseye	2.00
50	Elisha Otis	2.00
51	Martin Luther King	4.00
52	Malcom X	2.00
53	Harriet Tubman	2.00
54	Frederick Douglass	2.00
55	Barbara Rose Johns	2.00
56	Susan B. Anthony	2.00
57	Cesar Chavez	2.00
58	W.E.B. DuBois	2.00
59	Booker T. Washington	2.00
60	Elizabeth Jennings Graham	2.00
61	Thomas Eakins	2.00
62	Ansel Adams	2.00
63	Frederic Remington	2.00
64	Georgia O'Keefe	2.00
65	Jackson Pollack	2.00
66	Norman Rockwell	2.00
67	Andy Warhol	2.00
68	Matthew Brady	2.00
69	Thomas Nast	2.00
70	Frederic Edwin Church	2.00
71	Henry Clay	2.00
72	John C. Calhoun	2.00
73	Robert F. Kennedy	5.00
74	Daniel Webster	2.00
75	John Jay	2.00
76	Ron Livingston	2.00
77	Charles Sumner	2.00
78	Thurgood Marshall	2.00
79	William Jennings Bryan	2.00
80	Henry Cabot Lodge	2.00
81	Wild Bill Cody	2.00
82	P.T. Barnum	2.00
83	George & Ira Gershwin	2.00
84	Harry Houdini	2.00
85	Buster Keaton	2.00
86	Duke Ellington	2.00
87	Joe Namath	4.00
88	Tony Pastor	2.00
89	Will Rogers	2.00
90	Clara Bow	2.00
91	John D. Rockefeller	2.00
92	Henry Ford	2.00
93	John Paul Getty	2.00
94	J.P. Morgan	2.00
95	Samuel Colt	2.00
96	William Randolph Hearst	2.00
97	John Deere	2.00
98	Estee Lauder	2.00
99	Frank Woolworth	2.00
100	Andrew Carnegie	2.00

Icons

NM/M
Common Icon: 8.00
Production 99 Sets

1	Babe Ruth	20.00
2	Jackie Robinson	15.00
3	Lou Gehrig	20.00
4	Honus Wagner	15.00
5	Ty Cobb	12.00
6	Cy Young	12.00
7	Roy Campanella	15.00
8	Walter Johnson	12.00
9	Johnny Mize	8.00
10	Christy Mathewson	10.00

Leg. & Presidents Dual Cut

Production One Set

Monuments/Presidents Relic

JOHN F. KENNEDY

NM/M
Common Relic:

GC	Grover Cleveland/ Handkerchief/75	20.00
USSC	U.S.S. Constitution	30.00
ZT	Zachary Taylor WH Roof/30	30.00
JT	John Tyler WH Roof/30	35.00
WM	William McKinley WH Roof/30	30.00
WHT	William Taft/Seat	20.00
WT	William Taft	2.00
WW	Woodrow Wilson/Seat	15.00
WGH	Warren G. Harding WH Roof/30	15.00
CC	Calvin Coolidge/Seat	15.00
HH	Herbert Hoover/Seat	15.00
HST	Harry S. Truman/Seat	15.00
HT	Harry S. Truman/ WH Floor/100	40.00
FDR	Franklin D. Roosevelt/ Seat	15.00
ER	Eleanor Roosevelt/ Pillow/200	25.00
FR	Franklin D. Roosevelt/ Pillow/200	40.00
FDR2	Franklin D. Roosevelt/ WH floor/100	30.00
JFK	John F. Kennedy/ Sweater/200	70.00
JK	John F. Kennedy/Seat	25.00
GWB	George W. Bush/Seat	25.00
GB	George W. Bush/Wall	25.00
GB2	George W. Bush/ Tie/100	70.00
RN	Richard Nixon/Seat	15.00
DEE	Duke Ellington/Seat	20.00
JPS	John Phillips Sousa/ Seat	15.00
BC	Bill Clinton/seat	20.00
BC1	Bill Clinton/Wall/175	20.00
RR	Ronald Reagan/Seat	20.00
GHB	George H.W. Bush/Seat	15.00
PBXVI	Pope Benedict XVI/Wall	20.00
PJPII	Pope John Paul II/ Wall/175	20.00
RG	Rudy Giuliani/Seat	20.00
MB	Michael Bloomberg/ Wall/175	20.00
JN	Joe Namath/seat	20.00

Presidential Patches

NM/M
Common Patch:
Production 50 Sets

GW	George Washington	30.00
JA	John Adams	20.00
TJ	Thomas Jefferson	20.00
JMR	James Madison	20.00
JM	James Monroe	20.00
JQA	John Quincy Adams	20.00
AJ	Andrew Jackson	20.00
MB	Martin Van Buren	15.00
WHH	William H. Harrison	15.00
JT	John Tyler	15.00
JP	James K. Polk	15.00
ZT	Zachary Taylor	15.00
MF	Millard Fillmore	15.00
FP	Franklin Pierce	15.00
AL	Abraham Lincoln	25.00
AJ2	Andrew Johnson	20.00
UG	Ulysses S. Grant	20.00
RH	Rutherford B. Hayes	15.00
JG	James A. Garfield	15.00
CA	Chester Arthur	15.00
GC	Grover Cleveland	15.00
BH	Benjamin Harrison	15.00
WK	William McKinley	15.00
TR	Theodore Roosevelt	20.00
WT	William Taft	15.00
WW	Woodrow Wilson	15.00
WH	Warren G. Harding	15.00
CC	Calvin Coolidge	15.00
HH	Herbert Hoover	15.00
FR	Franklin D. Roosevelt	20.00
HT	Harry S. Truman	15.00
DE	Dwight D. Eisenhower	15.00
JK	John F. Kennedy	30.00
LJ	Lyndon B. Johnson	20.00
RN	Richard Nixon	20.00
GF	Gerald R. Ford	15.00
JC	Jimmy Carter	15.00
RR	Ronald Reagan	15.00
GB	George Bush	20.00
BC	Bill Clinton	20.00
GWB	George W. Bush	20.00
BO	Barack Obama	100.00
JB	James Buchanan	15.00

Presidents

NM/M
Common President: 2.00

1	George Washington	8.00
2	John Adams	4.00
3	Thomas Jefferson	6.00
4	James Madison	4.00
5	James Monroe	3.00
6	John Quincy Adams	3.00
7	Andrew Jackson	4.00
8	Martin Van Buren	2.00
9	William H. Harrison	2.00
10	John Tyler	2.00
11	James K. Polk	2.00
12	Zachary Taylor	2.00
13	Millard Fillmore	2.00
14	Franklin Pierce	2.00
15	James Buchanan	2.00
16	Abraham Lincoln	8.00
17	Andrew Johnson	2.00
18	Ulysses S. Grant	4.00
19	Rutherford B. Hayes	2.00
20	James A. Garfield	2.00
21	Chester Arthur	2.00
22	Grover Cleveland	2.00
23	Benjamin Harrison	2.00
24	Grover Cleveland	2.00
25	William McKinley	2.00
26	Theodore Roosevelt	4.00
27	William Taft	2.00
28	Woodrow Wilson	2.00
29	Warren G. Harding	2.00
30	Calvin Coolidge	2.00
31	Herbert Hoover	2.00
32	Franklin D. Roosevelt	4.00
33	Harry S. Truman	4.00
34	Dwight D. Eisenhower	2.00
35	John F. Kennedy	8.00
36	Lyndon B. Johnson	2.00
37	Richard Nixon	2.00
38	Gerald R. Ford	2.00
39	Jimmy Carter	2.00
40	Ronald Reagan	4.00
41	George Bush	2.00
42	Bill Clinton	4.00
43	George W. Bush	4.00
44	Barack Obama	40.00

Presidential Cut Sigs.

Production One Set

2009 Topps American Heritage Heroes

D-DAY

NM/M
Complete Set (150): 50.00
Common (1-125): .25
Common SP (126-150): 4.00
Inserted 1:4
Pack (8): 3.50
Box (24): 65.00

1	George Washington	1.00
2	Molly Pitcher	.75
3	John McCain	.75
4	Norman Schwarzkopf	.50
5	Ulysses S. Grant	.50
6	Boyd "Buzz" Wagner	.25
7	George McClellan	.25
8	Col. Gordon R. Roberts	.25
9	Bud Day	.25
10	Jimmy Stewart	.50
11	Thomas Jefferson	.50
12	James Madison	.50
13	George Mason	.25
14	Claiborne Pell	.25
15	Horace Mann	.25
16	Hiram Rhodes Revels	.25
17	Charles Weltner	.25
18	Abraham Lincoln	1.00
19	Ronald Reagan	.50
20	Barack Obama	4.00
21	Elizabeth Cady Stanton	.25
22	Medgar Evers	.25
23	Sojourner Truth	.25
24	Frank Robinson	.50
25	Lucy Stone	.25
26	Jackie Robinson	1.00
27	Mary McLeod Bethune	.25
28	Emma Willard	.25
29	Mother Jones	.25
30	Samuel Gompers	.25
31	Benjamin Franklin	.25
32	Red Adair	.25
33	Ed Pulaski	.25
34	Edward Croker	.25
35	Dennis Smith	.25
36	Alexander Shaler	.25
37	John Finn	.25
38	Fire Fighter	.50
39	Paul Revere	.50
40	Alexander Hamilton	.50
41	Eliot Ness	.25
42	Wyatt Earp	.25
43	Det. Frank Serpico	.25
44	John Flynn	.25
45	Joe Petrosino	.25
46	Theodore Roosevelt	.50
47	J. Edgar Hoover	.25
48	John Moran	.25
49	David Lim	.25
50	Justin Garner	.25
51	Civil Rights Movement	.25
52	NAACP	.25
53	National Audubon Society	.25
54	Navajo Code Talkers	.25
55	Women's Suffrage	.25
56	USO	.25
57	American Red Cross	.25
58	VFW	.25
59	APCA	.25
60	ACLU	.25
61	Jonas Salk	.25
62	Charles Drew	.25
63	Mary Edwards Walker	.25
64	Susie Walking Bear Yellowtail	.25
65	Joseph Goldberger	.25
66	Robert Jarvik	.25
67	Charles Mayo	.25
68	Elizabeth Blackwell	.25
69	Norman Shumway	.25
70	Paul Zoll	.25
71	Henry Bergh	.25
72	Norman Borlaug	.25
73	Clara Barton	.25
74	Jimmy Carter	.25
75	Helen Keller	.25
76	Florence Kelley	.25
77	Herbert Hoover	.25
78	Jane Addams	.25
79	Erin Brockovich	.25
80	Eleanor Roosevelt	.25
81	Harry S. Truman	.50
82	George Marshall	.25
83	James Monroe	.50
84	John Adams	.50
85	John Hay	.25
86	Dwight D. Eisenhower	.50
87	Silas Deane	.25
88	Woodrow Wilson	.25
89	John Quincy Adams	.25
90	Dean Acheson	.25
91	Jacob Riis	.25
92	Upton Sinclair	.25
93	August Wilson	.25
94	Nellie Bly	.25
95	John Steinbeck	.25
96	Ida Tarbell	.25
97	William Lloyd Garrison	.25
98	Rachel Carson	.25
99	Ralph Ellison	.25
100	Carl Sagan	.25
101	Boston Tea Party	.50
102	Paul Revere's Midnight Ride	.50
103	Battles of Lexington and Concord	.50
104	Battle of Bunker Hill	.50
105	to give my country."	.50
106	Washington Crosses the Delaware	.50
107	Battles of Saratoga	.50
108	The Underground Railroad	.50
109	Siege of Yorktown	.50
110	Lewis & Clark Expedition	.50
111	Seneca Falls Convention	.50
112	Battle of Gettysburg	.50
113	Battle of Appomattox Courthouse	.50
114	The Wright Brothers' First Flight	.50
115	Battle of Belleau Wood	.50
116	Doolittle Raid	.50
117	Battle of Midway	.50
118	Battle of Guadalcanal	.50
119	D-Day	.50
120	Battle of the Bulge	.50
121	Battle of Iwo Jima	.50
122	Jackie Robinson Breaks Color Barrier	1.00
123	First American Spaceflight	.50
124	March to Montgomery	.50
125	Flight 93	.50
126-150	Abraham Lincoln/ Barack Obama	4.00

A Hero's Journey

NM/M
Common Lincoln: 2.00
Inserted 1:8
1-15 Abraham Lincoln 2.00

Amer. Heroes Cut Sig.

Production One Set

Autographs

NM/M
Inserted 1:303

BD	Col. Bud Day	40.00
DL	David Lim	30.00
DS	Dennis Smith	15.00
EB	Erin Brockovich	30.00
FS	Det. Frank Serpico	40.00
GRR	Col. Gordon R. Roberts	25.00
JF	John Flynn	15.00
JFI	John Finn	15.00
JG	Justin Garner	25.00
JM	John Moran	20.00
RJ	Robert Jarvik	30.00
WA	Wesley Autrey	15.00

Chrome

NM/M
Production 1,776 Sets
Refractors: 6-10X
Production 76 Sets

1	George Washington	3.00
2	Molly Pitcher	2.00
3	John McCain	2.00
4	Norman Schwarzkopf	3.00
5	Ulysses S. Grant	1.50
6	Boyd "Buzz" Wagner	.50
7	George McClellan	1.00
8	Col. Gordon R. Roberts	1.50
9	Bud Day	.50
10	Jimmy Stewart	1.50
11	Thomas Jefferson	1.50
12	James Madison	2.00
13	George Mason	.50
14	Claiborne Pell	.50
15	Horace Mann	.50
16	Hiram Rhodes Revels	.50
17	Charles Weltner	.50
18	Abraham Lincoln	3.00
19	Ronald Reagan	2.00
20	Barack Obama	8.00
21	Elizabeth Cady Stanton	.50
22	Medgar Evers	.50
23	Sojourner Truth	.50
24	Frank Robinson	3.00
25	Lucy Stone	.50
26	Jackie Robinson	4.00
27	Mary McLeod Bethune	.50
28	Emma Willard	.50
29	Mother Jones	.50
30	Samuel Gompers	.50
31	Benjamin Franklin	2.00
32	Red Adair	.50
33	Ed Pulaski	.50
34	Edward Croker	.50
35	Dennis Smith	.50
36	Alexander Shaler	.50
37	John Finn	.50
38	Fire Fighter	.50
39	Paul Revere	2.00
40	Alexander Hamilton	2.00
41	Eliot Ness	1.00
42	Wyatt Earp	1.00
43	Det. Frank Serpico	.50
44	John Flynn	.50
45	Joe Petrosino	.50
46	Theodore Roosevelt	2.00
47	J. Edgar Hoover	1.00
48	John Moran	.50
49	David Lim	.50
50	Justin Garner	.50
51	Civil Rights Movement	.50
52	NAACP	.50
53	National Audubon Society	.50
54	Navajo Code Talkers	.50
55	Women's Suffrage	.50
56	USO	.50
57	American Red Cross	.50
58	VFW	.50
59	ASPCA	.50
60	ACLU	.50
61	Jonas Salk	.50
62	Charles Drew	.50
63	Mary Edwards Walker	.50
64	Susie Walking Bear Yellowtail	.50
65	Joseph Goldberger	.50
66	Robert Jarvik	.50
67	Charles Mayo	.50
68	Elizabeth Blackwell	.50
69	Norman Shumway	.50
70	Paul Zoll	.50
71	Henry Bergh	.50
72	Norman Borlaug	.50
73	Clara Barton	.50
74	Jimmy Carter	1.50
75	Helen Keller	.50
76	Florence Kelley	.50
77	Herbert Hoover	1.00
78	Jane Addams	.50
79	Erin Brockovich	.50
80	Eleanor Roosevelt	1.00
81	Harry S. Truman	2.00
82	George Marshall	.50
83	James Monroe	1.50
84	John Adams	2.00
85	John Hay	.50
86	Dwight D. Eisenhower	2.00
87	Silas Deane	.50
88	Woodrow Wilson	1.00
89	John Quincy Adams	1.00
90	Dean Acheson	.50
91	Jacob Riis	.50
92	Upton Sinclair	.50
93	August Wilson	.50
94	Nellie Bly	.50
95	John Steinbeck	.50
96	Ida Tarbell	.50
97	William Lloyd Garrison	.50
98	Rachel Carson	.50
99	Ralph Ellison	.50
100	Carl Sagan	.50

Dual Cut Sigs.

Production One Set

Heroes of Sport

NM/M
Common Player: 1.00
Inserted 1:4
Gold: 4-8X
Production 199
Platinum: 10-20X
Production 25 Sets

1	Jackie Robinson	1.50
2	Babe Ruth	4.00
3	James J. Braddock	1.50
4	Cy Young	1.50
5	Larry Bird	2.00
6	Tris Speaker	1.50
7	Mickey Mantle	4.00
8	Thurman Munson	1.50
9	Tony Dorsett	1.50
10	Frank Robinson	1.50
11	Christy Mathewson	1.50

12	Roy Campanella	1.00
13	Dan Marino	2.00
14	Lou Gehrig	2.50
15	Bill Russell	2.00
16	Rogers Hornsby	1.50
17	Stan Musial	1.50
18	Honus Wagner	1.50
19	Jimmie Foxx	1.50
20	Walter Johnson	1.50
21	Jim Brown	2.00
22	Reggie Jackson	1.00
23	Ty Cobb	1.50
24	Magic Johnson	2.00
25	George Sisler	1.00

Heros of Sport Auto.
NM/M
Inserted 1:6,000
| BR | Bill Russell | 180.00 |
| TD | Tony Dorsett | 50.00 |

Hereos of Sport Cut Sigs.
Production One Set

Heros Journey Relic
NM/M
Inserted 1:12,100
| 2 | Abraham Lincoln Law Office Wood/20 | 400.00 |

Heros Journey Stamp
NM/M
Common Lincoln Stamp: 35.00
Production 100 Sets
| 1-20 | Abraham Lincoln | 35.00 |

Heroes of Sport 8
NM/M
One set produced.

Heroes of Sport Dual Relic
NM/M
Production 20 Sets
| R3 | Babe Ruth, Ty Cobb | 275.00 |

Hereos of Sport Relics
NM/M
Inserted 1:234
R1	Jackie Robinson/Bat	25.00
R2	Babe Ruth/Bat	140.00
R2	Babe Ruth/Jsy	160.00
R3	Mickey Mantle/Pants	70.00
R4	Johnny Mize/Bat	20.00
R5	Magic Johnson/Jsy	20.00
R6	Jim Brown/Jsy	20.00
R7	Rogers Hornsby/Bat	25.00
R8	Larry Bird/Jsy	20.00
R9	Jimmie Foxx/Bat	35.00
R10	Ty Cobb/Bat	75.00
R11	Lou Gehrig/Pants	90.00
R12	Frank Robinson/Bat	10.00
R13	Dan Marino/Jsy	30.00
R14	Bill Russell/Jsy	20.00
R15	Terry Bradshaw/Jsy	20.00

Heroism Relics
NM/M
Some not priced.
EA	Elmore Austin Span./ Amer. War Boots	40.00
ER	Eleanor Roosevelt Belt	40.00
KW	30th Infantry Korean War Uniform	15.00
LP	Libby Confederate War Prison Wood	20.00
RR	F. D. Roosevelt Pillow Liner	20.00
HST	Harry S. Truman Oval Office floor	30.00
LBJ	Lyndon B. Johnson Sofa	30.00
FDR1	F. D. Roosevelt Oval Office Floor	40.00
WWI1	105th Machine Gun Battery Blanket	15.00
WWI2	WWI Engineer Uniform	15.00
WWI3	WWI Signal Flag	15.00
WWI4	WWI Flag Kit	15.00
WWI5	WWI Soldier Leggings	25.00
USSME	U.S.S. Maine Deck Wood	80.00
USSMO	U.S.S. Missouri Teak Decking	60.00
USSNC	U.S.S. North Car. Deck Wood	40.00
WWII1	11th Airborne Paratrooper Uni.	15.00
WWII2	76th Infantry Uniform	15.00
WWII3	22nd Infantry D-Day Uniform	15.00
WWII4	12th Armored Captain's Uni.	15.00
WWII5	36th Infantry POW Uniform	15.00
WWII6	76th Infantry Medic's Uni.	15.00
WWII7	101st Airborne Paratrooper Uni.	15.00

Medal of Honor
NM/M
Common Card: .50
Inserted 1:2
1	Eugene Asa Carr	.50
2	Frank Baldwin	.50
3	Thomas Custer	.50
4	Orion P. Howe	.50
5	Joshua Chamberlain	.50
6	William Joyce Sewell	.50
7	Francis E. Brownell	.50
8	James Thompson	.50
9	Allen Thompson	.50
10	John C. Black	.50
11	William McBryar	.50
12	Arthur MacArthur Jr.	.50
13	Daniel Sickles	.50
14	Richmond Pearson Hobson	.50
15	William Harvey Carney	.50
16	Mary Edwards Walker	.50
17	Powhatan Beaty	.50
18	George Lewis Gillespie Jr.	.50
19	Billy Dixon	.50
20	Benjamin Brown	.50
21	Isaiah Mays	.50
22	William F. Cody	.50
23	Bernard J.D. Irwin	.50
24	William F. Lukes	.50
25	Theodore Roosevelt	2.00
26	Albert Leopold Mills	.50
27	Dennis Bell	.50
28	Ira Clinton Welborn	.50
29	Henry L. Hulbert	.50
30	Hiram I. Bearss	.50
31	Webb Hayes	.50
32	George F. Shiels	.50
33	Daniel Daly	.50
34	Smedley Butler	.50
35	Julien Edmund Victor Gaujot	.50
36	Louis Cukela	.50
37	John J. Kelly	.50
38	David Dixon Porter	.50
39	Christian Fleetwood	.50
40	Col. Gordon R. Roberts	.50
41	James Jonas Madison	.50
42	Floyd Bennett	.50
43	William Halford	.50
44	Bud Day	.50
45	J. Franklin Bell	.50
46	Edward Bancroft Williston	.50
47	Jason Dunham	.50
48	Matthias W. Day	.50
49	Orland B. Willcox	.50
50	Daniel Augustus Joseph Sullivan	.50

Medal of Freedom
NM/M
Common Card: 1.00
Inserted 1:4
1	Jesse Jackson	1.00
2	Jonas Salk	1.00
3	Mother Teresa	1.00
4	Billy Graham	1.00
5	David Brinkley	1.00
6	Carol Burnett	1.00
7	Wesley Clark	1.00
8	Bill Cosby	1.00
9	Jimmy Doolittle	1.00
10	Duke Ellington	1.00
11	Gerald Ford	1.00
12	Aretha Franklin	1.00
13	Harper Lee	1.00
14	Charlton Heston	1.00
15	Jimmy Stewart	1.00
16	Richard Petty	1.00
17	Jack Nicklaus	2.00
18	Arnold Palmer	1.00
19	Andy Griffith	1.00
20	Colin Powell	1.00
21	Ronald Reagan	1.00
22	Elliot Richardson	1.00
23	Frank Robinson	1.00
24	Fred Rogers	1.00
25	William Safire	1.00

Quad Cut Signature
NM/M
Production One Set

Relics
NM/M
Common Relic: 5.00
BD	Col. Bud Day	15.00
DL	David Lim	5.00
DS	Dennis Smith	5.00
EB	Erin Brockovich	8.00
FS	Det. Frank Serpico	10.00
GRR	Col. Gordon R. Roberts	8.00
JF	John Flynn	5.00
JFI	John Finn	5.00
JG	Justin Garner	5.00
JM	John Moran	5.00
RJ	Robert Jarvik	6.00
WA	Wesley Autrey	5.00
S1	Shana Leash	25.00
S2	Shana Bedding	10.00

Spaceflight
NM/M
Common Spaceflight: 2.50
Inserted 1:6
1	Freedom 7	2.50
2	Liberty Bell 7	2.50
3	Friendship 7	2.50
4	Aurora 7	2.50
5	Sigma 7	2.50
6	Faith 7	2.50
7	Gemini III	2.50
8	Gemini IV	2.50
9	Gemini V	2.50
10	Gemini VII	2.50
11	Gemini VI-A	2.50
12	Gemini VIII	2.50
13	Gemini IX-A	2.50
14	Gemini X	2.50
15	Gemini XI	2.50
16	Gemini XII	2.50
17	Apollo 1	2.50
18	Apollo 7	2.50
19	Apollo 8	2.50
20	Apollo 9	2.50
21	Apollo 10	2.50
22	Apollo 11	2.50
23	Apollo 12	2.50
24	Apollo 13	2.50
25	Apollo 14	2.50
26	Apollo 15	2.50
27	Apollo 16	2.50
28	Apollo 17	2.50

Spaceflight Cut Sig.
Production One Set

Spaceflight Relics
NM/M
Some not priced.
AS	Apollo Soyuz Test Project	250.00
SL	Spacelab Wiring	30.00
SSA	Space Shuttle Atlantis	40.00
SSC	Space Shuttle Columbia	40.00
SSD	Space Shuttle Discovery	40.00
SSE	Space Shuttle Endeavour	40.00
SSA1-6	Space Shuttle Atlantis Bay Liner	30.00
SSA7	Space Shuttle Atlantis Thermal Blanket	35.00
SSC1-6	Space Shuttle Columbia Bay Liner	30.00
SSC7	Space Shuttle Columbia Thermal Blanket	30.00
SSD1-6	Space Shuttle Discovery Bay Liner	30.00
SSD7	Space Shuttle Discovery Thermal Blanket	25.00
SSD8	Space Shuttle Discovery Bay Blanket	25.00
SSD9	Space Shuttle Discovery Clamp Seal	40.00
SSE1-6	Space Shuttle Endeavour Bay Liner	30.00
SSE7	Space Shuttle Endeavour Thermal Blanket	30.00

Spaceflight Patches
NM/M
Production 61 Sets
P1	Freedom 7	100.00
P2	Liberty Bell 7	80.00
P3	Friendship 7	100.00
P4	Aurora 7	80.00
P5	Sigma 7	80.00
P6	Faith 7	60.00
P7	Gemini III	100.00
P8	Gemini IV	100.00
P9	Gemini V	100.00
P10	Gemini VII	100.00
P11	Gemini VI-A	100.00
P12	Gemini VIII	100.00
P13	Gemini IX-A	100.00
P14	Gemini X	100.00
P15	Gemini XI	100.00
P16	Gemini XII	100.00
P17	Apollo 1	100.00
P18	Apollo 7	80.00
P19	Apollo 8	150.00
P20	Apollo 9	80.00
P21	Apollo 10	80.00
P22	Apollo 11	80.00
P23	Apollo 12	100.00
P24	Apollo 13	100.00
P25	Apollo 14	80.00
P26	Apollo 15	100.00
P27	Apollo 16	80.00
P28	Apollo 17	100.00

2009 Topps Chrome

NM/M
Common Player (1-170): .25
Common RC (171-220): 1.00
Common RC Auto. (221-243): 8.00
Hobby Pack (4): 4.00
Hobby Box (24): 75.00
1	Alex Rodriguez	1.50
2	Kerry Wood	.25
3	Dan Uggla	.40
4	Nate McLouth	.40
5	Brad Lidge	.25
6	Jon Lester	.50
7	Mickey Mantle	4.00
8	Jason Giambi	.40
9	Mike Lowell	.50
10	Ken Griffey Jr.	1.50
11	Erick Aybar	.25
12	Stephen Drew	.40
13	Geoff Jenkins	.25
14	Aubrey Huff	.25
15	Kazuo Matsui	.25
16	David Ortiz	.75
17	Mariano Rivera	.75
18	Jermaine Dye	.40
19	Rich Harden	.40
20	Brian McCann	.50
21	Brad Hawpe	.25
22	Justin Morneau	.75
23	Akinori Iwamura	.25
24	David Wright	1.00
25	Garrett Atkins	.25
26	David DeJesus	.25
27	Francisco Liriano	.40
28	George Sherrill	.25
29	Hideki Matsui	.75
30	Chris Young	.25
31	Kevin Youkilis	.75
32	Mark Teixeira	.50
33	Roy Oswalt	.50
34	Orlando Hudson	.25
35	Vladimir Guerrero	.75
36	Juan Pierre	.25
37	Carlos Delgado	.50
38	Tim Hudson	.25
39	Brandon Webb	.25
40	Alex Gordon	.40
41	Glen Perkins	.25
42	Kosuke Fukudome	.75
43	Ian Stewart	.25
44	A.J. Pierzynski	.25
44	Barack Obama/SP	15.00
45	Roy Halladay	.50
46	Carlos Pena	.50
47	Evan Longoria	1.50
48	Matt Kemp	.50
49	C.C. Sabathia	.75
50	Yadier Molina	.25
51	James Shields	.25
52	Jeff Samardzija	.25
53	Rafael Furcal	.40
54	Cliff Lee	.50
55	Daniel Murphy RC	2.00
56	Randy Johnson	.75
57	Jon Garland	.25
58	Chien-Ming Wang	.75
59	Zack Greinke	.50
60	Tim Lincecum	1.00
61	Conor Jackson	.25
62	Chase Utley	.75
63	Andrew Sonnanstine	.25
64	Miguel Tejada	.50
65	Geovany Soto	.50
66	Jeremy Sowers	.25
67	Ian Kinsler	.75
68	Jay Bruce	.75
69	Max Scherzer	.50
70	Scott Rolen	.50
71	Justin Upton	.50
72	Xavier Nady	.25
73	Erik Bedard	.25
74	Chad Billingsley	.50
75	Ryan Braun	1.00
76	Pat Burrell	.40
77	Edgar Renteria	.25
78	Joe Crede	.25
79	Manny Ramirez	.75
80	Carlos Zambrano	.25
81	Hunter Pence	.50
82	Grady Sizemore	.75
83	Brian Roberts	.50
84	Alex Rios	.40
85	Joe Saunders	.25
86	Albert Pujols	2.00
87	Derrek Lee	.50
88	Ichiro Suzuki	1.50
89	Javier Vazquez	.50
90	Johan Santana	.75
91	Miguel Cabrera	.75
92	Daisuke Matsuzaka	1.00
93	Chris Young	.25
94	Joe Mauer	.75
95	Stephen Drew	.50
96	Justin Masterson	.50
97	Dustin Pedroia	1.00
98	Derek Jeter	2.00
99	John Smoltz	.50
100	Jason Varitek	.50
101	Jorge Posada	.50
102	Mark Buehrle	.40
103	Bobby Abreu	.50
104	Victor Martinez	.50
105	Jeff Francis	.25
106	Rickie Weeks	.40
107	Carlos Quentin	.50
108	Howie Kendrick	.25
109	Aramis Ramirez	.25
110	Jonathan Papelbon	.50
111	Dan Haren	.50
112	Barry Zito	.25
113	Magglio Ordonez	.50
114	Alfonso Soriano	.50
115	Todd Helton	.50
116	Troy Tulowitzki	.50
117	Josh Beckett	.75
118	Andy Pettitte	.25
119	Hank Blalock	.25
120	Curtis Granderson	.75
121	Francisco Rodriguez	.25
122	Carlos Lee	.50
123	Gavin Floyd	.25
124	Joe Nathan	.25
125	Matt Holliday	.50
126	Hanley Ramirez	1.00
127	Javier Valentin	.25
128	John Maine	.25
129	Jeremy Bonderman	.25
130	Nick Markakis	.50
131	Troy Glaus	.25
132	Derek Lowe	.25
133	Lance Berkman	.50
134	Jered Weaver	.25
135	Chipper Jones	.75
136	Prince Fielder	1.00
137	Travis Hafner	.25
138	Joba Chamberlain	1.00
139	Ryan Howard	1.00
140	Paul Konerko	.50
141	Kenji Johjima	.25
142	Yovani Gallardo	.50
143	Adrian Gonzalez	.75
144	Jimmy Rollins	.75
145	Nick Swisher	.25
146	Felix Hernandez	.50
147	Garret Anderson	.25
148	Russell Martin	.40
149	Jason Bay	.50
150	Fausto Carmona	.25
151	Matt Garza	.25
152	Matt Cain	.50
153	Ryan Freel	.25
154	Rocco Baldelli	.25
155	Scott Kazmir	.40
156	Alexei Ramirez	.50
157	Adam Dunn	.50
158	Johnny Damon	.50
159	Jake Peavy	.50
160	Jose Reyes	.75
161	Rick Ankiel	.40
162	Michael Young	.40
163	Robinson Cano	.50
164	Ryan Zimmerman	.50
165	Jim Thome	.50
166	A.J. Burnett	.40
167	Joakim Soria	.40
168	J.D. Drew	.40
169	Cole Hamels	1.00
170	Jacoby Ellsbury	1.00
171	Travis Snider RC	3.00
172	Josh Outman RC	1.50
173	Dexter Fowler (RC)	2.00
174	Matt Tuiasosopo (RC)	1.00
175	Bobby Parnell RC	2.00
176	Jason Motte (RC)	1.00
177	James McDonald RC	2.50
178	Scott Lewis (RC)	1.00
179	George Kottaras (RC)	1.00
180	Phil Coke RC	2.00
181	Jordan Schafer (RC)	1.50
182	Joe Martinez RC	1.50
183	Trevor Crowe RC	2.00
184	Shairon Martis RC	1.50
185	Everth Cabrera RC	1.50
186	Trevor Cahill RC	3.00
187	Jesse Chavez RC	1.00
188	Josh Whitesell RC	1.50
189	Brian Duensing RC	1.50
190	Andrew Bailey RC	2.00
191	Ryan Perry RC	1.50
192	Brett Anderson RC	2.50
193	Ricky Romero (RC)	1.50
194	Elvis Andrus RC	3.00
195	Kenshin Kawakami (RC)	3.00
196	Colby Rasmus (RC)	2.50
197	David Patton RC	1.50
198	David Hernandez RC	1.50
199	David Freese RC	1.50
200	Rick Porcello RC	4.00
201	Fernando Martinez RC	3.00
202	Edwin Moreno (RC)	1.00
203	Koji Uehara RC	3.00
204	Jason Jaramillo (RC)	1.00
205	Ramiro Pena (RC)	2.00
206	Brad Nelson (RC)	1.00
207	Michael Hinckley (RC)	1.00
208	Ronald Belisario (RC)	1.00
209	Chris Jakubauskas RC	1.50
210	Hunter Jones RC	1.00
211	Walter Silva RC	1.00
212	Jordan Zimmerman RC	3.00
213	Andrew McCutchen (RC)	3.00
214	Gordon Beckham RC	3.00
215	Anthony Claggett RC	1.50
216	Mark Melancon (RC)	1.00
217	Brett Cecil RC	2.00
218	Derek Holland RC	4.00
219	Greg Golson (RC)	1.00
220	Bobby Scales RC	1.50
221	Jordan Schäfer/Auto.	12.00
222	Trevor Crowe/Auto.	8.00
223	Ramiro Pena/Auto.	15.00
224	Trevor Cahill/Auto.	15.00
225	Ryan Perry/Auto.	12.00
226	Brett Anderson/Auto.	15.00
227	Elvis Andrus/Auto.	20.00
229	Michael Bowden/ Auto. (RC)	15.00
230	David Freese/Auto.	12.00
231	Nolan Reimold/ Auto. (RC)	20.00
233	Jason Jaramillo/Auto.	8.00
234	Ricky Romero/Auto.	15.00
235	Jordan Zimmerman/ Auto.	15.00
236	Derek Holland/Auto.	20.00
237	George Kottaras/Auto.	8.00
239	Sergio Escalona/ Auto. RC	8.00
240	Brian Duensing/Auto.	8.00
241	Everth Cabrera/Auto.	10.00
242	Andrew Bailey/Auto.	10.00
243	Chris Jakubauskas/ Auto.	8.00
	Tommy Hanson/ Auto. RC	50.00
	Mark Melancon/Auto.	12.00
	Will Venable/Auto. RC	10.00

Blue Refractors
Blue (1-170): 3-5X
Blue RC (171-220): 2-3X
Blue Auto. RC: 1-1.5X
Production 199 Sets

Gold Refractors
Gold (1-170): 5-10X
Gold RC (171-220): 3-5X
Gold Auto. RC: 2-4X
Production 50 Sets

Refractors
Refractor (1-170): 2-3X
Refractor RC (171-220): 1-1.5X
Refractor Auto. RC: 1-1.2X
Inserted 1:3
Refract. RC Autos. #'d to 499

Red Refractors
No Pricing
Production 25 Sets

SuperFractors
Production One Set

X-Fractors
X-fractor (1-170): 2-4X
X-fractor RC (171-220): 1-2X

Printing Plates
Production one set per color.

World Baseball Classic

Common Player:		.75
Inserted 1:4		
Refractors:		1-2X
Production 500 Sets		
Blue Refractors:		2-4X
Production 199 Sets		
Gold Refractor:		4-6X
Production 50 Sets		
Red Refractor:		No Pricing
Production 25 Sets		
SuperFractor:		No Pricing
Production One Set		

1	Yu Darvish	4.00
2	Yulieski Gourriel	.75
3	Yi-Chuan Lin	.75
4	Ichiro Suzuki	3.00
5	Hung-Wen Chen	.75
6	Yuneiski Maya	.75
7	Chih-Hsien Chiang	.75
8	Kenji Johjima	.75
9	Hanley Ramirez	2.50
10	Chenhao Li	.75
11	Yoennis Cespedes	.75
12	Dae Ho Lee	.75
13	Alex Rodriguez	3.00
14	Luis Durango	.75
15	Chipper Jones	2.00
16	Dennis Neuman	.75
17	Carlos Lee	1.50
18	Tae Kyun Kim	.75
19	Adrian Gonzalez	1.50
20	Michel Enriquez	.75
21	Miguel Cabrera	1.50
22	Hisashi Iwakuma	2.00
23	Aroldis Chapman	2.00
24	Daisuke Matsuzaka	2.50
25	Chris Denorfia	.75
26	David Wright	2.50
27	Alex Rios	1.00
28	Michihiro Ogasawara	.75
29	Frederich Cepeda	1.00
30	Chen-Chang Lee	1.00
31	Shunsuke Watanabe	2.00
32	Luca Panerati	.75
33	David Ortiz	1.50
34	Tetsuya Yamaguchi	1.00
35	Jin Young Lee	.75
36	Tom Stuifbergen	.75
37	Masahiro Tanaka	1.00
38	Cheng-Ming Peng	.75
39	Yoshiyuki Ishihara	.75
40	Manuel Corpas	.75
41	Yi-Feng Kuo	.75
42	Ruben Tejada	.75
43	Kenley Jansen	.75
44	Shinnosuke Abe	1.00
45	Shuichi Murata	2.00
46	Yolexis Ulacia	.75
47	Yueh-Ping Lin	1.00
48	James Beresford	.75
49	Justin Morneau	1.50
50	Bradley Harman	.75
51	Juan Carlos Sulbaran	.75
52	Ubaldo Jimenez	1.00
53	Joel Naughton	.75
54	Rafael Diaz	.75
55	Russell Martin	1.00
56	Concepcion Rodriguez	.75
57	Po Yu Lin	.75
58	Chih-Kang Kao	.75
59	Gregor Blanco	.75
60	Justin Erasmus	.75
61	Kosuke Fukudome	2.00
62	Hiroyuki Nakajima	2.00
63	Luke Hughes	.75
64	Sidney de Jong	.75
65	Greg Halman	1.00
66	Seiichi Uchikawa	1.00
67	Tao Bu	.75
68	Pedro Martinez	1.50
69	Jingchao Wang	.75
70	Arquimedes Nieto	.75
71	Yang Yang	.75
72	Alex Liddi	1.00
73	Fei Feng	.75
74	Pedro Lazo	.75
75	Magglio Ordonez	1.00
76	Bryan Engelhardt	.75
77	Yen-Wen Kuo	.75
78	Norichika Aoki	1.00
79	Jose Reyes	2.00
80	Kangan Xia	.75
81	Shin-Soo Choo	1.00
82	Frank Catalanotto	.75
83	Ray Chang	.75
84	Nelson Cruz	1.00
85	Fu-Te Ni	.75
86	Hein Robb	.75
87	Hyun-Soo Kim	.75
88	Tai-Chi Kuo	.75
89	Akinori Iwamura	1.00
90	Chi-Hung Cheng	.75
91	Fujia Chu	.75
92	Gift Ngoepe	.75
93	Zhenwang Zhang	.75
94	Bernie Williams	1.00
95	Dustin Pedroia	2.50
96	Dylan Lindsay	1.00
97	Max Ramirez	.75
98	Yadier Molina	1.00
99	Phillippe Aumont	2.00
100	Derek Jeter	5.00

2009 Topps Heritage

		NM/M
Complete Set (500):		
Common Player (1-425):		.25
Common SP (426-500):		5.00
Inserted 1:3		
Hobby pack (8):		.25
Hobby box (24):		90.00

1	Mark Buehrle	.25
2	Nyjer Morgan	.25
3	Casey Kotchman	.25
4	Edinson Volquez	.50
5	Andre Ethier	.50
6	Brandon Inge	.25
7	Tim Lincecum, Bruce Bochy	.50
8	Gil Meche	.25
9	Brad Hawpe	.25
10	Hanley Ramirez	1.00
11	Ross Gload	.25
12	Jeremy Guthrie	.25
13	Garret Anderson	.25
14	Jeremy Sowers	.25
15	Dustin Pedroia	1.00
16	Chris Perez	.25
17	Adam Lind	.25
18	Los Angeles Dodgers	.25
19	Stephen Drew	.40
20	Matt Capps	.25
21	Mike Napoli	.25
22	Khalil Greene	.25
23	Andrew Sonnanstine	.25
24	Marco Scutaro	.25
25	Paul Konerko	.25
26	Miguel Tejada	.25
27	Nick Blackburn	.25
28	Nick Markakis	.75
29	Johan Santana	1.00
30	Grady Sizemore	.75
31	Raul Ibanez	.25
32	Jay Bruce, Johnny Cueto	.75
33	Randy Johnson	1.00
34	Ian Kinsler	.75
35	Andy Pettitte	.50
36	Lyle Overbay	.25
37	Jeff Francoeur	.25
38	Justin Duchscherer	.25
39	Mike Cameron	.25
40	Ryan Ludwick	.50
41	David Bush	.25
42	Pablo Sandoval RC	1.00
43	Washington Nationals	.25
44	Dana Eveland	.25
45	Jeff Keppinger	.25
46	Brandon Backe	.25
47	Ryan Theriot	.25
48	Vernon Wells	.50
49	Doug Davis	.25
50	Curtis Granderson	.75
51	Aaron Laffey	.25
52	Chris Young	.50
53	Adam Jones	.50
54	Jonathan Papelbon	.75
55	Nate McLouth	.50
56	Hunter Pence	.50
57	Scot Shields	.25
58	Conor Jackson	.25
58	Conor Jackson	
59	Rays Logo/SP	200.00
59	John Maine	.25
60	Ramon Hernandez	.25
61	Jorge De La Rosa	.25
62	Greg Maddux	1.00
63	Carlos Beltran	.75
64	Matt Harrison RC	.75
65	Ivan Rodriguez	.50
66	Jesse Litsch	.25
67	Omar Vizquel	.25
68	Edwin Jackson	.25
69	Ray Durham	.25
70	Tom Glavine	.50
70	Tom Glavine UER name spelled Thom	200.00
71	Darin Erstad	.25
72	Detroit Tigers	.25
73	David Price RC	3.00
74	Marlon Byrd	.25
75	Ryan Garko	.25
76	Jered Weaver	.50
77	Kelly Shoppach	.25
78	Joe Saunders	.25
79	Carlos Pena	.50
80	Brian Wilson	.25
81	Carlos Gonzalez	.25
82	Scott Baker	.25
83	Derek Jeter	2.50
84	Yadier Molina	.25
85	Justin Verlander	.50
86	Jose Lopez	.25
87	Jarrod Washburn	.25
88	Russell Martin	.25
89	Garrett Olson	.25
90	Erick Aybar	.25
91	Kevin Millwood	.25
92	Jose Guillen	.25
93	Rickie Weeks	.40
94	Yovani Gallardo	.50
95	Aramis Ramirez	.50
96	Phil Hughes	.50
97	Kevin Kouzmanoff	.25
98	Shaun Marcum	.25
99	Lastings Milledge	.25
100	Jair Jurrjens	.40
101	Gio Gonzalez	.25
102	Adrian Gonzalez	.25
102	Adrian Gonzalez	
	Rangers Logo/SP	200.00
103	Brad Lidge	.25
104	Chris Davis	.25
105	Brad Penny	.25
106	David Eckstein	.25
107	Jo Jo Reyes	.25
108	John Buck	.25
109	Delmon Young	.40
110	Johnny Cueto	.50
111	Kevin Youkilis	.25
112	Scott Lewis RC	.75
113	Brandon Moss	.25
114	Alexi Casilla	.25
115	Jonathan Papelbon, Tim Wakefield	.50
116	Emil Brown	.25
117	Michael Bowden RC	1.50
118	Chris Lambert RC	.25
119	Wilkin Castillo RC	.25
120	Fernando Perez RC	1.00
121	Angel Salome RC	.25
122	Dexter Fowler RC	1.50
123	Will Venable RC	.75
124	Jason Motte RC	1.00
125	Jesus Delgado RC	1.00
126	Alfredo Simon RC	.50
127	Gaby Sanchez RC	.25
128	Scott Elbert RC	1.00
129	James Parr RC	.25
130	Greg Golson RC	.75
131	Jon Niese RC	.75
132	Mat Gamel RC	3.00
133	Luis Cruz RC	.25
134	Phil Coke RC	1.00
135	Devon Lowery RC	.75
136	Matt Tuiasosopo RC	.25
137	Kila Ka'aihue RC	1.00
138	Andrew Carpenter RC	1.00
139	Jensen Lewis RC	1.50
140	Lou Marson RC	1.00
141	Wade LeBlanc RC	.75
142	Juan Miranda RC	.25
143	Alcides Escobar RC	1.50
144	Matt Antonelli RC	1.00
145	Jesse Chavez RC	1.00
146	Ramon Ramirez RC	.75
147	Aaron Cunningham RC	1.00
148	Travis Snider RC	3.00
149	Adam Dunn	.50
150	John Danks	.50
151	San Francisco Giants	.25
152	Jorge Cantu	.25
153	Jacoby Ellsbury	.75
154	Rich Aurilia	.25
155	Jeff Kent	.50
156	Salomon Torres	.25
157	Juan Uribe	.25
158	Gregor Blanco	.25
159	Shin-Soo Choo	.25
160	David Wright, Alex Rodriguez	.75
161	Jose Valverde	.25
162	B.J. Upton	.50
163	Johnny Damon	.50
164	Cincinnati Reds	.25
165	Tim Lincecum	1.00
166	Carl Crawford	.50
167	Jeff Mathis	.25
168	Felipe Lopez	.25
169	Joe Nathan	.25
170	Brian McCann	.50
171	Matt Joyce	.25
172	Cameron Maybin	.25
173	Brandon Phillips	.50
174	Cleveland Indians	.25
175	Tim Redding	.25
176	Corey Patterson	.25
177	Joakim Soria	.25
178	Jhonny Peralta	.40
179	Daniel Murphy RC	1.00
180	Ryan Church	.25
181	Josh Johnson	.25
182	Carlos Zambrano	.50
183	Pittsburgh Pirates	.25
184	Boston Red Sox	.50
185	Kyle Kendrick	.25
186	Joel Zumaya	.25
187	Bronson Arroyo	.25
188	Joey Gathright	.25
189	Mike Gonzalez	.25
190	Luke Scott	.25
191	Jonathan Broxton	.25
192	Jeff Baker	.25
193	Brian Fuentes	.25
194	Pat Burrell	.50
195	Ryan Franklin	.25
196	Alex Gordon	.50
197	Orlando Hudson	.25
198	Chris Dickerson	.25
199	David Purcey	.25
200	Ken Griffey Jr.	2.00
201	Chad Tracy	.25
202	Troy Percival	.25
203	Chris Iannetta	.25
204	Baltimore Orioles	.25
205	Yunel Escobar	.25
206	Dan Haren	.25
207	Aubrey Huff	.25
208	Chicago White Sox	.25
209	Randy Wolf	.25
210	Ryan Zimmerman	.50
211	Manny Parra	.40
212	Manny Acta	.25
213	Dusty Baker	.25
214	Bruce Bochy	.25
215	Bobby Cox	.25
216	Terry Francona	.25
217	Joe Girardi	.25
218	Ozzie Guillen	.25
219	Bob Geren	.25
220	Tony LaRussa	.25
221	Jim Leyland	.25
222	Charlie Manuel	.25
223	Lou Piniella	.25
224	John Russell	.25
225	Joe Torre	.50
226	Dave Trembley	.25
227	Eric Wedge	.25
228	Jeff Suppan	.25
229	Kazuo Matsui	.25
230	Josh Beckett, Daisuke Matsuzaka, Jon Lester	1.00
231	Mark Reynolds	.25
232	Jay Payton	.25
233	Kerry Wood	.25
234	Juan Pierre	.25
235	Ryan Freel	.25
236	Ryan Feierabend	.25
237	Xavier Nady	.25
238	Ronny Paulino	.25
239	A.J. Burnett	.25
240	Orlando Cabrera	.25
241	Corey Hart	.40
242	St. Louis Cardinals	.25
243	Andy Marte	.25
244	Trevor Hoffman	.25
245	Carlos Guillen	.25
246	Brandon Jones	.25
247	Hideki Matsui	.75
248	Henry Blanco	.25
249	Jon Lester	.50
250	Albert Pujols	2.50
251	Manny Ramirez	1.00
252	Brian Bannister	.25
253	Alex Cintron	.25
254	Brandon Lyon	.25
255	Blake DeWitt	.25
256	Luis Castillo	.25
257	Mark Teixeira	.75
258	Jack Wilson	.25
259	Kosuke Fukudome	.50
260	Manny Ramirez, Andre Ethier	.50
261	Scott Kazmir	.25
262	Mark Teahen	.25
263	Dioner Navarro	.25
264	Cole Hamels	.25
265	Justin Upton	.50
266	Ricky Nolasco	.25
267	Hank Blalock	.40
268	John Lackey	.40
269	Jeremy Hermida	.25
270	Chien-Ming Wang	.75
271	Lance Berkman	.50
272	Scott Olsen	.25
273	Alex Rios	.25
274	Matt Garza	.50
275	Skip Schumaker	.25
276	Greg Smith	.25
277	Bobby Crosby	.25
278	Hiroki Kuroda	.50
279	Gary Matthews Jr.	.25
280	Tim Wakefield	.25
281	Mike Jacobs	.25
282	Chris Volstad	.25
283	Jeff Clement	.25
284	Max Scherzer	.50
285	Chase Headley	.25
286	Francisco Rodriguez	.50
287	Moises Alou	.25
288	Jeff Francis	.25
289	Carlos Delgado	.75
290	Jose Reyes	1.00
291	Ubaldo Jimenez	.25
292	Kelly Shoppach	
	Victor Martinez	.25
293	Joe Blanton	.25
294	Mark DeRosa	.25
295	Casey Blake	.25
296	Mike Pelfrey	.25
297	Aaron Boone	.25
298	Aaron Cook	.25
299	Daric Barton	.25
300	Ryan Howard	1.50
301	Ty Wigginton	.25
302	Philadelphia Phillies	.25
303	Barry Zito	.25
304	Jake Peavy	.50
305	Alfonso Soriano	.75
306	Scott Linebrink	.25
307	Torii Hunter	.50
308	Zack Greinke	.40
309	Ryan Sweeney	.25
310	Mike Lowell	.25
311	Jason Marquis	.25
312	Aaron Rowand	.25
313	Brandon Morrow	.40
314	Edgar Renteria	.40
315	Mariano Rivera	.50
316	Wilson Betemit	.25
317	Joey Votto	.50
318	Evan Longoria	1.00
319	Mike Aviles	.25
320	Jay Bruce	.75
321	Denard Span	.25
322	David Murphy	.25
323	Geovany Soto	.50
324	John Lannan	.25
325	Brad Ziegler	.25
326	Ichiro Suzuki	1.50
327	Kyle Lohse	.25
328	Jesus Flores	.25
329	Edwin Encarnacion	.25
330	Franklin Gutierrez	.25
331	Troy Glaus	.40
332	David Ortiz	1.00
333	Anibal Sanchez	.25
334	Jimmy Rollins	.75
335	Kelly Johnson	.25
336	Paul Byrd	.25
337	Akinori Iwamura	.25
338	Milton Bradley	.25
339	Miguel Olivo	.25
340	Ian Snell	.25
341	Vladimir Guerrero	.75
342	Asdrubal Cabrera	.25
343	Clayton Kershaw	.50
344	Rafael Furcal	.25
345	Aaron Harang	.25
346	Fred Lewis	.25
346	Fred Lewis/SP	
	Randy Winn Pictured	180.00
347	Jack Cust	.25
348	Todd Helton	.50
349	Steve Pearce	.25
350	Javier Vazquez	.40
351	Ben Sheets	.40
352	Joey Votto, Edwin Encarnacion, Jay Bruce	.50
353	Luke Hochevar	.25
354	Chris Snyder	.25
355	Rick Ankiel	.50
356	Emmanuel Burriss	.25
357	Vicente Padilla	.25
358	Yuniesky Betancourt	.25
359	Willy Taveras	.25
360	Gavin Floyd	.25
361	Gerald Laird	.25
362	Roy Oswalt	.50
363	Coco Crisp	.25
364	Felix Hernandez	.50
365	Carlos Quentin	.50
366	Ervin Santana	.40
367	David DeJesus	.25
368	Aaron Miles	.25
369	B.J. Ryan	.25
370	Jason Giambi	.50
371	J.J. Putz	.25
372	Brian Schneider	.25
373	Andy LaRoche	.25
374	Tim Hudson	.25
375	Garrett Atkins	.50
376	James Shields	.40
377	Alex Rodriguez	2.50
378	James Hardy	.25
379	Michael Young	.40
380	Prince Fielder	.50
381	Atlanta Braves	.25
382	Chone Figgins	.25
383	David Wright	1.50
384	Brian Giles	.25
385	Chase Utley	1.00
386	Eric Bruntlett	.25
387	Carlos Ruiz	.25
388	Ryan Howard	1.00
389	Jayson Werth	.50
390	B.J. Upton	.50
391	Brad Lidge	.25
392	Chad Cordero	.25
393	Ryan Doumit	.25
394	James Loney	.50
395	George Sherrill	.25
396	Gary Sheffield	.50
397	Chicago Cubs	.25
398	Rich Harden	.25
399	Scott Kazmir, David Price, James Shields	1.00
400	Magglio Ordonez	.40
401	Dan Uggla	.50
402	Adam LaRoche	.25
403	Taylor Teagarden	.40
404	Chris Young	.50
405	Robinson Cano	.50
406	Dustin McGowan	.25
407	Randy Winn	.25
407	Randy Winn/SP Fred Lewis Pictured	150.00
408	Carlos Lee	.50
409	Kurt Suzuki	.25
410	Matt Cain	.50
411	Paul Bako	.25
412	Ted Lilly	.25
413	Kansas City Royals	.25
414	Miguel Cabrera	.75
415	Jayson Werth	.25
416	J.C. Romero	.25
417	Martin Prado	.25
418	Armando Galarraga	.25
419	Brian Roberts	.50
420	Chipper Jones	1.00
421	Bengie Molina	.25
422	Matt Kemp	.75
423	Brian Buscher	.25
424	Erik Bedard	.25
425	Chad Billingsley	.50
426	Scott Rolen/SP	5.00
427	Ben Francisco/SP	5.00
428	Jermaine Dye/SP	5.00
429	Dustin Pedroia, Ichiro Suzuki/SP	8.00
430	Kevin Slowey/SP	5.00
431	Jason Bartlett/SP	5.00
432	Glen Perkins/SP	5.00
433	Carlos Gomez/SP	5.00
434	Jon Garland/SP	5.00
435	Joe Crede/SP	5.00
436	Billy Butler/SP	5.00
437	Zach Duke/SP	5.00
438	Chris Coste/SP	5.00
439	Daisuke Matsuzaka/SP	8.00
440	Elijah Dukes/SP	5.00
441	Fausto Carmona/SP	5.00
442	Joe Mauer/SP	6.00
443	Marcus Thames/SP	5.00
444	Mike Fontenot/SP	5.00
445	John Smoltz/SP Braves	6.00
445	John Smoltz/SP Red Sox	150.00
446	Pedro Martinez/SP	6.00
447	Adrian Beltre/SP	6.00
448	Kevin Millar/SP	5.00
449	Nick Swisher/SP	5.00
450	Justin Morneau/SP	6.00
451	Shane Victorino/SP	5.00
452	Placido Polanco/SP	5.00
453	Ryan Dempster/SP	5.00
454	Frank Thomas/SP	8.00
455	Orioles Coaches/SP	5.00
456	Boston Red Sox Coaches/SP	5.00
457	Chicago Cubs Coaches/SP	5.00
458	Chicago White Sox Coaches/SP	5.00
459	Cincinnati Reds Coaches/SP	5.00
460	Cleveland Indians Coaches/SP	5.00
461	Detroit Tigers Coaches/SP	5.00
462	Tampa Bay Rays Coaches/SP	5.00
463	L.A. Dodgers Coaches/SP	5.00
464	Atlanta Braves Coaches/SP	5.00
465	New York Yankees Coaches/SP	5.00
466	Philadelphia Phillies Coaches/SP	5.00
467	Pittsburgh Pirates Coaches/SP	5.00
468	St. Louis Cardinals Coaches/SP	5.00
469	New York Mets Coaches/SP	5.00
470	Washington Nationals Coaches/SP	5.00
471	Brad Ausmus/SP	5.00
472	Melvin Mora/SP	5.00
473	Austin Kearns/SP	5.00
474	Josh Willingham/SP	5.00
475	Derek Lowe/SP	5.00
476	Nick Punto/SP	5.00
477	A.J. Pierzynski/SP	5.00
478	Troy Tulowitzki/SP	6.00
479	C.C. Sabathia/SP	8.00
480	Jorge Posada/SP	6.00
481	Kevin Youkilis/SP	6.00
482	Lance Berkman/SP	6.00
483	Dustin Pedroia/SP	8.00
484	Chase Utley/SP	8.00
485	Alex Rodriguez/SP	12.00
486	Chipper Jones/SP	8.00
487	Derek Jeter/SP	15.00
488	Hanley Ramirez/SP Marlins	8.00
488	Hanley Ramirez/SP Red Sox	200.00
489	Josh Hamilton/SP	8.00
490	Ryan Braun/SP	8.00
491	Manny Ramirez/SP	8.00
492	Kosuke Fukudome/SP	8.00
493	Ichiro Suzuki/SP	10.00
494	Matt Holliday/SP	6.00
495	Joe Mauer/SP	6.00
496	Geovany Soto/SP	5.00
497	Roy Halladay/SP	5.00
498	Ben Sheets/SP	5.00
499	Cliff Lee/SP	5.00
500	Billy Wagner/SP	5.00

Advertising Panels

		NM/M
Common Panel:		2.00
Inserted 1:Box		
	Aaron Boone, James Loney, Gerald Laird	2.00
	Aaron Laffey, Hanley Ramirez, Scott Olsen	3.00
	Albert Pujols, Dan Haren, John Danks	4.00

SCOTT OLSEN

RYAN FRANKLIN

EMIL BROWN

Andre Ethier, Kelly Shoppach,
Victor Martinez,
Ronny Paulino,
Mike Gonzalez 2.00
Aubrey Huff, Rich Aurilia,
Scott Baker 2.00
Brad Hawpe, Roy Oswalt,
Mike Jacobs 2.00
Brandon Backe, Shin-
Soo Choo, Ozzie Guillen 2.00
Brian Wilson,
Gary Mathews Jr.,
Ubaldo Jimenez 2.00
Bronson Arroyo, Matt Cain,
Detroit Tigers 2.00
Carlos Beltran, Andre Ethier,
Kelly Shoppach,
Victor Martinez 2.00
Carlos Zambrano,
Edgar Renteria,
Dave Tremblay
Chien-Ming Wang,
Corey Hart, Aubrey Huff 2.00
Chris Lambert,
Carlos Zambrano,
Dave Tremblay 2.00
Cole Hamels, Juan Pierre,
Yunel Escobar 3.00
Corey Hart, Aubrey Huff,
Rich Aurilia 2.00
Corey Patterson, Pat Burrell,
Brian Bannister 2.00
Dan Haren, John Danks,
Carlos Beltran
Daniel Murphy, Hideki Matsui,
Ty Wigginton 2.00
Edgar Renteria, Brian Giles,
Dave Tremblay
David Price, Luke Scott,
Jeff Suppan 2.00
David Wright, Matt Antonelli,
Alex Rodriguez 4.00
Matt Cain, Jeff Francis,
Detroit Tigers 2.00
Edgar Renteria, Brian Giles,
Greg Smith 2.00
Emil Brown, Scot Shields,
Francisco Rodriguez,
David Murphy 2.00
Fernando Perez,
Jeremy Guthrie,
Nick Blackburn 2.00
Gaby Sanchez, Vernon Wells,
Ross Gload 2.00
Garret Anderson,
Brandon Backe,
Shin-Soo Choo 2.00
Gerald Laird, Chien-
Ming Wang, Corey Hart 3.00
Gil Meche, David Price,
Luke Scott 3.00
Hanley Ramirez, Scott Olsen,
Ryan Franklin 2.00
Hideki Matsui, Ty Wigginton,
Vicente Padilla 2.00
Jack Wilson,
Dustin McGowan,
Cincinnati Reds 2.00
James Loney, Gerald Laird,
Chien-Ming Wang 2.00
Jeff Clement,
Bronson Arroyo,
Detroit Tigers 2.00
Jeremy Guthrie,
Nick Blackburn,
Scott Lewis 2.00
Jesus Delgado, Brian Wilson,
Gary Mathews Jr. 2.00
John Danks, Carlos Beltran,
Andre Ethier 2.00
John Lackey, Lyle Overbay,
Chris Lambert 2.00
Jonathan Papelbon,
Tim Wakefield,
Corey Patterson,
Pat Burrell 2.00
Juan Pierre, Yunel Escobar,
Gaby Sanchez 2.00

Kelly Shoppach,
Victor Martinez,
Ronny Paulino,
Mike Gonzalez 2.00
Kerry Wood, Scott Elbert,
Fernando Perez 2.00
Khalil Greene, Cole Hamels,
Juan Pierre 2.00
Jesus Delgado, Brian Wilson,
L.A. Dodgers 2.00
Lou Piniella, Scott Kazmir,
Jeff Clement 2.00
Lyle Overbay, Chris Lambert,
Carlos Zambrano 2.00
Matt Antonelli, David Wright,
Alex Rodriguez,
Alfredo Simon 4.00
Miguel Tejada, Matt Harrison,
James Parr 2.00
Mike Cameron, Ted Lilly,
John Lackey 2.00
Mike Jacobs, Terry Francona,
Jacoby Ellsbury 2.00
Mike Napoli, David Wright,
Matt Antonelli 3.00
Nick Blackburn, Scott Lewis,
Ramon Ramirez 2.00
Pat Burrell, Brian Bannister,
Jesus Flores 2.00
Ross Gload, Miguel Tejada,
Matt Harrison 2.00
Roy Oswalt, Mike Jacobs,
Terry Francona 2.00
Ryan Franklin, Emil Brown,
Scot Shields 2.00
Francisco Rodriguez 2.00
Scott Elbert, Fernando Perez,
Jeremy Guthrie 2.00
Scott Kazmir, Jeff Clement,
Bronson Arroyo 2.00
Scott Olsen, Ryan Franklin,
Emil Brown 2.00
Shin-Soo Choo, Ozzie Guillen,
Mike Aviles 2.00
Stephen Drew, Andy Pettitte,
R. Feirebrand 2.00
Ted Lilly, John Lackey,
Lyle Overbay 2.00
Ty Wigginton, Vicente Padilla,
Brad Hawpe 2.00
Vernon Wells, Ross Gload,
Miguel Tejada 2.00
Vicente Padilla, Brad Hawpe,
Roy Oswalt 2.00
Yunel Escobar,
Gaby Sanchez,
Vernon Wells 2.00

Chrome

STEPHEN DREW

		NM/M
Common Chrome (1-100):		3.00
Production 1,960 Sets		
Refractor:		2X
Production 560 Sets		
Black Refractor:		4-6X
Production 60 Sets		
1	Manny Ramirez	4.00
2	Andre Ethier	4.00
3	Miguel Tejada	3.00
4	Nick Markakis	4.00
5	Johan Santana	4.00
6	Grady Sizemore	4.00
7	Ian Kinsler	4.00
8	Ryan Ludwick	3.00
9	Jonathan Papelbon	4.00
10	Albert Pujols	10.00
11	Carlos Beltran	4.00
12	David Price	6.00
13	Carlos Pena	4.00
14	Derek Jeter	12.00
15	Mark Teixeira	4.00
16	Aramis Ramirez	3.00
17	Dexter Fowler	4.00
18	Brad Lidge	3.00
19	Johnny Cueto	3.00
20	David Wright	8.00
21	Mat Gamel	6.00
22	B.J. Upton	4.00
23	Carl Crawford	3.00
24	Mariano Rivera	4.00
25	Scott Kazmir	4.00
26	Vladimir Guerrero	4.00
27	Clayton Kershaw	6.00
28	Ben Sheets	3.00
29	Rick Ankiel	4.00
30	Nate McLouth	3.00
31	Roy Oswalt	4.00
32	Felix Hernandez	4.00
33	Ervin Santana	3.00
34	Prince Fielder	5.00
35	Cole Hamels	4.00
36	Jon Lester	4.00
37	Kosuke Fukudome	3.00
38	Justin Upton	4.00
39	John Lackey	3.00
40	Lance Berkman	4.00
41	Chien-Ming Wang	5.00

42	Alex Rios	4.00
43	Carlos Delgado	4.00
44	Jake Peavy	4.00
45	Hanley Ramirez	6.00
46	Alfonso Soriano	4.00
47	Jimmy Rollins	5.00
48	J.J. Hardy	3.00
49	James Loney	3.00
50	Ryan Howard	6.00
51	Rich Harden	4.00
52	Dan Uggla	4.00
53	Miguel Cabrera	6.00
54	Matt Kemp	4.00
55	Russell Martin	4.00
56	Chipper Jones	5.00
57	Stephen Drew	4.00
58	Randy Johnson	4.00
59	Andy Pettitte	3.00
60	Francisco Rodriguez	3.00
61	Vernon Wells	3.00
62	Ivan Rodriguez	3.00
63	Joe Saunders	3.00
64	Yadier Molina	3.00
65	Ken Griffey Jr.	8.00
66	Justin Verlander	3.00
67	Edinson Volquez	3.00
68	Phil Hughes	3.00
69	Yovani Gallardo	3.00
70	Jose Reyes	6.00
71	Gio Gonzalez	3.00
72	Adrian Gonzalez	4.00
73	Chris Davis	3.00
74	Brad Penny	4.00
75	Dustin Pedroia	5.00
76	Kevin Youkilis	4.00
77	Angel Salome	3.00
78	Kila Ka'aihue	3.00
79	Lou Marson	3.00
80	Ichiro Suzuki	6.00
81	Alcides Escobar	3.00
82	Travis Snider	4.00
83	Adam Dunn	4.00
84	Jacoby Ellsbury	4.00
85	Jay Bruce	5.00
86	Ryan Doumit	3.00
87	Tim Lincecum	5.00
88	Joe Nathan	3.00
89	Brian McCann	3.00
90	Evan Longoria	8.00
91	Carlos Zambrano	3.00
92	Pat Burrell	3.00
93	Alex Gordon	4.00
94	Ryan Zimmerman	3.00
95	Carlos Quentin	3.00
96	Xavier Nady	3.00
97	Max Scherzer	4.00
98	Hiroki Kuroda	3.00
99	Carlos Lee	4.00
100	Alex Rodriguez	8.00

Clubhouse Collection Relics

★ Clubhouse Collection ★
KURT SUZUKI

		NM/M
Common Relic:		4.00
DW	David Wright	10.00
DJ	Dan Johnson	4.00
LM	Lastings Milledge	4.00
BU	B.J. Upton	6.00
CU	Chase Utley	10.00
VW	Vernon Wells	4.00
DP	Dustin Pedroia	15.00
KS	Kurt Suzuki	4.00
CM	Cameron Maybin	6.00
MR	Manny Ramirez	10.00
DU	Dan Uggla	6.00
SP	Scott Podsednik	4.00
DW	Dontrelle Willis	4.00
KM	Kevin Millwood	4.00
KM	Kevin Mench	4.00
CT	Curtis Thigpen	4.00
MT	Miguel Tejada	4.00
CC	Carl Crawford	6.00
JD	J.D. Drew	4.00
JL	Jon Lester	8.00
RB	Rocco Baldelli	4.00
KY	Kevin Youkilis	8.00
AR	Aramis Ramirez	4.00
CB	Clay Buchholz	6.00

Clubhouse Collection Relic Auto.

Production 25 Sets

Clubhouse Collection Dual Auto.

Production 10 Sets

Clubhouse Collection Dual Relic

		NM/M
Common Duo:		
Production 60 Sets		
BR	Jay Bruce,	
	Frank Robinson	50.00
PM	Albert Pujols,	
	Stan Musial	140.00
RM	Alex Rodriguez,	
	Mickey Mantle	200.00
SB	Alfonso Soriano,	
	Ernie Banks	150.00
TM	Mark Teixeira,	
	Mickey Mantle	180.00

Flashbacks

MICKEY MANTLE
NEW YORK YANKEES

		NM/M
Complete Set (10):		10.00
Common Player:		.50
1	Mickey Mantle	3.00
2	Bill Mazeroski	.50
3	Juan Marichal	1.00
4	Paul Richards	.50
5	Luis Aparicio	.50
6	Ted Williams	2.00
7	Roger Maris	1.50
8	Ernie Banks	1.50
9	Mickey Mantle	3.00
10	Bobby Richardson	.50

Flashback Autographs

Production 25 Sets

Flashback Dual Stadium Relic

Production 10 Sets

Flashback Stadium Relic

		NM/M
Common Stadium Relic:		
EB	Ernie Banks	20.00
MM	Mickey Mantle	50.00
MM2	Mickey Mantle	50.00
SM	Stan Musial	30.00
FR	Frank Robinson	20.00
BM	Bill Mazeroski	25.00
BR	Brooks Robinson	20.00
AK	Al Kaline	25.00
LA	Luis Aparicio	20.00
BRI	Bobby Richardson	20.00

Flashback Stadium Relic Autos.

Production 25 Sets

Mayo

		NM/M
Common Player:		1.50
AP	Albert Pujols	6.00
AR	Alex Rodriguez	6.00
AR	Alex Rios	1.50
AS	Alfonso Soriano	2.00
CJ	Chipper Jones	3.00
DM	Daisuke Matsuzaka	3.00
DO	David Ortiz	4.00
DP	Dustin Pedroia	4.00
DW	David Wright	5.00
EL	Evan Longoria	5.00
GS	Grady Sizemore	4.00
HR	Hanley Ramirez	3.00
IS	Ichiro Suzuki	4.00
JH	Josh Hamilton	4.00
JS	Johan Santana	2.00
MR	Manny Ramirez	3.00
RB	Ryan Braun	3.00
RH	Ryan Howard	4.00
TL	Tim Lincecum	3.00
VG	Vladimir Guerrero	3.00

New Age Performers

		NM/M
Complete Set (15):		25.00
Common Player:		1.00
1	David Wright	3.00
2	Manny Ramirez	1.50
3	Mark Teixeira	1.50
4	Josh Hamilton	2.50
5	Chase Utley	2.50
6	Tim Lincecum	2.50
7	Stephen Drew	1.00
8	Cliff Lee	1.00
9	Carlos Quentin	1.00
10	Ryan Braun	2.50
11	Cole Hamels	1.50
12	Dustin Pedroia	3.00
13	Geovany Soto	1.50

NEW AGE PERFORMERS
SECOND BASE
DUSTIN PEDROIA
BOSTON RED SOX

14	Scott Kazmir	1.00
15	Evan Longoria	4.00

News Flashbacks

		NM/M
Complete Set (10):		10.00
Common Card:		1.00
1	Aswan High Dam	1.00
2	Bathyscaphe Trieste	1.00
3	Weather Satellite - TIROS	1.00
4	Civil Rights Act 1960	1.00
5	Fifty Star Flag	1.00
6	USS Seadragon	1.00
7	Marshall Space Flight Center	1.00
8	Presidential Debate	2.00
9	John F. Kennedy	2.00
10	Polaris Missile	1.00

Real One Autographs

		NM/M
Common Auto:		
Red Ink:		1.5X
Production 60 Sets		
NC	Nelson Chittum	30.00
AC	Art Ceccarelli	40.00
DG	Dick Gray	50.00
JG	Johnny Groth	40.00
BG	Buddy Gilbert	40.00
BJ	Ben Johnson	40.00
SK	Steve Korcheck	40.00
ML	Mike Lee	40.00
WL	Whitey Lockman	50.00
CM	Carl Mathias	35.00
GM	Gil McDougald	50.00
CN	Cal Neeman	50.00
IN	Irv Noren	50.00
TP	Taylor Phillips	50.00
JP	Jim Proctor	40.00
CR	Curt Raydon	50.00
JR	John Romonosky	30.00
RS	Ron Samford	40.00
AS	Art Schult	50.00
JS	Joe Shipley	50.00
JSS	Jake Striker	40.00
WT	Wayne Terwilliger	50.00
JH	Jack Harshman	50.00
BTH	Bill Harris	40.00
BR	Bob Rush	50.00
SL	Stan Lopata	50.00
RW	Ray Webster	50.00
TW	Ted Wieand	50.00
DW	Don Williams	40.00
RW	Red Wilson	50.00
JM	Justin Masterson	50.00
JB	Jay Bruce	60.00
FC	Fausto Carmona	35.00
MG	Mat Gamel	40.00
CK	Clayton Kershaw	40.00

Real One Dual Autographs

Production 25 Sets

Then & Now

WHITEY FORD
THEN AND NOW
CC SABATHIA

		NM/M
Complete Set (10):		15.00
Common duo:		1.00
1	Ernie Banks, Ryan Howard	3.00
2	Roger Maris, Ryan Howard	3.00
3	Roberto Clemente, Chipper Jones	3.00
4	Luis Aparicio, Willy Taveras	1.00
5	Mickey Mantle, Adam Dunn	3.00
6	Jim Bunning, Tim Lincecum	2.00
7	Jim Bunning, Tim Lincecum	2.00
8	Lew Burdette, Cliff Lee	
9	Lew Burdette, Roy Halladay	3.00
10	Whitey Ford, C.C. Sabathia	1.50

1960 Buybacks

No Pricing

1960 Cut Signatures

Production One Set

2009 Topps Heritage High

Common Player:		.25
Common SP (686-720):		5.00
High # Pack (8):		3.00
High # Box (24):		60.00
501	Shane Robinson RC	1.00
502	Mat Latos RC	1.50
503	Aaron Poreda RC	1.00
504	Takashi Saito	.40
505	Adam Everett	.40
506	Adam Kennedy	.40
507	John Smoltz	1.00
508	Alex Cora	.40
509	Alfredo Aceves	.60
510	Alfredo Figaro RC	1.00
511	Andrew Bailey RC	2.50
512	Jhoulys Chacin RC	1.50
513	Andruw Jones	.40
514	Anthony Swarzak (RC)	1.00
515	Antonio Bastardo RC	1.00
516	Bartolo Colon	.40
517	Michael Saunders RC	1.50
518	Blake Hawksworth (RC)	1.00
519	Bud Norris RC	1.00
520	Bobby Scales RC	1.50
521	Nick Evans	.40
522	Brad Bergensen (RC)	1.00
523	Brad Mills RC	1.00
524	Brad Penny	.25
525	Braden Looper	.40
526	Brandon Lyon	.40
527	Brandon Wood	.40
528	Aaron Bates RC	1.00
529	Brett Cecil RC	1.00
530	Brett Gardner	.40
531	Brett Hayes (RC)	1.00
532	C.J. Wilson	.40
533	Carl Pavano	.40
534	Cesar Izturis	.40
535	Chad Qualls	.40
536	Marc Rzepczynski RC	1.50
537	Chris Gimenez RC	1.00
538	Chris Jakubauskas RC	1.50
539	Chris Perez	.40
540	Clay Zavada RC	1.00
541	Clayton Mortensen RC	1.00
542	Clayton Richard	.40
543	Cliff Floyd	.40
544	Coco Crisp	.40
545	Neftali Feliz RC	2.50
545	N. Feliz Black and White Photo	150.00
546	Craig Counsell	.40
547	Craig Stammen RC	1.00
548	Cristian Guzman	.40
549	Dallas Braden	.40
550	Daniel Bard RC	1.00
551	Jack Wilson	.25
552	Daniel Schlereth RC	1.00
553	David Aardsma	.40
554	David Eckstein	.40
555	David Freese RC	2.50
556	David Hernandez RC	1.00
557	David Huff RC	1.00
558	David Ross	.40
559	Delwyn Young	.60
560	Derek Holland RC	1.50
561	Derek Lowe	.40
562	Diory Hernandez RC	1.00
563a	Pedro Martinez	.60
563	P. Martinez Black and White Photo	250.00
564	Emilio Bonifacio	.40
565	Endy Chavez	.40
566	Eric Byrnes	.40
567	Eric Hinske	.40
568	Everth Cabrera RC	.40
569a	Alex Rios	.40
569	Alex Rios Black and White Photo	150.00
570	Fernando Nieve	.40
571	Francisco Cervelli RC	2.50
572	Frank Catalanotto	.40
573	Fu-Te Ni RC	1.00
574	Gabe Kapler	.40
575	Scott Rolen	.60
576	Garrett Olson	.40
577	Adam LaRoche	.40
578	Gerardo Parra RC	1.50
579	George Sherrill	.40
580	Graham Taylor RC	1.50
581	Gregg Zaun	.40
582	Homer Bailey	.40
583	Garrett Jones	.60
584	Julio Lugo	.40
585	J.A. Happ	.60
586	J.J. Putz	.40
587	J.P. Howell	.40
588	Jake Fox	.60
589	Jamey Carroll	.40
590	Jarrett Hoffpauir (RC)	.40
591	Felipe Lopez	.40
592	Cliff Lee	.60
593	Jason Giambi	.60
594	Jason Jaramillo (RC)	.40
595	Jason Kubel	.40
596	Jason Marquis	.40
597	Jason Vargas	.40
598	Jeff Baker	.40
599	Jeff Francoeur	.60
600	Jeremy Reed	.40
601	Jerry Hairston	.40

#	Player	Price
602	Jesus Guzman RC	1.00
603	Jody Gerut	.40
604	Joe Crede	.60
605	Alex Gonzalez	.40
606	Joel Hanrahan	.40
607	John Mayberry Jr. (RC)	1.00
608	Jon Garland	.40
609	Jonny Gomes	.40
610	Jordan Schafer (RC)	1.50
611	Victor Martinez	.60
612	Jose Contreras	.40
613	Josh Bard	.40
614	Josh Outman	.60
615	Juan Rivera	.40
616	Juan Uribe	.40
617	Julio Borbon RC	1.50
618	Jarrod Washburn	.40
619	Justin Masterson	.40
620	Kenshin Kawakami RC	1.50
621	Kevin Correia	.40
622	Kevin Gregg	.40
623	Kevin Millar	.40
624	Koji Uehara RC	1.50
625	Kris Medlen RC	1.50
626	Tim Redding	.40
627	Kyle Farnsworth	.40
628	Landon Powell (RC)	1.00
629	Lastings Milledge	.40
630	LaTroy Hawkins	.40
631	Laynce Nix	.40
632	Billy Wagner	.40
633	Tony Gwynn Jr.	.40
634	Mark Loretta	.40
635	Matt Diaz	.40
636	Ben Francisco	.40
637	Travis Ishikawa	.40
638	Matt Maloney (RC)	1.00
639	Scott Kazmir	.40
640	Melky Cabrera	.40
641	Micah Hoffpauir	.40
642	Micah Owings	.40
643	Mike Carp (RC)	1.00
644	Mike Hampton	.40
645	Mike Sweeney	.40
646	Milton Bradley	.40
647	Mitch Jones (RC)	1.00
648	Trevor Crowe RC	1.00
649	Ty Wigginton	.60
650	Jim Thome	.60
651	Nick Green	.40
652	Tyler Greene (RC)	1.00
653	Nyjer Morgan	.40
654	Omar Vizquel	.60
655	Omir Santos RC	1.00
656	Orlando Cabrera	.40
657	Vin Mazzaro RC	.40
658	Pat Burrell	.60
659	Rafael Soriano	.40
660	Ramiro Pena RC	1.50
661	Freddy Sanchez	.40
662	Ramon Ramirez	.40
663	Wilkin Ramirez RC	1.00
664	Randy Wells	.40
665	Randy Wolf	.40
666	Rich Hill	.40
667	Willy Taveras	.40
668	Xavier Paul (RC)	1.00
669	Rocco Baldelli	.40
670	Ross Detwiler	.40
671	Ross Gload	.40
672	Aubrey Huff	.40
673	Yuniesky Betancourt	.40
674	Ryan Church	.40
675	Ryan Garko	.40
676	Ryan Perry RC	2.50
677	Ryan Sadowski RC	1.00
678	Ryan Spilborghs	.40
679	Scott Downs	.40
680	Scott Hairston	.40
681	Scott Olsen	.40
682	Scott Podsednik	.40
683	Bill Hall	.40
684	Sean O'Sullivan RC	1.00
685	Sean West (RC)	1.00
686	Aaron Hill	6.00
687	Adam Dunn	10.00
688	Andrew McCutchen (RC)	8.00
689	Ben Zobrist	6.00
690	Chris Tillman RC	10.00
691	Bobby Abreu	6.00
692	Brett Anderson RC	6.00
693	Chris Coghlan RC	8.00
694	Colby Rasmus (RC)	8.00
695	Elvis Andrus RC	8.00
696	Fernando Martinez RC	15.00
697	Garret Anderson	6.00
698	Gary Sheffield	6.00
699	Gordon Beckham RC	6.00
700	Huston Street	6.00
701	Ivan Rodriguez	8.00
702	Jason Bay	8.00
703	Jordan Zimmermann RC	6.00
704	Ken Griffey Jr.	10.00
705	Kendry Morales	6.00
706	Kyle Blanks RC	10.00
707	Tommy Hanson RC	8.00
708	Mark DeRosa	6.00
709	Matt Holliday	8.00
710	Matt LaPorta RC	8.00
711	Trevor Cahill RC	8.00
712	Nate McLouth	6.00
713	Trevor Hoffman	6.00
714	Nelson Cruz	6.00
715	Nolan Reimold (RC)	6.00
716	Randy Johnson	8.00
717	Rick Porcello RC	8.00
718	Ricky Romero (RC)	8.00
719	Ricky Romero (RC)	8.00
720	Russell Branyan	6.00

Chrome
Production 1960 Sets
Refractor: 2X
Production 560 Sets
Black Refractor: 4-6X
Production 60 Sets

#	Player	Price
CHR101	Chad Qualls	4.00
CHR102	Daniel Schlereth	4.00
CHR103	Derek Lowe	4.00
CHR104	Jason Giambi	4.00
CHR105	Jason Marquis	4.00
CHR106	Kevin Correia	4.00
CHR107	Koji Uehara	5.00
CHR108	Matt Diaz	4.00
CHR109	Melky Cabrera	4.00
CHR110	Milton Bradley	4.00
CHR111	Rafael Soriano	4.00
CHR112	Scott Downs	4.00
CHR113	David Aardsma	4.00
CHR114	Eric Byrnes	4.00
CHR115	Gerardo Parra	5.00
CHR116	Homer Bailey	4.00
CHR117	J.P. Howell	4.00
CHR118	Joe Crede	5.00
CHR119	John Mayberry Jr	4.00
CHR120	Josh Outman	5.00
CHR121	Lastings Milledge	4.00
CHR122	Mike Hampton	4.00
CHR123	Orlando Cabrera	4.00
CHR124	Randy Wells	4.00
CHR125	Michael Saunders	6.00
CHR126	Tony Gwynn Jr.	4.00
CHR127	Trevor Crowe	3.00
CHR128	Vin Mazzaro	4.00
CHR129	Andruw Jones	4.00
CHR130	Brad Penny	4.00
CHR131	Brandon Wood	4.00
CHR132	Cristian Guzman	4.00
CHR133	David Huff	4.00
CHR134	J.A. Happ	5.00
CHR135	Jason Kubel	4.00
CHR136	Ryan Garko	4.00
CHR137	Jose Contreras	4.00
CHR138	Juan Rivera	4.00
CHR139	Jhoulys Chacin	5.00
CHR140	Randy Wolf	4.00
CHR141	Aaron Hill	4.00
CHR142	Adam Dunn	6.00
CHR143	Andrew Bailey	6.00
CHR144	Andrew McCutchen	6.00
CHR145	Ben Zobrist	4.00
CHR146	Bobby Abreu	4.00
CHR147	Brett Anderson	4.00
CHR148	Chris Coghlan	6.00
CHR149	Colby Rasmus	5.00
CHR150	Elvis Andrus	5.00
CHR151	Fernando Martinez	10.00
CHR152	Garret Anderson	4.00
CHR153	Gary Sheffield	4.00
CHR154	Gordon Beckham	8.00
CHR155	Huston Street	4.00
CHR156	Ivan Rodriguez	5.00
CHR157	Jason Bay	5.00
CHR158	Jeff Francoeur	5.00
CHR159	Jordan Zimmermann	.40
CHR160	Ken Griffey Jr.	8.00
CHR161	Kendry Morales	4.00
CHR162	Kyle Blanks	6.00
CHR163	Mark DeRosa	4.00
CHR164	Matt Holliday	5.00
CHR165	Matt LaPorta	6.00
CHR166	Nate McLouth	4.00
CHR167	Nelson Cruz	4.00
CHR168	Nolan Reimold	4.00
CHR169	Orlando Hudson	4.00
CHR170	Randy Johnson	5.00
CHR171	Rick Porcello	6.00
CHR172	Ricky Romero	5.00
CHR173	Russell Branyan	4.00
CHR174	Tommy Hanson	8.00
CHR175	Trevor Cahill	5.00
CHR176	Trevor Hoffman	4.00
CHR177	Aaron Poreda	4.00
CHR178	John Smoltz	5.00
CHR179	Brad Mills	4.00
CHR180	Brett Gardner	4.00
CHR181	Carl Pavano	4.00
CHR182	Daniel Bard	4.00
CHR183	David Hernandez	4.00
CHR184	Fu-Te Ni	4.00
CHR185	Jerry Hairston	4.00
CHR186	Jordan Schafer	5.00
CHR187	Julio Borbon	5.00
CHR188	Kris Medlen	5.00
CHR189	Micah Hoffpauir	4.00
CHR190	Nyjer Morgan	4.00
CHR191	Derek Holland	5.00
CHR192	Jack Wilson	4.00
CHR193	Cliff Lee	5.00
CHR194	Freddy Sanchez	4.00
CHR195	Pat Burrell	4.00
CHR196	Ryan Spilborghs	4.00
CHR197	Takashi Saito	4.00
CHR198	Bud Norris	5.00
CHR199	Chris Tillman	5.00
CHR200	Mat Latos	5.00

Clubhouse Collection Relics
Common Relic: 4.00
Inserted 1:26

#	Player	Price
AG	Adrian Gonzalez HN	6.00
AJ	Adam Jones HN	6.00
AR	Aramis Ramirez HN	6.00
AS	Alfonso Soriano HN	6.00
BM	Brian McCann HN	6.00
BR	Brooks Robinson HN	75.00
CB	Chad Billingsley HN	6.00
H	Cole Hamels HN	10.00
CJ	Chipper Jones HN	10.00
CQ	Carlos Quentin HN	6.00
CU	Chase Utley HN	12.00
DS	Duke Snider HN	50.00
DW	David Wright HN	10.00
EB	Ernie Banks HN	100.00
EL	Evan Longoria HN	12.00
FH	Felix Hernandez HN	6.00
FR	Frank Robinson HN	80.00
GS	Giovany Soto HN	10.00
HR	Hanley Ramirez HN	6.00
IK	Ian Kinsler HN	6.00
JB	Jay Bruce HN	10.00
JM	Joe Mauer HN	10.00
JR	Jimmy Rollins HN	6.00
JS	Joakim Soria HN	6.00
JU	Justin Upton HN	6.00
KK	Kenshin Kawakami HN	10.00
KU	Koji Uehara HN	10.00
MH	Matt Holliday HN	6.00
MM	Mickey Mantle HN	120.00
NM	Nick Markakis HN	N/A
RB	Ryan Braun HN	10.00
RH	Ryan Howard HN	10.00
RM	Roger Maris HN	100.00
SM	Stan Musial HN	80.00
TL	Tim Lincecum HN	12.00
WM	Willie McCovey HN	100.00
ALR	Alexei Ramirez HN	N/A
BJU	B.J. Upton HN	6.00
EVL	Evan Longoria HN	12.00
GRS	Grady Sizemore HN	N/A
JAB	Jay Bruce HN	6.00
MIC	Miguel Cabrera HN	10.00

Clubhouse Collection Relic Autographs
Production 25 Sets
No Pricing

Milton Bradley Clubhouse Collection Relic Dual
Production 60 Sets

#	Players	Price
HM	Matt Holliday / Stan Musial HN	150.00
LM	Tim Lincecum / Juan Marichal HN	120.00
MR	Nick Markakis / Brooks Robinson HN	120.00
PM	Jorge Posada / Mickey Mantle HN	150.00
SK	Duke Snider / Matt Kemp HN	150.00

Clubhouse Collection Relic Dual Autograph
Production 10 Sets
No Pricing

Flashback Stadium Relics
Inserted 1:925
No Pricing

Flashbacks
Inserted 1:12

#	Player	Price
FB01	Jonathan Sanchez	1.25
FB02	Jason Giambi	1.25
FB03	Randy Johnson	2.00
FB04	Ian Kinsler	2.00
FB05	Carl Crawford	2.00
FB06	Albert Pujols	8.00
FB07	Todd Helton	2.00
FB08	Mariano Rivera	2.00
FB09	Gary Sheffield	1.25
FB10	Ichiro Suzuki	5.00

Rookie Performers
Inserted 1:12

#	Player	Price
RP01	Colby Rasmus	4.00
RP02	Tommy Hanson	6.00
RP03	Andrew McCutchen	4.00
RP04	Rick Porcello	5.00
RP05	Nolan Reimold	1.50
RP06	Mat Latos	2.50
RP07	Gordon Beckham	5.00
RP08	Brett Anderson	1.50
RP09	Chris Coghlan	4.00
RP10	Jordan Zimmermann	1.50
RP11	Brad Bergesen	1.50
RP12	Elvis Andrus	2.50
RP13	Ricky Romero	2.50
RP14	Dexter Fowler	5.00
RP15	David Price	4.00

Then & Now
Inserted 1:12

#	Players	Price
TN01	Dustin Pedroia / Roger Maris	3.00
TN02	Jimmy Rollins / Ernie Banks	2.50
TN03	Adrian Beltre / Brooks Robinson	1.50
TN04	Michael Young / Ernie Banks	2.50
TN05	Ichiro Suzuki / Roger Maris	3.00
TN06	Grady Sizemore / Roger Maris	2.50
TN07	Albert Pujols / Roger Maris	6.00
TN08	David Wright / Brooks Robinson	3.00
TN09	Cole Hamels / Bobby Richardson	2.50
TN10	Torii Hunter / Roger Maris	2.50

Real One Autographs
Inserted 1:372
Red Ink: 1.5X
Production 60 Sets

#	Player	Price
AD	Alvin Dark HN	60.00
BB	Brian Barton HN	25.00
BJ	Bob Johnson HN	50.00
CK	Clayton Kershaw HN	60.00
CP	Cliff Pennington HN	50.00
DB	Dick Burwell HN	50.00
GB	Gordon Beckham HN	120.00
GC	Gio Gonzalez HN	50.00
IN	Irv Noren HN	50.00
JB	Jay Bruce HN	50.00
MB	Milton Bradley HN	25.00
RI	Raul Ibanez HN	50.00
BWI	Bobby Wine HN	50.00

Real One Autographs Dual
Production 25 Sets
No Pricing

2009 Topps Sterling
Common Player: 2.00
Production 250 Sets
Box (6 cards): 225.00

#	Player	Price
1	Babe Ruth	10.00
2	Bob Feller	3.00
3	Orlando Cepeda	2.00
4	Curt Schilling	3.00
5	Mickey Mantle	10.00
6	Joey Votto	3.00
7	Koji Uehara RC	3.00
8	Mel Ott	4.00
9	Miguel Cabrera	4.00
10	Prince Fielder	4.00
11	Jose Reyes	4.00
12	Carlos Beltran	2.50
13	David Price RC	5.00
14	Tommy Hanson RC	10.00
15	Roger Maris	5.00
16	Roger Maris	5.00
17	Mike Schmidt	6.00
18	Lou Gehrig	8.00
19	Ozzie Smith	5.00
20	Reggie Jackson	3.00
21	Reggie Jackson	3.00
22	Reggie Jackson	3.00
23	Tim Lincecum	6.00
24	Warren Spahn	3.00
25	Duke Snider	4.00
26	Yogi Berra	5.00
27	Ty Cobb	8.00
28	Stan Musial	5.00
29	Jimmie Foxx	5.00
30	Jimmie Foxx	5.00
31	Rick Porcello RC	8.00
32	Dwight Gooden	2.00
33	Ichiro Suzuki	5.00
34	CC Sabathia	3.00
35	Willie McCovey	3.00
36	Albert Pujols	10.00
37	Gary Sheffield	2.00
38	Cal Ripken Jr.	15.00
39	Daisuke Matsuzaka	5.00
40	Gary Carter	3.00
41	Josh Hamilton	4.00
42	Joe Mauer	4.00
43	Pedro Martinez	3.00
44	Whitey Ford	3.00
45	Johnny Damon	3.00
46	Frank Thomas	4.00
47	Dale Murphy	2.00
48	George Sisler	3.00
49	Roger Clemens	5.00
50	Lou Brock	3.00
51	Paul Molitor	4.00
52	David Ortiz	4.00
53	Tris Speaker	3.00
54	Tris Speaker	3.00
55	Carl Yastrzemski	4.00
56	Nolan Ryan	12.00
57	Nolan Ryan	12.00
58	Nolan Ryan	12.00
60	Joe Morgan	4.00
61	Honus Wagner	4.00
62	Andre Dawson	3.00
63	Justin Morneau	3.00
64	Manny Ramirez	4.00
65	Manny Ramirez	4.00
66	Manny Ramirez	4.00
67	Vladimir Guerrero	4.00
68	Hanley Ramirez	5.00
69	Ryan Braun	5.00
70	Dan Haren	2.00
71	Dave Winfield	4.00
72	Robin Yount	5.00
73	Ryne Sandberg	8.00
74	Johnny Mize	3.00
75	Johnny Mize	3.00
76	Johnny Mize	3.00
77	Don Mattingly	8.00
78	Ivan Rodriguez	4.00
79	Ralph Kiner	3.00
80	Steve Garvey	2.00
81	Carlos Delgado	2.00
82	Dustin Pedroia	5.00
83	Hank Greenberg	4.00
84	Al Kaline	4.00
85	Fergie Jenkins	3.00
86	David Wright	6.00
87	Frank Robinson	3.00
88	Brandon Webb	3.00
89	Colby Rasmus (RC)	4.00
90	Alfonso Soriano	3.00
91	Jackie Robinson	5.00
92	Lance Berkman	4.00
93	Chase Utley	5.00
94	Mark Teixeira	4.00
95	Mike Piazza	4.00
96	Johan Santana	4.00
97	Rogers Hornsby	3.00
98	Rogers Hornsby	3.00
99	Dennis Eckersley	2.00
100	Evan Longoria	6.00
101	Bob Gibson	3.00
102	Tom Seaver	3.00
103	Tony Gwynn	4.00
104	Johnny Bench	5.00
105	Carlton Fisk	3.00
106	Ernie Banks	5.00
107	Mariano Rivera	3.00
108	Tony Perez	2.00
109	Roy Campanella	4.00
110	Francisco Rodriguez	2.00
111	Luis Aparicio	2.00
112	Monte Irvin	3.00
113	Zack Greinke	4.00
114	Jim Thome	3.00
115	Jimmy Piersall	2.00
116	Eddie Murray	4.00
117	Jim Palmer	2.00
118	Carl Erskine	2.00
119	Juan Marichal	3.00
120	Joba Chamberlain	5.00
121	Chipper Jones	5.00
122	Johnny Podres	2.00
123	Wade Boggs	3.00
124	Michael Young	2.00
125	Steve Carlton	2.00
126	Ryan Howard	4.00
127	Jay Bruce	3.00
128	Alex Rodriguez	8.00
129	Alex Rodriguez	8.00
130	Alex Rodriguez	8.00

Framed Burgundy
No Pricing
Production 10 Sets

Framed Cherry Wood
Production One Set

Framed Gold
No Pricing
Production 5 Sets

Framed Sterling Silver
Production One Set

Framed White
White: 1-2X
Production 50 Sets

Bat Barrel Autographs
Production One Set
No Pricing

Bat Barrels
Production One Set
No Pricing

Career Chronicles Relic Five Autos.
Production 10 Sets
Sterling Silver 1 of 1's exist
No Pricing

Career Chronicles Relic Quad Autos.
Production 10 Sets
Sterling Silver 1 of 1's exist
No Pricing

Career Chronicles Relic Triple Autos.
Production 10 Sets
Sterling Silver 1 of 1's exist
No Pricing

Career Chronicles Five Relics
Production 25 Sets
Parallel/ 10: No Pricing
Production 10 Sets
Sterling Silver 1 of 1's exist

#	Player	Price
1	Babe Ruth	300.00
2	Ichiro Suzuki	50.00
3	Jackie Robinson	60.00
4	Cal Ripken Jr.	60.00
5	David Ortiz	20.00
6	Vladimir Guerrero	15.00
7	Reggie Jackson	25.00
8	Prince Fielder	20.00
9	Chase Utley	40.00
10	Francisco Rodriguez	15.00
11	Carl Yastrzemski	25.00
12	Jimmie Foxx	50.00
13	Eddie Mathews	40.00
14	Yogi Berra	40.00
15	Mike Schmidt	35.00
16	Tim Lincecum	40.00
17	Mark Teixeira	20.00
18	Ernie Banks	35.00
19	Al Kaline	25.00
20	Carlos Beltran	15.00
21	Mel Ott	40.00
22	Albert Pujols	40.00
23	Albert Pujols	40.00
24	Chipper Jones	40.00
25	Daisuke Matsuzaka	25.00
26	Carlos Delgado	15.00
27	Joba Chamberlain	15.00
28	Dennis Eckersley	15.00
29	CC Sabathia	30.00
30	CC Sabathia	30.00
31	Evan Longoria	40.00
32	Honus Wagner	125.00
33	Ryan Howard	35.00
34	Mariano Rivera	40.00
35	Ty Cobb	100.00
36	Nolan Ryan	50.00
37	Lou Gehrig	150.00
38	Dale Murphy	40.00
39	Eddie Murray	20.00
40	Don Mattingly	35.00
41	Johnny Bench	35.00
42	Joe Mauer	40.00
43	Dave Winfield	25.00
44	David Wright	25.00
45	Carlton Fisk	25.00
46	Frank Robinson	25.00
47	Johan Santana	30.00
48	Duke Snider	30.00
49	Bob Gibson	30.00
50	Tom Seaver	30.00
51	Warren Spahn	30.00
52	Paul Molitor	20.00
53	Orlando Cepeda	20.00
54	Roger Maris	65.00
55	Tris Speaker	40.00
56	Manny Ramirez	40.00
57	Hank Greenberg	40.00
58	Rogers Hornsby	50.00
59	Tony Gwynn	40.00
60	Ozzie Smith	40.00
61	Stan Musial	40.00
62	George Sisler	40.00
63	Roy Campanella	30.00
64	Jim Palmer	30.00
65	Ryan Braun	25.00
66	Johnny Mize	25.00
67	Ryne Sandberg	35.00
68	Robin Yount	30.00
69	Juan Marichal	25.00
70	Alex Rodriguez	40.00

Career Chronicles Relic Quad
Production 25 Sets
Parallel 10: No Pricing
Production 10 Sets
Sterling Silver 1 of 1's exist

#	Player	Price
1	Babe Ruth	300.00
2	Ichiro Suzuki	50.00
3	Ichiro Suzuki	50.00
4-5	Jackie Robinson	60.00
6-7	Cal Ripken Jr.	60.00
8-9	David Ortiz	15.00
10-11	Vladimir Guerrero	15.00
12-13	Reggie Jackson	25.00
14-15	Prince Fielder	25.00
16-17	Chase Utley	25.00
18-19	Francisco Rodriguez	15.00
20-21	Lou Brock	25.00
22-23	Carl Yastrzemski	25.00
24-25	Jimmie Foxx	50.00
26-27	Eddie Mathews	40.00
28-29	Yogi Berra	40.00
30-31	Mike Schmidt	40.00
32-33	Tim Lincecum	40.00
34-35	Mark Teixeira	20.00
36-37	Ernie Banks	35.00
38-39	Joe Morgan	25.00
40-41	Al Kaline	25.00
42-43	Carlos Beltran	15.00
44	Mel Ott	40.00
45-46	Mickey Mantle	100.00
47-48	Albert Pujols	50.00
49-50	Chipper Jones	25.00
51-52	Daisuke Matsuzaka	25.00
53-54	Carlos Delgado	15.00
55-56	Joba Chamberlain	15.00
57-58	Dennis Eckersley	15.00
59-60	Luis Aparicio	20.00
61-62	CC Sabathia	25.00
63-64	Evan Longoria	25.00
65	Honus Wagner	125.00
66-67	Ryan Howard	25.00
68-69	Mariano Rivera	25.00
70	Ty Cobb	100.00
71-72	Nolan Ryan	25.00
73	Lou Gehrig	150.00
74-75	Dale Murphy	40.00
76-77	Eddie Murray	20.00
78-79	Don Mattingly	35.00
80-81	Johnny Bench	20.00
82-83	Joe Mauer	35.00
84-85	Dave Winfield	20.00
86-87	David Wright	20.00
88-89	Carlton Fisk	20.00
90-91	Frank Robinson	25.00
92-93	Johan Santana	25.00
94-95	Duke Snider	25.00
96-97	Bob Gibson	25.00
98-99	Tom Seaver	25.00
100-101	Warren Spahn	30.00
102-103	Paul Molitor	20.00
104-105	Orlando Cepeda	15.00
106-107	Roger Maris	65.00
108	Tris Speaker	40.00
109-110	Manny Ramirez	25.00
111-112	Hank Greenberg	25.00
113	Rogers Hornsby	50.00
114-115	Tony Gwynn	25.00
116-117	Ozzie Smith	40.00
118-119	Stan Musial	40.00
120	George Sisler	40.00
121-122	Roy Campanella	30.00
123-124	Jim Palmer	25.00
125-126	Ryan Braun	25.00
127-128	Johnny Mize	20.00
129-130	Ryne Sandberg	30.00
131-132	Robin Yount	30.00
133-134	Juan Marichal	20.00
135-136	Jackie Robinson	30.00

Career Chronicles Relic Triple
Production 25 Sets
Parallel 10: No Pricing
Production 10 Sets

2009 Topps Sterling

Sterling Silver 1 of 1's exist

#	Player	Price
1-3	Babe Ruth	250.00
4-6	Ichiro Suzuki	40.00
7-9	Jackie Robinson	50.00
10-12	Cal Ripken Jr.	50.00
13-15	David Ortiz	10.00
16-18	Vladimir Guerrero	10.00
19-21	Reggie Jackson	20.00
22-23	Prince Fielder	10.00
24-25	Chase Utley	30.00
26-27	Francisco Rodriguez	10.00
28-29	Lou Brock	25.00
30-32	Carl Yastrzemski	20.00
33-34	Jimmie Foxx	40.00
35-36	Eddie Mathews	25.00
37-39	Yogi Berra	30.00
40-42	Mike Schmidt	25.00
43-45	Tim Lincecum	30.00
46-47	Mark Teixeira	15.00
48-50	Ernie Banks	15.00
51-52	Joe Morgan	15.00
53-54	Al Kaline	25.00
55-56	Carlos Beltran	10.00
57-59	Mel Ott	30.00
60-62	Mickey Mantle	85.00
63-65	Albert Pujols	35.00
66-67	Chipper Jones	25.00
68-70	Daisuke Matsuzaka	20.00
71-72	Carlos Delgado	10.00
73-75	Joba Chamberlain	15.00
76-77	Dennis Eckersley	15.00
78-79	Luis Aparicio	15.00
80-81	CC Sabathia	20.00
82-83	Evan Longoria	25.00
84-86	Honus Wagner	100.00
87-89	Ryan Howard	25.00
90-92	Mariano Rivera	25.00
93-95	Ty Cobb	80.00
96-98	Nolan Ryan	40.00
99-101	Lou Gehrig	125.00
102-104	Dale Murphy	35.00
105-106	Eddie Murray	20.00
107-109	Don Mattingly	30.00
110-112	Johnny Bench	25.00
113-114	Joe Mauer	20.00
115-116	Dave Winfield	20.00
117-118	David Wright	20.00
119-120	Carlton Fisk	20.00
121-123	Frank Robinson	15.00
124-125	Johan Santana	20.00
126-127	Duke Snider	25.00
128-130	Bob Gibson	20.00
131-133	Tom Seaver	20.00
134-135	Warren Spahn	25.00
136-137	Paul Molitor	20.00
138-139	Orlando Cepeda	15.00
140-142	Roger Maris	60.00
143-145	Tris Speaker	50.00
146-148	Manny Ramirez	25.00
149-150	Hank Greenberg	40.00
151-153	Rogers Hornsby	25.00
154-155	Tony Gwynn	25.00
156-158	Ozzie Smith	25.00
159-161	Stan Musial	30.00
162-164	George Sisler	35.00
165-167	Roy Campanella	25.00
168-169	Jim Palmer	20.00
170-171	Ryan Braun	25.00
172-173	Johnny Mize	25.00
174-176	Ryne Sandberg	25.00
177-178	Robin Yount	25.00
179-180	Juan Marichal	15.00
181-183	Alex Rodriguez	35.00

Cut Signatures
No Pricing

Jumbo Swatch Relic Autos.
Production 10 Sets
No Pricing

Moments Relics Autographs
Production 10 Sets
Sterling Silver 1 of 1's exist
No Pricing

Moments Relics
Production 10 Sets
Sterling Silver 1 of 1's exist
No Pricing

Pairs Relic Autographs
Production 10 Sets
Sterling Silver 1 of 1's exist
No Pricing

Pairs Relics
Production 10 Sets
Sterling Silver 1 of 1's exist
No Pricing

Season Relic Autographs
Production 10 Sets
Sterling Silver 1 of 1's exist
No Pricing

Season Relics
Production 10 Sets
Sterling Silver 1 of 1's exist
No Pricing

Spectator Relics
Production 10 Sets
Sterling Silver 1 of 1's exist
No Pricing

2009 Topps Tribute
Complete Set (100): 150.00
Common Player: 1.00
Common RC: 2.00
Pack (5): 50.00
Box (6): 280.00

#	Player	Price
1	Babe Ruth	8.00
2	Christy Mathewson	3.00
3	Don Zimmer	1.00
4	Nolan Ryan	10.00
5	Dennis Eckersley	1.00
6	Carl Yastrzemski	4.00
7	Mickey Mantle	10.00
8	Tony Perez	1.50
9	Cal Ripken Jr.	12.00
10	Derek Jeter	8.00
11	Wade Boggs	2.00
12	Tom Seaver	2.50
13	Willie McCovey	2.50
14	Walter Johnson	3.00
15	Steve Garvey	1.00
16	George Sisler	2.00
17	Joe Morgan	1.50
18	Don Larsen	1.50
19	Reggie Jackson	2.50
20	Thurman Munson	4.00
21	Howard Johnson	1.00
22	Johnny Bench	3.00
23	Bo Jackson	2.50
24	Ray Knight	1.00
25	Cy Young	3.00
26	Bruce Sutter	1.00
27	Mike Schmidt	5.00
28	Roy Campanella	3.00
29	John Smoltz	3.00
30	Bob Gibson	2.50
31	Roy Halladay	2.50
32	Tris Speaker	2.50
33	Tony Gwynn	3.00
34	Whitey Ford	2.50
35	Carlos Beltran	1.50
36	Manny Ramirez	3.00
37	Frank Thomas	2.50
38	Honus Wagner	4.00
39	Josh Beckett	2.00
40	Hanley Ramirez	3.00
41	Ty Cobb	5.00
42	Darryl Strawberry	1.00
43	Stan Musial	5.00
44	Duke Snider	2.00
45	Rollie Fingers	1.00
46	Juan Marichal	1.50
47	Eddie Mathews	3.00
48	Paul Molitor	3.00
49	Pee Wee Reese	1.50
50	Ryan Howard	4.00
51	Johnny Podres	2.00
52	Randy Johnson	2.50
53	Rogers Hornsby	2.50
54	Dwight Gooden	1.00
55	Ryne Sandberg	6.00
56	Robin Yount	3.00
57	Greg Maddux	4.00
58	Jackie Robinson	3.00
59	Adrian Gonzalez	2.00
60	Jim Palmer	1.50
61	David Wright	5.00
62	Ernie Banks	4.00
63	Chipper Jones	4.00
64	Gary Carter	1.50
65	Aramis Ramirez	1.50
66	Jimmie Foxx	4.00
67	Joe Mauer	3.00
68	Ozzie Smith	5.00
69	George Kell	1.00
70	Derrek Lee	2.00
71	Hank Greenberg	3.00
72	Joey Votto	2.00
73	Mel Ott	3.00
74	Clayton Kershaw	2.50
75	Josh Hamilton	3.00
76	Tommy Hanson RC	8.00
77	Alex Rodriguez	6.00
78	Andre Dawson	2.50
79	Johnny Mize	2.50
80	Sal Bando	1.00
81	Justin Morneau	2.00
82	Keith Hernandez	1.00
83	Lou Gehrig	6.00
84	Dustin Pedroia	4.00
85	Mark Teixeira	2.00
86	Jay Bruce	2.00
87	Chase Utley	4.00
88	Lance Berkman	2.00
89	Frank Robinson	2.50
90	Matt LaPorta (RC)	5.00
91	Albert Pujols	8.00
92	Mike Piazza	3.00
93	Robin Roberts	1.50
94	Evan Longoria	5.00
95	Ryan Braun	4.00
96	Rick Porcello RC	8.00
97	CC Sabathia	2.50
98	Brooks Robinson	2.50
99	Ichiro Suzuki	5.00
100	Ken Griffey Jr.	6.00

Black
Black (1-100): 1-2X
Production 99 Sets

Blue
Blue (1-100): 1.5X
Production 219 Sets

Gold
Gold (1-100): 2-4X
Gold RC: 2-3X
Production 50 Sets

Red
Production One Set
Printing Plates
Production one set per color.

Autograph Dual Relics
Production 99 Sets
Black: 1-1.2X
Production 50 Sets
Blue: 1X
Production 75 Sets
Gold: 1.5X
Production 25 Sets
Red 1 of 1's exist

Code	Player	Price
AI	Akinori Iwamura	15.00
AR	Aramis Ramirez	20.00
BJ	Bo Jackson	40.00
DG	Dwight Gooden	20.00
DP	Dustin Pedroia	40.00
DS	Duke Snider	30.00
DS	Darryl Strawberry	20.00
DW	David Wright	40.00
EL	Evan Longoria	40.00
GC	Gary Carter	20.00
JB	Jay Bruce	20.00
MC	Melky Cabrera	15.00
PF	Prince Fielder	30.00
RP	Rick Porcello	30.00
DW2	David Wright	40.00
EL2	Evan Longoria	40.00
RC1	Robinson Cano	25.00
RC2	Robinson Cano	25.00

Autograph Relics
Production 99 Sets
Variations same value
Black: 1.2X
Production 50 Sets
Blue: 1X
Production 75 Sets
Gold: 1.5X
Production 25 Sets
Red 1 of 1's exist

Code	Player	Price
JH	Josh Hamilton	25.00
JM	Juan Marichal	20.00
TS	Tom Seaver	30.00
AD1-2	Andre Dawson	30.00
CC1-2	Carl Crawford	15.00
CK1-4	Clayton Kershaw	20.00
DP1-4	Dustin Pedroia	40.00
DS1-4	Duke Snider	25.00
DW1-4	David Wright	40.00
EL1-4	Evan Longoria	40.00
GC1-4	Gary Carter	20.00
JB1-4	Jay Bruce	20.00
JP1-2	Johnny Podres	20.00
KH1-4	Keith Hernandez	15.00
ML1	Matt LaPorta	25.00
RB1-4	Ryan Braun	30.00
RP1-4	Rick Porcello	30.00
SB1-4	Sal Bando	15.00
TH1-2	Tommy Hanson	50.00

Autograph Triple Relics
Production 99 Sets
Black: 1.2X
Production 50 Sets
Blue: 1X
Production 75 Sets
Gold: 1.5X
Production 25 Sets
Red 1 of 1's exist

Code	Player	Price
AP	Albert Pujols	200.00
CJ	Chipper Jones	60.00
DM	Don Mattingly	60.00
DW	David Wright	50.00
RH	Ryan Howard	60.00

Franchise Tribute Dual Relic Auto.
Production 99 Sets
Black: 1.2X
Production 50 Sets
Blue: 1X
Production 75 Sets
Gold: 1.5X
Production 25 Sets
Red 1 of 1's exist

Code	Players	Price
BB	Johnny Bench / Jay Bruce	80.00
BM	Johnny Bench / Joe Morgan	100.00
MC	Juan Marichal / Matt Cain	75.00
PO	Dustin Pedroia / David Ortiz	100.00
PR	Jim Palmer / Cal Ripken	120.00
RR	Cal Ripken / Brooks Robinson	140.00
SC	Mike Schmidt / Steve Carlton	125.00
SR	Tom Seaver / Nolan Ryan	200.00
SW	Tom Seaver / David Wright	125.00
WB	David Wright / Carlos Beltran	75.00

Franchise Tribute Quad Relic Autos
Production One Set
Red 1 of 1's also exist
No Pricing

Franchise Tribute Quad Relics
Production 5 Sets
Red 1 of 1's exist
No Pricing

Jumbo Dual Relics
Production 25 Sets
Red 1 of 1's exist

Code	Players	Price
CYCR	Carl Yastrzemski / Cal Ripken Jr.	100.00
JPEM	Jim Palmer / Eddie Murray	65.00
MSJM	Mike Schmidt / Johnny Mize	65.00
NRJB	Nolan Ryan / Johnny Bench	100.00
PMAD	Paul Molitor / Andre Dawson	60.00
RCPR	Roy Campanella / Pee Wee Reese	125.00
RJTM	Reggie Jackson / Thurman Munson	75.00
SGTG	Steve Garvey / Tony Gwynn	100.00
SMMM	Stan Musial / Mickey Mantle	300.00
TSGS	Tris Speaker / George Sisler	140.00

Relics
Production 99 Sets
Black: 1.2X
Production 50 Sets
Blue: 1X
Production 75 Sets
Gold: 1.5X
Production 25 Sets
Red 1 of 1's exist

#	Player	Price
1	Babe Ruth	120.00
6	Nolan Ryan	30.00
7	Carl Yastrzemski	12.00
9	Mickey Mantle	100.00
11	Cal Ripken Jr.	25.00
12	Tom Seaver	15.00
18	Don Larsen	10.00
19	Reggie Jackson	15.00
20	Thurman Munson	20.00
22	Johnny Bench	12.00
25	Bo Jackson	15.00
27	Mike Schmidt	15.00
28	Roy Campanella	20.00
32	Bob Gibson	12.00
33	Tony Gwynn	12.00
34	Whitey Ford	20.00
36	Manny Ramirez	10.00
40	Hanley Ramirez	8.00
41	Ty Cobb	50.00
44	Duke Snider	15.00
46	Juan Marichal	8.00
47	Eddie Mathews	15.00
49	Pee Wee Reese	15.00
50	Ryan Howard	15.00
58	Jackie Robinson	50.00
61	David Wright	15.00
63	Chipper Jones	12.00
67	Joe Mauer	12.00
68	Ozzie Smith	12.00
72	Joey Votto	10.00
74	Clayton Kershaw	8.00
75	Josh Hamilton	10.00
76	Tommy Hanson	12.00
77	Alex Rodriguez	25.00
83	Justin Morneau	12.00
83	Lou Gehrig	100.00
84	Dustin Pedroia	10.00
85	Mark Teixeira	15.00
87	Chase Utley	15.00
88	Lance Berkman	8.00
91	Albert Pujols	15.00
92	Mike Piazza	15.00
94	Evan Longoria	12.00
95	Ryan Braun	12.00
96	Rick Porcello	8.00
98	CC Sabathia	8.00
99	Ichiro Suzuki	30.00

Relics Dual
Production 99 Sets
Black: 1.2X
Production 50 Sets
Blue: 1X
Production 75 Sets
Gold: 1.5X
Production 25 Sets
Red 1 of 1's exist

#	Player	Price
1	Babe Ruth	150.00
9	Cal Ripken Jr.	30.00
19	Reggie Jackson	15.00
22	Johnny Bench	15.00
27	Mike Schmidt	25.00
33	Tony Gwynn	15.00
36	Manny Ramirez	12.00
41	Ty Cobb	75.00
44	Duke Snider	20.00
50	Ryan Howard	20.00
61	David Wright	15.00
72	Tommy Hanson	15.00
94	Evan Longoria	15.00
95	Ryan Braun	15.00
99	Ichiro Suzuki	30.00

Relics Triple
Production 99 Sets
Black: 1.2X
Production 50 Sets
Blue: 1X
Production 75 Sets
Gold: 1.5X
Production 25 Sets
Red 1 of 1's exist

#	Player	Price
1	Babe Ruth	250.00
7	Mickey Mantle	120.00
58	Jackie Robinson	50.00
77	Alex Rodriguez	25.00
91	Albert Pujols	30.00

2009 Topps Ticket to Stardom
NM/M
Common Player (1-200): .25
Common RC (201-225): 4.00
Production 199
Pack (12): 4.00
Box (20): 75.00

#	Player	Price
1	Albert Pujols	2.00
2	Ichiro Suzuki	1.50
3	Aubrey Huff	.25
4	Kevin Youkilis	.50
5	David Wright	1.00
6	Ryan Howard	1.00
7	Jimmy Rollins	.75
8	Justin Morneau	.50
9	Joe Saunders	.25
10	David DeJesus	.25
11	Grady Sizemore	.75
12	Brian Roberts	.40
13	Alex Rodriguez	1.50
14	Alex Rios	.40
15	Brad Hawpe	.40
16	Gary Matthews Jr.	.25
17	Glen Perkins	.25
18	Erick Aybar	.25
19	Manny Ramirez	.75
20	Kosuke Fukudome	.50
21	David Ortiz	.50
22	Hunter Pence	.40
23	Edgar Renteria	.25
24	Ken Griffey Jr.	1.50
25	Joe Mauer	.75
26	Adrian Gonzalez	.50
27	Brian McCann	.40
28	Paul Konerko	.40
29	Francisco Liriano	.40
30	Pat Burrell	.40
31	Stephen Drew	.40
32	Chris Young	.25
33	Carlos Pena	.40
34	Rich Harden	.25
35	Felix Hernandez	.50
36	Geoff Jenkins	.25
37	Kenji Johjima	.25
38	Yovani Gallardo	.50
39	Max Scherzer	.40
40	Joe Crede	.25
41	Miguel Tejada	.50
42	Nick Swisher	.40
43	Tim Lincecum	1.00
44	Mat Latos RC	1.00
45	Alex Gordon	.25
46	Jeff Francoeur	.25
47	Jay Bruce	.75
48	George Sherrill	.25
49	Zack Greinke	.75
50	Jeremy Guthrie	.25
51	Chris Young	.25
52	Melvin Mora	.25
53	Tim Wakefield	.25
54	Victor Martinez	.40
55	Nick Markakis	.50
56	Carlos Zambrano	.40
57	Ryan Garko	.25
58	Hideki Okajima	.25
59	Ubaldo Jimenez	.40
60	Justin Verlander	.50
61	Brad Penny	.25
62	Cameron Maybin	.40
63	Milton Bradley	.25
64	Hideki Matsui	.50
65	Jorge Cantu	.25
66	Jose Contreras	.25
67	Jon Lester	.40
68	Torii Hunter	.50
69	Jermaine Dye	.25
70	Roy Halladay	.50
71	Carlos Marmol	.25
72	Kerry Wood	.25
73	Josh Fields	.25
74	Evan Longoria	1.00
75	Andrew McCutchen (RC)	1.00
76	Freddy Sanchez	.25
77	Mike Cameron	.25
78	Josh Hamilton	.75
79	A.J. Pierzynski	.25
80	Scott Rolen	.40
81	Joey Votto	.50
82	Brandon Inge	.25
83	Vernon Wells	.40
84	Armando Galarraga	.25
85	Mark Teixeira	.75
86	Austin Kearns	.25
87	Jason Giambi	.25
88	Kevin Millwood	.25
89	Josh Willingham	.25
90	Ryan Braun	1.00
91	Chris Davis	.40
92	Erik Bedard	.25
93	Fred Perez	.75
94	Kurt Suzuki	.25
95	Ryan Doumit	.25
96	Bill Hall	.25
97	Jack Wilson	.25
98	Tim Hudson	.25
99	Paul Maholm	.25
100	Adrian Beltre	.25
101	Curtis Granderson	.50
102	Travis Hafner	.25
103	Edinson Volquez	.25
104	Mike Lowell	.40
105	Justin Upton	.50
106	Eric Chavez	.25
107	Bobby Abreu	.40
108	Joba Chamberlain	.50
109	Gary Sheffield	.40
110	Chad Billingsley	.40
111	Carlos Beltran	.40
112	Rickie Weeks	.25
113	Jeremy Hermida	.25
114	Bronson Arroyo	.25
115	Mark Buehrle	.25
116	Jorge Posada	.50
117	Derrek Lee	.50
118	Dustin Pedroia	.75
119	Javier Vazquez	.40
120	Derek Jeter	2.00
121	Johan Santana	.50
122	J.J. Hardy	.25
123	Miguel Cabrera	.50
124	Daisuke Matsuzaka	.50
125	Geovany Soto	.40
126	Jason Varitek	.25
127	Magglio Ordonez	.40
128	Carlos Quentin	.40
129	Brandon Webb	.40
130	Jonathan Papelbon	.40
131	Josh Beckett	.50
132	Dan Haren	.40
133	Alfonso Soriano	.25
134	Yadier Molina	.25
135	John Maine	.50
136	Todd Helton	.50
137	Troy Tulowitzki	.40
138	Luis Castillo	.25
139	Andy Pettitte	.40
140	Hank Blalock	.25
141	Jeremy Sowers	.25
142	Nate McLouth	.25
143	Carlos Lee	.40
144	Gavin Floyd	.25
145	Joe Nathan	.25
146	Matt Holliday	.50
147	Hanley Ramirez	.75
148	Akinori Iwamura	.25
149	Jeremy Bonderman	.25
150	Johnny Damon	.50
151	Derek Lowe	.25
152	Matt Kemp	.75
153	Troy Glaus	.25
154	Fausto Carmona	.25
155	Jered Weaver	.40
156	Orlando Hudson	.25
157	Garret Anderson	.25
158	Jason Bay	.50
159	Lance Berkman	.50
160	Randy Johnson	.50
161	Chipper Jones	.75
162	Conor Jackson	.25
163	Adam Dunn	.50
164	Jake Peavy	.50
165	Vladimir Guerrero	.50
166	Jacoby Ellsbury	.75
167	Cole Hamels	.75
168	J.D. Drew	.50
169	Cliff Lee	.50
170	Russell Martin	.25
171	Derek Holland	.25
172	Joakim Soria	.25
173	Dan Uggla	.40
174	Carlos Delgado	.50
175	Jose Reyes	.75
176	Chase Utley	.75
177	Alexei Ramirez	.40
178	Roy Oswalt	.40
179	Matt Garza	.40
180	Matt Cain	.40
181	Chien-Ming Wang	.25
182	Gordon Beckham RC	5.00
183	Johnny Cueto	.25
184	Ryan Freel	.25
185	James Shields	.40
186	Rick Ankiel	.25
187	A.J. Burnett	.25
188	Adam Jones	.50
189	Jim Thome	.50
190	Andrew Sonnanstine	.25
191	Ryan Zimmerman	.40
192	Jon Garland	.25
193	Robinson Cano	.50
194	Michael Young	.40
195	Xavier Nady	.25
196	B.J. Upton	.40
197	Ian Kinsler	.75
198	Scott Kazmir	.40
199	C.C. Sabathia	.50
200	Justin Masterson	.25
201	Colby Rasmus (RC)	5.00
202	Jordan Schafer (RC)	5.00
203	Ryan Perry RC	4.00
204	Brett Anderson RC	5.00
205	David Hernandez RC	15.00
206	Brian Duensing RC	5.00
207	Rick Porcello RC	15.00
208	Koji Uehara RC	5.00
209	Trevor Crowe RC	5.00
210	Andrew Bailey RC	5.00
211	David Price RC	10.00
212	Travis Snider RC	10.00
213	David Patton RC	4.00

#	Player	Price
214	Dexter Fowler (RC)	6.00
215	Phil Coke RC	6.00
216	Bobby Parnell RC	4.00
217	Ricky Romero (RC)	4.00
218	Everth Cabrera RC	5.00
219	Bobby Scales RC	5.00
220	Michael Bowden (RC)	6.00
221	Jordan Zimmermann RC	6.00
222	Fernando Martinez RC	8.00
223	David Freese RC	5.00
224	Elvis Andrus RC	10.00
225	Kenshin Kawakami RC	5.00

Blue
Blue (1-200): 3-5X
Blue RC (201-225): 1X
Production 99 Sets

Gold
Gold (1-200): 4-6X
Gold RC (201-225): 1-1.5X
Production 50 Sets

Red
Production One Set

Perforated
Perforated (1-200): 1-2X
Perforated (201-225): .5X
Inserted 1:1

Printing Plates
Production one set per color.

Autographed Relics
NM/M
Common Auto. Relic: 10.00
Gold: No Pricing
Production 10 sets
Red 1 of 1's exist

Code	Player	Price
MB	Michael Bowden/489	15.00
EL	Evan Longoria/489	60.00
CK	Clayton Kershaw/489	25.00
TT	Troy Tulowitzki/489	15.00
JC	Joba Chamberlain/489	35.00
JB	Jay Bruce/489	75.00
SK	Scott Kazmir/489	15.00
JW	Jayson Werth/489	35.00
NS	Nick Swisher/489	30.00
DP	Dustin Pedroia/489	40.00
BD	Blake DeWitt/489	10.00
MG	Mat Gamel/489	10.00
CAJ	Conor Jackson/489	10.00
AE	Andre Ethier/489	20.00
JCC	Johnny Cueto/489	15.00
MC	Matt Cain/489	15.00
GA	Garrett Atkins/489	8.00
ES	Ervin Santana/489	10.00
UJ	Ubaldo Jimenez/489	10.00
JM	Justin Masterson/489	15.00
VG	Vladimir Guerrero/89	50.00
RH	Ryan Howard/89	75.00
DW	David Wright/89	100.00
ML	Mike Lowell/99	40.00
CJ	Chipper Jones/89	100.00

Autographed Relics Dual
NM/M
Some not priced due to scarcity.
Gold: No Pricing
Production 10 sets
Red 1 of 1's exist

Code	Player	Price
CKMK	Clayton Kershaw, Matt Kemp/39	40.00
ELMH	Evan Longoria, Matt Holliday/39	65.00
MLJP	Mike Lowell, Jonathan Papelbon/39	50.00
RCJC	Robinson Cano, Joba Chamberlain/39	50.00
CPEL	Carlos Pena, Evan Longoria/39	120.00
AGCY	Adrian Gonzalez, Chris Young/39	50.00
MGPF	Mat Gamel, Prince Fielder/39	75.00
BUCP	B.J. Upton, Carlos Pena/39	40.00
NMJG	Nick Markakis, Jeremy Guthrie/39	35.00
MGJH	Mat Gamel, J.J. Hardy/39	20.00

Big Tickets
NM/M
Common Player: 1.00
Blue: 1-2X
Production 99 Sets
Gold: 2-3X
Production 50 Sets
Red 1 of 1's exist

#	Player	Price
1	Ichiro Suzuki	3.00
2	Josh Hamilton	1.50
3	Ryan Braun	2.00
4	Albert Pujols	5.00
5	David Wright	3.00
6	Dustin Pedroia	3.00
7	Jose Reyes	2.00
8	Grady Sizemore	1.50
9	Tim Lincecum	3.00
10	Alex Rodriguez	3.00
11	Lance Berkman	1.50
12	Miguel Cabrera	1.50
13	Brandon Webb	1.00
14	Hanley Ramirez	2.00
15	C.C. Sabathia	1.50

Opening Day Ticket Stubs
NM/M
Common Stub: 1.00
Inserted 1:120 Hobby

Varying quantities produced.

Code	Player	Price
MH	Matt Holliday/52	20.00
BW	Brandon Webb/50	20.00
CQ	Carlos Quentin/78	15.00
DM	Daisuke Matsuzaka/30	30.00
EL	Evan Longoria/50	60.00
GS	Grady Sizemore/50	20.00
HR	Hanley Ramirez/50	20.00
JP	Jake Peavy/50	15.00
JB	Jay Bruce/50	30.00
JH	Josh Hamilton	40.00
JM	Justin Morneau	40.00
KJ	Kenji Johjima/262	15.00
LB	Lance Berkman	25.00
MT	Mark Teixeira	40.00
MC	Miguel Cabrera/55	25.00
NM	Nick Markakis/50	15.00
PF	Prince Fielder/99	20.00
RHH	Ryan Howard/102	30.00
RZ	Ryan Zimmerman/100	30.00
TL	Tim Lincecum/50	40.00
VG	Vladimir Guerrero/76	15.00
TH	Todd Helton/50	20.00
MR	Manny Ramirez/54	40.00
AS	Alfonso Soriano/50	20.00
AP	Albert Pujols/55	40.00
NMM	Nate McLouth/41	15.00

Seasoned Vets
NM/M
Common Player: .75
Blue: 1-2X
Production 99 Sets
Gold: 2-3X
Production 50 Sets
Red 1 of 1's exist.

#	Player	Price
1	Alex Rodriguez	3.00
2	David Wright	2.50
3	Manny Ramirez	2.00
4	Albert Pujols	5.00
5	Ryan Howard	3.00
6	Vladimir Guerrero	2.00
7	Alfonso Soriano	1.00
8	Magglio Ordonez	.75
9	Ryan Braun	2.50
10	David Ortiz	1.50

Ticket to Stardom
NM/M
Common Player: 1.00
Inserted 1:4
Blue: 1-2X
Production 99 Sets
Gold: 2-3X
Production 50 Sets
Red 1 of 1's exist

#	Player	Price
1	David Price	3.00
2	Travis Snider	3.00
3	Colby Rasmus	1.50
4	Cameron Maybin	1.00
5	Matt Kemp	2.00
6	Jay Bruce	1.50
7	Prince Fielder	2.00
8	Joba Chamberlain	1.50
9	Grady Sizemore	1.50
10	Evan Longoria	3.00
11	Joe Mauer	2.00
12	Joey Votto	1.50
13	Nick Markakis	1.50
14	Jacoby Ellsbury	2.50
15	Kenshin Kawakami	1.50

Ticket Stubs
NM/M
Common Ticket Stub: 5.00
Some not priced.
Varying quantities produced.
Gold: No Pricing
Production 10 Sets

#	Player	Price
TS1	Alex Rodriguez/110	20.00
TS2	Adrian Gonzalez/110	10.00
TS3	Carlos Beltran/110	10.00
TS4	Chad Billingsley	10.00
TS5	David Wright/110	15.00
TS6	Felix Hernandez/110	15.00
TS7	Ichiro Suzuki/110	20.00
TS9	Albert Pujols/110	20.00
TS10	Blake DeWitt/107	10.00
TS11	Brandon Webb/110	10.00
TS12	Alexei Ramirez/110	15.00
TS13	Chris Young/110	8.00
TS14	Carlos Delgado/110	10.00
TS15	Brian Fuentes/110	5.00
TS16	Grady Sizemore/110	12.00
TS17	Johan Santana/110	15.00
TS18	Kevin Kouzmanoff/110	8.00
TS19	Manny Ramirez/110	15.00
TS20	Prince Fielder/110	12.00
TS21	Ryan Howard/110	20.00
TS23	Jose Reyes/110	15.00
TS24	Robinson Cano/110	15.00
TS25	Vladimir Guerrero/110	12.00
TS26	Evan Longoria/63	20.00
TS27	Jake Peavy/110	8.00
TS30	Jon Lester/102	15.00
TS31	Chipper Jones/110	12.00
TS32	Josh Hamilton/110	12.00
TS34	Prince Fielder/110	10.00
TS35	J. Saltalamacchia/110	10.00
TS36	Joey Votto/110	10.00
TS37	Kyle Lohse/110	5.00
TS39	J.J. Hardy/110	5.00
TS42	Erick Aybar/110	8.00
TS43	Bobby Crosby/110	5.00
TS44	Miguel Cabrera/110	12.00
TS45	Fred Lewis/110	5.00
TS46	Chris Davis/110	8.00
TS48	Jack Cust/110	5.00
TS49	Russell Martin/110	8.00
TS50	Adam Wainwright/110	15.00
TS52	Corey Hart/110	5.00
TS53	Kurt Suzuki/110	8.00
TS57	Justin Duchscherer/110	5.00
TS58	Daric Barton/110	5.00
TS59	Tim Lincecum/110	25.00
TS61	Ryan Braun/110	15.00
TS62	Joba Chamberlain/110	15.00
TS64	Chone Figgins/110	8.00
TS65	Jermaine Dye/110	8.00
TS67	Brian Giles/110	5.00
TS68	Nate McLouth/110	8.00
TS70	John Lackey/110	8.00
TS71	Rick Ankiel/110	8.00
TS72	Ryan Braun/110	15.00
TS74	Jose Reyes/110	12.00
TS75	Nate McLouth/110	8.00
TS79	Justin Duchscherer/110	8.00
TS80	J.J. Hardy/110	5.00
TS81	Chris Young/110	8.00
TS82	Chad Billingsley/105	8.00
TS83	David Wright/110	15.00
TS84	Daric Barton/110	5.00
TS85	Ichiro Suzuki/110	20.00
TS86	Blake DeWitt/106	10.00
TS87	Jarrod Saltalamacchia/110	5.00
TS88	Erick Aybar/95	8.00
TS89	Albert Pujols/110	25.00
TS90	Corey Hart/110	8.00
TS91	Adam Wainwright/110	15.00
TS93	Carlos Delgado/110	10.00
TS95	Jose Reyes/110	15.00
TS96	Russell Martin/110	8.00
TS97	Felix Hernandez/110	15.00
TS98	Ichiro Suzuki/110	20.00
TS100	Ichiro Suzuki/110	20.00

Ticket Stubs Plus Dual
NM/M
Production 14-239
Gold: No Pricing
Production 10 Sets
Red: No Pricing

#	Player	Price
1	Ichiro Suzuki/239	20.00
2	Ichiro Suzuki/228	20.00
3	Ichiro Suzuki/36	30.00
4	David Wright/239	20.00
5	David Wright/239	20.00
6	David Wright	20.00
8	Howie Kendrick/224	8.00
9	Corey Hart/224	5.00
10	Mike Napoli/224	6.00
11	Jake Peavy/61	10.00
12	J.J. Hardy/239	6.00
13	J.J. Hardy/224	6.00
14	J.J. Hardy/221	5.00
15	Josh Hamilton/224	10.00
16	Michael Young/224	5.00
17	Robinson Cano/224	15.00
18	Vladimir Guerrero/228	8.00
19	Vladimir Guerrero	15.00
20	Travis Buck/224	6.00
21	Prince Fielder/239	20.00
22	Prince Fielder/228	10.00
23	Prince Fielder/14	25.00
24	Eric Chavez/224	6.00
25	Jose Reyes/239	20.00
26	Jose Reyes/210	20.00
27	Trevor Hoffman/224	8.00
29	Jack Cust/239	5.00
30	Russell Martin/223	5.00
31	Jake Peavy/116	5.00
32	Alex Rios/180	10.00
33	Matt Kemp/239	15.00
34	Matt Kemp/40	20.00
35	Nick Markakis	15.00
36	Johnny Damon/85	15.00
37	Bobby Crosby/224	5.00
38	James Loney/79	8.00
39	Carlos Delgado/81	12.00
41	Conor Jackson/81	6.00
41	Aaron Rowand/79	8.00
42	Ryan Braun/126	15.00
43	Kosuke Fukudome/90	25.00
44	Chin-Lung Hu/77	10.00
45	Wladimir Balentien	5.00
46	Wladimir Balentien	5.00
47	Wladimir Balentien/185	6.00
48	Adrian Beltre/53	8.00
49	Kevin Kouzmanoff/239	5.00
50	Kevin Kouzmanoff/228	5.00
51	Kevin Kouzmanoff/200	5.00
52	Kevin Kouzmanoff	5.00
53	Bobby Crosby	5.00
54	Trevor Hoffman/162	5.00
55	Wladimir Balentien	5.00
56	Jack Cust/235	5.00
57	Jack Cust/89	6.00
58	Eric Chavez/239	5.00
59	Eric Chavez/75	8.00
60	Wladimir Balentien/228	5.00
61	Wladimir Balentien	5.00
62	Travis Buck/224	5.00
63	Daric Barton/224	5.00

Ticket Stubs Plus
NM/M
Inserted 1:22
Gold: No Pricing
Production 10 Sets
Red 1 of 1's exist

#	Player	Price
1	David Wright/224	15.00
2	Bobby Crosby/224	5.00
3	Albert Pujols/239	25.00
4	Chad Billingsley/225	8.00
5	Blake DeWitt/228	8.00
6	Carlos Beltran/239	10.00
7	Ichiro Suzuki/225	20.00
8	Michael Young/224	8.00
9	Nate McLouth/239	10.00
10	Kevin Kouzmanoff/224	5.00
11	Ryan Braun/224	15.00
12	Josh Hamilton/225	12.00
13	Robinson Cano/224	15.00
14	Trevor Hoffman/224	8.00
15	Eric Chavez/225	5.00
16	Adrian Gonzalez/224	5.00
17	Nick Swisher/224	8.00
18	Manny Ramirez/239	15.00
19	Troy Glaus/160	10.00
20	Jermaine Dye/151	5.00
21	Magglio Ordonez/90	5.00
22	Rich Harden/225	5.00
23	Alex Rodriguez/33	20.00
24	Greg Maddux	20.00
25	Hanley Ramirez/90	15.00
26	Ryan Zimmerman	10.00
27	Conor Jackson/81	5.00
28	Ubaldo Jimenez/79	5.00
29	Alfonso Soriano	8.00
30	Aramis Ramirez/79	8.00
31	Travis Buck/224	5.00
32	Brian McCann/79	8.00
33	Hunter Pence/79	8.00
35	Clayton Kershaw/79	15.00
36	Ichiro Suzuki/225	20.00
37	Cliff Lee	10.00
39	Ichiro Suzuki/225	20.00
40	Adrian Gonzalez/161	8.00
41	Bobby Crosby/224	4.00
42	Jack Cust/239	4.00
43	Ichiro Suzuki/225	20.00
44	Adrian Gonzalez/161	8.00
45	Kevin Kouzmanoff/224	4.00
46	Josh Hamilton/225	12.00
47	Brian Giles/224	5.00
48	Travis Buck/224	4.00
49	Hanley Ramirez/90	15.00
50	Miguel Tejada/110	8.00
51	Jose Reyes	15.00
52	Pedro Martinez/110	8.00
53	Geovany Soto/110	10.00
54	Bernie Williams/110	8.00
55	Jonathan Sanchez	5.00
56	J.C. Romero/110	8.00
57	Michel Enriquez/110	20.00
58	Yulieski Gourriel/110	15.00
59	Yoennis Cespedes/110	15.00
60	Frederich Cepeda/110	20.00
61	Jimmy Rollins/110	15.00
62	Roy Oswalt/110	8.00
63	Adam Dunn/110	8.00
64	Kosuke Fukudome/90	20.00
65	Yu Darvish/90	50.00
67	Shinnosuke Abe/90	20.00
68	Norichika Aoki/90	40.00
69	Kwang Ung Kim/90	10.00
70	Tae Kyun Kim/90	20.00
71	Jin Young Lee/90	12.00
72	Shin-Soo Choo	15.00

2009 Topps Update
NM/M
Complete Set (330): 40.00
Common Player: .15
Common SP: 10.00
Inserted 1:32 Hobby
Common RC: .50
Hobby Pack (10): 2.00
Hobby Box (36): 50.00

#	Player	Price
1	Ivan Rodriguez	.25
2	Felipe Lopez	.15
3	Michael Saunders RC	.50
4	David Hernandez RC	1.00
5	Brian Fuentes	.15
6	Josh Barfield	.15
7	Brayan Pena	.15
8	Lance Broadway	.15
9	Jonathan Broxton	.25
10	Tommy Hanson RC	4.00
11	Dan Schlereth RC	.50
12	Edwin Maysonet	.15
13	Scott Hairston	.15
14	Yadier Molina	.15
15	Jacoby Ellsbury	.50
16	Brian Buscher	.15
17	Derek Jeter, David Wright	1.00
18	John Grabow	.15
19	Nelson Cruz	.15
20	Gordon Beckham RC	4.00
21	Matt Diaz	.15
22	Brett Gardner	.15
23	Sean O'Sullivan RC	.50
24	Gabe Gross	.15
25	Orlando Hudson	.15
26	Ryan Howard	.25
27	Josh Reddick RC	1.00
28	Matt Murton	.15
29	Rich Hill	.15
30	J.A. Happ	.15
31	Adam Jones	.25
32	Kris Medlen RC	1.00
33	Daniel Bard RC	1.00
34	Laynce Nix	.15
35	Tom Gorzelanny	.15
36	Paul Konerko	.25
36	Jermaine Dye	.15
37	Adam Kennedy	.15
38	Justin Upton	.40
39	Jake Fox	.15
40	Carl Pavano	.15
41	Xavier Paul (RC)	.50
42	Eric Hinske	.15
43	Koyie Hill	.15
44	Seth Smith	.15
45	Brad Ausmus	.15
46	Clayton Richard	.15
47	Carlos Beltran	.25
48	Duke Snider/SP	12.00
48	Albert Pujols	1.50
49	Roger Maris/SP	15.00
49	Edwin Jackson	.15
50	Gary Sheffield	.25
51	Jesus Guzman RC	.50
52	Kyle Blanks RC	.50
52	Bo Jackson/SP	12.00
53	Clete Thomas	.15
54	Vin Mazzaro RC	.15
55	Ben Zobrist	.15
56	Wes Helms	.15
57	Juan Uribe	.15
58	Omar Quintanilla	.15
59	David Ross	.15
60	Brandon Inge	.15
61	Jamie Hoffman RC	.50
62	Russell Branyan	.15
63	Mark Rzepczynski RC	.50
64	Alex Gonzalez	.15
65	Joe Mauer	.75
66	Paul Molitor/SP	10.00
67	Jhoulys Chacin RC	.75
68	Brandon McCarthy	.15
69	David Eckstein	.15
69	Joe Girardi, Derek Jeter	1.50
70	Wilkin Ramirez RC	.15
71	Chase Utley	.50
71	Rogers Hornsby/SP	12.00
72	Ryne Sandberg/SP	12.00
73	John Mayberry Jr.	.15
74	Sean West (RC)	.50
75	Mitch Maier	.15
76	Matt Lindstrom	.15
77	Scott Rolen	.25
78	Jeremy Reed	.15
79	LaTroy Hawkins	.15
80	Robert Andino	.15
81	Matt Stairs	.15
82	Mark Teixeira	.15
83	David Wright	.75
84	Emilio Bonifacio	.15
85	Gerardo Parra RC	1.00
86	Joe Crede	.15
87	Carlos Pena	.40
88	Jake Peavy	.40
89	Jim Leyland	.15
90	Phil Hughes	.25
91	Orlando Cabrera	.15
92	Anderson Hernandez	.15
93	Edwin Encarnacion	.15
94	Pedro Martinez	.25
95	Jarrod Washburn	.15
96	Ryan Freel	.15
97	Tony Gwynn	.15
98	Juan Castro	.15
99	Hanley Ramirez	.75
99	Honus Wagner/SP	10.00
100	Kevin Gregg	.15
101	C.C. Sabathia	.50
102	Nick Green	.15
102	Brett Hayes (RC)	.50
103	Evan Longoria	1.00
103	Wade Boggs/SP	10.00
104	Geoff Blum	.15
105	Luis Valbuena	.15
106	Jonny Gomes	.15
107	Anthony Swarzak (RC)	.50
108	Chris Tillman RC	1.00
109	Orlando Hudson	.15
110	Justin Masterson	.15
111	Livan Hernandez	.15
112	Kyle Farnsworth	.15
113	Francisco Rodriguez	.25
114	Chris Coghlan RC	1.00
115	Jeff Weaver	.15
116	Alfredo Figaro RC	.50
117	Alex Rios	.15
118	Blake Hawksworth (RC)	.50
119	Bud Norris RC	.50
120	Aaron Poreda RC	.50
121	Brandon Inge.	.15
122	Kevin Youkilis, David Wright, Derek Jeter, Shane Victorino	1.00
123	Ryan Braun	.75
124	Delwyn Young	.15
125	Fernando Martinez RC	1.00
126	Matt Tolbert	.15
127	Shane Robinson	.50
128	Chone Figgins	.25
129	Shane Victorino	.25
130	Randy Johnson	.40
131	Derek Jeter	.15
132	Joe Thurston	.15
133	Graham Taylor RC	.50
134	Derek Holland RC	1.00
135	Ryan Perry, Rick Porcello	1.00
136	Raul Ibanez	.25
137	Ross Ohlendorf	.15
138	Ryan Church	.15
139	Brian Moehler	.15
140	Jack Wilson	.15
141	Jason Hammel	.15
142	Jorge Posada	.25
143	Matt Maloney (RC)	.50
144	Ronny Cedeno	.15
145	Micah Hoffpauir	.15
146	Juan Cruz	.15
147	Jayson Nix	.15
148	Jason Bay	.25
148	Tris Speaker/SP	12.00
149	Joel Hanrahan	.15
150	Raul Ibanez	.25
150	Ty Cobb/SP	15.00
151	Jayson Werth	.25
152	Barbaro Canizares RC	.50
153	Ichiro Suzuki	1.00
153	George Sisler/SP	10.00
154	Gerardo Parra	.15
155	Andrew McCutchen (RC)	1.00
156	Heath Bell	.15
157	Josh Hamilton	.15
158	Wilson Valdez	.15
159	Chad Billingsley	.15
160	Edgar Renteria	.15
161	Andrew Bailey	.25
162	Chris Perez	.15
163	Alejandro De Aza	.15
164	Brett Tomko	.15
165	Maicer Izturis	.15
166	Mike Redmond	.15
167	Julio Borbon RC	.75
168	Paul Phillips	.15
169	Mark Kotsay	.15
170	Jason Giambi	.15
171	Trevor Hoffman	.15
172	Tyler Greene (RC)	.50
173	David Robertson	.15
174	Omar Vizquel	.15
175	Jody Gerut	.15
176	Diory Hernandez RC	.50
177	Neftali Feliz RC	1.50
178	Josh Beckett	.40
179	Carl Crawford	.40
180	Mariano Rivera	.75
181	Zach Duke	.15
182	Mark Buehrle	.15
183	Guillermo Quiroz	.15
184	Francisco Cordero	.15
185	Kevin Correia	.15
186	Zack Greinke	.40
186	Christy Mathewson/SP	15.00
187	Ryan Franklin	.15
188	Jeff Francoeur	.15
189	Michael Young, Josh Hamilton, Ian Kinsler	.50
190	Ken Griffey Jr.	1.00
191	Ben Zobrist	.15
192	Prince Fielder	.50
193	Landon Powell (RC)	.50
194	Ty Wigginton	.15
195	P.J. Walters RC	.50
196	Brian Fuentes	.15
197	Dan Haren	.25
198	Roy Halladay	.40
198	Cy Young/SP	12.00
199	Mike Rivera	.15
200	Randy Johnson	.15
200	Jordan Zimmermann RC	1.00
202	Angel Berroa	.15
203	Ben Francisco	.15
204	Brian Barden	.15
205	Dallas Braden	.15
206	Chris Burke	.15
207	Garrett Jones	.15
208	Chad Gaudin	.15
209	Andruw Jones	.15
210	Jason Vargas	.15
211	Bradley Bergesen (RC)	.50
212	Ian Kinsler	.15
213	Josh Johnson	.15
214	Jason Grilli	.15
215	Felix Hernandez	.40
216	Mat Latos RC	.75
217	Craig Stammen RC	.15
218	Cliff Lee	.40
219	Ken Takahashi RC	.15
220	Matt LaPorta RC	1.50
221	Adrian Gonzalez	.50
222	Ted Lilly	.15
223	Jack Hannahan	.15
224	Takashi Saito	.15
225	Gregorio Petit	.15
226	Kevin Hart	.15
227	Edwin Jackson	.15
228	Jason LaRue	.15
229	Kevin Millar	.15
230	Freddy Sanchez	.15
231	Josh Bard	.15
232	Tim Lincecum	.75
232	Nolan Ryan/SP Angels	15.00
232	Nolan Ryan/SP Mets	15.00
233	Ramon Santiago	.15
234	Mike Sweeney	.15
235	Joe Nathan	.15
236	Kris Benson	.15
237	Dustin Pedroia	.75
238	Kevin Cash	.15
239	George Sherrill	.15
240	Jason Marquis	.15
241	Dewayne Wise	.15
242	Randy Wells	.15
243	Jonathan Papelbon	.25
244	Johan Santana	.50
245	Mariano Rivera	.40
246	Javier Vazquez	.15
247	Lastings Milledge	.15
248	Chan Ho Park	.15
249	Brian McCann	.25
250	Mark Teixeira	.15
250	Johnny Mize/SP NYG	10.00
251	Johnny Mize/SP NYY	10.00
251	Ian Snell	.15
252	Justin Verlander	.15
253	Prince Fielder	.50
253	Reggie Jackson/SP Cal	10.00

253	Reggie Jackson/ SP NYY	10.00
254	Cesar Izturis	.15
255	Omir Santos RC	.50
256	Tim Wakefield	.15
257	Adrian Gonzalez	.50
258	Nyjer Morgan	.15
259	Victor Martinez	.25
260	Ryan Howard	.75
260	Willie McCovey/SP	10.00
261	Aaron Bates RC	.50
262	Jeff Niemann	.15
263	Matt Holliday	.25
264	Adam LaRoche	.15
265	Justin Morneau	.40
266	Jonathan Broxton	.15
267	Miguel Cairo	.15
268	Chris Getz	.15
269	Cliff Floyd	.15
270	David Ortiz, Alex Rodriguez	.75
271	Frank Catalanotto	.15
272	Carlos Pena	.25
273	Mark Lowe	.15
274	Joe Mauer	.75
275	Ryan Garko	.15
276	Brad Penny	.15
277	Orlando Hudson	.15
278	Gaby Sanchez RC	.75
279	Ross Detwiler	.15
280	Mark DeRosa	.40
281	Kevin Youkilis	.40
281	Jimmie Foxx/SP	12.00
282	Victor Martinez	.25
283	Freddy Sanchez	.15
284	Mark Melancon RC	.50
285	Ryan Franklin	.15
286	Sidney Ponson	.15
287	Matt Joyce	.15
288	Jon Garland	.15
289	Nick Johnson	.15
290	Jason Michaels	.15
291	Ross Gload	.15
292	Yuniesky Betancourt	.15
293	Aaron Hill	.15
294	Josh Anderson	.15
295	Miguel Tejada	.40
296	Casey McGehee	.15
297	Brett Cecil RC	.15
298	Jason Bartlett	.15
299	Ryan Langerhans	.15
300	Albert Pujols	1.50
301	Ryan Zimmerman	.40
302	Casey Kotchman	.15
303	Luke French (RC)	.50
304	Nick Swisher, Johnny Damon	.25
305	Michael Young	.15
306	Endy Chavez	.15
307	Heath Bell	.15
308	Matt Cain	.25
309	Scott Podsednik	.15
310	Scott Richmond	.15
311	David Huff RC	.50
312	Ryan Hanigan	.15
313	Jeff Baker	.15
314	Brad Hawpe	.15
315	Jerry Hairston	.15
316	Hunter Pence, Ryan Braun	.75
317	Nelson Cruz	.25
318	Carl Crawford	.25
318	Rickey Henderson/SP	10.00
319	Ramon Castro	.15
320	Dan Schlereth, Mark Schlereth	.15
321	Hunter Pence	.15
322	Sean Marshall	.15
323	Ramon Ramirez	.15
324	Nolan Reimold (RC)	1.00
325	Torii Hunter	.25
325	Frank Robinson/SP	12.00
326	Nate McLouth	.25
327	Julio Lugo	.15
328	Matt Palmer	.15
329	Curtis Granderson	.25
330	Ken Griffey Jr.	1.00
330	Babe Ruth/SP Braves	20.00
330	Babe Ruth/SP Sox	20.00

Black

Stars: 15-25X
RC's: 8-15X
Production 58 Sets

Gold

Gold Stars: 4-6X
Gold RC's: 2-3X
Production 2009 Sets

Platinum

Production One Set

Printing Plates

Production one set per color.

All-Star Jumbo Patches

No Pricing
Production 6 Sets

All-Star Jumbo Patches Autographs

No Pricing
Production 6 Sets

All-Star Stitches

NM/M
Common Player: 5.00
Inserted 1:58 Hobby

Gold: 1-2X
Production 50 Sets

1	Chase Utley	12.00
2	Nelson Cruz	6.00
3	Adam Jones	10.00
4	Justin Upton	6.00
5	Albert Pujols	35.00
6	Ben Zobrist	8.00
7	Joe Mauer	12.00
8	Yadier Molina	20.00
9	Mark Teixeira	15.00
10	David Wright	15.00
11	Carlos Pena	8.00
12	Hanley Ramirez	12.00
13	Adrian Gonzalez	10.00
14	Francisco Rodriguez	8.00
15	Evan Longoria	8.00
16	Brandon Inge	8.00
17	Shane Victorino	15.00
18	Raul Ibanez	15.00
19	Jason Bay	8.00
20	Jayson Werth	15.00
21	Ichiro Suzuki	25.00
22	Heath Bell	5.00
23	Andrew Bailey	5.00
24	Chad Billingsley	8.00
25	Josh Hamilton	12.00
26	Trevor Hoffman	8.00
27	Josh Beckett	10.00
28	Zach Duke	5.00
29	Mark Buehrle	8.00
30	Zack Greinke	12.00
31	Francisco Cordero	5.00
32	Ryan Franklin	25.00
33	Brian Fuentes	8.00
34	Dan Haren	8.00
35	Roy Halladay	8.00
36	Josh Johnson	5.00
37	Felix Hernandez	10.00
38	Ted Lilly	5.00
39	Edwin Jackson	8.00
40	Tim Lincecum	15.00
41	Joe Nathan	8.00
42	Jason Marquis	8.00
43	Jonathan Papelbon	8.00
44	Johan Santana	10.00
45	Mariano Rivera	12.00
46	Brian McCann	15.00
47	Justin Verlander	12.00
48	Prince Fielder	12.00
49	Tim Wakefield	8.00
50	Ryan Braun	12.00
51	Victor Martinez	8.00
52	Ryan Zimmerman	10.00
53	Orlando Hudson	5.00
54	Kevin Youkilis	8.00
55	Freddy Sanchez	5.00
56	Aaron Hill	5.00
57	Miguel Tejada	8.00
58	Jason Bartlett	8.00
59	Ryan Howard	15.00
60	Michael Young	5.00
61	Brad Hawpe	8.00
62	Carl Crawford	8.00
63	Hunter Pence	8.00
64	Curtis Granderson	10.00
65	Jonathan Broxton	8.00
66	Matt Cain	8.00

All-Star Stitches Autographs

NM/M
Production 25 Sets

DW	David Wright	60.00
EL	Evan Longoria	125.00
NC	Nelson Cruz	40.00
OH	Orlando Hudson	25.00
PF	Prince Fielder	60.00
ZG	Zack Greinke	40.00

All-Star Stitches Dual

NM/M
Production 25 Sets

2	Mariano Rivera, Francisco Rodriguez	20.00
3	Mark Teixeira, Prince Fielder	35.00
4	Ryan Howard, Chase Utley	50.00
5	David Wright, Evan Longoria	50.00
6	Tim Lincecum, Roy Halladay	40.00
7	Justin Upton, Adam Jones	40.00
8	Albert Pujols, Joe Mauer	50.00

All-Star Stitches Triple

NM/M
Production 25 Sets

1	Evan Longoria, Carl Crawford, Ben Zobrist	35.00
2	Chase Utley, Ryan Howard, Raul Ibanez	50.00
4	Kevin Youkilis, Jason Bay, Josh Beckett	35.00
5	Johan Santana, Tim Lincecum, Roy Halladay	40.00
6	Felix Hernandez, Dan Haren, Chad Billingsley	40.00
7	Mark Teixeira, Carlos Pena, Adrian Gonzalez	25.00
8	Albert Pujols, Ryan Howard, Prince Fielder	50.00
9	Adam Jones, Ryan Braun, Justin Upton	40.00
10	Mariano Rivera, Jonathan Papelbon, Francisco Rodriguez	40.00

Career Best Autographs

NM/M
Inserted 1:352 Hobby

AE	Andre Ethier	15.00
AJ	Andruw Jones	10.00
BZ	Ben Zobrist	20.00
GS	Gary Sheffield	30.00
HB	Heath Bell	5.00
IR	Ivan Rodriguez	35.00
JG	Jason Giambi	30.00
JN	Jayson Nix	5.00
KG	Kevin Gregg	5.00
MB	Milton Bradley	10.00
MH	Matt Holliday	40.00
OH	Orlando Hudson	10.00
PM	Peter Moylan	5.00
RH	Rich Hill	5.00
RI	Raul Ibanez	40.00
RO	Roy Oswalt	20.00
VG	Vladimir Guerrero	30.00

Career Quest Autographs

NM/M
Inserted 1:546 Hobby

AM	Andrew McCutchen	20.00
DH	David Hernandez	8.00
DS	Dan Schlereth	6.00
GB	Gordon Beckham	60.00
JZ	Jordan Zimmermann	15.00
KU	Koji Uehara	40.00
MG	Mat Gamel	15.00
RB	Reid Brignac	10.00
RP	Ryan Perry	12.00
TH	Tommy Hanson	30.00
VM	Vin Mazzaro	10.00
RPO	Rick Porcello	35.00

Legends of the Game

NM/M
Common Player: 1.00
Gold: 2-4X
Production 99 Sets
Platinum: 6-10X
Production 25 Sets

1	Cy Young	1.50
2	Honus Wagner	2.00
3	Christy Mathewson	1.50
4	Ty Cobb	1.50
5	Tris Speaker	1.50
6	Babe Ruth	4.00
7	George Sisler	1.00
8	Rogers Hornsby	1.50
9	Jimmie Foxx	2.00
10	Johnny Mize	1.00
11	Nolan Ryan	4.00
12	Juan Marichal	1.00
13	Steve Carlton	1.00
14	Reggie Jackson	1.50
15	Frank Robinson	1.50
16	Wade Boggs	1.00
17	Paul Molitor	1.00
18	Babe Ruth	4.00
19	Nolan Ryan	4.00
20	Frank Robinson	1.50
21	Reggie Jackson	1.50
22	Wade Boggs	1.00
23	Rogers Hornsby	1.50
24	Paul Molitor	1.50
25	Johnny Mize	1.00

Legends of the Game Team Name Letter

NM/M
Common Letter Patch: 10.00
Each Letter #'d to 50:

BR	Babe Ruth (Red Sox)	25.00
BR2	Babe Ruth (New York)	25.00
CM	Christy Mathewson	15.00
CY	Cy Young	10.00
GS	George Sisler	10.00
HW	Honus Wagner	15.00
JF	Jimmie Foxx	15.00
JM	Johnny Mize	10.00
JR	Jackie Robinson	15.00
LG	Lou Gehrig	20.00
MM	Mickey Mantle	30.00
PR	Pee Wee Reese	15.00
RC	Roy Campanella	15.00
RH	Rogers Hornsby	15.00
TC	Ty Cobb	15.00
TM	Thurman Munson	15.00
TS	Tris Speaker	10.00
WJ	Walter Johnson	12.00

Legends of the Game Autographs

Production One Set

Legends of the Game Cut Signature

Production One Set

Propaganda Poster

NM/M
Common Card: .50
Inserted 1:6

1	Adam Dunn	.75
2	Adrian Gonzalez	.75
3	Albert Pujols	3.00
4	Andrew McCutchen	.75
5	Alfonso Soriano	.75
6	Carlos Quentin	.75
7	Chipper Jones	1.50
8	David Wright	2.00
9	Dustin Pedroia	1.50
10	Evan Longoria	2.00
11	Grady Sizemore	1.00
12	Hanley Ramirez	1.00
13	Hunter Pence	.50
14	Ichiro Suzuki	2.00
15	Andrew Bailey	.50
16	Jay Bruce	1.00
17	Joe Mauer	1.00
18	Josh Hamilton	.75
19	Justin Upton	.75
20	Manny Ramirez	.75
21	Mark Teixeira	.75
22	Miguel Cabrera	.75
23	Nick Markakis	.75
24	Roy Halladay	.75
25	Ryan Braun	1.00
26	Ryan Howard	1.00
27	Tim Lincecum	1.50
28	Todd Helton	.50
29	Vladimir Guerrero	.75
30	Zack Greinke	.50

Ring of Honor

NM/M
Common (76-100): .50

76	Babe Ruth	4.00
77	Jackie Robinson	2.00
78	Chris Duncan	.50
79	Christy Mathewson	1.50
80	Cy Young	1.50
81	Jermaine Dye	.50
82	Honus Wagner	2.00
83	Chone Figgins	.50
84	Walter Johnson	1.50
85	Jon Garland	.50
86	Mel Ott	1.50
87	Jimmie Foxx	1.50
88	Hideki Okajima	.50
89	Johnny Mize	1.00
90	Rogers Hornsby	1.00
91	Miguel Cabrera	1.00
92	Pee Wee Reese	1.00
93	Darin Erstad	.50
94	Tris Speaker	1.00
95	Steve Garvey	.50
96	Lou Gehrig	3.00
97	Babe Ruth	4.00
98	David Ortiz	1.00
99	Thurman Munson	1.50
100	Roy Campanella	1.00

Ring of Honor Autographs

NM/M
Inserted 1:3,900 Hobby

BS	Bruce Sutter	40.00
CD	Chris Duncan	30.00
JD	Jermaine Dye	40.00
RK	Ray Knight	35.00
SG	Steve Garvey	50.00

Rookie Chrome Refractors

NM/M
Common Refractor: 4.00
Box Topper: 1:Box

1	Michael Saunders	6.00
2	David Hernandez	4.00
3	Tommy Hanson	15.00
4	Dan Schlereth	4.00
5	Gordon Beckham	20.00
6	Sean O'Sullivan	4.00
7	Josh Reddick	6.00
8	Kris Medlen	6.00
9	Daniel Bard	6.00
10	Xavier Paul	4.00
11	Jesus Guzman	6.00
12	Kyle Blanks	6.00
13	Vin Mazzaro	6.00
14	Jamie Hoffman	5.00
15	Mark Rzepczynski	4.00
16	Jhoulys Chacin	4.00
17	Wilkin Ramirez	4.00
18	John Mayberry Jr.	4.00
19	Sean West	4.00
20	Gerardo Parra	6.00
21	Brett Hayes	4.00
22	Anthony Swarzak	4.00
23	Chris Tillman	8.00
24	Chris Coghlan	4.00
25	Alfredo Figaro	4.00
26	Blake Hawksworth	4.00
27	Bud Norris	4.00
28	Aaron Poreda	4.00
29	Fernando Martinez	8.00
30	Shane Robinson	4.00
31	Graham Taylor	15.00
32	Derek Holland	6.00
33	Matt Maloney	4.00
34	Barbaro Canizares	6.00
35	Andrew McCutchen	10.00
36	Julio Borbon	6.00
37	Tyler Greene	4.00
38	Diory Hernandez	4.00
39	Neftali Feliz	10.00
40	Landon Powell	4.00
41	P.J. Walters	4.00
42	Jordan Zimmermann	6.00
43	Brad Bergesen	4.00
44	Mat Latos	6.00
45	Craig Stammen	4.00
46	Ken Takahashi	8.00
47	Matt LaPorta	8.00
48	Omir Santos	4.00
49	Aaron Bates	6.00
50	Gaby Sanchez	6.00
51	Mark Melancon	6.00
52	Brett Cecil	6.00
53	Luke French	4.00
54	David Huff	4.00
55	Nolan Reimold	8.00

Sketch

No Pricing
Inserted 1:8,100 Hobby

Stadium Stamp

NM/M
Production 90 Sets

1	Polo Grounds	30.00
2	Forbes Field	30.00
3	Wrigley Field	40.00
4	Yankee Stadium	40.00
5	Tiger Stadium	30.00
6	Shibe Park	25.00
7	Crosley Field	20.00
8	Comiskey Park	25.00
9	Fenway Park	30.00
10	Ebbets Field	25.00

Turkey Red

NM/M
Common Player: .50

101	Ty Cobb	1.50
102	David Price	3.00
103	Jorge Posada	.75
104	Brian Roberts	.75
105	Tris Speaker	1.00
106	John Lackey	.50
107	Miguel Tejada	.50
108	Dan Haren	.50
109	Troy Tulowitzki	.75
110	Yunel Escobar	.50
111	Koji Uehara	.75
112	Vernon Wells	.50
113	Jimmie Foxx	1.00
114	C.C. Sabathia	1.00
115	Alexei Ramirez	.75
116	Rick Porcello	3.00
117	Gary Sheffield	.75
118	Ryan Dempster	.50
119	Shin-Soo Choo	.75
120	Adam Dunn	.75
121	Edinson Volquez	.50
122	Kevin Youkilis	1.00
123	Roy Halladay	.75
124	Justin Verlander	.75
125	Max Scherzer	.50
126	Jorge Cantu	.50
127	Roy Oswalt	.75
128	Tommy Hanson	3.00
129	Raul Ibanez	.50
130	Johan Santana	.75
131	Jermaine Dye	.50
132	Mariano Rivera	.75
133	Rogers Hornsby	1.00
134	Daisuke Matsuzaka	2.00
135	Andrew McCutchen	1.50
136	Jake Peavy	.75
137	Jason Bay	1.00
138	Ken Griffey Jr.	2.50
139	Chris Carpenter	1.00
140	Carl Crawford	.75
141	Victor Martinez	.75
142	Brad Hawpe	.50
143	Aaron Hill	.50
144	Randy Johnson	1.00
145	Gordon Beckham	3.00
146	Jordan Zimmermann	1.00
147	Freddy Sanchez	.50
148	Carlos Pena	1.00
149	Johnny Cueto	.50
150	Babe Ruth	4.00

WBC Stitches Dual

NM/M
Production 25 Sets

AA	Norichika Aoki, Shinnosuke Abe	75.00
CK	Hung-Wen Chen, Po-Hsuan Keng	20.00
COR	Miguel Cabrera, Magglio Ordonez	50.00
CP	Francisco Cervelli, Nick Punto	15.00
DH	Yurendell De Caster, Greg Halman	15.00
EN	Justin Erasmus, Gift Ngoepe	20.00
ER	Damaso Espino, Carlos Ruiz	20.00
GCE	Yulieski Gourriel, Frederich Cepeda	30.00
LK	Jae Woo Lee, Kwang-Hyun Kim	35.00
LL	Kai Liu, Chenhao Li	20.00
NH	Drew Naylor, Luke Hughes	20.00
RL	Hein Robb, Dylan Lindsay	15.00
RR	Jose Reyes, Hanley Ramirez	25.00
WA	Nick Weglarz, Phillippe Aumont	15.00
ZF	Xiaotian Zhang, Fei Feng	20.00

WBC Stitches Triple

NM/M
Production 25 Sets

CHR	Francisco Cervelli, Ramon Hernandez, Carlos Ruiz	20.00
COH	Johnny Cueto, Roy Oswalt, Felix Hernandez	20.00
DMC	Adam Dunn, Alexander Mayeta, Miguel Cabrera	20.00
DWR	Adam Dunn, David Wright, Jimmy Rollins	40.00
FTA	Kosuke Fukudome, Masahiro Tanaka, Norichika Aoki	180.00
GCC	Yulieski Gourriel, Frederich Cepeda, Yoennis Cespedes	40.00
IDA	Ichiro Suzuki, Yu Darvish, Shinnosuke Abe	200.00
KRL	Tae Kyun Kim, HyunJin Ryu, Jae Woo Lee	40.00
MSR	Russell Martin, Geovany Soto, Carlos Ruiz	20.00
PCO	Nick Punto, Francisco Cervelli, Adam Ottavino	15.00
RRR	Jose Reyes, Jimmy Rollins, Hanley Ramirez	30.00
RRT	Jose Reyes, Hanley Ramirez, Miguel Tejada	25.00
SOH	Carlos Silva, Magglio Ordonez, Ramon Hernandez	20.00
SSR	Jonathan Sanchez, Geovany Soto, J.C. Romero	15.00

2009 Topps World Baseball Classic Boxed Set

NM/M
Complete Set (55): 25.00
Common Player: .50

1	Yu Darvish	2.00
2	Derek Jeter	3.00
3	Ryan Braun	1.50
4	Michel Enriquez	.50
5	Phillippe Aumont	.50
6	Yulieski Gourriel	.50
7	Shinnosuke Abe	.50
8	Hanley Ramirez	1.00
9	Daisuke Matsuzaka	1.50
10	Justin Erasmus	.50
11	Frank Catalanotto	.50
12	Travis Blackley	.50
13	Alex Rodriguez	2.00
14	Brian McCann	.75
15	Arquimedes Nieto	.50
16	Joakim Soria	.50
17	Justin Morneau	.75
18	Geovany Soto	.75
19	Alex Liddi	.50
20	Cheng-Min Peng	.50
21	Luke Hughes	.50
22	Manny Corpas	.50
23	Chipper Jones	1.00
24	Drew Naylor	.50
25	Jimmy Rollins	1.00
26	Kosuke Fukudome	1.00
27	Jose Reyes	1.00
28	David Wright	1.50
29	Ichiro Suzuki	2.00
30	Carlos Lee	.50
31	Joey Votto	.75
32	Jin Young Lee	.50
33	Jonathan Sanchez	.50
34	Lenny DiNardo	.50
35	Miguel Cabrera	1.00
36	Rick Vanden Hurk	.50
37	David Ortiz	1.00
38	Jason Bay	.75
39	Dylan Lindsay	.50
40	Chris Denorfia	.50
41	Bernie Williams	.50
42	Akinori Iwamura	.50
43	Pedro Martinez	.75
44	Gift Ngoepe	.50
45	Chenhao Li	.50
46	Roy Oswalt	.50
47	Dustin Pedroia	1.00
48	Tao Bu	.50
49	Greg Halman	1.00
50	Adrian Gonzalez	.75
51	Carlos Beltran	.75
52	Pedro Lazo	.50
53	Jorge Cantu	.50
54	Kenji Johjima	.50
55	Fu-Te Ni	.50

2009 Topps Unique

Common Player (1-150): .25
Common RC (151-200): 2.00
Production 26
99Pack (7): 5.00
Box (24): 100.00

#	Player	Price
1	Nick Markakis	0.75
2	Geovany Soto	0.75
3	Brandon Phillips	0.50
4	Torii Hunter	0.50
5	Jay Bruce	0.75
6	Cliff Lee	0.75
7	Jose Reyes	0.75
8	Justin Masterson	0.50
9	Jermaine Dye	0.50
10	Ryan Braun	1.50
11	Ubaldo Jimenez	0.50
12	Carlos Lee	0.50
13	Alex Rodriguez	2.00
14	Jon Lester	0.75
15	Chipper Jones	1.25
16	Justin Morneau	0.75
17	Dan Haren	0.75
18	Andre Ethier	0.75
19	Felix Hernandez	0.75
20	Grady Sizemore	0.75
21	Rick Ankiel	0.50
22	Ryan Dempster	0.50
23	Justin Verlander	0.75
24	Chase Utley	1.25
25	David Wright	1.50
26	Matt Cain	0.50
27	Brad Hawpe	0.50
28	John Lackey	0.50
29	Roy Oswalt	0.75
30	Alfonso Soriano	0.75
31	Braden Looper	0.50
32	Jayson Werth	0.75
33	Edinson Volquez	0.50
34	Matt Kemp	0.75
35	Adam Jones	0.75
36	Joba Chamberlain	1.50
37	Jason Giambi	0.75
38	Chris Carpenter	0.75
39	Jim Thome	0.75
40	Daisuke Matsuzaka	2.00
41	Kevin Millwood	0.50
42	Francisco Liriano	0.75
43	Joey Votto	0.75
44	Aramis Ramirez	0.50
45	Hanley Ramirez	1.25
46	Johan Santana	1.25
47	Hank Blalock	0.50
48	Joe Saunders	0.50
49	Carlos Quentin	0.75
50	Ryan Howard	1.50
51	Aaron Rowand	0.50
52	Aaron Cook	0.50
53	Curtis Granderson	0.75
54	Max Scherzer	0.75
55	Manny Ramirez	1.25
56	Carlos Delgado	0.50
57	Garrett Atkins	0.50
58	Josh Johnson	0.50
59	Gary Sheffield	0.75
60	Victor Martinez	0.75
61	Miguel Tejada	0.75
62	Roy Halladay	0.75
63	Kevin Kouzmanoff	0.50
64	Javier Vazquez	0.50
65	Joe Mauer	1.25
66	Lance Berkman	0.75
67	Ryan Zimmerman	0.75
68	Ryan Ludwick	0.50
69	Randy Johnson	0.75
70	Jimmy Rollins	0.75
71	A.J. Burnett	0.75
72	Adrian Beltre	0.50
73	Nelson Cruz	0.50
74	Bobby Abreu	0.50
75	Miguel Cabrera	0.75
76	Chad Billingsley	0.50
77	Freddy Sanchez	0.50
78	Scott Kazmir	0.50
79	Magglio Ordonez	0.75
80	Brandon Webb	0.75
81	Hunter Pence	0.75
82	Adam Dunn	0.50
83	Dan Uggla	0.50
84	Jair Jurrjens	0.50
85	Prince Fielder	1.25
86	Melvin Mora	0.50
87	Jason Bay	0.75
88	Clayton Kershaw	0.75
89	Akinori Iwamura	0.50
90	Zack Greinke	1.25
91	Yunel Escobar	0.50
92	Russell Martin	0.75
93	Derek Lee	0.75
94	Mike Pelfrey	0.50
95	Tim Lincecum	1.50
96	Carlos Pena	0.75
97	Justin Upton	0.75
98	Denard Span	0.50
99	Paul Konerko	0.50
100	Albert Pujols	3.00
101	Kurt Suzuki	0.50
102	Corey Hart	0.50
103	Aubrey Huff	0.50
104	Scott Rolen	0.75
105	Ken Griffey Jr.	1.50
106	Stephen Drew	0.50
107	Carlos Zambrano	0.75
108	Dustin Pedroia	1.50
109	Derek Jeter	3.00
110	Carl Crawford	0.75
111	Carlos Zambrano	0.75
112	Yovani Gallardo	0.50
113	Raul Ibanez	0.75
114	Vernon Wells	0.50
115	Vladimir Guerrero	1.25
116	Adam LaRoche	0.50
117	Carlos Guillen	0.50
118	Todd Helton	0.75
119	Brian McCann	0.75
120	Jake Peavy	0.75
121	David Ortiz	0.75
122	Mark Buehrle	0.50
123	CC Sabathia	0.75
124	Jorge Cantu	0.50
125	Ichiro Suzuki	2.00
126	Josh Hamilton	1.25
127	Nate McLouth	0.50
128	B.J. Upton	0.75
129	Alex Gordon	0.75
130	Cole Hamels	1.25
131	Josh Beckett	0.75
132	James Shields	0.75
133	Alexei Ramirez	0.75
134	Kosuke Fukudome	1.25
135	Adrian Gonzalez	0.75
136	Ian Kinsler	0.75
137	Johnny Cueto	0.50
138	Jacoby Ellsbury	1.25
139	Jorge Posada	0.75
140	Alex Rios	0.50
141	Matt Holliday	0.75
142	Michael Young	0.75
143	Robinson Cano	0.75
144	Mike Lowell	0.50
145	Evan Longoria	2.00
146	John Maine	0.50
147	Jose Lopez	0.50
148	Aaron Hill	0.50
149	Garret Anderson	0.50
150	Mark Teixeira	1.25
151	Fernando Martinez RC	4.00
152	David Hernandez RC	1.50
153	Chris Coghlan RC	4.00
154	Brett Anderson RC	1.50
155	Tyler Greene (RC)	1.50
156	Michael Bowden (RC)	2.50
157	Wilkin Ramirez RC	1.50
158	Trevor Cahill RC	2.50
159	Dexter Fowler (RC)	2.50
160	Bud Norris RC	1.50
161	Francisco Cervelli RC	4.00
162	Brett Cecil RC	1.50
163	Mat Latos RC	2.50
164	Derek Holland RC	2.50
165	Mat Gamel RC	2.50
166	Kenshin Kawakami RC	2.50
167	Matt LaPorta RC	4.00
168	Kris Medlen RC	2.50
169	Gerardo Parra RC	2.50
170	Josh Outman RC	2.50
171	Trevor Crowe RC	1.50
172	Ryan Perry RC	4.00
173	Colby Rasmus (RC)	4.00
174	Rick Porcello (RC)	5.00
175	Nolan Reimold (RC)	1.50
176	David Price RC	5.00
177	Omir Santos RC	1.50
178	Ricky Romero (RC)	2.50
179	Jordan Schafer (RC)	2.50
180	Anthony Swarzak (RC)	1.50
181	Travis Snider RC	4.00
182	Koji Uehara RC	2.50
183	Jesus Guzman RC	1.50
184	Sean West (RC)	1.50
185	Neftali Feliz RC	4.00
186	Vin Mazzaro RC	1.50
187	Gordon Beckham RC	6.00
188	Jordan Zimmermann RC	1.50
189	Chris Tillman RC	2.50
190	Tommy Hanson RC	6.00
191	Josh Reddick RC	2.50
192	Michael Saunders RC	2.50
193	Alfredo Aceves RC	2.50
194	Kyle Blanks RC	2.50
195	Elvis Andrus RC	2.50
196	Andrew McCutchen (RC)	4.00
197	Will Venable RC	1.50
198	David Huff RC	1.50
199	Aaron Bates RC	1.50
200	Jhoulys Chacin RC	2.50

Bronze
Bronze (1-150): 3-5X
Bronze RC (151-200): 1-2X
Production 99 Sets

Gold
No Pricing
Production 25 Sets

Platinum
Production One Set

Red
Red (1-150): 1-2X
Red RC (151-200): 1X
Production 1,199

Alone at the Top
Common Player: 1.00
Bronze: 1.5X
Production 99 Sets
Gold: 2-4X
Production 25 Sets
Platinum 1 of 1's exist

AT01	Chipper Jones	2.50
AT02	Albert Pujols	5.00
AT03	Hanley Ramirez	2.50
AT04	Ryan Howard	3.00
AT05	Adam Dunn	1.50
AT06	Willy Taveras	1.00
AT07	Johan Santana	2.50

ALONE AT THE TOP
CARDINALS — ALBERT PUJOLS

AT08	Tim Lincecum	3.00
AT09	Francisco Rodriguez	1.00
AT10	Roy Halladay	1.50

Autentic Tag
Production One Set
No Pricing

Barrels
Production One Set
No Pricing

Bat Barrel Autographs
Production One Set
No Pricing

Bat Knob Autographs
No Pricing

Bat Knobs
Production One Set
No Pricing

Button Autographs
No Pricing
Production 6 Sets

Buttons
No Pricing
Production 6 Sets

Dual Distinction Autograph Relics
Production 10 Sets
No Pricing

Dual Distinction Autographs
Production 25 Sets

PB	Jake Peavy / Gordon Beckham	150.00
PP	Rick Porcello / David Price	60.00
SS	Joe Saunders / Ervin Santana	20.00
VB	Joey Votto / Jay Bruce	60.00

Dual Distinction Relics
Common Duo:
Production 99 Sets

BF	Ryan Braun / Prince Fielder	15.00
BP	Lance Berkman / Hunter Pence	10.00
CL	Matt Cain / Tim Lincecum	15.00
CP	Miguel Cabrera / Albert Pujols	25.00
EP	Jacoby Ellsbury / Dustin Pedroia	20.00
GH	Vladimir Guerrero / Torii Hunter	8.00
GP	Adrian Gonzalez / Albert Pujols	20.00
HB	Roy Halladay / Josh Beckett	8.00
HK	Josh Hamilton / Ian Kinsler	10.00
HU	Ryan Howard / Chase Utley	30.00
IM	Ichiro Suzuki / Daisuke Matsuzaka	25.00
JM	Chipper Jones / Brian McCann	10.00
KR	Matt Kemp / Manny Ramirez	10.00
LC	Evan Longoria / Carl Crawford	15.00
MJ	Nick Markakis / Adam Jones	20.00
MM	Joe Mauer / Justin Morneau	15.00
OY	David Ortiz / Kevin Youkilis	10.00
PR	Jorge Posada / Mariano Rivera	20.00
RU	Hanley Ramirez / Dan Uggla	8.00
SH	Johan Santana / Cole Hamels	10.00
SR	Alfonso Soriano / Aramis Ramirez	8.00
SS	Grady Sizemore / Ichiro Suzuki	15.00
TR	Mark Teixeira / Alex Rodriguez	20.00
VP	Justin Verlander / Rick Porcello	10.00
WR	David Wright / Jose Reyes	10.00

Jumbo Patch Autographs
Production 15 Sets
No Pricing

Jumbo Patches
Some not priced due to scarcity

AR	Anthony Reyes	
BM	Brian McCann/40	20.00
CL	Che-Hsuan Lin/40	30.00
CS	CC Sabathia/40	60.00
DC	David Cortes/40	10.00
DE	Damaso Espino	
DU	Dan Uggla	60.00
FC	Francisco Cervelli	10.00
FH	Felix Hernandez	460.00
GS	Grady Sizemore/13	150.00
HR	Hein Robb/40	20.00
JE	Justin Erasmus	12.00
JU	Justin Upton/15	125.00
JW	Jered Weaver	40.00
MO	Magglio Ordonez/22	30.00
MT	Mark Teixeira	50.00
RA	Rick Ankiel	20.00
RJ	Randy Johnson	50.00
RL	Ryan Ludwick/40	50.00
YG	Yovani Gallardo/22	100.00
CSM	Curt Smith/40	20.00
HJR	Hyun-Jin Ryu/40	40.00
JWE	Jeff Weaver	30.00
MO2	Magglio Ordonez	60.00

Majestic Tag
Production One Set
No Pricing

Majestic Tag Autographs
Production One Set
No Pricing

MLB Logo Man Autographs
Production One Set
No Pricing

MLB Logo Patch
Production One Set
No Pricing

Presidential Plates
Common Plate: 30.00
Platinum 1 of 1's exist

PP1	George Washington	80.00
PP2	John Adams	50.00
PP3	Thomas Jefferson	80.00
PP4	James Madison	30.00
PP5	James Monroe	30.00
PP6	John Quincy Adams	30.00
PP7	Andrew Jackson	30.00
PP8	Martin Van Buren	30.00
PP9	William Henry Harrison	30.00
PP10	John Tyler	30.00
PP11	James K. Polk	40.00
PP12	Zachary Taylor	30.00
PP13	Millard Fillmore	30.00
PP14	Franklin Pierce	30.00
PP15	James Buchanan	30.00
PP16	Abraham Lincoln	100.00
PP17	Andrew Johnson	30.00
PP18	Ulysses S. Grant	50.00
PP19	Rutherford B. Hayes	40.00
PP20	James A. Garfield	30.00
PP21	Chester A. Arthur	40.00
PP22	Grover Cleveland	40.00
PP23	Benjamin Harrison	30.00
PP24	Grover Cleveland	40.00
PP25	William McKinley	40.00
PP26	Theodore Roosevelt	50.00
PP27	William Howard Taft	40.00
PP28	Woodrow Wilson	50.00
PP29	Warren G. Harding	30.00
PP30	Calvin Coolidge	40.00
PP32	Franklin D. Roosevelt	50.00
PP33	Harry S Truman	50.00
PP34	Dwight D. Eisenhower	50.00
PP35	John F. Kennedy	100.00
PP36	Lyndon B. Johnson	50.00
PP37	Richard Nixon	50.00
PP38	Gerald R. Ford	40.00
PP39	Ronald Reagan	50.00
PP40	George Bush	50.00
PP41	Bill Clinton	50.00
PP42	George W. Bush	50.00
PP43	Barack Obama	80.00

Primetime Patches
Common Patch: 10.00

PTP1	Adam Dunn	10.00
PTP2	Adrian Beltre	10.00
PTP3	Albert Pujols	30.00
PTP4	Alex Gordon	20.00
PTP6	Alex Rodriguez	20.00
PTP7	Andrew Miller	10.00
PTP8	Anthony Reyes	10.00
PTP9	Barry Zito	10.00
PTP10	Brad Lidge	10.00
PTP11	Brett Myers	10.00
PTP12	Carlos Beltran	15.00
PTP13	Carlos Delgado	15.00
PTP14	CC Sabathia	15.00
PTP16	Chase Utley	40.00
PTP17	Chipper Jones	15.00
PTP18	David Ortiz	15.00
PTP19	David Ortiz	10.00
PTP20	Edinson Volquez	10.00
PTP21	Ervin Santana	10.00
PTP22	Freddy Sanchez	10.00
PTP23	Hank Blalock	10.00
PTP24	Hideki Okajima	10.00
PTP25	Howie Kendrick	10.00
PTP26	Ian Kinsler	10.00
PTP27	Ivan Rodriguez	10.00
PTP28	J.D. Drew	10.00
PTP29	J.J. Hardy	10.00
PTP30	Jacoby Ellsbury	20.00
PTP31	Jason Giambi	10.00
PTP33	Jim Thome	10.00
PTP35	Joey Votto	15.00
PTP36	John Smoltz	10.00
PTP37	Johnny Damon	10.00
PTP38	Jorge Posada	20.00
PTP39	Jose Reyes	10.00
PTP40	Josh Hamilton	12.00
PTP41	Kevin Millwood	10.00
PTP42	Kevin Youkilis	15.00
PTP43	Lance Berkman	10.00
PTP44	Magglio Ordonez	10.00
PTP45	Manny Ramirez	12.00
PTP46	Mark Teixeira	15.00
PTP47	Matt Holliday	10.00
PTP48	Michael Young	10.00
PTP49	Miguel Cabrera	12.00
PTP50	Miguel Tejada	10.00
PTP51	Mike Lowell	10.00
PTP52	Mike Napoli	15.00
PTP53	Pablo Sandoval	40.00
PTP54	Pat Burrell	10.00
PTP55	Pedro Martinez	12.00
PTP56	Phil Hughes	12.00
PTP57	Prince Fielder	15.00
PTP58	Rafael Furcal	10.00
PTP59	Robinson Cano	15.00
PTP60	Rocco Baldelli	10.00
PTP61	Roy Oswalt	10.00
PTP62	Scott Rolen	12.00
PTP63	Todd Helton	10.00
PTP64	Torii Hunter	10.00
PTP65	Trevor Hoffman	10.00
PTP66	Vernon Wells	10.00
PTP67	Victor Martinez	10.00
PTP68	Vladimir Guerrero	10.00
PTP69	Wladimir Balentien	10.00
PTP70	Yovani Gallardo	12.00
PTP71	Anthony Reyes	10.00
PTP72	Carlos Delgado	20.00
PTP73	Jason Giambi	10.00
PTP74	Jim Thome	12.00
PTP76	Johnny Damon	10.00
PTP77	Mark Teixeira	15.00
PTP78	Pablo Sandoval	40.00
PTP79	Prince Fielder	15.00
PTP80	Albert Pujols	40.00
PTP81	Andrew Miller	10.00
PTP82	Brett Myers	10.00
PTP83	Carlos Beltran	10.00
PTP84	Edinson Volquez	10.00
PTP85	Freddy Sanchez	10.00
PTP86	Josh Hamilton	15.00
PTP87	Miguel Cabrera	15.00
PTP88	Mike Lowell	10.00
PTP89	Mike Napoli	15.00
PTP90	Vladimir Guerrero	10.00
PTP91	Adrian Beltre	10.00
PTP92	Barry Zito	10.00
PTP93	David Ortiz	15.00
PTP94	Hank Blalock	10.00
PTP95	Ivan Rodriguez	10.00
PTP96	Jose Reyes	12.00
PTP97	Magglio Ordonez	15.00
PTP98	Michael Young	10.00
PTP99	Miguel Tejada	10.00
PTP100	Pedro Martinez	12.00
PTP101	Rocco Baldelli	10.00
PTP102	Roy Oswalt	10.00
PTP103	Scott Rolen	12.00
PTP104	Wladimir Balentien	10.00
PTP105	Kevin Millwood	10.00
PTP106	Kevin Millwood	12.00
PTP107-108	Torii Hunter	10.00
PTP109-111	Adam Dunn	10.00
PTP112	Chipper Jones	15.00
PTP113-114	Chipper Jones	15.00
PTP115-117	Lance Berkman	10.00
PTP118-120	Todd Helton	10.00

Russell Logo
Production One Set
No Pricing

Russell Logo Autographs
Production One Set
No Pricing

Solo Shot Relics
Common Player: 5.00
Production 275 Sets

AG	Adrian Gonzalez	6.00
AP	Albert Pujols	15.00
AR	Alex Rodriguez	15.00
AS	Alfonso Soriano	5.00
CJ	Chipper Jones	10.00
CU	Chase Utley	5.00
DO	David Ortiz	5.00
DW	David Wright	10.00
EL	Evan Longoria	10.00
GS	Grady Sizemore	10.00
HR	Hanley Ramirez	10.00
IS	Ichiro Suzuki	15.00
JH	Josh Hamilton	8.00
JM	Joe Mauer	8.00
JR	Jimmy Rollins	8.00
MC	Miguel Cabrera	8.00
MH	Matt Holliday	8.00
MR	Manny Ramirez	8.00
MT	Mark Teixeira	15.00
NM	Nick Markakis	8.00
PF	Prince Fielder	8.00
RB	Ryan Braun	10.00
RH	Ryan Howard	15.00
VG	Vladimir Guerrero	8.00
JMO	Justin Morneau	5.00

Solo Shots Autograph Relics
Production 25 Sets

DP	Dustin Pedroia	30.00
DW	David Wright	65.00
EL	Evan Longoria	60.00
JH	Josh Hamilton	50.00
JM	Justin Morneau	40.00
NM	Nick Markakis	30.00
RB	Ryan Braun	40.00
DPR	David Price	25.00

Solo Shots Autographs
Some not priced

AE	Andre Ethier	12.00
AG	Adrian Gonzalez	12.00
AL	Adam Lind	8.00
CB	Chad Billingsley	10.00
CG	Curtis Granderson	15.00
DP	David Price	20.00
DU	Dan Uggla	8.00
GB	Gordon Beckham	200.00
JB	Jay Bruce	15.00
JC	Johnny Cueto	10.00
JJ	Josh Johnson	8.00
MB	Milton Bradley	8.00
MC	Melky Cabrera	20.00
MK	Matt Kemp	10.00
MS	Max Scherzer	8.00
NM	Nick Markakis	30.00
PH	Phil Hughes	12.00
RB	Ryan Braun	40.00
RC	Ryan Church	8.00
RH	Rich Hill	8.00
RI	Raul Ibanez	20.00
RP	Rick Porcello	40.00
TL	Tim Lincecum	85.00
ZG	Zack Greinke	25.00
DPE	Dustin Pedroia	30.00
JCH	Joba Chamberlain	20.00
JCU	Jack Cust	8.00
MCA	Matt Cain	12.00

Triple Threat Autograph Relics
Production 5 Sets
No Pricing

Triple Threat Autographs
Production 10 Sets
No Pricing

Triple Threat Relics
Production 25 Sets

LCJ	Tim Lincecum / Matt Cain / Randy Johnson	40.00

Unique Unis

TOPPS unique — PITTSBURGH PIRATES

Common Player: 1.00
Bronze: 1.5X
Production 99 Sets
Gold: 2-4X
Production 25 Sets
Platinum 1 of 1's exist

UU01	Chipper Jones	2.50
UU02	Ryan Braun	3.00
UU03	Alexei Ramirez	1.50
UU04	Andrew McCutchen	1.50
UU05	Ben Sheets	1.00
UU06	Jermaine Dye	1.50
UU07	Prince Fielder	2.50
UU08	Evan Longoria	4.00
UU09	Jason Giambi	1.00
UU10	Jose Reyes	1.50
UU11	Curtis Granderson	1.50
UU12	Jason Bay	1.50
UU13	Jimmy Rollins	1.50
UU14	Justin Verlander	1.50
UU15	Roy Halladay	1.50
UU16	David Wright	3.00
UU17	Carl Crawford	1.50
UU18	Gil Meche	1.50
UU19	Kevin Youkilis	1.50
UU20	Ryan Zimmerman	1.50

Unparalleled Performances
Common Player: 1.00
Bronze: 1.5X
Production 99 Sets
Gold: 2-4X
Production 25 Sets
Platinum 1 of 1's exist

UP01	Ian Kinsler	1.50

RANDY JOHNSON
ARIZONA DIAMONDBACKS

UNPARALLELED PERFORMANCES

UP02	Carlos Delgado	1.00
UP03	Randy Johnson	1.50
UP04	Alex Rodriguez	4.00
UP05	Orlando Hudson	1.00
UP06	Carl Crawford	1.50
UP07	Mariano Rivera	1.00
UP08	Alfonso Soriano	1.00
UP09	Dexter Fowler	1.50
UP10	Fernando Tatis	1.00
UP11	Adam LaRoche	1.00
UP12	Raul Ibanez	1.50
UP13	Carlos Beltran	1.00
UP14	James Loney	1.50
UP15	Bronson Arroyo	1.00
UP16	Aaron Hill	1.00
UP17	Jeremy Hermida	1.00
UP18	Randy Johnson	1.50
UP19	Micah Owings	1.00
UP20	Johnny Cueto	1.00

0256/1350
ALEX RODRIGUEZ
THIRD BASE

2009 Topps Triple Threads

Common (1-100):		1.00
Production 1,350		
Common RC Jsy Auto.		
(101-138):		10.00
Pack:		85.00
Box (2):		160.00
1	Justin Upton	1.50
2	Brian McCann	1.50
3	Babe Ruth	6.00
4	Alfonso Soriano	1.50
5	Albert Pujols	6.00
6	Edinson Volquez	1.00
7	Todd Helton	1.50
8	Hanley Ramirez	2.50
9	Mickey Mantle	8.00
10	Manny Ramirez	2.50
11	Francisco Liriano	1.00
12	Lou Gehrig	5.00
13	Carlos Delgado	1.00
14	Walter Johnson	2.50
15	Alex Rodriguez	4.00
16	Ryan Howard	3.00
17	Nate McLouth	1.00
18	Cy Young	2.50
19	Ichiro Suzuki	4.00
20	Jorge Posada	1.50
21	Scott Kazmir	1.00
22	Michael Young	1.50
23	Brandon Webb	1.50
24	George Sisler	1.50
25	Chipper Jones	2.50
26	Adam Jones	1.50
27	David Ortiz	1.50
28	Geovany Soto	1.50
29	Tony Gwynn	2.50
30	Victor Martinez	1.50
31	Jose Lopez	1.00
32	Lance Berkman	1.50
33	Russell Martin	1.50
34	Cal Ripken	10.00
35	Dan Haren	1.00
36	Jose Reyes	1.50
37	Rogers Hornsby	1.50
38	Mark Teixeira	2.50
39	Ernie Banks	2.50
40	Jimmy Rollins	1.50
41	Jake Peavy	1.50
42	Jackie Robinson	2.50
43	B.J. Upton	1.50
44	Roy Halladay	1.50
45	Jimmie Foxx	2.50
46	Randy Johnson	1.50
47	Mel Ott	2.50
48	Carlos Lee	1.00
49	Nick Markakis	1.50
50	Dustin Pedroia	3.00
51	Nolan Ryan	8.00
52	Matt Cain	1.00
53	Grady Sizemore	1.50

54	Christy Mathewson	2.50
55	Miguel Cabrera	1.50
56	Roy Campanella	2.50
57	Prince Fielder	2.50
58	Ty Cobb	4.00
59	Carlos Beltran	1.00
60	Pee Wee Reese	1.50
61	A.J. Burnett	1.50
62	Carl Crawford	1.50
63	Chase Utley	2.50
64	Adrian Gonzalez	1.50
65	Thurman Munson	2.50
66	Felix Hernandez	1.50
67	Chris Carpenter	1.50
68	Carl Yastrzemski	4.00
69	Ian Kinsler	1.50
70	Vernon Wells	1.50
71	Matt Holliday	1.50
72	Tris Speaker	1.50
73	Roy Oswalt	1.50
74	Ozzie Smith	4.00
75	Daisuke Matsuzaka	4.00
76	David Wright	3.00
77	Kosuke Fukudome	2.50
78	Johan Santana	2.50
79	Curtis Granderson	1.50
80	Johnny Mize	1.50
81	Derek Jeter	6.00
82	Vladimir Guerrero	2.50
83	Dan Uggla	1.50
84	Hank Greenberg	2.50
85	Justin Morneau	1.50
86	CC Sabathia	1.50
87	Mike Schmidt	4.00
88	Cole Hamels	2.50
89	Alex Rios	1.00
90	Ryne Sandberg	5.00
91	Ryan Ludwick	1.50
92	Tim Lincecum	3.00
93	Honus Wagner	2.50
94	Carlos Quentin	1.50
95	Alexei Ramirez	1.50
96	Joe Mauer	2.50
97	Bob Gibson	1.50
98	Reggie Jackson	1.50
99	Carlos Zambrano	1.50
100	Stan Musial	4.00
101	Ryan Braun/Jsy Auto.	30.00
102	Jay Bruce/Jsy Auto.	25.00
103	Fausto Carmona/ Jsy Auto.	15.00
104	Matt Kemp/Jsy Auto.	30.00
105	Cameron Maybin/ Jsy Auto.	20.00
106	Johnny Cueto/ Jsy Auto.	15.00
107	Josh Hamilton/ Jsy Auto.	40.00
108	Ubaldo Jimenez/ Jsy Auto.	15.00
109	Geovany Soto/ Jsy Auto.	25.00
110	Jon Lester/Jsy Auto.	40.00
111	Clayton Kershaw/ Jsy Auto.	30.00
112	Luke Hochevar/ Jsy Auto.	15.00
113	Evan Longoria/ Jsy Auto.	80.00
114	Justin Masterson/ Jsy Auto.	25.00
115	Blake DeWitt/ Jsy Auto.	15.00
116	Daniel Murphy/ Jsy Auto.	25.00
117	Chad Billingsley/ Jsy Auto.	20.00
118	Dustin Pedroia/ Jsy Auto.	50.00
119	Hunter Pence/ Jsy Auto.	25.00
120	Joakim Soria/ Jsy Auto.	20.00
121	Justin Upton/Jsy Auto.	40.00
122	Fernando Martinez/ Jsy Auto. RC	25.00
123	Nolan Reimold/ Jsy Auto. (RC)	40.00
124	Mat Gamel/ Jsy Auto. RC	25.00
125	Michael Bowden/ Jsy Auto. (RC)	20.00
126	Derek Holland/ Jsy Auto. RC	20.00
127	Elvis Andrus/ Jsy Auto. RC	30.00
128	Trevor Cahill/ Jsy Auto. RC	20.00
129	Ryan Perry/ Jsy Auto. RC	20.00
130	Jordan Zimmermann/ Jsy Auto. RC	20.00
131	Tommy Hanson/ Jsy Auto. RC	100.00
132	David Price/ Jsy Auto. RC	50.00
133	Colby Rasmus/ Jsy Auto. (RC)	40.00
134	Rick Porcello/ Jsy Auto. RC	60.00
135	Brett Anderson/ Jsy Auto. RC	20.00
136	Koji Uehara/ Jsy Auto. RC	60.00
137	Lou Marson/ Jsy Auto. (RC)	15.00
138	Matt Tolbert/ Jsy Auto.	15.00

Printing Plates
Production one set per color.

All-Star Triple Patches
No Pricing
Production 9 Sets
Dual Patch Logo Man: No Pricing
Production One Set
Platinum: No Pricing
Production One Set
No Pricing

Bat Knobs
No Pricing
Production One Set
No Pricing

Bat Barrels
No Pricing
Production One Set
No Pricing

Camelot Relic
Production 5
No Pricing

Cut Above
No Pricing
Production One Set
No Pricing

Cut Above Dual
Production One Set
No Pricing

Cut Above Presidential
Production One Set
No Pricing

Cut Above Triple
Production One Set
No Pricing

Jumbo Patch Combos
Production One Set
No Pricing

Jumbo Plus Relic
Production 3 Sets
Platinum 1 of 1's exist
No Pricing

Legend Relic
Production 36 Sets
Sepia: 1X
Production 27 Sets
Emerald: 1.25X
Production 18 Sets
Gold: No Pricing
Production 9 Sets
Platinum 1 of 1's exist
Sapphire: No Pricing
Production 3 Sets

1	Babe Ruth	250.00
2	Rogers Hornsby	60.00
3	Pee Wee Reese	25.00
4	Lou Gehrig	200.00
5	Jimmie Foxx	60.00
6	Honus Wagner	125.00
7	Roy Campanella	35.00
8	Mickey Mantle	120.00
9	Mel Ott	60.00
10	Tris Speaker	60.00
11	Jackie Robinson	80.00
12	George Sisler	50.00
13	Ty Cobb	100.00
14	Thurman Munson	50.00
15	Johnny Mize	40.00

Letter Plus Relics
Production 3 Sets
Platinum 1 of 1's exist
No Pricing

Letter Number Logo
Production One Set
No Pricing

Relic Autographs
Production 18 Sets
Gold: 1.25X
Production 9 Sets
Sapphire: No Pricing
Production 3 Sets
Platinum 1 of 1's exist
Wood 1 of 1's exist

1-3	David Wright	100.00
4-6	David Ortiz	60.00
7-9	Jose Reyes	50.00
10-12	Zack Greinke	40.00
13-15	Miguel Cabrera	50.00
16-18	Matt Cain	25.00
19-21	Robinson Cano	40.00
22-24	Andre Ethier	40.00
25-27	Curtis Granderson	50.00
28-30	Manny Ramirez	150.00
31-33	Nick Markakis	25.00
34-36	Vladimir Guerrero	60.00
37-39	Matt Holliday	30.00
40-42	Ryan Howard	80.00
43-45	Chipper Jones	75.00
46-48	Scott Kazmir	20.00
49-51	Joba Chamberlain	40.00
52-54	Alfonso Soriano	30.00
55-57	Nick Swisher	40.00
58-60	Prince Fielder	50.00
61-63	Ryan Zimmerman	40.00
64-66	Johnny Podres	40.00
67-69	George Kell	40.00
70-72	Gary Carter	40.00
73-75	Whitey Ford	60.00
76-78	Bob Gibson	60.00
79-81	Juan Marichal	40.00
82-84	Duke Snider	50.00

85-87	Robin Yount	50.00
88-90	Jim Palmer	30.00
91-93	Bo Jackson	70.00
94-96	Don Larsen	50.00
97-99	Tony Gwynn	60.00
100-102	Brian McCann	30.00
103-105	Shane Victorino	50.00
106-108	Adrian Gonzalez	25.00
109-111	Garrett Atkins	15.00
112-114	Carl Yastrzemski	60.00
115-117	Carlos Delgado	20.00
118-120	Jason Varitek	40.00
121-123	Tom Seaver	60.00
124-126	Rich Harden	20.00
127-129	Aramis Rairez	30.00
130-132	Chien-Ming Wang	100.00
133-135	Jayson Werth	60.00
136-138	Jonathan Papelbon	25.00
139-141	Alex Rodriguez	200.00
145-147	Mark Teixeira	100.00
148-150	Dan Haren	25.00
151-153	Ernie Banks	50.00
154-156	Lance Berkman	30.00
157-159	Cal Ripken	200.00
160-162	Paul Mollitor	50.00
163-165	Mike Lowell	30.00
166-168	Dan Uggla	15.00
169-171	Aaron Hill	25.00
172-174	Johnny Damon	100.00

Relic Autographs Pairs
Production 18 Sets
Gold: No Pricing
Production 9 Sets
Sapphire: No Pricing
Production 3 Sets
Platinum 1 of 1's exist

1	Dustin Pedroia Ryan Howard	75.00

Relic Triple Autographs
Production 36 Sets
Sepia: 1X
Production 27 Sets
Emerald: 1.25X
Production 18 Sets
Gold: No Pricing
Production 9 Sets
Sapphire: No Pricing
Productoin 3 Sets
Platinum 1 of 1's exist
Wood 1 of 1's exist

1	Geovany Soto Brian McCann Russell Martin	30.00
2	Hanley Ramirez Jose Reyes Miguel Tejada	50.00
3	Johnny Cueto Carlos Silva Joakim Soria	25.00
4	Roy Halladay Brandon Webb Chien-Ming Wang	80.00
5	Manny Ramirez Matt Kemp Andre Ethier	100.00
6	Frank Robinson Jim Palmer Eddie Murray	60.00
7	Scott Kazmir Joba Chamberlain Jon Lester	40.00
8	Ryan Howard Albert Pujols Miguel Cabrera	200.00
9	Reggie Jackson Alex Rodriguez Robinson Cano	180.00
10	Paul Molitor Robin Yount Ryan Braun	100.00
11	Jon Lester Justin Masterson JonathanPapelbon	40.00
12	Jay Bruce Josh Hamilton Hunter Pence	40.00
13	David Ortiz Jason Varitek Jonathan Papelbon	60.00
14	Duke Snider Manny Ramirez Matt Kemp	100.00
15	Brian Roberts Dustin Pedroia Robinson Cano	40.00
16	Alfonso Soriano Aramis Ramirez Ryne Sandberg	60.00
17	David Wright Hanley Ramirez Albert Pujols	200.00
18	Ryan Howard Scott Kazmir Evan Longoria David Price	60.00
19	Mark Teixeira Robinson Cano Alex Rodriguez	200.00
20	Jonathan Papelbon Joakim Soria Joe Nathan	40.00
21	Torii Hunter Vladimir Guerrero Reggie Jackson	70.00

Relic Combo Double Autographs
Production 3 Sets
Platinum 1 of 1's exist
No Pricing

Relic Combos
Production 36 Sets
Sepia: 1X
Production 27 Sets
Emerald: 1.25X
Production 18 Sets
Gold: No Pricing
Production 9 Sets
Sapphire: No Pricing
Production 3 Sets
Platinum 1 of 1's exist

1	Tom Seaver Nolan Ryan Johan Santana	40.00
2	Ryan Howard Mike Schmidt Chase Utley	60.00
3	Jorge Posada Mickey Mantle Mark Teixeira	80.00
4	Josh Beckett Jon Lester John Smoltz	25.00
5	Jose Reyes Gary Carter David Wright	40.00
6	Albert Pujols Miguel Cabrera Ryan Howard	25.00
7	Ryne Sandberg Mike Schmidt Ozzie Smith	30.00
8	Daisuke Matsuzaka Ichiro Suzuki Hideki Matsui	50.00
9	Kenshin Kawakami Daisuke Matsuzaka Koji Uehara	40.00
10	Manny Ramirez Carlos Beltran Alfonso Soriano	20.00
11	Josh Hamilton Ian Kinsler Michael Young	20.00
12	Grady Sizemore Josh Hamilton Ichiro Suzuki	25.00
13	Hanley Ramirez Jimmy Rollins Jose Reyes	20.00
14	Dustin Pedroia Ryne Sandberg Ian Kinsler	20.00
15	Evan Longoria Alex Rodriguez Chipper Jones	30.00
16	Manny Ramirez Albert Pujols Ryan Howard	25.00
17	Jim Thome Manny Ramirez Gary Sheffield	20.00
18	Mickey Mantle Babe Ruth Lou Gehrig	400.00
19	Stan Musial Duke Snider Frank Robinson	75.00
20	Mickey Mantle Frank Robinson Carl Yastrzemski	85.00
21	Pee Wee Reese Jackie Robinson Roy Campanella	60.00
22	Carlos Beltran Carlos Delgado David Wright	25.00
23	Ryan Zimmerman David Wright Evan Longoria	25.00
24	Joe Mauer Johnny Bench Brian McCann	25.00
25	Ryan Howard Alex Rodriguez David Wright	30.00
26	Tim Lincecum Jake Peavy Brandon Webb	25.00
27	Kevin Youkilis David Ortiz Jason Varitek	25.00
28	Russell Martin Manny Ramirez Matt Kemp	25.00
29	Geovany Soto Ryan Braun Hanley Ramirez	25.00
30	Albert Pujols Ryan Howard Hanley Ramirez	30.00
31	Adrian Gonzalez Jimmy Rollins David Wright	25.00
32	Cal Ripken Alex Rodriguez Chipper Jones	50.00
33	Ernie Banks Ozzie Smith Hanley Ramirez	25.00
34	Adrian Gonzalez Tony Gwynn Jake Peavy	25.00
35	Ernie Banks Ozzie Smith Cal Ripken	40.00
36	Chase Utley	

	Jimmy Rollins Ryan Howard	
37	Reggie Jackson Reggie Jackson Reggie Jackson	40.00
38	Nolan Ryan Nolan Ryan Nolan Ryan	50.00
39	Prince Fielder Albert Pujols Lance Berkman	25.00
40	Jorge Cantu Joakim Soria Edgar Gonzalez	20.00
41	Felix Hernandez Magglio Ordonez Miguel Cabrera	25.00
42	Jimmy Rollins Roy Oswalt Adam Dunn	20.00
43	Dae Ho Lee Jin Young Lee Shin-Soo Choo	40.00
44	Phillippe Aumont Aroldis Chapman Dylan Lindsay	25.00
45	Frederich Cepeda Yulieski Gourriel Yoennis Cespedes	20.00
46	Ichiro Suzuki Yu Darvish Norichika Aoki	100.00

Relic Combos Double
Production 36 Sets
Sepia: 1X
Production 27 Sets
Emerald: 1.25X
Production 18 Sets
Gold: No Pricing
Production 9 Sets
Sapphire: No Pricing
Production 3 Sets
Platinum 1 of 1's exist

1	Mike Schmidt Ryan Howard	50.00
2	Yulieski Gourriel Yu Darvish	60.00
3	Ryan Howard Dustin Pedroia	40.00
4	Ryan Howard Dustin Pedroia	30.00
5	Cal Ripken Alex Rodriguez	60.00
6	Jake Peavy Tim Lincecum	30.00
7	Ichiro Daisuke Matsuzaka	50.00
8	Manny Ramirez Alfonso Soriano Ryan Howard Evan Longoria Carlos Quentin Vladimir Guerrero	40.00
9	Mariano Rivera Jonathan Papelbon Trevor Hoffman Joe Nathan Francisco Rodriguez Dennis Eckersley	50.00
10	Alex Rodriguez Evan Longoria Kevin Youkilis Alex Rios Nick Markakis Wade Boggs	40.00
11	Albert Pujols David Wright Hanley Ramirez Alex Rodriguez Josh Hamilton Evan Longoria	60.00
12		

Relics
Production 36 Sets
Sepia: 1X
Production 27 Sets
Emerald: 1.25X
Production 18 Sets
Gold: No Pricing
Production 9 Sets
Sapphire: No Pricing
Productoin 3 Sets
Platinum 1 of 1's exist

1-3	Tim Lincecum	25.00
4-6	David Wright	25.00
7-9	Albert Pujols	50.00
10-12	Alex Rodriguez	40.00
13-15	David Ortiz	25.00
16-18	Manny Ramirez	25.00
19-21	Ichiro Suzuki	40.00
22-24	Vladimir Guerrero	15.00
25-27	Ryan Braun	25.00
28-30	Chipper Jones	25.00
31-33	Evan Longoria	30.00
34-36	Dustin Pedroia	25.00
37-39	Alfonso Soriano	15.00
40-42	Miguel Cabrera	20.00
43-45	Nick Markakis	15.00
46-48	Josh Hamilton	20.00
49-51	Jose Reyes	20.00
52-54	Bob Gibson	25.00
55-57	Frank Robinson	25.00
58-60	Paul Molitor	25.00
61-63	Tom Seaver	25.00
64-66	Gary Carter	25.00

67-69	Stan Musial	40.00
70-72	Ryne Sandberg	40.00
73-75	Carl Yastrzemski	25.00
76-78	Duke Snider	30.00
79-81	Whitey Ford	40.00
82-84	Mike Schmidt	40.00
85-87	Daisuke Matsuzaka	40.00
88-90	Grady Sizemore	15.00
91-93	Chase Utley	30.00
94-96	Josh Beckett	20.00
97-99	Hanley Ramirez	20.00
100-102	Johan Santana	20.00
103-105	Ryan Howard	30.00
106-108	Bo Jackson	20.00
109-111	Carlos Quentin	15.00
112-114	Hideki Matsui	30.00
115-117	Rickey Henderson	50.00

Rookie/Rising Stars Relic Autographs

Production 18 Sets	
Gold:	No Pricing
Production 9 Sets	
Sapphire:	No Pricing
Production 3 Sets	
Platinum 1 of 1's exist	
No Pricing	

WBC Dual Patch Logo

Production One Set	
Triple Patch:	No Pricing
Production One Set	
Plaitinum 1 of 1's exist	
No Pricing	

WBC Relic Autographs

Production 36 Sets	
Sepia:	1X
Production 27 Sets	
Emerald:	1.25X
Production 18 Sets	
Gold:	No Pricing
Production 9 Sets	
Sapphire:	No Pricing
Productoin 3 Sets	
Platinum 1 of 1's exist	
Wood 1 of 1's exist	
1	Miguel Tejada	20.00
2	Jose Reyes	40.00
3	Geovany Soto	25.00
4	David Wright	80.00
5	Roy Oswalt	25.00
6	Miguel Cabrera	40.00

XXIV Legends Relic

Production 18 Sets	
No Pricing	

XXIV Relics

Production 18 Sets	
Gold:	No Pricing
Production 9 Sets	
Sapphire:	No Pricing
Production 3 Sets	
Platinum 1 of 1's exist	
No Pricing	

2010 Topps

Common Player:		.15
Common SP:		
1a	Prince Fielder	.50
1b	Hank Greenberg/SP	20.00
2	Buster Posey RC	4.00
3	Derek Lee	.25
4	Hanley Ramirez	
	Pablo Sandoval	
	Albert Pujols	.75
5	Texas Rangers	.15
6	Chicago White Sox	.15
7	Mickey Mantle	2.00
8	Joe Mauer	.75
	Ichiro Suzuki	
	Derek Jeter	
9	Tim Lincecum NL CY	.75
10	Clayton Kershaw	.40
11	Orlando Cabrera	.15
12	Doug Davis	.15
13	Melvin Mora	.15
14	Ted Lilly	.15
15	Bobby Abreu	.25
16	Johnny Cueto	.15
17	Dexter Fowler	.15
18	Tim Stauffer	.15
19	Felipe Lopez	.15
20	Tommy Hanson	.50
21	Cristian Guzman	.15
22	Anthony Swarzak	.15
23	Shane Victorino	.25
24	John Maine	.15

25	Adam Jones	.25
26	Zach Duke	.15
27	Lance Berkman	.25
	Mike Hampton	
28	Jonathan Sanchez	.15
29	Aubrey Huff	.15
	Victor Martinez	.25
31	Jason Grilli	.15
32	Cincinnati Reds	.15
33	Adam Moore RC	.50
34	Michael Dunn RC	.50
35	Rick Porcello	.25
36	Tobi Stoner RC	.50
37	Garret Anderson	.15
38	Houston Astros	.15
39	Jeff Baker	.15
40	Josh Johnson	.15
41	Los Angeles Dodgers	.25
42	Prince Fielder	.75
	Ryan Howard	
	Albert Pujols	
43	Marco Scutaro	.15
44	Howie Kendrick	.15
45	David Hernandez	.15
46	Chad Tracy	.15
47	Brad Penny	.15
48	Joey Votto	.40
49	Jorge De La Rosa	.15
50	Zack Greinke	.40
51	Eric Young Jr.	.15
52	Billy Butler	.15
53	Craig Counsell	.15
54	John Lackey	.25
55	Manny Ramirez	.50
56	Andy Pettitte	.25
57	CC Sabathia	.50
58	Kyle Blanks	.15
59	Kevin Gregg	.15
60	David Wright	.75
61	Skip Schumaker	.15
62	Kevin Millwood	.15
63	Josh Bard	.15
64	Drew Stubbs RC	.50
65	Nick Swisher	.15
65b	Nick Swisher/SP	
	Pie in face	100.00
66	Kyle Phillips RC	.50
67	Matt LaPorta	.25
68	Brandon Inge	.15
69	Kansas City Royals	.15
70	Cole Hamels	.25
71	Mike Hampton	.15
72	Milwaukee Brewers	.15
73	Adam Wainwright	
	Chris Carpenter	
	Jorge De La Rosa	
74	Casey Blake	.15
75	Adrian Gonzalez	.40
76	Joe Saunders	.15
77	Kenshin Kawakami	.15
78	Cesar Izturis	.15
79	Francisco Cordero	.15
80	Tim Lincecum	.75
81	Ryan Theriot	.15
82	Jason Marquis	.15
83	Mark Teahen	.15
84	Nate Robertson	.15
85	Ken Griffey Jr.	1.00
86	Gil Meche	.15
87	Darin Erstad	.15
88	Jerry Hairston Jr.	.15
88b	Jerry Hairston Jr./SP	
	Pie in face	50.00
89	J.A. Happ	.25
90	Ian Kinsler	.40
91	Erik Bedard	.15
92	David Eckstein	.15
93	Joe Nathan	.15
94a	Ivan Rodriguez	.25
94b	Carlton Fisk/SP	15.00
95	Carl Crawford	.25
96	Jon Garland	.15
97	Luis Durango RC	.50
98	Cesar Ramos (RC)	.50
99	Garrett Jones	.15
100	Albert Pujols	1.50
101	Scott Baker	.15
102	Minnesota Twins	.15
103	Daniel Murphy	.15
104	New York Mets	.15
105	Madison Bumgarner RC	1.00
106	Chris Carpenter	.50
	Tim Lincecum	
	Jair Jurrjens	
107	Scott Hairston	.15
108	Erick Aybar	.15
109	Justin Masterson	.15
110	Andrew McCutchen	.25
111	Ty Wigginton	.15
112	Kevin Correia	.15
113	Willy Taveras	.15
114	Chris Iannetta	.15
115	Gordon Beckham	1.00
116a	Carlos Gomez	.15
116b	Robin Yount/SP	15.00
117	David DeJesus	.25
118	Brandon Morrow	.15
119	Wilkin Ramirez	.15
120	Jorge Posada	.25
120b	Jorge Posada	
	Pie in the face	100.00
121	Brett Anderson	.25
122	Carlos Ruiz	.15
123	Jeff Samardzija	.15
124	Rickie Weeks	.25
125	Ichiro Suzuki	1.00
126	John Smoltz	.25
127	Hank Blalock	.15
128	Garrett Mock	.15

129	Reid Gorecki (RC)	.50
130	Vladimir Guerrero	.25
131	Dustin Richardson RC	.50
132	Cliff Lee	.25
133	Freddy Sanchez	.15
134	Philadelphia Phillies	.25
135	Ryan Dempster	.15
136	Adam Wainwright	.25
137	Oakland Athletics	.15
138	Carlos Pena	.25
	Mark Teixeira	
	Jason Bay	
139	Frank Francisco	.15
140	Matt Holliday	.25
141	Chone Figgins	.15
142	Tim Hudson	.15
143	Omar Vizquel	.15
144	Rich Harden	.15
145	Justin Upton	.25
146	Yunel Escobar	.15
147	Huston Street	.15
148	Cody Ross	.15
149	Jose Guillen	.15
150	Joe Mauer	.50
151	Mat Gamel	.15
152	Nyjer Morgan	.15
153	Justin Duchscherer	.15
154	Pedro Feliz	.15
155	Zack Greinke AL CY	.25
156	Tony Gwynn Jr.	.15
157	Mike Sweeney	.15
158	Jeff Niemann	.15
159	Vernon Wells	.15
160	Miguel Tejada	.15
161	Denard Span	.25
162	Wade Davis (RC)	.50
163	Josh Butler RC	.50
164	Carlos Carrasco (RC)	.50
165	Brandon Phillips	.25
166	Eric Byrnes	.15
167	San Diego Padres	.15
168	Brad Kilby RC	.50
169	Pittsburgh Pirates	.15
170	Jason Bay	.25
171	Felix Hernandez	.15
	CC Sabathia	
172	Joe Mauer AL MVP	.50
173	Kendry Morales	.15
174	Mike Gonzalez	.15
175	Josh Hamilton	.40
176	Yovani Gallardo	.15
177	Adam Lind	.15
178	Kerry Wood	.15
179	Ryan Spilborghs	.15
180	Jayson Nix	.15
181	Nick Johnson	.15
182	Coco Crisp	.15
183	Jonathan Papelbon	.25
184	Jeff Francoeur	.25
185	Hideki Matsui	.40
185b	Hideki Matsui/SP	125.00
	Pie in face	
186	Andrew Bailey	.15
187	Will Venable	.15
188	Joe Blanton	.15
189	Adrian Beltre	.25
190	Pablo Sandoval	.40
191	Mat Latos	.15
192	Andruw Jones	.15
193	Shairon Martis	.15
194	Neill Walker (RC)	.50
195	James Shields	.25
196	Ian Desmond (RC)	.50
197	Cleveland Indians	.15
198	Florida Marlins	.15
199	Seattle Mariners	.15
200	Roy Halladay	.40
201	Detroit Tigers	.15
202	San Francisco Giants	.15
203	Zack Greinke	.25
	Felix Hernandez	
	Roy Halladay	
204	Elvis Andrus	.25
	Ian Kinsler	
205	Chris Coghlan	.25
206	Albert Pujols	1.00
	Prince Fielder	
	Ryan Howard	
207	Colby Rasmus	.15
208	Tim Wakefield	.15
209	Alexei Ramirez	.25
210	Josh Beckett	.40
211	Kelly Shoppach	.15
212	Magglio Ordonez	.15
213	Ricky Nolasco	.15
214	Matt Kemp	.50
215	Max Scherzer	.15
216	Mike Cameron	.15
217	Gio Gonzalez	.15
218	Fernando Martinez	.25
219	Kevin Hart	.15
220	Randy Johnson	.40
221	Russell Branyan	.15
222	Curtis Granderson	.25
223	Ryan Church	.15
224	Rod Barajas	.15
225	David Price	.25
226	Juan Rivera	.15
227	Josh Thole RC	.50
228	Chris Pettit RC	.50
229	Daniel McCutchen (RC)	.50
230	Jonathan Broxton	.25
231	Luke Scott	.15
232	St. Louis Cardinals	.15
233	Mark Teixeira	.25
	Jason Bay	
	Adam Lind	
234	Tampa Bay Rays	.15
235	Neftali Feliz	.25

236	Andrew Bailey AL ROY	.15
237	Ryan Braun	.50
	Prince Fielder	
238	Ian Stewart	.15
239	Juan Uribe	.15
240	Ricky Romero	.15
241	Rocco Baldelli	.15
242	Bobby Jenks	.15
243	Asdrubal Cabrera	.15
244	Barry Zito	.15
245	Lance Berkman	.25
246	Leo Nunez	.15
247	Andre Ethier	.25
248	Jason Kendall	.15
249	Jon Niese	.15
250	Mark Teixeira	.40
250b	Mark Teixeira/SP	120.00
	Pie in face	
251	John Lannan	.15
252	Ronny Cedeno	.15
253	Bengie Molina	.15
254	Edwin Jackson	.15
255	Chris Davis	.15
256	Akinori Iwamura	.15
257	Bobby Crosby	.15
258	Edwin Encarnacion	.15
259	Daniel Hudson RC	.50
260	New York Yankees	.50
261	Matt Carson (RC)	.50
262	Homer Bailey	.15
263	Placido Polanco	.15
264	Arizona Diamondbacks	.15
265	Los Angeles Angels	.15
266	Humberto Quintero	.15
267	Toronto Blue Jays	.15
268	Juan Pierre	.15
269	Alex Rodriguez	1.00
	Derek Jeter	
	Robinson Cano	
270	Michael Brantley RC	.50
271	Jermaine Dye	.25
272	Jair Jurrjens	.15
273	Pat Neshek	.15
274	Stephen Drew	.15
275	Chris Coghlan NL ROY	.25
276	Matt Lindstrom	.15
277	Jarrod Washburn	.15
278	Carlos Delgado	.15
279	Randy Wolf	.15
280	Mark DeRosa	.15
281	Braden Looper	.15
282	Washington Nationals	.15
283	Adam Kennedy	.15
284	Ross Ohlendorf	.15
285	Kurt Suzuki	.15
286	Javier Vazquez	.15
287	Jhonny Peralta	.15
288	Boston Red Sox	.50
289	Lyle Overbay	.15
290	Orlando Hudson	.15
291	Austin Kearns	.15
292	Tommy Manzella (RC)	.50
293	Brent Dlugach (RC)	.50
294	Adam Dunn	.25
295	Kevin Youkilis	.40
296	Atlanta Braves	.15
297	Ben Zobrist	.15
298	Baltimore Orioles	.15
299	Gary Sheffield	.25
300a	Chase Utley	.50
300b	Ryne Sandberg/SP	15.00
301	Jack Cust	.15
302	Kevin Youkilis	.25
	David Ortiz	
303	Chris Snyder	.15
304	Adam LaRoche	.15
305	Juan Francisco (RC)	.50
306	Milton Bradley	.15
307	Henry Rodriguez RC	.50
308	Robinson Diaz	.15
309	Gerald Laird	.15
310	Elvis Andrus	.25
311	Jose Valverde	.15
312	Tyler Flowers RC	.50
313	Jason Kubel	.15
314	Angel Pagan	.15
315	Scott Kazmir	.25
316	Chris Young	.25
317	Ryan Doumit	.15
318	Nate Schierholtz	.15
319	Ryan Franklin	.15
320	Brian McCann	.25
321	Pat Burrell	.15
322	Travis Buck	.15
323	Jim Thome	.25
324	Alex Rios	.15
325	Julio Lugo	.15
326	Tyler Colvin RC	.50
327	Albert Pujols NL MVP	1.00
328	Chicago Cubs	.25
329	Colorado Rockies	.15
330	Brandon Allen (RC)	.25
370b	Robinson Cano	50.00
	Pie in face	
370c	Robinson Cano	50.00
	Pie in face	
400b	Alex Rodriguez	60.00
	Pie in face	
400c	Alex Rodriguez	120.00
	Pie in face	
422b	Francisco Cervelli	60.00
	Pie in face	
475b	Johnny Damon	60.00
	Pie in face	
579b	Juan Miranda	60.00
	Pie in face	

Series 2

331a	Ryan Braun	1.00
331b	Eddie Mathews/SP	15.00
332	Brad Hawpe	.25
333	Ryan Ludwick	.25

334	Jayson Werth	.40
335	Jordan Norberto RC	.75
336	C.J. Wilson	.15
337	Carlos Zambrano	.15
338	Brett Cecil	.15
339	Jose Reyes	.50
340	John Buck	.15
341	Texas Rangers	.25
342	Melky Cabrera	.15
343	Brian Bruney	.15
344	Brett Myers	.15
345	Chris Volstad	.15
346	Taylor Teagarden	.15
347	Aaron Harang	.15
348	Jordan Zimmermann	.15
349	Felix Pie	.15
350	Prince Fielder Ryan Braun	.50
351	Koji Uehara	.15
352	Cameron Maybin	.15
353a	Jason Heyward	5.00
353b	Jason Heyward	
	Pie in face	100.00
354a	Evan Longoria	1.00
354b	Johnny Mize/SP	15.00
355	James Russell RC	2.00
356	Los Angeles Angels	.25
357	Scott Downs	.15
358	Mark Buehrle	.15
359	Aramis Ramirez	.25
360	Justin Morneau	.40
361	Washington Nationals	.15
362	Travis Snider	.25
363	Joba Chamberlain	.25
364	Trevor Hoffman	.25
365	Logan Ondrusek RC	.75
366	Hiroki Kuroda	.15
367	Wandy Rodriguez	.15
368	Wade LeBlanc	.15
369a	David Ortiz	.25
369b	Jimmie Foxx	15.00
370a	Robinson Cano	.50
370d	Mel Ott/SP	15.00
371	Nick Hundley	.15
372	Philadelphia Phillies	.25
373	Clint Barmes	.15
374	Scott Feldman	.15
375	Mike Leake RC	3.00
376	Esmil Rogers RC	.50
377a	Felix Hernandez	.40
377b	Tom Seaver/SP	20.00
378	George Sherrill	.15
379	Phil Hughes	.40
380	J.D. Drew	.25
381	Miguel Montero	.15
382	Kyle Davies	.15
383	Derek Lowe	.15
384	Chris Johnson RC	.75
385	Torii Hunter	.40
386	Dan Haren	.25
387	Josh Fields	.15
388	Joel Pineiro	.15
389	Troy Tulowitzki	.40
390	Ervin Santana	.15
391	Manny Parra	.15
392	Carlos Monasterios RC	.50
393	Jason Frasor	.15
394	Luis Castillo	.15
395	Jenrry Mejia RC	.50
396	Jake Westbrook	.15
397	Colorado Rockies	.25
398	Carlos Gonzalez	.25
399	Matt Garza	.25
400a	Alex Rodriguez	1.50
400d	Frank Robinson/SP	20.00
401	Chad Billingsley	.15
402	J.P. Howell	.15
403a	Jimmy Rollins	.40
403b	Ozzie Smith/SP	15.00
404	Mariano Rivera	.50
405	Dustin McGowan	.15
406	Jeff Francis	.15
407	Nick Punto	.15
408	Detroit Tigers	.25
409a	Kosuke Fukudome	.25
409b	Richie Ashburn/SP	20.00
410	Oakland Athletics	.25
411	Jack Wilson	.15
412	San Francisco Giants	.25
413	J.J. Hardy	.15
414	Sean West	.15
415	Cincinnati Reds	.25
416	Ruben Tejada RC	.75
417	Dallas Braden	.25
418	Aaron Laffey	.15
419	David Aardsma	.15
420	Shin-Soo Choo	.25
421	Doug Fister	.15
422	Vin Mazzaro	.15
423	Brad Bergesen	.15
424	David Herndon RC	.50
425	Dontrelle Willis	.15
426	Mark Reynolds	.25
427	Brandon Webb	.15
428	Baltimore Orioles	.25
429	Seth Smith	.15
430	Kazuo Matsui	.15
431	John Raynor RC	.50
432	A.J. Burnett	.25
433	Julio Borbon	.15
434	Kevin Slowey	.15
435a	Nelson Cruz	.25
435b	Nelson Cruz	
	Pie in the face	50.00
436	New York Mets	.50
437	Luke Hochevar	.15
438	Jason Bartlett	.15
439	Emilio Bonifacio	.15
440	Willie Harris	.15

441	Clete Thomas	.15
442	Dan Runzler RC	.50
443	Jason Hammel	.15
444	Yuniesky Betancourt	.15
445	Miguel Olivo	.15
446	Gavin Floyd	.15
447	Jeremy Guthrie	.15
448	Joakim Soria	.15
449	Ryan Sweeney	.15
450	Omir Santos	.15
451	Michael Saunders	.15
452	Allen Craig RC	.50
453	Jesse English (RC)	.50
454	James Loney	.25
455	St. Louis Cardinals	.50
456	Clayton Richard	.15
457	Kanekoa Texeira RC	.50
458	Todd Wellemeyer	.15
459	Joel Zumaya	.15
460	Aaron Cunningham	.15
461	Tyson Ross	.50
462	Alcides Escobar	.25
463	Carlos Marmol	.25
464	Francisco Liriano	.25
465	Chien-Ming Wang	.25
466	Jered Weaver	.25
467a	Fausto Carmona	.15
467b	Mitch Talbot	
	Pie in the face	50.00
468	Delmon Young	.15
469	Alex Burnett RC	.50
470	New York Yankees	.50
471	Drew Butera (RC)	.50
472	Toronto Blue Jays	.25
473	Jason Varitek	.25
474	Kyle Kendrick	.15
475a	Johnny Damon	.40
476a	Yadier Molina	.25
476b	Thurman Munson/SP	20.00
477	Nate McLouth	.15
478	Conor Jackson	.15
479a	Chris Carpenter	.50
479b	Dizzy Dean/SP	20.00
480	Boston Red Sox	.50
481	Scott Rolen	.25
482	Mike McCoy RC	.25
483	Daisuke Matsuzaka	.25
484	Mike Fontenot	.15
485	Jesus Flores	.15
486	Raul Ibanez	.25
487	Dan Uggla	.25
488	Delwyn Young	.15
489a	Russell Martin	.25
489b	Roy Campanella/SP	15.00
490	Michael Bourn	.15
491	Rafael Furcal	.25
492	Brian Wilson	.25
493	Travis Ishikawa	.15
494	Andrew Miller	.15
495	Carlos Pena	.25
496	Rajai Davis	.15
497	Edgar Renteria	.25
498	Sergio Santos (RC)	.50
499	Michael Bowden	.15
500	Brad Lidge	.25
501	Jake Peavy	.40
502	Jhoulys Chacin	.15
503	Austin Jackson RC	2.50
504	Jeff Mathis	.15
505	Andy Marte	.15
506	Jose Lopez	.25
507	Francisco Rodriguez	.25
508	Chris Getz	.15
509a	Todd Helton	.25
509b	Ike Davis	
	Pie in the face	65.00
510	Justin Upton	
	Mark Reynolds	.40
511	Chicago Cubs	.50
512	Scot Shields	.15
513	Scott Sizemore RC	1.00
514	Rafael Soriano	.15
515	Seattle Mariners	.15
516	Marlon Byrd	.15
517	Cliff Pennington	.15
518	Corey Hart	.15
519	Alexi Casilla	.15
520	Randy Wells	.15
521	Jeremy Bonderman	.15
522	Jordan Schafer	.15
523	Phil Coke	.15
524	Dusty Hughes RC	.50
525	David Huff	.15
526	Carlos Guillen	.15
527	Brandon Wood	.15
528	Brian Bannister	.15
529	Carlos Lee	.25
530	Steve Pearce	.15
531	Matt Cain	.25
532a	Hunter Pence	.25
532b	Dale Murphy/SP	15.00
533	Gary Matthews Jr.	.15
534	Hideki Okajima	.15
535	Andy Sonnanstine	.15
536	Matt Palmer	.15
537	Michael Cuddyer	.25
538	Travis Hafner	.15
539	Arizona Diamondbacks	.25
540	Sean Rodriguez	.25
541	Jason Motte	.15
542	Heath Bell	.15
543	Adam Jones	
	Nick Markakis	.25
544	Kevin Kouzmanoff	.15
545	Fred Lewis	.15
546	Bud Norris	.15
547	Brett Gardner	.25
548	Minnesota Twins	.25

549a	Derek Jeter	1.50
549b	Pee Wee Reese/SP	15.00
550	Freddy Garcia	.15
551	Everth Cabrera	.15
552	Chris Tillman	.25
553	Florida Marlins	.25
554	Ramon Hernandez	.15
555	B.J. Upton	.25
556	Chicago White Sox	.25
557	Aaron Hill	.15
558	Ronny Paulino	.15
559a	Nick Markakis	.25
559b	Eddie Murray/SP	15.00
560	Ryan Rowland-Smith	.15
561	Ryan Zimmerman	.40
562	Carlos Quentin	.25
563	Bronson Arroyo	.25
564	Houston Astros	.25
565	Franklin Morales	.15
566	Maicer Izturis	.15
567	Mike Pelfrey	.15
568	Jarrod Saltalamacchia	.15
569a	Jacoby Ellsbury	.40
569b	Tris Speaker/SP	15.00
570	Josh Willingham	.15
571	Brandon Lyon	.15
572	Clay Buchholz	.25
573	Johan Santana	.40
574	Milwaukee Brewers	.25
575	Ryan Perry	.15
576	Paul Maholm	.15
577	Jason Jaramillo	.15
578	Aaron Rowand	.15
579a	Trevor Cahill	.15
580	Ian Snell	.15
581	Chris Dickerson	.15
582	Martin Prado	.25
583	Anibal Sanchez	.15
584	Matt Capps	.15
585	Dioner Navarro	.15
586	Roy Oswalt	.25
587	David Murphy	.15
588	Landon Powell	.15
589	Edinson Volquez	.25
590a	Ryan Howard	1.00
590b	Ernie Banks/SP	15.00
591	Fernando Rodney	.15
592	Brian Roberts	.25
593	Derek Holland	.15
594	Andy LaRoche	.15
595	Mike Lowell	.25
596	Brendan Ryan	.15
597	J.R. Towles	.15
598	Alberto Callaspo	.15
599	Jay Bruce	.25
600a	Hanley Ramirez	.75
600b	Honus Wagner/SP	15.000
601	Blake DeWitt	.15
602	Kansas City Royals	.25
603	Gerardo Parra	.15
604	Atlanta Braves	.25
605	A.J. Pierzynski	.15
606	Chad Qualls	.15
607	Ubaldo Jimenez	.40
608	Pittsburgh Pirates	.25
609	Jeff Suppan	.15
610	Alex Gordon	.15
611	Josh Outman	.15
612	Lastings Milledge	.15
613	Eric Chavez	.15
614	Kelly Johnson	.15
615a	Justin Verlander	.40
615b	Nolan Ryan/SP	20.00
616	Franklin Gutierrez	.15
617	Luis Valbuena	.15
618	Jorge Cantu	.25
619	Mike Napoli	.15
620	Geovany Soto	.15
621	Aaron Cook	.15
622	Cleveland Indians	.25
623	Miguel Cabrera	.40
624	Carlos Beltran	.25
625	Grady Sizemore	.25
626	Glen Perkins	.15
627	Jeremy Hermida	.15
628	Ross Detwiler	.15
629	Oliver Perez	.15
630	Ben Francisco	.15
631	Marc Rzepczynski	.15
632	Daric Barton	.15
633	Daniel Bard	.15
634	Casey Kotchman	.15
635	Carl Pavano	.15
636	Evan Longoria ... B.J. Upton	.15
637	Babe Ruth/Lou Gehrig	.50
638	Paul Konerko	.25
639	Los Angeles Dodgers	.50
640	Matt Diaz	.15
641	Chase Headley	.15
642	San Diego Padres	.25
643	Michael Young	.25
644	David Purcey	.15
645	Texas Rangers	.25
646	Trevor Crowe	.15
647	Alfonso Soriano	.15
648	Brian Fuentes	.15
649	Casey McGehee	.25
650a	Dustin Pedroia	.50
650b	Ty Cobb/SP	20.00
651	Mike Aviles	.15
652a	Chipper Jones	.75
652b	Mickey Mantle/SP	25.00
653	Nolan Reimold	.15
654	Collin Balester	.15
655	Ryan Madson	.15
656	Jon Lester	.40
657	Chris Young	.15

658	Tommy Hunter	.15
659	Nick Blackburn	.15
660	Brandon McCarthy	.15

20/20

Common Player:		.75
T1	Ryan Braun	2.50
T2	Gordon Beckham	1.00
T3	Andre Ethier	1.50
T4	David Price	1.50
T5	Justin Upton	1.50
T6	Hunter Pence	.75
T7	Ryan Howard	2.50
T8	Buster Posey	2.00
T9	Madison Bumgarner	1.00
T10	Evan Longoria	2.50
T11	Joe Mauer	1.50
T12	Chris Coghlan	.75
T13	Andrew McCutchen	1.00
T14	Ubaldo Jimenez	1.50
T15	Pablo Sandoval	1.50
T16	David Wright	2.00
T17	Tommy Hanson	1.50
T18	Clayton Kershaw	1.00
T19	Zack Greinke	1.00
T20	Matt Kemp	1.00

Baseball Legends Cut Sigs.
Production One Set
No Pricing

Blue Back

Common Player:		
WalMart Exclusive		
1	Babe Ruth	5.00
2	Stan Musial	3.00
3	George Sisler	1.50
4	Tim Lincecum	2.00
5	Ichiro Suzuki	3.00
6	Roy Halladay	2.00
7	Walter Johnson	2.00
8	Nolan Ryan	6.00
9	Hanley Ramirez	1.50
10	Derek Jeter	5.00
11	Tom Seaver	1.00
12	Roger Maris	2.00
13	Honus Wagner	2.00
14	Vladimir Guerrero	1.50
15	Mel Ott	2.00
16	Mickey Mantle	6.00
17	Cal Ripken Jr.	5.00
18	Cy Young	2.00
19	Jackie Robinson	2.50
20	Jimmie Foxx	2.50
21	Lou Gehrig	3.00
22	Rogers Hornsby	2.00
23	Ty Cobb	3.00
24	Dizzy Dean	1.5.0
25	Reggie Jackson	1.50
26	Warren Spahn	1.50
27	Albert Pujols	5.00
28	Chipper Jones	2.50
29	Mariano Rivera	2.00
30	David Wright	2.00

Black
Black:	20-30X
Black RC's:	6-10X
Production 59 Sets	

Gold
Gold:	4-8X
Gold RC:	2-4X
Production 2010 Sets	

Platinum
Production One Set

Printing Plates
Production one set per color.

Cards Your Mom Threw Out

Common Player:		.50
Inserted 1:3		
Original Back:		1.5X
Inserted 1:36		
1	Mickey Mantle	5.00
2	Jackie Robinson	1.50
3	Ernie Banks	1.50
4	Duke Snider	1.00
5	Luis Aparicio	.50
6	Frank Robinson	1.00
7	Orlando Cepeda	.50
8	Bob Gibson	1.00
9	Carl Yastrzemski	2.00
10	Roger Maris	1.50
11	Mickey Mantle	5.00
12	Stan Musial	2.50
13	Brooks Robinson	1.00
14	Juan Marichal	.50
15	Jim Palmer	.50
16	Willie McCovey	1.00
17	Mickey Mantle	5.00
18	Reggie Jackson	1.50
19	Steve Carlton	.50
20	Thurman Munson	2.00
21	Tom Seaver	1.00
22	Johnny Bench	1.50
23	Dave Winfield	.50
24	Robin Yount	1.50
25	Mike Schmidt	2.00
26	Reggie Jackson	1.50
27	Nolan Ryan	4.00
28	Ozzie Smith	2.00
29	Rickey Henderson	1.00
30	Eddie Murray	1.00
31	Paul Molitor	1.50
32	Ryne Sandberg	3.00
33	Don Mattingly	3.00
34	Dwight Gooden	.50
35	Tony Gwynn	1.50
36	Bo Jackson	1.50
37	Nolan Ryan	4.00
38	Gary Sheffield	.50
39	Frank Thomas	1.00
40	Manny Ramirez	1.50
41	Manny Ramirez	1.50
42	Derek Jeter	4.00
43	Tony Gwynn	1.50
44	Mike Piazza	1.50
45	Cal Ripken	5.00
46	Pedro Martinez	1.00
47	Alex Rodriguez	3.00
48	Ivan Rodriguez	.75
49	Randy Johnson	1.00
50	Ichiro Suzuki	2.00
51	Albert Pujols	4.00
52	Kevin Youkilis	1.00
53	Alfonso Soriano	1.00
54	Ryan Howard	2.50
55	Alex Gordon	.50
56	Dustin Pedroia	1.50
57	Tim Lincecum	2.00
58	Evan Longoria	2.00
59	Phil Rizzuto	1.00
60	Mickey Mantle	5.00
61	Al Kaline	1.00
62	Yogi Berra	1.50
63	Ernie Banks	1.50
64	Whitey Ford	1.00
65	Duke Snider	1.00
66	Warren Spahn	1.00
67	Willie McCovey	1.00
68	Brooks Robinson	1.00
69	Roger Maris	1.50
70	Harmon Killebrew	1.50
71	Eddie Mathews	1.50
72	Carl Yastrzemski	1.00
73	Gaylord Perry	.50
74	Jim Bunning	.50
75	Rod Carew	1.00
76	Nolan Ryan	4.00
77	Johnny Bench	2.00
78	Frank Robinson	1.00
79	Juan Marichal	1.00
80	Reggie Jackson	1.00
81	Willie McCovey	1.00
82	George Brett	2.00
83	Dennis Eckersley	.50
84	Tom Seaver	1.50
85	Eddie Murray	1.00
86	Paul Molitor	1.00
87	Joe Morgan	.75
88	Rickey Henderson	1.00
89	Steve Carlton	.50
90	Tony Gwynn	1.00
91	Ryne Sandberg	2.00
92	Robin Yount	1.50
93	Mike Schmidt	2.00
94	Don Mattingly	2.00
95	Darryl Strawberry	1.00
96	Randy Johnson	1.00
97	Frank Thomas	1.00
98	Ken Griffey Jr.	2.50
99	Cal Ripken	4.00
100	Ozzie Smith	1.50
101	Bo Jackson	1.50
102	Babe Ruth	4.00
103	Manny Ramirez	1.50
104	John Smoltz	.50
105	Derek Jeter	4.00
106	Alex Rodriguez	3.00
107	Chipper Jones	1.50
108	Mariano Rivera	1.00
109	Joe Mauer	1.50
110	Cole Hamels	.50
111	Ichiro Suzuki ... Albert Pujols	1.50
112	Andre Ethier	1.00
113	Justin Verlander	1.00

114	Derek Jeter	4.00
115	Ryan Zimmerman	1.50
116	Rick Porcello	.50

Commemorative Patch

1	Tris Speaker	10.00
2	Babe Ruth	20.00
3	Babe Ruth	20.00
4	Mel Ott	10.00
5	Dizzy Dean	15.00
6	Jimmie Foxx	12.00
7	Hank Greenberg	12.00
8	Lou Gehrig	15.00
9	Lou Gehrig	15.00
10	Ralph Kiner	10.00
11	Johnny Mize	10.00
12	Robin Roberts	8.00
13	Monte Irvin	10.00
14	Duke Snider	15.00
15	Eddie Mathews	15.00
16	Mickey Mantle	20.00
17	Roger Maris	15.00
18	Johnny Podres	8.00
19	Bob Gibson	15.00
20	Juan Marichal	10.00
21	Orlando Cepeda	8.00
22	Al Kaline	15.00
23	Frank Robinson	10.00
24	Bobby Murcer	8.00
25	Willie Stargell	12.00
26	Johnny Bench	15.00
27	Ozzie Smith	15.00
28	Eddie Murray	10.00
29	Gary Carter	10.00
30	Dennis Eckersley	10.00
31	Ryne Sandberg	10.00
32	Gary Sheffield	8.00
33	Frank Thomas	12.00
34	Vladimir Guerrero	10.00
35	Ichiro Suzuki	12.00
36	Curt Schilling	10.00
37	Chipper Jones	12.00
38	Ryan Zimmerman	10.00
39	Roy Halladay	12.00
40	Grady Sizemore	10.00
41	Manny Ramirez	12.00
42	Tim Lincecum	15.00
43	Evan Longoria	15.00
44	David Wright	15.00
45	Chase Utley	15.00
46	Mariano Rivera	15.00
47	Joe Mauer	15.00
48	Albert Pujols	20.00
49	Ichiro Suzuki	15.00
50	Mark Teixeira	15.00
51	Richie Ashburn	10.00
52	Johnny Bench	15.00
53	Yogi Berra	12.00
54	Rod Carew	10.00
55	Orlando Cepeda	8.00
56	Rickey Henderson	10.00
57	Bob Feller	10.00
58	Rollie Fingers	8.00
59	Carlton Fisk	10.00
60	Catfish Hunter	8.00
61	Monte Irvin	10.00
62	Reggie Jackson	10.00
63	Fergie Jenkins	8.00
64	Al Kaline	12.00
65	George Kell	10.00
66	Harmon Killebrew	12.00
67	Ralph Kiner	10.00
68	Juan Marichal	10.00
69	Eddie Mathews	15.00
70	Bill Mazeroski	10.00
71	Willie McCovey	10.00
72	Joe Morgan	10.00
73	Eddie Murray	12.00
74	Ryne Sandberg	15.00
75	Tom Seaver	15.00
76	Hal Newhouser	8.00
77	Phil Niekro	8.00
78	Jim Palmer	10.00
79	Tony Perez	10.00
80	Phil Rizzuto	12.00
81	Robin Roberts	10.00
82	Brooks Robinson	15.00
83	Mike Schmidt	15.00
84	Red Schoendienst	10.00
85	Ozzie Smith	15.00
86	Warren Spahn	15.00
87	Willie Stargell	12.00
88	Hoyt Wilhelm	10.00
89	Jimmie Foxx	15.00
90	Mickey Mantle	20.00
91	Jackie Robinson	15.00
92	Lou Gehrig	15.00
93	Babe Ruth	20.00
94	Albert Pujols	15.00
95	David Wright	15.00
96	Mariano Rivera	15.00
97	Ryan Howard	15.00
98	Ryan Braun	15.00
99	Joe Mauer	15.00
100	CC Sabathia	15.00

History of the World Series

Common Player:		.50
1	Christy Mathewson	.75
2	Walter Johnson	.75
3	Babe Ruth	2.50
4	Rogers Hornsby	.75
5	Babe Ruth	2.50
6	Mickey Mantle	3.00
7	Mel Ott	.75
8	Enos Slaughter	.50
9	Bob Feller	.75
10	Whitey Ford	.75

11	Johnny Podres	.50
12	Yogi Berra	1.00
13	Yogi Berra	1.00
14	Jim Palmer	.50
15	Bob Gibson	1.00
16	Brooks Robinson	.75
17	Dennis Eckersley	.50
18	Paul Molitor	.75
19	Jason Varitek	.50
20	Edgar Renteria	.50
21	Derek Jeter	3.00
22	Alex Gonzalez	.50
23	Cole Hamels	.75
24	Chase Utley	1.00
25	New York Yankees	2.00

Hat Logos

Common Player:		
Production 99 Sets		
1-2	Babe Ruth	50.00
3-4	George Sisler	20.00
5	Honus Wagner	35.00
6	Jackie Robinson	40.00
7-8	Jimmie Foxx	25.00
9-11	Johnny Mize	25.00
12	Lou Gehrig	40.00
13	Mel Ott	20.00
14-15	Rogers Hornsby	30.00
16	Roy Campanella	25.00
17	Thurman Munson	35.00
18	Tris Speaker	20.00
19-20	Ty Cobb	35.00
21	Mickey Mantle	70.00
22	Richie Ashburn	30.00
23-24	Bo Jackson	40.00
25-27	Paul Molitor	20.00
28-30	Tony Gwynn	25.00
31	Al Kaline	35.00
32-33	Andre Dawson	30.00
34	Bob Feller	30.00
35	Bob Gibson	30.00
36	Bobby Murcer	25.00
37-38	Carl Erskine	20.00
39-41	Curt Schilling	20.00
42-43	Dale Murphy	50.00
44-45	Dizzy Dean	25.00
47-48	Duke Snider	25.00
49-50	Dwight Gooden	20.00
51-52	Eddie Mathews	35.00
53-56	Eddie Murray	20.00
57-58	Fergie Jenkins	15.00
59-60	Frank Robinson	20.00
61-63	Frank Thomas	40.00
64-65	Gary Carter	30.00
66	George Kell	25.00
67	Hank Greenberg	30.00
68-70	Jim Palmer	25.00
71	Jimmy Piersall	15.00
72-73	Johnny Bench	30.00
74-75	Johnny Podres	15.00
76-77	Juan Marichal	20.00
78	Monte Irvin	25.00
79-82	Nolan Ryan	40.00
83-84	Orlando Cepeda	20.00
85-86	Ozzie Smith	40.00
87	Ralph Kiner	20.00
88-92	Reggie Jackson	30.00
93	Robin Roberts	25.00
94-95	Robin Yount	40.00
96-98	Roger Maris	35.00
100-101	Steve Carlton	25.00
102-103	Tom Seaver	25.00
104	Tony Perez	25.00
105-106	Warren Spahn	30.00
107-108	Willie McCovey	25.00
109	Willie Stargell	30.00
110-113	Rickey Henderson	50.00
114-115	Carlton Fisk	20.00
116-117	Dennis Eckersley	20.00
118-119	Ryne Sandberg	30.00
120	Lou Brock	30.00
121	Carl Yastrzemski	25.00
122	Ernie Banks	35.00
123	Mike Schmidt	50.00
124-126	Alex Rodriguez	40.00
127	Kevin Youkilis	20.00
128-129	Vladimir Guerrero	20.00
130	Chipper Jones	40.00
131	Dustin Pedroia	30.00
132	Ian Kinsler	20.00
133	Dustin Pedroia	30.00
134	Ryan Howard	50.00
135	Prince Fielder	25.00
136	David Wright	40.00
137	Carl Crawford	20.00
138	Justin Upton	20.00
139	Dan Haren	20.00

140-145	Randy Johnson	25.00
146	David Ortiz	20.00
147	Roy Halladay	25.00
148	Tim Lincecum	50.00
149	Pablo Sandoval	50.00
150	Albert Pujols	75.00
151	Hanley Ramirez	25.00
152	Nick Markakis	30.00
153	Ichiro Suzuki	50.00
154	Adam Jones	25.00
155	Evan Longoria	30.00
156	Joe Mauer	50.00
157	Matt Kemp	25.00
158	Justin Verlander	30.00
159	Zack Greinke	30.00
160	Miguel Cabrera	30.00
161	Chase Utley	50.00
162	Adam Dunn	25.00
163-164	Manny Ramirez	25.00
165	Grady Sizemore	25.00
166	Felix Hernandez	20.00
167	Mark Teixeira	40.00
168	Joey Votto	25.00
169	Ryan Braun	25.00
170	Mariano Rivera	40.00
171	Tommy Hanson	30.00
172	Matt Cain	20.00
173	Josh Johnson	15.00
174	Clayton Kershaw	25.00
175	Jon Lester	30.00
176	Elvis Andrus	15.00
177	Dexter Fowler	15.00
178	Rick Porcello	35.00
179	Andrew McCutchen	20.00
180	Colby Rasmus	25.00
181	Chris Coghlan	20.00
182	Nolan Reimold	15.00
183	Buster Posey	35.00
185	Madison Bumgarner	30.00
186	Neftali Feliz	20.00
187	Mark Teixeira	25.00
188	Vladimir Guerrero	15.00
189	Joe Mauer	25.00
190	Max Scherzer	15.00
191	Adrian Gonzalez	20.00
192	Josh Beckett	15.00
193	Jose Reyes	20.00
194	Ryan Braun	25.00
195	Cliff Lee	15.00
196	Kendry Morales	15.00
197	Tim Lincecum	40.00
198	Prince Fielder	20.00
199	Ichiro Suzuki	35.00
200	Chipper Jones	30.00
201	Chase Utley	30.00
202	Felix Hernandez	20.00
203	Nolan Reimold	15.00
204	Albert Pujols	75.00
205	Torii Hunter	15.00
206	Evan Longoria	30.00
207	CC Sabathia	25.00
208	Mariano Rivera	25.00
209	B.J. Upton	15.00
210	Justin Upton	20.00
211	Ivan Rodriguez	25.00
212	Curtis Granderson	20.00
213	Josh Hamilton	25.00
214	Tim Hudson	15.00
215	Neftali Feliz	15.00
216	Babe Ruth	50.00
217	Adam Lind	15.00
218	David Price	20.00
219	Tommy Hanson	20.00
220	Andrew McCutchen	25.00
221	Adam Dunn	15.00
222	Victor Martinez	20.00
223	Pablo Sandoval	20.00
224	Ricky Romero	15.00
225	Brian McCann	15.00
226	Jered Weaver	15.00
227	Andrew Bailey	15.00
228	Joe Saunders	15.00
229	Colby Rasmus	25.00
230	Nick Markakis	20.00
231	Mark Reynolds	15.00
232	Ryan Howard	25.00
233	Stephen Drew	15.00
234	David Ortiz	15.00
235	Kenshin Kawakami	15.00
236	Michael Young	15.00
237	Jayson Werth	20.00
238	John Lackey	15.00
239	Dustin Pedroia	20.00
240	Travis Snider	15.00
241	Rajai Davis	15.00
242	Edgar Renteria	15.00
243	Justin Morneau	25.00
244	Jimmy Rollins	15.00
245	Elvis Andrus	15.00
246	David Wright	25.00
247	Javier Vazquez	15.00
248	Jorge Posada	25.00
249	Carlos Beltran	15.00
250	Jonathan Broxton	15.00
251	Adam Jones	20.00
252	Alex Rodriguez	35.00
253	Koji Uehara	15.00
254	Brandon Webb	15.00
255	Kevin Kouzmanoff	15.00
256	Ryan Zimmerman	20.00
257	Brian Roberts	15.00
258	Alfonso Soriano	15.00
259	Jason Varitek	15.00
260	Aramis Ramirez	15.00
261	Jeremy Guthrie	15.00
262	Johnny Cueto	15.00
263	Jacoby Ellsbury	20.00
264	Carlos Quentin	15.00

265	Kosuke Fukudome	20.00
266	Grady Sizemore	20.00
267	Troy Tulowitzki	25.00
268	Alexei Ramirez	15.00
269	Jeff Francis	15.00
270	Jay Bruce	20.00
271	Rick Porcello	20.00
272	Gordon Beckham	25.00
273	Justin Verlander	20.00
274	Magglio Ordonez	20.00
275	Miguel Cabrera	25.00
276	Jake Peavy	15.00
277	Ryan Ludwick	15.00
278	Todd Helton	20.00
279	Carlos Lee	15.00
280	Mark Buehrle	15.00
281	Billy Butler	15.00
282	Chris Coghlan	15.00
283	Brett Anderson	15.00
284	Lance Berkman	15.00
285	Chone Figgins	15.00
286	Ubaldo Jimenez	20.00
287	Jason Kubel	15.00
288	Manny Ramirez	25.00
289	Joe Nathan	15.00
290	Jimmie Foxx	25.00
291	J.J. Hardy	15.00
292	Mike Cameron	15.00
293	Roy Oswalt	15.00
294	Carlos Delgado	15.00
295	Rogers Hornsby	15.00
296	Hunter Pence	15.00
297	Scott Kazmir	15.00
298	Tris Speaker	20.00
299	Jhoulys Chacin	15.00
300	Michael Cuddyer	15.00
301	Zack Greinke	20.00
302	Jeff Francoeur	15.00
303	Matt Kemp	20.00
304	Dan Haren	15.00
305	Andy Pettitte	20.00
306	David DeJesus	15.00
307	A.J. Burnett	15.00
308	Ty Cobb	25.00
309	Johnny Mize	20.00
310	Joakim Soria	15.00
311	Chris Carpenter	30.00
312	Asdrubal Cabrera	15.00
313	Shane Victorino	20.00
314	Andre Ethier	20.00
315	Kurt Suzuki	15.00
316	Honus Wagner	20.00
317	Clayton Kershaw	20.00
318	Zach Duke	15.00
319	Shin-Soo Choo	25.00
320	Matt Cain	20.00
321	Russell Martin	15.00
322	Joba Chamberlain	25.00
323	Jason Bay	20.00
324	Delmon Young	15.00
325	Matt Holliday	20.00
326	Scott Rolen	20.00
327	Adam Wainwright	25.00
328	Hanley Ramirez	20.00
329	Cal Ripken Jr.	60.00
330	Mickey Mantle	60.00
331	Chase Headley	15.00
332	Rich Harden	15.00
333	Garrett Jones	15.00
334	Dexter Fowler	15.00
335	Ian Kinsler	20.00
336	Raul Ibanez	20.00
337	Roy Halladay	30.00
338	Ryan Spilborghs	15.00
339	Cole Hamels	15.00
340	Thurman Munson	30.00
341	Robinson Cano	25.00
342	Matt LaPorta	15.00
343	Travis Hafner	15.00
344	Lou Gehrig	35.00
345	Nelson Cruz	20.00
346	Derrek Lee	15.00
347	Juan Marichal	20.00
348	Rollie Fingers	15.00
349	Carl Yastrzemski	20.00
350	Frank Robinson	20.00
351	Joe Morgan	25.00
352	Steve Carlton	15.00
353	Catfish Hunter	15.00
354	Willie Stargell	25.00
355	Early Wynn	15.00
356	Larry Doby	15.00
357	Bill Mazeroski	25.00
358	Carlton Fisk	20.00
359	Dave Winfield	20.00
360	Enos Slaughter	15.00
361	Ernie Banks	25.00
362	Joe Morgan	20.00
363	Rollie Fingers	15.00
364	Phil Rizzuto	25.00
365	Bo Jackson	20.00
366	Dave Winfield	20.00
367	Babe Ruth	50.00
368	Luis Aparicio	20.00
369	Duke Snider	20.00
370	Richie Ashburn	30.00
371	Early Wynn	15.00
372	Yogi Berra	20.00
373	Lou Brock	25.00
374	Roger Maris	30.00
375	Orlando Cepeda	20.00
376	Catfish Hunter	15.00
377	Ralph Kiner	15.00
378	Bob Gibson	25.00
379	Robin Yount	30.00
380	Harmon Killebrew	20.00
381	Orlando Cepeda	20.00
382	Steve Carlton	15.00
383	Bob Feller	20.00
384	Dennis Eckersley	15.00
385	Robin Roberts	20.00
386	Willie McCovey	20.00
387	Hank Greenberg	25.00
388	Johnny Bench	25.00
389	Eddie Murray	20.00
390	Red Schoendienst	20.00
391	Roger Maris	30.00
392	Tris Speaker	20.00
393	Dale Murphy	25.00
394	Fergie Jenkins	20.00
395	Frank Robinson	20.00
396	Willie McCovey	20.00
397	George Kell	20.00
398	Dave Winfield	20.00
399	Ozzie Smith	35.00
400	Rogers Hornsby	25.00
401	Jim Palmer	20.00
402	Carlton Fisk	20.00
403	Duke Snider	20.00
404	Gary Carter	15.00
405	Luis Aparicio	15.00
406	Andre Dawson	20.00
407	Hal Newhouser	15.00
408	Al Kaline	25.00
409	Bo Jackson	20.00
410	Johnny Mize	20.00
411	Mike Schmidt	35.00
412	Jim Bunning	15.00
413	Tony Perez	15.00
414	Dizzy Dean	25.00
415	Frank Thomas	20.00
416	Stan Musial	35.00

MLB Logoman Patch
Production 50 Sets

LM1	Albert Pujols	100.00
LM2	Hanley Ramirez	50.00
LM3	Mike Schmidt	100.00
LM4	Nick Markakis	50.00
LM5	CC Sabathia	50.00
LM6	Babe Ruth	80.00
LM8	Gordon Beckham	80.00
LM9	Adrian Gonzalez	50.00
LM36	Frank Robinson	50.00
LM37	Johnny Bench	75.00
LM38	Ryne Sandberg	50.00
LM39	Reggie Jackson	50.00
LM40	Nolan Ryan	100.00

Million Card Giveaway
Prices for unused redempt.

1	Roy Campanella	4.00
2	Gary Carter	4.00
3	Bob Gibson	4.00
4	Ichiro Suzuki	4.00
5	Mickey Mantle	4.00
6	Mickey Mantle	4.00
7	Roger Maris	4.00
8	Thurman Munson	4.00
9	Mike Schmidt	4.00
10	Carl Yastrzemski	4.00

History of the Game
Common Card: .50
Inserted 1:6

1	Baseball Invented Game Played	1.00
2	First Professional Baseball Game Played	.50
3	National League Created	.50
4	American League Elevated to Major League Status	.50
5	First World Series Game Played	.50
6	President Taft Attends Opening Day	.50
7	Ruth Sold to the Yankees	2.00
8	Baseball hits the Airwaves	.50
9	Lou Gehrig Replaces Wally Pipp	2.00
10	Ruth Sets New Single Season HR Mark	2.00
11	First MLB All-Star Game is Played	.50
12	First Night Game Played in MLB History	.50
13	Ruth Retires with 715 Career Homeruns	2.00
14	First Hall of Fame Class is Inducted	.50
15	Jackie Robinson Plays in first MLB game	2.00
16	First Televised Baseball Game	.50
17	Dodgers & Giants move to California	.50
18	Roger Maris Breaks Ruth Single Season HR Record	1.00
19	First MLB Draft	.50
20	MLBPA Created	.50
21	DH rule created	.50
22	Ryan Throws 7th No-Hitter	2.00
23	Ripken Breaks Gehrig Games Played Streak	3.00
24	Interleague Play Introduced	.50
25	1st MLB game played in Japan	.50

In the Name Letter Relics
Production One Set
No Pricing

Legendary Lineage
Common Duo: .75
Inserted 1:4

1	Willie McCovey / Ryan Howard	2.00
2	Mickey Mantle / Chipper Jones	4.00
3	Babe Ruth / Alex Rodriguez	4.00
4	Lou Gehrig / Mark Teixeira	3.00
5	Ty Cobb / Curtis Granderson	2.00
6	Jimmie Foxx / Manny Ramirez	1.50
7	George Sisler / Ichiro Suzuki	2.50
8	Grady Sizemore	.75
9	Honus Wagner / Hanley Ramirez	1.00
10	Johnny Bench / Ivan Rodriguez	1.00
11	Mike Schmidt / Evan Longoria	2.00
12	Ozzie Smith / Jose Reyes	2.00
13	Reggie Jackson / Adam Dunn	1.00
14	Warren Spahn / Tommy Hanson	1.50
15	Duke Snider / Andre Ethier	1.00
16	Stan Musial / Albert Pujols	3.00
17	Cal Ripken / Derek Jeter	4.00
18	Gary Carter / David Wright	1.50
19	Whitey Ford / CC Sabathia	.75
20	Frank Thomas / Prince Fielder	1.50
21	Hank Greenberg / Ryan Braun	1.50
22	Frank Robinson / Vladimir Guerrero	1.00
23	Jackie Robinson / Matt Kemp	1.00
24	Bob Gibson / Tim Lincecum	2.00
25	Tom Seaver / Roy Halladay	.75
26	Dennis Eckersley / Mariano Rivera	1.50
27	Tony Gwynn / Joe Mauer	1.00
28	Nolan Ryan / Zack Greinke	4.00
29	Carl Yastrzemski / Kevin Youkilis	2.00
30	Rickey Henderson / Carl Crawford	1.00
31	Joe Mauer / Johnny Bench	1.50
32	Orlando Cepeda / Pablo Sandoval	1.00
33	Carlton Fisk / Victor Martinez	.75
34	Eddie Mathews / Chipper Jones	1.50
35	Al Kaline / Miguel Cabrera	1.50
36	Andre Dawson / Alfonso Soriano	.75
37	Jackie Robinson / Ichiro Suzuki	1.50
38	Cal Ripken Jr. / Hanley Ramirez	3.00
39	Phil Rizzuto / Derek Jeter	3.00
40	Harmon Killebrew / Justin Morneau	1.00
41	Jimmie Foxx / Prince Fielder	1.50
42	Lou Gehrig / Albert Pujols	3.00
43	Mike Schmidt / Alex Rodriguez	2.50
44	Bo Jackson / Justin Upton	1.00
45	Babe Ruth / Ryan Howard	3.00
46	Luis Aparicio / Alexei Ramirez	.75
47	Frank Robinson / Ryan Braun	1.50
48	Stan Musial / Matt Holliday	1.50
49	Lou Brock / Carl Crawford	.75
50	Tris Speaker / Jacoby Ellsbury	1.50
51	Juan Marichal / Tim Lincecum	1.50
52	Dale Murphy / Matt Kemp	.75
53	Nolan Ryan / Justin Verlander	2.50
54	Ozzie Smith / Elvis Andrus	1.50
55	Rickey Henderson / B.J. Upton	1.00
56	Brooks Robinson / Ryan Zimmerman	1.00
57	Yogi Berra / Jorge Posada	1.00
58	Honus Wagner / Andrew McCutchen	1.00
59	Mickey Mantle / Mark Teixeira	3.00
60	Ryne Sandberg / Chase Utley	1.50

Legendary Lineage Relics
Production 50 Sets

BC	Lou Brock / Carl Crawford	30.00
BM	Yogi Berra / Jorge Posada	75.00
CS	Orlando Cepeda / Pablo Sandoval	50.00
FR	Jimmie Foxx / Manny Ramirez	60.00
HU	Rickey Henderson / B.J. Upton	50.00
KC	Al Kaline / Miguel Cabrera	60.00
KM	Harmon Killebrew / Justin Morneau	30.00
MH	Willie McCovey / Ryan Howard	30.00
MJ	Eddie Mathews / Chipper Jones	75.00
MK	Dale Murphy / Matt Kemp	50.00
MT	Mickey Mantle / Mark Teixeira	120.00
RB	Frank Robinson / Ryan Braun	50.00
RR	Cal Ripken Jr. / Hanley Ramirez	60.00
SR	Mike Schmidt / Alex Rodriguez	65.00
SU	Ryne Sandberg / Chase Utley	50.00
BMA	Johnny Bench / Joe Mauer	70.00

Legends Gold Chrome Target Cereal
Common Player: 3.00
Target Exclusive

1	Babe Ruth	12.00
2	Honus Wagner	5.00
3	Ichiro Suzuki	6.00
4	Nolan Ryan	12.00
5	Jackie Robinson	6.00
6	Tom Seaver	3.00
7	Derek Jeter	12.00
8	George Sisler	3.00
9	Roger Maris	5.00
10	Lou Gehrig	8.00
11	Mickey Mantle	15.00
12	Willie McCovey	3.00
13	Ty Cobb	5.00
14	Warren Spahn	3.00
15	Albert Pujols	10.00
16	Lou Gehrig	8.00
17	Mariano Rivera	5.00
18	Jimmie Foxx	5.00
19	Babe Ruth	12.00
20	Honus Wagner	5.00

Legends Platinum Chrome Wal-Mart Cereal
Common Player: 3.00
Wal-Mart Exclusive

PC1	Mickey Mantle	15.00
PC2	Jackie Robinson	6.00
PC3	Ty Cobb	5.00
PC4	Warren Spahn	3.00
PC5	Albert Pujols	10.00
PC6	Lou Gehrig	8.00
PC7	Mariano Rivera	5.00
PC8	Jimmie Foxx	5.00
PC9	Cy Young	4.00
PC10	Honus Wagner	5.00
PC11	Babe Ruth	12.00
PC12	Mickey Mantle	15.00
PC13	Ichiro Suzuki	6.00
PC14	Nolan Ryan	12.00
PC15	Jackie Robinson	6.00
PC16	Tom Seaver	3.00
PC17	Derek Jeter	12.00
PC18	Ty Cobb	5.00
PC19	Roger Maris	5.00
PC20	Lou Gehrig	8.00

Legendary Lineage Relics
Production 50 Sets

CR	Johnny Bench / Ivan Rodriguez	25.00
CW	Gary Carter / David Wright	35.00
ER	Dennis Eckersley / Mariano Rivera	30.00
GB	Hank Greenberg / Ryan Braun	50.00
MJ	Mickey Mantle / Chipper Jones	100.00
MP	Stan Musial / Albert Pujols	120.00
SE	Duke Snider / Andre Ethier	60.00
SH	Warren Spahn / Tommy Hanson	120.00
SL	Mike Schmidt / Evan Longoria	50.00
SS	George Sisler / Ichiro Suzuki	120.00
TF	Frank Thomas / Prince Fielder	80.00
WR	Honus Wagner / Hanley Ramirez	60.00
SSI	Tris Speaker / Grady Sizemore	50.00

Mickey Mantle Reprint Relics
Production 61

MMR61	Mickey Mantle	250.00

Peak Performance

Common Player: .50
Inserted 1:4

1	Albert Pujols	3.00
2	Tim Lincecum	2.00
3	Honus Wagner	1.00
4	Walter Johnson	1.00
5	Babe Ruth	3.00
6	Steve Carlton	.50
7	Grady Sizemore	1.00
8	Justin Morneau	.75
9	Bob Gibson	1.00
10	Christy Mathewson	1.00
11	Mel Ott	1.00
12	Lou Gehrig	2.50
13	Mariano Rivera	.75
14	Raul Ibanez	.50
15	Alex Rodriguez	2.50
16	Vladimir Guerrero	.75
17	Reggie Jackson	1.00
18	Mickey Mantle	4.00
19	Tris Speaker	1.00
20	Mark Teixeira	1.00
21	Jimmie Foxx	.50
22	George Sisler	.75
23	Stan Musial	2.00
24	Willie Stargell	01.00
25	Chase Utley	1.00
26	Joe Mauer	1.00
27	Tom Seaver	.75
28	Johnny Mize	.75
29	Roy Campanella	1.00
30	Prince Fielder	1.00
31	Manny Ramirez	1.50
32	Ryan Howard	1.50
33	Cy Young	1.00
34	Ichiro Suzuki	2.00
35	Miguel Cabrera	.75
36	Dizzy Dean	.50
37	Hanley Ramirez	.75
38	David Ortiz	.75
39	Chipper Jones	1.50
40	Alfonso Soriano	.75
41	David Wright	1.50
42	Ryan Braun	1.50
43	Dustin Pedroia	1.00
44	Roy Halladay	1.00
45	Jackie Robinson	1.00
46	Rogers Hornsby	.75
47	Roger Maris	1.00
48	Curt Schilling	.50
49	Evan Longoria	2.00
50	Ty Cobb	2.00
51	Luis Aparicio	.50
52	Lance Berkman	.50
53	Ubaldo Jimenez	1.00
54	Ian Kinsler	1.00
55	George Kell	.50
56	Felix Hernandez	.50
57	Max Scherzer	.50
58	Magglio Ordonez	.50
59	Derek Jeter	3.00
60	Mike Schmidt	1.50
61	Hunter Pence	.50
62	Jason Bay	.50
63	Clay Buchholz	.50
64	Josh Hamilton	.75
65	Willie McCovey	.50
66	Aaron Hill	.50
67	Derrek Lee	.50
68	Andre Ethier	.75
69	Ryan Zimmerman	.75
70	Joe Morgan	.75
71	Carlos Lee	.50
72	Chad Billingsley	.50
73	Adam Dunn	.50
74	Dan Uggla	.50
75	Jermaine Dye	.50
76	Monte Irvin	.75
77	Curtis Granderson	.75
78	Mark Reynolds	.50
79	Matt Kemp	.75
80	Ozzie Smith	1.50
81	Brandon Phillips	.50
82	Yogi Berra	1.00
83	Bobby Abreu	.50
84	Catfish Hunter	.50
85	Justin Upton	.75
86	Justin Verlander	.75
87	Troy Tulowitzki	.75
88	Phil Rizzuto	.75
89	B.J. Upton	.50
90	Richie Ashburn	.50
91	Matt Cain	.75
92	Joey Votto	1.00
93	Robin Roberts	.75
94	Nick Markakis	.50
95	Al Kaline	1.00
96	Dan Haren	.50
97	Thurman Munson	.75
98	Victor Martinez	.50
99	Brian McCann	.50
100	Zack Greinke	.75

Peak Performance Dual Relic
Production 50 Sets

BR	Gordon Beckham / Alexei Ramirez	30.00
HP	Ryan Howard / Albert Pujols	50.00
IF	Ichiro Suzuki / Kosuke Fukudome	40.00
KE	Matt Kemp / Andre Ethier	35.00
LS	Tim Lincecum / Pablo Sandoval	65.00
SU	Ryne Sandberg / Chase Utley	45.00
UU	B.J. Upton / Justin Upton	25.00
RTU	Hanley Ramirez / Troy Tulowitzki	50.00

Peak Performance Jumbo Relics
Production 20 Sets

AG	Adrian Gonzalez	40.00
AH	Aaron Hill	20.00
AS	Alfonso Soriano	40.00
BP	Buster Posey	100.00
CJ	Chipper Jones	60.00
CR	Colby Rasmus	30.00
DP	David Price	40.00
FH	Felix Hernandez	40.00
GB	Gordon Beckham	40.00
HR	Hanley Ramirez	50.00
IK	Ian Kinsler	40.00
JH	Josh Hamilton	40.00
JM	Justin Morneau	40.00
JV	Joey Votto	40.00
KK	Kenshin Kawakami	
MC	Matt Cain	50.00
NF	Neftali Feliz	
RP	Rick Porcello	40.00
TT	Troy Tulowitzki	
ZG	Zack Greinke	40.00

Peak Performance Relics

Blue: 1-1.5X
Production 99 Sets

AG	Adrian Gonzalez	6.00
AH	Aaron Hill	5.00
AJ	Adam Jones	6.00
AK	Al Kaline	12.00
AP	Andy Pettitte	10.00
AR	Alexei Ramirez	5.00
AS	Alfonso Soriano	6.00
BP	Buster Posey	12.00
CC	Chris Coghlan	5.00
CH	Catfish Hunter	10.00
CJ	Chipper Jones	8.00
CR	Colby Rasmus	6.00
CS	CC Sabathia	8.00
CZ	Carlos Zambrano	5.00
DH	Dan Haren	5.00
DL	Derrek Lee	5.00
DO	David Ortiz	8.00
DP	David Price	8.00
DU	Dan Uggla	5.00
FH	Felix Hernandez	6.00
GB	Gordon Beckham	10.00
GK	George Kell	15.00
GS	Grady Sizemore	8.00
HR	Hanley Ramirez	8.00
HW	Honus Wagner	60.00
IK	Ian Kinsler	5.00
IS	Ichiro Suzuki	15.00
JH	Josh Hamilton	8.00
JM	Justin Morneau	8.00
JP	Willie Stargell	15.00
JV	Joey Votto	8.00
KF	Kosuke Fukudome	6.00
KK	Kenshin Kawakami	5.00
LB	Lance Berkman	5.00
MC	Matt Cain	5.00
MF	Mike Fontenot	5.00
MI	Monte Irvin	10.00
MO	Mel Ott	10.00
MT	Mark Teixeira	8.00
NF	Neftali Feliz	6.00
NM	Nick Markakis	6.00

NS	Nick Swisher	6.00
OS	Ozzie Smith	20.00
PF	Prince Fielder	8.00
PH	Phil Hughes	6.00
RA	Richie Ashburn	20.00
RC	Roy Campanella	15.00
RD	Ryan Dempster	5.00
RH	Ryan Howard	10.00
RP	Rick Porcello	6.00
RR	Robin Roberts	15.00
RT	Ryan Theriot	5.00
TL	Ted Lilly	5.00
TM	Thurman Munson	15.00
TS	Tris Speaker	25.00
TT	Troy Tulowitzki	6.00
UJ	Ubaldo Jimenez	8.00
YB	Yogi Berra	25.00
YG	Yovani Gallardo	6.00
ZG	Zack Greinke	8.00
ARA	Aramis Ramirez	5.00
GSI	George Sisler	25.00
GSO	Geovany Soto	5.00
JMI	Johnny Mize	10.00
PWR	Pee Wee Reese	20.00
RCA	Robinson Cano	8.00
RHO	Rogers Hornsby	25.00

Red Back
Common Player:
Target Exclusive

1	Mickey Mantle	6.00
2	Rogers Hornsby	1.00
3	Warren Spahn	1.00
4	Jackie Robinson	2.00
5	Ty Cobb	2.50
6	Cy Young	1.50
7	Albert Pujols	4.00
8	Mariano Rivera	2.00
9	Jimmie Foxx	2.00
10	Reggie Jackson	1.50
11	Lou Gehrig	3.00
12	Dizzy Dean	1.00
13	Chipper Jones	2.00
14	Cal Ripken Jr.	6.00
15	David Wright	2.50
16	Babe Ruth	5.00
17	Honus Wagner	3.00
18	Ichiro Suzuki	2.50
19	Nolan Ryan	4.00
20	Stan Musial	3.00
21	Tom Seaver	2.50
22	Derek Jeter	4.00
23	Roy Halladay	2.50
24	Mel Ott	2.00
25	George Sisler	1.50
26	Roger Maris	2.50
27	Walter Johnson	1.50
28	Vladimir Guerrero	1.00
29	Tim Lincecum	2.50
30	Hanley Ramirez	2.00

Red Hot Rookie Redemption
No Pricing

Peak Performance Relic Autographs
Production 50 Sets

CG	Curtis Granderson	40.00
DO	David Ortiz	50.00
DW	David Wright	65.00
GB	Gordon Beckham	125.00
JJ	Josh Johnson	20.00
PF	Prince Fielder	50.00
RB	Ryan Braun	50.00
RH	Ryan Howard	75.00

Series 2
Production 50 Sets

CB	Chad Billingsley	40.00
DW	David Wright	75.00
FH	Felix Hernandez	30.00
HP	Hunter Pence	25.00
HR	Hanley Ramirez	30.00
JU	Justin Upton	40.00
MK	Matt Kemp	40.00
PF	Prince Fielder	40.00
RH	Ryan Howard	75.00

Peak Performance Autos.
Some not priced due to scarcity.

AB	Andrew Bailey	
AP	Albert Pujols	250.00
AR	Alex Rodriguez	150.00
AS	Alfonso Soriano	40.00
BP	Buster Posey	40.00
CB	Collin Balester	8.00
CK	Clayton Kershaw	15.00
CY	Chris Young	8.00
DB	Daniel Bard	15.00
DP	Dustin Pedroia	25.00
DS	Daniel Schlereth	8.00
DW	David Wright	75.00
FJ	Fergie Jenkins	30.00
FM	Franklin Morales D	5.00
GB	Gordon Beckham	40.00
GC	Gary Carter	25.00
HR	Hanley Ramirez B	20.00
JB	Jay Bruce	20.00
JC	Johnny Cueto	10.00
JJ	Josh Johnson	12.00
KS	Kurt Suzuki	8.00
LS	Lee Smith	20.00
MB	Milton Bradley	10.00
MG	Matt Gamel	8.00
MR	Manny Ramirez	150.00
MS	Max Scherzer	12.00
MT	Matt Tolbert	8.00
PF	Prince Fielder	40.00
PH	Phil Hughes	20.00
RB	Ryan Braun	30.00
RC	Robinson Cano	20.00
RH	Ryan Howard	50.00
RP	Ryan Perry	10.00
RR	Randy Ruiz	15.00
SV	Shane Victorino	20.00
TH	Tommy Hanson	35.00
TT	Troy Tulowitzki	15.00
VG	Vladimir Guerrero	50.00
WD	Wade Davis	15.00
BPA	Bobby Parnell	8.00
JMI	Jose Mijares	8.00

Series 2
Common Auto.: 8.00

AB	Andrew Bailey	10.00
AE	Andre Ethier	30.00
AH	Aaron Hill	8.00
BM	Brian McCann	20.00
CB	Clay Buchholz	15.00
CM	Cameron Maybin	8.00
CR	Carlos Ruiz	8.00
CR	Cal Ripken Jr	125.00
CV	Chris Volstad	8.00
DB	Dallas Braden	10.00
DM	Daniel Murphy	8.00
DP	Dustin Pedroia	25.00
DS	Denard Span	12.00
DW	David Wright	65.00
EC	Everth Cabrera	8.00
EV	Edinson Volquez	8.00
FC	Fausto Carmona	8.00
GG	Gio Gonzalez	8.00
GK	George Kell	25.00
HK	Howie Kendrick	10.00
HP	Hunter Pence	20.00
HR	Hanley Ramirez	20.00
JB	Jason Bartlett	12.00
JD	Jermaine Dye	10.00
JF	Jeff Francoeur	12.00
JL	Jon Lester	20.00
JM	Joe Morgan	20.00
JO	Josh Outman	8.00
JP	Jhonny Peralta	8.00
JR	Juan Rivera	8.00
JS	Joe Saunders	10.00
JU	Justin Upton	30.00
KU	Koji Uehara	15.00
LA	Luis Aparicio	35.00
LM	Lou Marson	8.00
MN	Mike Napoli	10.00
MR	Manny Ramirez	100.00
MT	Matt Tolbert	10.00
MY	Michael Young	15.00
NE	Nick Evans	10.00
NS	Nick Swisher	30.00
OS	Ozzie Smith	75.00
PF	Prince Fielder	30.00
PH	Phil Hughes	25.00
RC	Robinson Cano	30.00
RH	Ryan Howard	60.00
RI	Raul Ibanez	15.00
RP	Ryan Perry	8.00
RW	Randy Wells	10.00
TC	Trevor Cahill	10.00
TH	Torii Hunter	25.00
TS	Travis Snider	12.00
UJ	Ubaldo Jimenez	30.00
WD	Wade Davis	12.00
WM	Willie McCovey	50.00
CBI	Chad Billingsley	12.00
CGE	Chris Getz	8.00
CGO	Carlos Gomez	12.00
DMC	Dustin McGowan	8.00
JDE	Joey Devine	8.00
JFR	Jeff Francis	8.00
JLM	Jason Motte	8.00
JMO	Justin Morneau	25.00
JRE	Josh Reddick	10.00
JSO	Joakim Soria	10.00
MSC	Max Scherzer	10.00

Peak Performance Relics
Common Relic:

AC	Asdrubal Cabrera	8.00
AE	Alcides Escobar	8.00
AJ	Adam Jones	8.00
AL	Adam LaRoche	5.00
AP	Albert Pujols	20.00
AR	Aramis Ramirez	6.00
BG	Bob Gibson	25.00
BM	Brian McCann	5.00
BR	Brad Lidge	6.00
CF	Carlton Fisk	20.00
CH	Cole Hamels	8.00
CJ	Chipper Jones	10.00
CL	Cliff Lee	6.00
CR	Cal Ripken Jr.	20.00
CU	Chase Utley	10.00
DE	Dennis Eckersley	5.00
DG	Dwight Gooden	5.00
DL	Derek Lee	6.00
DM	Daniel Murphy	5.00
DO	David Ortiz	8.00
DP	Dustin Pedroia	8.00
DU	Dan Uggla	4.00
DW	David Wright	10.00
DW	Dave Winfield	10.00
DY	Delmon Young	5.00
EL	Evan Longoria	8.00
FC	Fausto Carmona	5.00
FH	Felix Hernandez	6.00
GS	Gary Sheffield	6.00
HG	Hank Greenberg	20.00
HM	Hideki Matsui	15.00
HW	Honus Wagner	100.00
IS	Ichiro Suzuki	20.00
JB	Jason Bulger	5.00
JD	J.D. Drew	5.00
JE	Jacoby Ellsbury	10.00
JG	Jody Gerut	5.00
JH	Jeremy Hermida	5.00
JM	Johnny Mize	30.00
JP	Jonathan Papelbon	6.00
JR	Jose Reyes	8.00
JS	Joakim Soria	5.00
JW	Jayson Werth	15.00
JZ	Jordan Zimmermann	6.00
KF	Kosuke Fukudome	5.00
KJ	Kenji Johjima	5.00
MC	Matt Cain	6.00
MG	Matt Gamel	6.00
MK	Matt Kemp	6.00
MM	Melvin Mora	5.00
MO	Mel Ott	30.00
MP	Manny Parra	6.00
MS	Mike Schmidt	30.00
MY	Michael Young	5.00
NS	Nick Swisher	5.00
PF	Prince Fielder	8.00
PM	Paul Molitor	10.00
RA	Rick Ankiel	6.00
RB	Ryan Braun	10.00
RH	Rich Harden	5.00
RW	Rickie Weeks	5.00
SC	Shin-Soo Choo	8.00
TG	Tony Gwynn	8.00
TH	Tim Hudson	5.00
TM	Thurman Munson	40.00
TS	Tris Speaker	40.00
TT	Troy Tulowitzki	6.00
YG	Yovani Gallardo	6.00
AH1	Aaron Hill	5.00
GSI	George Sisler	35.00
GSO	Geovany Soto	8.00
JBO	Jeremy Bonderman	5.00
JPO	Jorge Posada	8.00
JV1	Joey Votto	8.00
JWI	Josh Willingham	5.00
KY1	Kevin Youkilis	8.00
MCA	Melky Cabrera	5.00
MMA	Mickey Mantle	85.00
PWR	Pee Wee Reese	40.00
RHE	Rickey Henderson	10.00
RHO	Ryan Howard	10.00
SK1	Scott Kazmir	5.00
SK2	Scott Kazmir	5.00
THA	Tommy Hanson	10.00

Silk Collection
Production 50 Sets

S1	Prince Fielder	25.00
S3	Derek Lee	15.00
S4	Mickey Mantle	65.00
S5	Clayton Kershaw	20.00
S6	Bobby Abreu	10.00
S7	Johnny Cueto	10.00
S8	Dexter Fowler	10.00
S9	Felipe Lopez	10.00
S10	Tommy Hanson	25.00
S11	Shane Victorino	20.00
S12	Adam Jones	20.00
S13	Victor Martinez	15.00
S14	Rick Porcello	20.00
S15	Garret Anderson	10.00
S16	Josh Johnson	30.00
S17	Marco Scutaro	10.00
S18	Howie Kendrick	10.00
S19	Joey Votto	25.00
S20	Jorge De La Rosa	10.00
S21	Zack Greinke	20.00
S23	Billy Butler	10.00
S24	John Lackey	15.00
S25	Manny Ramirez	20.00
S26	CC Sabathia	20.00
S27	David Wright	30.00
S28	Nick Swisher	15.00
S29	Matt LaPorta	20.00
S30	Brandon Inge	15.00
S31	Cole Hamels	25.00
S32	Adrian Gonzalez	15.00
S33	Joe Saunders	10.00
S34	Tim Lincecum	40.00
S35	Ken Griffey Jr	40.00
S36	J.A. Happ	15.00
S37	Ian Kinsler	15.00
S38	Ivan Rodriguez	15.00
S39	Carl Crawford	15.00
S40	Jon Garland	10.00
S41	Albert Pujols	50.00
S43	Andrew McCutchen	15.00
S44	Gordon Beckham	35.00
S45	Jorge Posada	20.00
S46	Ichiro Suzuki	40.00
S47	Vladimir Guerrero	20.00
S48	Cliff Lee	15.00
S49	Freddy Sanchez	10.00
S50	Ryan Dempster	10.00
S51	Adam Wainwright	20.00
S52	Matt Holliday	25.00
S53	Chone Figgins	10.00
S54	Tim Hudson	10.00
S55	Rich Harden	10.00
S56	Justin Upton	15.00
S57	Joe Mauer	35.00
S58	Vernon Wells	10.00
S59	Miguel Tejada	15.00
S60	Denard Span	10.00
S61	Brandon Phillips	15.00
S62	Jason Bay	15.00
S63	Kendry Morales	10.00
S64	Josh Hamilton	20.00
S65	Yovani Gallardo	15.00
S66	Adam Lind	15.00
S67	Hideki Matsui	30.00
S68	Will Venable	10.00
S69	Joe Blanton	10.00
S70	Adrian Beltre	10.00
S71	Pablo Sandoval	20.00
S72	Roy Halladay	20.00
S73	Chris Coghlan	15.00
S74	Colby Rasmus	30.00
S75	Alexei Ramirez	10.00
S76	Josh Beckett	15.00
S77	Matt Kemp	15.00
S78	Max Scherzer	10.00
S79	Randy Johnson	20.00
S80	Curtis Granderson	20.00
S81	David Price	20.00
S82	Neftali Feliz	20.00
S83	Ricky Romero	15.00
S84	Lance Berkman	15.00
S85	Andre Ethier	15.00
S86	Mark Teixeira	25.00
S87	Edwin Jackson	10.00
S88	Akinori Iwamura	10.00
S90	Jair Jurrjens	10.00
S91	Stephen Drew	15.00
S92	Javier Vazquez	10.00
S93	Orlando Hudson	10.00
S94	Adam Dunn	15.00
S95	Kevin Youkilis	15.00
S96	Chase Utley	35.00
S97	Brian McCann	20.00
S98	Jim Thome	15.00
S99	Alex Rios	15.00
S100	Alex Rios	15.00

Series 2
Production 50 Sets

101	Geovany Soto	10.00
102	Joakim Soria	10.00
103	Chad Billingsley	10.00
104	Jacoby Ellsbury	15.00
105	Justin Morneau	20.00
106	Jeff Francis	10.00
107	Francisco Rodriguez	10.00
108	Torii Hunter	10.00
109	A.J Burnett	10.00
110	Chris Young	10.00
111	Bud Norris	10.00
112	Todd Helton	15.00
113	Shin-Soo Choo	20.00
114	Matt Cain	15.00
115	Jered Weaver	10.00
116	Jason Bartlett	10.00
117	Chris Carpenter	15.00
118	Kosuke Fukudome	20.00
119	Roy Oswalt	12.00
120	Alex Rodriguez	40.00
121	Dan Haren	15.00
122	Hiroki Kuroda	10.00
123	Hunter Pence	15.00
124	Jeremy Guthrie	10.00
125	Grady Sizemore	15.00
126	Mark Reynolds	10.00
127	Johnny Damon	20.00
128	Aaron Rowand	10.00
129	Carlos Beltran	12.00
130	Alfonso Soriano	15.00
131	Nelson Cruz	10.00
132	Edinson Volquez	10.00
133	Jayson Werth	20.00
134	Mariano Rivera	20.00
135	Brandon Webb	15.00
136	Jordan Zimmermann	15.00
137	Michael Young	10.00
138	Daisuke Matsuzaka	15.00
139	Ubaldo Jimenez	15.00
140	Evan Longoria	30.00
141	Brad Lidge	10.00
142	Carlos Zambrano	15.00
143	Heath Bell	10.00
144	Trevor Cahill	10.00
145	Carlos Gonzalez	15.00
146	Jose Reyes	15.00
147	Ian Snell	10.00
148	Manny Parra	10.00
149	Michael Cuddyer	10.00
150	Melky Cabrera	10.00
151	Justin Verlander	15.00
152	Delmon Young	10.00
153	Kelly Johnson	10.00
154	Derek Lowe	10.00
155	Derek Jeter	60.00
156	Paul Maholm	10.00
157	Mike Napoli	10.00
158	Aramis Ramirez	15.00
159	Alex Gordon	10.00
160	Jorge Cantu	10.00
161	Brad Hawpe	15.00
162	Troy Tulowitzki	20.00
163	Casey Kotchman	10.00
164	Carlos Guillen	10.00
165	J.D. Drew	10.00
166	Dustin Pedroia	25.00
167	Francisco Liriano	10.00
168	Jimmy Rollins	15.00
169	Wade LeBlanc	10.00
170	Miguel Cabrera	20.00
171	Jeremy Hermida	10.00
172	Koji Uehara	10.00
173	Tommy Hunter	10.00
174	Dustin McGowan	10.00
175	Corey Hart	10.00
176	Jake Peavy	15.00
177	Jason Varitek	10.00
178	Chris Dickerson	10.00
179	Robinson Cano	20.00
180	Michael Bourn	10.00
181	Chris Volstad	10.00
182	Mark Buehrle	10.00
183	Jarrod Saltalamacchia	10.00
184	Aaron Hill	10.00
185	Carlos Pena	15.00
186	Luke Hochevar	10.00
187	Derek Holland	15.00
188	Carlos Quentin	10.00
189	J.J. Hardy	15.00
190	Ryan Zimmerman	15.00
191	Travis Snider	15.00
192	Russell Martin	15.00
193	Brian Roberts	15.00
194	Ryan Ludwick	15.00
195	Aaron Cook	10.00
196	Jay Bruce	15.00
197	Kevin Slowey	10.00
198	Johan Santana	15.00
199	Carlos Lee	10.00
200	David Ortiz	15.00

Tales of the Game
Common Card: 1.00
Inserted 1:6

1	Spikes Up	1.50
2	The Curse of the Bambino	2.00
3	Ruth Calls His Shot	3.00
4	Topps Dumps 1952 Cards in the River	1.00
5	Jackie Robinson Steals Home in World Series	2.00
6	Let's Play Two	1.50
7	Mazeroski Hits World Series Walk-Off	1.00
8	Maris Chases #61	2.00
9	Mantle Homers Off Yankee Stadium Façade	3.00
10	Piersall Runs Backwards for HR #100	1.00
11	1969 Amazin' Mets	1.00
12	Reggie has Light Tower Power	1.00
13	Carlton Fisk: The Wave	1.00
14	Reggie's World Series HR Hat Trick	1.50
15	Ozzie Smith Flips Out	1.50
16	Bo Knows Wall Climbing	1.50
17	Wade Boggs: Who You Calling Chicken?	1.50
18	Prince: BP HR at Age 12	1.50
19	Old Cal Clutch	3.00
20	Jeter: The Flip	3.00
21	Schilling's Bloody Sock	1.00
22	Pesky's Pole	1.00
23	Manny Being Manny	1.50
24	The Great Ham-Bino	1.50
25	Yankees Dig Up Ortiz' Jersey	1.00

Ticket to Topps Town
Common Player: .50
Gold: 1-2X

1	Joe Mauer	.75
2	David Wright	1.00
3	Hanley Ramirez	1.00
4	Adrian Gonzalez	.75
5	Evan Longoria	1.50
6	Ichiro Suzuki	1.50
7	Josh Hamilton	.75
8	Zack Greinke	.75
9	Roy Halladay	.75
10	Tim Lincecum	1.50
11	Brian McCann	.75
12	Miguel Tejada	.75
13	Ryan Howard	1.00
14	Albert Pujols	2.00
15	Miguel Cabrera	0.75
16	Kevin Youkilis	.50
17	Todd Helton	.50
18	Vladimir Guerrero	.75
19	Justin Upton	.50
20	Adam Jones	.50
21	Adam Dunn	.50
22	Andrew McCutchen	.50
23	CC Sabathia	.50
24	Ryan Braun	1.00
25	Manny Ramirez	.75

Turkey Red

Common Player: .50
Inserted 1:4

1	Ryan Howard	2.50
2	Miguel Tejada	.75
3	Nolan Ryan	4.00
4	Albert Pujols	4.00
5	Josh Beckett	.75
6	Justin Upton	.75
7	Andre Ethier	.75
8	Tommy Hanson	1.50
9	Josh Johnson	.50
10	Jonathan Papelbon	.75
11	Cole Hamels	1.50
12	Manny Ramirez	1.50
13	Yovani Gallardo	.50
14	Kevin Youkilis	.75
15	Hank Greenberg	1.00
16	Ozzie Smith	1.50
17	Derrek Lee	.75
18	Ryan Braun	2.00
19	Cal Ripken Jr.	5.00
20	CC Sabathia	.75
21	Johnny Bench	1.50
22	Tim Lincecum	2.00
23	Mike Schmidt	2.00
24	Clayton Kershaw	.75
25	Ernie Banks	1.50
26	Dexter Fowler	.50
27	Edwin Jackson	.50
28	Mickey Mantle	5.00
29	Gordon Beckham	1.50
30	Victor Martinez	.75
31	Mel Ott	1.50
32	Zack Greinke	1.50
33	Roy Halladay	.75
34	David Wright	2.00
35	Stephen Drew	.50
36	Matt Holliday	1.00
37	Chase Utley	1.50
38	Rick Porcello	1.00
39	Vladimir Guerrero	1.00
40	Mark Teixeira	1.50
41	Evan Longoria	2.50
42	Ian Kinsler	.75
43	Adrian Gonzalez	1.00
44	Matt Kemp	1.00
45	Ryne Sandberg	2.50
46	Babe Ruth	4.00
47	Curtis Granderson	1.50
48	Willie McCovey	1.00
49	Josh Hamilton	1.00
50	Pablo Sandoval	1.00

Series 2
Common Player: .50

51	Torii Hunter	.50
52	Adam Dunn	.50
53	Alexei Ramirez	.50
54	Andrew McCutchen	1.00
55	Aaron Hill	.50
56	Alcides Escobar	.50
57	Jimmie Foxx	1.50
58	Joey Votto	1.50
59	Jose Reyes	1.50
60	Al Kaline	1.50
61	Felix Hernandez	.75
62	Troy Tulowitzki	1.50
63	Nate McLouth	.50
64	Justin Morneau	1.00
65	Prince Fielder	1.00
66	Nelson Cruz	1.00
67	Grady Sizemore	1.00
68	Hanley Ramirez	1.50
69	Brooks Robinson	1.50
70	Jackie Robinson	2.00
71	Nick Markakis	.75
72	Roy Oswalt	.75
73	Chad Billingsley	.50
74	Tom Seaver	1.50
75	B.J. Upton	.50
76	Chris Coghlan	.50
77	Luis Aparicio	.75
78	Dan Haren	.50
79	Raul Ibanez	.50
80	Kosuke Fukudome	.50
81	Denard Span	.50
82	Joe Morgan	1.00
83	Yogi Berra	2.50
84	Dustin Pedroia	2.00
85	Lou Gehrig	3.00
86	Billy Butler	.50
87	Jake Peavy	.75
88	Eddie Mathews	1.50
89	Ubaldo Jimenez	1.50
90	Johan Santana	1.50
91	Buster Posey	3.00
92	George Sisler	2.00
93	Ian Desmond	.50
94	Kurt Suzuki	.50
95	Ty Cobb	3.00
96	Magglio Ordonez	.50
97	Chase Headley	.50
98	Hunter Pence	.75
99	Ryan Ludwick	.75
100	Derek Jeter	4.00

Vintage Legends Collection

Common Player: .50

1	Lou Gehrig	3.00
2	Johnny Mize	

#	Player	Price
3	Reggie Jackson	1.00
4*	Tris Speaker	1.00
5	George Sisler	1.00
6	Willie McCovey	1.00
7	Tom Seaver	1.00
8	Walter Johnson	1.00
9	Ozzie Smith	1.50
10	Babe Ruth	3.00
11	Christy Mathewson	1.00
12	Jackie Robinson	2.00
13	Eddie Murray	1.00
14	Mel Ott	1.00
15	Jimmie Foxx	1.50
16	Thurman Munson	1.50
17	Mike Schmidt	2.00
18	Johnny Bench	1.50
19	Rogers Hornsby	1.00
20	Ty Cobb	2.00
21	Nolan Ryan	3.00
22	Roy Campanella	1.00
23	Cy Young	1.00
24	Pee Wee Reese	.50
25	Honus Wagner	1.50

WalMart Black Border
Singles: 1-1.25X

When They Were Young
Common Player: .50
Inserted 1:6

	Player	Price
AP	Aaron Poreda	.50
AR	Alex Rodriguez	3.00
BR	Brian Roberts	.50
CM	Charlie Morton	.50
CR	Cody Ross	.50
CS	Clint Sammons	.50
DM	Daniel McCutchen	1.00
DO	David Ortiz	1.00
DW	David Wright	2.00
GB	Gordon Beckham	2.00
JB	Jason Berken	.50
JD	Johnny Damon	.75
JV	Justin Verlander	.75
RD	Ryan Doumit	.75
RM	Russell Martin	.75
RN	Ricky Nolasco	.50
SO	Scott Olsen	.50
YM	Yadier Molina	.50

World Champion Autograph Relics
Production 50 Sets

	Player	Price
AR	Alex Rodriguez	225.00
CS	CC Sabathia	200.00
MC	Melky Cabrera	50.00
MR	Mariano Rivera	180.00
RC	Robinson Cano	85.00

World Champion Autographs
Production 50 Sets

	Player	Price
AR	Alex Rodriguez	185.00
CS	CC Sabathia	180.00
MC	Melky Cabrera	35.00
MR	Mariano Rivera	175.00
RC	Robinson Cano	75.00

World Champion Relics
Production 100 Sets

	Player	Price
AP	Andy Pettitte	50.00
AR	Alex Rodriguez	75.00
BG	Brett Gardner	30.00
CS	CC Sabathia	50.00
EH	Eric Hinske	20.00
HM	Hideki Matsui	65.00
JD	Johnny Damon	40.00
JG	Joe Girardi	35.00
JH	Jerry Hairston Jr.	20.00
JP	Jorge Posada	40.00
MC	Melky Cabrera	25.00
MR	Mariano Rivera	50.00
MT	Mark Teixeira	50.00
NS	Nick Swisher	35.00
RC	Robinson Cano	40.00

2010 Topps Heritage

CHIPPER JONES — Atlanta Braves — Third Base

Common (1-425): .25
Common RC: .25
Common Dice: 5.00
Inserted 1:72
Common SP (426-500): 5.00
Inserted 1:3
Pack (8): 4.00
Box (24): 85.00

#	Player	Price
1	Albert Pujols	2.50
1	Albert Pujols Dice Back/SP	15.00
1	Albert Pujols Black Nameplate/SP	100.00
2	Joe Mauer	.75
2	Joe Mauer Dice Back/SP	8.00
2	Joe Mauer All Black Nameplate/SP	50.00
3	Joe Blanton	.25
4	Delmon Young	.50
5	Kelly Shoppach	.25
6	Ronald Belisario	.25
7	Chicago White Sox	.25
8	Rajai Davis	.25
9	Aaron Harang	.25
10	Brian Roberts	.40
11	Adam Wainwright	.50
12	Geovany Soto	.40
13	Ramon Santiago	.25
14	Albert Callaspo	.25
15	Grady Sizemore	.50
15	Grady Sizemore Dice Back/SP	6.00
15	Grady Sizemore Red-Green Nameplate/SP	50.00
16	Clay Buchholz	.40
17	Checklist	.25
18	David Huff	.25
19	Alex Rodriguez	1.50
20	Cole Hamels	.50
21	Orlando Cabrera	.25
22	Ross Ohlendorf	.25
23	Matt Kemp	.50
23	Matt Kemp Dice Back/SP	6.00
24	Andrew Bailey	.40
25	Juan Francisco Jay Bruce Joey Votto	.50
26	Chris Tillman	.40
27	Mike Fontenot	.25
28	Melky Cabrera	.25
29	Reid Gorecki (RC)	1.00
30	Jayson Nix	.25
31	Bengie Molina	.25
32	Chris Carpenter	.50
33	Jason Bay	.25
34	Fausto Carmona	.25
35	Gordon Beckham	1.00
36	Glen Perkins	.25
37	Curtis Granderson	.50
38	Rafael Furcal	.40
39	Matt Carson (RC)	.50
40	A.J. Burnett	.25
41	Hanley Ramirez/ Pablo Sandoval/ Albert Pujols/ Todd Helton	1.00
42	Joe Mauer/ Ichiro Suzuki/ Derek Jeter/ Miguel Cabrera	1.00
43	Albert Pujols/ Prince Fielder/ Ryan Howard/ Mark Reynolds	1.00
44	Carlos Pena/ Mark Teixeira/ Jason Bay/Aaron Hill	.50
45	Chris Carpenter/ Tim Lincecum/ Jair Jurrjens/ Adam Wainwright	.50
46	Zack Greinke/ Felix Hernandez/ Roy Halladay/CC Sabathia	.50
47	Adam Wainwright/ Chris Carpenter/ Jorge De La Rosa/ Bronson Arroyo	.40
48	Felix Hernandez/ CC Sabathia/ Justin Verlander/ Josh Beckett	.40
49	Tim Lincecum/ Javier Vazquez/ Dan Haredam Wainwright	.50
50	Justin Verlander/ Zack Greinke/Jon Lester/ Felix Hernandez	.50
51	Detroit Tigers	.25
52	Ronny Cedeno	.25
53	Jason Varitek	.25
54	Daniel McCutchen RC	1.00
55	Pablo Sandoval	.50
55	Pablo Sandoval Yellow-Green Nameplate/SP	50.00
56	Jake Peavy	.50
56	Mickey Mantle SP	50.00
57	Billy Butler	.40
58	Ryan Dempster	.25
59	Neil Walker (RC)	.50
60a	Asdrubal Cabrera	.25
60b	Babe Ruth/SP	40.00
61a	Ryan Church	.25
61b	Roger Maris/SP	40.00
62	Nick Markakis	.25
63	Nick Blackburn	.25
64	Mark DeRosa	.25
65	Paul Konerko	.25
66	Daniel Ray Herrera	.25
67	Brandon Inge	.40
68	Josh Thole RC	1.00
69	Josh Beckett	.50
70	Lastings Milledge	.25
71	Robert Andino	.25
72	Matt Cain	.50
73	Nate McLouth	.40
74	Russell Martin	.40
75	Albert Pujols	
76	David Wright	1.50
77	Jay Bruce	.50
77a	J.A. Happ	.50
77b	J.A. Happ Orange-Blue Nameplate/SP	50.00
78	Jayson Werth	.25
79	A.J. Pierzynski	.25
80	Michael Cuddyer	.25
81	Dustin Richardson RC	.25
82a	Justin Upton	.50
82b	Justin Upton Dice Back/SP	8.00
83	Rick Porcello	.50
84	Garret Anderson	.25
85	Jeremy Guthrie	.25
86	Los Angeles Dodgers	.25
87	Juan Uribe	.25
88	Alfonso Soriano	.50
89	Martin Prado	.25
90	Gavin Floyd	.25
91	Colby Rasmus	.50
92a	Mark Teixeira	.75
92b	Mark Teixeira Dice Back/SP	8.00
93	Raul Ibanez	.50
94a	Zack Greinke	.50
94b	Zack Greinke Yellow-Blue Nameplate/SP	50.00
95	Miguel Cabrera	.75
96	Randy Johnson	.75
97	Chris Dickerson	.25
98	Checklist	.25
99	Jed Lowrie	.25
100	Zach Duke	.25
101	Jhonny Peralta	.25
102	Nolan Reimold	.40
103	Jimmy Rollins	.50
104	Jorge Posada	.50
105	Tim Hudson	.40
106	Scott Hairston	.25
107	Rich Harden	.25
108	Jason Kubel	.40
109	Clayton Kershaw	.75
110	Willy Taveras	.25
111	Brett Myers	.25
112	Adam Everett	.25
113	Jonathan Papelbon	.40
114	Buster Posey	5.00
115	Kerry Wood	.25
116	Jerry Hairston Jr.	.25
117	Adam Dunn	.40
118	Yadier Molina	.40
119	David DeJesus Alex Gordon	.25
120a	Chipper Jones	1.00
120b	Chipper Jones Dice Back/SP	8.00
121	John Lackey	.40
122	Chicago Cubs	.50
123	Nick Punto	.25
124	Daniel Hudson RC	1.00
125	David Hernandez	.25
126	Garrett Jones	.40
127	Joel Pineiro	.25
128	Jacoby Ellsbury	.75
129	Ian Desmond (RC)	.75
130	James Loney	.40
131	Dave Trembley	.25
132	Ozzie Guillen	.25
133	Joe Girardi	.25
134	Jim Riggleman	.25
135	Dusty Baker	.25
136	Joe Torre	.50
137	Bobby Cox	.25
138	John Russell	.25
139	Tony LaRussa	.40
140	Jarrod Saltalamacchia	.25
141	Kosuke Fukudome	.40
142	Mariano Rivera	.50
143	David DeJesus	.25
144	Jon Niese	.25
145	Jair Jurrjens	.25
146	Josh Willingham	.25
147	Chris Pettit RC	.50
148	Chris Getz	.25
149	Ryan Doumit	.25
150	Aaron Rowand	.25
151	Brad Kilby RC	.50
152	Prince Fielder	.75
153	Scott Baker	.25
154	Shane Victorino	.50
155	Luis Valbuena	.25
156	Drew Stubbs RC	1.00
157	Mark Buehrle	.40
158	Josh Bard	.25
159	Baltimore Orioles	.25
160	Andy Pettitte	.50
161	Madison Bumgarner RC	3.00
162	Johnny Cueto	.25
163	Jeff Mathis	.25
164	Yunel Escobar	.25
165	Steve Pearce	.25
166	Ramon Hernandez	.25
167	San Francisco Giants	.25
168	Chris Coghlan	.50
169	Ted Lilly	.25
170	Alex Rios	.50
171	Justin Verlander	.50
172	Michael Brantley RC	1.00
173	Dustin Pedroia	.25
	Jacoby Ellsbury	.75
174	Craig Stammen	.25
175	Scott Rolen	.40
176	Howie Kendrick	.40
177	Trevor Cahill	.25
178	Matt Holliday	.75
179a	Chase Utley	1.00
179b	Chase Utley Dice Back/SP	8.00
180	Robinson Cano	.50
181	Paul Maholm	.25
182a	Adam Jones	.50
182b	Adam Jones Dice Back/SP	8.00
183	Felipe Lopez	.25
184	Kendry Morales	.40
185	John Danks	.40
186	Denard Span	.40
187	Nyjer Morgan	.25
188	Adrian Gonzalez	.50
189	Checklist	.25
190	Chad Billingsley	.40
191	Travis Hafner	.25
192	Gerald Laird	.25
193a	Daisuke Matsuzaka	.50
193b	Daisuke Matsuzaka Dice Back/SP	8.00
194	Joey Votto	.75
195	Jered Weaver	.40
196	Ryan Theriot	.40
197	Gio Gonzalez	.25
198	Chris Iannetta	.25
199	Mike Jacobs	.25
19b	Alex Rodriguez Dice Back/SP	8.00
200	Javier Vasquez	.40
201	Josh Beckett	
202	Torii Hunter	.40
203	Juan Rivera	.25
204	Brandon Phillips	.40
205	Edwin Jackson	.25
206	Lance Berkman	.50
207	Gil Meche	.25
208	Jorge Cantu	.25
209	Eric Young Jr. (RC)	.50
210	Andre Ethier	.50
211	Rickie Weeks	.40
212	Omir Santos	.25
213	Mat Latos	.25
214	Tyler Colvin RC	1.50
215	Derek Jeter	2.50
215	Derek Jeter Dice Back/SP	15.00
215	Derek Jeter Red-Yellow Nameplate	100.00
216	Carlos Pena	.50
217	Carlos Ruiz	.25
218	Jason Marquis	.25
219	Charlie Manuel	.25
220	Bruce Bochy	.25
221	Terry Francona	.25
222	Manny Acta	.25
223	Jim Leyland	.25
224	Bob Geren	.25
225	Mike Scioscia	.25
226	Ron Gardenhire	.25
227	Luis Castillo	.25
228	New York Mets	.50
229	Carlos Carrasco (RC)	1.50
230	Chone Figgins	.40
231	Johan Santana	.75
232	Max Scherzer	.25
233a	Ian Kinsler	.50
233b	Ian Kinsler Dice Back/SP	8.00
234	Jeff Samardzija	.25
235	Will Venable	.25
236	Cristian Guzman	.25
237	Alexei Ramirez	.25
238	B.J. Upton	.40
239	Derek Lowe	.25
240	Elvis Andrus	.40
241	Joakim Soria	.25
242	Chase Headley	.25
243	Adam Lind	.40
244a	Ichiro Suzuki	1.50
244b	Ichiro Suzuki Dice Back/SP	10.00
245	Ryan Howard	1.00
246	Johnny Damon	.50
247	Casey Blake	.25
248	Kevin Millwood	.25
249	Cincinnati Reds	.25
250	Andrew McCutchen Garrett Jones	.50
251	Jarrod Washburn	.25
252	Dan Uggla	.50
253	Cliff Lee	.50
254	Chris Davis	.25
255	Jordan Zimmermann	.40
256	Pedro Feliz	.25
257	Carlos Quentin	.50
258	Derek Holland	.25
259	Jose Reyes	.75
260	Manny Ramirez	.75
261	David Ortiz	.50
262	Andrew McCutchen	.50
263	Brian Fuentes	.25
264	Nelson Cruz	.25
265	Dexter Fowler	.40
266	Carlos Beltran	.25
267	Michael Young	.40
268	Chris Young	.25
269	Edgar Renteria	.25
270	Vin Mazzaro	.25
271	Gary Sheffield	.25
272	Roy Oswalt	.50
273	Checklist	.25
274	Stephen Drew	.40
275	John Lannan	.25
276	Tyler Flowers RC	.75
277	Coco Crisp	.25
278	Luis Durango RC	.50
279	Erick Aybar	.25
280	Tobi Stoner RC	1.00
281	Cody Ross	.25
282	Koji Uehara	.25
283	Cleveland Indians	.25
284	Yovani Gallardo	.25
285	Wilkin Ramirez	.25
286	Roy Halladay	.50
287	Juan Francisco RC	1.00
288	Carlos Zambrano	.50
289	Carl Crawford	.50
290	Joba Chamberlain	.75
291	Fernando Martinez	.25
292	Jhoulys Chacin	.25
293	Felix Hernandez	.50
294	Josh Hamilton	.75
295	Rick Ankiel	.40
296	Hiroki Kuroda	.25
297	Oakland Athletics	.25
298	Wade Davis (RC)	1.00
299	Derek Lee	.50
300a	Hanley Ramirez	1.00
300b	Hanley Ramirez Dice Back/SP	8.00
301	Chris Iannetta	.25
302	Adrian Beltre	.40
303	James Shields	.25
304	Alex Gordon	.40
305	Brad Bergesen	.25
306	Lee Dominates	.25
307	Burnett Outduels Pedro	.50
308	Replay AROD Homer	1.00
309	Damon Steals 2 Bags on 1 Pitch	.25
310	Utley Ties Reggie	.75
311	Matsui Knocks in 6	.50
312	Matsui Named MVP	.50
313	The Winners Celebrate	.50
314	Hanley Ramirez Evan Longoria	.50
315	Brandon Webb	.25
316	Kevin Youkilis	.25
317	Brent Dlugach (RC)	.50
318	Aubrey Huff	.40
319	John Maine	.25
320	Pittsburgh Pirates	.25
321	Aramis Ramirez	.25
322	Michael Dunn RC	1.00
323	Shin-Soo Choo	.25
324	Mike Pelfrey	.25
325	Brett Gardner	.25
326	Nick Johnson	.25
327	Henry Rodriguez RC	1.50
328	Joe Nathan	.25
329	Mike Napoli	.25
330	Jamie Moyer	.25
331	Kyle Blanks	.40
332	Ryan Langerhans	.25
333	Travis Snider	.40
334	Wandy Rodriguez	.25
335	Carlos Gonzalez	.40
336	Francisco Rodriguez	.25
337	Mark BuehrleJake Peavy	.40
338	Ryan Zimmerman	.50
339	Michael Bourn	.25
340	Magglio Ordonez	.40
341	Brandon Morrow	.25
342	Daniel Murphy	.25
343	Ricky Romero	.25
344	Homer Bailey	.25
345	Nick Swisher	.40
346	Akinori Iwamura	.25
347	St. Louis Cardinals	.50
348	Julio Borbon	.25
349	Jose Guillen	.25
350	Scott Podsednik	.25
351	Bobby Crosby	.25
352	Ryan Ludwick	.40
353	Brett Cecil	.25
354	Minnesota Twins	.25
355	Ben Zobrist	.25
356	Dan Haren	.40
357	Vernon Wells	.40
358	Skip Schumaker	.25
359	Jose Lopez	.40
360	Vladimir Guerrero	.25
360	Vladimir Guerrero Dice Back/SP	5.00
361	Checklist	.25
362	Brandon Allen (RC)	1.00
363	Joe Mauer	.25
364	Roy Halladay	.50
364	Todd Helton	.25
365	J.J. Hardy	.25
366	CC Sabathia	.50
366	CC Sabathia Green-Yellow Nameplate/SP	50.00
367	Yuniesky Betancourt	.25
368	Placido Polanco	.25
369	Josh Johnson	.40
370	Mark Reynolds	.40
371	Victor Martinez	.40
371	Victor Martinez Dice Back/SP	5.00
372	Ian Stewart	.25
373	Boston Red Sox	.25
374	Brad Hawpe	.25
375	Ricky Nolasco	.25
376	Marco Scutaro	.25
377	Troy Tulowitzki	.50
378	Francisco Liriano	.25
379	Randy Wells	.25
380	Jeff Francoeur	.25
381	Mike Lowell	.25
382	Hunter Pence	.50
383	Tim Lincecum	
384	Matt Cain	1.00
	Scott Kazmir	.40
385	Hideki Matsui	.75
386	Tim Wakefield	.25
387	Jeff Niemann	.40
388	John Smoltz	.50
389	Franklin Gutierrez	.25
390	Matt LaPorta	.25
391	Melvin Mora	.25
392	Jeremy Bonderman	.25
393a	Ryan Braun	.50
393b	Ryan Braun Blue-Orange Nameplate/SP	60.00
394	Emilio Bonifacio	.25
395	Tommy Hanson	1.00
396	Aaron Hill	.40
397	Micah Owings	.25
398	Jack Cust	.25
399	Jason Bartlett	.25
400	Brian McCann	.50
401	Babe Ruth	2.00
402	George Sisler	.50
403	Jackie Robinson	1.00
404	Rogers Hornsby	.50
405	Lou Gehrig	1.50
406	Mickey Mantle	2.50
407	Ty Cobb	1.00
408	Christy Mathewson	.75
409	Walter Johnson	.75
410	Honus Wagner	1.00
411	Andy Pettitte Jorge Posada Derek Jeter Mariano Rivera	1.50
412	Joe Saunders	.25
413	Andrew Miller	.25
414	Alcides Escobar	.25
415	Luke Hochevar	.25
416	Gerardo Parra	.25
417	Garrett Atkins	.25
418	Jim Thome	.40
419	Michael Saunders	.25
420	Justin Morneau	.50
421	Dustin Pedroia	.25
422	Dioner Navarro	.25
423	Checklist	.25
424	Chien-Ming Wang	.50
425	Marcus Thames	.25
426	David Price/SP	6.00
427a	David Wright/SP	8.00
427b	David Wright Green-Yellow Nameplate/SP	50.00
428	Tommy Manzella/ SP (RC)	5.00
429a	Tim Lincecum/SP	10.00
429b	Tim Lincecum Dice Back/SP	5.00
430	Ken Griffey Jr./SP	8.00
431	Justin Masterson/SP	5.00
432	Jermaine Dye/SP	5.00
433	Casey McGehee/SP	5.00
434	Brett Anderson/SP	6.00
435	Matt Garza/SP	5.00
436	Miguel Tejada/SP	5.00
437	Checklist/SP	5.00
438	Kurt Suzuki/SP	5.00
439	Evan Longoria/SP	10.00
440	Edinson Volquez/SP	5.00
441	Doug Fister/SP	5.00
442	Carlos Delgado/SP	5.00
443	Philadelphia Phillies/SP	5.00
444	Justin Duchscherer/SP	5.00
445	Chris Volstad/SP	5.00
446	Freddy Sanchez/SP	5.00
447	Carlos Lee/SP	5.00
448	Carlos Guillen/SP	5.00
449	Hank Blalock/SP	6.00
450	Ubaldo Jimenez/SP	6.00
451	Derek Jeter Jason Bartlett/SP	10.00
452	Cliff Pennington/SP	5.00
453	Miguel Montero/SP	5.00
454	Corey Hart/SP	5.00
455	Bronson Arroyo/SP	5.00
456	Carlos Gomez/SP	5.00
457	J.D. Drew/SP	5.00
458	Kenshin Kawakami/SP	6.00
459	Neftali Feliz/SP	5.00
460	Bobby Abreu/SP	5.00
461	Joe Maddon/SP	5.00
462	Charlie Manuel/SP	5.00
463a	Mark Teixeira/SP	8.00
463b	Atlanta Braves/SP	40.00
464	Albert Pujols/SP	10.00
465	Aaron Hill/SP	5.00
466	Chase Utley/SP	8.00
467	Michael Young/SP	5.00
468	David Wright/SP	8.00
469	Derek Jeter/SP	12.00
470	Hanley Ramirez/SP	8.00
471	Jason Giambi/SP	5.00
472	Ichiro Suzuki/SP	8.00
473	Miguel Tejada/SP	5.00
474	Alex Rodriguez/SP	10.00
475	Justin Morneau/SP	6.00
476	Dustin Pedroia/SP	6.00
477	Albert Pujols/SP	12.00
478	Jimmy Rollins/SP	5.00
479	Ryan Howard/SP	10.00
480	Cole Hamels/SP	6.00
481	Manny Ramirez/SP	5.00
482	Jermaine Dye/SP	5.00
483	Mariano Rivera/SP	8.00
484	Roy Oswalt/SP	6.00
485	Matt Garza/SP	5.00

486	Derek Jeter/SP	12.00
487	Ichiro Suzuki/SP	8.00
488	Raul Ibanez/SP	6.00
489	Josh Hamilton/SP	6.00
490	Shane Victorino/SP	6.00
491	Jason Bay/SP	6.00
492	Ryan Braun/SP	8.00
493	Joe Mauer/SP	8.00
494	Yadier Molina/SP	5.000
495	Roy Halladay/SP	8.00
496	Tim Lincecum/SP	10.00
497	Mark Buehrle/SP	6.00
498	Johan Santana/SP	6.00
499	Mariano Rivera/SP	6.00
500	Francisco Rodriguez/SP	6.00

1961 Buybacks
See 1961 Topps pricing.

Baseball Flashbacks
Common Player: 1.00
Inserted 1:12

1	Roger Maris	2.50
2	Warren Spahn	1.50
3	Whitey Ford	1.50
4	Frank Robinson	2.00
5	Whitey Ford	1.50
6	Candlestick Park	1.00
7	Carl Yastrzemski	2.50
8	Luis Aparicio	1.00
9	Al Kaline	2.00
10	Angels/Senators	1.00

Chase 61 Dual Relic
Production 5
No Pricing

Chase 61 Triple Relic
Production 5
No Pricing

Chrome
Common Player: 3.00
Production 1,961 Sets
Refractor: 2X
Production 561 Sets
Black Refractor: 6-8X
Production 61 Sets

C1	Albert Pujols	10.00
C2	Joe Mauer	5.00
C3	Rajai Davis	3.00
C4	Adam Wainwright	4.00
C5	Grady Sizemore	4.00
C6	Alex Rodriguez	8.00
C7	Cole Hamels	5.00
C8	Matt Kemp	5.00
C9	Chris Tillman	3.00
C10	Reid Gorecki	3.00
C11	Chris Carpenter	4.00
C12	Jason Bay	4.00
C13	Gordon Beckham	6.00
C14	Curtis Granderson	4.00
C15	Daniel McCutchen	3.00
C16	Pablo Sandoval	4.00
C17	Jake Peavy	4.00
C18	Ryan Church	3.00
C19	Nick Markakis	4.000
C20	Josh Beckett	4.00
C21	Matt Cain	4.00
C22	Nate McLouth	3.00
C23	J.A. Happ	4.00
C24	Justin Upton	4.00
C25	Rick Porcello	5.00
C26	Mark Teixeira	5.00
C27	Raul Ibanez	4.00
C28	Zack Greinke	5.00
C29	Nolan Reimold	4.00
C30	Jimmy Rollins	5.00
C31	Jorge Posada	4.00
C32	Clayton Kershaw	5.00
C33	Buster Posey	10.00
C34	Adam Dunn	3.00
C35	Chipper Jones	6.00
C36	John Lackey	3.00
C37	Daniel Hudson	3.00
C38	Jacoby Ellsbury	5.00
C39	Mariano Rivera	6.00
C40	Jair Jurrjens	3.00
C41	Prince Fielder	6.00
C42	Shane Victorino	4.00
C43	Mark Buehrle	3.00
C44	Madison Bumgarner	6.00
C45	Yunel Escobar	3.00
C46	Chris Coghlan	4.00
C47	Justin Verlander	4.00
C48	Michael Brantley	4.00
C49	Matt Holliday	5.00
C50	Chase Utley	6.00
C51	Adam Jones	5.00
C52	Kendry Morales	3.00
C53	Denard Span	3.00
C54	Nyjer Morgan	3.00
C55	Adrian Gonzalez	6.00
C56	Daisuke Matsuzaka	4.00
C57	Joey Votto	6.00
C58	Jered Weaver	3.00
C59	Lance Berkman	4.00
C60	Andre Ethier	6.00
C61	Mat Latos	3.00
C62	Derek Jeter	12.00
C63	Johan Santana	5.00
C64	Max Scherzer	4.00
C65	Ian Kinsler	4.00
C66	Elvis Andrus	5.00
C67	Adam Lind	4.00
C68	Ichiro Suzuki	8.00
C69	Ryan Howard	6.00
C70	Dan Uggla	4.00
C71	Cliff Lee	4.00
C72	Andrew McCutchen	5.00
C73	Nelson Cruz	4.00
C74	Stephen Drew	4.00
C75	Koji Uehara	4.00
C76	Roy Halladay	5.00
C77	Felix Hernandez	5.00
C78	Josh Hamilton	5.00
C79	Hanley Ramirez	6.00
C80	Kevin Youkilis	3.00
C81	Kyle Blanks	3.00
C82	Ryan Zimmerman	4.00
C83	Ricky Romero	4.00
C84	Julio Borbon	3.00
C85	Ben Zobrist	3.00
C86	Vladimir Guerrero	4.00
C87	CC Sabathia	5.00
C88	Josh Johnson	4.00
C89	Mark Reynolds	4.00
C90	Troy Tulowitzki	6.00
C91	Hunter Pence	4.00
C92	Ryan Braun	6.00
C93	Tommy Hanson	6.00
C94	Aaron Hill	3.00
C95	Brian McCann	4.00
C96	David Wright	5.00
C97	Tim Lincecum	5.00
C98	Evan Longoria	4.00
C99	Ubaldo Jimenez	3.00
C100	Neftali Feliz	4.00

Clubhouse Collection Dual Relic Autos.
Production 10 Sets
No Pricing

Clubhouse Collection Dual Relics
Production 61 Sets

AR	Luis Aparicio / Alexei Ramirez	100.00
BM	Brooks Robinson / Nick Markakis	100.00
MR	Roger Maris / Alex Rodriguez	200.00
MT	Mickey Mantle / Mark Teixeira	180.00
YE	Carl Yastrzemski / Jacoby Ellsbury	150.00

Clubhouse Collection Relic Autos.
Production 25 Sets

BG	Bob Gibson	125.00
DP	Dustin Pedroia	150.00
FR	Frank Robinson	100.00
GB	Gordon Beckham	150.00
RH	Ryan Howard	125.00

Clubhouse Collection Relics
Common Player: 4.00
Inserted 1:29

AE	Andre Ethier	6.00
AK	Adam Kennedy	4.00
AL	Adam Lind	6.00
AP	Albert Pujols	20.00
AR	Aramis Ramirez	6.00
AW	Adam Wainwright	6.00
BJ	Bobby Jenks	4.00
BW	Billy Wagner	4.00
CB	Clay Buchholz	4.00
CG	Cristian Guzman	4.00
CH	Cole Hamels	6.00
CM	Carlos Marmol	4.00
CS	CC Sabathia	4.00
CZ	Carlos Zambrano	4.00
DH	Dan Haren	4.00
DN	Dioner Navarro	4.00
DO	David Ortiz	6.00
DU	Dan Uggla	4.00
EL	Evan Longoria	8.00
EV	Edinson Volquez	4.00
GB	Gordon Beckham	15.00
GS	Grady Sizemore	6.00
HK	Hiroki Kuroda	4.00
JB	Jason Bulger	4.00
JC	Jose Contreras	4.00
JD	Jermaine Dye	4.00
JF	Jeff Francis	4.00
JL	James Loney	4.00
JV	Joey Votto	6.00
JW	Jered Weaver	4.00
KJ	Kenji Johjima	4.00
KM	Kendry Morales	4.00
KW	Kerry Wood	4.00
LB	Lance Berkman	6.00
MB	Mark Buehrle	4.00
MK	Matt Kemp	8.00
MT	Miguel Tejada	4.00
MY	Michael Young	4.00
NM	Nate McLouth	4.00
PK	Paul Konerko	4.00
PS	Pablo Sandoval	8.00
RB	Rocco Baldelli	4.00
RD	Ryan Dempster	4.00
RH	Ryan Howard	8.00
RL	Ryan Ludwick	4.00
RM	Russell Martin/SP	15.00
VG	Vladimir Guerrero	6.00
AJP	A.J. Pierzynski	4.00
ARA	Alexei Ramirez	6.00
BWE	Brandon Webb	6.00
CHE	Chase Headley	4.00
HCK	Hong-Chih Kuo	4.00
JCR	Joe Crede	4.00
KMI	Kevin Millwood	4.00

Cut Signatures
Production One Set
No Pricing

Flashback Autographs
Production 25 Sets

BG	Bob Gibson	150.00
JM	Juan Marichal	80.00
LA	Luis Aparicio	90.00
RS	Red Schoendienst	150.00

Flashback Stadium Dual Relics
Production 10 Sets

Flashback Stadium Relic Autos.
Production 25 Sets

JM	Juan Marichal	80.00
LA	Luis Aparicio	100.00

Flashback Stadium Relics
Common Player: 10.00
Inserted 1:475

AK	Al Kaline	15.00
BG	Bob Gibson	30.00
EB	Ernie Banks	25.00
JP	Jim Piersall	10.00
LA	Luis Aparicio	40.00
MM	Mickey Mantle	50.00
RM	Roger Maris	40.00
RS	Brooks Robinson	15.00
SM	Stan Musial	30.00

Framed Buyback Stamps
Production One Set
No Pricing

Framed Dual Stamps
Production 50 Sets

AH	Bronson Arroyo / Luke Hochevar	10.00
AP	Garret Anderson / Andy Pettitte	15.00
BA	Casey Blake / Elvis Andrus	15.00
BF	Ryan Braun / Gavin Floyd	20.00
BL	Carlos Beltran / John Lackey	15.00
BU	Kyle Blanks / B.J. Upton	15.00
CE	Michael Cuddyer / Andre Ethier	15.00
CG	Johnny Cueto / Zack Greinke	15.00
CH1	Miguel Cabrera / Felix Hernandez	20.00
CH2	Chris Coghlan / Felix Hernandez	15.00
CK	Matt Cain / Paul Konerko	15.00
CL	Melky Cabrera / Mat Latos	10.00
CM	Orlando Cabrera / Yadier Molina	20.00
CR	Shin-Soo Choo / Francisco Rodriguez	15.00
DA	Adam Dunn / Bobby Abreu	15.00
DF	Zach Duke / Tyler Flowers	25.00
DG	David DeJesus / Reid Gorecki	10.00
DI	Johnny Damon / Raul Ibanez	15.00
DR	Rajai Davis / Mark Reynolds	15.00
DY	Ryan Dempster / Michael Young	15.00
EC	Andre Ethier / Robinson Cano	20.00
FB	Pedro Feliz / Adrian Beltre	15.00
FG	Jeff Francoeur / Carlos Guillen	10.00
GB	Cristian Guzman / Chad Billingsley	15.00
GC	Adrian Gonzalez / Carl Crawford	15.00
GF	Matt Garza / Prince Fielder	25.00
GG	Curtis Granderson / Adrian Gonzalez	15.00
GH	Carlos Guillen / Rich Harden	10.00
GR	Zack Greinke / Hanley Ramirez	20.00
GS	Reid Gorecki / Joe Saunders	25.00
GW	Vladimir Guerrero / David Wright	15.00
HA	Orlando Hudson / Erick Aybar	10.00
HB	Rich Harden / Marlon Byrd	10.00
HC	J.A. Happ / Miguel Cabrera	15.00
HM	Matt Holliday / Justin Morneau	20.00
HR	Aaron Hill / Jimmy Rollins	20.00
HU	Roy Halladay / Justin Upton	20.00
IL	Raul Ibanez / Jon Lester	15.00
IU	Ian Kinsler / Chase Utley	30.00
JL	Jair Jurrjens / Adam Lind	20.00
JM	Josh Johnson / Victor Martinez	10.00
JN	Garrett Jones / Jeff Niemann	15.00
JO	Ubaldo Jimenez / Magglio Ordonez	15.00
JZ	Adam Jones / Ryan Zimmerman	15.00
KA	Howie Kendrick / Bronson Arroyo	15.00
KD	Jason Kubel / Stephen Drew	15.00
KJ	Paul Konerko / Ubaldo Jimenez	15.00
KK	Matt Kemp / Scott Kazmir	20.00
KM	Scott Kazmir / Nate McLouth	15.00
KP	Hiroki Kuroda / Chris Pettit	10.00
KQ	Kenshin Kawakami / Carlos Quentin	10.00
KR	Clayton Kershaw / Alexi Ramirez	15.00
LC	Derek Lowe / Orlando Cabrera	15.00
LG	Tim Lincecum / Matt Garza	30.00
LL	Adam Lind / Felipe Lopez	15.00
LM	Cliff Lee / Hideki Matsui	15.00
LT	Mat Latos / Chris Tillman	15.00
LW	Jon Lester / Jayson Werth	20.00
LZ	Jose Lopez / Jordan Zimmermann	15.00
MB	Kevin Millwood / Casey Blake	10.00
MD	Yadier Molina / David DeJesus	15.00
ME	Nate McLouth / Jacoby Ellsbury	15.00
MG	Miguel Montero / Ken Griffey Jr.	25.00
ML	Hideki Matsui / James Loney	15.00
MM	Kendry Morales / Andrew McCutchen	15.00
MU	Justin Morneau / Dan Uggla	15.00
MV	Andrew McCutchen / Justin Verlander	25.00
NF	Ricky Nolasco / Scott Feldman	15.00
NG	Jeff Niemann / Cristian Guzman	10.00
NL	Joe Nathan / Derek Lowe	10.00
OA	Roy Oswalt / Brett Anderson	15.00
OO	Magglio Ordonez / Roy Oswalt	15.00
OW	David Ortiz / Brandon Webb	15.00
PB	Dustin Pedroia / Carlos Beltran	15.00
PF	Andy Pettitte / Pedro Feliz	15.00
PG	Hunter Pence / Franklin Gutierrez	15.00
PR	Mike Pelfrey / Dustin Richardson	15.00
PS	David Price / Max Scherzer	20.00
QP	Carlos Quentin / Gerardo Parra	15.00
RB	Manny Ramirez / Gordon Beckham	25.00
RJ	Hanley Ramirez / Adam Jones	20.00
RL	Alex Rodriguez / Tim Lincecum	25.00
RM	Dustin Richardson / Brian McCann	15.00
RR	Jose Reyes / Alex Rodriguez	30.00
RT	Mark Reynolds / Mark Teixeira	15.00
SB	Ichiro Suzuki / Ryan Braun	40.00
SC	Grady Sizemore / Johnny Cueto	15.00
SD	Johan Santana / Rajai Davis	20.00
SG	Pablo Sandoval / Vladimir Guerrero	15.00
SJ	Denard Span / Jair Jurrjens	15.00
SK	Kurt Suzuki / Clayton Kershaw	15.00
SY	Nick Swisher / Eric Young Jr.	15.00
TD	Ryan Theriot / Johnny Damon	15.00
TS	Troy Tulowitzki / Grady Sizemore	20.00
TZ	Chris Tillman / Carlos Zambrano	15.00
UC	Koji Uehara / Jorge Cantu	15.00
UH	Dan Uggla / Torii Hunter	15.00
UK	Justin Upton / Ian Kinsler	20.00
UM	B.J. Upton / Miguel Montero	15.00
UY	Chase Utley / Kevin Youkilis	25.00
VH	Justin Verlander / Ryan Howard	30.00
VM	Joey Votto / Nick Markakis	20.00
VR	Shane Victorino / Brian Roberts	15.00
WF	Jered Weaver / Dexter Fowler	15.00
WL	Jayson Werth / Jose Lopez	15.00
WR	Brandon Webb / Nolan Reimold	15.00
YC	Eric Young Jr. / Melky Cabrera	15.00
YH	Michael Young / Matt Holliday	15.00
YT	Kevin Youkilis / Troy Tulowitzki	20.00
ZL	Ryan Zimmerman / Evan Longoria	20.00
ZO	Carlos Zambrano / David Ortiz	15.00
ZU	Jordan Zimmermann / Koji Uehara	15.00
AR1	Elvis Andrus / Colby Rasmus	15.00
AR2	Erick Aybar / Jorge De La Rosa	15.00
AV1	Bobby Abreu / Shane Victorino	15.00
AV2	Brandon Allen / Will Venable	15.00
BB1	Jason Bay / Lance Berkman	15.00
BB2	Adrian Beltre / Kyle Blanks	15.00
BB3	Chad Billingsley / Nick Blackburn	15.00
BH1	Scott Baker / Dan Haren	15.00
BH2	Gordon Beckham / Tommy Hanson	30.00
BM1	Jason Bartlett / Daniel McCutchen	15.00
BM2	Lance Berkman / Daisuke Matsuzaka	15.00
BP1	Josh Beckett / Hunter Pence	15.00
BP2	A.J. Burnett / Joel Pineiro	15.00
BV1	Nick Blackburn / Joey Votto	15.00
BV2	Billy Butler / Javier Vazquez	10.00
CD1	Robinson Cano / Carlos Delgado	15.00
CD2	Carl Crawford / Ryan Dempster	10.00
DB1	Jorge De La Rosa / Jason Bartlett	10.00
DB2	Carlos Delgado / Billy Butler	15.00
DS1	Mark Derosa / James Shields	10.00
DS2	Stephen Drew / CC Sabathia	15.00
EP1	Jacoby Ellsbury / Buster Posey	50.00
EP2	Yunel Escobar / Rick Porcello	15.00
FM1	Prince Fielder / Kendry Morales	20.00
FM2	Tyler Flowers / Daniel Murphy	15.00
FS1	Gavin Floyd / Alfonso Soriano	15.00
FS2	Dexter Fowler / Denard Span	15.00
FT1	Scott Feldman / Ryan Theriot	15.00
FT2	Chone Figgins / Miguel Tejada	15.00
GD1	Ken Griffey Jr. / Zach Duke	25.00
GD2	Franklin Gutierrez / Mark Derosa	15.00
HF1	Tommy Hanson / Chone Figgins	25.00
HF2	Luke Hochevar / Jeff Francoeur	10.00
HH1	Brad Hawpe / Daniel Hudson	15.00
HH2	Felix Hernandez / Orlando Hudson	15.00
HJ1	Josh Hamilton / Chipper Jones	15.00
HJ2	Daniel Hudson / Nick Johnson	15.00
HK1	Cole Hamels / Jason Kubel	15.00
HK2	Todd Helton / Howie Kendrick	15.00
HK3	Torii Hunter Matt Kemp	15.00
HP1	Dan Haren / Placido Polanco	15.00
HP2	Ryan Howard / Dustin Pedroia	30.00
JS1	Derek Jeter / Pablo Sandoval	50.00
JS2	Nick Johnson / Nick Swisher	15.00
JS3	Chipper Jones / Ichiro Suzuki	50.00
LB1	John Lackey / Jay Bruce	15.00
LB2	Derek Lee / Mark Buehrle	15.00
LB3	Felipe Lopez / A.J. Burnett	15.00
LR1	Evan Longoria / Jose Reyes	35.00
LR2	James Loney / Juan Rivera	15.00
MP1	Nick Markakis / David Price	20.00
MP2	Joe Mauer / Albert Pujols	40.00
MR1	Victor Martinez / Manny Ramirez	15.00
MR2	Daisuke Matsuzaka / Aramis Ramirez	15.00
MR3	Brian McCann / Mariano Rivera	20.00
MR4	Daniel Murphy / Ricky Romero	15.00
MW1	John Maine / Vernon Wells	15.00
MW2	Daniel McCutchen / Jered Weaver	15.00
PA1	Jake Peavy / Garret Anderson	15.00
PA2	Rick Porcello / Brandon Allen	15.00
PC1	Carlos Pena / Matt Cain	15.00
PC2	Joel Pineiro / Shin-Soo Choo	15.00
PJ1	Jorge Posada / Josh Johnson	15.00
PJ2	Albert Pujols / Derek Jeter	100.00
PM1	Chris Pettit / John Maine	15.00
PM2	Placido Polanco / Kevin Millwood	15.00
PP1	Gerardo Parra / Jake Peavy	15.00
PP2	Buster Posey / Jorge Posada	20.00
RH1	Alexi Ramirez / Brad Hawpe	15.00
RH2	Colby Rasmus / J.A. Happ	15.00
RK1	Nolan Reimold / Kenshin Kawakami	15.00
RK2	Ricky Romero / Hiroki Kuroda	15.00
RN1	Juan Rivera / Ricky Nolasco	15.00
RN2	Francisco Rodriguez / Joe Nathan	15.00
RP1	Aramis Ramirez / Carlos Pena	15.00
RP2	Brian Roberts / Mike Pelfrey	15.00
RS1	Mariano Rivera / Johan Santana	20.00
RS2	Jimmy Rollins / Kurt Suzuki	15.00
SH1	Max Scherzer / Aaron Hill	15.00
SH2	James Shields / Cole Hamels	20.00
SH3	Alfonso Soriano / Roy Halladay	20.00
SL1	CC Sabathia / Derek Lee	20.00
SL2	Joe Saunders / Cliff Lee	15.00
TC1	Mark Teixeira / Chris Coghlan	15.00
TC2	Miguel Tejada / Michael Cuddyer	15.00
VB1	Javier Vazquez / Josh Beckett	15.00
VB2	Will Venable / Jason Bay	15.00
WH1	Vernon Wells / Todd Helton	15.00
WH2	David Wright / Josh Hamilton	25.00

Mantle Chase '61
Common Mantle: 8.00
Exclusive in Target packs
Relics: No Pricing
Production 7 Sets
MM1-15 Mickey Mantle 8.00

Maris Chase '61
Common Maris: 8.00
Exclusive in Wal-Mart packs:
Relics: No Pricing
Production 9 Sets
RM1-15 Roger Maris 8.00

New Age Performers
Common Player: 1.50
Inserted 1:15

NA1	Justin Upton	1.50
NA2	Jacoby Ellsbury	1.50
NA3	Gordon Beckham	2.50
NA4	Tommy Hanson	2.50
NA5	Hanley Ramirez	2.00
NA6	Joe Mauer	3.00
NA7	Ichiro Suzuki	3.00
NA8	Derek Jeter	5.00
NA9	Albert Pujols	3.00
NA10	Ryan Howard	3.00
NA11	Zack Greinke	1.50
NA12	Matt Kemp	1.50
NA13	Miguel Cabrera	1.50
NA14	Mark Reynolds	2.00
NA15	Prince Fielder	2.00

News Flashbacks
Common Card: 1.00 Inserted 1:12
NF1 Peace Corps 1.00
NF2 John F. Kennedy

NF3 Ham the Chimp 1.00
NF4 Venera 1 1.00
NF5 Hassan II 1.00
NF6 Twenty Third Amendment 1.00
NF7 Apollo Program Announce 1.00
NF8 Berlin Wall 1.00
NF9 Vostok 1 1.00
NF10 Ty Cobb 2.50

Real One Autographs
Common Auto:
Inserted 1:357
Red Ink: 1.5X
Production 61 Sets

AN Al Neiger 40.00
AR Al Rosen 50.00
BG Bob Gibson 75.00
BH Billy Harrell 30.00
BM Bobby Malkmus 40.00
BP Buster Posey 80.00
CB Collin Balester 25.00
DK Danny Kravitz 35.00
DP Dustin Pedroia 40.00
FR Frank Robinson 80.00
GB Gordon Beckham 100.00
GL Gene Leek 35.00
JB Julio Becquer 30.00
JB Jay Bruce 40.00
JC Jerry Casale 30.00
JD Joe DeMaestri 40.00
JG Joe Ginsberg 50.00
JJ Johnny James 40.00
JR Jim Rivera 40.00
JU Justin Upton 50.00
JW Jim Woods 40.00
LA Luis Aparicio 75.00
MH Matt Holliday 80.00
NG Ned Garver 40.00
RB Reno Bertoia 40.00
RB Rocky Bridges 40.00
RI Raul Ibanez 40.00
RL Ralph Lumenti 40.00
RS R.C. Stevens 40.00
RS Ray Semproch 40.00
RS Red Schoendienst 70.00
TB Tom Borland 30.00
TB Tom Brewer 40.00
TL Ted Lepcio 40.00
WD Walt Dropo 40.00
BHA Bob Hale 40.00

Real One Dual Autographs
Production 25 Sets
GH Bob Gibson/ Matt Holliday 180.00
MP Juan Marichal/ Buster Posey 140.00
RU Frank Robinson/ Justin Upton 225.00

Ruth Chase '61
Common Ruth: 2.00
Relics: No Pricing
Production 3 Sets
BR1-15 Babe Ruth 2.00

Then & Now

Common Duo: 1.50
Inserted 1:15
TN1 Roger Maris / Albert Pujols 4.00
TN2 Roger Maris / Prince Fielder 2.50
TN3 Al Kaline / Joe Mauer 2.50
TN4 Luis Aparicio / Jacoby Ellsbury 2.00
TN5 Mickey Mantle / Adrian Gonzalez 4.00
TN6 Whitey Ford / Zack Greinke 1.50
TN7 Whitey Ford / Justin Verlander 1.50
TN8 Whitey Ford / Felix Hernandez 1.50
TN9 Whitey Ford / Justin Verlander 1.50
TN10 Whitey Ford / Roy Halladay 1.50

2010 Topps National Chicle
Common Player (1-255): .25
Common RC (256-275): .50
Common SP (276-329): 1.00
Inserted 1:4
Hobby Pack (8): 4.00
Hobby Box (24): 80.00

LOU BROCK

1 Albert Pujols 2.00
2 Grady Sizemore .50
3 Ichiro Suzuki 1.50
4 Daisuke Matsuzaka .50
5 Prince Fielder .75
6 Joba Chamberlain .50
7 Joe Mauer .75
8 Jason Bartlett .25
9 Brandon Webb .50
10 Manny Ramirez .50
11 CC Sabathia .50
12 Raul Ibanez .50
13 Dan Uggla .50
14 Mariano Rivera .75
15 Brad Hawpe .25
16 James Loney .50
17 Ken Griffey Jr. 1.00
18 Josh Johnson .50
19 Jay Bruce .50
20 David DeJesus .25
21 J.A. Happ .50
22 Tim Wakefield .50
23 Shane Victorino .50
24 Kevin Kouzmanoff .25
25 Aaron Hill .25
26 Rick Porcello .50
27 Jacoby Ellsbury .75
28 Andrew McCutchen .75
29 Hunter Pence .50
30 Michael Cuddyer .25
31 Jayson Werth .75
32 Andy Pettitte .50
33 Evan Longoria 1.50
34 David Wright 1.00
35 Justin Morneau .50
36 Derek Jeter 2.00
37 Ryan Howard 1.00
38 Russell Martin .25
39 Michael Young .50
40 Johnny Damon .50
41 Carlos Pena .50
42 Robinson Cano .75
43 Ian Kinsler .50
44 Jason Bay .50
45 Adam Lind .50
46 Kevin Youkilis .50
47 Brandon Inge .25
48 Jason Kubel .25
49 Adrian Gonzalez .75
50 David Ortiz .75
51 Joey Votto .75
52 Nick Swisher .50
53 Marco Scutaro .25
54 Yunel Escobar .25
55 Carl Crawford .50
56 B.J. Upton .50
57 Kosuke Fukudome .50
58 Matt Cain .50
59 Wandy Rodriguez .25
60 J.J. Hardy .25
61 Gordon Beckham .75
62 Chad Billingsley .50
63 Aramis Ramirez .25
64 Alex Rodriguez 1.50
65 Clayton Kershaw .75
66 Johan Santana .75
67 Mark Buehrle .25
68 Vladimir Guerrero .50
69 Jose Reyes .50
70 Cliff Lee .50
71 Miguel Cabrera .75
72 Jorge Posada .50
73 Nick Markakis .50
74 Ryan Zimmerman .50
75 Kendry Morales .50
76 Victor Martinez .50
77 Carlos Lee .50
78 Bobby Abreu .50
79 Russell Branyan .25
80 Jermaine Dye .50
81 Hideki Matsui .75
82 Josh Beckett .50
83 Brian Roberts .50
84 Hanley Ramirez .75
85 Justin Verlander .50
86 Adam Jones .50
87 Ted Lilly .25
88 Jorge Cantu .25
89 Chone Figgins .25
90 Miguel Tejada .50
91 Asdrubal Cabrera .25
92 Cole Hamels .50
93 Roy Oswalt .50
94 Nyjer Morgan .25
95 Ryan Braun 1.00
96 Derrek Lee .50
97 Matt Kemp .50
98 Troy Tulowitzki .50
99 Alexei Ramirez .25
100 Adam Dunn .50
101 Torii Hunter .50
102 Adam Wainwright .50
103 Pablo Sandoval .50
104 Justin Upton .50
105 Mark Reynolds .50
106 Todd Helton .50
107 Mark Teixeira .50
108 Josh Hamilton .50
109 Nelson Cruz .50
110 Curtis Granderson .50
111 Paul Konerko .50
112 Dustin Pedroia .75
113 Billy Butler .50
114 Felix Hernandez .50
115 Lance Berkman .50
116 Carlos Beltran .50
117 Jason Marquis .25
118 Ubaldo Jimenez .50
119 Jose Lopez .25
120 Tommy Hanson .75
121 Yovani Gallardo .50
122 Roy Halladay .75
123 Brian McCann .50
124 Carlos Zambrano .50
125 Luis Castillo .25
126 Melky Cabrera .25
127 Kyle Blanks .50
128 Michael Bowden .25
129 Nolan Reimold .50
130 Elvis Andrus .50
131 David Price .75
132 Bengie Molina .25
133 Andrew Bailey .50
134 Felix Pie .25
135 Chris Carpenter .50
136 Julio Borbon .50
137 Zack Greinke .75
138 Scott Kazmir .25
139 Yadier Molina .50
140 Javier Vazquez .25
141 Brett Anderson .25
142 Colby Rasmus .50
143 Chris Coghlan .50
144 Jhoulys Chacin .25
145 Kurt Suzuki .50
146 Scott Feldman .25
147 Jon Lester .50
148 Chris Young .25
149 Trevor Cahill .25
150 Zach Duke .25
151 Michael Bourn .50
152 Rick Ankiel .50
153 Alex Gordon .50
154 Derek Lowe .50
155 Vernon Wells .50
156 Luke Scott .25
157 Jimmy Rollins .50
158 Stephen Drew .50
159 Kenshin Kawakami .25
160 Jonathan Sanchez .25
161 Juan Pierre .50
162 Jonathan Papelbon .50
163 Erick Aybar .25
164 Andre Ethier .75
165 Jed Lowrie .25
166 Duke Snider .50
167 Ryan Ludwick .25
168 Jake Peavy .50
169 Denard Span .25
170 Jair Jurrjens .25
171 Mike Cameron .25
172 Gavin Floyd .25
173 Jonathan Broxton .25
174 Marlon Byrd .25
175 Dexter Fowler .50
176 Aaron Rowand .25
177 Koji Uehara .25
178 Joel Pineiro .25
179 Carlos Quentin .50
180 Freddy Sanchez .25
181 John Maine .25
182 Neftali Feliz .50
183 Nate McLouth .25
184 Phil Hughes .50
185 Travis Snider .50
186 Alfonso Soriano .50
187 Joe Saunders .25
188 Rich Harden .25
189 Mat Gamel .25
190 Orlando Hudson .25
191 Chase Utley .75
192 J.D. Drew .50
193 Marc Rzepczynski .25
194 Tim Lincecum 1.50
195 Alex Rios .50
196 Will Venable .25
197 Dan Haren .25
198 Michael Saunders .25
199 Trevor Crowe .25
200 A.J. Burnett .50
201 Ian Stewart .25
202 Edinson Volquez .25
203 Carlos Gonzalez .50
204 John Danks .25
205 Hank Greenberg .50
206 Johnny Bench .75
207 Luis Aparicio .50
208 Juan Marichal .50
209 Robin Yount .50
210 Jim Palmer .50
211 Ozzie Smith 1.00
212 Paul Molitor .75
213 Warren Spahn .50
214 Orlando Cepeda .50
215 Bob Gibson .75
216 Bob Gibson .75
217 Frank Robinson .50
218 Carlton Fisk .50
219 Eddie Murray .75
220 Dale Murphy .50
221 Dennis Eckersley .50
222 Lou Brock .50
223 Carl Yastrzemski .50
224 Al Kaline .75
225 Mike Schmidt 1.00
226 Phil Rizzuto .50
227 Rogers Hornsby .50
228 Pee Wee Reese .50
229 Lou Gehrig 1.50
230 Jimmie Foxx .50
231 Honus Wagner .75
232 Roy Campanella .75
233 Mel Ott .50
234 Tris Speaker .50
235 Jackie Robinson 1.00
236 George Sisler .50
237 Thurman Munson .50
238 Johnny Mize .50
239 Walter Johnson .75
240 Cy Young .75
241 Christy Mathewson .75
242 Mickey Mantle 2.50
243 Stan Musial 1.00
244 Eddie Mathews .75
245 Whitey Ford .50
246 Willie McCovey .50
247 Reggie Jackson .50
248 Tom Seaver .50
249 Nolan Ryan 2.50
250 Joe Morgan .25
251 Richie Ashburn .50
252 Duke Snider .50
253 Ryne Sandberg 1.50
254 Ernie Banks .75
255 Babe Ruth 2.00
256 Tyler Flowers RC .50
257 Madison Bumgarner RC 3.00
258 Gordon Beckham .50
259 Henry Rodriguez RC 1.00
260 Drew Stubbs RC .50
261 Kevin Richardson RC 1.00
262 Reid Gorecki RC 1.00
263 Eric Young Jr. (RC) .50
264 Josh Thole RC 1.00
265 Neil Walker (RC) .50
266 Carlos Carrasco (RC) 1.50
267 Tobi Stoner RC 1.00
268 Luis Durango (RC) .50
269 Tommy Manzella (RC) .50
270 Adam Moore RC .50
271 Brent Dlugach (RC) .50
272 Michael Brantley RC .75
273 Juan Francisco RC 1.00
274 Ian Desmond (RC) .50
275 Buster Posey RC 4.00
276 Babe Ruth/SP 8.00
277 Rogers Hornsby/SP 3.00
278 Pee Wee Reese/SP 3.00
279 Lou Gehrig/SP 3.00
280 Jimmie Foxx/SP 4.00
281 Honus Wagner/SP 4.00
282 Roy Campanella/SP 4.00
283 Mel Ott/SP 4.00
284 Tris Speaker/SP 2.00
285 Jackie Robinson/SP 5.00
286 George Sisler/SP 3.00
287 Ty Cobb/SP 5.00
288 Thurman Munson/SP 4.00
289 Johnny Mize/SP 3.00
290 Walter Johnson/SP 4.00
291 Cy Young/SP 4.00
292 Christy Mathewson/SP 4.00
293 Mickey Mantle/SP 10.00
294 Stan Musial/SP 6.00
295 Eddie Mathews/SP 5.00
296 Ernie Banks/SP 8.00
297 Ryne Sandberg/SP 8.00
298 Joe Morgan/SP 4.00
299 Reggie Jackson/SP 4.00
300 Ian Desmond/SP 3.00
301 Albert Pujols/SP 8.00
302 Ichiro Suzuki/SP 6.00
303 Alex Rodriguez/SP 5.00
304 Ryan Howard/SP 5.00
305 Lance Berkman/SP 4.00
306 Chipper Jones/SP 4.00
307 Manny Ramirez/SP 4.00
308 Dustin Pedroia/SP 5.00
309 Ryan Zimmerman/SP 4.00
310 Joe Mauer/SP 4.00
311 Buster Posey/SP 8.00
312 Tyler Flowers/SP 4.00
313 Madison Bumgarner/SP 5.00
314 Adam Moore/SP 4.00
315 Henry Rodriguez/SP 4.00
316 Drew Stubbs/SP 4.00
317 Kevin Richardson/SP 4.00
318 Reid Gorecki/SP 4.00
319 Eric Young Jr./SP 4.00
320 Josh Thole/SP 4.00
321 Neil Walker/SP 4.00
322 Carlos Carrasco/SP 4.00
323 Tobi Stoner/SP 4.00
324 Matt Carson/SP 4.00
325 Tommy Manzella/SP 4.00
326 Michael Dunn/SP 4.00
327 Brent Dlugach/SP 4.00
328 Michael Brantley/SP 4.00
329 Juan Francisco/SP 4.00

Bazooka Back
Bazooka (1-255): 3-5X
Bazooka RC (256-275): 1-2X
Inserted 1:8
Bazooka (276-329): 1-1.5X
Inserted 1:100

National Chicle Back
Chicle Back (1-255): 2-3X
Chicle Back RC (256-275): 1-1.5X
Inserted 1:4
Chicle Back (276-329): 1X
Inserted 1:50

Umbrella Black Back
Black (1-255): 4-8X
RC's (256-275): 2-4X
Production 25 Sets

Umbrella Red Back
Production One Set
Printing Plates
Production one set per color.

Artist's Proofs Signatures
Production 10 Sets
No Pricing

Autographs

NEIL WALKER

Common Auto.: 8.00
Bazooka RC: 1.25X
Production 99 Sets
National Chicle Back: 1X
Production 199 Sets
Black Back: 1-2X
Production 25 Sets
Red Back 1 of 1's exist

AB Andrew Bailey 10.00
BD Brent Dlugach 8.00
CC Carlos Carrasco 8.00
CR Colby Rasmus B 40.00
CY Carl Yastrzemski 50.00
DS Denard Span 10.00
GB Gordon Beckham 50.00
HR Henry Rodriguez 8.00
ID Ian Desmond 10.00
JB Jason Bartlett 8.00
JF Juan Francisco 10.00
JT Josh Thole 10.00
KU Koji Uehara 10.00
LD Luis Durango 8.00
MB Madison Bumgarner 15.00
NF Neftali Feliz 15.00
NM Nate McLouth 8.00
NW Neil Walker 8.00
PS Pablo Sandoval 20.00
RH Ryan Howard 60.00
RP Rick Porcello 30.00
SM Stan Musial 100.00
TH Tommy Hanson 40.00
TM Tommy Manzella 8.00
TS Tobi Stoner 8.00
DST Drew Stubbs 10.00
MBR Michael Brantley 10.00

Dual Autographs
Production 25 Sets
BK Ryan Braun / Matt Kemp 75.00
CH Miguel Cabrera / Ryan Howard 100.00
LB Evan Longoria / Gordon Beckham 200.00
MY Stan Musial / Carl Yastrzemski 180.00
PP Dustin Pedroia / Jonathan Papelbon 60.00
SG Alfonso Soriano / Vladimir Guerrero 60.00
TP Troy Tulowitzki / Dustin Pedroia 100.00
ZF Ryan Zimmerman / Chone Figgins 50.00

Cabinet
Inserted 1:Box
BR Babe Ruth 10.00
CM Christy Mathewson 5.00
CY Cy Young 5.00
EM Eddie Mathews 5.00
GS George Sisler 5.00
HW Honus Wagner 5.00
JF Jimmie Foxx 5.00
JM Johnny Mize 3.00
JR Jackie Robinson 5.00
LG Lou Gehrig 5.00
MM Mickey Mantle 10.00
MO Mel Ott 5.00
NR Nolan Ryan 5.00
RC Roy Campanella 4.00
RH Rogers Hornsby 4.00
RJ Reggie Jackson 3.00
SM Stan Musial 8.00
TC Ty Cobb 8.00
TM Thurman Munson 5.00
TS Tris Speaker 3.00
WF Whitey Ford 4.00
WJ Walter Johnson 5.00
CYA Carl Yastrzemski 5.00
PWR Pee Wee Reese 3.00
TSE Tom Seaver 4.00

Cabinet Artist Autographs
Production 50 Sets
BR Babe Ruth / Dave Hobrecht 40.00
CM Christy Mathewson / Jeff Zachowski 15.00
CY Cy Young / Monty Sheldon 20.00
EM Eddie Mathews / Paul Lempa 20.00
JF Jimmie Foxx / Monty Sheldon 25.00
JM Johnny Mize / Jason Davies 20.00
JR Jackie Robinson / Brian Kong 30.00
LG Lou Gehrig / Jason Davies 40.00
MM Mickey Mantle / Jason Davies 40.00
MO Mel Ott / Dave Hobrecht 15.00
NR Nolan Ryan / Paul Lempa 40.00
RC Roy Campanella / Monty Sheldon 20.00
RH Rogers Hornsby / Monty Sheldon 20.00
RJ Reggie Jackson / Brian Kong 20.00
SM Stan Musial / Monty Sheldon 20.00
TC Ty Cobb / Dave Hobrecht 20.00
TM Thurman Munson / Paul Lempa 25.00
TS Tris Speaker / Mike Kupka 20.00
WF Whitey Ford / Jason Davies 15.00
WJ Walter Johnson / Mike Kupka 25.00
CYA Carl Yastrzemski / Paul Lempa 15.00
PWR Pee Wee Reese / Mike Kupka 15.00
TSE Tom Seaver / Paul Lempa 20.00

Cowhide
Production One Set

Relics

CARLOS BELTRAN
Game-Used Bat

Common Player: 5.00
Bazooka Back: 1.5X
Production 99 Sets
National Chicle Back: 1.2X
Production 199 Sets
Umbrella Black Back: 1-2X
Production 25 Sets
Umbrella Red Back 1 of 1's exist

AE Andre Ethier 6.00
AP Albert Pujols 15.00
AR Alex Rodriguez 12.00
AS Alfonso Soriano 5.00
BR Babe Ruth 125.00
CB Carlos Beltran 5.00
CJ Chipper Jones 8.00
CR Colby Rasmus 8.00
DM Dale Murphy 8.00
DO David Ortiz 6.00
DP Dustin Pedroia 6.00
EA Elvis Andrus 6.00
EL Evan Longoria 10.00
EM Eddie Murray 8.00
HG Hank Greenberg 20.00
JC Joba Chamberlain 6.00
JH Josh Hamilton 6.00
JM Justin Morneau 6.00
KF Kosuke Fukudome 6.00
LG Lou Gehrig 75.00
MM Mickey Mantle 75.00
MR Manny Ramirez 8.00
MT Mark Teixeira 8.00
NM Nick Markakis 8.00
NR Nolan Ryan 25.00
NS Nick Swisher 5.00
OS Ozzie Smith 8.00
PF Prince Fielder 6.00
PH Phil Hughes 6.00
PM Paul Molitor 8.00
PR Phil Rizzuto 10.00

PS	Pablo Sandoval	6.00
RC	Robinson Cano	8.00
TM	Thurman Munson	15.00
VG	Vladimir Guerrero	6.00
WF	Whitey Ford	12.00
JPA	Jim Palmer	6.00
PWR	Pee Wee Reese	10.00

2010 Topps Opening Day

Complete Set (220): 30.00
Common Player: .15
Pack (7): 1.00
Box (36): 30.00

1	Prince Fielder	.50
2	Derrek Lee	.40
3	Clayton Kershaw	.50
4	Orlando Cabrera	.15
5	Ted Lilly	.15
6	Bobby Abreu	.25
7	Mickey Mantle	2.00
8	Johnny Cueto	.15
9	Dexter Fowler	.15
10	Felipe Lopez	.15
11	Tommy Hanson	.50
12	Cristian Guzman	.15
13	Shane Victorino	.40
14	John Maine	.15
15	Adam Jones	.40
16	Aubrey Huff	.15
17	Victor Martinez	.25
18	Rick Porcello	.25
19	Garret Anderson	.15
20	Josh Johnson	.25
21	Marco Scutaro	.15
22	Howie Kendrick	.15
23	Joey Votto	.50
24	Jorge De La Rosa	.25
25	Zack Greinke	.50
26	Eric Young Jr	.15
27	Billy Butler	.25
28	John Lackey	.25
29	Manny Ramirez	.50
30	CC Sabathia	.50
31	Kyle Blanks	.15
32	David Wright	.75
33	Kevin Millwood	.15
34	Nick Swisher	.25
35	Matt LaPorta	.25
36	Brandon Inge	.15
37	Cole Hamels	.50
38	Adrian Gonzalez	.50
39	Joe Saunders	.15
40	Kenshin Kawakami	.15
41	Tim Lincecum	1.00
42	Ken Griffey Jr.	1.00
43	Ian Kinsler	.40
44	Ivan Rodriguez	.25
45	Carl Crawford	.40
46	Jon Garland	.15
47	Albert Pujols	2.00
48	Daniel Murphy	.15
49	Scott Hairston	.15
50	Justin Masterson	.15
51	Andrew McCutchen	.50
52	Gordon Beckham	.50
53	David DeJesus	.15
54	Jorge Posada	.25
55	Brett Anderson	.25
56	Ichiro Suzuki	1.00
57	Hank Blalock	.15
58	Vladimir Guerrero	.50
59	Cliff Lee	.40
60	Freddy Sanchez	.15
61	Ryan Dempster	.15
62	Adam Wainwright	.40
63	Matt Holliday	.50
64	Chone Figgins	.15
65	Tim Hudson	.25
66	Rich Harden	.15
67	Justin Upton	.25
68	Yunel Escobar	.15
69	Joe Mauer	.25
70	Jeff Niemann	.15
71	Vernon Wells	.25
72	Miguel Tejada	.25
73	Denard Span	.25
74	Brandon Phillips	.25
75	Jason Bay	.25
76	Kendry Morales	.50
77	Josh Hamilton	.50
78	Yovani Gallardo	.25
79	Adam Lind	.40
80	Nick Johnson	.15
81	Coco Crisp	.15
82	Jeff Francoeur	.15
83	Hideki Matsui	.15
84	Will Venable	.15
85	Adrian Beltre	.25
86	Pablo Sandoval	.40
87	Mat Latos	.25
88	James Shields	.25
89	Roy Halladay Error #32	4.00
90	Chris Coghlan	.40
91	Colby Rasmus	.40
92	Alexei Ramirez	.25
93	Josh Beckett	.40
94	Kelly Shoppach	.15
95	Magglio Ordonez	.25
96	Matt Kemp	.40
97	Max Scherzer	.25
98	Curtis Granderson	.25
99	David Price	.50
100	Neftali Feliz	.25
101	Ian Stewart	.25
102	Ricky Romero	.25
103	Barry Zito	.25
104	Lance Berkman	.40
105	Andre Ethier	.50
106	Mark Teixeira	.50
107	Bengie Molina	.15
108	Edwin Jackson	.15
109	Akinori Iwamura	.15
110	Jermaine Dye	.15
111	Jair Jurrjens	.25
112	Stephen Drew	.25
113	Carlos Delgado	.25
114	Mark DeRosa	.15
115	Kurt Suzuki	.15
116	Javier Vazquez	.15
117	Lyle Overbay	.15
118	Orlando Hudson	.15
119	Adam Dunn	.25
120	Kevin Youkilis	.40
121	Ben Zobrist	.15
122	Chase Utley	.50
123	Jack Cust	.15
124	Gerald Laird	.15
125	Elvis Andrus	.25
126	Jason Kubel	.25
127	Scott Kazmir	.15
128	Ryan Doumit	.25
129	Brian McCann	.40
130	Jim Thome	.25
131	Alex Rios	.25
132	Jered Weaver	.25
133	Carlos Lee	.25
134	Mark Buehrle	.25
135	Chipper Jones	.50
136	Robinson Cano	.50
137	Mark Reynolds	.25
138	David Ortiz	.40
139	Carlos Gonzalez	.25
140	Torii Hunter	.25
141	Nick Markakis	.25
142	Jose Reyes	.50
143	Johnny Damon	.25
144	Roy Oswalt	.25
145	Alfonso Soriano	.25
146	Jimmy Rollins	.50
147	Matt Garza	.25
148	Michael Cuddyer	.25
149	Rick Ankiel	.25
150	Miguel Cabrera	.50
151	Mike Napoli	.15
152	Josh Willingham	.25
153	Chris Carpenter	.25
154	Paul Konerko	.25
155	Jake Peavy	.25
156	Nate McLouth	.15
157	Daisuke Matsuzaka	.50
158	Brad Hawpe	.25
159	Johan Santana	.50
160	Grady Sizemore	.40
161	Chad Billingsley	.25
162	Corey Hart	.15
163	A.J. Burnett	.25
164	Kosuke Fukudome	.40
165	Justin Verlander	.40
166	Jayson Werth	.40
167	Matt Cain	.40
168	Carlos Pena	.40
169	Hunter Pence	.25
170	Russell Martin	.25
171	Carlos Quentin	.25
172	Jacoby Ellsbury	.50
173	Todd Helton	.25
174	Derek Jeter	2.00
175	Dan Haren	.40
176	Nelson Cruz	.40
177	Jose Lopez	.25
178	Carlos Zambrano	.25
179	Hanley Ramirez	.75
180	Aaron Hill	.15
181	Ubaldo Jimenez	.50
182	Brian Roberts	.25
183	Jon Lester	.40
184	Ryan Braun	1.00
185	Jay Bruce	.25
186	Aramis Ramirez	.25
187	Dustin Pedroia	.75
188	Troy Tulowitzki	.50
189	Justin Morneau	.40
190	Jorge Cantu	.15
191	Scott Rolen	.25
192	B.J. Upton	.40
193	Yadier Molina	.15
194	Alex Rodriguez	1.50
195	Felix Hernandez	.40
196	Raul Ibanez	.25
197	Travis Snider	.40
198	Brandon Webb	.40
199	Ryan Howard	1.00
200	Michael Young	.15
201	Rajai Davis	.15
202	Ryan Zimmerman	.40
203	Carlos Beltran	.25
204	Evan Longoria	1.00
205	Dan Uggla	.25
206	Brandon Allen (RC)	.50
207	Buster Posey RC	2.50
208	Drew Stubbs RC	.50
209	Madison Bumgarner RC	2.00
210	Reid Gorecki (RC)	.50
211	Wade Davis (RC)	.25
212	Neil Walker (RC)	.25
213	Ian Desmond (RC)	.50
214	Josh Thole RC	.25
215	Chris Pettit RC	.25
216	Daniel McCutchen RC	.25
217	Daniel Hudson RC	.25
218	Michael Brantley RC	.25
219	Tyler Flowers RC	.25
220	Checklist	.15

Blue

Blue (1-220): 2-4X
Production 2010 Sets

Printing Plates

Production one set per color.

Attax

Common Player:
Inserted 1:6

1	Tim Lincecum	2.00
2	Ichiro Suzuki	2.00
3	Miguel Cabrera	.75
4	Ryan Braun	2.00
5	Zack Greinke	1.00
6	Alex Rodriguez	2.50
7	Albert Pujols	3.00
8	Evan Longoria	2.50
9	Roy Halladay	1.00
10	Ryan Howard	2.00
11	Josh Beckett	2.00
12	Hanley Ramirez	2.00
13	Lance Berkman	.75
14	Dan Haren	.50
15	Joe Mauer	1.50
16	Adrian Gonzalez	1.00
17	Vladimir Guerrero	1.00
18	Felix Hernandez	1.00
19	Matt Kemp	1.00
20	Mariano Rivera	1.50
21	Grady Sizemore	1.00
22	Nick Markakis	1.00
23	CC Sabathia	1.00
24	Ian Kinsler	1.00
25	David Wright	2.00

Autographs

Common Player: 8.00
Inserted 1:746

AC	Aaron Cunningham	8.00
CP	Cliff Pennington	10.00
CV	Chris Volstad	10.00
DS	Denard Span	15.00
GP	Gerardo Parra	10.00
MT	Matt Tolbert	15.00
RR	Ricky Romero	15.00
DSC	Daniel Schlereth	12.00

Mascots

Common Mascot: .50

M1	Baxter the Bobcat	.50
M2	Homer the Brave	.50
M3	The Oriole Bird	.50
M4	Wally the Green Monster	.50
M5	Southpaw	.50
M6	Gapper	.50
M7	Slider	.50
M8	Dinger	.50
M9	Paws	.50
M10	Billy the Marlin	.50
M11	Junction Jack	.50
M12	Sluggerrr	.50
M13	Bernie Brewer	.50
M14	TC the Bear	.50
M15	Mr. Met	.50
M16	Stomper	.50
M17	Phillie Phanatic	.50
M18	The Pirate Parrot	.50
M19	The Swinging Friar	.50
M20	Mariner Moose	.50
M21	Fredbird	.50
M22	Raymond	.50
M23	Rangers Captain	.50
M24	ACE	.50
M25	Screech the Eagle	.50

Superstar Celebrations

Common Player: .50

1	Ryan Braun	1.00
2	Mark Buehrle	.50
3	Alex Rodriguez	2.00
4	Ichiro Suzuki	1.50
5	Ryan Zimmerman	.75
6	Colby Rasmus	.50
7	Andre Ethier	.75
8	Michael Young	.50
9	Evan Longoria	2.00
10	Aramis Ramirez	.50

Topps Town Stars

Common Player: .25
Inserted 1:3

1	Vladimir Guerrero	.50
2	Justin Upton	.75
3	Chipper Jones	.50
4	Nick Markakis	.50
5	David Ortiz	.50
6	Alfonso Soriano	.50
7	Jake Peavy	.50
8	Jay Bruce	.50
9	Grady Sizemore	.50
10	Troy Tulowitzki	.50
11	Miguel Cabrera	.50
12	Hanley Ramirez	.75
13	Hunter Pence	.75
14	Zack Greinke	.75
15	Manny Ramirez	.75
16	Prince Fielder	.75
17	Joe Mauer	.75
18	David Wright	1.00
19	Mark Teixeira	1.00
20	Evan Longoria	1.00
21	Ryan Howard	1.00
22	Albert Pujols	2.00
23	Adrian Gonzalez	.50
24	Tim Lincecum	1.00
25	Ichiro Suzuki	1.00

Where'd you go Bazooka Joe?

Common Player:

1	David Wright	1.50
2	Ryan Howard	1.50
3	Miguel Cabrera	.75
4	Albert Pujols	3.00
5	CC Sabathia	.75
6	Prince Fielder	1.00
7	Evan Longoria	1.50
8	Chipper Jones	1.00
9	Grady Sizemore	.50
10	Ian Kinsler	.50

1984 Toronto Blue Jays Fire Safety

TONY FERNANDEZ
1
infielder

This 35-card set was issued in conjuction with the Toronto Sun newspaper and various Ontario area fire departments. The cards feature full-color action photos on the fronts, along with the player name, number and position. Rather than the customary wide white border on front, the Blue Jays fire safety set features bright blue borders. The card backs include brief player biographies and a fire safety tip. The 2-1/2" x 3-1/2" cards were distributed five at a time at two-week intervals during the summer of 1984.

NM/M
Complete Set (35): 6.00
Common Player: .25

1	Tony Fernandez	.30
3	Jimmy Williams	.25
4	Alfredo Griffin	.25
5	Rance Mulliniks	.25
6	Bobby Cox	.50
7	Damaso Garcia	.25
8	John Sullivan	.25
9	Rick Leach	.25
10	Dave Collins	.25
11	George Bell	.40
12	Ernie Whitt	.25
13	Buck Martinez	.25
15	Lloyd Moseby	.25
16	Garth Iorg	.25
17	Kelly Gruber	.25
18	Jim Clancy	.25
23	Mitch Webster	.25
24	Willie Aikens	.25
25	Roy Lee Jackson	.25
26	Willie Upshaw	.25
29	Jimmy Key	.50
31	Jesse Barfield	.25
33	Jim Acker	.25
34	Doyle Alexander	.25
35	Stan Clarke	.25
36	Bryan Clark	.25
37	Dave Stieb	.40
38	Jim Gott	.25
41	Al Widmar	.25
42	Billy Smith	.25
43	Cito Gaston	.25
44	Cliff Johnson	.25
48	Luis Leal	.25
53	Dennis Lamp	.25
---	Team Logo/Checklist	.25

1985 Toronto Blue Jays Fire Safety

JESSE BARFIELD
29
outfielder

The Toronto Blue Jays issued a 35-card fire safety set for the second year in a row in 1985. Cards feature players, coaches, manager, checklist and team picture. The full-color photos are on the card fronts with a blue border. The backs feature player stats and a safety tip. The cards measure 2-1/2" x 3-1/2" and were distributed throughout the Province of Ontario, Canada.

NM/M
Complete Set (36): 5.00
Common Player: .25

1	Tony Fernandez	.30
3	Jimmy Williams	.25
4	Manny Lee	.25
5	Rance Mulliniks	.25
7	Bobby Cox	.40
8	Damaso Garcia	.25
9	John Sullivan	.25
11	George Bell	.30
12	Ernie Whitt	.25
13	Buck Martinez	.25
15	Lloyd Moseby	.25
16	Garth Iorg	.25
17	Kelly Gruber	.25
18	Jim Clancy	.25
22	Jimmy Key	.35
23	Mitch Webster	.25
24	Willie Aikens	.25
25	Len Matuszek	.25
26	Willie Upshaw	.25
28	Lou Thornton	.25
29	Jesse Barfield	.25
30	Ron Musselman	.25
31	Jim Acker	.25
34	Doyle Alexander	.25
36	Bill Caudill	.25
37	Dave Stieb	.30
41	Al Widmar	.25
42	Billy Smith	.25
43	Cito Gaston	.25
44	Jeff Burroughs	.25
45	Gary Lavelle	.25
48	Luis Leal	.25
51	Tom Henke	.30
53	Dennis Lamp	.25
---	Team Logo/Checklist	.25
---	Team Photo/Schedule	.25

1986 Toronto Blue Jays Fire Safety

LLOYD MOSEBY
15
outfielder

This was the third consecutive year the Toronto Blue Jays issued a fire safety set of 36 baseball cards. The cards were given out at many fire stations in Ontario, Canada. The cards are printed in full color and include players and other personel. The set was co-sponsored by the local fire departments, Bubble Yum and the Toronto Star. The cards measure 2-1/2" x 3-1/2".

NM/M
Complete Set (36): 6.00
Common Player: .25

1	Tony Fernandez	.30
3	Jimmy Williams	.25
5	Rance Mulliniks	.25
8	Damaso Garcia	.25
9	John Sullivan	.25
11	George Bell	.30
12	Ernie Whitt	.25
13	Buck Martinez	.25
15	Lloyd Moseby	.25
16	Garth Iorg	.25
17	Kelly Gruber	.25
18	Jim Clancy	.25
22	Jimmy Key	.30
23	Cecil Fielder	2.00
24	John McLaren	.25
25	Steve Davis	.25
26	Willie Upshaw	.25
29	Jesse Barfield	.25
31	Jim Acker	.25
33	Doyle Alexander	.25
36	Bill Caudill	.25
37	Dave Stieb	.30
38	Mark Eichhorn	.25
40	Don Gordon	.25
41	Al Widmar	.25
42	Billy Smith	.25
43	Cito Gaston	.25
44	Cliff Johnson	.25
45	Gary Lavelle	.25
49	Tom Filer	.25
51	Tom Henke	.25
53	Dennis Lamp	.25
54	Jeff Hearron	.25
---	Team Photo	.25
---	10th Anniversary	.25
---	Logo Card	.25

1987 Toronto Blue Jays Fire Safety

JESSE BARFIELD
29
outfielder

For the fourth consecutive year, the Toronto Blue Jays issued a fire safety set of 36 cards. As in 1986, the set was sponsored by the local fire departments and governing agencies, Bubble Yum and the Toronto Star. The card fronts feature a full-color photo surrounded by a white border. The backs carry a fire safety tip and logos of all sponsors, plus player personal data and statistics. Produced on thin stock, cards in the set are the standard 2-1/2" x 3-1/2" size.

NM/M
Complete Set (36): 6.00
Common Player: .25

1	Tony Fernandez	.30
3	Jimmy Williams	.25
5	Rance Mulliniks	.25
8	John Sullivan	.25
9	Rick Leach	.25
10	Mike Sharperson	.25
11	George Bell	.30
12	Ernie Whitt	.25
15	Lloyd Moseby	.25
16	Garth Iorg	.25
17	Kelly Gruber	.25
18	Jim Clancy	.25
19	Fred McGriff	2.00
22	Jimmy Key	.30
23	Cecil Fielder	.50
24	John McLaren	.25
26	Willie Upshaw	.25
29	Jesse Barfield	.25
31	Duane Ward	.25
32	Joe Johnson	.25
35	Jeff Musselman	.25
37	Dave Stieb	.30
38	Mark Eichhorn	.25
40	Rob Ducey	.25
41	Al Widmar	.25
42	Billy Smith	.25
43	Cito Gaston	.25
45	Jose Nunez	.25
47	Gary Lavelle	.25
48	Matt Stark	.25
49	Craig McMurtry	.25
50	Tom Henke	.25
54	Jeff Hearron	.25
55	John Cerutti	.25
---	Logo/Won-Loss Record	.25
---	Team Photo/Checklist	.25

1988 Toronto Blue Jays Fire Safety

PAT BORDERS
catcher
(10)

This 36-card set features action photos on 3-1/2" x 5" cards with white borders. Card numbers (player's uniform #) appear lower-left; team logo lower-right; player's name and position are printed bottom center. Card backs are blue on white and include personal and career info, 1987 and career stats, sponsor logos and a fire safety tip. The set includes 34 player cards, a team photo checklist card and a team logo card with a year-by-year won/loss record. The set was sponsored by the Ontario Fire Chief Association, Ontario's Solicitor General, The Toronto Star and Bubble Yum and was distributed free as part of a community service project. At least some of the cards have been seen in a blank-back version, apparently used to answer fans autograph requests.

		NM/M
Complete Set (36):		5.00
Common Player:		.25
1	Tony Fernandez	.30
2	Nelson Liriano	.25
3	Jimy Williams	.25
4	Manny Lee	.25
5	Rance Mulliniks	.25
6	Silvestre Campusano	.25
7	John McLaren	.25
8	John Sullivan	.25
9	Rick Leach	.25
10	Pat Borders	.30
11	George Bell	.30
12	Ernie Whitt	.25
13	Jeff Musselman	.25
15	Lloyd Moseby	.25
16	Todd Stottlemyre	.75
17	Kelly Gruber	.25
18	Jim Clancy	.25
19	Fred McGriff	.75
21	Juan Beniquez	.25
22	Jimmy Key	.30
23	Cecil Fielder	.30
29	Jesse Barfield	.25
31	Duane Ward	.25
36	David Wells	1.00
37	Dave Stieb	.30
38	Mark Eichhorn	.25
40	Rob Ducey	.25
41	Al Widmar	.25
42	Billy Smith	.25
43	Cito Gaston	.25
46	Mike Flanagan	.25
50	Tom Henke	.25
55	John Cerutti	.25
57	Winston Llenas	.25
---	Team Photo	.25
---	Team Logo	.25

1989 Toronto Blue Jays Fire Safety

The 1989 Blue Jays safety set consists of 36 standard-size cards co-sponsored by the Ontario Association of Fire Chiefs, Oh Henry! candy bars and A&P supermarkets. Card fronts feature color photos with the player's uniform number in large type in the upper left corner. His name and position are to the right above the photo. The Blue Jays "On the Move" logo is centered at the bottom. The backs of the cards include fire safety messages.

		NM/M
Complete Set (36):		6.00
Common Player:		.25
1	Tony Fernandez	.30
2	Nelson Liriano	.25
3	Jimy Williams	.25
4	Manny Lee	.25
5	Rance Mulliniks	.25
6	Silvestre Campusano	.25
7	John McLaren	.25
8	John Sullivan	.25
9	Bob Brenly	.25
10	Pat Borders	.25
11	George Bell	.30
12	Ernie Whitt	.25
13	Jeff Musselman	.25
15	Lloyd Moseby	.25
16	Greg Myers	.25
17	Kelly Gruber	.25
18	Tom Lawless	.25
19	Fred McGriff	.50
22	Jimmy Key	.25
25	Mike Squires	.25
26	Sal Butera	.25
29	Jesse Barfield	.25
30	Todd Stottlemyre	.35

1990 Toronto Blue Jays Fire Safety

19 FRED McGRIFF
Infielder

This 35-card set was co-sponsored by the Ontario Association of Fire Chiefs, The Ministry of the Solicitor General, A & P/Dominion, Oh Henry, and the Toronto Blue Jays. The card fronts feature full-color photos on white stock and display a special Blue Jays fan club logo in the upper left corner. The flip sides feature biographical information, statistics, and a fire fact. The cards are checklisted here by uniform number.

		NM/M
Complete Set (35):		6.00
Common Player:		.25
1	Tony Fernandez	.30
2	Nelson Liriano	.25
3	Mookie Wilson	.25
4	Manny Lee	.25
5	Rance Mulliniks	.25
7	John McLaren	.25
8	John Sullivan	.25
9	John Olerud	2.00
10	Pat Borders	.25
11	George Bell	.30
12	Gene Tenace	.25
18	Tom Lawless	.25
19	Fred McGriff	.50
21	Greg Myers	.25
22	Jimmy Key	.30
23	Alex Sanchez	.25
24	Glenallen Hill	.25
25	Mike Squires	.25
26	Ozzie Virgil	.25
27	Willie Blair	.25
28	Al Leiter	.30
30	Todd Stottlemyre	.25
31	Duane Ward	.25
34	Jim Acker	.25
36	David Wells	.50
37	Dave Stieb	.30
39	Paul Kilgus	.25
42	Galen Cisco	.25
43	Cito Gaston	.25
44	Frank Wills	.25
47	Junior Felix	.25
50	Tom Henke	.25
55	John Cerutti	.25
---	Skydome/Checklist	.25
---	Logo/Schedule	.25

1991 Toronto Blue Jays Fire Safety

29 JOE CARTER
Outfielder

The Blue Jays played host to the 1991 All-Star Game and the team's annual fire safety set prominently featured that honor. A head-

ercard with the Jays All-Star logo was included in the set and each card carried the logo in full color on the front. The 2-1/2" x 3-1/2" cards have a color action photo at top which bleeds off the top and sides. Beneath the photo is a white border with the player's name, position and uniform number. Backs are printed in black-and-white and have a few biographical notes, 1990 and career stats, a Fire Fact safety message and logos of the cards' sponsors.

		NM/M
Complete Set (36):		6.00
Common Player:		.25
3	Mookie Wilson	.25
4	Manuel Lee	.25
5	Rance Mulliniks	.25
6	Mike Squires	.25
7	Rich Hacker	.25
8	John Sullivan	.25
9	John Olerud	.50
10	Pat Borders	.25
12	Roberto Alomar	3.00
14	Kenny Williams	.25
15	Pat Tabler	.25
17	Kelly Gruber	.25
18	Gene Tenace	.25
20	Rob Ducey	.25
21	Greg Myers	.25
22	Jimmy Key	.30
23	Mark Whiten	.25
24	Glenallen Hill	.25
28	Devon White	.35
29	Al Leiter	.30
30	Joe Carter	.50
32	Todd Stottlemyre	.30
31	Duane Ward	.25
34	Jim Acker	.25
35	Denis Boucher	.25
36	David Wells	.45
37	Dave Stieb	.30
42	Galen Cisco	.25
43	Cito Gaston	.25
44	Frank Wills	.25
46	Ken Dayley	.25
50	Tom Henke	.25
56	Hector Torres	.25
88	Rene Gonzales	.25
---	BJ Birdy (Mascot)	.25
---	All-Star Season Header/Checklist Card	.25

1992 Toronto Blue Jays Fire Safety

10 PAT BORDERS
CATCHER

Hidden amid the myriad sponsors' logos on the backs of these cards is a fire safety message. The 2-1/2" x 3-1/2" cards are printed on thin cardboard and feature color player photos on front, along with a red, white and blue "Toronto Blue Jays Fanatic" logo. Fronts also carry uniform numbers, by which the set is checklisted here. Backs are printed in black-and-white with a few biographical details, 1991 and career stats.

		NM/M
Complete Set (36):		8.00
Common Player:		.25
1	Eddie Zosky	.25
2	Manuel Lee	.25
3	Bob Bailor	.25
4	Alfredo Griffin	.25
5	Rance Mulliniks	.25
7	Rich Hacker	.25
8	John Sullivan	.25
9	John Olerud	.50
10	Pat Borders	.25
12	Roberto Alomar	1.00
14	Derek Bell	.25
15	Pat Tabler	.25
17	Kelly Gruber	.25
18	Gene Tenace	.25
20	Rob Ducey	.25
21	Greg Myers	.25
22	Jimmy Key	.35
23	Candy Maldonado	.25
24	Turner Ward	.25

25	Devon White	.30
29	Joe Carter	.35
30	Todd Stottlemyre	.30
31	Duane Ward	.25
32	Dave Winfield	1.50
36	David Wells	.45
37	Dave Stieb	.25
39	Larry Hisle	.25
40	Mike Timlin	.25
42	Galen Cisco	.25
43	Cito Gaston	.25
45	Bob MacDonald	.25
46	Ken Dayley	.25
47	Jack Morris	.25
50	Tom Henke	.25
66	Juan Guzman	.25
---	Checklist	.25

1993 Toronto Blue Jays Fire Safety

The Blue Jays produced a fire safety set for the 10th year in a row in 1993. In the first year of offering the item as a boxed set, the cards feature a full-bleed color photo on the front, with the player's name printed in white over a blue stripe across the top of the card. The Blue Jay's 1992 World Champions logo appears in the upper left corner. Cards are checklisted here by uniform number.

		NM/M
Complete Set (36):		6.00
Common Player:		.25
1	Eddie Zosky	.25
2	Luis Sojo	.25
3	Bob Bailor	.25
4	Alfredo Griffin	.25
5	Domingo Martinez	.25
7	Rich Hacker	.25
8	John Sullivan	.25
9	John Olerud	.40
10	Pat Borders	.25
11	Darnell Coles	.25
12	Roberto Alomar	.75
14	Darrin Jackson	.25
16	Tom Quinlin	.25
18	Gene Tenace	.25
19	Paul Molitor	1.50
22	Dick Schofield	.25
24	Turner Ward	.25
25	Devon White	.30
27	Randy Knorr	.25
28	Al Leiter	.30
29	Joe Carter	.35
30	Todd Stottlemyre	.30
31	Duane Ward	.25
33	Ed Sprague	.25
34	Dave Stewart	.25
39	Larry Hisle	.25
40	Mike Timlin	.25
41	Pat Hentgen	.25
42	Galen Cisco	.25
43	Cito Gaston	.25
46	Ken Davley	.25
47	Jack Morris	.25
48	Mark Eichhorn	.25
24	Danny Cox	.25
66	Juan Guzman	.25
---	World's Champion Trophy/Checklist	.25

2002 Toronto Blue Jays Team Issue

JOE LAWRENCE
INFIELDER

This boxed set was a stadium giveaway. It features current players, coaches and a handful of "alumni." Backs have Major League stats, biographical data and either 2001 highlights or a short biography.

		NM/M
Complete Set (34):		10.00
Common Player:		.35
2	Dave Berg	.35
5	Chris Woodward	.35
6	Joe Lawrence	.35
7	Felipe Lopez	.35
9	Darrin Fletcher	.35
10	Vernon Wells	.50
11	Eric Hinske	.50
14	Carlos Tosca	.35
15	Tom Wilson	.35
19	Cliff Politte	.35
20	Ken Huckaby	.35
21	Esteban Loaiza	.35
23	Jose Cruz Jr.	.35
24	Shannon Stewart	.45
25a	Carlos Delgado	.50
25b	Devon White	.35
26	Cris Carpenter	.35
29	Scott Eyre	.35
32	Roy Halladay	.35
35	Corey Thurman	.35
39	Steve Parris	.35
40	Scott Cassidy	.35
41	Pete Walker	.35
43	Cito Gaston	.35
44	Luke Prokopec	.35
45	Kelvim Escobar	.35
47a	Jack Morris	.35
47b	Gil Patterson	.35
49	Felix Heredia	.35
50	Tom Henke	.35
52	Bruce Walton	.35
53	John Gibbons	.35
55	Brian Butterfield	.35
56	Mike Barnett	.35

1987 Toys "R" Us

JOHN CERUTTI JR.

Marked as a collectors' edition set and titled "Baseball Rookies," the 1987 Toys "R" Us issue was produced by Topps for the toy store chain. The set is comprised of 33 glossy-coated cards, each measuring 2-1/2" x 3-1/2". The card fronts are very colorful, employing nine different colors including deep black borders. The backs, printed in blue and orange, contain career highlights and composite minor and major league statistics. The set was distributed in a specially designed box and sold for $1.99 in retail outlets.

		NM/M
Complete Set (33):		15.00
Common Player:		.10
1	Andy Allanson	.10
2	Paul Assenmacher	.10
3	Scott Bailes	.10
4	Barry Bonds	12.50
5	Jose Canseco	.50
6	John Cerutti	.10
7	Will Clark	.10
8	Kal Daniels	.10
9	Jim Deshaies	.10
10	Mark Eichhorn	.10
11	Ed Hearn	.10
12	Pete Incaviglia	.10
13	Bo Jackson	.50
14	Wally Joyner	.10
15	Charlie Kerfeld	.10
16	Eric King	.10
17	John Kruk	.10
18	Barry Larkin	.10
19	Mike LaValliere	.10
20	Greg Mathews	.10
21	Kevin Mitchell	.10
22	Dan Plesac	.10
23	Bruce Ruffin	.10
24	Ruben Sierra	.10
25	Cory Snyder	.10
26	Kurt Stillwell	.10
27	Dale Sveum	.10
28	Danny Tartabull	.10
29	Andres Thomas	.10

30	Robby Thompson	.10
31	Jim Traber	.10
32	Mitch Williams	.10
33	Todd Worrell	.10

1988 Toys "R" Us Rookies

This 33-card boxed edition was produced by Topps for exclusive distribution at Toys "R" Us stores. The glossy standard-size cards spotlight rookies in both close-ups and action photos on a bright blue background inlaid with yellow. The Toys "R" Us logo frames the top left corner, above a curving white banner that reads "Topps 1988 Collectors' Edition Rookies." A black Topps logo hugs the upper right-hand edge of the photo. The player name, red-lettered on a tube of yellow, frames the bottom. Card backs are horizontal, blue and pink on a bright pink background and include the player name, personal information and career highlights and stats.

		NM/M
Complete Set (33):		3.00
Common Player:		.10
1	Todd Benzinger	.10
2	Bob Brower	.10
3	Jerry Browne	.10
4	DeWayne Buice	.10
5	Ellis Burks	.10
6	Ken Caminiti	.10
7	Casey Candaele	.10
8	Dave Cone	.10
9	Kelly Downs	.10
10	Mike Dunne	.10
11	Ken Gerhart	.10
12	Mike Greenwell	.10
13	Mike Henneman	.10
14	Sam Horn	.10
15	Joe Magrane	.10
16	Fred Manrique	.10
17	John Marzano	.10
18	Fred McGriff	.10
19	Mark McGwire	2.50
20	Jeff Musselman	.10
21	Randy Myers	.10
22	Matt Nokes	.10
23	Al Pedrique	.10
24	Luis Polonia	.10
25	Billy Ripken	.10
26	Benny Santiago	.10
27	Kevin Seitzer	.10
28	John Smiley	.10
29	Mike Stanley	.10
30	Terry Steinbach	.10
31	B.J. Surhoff	.10
32	Bobby Thigpen	.10
33	Devon White	.10

1989 Toys "R" Us Rookies

MARK GRACE

This glossy set of 33 top rookies was produced by Topps for the Toys "R" Us chain and was sold in a special box. Each player's name and position appear below the full-color photo, while the Toys "R" Us logo and Topps 1989 Collector's Edition appear along the top. Major and minor league stats are on the back. The set is numbered alphabetically.

		NM/M
Complete Set (33):		3.00
Common Player:		.10
1	Roberto Alomar	.50
2	Brady Anderson	.10
3	Tim Belcher	.10
4	Damon Berryhill	.10
5	Jay Buhner	.10
6	Sherman Corbett	.10
7	Kevin Elster	.10
8	Cecil Espy	.10
9	Dave Gallagher	.10
10	Ron Gant	.10
11	Paul Gibson	.10
12	Mark Grace	.50
13	Bryan Harvey	.10
14	Darrin Jackson	.10
15	Gregg Jefferies	.10
16	Ron Jones	.10
17	Ricky Jordan	.10
18	Roberto Kelly	.10
19	Al Leiter	.10
20	Jack McDowell	.10
21	Melido Perez	.10
22	Jeff Pico	.10
23	Jody Reed	.10
24	Chris Sabo	.10
25	Nelson Santovenia	.10
26	Mackey Sasser	.10
27	Mike Schooler	.10
28	Gary Sheffield	1.50
29	Pete Smith	.10
30	Pete Stanicek	.10
31	Jeff Treadway	.10
32	Walt Weiss	.10
33	Dave West	.10

1990 Toys "R" Us Rookies

This 33-card set marks the fourth straight year that Topps has produced a set to be sold exclusively at Toys "R" Us stores. The card fronts contain full-color photos of 1989 rookies. The flip sides are horizontal and provide both minor and major league totals. The complete set is packaged in a special box which features a checklist on the back.

		NM/M
Complete Set (33):		3.00
Common Player:		.10
1	Jim Abbott	.10
2	Eric Anthony	.10
3	Joey Belle	.50
4	Andy Benes	.10
5	Greg Briley	.10
6	Kevin Brown	.10
7	Mark Carreon	.10
8	Mike Devereaux	.10
9	Junior Felix	.10
10	Mark Gardner	.10
11	Bob Geren	.10
12	Tom Gordon	.10
13	Ken Griffey Jr.	2.50
14	Pete Harnisch	.10
15	Ken Hill	.10
16	Gregg Jefferies	.10
17	Derek Lilliquist	.10
18	Carlos Martinez	.10
19	Ramon Martinez	.10
20	Bob Milacki	.10
21	Gregg Olson	.10
22	Kenny Rogers	.10
23	Alex Sanchez	.10
24	Gary Sheffield	.10
25	Dwight Smith	.10
26	Billy Spiers	.10
27	Greg Vaughn	.10
28	Robin Ventura	.10
29	Jerome Walton	.10
30	Dave West	.10
31	John Wetteland	.10
32	Craig Worthington	.10
33	Todd Zeile	.10

1991 Toys "R" Us Rookies

Produced by Topps, this 33-card set features young players. The cards are styled much like past Toys "R" Us issues

featuring glossy photos. The backs are printed horizontally and include player information and statistics. This set is the fifth of its kind produced by Topps for Toys "R" Us.

		NM/M
Complete Set (33):		3.00
Common Player:		.10
1	Sandy Alomar, Jr.	.10
2	Kevin Appier	.10
3	Steve Avery	.10
4	Carlos Baerga	.10
5	Alex Cole	.10
6	Pat Combs	.10
7	Delino DeShields	.10
8	Travis Fryman	.10
9	Marquis Grissom	.10
10	Mike Harkey	.10
11	Glenallen Hill	.10
12	Jeff Huson	.10
13	Felix Jose	.10
14	Dave Justice	.50
15	Dana Kiecker	.10
16	Kevin Maas	.10
17	Ben McDonald	.10
18	Brian McRae	.10
19	Kent Mercker	.10
20	Hal Morris	.10
21	Chris Nabholz	.10
22	Tim Naehring	.10
23	Jose Offerman	.10
24	John Olerud	.25
25	Scott Radinsky	.10
26	Bill Sampen	.10
27	Frank Thomas	1.50
28	Randy Tomlin	.10
29	Greg Vaughn	.10
30	Robin Ventura	.10
31	Larry Walker	.50
32	Wally Whitehurst	.10
33	Todd Zeile	.10

1993 Toys "R" Us Topps Stadium Club

Featuring subsets labeled "Young Stars," "Future Stars" and "Rookie Stars," this 100-card set was sold in a plastic replica of a Toys "R" Us store, packaged with a dozen "Master Photos." Similar to regular 1993 Topps Stadium Club cards, the Toys "R" Us version features full-bleed photos on front, highlighted with goil-foil and a color Toys "R" Us logo in one of the upper corners. Backs have a background of a cloud-filled blue sky and green grass. A small player photo is at upper-right. Back information offers a few personal details, 1992 and career stats and a few career highlights. At bottom are the logos of all involved parties. The cards are UV-coated front and back. Each card is designated on the front as "Rookie Star," "Young Star" or "Future Star" in gold foil.

		NM/M
Unopened Set (100+12):		10.00
Unopened Set (100):		6.00
Common Player:		.05
1	Ken Griffey Jr.	1.50
2	Chad Curtis	.05

3	Mike Bordick	.05
4	Ryan Klesko	.05
5	Pat Listach	.05
6	Jim Bullinger	.05
7	Tim Laker	.05
8	Mike Devereaux	.05
9	Kevin Young	.05
10	John Valentin	.05
11	Pat Mahomes	.05
12	Todd Hundley	.05
13	Roberto Alomar	.25
14	David Justice	.25
15	Mike Perez	.05
16	Royce Clayton	.05
17	Ryan Thompson	.05
18	Dave Hollins	.05
19	Brien Taylor	.05
20	Melvin Nieves	.05
21	Rheal Cormier	.05
22	Mike Piazza	1.50
23	Larry Walker	.05
24	Tim Wakefield	.05
25	Tim Costo	.05
26	Pedro Munoz	.05
27	Reggie Sanders	.05
28	Arthur Rhodes	.05
29	Scott Cooper	.05
30	Marquis Grissom	.05
31	Dave Nilsson	.05
32	John Patterson	.05
33	Ivan Rodriguez	.50
34	Andy Stankiewicz	.05
35	Bret Boone	.05
36	Gerald Williams	.05
37	Mike Mussina	.45
38	Henry Rodriguez	.05
39	Chuck Knoblauch	.05
40	Bob Wickman	.05
41	Donovan Osborne	.05
42	Mike Timlin	.05
43	Damion Easley	.05
44	Pedro Astacio	.05
45	David Segui	.05
46	Willie Greene	.05
47	Mike Trombley	.05
48	Bernie Williams	.05
49	Eric Anthony	.05
50	Tim Naehring	.05
51	Carlos Baerga	.05
52	Brady Anderson	.05
53	Mo Vaughn	.05
54	Willie Banks	.05
55	Mark Wohlers	.05
56	Jeff Bagwell	.75
57	Frank Seminara	.05
58	Robin Ventura	.05
59	Alan Embree	.05
60	Rey Sanchez	.05
61	Delino DeShields	.05
62	Todd Van Poppel	.05
63	Eric Karros	.05
64	Gary Sheffield	.35
65	Dan Wilson	.05
66	Frank Thomas	.75
67	Tim Salmon	.05
68	Dan Smith	.05
69	Kenny Lofton	.05
70	Carlos Garcia	.05
71	Scott Livingstone	.05
72	Sam Militello	.05
73	Juan Guzman	.05
74	Greg Colbrunn	.05
75	David Hulse	.05
76	Rusty Meacham	.05
77	Dave Fleming	.05
78	Rene Arocha	.05
79	Derrick May	.05
80	Cal Eldred	.05
81	Bernard Gilkey	.05
82	Deion Sanders	.05
83	Reggie Jefferson	.05
84	Jeff Kent	.05
85	Juan Gonzalez	.35
86	Bill Ashley	.05
87	Travis Fryman	.05
88	Roberto Hernandez	.05
89	Hipolito Pichardo	.05
90	Wil Cordero	.05
91	John Jaha	.05
92	Javy Lopez	.05
93	Derek Bell	.05
94	Jeff Juden	.05
95	Steve Avery	.05
96	Moises Alou	.05
97	Brian Jordan	.05
98	Brian Williams	.05
99	Bob Zupcic	.05
100	Ray Lankford	.05

Master Photos

Each boxed set of Toys "R" Us Stadium Club cards comes with a set of 12 Master Photos. Similar to the regular 1993 S.C. Master Photos, they feature at center a larger 2-3/4" x 3-3/4", uncropped version of the photo used on the Toys "R" Us card. A gold holographic box on the photo delineates the dimensions of the regular card, while another separates the photo from the 5" by 7" white background. Topps, Toys "R" Us, and Master Photo logos appear at

the top of the card. Blank white backs have a few logos and copyrights printed in black.

		NM/M
Complete Set (12):		4.00
Common Player:		.25
(1)	Willie Greene	.25
(2)	Frank Thomas	1.00
(3)	Chuck Knoblauch	.25
(4)	Marquis Grissom	.25
(5)	Scott Livingstone	.25
(6)	Ken Griffey Jr.	2.00
(7)	Carlos Baerga	.25
(8)	Ivan Rodriguez	.75
(9)	Moises Alou	.25
(10)	Sam Militello	.25
(11)	Eric Anthony	.25
(12)	Gary Sheffield	.50

Ty Cobb

This special gold-foil bordered card was available exclusively at TRU stores as part of a package of 65 plastic sheets sold by Megacards. The card is in the design of the contemporary Conlon Collection issue from Megacards and features on its front the classic photo of Cobb sliding into base. On the back, Conlon describes how he came to take the photo.

		NM/M
Ty Cobb		4.00

1992 Triple Play Previews

To introduce its base-brand Triple Play set in 1992, Donruss issued these preview cards. The format and photos on the previews are exactly like the issued versions; backs, however, differ in the numbering "X of 8" and the appearance of the word "PREVIEW" between the MLBPA and MLB logos at bottom.

		NM/M
Complete Set (8):		25.00
Common Player:		1.00
1	Ken Griffey Jr.	9.00
2	Darryl Strawberry	1.00
3	Andy Van Slyke (Little Hotshots)	1.00
4	Don Mattingly	7.50
5	Awesome Action (Gary Carter, Steve Finley)	1.00
6	Frank Thomas	5.00
7	Kirby Puckett	6.00
8	Fun at the Ballpark	1.00

1992 Triple Play

This set was released only in wax pack form. Cards feature red borders. Boyhood photos, mascots

and ballparks are among the featured cards. This set was designed to give collectors an alternative product to the high-end card sets. The cards are standard size.

		NM/M
Complete Set (264):		6.00
Common Player:		.05
Wax Pack (12):		.40
Wax Box (36):		7.50
1	SkyDome	.05
2	Tom Foley	.05
3	Scott Erickson	.05
4	Matt Williams	.05
5	Dave Valle	.05
6	Andy Van Slyke (Little Hotshot)	.05
7	Tom Glavine	.25
8	Kevin Appier	.05
9	Pedro Guerrero	.05
10	Terry Steinbach	.05
11	Terry Mulholland	.05
12	Mike Boddicker	.05
13	Gregg Olson	.05
14	Tim Burke	.05
15	Candy Maldonado	.05
16	Orlando Merced	.05
17	Robin Ventura	.05
18	Eric Anthony	.05
19	Greg Maddux	.60
20	Erik Hanson	.05
21	Bob Ojeda	.05
22	Nolan Ryan	1.00
23	Dave Righetti	.05
24	Reggie Jefferson	.05
25	Jody Reed	.05
26	Awesome Action (Steve Finley, Gary Carter)	.10
27	Chili Davis	.05
28	Hector Villanueva	.05
29	Cecil Fielder	.05
30	Hal Morris	.05
31	Barry Larkin	.05
32	Bobby Thigpen	.05
33	Andy Benes	.05
34	Harold Baines	.05
35	David Cone	.05
36	Mark Langston	.05
37	Bryan Harvey	.05
38	John Kruk	.05
39	Scott Sanderson	.05
40	Lonnie Smith	.05
41	Awesome Action (Rex Hudler)	.05
42	George Bell	.05
43	Steve Finley	.05
44	Mickey Tettleton	.05
45	Robby Thompson	.05
46	Pat Kelly	.05
47	Marquis Grissom	.05
48	Tony Pena	.05
49	Alex Cole	.05
50	Steve Buechele	.05
51	Ivan Rodriguez	.45
52	John Smiley	.05
53	Gary Sheffield	.25
54	Greg Olson	.05
55	Ramon Martinez	.05
56	B.J. Surhoff	.05
57	Bruce Hurst	.05
58	Todd Stottlemyre	.05
59	Brett Butler	.05
60	Glenn Davis	.05
61	Awesome Action (Glenn Braggs, Kirt Manwaring)	.05
62	Lee Smith	.05
63	Rickey Henderson	.45
64	Fun at the Ballpark (David Cone, Jeff Innis, John Franco)	.05
65	Rick Aguilera	.05
66	Kevin Elster	.05
67	Dwight Evans	.05
68	Andujar Cedeno	.05
69	Brian McRae	.05
70	Benito Santiago	.05
71	Randy Johnson	.45
72	Roberto Kelly	.05
73	Awesome Action (Juan Samuel)	.05
74	Alex Fernandez	.05
75	Felix Jose	.05
76	Brian Harper	.05
77	Scott Sanderson (Little Hotshot)	.05
78	Ken Caminiti	.05

79	Mo Vaughn	.05
80	Roger McDowell	.05
81	Robin Yount	.45
82	Dave Magadan	.05
83	Julio Franco	.05
84	Roberto Alomar	.25
85	Steve Avery	.05
86	Travis Fryman	.05
87	Fred McGriff	.05
88	Dave Stewart	.05
89	Larry Walker	.05
90	Chris Sabo	.05
91	Chuck Finley	.05
92	Dennis Martinez	.05
93	Jeff Johnson	.05
94	Len Dykstra	.05
95	Mark Whiten	.05
96	Wade Taylor	.05
97	Lance Dickson	.05
98	Kevin Tapani	.05
99	Awesome Action (Luis Polonia, Tony Phillips)	.05
100	Milt Cuyler	.05
101	Willie McGee	.05
102	Awesome Action (Tony Fernandez, Ryne Sandberg)	.15
103	Albert Belle	.05
104	Todd Hundley	.05
105	Ben McDonald	.05
106	Doug Drabek	.05
107	Tim Raines	.05
108	Joe Carter	.05
109	Reggie Sanders	.05
110	John Olerud	.05
111	Darren Lewis	.05
112	Juan Gonzalez	.25
113	Awesome Action (Andre Dawson)	.05
114	Mark Grace	.05
115	George Brett	.65
116	Barry Bonds	1.00
117	Lou Whitaker	.05
118	Jose Oquendo	.05
119	Lee Stevens	.05
120	Phil Plantier	.05
121	Awesome Action (Devon White, Matt Merullo)	.05
122	Greg Vaughn	.05
123	Royce Clayton	.05
124	Bob Welch	.05
125	Juan Samuel	.05
126	Ron Gant	.05
127	Edgar Martinez	.05
128	Andy Ashby	.05
129	Jack McDowell	.05
130	Awesome Action (Dave Henderson, Jerry Browne)	.05
131	Leo Gomez	.05
132	Checklist 1-88	.05
133	Phillie Phanatic	.05
134	Bret Barbarie	.05
135	Kent Hrbek	.05
136	Hall of Fame	.05
137	Omar Vizquel	.05
138	The Famous Chicken	.05
139	Terry Pendleton	.05
140	Jim Eisenreich	.05
141	Todd Zeile	.05
142	Todd Van Poppel	.05
143	Darren Daulton	.05
144	Mike Macfarlane	.05
145	Luis Mercedes	.05
146	Trevor Wilson	.05
147	Dave Steib	.05
148	Andy Van Slyke	.05
149	Carlton Fisk	.45
150	Craig Biggio	.05
151	Joe Girardi	.05
152	Ken Griffey Jr.	.65
153	Jose Offerman	.05
154	Bobby Witt	.05
155	Will Clark	.05
156	Steve Olin	.05
157	Greg Harris	.05
158	Dale Murphy (Little Hotshot)	.05
159	Don Mattingly	.65
160	Shawon Dunston	.05
161	Bill Gullickson	.05
162	Paul O'Neill	.05
163	Norm Charlton	.05
164	Bo Jackson	.10
165	Tony Fernandez	.05
166	Dave Henderson	.05
167	Dwight Gooden	.05
168	Junior Felix	.05
169	Lance Parrish	.05
170	Pat Combs	.05
171	Chuck Knoblauch	.05
172	John Smoltz	.05
173	Wrigley Field	.05
174	Andre Dawson	.25
175	Pete Harnisch	.05
176	Alan Trammell	.05
177	Kirk Dressendorfer	.05
178	Matt Nokes	.05
179	Wil Cordero	.05
180	Scott Cooper	.05
181	Glenallen Hill	.05
182	John Franco	.05
183	Rafael Palmeiro	.40
184	Jay Bell	.05
185	Bill Wegman	.05
186	Deion Sanders	.05

#	Player	Price
187	Darryl Strawberry	.05
188	Jaime Navarro	.05
189	Darren Jackson	.05
190	Eddie Zosky	.05
191	Mike Scioscia	.05
192	Chito Martinez	.05
193	Awesome Action (Pat Kelly, Ron Tingley)	.05
194	Ray Lankford	.05
195	Dennis Eckersley	.35
196	Awesome Action (Ivan Calderon, Mike Maddux)	.05
197	Shane Mack	.05
198	Checklist 89-176	.05
199	Cal Ripken, Jr.	1.00
200	Jeff Bagwell	.45
201	David Howard	.05
202	Kirby Puckett	.60
203	Harold Reynolds	.05
204	Jim Abbott	.05
205	Mark Lewis	.05
206	Frank Thomas	.45
207	Rex Hudler	.05
208	Vince Coleman	.05
209	Delino DeShields	.05
210	Luis Gonzalez	.05
211	Wade Boggs	.60
212	Orel Hershiser	.05
213	Cal Eldred	.05
214	Jose Canseco	.25
215	Jose Guzman	.05
216	Roger Clemens	.65
217	Dave Justice	.05
218	Tony Phillips	.05
219	Tony Gwynn	.60
220	Mitch Williams	.05
221	Bill Sampen	.05
222	Billy Hatcher	.05
223	Gary Gaetti	.05
224	Tim Wallach	.05
225	Kevin Maas	.05
226	Kevin Brown	.05
227	Sandy Alomar	.05
228	John Habyan	.05
229	Ryne Sandberg	.60
230	Greg Gagne	.05
231	Autographs (Mark McGwire)	.40
232	Mike LaValliere	.05
233	Mark Gubicza	.05
234	Lance Parrish (Little Hotshot)	.05
235	Carlos Baerga	.05
236	Howard Johnson	.05
237	Mike Mussina	.25
238	Ruben Sierra	.05
239	Lance Johnson	.05
240	Devon White	.05
241	Dan Wilson	.05
242	Kelly Gruber	.05
243	Brett Butler (Little Hotshot)	.05
244	Ozzie Smith	.60
245	Chuck McElroy	.05
246	Shawn Boskie	.05
247	Mark Davis	.05
248	Bill Landrum	.05
249	Frank Tanana	.05
250	Darryl Hamilton	.05
251	Gary DiSarcina	.05
252	Mike Greenwell	.05
253	Cal Ripken, Jr. (Little Hotshot)	.35
254	Paul Molitor	.45
255	Tim Teufel	.05
256	Chris Hoiles	.05
257	Rob Dibble	.05
258	Sid Bream	.05
259	Chito Martinez	.05
260	Dale Murphy	.15
261	Greg Hibbard	.05
262	Mark McGwire	.75
263	Oriole Park	.05
264	Checklist 177-264	.05

Gallery of Stars

Two levels of scarcity are represented in this insert set. Cards #1-6 (all cards have a GS prefix to the card number) feature in their new uniforms players who changed teams for 1993. Those inserts were found in the standard Triple Play foil packs and are somewhat more common than cards #7-12, which were found only in jumbo packs and which feature a better selection of established stars and rookies. All of the inserts feature the artwork of Dick Perez, with player portraits set against a colorful background. Silver-foil accents highlight the front design. Backs are red with a white "tombstone" containing a career summary.

		NM/M
	Complete Set (12):	4.00
	Common Player:	.15
1	Bobby Bonilla	.15
2	Wally Joyner	.15
3	Jack Morris	.15
4	Steve Sax	.15
5	Danny Tartabull	.15
6	Frank Viola	.15
7	Jeff Bagwell	.60
8	Ken Griffey Jr.	1.00
9	David Justice	.15
10	Ryan Klesko	.15
11	Cal Ripken, Jr.	1.50
12	Frank Thomas	.75

1993 Triple Play Promos

This set was given to dealers to preview the 1993 Donruss Triple Play issue. Cards are virtually identical to the regular-issue cards except for a large promotional sample notation printed on back.

		NM/M
	Complete Set (12):	100.00
	Common Player:	5.00
1	Ken Griffey Jr.	25.00
2	Roberto Alomar	6.00
3	Cal Ripken, Jr.	40.00
4	Eric Karros	5.00
5	Cecil Fielder	5.00
6	Gary Sheffield	7.50
7	Darren Daulton	5.00
8	Andy Van Slyke	5.00
9	Dennis Eckersley	10.00
10	Ryne Sandberg	25.00
11	Mark Grace (Little Hotshots)	5.00
12	Awesome Action #1 (Luis Polonia, David Segui)	5.00

1993 Triple Play

MARK LEMKE 2B

For the second year, Leaf-Donruss used the "Triple Play" brand name for its base-level card set aimed at the younger collector. The 264-card set was available in several types of retail packaging and included a number of special subsets, such as childhood photos (labeled LH - Little Hotshots - in the checklist) and insert sets. Checklist card #264 incorrectly shows card #129, Joe Robbie Stadium, as #259. There is a second card, "Equipment," which also bears #129. An "Action Baseball" scratch-off game card was included in each foil pack.

		NM/M
	Complete Set (264):	10.00
	Common Player:	.05
	Wax Pack (12):	.60
	Wax Box (36):	15.00
1	Ken Griffey Jr.	.50
2	Roberto Alomar	.10
3	Cal Ripken, Jr.	.75
4	Eric Karros	.05
5	Cecil Fielder	.05
6	Gary Sheffield	.05
7	Darren Daulton	.05
8	Andy Van Slyke	.05
9	Dennis Eckersley	.20
10	Ryne Sandberg	.35
11	Mark Grace (Little Hotshots)	.05
12	Awesome Action #1 (Luis Polonia, David Segui)	.05
13	Mike Mussina	.15
14	Vince Coleman	.05
15	Rafael Belliard	.05
16	Ivan Rodriguez	.05
17	Eddie Taubensee	.05
18	Cal Eldred	.05
19	Rick Wilkins	.05
20	Edgar Martinez	.05
21	Brian McRae	.05
22	Darren Holmes	.05
23	Mark Whiten	.05
24	Todd Zeile	.05
25	Scott Cooper	.05
26	Frank Thomas	.25
27	Wil Cordero	.05
28	Juan Guzman	.05
29	Pedro Astacio	.05
30	Steve Avery	.05
31	Barry Larkin	.05
32	President Clinton	2.00
33	Scott Erickson	.05
34	Mike Devereaux	.05
35	Tino Martinez	.05
36	Brent Mayne	.05
37	Tim Salmon	.05
38	Dave Hollins	.05
39	Royce Clayton	.05
40	Shawon Dunston	.05
41	Eddie Murray	.25
42	Larry Walker	.25
43	Jeff Bagwell	.25
44	Milt Cuyler	.05
45	Mike Bordick	.05
46	Mike Greenwell	.05
47	Steve Sax	.05
48	Chuck Knoblauch	.05
49	Charles Nagy	.05
50	Tim Wakefield	.05
51	Tony Gwynn	.35
52	Rob Dibble	.05
53	Mickey Morandini	.05
54	Steve Hosey	.05
55	Mike Piazza	.50
56	Bill Wegman	.05
57	Kevin Maas	.05
58	Gary DiSarcina	.05
59	Travis Fryman	.05
60	Ruben Sierra	.05
61	Awesome Action #2 (Ken Caminiti)	.05
62	Brian Jordan	.05
63	Scott Chiamparino	.05
64	Awesome Action #3 (Mike Bordick, George Brett)	.05
65	Carlos Garcia	.05
66	Checklist 1-66	.05
67	John Smoltz	.05
68	Awesome Action #4 (Mark McGwire, Brian Harper)	.20
69	Kurt Stillwell	.05
70	Chad Curtis	.05
71	Rafael Palmeiro	.20
72	Kevin Young	.05
73	Glenn Davis	.05
74	Dennis Martinez	.05
75	Sam Militello	.05
76	Mike Morgan	.05
77	Frank Thomas (Little Hotshots)	.20
78	Staying Fit (Bip Roberts, Mike Devereaux)	.05
79	Steve Buechele	.05
80	Carlos Baerga	.05
81	Robby Thompson	.05
82	Kirk McCaskill	.05
83	Lee Smith	.05
84	Gary Scott	.05
85	Tony Pena	.05
86	Howard Johnson	.05
87	Mark McGwire	.60
88	Bip Roberts	.05
89	Devon White	.05
90	John Franco	.05
91	Tom Browning	.05
92	Mickey Tettleton	.05
93	Jeff Conine	.05
94	Albert Belle	.05
95	Fred McGriff	.05
96	Nolan Ryan	.75
97	Paul Molitor (Little Hotshots)	.10
98	Juan Bell	.05
99	Dave Fleming	.05
100	Craig Biggio	.05
101a	Andy Stankiewicz (White name on front.)	.05
101b	Andy Stankiewicz (Red name on front.)	.25
102	Delino DeShields	.05
103	Damion Easley	.05
104	Kevin McReynolds	.05
105	David Nied	.05
106	Rick Sutcliffe	.05
107	Will Clark	.05
108	Tim Raines	.05
109	Eric Anthony	.05
110	Mike LaValliere	.05
111	Dean Palmer	.05
112	Eric Davis	.05
113	Damon Berryhill	.05
114	Felix Jose	.05
115	Ozzie Guillen	.05
116	Pat Listach	.05
117	Tom Glavine	.15
118	Roger Clemens	.40
119	Dave Henderson	.05
120	Don Mattingly	.40
121	Orel Hershiser	.05
122	Ozzie Smith	.35
123	Joe Carter	.05
124	Bret Saberhagen	.05
125	Mitch Williams	.05
126	Jerald Clark	.05
127	Mile High Stadium	.05
128	Kent Hrbek	.05
129a	Equipment (Curt Schilling, Mark Whiten)	.05
129b	Joe Robbie Stadium	.05
130	Gregg Jefferies	.05
131	John Orton	.05
132	Checklist 67-132	.05
133	Bret Boone	.05
134	Pat Borders	.05
135	Gregg Olson	.05
136	Brett Butler	.05
137	Rob Deer	.05
138	Darrin Jackson	.05
139	John Kruk	.05
140	Jay Bell	.05
141	Bobby Witt	.05
142	New Cubs (Dan Plesac, Randy Myers, Jose Guzman)	.05
143	Wade Boggs (Little Hotshots)	.15
144	Awesome Action #5 (Kenny Lofton)	.05
145	Ben McDonald	.05
146	Dwight Gooden	.05
147	Terry Pendleton	.05
148	Julio Franco	.05
149	Ken Caminiti	.05
150	Greg Vaughn	.05
151	Sammy Sosa	.05
152	David Valle	.05
153	Wally Joyner	.05
154	Dante Bichette	.05
155	Mark Lewis	.05
156	Bob Tewksbury	.05
157	Billy Hatcher	.05
158	Jack McDowell	.05
159	Marquis Grissom	.05
160	Jack Morris	.05
161	Ramon Martinez	.05
162	Deion Sanders	.05
163	Tim Belcher	.05
164	Mascots	.05
165	Scott Leius	.05
166	Brady Anderson	.05
167	Randy Johnson	.25
168	Mark Gubicza	.05
169	Chuck Finley	.05
170	Terry Mulholland	.05
171	Matt Williams	.05
172	Dwight Smith	.05
173	Bobby Bonilla	.05
174	Ken Hill	.05
175	Doug Jones	.05
176	Tony Phillips	.05
177	Terry Steinbach	.05
178	Frank Viola	.05
179	Robin Ventura	.05
180	Shane Mack	.05
181	Kenny Lofton	.05
182	Jeff King	.05
183	Tim Teufel	.05
184	Chris Sabo	.05
185	Lenny Dykstra	.05
186	Trevor Wilson	.05
187	Darryl Strawberry	.05
188	Robin Yount	.25
189	Bob Wickman	.05
190	Luis Polonia	.05
191	Alan Trammell	.05
192	Bob Welch	.05
193	Awesome Action #6 Tom Pagnozzi	.05
194	Tom Pagnozzi	.05
195	Bret Barberie	.05
196	Awesome Action #7 (Mike Scioscia)	.05
197	Randy Tomlin	.05
198	Checklist 133-198	.05
199	Ron Gant	.05
200	Awesome Action #8 (Roberto Alomar)	.05
201	Andy Benes	.05
202	Pepper	.05
203	Steve Finley	.05
204	Steve Olin	.05
205	Chris Hoiles	.05
206	John Wetteland	.05
207	Danny Tartabull	.05
208	Bernard Gilkey	.05
209	Tom Glavine (Little Hotshots)	.05
210	Benito Santiago	.05
211	Mark Grace	.05
212	Glenallen Hill	.05
213	Jeff Brantley	.05
214	George Brett	.40
215	Mark Lemke	.05
216	Ron Karkovice	.05
217	Tom Brunansky	.05
218	Todd Hundley	.05
219	Rickey Henderson	.25
220	Joe Oliver	.05
221	Juan Gonzalez	.15
222	John Olerud	.05
223	Hal Morris	.05
224	Lou Whitaker	.05
225	Bryan Harvey	.05
226	Mike Gallego	.05
227	Willie McGee	.05
228	Jose Oquendo	.05
229	Darren Daulton (Little Hotshots)	.05
230	Curt Schilling	.10
231	Jay Buhner	.05
232	New Astros (Doug Drabek, Greg Swindell)	.05
233	Jaime Navarro	.05
234	Kevin Appier	.05
235	Mark Langston	.05
236	Jeff Montgomery	.05
237	Joe Girardi	.05
238	Ed Sprague	.05
239	Dan Walters	.05
240	Kevin Tapani	.05
241	Pete Harnisch	.05
242	Al Martin	.05
243	Jose Canseco	.15
244	Moises Alou	.05
245	Mark McGwire (Little Hotshots)	.05
246	Luis Rivera	.05
247	George Bell	.05
248	B.J. Surhoff	.05
249	Dave Justice	.05
250	Brian Harper	.05
251	Sandy Alomar, Jr.	.05
252	Kevin Brown	.05
253	New Dodgers (Tim Wallach, Jody Reed, Todd Worrell)	.05
254	Ray Lankford	.05
255	Derek Bell	.05
256	Joe Grahe	.05
257	Charlie Hayes	.05
258	New Yankees (Wade Boggs, Jim Abbott)	.25
259	Joe Robbie Stadium	.05
260	Kirby Puckett	.35
261	Fun at the Ballpark (Jay Bell, Vince Coleman)	.05
262	Bill Swift	.05
263	Fun at the Ballpark (Roger McDowell)	.05
264	Checklist 199-264	.05

Action Baseball

These game folders were inserted in each 1993 Triple Play foil pack. Because collation of the folders was very bad, few collectors bothered to save them. Measuring 2-1/2" x 5", fronts have an action photo of an unnamed player. Printed over the bottom of the photo are two full-color team logos, with a white "Versus" between. Inside the folder is a baseball diamond diagram, a three-inning scoreboard, rules for playing the game and 32 scratch-off squares for playing. Backs have a number designating the folder as "of 30."

		NM/M
	Complete Set (30):	3.00
	Common Player:	.10
1	Andy Van Slyke	.10
2	Bobby Bonilla	.10
3	Ozzie Smith	.30
4	Ryne Sandberg	.30
5	Darren Daulton	.10
6	Larry Walker	.10
7	Eric Karros	.10
8	Barry Larkin	.10
9	Deion Sanders	.10
10	Gary Sheffield	.20
11	Will Clark	.10
12	Jeff Bagwell	.25
13	Roberto Alomar	.15
14	Roger Clemens	.35
15	Cecil Fielder	.10
16	Robin Yount	.25
17	Cal Ripken, Jr.	.50
18	Carlos Baerga	.10
19	Don Mattingly	.35
20	Kirby Puckett	.30
21	Frank Thomas	.25
22	Juan Gonzalez	.15
23	Mark McGwire	.45
24	Ken Griffey Jr.	.40
25	Wally Joyner	.10
26	Chad Curtis	.10
27	Batting glove	.10
28	Juan Guzman	.10
29	Dave Justice	.10
30	Joe Carter	.10

Gallery

The Gallery of Stars cards were found as random inserts in Triple Play jumbo packs. The cards feature Dick Perez painted representations of the players.

		NM/M
	Complete Set (10):	7.00
	Common Player:	.50
1	Barry Bonds	3.00
2	Andre Dawson	.65
3	Wade Boggs	1.50
4	Greg Maddux	1.50
5	Dave Winfield	1.00
6	Paul Molitor	1.00
7	Jim Abbott	.50
8	J.T. Snow	.50
9	Benito Santiago	.50
10	David Nied	.50

League Leaders

These "double-headed" cards feature one player on each side. The six cards were random inserts in Triple Play retail packs.

		NM/M
	Complete Set (6):	7.00
	Common Player:	.50
1	Barry Bonds, Dennis Eckersley	3.50
2	Greg Maddux, Dennis Eckersley	2.00
3	Eric Karros, Pat Listach	.50
4	Fred McGriff, Juan Gonzalez	.75
5	Darren Daulton, Cecil Fielder	.50
6	Gary Sheffield, Edgar Martinez	.65

Nicknames

Popular nicknames of 10 of the game's top stars are featured in silver foil on this insert set found in Triple Play foil packs.

		NM/M
	Complete Set (10):	10.00
	Common Player:	.75
1	Frank Thomas (Big Hurt)	1.25
2	Roger Clemens (Rocket)	2.00
3	Ryne Sandberg (Ryno)	1.50
4	Will Clark (Thrill)	.75
5	Ken Griffey Jr. (Junior)	3.00
6	Dwight Gooden (Doc)	.75
7	Nolan Ryan (Express)	4.00

8	Deion Sanders (Prime Time)	.75
9	Ozzie Smith (Wizard)	1.50
10	Fred McGriff (Crime Dog)	.75

1994 Triple Play Promos

PIAZZA

This set was given to dealers to preview the 1994 Donruss Triple Play issue. Cards are virtually identical to the regular-issue cards except for a large black "Promotional Sample" printed diagonally in black on both front and back. Cards are numbered as "X of 10" on the promos.

		NM/M
Complete Set (10):		9.00
Common Player:		.50
1	Juan Gonzalez	.60
2	Frank Thomas	.85
3	Barry Bonds	3.00
4	Ken Griffey Jr.	1.50
5	Paul Molitor	.75
6	Mike Piazza	1.50
7	Tim Salmon	.75
8	Lenny Dykstra	.50
9	Don Mattingly	1.25
10	Greg Maddux	1.00

1994 Triple Play

LANGSTON

Triple Play cards returned for a third year in 1994, this time with a borderless design. According to company officials, production was less than 1994 Donruss Series I baseball, which was roughly 17,500 20-box cases. In the regular-issue 300-card set, 10 players from each team were featured, along with a 17-card Rookie Review subset and several insert sets.

		NM/M
Complete Set (300):		7.50
Common Player:		.05
Wax Pack (12):		.50
Wax Box (36):		12.00
1	Mike Bordick	.05
2	Dennis Eckersley	.35
3	Brent Gates	.05
4	Rickey Henderson	.40
5	Mark McGwire	.65
6	Troy Neel	.05
7	Craig Paquette	.05
8	Ruben Sierra	.05
9	Terry Steinbach	.05
10	Bobby Witt	.05
11	Chad Curtis	.05
12	Chili Davis	.05
13	Gary DiSarcina	.05
14	Damion Easley	.05
15	Chuck Finley	.05
16	Joe Grahe	.05
17	Mark Langston	.05
18	Eduardo Perez	.05
19	Tim Salmon	.05
20	J.T. Snow	.05
21	Jeff Bagwell	.40
22	Craig Biggio	.05
23	Ken Caminiti	.05
24	Andujar Cedeno	.05
25	Doug Drabek	.05
26	Steve Finley	.05
27	Luis Gonzalez	.05
28	Pete Harnisch	.05
29	Darryl Kile	.75
30	Mitch Williams	.05
31	Roberto Alomar	.20
32	Joe Carter	.05
33	Juan Guzman	.05
34	Pat Hentgen	.05
35	Paul Molitor	.40
36	John Olerud	.05
37	Ed Sprague	.05
38	Dave Stewart	.05
39	Duane Ward	.05
40	Devon White	.05
41	Steve Avery	.05
42	Jeff Blauser	.05
43	Ron Gant	.05
44	Tom Glavine	.20
45	Dave Justice	.05
46	Greg Maddux	.45
47	Fred McGriff	.05
48	Terry Pendleton	.05
49	Deion Sanders	.05
50	John Smoltz	.05
51	Ricky Bones	.05
52	Cal Eldred	.05
53	Darryl Hamilton	.05
54	John Jaha	.05
55	Pat Listach	.05
56	Jaime Navarro	.05
57	Dave Nilsson	.05
58	B.J. Surhoff	.05
59	Greg Vaughn	.05
60	Robin Yount	.40
61	Bernard Gilkey	.05
62	Gregg Jefferies	.05
63	Brian Jordan	.05
64	Ray Lankford	.05
65	Tom Pagnozzi	.05
66	Ozzie Smith	.45
67	Bob Tewksbury	.05
68	Allen Watson	.05
69	Mark Whiten	.05
70	Todd Zeile	.05
71	Steve Buechele	.05
72	Mark Grace	.05
73	Jose Guzman	.05
74	Derrick May	.05
75	Mike Morgan	.05
76	Randy Myers	.05
77	Ryne Sandberg	.45
78	Sammy Sosa	.50
79	Jose Vizcaino	.05
80	Rick Wilkins	.05
81	Pedro Astacio	.05
82	Brett Butler	.05
83	Delino DeShields	.05
84	Orel Hershiser	.05
85	Eric Karros	.05
86	Ramon Martinez	.05
87	Jose Offerman	.05
88	Mike Piazza	.05
89	Darryl Strawberry	.05
90	Tim Wallach	.05
91	Moises Alou	.05
92	Wil Cordero	.05
93	Jeff Fassero	.05
94	Darrin Fletcher	.05
95	Marquis Grissom	.05
96	Ken Hill	.05
97	Mike Lansing	.05
98	Kirk Rueter	.05
99	Larry Walker	.05
100	John Wetteland	.05
101	Rod Beck	.05
102	Barry Bonds	.75
103	John Burkett	.05
104	Royce Clayton	.05
105	Darren Lewis	.05
106	Kirt Manwaring	.05
107	Willie McGee	.05
108	Bill Swift	.05
109	Robby Thompson	.05
110	Matt Williams	.05
111	Sandy Alomar Jr.	.05
112	Carlos Baerga	.05
113	Albert Belle	.05
114	Wayne Kirby	.05
115	Kenny Lofton	.05
116	Jose Mesa	.05
117	Eddie Murray	.40
118	Charles Nagy	.05
119	Paul Sorrento	.05
120	Jim Thome	.35
121	Rich Amaral	.05
122	Eric Anthony	.05
123	Mike Blowers	.05
124	Chris Bosio	.05
125	Jay Buhner	.05
126	Dave Fleming	.05
127	Ken Griffey Jr.	.50
128	Randy Johnson	.40
129	Edgar Martinez	.05
130	Tino Martinez	.05
131	Bret Barberie	.05
132	Ryan Bowen	.05
133	Chuck Carr	.05
134	Jeff Conine	.05
135	Orestes Destrade	.05
136	Chris Hammond	.05
137	Bryan Harvey	.05
138	Dave Magadan	.05
139	Benito Santiago	.05
140	Gary Sheffield	.30
141	Bobby Bonilla	.05
142	Jeromy Burnitz	.05
143	Dwight Gooden	.05
144	Todd Hundley	.05
145	Bobby Jones	.05
146	Jeff Kent	.05
147	Joe Orsulak	.05
148	Bret Saberhagen	.05
149	Pete Schourek	.05
150	Ryan Thompson	.05
151	Brady Anderson	.05
152	Harold Baines	.05
153	Mike Devereaux	.05
154	Chris Hoiles	.05
155	Ben McDonald	.05
156	Mark McLemore	.05
157	Mike Mussina	.25
158	Rafael Palmeiro	.40
159	Cal Ripken, Jr.	.75
160	Chris Sabo	.05
161	Brad Ausmus	.05
162	Derek Bell	.05
163	Andy Benes	.05
164	Doug Brocail	.05
165	Archi Cianfrocco	.05
166	Ricky Gutierrez	.05
167	Tony Gwynn	.45
168	Gene Harris	.05
169	Pedro Martinez	.40
170	Phil Plantier	.05
171	Darren Daulton	.05
172	Mariano Duncan	.05
173	Len Dykstra	.05
174	Tommy Greene	.05
175	Dave Hollins	.05
176	Danny Jackson	.05
177	John Kruk	.05
178	Terry Mulholland	.05
179	Curt Schilling	.20
180	Kevin Stocker	.05
181	Jay Bell	.05
182	Steve Cooke	.05
183	Carlos Garcia	.05
184	Joel Johnston	.05
185	Jeff King	.05
186	Al Martin	.05
187	Orlando Merced	.05
188	Don Slaught	.05
189	Andy Van Slyke	.05
190	Kevin Young	.05
191	Kevin Brown	.05
192	Jose Canseco	.25
193	Will Clark	.05
194	Juan Gonzalez	.20
195	Tom Henke	.05
196	David Hulse	.05
197	Dean Palmer	.05
198	Roger Pavlik	.05
199	Ivan Rodriguez	.35
200	Kenny Rogers	.05
201	Roger Clemens	.45
202	Scott Cooper	.05
203	Andre Dawson	.20
204	Mike Greenwell	.05
205	Billy Hatcher	.05
206	Jeff Russell	.05
207	Aaron Sele	.05
208	John Valentin	.05
209	Mo Vaughn	.05
210	Frank Viola	.05
211	Rob Dibble	.05
212	Willie Greene	.05
213	Roberto Kelly	.05
214	Barry Larkin	.05
215	Kevin Mitchell	.05
216	Hal Morris	.05
217	Joe Oliver	.05
218	Jose Rijo	.05
219	Reggie Sanders	.05
220	John Smiley	.05
221	Dante Bichette	.05
222	Ellis Burks	.05
223	Andres Galarraga	.05
224	Joe Girardi	.05
225	Charlie Hayes	.05
226	Darren Holmes	.05
227	Howard Johnson	.05
228	Roberto Mejia	.05
229	David Nied	.05
230	Armando Reynoso	.05
231	Kevin Appier	.05
232	David Cone	.05
233	Greg Gagne	.05
234	Tom Gordon	.05
235	Felix Jose	.05
236	Wally Joyner	.05
237	Jose Lind	.05
238	Brian McRae	.05
239	Mike MacFarlane	.05
240	Jeff Montgomery	.05
241	Eric Davis	.05
242	John Doherty	.05
243	Cecil Fielder	.05
244	Travis Fryman	.05
245	Bill Gullickson	.05
246	Mike Henneman	.05
247	Tony Phillips	.05
248	Mickey Tettleton	.05
249	Alan Trammell	.05
250	Lou Whitaker	.05
251	Rick Aguilera	.05
252	Scott Erickson	.05
253	Kent Hrbek	.05
254	Chuck Knoblauch	.05
255	Shane Mack	.05
256	Dave McCarty	.05
257	Pat Meares	.05
258	Kirby Puckett	.45
259	Kevin Tapani	.05
260	Dave Winfield	.40
261	Wilson Alvarez	.05
262	Jason Bere	.05
263	Alex Fernandez	.05
264	Ozzie Guillen	.05
265	Roberto Hernandez	.05
266	Lance Johnson	.05
267	Jack McDowell	.05
268	Tim Raines	.05
269	Frank Thomas	.40
270	Robin Ventura	.05
271	Jim Abbott	.05
272	Wade Boggs	.45
273	Mike Gallego	.05
274	Pat Kelly	.05
275	Jimmy Key	.05
276	Don Mattingly	.50
277	Paul O'Neill	.05
278	Mike Stanley	.05
279	Danny Tartabull	.05
280	Bernie Williams	.05
281	Chipper Jones	.50
282	Ryan Klesko	.05
283	Javier Lopez	.05
284	Jeffrey Hammonds	.05
285	Jeff McNeely	.05
286	Manny Ramirez	.40
287	Billy Ashley	.05
288	Raul Mondesi	.05
289	Cliff Floyd	.05
290	Rondell White	.05
291	Steve Karsay	.05
292	Midre Cummings	.05
293	Salomon Torres	.05
294	J.R. Phillips	.05
295	Marc Newfield	.05
296	Carlos Delgado	.30
297	Butch Huskey	.05
298	Checklist (Frank Thomas)	.05
299	Checklist (Barry Bonds)	.05
300	Checklist (Juan Gonzalez)	.05

Bomb Squad

DAVID JUSTICE

Ten of the top major league home run hitters are included in this insert set. Fronts feature sepia-toned player photos within a wide brown frame. Gold foil enhances the typography. Backs have a white background with representations of vintage airplanes. A bar chart at left gives the player's home run totals by year. A small color portrait photo is at upper-right. Below are a few words about his homer history.

		NM/M
Complete Set (10):		5.00
Common Player:		.25
1	Frank Thomas	1.00
2	Cecil Fielder	.25
3	Juan Gonzalez	.45
4	Barry Bonds	2.50
5	Dave Justice	.25
6	Fred McGriff	.25
7	Ron Gant	.25
8	Ken Griffey Jr.	1.50
9	Albert Belle	.25
10	Matt Williams	.25

Medalists

Statistical performance over the 1992-93 seasons was used to rank the players appearing in the Medalists insert set. Horizontal format cards have photos of the first, second and third place winners in appropriate boxes of gold, silver and bronze foil. "Medalists," the "medals" and "Triple Play 94" are embossed on the front. Backs have color action photos of each player along with team logos and a few stats.

	NM/M
Complete Set (15):	10.00
Common Player:	.50
1 A.L. Catchers (Chris Hoiles, Mickey Tettleton, Brian Harper)	.50
2 N.L. Catchers (Darren Daulton, Rick Wilkins, Kirt Manwaring)	.50
3 A.L. First Basemen (Frank Thomas, Rafael Palmeiro, John Olerud)	1.00
4 N.L. First Basemen (Mark Grace, Fred McGriff, Jeff Bagwell)	1.00
5 A.L. Second Basemen (Roberto Alomar, Carlos Baerga, Lou Whitaker)	.50
6 N.L. Second Basemen (Ryne Sandberg, Craig Biggio, Robby Thompson)	1.25
7 A.L. Shortstops (Tony Fernandez, Cal Ripken, Jr., Alan Trammell)	2.00
8 N.L. Shortstops (Barry Larkin, Jay Bell, Jeff Blauser)	.50
9 A.L. Third Basemen (Robin Ventura, Travis Fryman, Wade Boggs)	1.25
10 N.L. Third Basemen (Terry Pendleton, Dave Hollins, Gary Sheffield)	.50
11 A.L. Outfielders (Ken Griffey Jr., Kirby Puckett, Albert Belle)	1.50
12 N.L. Outfielders (Barry Bonds, Andy Van Slyke, Len Dykstra)	2.00
13 A.L. Starters (Jack McDowell, Kevin Brown, Randy Johnson)	.60
14 N.L. Starters (Greg Maddux, Jose Rijo, Billy Swift)	1.25
15 Designated Hitters (Paul Molitor, Dave Winfield, Harold Baines)	.60

Nicknames

ST LOUIS

Eight of baseball's most colorful team nicknames are featured in this insert set. Fronts feature a background photo representative of the nickname, with a player photo superimposed over that. Backs have another player photo and a history of the team's nickname.

		NM/M
Complete Set (8):		10.00
Common Player:		.75
1	Cecil Fielder	.75
2	Ryne Sandberg	1.50
3	Gary Sheffield	.90
4	Joe Carter	.75
5	John Olerud	.75
6	Cal Ripken, Jr.	3.00
7	Mark McGwire	2.50
8	Gregg Jefferies	.75

1990 Tropicana Team Mets

In 1990, Tropicana orange juice took over as sponsor of the junior Mets fan club. One of the membership perks was a nine-card sheet. Action photos were surrounded by team-color stripes of blue and orange and a white outer border. Backs have Team Mets and Tropicana logos, 1989 highlights and stats, career numbers and personal data. Individual cards measure 2-1/2" x 3-1/2", though they are not often sold other than as an original 7-1/2" x 10-1/2" sheet. Cards are checklisted here on the basis of uniform numbers found on the cards' fronts.

		NM/M
Complete Set (9):		4.00
Common Player:		.50
9	Gregg Jefferies	.50
16	Dwight Gooden	.50
18	Darryl Strawberry	.50
20	Howard Johnson	.50
21	Kevin Elster	.50
25	Keith Miller	.50
29	Frank Viola	.50
44	David Cone	.50
50	Sid Fernandez	.50

1991 Tropicana Team Mets

JOHN FRANCO #31 Pitcher

This nine-card sheet was a perk for members of the junior Mets fan club - Team Mets. Sponsored by Tropicana fruit juices for the second straight year, the 2-1/2" x 3-1/2" individual cards on the 7-1/2" x 10-1/2" sheet feature color action photos of the players, surrounded by team-color blue and orange stripes and an outer white border. Backs have 1990 highlights and stats, career stats and biographical details, along with the Team Mets and Tropicana logos. Cards are checklisted here according to the uniform numbers found on the front.

		NM/M
Complete Set (9):		4.00
Common Player:		.50
2	Mackey Sasser	.50
9	Gregg Jefferies	.50
10	Dave Magadan	.50
16	Dwight Gooden	.50
20	Howard Johnson	.50
22	Kevin McReynolds	.50
29	Frank Viola	.50
31	John Franco	.50
44	David Cone	.50

1983 True Value White Sox

HAROLD BAINES Right Field 3

Issued by the White Sox and True Value hardware stores, these 2-5/8" x 4-1/8" cards are among the scarcer early 1980s regional sets. The issue was originally scheduled as part of a promotion in which cards were given out at special

Tuesday night games. The idea was sound, but rainouts forced the cancellation of some games so those scheduled cards were never given out. They were, however, smuggled out to hobby channels making it possible, although not easy, to assemble complete sets. The cards feature a large color photo with a wide white border. A team logo is at lower-left while the player's name, position and uniform number are in the lower-right. Backs feature a True Value ad along with statistics. The three cards which were never given out through the normal channels are considered scarcer than the others. They are Marc Hill, Harold Baines and Salome Barojas.

		NM/M
Complete Set (23):		12.00
Common Player:		.25
1	Scott Fletcher	.25
2	Harold Baines	3.50
5	Vance Law	.25
7	Marc Hill	2.00
10	Tony LaRussa	.40
11	Rudy Law	.25
14	Tony Bernazard	.25
17	Jerry Hairston Sr.	.25
19	Greg Luzinski	.25
24	Floyd Bannister	.25
25	Mike Squires	.25
30	Salome Barojas	2.00
31	LaMarr Hoyt	.25
34	Richard Dotson	.25
36	Jerry Koosman	.25
40	Britt Burns	.25
41	Dick Tidrow	.25
44	Ron Kittle	.25
44	Tom Paciorek	.25
45	Kevin Hickey	.25
53	Dennis Lamp	.25
67	Jim Kern	.25
72	Carlton Fisk	1.50

1984 True Value White Sox

CARLTON FISK
Catcher 72

True Value hardware stores and the White Sox gave the Tuesday night baseball card promotion at Comiskey Park another try in 1984. The cards measure 2-5/8" x 4-1/8". In addition to the players, there are cards for manager Tony LaRussa, the coaching staff, and former Sox greats Luis Aparicio and Minnie Minoso. Card design is very similar to the 1983 cards. As the cards were given out two at a time, it was very difficult to acquire a complete set. Additionally, as numbers available vary because of attendance, some cards are scarcer than others.

		NM/M
Complete Set (30):		25.00
Common Player:		.50
1	Scott Fletcher	.50
3	Harold Baines	1.00
5	Vance Law	.50
7	Marc Hill	.50
8	Dave Stegman	.50
10	Tony LaRussa	1.00
11	Rudy Law	.50
16	Julio Cruz	.50
17	Jerry Hairston Sr.	.50
19	Greg Luzinski	.50
20	Jerry Dybzinski	.50
24	Floyd Bannister	.50
25	Mike Squires	.50
27	Ron Reed	.50
29	Greg Walker	.50
30	Salome Barojas	.50
31	LaMarr Hoyt	.50
32	Tim Hulett	.50
34	Richard Dotson	.50
40	Britt Burns	.50
72	Tom Seaver	5.00

42	Ron Kittle	.50
44	Tom Paciorek	.50
50	Juan Agosto	.50
59	Tom Brennan	.50
72	Carlton Fisk	3.00
---	Minnie Minoso	3.00
---	Luis Aparicio	3.00
---	Nancy Faust (organist)	1.00
---	The Coaching Staff (Ed Brinkman, Dave Duncan, Art Kusnyer, Tony LaRussa, Jim Leyland, Dave Nelson, Joe Nossek)	.50

1986 True Value

A 30-card set of 2-1/2" x 3-1/2" cards was available in three-card folders at True Value hardware stores with a purchase of $5 or more. Fronts feature a portrait flanked by stars with balls and bats at the bottom. The player's ID and a Major League Players Association logo are at bottom. Team insignia have been removed from the uniforms. Backs feature some personal information and brief 1985 statistics. Along with the player cards, the folders contained a sweepstakes card offering trips to postseason games and other prizes.

		NM/M
Complete Panel Set (10):		6.00
Complete Singles Set (30):		5.00
Common Player:		.05
Panel (1)		.50
1	Pedro Guerrero	.05
2	Steve Garvey	.10
3	Eddie Murray	.25
Panel (2)		1.25
4	Pete Rose	.60
5	Don Mattingly	.50
6	Fernando Valenzuela	.05
Panel (3)		.50
7	Jim Rice	.15
8	Kirk Gibson	.05
9	Ozzie Smith	.35
Panel (4)		.75
10	Dale Murphy	.15
11	Robin Yount	.25
12	Tom Seaver	.25
Panel (5)		.75
13	Reggie Jackson	.35
14	Ryne Sandberg	.35
15	Bruce Sutter	.25
Panel (6)		.75
16	Gary Carter	.25
17	George Brett	.50
18	Rick Sutcliffe	.05
Panel (7)		.25
19	Dave Steib	.05
20	Buddy Bell	.05
21	Alvin Davis	.05
Panel (8)		1.00
22	Cal Ripken Jr.	.75
23	Bill Madlock	.05
24	Kent Hrbek	.05
Panel (9)		1.00
25	Lou Whitaker	.05
26	Nolan Ryan	.75
27	Dwayne Murphy	.05
Panel (10)		1.00
28	Mike Schmidt	.50
29	Andre Dawson	.15
30	Wade Boggs	.35

1991 Ultra

This 400-card set was originally going to be called the Elite set, but Fleer chose to use the Ultra

GEORGE BELL CUBS OUTFIELD

label. The card fronts feature gray borders surrounding full-color action photos. The backs feature three player photos and statistics. Hot Prospects and Great Performers are among the special cards featured within the set.

		NM/M
Complete Set (400):		12.00
Common Player:		.05
Wax Pack (14):		.50
Wax Box (36):		9.00
1	Steve Avery	.05
2	Jeff Blauser	.05
3	Francisco Cabrera	.05
4	Ron Gant	.05
5	Tom Glavine	.25
6	Tommy Gregg	.05
7	Dave Justice	.05
8	Oddibe McDowell	.05
9	Greg Olson	.05
10	Terry Pendleton	.05
11	Lonnie Smith	.05
12	John Smoltz	.05
13	Jeff Treadway	.05
14	Glenn Davis	.05
15	Mike Devereaux	.05
16	Leo Gomez	.05
17	Chris Hoiles	.05
18	Dave Johnson	.05
19	Ben McDonald	.05
20	Randy Milligan	.05
21	Gregg Olson	.05
22	Joe Orsulak	.05
23	Bill Ripken	.05
24	Cal Ripken, Jr.	1.50
25	David Segui	.05
26	Craig Worthington	.05
27	Wade Boggs	.60
28	Tom Bolton	.05
29	Tom Brunansky	.05
30	Ellis Burks	.05
31	Roger Clemens	.65
32	Mike Greenwell	.05
33	Greg Harris	.05
34	Daryl Irvine	.05
35	Mike Marshall	.05
36	Tim Naehring	.05
37	Tony Pena	.05
38	Phil Plantier **RC**	.05
39	Carlos Quintana	.05
40	Jeff Reardon	.05
41	Jody Reed	.05
42	Luis Rivera	.05
43	Jim Abbott	.05
44	Chuck Finley	.05
45	Bryan Harvey	.05
46	Donnie Hill	.05
47	Jack Howell	.05
48	Wally Joyner	.05
49	Mark Langston	.05
50	Kirk McCaskill	.05
51	Lance Parrish	.05
52	Dick Schofield	.05
53	Lee Stevens	.05
54	Dave Winfield	.50
55	George Bell	.05
56	Damon Berryhill	.05
57	Mike Bielecki	.05
58	Andre Dawson	.25
59	Shawon Dunston	.05
60	Joe Girardi	.05
61	Mark Grace	.05
62	Mike Harkey	.05
63	Les Lancaster	.05
64	Greg Maddux	.60
65	Derrick May	.05
66	Ryne Sandberg	.60
67	Luis Salazar	.05
68	Dwight Smith	.05
69	Hector Villanueva	.05
70	Jerome Walton	.05
71	Mitch Williams	.05
72	Carlton Fisk	.50
73	Scott Fletcher	.05
74	Ozzie Guillen	.05
75	Greg Hibbard	.05
76	Lance Johnson	.05
77	Steve Lyons	.05
78	Jack McDowell	.05
79	Dan Pasqua	.05
80	Melido Perez	.05
81	Tim Raines	.05
82	Sammy Sosa	.60
83	Cory Snyder	.05
84	Bobby Thigpen	.05
85	Frank Thomas	.50
86	Robin Ventura	.05
87	Todd Benzinger	.05
88	Glenn Braggs	.05
89	Tom Browning	.05
90	Norm Charlton	.05
91	Eric Davis	.05
92	Rob Dibble	.05
93	Bill Doran	.05
94	Mariano Duncan	.05
95	Billy Hatcher	.05
96	Barry Larkin	.05
97	Randy Myers	.05
98	Hal Morris	.05
99	Joe Oliver	.05
100	Paul O'Neill	.05
101a	Jeff Reed	.05
101b	Beau Allred (Should be #104.)	.05
102	Jose Rijo	.05

103a	Chris Sabo	.05
103b	Carlos Baerga (Should be #106.)	.05
105	Sandy Alomar, Jr.	.05
107	Albert Belle	.05
108	Jerry Browne	.05
109	Tom Candiotti	.05
110	Alex Cole	.05
111a	John Farrell	.05
111b	Chris James (Should be #114.)	.05
112	Felix Fermin	.05
113	Brook Jacoby	.05
115	Doug Jones	.05
116a	Steve Olin	.05
116b	Mitch Webster (Should be #119.)	.05
117	Greg Swindell	.05
118	Turner Ward	.05
120	Dave Bergman	.05
121	Cecil Fielder	.05
122	Travis Fryman	.05
123	Mike Henneman	.05
124	Lloyd Moseby	.05
125	Dan Petry	.05
126	Tony Phillips	.05
127	Mark Salas	.05
128	Frank Tanana	.05
129	Alan Trammell	.05
130	Lou Whitaker	.05
131	Eric Anthony	.05
132	Craig Biggio	.05
133	Ken Caminiti	.05
134	Casey Candaele	.05
135	Andujar Cedeno	.05
136	Mark Davidson	.05
137	Jim Deshaies	.05
138	Mark Portugal	.05
139	Rafael Ramirez	.05
140	Mike Scott	.05
141	Eric Yelding	.05
142	Gerald Young	.05
143	Kevin Appier	.05
144	George Brett	.65
145	Jeff Conine **RC**	.40
146	Jim Eisenreich	.05
147	Tom Gordon	.05
148	Mark Gubicza	.05
149	Bo Jackson	.10
150	Brent Mayne	.05
151	Mike Macfarlane	.05
152	Brian McRae **RC**	.10
153	Jeff Montgomery	.05
154	Bret Saberhagen	.05
155	Kevin Seitzer	.05
156	Terry Shumpert	.05
157	Kurt Stillwell	.05
158	Danny Tartabull	.05
159	Tim Belcher	.05
160	Kal Daniels	.05
161	Alfredo Griffin	.05
162	Lenny Harris	.05
163	Jay Howell	.05
164	Ramon Martinez	.05
165	Mike Morgan	.05
166	Eddie Murray	.50
167	Jose Offerman	.05
168	Juan Samuel	.05
169	Mike Scioscia	.05
170	Mike Sharperson	.05
171	Darryl Strawberry	.05
172	Greg Brock	.05
173	Chuck Crim	.05
174	Jim Gantner	.05
175	Ted Higuera	.05
176	Mark Knudson	.05
177	Tim McIntosh	.05
178	Paul Molitor	.50
179	Dan Plesac	.05
180	Gary Sheffield	.35
181	Bill Spiers	.05
182	B.J. Surhoff	.05
183	Greg Vaughn	.05
184	Robin Yount	.50
185	Rick Aguilera	.05
186	Greg Gagne	.05
187	Dan Gladden	.05
188	Brian Harper	.05
189	Kent Hrbek	.05
190	Gene Larkin	.05
191	Shane Mack	.05
192	Pedro Munoz	.05
193	Al Newman	.05
194	Junior Ortiz	.05
195	Kirby Puckett	.60
196	Kevin Tapani	.05
197	Dennis "Oil Can" Boyd	.05
198	Tim Burke	.05
199	Ivan Calderon	.05
200	Delino DeShields	.05
201	Mike Fitzgerald	.05
202	Steve Frey	.05
203	Andres Galarraga	.05
204	Marquis Grissom	.05
205	Dave Martinez	.05
206	Dennis Martinez	.05
207	Junior Noboa	.05
208	Spike Owen	.05
209	Scott Ruskin	.05
210	Tim Wallach	.05
211	Daryl Boston	.05
212	Vince Coleman	.05
213	David Cone	.05
214	Ron Darling	.05
215	Kevin Elster	.05
216	Sid Fernandez	.05
217	John Franco	.05
218	Dwight Gooden	.05

219	Tom Herr	.05
220	Todd Hundley	.05
221	Gregg Jefferies	.05
222	Howard Johnson	.05
223	Dave Magadan	.05
224	Kevin McReynolds	.05
225	Keith Miller	.05
226	Mackey Sasser	.05
227	Frank Viola	.05
228	Jesse Barfield	.05
229	Greg Cadaret	.05
230	Alvaro Espinoza	.05
231	Bob Geren	.05
232	Lee Guetterman	.05
233	Mel Hall	.05
234	Andy Hawkins	.05
235	Roberto Kelly	.05
236	Tim Leary	.05
237	Jim Leyritz	.05
238	Kevin Maas	.05
239	Don Mattingly	.65
240	Hensley Meulens	.05
241	Eric Plunk	.05
242	Steve Sax	.05
243	Todd Burns	.05
244	Jose Canseco	.35
245	Dennis Eckersley	.05
246	Mike Gallego	.05
247	Dave Henderson	.05
248	Rickey Henderson	.50
249	Rick Honeycutt	.05
250	Carney Lansford	.05
251	Mark McGwire	1.00
252	Mike Moore	.05
253	Terry Steinbach	.05
254	Dave Stewart	.05
255	Walt Weiss	.05
256	Bob Welch	.05
257	Curt Young	.05
258	Wes Chamberlain	.05
259	Pat Combs	.05
260	Darren Daulton	.05
261	Jose DeJesus	.05
262	Len Dykstra	.05
263	Charlie Hayes	.05
264	Von Hayes	.05
265	Ken Howell	.05
266	John Kruk	.05
267	Roger McDowell	.05
268	Mickey Morandini	.05
269	Terry Mulholland	.05
270	Dale Murphy	.15
271	Randy Ready	.05
272	Dickie Thon	.05
273	Stan Belinda	.05
274	Jay Bell	.05
275	Barry Bonds	1.50
276	Bobby Bonilla	.05
277	Doug Drabek	.05
278	Carlos Garcia **RC**	.05
279	Neal Heaton	.05
280	Jeff King	.05
281	Bill Landrum	.05
282	Mike LaValliere	.05
283	Jose Lind	.05
284	Orlando Merced **RC**	.10
285	Gary Redus	.05
286	Don Slaught	.05
287	Andy Van Slyke	.05
288	Jose DeLeon	.05
289	Pedro Guerrero	.05
290	Ray Lankford	.05
291	Joe Magrane	.05
292	Jose Oquendo	.05
293	Tom Pagnozzi	.05
294	Bryn Smith	.05
295	Lee Smith	.05
296	Ozzie Smith	.60
297	Milt Thompson	.05
298	Craig Wilson **RC**	.05
299	Todd Zeile	.05
300	Shawn Abner	.05
301	Andy Benes	.05
302	Paul Faries	.05
303	Tony Gwynn	.60
304	Greg Harris	.05
305	Thomas Howard	.05
306	Bruce Hurst	.05
307	Craig Lefferts	.05
308	Fred McGriff	.05
309	Dennis Rasmussen	.05
310	Bip Roberts	.05
311	Benito Santiago	.05
312	Garry Templeton	.05
313	Ed Whitson	.05
314	Dave Anderson	.05
315	Kevin Bass	.05
316	Jeff Brantley	.05
317	John Burkett	.05
318	Will Clark	.05
319	Steve Decker	.05
320	Scott Garrelts	.05
321	Terry Kennedy	.05
322	Mark Leonard	.05
323	Darren Lewis	.05
324	Greg Litton	.05
325	Willie McGee	.05
326	Kevin Mitchell	.05
327	Don Robinson	.05
328	Andres Santana	.05
329	Robby Thompson	.05
330	Jose Uribe	.05
331	Matt Williams	.05
332	Scott Bradley	.05
333	Henry Cotto	.05
334	Alvin Davis	.05
335	Ken Griffey Sr.	.05
336	Ken Griffey Jr.	.75

337	Erik Hanson	.05
338	Brian Holman	.05
339	Randy Johnson	.50
340	Edgar Martinez	.05
341	Tino Martinez	.05
342	Pete O'Brien	.05
343	Harold Reynolds	.05
344	David Valle	.05
345	Omar Vizquel	.05
346	Brad Arnsberg	.05
347	Kevin Brown	.05
348	Julio Franco	.05
349	Jeff Huson	.05
350	Rafael Palmeiro	.40
351	Geno Petralli	.05
352	Gary Pettis	.05
353	Kenny Rogers	.05
354	Jeff Russell	.05
355	Nolan Ryan	1.50
356	Ruben Sierra	.05
357	Bobby Witt	.05
358	Roberto Alomar	.15
359	Pat Borders	.05
360	Joe Carter	.05
361	Kelly Gruber	.05
362	Tom Henke	.05
363	Glenallen Hill	.05
364	Jimmy Key	.05
365	Manny Lee	.05
366	Rance Mulliniks	.05
367	John Olerud	.05
368	Dave Stieb	.05
369	Duane Ward	.05
370	David Wells	.05
371	Mark Whiten	.05
372	Mookie Wilson	.05
373	Willie Banks	.05
374	Steve Carter	.05
375	Scott Chiamparino	.05
376	Steve Chitren	.05
377	Darrin Fletcher	.05
378	Rich Garces	.05
379	Reggie Jefferson	.05
380	Eric Karros **RC**	.50
381	Pat Kelly	.05
382	Chuck Knoblauch	.05
383	Denny Neagle	.05
384	Dan Opperman	.05
385	John Ramos	.05
386	Henry Rodriguez **RC**	.05
387	Mo Vaughn	.05
388	Gerald Williams	.05
389	Mike York	.05
390	Eddie Zosky	.05
391	Barry Bonds (Great Performer)	.75
392	Cecil Fielder (Great Performer)	.05
393	Rickey Henderson (Great Performer)	.25
394	Dave Justice (Great Performer)	.05
395	Nolan Ryan (Great Performer)	.75
396	Bobby Thigpen (Great Performer)	.05
397	Checklist	.05
398	Checklist	.05
399	Checklist	.05
400	Checklist	.05

Gold

BO JACKSON
KANSAS CITY ROYALS • OUTFIELD

A pair of action photos flanking and below a portrait in a home plate frame at top-center are featured on these cards. Background is a graduated gold coloring. The Fleer Ultra Team logo is in the upper-left corner. Backs have narrative career information. The Puckett and Sandberg cards feature incorrect historical information on the backs.

		NM/M
Complete Set (10):		5.00
Common Player:		.15
1	Barry Bonds	2.50
2	Will Clark	.15
3	Doug Drabek	.15
4	Ken Griffey Jr.	1.50
5	Rickey Henderson	.75
6	Bo Jackson	.25
7	Ramon Martinez	.15
8	Kirby Puckett	1.00
9	Chris Sabo	.15
10	Ryne Sandberg	1.00

Update

RICK WILKINS CUBS CATCHER

This 120-card set was produced as a supplement to the premier Fleer Ultra set. Cards feature the same style as the regular Fleer Ultra cards. The cards were sold only as complete sets in full color, shrinkwrapped boxes.

		NM/M
Complete Set (120):		15.00
Common Player:		.05
1	Dwight Evans	.05
2	Chito Martinez	.05
3	Bob Melvin	.05
4	Mike Mussina RC	3.00
5	Jack Clark	.05
6	Dana Kiecker	.05
7	Steve Lyons	.05
8	Gary Gaetti	.05
9	Dave Gallagher	.05
10	Dave Parker	.05
11	Luis Polonia	.05
12	Luis Sojo	.05
13	Wilson Alvarez	.05
14	Alex Fernandez	.05
15	Craig Grebeck	.05
16	Ron Karkovice	.05
17	Warren Newson	.05
18	Scott Radinsky	.05
19	Glenallen Hill	.05
20	Charles Nagy	.05
21	Mark Whiten	.05
22	Milt Cuyler	.05
23	Paul Gibson	.05
24	Mickey Tettleton	.05
25	Todd Benzinger	.05
26	Storm Davis	.05
27	Kirk Gibson	.05
28	Bill Pecota	.05
29	Gary Thurman	.05
30	Darryl Hamilton	.05
31	Jaime Navarro	.05
32	Willie Randolph	.05
33	Bill Wegman	.05
34	Randy Bush	.05
35	Chili Davis	.05
36	Scott Erickson	.05
37	Chuck Knoblauch	.05
38	Scott Leius	.05
39	Jack Morris	.05
40	John Habyan	.05
41	Pat Kelly	.05
42	Matt Nokes	.05
43	Scott Sanderson	.05
44	Bernie Williams	.05
45	Harold Baines	.05
46	Brook Jacoby	.05
47	Ernest Riles	.05
48	Willie Wilson	.05
49	Jay Buhner	.05
50	Rich DeLucia	.05
51	Mike Jackson	.05
52	Bill Krueger	.05
53	Bill Swift	.05
54	Brian Downing	.05
55	Juan Gonzalez	.75
56	Dean Palmer	.05
57	Kevin Reimer	.05
58	Ivan Rodriguez RC	6.00
59	Tom Candiotti	.05
60	Juan Guzman	.05
61	Bob MacDonald	.05
62	Greg Myers	.05
63	Ed Sprague	.05
64	Devon White	.05
65	Rafael Belliard	.05
66	Juan Berenguer	.05
67	Brian Hunter	.05
68	Kent Mercker	.05
69	Otis Nixon	.05
70	Danny Jackson	.05
71	Chuck McElroy	.05
72	Gary Scott	.05
73	Heathcliff Slocumb	.05
74	Chico Walker	.05
75	Rick Wilkins	.05
76	Chris Hammond	.05
77	Luis Quinones	.05
78	Herm Winningham	.05
79	Jeff Bagwell RC	6.00
80	Jim Corsi	.05
81	Steve Finley	.05
82	Luis Gonzalez RC	1.00
83	Pete Harnisch	.05
84	Darryl Kile	.05
85	Brett Butler	.05
86	Gary Carter	1.00
87	Tim Crews	.05
88	Orel Hershiser	.05
89	Bob Ojeda	.05
90	Bret Barberie	.05
91	Barry Jones	.05
92	Gilberto Reyes	.05
93	Larry Walker	.05
94	Hubie Brooks	.05
95	Tim Burke	.05
96	Rick Cerone	.05
97	Jeff Innis	.05
98	Wally Backman	.05
99	Tommy Greene	.05
100	Ricky Jordan	.05
101	Mitch Williams	.05
102	John Smiley	.05
103	Randy Tomlin	.05
104	Gary Varsho	.05
105	Cris Carpenter	.05
106	Ken Hill	.05
107	Felix Jose	.05
108	Omar Oliveras RC	.05
109	Gerald Perry	.05
110	Jerald Clark	.05
111	Tony Fernandez	.05
112	Darrin Jackson	.05
113	Mike Maddux	.05
114	Tim Teufel	.05
115	Bud Black	.05
116	Kelly Downs	.05
117	Mike Felder	.05
118	Willie McGee	.05
119	Trevor Wilson	.05
120	Checklist	.05

1992 Ultra Pre-Production Samples

ROGER CLEMENS

These cards were produced and distributed to hobby dealers to give them a preview of Ultra's second-year offering. Cards are virtually identical to the issued versions except for a white oval on back which has a "1992 / PRE-PRODUCTION / SAMPLE" notice printed in black. Each card (except the Gwynn) can also be found in a version with no card number on back; they are worth a small premium over the numbered promos. Two strips were issued, each with a different Gwynn card.

		NM/M
Uncut Strip:		25.00
Complete Set (6):		25.00
Common Player:		1.00
118	Todd Van Poppel	1.00
180	Rey Sanchez	1.00
271	Ozzie Smith	7.50
288	Royce Clayton	1.00
6/25	Roger Clemens (Award Winners)	10.00
2/10	Tony Gwynn (Commermorative Series)	7.50
7/10	Tony Gwynn (Commemorative Series)	7.50

1992 Ultra

JOE CARTER TORONTO BLUE JAYS • OUTFIELD

Fleer released its second annual Ultra set in 1992. Card fronts feature full-color action photos with a marble accent at the card bottom. The flip sides are horizontal with two additional player photos. Many insert sets were randomly included in foil packs as premiums. These included rookie, All-Star and award winners, among others. A two-card Tony Gwynn send-away set was also available through an offer from Fleer. For $1 and 10 Ultra wrappers, collectors could receive the Gwynn cards. The set is numbered by team; cards #1-300 comprise Series I, cards #301-600 are Series II.

		NM/M
Complete Set (600):		12.00
Common Player:		.05
Ser. 1 or 2 Pack (14):		.60
Ser. 1 or 2 Box (36):		12.50
Tony Gwynn Auto.		60.00
1	Glenn Davis	.05
2	Mike Devereaux	.05
3	Dwight Evans	.05
4	Leo Gomez	.05
5	Chris Hoiles	.05
6	Sam Horn	.05
7	Chito Martinez	.05
8	Randy Milligan	.05
9	Mike Mussina	.30
10	Billy Ripken	.05
11	Cal Ripken, Jr.	1.00
12	Tom Brunansky	.05
13	Ellis Burks	.05
14	Jack Clark	.05
15	Roger Clemens	.60
16	Mike Greenwell	.05
17	Joe Hesketh	.05
18	Tony Pena	.05
19	Carlos Quintana	.05
20	Jeff Reardon	.05
21	Jody Reed	.05
22	Luis Rivera	.05
23	Mo Vaughn	.75
24	Gary DiSarcina	.05
25	Chuck Finley	.05
26	Gary Gaetti	.05
27	Bryan Harvey	.05
28	Lance Parrish	.05
29	Luis Polonia	.05
30	Dick Schofield	.05
31	Luis Sojo	.05
32	Wilson Alvarez	.05
33	Carlton Fisk	.40
34	Craig Grebeck	.05
35	Ozzie Guillen	.05
36	Greg Hibbard	.05
37	Charlie Hough	.05
38	Lance Johnson	.05
39	Ron Karkovice	.05
40	Jack McDowell	.05
41	Donn Pall	.05
42	Melido Perez	.05
43	Tim Raines	.05
44	Frank Thomas	.40
45	Sandy Alomar, Jr.	.05
46	Carlos Baerga	.05
47	Albert Belle	.05
48	Jerry Browne	.05
49	Felix Fermin	.05
50	Reggie Jefferson	.05
51	Mark Lewis	.05
52	Carlos Martinez	.05
53	Steve Olin	.05
54	Jim Thome	.35
55	Mark Whiten	.05
56	Dave Bergman	.05
57	Milt Cuyler	.05
58	Rob Deer	.05
59	Cecil Fielder	.05
60	Travis Fryman	.05
61	Scott Livingstone	.05
62	Tony Phillips	.05
63	Mickey Tettleton	.05
64	Alan Trammell	.05
65	Lou Whitaker	.05
66	Kevin Appier	.05
67	Mike Boddicker	.05
68	George Brett	.60
69	Jim Eisenreich	.05
70	Mark Gubicza	.05
71	David Howard	.05
72	Joel Johnston	.05
73	Mike Macfarlane	.05
74	Brent Mayne	.05
75	Brian McRae	.05
76	Jeff Montgomery	.05
77	Terry Shumpert	.05
78	Don August	.05
79	Dante Bichette	.05
80	Ted Higuera	.05
81	Paul Molitor	.40
82	Jamie Navarro	.05
83	Gary Sheffield	.30
84	Bill Spiers	.05
85	B.J. Surhoff	.05
86	Greg Vaughn	.05
87	Robin Yount	.40
88	Rick Aguilera	.05
89	Chili Davis	.05
90	Scott Erickson	.05
91	Brian Harper	.05
92	Kent Hrbek	.05
93	Chuck Knoblauch	.05
94	Scott Leius	.05
95	Shane Mack	.05
96	Mike Pagliarulo	.05
97	Kirby Puckett	.50
98	Kevin Tapani	.05
99	Jesse Barfield	.05
100	Alvaro Espinoza	.05
101	Mel Hall	.05
102	Pat Kelly	.05
103	Roberto Kelly	.05
104	Kevin Maas	.05
105	Don Mattingly	.60
106	Hensley Meulens	.05
107	Matt Nokes	.05
108	Steve Sax	.05
109	Harold Baines	.05
110	Jose Canseco	.30
111	Ron Darling	.05
112	Mike Gallego	.05
113	Dave Henderson	.05
114	Rickey Henderson	.40
115	Mark McGwire	.05
116	Terry Steinbach	.05
117	Dave Stewart	.05
118	Todd Van Poppel	.05
119	Bob Welch	.05
120	Greg Briley	.05
121	Jay Buhner	.05
122	Rich DeLucia	.05
123	Ken Griffey Jr.	.65
124	Erik Hanson	.05
125	Randy Johnson	.40
126	Edgar Martinez	.05
127	Tino Martinez	.05
128	Pete O'Brien	.05
129	Harold Reynolds	.05
130	Dave Valle	.05
131	Julio Franco	.05
132	Juan Gonzalez	.20
133	Jeff Huson	.05
134	Mike Jeffcoat	.05
135	Terry Mathews	.05
136	Rafael Palmeiro	.35
137	Dean Palmer	.05
138	Geno Petralli	.05
139	Ivan Rodriguez	.35
140	Jeff Russell	.05
141	Nolan Ryan	1.00
142	Ruben Sierra	.05
143	Roberto Alomar	.15
144	Pat Borders	.05
145	Joe Carter	.05
146	Kelly Gruber	.05
147	Jimmy Key	.05
148	Manny Lee	.05
149	Rance Mullinks	.05
150	Greg Myers	.05
151	John Olerud	.05
152	Dave Stieb	.05
153	Todd Stottlemyre	.05
154	Duane Ward	.05
155	Devon White	.05
156	Eddie Zosky	.05
157	Steve Avery	.05
158	Rafael Belliard	.05
159	Jeff Blauser	.05
160	Sid Bream	.05
161	Ron Gant	.05
162	Tom Glavine	.25
163	Brian Hunter	.05
164	Dave Justice	.05
165	Mark Lemke	.05
166	Greg Olson	.05
167	Terry Pendleton	.05
168	Lonnie Smith	.05
169	John Smoltz	.05
170	Mike Stanton	.05
171	Jeff Treadway	.05
172	Paul Assenmacher	.05
173	George Bell	.05
174	Shawon Dunston	.05
175	Mark Grace	.05
176	Danny Jackson	.05
177	Les Lancaster	.05
178	Greg Maddux	.50
179	Luis Salazar	.05
180	Rey Sanchez	.05
181	Ryne Sandberg	.50
182	Jose Vizcaino	.05
183	Chico Walker	.05
184	Jerome Walton	.05
185	Glenn Braggs	.05
186	Tom Browning	.05
187	Rob Dibble	.05
188	Bill Doran	.05
189	Chris Hammond	.05
190	Billy Hatcher	.05
191	Barry Larkin	.05
192	Hal Morris	.05
193	Joe Oliver	.05
194	Paul O'Neill	.05
195	Jeff Reed	.05
196	Jose Rijo	.05
197	Chris Sabo	.05
198	Jeff Bagwell	.40
199	Craig Biggio	.05
200	Ken Caminiti	.05
201	Andujar Cedeno	.05
202	Steve Finley	.05
203	Luis Gonzalez	.05
204	Pete Harnisch	.05
205	Xavier Hernandez	.05
206	Darryl Kile	.05
207	Al Osuna	.05
208	Curt Schilling	.25
209	Brett Butler	.05
210	Kal Daniels	.05
211	Lenny Harris	.05
212	Stan Javier	.05
213	Ramon Martinez	.05
214	Roger McDowell	.05
215	Jose Offerman	.05
216	Juan Samuel	.05
217	Mike Scioscia	.05
218	Mike Sharperson	.05
219	Darryl Strawberry	.05
220	Delino DeShields	.05
221	Tom Foley	.05
222	Steve Frey	.05
223	Dennis Martinez	.05
224	Spike Owen	.05
225	Gilberto Reyes	.05
226	Tim Wallach	.05
227	Daryl Boston	.05
228	Tim Burke	.05
229	Vince Coleman	.05
230	David Cone	.05
231	Kevin Elster	.05
232	Dwight Gooden	.05
233	Todd Hundley	.05
234	Jeff Innis	.05
235	Howard Johnson	.05
236	Dave Magadan	.05
237	Mackey Sasser	.05
238	Anthony Young	.05
239	Wes Chamberlain	.05
240	Darren Daulton	.05
241	Len Dykstra	.05
242	Tommy Greene	.05
243	Charlie Hayes	.05
244	Dave Hollins	.05
245	Ricky Jordan	.05
246	John Kruk	.05
247	Mickey Morandini	.05
248	Terry Mulholland	.05
249	Dale Murphy	.25
250	Jay Bell	.05
251	Barry Bonds	1.00
252	Steve Buechele	.05
253	Doug Drabek	.05
254	Mike LaValliere	.05
255	Jose Lind	.05
256	Lloyd McClendon	.05
257	Orlando Merced	.05
258	Don Slaught	.05
259	John Smiley	.05
260	Zane Smith	.05
261	Randy Tomlin	.05
262	Andy Van Slyke	.05
263	Pedro Guerrero	.05
264	Felix Jose	.05
265	Ray Lankford	.05
266	Omar Olivares	.05
267	Jose Oquendo	.05
268	Tom Pagnozzi	.05
269	Bryn Smith	.05
270	Lee Smith	.05
271	Ozzie Smith	.50
272	Milt Thompson	.05
273	Todd Zeile	.05
274	Andy Benes	.05
275	Jerald Clark	.05
276	Tony Fernandez	.05
277	Tony Gwynn	.50
278	Greg Harris	.05
279	Thomas Howard	.05
280	Bruce Hurst	.05
281	Mike Maddux	.05
282	Fred McGriff	.05
283	Benito Santiago	.05
284	Kevin Bass	.05
285	Jeff Brantley	.05
286	John Burkett	.05
287	Will Clark	.05
288	Royce Clayton	.05
289	Steve Decker	.05
290	Kelly Downs	.05
291	Mike Felder	.05
292	Darren Lewis	.05
293	Kirt Manwaring	.05
294	Willie McGee	.05
295	Robby Thompson	.05
296	Matt Williams	.05
297	Trevor Wilson	.05
298	Checklist 1-108 (Sandy Alomar, Jr.)	.05
299	Checklist 109-208 (Rey Sanchez)	.05
300	Checklist 209-300 (Nolan Ryan)	.25
301	Brady Anderson	.05
302	Todd Frohwirth	.05
303	Ben McDonald	.05
304	Mark McLemore	.05
305	Jose Mesa	.05
306	Bob Milacki	.05
307	Gregg Olson	.05
308	David Segui	.05
309	Rick Sutcliffe	.05
310	Jeff Tackett	.05
311	Wade Boggs	.50
312	Scott Cooper	.05
313	John Flaherty	.05
314	Wayne Housie	.05
315	Peter Hoy	.05
316	John Marzano	.05
317	Tim Naehring	.05
318	Phil Plantier	.05
319	Frank Viola	.05
320	Matt Young	.05
321	Jim Abbott	.05
322	Hubie Brooks	.05
323	Chad Curtis RC	.25
324	Alvin Davis	.05
325	Junior Felix	.05
326	Von Hayes	.05
327	Mark Langston	.05
328	Scott Lewis	.05
329	Don Robinson	.05
330	Bobby Rose	.05
331	Lee Stevens	.05
332	George Bell	.05
333	Esteban Beltre	.05
334	Joey Cora	.05
335	Alex Fernandez	.05
336	Roberto Hernandez	.05
337	Mike Huff	.05
338	Kirk McCaskill	.05
339	Dan Pasqua	.05
340	Scott Radinsky	.05
341	Steve Sax	.05
342	Bobby Thigpen	.05
343	Robin Ventura	.05
344	Jack Armstrong	.05
345	Alex Cole	.05
346	Dennis Cook	.05
347	Glenallen Hill	.05
348	Thomas Howard	.05
349	Brook Jacoby	.05
350	Kenny Lofton	.05
351	Charles Nagy	.05
352	Rod Nichols	.05
353	Junior Ortiz	.05
354	Dave Otto	.05
355	Tony Perezchica	.05
356	Scott Scudder	.05
357	Paul Sorrento	.05
358	Skeeter Barnes	.05
359	Mark Carreon	.05
360	John Doherty	.05
361	Dan Gladden	.05
362	Bill Gullickson	.05
363	Shawn Hare	.05
364	Mike Henneman	.05
365	Chad Kreuter	.05
366	Mark Leiter	.05
367	Mike Munoz	.05
368	Kevin Ritz	.05
369	Mark Davis	.05
370	Tom Gordon	.05
371	Chris Gwynn	.05
372	Gregg Jefferies	.05
373	Wally Joyner	.05
374	Kevin McReynolds	.05
375	Keith Miller	.05
376	Rico Rossy	.05
377	Curtis Wilkerson	.05
378	Ricky Bones	.05
379	Chris Bosio	.05
380	Cal Eldred	.05
381	Scott Fletcher	.05
382	Jim Gantner	.05
383	Darryl Hamilton	.05
384	Doug Henry	.05
385	Pat Listach RC	.05
386	Tim McIntosh	.05
387	Edwin Nunez	.05
388	Dan Plesac	.05
389	Kevin Seitzer	.05
390	Franklin Stubbs	.05
391	William Suero	.05
392	Bill Wegman	.05
393	Willie Banks	.05
394	Jarvis Brown	.05
395	Greg Gagne	.05
396	Mark Guthrie	.05
397	Bill Krueger	.05
398	Pat Mahomes RC	.05
399	Pedro Munoz	.05
400	John Smiley	.05
401	Gary Wayne	.05
402	Lenny Webster	.05
403	Carl Willis	.05
404	Greg Cadaret	.05
405	Steve Farr	.05
406	Mike Gallego	.05
407	Charlie Hayes	.05
408	Steve Howe	.05
409	Dion James	.05
410	Jeff Johnson	.05
411	Tim Leary	.05
412	Jim Leyritz	.05
413	Melido Perez	.05
414	Scott Sanderson	.05
415	Andy Stankiewicz	.05
416	Mike Stanley	.05
417	Danny Tartabull	.05
418	Lance Blankenship	.05
419	Mike Bordick	.05
420	Scott Brosius RC	.05
421	Dennis Eckersley	.35
422	Scott Hemond	.05
423	Carney Lansford	.05
424	Henry Mercedes	.05
425	Mike Moore	.05
426	Gene Nelson	.05
427	Randy Ready	.05
428	Bruce Walton	.05
429	Willie Wilson	.05
430	Rich Amaral	.05
431	Dave Cochrane	.05
432	Henry Cotto	.05
433	Calvin Jones	.05
434	Kevin Mitchell	.05
435	Clay Parker	.05
436	Omar Vizquel	.05
437	Floyd Bannister	.05
438	Kevin Brown	.05
439	John Cangelosi	.05
440	Brian Downing	.05
441	Monty Fariss	.05
442	Jose Guzman	.05
443	Donald Harris	.05
444	Kevin Reimer	.05
445	Kenny Rogers	.05
446	Wayne Rosenthal	.05

447	Dickie Thon	.05
448	Derek Bell	.05
449	Juan Guzman	.05
450	Tom Henke	.05
451	Candy Maldonado	.05
452	Jack Morris	.05
453	David Wells	.05
454	Dave Winfield	.40
455	Juan Berenguer	.05
456	Damon Berryhill	.05
457	Mike Bielecki	.05
458	Marvin Freeman	.05
459	Charlie Leibrandt	.05
460	Kent Mercker	.05
461	Otis Nixon	.05
462	Alejandro Pena	.05
463	Ben Rivera	.05
464	Deion Sanders	.10
465	Mark Wohlers	.05
466	Shawn Boskie	.05
467	Frank Castillo	.05
468	Andre Dawson	.25
469	Joe Girardi	.05
470	Chuck McElroy	.05
471	Mike Morgan	.05
472	Ken Patterson	.05
473	Bob Scanlan	.05
474	Gary Scott	.05
475	Dave Smith	.05
476	Sammy Sosa	.50
477	Hector Villanueva	.05
478	Scott Bankhead	.05
479	Tim Belcher	.05
480	Freddie Benavides	.05
481	Jacob Brumfield	.05
482	Norm Charlton	.05
483	Dwayne Henry	.05
484	Dave Martinez	.05
485	Bip Roberts	.05
486	Reggie Sanders	.05
487	Greg Swindell	.05
488	Ryan Bowen	.05
489	Casey Candaele	.05
490	Juan Guerrero	.05
491	Pete Incaviglia	.05
492	Jeff Juden	.05
493	Rob Murphy	.05
494	Mark Portugal	.05
495	Rafael Ramirez	.05
496	Scott Servais	.05
497	Ed Taubensee	.05
498	Brian Williams	.05
499	Todd Benzinger	.05
500	John Candelaria	.05
501	Tom Candiotti	.05
502	Tim Crews	.05
503	Eric Davis	.05
504	Jim Gott	.05
505	Dave Hansen	.05
506	Carlos Hernandez	.05
507	Orel Hershiser	.05
508	Eric Karros	.05
509	Bob Ojeda	.05
510	Steve Wilson	.05
511	Moises Alou	.05
512	Bret Barberie	.05
513	Ivan Calderon	.05
514	Gary Carter	.40
515	Archi Cianfrocco	.05
516	Jeff Fassero	.05
517	Darrin Fletcher	.05
518	Marquis Grissom	.05
519	Chris Haney	.05
520	Ken Hill	.05
521	Chris Nabholz	.05
522	Bill Sampen	.05
523	John VanderWal	.05
524	David Wainhouse	.05
525	Larry Walker	.05
526	John Wetteland	.05
527	Bobby Bonilla	.05
528	Sid Fernandez	.05
529	John Franco	.05
530	Dave Gallagher	.05
531	Paul Gibson	.05
532	Eddie Murray	.40
533	Junior Noboa	.05
534	Charlie O'Brien	.05
535	Bill Pecota	.05
536	Willie Randolph	.05
537	Bret Saberhagen	.05
538	Dick Schofield	.05
539	Pete Schourek	.05
540	Ruben Amaro	.05
541	Andy Ashby	.05
542	Kim Batiste	.05
543	Cliff Brantley	.05
544	Mariano Duncan	.05
545	Jeff Grotewold	.05
546	Barry Jones	.05
547	Julio Peguero	.05
548	Curt Schilling	.25
549	Mitch Williams	.05
550	Stan Belinda	.05
551	Scott Bullett	.05
552	Cecil Espy	.05
553	Jeff King	.05
554	Roger Mason	.05
555	Paul Miller	.05
556	Denny Neagle	.05
557	Vocente Palacios	.05
558	Bob Patterson	.05
559	Tom Prince	.05
560	Gary Redus	.05
561	Gary Varsho	.05
562	Juan Agosto	.05
563	Cris Carpenter	.05
564	Mark Clark RC	.05

565	Jose DeLeon	.05
566	Rich Gedman	.05
567	Bernard Gilkey	.05
568	Rex Hudler	.05
569	Tim Jones	.05
570	Donovan Osborne	.05
571	Mike Perez	.05
572	Gerald Perry	.05
573	Bob Tewksbury	.05
574	Todd Worrell	.05
575	Dave Eiland	.05
576	Jeremy Hernandez	.05
577	Craig Lefferts	.05
578	Jose Melendez	.05
579	Randy Myers	.05
580	Gary Pettis	.05
581	Rich Rodriguez	.05
582	Gary Sheffield	.30
583	Craig Shipley	.05
584	Kurt Stillwell	.05
585	Tim Teufel	.05
586	Rod Beck RC	.05
587	Dave Burba	.05
588	Craig Colbert	.05
589	Bryan Hickerson	.05
590	Mike Jackson	.05
591	Mark Leonard	.05
592	Jim McNamara	.05
593	John Patterson	.05
594	Dave Righetti	.05
595	Cory Snyder	.05
596	Bill Swift	.05
597	Ted Wood	.05
598	Checklist 301-403 (Scott Sanderson)	.05
599	Checklist 404-498 (Junior Ortiz)	.05
600	Checklist 499-600 (Mike Morgan)	.05

All-Rookies

The 10 promising rookies in this set could be found on special cards inserted in Ultra Series 2 foil packs.

		NM/M
Complete Set (10):		2.00
Common Player:		.25
1	Eric Karros	.35
2	Andy Stankiewicz	.25
3	Gary DiSarcina	.25
4	Archi Cianfrocco	.25
5	Jim McNamara	.25
6	Chad Curtis	.25
7	Kenny Lofton	.35
8	Reggie Sanders	.25
9	Pat Mahomes	.25
10	Donovan Osborne	.25

All-Stars

An All-Star team from each league, with two pitchers, could be assembled by collecting these inserts from Ultra Series 2 foil packs.

		NM/M
Complete Set (20):		7.50
Common Player:		.15
1	Mark McGwire	1.25
2	Roberto Alomar	.30
3	Cal Ripken, Jr.	1.50
4	Wade Boggs	.75
5	Mickey Tettleton	.15
6	Ken Griffey Jr.	1.00
7	Roberto Kelly	.15
8	Kirby Puckett	.75
9	Frank Thomas	.65
10	Jack McDowell	.15
11	Will Clark	.15
12	Ryne Sandberg	.75
13	Barry Larkin	.15
14	Gary Sheffield	.35
15	Tom Pagnozzi	.15
16	Barry Bonds	1.50
17	Deion Sanders	.15
18	Darryl Strawberry	.15
19	David Cone	.15
20	Tom Glavine	.30

Award Winners

The 25 cards in this insert issue were randomly packaged with Series 1 Ultra. One of the Cal Ripken cards (#21) can be found with a photo made from a reversed negative, as well as with the proper orientation. Neither version carries a premium.

		NM/M
Complete Set (26):		10.00
Common Player:		.20
1	Jack Morris	.20
2	Chuck Knoblauch	.20
3	Jeff Bagwell	.75
4	Terry Pendleton	.20
5	Cal Ripken, Jr.	2.00
6	Roger Clemens	1.25
7	Tom Glavine	.35
8	Tom Pagnozzi	.20
9	Ozzie Smith	1.00
10	Andy Van Slyke	.20
11	Barry Bonds	2.00
12	Tony Gwynn	1.00
13	Matt Williams	.20
14	Will Clark	.20
15	Robin Ventura	.20
16	Mark Langston	.20
17	Devon White	.20
18	Don Mattingly	1.25
19	Roberto Alomar	.40
21a	Cal Ripken, Jr. (Reversed negative.)	2.00
21b	Cal Ripken, Jr. (Correct)	2.00
22	Ken Griffey Jr.	1.50
23	Kirby Puckett	1.00
24	Greg Maddux	1.00
25	Ryne Sandberg	1.00

Tony Gwynn

This 12-card subset of Ultra's spokesman features 10 cards which were available as inserts in Series I foil packs, plus two cards labeled "Special No. 1" and "Special No. 2" which could only be obtained in a send-away offer. Some 2,000 of these cards carry a "certified" Gwynn autograph. Not part of the issue, but similar in format were a pair of extra Tony Gwynn cards. One pictures him with Fleer CEO Paul Mullan and the other shows him with the poster child for Casa de Amparo, a children's shelter in San Diego County.

		NM/M
Complete Set (12):		9.00
Common Card:		.75
Certified Autograph Card:		60.00
1	Tony Gwynn/Fldg	.75
2	Tony Gwynn/Btg	.75
3	Tony Gwynn/Fldg	.75
4	Tony Gwynn/Btg	.75
5	Tony Gwynn/ Base-Running	.75
6	Tony Gwynn/Awards	.75
7	Tony Gwynn/Bunting	.75
8	Tony Gwynn/Btg	.75
9	Tony Gwynn (Running)	.75
10	Tony Gwynn/Btg	.75
1	Tony Gwynn/Btg	2.00
2	Tony Gwynn/Fldg	2.00
---	Tony Gwynn, Paul Mullan	3.00
---	Tony Gwynn (Casa de Amparo)	7.50

1993 Ultra

The first series of 300 cards retains Fleer's successful features from 1992, including additional gold foil stamping, UV coating, and team color-coded marbled bars on the fronts. The backs feature a stylized ballpark background, which creates a 3-D effect, stats and portrait and an action photo. Dennis Eckersley is featured in a limited-edition "Career Highlights" set and personally autographed more than 2,000 of his cards, to be randomly inserted into both series' packs. A 10-card Home Run Kings subset and 25-card Ultra Awards Winners subset were also randomly inserted in packs. Ultra Rookies cards are included in both series. Ultra's second series has three limited-edition subsets: Ultra All-Stars, Ultra All-Rookie Team, and Strikeout Kings, plus cards featuring Colorado Rockies and Florida Marlins players.

		NM/M
Complete Set (650):		15.00
Common Player:		.05
Series 1 or 2 Pack (14):		.75
Series 1 or 2 Wax Box (36):		15.00
1	Steve Avery	.05
2	Rafael Belliard	.05
3	Damon Berryhill	.05
4	Sid Bream	.05
5	Ron Gant	.05
6	Tom Glavine	.20
7	Ryan Klesko	.05
8	Mark Lemke	.05
9	Javier Lopez	.05
10	Greg Olson	.05
11	Terry Pendleton	.05
12	Deion Sanders	.05
13	Mike Stanton	.05
14	Paul Assenmacher	.05
15	Steve Buechele	.05
16	Frank Castillo	.05
17	Shawon Dunston	.05
18	Mark Grace	.05
19	Derrick May	.05
20	Chuck McElroy	.05
21	Mike Morgan	.05
22	Bob Scanlan	.05
23	Dwight Smith	.05
24	Sammy Sosa	.60
25	Rick Wilkins	.05
26	Tim Belcher	.05
27	Jeff Branson	.05
28	Bill Doran	.05
29	Chris Hammond	.05
30	Barry Larkin	.05
31	Hal Morris	.05
32	Joe Oliver	.05
33	Jose Rijo	.05
34	Bip Roberts	.05
35	Chris Sabo	.05
36	Reggie Sanders	.05
37	Craig Biggio	.05
38	Ken Caminiti	.05
39	Steve Finley	.05
40	Luis Gonzalez	.05
41	Juan Guerrero	.05
42	Pete Harnisch	.05
43	Xavier Hernandez	.05
44	Doug Jones	.05
45	Al Osuna	.05
46	Eddie Taubensee	.05
47	Scooter Tucker	.05
48	Brian Williams	.05
49	Pedro Astacio	.05

50	Rafael Bournigal	.05
51	Brett Butler	.05
52	Tom Candiotti	.05
53	Eric Davis	.05
54	Lenny Harris	.05
55	Orel Hershiser	.05
56	Eric Karros	.05
57	Pedro Martinez	.50
58	Roger McDowell	.05
59	Jose Offerman	.05
60	Mike Piazza	.75
61	Moises Alou	.05
62	Kent Bottenfield	.05
63	Archi Cianfrocco	.05
64	Greg Colbrunn	.05
65	Wil Cordero	.05
66	Delino DeShields	.05
67	Darrin Fletcher	.05
68	Ken Hill	.05
69	Chris Nabholz	.05
70	Mel Rojas	.05
71	Larry Walker	.05
72	Sid Fernandez	.05
73	John Franco	.05
74	Dave Gallagher	.05
75	Todd Hundley	.05
76	Howard Johnson	.05
77	Jeff Kent	.05
78	Eddie Murray	.50
79	Bret Saberhagen	.05
80	Chico Walker	.05
81	Anthony Young	.05
82	Kyle Abbott	.05
83	Ruben Amaro Jr.	.05
84	Juan Bell	.05
85	Wes Chamberlain	.05
86	Darren Daulton	.05
87	Mariano Duncan	.05
88	Dave Hollins	.05
89	Ricky Jordan	.05
90	John Kruk	.05
91	Mickey Morandini	.05
92	Terry Mulholland	.05
93	Ben Rivera	.05
94	Mike Williams	.05
95	Stan Belinda	.05
96	Jay Bell	.05
97	Jeff King	.05
98	Mike LaValliere	.05
99	Lloyd McClendon	.05
100	Orlando Merced	.05
101	Zane Smith	.05
102	Randy Tomlin	.05
103	Andy Van Slyke	.05
104	Tim Wakefield	.05
105	John Wehner	.05
106	Bernard Gilkey	.05
107	Brian Jordan	.05
108	Ray Lankford	.05
109	Donovan Osborne	.05
110	Tom Pagnozzi	.05
111	Mike Perez	.05
112	Lee Smith	.05
113	Ozzie Smith	.60
114	Bob Tewksbury	.05
115	Todd Zeile	.05
116	Andy Benes	.05
117	Greg Harris	.05
118	Darrin Jackson	.05
119	Fred McGriff	.05
120	Rich Rodriguez	.05
121	Frank Seminara	.05
122	Gary Sheffield	.35
123	Craig Shipley	.05
124	Kurt Stillwell	.05
125	Dan Walters	.05
126	Rod Beck	.05
127	Mike Benjamin	.05
128	Jeff Brantley	.05
129	John Burkett	.05
130	Will Clark	.05
131	Royce Clayton	.05
132	Steve Hosey	.05
133	Mike Jackson	.05
134	Darren Lewis	.05
135	Kirt Manwaring	.05
136	Bill Swift	.05
137	Robby Thompson	.05
138	Brady Anderson	.05
139	Glenn Davis	.05
140	Leo Gomez	.05
141	Chito Martinez	.05
142	Ben McDonald	.05
143	Alan Mills	.05
144	Mike Mussina	.30
145	Gregg Olson	.05
146	David Segui	.05
147	Jeff Tackett	.05
148	Jack Clark	.05
149	Scott Cooper	.05
150	Danny Darwin	.05
151	John Dopson	.05
152	Mike Greenwell	.05
153	Tim Naehring	.05
154	Tony Pena	.05
155	Paul Quantrill	.05
156	Mo Vaughn	.05
157	Frank Viola	.05
158	Bob Zupcic	.05
159	Chad Curtis	.05
160	Gary DiSarcina	.05
161	Damion Easley	.05
162	Chuck Finley	.05
163	Tim Fortugno	.05
164	Rene Gonzales	.05
165	Joe Grahe	.05
166	Mark Langston	.05
167	John Orton	.05

168	Luis Polonia	.05
169	Julio Valera	.05
170	Wilson Alvarez	.05
171	George Bell	.05
172	Joey Cora	.05
173	Alex Fernandez	.05
174	Lance Johnson	.05
175	Ron Karkovice	.05
176	Jack McDowell	.05
177	Scott Radinsky	.05
178	Tim Raines	.05
179	Steve Sax	.05
180	Bobby Thigpen	.05
181	Frank Thomas	.50
182	Sandy Alomar Jr.	.05
183	Carlos Baerga	.05
184	Felix Fermin	.05
185	Thomas Howard	.05
186	Mark Lewis	.05
187	Derek Lilliquist	.05
188	Carlos Martinez	.05
189	Charles Nagy	.05
190	Scott Scudder	.05
191	Paul Sorrento	.05
192	Jim Thome	.40
193	Mark Whiten	.05
194	Milt Cuyler	.05
195	Rob Deer	.05
196	John Doherty	.05
197	Travis Fryman	.05
198	Dan Gladden	.05
199	Mike Henneman	.05
200	John Kiely	.05
201	Chad Kreuter	.05
202	Scott Livingstone	.05
203	Tony Phillips	.05
204	Alan Trammell	.05
205	Mike Boddicker	.05
206	George Brett	.65
207	Tom Gordon	.05
208	Mark Gubicza	.05
209	Gregg Jefferies	.05
210	Wally Joyner	.05
211	Kevin Koslofski	.05
212	Brent Mayne	.05
213	Brian McRae	.05
214	Kevin McReynolds	.05
215	Rusty Meacham	.05
216	Steve Shifflett	.05
217	James Austin	.05
218	Cal Eldred	.05
219	Darryl Hamilton	.05
220	Doug Henry	.05
221	John Jaha	.05
222	Dave Nilsson	.05
223	Jesse Orosco	.05
224	B.J. Surhoff	.05
225	Greg Vaughn	.05
226	Bill Wegman	.05
227	Robin Yount	.50
228	Rick Aguilera	.05
229	J.T. Bruett	.05
230	Scott Erickson	.05
231	Kent Hrbek	.05
232	Terry Jorgensen	.05
233	Scott Leius	.05
234	Pat Mahomes	.05
235	Pedro Munoz	.05
236	Kirby Puckett	.60
237	Kevin Tapani	.05
238	Lenny Webster	.05
239	Carl Willis	.05
240	Mike Gallego	.05
241	John Habyan	.05
242	Pat Kelly	.05
243	Kevin Maas	.05
244	Don Mattingly	.65
245	Hensley Meulens	.05
246	Sam Militello	.05
247	Matt Nokes	.05
248	Melido Perez	.05
249	Andy Stankiewicz	.05
250	Randy Velarde	.05
251	Bob Wickman	.05
252	Bernie Williams	.05
253	Lance Blankenship	.05
254	Mike Bordick	.05
255	Jerry Browne	.05
256	Ron Darling	.05
257a	Dennis Eckersley	.40
257b	Dennis Eckersley (Wt. 195; no "MLBPA" on back - unmarked sample card.)	1.50
257c	Dennis Eckersley (Wt. 195; no "Printed in USA" on back - unmarked sample card.)	1.50
258	Rickey Henderson	.50
259	Vince Horsman	.05
260	Troy Neel	.05
261	Jeff Parrett	.05
262	Terry Steinbach	.05
263	Bob Welch	.05
264	Bobby Witt	.05
265	Rich Amaral	.05
266	Bret Boone	.05
267	Jay Buhner	.05
268	Dave Fleming	.05
269	Randy Johnson	.50
270	Edgar Martinez	.05
271	Mike Schooler	.05
272	Russ Swan	.05
273	Dave Valle	.05
274	Omar Vizquel	.05
275	Kerry Woodson	.05
276	Kevin Brown	.05
277	Julio Franco	.05
278	Jeff Frye	.05
279	Juan Gonzalez	.25

No	Player	Price
280	Jeff Huson	.05
281	Rafael Palmeiro	.40
282	Dean Palmer	.05
283	Roger Pavlik	.05
284	Ivan Rodriguez	.40
285	Kenny Rogers	.05
286	Derek Bell	.05
287	Pat Borders	.05
288	Joe Carter	.05
289	Bob MacDonald	.05
290	Jack Morris	.05
291	John Olerud	.05
292	Ed Sprague	.05
293	Todd Stottlemyre	.05
294	Mike Timlin	.05
295	Duane Ward	.05
296	David Wells	.05
297	Devon White	.05
298	Checklist (Ray Lankford)	.05
299	Checklist (Bobby Witt)	.05
300	Checklist (Mike Piazza)	.40
301	Steve Bedrosian	.05
302	Jeff Blauser	.05
303	Francisco Cabrera	.05
304	Marvin Freeman	.05
305	Brian Hunter	.05
306	Dave Justice	.05
307	Greg Maddux	.60
308	Greg McMichael RC	.05
309	Kent Mercker	.05
310	Otis Nixon	.05
311	Pete Smith	.05
312	John Smoltz	.05
313	Jose Guzman	.05
314	Mike Harkey	.05
315	Greg Hibbard	.05
316	Candy Maldonado	.05
317	Randy Myers	.05
318	Dan Plesac	.05
319	Rey Sanchez	.05
320	Ryne Sandberg	.60
321	Tommy Shields RC	.05
322	Jose Vizcaino	.05
323	Matt Walbeck RC	.05
324	Willie Wilson	.05
325	Tom Browning	.05
326	Tim Costo	.05
327	Rob Dibble	.05
328	Steve Foster	.05
329	Roberto Kelly	.05
330	Randy Milligan	.05
331	Kevin Mitchell	.05
332	Tim Pugh RC	.05
333	Jeff Reardon	.05
334	John Roper RC	.05
335	Juan Samuel	.05
336	John Smiley	.05
337	San Wilson	.05
338	Scott Aldred	.05
339	Andy Ashby	.05
340	Freddie Benavides	.05
341	Dante Bichette	.05
342	Willie Blair	.05
343	Daryl Boston	.05
344	Vinny Castilla	.05
345	Jerald Clark	.05
346	Alex Cole	.05
347	Andres Galarraga	.05
348	Joe Girardi	.05
349	Ryan Hawblitzel RC	.05
350	Charlie Hayes	.05
351	Butch Henry	.05
352	Darren Holmes	.05
353	Dale Murphy	.20
354	David Nied	.05
355	Jeff Parrett	.05
356	Steve Reed RC	.05
357	Bruce Ruffin	.05
358	Danny Sheaffer RC	.05
359	Bryn Smith	.05
360	Jim Tatum RC	.05
361	Eric Young	.05
362	Gerald Young	.05
363	Luis Aquino	.05
364	Alex Arias RC	.05
365	Jack Armstrong	.05
366	Bret Barberie	.05
367	Ryan Bowen	.05
368	Greg Briley	.05
369	Cris Carpenter	.05
370	Chuck Carr	.05
371	Jeff Conine RC	.25
372	Steve Decker	.05
373	Orestes Destrade	.05
374	Monty Fariss	.05
375	Junior Felix	.05
376	Chris Hammond	.05
377	Bryan Harvey	.05
378	Trevor Hoffman RC	.25
379	Charlie Hough	.05
380	Joe Klink	.05
381	Richie Lewis RC	.05
382	Dave Magadan	.05
383	Bob McClure	.05
384	Scott Pose RC	.05
385	Rich Renteria RC	.05
386	Benito Santiago	.05
387	Walt Weiss	.05
388	Nigel Wilson	.05
389	Eric Anthony	.05
390	Jeff Bagwell	.50
391	Andujar Cedeno	.05
392	Doug Drabek	.05
393	Darryl Kile	.05
394	Mark Portugal	.05
395	Karl Rhodes	.05
396	Scott Servais	.05
397	Greg Swindell	.05
398	Tom Goodwin	.05
399	Kevin Gross	.05
400	Carlos Hernandez	.05
401	Ramon Martinez	.05
402	Raul Mondesi	.05
403	Jody Reed	.05
404	Mike Sharperson	.05
405	Cory Snyder	.05
406	Darryl Strawberry	.05
407	Rick Trlicek RC	.05
408	Tim Wallach	.05
409	Todd Worrell	.05
410	Tavo Alvarez	.05
411	Sean Berry RC	.05
412	Frank Bolick RC	.05
413	Cliff Floyd	.05
414	Mike Gardiner	.05
415	Marquis Grissom	.05
416	Tim Laker RC	.05
417	Mike Lansing RC	.10
418	Dennis Martinez	.05
419	John Vander Wal	.05
420	John Wetteland	.05
421	Rondell White	.05
422	Bobby Bonilla	.05
423	Jeromy Burnitz	.05
424	Vince Burnitz RC	.05
425	Mike Draper RC	.05
426	Tony Fernandez	.05
427	Dwight Gooden	.05
428	Jeff Innis	.05
429	Bobby Jones	.05
430	Mike Maddux	.05
431	Charlie O'Brien	.05
432	Joe Orsulak	.05
433	Pete Schourek	.05
434	Frank Tanana	.05
435	Ryan Thompson RC	.05
436	Kim Batiste	.05
437	Mark Davis	.05
438	Jose DeLeon	.05
439	Len Dykstra	.05
440	Jim Eisenreich	.05
441	Tommy Greene	.05
442	Pete Incaviglia	.05
443	Danny Jackson	.05
444	Todd Pratt RC	.05
445	Curt Schilling	.20
446	Milt Thompson	.05
447	David West	.05
448	Mitch Williams	.05
449	Steve Cooke	.05
450	Carlos Garcia	.05
451	Al Martin	.05
452	Blas Minor RC	.05
453	Denny Moeller	.05
454	Denny Neagle	.05
455	Don Slaught	.05
456	Lonnie Smith	.05
457	Paul Wagner	.05
458	Bob Walk	.05
459	Kevin Young	.05
460	Rene Arocha RC	.05
461	Brian Barber	.05
462	Rheal Cormier	.05
463	Gregg Jefferies	.05
464	Joe Magrane	.05
465	Omar Olivares	.05
466	Geronimo Pena	.05
467	Allen Watson	.05
468	Mark Whiten	.05
469	Derek Bell	.05
470	Phil Clark	.05
471	Pat Gomez RC	.05
472	Tony Gwynn	.60
473	Jeremy Hernandez	.05
474	Bruce Hurst	.05
475	Phil Plantier	.05
476	Scott Sanders RC	.05
477	Tim Scott RC	.05
478	Darrell Sherman RC	.05
479	Guillermo Velasquez	.05
480	Tim Worrell RC	.05
481	Todd Benzinger	.05
482	Bud Black	.05
483	Barry Bonds	1.50
484	Dave Burba	.05
485	Bryan Hickerson	.05
486	Dave Martinez	.05
487	Willie McGee	.05
488	Jeff Reed	.05
489	Kevin Rogers	.05
490	Matt Williams	.05
491	Trevor Wilson	.05
492	Harold Baines	.05
493	Mike Devereaux	.05
494	Todd Frohwirth	.05
495	Chris Hoiles	.05
496	Luis Mercedes	.05
497	Sherman Obando RC	.05
498	Brad Pennington RC	.05
499	Harold Reynolds	.05
500	Arthur Rhodes	.05
501	Cal Ripken, Jr.	1.50
502	Rick Sutcliffe	.05
503	Fernando Valenzuela	.05
504	Mark Williamson	.05
505	Scott Bankhead	.05
506	Greg Blosser	.05
507	Ivan Calderon	.05
508	Roger Clemens	.65
509	Andre Dawson	.05
510	Scott Fletcher	.05
511	Greg Harris	.05
512	Billy Hatcher	.05
513	Bob Melvin	.05
514	Carlos Quintana	.05
515	Luis Rivera	.05
516	Jeff Russell	.05
517	Ken Ryan RC	.05
518	Chili Davis	.05
519	Jim Edmonds RC	1.50
520	Gary Gaetti	.05
521	Torey Lovullo	.05
522	Tony Percival RC	.05
523	Tim Salmon	.05
524	Scott Sanderson	.05
525	J.T. Snow RC	.75
526	Jerome Walton	.05
527	Jason Bere	.05
528	Rod Bolton RC	.05
529	Ellis Burks	.05
530	Carlton Fisk	.50
531	Craig Grebeck	.05
532	Ozzie Guillen	.05
533	Roberto Hernandez	.05
534	Bo Jackson	.10
535	Kirk McCaskill	.05
536	Dave Stieb	.05
537	Robin Ventura	.05
538	Albert Belle	.05
539	Mike Bielecki	.05
540	Glenallen Hill	.05
541	Reggie Jefferson	.05
542	Kenny Lofton	.05
543	Jeff Mutis RC	.05
544	Junior Ortiz	.05
545	Manny Ramirez	.50
546	Jeff Treadway	.05
547	Kevin Wickander	.05
548	Cecil Fielder	.05
549	Kirk Gibson	.05
550	Greg Gohr RC	.05
551	David Haas	.05
552	Bill Krueger	.05
553	Mike Moore	.05
554	Mickey Tettleton	.05
555	Lou Whitaker	.05
556	Kevin Appier	.05
557	Billy Brewer RC	.05
558	David Cone	.05
559	Greg Gagne	.05
560	Mark Gardner	.05
561	Phil Hiatt	.05
562	Felix Jose	.05
563	Jose Lind	.05
564	Mike Macfarlane	.05
565	Keith Miller	.05
566	Jeff Montgomery	.05
567	Hipolito Pechardo	.05
568	Ricky Bones	.05
569	Tom Brunansky	.05
570	Joe Kmak RC	.05
571	Pat Listach	.05
572	Graeme Lloyd RC	.05
573	Carlos Maldonado RC	.05
574	Josias Manzanillo	.05
575	Matt Mieske	.05
576	Kevin Reimer	.05
577	Bill Spiers	.05
578	Dickie Thon	.05
579	Willie Banks	.05
580	Jim Deshaies	.05
581	Mark Guthrie	.05
582	Brian Harper	.05
583	Chuck Knoblauch	.05
584	Gene Larkin	.05
585	Shane Mack	.05
586	David McCarty	.05
587	Mike Pagliarulo	.05
588	Mike Trombley	.05
589	Dave Winfield	.50
590	Jim Abbott	.05
591	Wade Boggs	.60
592	Russ Davis RC	.05
593	Steve Farr	.05
594	Steve Howe	.05
595	Mike Humphreys RC	.05
596	Jimmy Key	.05
597	Jim Leyritz	.05
598	Bobby Munoz RC	.05
599	Paul O'Neill	.05
600	Spike Owen	.05
601	Mike Stanley	.05
602	Danny Tartabull	.05
603	Scott Brosius	.05
604	Storm Davis	.05
605	Eric Fox	.05
606	Goose Gossage	.05
607	Scott Hammond	.05
608	Dave Henderson	.05
609	Mark McGwire	1.00
610	Mike Mohler RC	.05
611	Edwin Nunez	.05
612	Kevin Seitzer	.05
613	Ruben Sierra	.05
614	Chris Bosio	.05
615	Norm Charlton	.05
616	Jim Converse RC	.05
617	John Cummings RC	.05
618	Mike Felder	.05
619	Ken Griffey Jr.	.75
620	Mike Hampton	.05
621	Erik Hanson	.05
622	Bill Haselman	.05
623	Tino Martinez	.05
624	Lee Tinsley	.05
625	Fernando Vina RC	.05
626	David Wainhouse RC	.05
627	Jose Canseco	.30
628	Benji Gil	.05
629	Tom Henke	.05
630	David Hulse RC	.05
631	Manuel Lee	.05
632	Craig Lefferts	.05
633	Robb Nen RC	.05
634	Gary Redus	.05
635	Bill Ripken	.05
636	Nolan Ryan	1.50
637	Dan Smith	.05
638	Matt Whiteside RC	.05
639	Roberto Alomar	.25
640	Juan Guzman	.05
641	Pat Hentgen	.05
642	Darrin Jackson	.05
643	Randy Knorr	.05
644	Domingo Martinez RC	.05
645	Paul Molitor	.50
646	Dick Schofield	.05
647	Dave Stewart	.05
648	Checklist (Rey Sanchez)	.05
649	Checklist (Jeremy Hernandez)	.05
650	Checklist (Junior Ortiz)	.05

Award Winners

This insert set features 18 Top Glove players (nine from each league), two rookies of the year, three MVPs (both leagues and World Series), both Cy Young Award winners and one Player of the Year. All cards are UV coated and foil stamped on both sides and were found in Series I packs. Two formats are seen. Cards #1-18 are horizontal with player portrait and action photos on a marbled black background. Gold-foil graphics identify the player. Cards #19-25 are verticial with a black background that has "Fleer Ultra Award Winners" splashed around in trendy colors. The Ultra logo, player's name and his award are spelled out in gold foil. Horizontally arranged backs share many of their respective front elements, and have a summary of the season's performance which led to the award. There is a close-up player photo, as well.

		NM/M
Complete Set (25):		12.00
Common Card:		.25
1	Greg Maddux	.75
2	Tom Pagnozzi	.25
3	Mark Grace	.25
4	Jose Lind	.25
5	Terry Pendleton	.25
6	Ozzie Smith	.75
7	Barry Bonds	2.00
8	Andy Van Slyke	.25
9	Larry Walker	.25
10	Mark Langston	.25
11	Ivan Rodriguez	.60
12	Don Mattingly	.75
13	Roberto Alomar	.35
14	Robin Ventura	.25
15	Cal Ripken, Jr.	2.00
16	Ken Griffey Jr.	1.00
17	Kirby Puckett	.75
18	Devon White	.25
19	Pat Listach	.25
20	Eric Karros	.25
21	Pat Borders	.25
22	Greg Maddux	.75
23	Dennis Eckersley	.60
24	Barry Bonds	2.00
25	Gary Sheffield	.45

All-Rookies

These insert cards are foil stamped on both sides and were randomly inserted into Series 2 packs. The cards have black fronts, with six different colors of type. The player's uniform number and position are located in the upper-right corner. The player's name and Ultra logo are gold-foil stamped. Backs have a black background with a player photo and career summary.

		NM/M
Complete Set (10):		4.00
Common Player:		.25
1	Rene Arocha	.25
2	Jeff Conine	.25
3	Phil Hiatt	.25
4	Mike Lansing	.25
5	Al Martin	.25
6	David Nied	.25
7	Mike Piazza	3.00
8	Tim Salmon	.50
9	J.T. Snow	.45
10	Kevin Young	.25

All-Stars

This 20-card set features 10 of the top players from each league. Cards were randomly inserted into Series II packs and are foil stamped on both sides.

		NM/M
Complete Set (20):		17.50
Common Player:		.25
1	Darren Daulton	.25
2	Will Clark	.35
3	Ryne Sandberg	1.50
4	Barry Larkin	.25
5	Gary Sheffield	.40
6	Barry Bonds	3.00
7	Ray Lankford	.25
8	Larry Walker	.25
9	Greg Maddux	1.50
10	Lee Smith	.25
11	Ivan Rodriguez	.75
12	Mark McGwire	2.50
13	Carlos Baerga	.25
14	Cal Ripken, Jr.	3.00
15	Edgar Martinez	.25
16	Juan Gonzalez	1.00
17	Ken Griffey Jr.	2.00
18	Kirby Puckett	1.50
19	Frank Thomas	1.25
20	Mike Mussina	.65

1993 Ultra Career Highlights Promo Sheet

To introduce its "Career Highlights" insert cards in Fleer and Fleer Ultra, the company distributed this promo sheet picturing one card each from the Tom Glavine and Dennis Eckersley sets, overprinted with a gray "PROMOTIONAL SAMPLE" across front and back. A third panel on the sheet provides details of the mail-in offer through which additional cards from the sets could be ordered. The sheet measures 7-1/2"x3-1/2".

	NM/M
Three-Panel Strip:	2.50

Dennis Eckersley Career Highlights

This limited-edition subset chronicles Dennis Eckersley's illustrious career. Cards, which are UV coated and silver foil-stamped on both sides, were randomly inserted into both series' packs. Eckersley autographed more than 2,000 of the cards, which were also randomly inserted in packs. By sending in 10 Fleer Ultra wrappers plus $1, collectors could receive two additional Eckersley cards which were not available in regular packs. Card fronts have a

color action photo, the background of which has been colorized into shades of purple. A black marble strip at bottom has the city name and years he was with the team in silver foil. A large black marble box in one corner has the "Dennis Eckersley Career Highlights" logo in silver foil. On back, a purple box is dropped out of a color photo, and silver-foil typography describes some phrase of Eck's career.

		NM/M
Complete Set (12):		6.00
Common Card:		.50
Autographed Card:		35.00
1	"Perfection" (A's 1987-92)	.50
2	"The Kid" (Indians 1975-77)	.50
3	"The Warrior" (Indians 1975-77)	.50
4	"Beantown Blazer" (Red Sox 1978-84)	.50
5	"Eckspeak" (Red Sox 1978-84)	.50
6	"Down to Earth" (Red Sox 1978-84)	.50
7	"Wrigley Bound" (Cubs 1984-86)	.50
8	"No Relief" (A's 1987-92)	.50
9	"In Control" (A's 1987-92)	.50
10	"Simply the Best" (A's 1987-92)	.50
11	"Reign of Perfection" (A's 1987-92)	.50
12	"Leaving His Mark" (A's 1987-92)	.50

1993 Ultra Commemorative

Photos of Fleer's CEO and the company's spokesman, 1992 Cy Young/MVP winner Dennis Eckersley are superimposed on a background of Oakland-Alameda County Stadium on this promo card. The back gives details of the forthcoming 1993 Fleer Ultra issue.

	NM/M
Dennis Eckersley, Paul Mullan	5.00

Home Run Kings

This insert set features top home run kings. Cards, which are UV coated and have gold foil stamping on both sides, were inserts in Series I packs.

		NM/M
	Complete Set (10):	8.00
	Common Player:	.50
1	Juan Gonzalez	.65
2	Mark McGwire	2.50
3	Cecil Fielder	.50
4	Fred McGriff	.50
5	Albert Belle	.50
6	Barry Bonds	2.50
7	Joe Carter	.50
8	Gary Sheffield	.65
9	Darren Daulton	.50
10	Dave Hollins	.50

Performers

An Ultra Performers set of Fleer Ultra baseball cards was offered directly to collectors in 1993. The set, available only by mail, was limited to 150,000 sets. The cards featured gold-foil stamping and UV coating on each side and a six-photo design, including five on the front of the card. Each card was identified on the back by set serial number jet-printed in black in a strip at bottom.

		NM/M
	Complete Set (10):	5.00
	Common Player:	.25
1	Barry Bonds	2.50
2	Juan Gonzalez	.30
3	Ken Griffey Jr.	1.00
4	Eric Karros	.25
5	Pat Listach	.25
6	Greg Maddux	.75
7	David Nied	.25
8	Gary Sheffield	.40
9	J.T. Snow	.25
10	Frank Thomas	.65

Strikeout Kings

Five of baseball's top strikeout pitchers are featured in this second-series Ultra insert set. Cards are UV coated and foil stamped on both sides. Each card front has a picture of a pitcher winding up to throw. A baseball is in the background, with the pitcher in the forefront.

		NM/M
	Complete Set (5):	7.50
	Common Player:	.25
1	Roger Clemens	2.50
2	Juan Guzman	.25
3	Randy Johnson	1.25
4	Nolan Ryan	5.00
5	John Smoltz	.50

1994 Ultra

Issued in two series of 300 cards each, Ultra for 1994 represented a new highwater mark in production values for a mid-priced brand. Each side of the basic cards

is UV coated and gold-foil embossed. Fronts feature full-bleed action photos. At bottom the player name, team, position and Fleer Ultra logo appear in gold foil above a gold-foil strip. Some rookie cards are specially designated with a large gold "ROOKIE" above the Ultra logo. Backs feature a basic background that is team color coordinated. Three more player action photos are featured on the back, along with a team logo and a modicum of stats and personal data. There is a gold stripe along the left edge and the player's name and card number appear in gold in the lower-left corner. The set features seven types of insert cards, packaged one per pack.

		NM/M
	Complete Set (600):	15.00
	Common Player:	.05
	Series 1 or 2 Pack (14):	.50
	Series 1 or 2 Wax Box (36):	15.00

No.	Player	Price
1	Jeffrey Hammonds	.05
2	Chris Hoiles	.05
3	Ben McDonald	.05
4	Mark McLemore	.05
5	Alan Mills	.05
6	Jamie Moyer	.05
7	Brad Pennington	.05
8	Jim Poole	.05
9	Cal Ripken, Jr.	1.50
10	Jack Voigt	.05
11	Roger Clemens	.65
12	Danny Darwin	.05
13	Andre Dawson	.25
14	Scott Fletcher	.05
15	Greg Harris	.05
16	Billy Hatcher	.05
17	Jeff Russell	.05
18	Aaron Sele	.05
19	Mo Vaughn	.75
20	Mike Butcher	.05
21	Rod Correia	.05
22	Steve Frey	.05
23	Phil Leftwich RC	.05
24	Torey Lovullo	.05
25	Ken Patterson	.05
26	Eduardo Perez	.05
27	Tim Salmon	.25
28	J.T. Snow	.05
29	Chris Turner	.05
30	Wilson Alvarez	.05
31	Jason Bere	.05
32	Joey Cora	.05
33	Alex Fernandez	.05
34	Roberto Hernandez	.05
35	Lance Johnson	.05
36	Ron Karkovice	.05
37	Kirk McCaskill	.05
38	Jeff Schwarz	.05
39	Frank Thomas	.50
40	Sandy Alomar Jr.	.05
41	Albert Belle	.25
42	Felix Fermin	.05
43	Wayne Kirby	.05
44	Tom Kramer	.05
45	Kenny Lofton	.25
46	Jose Mesa	.05
47	Eric Plunk	.05
48	Paul Sorrento	.05
49	Jim Thome	.35
50	Bill Wertz	.05
51	John Doherty	.05
52	Cecil Fielder	.05
53	Travis Fryman	.05
54	Chris Gomez	.05
55	Mike Henneman	.05
56	Chad Kreuter	.05
57	Bob MacDonald	.05
58	Mike Moore	.05
59	Tony Phillips	.05
60	Lou Whitaker	.05
61	Kevin Appier	.05
62	Greg Gagne	.05
63	Chris Gwynn	.05
64	Bob Hamelin	.05
65	Chris Haney	.05
66	Phil Hiatt	.05
67	Felix Jose	.05
68	Jose Lind	.05
69	Mike Macfarlane	.05
70	Jeff Montgomery	.05
71	Hipolito Pichardo	.05
72	Juan Bell	.05
73	Cal Eldred	.05
74	Darryl Hamilton	.05
75	Doug Henry	.05
76	Mike Ignasiak	.05
77	John Jaha	.05
78	Graeme Lloyd	.05
79	Angel Miranda	.05
80	Dave Nilsson	.05
81	Troy O'Leary	.05
82	Kevin Reimer	.05
83	Willie Banks	.05
84	Larry Casian	.05
85	Scott Erickson	.05
86	Eddie Guardado	.05
87	Kent Hrbek	.05
88	Terry Jorgensen	.05
89	Chuck Knoblauch	.05
90	Pat Meares	.05
91	Mike Trombley	.05
92	Dave Winfield	.50
93	Wade Boggs	.60
94	Scott Kamieniecki	.05
95	Pat Kelly	.05
96	Jimmy Key	.05
97	Jim Leyritz	.05
98	Bobby Munoz	.05
99	Paul O'Neill	.05
100	Melido Perez	.05
101	Mike Stanley	.05
102	Danny Tartabull	.05
103	Bernie Williams	.05
104	Kurt Abbott RC	.05
105	Mike Bordick	.05
106	Ron Darling	.05
107	Brent Gates	.05
108	Miguel Jimenez	.05
109	Steve Karsay	.05
110	Scott Lydy	.05
111	Mark McGwire	1.00
112	Troy Neel	.05
113	Craig Paquette	.05
114	Bob Welch	.05
115	Bobby Witt	.05
116	Rich Amaral	.05
117	Mike Blowers	.05
118	Jay Buhner	.05
119	Dave Fleming	.05
120	Ken Griffey Jr.	.75
121	Tino Martinez	.05
122	Marc Newfield	.05
123	Ted Power	.05
124	Mackey Sasser	.05
125	Omar Vizquel	.05
126	Kevin Brown	.05
127	Juan Gonzalez	.25
128	Tom Henke	.05
129	David Hulse	.05
130	Dean Palmer	.05
131	Roger Pavlik	.05
132	Ivan Rodriguez	.40
133	Kenny Rogers	.05
134	Doug Strange	.05
135	Pat Borders	.05
136	Joe Carter	.05
137	Darnell Coles	.05
138	Pat Hentgen	.05
139	Al Leiter	.05
140	Paul Molitor	.50
141	John Olerud	.05
142	Ed Sprague	.05
143	Dave Stewart	.05
144	Mike Timlin	.05
145	Duane Ward	.05
146	Devon White	.05
147	Steve Avery	.05
148	Steve Bedrosian	.05
149	Damon Berryhill	.05
150	Jeff Blauser	.05
151	Tom Glavine	.20
152	Chipper Jones	.75
153	Mark Lemke	.05
154	Fred McGriff	.05
155	Greg McMichael	.05
156	Deion Sanders	.05
157	John Smoltz	.05
158	Mark Wohlers	.05
159	Jose Bautista	.05
160	Steve Buechele	.05
161	Mike Harkey	.05
162	Greg Hibbard	.05
163	Chuck McElroy	.05
164	Mike Morgan	.05
165	Kevin Roberson	.05
166	Ryne Sandberg	.60
167	Jose Vizcaino	.05
168	Rick Wilkins	.05
169	Willie Wilson	.05
170	Willie Greene	.05
171	Roberto Kelly	.05
172	Larry Luebbers	.05
173	Kevin Mitchell	.05
174	Joe Oliver	.05
175	John Roper	.05
176	Johnny Ruffin	.05
177	Reggie Sanders	.05
178	John Smiley	.05
179	Jerry Spradlin	.05
180	Freddie Benavides	.05
181	Dante Bichette	.05
182	Willie Blair	.05
183	Kent Bottenfield	.05
184	Jerald Clark	.05
185	Joe Girardi	.05
186	Roberto Mejia	.05
187	Steve Reed	.05
188	Armando Reynoso	.05
189	Bruce Ruffin	.05
190	Eric Young	.05
191	Luis Aquino	.05
192	Bret Barberie	.05
193	Ryan Bowen	.05
194	Chuck Carr	.05
195	Orestes Destrade	.05
196	Richie Lewis	.05
197	Dave Magadan	.05
198	Bob Natal	.05
199	Gary Sheffield	.30
200	Matt Turner	.05
201	Darrell Whitmore	.05
202	Eric Anthony	.05
203	Jeff Bagwell	.50
204	Andujar Cedeno	.05
205	Luis Gonzalez	.05
206	Xavier Hernandez	.05
207	Doug Jones	.05
208	Darryl Kile	.05
209	Scott Servais	.05
210	Greg Swindell	.05
211	Brian Williams	.05
212	Pedro Astacio	.05
213	Brett Butler	.05
214	Omar Daal	.05
215	Jim Gott	.05
216	Raul Mondesi	.05
217	Jose Offerman	.05
218	Mike Piazza	.75
219	Cory Snyder	.05
220	Tim Wallach	.05
221	Todd Worrell	.05
222	Moises Alou	.05
223	Sean Berry	.05
224	Wil Cordero	.05
225	Jeff Fassero	.05
226	Darrin Fletcher	.05
227	Cliff Floyd	.05
228	Marquis Grissom	.05
229	Ken Hill	.05
230	Mike Lansing	.05
231	Kirk Rueter	.05
232	John Wetteland	.05
233	Rondell White	.05
234	Tim Bogar	.05
235	Jeromy Burnitz	.05
236	Dwight Gooden	.05
237	Todd Hundley	.05
238	Jeff Kent	.05
239	Josias Manzanillo	.05
240	Joe Orsulak	.05
241	Ryan Thompson	.05
242	Kim Batiste	.05
243	Darren Daulton	.05
243a	Darren Daulton (Promotional Sample)	1.00
244	Tommy Greene	.05
245	Dave Hollins	.05
246	Pete Incaviglia	.05
247	Danny Jackson	.05
248	Ricky Jordan	.05
249	John Kruk	.05
249a	John Kruk (Promotional Sample)	1.00
250	Mickey Morandini	.05
251	Terry Mulholland	.05
252	Ben Rivera	.05
253	Kevin Stocker	.05
254	Jay Bell	.05
255	Steve Cooke	.05
256	Jeff King	.05
257	Al Martin	.05
258	Danny Micelli	.05
259	Blas Minor	.05
260	Don Slaught	.05
261	Paul Wagner	.05
262	Tim Wakefield	.05
263	Kevin Young	.05
264	Rene Arocha	.05
265	Richard Batchelor RC	.05
266	Gregg Jefferies	.05
267	Brian Jordan	.05
268	Jose Oquendo	.05
269	Donovan Osborne	.05
270	Erik Pappas	.05
271	Mike Perez	.05
272	Bob Tewksbury	.05
273	Mark Whiten	.05
274	Todd Zeile	.05
275	Andy Ashby	.05
276	Brad Ausmus	.05
277	Phil Clark	.05
278	Jeff Gardner	.05
279	Ricky Gutierrez	.05
280	Tony Gwynn	.60
281	Tim Mauser	.05
282	Scott Sanders	.05
283	Frank Seminara	.05
284	Wally Whitehurst	.05
285	Rod Beck	.05
286	Barry Bonds	1.50
287	Dave Burba	.05
288	Mark Carreon	.05
289	Royce Clayton	.05
290	Mike Jackson	.05
291	Darren Lewis	.05
292	Kirt Manwaring	.05
293	Dave Martinez	.05
294	Billy Swift	.05
295	Salomon Torres	.05
296	Matt Williams	.05
297	Checklist 1-103 (Joe Orsulak)	.05
298	Checklist 104-201 (Pete Incaviglia)	.05
299	Checklist 202-300 (Todd Hundley)	.05
300	Checklist - Inserts (John Doherty)	.05
301	Brady Anderson	.05
302	Harold Baines	.05
303	Damon Buford	.05
304	Mike Devereaux	.05
305	Sid Fernandez	.05
306	Rick Krivda	.05
307	Mike Mussina	.30
308	Rafael Palmeiro	.40
309	Arthur Rhodes	.05
310	Chris Sabo	.05
311	Lee Smith	.05
312	Gregg Zaun RC	.05
313	Scott Cooper	.05
314	Mike Greenwell	.05
315	Tim Naehring	.05
316	Otis Nixon	.05
317	Paul Quantrill	.05
318	John Valentin	.05
319	Dave Valle	.05
320	Frank Viola	.05
321	Brian Anderson RC	.10
322	Garret Anderson	.05
323	Chad Curtis	.05
324	Chili Davis	.05
325	Gary DiSarcina	.05
326	Damion Easley	.05
327	Jim Edmonds	.05
328	Chuck Finley	.05
329	Joe Grahe	.05
330	Bo Jackson	.10
331	Mark Langston	.05
332	Harold Reynolds	.05
333	James Baldwin	.05
334	Ray Durham RC	.50
335	Julio Franco	.05
336	Craig Grebeck	.05
337	Ozzie Guillen	.05
338	Joe Hall	.05
339	Darrin Jackson	.05
340	Jack McDowell	.05
341	Tim Raines	.05
342	Robin Ventura	.05
343	Carlos Baerga	.05
344	Derek Lilliquist	.05
345	Dennis Martinez	.05
346	Jack Morris	.05
347	Eddie Murray	.50
348	Chris Nabholz	.05
349	Charles Nagy	.05
350	Chad Ogea	.05
351	Manny Ramirez	.50
352	Omar Vizquel	.05
353	Tim Belcher	.05
354	Eric Davis	.05
355	Kirk Gibson	.05
356	Rick Greene	.05
357	Mickey Tettleton	.05
358	Alan Trammell	.05
359	David Wells	.05
360	Stan Belinda	.05
361	Vince Coleman	.05
362	David Cone	.05
363	Gary Gaetti	.05
364	Tom Gordon	.05
365	Dave Henderson	.05
366	Wally Joyner	.05
367	Brent Mayne	.05
368	Brian McRae	.05
369	Michael Tucker	.05
370	Ricky Bones	.05
371	Brian Harper	.05
372	Tyrone Hill	.05
373	Mark Kiefer	.05
374	Pat Listach	.05
375	Mike Matheny RC	.10
376	Jose Mercedes RC	.05
377	Jody Reed	.05
378	Kevin Seitzer	.05
379	B.J. Surhoff	.05
380	Greg Vaughn	.05
381	Turner Ward	.05
382	Wes Weger RC	.05
383	Bill Wegman	.05
384	Rick Aguilera	.05
385	Rich Becker	.05
386	Alex Cole	.05
387	Steve Dunn	.05
388	Keith Garagozzo RC	.05
389	LaTroy Hawkins RC	.05
390	Shane Mack	.05
391	David McCarty	.05
392	Pedro Munoz	.05
393	Derek Parks RC	.05
394	Kirby Puckett	.60
395	Kevin Tapani	.05
396	Matt Walbeck	.05
397	Jim Abbott	.05
398	Mike Gallego	.05
399	Xavier Hernandez	.05
400	Don Mattingly	.65
401	Terry Mulholland	.05
402	Matt Nokes	.05
403	Luis Polonia	.05
404	Bob Wickman	.05
405	Mark Acre	.05
406	Fausto Cruz RC	.05
407	Dennis Eckersley	.45
408	Rickey Henderson	.50
409	Stan Javier	.05
410	Carlos Reyes RC	.05
411	Ruben Sierra	.05
412	Terry Steinbach	.05
413	Bill Taylor	.05
414	Todd Van Poppel	.05
415	Eric Anthony	.05
416	Bobby Ayala	.05
417	Chris Bosio	.05
418	Tim Davis	.05
419	Randy Johnson	.50
420	Kevin King	.05
421	Anthony Manahan RC	.05
422	Edgar Martinez	.05
423	Keith Mitchell	.05
424	Roger Salkeld	.05
425	Mac Suzuki RC	.05
426	Dan Wilson	.05
427	Duff Brumley RC	.05
428	Jose Canseco	.30
429	Will Clark	.05
430	Steve Dreyer	.05
431	Rick Helling	.05
432	Chris James	.05
433	Matt Whiteside	.05
434	Roberto Alomar	.20
435	Scott Brow	.05
436	Domingo Cedeno RC	.05
437	Carlos Delgado	.35
438	Juan Guzman	.05
439	Paul Spoljaric	.05
440	Todd Stottlemyre	.05
441	Woody Williams	.05
442	Dave Justice	.05
443	Mike Kelly	.05
444	Ryan Klesko	.05
445	Javier Lopez	.05
446	Greg Maddux	.60
447	Kent Mercker	.05
448	Charlie O'Brien	.05
449	Terry Pendleton	.05
450	Mike Stanton	.05
451	Tony Tarasco	.05
452	Terrell Wade RC	.05
453	Willie Banks	.05
454	Shawon Dunston	.05
455	Mark Grace	.05
456	Jose Guzman	.05
457	Jose Hernandez	.05
458	Glenallen Hill	.05
459	Blaise Ilsley	.05
460	Brooks Kieschnick RC	.05
461	Derrick May	.05
462	Randy Myers	.05
463	Karl Rhodes	.05
464	Sammy Sosa	.60
465	Steve Trachsel RC	.10
466	Anthony Young	.05
467	Eddie Zambrano RC	.05
468	Bret Boone	.05
469	Tom Browning	.05
470	Hector Carrasco RC	.05
471	Rob Dibble	.05
472	Erik Hanson	.05
473	Thomas Howard	.05
474	Barry Larkin	.05
475	Hal Morris	.05
476	Jose Rijo	.05
477	John Burke	.05
478	Ellis Burks	.05
479	Marvin Freeman	.05
480	Andres Galarraga	.05
481	Greg Harris	.05
482	Charlie Hayes	.05
483	Darren Holmes	.05
484	Howard Johnson	.05
485	Marcus Moore RC	.05
486	David Nied	.05
487	Mark Thompson	.05
488	Walt Weiss	.05
489	Kurt Abbott	.05
490	Matias Carrillo	.05
491	Jeff Conine	.05
492	Chris Hammond	.05
493	Bryan Harvey	.05
494	Charlie Hough	.05
495	Yorkis Perez RC	.05
496	Pat Rapp	.05
497	Benito Santiago	.05
498	David Weathers	.05
499	Craig Biggio	.05
500	Ken Caminiti	.05
501	Doug Drabek	.05
502	Tony Eusebio RC	.10
503	Steve Finley	.05
504	Pete Harnisch	.05
505	Brian Hunter	.05
506	Domingo Jean	.05
507	Todd Jones	.05
508	Orlando Miller	.05
509	James Mouton	.05
510	Roberto Petagine	.05
511	Shane Reynolds	.05
512	Mitch Williams	.05
513	Billy Ashley	.05
514	Tom Candiotti	.05
515	Delino DeShields	.05
516	Kevin Gross	.05
517	Orel Hershiser	.05
518	Eric Karros	.05
519	Ramon Martinez	.05
520	Chan Ho Park RC	.75
521	Henry Rodriguez	.05
522	Joey Eischen	.05
523	Rod Henderson	.05
524	Pedro Martinez	.50
525	Mel Rojas	.05
526	Larry Walker	.05
527	Gabe White RC	.10
528	Bobby Bonilla	.05
529	Jonathan Hurst	.05
530	Bobby Jones	.05
531	Kevin McReynolds	.05
532	Bill Pulsipher	.05
533	Bret Saberhagen	.05
534	David Segui	.05

535	Pete Smith	.05
536	Kelly Stinnett RC	.05
537	Dave Telgheder RC	.05
538	Quilvio Veras RC	.05
539	Jose Vizcaino	.05
540	Pete Walker	.05
541	Ricky Bottalico	.05
542	Wes Chamberlain	.05
543	Mariano Duncan	.05
544	Len Dykstra	.05
545	Jim Eisenreich	.05
546	Phil Geisler RC	.05
547	Wayne Gomes RC	.10
548	Doug Jones	.05
549	Jeff Juden	.05
550	Mike Lieberthal	.05
551	Tony Longmire RC	.05
552	Tom Marsh	.05
553	Bobby Munoz	.05
554	Curt Schilling	.15
555	Carlos Garcia	.05
556	Ravelo Manzanillo RC	.05
557	Orlando Merced	.05
558	Will Pennyfeather RC	.05
559	Zane Smith	.05
560	Andy Van Slyke	.05
561	Rick White	.05
562	Luis Alicea	.05
563	Brian Barber RC	.05
564	Clint Davis RC	.05
565	Bernard Gilkey	.05
566	Ray Lankford	.05
567	Tom Pagnozzi	.05
568	Ozzie Smith	.60
569	Rick Sutcliffe	.05
570	Allen Watson	.05
571	Dmitri Young	.05
572	Derek Bell	.05
573	Andy Benes	.05
574	Archi Cianfrocco	.05
575	Joey Hamilton	.05
576	Gene Harris	.05
577	Trevor Hoffman	.05
578	Tim Hyers RC	.05
579	Brian Johnson RC	.05
580	Keith Lockhart RC	.05
581	Pedro Martinez	.05
582	Ray McDavid	.05
583	Phil Plantier	.05
584	Bip Roberts	.05
585	Dave Staton	.05
586	Todd Benzinger	.05
587	John Burkett	.05
588	Bryan Hickerson	.05
589	Willie McGee	.05
590	John Patterson	.05
591	Mark Portugal	.05
592	Kevin Rogers	.05
593	Joe Rosselli RC	.05
594	Steve Soderstrom RC	.05
595	Robby Thompson	.05
596	125th Anniversary card	.05
597	Checklist	.05
598	Checklist	.05
599	Checklist	.05
600	Checklist	.05

All-Rookie Team

A stylized sunrise landscape is the background for this insert set featuring top rookies and inserted into Ultra Series II packs at the rate of about one per 10. Backs repeat the motif with an action photo. Both sides are gold-foil enhanced and UV-coated.

		NM/M
Complete Set (10):		4.00
Common Player:		.35
1	Kurt Abbott	.35
2	Carlos Delgado	3.00
3	Cliff Floyd	.35
4	Jeffrey Hammonds	.35
5	Ryan Klesko	.35
6	Javier Lopez	.35
7	Raul Mondesi	.35
8	James Mouton	.35
9	Chan Ho Park	.50
10	Dave Staton	.35

1994 Ultra All-Rookie Team Supers

This super-size (3-1/2" x5-1/2") version of the Fleer Ultra II insert set featuring top rookies was included one per case of hobby packaging.

Cards are identical to the smaller version. Both sides are gold-foil enhanced and UV-coated.

		NM/M
Complete Set (10):		5.00
Common Player:		.50
1	Kurt Abbott	.50
2	Carlos Delgado	3.00
3	Cliff Floyd	.50
4	Jeffrey Hammonds	.50
5	Ryan Klesko	.50
6	Javier Lopez	.50
7	Raul Mondesi	.50
8	James Mouton	.50
9	Chan Ho Park	.75
10	Dave Staton	.50

All-Stars

Fleer's opinion of the top 20 players in 1994 are featured in this most common of the Series II Ultra insert sets. Silver-foil highlights enhance the chase cards, found, according to stated odds, once per three packs, on average. National Leaguers have purple backgrounds front and back, American Leaguers have red.

		NM/M
Complete Set (20):		5.00
Common Player:		.15
1	Chris Hoiles	.15
2	Frank Thomas	.35
3	Roberto Alomar	.20
4	Cal Ripken, Jr.	1.00
5	Robin Ventura	.15
6	Albert Belle	.15
7	Juan Gonzalez	.20
8	Ken Griffey Jr.	.50
9	John Olerud	.15
10	Jack McDowell	.15
11	Mike Piazza	.50
12	Fred McGriff	.15
13	Ryne Sandberg	.40
14	Jay Bell	.15
15	Matt Williams	.15
16	Barry Bonds	1.00
17	Len Dykstra	.15
18	Dave Justice	.15
19	Tom Glavine	.20
20	Greg Maddux	.40

Award Winners

The most common of the Fleer Ultra insert sets for 1994 is the 25-card "Award Winners." Horizontal format cards feature front and back background with a gold-embossed look. A player action photo appears on the front. A gold-foil seal on the front has a symbolic player representation flanked by the pictured player's name and award. A gold Fleer Ultra logo is at top. Backs have a player portrait photo and a write-up about the award. The name of the award and the player's name appear in gold foil at the top. Stated odds of finding an Award Winners card were one in three packs.

		NM/M
Complete Set (25):		5.00
Common Player:		.10
1	Ivan Rodriguez	.25
2	Don Mattingly	.45
3	Roberto Alomar	.20
4	Robin Ventura	.10
5	Omar Vizquel	.10
6	Ken Griffey Jr.	.50
7	Kenny Lofton	.10
8	Devon White	.10
9	Mark Langston	.10
10	Kirt Manwaring	.10
11	Mark Grace	.10
12	Robby Thompson	.10
13	Matt Williams	.10
14	Jay Bell	.10
15	Barry Bonds	.60
16	Marquis Grissom	.10
17	Larry Walker	.10
18	Greg Maddux	.40
19	Frank Thomas	.35
20	Barry Bonds	.60
21	Paul Molitor	.35
22	Jack McDowell	.10
23	Greg Maddux	.40
24	Tim Salmon	.10
25	Mike Piazza	.50

Career Achievement Awards

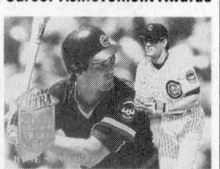

The outstanding careers of five of baseball's top veteran stars are recognized in this chase set, inserted on average once every 21 packs of Ultra Series II. The gold-highlighted horizontal fronts combine a current color photo with a background single-tint photo from the player's earlier days. Backs flip-flop the photo use, with the current photo in the background and the earlier photo in full color in the foreground. The gold Ultra Career Achievement Award seal is repeated on back, as well.

		NM/M
Complete Set (5):		4.00
Common Player:		.50
1	Joe Carter	.50
2	Paul Molitor	.75
3	Cal Ripken, Jr.	2.00
4	Ryne Sandberg	1.00
5	Dave Winfield	.75

Firemen

Ten of the major leagues' leading relief pitchers are featured in this Ultra insert set. Cards have an action photo of the player superimposed over a background photo of a fire truck. A shield at top, in gold foil, has a smoke-eater's helmet, stylized flames and proclaims the player an "Ultra Fireman." Backs are horizontal in format and feature the pumper's control panel in the background photo. A color player portrait photo appears on one side, with a description of his relief role and successes in a whit-ened box. Fireman cards are found, on average, once per 11 packs, according to stated odds.

		NM/M
Complete Set (10):		2.00
Common Player:		.25
1	Jeff Montgomery	.25
2	Duane Ward	.25
3	Tom Henke	.25
4	Roberto Hernandez	.25
5	Dennis Eckersley	1.25
6	Randy Myers	.25
7	Rod Beck	.25
8	Bryan Harvey	.25
9	John Wetteland	.25
10	Mitch Williams	.25

Hitting Machines

A heavy metal background of gears and iron-letter logo is featured in this insert set honoring the game's top hitters. The cards turn up about once in every five packs of Ultra Series II. Both front and back are highlighted in silver foil.

		NM/M
Complete Set (10):		4.00
Common Player:		.15
1	Roberto Alomar	.15
2	Carlos Baerga	.15
3	Barry Bonds	2.00
4	Andres Galarraga	.15
5	Juan Gonzalez	.25
6	Tony Gwynn	.50
7	Paul Molitor	.40
8	John Olerud	.15
9	Mike Piazza	.75
10	Frank Thomas	.40

Home Run Kings

One of two high-end insert sets in '94 Ultra is the 12-card "Home Run Kings" found exclusively in 14-card foil packs, on an average of once per 36-pack box. Featuring the technology Fleer calls "etched metallization," the cards have a black background with a red and blue foil representation of a batter. An action photo of a player taking a mighty cut or starting his home-run trot is featured. A large gold-foil "Home Run King" crown-and-shield device are in an upper corner, while the Ultra logo and player name are in gold foil at bottom. Backs have a white background with the red and blue batter symbol. The player's name appears in gold foil at the top, along with a portrait photo and a summary of his home run prowess.

		NM/M
Complete Set (12):		15.00
Common Player:		.75
1	Juan Gonzalez	1.00
2	Ken Griffey Jr.	2.50
3	Frank Thomas	2.00
4	Albert Belle	.75
5	Rafael Palmeiro	1.50
6	Joe Carter	.75
7	Barry Bonds	4.00
8	Dave Justice	.75
9	Matt Williams	.75
10	Fred McGriff	.75
11	Ron Gant	.75
12	Mike Piazza	2.50

League Leaders

Arguably the least attractive of the '94 Ultra inserts are the "League Leaders." Fronts feature a full-bleed action photo on which the bottom has been re-colored to a team hue giving the effect of teal, purple and magenta miasmas rising from the turf. An Ultra logo appears in gold foil in an upper corner, with the player's name in gold foil at about the dividing line between the natural color and colorized portions of the photo. A large "League Leader" appears in the bottom half of the photo, with the category led printed in the lower-left. Backs repeat the team color at top, fading to white at the bottom. In gold foil are "League Leader" and the category. A portrait photo appears at bottom. Several paragraphs detail the league leading performance of the previous season.

		NM/M
Complete Set (10):		3.00
Common Player:		.25
1	John Olerud	.25
2	Rafael Palmeiro	1.00
3	Kenny Lofton	.25
4	Jack McDowell	.25
5	Randy Johnson	1.50
6	Andres Galarraga	.25
7	Len Dykstra	.25
8	Chuck Carr	.25
9	Tom Glavine	.35
10	Jose Rijo	.25

On-Base Leaders

One of the lesser-known, but most valuable, stats - on-base percentage - is featured in this subset found exclusively in 17-card packs, at the rate of about one per 37 packs. The fronts feature color photos against a stat-filled printed-foil background.

		NM/M
Complete Set (12):		25.00
Common Player:		1.50
1	Roberto Alomar	2.00
2	Barry Bonds	6.50
3	Len Dykstra	1.50
4	Andres Galarraga	1.50
5	Mark Grace	1.50
6	Ken Griffey Jr.	5.00
7	Gregg Jefferies	1.50
8	Orlando Merced	1.50
9	Paul Molitor	3.50
10	John Olerud	1.50
11	Tony Phillips	1.50
12	Frank Thomas	3.50

Phillies Finest

As a tribute to two of Fleer's home-team heroes, the Philadelphia-based card company created an Ultra insert set featuring 12 cards each of "Phillies Finest," John Kruk and Darren Daulton. Twenty of the cards were issued as Series 1 and 2 inserts, about one in every eight packs, while four were available only by a mail-in offer.

Leaders." Fronts feature a full-bleed action photo on which the bottom has been re-colored to a team hue giving the effect of teal, purple and magenta miasmas rising from the turf. An Ultra logo appears in gold foil in an upper corner, with the player's name in gold foil at about the dividing line between the natural color and colorized portions of the photo. A large "League Leader" appears in the bottom half of the photo, with the category led printed in the lower-left. Backs repeat the team color at top, fading to white at the bottom. In gold foil are "League Leader" and the category. A portrait photo appears at bottom. Several paragraphs detail the league leading performance of the previous season.

		NM/M
Complete Set (24):		4.00
Common Player:		.25
Autographed Daulton:		45.00
Autographed Kruk:		30.00
1-5	Darren Daulton	.25
6-10	John Kruk	.25
11-15	Darren Daulton	.25
16-20	John Kruk	.25
9a	John Kruk(PROMOTIONAL SAMPLE)	1.50
1M, 3M	Darren Daulton	.75
2M, 4M	John Kruk	.75

RBI Kings

Exclusive to the 19-card jumbo packs of Fleer Ultra are a series of 12 "RBI Kings" insert cards, found, according to stated odds, one per 36 packs. The horizontal-format card front uses Fleer's "etched metallized" technology to produce a sepia-toned background action photo, in front of which is a color player photo. An Ultra logo appears in gold foil in an upper corner while a fancy shield-and-scroll "RBI King" logo and the player's name are in gold at the bottom. Backs repeat the basic front motif and include a color player portrait photo, his name in gold foil and a paragraph justifying his selection as an RBI King.

		NM/M
Complete Set (12):		16.00
Common Player:		1.00
1	Albert Belle	1.00
2	Frank Thomas	2.50
3	Joe Carter	1.00
4	Juan Gonzalez	1.25
5	Cecil Fielder	1.00
6	Carlos Baerga	1.00
7	Barry Bonds	5.00
8	David Justice	1.00
9	Ron Gant	1.00
10	Mike Piazza	3.50
11	Matt Williams	1.00
12	Darren Daulton	1.00

Rising Stars

An outer space background printed on metallic foil sets this chase set apart from most of the rest of the Ultra Series II inserts. The silver-foil enhanced cards of projected superstars of tomorrow are found on average once every 37 packs.

		NM/M
Complete Set (12):		15.00
Common Player:		1.00
1	Carlos Baerga	1.00
2	Jeff Bagwell	5.00
3	Albert Belle	1.00
4	Cliff Floyd	1.00
5	Travis Fryman	1.00
6	Marquis Grissom	1.00

1995 Ultra

7	Kenny Lofton	1.00
8	John Olerud	1.00
9	Mike Piazza	7.50
10	Kirk Rueter	1.00
11	Tim Salmon	1.00
12	Aaron Sele	1.00

Second Year Standouts

Approximately once every 11 packs, the Ultra insert find is a "Second Year Standout" card. Ten of the game's sophomore stars are featured. Fronts feature a pair of action photos against a team-color background. Gold-foil highlights are the Ultra logo, the player's name and a "Second Year Standout" shield. The shield and player name are repeated in gold foil on the back, as is the team color background. There is a player portrait photo at bottom and a summary of the player's 1993 season.

		NM/M
Complete Set (10):		5.00
Common Player:		.25
1	Jason Bere	.25
2	Brent Gates	.25
3	Jeffrey Hammonds	.25
4	Tim Salmon	.50
5	Aaron Sele	.25
6	Chuck Carr	.25
7	Jeff Conine	.25
8	Greg McMichael	.25
9	Mike Piazza	4.00
10	Kevin Stocker	.25

Strikeout Kings

A gold-foil "Strikeout Kings" crown-and-shield logo is featured on the front of this chase set. Cards are found on average once per seven packs. Each of the cards features the K-king in sequential action photos. Backs have a larger action photo with a large version of the Strikeout King shield in the background.

		NM/M
Complete Set (5):		2.00
Common Player:		.25
1	Randy Johnson	.75
2	Mark Langston	.25
3	Greg Maddux	1.00
4	Jose Rijo	.25
5	John Smoltz	.25

A clean design enhanced with three different colors of metallic foil graphics is featured on the basic cards of 1995 Fleer Ultra. Two series of 250 cards each were issued with cards arranged alphabetically within team, also sequenced alphabetically. Fronts have a gold-foil Ultra logo in an upper corner, with the player's name and team logo in a team-color coded foil at bottom. There are no other graphic elements on the borderless fronts. Backs have a large photo rendered in a single color, again team-coded. A postage-stamp sized color photo in one corner is flanked by a few vital stats in silver foil. Career and '94 stats are printed at bottom, enhanced by the foil color from the front. Cards were issued in 12-card retail and hobby packs at $1.99 and jumbo pre-priced ($2.69) magazine packs. Each pack contains one of the several insert series from the appropriate series.

		NM/M
Complete Set (450):		10.00
Common Player:		.05
Gold Medallion:		2X
Series 1 or 2 Pack (12):		.50
Series 1 or 2 Wax Box (36):		12.50
1	Brady Anderson	.05
2	Sid Fernandez	.05
3	Jeffrey Hammonds	.05
4	Chris Hoiles	.05
5	Ben McDonald	.05
6	Mike Mussina	.35
7	Rafael Palmeiro	.65
8	Jack Voigt	.05
9	Wes Chamberlain	.05
10	Roger Clemens	1.00
11	Chris Howard	.05
12	Tim Naehring	.05
13	Otis Nixon	.05
14	Rich Rowland	.05
15	Ken Ryan	.05
16	John Valentin	.05
17	Mo Vaughn	.05
18	Brian Anderson	.05
19	Chili Davis	.05
20	Damion Easley	.05
21	Jim Edmonds	.05
22	Mark Langston	.05
23	Tim Salmon	.05
24	J.T. Snow	.05
25	Chris Turner	.05
26	Wilson Alvarez	.05
27	Joey Cora	.05
28	Alex Fernandez	.05
29	Roberto Hernandez	.05
30	Lance Johnson	.05
31	Ron Karkovice	.05
32	Kirk McCaskill	.05
33	Tim Raines	.05
34	Frank Thomas	.75
35	Sandy Alomar	.05
36	Albert Belle	.75
37	Mark Clark	.05
38	Kenny Lofton	.75
39	Eddie Murray	.75
40	Eric Plunk	.05
41	Manny Ramirez	.75
42	Jim Thome	.60
43	Omar Vizquel	.05
44	Danny Bautista	.05
45	Junior Felix	.05
46	Cecil Fielder	.05
47	Chris Gomez	.05
48	Chad Kreuter	.05
49	Mike Moore	.05
50	Tony Phillips	.05
51	Alan Trammell	.05
52	David Wells	.05
53	Kevin Appier	.05
54	Billy Brewer	.05
55	David Cone	.05
56	Greg Gagne	.05
57	Bob Hamelin	.05
58	Jose Lind	.05
59	Brent Mayne	.05
60	Brian McRae	.05

61	Terry Shumpert	.05
62	Ricky Bones	.05
63	Mike Fetters	.05
64	Darryl Hamilton	.05
65	John Jaha	.05
66	Graeme Lloyd	.05
67	Matt Mieske	.05
68	Kevin Seitzer	.05
69	Jose Valentin	.05
70	Turner Ward	.05
71	Rick Aguilera	.05
72	Rich Becker	.05
73	Alex Cole	.05
74	Scott Leius	.05
75	Pat Meares	.05
76	Kirby Puckett	1.00
77	Dave Stevens	.05
78	Kevin Tapani	.05
79	Matt Walbeck	.05
80	Wade Boggs	1.00
81	Scott Kamieniecki	.05
82	Pat Kelly	.05
83	Jimmy Key	.05
84	Paul O'Neill	.05
85	Luis Polonia	.05
86	Mike Stanley	.05
87	Danny Tartabull	.05
88	Bob Wickman	.05
89	Mark Acre	.05
90	Geronimo Berroa	.05
91	Mike Bordick	.05
92	Ron Darling	.05
93	Stan Javier	.05
94	Mark McGwire	1.50
95	Troy Neel	.05
96	Ruben Sierra	.05
97	Terry Steinbach	.05
98	Eric Anthony	.05
99	Chris Bosio	.05
100	Dave Fleming	.05
101	Ken Griffey Jr.	1.25
102	Reggie Jefferson	.05
103	Randy Johnson	.75
104	Edgar Martinez	.05
105	Bill Risley	.05
106	Dan Wilson	.05
107	Cris Carpenter	.05
108	Will Clark	.05
109	Juan Gonzalez	.40
110	Rusty Greer	.05
111	David Hulse	.05
112	Roger Pavlik	.05
113	Ivan Rodriguez	.75
114	Doug Strange	.05
115	Matt Whiteside	.05
116	Roberto Alomar	.20
117	Brad Cornett	.05
118	Carlos Delgado	.45
119	Alex Gonzalez	.05
120	Darren Hall	.05
121	Pat Hentgen	.05
122	Paul Molitor	.75
123	Ed Sprague	.05
124	Devon White	.05
125	Tom Glavine	.25
126	Dave Justice	.05
127	Roberto Kelly	.05
128	Mark Lemke	.05
129	Greg Maddux	1.00
130	Charles Johnson	.05
131	Kent Mercker	.05
132	Charlie O'Brien	.05
133	John Smoltz	.05
134	Willie Banks	.05
135	Steve Buechele	.05
136	Kevin Foster	.05
137	Glenallen Hill	.05
138	Ray Sanchez	.05
139	Sammy Sosa	1.00
140	Steve Trachsel	.05
141	Rick Wilkins	.05
142	Jeff Brantley	.05
143	Hector Carrasco	.05
144	Kevin Jarvis	.05
145	Barry Larkin	.05
146	Chuck McElroy	.05
147	Jose Rijo	.05
148	Johnny Ruffin	.05
149	Deion Sanders	.05
150	Eddie Taubensee	.05
151	Dante Bichette	.05
152	Ellis Burks	.05
153	Joe Girardi	.05
154	Charlie Hayes	.05
155	Mike Kingery	.05
156	Steve Reed	.05
157	Kevin Ritz	.05
158	Bruce Ruffin	.05
159	Eric Young	.05
160	Kurt Abbott	.05
161	Chuck Carr	.05
162	Chris Hammond	.05
163	Bryan Harvey	.05
164	Terry Mathews	.05
165	Yorkis Perez	.05
166	Pat Rapp	.05
167	Gary Sheffield	.40
168	Dave Weathers	.05
169	Jeff Bagwell	.75
170	Ken Caminiti	.05
171	Doug Drabek	.05
172	Steve Finley	.05
173	John Hudek	.05
174	Todd Jones	.05
175	James Mouton	.05
176	Shane Reynolds	.05
177	Scott Servais	.05
178	Tom Candiotti	.05

179	Omar Daal	.05
180	Darren Dreifort	.05
181	Eric Karros	.05
182	Ramon Martinez	.05
183	Raul Mondesi	.05
184	Henry Rodriguez	.05
185	Todd Worrell	.05
186	Moises Alou	.05
187	Sean Berry	.05
188	Wil Cordero	.05
189	Jeff Fassero	.05
190	Darrin Fletcher	.05
191	Butch Henry	.05
192	Ken Hill	.05
193	Mel Rojas	.05
194	John Wetteland	.05
195	Bobby Bonilla	.05
196	Rico Brogna	.05
197	Bobby Jones	.05
198	Jeff Kent	.05
199	Josias Manzanillo	.05
200	Kelly Stinnett	.05
201	Ryan Thompson	.05
202	Jose Vizcaino	.05
203	Lenny Dykstra	.05
204	Jim Eisenreich	.05
205	Dave Hollins	.05
206	Mike Lieberthal	.05
207	Mickey Morandini	.05
208	Bobby Munoz	.05
209	Curt Schilling	.20
210	Heathcliff Slocumb	.05
211	David West	.05
212	Dave Clark	.05
213	Steve Cooke	.05
214	Midre Cummings	.05
215	Carlos Garcia	.05
216	Jeff King	.05
217	Jon Lieber	.05
218	Orlando Merced	.05
219	Don Slaught	.05
220	Rick White	.05
221	Rene Arocha	.05
222	Bernard Gilkey	.05
223	Brian Jordan	.05
224	Tom Pagnozzi	.05
225	Vicente Palacios	.05
226	Geronimo Pena	.05
227	Ozzie Smith	1.00
228	Allen Watson	.05
229	Mark Whiten	.05
230	Brad Ausmus	.05
231	Derek Bell	.05
232	Andy Benes	.05
233	Tony Gwynn	1.00
234	Joey Hamilton	.05
235	Luis Lopez	.05
236	Pedro A. Martinez	.05
237	Scott Sanders	.05
238	Eddie Williams	.05
239	Rod Beck	.05
240	Dave Burba	.05
241	Darren Lewis	.05
242	Kirt Manwaring	.05
243	Mark Portugal	.05
244	Darryl Strawberry	.05
245	Robby Thompson	.05
246	William Van Landingham	.05
247	Matt Williams	.05
248	Checklist	.05
249	Checklist	.05
250	Checklist	.05
251	Harold Baines	.05
252	Bret Barberie	.05
253	Armando Benitez	.05
254	Mike Devereaux	.05
255	Leo Gomez	.05
256	Jamie Moyer	.05
257	Arthur Rhodes	.05
258	Cal Ripken Jr.	2.00
259	Luis Alicea	.05
260	Jose Canseco	.45
261	Scott Cooper	.05
262	Andre Dawson	.25
263	Mike Greenwell	.05
264	Aaron Sele	.05
265	Garret Anderson	.05
266	Chad Curtis	.05
267	Gary DiSarcina	.05
268	Chuck Finley	.05
269	Rex Hudler	.05
270	Andrew Lorraine	.05
271	Spike Owen	.05
272	Lee Smith	.05
273	Jason Bere	.05
274	Ozzie Guillen	.05
275	Norberto Martin	.05
276	Scott Ruffcorn	.05
277	Robin Ventura	.05
278	Carlos Baerga	.05
279	Jason Grimsley	.05
280	Dennis Martinez	.05
281	Charles Nagy	.05
282	Paul Sorrento	.05
283	Dave Winfield	.75
284	John Doherty	.05
285	Travis Fryman	.05
286	Kirk Gibson	.05
287	Lou Whitaker	.05
288	Gary Gaetti	.05
289	Tom Gordon	.05
290	Mark Gubicza	.05
291	Wally Joyner	.05
292	Mike Macfarlane	.05
293	Jeff Montgomery	.05
294	Jeff Cirillo	.05
295	Cal Eldred	.05
296	Pat Listach	.05

297	Jose Mercedes	.05
298	Dave Nilsson	.05
299	Duane Singleton	.05
300	Greg Vaughn	.05
301	Scott Erickson	.05
302	Denny Hocking	.05
303	Chuck Knoblauch	.05
304	Pat Mahomes	.05
305	Pedro Munoz	.05
306	Erik Schullstrom	.05
307	Jim Abbott	.05
308	Tony Fernandez	.05
309	Sterling Hitchcock	.05
310	Jim Leyritz	.05
311	Don Mattingly	1.00
312	Jack McDowell	.05
313	Melido Perez	.05
314	Bernie Williams	.05
315	Scott Brosius	.05
316	Dennis Eckersley	.65
317	Brent Gates	.05
318	Rickey Henderson	.75
319	Steve Karsay	.05
320	Steve Ontiveros	.05
321	Bill Taylor	.05
322	Todd Van Poppel	.05
323	Bob Welch	.05
324	Bobby Ayala	.05
325	Mike Blowers	.05
326	Jay Buhner	.05
327	Felix Fermin	.05
328	Tino Martinez	.05
329	Marc Newfield	.05
330	Greg Pirkl	.05
331	Alex Rodriguez	1.50
332	Kevin Brown	.05
333	John Burkett	.05
334	Jeff Frye	.05
335	Kevin Gross	.05
336	Dean Palmer	.05
337	Joe Carter	.05
338	Shawn Green	.35
339	Juan Guzman	.05
340	Mike Huff	.05
341	Al Leiter	.05
342	John Olerud	.05
343	Dave Stewart	.05
344	Todd Stottlemyre	.05
345	Steve Avery	.05
346	Jeff Blauser	.05
347	Chipper Jones	1.00
348	Mike Kelly	.05
349	Ryan Klesko	.05
350	Javier Lopez	.05
351	Fred McGriff	.05
352	Jose Oliva	.05
353	Terry Pendleton	.05
354	Mike Stanton	.05
355	Tony Tarasco	.05
356	Mark Wohlers	.05
357	Jim Bullinger	.05
358	Shawon Dunston	.05
359	Mark Grace	.05
360	Derrick May	.05
361	Randy Myers	.05
362	Karl Rhodes	.05
363	Bret Boone	.05
364	Brian Dorsett	.05
365	Ron Gant	.05
366	Brian R. Hunter	.05
367	Hal Morris	.05
368	Jack Morris	.05
369	John Roper	.05
370	Reggie Sanders	.05
371	Pete Schourek	.05
372	John Smiley	.05
373	Marvin Freeman	.05
374	Andres Galarraga	.05
375	Mike Munoz	.05
376	David Nied	.05
377	Walt Weiss	.05
378	Greg Colbrunn	.05
379	Jeff Conine	.05
380	Charles Johnson	.05
381	Kurt Miller	.05
382	Robb Nen	.05
383	Benito Santiago	.05
384	Craig Biggio	.05
385	Tony Eusebio	.05
386	Luis Gonzalez	.05
387	Brian L. Hunter	.05
388	Darryl Kile	.05
389	Orlando Miller	.05
390	Phil Plantier	.05
391	Greg Swindell	.05
392	Billy Ashley	.05
393	Pedro Astacio	.05
394	Brett Butler	.05
395	Delino DeShields	.05
396	Orel Hershiser	.05
397	Garey Ingram	.05
398	Chan Ho Park	.05
399	Mike Piazza	1.25
400	Ismael Valdes	.05
401	Tim Wallach	.05
402	Cliff Floyd	.05
403	Marquis Grissom	.05
404	Mike Lansing	.05
405	Pedro Martinez	.05
406	Kirk Rueter	.75
407	Tim Scott	.05
408	Jeff Shaw	.05
409	Larry Walker	.05
410	Rondell White	.05
411	John Franco	.05
412	Todd Hundley	.05
413	Jason Jacome	.05
414	Joe Orsulak	.05

415	Bret Saberhagen	.05
416	David Segui	.05
417	Darren Daulton	.05
418	Mariano Duncan	.05
419	Gregg Jefferies	.05
420	John Kruk	.05
421	Kevin Stocker	.05
422	Jay Bell	.05
423	Al Martin	.05
424	Denny Neagle	.05
425	Zane Smith	.05
426	Andy Van Slyke	.05
427	Paul Wagner	.05
428	Tom Henke	.05
429	Danny Jackson	.05
430	Ray Lankford	.05
431	John Mabry	.05
432	Bob Tewksbury	.05
433	Todd Zeile	.05
434	Andy Ashby	.05
435	Andujar Cedeno	.05
436	Donnie Elliott	.05
437	Bryce Florie	.05
438	Trevor Hoffman	.05
439	Melvin Nieves	.05
440	Bip Roberts	.05
441	Barry Bonds	2.00
442	Royce Clayton	.05
443	Mike Jackson	.05
444	John Patterson	.05
445	J.R. Phillips	.05
446	Bill Swift	.05
447	Checklist	.05
448	Checklist	.05
449	Checklist	.05
450	Checklist	.05

1995 Ultra Gold Medallion

Less than 10 percent of the production run of Fleer Ultra (regular and insert sets) was produced in a special parallel Gold Medallion edition. On these special cards an embossed round gold seal replaces the Fleer Ultra logo in the upper corner. One Gold Medallion card was inserted into each Ultra foil pack.

		NM/M
Complete Set (450):		60.00
Common Player:		.25
Stars/Rookies:		2X

All-Rookies

Enlarged pieces of the central color action photo, set on a white background, make up the front design on these inserts. The player's name, card title and Ultra logo are printed in silver foil. Horizontal backs have another color photo, which is also repeated in single-color fashion. A career summary is printed over the larger photo. The All-Rookie inserts are found only in 12-card packs, at the rate of about one per four packs.

		NM/M
Complete Set (10):		2.25
Common Player:		.15
Gold Medallion:		2X
1	Cliff Floyd	.15
2	Chris Gomez	.15
3	Rusty Greer	.15
4	Bob Hamelin	.15

5	Joey Hamilton	.15
6	John Hudek	.15
7	Ryan Klesko	.15
8	Raul Mondesi	.15
9	Manny Ramirez	2.00
10	Steve Trachsel	.15

All-Stars

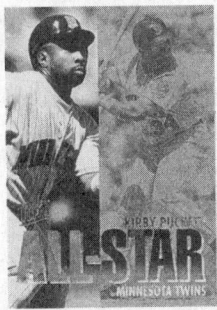

Twenty of the top players in the majors were chosen as Ultra All-Stars in this Series II chase set. Fronts have a color player photo at left. At right is a second photo, printed in only one color. A large "ALL-STAR" is at bottom, with the player's name above and team below in silver foil. An Ultra logo is at left. Backs have another color photo, with a '94 season summary printed in a black panel at right. These cards were found one per five packs, on average.

		NM/M
Complete Set (20):		7.50
Common Player:		.15
Gold Medallion:		2X
1	Moises Alou	.15
2	Albert Belle	.15
3	Craig Biggio	.15
4	Wade Boggs	.60
5	Barry Bonds	1.50
6	David Cone	.15
7	Ken Griffey Jr.	.75
8	Tony Gwynn	.60
9	Chuck Knoblauch	.15
10	Barry Larkin	.15
11	Kenny Lofton	.15
12	Greg Maddux	.60
13	Fred McGriff	.15
14	Paul O'Neill	.15
15	Mike Piazza	.75
16	Kirby Puckett	.60
17	Cal Ripken Jr.	1.50
18	Ivan Rodriguez	.45
19	Frank Thomas	.50
20	Matt Williams	.15

Award Winners

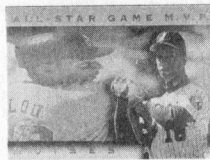

Various official and unofficial award winners from the 1994 season are featured in this Series I insert set. Horizontal cards have a color player photo on the right side, with a single-color, vertically compressed action photo at left. The player's award is printed in a white strip at top, while his name and team logo, along with the Ultra logo, are at bottom. All front typography is in gold foil. Backs repeat the compressed photo at left, combined with another color photo at right. A season summary is printed over the photo at left. The Award Winners inserts were common to all types of packaging, found at the rate of about one per four packs.

		NM/M
Complete Set (25):		6.00
Common Player:		.10
Gold Medallion:		2X
1	Ivan Rodriguez	.30
2	Don Mattingly	.65
3	Roberto Alomar	.20
4	Wade Boggs	.60
5	Omar Vizquel	.10
6	Ken Griffey Jr.	.75
7	Kenny Lofton	.10
8	Devon White	.10
9	Mark Langston	.10

10	Tom Pagnozzi	.10
11	Jeff Bagwell	.45
12	Craig Biggio	.10
13	Matt Williams	.10
14	Barry Larkin	.10
15	Barry Bonds	1.00
16	Marquis Grissom	.10
17	Darren Lewis	.10
18	Greg Maddux	.60
19	Frank Thomas	.45
20	Jeff Bagwell	.45
21	David Cone	.10
22	Greg Maddux	.60
23	Bob Hamelin	.10
24	Raul Mondesi	.10
25	Moises Alou	.10

Golden Prospects

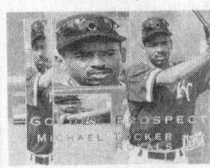

A hobby-pack exclusive, found at the rate of one per eight packs on average in Series I. Fronts feature a player photo at right, with three horizontally and vertically compressed versions of the same photo at right. The photo's background has been rendered in a single color. All typography - Ultra logo, card title, name and team - is in gold foil. Backs are also horizontal and have a color player photo and career summary.

		NM/M
Complete Set (10):		5.00
Common Player:		.15
Gold Medallion:		2X
1	James Baldwin	.10
2	Alan Benes	.10
3	Armando Benitez	.10
4	Ray Durham	.10
5	LaTroy Hawkins	.10
6	Brian Hunter	.10
7	Derek Jeter	3.00
8	Charles Johnson	.10
9	Alex Rodriguez	2.00
10	Michael Tucker	.10

1995 Ultra Gold Medallion Rookies Mail-in

This set of 20 was available only by mailing in 10 Fleer Ultra wrappers plus $5.95. A reported 100,000 sets were produced. The cards are in the same format as the regular-issue Fleer Ultra. Each card has a team logo, player name and "ROOKIE" notation in gold foil at bottom, and the round Gold Medallion seal in an upper-corner of the borderless game-action photo front. Backs have two more action photos, a large one in one-color and a small one in full-color. Much of the typography on back is rendered in gold foil. Card numbers have an M prefix.

		NM/M
Complete Set (20):		3.00
Common Player:		.10
M-1	Manny Alexander	.10
M-2	Edgardo Alfonzo	.10
M-3	Jason Bates	.10
M-4	Andres Berumen	.10
M-5	Darren Bragg	.10
M-6	Jamie Brewington	.10
M-7	Jason Christiansen	.10
M-8	Brad Clontz	.10
M-9	Marty Cordova	.10
M-10	Johnny Damon	1.50
M-11	Vaughn Eshelman	.10
M-12	Chad Fonville	.10
M-13	Curtis Goodwin	.10

M-14	Tyler Green	.10
M-15	Bob Higginson	.10
M-16	Jason Isringhausen	.10
M-17	Hideo Nomo	1.50
M-18	Jon Nunnally	.10
M-19	Carlos Perez	.10
M-20	Julian Tavarez	.10

Hitting Machines

Various mechanical devices and dynamics make up the letters of "HITTING MACHINE" behind the color player action photo in this insert set. Both of those elements, along with the gold-foil player name, team and Ultra logo are in UV-coated contrast to the matte-finish gray background. Backs are also horizontal in format and feature a portrait photo at right, against a gray-streaked background. A career summary is printed at right. The Hitting Machines series is found only in Series II Ultra retail packs, at the rate of one card per eight packs, on average.

		NM/M
Complete Set (10):		6.00
Common Player:		.40
Gold Medallion:		2X
1	Jeff Bagwell	.65
2	Albert Belle	.25
3	Dante Bichette	.25
4	Barry Bonds	2.50
5	Jose Canseco	.50
6	Ken Griffey Jr.	1.00
7	Tony Gwynn	.75
8	Fred McGriff	.25
9	Mike Piazza	1.00
10	Frank Thomas	.65

Home Run Kings

Retail packaging of Fleer Ultra Series I was the hiding place for this sluggers' chase set. An average of one out of eight packs yielded a Home Run King insert. Fronts have a photo of the player's home run cut, while large letters "H," "R" and "K" are stacked vertically down one side. All front typography is in gold foil. Backs have another batting photo and a couple of sentences of recent career slugging prowess.

		NM/M
Complete Set (10):		7.50
Common Player:		.25
Gold Medallion:		2X
1	Ken Griffey Jr.	2.00
2	Frank Thomas	.75
3	Albert Belle	.25
4	Jose Canseco	.50
5	Cecil Fielder	.25
6	Matt Williams	.25
7	Jeff Bagwell	.75
8	Barry Bonds	3.00
9	Fred McGriff	.25
10	Andres Galarraga	.25

League Leaders

Top performers in major statistical categories are featured in this Series I insert. Cards were seeded in all types of Ultra packaging, at the rate of about one card per three packs. Cards have a horizontal orientation with a color player action photo printed over a black logo of the appropriate league. American Leaguers' cards have a light brown overall background color, National Leaguers have dark green. The player's name, team and Ultra logos, and box with his league-leading category are printed in silver foil. The background from the front is carried over to the back, where a color portrait photo is at left, and a '94 season summary printed at right.

		NM/M
Complete Set (10):		2.50
Common Player:		.15
Gold Medallion:		2X
1	Paul O'Neill	.15
2	Kenny Lofton	.15
3	Jimmy Key	.15
4	Randy Johnson	.50
5	Lee Smith	.15
6	Tony Gwynn	.75
7	Craig Biggio	.15
8	Greg Maddux	.75
9	Andy Benes	.15
10	John Franco	.15

On-Base Leaders

Numerous smaller versions in several sizes of the central action photo against a graduated color background from the front design of this Series II insert set. The player name, card title and Ultra logo are printed in gold foil down one side. Backs have a horizontal player photo with a large team logo at top, a smaller version at bottom and a 1994 season summary. One out of eight (on average) pre-priced packs yielded an On-Base Leaders insert.

		NM/M
Complete Set (10):		15.00
Common Player:		1.00
Gold Medallion:		2X
1	Jeff Bagwell	2.00
2	Albert Belle	1.00
3	Craig Biggio	1.00
4	Wade Boggs	2.50
5	Barry Bonds	6.00
6	Will Clark	1.00
7	Tony Gwynn	2.50
8	Dave Justice	1.00
9	Paul O'Neill	1.00
10	Frank Thomas	2.00

Power Plus

The scarcest of the Series I Ultra inserts are the Power Plus cards, printed on 100% etched foil and inserted at the rate of less than one per box. Fronts have a player action photo overprinted on a background of "POWER PLUS" logos in various metallic colors. A team logo and player name are at bottom in gold foil, as is the Ultra logo at top. Backs are conventionally printed and have a player photo on one side and season summary on the other.

		NM/M
Complete Set (6):		7.50
Common Player:		.50
Gold Medallion:		2X
1	Albert Belle	.50
2	Ken Griffey Jr.	2.00
3	Frank Thomas	1.00
4	Jeff Bagwell	1.00
5	Barry Bonds	4.00
6	Matt Williams	.50

RBI Kings

A bright aura surrounds the central player action photo on these cards, separating the player image from an indistinct colored background. At center is a large gold-foil "RBI KING" with the player's name above and team below. Backs have a similar design with a white box at bottom covering the player's RBI abilities. This set is found only in Series I jumbo packs, at an average rate of one per eight packs.

		NM/M
Complete Set (10):		12.00
Common Player:		.50
Gold Medallion:		2X
1	Kirby Puckett	3.00
2	Joe Carter	.50
3	Albert Belle	.50
4	Frank Thomas	2.00
5	Julio Franco	.50
6	Jeff Bagwell	2.00
7	Matt Williams	.50
8	Dante Bichette	.50
9	Fred McGriff	.50
10	Mike Piazza	4.00

Rising Stars

The top of the line among Series II chase cards is this set printed on 100% etched foil and seeded at the rate of less than one per box, on average. Horizontal-format cards have two player photos on a background of multi-colored rays. The Ultra logo, card title, player name and team are printed in gold foil. Backs repeat the colored rays, have another player photo and a career summary.

		NM/M
Complete Set (9):		7.00
Common Player:		.50
Gold Medallion:		2X
1	Moises Alou	.50
2	Jeff Bagwell	1.50
3	Albert Belle	.65
4	Juan Gonzalez	1.50
5	Chuck Knoblauch	.50
6	Kenny Lofton	.50
7	Raul Mondesi	.50
8	Mike Piazza	2.50
9	Frank Thomas	1.50

Second Year Standouts

Fifteen of the game's sophomore stars are featured in this Series I insert set. Horizontal-format cards have player action photos front and

back set against a background of orange and yellow rays. Besides the player name, card title and Ultra logo in gold-foil, the front features a pair of leafed branches flanking a team logo, all in embossed gold-foil. Backs have a career summary. The series was seeded at the average rate of one per six packs.

		NM/M
Complete Set (15):		3.50
Common Player:		.15
Gold Medallion:		2X
1	Cliff Floyd	.15
2	Chris Gomez	.15
3	Rusty Greer	.15
4	Darren Hall	.15
5	Bob Hamelin	.15
6	Joey Hamilton	.15
7	Jeffrey Hammonds	.15
8	John Hudek	.15
9	Ryan Klesko	.15
10	Raul Mondesi	.15
11	Manny Ramirez	3.00
12	Bill Risley	.15
13	Steve Trachsel	.15
14	William Van Landingham	.15
15	Rondell White	.15

Strikeout Kings

A purple background with several types of concentric and overlapping circular designs in white are the background of this Series II chase set. An action color photo of the K-King is at center, while down one side are stacked photos of the grips used for various pitches. The player name, card title and Ultra logo are in silver foil. Backs have a portrait photo and career summary with purple circles behind and a black background. Stated odds of finding a Strikeout King card are one in five packs, on average.

		NM/M
Complete Set (6):		3.00
Common Player:		.10
Gold Medallion:		2X
1	Andy Benes	.10
2	Roger Clemens	1.50
3	Randy Johnson	.75
4	Greg Maddux	.75
5	Pedro Martinez	.75
6	Jose Rijo	.10

1996 Ultra Promotional Samples

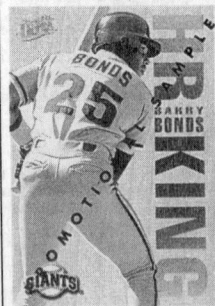

A six-page glossy folder which was die-cut to hold three sample cards introduced Fleer's

Ultra line for 1996. The fronts of all three cards are similar in format to the issued versions, but only the back of the basic-card sample replicates the issued version. Backs of the chase card samples contained product information.

	NM/M
Complete Set (8):	7.50
Common Player:	1.00
(1) Ken Griffey Jr. (Basic Card)	1.50
(2) Matt Williams (Basic Card)	1.00
(3) Barry Bonds (HR King)	2.50
(4) Frank Thomas (HR King)	1.25
(5) Roberto Alomar (Prime Leather)	1.00
(6) Cal Ripken Jr. (Prime Leather)	2.50
2 Tony Gwynn (Season Crown)	1.50
4 Kenny Lofton (Season Crown)	1.00

1996 Ultra

A 40% thicker cardboard stock and silver-foil highlights are featured in this year's edition. Fronts are very basic with a borderless action photo and silver-foil graphics. Backs feature a three-photo montage along with 1995 and career stats. The set was released in two 300-card series; each card is also reprinted as part of a limited-edition Gold Medallion parallel set. One Gold Medallion card is found in every pack. Each series has eight insert sets. Series 1 inserts are RBI Kings, Home Run Kings, Fresh Foundations, Diamond Producers, Power Plus, Season Crowns, Golden Prospects and Prime Leather. Series 2 inserts are Call to Honor, Golden Prospects, Hitting Machines, On-Base Leaders, RESPECT, Rawhide, Rising Stars and Thunderclap. Checklist cards were also randomly inserted into packs from both series.

	NM/M
Complete Set (600):	22.50
Common Player:	.05
Gold Medallions:	2X
Series 1 or 2 Pack (12):	1.25
Series 1 or 2 Wax Box (24):	20.00

#	Player	Price
1	Manny Alexander	.05
2	Brady Anderson	.05
3	Bobby Bonilla	.05
4	Scott Erickson	.05
5	Curtis Goodwin	.05
6	Chris Hoiles	.05
7	Doug Jones	.05
8	Jeff Manto	.05
9	Mike Mussina	.35
10	Rafael Palmeiro	.50
11	Cal Ripken Jr.	1.50
12	Rick Aguilera	.05
13	Luis Alicea	.05
14	Stan Belinda	.05
15	Jose Canseco	.40
16	Roger Clemens	.85
17	Mike Greenwell	.05
18	Mike Macfarlane	.05
19	Tim Naehring	.05
20	Troy O'Leary	.05
21	John Valentin	.05
22	Mo Vaughn	.25
23	Tim Wakefield	.05
24	Brian Anderson	.05
25	Garret Anderson	.05
26	Chili Davis	.05
27	Gary DiSarcina	.05
28	Jim Edmonds	.05
29	Jorge Fabregas	.05
30	Chuck Finley	.05
31	Mark Langston	.05
32	Troy Percival	.05
33	Tim Salmon	.05
34	Lee Smith	.05
35	Wilson Alvarez	.05
36	Ray Durham	.05
37	Alex Fernandez	.05
38	Ozzie Guillen	.05
39	Roberto Hernandez	.05
40	Lance Johnson	.05
41	Ron Karkovice	.05
42	Lyle Mouton	.05
43	Tim Raines	.05
44	Frank Thomas	.60
45	Carlos Baerga	.05
46	Albert Belle	.05
47	Orel Hershiser	.05
48	Kenny Lofton	.05
49	Dennis Martinez	.05
50	Jose Mesa	.05
51	Eddie Murray	.60
52	Chad Ogea	.05
53	Manny Ramirez	.60
54	Jim Thome	.50
55	Omar Vizquel	.05
56	Dave Winfield	.60
57	Chad Curtis	.05
58	Cecil Fielder	.05
59	John Flaherty	.05
60	Travis Fryman	.05
61	Chris Gomez	.05
62	Bob Higginson	.05
63	Felipe Lira	.05
64	Brian Maxcy	.05
65	Alan Trammell	.05
66	Lou Whitaker	.05
67	Kevin Appier	.05
68	Gary Gaetti	.05
69	Tom Goodwin	.05
70	Tom Gordon	.05
71	Jason Jacome	.05
72	Wally Joyner	.05
73	Brent Mayne	.05
74	Jeff Montgomery	.05
75	Jon Nunnally	.05
76	Joe Vitiello	.05
77	Ricky Bones	.05
78	Jeff Cirillo	.05
79	Mike Fetters	.05
80	Darryl Hamilton	.05
81	David Hulse	.05
82	Dave Nilsson	.05
83	Kevin Seitzer	.05
84	Steve Sparks	.05
85	B.J. Surhoff	.05
86	Jose Valentin	.05
87	Greg Vaughn	.05
88	Marty Cordova	.05
89	Chuck Knoblauch	.05
90	Pat Meares	.05
91	Pedro Munoz	.05
92	Kirby Puckett	.75
93	Brad Radke	.05
94	Scott Stahoviak	.05
95	Dave Stevens	.05
96	Mike Trombley	.05
97	Matt Walbeck	.05
98	Wade Boggs	.75
99	Russ Davis	.05
100	Jim Leyritz	.05
101	Don Mattingly	.85
102	Jack McDowell	.05
103	Paul O'Neill	.05
104	Andy Pettitte	.30
105	Mariano Rivera	.15
106	Ruben Sierra	.05
107	Darryl Strawberry	.05
108	John Wetteland	.05
109	Bernie Williams	.05
110	Geronimo Berroa	.05
111	Scott Brosius	.05
112	Dennis Eckersley	.50
113	Brent Gates	.05
114	Rickey Henderson	.60
115	Mark McGwire	1.25
116	Ariel Prieto	.05
117	Terry Steinbach	.05
118	Todd Stottlemyre	.05
119	Todd Van Poppel	.05
120	Steve Wojciechowski	.05
121	Rich Amaral	.05
122	Bobby Ayala	.05
123	Mike Blowers	.05
124	Chris Bosio	.05
125	Joey Cora	.05
126	Ken Griffey Jr.	1.00
127	Randy Johnson	.05
128	Edgar Martinez	.05
129	Tino Martinez	.05
130	Alex Rodriguez	1.25
131	Dan Wilson	.05
132	Will Clark	.05
133	Jeff Frye	.05
134	Benji Gil	.05
135	Juan Gonzalez	.30
136	Rusty Greer	.05
137	Mark McLemore	.05
138	Roger Pavlik	.05
139	Ivan Rodriguez	.50
140	Kenny Rogers	.05
141	Mickey Tettleton	.05
142	Roberto Alomar	.20
143	Joe Carter	.05
144	Tony Castillo	.05
145	Alex Gonzalez	.05
146	Shawn Green	.35
147	Pat Hentgen	.05
148	Sandy Martinez RC	.05
149	Paul Molitor	.60
150	John Olerud	.05
151	Ed Sprague	.05
152	Jeff Blauser	.05
153	Brad Clontz	.05
154	Tom Glavine	.30
155	Marquis Grissom	.05
156	Chipper Jones	.75
157	David Justice	.05
158	Ryan Klesko	.05
159	Javier Lopez	.05
160	Greg Maddux	.75
161	John Smoltz	.05
162	Mark Wohlers	.05
163	Jim Bullinger	.05
164	Frank Castillo	.05
165	Shawon Dunston	.05
166	Kevin Foster	.05
167	Luis Gonzalez	.05
168	Mark Grace	.05
169	Rey Sanchez	.05
170	Scott Servais	.05
171	Sammy Sosa	.75
172	Ozzie Timmons	.05
173	Steve Trachsel	.05
174	Bret Boone	.05
175	Jeff Branson	.05
176	Jeff Brantley	.05
177	Dave Burba	.05
178	Ron Gant	.05
179	Barry Larkin	.05
180	Darren Lewis	.05
181	Mark Portugal	.05
182	Reggie Sanders	.05
183	Pete Schourek	.05
184	John Smiley	.05
185	Jason Bates	.05
186	Dante Bichette	.05
187	Ellis Burks	.05
188	Vinny Castilla	.05
189	Andres Galarraga	.05
190	Darren Holmes	.05
191	Armando Reynoso	.05
192	Kevin Ritz	.05
193	Bill Swift	.05
194	Larry Walker	.05
195	Kurt Abbott	.05
196	John Burkett	.05
197	Greg Colbrunn	.05
198	Jeff Conine	.05
199	Andre Dawson	.25
200	Chris Hammond	.05
201	Charles Johnson	.05
202	Robb Nen	.05
203	Terry Pendleton	.05
204	Quilvio Veras	.05
205	Jeff Bagwell	.60
206	Derek Bell	.05
207	Doug Drabek	.05
208	Tony Eusebio	.05
209	Mike Hampton	.05
210	Brian Hunter	.05
211	Todd Jones	.05
212	Orlando Miller	.05
213	James Mouton	.05
214	Shane Reynolds	.05
215	Dave Veres	.05
216	Billy Ashley	.05
217	Brett Butler	.05
218	Chad Fonville	.05
219	Todd Hollandsworth	.05
220	Eric Karros	.05
221	Ramon Martinez	.05
222	Raul Mondesi	.05
223	Hideo Nomo	.30
224	Mike Piazza	1.00
225	Kevin Tapani	.05
226	Ismael Valdes	.05
227	Todd Worrell	.05
228	Moises Alou	.05
229	Wil Cordero	.05
230	Jeff Fassero	.05
231	Darrin Fletcher	.05
232	Mike Lansing	.05
233	Pedro Martinez	.60
234	Carlos Perez	.05
235	Mel Rojas	.05
236	David Segui	.05
237	Tony Tarasco	.05
238	Rondell White	.05
239	Edgardo Alfonzo	.05
240	Rico Brogna	.05
241	Carl Everett	.05
242	Todd Hundley	.05
243	Butch Huskey	.05
244	Jason Isringhausen	.05
245	Bobby Jones	.05
246	Jeff Kent	.05
247	Bill Pulsipher	.05
248	Jose Vizcaino	.05
249	Ricky Bottalico	.05
250	Darren Daulton	.05
251	Jim Eisenreich	.05
252	Tyler Green	.05
253	Charlie Hayes	.05
254	Gregg Jefferies	.05
255	Tony Longmire	.05
256	Michael Mimbs	.05
257	Mickey Morandini	.05
258	Paul Quantrill	.05
259	Heathcliff Slocumb	.05
260	Jay Bell	.05
261	Jacob Brumfield	.05
262	Angelo Encarnacion RC	.05
263	John Ericks	.05
264	Mark Johnson	.05
265	Esteban Loaiza	.05
266	Al Martin	.05
267	Orlando Merced	.05
268	Dan Miceli	.05
269	Denny Neagle	.05
270	Brian Barber	.05
271	Scott Cooper	.05
272	Tripp Cromer	.05
273	Bernard Gilkey	.05
274	Tom Henke	.05
275	Brian Jordan	.05
276	John Mabry	.05
277	Tom Pagnozzi	.05
278	Mark Petkovsek RC	.05
279	Ozzie Smith	.75
280	Andy Ashby	.05
281	Brad Ausmus	.05
282	Ken Caminiti	.05
283	Glenn Dishman	.05
284	Tony Gwynn	.75
285	Joey Hamilton	.05
286	Trevor Hoffman	.05
287	Phil Plantier	.05
288	Jody Reed	.05
289	Eddie Williams	.05
290	Barry Bonds	1.50
291	Jamie Brewington	.05
292	Mark Carreon	.05
293	Royce Clayton	.05
294	Glenallen Hill	.05
295	Mark Leiter	.05
296	Kirt Manwaring	.05
297	J.R. Phillips	.05
298	Deion Sanders	.05
299	William Van Landingham	.05
300	Matt Williams	.05
301	Roberto Alomar	.20
302	Armando Benitez	.05
303	Mike Devereaux	.05
304	Jeffrey Hammonds	.05
305	Jimmy Haynes	.05
306	Scott McClain RC	.05
307	Kent Mercker RC	.05
308	Randy Myers	.05
309	B.J. Surhoff	.05
310	Tony Tarasco	.05
311	David Wells	.05
312	Wil Cordero	.05
313	Alex Delgado	.05
314	Tom Gordon	.05
315	Dwayne Hosey	.05
316	Jose Malave	.05
317	Kevin Mitchell	.05
318	Jamie Moyer	.05
319	Aaron Sele	.05
320	Heathcliff Slocumb	.05
321	Mike Stanley	.05
322	Jeff Suppan	.05
323	Jim Abbott	.05
324	George Arias	.05
325	Todd Greene	.05
326	Bryan Harvey	.05
327	J.T. Snow	.05
328	Randy Velarde	.05
329	Tim Wallach	.05
330	Harold Baines	.05
331	Jason Bere	.05
332	Darren Lewis	.05
333	Norberto Martin	.05
334	Tony Phillips	.05
335	Bill Simas	.05
336	Chris Snopek	.05
337	Kevin Tapani	.05
338	Danny Tartabull	.05
339	Robin Ventura	.05
340	Sandy Alomar	.05
341	Julio Franco	.05
342	Jack McDowell	.05
343	Charles Nagy	.05
344	Julian Tavarez	.05
345	Kimera Bartee	.05
346	Greg Keagle	.05
347	Mark Lewis	.05
348	Jose Lima	.05
349	Melvin Nieves	.05
350	Mark Parent	.05
351	Eddie Williams	.05
352	Johnny Damon	.30
353	Sal Fasano	.05
354	Mark Gubicza	.05
355	Bob Hamelin	.05
356	Chris Haney	.05
357	Keith Lockhart	.05
358	Mike Macfarlane	.05
359	Jose Offerman	.05
360	Bip Roberts	.05
361	Michael Tucker	.05
362	Chuck Carr	.05
363	Bobby Hughes	.05
364	John Jaha	.05
365	Mark Loretta	.05
366	Mike Matheny	.05
367	Ben McDonald	.05
368	Matt Mieske	.05
369	Angel Miranda	.05
370	Fernando Vina	.05
371	Rick Aguilera	.05
372	Rich Becker	.05
373	LaTroy Hawkins	.05
374	Dave Hollins	.05
375	Roberto Kelly	.05
376	Matt Lawton RC	.25
377	Paul Molitor	.60
378	Dan Naulty RC	.05
379	Rich Robertson	.05
380	Frank Rodriguez	.05
381	David Cone	.05
382	Mariano Duncan	.05
383	Andy Fox RC	.05
384	Joe Girardi	.05
385	Dwight Gooden	.05
386	Derek Jeter	1.50
387	Pat Kelly	.05
388	Jimmy Key	.05
389	Matt Luke RC	.05
390	Tino Martinez	.05
391	Jeff Nelson	.05
392	Melido Perez	.05
393	Tim Raines	.05
394	Ruben Rivera	.05
395	Kenny Rogers	.05
396	Tony Batista RC	.25
397	Allen Battle	.05
398	Mike Bordick	.05
399	Steve Cox	.05
400	Jason Giambi	.40
401	Doug Johns	.05
402	Pedro Munoz	.05
403	Phil Plantier	.05
404	Scott Spiezio	.05
405	George Williams	.05
406	Ernie Young	.05
407	Darren Bragg	.05
408	Jay Buhner	.05
409	Norm Charlton	.05
410	Russ Davis	.05
411	Sterling Hitchcock	.05
412	Edwin Hurtado	.05
413	Raul Ibanez RC	2.00
414	Mike Jackson	.05
415	Luis Sojo	.05
416	Paul Sorrento	.05
417	Bob Wolcott	.05
418	Damon Buford	.05
419	Kevin Gross	.05
420	Darryl Hamilton	.05
421	Mike Henneman	.05
422	Ken Hill	.05
423	Dean Palmer	.05
424	Bobby Witt	.05
425	Tilson Brito	.05
426	Giovanni Carrara	.05
427	Domingo Cedeno	.05
428	Felipe Crespo	.05
429	Carlos Delgado	.40
430	Juan Guzman	.05
431	Erik Hanson	.05
432	Marty Janzen RC	.05
433	Otis Nixon	.05
434	Robert Perez	.05
435	Paul Quantrill	.05
436	Bill Risley	.05
437	Steve Avery	.05
438	Jermaine Dye	.05
439	Mark Lemke	.05
440	Marty Malloy RC	.05
441	Fred McGriff	.05
442	Greg McMichael	.05
443	Wonderful Monds	.05
444	Eddie Perez	.05
445	Jason Schmidt	.05
446	Terrell Wade	.05
447	Terry Adams	.05
448	Scott Bullett	.05
449	Robin Jennings RC	.05
450	Doug Jones	.05
451	Brooks Kieschnick	.05
452	Dave Magadan	.05
453	Jason Maxwell RC	.05
454	Brian McRae	.05
455	Rodney Myers	.05
456	Jaime Navarro	.05
457	Ryne Sandberg	.75
458	Vince Coleman	.05
459	Eric Davis	.05
460	Steve Gibralter	.05
461	Thomas Howard	.05
462	Mike Kelly	.05
463	Hal Morris	.05
464	Eric Owens	.05
465	Jose Rijo	.05
466	Chris Sabo	.05
467	Eddie Taubensee	.05
468	Trenidad Hubbard	.05
469	Curt Leskanic	.05
470	Quinton McCracken	.05
471	Jayhawk Owens	.05
472	Steve Reed	.05
473	Bryan Rekar	.05
474	Bruce Ruffin	.05
475	Bret Saberhagen	.05
476	Walt Weiss	.05
477	Eric Young	.05
478	Kevin Brown	.05
479	Al Leiter	.05
480	Pat Rapp	.05
481	Gary Sheffield	.35
482	Devon White	.05
483	Bob Abreu	.05
484	Sean Berry	.05
485	Craig Biggio	.05
486	Jim Dougherty	.05
487	Richard Hidalgo	.05
488	Darryl Kile	.05
489	Derrick May	.05
490	Greg Swindell	.05
491	Rick Wilkins	.05
492	Mike Blowers	.05
493	Tom Candiotti	.05
494	Roger Cedeno	.05
495	Delino DeShields	.05
496	Greg Gagne	.05
497	Karim Garcia	.10
498	Wilton Guerrero RC	.05
499	Chan Ho Park	.05
500	Israel Alcantara	.05
501	Shane Andrews	.05
502	Yamil Benitez	.05
503	Cliff Floyd	.05
504	Mark Grudzielanek	.05
505	Ryan McGuire	.05
506	Sherman Obando	.05
507	Jose Paniagua	.05
508	Henry Rodriguez	.05
509	Kirk Rueter	.05
510	Juan Acevedo	.05
511	John Franco	.05
512	Bernard Gilkey	.05
513	Lance Johnson	.05
514	Rey Ordonez	.05
515	Robert Person	.05
516	Paul Wilson	.05
517	Toby Borland	.05
518	David Doster RC	.05
519	Lenny Dykstra	.05
520	Sid Fernandez	.05
521	Mike Grace RC	.05
522	Rich Hunter RC	.05
523	Benito Santiago	.05
524	Gene Schall	.05
525	Curt Schilling	.15
526	Kevin Sefcik RC	.05
527	Lee Tinsley	.05
528	David West	.05
529	Mark Whiten	.05
530	Todd Zeile	.05
531	Carlos Garcia	.05
532	Charlie Hayes	.05
533	Jason Kendall	.05
534	Jeff King	.05
535	Mike Kingery	.05
536	Nelson Liriano	.05
537	Dan Plesac	.05
538	Paul Wagner	.05
539	Luis Alicea	.05
540	David Bell	.05
541	Alan Benes	.05
542	Andy Benes	.05
543	Mike Busby RC	.05
544	Royce Clayton	.05
545	Dennis Eckersley	.50
546	Gary Gaetti	.05
547	Ron Gant	.05
548	Aaron Holbert	.05
549	Ray Lankford	.05
550	T.J. Mathews	.05
551	Willie McGee	.05
552	Miguel Mejia RC	.05
553	Todd Stottlemyre	.05
554	Sean Bergman	.05
555	Willie Blair	.05
556	Andujar Cedeno	.05
557	Steve Finley	.05
558	Rickey Henderson	.60
559	Wally Joyner	.05
560	Scott Livingstone	.05
561	Marc Newfield	.05
562	Bob Tewksbury	.05
563	Fernando Valenzuela	.05
564	Rod Beck	.05
565	Doug Creek	.05
566	Shawon Dunston	.05
567	Osvaldo Fernandez RC	.20
568	Stan Javier	.05
569	Marcus Jensen	.05
570	Steve Scarsone	.05
571	Robby Thompson	.05
572	Allen Watson	.05
573	Roberto Alomar (Ultra Stars)	.10
574	Jeff Bagwell (Ultra Stars)	.30
575	Albert Belle (Ultra Stars)	.40
576	Wade Boggs (Ultra Stars)	.40
577	Barry Bonds (Ultra Stars)	.75
578	Juan Gonzalez (Ultra Stars)	.15
579	Ken Griffey Jr. (Ultra Stars)	.50
580	Tony Gwynn (Ultra Stars)	.40
581	Randy Johnson (Ultra Stars)	.30
582	Chipper Jones (Ultra Stars)	.40
583	Barry Larkin (Ultra Stars)	.05
584	Kenny Lofton (Ultra Stars)	.05
585	Greg Maddux (Ultra Stars)	.40
586	Raul Mondesi (Ultra Stars)	.05
587	Mike Piazza (Ultra Stars)	.50
588	Cal Ripken Jr. (Ultra Stars)	.75
589	Tim Salmon (Ultra Stars)	.05
590	Frank Thomas (Ultra Stars)	.35
591	Mo Vaughn (Ultra Stars)	.05
592	Matt Williams (Ultra Stars)	.05
593	Marty Cordova (Raw Power)	.05
594	Jim Edmonds (Raw Power)	.05
595	Cliff Floyd (Raw Power)	.05
596	Chipper Jones (Raw Power)	.40
597	Ryan Klesko (Raw Power)	.05
598	Raul Mondesi (Raw Power)	.05
599	Manny Ramirez (Raw Power)	.30
600	Ruben Rivera (Raw Power)	.05

1996 Ultra Gold Medallion

Limited to less than 10 percent of the regular edition's production, the Gold Medallion parallel set replaces the front photo's background with gold foil featuring a large embossed Fleer Ultra

Gold Medallion seal at center. One Gold Medallion card is found in each foil pack.

	NM/M
Complete Set (600):	75.00
Common Player:	.25

Call to the Hall

Ten probable future Hall of Famers are featured on these cards, which use classic style original illustrations of the players. The cards were seeded one per every 24 Series 2 packs.

		NM/M
Complete Set (10):		10.00
Common Player:		1.00
Gold Medallion Edition:		2X
1	Barry Bonds	3.00
2	Ken Griffey Jr.	2.00
3	Tony Gwynn	1.25
4	Rickey Henderson	1.00
5	Greg Maddux	1.25
6	Eddie Murray	1.00
7	Cal Ripken Jr.	3.00
8	Ryne Sandberg	1.25
9	Ozzie Smith	1.25
10	Frank Thomas	1.00

Checklists

Fleer Ultra featured 10 checklist cards that were inserted every four packs. These cards feature a superstar player on the front and, throughout the set, a full checklist of all cards in the 1996 Ultra set on the back.

		NM/M
Complete Set (20):		9.00
Common Player:		.15
1	Jeff Bagwell	.50
2	Barry Bonds	1.00
3	Juan Gonzalez	.25
4	Ken Griffey Jr.	.65
5	Chipper Jones	.60
6	Mike Piazza	.65
7	Manny Ramirez	.65
8	Cal Ripken Jr.	1.00
9	Frank Thomas	.50
10	Matt Williams	.15
1	Albert Belle	.15
2	Cecil Fielder	.15
3	Ken Griffey Jr.	.65
4	Tony Gwynn	.60
5	Derek Jeter	.65

6	Jason Kendall	.15
7	Ryan Klesko	.15
8	Greg Maddux	.60
9	Cal Ripken Jr.	1.00
10	Frank Thomas	.50

1996 Ultra Diamond Dust

This card commemorates Cal Ripken's history-making 1995 record of playing in 2,131 consecutive regular-season games. Horizontal in format, the front has a color action photo of Ripken on a simulated leather background. Back has a photo of Ripken on the night he set the new record. Sandwiched between front and back is a dime-sized plastic capsule of dirt certified, according to the facsimile autograph of the team's head groundskeeper, to have been used on the infield at Oriole Park in Camden Yards during the 1995 season. Two versions of the card were made. A hand-numbered version limited to 2,131 was offered direct to dealers for $39.99. An unnumbered version was available to collectors as a wrapper redemption for $24.99.

	NM/M
Cal Ripken Jr. (Numbered)	40.00
Cal Ripken Jr. (Unnumbered)	20.00

Diamond Producers

A horizontal layout and two versions of the same photo printed on holographic foil are featured in this insert set. Stated odds of finding a Diamond Producers card are one per every 20 Series I packs.

		NM/M
Complete Set (12):		15.00
Common Player:		.50
Gold Medallions:		2X
1	Albert Belle	.50
2	Barry Bonds	3.00
3	Ken Griffey Jr.	2.00
4	Tony Gwynn	1.50
5	Greg Maddux	1.50
6	Hideo Nomo	.75
7	Mike Piazza	2.00
8	Kirby Puckett	1.50
9	Cal Ripken Jr.	3.00
10	Frank Thomas	1.25
11	Mo Vaughn	.50
12	Matt Williams	.50

Fresh Foundations

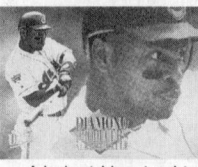

Rising stars who can carry their teams' fortunes into the next century are featured in this foil-printed insert set, found on average of one card per every three Series I foil packs.

		NM/M
Complete Set (10):		2.00
Common Player:		.15
Gold Medallions:		2X
1	Albert Belle	2.00
2	Barry Bonds	12.00

1	Garret Anderson	.15
2	Marty Cordova	.15
3	Jim Edmonds	.15
4	Brian Hunter	.15
5	Chipper Jones	.50
6	Ryan Klesko	.15
7	Raul Mondesi	.15
8	Hideo Nomo	.25
9	Manny Ramirez	.40
10	Rondell White	.15

Golden Prospects, Series 1

A hobby-pack-only insert, these horizontal format cards have rainbow foil ballpark backgrounds and feature 1996's rookie crop. They are found on average of one per every five Series I packs.

		NM/M
Complete Set (10):		7.00
Common Player:		.25
Gold Medallions:		2X
1	Yamil Benitez	.25
2	Alberto Castillo	.25
3	Roger Cedeno	.25
4	Johnny Damon	1.00
5	Micah Franklin	.25
6	Jason Giambi	1.00
7	Jose Herrera	.25
8	Derek Jeter	5.00
9	Kevin Jordan	.25
10	Ruben Rivera	.25

Golden Prospects, Series 2

The Golden Prospects insert series continued with 15 more young stars found exclusively in Series 2 hobby packs, though in much lower numbers than the Series 1 inserts.

		NM/M
Complete Set (15):		10.00
Common Player:		1.00
Gold Medallions:		2X
1	Bob Abreu	1.50
2	Israel Alcantara	1.00
3	Tony Batista	1.00
4	Mike Cameron	1.00
5	Steve Cox	1.00
6	Jermaine Dye	1.00
7	Wilton Guerrero	1.00
8	Richard Hidalgo	1.00
9	Raul Ibanez	1.00
10	Marty Janzen	1.00
11	Robin Jennings	1.00
12	Jason Maxwell	1.00
13	Scott McClain	1.00
14	Wonderful Monds	1.00
15	Chris Singleton	1.00

Hitting Machines

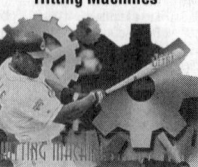

These die-cut 1996 Fleer Ultra Series II insert cards showcase the heaviest hitters on cards featuring a machine-gear design. The cards were seeded one per every 288 Series II packs.

		NM/M
Complete Set (10):		35.00
Common Player:		2.00
Gold Medallion:		2X
1	Albert Belle	2.00
2	Barry Bonds	12.00

3	Juan Gonzalez	2.50
4	Ken Griffey Jr.	6.00
5	Edgar Martinez	2.00
6	Rafael Palmeiro	3.00
7	Mike Piazza	6.00
8	Tim Salmon	2.00
9	Frank Thomas	4.00
10	Matt Williams	2.00

1996 Ultra Home Run Kings Exchange Cards

Printed on cardboard, these super-scarce inserts are found at the rate of only one per 75 packs. Because of quality control problems, the cards were initially released as exchange cards, with instructions on back for a mail-in redemption offer for the actual wooden card. The redemption period expired Dec. 1, 1996.

		NM/M
Complete Set (12):		20.00
Common Player:		.75
1	Albert Belle	.75
2	Dante Bichette	.75
3	Barry Bonds	5.00
4	Jose Canseco	1.50
5	Juan Gonzalez	1.25
6	Ken Griffey Jr.	3.00
7	Mark McGwire	4.00
8	Manny Ramirez	2.50
9	Tim Salmon	.75
10	Frank Thomas	2.50
11	Mo Vaughn	.75
12	Matt Williams	.75

Home Run Kings

Printed on a thin wood veneer, these super-scarce inserts are seeded one per every 75 Series 1 packs. Because of quality control problems, the cards were initially released as exchange cards, with instructions on back for a mail-in redemption offer for the actual wooden card.

		NM/M
Complete Set (12):		50.00
Common Player:		2.50
Gold Medallions:		2X
1	Albert Belle	2.50
2	Dante Bichette	2.50
3	Barry Bonds	12.50
4	Jose Canseco	5.00
5	Juan Gonzalez	3.00
6	Ken Griffey Jr.	9.00
7	Mark McGwire	10.00
8	Manny Ramirez	6.50
9	Tim Salmon	2.50
10	Frank Thomas	6.50
11	Mo Vaughn	2.50
12	Matt Williams	2.50

On-Base Leaders

These 1996 Fleer Ultra Series II insert cards feature 10 of the game's top on-base leaders. The cards were seeded one per every four packs.

		NM/M
Complete Set (10):		4.50
Common Player:		.25
Gold Medallion:		2X
1	Roberto Alomar	.65
2	Wade Boggs	.75

2	Barry Bonds	2.00
3	Tony Gwynn	.75
4	Rickey Henderson	.60
5	Chuck Knoblauch	.25
6	Edgar Martinez	.25
7	Mike Piazza	1.00
8	Tim Salmon	.25
9	Frank Thomas	.60
10	Jim Thome	.50

Power Plus

Etched-foil backgrounds, multiple player photos and a horizontal format are featured in this chase set. Stated odds of finding one of the dozen Power Plus cards are one per every 10 Series I packs.

		NM/M
Complete Set (12):		10.00
Common Player:		.40
Gold Medallions:		2X
1	Jeff Bagwell	1.25
2	Barry Bonds	3.00
3	Ken Griffey Jr.	2.00
4	Raul Mondesi	.40
5	Rafael Palmeiro	1.00
6	Mike Piazza	2.00
7	Manny Ramirez	1.25
8	Tim Salmon	.40
9	Reggie Sanders	.40
10	Frank Thomas	1.25
11	Larry Walker	.40
12	Matt Williams	.40

Prime Leather

An embossed leather-feel background is featured on these cards of top fielders, seeded one per every eight Series I packs, on average.

		NM/M
Complete Set (18):		17.50
Common Player:		.50
Gold Medallions:		2X
1	Ivan Rodriguez	1.50
2	Will Clark	.50
3	Roberto Alomar	.65
4	Cal Ripken Jr.	4.00
5	Wade Boggs	2.00
6	Ken Griffey Jr.	2.50
7	Kenny Lofton	.50
8	Kirby Puckett	2.00
9	Tim Salmon	.65
10	Mike Piazza	2.50
11	Mark Grace	.50
12	Craig Biggio	.50
13	Barry Larkin	.50
14	Matt Williams	.50
15	Barry Bonds	4.00
16	Tony Gwynn	2.00
17	Brian McRae	.50
18	Raul Mondesi	.50

Rawhide

Ten top fielders are featured on these 1996 Fleer Ultra Series II inserts. The cards were seeded one per every eight packs.

		NM/M
Complete Set (10):		10.00
Common Player:		.45
Gold Medallion:		2X
1	Roberto Alomar	.65
2	Barry Bonds	3.00

3	Mark Grace	.45
4	Ken Griffey Jr.	1.50
5	Kenny Lofton	.45
6	Greg Maddux	1.00
7	Raul Mondesi	.45
8	Mike Piazza	1.50
9	Cal Ripken Jr.	3.00
10	Matt Williams	.45

RBI Kings

Retail packs are the exclusive provenance of this 10-card set of top RBI men. Stated odds of finding an RBI King card are one per every five Series I packs.

		NM/M
Complete Set (10):		4.00
Common Player:		.10
Gold Medallions:		2X
1	Derek Bell	.10
2	Albert Belle	.10
3	Dante Bichette	.10
4	Barry Bonds	2.00
5	Jim Edmonds	.15
6	Manny Ramirez	1.00
7	Reggie Sanders	.10
8	Sammy Sosa	.10
9	Frank Thomas	1.00
10	Mo Vaughn	.10

R-E-S-P-E-C-T

These cards feature 10 players held in high esteem by their major league peers. The cards were seeded one per every 18 1996 Ultra Series II packs.

		NM/M
Complete Set (10):		20.00
Common Player:		.50
Gold Medallion:		2X
1	Joe Carter	.50
2	Ken Griffey Jr.	3.00
3	Tony Gwynn	2.50
4	Greg Maddux	2.50
5	Eddie Murray	2.00
6	Kirby Puckett	2.50
7	Cal Ripken Jr.	5.00
8	Ryne Sandberg	2.50
9	Frank Thomas	2.50
10	Mo Vaughn	.50

Rising Stars

Ten of baseball's best young players are spotlighted on these 1996 Fleer Ultra Series II inserts.

Cards were seeded one per every four packs.

		NM/M
Complete Set (10):		4.00
Common Player:		.20
Gold Medallion:		2X
1	Garret Anderson	.20
2	Marty Cordova	.20
3	Jim Edmonds	.35
4	Cliff Floyd	.20
5	Brian Hunter	.20
6	Chipper Jones	2.00
7	Ryan Klesko	.20
8	Hideo Nomo	.65
9	Manny Ramirez	1.25
10	Rondell White	.20

Season Crowns

Large coats-of-arms printed on "Ultra Crystal" clear plastic are the background for player action photos in this insert set. Odds of one per every 10 Series II packs were stated.

		NM/M
Complete Set (10):		12.50
Common Player:		.75
Gold Medallions:		2X
1	Barry Bonds	4.00
2	Tony Gwynn	2.00
3	Randy Johnson	1.25
4	Kenny Lofton	.75
5	Greg Maddux	2.00
6	Edgar Martinez	.75
7	Hideo Nomo	1.00
8	Cal Ripken Jr.	4.00
9	Frank Thomas	1.25
10	Tim Wakefield	.75

Thunderclap

The active career home run leaders are featured in this retail-exclusive Ultra insert set. Seeded only one per 72 packs, the Thunderclap cards have action photos on front with simulated lightning in the background and other graphic highlights rendered in holographic foil. Backs have a large portrait photo and career summary. Each of these scarce retail inserts can also be found in an even more elusive Gold Medallion version.

		NM/M
Complete Set (20):		45.00
Common Player:		1.00
Gold Medallion:		2X
1	Albert Belle	1.00
2	Barry Bonds	7.50
3	Bobby Bonilla	1.00
4	Jose Canseco	1.50
5	Joe Carter	1.00
6	Will Clark	1.00
7	Andre Dawson	1.50
8	Cecil Fielder	1.00
9	Andres Galarraga	1.00
10	Juan Gonzalez	1.50
11	Ken Griffey Jr.	5.00
12	Fred McGriff	1.00
13	Mark McGwire	6.00
14	Eddie Murray	2.50
15	Rafael Palmeiro	2.00
16	Kirby Puckett	4.00
17	Cal Ripken Jr.	7.50
18	Ryne Sandberg	4.00
19	Frank Thomas	2.50
20	Matt Williams	1.00

1997 Ultra Promo Strip

To introduce the concept of its new non-parallel parallel set, Fleer issued this three-card promo strip picturing regular (left), Gold Medallion (center) and Platinum Medallion (right) Cal Ripken, Jr., cards. Fronts have a "PROMOTIONAL SAMPLE," overprint in foil to match the cards' graphic highlights (silver, gold and prismatic). Backs, which have stats only through the 1995 season, have the same overprint in red.

	NM/M
Three-Card Strip:	10.00

1997 Ultra

Ultra was issued in a 300-card Series 1 and 252-card Series 2, each with two parallel editions, Gold and Platinum, which feature "G" and "P" prefixes on the card number, respectively. Cards were issued in 10-card packs. Player names and the Ultra logo are in silver holographic foil. Backs contains complete year-by-year statistics, plus two photos of the player. This also marked the first time that the Gold and Platinum parallel sets displayed a different photo than the base card. Inserts in Ultra included: Rookie Reflections, Double Trouble, Checklists, Season Crowns, RBI Kings, Power Plus, Fielder's Choice, Diamond Producers, HR Kings, and Baseball Rules.

		NM/M
Complete Set (553):		80.00
Common Player:		.05
Gold Medallion:		3X
Platinum Medallion:		25X
Series 1 Wax Pack (10):		1.25
Series 1 Wax Box (24):		20.00
Series 2 Wax Pack (10):		5.00
Series 2 Wax Box (24):		90.00
1	Roberto Alomar	.25
2	Brady Anderson	.05
3	Rocky Coppinger	.05
4	Jeffrey Hammonds	.05
5	Chris Hoiles	.05
6	Eddie Murray	.75
7	Mike Mussina	.45
8	Jimmy Myers	.05
9	Randy Myers	.05
10	Arthur Rhodes	.05
11	Cal Ripken Jr.	2.50
12	Jose Canseco	.50
13	Roger Clemens	1.25
14	Tom Gordon	.05
15	Jose Malave	.05
16	Tim Naehring	.05
17	Troy O'Leary	.05
18	Bill Selby	.05
19	Heathcliff Slocumb	.05
20	Mike Stanley	.05
21	Mo Vaughn	.05
22	Garret Anderson	.05
23	George Arias	.05
24	Chili Davis	.05
25	Jim Edmonds	.05
26	Darin Erstad	.25
27	Chuck Finley	.05
28	Todd Greene	.05
29	Troy Percival	.05
30	Tim Salmon	.05
31	Jeff Schmidt	.05
32	Randy Velarde	.05
33	Shad Williams	.05
34	Wilson Alvarez	.05
35	Harold Baines	.05
36	James Baldwin	.05
37	Mike Cameron	.05
38	Ray Durham	.05
39	Ozzie Guillen	.05
40	Roberto Hernandez	.05
41	Darren Lewis	.05
42	Jose Munoz	.05
43	Tony Phillips	.05
44	Frank Thomas	.75
45	Sandy Alomar Jr.	.05
46	Albert Belle	.05
47	Mark Carreon	.05
48	Julio Franco	.05
49	Orel Hershiser	.05
50	Kenny Lofton	.05
51	Jack McDowell	.05
52	Jose Mesa	.05
53	Charles Nagy	.05
54	Manny Ramirez	.75
55	Julian Tavarez	.05
56	Omar Vizquel	.05
57	Raul Casanova	.05
58	Tony Clark	.05
59	Travis Fryman	.05
60	Bob Higginson	.05
61	Melvin Nieves	.05
62	Curtis Pride	.05
63	Justin Thompson	.05
64	Alan Trammell	.05
65	Kevin Appier	.05
66	Johnny Damon	.35
67	Keith Lockhart	.05
68	Jeff Montgomery	.05
69	Jose Offerman	.05
70	Bip Roberts	.05
71	Jose Rosado	.05
72	Chris Stynes	.05
73	Mike Sweeney	.05
74	Jeff Cirillo	.05
75	Jeff D'Amico	.05
76	John Jaha	.05
77	Scott Karl	.05
78	Mike Matheny	.05
79	Ben McDonald	.05
80	Matt Mieske	.05
81	Marc Newfield	.05
82	Dave Nilsson	.05
83	Jose Valentin	.05
84	Fernando Vina	.05
85	Rick Aguilera	.05
86	Marty Cordova	.05
87	Chuck Knoblauch	.05
88	Matt Lawton	.05
89	Pat Meares	.05
90	Paul Molitor	.75
91	Greg Myers	.05
92	Dan Naulty	.05
93	Kirby Puckett	1.00
94	Frank Rodriguez	.05
95	Wade Boggs	1.00
96	Cecil Fielder	.05
97	Joe Girardi	.05
98	Dwight Gooden	.05
99	Derek Jeter	2.50
100	Tino Martinez	.05
101	Ramiro Mendoza RC	.05
102	Andy Pettitte	.20
103	Mariano Rivera	.15
104	Ruben Rivera	.05
105	Kenny Rogers	.05
106	Darryl Strawberry	.05
107	Bernie Williams	.05
108	Tony Batista	.05
109	Geronimo Berroa	.05
110	Bobby Chouinard	.05
111	Brent Gates	.05
112	Jason Giambi	.60
113	Damon Mashore RC	.05
114	Mark McGwire	2.00
115	Scott Spiezio	.05
116	John Wasdin	.05
117	Steve Wojciechowski	.05
118	Ernie Young	.05
119	Norm Charlton	.05
120	Joey Cora	.05
121	Ken Griffey Jr.	1.50
122	Sterling Hitchcock	.05
123	Raul Ibanez	.05
124	Randy Johnson	.75
125	Edgar Martinez	.05
126	Alex Rodriguez	2.00
127	Matt Wagner	.05
128	Bob Wells	.05
129	Dan Wilson	.05
130	Will Clark	.05
131	Kevin Elster	.05
132	Juan Gonzalez	.40
133	Rusty Greer	.05
134	Darryl Hamilton	.05
135	Mike Henneman	.05
136	Ken Hill	.05
137	Mark McLemore	.05
138	Dean Palmer	.05
139	Roger Pavlik	.05
140	Ivan Rodriguez	.65
141	Joe Carter	.05
142	Carlos Delgado	.50
143	Alex Gonzalez	.05
144	Juan Guzman	.05
145	Pat Hentgen	.05
146	Marty Janzen	.05
147	Otis Nixon	.05
148	Charlie O'Brien	.05
149	John Olerud	.05
150	Robert Perez	.05
151	Jermaine Dye	.05
152	Tom Glavine	.30
153	Andruw Jones	.75
154	Chipper Jones	1.00
155	Ryan Klesko	.05
156	Javier Lopez	.05
157	Greg Maddux	1.00
158	Fred McGriff	.05
159	Wonderful Monds	.05
160	John Smoltz	.05
161	Terrell Wade	.05
162	Mark Wohlers	.05
163	Brant Brown	.05
164	Mark Grace	.05
165	Tyler Houston	.05
166	Robin Jennings	.05
167	Jason Maxwell	.05
168	Ryne Sandberg	1.00
169	Sammy Sosa	1.00
170	Amaury Telemaco	.05
171	Steve Trachsel	.05
172	Pedro Valdes RC	.05
173	Tim Belk	.05
174	Bret Boone	.05
175	Jeff Brantley	.05
176	Eric Davis	.05
177	Barry Larkin	.05
178	Chad Mottola	.05
179	Mark Portugal	.05
180	Reggie Sanders	.05
181	John Smiley	.05
182	Eddie Taubensee	.05
183	Dante Bichette	.05
184	Ellis Burks	.05
185	Andres Galarraga	.05
186	Curt Leskanic	.05
187	Quinton McCracken	.05
188	Jeff Reed	.05
189	Kevin Ritz	.05
190	Walt Weiss	.05
191	Jamey Wright	.05
192	Eric Young	.05
193	Kevin Brown	.05
194	Luis Castillo	.05
195	Jeff Conine	.05
196	Andre Dawson	.25
197	Charles Johnson	.05
198	Al Leiter	.05
199	Ralph Milliard	.05
200	Robb Nen	.05
201	Edgar Renteria	.05
202	Gary Sheffield	.40
203	Bob Abreu	.10
204	Jeff Bagwell	.75
205	Derek Bell	.05
206	Sean Berry	.05
207	Richard Hidalgo	.05
208	Todd Jones	.05
209	Darryl Kile	.05
210	Orlando Miller	.05
211	Shane Reynolds	.05
212	Billy Wagner	.05
213	Donne Wall	.05
214	Roger Cedeno	.05
215	Greg Gagne	.05
216	Karim Garcia	.10
217	Wilton Guerrero	.05
218	Todd Hollandsworth	.05
219	Ramon Martinez	.05
220	Raul Mondesi	.05
221	Hideo Nomo	.40
222	Chan Ho Park	.05
223	Mike Piazza	1.50
224	Ismael Valdes	.05
225	Moises Alou	.05
226	Derek Aucoin	.05
227	Yamil Benitez	.05
228	Jeff Fassero	.05
229	Darrin Fletcher	.05
230	Mark Grudzielanek	.05
231	Barry Manuel	.05
232	Pedro Martinez	.75
233	Henry Rodriguez	.05
234	Ugueth Urbina	.05
235	Rondell White	.05
236	Carlos Baerga	.05
237	John Franco	.05
238	Bernard Gilkey	.05
239	Todd Hundley	.05
240	Butch Huskey	.05
241	Jason Isringhausen	.05
242	Lance Johnson	.05
243	Bobby Jones	.05
244	Alex Ochoa	.05
245	Rey Ordonez	.05
246	Paul Wilson	.05
247	Ron Blazier	.05
248	David Doster	.05
249	Jim Eisenreich	.05
250	Mike Grace	.05
251	Mike Lieberthal	.05
252	Wendell Magee	.05
253	Mickey Morandini	.05
254	Ricky Otero	.05
255	Scott Rolen	.60
256	Curt Schilling	.20
257	Todd Zeile	.05
258	Jermaine Allensworth	.05
259	Trey Beamon	.05
260	Carlos Garcia	.05
261	Mark Johnson	.05
262	Jason Kendall	.05
263	Jeff King	.05
264	Al Martin	.05
265	Denny Neagle	.05
266	Matt Ruebel	.05
267	Marc Wilkins RC	.05
268	Alan Benes	.05
269	Dennis Eckersley	.65
270	Ron Gant	.05
271	Aaron Holbert	.05
272	Brian Jordan	.05
273	Ray Lankford	.05
274	John Mabry	.05
275	T.J. Mathews	.05
276	Ozzie Smith	1.00
277	Todd Stottlemyre	.05
278	Mark Sweeney	.05
279	Andy Ashby	.05
280	Steve Finley	.05
281	John Flaherty	.05
282	Chris Gomez	.05
283	Tony Gwynn	1.00
284	Joey Hamilton	.05
285	Rickey Henderson	.75
286	Trevor Hoffman	.05
287	Jason Thompson	.05
288	Fernando Valenzuela	.05
289	Greg Vaughn	.05
290	Barry Bonds	2.50
291	Jay Canizaro	.05
292	Jacob Cruz	.05
293	Shawon Dunston	.05
294	Shawn Estes	.05
295	Mark Gardner	.05
296	Marcus Jensen	.05
297	Bill Mueller RC	.35
298	Chris Singleton	.05
299	Allen Watson	.05
300	Matt Williams	.05
301	Rod Beck	.05
302	Jay Bell	.05
303	Shawon Dunston	.05
304	Reggie Jefferson	.05
305	Darren Oliver	.05
306	Benito Santiago	.05
307	Gerald Williams	.05
308	Damon Buford	.05
309	Jeromy Burnitz	.05
310	Sterling Hitchcock	.05
311	Dave Hollins	.05
312	Mel Rojas	.05
313	Robin Ventura	.05
314	David Wells	.05
315	Cal Eldred	.05
316	Gary Gaetti	.05
317	John Hudek	.05
318	Brian Johnson	.05
319	Denny Neagle	.05
320	Larry Walker	.05
321	Russ Davis	.05
322	Delino DeShields	.05
323	Charlie Hayes	.05
324	Jermaine Dye	.05
325	John Ericks	.05
326	Jeff Fassero	.05
327	Nomar Garciaparra	1.00
328	Willie Greene	.05
329	Greg McMichael	.05
330	Damion Easley	.05
331	Ricky Bones	.05
332	John Burkett	.05
333	Royce Clayton	.05
334	Greg Colbrunn	.05
335	Tony Eusebio	.05
336	Gregg Jefferies	.05
337	Wally Joyner	.05
338	Jim Leyritz	.05
339	Paul O'Neill	.05
340	Bruce Ruffin	.05
341	Michael Tucker	.05
342	Andy Benes	.05
343	Craig Biggio	.05
344	Rex Hudler	.05
345	Brad Radke	.05
346	Deion Sanders	.05
347	Moises Alou	.05
348	Brad Ausmus	.05
349	Armando Benitez	.05
350	Mark Gubicza	.05
351	Terry Steinbach	.05
352	Mark Whiten	.05
353	Ricky Bottalico	.05
354	Brian Giles RC	.75
355	Eric Karros	.05
356	Jimmy Key	.05
357	Carlos Perez	.05
358	Alex Fernandez	.05
359	J.T. Snow	.05
360	Bobby Bonilla	.05
361	Scott Brosius	.05
362	Greg Swindell	.05
363	Jose Vizcaino	.05
364	Matt Williams	.05
365	Darren Daulton	.05
366	Shawn Andrews	.05
367	Jim Eisenreich	.05
368	Ariel Prieto	.05
369	Bob Tewksbury	.05
370	Mike Bordick	.05
371	Rheal Cormier	.05
372	Cliff Floyd	.05
373	David Justice	.05
374	John Wetteland	.05
375	Mike Blowers	.05
376	Jose Canseco	.50
377	Roger Clemens	1.25
378	Kevin Mitchell	.05
379	Todd Zeile	.05
380	Jim Thome	.60
381	Turk Wendell	.05
382	Rico Brogna	.05
383	Eric Davis	.05
384	Mike Lansing	.05
385	Devon White	.05
386	Marquis Grissom	.05
387	Todd Worrell	.05
388	Jeff Kent	.05
389	Mickey Tettleton	.05
390	Steve Avery	.05
391	David Cone	.05
392	Scott Cooper	.05
393	Lee Stevens	.05
394	Kevin Elster	.05
395	Tom Goodwin	.05
396	Shawn Green	.25
397	Pete Harnisch	.05
398	Eddie Murray	.75
399	Joe Randa	.05
400	Scott Sanders	.05
401	John Valentin	.05
402	Todd Jones	.05
403	Terry Adams	.05
404	Brian Hunter	.05
405	Pat Listach	.05
406	Kenny Lofton	.05
407	Hal Morris	.05
408	Ed Sprague	.05
409	Rich Becker	.05
410	Edgardo Alfonzo	.05
411	Albert Belle	.05
412	Jeff King	.05
413	Kirt Manwaring	.05
414	Jason Schmidt	.05
415	Allen Watson	.05
416	Lee Tinsley	.05
417	Brett Butler	.05
418	Carlos Garcia	.05
419	Mark Lemke	.05
420	Jaime Navarro	.05
421	David Segui	.05
422	Ruben Sierra	.05
423	B.J. Surhoff	.05
424	Julian Tavarez	.05
425	Billy Taylor	.05
426	Ken Caminiti	.05
427	Chuck Carr	.05
428	Benji Gil	.05
429	Terry Mulholland	.05
430	Mike Stanton	.05
431	Wil Cordero	.05
432	Chili Davis	.05
433	Mariano Duncan	.05
434	Orlando Merced	.05
435	Kent Mercker	.05
436	John Olerud	.05
437	Quilvio Veras	.05
438	Mike Fetters	.05
439	Glenallen Hill	.05
440	Bill Swift	.05
441	Tim Wakefield	.05
442	Pedro Astacio	.05
443	Vinny Castilla	.05
444	Doug Drabek	.05
445	Alan Embree	.05
446	Lee Smith	.05
447	Darryl Hamilton	.05
448	Brian McRae	.05
449	Mike Timlin	.05
450	Bob Wickman	.05
451	Jason Dickson	.05
452	Chad Curtis	.05
453	Mark Leiter	.05
454	Damon Berryhill	.05
455	Kevin Orie	.05
456	Dave Burba	.05
457	Chris Holt	.05
458	Ricky Ledee RC	.10
459	Mike Devereaux	.05
460	Pokey Reese	.05
461	Tim Raines	.05
462	Ryan Jones	.05
463	Shane Mack	.05
464	Darren Dreifort	.05
465	Mark Parent	.05
466	Mark Portugal	.05
467	Dante Powell	.05
468	Craig Grebeck	.05
469	Ron Villone	.05
470	Dmitri Young	.05
471	Shannon Stewart	.05
472	Rick Helling	.05
473	Bill Haselman	.05
474	Albie Lopez	.05
475	Glendon Rusch	.05
476	Derrick May	.05
477	Chad Ogea	.05
478	Kirk Reuter	.05
479	Chris Hammond	.05
480	Russ Johnson	.05
481	James Mouton	.05
482	Mike Macfarlane	.05
483	Scott Ruffcorn	.05
484	Jeff Frye	.05

485	Richie Sexson	.05
486	Emil Brown **RC**	.05
487	Desi Wilson	.05
488	Brent Gates	.05
489	Tony Graffanino	.05
490	Dan Miceli	.05
491	Orlando Cabrera **RC**	.65
492	Tony Womack **RC**	.05
493	Jerome Walton	.05
494	Mark Thompson	.05
495	Jose Guillen	.05
496	Willie Blair	.05
497	T.J. Staton **RC**	.05
498	Scott Kamieniecki	.05
499	Vince Coleman	.05
500	Jeff Abbott	.05
501	Chris Widger	.05
502	Kevin Tapani	.05
503	Carlos Castillo **RC**	.05
504	Luis Gonzalez	.05
505	Tim Belcher	.05
506	Armando Reynoso	.05
507	Jamie Moyer	.05
508	Randall Simon **RC**	.05
509	Vladimir Guerrero	.75
510	Wady Almonte **RC**	.05
511	Dustin Hermanson	.05
512	Deivi Cruz **RC**	.25
513	Luis Alicea	.05
514	Felix Heredia **RC**	.15
515	Don Slaught	.05
516	Shigetosi Hasegawa	.05
517	Matt Walbeck	.05
518	David Arias **RC** (Last name actually Ortiz.)	40.00
519	Brady Raggio **RC**	.05
520	Rudy Pemberton	.05
521	Wayne Kirby	.05
522	Calvin Maduro	.05
523	Mark Lewis	.05
524	Mike Jackson	.05
525	Sid Fernandez	.05
526	Mike Bielecki	.05
527	Bubba Trammell **RC**	.05
528	Brent Brede **RC**	.05
529	Matt Morris	.05
530	Joe Borowski	.05
531	Orlando Miller	.05
532	Jim Bullinger	.05
533	Robert Person	.05
534	Doug Glanville	.05
535	Terry Pendleton	.05
536	Jorge Posada	.05
537	Marc Sagmoen **RC**	.05
538	Fernando Tatis **RC**	.20
539	Aaron Sele	.05
540	Brian Banks	.05
541	Derrek Lee	.50
542	John Wasdin	.05
543	Justin Towle **RC**	.05
544	Pat Cline	.05
545	Dave Magadan	.05
546	Jeff Blauser	.05
547	Phil Nevin	.05
548	Todd Walker	.05
549	Elieser Marrero	.05
550	Bartolo Colon	.05
551	Jose Cruz Jr. **RC**	.50
552	Todd Dunwoody	.05
553	Hideki Irabu **RC**	.25

1997 Ultra Gold Medallion Edition

A new concept in parallel editions was debuted by Ultra in Series I. While sharing the card numbers with regular-issue Ultra cards, the Gold Medallion Edition features a "G" prefix to the card number and gold-foil highlights on front. Unlike past parallels, however, the '97 Ultra Gold Medallion and Platinum Medallion inserts share a photograph which is entirely different from the regular Ultra base cards. Gold Medallion Edition cards are identified as such in the lower-right corner and were inserted at a rate of one per pack.

	NM/M
Complete Set (553):	100.00
Common Player:	.25
Stars/Rookies:	3X

1997 Ultra Platinum Medallion Edition

A new concept in parallel editions was debuted by Ultra in Series I. While sharing the card numbers with regular-issue Ultra cards, the Platinum Medallion Edition features a "P" prefix to the card number and holographic-foil highlights on front. Unlike past parallels, however, the '97 Ultra Gold Medallion and Platinum Medallion inserts share a photograph which is entirely different from the regular Ultra base cards and are identified as such in the lower-right corner and were inserted at a rate of one per 100 packs.

	NM/M
Common Player:	2.00
Stars/Rookies:	25X

Baseball Rules!

Baseball Rules was a 10-card insert that was found only in retail packs at a rate of one per 36 packs. The cards are die-cut with a player in front of a mound of baseballs with embossed seams on the front, while each card back explains a baseball term or rule.

		NM/M
Complete Set (10):		45.00
Common Player:		.50
1	Barry Bonds	10.00
2	Ken Griffey Jr.	6.00
3	Derek Jeter	10.00
4	Chipper Jones	5.00
5	Greg Maddux	5.00
6	Mark McGwire	7.50
7	Troy Percival	.50
8	Mike Piazza	
9	Cal Ripken Jr.	10.00
10	Frank Thomas	4.00

Checklists

There are 10 Checklist cards in each series of Ultra baseball covering all regular-issue cards and inserts. The front of the card features a superstar, while the back contains a portion of the set checklist. The cards have the player's name and "CHECKLIST" in bold, all caps across the bottom in silver foil.

		NM/M
Complete Set (20):		5.00
Common Player:		.05
1	Dante Bichette	.05
2	Barry Bonds	.75
3	Ken Griffey Jr.	.35
4	Greg Maddux	.25
5	Mark McGwire	.50
6	Mike Piazza	.35
7	Cal Ripken Jr.	.75
8	John Smoltz	.05
9	Sammy Sosa	.25
10	Frank Thomas	.20
1	Andruw Jones	.20
2	Ken Griffey Jr.	.35
3	Frank Thomas	.20
4	Alex Rodriguez	.60
5	Cal Ripken Jr.	.75
6	Mike Piazza	.35
7	Greg Maddux	.25
8	Chipper Jones	.25
9	Derek Jeter	.75
10	Juan Gonzalez	.10

Diamond Producers

Printed on textured, uniform-like matterial, this 12-card insert contains some of the most consistent producers in baseball. Horizontal backs are conventionally printed with another color player photo on a pin-striped background and a few words about him. This was the most difficult insert Ultra foil-pack insert, with a ratio of one per 288.

		NM/M
Complete Set (12):		110.00
Common Player:		2.50
1	Jeff Bagwell	7.00
2	Barry Bonds	20.00
3	Ken Griffey Jr.	12.50
4	Chipper Jones	10.00
5	Kenny Lofton	2.50
6	Greg Maddux	10.00
7	Mark McGwire	15.00
8	Mike Piazza	12.50
9	Cal Ripken Jr.	20.00
10	Alex Rodriguez	15.00
11	Frank Thomas	7.50
12	Matt Williams	2.50

Double Trouble

Double Trouble is a 20-card, team color coded set pairing two stars from the same team on a horizontal front. These inserts were found every four packs.

		NM/M
Complete Set (20):		10.00
Common Player:		.15
1	Roberto Alomar, Cal Ripken Jr.	1.50
2	Mo Vaughn, Jose Canseco	.40
3	Jim Edmonds, Tim Salmon	.15
4	Harold Baines, Frank Thomas	
5	Albert Belle, Kenny Lofton	.15
6	Chuck Knoblauch, Marty Cordova	.15
7	Andy Pettitte, Derek Jeter	1.50
8	Jason Giambi, Mark McGwire	1.00
9	Ken Griffey Jr., Alex Rodriguez	1.00
10	Juan Gonzalez, Will Clark	.30
11	Greg Maddux, Chipper Jones	.75
12	Mark Grace, Sammy Sosa	.60

13	Dante Bichette, Andres Galarraga	.15
14	Jeff Bagwell, Derek Bell	.50
15	Hideo Nomo, Mike Piazza	.75
16	Henry Rodriguez, Moises Alou	
17	Rey Ordonez, Alex Ochoa	.15
18	Ray Lankford, Ron Gant	.15
19	Tony Gwynn, Rickey Henderson	.60
20	Barry Bonds, Matt Williams	1.50

Fame Game

This eight-card hobby-exclusive insert showcases players who have displayed Hall of Fame potential. The player photo on front and Fame Game logo are embossed and highlighted in gold and silver foil. Backs have a color portrait photo and a few words about the player. Cards were inserted 1:8 packs.

		NM/M
Complete Set (18):		20.00
Common Player:		.35
1	Ken Griffey Jr.	1.75
2	Frank Thomas	1.00
3	Alex Rodriguez	2.00
4	Cal Ripken Jr.	3.00
5	Mike Piazza	1.75
6	Greg Maddux	1.25
7	Derek Jeter	3.00
8	Jeff Bagwell	1.00
9	Juan Gonzalez	.50
10	Albert Belle	.35
11	Tony Gwynn	1.25
12	Mark McGwire	2.00
13	Andy Pettitte	.45
14	Kenny Lofton	.35
15	Roberto Alomar	.40
16	Ryne Sandberg	1.25
17	Barry Bonds	3.00
18	Eddie Murray	1.00

Fielder's Choice

Fielder's Choice highlights 18 of the top defensive players in baseball. Fronts of the horizontal cards have a leather look and feel and are highlighted in gold foil. Backs are conventionally printed with another player photo and some words about his fielding ability. Fielder's Choice inserts were found every 144 packs.

		NM/M
Complete Set (18):		80.00
Common Player:		1.00
1	Roberto Alomar	1.50
2	Jeff Bagwell	6.00
3	Wade Boggs	7.50
4	Barry Bonds	15.00
5	Mark Grace	1.00
6	Ken Griffey Jr.	10.00
7	Marquis Grissom	1.00
8	Charles Johnson	1.00
9	Chuck Knoblauch	1.00
10	Barry Larkin	1.00
11	Kenny Lofton	1.00
12	Greg Maddux	7.50
13	Raul Mondesi	1.00
14	Rey Ordonez	1.00
15	Cal Ripken Jr.	15.00
16	Alex Rodriguez	12.50
17	Ivan Rodriguez	5.00
18	Matt Williams	1.00

Golden Prospects

This 10-card set was exclusive to hobby shop packs and highlighted the top young players in baseball. Action photos on front

and portraits on back are set on a sepia background. Cards were inserted 1:4 packs.

		NM/M
Complete Set (10):		3.00
Common Player:		.25
1	Andruw Jones	1.50
2	Vladimir Guerrero	1.50
3	Todd Walker	.25
4	Karim Garcia	.25
5	Kevin Orie	.25
6	Brian Giles	.25
7	Jason Dickson	.25
8	Jose Guillen	.25
9	Ruben Rivera	.25
10	Derrek Lee	1.00

Hitting Machines

This 36-card insert was only found in hobby packs and showcases the game's top hitters. Cards were inserted at a ratio of 1:36 packs.

		NM/M
Complete Set (18):		60.00
Common Player:		1.00
1	Andruw Jones	3.00
2	Ken Griffey Jr.	5.00
3	Frank Thomas	3.00
4	Alex Rodriguez	6.50
5	Cal Ripken Jr.	9.00
6	Mike Piazza	5.00
7	Derek Jeter	9.00
8	Albert Belle	1.00
9	Tony Gwynn	4.00
10	Jeff Bagwell	3.00
11	Mark McGwire	6.50
12	Kenny Lofton	1.00
13	Manny Ramirez	3.00
14	Roberto Alomar	1.25
15	Ryne Sandberg	4.00
16	Eddie Murray	3.00
17	Sammy Sosa	4.00
18	Ken Caminiti	1.00

HR Kings

HR Kings are printed on clear plastic with transparent refractive holofoil crowns and other objects in the plastic. Backs contain a white silhouette of the player with career summary and logos within the figure. Stated odds of finding an HR King card were one per 36 packs.

	NM/M
Complete Set (12):	30.00

Common Player:		1.00
1	Albert Belle	1.00
2	Barry Bonds	7.50
3	Juan Gonzalez	1.50
4	Ken Griffey Jr.	4.50
5	Todd Hundley	1.00
6	Ryan Klesko	1.00
7	Mark McGwire	6.00
8	Mike Piazza	4.50
9	Sammy Sosa	3.50
10	Frank Thomas	2.50
11	Mo Vaughn	1.00
12	Matt Williams	1.00

Leather Shop

Baseball's best fielders are honored in this 12-card hobby-exclusive insert. Cards were inserted at a ratio of 1:6 packs and feature an embossed grain-like finish on the fronts.

		NM/M
Complete Set (12):		9.00
Common Player:		.25
1	Ken Griffey Jr.	1.25
2	Alex Rodriguez	1.50
3	Cal Ripken Jr.	2.00
4	Derek Jeter	2.00
5	Juan Gonzalez	.45
6	Tony Gwynn	1.00
7	Jeff Bagwell	.75
8	Roberto Alomar	.40
9	Ryne Sandberg	1.00
10	Ken Caminiti	.25
11	Kenny Lofton	.25
12	John Smoltz	.25

Power Plus Series 1

Series 1 Power Plus is a 12-card insert utilizing silver rainbow holofoil in the background, with the featured player in the foreground. Backs have another action photo and the player's credentials. The insert captures power hitters that also excel in other areas of the game. Power Plus inserts can be found every 24 packs.

		NM/M
Complete Set (12):		15.00
Common Player:		.50
1	Jeff Bagwell	.75
2	Barry Bonds	3.00
3	Juan Gonzalez	.60
4	Ken Griffey Jr.	1.50
5	Chipper Jones	1.50
6	Mark McGwire	2.00
7	Mike Piazza	1.50
8	Cal Ripken Jr.	2.00
9	Alex Rodriguez	2.00
10	Sammy Sosa	1.00
11	Frank Thomas	.75
12	Matt Williams	.50

Power Plus Series 2

Similar in design to the Power Plus insert in Series I, this 12-card insert salutes the game's top sluggers and was found only in hobby packs. Cards were inserted at a ratio of 1:8 packs. Front design features gold holographic foil graphics. Backs have another photo and a description of the player's skills.

		NM/M
Complete Set (12):		6.50
Common Player:		.25
1	Ken Griffey Jr.	.75
2	Frank Thomas	.50
3	Alex Rodriguez	1.00
4	Cal Ripken Jr.	1.50
5	Mike Piazza	.75
6	Chipper Jones	.75
7	Albert Belle	.25
8	Juan Gonzalez	.35
9	Jeff Bagwell	.50
10	Mark McGwire	1.00
11	Mo Vaughn	.25
12	Barry Bonds	1.50

RBI Kings

Ten different players are featured in RBI Kings, which contain a metallic paisley background, with an English shield of armor and latin words in the background. RBI Kings were inserted every 18 packs of Series I.

		NM/M
Complete Set (10):		12.50
Common Player:		.75
1	Jeff Bagwell	1.50
2	Albert Belle	.75
3	Dante Bichette	.75
4	Barry Bonds	4.00
5	Jay Buhner	.75
6	Juan Gonzalez	1.00
7	Ken Griffey Jr.	2.50
8	Sammy Sosa	2.00
9	Frank Thomas	1.50
10	Mo Vaughn	.75

Rookie Reflections

Rookie Reflections features 10 of the 1996 season's top first-year stars. Cards are inserted every four packs. Front features an action photo on a black-and-silver starburst pattern. Horizontal backs have another photo and a career summary of the prospect.

		NM/M
Complete Set (10):		3.50
Common Player:		.25
1	James Baldwin	.25
2	Jermaine Dye	.25

3	Darin Erstad	.40
4	Todd Hollandsworth	.25
5	Derek Jeter	3.00
6	Jason Kendall	.25
7	Alex Ochoa	.25
8	Rey Ordonez	.25
9	Edgar Renteria	.25
10	Scott Rolen	.50

Season Crowns

Season Crowns were found at a rate of one per eight packs of Ultra I Baseball. This etched, silver-foil insert contained 12 statistical leaders and award winners from the 1996 season.

		NM/M
Complete Set (12):		10.00
Common Player:		.50
1	Albert Belle	.50
2	Dante Bichette	.50
3	Barry Bonds	3.00
4	Kenny Lofton	.50
5	Edgar Martinez	.50
6	Mark McGwire	2.00
7	Andy Pettitte	.50
8	Mike Piazza	1.50
9	Alex Rodriguez	2.00
10	John Smoltz	.50
11	Sammy Sosa	1.25
12	Frank Thomas	1.00

Starring Role

Another hobby-exclusive insert, these 12 cards salute baseball's clutch performers and were found 1:288 packs.

		NM/M
Complete Set (12):		175.00
Common Player:		7.50
1	Andruw Jones	12.00
2	Ken Griffey Jr.	20.00
3	Frank Thomas	12.00
4	Alex Rodriguez	25.00
5	Cal Ripken Jr.	30.00
6	Mike Piazza	20.00
7	Greg Maddux	15.00
8	Chipper Jones	15.00
9	Derek Jeter	30.00
10	Juan Gonzalez	9.00
11	Albert Belle	7.50
12	Tony Gwynn	15.00

Thunderclap

This 10-card hobby-exclusive insert showcases hitters who strike fear in opposing pitchers. Cards were inserted 1:18 packs. Fronts are highlighted by streaks of gold prismatic foil lightning in a stormy sky. Backs have another player photo and a few words about him.

		NM/M
Complete Set (10):		20.00
Common Player:		.75
1	Barry Bonds	5.00
2	Mo Vaughn	.75
3	Mark McGwire	4.00
4	Jeff Bagwell	1.50
5	Juan Gonzalez	1.00
6	Alex Rodriguez	4.00
7	Chipper Jones	2.50
8	Ken Griffey Jr.	3.00
9	Mike Piazza	3.00
10	Frank Thomas	2.00

Top 30

This 30-card insert was found only in retail store packs and salutes the 30 most collectible players in the game. Cards were inserted one per pack. A Top 30 Gold Medallion parallel set, die-cut around the top, was also produced and inserted 1:18 packs.

		NM/M
Complete Set (30):		12.00
Common Player:		.20
Gold Medallions:		6X
1	Andruw Jones	.75
2	Ken Griffey Jr.	1.25
3	Frank Thomas	.75
4	Alex Rodriguez	1.50
5	Cal Ripken Jr.	2.00
6	Mike Piazza	1.25
7	Greg Maddux	1.00
8	Chipper Jones	1.00
9	Derek Jeter	2.00
10	Juan Gonzalez	.40
11	Albert Belle	.20
12	Tony Gwynn	1.00
13	Jeff Bagwell	.75
14	Mark McGwire	1.50
15	Andy Pettitte	.30
16	Mo Vaughn	.20
17	Kenny Lofton	.20
18	Manny Ramirez	.75
19	Roberto Alomar	.40
20	Ryne Sandberg	1.00
21	Hideo Nomo	.40
22	Barry Bonds	2.00
23	Eddie Murray	.75
24	Ken Caminiti	.20
25	John Smoltz	.20
26	Pat Hentgen	.20
27	Todd Hollandsworth	.20
28	Matt Williams	.20
29	Bernie Williams	.20
30	Brady Anderson	.20

1997 Ultra FanFest Larry Doby

In the same basic style as its regular-issue Ultra baseball series of 1997, Fleer issued a special Larry Doby card in conjunction with the All-Star FanFest in Cleve-

land, recognizing Doby's 50th anniversary of breaking the American League color barrier. The card has a black-and-white batting pose of Doby on front with his name, team and Fleer Ultra logo in red-shaded silver holographic foil. A color All-Star Game logo also appears on front. Backs have a red duotone photo of Doby fielding, his career stats and a few words about his career.

	NM/M
Larry Doby	4.00

1998 Ultra

Ultra was released in two series with a total of 501 cards; 250 in Series 1 and 251 in Series 2. Ten-card packs carried an SRP of $2.59. There were three parallel sets: Gold Medallion, Platinum Medallion and Masterpieces. Series 1 has 210 regular cards, 25 Prospects (seeded 1:4 packs), 10 Season's Crowns (1:12) and five Checklists (1:8). Series 2 has 202 regular cards, 25 Pizzazz (1:4), 20 New Horizons and three checklists. Series 2 also added a Mike Piazza N.Y. Mets card as #501, inserted every 20 packs. Inserts in Series 1 include: Big Shots, Double Trouble, Kid Gloves, Back to the Future, Artistic Talents, Fall Classics, Power Plus, Prime Leather, Diamond Producers, Diamond Ink and Million Dollar Moments. Series 2 included: Notables, Rocket to Stardom, Millennium Men, Win Now, Ticket Studs, Diamond Immortals, Diamond Ink, Top 30 and 750 sequentially numbered Alex Rodriguez autographed promo cards.

		NM/M
Complete Set (501):		75.00
Common Player:		.05
Alex Rodriguez		
Autograph (750):		50.00
Pack (10):		1.25
Wax Box (24):		20.00
1	Ken Griffey Jr.	1.25
2	Matt Morris	.05
3	Roger Clemens	1.00
4	Matt Williams	.05
5	Roberto Hernandez	.05
6	Rondell White	.05
7	Tim Salmon	.05
8	Brad Radke	.05
9	Brett Butler	.05
10	Carl Everett	.05
11	Chili Davis	.05
12	Chuck Finley	.05
13	Darryl Kile	.05
14	Deivi Cruz	.05
15	Gary Gaetti	.05
16	Matt Stairs	.05
17	Pat Meares	.05
18	Will Cunnane	.05
19	Steve Woodard RC	.15
20	Andy Ashby	.05
21	Bobby Higginson	.05
22	Brian Jordan	.05
23	Craig Biggio	.05
24	Jim Edmonds	.05
25	Ryan McGuire	.05
26	Scott Hatteberg	.05
27	Willie Greene	.05
28	Albert Belle	.05
29	Ellis Burks	.05
30	Hideo Nomo	.40
31	Jeff Bagwell	.75
32	Kevin Brown	.05
33	Nomar Garciaparra	1.00
34	Pedro Martinez	.75
35	Raul Mondesi	.05
36	Ricky Bottalico	.05
37	Shawn Estes	.05
38	Shawon Dunston	.05

39	Terry Steinbach	.05
40	Tom Glavine	.25
41	Todd Dunwoody	.05
42	Deion Sanders	.05
43	Gary Sheffield	.45
44	Mike Lansing	.05
45	Mike Lieberthal	.05
46	Paul Sorrento	.05
47	Paul O'Neill	.05
48	Tom Goodwin	.05
49	Andruw Jones	.75
50	Barry Bonds	2.00
51	Bernie Williams	.05
52	Jeremi Gonzalez	.05
53	Mike Piazza	1.25
54	Russ Davis	.05
55	Vinny Castilla	.05
56	Rod Beck	.05
57	Andres Galarraga	.05
58	Ben McDonald	.05
59	Billy Wagner	.05
60	Charles Johnson	.05
61	Fred McGriff	.05
62	Dean Palmer	.05
63	Frank Thomas	.75
64	Ismael Valdes	.05
65	Mark Bellhorn	.05
66	Jeff King	.05
67	John Wetteland	.05
68	Mark Grace	.05
69	Mark Kotsay	.05
70	Scott Rolen	.60
71	Todd Hundley	.05
72	Todd Worrell	.05
73	Wilson Alvarez	.05
74	Bobby Jones	.05
75	Jose Canseco	.50
76	Kevin Appier	.05
77	Neifi Perez	.05
78	Paul Molitor	.75
79	Quilvio Veras	.05
80	Randy Johnson	.75
81	Glendon Rusch	.05
82	Curt Schilling	.15
83	Alex Rodriguez	1.50
84	Rey Ordonez	.05
85	Jeff Juden	.05
86	Mike Cameron	.05
87	Ryan Klesko	.05
88	Trevor Hoffman	.05
89	Chuck Knoblauch	.05
90	Larry Walker	.05
91	Mark McLemore	.05
92	B.J. Surhoff	.05
93	Darren Daulton	.05
94	Ray Durham	.05
95	Sammy Sosa	1.00
96	Eric Young	.05
97	Gerald Williams	.05
98	Javy Lopez	.05
99	John Smiley	.05
100	Juan Gonzalez	.40
101	Shawn Green	.30
102	Charles Nagy	.05
103	David Justice	.05
104	Joey Hamilton	.05
105	Pat Hentgen	.05
106	Raul Casanova	.05
107	Tony Phillips	.05
108	Tony Gwynn	1.00
109	Will Clark	.05
110	Jason Giambi	.50
111	Jay Bell	.05
112	Johnny Damon	.30
113	Alan Benes	.05
114	Jeff Suppan	.05
115	Kevin Polcovich RC	.05
116	Shigetosi Hasegawa	.05
117	Steve Finley	.05
118	Tony Clark	.05
119	David Cone	.05
120	Jose Guillen	.05
121	Kevin Millwood RC	1.00
122	Greg Maddux	1.00
123	Dave Nilsson	.05
124	Hideki Irabu	.05
125	Jason Kendall	.05
126	Jim Thome	.60
127	Delino DeShields	.05
128	Edgar Renteria	.05
129	Edgardo Alfonzo	.05
130	J.T. Snow	.05
131	Jeff Abbott	.05
132	Jeffrey Hammonds	.05
133	Rich Loiselle	.05
134	Vladimir Guerrero	.75
135	Jay Buhner	.05
136	Jeff Cirillo	.05
137	Jeromy Burnitz	.05
138	Mickey Morandini	.05
139	Tino Martinez	.05
140	Jeff Shaw	.05
141	Rafael Palmeiro	.65
142	Bobby Bonilla	.05
143	Cal Ripken Jr.	2.00
144	Chad Fox RC	.05
145	Dante Bichette	.05
146	Dennis Eckersley	.05
147	Mariano Rivera	.15
148	Mo Vaughn	.05
149	Reggie Sanders	.05
150	Derek Jeter	2.00
151	Rusty Greer	.05
152	Brady Anderson	.05
153	Brett Tomko	.05
154	Jaime Navarro	.05
155	Kevin Orie	.05
156	Roberto Alomar	.20

157	Edgar Martinez	.05
158	John Olerud	.05
159	John Smoltz	.05
160	Ryne Sandberg	1.00
161	Billy Taylor	.05
162	Chris Holt	.05
163	Damion Easley	.05
164	Darin Erstad	.25
165	Joe Carter	.05
166	Kelvim Escobar	.05
167	Ken Caminiti	.05
168	Pokey Reese	.05
169	Ray Lankford	.05
170	Livan Hernandez	.05
171	Steve Kline	.05
172	Tom Gordon	.05
173	Travis Fryman	.05
174	Al Martin	.05
175	Andy Pettitte	.05
176	Jeff Kent	.05
177	Jimmy Key	.05
178	Mark Grudzielanek	.05
179	Tony Saunders	.05
180	Barry Larkin	.05
181	Bubba Trammell	.05
182	Carlos Delgado	.50
183	Carlos Baerga	.05
184	Derek Bell	.05
185	Henry Rodriguez	.05
186	Jason Dickson	.05
187	Ron Gant	.05
188	Tony Womack	.05
189	Justin Thompson	.05
190	Fernando Tatis	.05
191	Mark Wohlers	.05
192	Takashi Kashiwada	.05
193	Garret Anderson	.05
194	Jose Cruz, Jr.	.05
195	Ricardo Rincon	.05
196	Tim Naehring	.05
197	Moises Alou	.05
198	Eric Karros	.05
199	John Jaha	.05
200	Marty Cordova	.05
201	Travis Lee	.10
202	Mark Davis	.05
203	Vladimir Nunez	.05
204	Stanton Cameron	.05
205	Mike Stoner RC	.05
206	Rolando Arrojo RC	.40
207	Rick White	.05
208	Luis Polonia	.05
209	Greg Blosser	.05
210	Cesar Devarez	.05
211	Jeff Bagwell	
	(Season Crown)	1.00
212	Barry Bonds	
	(Season Crown)	3.00
213	Roger Clemens	
	(Season Crown)	1.75
214	Nomar Garciaparra	
	(Season Crown)	1.50
215	Ken Griffey Jr.	
	(Season Crown)	2.00
216	Tony Gwynn	
	(Season Crown)	1.50
217	Randy Johnson	
	(Season Crown)	1.00
218	Mark McGwire	
	(Season Crown)	3.00
219	Scott Rolen	
	(Season Crown)	.75
220	Frank Thomas	
	(Season Crown)	1.25
221	Matt Perisho (Prospect)	.25
222	Wes Helms (Prospect)	.25
223	David Dellucci RC	
	(Prospect)	.25
224	Todd Helton (Prospect)	1.00
225	Brian Rose (Prospect)	.25
226	Aaron Boone (Prospect)	.25
227	Keith Foulke (Prospect)	.25
228	Homer Bush (Prospect)	.25
229	Shannon Stewart	
	(Prospect)	.25
230	Richard Hidalgo	
	(Prospect)	.25
231	Russ Johnson (Prospect)	.25
232	Henry Blanco RC	
	(Prospect)	.25
233	Paul Konerko (Prospect)	.35
234	Antone Williamson	
	(Prospect)	.25
235	Shane Bowers RC	
	(Prospect)	.25
236	Jose Vidro (Prospect)	.25
237	Derek Wallace (Prospect)	.25
238	Ricky Ledee (Prospect)	.25
239	Ben Grieve (Prospect)	.25
240	Lou Collier (Prospect)	.25
241	Derrek Lee (Prospect)	.65
242	Ruben Rivera (Prospect)	.25
243	Jorge Velandia (Prospect)	.25
244	Andrew Vessel (Prospect)	.25
245	Chris Carpenter (Prospect)	.25
246	Checklist (Ken Griffey Jr.)	.65
247	Checklist (Andruw Jones)	.50
248	Checklist (Alex Rodriguez)	.75
249	Checklist (Frank Thomas)	.60
250	Checklist (Cal Ripken Jr.)	.60
251	Carlos Perez	.05
252	Larry Sutton	.05
253	Brad Rigby	.05
254	Wally Joyner	.05
255	Todd Stottlemyre	.05
256	Nerio Rodriguez	.05
257	Jeff Frye	.05
258	Pedro Astacio	.05

259	Cal Eldred	.05
260	Chili Davis	.05
261	Freddy Garcia	.05
262	Bobby Witt	.05
263	Michael Coleman	.05
264	Mike Caruso	.05
265	Mike Lansing	.05
266	Dennis Reyes	.05
267	F.P. Santangelo	.05
268	Darryl Hamilton	.05
269	Mike Fetters	.05
270	Charlie Hayes	.05
271	Royce Clayton	.05
272	Doug Drabek	.05
273	James Baldwin	.05
274	Brian Hunter	.05
275	Chan Ho Park	.05
276	John Franco	.05
277	David Wells	.05
278	Eli Marrero	.05
279	Kerry Wood	.40
280	Donnie Sadler	.05
281	Scott Winchester RC	.05
282	Hal Morris	.05
283	Brad Fullmer	.05
284	Bernard Gilkey	.05
285	Ramiro Mendoza	.05
286	Kevin Brown	.05
287	David Segui	.05
288	Willie McGee	.05
289	Darren Oliver	.05
290	Antonio Alfonseca	.05
291	Eric Davis	.05
292	Mickey Morandini	.05
293	Frank Catalanotto RC	.20
294	Derrek Lee	.50
295	Todd Zeile	.05
296	Chuck Knoblauch	.05
297	Wilson Delgado	.05
298	Raul Ibanez	.05
299	Orel Hershiser	.05
300	Ozzie Guillen	.05
301	Aaron Sele	.05
302	Joe Carter	.05
303	Darryl Kile	.05
304	Shane Reynolds	.05
305	Todd Dunn	.05
306	Bob Abreu	.10
307	Doug Strange	.05
308	Jose Canseco	.50
309	Lance Johnson	.05
310	Harold Baines	.05
311	Todd Pratt	.05
312	Greg Colbrunn	.05
313	Masato Yoshii RC	.25
314	Felix Heredia	.05
315	Dennis Martinez	.05
316	Geronimo Berroa	.05
317	Darren Lewis	.05
318	Billy Ripken	.05
319	Enrique Wilson	.05
320	Alex Ochoa	.05
321	Doug Glanville	.05
322	Mike Stanley	.05
323	Gerald Williams	.05
324	Pedro Martinez	.75
325	Jaret Wright	.05
326	Terry Pendleton	.05
327	LaTroy Hawkins	.05
328	Emil Brown	.05
329	Walt Weiss	.05
330	Omar Vizquel	.05
331	Carl Everett	.05
332	Fernando Vina	.05
333	Mike Blowers	.05
334	Dwight Gooden	.05
335	Mark Lewis	.05
336	Jim Leyritz	.05
337	Kenny Lofton	.05
338	John Halama RC	.05
339	Jose Valentin	.05
340	Desi Relaford	.05
341	Dante Powell	.05
342	Ed Sprague	.05
343	Reggie Jefferson	.05
344	Mike Hampton	.05
345	Marquis Grissom	.05
346	Heathcliff Slocumb	.05
347	Francisco Cordova	.05
348	Ken Cloude	.05
349	Benito Santiago	.05
350	Denny Neagle	.05
351	Sean Casey	.15
352	Robb Nen	.05
353	Orlando Merced	.05
354	Adrian Brown	.05
355	Gregg Jefferies	.05
356	Otis Nixon	.05
357	Michael Tucker	.05
358	Eric Milton	.05
359	Travis Fryman	.05
360	Gary DiSarcina	.05
361	Mario Valdez	.05
362	Craig Counsell	.05
363	Jose Offerman	.05
364	Tony Fernandez	.05
365	Jason McDonald	.05
366	Sterling Hitchcock	.05
367	Donovan Osborne	.05
368	Troy Percival	.05
369	Henry Rodriguez	.05
370	Dmitri Young	.05
371	Jay Powell	.05
372	Jeff Conine	.05
373	Orlando Cabrera	.10
374	Butch Huskey	.05
375	Mike Lowell RC	1.00
376	Kevin Young	.05

377	Jamie Moyer	.05
378	Jeff D'Amico	.05
379	Scott Erickson	.05
380	Magglio Ordonez RC	2.50
381	Melvin Nieves	.05
382	Ramon Martinez	.05
383	A.J. Hinch	.05
384	Jeff Brantley	.05
385	Kevin Elster	.05
386	Allen Watson	.05
387	Moises Alou	.05
388	Jeff Blauser	.05
389	Pete Harnisch	.05
390	Shane Andrews	.05
391	Rico Brogna	.05
392	Stan Javier	.05
393	David Howard	.05
394	Darryl Strawberry	.05
395	Kent Mercker	.05
396	Juan Encarnacion	.05
397	Sandy Alomar	.05
398	Al Leiter	.05
399	Tony Graffanino	.05
400	Terry Adams	.05
401	Bruce Aven	.05
402	Derrick Gibson	.05
403	Jose Cabrera	.05
404	Rich Becker	.05
405	David Ortiz	.50
406	Brian McRae	.05
407	Bobby Estalella	.05
408	Bill Mueller	.05
409	Dennis Eckersley	.65
410	Sandy Martinez	.05
411	Jose Vizcaino	.05
412	Jermaine Allensworth	.05
413	Miguel Tejada	.20
414	Turner Ward	.05
415	Glenallen Hill	.05
416	Lee Stevens	.05
417	Cecil Fielder	.05
418	Ruben Sierra	.05
419	Jon Nunnally	.05
420	Rod Myers	.05
421	Dustin Hermanson	.05
422	James Mouton	.05
423	Dan Wilson	.05
424	Roberto Kelly	.05
425	Antonio Osuna	.05
426	Jacob Cruz	.05
427	Brent Mayne	.05
428	Matt Karchner	.05
429	Damian Jackson	.05
430	Roger Cedeno	.05
431	Rickey Henderson	.75
432	Joe Randa	.05
433	Greg Vaughn	.05
434	Andres Galarraga	.05
435	Rod Beck	.05
436	Curtis Goodwin	.05
437	Brad Ausmus	.05
438	Bob Hamelin	.05
439	Todd Walker	.05
440	Scott Brosius	.05
441	Lenny Dykstra	.05
442	Abraham Nunez	.05
443	Brian Johnson	.05
444	Randy Myers	.05
445	Bret Boone	.15
446	Oscar Henriquez	.05
447	Mike Sweeney	.05
448	Kenny Rogers	.05
449	Mark Langston	.05
450	Luis Gonzalez	.05
451	John Burkett	.05
452	Bip Roberts	.05
453	Travis Lee (New Horizons)	.15
454	Felix Rodriguez (New Horizons)	.05
455	Andy Benes (New Horizons)	.05
456	Willie Blair (New Horizons)	.05
457	Brian Anderson (New Horizons)	.05
458	Jay Bell (New Horizons)	.05
459	Matt Williams (New Horizons)	.05
460	Devon White (New Horizons)	.05
461	Karim Garcia (New Horizons)	.10
462	Jorge Fabregas (New Horizons)	.05
463	Wilson Alvarez (New Horizons)	.05
464	Roberto Hernandez (New Horizons)	.05
465	Tony Saunders (New Horizons)	.05
466	Rolando Arrojo RC (New Horizons)	.35
467	Wade Boggs (New Horizons)	1.00
468	Fred McGriff (New Horizons)	.05
469	Paul Sorrento (New Horizons)	.05
470	Kevin Stocker (New Horizons)	.05
471	Bubba Trammell (New Horizons)	.05
472	Quinton McCracken (New Horizons)	.05
473	Checklist (Ken Griffey Jr.)	.60
474	Checklist (Cal Ripken Jr.)	1.00
475	Checklist (Frank Thomas)	.60
476	Ken Griffey Jr. (Pizzazz)	1.75

477	Cal Ripken Jr. (Pizzazz)	3.00
478	Frank Thomas (Pizzazz)	1.25
479	Alex Rodriguez (Pizzazz)	2.00
480	Nomar Garciaparra (Pizzazz)	1.50
481	Derek Jeter (Pizzazz)	3.00
482	Andruw Jones (Pizzazz)	1.50
483	Chipper Jones (Pizzazz)	1.50
484	Greg Maddux (Pizzazz)	1.50
485	Mike Piazza (Pizzazz)	1.75
486	Juan Gonzalez (Pizzazz)	.60
487	Jose Cruz (Pizzazz)	.50
488	Jaret Wright (Pizzazz)	.50
489	Hideo Nomo (Pizzazz)	.50
490	Scott Rolen (Pizzazz)	.65
491	Tony Gwynn (Pizzazz)	1.50
492	Roger Clemens (Pizzazz)	1.60
493	Darin Erstad (Pizzazz)	.50
494	Mark McGwire (Pizzazz)	2.00
495	Jeff Bagwell (Pizzazz)	.50
496	Mo Vaughn (Pizzazz)	.50
497	Albert Belle (Pizzazz)	.50
498	Kenny Lofton (Pizzazz)	.50
499	Ben Grieve (Pizzazz)	.50
500	Barry Bonds (Pizzazz)	2.50
501	Mike Piazza (Mets)	1.50

1998 Ultra Gold Medallion

This parallel to the Ultra set is found seeded on a one per pack ratio. Cards are similar to the regular-issue Ultra except for a gold presentation of the embossed player name on front and a shower of gold specks in the photo background. Backs have a "G" suffix to the card number and a "GOLD MEDALLION EDITION" notation at bottom. The short-printed subset cards from the regular Ultra edition are not short-printed in Gold Medallion.

	NM/M
Common Player:	.25
Stars/RC's:	2X
Checklists:	2X
Season Crowns:	1X
Prospects:	1X
Pizzazz:	1X

1998 Ultra Platinum Medallion

Insertion odds on this superscarce insert set are not given but each card is produced and serially numbered in an edition of only 100 (Series 1) or 98 (Series 2). Fronts are similar to regular Ultra cards except the photo is black-and-white and the name is rendered in silver prismatic foil. Backs are in color with the serial number printed in silver foil at bottom. Series 2 checklist cards #473-475 were not printed in Platinum, and the short-prints from the regular issue are not short-printed in this parallel edition.

	NM/M
Common Player:	5.00
Stars/RC's:	25X
Checklists:	25X
Season Crowns:	8X
Prospects:	8X
Pizzazz:	8X

Masterpiece

This top of the line parallel to '98 Ultra consists of a 1 of 1 version of each regular card.

	NM/M
Common Player:	50.00

Artistic Talents

This 18-card insert featured top players in the game on a canvas-like surface with the insert name in silver holographic letters across the top. The backs are done in black and white and numbered with an "AT" suffix.

		NM/M
Complete Set (18):		12.00
Common Player:		.40
Inserted 1:8		
1	Ken Griffey Jr.	1.00
2	Andruw Jones	.60
3	Alex Rodriguez	1.25
4	Frank Thomas	.60
5	Cal Ripken Jr.	1.50
6	Derek Jeter	1.50
7	Chipper Jones	.75
8	Greg Maddux	.75
9	Mike Piazza	1.00
10	Albert Belle	.40
11	Darin Erstad	.50
12	Juan Gonzalez	.50
13	Jeff Bagwell	.60
14	Tony Gwynn	.75
15	Mark McGwire	1.25
16	Scott Rolen	.50
17	Barry Bonds	1.50
18	Kenny Lofton	.40

Back to the Future

This 15-card insert was printed in a horizontal format with a baseball field background. Cards were numbered with a "BF" suffix.

		NM/M
Complete Set (15):		4.00
Common Player:		.10
Inserted 1:6		
1	Andruw Jones	.50
2	Alex Rodriguez	1.00
3	Derek Jeter	1.50
4	Darin Erstad	.25
5	Mike Cameron	.10
6	Scott Rolen	.35
7	Nomar Garciaparra	.75
8	Hideki Irabu	.10
9	Jose Cruz, Jr.	.25
10	Vladimir Guerrero	.50
11	Mark Kotsay	.10
12	Tony Womack	.10
13	Jason Dickson	.10
14	Jose Guillen	.10
15	Tony Clark	.10

Diamond Producers

Big Shots

Big Shots is a 15-card insert displaying some of the top home run hitters in baseball. A generic stadium is pictured across the bottom with the insert name running up the left side. Cards are numbered with a "BS" suffix and inserted one per four Series 1 packs.

		NM/M
Complete Set (15):		4.00
Common Player:		.10
Inserted 1:4		
1	Ken Griffey Jr.	.75
2	Frank Thomas	.35
3	Chipper Jones	.50
4	Albert Belle	.10
5	Juan Gonzalez	.25
6	Jeff Bagwell	.35
7	Mark McGwire	1.00
8	Barry Bonds	1.50
9	Manny Ramirez	.10
10	Mo Vaughn	.10
11	Matt Williams	.10
12	Jim Thome	.30
13	Tino Martinez	.10
14	Mike Piazza	.75
15	Tony Clark	.10

Diamond Immortals

This Series 2 insert showcases 15 top players on an intricate silver holographic foil design. Cards are numbered with a "DI" suffix.

		NM/M
Complete Set (15):		330.00
Common Player:		7.50
Inserted 1:288		
1	Ken Griffey Jr.	30.00
2	Frank Thomas	12.50
3	Alex Rodriguez	40.00
4	Cal Ripken Jr.	50.00
5	Mike Piazza	30.00
6	Mark McGwire	40.00
7	Greg Maddux	20.00
8	Andruw Jones	12.50
9	Chipper Jones	20.00
10	Derek Jeter	50.00
11	Tony Gwynn	20.00
12	Juan Gonzalez	9.00
13	Jose Cruz	7.50
14	Roger Clemens	25.00
15	Barry Bonds	50.00

Diamond Producers

1	Andruw Jones	.50
2	Alex Rodriguez	1.00
3	Derek Jeter	1.50
4	Darin Erstad	.25
5	Mike Cameron	.10
6	Scott Rolen	.35
7	Nomar Garciaparra	.75
8	Hideki Irabu	.10
9	Jose Cruz, Jr.	.25
10	Vladimir Guerrero	.50
11	Mark Kotsay	.10
12	Tony Womack	.10
13	Jason Dickson	.10
14	Jose Guillen	.10
15	Tony Clark	.10

This 15-card insert...

This 15-card insert captures players on a prismatic silver design, with a wood backdrop and a black felt frame around the border. Cards were seeded one per 288 Series 1 packs and numbered with a "DP" suffix.

		NM/M
Complete Set (15):		180.00
Common Player:		7.50
Inserted 1:288		
1	Ken Griffey Jr.	30.00
2	Andruw Jones	12.50
3	Alex Rodriguez	40.00
4	Frank Thomas	12.50
5	Cal Ripken Jr.	50.00
6	Derek Jeter	50.00
7	Chipper Jones	20.00
8	Greg Maddux	30.00
9	Mike Piazza	30.00
10	Juan Gonzalez	9.00
11	Jeff Bagwell	12.50
12	Tony Gwynn	20.00
13	Mark McGwire	40.00
14	Barry Bonds	50.00
15	Jose Cruz, Jr.	7.50

Double Trouble

Double Trouble includes 20 cards and pairs teammates on a horizontal format with the team's logo and the insert name featured in a silver holographic circle in the middle. These are numbered with a "DT" suffix and exclusive to Series 1 packs.

		NM/M
Complete Set (20):		12.00
Common Player:		.15
Inserted 1:4		
1	Ken Griffey Jr., Alex Rodriguez	1.25
2	Vladimir Guerrero, Pedro Martinez	.60
3	Andruw Jones, Kenny Lofton	.60
4	Chipper Jones, Greg Maddux	.75
5	Derek Jeter, Tino Martinez	1.50
6	Frank Thomas, Albert Belle	.60
7	Cal Ripken Jr., Roberto Alomar	1.50
8	Mike Piazza, Hideo Nomo	1.00
9	Darin Erstad, Jason Dickson	.15
10	Juan Gonzalez, Ivan Rodriguez	.60
11	Jeff Bagwell, Darryl Kile	.60
12	Tony Gwynn, Steve Finley	.75
13	Mark McGwire, Ray Lankford	1.00
14	Barry Bonds, Jeff Kent	1.50
15	Andy Pettitte, Bernie Williams	.25
16	Mo Vaughn, Nomar Garciaparra	.65
17	Matt Williams, Jim Thome	.15
18	Hideki Irabu, Mariano Rivera	.25
19	Roger Clemens, Jose Cruz, Jr.	.75
20	Manny Ramirez, David Justice	.60

Fall Classics

This Series 1 insert pictures 15 stars on a green holographic background. They are numbered with a "FC" suffix.

	NM/M
Complete Set (15):	35.00
Common Player:	1.00

Inserted 1:18
1	Ken Griffey Jr.	3.00
2	Andruw Jones	1.50
3	Alex Rodriguez	4.00
4	Frank Thomas	1.50
5	Cal Ripken Jr.	5.00
6	Derek Jeter	5.00
7	Chipper Jones	2.00
8	Greg Maddux	2.00
9	Mike Piazza	4.00
10	Albert Belle	1.00
11	Juan Gonzalez	1.00
12	Jeff Bagwell	1.50
13	Tony Gwynn	2.00
14	Mark McGwire	3.00
15	Barry Bonds	5.00

Kid Gloves

Kid Gloves features top fielders on an embossed glove background. Exclusive to Series 1 packs, they are numbered with a "KG" suffix.

		NM/M
Complete Set (12):		9.00
Common Player:		.25
Inserted 1:8		
1	Andruw Jones	.75
2	Alex Rodriguez	2.00
3	Derek Jeter	3.00
4	Chipper Jones	1.00
5	Darin Erstad	.35
6	Todd Walker	.25
7	Scott Rolen	.65
8	Nomar Garciaparra	.75
9	Jose Cruz, Jr.	.25
10	Charles Johnson	.25
11	Rey Ordonez	.25
12	Vladimir Guerrero	.75

Millennium Men

Millenium Men is a hobby-only insert exclusive to Series 2 packs. The tri-fold cards feature an embossed wax seal design and can be unfolded to reveal another shot of the player, team logo and statistics. They are numbered with a "MM" suffix.

		NM/M
Complete Set (15):		30.00
Common Player:		.75
Inserted 1:35		
1	Jose Cruz	.75
2	Ken Griffey Jr.	3.50
3	Cal Ripken Jr.	6.00
4	Derek Jeter	6.00
5	Andruw Jones	2.00
6	Alex Rodriguez	4.50
7	Chipper Jones	2.50
8	Scott Rolen	1.00
9	Nomar Garciaparra	2.50
10	Frank Thomas	2.00
11	Mike Piazza	3.50
12	Greg Maddux	2.50
13	Juan Gonzalez	1.00
14	Ben Grieve	.75
15	Jaret Wright	.75

Notables

This insert pictures a player on a holographic background with either an American League or National

League logo in the background. Notables were seeded in Series 2 packs and numbered with a "N" suffix.

		NM/M
Complete Set (20):		13.50
Common Player:		.20
Inserted 1:4		
1	Frank Thomas	.50
2	Ken Griffey Jr.	1.25
3	Edgar Renteria	.20
4	Albert Belle	.20
5	Juan Gonzalez	.30
6	Jeff Bagwell	.50
7	Mark McGwire	1.50
8	Barry Bonds	2.25
9	Scott Rolen	.40
10	Mo Vaughn	.20
11	Andruw Jones	.50
12	Chipper Jones	.75
13	Tino Martinez	.20
14	Mike Piazza	1.25
15	Tony Clark	.20
16	Jose Cruz	.20
17	Nomar Garciaparra	.75
18	Cal Ripken Jr.	2.25
19	Alex Rodriguez	1.50
20	Derek Jeter	2.25

Power Plus

This insert is exclusive to Series 1 packs. Cards picture the player on an embossed blue background featuring plus signs. These are numbered with a "PP" suffix.

		NM/M
Complete Set (10):		16.00
Common Player:		1.00
Inserted 1:36		
1	Ken Griffey Jr.	4.00
2	Andruw Jones	2.00
3	Alex Rodriguez	3.00
4	Frank Thomas	2.00
5	Mike Piazza	3.00
6	Albert Belle	1.00
7	Juan Gonzalez	1.25
8	Jeff Bagwell	2.00
9	Barry Bonds	5.00
10	Jose Cruz, Jr.	1.00

Prime Leather

This insert features top fielders on a leather-like card stock, with a large baseball in the background. Cards are seeded in Series 1 packs and numbered with a "PL" suffix.

		NM/M
Complete Set (18):		135.00
Common Player:		2.00
Inserted 1:144		
1	Ken Griffey Jr.	12.50
2	Andruw Jones	7.50
3	Alex Rodriguez	15.00
4	Frank Thomas	7.50
5	Cal Ripken Jr.	20.00
6	Derek Jeter	20.00
7	Chipper Jones	10.00
8	Greg Maddux	10.00
9	Mike Piazza	12.50
10	Albert Belle	2.00
11	Darin Erstad	3.00
12	Juan Gonzalez	3.00
13	Jeff Bagwell	7.50
14	Tony Gwynn	10.00
15	Roberto Alomar	2.50
16	Barry Bonds	20.00
17	Kenny Lofton	2.00
18	Jose Cruz, Jr.	2.00

Rocket to Stardom

This insert set is exclusive to Series 2 packs. Cards are in black-and-white and are die-cut, embossed and numbered with an "RS" suffix.

		NM/M
Complete Set (15):		15.00
Common Player:		.75
Inserted 1:20		
1	Ben Grieve	.75
2	Magglio Ordonez	4.00
3	Travis Lee	1.00
4	Carl Pavano	.75
5	Brian Rose	.75
6	Brad Fullmer	.75
7	Michael Coleman	.75
8	Juan Encarnacion	.75
9	Karim Garcia	1.00
10	Todd Helton	7.50
11	Richard Hildalgo	.75
12	Paul Konerko	1.50
13	Rod Myers	.75
14	Jaret Wright	.75
15	Miguel Tejada	1.50

Ticket Studs

Fifteen players are featured on fold-out ticket-like cards in Ticket Studs. The cards arrive folded across the middle and open to reveal a full-length shot of the player with prismatic team color stripes over a white background that has section, seat and row numbers. Cards are inserted in Series 2 packs and are numbered with a "TS" suffix.

		NM/M
Complete Set (15):		150.00
Common Player:		2.50
Inserted 1:144		
1	Travis Lee	3.00
2	Tony Gwynn	12.00
3	Scott Rolen	6.00
4	Nomar Garciaparra	12.00
5	Mike Piazza	15.00
6	Mark McGwire	17.50
7	Ken Griffey Jr.	15.00
8	Juan Gonzalez	5.00
9	Jose Cruz	2.50
10	Frank Thomas	9.00
11	Derek Jeter	20.00
12	Chipper Jones	12.00
13	Cal Ripken Jr.	20.00
14	Andruw Jones	9.00
15	Alex Rodriguez	17.50

Top 30

Top 30 is a retail-only insert found only in Series 2.

		NM/M
Complete Set (30):		20.00
Common Player:		.15
Inserted 1:1 R		
1	Barry Bonds	2.00
2	Ivan Rodriguez	.65
3	Kenny Lofton	.15
4	Albert Belle	.15
5	Mo Vaughn	.15
6	Jeff Bagwell	.75
7	Mark McGwire	1.50
8	Darin Erstad	.35
9	Roger Clemens	1.00
10	Tony Gwynn	1.00
11	Scott Rolen	.45
12	Hideo Nomo	.35
13	Juan Gonzalez	.35
14	Mike Piazza	1.25
15	Greg Maddux	1.00
16	Chipper Jones	1.00
17	Andruw Jones	.75
18	Derek Jeter	2.00
19	Nomar Garciaparra	1.00
20	Alex Rodriguez	1.50
21	Frank Thomas	1.00
22	Cal Ripken Jr.	2.00
23	Ken Griffey Jr.	1.25
24	Jose Cruz Jr.	.15
25	Jaret Wright	.15
26	Travis Lee	.30
27	Wade Boggs	1.00
28	Chuck Knoblauch	.15
29	Joe Carter	.15
30	Ben Grieve	.15

Win Now

This Series 2 insert has top players printed on plastic card stock, with a color shot of the player on the left side and a close-up shot on the right with black lines through it. Cards are numbered with a "WN" suffix.

		NM/M
Complete Set (20):		100.00
Common Player:		2.50
Inserted 1:72		
1	Alex Rodriguez	10.00
2	Andruw Jones	4.00
3	Cal Ripken Jr.	12.50
4	Chipper Jones	5.00
5	Darin Erstad	3.00
6	Derek Jeter	12.50
7	Frank Thomas	4.00
8	Greg Maddux	3.00
9	Hideo Nomo	3.00
10	Jeff Bagwell	4.00
11	Jose Cruz	2.50
12	Juan Gonzalez	3.00
13	Ken Griffey Jr.	7.50
14	Mark McGwire	10.00
15	Mike Piazza	7.50
16	Mo Vaughn	2.50
17	Nomar Garciaparra	5.00
18	Roger Clemens	6.00
19	Scott Rolen	3.00
20	Tony Gwynn	5.00

1999 Ultra Sample Sheet

This six-card sheet was issued to introduce potential customers to '99 Ultra's base cards. The sheet measures 7-1/2" x 7". Cards are virtually identical to the issued version, except for the diagonal black-and-white "PROMOTIONAL SAMPLE" overprint on front and back.

	NM/M
Complete Sheet:	5.00

1999 Ultra

Base cards feature the full career stats by year in 15 categories and career highlights. There are short-printed subsets including Season Crowns (216-225) found 1:8 packs and Prospects (226-250) found 1:4 packs. Card fronts feature full bleed photography, and metallic foil stamping. There are three parallel versions Gold Medallion seeded 1 per pack with Prospects 1:40 and Season Crowns 1:80. Platinum Medallions are numbered to 99 with Prospects numbered to 65 and Season Crowns numbered to 50 sets. One of One Masterpiece parallels also exist. Packs consist of 10 cards with a S.R.P. of $2.69.

		NM/M
Complete Set (250):		35.00
Common Player:		.05
Common Season Crown:		.25
Inserted 1:8		
Common Prospect:		.25
Inserted 1:4		
Gold Medallion (1-215):		2X
Inserted 1:1		
Gold Medall. Prospect:		4X
Inserted 1:40		
Gold Medall. Season Crown:		3X
Inserted 1:80		
Platinums (1-215):		25X
Production 99 Sets		
Platinum Prospects:		6X
Production 65 Sets		
Platinum Season Crowns:		20X
Production 50 Sets		
Pack (10):		1.50
Wax Box (24):		25.00
1	Greg Maddux	1.00
2	Greg Vaughn	.05
3	John Wetteland	.05
4	Tino Martinez	.05
5	Todd Walker	.05
6	Troy O'Leary	.05
7	Barry Larkin	.05
8	Mike Lansing	.05
9	Delino DeShields	.05
10	Brett Tomko	.05
11	Carlos Perez	.05
12	Mark Langston	.05
13	Jamie Moyer	.05
14	Jose Guillen	.05
15	Bartolo Colon	.05
16	Brady Anderson	.05
17	Walt Weiss	.05
18	Shane Reynolds	.05
19	David Segui	.05
20	Vladimir Guerrero	.75
21	Freddy Garcia	.05
22	Carl Everett	.05
23	Jose Cruz Jr.	.05
24	David Ortiz	.40
25	Andruw Jones	.75
26	Darren Lewis	.05
27	Ray Lankford	.05
28	Wally Joyner	.05
29	Charles Johnson	.05
30	Derek Jeter	2.00
31	Sean Casey	.10
32	Bobby Bonilla	.05
33	Todd Zeile	.05
34	Todd Helton	.65
35	David Wells	.05
36	Darin Erstad	.30
37	Ivan Rodriguez	.65
38	Antonio Osuna	.05
39	Mickey Morandini	.05
40	Rusty Greer	.05
41	Rod Beck	.05
42	Larry Sutton	.05
43	Edgar Renteria	.05
44	Otis Nixon	.05
45	Eli Marrero	.05
46	Reggie Jefferson	.05
47	Trevor Hoffman	.05
48	Andres Galarraga	.05
49	Scott Brosius	.05
50	Vinny Castilla	.05
51	Bret Boone	.05
52	Masato Yoshii	.05
53	Matt Williams	.05
54	Robin Ventura	.05
55	Jay Powell	.05
56	Dean Palmer	.05
57	Eric Milton	.05
58	Willie McGee	.05
59	Tony Gwynn	1.00
60	Tom Gordon	.05
61	Dante Bichette	.05
62	Jaret Wright	.05
63	Devon White	.05
64	Frank Thomas	.75
65	Mike Piazza	1.25
66	Jose Offerman	.05
67	Pat Meares	.05
68	Brian Meadows	.05
69	Nomar Garciaparra	1.00
70	Mark McGwire	1.50
71	Tony Graffanino	.05
72	Ken Griffey Jr.	1.25
73	Ken Caminiti	.05
74	Todd Jones	.05
75	A.J. Hinch	.05
76	Marquis Grissom	.05
77	Jay Buhner	.05
78	Albert Belle	.05
79	Brian Anderson	.05
80	Quinton McCracken	.05
81	Omar Vizquel	.05
82	Todd Stottlemyre	.05
83	Cal Ripken Jr.	2.00
84	Magglio Ordonez	.30
85	John Olerud	.05
86	Hal Morris	.05
87	Derek Lee	.40
88	Doug Glanville	.05
89	Marty Cordova	.05
90	Kevin Brown	.05
91	Kevin Young	.05
92	Rico Brogna	.05
93	Wilson Alvarez	.05
94	Bob Wickman	.05
95	Jim Thome	.50
96	Mike Mussina	.35
97	Al Leiter	.05
98	Travis Lee	.10
99	Jeff King	.05
100	Kerry Wood	.40
101	Cliff Floyd	.05
102	Jose Valentin	.05
103	Manny Ramirez	.75
104	Butch Huskey	.05
105	Scott Erickson	.05
106	Ray Durham	.05
107	Johnny Damon	.30
108	Craig Counsell	.05
109	Rolando Arrojo	.05
110	Bob Abreu	.05
111	Tony Womack	.05
112	Mike Stanley	.05
113	Kenny Lofton	.05
114	Eric Davis	.05
115	Jeff Conine	.05
116	Carlos Baerga	.05
117	Rondell White	.05
118	Billy Wagner	.05
119	Ed Sprague	.05
120	Jason Schmidt	.05
121	Edgar Martinez	.05
122	Travis Fryman	.05
123	Armando Benitez	.05
124	Matt Stairs	.05
125	Roberto Hernandez	.05
126	Jay Bell	.05
127	Justin Thompson	.05
128	John Jaha	.05

129	Mike Caruso	.05
130	Miguel Tejada	.20
131	Geoff Jenkins	.05
132	Wade Boggs	1.00
133	Andy Benes	.05
134	Aaron Sele	.05
135	Bret Saberhagen	.05
136	Mariano Rivera	.15
137	Neifi Perez	.05
138	Paul Konerko	.15
139	Barry Bonds	2.00
140	Garret Anderson	.05
141	Bernie Williams	.05
142	Gary Sheffield	.40
143	Rafael Palmeiro	.65
144	Orel Hershiser	.05
145	Craig Biggio	.05
146	Dmitri Young	.05
147	Damion Easley	.05
148	Henry Rodriguez	.05
149	Brad Radke	.05
150	Pedro Martinez	.75
151	Mike Lieberthal	.05
152	Jim Leyritz	.05
153	Chuck Knoblauch	.05
154	Darryl Kile	.05
155	Brian Jordan	.05
156	Chipper Jones	1.00
157	Pete Harnisch	.05
158	Moises Alou	.05
159	Ismael Valdes	.05
160	Stan Javier	.05
161	Mark Grace	.05
162	Jason Giambi	.40
163	Chuck Finley	.05
164	Juan Encarnacion	.05
165	Chan Ho Park	.05
166	Randy Johnson	.75
167	J.T. Snow	.05
168	Tim Salmon	.05
169	Brian Hunter	.05
170	Rickey Henderson	.75
171	Cal Eldred	.05
172	Curt Schilling	.25
173	Alex Rodriguez	1.50
174	Dustin Hermanson	.05
175	Mike Hampton	.05
176	Shawn Green	.30
177	Roberto Alomar	.20
178	Sandy Alomar Jr.	.05
179	Larry Walker	.05
180	Mo Vaughn	.05
181	Raul Mondesi	.05
182	Hideki Irabu	.05
183	Jim Edmonds	.05
184	Shawn Estes	.05
185	Tony Clark	.05
186	Dan Wilson	.05
187	Michael Tucker	.05
188	Jeff Shaw	.05
189	Mark Grudzielanek	.05
190	Roger Clemens	1.00
191	Juan Gonzalez	.40
192	Sammy Sosa	1.00
193	Troy Percival	.05
194	Robb Nen	.05
195	Bill Mueller	.05
196	Ben Grieve	.05
197	Luis Gonzalez	.05
198	Will Clark	.05
199	Jeff Cirillo	.05
200	Scott Rolen	.50
201	Reggie Sanders	.05
202	Fred McGriff	.05
203	Denny Neagle	.05
204	Brad Fullmer	.05
205	Royce Clayton	.05
206	Jose Canseco	.50
207	Jeff Bagwell	.75
208	Hideo Nomo	.40
209	Karim Garcia	.05
210	Kenny Rogers	.05
211	Checklist (Kerry Wood)	.25
212	Checklist (Alex Rodriguez)	.75
213	Checklist (Cal Ripken Jr.)	1.00
214	Checklist (Frank Thomas)	.50
215	Checklist (Ken Griffey Jr.)	.65
216	Alex Rodriguez (Season Crowns)	1.00
217	Greg Maddux (Season Crowns)	.50
218	Juan Gonzalez (Season Crowns)	.20
219	Ken Griffey Jr. (Season Crowns)	.75
220	Kerry Wood (Season Crowns)	.25
221	Mark McGwire (Season Crowns)	1.00
222	Mike Piazza (Season Crowns)	.75
223	Rickey Henderson (Season Crowns)	.40
224	Sammy Sosa (Season Crowns)	.50
225	Travis Lee (Season Crowns)	.25
226	Gabe Alvarez (Prospects)	.25
227	Matt Anderson (Prospects)	.25
228	Adrian Beltre (Prospects)	.35
229	Orlando Cabrera (Prospects)	.35
230	Orlando Hernandez (Prospects)	.25
231	Aramis Ramirez (Prospects)	.25
232	Troy Glaus (Prospects)	1.00
233	Gabe Kapler (Prospects)	.25
234	Jeremy Giambi (Prospects)	.25

235	Derrick Gibson (Prospects)	.25
236	Carlton Loewer (Prospects)	.25
237	Mike Frank (Prospects)	.25
238	Carlos Guillen (Prospects)	.25
239	Alex Gonzalez (Prospects)	.25
240	Enrique Wilson (Prospects)	.25
241	J.D. Drew (Prospects)	.75
242	Bruce Chen (Prospects)	.25
243	Ryan Minor (Prospects)	.25
244	Preston Wilson (Prospects)	.35
245	Josh Booty (Prospects)	.25
246	Luis Ordaz (Prospects)	.25
247	George Lombard (Prospects)	.25
248	Matt Clement (Prospects)	.25
249	Eric Chavez (Prospects)	.35
250	Corey Koskie (Prospects)	.30

Gold Medallion

The basic cards (#1-215) in this parallel set are found one per pack, while the short-printed versions are seen one per 40 packs (Prospects) or one per 80 packs (Season Crowns). Sharing the photos and format of the regular-issue cards, these inserts have a gold-foil background on front. On back, "GOLD MEDALLION EDITION" is printed in gold foil.

	NM/M
Common Player (1-215):	.25
Stars/RC's:	2X
Season Crowns (216-225):	4X
Prospects (226-250):	3X

Platinum Medallion

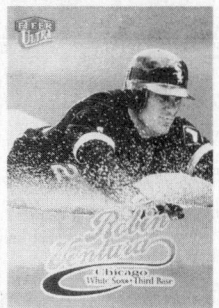

The basic cards (#1-215) in this parallel set are found in an individually serial numbered edition of 99. The short-printed cards were released in editions of 65 (Prospects) and 50 (Season Crowns). Sharing the photos and format of the regular-issue cards, these inserts have a silver-foil background on front. On back, "PLATINUM MEDALLION" is printed in silver foil along with the serial number.

	NM/M
Common Player (1-215):	5.00
Stars/RC's:	25X
Season Crowns (216-225):	20X
Prospects (226-250):	6X

Masterpiece

This top of the line parallel to '99 Ultra consists of a 1 of 1 version of each regular card.

	NM/M
Common Player:	50.00

Book On

This set features insider scouting reports on the game's best players, utilizing embossing and gold foil stamping.

		NM/M
Complete Set (20):		13.50
Common Player:		.25
Inserted 1:6		
1	Kerry Wood	.35
2	Ken Griffey Jr.	1.00
3	Frank Thomas	.65
4	Albert Belle	.25
5	Juan Gonzalez	.35
6	Jeff Bagwell	.65
7	Mark McGwire	1.25
8	Barry Bonds	1.50
9	Andruw Jones	.65
10	Mo Vaughn	.25
11	Scott Rolen	.40
12	Travis Lee	.25
13	Tony Gwynn	.75
14	Greg Maddux	.75
15	Mike Piazza	1.00
16	Chipper Jones	.75
17	Nomar Garciaparra	.75
18	Cal Ripken Jr.	1.50
19	Derek Jeter	1.50
20	Alex Rodriguez	1.25

Damage Inc.

This insert set has a buisness card design, for players who mean business.

		NM/M
Complete Set (15):		50.00
Common Player:		1.00
Inserted 1:72		
1	Alex Rodriguez	5.00
2	Greg Maddux	3.50
3	Cal Ripken Jr.	7.50
4	Chipper Jones	4.00
5	Derek Jeter	7.50
6	Frank Thomas	2.50
7	Juan Gonzalez	1.50
8	Ken Griffey Jr.	4.00
9	Kerry Wood	1.25
10	Mark McGwire	5.00
11	Mike Piazza	4.00
12	Nomar Garciaparra	3.50
13	Scott Rolen	1.50
14	Tony Gwynn	3.50
15	Travis Lee	1.00

Diamond Producers

This die-cut set uses full-foil plastic with custom embossing.

		NM/M
Complete Set (10):		140.00
Common Player:		6.00
Inserted 1:288		
1	Ken Griffey Jr.	17.50
2	Frank Thomas	12.00
3	Alex Rodriguez	20.00
4	Cal Ripken Jr.	25.00
5	Mike Piazza	17.50
6	Mark McGwire	20.00
7	Greg Maddux	15.00
8	Kerry Wood	6.00
9	Chipper Jones	15.00
10	Derek Jeter	25.00

RBI Kings

Found exclusively in retail packs, this set showcases baseball's top run producers.

		NM/M
Complete Set (30):		12.00
Common Player:		.15
Inserted 1:1 R		
1	Rafael Palmeiro	.40
2	Mo Vaughn	.15
3	Ivan Rodriguez	.40
4	Barry Bonds	.75
5	Albert Belle	.15
6	Jeff Bagwell	.45
7	Mark McGwire	1.00
8	Darin Erstad	.15
9	Manny Ramirez	.45
10	Chipper Jones	.75
11	Jim Thome	.45
12	Scott Rolen	.35
13	Tony Gwynn	.60
14	Juan Gonzalez	.25
15	Mike Piazza	.60
16	Sammy Sosa	.60
17	Andruw Jones	.45
18	Derek Jeter	1.25
19	Nomar Garciaparra	.60
20	Alex Rodriguez	1.00
21	Frank Thomas	.45
22	Cal Ripken Jr.	1.25
23	Ken Griffey Jr.	.75
24	Travis Lee	.25
25	Paul O'Neill	.15
26	Greg Vaughn	.15
27	Andres Galarraga	.15
28	Tino Martinez	.15
29	Jose Canseco	.30
30	Ben Grieve	.15

Thunderclap

This set highlights the top hitters in the game. Card fronts feature a lightning bolt in the background.

		NM/M
Complete Set (15):		35.00
Common Player:		.75
Inserted 1:36		
1	Alex Rodriguez	4.00
2	Andruw Jones	1.50
3	Cal Ripken Jr.	6.00
4	Chipper Jones	2.50
5	Darin Erstad	.75
6	Derek Jeter	6.00
7	Frank Thomas	1.50
8	Jeff Bagwell	1.50
9	Juan Gonzalez	.75
10	Ken Griffey Jr.	3.00
11	Mark McGwire	4.00
12	Mike Piazza	3.00
13	Travis Lee	.75
14	Nomar Garciaparra	2.50
15	Scott Rolen	1.00

World Premiere

This set highlights rookies who made debuts in 1998.

		NM/M
Complete Set (15):		8.00
Common Player:		.10
Inserted 1:18		
1	Gabe Alvarez	.50
2	Kerry Wood	1.50
3	Orlando Hernandez	.60
4	Mike Caruso	.50
5	Matt Anderson	.50

6	Randall Simon	.50
7	Adrian Beltre	.65
8	Scott Elarton	.50
9	Karim Garcia	.60
10	Mike Frank	.50
11	Richard Hidalgo	.60
12	Paul Konerko	.60
13	Travis Lee	.65
14	J.D. Drew	1.50
15	Miguel Tejada	.75

2000 Ultra Sample

Product spokesman Alex Rodriguez is featured on the promo card for 2000 Ultra. Virtually identical in format to the issued version, the card has a "PROMOTIONAL SAMPLE" overprint diagonally on front and back.

		NM/M
1	Alex Rodriguez	2.00

2000 Ultra

The 300-card base set features a borderless design with silver holographic foil stamping on the card front. Card backs have an action image along with complete year-by-year statistics. The base set includes a 50-card short-printed Prospects (1:4) subset. A Masterpiece one-of-one parallel was produced.

	NM/M
Complete Set (300):	35.00
Common Player:	.10
Common Player (251-300):	.50
Inserted 1:4	
Pack (10):	2.00
Wax Box (24):	35.00

1	Alex Rodriguez	1.50
2	Shawn Green	.25
3	Magglio Ordonez	.25
4	Tony Gwynn	.75
5	Joe McEwing	.10
6	Jose Rosado	.10
7	Sammy Sosa	1.00
8	Gary Sheffield	.25
9	Mickey Morandini	.10
10	Mo Vaughn	.15
11	Todd Hollandsworth	.10
12	Tom Gordon	.10
13	Charles Johnson	.10
14	Derek Bell	.10
15	Kevin Young	.10
16	Jay Buhner	.15

17	J.T. Snow	.10
18	Jay Bell	.10
19	John Rocker	.10
20	Ivan Rodriguez	.40
21	Pokey Reese	.10
22	Paul O'Neill	.20
23	Ronnie Belliard	.10
24	Ryan Rupe	.10
25	Travis Fryman	.20
26	Trot Nixon	.10
27	Wally Joyner	.10
28	Andy Pettitte	.20
29	Dan Wilson	.10
30	Orlando Hernandez	.20
31	Dmitri Young	.10
32	Edgar Renteria	.10
33	Eric Karros	.20
34	Fernando Seguignol	.10
35	Jason Kendall	.10
36	Jeff Shaw	.10
37	Matt Lawton	.10
38	Robin Ventura	.20
39	Scott Williamson	.10
40	Ben Grieve	.20
41	Billy Wagner	.10
42	Javy Lopez	.20
43	Joe Randa	.10
44	Neifi Perez	.10
45	David Justice	.20
46	Ray Durham	.10
47	Dustin Hermanson	.10
48	Andres Galarraga	.20
49	Brad Fullmer	.10
50	Nomar Garciaparra	1.50
51	David Cone	.15
52	David Nilsson	.10
53	David Wells	.10
54	Miguel Tejada	.20
55	Ismael Valdes	.10
56	Jose Lima	.10
57	Juan Encarnacion	.10
58	Fred McGriff	.20
59	Kenny Rogers	.10
60	Vladimir Guerrero	.75
61	Benito Santiago	.10
62	Chris Singleton	.10
63	Carlos Lee	.20
64	Sean Casey	.20
65	Tom Goodwin	.10
66	Todd Hundley	.10
67	Ellis Burks	.10
68	Tim Hudson	.20
69	Matt Stairs	.10
70	Chipper Jones	1.00
71	Craig Biggio	.20
72	Brian Rose	.10
73	Carlos Delgado	.40
74	Eddie Taubensee	.10
75	John Smoltz	.20
76	Ken Caminiti	.15
77	Rafael Palmeiro	.20
78	Sidney Ponson	.10
79	Todd Helton	.50
80	Juan Gonzalez	.20
81	Bruce Aven	.10
82	Desi Relaford	.10
83	Johnny Damon	.20
84	Albert Belle	.10
85	Mark McGwire	1.50
86	Rico Brogna	.10
87	Tom Glavine	.20
88	Harold Baines	.10
89	Chad Allen	.10
90	Barry Bonds	2.00
91	Mark Grace	.20
92	Paul Byrd	.10
93	Roberto Alomar	.40
94	Roberto Hernandez	.10
95	Steve Finley	.10
96	Bret Boone	.20
97	Charles Nagy	.10
98	Eric Chavez	.20
99	Jamie Moyer	.10
100	Ken Griffey Jr.	1.00
101	J.D. Drew	.10
102	Todd Stottlemyre	.10
103	Tony Fernandez	.10
104	Jeromy Burnitz	.10
105	Jeremy Giambi	.10
106	Livan Hernandez	.10
107	Marlon Anderson	.10
108	Troy Glaus	.50
109	Troy O'Leary	.10
110	Scott Rolen	.50
111	Bernard Gilkey	.10
112	Brady Anderson	.10
113	Chuck Knoblauch	.20
114	Jeff Weaver	.10
115	B.J. Surhoff	.10
116	Alex Gonzalez	.10
117	Vinny Castilla	.10
118	Tim Salmon	.20
119	Brian Jordan	.10
120	Corey Koskie	.10
121	Dean Palmer	.10
122	Gabe Kapler	.15
123	Jim Edmonds	.25
124	John Jaha	.10
125	Mark Grudzielanek	.10
126	Mike Bordick	.10
127	Mike Lieberthal	.10
128	Pete Harnisch	.10
129	Russ Ortiz	.10
130	Kevin Brown	.20
131	Troy Percival	.10
132	Alex Gonzalez	.10
133	Bartolo Colon	.10
134	John Valentin	.10

135	Jose Hernandez	.10
136	Marquis Grissom	.10
137	Wade Boggs	.25
138	Dante Bichette	.10
139	Bobby Higginson	.10
140	Frank Thomas	.50
141	Geoff Jenkins	.20
142	Jason Giambi	.50
143	Jeff Cirillo	.10
144	Sandy Alomar Jr.	.10
145	Luis Gonzalez	.20
146	Preston Wilson	.20
147	Carlos Beltran	.10
148	Greg Vaughn	.10
149	Carlos Febles	.10
150	Jose Canseco	.40
151	Kris Benson	.10
152	Chuck Finley	.10
153	Michael Barrett	.10
154	Rey Ordonez	.10
155	Adrian Beltre	.20
156	Andruw Jones	.50
157	Barry Larkin	.20
158	Brian Giles	.20
159	Carl Everett	.10
160	Manny Ramirez	.50
161	Darryl Kile	.10
162	Edgar Martinez	.15
163	Jeff Kent	.20
164	Matt Williams	.20
165	Mike Piazza	1.00
166	Pedro J. Martinez	.75
167	Ray Lankford	.10
168	Roger Cedeno	.10
169	Ron Coomer	.10
170	Cal Ripken Jr.	2.00
171	Jose Offerman	.10
172	Kenny Lofton	.20
173	Kent Bottenfield	.10
174	Kevin Millwood	.20
175	Omar Daal	.10
176	Orlando Cabrera	.10
177	Pat Hentgen	.10
178	Tino Martinez	.20
179	Tony Clark	.10
180	Roger Clemens	1.25
181	Brad Radke	.10
182	Darin Erstad	.20
183	Jose Jimenez	.10
184	Jim Thome	.50
185	John Wetteland	.10
186	Justin Thompson	.10
187	John Hamala	.10
188	Lee Stevens	.10
189	Miguel Cairo	.10
190	Mike Mussina	.40
191	Raul Mondesi	.15
192	Armando Rios	.10
193	Trevor Hoffman	.10
194	Tony Batista	.10
195	Will Clark	.40
196	Brad Ausmus	.10
197	Chili Davis	.10
198	Cliff Floyd	.10
199	Curt Schilling	.25
200	Derek Jeter	2.00
201	Henry Rodriguez	.10
202	Jose Cruz Jr.	.10
203	Omar Vizquel	.20
204	Randy Johnson	.75
205	Reggie Sanders	.10
206	Al Leiter	.10
207	Damion Easley	.10
208	David Bell	.10
209	Fernando Tatis	.10
210	Kerry Wood	.25
211	Kevin Appier	.10
212	Mariano Rivera	.20
213	Mike Caruso	.10
214	Moises Alou	.20
215	Randy Winn	.10
216	Roy Halladay	.20
217	Shannon Stewart	.10
218	Todd Walker	.10
219	Jim Parque	.10
220	Travis Lee	.10
221	Andy Ashby	.10
222	Ed Sprague	.10
223	Larry Walker	.20
224	Rick Helling	.10
225	Rusty Greer	.10
226	Todd Zeile	.10
227	Freddy Garcia	.15
228	Hideo Nomo	.20
229	Marty Cordova	.10
230	Greg Maddux	1.00
231	Rondell White	.20
232	Paul Konerko	.15
233	Warren Morris	.10
234	Bernie Williams	.40
235	Bobby Abreu	.20
236	John Olerud	.25
237	Doug Glanville	.10
238	Eric Young	.10
239	Robb Nen	.10
240	Jeff Bagwell	.50
241	Sterling Hitchcock	.10
242	Todd Greene	.10
243	Bill Mueller	.10
244	Rickey Henderson	.25
245	Chan Ho Park	.10
246	Jason Schmidt	.10
247	Jeff Zimmerman	.10
248	Jermaine Dye	.10
249	Randall Simon	.10
250	Richie Sexson	.40
251	Micah Bowie	.50
252	Joe Nathan	.50
253	Chris Woodward	.50
254	Lance Berkman	.75
255	Ruben Mateo	.50

256	Russell Branyan	.50
257	Randy Wolf	.75
258	A.J. Burnett	.75
259	Mark Quinn	.50
260	Buddy Carlyle	.50
261	Ben Davis	.50
262	Yamid Haad	.50
263	Mike Colangelo	.50
264	Rick Ankiel	.75
265	Jacque Jones	.75
266	Kelly Dransfeldt	.50
267	Matt Riley	.50
268	Adam Kennedy	.50
269	Octavio Dotel	.50
270	Francisco Cordero	.50
271	Wilton Veras	.50
272	Calvin Pickering	.50
273	Alex Sanchez	.50
274	Tony Armas Jr.	.50
275	Pat Burrell	1.00
276	Chad Meyers	.50
277	Ben Petrick	.50
278	Ramon Hernandez	.50
279	Ed Yarnall	.50
280	Erubiel Durazo	.50
281	Vernon Wells	1.00
282	Gary Matthews	.50
283	Kip Wells	.50
284	Peter Bergeron	.50
285	Travis Dawkins	.50
286	Jorge Toca	.50
287	Cole Liniak	.50
288	Chad Hermansen	.50
289	Eric Gagne	.50
290	Chad Hutchinson	.50
291	Eric Munson	.50
292	Wiki Gonzalez	.50
293	Alfonso Soriano	1.50
294	Trent Durrington	.50
295	Ben Molina	.50
296	Aaron Myette	.50
297	Willi Mo Pena	.75
298	Kevin Barker	.50
299	Geoff Blum	.50
300	Josh Beckett	.75

Gold Medallion

A parallel to the 300-card base set these have gold foil stamping over a metallic gold background. Cards 1-250 are seeded one per pack, Prospects 251-300 are seeded 1:24 packs. Card backs are numbered with a "G" suffix.

Stars:	2X
Inserted 1:1	
Prospects (251-300):	2-4X
Inserted 1:24	

Platinum Medallion

Platinum Medallion are a parallel to the 300-card base set and are die-cut like the Gold Medallion parallel inserts. Card fronts are stamped with silver foil over a metallic silver background. Card backs are serially numbered with cards 1-250 limited to 50 sets and Prospects limited to 25 numbered sets. Card backs are numbered with a "P" suffix.

Stars:	15-30X
Production 50 Sets	
Prospects (251-300):	4-8X
Production 25 Sets	

Masterpiece Edition

Masterpiece Edition is a 1 of 1 parallel to the 300-card base set and are "tombstone" die-cut like the Gold and Platinum Medallion inserts. Card fronts are stamped with purple foil over a metallic purple background. Card backs are overprinted with "The only 1 of 1 Masterpiece."

Club 3000

This three-card set is die-cut around the number 3,000 and commemorates 3,000 hit club members Wade Boggs, Tony Gwynn and Carl Yastrzemski. These were seeded 1:24 packs.

		NM/M
Common Player:		3.00
Inserted 1:24		
	Wade Boggs	2.00
	Tony Gwynn	3.00
	Carl Yastrzemski	3.00

Club 3000 Memorabilia

Each featured player has a total of four different memorabilia based inserts: hat, jersey, bat/jersey and bat/hat/jersey.

	NM/M
Wade Boggs/Bat/250	20.00
Wade Boggs/Hat/100	40.00
Wade Boggs/Jsy/440	20.00
Wade Boggs/ Bat/Jsy/100	40.00
Wade Boggs/ Bat, Hat, Jsy/25	150.00
Tony Gwynn/Bat/260	40.00
Tony Gwynn/Hat/115	40.00
Tony Gwynn/Jsy/450	25.00
Tony Gwynn/ Bat, Jsy/100	65.00
Tony Gwynn/ Bat, Hat, Jsy/25	375.00
Carl Yastrzemski/ Bat/250	40.00
Carl Yastrzemski/ Hat/100	60.00
Carl Yastrzemski/ Jsy/440	25.00
Carl Yastrzemski/ Bat, Jsy/100	75.00
Carl Yastrzemski/ Bat, Hat, Jsy/25	300.00

Crunch Time

This 15-card insert set is printed on suede stock with gold foil stamping. These were seeded 1:72 packs and numbered with a "CT" suffix on the card back.

	NM/M
Complete Set (15):	50.00
Common Player:	2.00
Inserted 1:72	
1 Nomar Garciaparra	8.00
2 Ken Griffey Jr.	5.00
3 Mark McGwire	8.00
4 Alex Rodriguez	8.00
5 Derek Jeter	8.00
6 Sammy Sosa	6.00
7 Mike Piazza	5.00
8 Cal Ripken Jr.	10.00
9 Frank Thomas	3.00
10 Juan Gonzalez	3.00
11 J.D. Drew	2.00
12 Greg Maddux	5.00
13 Tony Gwynn	3.00
14 Vladimir Guerrero	3.00
15 Ben Grieve	2.00

Diamond Mine

GREG MADDUX

These were printed on a silver foil card front with Diamond Mine stamped in the background of the player image. These were inserted 1:6 packs and numbered with a "DM" suffix on the card back.

	NM/M
Complete Set (15):	20.00
Common Player:	1.00
Inserted 1:6	
1 Greg Maddux	1.50
2 Mark McGwire	1.50
3 Ken Griffey Jr.	1.50
4 Cal Ripken Jr.	2.00
5 Nomar Garciaparra	2.50
6 Mike Piazza	2.00
7 Alex Rodriguez	2.50
8 Frank Thomas	1.00
9 Juan Gonzalez	1.00
10 Derek Jeter	2.50
11 Tony Gwynn	1.00
12 Chipper Jones	1.50
13 Sammy Sosa	2.00
14 Roger Clemens	1.50
15 Vladimir Guerrero	1.00

Feel the Game

These memorabilia based inserts have a piece of game worn jersey or batting glove embedded into the card front.

	NM/M
Common Player:	5.00
Roberto Alomar	10.00
J.D. Drew	10.00
Tony Gwynn/SP	40.00
Randy Johnson	20.00
Greg Maddux	20.00
Edgar Martinez	10.00
Pedro Martinez	20.00
Kevin Millwood	10.00
Cal Ripken Jr.	40.00
Alex Rodriguez	25.00
Scott Rolen	10.00
Curt Schilling	10.00
Chipper Jones	20.00
Frank Thomas/SP	40.00
Robin Ventura	5.00

Fresh Ink

These autographed cards have the words "Fresh Ink" printed continually in the background image of the player. The signature

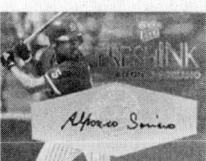

is in a designated blank box intended for the autograph. Production numbers vary from player to player and are listed in parentheses after the player name.

		NM/M
Common Player:		5.00
1	Bobby Abreu/400	10.00
2	Chad Allen/1,000	5.00
3	Marlon Anderson/1,000	5.00
4	Glen Barker/1,000	5.00
5	Michael Barrett/1,000	5.00
6	Carlos Beltran/1,000	15.00
7	Adrian Beltre/1,000	8.00
8	Wade Boggs/500	40.00
9	Barry Bonds/250	150.00
10	Peter Bergeron/1,000	5.00
11	Pat Burrell/500	20.00
12	Roger Cedeno/500	5.00
13	Eric Chavez/750	10.00
14	Bruce Chen/600	5.00
15	Johnny Damon/750	8.00
16	Ben Davis/1,000	5.00
17	Carlos Delgado/300	10.00
18	Einar Diaz/1,000	5.00
19	Octavio Dotel/1,000	6.00
20	J.D. Drew/600	8.00
21	Scott Elarton/1,000	5.00
22	Freddy Garcia/500	8.00
23	Jeremy Giambi/1,000	5.00
24	Troy Glaus/500	20.00
25	Shawn Green/350	30.00
26	Tony Gwynn/250	50.00
27	Richard Hidalgo/500	8.00
28	Bobby Higginson/1,000	6.00
29	Tim Hudson/1,000	10.00
30	Norm Hutchins/1,000	5.00
31	Derek Jeter/95	200.00
32	Randy Johnson/150	50.00
33	Gabe Kapler/750	8.00
34	Jason Kendall/400	8.00
35	Paul Konerko/500	8.00
36	Matt Lawton/1,000	8.00
37	Carlos Lee/1,000	8.00
38	Jose Macias/1,000	5.00
39	Greg Maddux/250	65.00
40	Ruben Mateo/250	8.00
41	Kevin Millwood/500	10.00
42	Warren Morris/1,000	5.00
43	Eric Munson/1,000	6.00
44	Heath Murray/1,000	5.00
45	Joe Nathan/1,000	5.00
46	Magglio Ordonez/350	10.00
47	Angel Pena/1,000	5.00
48	Cal Ripken Jr./350	125.00
49	Alex Rodriguez/350	80.00
50	Scott Rolen/250	35.00
51	Ryan Rupe/1,000	5.00
52	Curt Schilling/375	25.00
53	Randall Simon/1,000	5.00
54	Alfonso Soriano/1,000	60.00
55	Shannon Stewart/300	5.00
56	Miguel Tejada/1,000	25.00
57	Frank Thomas/150	60.00
58	Jeff Weaver/1,000	6.00
59	Randy Wolf/1,000	8.00
60	Ed Yarnall/1,000	5.00
61	Kevin Young/1,000	5.00
62	Tony Gwynn, Wade Boggs, Nolan Ryan/100	450.00
63	Rick Ankiel/500	10.00

Swing King

Printed on a clear, plastic stock this 10-card set features the top hitters in the game. Card fronts also utilize silver foil stamping. These were seeded 1:24 packs and are numbered on the card back with a "SK" suffix.

	NM/M
Complete Set (10):	20.00
Common Player:	1.00
Inserted 1:24	
1 Cal Ripken Jr.	4.00

2	Nomar Garciaparra	3.00
3	Frank Thomas	1.00
4	Tony Gwynn	1.50
5	Ken Griffey Jr.	2.00
6	Chipper Jones	2.00
7	Mark McGwire	3.00
8	Sammy Sosa	2.50
9	Derek Jeter	3.00
10	Alex Rodriguez	3.00

Ultra Talented

ULTRA TALENTED

Available exclusively in hobby packs these were printed on a holofoil background with gold foil stamping. Each card is serially numbered to 100 and are numbered on the card back with a "UT" suffix.

		NM/M
Common Player:		5.00
Production 100 Sets		
1	Sammy Sosa	15.00
2	Derek Jeter	20.00
3	Alex Rodriguez	20.00
4	Mike Piazza	15.00
5	Ken Griffey Jr.	15.00
6	Nomar Garciaparra	20.00
7	Mark McGwire	20.00
8	Cal Ripken Jr.	25.00
9	Frank Thomas	8.00
10	J.D. Drew	5.00

World Premiere

This insert set highlights ten young potential stars on a die-cut, silver foil etched design. These were inserted 1:12 packs and are numbered with a "WP" suffix on the card back.

		NM/M
Complete Set (10):		5.00
Common Player:		.50
Inserted 1:12		
1	Ruben Mateo	.50
2	Lance Berkman	1.00
3	Octavio Dotel	.50
4	Ben Davis	.50
5	Warren Morris	.50
6	Carlos Beltran	.75
7	Rick Ankiel	.50
8	Adam Kennedy	.50
9	Tim Hudson	1.00
10	Jorge Toca	.50

2001 Ultra

BRIAN JORDAN

	NM/M
Complete Set (275):	65.00

Common Player: .15
Common Prospect (251-275): 1.00
Inserted 1:4
Pack (10): 3.00
Box (24): 55.00

1 Pedro Martinez .75
2 Derek Jeter 2.00
3 Cal Ripken Jr. 2.00
4 Alex Rodriguez 1.50
5 Vladimir Guerrero .75
6 Troy Glaus .40
7 Sammy Sosa 1.25
8 Mike Piazza 1.00
9 Tony Gwynn .75
10 Tim Hudson .25
11 John Flaherty .15
12 Jeff Cirillo .15
13 Ellis Burks .15
14 Carlos Lee .15
15 Carlos Beltran .25
16 Ruben Rivera .15
17 Richard Hidalgo .15
18 Omar Vizquel .15
19 Michael Barrett .15
20 Jose Canseco .40
21 Jason Giambi .50
22 Greg Maddux 1.00
23 Charles Johnson .15
24 Sandy Alomar .15
25 Rick Ankiel .25
26 Richie Sexson .40
27 Matt Williams .15
28 Joe Girardi .15
29 Jason Kendall .25
30 Brad Fullmer .15
31 Alex Gonzalez .15
32 Rick Helling .15
33 Mike Mussina .50
34 Joe Randa .15
35 J.T. Snow .15
36 Edgardo Alfonzo .15
37 Dante Bichette .15
38 Brad Ausmus .15
39 Bobby Abreu .25
40 Warren Morris .15
41 Tony Womack .15
42 Russell Branyan .15
43 Mike Lowell .25
44 Mark Grace .40
45 Jeromy Burnitz .15
46 J.D. Drew .25
47 David Justice .25
48 Alex Gonzalez .15
49 Tino Martinez .25
50 Raul Mondesi .25
51 Rafael Furcal .25
52 Marquis Grissom .15
53 Kevin Young .15
54 Jon Lieber .15
55 Henry Rodriguez .15
56 Dave Burba .15
57 Shannon Stewart .15
58 Preston Wilson .15
59 Paul O'Neill .25
60 Jimmy Haynes .15
61 Darryl Kile .15
62 Bret Boone .25
63 Bartolo Colon .25
64 Andres Galarraga .25
65 Trot Nixon .15
66 Steve Finley .15
67 Shawn Green .30
68 Robert Person .15
69 Kenny Rogers .15
70 Bobby Higginson .15
71 Barry Larkin .30
72 Al Martin .15
73 Tom Glavine .40
74 Rondell White .15
75 Ray Lankford .15
76 Moises Alou .25
77 Matt Clement .15
78 Geoff Jenkins .15
79 David Wells .15
80 Chuck Finley .15
81 Andy Pettitte .25
82 Travis Fryman .25
83 Ron Coomer .15
84 Mark McGwire 1.50
85 Kerry Wood .25
86 Jorge Posada .40
87 Jeff Bagwell .50
88 Andruw Jones .50
89 Ryan Klesko .25
90 Mariano Rivera .25
91 Lance Berkman .25
92 Kenny Lofton .25
93 Jacque Jones .15
94 Eric Young .15
95 Edgar Renteria .15
96 Chipper Jones 1.00
97 Todd Helton .50
98 Shawn Estes .15
99 Mark Mulder .25
100 Lee Stevens .15
101 Jermaine Dye .15
102 Greg Vaughn .15
103 Chris Singleton .15
104 Brady Anderson .15
105 Terrence Long .15
106 Quilvio Veras .15
107 Magglio Ordonez .40
108 Johnny Damon .25
109 Jeffrey Hammonds .15
110 Fred McGriff .25
111 Carl Pavano .15
112 Bobby Estalella .15
113 Todd Hundley .15

114 Scott Rolen .75
115 Robin Ventura .25
116 Pokey Reese .15
117 Luis Gonzalez .25
118 Jose Offerman .15
119 Edgar Martinez .25
120 Dean Palmer .15
121 David Segui .15
122 Troy O'Leary .15
123 Tony Batista .15
124 Todd Zeile .15
125 Randy Johnson .75
126 Luis Castillo .15
127 Kris Benson .15
128 John Olerud .25
129 Eric Karros .25
130 Eddie Taubensee .15
131 Neifi Perez .15
132 Matt Stairs .15
133 Luis Alicea .15
134 Jeff Kent .25
135 Javier Vazquez .15
136 Garret Anderson .25
137 Frank Thomas .50
138 Carlos Febles .15
139 Albert Belle .25
140 Tony Clark .15
141 Pat Burrell .50
142 Mike Sweeney .15
143 Jay Buhner .15
144 Gabe Kapler .15
145 Derek Bell .15
146 B.J. Surhoff .15
147 Adam Kennedy .15
148 Aaron Boone .15
149 Todd Stottlemyre .15
150 Roberto Alomar .40
151 Orlando Hernandez .25
152 Jason Varitek .25
153 Gary Sheffield .40
154 Cliff Floyd .15
155 Chad Hermansen .15
156 Carlos Delgado .50
157 Aaron Sele .15
158 Sean Casey .15
159 Ruben Mateo .15
160 Mike Bordick .15
161 Mike Cameron .15
162 Doug Glanville .15
163 Damion Easley .15
164 Carl Everett .15
165 Bengie Molina .15
166 Adrian Beltre .25
167 Tom Goodwin .15
168 Rickey Henderson .40
169 Mo Vaughn .15
170 Mike Lieberthal .15
171 Ken Griffey Jr. 1.00
172 Juan Gonzalez .50
173 Ivan Rodriguez .50
174 Al Leiter .15
175 Vinny Castilla .15
176 Peter Bergeron .15
177 Pedro Astacio .15
178 Paul Konerko .15
179 Mitch Meluskey .15
180 Kevin Millwood .25
181 Ben Grieve .15
182 Barry Bonds 2.00
183 Rusty Greer .15
184 Miguel Tejada .40
185 Mark Quinn .15
186 Larry Walker .25
187 Jose Valentin .15
188 Jose Vidro .15
189 Delino DeShields .15
190 Darin Erstad .25
191 Bill Mueller .15
192 Ray Durham .15
193 Ken Caminiti .15
194 Jim Thome .75
195 Javy Lopez .15
196 Fernando Vina .15
197 Eric Chavez .15
198 Eric Owens .15
199 Brad Radke .15
200 Travis Lee .15
201 Tim Salmon .25
202 Rafael Palmeiro .50
203 Nomar Garciaparra 1.50
204 Mike Hampton .25
205 Kevin Brown .25
206 Juan Encarnacion .15
207 Danny Graves .15
208 Carlos Guillen .15
209 Phil Nevin .25
210 Matt Lawton .15
211 Manny Ramirez .50
212 James Baldwin .15
213 Fernando Tatis .15
214 Craig Biggio .25
215 Brian Jordan .15
216 Bernie Williams .40
217 Ryan Dempster .15
218 Roger Clemens 1.50
219 Jose Cruz Jr. .15
220 John Valentin .15
221 Dmitri Young .15
222 Curt Schilling .25
223 Jim Edmonds .30
224 Chan Ho Park .15
225 Brian Giles .15
226 Jimmy Anderson .15
227 Adam Piatt .15
228 Kenny Kelly .15
229 Randy Choate .15
230 Eric Cammack .15
231 Yovanny Lara .15

232 Wayne Franklin .15
233 Cameron Cairncross .15
234 J.C. Romero .15
235 Geraldo Guzman .15
236 Morgan Burkhart .15
237 Pascual Coco .15
238 John Parrish .15
239 Keith McDonald .15
240 Carlos Casimiro .15
241 Daniel Garibay .15
242 Sang-Hoon Lee .15
243 Hector Ortiz .15
244 Jeff Sparks .15
245 Jason Boyd .15
246 Mark Buehrle .15
247 Adam Melhuse .15
248 Kane Davis .15
249 Mike Darr .15
250 Vicente Padilla .15
251 Barry Zito (Prospects) 4.00
252 Tim Drew (Prospects) 1.00
253 Luis Matos (Prospects) 2.00
254 Alex Cabrera (Prospects) 1.00
255 Jon Garland (Prospects) 1.00
256 Milton Bradley (Prospects) 1.50
257 Juan Pierre (Prospects) 2.00
258 Ismael Villegas (Prospects) 1.00
259 Eric Munson (Prospects) 1.00
260 Tomas De La Rosa (Prospects) 1.00
261 Chris Richard (Prospects) 1.00
262 Jason Tyner (Prospects) 1.00
263 B.J. Waszgis (Prospects) 1.00
264 Jason Marquis (Prospects) 1.00
265 Dusty Allen (Prospects) 1.00
266 Corey Patterson (Prospects) 2.00
267 Eric Byrnes (Prospects) 2.00
268 Xavier Nady (Prospects) 2.00
269 George Lombard (Prospects) 1.00
270 Timoniel Perez (Prospects) 1.00
271 Gary Matthews Jr. (Prospects) 1.00
272 Chad Durbin (Prospects) 1.00
273 Tony Armas Jr. (Prospects) 2.00
274 Francisco Cordero (Prospects) 1.00
275 Alfonso Soriano (Prospects) 5.00

Gold Medallion

Stars (1-250): 1-2X
Inserted 1:1
Prospects (251-275): 1-2X
Inserted 1:24

Platinum Medallion

Stars (1-250): 15-25X
Production 50 Sets
Prospects (251-275): 5-10X
Production 25 Sets

Autographics

	NM/M
Common Player:	5.00

Inserted 1:48
Silvers: 1-1.5X
Production 250 Sets

1 Roberto Alomar 25.00
2 Jimmy Anderson 5.00
3 Lance Berkman 15.00
4 Barry Bonds 150.00
5 Roosevelt Brown 5.00
6 Jeromy Burnitz 5.00
7 Pat Burrell 10.00
8 Alex Cabrera 5.00
9 Eric Chavez 10.00
10 Joe Crede 5.00
11 Johnny Damon 30.00
12 Carlos Delgado 10.00
13 Adam Dunn 20.00
14 Jim Edmonds 15.00
15 Chad Green 5.00
16 Dustin Hermanson 5.00
17 Randy Johnson 50.00
18 Corey Lee 5.00
19 Derek Lee 25.00
20 Terrence Long 5.00
21 Julio Lugo 5.00
22 Edgar Martinez 20.00
23 Justin Miller 5.00
24 Russ Ortiz 5.00
25 Pablo Ozuna 5.00
26 Adam Piatt 5.00
27 Mark Redman 5.00
28 Richie Sexson 15.00
29 Gary Sheffield 15.00
30 Alfonso Soriano 25.00
31 Jose Vidro 8.00
32 Vernon Wells 10.00
33 Preston Wilson 10.00
34 Jamey Wright 5.00
35 Julio Zuleta 5.00

Decade of Dominance

	NM/M
Complete Set (15):	15.00
Common Player:	.50

Inserted 1:8
1 Barry Bonds 3.00
2 Mark McGwire 2.00
3 Sammy Sosa 2.00
4 Ken Griffey Jr. 1.50
5 Cal Ripken Jr. 3.00
6 Tony Gwynn 1.00
7 Albert Belle .50
8 Frank Thomas 1.00
9 Randy Johnson .75
10 Juan Gonzalez .75
11 Greg Maddux 1.50
12 Craig Biggio .50
13 Edgar Martinez .50
14 Roger Clemens 2.00
15 Andres Galarraga .50

Fall Classics

	NM/M
Complete Set (37):	150.00
Common Player:	2.00

Inserted 1:20
1 Jackie Robinson 8.00
2 Enos Slaughter 2.00
3 Mariano Rivera 2.00
4 Hank Bauer 2.00
5 Cal Ripken Jr. 12.00
6 Babe Ruth 15.00
7 Thurman Munson 5.00
8 Tom Glavine 3.00
9 Fred Lynn 2.00
10 Johnny Bench 6.00
11 Tony Lazzeri 2.00
12 Al Kaline 5.00
13 Reggie Jackson 5.00
14 Derek Jeter 10.00
15 Willie Stargell 3.00
16 Roy Campanella 4.00
17 Phil Rizzuto 4.00
18 Roberto Clemente 12.00
19 Carlton Fisk 4.00
20 Duke Snider 4.00
21 Ted Williams 12.00
22 Bill Skowron 2.00
23 Bucky Dent 2.00
24 Mike Schmidt 8.00
25 Lou Brock 5.00
26 Whitey Ford 5.00
27 Brooks Robinson 4.00
28 Roberto Alomar 3.00
29 Yogi Berra 5.00
30 Joe Carter 4.00
31 Bill Mazeroski 2.00
32 Bob Gibson 3.00
33 Hank Greenberg 4.00
34 Andruw Jones 4.00
35 Bernie Williams 3.00
36 Don Larsen 3.00
37 Billy Martin 3.00

Fall Classics Memorabilia

	NM/M
Common Player:	10.00

Inserted 1:288
1 Jackie Robinson/Pants 80.00
2 Enos Slaughter/Bat 15.00
3 Mariano Rivera/Jsy 15.00
4 Hank Bauer/Bat 15.00
5 Cal Ripken Jr./Jsy 40.00
6 Thurman Munson/Bat 25.00
7 Tom Glavine/Jsy 15.00
8 Fred Lynn/Bat 10.00
9 Babe Ruth/Bat 200.00
10 Tony Lazzeri/Bat 10.00
11 Al Kaline/Jersey 10.00
12 Reggie Jackson/Jsy 20.00
13 Derek Jeter/Bat 40.00
14 Willie Stargell/Bat 15.00
15 Roy Campanella/Bat 50.00
16 Phil Rizzuto/Bat 15.00
17 Roberto Clemente/Bat 120.00
18 Carlton Fisk/Jsy 20.00
19 Duke Snider/Bat 25.00
20 Ted Williams/Bat 120.00
21 Bill Skowron/Bat 10.00
22 Bucky Dent/Bat 10.00
23 Mike Schmidt/Jsy 40.00
24 Lou Brock/Jsy 15.00
25 Brooks Robinson/Bat 20.00
26 Johnny Bench/Jsy 25.00

Fall Classics Memorabilia Autographs

No pricing due to scarcity.

Feel the Game

	NM/M
Common Player:	5.00

Inserted 1:48
Golds: 2X
Production 50 Sets
1 Moises Alou 5.00
2 Brady Anderson 5.00
3 Adrian Beltre 5.00
4 Carlos Delgado 8.00
5 J.D. Drew 5.00
6 Jermaine Dye 5.00
7 Jason Giambi 5.00
8 Richard Hidalgo 5.00
9 Chipper Jones 10.00
10 Eric Karros 5.00
11 Raul Mondesi 5.00
12 Chan Ho Park 5.00
13 Ivan Rodriguez 8.00
14 Matt Stairs 5.00
15 Frank Thomas 8.00
16 Jose Vidro 5.00
17 Matt Williams 5.00
18 Preston Wilson 5.00

Power Plus

	NM/M
Complete Set (10):	15.00
Common Player:	1.00

Inserted 1:24
1 Vladimir Guerrero 1.50
2 Mark McGwire 2.00
3 Mike Piazza 2.00

4 Derek Jeter 4.00
5 Chipper Jones 2.00
6 Carlos Delgado 1.00
7 Sammy Sosa 2.00
8 Ken Griffey Jr. 2.00
9 Nomar Garciaparra 2.50
10 Alex Rodriguez 3.00

Season Pass

Complete Set (6):
Common Player:

The Greatest Hits of ...

	NM/M
Complete Set (10):	10.00
Common Player:	.50

Inserted 1:12
1 Mark McGwire 2.00
2 Alex Rodriguez 2.00
3 Ken Griffey Jr. 1.50
4 Ivan Rodriguez .75
5 Cal Ripken Jr. 3.00
6 Todd Helton .75
7 Derek Jeter 3.00
8 Pedro Martinez 1.00
9 Tony Gwynn 1.00
10 Jim Edmonds .50

Tomorrow's Legends

	NM/M
Complete Set (15):	10.00
Common Player:	.25

Inserted 1:4
1 Rick Ankiel .25
2 J.D. Drew .40
3 Carlos Delgado .75
4 Todd Helton .75
5 Andruw Jones .75
6 Troy Glaus .75
7 Jermaine Dye .25
8 Vladimir Guerrero 1.00
9 Brian Giles .25
10 Scott Rolen .75
11 Darin Erstad .40
12 Derek Jeter 3.00
13 Alex Rodriguez 3.00
14 Pat Burrell .50
15 Nomar Garciaparra 2.00

2002 Ultra

	NM/M
Complete Set (285):	100.00
Common Player:	.15
Common SP (201-285):	.50

Inserted 1:4
Pack (10): 2.00
Box (24): 40.00
1 Jeff Bagwell .50
2 Derek Jeter 2.00
3 Alex Rodriguez 1.50
4 Eric Chavez .40
5 Tsuyoshi Shinjo .15
6 Chris Stynes .15
7 Ivan Rodriguez .50
8 Cal Ripken Jr. 2.00
9 Freddy Garcia .15
10 Chipper Jones .75
11 Hideo Nomo .50
12 Rafael Furcal .15

#	Player	Price
13	Preston Wilson	.15
14	Jimmy Rollins	.25
15	Cristian Guzman	.15
16	Garret Anderson	.40
17	Todd Helton	.50
18	Moises Alou	.25
19	Tony Gwynn	.75
20	Jorge Posada	.40
21	Sean Casey	.25
22	Kazuhiro Sasaki	.15
23	Ray Lankford	.15
24	Manny Ramirez	.50
25	Barry Bonds	2.00
26	Fred McGriff	.25
27	Vladimir Guerrero	.75
28	Jermaine Dye	.15
29	Adrian Beltre	.15
30	Ken Griffey Jr.	1.00
31	Ramon Hernandez	.15
32	Kerry Wood	.75
33	Greg Maddux	1.00
34	Rondell White	.15
35	Mike Mussina	.50
36	Jim Edmonds	.40
37	Scott Rolen	.75
38	Mike Lowell	.25
39	Al Leiter	.15
40	Tony Clark	.15
41	Joe Mays	.15
42	Mo Vaughn	.15
43	Geoff Jenkins	.25
44	Curt Schilling	.50
45	Pedro Martinez	.75
46	Andy Pettitte	.40
47	Tim Salmon	.25
48	Carl Everett	.15
49	Lance Berkman	.15
50	Troy Glaus	.40
51	Ichiro Suzuki	1.00
52	Alfonso Soriano	.75
53	Tomo Ohka	.15
54	Dean Palmer	.15
55	Kevin Brown	.25
56	Albert Pujols	1.50
57	Homer Bush	.15
58	Tim Hudson	.40
59	Frank Thomas	.50
60	Joe Randa	.15
61	Chan Ho Park	.15
62	Bobby Higginson	.15
63	Bartolo Colon	.40
64	Aramis Ramirez	.15
65	Jeff Cirillo	.15
66	Roberto Alomar	.50
67	Mark Kotsay	.15
68	Mike Cameron	.15
69	Mike Hampton	.15
70	Trot Nixon	.15
71	Juan Gonzalez	.50
72	Damian Rolls	.15
73	Brad Fullmer	.15
74	David Ortiz	.25
75	Brandon Inge	.15
76	Orlando Hernandez	.15
77	Matt Stairs	.15
78	Jay Gibbons	.15
79	Greg Vaughn	.15
80	Brady Anderson	.15
81	Jim Thome	.75
82	Ben Sheets	.40
83	Rafael Palmeiro	.50
84	Edgar Renteria	.25
85	Doug Mientkiewicz	.15
86	Raul Mondesi	.15
87	Shane Reynolds	.15
88	Steve Finley	.15
89	Jose Cruz Jr.	.15
90	Edgardo Alfonzo	.15
91	Jose Valentin	.15
92	Mark McGwire	2.00
93	Mark Grace	.40
94	Mike Lieberthal	.15
95	Barry Larkin	.25
96	Chuck Knoblauch	.15
97	Deivi Cruz	.15
98	Jeromy Burnitz	.15
99	Shannon Stewart	.15
100	David Wells	.15
101	Brook Fordyce	.15
102	Rusty Greer	.15
103	Andruw Jones	.50
104	Jason Kendall	.15
105	Nomar Garciaparra	1.25
106	Shawn Green	.25
107	Craig Biggio	.25
108	Masato Yoshii	.15
109	Ben Petrick	.15
110	Gary Sheffield	.40
111	Travis Lee	.15
112	Matt Williams	.25
113	Billy Wagner	.15
114	Robin Ventura	.15
115	Jerry Hairston Jr.	.15
116	Paul LoDuca	.15
117	Darin Erstad	.25
118	Ruben Sierra	.15
119	Ricky Gutierrez	.15
120	Bret Boone	.25
121	John Rocker	.15
122	Roger Clemens	1.50
123	Eric Karros	.15
124	J.D. Drew	.25
125	Carlos Delgado	.40
126	Jeffrey Hammonds	.15
127	Jeff Kent	.25
128	David Justice	.25
129	Cliff Floyd	.15
130	Omar Vizquel	.25
131	Matt Morris	.25
132	Rich Aurilia	.15
133	Larry Walker	.25
134	Miguel Tejada	.25
135	Eric Young	.15
136	Aaron Sele	.15
137	Eric Milton	.15
138	Travis Fryman	.15
139	Magglio Ordonez	.25
140	Sammy Sosa	1.50
141	Pokey Reese	.15
142	Adam Eaton	.15
143	Adam Kennedy	.15
144	Mike Piazza	1.00
145	Larry Barnes	.15
146	Darryl Kile	.15
147	Tom Glavine	.25
148	Ryan Klesko	.15
149	Jose Vidro	.15
150	Joe Kennedy	.15
151	Bernie Williams	.40
152	C.C. Sabathia	.15
153	Alex Ochoa	.15
154	A.J. Pierzynski	.15
155	Johnny Damon	.25
156	Omar Daal	.15
157	A.J. Burnett	.15
158	Eric Munson	.15
159	Fernando Vina	.15
160	Chris Singleton	.15
161	Juan Pierre	.15
162	John Olerud	.25
163	Randy Johnson	.75
164	Paul Konerko	.25
165	Tino Martinez	.25
166	Richard Hidalgo	.15
167	Luis Gonzalez	.25
168	Ben Grieve	.15
169	Matt Lawton	.15
170	Gabe Kapler	.15
171	Mariano Rivera	.25
172	Kenny Lofton	.25
173	Brian Jordan	.15
174	Brian Giles	.25
175	Mark Quinn	.15
176	Neifi Perez	.15
177	Ellis Burks	.15
178	Bobby Abreu	.40
179	Jeff Weaver	.15
180	Andres Galarraga	.25
181	Javy Lopez	.25
182	Todd Walker	.15
183	Fernando Tatis	.15
184	Charles Johnson	.15
185	Pat Burrell	.40
186	Jay Bell	.15
187	Aaron Boone	.15
188	Jason Giambi	.50
189	Jay Payton	.15
190	Carlos Lee	.15
191	Phil Nevin	.15
192	Mike Sweeney	.15
193	J.T. Snow	.15
194	Dmitri Young	.15
195	Richie Sexson	.40
196	Derrek Lee	.25
197	Corey Koskie	.15
198	Edgar Martinez	.25
199	Wade Miller	.15
200	Tony Batista	.15
201	John Olerud	.50
202	Bret Boone	.50
203	Cal Ripken Jr.	3.00
204	Alex Rodriguez	2.50
205	Ichiro Suzuki	2.00
206	Manny Ramirez	.75
207	Juan Gonzalez	.75
208	Ivan Rodriguez	.75
209	Roger Clemens	2.00
210	Edgar Martinez	.50
211	Todd Helton	.75
212	Jeff Kent	.50
213	Chipper Jones	1.00
214	Rich Aurilia	.50
215	Barry Bonds	3.00
216	Sammy Sosa	2.00
217	Luis Gonzalez	.50
218	Mike Piazza	2.00
219	Randy Johnson	1.00
220	Larry Walker	.50
221	Todd Helton, Juan Uribe	.50
222	Pat Burrell, Eric Valent	.50
223	Edgar Martinez	.50
224	Ben Grieve, Jason Tyner	.50
225	Mark Quinn, Dee Brown	.50
226	Cal Ripken Jr., Brian Roberts	3.00
227	Cliff Floyd, Abraham Nunez	.50
228	Jeff Bagwell, Adam Everett	.75
229	Mark McGwire, Albert Pujols	3.00
230	Doug Mientkiewicz, Luis Rivas	.50
231	Juan Gonzalez, Danny Peoples	.75
232	Kevin Brown, Luke Prokopec	.50
233	Richie Sexson, Ben Sheets	.50
234	Jason Giambi, Jason Hart	.75
235	Barry Bonds, Carlos Valderrama	3.00
236	Tony Gwynn, Cesar Crespo	1.00
237	Ken Griffey Jr., Adam Dunn	1.50
238	Frank Thomas, Joe Crede	.75
239	Derek Jeter, Drew Henson	3.00
240	Chipper Jones, Wilson Betemit	1.00
241	Luis Gonzalez, Junior Spivey	.50
242	Bobby Higginson, Andres Torres	.50
243	Carlos Delgado, Vernon Wells	.50
244	Sammy Sosa, Corey Patterson	2.00
245	Nomar Garciaparra, Shea Hillenbrand	2.00
246	Alex Rodriguez, Jason Romano	2.50
247	Troy Glaus, David Eckstein	.75
248	Mike Piazza, Alex Escobar	2.00
249	Brian Giles, Jack Wilson	.50
250	Vladimir Guerrero, Scott Hodges	1.00
251	Bud Smith	1.00
252	Juan Diaz	1.00
253	Wilkin Ruan	1.00
254	Chris Spurling RC	1.00
255	Toby Hall	1.00
256	Jason Jennings	1.00
257	George Perez	1.00
258	D'Angelo Jimenez	1.00
259	Jose Acevedo	1.00
260	Josue Perez	1.00
261	Brian Rogers	1.00
262	Carlos Maldonado	1.00
263	Travis Phelps	1.00
264	Rob Mackowiak	1.50
265	Ryan Drese	1.00
266	Carlos Garcia	1.00
267	Alexis Gomez	1.00
268	Jeremy Affeldt	1.00
269	Scott Podsednik	3.00
270	Adam Johnson	1.00
271	Pedro Santana	1.00
272	Les Walrond	1.00
273	Jackson Melian	1.00
274	Carlos Hernandez	1.00
275	Mark Nussbeck RC	1.00
276	Cory Aldridge	1.00
277	Troy Mattes	1.00
278	Brent Abernathy	1.00
279	J.J. Davis	1.00
280	Brandon Duckworth	1.00
281	Kyle Lohse	1.00
282	Justin Kaye	1.00
283	Cody Ransom	1.00
284	Dave Williams	1.00
285	Luis Lopez	1.00

Gold Medallion

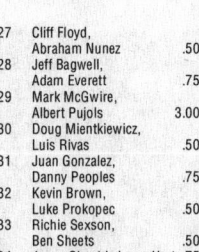

Stars (1-200):	2-3X
Inserted 1:1	
Stars (201-250):	2-4X
Inserted 1:24	
Prospects (251-285):	4-8X
Production 100	

Fall Classic

NM/M
Complete Set (39): 180.00
Common Player: 2.50
Inserted 1:20

#	Player	Price
1FC	Ty Cobb	10.00
2FC	Lou Gehrig	10.00
3FC	Babe Ruth	15.00
4FC	Stan Musial	8.00
5FC	Ted Williams	12.00
6FC	Dizzy Dean	6.00
7FC	Mickey Cochrane	2.50
8FC	Jimmie Foxx	8.00
9FC	Mel Ott	5.00
10FC	Rogers Hornsby	6.00
11FC	Hank Aaron	10.00
12FC	Clete Boyer	2.50
13FC	George Brett	10.00
14FC	Bob Gibson	5.00
15FC	Carlton Fisk	4.00
16FC	Johnny Bench	8.00
17FC	Rusty Staub	2.50
18FC	Willie McCovey	2.50
19FC	Paul Molitor	5.00
20FC	Jim Palmer	4.00
21FC	Frank Robinson	5.00
22FC	Derek Jeter	10.00
23FC	Earl Weaver	2.50
24FC	Lefty Grove	2.50
25FC	Tony Perez	2.50
26FC	Reggie Jackson	5.00
27FC	Sparky Anderson	2.50
28FC	Casey Stengel	2.50
29FC	Roy Campanella	6.00
30FC	Roberto Clemente	10.00
31FC	Don Drysdale	6.00
32FC	Joe Morgan	4.00
33FC	Eddie Murray	5.00
34FC	Nolan Ryan	15.00
35FC	Tom Seaver	8.00
36FC	Bill Mazeroski	2.50
37FC	Jackie Robinson	8.00
38FC	Kirk Gibson	2.50
39FC	Robin Yount	8.00

Fall Classic Autographs

NM/M
Common Autograph: 10.00
Inserted 1:240

#	Player	Price
1	Sparky Anderson	15.00
2	Johnny Bench/SP	40.00
3	George Brett/SP	80.00
4	Carlton Fisk	25.00
5	Bob Gibson	25.00
6	Kirk Gibson	15.00
7	Reggie Jackson/SP	40.00
8	Willie McCovey/SP	30.00
9	Bill Mazeroski	15.00
10	Joe Morgan	15.00
11	Eddie Murray/SP	40.00
12	Jim Palmer	15.00
13	Tony Perez	15.00
14	Frank Robinson	20.00
15	Nolan Ryan/SP	175.00
16	Tom Seaver/SP	30.00
17	Earl Weaver	10.00
18	Robin Yount/SP	50.00

Fall Classic Game-Used

Twenty-six players or managers who have had a role in World Series history are included in this insert series found at the announced rate of about one per 113 packs. Some players' cards can be found with more than one type of game-used memorabilia and in varying rates of production (some with as few as 21 pieces reported by the manufacturer and shown here). Players are checklisted alphabetically.

NM/M
Inserted 1:113

Player	Price
Sparky Anderson/Pants	5.00
Johnny Bench/Jsy	15.00
Johnny Bench/Pants	15.00
George Brett/Bat	15.00
George Brett/Blue Jsy/65	45.00
George Brett/White Jsy	15.00
Roy Campanella/Bat/21	225.00
Carlton Fisk/Bat/42	35.00
Carlton Fisk/Jersey	35.00
Jimmie Foxx/Bat	35.00
Bob Gibson/Jsy	10.00
Kirk Gibson/Bat	5.00
Reggie Jackson/Bat	10.00
Reggie Jackson/Jsy/73	20.00
Derek Jeter/Pants	30.00
Willie McCovey/Jsey	10.00
Paul Molitor/Bat	10.00
Paul Molitor/Jsy	10.00
Joe Morgan/Bat	8.00
Joe Morgan/Jersey	8.00
Eddie Murray/Bat	10.00
Eddie Murray/Jsy/91	35.00
Jim Palmer/Gray Jsy/85	20.00
Jim Palmer/White Jsy	10.00
Tony Perez/Bat	8.00
Frank Robinson/Bat/40	25.00
Jackie Robinson/Jsy	50.00
Babe Ruth/Bat/44	200.00
Nolan Ryan/Pants	30.00
Tom Seaver/Jsy	10.00
Earl Weaver/Jsy	5.00
Ted Williams/Bat/30	200.00
Ted Williams/Jsy	75.00
Robin Yount/Bat	10.00
Robin Yount/Gray Jsy	10.00
Robin Yount/White Jsy/30	30.00

Glove Works

NM/M
Complete Set (15): 25.00
Common Player: 1.00
Inserted 1:20

#	Player	Price
1GW	Andruw Jones	1.50
2GW	Derek Jeter	6.00
3GW	Cal Ripken Jr.	8.00
4GW	Larry Walker	1.00
5GW	Chipper Jones	2.00
6GW	Barry Bonds	6.00
7GW	Scott Rolen	2.00
8GW	Jim Edmonds	1.00
9GW	Robin Ventura	1.00
10GW	Darin Erstad	1.00
11GW	Barry Larkin	1.00
12GW	Raul Mondesi	1.00
13GW	Mark Grace	1.50
14GW	Bernie Williams	1.50
15GW	Ivan Rodriguez	1.50

Glove Works Game Worn

NM/M
Common Player: 10.00
Production 450 Sets
Platinum (25 Sets) randomly inserted.

Player	Price
Derek Jeter	35.00
Cal Ripken Jr.	50.00
Barry Bonds	40.00
Robin Ventura	10.00
Barry Larkin/SP	15.00
Raul Mondesi	10.00
Ivan Rodriguez	15.00

Hitting Machine

NM/M
Complete Set (25): 60.00
Common Player: 1.00
Inserted 1:20

#	Player	Price
1HM	Frank Thomas	2.00
2HM	Derek Jeter	8.00
3HM	Vladimir Guerrero	3.00
4HM	Jim Edmonds	1.50
5HM	Mike Piazza	5.00
6HM	Ivan Rodriguez	2.00
7HM	Chipper Jones	3.00
8HM	Tony Gwynn	3.00
9HM	Manny Ramirez	2.00
10HM	Andruw Jones	2.00
11HM	Carlos Delgado	1.50
12HM	Bernie Williams	1.50
13HM	Larry Walker	1.00
14HM	Juan Gonzalez	2.00
15HM	Ichiro Suzuki	5.00
16HM	Albert Pujols	6.00
17HM	Barry Bonds	8.00
18HM	Cal Ripken Jr.	8.00
19HM	Edgar Martinez	1.50
20HM	Luis Gonzalez	1.00
21HM	Moises Alou	1.50
22HM	Roberto Alomar	2.00
23HM	Todd Helton	2.00
24HM	Rafael Palmeiro	2.00
25HM	Bobby Abreu	1.50

Hitting Machine Game Worn

NM/M
Common Player: 8.00
Inserted 1:81
Platinum (25 Sets) randomly inserted.

Player	Price
Frank Thomas	15.00
Derek Jeter	25.00
Jim Edmonds	10.00
Mike Piazza	15.00
Ivan Rodriguez	15.00
Chipper Jones	15.00
Tony Gwynn	15.00
Manny Ramirez	10.00
Andruw Jones	10.00
Carlos Delgado	10.00
Bernie Williams	10.00
Larry Walker	8.00
Juan Gonzalez	10.00
Albert Pujols	30.00
Barry Bonds	25.00
Cal Ripken Jr.	40.00
Edgar Martinez	10.00
Luis Gonzalez	8.00
Moises Alou	10.00
Roberto Alomar	15.00
Todd Helton	15.00
Rafael Palmeiro	10.00
Bobby Abreu	10.00

On the Road Game Used

NM/M
Common Player: 10.00
Inserted 1:93
Platinum (25 Sets) randomly inserted.

Player	Price
Derek Jeter	30.00
Ivan Rodriguez	10.00
Carlos Delgado	8.00
Larry Walker	8.00
Roberto Alomar	15.00
Tony Gwynn	15.00
Greg Maddux	20.00
Barry Bonds	30.00
Todd Helton	15.00
Kazuhiro Sasaki	10.00
Jeff Bagwell	15.00
Omar Vizquel	8.00
Chan Ho Park	10.00
Tom Glavine	10.00

Rising Stars

NM/M
Complete Set (15): 15.00
Common Player: .50
Inserted 1:12

#	Player	Price
1RS	Ichiro Suzuki	2.50
2RS	Derek Jeter	4.00
3RS	Albert Pujols	3.00
4RS	Jimmy Rollins	1.00
5RS	Adam Dunn	1.00
6RS	Sean Casey	1.00
7RS	Kerry Wood	2.00
8RS	Tsuyoshi Shinjo	.50
9RS	Shea Hillenbrand	.50
10RS	Pat Burrell	1.00
11RS	Ben Sheets	1.00
12RS	Alfonso Soriano	1.50
13RS	J.D. Drew	1.00
14RS	Kazuhiro Sasaki	.50
15RS	Corey Patterson	.75

Rising Stars Game Worn

NM/M
Common Player: 20.00
Production 100 Sets
Platinum (25 Sets) randomly seeded.

Player	Price
Derek Jeter	75.00
Albert Pujols	50.00
Tsuyoshi Shinjo	25.00
Alfonso Soriano	25.00
J.D. Drew	25.00
Kazuhiro Sasaki	20.00

2003 Ultra

NM/M
Complete Set (250): 75.00
Common Player: .15
Common SP (201-250): .50
Inserted 1:4
Hobby Pack (10): 2.00
Hobby Box (24): 35.00

#	Player	Price
1	Barry Bonds	2.00
2	Derek Jeter	2.50
3	Ichiro Suzuki	1.50
4	Mike Lowell	.50
5	Hideo Nomo	.50
6	Javier Vazquez	.15
7	Jeremy Giambi	.15
8	Jamie Moyer	.15
9	Rafael Palmeiro	.40
10	Magglio Ordonez	.25

11	Trot Nixon	.15
12	Luis Castillo	.15
13	Paul Byrd	.15
14	Adam Kennedy	.15
15	Trevor Hoffman	.15
16	Matt Morris	.15
17	Nomar Garciaparra	1.50
18	Matt Lawton	.15
19	Carlos Beltran	.15
20	Jason Giambi	1.25
21	Brian Giles	.25
22	Jim Edmonds	.25
23	Garret Anderson	.25
24	Tony Batista	.15
25	Aaron Boone	.15
26	Mike Hampton	.15
27	Billy Wagner	.15
28	Kazuhisa Ishii	.15
29	Al Leiter	.25
30	Pat Burrell	.40
31	Jeff Kent	.25
32	Randy Johnson	.75
33	Ray Durham	.15
34	Josh Beckett	.15
35	Cristian Guzman	.15
36	Roger Clemens	1.25
37	Freddy Garcia	.15
38	Roy Halladay	.15
39	David Eckstein	.15
40	Jerry Hairston Jr.	.15
41	Barry Larkin	.25
42	Larry Walker	.25
43	Craig Biggio	.25
44	Edgardo Alfonzo	.15
45	Marlon Byrd	.15
46	J.T. Snow	.15
47	Juan Gonzalez	.50
48	Ramon Ortiz	.15
49	Jay Gibbons	.15
50	Adam Dunn	.60
51	Juan Pierre	.15
52	Jeff Bagwell	.60
53	Kevin Brown	.15
54	Pedro Astacio	.15
55	Mike Lieberthal	.15
56	Johnny Damon	.15
57	Tim Salmon	.25
58	Mike Bordick	.15
59	Ken Griffey Jr.	1.50
60	Jason Jennings	.15
61	Lance Berkman	.50
62	Jeromy Burnitz	.15
63	Jimmy Rollins	.25
64	Tsuyoshi Shinjo	.15
65	Alex Rodriguez	2.00
66	Greg Maddux	1.25
67	Mark Prior	.40
68	Mike Maroth	.15
69	Geoff Jenkins	.15
70	Tony Armas Jr.	.15
71	Jermaine Dye	.15
72	Albert Pujols	.75
73	Shannon Stewart	.15
74	Troy Glaus	.60
75	Brook Fordyce	.15
76	Juan Encarnacion	.15
77	Todd Hollandsworth	.15
78	Roy Oswalt	.25
79	Paul LoDuca	.15
80	Mike Piazza	1.50
81	Bobby Abreu	.15
82	Sean Burroughs	.15
83	Randy Winn	.15
84	Curt Schilling	.50
85	Chris Singleton	.15
86	Sean Casey	.25
87	Todd Zeile	.15
88	Richard Hidalgo	.15
89	Roberto Alomar	.50
90	Tim Hudson	.25
91	Ryan Klesko	.25
92	Greg Vaughn	.15
93	Tony Womack	.15
94	Fred McGriff	.25
95	Tom Glavine	.40
96	Todd Walker	.15
97	Travis Fryman	.15
98	Shane Reynolds	.15
99	Shawn Green	.25
100	Mo Vaughn	.25
101	Adam Piatt	.15
102	Deivi Cruz	.15
103	Steve Cox	.15
104	Luis Gonzalez	.15
105	Russell Branyan	.15
106	Daryle Ward	.15
107	Mariano Rivera	.50
108	Phil Nevin	.15

109	Ben Grieve	.15
110	Moises Alou	.15
111	Omar Vizquel	.25
112	Joe Randa	.15
113	Jorge Posada	.40
114	Mark Kotsay	.15
115	Ryan Rupe	.15
116	Javy Lopez	.15
117	Corey Patterson	.15
118	Bobby Higginson	.15
119	Jose Vidro	.15
120	Barry Zito	.25
121	Matt Morris	.15
122	Gary Sheffield	.25
123	Kerry Wood	.15
124	Brandon Inge	.15
125	Jose Hernandez	.15
126	Michael Barrett	.15
127	Miguel Tejada	.40
128	Edgar Renteria	.15
129	Junior Spivey	.15
130	Jose Valentin	.15
131	Derrek Lee	.15
132	A.J. Pierzynski	.15
133	Mike Mussina	.50
134	Bret Boone	.15
135	Chan Ho Park	.15
136	Steve Finley	.15
137	Mark Buehrle	.15
138	A.J. Burnett	.15
139	Ben Sheets	.15
140	David Ortiz	.15
141	Nick Johnson	.15
142	Randall Simon	.15
143	Carlos Delgado	.40
144	Darin Erstad	.25
145	Shea Hillenbrand	.15
146	Todd Helton	.40
147	Preston Wilson	.15
148	Eric Gagne	.15
149	Vladimir Guerrero	.75
150	Brandon Duckworth	.15
151	Rich Aurilia	.15
152	Ivan Rodriguez	.50
153	Andruw Jones	.50
154	Carlos Lee	.15
155	Robert Fick	.15
156	Jacque Jones	.15
157	Bernie Williams	.50
158	John Olerud	.25
159	Eric Hinske	.15
160	Matt Clement	.15
161	Dmitri Young	.15
162	Torii Hunter	.15
163	Carlos Pena	.15
164	Mike Cameron	.15
165	Raul Mondesi	.15
166	Pedro J. Martinez	.75
167	Bob Wickman	.15
168	Mike Sweeney	.15
169	David Wells	.15
170	Jason Kendall	.15
171	Tino Martinez	.15
172	Matt Williams	.15
173	Frank Thomas	.60
174	Cliff Floyd	.15
175	Corey Koskie	.15
176	Orlando Hernandez	.15
177	Edgar Martinez	.15
178	Richie Sexson	.25
179	Manny Ramirez	.60
180	Jim Thome	.50
181	Andy Pettitte	.40
182	Aramis Ramirez	.15
183	J.D. Drew	.25
184	Brian Jordan	.15
185	Sammy Sosa	1.25
186	Jeff Weaver	.15
187	Jeffrey Hammonds	.15
188	Eric Milton	.15
189	Eric Chavez	.25
190	Kazuhiro Sasaki	.15
191	Jose Cruz Jr.	.15
192	Derek Lowe	.15
193	C.C. Sabathia	.15
194	Adrian Beltre	.15
195	Alfonso Soriano	1.00
196	Jack Wilson	.15
197	Fernando Vina	.15
198	Chipper Jones	1.25
199	Paul Konerko	.15
200	Rusty Greer	.15
201	Jason Giambi	2.00
202	Alfonso Soriano	2.00
203	Shea Hillenbrand	.50
204	Alex Rodriguez	3.00
205	Jorge Posada	.60
206	Ichiro Suzuki	3.00
207	Manny Ramirez	1.00
208	Torii Hunter	.50
209	Todd Helton	.75
210	Roberto Alomar	.75
211	Scott Rolen	.75
212	Jimmy Rollins	.50
213	Mike Piazza	3.00
214	Barry Bonds	3.00
215	Sammy Sosa	2.00
216	Vladimir Guerrero	1.50
217	Lance Berkman	.75
218	Derek Jeter	4.00
219	Nomar Garciaparra	3.00
220	Luis Gonzalez	.75
221	Kazuhisa Ishii	1.00
222	Satoru Komiyama	.50
223	So Taguchi	.50
224	Jorge Padilla	.50
225	Ben Howard	.50
226	Jason Simontacchi	.50

227	Barry Wesson	.50
228	Howie Clark	.50
229	Aaron Guiel	.50
230	Oliver Perez	.75
231	David Ross	.50
232	Julius Matos	.50
233	Chris Snelling	.50
234	Rodrigo Lopez	.50
235	Wilbert Nieves	.50
236	Brendan Donnelly	.50
237	Aaron Cook	.50
238	Anderson Machado	.50
239	Corey Thurman	.50
240	Tyler Yates	.50
241	Coco Crisp	4.00
242	Andy Van Hekken	1.50
243	Jim Rushford	2.00
244	Jeriome Robertson	1.00
245	Shane Nance	1.00
246	Kevin Cash	.50
247	Kirk Saarloos	1.50
248	Josh Bard	2.00
249	David Pember **RC**	1.00
250	Freddy Sanchez	1.50

Gold Medallion

Stars (1-200):		2-3X
Inserted 1:1		
Stars (201-220):		3-4X
Inserted 1:24		
Rookies (221-250):		1-30X
Inserted 1:24		

Back 2 Back

		NM/M
Complete Set (17):		60.00
Common Player:		2.00
Production 1,000 Sets		
1B2B	Derek Jeter	10.00
2B2B	Barry Bonds	8.00
3B2B	Mike Piazza	6.00
4B2B	Alex Rodriguez	8.00
5B2B	Todd Helton	2.00
6B2B	Edgar Martinez	2.00
7B2B	Chipper Jones	5.00
8B2B	Shawn Green	2.00
9B2B	Chan Ho Park	2.00
10B2B	Preston Wilson	2.00
11B2B	Manny Ramirez	3.00
12B2B	Aramis Ramirez	2.00
13B2B	Pedro J. Martinez	4.00
14B2B	Ivan Rodriguez	2.00
15B2B	Ichiro Suzuki	6.00
16B2B	Sammy Sosa	5.00
17B2B	Jason Giambi	5.00

Back 2 Back Memorabilia

		NM/M
Common Player:		5.00
Production 500 Sets		
Golds:		1.5-3X
Production 50 Sets		
	Derek Jeter	25.00
	Barry Bonds/Bat	20.00
	Mike Piazza/Jsy	12.00
	Alex Rodriguez/Jsy	12.00
	Todd Helton/Jsy	8.00
	Edgar Martinez/Jsy	6.00
	Chipper Jones/Jsy	15.00
	Shawn Green/Jsy	6.00
	Chan Ho Park/Bat	6.00
	Preston Wilson/Jsy	5.00
	Manny Ramirez/Jsy	8.00
	Aramis Ramirez/Jsy	5.00
	Pedro Martinez/Jsy	8.00
	Ivan Rodriguez/Jsy	8.00
	Ichiro Suzuki/Base	15.00
	Sammy Sosa/Base	10.00
	Jason Giambi/Base	8.00

Double Up

		NM/M
Complete Set (16):		30.00
Common Card:		1.00
Inserted 1:8		
1DU	Derek Jeter, Mike Piazza	4.00
2DU	Barry Bonds, Rafael Palmeiro	3.00
3DU	Chipper Jones, Andruw Jones	2.00
4DU	Derek Jeter, Alex Rodriguez	4.00
5DU	Nomar Garciaparra, Derek Jeter	4.00
6DU	Barry Bonds, Jason Giambi	3.00
7DU	Ichiro Suzuki, Hideo Nomo	3.00

8DU	Randy Johnson, Curt Schilling	1.00
9DU	Pedro J. Martinez, Nomar Garciaparra	2.50
10DU	Roger Clemens, Kevin Brown	2.00
11DU	Nomar Garciaparra, Manny Ramirez	2.50
12DU	Kazuhiro Sasaki, Hideo Nomo	1.00
13DU	Mike Piazza, Ivan Rodriguez	3.00
14DU	Ichiro Suzuki, Ken Griffey Jr.	3.00
15DU	Barry Bonds, Sammy Sosa	3.00
16DU	Alfonso Soriano, Roberto Alomar	2.00

Double Up Memorabilia

	NM/M
Common Card:	15.00
Production 100 Sets	
Derek Jeter, Mike Piazza	50.00
Alex Rodriguez, Rafael Palmeiro	25.00
Chipper Jones, Andruw Jones	15.00
Derek Jeter, Alex Rodriguez	50.00
Nomar Garciaparra, Derek Jeter	50.00
Barry Bonds, Jason Giambi	30.00
Ichiro Suzuki, Hideo Nomo	80.00
Randy Johnson, Curt Schilling	20.00
Pedro J. Martinez, Nomar Garciaparra	30.00
Roger Clemens, Kevin Brown	25.00
Nomar Garciaparra, Manny Ramirez	25.00
Kazuhiro Sasaki, Hideo Nomo	50.00
Mike Piazza, Ivan Rodriguez	25.00
Ichiro Suzuki, Ken Griffey Jr.	50.00
Barry Bonds, Sammy Sosa	40.00
Alfonso Soriano, Roberto Alomar	25.00

Moonshots

		NM/M
Complete Set (20):		30.00
Common Player:		.75
Inserted 1:12		
1M	Mike Piazza	4.00
2M	Alex Rodriguez	4.00
3M	Manny Ramirez	1.50
4M	Ivan Rodriguez	1.00
5M	Luis Gonzalez	.75
6M	Shawn Green	.75
7M	Barry Bonds	5.00
8M	Jason Giambi	3.00
9M	Nomar Garciaparra	4.00
10M	Edgar Martinez	.75
11M	Mo Vaughn	.75
12M	Chipper Jones	3.00
13M	Todd Helton	1.00
14M	Raul Mondesi	.75
15M	Preston Wilson	.75
16M	Rafael Palmeiro	1.00
17M	Jim Edmonds	1.00
18M	Bernie Williams	1.00

19M	Vladimir Guerrero	2.00
20M	Alfonso Soriano	2.00

Moonshots Memorabilia

	NM/M
Common Player:	4.00
Inserted 1:20	
Mike Piazza/Jsy	12.00
Alex Rodriguez/Jsy	12.00
Manny Ramirez/Jsy	5.00
Ivan Rodriguez/Jsy	5.00
Luis Gonzalez/Jsy	4.00
Shawn Green/Jsy	4.00
Barry Bonds/Jsy	12.00
Jason Giambi/Base	8.00
Nomar Garciaparra/Jsy	12.00
Edgar Martinez/Jsy	5.00
Mo Vaughn/Jsy	4.00
Chipper Jones/Jsy	8.00
Todd Helton/Jsy	6.00
Raul Mondesi/Jsy	5.00
Preston Wilson/Jsy	4.00
Rafael Palmeiro/Jsy	5.00
Jim Edmonds/Jsy	5.00
Bernie Williams/Jsy	6.00
Vladimir Guerrero/Base	5.00
Alfonso Soriano/Jsy	5.00

Photo Effex

Vladimir Guerrero
Montreal Expos™

◆ **Photo Effex**

	NM/M
Complete Set (20):	45.00
Common Player:	1.00
Inserted 1:12	
Golds:	6-12X
Production 25 Sets	
1PE	Derek Jeter	6.00
2PE	Barry Bonds	5.00
3PE	Sammy Sosa	3.00
4PE	Troy Glaus	1.50
5PE	Albert Pujols	2.00
6PE	Alex Rodriguez	5.00
7PE	Ichiro Suzuki	4.00
8PE	Greg Maddux	3.00
9PE	Nomar Garciaparra	4.00
10PE	Jeff Bagwell	1.50
11PE	Chipper Jones	3.00
12PE	Mike Piazza	4.00
13PE	Randy Johnson	2.00
14PE	Vladimir Guerrero	3.00
15PE	Alfonso Soriano	3.00
16PE	Lance Berkman	1.00
17PE	Todd Helton	1.00
18PE	Mike Lowell	1.00
19PE	Carlos Delgado	1.00
20PE	Jason Giambi	3.00

When it was a Game

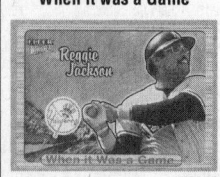

Reggie Jackson

When it Was a Game

		NM/M
Complete Set (40):		125.00
Common Player:		.75
Inserted 1:20		
1WG	Derek Jeter	10.00
2WG	Barry Bonds	8.00
3WG	Luis Aparicio	2.00
4WG	Richie Ashburn	3.00
5WG	Ernie Banks	5.00
6WG	Enos Slaughter	2.00
7WG	Yogi Berra	5.00
8WG	Lou Boudreau	2.00
9WG	Lou Brock	4.00
10WG	Jim Bunning	4.00
11WG	Rod Carew	4.00
12WG	Orlando Cepeda	4.00
13WG	Larry Doby	4.00
14WG	Bobby Doerr	2.00
15WG	Bob Feller	3.00
16WG	Brooks Robinson	5.00
17WG	Rollie Fingers	2.00
18WG	Whitey Ford	3.00
19WG	Bob Gibson	4.00
20WG	Jim "Catfish" Hunter	3.00
21WG	Nolan Ryan	15.00
22WG	Reggie Jackson	5.00
23WG	Fergie Jenkins	3.00
24WG	Al Kaline	6.00
25WG	Mike Schmidt	8.00
26WG	Harmon Killebrew	8.00
27WG	Ralph Kiner	4.00
28WG	Willie Stargell	4.00
29WG	Billy Williams	4.00
30WG	Tom Seaver	5.00
31WG	Juan Marichal	3.00
32WG	Eddie Mathews	6.00
33WG	Willie McCovey	4.00
34WG	Joe Morgan	4.00
35WG	Stan Musial	8.00
36WG	Robin Roberts	4.00
37WG	Robin Yount	8.00
38WG	Jim Palmer	4.00
39WG	Phil Rizzuto	4.00
40WG	Pee Wee Reese	4.00

When it was a Game Autograph

No Pricing

When it was a Game Memorabilia

	NM/M
Common Player:	
Varying quantities produced.	
Derek Jeter/Jsy/200	35.00
Barry Bonds/Bat/200	25.00
Yogi Berra/100	35.00
Larry Doby/Bat/150	20.00
Catfish Hunter/Jsy	8.00
Reggie Jackson/Bat	12.00
Tom Seaver/Jsy	15.00
Juan Marichal/Jsy	8.00
Eddie Mathews/Bat	25.00
Willie McCovey/Jsy/150	15.00
Joe Morgan/Jsy/200	10.00
Jim Palmer/Jsy/300	10.00

2003 Ultra All-Vet Phillies Team

John Kruk • Phillies • 1B

At the Phillies Sept. 28 final game at Veterans Stadium, this cello-wrapped set of the greatest players to appear for the home team in that era was issued as a stadium give away. Fronts have gold-foil highlights on borderless, game-action photos. Backs have personal data, full or partial major league stats and an assortment of licensor and sponsor logos.

		NM/M
Complete Set (13):		6.00
Common Player:		.50
1	Steve Carlton	1.00
2	Darren Daulton	.50
3	John Kruk	.50
4	Juan Samuel	.50
5	Mike Schmidt	3.00
6	Larry Bowa	.50
7	Greg Luzinski	.50
8	Garry Maddox	.50
9	Bobby Abreu	.50
10	Tug McGraw	.50
11	Curt Schilling	.50
12	Dallas Green	.50
---	Header Card	.50

2004 Ultra

	NM/M
Complete Set (220):	45.00
Common Player:	.50
Common All-Rookie (201-220):	.50
Common Player (221-295):	.50
Minor Stars (221-295):	.40
Unlisted Stars (221-295):	.60
Common Player (296-382):	.50

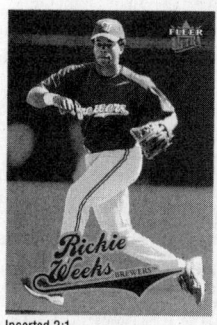

Inserted 2:1
Common Player (383-395): 15.00
Production 500 Sets
Pack (8): 3.00
Box (24): 60.00

#	Player	Price
1	Magglio Ordonez	.40
2	Bobby Abreu	.25
3	Eric Munson	.15
4	Eric Byrnes	.15
5	Bartolo Colon	.25
6	Juan Encarnacion	.15
7	Jody Gerut	.15
8	Eddie Guardado	.15
9	Shea Hillenbrand	.15
10	Andruw Jones	.50
11	Carlos Lee	.15
12	Pedro J. Martinez	.75
13	Barry Larkin	.25
14	Angel Berroa	.15
15	Edgar Martinez	.25
16	Sidney Ponson	.15
17	Mariano Rivera	.25
18	Richie Sexson	.40
19	Frank Thomas	.50
20	Jerome Williams	.15
21	Barry Zito	.40
22	Roberto Alomar	.50
23	Rocky Biddle	.15
24	Orlando Cabrera	.25
25	Placido Polanco	.15
26	Morgan Ensberg	.15
27	Jason Giambi	.75
28	Jim Thome	.75
29	Vladimir Guerrero	.75
30	Tim Hudson	.40
31	Jacque Jones	.15
32	Derrek Lee	.25
33	Rafael Palmeiro	.40
34	Mike Mussina	.40
35	Corey Patterson	.15
36	Mike Cameron	.15
37	Ivan Rodriguez	.50
38	Ben Sheets	.15
39	Woody Williams	.15
40	Ichiro Suzuki	1.00
41	Moises Alou	.25
42	Craig Biggio	.25
43	Jorge Posada	.40
44	Craig Monroe	.15
45	Darin Erstad	.25
46	Jay Gibbons	.25
47	Aaron Guiel	.15
48	Travis Lee	.15
49	Jorge Julio	.15
50	Torii Hunter	.25
51	Luis Matos	.15
52	Brett Myers	.15
53	Sean Casey	.15
54	Mark Prior	1.50
55	Alex Rodriguez	1.50
56	Gary Sheffield	.40
57	Jason Varitek	.15
58	Dontrelle Willis	.40
59	Garret Anderson	.25
60	Casey Blake	.15
61	Jay Payton	.15
62	Carl Crawford	.15
63	Carl Everett	.15
64	Marcus Giles	.15
65	Jose Guillen	.15
66	Eric Karros	.15
67	Mike Lieberthal	.15
68	Hideki Matsui	3.00
69	Xavier Nady	.15
70	Hank Blalock	.40
71	Albert Pujols	1.50
72	Jose Cruz Jr.	.15
73	Randall Simon	.15
74	Javier Vazquez	.15
75	Preston Wilson	.15
76	Danys Baez	.15
77	Alex Cintron	.15
78	Jake Peavy	.25
79	Scott Rolen	.50
80	Robert Fick	.15
81	Brian Giles	.25
82	Roy Halladay	.25
83	Kazuhisa Ishii	.15
84	Austin Kearns	.40
85	Paul LoDuca	.15
86	Darrell May	.15
87	Phil Nevin	.15
88	Carlos Pena	.15
89	Manny Ramirez	.50
90	C.C. Sabathia	.15
91	John Smoltz	.25
92	Jose Vidro	.15
93	Randy Wolf	.15

#	Player	Price
94	Jeff Bagwell	.50
95	Barry Bonds	2.00
96	Frank Catalanotto	.15
97	Zach Day	.15
98	David Ortiz	.15
99	Troy Glaus	.40
100	Bo Hart	.15
101	Geoff Jenkins	.25
102	Jason Kendall	.15
103	Esteban Loaiza	.15
104	Doug Mientkiewicz	.15
105	Trot Nixon	.15
106	Troy Percival	.15
107	Aramis Ramirez	.15
108	Alex Sanchez	.15
109	Alfonso Soriano	.75
110	Omar Vizquel	.15
111	Kerry Wood	.50
112	Rocco Baldelli	.15
113	Bret Boone	.25
114	Shawn Chacon	.15
115	Carlos Delgado	.50
116	Shawn Green	.40
117	Tim Worrell	.15
118	Tom Glavine	.25
119	Shigetoshi Hasegawa	.15
120	Derek Jeter	2.00
121	Jeff Kent	.25
122	Braden Looper	.15
123	Kevin Millwood	.25
124	Hideo Nomo	.40
125	Jason Phillips	.15
126	Tim Redding	.15
127	Reggie Sanders	.15
128	Sammy Sosa	1.25
129	Billy Wagner	.15
130	Miguel Batista	.15
131	Milton Bradley	.15
132	Eric Chavez	.25
133	J.D. Drew	.15
134	Keith Foulke	.15
135	Luis Gonzalez	.25
136	LaTroy Hawkins	.15
137	Randy Johnson	.75
138	Byung-Hyun Kim	.15
139	Javy Lopez	.25
140	Melvin Mora	.15
141	Aubrey Huff	.25
142	Mike Piazza	1.00
143	Mark Redman	.15
144	Kazuhiro Sasaki	.15
145	Shannon Stewart	.15
146	Larry Walker	.25
147	Dmitri Young	.15
148	Josh Beckett	.50
149	Jae Weong Seo	.15
150	Hee Seop Choi	.15
151	Adam Dunn	.40
152	Rafael Furcal	.25
153	Juan Gonzalez	.50
154	Todd Helton	.50
155	Carlos Zambrano	.15
156	Ryan Klesko	.25
157	Mike Lowell	.25
158	Jamie Moyer	.15
159	Russ Ortiz	.15
160	Juan Pierre	.15
161	Edgar Renteria	.15
162	Curt Schilling	.40
163	Mike Sweeney	.15
164	Brandon Webb	.15
165	Michael Young	.15
166	Carlos Beltran	.25
167	Sean Burroughs	.15
168	Luis Castillo	.15
169	David Eckstein	.15
170	Eric Gagne	.25
171	Chipper Jones	1.00
172	Livan Hernandez	.15
173	Nick Johnson	.15
174	Corey Koskie	.15
175	Jason Schmidt	.15
176	Bill Mueller	.15
177	Steve Finley	.15
178	A.J. Pierzynski	.15
179	Rene Reyes	.15
180	Jason Johnson	.15
181	Mark Teixeira	.15
182	Kip Wells	.15
183	Mike MacDougal	.15
184	Lance Berkman	.25
185	Victor Zambrano	.15
186	Roger Clemens	1.50
187	Jim Edmonds	.25
188	Nomar Garciaparra	1.50
189	Ken Griffey Jr.	1.00
190	Richard Hidalgo	.15
191	Cliff Floyd	.15
192	Greg Maddux	1.00
193	Mark Mulder	.25
194	Roy Oswalt	.25
195	Marlon Byrd	.15
196	Jose Reyes	.25
197	Kevin Brown	.25
198	Miguel Tejada	.25
199	Vernon Wells	.25
200	Joel Pineiro	.15
201	Rickie Weeks	5.00
202	Chad Gaudin	1.50
203	Ryan Wagner	1.50
204	Chris Bootcheck	.50
205	Koyie Hill	1.00
206	Jeff Duncan	1.00
207	Rich Harden	.50
208	Edwin Jackson	.50
209	Robby Hammock	.50
210	Khalil Greene	.50
211	Chien-Ming Wang	.50

#	Player	Price
212	Prentice Redman	.50
213	Todd Wellemeyer	.50
214	Clint Barmes	1.00
215	Matt Kata	.50
216	Jon Leicester	.50
217	Jeremy Guthrie	.50
218	Chin-Hui Tsao	1.50
219	Dan Haren	1.00
220	Delmon Young	5.00
221	Vladimir Guerrero	1.00
222	Andy Pettitte	.60
223	Gary Sheffield	.60
224	Javier Vazquez	.25
225	Alex Rodriguez	2.50
226	Billy Wagner	.25
227	Miguel Tejada	.25
228	Greg Maddux	1.50
229	Ivan Rodriguez	.60
230	Roger Clemens	2.50
231	Alfonso Soriano	1.00
232	Miguel Cabrera	.75
233	Javy Lopez	.40
234	David Wells	.25
235	Eric Milton	.25
236	Armando Benitez	.25
237	Mike Cameron	.25
238	J.D. Drew	.40
239	Carlos Beltran	.60
240	Bartolo Colon	.40
241	Jose Guillen	.25
242	Kevin Brown	.40
243	Carlos Guillen	.25
244	Kenny Lofton	.25
245	Pokey Reese	.25
246	Rafael Palmeiro	.75
247	Nomar Garciaparra	2.50
248	Hee Seop Choi	.25
249	Juan Uribe	.25
250	Nick Johnson	.25
251	Scott Podsednik	.25
252	Richie Sexson	.60
253	Keith Foulke	.25
254	Jaret Wright	.25
255	Johnny Estrada	.25
256	Michael Barrett	.25
257	Bernie Williams	.60
258	Octavio Dotel	.25
259	Jeromy Burnitz	.25
260	Kevin Youkilis	.25
261	Derek Lee	.40
262	Jack Wilson	.25
263	Craig Wilson	.25
264	Richard Hidalgo	.25
265	Royce Clayton	.25
266	Curt Schilling	.60
267	Joe Mauer	.75
268	Bobby Crosby	.25
269	Zack Greinke	.25
270	Victor Martinez	.25
271	Pedro Feliz	.25
272	Tony Batista	.25
273	Casey Kotchman	.25
274	Freddy Garcia	.25
275	Adam Everett	.25
276	Alexis Rios	.25
277	Lew Ford	.25
278	Adam LaRoche	.25
279	Lyle Overbay	.25
280	Juan Gonzalez	.40
281	A.J. Pierzynski	.25
282	Scott Hairston	.25
283	Danny Bautista	.25
284	Brad Penny	.25
285	Paul Konerko	.25
286	Matt Lawton	.25
287	Carl Pavano	.25
288	Pat Burrell	.40
289	Kenny Rogers	.25
290	Laynce Nix	.25
291	Johnny Damon	.40
292	Paul Wilson	.25
293	Vinny Castilla	.25
294	Aaron Miles	.25
295	Ken Harvey	.25
296	Onil Joseph RC	2.00
297	Kazuhito Tadano RC	3.00
298	Jeff Bennett RC	2.00
299	Chad Bentz RC	2.00
300	Akinori Otsuka RC	2.00
301	Jon Knott RC	3.00
302	Ian Snell RC	3.00
303	Fernando Nieve RC	2.00
304	Mike Rouse RC	2.00
305	Dennis Sarfate RC	2.00
306	Josh Labandeira RC	3.00
307	Chris Oxspring RC	2.00
308	Alfredo Simon RC	2.00
309	Rusty Tucker RC	2.00
310	Lincoln Holdzkom RC	2.00
311	Justin Leone RC	2.00
312	Jorge Sequea RC	2.00
313	Brian Dallimore RC	2.00
314	Tim Bittner RC	2.00
315	Ronny Cedeno RC	2.00
316	Justin Hampson RC	2.00
317	Ryan Wing RC	2.00
318	Mariano Gomez RC	2.00
319	Carlos Vasquez RC	2.00
320	Casey Daigle RC	2.00
321	Renyel Pinto RC	2.00
322	Chris Shelton RC	4.00
323	Mike Gosling RC	2.00
324	Aarom Baldiris RC	2.00
325	Ramon Ramirez RC	2.00
326	Roberto Novoa RC	2.00
327	Sean Henn RC	2.00
328	Nick Regilio RC	2.00
329	David Crouthers RC	2.00

#	Player	Price
330	Greg Dobbs RC	2.00
331	Angel Chavez RC	2.00
332	Luis A. Gonzalez RC	2.00
333	Justin Knoedler RC	2.00
334	Jason Frasor RC	2.00
335	Jerry Gil RC	2.00
336	Carlos Hines RC	2.00
337	Ivan Ochoa RC	3.00
338	Jose Capellan RC	3.00
339	Hector Gimenez RC	2.00
340	Shawn Hill RC	3.00
341	Freddy Guzman RC	2.00
342	Scott Proctor RC	2.00
343	Frank Francisco RC	2.00
344	Brandon Medders RC	2.00
345	Andy Green RC	2.00
346	Eddy Rodriguez RC	2.00
347	Tim Hamulack RC	2.00
348	Mike Wuertz RC	2.00
349	Arnie Munoz RC	2.00
350	Enemencio Pacheco RC	2.00
351	Dusty Bergman RC	2.00
352	Charles Thomas RC	5.00
353	William Bergolla RC	2.00
354	Ramon Castro RC	2.00
355	Justin Lehr RC	2.00
356	Lino Urdaneta RC	2.00
357	Donnie Kelly RC	2.00
358	Kevin Cave RC	2.00
359	Franklyn Gracesqui RC	2.00
360	Chris Aguila RC	2.00
361	Jorge Vasquez RC	2.00
362	Andres Blanco RC	2.00
363	Orlando Rodriguez RC	2.00
364	Colby Miller RC	2.00
365	Shawn Camp RC	2.00
366	Jake Woods RC	2.00
367	George Sherrill RC	2.00
368	Justin Huisman RC	2.00
369	Jimmy Serrano RC	3.00
370	Mike Johnston RC	3.00
371	Ryan Meaux RC	2.00
372	Scott Dohmann RC	2.00
373	Brad Halsey RC	5.00
374	Joey Gathright RC	3.00
375	Yadier Molina RC	3.00
376	Travis Blackley RC	2.00
377	Steve Andrade RC	2.00
378	Phil Stockman RC	2.00
379	Roman Colon RC	2.00
380	Jesse Crain RC	2.00
381	Edwardo Sierra RC	2.00
382	Justin Germano RC	2.00
383	Kazuo Matsui SI	20.00
384	Shingo Takatsu SI	10.00
385	John Gall SI	15.00
386	Chris Saenz RC	15.00
387	Merkin Valdez RC	20.00
388	Jamie Brown RC	15.00
389	Jason Bartlett RC	20.00
390	David Aardsma RC	20.00
391	Scott Kazmir RC	20.00
392	David Wright RC	40.00
393	Dioner Navarro RC	10.00
394	B.J. Upton RC	25.00
395	Gavin Floyd RC	20.00

Gold Medallion

Cards (1-200): 2-3X
Inserted 1:1
All-Rookies (201-220): 3-4X
Inserted 1:8
Cards (221-295): .75-1.5X
Inserted 1:1
Cards (296-382): .75-1.25X
Cards (383-395): .25-.75X
Inserted 1:4

Platinum Medallion

Cards (1-200): 8-15X
All-Rookies (201-220): 5-10X
Production 66 Sets
Cards (221-295): 4-8X
Cards (296-382): 2-4X
Production 100 Sets
Cards (383-395): No Pricing
Production 13 Sets

Diamond Producers

		NM/M
Complete Set (10):		60.00
Common Player:		4.00
Inserted 1:144		
1DP	Greg Maddux	8.00
2DP	Dontrelle Willis	4.00
3DP	Jim Thome	5.00
4DP	Alfonso Soriano	6.00
5DP	Alex Rodriguez	10.00

6DP	Sammy Sosa	10.00
7DP	Nomar Garciaparra	10.00
8DP	Derek Jeter	15.00
9DP	Adam Dunn	4.00
10DP	Mark Prior	8.00

Diamond Producers Memorabilia

	NM/M
Production 1,000 Sets	
Dontrelle Willis	15.00
Alfonso Soriano	10.00
Alex Rodriguez	10.00
Sammy Sosa	10.00
Nomar Garciaparra	10.00
Derek Jeter	15.00
Mark Prior	10.00

Diamond Producers UltraSwatch

	NM/M
Numbered to Jersey #.	
Dontrelle Willis/35	25.00

Hitting Machines

		NM/M
Common Player:		3.00
Inserted 1:12		
Die-Cut:		1-2X
1HM	Albert Pujols	6.00
2HM	Ken Griffey Jr.	4.00
3HM	Vladimir Guerrero	3.50
4HM	Mike Piazza	4.00
5HM	Ichiro Suzuki	5.00
6HM	Miguel Cabrera	3.00
7HM	Hideki Matsui	6.00
8HM	Nomar Garciaparra	6.00
9HM	Derek Jeter	8.00
10HM	Chipper Jones	4.00

Hitting Machines Game-Used Silver

		NM/M
Common Player:		8.00
Inserted 1:74		
Gold:		1-30X
Production 50 Sets		
Platinum:		No Pricing
Production 10 Sets		
JB	Jeff Bagwell	10.00
MC	Miguel Cabrera	10.00
AD	Adam Dunn	8.00
VG	Vladimir Guerrero	10.00
TH	Todd Helton	10.00
CJ	Chipper Jones	12.00
HM	Hideki Matsui	20.00
MP	Mike Piazza	12.00
AP	Albert Pujols	12.00
FT	Frank Thomas	10.00

HR Kings

		NM/M
Complete Set (10):		35.00
Inserted 1:96		
Golds:		2-3X
Production 50 Sets		
1HK	Barry Bonds	8.00
2HK	Albert Pujols	6.00
3HK	Jason Giambi	3.00
4HK	Jeff Bagwell	2.00
5HK	Ken Griffey Jr.	4.00
6HK	Alex Rodriguez	6.00
7HK	Sammy Sosa	5.00
8HK	Alfonso Soriano	3.00

9HK	Chipper Jones	4.00
10HK	Mike Piazza	4.00

Legendary 13 Memorabilia

Numbered to 13 each.
Each player's jersey swatch on each card.
Masterpiece 1/1 auto. by named player.
Inserted 1:192 Series 2 Hobby

Legendary 13 Memorabilia Autographs

	NM/M
Numbered to five each.	
Masterpiece: 1/1	
Numbered with "L13A-" prefix.	
Limited pricing due to scarcity.	
TW Ted Williams	900.00

Legendary 13 Memorabilia Gold

Numbered to uniform #.
Jersey, patch or bat swatch on each.
Masterpiece: 1/1
No pricing due to scarcity.

Legendary 13 Dual Memorabilia Autographs

Numbered to three each.
Masterpiece 1/1
No pricing due to scarcity.

Legendary 13 Dual Memorabilia Gold

Numbered to 22 each.
Jersey, patch or bat swatches on each.
Platinum numbered to 10 each.
Masterpiece 1/1
Numbered with "L13D-" prefix.
No pricing due to scarcity.

Performers

		NM/M
Complete Set (15):		12.00
Common Player:		.50
Inserted 1:6		
1UP	Ichiro Suzuki	1.50
2UP	Albert Pujols	2.00
3UP	Barry Bonds	3.00
4UP	Hideki Matsui	2.00
5UP	Randy Johnson	1.00
6UP	Jason Giambi	1.00
7UP	Pedro J. Martinez	1.00
8UP	Hank Blalock	.50
9UP	Chipper Jones	1.50
10UP	Mike Piazza	1.50
11UP	Derek Jeter	3.00
12UP	Vladimir Guerrero	1.00
13UP	Barry Zito	.75
14UP	Rocco Baldelli	.75
15UP	Hideo Nomo	.75

Performers Memorabilia

	NM/M
Common Player:	6.00
Production 500 Sets	
Albert Pujols	15.00
Barry Bonds/base	15.00
Randy Johnson	8.00
Jason Giambi	8.00
Pedro J. Martinez	10.00
Hank Blalock	6.00
Chipper Jones	10.00
Mike Piazza	10.00
Derek Jeter	15.00
Vladimir Guerrero	8.00

Rocco Baldelli	10.00
Hideo Nomo	15.00

Performers UltraSwatch

NM/M

Numbered to Jersey #.

Randy Johnson/51	15.00
Pedro Martinez/45	20.00
Mike Piazza/31	25.00
Vladimir Guerrero/27	20.00

RBI Kings

Complete Set (10):	15.00
Inserted 1:32	
Golds:	3-4X
Production 50 Sets	
1RK Hideki Matsui	4.00
2RK Albert Pujols	4.00
3RK Todd Helton	1.50
4RK Jim Thome	1.50
5RK Carlos Delgado	1.50
6RK Alex Rodriguez	4.00
7RK Barry Bonds	5.00
8RK Manny Ramirez	1.50
9RK Vladimir Guerrero	1.50
10RK Nomar Garciaparra	4.00

Season Crowns Autograph

NM/M

Common Player:	15.00
Production 150 Sets	
Golds:	No Pricing
Production 25 Sets	
Rocco Baldelli	35.00
Hank Blalock	15.00
Bo Hart	30.00
Aubrey Huff	15.00
Chipper Jones	60.00
Austin Kearns	15.00
Mike Lowell	15.00
Corey Patterson	20.00
Carlos Pena	15.00
Jose Reyes	30.00
Scott Rolen	20.00
Miguel Tejada	25.00
Brandon Webb	15.00
Rickie Weeks	30.00
Dontrelle Willis	35.00

Season Crowns Memorabilia

Common Player:	4.00
Production 399 Sets	
Golds:	1-2X
Production 99 Sets	
Platinums:	No Pricing
Production 25 Sets	
Adam Dunn	6.00
Carlos Pena	4.00
Torii Hunter	8.00
Gary Sheffield	8.00
Sean Casey	4.00
Lance Berkman	4.00
Tom Glavine	6.00
Sean Burroughs	4.00
Shawn Green	6.00
Jason Kendall	4.00
Vladimir Guerrero	10.00
Todd Helton	8.00
Tim Hudson	8.00
Troy Glaus	6.00
Larry Walker	4.00
Carlos Beltran	6.00
Hideo Nomo	10.00
Kazuhiro Sasaki	4.00
Mike Piazza	10.00
Scott Rolen	8.00
Carlos Delgado	6.00
Andruw Jones	8.00
Alfonso Soriano	10.00
Angel Berroa	6.00
Brandon Webb	6.00
Jason Giambi	8.00
Pedro J. Martinez	10.00
Manny Ramirez	8.00

Alex Rodriguez	10.00
Derek Jeter	15.00
Mark Mulder	6.00
Greg Maddux	15.00
Sammy Sosa	15.00
Jim Thome	10.00
Hank Blalock	6.00
Roberto Alomar	8.00
Omar Vizquel	5.00
Austin Kearns	8.00
Jeff Bagwell	8.00
Frank Thomas	8.00
Randy Johnson	8.00
Rocco Baldelli	12.00
Albert Pujols	15.00
Jose Reyes	8.00
Dontrelle Willis	12.00
Hideki Matsui/Base	20.00
Barry Bonds/Base	15.00
Ichiro Suzuki/Base	15.00
Chipper Jones	10.00
Roger Clemens	15.00

Strikeout Kings

Complete Set (10):		10.00
Common Player:		.75
Inserted 1:24		
Golds:		3-5X
Production 50 Sets		
1KK	Randy Johnson	1.50
2KK	Pedro J. Martinez	1.50
3KK	Curt Schilling	1.00
4KK	Roger Clemens	3.00
5KK	Mike Mussina	1.00
6KK	Roy Halladay	.75
7KK	Kerry Wood	1.00
8KK	Dontrelle Willis	1.00
9KK	Greg Maddux	2.00
10KK	Mark Prior	2.00

Turn Back the Clock

Common Player:		1.50
Inserted 1:6		
1	Roger Clemens	5.00
2	Alex Rodriguez	5.00
3	Randy Johnson	2.00
4	Pedro Martinez	2.00
5	Alfonso Soriano	2.00
6	Curt Schilling	1.50
7	Miguel Tejada	1.50
8	Scott Rolen	2.00
9	Jim Thome	2.00
10	Manny Ramirez	1.50
11	Vladimir Guerrero	2.00
12	Tom Glavine	1.50
13	Andy Pettitte	1.50
14	Ivan Rodriguez	1.50
15	Jason Giambi	2.00
16	Rafael Palmeiro	2.00
17	Greg Maddux	3.00
18	Hideo Nomo	1.50
19	Mike Mussina	1.50
20	Sammy Sosa	4.00

Turn Back the Clock Game-Used Copper

NM/M

Common Player:		8.00
Production 399 Sets		
Silver:		.75-1.5X
Production 199 Sets		
Gold:		1-2X
Production 99 Sets		
Platinum Patch:		2-5X
Production 29 Sets		
RC	Roger Clemens	12.00
JG	Jason Giambi	10.00
TG	Tom Glavine	8.00
VG	Vladimir Guerrero	10.00
RJ	Randy Johnson	8.00
GM	Greg Maddux	12.00
PR	Pedro Martinez	10.00
MM	Mike Mussina	8.00
HM	Hideo Nomo	8.00
RP	Rafael Palmeiro	10.00

AP	Andy Pettitte	8.00
MR	Manny Ramirez	10.00
IR	Ivan Rodriguez	8.00
SR	Scott Rolen	10.00
CS	Curt Schilling	8.00
AS	Alfonso Soriano	10.00
SS	Sammy Sosa	12.00
MT	Miguel Tejada	8.00
JT	Jim Thome	10.00

3 Kings

NM/M

Production 33 Sets	
Mike Piazza, Roger Clemens, Alex Rodriguez	70.00
Albert Pujols, Mark Prior, Todd Helton	50.00
Alfonso Soriano, Dontrelle Willis, Albert Pujols	60.00
P. Martinez, Sammy Sosa, Albert Pujols	70.00
Randy Johnson, Albert Pujols, Todd Helton	50.00
Dontrelle Willis, Chipper Jones, Albert Pujols	60.00
Dontrelle Willis, Jeff Bagwell, Jim Thome	40.00
Greg Maddux, Jason Giambi, Manny Ramirez	50.00

2005 Ultra

Common Player (1-200):	.15
Minor Stars (1-200):	.25
Unlisted Stars (1-200):	.50
Common Player (201-220):	2.00
Minor Stars (201-220):	3.00
Inserted 1:4	
Pack (8):	3.50
Box (24):	75.00
1 Andy Pettitte	.25
2 Jose Cruz	.15
3 Cliff Floyd	.25
4 Paul Konerko	.25
5 Joe Mauer	.75
6 Scott Spiezio	.15
7 Ben Sheets	.25
8 Kerry Wood	.50
9 Carl Pavano	.15
10 Matt Morris	.15
11 Kazuo Matsui	.75
12 Ivan Rodriguez	.40
13 Victor Martinez	.15
14 Justin Morneau	.25
15 Adam Everett	.15
16 Carl Crawford	.25
17 David Ortiz	.25
18 Jason Giambi	.25
19 Derek Lee	.25
20 Magglio Ordonez	.25
21 Bobby Abreu	.25
22 Milton Bradley	.15
23 Jeff Bagwell	.50
24 Jim Edmonds	.25
25 Garret Anderson	.25
26 Jacque Jones	.15
27 Ted Lilly	.15
28 Greg Maddux	1.00
29 Jermaine Dye	.15
30 Bill Mueller	.15
31 Roy Oswalt	.25
32 Tony Womack	.15
33 Andruw Jones	.50
34 Tom Glavine	.25
35 Mariano Rivera	.25
36 Sean Casey	.15
37 Edgardo Alfonzo	.15
38 Brad Penny	.15
39 Johan Santana	.25
40 Mark Teixeira	.25
41 Manny Ramirez	.50
42 Gary Sheffield	.40
43 Matt Lawton	.15
44 Troy Percival	.15
45 Rocco Baldelli	.40
46 Doug Mientkiewicz	.15
47 Corey Patterson	.15
48 Austin Kearns	.15
49 Edgar Martinez	.25
50 Brad Radke	.15
51 Barry Larkin	.25
52 Chone Figgins	.15
53 Alexis Rios	.15
54 Alex Rodriguez	1.50
55 Vinny Castilla	.15

56 Javier Vazquez	.15
57 Javy Lopez	.25
58 Mike Cameron	.25
59 Brian Giles	.25
60 Dontrelle Willis	.25
61 Rafael Furcal	.15
62 Trot Nixon	.15
63 Mark Mulder	.25
64 Josh Beckett	.50
65 J.D. Drew	.25
66 Brandon Webb	.15
67 Wade Miller	.15
68 Lyle Overbay	.15
69 Pedro J. Martinez	.75
70 Rich Harden	.15
71 Al Leiter	.15
72 Adam Eaton	.15
73 Mike Sweeney	.15
74 Steve Finley	.15
75 Kris Benson	.15
76 Jim Thome	.75
77 Juan Pierre	.15
78 Bartolo Colon	.25
79 Carlos Delgado	.50
80 Jack Wilson	.15
81 Ken Harvey	.15
82 Nomar Garciaparra	1.50
83 Paul LoDuca	.15
84 Cesar Izturis	.15
85 Adrian Beltre	.25
86 Brian Roberts	.15
87 David Eckstein	.15
88 Jimmy Rollins	.25
89 Roger Clemens	1.00
90 Randy Johnson	.75
91 Orlando Hudson	.15
92 Tim Hudson	.25
93 Dmitri Young	.15
94 Chipper Jones	1.00
95 John Smoltz	.25
96 Billy Wagner	.15
97 Hideo Nomo	.25
98 Sammy Sosa	1.25
99 Darin Erstad	.15
100 Todd Helton	.50
101 Aubrey Huff	.15
102 Alfonso Soriano	.75
103 Jose Vidro	.15
104 Carlos Lee	.15
105 Corey Koskie	.15
106 Bret Boone	.25
107 Torii Hunter	.40
108 Aramis Ramirez	.15
109 Chase Utley	.15
110 Reggie Sanders	.15
111 Livan Hernandez	.15
112 Jeromy Burnitz	.15
113 Carlos Zambrano	.15
114 Hank Blalock	.40
115 Sidney Ponson	.15
116 Zack Greinke	.15
117 Trevor Hoffman	.15
118 Jeff Kent	.25
119 Richie Sexson	.40
120 Melvin Mora	.15
121 Eric Chavez	.25
122 Miguel Cabrera	.50
123 Ryan Freel	.15
124 Russ Ortiz	.15
125 Craig Wilson	.15
126 Craig Biggio	.25
127 Curt Schilling	.40
128 Kazuhisa Ishii	.15
129 Marquis Grissom	.15
130 Bernie Williams	.40
131 Travis Hafner	.15
132 Hee Seop Choi	.15
133 Scott Rolen	.15
134 Tony Batista	.75
135 Frank Thomas	.15
136 Jason Varitek	.50
137 Ichiro Suzuki	1.25
138 Junior Spivey	.15
139 Adam Dunn	.40
140 Jorge Posada	.40
141 Edgar Renteria	.15
142 Hideki Matsui	1.50
143 Carlos Guillen	.15
144 Jody Gerut	.15
145 Wily Mo Pena	.15
146 Derek Jeter	2.00
147 C.C. Sabathia	.15
148 Geoff Jenkins	.25
149 Albert Pujols	1.50
150 Eric Munson	.15
151 Moises Alou	.15
152 Jerry Hairston	.15
153 Ray Durham	.15
154 Mike Piazza	1.00
155 Omar Vizquel	.25
156 A.J. Pierzynski	.15
157 Michael Young	.15
158 Jason Bay	.25
159 Mark Loretta	.15
160 Shawn Green	.25
161 Luis Gonzalez	.25
162 Johnny Damon	.25
163 Eric Milton	.15
164 Mike Lowell	.15
165 Jose Guillen	.15
166 Eric Hinske	.15
167 Jason Kendall	.15
168 Carlos Beltran	.25
169 Johnny Estrada	.15
170 Scott Hatteberg	.15
171 Laynce Nix	.15
172 Eric Gagne	.25
173 Richard Hidalgo	.15

174 Bobby Crosby	.15
175 Woody Williams	.15
176 Justin Leone	.15
177 Orlando Cabrera	.15
178 Mark Prior	1.50
179 Jorge Julio	.15
180 Jamie Moyer	.15
181 Jose Reyes	.40
182 Ken Griffey Jr.	1.00
183 Mike Lieberthal	.15
184 Kenny Rogers	.15
185 Mike Mussina	.40
186 Preston Wilson	.15
187 Khalil Greene	.50
188 Angel Berroa	.15
189 Miguel Tejada	.40
190 Freddy Garcia	.15
191 Pat Burrell	.25
192 Luis Castillo	.15
193 Vladimir Guerrero	.75
194 Roy Halladay	.15
195 Barry Zito	.40
196 Lance Berkman	.25
197 Rafael Palmeiro	.50
198 Nate Robertson	.15
199 Jason Schmidt	.25
200 Scott Podsednik	.15
201 Casey Kotchman	3.00
202 Scott Kazmir	4.00
203 Bucky Jacobsen	4.00
204 Jeff Keppinger	3.00
205 David Bush	3.00
206 Gavin Floyd	5.00
207 David Wright	8.00
208 B.J. Upton	3.00
209 David Aardsma	2.00
210 Jason Bartlett	3.00
211 Dioner Navarro	3.00
212 Jason Kubel	3.00
213 Ryan Howard	3.00
214 Charles Thomas RC	2.00
215 Freddy Guzman	2.00
216 Brad Halsey	3.00
217 Joey Gathright	2.00
218 Jeff Francis	2.00
219 Terry Tiffee	2.00
220 Nick Swisher	5.00

Gold

Cards 1-200:	1-30X
Inserted 1:1	
Cards 201-220:	.5-1X
Inserted 1:8	

Platinum

Cards 1-200:	5-8X
Cards 201-220:	3-5X
Production 50 Sets	

Follow the Leader

NM/M

Common Player:	1.50
Inserted 1:6	
Copper Game-Used:	3-5X
Inserted 1:72 (Hobby Only)	
Red Game-Used:	2-4X
Inserted 1:48 (Retail Only)	
Gold Game-Used:	4-6X
Production 250 Sets	
Platinum Game-Used:	5-8X
Production 99 Sets	
Ultra Game-Used:	
Numbered 26-51:	5-10X
Numbered 25 or less:	No Pricing
Production to player's jersey number.	
1 Roger Clemens	3.00
2 Albert Pujols	3.00
3 Sammy Sosa	2.50
4 Manny Ramirez	1.50
5 Vladimir Guerrero	2.00
6 Ivan Rodriguez	1.50
7 Mike Piazza	2.00
8 Scott Rolen	2.00
9 Ichiro Suzuki	2.50
10 Randy Johnson	2.00
11 Mark Prior	2.00
12 Jim Thome	2.00
13 Greg Maddux	2.50

14 Pedro J. Martinez	2.00
15 Miguel Cabrera	1.50

HR Kings

NM/M

Common Player:	2.50
Inserted 1:96	
Ultra Kings Gold:	1-30X
Production 50 Sets	
1 Jim Thome	4.00
2 David Ortiz	3.00
3 Adam Dunn	3.00
4 Albert Pujols	8.00
5 Manny Ramirez	3.50
6 Vladimir Guerrero	4.00
7 Miguel Tejada	3.50
8 Rafael Palmeiro	3.50
9 Mark Teixeira	2.50
10 Sammy Sosa	6.00
11 Frank Thomas	3.50
12 Pat Burrell	2.50
13 Adrian Beltre	2.50
14 Miguel Cabrera	3.50
15 Gary Sheffield	3.00

RBI Kings

NM/M

Common Player:	2.50
Inserted 1:32	
Ultra Kings Gold:	2-4X
Production 50 Sets	
1 Sean Casey	2.50
2 Ivan Rodriguez	2.50
3 Mike Piazza	4.00
4 Todd Helton	3.00
5 Scott Rolen	3.50
6 Hideki Matsui	6.00
7 Gary Sheffield	2.50
8 Alfonso Soriano	3.50
9 Bobby Abreu	2.50
10 Lance Berkman	2.50
11 Miguel Tejada	2.50
12 Travis Hafner	2.50
13 Hank Blalock	2.50
14 Jeff Bagwell	3.00
15 Chipper Jones	4.00

Season Crown Autographs Copper

NM/M

Common Player:	20.00
Stated Production 199 Sets	
All 199 cards not released for some players.	
31 Roy Oswalt/50	25.00
80 Jack Wilson/199	20.00
125 Craig Wilson/130	20.00
157 Michael Young/150	20.00

Season Crown Autographs Gold

NM/M

Common Player:	20.00
Stated Production 99 Sets	
All 99 cards not released for some players.	
21 Roy Oswalt/99	20.00
50 Brad Radke/89	20.00
51 Barry Larkin/99	25.00
62 Trot Nixon/37	25.00
70 Rich Harden/41	20.00
80 Jack Wilson/99	20.00
88 Jimmy Rollins/45	25.00
121 Eric Chavez/69	20.00
125 Craig Wilson/99	20.00
157 Michael Young/99	20.00
200 Scott Podsednik/99	20.00

Season Crown Autographs Platinum

NM/M

Common Player:	25.00
Stated Production 50 Sets	
All 50 cards not released for some players.	
Masterpiece:	No Pricing
Production One Set	
20 Magglio Ordonez/50	25.00
25 Garret Anderson/50	25.00
31 Roy Oswalt/50	25.00
40 Mark Teixeira/50	30.00
50 Brad Radke/50	25.00
51 Barry Larkin/50	30.00
62 Trot Nixon/50	25.00
70 Rich Harden/50	25.00
80 Jack Wilson/50	25.00
87 David Eckstein/45	25.00
88 Jimmy Rollins/50	25.00
96 Billy Wagner/50	30.00
116 Zack Greinke/49	25.00
121 Eric Chavez/50	25.00
125 Craig Wilson/50	25.00
157 Michael Young/50	25.00
161 Luis Gonzalez/50	25.00
185 Mike Mussina/50	30.00
195 Barry Zito/50	25.00

199 Jason Schmidt/50 25.00
200 Scott Podsednik/50 25.00
201 Casey Kotchman/50 25.00

Season Crowns Copper Game-Used

		NM/M
Common Player:		5.00
Production 399 Sets		
Gold:		.75-1.5X
Production 99 Sets		
Platinum:		No Pricing
Production 25 Sets		
1	Andy Pettitte/Jsy	8.00
3	Cliff Floyd/Jsy	5.00
7	Ben Sheets/Jsy	5.00
8	Kerry Wood/Jsy	8.00
11	Kazuo Matsui/Jsy	15.00
13	Victor Martinez/Jsy	8.00
17	David Carr/Jsy	8.00
20	Magglio Ordonez/Bat	5.00
21	Bobby Abreu/Bat	5.00
24	Jim Edmonds/Jsy	5.00
31	Roy Oswalt/Jsy	5.00
33	Andruw Jones/Jsy	8.00
34	Tom Glavine/Bat	5.00
36	Sean Casey/Jsy	5.00
41	Edgardo Alfonzo/Bat	8.00
42	Manny Ramirez/Bat	8.00
45	Gary Sheffield/Bat	8.00
48	Rocco Baldelli/Jsy	8.00
49	Austin Kearns/Jsy	5.00
60	Edgar Martinez/Jsy	5.00
65	J.D. Drew/Jsy	5.00
70	Rich Harden/Jsy	5.00
71	Al Leiter/Jsy	5.00
80	Jack Wilson/Bat	5.00
93	Dmitri Young/Bat	5.00
94	Chipper Jones/Bat	10.00
97	Hideo Nomo/Jsy	8.00
98	Sammy Sosa/Bat	12.00
100	Todd Helton/Bat	8.00
102	Alfonso Soriano/Bat	8.00
114	Hank Blalock/Bat	8.00
119	Richie Sexson/Jsy	5.00
121	Eric Chavez/Jsy	5.00
130	Bernie Williams/Bat	8.00
139	Frank Thomas/Bat	8.00
142	Adam Dunn/Bat	8.00
144	Hideki Matsui/Bat	15.00
158	Jody Gerut/Bat	8.00
162	Mike Piazza/Bat	10.00
168	Johnny Damon/Bat	10.00
173	Carlos Beltran/Bat	8.00
181	Richard Hidalgo/Jsy	8.00
187	Jose Reyes/Bat	6.00
191	Khalil Greene/Jsy	15.00
193	Pat Burrell/Bat	8.00
197	Vladimir Guerrero/Bat	8.00
197	Rafael Palmeiro/Jsy	8.00

Strikeout Kings

		NM/M
Common Player:		2.50
Inserted 1:24		
Ultra Kings Gold:		2-4X
Production 50 Sets		
1	Pedro J. Martinez	3.50
2	Randy Johnson	3.50
3	Mark Mulder	2.50
4	Barry Zito	2.50
5	Roger Clemens	6.00
6	Mark Prior	5.00
7	Ben Sheets	2.50
8	Curt Schilling	2.50
9	Billy Wagner	2.50
10	Eric Gagne	2.50
11	Josh Beckett	3.00
12	Kerry Wood	2.50
13	Jason Schmidt	2.50
14	Roy Halladay	2.50
15	Greg Maddux	4.00

Ultra Kings Game-Used Gold

		NM/M
Common Player:		8.00
Production 150 Sets		
Ultra Swatch		
Numbered 51-75:		.75-1.5X
Numbered 26-50:		1-2X
Numbered 25 or less:		No Pricing
Production to player's jersey number.		
Platinum:		No Pricing
Production 25 Sets		
1	Pedro J. Martinez	12.00
2	Randy Johnson	12.00
3	Mark Mulder	8.00
4	Barry Zito	8.00
5	Roger Clemens	25.00
6	Mark Prior	20.00
7	Ben Sheets	8.00
8	Curt Schilling	8.00
9	Billy Wagner	8.00
10	Eric Gagne	8.00
11	Josh Beckett	10.00
12	Kerry Wood	10.00
13	Jason Schmidt	8.00
14	Roy Halladay	8.00
15	Greg Maddux	15.00
16	Sean Casey	8.00
17	Ivan Rodriguez	8.00
18	Mike Piazza	15.00
19	Todd Helton	10.00
20	Scott Rolen	12.00
21	Hideki Matsui	30.00
22	Gary Sheffield	8.00
23	Alfonso Soriano	12.00
24	Bobby Abreu	8.00
25	Lance Berkman	8.00
26	Miguel Tejada	8.00
27	Travis Hafner	8.00
28	Hank Blalock	8.00
29	Jeff Bagwell	10.00
30	Chipper Jones	15.00
31	Jim Thome	12.00
32	David Ortiz	8.00
33	Adam Dunn	8.00
34	Albert Pujols	25.00
35	Manny Ramirez	10.00
36	Vladimir Guerrero	12.00
37	Miguel Tejada	8.00
38	Rafael Palmeiro	10.00
39	Mark Teixeira	8.00
40	Sammy Sosa	20.00
41	Frank Thomas	10.00
42	Pat Burrell	8.00
43	Adrian Beltre	8.00
44	Miguel Cabrera	10.00
45	Gary Sheffield	8.00

Ultra 3 Kings Triple Swatch

		NM/M
Common Card:		40.00
Production 33 Sets		
1	Greg Maddux, Mark Prior, Kerry Wood	75.00
2	Mark Teixeira, Hank Blalock, Alfonso Soriano	40.00
3	Jeff Bagwell, Roger Clemens, Lance Berkman	60.00
4	Jim Thome, Pat Burrell, Billy Wagner	40.00
5	Gary Sheffield, Hideki Matsui, Mike Piazza	75.00
6	Scott Rolen, Chipper Jones, Adrian Beltre	40.00
7	Albert Pujols, Adam Dunn, Miguel Cabrera	50.00
8	Curt Schilling, Pedro J. Martinez, Manny Ramirez	60.00
9	Randy Johnson, Greg Maddux, Pedro J. Martinez	50.00
10	Josh Beckett, Miguel Cabrera, Ivan Rodriguez	40.00

2006 Ultra

		NM/M
Complete Set (251):		60.00
Common Player:		.15
Common SP (201-250):		.50
Inserted 1:4		
Production 5,000 for #251		
Pack (8):		2.50
Box (8):		50.00
1	Vladimir Guerrero	.75
2	Bartolo Colon	.15
3	Francisco Rodriguez	.15
4	Darin Erstad	.15
5	Chone Figgins	.25
6	Bengie Molina	.15
7	Roger Clemens	2.00
8	Lance Berkman	.50
9	Morgan Ensberg	.15
10	Roy Oswalt	.25
11	Andy Pettitte	.25
12	Craig Biggio	.25
13	Eric Chavez	.25
14	Barry Zito	.25
15	Huston Street	.15
16	Bobby Crosby	.15
17	Nick Swisher	.25
18	Rich Harden	.15
19	Vernon Wells	.25
20	Roy Halladay	.25
21	Alex Rios	.15
22	Orlando Hudson	.15
23	Shea Hillenbrand	.15
24	Gustavo Chacin	.15
25	Chipper Jones	.50
26	Andruw Jones	.50
27	Jeff Francoeur	.50
28	John Smoltz	.25
29	Tim Hudson	.25
30	Marcus Giles	.15
31	Carlos Lee	.25
32	Ben Sheets	.25
33	Rickie Weeks	.25
34	Chris Capuano	.15
35	Geoff Jenkins	.15
36	Brady Clark	.15
37	Albert Pujols	2.00
38	Jim Edmonds	.25
39	Chris Carpenter	.25
40	Mark Mulder	.25
41	Yadier Molina	.15
42	Scott Rolen	.25
43	Derek Lee	.50
44	Mark Prior	.75
45	Aramis Ramirez	.40
46	Carlos Zambrano	.25
47	Greg Maddux	1.50
48	Nomar Garciaparra	.50
49	Jonny Gomes	.25
50	Carl Crawford	.25
51	Scott Kazmir	.15
52	Jorge Cantu	.15
53	Julio Lugo	.15
54	Aubrey Huff	.15
55	Luis Gonzalez	.15
56	Brandon Webb	.50
57	Troy Glaus	.25
58	Shawn Green	.15
59	Craig Counsell	.15
60	Conor Jackson RC	.25
61	Jeff Kent	.25
62	Eric Gagne	.15
63	J.D. Drew	.25
64	Milton Bradley	.15
65	Jeff Weaver	.15
66	Cesar Izturis	.15
67	Jason Schmidt	.25
68	Moises Alou	.15
69	Pedro Feliz	.15
70	Randy Winn	.15
71	Omar Vizquel	.15
72	Noah Lowry	.15
73	Travis Hafner	.40
74	Victor Martinez	.25
75	C.C. Sabathia	.40
76	Grady Sizemore	.40
77	Coco Crisp	.15
78	Cliff Lee	.25
79	Raul Ibanez	.15
80	Ichiro Suzuki	1.00
81	Richie Sexson	.25
82	Felix Hernandez	.25
83	Adrian Beltre	.25
84	Jamie Moyer	.15
85	Miguel Cabrera	.75
86	A.J. Burnett	.15
87	Juan Pierre	.15
88	Carlos Delgado	.50
89	Dontrelle Willis	.25
90	Juan Encarnacion	.15
91	Carlos Beltran	.50
92	Jose Reyes	.75
93	David Wright	.75
94	Tom Glavine	.25
95	Mike Piazza	.75
96	Pedro Martinez	.75
97	Ryan Zimmerman RC	2.00
98	Nick Johnson	.15
99	Jose Vidro	.15
100	Jose Guillen	.15
101	Livan Hernandez	.15
102	John Patterson	.15
103	Miguel Tejada	.25
104	Melvin Mora	.15
105	Brian Roberts	.25
106	Erik Bedard	.25
107	Javy Lopez	.25
108	Rodrigo Lopez	.15
109	Jake Peavy	.50
110	Mike Cameron	.15
111	Mark Loretta	.15
112	Brian Giles	.25
113	Trevor Hoffman	.15
114	Ramon Hernandez	.15
115	Bobby Abreu	.25
116	Chase Utley	.75
117	Pat Burrell	.25
118	Jimmy Rollins	.75
119	Ryan Howard	.75
120	Billy Wagner	.15
121	Jason Bay	.40
122	Oliver Perez	.15
123	Jack Wilson	.15
124	Zach Duke	.15
125	Robert Mackowiak	.15
126	Freddy Sanchez	.15
127	Mark Teixeira	.50
128	Michael Young	.25
129	Alfonso Soriano	.50
130	Hank Blalock	.25
131	Kenny Rogers	.15
132	Kevin Mench	.15
133	Manny Ramirez	.75
134	Josh Beckett	.50
135	David Ortiz	.75
136	Johnny Damon	.50
137	Edgar Renteria	.25
138	Curt Schilling	.75
139	Ken Griffey Jr.	1.50
140	Adam Dunn	.50
141	Felipe Lopez	.15
142	Wily Mo Pena	.15
143	Aaron Harang	.25
144	Sean Casey	.15
145	Todd Helton	.50
146	Garrett Atkins	.25
147	Matt Holliday	.40
148	Jeff Francis	.15
149	Clint Barmes	.15
150	Luis Gonzalez	.15
151	Mike Sweeney	.15
152	Zack Greinke	.25
153	Angel Berroa	.15
154	Emil Brown	.15
155	David DeJesus	.15
156	Ivan Rodriguez	.50
157	Jeremy Bonderman	.15
158	Brandon Inge	.15
159	Craig Monroe	.15
160	Chris Shelton	.15
161	Dmitri Young	.15
162	Johan Santana	.50
163	Joe Mauer	.50
164	Torii Hunter	.25
165	Shannon Stewart	.15
166	Scott Baker	.15
167	Brad Radke	.15
168	Jon Garland	.15
169	Tadahito Iguchi	.25
170	Paul Konerko	.25
171	Scott Podsednik	.15
172	Mark Buehrle	.25
173	Joe Crede	.15
174	Derek Jeter	2.00
175	Alex Rodriguez	1.50
176	Hideki Matsui	1.00
177	Randy Johnson	.75
178	Gary Sheffield	.40
179	Mariano Rivera	.40
180	Jason Giambi	.40
181	Joey Devine RC	.50
182	Alejandro Freire RC	.75
183	Craig Hansen RC	.50
184	Robert Andino RC	.50
185	Ryan Jorgensen RC	.50
186	Chris Demaria RC	.50
187	Jonah Bayliss RC	.50
188	Ryan Theriot RC	1.00
189	Steve Stemle RC	.50
190	Brian Myrow RC	.50
191	Chris Heintz RC	.50
192	Ron Flores RC	.50
193	Danny Sandoval RC	.50
194	Craig Breslow RC	.50
195	Jeremy Accardo RC	.50
196	Jeff Harris RC	.50
197	Tim Corcoran RC	.50
198	Scott Feldman RC	1.00
199	Robinson Cano RC	1.00
200	Jason Bergmann RC	.50
201	Ken Griffey Jr.	4.00
202	Frank Thomas	1.00
203	Chipper Jones	2.00
204	Tony Clark	.50
205	Mike Lieberthal	.50
206	Manny Ramirez	2.00
207	Phil Nevin	.50
208	Derek Jeter	6.00
209	Preston Wilson	.50
210	Billy Wagner	.50
211	Alex Rodriguez	6.00
212	Trot Nixon	1.00
213	Jaret Wright	.50
214	Nomar Garciaparra	1.50
215	Paul Konerko	1.00
216	Paul Wilson	.50
217	Dustin Hermanson	.50
218	Todd Walker	.50
219	Matt Morris	.50
220	Darin Erstad	.50
221	Todd Helton	1.50
222	Geoff Jenkins	.50
223	Eric Chavez	.50
224	Kris Benson	.50
225	Jon Garland	.50
226	Troy Glaus	1.00
227	Vernon Wells	1.00
228	Michael Cuddyer	.50
229	Justin Verlander RC	2.00
230	Pat Burrell	2.00
231	Mark Mulder	.50
232	Corey Patterson	.50
233	J.D. Drew	1.00
234	Austin Kearns	.50
235	Felipe Lopez	.50
236	Sean Burroughs	.50
237	Ben Sheets	1.00
238	Brett Myers	.50
239	Josh Beckett	1.50
240	Barry Zito	.75
241	Adrian Gonzalez	1.00
242	Rocco Baldelli	.50
243	Chris Burke	.50
244	Joe Mauer	1.50
245	Mark Prior	1.00
246	Mark Teixeira	2.00
247	Khalil Greene	.50
248	Zack Greinke	.50
249	Prince Fielder RC	6.00
250	Rickie Weeks	1.00
251	Kenji Johjima RC	10.00

Gold

Gold (1-200):	2-3X
Inserted 1:1	
Gold (201-251):	2-3X
Inserted 1:13	

AUTOGRAPHics

Inserted 1:576 Hobby
No Pricing

Diamond Producers

		NM/M
Complete Set (25):		15.00
Common Player:		.50
DP1	Derek Jeter	3.00
DP2	Chipper Jones	1.00
DP3	Jim Edmonds	.75
DP4	Ken Griffey Jr.	2.00
DP5	David Ortiz	1.00
DP6	Manny Ramirez	.75
DP7	Mark Teixeira	.75
DP8	Alex Rodriguez	3.00
DP9	Jeff Kent	.50
DP10	Albert Pujols	3.00
DP11	Todd Helton	.75
DP12	Miguel Cabrera	1.00
DP13	Hideki Matsui	1.00
DP14	Derek Lee	.75
DP15	Vladimir Guerrero	1.00
DP16	Miguel Tejada	.75
DP17	Jorge Cantu	.50
DP18	Travis Hafner	.75
DP19	Pat Burrell	.50
DP20	Bobby Abreu	.50
DP21	David Wright	2.00
DP22	Jason Bay	.75
DP23	Adam Dunn	.75
DP24	Eric Chavez	.50
DP25	Paul Konerko	.50

Feel the Game

		NM/M
Common Player:		4.00
BA	Bobby Abreu	6.00
JB	Josh Beckett	6.00
CB	Carlos Beltran	8.00
AB	Adrian Beltre	6.00
EC	Eric Chavez	4.00
MC	Matt Clement/SP	8.00
CD	Carlos Delgado	6.00
BG	Brian Giles	4.00
TG	Troy Glaus	6.00
SG	Shawn Green	4.00
KG	Ken Griffey Jr.	20.00
VG	Vladimir Guerrero	8.00
FH	Felix Hernandez	8.00
DJ	Derek Jeter	20.00
RJ	Randy Johnson/SP	10.00
AJ	Andruw Jones	8.00
CJ	Chipper Jones	8.00
GM	Greg Maddux	10.00
MO	Magglio Ordonez	4.00
MP	Mike Piazza	10.00
AP	Albert Pujols	20.00
MR	Manny Ramirez	10.00
JR	Jose Reyes/SP	8.00
IR	Ivan Rodriguez	6.00
RS	Richie Sexson	4.00
AS	Alfonso Soriano	8.00
MT	Miguel Tejada	8.00
FT	Frank Thomas/SP	40.00
PW	Preston Wilson	4.00
DW	David Wright	15.00

Home Run Kings

		NM/M
Complete Set (15):		10.00
Common Player:		.50
HRK1	Albert Pujols	3.00
HRK2	Ken Griffey Jr.	2.00
HRK3	Andruw Jones	1.00
HRK4	Alex Rodriguez	3.00
HRK5	David Ortiz	3.00
HRK6	Manny Ramirez	1.00
HRK7	Derek Lee	.75
HRK8	Mark Teixeira	.75
HRK9	Adam Dunn	.75
HRK10	Paul Konerko	.50
HRK11	Richie Sexson	.50
HRK12	Alfonso Soriano	.75
HRK13	Vladimir Guerrero	1.00
HRK14	Gary Sheffield	.75
HRK15	Mike Piazza	1.00

Midsummer Classic Kings

		NM/M
Complete Set (10):		10.00
Common Player:		.50
MCK1	Ken Griffey Jr.	2.00
MCK2	Mike Piazza	1.00
MCK3	Derek Jeter	3.00
MCK4	Roger Clemens	3.00
MCK5	Randy Johnson	1.00
MCK6	Miguel Tejada	.75
MCK7	Alfonso Soriano	.75
MCK8	Garret Anderson	.50
MCK9	Pedro Martinez	1.00
MCK10	Ivan Rodriguez	.75

RBI Kings

		NM/M
Complete Set (20):		15.00
Common Player:		.50
RBI1	Ken Griffey Jr.	2.00
RBI2	David Ortiz	1.00
RBI3	Manny Ramirez	1.00
RBI4	Mark Teixeira	.75
RBI5	Alex Rodriguez	3.00
RBI6	Andruw Jones	1.00
RBI7	Jeff Bagwell	.75
RBI8	Gary Sheffield	.75
RBI9	Richie Sexson	.50
RBI10	Jeff Kent	.50
RBI11	Albert Pujols	3.00
RBI12	Todd Helton	.75
RBI13	Miguel Cabrera	1.00
RBI14	Hideki Matsui	2.00
RBI15	Carlos Delgado	.75
RBI16	Carlos Lee	.50
RBI17	Derek Lee	.75
RBI18	Vladimir Guerrero	1.00
RBI19	Luis Gonzalez	.50
RBI20	Mike Piazza	1.00

Strikeout Kings

		NM/M
Complete Set (10):		8.00
Common Player:		.50
SOK1	Roger Clemens	3.00
SOK2	Johan Santana	1.00
SOK3	Jake Peavy	.50
SOK4	Randy Johnson	1.00
SOK5	Curt Schilling	.50
SOK6	Chris Carpenter	.75
SOK7	Pedro Martinez	1.00
SOK8	Mark Prior	.50
SOK9	Carlos Zambrano	.50
SOK10	John Smoltz	.50

Fine Fabrics

		NM/M
BA	Bobby Abreu	6.00
JB	Josh Beckett	6.00
CB	Carlos Beltran	8.00

AB	Adrian Beltre	6.00
HB	Hank Blalock	6.00
SB	Sean Burroughs	4.00
EC	Eric Chavez	4.00
RC	Roger Clemens/SP	15.00
MC	Matt Clement	4.00
BC	Bobby Crosby	6.00
CD	Carlos Delgado	4.00
JD	J.D. Drew	4.00
AD	Adam Dunn	8.00
SF	Steve Finley	4.00
JG	Jason Giambi	10.00
BG	Brian Giles	4.00
TG	Troy Glaus	4.00
SG	Shawn Green	4.00
KH	Khalil Greene/SP	4.00
KG	Ken Griffey Jr.	20.00
VG	Vladimir Guerrero	8.00
TH	Travis Hafner	8.00
FH	Felix Hernandez	8.00
RH	Ramon Hernandez	4.00
RY	Ryan Howard	15.00
DJ	Derek Jeter	20.00
RJ	Randy Johnson/SP	10.00
AJ	Andruw Jones	8.00
CJ	Chipper Jones	8.00
JK	Jeff Kent	4.00
RK	Ryan Klesko	4.00
DL	Derek Lee	8.00
GM	Greg Maddux	10.00
MO	Magglio Ordonez	4.00
DO	David Ortiz	8.00
CP	Corey Patterson	6.00
MP	Mike Piazza	8.00
JP	Jorge Posada	4.00
AP	Albert Pujols	20.00
MR	Manny Ramirez	10.00
JR	Jose Reyes	8.00
BR	Brian Roberts	6.00
IR	Ivan Rodriguez	6.00
SR	Scott Rolen	10.00
RS	Richie Sexson	6.00
JS	John Smoltz	8.00
AS	Alfonso Soriano	6.00
SS	Sammy Sosa	10.00
HS	Huston Street	4.00
TX	Mark Teixeira	8.00
MT	Miguel Tejada	8.00
FT	Frank Thomas	8.00
CU	Chase Utley	15.00
VW	Vernon Wells	6.00
BW	Bernie Williams	6.00
WI	Dontrelle Willis	6.00
PW	Preston Wilson	4.00
KW	Kerry Wood	6.00
DW	David Wright	15.00
BZ	Barry Zito	6.00

Rising Stars

		NM/M
Complete Set (10):		10.00
Common Player:		.50
URS1	Ryan Howard	3.00
URS2	Huston Street	.50
URS3	Jeff Francoeur	.75
URS4	Felix Hernandez	1.50
URS5	Chase Utley	2.00
URS6	Robinson Cano	1.00
URS7	Zachary Duke	.50
URS8	Scott Kazmir	1.00
URS9	Willy Taveras	.50
URS10	Tadahito Iguchi	1.00

2007 Ultra

		NM/M
Complete Set (250):		
Common Player (1-200):		.15
Common RC (201-250):		1.00
Hobby SE Pack (15):		12.00
Hobby SE Box (5):		55.00
1	Brandon Webb	.25
2	Randy Johnson	.75
3	Conor Jackson	.15
4	Stephen Drew	.25
5	Eric Byrnes	.25
6	Carlos Quentin	.25
7	Andruw Jones	.50
8	Chipper Jones	.75

9	Jeff Francoeur	.50
10	Tim Hudson	.25
11	John Smoltz	.50
12	Ed Renteria	.25
13	Erik Bedard	.25
14	Kris Benson	.15
15	Miguel Tejada	.50
16	Nicholas Markakis	.25
17	Brian Roberts	.25
18	Melvin Mora	.15
19	Aubrey Huff	.15
20	Curt Schilling	.75
21	Jonathan Papelbon	1.00
22	Josh Beckett	.50
23	Jason Varitek	.25
24	David Ortiz	1.00
25	Manny Ramirez	.75
26	J.D. Drew	.25
27	Carlos Zambrano	.25
28	Derrek Lee	.50
29	Aramis Ramirez	.50
30	Alfonso Soriano	.75
31	Rich Hill	.15
32	Jacque Jones	.15
33	A.J. Pierzynski	.15
34	Jermaine Dye	.25
35	Paul Konerko	.25
36	Bobby Jenks	.15
37	Jon Garland	.15
38	Mark Buehrle	.25
39	Tadahito Iguchi	.15
40	Adam Dunn	.50
41	Ken Griffey Jr.	1.50
42	Aaron Harang	.15
43	Bronson Arroyo	.15
44	Ryan Freel	.15
45	Brandon Phillips	.25
46	Grady Sizemore	1.00
47	Travis Hafner	.25
48	Victor Martinez	.25
49	Jhonny Peralta	.25
50	C.C. Sabathia	.25
51	Jeremy Sowers	.15
52	Ryan Garko	.15
53	Garrett Atkins	.25
54	Willy Taveras	.15
55	Todd Helton	.50
56	Jeff Francis	.15
57	Brad Hawpe	.15
58	Matt Holliday	.50
59	Justin Verlander	.75
60	Jeremy Bonderman	.50
61	Magglio Ordonez	.50
62	Ivan Rodriguez	.50
63	Gary Sheffield	.25
64	Kenny Rogers	.15
65	Brandon Inge	.15
66	Anibal Sanchez	.15
67	Scott Olsen	.15
68	Dontrelle Willis	.50
69	Dan Uggla	.25
70	Hanley Ramirez	1.00
71	Miguel Cabrera	1.00
72	Jeremy Hermida	.15
73	Roy Oswalt	.50
74	Brad Lidge	.15
75	Lance Berkman	.50
76	Carlos Lee	.50
77	Morgan Ensberg	.15
78	Craig Biggio	.50
79	Reggie Sanders	.15
80	Mike Sweeney	.15
81	Mark Teahen	.15
82	John Buck	.15
83	Mark Grudzielanek	.15
84	Gary Matthews	.15
85	Vladimir Guerrero	1.00
86	Garret Anderson	.25
87	Howie Kendrick	.25
88	Jered Weaver	.50
89	Chone Figgins	.15
90	Bartolo Colon	.15
91	Francisco Rodriguez	.25
92	Nomar Garciaparra	.75
93	Andre Ethier	.15
94	Rafael Furcal	.25
95	Jeff Kent	.50
96	Derek Lowe	.25
97	Jason Schmidt	.25
98	Takashi Saito	.25
99	Ben Sheets	.25
100	Prince Fielder	1.00
101	Bill Hall	.15
102	Rickie Weeks	.25
103	Francisco Cordero	.15
104	J.J. Hardy	.25
105	Johan Santana	.75
106	Justin Morneau	.50

107	Joe Mauer	.25
108	Joe Nathan	.15
109	Torii Hunter	.25
110	Michael Cuddyer	.15
111	Boof Bonser	.15
112	Tom Glavine	.50
113	Pedro Martinez	.75
114	Billy Wagner	.15
115	Jose Reyes	1.00
116	David Wright	1.00
117	Carlos Delgado	.50
118	Carlos Beltran	.50
119	Alex Rodriguez	2.00
120	Chien-Ming Wang	1.00
121	Mariano Rivera	.50
122	Bobby Abreu	.50
123	Hideki Matsui	1.50
124	Johnny Damon	.75
125	Robinson Cano	.75
126	Derek Jeter	2.00
127	Nick Swisher	.25
128	Eric Chavez	.15
129	Jason Kendall	.15
130	Bobby Crosby	.15
131	Huston Street	.15
132	Danny Haren	.15
133	Rich Harden	.15
134	Mike Piazza	.75
135	Chase Utley	1.00
136	Jimmy Rollins	.75
137	Aaron Rowand	.25
138	Jamie Moyer	.15
139	Cole Hamels	.50
140	Pat Burrell	.25
141	Ryan Howard	1.50
142	Freddy Sanchez	.15
143	Zachary Duke	.15
144	Ian Snell	.15
145	Jack Wilson	.15
146	Jason Bay	.25
147	Albert Pujols	2.00
148	Scott Rolen	.50
149	Jim Edmonds	.25
150	Chris Carpenter	.25
151	Yadier Molina	.50
152	Adam Wainwright	.25
153	David Eckstein	.15
154	Trevor Hoffman	.15
155	Brian Giles	.15
156	Adrian Gonzalez	.25
157	Jake Peavy	.50
158	Khalil Greene	.15
159	Chris Young	.15
160	Greg Maddux	1.00
161	Mike Cameron	.15
162	Matt Cain	.15
163	Matt Morris	.15
164	Pedro Feliz	.15
165	Omar Vizquel	.15
166	Randy Winn	.15
167	Barry Zito	.25
168	Adrian Beltre	.15
169	Yuniesky Betancourt	.15
170	Richie Sexson	.25
171	Raul Ibanez	.15
172	Kenji Johjima	.25
173	Ichiro Suzuki	1.50
174	Felix Hernandez	.50
175	Scott Kazmir	.25
176	Carl Crawford	.25
177	B.J. Upton	.25
178	James Shields	.15
179	Rocco Baldelli	.15
180	Jorge Cantu	.15
181	Ty Wigginton	.15
182	Mark Teixeira	.50
183	Hank Blalock	.25
184	Ian Kinsler	.25
185	Michael Young	.25
186	Vicente Padilla	.15
187	Akinori Otsuka	.15
188	Kenny Lofton	.15
189	A.J. Burnett	.15
190	Roy Halladay	.25
191	B.J. Ryan	.15
192	Vernon Wells	.25
193	Alex Rios	.50
194	Troy Glaus	.25
195	Frank Thomas	.75
196	Ryan Zimmerman	.50
197	Michael O'Connor	.15
198	Chad Cordero	.15
199	Nick Johnson	.15
200	Felipe Lopez	.15
201	Miguel Montero	1.00
202	Doug Slaten RC	1.00
203	Joseph Bisenius RC	1.00
204	Jared Burton RC	1.00
205	Kevin Cameron RC	1.00
206	Matt Chico (RC)	1.00
207	Chris Stewart RC	1.00
208	Josh Smith RC	2.00
209	Zack Segovia (RC)	1.00
210	John Danks (RC)	2.00
211	Lee Gardner (RC)	1.00
212	Jeff Baker (RC)	2.00
213	Jamie Burke (RC)	1.00
214	Phil Hughes (RC)	3.00
215	Mike Rabelo RC	1.00
216	Jose Garcia RC	1.00
217	Hector Gimenez (RC)	1.00
218	Jesus Flores RC	1.00
219	Brandon Morrow RC	3.00
220	Hideki Okajima RC	1.00
221	Jay Marshall RC	1.00
222	Matt Lindstrom (RC)	1.00
223	Juan Salas (RC)	1.00
224	Juan Perez RC	1.00

225	Sean Henn (RC)	1.00
226	Travis Buck (RC)	1.00
227	Gustavo Molina RC	1.00
228	Hunter Pence (RC)	3.00
229	Michael Bourn (RC)	1.00
230	Brian Barden RC	1.00
231	Donald Kelly (RC)	1.00
232	Joakim Soria RC	2.00
233	Cesar Jimenez RC	1.00
234	Levale Speigner RC	2.00
235	Micah Owings (RC)	1.00
236	Brian Stokes (RC)	1.00
237	Joaquin Arias (RC)	1.00
238	Josh Hamilton (RC)	2.00
239	Daisuke Matsuzaka RC	4.00
240	Alejandro De Aza RC	1.00
241	Kory Casto (RC)	1.00
242	Troy Tulowitzki (RC)	4.00
243	Akinori Iwamura RC	2.00
244	Angel Sanchez RC	1.00
245	Ryan Braun (RC)	8.00
246	Alex Gordon RC	2.00
247	Elijah Dukes RC	1.00
248	Kei Igawa RC	1.00
249	Kevin Kouzmanoff (RC)	1.00
250	Delmon Young (RC)	1.00

Printing Plates

Production one set per color.

Gold

Gold (1-200):	2-3X
Gold RC (201-250):	1X
Inserted 1:10 Hobby	

Retail

Retail (1-200):	.5X
Retail RC (201-250):	.5X

Iron Man

	NM/M
Common Ripken (1-50):	5.00
Autograph:	No Pricing
Production 10 Sets	

Autographics

		NM/M
Common Auto.:		3.00
AG	Alex Gordon/499	30.00
AH	Aaron Harang/499	15.00
CH	Clay Hensley/499	10.00
JA	Jason Bay/499	15.00
JB	Joe Blanton/499	10.00
JE	Johnny Estrada/132	10.00
JS	Johan Santana/173	30.00
KG	Khalil Greene/499	15.00
KI	Kei Igawa/199	25.00

Dual Materials

		NM/M
Common Player:		5.00
Production 160 unless noted.		
Gold:		1-1.5x
Production 20-75		
Patch:		No Pricing
Production 25 Sets		
AB	A.J. Burnett	5.00
AE	Andre Ethier	5.00
AJ	Andruw Jones	8.00
AK	Austin Kearns	5.00
AL	Adam LaRoche	5.00
AN	Garret Anderson	5.00
AP	Albert Pujols	20.00
AS	Anibal Sanchez	5.00
BA	Bobby Abreu	5.00
BC	Bobby Crosby	5.00
BE	Adrian Beltre	5.00
BG	Brian Giles	5.00
BI	Craig Biggio	8.00
BJ	Bobby Jenks	5.00
BL	Brad Lidge	5.00
BM	Brandon McCarthy	5.00
BR	Brian Roberts	5.00
BS	Ben Sheets	5.00
BW	Brandon Webb	5.00
CA	Carlos Beltran	10.00
CB	Chris Burke	5.00
CC	Carl Crawford	8.00
CF	Chone Figgins	5.00
CH	Chris Carpenter	5.00
CJ	Conor Jackson	5.00
CK	Casey Kotchman	5.00
CL	Carlos Lee	8.00
CP	Corey Patterson	5.00
CR	Coco Crisp	5.00
CS	C.C. Sabathia	8.00
CU	Curt Schilling	10.00
DJ	Derek Jeter	20.00

DL	Derek Lowe	8.00
DO	David Ortiz	10.00
DR	J.D. Drew	5.00
DU	Dan Uggla	5.00
DW	David Wells	5.00
ED	Jim Edmonds	5.00
ES	Ervin Santana	5.00
FG	Freddy Garcia	5.00
FH	Felix Hernandez	10.00
GA	Garrett Atkins	5.00
GJ	Geoff Jenkins	5.00
GM	Greg Maddux	15.00
GS	Gary Sheffield	10.00
HE	Todd Helton	8.00
HO	Trevor Hoffman	8.00
HR	Hanley Ramirez	10.00
HU	Torii Hunter	8.00
IS	Ian Snell	5.00
JB	Jeremy Bonderman	5.00
JC	Chipper Jones	10.00
JD	Jermaine Dye	5.00
JG	Jonny Gomes	5.00
JH	J.J. Hardy	8.00
JJ	Josh Johnson	5.00
JK	Jeff Kent	8.00
JM	Justin Morneau	10.00
JN	Joe Nathan	5.00
JO	Josh Beckett	15.00
JP	Jorge Posada	10.00
JS	James Shields	8.00
JV	Jason Varitek	10.00
JW	Josh Willingham	5.00
KG	Khalil Greene	8.00
KW	Kerry Wood	5.00
LB	Lance Berkman	8.00
LE	Derrek Lee	10.00
LG	Luis Gonzalez	5.00
LM	Lastings Milledge	5.00
LS	Luke Scott	5.00
MC	Matt Cain	5.00
ME	Melky Cabrera	10.00
MH	Matt Holliday	5.00
MI	Mike Mussina	10.00
MM	Melvin Mora	5.00
MO	Magglio Ordonez	8.00
MR	Manny Ramirez	10.00
MS	Mike Sweeney	5.00
MT	Miguel Tejada	8.00
MU	Mark Mulder	5.00
PE	Andy Pettitte	8.00
PF	Prince Fielder	15.00
PJ	Jhonny Peralta	5.00
RH	Rich Harden	5.00
SC	Jason Schmidt	5.00
SI	Grady Sizemore	20.00
SO	Scott Olsen	5.00
TE	Mark Teixeira	10.00
TH	Travis Hafner	8.00
TW	Tim Wakefield	5.00
VG	Vladimir Guerrero	10.00
VM	Victor Martinez	8.00
VW	Vernon Wells	5.00
WI	Dontrelle Willis	5.00
ZD	Zachary Duke	5.00

Faces of the Game Materials

		NM/M
Common Jersey:		5.00
AB	Adrian Beltre	5.00
AJ	Andruw Jones	8.00
BS	Ben Sheets	5.00
CJ	Chipper Jones	8.00
CS	C.C. Sabathia	5.00
CU	Chase Utley	10.00
DJ	Derek Jeter	20.00
FR	Francisco Rodriguez	5.00
GM	Greg Maddux	10.00
HU	Torii Hunter	5.00
JB	Jason Bay	5.00
JG	Jason Giambi	8.00
KG	Ken Griffey Jr.	15.00
LG	Luis Gonzalez	5.00
MC	Miguel Cabrera	8.00
MP	Mike Piazza	8.00
MR	Mariano Rivera	10.00
OV	Omar Vizquel	5.00
TG	Tom Glavine	5.00
TH	Trevor Hoffman	5.00

Feel the Game Materials

		NM/M
Common Jersey:		5.00
AP	Albert Pujols	20.00
BA	Bobby Abreu	5.00
BR	Brian Roberts	5.00
BW	Brandon Webb	5.00

CC	Chris Carpenter	8.00
CJ	Chipper Jones	8.00
CR	Carl Crawford	5.00
CS	Curt Schilling	8.00
CU	Chase Utley	10.00
CZ	Carlos Zambrano	8.00
DJ	Derek Jeter	20.00
DW	Dontrelle Willis	5.00
EC	Eric Chavez	5.00
GS	Grady Sizemore	10.00
HR	Hanley Ramirez	8.00
IR	Ivan Rodriguez	8.00
JM	Justin Morneau	8.00
JP	Jonathan Papelbon	10.00
JR	Jose Reyes	10.00
JS	John Smoltz	8.00
KJ	Ken Griffey Jr.	15.00
KJ	Kenji Johjima	8.00
LB	Lance Berkman	5.00
LG	Luis Gonzalez	5.00
MC	Miguel Cabrera	8.00
RC	Robinson Cano	10.00
RJ	Randy Johnson	8.00
SA	Johan Santana	8.00
SC	Jason Schmidt	5.00
VG	Vladimir Guerrero	8.00

Hitting Machines Materials

		NM/M
Common Jersey:		5.00
AR	Aramis Ramirez	8.00
AS	Alfonso Soriano	8.00
BI	Craig Biggio	8.00
CB	Carlos Beltran	8.00
DO	David Ortiz	8.00
FS	Freddy Sanchez	5.00
FT	Frank Thomas	10.00
JK	Jeff Kent	5.00
JM	Joe Mauer	8.00
JT	Jim Thome	8.00
MT	Mark Teixeira	8.00
NS	Nick Swisher	5.00
TE	Miguel Tejada	5.00
TG	Troy Glaus	5.00
TH	Todd Helton	8.00

Strike Zone Materials

		NM/M
Common Player:		5.00
BZ	Barry Zito	5.00
CC	C.C. Sabathia	5.00
CZ	Carlos Zambrano	8.00
DW	Dontrelle Willis	5.00
JS	Johan Santana	8.00
JV	Justin Verlander	8.00
MM	Mike Mussina	8.00
PM	Pedro Martinez	8.00
RH	Roy Halladay	8.00
RO	Roy Oswalt	8.00

Swing Kings Materials

		NM/M
Common Player:		5.00
AD	Adam Dunn	8.00
AJ	Andruw Jones	8.00
AP	Albert Pujols	20.00
AR	Aramis Ramirez	8.00
AS	Alfonso Soriano	8.00
CB	Carlos Beltran	8.00
CL	Carlos Lee	5.00
DJ	Derek Jeter	20.00
DO	David Ortiz	8.00
FT	Frank Thomas	10.00
GS	Gary Sheffield	8.00
HE	Todd Helton	8.00
JM	Joe Mauer	8.00
JR	Jose Reyes	10.00
JT	Jim Thome	8.00
KG	Ken Griffey Jr.	15.00
MC	Miguel Cabrera	8.00
MR	Manny Ramirez	8.00
MT	Miguel Tejada	5.00
NG	Nomar Garciaparra	5.00
PB	Pat Burrell	5.00
TE	Mark Teixeira	8.00
TH	Travis Hafner	5.00
VG	Vladimir Guerrero	8.00
VW	Vernon Wells	5.00

Ultragraphs

		NM/M
Common Auto.:		8.00
AK	Austin Kearns/499	8.00
AL	Adam LaRoche/499	8.00
AN	Garret Anderson/499	10.00
BB	Boof Bonser/499	8.00
GA	Garrett Atkins/499	8.00
JG	Jorge Julio/499	8.00
JN	Joe Nathan/299	10.00
JW	Jered Weaver/499	10.00
MM	Mark Mulder/319	8.00
RW	Rickie Weeks/499	10.00
TH	Travis Hafner/499	10.00
ZG	Zack Greinke/199	20.00

Faces of the Game

		NM/M
Common Player:		.50
AB	Adrian Beltre	.50
AJ	Andruw Jones	.75
BS	Ben Sheets	.50
CJ	Chipper Jones	1.00
CS	C.C. Sabathia	.75
CU	Chase Utley	1.00
DJ	Derek Jeter	3.00
FR	Francisco Rodriguez	.50
GM	Greg Maddux	2.00
HO	Trevor Hoffman	.50

Swing Kings

		NM/M
	Common Player:	.50
AD	Adam Dunn	.75
AJ	Andruw Jones	1.00
AP	Albert Pujols	3.00
AR	Aramis Ramirez	.75
AS	Alfonso Soriano	1.00
CB	Carlos Beltran	.75
CL	Carlos Lee	.75
DJ	Derek Jeter	3.00
DO	David Ortiz	1.00
FT	Frank Thomas	1.00
GS	Gary Sheffield	.75
HE	Todd Helton	.75
JM	Joe Mauer	.75
JR	Jose Reyes	2.00
JT	Jim Thome	.75
KG	Ken Griffey Jr.	2.00
MC	Miguel Cabrera	1.00
MR	Manny Ramirez	1.00
MT	Miguel Tejada	.75
NG	Nomar Garciaparra	1.00
PB	Pat Burrell	.75
TE	Mark Teixeira	.75
TH	Travis Hafner	.75
VG	Vladimir Guerrero	1.00
VW	Vernon Wells	.50

Rookies Auto.

		NM/M
	Production 299 unless noted.	
	Parallel:	1x
	Production 99-349	
201	Miguel Montero	10.00
202	Doug Slaten	10.00
203	Joseph Bisenius	10.00
204	Jared Burton	10.00
205	Kevin Cameron	10.00
206	Matt Chico	10.00
207	Chris Stewart	10.00
209	Zack Segovia	15.00
210	John Danks	10.00
213	Jamie Burke	15.00
215	Mike Rabelo	10.00
217	Hector Gimenez	10.00
219	Brandon Morrow	25.00
221	Jay Marshall	10.00
225	Sean Henn	10.00
226	Travis Buck	15.00
227	Gustavo Molina	10.00
229	Michael Bourn	15.00
232	Joakim Soria	25.00
234	Levale Speigner	10.00
236	Brian Stokes	10.00
237	Joaquin Arias	10.00

Rookies Auto.-Retail

		NM/M
	Common Autograph:	10.00
201	Miguel Montero	10.00
202	Doug Slaten	10.00
204	Jared Burton/SP	10.00
205	Kevin Cameron/SP	10.00
206	Matt Chico	10.00
207	Chris Stewart	10.00
209	Zack Segovia	10.00
215	Mike Rabelo	15.00
217	Hector Gimenez	10.00
225	Sean Henn	10.00
229	Michael Bourn/SP	15.00
234	Levale Speigner	10.00
236	Brian Stokes	10.00
237	Joaquin Arias	10.00

1989 Upper Deck Promos

WALLY JOYNER

In 1988 Upper Deck produced a two-card test set to be distributed as samples for the 1989 set; 18,000 of each card were produced. The cards were distributed to dealers at the 1988 National Sports Collectors Convention. Two other variations of the promo cards exist. Both variations involve differences in where the hologram was placed. Fewer than 5,000 of one of the hologram variations exist, while less than 1,000 of the third variation exist. Joyner and Buice were selected for the promo cards because of a reported investment interest in Upper Deck; they were later required to sell their interest in the card company due to their active-player status.

		NM/M
	Complete Set A (2):	5.00
	Complete Set B (2):	9.00
	Complete Set C (2):	15.00
1a	DeWayne Buice (1/2" x 3/16" hologram at bottom)	2.00
1b	DeWayne Buice (Hologram extends to bottom edge.)	3.00
1c	DeWayne Buice (Hologram at top.)	5.00
700a	Wally Joyner (1/2" x 3/16" hologram at bottom)	2.50
700b	Wally Joyner (Hologram extends to bottom edge.)	6.00
700c	Wally Joyner (Hologram at top.)	10.00

1989 Upper Deck Show Samples

Tommy John

At the Nov. 26-27, 1988 Anaheim card show, Upper Deck distributed samples of its forthcoming premiere set. While card fronts are nearly identical to the same players' issued versions (except they lack the position indicator at top-right), the backs are blank, also lacking the hologram. All cards in this sample distribution are from the range of card numbers between 206-250, in five contiguous groups of five, with gaps of five between them. The samples are listed here in alphabetical order. Uncut sheets of the samples were reported to be widely available at the show.

		NM/M
	Complete Set (25):	90.00
	Common Player:	3.00
	Uncut Sheet (25):	100.00
	Mike Aldrete	3.00
	Andy Allanson	3.00
	Scott Bailes	3.00
	Phil Bradley	3.00
	Scott Bradley	3.00
	Jay Buhner	3.00
	Brett Butler	3.00
	John Candelaria	3.00
	Bruce Fields	3.00
	Von Hayes	3.00
	Rickey Henderson	15.00
	Steve Jeltz	3.00
	Tommy John	4.50
	Ron Kittle	3.00
	Bob Melvin	3.00
	Lance Parrish	3.00
	Willie Randolph	4.50
	Harold Reynolds	3.00
	Rafael Santana	3.00
	Rod Scurry	3.00
	Chris Speier	3.00
	Greg Swindell	3.00
	Kent Tekulve	3.00
	Matt Williams	3.00
	Paul Zuvella	3.00

1989 Upper Deck

This premiere "Collector's Choice" issue from Upper Deck contains 700 cards (2-1/2" x 3-1/2")

Dale Murphy

with full-color photos on both sides. The first 26 cards feature Star Rookies. The set also includes 26 special portrait cards with team checklist backs and seven numerical checklist cards. Major 1988 award winners (Cy Young, Rookie of Year, MVP) are honored on 10 cards in the set, in addition to their individual player cards. There are also special cards for the Most Valuable Players in both League Championship series and the World Series. The card fronts feature player photos framed by a white border. A vertical brown and green artist's rendition of the runner's lane that leads from home plate to first base is found along the right margin. Backs carry full-color action poses that fill the card back, except for a compact (yet complete) stats chart. A high-number series, cards 701-800, featuring rookies and traded players, was released in mid-season in foil packs mixed within the complete set, in boxed complete sets and in high number set boxes.

		NM/M
	Unopened Fact. Set (800):	80.00
	Complete Set (800):	45.00
	Complete Low Set (700):	40.00
	Complete High Set (100):	5.00
	Common Player:	.05
	Low Foil Pack (15):	4.00
	Low Foil Box (36):	100.00
	High Foil Pack (15):	2.00
	High Foil Box (36):	60.00
1	Ken Griffey Jr. RC	40.00
2	Luis Medina RC	.05
3	Tony Chance RC	.05
4	Dave Otto RC	.05
5	Sandy Alomar, Jr. RC	1.00
6	Rolando Roomes RC	.05
7	David West RC	.05
8	Cris Carpenter RC	.05
9	Gregg Jefferies	.25
10	Doug Dascenzo RC	.05
11	Ron Jones RC	.05
12	Luis de los Santos RC	.05
13a	Gary Sheffield RC ("SS" upside-down)	8.00
13b	Gary Sheffield RC ("SS" correct)	8.00
14	Mike Harkey RC	.05
15	Lance Blankenship RC	.05
16	William Brennan RC	.05
17	John Smoltz	.60
18	Ramon Martinez RC	.25
19	Mark Lemke RC	.05
20	Juan Bell RC	.05
21	Rey Palacios RC	.05
22	Felix Jose RC	.05
23	Van Snider RC	.05
24	Dante Bichette RC	.75
25	Randy Johnson RC	10.00
26	Carlos Quintana RC	.05
27	Star Rookie Checklist 1-26	.05
28	Mike Schooler RC	.05
29	Randy St. Claire	.05
30	Jerald Clark RC	.05
31	Kevin Gross	.05
32	Dan Firova RC	.05
33	Jeff Calhoun	.05
34	Tommy Hinzo	.05
35	Ricky Jordan RC	.05
36	Larry Parrish	.05
37	Bret Saberhagen	.05
38	Mike Smithson	.05
39	Dave Dravecky	.05
40	Ed Romero	.05
41	Jeff Musselman	.05
42	Ed Hearn	.05
43	Rance Mulliniks	.05
44	Jim Eisenreich	.05
45	Sil Campusano RC	.05
46	Mike Krukow	.05
47	Paul Gibson RC	.05
48	Mike LaCoss	.05
49	Larry Herndon	.05
50	Scott Garrelts	.05
51	Dwayne Henry	.05
52	Jim Acker	.05
53	Steve Sax	.05
54	Pete O'Brien	.05
55	Paul Runge	.05
56	Rick Rhoden	.05
57	John Dopson RC	.05
58	Casey Candaele	.05
59	Dave Righetti	.05
60	Joe Hesketh	.05
61	Frank DiPino	.05
62	Tim Laudner	.05
63	Jamie Moyer	.05
64	Fred Toliver	.05
65	Mitch Webster	.05
66	John Tudor	.05
67	John Cangelosi	.05
68	Mike Devereaux	.05
69	Brian Fisher	.05
70	Mike Marshall	.05
71	Zane Smith	.05
72a	Brian Holton (Ball not visible on card front, photo actually Shawn Hillegas.)	.75
72b	Brian Holton (Ball visible, correct photo.)	.05
73	Jose Guzman	.05
74	Rick Mahler	.05
75	John Shelby	.05
76	Jim Deshaies	.05
77	Bobby Meacham	.05
78	Bryn Smith	.05
79	Joaquin Andujar	.05
80	Richard Dotson	.05
81	Charlie Lea	.05
82	Calvin Schiraldi	.05
83	Les Straker	.05
84	Les Lancaster	.05
85	Allan Anderson	.05
86	Junior Ortiz	.05
87	Jesse Orosco	.05
88	Felix Fermin	.05
89	Dave Anderson	.05
90	Rafael Belliard	.05
91	Franklin Stubbs	.05
92	Cecil Espy	.05
93	Albert Hall	.05
94	Tim Leary	.05
95	Mitch Williams	.05
96	Tracy Jones	.05
97	Danny Darwin	.05
98	Gary Ward	.05
99	Neal Heaton	.05
100	Jim Pankovits	.05
101	Bill Doran	.05
102	Tim Wallach	.05
103	Joe Magrane	.05
104	Ozzie Virgil	.05
105	Alvin Davis	.05
106	Tom Brookens	.05
107	Shawon Dunston	.05
108	Tracy Woodson	.05
109	Nelson Liriano	.05
110	Devon White	.05
111	Steve Balboni	.05
112	Buddy Bell	.05
113	German Jimenez RC	.05
114	Ken Dayley	.05
115	Andres Galarraga	.05
116	Mike Scioscia	.05
117	Gary Pettis	.05
118	Ernie Whitt	.05
119	Bob Boone	.05
120	Ryne Sandberg	1.50
121	Bruce Benedict	.05
122	Hubie Brooks	.05
123	Mike Moore	.05
124	Wallace Johnson	.05
125	Bob Horner	.05
126	Chili Davis	.05
127	Manny Trillo	.05
128	Chet Lemon	.05
129	John Cerutti	.05
130	Orel Hershiser	.05
131	Terry Pendleton	.05
132	Jeff Blauser	.05
133	Mike Fitzgerald	.05
134	Henry Cotto	.05
135	Gerald Young	.05
136	Luis Salazar	.05
137	Alejandro Pena	.05
138	Jack Howell	.05
139	Tony Fernandez	.05
140	Mark Grace	.05
141	Ken Caminiti	.05
142	Mike Jackson	.05
143	Larry McWilliams	.05
144	Andres Thomas	.05
145	Nolan Ryan	2.00
146	Mike Davis	.05
147	DeWayne Buice	.05
148	Jody Davis	.05
149	Jesse Barfield	.05
150	Matt Nokes	.05
151	Jerry Reuss	.05
152	Rick Cerone	.05
153	Storm Davis	.05
154	Marvell Wynne	.05
155	Will Clark	.60
156	Luis Aguayo	.05
157	Willie Upshaw	.05
158	Randy Bush	.05
159	Ron Darling	.05
160	Kal Daniels	.05
161	Spike Owen	.05
162	Luis Polonia	.05
163	Kevin Mitchell	.05
164	Dave Gallagher RC	.05
165	Benito Santiago	.05
166	Greg Gagne	.05
167	Ken Phelps	.05
168	Sid Fernandez	.05
169	Bo Diaz	.05
170	Cory Snyder	.05
171	Eric Show	.05
172	Robby Thompson	.05
173	Marty Barrett	.05
174	Dave Henderson	.05
175	Ozzie Guillen	.05
176	Barry Lyons	.05
177	Kelvin Torve RC	.05
178	Don Slaught	.05
179	Steve Lombardozzi	.05
180	Chris Sabo RC	.05
181	Jose Uribe	.05
182	Shane Mack	.05
183	Ron Karkovice	.05
184	Todd Benzinger	.05
185	Dave Stewart	.05
186	Julio Franco	.05
187	Ron Robinson	.05
188	Wally Backman	.05
189	Randy Velarde	.05
190	Joe Carter	.05
191	Bob Welch	.05
192	Kelly Paris	.05
193	Chris Brown	.05
194	Rick Reuschel	.05
195	Roger Clemens	1.60
196	Dave Concepcion	.05
197	Al Newman	.05
198	Brook Jacoby	.05
199	Mookie Wilson	.05
200	Don Mattingly	1.60
201	Dick Schofield	.05
202	Mark Gubicza	.05
203	Gary Gaetti	.05
204	Dan Pasqua	.05
205	Andre Dawson	.35
206	Chris Speier	.05
207	Kent Tekulve	.05
208	Rod Scurry	.05
209	Scott Bailes	.05
210	Rickey Henderson	1.00
211	Harold Baines	.05
212	Tony Armas	.05
213	Kent Hrbek	.05
214	Darrin Jackson	.05
215	George Brett	1.60
216	Rafael Santana	.05
217	Andy Allanson	.05
218	Brett Butler	.05
219	Steve Jeltz	.05
220	Jay Buhner	.05
221	Bo Jackson	.15
222	Angel Salazar	.05
223	Kirk McCaskill	.05
224	Steve Lyons	.05
225	Bert Blyleven	.05
226	Scott Bradley	.05
227	Bob Melvin	.05
228	Ron Kittle	.05
229	Phil Bradley	.05
230	Tommy John	.05
231	Greg Walker	.05
232	Juan Berenguer	.05
233	Pat Tabler	.05
234	Terry Clark RC	.05
235	Rafael Palmeiro	.75
236	Paul Zuvella	.05
237	Willie Randolph	.05
238	Bruce Fields	.05
239	Mike Aldrete	.05
240	Lance Parrish	.05
241	Greg Maddux	1.50
242	John Moses	.05
243	Melido Perez	.05
244	Willie Wilson	.05
245	Mark McLemore	.05
246	Von Hayes	.05
247	Matt Williams	.05
248	John Candelaria	.05
249	Harold Reynolds	.05
250	Greg Swindell	.05
251	Juan Agosto	.05
252	Mike Felder	.05
253	Vince Coleman	.05
254	Larry Sheets	.05
255	George Bell	.05
256	Terry Steinbach	.05
257	Jack Armstrong RC	.05
258	Dickie Thon	.05
259	Ray Knight	.05
260	Darryl Strawberry	.05
261	Doug Sisk	.05
262	Alex Trevino	.05
263	Jeff Leonard	.05
264	Tom Henke	.05
265	Ozzie Smith	1.50
266	Dave Bergman	.05
267	Tony Phillips	.05
268	Mark Davis	.05
269	Kevin Elster	.05
270	Barry Larkin	.05
271	Manny Lee	.05
272	Tom Brunansky	.05
273	Craig Biggio	.05
274	Jim Gantner	.05
275	Eddie Murray	1.00
276	Jeff Reed	.05
277	Tim Teufel	.05
278	Rick Honeycutt	.05
279	Guillermo Hernandez	.05
280	John Kruk	.05
281	Luis Alicea RC	.15
282	Jim Clancy	.05
283	Billy Ripken	.05

Feel the Game

		NM/M
	Common Player:	.50
AP	Albert Pujols	3.00
BA	Bobby Abreu	.50
BR	Brian Roberts	.50
BW	Brandon Webb	.50
CC	Chris Carpenter	.75
CJ	Chipper Jones	1.00
CR	Carl Crawford	.50
CS	Curt Schilling	1.00
CZ	Carlos Zambrano	.50
DJ	Derek Jeter	3.00
DW	Dontrelle Willis	.50
EC	Eric Chavez	.50
GS	Grady Sizemore	1.00
HR	Hanley Ramirez	1.00
IR	Ivan Rodriguez	.75
JM	Justin Morneau	.75
JP	Jonathan Papelbon	.75
JR	Jose Reyes	2.00
JS	John Smoltz	.75
KG	Ken Griffey Jr.	2.00
KJ	Kenji Johjima	.50
LB	Lance Berkman	.50
LG	Luis Gonzalez	.50
MC	Miguel Cabrera	1.00
RC	Robinson Cano	1.00
RJ	Randy Johnson	1.00
SA	Johan Santana	1.00
SC	Jason Schmidt	.50
VG	Vladimir Guerrero	1.00

Hitting Machines

		NM/M
	Common Player:	.50
AR	Aramis Ramirez	.75
AS	Alfonso Soriano	.50
BI	Craig Biggio	.50
CB	Carlos Beltran	1.00
DO	David Ortiz	1.00
FS	Freddy Sanchez	.50
FT	Frank Thomas	1.00
JK	Jeff Kent	.50
JM	Joe Mauer	.75
JT	Jim Thome	.75
MT	Mark Teixeira	1.00
NS	Nick Swisher	.50
TE	Miguel Tejada	.75
TG	Troy Glaus	.75
TH	Todd Helton	.75

Lucky 13 Rookies Auto

		NM/M
	Quantity Produced Listed	10.00
	Parallel:	1-1.5X
	Production 99 or 199	
238	Josh Hamilton/499	35.00
241	Kory Casto/499	10.00
242	Troy Tulowitzki/499	30.00
245	Ryan Braun/499	100.00
246	Alex Gordon/499	30.00
248	Kei Igawa/299	40.00
249	Kevin Kouzmanoff/499	15.00

Lucky 13 Rookies Auto.-Retail

		NM/M
	Common Autograph:	10.00
238	Josh Hamilton	35.00
241	Kory Casto	10.00
242	Troy Tulowitzki	30.00
246	Alex Gordon/SP	30.00
248	Kei Igawa/SP	40.00
249	Kevin Kouzmanoff	15.00

Stike Zone

		NM/M
	Common Player:	.50
BZ	Barry Zito	.50
CC	C.C. Sabathia	.75
CZ	Carlos Zambrano	.75
DW	Dontrelle Willis	.75
JS	Johan Santana	1.00
JV	Justin Verlander	.75
MM	Mike Mussina	.75
PM	Pedro Martinez	1.00

(top of first column, above Feel the Game — team players list)

JB	Jason Bay	.75
JG	Jason Giambi	.75
KG	Ken Griffey Jr.	2.00
LG	Luis Gonzalez	.50
MC	Miguel Cabrera	1.00
MP	Mike Piazza	1.00
MR	Mariano Rivera	.75
OV	Omar Vizquel	.50
TG	Tom Glavine	.75
TH	Torii Hunter	.50

RH	Roy Halladay	.75
RO	Roy Oswalt	.75

#	Player	Price
284	Craig Reynolds	.05
285	Robin Yount	1.00
286	Jimmy Jones	.05
287	Ron Oester	.05
288	Terry Leach	.05
289	Dennis Eckersley	.75
290	Alan Trammell	.05
291	Jimmy Key	.05
292	Chris Bosio	.05
293	Jose DeLeon	.05
294	Jim Traber	.05
295	Mike Scott	.05
296	Roger McDowell	.05
297	Garry Templeton	.05
298	Doyle Alexander	.05
299	Nick Esasky	.05
300	Mark McGwire	1.75
301	Darryl Hamilton RC	.05
302	Dave Smith	.05
303	Rick Sutcliffe	.05
304	Dave Stapleton	.05
305	Alan Ashby	.05
306	Pedro Guerrero	.05
307	Ron Guidry	.05
308	Steve Farr	.05
309	Curt Ford	.05
310	Claudell Washington	.05
311	Tom Prince	.05
312	Chad Kreuter RC	.15
313	Ken Oberkfell	.05
314	Jerry Browne	.05
315	R.J. Reynolds	.05
316	Scott Bankhead	.05
317	Milt Thompson	.05
318	Mario Diaz	.05
319	Bruce Ruffin	.05
320	Dave Valle	.05
321a	Gary Varsho RC (Batting righty on card back, photo actually Mike Bielecki.)	1.00
321b	Gary Varsho RC (Batting lefty on card back, correct photo.)	.05
322	Paul Mirabella	.05
323	Chuck Jackson	.05
324	Drew Hall	.05
325	Don August	.05
326	Israel Sanchez RC	.05
327	Denny Walling	.05
328	Joel Skinner	.05
329	Danny Tartabull	.05
330	Tony Pena	.05
331	Jim Sundberg	.05
332	Jeff Robinson	.05
333	Odibbe McDowell	.05
334	Jose Lind	.05
335	Paul Kilgus	.05
336	Juan Samuel	.05
337	Mike Campbell	.05
338	Mike Maddux	.05
339	Darnell Coles	.05
340	Bob Dernier	.05
341	Rafael Ramirez	.05
342	Scott Sanderson	.05
343	B.J. Surhoff	.05
344	Billy Hatcher	.05
345	Pat Perry	.05
346	Jack Clark	.05
347	Gary Thurman	.05
348	Timmy Jones RC	.05
349	Dave Winfield	1.00
350	Frank White	.05
351	Dave Collins	.05
352	Jack Morris	.25
353	Eric Plunk	.05
354	Leon Durham	.05
355	Ivan DeJesus	.05
356	Brian Holman RC	.05
357a	Dale Murphy (Reversed negative.)	25.00
357b	Dale Murphy (Corrected)	.25
358	Mark Portugal	.05
359	Andy McGaffigan	.05
360	Tom Glavine	.25
361	Keith Moreland	.05
362	Todd Stottlemyre	.05
363	Dave Leiper	.05
364	Cecil Fielder	.05
365	Carmelo Martinez	.05
366	Dwight Evans	.05
367	Kevin McReynolds	.05
368	Rich Gedman	.05
369	Len Dykstra	.05
370	Jody Reed	.05
371	Jose Canseco	.60
372	Rob Murphy	.05
373	Mike Henneman	.05
374	Walt Weiss	.05
375	Rob Dibble RC	.05
376	Kirby Puckett	1.50
377	Denny Martinez	.05
378	Ron Gant	.05
379	Brian Harper	.05
380	Nelson Santovenia RC	.05
381	Lloyd Moseby	.05
382	Lance McCullers	.05
383	Dave Stieb	.05
384	Tony Gwynn	1.50
385	Mike Flanagan	.05
386	Bob Ojeda	.05
387	Bruce Hurst	.05
388	Dave Magadan	.05
389	Wade Boggs	1.50
390	Gary Carter	1.00
391	Frank Tanana	.05
392	Curt Young	.05
393	Jeff Treadway	.05
394	Darrell Evans	.05
395	Glenn Hubbard	.05
396	Chuck Cary	.05
397	Frank Viola	.05
398	Jeff Parrett	.05
399	Terry Blocker RC	.05
400	Dan Gladden	.05
401	Louie Meadows RC	.05
402	Tim Raines	.05
403	Joey Meyer	.05
404	Larry Andersen	.05
405	Rex Hudler	.05
406	Mike Schmidt	1.60
407	John Franco	.05
408	Brady Anderson	.05
409	Don Carman	.05
410	Eric Davis	.05
411	Bob Stanley	.05
412	Pete Smith	.05
413	Jim Rice	.25
414	Bruce Sutter	.75
415	Dennis "Oil Can" Boyd	.05
416	Ruben Sierra	.05
417	Mike LaValliere	.05
418	Steve Buechele	.05
419	Gary Redus	.05
420	Scott Fletcher	.05
421	Dale Sveum	.05
422	Bob Knepper	.05
423	Luis Rivera	.05
424	Ted Higuera	.05
425	Kevin Bass	.05
426	Ken Gerhart	.05
427	Shane Rawley	.05
428	Paul O'Neill	.05
429	Joe Orsulak	.05
430	Jackie Gutierrez	.05
431	Gerald Perry	.05
432	Mike Greenwell	.05
433	Jerry Royster	.05
434	Ellis Burks	.05
435	Ed Olwine	.05
436	Dave Rucker	.05
437	Charlie Hough	.05
438	Bob Walk	.05
439	Bob Brower	.05
440	Barry Bonds	2.00
441	Tom Foley	.05
442	Rob Deer	.05
443	Glenn Davis	.05
444	Dave Martinez	.05
445	Bill Wegman	.05
446	Lloyd McClendon	.05
447	Dave Schmidt	.05
448	Darren Daulton	.05
449	Frank Williams	.05
450	Don Aase	.05
451	Lou Whitaker	.05
452	Goose Gossage	.05
453	Ed Whitson	.05
454	Jim Walewander	.05
455	Damon Berryhill	.05
456	Tim Burke	.05
457	Barry Jones	.05
458	Joel Youngblood	.05
459	Floyd Youmans	.05
460	Mark Salas	.05
461	Jeff Russell	.05
462	Darrell Miller	.05
463	Jeff Kunkel	.05
464	Sherman Corbett RC	.05
465	Curtis Wilkerson	.05
466	Bud Black	.05
467	Cal Ripken, Jr.	2.00
468	John Farrell	.05
469	Terry Kennedy	.05
470	Tom Candiotti	.05
471	Roberto Alomar	.20
472	Jeff Robinson	.05
473	Vance Law	.05
474	Randy Ready	.05
475	Walt Terrell	.05
476	Kelly Downs	.05
477	Johnny Paredes RC	.05
478	Shawn Hillegas	.05
479	Bob Brenly	.05
480	Otis Nixon	.05
481	Johnny Ray	.05
482	Geno Petralli	.05
483	Stu Cliburn	.05
484	Pete Incaviglia	.05
485	Brian Downing	.05
486	Jeff Stone	.05
487	Carmen Castillo	.05
488	Tom Niedenfuer	.05
489	Jay Bell	.05
490	Rick Schu	.05
491	Jeff Pico RC	.05
492	Mark Parent RC	.05
493	Eric King	.05
494	Al Nipper	.05
495	Andy Hawkins	.05
496	Daryl Boston	.05
497	Ernie Riles	.05
498	Pascual Perez	.05
499	Bill Long	.05
500	Kirt Manwaring	.05
501	Chuck Crim	.05
502	Candy Maldonado	.05
503	Dennis Lamp	.05
504	Glenn Braggs	.05
505	Joe Price	.05
506	Ken Williams	.05
507	Bill Pecota	.05
508	Rey Quinones	.05
509	Jeff Bittiger RC	.05
510	Kevin Seitzer	.05
511	Steve Bedrosian	.05
512	Todd Worrell	.05
513	Chris James	.05
514	Jose Oquendo	.05
515	David Palmer	.05
516	John Smiley	.05
517	Dave Clark	.05
518	Mike Dunne	.05
519	Ron Washington	.05
520	Bob Kipper	.05
521	Lee Smith	.05
522	Juan Castillo	.05
523	Don Robinson	.05
524	Kevin Romine	.05
525	Paul Molitor	1.00
526	Mark Langston	.05
527	Donnie Hill	.05
528	Larry Owen	.05
529	Jerry Reed	.05
530	Jack McDowell	.05
531	Greg Mathews	.05
532	John Russell	.05
533	Dan Quisenberry	.05
534	Greg Gross	.05
535	Danny Cox	.05
536	Terry Francona	.05
537	Andy Van Slyke	.05
538	Mel Hall	.05
539	Jim Gott	.05
540	Doug Jones	.05
541	Criag Lefferts	.05
542	Mike Boddicker	.05
543	Greg Brock	.05
544	Atlee Hammaker	.05
545	Tom Bolton	.05
546	Mike Macfarlane RC	.25
547	Rich Renteria RC	.05
548	John Davis	.05
549	Floyd Bannister	.05
550	Mickey Brantley	.05
551	Duane Ward	.05
552	Dan Petry	.05
553	Mickey Tettleton	.05
554	Rick Leach	.05
555	Mike Witt	.05
556	Sid Bream	.05
557	Bobby Witt	.05
558	Tommy Herr	.05
559	Randy Milligan	.05
560	Jose Cecena RC	.05
561	Mackey Sasser	.05
562	Carney Lansford	.05
563	Rick Aguilera	.05
564	Ron Hassey	.05
565	Dwight Gooden	.05
566	Paul Assenmacher	.05
567	Neil Allen	.05
568	Jim Morrison	.05
569	Mike Pagliarulo	.05
570	Ted Simmons	.05
571	Mark Thurmond	.05
572	Fred McGriff	.05
573	Wally Joyner	.05
574	Jose Bautista RC	.05
575	Kelly Gruber	.05
576	Cecilio Guante	.05
577	Mark Davidson	.05
578	Bobby Bonilla	.05
579	Mike Stanley	.05
580	Gene Larkin	.05
581	Stan Javier	.05
582	Howard Johnson	.05
583a	Mike Gallego (Photo on card back reversed.)	.75
583b	Mike Gallego (Correct photo.)	.05
584	David Cone	.05
585	Doug Jennings RC	.05
586	Charlie Hudson	.05
587	Dion James	.05
588	Al Leiter	.05
589	Charlie Puleo	.05
590	Roberto Kelly	.05
591	Thad Bosley	.05
592	Pete Stanicek	.05
593	Pat Borders RC	.25
594	Bryan Harvey RC	.05
595	Jeff Ballard	.05
596	Jeff Reardon	.05
597	Doug Drabek	.05
598	Edwin Correa	.05
599	Keith Atherton	.05
600	Dave LaPoint	.05
601	Don Baylor	.05
602	Tom Pagnozzi	.05
603	Tim Flannery	.05
604	Gene Walter	.05
605	Dave Parker	.05
606	Mike Diaz	.05
607	Chris Gwynn	.05
608	Odell Jones	.05
609	Carlton Fisk	1.00
610	Jay Howell	.05
611	Tim Crews	.05
612	Keith Hernandez	.05
613	Willie Fraser	.05
614	Jim Eppard	.05
615	Jeff Hamilton	.05
616	Kurt Stillwell	.05
617	Tom Browning	.05
618	Jeff Montgomery	.05
619	Jose Rijo	.05
620	Jamie Quirk	.05
621	Willie McGee	.05
622	Mark Grant	.05
623	Bill Swift	.05
624	Orlando Mercado	.05
625	John Costello RC	.05
626	Jose Gonzalez	.05
627a	Bill Schroeder (Putting on shin guards on card back, photo actually Ronn Reynolds.)	.75
627b	Bill Schroeder (Arms crossed on card back, correct photo.)	.05
628a	Fred Manrique (Throwing on card back, photo actually Ozzie Guillen.)	.05
628b	Fred Manrique (Batting on card back, correct photo.)	.05
629	Ricky Horton	.05
630	Dan Plesac	.05
631	Alfredo Griffin	.05
632	Chuck Finley	.05
633	Kirk Gibson	.05
634	Randy Myers	.05
635	Greg Minton	.05
636	Herm Winningham	.05
637	Charlie Leibrandt	.05
638	Tim Birtsas	.05
639	Bill Buckner	.05
640	Danny Jackson	.05
641	Greg Booker	.05
642	Jim Presley	.05
643	Gene Nelson	.05
644	Rod Booker	.05
645	Dennis Rasmussen	.05
646	Juan Nieves	.05
647	Bobby Thigpen	.05
648	Tim Belcher	.05
649	Mike Young	.05
650	Ivan Calderon	.05
651	Oswaldo Peraza RC	.05
652a	Pat Sheridan (No position on front.)	8.00
652b	Pat Sheridan (Position on front.)	.05
653	Mike Morgan	.05
654	Mike Heath	.05
655	Jay Tibbs	.05
656	Fernando Valenzuela	.05
657	Lee Mazzilli	.05
658	Frank Viola	.05
659	Jose Canseco	.60
660	Walt Weiss	.05
661	Orel Hershiser	.05
662	Kirk Gibson	.05
663	Chris Sabo	.05
664	Dennis Eckersley	.75
665	Orel Hershiser	.05
666	Kirk Gibson	.05
667	Orel Hershiser	.05
668	Wally Joyner (TC)	.05
669	Nolan Ryan (TC)	1.00
670	Jose Canseco (TC)	.30
671	Fred McGriff (TC)	.05
672	Dale Murphy (TC)	.20
673	Paul Molitor (TC)	.50
674	Ozzie Smith (TC)	.75
675	Ryne Sandberg (TC)	.40
676	Kirk Gibson (TC)	.05
677	Andres Galarraga (TC)	.05
678	Will Clark (TC)	.05
679	Cory Snyder (TC)	.05
680	Alvin Davis (TC)	.05
681	Darryl Strawberry (TC)	.05
682	Cal Ripken, Jr. (TC)	1.00
683	Tony Gwynn (TC)	.40
684	Mike Schmidt (TC)	.85
685	Andy Van Slyke (TC)	.05
686	Ruben Sierra (TC)	.05
687	Wade Boggs (TC)	.40
688	Eric Davis (TC)	.05
689	George Brett (TC)	.85
690	Alan Trammell (TC)	.05
691	Frank Viola (TC)	.05
692	Harold Baines (TC)	.05
693	Don Mattingly (TC)	.85
694	Checklist 1-100	.05
695	Checklist 101-200	.05
696	Checklist 201-300	.05
697	Checklist 301-400	.05
698	Checklist 401-500	.05
699	Checklist 501-600	.05
700	Checklist 601-700	.05
701	Checklist 701-800	.05
702	Jessie Barfield	.05
703	Walt Terrell	.05
704	Dickie Thon	.05
705	Al Leiter	.05
706	Dave LaPoint	.05
707	Charlie Hayes RC	.05
708	Andy Hawkins	.05
709	Mickey Hatcher	.05
710	Lance McCullers	.05
711	Ron Kittle	.05
712	Bert Blyleven	.05
713	Rick Dempsey	.05
714	Ken Williams	.05
715	Steve Rosenberg RC	.05
716	Joe Skalski RC	.05
717	Spike Owen	.05
718	Todd Burns	.05
719	Kevin Gross	.05
720	Tommy Herr	.05
721	Rob Ducey	.05
722	Gary Green RC	.05
723	Gregg Olson RC	.10
724	Greg Harris RC	.05
725	Craig Worthington RC	.05
726	Tom Howard RC	.05
727	Dale Mohorcic	.05
728	Rich Yett	.05
729	Mel Hall	.05
730	Floyd Youmans	.05
731	Lonnie Smith	.05
732	Wally Backman	.05
733	Trevor Wilson	.05
734	Jose Alvarez	.05
735	Bob Milacki RC	.05
736	Tom Gordon RC	.50
737	Wally Whitehurst RC	.05
738	Mike Aldrete	.05
739	Keith Miller	.05
740	Randy Milligan	.05
741	Jeff Parrett	.05
742	Steve Finley RC	.75
743	Junior Felix RC	.05
744	Pete Harnisch RC	.25
745	Bill Spiers RC	.05
746	Hensley Meulens RC	.05
747	Juan Bell	.05
748	Steve Sax	.05
749	Phil Bradley	.05
750	Rey Quinones	.05
751	Tommy Gregg RC	.05
752	Kevin Brown RC	.25
753	Derek Lilliquist RC	.05
754	Todd Zeile RC	.75
755	Jim Abbott	.05
756	Ozzie Canseco RC	.05
757	Nick Esasky	.05
758	Mike Moore	.05
759	Rob Murphy	.05
760	Rick Mahler	.05
761	Fred Lynn	.05
762	Kevin Blankenship RC	.05
763	Eddie Murray	1.00
764	Steve Searcy RC	.05
765	Jerome Walton RC	.05
766	Erik Hanson RC	.05
767	Bob Boone	.05
768	Edgar Martinez	.05
769	Jose DeJesus RC	.05
770	Greg Briley RC	.05
771	Steve Peters RC	.05
772	Rafael Palmeiro	.75
773	Jack Clark	.05
774	Nolan Ryan	2.00
775	Lance Parrish	.05
776	Joe Girardi RC	.30
777	Willie Randolph	.05
778	Mitch Williams	.05
779	Dennis Cook RC	.05
780	Dwight Smith RC	.05
781	Lenny Harris RC	.10
782	Torey Lovullo RC	.05
783	Norm Charlton RC	.15
784	Chris Brown	.05
785	Todd Benzinger	.05
786	Shane Rawley	.05
787	Omar Vizquel RC	2.00
788	LaVel Freeman RC	.05
789	Jeffrey Leonard	.05
790	Eddie Williams RC	.05
791	Jamie Moyer	.05
792	Bruce Hurst	.05
793	Julio Franco	.05
794	Claudell Washington	.05
795	Jody Davis	.05
796	Oddibe McDowell	.05
797	Paul Kilgus	.05
798	Tracy Jones	.05
799	Steve Wilson RC	.05
800	Pete O'Brien	.05

Complete Set (800):		15.00
Complete Low Set (700):		12.00
Complete High Set (100):		5.00
Common Player:		.05
Low or High Foil Pack (15):		.50
Low or High Foil Box (36):		12.00
1	Star Rookie Checklist	.05
2	Randy Nosek RC	.05
3	Tom Drees RC	.05
4	Curt Young	.05
5	Angels checklist (Devon White)	.05
6	Luis Salazar	.05
7	Phillies checklist (Von Hayes)	.05
8	Jose Bautista	.05
9	Marquis Grissom RC	.50
10	Dodgers checklist (Orel Hershiser)	.05
11	Rick Aguilera	.05
12	Padres checklist (Benito Santiago)	.05
13	Deion Sanders	.10
14	Marvell Wynne	.05
15	David West	.05
16	Pirates checklist (Bobby Bonilla)	.05
17	Sammy Sosa RC	5.00
18	Yankees checklist (Steve Sax)	.05
19	Jack Howell	.05
20	Mike Schmidt Retires (Mike Schmidt)	.75
21	Robin Ventura	.05
22	Brian Meyer RC	.05
23	Blaine Beatty RC	.05
24	Mariners checklist (Ken Griffey Jr.)	.50
25	Greg Vaughn	.05
26	Xavier Hernandez RC	.05
27	Jason Grimsley RC	.05
28	Eric Anthony RC	.05
29	Expos checklist (Tim Raines)	.05
30	David Wells	.05
31	Hal Morris RC	.05
32	Royals checklist (Bo Jackson)	.10
33	Kelly Mann RC	.05
34	Nolan Ryan 5000 Strikeouts (Nolan Ryan)	1.00
35	Scott Service RC	.05
36	Athletics checklist (Mark McGwire)	.50
37	Tino Martinez	.05
38	Chili Davis	.05
39	Scott Sanderson	.05
40	Giants checklist (Kevin Mitchell)	.05
41	Tigers checklist (Lou Whitaker)	.05
42	Scott Coolbaugh RC	.05
43	Jose Cano RC	.05
44	Jose Vizcaino RC	.10
45	Bob Hamelin RC	.05
46	Jose Offerman RC	.15
47	Kevin Blankenship	.05
48	Twins checklist (Kirby Puckett)	.40
49	Tommy Greene RC	.05
50	N.L. Top Vote Getter (Will Clark)	.05
51	Rob Nelson RC	.05
52	Chris Hammond RC	.15
53	Indians checklist (Joe Carter)	.05
54a	Ben McDonald RC (Orioles Logo)	1.00
54b	Ben McDonald RC (Star Rookie logo)	.25
55	Andy Benes	.05
56	John Olerud RC	1.00
57	Red Sox checklist (Roger Clemens)	.45
58	Tony Armas	.05
59	George Canale RC	.05
60a	Orioles checklist (Mickey Tettleton) (#683 Jamie Weston))	1.00
60b	Orioles checklist (Mickey Tettleton) (#683 Jamie Weston)	.05
61	Mike Stanton RC	.05
62	Mets checklist (Dwight Gooden)	.05
63	Kent Mercker RC	.10
64	Francisco Cabrera RC	.05
65	Steve Avery	.05
66	Jose Canseco	.35
67	Matt Merullo RC	.05
68	Cardinals checklist (Vince Coleman)	.05
69	Ron Karkovice	.05
70	Kevin Maas RC	.05
71	Dennis Cook	.05
72	Juan Gonzalez RC	2.00
73	Cubs checklist (Andre Dawson)	.05
74	Dean Palmer RC	.25
75	A.L. Top Vote Getter (Bo Jackson)	.10
76	Rob Richie RC	.05
77	Bobby Rose RC	.05
78	Brian DuBois RC	.05
79	White Sox checklist (Ozzie Guillen)	.05
80	Gene Nelson	.05
81	Bob McClure	.05

1990 Upper Deck

Tom Gordon

Following the success of its first issue, Upper Deck released another 800-card set in 1990. The cards feature full-color photos on both sides in the standard 2-1/2" x 3-1/2" format. The artwork of Vernon Wells Sr. is featured on the front of all team checklist cards. The 1990 set also introduces two new Wells illustrations - a tribute to Mike Schmidt upon his retirement and one commemorating Nolan Ryan's 5,000 career strikeouts. The cards are similar in design to the 1989 issue. The high-number series (701-800) was released as a boxed set, in factory sets and in foil packs at mid-season. Cards #101-199 can be found either with or without the copyright line on back; no premium attaches to either.

	NM/M
Unopened Factory Set (800):	20.00

No.	Player	Price
82	Rangers checklist (Julio Franco)	.05
83	Greg Minton	.05
84	Braves checklist (John Smoltz)	.05
85	Willie Fraser	.05
86	Neal Heaton	.05
87	Kevin Tapani RC	.05
88	Astros Checklist (Mike Scott)	.05
89a	Jim Gott (Incorrect photo.)	1.00
89b	Jim Gott (Correct photo.)	.05
90	Lance Johnson	.05
91	Brewers checklist (Robin Yount)	.35
92	Jeff Parrett	.05
93	Julio Machado RC	.05
94	Ron Jones	.05
95	Blue Jays checklist (George Bell)	.05
96	Jerry Reuss	.05
97	Brian Fisher	.05
98	Kevin Ritz RC	.05
99	Reds Checklist (Barry Larkin)	.05
100	Checklist 1-100	.05
101	Gerald Perry	.05
102	Kevin Appier	.05
103	Julio Franco	.05
104	Craig Biggio	.05
105	Bo Jackson	.10
106	Junior Felix RC	.05
107	Mike Harkey RC	.05
108	Fred McGriff	.05
109	Rick Sutcliffe	.05
110	Pete O'Brien	.05
111	Kelly Gruber	.05
112	Pat Borders	.05
113	Dwight Evans	.05
114	Dwight Gooden	.05
115	Kevin Batiste RC	.05
116	Eric Davis	.05
117	Kevin Mitchell	.05
118	Ron Oester	.05
119	Brett Butler	.05
120	Danny Jackson	.05
121	Tommy Gregg	.05
122	Ken Caminiti	.05
123	Kevin Brown	.05
124	George Brett	.85
125	Mike Scott	.05
126	Cory Snyder	.05
127	George Bell	.05
128	Mark Grace	.05
129	Devon White	.05
130	Tony Fernandez	.05
131	Don Aase	.05
132	Rance Mulliniks	.05
133	Marty Barrett	.05
134	Nelson Liriano	.05
135	Mark Carreon RC	.05
136	Candy Maldonado	.05
137	Tim Birtsas	.05
138	Tom Brookens	.05
139	John Franco	.05
140	Mike LaCoss	.05
141	Jeff Treadway	.05
142	Pat Tabler	.05
143	Darrell Evans	.05
144	Rafael Ramirez	.05
145	Oddibe McDowell	.05
146	Brian Downing	.05
147	Curtis Wilkerson	.05
148	Ernie Whitt	.05
149	Bill Schroeder	.05
150	Domingo Ramos	.05
151	Rick Honeycutt	.05
152	Don Slaught	.05
153	Mitch Webster	.05
154	Tony Phillips	.05
155	Paul Kilgus	.05
156	Ken Griffey Jr.	1.50
157	Gary Sheffield	.35
158	Wally Backman	.05
159	B.J. Surhoff	.05
160	Louie Meadows	.05
161	Paul O'Neill	.05
162	Jeff McKnight RC	.05
163	Alvaro Espinoza RC	.05
164	Scott Scudder RC	.05
165	Jeff Reed	.05
166	Gregg Jefferies	.05
167	Barry Larkin	.05
168	Gary Carter	.60
169	Robby Thompson	.05
170	Rolando Roomes	.05
171	Mark McGwire	1.50
172	Steve Sax	.05
173	Mark Williamson	.05
174	Mitch Williams	.05
175	Brian Holton	.05
176	Rob Deer	.05
177	Tim Raines	.05
178	Mike Felder	.05
179	Harold Reynolds	.05
180	Terry Francona	.05
181	Chris Sabo	.05
182	Darryl Strawberry	.05
183	Willie Randolph	.05
184	Billy Ripken	.05
185	Mackey Sasser	.05
186	Todd Benzinger	.05
187	Kevin Elster	.05
188	Jose Uribe	.05
189	Tom Browning	.05
190	Keith Miller	.05
191	Don Mattingly	.85
192	Dave Parker	.05
193	Roberto Kelly	.05
194	Phil Bradley	.05
195	Ron Hassey	.05
196	Gerald Young	.05
197	Hubie Brooks	.05
198	Bill Doran	.05
199	Al Newman	.05
200	Checklist 101-200	.05
201	Terry Puhl	.05
202	Frank DiPino	.05
203	Jim Clancy	.05
204	Bob Ojeda	.05
205	Alex Trevino	.05
206	Dave Henderson	.05
207	Henry Cotto	.05
208	Rafael Belliard	.05
209	Stan Javier	.05
210	Jerry Reed	.05
211	Doug Dascenzo	.05
212	Andres Thomas	.05
213	Greg Maddux	.75
214	Mike Schooler	.05
215	Lonnie Smith	.05
216	Jose Rijo	.05
217	Greg Gagne	.05
218	Jim Gantner	.05
219	Allan Anderson	.05
220	Rick Mahler	.05
221	Jim Deshaies	.05
222	Keith Hernandez	.05
223	Vince Coleman	.05
224	David Cone	.05
225	Ozzie Smith	.75
226	Matt Nokes	.05
227	Barry Bonds	2.00
228	Felix Jose	.05
229	Dennis Powell	.05
230	Mike Gallego	.05
231	Shawon Dunston	.05
232	Ron Gant	.05
233	Omar Vizquel	.05
234	Derek Lilliquist	.05
235	Erik Hanson	.05
236	Kirby Puckett	.75
237	Bill Spiers	.05
238	Dan Gladden	.05
239	Bryan Clutterbuck RC	.05
240	John Moses	.05
241	Ron Darling	.05
242	Joe Magrane	.05
243	Dave Magadan	.05
244	Pedro Guerrero	.05
245	Glenn Davis	.05
246	Terry Steinbach	.05
247	Fred Lynn	.05
248	Gary Redus	.05
249	Kenny Williams	.05
250	Sid Bream	.05
251	Bob Welch	.05
252	Bill Buckner	.05
253	Carney Lansford	.05
254	Paul Molitor	.60
255	Jose DeJesus	.05
256	Orel Hershiser	.05
257	Tom Brunansky	.05
258	Mike Davis	.05
259	Jeff Ballard	.05
260	Scott Terry	.05
261	Sid Fernandez	.05
262	Mike Marshall	.05
263	Howard Johnson	.05
264	Kirk Gibson	.05
265	Kevin McReynolds	.05
266	Cal Ripken, Jr.	2.00
267	Ozzie Guillen	.05
268	Jim Traber	.05
269	Bobby Thigpen	.05
270	Joe Orsulak	.05
271	Bob Boone	.05
272	Dave Stewart	.05
273	Tim Wallach	.05
274	Luis Aquino	.05
275	Mike Moore	.05
276	Tony Pena	.05
277	Eddie Murray	.60
278	Milt Thompson	.05
279	Alejandro Pena	.05
280	Ken Dayley	.05
281	Carmen Castillo	.05
282	Tom Henke	.05
283	Mickey Hatcher	.05
284	Roy Smith RC	.05
285	Manny Lee	.05
286	Dan Pasqua	.05
287	Larry Sheets	.05
288	Garry Templeton	.05
289	Eddie Williams	.05
290	Brady Anderson	.05
291	Spike Owen	.05
292	Storm Davis	.05
293	Chris Bosio	.05
294	Jim Eisenreich	.05
295	Don August	.05
296	Jeff Hamilton	.05
297	Mickey Tettleton	.05
298	Mike Scioscia	.05
299	Kevin Hickey RC	.05
300	Checklist 201-300	.05
301	Shawn Abner	.05
302	Kevin Bass	.05
303	Bip Roberts RC	.05
304	Joe Girardi RC	.05
305	Danny Darwin	.05
306	Mike Heath	.05
307	Mike Macfarlane	.05
308	Ed Whitson	.05
309	Tracy Jones	.05
310	Scott Fletcher	.05
311	Darnell Coles	.05
312	Mike Brumley	.05
313	Bill Swift	.05
314	Charlie Hough	.05
315	Jim Presley	.05
316	Luis Polonia	.05
317	Mike Morgan	.05
318	Lee Guetterman	.05
319	Jose Oquendo	.05
320	Wayne Tolleson	.05
321	Jody Reed	.05
322	Damon Berryhill	.05
323	Roger Clemens	.85
324	Ryne Sandberg	.75
325	Benito Santiago	.05
326	Bret Saberhagen	.05
327	Lou Whitaker	.05
328	Dave Gallagher	.05
329	Mike Pagliarulo	.05
330	Doyle Alexander	.05
331	Jeffrey Leonard	.05
332	Torey Lovullo	.05
333	Pete Incaviglia	.05
334	Rickey Henderson	.60
335	Rafael Palmeiro	.50
336	Ken Hill RC	.05
337	Dave Winfield	.60
338	Alfredo Griffin	.05
339	Andy Hawkins	.05
340	Ted Power	.05
341	Steve Wilson	.05
342	Jack Clark	.05
343	Ellis Burks	.05
344	Tony Gwynn	.75
345	Jerome Walton	.05
346	Roberto Alomar	.20
347	Carlos Martinez RC	.05
348	Chet Lemon	.05
349	Willie Wilson	.05
350	Greg Walker	.05
351	Tom Bolton	.05
352	German Gonzalez RC	.05
353	Harold Baines	.05
354	Mike Greenwell	.05
355	Ruben Sierra	.05
356	Andres Galarraga	.05
357	Andre Dawson	.25
358	Jeff Brantley RC	.05
359	Mike Bielecki	.05
360	Ken Oberkfell	.05
361	Kurt Stillwell	.05
362	Brian Holman	.05
363	Kevin Seitzer	.05
364	Alvin Davis	.05
365	Tom Gordon	.05
366	Bobby Bonilla	.05
367	Carlton Fisk	.60
368	Steve Carter RC	.05
369	Joel Skinner	.05
370	John Cangelosi	.05
371	Cecil Espy	.05
372	Gary Wayne RC	.05
373	Jim Rice	.20
374	Mike Dyer RC	.05
375	Joe Carter	.05
376	Dwight Smith	.05
377	John Wetteland RC	.15
378	Ernie Riles	.05
379	Otis Nixon	.05
380	Vance Law	.05
381	Dave Bergman	.05
382	Frank White	.05
383	Scott Bradley	.05
384	Israel Sanchez	.05
385	Gary Pettis	.05
386	Donn Pall RC	.05
387	John Smiley	.05
388	Tom Candiotti	.05
389	Junior Ortiz	.05
390	Steve Lyons	.05
391	Brian Harper	.05
392	Fred Manrique	.05
393	Lee Smith	.05
394	Jeff Kunkel	.05
395	Claudell Washington	.05
396	John Tudor	.05
397	Terry Kennedy	.05
398	Lloyd McClendon	.05
399	Craig Lefferts	.05
400	Checklist 301-400	.05
401	Keith Moreland	.05
402	Rich Gedman	.05
403	Jeff Robinson	.05
404	Randy Ready	.05
405	Rick Cerone	.05
406	Jeff Blauser	.05
407	Larry Andersen	.05
408	Joe Boever	.05
409	Felix Fermin	.05
410	Glenn Wilson	.05
411	Rex Hudler	.05
412	Mark Grant	.05
413	Dennis Martinez	.05
414	Darrin Jackson	.05
415	Mike Aldrete	.05
416	Roger McDowell	.05
417	Jeff Reardon	.05
418	Darren Daulton	.05
419	Tim Laudner	.05
420	Don Carman	.05
421	Lloyd Moseby	.05
422	Doug Drabek	.05
423	Lenny Harris	.05
424	Jose Lind	.05
425	Dave Johnson RC	.05
426	Jerry Browne	.05
427	Eric Yelding RC	.05
428	Brad Komminsk RC	.05
429	Jody Davis	.05
430	Mariano Duncan RC	.05
431	Mark Davis	.05
432	Nelson Santovenia	.05
433	Bruce Hurst	.05
434	Jeff Huson RC	.05
435	Chris James	.05
436	Mark Guthrie RC	.05
437	Charlie Hayes RC	.05
438	Shane Rawley	.05
439	Dickie Thon	.05
440	Juan Berenguer	.05
441	Kevin Romine	.05
442	Bill Landrum	.05
443	Todd Frohwirth	.05
444	Craig Worthington	.05
445	Fernando Valenzuela	.05
446	Albert Belle	.05
447	Ed Whited RC	.05
448	Dave Smith	.05
449	Dave Clark	.05
450	Juan Agosto	.05
451	Dave Valle	.05
452	Kent Hrbek	.05
453	Von Hayes	.05
454	Gary Gaetti	.05
455	Greg Briley	.05
456	Glenn Braggs	.05
457	Kirt Manwaring	.05
458	Mel Hall	.05
459	Brook Jacoby	.05
460	Pat Sheridan	.05
461	Rob Murphy	.05
462	Jimmy Key	.05
463	Nick Esasky	.05
464	Rob Ducey	.05
465	Carlos Quintana	.05
466	Larry Walker RC	1.00
467	Todd Worrell	.05
468	Kevin Gross	.05
469	Terry Pendleton	.05
470	Dave Martinez	.05
471	Gene Larkin	.05
472	Len Dykstra	.05
473	Barry Lyons	.05
474	Terry Mulholland RC	.05
475	Chip Hale RC	.05
476	Jesse Barfield	.05
477	Dan Plesac	.05
478a	Scott Garrelts (Photo actually Bill Bathe.)	1.00
478b	Scott Garrelts (Correct photo.)	.05
479	Dave Righetti	.05
480	Gus Polidor	.05
481	Mookie Wilson	.05
482	Luis Rivera	.05
483	Mike Flanagan	.05
484	Dennis "Oil Can" Boyd	.05
485	John Cerutti	.05
486	John Costello	.05
487	Pascual Perez	.05
488	Tommy Herr	.05
489	Tom Foley	.05
490	Curt Ford	.05
491	Steve Lake	.05
492	Tim Teufel	.05
493	Randy Bush	.05
494	Mike Jackson	.05
495	Steve Jeltz	.05
496	Paul Gibson	.05
497	Steve Balboni	.05
498	Bud Black	.05
499	Dale Sveum	.05
500	Checklist 401-500	.05
501	Timmy Jones	.05
502	Mark Portugal	.05
503	Ivan Calderon	.05
504	Rick Rhoden	.05
505	Willie McGee	.05
506	Kirk McCaskill	.05
507	Dave LaPoint	.05
508	Jay Howell	.05
509	Johnny Ray	.05
510	Dave Anderson	.05
511	Chuck Crim	.05
512	Joe Hesketh	.05
513	Dennis Eckersley	.40
514	Greg Brock	.05
515	Tim Burke RC	.05
516	Frank Tanana	.05
517	Jay Bell	.05
518	Guillermo Hernandez	.05
519	Randy Kramer RC	.05
520	Charles Hudson	.05
521	Jim Corsi RC	.05
522	Steve Rosenberg	.05
523	Cris Carpenter	.05
524	Matt Winters RC	.05
525	Melido Perez	.05
526	Chris Gwynn RC	.05
527	Bert Blyleven	.05
528	Chuck Cary RC	.05
529	Daryl Boston	.05
530	Dale Mohorcic	.05
531	Geronimo Berroa RC	.05
532	Edgar Martinez	.05
533	Dale Murphy	.20
534	Jay Buhner	.05
535	John Smoltz	.05
536	Andy Van Slyke	.05
537	Mike Henneman RC	.05
538	Miguel Garcia RC	.05
539	Frank Williams RC	.05
540	R.J. Reynolds	.05
541	Shawn Hillegas RC	.05
542	Walt Weiss	.05
543	Greg Hibbard RC	.05
544	Nolan Ryan	2.00
545	Todd Zeile	.05
546	Hensley Meulens	.05
547	Tim Belcher RC	.05
548	Mike Witt	.05
549	Greg Cadaret RC	.05
550	Franklin Stubbs	.05
551	Tony Castillo RC	.05
552	Jeff Robinson	.05
553	Steve Olin RC	.05
554	Alan Trammell	.05
555	Wade Boggs	.75
556	Will Clark	.05
557	Jeff King	.05
558	Mike Fitzgerald	.05
559	Ken Howell	.05
560	Bob Kipper	.05
561	Scott Bankhead RC	.05
562a	Jeff Innis RC (Photo actually David West.)	1.00
562b	Jeff Innis RC (Correct photo.)	.05
563	Randy Johnson	.60
564	Wally Whithurst RC	.05
565	Gene Harris RC	.05
566	Norm Charlton RC	.05
567	Robin Yount	.60
568	Joe Oliver RC	.05
569	Mark Parent	.05
570	John Farrell RC	.05
571	Tom Glavine	.20
572	Rod Nichols RC	.05
573	Jack Morris	.05
574	Greg Swindell RC	.05
575	Steve Searcy RC	.05
576	Ricky Jordan RC	.05
577	Matt Williams	.05
578	Mike LaValliere RC	.05
579	Bryn Smith	.05
580	Bruce Ruffin RC	.05
581	Randy Myers	.05
582	Rick Wrona RC	.05
583	Juan Samuel	.05
584	Les Lancaster RC	.05
585	Jeff Musselman	.05
586	Rob Dibble RC	.05
587	Eric Show	.05
588	Jesse Orosco	.05
589	Herm Winningham	.05
590	Andy Allanson	.05
591	Dion James	.05
592	Carmelo Martinez RC	.05
593	Luis Quinones RC	.05
594	Dennis Rasmussen RC	.05
595	Rich Yett	.05
596	Bob Walk RC	.05
597a	Andy McGaffigan (Player #48, photo actually Rich Thompson.)	1.00
597b	Andy McGaffigan (Player #27, correct photo.)	.05
598	Billy Hatcher RC	.05
599	Bob Knepper	.05
600	Checklist 501-600	.05
601	Joey Cora	.05
602	Steve Finley RC	.20
603	Kal Daniels	.05
604	Gregg Olson	.05
605	Dave Steib	.05
606	Kenny Rogers RC	.05
607	Zane Smith	.05
608	Bob Geren RC	.05
609	Chad Kreuter	.05
610	Mike Smithson RC	.05
611	Jeff Wetherby RC	.05
612	Gary Mielke RC	.05
613	Pete Smith	.05
614	Jack Daugherty RC	.05
615	Lance McCullers	.05
616	Don Robinson RC	.05
617	Jose Guzman	.05
618	Steve Bedrosian RC	.05
619	Jamie Moyer	.05
620	Atlee Hammaker RC	.05
621	Rick Luecken RC	.05
622	Greg W. Harris RC	.05
623	Pete Harnisch	.05
624	Jerald Clark RC	.05
625	Jack McDowell	.05
626	Frank Viola	.05
627	Ted Higuera	.05
628	Marty Pevey RC	.05
629	Bill Wegman	.05
630	Eric Plunk RC	.05
631	Drew Hall	.05
632	Doug Jones RC	.05
633	Geno Petralli	.05
634	Jose Alvarez RC	.05
635	Bob Milacki	.05
636	Bobby Witt RC	.05
637	Trevor Wilson	.05
638	Jeff Russell RC	.05
639	Mike Krukow	.05
640	Rick Leach RC	.05
641	Dave Schmidt	.05
642	Terry Leach RC	.05
643	Calvin Schiraldi	.05
644	Bob Melvin RC	.05
645	Jim Abbott	.05
646	Jaime Navarro RC	.05
647	Mark Langston	.05
648	Juan Nieves RC	.05
649	Damaso Garcia	.05
650	Charlie O'Brien RC	.05
651	Eric King	.05
652	Mike Boddicker	.05
653	Duane Ward	.05
654	Bob Stanley	.05
655	Sandy Alomar, Jr.	.05
656	Danny Tartabull	.05
657	Randy McCament	.05
658	Charlie Leibrandt	.05
659	Dan Quisenberry	.05
660	Paul Assenmacher RC	.05
661	Walt Terrell	.05
662	Tim Leary	.05
663	Randy Milligan	.05
664	Bo Diaz RC	.05
665	Mark Lemke	.05
666	Jose Gonzalez RC	.05
667	Chuck Finley	.05
668	John Kruk	.05
669	Dick Schofield	.05
670	Tim Crews	.05
671	John Dopson	.05
672	John Orton RC	.05
673	Eric Hetzel RC	.05
674	Lance Parrish	.05
675	Ramon Martinez	.05
676	Mark Gubicza	.05
677	Greg Litton	.05
678	Greg Mathews	.05
679	Dave Dravecky	.05
680	Steve Farr	.05
681	Mike Devereaux	.05
682	Ken Griffey Sr.	.05
683a	Jamie Weston RC (First name incorrect.)	1.00
683b	Mickey Weston RC (Corrected.)	.05
684	Jack Armstrong	.05
685	Steve Buechele	.05
686	Bryan Harvey	.05
687	Lance Blankenship	.05
688	Dante Bichette	.05
689	Todd Burns RC	.05
690	Dan Petry	.05
691	Kent Anderson RC	.05
692	Todd Stottlemyre	.05
693	Wally Joyner	.05
694	Mike Rochford RC	.05
695	Floyd Bannister	.05
696	Rick Reuschel	.05
697	Jose DeLeon	.05
698	Jeff Montgomery	.05
699	Kelly Downs	.05
700a	Checklist 601-700 (#683 Jamie Weston)	.05
700b	Checklist 601-700 (# 683 Mickey Weston)	.05
701	Jim Gott	.05
702	"Rookie Threats" (Delino DeShields, Larry Walker, Marquis Grissom)	.25
703	Alejandro Pena	.05
704	Willie Randolph	.05
705	Tim Leary	.05
706	Chuck McElroy RC	.05
707	Gerald Perry RC	.05
708	Tom Brunansky	.05
709	John Franco	.05
710	Mark Davis	.05
711	Dave Justice RC	1.50
712	Storm Davis	.05
713	Scott Ruskin RC	.05
714	Glenn Braggs	.05
715	Kevin Bearse RC	.05
716	Jose Nunez RC	.05
717	Tim Layana RC	.05
718	Greg Myers RC	.05
719	Pete O'Brien	.05
720	John Candelaria	.05
721	Craig Grebeck RC	.05
722	Shawn Boskie RC	.05
723	Jim Leyritz RC	.10
724	Bill Sampen RC	.05
725	Scott Radinsky RC	.05
726	Todd Hundley RC	.25
727	Scott Hemond RC	.05
728	Lenny Webster RC	.05
729	Jeff Reardon	.05
730	Mitch Webster	.05
731	Brian Bohanon RC	.05
732	Rick Parker RC	.05
733	Terry Shumpert RC	.05
734a	Nolan Ryan (300-win stripe on front)	1.50
734b	Nolan Ryan (No stripe.)	4.00
735	John Burkett	.05
736	Derrick May RC	.05
737	Carlos Baerga RC	.05
738	Greg Smith RC	.05
739	Joe Kraemer RC	.05
740	Scott Sanderson RC	.05
741	Hector Villanueva RC	.05
742	Mike Fetters RC	.05
743	Mark Gardner RC	.05
744	Matt Nokes RC	.05
745	Dave Winfield	.60
746	Delino DeShields RC	.15
747	Dann Howitt RC	.05
748	Tony Pena	.05
749	Dennis "Oil Can" Boyd	.05
750	Mike Benjamin RC	.05
751	Alex Cole RC	.05
752	Eric Gunderson RC	.05
753	Howard Farmer RC	.05
754	Joe Carter	.05
755	Ray Lankford RC	.25
756	Sandy Alomar, Jr.	.05
757	Alex Sanchez RC	.05
758	Nick Esasky	.05
759	Stan Belinda RC	.05
760	Jim Presley RC	.05

761	Gary DiSarcina RC	.05	
762	Wayne Edwards RC	.05	
763	Pat Combs RC	.05	
764	Mickey Pina RC	.05	
765	Wilson Alvarez RC	.25	
766	Dave Parker RC	.05	
767	Mike Blowers RC	.05	
768	Tony Phillips	.05	
769	Pascual Perez	.05	
770	Gary Pettis	.05	
771	Fred Lynn	.05	
772	Mel Rojas RC	.10	
773	David Segui RC	.25	
774	Gary Carter	.60	
775	Rafael Valdez RC	.05	
776	Glenallen Hill RC	.05	
777	Keith Hernandez	.05	
778	Billy Hatcher	.05	
779	Marty Clary RC	.05	
780	Candy Maldonado RC	.05	
781	Mike Marshall	.05	
782	Billy Jo Robidoux RC	.05	
783	Mark Langston	.05	
784	Paul Sorrento RC	.05	
785	Dave Hollins RC	.05	
786	Cecil Fielder	.05	
787	Matt Young	.05	
788	Jeff Huson	.05	
789	Lloyd Moseby	.05	
790	Ron Kittle	.05	
791	Hubie Brooks	.05	
792	Craig Lefferts	.05	
793	Kevin Bass	.05	
794	Bryn Smith RC	.05	
795	Juan Samuel	.05	
796	Sam Horn	.05	
797	Randy Myers	.05	
798	Chris James	.05	
799	Bill Gullickson	.05	
800	Checklist 701-800	.05	

NM/M
702 Mike Witt 450.00
800 Checklist 701-800 250.00

1991 Upper Deck

Shawn Abner

More than 110 rookies are included among the first 700 cards in the 1991 Upper Deck set. A 100-card high-number series was released in late summer. Cards feature top quality white stock and color photos on front and back. A nine-card "Baseball Heroes" bonus set honoring Nolan Ryan, is among the many insert specials in the '91 UD set. Others include a card of Chicago Bulls superstar Michael Jordan. Along with the Ryan bonus cards, 2,500 cards personally autographed and numbered by Ryan were randomly inserted. Upper Deck cards are packaged in tamper-proof foil packs. Each pack contains 15 cards and a 3-1/2" x 2-1/2" 3-D team logo hologram sticker.

NM/M
Unopened Factory Set (800): 20.00
Complete Set (800): 10.00
Complete Low Series (700): 9.00
Complete High Series (100): 1.00
Common Player: .05
Low or High Wax Pack (15): .60
Low or High Wax Box (36): 13.50
1 Star Rookie Checklist .05
2 Phil Plantier RC .05
3 D.J. Dozier RC .05
4 Dave Hansen RC .05
5 Mo Vaughn RC .10
6 Leo Gomez RC .05
7 Scott Aldred RC .05
8 Scott Chiamparino RC .05
9 Lance Dickson RC .05
10 Sean Berry RC .05
11 Bernie Williams RC .25
12 Brian Barnes RC .05
13 Narciso Elvira RC .05
14 Mike Gardiner RC .05
15 Greg Colbrunn RC .05
16 Bernard Gilkey RC .05
17 Mark Lewis RC .05
18 Mickey Morandini RC .05
19 Charles Nagy RC .15
20 Geronimo Pena RC .05
21 Henry Rodriguez RC .05
22 Scott Cooper RC .05
23 Andujar Cedeno RC .05
24 Eric Karros RC .25
25 Steve Decker RC .05
26 Kevin Belcher RC .05
27 Jeff Conine RC .25
28 Oakland Athletics Checklist
   (Dave Stewart) .05
29 Chicago White Sox Checklist
   (Carlton Fisk) .20
30 Texas Rangers Checklist
   (Rafael Palmeiro) .20
31 California Angels Checklist
   (Chuck Finley) .05
32 Seattle Mariners Checklist
   (Harold Reynolds) .05
33 Kansas City Royals Checklist
   (Bret Saberhagen) .05

Baseball Heroes Reggie Jackson

This Baseball Heroes set is devoted to Reggie Jackson. The cards, numbered 1-9, are the first in a continuing series of cards issued in subsequent years. An un-numbered cover card that says "Baseball Heroes" was also issued. The Jackson cards were randomly inserted in high number foil packs only. Jackson also autographed 2,500 numbered cards, which were randomly included in high number packs.

NM/M
Complete Set (10): 5.00
Common Player: .50
Autographed Card: 100.00
1 1969 Emerging Superstar
  (Reggie Jackson) .50
2 1973 An MVP Year
  (Reggie Jackson) .50
3 1977 "Mr. October"
  (Reggie Jackson) .50
4 1978 Jackson vs. Welch
  (Reggie Jackson) .50
5 1982 Under the Halo
  (Reggie Jackson) .50
6 1984 500!
  (Reggie Jackson) .50
7 1986 Moving Up the List
  (Reggie Jackson) .50
8 1987 A Great Career Ends
  (Reggie Jackson) .50
9 Heroes Checklist 1-9
  (Reggie Jackson) .50
---- Header Card .50

1990 Upper Deck Black-Box Variations

It appears that card #702 in 1990 UD was originally intended to be Mike Witt, but that it was replaced by a "Rookie Threats" card picturing three Expos. At least a few examples of the Witt card, factory cancelled with a large black ink box on back, have made their way into the market, along with a #800 checklist card naming Witt as #702.

34 Minnesota Twins Checklist
   (Gary Gaetti) .05
35 Scott Leius .05
36 Neal Heaton .05
37 Terry Lee RC .05
38 Gary Redus .05
39 Barry Jones .05
40 Chuck Knoblauch .05
41 Larry Andersen .05
42 Darryl Hamilton .05
43 Boston Red Sox Checklist
   (Mike Greenwell) .05
44 Toronto Blue Jays Checklist
   (Kelly Gruber) .05
45 Detroit Tigers Checklist
   (Jack Morris) .05
46 Cleveland Indians Checklist
   (Sandy Alomar Jr.) .05
47 Baltimore Orioles Checklist
   (Gregg Olson) .05
48 Milwaukee Brewers Checklist
   (Dave Parker) .05
49 New York Yankees Checklist
   (Roberto Kelly) .05
50 Top Prospect '91 checklist .05
51 Kyle Abbott RC
   (Top Prospect) .10
52 Jeff Juden RC
   (Top Prospect) .05
53 Todd Van Poppel RC
   (Top Prospect) .10
54 Steve Karsay RC
   (Top Prospect) .10
55 Chipper Jones RC
   (Top Prospect) 6.00
56 Chris Johnson RC
   (Top Prospect) .05
57 John Ericks RC
   (Top Prospect) .05
58 Gary Scott RC
   (Top Prospect) .05
59 Kiki Jones RC
   (Top Prospect) .05
60 Wil Cordero RC
   (Top Prospect) .05
61 Royce Clayton RC
   (Top Prospect) .05
62 Tim Costo RC
   (Top Prospect) .05
63 Roger Salkeld RC
   (Top Prospect) .05
64 Brook Fordyce RC
   (Top Prospect) .05
65 Mike Mussina RC
   (Top Prospect) 1.00
66 Dave Staton RC
   (Top Prospect) .05
67 Mike Lieberthal RC
   (Top Prospect) .50
68 Kurt Miller RC
   (Top Prospect) .05
69 Dan Peltier RC
   (Top Prospect) .05
70 Greg Blosser RC
   (Top Prospect) .05
71 Reggie Sanders RC
   (Top Prospect) .25
72 Brent Mayne RC
   (Top Prospect) .05
73 Rico Brogna RC
   (Top Prospect) .05
74 Willie Banks RC
   (Top Prospect) .05
75 Len Brutcher RC
   (Top Prospect) .05
76 Pat Kelly RC
   (Top Prospect) .05
77 Cincinnati Reds Checklist
   (Chris Sabo) .05
78 Los Angeles Dodgers Checklist
   (Ramon Martinez) .05
79 San Francisco Giants Checklist (Matt Williams) .05
80 San Diego Padres Checklist
   (Roberto Alomar) .05
81 Houston Astros checklist
   (Glenn Davis) .05
82 Atlanta Braves checklist
   (Ron Gant) .05
83 "Fielder's Feat"
   (Cecil Fielder) .05
84 Orlando Merced RC .10
85 Domingo Ramos .05
86 Tom Bolton .05
87 Andres Santana RC .05
88 John Dopson RC .05
89 Kenny Williams .05
90 Marty Barrett .05
91 Tom Pagnozzi .05
92 Carmelo Martinez .05
93 "Save Master"
   (Bobby Thigpen) .05
94 Pittsburgh Pirates Checklist
   (Barry Bonds) .50
95 New York Mets Checklist
   (Gregg Jefferies) .05
96 Montreal Expos Checklist
   (Tim Wallach) .05
97 Philadelphia Phillies Checklist
   (Lenny Dykstra) .05
98 St. Louis Cardinals Checklist
   (Pedro Guerrero) .05
99 Chicago Cubs Checklist
   (Mark Grace) .05
100 Checklist 1-100 .05
101 Kevin Elster .05
102 Tom Brookens .05

103 Mackey Sasser .05
104 Felix Fermin RC .05
105 Kevin McReynolds .05
106 Dave Steib .05
107 Jeffrey Leonard .05
108 Dave Henderson .05
109 Sid Bream .05
110 Henry Cotto .05
111 Shawon Dunston .05
112 Mariano Duncan RC .05
113 Joe Girardi .05
114 Billy Hatcher .05
115 Greg Maddux .50
116 Jerry Browne RC .05
117 Juan Samuel .05
118 Steve Olin .05
119 Alfredo Griffin .05
120 Mitch Webster RC .05
121 Joel Skinner .05
122 Frank Viola .05
123 Cory Snyder .05
124 Howard Johnson .05
125 Carlos Baerga .05
126 Tony Fernandez .05
127 Dave Stewart .05
128 Jay Buhner .05
129 Mike LaValliere .05
130 Scott Bradley .05
131 Tony Phillips .05
132 Ryne Sandberg .50
133 Paul O'Neill .05
134 Mark Grace .05
135 Chris Sabo .05
136 Ramon Martinez .05
137 Brook Jacoby .05
138 Candy Maldonado .05
139 Mike Scioscia .05
140 Chris James RC .05
141 Craig Worthington .05
142 Manny Lee .05
143 Tim Raines .05
144 Sandy Alomar, Jr. .05
145 John Olerud .05
146 Ozzie Canseco RC .05
147 Pat Borders .05
148 Harold Reynolds .05
149 Tom Henke .05
150 R.J. Reynolds .05
151 Mike Gallego .05
152 Bobby Bonilla .05
153 Terry Steinbach .05
154 Barry Bonds 1.00
155 Jose Canseco .30
156 Gregg Jefferies .05
157 Matt Williams .05
158 Craig Biggio .05
159 Daryl Boston .05
160 Ricky Jordan .05
161 Stan Belinda .05
162 Ozzie Smith .50
163 Tom Brunansky .05
164 Todd Zeile .05
165 Mike Greenwell .05
166 Kal Daniels .05
167 Kent Hrbek .05
168 Franklin Stubbs .05
169 Dick Schofield .05
170 Junior Ortiz .05
171 Hector Villanueva RC .05
172 Dennis Eckersley .35
173 Mitch Williams .05
174 Mark McGwire .75
175 Fernando Valenzuela .05
176 Gary Carter .40
177 Dave Magadan .05
178 Robby Thompson .05
179 Bob Ojeda .05
180 Ken Caminiti .05
181 Don Slaught .05
182 Luis Rivera .05
183 Jay Bell .05
184 Jody Reed .05
185 Wally Backman .05
186 Dave Martinez .05
187 Luis Polonia .05
188 Shane Mack .05
189 Spike Owen .05
190 Scott Bailes .05
191 John Russell .05
192 Walt Weiss .05
193 Jose Oquendo .05
194 Carney Lansford .05
195 Jeff Huson .05
196 Keith Miller .05
197 Eric Yelding .05
198 Ron Darling .05
199 John Kruk .05
200 Checklist 101-200 .05
201 John Shelby .05
202 Bob Geren .05
203 Lance McCullers .05
204 Alvaro Espinoza .05
205 Mark Salas .05
206 Mike Pagliarulo .05
207 Jose Uribe .05
208 Jim Deshaies RC .05
209 Ron Karkovice .05
210 Rafael Ramirez .05
211 Donnie Hill .05
212 Brian Harper RC .05
213 Jack Howell .05
214 Wes Gardner .05
215 Tim Burke .05
216 Doug Jones RC .05
217 Hubie Brooks .05
218 Tom Candiotti .05
219 Gerald Perry .05
220 Jose DeLeon RC .05

221 Wally Whitehurst .05
222 Alan Mills RC .05
223 Alan Trammell .05
224 Dwight Gooden .05
225 Travis Fryman .05
226 Joe Carter .05
227 Julio Franco .05
228 Craig Lefferts .05
229 Gary Pettis .05
230 Dennis Rasmussen .05
231a Brian Downing
   (No position on front.) 2.00
231b Brian Downing
   (DH on front) .05
232 Carlos Quintana RC .05
233 Gary Gaetti .05
234 Mark Langston .05
235 Tim Wallach .05
236 Greg Swindell .05
237 Eddie Murray .40
238 Jeff Manto RC .05
239 Lenny Harris .05
240 Jesse Orosco .05
241 Scott Lusader .05
242 Sid Fernandez .05
243 Jim Leyritz .05
244 Cecil Fielder .05
245 Darryl Strawberry .05
246 Frank Thomas .50
247 Kevin Mitchell .05
248 Lance Johnson RC .05
249 Rick Rueschel .05
250 Mark Portugal .05
251 Derek Lilliquist .05
252 Brian Holman RC .05
253 Rafael Valdez .05
254 B.J. Surhoff .05
255 Tony Gwynn .50
256 Andy Van Slyke .05
257 Todd Stottlemyre .05
258 Jose Lind .05
259 Greg Myers .05
260 Jeff Ballard RC .05
261 Bobby Thigpen .05
262 Jimmy Kremers RC .05
263 Robin Ventura .05
264 John Smoltz .05
265 Sammy Sosa .50
266 Gary Sheffield .30
267 Len Dykstra .05
268 Bill Spiers .05
269 Charlie Hayes .05
270 Brett Butler .05
271 Bip Roberts .05
272 Rob Deer .05
273 Fred Lynn .05
274 Dave Parker .05
275 Andy Benes .05
276 Glenallen Hill RC .05
277 Steve Howard RC .05
278 Doug Drabek .05
279 Joe Oliver .05
280 Todd Benzinger .05
281 Eric King .05
282 Jim Presley .05
283 Ken Patterson RC .05
284 Jack Daugherty RC .05
285 Ivan Calderon .05
286 Edgar Diaz RC .05
287 Kevin Bass .05
288 Don Carman RC .05
289 Greg Brock .05
290 John Franco .05
291 Joey Cora .05
292 Bill Wegman .05
293 Eric Show .05
294 Scott Bankhead .05
295 Garry Templeton .05
296 Mickey Tettleton .05
297 Luis Sojo .05
298 Jose Rijo .05
299 Dave Johnson .05
300 Checklist 201-300 .05
301 Mark Grant .05
302 Pete Harnisch .05
303 Greg Olson .05
304 Anthony Telford RC .05
305 Lonnie Smith .05
306 Chris Hoiles .05
307 Bryn Smith .05
308 Mike Devereaux .05
309a Milt Thompson
   ("86" in stats obscured by
   "bull's eye") .50
309b Milt Thompson
   ("86" visible) .05
310 Bob Melvin .05
311a Luis Salazar (Circled dot over
   "i" in Luis on back.) 2.00
311b Luis Salazar (Corrected) .05
312 Ed Whitson RC .05
313 Charlie Hough .05
314 Dave Clark .05
315 Eric Gunderson RC .05
316 Dan Petry .05
317 Dante Bichette .05
318 Mike Heath .05
319 Damon Berryhill .05
320 Walt Terrell .05
321 Scott Fletcher .05
322 Dan Plesac .05
323 Jack McDowell .05
324 Paul Molitor .40
325 Ozzie Guillen .05
326 Gregg Olson .05
327 Pedro Guerrero .05
328 Bob Milacki RC .05
329 John Tudor .05

330 Steve Finley .05
331 Jack Clark .05
332 Jerome Walton .05
333 Andy Hawkins .05
334 Derrick May .05
335 Roberto Alomar .20
336 Jack Morris .05
337 Dave Winfield .40
338 Steve Searcy .05
339 Chili Davis .05
340 Larry Sheets .05
341 Ted Higuera .05
342 David Segui RC .10
343 Greg Cadaret .05
344 Robin Yount .40
345 Nolan Ryan 1.00
346 Ray Lankford .05
347 Cal Ripken, Jr. 1.00
348 Lee Smith .05
349 Brady Anderson .05
350 Frank DiPino .05
351 Hal Morris .05
352 Deion Sanders .10
353 Barry Larkin .05
354 Don Mattingly .60
355 Eric Davis .05
356 Jose Offerman .05
357 Mel Rojas .05
358 Rudy Seanez RC .05
359 Dennis "Oil Can" Boyd .05
360 Nelson Liriano .05
361 Ron Gant .05
362 Howard Farmer RC .05
363 Dave Justice .05
364 Delino DeShields .05
365 Steve Avery .05
366 David Cone .05
367 Lou Whitaker .05
368 Von Hayes .05
369 Frank Tanana .05
370 Tim Teufel .05
371 Randy Myers .05
372 Roberto Kelly .05
373 Jack Armstrong .05
374 Kelly Gruber .05
375 Kevin Maas .05
376 Randy Johnson .40
377 David West .05
378 Brent Knackert RC .05
379 Rick Honeycutt .05
380 Kevin Gross .05
381 Tom Foley .05
382 Jeff Blauser .05
383 Scott Ruskin RC .05
384 Andres Thomas RC .05
385 Dennis Martinez .05
386 Mike Henneman .05
387 Felix Jose .05
388 Alejandro Pena .05
389 Chet Lemon .05
390 Craig Wilson RC .05
391 Chuck Crim .05
392 Mel Hall .05
393 Mark Knudson .05
394 Norm Charlton .05
395 Mike Felder .05
396 Tim Layana RC .05
397 Steve Frey RC .05
398 Bill Doran .05
399 Dion James .05
400 Checklist 301-400 .05
401 Ron Hassey .05
402 Don Robinson .05
403 Gene Nelson .05
404 Terry Kennedy .05
405 Todd Burns .05
406 Roger McDowell .05
407 Bob Kipper .05
408 Darren Daulton .05
409 Chuck Cary .05
410 Bruce Ruffin .05
411 Juan Berenguer .05
412 Gary Ward .05
413 Al Newman .05
414 Danny Jackson .05
415 Greg Gagne .05
416 Tom Herr .05
417 Jeff Parrett .05
418 Jeff Reardon .05
419 Mark Lemke .05
420 Charlie O'Brien RC .05
421 Willie Randolph .05
422 Steve Bedrosian .05
423 Mike Moore .05
424 Jeff Brantley RC .05
425 Bob Welch .05
426 Terry Mulholland .05
427 Willie Blair RC .05
428 Darrin Fletcher RC .05
429 Mike Witt .05
430 Joe Boever .05
431 Tom Gordon .05
432 Pedro Munoz RC .05
433 Kevin Seitzer .05
434 Kevin Tapani .05
435 Bret Saberhagen .05
436 Ellis Burks .05
437 Chuck Finley .05
438 Mike Boddicker .05
439 Francisco Cabrera .05
440 Todd Hundley .05
441 Kelly Downs .05
442 Dann Howitt RC .05
443 Scott Garrelts .05
444 Rickey Henderson .40
445 Will Clark .05
446 Ben McDonald .05
447 Dale Murphy .20

448	Dave Righetti	.05
449	Dickie Thon	.05
450	Ted Power	.05
451	Scott Coolbaugh	.05
452	Dwight Smith	.05
453	Pete Incaviglia	.05
454	Andre Dawson	.25
455	Ruben Sierra	.05
456	Andres Galarraga	.05
457	Alvin Davis	.05
458	Tony Castillo	.05
459	Pete O'Brien	.05
460	Charlie Leibrandt	.05
461	Vince Coleman	.05
462	Steve Sax	.05
463	Omar Oliveras RC	.05
464	Oscar Azocar RC	.05
465	Joe Magrane RC	.05
466	Karl Rhodes RC	.05
467	Benito Santiago	.05
468	Joe Klink RC	.05
469	Sil Campusano RC	.05
470	Mark Parent	.05
471	Shawn Boskie RC	.05
472	Kevin Brown	.05
473	Rick Sutcliffe	.05
474	Rafael Palmeiro	.35
475	Mike Harkey	.05
476	Jaime Navarro	.05
477	Marquis Grissom	.05
478	Marty Clary	.05
479	Greg Briley RC	.05
480	Tom Glavine	.25
481	Lee Guetterman	.05
482	Rex Hudler	.05
483	Dave LaPoint RC	.05
484	Terry Pendleton	.05
485	Jesse Barfield	.05
486	Jose DeJesus	.05
487	Paul Abbott RC	.05
488	Ken Howell	.05
489	Greg W. Harris	.05
490	Roy Smith	.05
491	Paul Assenmacher	.05
492	Geno Petralli	.05
493	Steve Wilson	.05
494	Kevin Reimer RC	.05
495	Bill Long	.05
496	Mike Jackson RC	.05
497	Oddibe McDowell	.05
498	Bill Swift	.05
499	Jeff Treadway	.05
500	Checklist 401-500	.05
501	Gene Larkin	.05
502	Bob Boone	.05
503	Allan Anderson	.05
504	Luis Aquino RC	.05
505	Mark Guthrie	.05
506	Joe Orsulak	.05
507	Dana Kiecker RC	.05
508	Dave Gallagher RC	.05
509	Greg A. Harris	.05
510	Mark Williamson	.05
511	Casey Candaele	.05
512	Mookie Wilson	.05
513	Dave Smith	.05
514	Chuck Carr RC	.05
515	Glenn Wilson	.05
516	Mike Fitzgerald RC	.05
517	Devon White	.05
518	Dave Hollins	.05
519	Mark Eichhorn	.05
520	Otis Nixon	.05
521	Terry Shumpert RC	.05
522	Scott Erickson RC	.15
523	Danny Tartabull	.05
524	Orel Hershiser	.05
525	George Brett	.60
526	Greg Vaughn	.05
527	Tim Naehring RC	.05
528	Curt Schilling RC	.25
529	Chris Bosio	.05
530	Sam Horn	.05
531	Mike Scott	.05
532	George Bell	.05
533	Eric Anthony	.05
534	Julio Valera RC	.05
535	Glenn Davis	.05
536	Larry Walker	.05
537	Pat Combs	.05
538	Chris Nabholz RC	.05
539	Kirk McCaskill	.05
540	Randy Ready	.05
541	Mark Gubicza	.05
542	Rick Aguilera	.05
543	Brian McRae RC	.05
544	Kirby Puckett	.50
545	Bo Jackson	.10
546	Wade Boggs	.50
547	Tim McIntosh RC	.05
548	Randy Milligan RC	.05
549	Dwight Evans	.05
550	Billy Ripken	.05
551	Erik Hanson	.05
552	Lance Parrish	.05
553	Tino Martinez	.05
554	Jim Abbott	.05
555	Ken Griffey Jr.	.65
556	Milt Cuyler RC	.05
557	Mark Leonard RC	.05
558	Jay Howell	.05
559	Lloyd Moseby	.05
560	Chris Gwynn	.05
561	Mark Whiten RC	.05
562	Harold Baines	.05
563	Junior Felix	.05
564	Darren Lewis	.05
565	Fred McGriff	.05

566	Kevin Appier	.05
567	Luis Gonzalez RC	1.00
568	Frank White	.05
569	Juan Agosto	.05
570	Mike Macfarlane	.05
571	Bert Blyleven	.05
572	Ken Griffey Sr.	.05
573	Lee Stevens RC	.05
574	Edgar Martinez	.05
575	Wally Joyner	.05
576	Tim Belcher	.05
577	John Burkett	.05
578	Mike Morgan	.05
579	Paul Gibson	.05
580	Jose Vizcaino RC	.05
581	Duane Ward	.05
582	Scott Sanderson	.05
583	David Wells	.05
584	Willie McGee	.05
585	John Cerutti	.05
586	Danny Darwin	.05
587	Kurt Stillwell	.05
588	Rich Gedman	.05
589	Mark Davis	.05
590	Bill Gullickson	.05
591	Matt Young	.05
592	Bryan Harvey RC	.05
593	Omar Vizquel	.05
594	Scott Lewis RC	.05
595	Dave Valle	.05
596	Tim Crews RC	.05
597	Mike Bielecki	.05
598	Mike Sharperson	.05
599	Dave Bergman	.05
600	Checklist 501-600	.05
601	Steve Lyons	.05
602	Bruce Hurst	.05
603	Donn Pall	.05
604	Jim Vatcher RC	.05
605	Dan Pasqua	.05
606	Kenny Rogers	.05
607	Jeff Schulz RC	.05
608	Brad Arnsberg RC	.05
609	Willie Wilson	.05
610	Jamie Moyer	.05
611	Ron Oester	.05
612	Dennis Cook RC	.05
613	Rick Mahler	.05
614	Bill Landrum	.05
615	Scott Scudder	.05
616	Tom Edens RC	.05
617	"1917 Revisited" (Chicago White Sox team photo.)	.05
618	Jim Gantner	.05
619	Darrel Akerfelds RC	.05
620	Ron Robinson	.05
621	Scott Radinsky RC	.05
622	Pete Smith	.05
623	Melido Perez	.05
624	Jerald Clark RC	.05
625	Carlos Martinez	.05
626	Wes Chamberlain RC	.05
627	Bobby Witt	.05
628	Ken Dayley RC	.05
629	John Barfield RC	.05
630	Bob Tewksbury	.05
631	Glenn Braggs	.05
632	Jim Neidlinger RC	.05
633	Tom Browning	.05
634	Kirk Gibson	.05
635	Rob Dibble	.05
636	"Stolen Base Leaders" (Lou Brock, Rickey Henderson)	.15
637	Jeff Montgomery	.05
638	Mike Schooler	.05
639	Storm Davis	.05
640	Rich Rodriguez RC	.05
641	Phil Bradley	.05
642	Kent Mercker	.05
643	Carlton Fisk	.40
644	Mike Bell	.05
645	Alex Fernandez RC	.05
646	Juan Gonzalez	.30
647	Ken Hill	.05
648	Jeff Russell	.05
649	Chuck Malone RC	.05
650	Steve Buechele	.05
651	Mike Benjamin	.05
652	Tony Pena	.05
653	Trevor Wilson	.05
654	Alex Cole	.05
655	Roger Clemens	.60
656	"The Bashing Years" (Mark McGwire)	.50
657	Joe Grahe RC	.05
658	Jim Eisenreich	.05
659	Dan Gladden	.05
660	Steve Farr RC	.05
661	Bill Sampen RC	.05
662	Dave Rohde RC	.05
663	Mark Gardner	.05
664	Mike Simms RC	.05
665	Moises Alou	.05
666	Mickey Hatcher	.05
667	Jimmy Key	.05
668	John Wetteland	.05
669	John Smiley	.05
670	Jim Acker	.05
671	Pascual Perez	.05
672	Reggie Harris RC	.05
673	Matt Nokes	.05
674	Rafael Novoa RC	.05
675	Hensley Meulens	.05
676	Jeff M. Robinson RC	.05
677	"Ground Breaking" (New Comiskey Park)	.15
678	Johnny Ray	.05

679	Greg Hibbard	.05
680	Paul Sorrento	.05
681	Mike Marshall	.05
682	Jim Clancy	.05
683	Rob Murphy	.05
684	Dave Schmidt RC	.05
685	Jeff Gray RC	.05
686	Mike Hartley RC	.05
687	Jeff King	.05
688	Stan Javier RC	.05
689	Bob Walk	.05
690	Jim Gott	.05
691	Mike LaCoss	.05
692	John Farrell	.05
693	Tim Leary	.05
694	Mike Walker RC	.05
695	Eric Plunk	.05
696	Mike Fetters	.05
697	Wayne Edwards	.05
698	Tim Drummond RC	.05
699	Willie Fraser	.05
700	Checklist 601-700	.05
701	Mike Heath	.05
702	"Rookie Threats" (Luis Gonzalez, Karl Rhodes, Jeff Bagwell)	.45
703	Jose Mesa	.05
704	Dave Smith RC	.05
705	Danny Darwin	.05
706	Rafael Belliard	.05
707	Rob Murphy	.05
708	Terry Pendleton	.05
709	Mike Pagliarulo	.05
710	Sid Bream	.05
711	Junior Felix	.05
712	Dante Bichette	.05
713	Kevin Gross	.05
714	Luis Sojo	.05
715	Bob Ojeda	.05
716	Julio Machado RC	.05
717	Steve Farr	.05
718	Franklin Stubbs	.05
719	Mike Boddicker	.05
720	Willie Randolph	.05
721	Willie McGee	.05
722	Chili Davis	.05
723	Danny Jackson	.05
724	Cory Snyder	.05
725	"MVP Lineup" (Andre Dawson, George Bell, Ryne Sandberg)	.20
726	Rob Deer	.05
727	Rich DeLucia RC	.05
728	Mike Perez RC	.05
729	Mickey Tettleton	.05
730	Mike Blowers	.05
731	Gary Gaetti	.05
732	Brett Butler	.05
733	Dave Parker	.05
734	Eddie Zosky RC	.05
735	Jack Clark	.05
736	Jack Morris	.05
737	Kirk Gibson	.05
738	Steve Bedrosian	.05
739	Candy Maldonado	.05
740	Matt Young	.05
741	Rich Garces RC	.05
742	George Bell	.05
743	Deion Sanders	.10
744	Bo Jackson	.05
745	Luis Mercedes RC	.05
746	Reggie Jefferson RC	.05
747	Pete Incaviglia	.05
748	Chris Hammond	.05
749	Mike Stanton	.05
750	Scott Sanderson	.05
751	Paul Faries RC	.05
752	Al Osuna RC	.05
753	Steve Chitren RC	.05
754	Tony Fernandez	.05
755	Jeff Bagwell RC	1.50
756	Kirk Dressendorfer RC	.05
757	Glenn Davis	.05
758	Gary Carter	.40
759	Zane Smith	.05
760	Vance Law	.05
761	Denis Boucher RC	.05
762	Turner Ward RC	.05
763	Roberto Alomar	.20
764	Albert Belle	.05
765	Joe Carter	.05
766	Pete Schourek RC	.05
767	Heathcliff Slocumb RC	.05
768	Vince Coleman	.05
769	Mitch Williams	.05
770	Brian Downing	.05
771	Dana Allison RC	.05
772	Pete Harnisch	.05
773	Tim Raines	.05
774	Darryl Kile RC	.05
775	Fred McGriff	.05
776	Dwight Evans	.05
777	Joe Slusarski	.05
778	Dave Righetti	.05
779	Jeff Hamilton	.05
780	Ernest Riles	.05
781	Ken Dayley	.05
782	Eric King	.05
783	Devon White	.05
784	Beau Allred RC	.05
785	Mike Timlin RC	.05
786	Ivan Calderon	.05
787	Hubie Brooks	.05
788	Juan Agosto RC	.05
789	Barry Jones	.05
790	Wally Backman	.05
791	Jim Presley	.05
792	Charlie Hough	.05

793	Larry Andersen	.05
794	Steve Finley	.05
795	Shawn Abner	.05
796	Jeff M. Robinson	.05
797	Joe Bitker RC	.05
798	Eric Show	.05
799	Bud Black	.05
800	Checklist 701-800	.05
SP1	Michael Jordan	3.00
SP2	"A Day to Remember" (Rickey Henderson, Nolan Ryan)	1.00
HH1	Hank Aaron (Hologram)	1.00

This four-card set features three members of Baseball's Hall of Fame: Harmon Killebrew, Gaylord Perry and Ferguson Jenkins. Each has a card for himself, plus there's a card which features all three players. The cards were found in specially-marked low number foil packs. The cards are numbered H1-H4. Upper Deck also produced 3,000 autographed and numbered cards for each player.

	NM/M
Complete Set (4):	7.00
Common Card:	2.00
1 Harmon Killebrew	2.00
1a Harmon Killebrew/Auto.	10.00
2 Gaylord Perry	2.00
2a Gaylord Perry/Auto.	10.00
3 Ferguson Jenkins	2.00
3a Ferguson Jenkins/Auto.	10.00
4 Gaylord Perry, Ferguson Jenkins, Harmon Killebrew	2.00

Baseball Heroes Hank Aaron

This set devoted to Hank Aaron is numbered 19-27 and includes an unnumbered "Baseball Heroes" cover card. The cards are found in foil and jumbo packs of Upper Deck high-number cards.

	NM/M
Complete Set (10):	4.00
Common Aaron:	.50
Autographed Card:	180.00
Aaron Header:	1.00
19 1954 Rookie Year	.50
20 1957 MVP	.50
21 1966 Move to Atlanta	.50
22 1970 3,000	.50
23 1974 715	.50
24 1975 Return to Milwaukee	.50
25 1976 755	.50
26 1982 Hall of Fame	.50
27 Checklist - Heroes 19-27	.50

Baseball Heroes Nolan Ryan

This set devoted to Nolan Ryan is numbered 10-18 and includes an unnumbered "Baseball Heroes" cover card. The cards are found in low-number foil and jumbo boxes. One out of every hundred of the autographed cards was specially inscribed "Strike Out King."

	NM/M
Complete Set (10):	3.00
Common Player:	.50
Ryan Header Card:	1.00
Autographed Card:	200.00
"Strike Out King" Auto.	575.00
10 1968 Victory #1	.50
11 1973 A Career Year	.50
12 1975 Double Milestone	.50
13 1979 Back Home	.50
14 1981 All-Time Leader	.50
15 1989 5,000	.50
16 1990 The Sixth	.50
17 1990 ... and Still Counting	.50
18 Checklist - Heroes 10-18	.50

1991 Upper Deck Heroes of Baseball

Silver Sluggers

Alan Trammell

Each year the "Silver Slugger" award is presented to the player at each position with the highest batting average in each league. Upper Deck produced special cards in honor of the 1990 season award winners. The cards were randomly inserted in jumbo packs of Upper Deck. The cards feature a "SS" designation along with the card number. The cards are designed like the regular issue Upper Deck cards from 1991, but feature a Silver Slugger bat along the left border of the card.

	NM/M
Complete Set (18):	5.00
Common Player:	.15
1 Julio Franco	.15
2 Alan Trammell	.15
3 Rickey Henderson	.75
4 Jose Canseco	.50
5 Barry Bonds	2.00
6 Eddie Murray	.75
7 Kelly Gruber	.15
8 Ryne Sandberg	1.00
9 Darryl Strawberry	.15
10 Ellis Burks	.15
11 Lance Parrish	.15
12 Cecil Fielder	.15
13 Matt Williams	.15
14 Dave Parker	.15
15 Bobby Bonilla	.15
16 Don Robinson	.15
17 Benito Santiago	.15
18 Barry Larkin	.15

Final Edition

Oil Can Boyd

Upper Deck surprised the hobby with the late-season release of this 100-card boxed set. The cards are numbered with an "F" designation. A special "Minor League Diamond Skills" subset (cards #1-21) features several top prospects. An All-Star subset (cards #79-99) is also included in this set. The cards are styled like the regular 1991 Upper Deck issue Special team hologram cards are included with the set.

		NM/M
Complete Set (100):		9.00
Common Player:		.05
1	Ryan Klesko, Reggie Sanders (Minor League Diamond Skills Checklist)	.10
2	Pedro Martinez RC	5.00
3	Lance Dickson RC	.05
4	Royce Clayton	.05
5	Scott Bryant RC	.05
6	Dan Wilson RC	.05
7	Dmitri Young RC	.50
8	Ryan Klesko RC	.50
9	Tom Goodwin RC	.05
10	Rondell White RC	.25
11	Reggie Sanders	.05
12	Todd Van Poppel	.05
13	Arthur Rhodes RC	.05
14	Eddie Zosky	.05
15	Gerald Williams RC	.05
16	Robert Eenhoorn RC	.05
17	Jim Thome RC	3.00
18	Marc Newfield RC	.05
19	Kerwin Moore RC	.05
20	Jeff McNeely RC	.05
21	Frankie Rodriguez RC	.05
22	Andy Mota RC	.05
23	Chris Haney RC	.05
24	Kenny Lofton RC	.05
25	Dave Nilsson RC	.05
26	Derek Bell	.05
27	Frank Castillo RC	.05
28	Candy Maldonado	.05
29	Chuck McElroy	.05
30	Chito Martinez RC	.05
31	Steve Howe RC	.05
32	Freddie Benavides RC	.05
33	Scott Kamieniecki RC	.05
34	Denny Neagle RC	.05
35	Mike Humphreys RC	.05
36	Mike Remlinger RC	.05
37	Scott Coolbaugh	.05
38	Darren Lewis	.05
39	Thomas Howard RC	.05
40	John Candelaria	.05
41	Todd Benzinger	.05
42	Wilson Alvarez RC	.05
43	Patrick Lennon RC	.05
44	Rusty Meacham RC	.05
45	Ryan Bowen RC	.05
46	Rick Wilkins RC	.10
47	Ed Sprague RC	.05
48	Bob Scanlan RC	.05
49	Tom Candiotti	.05
50	Dennis Martinez (Perfecto)	.05
51	Dennis "Oil Can" Boyd	.05
52	Glenallen Hill	.05
53	Scott Livingstone RC	.05
54	Brian Hunter RC	.05
55	Ivan Rodriguez RC	1.50
56	Keith Mitchell RC	.05
57	Roger McDowell	.05
58	Otis Nixon	.05
59	Juan Bell RC	.05
60	Bill Krueger	.05
61	Chris Donnels RC	.05
62	Tommy Greene	.05
63	Doug Simons RC	.05
64	Andy Ashby RC	.15
65	Anthony Young RC	.05
66	Kevin Morton RC	.05
67	Bret Barberie RC	.05
68	Scott Servais RC	.05
69	Ron Darling	.05
70	Vicente Palacios	.05
71	Tim Burke RC	.05
72	Gerald Alexander RC	.05
73	Reggie Jefferson	.05
74	Dean Palmer	.05
75	Mark Whiten	.05
76	Randy Tomlin RC	.05
77	Mark Wohlers RC	.05
78	Brook Jacoby	.05
79	Ken Griffey Jr., Ryne Sandberg (All-Star Checklist)	.25
80	Jack Morris/AS	.05
81	Sandy Alomar, Jr./AS	.05
82	Cecil Fielder/AS	.05
83	Roberto Alomar/AS	.10
84	Wade Boggs/AS	.25
85	Cal Ripken, Jr./AS	.60
86	Rickey Henderson/AS	.15
87	Ken Griffey Jr./AS	.60
88	Dave Henderson/AS	.05
89	Danny Tartabull/AS	.05
90	Tom Glavine/AS	.10
91	Benito Santiago/AS	.05
92	Will Clark/AS	.05
93	Ryne Sandberg/AS	.50
94	Chris Sabo/AS	.05
95	Ozzie Smith/AS	.50
96	Ivan Calderon/AS	.05
97	Tony Gwynn/AS	.25
98	Andre Dawson/AS	.05
99	Bobby Bonilla/AS	.05
100	Checklist	.05

1991 Upper Deck Comic Ball 2 Promos

Among the most sought-after promo cards in the promocard mania that marked the 1991 National Sports Collectors Convention in Anaheim, Calif., was this set of Upper Deck preview cards for its Comic Ball 2 set. One card was given out each day of the National, from July 4-7, with the give-away date noted in a banner at top. Fronts picture Reggie Jackson and Nolan Ryan with various Looney Tunes cartoon characters. Backs have information on the upcoming Comic Ball 2 issue against a cartoon puzzle background.

	NM/M
Complete Set (4):	6.00
Common Player:	1.00
7/4/91 Nolan Ryan (w/Bugs Bunny, Daffy Duck)	2.50
7/5/91 Reggie Jackson (w/Taz)	1.00
7/6/91 Nolan Ryan (w/Speedy Gonzalez)	2.50
7/7/91 Reggie Jackson (w/Sylvester, Elmer Fudd)	1.00

1991 Upper Deck Comic Ball 2

Despite featuring two popular superstars on dozens of the cards, this 198-piece issue has found little favor with collectors. Most cards are arranged in 18-card sequences which tell a baseball-related cartoon tale starring Bugs Bunny, Daffy Duck, Wile E. Coyote and the rest of the Looney Tune characters. Actual-card "guest appearances" by Nolan Ryan and Reggie Jackson highlight these presentations. There are also "Seventh Inning Stretch' cards featuring the ballplayers in scenes with the cartoon figures. When arranged in nine-pocket plastic sheets, card backs form a cartoon picture puzzle. Cards are typical Upper Deck quality with semi-gloss front and back surfaces and a circular hologram on the backs in the standard 2-1/2" x 3-1/2" format. Nine hologram stickers featuring Ryan and Jackson along with the cartoon characters were produced as random pack inserts. Because the cards are licensed by Major League Baseball, the players and cartoon critters are depicted in Major League uniforms.

	NM/M
Complete Set (198):	5.00
Common Card, Cartoon:	.05
Common Card, Ryan/Jackson:	.10
Hologram Sticker:	2.00
Wax Pack:	.50
Wax Box (36):	7.50

1991 Upper Deck Comic Ball 2 Holograms

Nine silver-foil hologram stickers combine photos of Reggie Jackson and/or Nolan Ryan with various Warner Brothers cartoon stars and were issued as random pack inserts in Comic Ball 2. The 2-1/2" x 3-1/2" round-cornered stickers are blank-backed and unnumbered.

	NM/M
Complete Set (9):	17.50
Common Player:	3.00

No.	Card	Price
(1)	Reggie Jackson (w/Daffy)	3.00
(2)	Reggie Jackson (w/Speedy)	3.00
(3)	Reggie Jackson (w/Sylvester)	3.00
(4)	Reggie Jackson (w/Taz)	3.00
(5)	Reggie Jackson, Nolan Ryan (w/Roadrunner & Wile)	3.00
(6)	Nolan Ryan (w/Bugs)	3.00
(7)	Nolan Ryan (w/Sylvester)	3.00
(8)	Nolan Ryan (w/?)	3.00
(9)	Nolan Ryan (w/?)	3.00

1992 Upper Deck

Upper Deck introduced a new look in 1992. The baseline style was no longer used. The cards feature full-color action photos on white stock, with the player's name and the Upper Deck logo along the top border. The team name in the photo's bottom-right corner. Once again a 100-card high number series was released in late summer. Ted Williams autographed 2,500 Baseball Heroes cards which were randomly inserted into packs. Subsets featured in the 1992 issue include Star Rookies and Top Prospects. Cards originating from factory sets have gold-foil holograms on back, rather than silver.

	NM/M
Unopened Fact. Set (800):	20.00
Complete Set (800):	15.00
Common Player:	.05
Low or High Pack (15):	.50
Low or High Box (36):	12.50
Jumbo Pack (27):	1.00
Jumbo Box (20):	16.00
Bench/Morgan Auto.	75.00
Ted Williams Auto.	425.00

No.	Player	Price
1	Star Rookie Checklist (Ryan Klesko, Jim Thome)	.25
2	Royce Clayton/SR	.05
3	Brian Jordan/SR RC	.30
4	Dave Fleming/SR RC	.05
5	Jim Thome/SR	.40
6	Jeff Juden/SR	.05
7	Roberto Hernandez/SR RC	.15
8	Kyle Abbott/SR RC	.05
9	Chris George/SR RC	.05
10	Rob Maurer/SR RC	.05
11	Donald Harris/SR RC	.05
12	Ted Wood/SR RC	.05
13	Patrick Lennon/SR RC	.05
14	Willie Banks/SR	.05
15	Roger Salkeld/SR RC	.05
16	Wil Cordero/SR	.05
17	Arthur Rhodes/SR RC	.05
18	Pedro Martinez/SR RC	.40
19	Andy Ashby/SR RC	.10
20	Tom Goodwin/SR	.05
21	Braulio Castillo/SR RC	.05
22	Todd Van Poppel/SR	.05
23	Brian Williams/SR RC	.05
24	Ryan Klesko/SR	.05
25	Kenny Lofton/SR	.05
26	Derek Bell/SR	.05
27	Reggie Sanders/SR	.05
28	Dave Winfield (Winfield's 400th)	.25
29	Atlanta Braves Checklist (Dave Justice)	.05
30	Cincinnati Reds Checklist (Rob Dibble)	.05
31	Houston Astros Checklist (Craig Biggio) RC	.05
32	Los Angeles Dodgers Checklist (Eddie Murray)	.20
33	San Diego Padres Checklist (Fred McGriff)	.05
34	San Francisco Giants Checklist (Willie McGee)	.05
35	Chicago Cubs Checklist (Shawon Dunston)	.05
36	Montreal Expos Checklist (Delino DeShields)	.05
37	New York Mets Checklist (Howard Johnson)	.05
38	Philadelphia Phillies Checklist (John Kruk)	.05
39	Pittsburgh Pirates Checklist (Doug Drabek)	.05
40	St. Louis Cardinals Checklist (Todd Zeile)	.05
41	Steve Avery (Playoff Perfection)	.05
42	Jeremy Hernandez RC	.05
43	Doug Henry RC	.05
44	Chris Donnels RC	.05
45	Mo Sanford RC	.05
46	Scott Kamieniecki RC	.10
47	Mark Lemke	.05
48	Steve Farr	.05
49	Francisco Oliveras	.05
50	Ced Landrum RC	.05
51	Top Prospect Checklist (Rondell White, Marc Newfield)	.05
52	Eduardo Perez RC (Top Prospect)	.10
53	Tom Nevers RC (Top Prospect)	.05
54	David Zancanaro RC (Top Prospect)	.05
55	Shawn Green RC (Top Prospect)	1.50
56	Mark Wohlers RC (Top Prospect)	.05
57	Dave Nilsson (Top Prospect)	.05
58	Dmitri Young (Top Prospect)	.05
59	Ryan Hawblitzel RC (Top Prospect)	.05
60	Raul Mondesi (Top Prospect)	.05
61	Rondell White (Top Prospect)	.05
62	Steve Hosey (Top Prospect)	.05
63	Manny Ramirez RC (Top Prospect)	2.00
64	Marc Newfield (Top Prospect)	.05
65	Jeromy Burnitz (Top Prospect)	.05
66	Mark Smith RC (Top Prospect)	.05
67	Joey Hamilton RC (Top Prospect)	.10
68	Tyler Green RC (Top Prospect)	.05
69	John Farrell RC (Top Prospect)	.05
70	Kurt Miller RC (Top Prospect)	.05
71	Jeff Plympton RC (Top Prospect)	.05
72	Dan Wilson (Top Prospect)	.05
73	Joe Vitiello RC (Top Prospect)	.05
74	Rico Brogna (Top Prospect)	.05
75	David McCarty RC (Top Prospect)	.05
76	Bob Wickman RC (Top Prospect)	.05
77	Carlos Rodriguez RC (Top Prospect)	.05
78	Jim Abbott (Stay in School)	.05
79	Bloodlines (Pedro Martinez, Ramon Martinez)	.25
80	Bloodlines (Kevin Mitchell, Keith Mitchell)	.05
81	Bloodlines (Sandy Jr. & Roberto Alomar, Sandy Jr. & Roberto Alomar)	.10
82	Bloodlines (Cal Jr. & Billy Ripken, Cal Jr. & Billy Ripken)	.40
83	Bloodlines (Tony & Chris Gwynn, Tony & Chris Gwynn)	.20
84	Bloodlines (Dwight Gooden, Gary Sheffield)	.15
85	Bloodlines (Ken, Sr.; Ken, Jr.; & Craig Griffey, Ken, Sr.; Ken, Jr.; & Craig Griffey, Ken, Sr.; Ken, Jr.; & Craig Griffey)	.30
86	California Angels Checklist (Jim Abbott)	.05
87	Chicago White Sox Checklist (Frank Thomas)	.25
88	Kansas City Royals Checklist (Danny Tartabull)	.05
89	Minnesota Twins Checklist (Scott Erickson)	.05
90	Oakland Athletics Checklist (Rickey Henderson)	.25
91	Seattle Mariners Checklist (Edgar Martinez)	.05
92	Texas Rangers Checklist (Nolan Ryan)	.50
93	Baltimore Orioles Checklist (Ben McDonald)	.05
94	Boston Red Sox Checklist (Ellis Burks)	.05
95	Cleveland Indians Checklist (Greg Swindell)	.05
96	Detroit Tigers Checklist (Cecil Fielder)	.05
97	Milwaukee Brewers Checklist (Greg Vaughn)	.05
98	New York Yankees Checklist (Kevin Maas)	.05
99	Toronto Blue Jays Checklist (Dave Stieb)	.05
100	Checklist 1-100	.05
101	Joe Oliver	.05
102	Hector Villanueva	.05
103	Ed Whitson	.05
104	Danny Jackson	.05
105	Chris Hammond	.05
106	Ricky Jordan	.05
107	Kevin Bass	.05
108	Darrin Fletcher	.05
109	Junior Ortiz	.05
110	Tom Bolton	.05
111	Jeff King	.05
112	Dave Magadan	.05
113	Mike LaValliere	.05
114	Hubie Brooks	.05
115	Jay Bell	.05
116	David Wells	.05
117	Jim Leyritz	.05
118	Manuel Lee	.05
119	Alvaro Espinoza	.05
120	B.J. Surhoff	.05
121	Hal Morris	.05
122	Shawon Dunston	.05
123	Chris Sabo	.05
124	Andre Dawson	.25
125	Eric Davis	.05
126	Chili Davis	.05
127	Dale Murphy	.15
128	Kirk McCaskill	.05
129	Terry Mulholland	.05
130	Rick Aguilera	.05
131	Vince Coleman	.05
132	Andy Van Slyke	.05
133	Gregg Jefferies	.05
134	Barry Bonds	1.00
135	Dwight Gooden	.05
136	Dave Stieb	.05
137	Albert Belle	.05
138	Teddy Higuera	.05
139	Jesse Barfield	.05
140	Pat Borders	.05
141	Bip Roberts	.05
142	Rob Dibble	.05
143	Mark Grace	.05
144	Barry Larkin	.05
145	Ryne Sandberg	.50
146	Scott Erickson	.05
147	Luis Polonia	.05
148	John Burkett	.05
149	Luis Sojo	.05
150	Dickie Thon	.05
151	Walt Weiss	.05
152	Mike Scioscia	.05
153	Mark McGwire	.75
154	Matt Williams	.05
155	Rickey Henderson	.40
156	Sandy Alomar, Jr.	.05
157	Brian McRae	.05
158	Harold Baines	.05
159	Kevin Appier	.05
160	Felix Fermin	.05
161	Leo Gomez	.05
162	Craig Biggio	.05
163	Ben McDonald	.05
164	Randy Johnson	.40
165	Cal Ripken, Jr.	1.00
166	Frank Thomas	.40
167	Delino DeShields	.05
168	Greg Gagne	.05
169	Ron Karkovice	.05
170	Charlie Leibrandt	.05
171	Dave Righetti	.05
172	Dave Henderson	.05
173	Steve Decker	.05
174	Darryl Strawberry	.05
175	Will Clark	.05
176	Ruben Sierra	.05
177	Ozzie Smith	.50
178	Charles Nagy	.05
179	Gary Pettis	.05
180	Kirk Gibson	.05
181	Randy Milligan	.05
182	Dave Valle	.05
183	Chris Hoiles	.05
184	Tony Phillips	.05
185	Brady Anderson	.05
186	Scott Fletcher	.05
187	Gene Larkin	.05
188	Lance Johnson	.05
189	Greg Olson	.05
190	Melido Perez	.05
191	Lenny Harris	.05
192	Terry Kennedy	.05
193	Mike Gallego	.05
194	Willie McGee	.05
195	Juan Samuel	.05
196	Jeff Huson	.05
197	Alex Cole	.05
198	Ron Robinson	.05
199	Joel Skinner	.05
200	Checklist 101-200	.05
201	Kevin Reimer	.05
202	Stan Belinda	.05
203	Pat Tabler	.05
204	Jose Guzman	.05
205	Jose Lind	.05
206	Spike Owen	.05
207	Joe Orsulak	.05
208	Charlie Hayes	.05
209	Mike Devereaux	.05
210	Mike Fitzgerald	.05
211	Willie Randolph	.05
212	Rod Nichols	.05
213	Mike Boddicker	.05
214	Bill Spiers	.05
215	Steve Olin	.05
216	David Howard RC	.05
217	Gary Varsho	.05
218	Mike Harkey	.05
219	Luis Aquino	.05
220	Chuck McElroy RC	.05
221	Doug Drabek	.05
222	Dave Winfield	.40
223	Rafael Palmeiro	.35
224	Joe Carter	.05
225	Bobby Bonilla	.05
226	Ivan Calderon	.05
227	Gregg Olson	.05
228	Tim Wallach	.05
229	Terry Pendleton	.05
230	Gilberto Reyes RC	.05
231	Carlos Baerga	.05
232	Greg Vaughn	.05
233	Bret Saberhagen	.05
234	Gary Sheffield	.30
235	Mark Lewis	.05
236	George Bell	.05
237	Danny Tartabull	.05
238	Willie Wilson	.05
239	Doug Dascenzo	.05
240	Bill Pecota	.05
241	Julio Franco	.05
242	Ed Sprague	.05
243	Juan Gonzalez	.20
244	Chuck Finley	.05
245	Ivan Rodriguez	.35
246	Len Dykstra	.05
247	Deion Sanders	.10
248	Dwight Evans	.05
249	Larry Walker	.05
250	Billy Ripken	.05
251	Mickey Tettleton	.05
252	Tony Pena	.05
253	Benito Santiago	.05
254	Kirby Puckett	.50
255	Cecil Fielder	.05
256	Howard Johnson	.05
257	Andujar Cedeno	.05
258	Jose Rijo	.05
259	Al Osuna	.05
260	Todd Hundley	.05
261	Orel Hershiser	.05
262	Ray Lankford	.05
263	Robin Ventura	.05
264	Felix Jose	.05
265	Eddie Murray	.40
266	Kevin Mitchell	.05
267	Gary Carter	.40
268	Mike Benjamin	.05
269	Dick Schofield	.05
270	Jose Uribe	.05
271	Pete Incaviglia	.05
272	Tony Fernandez	.05
273	Alan Trammell	.05
274	Tony Gwynn	.50
275	Mike Greenwell	.05
276	Jeff Bagwell	.40
277	Frank Viola	.05
278	Randy Myers	.05
279	Ken Caminiti	.05
280	Bill Doran	.05
281	Dan Pasqua	.05
282	Alfredo Griffin	.05
283	Jose Oquendo	.05
284	Kal Daniels	.05
285	Bobby Thigpen	.05
286	Robby Thompson	.05
287	Mark Eichhorn	.05
288	Mike Felder	.05
289	Dave Gallagher	.05
290	Dave Anderson	.05
291	Mel Hall	.05
292	Jerald Clark	.05
293	Al Newman	.05
294	Rob Deer	.05
295	Matt Nokes	.05
296	Jack Armstrong	.05
297	Jim Deshaies	.05
298	Jeff Innis	.05
299	Jeff Reed	.05
300	Checklist 201-300	.05
301	Lonnie Smith	.05
302	Jimmy Key	.05
303	Junior Felix	.05
304	Mike Heath	.05
305	Mark Langston	.05
306	Greg W. Harris	.05
307	Brett Butler	.05
308	Luis Rivera RC	.05
309	Bruce Ruffin	.05
310	Paul Faries	.05
311	Terry Leach	.05
312	Scott Brosius RC	.10
313	Scott Leius	.05
314	Harold Reynolds	.05
315	Jack Morris	.05
316	David Segui	.05
317	Bill Gullickson	.05
318	Todd Frohwirth	.05
319	Mark Leiter RC	.05
320	Jeff M. Robinson	.05
321	Gary Gaetti	.05
322	John Smoltz	.05
323	Andy Benes	.05
324	Kelly Gruber	.05
325	Jim Abbott	.05
326	John Kruk	.05
327	Kevin Seitzer	.05
328	Darrin Jackson	.05
329	Kurt Stillwell RC	.05
330	Mike Maddux	.05
331	Dennis Eckersley	.35
332	Dan Gladden	.05
333	Jose Canseco	.30
334	Kent Hrbek	.05
335	Ken Griffey Sr.	.05
336	Greg Swindell	.05
337	Trevor Wilson RC	.05
338	Sam Horn	.05
339	Mike Henneman	.05
340	Jerry Browne	.05
341	Glenn Braggs	.05
342	Tom Glavine	.20
343	Wally Joyner	.05
344	Fred McGriff	.05
345	Ron Gant	.05
346	Ramon Martinez	.05
347	Wes Chamberlain	.05
348	Terry Shumpert	.05
349	Tim Teufel	.05
350	Wally Backman	.05
351	Joe Girardi	.05
352	Devon White	.05
353	Greg Maddux	.50
354	Ryan Bowen RC	.05
355	Roberto Alomar	.20
356	Don Mattingly	.60
357	Pedro Guerrero	.05
358	Steve Sax	.05
359	Joey Cora	.05
360	Jim Gantner	.05
361	Brian Barnes RC	.05
362	Kevin McReynolds	.05
363	Bret Barberie RC	.05
364	David Cone	.05
365	Dennis Martinez	.05
366	Brian Hunter RC	.05
367	Edgar Martinez	.05
368	Steve Finley	.05
369	Greg Briley	.05
370	Jeff Blauser	.05
371	Todd Stottlemyre	.05
372	Luis Gonzalez	.05
373	Rick Wilkins	.05
374	Darryl Kile RC	.05
375	John Olerud	.05
376	Lee Smith	.05
377	Kevin Maas	.05
378	Dante Bichette	.05
379	Tom Pagnozzi	.05
380	Mike Flanagan	.05
381	Charlie O'Brien	.05
382	Dave Martinez	.05
383	Keith Miller	.05
384	Scott Ruskin	.05
385	Kevin Elster	.05
386	Alvin Davis	.05
387	Casey Candaele	.05
388	Pete O'Brien	.05
389	Jeff Treadway RC	.05
390	Scott Bradley	.05
391	Mookie Wilson	.05
392	Jimmy Jones	.05
393	Candy Maldonado	.05
394	Eric Yelding	.05
395	Tom Henke	.05
396	Franklin Stubbs	.05
397	Milt Thompson	.05
398	Mark Carreon	.05
399	Randy Velarde	.05
400	Checklist 301-400	.05
401	Omar Vizquel	.05
402	Joe Boever	.05
403	Bill Krueger	.05
404	Jody Reed	.05
405	Mike Schooler RC	.05
406	Jason Grimsley	.05
407	Greg Myers	.05
408	Randy Ready	.05
409	Mike Timlin RC	.15
410	Mitch Williams	.05
411	Garry Templeton	.05
412	Greg Cadaret	.05
413	Donnie Hill	.05
414	Wally Whitehurst	.05
415	Scott Sanderson	.05
416	Thomas Howard	.05
417	Neal Heaton	.05
418	Charlie Hough	.05
419	Jack Howell	.05
420	Greg Hibbard	.05
421	Carlos Quintana	.05
422	Kim Batiste RC	.05
423	Paul Molitor	.05
424	Ken Griffey Jr.	.65
425	Phil Plantier	.05
426	Denny Neagle	.05
427	Von Hayes	.05

428	Shane Mack	.05	
429	Darren Daulton	.05	
430	Dwayne Henry	.05	
431	Lance Parrish	.05	
432	Mike Humphreys RC	.05	
433	Tim Burke	.05	
434	Bryan Harvey	.05	
435	Pat Kelly	.05	
436	Ozzie Guillen	.05	
437	Bruce Hurst	.05	
438	Sammy Sosa	.50	
439	Dennis Rasmussen	.05	
440	Ken Patterson	.05	
441	Jay Buhner	.05	
442	Pat Combs	.05	
443	Wade Boggs	.50	
444	George Brett	.60	
445	Mo Vaughn	.05	
446	Chuck Knoblauch	.05	
447	Tom Candiotti	.05	
448	Mark Portugal	.05	
449	Mickey Morandini	.05	
450	Duane Ward	.05	
451	Otis Nixon	.05	
452	Bob Welch	.05	
453	Rusty Meacham	.05	
454	Keith Mitchell	.05	
455	Marquis Grissom	.05	
456	Robin Yount	.40	
457	Harvey Pulliam RC	.05	
458	Jose DeLeon RC	.05	
459	Mark Gubicza	.05	
460	Darryl Hamilton	.05	
461	Tom Browning	.05	
462	Monty Fariss	.05	
463	Jerome Walton	.05	
464	Paul O'Neill	.05	
465	Dean Palmer	.05	
466	Travis Fryman	.05	
467	John Smiley	.05	
468	Lloyd Moseby	.05	
469	John Wehner RC	.05	
470	Skeeter Barnes RC	.05	
471	Steve Chitren	.05	
472	Kent Mercker	.05	
473	Terry Steinbach	.05	
474	Andres Galarraga	.05	
475	Steve Avery	.05	
476	Tom Gordon	.05	
477	Cal Eldred	.05	
478	Omar Olivares RC	.05	
479	Julio Machado	.05	
480	Bob Milacki	.05	
481	Les Lancaster	.05	
482	John Candelaria	.05	
483	Brian Downing	.05	
484	Roger McDowell	.05	
485	Scott Scudder	.05	
486	Zane Smith	.05	
487	John Cerutti	.05	
488	Steve Buechele	.05	
489	Paul Gibson	.05	
490	Curtis Wilkerson	.05	
491	Marvin Freeman	.05	
492	Tom Foley	.05	
493	Juan Berenguer	.05	
494	Ernest Riles	.05	
495	Sid Bream	.05	
496	Chuck Crim	.05	
497	Mike Macfarlane	.05	
498	Dale Sveum	.05	
499	Storm Davis	.05	
500	Checklist 401-500	.05	
501	Jeff Reardon	.05	
502	Shawn Abner	.05	
503	Tony Fossas	.05	
504	Cory Snyder	.05	
505	Matt Young	.05	
506	Allan Anderson RC	.05	
507	Mark Lee	.05	
508	Gene Nelson	.05	
509	Mike Pagliarulo	.05	
510	Rafael Belliard	.05	
511	Jay Howell	.05	
512	Bob Tewksbury	.05	
513	Mike Morgan	.05	
514	John Franco	.05	
515	Kevin Gross	.05	
516	Lou Whitaker	.05	
517	Orlando Merced	.05	
518	Todd Benzinger	.05	
519	Gary Redus	.05	
520	Walt Terrell	.05	
521	Jack Clark	.05	
522	Dave Parker	.05	
523	Tim Naehring	.05	
524	Mark Whiten	.05	
525	Ellis Burks	.05	
526	Frank Castillo RC	.05	
527	Brian Harper	.05	
528	Brook Jacoby	.05	
529	Rick Sutcliffe	.05	
530	Joe Klink	.05	
531	Terry Bross	.05	
532	Jose Offerman	.05	
533	Todd Zeile	.05	
534	Eric Karros	.05	
535	Anthony Young RC	.05	
536	Milt Cuyler	.05	
537	Randy Tomlin	.05	
538	Scott Livingstone RC	.05	
539	Jim Eisenreich	.05	
540	Don Slaught	.05	
541	Scott Cooper	.05	
542	Joe Grahe RC	.05	
543	Tom Brunansky	.05	
544	Eddie Zosky	.05	
545	Roger Clemens	.60	

546	Dave Justice	.05	
547	Dave Stewart	.05	
548	David West	.05	
549	Dave Smith	.05	
550	Dan Plesac	.05	
551	Alex Fernandez	.05	
552	Bernard Gilkey	.05	
553	Jack McDowell	.05	
554	Tino Martinez	.05	
555	Bo Jackson	.10	
556	Bernie Williams	.05	
557	Mark Gardner	.05	
558	Glenallen Hill	.05	
559	Dennis "Oil Can" Boyd	.05	
560	Chris James	.05	
561	Scott Servais RC	.05	
562	Rey Sanchez RC	.05	
563	Paul McClellan RC	.05	
564	Andy Mota RC	.05	
565	Darren Lewis	.05	
566	Jose Melendez RC	.05	
567	Tommy Greene	.05	
568	Rich Rodriguez	.05	
569	Heathcliff Slocumb RC	.05	
570	Joe Hesketh RC	.05	
571	Carlton Fisk	.40	
572	Erik Hanson	.05	
573	Wilson Alvarez	.05	
574	Rheal Cormier RC	.05	
575	Tim Raines	.05	
576	Bobby Witt	.05	
577	Roberto Kelly	.05	
578	Kevin Brown	.05	
579	Chris Nabholz	.05	
580	Jesse Orosco	.05	
581	Jeff Brantley	.05	
582	Rafael Ramirez	.05	
583	Kelly Downs	.05	
584	Mike Simms	.05	
585	Mike Remlinger RC	.05	
586	Dave Hollins	.05	
587	Larry Andersen	.05	
588	Mike Gardiner	.05	
589	Craig Lefferts	.05	
590	Paul Assenmacher RC	.05	
591	Bryn Smith	.05	
592	Donn Pall	.05	
593	Mike Jackson	.05	
594	Scott Radinsky	.05	
595	Brian Holman	.05	
596	Geronimo Pena	.05	
597	Mike Jeffcoat	.05	
598	Carlos Martinez RC	.05	
599	Geno Petralli	.05	
600	Checklist 501-600	.05	
601	Jerry Don Gleaton	.05	
602	Adam Peterson RC	.05	
603	Craig Grebeck	.05	
604	Mark Guthrie	.05	
605	Frank Tanana	.05	
606	Hensley Meulens RC	.05	
607	Mark Davis	.05	
608	Eric Plunk	.05	
609	Mark Williamson	.05	
610	Lee Guetterman RC	.05	
611	Bobby Rose	.05	
612	Bill Wegman	.05	
613	Mike Hartley	.05	
614	Chris Beasley RC	.05	
615	Chris Bosio	.05	
616	Henry Cotto	.05	
617	Chico Walker RC	.05	
618	Russ Swan RC	.05	
619	Bob Walk	.05	
620	Billy Swift	.05	
621	Warren Newson RC	.05	
622	Steve Bedrosian RC	.05	
623	Ricky Bones RC	.05	
624	Kevin Tapani	.05	
625	Juan Guzman RC	.05	
626	Jeff Johnson RC	.05	
627	Jeff Montgomery	.05	
628	Ken Hill	.05	
629	Gary Thurman	.05	
630	Steve Howe RC	.05	
631	Jose DeJesus	.05	
632	Bert Blyleven	.05	
633	Jaime Navarro	.05	
634	Lee Stevens RC	.05	
635	Pete Harnisch	.05	
636	Bill Landrum	.05	
637	Rich DeLucia	.05	
638	Luis Salazar RC	.05	
639	Rob Murphy	.05	
640	A.L. Diamond Skills Checklist (Rickey Henderson, Jose Canseco)	.05	
641	Roger Clemens (Diamond Skills)	.40	
642	Jim Abbott (Diamond Skills)	.05	
643	Travis Fryman (Diamond Skills)	.05	
644	Jesse Barfield (Diamond Skills)	.05	
645	Cal Ripken, Jr. (Diamond Skills)	.50	
646	Wade Boggs (Diamond Skills)	.35	
647	Cecil Fielder (Diamond Skills)	.05	
648	Rickey Henderson (Diamond Skills)	.20	
649	Jose Canseco (Diamond Skills)	.15	
650	Ken Griffey Jr. (Diamond Skills)	.45	
651	Kenny Rogers	.05	

652	Luis Mercedes RC	.05	
653	Mike Stanton	.05	
654	Glenn Davis	.05	
655	Nolan Ryan	1.00	
656	Reggie Jefferson	.05	
657	Javier Ortiz RC	.05	
658	Greg A. Harris	.05	
659	Mariano Duncan	.05	
660	Jeff Shaw	.05	
661	Mike Moore	.05	
662	Chris Haney RC	.05	
663	Joe Slusarski RC	.05	
664	Wayne Housie RC	.05	
665	Carlos Garcia	.05	
666	Bob Ojeda	.05	
667	Bryan Hickerson RC	.05	
668	Tim Belcher	.05	
669	Ron Darling	.05	
670	Rex Hudler RC	.05	
671	Sid Fernandez	.05	
672	Chito Martinez RC	.05	
673	Pete Schourek RC	.05	
674	Armando Renoso RC	.05	
675	Mike Mussina	.30	
676	Kevin Morton RC	.20	
677	Norm Charlton	.05	
678	Danny Darwin	.05	
679	Eric King	.05	
680	Ted Power	.05	
681	Barry Jones	.05	
682	Carney Lansford	.05	
683	Mel Rojas	.05	
684	Rick Honeycutt	.05	
685	Jeff Fassero RC	.05	
686	Cris Carpenter RC	.05	
687	Tim Crews	.05	
688	Scott Terry	.05	
689	Chris Gwynn	.05	
690	Gerald Perry	.05	
691	John Barfield	.05	
692	Bob Melvin	.05	
693	Juan Agosto	.05	
694	Alejandro Pena RC	.05	
695	Jeff Russell	.05	
696	Carmelo Martinez	.05	
697	Bud Black	.05	
698	Dave Otto RC	.05	
699	Billy Hatcher	.05	
700	Checklist 601-700	.05	
701	Clemente Nunez RC	.05	
702	"Rookie Threats" (Donovan Osborne, Brian Jordan, Mark Clark)	.05	
703	Mike Morgan	.05	
704	Keith Miller	.05	
705	Kurt Stillwell	.05	
706	Damon Berryhill	.05	
707	Von Hayes	.05	
708	Rick Sutcliffe	.05	
709	Hubie Brooks	.05	
710	Ryan Turner RC	.05	
711	N.L. Diamond Skills Checklist (Barry Bonds, Andy Van Slyke)	.30	
712	Jose Rijo (Diamond Skills)	.05	
713	Tom Glavine (Diamond Skills)	.05	
714	Shawon Dunston (Diamond Skills)	.05	
715	Andy Van Slyke (Diamond Skills)	.05	
716	Ozzie Smith (Diamond Skills)	.35	
717	Tony Gwynn (Diamond Skills)	.35	
718	Will Clark (Diamond Skills)	.05	
719	Marquis Grissom (Diamond Skills)	.05	
720	Howard Johnson (Diamond Skills)	.05	
721	Barry Bonds (Diamond Skills)	.50	
722	Kirk McCaskill	.05	
723	Sammy Sosa	.50	
724	George Bell	.05	
725	Gregg Jefferies	.05	
726	Gary DiSarcina RC	.05	
727	Mike Bordick	.05	
728	Eddie Murray (400 Home Run Club)	.20	
729	Rene Gonzales	.05	
730	Mike Bielecki	.05	
731	Calvin Jones RC	.05	
732	Jack Morris	.05	
733	Frank Viola	.05	
734	Dave Winfield	.40	
735	Kevin Mitchell	.05	
736	Billy Swift	.05	
737	Dan Gladden	.05	
738	Mike Jackson	.05	
739	Mark Carreon	.05	
740	Kirt Manwaring	.05	
741	Randy Myers	.05	
742	Kevin McReynolds	.05	
743	Steve Sax	.05	
744	Wally Joyner	.05	
745	Gary Sheffield	.25	
746	Danny Tartabull	.05	
747	Julio Valera	.05	
748	Denny Neagle	.05	
749	Lance Blankenship	.05	
750	Mike Gallego	.05	
751	Bret Saberhagen	.05	
752	Ruben Amaro RC	.05	
753	Eddie Murray	.40	
754	Kyle Abbott RC	.05	
755	Bobby Bonilla	.05	

756	Eric Davis	.05	
757	Eddie Taubensee RC	.05	
758	Andres Galarraga	.05	
759	Pete Incaviglia	.05	
760	Tom Candiotti	.05	
761	Tim Belcher	.05	
762	Ricky Bones	.05	
763	Bip Roberts	.05	
764	Pedro Munoz	.05	
765	Greg Swindell	.05	
766	Kenny Lofton	.05	
767	Gary Carter	.40	
768	Charlie Hayes	.05	
769	Dickie Thon	.05	
770	Diamond Debuts Checklist (Donovan Osborne)	.05	
771	Bret Boone (Diamond Debuts)	.10	
772	Archi Cianfrocco RC (Diamond Debuts)	.05	
773	Mark Clark RC (Diamond Debuts)	.05	
774	Chad Curtis RC (Diamond Debuts)	.20	
775	Pat Listach RC (Diamond Debuts)	.05	
776	Pat Mahomes RC (Diamond Debuts)	.05	
777	Donovan Osborne RC (Diamond Debuts)	.05	
778	John Patterson RC (Diamond Debuts)	.05	
779	Andy Stankiewicz RC (Diamond Debuts)	.05	
780	Turk Wendell RC (Diamond Debuts)	.10	
781	Bill Krueger	.05	
782	Rickey Henderson (Grand Theft)	.20	
783	Kevin Seitzer	.05	
784	Dave Martinez	.05	
785	John Smiley	.05	
786	Matt Stairs	.05	
787	Scott Scudder	.05	
788	John Wetteland	.05	
789	Jack Armstrong	.05	
790	Ken Hill	.05	
791	Dick Schofield	.05	
792	Mariano Duncan	.05	
793	Bill Pecota	.05	
794	Mike Kelly RC	.05	
795	Willie Randolph	.05	
796	Butch Henry RC	.05	
797	Carlos Hernandez RC	.05	
798	Doug Jones	.05	
799	Melido Perez	.05	
800	Checklist	.05	
SP3	"Prime Time's Two" (Deion Sanders)		
SP4	"Mr. Baseball" (Tom Selleck, Frank Thomas)	2.00	
HH2	Ted Williams (Hologram)	2.00	

Baseball Heroes Bench/Morgan

This set is devoted to two of the vital cogs in Cincinnati's Big Red Machine: Hall of Famers Johnny Bench and Joe Morgan. Cards, numbered 37-45, were included in high number packs. An unnumbered cover card was also produced. Both players autographed 2,500 of card #45, the painting of the Reds duo by sports artist Vernon Wells.

		NM/M
Complete Set (10):		4.00
Common Card:		.50
Autographed Card:		65.00
---	Header Card	.75
37	1968 Rookie of the Year (Johnny Bench)	.75
38	1968-77 Ten Straight Gold Gloves (Johnny Bench)	.75
39	1970 & 1972 MVP (Johnny Bench)	.75
40	1965 Rookie Year (Joe Morgan)	.50
41	1975-76 Back-to-Back MVP (Joe Morgan)	.50
42	1980-83 The Golden Years (Joe Morgan)	.50
43	1972-79 Big Red Machine (Johnny Bench, Joe Morgan)	.60
44	1989 & 1990 Hall of Fame (Johnny Bench, Joe Morgan)	.60
45	Checklist - Heroes 37-45 (Johnny Bench, Joe Morgan)	.60

Foil-pack boxes of low-number 1992 Upper Deck baseball featured on their bottom an oversize reproduction of the front of one of the Ted Williams "Baseball Heroes" insert cards. Eight different box-bottom cards were produced, mea-

Bench-Morgan Box Bottoms

The eight Heroes of Baseball high-number cards featuring Johnny Bench and/or Joe Morgan were also issued in a box-bottom version measuring about 5" x 7". The blank-back box bottoms are listed here according to the corresponding number of the regular-size cards.

		NM/M
Complete Set (8):		7.00
Common Card:		1.00
(37)	1968 Rookie of the Year (Johnny Bench)	1.00
(38)	1968-77 Ten Straight Gold Gloves (Johnny Bench)	1.00
(39)	1970 & 1972 MVP (Johnny Bench)	1.00
(40)	1965 Rookie Year (Joe Morgan)	1.00
(41)	1975-76 Back-to-Back MVP (Joe Morgan)	1.00
(42)	1980-83 The Golden Years (Joe Morgan)	1.00
(43)	1972-79 Big Red Machine (Johnny Bench, Joe Morgan)	1.00
(44)	1989 & 1990 Hall of Fame (Johnny Bench, Joe Morgan)	1.00

Baseball Heroes Ted Williams

This Baseball Heroes set devoted to Ted Williams continues where previous efforts left off by numbering it from 28-36. An unnumbered "Baseball Heroes" cover card was also included. Cards were found in low-number foil and jumbo packs. Williams also autographed 2,500 cards, which were numbered and randomly inserted in low-number packs.

		NM/M
Complete Set (10):		3.00
Common Player:		.50
Autographed Card:		425.00
---	Header Card	.75
28	1939 Rookie Year (Ted Williams)	.50
29	1941 .406! (Ted Williams)	.50
30	1942 Triple Crown Year (Ted Williams)	.50
31	1946 & 1949 MVP (Ted Williams)	.50
32	1947 Second Triple Crown (Ted Williams)	.50
33	1950s Player of the Decade (Ted Williams)	.50
34	1960 500 Home Run Club (Ted Williams)	.50
35	1966 Hall of Fame (Ted Williams)	.50
36	Checklist - Heroes 28-36 (Ted Williams)	.50

Ted Williams Box Bottoms

suring 5" x 7" and printed on a mottled orange background. The box-bottom cards are blank-backed and unnumbered. They are checklisted here according to the card numbers of the regular-size version.

		NM/M
Complete Set (8):		6.00
Common Player:		1.00
(28)	1939 - Rookie Year (Ted Williams)	1.00
(29)	1941 - .406 (Ted Williams)	1.00
(30)	1942 - Triple Crown Year (Ted Williams)	1.00
(31)	1946, 1949 - MVP (Ted Williams)	1.00
(32)	1947 - Second Triple Crown (Ted Williams)	1.00
(33)	1950s - Player of the Decade (Ted Williams)	1.00
(34)	1960 - 500 Hokme Run Club (Ted Williams)	1.00
(35)	1966 - Hall of Fame (Ted Williams)	1.00

College POY Holograms

This three-card hologram set features the College Player of the Year winners from 1989-91. Cards were randomly inserted in high number foil packs and have a CP prefix for numbering.

		NM/M
Complete Set (3):		.75
Common Player:		.25
1	David McCarty	.25
2	Mike Kelly	.25
3	Ben McDonald	.25

Hall of Fame Heroes

This set features three top players from the 1970s: Vida Blue, Lou Brock and Rollie Fingers. The cards continue from last year's set by using numbers H5-H8. The three players are each on one card; the fourth card features all three. They were found in low-number foil packs and specially-marked jumbo packs. Both types of packs could also contain autographed cards; each player signed 3,000 cards.

		NM/M
Complete Set (4):		2.50
Common Player:		.50
5	Vida Blue	.50
5a	Vida Blue/Auto.	20.00
6	Lou Brock	1.00
6a	Lou Brock/Auto.	35.00
7	Rollie Fingers	.50
7a	Rollie Fingers/Auto.	30.00
8	Vida Blue, Lou Brock, Rollie Fingers	1.00

Heroes Highlights

Special packaging of 1992 Upper Deck high numbers produced for sales to dealers at its Heroes of Baseball show series included these cards of former players as inserts. Cards have a Heroes

Highlights banner including the player's name and the date of his career highlight beneath the photo. In a tombstone frame on back, the highlight is chronicled. Cards are numbered alphabetically by player name, with the card number carrying an HI prefix.

		NM/M
Complete Set (10):		4.00
Common Player:		.45
1	Bobby Bonds	.45
2	Lou Brock	.45
3	Rollie Fingers	.45
4	Bob Gibson	.45
5	Reggie Jackson	.75
6	Gaylord Perry	.45
7	Robin Roberts	.45
8	Brooks Robinson	.45
9	Billy Williams	.45
10	Ted Williams	2.00

Home Run Heroes

This 26-card set features a top home run hitter from each major league team. The cards, numbered HR1-HR26, were found in low-number jumbo packs, one per pack.

		NM/M
Complete Set (26):		5.00
Common Player:		.15
1	Jose Canseco	.45
2	Cecil Fielder	.15
3	Howard Johnson	.15
4	Cal Ripken, Jr.	1.50
5	Matt Williams	.15
6	Joe Carter	.15
7	Ron Gant	.15
8	Frank Thomas	.75
9	Andre Dawson	.40
10	Fred McGriff	.15
11	Danny Tartabull	.15
12	Chili Davis	.15
13	Albert Belle	.15
14	Jack Clark	.15
15	Paul O'Neill	.15
16	Darryl Strawberry	.15
17	Dave Winfield	.75
18	Jay Buhner	.15
19	Juan Gonzalez	.25
20	Greg Vaughn	.15
21	Barry Bonds	1.50
22	Matt Nokes	.15
23	John Kruk	.15
24	Ivan Calderon	.15
25	Jeff Bagwell	.75
26	Todd Zeile	.15

Scouting Report

These cards were randomly inserted in Upper Deck high-number jumbo packs. The set is numbered SR1-SR25 and features 25 top prospects, including 1992 Rookies of the Year Pat Listach and Eric Karros. "Scouting Report" is written down the side on the front in silver lettering. The back features a clipboard which shows a photo, a player profile and a major league scouting report.

	NM/M
Complete Set (25):	2.00

		NM/M
Common Player:		.25
1	Andy Ashby	.25
2	Willie Banks	.25
3	Kim Batiste	.25
4	Derek Bell	.25
5	Archi Cianfrocco	.25
6	Royce Clayton	.25
7	Gary DiSarcina	.25
8	Dave Fleming	.25
9	Butch Henry	.25
10	Todd Hundley	.25
11	Brian Jordan	.25
12	Eric Karros	.25
13	Pat Listach	.25
14	Scott Livingstone	.25
15	Kenny Lofton	.25
16	Pat Mahomes	.25
17	Denny Neagle	.25
18	Dave Nilsson	.25
19	Donovan Osborne	.25
20	Reggie Sanders	.25
21	Andy Stankiewicz	.25
22	Jim Thome	1.50
23	Julio Valera	.25
24	Mark Wohlers	.25
25	Anthony Young	.25

Ted Williams' Best Hitters/Future

Twenty of the best hitters in baseball according to legend Ted Williams are featured in this special insert set from Upper Deck. The cards are styled much like the 1992 FanFest cards and showcase each chosen player. Each card is numbered with a "T" designation.

		NM/M
Complete Set (20):		3.00
Common Player:		.12
1	Wade Boggs	.50
2	Barry Bonds	1.00
3	Jose Canseco	.25
4	Will Clark	.10
5	Cecil Fielder	.10
6	Tony Gwynn	.50
7	Rickey Henderson	.40
8	Fred McGriff	.10
9	Kirby Puckett	.50
10	Ruben Sierra	.10
11	Roberto Alomar	.20
12	Jeff Bagwell	.40
13	Albert Belle	.10
14	Juan Gonzalez	.20
15	Ken Griffey Jr.	.75
16	Chris Hoiles	.10
17	Dave Justice	.10
18	Phil Plantier	.10
19	Frank Thomas	.40
20	Robin Ventura	.10

FanFest

This 54-card boxed set was made available through special offers at the 1992 National Sports Collectors Convention and at the 1992 All-Star FanFest in San Diego. Card fronts feature a glossy UV finish, silver-foil stamping and the All-Star FanFest logo. The card backs include a player profile. Both "Future Heroes" and past and present "All-Star Heroes" are fea-

---

tured. The complete set was packaged in an attractive blue box with white pinstripes.

		NM/M
Complete Set (54):		6.00
Common Player:		.10
1	Steve Avery	.10
2	Ivan Rodriguez	.60
3	Jeff Bagwell	.75
4	Delino DeShields	.10
5	Royce Clayton	.10
6	Robin Ventura	.10
7	Phil Plantier	.10
8	Ray Lankford	.10
9	Juan Gonzalez	.40
10	Frank Thomas	.75
11	Roberto Alomar	.30
12	Sandy Alomar, Jr.	.10
13	Wade Boggs	1.25
14	Barry Bonds	2.50
15	Bobby Bonilla	.10
16	George Brett	1.50
17	Jose Canseco	.60
18	Will Clark	.10
19	Roger Clemens	1.50
20	Eric Davis	.10
21	Rob Dibble	.10
22	Cecil Fielder	.10
23	Dwight Gooden	.10
24	Ken Griffey Jr.	2.00
25	Tony Gwynn	1.25
26	Bryan Harvey	.10
27	Rickey Henderson	.75
28	Howard Johnson	.10
29	Wally Joyner	.10
30	Barry Larkin	.10
31	Don Mattingly	1.50
32	Mark McGwire	2.25
33	Dale Murphy	.30
34	Rafael Palmeiro	.60
35	Kirby Puckett	1.25
36	Cal Ripken, Jr.	2.50
37	Nolan Ryan	2.50
38	Chris Sabo	.10
39	Ryne Sandberg	1.25
40	Benito Santiago	.10
41	Ruben Sierra	.10
42	Ozzie Smith	1.25
43	Darryl Strawberry	.10
44	Robin Yount	.75
45	Rollie Fingers	.10
46	Reggie Jackson	1.25
47	Billy Williams	.20
48	Lou Brock	.20
49	Gaylord Perry	.20
50	Ted Williams	2.00
51	Brooks Robinson	.50
52	Bob Gibson	.20
53	Bobby Bonds	.10
54	Robin Roberts	.20

FanFest Gold

One out of every 60 sets of Upper Deck FanFest All-Stars was produced with gold-foil printing highlights rather than silver. The sets were randomly inserted into cases.

	NM/M
Complete Set (54):	30.00
Common Player:	.25

FanFest Ted Williams Super

This large-format (8-1/2" x 11") card is essentially an enlargement of Ted Williams' card issued with the FanFest All-Star Heroes

---

boxed set by UD. The Williams super cards were distributed at the FanFest event and are serially numbered on back within an edition of 2,500.

	NM/M
Ted Williams	25.00

MVP Holograms

State of the art holography is presented in this 54-card plastic-cased set featuring a top pitcher and a top position player from each major league team, plus 1991 MVPs Terry Pendleton and Cal Ripken, Jr. The hologram on the front of each card feature a close-up and a field-action photo of the player; his name and position are in a strip at bottom. Full-color backs have a player photo on the right and career summary on the left. A custom album for the set was available via a mail offer for $10. Each set includes a numbered certificate of authenticity, verifying its position within a total issue of 216,000 sets.

		NM/M
Complete Set (54):		6.00
Common Player:		.10
1	A.L. Checklist (Cal Ripken, Jr.)	.40
2	N.L. Checkklist (Terry Pendleton)	.10
3	Jim Abbott	.10
4	Roberto Alomar	.25
5	Kevin Appier	.10
6	Steve Avery	.10
7	Jeff Bagwell	.40
8	Albert Belle	.10
9	Andy Benes	.10
10	Wade Boggs	.50
11	Barry Bonds	1.00
12	George Brett	.60
13	Ivan Calderon	.10
14	Jose Canseco	.30
15	Will Clark	.10
16	Roger Clemens	.60
17	David Cone	.10
18	Doug Drabek	.10
19	Dennis Eckersley	.35
20	Scott Erickson	.10
21	Cecil Fielder	.10
22	Ken Griffey Jr.	.75
23	Bill Gullickson	.10
24	Juan Guzman	.10
25	Pete Harnisch	.10
26	Howard Johnson	.10
27	Randy Johnson	.40
28	John Kruk	.10
29	Barry Larkin	.10
30	Greg Maddux	.50
31	Dennis Martinez	.10
32	Ramon Martinez	.10
33	Don Mattingly	.60
34	Jack McDowell	.10
35	Fred McGriff	.10
36	Paul Molitor	.40
37	Charles Nagy	.10
38	Gregg Olson	.10
39	Terry Pendleton	.10
40	Luis Polonia	.10
41	Kirby Puckett	.50
42	Dave Righetti	.10
43	Jose Rijo	.10
44	Cal Ripken, Jr.	1.00
45	Nolan Ryan	1.00
46	Ryne Sandberg	.50
47	Scott Sanderson	.10
48	Ruben Sierra	.10
49	Lee Smith	.10
50	Ozzie Smith	.50
51	Darryl Strawberry	.10
52	Frank Thomas	.40
53	Bill Wegman	.10
54	Mitch Williams	.10

Comic Ball 3

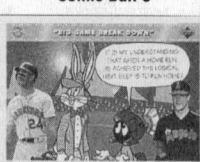

The third series of Comic Ball cards was issued in 1992 and was the second to combine photos of

---

real ballplayers with Looney Tune cartoon characters in several cartoon strip-style series. Players featured in the set with Bugs, Taz and the gang were Jim Abbott and the Ken Griffeys, Sr. and Jr. Each of the 198 regular cards features a puzzle-piece back. A special album to house the set was sold separately. A series of holograms which also combined the players and cartoon figures was issued as pack inserts.

	NM/M
Complete Set (198):	6.00
Common Card:	.05
Hologram:	1.00

Holograms

These blank-back holograms which combine player pictures with those of cartoon characters were issued as inserts in Comic Ball 3 foil packs.

		NM/M
Common Hologram:		.50
(1)	Jim Abbott (w/Tweety)	1.00
(2)	Jim Abbott (w/Taz)	1.00
(3)	Ken Griffey Jr. (w/Bugs)	2.00
(4)	Ken Griffey Jr. (w/Wile E. Coyote)	2.00
(5)	Chuck Jones (Artist) (w/Bugs)	.50

1993 Upper Deck

Upper Deck introduced its 1993 set in a two-series format to adjust to expansion. Cards 1-420 make up the first series. Special subsets in Series 1 include rookies, teammates and community heroes. Fronts feature color player photos surrounded by a white border. Backs feature vertical photos, a change from the past, and more complete statistics than Upper Deck had in the past. The hologram appears in the lower-left corner on the card back. One out of 20 factory sets featured cards with gold, rather than silver, holograms.

		NM/M
Unopened Fact. Set (840):		30.00
Complete Set (840):		25.00
Common Player:		.05
Gold Hologram:		4X
Series 1 or 2 Pack (15):		.75
Series 1 or 2 Wax Box (36):		17.50
Jumbo Pack, USA (27):		1.50
Jumbo Box, USA (20):		17.50
Jumbo Pack, Canada (23):		2.00
Jumbo Box, Canada (20):		20.00
1	Tim Salmon (Checklist)	
2	Mike Piazza/SR	1.25
3	Rene Arocha/SR RC	.05
4	Willie Greene/SR RC	.05
5	Manny Alexander/SR RC	.05
6	Dan Wilson/SR	.05
7	Dan Smith/SR RC	.05
8	Kevin Rogers/SR RC	.05
9	Nigel Wilson/SR RC	.05
10	Joe Vitko/SR RC	.05
11	Tim Costo/SR RC	.05
12	Alan Embree/SR	.05
13	Jim Tatum/SR RC	.05
14	Cris Colon/SR RC	.05
15	Steve Hosey/SR RC	.05
16	Sterling Hitchcock/SR RC	.15
17	Dave Mlicki/SR	.05
18	Jessie Hollins/SR RC	.05
19	Bobby J. Jones/SR RC	.05
20	Kurt Miller/SR RC	.05
21	Melvin Nieves/SR RC	.05
22	Billy Ashley/SR RC	.05
23	J.T. Snow/SR RC	.50
24	Chipper Jones/SR RC	1.00
25	Tim Salmon/SR	.25
26	Tim Pugh/SR RC	.05
27	David Nied/SR	.05
28	Mike Trombley/SR RC	.05
29	Javier Lopez/SR)	.05

30	Community Heroes Checklist (Jim Abbott)	.05
31	Jim Abbott (Community Heroes)	.05
32	Dale Murphy (Community Heroes)	.10
33	Tony Pena (Community Heroes)	.05
34	Kirby Puckett (Community Heroes)	.40
35	Harold Reynolds (Community Heroes)	.05
36	Cal Ripken, Jr. (Community Heroes)	.65
37	Nolan Ryan (Community Heroes)	.65
38	Ryne Sandberg (Community Heroes)	.35
39	Dave Stewart (Community Heroes)	.05
40	Dave Winfield (Community Heroes)	.25
41	Teammates Checklist (Joe Carter, Mark McGwire)	.50
42	Blockbuster Trade (Joe Carter, Roberto Alomar)	.50
43	Brew Crew (Pat Listach, Robin Yount, Paul Molitor)	.15
44	Iron and Steal (Brady Anderson, Cal Ripken, Jr.)	.35
45	Youthful Tribe (Albert Belle, Sandy Alomar Jr., Jim Thome, Carlos Baerga, Kenny Lofton)	.25
46	Motown Mashers (Cecil Fielder, Mickey Tettleton)	.45
47	Yankee Pride (Roberto Kelly, Don Mattingly)	.45
48	Boston Cy Sox (Frank Viola, Roger Clemens)	.30
49	Bash Brothers (Ruben Sierra, Mark McGwire)	.50
50	Twin Titles (Kent Hrbek, Kirby Puckett)	.30
51	Southside Sluggers (Robin Ventura, Frank Thomas)	.35
52	Latin Stars (Jose Canseco, Ivan Rodriguez, Rafael Palmeiro, Juan Gonzalez)	.35
53	Lethal Lefties (Mark Langston, Jim Abbott, Chuck Finley)	.10
54	Royal Family (Gregg Jefferies, George Brett, Wally Joyner)	.35
55	Pacific Sox Exchange (Kevin Mitchell, Jay Buhner, Ken Griffey Jr.)	.40
56	George Brett	.85
57	Scott Cooper	.05
58	Mike Maddux	.05
59	Rusty Meacham RC	.05
60	Wil Cordero	.05
61	Tim Teufel	.05
62	Jeff Montgomery	.05
63	Scott Livingstone RC	.05
64	Doug Dascenzo	.05
65	Bret Boone	.05
66	Tim Wakefield RC	.10
67	Curt Schilling	.05
68	Frank Tanana	.05
69	Len Dykstra	.05
70	Derek Lilliquist	.05
71	Anthony Young RC	.05
72	Hipolito Pichardo RC	.05
73	Rod Beck RC	.05
74	Kent Hrbek	.05
75	Tom Glavine	.20
76	Kevin Brown	.05
77	Chuck Finley	.05
78	Bob Walk	.05
79	Rheal Cormier	.05
80	Rick Sutcliffe	.05
81	Harold Baines	.05
82	Lee Smith	.05
83	Geno Petralli	.05
84	Jose Oquendo	.05
85	Mark Gubicza	.05
86	Mickey Tettleton	.05
87	Bobby Witt	.05
88	Mark Lewis	.05
89	Kevin Appier	.05
90	Mike Stanton	.05
91	Rafael Belliard	.05
92	Kenny Rogers	.05
93	Randy Velarde	.05
94	Luis Sojo	.05
95	Mark Leiter	.05
96	Jody Reed	.05
97	Pete Harnisch	.05
98	Tom Candiotti	.05
99	Mark Portugal	.05
100	Dave Valle	.05
101	Shawon Dunston	.05
102	B.J. Surhoff	.05
103	Jay Bell	.05
104	Sid Bream	.05
105	Checklist 1-105 (Frank Thomas)	.05
106	Mike Morgan	.05
107	Bill Doran	.05
108	Lance Blankenship	.05

#	Player	Price
109	Mark Lemke	.05
110	Brian Harper	.05
111	Brady Anderson	.05
112	Bip Roberts	.05
113	Mitch Williams	.05
114	Craig Biggio	.05
115	Eddie Murray	.65
116	Matt Nokes	.05
117	Lance Parrish	.05
118	Bill Swift	.05
119	Jeff Innis	.05
120	Mike LaValliere	.05
121	Hal Morris	.05
122	Walt Weiss	.05
123	Ivan Rodriguez	.60
124	Andy Van Slyke	.05
125	Roberto Alomar	.20
126	Robby Thompson	.05
127	Sammy Sosa	.75
128	Mark Langston	.05
129	Jerry Browne	.05
130	Chuck McElroy	.05
131	Frank Viola	.05
132	Leo Gomez	.05
133	Ramon Martinez	.05
134	Don Mattingly	.85
135	Roger Clemens	.85
136	Rickey Henderson	.65
137	Darren Daulton	.05
138	Ken Hill	.05
139	Ozzie Guillen	.05
140	Jerald Clark	.05
141	Dave Fleming	.05
142	Delino DeShields	.05
143	Matt Williams	.05
144	Larry Walker	.05
145	Ruben Sierra	.05
146	Ozzie Smith	.75
147	Chris Sabo	.05
148	Carlos Hernandez RC	.05
149	Pat Borders	.05
150	Orlando Merced	.05
151	Royce Clayton	.05
152	Kurt Stillwell	.05
153	Dave Hollins	.05
154	Mike Greenwell	.05
155	Nolan Ryan	1.50
156	Felix Jose	.05
157	Junior Felix	.05
158	Derek Bell	.05
159	Steve Buechele	.05
160	John Burkett	.05
161	Pat Howell RC	.05
162	Milt Cuyler	.05
163	Terry Pendleton	.05
164	Jack Morris	.05
165	Tony Gwynn	.75
166	Deion Sanders	.10
167	Mike Devereaux	.05
168	Ron Darling	.05
169	Orel Hershiser	.05
170	Mike Jackson	.05
171	Doug Jones	.05
172	Dan Walters RC	.05
173	Carlos Lewis	.05
174	Carlos Baerga	.05
175	Ryne Sandberg	.75
176	Gregg Jefferies	.05
177	John Jaha	.05
178	Luis Polonia	.05
179	Kirt Manwaring	.05
180	Mike Magnante	.05
181	Billy Ripken	.05
182	Mike Moore	.05
183	Eric Anthony	.05
184	Lenny Harris	.05
185	Tony Pena	.05
186	Mike Felder	.05
187	Greg Olson	.05
188	Rene Gonzales	.05
189	Mike Bordick	.05
190	Mel Rojas	.05
191	Todd Frohwirth	.05
192	Darryl Hamilton	.05
193	Mike Fetters	.05
194	Omar Olivares RC	.05
195	Tony Phillips	.05
196	Paul Sorrento	.05
197	Trevor Wilson	.05
198	Kevin Gross	.05
199	Ron Karkovice	.05
200	Brook Jacoby	.05
201	Mariano Duncan	.05
202	Dennis Cook	.05
203	Daryl Boston	.05
204	Mike Perez	.05
205	Manuel Lee	.05
206	Steve Olin	.05
207	Charlie Hough	.05
208	Scott Scudder	.05
209	Charlie O'Brien	.05
210	Checklist 106-210 (Barry Bonds)	.60
211	Jose Vizcaino	.05
212	Scott Leius	.05
213	Kevin Mitchell	.05
214	Brian Barnes	.05
215	Pat Kelly	.05
216	Chris Hammond	.05
217	Rob Deer	.05
218	Cory Snyder	.05
219	Gary Carter	.65
220	Danny Darwin	.05
221	Tom Gordon	.05
222	Gary Sheffield	.40
223	Joe Carter	.05
224	Jay Bell	.05
225	Jose Offerman	.05
226	Jose Rijo	.05
227	Mark Whiten	.05
228	Randy Milligan	.05
229	Bud Black	.05
230	Gary DiSarcina	.05
231	Steve Finley	.05
232	Dennis Martinez	.05
233	Mike Mussina	.30
234	Joe Oliver	.05
235	Chad Curtis	.05
236	Shane Mack	.05
237	Jaime Navarro	.05
238	Brian McRae	.05
239	Chili Davis	.05
240	Jeff King	.05
241	Dean Palmer	.05
242	Danny Tartabull	.05
243	Charles Nagy	.05
244	Ray Lankford	.05
245	Barry Larkin	.05
246	Steve Avery	.05
247	John Kruk	.05
248	Derrick May	.05
249	Stan Javier	.05
250	Roger McDowell	.05
251	Dan Gladden	.05
252	Wally Joyner	.05
253	Pat Listach	.05
254	Chuck Knoblauch	.05
255	Sandy Alomar Jr.	.05
256	Jeff Bagwell	.65
257	Andy Stankiewicz	.05
258	Darrin Jackson	.05
259	Brett Butler	.05
260	Joe Orsulak	.05
261	Andy Benes	.05
262	Kenny Lofton	.05
263	Robin Ventura	.05
264	Ron Gant	.05
265	Ellis Burks	.05
266	Juan Guzman	.05
267	Wes Chamberlain	.05
268	John Smiley	.05
269	Franklin Stubbs	.05
270	Tom Browning	.05
271	Dennis Eckersley	.60
272	Carlton Fisk	.65
273	Lou Whitaker	.05
274	Phil Plantier	.05
275	Bobby Bonilla	.05
276	Ben McDonald	.05
277	Bob Zupcic	.05
278	Terry Steinbach	.05
279	Terry Mulholland	.05
280	Lance Johnson	.05
281	Willie McGee	.05
282	Bret Saberhagen	.05
283	Randy Myers	.05
284	Randy Tomlin	.05
285	Mickey Morandini	.05
286	Brian Williams	.05
287	Tino Martinez	.05
288	Jose Melendez	.05
289	Jeff Huson	.05
290	Joe Grahe	.05
291	Mel Hall	.05
292	Otis Nixon	.05
293	Todd Hundley	.05
294	Casey Candaele	.05
295	Kevin Seitzer	.05
296	Eddie Taubensee	.05
297	Moises Alou	.05
298	Scott Radinsky	.05
299	Thomas Howard	.05
300	Kyle Abbott	.05
301	Omar Vizquel	.05
302	Keith Miller	.05
303	Rick Aguilera	.05
304	Bruce Hurst	.05
305	Ken Caminiti	.05
306	Mike Pagliarulo	.05
307	Frank Seminara	.05
308	Andre Dawson	.30
309	Jose Lind	.05
310	Joe Boever	.05
311	Jeff Parrett RC	.05
312	Alan Mills	.05
313	Kevin Tapani	.05
314	Darryl Kile	.05
315	Checklist 211-315 (Will Clark)	.05
316	Mike Sharperson	.05
317	John Orton	.05
318	Bob Tewksbury	.05
319	Xavier Hernandez	.05
320	Paul Assenmacher	.05
321	John Franco	.05
322	Mike Timlin	.05
323	Jose Guzman	.05
324	Pedro Martinez	.65
325	Bill Spiers	.05
326	Melido Perez	.05
327	Mike Macfarlane	.05
328	Ricky Bones	.05
329	Scott Bankhead	.05
330	Rich Rodriguez	.05
331	Geronimo Pena	.05
332	Bernie Williams	.05
333	Paul Molitor	.65
334	Roger Mason	.05
335	David Cone	.05
336	Randy Johnson	.65
337	Pat Mahomes	.05
338	Erik Hanson	.05
339	Duane Ward	.05
340	Al Martin	.05
341	Pedro Munoz	.05
342	Greg Colbrunn	.05
343	Julio Valera	.05
344	John Olerud	.05
345	George Bell	.05
346	Devon White	.05
347	Donovan Osborne	.05
348	Mark Gardner	.05
349	Zane Smith	.05
350	Wilson Alvarez	.05
351	Kevin Koslofski RC	.05
352	Roberto Hernandez	.05
353	Glenn Davis	.05
354	Reggie Sanders	.05
355	Ken Griffey Jr.	1.00
355a	Ken Griffey Jr. (Promo, 1992-dated hologram on back.)	3.00
355b	Ken Griffey Jr. (8-1/2" x 11" limited edition of 1,000)	15.00
356	Marquis Grissom	.05
357	Jack McDowell	.05
358	Jimmy Key	.05
359	Stan Belinda	.05
360	Gerald Williams	.05
361	Sid Fernandez	.05
362	Alex Fernandez	.05
363	John Smoltz	.05
364	Travis Fryman	.05
365	Jose Canseco	.50
366	Dave Justice	.05
367	Pedro Astacio RC	.10
368	Tim Belcher	.05
369	Steve Sax	.05
370	Gary Gaetti	.05
371	Jeff Frye	.05
372	Bob Wickman	.05
373	Ryan Thompson RC	.05
374	David Hulse RC	.05
375	Cal Eldred	.05
376	Ryan Klesko	.05
377	Damion Easley RC	.05
378	John Kiely RC	.05
379	Jim Bullinger RC	.05
380	Brian Bohanon	.05
381	Rod Brewer	.05
382	Fernando Ramsey RC	.05
383	Sam Militello	.05
384	Arthur Rhodes	.05
385	Eric Karros	.05
386	Rico Brogna	.05
387	John Valentin RC	.10
388	Kerry Woodson RC	.05
389	Ben Rivera RC	.05
390	Matt Whiteside RC	.05
391	Henry Rodriguez	.05
392	John Wetteland	.05
393	Kent Mercker	.05
394	Bernard Gilkey	.05
395	Doug Henry	.05
396	Mo Vaughn	.05
397	Scott Erickson	.05
398	Bill Gullickson	.05
399	Mark Guthrie	.05
400	Dave Martinez	.05
401	Jeff Kent RC	.50
402	Chris Hoiles	.05
403	Mike Henneman	.05
404	Chris Nabholz	.05
405	Tom Pagnozzi	.05
406	Kelly Gruber	.05
407	Bob Welch	.05
408	Frank Castillo	.05
409	John Dopson	.05
410	Steve Farr	.05
411	Henry Cotto	.05
412	Bob Patterson	.05
413	Todd Stottlemyre	.05
414	Greg A. Harris	.05
415	Denny Neagle	.05
416	Bill Wegman	.05
417	Willie Wilson	.05
418	Terry Leach	.05
419	Willie Randolph	.05
420	Checklist 316-420 (Mark McGwire)	.65
421	Calvin Murray (Top Prospects Checklist)	.05
422	Pete Janicki RC (Top Prospect)	.05
423	Todd Jones RC (Top Prospect)	.05
424	Mike Neill (Top Prospect)	.05
425	Carlos Delgado (Top Prospect)	.40
426	Jose Oliva (Top Prospect)	.05
427	Tyrone Hill (Top Prospect)	.05
428	Dmitri Young (Top Prospect)	.05
429	Derek Wallace RC (Top Prospect)	.05
430	Michael Moore RC (Top Prospect)	.05
431	Cliff Floyd (Top Prospect)	.05
432	Calvin Murray (Top Prospect)	.05
433	Manny Ramirez (Top Prospect)	.75
434	Marc Newfield (Top Prospect)	.05
435	Charles Johnson (Top Prospect)	.05
436	Butch Huskey (Top Prospect)	.05
437	Brad Pennington (Top Prospect)	.05
438	Ray McDavid RC (Top Prospect)	.05
439	Chad McConnell (Top Prospect)	.05
440	Midre Cummings RC (Top Prospect)	.05
441	Benji Gil (Top Prospect)	.05
442	Frank Rodriguez (Top Prospect)	.05
443	Chad Mottola RC (Top Prospect)	.05
444	John Burke RC (Top Prospect)	.05
445	Michael Tucker (Top Prospect)	.05
446	Rick Greene (Top Prospect)	.05
447	Rich Becker (Top Prospect)	.05
448	Mike Robertson (Top Prospect)	.05
449	Derek Jeter RC (Top Prospect)	10.00
450	Checklist 451-470 Inside the Numbers (David McCarty, Ivan Rodriguez)	.05
451	Jim Abbott (Inside the Numbers)	.05
452	Jeff Bagwell (Inside the Numbers)	.40
453	Jason Bere (Inside the Numbers)	.05
454	Delino DeShields (Inside the Numbers)	.05
455	Travis Fryman (Inside the Numbers)	.05
456	Alex Gonzalez (Inside the Numbers)	.05
457	Phil Hiatt (Inside the Numbers)	.05
458	Dave Hollins (Inside the Numbers)	.05
459	Chipper Jones (Inside the Numbers)	.75
460	Dave Justice (Inside the Numbers)	.05
461	Ray Lankford (Inside the Numbers)	.05
462	David McCarty (Inside the Numbers)	.05
463	Mike Mussina (Inside the Numbers)	.15
464	Jose Offerman (Inside the Numbers)	.05
465	Dean Palmer (Inside the Numbers)	.05
466	Geronimo Pena (Inside the Numbers)	.05
467	Eduardo Perez (Inside the Numbers)	.05
468	Ivan Rodriguez (Inside the Numbers)	.25
469	Reggie Sanders (Inside the Numbers)	.05
470	Bernie Williams (Inside the Numbers)	.05
471	Checklist 472-485 Team Stars (Matt Williams, Will Clark, Barry Bonds)	.45
472	Strike Force (John Smoltz, Steve Avery, Greg Maddux, Tom Glavine)	.10
473	Red October (Jose Rijo, Rob Dibble, Roberto Kelly, Reggie Sanders, Barry Larkin)	.05
474	Four Corners (Gary Sheffield, Phil Plantier, Tony Gwynn, Fred McGriff)	.20
475	Shooting Stars (Doug Drabek, Craig Biggio, Jeff Bagwell)	.15
476	Giant Sticks (Will Clark, Barry Bonds, Matt Williams)	.40
477	Boyhood Friends (Darryl Strawberry, Eric Davis)	.05
478	Rock Solid (Dante Bichette, David Nied, Andres Galarraga)	.05
479	Inaugural Catch (Dave Magadan, Orestes Destrade, Bret Barbarie, Jeff Conine)	.05
480	Steel City Champions (Tim Wakefield, Andy Van Slyke, Jay Bell)	.05
481	"Les Grandes Etoiles" (Marquis Grissom, Delino DeShields, Dennis Martinez, Larry Walker)	.05
482	Runnin' Redbirds (Geronimo Pena, Ray Lankford, Ozzie Smith, Bernard Gilkey)	.10
483	Ivy Leaguers (Ryne Sandberg, Mark Grace, Randy Myers)	.15
484	Big Apple Power Switch (Eddie Murray, Bobby Bonilla, Howard Johnson)	.10
485	Hammers & Nails (John Kruk, Dave Hollins, Darren Daulton, Len Dykstra)	.05
486	Barry Bonds (Award Winners)	.60
487	Dennis Eckersley (Award Winners)	.30
488	Greg Maddux (Award Winners)	.40
489	Dennis Eckersley (Award Winners)	.30
490	Eric Karros (Award Winners)	.05
491	Pat Listach (Award Winners)	.05
492	Gary Sheffield (Award Winners)	.10
493	Mark McGwire (Award Winners)	.75
494	Gary Sheffield (Award Winners)	.10
495	Edgar Martinez (Award Winners)	.05
496	Fred McGriff (Award Winners)	.05
497	Juan Gonzalez (Award Winners)	.20
498	Darren Daulton (Award Winners)	.05
499	Cecil Fielder (Award Winners)	.05
500	Checklist 501-510 Diamond Debuts (Brent Gates)	.05
501	Tavo Alvarez (Diamond Debuts)	.05
502	Rod Bolton (Diamond Debuts)	.05
503	John Cummings RC (Diamond Debuts)	.05
504	Brent Gates (Diamond Debuts)	.05
505	Tyler Green (Diamond Debuts)	.05
506	Jose Martinez RC (Diamond Debuts)	.05
507	Troy Percival (Diamond Debuts)	.05
508	Kevin Stocker (Diamond Debuts)	.05
509	Matt Walbeck RC (Diamond Debuts)	.10
510	Rondell White (Diamond Debuts)	.05
511	Billy Ripken	.05
512	Mike Moore	.05
513	Jose Lind	.05
514	Chito Martinez	.05
515	Jose Guzman	.05
516	Kim Batiste	.05
517	Jeff Tackett	.05
518	Charlie Hough	.05
519	Marvin Freeman	.05
520	Carlos Martinez	.05
521	Eric Young	.05
522	Pete Incaviglia	.05
523	Scott Fletcher	.05
524	Orestes Destrade	.05
525	Checklist 421-525 (Ken Griffey Jr.)	.40
526	Ellis Burks	.05
527	Juan Samuel	.05
528	Dave Magadan	.05
529	Jeff Parrett	.05
530	Bill Krueger	.05
531	Frank Bolick	.05
532	Alan Trammell	.05
533	Walt Weiss	.05
534	David Cone	.05
535	Greg Maddux	.75
536	Kevin Young	.05
537	Dave Hansen	.05
538	Alex Cole	.05
539	Greg Hibbard	.05
540	Gene Larkin	.05
541	Jeff Reardon	.05
542	Felix Jose	.05
543	Jimmy Key	.05
544	Reggie Jefferson	.05
545	Gregg Jefferies	.05
546	Dave Stewart	.05
547	Tim Wallach	.05
548	Spike Owen	.05
549	Tommy Greene	.05
550	Fernando Valenzuela	.05
551	Rich Amaral	.05
552	Bret Barberie	.05
553	Edgar Martinez	.05
554	Jim Abbott	.05
555	Frank Thomas	.65
556	Wade Boggs	.75
557	Tom Henke	.05
558	Milt Thompson	.05
559	Lloyd McClendon	.05
560	Vinny Castilla	.05
561	Ricky Jordan	.05
562	Andujar Cedeno	.05
563	Greg Vaughn	.05
564	Cecil Fielder	.05
565	Kirby Puckett	.75
566	Mark McGwire	1.25
567	Barry Bonds	1.50
568	Jody Reed	.05
569	Todd Zeile	.05
570	Mark Carreon	.05
571	Joe Girardi	.05
572	Luis Gonzalez	.05
573	Mark Grace	.05
574	Rafael Palmeiro	.60
575	Darryl Strawberry	.05
576	Will Clark	.05
577	Fred McGriff	.05
578	Kevin Reimer	.05
579	Dave Righetti	.05
580	Juan Bell	.05
581	Jeff Branson	.05
582	Brian Hunter	.05
583	Tim Naehring	.05
584	Glenallen Hill	.05
585	Cal Ripken, Jr.	1.50
586	Albert Belle	.05
587	Robin Yount	.65
588	Chris Bosio	.05
589	Pete Smith	.05
590	Chuck Carr	.05
591	Jeff Blauser	.05
592	Kevin McReynolds	.05
593	Andres Galarraga	.05
594	Kevin Maas	.05
595	Eric Davis	.05
596	Brian Jordan	.05
597	Tim Raines	.05
598	Rick Wilkins	.05
599	Steve Cooke	.05
600	Mike Gallego	.05
601	Mike Munoz	.05
602	Luis Rivera	.05
603	Junior Ortiz	.05
604	Brent Mayne	.05
605	Luis Alicea	.05
606	Damon Berryhill	.05
607	Dave Henderson	.05
608	Kirk McCaskill	.05
609	Jeff Fassero	.05
610	Mike Harkey	.05
611	Francisco Cabrera	.05
612	Rey Sanchez	.05
613	Scott Servais	.05
614	Darrin Fletcher	.05
615	Felix Fermin	.05
616	Kevin Seitzer	.05
617	Bob Scanlan	.05
618	Billy Hatcher	.05
619	John Vander Wal	.05
620	Joe Hesketh	.05
621	Hector Villanueva	.05
622	Randy Milligan	.05
623	Tony Tarasco RC	.05
624	Russ Swan	.05
625	Willie Wilson	.05
626	Frank Tanana	.05
627	Pete O'Brien	.05
628	Lenny Webster	.05
629	Mark Clark	.05
630	Checklist 526-630 (Roger Clemens)	.40
631	Alex Arias	.05
632	Chris Gwynn	.05
633	Tom Bolton	.05
634	Greg Briley	.05
635	Kent Bottenfield	.05
636	Kelly Downs	.05
637	Manuel Lee	.05
638	Al Leiter	.05
639	Jeff Gardner	.05
640	Mike Gardiner	.05
641	Mark Gardner	.05
642	Jeff Branson	.05
643	Paul Wagner	.05
644	Sean Berry	.05
645	Phil Hiatt	.05
646	Kevin Mitchell	.05
647	Charlie Hayes	.05
648	Jim Deshaies	.05
649	Dan Pasqua	.05
650	Mike Maddux	.05
651	Domingo Martinez RC	.05
652	Greg McMichael RC	.05
653	Eric Wedge RC	.05
654	Mark Whiten	.05
655	Bobby Kelly	.05
656	Julio Franco	.05
657	Gene Harris	.05
658	Pete Schourek	.05
659	Mike Bielecki	.05
660	Ricky Gutierrez	.05
661	Chris Hammond	.05
662	Tim Scott	.05
663	Norm Charlton	.05
664	Doug Drabek	.05
665	Dwight Gooden	.05
666	Jim Gott	.05
667	Randy Myers	.05
668	Darren Holmes	.05
669	Tim Spehr	.05
670	Bruce Ruffin	.05
671	Bobby Thigpen	.05
672	Tony Fernandez	.05
673	Darrin Jackson	.05
674	Gregg Olson	.05
675	Rob Dibble	.05
676	Howard Johnson	.05
677	Mike Lansing RC	.15
678	Charlie Leibrandt	.05
679	Kevin Bass	.05
680	Hubie Brooks	.05
681	Scott Brosius	.05
682	Randy Knorr	.05
683	Dante Bichette	.05
684	Bryan Harvey	.05
685	Greg Gohr	.05
686	Willie Banks	.05
687	Robb Nen	.05
688	Mike Scioscia	.05
689	John Farrell	.05
690	John Candelaria	.05
691	Damon Buford	.05
692	Todd Worrell	.05
693	Pat Hentgen	.05
694	John Smiley	.05
695	Greg Swindell	.05
696	Derek Bell	.05
697	Terry Jorgensen	.05
698	Jimmy Jones	.05
699	David Wells	.05
700	Steve Martinez	.05
701	Steve Bedrosian	.05
702	Jeff Russell	.05

703	Joe Magrane	.05
704	Matt Mieske	.05
705	Paul Molitor	.65
706	Dale Murphy	.15
707	Steve Howe	.05
708	Greg Gagne	.05
709	Dave Eiland	.05
710	David West	.05
711	Luis Aquino	.05
712	Joe Orsulak	.05
713	Eric Plunk	.05
714	Mike Felder	.05
715	Joe Klink	.05
716	Lonnie Smith	.05
717	Monty Fariss	.05
718	Craig Lefferts	.05
719	John Habyan	.05
720	Willie Blair	.05
721	Darnell Coles	.05
722	Mark Williamson	.05
723	Bryn Smith	.05
724	Greg W. Harris	.05
725	Graeme Lloyd RC	.05
726	Cris Carpenter	.05
727	Chico Walker	.05
728	Tracy Woodson	.05
729	Jose Uribe	.05
730	Stan Javier	.05
731	Jay Howell	.05
732	Freddie Benavides	.05
733	Jeff Reboulet	.05
734	Scott Sanderson	.05
735	Checklist 631-735 (Ryne Sandberg)	.20
736	Archi Cianfrocco	.05
737	Daryl Boston	.05
738	Craig Grebeck	.05
739	Doug Dascenzo	.05
740	Gerald Young	.05
741	Candy Maldonado	.05
742	Joey Cora	.05
743	Don Slaught	.05
744	Steve Decker	.05
745	Blas Minor	.05
746	Storm Davis	.05
747	Carlos Quintana	.05
748	Vince Coleman	.05
749	Todd Burns	.05
750	Steve Frey	.05
751	Ivan Calderon	.05
752	Steve Reed RC	.05
753	Danny Jackson	.05
754	Jeff Conine	.05
755	Juan Gonzalez	.35
756	Mike Kelly	.05
757	John Doherty	.05
758	Jack Armstrong	.05
759	John Wehner	.05
760	Scott Bankhead	.05
761	Jim Tatum	.05
762	Scott Pose RC	.05
763	Andy Ashby	.05
764	Ed Sprague	.05
765	Harold Baines	.05
766	Kirk Gibson	.05
767	Troy Neel	.05
768	Dick Schofield	.05
769	Dickie Thon	.05
770	Butch Henry	.05
771	Junior Felix	.05
772	Ken Ryan RC	.05
773	Trevor Hoffman	.05
774	Phil Plantier	.05
775	Bo Jackson	.10
776	Benito Santiago	.05
777	Andre Dawson	.25
778	Bryan Hickerson	.05
779	Dennis Moeller	.05
780	Ryan Bowen	.05
781	Eric Fox	.05
782	Joe Kmak	.05
783	Mike Hampton	.05
784	Darrell Sherman RC	.05
785	J.T. Snow	.65
786	Dave Winfield	.65
787	Jim Austin	.05
788	Craig Shipley	.05
789	Greg Myers	.05
790	Todd Benzinger	.05
791	Cory Snyder	.05
792	David Segui	.05
793	Armando Reynoso	.05
794	Chili Davis	.05
795	Dave Nilsson	.05
796	Paul O'Neill	.05
797	Jerald Clark	.05
798	Jose Mesa	.05
799	Brian Holman	.05
800	Jim Eisenreich	.05
801	Mark McLemore	.05
802	Luis Sojo	.05
803	Harold Reynolds	.05
804	Dan Plesac	.05
805	Dave Stieb	.05
806	Tom Brunansky	.05
807	Kelly Gruber	.05
808	Bob Ojeda	.05
809	Dave Burba	.05
810	Joe Boever	.05
811	Jeremy Hernandez	.05
812	Angels Checklist (Tim Salmon)	.05
813	Astros Checklist (Jeff Bagwell)	.35
814	Athletics Checklist (Mark McGwire)	.75
815	Blue Jays Checklist (Roberto Alomar)	.10
816	Braves Checklist (Steve Avery)	.05
817	Brewers Checklist (Pat Listach)	.05
818	Cardinals Checklist (Gregg Jefferies)	.05
819	Cubs Checklist (Sammy Sosa)	.40
820	Dodgers Checklist (Darryl Strawberry)	.05
821	Expos Checklist (Dennis Martinez)	.05
822	Giants Checklist (Robby Thompson)	.05
823	Indians Checklist (Albert Belle)	.05
824	Mariners Checklist (Randy Johnson)	.30
825	Marlins Checklist (Nigel Wilson)	.05
826	Mets Checklist (Bobby Bonilla)	.05
827	Orioles Checklist (Glenn Davis)	.05
828	Padres Checklist (Gary Sheffield)	.10
829	Phillies Checklist (Darren Daulton)	.05
830	Pirates Checklist (Jay Bell)	.05
831	Rangers Checklist (Juan Gonzalez)	.20
832	Red Sox Checklist (Andre Dawson)	.10
833	Reds Checklist (Hal Morris)	.05
834	Rockies Checklist (David Nied)	.05
835	Royals Checklist (Felix Jose)	.05
836	Tigers Checklist (Travis Fryman)	.05
837	Twins Checklist (Shane Mack)	.05
838	White Sox Checklist (Robin Ventura)	.05
839	Yankees Checklist (Danny Tartabull)	.05
840	Checklist 736-840 (Roberto Alomar)	.10
SP5	3,000 Hits (Robin Yount, George Brett)	
SP6	Nolan Ryan	1.50

Gold Holograms

Unlike 1992, when gold holograms were found on the back of every card originating in a factory set, in 1993 the use of gold holograms was limited to just one factory set per 20-set case, creating a scarce parallel version.

	NM/M
Complete Fact. Set (840):	200.00
Common Player:	.50

Baseball Heroes Reggie Jackson Supers

Upper Deck issued a large version of its 1990 Heroes Reggie Jackson cards that was available in retail outlets. Just as in the case of the regular issue Jackson insert cards, there are 10 cards (nine numbered and one unnumbered header card). The cards are 3-1/2"

x 5" and identical to the smaller Heroes cards in every other respect. Each of the individual cards carries a sequential number out of a limit of 10,000. The cards were sold one to a package that also included two packs of 1993 Upper Deck cards for about $5.

		NM/M
Complete Set (10):		25.00
Common Card:		3.00
1	1969 Emerging Superstar (Reggie Jackson)	3.00
2	1973 An MVP Year (Reggie Jackson)	3.00
3	1977 "Mr. October" (Reggie Jackson)	3.00
4	1978 Jackson vs. Welch (Reggie Jackson)	3.00
5	1982 Under the Halo (Reggie Jackson)	3.00
6	1984 500! (Reggie Jackson)	3.00
7	1986 Moving Up the List (Reggie Jackson)	3.00
8	1987 A Great Career Ends (Reggie Jackson)	3.00
9	Heroes Checklist (Reggie Jackson)	3.00
---	Header Card	3.00

Baseball Heroes Willie Mays

This 10-card insert set includes eight individually-titled cards, an illustrated checklist and one header card. The set is a continuation of Upper Deck's previous Heroes efforts, honoring greats such as Hank Aaron, Nolan Ryan and Reggie Jackson, and is numbered 46-54. Cards were randomly inserted into Series 1 foil packs.

		NM/M
Complete Set (10):		4.00
Common Card:		.50
Header Card:		1.00
46	1951 Rookie-of-the-Year	.50
47	1954 The Catch	.50
48	1956-57 30-30 Club	.50
49	1961 Four-Homer Game	.50
50	1965 Most Valuable Player	.50
51	1969 600-Home Run Club	.50
52	1972 New York Homecoming	.50
53	1979 Hall of Fame	.50
54	Checklist - Heroes 46-54	.50

Clutch Performers

Reggie Jackson has selected the players who perform the best under pressure for this 20-card insert set. Cards were available only in Series II retail packs and use the prefix "R" for numbering. Fronts have a black bottom panel with "Clutch Performers" printed in dark gray. Jackson's facsimile autograph is overprinted in gold foil. On back, under a second player photo, is Jackson's picture and his assessment of the player. There are a few lines of stats to support the player's selection to this exclusive company.

		NM/M
Complete Set (20):		8.00
Common Player:		.25
1	Roberto Alomar	.30
2	Wade Boggs	1.00
3	Barry Bonds	2.50
4	Jose Canseco	.40
5	Joe Carter	.25
6	Will Clark	.25
7	Roger Clemens	1.25
8	Dennis Eckersley	.60
9	Cecil Fielder	.25
10	Juan Gonzalez	.60
11	Ken Griffey Jr.	2.00
12	Rickey Henderson	.75
13	Barry Larkin	.25
14	Don Mattingly	1.25
15	Fred McGriff	.25
16	Terry Pendleton	.25
17	Kirby Puckett	1.00
18	Ryne Sandberg	1.00
19	John Smoltz	.25
20	Frank Thomas	.75

Future Heroes

This insert set includes eight player cards, a checklist and an unnumbered header card. The cards are numbered 55-63 as a continuation of previous Heroes sets, but this one features more than one player; previous sets featured only one player. Card fronts have a Future Heroes logo and a facsimile autograph. The player's name is revealed using a peeled-back paper effect. Cards were randomly inserted in Series II foil packs.

		NM/M
Complete Set (10):		5.00
Common Player:		.50
Header Card:		.25
55	Roberto Alomar	.50
56	Barry Bonds	2.50
57	Roger Clemens	1.00
58	Juan Gonzalez	.50
59	Ken Griffey Jr.	1.50
60	Mark McGwire	2.00
61	Kirby Puckett	.85
62	Frank Thomas	.75
63	Checklist	.05

Highlights

These 20 insert cards commemorate highlights from the 1992 season. Cards, which were randomly inserted in Series II packs, have a '92 Season Highlights logo on the bottom, with the player's name inside a banner trailing from the logo. The date of the significant event is under the player's name. Card backs have the logo at the top and are numbered with an "HI" prefix. A headline describes what highlight occurred, while the text describes the event.

		NM/M
Complete Set (20):		20.00
Common Player:		.25
1	Roberto Alomar	.50
2	Steve Avery	.25
3	Harold Baines	.25
4	Damon Berryhill	.25
5	Barry Bonds	7.50
6	Bret Boone	.25
7	George Brett	4.00
8	Francisco Cabrera	.25
9	Ken Griffey Jr.	5.00
10	Rickey Henderson	2.00
11	Kenny Lofton	.25
12	Mickey Morandini	.25
13	Eddie Murray	2.00
14	David Nied	.25
15	Jeff Reardon	.25
16	Bip Roberts	.25
17	Nolan Ryan	7.50
18	Ed Sprague	.25
19	Dave Winfield	2.00
20	Robin Yount	2.00

Home Run Heroes

This 28-card insert set features the top home run hitters from each team for 1992. Cards, inserted in Series I jumbo packs, are numbered with an "HR" prefix. The card fronts have "Home Run Heroes" printed vertically at the left edge and an embossed bat with the player's name and Upper Deck trademark at bottom. Backs have a purple or pink posterized photo and a few words about the player.

		NM/M
Complete Set (28):		7.50
Common Player:		.15
1	Juan Gonzalez	.50
2	Mark McGwire	2.25
3	Cecil Fielder	.15
4	Fred McGriff	.15
5	Albert Belle	.15
6	Barry Bonds	2.50
7	Joe Carter	.15
8	Darren Daulton	.15
9	Ken Griffey Jr.	2.00
10	Dave Hollins	.15
11	Ryne Sandberg	1.00
12	George Bell	.15
13	Danny Tartabull	.15
14	Mike Devereaux	.15
15	Greg Vaughn	.15
16	Larry Walker	.15
17	Dave Justice	.15
18	Terry Pendleton	.15
19	Eric Karros	.15
20	Ray Lankford	.15
21	Matt Williams	.15
22	Eric Anthony	.15
23	Bobby Bonilla	.15
24	Kirby Puckett	1.00
25	Mike Macfarlane	.15
26	Tom Brunansky	.15
27	Paul O'Neill	.15
28	Gary Gaetti	.15

Iooss Collection

Sports photographer Walter Iooss Jr. has captured 26 current players in this insert set featuring their candid portraits. Cards have full-bleed photos and gold foil stamping. Backs have biographical sketches and are numbered using a WI prefix. They are available in Series I retail packs.

		NM/M
Complete Set (27):		10.00
Common Player:		.25
Header Card:		.25
1	Tim Salmon	.25
2	Jeff Bagwell	.75
3	Mark McGwire	1.50
4	Roberto Alomar	.35

Iooss Collection Supers

Upper Deck issued a series of 27 individually numbered oversized cards identical to the Iooss Collection inserts from the regular 1993 Upper Deck set. The cards are 3-1/2" x 5" and each is numbered on back to a limit of 10,000. The cards were available in retail outlets such as WalMart, packaged in blister packs with two foil packs of 1993 Upper Deck cards for around $5. Authentically autographed and numbered (on card fronts) of some players' cards were sold by Upper Deck Authenticated.

	NM/M
Complete Set (27):	20.00
Common Player:	.50
Header Card:	.25
1	Tim Salmon	.50
2	Jeff Bagwell	1.00
3	Mark McGwire	2.00
4	Roberto Alomar	.75
5	Steve Avery	.50
6	Paul Molitor	1.00
7	Ozzie Smith	1.25
8	Mark Grace	.50
9	Eric Karros	.50
10	Delino DeShields	.50
11	Will Clark	.50
12	Albert Belle	.50
13	Ken Griffey Jr.	2.00
14	Howard Johnson	.50
15	Cal Ripken, Jr.	2.50
16	Fred McGriff	.50
17	Darren Daulton	.50
18	Andy Van Slyke	.50
19	Nolan Ryan	2.50
20	Wade Boggs	1.25
21	Barry Larkin	.50
22	George Brett	1.50
23	Cecil Fielder	.50
24	Kirby Puckett	1.25
25	Frank Thomas	1.00
26	Don Mattingly	1.50

On Deck

These UV-coated cards feature 25 of the game's top players. Each card has a full-bleed photo on the front and questions and answers on the back. Available only in Series II jumbo packs, the cards have a D prefix for numbering.

		NM/M
Complete Set (25):		10.00
Common Player:		.15
1	Jim Abbott	.15
2	Roberto Alomar	.25
3	Carlos Baerga	.15
4	Albert Belle	.15
5	Wade Boggs	1.00
6	George Brett	1.25
7	Jose Canseco	.45
8	Will Clark	.15
9	Roger Clemens	1.25
10	Dennis Eckersley	.65
11	Cecil Fielder	.15
12	Juan Gonzalez	.40
13	Ken Griffey Jr.	

Secondary Home Run Heroes-era lists:

		NM/M
5	Joe Carter	.25
6	Will Clark	.25
7	Roger Clemens	1.25
8	Dennis Eckersley	.60
9	Cecil Fielder	.25
10	Juan Gonzalez	.60
11	Ken Griffey Jr.	2.00
12	Rickey Henderson	.75
13	Barry Larkin	.25
14	Don Mattingly	1.25
15	Fred McGriff	.25
16	Terry Pendleton	.25
17	Kirby Puckett	1.00
18	Ryne Sandberg	1.00
19	John Smoltz	.25
20	Frank Thomas	.75

Iooss Collection continued list:

		NM/M
5	Steve Avery	.25
6	Paul Molitor	.75
7	Ozzie Smith	.25
8	Mark Grace	.25
9	Eric Karros	.25
10	Delino DeShields	.25
11	Will Clark	.35
12	Albert Belle	.35
13	Ken Griffey Jr.	1.50
14	Howard Johnson	.25
15	Cal Ripken, Jr.	2.00
16	Fred McGriff	.25
17	Darren Daulton	.25
18	Andy Van Slyke	.25
19	Nolan Ryan	.25
20	Wade Boggs	1.00
21	Barry Larkin	.25
22	George Brett	1.25
23	Cecil Fielder	.25
24	Kirby Puckett	1.00
25	Frank Thomas	.75
26	Don Mattingly	

14	Tony Gwynn	1.00
15	Bo Jackson	.20
16	Chipper Jones	1.00
17	Eric Karros	.15
18	Mark McGwire	2.00
19	Kirby Puckett	1.00
20	Nolan Ryan	2.50
21	Tim Salmon	.15
22	Ryne Sandberg	1.00
23	Darryl Strawberry	.15
24	Frank Thomas	.75
25	Andy Van Slyke	.15

Supers

A series of six 1993 Upper Deck cards and one from 1991 was re-issued in an 8-1/2" x 11" format, though the manner of distribution is unclear. The cards are virtually identical in design to the regularly issued versions, except for the size, the lack of a hologram on back, and a 1993 dated seal with an individual serial number. The Ryan card was issued in an edition of 5,000, the Karros and Finley cards were issued in an edition of 2,500, the others were limited to 1,000 each.

		NM/M
Complete Set (7):		24.00
Common Card:		3.00
6	Kirby Puckett (Triple Crown Contender)	4.50
10	Barry Bonds/SP	7.50
24	Eric Karros/1991	3.00
75	Tom Glavine/1993	3.00
77	Chuck Finley	3.00
155	Nolan Ryan	7.50
199	Roger Clemens/SP	5.00

Then And Now

This 18-card lithogram set features both Hall of Famers and current players. The cards feature a combination of four-color player photos and a holographic background. They were random inserts in both Series I and Series II packs. Numbering includes the prefix TN. A limited edition of 2,500 supersize 5" by 7" Mickey Mantle Then And Now cards was created for sale through Upper Deck Authenticated.

		NM/M
Complete Set (18):		30.00
Common Player:		.75
1	Wade Boggs	2.00
2	George Brett	2.50
3	Rickey Henderson	1.25
4	Cal Ripken, Jr.	4.00
5	Nolan Ryan	4.00
6	Ryne Sandberg	2.00
7	Ozzie Smith	2.00
8	Darryl Strawberry	.75
9	Dave Winfield	1.25
10	Dennis Eckersley	1.00
11	Tony Gwynn	2.00
12	Howard Johnson	.75
13	Don Mattingly	2.50
14	Eddie Murray	1.25
15	Robin Yount	1.25
16	Reggie Jackson	2.00
17	Mickey Mantle	6.00
17a	Mickey Mantle (5" x 7")	13.50
18	Willie Mays	3.00

Triple Crown Contenders

These insert cards were available in 1993 Upper Deck Series I foil packs sold by hobby dealers. The set features 10 players who are candidates to win baseball's Triple Crown. Card fronts have a crown

and the player's name at the bottom. Backs put that material at the top and explain why the player might lead the league in home runs, batting average and runs batted in.

		NM/M
Complete Set (10):		6.00
Common Player:		.25
1	Barry Bonds	1.50
2	Jose Canseco	.45
3	Will Clark	.25
4	Ken Griffey Jr.	1.25
5	Fred McGriff	.25
6	Kirby Puckett	.60
7	Cal Ripken, Jr.	1.50
8	Gary Sheffield	.35
9	Frank Thomas	.60
10	Larry Walker	.25

5th Anniversary

This 15-card insert set replicates 15 of Upper Deck's most popular cards from its first five years. Foil stamping and a fifth-anniversary logo appear on the cards, which are otherwise reproductions of the originals. The prefix A appears before each card number. The cards were available in Series II hobby packs only.

		NM/M
Complete Set (15):		7.00
Common Player:		.25
1	Ken Griffey Jr.	1.50
2	Gary Sheffield	.35
3	Roberto Alomar	.35
4	Jim Abbott	.25
5	Nolan Ryan	2.00
6	Juan Gonzalez	.35
7	Dave Justice	.25
8	Carlos Baerga	.25
9	Reggie Jackson	1.00
10	Eric Karros	.25
11	Chipper Jones	1.00
12	Ivan Rodriguez	.50
13	Pat Listach	.25
14	Frank Thomas	.90
15	Tim Salmon	.25

1993 Upper Deck 5th Anniversary Supers

This set of oversized (3-1/2" x 5") cards is simply an enlarged version of the Upper Deck 5th An-

niversary subset that was inserted with the company's 1993 cards. There are 15 cards in the set, which are reprinted versions of some of the most popular cards in the last five years from Upper Deck. Each of the cards carries a number on the back out of an edition of 10,000. The cards were sold individually in blister packs at retail outlets along with two packs of 1993 Upper Deck.

		NM/M
Complete Set (15):		17.50
Common Player:		1.00
1	Ken Griffey Jr.	2.50
2	Gary Sheffield	1.25
3	Roberto Alomar	1.25
4	Jim Abbott	1.00
5	Nolan Ryan	3.00
6	Juan Gonzalez	1.25
7	David Justice	1.00
8	Carlos Baerga	1.00
9	Reggie Jackson	2.00
10	Eric Karros	1.00
11	Chipper Jones	2.00
12	Ivan Rodriguez	1.50
13	Pat Listach	1.00
14	Frank Thomas	1.75
15	Tim Salmon	1.00

1993 Upper Deck Heroes of Baseball Previews

This four-card preview set was produced in conjunction with the All-Star FanFest in Baltimore to re-introduce the concept of T202-style "triplefolder" baseball cards. The preview set came in a specially decorated box. The 5-1/4" x 2-1/4" cards feature Ted Williams, Mickey Mantle and Reggie Jackson in various combinations of photos and artwork on each card. Backs are printed in red and gold and include an infield-shaped hologram. Written summaries of the players and their careers are featured. Cards have an "HOB" prefix to their number. A special offering of uncut 27" x 20" sheets containing eight complete sets of the preview cards was sold by UD Authenticated in a numbered edition of 2,000.

		NM/M
Complete Set (4):		5.00
Common Card:		1.00
Uncut UDA Sheet:		20.00
1	Triple Threat (Mickey Mantle, Ted Williams)	2.00
2	Changing of the Guard (Mickey Mantle, Reggie Jackson)	1.50
3	Night and Day (Reggie Jackson, Ted Williams)	1.00
4	Hall-of-Fame Trio (Reggie Jackson, Mickey Mantle, Ted Williams)	1.50

1993UD All-Time Heroes

This 1993 set pays homage to one of the classiest, turn-of-the-century card sets, the T202 Hassan Triple Folders. The All-Time Heroes cards are 2-1/4" x 5-1/4" and feature two side panels and a larger middle panel, which features an action shot of the player. A portrait of the player and the Baseball Assistance Team (BAT) logo flank the action photo. Card backs have a biography and career summary. A Classic Combinations subset of 35 cards features artwork or photographs of two or more great players together, plus individual photos on the side panels. Production was limited to 5,140 numbered cases of 12-card foil packs. Ten T202 reprints were also produced and were randomly inserted in the foil packs.

		NM/M
Complete Set (165):		35.00
Common Player:		.10
Wax Pack (12):		2.00
Wax Box (24):		30.00
1	Hank Aaron	2.00
2	Tommie Agee	.10
3	Bob Allison	.10
4	Matty Alou	.10
5	Sal Bando	.10
6	Hank Bauer	.15
7	Don Baylor	.15
8	Glenn Beckert	.10
9	Yogi Berra	.50
10	Buddy Biancalana	.10
11	Jack Billingham	.10
12	Joe Black	.10
13	Paul Blair	.10
14	Steve Blass	.10
15	Ray Boone	.10
16	Lou Boudreau	.15
17	Ken Brett	.10
18	Nellie Briles	.10
19	Bobby Brown	.10
20	Bill Buckner	.15
21	Don Buford	.10
22	Al Bumbry	.10
23	Lew Burdette	.10
24	Jeff Burroughs	.10
25	Johnny Callison	.10
26	Bert Campaneris	.10
27	Rico Carty	.10
28	Dave Cash	.10
29	Cesar Cedeno	.10
30	Frank Chance	.25
31	Joe Charboneau	.15
32	Ty Cobb	2.00
33	Jerry Coleman	.10
34	Cecil Cooper	.10
35	Frankie Crossetti	.10
36	Alvin Dark	.10
37	Tommy Davis	.10
38	Dizzy Dean	.25
39	Doug DeCinces	.10
40	Bucky Dent	.10
41	Larry Dierker	.10
42	Larry Doby	.20
43	Moe Drabowsky	.10
44	Dave Dravecky	.15
45	Del Ennis	.10
46	Carl Erskine	.10
47	Johnny Evers	.25
48	Elroy Face	.10
49	Rick Ferrell	.10
50	Mark Fidrych	.15
51	Curt Flood	.10
52	Whitey Ford	.50
53	George Foster	.10
54	Jimmie Foxx	.25
55	Jim Fregosi	.10
56	Phil Garner	.10
57	Ralph Garr	.10
58	Lou Gehrig	2.00
59	Bobby Grich	.10
60	Jerry Grote	.10
61	Harvey Haddix	.10
62	Toby Harrah	.10
63	Bud Harrelson	.10
64	Jim Hegan	.10
65	Gil Hodges	.25
66	Ken Holtzman	.10
67	Bob Horner	.10
68	Rogers Hornsby	.25
69	Carl Hubbell	.25
70	Ron Hunt	.10
71	Monte Irvin	.10
72a	Reggie Jackson (Regular issue, black printing on back.)	.50
72b	Reggie Jackson (Dealer promo, red printing on back.)	6.00
73	Larry Jansen	.10
74	Ferguson Jenkins	.10
75	Tommy John	.10
76	Cliff Johnson	.10
77	Davey Johnson	.10
78	Walter Johnson	.45
79	George Kell	.10
80	Don Kessinger	.10
81	Vern Law	.10
82	Dennis Leonard	.10
83	Johnny Logan	.10
84	Mickey Lolich	.10
85	Jim Lonborg	.10
86	Bill Madlock	.10
87	Mickey Mantle	4.00
88	Billy Martin	.25
89	Christy Mathewson	.45
90	Lee May	.10
91	Willie Mays	2.00
92	Bill Mazeroski	.25
93	Gil McDougald	.15
94	Sam McDowell	.15
95	Minnie Minoso	.15
96	Johnny Mize	.25
97	Rick Monday	.10
98	Wally Moon	.10
99	Manny Mota	.10
100	Bobby Murcer	.10
101	Ron Necciai	.10
102	Al Oliver	.10
103	Mel Ott	.25
104	Mel Parnell	.10
105	Jimmy Piersall	.10
106	Johnny Podres	.15
107	Bobby Richardson	.15
108	Robin Roberts	.15
109	Al Rosen	.10
110	Babe Ruth	3.00
111	Joe Sambito	.10
112	Manny Sanguillen	.10
113	Ron Santo	.10
114	Bill Skowron	.15
115	Enos Slaughter	.15
116	Warren Spahn	.20
117	Tris Speaker	.20
118	Frank Thomas	.10
119	Bobby Thomson	.10
120	Andre Thornton	.10
121	Marv Throneberry	.10
122	Luis Tiant	.10
123	Joe Tinker	.25
124	Honus Wagner	.50
125	Bill White	.10
126	Ted Williams	1.00
127	Earl Wilson	.10
128	Joe Wood	.10
129	Cy Young	.40
130	Richie Zisk	.10
131	Babe Ruth, Lou Gehrig	2.00
132	Ted Williams, Rogers Hornsby	1.00
133	Lou Gehrig, Babe Ruth	2.00
134	Babe Ruth, Mickey Mantle	3.00
135	Mickey Mantle, Reggie Jackson	1.00
136	Mel Ott, Carl Hubbell	.15
137	Mickey Mantle, Willie Mays	2.00
138	Cy Young, Walter Johnson	.25
139	Honus Wagner, Rogers Hornsby	.25
140	Mickey Mantle, Whitey Ford	2.00
141	Mickey Mantle, Billy Martin	2.00
142	Cy Young, Walter Johnson	.25
143	Christy Mathewson, Walter Johnson	.25
144	Warren Spahn, Christy Mathewson	.15
145	Honus Wagner, Ty Cobb	.50
146	Babe Ruth, Ty Cobb	1.00
147	Joe Tinker, Johnny Evers	.15
148	Johnny Evers, Frank Chance	.10
149	Hank Aaron, Babe Ruth	1.00
150	Willie Mays, Hank Aaron	1.00
151	Babe Ruth, Willie Mays	1.00
152	Babe Ruth, Whitey Ford	1.00
153	Larry Doby, Minnie Minoso	.25
154	Joe Black, Monte Irvin	.10
155	Joe Wood, Christy Mathewson	.15
156	Christy Mathewson, Cy Young	.25
157	Cy Young, Joe Wood	.25
158	Cy Young, Whitey Ford	.20
159	Cy Young, Ferguson Jenkins	.15
160	Ty Cobb, Rogers Hornsby	.45
161	Tris Speaker, Ted Williams	1.00
162	Rogers Hornsby, Ted Williams	1.00
163	Willie Mays, Monte Irvin	.50
164	Willie Mays, Bobby Thomson	.50
165	Reggie Jackson, Mickey Mantle	2.00

All-Time Heroes T202 Reprints

A series of 10 reprints of the classic 1912 Hassan "Triplefolders" baseball cards on which the All-Time Heroes set was patterned was included as random inserts in the Upper Deck Old-Timers set. The reprints measure 5-1/4" x 2-1/4" (same as the originals). The Hassan cigarette ads on the backs of the originals have been replaced on the reprints by an Upper Deck hologram and the logos of the card company, B.A.T., Major League Baseball and the Cooperstown Collection. The Hassan cards are known as T202, their designation in the "American Card Catalog." The reprints are unnumbered and are checklisted here alphabetically in order of the player appearing on the left end of each card.

		NM/M
Complete Set (10):		10.00
Common Player:		.50
(1)	Art Devlin, Christy Mathewson	
(2)	Hugh Jennings, Ty Cobb	2.00
(3)	John Kling, Cy Young	1.00
(4)	Jack Knight, Walter Johnson	.75
(5)	John McGraw, Hugh Jennings	.50
(6)	George Moriarty, Ty Cobb	
(7)	Charley O'Leary, Ty Cobb	2.00
(8)	Charley O'Leary, Ty Cobb	2.00
(9)	Joe Tinker, Frank Chance	1.00
(10)	Joe Wood, Tris Speaker	.50

1993 Upper Deck Diamond Gallery

Utilizing something the company calls lithogram technology, Upper Deck produced a 36-card set that combines four-color photography and a holographic image. The set features one star from each of the 28 teams, along with a subset spotlighting top rookies from 1993 and cards saluting Nolan Ryan, Rickey Henderson and Ozzie Smith. The set comes in a specially-designed box, with a numbered checklist card. The set was limited to a total of 123,600.

		NM/M
Complete Set (36):		6.00
Common Player:		.10
1	Tim Salmon	.10
2	Jeff Bagwell	.30
3	Mark McGwire	.75
4	Roberto Alomar	.10
5	Terry Pendleton	.10
6	Robin Yount	.30
7	Ray Lankford	.10
8	Ryne Sandberg	.40
9	Darryl Strawberry	.10
10	Marquis Grissom	.10
11	Barry Bonds	.10
12	Carlos Baerga	.10
13	Ken Griffey Jr.	.65
14	Benito Santiago	.10
15	Dwight Gooden	.10
16	Cal Ripken, Jr.	1.00
17	Tony Gwynn	.40
18	Dave Hollins	.10
19	Andy Van Slyke	.10
20	Juan Gonzalez	.50
21	Roger Clemens	.50
22	Barry Larkin	.10
23	Dave Nied	.10
24	George Brett	.50
25	Travis Fryman	.10
26	Kirby Puckett	.40
27	Frank Thomas	.30
28	Don Mattingly	.50
29	Rickey Henderson	.30
30	Nolan Ryan	1.00
31	Ozzie Smith	.40
32	Wil Cordero	.10
33	Phil Hiatt	.10
34	Mike Piazza	.65
35	J.T. Snow	.10
36	Kevin Young	.10

1993 Upper Deck Fun Packs

Aimed at the younger audience, this product features 150 "regular" player cards and 75 specialty cards in a variety of subsets, plus two different types of insert cards. Basic player cards feature a photo (generally in action) on a background of purple, green and red, highlighted by yellow and orange stripes. On back is a white panel on red, yellow and orange blended stripes. In the panel are a cartoon, a trivia question and answer, brief biographical details, stats, and career summary. The basic player cards are arranged within the set alphabetically by team. The teams are also arranged alphabetically by nickname. Leading off each team's roster is a "Glow Stars" sticker, featuring a player photo against a parti-colored background. The area around the photo is die-cut to allow the picture to be separated from the background and stuck to a wall, where the white and green outlines glow in the dark. Cards #1-9 are designated "Stars of Tomorrow." Both front and back have a background of a star-studded purple sky. Cards #10-21 are "Hot Shots" - heat-sensitive cards. When touched the black textured ink surrounding the player photo turns clear, revealing a colored pattern beneath. The Hot Shot cards were available only via mail-in redemption. Cards #22-27 are "Kid Stars" and feature a childhood photo. Cards #28-37 are checklisted as "Upper Deck Heroes," though that designation does not appear on the cards. The subset is done in comic-book art style. Cards #216-220 are double-size (2-1/2"x7") "Fold-outs." The five checklist cards which conclude the set have player photos on front.

	NM/M
Complete Set (225):	15.00
Common Player:	.05
Wax Pack (6):	.50
Wax Box (36):	15.00

1	Wil Cordero (Stars of Tomorrow)	.05
2	Brent Gates (Stars of Tomorrow)	.05
3	Benji Gil (Stars of Tomorrow)	.05
4	Phil Hiatt (Stars of Tomorrow)	.05
5	David McCarty (Stars of Tomorrow)	.05
6	Mike Piazza (Stars of Tomorrow)	1.50
7	Tim Salmon (Stars of Tomorrow)	.05
8	J.T. Snow RC (Stars of Tomorrow)	.50
9	Kevin Young (Stars of Tomorrow)	.05
10	Roberto Alomar (Hot Shots)	.25
11	Barry Bonds (Hot Shots)	1.50
12	Jose Canseco (Hot Shots)	.35
13	Will Clark (Hot Shots)	.10
14	Roger Clemens (Hot Shots)	.75
15	Juan Gonzalez (Hot Shots)	.25
16	Ken Griffey Jr. (Hot Shots)	1.00
17	Mark McGwire (Hot Shots)	1.25
18	Nolan Ryan (Hot Shots)	1.50
19	Ryne Sandberg (Hot Shots)	.65
20	Gary Sheffield (Hot Shots)	.30
21	Frank Thomas (Hot Shots)	.60
22	Roberto Alomar (Kid Stars)	.10
23	Roger Clemens (Kid Stars)	.45
24	Ken Griffey Jr. (Kid Stars)	.50
25	Gary Sheffield (Kid Stars)	.15
26	Nolan Ryan (Kid Stars)	.75
27	Frank Thomas (Kid Stars)	.40
28	Reggie Jackson (Heroes)	.45
29	Roger Clemens (Heroes)	.45
30	Ken Griffey Jr. (Heroes)	.50
31	Bo Jackson (Heroes)	.10
32	Cal Ripken, Jr. (Heroes)	.45
33	Nolan Ryan (Heroes)	.75
34	Deion Sanders (Heroes)	.10
35	Ozzie Smith (Heroes)	.40
36	Frank Thomas (Heroes)	.35
37	Tim Salmon (Glow Stars)	.05
38	Chili Davis	.05
39	Chuck Finley	.05
40	Mark Langston	.05
41	Luis Polonia	.05
42	Jeff Bagwell (Glow Stars)	.30
43	Jeff Bagwell	.50
44	Craig Biggio	.05
45	Ken Caminiti	.05
46	Doug Drabek	.05
47	Steve Finley	.05
48	Mark McGwire (Glow Stars)	.65
49	Dennis Eckersley	.45
50	Rickey Henderson	.50
51	Mark McGwire	1.25
52	Ruben Sierra	.05
53	Terry Steinbach	.05
54	Roberto Alomar (Glow Stars)	.10

55	Roberto Alomar	.20
56	Joe Carter	.05
57	Juan Guzman	.05
58	Paul Molitor	.50
59	Jack Morris	.05
60	John Olerud	.05
61	Tom Glavine (Glow Stars)	.10
62	Steve Avery	.05
63	Tom Glavine	.20
64	Dave Justice	.05
65	Greg Maddux	.65
66	Terry Pendleton	.05
67	Deion Sanders	.10
68	John Smoltz	.05
69	Robin Yount (Glow Stars)	.30
70	Cal Eldred	.05
71	Pat Listach	.05
72	Greg Vaughn	.05
73	Robin Yount	.50
74	Ozzie Smith (Glow Stars)	.45
75	Gregg Jefferies	.05
76	Ray Lankford	.05
77	Lee Smith	.05
78	Ozzie Smith	.65
79	Bob Tewksbury	.05
80	Ryne Sandberg (Glow Stars)	.35
81	Mark Grace	.05
82	Mike Morgan	.05
83	Randy Myers	.05
84	Ryne Sandberg	.65
85	Sammy Sosa	.65
86	Eric Karros (Glow Stars)	.05
87	Brett Butler	.05
88	Orel Hershiser	.05
89	Eric Karros	.05
90	Ramon Martinez	.05
91	Jose Offerman	.05
92	Darryl Strawberry	.05
93	Marquis Grissom (Glow Stars)	.05
94	Delino DeShields	.05
95	Marquis Grissom	.05
96	Ken Hill	.05
97	Dennis Martinez	.05
98	Larry Walker	.05
99	Barry Bonds (Glow Stars)	.65
100	Barry Bonds	1.50
101	Will Clark	.05
102	Bill Swift	.05
103	Robby Thompson	.05
104	Matt Williams	.05
105	Carlos Baerga (Glow Stars)	.05
106	Sandy Alomar, Jr.	.05
107	Carlos Baerga	.05
108	Albert Belle	.05
109	Kenny Lofton	.05
110	Charles Nagy	.05
111	Ken Griffey Jr. (Glow Stars)	.50
112	Jay Buhner	.05
113	Dave Fleming	.05
114	Ken Griffey Jr.	1.00
115	Randy Johnson	.50
116	Edgar Martinez	.05
117	Benito Santiago (Glow Stars)	.05
118	Bret Barberie	.05
119	Jeff Conine	.05
120	Brian Harvey	.05
121	Benito Santiago	.05
122	Walt Weiss	.05
123	Dwight Gooden (Glow Stars)	.50
124	Bobby Bonilla	.05
125	Tony Fernandez	.05
126	Dwight Gooden	.05
127	Howard Johnson	.05
128	Eddie Murray	.50
129	Bret Saberhagen	.05
130	Cal Ripken, Jr. (Glow Stars)	.75
131	Brady Anderson	.05
132	Mike Devereaux	.05
133	Ben McDonald	.05
134	Mike Mussina	.30
135	Cal Ripken, Jr.	1.50
136	Fred McGriff (Glow Stars)	.05
137	Andy Benes	.05
138	Tony Gwynn	.65
139	Fred McGriff	.05
140	Phil Plantier	.05
141	Gary Sheffield	.25
142	Darren Daulton (Glow Stars)	.05
143	Darren Daulton	.05
144	Len Dykstra	.05
145	Dave Hollins	.05
146	John Kruk	.05
147	Mitch Williams	.05
148	Andy Van Slyke (Glow Stars)	.05
149	Jay Bell	.05
150	Zane Smith	.05
151	Andy Van Slyke	.05
152	Tim Wakefield	.05
153	Juan Gonzalez (Glow Stars)	.15
154	Kevin Brown	.05
155	Jose Canseco	.35
156	Juan Gonzalez	.25
157	Rafael Palmeiro	.05
158	Dean Palmer	.05
159	Ivan Rodriguez	.45
160	Nolan Ryan	1.50
161	Roger Clemens (Glow Stars)	.50

162	Roger Clemens	.75
163	Andre Dawson	.25
164	Mike Greenwell	.05
165	Tony Pena	.05
166	Frank Viola	.05
167	Barry Larkin (Glow Stars)	.05
168	Rob Dibble	.05
169	Roberto Kelly	.05
170	Barry Larkin	.05
171	Kevin Mitchell	.05
172	Bip Roberts	.05
173	Andres Galarraga (Glow Stars)	.05
174	Dante Bichette	.05
175	Jerald Clark	.05
176	Andres Galarraga	.05
177	Charlie Hayes	.05
178	David Nied	.05
179	David Cone (Glow Stars)	.05
180	Kevin Appler	.05
181	George Brett	.75
182	David Cone	.05
183	Felix Jose	.05
184	Wally Joyner	.05
185	Cecil Fielder (Glow Stars)	.05
186	Cecil Fielder	.05
187	Travis Fryman	.05
188	Tony Phillips	.05
189	Mickey Tettleton	.05
190	Lou Whitaker	.05
191	Kirby Puckett (Glow Stars)	.35
192	Scott Erickson	.05
193	Chuck Knoblauch	.05
194	Shane Mack	.05
195	Kirby Puckett	.65
196	Dave Winfield	.50
197	Frank Thomas (Glow Stars)	.40
198	George Bell	.05
199	Bo Jackson	.10
200	Jack McDowell	.05
201	Tim Raines	.05
202	Frank Thomas	.50
203	Robin Ventura	.05
204	Jim Abbott (Glow Stars)	.05
205	Jim Abbott	.05
206	Wade Boggs	.65
207	Jimmy Key	.05
208	Don Mattingly	.75
209	Danny Tartabull	.05
210	Brett Butler (All-Star Advice)	.05
211	Tony Gwynn (All-Star Advice)	.35
212	Rickey Henderson (All-Star Advice)	.25
213	Ramon Martinez (All-Star Advice)	.05
214	Nolan Ryan (All-Star Advice)	.75
215	Ozzie Smith (All-Star Advice)	.35
216	Marquis Grissom (Fold-Out)	.05
217	Dean Palmer (Fold-Out)	.05
218	Cal Ripken, Jr. (Fold-Out)	.75
219	Deion Sanders (Fold-Out)	.05
220	Darryl Strawberry (Fold-Out)	.05
221	David McCarty (Checklist)	.05
222	Barry Bonds (Checklist)	.65
223	Juan Gonzalez (Checklist)	.15
224	Ken Griffey Jr. (Checklist)	.05
225	Frank Thomas (Checklist)	.25
	Trade Upper Deck ("Hot Shots" redemption card)	.05

Fun Packs Mascot Madness

Upper Deck's high-tech lithogram process of combining color photos and holograms was used to create the five-card "Mascot Madness" inserts which were randomly found in Fun Packs. Backs have a description of the mascot and explain his role with the team.

	NM/M
Complete Set (5):	2.50
Common Card:	.50
1	Phillie Phanatic	.50
2	Pirate Parrot	.50
3	Fredbird	.50
4	BJ Birdy	.50
5	Youppi (Mascot)	.50

Fun Packs All-Star Scratch-Off

Randomly inserted into Fun Packs was a series of nine "All-Star Scratch-Off" game cards. Fronts and backs have a star-studded blue background. Inside the folded, double-size (2-1/2" x 7") cards are American and National

League line-ups which can be used to play a baseball game, the rules of which are explained on the card backs. On front are photos of two of the players in the line-up, matched by position from each league. The inserts are numbered with an "AS" prefix.

	NM/M
Complete Set (9):	5.00
Common Player:	.25
1	Fred McGriff, Frank Thomas	.45
2	Darren Daulton, Ivan Rodriguez	.35
3	Mark McGwire, Will Clark	1.25
4	Ryne Sandberg, Roberto Alomar	.50
5	Robin Ventura, Terry Pendleton	.25
6	Cal Ripken Jr., Ozzie Smith	1.50
7	Barry Bonds, Juan Gonzalez	1.50
8	Marquis Grissom, Ken Griffey Jr.	1.00
9	Tony Gwynn, Kirby Puckett	.50

1994 Upper Deck

Upper Deck's 1994 offering was a typical presentation, combining high-quality regular-issue cards with innovative subsets and high-tech chase cards. Series 1, besides the standard player cards, features subsets including Star Rookies with metallic borders, "Fantasy Team" stars, Home Field Advantage cards showcasing National League stadiums, and, stars under the age of 25 in a subset titled, "The Future is Now." Regular-issue cards feature a color photo on front and a second, black-and-white version of the same photo at left in a vertically stretched format. The player's name, team and Upper Deck logo appear on front in copper foil. Backs have a color photo, stats and an infield-shaped hologram. Series 2 offered in addition to regular cards, subsets of American League Home Field Advantage cards, a group of "Classic Alumni" minor league players, a selection of "Diamond Debuts" cards and a group of "Top Prospects." Series 1 retail packaging contained a special Mickey Mantle/Ken Griffey, Jr. card that could be found bearing either one or both of the players' autographs in an edition of 1,000 each. Series 2 retail packs offered a chance to find an autographed version of Alex Rodriguez' Classic Alumni card.

	NM/M
Complete Set (550):	30.00
Complete Series 1 (280):	25.00

Complete Series 2 (270):		5.00
Common Player:		.05
Series 1 Hobby Pack (12):		2.50
Series 1 Hobby Box (36):		65.00
Series 1 Retail Pack (12):		2.00
Series 1 Retail Box (36):		40.00
Series 2 Hobby Pack (12):		.75
Series 2 Hobby Box (36):		20.00
Series 2 Retail Pack (12):		1.25
Series 2 Retail Box (36):		25.00
1	Brian Anderson/SR RC	.15
2	Shane Andrews/SR	.05
3	James Baldwin/SR	.05
4	Rich Becker/SR	.05
5	Greg Blosser/SR	.05
6	Ricky Bottalico/SR RC	.05
7	Midre Cummings/SR	.05
8	Carlos Delgado/SR	.50
9	Steve Dreyer/SR RC	.05
10	Joey Eischen/SR RC	.05
11	Carl Everett/SR	.05
12	Cliff Floyd/SR	.05
13	Alex Gonzalez/SR	.05
14	Jeff Granger/SR	.05
15	Shawn Green/SR	.35
16	Brian Hunter/SR	.05
17	Butch Huskey/SR	.05
18	Mark Hutton/SR	.05
19	Michael Jordan/SR RC	5.00
20	Steve Karsay/SR	.05
21	Jeff McNeely/SR	.05
22	Marc Newfield/SR	.05
23	Manny Ramirez/SR	.45
24	Alex Rodriguez/SR RC	20.00
25	Scott Ruffcorn/SR	.05
26	Paul Spoljaric/SR	.05
27	Salomon Torres/SR RC	.05
28	Steve Trachsel/SR	.05
29	Chris Turner/SR RC	.05
30	Gabe White/SR	.05
31	Randy Johnson (Fantasy Team)	.40
32	John Wetteland (Fantasy Team)	.05
33	Mike Piazza (Fantasy Team)	.65
34	Rafael Palmeiro (Fantasy Team)	.35
35	Roberto Alomar (Fantasy Team)	.10
36	Matt Williams (Fantasy Team)	.05
37	Travis Fryman (Fantasy Team)	.05
38	Barry Bonds (Fantasy Team)	1.00
39	Marquis Grissom (Fantasy Team)	.05
40	Albert Belle (Fantasy Team)	.05
41	Steve Avery (Future/Now)	.05
42	Jason Bere (Future/Now)	.05
43	Alex Fernandez (Future/Now)	.05
44	Mike Mussina (Future/Now)	.15
45	Aaron Sele (Future/Now)	.05
46	Rod Beck (Future/Now)	.05
47	Mike Piazza (Future/Now)	.65
48	John Olerud (Future/Now)	.05
49	Carlos Baerga (Future/Now)	.05
50	Gary Sheffield (Future/Now)	.20
51	Travis Fryman (Future/Now)	.05
52	Juan Gonzalez (Future/Now)	.20
53	Ken Griffey Jr. (Future/Now)	.65
54	Tim Salmon (Future/Now)	.05
55	Frank Thomas (Future/Now)	.45
56	Tony Phillips	.05
57	Julio Franco	.05
58	Kevin Mitchell	.05
59	Raul Mondesi	.05
60	Rickey Henderson	.75
61	Jay Buhner	.05
62	Bill Swift	.05
63	Brady Anderson	.05
64	Ryan Klesko	.05
65	Darren Daulton	.05
66	Damion Easley	.05
67	Mark McGwire	1.50
68	John Roper	.05
69	Dave Telgheder	.05
70	Dave Nied	.05
71	Mo Vaughn	.05
72	Tyler Green	.05
73	Dave Magadan	.05
74	Chili Davis	.05
75	Archi Cianfrocco	.05
76	Joe Girardi	.05
77	Chris Hoiles	.05
78	Ryan Bowen	.05
79	Greg Gagne	.05
80	Aaron Sele	.05
81	Dave Winfield	.75
82	Chad Curtis	.05
83	Andy Van Slyke	.05
84	Kevin Stocker	.05
85	Deion Sanders	.05
86	Bernie Williams	.05
87	John Smoltz	.05
88	Ruben Santana RC	.05
89	Dave Stewart	.05
90	Don Mattingly	1.00

91	Joe Carter	.05
92	Ryne Sandberg	.90
93	Chris Gomez	.05
94	Tino Martinez	.05
95	Terry Pendleton	.05
96	Andre Dawson	.25
97	Wil Cordero	.05
98	Kent Hrbek	.05
99	John Olerud	.05
100	Kirt Manwaring	.05
101	Tim Bogar	.05
102	Mike Mussina	.30
103	Nigel Wilson	.05
104	Ricky Gutierrez	.05
105	Roberto Mejia	.05
106	Tom Pagnozzi	.05
107	Mike Macfarlane	.05
108	Jose Bautista	.05
109	Luis Ortiz	.05
110	Brent Gates	.05
111	Tim Salmon	.05
112	Wade Boggs	.90
113	Tripp Cromer RC	.05
114	Denny Hocking	.05
115	Carlos Baerga	.05
116	J.R. Phillips RC	.05
117	Bo Jackson	.10
118	Lance Johnson	.05
119	Bobby Jones	.05
120	Bobby Witt	.05
121	Ron Karkovice	.05
122	Jose Vizcaino	.05
123	Danny Darwin	.05
124	Eduardo Perez	.05
125	Brian Looney	.05
126	Pat Hentgen	.05
127	Frank Viola	.05
128	Darren Holmes	.05
129	Wally Whitehurst	.05
130	Matt Walbeck	.05
131	Albert Belle	.05
132	Steve Cooke	.05
133	Kevin Appier	.05
134	Joe Oliver	.05
135	Benji Gil	.05
136	Steve Buechele	.05
137	Devon White	.05
138	Sterling Hitchcock	.05
139	Phil Leftwich RC	.05
140	Jose Canseco	.45
141	Rick Aguilera	.05
142	Rod Beck	.05
143	Jose Rijo	.05
144	Tom Glavine	.25
145	Phil Plantier	.05
146	Jason Bere	.05
147	Jamie Moyer	.05
148	Wes Chamberlain	.05
149	Glenallen Hill	.05
150	Mark Whiten	.05
151	Bret Barberie	.05
152	Chuck Knoblauch	.05
153	Trevor Hoffman	.05
154	Rick Wilkins	.05
155	Juan Gonzalez	.40
156	Ozzie Guillen	.05
157	Jim Eisenreich	.05
158	Pedro Astacio	.05
159	Joe Magrane	.05
160	Ryan Thompson	.05
161	Jose Lind	.05
162	Jeff Conine	.05
163	Todd Benzinger	.05
164	Roger Salkeld	.05
165	Gary DiSarcina	.05
166	Kevin Gross	.05
167	Charlie Hayes	.05
168	Tim Costo	.05
169	Wally Joyner	.05
170	Johnny Ruffin	.05
171	Kirk Rueter RC	.10
172	Len Dykstra	.05
173	Ken Hill	.05
174	Mike Bordick	.05
175	Billy Hall	.05
176	Rob Butler	.05
177	Jay Bell	.05
178	Jeff Kent	.05
179	David Wells	.05
180	Dean Palmer	.05
181	Mariano Duncan	.05
182	Orlando Merced	.05
183	Brett Butler	.05
184	Milt Thompson	.05
185	Chipper Jones	1.00
186	Paul O'Neill	.05
187	Mike Greenwell	.05
188	Harold Baines	.05
189	Todd Stottlemyre	.05
190	Jeromy Burnitz	.05
191	Rene Arocha	.05
192	Jeff Fassero	.05
193	Robby Thompson	.05
194	Greg W. Harris	.05
195	Todd Van Poppel	.05
196	Jose Guzman	.05
197	Shane Mack	.05
198	Carlos Garcia	.05
199	Kevin Roberson	.05
200	David McCarty	.05
201	Alan Trammell	.05
202	Chuck Carr	.05
203	Tommy Greene	.05
204	Wilson Alvarez	.05
205	Dwight Gooden	.05
206	Tony Tarasco	.05
207	Darren Lewis	.05
208	Eric Karros	.05

Checklist (continued)

#	Player	Price
209	Chris Hammond	.05
210	Jeffrey Hammonds	.05
211	Rich Amaral	.05
212	Danny Tartabull	.05
213	Jeff Russell	.05
214	Dave Staton	.05
215	Kenny Lofton	.05
216	Manuel Lee	.05
217	Brian Koelling	.05
218	Scott Lydy	.05
219	Tony Gwynn	.90
220	Cecil Fielder	.05
221	Royce Clayton	.05
222	Reggie Sanders	.05
223	Brian Jordan	.05
224	Ken Griffey Jr.	1.25
224a	Ken Griffey Jr. (Promo Card)	3.00
225	Fred McGriff	.05
226	Felix Jose	.05
227	Brad Pennington	.05
228	Chris Bosio	.05
229	Mike Stanley	.05
230	Willie Greene	.05
231	Alex Fernandez	.05
232	Brad Ausmus	.05
233	Darrell Whitmore	.05
234	Marcus Moore	.05
235	Allen Watson	.05
236	Jose Offerman	.05
237	Rondell White	.05
238	Jeff King	.05
239	Luis Alicea	.05
240	Dan Wilson	.05
241	Ed Sprague	.05
242	Todd Hundley	.05
243	Al Martin	.05
244	Mike Lansing	.05
245	Ivan Rodriguez	.65
246	Dave Fleming	.05
247	John Doherty	.05
248	Mark McLemore	.05
249	Bob Hamelin	.05
250	Curtis Pride RC	.05
251	Zane Smith	.05
252	Eric Young	.05
253	Brian McRae	.05
254	Tim Raines	.05
255	Javier Lopez	.05
256	Melvin Nieves	.05
257	Randy Myers	.05
258	Willie McGee	.05
259	Jimmy Key	.05
260	Tom Candiotti	.05
261	Eric Davis	.05
262	Craig Paquette	.05
263	Robin Ventura	.05
264	Pat Kelly	.05
265	Gregg Jefferies	.05
266	Cory Snyder	.05
267	Dave Justice (Home Field Advantage)	.05
268	Sammy Sosa (Home Field Advantage)	.45
269	Barry Larkin (Home Field Advantage)	.05
270	Andres Galarraga (Home Field Advantage)	.05
271	Gary Sheffield (Home Field Advantage)	.20
272	Jeff Bagwell (Home Field Advantage)	.40
273	Mike Piazza (Home Field Advantage)	.65
274	Larry Walker (Home Field Advantage)	.05
275	Bobby Bonilla (Home Field Advantage)	.05
276	John Kruk (Home Field Advantage)	.05
277	Jay Bell (Home Field Advantage)	.05
278	Ozzie Smith (Home Field Advantage)	.45
279	Tony Gwynn (Home Field Advantage)	.45
280	Barry Bonds (Home Field Advantage)	1.00
281	Cal Ripken, Jr. (Home Field Advantage)	1.00
282	Mo Vaughn (Home Field Advantage)	.05
283	Tim Salmon (Home Field Advantage)	.05
284	Frank Thomas (Home Field Advantage)	.40
285	Albert Belle (Home Field Advantage)	.05
286	Cecil Fielder (Home Field Advantage)	.05
287	Wally Joyner (Home Field Advantage)	.05
288	Greg Vaughn (Home Field Advantage)	.05
289	Kirby Puckett (Home Field Advantage)	.45
290	Don Mattingly (Home Field Advantage)	.50
291	Terry Steinbach (Home Field Advantage)	.05
292	Ken Griffey Jr. (Home Field Advantage)	.90
293	Juan Gonzalez (Home Field Advantage)	.20
294	Paul Molitor (Home Field Advantage)	.40
295	Tavo Alvarez (Classic Alumni)	.05
296	Matt Brunson (Classic Alumni)	.05
297	Shawn Green (Classic Alumni)	.20
298	Alex Rodriguez (Classic Alumni)	2.00
299	Shannon Stewart (Classic Alumni)	.05
300	Frank Thomas	.75
301	Mickey Tettleton	.05
302	Pedro Munoz	.05
303	Jose Valentin	.05
304	Orestes Destrade	.05
305	Pat Listach	.05
306	Scott Brosius	.05
307	Kurt Miller RC	.05
308	Rob Dibble	.05
309	Mike Blowers	.05
310	Jim Abbott	.05
311	Mike Jackson	.05
312	Craig Biggio	.05
313	Kurt Abbott RC	.05
314	Chuck Finley	.05
315	Andres Galarraga	.05
316	Mike Moore	.05
317	Doug Strange	.05
318	Pedro J. Martinez	.75
319	Kevin McReynolds	.05
320	Greg Maddux	.90
321	Mike Henneman	.05
322	Scott Leius	.05
323	John Franco	.05
324	Jeff Blauser	.05
325	Kirby Puckett	.90
326	Darryl Hamilton	.05
327	John Smiley	.05
328	Derrick May	.05
329	Jose Vizcaino	.05
330	Randy Johnson	.75
331	Jack Morris	.05
332	Graeme Lloyd	.05
333	Dave Valle	.05
334	Greg Myers	.05
335	Kevin Wetteland	.05
336	Jim Gott	.05
337	Tim Naehring	.05
338	Mike Kelly	.05
339	Jeff Montgomery	.05
340	Rafael Palmeiro	.65
341	Eddie Murray	.25
342	Xavier Hernandez	.05
343	Bobby Munoz	.05
344	Bobby Bonilla	.05
345	Travis Fryman	.05
346	Steve Finley	.05
347	Chris Sabo	.05
348	Armando Reynoso	.05
349	Ramon Martinez	.05
350	Will Clark	.05
351	Moises Alou	.05
352	Jim Thome	.50
353	Bob Tewksbury	.05
354	Andujar Cedeno	.05
355	Orel Hershiser	.05
356	Mike Devereaux	.05
357	Mike Perez	.05
358	Dennis Martinez	.05
359	Dave Nilsson	.05
360	Ozzie Smith	.90
361	Eric Anthony	.05
362	Scott Sanders	.05
363	Paul Sorrento	.05
364	Tim Belcher	.05
365	Dennis Eckersley	.60
366	Mel Rojas	.05
367	Tom Henke	.05
368	Randy Tomlin	.05
369	B.J. Surhoff	.05
370	Joey Cora	.05
371	Mike Harkey	.05
372	John Valentin	.05
373	Doug Jones	.05
374	Dave Justice	.05
375	Vince Coleman	.05
376	David Hulse	.05
377	Kevin Seitzer	.05
378	Pete Harnisch	.05
379	Ruben Sierra	.05
380	Mark Lewis	.05
381	Bip Roberts	.05
382	Paul Wagner	.05
383	Stan Javier	.05
384	Barry Larkin	.05
385	Mark Portugal	.05
386	Roberto Kelly	.05
387	Andy Benes	.05
388	Felix Fermin	.05
389	Marquis Grissom	.05
390	Troy Neel	.05
391	Chad Kreuter	.05
392	Gregg Olson	.05
393	Charles Nagy	.05
394	Jack McDowell	.05
395	Luis Gonzalez	.05
396	Benito Santiago	.05
397	Chris James	.05
398	Terry Mulholland	.05
399	Barry Bonds	2.00
400	Joe Grahe	.05
401	Duane Ward	.05
402	John Burkett	.05
403	Scott Servais	.05
404	Bryan Harvey	.05
405	Bernard Gilkey	.05
406	Greg McMichael	.05
407	Tim Wallach	.05
408	Ken Caminiti	.05
409	Ken Caminiti	.05
410	John Kruk	.05
411	Darrin Jackson	.05
412	Mike Gallego	.05
413	David Cone	.05
414	Lou Whitaker	.05
415	Sandy Alomar Jr.	.05
416	Bill Wegman	.05
417	Pat Borders	.05
418	Roger Pavlik	.05
419	Pete Smith	.05
420	Steve Avery	.05
421	David Segui	.05
422	Rheal Cormier	.05
423	Harold Reynolds	.05
424	Edgar Martinez	.05
425	Cal Ripken, Jr.	2.00
426	Jaime Navarro	.05
427	Sean Berry	.05
428	Bret Saberhagen	.05
429	Bob Welch	.05
430	Juan Guzman	.05
431	Cal Eldred	.05
432	Dave Hollins	.05
433	Sid Fernandez	.05
434	Willie Banks	.05
435	Darryl Kile	.05
436	Henry Rodriguez	.05
437	Tony Fernandez	.05
438	Walt Weiss	.05
439	Kevin Tapani	.05
440	Mark Grace	.05
441	Brian Harper	.05
442	Kent Mercker	.05
443	Anthony Young	.05
444	Todd Zeile	.05
445	Greg Vaughn	.05
446	Ray Lankford	.05
447	David Weathers	.05
448	Bret Boone	.05
449	Charlie Hough	.05
450	Roger Clemens	1.00
451	Mike Morgan	.05
452	Doug Drabek	.05
453	Danny Jackson	.05
454	Dante Bichette	.05
455	Roberto Alomar	.20
456	Ben McDonald	.05
457	Kenny Rogers	.05
458	Bill Gullickson	.05
459	Darrin Fletcher	.05
460	Curt Schilling	.20
461	Billy Hatcher	.05
462	Howard Johnson	.05
463	Mickey Morandini	.05
464	Frank Castillo	.05
465	Delino DeShields	.05
466	Gary Gaetti	.05
467	Steve Farr	.05
468	Roberto Hernandez	.05
469	Jack Armstrong	.05
470	Paul Molitor	.75
471	Melido Perez	.05
472	Greg Hibbard	.05
473	Jody Reed	.05
474	Tom Gordon	.05
475	Gary Sheffield	.35
476	John Jaha	.05
477	Shawon Dunston	.05
478	Reggie Jefferson	.05
479	Don Slaught	.05
480	Jeff Bagwell	.75
481	Tim Pugh	.05
482	Kevin Young	.05
483	Ellis Burks	.05
484	Greg Swindell	.05
485	Mark Langston	.05
486	Omar Vizquel	.05
487	Kevin Brown	.05
488	Terry Steinbach	.05
489	Mark Lemke	.05
490	Matt Williams	.05
491	Pete Incaviglia	.05
492	Karl Rhodes	.05
493	Shawn Green	.30
494	Hal Morris	.05
495	Derek Bell	.05
496	Luis Polonia	.05
497	Otis Nixon	.05
498	Ron Darling	.05
499	Mitch Williams	.05
500	Mike Piazza	1.25
501	Pat Meares	.05
502	Scott Cooper	.05
503	Scott Erickson	.05
504	Jeff Juden	.05
505	Lee Smith	.05
506	Bobby Ayala	.05
507	Dave Henderson	.05
508	Erik Hanson	.05
509	Bob Wickman	.05
510	Sammy Sosa	.90
511	Hector Carrasco (Diamond Debuts)	.05
512	Tim Davis (Diamond Debuts)	.05
513	Joey Hamilton (Diamond Debuts)	.05
514	Robert Eenhoorn (Diamond Debuts)	.05
515	Jorge Fabregas (Diamond Debuts)	.05
516	Tim Hyers (Diamond Debuts)	.05
517	John Hudek (Diamond Debuts)	.05
518	James Mouton RC (Diamond Debuts)	.05
519	Herbert Perry (Diamond Debuts)	.05
520	Chan Ho Park RC (Diamond Debuts)	.75
521	Bill VanLandingham (Diamond Debuts)	.05
522	Paul Shuey (Diamond Debuts)	.05
523	Ryan Hancock RC (Top Prospects)	.05
524	Billy Wagner RC (Top Prospects)	.25
525	Jason Giambi (Top Prospects)	.50
526	Jose Silva RC (Top Prospects)	.05
527	Terrell Wade RC (Top Prospects)	.05
528	Todd Dunn (Top Prospects)	.05
529	Alan Benes RC (Top Prospects)	.05
530	Brooks Kieschnick RC (Top Prospects)	.05
531	Todd Hollandsworth (Top Prospects)	.05
532	Brad Fullmer RC (Top Prospects)	.15
533	Steve Soderstrom RC (Top Prospects)	.05
534	Daron Kirkreit (Top Prospects)	.05
535	Arquimedez Pozo RC (Top Prospects)	.05
536	Charles Johnson (Top Prospects)	.05
537	Preston Wilson (Top Prospects)	.10
538	Alex Ochoa (Top Prospects)	.05
539	Derrek Lee RC (Top Prospects)	3.00
540	Wayne Gomes RC (Top Prospects)	.05
541	Jermaine Allensworth RC (Top Prospects)	.05
542	Mike Bell RC (Top Prospects)	.05
543	Trot Nixon RC (Top Prospects)	1.25
544	Pokey Reese (Top Prospects)	.05
545	Neifi Perez RC (Top Prospects)	.05
546	Johnny Damon (Top Prospects)	.30
547	Matt Brunson (Top Prospects)	.05
548	LaTroy Hawkins RC (Top Prospects)	.05
549	Eddie Pearson RC (Top Prospects)	.05
550	Derek Jeter (Top Prospects)	2.00

Electric Diamond

Each of the regular-issue and subset cards from 1994 Upper Deck was also produced in a limited edition premium insert "Electric Diamond" version. Where the regular cards have the Upper Deck logo, player and team name in copper foil, the Electric Diamond version has these elements in a silver prismatic foil, along with an "Electric Diamond" identification line next to the UD logo. Backs are identical to the regular cards. (Forty-five of the first series cards can be found with player names on back in either silver or copper.) Electric Diamond cards are found, on average, about every other pack.

	NM/M
Complete Set (550):	75.00
Common Player:	.25
Stars:	1.5X

Baseball Heroes Mickey Mantle

Mickey Mantle Baseball Hero is a 10-card set that chronicles his career. The cards, which include an unnumbered header card, were randomly inserted into both hobby and retail packs of Series II Upper Deck Baseball. This set starts with his rookie season in 1951 and concludes with his induction into The Hall of Fame. It is numbered 64-72 and was the eighth in the continuing "Baseball Heroes" series, which began in 1990.

		NM/M
Complete Set (10):		25.00
Common Card:		3.00
64	1951 - The Early Years (Mickey Mantle)	3.00
65	1953 - Tape Measure Home Runs (Mickey Mantle)	3.00
66	1956 - Triple Crown Season (Mickey Mantle)	3.00
67	1957 - 2nd Consecutive MVP (Mickey Mantle)	3.00
68	1961 - Chases The Babe (Mickey Mantle)	3.00
69	1964 - Series Home Run Record (Mickey Mantle)	3.00
70	1967 - 500th Home Run (Mickey Mantle)	3.00
71	1974: Hall of Fame (Mickey Mantle)	3.00
72	Mickey Mantle/Portrait (Mickey Mantle)	3.00
----	Header Card (Mickey Mantle)	5.00

Diamond Collection

The premium chase cards in 1994 Upper Deck are a series of Diamond Collection cards issued in regional subsets. Ten cards are found unique to each of three geographic areas of distribution. Western region cards carry a "W" prefix to the card number, Central cards have a "C" prefix and Eastern cards have an "E" prefix. The region is also indicated in silver-foil printing on the front of the card, with a large "W," "C" or "E" in a compass design. The player's name and team are presented in a foil strip at bottom. A "Diamond Collection" logo is shown in embossed-look typography in the background. Diamond Collection cards are inserted only in hobby packs.

		NM/M
Complete Set (30):		40.00
Common Player:		.50
Complete Central (10):		20.00
1	Michael Jordan	10.00
2	Jeff Bagwell	2.00
3	Barry Larkin	1.00
4	Kirby Puckett	4.00
5	Manny Ramirez	3.00
6	Ryne Sandberg	3.00
7	Ozzie Smith	3.00
8	Frank Thomas	3.00
9	Andy Van Slyke	.50
10	Robin Yount	3.00
Complete East (10):		12.00
1	Roberto Alomar	1.00
2	Roger Clemens	.50
3	Len Dykstra	.50
4	Cecil Fielder	.50
5	Cliff Floyd	.50
6	Dwight Gooden	.50
7	Dave Justice	.50
8	Don Mattingly	3.00
9	Cal Ripken, Jr.	6.00
10	Gary Sheffield	.50
Complete West (10):		15.00
1	Barry Bonds	5.00
2	Andres Galarraga	.50
3	Juan Gonzalez	1.00
4	Ken Griffey Jr.	4.00
5	Tony Gwynn	2.50
6	Rickey Henderson	1.50
7	Bo Jackson	1.00
8	Mark McGwire	3.00
9	Mike Piazza	3.00
10	Tim Salmon	.50

Jumbo Checklists

Each hobby foil box of 1994 Upper Deck cards contains one jumbo checklist card. Each of the 5" x 7" cards features Ken Griffey, Jr. There is a large color action photo along with a hologram of the player on front, highlighted by copper-foil printing. Backs have one of four checklists and are numbered with a "CL" prefix.

		NM/M
Complete Set (4):		4.00
Common Card:		1.00
1	Numerical Checklist (Ken Griffey Jr.)	1.00
2	Alphabetical Checklist (Ken Griffey Jr.)	1.00
3	Team Checklist (Ken Griffey Jr.)	1.00
4	Insert Checklist (Ken Griffey Jr.)	1.00

Mickey Mantle's Long Shots

Retail packaging was the exclusive venue for this insert set of contemporary long-ball sluggers. Horizontal fronts feature game-action photos with holographic foil rendering of the background. In one of the lower corners appears the logo "1994 Mickey Mantle's Long Shots." Backs have a color player photo at top, with a photo of Mantle beneath and a statement by him about the featured player. Previous season and career stats are included. Cards are numbered with an "MM" prefix. Besides the 20 current player cards there is a Mickey Mantle card and two trade cards which could be redeemed for complete insert card sets.

		NM/M
Complete Set (21):		20.00
Common Player:		.50
Electric Diamonds:		1X
(1)	Mickey Mantle Trade Card (Silver): (Redeemable for 21-card Mantle Long Shots set.)	4.00
(2)	Mickey Mantle Trade Card (Blue): (Redeemable for Electric Diamond version Mantle Long Shots set.)	4.00
1	Jeff Bagwell	1.50
2	Albert Belle	.50
3	Barry Bonds	4.00
4	Jose Canseco	.75
5	Joe Carter	.50
6	Carlos Delgado	.75
7	Cecil Fielder	.50
8	Cliff Floyd	.50
9	Juan Gonzalez	.75
10	Ken Griffey Jr.	2.50
11	David Justice	.50
12	Fred McGriff	.50
13	Mark McGwire	3.00
14	Dean Palmer	.50
15	Mike Piazza	2.50
16	Manny Ramirez	1.50
17	Tim Salmon	.50
18	Frank Thomas	1.50
19	Mo Vaughn	.50
20	Matt Williams	.50
21	Header (Mickey Mantle)	4.00

Mantle-Griffey Autographed Inserts

First series retail packs of '94 UD were the exclusive venue for a special card featuring spokesmen Ken Griffey Jr. and Mickey Mantle.

The front has a painting of the two stars. On back are career highlights and a comparison of the players' first five seasons. A large numbered elliptical hologram on back authenticates the autographs. One thousand cards were issued with either or both signatures.

		NM/M
KG1	Ken Griffey Jr., Mickey Mantle (Griffey Autograph)	250.00
MM1	Ken Griffey Jr., Mickey Mantle (Mantle Autograph)	650.00
GM1	Ken Griffey Jr., Mickey Mantle (Both Autographs)	1,150

Next Generation

Next Generation linked 18 top stars with all-time greats, using the HoloView printing technology. Next Generation Electric Diamond Trade Cards could be redeemed for a complete set of Electic Diamond versions of the Next Generation set. The insert cards were a retail-only find at a rate of one per 20 packs, while the Electric Diamond Trade card was inserted one per case.

		NM/M
Complete Set (18):		100.00
Common Player:		1.50
Electric Diamond		
Complete Set (18):		
Electric Diamond Singles (1.5X)		
1	Roberto Alomar	2.50
2	Carlos Delgado	4.00
3	Cliff Floyd	1.50
4	Alex Gonzalez	1.50
5	Juan Gonzalez	3.00
6	Ken Griffey Jr.	10.00
7	Jeffrey Hammonds	1.50
8	Michael Jordan	30.00
9	Dave Justice	1.50
10	Ryan Klesko	1.50
11	Javier Lopez	1.50
12	Raul Mondesi	1.50
13	Mike Piazza	10.00
14	Kirby Puckett	7.50
15	Manny Ramirez	6.50
16	Alex Rodriguez	30.00
17	Tim Salmon	1.50
18	Gary Sheffield	4.00
	ED Trade Card (Ken Griffey Jr.)	30.00

Alex Rodriguez Autograph

Available exclusively in Series 2 retail packaging was this special version of A-Rod's Classic Alumni card. The card is authentically signed in blue Sharpie and carries on its back an authentication hologram.

		NM/M
A298	Alex Rodriguez/Auto. (Classic Alumni)	500.00

SP Insert

Fifteen SP Preview cards were inserted into Series II packs of Upper Deck baseball. The cards

were inserted with regional distribution and gave collectors a chance to see what the SP super-premium cards would look like. There were five cards available in the East, Central and West and were inserted at a rate of about one per 36 packs. Most of the preview inserts have different front and back photos than the regularly issued SPs, along with other differences in typography and graphics elements.

		NM/M
Complete Set (15):		60.00
Common Player:		.50
EASTERN REGION		
1	Roberto Alomar	1.00
2	Cliff Floyd	.50
3	Javier Lopez	.50
4	Don Mattingly	6.00
5	Cal Ripken, Jr.	10.00
CENTRAL REGION		
1	Jeff Bagwell	3.00
2	Michael Jordan	10.00
3	Kirby Puckett	6.00
4	Manny Ramirez	3.00
5	Frank Thomas	4.00
WESTERN REGION		
1	Barry Bonds	10.00
2	Juan Gonzalez	1.50
3	Ken Griffey Jr.	5.00
4	Mike Piazza	5.00
5	Tim Salmon	.50

Ken Griffey Jr. 5th Anniversary Jumbo

The origins of this card are unknown. Besides producing 15-card sets of top players in a black-bordered 5th Anniversary insert set in regular and 3-1/2" x 5-1/2" formats, UD issued an 8-1/2" x 11" 5th Anniversary card of Griffey. In virtually all respects except size, the jumbo card is identical to the others. It is, however, numbered on back from within an edition of 5,000.

	NM/M
Ken Griffey Jr.	20.00

All-Stars

Produced in commemoration of the 1994 All-Star Game, this boxed set features photography by Walter Iooss, Jr. on most cards, shown to its best advantage on a large 3-1/2" x 5" format. The front of each card has a foil seal of the Pittsburgh All-Star Game logo. On most sets, the seal is in green foil; every 40th set has the seals in gold. The left side of the card backs features a smaller version of the front photo and a few sentences about the player. Some cards feature a second, larger photo on back, but most have a photo and write-up of a teammate. The last six cards in the set honor the 125th anniversary of profes-

sional baseball. An album to house the set was made available for $10 via a mail-in offer card in the set.

		NM/M
Complete Set (48):		9.00
Common Player:		.15
Gold:		4X
1	Ken Griffey Jr.	1.00
2	Ruben Sierra, Todd Van Poppel	.15
3	Bryan Harvey, Gary Sheffield	.35
4	Gregg Jefferies, Brian Jordan	.15
5	Ryne Sandberg	.75
6	Matt Williams, John Burkett	.15
7	Darren Daulton, John Kruk	.15
8	Don Mattingly, Wade Boggs	.75
9	Pat Listach, Greg Vaughn	.15
10	Tim Salmon, Eduardo Perez	.25
11	Fred McGriff, Tom Glavine	.25
12	Mo Vaughn, Andre Dawson	.35
13	Brian McRae, Kevin Appier	.15
14	Kirby Puckett, Kent Hrbek	.75
15	Cal Ripken, Jr.	2.00
16	Roberto Alomar, Paul Molitor	.65
17	Tony Gwynn, Phil Plantier	.75
18	Greg Maddux, Steve Avery	.75
19	Mike Mussina, Chris Hoiles	.50
20	Randy Johnson	.65
21	Roger Clemens, Aaron Sele	.75
22	Will Clark, Dean Palmer	.25
23	Cecil Fielder, Travis Fryman	.15
24	John Olerud, Joe Carter	.15
25	Juan Gonzalez	.65
26	Jose Rijo, Barry Larkin	.15
27	Andy Van Slyke, Jeff King	.15
28	Larry Walker, Marquis Grissom	.15
29	Kenny Lofton, Albert Belle	.25
30	Mark Grace, Sammy Sosa	1.00
31	Mike Piazza	1.00
32	Ramon Martinez, Orel Hershiser	.15
33	Dave Justice, Terry Pendleton	.15
34	Ivan Rodriguez, Jose Canseco	.50
35	Barry Bonds	2.00
36	Jeff Bagwell, Craig Biggio	.65
37	Jay Bell, Orlando Merced	.15
38	Jeff Kent, Dwight Gooden	.15
39	Andres Galarraga, Charlie Hayes	.15
40	Frank Thomas	.70
41	Bobby Bonilla	.15
42	Jack McDowell, Tim Raines	.15
43	1869 Red Stockings	.15
44	Ty Cobb	.50
45	Babe Ruth	1.50
46	Mickey Mantle	2.50
47	Reggie Jackson	.50
48	Ken Griffey Jr.	1.00
48a	Ken Griffey Jr. (Promo Card)	1.00

1994 UD All-Time Heroes

The All-Time Heroes set provided collectors with both Ted Williams cards from Topps 1954 reprint set, from which they were absent due to a contractual obligation between Ted Williams and the Upper Deck Co. An agreement between Topps and Upper Deck allowed both Williams' cards to be offered in the All-Time Heroes set. There is also a 1954 Mickey Mantle inserted that has no number, but bears the same design as original 1954 Topps cards. The basic All-Time Heroes of Baseball set contains 225 cards. The cards were patterned after cards from the early 60's, with black bor-

ders across the top and bottom. Black-and-white photographs give the 2-1/2" x 3-1/2" cards a nostalgic appearance. All-Time Heroes also has autographed cards of Mantle, Brett, Jackson and Seaver, along with a Next in Line insert set and a parallel, bronze-foil 125th anniversary set. Cards #1-18 comprise an Off the Wire subset. Cards #101-125 are a Major League 125th Anniversary subset. Cards #151-177 are a Diamond Legends subset. Cards #208-224 are a subset titled Heroes of Baseball.

		NM/M
Complete Set (225):		20.00
Common Player:		.10
Wax Box:		65.00
1	Ted Williams (OTW)	.75
2	Johnny Vander Meer (OTW)	.10
3	Lou Brock (OTW)	.10
4	Lou Gehrig (OTW)	.75
5	Hank Aaron (OTW)	.50
6	Tommie Agee (OTW)	.10
7	Mickey Mantle (OTW)	1.50
8	Bill Mazeroski (OTW)	.30
9	Reggie Jackson, Bud Harrelson (OTW)	.20
10	Willie Mays, Mickey Mantle (OTW)	1.25
11	Roy Campanella (OTW)	.10
12	Harvey Haddix (OTW)	.10
13	Jimmy Piersall (OTW)	.10
14	Enos Slaughter (OTW)	.10
15	Nolan Ryan (OTW)	.75
16	Bobby Thomson (OTW)	.10
17	Willie Mays (OTW)	.50
18	Bucky Dent (OTW)	.10
19	Joe Garagiola	.20
20	George Brett	.75
21	Cecil Cooper	.10
22	Ray Boone	.10
23	King Kelly	.10
24	Willie Mays	1.00
25	Napoleon Lajoie	.10
26	Gil McDougald	.10
27	Nelson Briles	.10
28	Bucky Dent	.10
29	Manny Sanguillen	.10
30	Ty Cobb	1.00
31	Jim Grant	.10
32	Del Ennis	.10
33	Ron Hunt	.10
34	Nolan Ryan	1.50
35	Christy Mathewson	.75
36	Robin Roberts	.10
37	Frank Crosetti	.10
38	Johnny Vander Meer	.10
39	Virgil Trucks	.10
40	Lou Gehrig	1.50
41	Luke Appling	.10
42	Rico Petrocelli	.10
43	Harry Walker	.10
44	Reggie Jackson	.65
44a	Reggie Jackson (Promo card.)	4.00
45	Mel Ott	.10
46	Phil Cavaretta	.10
47	Larry Doby	.10
48	Johnny Mize	.10
49	Ralph Kiner	.10
50	Ted Williams	1.50
51	Bobby Thomson	.10
52	Joe Black	.10
53	Monte Irvin	.10
54	Bill Virdon	.10
55	Honus Wagner	1.00
56	Herb Score	.10
57	Jerry Coleman	.10
58	Jimmie Foxx	.30
59	Elroy Face	.10
60	Babe Ruth	2.00
61	Jimmy Piersall	.10
62	Ed Charles	.10
63	Johnny Podres	.10
64	Charlie Neal	.10
65	Bill White	.10
66	Bill Skowron	.10
67	Al Rosen	.10
68	Eddie Lopat	.10
69	Bud Harrelson	.10
70	Steve Carlton	.10
71	Vida Blue	.10
72	Don Newcombe	.10
73	Al Bumbry	.10
74	Bill Madlock	.10
(75)	Checklist 1-75 (Hank Aaron)	.50
76	Bill Mazeroski	.50
77	Ron Cey	.10
78	Tommy John	.10
79	Lou Brock	.75
80	Walter Johnson	.75
81	Harvey Haddix	.10
82	Al Oliver	.10
83	Johnny Logan	.10
84	Dave Dravecky	.10
85	Tony Oliva	.10
86	Dave Kingman	.10
87	Luis Tiant	.10
88	Sal Bando	.10
89	Cesar Cedeno	.10
90	Warren Spahn	.10

		NM/M
91	Mickey Lolich	.10
92	Lew Burdette	.10
93	Hank Bauer	.10
94	Marv Throneberry	.10
95	Willie Stargell	.10
96	George Kell	.10
97	Fergie Jenkins	.10
98	Al Kaline	.10
99	Billy Martin	.10
100	Mickey Mantle	3.00
101	1869 - Red Stockings (125th)	.10
102	1892 (King Kelly (125th))	.10
103	1901 (Nap Lajoie (125th))	.10
104	1905 (Christy Mathewson (125th))	.40
105	1910 (Cy Young (125th))	.10
106	1915 (Ty Cobb (125th))	.40
(107)	Checklist 136-180 (Reggie Jackson)	.40
108	1924 (Rogers Hornsby (125th))	.10
109	1926 (Walter Johnson (125th))	.40
110	1927 (Babe Ruth (125th))	1.00
111	1930 (Hack Wilson (125th))	.10
112	1939 (Lou Gehrig (125th))	.75
113	1941 (Ted Williams (125th))	.75
113a	1941 (Ted Williams (125th)(Autographed edition of 2,500.))	250.00
114	1949 (Yogi Berra (125th))	.30
115	1951 (Bobby Thomson (125th))	.10
116	1953 (Mickey Mantle (125th))	1.50
117	1954 (Willie Mays (125th))	.50
118	1960 (Bill Mazeroski (125th))	.30
119	1967 (Bob Gibson (125th))	.10
120	1969 Miracle Mets (125th)	.50
121	1974 (Hank Aaron (125th))	.50
122	1977 (Reggie Jackson (125th))	.40
123	1980 (George Brett (125th))	.20
124	1982 (Steve Carlton (125th))	.10
125	1991 (Nolan Ryan (125th))	.75
126	Frank Thomas	.10
127	Sam McDowell	.10
128	Jim Lonberg	.10
129	Bert Campaneris	.10
130	Bob Gibson	.10
131	Bobby Richardson	.10
132	Bobby Grich	.10
133	Billy Pierce	.10
134	Enos Slaughter	.10
(135)	Checklist 181-225 (Honus Wagner)	.50
136	Orlando Cepeda	.10
137	Rennie Stennett	.10
138	Gene Alley	.10
139	Manny Mota	.10
140	Rogers Hornsby	.10
141	Joe Charboneau	.20
142	Rick Farrell	.10
143	Toby Harrah	.10
144	Hank Aaron	1.00
145	Yogi Berra	.50
146	Whitey Ford	.50
147	Roy Campanella	.50
148	Graig Nettles	.10
149	Bobby Brown	.10
150	Checklist 76-150 (Willie Mays)	.50
151	Cy Young (DL)	.40
152	Walter Johnson (DL)	.40
153	Christy Mathewson (DL)	.40
154	Warren Spahn (DL)	.10
155	Steve Carlton (DL)	.10
156	Bob Gibson (DL)	.10
157	Whitey Ford (DL)	.30
158	Yogi Berra (DL)	.30
159	Roy Campanella (DL)	.30
160	Lou Gehrig (DL)	.75
161	Johnny Mize (DL)	.10
162	Rogers Hornsby (DL)	.10
163	Honus Wagner (DL)	.50
164	Hank Aaron (DL)	.50
165	Babe Ruth (DL)	1.00
166	Willie Mays (DL)	.50
167	Reggie Jackson (DL)	.40
168	Mickey Mantle (DL)	1.50
169	Jimmie Foxx (DL)	.10
170	Ted Williams (DL)	.75
171	Mel Ott (DL)	.10
172	Willie Stargell (DL)	.10
173	Al Kaline (DL)	.10
174	Ty Cobb (DL)	.75
175	Napoleon Lajoie (DL)	.10
176	Lou Brock (DL)	.50
177	Tom Seaver (DL)	.30
178	Mark Fidrych	.20
179	Don Baylor	.10
180	Tom Seaver	.10
181	Jerry Grote	.10
182	George Foster	.10
183	Buddy Bell	.10
184	Ralph Garr	.10
185	Steve Garvey	.10

		NM/M
186	Joe Torre	.10
187	Carl Erskine	.10
188	Tommy Davis	.10
189	Bill Buckner	.10
190	Hack Wilson	.10
191	Steve Bass	.10
192	Ken Brett	.10
193	Lee May	.10
194	Bob Horner	.10
195	Boog Powell	.10
196	Darrell Evans	.10
197	Paul Blair	.10
198	Johnny Callison	.10
199	Jimmie-Reese	.10
200	Cy Young	.75
201	Ron Santo	.10
202	Rico Carty	.10
203	Ron Necciai	.10
204	Lou Boudreau	.10
205	Minnie Minoso	.10
206	Eddie Yost	.10
207	Tommie Agee	.10
208	Dave Kingman (Heroes)	.10
209	Tony Oliva (Heroes)	.10
210	Reggie Jackson (Heroes)	.40
211	Paul Blair (Heroes)	.10
212	Fergie Jenkins (Heroes)	.10
213	Steve Garvey (Heroes)	.10
214	Bert Campaneris (Heroes)	.10
215	Orlando Cepeda (Heroes)	.10
216	Bill Madlock (Heroes)	.10
217	Rennie Stennett (Heroes)	.10
218	Frank Thomas (Heroes)	.10
219	Bob Gibson (Heroes)	.10
220	Lou Brock (Heroes)	.10
221	Rico Carty (Heroes)	.10
222	Mickey Mantle (Heroes)	1.50
223	Robin Roberts (Heroes)	.10
224	Manny Sanguillen (Heroes)	.10
225	Checklist 151-225 (Mickey Mantle)	1.50

1994 Upper Deck All-Time Heroes 125th Anniversary

This parallel set was issued at the rate of one card per pack of Upper Deck All-Time Heroes cards. They are identical to the regular-issue version except for the presence of bronze-foil stamping which reads, "Major League Baseball / 125th Anniversary."

		NM/M
Complete Set (225):		40.00
Common Player:		.25
Stars:		2X
15	Nolan Ryan (OTW) (Overprint at left.)	1.00
15	Nolan Ryan (OTW) (Overprint at right.)	1.00

All-Time Heroes Autographs

Four players' autographed cards were randomly inserted into packs of All-Time Heroes at a reported rate of about 1:385. Seaver, Jackson and Mantle signed 1,000 each, Brett signed 2,000.

		NM/M
Complete Set (4):		650.00
Common Player:		45.00
(1)	Mickey Mantle	550.00
(2)	Reggie Jackson	40.00
(3)	George Brett	60.00
(4)	Tom Seaver	25.00

All-Time Heroes Next In Line

The Next in Line insert set includes 20 top minor leaguers. These cards were randomly inserted into every 39 packs with only 2,500 of each card produced.

		NM/M
Complete Set (20):		40.00
Common Player:		1.00
1	Mike Bell	1.00
2	Alan Benes	1.00
3	D.J. Boston	1.00
4	Johnny Damon	5.00
5	Brad Fullmer	1.00
6	LaTroy Hawkins	1.00
7	Derek Jeter	25.00
8	Daron Kirkreit	1.00
9	Trot Nixon	3.00
10	Alex Ochoa	1.00
11	Kirk Presley	1.00
12	Jose Silva	1.00
13	Terrell Wade	1.00
14	Billy Wagner	1.50
15	Glenn Williams	1.00
16	Preston Wilson	1.50
17	Wayne Gomes	1.00
18	Ben Grieve	1.00
19	Dustin Hermanson	1.00
20	Paul Wilson	1.00

All-Time Heroes 1954 Topps Archives

Two cards that were not included in the Topps 1954 Archives Set and one that wasn't even in the original 1954 set were randomly inserted into All-Time Heroes foil packs. Both Ted Williams cards, numbers 1 and 250, were left out of the Archives set because of contractual obligations of Williams with Upper Deck. In addition, a Mickey Mantle card with the original 1954 design was randomly inserted. Mantle was signed exclusively with Bowman in 1954 and 1955, and therefore, was not in either Topps set.

		NM/M
Complete Set (3):		150.00
1	Ted Williams	50.00
250	Ted Williams	50.00
259	Mickey Mantle	75.00

American Epic

Baseball, The American Epic traces the history of the game, highlighting players, personalities, events and stadiums that have contributed to the national pastime. The set was patterned after a 1994 18-hour TV documentary. This boxed set contains 80 cards. It explains the roots of the game and showcases some of baseball's great players and events. Each set contains a randomly inserted card of either Michael Jordan, Babe Ruth or Mickey Mantle. Cards from the regular set are in black-and-white, with the player name and the featured year running down the left side in white print. Card backs contain half color, depending on what "inning" the card is from, and half white. The color side tells a story, the white side gives statistics and highlights.

		NM/M
Complete Set (81):		12.50
Common Player:		.15
1	1880s - Our Game	.15
2	1845 - Alexander Cartwright	.15
3	1857 - Henry Chadwick	.15
4	1866 - The Fair Sex	.15
5	1869 - Harry Wright	.15
6	1876 - Albert Goodwill Spalding	.15
7	1883 - Cap Anson	.15
8	1884 - Moses Fleetwood Walker	.25
9	1886 - King Kelly	.15
10	1890 - John Montgomery Ward	.15
11	1909 - Ty Cobb	.75
12	1904 - John McGraw	.15
13	1904 - Rube Waddell	.15
14	1905 - Christy Mathewson	.25
15	1907 - Walter Johnson	.25
16	1908 - Alta Weiss	.15
17	1908 - Fred Merkle	.15
18	1908 - Take Me Out To The Ball Game	.15
19	1909 - John Henry Lloyd	.15
20	1909 - Honus Wagner	.40
21	1915 - Woodrow Wilson	.15
22	1910 - Napoleon Lajoie	.15
23	1911 - Addie Joss	.15
24	1912 - Joe Wood	.15
25	1912 - Royal Rooters	.15
26	1913 - Ebbets Field	.15
27	1914 - Johnny Evers	.15
28	1918 - World War II	.15
29	1919 - Joe Jackson	.75
30	1927 - Babe Ruth	1.50
31	1920 - Rube Foster	.15
32	1920 - Ray Chapman	.15
33	1921 - Kenesaw M. Landis	.15
34	1923 - Yankee Stadium	.15
35	1924 - Rogers Hornsby	.15
36	1923 - Warren G. Harding	.15
37	1925 - Lou Gehrig	.75
38	1926 - Grover C. Alexander	.15
39	1929 - House of David	.15
40	1933 - Satchel Paige	.40
41	1931 - Lefty Grove	.15
42	1932 - Jimmie Foxx	.15
43	1932 - Connie Mack	.15
44	1937 - Josh Gibson	.15
45	1934 - Dizzy Dean	.15
46	1934 - Carl Hubbell	.15
47	1937 - Franklin D. Roosevelt	.15
48	1938 - Bob Feller	.15
49	1939 - Cool Papa Bell	.15
50	1947 - Jackie Robinson	.75
51	1941 - Ted Williams	.75
52	1941 - Sym-Phony Band	.15
53	1944 - Annabel Lee	.15
54	1945 - Hank Greenberg	.15
55	1947 - Branch Rickey	.15
56	1948 - Harry S. Truman	.15
57	1953 - Casey Stengel	.15
58	1951 - Bobby Thomson	.15
59	1952 - Dwight D. Eisenhower	.15
60	1952 - Mario Cuomo	.15
61	1952 - Buck O'Neil	.15
62	1955 - Yogi Berra	.25
63	1956 - Mickey Mantle	2.00
64	1956 - Don Larsen	.15
65	1961 - John F. Kennedy	.15
66	1960 - Bill Mazeroski	.15
67	1961 - Roger Maris	.25
68	1966 - Frank Robinson	.15
69	1969 - Bob Gibson	.15
70	1970 - Tom Seaver	.15
71	1969 - Curt Flood	.15
72	1972 - Roberto Clemente	.75
73	1975 - Luis Tiant	.15
74	1975 - Marvin Miller	.15
75	1977 - Reggie Jackson	.15
76	1979 - Willie Stargell	.15
77	1985 - Pete Rose	.75
78	1994 - Bill Clinton	.15
79	1991 - Nolan Ryan	.75
80	1993 - George Brett	.25
----	Checklist	.08

American Epic Inserts

In addition to the regular 80-card set, each boxed set contains one special insert card, depending on where it was purchased. At retail locations, an additional Babe Ruth card was included. Michael Jordan was included in sets purchased through direct mail outlets. Mickey Mantle was featured in sets purchased from QVC (sets purchased from Upper Deck Authenticated included an autographed card of Mantle). The inserts are numbered BC1- BC3.

		NM/M
Complete Set (3):		6.00
Common Player:		2.00
1	Mickey Mantle	2.00
2	Michael Jordan	2.00
3	Babe Ruth	2.00

American Epic Little Debbie Mail-in

Fifteen of the cards from Upper Deck's "An American Epic" card set were chosen for use in a mail-in promotion with Little Debbie snack cakes. These cards are identical to the Epic versions except for the card numbers, which include an "LD" prefix. The back of card LD1 is a checklist for the set and includes a Little Debbie logo. Sets sold for about $4, with proofs of purchase.

		NM/M
Complete Set (15):		4.50
Common Player:		.25
1	Our Game/Checklist	.05
2	Alexander Cartwright	.25
3	King Kelly	.25
4	John McGraw	.25
5	Christy Mathewson	.40
6	Walter Johnson	.40
7	Ted Williams	.75
8	Annabel Lee	.25
9	Jackie Robinson	.50
10	Bobby Thomson	.25
11	Buck O'Neil	.25
12	Mickey Mantle	1.50
13	Bob Gibson	.25
14	Curt Flood	.25
15	Reggie Jackson	.40

1994 Upper Deck Fun Packs

In its second year this product aimed at the young collector again offered a basic set of some 160 players, surrounded by several special subsets. The first nine cards feature Stars of Tomorrow. There is a group of 18 Stand Out cards on which the background can be folded to create a player figure. Profiles cards feature playing tips from six young stars. A group of nine Headline Stars cards features two players on each which fold back to reveal a holographic photo. What's the Call cards offer game problems and cartoon caricatures of nine players. There are nine Fold Outs cards which open to reveal action photos. The subsets concluded with seven heat-activated Fun Cards on which the background temporarily appears when body heat is applied. Each five-card foil pack also includes a scratch-off game card; one for each major league team and one All-Star team for each league.

		NM/M
Complete Set (240):		35.00
Common Player:		.05
Wax Box:		15.00
1	Manny Ramirez (Stars of Tomorrow)	.75
2	Cliff Floyd (Stars of Tomorrow)	.05
3	Rondell White (Stars of Tomorrow)	.05
4	Carlos Delgado (Stars of Tomorrow)	.50
5	Chipper Jones (Stars of Tomorrow)	1.25
6	Javier Lopez (Stars of Tomorrow)	.05
7	Ryan Klesko (Stars of Tomorrow)	.05
8	Steve Karsay (Stars of Tomorrow)	.05
9	Rich Becker (Stars of Tomorrow)	.05
10	Gary Sheffield	.35
11	Jeffrey Hammonds	.05
12	Roberto Alomar	.20
13	Brent Gates	.05
14	Andres Galarraga	.05
15	Tim Salmon	.05
16	Dwight Gooden	.05
17	Mark Grace	.05
18	Andy Van Slyke	.05
19	Juan Gonzalez	.40
20	Mickey Tettleton	.05
21	Roger Clemens	1.25
22	Will Clark	.05
23	Dave Justice	.05
24	Ken Griffey Jr.	1.50
24a	Ken Griffey Jr. (Promo Card)	1.50
25	Barry Bonds	2.50
26	Bill Swift	.05
27	Fred McGriff	.05
28	Randy Myers	.05
29	Joe Carter	.05
30	Nigel Wilson	.05
31	Mike Piazza	1.50
32	Dave Winfield	.75
33	Steve Avery	.05
34	Kirby Puckett	.90
35	Frank Thomas	.75
36	Aaron Sele	.05
37	Ricky Gutierrez	.05
38	Curt Schilling	.25
39	Mike Greenwell	.05
40	Andy Benes	.05
41	Kevin Brown	.05
42	Mo Vaughn	.05
43	Dennis Eckersley	.60
44	Ken Hill	.05
45	Cecil Fielder	.05
46	Bobby Jones	.05
47	Tom Glavine	.25
48	Wally Joyner	.05
49	Ellis Burks	.05
50	Jason Bere	.05
51	Randy Johnson	.75
52	Darryl Kile	.05
53	Jeff Montgomery	.05
54	Alex Fernandez	.05
55	Kevin Appier	.05
56	Brian McRae	.05
57	John Wetteland	.05
58	Bob Tewksbury	.05
59	Todd Van Poppel	.05
60	Ryne Sandberg	.90
61	Bret Barberie	.05
62	Phil Plantier	.05
63	Chris Hoiles	.05
64	Tony Phillips	.05
65	Salomon Torres	.05
66	Juan Guzman	.05
67	Paul O'Neill	.05
68	Dante Bichette	.05
69	Len Dykstra	.05
70	Ivan Rodriguez	.65
71	Dean Palmer	.05
72a	Brett Butler	.05
72b	Phil Hiatt (Checklisted as #172.)	.05
73	Rick Aguilera	.05
74	Robby Thompson	.05
75	Jim Abbott	.05
76	Al Martin	.05
77	Roberto Hernandez	.05
78	Jay Buhner	.05
79	Devon White	.05
80	Travis Fryman	.05
81	Jeromy Burnitz	.05
82	John Burkett	.05
83	Orlando Merced	.05
84	Jose Rijo	.05
85	Eddie Murray	.75
86	Howard Johnson	.05
87	Chuck Carr	.05
88	Pedro J. Martinez	.75
89	Charlie Hayes	.05
90	Matt Williams	.05
91	Steve Finley	.05
92	Pat Listach	.05
93	Sandy Alomar, Jr.	.05
94	Delino DeShields	.05
95	Rod Beck	.05
96	Todd Zeile (Checklisted as #96.)	.05
98a	Darryl Hamilton	.05
98b	Duane Ward (Checklisted as #97.)	
99	John Olerud	.05
100	Andre Dawson	.25
101	Ozzie Smith	.90
102	Rick Wilkins	.05
103	Alan Trammell	.05
104	Jeff Blauser	.05
105	Bret Boone	.05
106	J.T. Snow	.05
107	Kenny Lofton	.05
108	Cal Ripken, Jr.	2.50
109	Carlos Baerga	.05
110	Bip Roberts	.05
111	Barry Larkin	.05
112	Mark Langston	.05
113	Ozzie Guillen	.05
114	Chad Curtis	.05
115	Dave Hollins	.05
116	Reggie Sanders	.05
117	Jeff Conine	.05
118	Mark Whiten	.05
119	Tony Gwynn	.90
120	John Kruk	.05
121	Eduardo Perez	.05
122	Walt Weiss	.05
123	Don Mattingly	1.00
124	Rickey Henderson	.75
125	Mark McGwire	2.00
126	Wade Boggs	.90
127	Bobby Bonilla	.05
128	Jeff King	.05
129	Jack McDowell	.05
130	Albert Belle	.05
131	Greg Maddux	.90
132	Dennis Martinez	.05
133	Jose Canseco	.40
134	Bryan Harvey	.05
135	Dave Fleming	.05
136	Larry Walker	.05
137	Ken Caminiti	.05
138	Doug Drabek	.05
139	Ron Gant	.05
140	Darren Daulton	.05
141	Ruben Sierra	.05
142	Kirk Rueter	.05
143	Raul Mondesi	.05
144	Greg Vaughn	.05
145	Danny Tartabull	.05
146	Eric Karros	.05
147	Chuck Knoblauch	.05
148	Mike Mussina	.30
149	Brady Anderson	.05
150	Paul Molitor	.75
151	Bo Jackson	.10
152	Jeff Bagwell	.75
153	Gregg Jefferies	.05
154	Rafael Palmeiro	.65
155	Orel Hershiser	.05
156	Derek Bell	.05
157	Jeff Kent	.05
158	Craig Biggio	.05
159	Marquis Grissom	.05
160	Matt Mieske	.05
161	Jay Bell	.05
162	Sammy Sosa	.90
163	Robin Ventura	.05
164	Deion Sanders	.05
165	Jimmy Key	.05
166	Cal Eldred	.05
167	David McCarty	.05
168	Carlos Garcia	.05
169	Willie Greene	.05
170	Michael Jordan RC	2.50
171	Roberto Mejia	.05
173	Marc Newfield	.05
174	Kevin Stocker	.05
175	Randy Johnson (Standouts)	.40
176	Ivan Rodriguez (Standouts)	.30
177	Frank Thomas (Standouts)	.45
178	Roberto Alomar (Standouts)	.05
179	Travis Fryman (Standouts)	.05
180	Cal Ripken, Jr. (Standouts)	1.25
181	Juan Gonzalez (Standouts)	.30
182	Ken Griffey Jr. (Standouts)	.75
183	Albert Belle (Standouts)	.05
184	Greg Maddux (Standouts)	.50
185	Mike Piazza (Standouts)	.75
186	Fred McGriff (Standouts)	.05
187	Robby Thompson (Standouts)	.05
188	Matt Williams (Standouts)	.05
189	Jeff Blauser (Standouts)	.05
190	Barry Bonds (Standouts)	1.25
191	Len Dykstra (Standouts)	.05
192	Dave Justice (Standouts)	.05
193	Ken Griffey Jr. (Profiles)	.75
194	Barry Bonds (Profiles)	1.25
195	Frank Thomas (Profiles)	.45
196	Juan Gonzalez (Profiles)	.30
197	Randy Johnson (Profiles)	.40
198	Chuck Carr (Profiles)	.05
199	Barry Bonds, Juan Gonzalez (Headline Stars)	1.00
200	Ken Griffey Jr., Don Mattingly (Headline Stars)	.75
201	Roberto Alomar, Carlos Baerga (Headline Stars)	.10
202	Dave Winfield, Robin Yount (Headline Stars)	.40
203	Mike Piazza, Tim Salmon (Headline Stars)	.75
204	Albert Belle, Frank Thomas (Headline Stars)	.45
205	Cliff Floyd, Rondell White (Headline Stars)	.05
206	Kirby Puckett, Tony Gwynn (Headline Stars)	.50
207	Roger Clemens, Greg Maddux (Headline Stars)	.50
208	Mike Piazza (What's The Call)	.75
209	Jose Canseco (What's The Call)	.20
210	Frank Thomas (What's The Call)	.45
211	Roberto Alomar (What's The Call)	.10
212	Barry Bonds (What's The Call)	1.25
213	Rickey Henderson (What's The Call)	.40
214	John Kruk (What's The Call)	.05
215	Juan Gonzalez (What's The Call)	.40
216	Ken Griffey Jr. (What's The Call)	.75
217	Roberto Alomar (Foldouts)	.10
218	Craig Biggio (Foldouts)	.05
219	Cal Ripken, Jr. (Foldouts)	1.25
220	Mike Piazza (Foldouts)	.75
221	Brent Gates (Foldouts)	.05
222	Walt Weiss (Foldouts)	.05
223	Bobby Bonilla (Foldouts)	.05
224	Ken Griffey Jr. (Foldouts)	.75
225	Barry Bonds (Foldouts)	1.25
226	Barry Bonds (Fun Cards)	1.25
227	Joe Carter (Fun Cards)	.05
228	Mike Greenwell (Fun Cards)	.05
229	Ken Griffey Jr. (Fun Cards)	.75
230	John Kruk (Fun Cards)	.05
231	Mike Piazza (Fun Cards)	.75
232	Kirby Puckett (Fun Cards)	.50
233	John Smoltz (Fun Cards)	.05
234	Rick Wilkins (Fun Cards)	.05
235	Checklist 1-40 (Ken Griffey Jr.)	.65
236	Checklist 41-80 (Frank Thomas)	.45
237	Checklist 81-120 (Barry Bonds)	1.00
238	Checklist 121-160 (Mike Piazza)	.65
239	Checklist 161-200 (Tim Salmon)	.05
240	Checklist 201-240 (Juan Gonzalez)	.35

Scratch-off Game Cards:

(1)	National League	.05
(2)	Atlanta Braves	.05
(3)	Chicago Cubs	.05
(4)	Cincinnati Reds	.05
(5)	Colorado Rockies	.05
(6)	Florida Marlins	.05
(7)	Houston Astros	.05
(8)	Los Angeles Dodgers	.05
(9)	Montreal Expos	.05
(10)	New York Mets	.05
(11)	Philadelphia Phillies	.05
(12)	Pittsburgh Pirates	.05
(13)	St. Louis Cardinals	.05
(14)	San Diego Padres	.05
(15)	San Francisco Giants	.05

GM "Baseball" Previews

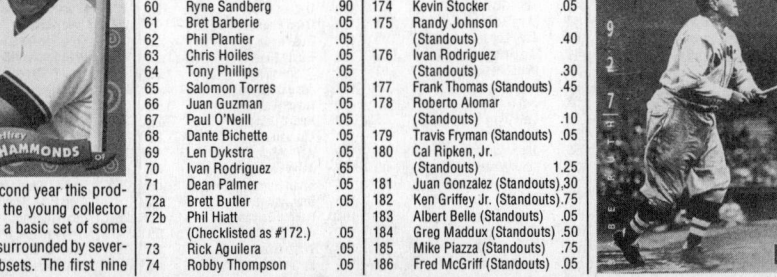

This nine-card set is closely related to the 80-card issue subsequently released in conjunction with the public television series "Baseball" by Ken Burns. This preview issue, carrying the logo of General Motors (principal sponsor of the TV series), was issued in cello and foil packs and was available, generally with a test drive, at GM automobile dealerships. Card backs have some biographical and statistical highlights and a career summary.

		NM/M
Complete Set (9):		6.00
Common Player:		.50
1	Hank Aaron	1.25
2	Roberto Clemente	1.50
3	Ty Cobb	.50
4	Hank Greenberg	.50
5	Mickey Mantle	3.00
6	Satchel Paige	.50
7	Jackie Robinson	.75
8	Babe Ruth	2.00
9	Ted Williams	1.00

GTS Mickey Mantle Phone Cards

Upper Deck and Global Telecommunication Solutions combined to produce this set of phone cards paralleling the Mantle Heroes insert cards found in the regular UD issue. The phone cards were sold in two series of five cards each for $59.95 per series. Fronts of the 2-1/8" x 3-3/8" plastic cards feature black-and-white or color photos of Mantle, along with mention of a career highlight. Backs are printed in black and have instructions for use of the card. A card picturing the 1869 Cincinnati Red Stockings was included as a random insert in the first series of Mantle phone card sets.

		NM/M
Complete Set (10):		20.00
Common Player:		3.00
(1)	Mickey Mantle/Portrait	3.00
(2)	Mickey Mantle (1951: The Early Years)	3.00
(3)	Mickey Mantle (1953: Tape Measure Home Runs)	3.00
(4)	Mickey Mantle (1956: Triple Crown Season)	3.00
(5)	Mickey Mantle (1957: Second Consecutive MVP)	3.00
(6)	Mickey Mantle (1961: Chasing the Babe)	3.00
(7)	Mickey Mantle (1964: Series Home Run Record)	3.00
(8)	Mickey Mantle (1967: 500th Home Run)	3.00
(9)	Mickey Mantle (1974: Hall of Fame)	3.00
(10)	Mickey Mantle/Portrait	3.00
(11)	1869 Cincinnati Red Stockings	10.00

1995 Upper Deck

Issued in two series of 225 base cards each, with loads of subsets and inserts, the 1995 Upper Deck set was a strong collector favorite from the outset. Basic cards feature a borderless front photo with the player's name and UD logo in bronze foil. Backs have another large color photo, recent stats and career totals and appropriate logos, along with the infield-shaped hologram. Subsets in each series include Star Rookies and Top Prospects, each with special designs highlighting the game's young stars. Series I has a "'90s

Midpoint Analysis" subset studying the decade's superstars, and Series II has another hot rookies' subset, Diamond Debuts. The set closes with a five-card "Final Tribute" subset summarizing the careers of five recently retired superstars. Retail and hobby versions were sold with each featuring some unique insert cards. Basic packaging of each type was the 12-card foil pack at $1.99, though several other configurations were also released.

		NM/M
Complete Set (450):		20.00
Common Player:		.05
Electric Diamond:		2X
Electric Diamond Golds:		8X
Series 1 or 2 Pack (12):		.85
Series 1 or 2 Wax Box (36):		20.00
1	Ruben Rivera (Top Prospect)	.05
2	Bill Pulsipher (Top Prospect)	.05
3	Ben Grieve (Top Prospect)	.05
4	Curtis Goodwin (Top Prospect)	.05
5	Damon Hollins (Top Prospect)	.05
6	Todd Greene (Top Prospect)	.05
7	Glenn Williams (Top Prospect)	.05
8	Bret Wagner (Top Prospect)	.05
9	Karim Garcia RC (Top Prospect)	.50
10	Nomar Garciaparra (Top Prospect)	1.00
11	Raul Casanova RC (Top Prospect)	.10
12	Matt Smith (Top Prospect)	.05
13	Paul Wilson (Top Prospect)	.05
14	Jason Isringhausen (Top Prospect)	.05
15	Reid Ryan (Top Prospect)	.05
16	Lee Smith	.05
17	Chili Davis	.05
18	Brian Anderson	.05
19	Gary DiSarcina	.05
20	Bo Jackson	.10
21	Chuck Finley	.05
22	Darryl Kile	.05
23	Shane Reynolds	.05
24	Tony Eusebio	.05
25	Craig Biggio	.05
26	Doug Drabek	.05
27	Brian L. Hunter	.05
28	James Mouton	.05
29	Geronimo Berroa	.05
30	Rickey Henderson	.75
31	Steve Karsay	.05
32	Steve Ontiveros	.05
33	Ernie Young	.05
34	Dennis Eckersley	.65
35	Mark McGwire	1.50
36	Dave Stewart	.05
37	Pat Hentgen	.05
38	Carlos Delgado	.45
39	Joe Carter	.05
40	Roberto Alomar	.20
41	John Olerud	.05
42	Devon White	.05
43	Roberto Kelly	.05
44	Jeff Blauser	.05
45	Fred McGriff	.05
46	Tom Glavine	.25
47	Mike Kelly	.05
48	Javy Lopez	.05
49	Greg Maddux	1.00
50	Matt Mieske	.05
51	Troy O'Leary	.05
52	Jeff Cirillo	.05
53	Cal Eldred	.05
54	Pat Listach	.05
55	Jose Valentin	.05
56	John Mabry	.05
57	Bob Tewksbury	.05
58	Brian Jordan	.05
59	Gregg Jefferies	.05
60	Ozzie Smith	1.00
61	Geronimo Pena	.05
62	Mark Whiten	.05
63	Rey Sanchez	.05
64	Willie Banks	.05
65	Mark Grace	.05
66	Randy Myers	.05
67	Steve Trachsel	.05
68	Derrick May	.05
69	Brett Butler	.05
70	Eric Karros	.05
71	Tim Wallach	.05
72	Delino DeShields	.05
73	Darren Dreifort	.05
74	Orel Hershiser	.05
75	Billy Ashley	.05
76	Sean Berry	.05
77	Ken Hill	.05
78	John Wetteland	.05
79	Moises Alou	.05
80	Cliff Floyd	.05
81	Marquis Grissom	.05
82	Larry Walker	.05
83	Rondell White	.05
84	William VanLandingham	.05
85	Matt Williams	.05
86	Rod Beck	.05
87	Darren Lewis	.05
88	Robby Thompson	.05
89	Darryl Strawberry	.05
90	Kenny Lofton	.05
91	Charles Nagy	.05
92	Sandy Alomar Jr.	.05
93	Mark Clark	.05
94	Dennis Martinez	.05
95	Dave Winfield	.75
96	Jim Thome	.60
97	Manny Ramirez	.75
98	Goose Gossage	.05
99	Tino Martinez	.05
100	Ken Griffey Jr.	1.25
100a	Ken Griffey Jr./OPS	2.00
101	Greg Maddux (Analysis: '90s Midpoint)	.50
102	Randy Johnson (Analysis: '90s Midpoint)	.40
103	Barry Bonds (Analysis: '90s Midpoint)	1.00
104	Juan Gonzalez (Analysis: '90s Midpoint)	.20
105	Frank Thomas (Analysis: '90s Midpoint)	.40
106	Matt Williams (Analysis: '90s Midpoint)	.05
107	Paul Molitor (Analysis: '90s Midpoint)	.40
108	Fred McGriff (Analysis: '90s Midpoint)	.05
109	Carlos Baerga (Analysis: '90s Midpoint)	.05
110	Ken Griffey Jr. (Analysis: '90s Midpoint)	.65
111	Reggie Jefferson	.05
112	Randy Johnson	.75
113	Marc Newfield	.05
114	Robb Nen	.05
115	Jeff Conine	.05
116	Kurt Abbott	.05
117	Charlie Hough	.05
118	Dave Weathers	.05
119	Juan Castillo	.05
120	Bret Saberhagen	.05
121	Rico Brogna	.05
122	John Franco	.05
123	Todd Hundley	.05
124	Jason Jacome	.05
125	Bobby Jones	.05
126	Bret Barberie	.05
127	Ben McDonald	.05
128	Harold Baines	.05
129	Jeffrey Hammonds	.05
130	Mike Mussina	.30
131	Chris Hoiles	.05
132	Brady Anderson	.05
133	Eddie Williams	.05
134	Andy Benes	.05
135	Tony Gwynn	1.00
136	Bip Roberts	.05
137	Joey Hamilton	.05
138	Luis Lopez	.05
139	Ray McDavid	.05
140	Lenny Dykstra	.05
141	Mariano Duncan	.05
142	Fernando Valenzuela	.05
143	Bobby Munoz	.05
144	Kevin Stocker	.05
145	John Kruk	.05
146	Jon Lieber	.05
147	Zane Smith	.05
148	Steve Cooke	.05
149	Andy Van Slyke	.05
150	Jay Bell	.05
151	Carlos Garcia	.05
152	John Dettmer	.05
153	Darren Oliver	.05
154	Dean Palmer	.05
155	Otis Nixon	.05
156	Rusty Greer	.05
157	Rick Helling	.05
158	Jose Canseco	.40
159	Roger Clemens	1.00
160	Andre Dawson	.25
161	Mo Vaughn	.05
162	Aaron Sele	.05
163	John Valentin	.05
164	Brian Hunter	.05
165	Bret Boone	.05
166	Hector Carrasco	.05
167	Pete Schourek	.05
168	Willie Greene	.05
169	Kevin Mitchell	.05
170	Deion Sanders	.05
171	John Roper	.05
172	Charlie Hayes	.05
173	David Nied	.05
174	Ellis Burks	.05
175	Dante Bichette	.05
176	Marvin Freeman	.05
177	Eric Young	.05
178	David Cone	.05
179	Greg Gagne	.05
180	Bob Hamelin	.05
181	Wally Joyner	.05
182	Jeff Montgomery	.05
183	Jose Lind	.05
184	Chris Gomez	.05
185	Travis Fryman	.05
186	Kirk Gibson	.05
187	Mike Moore	.05
188	Lou Whitaker	.05
189	Sean Bergman	.05
190	Shane Mack	.05
191	Rick Aguilera	.05
192	Denny Hocking	.05
193	Chuck Knoblauch	.05
194	Kevin Tapani	.05
195	Kent Hrbek	.05
196	Ozzie Guillen	.05
197	Wilson Alvarez	.05
198	Tim Raines	.05
199	Scott Ruffcorn	.05
200	Michael Jordan	2.00
201	Robin Ventura	.05
202	Jason Bere	.05
203	Darrin Jackson	.05
204	Russ Davis	.05
205	Jimmy Key	.05
206	Jack McDowell	.05
207	Jim Abbott	.05
208	Paul O'Neill	.05
209	Bernie Williams	.05
210	Don Mattingly	1.00
211	Orlando Miller/SR	.05
212	Alex Gonzalez/SR	.05
213	Terrell Wade/SR	.05
214	Jose Oliva/SR	.05
215	Alex Rodriguez/SR	1.50
216	Garret Anderson/SR	.05
217	Alan Benes/SR	.05
218	Armando Benitez/SR	.05
219	Dustin Hermanson/SR	.05
220	Charles Johnson/SR	.05
221	Julian Tavarez/SR	.05
222	Jason Giambi/SR	.50
223	LaTroy Hawkins/SR	.25
224	Todd Hollandsworth/SR	.05
225	Derek Jeter/SR	2.00
226	Hideo Nomo/SR RC	2.00
227	Tony Clark/SR	.05
228	Roger Cedeno/SR	.05
229	Scott Stahoviak/SR	.05
230	Michael Tucker/SR	.05
231	Joe Rosselli/SR	.05
232	Antonio Osuna/SR	.05
233	Bobby Higginson/SR RC	.25
234	Mark Grudzielanek/SR RC	.25
235	Ray Durham/SR	.05
236	Frank Rodriguez/SR	.05
237	Quilvio Veras/SR	.05
238	Darren Bragg/SR	.05
239	Ugueth Urbina/SR	.05
240	Jason Bates/SR	.05
241	David Bell (Diamond Debuts)	.05
242	Ron Villone (Diamond Debuts)	.05
243	Joe Randa (Diamond Debuts)	.05
244	Carlos Perez RC (Diamond Debuts)	.05
245	Brad Clontz (Diamond Debuts)	.05
246	Steve Rodriguez (Diamond Debuts)	.05
247	Joe Vitiello (Diamond Debuts)	.05
248	Ozzie Timmons (Diamond Debuts)	.05
249	Rudy Pemberton (Diamond Debuts)	.05
250	Marty Cordova (Diamond Debuts)	.05
251	Tony Graffanino (Top Prospect)	.05
252	Mark Johnson RC (Top Prospect)	.05
253	Tomas Perez RC (Top Prospect)	.05
254	Jimmy Hurst (Top Prospect)	.05
255	Edgardo Alfonzo (Top Prospect)	.05
256	Jose Malave (Top Prospect)	.05
257	Brad Radke RC (Top Prospect)	.30
258	Jon Nunnally (Top Prospect)	.05
259	Dilson Torres (Top Prospect)	.05
260	Esteban Loaiza (Top Prospect)	.05
261	Freddy Garcia RC (Top Prospect)	.05
262	Don Wengert (Top Prospect)	.05
263	Robert Person RC (Top Prospect)	.05
264	Tim Unroe RC (Top Prospect)	.05
265	Juan Acevedo (Top Prospect)	.05
266	Eduardo Perez	.05
267	Tony Phillips	.05
268	Jim Edmonds	.05
269	Jorge Fabregas	.05
270	Tim Salmon	.05
271	Mark Langston	.05
272	J.T. Snow	.05
273	Phil Plantier	.05
274	Derek Bell	.05
275	Jeff Bagwell	.75
276	Luis Gonzalez	.05
277	John Hudek	.05
278	Todd Stottlemyre	.05
279	Mark Acre	.05
280	Ruben Sierra	.05
281	Mike Bordick	.05
282	Ron Darling	.05
283	Brent Gates	.05
284	Todd Van Poppel	.05
285	Paul Molitor	.75
286	Ed Sprague	.05
287	Juan Guzman	.05
288	David Cone	.05
289	Shawn Green	.30
290	Marquis Grissom	.05
291	Kent Mercker	.05
292	Steve Avery	.05
293	Chipper Jones	1.00
294	John Smoltz	.05
295	Dave Justice	.05
296	Ryan Klesko	.05
297	Joe Oliver	.05
298	Ricky Bones	.05
299	John Jaha	.05
300	Greg Vaughn	.05
301	Dave Nilsson	.05
302	Kevin Seitzer	.05
303	Bernard Gilkey	.05
304	Allen Battle	.05
305	Ray Lankford	.05
306	Tom Pagnozzi	.05
307	Allen Watson	.05
308	Danny Jackson	.05
309	Ken Hill	.05
310	Todd Zeile	.05
311	Kevin Roberson	.05
312	Steve Buechele	.05
313	Rick Wilkins	.05
314	Kevin Foster	.05
315	Sammy Sosa	1.00
316	Howard Johnson	.05
317	Greg Hansell	.05
318	Pedro Astacio	.05
319	Rafael Bournigal	.05
320	Mike Piazza	1.25
321	Ramon Martinez	.05
322	Raul Mondesi	.05
323	Ismael Valdes	.05
324	Wil Cordero	.05
325	Tony Tarasco	.05
326	Roberto Kelly	.05
327	Jeff Fassero	.05
328	Mike Lansing	.05
329	Pedro J. Martinez	.75
330	Kirk Rueter	.05
331	Glenallen Hill	.05
332	Kirt Manwaring	.05
333	Royce Clayton	.05
334	J.R. Phillips	.05
335	Barry Bonds	2.00
336	Mark Portugal	.05
337	Terry Mulholland	.05
338	Omar Vizquel	.05
339	Carlos Baerga	.05
340	Albert Belle	.05
341	Eddie Murray	.75
342	Wayne Kirby	.05
343	Chad Ogea	.05
344	Tim Davis	.05
345	Jay Buhner	.05
346	Bobby Ayala	.05
347	Mike Blowers	.05
348	Dave Fleming	.05
349	Edgar Martinez	.05
350	Andre Dawson	.30
351	Darrell Whitmore	.05
352	Chuck Carr	.05
353	John Burkett	.05
354	Chris Hammond	.05
355	Gary Sheffield	.40
356	Pat Rapp	.05
357	Greg Colbrunn	.05
358	David Segui	.05
359	Jeff Kent	.05
360	Bobby Bonilla	.05
361	Pete Harnisch	.05
362	Ryan Thompson	.05
363	Jose Vizcaino	.05
364	Brett Butler	.05
365	Cal Ripken Jr.	2.00
366	Rafael Palmeiro	.65
367	Leo Gomez	.05
368	Andy Van Slyke	.05
369	Arthur Rhodes	.05
370	Ken Caminiti	.05
371	Steve Finley	.05
372	Melvin Nieves	.05
373	Andujar Cedeno	.05
374	Trevor Hoffman	.05
375	Fernando Valenzuela	.05
376	Ricky Bottalico	.05
377	Dave Hollins	.05
378	Charlie Hayes	.05
379	Tommy Greene	.05
380	Darren Daulton	.05
381	Curt Schilling	.25
382	Midre Cummings	.05
383	Al Martin	.05
384	Jeff King	.05
385	Orlando Merced	.05
386	Denny Neagle	.05
387	Don Slaught	.05
388	Dave Clark	.05
389	Kevin Gross	.05
390	Will Clark	.05
391	Ivan Rodriguez	.65
392	Benji Gil	.05
393	Jeff Frye	.05
394	Kenny Rogers	.05
395	Juan Gonzalez	.40
396	Mike Macfarlane	.05
397	Lee Tinsley	.05
398	Tim Naehring	.05
399	Tim Vanegmond	.05
400	Mike Greenwell	.05
401	Ken Ryan	.05
402	John Smiley	.05
403	Tim Pugh	.05
404	Reggie Sanders	.05
405	Barry Larkin	.05
406	Hal Morris	.05
407	Jose Rijo	.05
408	Lance Painter	.05
409	Joe Girardi	.05
410	Andres Galarraga	.05
411	Mike Kingery	.05
412	Roberto Mejia	.05
413	Walt Weiss	.05
414	Bill Swift	.05
415	Larry Walker	.05
416	Billy Brewer	.05
417	Pat Borders	.05
418	Tom Gordon	.05
419	Kevin Appier	.05
420	Gary Gaetti	.05
421	Greg Gohr	.05
422	Felipe Lira	.05
423	John Doherty	.05
424	Chad Curtis	.05
425	Cecil Fielder	.05
426	Alan Trammell	.05
427	David McCarty	.05
428	Scott Erickson	.05
429	Pat Mahomes	.05
430	Kirby Puckett	1.00
431	Dave Stevens	.05
432	Pedro Munoz	.05
433	Chris Sabo	.05
434	Alex Fernandez	.05
435	Frank Thomas	.75
436	Roberto Hernandez	.05
437	Lance Johnson	.05
438	Jim Abbott	.05
439	John Wetteland	.05
440	Melido Perez	.05
441	Tony Fernandez	.05
442	Pat Kelly	.05
443	Mike Stanley	.05
444	Danny Tartabull	.05
445	Wade Boggs	1.00
446	Robin Yount (Final Tribute)	.75
447	Ryne Sandberg (Final Tribute)	1.00
448	Nolan Ryan (Final Tribute)	1.00
449	George Brett (Final Tribute)	1.00
450	Mike Schmidt (Final Tribute)	1.00

Electric Diamond

Included as an insert at the rate of one per retail foil pack and two per jumbo pack, this set parallels the regular issue. The only differences are that the Electric Diamond cards utilize silver-foil highlights on front, compared to the copper foil on the regular cards. The Electric Diamond cards also include a home-plate shaped logo printed in silver foil in one of the upper corners.

	NM/M
Complete Set (1-450):	60.00
Common Player:	.05
Stars/Rookies:	2X

Electric Diamond Gold

David Justice — Atlanta Braves® — OF

A parallel set of a parallel set, the Electric Diamond Gold cards were found at an average rate of one per 36 retail packs. They differ from the standard ED inserts in that the home plate-shaped Electric Diamond logo in the upper corner and the player's name at bottom are printed in gold foil, rather than the silver of the ED cards or the copper of the regular-issue UD cards.

		NM/M
Complete Set (450):		650.00
Common Player:		2.00
Stars/Rookies:		8X

Update Trade Cards

Benito Santiago — TRADE CARD

Inserted into Series 2 at the rate of about one per 11 packs was this five-card series of trade cards. Each card could be mailed in with $2 to receive nine cards from a special UD Update set picturing traded or free agent players in the uniforms of their new teams. The front of each trade card pictures one of the traded players in his old uniform against a red and blue background. Backs have instructions for redeeming the trade cards. The mail-in offer expired Feb. 1, 1996. Cards are numbered with a "TC" prefix.

		NM/M
Complete Set (5):		6.00
Common Player:		1.00
1	Orel Hershiser	1.00
2	Terry Pendleton	1.00
3	Benito Santiago	1.00
4	Kevin Brown	1.00
5	Gregg Jefferies	1.00

Update

Orel Hershiser — Cleveland Indians® — P

These cards depicting traded and free agent players in the uniforms of their new 1995 teams were available only by redeeming trade cards found in Series 2 packs. Each trade-in card was good for one nine-card segment of the Update series when sent with $2 prior

to the Feb. 1, 1996 deadline. Update cards share the same format as the regular 1995 Upper Deck set.

		NM/M
Complete Set (45):		7.50
Common Player:		.25
451	Jim Abbott	.25
452	Danny Tartabull	.25
453	Ariel Prieto	.25
454	Scott Cooper	.25
455	Tom Henke	.25
456	Todd Zeile	.25
457	Brian McRae	.25
458	Luis Gonzalez	.25
459	Jaime Navarro	.25
460	Todd Worrell	.25
461	Roberto Kelly	.25
462	Chad Fonville	.25
463	Shane Andrews	.25
464	David Segui	.25
465	Deion Sanders	.50
466	Orel Hershiser	.25
467	Ken Hill	.25
468	Andy Benes	.25
469	Terry Pendleton	.25
470	Bobby Bonilla	.25
471	Scott Erickson	.25
472	Kevin Brown	.25
473	Glenn Dishman	.25
474	Phil Plantier	.25
475	Gregg Jefferies	.25
476	Tyler Green	.25
477	Heathcliff Slocumb	.25
478	Mark Whiten	.25
479	Mickey Tettleton	.25
480	Tim Wakefield	.25
481	Vaughn Eshelman	.25
482	Rick Aguilera	.25
483	Erik Hanson	.25
484	Willie McGee	.25
485	Troy O'Leary	.25
486	Benito Santiago	.25
487	Darren Lewis	.25
488	Dave Burba	.25
489	Ron Gant	.25
490	Bret Saberhagen	.25
491	Vinny Castilla	.25
492	Frank Rodriguez	.25
493	Andy Pettitte	5.00
494	Ruben Sierra	.25
495	David Cone	.25

Autograph Trade Cards

On the average of once every 72 packs (two boxes) of Series II hobby, a trade card good for an autographed player card could be found as an insert. The cards feature the player name, but no picture, on front, while the reverse has instructions for redeeming the card for a $5 fee. The autograph trade cards expired on Nov. 1, 1995.

		NM/M
Complete Set (5):		15.00
Common Player:		2.00
(1)	Roger Clemens	4.00
(2)	Reggie Jackson	3.00
(3)	Willie Mays	6.00
(4)	Raul Mondesi	2.00
(5)	Frank Robinson	3.00

Autograph Redemption Cards

New York Yankees® — OF

These cards were sent to collectors who redeemed Autograph Trade cards found in Series II Upper Deck baseball. A certificate of authenticity with a holographic serial number matching that on the card back was issued with each card.

		NM/M
Complete Set (5):		220.00
Common Player:		15.00
AC1	Reggie Jackson	20.00
AC2	Willie Mays	100.00
AC3	Frank Robinson	30.00
AC4	Roger Clemens	125.00
AC5	Raul Mondesi	10.00

Autographed Jumbos

By sending in quantities of foil wrappers from Upper Deck baseball cards, collectors could receive a jumbo 5" x 7" blow-up of a player's card. The offer was limited to 8,000 Roger Clemens cards (Series I) and 6,000 Alex Rodriguez cards (Series II). Each card bears a serial number hologram on back and comes with a matching Upper Deck Authenticated auhtenticity guarantee card.

		NM/M
Complete Set (2):		100.00
(1)	Roger Clemens	50.00
(2)	Alex Rodriguez	75.00

Award Winners Predictors (Hobby)

JOSE CANSECO — PREDICTOR

Candidates for 1995 MVP and Rookie of the Year in each league are featured in the interactive insert series called Predictors. Twenty potential award winners were released in each of Series 1 and 2 at the rate of one per 30 packs on average. Cards feature on front a player photo inside a diamond cutout on a rich looking black and marbled background. In gold foil are his name and team at top, and "PREDICTOR" and the category at bottom. Backs feature game rules and details for redeeming the card if the pictured player wins the specified award. Winners could trade in the card for a foil-enhanced set of Predictor cards. The trade-in offer expired at the end of 1995. Cards are numbered with a "H" prefix.

		NM/M
Complete Set (40):		50.00
Common Player:		.50
Winner Exchange Cards:		2X
1	Albert Belle	.50
2	Juan Gonzalez	1.50
3	Ken Griffey Jr.	3.00
4	Kirby Puckett	2.50
5	Frank Thomas	2.00
6	Jeff Bagwell	2.00
7	Barry Bonds	5.00
8	Mike Piazza	3.00
9	Matt Williams	.50
10	1995 MVP Long Shot (Winner)	.50
11	Armando Benitez	.50
12	Alex Gonzalez	.50
13	Shawn Green	1.50
14	Derek Jeter	5.00
15	Alex Rodriguez	4.00
16	Alan Benes	.50
17	Brian L. Hunter	.50
18	Charles Johnson	.50
19	Jose Oliva	.50
20	1995 ROY Long Shot	.50
21	Cal Ripken Jr.	5.00
22	Don Mattingly	2.75
23	Roberto Alomar	.75
24	Kenny Lofton	.50
25	Will Clark	.50
26	Mark McGwire	4.00
27	Greg Maddux	2.50
28	Fred McGriff	.50
29	Andres Galarraga	.50
30	Jose Canseco	1.50
31	Ray Durham	.50
32	Mark Grudzielanek	.50
33	Scott Ruffcorn	.50
34	Michael Tucker	.50
35	Garret Anderson	.50
36	Darren Bragg	.50
37	Quilvio Veras	.50
38	Hideo Nomo (Winner)	4.00
39	Chipper Jones	2.50
40	Marty Cordova (Winner)	1.50

Baseball Heroes Babe Ruth

NEW YORK

In the 100th anniversary year of his birth, Babe Ruth was the featured star in Upper Deck continuing "Heroes" insert set. Ten cards, including an unnumbered header, were issued in Series 2 packs. The cards featured colorized photos printed on metallic foil on the front. Backs have stats and/or biographical data. On average, one Babe Ruth Heroes card is found per 34 packs.

		NM/M
Complete Set (10):		45.00
Common Card:		6.00
73	1914-18 Pitching Career (Babe Ruth)	6.00
74	1919 - Move to Outfield (Babe Ruth)	6.00
75	1920 - Renaissance Man (Babe Ruth)	6.00
76	1923 - House That Ruth Built (Babe Ruth)	6.00
77	1927 - 60-Homer Season (Babe Ruth)	6.00
78	1928 - Three-homer Game (Babe Ruth)	6.00
79	1932 - The Called Shot (Babe Ruth)	6.00
80	1930-35 - Milestones (Babe Ruth)	6.00
81	1935 - The Last Hurrah (Babe Ruth)	6.00
---	Header Card	7.50

Checklists

JOHNSON — CHECKLIST 134-205

Upscale checklists for the 1995 UD set were part of the insert card program, seeded about one per 17 packs, on average. Horizontally formatted fronts are printed on metallic foil and include a career highlight of the pictured player. Backs have the checklist data. Five checklists were issued in each of Series I and Series II.

		NM/M
Complete Set (10):		3.00
Common Player:		.25
1	Checklist 1-75 (Montreal Expos)	.25
2	Checklist 76-150 (Fred McGriff)	.25
3	Checklist 151-225 (John Valentin (Unassisted triple play.))	.25
4	Special Edition Checklist (Greg Maddux)	.75
5	Special Edition Checklist 69-135 (Kenny Rogers (Perfect Game))	.25
1	Checklist 226-300 (Cecil Fielder)	.25
2	Checklist 301-375 (Tony Gwynn)	.75
3	Checklist 376-450 (Greg Maddux)	.75
4	Special Edition Checklist 136-203 (Randy Johnson)	.50
5	Special Edition Checklist 204-270 (Mike Schmidt)	.75

League Leaders Predictors (Retail)

Candidates for the Triple Crown categories of league leaders in hits, home runs and RBIs are featured in this retail-only insert set, found at the average rate of one per 30 packs in both Series 1 and 2. If the player pictured on the card front won the category specified on his card, it could be redeemed for a special foil-enhanced version of the subset prior to the Dec. 31, 1995 deadline. Cards are numbered with a "R" prefix.

		NM/M
Complete Set (60):		65.00
Common Player:		.50
Winner Exchange Cards:		2X
1	Albert Belle (Winner)	1.50
2	Jose Canseco	1.50
3	Juan Gonzalez	1.00
4	Ken Griffey Jr.	3.00
5	Frank Thomas	2.00
6	Jeff Bagwell	2.00
7	Barry Bonds	5.00
8	Fred McGriff	.50
9	Matt Williams	.50
10	1995 Home Run Long Shot (Winner)	.50
11	Albert Belle (Winner)	1.50
12	Joe Carter	.50
13	Cecil Fielder	.50
14	Kirby Puckett	2.50
15	Frank Thomas	2.00
16	Jeff Bagwell	2.00
17	Barry Bonds	5.00
18	Mike Piazza	3.00
19	Matt Williams	.50
20	1995 RBI Long Shot (Winner)	.50
21	Wade Boggs	2.50
22	Kenny Lofton	.50
23	Paul Molitor	2.00
24	Paul O'Neill	.50
25	Frank Thomas	2.00
26	Jeff Bagwell	2.00
27	Tony Gwynn (Winner)	5.00
28	Gregg Jefferies	.50
29	Hal Morris	.50
30	1995 Batting Long Shot (Winner)	.50
31	Joe Carter	.50
32	Cecil Fielder	.50
33	Rafael Palmeiro	1.50
34	Larry Walker	.50
35	Manny Ramirez	2.00
36	Tim Salmon	.50
37	Mike Piazza	3.00
38	Andres Galarraga	.50
39	Dave Justice	.50
40	Gary Sheffield	1.50
41	Juan Gonzalez	1.00
42	Jose Canseco	1.50
43	Will Clark	.50
44	Rafael Palmeiro	1.50
45	Ken Griffey Jr.	3.00
46	Ruben Sierra	.50
47	Larry Walker	.50
48	Fred McGriff	.50
49	Dante Bichette (Winner)	.50
50	Darren Daulton	.50
51	Will Clark	.50
52	Ken Griffey Jr.	3.00
53	Don Mattingly	2.75
54	John Olerud	.50
55	Kirby Puckett	2.50
56	Raul Mondesi	.50
57	Moises Alou	.50
58	Bret Boone	.50
59	Albert Belle	.50
60	Mike Piazza	3.00

Steal of a Deal

steal a DEAL

A horizontal format with an action photo printed over a green foil background and a large bronze seal indicating how the player was acquired are featured in this 15-card insert set. The front has a terra-cotta border, which is carried over to the back. A large green box on back details the transaction and describes why it can be categorized as a "steal" for the player's new team. These top-of-the-line chase cards were seeded in both hobby and retail packs of Series I at the average rate of one per 34 packs. Cards are numbered with a "SD" prefix.

		NM/M
Complete Set (15):		25.00
Common Player:		1.00
1	Mike Piazza	6.00
2	Fred McGriff	1.00
3	Kenny Lofton	1.00
4	Jose Oliva	1.00
5	Jeff Bagwell	3.00
6	Roberto Alomar, Joe Carter	1.00
7	Steve Karsay	1.00
8	Ozzie Smith	4.00
9	Dennis Eckersley	2.00
10	Jose Canseco	1.50
11	Carlos Baerga	1.00
12	Cecil Fielder	1.00
13	Don Mattingly	5.00
14	Bret Boone	1.00
15	Michael Jordan	10.00

Special Edition

SPECIAL EDITION

Printed on metallic foil on front, and inserted into hobby packs only at the rate of one per pack, this insert set is found in both Series 1 (#1-135) and Series 2 (#136-270). A silver stripe at top has the name of the issue and the issuer, while stacked black and silver bars at bottom have the player name, team and position. Backs are conventionally printed and have another color photo, career data and 1994 and lifetime stats.

		NM/M
Complete Set (270):		60.00
Common Player:		.10
Gold:		3X
1	Cliff Floyd	.10
2	Wil Cordero	.10
3	Pedro Martinez	1.50
4	Larry Walker	.10
5	Derek Jeter	4.00
6	Mike Stanley	.10
7	Melido Perez	.10
8	Jim Leyritz	.10
9	Danny Tartabull	.10
10	Wade Boggs	2.00
11	Ryan Klesko	.10
12	Steve Avery	.10
13	Damon Hollins	.10
14	Chipper Jones	2.00
15	Dave Justice	.10
16	Glenn Williams	.10
17	Jose Oliva	.10
18	Terrell Wade	.10
19	Alex Fernandez	.10
20	Frank Thomas	1.50
21	Ozzie Guillen	.10
22	Roberto Hernandez	.10
23	Albie Lopez	.10
24	Eddie Murray	1.50
25	Albert Belle	.10
26	Omar Vizquel	.10

27	Carlos Baerga	.10
28	Jose Rijo	.10
29	Hal Morris	.10
30	Reggie Sanders	.10
31	Jack Morris	.10
32	Raul Mondesi	.10
33	Karim Garcia	.15
34	Todd Hollandsworth	.10
35	Mike Piazza	2.50
36	Chan Ho Park	.10
37	Ramon Martinez	.10
38	Kenny Rogers	.10
39	Will Clark	.10
40	Juan Gonzalez	.75
41	Ivan Rodriguez	1.25
42	Orlando Miller	.10
43	John Hudek	.10
44	Luis Gonzalez	.10
45	Jeff Bagwell	1.50
46	Cal Ripken Jr.	4.00
47	Mike Oquist	.10
48	Armando Benitez	.10
49	Ben McDonald	.10
50	Rafael Palmeiro	1.25
51	Curtis Goodwin	.10
52	Vince Coleman	.10
53	Tom Gordon	.10
54	Mike Macfarlane	.10
55	Brian McRae	.10
56	Matt Smith	.10
57	David Segui	.10
58	Paul Wilson	.10
59	Bill Pulsipher	.10
60	Bobby Bonilla	.10
61	Jeff Kent	.10
62	Ryan Thompson	.10
63	Jason Isringhausen	.10
64	Ed Sprague	.10
65	Paul Molitor	1.50
66	Juan Guzman	.10
67	Alex Gonzalez	.10
68	Shawn Green	.50
69	Mark Portugal	.10
70	Barry Bonds	4.00
71	Robby Thompson	.10
72	Royce Clayton	.10
73	Ricky Bottalico	.10
74	Doug Jones	.10
75	Darren Daulton	.10
76	Gregg Jefferies	.10
77	Scott Cooper	.10
78	Nomar Garciaparra	2.00
79	Ken Ryan	.10
80	Mike Greenwell	.10
81	LaTroy Hawkins	.10
82	Rich Becker	.10
83	Scott Erickson	.10
84	Pedro Munoz	.10
85	Kirby Puckett	2.00
86	Orlando Merced	.10
87	Jeff King	.10
88	Midre Cummings	.10
89	Bernard Gilkey	.10
90	Ray Lankford	.10
91	Todd Zeile	.10
92	Alan Benes	.10
93	Bret Wagner	.10
94	Rene Arocha	.10
95	Cecil Fielder	.10
96	Alan Trammell	.10
97	Tony Phillips	.10
98	Junior Felix	.10
99	Brian Harper	.10
100	Greg Vaughn	.10
101	Ricky Bones	.10
102	Walt Weiss	.10
103	Lance Painter	.10
104	Roberto Mejia	.10
105	Andres Galarraga	.10
106	Todd Van Poppel	.10
107	Ben Grieve	.10
108	Brent Gates	.10
109	Jason Giambi	1.00
110	Ruben Sierra	.10
111	Terry Steinbach	.10
112	Chris Hammond	.10
113	Charles Johnson	.10
114	Jesus Tavarez	.10
115	Gary Sheffield	.40
116	Chuck Carr	.10
117	Bobby Ayala	.10
118	Randy Johnson	1.50
119	Edgar Martinez	.10
120	Alex Rodriguez	3.00
121	Kevin Foster	.10
122	Kevin Roberson	.10
123	Sammy Sosa	2.00
124	Steve Trachsel	.10
125	Eduardo Perez	.10
126	Tim Salmon	.10
127	Todd Greene	.10
128	Jorge Fabregas	.10
129	Mark Langston	.10
130	Mitch Williams	.10
131	Raul Casanova	.10
132	Mel Nieves	.10
133	Andy Benes	.10
134	Dustin Hermanson	.10
135	Trevor Hoffman	.10
136	Mark Grudzielanek	.10
137	Ugueth Urbina	.10
138	Moises Alou	.10
139	Roberto Kelly	.10
140	Rondell White	.10
141	Paul O'Neill	.10
142	Jimmy Key	.10
143	Jack McDowell	.10
144	Ruben Rivera	.10

145	Don Mattingly	2.25
146	John Wetteland	.10
147	Tom Glavine	.25
148	Marquis Grissom	.10
149	Javy Lopez	.10
150	Fred McGriff	.10
151	Greg Maddux	2.00
152	Chris Sabo	.10
153	Ray Durham	.10
154	Robin Ventura	.10
155	Jim Abbott	.10
156	Jimmy Hurst	.10
157	Tim Raines	.10
158	Dennis Martinez	.10
159	Kenny Lofton	.10
160	Dave Winfield	1.50
161	Manny Ramirez	1.50
162	Jim Thome	1.00
163	Barry Larkin	.10
164	Bret Boone	.10
165	Deion Sanders	.10
166	Ron Gant	.10
167	Benito Santiago	.10
168	Hideo Nomo	.75
169	Billy Ashley	.10
170	Roger Cedeno	.10
171	Ismael Valdes	.10
172	Eric Karros	.10
173	Rusty Greer	.10
174	Rick Helling	.10
175	Nolan Ryan	4.00
176	Dean Palmer	.10
177	Phil Plantier	.10
178	Darryl Kile	.10
179	Derek Bell	.10
180	Doug Drabek	.10
181	Craig Biggio	.10
182	Kevin Brown	.10
183	Harold Baines	.10
184	Jeffrey Hammonds	.10
185	Chris Hoiles	.10
186	Mike Mussina	.50
187	Bob Hamelin	.10
188	Jeff Montgomery	.10
189	Michael Tucker	.10
190	George Brett	2.25
191	Edgardo Alfonzo	.10
192	Brett Butler	.10
193	Bobby Jones	.10
194	Todd Hundley	.10
195	Bret Saberhagen	.10
196	Pat Hentgen	.10
197	Roberto Alomar	.30
198	David Cone	.10
199	Carlos Delgado	1.00
200	Joe Carter	.10
201	William Van Landingham	.10
202	Rod Beck	.10
203	J.R. Phillips	.10
204	Darren Lewis	.10
205	Matt Williams	.10
206	Lenny Dykstra	.10
207	Dave Hollins	.10
208	Mike Schmidt	2.25
209	Charlie Hayes	.10
210	Mo Vaughn	.10
211	Jose Malave	.10
212	Roger Clemens	2.25
213	Jose Canseco	.75
214	Mark Whiten	.10
215	Marty Cordova	.10
216	Rick Aguilera	.10
217	Kevin Tapani	.10
218	Chuck Knoblauch	.10
219	Al Martin	.10
220	Jay Bell	.10
221	Carlos Garcia	.10
222	Freddy Garcia	.10
223	Jon Lieber	.10
224	Danny Jackson	.10
225	Ozzie Smith	2.00
226	Brian Jordan	.10
227	Ken Hill	.10
228	Scott Cooper	.10
229	Chad Curtis	.10
230	Lou Whitaker	.10
231	Kirk Gibson	.10
232	Travis Fryman	.10
233	Jose Valentin	.10
234	Dave Nilsson	.10
235	Cal Eldred	.10
236	Matt Mieske	.10
237	Bill Swift	.10
238	Marvin Freeman	.10
239	Jason Bates	.10
240	Larry Walker	.10
241	David Nied	.10
242	Dante Bichette	.10
243	Dennis Eckersley	1.25
244	Todd Stottlemyre	.10
245	Rickey Henderson	1.50
246	Geronimo Berroa	.10
247	Mark McGwire	3.00
248	Quilvio Veras	.10
249	Terry Pendleton	.10
250	Andre Dawson	.30
251	Jeff Conine	.10
252	Kurt Abbott	.10
253	Jay Buhner	.10
254	Darren Bragg	.10
255	Ken Griffey Jr.	2.50
256	Tino Martinez	.10
257	Mark Grace	.10
258	Ryne Sandberg	2.00
259	Randy Myers	.10
260	Howard Johnson	.10
261	Lee Smith	.10
262	J.T. Snow	.10

263	Chili Davis	.10
264	Chuck Finley	.10
265	Eddie Williams	.10
266	Joey Hamilton	.10
267	Ken Caminiti	.10
268	Andujar Cedeno	.10
269	Steve Finley	.10
270	Tony Gwynn	2.00

Special Edition Gold

An insert set within an insert set, gold-foil enhanced versions of the Special Edition cards were seeded into hobby packs at the rate of about one per box. The substitution of gold ink for silver is also carried over onto the background of the card back.

	NM/M
Complete Set (270):	350.00
Common Player:	1.50
Stars/Rookies:	3X

Cal Ripken Commemorative Jumbo

To commemorate Cal Ripken's 2,131st consecutive game, UD issued this 5" x 3" die-cut card. Five thousand of the cards were issued with silver foil highlights; 2,131 with gold trim. Each card is serially numbered in the lower-right corner on back.

	NM/M
Cal Ripken Jr. (Silver edition of 5,000.)	10.00
Cal Ripken Jr. (Gold edition of 2,131.)	13.50

Sports Drink Reggie Jackson

UD partnered with Energy Foods to produce "Upper Deck Authentic Sports Drink." Each $2.99 six pack contained a cello-wrapped Reggie Jackson card. The cards are 2-1/2" x 3-1/2" and have a color photo on front on which the team logos have been removed. Backs has a subdued photo of a player swinging a bat with a stadium scene in the background. A few career highlights are presented along with the sports drink logo and UD hologram. Each card could also be found in a version with a gold-foil facsimile autograph on front.

	NM/M
Complete Set (3):	5.00
Common Card:	2.00
Gold:	1-1.5X

1/3	Reggie Jackson (Swinging bat.)	2.00
2/3	Reggie Jackson/Portrait	2.00
3/3	Reggie Jackson (Batting follow-thru.)	2.00

Eagle Snacks Ballpark Legends

Nine Hall of Famers comprise this set which was produced by UD for the Eagle snack food company. Sets were available via mail-in redemption for proofs of purchase and $1. Fronts have sepia photos on which uniform logos have been removed. The Eagle Ballpark Legends is at upper-left, the UD logo is at lower-left, followed by the player name. Backs of the 2-1/2" x 3-1/2" cards have career summary and personal data. Autographed cards of Harmon Killebrew were random inserts.

	NM/M
Complete Set (9):	3.00
Common Player:	.25

1	Nolan Ryan	1.00
2	Reggie Jackson	.50
3	Tom Seaver	.50
4	Harmon Killebrew	.25
4a	Harmon Killebrew (Autographed)	20.00
5	Ted Williams	.75
6	Whitey Ford	.50
7	Al Kaline	.50
8	Willie Stargell	.25
9	Bob Gibson	.25

GTS Phone Cards

In conjunction with Global Telecommunications Service, Upper Deck issued a series of 15 phone cards described as being the first licensed by Major League Baseball and the Player's Association. Measuring about 2-1/8" x 3-3/8" with round corners, the cards were printed on heavy plastic and utilized the basic format and photos from the players' 1994 Upper Deck baseball cards. Issue price, with phone time, was $12 each. Cards are numbered with a "MLB" prefix.

	NM/M
Complete Set (15):	21.00
Common Player:	1.00

01	Tony Gwynn	2.00
02	Fred McGriff	1.00
03	Frank Thomas	1.50
04	Ken Griffey Jr.	2.50
05	Cecil Fielder	1.00
06	Barry Bonds	3.00
07	Don Mattingly	2.25
08	Dave Justice	1.00
09	Roger Clemens	2.25
10	Cal Ripken Jr.	3.00
11	Roberto Alomar	1.25
12	Gary Sheffield	1.25
13	Jeff Bagwell	1.50
14	Kirby Puckett	2.00
15	Ozzie Smith	1.25

Metallic Impressions Michael Jordan

Michael Jordan's brief, highly publicized baseball career is chronicled in this metallic card set produced for UD by Metallic Impressions and sold in a special lithographed tin box. Each of the 2-5/8" x 3-9/16" cards has a gold-tone rolled edge. Fronts feature photos of Jordan in action. Backs have another photo and a career summary in a horizontal format. Cards are numbered with a "JT" prefix.

	NM/M
Complete Boxed Set (5):	7.50
Common Card:	1.50

1	Starting Out (Michael Jordan)	1.50
2	West to Arizona (Michael Jordan)	1.50
3	Hitting (Michael Jordan)	1.50
4	Baserunning (Michael Jordan)	1.50
5	Fielding (Michael Jordan)	1.50

Metallic Impressions Mickey Mantle

Sharing the card-front images with the UD phone cards of 1994, these metal cards trace the career of Mickey Mantle. Sold in an embossed metal box, the cards measure 2-5/8" x 3-9/16" and have rolled gold-tone metal borders. Fronts have black-and-white or color photos of Mantle. Backs have a career summary in a red box against a background of pin-striped flannel, along with a small color photo of Mantle. The issue was reportedly limited to 19,950 sets.

	NM/M
Complete Boxed Set (10):	17.50
Common Player:	3.00

1	The Commerce Comet (Mickey Mantle)	3.00
2	1951 - The Early Years (Mickey Mantle)	3.00
3	1953 - Tape-Measure Home Runs (Mickey Mantle)	3.00
4	1956 - Triple Crown Season (Mickey Mantle)	3.00
5	1957 - Second Consecutive MVP (Mickey Mantle)	3.00
6	1961 - Chasing the Babe (Mickey Mantle)	3.00
7	1964 - Series Home Run Record (Mickey Mantle)	3.00
8	1967 - 500th Home Run (Mickey Mantle)	3.00
9	1974 - Hall of Famer (Mickey Mantle)	3.00
10	Checklist (Mickey Mantle)	3.00

1996 Upper Deck Promo

To debut its 1996 issue, Upper Deck issued this sample card. It is identical in format to the regular-issue card, except that it is

numbered 100 and overprinted diagonally on each side, "For Promotional Use Only."

	NM/M
100	Ken Griffey Jr.	2.00

1996 Upper Deck

Upper Deck Series 1 consists of 240 base cards. There are 187 regular player cards plus subsets of Star Rookies, Young at Heart, Beat the Odds, Milestones, Postseason, checklists, and expansion logos. The issue was marketed in 10-card foil packs in hobby and retail versions Series 1 insert sets are Blue Chip Prospects, Future Shock and Power Driven. Cal Ripken Jr. Collection cards are inserted in both series, as are Retail Predictor (home runs, batting average and RBIs) and Hobby Predictor (Player of the Month, Pitcher of the Month and rookie hits leaders) cards. Series 2 has 240 cards, including subsets for Star Rookies, Diamond Debuts, Strange But True, Managerial Salutes and Best of a Generation. Insert sets include Hot Commodities, Hideo Nomo Highlights, Run Producers and the Lovero Collection. Factory sets comprising both regular series and the Update series were issued in two serially numbered versions, a regular boxed set in an edition of 15,000 and a wooden boxed set numbered to 500.

	NM/M
Unopened Wood Box Set (510):	40.00
Unopened Fact. Set (510):	35.00
Complete Set (480):	20.00
Common Player:	.05
Wax Pack (10):	.75
Wax Box (32):	17.50

1	Cal Ripken Jr. (Milestones)	1.00
2	Eddie Murray (Milestones)	.40
3	Mark Wohlers	.05
4	Dave Justice	.05
5	Chipper Jones	1.00
6	Javier Lopez	.05
7	Mark Lemke	.05
8	Marquis Grissom	.25
9	Tom Glavine	.25
10	Greg Maddux	1.00
11	Manny Alexander	.05
12	Curtis Goodwin	.05
13	Scott Erickson	.05
14	Chris Hoiles	.05
15	Rafael Palmeiro	.65
16	Rick Krivda	.05
17	Jeff Manto	.05
18	Mo Vaughn	.05
19	Tim Wakefield	.05
20	Roger Clemens	1.00
21	Tim Naehring	.05
22	Troy O'Leary	.05
23	Mike Greenwell	.05
24	Stan Belinda	.05
25	John Valentin	.05

No.	Player	Price
26	J.T. Snow	.05
27	Gary DiSarcina	.05
28	Mark Langston	.05
29	Brian Anderson	.05
30	Jim Edmonds	.05
31	Garret Anderson	.05
32	Orlando Palmeiro	.05
33	Brian McRae	.05
34	Kevin Foster	.05
35	Sammy Sosa	1.00
36	Todd Zeile	.05
37	Jim Bullinger	.05
38	Luis Gonzalez	.05
39	Lyle Mouton	.05
40	Ray Durham	.05
41	Ozzie Guillen	.05
42	Alex Fernandez	.05
43	Brian Keyser	.05
44	Robin Ventura	.05
45	Reggie Sanders	.05
46	Pete Schourek	.05
47	John Smiley	.05
48	Jeff Brantley	.05
49	Thomas Howard	.05
50	Bret Boone	.05
51	Kevin Jarvis	.05
52	Jeff Branson	.05
53	Carlos Baerga	.05
54	Jim Thome	.50
55	Manny Ramirez	.75
56	Omar Vizquel	.05
57	Jose Mesa	.05
58	Julian Tavarez	.05
59	Orel Hershiser	.05
60	Larry Walker	.05
61	Bret Saberhagen	.05
62	Vinny Castilla	.05
63	Eric Young	.05
64	Bryan Rekar	.05
65	Andres Galarraga	.05
66	Steve Reed	.05
67	Chad Curtis	.05
68	Bobby Higginson	.05
69	Phil Nevin	.05
70	Cecil Fielder	.05
71	Felipe Lira	.05
72	Chris Gomez	.05
73	Charles Johnson	.05
74	Quilvio Veras	.05
75	Jeff Conine	.05
76	John Burkett	.05
77	Greg Colbrunn	.05
78	Terry Pendleton	.05
79	Shane Reynolds	.05
80	Jeff Bagwell	.75
81	Orlando Miller	.05
82	Mike Hampton	.05
83	James Mouton	.05
84	Brian L. Hunter	.05
85	Derek Bell	.05
86	Kevin Appier	.05
87	Joe Vitiello	.05
88	Wally Joyner	.05
89	Michael Tucker	.05
90	Johnny Damon	.20
91	Jon Nunnally	.05
92	Jason Jacome	.05
93	Chad Fonville	.05
94	Chan Ho Park	.05
95	Hideo Nomo	.40
96	Ismael Valdes	.05
97	Greg Gagne	.05
98	Diamondbacks-Devil Rays (Expansion Card)	.10
99	Raul Mondesi	.05
100	Dave Winfield (Young at Heart)	.75
101	Dennis Eckersley (Young at Heart)	.35
102	Andre Dawson (Young at Heart)	.15
103	Dennis Martinez (Young at Heart)	.05
104	Lance Parrish (Young at Heart)	.05
105	Eddie Murray (Young at Heart)	.40
106	Alan Trammell (Young at Heart)	.05
107	Lou Whitaker (Young at Heart)	.05
108	Ozzie Smith (Young at Heart)	.50
109	Paul Molitor (Young at Heart)	.40
110	Rickey Henderson (Young at Heart)	.40
111	Tim Raines (Young at Heart)	.05
112	Harold Baines (Young at Heart)	.05
113	Lee Smith (Young at Heart)	.05
114	Fernando Valenzuela (Young at Heart)	.05
115	Cal Ripken Jr. (Young at Heart)	1.00
116	Tony Gwynn (Young at Heart)	.50
117	Wade Boggs (Young at Heart)	.50
118	Todd Hollandsworth	.05
119	Dave Nilsson	.05
120	Jose Valentin RC	.05
121	Steve Sparks	.05
122	Chuck Carr	.05
123	John Jaha	.05
124	Scott Karl	.05
125	Chuck Knoblauch	.05
126	Brad Radke	.05
127	Pat Meares	.05
128	Ron Coomer	.05
129	Pedro Munoz	.05
130	Kirby Puckett	1.00
131	David Segui	.05
132	Mark Grudzielanek	.05
133	Mike Lansing	.05
134	Sean Berry	.05
135	Rondell White	.05
136	Pedro Martinez	.75
137	Carl Everett	.05
138	Dave Mlicki	.05
139	Bill Pulsipher	.05
140	Jason Isringhausen	.05
141	Rico Brogna	.05
142	Edgardo Alfonzo	.05
143	Jeff Kent	.05
144	Andy Pettitte	.25
145	Mike Piazza (Beat the Odds)	.65
146	Cliff Floyd (Beat the Odds)	.05
147	Jason Isringhausen (Beat the Odds)	.05
148	Tim Wakefield (Beat the Odds)	.05
149	Chipper Jones (Beat the Odds)	.50
150	Hideo Nomo (Beat the Odds)	.20
151	Mark McGwire (Beat the Odds)	.75
152	Ron Gant (Beat the Odds)	.05
153	Gary Gaetti (Beat the Odds)	.05
154	Don Mattingly	1.00
155	Paul O'Neill	.05
156	Derek Jeter	2.00
157	Joe Girardi	.05
158	Ruben Sierra	.05
159	Jorge Posada	.05
160	Geronimo Berroa	.05
161	Steve Ontiveros	.05
162	George Williams	.05
163	Doug Johns	.05
164	Ariel Prieto	.05
165	Scott Brosius	.05
166	Mike Bordick	.05
167	Tyler Green	.05
168	Mickey Morandini	.05
169	Darren Daulton	.05
170	Gregg Jefferies	.05
171	Jim Eisenreich	.05
172	Heathcliff Slocumb	.05
173	Kevin Stocker	.05
174	Esteban Loaiza	.05
175	Jeff King	.05
176	Mark Johnson	.05
177	Denny Neagle	.05
178	Orlando Merced	.05
179	Carlos Garcia	.05
180	Brian Jordan	.05
181	Mike Morgan	.05
182	Mark Petkovsek	.05
183	Bernard Gilkey	.05
184	John Mabry	.05
185	Tom Henke	.05
186	Glenn Dishman	.05
187	Andy Ashby	.05
188	Bip Roberts	.05
189	Melvin Nieves	.05
190	Ken Caminiti	.05
191	Brad Ausmus	.05
192	Deion Sanders	.05
193	Jamie Brewington	.05
194	Glenallen Hill	.05
195	Barry Bonds	2.00
196	William Van Landingham	.05
197	Mark Carreon	.05
198	Royce Clayton	.05
199	Joey Cora	.05
200	Ken Griffey Jr.	1.25
201	Jay Buhner	.05
202	Alex Rodriguez	1.50
203	Norm Charlton	.05
204	Andy Benes	.05
205	Edgar Martinez	.05
206	Juan Gonzalez	.40
207	Will Clark	.05
208	Kevin Gross	.05
209	Roger Pavlik	.05
210	Ivan Rodriguez	.65
211	Rusty Greer	.05
212	Angel Martinez	.05
213	Tomas Perez	.05
214	Alex Gonzalez	.05
215	Joe Carter	.05
216	Shawn Green	.30
217	Edwin Hurtado	.05
218	Edgar Martinez, Tony Pena (Post Season Checklist)	.05
219	Chipper Jones, Barry Larkin (Post Season Checklist)	.25
220	Orel Hershiser (Post Season Checklist)	.05
221	Mike Devereaux (Post Season Checklist)	.05
222	Tom Glavine (Post Season Checklist)	.05
223	Karim Garcia/SR	.10
224	Arquimedez Pozo/SR	.05
225	Billy Wagner/SR	.05
226	John Wasdin/SR	.05
227	Jeff Suppan/SR	.05
228	Steve Gibralter/SR	.05
229	Jimmy Haynes/SR	.05
230	Ruben Rivera/SR	.05
231	Chris Snopek/SR	.05
232	Alex Ochoa/SR	.05
233	Shannon Stewart/SR	.05
234	Quinton McCracken/SR	.05
235	Trey Beamon/SR	.05
236	Billy McMillon/SR	.05
237	Steve Cox/SR	.05
238	George Arias/SR	.05
239	Yamil Benitez/SR	.05
240	Todd Greene/SR	.05
241	Jason Kendall/SR	.05
242	Brooks Kieschnick/SR	.05
243	Osvaldo Fernandez/SR RC	.15
244	Livan Hernandez/SR RC	.35
245	Rey Ordonez/SR	.05
246	Mike Grace/SR RC	.05
247	Jay Canizaro/SR	.05
248	Bob Wolcott/SR	.05
249	Jermaine Dye/SR	.05
250	Jason Schmidt/SR	.05
251	Marc Sweeney/SR RC	1.00
252	Marcus Jensen/SR	.05
253	Mendy Lopez/SR	.05
254	Wilton Guerrero/SR RC	.10
255	Paul Wilson/SR	.05
256	Edgar Renteria/SR	.05
257	Richard Hidalgo/SR	.05
258	Bob Abreu/SR	.10
259	Robert Smith RC (Diamond Debuts)	.05
260	Sal Fasano (Diamond Debuts)	.05
261	Enrique Wilson (Diamond Debuts)	.05
262	Rich Hunter RC (Diamond Debuts)	.05
263	Sergio Nunez (Diamond Debuts)	.05
264	Dan Serafini (Diamond Debuts)	.05
265	David Doster RC (Diamond Debuts)	.05
266	Ryan McGuire (Diamond Debuts)	.05
267	Scott Spiezio (Diamond Debuts)	.05
268	Rafael Orellano (Diamond Debuts)	.05
269	Steve Avery	.05
270	Fred McGriff	.05
271	John Smoltz	.05
272	Ryan Klesko	.05
273	Jeff Blauser	.05
274	Brad Clontz	.05
275	Roberto Alomar	.20
276	B.J. Surhoff	.05
277	Jeffrey Hammonds	.05
278	Brady Anderson	.05
279	Bobby Bonilla	.05
280	Cal Ripken Jr.	2.00
281	Mike Mussina	.30
282	Wil Cordero	.05
283	Mike Stanley	.05
284	Aaron Sele	.05
285	Jose Canseco	.40
286	Tom Gordon	.05
287	Heathcliff Slocumb	.05
288	Lee Smith	.05
289	Troy Percival	.05
290	Tim Salmon	.05
291	Chuck Finley	.05
292	Jim Abbott	.05
293	Chili Davis	.05
294	Steve Trachsel	.05
295	Mark Grace	.05
296	Rey Sanchez	.05
297	Scott Servais	.05
298	Jaime Navarro	.05
299	Frank Castillo	.05
300	Frank Thomas	.75
301	Jason Bere	.05
302	Danny Tartabull	.05
303	Darren Lewis	.05
304	Roberto Hernandez	.05
305	Tony Phillips	.05
306	Wilson Alvarez	.05
307	Jose Rijo	.05
308	Hal Morris	.05
309	Mark Portugal	.05
310	Barry Larkin	.05
311	Dave Burba	.05
312	Eddie Taubensee	.05
313	Sandy Alomar Jr.	.05
314	Dennis Martinez	.05
315	Albert Belle	.15
316	Eddie Murray	.75
317	Charles Nagy	.05
318	Chad Ogea	.05
319	Kenny Lofton	.05
320	Dante Bichette	.05
321	Armando Reynoso	.05
322	Walt Weiss	.05
323	Ellis Burks	.05
324	Kevin Ritz	.05
325	Bill Swift	.05
326	Jason Bates	.05
327	Tony Clark	.05
328	Travis Fryman	.05
329	Mark Parent	.05
330	Alan Trammell	.05
331	C.J. Nitkowski	.05
332	Jose Lima	.05
333	Phil Plantier	.05
334	Kurt Abbott	.05
335	Andre Dawson	.25
336	Chris Hammond	.05
337	Robb Nen	.05
338	Pat Rapp	.05
339	Al Leiter	.05
340	Gary Sheffield	.35
341	Todd Jones	.05
342	Doug Drabek	.05
343	Greg Swindell	.05
344	Tony Eusebio	.05
345	Craig Biggio	.05
346	Darryl Kile	.05
347	Mike Macfarlane	.05
348	Jeff Montgomery	.05
349	Chris Haney	.05
350	Bip Roberts	.05
351	Tom Goodwin	.05
352	Mark Gubicza	.05
353	Joe Randa	.05
354	Ramon Martinez	.05
355	Eric Karros	.05
356	Delino DeShields	.05
357	Brett Butler	.05
358	Todd Worrell	.05
359	Mike Blowers	.05
360	Mike Piazza	1.25
361	Ben McDonald	.05
362	Ricky Bones	.05
363	Greg Vaughn	.05
364	Matt Mieske	.05
365	Kevin Seitzer	.05
366	Jeff Cirillo	.05
367	LaTroy Hawkins	.05
368	Frank Rodriguez	.05
369	Rick Aguilera	.05
370	Roberto Alomar (Best of a Generation)	.15
371	Albert Belle (Best of a Generation)	.05
372	Wade Boggs (Best of a Generation)	.50
373	Barry Bonds (Best of a Generation)	1.00
374	Roger Clemens (Best of a Generation)	.65
375	Dennis Eckersley (Best of a Generation)	.35
376	Ken Griffey Jr. (Best of a Generation)	.65
377	Tony Gwynn (Best of a Generation)	.50
378	Rickey Henderson (Best of a Generation)	.40
379	Greg Maddux (Best of a Generation)	.50
380	Fred McGriff (Best of a Generation)	.05
381	Paul Molitor (Best of a Generation)	.40
382	Eddie Murray (Best of a Generation)	.40
383	Mike Piazza (Best of a Generation)	.65
384	Kirby Puckett (Best of a Generation)	.50
385	Cal Ripken Jr. (Best of a Generation)	1.00
386	Ozzie Smith (Best of a Generation)	.50
387	Frank Thomas (Best of a Generation)	.45
388	Matt Walbeck	.05
389	Dave Stevens	.05
390	Marty Cordova	.05
391	Darrin Fletcher	.05
392	Cliff Floyd	.05
393	Mel Rojas	.05
394	Shane Andrews	.05
395	Moises Alou	.05
396	Carlos Perez	.05
397	Jeff Fassero	.05
398	Bobby Jones	.05
399	Todd Hundley	.05
400	John Franco	.05
401	Jose Vizcaino	.05
402	Bernard Gilkey	.05
403	Pete Harnisch	.05
404	Pat Kelly	.05
405	David Cone	.05
406	Bernie Williams	.05
407	John Wetteland	.05
408	Scott Kamieniecki	.05
409	Tim Raines	.05
410	Wade Boggs	1.00
411	Terry Steinbach	.05
412	Jason Giambi	.40
413	Todd Van Poppel	.05
414	Pedro Munoz	.05
415	Eddie Murray-1990 (Strange But True)	.40
416	Dennis Eckersley-1990 (Strange But True)	.35
417	Bip Roberts-1992 (Strange But True)	.05
418	Glenallen Hill-1992 (Strange But True)	.05
419	John Hudek-1994 (Strange But True)	.05
420	Derek Bell-1995 (Strange But True)	.05
421	Larry Walker-1995 (Strange But True)	.05
422	Greg Maddux-1995 (Strange But True)	.50
423	Ken Caminiti-1995 (Strange But True)	.05
424	Brent Gates	.05
425	Mark McGwire	1.50
426	Mark Whiten	.05
427	Sid Fernandez	.05
428	Ricky Bottalico	.05
429	Mike Mimbs	.05
430	Lenny Dykstra	.05
431	Todd Zeile	.05
432	Benito Santiago	.05
433	Danny Miceli	.05
434	Al Martin	.05
435	Jay Bell	.05
436	Charlie Hayes	.05
437	Mike Kingery	.05
438	Paul Wagner	.05
439	Tom Pagnozzi	.05
440	Ozzie Smith	1.00
441	Ray Lankford	.05
442	Dennis Eckersley	.65
443	Ron Gant	.05
444	Alan Benes	.05
445	Rickey Henderson	.75
446	Jody Reed	.05
447	Trevor Hoffman	.05
448	Andujar Cedeno	.05
449	Steve Finley	.05
450	Tony Gwynn	1.00
451	Joey Hamilton	.05
452	Mark Leiter	.05
453	Rod Beck	.05
454	Kirt Manwaring	.05
455	Matt Williams	.05
456	Robby Thompson	.05
457	Shawon Dunston	.05
458	Russ Davis	.05
459	Paul Sorrento	.05
460	Randy Johnson	.75
461	Chris Bosio	.05
462	Luis Sojo	.05
463	Sterling Hitchcock	.05
464	Benji Gil	.05
465	Mickey Tettleton	.05
466	Mark McLemore	.05
467	Darryl Hamilton	.05
468	Ken Hill	.05
469	Dean Palmer	.05
470	Carlos Delgado	.40
471	Ed Sprague	.05
472	Otis Nixon	.05
473	Pat Hentgen	.05
474	Juan Guzman	.05
475	John Olerud	.05
476	Checklist (Buck Showalter)	.05
477	Checklist (Bobby Cox)	.05
478	Checklist (Tommy Lasorda)	.05
479	Checklist (Jim Leyland)	.05
480	Checklist (Sparky Anderson)	.05

Blue Chip Prospects

Twenty top young stars who could make a major impact in the major leagues in upcoming seasons are featured in this insert set. Each card is highlighted with blue-foil printing and double die-cut technology, which includes a zig-zag pattern around the top and a die-cut around both bottom corners. The cards are found one per 20 packs in Series 1 foil packs. Cards are numbered with a "BC" prefix.

		NM/M
Complete Set (20):		50.00
Common Player:		1.00
1	Hideo Nomo	4.00
2	Johnny Damon	3.50
3	Jason Isringhausen	1.00
4	Bill Pulsipher	1.00
5	Marty Cordova	1.00
6	Michael Tucker	1.00
7	John Wasdin	1.00
8	Karim Garcia	1.50
9	Ruben Rivera	1.00
10	Chipper Jones	10.00
11	Billy Wagner	1.00
12	Brooks Kieschnick	1.00
13	Alex Ochoa	1.00
14	Roger Cedeno	1.00
15	Alex Rodriguez	15.00
16	Jason Schmidt	1.00
17	Derek Jeter	20.00
18	Brian L. Hunter	1.00
19	Garret Anderson	1.00
20	Manny Ramirez	7.50

1996 Upper Deck Update

Available only via a mail-in wrapper redemption or in factory sets, this update set offers cards of players who changed teams after the base card set was issued, as well as a few rookies and others. Cards share the earlier issue's format and are numbered with a "U" suffix.

		NM/M
Complete Set (30):		8.00
Common Player:		.25
481	Randy Myers	.25
482	Kent Mercker	.25
483	David Wells	.35
484	Kevin Mitchell	.25
485	Randy Velarde	.25
486	Ryne Sandberg	4.00
487	Doug Jones	.25
488	Terry Adams	.25
489	Kevin Tapani	.25
490	Harold Baines	.25
491	Eric Davis	.25
492	Julio Franco	.25
493	Jack McDowell	.25
494	Devon White	.25
495	Kevin Brown	.35
496	Rick Wilkins	.25
497	Sean Berry	.25
498	Keith Lockhart	.25
499	Mark Loretta	.25
500	Paul Molitor	2.50
501	Roberto Kelly	.25
502	Lance Johnson	.25
503	Tino Martinez	.25
504	Kenny Rogers	.25
505	Todd Stottlemyre	.25
506	Gary Gaetti	.25
507	Royce Clayton	.25
508	Andy Benes	.25
509	Wally Joyner	.25
510	Erik Hanson	.25

A Cut Above

No Pricing

Diamond Destiny

This late-season release is found exclusively in retail foil packs labeled "Upper Deck Tech." They are inserted at a rate of one per pack, sold with eight regular 1996 Upper Deck cards at a suggested retail of around $3. The cards have three versions of the same action photo; in color and black-and-white on front, and in black-and-white on back. A large team logo also appears on front and back. In the upper half of the card is a 1-3/16" diameter round color transparency portrait of the player. The basic version of this chase set had bronze foil highlights. Parallel silver and gold versions are found on average of one per 35 and one per 143 packs, respectively. Cards are numbered with a "DD" prefix.

		NM/M
Complete Set (Bronze):		35.00
Common Player (Bronze):		.30
Silver:		6X
Gold:		12X
1	Chipper Jones	1.50
2	Fred McGriff	.30
3	Ryan Klesko	.30
4	John Smoltz	.30
5	Greg Maddux	1.50
6	Cal Ripken Jr.	3.00
7	Roberto Alomar	.45

8	Eddie Murray	1.25
9	Brady Anderson	.30
10	Mo Vaughn	.30
11	Roger Clemens	1.75
12	Darin Erstad	.60
13	Sammy Sosa	1.50
14	Frank Thomas	1.25
15	Barry Larkin	.30
16	Albert Belle	.30
17	Manny Ramirez	1.25
18	Kenny Lofton	.30
19	Dante Bichette	.30
20	Gary Sheffield	.75
21	Jeff Bagwell	1.25
22	Hideo Nomo	.65
23	Mike Piazza	2.00
24	Kirby Puckett	1.50
25	Paul Molitor	1.25
26	Chuck Knoblauch	.30
27	Wade Boggs	1.50
28	Derek Jeter	3.00
29	Rey Ordonez	.30
30	Mark McGwire	2.50
31	Ozzie Smith	1.50
32	Tony Gwynn	1.50
33	Barry Bonds	3.00
34	Matt Williams	.30
35	Ken Griffey Jr.	2.00
36	Jay Buhner	.30
37	Randy Johnson	1.25
38	Alex Rodriguez	2.00
39	Juan Gonzalez	.65
40	Joe Carter	.30

Future Stock

Future Stock inserts are found on average of one per six packs of Series 1, highlighting 20 top young stars on a die-cut design. Each card has a blue border, vertical photo and silver-foil stamping on the front. Cards are numbered with a "FS" prefix.

		NM/M
Complete Set (20):		4.00
Common Player:		.25
1	George Arias	.25
2	Brian Barnes	.25
3	Trey Beamon	.25
4	Yamil Benitez	.25
5	Jamie Brewington	.25
6	Tony Clark	.25
7	Steve Cox	.25
8	Carlos Delgado	.75
9	Chad Fonville	.25
10	Steve Gibralter	.25
11	Curtis Goodwin	.25
12	Todd Greene	.25
13	Jimmy Haynes	.25
14	Quinton McCracken	.25
15	Billy McMillon	.25
16	Chan Ho Park	.25
17	Arquimedez Pozo	.25
18	Chris Snopek	.25
19	Shannon Stewart	.25
20	Jeff Suppan	.25

Gameface

This insert was exclusive to $1.50 Wal-Mart retail packs. Fronts have an action photo vignetted in white with a gold-foil Gameface logo. Backs have another photo and a few sentences about the player. One Gameface card was found in each pack.

		NM/M
Complete Set (10):		6.00
Common Player:		.15
1	Ken Griffey Jr.	1.00
2	Frank Thomas	.65
3	Barry Bonds	1.50
4	Albert Belle	.15
5	Cal Ripken Jr.	1.50
6	Mike Piazza	1.00
7	Chipper Jones	.75
8	Matt Williams	.15
9	Hideo Nomo	.40
10	Greg Maddux	.75

Hobby Predictor

These inserts depict 60 top players as possible winners in the categories of Player of the Month, Pitcher of the Month and Rookie Hits Leader. If the pictured player won that category any month of the season the card was redeemable for a 10-card set with a different look, action photos and printed on silver-foil stock. Hobby Predictor inserts are found on average once per dozen packs in both series. Winning cards are indicated by (W).

		NM/M
Complete Set (60):		35.00
Common Player:		.40
H1	Albert Belle	.40
H2	Kenny Lofton	.40
H3	Rafael Palmeiro	.65
H4	Ken Griffey Jr.	2.00
H5	Tim Salmon	.40
H6	Cal Ripken Jr.	3.00
H7	Mark McGwire (W)	4.50
H8	Frank Thomas (W)	1.25
H9	Mo Vaughn (W)	.60
H10	Player of the Month Long Shot (W)	.40
H11	Roger Clemens	1.75
H12	David Cone	.40
H13	Jose Mesa	.40
H14	Randy Johnson	.75
H15	Steve Finley	.40
H16	Mike Mussina	.50
H17	Kevin Appier	.40
H18	Kenny Rogers	.40
H19	Lee Smith	.40
H20	Pitcher of the Month Long Shot (W)	.40
H21	George Arias	.40
H22	Jose Herrera	.40
H23	Tony Clark	.40
H24	Todd Greene	.40
H25	Derek Jeter (W)	6.00
H26	Arquimedez Pozo	.40
H27	Matt Lawton	.40
H28	Shannon Stewart	.40
H29	Chris Snopek	.40
H30	Rookie Hits Long Shot	.40
H31	Jeff Bagwell (W)	1.25
H32	Dante Bichette	.40
H33	Barry Bonds (W)	6.00
H34	Tony Gwynn	1.50
H35	Chipper Jones	1.50
H36	Eric Karros	.40
H37	Barry Larkin	.40
H38	Mike Piazza	2.00
H39	Matt Williams	.40
H40	Player of the Month Long Shot (W)	.40
H41	Osvaldo Fernandez	.40
H42	Tom Glavine	.60
H43	Jason Isringhausen	.40
H44	Greg Maddux	1.50
H45	Pedro Martinez	.75
H46	Hideo Nomo	.60
H47	Pete Schourek	.40
H48	Paul Wilson	.40
H49	Mark Wohlers	.40
H50	Pitcher of the Month Long Shot	.40
H51	Bob Abreu	.40
H52	Trey Beamon	.40
H53	Yamil Benitez	.40
H54	Roger Cedeno (W)	.60
H55	Todd Hollandsworth	.40
H56	Marvin Benard	.40
H57	Jason Kendall	.40
H58	Brooks Kieschnick	.40
H59	Rey Ordonez (W)	.60
H60	Rookie Hits Long Shot (W)	.40

Hobby Predictor Redemption

Persons who redeemed winning cards from UD's interactive Predictor insert series received a 10-card set of the top players in various statistical categories. The redemption cards are similar in format to the Predictor cards, but have fronts printed on silver-foil. In place of the contest rules found on the backs of Predictor cards, the redemption cards have a career summary.

		NM/M
Complete Set (60):		45.00
Common Player:		.50
H1	Albert Belle	.50
H2	Kenny Lofton	.50
H3	Rafael Palmeiro	.75
H4	Ken Griffey Jr.	2.50
H5	Tim Salmon	.50
H6	Cal Ripken Jr.	4.00
H7	Mark McGwire	3.00
H8	Frank Thomas	1.00
H9	Mo Vaughn	.50
H10	Player of the Month Long Shot	.50
H11	Roger Clemens	2.25
H12	David Cone	.50
H13	Jose Mesa	.50
H14	Randy Johnson	1.00
H15	Steve Finley	.50
H16	Mike Mussina	.65
H17	Kevin Appier	.50
H18	Kenny Rogers	.50
H19	Lee Smith	.50
H20	Pitcher of the Month Long Shot	.50
H21	George Arias	.50
H22	Jose Herrera	.50
H23	Tony Clark	.50
H24	Todd Greene	.50
H25	Derek Jeter	4.00
H26	Arquimedez Pozo	.50
H27	Matt Lawton	.50
H28	Shannon Stewart	.50
H29	Chris Snopek	.50
H30	Rookie Hits Long Shot	.50
H31	Jeff Bagwell	1.00
H32	Dante Bichette	.50
H33	Barry Bonds	4.00
H34	Tony Gwynn	2.00
H35	Chipper Jones	2.00
H36	Eric Karros	.50
H37	Barry Larkin	.50
H38	Mike Piazza	2.50
H39	Matt Williams	.50
H40	Player of the Month Long Shot	.50
H41	Osvaldo Fernandez	.50
H42	Tom Glavine	.65
H43	Jason Isringhausen	.50
H44	Greg Maddux	2.00
H45	Pedro Martinez	1.00
H46	Hideo Nomo	.65
H47	Pete Schourek	.50
H48	Paul Wilson	.50
H49	Mark Wohlers	.50
H50	Pitcher of the Month Long Shot	.50
H51	Bob Abreu	.50
H52	Trey Beamon	.50
H53	Yamil Benitez	.50
H54	Roger Cedeno	.50
H55	Todd Hollandsworth	.50
H56	Marvin Benard	.50
H57	Jason Kendall	.50
H58	Brooks Kieschnick	.50
H59	Rey Ordonez	.50
H60	Rookie Hits Long Shot	.50

Hot Commodities

These 20 die-cut cards were seeded one per every 37 1996 Upper Deck Series 2 packs. Cards are numbered with a "HC" prefix.

		NM/M
Complete Set (20):		30.00
Common Player:		.75
1	Ken Griffey Jr.	3.00
2	Hideo Nomo	1.50
3	Roberto Alomar	1.50
4	Paul Wilson	.75
5	Albert Belle	.75

6	Manny Ramirez	2.25
7	Kirby Puckett	2.50
8	Johnny Damon	2.00
9	Randy Johnson	2.25
10	Greg Maddux	2.50
11	Chipper Jones	2.50
12	Barry Bonds	5.00
13	Mo Vaughn	.75
14	Mike Piazza	3.00
15	Cal Ripken Jr.	5.00
16	Tim Salmon	.75
17	Sammy Sosa	2.50
18	Kenny Lofton	.75
19	Tony Gwynn	2.25
20	Frank Thomas	2.25

Lovero Collection

Every sixth pack of 1996 Upper Deck Series II has a V.J. Lovero insert card. This 20-card set features unique shots from Lovero, one of the most well-known photographers in the country. Some of the cards feature Randy Johnson wearing a conehead, Frank Thomas blowing a bubble while throwing the ball, and Jay Buhner and his child both chewing on a bat. Cards are numbered with a "VJ" prefix.

		NM/M
Complete Set (20):		17.50
Common Player:		.25
1	Rod Carew	1.00
2	Hideo Nomo	.50
3	Derek Jeter	3.00
4	Barry Bonds	3.00
5	Greg Maddux	1.50
6	Mark McGwire (W/Will Clark.)	2.50
7	Jose Canseco	.50
8	Ken Caminiti	.25
9	Raul Mondesi	.25
10	Ken Griffey Jr.	2.50
11	Jay Buhner	.25
12	Randy Johnson	1.00
13	Roger Clemens	2.00
14	Brady Anderson	.25
15	Frank Thomas	1.00
16	Angels Outfielders	.25
17	Mike Piazza	2.50
18	Dante Bichette	.25
19	Tony Gwynn	1.50
20	Jim Abbott	.25

Nomo Highlights

The 1995 rookie season of Los Angeles Dodgers' pitcher Hideo Nomo is recapped in this five-card 1996 Upper Deck insert set. The cards were seeded one per every 23 Series 2 packs. A 5" x 7" version of each card was also issued as a retail box insert. Values are the same as for small cards.

		NM/M
Complete Set (5):		3.00
Common Card:		.75
1-5	Hideo Nomo	.75

Power Driven

Twenty of the game's top power hitters are analyzed in depth by baseball writer Peter Gammons on these Series 1 insert cards. Found once per 36 packs, on average, the cards are printed on an embossed light F/X design. Cards are numbered with a "PD" prefix.

		NM/M
Complete Set (20):		24.00
Common Player:		.30
1	Albert Belle	.30
2	Barry Bonds	5.00
3	Jay Buhner	.30
4	Jose Canseco	.75
5	Cecil Fielder	.30
6	Juan Gonzalez	.75
7	Ken Griffey Jr.	3.00
8	Eric Karros	.30
9	Fred McGriff	.30
10	Mark McGwire	4.00
11	Rafael Palmeiro	1.25
12	Mike Piazza	3.00
13	Manny Ramirez	1.50
14	Tim Salmon	.30
15	Reggie Sanders	.30
16	Sammy Sosa	2.50
17	Frank Thomas	1.50
18	Mo Vaughn	.30
19	Larry Walker	.30
20	Matt Williams	.30

Retail Predictor

Retail Predictor inserts feature 60 possible winners in the categories of monthly leader in home runs, batting average and RBIs. If the pictured player led a category in any month, his card was redeemable for a 10-card set featuring action photos on silver foil. Retail Predictors are found on average once per 12 packs in each series. Winning cards are indicated by (W).

		NM/M
Complete Set (60):		40.00
Common Player:		.40
R1	Albert Belle (W)	.60
R2	Jay Buhner (W)	.60
R3	Juan Gonzalez	.50
R4	Ken Griffey Jr.	2.00
R5	Mark McGwire (W)	4.00
R6	Rafael Palmeiro	.65
R7	Tim Salmon	.40
R8	Frank Thomas	1.00
R9	Mo Vaughn	.60
R10	Home Run Long Shot (W)	.40
R11	Albert Belle (W)	.60
R12	Jay Buhner	.40
R13	Jim Edmonds	.40
R14	Cecil Fielder	.40
R15	Ken Griffey Jr.	2.00
R16	Edgar Martinez	.40
R17	Manny Ramirez	.75
R18	Frank Thomas	1.00
R19	Mo Vaughn	.60
R20	RBI Long Shot (W)	.40
R21	Roberto Alomar (W)	1.00
R22	Carlos Baerga	.40
R23	Wade Boggs	1.50
R24	Ken Griffey Jr.	2.00
R25	Chuck Knoblauch	.40
R26	Kenny Lofton	.40
R27	Edgar Martinez	.40
R28	Tim Salmon	.40
R29	Frank Thomas	1.00
R30	Batting Average Long Shot (W)	.40
R31	Dante Bichette	.40
R32	Barry Bonds (W)	4.50
R33	Ron Gant	.40
R34	Chipper Jones	1.50
R35	Fred McGriff	.40
R36	Mike Piazza	2.00
R37	Sammy Sosa	1.50
R38	Larry Walker	.40
R39	Matt Williams	.40
R40	Home Run Long Shot	.40
R41	Jeff Bagwell (W)	1.25
R42	Dante Bichette	.40
R43	Barry Bonds (W)	4.50
R44	Jeff Conine	.40
R45	Andres Galarraga	.40
R46	Mike Piazza	2.00
R47	Reggie Sanders	.40
R48	Sammy Sosa	1.50
R49	Matt Williams	.40
R50	RBI Long Shot	.40
R51	Jeff Bagwell	.75
R52	Derek Bell	.40
R53	Dante Bichette	.40
R54	Craig Biggio	.40
R55	Barry Bonds	2.50
R56	Bret Boone	.40
R57	Tony Gwynn	1.50
R58	Barry Larkin	.40
R59	Mike Piazza (W)	3.50
R60	AVG Long Shot	.40

Retail Predictor Redemption

Persons who redeemed winning cards from UD's interactive Predictor insert series received a 10-card set of the top players in various statistical categories. The redemption cards are similar in format to the Predictor cards, but have fronts printed on silver-foil. In place of the contest rules found on the backs of Predictor cards, the redemption cards have a career summary.

		NM/M
Complete Set (60):		25.00
Common Player:		.25
R1	Albert Belle	.25
R2	Jay Buhner	.25
R3	Juan Gonzalez	.35
R4	Ken Griffey Jr.	1.00
R5	Mark McGwire	1.50
R6	Rafael Palmeiro	.25
R7	Tim Salmon	.25
R8	Frank Thomas	.60
R9	Mo Vaughn	.25
R10	Home Run Long Shot	.25
R11	Albert Belle	.25
R12	Jay Buhner	.25
R13	Jim Edmonds	.25
R14	Cecil Fielder	.25
R15	Ken Griffey Jr.	1.00
R16	Edgar Martinez	.25
R17	Manny Ramirez	.60
R18	Frank Thomas	.60
R19	Mo Vaughn	.25
R20	RBI Long Shot	.25
R21	Roberto Alomar	.35
R22	Carlos Baerga	.25
R23	Wade Boggs	.75
R24	Ken Griffey Jr.	1.00
R25	Chuck Knoblauch	.25
R26	Kenny Lofton	.25
R27	Edgar Martinez	.25
R28	Tim Salmon	.25
R29	Frank Thomas	.60
R30	Batting Average Long Shot	.25
R31	Dante Bichette	.25
R32	Barry Bonds	2.00
R33	Ron Gant	.25
R34	Chipper Jones	.75
R35	Fred McGriff	.25
R36	Mike Piazza	1.00
R37	Sammy Sosa	.75
R38	Larry Walker	.25
R39	Matt Williams	.25
R40	Home Run Long Shot	.25
R41	Jeff Bagwell	.60
R42	Dante Bichette	.25
R43	Barry Bonds	2.00
R44	Jeff Conine	.25
R45	Andres Galarraga	.25
R46	Mike Piazza	1.00
R47	Reggie Sanders	.25
R48	Sammy Sosa	.75
R49	Matt Williams	.25
R50	RBI Long Shot	.25
R51	Jeff Bagwell	.60
R52	Derek Bell	.25
R53	Dante Bichette	.25

R54	Craig Biggio	.25
R55	Barry Bonds	2.00
R56	Bret Boone	.25
R57	Tony Gwynn	.75
R58	Barry Larkin	.25
R59	Mike Piazza	1.00
R60	AVG Long Shot	.25

Cal Ripken Collection

Part of a cross-brand insert set, four cards are included as Series I inserts at the rate of one per 24 packs. Five cards are also included in Series II, one per every 23 packs. They chronicle Cal Ripken's career and highlights.

		NM/M
	Complete Set (8):	12.50
	Common Card:	2.00
	Header:	2.00
5	Cal Ripken Jr.	2.00
6	Cal Ripken Jr.	2.00
7	Cal Ripken Jr.	2.00
8	Cal Ripken Jr.	2.00
13	Cal Ripken Jr.	2.00
14	Cal Ripken Jr.	2.00
15	Cal Ripken Jr.	2.00
16	Cal Ripken Jr.	2.00
17	Cal Ripken Jr.	2.00

Cal Ripken Collection Supers

The career of Cal Ripken Jr. to the point of his 2,131st consecutive major league game is chronicled in this boxed set of 3-1/2" x 5" cards. The tale is told in reverse order, with card #1 marking the record and #22 detailing Ripken's first major league experience. Fronts have photos of Ripken in various stages of his career and feature a gold-foil facsimile autograph. Backs have a green and black background with a portrait of Ripken at top. At center are a few sentences about his career and a season's stats.

		NM/M
	Complete Set (22):	10.00
	Common Card:	.75
1	Cal Ripken Jr.	.75
2	Cal Ripken Jr. (w/Barry Bonds)	1.00
3-21	Cal Ripken Jr.	.75
22	Cal Ripken Jr. (w/Eddie Murray)	.75

Run Producers

These double die-cut, embossed and color foil-stamped cards feature 20 of the game's top RBI men. The cards were seeded one per every 71 packs of 1996 Upper Deck Series II. Cards are numbered with a "RP" prefix.

		NM/M
	Complete Set (20):	50.00
	Common Player:	1.00
1	Albert Belle	1.00
2	Dante Bichette	1.00
3	Barry Bonds	10.00
4	Jay Buhner	1.00

5	Jose Canseco	2.00
6	Juan Gonzalez	1.50
7	Ken Griffey Jr.	6.00
8	Tony Gwynn	5.00
9	Kenny Lofton	1.00
10	Edgar Martinez	1.00
11	Fred McGriff	1.00
12	Mark McGwire	7.50
13	Rafael Palmeiro	2.50
14	Mike Piazza	6.00
15	Manny Ramirez	3.00
16	Tim Salmon	1.00
17	Sammy Sosa	3.00
18	Frank Thomas	5.00
19	Mo Vaughn	1.00
20	Matt Williams	1.00

All-Star Supers

The starting line-ups of the 1996 All-Star Game are featured in super-size (3-1/2" x 5") versions of their 1996 Upper Deck cards in this special boxed set sold at Wal-Mart late in the year for around $18. Other than a large silver-foil All-Star Game logo in the lower-left corner of each photo, these cards are identical to the regular-issue versions, right down to the silver- and bronze-foil highlights on front and the card numbers on back.

		NM/M
	Complete Set (18):	7.50
	Common Player:	.75
80	Jeff Bagwell	.75
195	Barry Bonds	2.00
200	Ken Griffey Jr.	1.25
271	John Smoltz	.25
275	Roberto Alomar	.45
280	Cal Ripken Jr.	2.00
300	Frank Thomas	.75
310	Barry Larkin	.25
313	Sandy Alomar Jr.	.25
315	Albert Belle	.25
317	Charles Nagy	.25
319	Kenny Lofton	.25
320	Dante Bichette	.25
345	Craig Biggio	.25
360	Mike Piazza	1.00
410	Wade Boggs	1.00
450	Tony Gwynn	1.00
455	Matt Williams	.25

Ken Griffey Jr. All-Star

Junior's seventh All-Star team selection was marked with the issue of this special jumbo (3-1/2" x 5") card. The front has an action photo with the 1996 All-Star Game logo and is highlighted in silver foil, including a reproduction of his autograph. The top is die-cut. On back is a portrait photo with Griffey's All-Star history overprinted, and a serial number from within an edition of 2,500. The card was an exclusive to a TV shopping network.

	NM/M
Ken Griffey Jr.	12.00

Ken Griffey Jr. 22kt Gold

This standard-size card has a gold-foil facsimile autograph on front and is serially numbered on back from within an edition of 5,000. A certificate of authenticity accompanied the card when sold new.

	NM/M
Ken Griffey Jr.	7.50

National Heroes

Two baseball stars are included in this series of collector issues believed to have been a TV shop-at-home exclusive. Measuring 3-1/2" x 5", the cards are die-cut to a torn ticket shape. Fronts have color action photos on a gold-foil background. Two versions of each card were issued, an edition of 5,000 unsigned cards and an autographed edition serially numbered on front to a limit of 250.

		NM/M
	Complete Set (2):	20.00
	Complete Set, Autographed (2):	190.00
(1)	Ken Griffey Jr.	7.50
(1a)	Ken Griffey Jr./Auto.	90.00
(2)	Cal Ripken Jr.	10.00
(2a)	Cal Ripken Jr./Auto.	100.00

Hideo Nomo R.O.Y.

The Japanese pitcher's 1995 Rookie of the Year season was commemorated with this large-format (3-1/2" x 5"), die-cut card sold only via TV shopping programs. The card has an action photo of Nomo on front and is highlighted in gold foil, including a replica of his autograph. On back is an action photo, major league career summary and stats and a serial number from within an edition of 5,000 pieces.

	NM/M
Hideo Nomo	15.00

Meet the Stars

These 7" x 5" cards were issued in conjunction with UD's "Meet the Stars" promotion.

		NM/M
	Complete Set (2):	12.00
(1)	Dynamic Debut/1989 (Ken Griffey Jr.)	5.00
(2)	Magic Memories/1995 (Ken Griffey Jr.)	5.00

Statistics Leaders Supers

National League and American League winners of important statistical categories, along with major award winners for the 1996 season are featured in this boxed set of large-format (3-1/2" x 5") cards. Besides the size, these cards differ from the regular-issue 1996 UD cards of the same players only in the addition of a silver-foil award shield on front and the card number on back. Players with multiple awards have identical cards. The set was sold only at retail outlets with a suggested price of about $20.

		NM/M
	Complete Set (23):	4.00
	Common Player:	.15
1	Alex Rodriguez (AL Batting)	1.50
2	Tony Gwynn (NL Batting)	.60
3	Mark McGwire (AL HR)	1.50
4	Andres Galarraga (NL HR)	.15
5	Albert Belle (AL RBI)	.15
6	Andres Galarraga (NL RBI)	.15
7	Kenny Lofton (AL Steals)	.15
8	Eric Young (NL Steals)	.15
9	Andy Pettitte (AL Wins)	.15
10	John Smoltz (NL Wins)	.15
11	Roger Clemens (AL Ks)	.75
12	John Smoltz (NL Ks)	.15
13	Juan Guzman (AL ERA)	.15
14	Kevin Brown (NL ERA)	.15
15	John Wetteland (AL Saves)	.15
16	Jeff Brantley (NL Saves)	.15
17	Todd Worrell (NL Saves)	.15
18	Derek Jeter (AL ROY)	2.00
19	Todd Hollandsworth (NL ROY)	.15
20	Juan Gonzalez (AL MVP)	.30
21	Ken Caminiti (NL MVP)	.15
22	Pat Hentgen (AL CY)	.15
23	John Smoltz (NL CY)	.15

1997 Upper Deck

The 520-card set was issued in two series in 12-card packs. Base card fronts feature a game-action shot with the player's name near the bottom edge above a

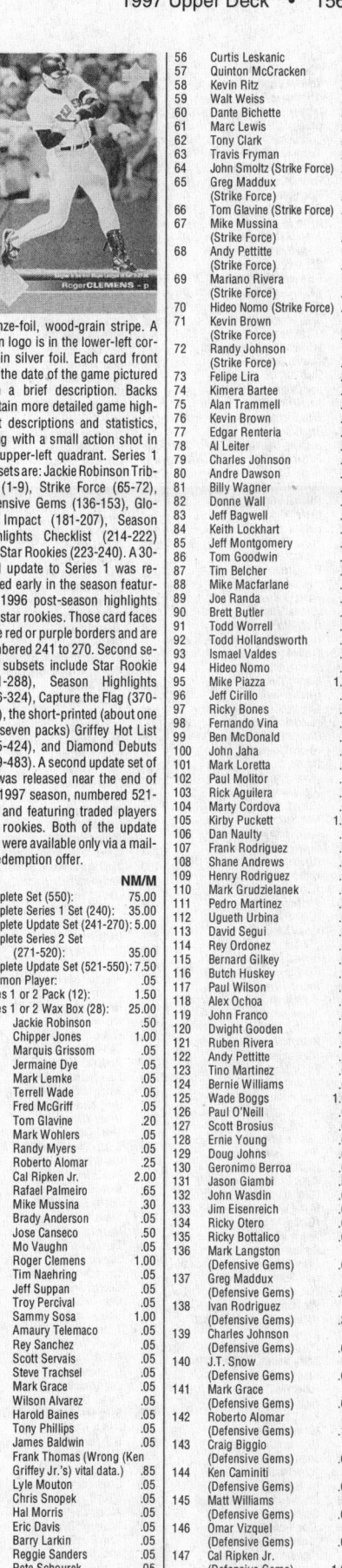

bronze-foil, wood-grain stripe. A team logo is in the lower-left corner in silver foil. Each card front has the date of the game pictured with a brief description. Backs contain more detailed game highlight descriptions and statistics, along with a small action shot in the upper-left quadrant. Series 1 subsets are: Jackie Robinson Tribute (1-9), Strike Force (65-72), Defensive Gems (136-153), Global Impact (181-207), Season Highlights Checklist (214-222) and Star Rookies (223-240). A 30-card update to Series 1 was released early in the season featuring 1996 post-season highlights and star rookies. Those card faces have red or purple borders and are numbered 241 to 270. Second series subsets include Star Rookie (271-288), Season Highlights (316-324), Capture the Flag (370-387), the short-printed (about one per seven packs) Griffey Hot List (415-424), and Diamond Debuts (469-483). A second update set of 30 was released near the end of the 1997 season, numbered 521-550 and featuring traded players and rookies. Both of the update sets were available only via a mail-in redemption offer.

		NM/M
	Complete Set (550):	75.00
	Complete Series 1 Set (240):	35.00
	Complete Update Set (241-270):	5.00
	Complete Series 2 Set (271-520):	35.00
	Complete Update Set (521-550):	7.50
	Common Player:	.05
	Series 1 or 2 Pack (12):	1.50
	Series 1 or 2 Wax Box (28):	25.00
1-9	Jackie Robinson	.50
10	Chipper Jones	1.00
11	Marquis Grissom	.05
12	Jermaine Dye	.05
13	Mark Lemke	.05
14	Terrell Wade	.05
15	Fred McGriff	.05
16	Tom Glavine	.20
17	Mark Wohlers	.05
18	Randy Myers	.05
19	Roberto Alomar	.25
20	Cal Ripken Jr.	2.00
21	Rafael Palmeiro	.65
22	Mike Mussina	.30
23	Brady Anderson	.05
24	Jose Canseco	.50
25	Mo Vaughn	.25
26	Roger Clemens	1.00
27	Tim Naehring	.05
28	Jeff Suppan	.05
29	Troy Percival	.05
30	Sammy Sosa	1.00
31	Amaury Telemaco	.05
32	Rey Sanchez	.05
33	Scott Servais	.05
34	Steve Trachsel	.05
35	Mark Grace	.05
36	Wilson Alvarez	.05
37	Harold Baines	.05
38	Tony Phillips	.05
39	James Baldwin	.05
40	Frank Thomas (Wrong (Ken Griffey Jr.'s) vital data.)	.85
41	Lyle Mouton	.05
42	Chris Snopek	.05
43	Hal Morris	.05
44	Eric Davis	.05
45	Barry Larkin	.05
46	Reggie Sanders	.05
47	Pete Schourek	.05
48	Lee Smith	.05
49	Charles Nagy	.05
50	Albert Belle	.05
51	Julio Franco	.05
52	Kenny Lofton	.05
53	Orel Hershiser	.05
54	Omar Vizquel	.05
55	Eric Young	.05
56	Curtis Leskanic	.05
57	Quinton McCracken	.05
58	Kevin Ritz	.05
59	Walt Weiss	.05
60	Dante Bichette	.05
61	Marc Lewis	.05
62	Tony Clark	.05
63	Travis Fryman	.05
64	John Smoltz (Strike Force)	.05
65	Greg Maddux (Strike Force)	.50
66	Tom Glavine (Strike Force)	.10
67	Mike Mussina (Strike Force)	.15
68	Andy Pettitte (Strike Force)	.15
69	Mariano Rivera (Strike Force)	.10
70	Hideo Nomo (Strike Force)	.20
71	Kevin Brown (Strike Force)	.05
72	Randy Johnson (Strike Force)	.40
73	Felipe Lira	.05
74	Kimera Bartee	.05
75	Alan Trammell	.05
76	Kevin Brown	.05
77	Edgar Renteria	.05
78	Al Leiter	.05
79	Charles Johnson	.05
80	Andre Dawson	.25
81	Billy Wagner	.05
82	Donne Wall	.05
83	Jeff Bagwell	.75
84	Keith Lockhart	.05
85	Jeff Montgomery	.05
86	Tom Goodwin	.05
87	Tim Belcher	.05
88	Mike Macfarlane	.05
89	Joe Randa	.05
90	Brett Butler	.05
91	Todd Worrell	.05
92	Todd Hollandsworth	.05
93	Ismael Valdes	.05
94	Hideo Nomo	.40
95	Mike Piazza	1.25
96	Jeff Cirillo	.05
97	Ricky Bones	.05
98	Fernando Vina	.05
99	Ben McDonald	.05
100	John Jaha	.05
101	Mark Loretta	.05
102	Paul Molitor	.75
103	Rick Aguilera	.05
104	Marty Cordova	.05
105	Kirby Puckett	1.00
106	Dan Naulty	.05
107	Frank Rodriguez	.05
108	Shane Andrews	.05
109	Henry Rodriguez	.05
110	Mark Grudzielanek	.05
111	Pedro Martinez	.75
112	Ugueth Urbina	.05
113	David Segui	.05
114	Rey Ordonez	.05
115	Bernard Gilkey	.05
116	Butch Huskey	.05
117	Paul Wilson	.05
118	Alex Ochoa	.05
119	John Franco	.05
120	Dwight Gooden	.05
121	Ruben Rivera	.05
122	Andy Pettitte	.20
123	Tino Martinez	.05
124	Bernie Williams	.05
125	Wade Boggs	1.00
126	Paul O'Neill	.05
127	Scott Brosius	.05
128	Ernie Young	.05
129	Doug Johns	.05
130	Geronimo Berroa	.05
131	Jason Giambi	.50
132	John Wasdin	.05
133	Jim Eisenreich	.05
134	Ricky Otero	.05
135	Ricky Bottalico	.05
136	Mark Langston (Defensive Gems)	.05
137	Greg Maddux (Defensive Gems)	.50
138	Ivan Rodriguez (Defensive Gems)	.35
139	Charles Johnson (Defensive Gems)	.05
140	J.T. Snow (Defensive Gems)	.05
141	Mark Grace (Defensive Gems)	.05
142	Roberto Alomar (Defensive Gems)	.15
143	Craig Biggio (Defensive Gems)	.05
144	Ken Caminiti (Defensive Gems)	.05
145	Matt Williams (Defensive Gems)	.05
146	Omar Vizquel (Defensive Gems)	.05
147	Cal Ripken Jr. (Defensive Gems)	1.00
148	Ozzie Smith (Defensive Gems)	.40
149	Rey Ordonez (Defensive Gems)	.05
150	Ken Griffey Jr. (Defensive Gems)	.65
151	Devon White (Defensive Gems)	.05

#	Player	Price
152	Barry Bonds (Defensive Gems)	1.00
153	Kenny Lofton (Defensive Gems)	.05
154	Mickey Morandini	.05
155	Gregg Jefferies	.05
156	Curt Schilling	.20
157	Jason Kendall	.05
158	Francisco Cordova	.05
159	Dennis Eckersley	.65
160	Ron Gant	.05
161	Ozzie Smith	1.00
162	Brian Jordan	.05
163	Jim Mabry	.05
164	Andy Ashby	.05
165	Steve Finley	.05
166	Fernando Valenzuela	.05
167	Archi Cianfrocco	.05
168	Wally Joyner	.05
169	Greg Vaughn	.05
170	Barry Bonds	2.00
171	William Van Landingham	.05
172	Marvin Benard	.05
173	Rich Aurilia	.05
174	Jay Canizaro	.05
175	Ken Griffey Jr.	1.25
176	Bob Wells	.05
177	Jay Buhner	.05
178	Sterling Hitchcock	.05
179	Edgar Martinez	.05
180	Rusty Greer	.05
181	Dave Nilsson (Global Impact)	.05
182	Larry Walker (Global Impact)	.05
183	Edgar Renteria (Global Impact)	.05
184	Rey Ordonez (Global Impact)	.05
185	Rafael Palmeiro (Global Impact)	.35
186	Osvaldo Fernandez (Global Impact)	.05
187	Raul Mondesi (Global Impact)	.05
188	Manny Ramirez (Global Impact)	.40
189	Sammy Sosa (Global Impact)	.50
190	Robert Eenhoorn (Global Impact)	.05
191	Devon White (Global Impact)	.05
192	Hideo Nomo (Global Impact)	.20
193	Mac Suzuki (Global Impact)	.05
194	Chan Ho Park (Global Impact)	.05
195	Fernando Valenzuela (Global Impact)	.05
196	Andruw Jones (Global Impact)	.40
197	Vinny Castilla (Global Impact)	.05
198	Dennis Martinez (Global Impact)	.05
199	Ruben Rivera (Global Impact)	.05
200	Juan Gonzalez (Global Impact)	.20
201	Roberto Alomar (Global Impact)	.30
202	Edgar Martinez (Global Impact)	.05
203	Ivan Rodriguez (Global Impact)	.35
204	Carlos Delgado (Global Impact)	.20
205	Andres Galarraga (Global Impact)	.05
206	Ozzie Guillen (Global Impact)	.05
207	Midre Cummings (Global Impact)	.05
208	Roger Pavlik	.05
209	Darren Oliver	.05
210	Dean Palmer	.05
211	Ivan Rodriguez	.65
212	Otis Nixon	.05
213	Pat Hentgen	.05
214	Ozzie Smith, Andre Dawson, Kirby Puckett CL (Season Highlights)	.10
215	Barry Bonds, Gary Sheffield, Brady Anderson (Checklist/Season Highlights)	.25
216	Ken Caminiti (Checklist/Season Highlights)	.05
217	John Smoltz (Checklist/Season Highlights)	.05
218	Eric Young (Checklist/Season Highlights)	.05
219	Juan Gonzalez (Checklist/Season Highlights)	.10
220	Eddie Murray (Checklist/Season Highlights)	.15
221	Tommy Lasorda (Checklist/Season Highlights)	.05
222	Paul Molitor (Checklist/Season Highlights)	.15
223	Luis Castillo	.05
224	Justin Thompson	.05
225	Rocky Coppinger	.05
226	Jermaine Allensworth	.05
227	Jeff D'Amico	.05
228	Jamey Wright	.05
229	Scott Rolen	.60
230	Darin Erstad	.25
231	Marty Janzen	.05
232	Jacob Cruz	.05
233	Raul Ibanez	.25
234	Nomar Garciaparra	1.00
235	Todd Walker	.05
236	Brian Giles RC	.75
237	Matt Beech	.05
238	Mike Cameron	.05
239	Jose Paniagua	.05
240	Andruw Jones	.75
241	Brant Brown/SR	.25
242	Robin Jennings/SR	.25
243	Willie Adams/SR	.25
244	Ken Caminiti/SR	.25
245	Brian Jordan (Division Series)	.25
246	Chipper Jones (Division Series)	2.50
247	Juan Gonzalez (Division Series)	1.00
248	Bernie Williams (Division Series)	.25
249	Roberto Alomar (Division Series)	.30
250	Bernie Williams (Post-Season)	.25
251	David Wells (Post-Season)	.05
252	Cecil Fielder (Post-Season)	.25
253	Darryl Strawberry (Post-Season)	.25
254	Andy Pettitte (Post-Season)	.40
255	Javier Lopez (Post-Season)	.25
256	Gary Gaetti (Post-Season)	.25
257	Ron Gant (Post-Season)	.25
258	Brian Jordan (Post-Season)	.25
259	John Smoltz (Post-Season)	.25
260	Greg Maddux (Post-Season)	2.50
261	Tom Glavine (Post-Season)	.45
262	Chipper Jones (World Series)	2.50
263	Greg Maddux (World Series)	2.50
264	David Cone (World Series)	.25
265	Jim Leyritz (World Series)	.25
266	Andy Pettitte (World Series)	.40
267	John Wetteland (World Series)	.25
268	Dario Veras/SR RC	.25
269	Neifi Perez/SR	.25
270	Bill Mueller/SR	.25
271	Vladimir Guerrero/SR	.75
272	Dmitri Young/SR	.05
273	Nerio Rodriguez/SR RC	.05
274	Kevin Orie/SR	.05
275	Felipe Crespo/SR	.05
276	Danny Graves/SR	.05
277	Roderick Myers/SR	.05
278	Felix Heredia/SR RC	.25
279	Ralph Milliard/SR	.05
280	Greg Norton/SR	.05
281	Derek Wallace/SR	.05
282	Trot Nixon/SR	.10
283	Bobby Chouinard/SR	.05
284	Jay Witasick/SR	.05
285	Travis Miller/SR	.05
286	Brian Bevil/SR	.05
287	Bobby Estalella/SR	.05
288	Steve Soderstrom/SR	.05
289	Mark Langston	.05
290	Tim Salmon	.25
291	Jim Edmonds	.05
292	Garret Anderson	.05
293	George Arias	.05
294	Gary DiSarcina	.05
295	Chuck Finley	.05
296	Todd Greene	.05
297	Randy Velarde	.05
298	David Justice	.05
299	Ryan Klesko	.05
300	John Smoltz	.05
301	Javier Lopez	.05
302	Greg Maddux	1.00
303	Denny Neagle	.05
304	B.J. Surhoff	.05
305	Chris Hoiles	.05
306	Eric Davis	.05
307	Scott Erickson	.05
308	Mike Bordick	.05
309	John Valentin	.05
310	Heathcliff Slocumb	.05
311	Tom Gordon	.05
312	Mike Stanley	.05
313	Reggie Jefferson	.05
314	Darren Bragg	.05
315	Troy O'Leary	.05
316	John Mabry (Season Highlight)	.05
317	Mark Whiten (Season Highlight)	.05
318	Edgar Martinez (Season Highlight)	.05
319	Alex Rodriguez (Season Highlight)	.75
320	Mark McGwire (Season Highlight)	.75
321	Hideo Nomo (Season Highlight)	.20
322	Todd Hundley (Season Highlight)	.05
323	Barry Bonds (Season Highlight)	1.00
324	Andruw Jones (Season Highlight)	.40
325	Ryne Sandberg	1.00
326	Brian McRae	.05
327	Frank Castillo	.05
328	Shawon Dunston	.05
329	Ray Durham	.05
330	Robin Ventura	.05
331	Ozzie Guillen	.05
332	Roberto Hernandez	.05
333	Albert Belle	.25
334	Dave Martinez	.05
335	Willie Greene	.05
336	Jeff Brantley	.05
337	Kevin Jarvis	.05
338	John Smiley	.05
339	Eddie Taubensee	.05
340	Bret Boone	.05
341	Kevin Seitzer	.05
342	Jack McDowell	.05
343	Sandy Alomar Jr.	.05
344	Chad Curtis	.05
345	Manny Ramirez	.75
346	Chad Ogea	.05
347	Jim Thome	.05
348	Mark Thompson	.05
349	Ellis Burks	.05
350	Andres Galarraga	.05
351	Vinny Castilla	.05
352	Kirt Manwaring	.05
353	Larry Walker	.05
354	Omar Olivares	.05
355	Bobby Higginson	.05
356	Melvin Nieves	.05
357	Brian Johnson	.05
358	Devon White	.05
359	Jeff Conine	.05
360	Gary Sheffield	.35
361	Robb Nen	.05
362	Mike Hampton	.05
363	Bob Abreu	.10
364	Luis Gonzalez	.05
365	Derek Bell	.05
366	Sean Berry	.05
367	Craig Biggio	.25
368	Darryl Kile	.05
369	Shane Reynolds	.05
370	Jeff Bagwell (Capture the Flag)	.40
371	Ron Gant (Capture the Flag)	.05
372	Andy Benes (Capture the Flag)	.05
373	Gary Gaetti (Capture the Flag)	.05
374a	Ramon Martinez (Capture the Flag)(Gold back.)	.25
374b	Ramon Martinez (Capture the Flag)(White back.))	.05
375	Raul Mondesi (Capture the Flag)	.05
376a	Steve Finley (Capture the Flag)(Gold back.)	.05
376b	Steve Finley (Capture the Flag)(White back.))	.05
377	Ken Caminiti (Capture the Flag)	.05
378	Tony Gwynn (Capture the Flag)	.40
379	Dario Veras (Capture the Flag)	.05
380	Andy Pettitte (Capture the Flag)	.10
381	Ruben Rivera (Capture the Flag)	.05
382	David Cone (Capture the Flag)	.05
383	Roberto Alomar (Capture the Flag)	.20
384	Edgar Martinez (Capture the Flag)	.05
385	Ken Griffey Jr. (Capture the Flag)	.65
386	Mark McGwire (Capture the Flag)	.75
387	Rusty Greer (Capture the Flag)	.05
388	Jose Rosado	.05
389	Kevin Appier	.05
390	Johnny Damon	.25
391	Jose Offerman	.05
392	Michael Tucker	.05
393	Craig Paquette	.05
394	Bip Roberts	.05
395	Ramon Martinez	.05
396	Greg Gagne	.05
397	Chan Ho Park	.05
398	Karim Garcia	.10
399	Wilton Guerrero	.05
400	Eric Karros	1.00
401	Raul Mondesi	.05
402	Matt Mieske	.05
403	Mike Fetters	.05
404	Dave Nilsson	.05
405	Jose Valentin	.05
406	Scott Karl	.05
407	Marc Newfield	.05
408	Cal Eldred	.05
409	Rich Becker	.05
410	Terry Steinbach	.05
411	Chuck Knoblauch	.05
412	Pat Meares	.05
413	Brad Radke	.05
415a	Kirby Puckett (Should be #414.)	1.00
415b	Andruw Jones (Griffey Hot List)	1.50
416	Chipper Jones (Griffey Hot List)	2.00
417	Mo Vaughn (Griffey Hot List)	.50
418	Frank Thomas (Griffey Hot List)	1.50
419	Albert Belle (Griffey Hot List)	.50
420	Mark McGwire (Griffey Hot List)	3.00
421	Derek Jeter (Griffey Hot List)	4.50
422	Alex Rodriguez (Griffey Hot List)	3.00
423	Juan Gonzalez (Griffey Hot List)	.75
424	Ken Griffey Jr. (Griffey Hot List)	2.50
425	Rondell White	.05
426	Darrin Fletcher	.05
427	Cliff Floyd	.05
428	Mike Lansing	.05
429	F.P. Santangelo	.05
430	Todd Hundley	.05
431	Mark Clark	.05
432	Pete Harnisch	.05
433	Jason Isringhausen	.05
434	Bobby Jones	.05
435	Lance Johnson	.05
436	Carlos Baerga	.05
437	Mariano Duncan	.05
438	David Cone	.05
439	Mariano Rivera	.15
440	Derek Jeter	2.00
441	Joe Girardi	.05
442	Charlie Hayes	.05
443	Tim Raines	.05
444	Darryl Strawberry	.05
445	Cecil Fielder	.05
446	Ariel Prieto	.05
447	Tony Batista	.05
448	Brent Gates	.05
449	Scott Spiezio	.05
450	Mark McGwire	1.50
451	Don Wengert	.05
452	Mike Lieberthal	.05
453	Lenny Dykstra	.05
454	Rex Hudler	.05
455	Darren Daulton	.05
456	Kevin Stocker	.05
457	Trey Beamon	.05
458	Midre Cummings	.05
459	Mark Johnson	.05
460	Al Martin	.05
461	Kevin Elster	.05
462	Jon Lieber	.05
463	Jason Schmidt	.05
464	Paul Wagner	.05
465	Andy Benes	.05
466	Alan Benes	.05
467	Royce Clayton	.05
468	Gary Gaetti	.05
469	Curt Lyons (Diamond Debuts)	.05
470	Eugene Kingsale (Diamond Debuts)	.05
471	Damian Jackson (Diamond Debuts)	.05
472	Wendell Magee (Diamond Dubuts)	.05
473	Kevin L. Brown (Diamond Debuts)	.05
474	Raul Casanova (Diamond Debuts)	*
475	Ramiro Mendoza RC (Diamond Debuts)	.05
476	Todd Dunn (Diamond Debuts)	.05
477	Chad Mottola (Diamond Debuts)	.05
478	Andy Larkin (Diamond Debuts)	.05
479	Jaime Bluma (Diamond Debuts)	.05
480	Mac Suzuki (Diamond Debuts)	.05
481	Brian Banks (Diamond Debuts)	.05
482	Desi Wilson (Diamond Debuts)	.05
483	Einar Diaz (Diamond Debuts)	.05
484	Tom Pagnozzi	.05
485	Ray Lankford	.05
486	Todd Stottlemyre	.05
487	Donovan Osborne	.05
488	Trevor Hoffman	.05
489	Chris Gomez	.05
490	Ken Caminiti	.05
491	John Flaherty	.05
492	Tony Gwynn	1.00
493	Joey Hamilton	.05
494	Rickey Henderson	.75
495	Glenallen Hill	.05
496	Rod Beck	.05
497	Osvaldo Fernandez	.05
498	Rick Wilkins	.05
499	Joey Cora	.05
500	Alex Rodriguez	1.50
501	Randy Johnson	.75
502	Paul Sorrento	.05
503	Dan Wilson	.05
504	Jamie Moyer	.05
505	Will Clark	.05
506	Mickey Tettleton	.05
507	John Burkett	.05
508	Ken Hill	.05
509	Mark McLemore	.05
510	Juan Gonzalez	.40
511	Bobby Witt	.05
512	Carlos Delgado	.40
513	Alex Gonzalez	.05
514	Shawn Green	.25
515	Joe Carter	.05
516	Juan Guzman	.05
517	Charlie O'Brien	.05
518	Ed Sprague	.05
519	Mike Timlin	.05
520	Roger Clemens	1.00
521	Eddie Murray	2.00
522	Jason Dickson	.25
523	Jim Leyritz	.25
524	Michael Tucker	.25
525	Kenny Lofton	.25
526	Jimmy Key	.25
527	Mel Rojas	.25
528	Deion Sanders	.25
529	Bartolo Colon	.25
530	Matt Williams	.25
531	Marquis Grissom	.25
532	David Justice	.25
533	Bubba Trammell RC	.35
534	Moises Alou	.25
535	Bobby Bonilla	.25
536	Alex Fernandez	.25
537	Jay Bell	.25
538	Chili Davis	.25
539	Jeff King	.25
540	Todd Zeile	.25
541	John Olerud	.25
542	Jose Guillen	.25
543	Derrek Lee	1.00
544	Dante Powell	.25
545	J.T. Snow	.25
546	Jeff Kent	.25
547	Jose Cruz Jr. RC	.75
548	John Wetteland	.25
549	Orlando Merced	.25
550	Hideki Irabu RC	.50

Amazing Greats

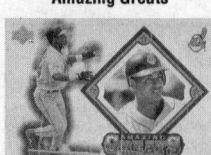

The 20-card, regular-sized insert set was included every 138 packs of 1997 Upper Deck baseball. The cards include real wood with two player shots imaged on the card front. The team logo appears in the upper right corner of the horizontal card. The cards are numbered with the "AG" prefix.

	NM/M
Complete Set (20):	140.00
Common Player:	2.50
1 Ken Griffey Jr.	12.50
2 Roberto Alomar	3.00
3 Alex Rodriguez	15.00
4 Paul Molitor	7.50
5 Chipper Jones	10.00
6 Tony Gwynn	10.00
7 Kenny Lofton	2.50
8 Albert Belle	2.50
9 Matt Williams	2.50
10 Frank Thomas	7.50
11 Greg Maddux	10.00
12 Sammy Sosa	10.00
13 Kirby Puckett	10.00
14 Jeff Bagwell	7.50
15 Cal Ripken Jr.	20.00
16 Manny Ramirez	7.50
17 Barry Bonds	20.00
18 Mo Vaughn	2.50
19 Eddie Murray	7.50
20 Mike Piazza	12.50

Blue Chip Prospects

This 20-card insert was found in packs of Series II and features a die-cut design. Cards appear to have a photo slide attached to them featuring a portrait shot of the promising youngster depicted

on the card. A total of 500 of each card were produced. Cards are numbered with a "BC" prefix.

	NM/M
Common Player:	6.00
Production 500 Sets	
1 Andruw Jones	25.00
2 Derek Jeter	60.00
3 Scott Rolen	15.00
4 Manny Ramirez	25.00
5 Todd Walker	6.00
6 Rocky Coppinger	6.00
7 Nomar Garciaparra	30.00
8 Darin Erstad	7.50
9 Jermaine Dye	6.00
10 Vladimir Guerrero	25.00
11 Edgar Renteria	6.00
12 Bob Abreu	7.50
13 Karim Garcia	6.00
14 Jeff D'Amico	6.00
15 Chipper Jones	30.00
16 Todd Hollandsworth	6.00
17 Andy Pettitte	9.00
18 Ruben Rivera	6.00
19 Jason Kendall	6.00
20 Alex Rodriguez	40.00

Game Jersey

The three-card, regular-sized set was inserted every 800 packs of Upper Deck Series I. The cards contained a square of the player's game-used jersey, and carried a "GJ" card number prefix.

	NM/M
Complete Set (3):	160.00
Common Player:	15.00
GJ1 Ken Griffey Jr.	150.00
GJ2 Tony Gwynn	25.00
GJ3 Rey Ordonez	15.00

Hot Commodities

This 20-card insert from Series II features a flame pattern behind the image of the player depicted on the front of the card. Odds of finding a card were 1:13 packs. Cards are numbered with a "HC" prefix.

	NM/M
Complete Set (20):	20.00
Common Player:	.30
1 Alex Rodriguez	2.00
2 Andruw Jones	1.00
3 Derek Jeter	2.50
4 Frank Thomas	1.00
5 Ken Griffey Jr.	1.50
6 Chipper Jones	1.25
7 Juan Gonzalez	.50
8 Cal Ripken Jr.	2.50
9 John Smoltz	.30
10 Mark McGwire	2.00
11 Barry Bonds	2.50
12 Albert Belle	.30
13 Mike Piazza	1.50
14 Manny Ramirez	.30
15 Mo Vaughn	.30
16 Tony Gwynn	1.25
17 Vladimir Guerrero	1.00
18 Hideo Nomo	.50
19 Greg Maddux	1.25
20 Kirby Puckett	1.25

Long Distance Connection

This 20-card insert from Series II features the top home run hitters in the game. Odds of finding a card were 1:35 packs. Cards are numbered with a "LD" prefix.

		NM/M
Complete Set (20):		32.50
Common Player:		.60
1	Mark McGwire	4.00
2	Brady Anderson	.60
3	Ken Griffey Jr.	3.00
4	Albert Belle	.60
5	Juan Gonzalez	1.25
6	Andres Galarraga	.60
7	Jay Buhner	.60
8	Mo Vaughn	.60
9	Barry Bonds	5.00
10	Gary Sheffield	1.25
11	Todd Hundley	.60
12	Frank Thomas	2.00
13	Sammy Sosa	2.50
14	Rafael Palmeiro	1.75
15	Alex Rodriguez	4.00
16	Mike Piazza	3.00
17	Ken Caminiti	.60
18	Chipper Jones	2.50
19	Manny Ramirez	2.00
20	Andruw Jones	2.00

Memorable Moments

This issue was a one per pack insert in special Series 1 and 2 Collector's Choice six-card retail packs. In standard 2-1/2" x 3-1/2", the cards are die-cut at top and bottom in a wave pattern. Fronts, highlighted in matte bronze foil, have action photos and a career highlight. Backs have another photo and a more complete explanation of the Memorable Moment.

		NM/M
Complete Set (20):		20.00
Common Player:		.50
1	Andruw Jones	.75
2	Chipper Jones	1.00
3	Cal Ripken Jr.	2.50
4	Frank Thomas	.75
5	Manny Ramirez	.75
6	Mike Piazza	1.50
7	Mark McGwire	2.00
8	Barry Bonds	2.50
9	Ken Griffey Jr.	1.50
10	Alex Rodriguez	2.00
1	Ken Griffey Jr.	1.50
2	Albert Belle	.50
3	Derek Jeter	2.50
4	Greg Maddux	1.00
5	Tony Gwynn	1.00
6	Ryne Sandberg	1.00
7	Juan Gonzalez	.60
8	Roger Clemens	1.25
9	Jose Cruz Jr.	2.00
10	Mo Vaughn	.50

Power Package

The 20-card, regular-sized, die-cut set was inserted every 23 packs of 1997 Upper Deck baseball. The player's name is printed in gold foil along the top border of the card face, which also features Light F/X. The die-cut cards have a silver-foil border and team-color frame with a "Power Package"

logo in gold foil centered on the bottom border. The card backs have a short highlight in a brown box bordered by team colors and are numbered with the "PP" prefix.

		NM/M
Complete Set (20):		30.00
Common Player:		1.00
1	Ken Griffey Jr.	3.50
2	Joe Carter	1.00
3	Rafael Palmeiro	1.75
4	Jay Buhner	1.00
5	Sammy Sosa	3.00
6	Fred McGriff	1.00
7	Jeff Bagwell	2.00
8	Albert Belle	1.00
9	Matt Williams	1.00
10	Mark McGwire	4.00
11	Gary Sheffield	1.25
12	Tim Salmon	1.00
13	Ryan Klesko	1.00
14	Manny Ramirez	2.00
15	Mike Piazza	3.50
16	Barry Bonds	5.00
17	Mo Vaughn	1.00
18	Jose Canseco	1.25
19	Juan Gonzalez	1.25
20	Frank Thomas	2.00

Power Package Jumbos

Unlike the regular Power Package inserts found in Series 1 packs, these jumbo versions are not die-cut. The 5"x 7" jumbos are found one per retail foil box of Series 1. Cards are numbered with a "PP" prefix.

		NM/M
Complete Set (20):		30.00
Common Player:		1.00
1	Ken Griffey Jr.	3.50
2	Joe Carter	1.00
3	Rafael Palmeiro	1.75
4	Jay Buhner	1.00
5	Sammy Sosa	3.00
6	Fred McGriff	1.00
7	Jeff Bagwell	2.00
8	Albert Belle	1.00
9	Matt Williams	1.00
10	Mark McGwire	4.00
11	Gary Sheffield	1.25
12	Tim Salmon	1.00
13	Ryan Klesko	1.00
14	Manny Ramirez	2.00
15	Mike Piazza	3.50
16	Barry Bonds	5.00
17	Mo Vaughn	1.00
18	Jose Canseco	1.25
19	Juan Gonzalez	1.25
20	Frank Thomas	2.00

Predictor

A new concept in interactive cards was UD's Series II Predictor inserts. Each player's card has four scratch-off baseball bats at the top-

right. Under each bat is printed a specific accomplishment - hit for cycle, CG shutout, etc. - If the player attained that goal during the '97 season, and if the collector had scratched off the correct bat among the four, the Predictor card could be redeemed (with $2) for a premium TV cel card of the player. Thus if the player made one of his goals, the collector had a 25 percent chance of choosing the right bat. Two goals gave a 50 percent chance, etc. The Predictor cards have color action photos of the players at the left end of the horizontal format. The background at left and bottom is a red scorecard motif. Behind the bats is a black-and-white stadium scene. Backs repeat the red scorecard design with contest rules printed in white. A (W) in the checklist here indicates the player won one or more of his goals, making his card eligible for redemption. The redemption period ended Nov. 22, 1997. Values shown are for unscratched cards.

		NM/M
Complete Set (30):		15.00
Common Player:		.10
Values for unscratched cards.
1	Andruw Jones	.40
2	Chipper Jones	.50
3	Greg Maddux (W)	1.00
4	Fred McGriff (W)	.25
5	John Smoltz (W)	.25
6	Brady Anderson (W)	.25
7	Cal Ripken Jr. (W)	2.00
8	Mo Vaughn (W)	.25
9	Sammy Sosa	.50
10	Albert Belle (W)	.25
11	Frank Thomas (W)	.40
12	Kenny Lofton (W)	.25
13	Jim Thome	.30
14	Dante Bichette (W)	.25
15	Andres Galarraga	.10
16	Gary Sheffield	.25
17	Hideo Nomo (W)	.40
18	Mike Piazza (W)	1.25
19	Derek Jeter (W)	2.00
20	Bernie Williams	.10
21	Mark McGwire (W)	1.50
22	Ken Caminiti (W)	.25
23	Tony Gwynn (W)	1.00
24	Barry Bonds (W)	2.00
25	Jay Buhner (W)	.25
26	Ken Griffey Jr. (W)	1.25
27	Alex Rodriguez (W)	1.50
28	Juan Gonzalez (W)	.40
29	Dean Palmer (W)	.25
30	Roger Clemens (W)	1.00

Predictor Prize Cards

Persons who redeemed winning Predictor scratch-off cards prior to the Nov. 22, 1997 deadline received a premium version of that player's card. A $2 per card handling fee was charged. The Predictor prize cards are in a format similar to the scratch-off cards, with a red background on front and back depicting the motif of a baseball score card. The prize cards are printed on plastic in 3-1/2" x 2-1/2" format. Fronts have a player portrait photo at left. At right is a large semi-circular mirrored window with an action photo visible when held to the light. Backs have a few stats, copyright data, logos, etc., with a reverse image in the window. Card fronts were covered with a sheet of peel-off protection plastic. The prize cards are numbered on back with a "P" prefix.

		NM/M
Complete Set (22):		35.00
Common Player:		.60
3	Greg Maddux	2.50
4	Fred McGriff	.60
5	John Smoltz	.60
6	Brady Anderson	.60
7	Cal Ripken Jr.	5.00
8	Mo Vaughn	.60
11	Frank Thomas	1.75
12	Kenny Lofton	.60

14	Dante Bichette	.60
17	Hideo Nomo	1.00
18	Mike Piazza	3.00
19	Derek Jeter	5.00
21	Mark McGwire	4.00
22	Ken Caminiti	.60
23	Tony Gwynn	2.50
24	Barry Bonds	5.00
25	Jay Buhner	.60
26	Ken Griffey Jr.	3.00
27	Alex Rodriguez	4.00
28	Juan Gonzalez	1.00
29	Dean Palmer	.60
30	Roger Clemens	2.75

Rock Solid Foundation

The 20-card, regular-sized set was inserted every seven packs of 1997 Upper Deck baseball. The card fronts feature rainbow foil with the player's name in silver foil along the top border. The team logo appears in gold foil in the lower right corner with "Rock Solid Foundation" also printed in gold foil over a marbled background. The card backs have the same marbled background with a close-up shot on the upper half. A short text is also included and the cards are numbered with the "RS" prefix.

		NM/M
Complete Set (20):		7.50
Common Player:		.15
1	Alex Rodriguez	1.50
2	Rey Ordonez	.15
3	Derek Jeter	2.00
4	Darin Erstad	.35
5	Chipper Jones	1.25
6	Johnny Damon	.35
7	Ryan Klesko	.15
8	Charles Johnson	.15
9	Andy Pettitte	.30
10	Manny Ramirez	.75
11	Ivan Rodriguez	.65
12	Jason Kendall	.15
13	Rondell White	.15
14	Alex Ochoa	.15
15	Javy Lopez	.15
16	Pedro Martinez	.75
17	Carlos Delgado	.50
18	Paul Wilson	.15
19	Alan Benes	.15
20	Raul Mondesi	.15

Run Producers

A 24-card insert found in Series II, Run Producers salutes the top offensive players in the game. Cards were inserted 1:69 packs. Die-cut into a shield shape, the cards have an action photo in a home-plate shaped center section and several colors of foil highlights. Backs have recent stats and career highlights. Cards are numbered with a "RP" prefix.

		NM/M
Complete Set (24):		45.00
Common Player:		.50
1	Ken Griffey Jr.	5.00
2	Barry Bonds	7.50
3	Albert Belle	.50
4	Mark McGwire	6.00

5	Frank Thomas	3.00
6	Juan Gonzalez	1.50
7	Brady Anderson	.50
8	Andres Galarraga	.50
9	Rafael Palmeiro	2.50
10	Alex Rodriguez	6.00
11	Jay Buhner	.50
12	Gary Sheffield	1.50
13	Sammy Sosa	4.00
14	Dante Bichette	.50
15	Mike Piazza	5.00
16	Manny Ramirez	3.00
17	Kenny Lofton	.50
18	Mo Vaughn	.50
19	Tim Salmon	.50
20	Chipper Jones	4.00
21	Jim Thome	2.00
22	Ken Caminiti	.50
23	Jeff Bagwell	3.00
24	Paul Molitor	3.00

Star Attractions

These die-cut cards were inserted one per pack of retail "Memorabila Madness" Collector's Choice (#11-20) and Upper Deck (#1-10) cards. Fronts have action photos, backs have portrait photos. A gold version of the inserts was exclusive to retail packaging.

		NM/M
Complete Set (20):		30.00
Common Player:		.30
Gold:		1.5X
1	Ken Griffey Jr.	3.00
2	Barry Bonds	5.00
3	Jeff Bagwell	2.00
4	Nomar Garciaparra	2.50
5	Tony Gwynn	2.50
6	Roger Clemens	2.75
7	Chipper Jones	2.50
8	Tino Martinez	.30
9	Albert Belle	.30
10	Kenny Lofton	.30
11	Alex Rodriguez	4.00
12	Mark McGwire	4.00
13	Cal Ripken Jr.	5.00
14	Larry Walker	.30
15	Mike Piazza	3.00
16	Frank Thomas	2.00
17	Juan Gonzalez	.65
18	Greg Maddux	2.50
19	Jose Cruz Jr.	.30
20	Mo Vaughn	.30

Ticket to Stardom

The 20-card, regular-sized, die-cut set was inserted every 34 packs of 1997 Upper Deck baseball. Card fronts have a gold-foil border on three sides with a portrait and action photo. Half of the player's league emblem appears on either the left or right border of the horizontal cards, as two cards can be placed together to form a "ticket." The card backs feature an in-depth text with the same headshot as the card front and are numbered with the "TS" prefix.

		NM/M
Complete Set (20):		35.00
Common Player:		.75
1	Chipper Jones	5.00
2	Jermaine Dye	.75
3	Rey Ordonez	.75
4	Alex Ochoa	.75
5	Derek Jeter	7.50
6	Ruben Rivera	.75
7	Billy Wagner	.75
8	Jason Kendall	.75
9	Darin Erstad	1.00
10	Alex Rodriguez	6.00
11	Bob Abreu	.75

12	Richard Hidalgo	.75
13	Karim Garcia	1.00
14	Andruw Jones	4.00
15	Carlos Delgado	1.50
16	Rocky Coppinger	.75
17	Jeff D'Amico	.75
18	Johnny Damon	2.00
19	John Wasdin	.75
20	Manny Ramirez	4.00

Ticket to Stardom Retail

Double-size "full ticket" versions of Upper Deck's Series 1 Ticket to Stardom inserts were produced as an incentive for collectors to buy a boxed three-pack of Collector's Choice cards in a special retail-only packaging. Unlike the insert Ticket cards which feature only one player and measure 3-1/2" x 2-1/2", the retail version measures 5" x 2-1/2" and features two players. The basic format of the retail cards follows the inserts, with gold-foil background, a vignetted player portrait at one end with an action photo toward center and a league logo at center. Arrangement of graphics on the retail ticket prevent unscrupulous persons from cutting them in half and passing them off as the more valuable insert cards. Backs repeat the player portrait photo and present a career summary. Cards are numbered in the upper-left corner. Seven players were dropped from the original Ticket checklist and replaced in the retail issue with new faces. Cards are numbered with a "TS" prefix.

		NM/M
Complete Set (10):		24.00
Common Player:		1.50
1	Chipper Jones,	
	Andruw Jones	4.00
2	Rey Ordonez, Kevin Orie	1.50
3	Derek Jeter,	
	Nomar Garciaparra	6.00
4	Billy Wagner,	
	Jason Kendall	1.50
5	Darin Erstad,	
	Alex Rodriguez	5.00
6	Bob Abreu, Jose Guillen	1.50
7	Wilton Guerrero,	
	Vladimir Guerrero	3.00
8	Carlos Delgado,	
	Rocky Coppinger	2.00
9	Jason Dickson,	
	Johnny Damon	2.00
10	Bartolo Colon,	
	Manny Ramirez	3.00

Ken Griffey Jr. Highlight Reel

Using its trademarked Diamond Vision technology to provide action scenes on these 5" x 3-1/2" plastic cards. Each card has two scenes which go into action as the angle of vision is changed. Cards were sold in retail outlets in plastic blister packs at a suggested $9.99 price.

		NM/M
Complete Set (5):		12.50
Common Card:		3.00
1	Record Setter	
	(Ken Griffey Jr.)	3.00
2	Long Distance Connection	
	(Ken Griffey Jr.)	3.00
3	Home Run Derby	
	(Ken Griffey Jr.)	3.00
4	Swing for the Ages	
	(Ken Griffey Jr.)	3.00
5	Postseason Power	
	(Ken Griffey Jr.)	3.00

Tony Gwynn Commemorative

Tony Gwynn's record-tying eighth batting title in 1997 is commemorated on this 3-1/2" x 4-7/8" card marketed by UD Authenticated. The card has a batting pose on front with a die-cut background of bats citing the year and average of each of his batting titles. The back has three color photos and is numbered within an edition of 2,500.

	NM/M
Tony Gwynn	7.50

Home Team Heroes

These large-format cards were issued both as a 12-card boxed set (original price about $20) and as a blister-pack insert to enhance the sales of special Collector's Choice team sets at Wal-Mart. Each $4.99 pack contains a 14-card team set and a Home Team Heroes card of one of 12 teams, plus a random assortment of Collector's Choice cards. The Heroes cards are 5" x 3-1/2" with a die-cut pattern at top. Fronts are rendered in team colors with two player action photos superimposed on a background of the players' home ballpark. The ballpark scene is executed in etched silver foil and there are silver-foil graphics around the card front. Backs are conventionally printed with small photos and a few sentences about each player.

	NM/M
Complete Set (12):	10.00
Common Player:	.50
1 Alex Rodriguez, Ken Griffey Jr.	2.00
2 Bernie Williams, Derek Jeter	2.50
3 Bernard Gilkey, Randy Hundley	.50
4 Hideo Nomo, Mike Piazza	1.50
5 Andruw Jones, Chipper Jones	1.00
6 John Smoltz, Greg Maddux	1.00
7 Mike Mussina, Cal Ripken Jr.	2.50
8 Andres Galarraga, Dante Bichette	.50
9 Juan Gonzalez, Ivan Rodriguez	.65
10 Albert Belle, Frank Thomas	.75
11 Jim Thome, Manny Ramirez	.75
12 Ken Caminiti, Tony Gwynn	1.00

Jackie Robinson Jumbos

The nine Jackie Robinson commemorative cards which lead off the '97 Upper Deck set were also issued in a large-format (3-

1/2" x 5") version as a complete boxed set. The jumbos are printed in sepia tones on gold-foil backgrounds and, like the standard-size cards, are highlighted with silver-foil graphics on front. Backs are also identical to the regular cards. Complete sets only were sold in a gold-foil stamped box with the 50th anniversary logo.

	NM/M
Complete Set (10):	13.50
Common Player:	2.00
1 The Beginnings (Jackie Robinson)	2.00
2 Breaking the Barrier (Jackie Robinson)	2.00
3 The MVP Season (Jackie Robinson)	2.00
4 The '51 Season (Jackie Robinson)	2.00
5 The '52 and '53 Seasons (Jackie Robinson)	2.00
6 The '54 Season (Jackie Robinson)	2.00
7 The '55 Season (Jackie Robinson)	2.00
8 The '56 Season (Jackie Robinson)	2.00
9 The Hall of Fame (Jackie Robinson)	2.00
-- Checklist	.10

Jackie Robinson Tribute

This retail exclusive card commemorates the 50th anniversary of Robinson's major league debut. The 5" x 3-1/2" card has a tombstone contour top edge and a sepia photo on front of Robinson at bat. Also on front are 50th anniversary and UD logos and a large gold-foil facsimile autograph. Back has a photo of Robinson sliding into home plate, his career stats and a serial number from within an edition of 5,000.

	NM/M
Jackie Robinson	3.50

1997 Upper Deck UD3

Released in April, this 60-card set is broken down into three different 20-card subsets, each utilizing a different print technology. There are 20 PROmotion cards (Light F/X cards featuring a special foil stock), 20 Future Impact cards (Cel-Chrome cards that feature a 3-D image on transparent chromium), and 20 Homerun Heroes (Electric Wood cards printed on an embossed wood/paper stock). Cards were sold in three-card packs (with one subset card per pack) for $3.99 each. Inserts include Superb Signatures, Generation Next and Marquee Attraction.

	NM/M
Complete Set (60):	30.00
Common Player:	.15
Pack (3):	1.50
Wax Box (24):	30.00
1 Mark McGwire	2.50
2 Brady Anderson	.15
3 Ken Griffey Jr.	2.00
4 Albert Belle	.15
5 Andres Galarraga	.15
6 Juan Gonzalez	.40
7 Jay Buhner	.15
8 Mo Vaughn	.15
9 Barry Bonds	3.00
10 Gary Sheffield	.40
11 Todd Hundley	.15
12 Ellis Burks	.15
13 Ken Caminiti	.15
14 Vinny Castilla	.15
15 Sammy Sosa	1.50
16 Frank Thomas	.75

17 Rafael Palmeiro	.65
18 Mike Piazza	2.00
19 Matt Williams	.15
20 Eddie Murray	.75
21 Roger Clemens	1.75
22 Tim Salmon	.15
23 Robin Ventura	.15
24 Ron Gant	.15
25 Cal Ripken Jr.	3.00
26 Bernie Williams	.15
27 Hideo Nomo	.40
28 Ivan Rodriguez	.65
29 John Smoltz	.15
30 Paul Molitor	.75
31 Greg Maddux	1.50
32 Raul Mondesi	.15
33 Roberto Alomar	.25
34 Barry Larkin	.15
35 Tony Gwynn	1.50
36 Jim Thome	.60
37 Kenny Lofton	.15
38 Jeff Bagwell	.75
39 Ozzie Smith	1.50
40 Kirby Puckett	1.50
41 Andruw Jones	.75
42 Vladimir Guerrero	.75
43 Edgar Renteria	.15
44 Luis Castillo	.15
45 Darin Erstad	.30
46 Nomar Garciaparra	1.50
47 Todd Greene	.15
48 Jason Kendall	.15
49 Rey Ordonez	.15
50 Alex Rodriguez	2.50
51 Manny Ramirez	.75
52 Todd Walker	.15
53 Ruben Rivera	.15
54 Andy Pettitte	.30
55 Derek Jeter	3.00
56 Todd Hollandsworth	.15
57 Rocky Coppinger	.15
58 Scott Rolen	.60
59 Jermaine Dye	.15
60 Chipper Jones	1.50

Generation Next

A 20-card insert saluting the game's up-and-coming stars with two different photos of the player on each card front. Odds of finding these cards were 1:11 packs. Cards are numbered with a "GN" prefix.

	NM/M
Complete Set (20):	35.00
Common Player:	1.00
1 Alex Rodriguez	5.00
2 Vladimir Guerrero	2.50
3 Luis Castillo	1.00
4 Rey Ordonez	1.00
5 Andruw Jones	2.50
6 Darin Erstad	1.25
7 Edgar Renteria	1.00
8 Jason Kendall	1.00
9 Jermaine Dye	1.00
10 Chipper Jones	3.00
11 Rocky Coppinger	1.00
12 Andy Pettitte	1.25
13 Todd Greene	1.00
14 Todd Hollandsworth	1.00
15 Derek Jeter	6.00
16 Ruben Rivera	1.00
17 Todd Walker	1.00
18 Nomar Garciaparra	3.00
19 Scott Rolen	2.00
20 Manny Ramirez	2.50

Marquee Attraction

The game's top names are featured in this insert set, inserted 1:144 packs. Cards featured a peel-off protector that would expose a holographic image on the card fronts. Cards are numbered with a "MA" prefix.

	NM/M
Complete Set (10):	40.00
Common Player:	1.25
1 Ken Griffey Jr.	6.00
2 Mark McGwire	7.50
3 Juan Gonzalez	1.75
4 Barry Bonds	9.00
5 Frank Thomas	2.50
6 Albert Belle	1.25
7 Mike Piazza	6.00

8 Cal Ripken Jr.	9.00
9 Mo Vaughn	1.25
10 Alex Rodriguez	7.50

Superb Signatures

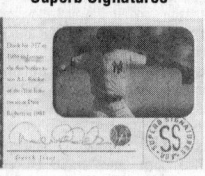

Autographed cards of Ken Griffey Jr., Ken Caminiti, Vladimir Guerrero, and Derek Jeter were inserted 1:1,500 packs.

	NM/M
Complete Set (4):	450.00
Common Autograph:	15.00
1 Ken Caminiti	45.00
2 Ken Griffey Jr.	150.00
3 Vladimir Guerrero	50.00
4 Derek Jeter	225.00

Pepsi Mariners Insert

Though unmarked as such, this set was sponsored by Pepsi with single cards inserted into 12-packs of soda in the Northwest. Format of the cards is similar to UD's regular 1996 issue, with borderless color photos on front and back. At bottom-front is a Mariners-blue foil area with the player identification. Backs differ from the regular '96 UD cards in the use of a "M" prefix to the card number.

	NM/M
Complete Set (19):	12.00
Common Player:	.25
1 Joey Cora	.25
2 Ken Griffey Jr.	5.00
3 Jay Buhner	.50
4 Alex Rodriguez	6.00
5 Norm Charlton	.25
6 Edgar Martinez	.50
7 Paul Sorrento	.25
8 Randy Johnson	2.00
9 Rich Amaral	.25
10 Russ Davis	.25
11 Bob Wolcott	.25
12 Jamie Moyer	.25
13 Bob Wells	.25
14 Makoto Suzuki	.25
15 Dan Wilson	.25
16 Tim Davis	.25
17 Bobby Ayala	.25
18 Salomon Torres	.25
19 Raul Ibanez	.25

1997 Upper Deck/Pepsi Mariners SGA

This team set, sponsored by Pepsi, was a stadium give-away to the first 20,000 fans attending the July 12 game at the Kingdome. Format of the cards is similar to UD's regular 1996 issue, with borderless color photos on front and back. At bottom-front is a Mariners-blue foil

area with the player identification. Backs differ from the regular '96 UD cards in the use of a "P" prefix to the card number and the inclusion of a Pepsi logo at lower-left.

	NM/M
Complete Set (21):	12.00
Common Player:	.25
1 Joey Cora	.25
2 Ken Griffey Jr.	5.00
3 Jay Buhner	.50
4 Alex Rodriguez	6.00
5 Norm Charlton	.25
6 Edgar Martinez	.50
7 Paul Sorrento	.25
8 Randy Johnson	2.00
9 Rich Amaral	.25
10 Russ Davis	.25
11 Greg McCarthy	.25
12 Jamie Moyer	.25
13 Jeff Fassero	.25
14 Scott Sanders	.25
15 Dan Wilson	.25
16 Mike Blowers	.25
17 Bobby Ayala	.25
18 Brent Gates	.25
19 John Marzano	.25
20 Lou Piniella	.25
--- Pepsi Header Card/Coupon	.05

Shimano

Two ballplayers are included with four professional fishermen in this set produced by Upper Deck as a premium with the purchase of Shimano fishing reels. Fronts have pictures of the fishermen displaying their trophy. Backs have a portrait photo, baseball and fishing stats and data.

	NM/M
5 Jay Buhner	3.00
6 Tony Gwynn	30.00

1998 Upper Deck

Upper Deck Baseball was released in three series. Series 1 consists of 270 base cards, with five subsets. Inserts included A Piece of the Action, Amazing Greats, National Pride, Ken Griffey Jr.'s Home Run Chronicles and 10th Anniversary Preview. The 270-card Series 2 also has five subsets. Inserts include Prime Nine, Ken Griffey Jr.'s Home Run Chronicles, Tape Measure Titans, Blue Chip Prospects, Clearly Dominant and A Piece of the Action. The third series, Upper Deck Rookie Edition, has a 210-card base set. Cards #601-630, the Eminent Prestige subset, are short-printed, about one per four packs. Mike Piazza's card in Series 3 can be found depicting him either as a Marlin or a Met. Insert sets were Ken Griffey Jr. Game Jersey, Game Jersey Rookie Cards, Unparalleled, Destination Stardom, All-Star Credentials and Retrospectives.

	NM/M
Complete Set (750):	100.00
Complete Series 1 Set (270):	25.00
Complete Series 2 Set (270):	25.00
Complete Series 3 Set (210):	75.00
Common Eminent Prestige (601-630):	.25
Common Player:	.05
Series 1 or 2 Pack (12):	1.50
Series 3 Pack (10):	1.50
Series 1 or 2 Wax Box (24):	35.00
Series 3 Wax Box (24):	35.00
1 Tino Martinez (History in the Making)	.05
2 Jimmy Key (History in the Making)	.05
3 Jay Buhner (History in the Making)	.05
4 Mark Gardner (History in the Making)	.05
5 Greg Maddux (History in the Making)	.05
6 Pedro Martinez (History in the Making)	.05
7 Hideo Nomo, Shigetoshi Hasegawa (History in the Making)	.25
8 Sammy Sosa (History in the Making)	.35
9 Mark McGwire (Griffey Hot List)	.50
10 Ken Griffey Jr. (Griffey Hot List)	.45
11 Larry Walker (Griffey Hot List)	.05
12 Tino Martinez (Griffey Hot List)	.05
13 Mike Piazza (Griffey Hot List)	.40
14 Jose Cruz, Jr. (Griffey Hot List)	.05
15 Tony Gwynn (Griffey Hot List)	.25
16 Greg Maddux (Griffey Hot List)	.25
17 Roger Clemens (Griffey Hot List)	.35
18 Alex Rodriguez (Griffey Hot List)	.50
19 Shigetoshi Hasegawa	.05
20 Eddie Murray	.50
21 Jason Dickson	.05
22 Darin Erstad	.25
23 Chuck Finley	.05
24 Dave Hollins	.05
25 Garret Anderson	.05
26 Michael Tucker	.05
27 Kenny Lofton	.25
28 Javier Lopez	.05
29 Fred McGriff	.05
30 Greg Maddux	.65
31 Jeff Blauser	.05
32 John Smoltz	.05
33 Mark Wohlers	.05
34 Scott Erickson	.05
35 Jimmy Key	.05
36 Harold Baines	.05
37 Randy Myers	.05
38 B.J. Surhoff	.05
39 Eric Davis	.05
40 Rafael Palmeiro	.35
41 Jeffrey Hammonds	.05
42 Mo Vaughn	.25
43 Tom Gordon	.05
44 Tim Naehring	.05
45 Darren Bragg	.05
46 Aaron Sele	.05
47 Troy O'Leary	.05
48 John Valentin	.05
49 Doug Glanville	.05
50 Ryne Sandberg	.65
51 Steve Trachsel	.05
52 Mark Grace	.25
53 Kevin Foster	.05
54 Kevin Tapani	.05
55 Kevin Orie	.05
56 Lyle Mouton	.05
57 Ray Durham	.05
58 Jaime Navarro	.05
59 Mike Cameron	.05
60 Albert Belle	.05
61 Doug Drabek	.05
62 Chris Snopek	.05
63 Eddie Taubensee	.05
64 Terry Pendleton	.05
65 Barry Larkin	.05
66 Willie Greene	.05
67 Deion Sanders	.05
68 Pokey Reese	.05
69 Jeff Shaw	.05
70 Jim Thome	.35
71 Orel Hershiser	.05
72 Omar Vizquel	.05
73 Brian Giles	.05
74 David Justice	.05
75 Bartolo Colon	.05
76 Sandy Alomar Jr.	.05
77 Neifi Perez	.05
78 Eric Young	.05
79 Vinny Castilla	.05
80 Dante Bichette	.05
81 Quinton McCracken	.05
82 Jamey Wright	.05
83 John Thomson	.05
84 Damion Easley	.05
85 Justin Thompson	.05
86 Willie Blair	.05

No.	Player	Price
87	Raul Casanova	.05
88	Bobby Higginson	.05
89	Bubba Trammell	.05
90	Tony Clark	.05
91	Livan Hernandez	.05
92	Charles Johnson	.05
93	Edgar Renteria	.05
94	Alex Fernandez	.05
95	Gary Sheffield	.30
96	Moises Alou	.05
97	Tony Saunders	.05
98	Robb Nen	.05
99	Darryl Kile	.05
100	Craig Biggio	.05
101	Chris Holt	.05
102	Bob Abreu	.10
103	Luis Gonzalez	.05
104	Billy Wagner	.05
105	Brad Ausmus	.05
106	Chili Davis	.05
107	Tim Belcher	.05
108	Dean Palmer	.05
109	Jeff King	.05
110	Jose Rosado	.05
111	Mike Macfarlane	.05
112	Jay Bell	.05
113	Todd Worrell	.05
114	Chan Ho Park	.05
115	Raul Mondesi	.05
116	Brett Butler	.05
117	Greg Gagne	.05
118	Hideo Nomo	.25
119	Todd Zeile	.05
120	Eric Karros	.05
121	Cal Eldred	.05
122	Jeff D'Amico	.05
123	Antone Williamson	.05
124	Doug Jones	.05
125	Dave Nilsson	.05
126	Gerald Williams	.05
127	Fernando Vina	.05
128	Ron Coomer	.05
129	Matt Lawton	.05
130	Paul Molitor	.50
131	Todd Walker	.05
132	Rick Aguilera	.05
133	Brad Radke	.05
134	Bob Tewksbury	.05
135	Vladimir Guerrero	.50
136	Tony Gwynn (Define The Game)	.25
137	Roger Clemens (Define The Game)	.35
138	Dennis Eckersley (Define The Game)	.15
139	Brady Anderson (Define The Game)	.05
140	Ken Griffey Jr. (Define The Game)	.40
141	Derek Jeter (Define The Game)	.75
142	Ken Caminiti (Define The Game)	.05
143	Frank Thomas (Define The Game)	.20
144	Barry Bonds (Define The Game)	.75
145	Cal Ripken Jr. (Define The Game)	.75
146	Alex Rodriguez (Define The Game)	.50
147	Greg Maddux (Define The Game)	.25
148	Kenny Lofton (Define The Game)	.05
149	Mike Piazza (Define The Game)	.40
150	Mark McGwire (Define The Game)	.50
151	Andruw Jones (Define The Game)	.20
152	Rusty Greer (Define The Game)	.05
153	F.P. Santangelo (Define The Game)	.05
154	Mike Lansing	.05
155	Lee Smith	.05
156	Carlos Perez	.05
157	Pedro Martinez	.50
158	Ryan McGuire	.05
159	F.P. Santangelo	.05
160	Rondell White	.05
161	Takashi Kashiwada RC	.05
162	Butch Huskey	.05
163	Edgardo Alfonzo	.05
164	John Franco	.05
165	Todd Hundley	.05
166	Rey Ordonez	.05
167	Armando Reynoso	.05
168	John Olerud	.05
169	Bernie Williams	.05
170	Andy Pettitte	.15
171	Wade Boggs	.65
172	Paul O'Neill	.05
173	Cecil Fielder	.05
174	Charlie Hayes	.05
175	David Cone	.05
176	Hideki Irabu	.05
177	Mark Bellhorn	.05
178	Steve Karsay	.05
179	Damon Mashore	.05
180	Jason McDonald	.05
181	Scott Spiezio	.05
182	Ariel Prieto	.05
183	Jason Giambi	.30
184	Wendell Magee	.05
185	Rico Brogna	.05
186	Garrett Stephenson	.05
187	Wayne Gomes	.05
188	Ricky Bottalico	.05
189	Mickey Morandini	.05
190	Mike Lieberthal	.05
191	Kevin Polcovich RC	.05
192	Francisco Cordova	.05
193	Kevin Young	.05
194	Jon Lieber	.05
195	Kevin Elster	.05
196	Tony Womack	.05
197	Lou Collier	.05
198	Mike Defelice RC	.05
199	Gary Gaetti	.05
200	Dennis Eckersley	.40
201	Alan Benes	.05
202	Willie McGee	.05
203	Ron Gant	.05
204	Fernando Valenzuela	.05
205	Mark McGwire	1.00
206	Archi Cianfrocco	.05
207	Andy Ashby	.05
208	Steve Finley	.05
209	Quilvio Veras	.05
210	Ken Caminiti	.05
211	Rickey Henderson	.50
212	Joey Hamilton	.05
213	Derek Lee	.30
214	Bill Mueller	.05
215	Shawn Estes	.05
216	J.T. Snow	.05
217	Mark Gardner	.05
218	Terry Mulholland	.05
219	Dante Powell	.05
220	Jeff Kent	.05
221	Jamie Moyer	.05
222	Joey Cora	.05
223	Jeff Fassero	.05
224	Dennis Martinez	.05
225	Ken Griffey Jr.	.75
226	Edgar Martinez	.05
227	Russ Davis	.05
228	Dan Wilson	.05
229	Will Clark	.40
230	Ivan Rodriguez	.40
231	Benji Gil	.05
232	Lee Stevens	.05
233	Mickey Tettleton	.05
234	Julio Santana	.05
235	Rusty Greer	.05
236	Bobby Witt	.05
237	Ed Sprague	.05
238	Pat Hentgen	.05
239	Kevin Escobar	.05
240	Joe Carter	.05
241	Carlos Delgado	.25
242	Shannon Stewart	.05
243	Benito Santiago	.05
244	Tino Martinez (Season Highlights)	.05
245	Ken Griffey Jr. (Season Highlights)	.40
246	Kevin Brown (Season Highlights)	.05
247	Ryne Sandberg (Season Highlights)	.35
248	Mo Vaughn (Season Highlights)	.05
249	Darryl Hamilton (Season Highlights)	.05
250	Randy Johnson (Season Highlights)	.20
251	Steve Finley (Season Highlights)	.05
252	Bobby Higginson (Season Highlights)	.05
253	Brett Tomko/SR	.05
254	Mark Kotsay/SR	.05
255	Jose Guillen/SR	.05
256	Elieser Marrero/SR	.05
257	Dennis Reyes/SR	.05
258	Richie Sexson/SR	.05
259	Pat Cline/SR	.05
260	Todd Helton/SR	.50
261	Juan Melo/SR	.05
262	Matt Morris/SR	.05
263	Jeremi Gonzalez/SR	.05
264	Jeff Abbott/SR	.05
265	Aaron Boone/SR	.05
266	Todd Dunwoody/SR	.05
267	Jaret Wright/SR	.05
268	Derrick Gibson/SR	.05
269	Mario Valdez/SR	.05
270	Fernando Tatis/SR	.05
271	Craig Counsell/SR	.05
272	Brad Rigby/SR	.05
273	Danny Clyburn/SR	.05
274	Brian Rose/SR	.05
275	Miguel Tejada/SR	.15
276	Jason Varitek/SR	.05
277	David Dellucci/SR RC	.15
278	Michael Coleman/SR	.05
279	Adam Riggs/SR	.05
280	Ben Grieve/SR	.05
281	Brad Fullmer/SR	.05
282	Ken Cloude/SR	.05
283	Tom Evans/SR	.05
284	Kevin Millwood/SR RC	.05
285	Paul Konerko/SR	.15
286	Juan Encarnacion/SR	.05
287	Chris Carpenter/SR	.05
288	Tom Fordham/SR	.05
289	Gary DiSarcina	.05
290	Tim Salmon	.05
291	Troy Percival	.05
292	Todd Greene	.05
293	Ken Hill	.05
294	Dennis Springer	.05
295	Jim Edmonds	.05
296	Allen Watson	.05
297	Brian Anderson	.05
298	Keith Lockhart	.05
299	Tom Glavine	.20
300	Chipper Jones	.75
301	Randall Simon	.05
302	Mark Lemke	.05
303	Ryan Klesko	.05
304	Denny Neagle	.05
305	Andruw Jones	.50
306	Mike Mussina	.30
307	Brady Anderson	.05
308	Chris Hoiles	.05
309	Mike Bordick	.05
310	Cal Ripken Jr.	1.50
311	Geronimo Berroa	.05
312	Armando Benitez	.05
313	Roberto Alomar	.25
314	Tim Wakefield	.05
315	Reggie Jefferson	.05
316	Jeff Frye	.05
317	Scott Hatteberg	.05
318	Steve Avery	.05
319	Robinson Checo	.05
320	Nomar Garciaparra	.65
321	Lance Johnson	.05
322	Tyler Houston	.05
323	Mark Clark	.05
324	Terry Adams	.05
325	Sammy Sosa	.65
326	Scott Servais	.05
327	Manny Alexander	.05
328	Norberto Martin	.05
329	Scott Eyre RC	.05
330	Frank Thomas	.50
331	Robin Ventura	.05
332	Matt Karchner	.05
333	Keith Foulke	.05
334	James Baldwin	.05
335	Chris Stynes	.05
336	Bret Boone	.05
337	Jon Nunnally	.05
338	Dave Burba	.05
339	Eduardo Perez	.05
340	Reggie Sanders	.05
341	Mike Remlinger	.05
342	Pat Watkins	.05
343	Chad Ogea	.05
344	Jon Smiley	.05
345	Kenny Lofton	.05
346	Jose Mesa	.05
347	Charles Nagy	.05
348	Bruce Aven	.05
349	Enrique Wilson	.05
350	Manny Ramirez	.50
351	Jerry DiPoto	.05
352	Ellis Burks	.05
353	Vinny Castilla	.05
354	Larry Walker	.05
355	Kevin Ritz	.05
356	Pedro Astacio	.05
357	Scott Sanders	.05
358	Deivi Cruz	.05
359	Brian L. Hunter	.05
360	Pedro Martinez (History in the Making)	.20
361	Tom Glavine (History in the Making)	.05
362	Willie McGee (History in the Making)	.05
363	J.T. Snow (History in the Making)	.05
364	Rusty Greer (History in the Making)	.05
365	Mike Grace (History in the Making)	.05
366	Alex Rodriguez (History in the Making)	.50
367	Tony Clark (History in the Making)	.05
368	Ben Grieve (History in the Making)	.05
369	Gary Sheffield (History in the Making)	.10
370	Joe Oliver	.05
371	Todd Jones	.05
372	Frank Catalanotto RC	.10
373	Brian Moehler	.05
374	Cliff Floyd	.05
375	Bobby Bonilla	.05
376	Al Leiter	.05
377	Josh Booty	.05
378	Darren Daulton	.05
379	Jay Powell	.05
380	Felix Heredia	.05
381	Jim Eisenreich	.05
382	Richard Hidalgo	.05
383	Mike Hampton	.05
384	Shane Reynolds	.05
385	Jeff Bagwell	.50
386	Derek Bell	.05
387	Ricky Gutierrez	.05
388	Bill Spiers	.05
389	Jose Offerman	.25
390	Johnny Damon	.25
391	Jermaine Dye	.05
392	Jeff Montgomery	.05
393	Glendon Rusch	.05
394	Mike Sweeney	.05
395	Kevin Appier	.05
396	Joe Vitiello	.05
397	Ramon Martinez	.05
398	Darren Dreifort	.05
399	Wilton Guerrero	.05
400	Mike Piazza	.75
401	Eddie Murray	.50
402	Ismael Valdes	.05
403	Todd Hollandsworth	.05
404	Mark Loretta	.05
405	Jeromy Burnitz	.05
406	Jeff Cirillo	.05
407	Scott Karl	.05
408	Mike Matheny	.05
409	Jose Valentin	.05
410	John Jaha	.05
411	Terry Steinbach	.05
412	Torii Hunter	.05
413	Pat Meares	.05
414	Marty Cordova	.05
415	Jaret Wright	.05
416	Mike Mussina (Postseason Headliners)	.10
417	John Smoltz (Postseason Headliners)	.05
418	Devon White (Postseason Headliners)	.05
419	Denny Neagle (Postseason Headliners)	.05
420	Livan Hernandez (Postseason Headliners)	.05
421	Kevin Brown (Postseason Headliners)	.05
422	Marquis Grissom (Postseason Headliners)	.05
423	Mike Mussina (Postseason Headliners)	.10
424	Eric Davis (Postseason Headliners)	.05
425	Tony Fernandez (Postseason Headliners)	.05
426	Moises Alou (Postseason Headliners)	.05
427	Sandy Alomar Jr. (Postseason Headliners)	.05
428	Gary Sheffield (Postseason Headliners)	.10
429	Jaret Wright (Postseason Headliners)	.05
430	Livan Hernandez (Postseason Headliners)	.05
431	Chad Ogea (Postseason Headliners)	.05
432	Edgar Renteria (Postseason Headliners)	.05
433	LaTroy Hawkins	.05
434	Rich Robertson	.05
435	Chuck Knoblauch	.05
436	Jose Vidro	.05
437	Dustin Hermanson	.05
438	Jim Bullinger	.05
439	Orlando Cabrera/SR	.10
440	Vladimir Guerrero	.50
441	Ugueth Urbina	.05
442	Brian McRae	.05
443	Matt Franco	.05
444	Bobby Jones	.05
445	Bernard Gilkey	.05
446	Dave Mlicki	.05
447	Brian Bohanon	.05
448	Mel Rojas	.05
449	Tim Raines	.05
450	Derek Jeter	1.50
451	Roger Clemens (Upper Echelon)	.35
452	Nomar Garciaparra (Upper Echelon)	.35
453	Mike Piazza (Upper Echelon)	.40
454	Mark McGwire (Upper Echelon)	.50
455	Ken Griffey Jr. (Upper Echelon)	.40
456	Larry Walker (Upper Echelon)	.05
457	Alex Rodriguez (Upper Echelon)	.50
458	Tony Gwynn (Upper Echelon)	.25
459	Frank Thomas (Upper Echelon)	.20
460	Tino Martinez	.05
461	Chad Curtis	.05
462	Ramiro Mendoza	.05
463	Joe Girardi	.05
464	David Wells	.05
465	Mariano Rivera	.15
466	Willie Adams	.05
467	George Williams	.05
468	Dave Telgheder	.05
469	Dave Magadan	.05
470	Matt Stairs	.05
471	Billy Taylor	.05
472	Jimmy Haynes	.05
473	Gregg Jefferies	.05
474	Midre Cummings	.05
475	Curt Schilling	.15
476	Mike Grace	.05
477	Mark Leiter	.05
478	Matt Beech	.05
479	Scott Rolen	.35
480	Jason Kendall	.05
481	Esteban Loaiza	.05
482	Jermaine Allensworth	.05
483	Mark Smith	.05
484	Jason Schmidt	.05
485	Jose Guillen	.05
486	Al Martin	.05
487	Delino DeShields	.05
488	Todd Stottlemyre	.05
489	Brian Jordan	.05
490	Ray Lankford	.05
491	Matt Morris	.05
492	Royce Clayton	.05
493	John Mabry	.05
494	Wally Joyner	.05
495	Trevor Hoffman	.05
496	Chris Gomez	.05
497	Sterling Hitchcock	.05
498	Pete Smith	.05
499	Greg Vaughn	.05
500	Tony Gwynn	.65
501	Will Cunnane	.05
502	Darryl Hamilton	.05
503	Brian Johnson	.05
504	Kirk Rueter	.05
505	Barry Bonds	1.50
506	Osvaldo Fernandez	.05
507	Stan Javier	.05
508	Julian Tavarez	.05
509	Rich Aurilia	.05
510	Alex Rodriguez	1.00
511	David Segui	.05
512	Rich Amaral	.05
513	Raul Ibanez	.25
514	Jay Buhner	.05
515	Randy Johnson	.50
516	Heathcliff Slocumb	.05
517	Tony Saunders	.05
518	Kevin Elster	.05
519	John Burkett	.05
520	Juan Gonzalez	.25
521	John Wetteland	.05
522	Domingo Cedeno	.05
523	Darren Oliver	.05
524	Roger Pavlik	.05
525	Jose Cruz Jr.	.05
526	Woody Williams	.05
527	Alex Gonzalez	.05
528	Robert Person	.05
529	Juan Guzman	.05
530	Roger Clemens	.70
531	Shawn Green	.20
532	Cordova, Ricon, Smith (Season Highlights)	.05
533	Nomar Garciaparra (Season Highlights)	.35
534	Roger Clemens (Season Highlights)	.35
535	Mark McGwire (Season Highlights)	.50
536	Larry Walker (Season Highlights)	.05
537	Mike Piazza (Season Highlights)	.40
538	Curt Schilling (Season Highlights)	.05
539	Tony Gwynn (Season Highlights)	.25
540	Ken Griffey Jr. (Season Highlights)	.40
541	Carl Pavano/SR	.05
542	Shane Monahan/SR	.05
543	Gabe Kapler/SR RC	.25
544	Eric Milton/SR	.05
545	Gary Matthews Jr./SR RC	.25
546	Mike Kinkade/SR RC	.25
547	Ryan Christenson/SR RC	.10
548	Corey Koskie/SR RC	.25
549	Norm Hutchins/SR	.05
550	Russell Branyan/SR	.25
551	Masato Yoshii/SR RC	.25
552	Jesus Sanchez/SR RC	.05
553	Anthony Sanders/SR	.05
554	Edwin Diaz/SR	.05
555	Gabe Alvarez/SR	.05
556	Carlos Lee/SR RC	.25
557	Mike Darr/SR	.05
558	Kerry Wood/SR	.20
559	Carlos Guillen/SR	.15
560	Sean Casey/SR	.15
561	Manny Aybar/SR RC	.05
562	Octavio Dotel/SR	.05
563	Jarrod Washburn/SR	.05
564	Mark L. Johnson/SR	.05
565	Ramon Hernandez/SR	.05
566	Rich Butler/SR RC	.05
567	Mike Caruso/SR	.05
568	Cliff Politte/SR	.05
569	Scott Elarton/SR	.05
570	Magglio Ordonez/SR RC	1.50
571	Adam Butler/SR RC	.05
572	Marlon Anderson/SR	.05
573	Julio Ramirez/SR RC	.05
574	Darron Ingram/SR RC	.05
575	Bruce Chen/SR	.05
576	Steve Woodard/SR RC	.05
577	Hiram Bocachica/SR	.05
578	Kevin Witt/SR	.05
579	Javier Vazquez/SR	.10
580	Alex Gonzalez/SR	.05
581	Brian Powell/SR	.05
582	Wes Helms/SR	.05
583	Ron Wright/SR	.05
584	Rafael Medina/SR	.05
585	Daryle Ward/SR	.05
586	Geoff Jenkins/SR	.05
587	Preston Wilson/SR	.10
588	Jim Chamblee/SR	.05
589	Mike Lowell/SR RC	2.00
590	A.J. Hinch/SR	.05
591	Francisco Cordero/SR RC	.10
592	Rolando Arrojo/SR RC	.25
593	Braden Looper/SR	.05
594	Sidney Ponson/SR	.05
595	Matt Clement/SR	.05
596	Carlton Loewer/SR	.05
597	Brian Meadows/SR	.05
598	Danny Klassen/SR	.05
599	Larry Sutton/SR	.05
600	Travis Lee/SR	.15
601	Randy Johnson (Eminent Prestige)	1.50
602	Greg Maddux (Eminent Prestige)	2.00
603	Roger Clemens (Eminent Prestige)	2.25
604	Jaret Wright (Eminent Prestige)	.25
605	Mike Piazza (Eminent Prestige)	2.50
606	Tino Martinez (Eminent Prestige)	.25
607	Frank Thomas (Eminent Prestige)	1.50
608	Mo Vaughn (Eminent Prestige)	.25
609	Todd Helton (Eminent Prestige)	1.00
610	Mark McGwire (Eminent Prestige)	3.00
611	Jeff Bagwell (Eminent Prestige)	1.50
612	Travis Lee (Eminent Prestige)	.40
613	Scott Rolen (Eminent Prestige)	1.00
614	Cal Ripken Jr. (Eminent Prestige)	4.00
615	Chipper Jones (Eminent Prestige)	2.00
616	Nomar Garciaparra (Eminent Prestige)	2.00
617	Alex Rodriguez (Eminent Prestige)	3.00
618	Derek Jeter (Eminent Prestige)	4.00
619	Tony Gwynn (Eminent Prestige)	2.00
620	Ken Griffey Jr. (Eminent Prestige)	2.50
621	Kenny Lofton (Eminent Prestige)	.25
622	Juan Gonzalez (Eminent Prestige)	.75
623	Jose Cruz Jr. (Eminent Prestige)	.25
624	Larry Walker (Eminent Prestige)	.25
625	Barry Bonds (Eminent Prestige)	4.00
626	Ben Grieve (Eminent Prestige)	.25
627	Andruw Jones (Eminent Prestige)	1.50
628	Vladimir Guerrero (Eminent Prestige)	1.50
629	Paul Konerko (Eminent Prestige)	.50
630	Paul Molitor (Eminent Prestige)	1.50
631	Cecil Fielder	.05
632	Jack McDowell	.05
633	Mike James	.05
634	Brian Anderson	.05
635	Jay Bell	.05
636	Devon White	.05
637	Andy Stankiewicz	.05
638	Tony Batista	.05
639	Omar Daal	.05
640	Matt Williams	.05
641	Brent Brede	.05
642	Jorge Fabregas	.05
643	Karim Garcia	.10
644	Felix Rodriguez	.05
645	Andy Benes	.05
646	Willie Blair	.05
647	Jeff Suppan	.05
648	Yamil Benitez	.05
649	Walt Weiss	.05
650	Andres Galarraga	.05
651	Doug Drabek	.05
652	Ozzie Guillen	.05
653	Joe Carter	.05
654	Dennis Eckersley	.40
655	Pedro Martinez	.50
656	Jim Leyritz	.05
657	Henry Rodriguez	.05
658	Rod Beck	.05
659	Mickey Morandini	.05
660	Jeff Blauser	.05
661	Ruben Sierra	.05
662	Mike Sirotka	.05
663	Pete Harnisch	.05
664	Damian Jackson	.05
665	Dmitri Young	.05
666	Steve Cooke	.05
667	Geronimo Berroa	.05
668	Shawon Dunston	.05
669	Mike Jackson	.05
670	Travis Fryman	.05
671	Dwight Gooden	.05
672	Paul Assenmacher	.05
673	Eric Plunk	.05
674	Mike Lansing	.05
675	Darryl Kile	.05
676	Luis Gonzalez	.05
677	Frank Castillo	.05
678	Joe Randa	.05
679	Bip Roberts	.05
680	Derrek Lee	.30
681a	Mike Piazza (Marlins)	2.00
681b	Mike Piazza (Mets)	1.00
682	Sean Berry	.05
683	Ramon Garcia	.05
684	Carl Everett	.05
685	Moises Alou	.05
686	Hal Morris	.05
687	Jeff Conine	.05
688	Gary Sheffield	.25
689	Jose Vizcaino	.05
690	Charles Johnson	.05
691	Bobby Bonilla	.05

692	Marquis Grissom	.05
693	Alex Ochoa	.05
694	Mike Morgan	.05
695	Orlando Merced	.05
696	David Ortiz	.30
697	Brent Gates	.05
698	Otis Nixon	.05
699	Trey Moore	.05
700	Derrick May	.05
701	Rich Becker	.05
702	Al Leiter	.05
703	Chili Davis	.05
704	Scott Brosius	.05
705	Chuck Knoblauch	.05
706	Kenny Rogers	.05
707	Mike Blowers	.05
708	Mike Fetters	.05
709	Tom Candiotti	.05
710	Rickey Henderson	.50
711	Bob Abreu	.05
712	Mark Lewis	.05
713	Doug Glanville	.05
714	Desi Relaford	.05
715	Kent Mercker	.05
716	J. Kevin Brown	.05
717	James Mouton	.05
718	Mark Langston	.05
719	Greg Myers	.05
720	Orel Hershiser	.05
721	Charlie Hayes	.05
722	Robb Nen	.05
723	Glenallen Hill	.05
724	Tony Saunders	.05
725	Wade Boggs	.65
726	Kevin Stocker	.05
727	Wilson Alvarez	.05
728	Albie Lopez	.05
729	Dave Martinez	.05
730	Fred McGriff	.05
731	Quinton McCracken	.05
732	Bryan Rekar	.05
733	Paul Sorrento	.05
734	Roberto Hernandez	.05
735	Bubba Trammell	.05
736	Miguel Cairo	.05
737	John Flaherty	.05
738	Terrell Wade	.05
739	Roberto Kelly	.05
740	Mark Mclemore (McLemore)	.05
741	Danny Patterson	.05
742	Aaron Sele	.05
743	Tony Fernandez	.05
744	Randy Myers	.05
745	Jose Canseco	.30
746	Darrin Fletcher	.05
747	Mike Stanley	.05
748	Marquis Grissom (Season Highlights)	.05
749	Fred McGriff (Season Highlights)	.05
750	Travis Lee (Season Highlights)	.05

Amazing Greats

The 30-card Amazing Greats insert is printed on acetate. The cards are labeled "One of 2,000." A die-cut parallel was sequentially numbered to 250. Amazing Greats was an insert in Upper Deck Series One packs. Cards carry an "AG" prefix.

		NM/M
Complete Set (30):		75.00
Common Player:		.60
Die-Cuts (250):		8X
1	Ken Griffey Jr.	5.00
2	Derek Jeter	7.50
3	Alex Rodriguez	6.00
4	Paul Molitor	3.00
5	Jeff Bagwell	3.00
6	Larry Walker	.60
7	Kenny Lofton	.60
8	Cal Ripken Jr.	7.50
9	Juan Gonzalez	1.50
10	Chipper Jones	4.00
11	Greg Maddux	4.00
12	Roberto Alomar	1.25
13	Mike Piazza	5.00
14	Andres Galarraga	.60
15	Barry Bonds	7.50
16	Andy Pettitte	1.25
17	Nomar Garciaparra	4.00
18	Hideki Irabu	.60
19	Tony Gwynn	4.00
20	Frank Thomas	3.00

21	Roger Clemens	4.50
22	Sammy Sosa	5.00
23	Jose Cruz, Jr.	.60
24	Manny Ramirez	3.00
25	Mark McGwire	6.00
26	Randy Johnson	3.00
27	Mo Vaughn	.60
28	Gary Sheffield	1.50
29	Andruw Jones	3.00
30	Albert Belle	.60

A Piece of the Action

A Piece of the Action was inserted in Series 1, 2 and 3 packs. Series 1 featured 10 cards: five with a piece of game-used jersey and five with a piece of game-used bat. Series 2 offered a piece of game-used bat and jersey on four cards. Series 3 inserts featured a piece of jersey only. The cards were inserted one per 2,500 packs in Series 1 and 2; the insertion rate in Series 3 was not revealed.

		NM/M
Complete Set (14):		250.00
Common Player:		5.00
Inserted 1:2,500		
(1)	Jay Buhner/Bat	20.00
(2)	Tony Gwynn/Bat	25.00
(3)	Tony Gwynn/Jsy	25.00
(4)	Todd Hollandsworth/Bat	5.00
(5)	Todd Hollandsworth/Jsy	5.00
(6)	Greg Maddux/Jsy	40.00
(7)	Alex Rodriguez/Bat	40.00
(8)	Alex Rodriguez/Jsy	40.00
(9)	Gary Sheffield/Bat	15.00
(10)	Gary Sheffield/Jsy	15.00
RA	Roberto Alomar	35.00
JB	Jay Buhner	10.00
AJ	Andruw Jones	20.00
GS	Gary Sheffield	15.00

Blue Chip Prospects

Inserted in Series 2 packs, these inserts are printed on die-cut acetate. The cards are sequentially numbered to 2,000. They carry a "BC" prefix.

		NM/M
Complete Set (30):		75.00
Common Player:		2.00
1	Nomar Garciaparra	8.00
2	Scott Rolen	5.00
3	Jason Dickson	2.00
4	Darin Erstad	3.00
5	Brad Fullmer	2.00
6	Jaret Wright	2.00
7	Justin Thompson	2.00
8	Matt Morris	2.00
9	Fernando Tatis	2.00
10	Alex Rodriguez	12.00
11	Todd Helton	6.50
12	Andy Pettitte	2.50
13	Jose Cruz Jr.	2.00
14	Mark Kotsay	2.00
15	Derek Jeter	15.00
16	Paul Konerko	3.00
17	Todd Dunwoody	2.00
18	Vladimir Guerrero	6.00
19	Miguel Tejada	5.00
20	Chipper Jones	8.00
21	Kevin Orie	2.00
22	Juan Encarnacion	6.00
23	Brian Rose	2.00
24	Andruw Jones	6.00
25	Livan Hernandez	2.00
26	Brian Giles	2.00
27	Brett Tomko	2.00
28	Jose Guillen	2.00
29	Aaron Boone	2.00
30	Ben Grieve	2.00

Clearly Dominant

Clearly Dominant was an insert in Series 2. Printed on Light F/X plastic stock, the 30-card set is sequentially numbered to 250. They carry a "CD" prefix.

		NM/M
Complete Set (30):		300.00
Common Player:		3.00
Production 250 Sets		
1	Mark McGwire	25.00
2	Derek Jeter	30.00
3	Alex Rodriguez	25.00
4	Paul Molitor	12.00
5	Jeff Bagwell	12.00
6	Ivan Rodriguez	10.00
7	Kenny Lofton	3.00
8	Cal Ripken Jr.	30.00
9	Albert Belle	3.00
10	Chipper Jones	15.00
11	Gary Sheffield	5.00
12	Roberto Alomar	4.00
13	Mo Vaughn	3.00
14	Andres Galarraga	3.00
15	Nomar Garciaparra	15.00
16	Randy Johnson	12.00
17	Mike Mussina	6.00
18	Greg Maddux	15.00
19	Tony Gwynn	15.00
20	Frank Thomas	12.00
21	Roger Clemens	17.50
22	Dennis Eckersley	10.00
23	Juan Gonzalez	6.00
24	Tino Martinez	3.00
25	Andruw Jones	12.00
26	Larry Walker	3.00
27	Ken Caminiti	3.00
28	Mike Piazza	20.00
29	Barry Bonds	30.00
30	Ken Griffey Jr.	20.00

Ken Griffey Jr.'s HR Chronicles

Griffey's Home Run Chronicles was inserted in both Series 1 and 2 packs. Series 1 had cards spotlighting one of Junior's first 30 home runs of the 1997 season. Series 2 had 26 cards highlighting the rest of his 1997 home run output. In both series, the cards were inserted one per nine packs. Cards are numbered "XX of 56" and printed on silver-metallic foil on front.

	NM/M
Complete Set (56):	45.00
Common Card:	1.00
Inserted 1:9	

National Pride

National Pride is a 42-card insert printed on die-cut rainbow foil. The set honors the nationality of the player with their country's flag in the background. The cards were inserted one per 24 packs. Cards are numbered with a "NP" prefix.

		NM/M
Complete Set (42):		65.00
Common Player:		.75
1	Dave Nilsson	.75
2	Larry Walker	.75
3	Edgar Renteria	.75
4	Jose Canseco	1.25
5	Rey Ordonez	.75
6	Rafael Palmeiro	2.50
7	Livan Hernandez	.75
8	Andruw Jones	3.00
9	Manny Ramirez	3.00
10	Sammy Sosa	4.00
11	Raul Mondesi	.75
12	Moises Alou	.75
13	Pedro Martinez	3.00
14	Vladimir Guerrero	3.00
15	Chili Davis	.75
16	Hideo Nomo	1.50
17	Hideki Irabu	.75
18	Shigetosi Hasegawa	.75
19	Takashi Kashiwada	.75
20	Chan Ho Park	.75
21	Fernando Valenzuela	.75
22	Vinny Castilla	.75
23	Armando Reynoso	.75
24	Karim Garcia	1.00
25	Marvin Benard	.75
26	Mariano Rivera	1.00
27	Juan Gonzalez	1.50
28	Roberto Alomar	1.00
29	Ivan Rodriguez	2.50
30	Carlos Delgado	1.00
31	Bernie Williams	.75
32	Edgar Martinez	.75
33	Frank Thomas	3.00
34	Barry Bonds	7.50
35	Mike Piazza	5.00
36	Chipper Jones	4.00
37	Cal Ripken Jr.	7.50
38	Alex Rodriguez	6.00
39	Ken Griffey Jr.	5.00
40	Andres Galarraga	.75
41	Omar Vizquel	.75
42	Ozzie Guillen	.75

Prime Nine

Nine of the most popular players are featured in this insert set. The cards are printed on silver-foil stock and inserted 1:5 in Series 2 packs.

	NM/M
Complete Set (60):	50.00
Common Griffey:	1.00
Common Piazza:	1.25
Common Thomas:	.60
Common McGwire:	1.25
Common Ripken:	1.75
Common Gonzalez:	.50
Common Gwynn:	.70
Common Bonds:	1.75
Common Maddux:	.70
Inserted 1:5	

PN1	Ken Griffey Jr./1989-1992	1.00
PN2	Ken Griffey Jr./1993	1.00
PN3	Ken Griffey Jr./1994	1.00
PN4	Ken Griffey Jr./1995	1.00
PN5	Ken Griffey Jr./1996	1.00
PN6	Ken Griffey Jr./1997	1.00
PN7	Ken Griffey Jr./1997	1.00
PN8	Mike Piazza/1991	1.00
PN9	Mike Piazza/1992	1.00
PN10	Mike Piazza/1993	1.00
PN11	Mike Piazza/1994	1.00
PN12	Mike Piazza/1995	1.00
PN13	Mike Piazza/1996	1.00
PN14	Mike Piazza/1997	1.00
PN15	Frank Thomas/1991	.60
PN16	Frank Thomas/1992	.60
PN17	Frank Thomas/1993	.60
PN18	Frank Thomas/1994	.60
PN19	Frank Thomas/1995	.60
PN20	Frank Thomas/1996	.60
PN21	Frank Thomas/1997	.60
PN22	Mark McGwire/1987	1.25
PN23	Mark McGwire/1988-1990	1.25
PN24	Mark McGwire/1992	1.25
PN25	Mark McGwire/1995-1996	1.25
PN26	Mark McGwire/1997	1.25
PN27	Mark McGwire/1997	1.25
PN28	Mark McGwire/1997	1.25
PN29	Cal Ripken Jr./1982	1.75
PN30	Cal Ripken Jr./1983	1.75
PN31	Cal Ripken Jr./1989	1.75
PN32	Cal Ripken Jr./1991	1.75
PN33	Cal Ripken Jr./1995	1.75
PN34	Cal Ripken Jr./1996	1.75
PN35	Cal Ripken Jr./1997	1.75
PN36	Juan Gonzalez/1992	.50
PN37	Juan Gonzalez/1993	.50
PN38	Juan Gonzalez/1994	.50
PN39	Juan Gonzalez/1995	.50
PN40	Juan Gonzalez/1996	.50
PN41	Juan Gonzalez/1996	.50
PN42	Juan Gonzalez/1997	.50
PN43	Tony Gwynn/1984	.75
PN44	Tony Gwynn/1987-1989	.75
PN45	Tony Gwynn/1990-1993	.75
PN46	Tony Gwynn/1994	.75
PN47	Tony Gwynn/1996	.75
PN48	Tony Gwynn/1997	.75
PN49	Tony Gwynn/1997	.75
PN50	Barry Bonds/1986-1992	1.75
PN51	Barry Bonds/1990-1993	1.75
PN52	Barry Bonds/1993	1.75
PN53	Barry Bonds/1994	1.75
PN54	Barry Bonds/1996	1.75
PN55	Barry Bonds/1997	1.75
PN56	Greg Maddux/1992	.75
PN57	Greg Maddux/1993-1994	.75
PN58	Greg Maddux/1995	.75
PN59	Greg Maddux/1996	.75
PN60	Greg Maddux/1997	.75

Tape Measure Titans

Tape Measure Titans is a 30-card insert seeded 1:23 in Series 2. The set honors the game's top home run hitters. A parallel gold version was also created with each card serially numbered to 2,667 on front.

		NM/M
Complete Set (30):		45.00
Common Player:		.40
Inserted 1:23		
Gold:		1.5X
1	Mark McGwire	5.00
2	Andres Galarraga	.40
3	Jeff Bagwell	.40
4	Larry Walker	.40
5	Frank Thomas	2.50
6	Rafael Palmeiro	1.50
7	Nomar Garciaparra	4.00
8	Mo Vaughn	.40
9	Albert Belle	.60
10	Ken Griffey Jr.	4.00
11	Manny Ramirez	2.00
12	Jim Thome	.40
13	Tony Clark	.40
14	Juan Gonzalez	2.00
15	Mike Piazza	4.00
16	Jose Canseco	1.00
17	Jay Buhner	.40
18	Alex Rodriguez	5.00
19	Jose Cruz Jr.	.40
20	Tino Martinez	.40
21	Carlos Delgado	.75
22	Andruw Jones	2.00
23	Chipper Jones	3.00
24	Fred McGriff	.40
25	Matt Williams	.40
26	Sammy Sosa	4.00
27	Vinny Castilla	.40
28	Tim Salmon	.60
29	Ken Caminiti	.40
30	Barry Bonds	6.00

10th Anniversary Preview

10th Anniversary Preview is a 60-card set. The foil cards have the same design as the 1989 Upper Deck base cards. The set was inserted one per five packs. Retail versions have the words "PREVIEW EDITION" stamped vertically in gold foil at left. While scarcer than the hobby version, they do not command a premium.

		NM/M
Complete Set (60):		45.00
Common Player:		.30
1	Greg Maddux	2.00
2	Mike Mussina	.50
3	Roger Clemens	2.25
4	Hideo Nomo	.75
5	David Cone	.45
6	Tom Glavine	.45
7	Andy Pettitte	.60
8	Jimmy Key	.30
9	Randy Johnson	1.00
10	Dennis Eckersley	1.00
11	Lee Smith	.30
12	John Franco	.30
13	Randy Myers	.30
14	Mike Piazza	2.50
15	Ivan Rodriguez	1.25
16	Todd Hundley	.30
17	Sandy Alomar Jr.	.30
18	Frank Thomas	1.50
19	Rafael Palmeiro	1.25
20	Mark McGwire	3.00
21	Mo Vaughn	.30
22	Fred McGriff	.30
23	Andres Galarraga	.30
24	Mark Grace	.30
25	Jeff Bagwell	1.50
26	Roberto Alomar	.45
27	Chuck Knoblauch	.30
28	Ryne Sandberg	2.00
29	Eric Young	.30
30	Craig Biggio	.30
31	Carlos Baerga	.30
32	Robin Ventura	.30
33	Matt Williams	.30
34	Wade Boggs	2.00
35	Dean Palmer	.30
36	Chipper Jones	2.00
37	Vinny Castilla	.30
38	Ken Caminiti	.30
39	Omar Vizquel	.30
40	Cal Ripken Jr.	3.50
41	Derek Jeter	3.50
42	Alex Rodriguez	3.00
43	Barry Larkin	.30
44	Mark Grudzielanek	.30
45	Albert Belle	.30
46	Manny Ramirez	1.50
47	Jose Canseco	.75
48	Ken Griffey Jr.	2.50
49	Juan Gonzalez	.75
50	Kenny Lofton	.30
51	Sammy Sosa	2.00
52	Larry Walker	.30
53	Gary Sheffield	.60
54	Rickey Henderson	1.50
55	Tony Gwynn	2.00
56	Barry Bonds	2.00
57	Paul Molitor	1.50
58	Edgar Martinez	.30
59	Chili Davis	.30
60	Eddie Murray	1.50

Jumbos

For $3 and 10 foil-pack wrappers, collectors could receive this set of large-format (3-1/2" x 5") cards in a mail-in redemption. The cards are identical to the standard-size versions.

		NM/M
Complete Set (15):		6.00
Common Player:		.25
27	Kenny Lofton	.25
30	Greg Maddux	.75
40	Rafael Palmeiro	.50
50	Ryne Sandberg	.75
60	Albert Belle	.40
65	Barry Larkin	.40
67	Deion Sanders	.40
95	Gary Sheffield	.40
130	Paul Molitor	.60
135	Vladimir Guerrero	.60
176	Hideki Irabu	.40
205	Mark McGwire	2.00
211	Rickey Henderson	.60
225	Ken Griffey Jr.	1.50
230	Ivan Rodriguez	.50

5x7 Inserts

Each box of specially marked Series 2 retail packs contains one of these oversize (5" x 7") versions of UD cards. Besides being four times the size of the regular cards, the jumbo versions do not have the metallic-foil highlights on front nor the hologram on back.

		NM/M
Complete Set (10):		30.00
Common Player:		1.00
310	Cal Ripken Jr.	6.00
320	Nomar Garciaparra	3.00
330	Frank Thomas	2.50
355	Larry Walker	1.00
385	Jeff Bagwell	2.50
400	Mike Piazza	3.00
450	Derek Jeter	6.00
500	Tony Gwynn	3.00
510	Alex Rodriguez	5.00
530	Roger Clemens	3.50

Richie Ashburn Tribute

As part of the company's participation at SportsFest in May 1998, the company issued a tribute card for Phillies Hall of Famer and broadcasting great Richie Ashburn. The card front features a color action photo, part of which is repeated on the back along with Ashburn's career stats and highlights.

		NM/M
1	Richie Ashburn	4.00

Ken Griffey Most Memorable Home Runs

This retail-exclusive boxed set features 11 large-format (3-1/2" x 5") cards depicting Junior's key home runs. The cards have brushed gold-foil graphic highlights on front and a large photo with details of the memorable home run on back. Each card in the set also exists in an autographed and numbered edition of 10 which were randomly inserted. The set was originally sold with a 4" x 6" lucite card holder for about $12.

		NM/M
Complete Set (11):		7.50
Common Card:		1.00
Autographed Card:		225.00
1	Ken Griffey Jr. (First ML HR)	1.00
2	Ken Griffey Jr. (Father-son HRs)	1.00

3	Ken Griffey Jr. (1992 All-Star HR)	1.00
4	Ken Griffey Jr. (HR in eight straight)	1.00
5	Ken Griffey Jr. (32 HR in June 1994)	1.00
6	Ken Griffey Jr. (Game-winning HR)	1.00
7	Ken Griffey Jr. (5th Divison Series HR)	1.00
8	Ken Griffey Jr. (April record)	1.00
9	Ken Griffey Jr. (50th HR in 1997)	1.00
10	Ken Griffey Jr. (56th in 1997)	1.00
11	Ken Griffey Jr. (300th)	1.00

Mark McGwire's Chase for 62

This boxed set chronicles the Cardinal slugger's quest for the single-season home run record. Sold only as a boxed set of 30 cards in standard 2-1/2" x 3-1/2" format, plus a 3-1/2" x 5" card picturing home runs No. 61 and 62, these sets were offered only on a television home shopping show (individually serial numbered red box) and in selected retail stores (unnumbered yellow box). The cards in each version are identical. Issue price was about $20. Card fronts have color poses or action photos at right; at left is a monochrome portrait photo in red. Backs repeat the large front photo, also in red monochrome, and have a few words about a McGwire homer or other highlight. Each card has a silver-foil UD logo on front and a diamond-shaped hologram on back.

		NM/M
Complete Boxed Set:		7.50
Common Card:		.50
1-30	Mark McGwire	.50
---	Mark McGwire (3-1/2" x 5" HR #61/62)	3.00

Mark McGwire - Sept. 8, 1998

This is one of many special issues from Upper Deck commemorating McGwire's record-breaking 1998 season. Most such cards were produced for retail-only sales, or for home shopping television shows. This blank-back, round-cornered card is 5" x 3" and has flicker-action scenes of Big Mac's home run swing and his salute to the crowd following his historic blast.

		NM/M
	Mark McGwire	6.00

Mark McGwire 70/62 Home Runs

This 3-1/2" x 5" die-cut card was one of many special issues from McGwire's record-breaking season in 1998. This card is highlighted on front with red foil and has a photo of the player with details of his 70th HR. On back in similar format is another photo and details of his 62nd HR, along with a serial number from within the edition of 17,000.

Mark McGwire

		NM/M
	Mark McGwire	4.00

PowerDeck Audio Card

A late-1990s reinvention of the "talking" baseball card, this was the first application of UD's "PowerDeck" technology to the trading card field. Specially marked hobby boxes of '98 UD baseball could contain one of three Ken Griffey, Jr., audio cards. The cards are standard 2-1/2" x 3-1/2" and were made to be inserted into a "dummy" plastic disc which could then be played in any audio CD, offering comments from Griffey, trivia, and career highlights. Insertion rate of each of the Griffey cards varies and is detailed in the listings.

		NM/M
Complete Set (3):		45.00
Common Card:		2.00
(1)	Ken Griffey Jr. (Gray jersey, 1:46 packs.)	3.00
(2)	Ken Griffey Jr. (Blue jersey, 1:500 packs.)	12.00
(3)	Ken Griffey Jr. (White jersey, 1:2,400 packs.)	35.00

Rookie Edition Preview

star rookie

		NM/M
Complete Set (10):		5.00
Common Player:		.50
1	Nomar Garciaparra	2.00
2	Scott Rolen	1.00
3	Mark Kotsay	.50
4	Todd Helton	1.50
5	Paul Konerko	.60
6	Juan Encarnacion	.50
7	Brad Fullmer	.50
8	Miguel Tejada	.65
9	Richard Hidalgo	.50
10	Ben Grieve	.50

Rookie Edition A Piece of the Action

ACTION

A Piece of the Action consists of five Game Jersey cards. Three rookie Game Jersey cards were sequentially numbered to 200, while a Ken Griffey Jr. Game Jersey card

---

was numbered to 300. Griffey also signed and hand-numbered 24 Game Jersey cards.

		NM/M
Common Card:		15.00
KG	Ken Griffey Jr./300	100.00
KGS	Ken Griffey Jr./Auto./24	300.00
BG	Ben Grieve/200	15.00
JC	Jose Cruz Jr./200	15.00
TL	Travis Lee/200	15.00

Rookie Edition All-Star Credentials

All-Star Credentials is a 30-card insert seeded 1:9. It features the game's top players.

		NM/M
Complete Set (30):		25.00
Common Player:		.25
Inserted 1:9		
AS1	Ken Griffey Jr.	1.50
AS2	Travis Lee	.40
AS3	Ben Grieve	.25
AS4	Jose Cruz Jr.	.25
AS5	Andruw Jones	.75
AS6	Craig Biggio	.25
AS7	Hideo Nomo	.40
AS8	Cal Ripken Jr.	2.50
AS9	Jaret Wright	.25
AS10	Mark McGwire	2.00
AS11	Derek Jeter	2.50
AS12	Scott Rolen	.60
AS13	Jeff Bagwell	.75
AS14	Manny Ramirez	.75
AS15	Alex Rodriguez	2.00
AS16	Chipper Jones	1.00
AS17	Larry Walker	.25
AS18	Barry Bonds	2.50
AS19	Tony Gwynn	1.00
AS20	Mike Piazza	1.50
AS21	Roger Clemens	1.25
AS22	Greg Maddux	1.00
AS23	Jim Thome	.60
AS24	Tino Martinez	.25
AS25	Nomar Garciaparra	1.00
AS26	Juan Gonzalez	.40
AS27	Kenny Lofton	.25
AS28	Randy Johnson	.75
AS29	Todd Helton	.65
AS30	Frank Thomas	.75

Rookie Edition Destination Stardom

Ricky Ledee
New York Yankees

This 60-card insert features top young players. Fronts are printed on a foil background. The insertion rate was one card per five packs. Cards have a "DS" prefix to the card number.

		NM/M
Complete Set (60):		40.00
Common Player:		.50
Inserted 1:5		
1	Travis Lee	.75
2	Nomar Garciaparra	3.50
3	Alex Gonzalez	.50
4	Richard Hidalgo	.50
5	Jaret Wright	.50
6	Mike Kinkade	.50
7	Matt Morris	.50
8	Gary Mathews Jr.	.50
9	Brett Tomko	.50
10	Todd Helton	2.00
11	Scott Elarton	.50
12	Scott Rolen	1.50
13	Jose Cruz Jr.	.50
14	Jarrod Washburn	.50
15	Sean Casey	.50
16	Magglio Ordonez	2.00
17	Gabe Alvarez	.50
18	Todd Dunwoody	.50
19	Kevin Witt	.50

20	Ben Grieve	.50
21	Daryle Ward	.50
22	Matt Clement	.50
23	Carlton Loewer	.50
24	Javier Vazquez	.50
25	Paul Konerko	.75
26	Preston Wilson	.60
27	Wes Helms	.50
28	Derek Jeter	5.00
29	Corey Koskie	.50
30	Russell Branyan	.50
31	Vladimir Guerrero	2.50
32	Ryan Christenson	.50
33	Carlos Lee	.60
34	David Dellucci	.50
35	Bruce Chen	.50
36	Ricky Ledee	.50
37	Ron Wright	.50
38	Derrek Lee	1.50
39	Miguel Tejada	.75
40	Brad Fullmer	.50
41	Rich Butler	.50
42	Chris Carpenter	.50
43	Alex Rodriguez	4.00
44	Darron Ingram	.50
45	Kerry Wood	1.50
46	Jason Varitek	.50
47	Ramon Hernandez	.50
48	Aaron Boone	.50
49	Juan Encarnacion	.50
50	A.J. Hinch	.50
51	Mike Lowell	1.00
52	Fernando Tatis	.50
53	Jose Guillen	.50
54	Mike Caruso	.50
55	Carl Pavano	.50
56	Chris Clemons	.50
57	Mark L. Johnson	.50
58	Ken Cloude	.50
59	Rolando Arrojo	.50
60	Mark Kotsay	.50

Rookie Edition Eminent Prestige 5x7

This 4X super-size (5" x 7") version is a partial parallel of the Rookie Edition Eminent Prestige subset. It was available only in specially marked retail packaging.

		NM/M
Complete Set (10):		25.00
Common Player:		2.00
605	Mike Piazza	3.50
607	Frank Thomas	2.50
610	Mark McGwire	4.00
611	Jeff Bagwell	2.50
612	Travis Lee	2.00
614	Cal Ripken Jr.	5.00
616	Nomar Garciaparra	3.00
617	Alex Rodriguez	4.00
619	Tony Gwynn	3.00
620	Ken Griffey Jr.	3.50

Rookie Edition Retrospectives

Retrospectives is a 30-card insert seeded 1:24. The cards offer a look back at the careers of baseball's top stars.

		NM/M
Complete Set (30):		55.00
Common Player:		.50
Inserted 1:24		
1	Dennis Eckersley	2.50
2	Rickey Henderson	3.00
3	Harold Baines	.50
4	Cal Ripken Jr.	7.50
5	Tony Gwynn	4.00
6	Wade Boggs	4.00
7	Orel Hershiser	.50
8	Joe Carter	.50
9	Roger Clemens	4.50
10	Barry Bonds	7.50
11	Mark McGwire	6.00
12	Greg Maddux	4.00
13	Fred McGriff	.50

14	Rafael Palmeiro	3.00
15	Craig Biggio	.50
16	Brady Anderson	.50
17	Randy Johnson	3.00
18	Gary Sheffield	1.00
19	Albert Belle	.50
20	Ken Griffey Jr.	5.00
21	Juan Gonzalez	1.50
22	Larry Walker	.50
23	Tino Martinez	.50
24	Frank Thomas	3.00
25	Jeff Bagwell	3.00
26	Kenny Lofton	.50
27	Mo Vaughn	.50
28	Mike Piazza	5.00
29	Alex Rodriguez	6.00
30	Chipper Jones	4.00

Rookie Edition Unparalleled

Unparalleled is a 20-card, hobby-only insert. The set consists of holo-pattern foil-stamped cards. They were inserted one per 72 packs.

		NM/M
Complete Set (20):		75.00
Common Player:		1.00
Inserted 1:72		
1	Ken Griffey Jr.	6.00
2	Travis Lee	1.50
3	Ben Grieve	1.00
4	Jose Cruz Jr.	1.00
5	Nomar Garciaparra	5.00
6	Hideo Nomo	1.75
7	Kenny Lofton	1.00
8	Cal Ripken Jr.	10.00
9	Roger Clemens	5.50
10	Mike Piazza	6.00
11	Jeff Bagwell	3.50
12	Chipper Jones	5.00
13	Greg Maddux	5.00
14	Randy Johnson	3.50
15	Alex Rodriguez	7.50
16	Barry Bonds	10.00
17	Frank Thomas	3.50
18	Juan Gonzalez	1.75
19	Tony Gwynn	5.00
20	Mark McGwire	7.50

1998 Upper Deck Special F/X

Special F/X is a retail-only product. The 150-card set consists of 125 regular cards, the 15-card Star Rookies subset and a 10-card subset called Ken Griffey Jr.'s Hot List. The base cards are printed on 20-point stock. The only insert is Power Zone which has four levels: Level One, Level Two - Octoberbest, Level Three - Power Driven and Level Four - Superstar Xcitement.

		NM/M
Complete Set (150):		30.00
Common Player:		.05
1	Ken Griffey Jr. (Griffey Hot List)	1.00
2	Mark McGwire (Griffey Hot List)	1.25
3	Alex Rodriguez (Griffey Hot List)	2.50
4	Larry Walker (Griffey Hot List)	.05
5	Tino Martinez (Griffey Hot List)	.05
6	Mike Piazza (Griffey Hot List)	2.50
7	Jose Cruz Jr. (Griffey Hot List)	.05
8	Greg Maddux (Griffey Hot List)	.75
9	Tony Gwynn (Griffey Hot List)	.75

#	Player	
10	Roger Clemens (Griffey Hot List)	1.75
11	Jason Dickson	.05
12	Darin Erstad	.25
13	Chuck Finley	.05
14	Dave Hollins	.05
15	Garret Anderson	.05
16	Michael Tucker	.05
17	Javier Lopez	.05
18	John Smoltz	.05
19	Mark Wohlers	.05
20	Greg Maddux	1.50
21	Scott Erickson	.05
22	Jimmy Key	.05
23	B.J. Surhoff	.05
24	Eric Davis	.05
25	Rafael Palmeiro	.75
26	Tim Naehring	.05
27	Darren Bragg	.05
28	Troy O'Leary	.05
29	John Valentin	.05
30	Mo Vaughn	.05
31	Mark Grace	.05
32	Kevin Foster	.05
33	Kevin Tapani	.05
34	Kevin Orie	.05
35	Albert Belle	.05
36	Ray Durham	.05
37	Jaime Navarro	.05
38	Mike Cameron	.05
39	Eddie Taubensee	.05
40	Barry Larkin	.05
41	Willie Greene	.05
42	Jeff Shaw	.05
43	Omar Vizquel	.05
44	Brian Giles	.05
45	Jim Thome	.60
46	David Justice	.05
47	Sandy Alomar Jr.	.05
48	Neifi Perez	.05
49	Dante Bichette	.05
50	Vinny Castilla	.05
51	John Thomson	.05
52	Damion Easley	.05
53	Justin Thompson	.05
54	Bobby Higginson	.05
55	Tony Clark	.05
56	Charles Johnson	.05
57	Edgar Renteria	.05
58	Alex Fernandez	.05
59	Gary Sheffield	.50
60	Livan Hernandez	.05
61	Craig Biggio	.05
62	Chris Holt	.05
63	Billy Wagner	.05
64	Brad Ausmus	.05
65	Dean Palmer	.05
66	Tim Belcher	.05
67	Jeff King	.05
68	Jose Rosado	.05
69	Chan Ho Park	.05
70	Raul Mondesi	.05
71	Hideo Nomo	.50
72	Todd Zeile	.05
73	Eric Karros	.05
74	Cal Eldred	.05
75	Jeff D'Amico	.05
76	Doug Jones	.05
77	Dave Nilsson	.05
78	Todd Walker	.05
79	Rick Aguilera	.05
80	Paul Molitor	1.00
81	Brad Radke	.05
82	Vladimir Guerrero	1.00
83	Carlos Perez	.05
84	F.P. Santangelo	.05
85	Rondell White	.05
86	Butch Huskey	.05
87	Edgardo Alfonzo	.05
88	John Franco	.05
89	John Olerud	.05
90	Todd Hundley	.05
91	Bernie Williams	.05
92	Andy Pettitte	.30
93	Paul O'Neill	.05
94	David Cone	.05
95	Jason Giambi	.50
96	Damon Mashore	.05
97	Scott Spiezio	.05
98	Ariel Prieto	.05
99	Rico Brogna	.05
100	Mike Lieberthal	.05
101	Garrett Stephenson	.05
102	Ricky Bottalico	.05
103	Kevin Polcovich	.05
104	Jon Lieber	.05
105	Kevin Young	.05
106	Tony Womack	.05
107	Gary Gaetti	.05
108	Alan Benes	.05
109	Willie McGee	.05
110	Mark McGwire	2.50
111	Ron Gant	.05
112	Andy Ashby	.05
113	Steve Finley	.05
114	Quilvio Veras	.05
115	Ken Caminiti	.05
116	Joey Hamilton	.05
117	Bill Mueller	.05
118	Mark Gardner	.05
119	Shawn Estes	.05
120	J.T. Snow	.05
121	Dante Powell	.05
122	Jeff Kent	.05
123	Jamie Moyer	.05
124	Joey Cora	.05
125	Ken Griffey Jr.	2.00
126	Jeff Fassero	.05
127	Edgar Martinez	.05
128	Will Clark	.05
129	Lee Stevens	.05
130	Ivan Rodriguez	.75
131	Rusty Greer	.05
132	Ed Sprague	.05
133	Pat Hentgen	.05
134	Shannon Stewart	.05
135	Carlos Delgado	.40
136	Brett Tomko/SR	.05
137	Jose Guillen/SR	.05
138	Elieser Marrero/SR	.05
139	Dennis Reyes/SR	.05
140	Mark Kotsay/SR	.05
141	Richie Sexson/SR	.05
142	Todd Helton/SR	.75
143	Jeremi Gonzalez/SR	.05
144	Jeff Abbott/SR	.05
145	Matt Morris/SR	.05
146	Aaron Boone/SR	.05
147	Todd Dunwoody/SR	.05
148	Mario Valdez/SR	.05
149	Fernando Tatis/SR	.05
150	Jaret Wright/SR	.05

OctoberBest

OctoberBest is Level Two of the Power Zone insert. This 20-card insert is die-cut and printed on silver foil. Inserted one per 34 packs, the set features the post-season exploits of 20 players from Power Zone Level One.

		NM/M
Complete Set (15):		40.00
Common Player:		1.00
Inserted 1:34		
PZ1	Frank Thomas	3.00
PZ2	Juan Gonzalez	1.50
PZ3	Mike Piazza	5.00
PZ4	Mark McGwire	6.00
PZ5	Jeff Bagwell	3.00
PZ6	Barry Bonds	7.50
PZ7	Ken Griffey Jr.	5.00
PZ8	John Smoltz	1.00
PZ9	Andruw Jones	3.00
PZ10	Greg Maddux	4.00
PZ11	Sandy Alomar Jr.	1.00
PZ12	Roberto Alomar	1.25
PZ13	Chipper Jones	4.00
PZ14	Kenny Lofton	1.00
PZ15	Tom Glavine	1.25

Power Driven

Power Driven is Level Three of the Power Zone insert. Inserted 1:69, the set features the top 10 power hitters from Power Zone Level Two. The cards feature gold Light F/X technology.

		NM/M
Complete Set (10):		40.00
Common Player:		1.50
Inserted 1:69		
PZ1	Frank Thomas	4.50
PZ2	Juan Gonzalez	2.50
PZ3	Mike Piazza	6.00
PZ4	Larry Walker	1.50
PZ5	Mark McGwire	7.50
PZ6	Jeff Bagwell	4.50
PZ7	Mo Vaughn	1.50
PZ8	Barry Bonds	10.00
PZ9	Tino Martinez	1.50
PZ10	Ken Griffey Jr.	6.00

Power Zone

Power Zone Level One is seeded one per seven packs. The cards are printed using silver Light F/X technology.

		NM/M
Complete Set (20):		40.00
Common Player:		.50
Inserted 1:7		
PZ1	Jose Cruz Jr.	.50
PZ2	Frank Thomas	2.50
PZ3	Juan Gonzalez	1.25
PZ4	Mike Piazza	4.50
PZ5	Mark McGwire	4.50
PZ6	Barry Bonds	6.00
PZ7	Greg Maddux	3.00
PZ8	Alex Rodriguez	4.50
PZ9	Nomar Garciaparra	3.00
PZ10	Ken Griffey Jr.	3.50
PZ11	John Smoltz	.50
PZ12	Andruw Jones	2.50
PZ13	Sandy Alomar Jr.	.50
PZ14	Roberto Alomar	1.00
PZ15	Chipper Jones	2.50
PZ16	Kenny Lofton	.50
PZ17	Larry Walker	.50
PZ18	Jeff Bagwell	2.50
PZ19	Mo Vaughn	.50
PZ20	Tom Glavine	1.00

Superstar Xcitement

Printed on Light F/X gold foil, this 10-card set features the same players as the Power Driven insert. This set is Power Zone Level Four and is sequentially numbered to 250.

		NM/M
Complete Set (10):		275.00
Common Player:		10.00
Production 250 Sets		
PZ1	Jose Cruz Jr.	10.00
PZ2	Frank Thomas	25.00
PZ3	Juan Gonzalez	10.00
PZ4	Mike Piazza	40.00
PZ5	Mark McGwire	45.00
PZ6	Barry Bonds	50.00
PZ7	Greg Maddux	35.00
PZ8	Alex Rodriguez	45.00
PZ9	Nomar Garciaparra	35.00
PZ10	Ken Griffey Jr.	40.00

1998 Upper Deck UD 3

The 270-card base set of UD 3 is actually three levels of the same 90 players. Light FX cards comprise #1-90. The first 30 cards are Future Impact players. Cards #31-60 are Power Corps and cards #61-90 are The Establishment. Cards #91-180 repeat the three subsets in Embossed technology while the final 90 cards repeat the basic sequence in Rainbow technology. Because each subset at each level is seeded at a different rate, few collectors bother to try to understand the relative scarcities and the issue is largely ignored. The insertion ratio for each tier is shown in the checklist. UD 3 was offered in three-card packs at an SRP of $3.99.

	NM/M
Complete Set (270):	200.00
Common Future Impact (1-30):	.50
Inserted 1:12	
Die-Cuts (2,000 Sets):	1X
Common Power Corps (31-60):	.25
Inserted 1:1	
Die-Cuts (2,000 Sets):	3X
Common Establishment (61-90):	.25
Inserted 1:6	
Die-Cuts (2,000 Sets):	2X
Common Future Impact Embossed (91-120):	.25
Inserted 1:6	
Die-Cuts (1,000 Sets):	3X
Common Power Corps Embossed (121-150):	.25
Inserted 1:4	
Die-Cuts (1,000 Sets):	6X
Common Establishment Embossed (151-180):	.25
Inserted 1:1	
Die-Cuts (1,000 Sets):	12X
Common Future Impact Rainbow (181-210):	.25
Inserted 1:1	
Die-Cuts (100 Sets):	15X
Common Power Corps Rainbow (211-240):	.50
Inserted 1:12	
Die-Cuts (100 Sets):	8X
Common Establishment Rainbow (241-270):	.75
Inserted 1:24	
Die-Cuts (100 Sets):	5X
Pack (3):	1.00
Wax Box (24):	20.00

#	Player	
1	Travis Lee	.50
2	A.J. Hinch	.50
3	Mike Caruso	.50
4	Miguel Tejada	.75
5	Brad Fullmer	.50
6	Eric Milton	.50
7	Mark Kotsay	.50
8	Darin Erstad	.75
9	Magglio Ordonez	1.00
10	Ben Grieve	.50
11	Brett Tomko	.50
12	Mike Kinkade RC	.75
13	Rolando Arrojo	.50
14	Todd Helton	1.00
15	Scott Rolen	1.00
16	Bruce Chen	.50
17	Daryle Ward	.50
18	Jaret Wright	.50
19	Sean Casey	.65
20	Paul Konerko	.65
21	Kerry Wood	1.00
22	Russell Branyan	.50
23	Gabe Alvarez	.50
24	Juan Encarnacion	.50
25	Andruw Jones	1.50
26	Vladimir Guerrero	1.50
27	Eli Marrero	.50
28	Matt Clement	.50
29	Gary Matthews Jr.	.50
30	Derek Lee	1.50
31	Ken Caminiti	.25
32	Gary Sheffield	.50
33	Jay Buhner	.25
34	Ryan Klesko	.25
35	Nomar Garciaparra	.75
36	Vinny Castilla	.25
37	Tony Clark	.25
38	Sammy Sosa	.75
39	Tino Martinez	.25
40	Mike Piazza	1.00
41	Manny Ramirez	.65
42	Larry Walker	.25
43	Jose Cruz Jr.	.25
44	Matt Williams	.25
45	Frank Thomas	.65
46	Jim Edmonds	.25
47	Raul Mondesi	.25
48	Alex Rodriguez	1.50
49	Albert Belle	.25
50	Mark McGwire	1.50
51	Tim Salmon	.25
52	Andres Galarraga	.25
53	Jeff Bagwell	.65
54	Jim Thome	.50
55	Barry Bonds	2.50
56	Carlos Delgado	.40
57	Mo Vaughn	.25
58	Chipper Jones	.75
59	Juan Gonzalez	.40
60	Ken Griffey Jr.	1.00
61	David Cone	.25
62	Hideo Nomo	.75
63	Edgar Martinez	.25
64	Fred McGriff	.25
65	Cal Ripken Jr.	4.00
66	Todd Hundley	.25
67	Barry Larkin	.25
68	Dennis Eckersley	1.00
69	Randy Johnson	1.50
70	Paul Molitor	1.50
71	Eric Karros	.25
72	Rafael Palmeiro	1.00
73	Chuck Knoblauch	.25
74	Ivan Rodriguez	1.25
75	Greg Maddux	2.00
76	Dante Bichette	.25
77	Brady Anderson	.25
78	Craig Biggio	.25
79	Derek Jeter	4.00
80	Roger Clemens	2.25
81	Roberto Alomar	.40
82	Wade Boggs	2.00
83	Charles Johnson	.25
84	Mark Grace	.25
85	Kenny Lofton	.25
86	Mike Mussina	1.00
87	Pedro Martinez	1.50
88	Curt Schilling	.50
89	Bernie Williams	.25
90	Tony Gwynn	2.00
91	Travis Lee	.40
92	A.J. Hinch	.25
93	Mike Caruso	.25
94	Miguel Tejada	.40
95	Brad Fullmer	.25
96	Eric Milton	.25
97	Mark Kotsay	.25
98	Darin Erstad	1.00
99	Magglio Ordonez	1.00
100	Ben Grieve	.25
101	Brett Tomko	.25
102	Mike Kinkade RC	.40
103	Rolando Arrojo	.25
104	Todd Helton	1.00
105	Scott Rolen	1.00
106	Bruce Chen	.25
107	Daryle Ward	.25
108	Jaret Wright	.25
109	Sean Casey	.25
110	Paul Konerko	.40
111	Kerry Wood	1.00
112	Russell Branyan	.25
113	Gabe Alvarez	.25
114	Juan Encarnacion	.25
115	Andruw Jones	1.50
116	Vladimir Guerrero	1.50
117	Eli Marrero	.25
118	Matt Clement	.25
119	Gary Matthews Jr.	.25
120	Derek Lee	1.00
121	Ken Caminiti	.25
122	Gary Sheffield	.50
123	Jay Buhner	.25
124	Ryan Klesko	.25
125	Nomar Garciaparra	1.50
126	Vinny Castilla	.25
127	Tony Clark	.25
128	Sammy Sosa	1.50
129	Tino Martinez	.25
130	Mike Piazza	2.00
131	Manny Ramirez	1.00
132	Larry Walker	.25
133	Jose Cruz Jr.	.25
134	Matt Williams	.25
135	Frank Thomas	1.00
136	Jim Edmonds	.25
137	Raul Mondesi	.25
138	Alex Rodriguez	3.00
139	Albert Belle	.25
140	Mark McGwire	3.00
141	Tim Salmon	.25
142	Andres Galarraga	.25
143	Jeff Bagwell	1.00
144	Jim Thome	.75
145	Barry Bonds	5.00
146	Carlos Delgado	.50
147	Mo Vaughn	.25
148	Chipper Jones	1.50
149	Juan Gonzalez	.50
150	Ken Griffey Jr.	2.00
151	David Cone	.25
152	Hideo Nomo	.40
153	Edgar Martinez	.25
154	Fred McGriff	.25
155	Cal Ripken Jr.	2.00
156	Todd Hundley	.25
157	Barry Larkin	.25
158	Dennis Eckersley	.65
159	Randy Johnson	.75
160	Paul Molitor	.75
161	Eric Karros	.25
162	Rafael Palmeiro	.65
163	Chuck Knoblauch	.25
164	Ivan Rodriguez	.65
165	Greg Maddux	1.00
166	Dante Bichette	.25
167	Brady Anderson	.25
168	Craig Biggio	.25
169	Derek Jeter	2.00
170	Roger Clemens	1.25
171	Roberto Alomar	.30
172	Wade Boggs	1.00
173	Charles Johnson	.25
174	Mark Grace	.25
175	Kenny Lofton	.25
176	Mike Mussina	.40
177	Pedro Martinez	.75
178	Curt Schilling	.40
179	Bernie Williams	.25
180	Tony Gwynn	1.00
181	Travis Lee	.40
182	A.J. Hinch	.25
183	Mike Caruso	.25
184	Miguel Tejada	.40
185	Brad Fullmer	.25
186	Eric Milton	.25
187	Mark Kotsay	.25
188	Darin Erstad	.50
189	Magglio Ordonez	1.25
190	Ben Grieve	.25
191	Brett Tomko	.25
192	Mike Kinkade RC	.40
193	Rolando Arrojo	.25
194	Todd Helton	.65
195	Scott Rolen	.60
196	Bruce Chen	.25
197	Daryle Ward	.25
198	Jaret Wright	.25
199	Sean Casey	.40
200	Paul Konerko	.60
201	Kerry Wood	.60
202	Russell Branyan	.25
203	Gabe Alvarez	.25
204	Juan Encarnacion	.25
205	Andruw Jones	1.50
206	Vladimir Guerrero	1.50
207	Eli Marrero	.25
208	Matt Clement	.25
209	Gary Matthews Jr.	.25
210	Derek Lee	1.00
211	Ken Caminiti	.50
212	Gary Sheffield	1.00
213	Jay Buhner	.50
214	Ryan Klesko	.50
215	Nomar Garciaparra	3.00
216	Vinny Castilla	.50
217	Tony Clark	.50
218	Sammy Sosa	3.00
219	Tino Martinez	.50
220	Mike Piazza	4.00
221	Manny Ramirez	2.00
222	Larry Walker	.50
223	Jose Cruz Jr.	.50
224	Matt Williams	.50
225	Frank Thomas	2.00
226	Jim Edmonds	.50
227	Raul Mondesi	.50
228	Alex Rodriguez	6.00
229	Albert Belle	.50
230	Mark McGwire	6.00
231	Tim Salmon	.50
232	Andres Galarraga	.50
233	Jeff Bagwell	2.00
234	Jim Thome	1.50
235	Barry Bonds	9.00
236	Carlos Delgado	.75
267	Mo Vaughn	.50
238	Chipper Jones	3.00
239	Juan Gonzalez	1.00
240	Ken Griffey Jr.	4.00
241	David Cone	.75
242	Hideo Nomo	1.50
243	Edgar Martinez	.75
244	Fred McGriff	.75
245	Cal Ripken Jr.	12.00
246	Todd Hundley	.75
247	Barry Larkin	.75
248	Dennis Eckersley	3.00
249	Randy Johnson	4.50
250	Paul Molitor	4.50
251	Eric Karros	.75
252	Rafael Palmeiro	3.50
253	Chuck Knoblauch	.75
254	Ivan Rodriguez	4.00
255	Greg Maddux	6.00
256	Dante Bichette	.75
257	Brady Anderson	.75
258	Craig Biggio	.75
259	Derek Jeter	12.00
260	Roger Clemens	6.50
261	Roberto Alomar	1.25
262	Wade Boggs	6.00
263	Charles Johnson	.75
264	Mark Grace	.75
265	Kenny Lofton	.75
266	Mike Mussina	1.25
267	Pedro Martinez	4.50
268	Curt Schilling	1.50
269	Bernie Williams	.75
270	Tony Gwynn	6.00

Die-Cut

Die-cut versions of all 270 cards in UD 3 were available in three sequentially numbered tiers. Light FX were numbered to 2,000 sets; Embossed cards were numbered to 1,000 and Rainbow cards were numbered to 100.

Light FX Die-Cuts (2,000 Each)	
Future Impact (1-30):	.75X
Power Corps (31-60):	3X
Establishment (61-90):	2X
Embossed Die-Cuts (1,000 Each)	
Future Impact (91-120):	1X
Power Corps (121-150):	3X
Establishment (151-180):	6X
Rainbow Die-Cuts (100 Each)	
Future Impact (181-210):	20X
Power Corps (211-240):	4X
Establishment (241-270):	12X

Power Corps Jumbos

Ten of the Power Corps cards from UD 3 were selected to be reproduced in jumbo 4X (5" x 7") format as box-toppers for special retail packaging of UD 3.

		NM/M
Complete Set (10):		60.00
Common Player:		2.50
35	Ken Griffey Jr.	7.50
38	Sammy Sosa	6.00
40	Mike Piazza	7.50
45	Frank Thomas	5.00
48	Alex Rodriguez	10.00
50	Mark McGwire	10.00
55	Barry Bonds	12.50
58	Chipper Jones	6.00
59	Juan Gonzalez	2.50
60	Ken Griffey Jr.	7.50

1998 UD Retro

The 129-card set is comprised of 99 regular player cards and 30 Futurama subset cards. Card fronts have a white border encasing the player photo. Retro is packaged in a lunchbox featuring one of six players. Each lunchbox contains 24 six-card packs.

		NM/M
Complete Set (129):		15.00
Common Player:		.05
Pack (6):		2.25
Lunchbox (24):		40.00
1	Jim Edmonds	.05
2	Darin Erstad	.25
3	Tim Salmon	.05
4	Jay Bell	.05
5	Matt Williams	.05
6	Andres Galarraga	.05
7	Andruw Jones	.60
8	Chipper Jones	.75
9	Greg Maddux	.75
10	Rafael Palmeiro	.50
11	Cal Ripken Jr.	2.00
12	Brooks Robinson	.15
13	Nomar Garciaparra	.75
14	Pedro Martinez	.60
15	Mo Vaughn	.05
16	Ernie Banks	.50
17	Mark Grace	.05
18	Gary Matthews	.05
19	Sammy Sosa	.75
20	Albert Belle	.05
21	Carlton Fisk	.15
22	Frank Thomas	.60
23	Ken Griffey Sr.	.05
24	Paul Konerko	.15
25	Barry Larkin	.05
26	Sean Casey	.10
27	Tony Perez	.05
28	Bob Feller	.05
29	Kenny Lofton	.05
30	Manny Ramirez	.60
31	Jim Thome	.45
32	Omar Vizquel	.05
33	Dante Bichette	.05
34	Larry Walker	.05
35	Tony Clark	.05
36	Damion Easley	.05
37	Cliff Floyd	.05
38	Livan Hernandez	.05
39	Jeff Bagwell	.60
40	Craig Biggio	.15
41	Al Kaline	.15
42	Johnny Damon	.20
43	Dean Palmer	.05
44	Charles Johnson	.05
45	Eric Karros	.05
46	Gaylord Perry	.05
47	Raul Mondesi	.05
48	Gary Sheffield	.30
49	Eddie Mathews	.15
50	Warren Spahn	.15
51	Jeromy Burnitz	.05
52	Jeff Cirillo	.05
53	Marquis Grissom	.05
54	Paul Molitor	.60
55	Kirby Puckett	.75
56	Brad Radke	.05
57	Todd Walker	.05
58	Vladimir Guerrero	.60
59	Brad Fullmer	.05
60	Rondell White	.05
61	Bobby Jones	.05
62	Hideo Nomo	.30
63	Mike Piazza	1.00
64	Tom Seaver	.15
65	Frank J. Thomas	.05
66	Yogi Berra	.50
67	Derek Jeter	2.00
68	Tino Martinez	.05
69	Paul O'Neill	.05
70	Andy Pettitte	.20
71	Rollie Fingers	.05
72	Rickey Henderson	.60
73	Matt Stairs	.05
74	Scott Rolen	.50
75	Curt Schilling	.25
76	Jose Guillen	.05
77	Jason Kendall	.05
78	Lou Brock	.10
79	Bob Gibson	.10
80	Ray Lankford	.05
81	Mark McGwire	1.50
83	Kevin Brown	.05
84	Ken Caminiti	.05
85	Tony Gwynn	.75
86	Greg Vaughn	.05
87	Barry Bonds	2.00
88	Willie Stargell	.10
89	Willie McCovey	.10
90	Ken Griffey Jr.	1.00
91	Randy Johnson	.60
92	Alex Rodriguez	1.50
93	Quinton McCracken	.05
94	Fred McGriff	.05
95	Juan Gonzalez	.30
96	Ivan Rodriguez	.05
97	Nolan Ryan	1.50
98	Jose Canseco	.45
99	Roger Clemens	.90
100	Jose Cruz Jr.	.05
101	Justin Baughman RC	.05
102	David Dellucci RC (Futurama)	.15
103	Travis Lee (Futurama)	.15
104	Troy Glaus RC (Futurama)	1.00
105	Kerry Wood (Futurama)	.40
106	Mike Caruso (Futurama)	.05
107	Jim Parque RC (Futurama)	.10
108	Brett Tomko (Futurama)	.05
109	Russell Branyan (Futurama)	.05
110	Jaret Wright (Futurama)	.05
111	Todd Helton (Futurama)	.60
112	Gabe Alvarez (Futurama)	.05
113	Matt Anderson RC (Futurama)	.10
114	Alex Gonzalez (Futurama)	.05
115	Mark Kotsay (Futurama)	.05
116	Derrek Lee (Futurama)	.50
117	Richard Hidalgo (Futurama)	.05
118	Adrian Beltre (Futurama)	.10
119	Geoff Jenkins (Futurama)	.05
120	Eric Milton (Futurama)	.05
121	Brad Fullmer (Futurama)	.05
122	Vladimir Guerrero (Futurama)	.60
123	Carl Pavano (Futurama)	.05
124	Orlando Hernandez RC (Futurama)	.25
125	Ben Grieve (Futurama)	.05
126	A.J. Hinch (Futurama)	.05
127	Matt Clement (Futurama)	.05
128	Gary Matthews Jr. RC (Futurama)	.05
129	Aramis Ramirez (Futurama)	.05
130	Rolando Arrojo (Futurama)	.05

Big Boppers

The game's heavy hitters are the focus of this insert set. Cards have a color action photo on a sepia background. Each card is individually serial numbered in red foil in the upper-right, within an edition of 500. Backs repeat part of the front photo, in sepia only, and have recent stats and hitting highlights. Cards are numbered with a "B" prefix.

		NM/M
Complete Set (30):		80.00
Common Player:		1.00
Production 500 Sets		
B1	Darin Erstad	1.50
B2	Rafael Palmeiro	3.00
B3	Cal Ripken Jr.	10.00
B4	Nomar Garciaparra	5.00
B5	Mo Vaughn	1.00
B6	Frank Thomas	4.00
B7	Albert Belle	1.00
B8	Jim Thome	2.50
B9	Manny Ramirez	4.00
B10	Tony Clark	1.00
B11	Tino Martinez	1.00
B12	Ben Grieve	1.00
B13	Ken Griffey Jr.	7.50
B14	Alex Rodriguez	7.50
B15	Jay Buhner	1.00
B16	Juan Gonzalez	2.00
B17	Jose Cruz Jr.	1.00
B18	Jose Canseco	2.50
B19	Travis Lee	1.50
B20	Chipper Jones	5.00
B21	Andres Galarraga	1.00
B22	Andruw Jones	2.00
B23	Sammy Sosa	5.00
B24	Vinny Castilla	1.00
B25	Larry Walker	1.00
B26	Jeff Bagwell	4.00
B27	Gary Sheffield	1.00
B28	Mike Piazza	6.00
B29	Mark McGwire	7.50
B30	Barry Bonds	10.00

Groovy Kind of Glove

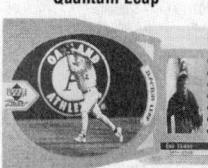

This 30-card set showcases baseball's top defensive players on a psychedelic, wavy and colorful background. They were inserted 1:7 packs.

		NM/M
Complete Set (30):		50.00
Common Player:		.60
Inserted 1:7		
G1	Roberto Alomar	1.00
G2	Cal Ripken Jr.	7.50
G3	Nomar Garciaparra	3.50
G4	Frank Thomas	2.25
G5	Robin Ventura	.60
G6	Omar Vizquel	.60
G7	Kenny Lofton	.60
G8	Ben Grieve	.60
G9	Alex Rodriguez	6.00
G10	Ken Griffey Jr.	7.50
G11	Ivan Rodriguez	1.50
G12	Travis Lee	.75
G13	Matt Williams	.60
G14	Greg Maddux	3.50
G15	Andres Galarraga	.60
G16	Andruw Jones	2.25
G17	Kerry Wood	1.25
G18	Mark Grace	.60
G19	Craig Biggio	.60
G20	Charles Johnson	.60
G21	Raul Mondesi	.60
G22	Mike Piazza	5.00
G23	Rey Ordonez	.60
G24	Derek Jeter	7.50
G25	Scott Rolen	1.25
G26	Mark McGwire	6.00
G27	Ken Caminiti	.60
G28	Tony Gwynn	3.50
G29	J.T. Snow	.60
G30	Barry Bonds	7.50

Legendary Cut

This insert features an actual Babe Ruth cut signature and is limited to a total of three cards.

		NM/M
LC	Babe Ruth (Three issued; 1/04 auction.)	9,500

New Frontier

This set spotlights 30 of baseball's top young prospects and is limited to 1,000 sequentially numbered sets.

	NM/M
Complete Set (30):	45.00

		NM/M
Common Player:		1.00
Production 1,000 Sets		
NF1	Justin Baughman	1.00
NF2	David Dellucci	1.00
NF3	Travis Lee	1.50
NF4	Troy Glaus	6.00
NF5	Mike Caruso	1.00
NF6	Jim Parque	1.00
NF7	Kerry Wood	2.00
NF8	Brett Tomko	1.00
NF9	Russell Branyan	1.00
NF10	Jaret Wright	1.00
NF11	Todd Helton	5.00
NF12	Gabe Alvarez	1.00
NF13	Matt Anderson	1.00
NF14	Alex Gonzalez	1.00
NF15	Mark Kotsay	1.00
NF16	Derrek Lee	3.00
NF17	Richard Hidalgo	1.00
NF18	Adrian Beltre	2.00
NF19	Geoff Jenkins	1.00
NF20	Eric Milton	1.00
NF21	Brad Fullmer	1.00
NF22	Vladimir Guerrero	6.00
NF23	Carl Pavano	1.00
NF24	Orlando Hernandez	1.25
NF25	Ben Grieve	1.00
NF26	A.J. Hinch	1.00
NF27	Matt Clement	1.00
NF28	Gary Matthews	1.00
NF29	Aramis Ramirez	1.00
NF30	Rolando Arrojo	1.00

Quantum Leap

This 30-card insert set highlights the technological advancements of Upper Deck products on a horizontal format. A total of 50 serially numbered sets were produced.

		NM/M
Common Player:		15.00
Production 50 Sets		
Q1	Darin Erstad	20.00
Q2	Cal Ripken Jr.	100.00
Q3	Nomar Garciaparra	50.00
Q4	Frank Thomas	40.00
Q5	Kenny Lofton	15.00
Q6	Ben Grieve	15.00
Q7	Ken Griffey Jr.	60.00
Q8	Alex Rodriguez	75.00
Q9	Juan Gonzalez	20.00
Q10	Jose Cruz Jr.	15.00
Q11	Roger Clemens	55.00
Q12	Travis Lee	15.00
Q13	Chipper Jones	50.00
Q14	Greg Maddux	50.00
Q15	Kerry Wood	20.00
Q16	Jeff Bagwell	40.00
Q17	Mike Piazza	60.00
Q18	Scott Rolen	20.00
Q19	Mark McGwire	75.00
Q20	Tony Gwynn	50.00
Q21	Larry Walker	15.00
Q22	Derek Jeter	100.00
Q23	Sammy Sosa	50.00
Q24	Barry Bonds	100.00
Q25	Mo Vaughn	15.00
Q26	Roberto Alomar	15.00
Q27	Todd Helton	30.00
Q28	Ivan Rodriguez	30.00
Q29	Vladimir Guerrero	40.00
Q30	Albert Belle	15.00

Sign of the Times

This retro-style autographed 31-card set features both retired legends and current players. They were inserted 1:36 packs.

		NM/M
Common Autograph:		7.50
Inserted 1:36		
EB	Ernie Banks/300	40.00
YB	Yogi Berra/150	60.00
RB	Russell Branyan/750	8.00
LB	Lou Brock/300	25.00
JC	Jose Cruz Jr./300	8.00
RF	Rollie Fingers/600	10.00
BF	Bob Feller/600	20.00
CF	Carlton Fisk/600	30.00
BGi	Bob Gibson/300	30.00
BGr	Ben Grieve/300	5.00
KGj	Ken Griffey Jr./100	185.00
KGs	Ken Griffey Sr./600	10.00
TG	Tony Gwynn/200	35.00
AK	Al Kaline/600	30.00
PK	Paul Konerko/750	15.00
TLe	Travis Lee/300	8.00
EM	Eddie Mathews/600	60.00
GMj	Gary Matthews Jr./750	8.00
GMs	Gary Matthews/600	8.00
WM	Willie McCovey/600	30.00
TP	Tony Perez/600	20.00
GP	Gaylord Perry/1,000	10.00
KP	Kirby Puckett/450	80.00
BR	Brooks Robinson/300	30.00
SR	Scott Rolen/300	20.00
NR	Nolan Ryan/500	100.00
TS	Tom Seaver/300	30.00
WS	Warren Spahn/600	40.00
WiS	Willie Stargell/600	50.00
FT	Frank Thomas/600	15.00
KW	Kerry Wood/200	25.00

Time Capsule

Another retro-styled card that featured current stars who were destined to earn a place in baseball history. They were inserted 1:2 packs.

		NM/M
Complete Set (50):		35.00
Common Player:		.25
Inserted 1:2		
TC1	Mike Mussina	.50
TC2	Rafael Palmeiro	.65
TC3	Cal Ripken Jr.	3.00
TC4	Nomar Garciaparra	1.50
TC5	Pedro Martinez	1.00
TC6	Mo Vaughn	.25
TC7	Albert Belle	.25
TC8	Frank Thomas	1.00
TC9	David Justice	.25
TC10	Kenny Lofton	.25
TC11	Manny Ramirez	1.00
TC12	Jim Thome	.60
TC13	Derek Jeter	3.00
TC14	Tino Martinez	.25
TC15	Ben Grieve	.25
TC16	Rickey Henderson	1.00
TC17	Ken Griffey Jr.	2.00
TC18	Randy Johnson	1.00
TC19	Alex Rodriguez	2.50
TC20	Wade Boggs	1.50
TC21	Fred McGriff	.25
TC22	Juan Gonzalez	.50
TC23	Ivan Rodriguez	.75
TC24	Nolan Ryan	2.50
TC25	Jose Canseco	.50
TC26	Roger Clemens	1.75
TC27	Jose Cruz Jr.	.25
TC28	Travis Lee	.40
TC29	Matt Williams	.25
TC30	Andres Galarraga	.25
TC31	Andruw Jones	1.00
TC32	Chipper Jones	1.50
TC33	Greg Maddux	1.50
TC34	Kerry Wood	.50
TC35	Barry Larkin	.25
TC36	Dante Bichette	.25
TC37	Larry Walker	.25
TC38	Livan Hernandez	.25
TC39	Jeff Bagwell	1.00
TC40	Craig Biggio	.25
TC41	Charles Johnson	.25
TC42	Gary Sheffield	.50
TC43	Marquis Grissom	.25
TC44	Mike Piazza	2.00
TC45	Scott Rolen	.65
TC46	Curt Schilling	.40
TC47	Mark McGwire	2.50
TC48	Ken Caminiti	.25
TC49	Tony Gwynn	1.50
TC50	Barry Bonds	3.00

Lunchbox

Lunchboxes were the form of packaging for UD Retro. Six different players are featured with each lunchbox containing 24 six-card packs, with a SRP of $4.99.

	NM/M
Complete Set (6):	40.00
Common Lunchbox:	4.00
Nomar Garciaparra	6.00
Ken Griffey Jr.	7.50
Chipper Jones	6.00
Travis Lee	4.00
Mark McGwire	10.00
Cal Ripken Jr.	12.00

1999 Upper Deck

Released in two series, base card fronts feature a textured silver border along the left and right sides. The player name and Upper Deck logo also are stamped in silver foil. Backs have a small photo, with stats and career highlights. Randomly seeded in packs are 100 Ken Griffey Jr. rookie cards that were bought back by Upper Deck from the hobby and autographed. Upper Deck also re-inserted one pack of '89 Upper Deck inside every hobby box. Ten-card hobby packs carry a S.R.P. of $2.99. Cards #256-265 were never produced.

		NM/M
Complete Set (525):		45.00
Complete Series 1 (255):		25.00
Complete Series 2 (270):		20.00
Common Player:		.05
Exclusive Stars/RC's:		15X
Production 100 each		
Pack (10):		1.50
Wax Box (24):		35.00
1	Troy Glaus/SR	.60
2	Adrian Beltre/SR	.25
3	Matt Anderson/SR	.05
4	Eric Chavez/SR	.15
5	Jin Cho/SR	.05
6	Robert Smith/SR RC	.05
7	George Lombard/SR	.05
8	Mike Kinkade/SR	.05
9	Seth Greisinger/SR	.05
10	J.D. Drew/SR	.50
11	Aramis Ramirez/SR	.05
12	Carlos Guillen/SR	.05
13	Justin Baughman/SR	.05
14	Jim Parque/SR	.05
15	Ryan Jackson/SR	.05
16	Ramon Martinez/SR	.05
17	Orlando Hernandez/SR	.05
18	Jeremy Giambi/SR	.05
19	Gary DiSarcina	.05
20	Darin Erstad	.25
21	Troy Glaus	.50
22	Chuck Finley	.05
23	Dave Hollins	.05
24	Troy Percival	.05
25	Tim Salmon	.05
26	Brian Anderson	.05
27	Jay Bell	.05
28	Andy Benes	.05
29	Brent Brede	.05
30	David Dellucci	.05
31	Karim Garcia	.10
32	Travis Lee	.20
33	Andres Galarraga	.05
34	Ryan Klesko	.05
35	Keith Lockhart	.05
36	Kevin Millwood	.05
37	Denny Neagle	.05
38	John Smoltz	.05
39	Michael Tucker	.05
40	Walt Weiss	.05
41	Dennis Martinez	.05
42	Javy Lopez	.05

43	Brady Anderson	.05
44	Harold Baines	.05
45	Mike Bordick	.05
46	Roberto Alomar	.20
47	Scott Erickson	.05
48	Mike Mussina	.30
49	Cal Ripken Jr.	2.00
50	Darren Bragg	.05
51	Dennis Eckersley	.50
52	Nomar Garciaparra	.75
53	Scott Hatteberg	.05
54	Troy O'Leary	.05
55	Bret Saberhagen	.05
56	John Valentin	.05
57	Rod Beck	.05
58	Jeff Blauser	.05
59	Brant Brown	.05
60	Mark Clark	.05
61	Mark Grace	.05
62	Kevin Tapani	.05
63	Henry Rodriguez	.05
64	Mike Cameron	.05
65	Mike Caruso	.05
66	Ray Durham	.05
67	Jaime Navarro	.05
68	Magglio Ordonez	.30
69	Mike Sirotka	.05
70	Sean Casey	.15
71	Barry Larkin	.05
72	Jon Nunnally	.05
73	Paul Konerko	.15
74	Chris Stynes	.05
75	Brett Tomko	.05
76	Dmitri Young	.05
77	Sandy Alomar	.05
78	Bartolo Colon	.05
79	Travis Fryman	.05
80	Brian Giles	.05
81	David Justice	.05
82	Omar Vizquel	.05
83	Jaret Wright	.05
84	Jim Thome	.40
85	Charles Nagy	.05
86	Pedro Astacio	.05
87	Todd Helton	.05
88	Darryl Kile	.05
89	Mike Lansing	.05
90	Neifi Perez	.05
91	John Thomson	.05
92	Larry Walker	.05
93	Tony Clark	.05
94	Deivi Cruz	.05
95	Damion Easley	.05
96	Brian L. Hunter	.05
97	Todd Jones	.05
98	Brian Moehler	.05
99	Gabe Alvarez	.05
100	Craig Counsell	.05
101	Cliff Floyd	.05
102	Livan Hernandez	.05
103	Andy Larkin	.05
104	Derrek Lee	.35
105	Brian Meadows	.05
106	Moises Alou	.05
107	Sean Berry	.05
108	Craig Biggio	.05
109	Ricky Gutierrez	.05
110	Mike Hampton	.05
111	Jose Lima	.05
112	Billy Wagner	.05
113	Hal Morris	.05
114	Johnny Damon	.30
115	Jeff King	.05
116	Jeff Montgomery	.05
117	Glendon Rusch	.05
118	Larry Sutton	.05
119	Bobby Bonilla	.05
120	Jim Eisenreich	.05
121	Eric Karros	.05
122	Matt Luke	.05
123	Ramon Martinez	.05
124	Gary Sheffield	.40
125	Eric Young	.05
126	Charles Johnson	.05
127	Jeff Cirillo	.05
128	Marquis Grissom	.05
129	Jeromy Burnitz	.05
130	Bob Wickman	.05
131	Scott Karl	.05
132	Mark Loretta	.05
133	Fernando Vina	.05
134	Matt Lawton	.05
135	Pat Meares	.05
136	Eric Milton	.05
137	Paul Molitor	.60
138	David Ortiz	.35
139	Todd Walker	.05
140	Shane Andrews	.05
141	Brad Fullmer	.05
142	Vladimir Guerrero	.60
143	Dustin Hermanson	.05
144	Ryan McGuire	.05
145	Ugueth Urbina	.05
146	John Franco	.05
147	Butch Huskey	.05
148	Bobby Jones	.05
149	John Olerud	.05
150	Rey Ordonez	.05
151	Mike Piazza	1.25
152	Hideo Nomo	.30
153	Masato Yoshii	.05
154	Derek Jeter	2.00
155	Chuck Knoblauch	.05
156	Paul O'Neill	.05
157	Andy Pettitte	.20
158	Mariano Rivera	.15
159	Darryl Strawberry	.05
160	David Wells	.05

161	Jorge Posada	.05
162	Ramiro Mendoza	.05
163	Miguel Tejada	.15
164	Ryan Christenson	.05
165	Rickey Henderson	.60
166	A.J. Hinch	.05
167	Ben Grieve	.05
168	Kenny Rogers	.05
169	Matt Stairs	.05
170	Bob Abreu	.05
171	Rico Brogna	.05
172	Doug Glanville	.05
173	Mike Grace	.05
174	Desi Relaford	.05
175	Scott Rolen	.40
176	Jose Guillen	.05
177	Francisco Cordova	.05
178	Al Martin	.05
179	Jason Schmidt	.05
180	Turner Ward	.05
181	Kevin Young	.05
182	Mark McGwire	1.50
183	Delino DeShields	.05
184	Eli Marrero	.05
185	Tom Lampkin	.05
186	Ray Lankford	.05
187	Willie McGee	.05
188	Matt Morris	.05
189	Andy Ashby	.05
190	Kevin Brown	.05
191	Ken Caminiti	.05
192	Trevor Hoffman	.05
193	Wally Joyner	.05
194	Greg Vaughn	.05
195	Danny Darwin	.05
196	Shawn Estes	.05
197	Orel Hershiser	.05
198	Jeff Kent	.05
199	Bill Mueller	.05
200	Robb Nen	.05
201	J.T. Snow	.05
202	Ken Cloude	.05
203	Russ Davis	.05
204	Jeff Fassero	.05
205	Ken Griffey Jr.	1.00
206	Shane Monahan	.05
207	David Segui	.05
208	Dan Wilson	.05
209	Wilson Alvarez	.05
210	Wade Boggs	.75
211	Miguel Cairo	.05
212	Bubba Trammell	.05
213	Quinton McCracken	.05
214	Paul Sorrento	.05
215	Kevin Stocker	.05
216	Will Clark	.05
217	Rusty Greer	.05
218	Rick Helling	.05
219	Mike McLemore	.05
220	Ivan Rodriguez	.50
221	John Wetteland	.05
222	Jose Canseco	.40
223	Roger Clemens	.85
224	Carlos Delgado	.25
225	Darrin Fletcher	.05
226	Alex Gonzalez	.05
227	Jose Cruz Jr.	.05
228	Shannon Stewart	.05
229	Rolando Arrojo (Foreign Focus)	.05
230	Livan Hernandez (Foreign Focus)	.05
231	Orlando Hernandez (Foreign Focus)	.05
232	Raul Mondesi (Foreign Focus)	.05
233	Moises Alou (Foreign Focus)	.05
234	Pedro Martinez (Foreign Focus)	.30
235	Sammy Sosa (Foreign Focus)	.50
236	Vladimir Guerrero (Foreign Focus)	.40
237	Bartolo Colon (Foreign Focus)	.05
238	Miguel Tejada (Foreign Focus)	.05
239	Ismael Valdes (Foreign Focus)	.05
240	Mariano Rivera (Foreign Focus)	.05
241	Jose Cruz Jr. (Foreign Focus)	.05
242	Juan Gonzalez (Foreign Focus)	.20
243	Ivan Rodriguez (Foreign Focus)	.15
244	Sandy Alomar (Foreign Focus)	.05
245	Roberto Alomar (Foreign Focus)	.10
246	Magglio Ordonez (Foreign Focus)	.05
247	Kerry Wood (Highlights Checklist)	.10
248	Mark McGwire (Highlights Checklist)	.75
249	David Wells (Highlights Checklist)	.05
250	Rolando Arrojo (Highlights Checklist)	.05
251	Ken Griffey Jr. (Highlights Checklist)	.65
252	Trevor Hoffman (Highlights Checklist)	.05
253	Travis Lee (Highlights Checklist)	.05

254	Roberto Alomar (Highlights Checklist)	.10
255	Sammy Sosa (Highlights Checklist)	.50
266	Pat Burrell/SR RC	2.00
267	Shea Hillenbrand/SR RC	.65
268	Robert Fick/SR	.05
269	Roy Halladay/SR	.05
270	Ruben Mateo/SR	.05
271	Bruce Chen/SR	.05
272	Angel Pena/SR	.05
273	Michael Barrett/SR	.05
274	Kevin Witt/SR	.05
275	Damon Minor/SR	.05
276	Ryan Minor/SR	.05
277	A.J. Pierzynski/SR	.05
278	A.J. Burnett/SR RC	.50
279	Dermal Brown/SR	.05
280	Joe Lawrence/SR	.05
281	Derrick Gibson/SR	.05
282	Carlos Febles/SR	.05
283	Chris Haas/SR	.05
284	Cesar King/SR	.05
285	Calvin Pickering/SR	.05
286	Mitch Meluskey/SR	.05
287	Carlos Beltran/SR	.50
288	Ron Belliard/SR	.05
289	Jerry Hairston Jr./SR	.05
290	Fernando Seguignol/SR	.05
291	Kris Benson/SR	.05
292	Chad Hutchinson/SR RC	.05
293	Jarrod Washburn	.05
294	Jason Dickson	.05
295	Mo Vaughn	.05
296	Garrett Anderson	.05
297	Jim Edmonds	.05
298	Ken Hill	.05
299	Shigetosi Hasegawa	.05
300	Todd Stottlemyre	.05
301	Randy Johnson	.60
302	Omar Daal	.05
303	Steve Finley	.05
304	Matt Williams	.05
305	Danny Klassen	.05
306	Tony Batista	.05
307	Brian Jordan	.05
308	Greg Maddux	.75
309	Chipper Jones	.75
310	Bret Boone	.05
311	Ozzie Guillen	.05
312	John Rocker	.05
313	Tom Glavine	.25
314	Andruw Jones	.60
315	Albert Belle	.05
316	Charles Johnson	.05
317	Will Clark	.05
318	B.J. Surhoff	.05
319	Delino DeShields	.05
320	Heathcliff Slocumb	.05
321	Sidney Ponson	.05
322	Juan Guzman	.05
323	Reggie Jefferson	.05
324	Mark Portugal	.05
325	Tim Wakefield	.05
326	Jason Varitek	.05
327	Jose Offerman	.05
328	Pedro Martinez	.60
329	Trot Nixon	.05
330	Kerry Wood	.30
331	Sammy Sosa	.75
332	Glenallen Hill	.05
333	Gary Gaetti	.05
334	Mickey Morandini	.05
335	Benito Santiago	.05
336	Jeff Blauser	.05
337	Frank Thomas	.65
338	Paul Konerko	.15
339	Jaime Navarro	.05
340	Carlos Lee	.05
341	Brian Simmons	.05
342	Mark Johnson	.05
343	Jeff Abbot	.05
344	Steve Avery	.05
345	Mike Cameron	.05
346	Michael Tucker	.05
347	Greg Vaughn	.05
348	Hal Morris	.05
349	Pete Harnisch	.05
350	Denny Neagle	.05
351	Manny Ramirez	.60
352	Roberto Alomar	.20
353	Dwight Gooden	.05
354	Kenny Lofton	.05
355	Mike Jackson	.05
356	Charles Nagy	.05
357	Enrique Wilson	.05
358	Russ Branyan	.05
359	Richie Sexson	.05
360	Vinny Castilla	.05
361	Dante Bichette	.05
362	Kirt Manwaring	.05
363	Darryl Hamilton	.05
364	Jamey Wright	.05
365	Curt Leskanic	.05
366	Jeff Reed	.05
367	Bobby Higginson	.05
368	Justin Thompson	.05
369	Brad Ausmus	.05
370	Dean Palmer	.05
371	Gabe Kapler	.05
372	Juan Encarnacion	.05
373	Karim Garcia	.10
374	Alex Gonzalez	.05
375	Braden Looper	.05
376	Preston Wilson	.05
377	Todd Dunwoody	.05
378	Alex Fernandez	.05
379	Mark Kotsay	.05

380	Mark Mantei	.05
381	Ken Caminiti	.05
382	Scott Elarton	.05
383	Jeff Bagwell	.60
384	Derek Bell	.05
385	Ricky Gutierrez	.05
386	Richard Hildalgo	.05
387	Shane Reynolds	.05
388	Carl Everett	.05
389	Scott Service	.05
390	Jeff Suppan	.05
391	Joe Randa	.05
392	Kevin Appier	.05
393	Shane Halter	.05
394	Chad Kreuter	.05
395	Mike Sweeney	.05
396	Kevin Brown	.05
397	Devon White	.05
398	Todd Hollandsworth	.05
399	Todd Hundley	.05
400	Chan Ho Park	.05
401	Mark Grudzielanek	.05
402	Raul Mondesi	.05
403	Ismael Valdes	.05
404	Rafael Roque	.05
405	Sean Berry	.05
406	Kevin Barker	.05
407	Dave Nilsson	.05
408	Geoff Jenkins	.05
409	Jim Abbott	.05
410	Bobby Hughes	.05
411	Corey Koskie	.05
412	Rick Aguilera	.05
413	LaTroy Hawkins	.05
414	Ron Coomer	.05
415	Denny Hocking	.05
416	Marty Cordova	.05
417	Terry Steinbach	.05
418	Rondell White	.05
419	Wilton Guerrero	.05
420	Shane Andrews	.05
421	Orlando Cabrera	.05
422	Carl Pavano	.05
423	Jeff Vasquez	.05
424	Chris Widger	.05
425	Robin Ventura	.05
426	Rickey Henderson	.60
427	Al Leiter	.05
428	Bobby Jones	.05
429	Brian McRae	.05
430	Roger Cedeno	.05
431	Bobby Bonilla	.05
432	Edgardo Alfonzo	.05
433	Bernie Williams	.05
434	Ricky Ledee	.05
435	Chili Davis	.05
436	Tino Martinez	.05
437	Scott Brosius	.05
438	David Cone	.05
439	Joe Girardi	.05
440	Roger Clemens	.85
441	Chad Curtis	.05
442	Hideki Irabu	.05
443	Jason Giambi	.40
444	Scott Spezio	.05
445	Tony Phillips	.05
446	Ramon Hernandez	.05
447	Mike Macfarlane	.05
448	Tom Candiotti	.05
449	Billy Taylor	.05
450	Bobby Estella	.05
451	Curt Schilling	.25
452	Carlton Loewer	.05
453	Marlon Anderson	.05
454	Kevin Jordan	.05
455	Ron Gant	.05
456	Chad Ogea	.05
457	Abraham Nunez	.05
458	Jason Kendall	.05
459	Pat Meares	.05
460	Brant Brown	.05
461	Brian Giles	.05
462	Chad Hermansen	.05
463	Freddy Garcia	.05
464	Edgar Renteria	.05
465	Fernando Tatis	.05
466	Eric Davis	.05
467	Darren Bragg	.05
468	Donovan Osborne	.05
469	Manny Aybar	.05
470	Jose Jimenez	.05
471	Kent Mercker	.05
472	Reggie Sanders	.05
473	Ruben Rivera	.05
474	Tony Gwynn	.75
475	Jim Leyritz	.05
476	Chris Gomez	.05
477	Matt Clement	.05
478	Carlos Hernandez	.05
479	Sterling Hitchcock	.05
480	Ellis Burks	.05
481	Barry Bonds	2.00
482	Marvin Bernard	.05
483	Kirk Rueter	.05
484	F.P. Santangelo	.05
485	Stan Javier	.05
486	Jeff Kent	.05
487	Alex Rodriguez	1.50
488	Tom Lampkin	.05
489	Jose Mesa	.05
490	Jay Buhner	.05
491	Edgar Martinez	.05
492	Butch Huskey	.05
493	John Mabry	.05
494	Jamie Moyer	.05
495	Roberto Hernandez	.05
496	Tony Saunders	.05
497	Fred McGriff	.05

498	Dave Martinez	.05
499	Jose Canseco	.40
500	Rolando Arrojo	.05
501	Esteban Yan	.05
502	Juan Gonzalez	.30
503	Rafael Palmeiro	.50
504	Aaron Sele	.05
505	Royce Clayton	.05
506	Todd Zeile	.05
507	Tom Goodwin	.05
508	Lee Stevens	.05
509	Esteban Loaiza	.05
510	Joey Hamilton	.05
511	Homer Bush	.05
512	Willie Greene	.05
513	Shawn Green	.25
514	David Wells	.05
515	Kelvim Escobar	.05
516	Tony Fernandez	.05
517	Pat Hentgen	.05
518	Mark McGwire (Arms Race)	.75
519	Ken Griffey Jr. (Arms Race)	.65
520	Sammy Sosa (Arms Race)	.50
521	Juan Gonzalez (Arms Race)	.20
522	J.D. Drew (Arms Race)	.10
523	Chipper Jones (Arms Race)	.50
524	Alex Rodriguez (Arms Race)	.75
525	Mike Piazza (Arms Race)	.65
526	Nomar Garciaparra (Arms Race)	.50
527	Season Highlights Checklist (Mark McGwire)	.75
528	Season Highlights Checklist (Sammy Sosa)	.50
529	Season Highlights Checklist (Scott Brosius)	.05
530	Season Highlights Checklist (Cal Ripken Jr.)	1.00
531	Season Highlights Checklist (Barry Bonds)	1.00
532	Season Highlights Checklist (Roger Clemens)	.40
533	Season Highlights Checklist (Ken Griffey Jr.)	.65
534	Season Highlights Checklist (Alex Rodriguez)	.75
535	Season Highlights Checklist (Curt Schilling)	.05

Exclusives

Randomly inserted into hobby packs, this parallel issue is individually serial numbered on back from within an edition of 100 of each card. Besides the serial number, the inserts are readily apparent by the use of copper metallic foil graphic highlights on front. Series 1 Exclusive cards have the serial number on back in gold foil; Series 2 Exclusives have the number ink-jetted in black. A green-foil parallel of the parallel was issued in quantities of just one card each for Series 1, and 10 cards each for Series 2.

	NM/M
Common Player:	3.00
Stars/Rookies:	15X
Greens (1-255):	Values Undetermined
Greens (266-535):	100X

Crowning Glory

These double-sided cards feature players who reached milestones during the '98 season. There are three cards in the set, with four different versions of each card. The regular version is seeded 1:23 packs. Doubles are numbered to 1,000, Triples are numbered to 25 and Home Runs are limited to one each.

	NM/M
Complete Set (3):	22.50
Common Player:	6.00
Inserted 1:23	
Doubles (1,000 Sets):	2X
Triples (25 Sets):	8X

Home Runs (1 Set): Values Undetermined

CG1	Roger Clemens, Kerry Wood	6.00
CG2	Mark McGwire, Barry Bonds	12.00
CG3	Ken Griffey Jr., Mark McGwire	7.50

Forte

This 30-card set features the top players in the game, highlighted by blue holofoil treatment. Numbers on card backs have an "F" prefix and are seeded 1:23 packs. There are also die-cut parallels to Forte: Double, Triple and Home Run. Doubles are sequentially numbered to 2,000 sets, Triples are limited to 100 numbered sets and Home Runs are limited to 10 numbered sets.

	NM/M
Complete Set (30):	50.00
Common Player:	.50
Inserted 1:23	
Doubles (2,000 Sets):	3X
Triples (100):	15X
Quadruples (10):	40X

1	Darin Erstad	1.50
2	Troy Glaus	1.50
3	Mo Vaughn	.50
4	Greg Maddux	2.50
5	Andres Galarraga	.50
6	Chipper Jones	2.50
7	Cal Ripken Jr.	5.00
8	Albert Belle	.50
9	Nomar Garciaparra	2.50
10	Sammy Sosa	2.50
11	Kerry Wood	1.00
12	Frank Thomas	2.50
13	Jim Thome	1.50
14	Jeff Bagwell	2.00
15	Vladimir Guerrero	2.00
16	Mike Piazza	3.00
17	Derek Jeter	5.00
18	Ben Grieve	.50
19	Eric Chavez	.50
20	Scott Rolen	1.50
21	Mark McGwire	4.00
22	J.D. Drew	1.00
23	Tony Gwynn	2.50
24	Barry Bonds	5.00
25	Alex Rodriguez	4.00
26	Ken Griffey Jr.	3.00
27	Ivan Rodriguez	1.50
28	Juan Gonzalez	1.00
29	Roger Clemens	2.75
30	Andruw Jones	.50

Game Jersey

A piece of game-worn jersey is framed by a baseball diamond schematic. A round portrait photo appears at top-right, along with the player's uniform number. A small action photo is at bottom center. Backs have another round portrait photo and a statement of authenticity. Game Jersey cards bearing an H1 or H2 designation were hobby-only inserts at a rate of one per 288 packs in the appropriate series. Cards with an HR1 or HR2 notation were found in both hobby and retail packs at a rate of 1:2,500. Autographed versions of some cards were produced, with the edition number noted.

		NM/M
Common Player:		6.00
AB	Adrian Beltre H1	10.00
EC	Eric Chavez H2	6.00
JD	J.D. Drew H2	10.00
JDs	J.D. Drew/Auto./8 H2	150.00
DE	Darin Erstad H1	10.00
BF	Brad Fullmer H2	4.50
JG	Juan Gonzalez HR1	15.00
BG	Ben Grieve H1	6.00
KG	Ken Griffey Jr. H1	20.00
KGs	Ken Griffey Jr./ Auto./24 H1	150.00
JR	Ken Griffey Jr. HR2	20.00
JRs	Ken Griffey Jr./ Auto./24 HR2	150.00
TGw	Tony Gwynn H2	15.00
TH	Todd Helton H2	15.00
CJ	Charles Johnson HR1	6.00
CJ	Chipper Jones H2	15.00
TL	Travis Lee H1	6.00
GM	Greg Maddux HR2	15.00
MP	Mike Piazza HR1	20.00
MR	Manny Ramirez H2	10.00
AR	Alex Rodriguez HR1	25.00
IR	Ivan Rodriguez H1	7.50
NRa	Nolan Ryan/Astros H2	25.00
NRas	Nolan Ryan H2/ Auto./34	450.00
NRb	Nolan Ryan/ Rangers HR2	25.00
SS	Sammy Sosa H2	20.00
BT	Bubba Trammell H2	6.00
FT	Frank Thomas HR2	15.00
KW	Kerry Wood HR1	15.00
KWs	Kerry Wood/ Auto./34 HR1	150.00

Grand Slam Record Breakers

These gold-foil accented cards were inserts in a limited distribution retail packaging.

		NM/M
Complete Set (10):		7.50
Common Player:		.50
G1	Mark McGwire	1.50
G2	Sammy Sosa	1.50
G3	Ken Griffey Jr.	1.50
G4	Roger Clemens	1.00
G5	Kerry Wood	.75
G6	Cal Ripken Jr.	2.00
G7	Barry Bonds	2.00
G8	David Wells	.50
G9	Sammy Sosa	1.50
G10	Mark McGwire	1.50

Homerun Heroes

These gold-foil enhanced cards were inserted one per specially marked five-card foil pack,

plus one as a topper in each tin can of this retail exclusive product. The first six players on the checklist were featured on the cans in which the cards were sold.

		NM/M
Complete Set (10):		10.00
Common Player:		.50
Complete Set Cans (6):		10.00
Common Player Can:		2.00
H1	Ken Griffey Jr.	1.25
H2	Mark McGwire	2.00
H3	Sammy Sosa	1.00
H4	Troy Glaus	.75
H5	Mike Piazza	2.00
H6	Chipper Jones	1.00
H7	Vladimir Guerrero	.75
H8	Frank Thomas	.75
H9	Juan Gonzalez	.50
H10	Alex Rodriguez	2.00
1	Ken Griffey Jr.	2.50
2	Mark McGwire	2.50
3	Sammy Sosa	2.00
4	Troy Glaus	1.50
5	Mike Piazza	2.50
6	Chipper Jones	2.00

Home Run Heroes

These cards were part of an unannounced multi-manufacturer (Fleer, Upper Deck, Topps, Pacific) insert program which was exclusive to Wal-Mart. Each company produced cards of Mark McGwire and Sammy Sosa, along with two other premier sluggers. Each company's cards share a "Power Elite" logo at top and "Home Run Heroes" logo vertically at right.

		NM/M
Complete Set (4):		5.00
Common Player:		1.00
5	Mark McGwire	2.00
6	Sammy Sosa	1.25
7	Ken Griffey Jr.	1.50
8	Frank Thomas	1.00

Immaculate Perception

Done in a horizontal format, this 27-card set features baseball's most celebrated players. Card fronts are enhanced with copper and silver foil stamping, encasing the player's image. The cards are numbered with an I prefix and are seeded 1:23 packs. There are also three parallel versions: Doubles numbered to 1,000, Triples numbered to 25 and Home Runs which are limited to one.

		NM/M
Complete Set (27):		45.00
Common Player:		.25
Inserted 1:23		
Doubles (1,000 Sets):		1.5X
Triples (25):		8X
Home Runs (1): Values Undetermined		
I1	Jeff Bagwell	2.00
I2	Craig Biggio	.25
I3	Barry Bonds	5.00
I4	Roger Clemens	2.75
I5	Jose Cruz Jr.	.25
I6	Nomar Garciaparra	2.50
I7	Tony Clark	.25
I8	Ben Grieve	.25
I9	Ken Griffey Jr.	3.00
I10	Tony Gwynn	2.50
I11	Randy Johnson	2.00
I12	Chipper Jones	2.50
I13	Travis Lee	.40
I14	Kenny Lofton	.25
I15	Greg Maddux	2.50

I16	Mark McGwire	4.00
I17	Hideo Nomo	1.00
I18	Mike Piazza	3.00
I19	Manny Ramirez	2.00
I20	Cal Ripken Jr.	5.00
I21	Alex Rodriguez	4.00
I22	Scott Rolen	1.50
I23	Frank Thomas	2.00
I24	Kerry Wood	1.00
I25	Larry Walker	.25
I26	Vinny Castilla	.25
I27	Derek Jeter	5.00

Opening Season Superstars

These gold-foil enhanced cards were inserted one per specially marked five-card foil pack, in limited retail-exclusive distribution.

		NM/M
Complete Set (10):		10.00
Common Player:		.50
S1	Ken Griffey Jr.	1.50
S2	Mark McGwire	1.50
S3	Sammy Sosa	1.00
S4	Cal Ripken Jr.	1.00
S5	Nomar Garciaparra	1.00
S6	Alex Rodriguez	1.50
S7	Kerry Wood	.50
S8	Juan Gonzalez	.50
S9	Derek Jeter	2.00
S10	Greg Maddux	1.00

Piece of History 500 Club Babe Ruth

Limited to a reported 50 pieces and inserted into Series 2 Upper Deck packs, this card differs from the Piece of History Ruth bat cards on the photos used and the 500 Club notation.

		NM/M
714HR	Babe Ruth/50	4,000

Babe Ruth Piece of History Bat

Limited to approximately 350, this card has an imbedded chip of a bat from an actual game-used Louisville Slugger swung by the Bambino himself. A "signed" version of this card also exists, which incorporates a cut signature of Ruth along with a piece of his game-used bat; only three exist.

		NM/M
PH	Babe Ruth/Bat	900.00
PHLC	Babe Ruth/Legendary Cut Auto.	25,000

Textbook Excellence

This 30-card set features the game's most fundamentally sound performers. Card fronts have a

photo of the featured player on a silver-foil stamped grid background. Vertically at left is player identification on a brown background. These are seeded 1:23 packs. Three hobby-only parallels were also issued: Double, Triple and Home Run. Doubles are numbered to 2,000 sets, Triples are limited to 100 numbered sets and Home Runs are limited to 10 numbered sets. Cards are numbered with a "T" prefix.

		NM/M
Complete Set (30):		12.50
Common Player:		.25
Inserted 1:4		
Doubles (2,000 Sets):		1.5X
Triples (100):		5X
Quadruples (10):		40X
T1	Mo Vaughn	.25
T2	Greg Maddux	.75
T3	Chipper Jones	.75
T4	Andruw Jones	.60
T5	Cal Ripken Jr.	2.00
T6	Albert Belle	.25
T7	Roberto Alomar	.30
T8	Nomar Garciaparra	.75
T9	Kerry Wood	.30
T10	Sammy Sosa	.75
T11	Greg Vaughn	.25
T12	Jeff Bagwell	.60
T13	Kevin Brown	.25
T14	Vladimir Guerrero	.60
T15	Mike Piazza	1.00
T16	Bernie Williams	.25
T17	Derek Jeter	2.00
T18	Ben Grieve	.25
T19	Eric Chavez	.25
T29	Scott Rolen	.50
T21	Mark McGwire	1.50
T22	David Wells	.25
T23	J.D. Drew	.50
T24	Tony Gwynn	.75
T25	Barry Bonds	2.00
T26	Alex Rodriguez	1.50
T27	Ken Griffey Jr.	1.00
T28	Juan Gonzalez	.30
T29	Ivan Rodriguez	.50
T30	Roger Clemens	.85

View to a Thrill

This 30-card set focuses on baseball's best overall athletes. There are two photos of the featured player on the card front, highlighted by silver foil and some embossing. These are inserted 1:7 packs. Numbered parallel sets were produced by: Doubles (2,000), Triples (100) and Quadruples (10).

		NM/M
Complete Set (30):		25.00
Common Player:		.35
Inserted 1:7		
Doubles (2,000 Sets):		1.5X
Triples (100):		4X
Quadruples (10):		30X
V1	Mo Vaughn	.35
V2	Darin Erstad	.40
V3	Travis Lee	.40
V4	Chipper Jones	1.50
V5	Greg Maddux	1.50
V6	Gabe Kapler	.35
V7	Cal Ripken Jr.	3.00
V8	Nomar Garciaparra	1.50
V9	Kerry Wood	.40
V10	Frank Thomas	1.00
V11	Manny Ramirez	1.00
V12	Larry Walker	.35
V13	Tony Clark	.35
V14	Jeff Bagwell	1.00
V15	Craig Biggio	.35
V16	Vladimir Guerrero	1.00
V17	Mike Piazza	2.00
V18	Bernie Williams	.35
V19	Derek Jeter	3.00
V20	Ben Grieve	.35
V21	Eric Chavez	.35
V22	Scott Rolen	.65
V23	Mark McGwire	3.00
V24	Tony Gwynn	1.50
V25	Barry Bonds	3.00

V26	Ken Griffey Jr.	2.00
V27	Alex Rodriguez	2.50
V28	J.D. Drew	.65
V29	Juan Gonzalez	.50
V30	Roger Clemens	1.75

Wonder Years

These inserts look like a throwback to the groovin' '70s, with brightly striped green and pink borders. "Wonder Years" is across the top of the front in yellow. Backs have the player's three best seasons' stats along with a mention of a milestone. The cards are numbered with a WY prefix and are seeded 1:7 packs. There are three parallel versions: Doubles numbered to 1,000, Triples numbered to 25 and Home Runs that are limited to one.

		NM/M
Complete Set (30):		30.00
Common Player:		.50
Inserted 1:7		
Doubles (2,000):		2.5X
Triples (50):		10X
Home Runs (1): Values Undetermined		
WY1	Kerry Wood	.75
WY2	Travis Lee	.65
WY3	Jeff Bagwell	1.50
WY4	Barry Bonds	4.00
WY5	Roger Clemens	2.25
WY6	Jose Cruz Jr.	.50
WY7	Andres Galarraga	.50
WY8	Nomar Garciaparra	.75
WY9	Juan Gonzalez	.75
WY10	Ken Griffey Jr.	2.50
WY11	Tony Gwynn	2.00
WY12	Derek Jeter	4.00
WY13	Randy Johnson	1.50
WY14	Andruw Jones	1.50
WY15	Chipper Jones	2.00
WY16	Kenny Lofton	.50
WY17	Greg Maddux	2.00
WY18	Tino Martinez	.50
WY19	Mark McGwire	3.00
WY20	Paul Molitor	1.50
WY21	Mike Piazza	2.50
WY22	Manny Ramirez	1.50
WY23	Cal Ripken Jr.	4.00
WY24	Alex Rodriguez	3.00
WY25	Sammy Sosa	3.00
WY26	Frank Thomas	1.50
WY27	Mo Vaughn	.50
WY28	Larry Walker	.50
WY29	Scott Rolen	1.00
WY30	Ben Grieve	.50

10th Anniversary Team

This 30-card set commemorates Upper Deck's 10th Anniversary, as collectors selected their favorite players for this set. Regular versions are seeded 1:4 packs. Doubles numbered to 4,000, Triples numbered to 100 and Home Runs which are limited to one set.

		NM/M
Complete Set (30):		20.00
Common Player:		.15
Inserted 1:4		
Doubles (4,000 Sets):		2X
Triples (100):		6X
Home Runs (1): Values Undetermined		

X1	Mike Piazza	1.50
X2	Mark McGwire	2.00
X3	Roberto Alomar	.30
X4	Chipper Jones	1.00
X5	Cal Ripken Jr.	3.00
X6	Ken Griffey Jr.	1.50
X7	Barry Bonds	3.00
X8	Tony Gwynn	1.00
X9	Nolan Ryan	3.00
X10	Randy Johnson	.75
X11	Dennis Eckersley	.65
X12	Ivan Rodriguez	.65
X13	Frank Thomas	.75
X14	Craig Biggio	.15
X15	Wade Boggs	1.00
X16	Alex Rodriguez	2.00
X17	Albert Belle	.15
X18	Juan Gonzalez	.40
X19	Rickey Henderson	.75
X20	Greg Maddux	1.00
X21	Tom Glavine	.35
X22	Randy Myers	.15
X23	Sandy Alomar	.15
X24	Jeff Bagwell	.75
X25	Derek Jeter	3.00
X26	Matt Williams	.15
X27	Kenny Lofton	.15
X28	Sammy Sosa	1.00
X29	Larry Walker	.15
X30	Roger Clemens	1.25

Ken Griffey Jr. Supers

These large-format (5" x 7") reproductions of each of Junior's regular-issue UD cards from 1989-98 were issued as a Wal-Mart exclusive in Series 1 UD baseball. Autographed versions of the super-sized Griffey cards were also found in the boxes. The supers were also distributed at the July 1999 National Sports Collectors Convention as a wrapper-redemption premium at the card company's booth. Other than the lack of a hologram on back, the cards are identical 4X blowups of the issued cards.

		NM/M
Complete Set (10):		15.00
Common Card:		2.00
Autographed Card:		75.00
1	Ken Griffey Jr./1989	5.00
156	Ken Griffey Jr./1990	2.00
555	Ken Griffey Jr./1991	2.00
424	Ken Griffey Jr./1992	2.00
355	Ken Griffey Jr./1993	2.00
224	Ken Griffey Jr./1994	2.00
100	Ken Griffey Jr./1995	2.00
200	Ken Griffey Jr./1996	2.00
175	Ken Griffey Jr./1997	2.00
225	Ken Griffey Jr./1998	2.00

Ken Griffey Jr. 1989 Buyback Autograph

One hundred authentically autographed 1989 Ken Griffey Jr. Upper Deck rookie cards were seeded into Series 1 packs. UD bought the cards on the open market, had them autographed by Griffey and added a diamond-shaped authentication hologram on back

	NM/M
Ken Griffey Jr./100	1,250

1999 Upper Deck Black Diamond

This 120-card base set features metallic foil fronts, while card backs have the featured player's vital information along with a close-up photo. The Diamond Debut subset (91-120) are short-printed and seeded 1:4 packs.

	NM/M
Complete Set (120):	30.00
Common Player:	.10
Common Diamond Debut (91-120):	.25
Inserted 1:4	
Double Diamonds (3,000 Each):	3X
Double Diamond Debuts (2,500):	2X
Triple Diamonds (1,500):	6X
Triple Diamond Debuts (1,000):	3X
Pack (6):	2.00
Wax Box (30):	40.00
1	Darin Erstad	.25
2	Tim Salmon	.10
3	Jim Edmonds	.10
4	Matt Williams	.10
5	David Dellucci	.10
6	Jay Bell	.10
7	Andres Galarraga	.10
8	Chipper Jones	1.00
9	Greg Maddux	1.00
10	Andruw Jones	.75
11	Cal Ripken Jr.	2.50
12	Rafael Palmeiro	.65
13	Brady Anderson	.10
14	Mike Mussina	.40
15	Nomar Garciaparra	1.00
16	Mo Vaughn	.10
17	Pedro Martinez	.75
18	Sammy Sosa	1.00
19	Henry Rodriguez	.10
20	Frank Thomas	.75
21	Magglio Ordonez	.40
22	Albert Belle	.10
23	Paul Konerko	.20
24	Sean Casey	.10
25	Jim Thome	.60
26	Kenny Lofton	.10
27	Sandy Alomar Jr.	.10
28	Jaret Wright	.10
29	Larry Walker	.10
30	Todd Helton	.65
31	Vinny Castilla	.10
32	Tony Clark	.10
33	Damion Easley	.10
34	Mark Kotsay	.10
35	Derek Lee	.50
36	Moises Alou	.10
37	Jeff Bagwell	.75
38	Craig Biggio	.10
39	Randy Johnson	.75
40	Dean Palmer	.10
41	Johnny Damon	.35
42	Chan Ho Park	.10
43	Raul Mondesi	.10
44	Gary Sheffield	.40
45	Jeromy Burnitz	.10
46	Marquis Grissom	.10
47	Jeff Cirillo	.10
48	Paul Molitor	.75
49	Todd Walker	.10
50	Vladimir Guerrero	.75
51	Brad Fullmer	.10
52	Mike Piazza	1.50
53	Hideo Nomo	.40
54	Carlos Baerga	.10
55	John Olerud	.10
56	Derek Jeter	2.50
57	Hideki Irabu	.10
58	Tino Martinez	.10
59	Bernie Williams	.10
60	Miguel Tejada	.25
61	Ben Grieve	.10
62	Jason Giambi	.55
63	Scott Rolen	.60
64	Doug Glanville	.10
65	Desi Relaford	.10
66	Tony Womack	.10
67	Jason Kendall	.10
68	Jose Guillen	.10
69	Tony Gwynn	1.00
70	Ken Caminiti	.10
71	Greg Vaughn	.10
72	Kevin Brown	.10

73	Barry Bonds	2.50
74	J.T. Snow	.10
75	Jeff Kent	.10
76	Ken Griffey Jr.	1.50
77	Alex Rodriguez	2.00
78	Edgar Martinez	.10
79	Jay Buhner	.10
80	Mark McGwire	2.00
81	Delino DeShields	.10
82	Brian Jordan	.10
83	Quinton McCracken	.10
84	Fred McGriff	.10
85	Juan Gonzalez	.40
86	Ivan Rodriguez	.65
87	Will Clark	.10
88	Roger Clemens	1.25
89	Jose Cruz Jr.	.10
90	Babe Ruth	2.00
91	Troy Glaus (Diamond Debut)	1.00
92	Jarrod Washburn (Diamond Debut)	.25
93	Travis Lee (Diamond Debut)	.75
94	Bruce Chen (Diamond Debut)	.25
95	Mike Caruso (Diamond Debut)	.25
96	Jim Parque (Diamond Debut)	.25
97	Kerry Wood (Diamond Debut)	.50
98	Jeremy Giambi (Diamond Debut)	.25
99	Matt Anderson (Diamond Debut)	.25
100	Seth Greisinger (Diamond Debut)	.25
101	Gabe Alvarez (Diamond Debut)	.25
102	Rafael Medina (Diamond Debut)	.25
103	Daryle Ward (Diamond Debut)	.25
104	Alex Cora (Diamond Debut)	.25
105	Adrian Beltre (Diamond Debut)	.50
106	Geoff Jenkins (Diamond Debut)	.25
107	Eric Milton (Diamond Debut)	.25
108	Carl Pavano (Diamond Debut)	.25
109	Eric Chavez (Diamond Debut)	.50
110	Orlando Hernandez (Diamond Debut)	.25
111	A.J. Hinch (Diamond Debut)	.25
112	Carlton Loewer (Diamond Debut)	.25
113	Aramis Ramirez (Diamond Debut)	.25
114	Cliff Politte (Diamond Debut)	.25
115	Matt Clement (Diamond Debut)	.25
116	Alex Gonzalez (Diamond Debut)	.25
117	J.D. Drew (Diamond Debut)	.75
118	Shane Monahan (Diamond Debut)	.25
119	Rolando Arrojo (Diamond Debut)	.25
120	George Lombard (Diamond Debut)	.25

Double Diamond

Double Diamonds are the most common parallels to the Black Diamond base set. Cards feature a red metallic-foil background or highlights. Regular-player cards (#1-90) are serially numbered on back from within an edition of 3,000 each. Diamond Debut cards (#91-120) are individually numbered within an edition of 2,500 each.

	NM/M
Complete Set (120):	200.00
Common Player (1-90):	.25
Common Diamond Debut (91-120):	1.00

Stars (1-90):	3X
Diamond Debuts (91-120):	2X

Triple Diamond

Triple Diamonds are the mid-level of scarcity among the parallel inserts to the Black Diamond base cards. They feature yellow metallic-foil backgrounds (1-90) and highlights (91-120). Regular-player cards are serially numbered on back from within an edition of 1,500 each. Diamond Debut cards are individually numbered within an edition of 1,000 each.

	NM/M
Common Player (1-90):	1.00
Common Diamond Debut (91-120):	1.50
Stars (1-90):	6X
Diamond Debuts (91-120):	3X

Quadruple Diamond

Quadruple Diamonds are the scarcest of the parallel inserts to the Black Diamond base cards. The regular player cards (#1-90) feature a green metallic-foil background and are serially numbered on back from within an edition of 150 each. Diamond Debut cards (#91-120) also feature green foil highlights on front and are individually numbered within an edition of 100 each. Quad Diamond cards of Sosa, Griffey and McGwire were limited to the number of home runs each hit the previous season.

	NM/M
Common Player (1-90):	4.00
Production 150 each.	
Common Diamond Debut (91-120):	6.00
Production 100 each.	
Stars (1-90):	25X
Diamond Debuts (91-120):	8X
18	Sammy Sosa/66	50.00
76	Ken Griffey Jr. /56	60.00
80	Mark McGwire/70	75.00

A Piece of History

This six-card set features green metallic foil fronts with a diamond-shaped piece of game-used bat from the featured player embedded on the card front. No insertion ratio was released.

	NM/M
Common Player:	5.00
JG	Juan Gonzalez	7.50
TG	Tony Gwynn	10.00
BW	Bernie Williams	5.00
MM	Mark McGwire	200.00
MV	Mo Vaughn	5.00
SS	Sammy Sosa	25.00

Diamond Dominance

This 30-card set features full-bleed metallic foil fronts and includes the top stars of the game along with Babe Ruth. Each card is numbered with a "D" prefix and is limited to 1,500 sequentially numbered sets.

	NM/M
Complete Set (30):	65.00
Common Player:	.50
Production 1,500 Sets	
D01	Kerry Wood	1.00
D02	Derek Jeter	6.00
D03	Alex Rodriguez	5.00
D04	Frank Thomas	2.00
D05	Jeff Bagwell	2.00
D06	Mo Vaughn	.50
D07	Ivan Rodriguez	1.50
D08	Cal Ripken Jr.	6.00
D09	Rolando Arrojo	.50
D10	Chipper Jones	3.00
D11	Kenny Lofton	.50
D12	Paul Konerko	.75
D13	Mike Piazza	4.00
D14	Ben Grieve	.50
D15	Nomar Garciaparra	3.00
D16	Travis Lee	.65
D17	Scott Rolen	1.00
D18	Juan Gonzalez	1.00
D19	Tony Gwynn	3.00
D20	Tony Clark	.50
D21	Roger Clemens	3.50
D22	Sammy Sosa	3.00
D23	Larry Walker	.50
D24	Ken Griffey Jr.	4.00
D25	Mark McGwire	5.00
D26	Barry Bonds	6.00
D27	Vladimir Guerrero	2.00
D28	Tino Martinez	.50
D29	Greg Maddux	3.00
D30	Babe Ruth	5.00

Mystery Numbers

The player's card number determines scarcity in this hobby-only insert set. The basic set has an action photo set against a silver-foil background of repeated numerals. Backs have a portrait photo and significant stat numbers from the 1998 season. Each base Mystery Numbers card is individually numbered within an edition of 100 cards times the card number within the 30-card set (i.e., card #24 has an edition of 2,400) for a total of 46,500 cards.

An emerald version of the Mystery Numbers cards has a total issue of 465 cards, with cards issued to a limit of the player's card number multiplied by 1.

	NM/M
Complete Set (30):	100.00
Common Player:	.75
M1	Babe Ruth/100	25.00
M2	Ken Griffey Jr./200	12.50
M3	Kerry Wood/300	4.00
M4	Mark McGwire/400	12.50
M5	Alex Rodriguez/500	12.50
M6	Chipper Jones/600	6.00
M7	Nomar Garciaparra/700	6.00
M8	Derek Jeter/800	10.00
M9	Mike Piazza/900	6.00
M10	Roger Clemens/1,000	4.50
M11	Greg Maddux/1,100	4.50
M12	Scott Rolen/1,200	1.25
M13	Cal Ripken Jr./1,300	7.50
M14	Ben Grieve/1,400	.75
M15	Troy Glaus/1,500	3.00
M16	Sammy Sosa/1,600	4.50
M17	Darin Erstad/1,700	1.25
M18	Juan Gonzalez/1,800	1.25
M19	Pedro Martinez/1,900	1.50
M20	Larry Walker/2,000	.75
M21	Vladimir Guerrero/2,100	1.50
M22	Jeff Bagwell/2,200	1.50
M23	Jaret Wright/2,300	.75
M24	Travis Lee/2,400	.75
M25	Barry Bonds/2,500	6.00
M26	Orlando Hernandez/2,600	.75
M27	Frank Thomas/2,700	1.50
M28	Tony Gwynn/2,800	2.00
M29	Andres Galarraga/2,900	.75
M30	Craig Biggio/3,000	.75

Piece of History 500 Club

A veneer of lumber from one of Mr. October's war clubs is included in this special insert card. A facsimile autograph is also featured on front. A premium version with an authentic autograph serially numbered from within an edition of 44 (his uniform number) was also issued. Backs have a congratulatory authentication message from Upper Deck CEO Richard McWilliam.

	NM/M
Reggie Jackson	165.00
Reggie Jackson/Auto.	500.00

1999 Upper Deck Century Legends

The first 47 cards in the 131-card set are taken from The Sporting News' list of Baseball's 100 Greatest Players. Each card bears a Sporting News photo of the featured player and his ranking in silver and copper foil. The next 50 cards tout Upper Deck's rankings of the Top 50 contemporary players. Rounding out the base set are two subsets: 21st Century Phenoms and Century Memories. Because of contractual problems, cards #11, 25, 26 and 126 were never issued. A die-cut parallel version of each card, serially numbered to 100 each, was produced as the "Century Collection."

	NM/M
Complete Set (131):	20.00
Common Player:	.10
Century Collection:	20X

Production 100 Sets		
Pack (5):		3.00
Wax Box (24):		60.00
1	Babe Ruth (Top 50)	2.00
1	Babe Ruth (SAMPLE overprint on back.)	2.00
2	Willie Mays (Top 50)	1.00
3	Ty Cobb (Top 50)	1.00
4	Walter Johnson (Top 50)	.40
5	Hank Aaron (Top 50)	1.00
6	Lou Gehrig (Top 50)	1.50
7	Christy Mathewson (Top 50)	.40
8	Ted Williams (Top 50)	1.25
9	Rogers Hornsby (Top 50)	.20
10	Stan Musial (Top 50)	.65
12	Grover Alexander (Top 50)	.20
13	Honus Wagner (Top 50)	.40
14	Cy Young (Top 50)	.40
15	Jimmie Foxx (Top 50)	.20
16	Johnny Bench (Top 50)	.50
17	Mickey Mantle (Top 50)	2.00
18	Josh Gibson (Top 50)	.25
19	Satchel Paige (Top 50)	.50
20	Roberto Clemente (Top 50)	1.50
21	Warren Spahn (Top 50)	.20
22	Frank Robinson (Top 50)	.20
23	Lefty Grove (Top 50)	.20
24	Eddie Collins (Top 50)	.10
25	Tris Speaker (Top 50)	.20
26	Mike Schmidt (Top 50)	.50
28	Napoleon LaJoie (Top 50)	.20
29	Steve Carlton (Top 50)	.25
30	Bob Gibson (Top 50)	.25
31	Tom Seaver (Top 50)	.25
32	George Sisler (Top 50)	.20
33	Barry Bonds (Top 50)	1.50
34	Joe Jackson (Top 50)	1.25
35	Bob Feller (Top 50)	.25
36	Hank Greenberg (Top 50)	.20
37	Ernie Banks (Top 50)	.40
38	Greg Maddux (Top 50)	.40
39	Yogi Berra (Top 50)	.40
40	Nolan Ryan (Top 50)	2.00
41	Mel Ott (Top 50)	.25
42	Al Simmons (Top 50)	.10
43	Jackie Robinson (Top 50)	1.25
44	Carl Hubbell (Top 50)	.25
45	Charley Gehringer (Top 50)	.10
46	Buck Leonard (Top 50)	.10
47	Reggie Jackson (Top 50)	.40
48	Tony Gwynn (Top 50)	.75
49	Roy Campanella (Top 50)	.40
50	Ken Griffey Jr. (Contemporaries)	1.00
51	Barry Bonds (Contemporaries)	1.50
52	Roger Clemens (Contemporaries)	.85
53	Tony Gwynn (Contemporaries)	.75
54	Cal Ripken Jr. (Contemporaries)	1.50
55	Greg Maddux (Contemporaries)	.75
56	Frank Thomas (Contemporaries)	.65
57	Mark McGwire (Contemporaries)	
58	Mike Piazza (Contemporaries)	1.00
59	Wade Boggs (Contemporaries)	.75
60	Alex Rodriguez (Contemporaries)	1.25
61	Juan Gonzalez (Contemporaries)	.30
62	Mo Vaughn (Contemporaries)	.10
63	Albert Belle (Contemporaries)	.10
64	Sammy Sosa (Contemporaries)	.75
65	Nomar Garciaparra (Contemporaries)	.75
66	Derek Jeter (Contemporaries)	1.50
67	Kevin Brown (Contemporaries)	.10
68	Jose Canseco (Contemporaries)	.35
69	Randy Johnson (Contemporaries)	.60
70	Tom Glavine (Contemporaries)	.10
71	Barry Larkin (Contemporaries)	.10
72	Curt Schilling (Contemporaries)	.25
73	Moises Alou (Contemporaries)	.10
74	Fred McGriff (Contemporaries)	.10
75	Pedro Martinez (Contemporaries)	.65
76	Andres Galarraga (Contemporaries)	
77	Will Clark (Contemporaries)	
78	Larry Walker (Contemporaries)	.10
79	Ivan Rodriguez (Contemporaries)	.50
80	Chipper Jones (Contemporaries)	

82	Jeff Bagwell (Contemporaries)	.60
83	Craig Biggio (Contemporaries)	.10
84	Kerry Wood (Contemporaries)	.35
85	Roberto Alomar (Contemporaries)	.20
86	Vinny Castilla (Contemporaries)	.10
87	Kenny Lofton (Contemporaries)	.10
88	Rafael Palmeiro (Contemporaries)	.50
89	Manny Ramirez (Contemporaries)	.60
90	David Wells (Contemporaries)	.10
91	Mark Grace (Contemporaries)	.10
92	Bernie Williams (Contemporaries)	.10
93	David Cone (Contemporaries)	.10
94	John Olerud (Contemporaries)	.10
95	John Smoltz (Contemporaries)	.10
96	Tino Martinez (Contemporaries)	.10
97	Raul Mondesi (Contemporaries)	.10
98	Gary Sheffield (Contemporaries)	.35
99	Orel Hershiser (Contemporaries)	.10
100	Rickey Henderson (Contemporaries)	.65
101	J.D. Drew (21st Century Phenoms)	.50
102	Troy Glaus (21st Century Phenoms)	.50
103	Nomar Garciaparra (21st Century Phenoms)	.75
104	Scott Rolen (21st Century Phenoms)	.45
105	Ryan Minor (21st Century Phenoms)	.10
106	Travis Lee (21st Century Phenoms)	.20
107	Roy Halladay (21st Century Phenoms)	.10
108	Carlos Beltran (21st Century Phenoms)	.50
109	Alex Rodriguez (21st Century Phenoms)	1.25
110	Eric Chavez (21st Century Phenoms)	.20
111	Vladimir Guerrero (21st Century Phenoms)	.60
112	Ben Grieve (21st Century Phenoms)	.15
113	Kerry Wood (21st Century Phenoms)	.30
114	Alex Gonzalez (21st Century Phenoms)	.10
115	Darin Erstad (21st Century Phenoms)	.30
116	Derek Jeter (21st Century Phenoms)	1.50
117	Jaret Wright (21st Century Phenoms)	.10
118	Jose Cruz Jr. (21st Century Phenoms)	.10
119	Chipper Jones (21st Century Phenoms)	.75
120	Gabe Kapler (21st Century Phenoms)	.10
121	Satchel Paige (Century Memories)	.50
122	Willie Mays (Century Memories)	1.00
123	Roberto Clemente (Century Memories)	1.50
124	Lou Gehrig (Century Memories)	1.50
125	Mark McGwire (Century Memories)	1.25
127	Bob Gibson (Century Memories)	.25
128	Johnny Vander Meer (Century Memories)	.10
129	Walter Johnson (Century Memories)	.25
130	Ty Cobb (Century Memories)	.75
131	Don Larsen (Century Memories)	.20
132	Jackie Robinson (Century Memories)	1.00
133	Tom Seaver (Century Memories)	.25
134	Johnny Bench (Century Memories)	.35
135	Frank Robinson (Century Memories)	.25

All-Century Team

This 10-card set highlights Upper Deck's all-time all-star team. These were seeded 1:23 packs.

		NM/M
	Complete Set (10):	30.00
	Common Player:	2.50
	Inserted 1:23	
1	Babe Ruth	7.50
2	Ty Cobb	3.50

Lou Gehrig • Yankees • First Base

ALL-CENTURY TEAM

3	Willie Mays	3.50
4	Lou Gehrig	6.00
5	Jackie Robinson	5.00
6	Mike Schmidt	2.50
7	Ernie Banks	2.50
8	Johnny Bench	2.50
9	Cy Young	2.50
10	Lineup Sheet	.25

Century Artifacts

A total of nine cards were inserted, redeemable for memorabilia from some of the top players of the century. Due to the limited nature of these one-of-one inserts and the fact that most or all were redeemed, no pricing is assigned. Each cut signature was framed with the player's Century Legends card.

Century MVPs

This collection selects 100 cards from Upper Deck's '99 MVP brand and adds a rainbow-foil shift to each card. These are limited to only one numbered set.

One Set Produced
Values Undetermined

Epic Milestones

HANK AARON Braves • OF

This nine-card set showcases nine of the most impressive milestones established in major league history. Each card is numbered with an "EM" prefix and are seeded 1:12 packs. Because of a contractual dispute, card #1 was never issued.

		NM/M
	Complete Set (9):	5.00
	Common Player:	.25
	Inserted 1:12	
2	Jackie Robinson	.75
3	Nolan Ryan	1.00
4	Mark McGwire	.75
5	Roger Clemens	.60
6	Sammy Sosa	.75
7	Cal Ripken Jr.	1.00
9	Rickey Henderson	.25
9	Hank Aaron	.75
10	Barry Bonds	1.00

Epic Signatures

BOB GIBSON

EPIC SIGNATURES

This 30-card set features autographs from retired and current stars on a horizonal format. A player portrait appears over a ballpark background on front. The portrait is repeated on back with a statement of authenticity. Cards are numbered with player initials. These autographed cards are seeded 1:24 packs. Exchange

---

cards of Fisk, Bench, Berra and McCovey were originally inserted into packs and had to be mailed in for the autographed card. They are valued about 10 percent of the corresponding signed card.

		NM/M
	Common Player:	10.00
	Inserted 1:24	
EB	Ernie Banks	65.00
JB	Johnny Bench	40.00
YB	Yogi Berra	50.00
BB	Barry Bonds	180.00
SC	Steve Carlton	20.00
BD	Bucky Dent	10.00
BF	Bob Feller	15.00
CF	Carlton Fisk	25.00
BG	Bob Gibson	25.00
JG	Juan Gonzalez	20.00
Jr.	Ken Griffey Jr.	100.00
Sr.	Ken Griffey Sr.	10.00
VG	Vladimir Guerrero	30.00
TG	Tony Gwynn	40.00
RJ	Reggie Jackson	40.00
HK	Harmon Killebrew	30.00
DL	Don Larsen	15.00
GM	Greg Maddux	100.00
EMa	Eddie Mathews	80.00
BM	Bill Mazeroski	30.00
WMc	Willie McCovey	20.00
SM	Stan Musial	80.00
FR	Frank Robinson	30.00
AR	Alex Rodriguez	150.00
NR	Nolan Ryan	150.00
MS	Mike Schmidt	50.00
TS	Tom Seaver	40.00
WS	Warren Spahn	60.00
FT	Frank Thomas	50.00
BT	Bobby Thomson	10.00

Century Epic Signatures

TED WILLIAMS   CENTURY EPIC SIGNATURES

This 32-card autographed set features signatures from retired and current stars. The cards have a horizontal format and have gold foil stamping. Each card is hand numbered to 100.

		NM/M
	Common Player:	20.00
	Production 100 Sets	
EB	Ernie Banks	85.00
JB	Johnny Bench	90.00
YB	Yogi Berra	75.00
BB	Barry Bonds	240.00
SC	Steve Carlton	50.00
BD	Bucky Dent	20.00
BF	Bob Feller	40.00
CF	Carlton Fisk	50.00
BG	Bob Gibson	60.00
JG	Juan Gonzalez	60.00
Jr.	Ken Griffey Jr.	165.00
Sr.	Ken Griffey Sr.	20.00
VG	Vladimir Guerrero	70.00
TG	Tony Gwynn	90.00
RJ	Reggie Jackson	60.00
HK	Harmon Killebrew	75.00
DL	Don Larsen	30.00
GM	Greg Maddux	150.00
EMa	Eddie Mathews	90.00
WM	Willie Mays	300.00
BM	Bill Mazeroski	25.00
WMc	Willie McCovey	50.00
SM	Stan Musial	100.00
FR	Frank Robinson	50.00
AR	Alex Rodriguez	200.00
NR	Nolan Ryan	200.00
MS	Mike Schmidt	125.00
TS	Tom Seaver	75.00
WS	Warren Spahn	80.00
FT	Frank Thomas	80.00
BT	Bobby Thomson	20.00
TW	Ted Williams	750.00

Jerseys of the Century

TONY GWYNN   JERSEYS OF THE CENTURY

This nine-card set features a swatch of game-worn jersey from the featured current and retired player.

		NM/M
	Common Player:	12.50
	Inserted 1:418	
GB	George Brett	25.00
RC	Roger Clemens	25.00
TG	Tony Gwynn	20.00

GM	Greg Maddux	20.00
EM	Eddie Murray	15.00
NR	Nolan Ryan	90.00
MS	Mike Schmidt	25.00
OZ	Ozzie Smith	20.00
DW	Dave Winfield	15.00

Legendary Cuts

A total of nine of these one-fo-one inserts exist. These are actual "cut" signatures from some of baseball's all-time greats.

		NM/M
	Values Undetermined	
CY	Cy Young	
	(11/00 Auction)	1,850

Memorable Shots

This 10-card insert set focuses on the most memorable home runs launched during this century. The player's image is framed in an embossed foil, frame-like design. These are seeded 1:12 packs, each card back is numbered with an "HR" prefix.

		NM/M
	Complete Set (10):	15.00
	Common Player:	.50
	Inserted 1:12	
1	Babe Ruth	5.00
2	Bobby Thomson	1.00
3	Kirk Gibson	.50
4	Carlton Fisk	.50
5	Bill Mazeroski	1.00
6	Bucky Dent	.50
7	Mark McGwire	2.00
8	Mickey Mantle	5.00
9	Joe Carter	.50
10	Mark McGwire	2.00

500 Club Piece History

This Jimmie Foxx insert has a piece of a game-used Louisville Slugger once swung by Foxx, embedded into the card front. An estimated 350 cards of this one exist.

		NM/M
JF	Jimmie Foxx	125.00

1999 Upper Deck Challengers for 70

Celebrating Mark McGwire's record-setting season of 1998, and featuring those who would chase his single-season home run crown in 1999, Upper Deck issued this specialty product. The base set of 90 cards is fractured into subsets of Power Elite (#1-10), Power Corps (#11-40), Rookie Power (#41-45), and Home Run

---

Highlights (#46-90). Several styles of inserts and numbered parallels were included in the 5-card foil packs. A parallel set with each card serially numbered to 600 was also issued, titled "Challengers Edition".

		NM/M
	Complete Set (90):	15.00
	Common Player:	.05
	Challenger's Edition (600 Sets):	5X
	Pack (5):	2.00
	Wax Box (20):	25.00
1	Mark McGwire (Power Elite)	1.50
2	Sammy Sosa (Power Elite)	1.00
3	Ken Griffey Jr. (Power Elite)	1.25
4	Alex Rodriguez (Power Elite)	1.50
5	Albert Belle (Power Elite)	.05
6	Mo Vaughn (Power Elite)	.05
7	Mike Piazza (Power Elite)	1.25
8	Frank Thomas (Power Elite)	.75
9	Juan Gonzalez (Power Elite)	.35
10	Barry Bonds (Power Elite)	2.00
11	Rafael Palmeiro (Power Corps)	.60
12	Jose Canseco (Power Corps)	.50
13	Nomar Garciaparra (Power Corps)	1.00
14	Carlos Delgado (Power Corps)	.20
15	Brian Jordan (Power Corps)	.05
16	Vladimir Guerrero (Power Corps)	.65
17	Vinny Castilla (Power Corps)	.05
18	Chipper Jones (Power Corps)	1.00
19	Jeff Bagwell (Power Corps)	.65
20	Moises Alou (Power Corps)	.05
21	Tony Clark (Power Corps)	.05
22	Jim Thome (Power Corps)	.50
23	Tino Martinez (Power Corps)	.05
24	Greg Vaughn (Power Corps)	.05
25	Javy Lopez (Power Corps)	.05
26	Jeromy Burnitz (Power Corps)	.05
27	Cal Ripken Jr. (Power Corps)	2.00
28	Manny Ramirez (Power Corps)	.65
29	Darin Erstad (Power Corps)	.25
30	Ken Caminiti (Power Corps)	.05
31	Edgar Martinez (Power Corps)	.05
32	Ivan Rodriguez (Power Corps)	.60
33	Larry Walker (Power Corps)	.05
34	Todd Helton (Power Corps)	.60
35	Andruw Jones (Power Corps)	.65
36	Ray Lankford (Power Corps)	.05
37	Travis Lee (Power Corps)	.10
38	Raul Mondesi (Power Corps)	.05
39	Scott Rolen (Power Corps)	.50
40	Ben Grieve (Power Corps)	.05
41	J.D. Drew (Rookie Power)	.50
42	Troy Glaus (Rookie Power)	.60
43	Eric Chavez (Rookie Power)	.10
44	Gabe Kapler (Rookie Power)	.05
45	Michael Barrett (Rookie Power)	.05
46	Mark McGwire (HR Highlights)	.75
47	Jose Canseco (HR Highlights)	.25
48	Greg Vaughn (HR Highlights)	.05
49	Albert Belle (HR Highlights)	.05
50	Mark McGwire (HR Highlights)	.75
51	Vinny Castilla (HR Highlights)	.05
52	Vladimir Guerrero (HR Highlights)	.35
53	Andres Galarraga (HR Highlights)	.05
54	Rafael Palmeiro (HR Highlights)	.30
55	Juan Gonzalez (HR Highlights)	.20
56	Ken Griffey Jr. (HR Highlights)	.60

57	Barry Bonds (HR Highlights)	1.00
58	Mo Vaughn (HR Highlights)	.05
59	Nomar Garciaparra (HR Highlights)	.50
60	Tino Martinez (HR Highlights)	.05
61	Mark McGwire (HR Highlights)	.75
62	Mark McGwire (HR Highlights)	.75
63	Mark McGwire (HR Highlights)	.75
64	Mark McGwire (HR Highlights)	.75
65	Mark McGwire (HR Highlights)	.75
66	Sammy Sosa (HR Highlights)	.50
67	Mark McGwire (HR Highlights)	.75
68	Mark McGwire (HR Highlights)	.75
69	Mark McGwire (HR Highlights)	.75
70	Mark McGwire (HR Highlights)	.75
71	Mark McGwire (HR Highlights)	.75
72	Scott Brosius (HR Highlights)	.05
73	Tony Gwynn (HR Highlights)	.40
74	Chipper Jones (HR Highlights)	.50
75	Jeff Bagwell (HR Highlights)	.35
76	Moises Alou (HR Highlights)	.05
77	Manny Ramirez (HR Highlights)	.35
78	Carlos Delgado (HR Highlights)	.05
79	Kerry Wood (HR Highlights)	.20
80	Ken Griffey Jr. (HR Highlights)	.60
81	Cal Ripken Jr. (HR Highlights)	1.00
82	Alex Rodriguez (HR Highlights)	.75
83	Barry Bonds (HR Highlights)	1.00
84	Ken Griffey Jr. (HR Highlights)	.60
85	Travis Lee (HR Highlights)	.15
86	George Lombard (HR Highlights)	.05
87	Michael Barrett (HR Highlights)	.05
88	Jeremy Giambi (HR Highlights)	.05
89	Troy Glaus (HR Highlights)	.30
90	J.D. Drew (HR Highlights)	.25

Challengers Insert

ALEX RODRIGUEZ

Found one per pack, this insert series identifies 30 top contenders for the 1999 home run crown. Action photos on front are highlighted by red graphics and silver-foil. Backs repeat a detail of the front photo and present a capsule of the player's 1998 season. Cards have a "C" prefix to the number. A parallel edition, utilizing refractive foil details on front, is serially numbered within an edition of 70 each.

		NM/M
	Complete Set (30):	9.00
	Common Player:	.15
	Parallel Edition (70 Sets):	15X
1	Mark McGwire	1.00
2	Sammy Sosa	.65
3	Ken Griffey Jr.	.75
4	Alex Rodriguez	1.00
5	Albert Belle	.15
6	Mo Vaughn	.15
7	Mike Piazza	.75
8	Frank Thomas	.50
9	Juan Gonzalez	.25
10	Barry Bonds	.65
11	Rafael Palmeiro	.35
12	Nomar Garciaparra	.65

		NM/M
13	Vladimir Guerrero	.45
14	Vinny Castilla	.15
15	Chipper Jones	.75
16	Jeff Bagwell	.45
17	Moises Alou	.15
18	Tony Clark	.15
19	Jim Thome	.35
20	Tino Martinez	.15
21	Greg Vaughn	.15
22	Manny Ramirez	.45
23	Darin Erstad	.25
24	Ken Caminiti	.15
25	Ivan Rodriguez	.35
26	Andruw Jones	.45
27	Travis Lee	.25
28	Scott Rolen	.35
29	Ben Grieve	.15
30	J.D. Drew	.35

Longball Legends

Top home-run threats are featured in this insert series. The action photos on front are repeated in a diffused version on back, where they are joined by a second photo and a bargraph of the player's home run production in recent seasons. Cards have an "L" prefix to the number. Stated odds of picking a Longball Legends card are one per 39 packs.

		NM/M
Complete Set (30):		20.00
Common Player:		.50
1	Ken Griffey Jr.	1.50
2	Mark McGwire	2.00
3	Sammy Sosa	1.00
4	Cal Ripken Jr.	2.50
5	Barry Bonds	2.50
6	Larry Walker	.50
7	Fred McGriff	.50
8	Alex Rodriguez	2.00
9	Frank Thomas	.75
10	Juan Gonzalez	.60
11	Jeff Bagwell	.75
12	Mo Vaughn	.50
13	Albert Belle	.50
14	Mike Piazza	1.50
15	Vladimir Guerrero	.75
16	Chipper Jones	1.00
17	Ken Caminiti	.50
18	Rafael Palmeiro	.65
19	Nomar Garciaparra	1.00
20	Jim Thome	.60
21	Edgar Martinez	.50
22	Ivan Rodriguez	.65
23	Andres Galarraga	.50
24	Scott Rolen	.60
25	Darin Erstad	.65
26	Moises Alou	.50
27	J.D. Drew	.65
28	Andruw Jones	.75
29	Manny Ramirez	.75
30	Tino Martinez	.50

Mark on History

The details of Mark McGwire's successful assault on the single-season home run record are captured in this 25-card insert set, found on average of one per five packs. Cards have action photos set against a split red-and-black background and are highlighted in red metallic foil. Backs have details

of the home run featured on front, a quote from McGwire and another photo. Cards have an "M" prefix to the number. A parallel edition numbered to 70 was also issued.

	NM/M
Complete Set (25):	25.00
Common McGwire:	1.50
Parallel:	8X
01-25 Mark McGwire	1.50

Piece of History 500

A piece of game-used bat from 500-HR club member Harmon Killebrew is featured on these inserts. Only 350 cards were issued, along with three (his uniform number) authentically autographed versions. Backs have an action photo and a congratulatory authentication message from UD CEO Richard McWilliam.

	NM/M
Harmon Killebrew	120.00
Harmon Killebrew/ Auto.	450.00

Swinging/Fences

Fifteen top sluggers are included in this insert set. The players' power swing is captured on a muted textured-look background. Back has a color portrait photo and an "S" prefix to the card number. Stated insertion rate is one per 19 packs.

		NM/M
Complete Set (15):		15.00
Common Player:		.50
1	Ken Griffey Jr.	1.50
2	Mark McGwire	2.00
3	Sammy Sosa	1.25
4	Alex Rodriguez	2.00
5	Nomar Garciaparra	1.25
6	J.D. Drew	.75
7	Vladimir Guerrero	1.00
8	Ben Grieve	.50
9	Chipper Jones	1.25
10	Gabe Kapler	.50
11	Travis Lee	.60
12	Todd Helton	.75
13	Juan Gonzalez	.60
14	Mike Piazza	1.50
15	Mo Vaughn	.50

Autographed Swinging

A total of 2,700 autographed versions of Swinging for the Fences inserts were featured in the Challengers for 70 issue. Only six of the 15 players' cards were included in this premium version.

	NM/M
Complete Set (6):	200.00
Common Player:	5.00
JR	Ken Griffey Jr.	95.00
VG	Vladimir Guerrero	25.00
TH	Todd Helton	15.00
GK	Gabe Kapler	5.00
TL	Travis Lee	7.50
AR	Alex Rodriguez	90.00

1999 Upper Deck UD Choice Previews

A month prior to the release of its new UD Choice brand baseball series, Upper Deck issued this 55-card Preview version. Sold in five-card cello packs for about 75 cents only at retail outlets, the cards are identical to the issued versions of the same players except for the appearance at top front of a gold foil-stamped "PREVIEW."

		NM/M
Complete Set (55):		16.00
Common Player:		.10
46	Tim Salmon	.10
48	Chuck Finley	.10
50	Matt Williams	.10
52	Travis Lee	.20
54	Andres Galarraga	.10
56	Greg Maddux	.75
58	Cal Ripken Jr.	1.50
60	Rafael Palmeiro	.50
62	Nomar Garciaparra	.75
64	Pedro Martinez	.60
66	Kerry Wood	.35
68	Sammy Sosa	.75
70	Albert Belle	.10
72	Frank Thomas	.60
74	Pete Harnisch	.10
76	Manny Ramirez	.60
78	Travis Fryman	.10
80	Kenny Lofton	.10
82	Larry Walker	.10
84	Gabe Alvarez	.10
86	Damion Easley	.10
88	Mark Kotsay	.10
90	Jeff Bagwell	.60
93	Craig Biggio	.10
94	Larry Sutton	.10
96	Johnny Damon	.30
98	Gary Sheffield	.35
100	Mark Grudzielanek	.10
102	Jeff Cirillo	.10
104	Mark Loretta	.10
106	David Ortiz	.40
108	Brad Fullmer	.10
110	Vladimir Guerrero	.60
112	Brian McRae	.10
114	Rey Ordonez	.10
115	Derek Jeter	1.50
118	Paul O'Neill	.10
120	A.J. Hinch	.10
122	Miguel Tejada	.15
124	Scott Rolen	.45
126	Bobby Abreu	.10
128	Jason Kendall	.10
130	Mark McGwire	1.25
132	Eli Marrero	.10
136	Kevin Brown	.10
137	Tony Gwynn	.75
138	Bill Mueller	.10
140	Barry Bonds	1.50
142	Ken Griffey Jr.	1.00
143	Alex Rodriguez	1.25
146	Rolando Arrojo	.10
148	Quinton McCracken	.10
150	Will Clark	.10
152	Juan Gonzalez	.30
154	Carlos Delgado	.25

1999 Upper Deck UD Choice

The 155-card base set consists of 110 regular player cards and two subsets, 27 Star Rookies and 18 Cover Glory subset cards. Card fronts have a white border, with the Upper Deck UD Choice logo on the bottom right of the front. Card backs have complete year-by-year stats along with some vital information. Each pack con-

tains 12 cards. A parallel version also exists, called Prime Choice Reserve and are numbered to 100.

		NM/M
Complete Set (155):		7.50
Common Player:		.03
Prime Choice Reserve Stars:		10X
Production 100 Sets		
Pack (12):		.50
Wax Box (36):		10.00
1	Gabe Kapler (Rookie Class)	.05
2	Jin Ho Cho (Rookie Class)	.05
3	Matt Anderson (Rookie Class)	.05
4	Ricky Ledee (Rookie Class)	.05
5	Bruce Chen (Rookie Class)	.05
6	Alex Gonzalez (Rookie Class)	.05
7	Ryan Minor (Rookie Class)	.05
8	Michael Barrett (Rookie Class)	.05
9	Carlos Beltran (Rookie Class)	.50
10	Ramon Martinez (Rookie Class)	.05
11	Dermal Brown (Rookie Class)	.05
12	Robert Fick (Rookie Class)	.05
13	Preston Wilson (Rookie Class)	.05
14	Orlando Hernandez (Rookie Class)	.05
15	Troy Glaus (Rookie Class)	.65
16	Calvin Pickering (Rookie Class)	.05
17	Corey Koskie (Rookie Class)	.05
18	Fernando Seguignol (Rookie Class)	.05
19	Carlos Guillen (Rookie Class)	.05
20	Kevin Witt (Rookie Class)	.05
21	Mike Kinkade (Rookie Class)	.05
22	Eric Chavez (Rookie Class)	.15
23	Mike Lowell (Rookie Class)	.10
24	Adrian Beltre (Rookie Class)	.10
25	George Lombard (Rookie Class)	.05
26	Jeremy Giambi (Rookie Class)	.05
27	J.D. Drew (Rookie Class)	.40
28	Mark McGwire (Cover Glory)	.60
29	Kerry Wood (Cover Glory)	.15
30	David Wells (Cover Glory)	.05
31	Juan Gonzalez (Cover Glory)	.15
32	Randy Johnson (Cover Glory)	.35
33	Derek Jeter (Cover Glory)	.75
34	Tony Gwynn (Cover Glory)	.45
35	Greg Maddux (Cover Glory)	.45
36	Cal Ripken Jr. (Cover Glory)	.75
37	Ken Griffey Jr. (Cover Glory)	.50
38	Bartolo Colon (Cover Glory)	.05
39	Troy Glaus (Cover Glory)	.30
40	Ben Grieve (Cover Glory)	.05
41	Roger Clemens (Cover Glory)	.50
42	Chipper Jones (Cover Glory)	.50
43	Scott Rolen (Cover Glory)	.25
44	Nomar Garciaparra (Cover Glory)	.45
45	Sammy Sosa (Cover Glory)	.45
46	Tim Salmon	.05
47	Darin Erstad	.25
48	Chuck Finley	.05
49	Garrett Anderson	.05
50	Matt Williams	.05
51	Jay Bell	.05
52	Travis Lee	.10
53	Andruw Jones	.25
54	Andres Galarraga	.05
55	Chipper Jones	.75
56	Greg Maddux	.75
57	Javy Lopez	.05
58	Cal Ripken Jr.	1.50

		NM/M
59	Brady Anderson	.05
60	Rafael Palmeiro	.50
61	B.J. Surhoff	.05
62	Nomar Garciaparra	.75
63	Troy O'Leary	.05
64	Pedro Martinez	.65
65	Jason Varitek	.05
66	Kerry Wood	.35
67	Sammy Sosa	.75
68	Mark Grace	.05
69	Mickey Morandini	.05
70	Albert Belle	.05
71	Mike Caruso	.05
72	Frank Thomas	.65
73	Sean Casey	.10
74	Pete Harnisch	.05
75	Dmitri Young	.05
76	Manny Ramirez	.65
77	Omar Vizquel	.05
78	Travis Fryman	.05
79	Jim Thome	.40
80	Kenny Lofton	.50
81	Todd Helton	.50
82	Larry Walker	.05
83	Vinny Castilla	.05
84	Gabe Alvarez	.05
85	Tony Clark	.05
86	Damion Easley	.05
87	Livan Hernandez	.05
88	Mark Kotsay	.05
89	Cliff Floyd	.05
90	Jeff Bagwell	.65
91	Moises Alou	.05
92	Randy Johnson	.65
93	Craig Biggio	.05
94	Larry Sutton	.05
95	Dean Palmer	.05
96	Johnny Damon	.20
97	Charles Johnson	.05
98	Gary Sheffield	.25
99	Raul Mondesi	.05
100	Mark Grudzielanek	.05
101	Jeromy Burnitz	.05
102	Jeff Cirillo	.05
103	Jose Valentin	.05
104	Mark Loretta	.05
105	Todd Walker	.05
106	David Ortiz	.35
107	Brad Radke	.05
108	Brad Fullmer	.05
109	Rondell White	.05
110	Vladimir Guerrero	.65
111	Mike Piazza	1.00
112	Brian McRae	.05
113	John Olerud	.05
114	Rey Ordonez	.05
115	Derek Jeter	1.50
116	Bernie Williams	.05
117	David Wells	.05
118	Paul O'Neill	.05
119	Tino Martinez	.05
120	A.J. Hinch	.05
121	Jason Giambi	.30
122	Miguel Tejada	.10
123	Ben Grieve	.05
124	Scott Rolen	.50
125	Desi Relaford	.05
126	Bobby Abreu	.10
127	Jose Guillen	.05
128	Jason Kendall	.05
129	Aramis Ramirez	.05
130	Mark McGwire	1.25
131	Ray Lankford	.05
132	Eli Marrero	.05
133	Wally Joyner	.05
134	Greg Vaughn	.05
135	Trevor Hoffman	.05
136	Kevin Brown	.05
137	Tony Gwynn	.75
138	Bill Mueller	.05
139	Ellis Burks	.05
140	Barry Bonds	1.50
141	Robb Nen	.05
142	Ken Griffey Jr.	1.00
143	Alex Rodriguez	1.25
144	Jay Buhner	.05
145	Edgar Martinez	.05
146	Rolando Arrojo	.05
147	Robert Smith	.05
148	Quinton McCracken	.05
149	Ivan Rodriguez	.50
150	Will Clark	.05
151	Mark McLemore	.05
152	Juan Gonzalez	.35
153	Jose Cruz Jr.	.05
154	Carlos Delgado	.25
155	Roger Clemens	.85

Prime Choice Reserve

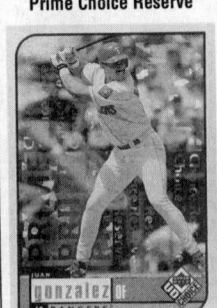

Each card in the UD Choice set is also found in a parallel version with the words "Prime Choice Reserve" repeated in the background of the photo in refractive foil. On back, the parallels are individually serial numbered within an edition of 100 each.

	NM/M
Common Player:	2.50
Stars:	10X

All-Star Game '99

These super-size (3-1/2" x 5") versions of 1999 UD Choice cards were issued as a boxed set exclusively for retail outlet sales. The cards are in a format identical to the regular-issue UD Choice except for a large All-Star Game logo in one of the upper corners. Fronts have game-action photos; backs have a small portrait, major league stats and career highlights. The set was sold in a green-foil enhanced box with a special card commemorating the 1999 game July 13 in Boston.

		NM/M
Complete Set (21):		12.50
Common Player:		.35
1	Kenny Lofton	.35
2	Pedro Martinez	.75
3	Nomar Garciaparra	1.00
4	Ken Griffey Jr.	1.25
5	Derek Jeter	2.00
6	Manny Ramirez	.75
7	Ivan Rodriguez	.65
8	Bernie Williams	.35
9	Cal Ripken Jr.	2.00
10	Jim Thome	.60
11	Mike Piazza	1.25
12	Jeff Bagwell	.75
13	Craig Biggio	.35
14	Mark McGwire	1.50
15	Matt Williams	.35
16	Chipper Jones	1.00
17	Tony Gwynn	1.00
18	Sammy Sosa	1.00
19	Raul Mondesi	.35
20	Larry Walker	.35
---	Header Card	.05

Mini Bobbing Head

Inserted 1:5 packs, some of the game's best players can be assembled into a miniature bobbing head figure by following the instructions on the card backs.

		NM/M
Complete Set (30):		15.00
Common Player:		.25
Inserted 1:5		
B1	Randy Johnson	.50
B2	Troy Glaus	.50
B3	Chipper Jones	.75
B4	Cal Ripken Jr.	1.50
B5	Nomar Garciaparra	.65
B6	Pedro Martinez	.50
B7	Kerry Wood	.35
B8	Sammy Sosa	.65
B9	Frank Thomas	.50
B10	Paul Konerko	.25
B11	Omar Vizquel	.25
B12	Kenny Lofton	.35
B13	Gabe Kapler	.25
B14	Adrian Beltre	.35
B15	Orlando Hernandez	.25
B16	Derek Jeter	1.50
B17	Mike Piazza	.75
B18	Tino Martinez	.25
B19	Ben Grieve	.25
B20	Rickey Henderson	.50

B21	Scott Rolen	.40
B22	Aramis Ramirez	.25
B23	Greg Vaughn	.25
B24	Tony Gwynn	.65
B25	Barry Bonds	1.50
B26	Alex Rodriguez	1.00
B27	Ken Griffey Jr.	.75
B28	Mark McGwire	1.00
B29	J.D. Drew	.45
B30	Juan Gonzalez	.30

Piece of History 500 Club

A piece from an Eddie Murray game-used bat was incorporated into each of these cards, which are limited to 350.

		NM/M
EM	Eddie Murray/350	150.00

StarQuest

This four-tiered 30-card set features four different colors for each of the levels. Singles are seeded one per pack and have blue foil etching, Doubles (1:8) have green foil etching, Triples (1:23) have red foil etching and Home Runs are limited to 100 numbered sets with gold foil etching.

		NM/M
Complete Set (30):		7.50
Common Player:		.10
Inserted 1:1		
Green (1:8):		1.5X
Red (1:23):		3X
Gold (100 Sets): 50X		
SQ1	Ken Griffey Jr.	.60
SQ2	Sammy Sosa	.50
SQ3	Alex Rodriguez	.75
SQ4	Derek Jeter	1.00
SQ5	Troy Glaus	.35
SQ6	Mike Piazza	.60
SQ7	Barry Bonds	1.00
SQ8	Tony Gwynn	.50
SQ9	Juan Gonzalez	.20
SQ10	Chipper Jones	.50
SQ11	Greg Maddux	.50
SQ12	Randy Johnson	.40
SQ13	Roger Clemens	.55
SQ14	Ben Grieve	.10
SQ15	Nomar Garciaparra	.50
SQ16	Travis Lee	.15
SQ17	Frank Thomas	.40
SQ18	Vladimir Guerrero	.40
SQ19	Scott Rolen	.30
SQ20	Ivan Rodriguez	.35
SQ21	Cal Ripken Jr.	1.00
SQ22	Mark McGwire	.75
SQ23	Jeff Bagwell	.40
SQ24	Tony Clark	.10
SQ25	Kerry Wood	.25
SQ26	Kenny Lofton	.10
SQ27	Adrian Beltre	.15
SQ28	Larry Walker	.10
SQ29	Curt Schilling	.25
SQ30	Jim Thome	.40

Yard Work

This 30-card set showcases the top power hitters in the game. The right side of the card is covered in bronze foil and stamped with Yard Work. They are numbered with a Y-prefix and seeded 1:13 packs.

		NM/M
Complete Set (30):		20.00
Common Player:		.35
Inserted 1:13		
Y1	Andres Galarraga	.35
Y2	Chipper Jones	1.50
Y3	Rafael Palmeiro	.75
Y4	Nomar Garciaparra	1.50

Y5	Sammy Sosa	1.50
Y6	Frank Thomas	1.00
Y7	J.D. Drew	.75
Y8	Albert Belle	.35
Y9	Jim Thome	.35
Y10	Manny Ramirez	1.00
Y11	Larry Walker	.35
Y12	Vinny Castilla	.35
Y13	Tony Clark	.35
Y14	Jeff Bagwell	1.00
Y15	Moises Alou	.35
Y16	Dean Palmer	.35
Y17	Gary Sheffield	.50
Y18	Vladimir Guerrero	1.00
Y19	Mike Piazza	1.75
Y20	Tino Martinez	.35
Y21	Ben Grieve	.35
Y22	Greg Vaughn	.35
Y23	Ken Caminiti	.35
Y24	Barry Bonds	3.00
Y25	Ken Griffey Jr.	1.75
Y26	Alex Rodriguez	2.25
Y27	Mark McGwire	2.25
Y28	Juan Gonzalez	.50
Y29	Jose Canseco	.50
Y30	Jose Cruz Jr.	.35

1999 Upper Deck Encore

Encore is a 180-card partial parallel of Upper Deck Series 1, utilizing a special holo-foil treatment on each card. The Encore set consists of 90 base cards and three short-printed subsets: 45 Star Rookies (1:4), 30 Homer Odyssey (1:6) and 15 Stroke of Genius (1:8).

		NM/M
Complete Set (180):		75.00
Common Player (1-90):		.05
Common Player (91-135):		.25
Inserted 1:4		
Common Player (136-165):		.35
Inserted 1:6		
Common Player (166-180):		.50
Inserted 1:8		
Gold (1-90):		10X
Gold (91-135):		1.5X
Gold (136-165):		3X
Gold (166-180):		4X
Production 125 Sets		
Pack (6):		1.50
Wax Box (24):		25.00
1	Darin Erstad	.25
2	Mo Vaughn	.25
3	Travis Lee	.15
4	Randy Johnson	.60
5	Matt Williams	.25
6	John Smoltz	.05
7	Greg Maddux	.75
8	Chipper Jones	.75
9	Tom Glavine	.25
10	Andruw Jones	.60
11	Cal Ripken Jr.	1.50
12	Mike Mussina	.30
13	Albert Belle	.05
14	Nomar Garciaparra	.75
15	Jose Offerman	.05
16	Pedro Martinez	.60
17	Trot Nixon	.10
18	Kerry Wood	.40
19	Sammy Sosa	.75
20	Frank Thomas	.60
21	Paul Konerko	.15
22	Sean Casey	.15
23	Barry Larkin	.05
24	Greg Vaughn	.05
25	Travis Fryman	.05
26	Jaret Wright	.05
27	Jim Thome	.45
28	Manny Ramirez	.60
29	Roberto Alomar	.20
30	Kenny Lofton	.05
31	Todd Helton	.60
32	Larry Walker	.05
33	Vinny Castilla	.05
34	Dante Bichette	.05
35	Tony Clark	.05
36	Dean Palmer	.05
37	Gabe Kapler	.05
38	Juan Encarnacion	.05
39	Alex Gonzalez	.05
40	Preston Wilson	.05
41	Mark Kotsay	.05
42	Moises Alou	.05
43	Craig Biggio	.05
44	Ken Caminiti	.05
45	Jeff Bagwell	.60
46	Johnny Damon	.30
47	Gary Sheffield	.25
48	Kevin Brown	.05
49	Raul Mondesi	.05
50	Jeff Cirillo	.05
51	Jeromy Burnitz	.05
52	Todd Walker	.05
53	Corey Koskie	.05
54	Brad Fullmer	.05
55	Vladimir Guerrero	.60
56	Mike Piazza	1.25
57	Robin Ventura	.05
58	Rickey Henderson	.60
59	Derek Jeter	1.50
60	Paul O'Neill	.05
61	Bernie Williams	.05
62	Tino Martinez	.05
63	Roger Clemens	.85
64	Ben Grieve	.05
65	Jason Giambi	.35
66	Bob Abreu	.10
67	Scott Rolen	.40
68	Curt Schilling	.25
69	Marlon Anderson	.05
70	Kevin Young	.05
71	Jason Kendall	.05
72	Brian Giles	.05
73	Mark McGwire	1.25
74	Fernando Tatis	.05
75	Eric Davis	.05
76	Trevor Hoffman	.05
77	Tony Gwynn	.75
78	Matt Clement	.05
79	Robb Nen	.05
80	Barry Bonds	1.50
81	Ken Griffey Jr.	1.00
82	Alex Rodriguez	1.25
83	Wade Boggs	.75
84	Fred McGriff	.05
85	Jose Canseco	.30
86	Ivan Rodriguez	.50
87	Juan Gonzalez	.30
88	Rafael Palmeiro	.50
89	Carlos Delgado	.25
90	David Wells	.05
91	Troy Glaus/SR	1.00
92	Adrian Beltre/SR	.50
93	Matt Anderson/SR	.25
94	Eric Chavez/SR	.40
95	Jeff Weaver/SR RC	.50
96	Warren Morris/SR	.25
97	George Lombard/SR	.25
98	Mike Kinkade/SR	.25
99	Kyle Farnsworth/SR RC	.25
100	J.D. Drew/SR	.50
101	Joe McEwing/SR RC	.50
102	Carlos Guillen/SR	.25
103	Kelly Dransfeldt/SR RC	.25
104	Eric Munson/SR RC	.50
105	Armando Rios/SR	.25
106	Ramon Martinez/SR	.25
107	Orlando Hernandez/SR	.45
108	Jeremy Giambi/SR	.25
109	Pat Burrell/SR RC	2.50
110	Shea Hillenbrand/SR RC	1.00
111	Billy Koch/SR	.25
112	Roy Halladay/SR	.35
113	Ruben Mateo/SR	.25
114	Bruce Chen/SR	.25
115	Angel Pena/SR	.25
116	Michael Barrett/SR	.25
117	Kevin Witt/SR	.25
118	Damon Minor/SR	.25
119	Ryan Minor/SR	.25
120	A.J. Pierzynski/SR	.25
121	A.J. Burnett/SR RC	.50
122	Christian Guzman/SR	.25
123	Joe Lawrence/SR	.25
124	Derrick Gibson/SR	.25
125	Carlos Febles/SR	.25
126	Chris Haas/SR	.25
127	Cesar King/SR	.25
128	Calvin Pickering/SR	.25
129	Mitch Meluskey/SR	.25
130	Carlos Beltran/SR	1.00
131	Ron Belliard/SR	.25
132	Jerry Hairston Jr./SR	.25
133	Fernando Seguignol/SR	.25
134	Kris Benson/SR	.25
135	Chad Hutchinson/SR RC	.25
136	Ken Griffey Jr. (Homer Odyssey)	1.50
137	Mark McGwire (Homer Odyssey)	2.00
138	Sammy Sosa (Homer Odyssey)	1.25
139	Albert Belle (Homer Odyssey)	.35
140	Mo Vaughn (Homer Odyssey)	.35
141	Alex Rodriguez (Homer Odyssey)	2.00
142	Manny Ramirez (Homer Odyssey)	.75
143	J.D. Drew (Homer Odyssey)	.50
144	Juan Gonzalez (Homer Odyssey)	.45
145	Vladimir Guerrero (Homer Odyssey)	.75
146	Fernando Tatis (Homer Odyssey)	.35
147	Mike Piazza (Homer Odyssey)	2.00
148	Barry Bonds (Homer Odyssey)	2.50
149	Ivan Rodriguez (Homer Odyssey)	.60
150	Jeff Bagwell (Homer Odyssey)	.75
151	Raul Mondesi (Homer Odyssey)	.35
152	Nomar Garciaparra (Homer Odyssey)	1.25
153	Jose Canseco (Homer Odyssey)	.50
154	Greg Vaughn (Homer Odyssey)	.35
155	Scott Rolen (Homer Odyssey)	.50
156	Vinny Castilla (Homer Odyssey)	.35
157	Troy Glaus (Homer Odyssey)	.65
158	Craig Biggio (Homer Odyssey)	.35
159	Tino Martinez (Homer Odyssey)	.35
160	Jim Thome (Homer Odyssey)	.60
161	Frank Thomas (Homer Odyssey)	1.00
162	Tony Clark (Homer Odyssey)	.35
163	Ben Grieve (Homer Odyssey)	.35
164	Matt Williams (Homer Odyssey)	.35
165	Derek Jeter (Homer Odyssey)	2.50
166	Ken Griffey Jr. (Strokes of Genius)	2.00
167	Tony Gwynn (Strokes of Genius)	1.50
168	Mike Piazza (Strokes of Genius)	2.00
169	Mark McGwire (Strokes of Genius)	2.50
170	Sammy Sosa (Strokes of Genius)	1.50
171	Juan Gonzalez (Strokes of Genius)	.60
172	Mo Vaughn (Strokes of Genius)	.50
173	Derek Jeter (Strokes of Genius)	3.00
174	Bernie Williams (Strokes of Genius)	.50
175	Ivan Rodriguez (Strokes of Genius)	.75
176	Barry Bonds (Strokes of Genius)	3.00
177	Scott Rolen (Strokes of Genius)	.75
178	Larry Walker (Strokes of Genius)	.50
179	Chipper Jones (Strokes of Genius)	1.50
180	Alex Rodriguez (Strokes of Genius)	2.50

FX Gold

This is a 180-card parallel to the base set featuring gold holo-foil treatment and limited to 125 sequentially numbered sets.

	NM/M
Common Player:	1.00
Gold (1-90):	10X
Gold (91-135):	1.5X
Gold (136-165):	3X
Gold (166-180):	4X

Batting Practice Caps

This 15-card set features actual swatch pieces of the highlight-

ed players' batting practice cap embedded into each card. These are seeded 1:750 packs.

		NM/M
Complete Set (15):		85.00
Common Player:		4.00
Inserted 1:750		
CB	Carlos Beltran	8.00
BB	Barry Bonds	30.00
VC	Vinny Castilla	4.00
EC	Eric Chavez	6.00
TC	Tony Clark	4.00
JD	J.D. Drew	6.00
VG	Vladimir Guerrero	8.00
TG	Tony Gwynn	15.00
TH	Todd Helton	8.00
GK	Gabe Kapler	4.00
JK	Jason Kendall	4.00
DP	Dean Palmer	4.00
BH	Frank Thomas	8.00
GV	Greg Vaughn	4.00
TW	Todd Walker	4.00

Driving Forces

This 15-card set is highlighted by holo-foil treatment on the card fronts on a thick card stock. Baseball's top performers are featured in this set and are seeded 1:23 packs. A Gold parallel exists and is limited to 10 sets.

		NM/M
Complete Set (15):		30.00
Common Player:		1.00
Inserted 1:23		
Gold (10 Sets):		30X
D1	Ken Griffey Jr.	3.00
D2	Mark McGwire	4.00
D3	Sammy Sosa	2.50
D4	Albert Belle	1.00
D5	Alex Rodriguez	4.00
D6	Mo Vaughn	1.00
D7	Juan Gonzalez	2.00
D8	Jeff Bagwell	2.00
D9	Mike Piazza	2.00
D10	Frank Thomas	2.00
D11	Barry Bonds	5.00
D12	Vladimir Guerrero	2.50
D13	Chipper Jones	2.50
D14	Tony Gwynn	2.50
D15	J.D. Drew	1.50

McGwired!

This 10-card set salutes baseball's reigning single season home run king. These are seeded 1:23 packs. A gold parallel also is randomly seeded and is limited to 500 sequentially numbered sets. A small photo of the pitcher McGwire hit the historic home run off of is pictured as well.

		NM/M
Complete Set (10):		12.50
Common Card:		1.50
Inserted 1:23		
Parallel:		2X
Production 500 Sets		
1	Mark McGwire, Carl Pavano	1.50
2	Mark McGwire, Michael Morgan	1.50
3	Mark McGwire, Steve Trachsel	1.50
4	Mark McGwire	2.50
5	Mark McGwire	2.50
6	Mark McGwire, Scott Elarton	1.50
7	Mark McGwire, Jim Parque	1.50
8	Mark McGwire	2.50
9	Mark McGwire, Rafael Roque	1.50
10	Mark McGwire, Jaret Wright	1.50

Pure Excitement

This 30-card set features Light F/X technology and includes the top players in baseball. These are seeded 1:7 packs.

		NM/M
Complete Set (30):		35.00
Common Player:		.50
Inserted 1:7		
1	Mo Vaughn	.50
2	Darin Erstad	.75
3	Travis Lee	.65
4	Chipper Jones	1.50
5	Greg Maddux	1.50
6	Gabe Kapler	.50
7	Cal Ripken Jr.	4.00
8	Nomar Garciaparra	1.50
9	Kerry Wood	.75
10	Frank Thomas	1.00
11	Manny Ramirez	1.00
12	Larry Walker	.50
13	Tony Clark	.50
14	Jeff Bagwell	1.00
15	Craig Biggio	.50
16	Vladimir Guerrero	1.00
17	Mike Piazza	2.00
18	Bernie Williams	.60
19	Derek Jeter	4.00
20	Ben Grieve	.60
21	Eric Chavez	.60
22	Scott Rolen	.75
23	Mark McGwire	3.00
24	Tony Gwynn	1.50
25	Barry Bonds	4.00
26	Ken Griffey Jr.	2.00
27	Alex Rodriguez	3.00
28	J.D. Drew	.75
29	Juan Gonzalez	.60
30	Roger Clemens	1.75

Rookie Encore

This 10-card set highlights the top rookie prospects in 1999, including J.D. Drew and Gabe Kapler. These are seeded 1:23 packs. A parallel version is also randomly seeded and limited to 500 sequentially numbered sets.

	NM/M
Complete Set (10):	17.50
Common Player:	1.50
Inserted 1:23	

FX Gold:		2X
Production 500 Sets		
1	J.D. Drew	2.00
2	Eric Chavez	1.00
3	Gabe Kapler	1.00
4	Bruce Chen	1.00
5	Carlos Beltran	3.00
6	Troy Glaus	5.00
7	Roy Halladay	1.00
8	Adrian Beltre	2.00
9	Michael Barrett	1.00
10	Pat Burrell	5.00

UD Authentics

This six-card autographed set features signatures of Griffey Jr. and Nomar Garciaparra. These are seeded 1:288 packs.

		NM/M
Complete Set (6):		130.00
Common Player:		5.00
Inserted 1:288		
MB	Michael Barrett	4.00
PB	Pat Burrell	10.00
JD	J.D. Drew	12.00
NG	Nomar Garciaparra	70.00
TG	Troy Glaus	12.00
JR	Ken Griffey Jr.	90.00

Upper Realm

This 15-card set focuses on the top stars of the game. Card fronts utilize holo-foil treatment, with the initials UR lightly foiled. Card backs are numbered with a "U" prefix and are seeded 1:11 packs.

		NM/M
Complete Set (15):		13.00
Common Player:		.30
Inserted 1:11		
1	Ken Griffey Jr.	1.25
2	Mark McGwire	1.50
3	Sammy Sosa	.75
4	Tony Gwynn	.75
5	Alex Rodriguez	1.50
6	Juan Gonzalez	.40
7	J.D. Drew	.50
8	Roger Clemens	.85
9	Greg Maddux	.75
10	Randy Johnson	.60
11	Mo Vaughn	.30
12	Derek Jeter	2.00
13	Vladimir Guerrero	.60
14	Cal Ripken Jr.	2.00
15	Nomar Garciaparra	.75

2K Countdown

This set recognizes the countdown to the next century with a salute to baseball's next century of superstars including Derek Jeter and Alex Rodriguez. These are done on a horizontal format and inserted 1:11 packs.

Ken Griffey Jr. Santa Hat Card

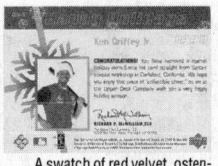

A swatch of red velvet, ostensibly from "a special holiday-worn Santa hat," is featured on this card given to customers and associates of UD. The standard-size card is highlighted in gold-foil front and back and features pictures of the spokesman in a Santa hat on each side, as well.

		NM/M
HH-1	Ken Griffey Jr.	40.00

1999 Upper Deck HoloGrFX Sample

Numbered 60, rather than 56 as in the regular-issue version, this card, which also bears a white "SAMPLE" notation on back, was issued to preview the new UD brand.

		NM/M
60	Ken Griffey Jr.	2.50

1999 Upper Deck HoloGrFX

HoloGrFX was distributed exclusively to retail and the base set is comprised of 60 base cards, each utilizing holographic technology. A parallel gold-enhanced AUsome version is found about once every eight packs.

		NM/M
Complete Set (60):		12.00
Common Player:		.10
AUsome:		1.5X
Inserted 1:8		
Pack (3):		1.00
Wax Box (36):		20.00
1	Mo Vaughn	.10
2	Troy Glaus	.60
3	Tim Salmon	.10
4	Randy Johnson	.65
5	Travis Lee	.25
6	Chipper Jones	.75
7	Greg Maddux	.75
8	Andruw Jones	.65
9	Tom Glavine	.25

10	Cal Ripken Jr.	1.50
11	Albert Belle	.10
12	Nomar Garciaparra	.75
13	Pedro J. Martinez	.65
14	Sammy Sosa	.75
15	Frank Thomas	.65
16	Greg Vaughn	.10
17	Kenny Lofton	.10
18	Jim Thome	.50
19	Manny Ramirez	.65
20	Todd Helton	.60
21	Larry Walker	.10
22	Tony Clark	.10
23	Juan Encarnacion	.10
24	Mark Kotsay	.10
25	Jeff Bagwell	.65
26	Craig Biggio	.10
27	Ken Caminiti	.10
28	Carlos Beltran	.50
29	Jeremy Giambi	.10
30	Raul Mondesi	.10
31	Kevin Brown	.10
32	Jeromy Burnitz	.10
33	Corey Koskie	.10
34	Todd Walker	.10
35	Vladimir Guerrero	.65
36	Mike Piazza	1.00
37	Robin Ventura	.10
38	Derek Jeter	1.50
39	Roger Clemens	.85
40	Bernie Williams	.10
41	Orlando Hernandez	.10
42	Ben Grieve	.10
43	Eric Chavez	.15
44	Scott Rolen	.45
45	Pat Burrell RC	1.50
46	Warren Morris	.10
47	Jason Kendall	.10
48	Mark McGwire	1.25
49	J.D. Drew	.50
50	Tony Gwynn	.75
51	Trevor Hoffman	.10
52	Barry Bonds	1.50
53	Ken Griffey Jr.	1.00
54	Alex Rodriguez	1.25
55	Jose Canseco	.35
56	Juan Gonzalez	.30
57	Ivan Rodriguez	.60
58	Rafael Palmeiro	.60
59	David Wells	.10
60	Carlos Delgado	.25

Future Fame

This six-card set focuses on players who are destined for Hall of Fame greatness. Card fronts feature a horizontal format on a die-cut design. These are seeded 1:34 packs. A parallel Gold (AU) version is also randomly seeded in every 1:432 packs.

		NM/M
Complete Set (6):		15.00
Common Player:		2.50
Gold:		2X
Inserted 1:34		
1	Tony Gwynn	2.50
2	Cal Ripken Jr.	5.00
3	Mark McGwire	4.00
4	Ken Griffey Jr.	3.50
5	Greg Maddux	2.50
6	Roger Clemens	3.00

Launchers

This 15-card set highlights the top home run hitters on holographic patterned foil fronts, including McGwire and Sosa. These are seeded 1:3 packs. A Gold (AU) parallel version is also seeded 1:105 packs.

		NM/M
Complete Set (15):		20.00
Common Player:		.50

		NM/M
Inserted 1:3		
Gold:		2X
Inserted 1:105		
1	Mark McGwire	3.00
2	Ken Griffey Jr.	2.50
3	Sammy Sosa	2.00
4	J.D. Drew	.75
5	Mo Vaughn	.50
6	Juan Gonzalez	.50
7	Mike Piazza	2.50
8	Alex Rodriguez	3.00
9	Chipper Jones	2.00
10	Nomar Garciaparra	2.50
11	Vladimir Guerrero	1.00
12	Albert Belle	.50
13	Barry Bonds	4.00
14	Frank Thomas	1.00
15	Jeff Bagwell	1.00

StarView

This nine-card set highlights the top players in the game on a rainbow foil, full bleed design. These are seeded 1:17 packs. A Gold parallel version is also randomly seeded 1:210 packs.

		NM/M
Complete Set (9):		25.00
Common Player:		2.50
Inserted 1:17		
Gold:		2X
Inserted 1:210		
1	Mark McGwire	5.00
2	Ken Griffey Jr.	4.00
3	Sammy Sosa	2.50
4	Nomar Garciaparra	2.50
5	Roger Clemens	3.00
6	Greg Maddux	2.50
7	Mike Piazza	4.00
8	Alex Rodriguez	5.00
9	Chipper Jones	2.50

UD Authentics

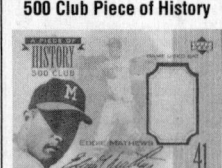

This autographed set is done on a horizontal format, with the player signature across the front of a shadow image of the featured player in the background.

		NM/M
Common Player:		4.00
Inserted 1:431		
CB	Carlos Beltran	25.00
BC	Bruce Chen	4.00
JD	J.D. Drew	12.00
AG	Alex Gonzalez	4.00
JR	Ken Griffey Jr.	80.00
CJ	Chipper Jones	50.00
GK	Gabe Kapler	6.00
MK	Mike Kinkade	4.00
CK	Corey Koskie	7.50
GL	George Lombard	4.00
RM	Ryan Minor	4.00
SM	Shane Monahan	4.00

500 Club Piece of History

This two card collection features game-used bat chips from bats swung by Willie McCovey and Eddie Mathews embedded into each card. 350 cards of each player exist. Each player also autographed these inserts to their respective jersey numbers: McCovey (44) and Mathews (41).

		NM/M
Eddie Mathews/350		150.00
Eddie Mathews/ Auto./41		550.00
Willie McCovey 350		120.00
Willie McCovey/ Auto./44		650.00

Hitter.Net Ted Williams

To promote Ted Williams; web site, UD issued this card to persons attending the 1999 All-Star Game July 13 at Fenway Park in Boston. Enclosed in a cellophane wrapper, the 2-1/2" x 3-1/2" card has a sepia photo of a young Williams superimposed on an aerial view of the ballpark. There is a facsimile autograph on front as well as the hitter.net logo. On back are various advertisements for the service, along with a photo of an autographed baseball.

		NM/M
9	Ted Williams	7.50

1999 UD Ionix

Ionix is a 90-card set that includes a 30-card "Techno" short-printed subset (1:4 packs). Four-card packs sold for $4.99. The first 60 cards of the set are included in a parallel set in which the photo from the back of the regular card was put on the front of a rainbow-foil Reciprocal card. These cards are sequentially numbered to 750. The Techno subset cards were also paralleled on a Reciprocal version sequentially numbered to 100. Due to an error, all Techno card numbers bear the "R" prefix intended for the Reciprocals; actual Reciprocal cards also bear a dot-matrix serial number on front.

		NM/M
Complete Set (90):		45.00
Common Player (1-60):		.25
Common Techno (61-90):		.50
Inserted 1:4		
Reciprocals (1-60):		3X
Production 750 Sets		
Techno Reciprocals (61-90):		1.5X
Production 100 Sets		
Pack (4):		2.00
Wax Box (20):		25.00
1	Troy Glaus	.60
2	Darin Erstad	.50
3	Travis Lee	.35
4	Matt Williams	.25
5	Chipper Jones	.75
6	Greg Maddux	.75
7	Andruw Jones	.65
8	Andres Galarraga	.25
9	Tom Glavine	.35
10	Cal Ripken Jr.	2.00
11	Ryan Minor	.25
12	Nomar Garciaparra	1.00
13	Mo Vaughn	.25
14	Pedro Martinez	.65
15	Sammy Sosa	.75
16	Kerry Wood	.50

17	Albert Belle	.25
18	Frank Thomas	.65
19	Sean Casey	.25
20	Kenny Lofton	.25
21	Manny Ramirez	.25
22	Jim Thome	.60
23	Bartolo Colon	.25
24	Jaret Wright	.25
25	Larry Walker	.25
26	Tony Clark	.25
27	Gabe Kapler	.25
28	Edgar Renteria	.25
29	Randy Johnson	.65
30	Craig Biggio	.65
31	Jeff Bagwell	.65
32	Moises Alou	.25
33	Johnny Damon	.50
34	Adrian Beltre	.35
35	Jeromy Burnitz	.25
36	Todd Walker	.25
37	Corey Koskie	.25
38	Vladimir Guerrero	.65
39	Mike Piazza	1.00
40	Hideo Nomo	.35
41	Derek Jeter	2.00
42	Tino Martinez	.25
43	Orlando Hernandez	.25
44	Ben Grieve	.25
45	Rickey Henderson	.65
46	Scott Rolen	.60
47	Curt Schilling	.25
48	Aramis Ramirez	.25
49	Tony Gwynn	.75
50	Kevin Brown	.25
51	Barry Bonds	2.00
52	Ken Griffey Jr.	1.00
53	Alex Rodriguez	1.50
54	Mark McGwire	1.50
55	J.D. Drew	.60
56	Rolando Arrojo	.25
57	Ivan Rodriguez	.60
58	Juan Gonzalez	.35
59	Roger Clemens	.75
60	Jose Cruz Jr.	.25
61	Travis Lee (Techno)	.65
62	Andres Galarraga (Techno)	.50
63	Andruw Jones (Techno)	1.50
64	Chipper Jones (Techno)	2.00
65	Greg Maddux (Techno)	2.00
66	Cal Ripken Jr. (Techno)	4.00
67	Nomar Garciaparra (Techno)	2.00
68	Mo Vaughn (Techno)	.50
69	Sammy Sosa (Techno)	2.00
70	Frank Thomas (Techno)	1.50
71	Kerry Wood (Techno)	.75
72	Kenny Lofton (Techno)	.50
73	Manny Ramirez (Techno)	1.50
74	Larry Walker (Techno)	.50
75	Jeff Bagwell (Techno)	1.50
76	Randy Johnson (Techno)	1.50
77	Paul Molitor (Techno)	1.50
78	Derek Jeter (Techno)	4.00
79	Tino Martinez (Techno)	.50
80	Mike Piazza (Techno)	2.50
81	Ben Grieve (Techno)	.50
82	Scott Rolen (Techno)	1.50
83	Mark McGwire (Techno)	3.00
84	Tony Gwynn (Techno)	2.00
85	Barry Bonds (Techno)	4.00
86	Ken Griffey Jr. (Techno)	3.00
87	Alex Rodriguez (Techno)	3.00
88	Juan Gonzalez (Techno)	.75
89	Roger Clemens (Techno)	2.25
90	J.D. Drew (Techno)	1.00
100	Ken Griffey Jr. (SAMPLE)	2.50

Reciprocal

Reciprocal is a parallel of the Ionix base set in which the front and back photos have been switched. Card numbers carry an "R" prefix. The first 60 Reciprocal parallels were produced in an edition of 750 each; the Techno subset Reciprocals (#61-90) are an edition of just 100 each.

Stars (1-60):		3X
Stars (61-90):		1.5X

Cyber

This insert set consisted of 25-cards of baseball's superstars and red-hot rookies. One card was inserted every 53 packs.

	NM/M
Complete Set (25):	125.00
Common Player:	2.00
C01 Ken Griffey Jr.	8.00
C02 Cal Ripken Jr.	12.50
C03 Frank Thomas	5.00
C04 Greg Maddux	6.50
C05 Mike Piazza	8.00
C06 Alex Rodriguez	10.00
C07 Chipper Jones	8.00
C08 Derek Jeter	12.50
C09 Mark McGwire	10.00
C10 Juan Gonzalez	2.50
C11 Kerry Wood	2.50
C12 Tony Gwynn	6.50
C13 Scott Rolen	4.00
C14 Nomar Garciaparra	6.50
C15 Roger Clemens	7.00
C16 Sammy Sosa	6.50
C17 Travis Lee	2.00
C18 Ben Grieve	2.00
C19 Jeff Bagwell	5.00
C20 Ivan Rodriguez	4.00
C21 Barry Bonds	12.50
C22 J.D. Drew	4.00
C23 Kenny Lofton	2.00
C24 Andruw Jones	5.00
C25 Vladimir Guerrero	5.00

HoloGrFX

This insert set consisted of 10-cards, and featured only the best players in the game. The cards in this set were holographically enhanced. These cards were rare with one card inserted every 1,500 packs.

	NM/M
Complete Set (10):	800.00
Common Player:	50.00
Inserted 1:1,500	
HG01 Ken Griffey Jr.	100.00
HG02 Cal Ripken Jr.	150.00
HG03 Frank Thomas	75.00
HG04 Greg Maddux	90.00
HG05 Mike Piazza	100.00
HG06 Alex Rodriguez	125.00
HG07 Chipper Jones	90.00
HG08 Derek Jeter	150.00
HG09 Mark McGwire	125.00
HG10 Juan Gonzalez	50.00

Hyper

This insert set featured the top players in baseball, and consisted of 20-cards. Hyper cards were inserted one per nine packs.

	NM/M
Complete Set (20):	37.00
Common Player:	.75
Inserted 1:9	
H01 Ken Griffey Jr.	3.00
H02 Cal Ripken Jr.	4.50
H03 Frank Thomas	1.50
H04 Greg Maddux	2.25
H05 Mike Piazza	3.00
H06 Alex Rodriguez	3.75
H07 Chipper Jones	2.50
H08 Derek Jeter	4.50
H09 Mark McGwire	3.75
H10 Juan Gonzalez	.75
H11 Kerry Wood	1.00
H12 Tony Gwynn	2.25
H13 Scott Rolen	1.00
H14 Nomar Garciaparra	2.25
H15 Roger Clemens	2.75
H16 Sammy Sosa	2.25
H17 Travis Lee	1.00
H18 Ben Grieve	.75
H19 Jeff Bagwell	1.50
H20 J.D. Drew	1.00

Nitro

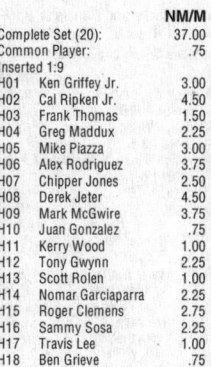

Baseball's ten most collectible players are featured in this 10-card insert set. Each card features Ionix technology with rainbow foil and a unique color pattern. Nitro cards were inserted one per 18 packs.

	NM/M
Complete Set (10):	18.00
Common Player:	1.00
Inserted 1:18	
N01 Ken Griffey Jr.	2.50
N02 Cal Ripken Jr.	4.00
N03 Frank Thomas	1.50
N04 Greg Maddux	2.00
N05 Mike Piazza	2.50
N06 Alex Rodriguez	3.00
N07 Chipper Jones	2.00
N08 Derek Jeter	4.00
N09 Mark McGwire	3.00
N10 J.D. Drew	1.00

Warp Zone

This 15-card insert set contained a special holographic foil enhancement. Warp Zone cards were inserted one per 216 packs.

	NM/M
Complete Set (15):	195.00
Common Player:	6.00
Inserted 1:216	
WZ1 Ken Griffey Jr.	20.00
WZ2 Cal Ripken Jr.	30.00
WZ3 Frank Thomas	10.00
WZ4 Greg Maddux	15.00
WZ5 Mike Piazza	20.00
WZ6 Alex Rodriguez	25.00
WZ7 Chipper Jones	15.00
WZ8 Derek Jeter	30.00
WZ9 Mark McGwire	25.00
WZ10 Juan Gonzalez	6.00
WZ11 Kerry Wood	6.00
WZ12 Tony Gwynn	15.00
WZ13 Scott Rolen	6.00
WZ14 Nomar Garciaparra	15.00
WZ15 J.D. Drew	6.00

500 Club Piece of History

These cards feature an actual piece of game-used bat from one

of Hall-of-Famer Frank Robinson's Louisville Sluggers. Approximately 350 were made. Robinson also autographed 20 of his Piece of History inserts.

	NM/M
FR Frank Robinson/350	165.00
FRA Frank Robinson/ Auto. 20	650.00

Mark McGwire Tribute Lunchbox

One of many special issues produced by Upper Deck in celebration of McGwire's short-lived season home run record, this 30-card set was sold in a metal lunchbox. Each 2-1/2" x 3-1/2" card has a large action photo on front and a small home run portrait, along with the card title. The back has the same photos, with the large photo in a ghosted image as a background for the description of the highlight presented on the card.

	NM/M
Complete Boxed Set (30):	10.00
Common Card:	.50
1-30 Mark McGwire	.50

Mark McGwire 70 HR - A New Record

This is one of many special issues from Upper Deck commemorating McGwire's record-breaking 1998 season. Most such cards were produced for retail-only sales, or for home shopping television shows. This blank-back, round-cornered card is 3-1/2" x 2-1/2" and has a flicker-action scene of Big Mac's home run swing.

	NM/M
Mark McGwire	4.00

Mark McGwire 500 Home Run Card Set

This TV-exclusive product depicts milestone home runs leading up to Big Mac's 500th career clout on Aug. 5, 1999. Sold in a shrink-wrapped decorative box, the basic design of the 2-1/2" x 3-1/2" cards has a central photo, usually an action shot, with a black pinstriped border at left and a red striped border at right. The word "MILESTONES" appears at the top of the picture. In a gray tab at left is a date or year, while his name is in a matching black tab at right. A silver-foil UD logo is at bottom. Backs have a grainy red monochromatic background photo on which are overprinted the details of the pictured blast, along with appropriate logos. Some cards have a silver-foil home run number printed on front. A special card pictures his 1st and 500th career homers. Issue price was about $30.

	NM/M
Complete Boxed Set (30):	7.00
Common Card:	.35
1-30 Mark McGwire	.35

1999 Upper Deck MVP Samples

	NM/M
S3 Ken Griffey Jr.	2.00
S3 Ken Griffey Jr. (Silver signature.)	2.00

1999 Upper Deck MVP

Card fronts of the 220-card set feature silver foil stamping and a white border. Backs feature year-by-year statistics, a small photo of the featured player and a brief career note. MVP was distributed in 36-pack boxes, with a SRP of $1.59 for 10-card packs.

	NM/M
Complete Set (220):	10.00
Common Player:	.05
Silver Script:	1X
Inserted 1:2	
Gold Script:	10X
Production 100 Sets	
Super Script:	30X
Production 25 Sets	
Pack (10):	1.00
Wax Box (36):	20.00
1 Mo Vaughn	.05
2 Tim Belcher	.05
3 Jack McDowell	.05
4 Troy Glaus	.60
5 Darin Erstad	.40
6 Tim Salmon	.15
7 Jim Edmonds	.05
8 Randy Johnson	.60
9 Steve Finley	.05
10 Travis Lee	.15
11 Matt Williams	.05
12 Todd Stottlemyre	.05
13 Jay Bell	.05
14 David Dellucci	.05
15 Chipper Jones	.75
16 Andruw Jones	.35
17 Greg Maddux	.75
18 Tom Glavine	.25
19 Javy Lopez	.05
20 Brian Jordan	.05
21 George Lombard	.05
22 John Smoltz	.05
23 Cal Ripken Jr.	1.50
24 Charles Johnson	.05
25 Albert Belle	.15
26 Brady Anderson	.05
27 Mike Mussina	.35
28 Calvin Pickering	.05
29 Ryan Minor	.05
30 Jerry Hairston Jr.	.05
31 Nomar Garciaparra	1.00
32 Pedro Martinez	.60
33 Jason Varitek	.05
34 Troy O'Leary	.05
35 Donnie Sadler	.05
36 Mark Portugal	.05
37 John Valentin	.05
38 Kerry Wood	.35
39 Sammy Sosa	1.00
40 Mark Grace	.10
41 Henry Rodriguez	.05
42 Rod Beck	.05
43 Benito Santiago	.05
44 Kevin Tapani	.05
45 Frank Thomas	.60
46 Mike Caruso	.05
47 Magglio Ordonez	.40
48 Paul Konerko	.05
49 Ray Durham	.05
50 Jim Parque	.05
51 Carlos Lee	.05
52 Denny Neagle	.05
53 Pete Harnisch	.05
54 Michael Tucker	.05
55 Sean Casey	.15
56 Eddie Taubensee	.05
57 Barry Larkin	.05
58 Pokey Reese	.05
59 Sandy Alomar	.05
60 Roberto Alomar	.25
61 Bartolo Colon	.05
62 Kenny Lofton	.05
63 Omar Vizquel	.05
64 Travis Fryman	.05
65 Jim Thome	.05
66 Manny Ramirez	.60
67 Jaret Wright	.05
68 Darryl Kile	.05
69 Kirt Manwaring	.05
70 Vinny Castilla	.05
71 Todd Helton	.60
72 Dante Bichette	.05
73 Larry Walker	.05
74 Derrick Gibson	.05
75 Gabe Kapler	.05
76 Dean Palmer	.05
77 Matt Anderson	.05
78 Bobby Higginson	.05
79 Damion Easley	.05
80 Tony Clark	.05
81 Juan Encarnacion	.05
82 Livan Hernandez	.05
83 Alex Gonzalez	.05
84 Preston Wilson	.05
85 Derrek Lee	.05
86 Mark Kotsay	.05
87 Todd Dunwoody	.05
88 Cliff Floyd	.05
89 Ken Caminiti	.05
90 Jeff Bagwell	.05
91 Moises Alou	.05
92 Craig Biggio	.05
93 Billy Wagner	.05
94 Richard Hidalgo	.05
95 Derek Bell	.05
96 Hipolito Pichardo	.05
97 Jeff King	.05
98 Carlos Beltran	.40
99 Jeremy Giambi	.05
100 Larry Sutton	.05
101 Johnny Damon	.20
102 Dee Brown	.05
103 Kevin Brown	.10
104 Chan Ho Park	.05
105 Raul Mondesi	.05
106 Eric Karros	.05
107 Adrian Beltre	.15
108 Devon White	.05
109 Gary Sheffield	.35
110 Sean Berry	.05
111 Alex Ochoa	.05
112 Marquis Grissom	.05
113 Fernando Vina	.05
114 Jeff Cirillo	.05
115 Geoff Jenkins	.05
116 Jeromy Burnitz	.05
117 Brad Radke	.05
118 Eric Milton	.05
119 A.J. Pierzynski	.05
120 Todd Walker	.05
121 David Ortiz	.05
122 Corey Koskie	.05
123 Vladimir Guerrero	.60
124 Rondell White	.05
125 Brad Fullmer	.05
126 Ugueth Urbina	.05
127 Dustin Hermanson	.05
128 Michael Barrett	.05
129 Fernando Seguignol	.05
130 Mike Piazza	1.00
131 Rickey Henderson	.60
132 Rey Ordonez	.05
133 John Olerud	.05
134 Robin Ventura	.05
135 Hideo Nomo	.60
136 Mike Kinkade	.05
137 Al Leiter	.05
138 Brian McRae	.05
139 Derek Jeter	1.50
140 Bernie Williams	.15
141 Paul O'Neill	.05
142 Scott Brosius	.05
143 Tino Martinez	.05
144 Roger Clemens	.85
145 Orlando Hernandez	.10
146 Mariano Rivera	.10
147 Ricky Ledee	.05
148 A.J. Hinch	.05
149 Ben Grieve	.10
150 Eric Chavez	.15
151 Miguel Tejada	.15
152 Matt Stairs	.05
153 Ryan Christenson	.05
154 Jason Giambi	.35
155 Curt Schilling	.25
156 Scott Rolen	.45
157 Pat Burrell RC	1.50
158 Doug Glanville	.05
159 Bobby Abreu	.05
160 Rico Brogna	.05
161 Ron Gant	.05
162 Jason Kendall	.05
163 Aramis Ramirez	.05
164 Jose Guillen	.05
165 Emil Brown	.05
166 Pat Meares	.05
167 Kevin Young	.05
168 Brian Giles	.05
169 Mark McGwire	1.25
170 J.D. Drew	.40
171 Edgar Renteria	.05
172 Fernando Tatis	.05
173 Matt Morris	.05
174 Eli Marrero	.05
175 Ray Lankford	.05
176 Tony Gwynn	.75
177 Sterling Hitchcock	.05
178 Ruben Rivera	.05
179 Wally Joyner	.05
180 Trevor Hoffman	.05
181 Jim Leyritz	.05
182 Carlos Hernandez	.05
183 Barry Bonds	1.50
184 Ellis Burks	.05
185 F.P. Santangelo	.05
186 J.T. Snow	.05
187 Ramon Martinez	.05
188 Jeff Kent	.05
189 Robb Nen	.05
190 Ken Griffey Jr.	1.00
191 Alex Rodriguez	1.25
192 Shane Monahan	.05
193 Carlos Guillen	.05
194 Edgar Martinez	.05
195 David Segui	.05
196 Jose Mesa	.05
197 Jose Canseco	.35
198 Rolando Arrojo	.05
199 Wade Boggs	.75
200 Fred McGriff	.05
201 Quinton McCracken	.05
202 Bobby Smith	.05
203 Bubba Trammell	.05
204 Juan Gonzalez	.60
205 Ivan Rodriguez	.45
206 Rafael Palmeiro	.45
207 Royce Clayton	.05
208 Rick Helling	.05
209 Todd Zeile	.05
210 Rusty Greer	.05
211 David Wells	.05
212 Roy Halladay	.05
213 Carlos Delgado	.25
214 Darrin Fletcher	.05
215 Shawn Green	.15
216 Kevin Witt	.05
217 Jose Cruz Jr.	.05
218 Checklist (Ken Griffey Jr.)	.45
219 Checklist (Sammy Sosa)	.45
220 Checklist (Mark McGwire)	.50

Scripts/Super Scripts

Three different parallels of the 220 base cards in MVP are inserted bearing a metallic-foil facsimile autograph on front. Silver Script cards are found about every other pack. Gold Script cards are hobby-only and serially numbered to 100 apiece. Also hobby-only are Super Script versions on which the autograph is in holographic foil and the cards are numbered on the back to 25 apiece.

Silver Script:	1X
Gold Script:	10X
Super Script:	30X

All-Star Game

In conjunction with FanFest held in Boston prior to the All-Star Game, UD issued a set of specially marked versions of its MVP issue. It was reported that 15,000 three-card packs were distributed at the show, with some cards reportedly short-printed. The cards have a format virtually identical to the regular-issue MVP cards, except for the presence on front of a bright silver-foil All-Star logo and an AS prefix to the card number on back.

		NM/M
Complete Set (30):		12.50
Common Player:		.25
1	Mo Vaughn	.25
2	Randy Johnson	.60
3	Chipper Jones	.75
4	Greg Maddux	.75
5	Cal Ripken Jr.	2.00
6	Albert Belle	.35
7	Nomar Garciaparra	1.00
8	Pedro Martinez	.60
9	Sammy Sosa	1.00
10	Frank Thomas	.60
11	Sean Casey	.35
12	Roberto Alomar	.30
13	Manny Ramirez	.60
14	Larry Walker	.25
15	Jeff Bagwell	.60
16	Craig Biggio	.25
17	Raul Mondesi	.25
18	Vladimir Guerrero	.60
19	Mike Piazza	1.00
20	Derek Jeter	2.00
21	Roger Clemens	.85
22	Scott Rolen	.40
23	Mark McGwire	1.50
24	Tony Gwynn	.75
25	Barry Bonds	2.00
26	Ken Griffey Jr.	1.00
27	Alex Rodriguez	1.50
28	Jose Canseco	.40
29	Juan Gonzalez	.60
30	Ivan Rodriguez	.50

Dynamics

This 15-card set features holofoil treatment on the card fronts with silver foil stamping. Card backs are numbered with a "D" prefix and are inserted 1:28 packs.

		NM/M
Complete Set (15):		17.50
Common Player:		.60
Inserted 1:28		
1	Ken Griffey Jr.	2.00
2	Alex Rodriguez	2.50
3	Nomar Garciaparra	2.00
4	Mike Piazza	2.00
5	Mark McGwire	2.25
6	Sammy Sosa	2.00
7	Chipper Jones	1.50
8	Mo Vaughn	.60
9	Tony Gwynn	1.50
10	Vladimir Guerrero	1.25
11	Derek Jeter	3.00
12	Jeff Bagwell	1.25
13	Cal Ripken Jr.	3.00
14	Juan Gonzalez	1.25
15	J.D. Drew	.90

Game-Used Souvenirs

This set has a piece of game-used bat from the featured player embedded into each card. These are found exclusively in hobby packs at a rate of 1:144 packs.

		NM/M
Complete Set (9):		75.00
Common Player:		5.00
Inserted 1:144		
JB	Jeff Bagwell	8.00
BB	Barry Bonds	20.00
JD	J.D. Drew	8.00
KGj	Ken Griffey Jr.	15.00
CJ	Chipper Jones	10.00
MP	Mike Piazza	15.00
CR	Cal Ripken Jr.	20.00
SR	Scott Rolen	8.00
MV	Mo Vaughn	5.00

Signed Game-Used Souvenirs

Ken Griffey Jr. and Chipper Jones both signed their Game Used Souvenir inserts to their jersey number, Griffey (24) and Jones (10). These were seeded exclusively in hobby packs.

		NM/M
KGj	Ken Griffey Jr.	300.00
CJ	Chipper Jones	200.00

Power Surge

This 15-card set features baseball's top home run hitters, utilizing rainbow-foil technology. Card backs are seeded with a "P" prefix and are seeded 1:9 packs.

		NM/M
Complete Set (15):		12.50
Common Player:		.50
Inserted 1:9		
1	Mark McGwire	1.50
2	Sammy Sosa	1.25
3	Ken Griffey Jr.	1.25
4	Alex Rodriguez	1.50
5	Juan Gonzalez	.75
6	Nomar Garciaparra	1.25
7	Vladimir Guerrero	.75
8	Chipper Jones	1.00
9	Albert Belle	.50
10	Frank Thomas	.75
11	Mike Piazza	1.25
12	Jeff Bagwell	.75
13	Manny Ramirez	.75
14	Mo Vaughn	.50
15	Barry Bonds	2.00

ProSign

This 30-card autographed set is randomly seeded exclusively in retail packs at a rate of 1:216 packs. Card backs are numbered with the featured player's initials.

		NM/M
Common Autograph:		5.00
Inserted 1:216 R		
MA	Matt Anderson	5.00
CB	Carlos Beltran	15.00
RB	Russ Branyan	5.00
EC	Eric Chavez	10.00
BC	Bruce Chen	5.00
BF	Brad Fuller	5.00
NG	Nomar Garciaparra	80.00
JG	Jeremy Giambi	5.00
DG	Derrick Gibson	5.00
CG	Chris Gomez	5.00
AG	Alex Gonzalez	5.00
BG	Ben Grieve	5.00
JR.	Ken Griffey Jr.	80.00
RH	Richard Hidalgo	5.00
SH	Shea Hillenbrand	10.00
CJ	Chipper Jones/SP	50.00
GK	Gabe Kapler	6.00
SK	Scott Karl	5.00
CK	Corey Koskie	7.50
RL	Ricky Ledee	5.00
ML	Mike Lincoln	5.00
GL	George Lombard	5.00
MLo	Mike Lowell	7.50
RM	Ryan Minor	5.00
SM	Shane Monahan	5.00
AN	Abraham Nunez	5.00
JP	Jim Parque	5.00
CP	Calvin Pickering	5.00
JRa	Jason Rakers	5.00
RR	Ruben Rivera	5.00
IR	Ivan Rodriguez/SP	50.00
KW	Kevin Witt	5.00

Scout's Choice

Utilizing Light F/X technology, this 15-card set highlights the top young prospects in the game. Card backs are numbered with an "SC" prefix and are seeded 1:9 packs.

		NM/M
Complete Set (15):		5.00
Common Player:		.25
Inserted 1:9		
1	J.D. Drew	.65
2	Ben Grieve	.35
3	Troy Glaus	1.50
4	Gabe Kapler	.35
5	Carlos Beltran	.45
6	Aramis Ramirez	.25
7	Pat Burrell	1.00
8	Kerry Wood	.65
9	Ryan Minor	.25
10	Todd Helton	1.00
11	Eric Chavez	.35
12	Russ Branyon	.25
13	Travis Lee	.35
14	Ruben Mateo	.25
15	Roy Halladay	.35

Super Tools

This 15-card insert set focuses on baseball's top stars and utilizes holo foil technology on the card fronts. Card backs are numbered with a "T" prefix and are seeded 1:14 packs.

		NM/M
Complete Set (15):		25.00
Common Player:		.50
Inserted 1:14		
1	Ken Griffey Jr.	2.50
2	Alex Rodriguez	3.00
3	Sammy Sosa	2.00
4	Derek Jeter	4.00
5	Vladimir Guerrero	1.50

6	Ben Grieve	.50
7	Mike Piazza	2.50
8	Kenny Lofton	.50
9	Barry Bonds	4.00
10	Darin Erstad	1.00
11	Nomar Garciaparra	2.00
12	Cal Ripken Jr.	4.00
13	J.D. Drew	1.00
14	Larry Walker	.50
15	Chipper Jones	2.00

Swing Time

This 12-card set focuses on top hitters in the game and points out three aspects why the featured player is such a successful hitter. Printed on a full foiled front these are seeded 1:6 packs. Cards are numbered with an "S" prefix.

		NM/M
Complete Set (12):		5.00
Common Player:		.35
Inserted 1:6		
1	Ken Griffey Jr.	.75
2	Mark McGwire	1.00
3	Sammy Sosa	.60
4	Tony Gwynn	.60
5	Alex Rodriguez	1.00
6	Nomar Garciaparra	.60
7	Barry Bonds	1.50
8	Frank Thomas	.45
9	Chipper Jones	.60
10	Ivan Rodriguez	.35
11	Mike Piazza	.75
12	Derek Jeter	1.50

500 Club Piece of History

This insert has a piece of game-used bat once swung by Mike Schmidt embedded into each card. A total of 350 of this insert was produced. Schmidt also signed 20 of the inserts.

	NM/M
Mike Schmidt/350	160.00
Mike Schmidt/Auto./20	1,250

1999 Upper Deck Ovation

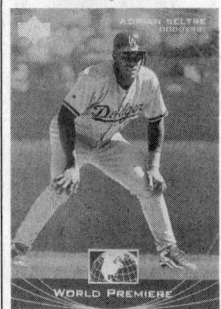

Cards 1-60 in the base set have the look and feel of an actual baseball. A player photo is in the foreground with a partial image of a baseball in the background on the card front. Cards 61-90 make up two subsets: World Premiere (61-80) is a 20-card collection consisting of 20 rookie prospects and Superstar Spotlight (81-90) is a 10-card lineup of baseball's biggest stars. Both subsets are short-printed, World Premiere are seeded

1:3.5 packs and Superstar Spotlight 1:6 packs. Five-card packs carry a S.R.P. of $3.99 per pack.

		NM/M
Complete Set (90):		20.00
Common Player:		.05
Common World Premiere:		.15
Inserted 1:3.5		
Common Superstar Spotlight:		.60
Inserted 1:6		
Pack (5):		2.00
Box (20):		30.00
1	Ken Griffey Jr.	1.50
2	Rondell White	.05
3	Tony Clark	.05
4	Barry Bonds	2.50
5	Larry Walker	.05
6	Greg Vaughn	.05
7	Mark Grace	.05
8	John Olerud	.05
9	Matt Williams	.05
10	Craig Biggio	.05
11	Quinton McCracken	.05
12	Kerry Wood	.35
13	Derek Jeter	2.50
14	Frank Thomas	.75
15	Tino Martinez	.05
16	Albert Belle	.05
17	Ben Grieve	.05
18	Cal Ripken Jr.	2.50
19	Johnny Damon	.30
20	Jose Cruz Jr.	.05
21	Barry Larkin	.05
22	Jason Giambi	.45
23	Sean Casey	.10
24	Scott Rolen	.60
25	Jim Thome	.45
26	Curt Schilling	.25
27	Moises Alou	.05
28	Alex Rodriguez	2.00
29	Mark Kotsay	.05
30	Darin Erstad	.05
31	Mike Mussina	.30
32	Todd Walker	.05
33	Nomar Garciaparra	1.00
34	Vladimir Guerrero	.75
35	Jeff Bagwell	.75
36	Mark McGwire	2.00
37	Travis Lee	.15
38	Dean Palmer	.05
39	Fred McGriff	.05
40	Sammy Sosa	1.00
41	Mike Piazza	1.50
42	Andres Galarraga	.05
43	Pedro Martinez	.75
44	Juan Gonzalez	.40
45	Greg Maddux	1.00
46	Jeromy Burnitz	.05
47	Roger Clemens	1.25
48	Vinny Castilla	.05
49	Kevin Brown	.05
50	Mo Vaughn	.05
51	Raul Mondesi	.05
52	Randy Johnson	.75
53	Ray Lankford	.05
54	Jaret Wright	.05
55	Tony Gwynn	1.00
56	Chipper Jones	1.00
57	Gary Sheffield	.40
58	Ivan Rodriguez	.65
59	Kenny Lofton	.05
60	Jason Kendall	.05
61	J.D. Drew (World Premiere)	.75
62	Gabe Kapler (World Premiere)	.15
63	Adrian Beltre (World Premiere)	.40
64	Carlos Beltran (World Premiere)	.50
65	Eric Chavez (World Premiere)	.35
66	Mike Lowell (World Premiere)	.25
67	Troy Glaus (World Premiere)	1.00
68	George Lombard (World Premiere)	.15
69	Alex Gonzalez (World Premiere)	.15
70	Mike Kinkade (World Premiere)	.15
71	Jeremy Giambi (World Premiere)	.15
72	Bruce Chen (World Premiere)	.15
73	Preston Wilson (World Premiere)	.25
74	Kevin Witt (World Premiere)	.15
75	Carlos Guillen (World Premiere)	.15
76	Ryan Minor (World Premiere)	.15
77	Corey Koskie (World Premiere)	.15
78	Robert Fick (World Premiere)	.15
79	Michael Barrett (World Premiere)	.15
80	Calvin Pickering (World Premiere)	.15
81	Ken Griffey Jr. (Superstar Spotlight)	1.00
82	Mark McGwire (Superstar Spotlight)	1.50
83	Cal Ripken Jr. (Superstar Spotlight)	2.00
84	Derek Jeter (Superstar Spotlight)	2.00
85	Chipper Jones (Superstar Spotlight)	.75
86	Nomar Garciaparra (Garciaparra) (Superstar Spotlight)	.75
87	Sammy Sosa (Superstar Spotlight)	.75
88	Juan Gonzalez (Superstar Spotlight)	.30
89	Mike Piazza (Superstar Spotlight)	1.00
90	Alex Rodriguez (Superstar Spotlight)	1.50

Standing Ovation

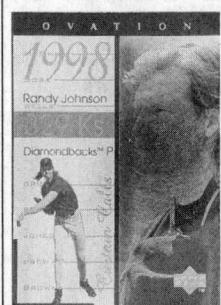

	NM/M
Stars (1-60):	3X
World Premiere (61-80):	1.5X
Superstar Spotlight (81-90):	2X
Production 500 Sets	

Curtain Calls

This 20-card set focuses on the most memorable accomplishments posted during the '98 season. Card fronts have two images of the player, one on the right half and a smaller image on the bottom left. Copper foil stamping is used to enhance the card front. These are numbered with a "R" prefix and are seeded 1:8 packs.

		NM/M
Complete Set (20):		20.00
Common Player:		.25
Inserted 1:8		
R1	Mark McGwire	2.00
R2	Sammy Sosa	1.00
R3	Ken Griffey Jr.	1.50
R4	Alex Rodriguez	2.00
R5	Roger Clemens	1.25
R6	Cal Ripken Jr.	2.50
R7	Barry Bonds	2.50
R8	Kerry Wood	.40
R9	Nomar Garciaparra	1.00
R10	Derek Jeter	2.50
R11	Juan Gonzalez	.50
R12	Greg Maddux	1.00
R13	Pedro Martinez	1.00
R14	David Wells	.25
R15	Moises Alou	.25
R16	Tony Gwynn	1.00
R17	Albert Belle	.25
R18	Mike Piazza	1.50
R19	Ivan Rodriguez	.75
R20	Randy Johnson	.75

Major Production

This 20-card set utilizes thermography technology to simulate the look and feel of home plate and highlights some of the game's most productive players. These are inserted 1:45 packs and are numbered with an "S" prefix.

		NM/M
Complete Set (20):		45.00
Common Player:		.75
Inserted 1:45		
S1	Mike Piazza	4.00
S2	Mark McGwire	5.00
S3	Chipper Jones	3.00

S4	Cal Ripken Jr.	6.00
S5	Ken Griffey Jr.	4.00
S6	Barry Bonds	6.00
S7	Tony Gwynn	3.00
S8	Randy Johnson	2.50
S9	Ivan Rodriguez	2.00
S10	Frank Thomas	2.50
S11	Alex Rodriguez	5.00
S12	Albert Belle	.75
S13	Juan Gonzalez	1.25
S14	Greg Maddux	3.00
S15	Jeff Bagwell	2.50
S16	Derek Jeter	6.00
S17	Matt Williams	.75
S18	Kenny Lofton	.75
S19	Sammy Sosa	3.00
S20	Roger Clemens	3.50

Piece of History

This 16-card set has actual pieces of game-used bat, from the featured player, imbedded into the card. These are inserted 1:247 packs. Ben Grieve autographed 25 versions of his Piece of History insert cards. Although there is no regular Piece of History Kerry Wood card, Upper Deck inserted 25 autographed Piece of History game-used baseball cards. These have a piece of one of Wood's game-hurled baseballs from the 1998 season.

		NM/M
Common Player:		5.00
Inserted 1:247		
BB	Barry Bonds	25.00
CJ	Chipper Jones	15.00
BW	Bernie Williams	5.00
KGj	Ken Griffey Jr.	20.00
NG	Nomar Garciaparra	15.00
JG	Juan Gonzalez	5.00
DJ	Derek Jeter	25.00
SS	Sammy Sosa	15.00
TG	Tony Gwynn	15.00
AR	Alex Rodriguez	20.00
CR	Cal Ripken Jr.	25.00
BG	Ben Grieve	5.00
VG	Vladimir Guerrero	10.00
MP	Mike Piazza	20.00
BGAU	Ben Grieve/Auto./25	30.00
KWAU	Kerry Wood/Auto./25	50.00

ReMarkable

This three-tiered 15-card insert showcases Mark McGwire's historic '98 season. Cards #1-5 are Bronze and inserted 1:9 packs; cards #6-10 are Silver and inserted 1:25 packs; and cards #11-15 are Gold and inserted 1:99 packs.

		NM/M
Complete Set (15):		20.00
Common #1-5:		1.50
Inserted 1:9		
Common #6-10:		2.25
Inserted 1:25		
Common # 11-15		3.00
Inserted 1:99		
MM1-5	Mark McGwire	1.50
MM6-10	Mark McGwire	3.00
MM11-15	Mark McGwire	5.00

500 Club Piece of History

Each of these cards actually has a piece of game-used Louisville Slugger, once swung by Mickey Mantle, embedded. Approximately 350 cards exist. There is also one card with a cut signature of Mantle and a piece of his game-used bat on it.

		NM/M
MIC-P	Mickey Mantle/350	600.00
	Mickey Mantle/Bat Auto.	8,000

1999 Upper Deck PowerDeck

This 25-card set is comprised of 25 digital PowerDeck interactive trading cards, complete with video and audio content. There is also a parallel "paper" version of the base set called Auxiliary Power. Each digital card includes 32 megabytes of information and is compatible with almost any internet ready computer. One PowerDeck digital card comes in every three-card pack.

		NM/M
Complete Set (25):		20.00
Common Player:		.50
Pack (3):		1.50
Wax Box (24):		20.00
1	Ken Griffey Jr.	2.00
2	Mark McGwire	2.50
3	Cal Ripken Jr.	3.00
4	Sammy Sosa	1.50
5	Derek Jeter	3.00
6	Mike Piazza	2.00
7	Nomar Garciaparra	1.50
8	Greg Maddux	1.50
9	Tony Gwynn	1.50
10	Roger Clemens	1.75
11	Scott Rolen	1.00
12	Alex Rodriguez	2.50
13	Manny Ramirez	1.25
14	Chipper Jones	1.50
15	Juan Gonzalez	.65
16	Ivan Rodriguez	1.00
17	Frank Thomas	1.25
18	Mo Vaughn	.50
19	Barry Bonds	3.00
20	Vladimir Guerrero	1.25
21	Jose Canseco	.65
22	Jeff Bagwell	1.25
23	Pedro Martinez	1.25
24	Gabe Kapler	.50
25	J.D. Drew	.75
---	Checklist	.10

Auxiliary Power

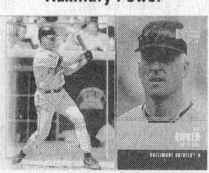

A "paper" parallel version of the 25-card digital set. These have a horizontal format with silver-foil graphics. Backs repeat the front portrait photo along with the player's past five years of statistics and a brief career highlight. Card numbers are prefixed with "AUX-."

		NM/M
Complete Set (25):		6.00
Common Player:		.10
1	Ken Griffey Jr.	.50
2	Mark McGwire	.60
3	Cal Ripken Jr.	.60
4	Sammy Sosa	.40
5	Derek Jeter	.75
6	Mike Piazza	.50
7	Nomar Garciaparra	.40
8	Greg Maddux	.40
9	Tony Gwynn	.40

10	Roger Clemens	.45
11	Scott Rolen	.25
12	Alex Rodriguez	.60
13	Manny Ramirez	.30
14	Chipper Jones	.40
15	Juan Gonzalez	.15
16	Ivan Rodriguez	.25
17	Frank Thomas	.30
18	Mo Vaughn	.10
19	Barry Bonds	.75
20	Vladimir Guerrero	.30
21	Jose Canseco	.20
22	Jeff Bagwell	.30
23	Pedro Martinez	.30
24	Gabe Kapler	.10
25	J.D. Drew	.25

Most Valuable Performances

This seven-card digital insert set consists of capturing true MVP performances from some of baseball's greatest players. These were seeded 1:287 packs.

		NM/M
Complete Set (7):		75.00
Common Player:		6.00
Inserted 1:287		
1	Sammy Sosa	10.00
2	Barry Bonds	20.00
3	Cal Ripken Jr.	20.00
4	Juan Gonzalez	6.00
5	Ken Griffey Jr.	12.50
6	Roger Clemens	10.00
7	Mark McGwire, Sammy Sosa	12.50

MVP Auxiliary

A "paper" parallel version of the digital set, these also were inserted 1:287 packs. They have a horizontal format using silver holofoil and also have different photos from the digital version.

		NM/M
Complete Set (7):		60.00
Common Player:		4.00
Inserted 1:287		
1	Sammy Sosa	7.50
2	Barry Bonds	15.00
3	Cal Ripken Jr.	15.00
4	Juan Gonzalez	4.00
5	Ken Griffey Jr.	10.00
6	Roger Clemens	7.50
7	Mark McGwire, Sammy Sosa	12.50

Powerful Moments

This six-card digital interactive set has game-action footage pinpointing specific milestones in each of the featured players' careers. These were inserted 1:7 packs.

		NM/M
Complete Set (6):		10.00
Common Player:		1.00
Inserted 1:7		
1	Mark McGwire	2.00
2	Sammy Sosa	1.00
3	Cal Ripken Jr.	3.00
4	Ken Griffey Jr.	1.50
5	Derek Jeter	3.00
6	Alex Rodriguez	2.00

Powerful Moments Auxiliary

This "paper" parallel version of the digital set is also inserted 1:7 packs on a horizontal format. Different photos were used from the digital set.

		NM/M
Complete Set (6):		10.00
Common Player:		1.00

Inserted 1:7		
Gold (One each.): Value Undetermined		
1	Mark McGwire	2.00
2	Sammy Sosa	1.00
3	Cal Ripken Jr.	3.00
4	Ken Griffey Jr.	1.50
5	Derek Jeter	3.00
6	Alex Rodriguez	2.00

Time Capsule

Six MLB Rookies of the Year are honored in this digital set with the digital content going back to the rookie seasons of the featured players. These were seeded 1:23 packs.

		NM/M
Complete Set (6):		12.50
Common Player:		1.00
Inserted 1:23		
1	Ken Griffey Jr.	2.50
2	Mike Piazza	2.50
3	Mark McGwire	3.00
4	Derek Jeter	4.00
5	Jose Canseco	1.00
6	Nomar Garciaparra	2.00

Time Capsule-Auxiliary Power

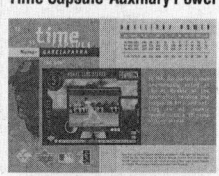

This "paper" parallel set of the digital version utilizes a similar design as the digital insert and uses different photos as well. Horizontal fronts have a thin vertical monochromatic portrait at left. At right is an action photos set on a metallized background. Backs repeat the front portrait and have a screen simulation along with stats and data. These were inserted 1:23 packs.

		NM/M
Complete Set (6):		15.00
Common Player:		1.00
Inserted 1:23		
Gold (One of each.): Values Undetermined		
1	Ken Griffey Jr.	2.50
2	Mike Piazza	2.50
3	Mark McGwire	3.00
4	Derek Jeter	4.00
5	Jose Canseco	1.00
6	Nomar Garciaparra	2.00

A Season to Remember

This special box-topper CD insert presents audio-visual highlights of the 1999 season, featuring players like David Cone, Ken Griffey, Jr., Mark McGwire, Tony Gwynn, Wade Boggs, Sammy Sosa and Cal Ripken, Jr. McGwire is pictured on this CD hitting his 500th home run.

		NM/M
	Mark McGwire	3.00

Athletes of the Century

Babe Ruth was baseball's representative in a four-sport set of CD "cards" produced by Upper Deck.

		NM/M
	Babe Ruth	1.00

World Series Power Deck

This CD-ROM card titled "Season to Remember" was distributed at Yankee Stadium during Game 4 of the 1999 World Series and features highlights of the Yankees championship season.

		NM/M
	Season to Remember (1999 Yankees)	12.00

1999 UD Retro

The 110-card base set is comprised of 88 current stars and 22 retired greats. Card fronts have a tan, speckled border while card backs have a year-by-year compilation of the player's stats along with a career note. Retro is packaged in lunchboxes, 24 packs to a box with an S.R.P. of $4.99 per six-card pack.

		NM/M
Complete Set (110):		15.00
Common Player:		.05
Gold:		12X
Production 250 Sets		
Platinum 1/1: Values Undetermined		
Wax Pack (6):		2.50
Lunchbox (24):		45.00
1	Mo Vaughn	.05
2	Troy Glaus	.65
3	Tim Salmon	.05
4	Randy Johnson	.75
5	Travis Lee	.15
6	Matt Williams	.05
7	Greg Maddux	.85
8	Chipper Jones	1.00
9	Andruw Jones	.75
10	Tom Glavine	.25
11	Javy Lopez	.05
12	Albert Belle	.05
13	Cal Ripken Jr.	2.00
14	Brady Anderson	.05
15	Nomar Garciaparra	.85
16	Pedro J. Martinez	.75
17	Sammy Sosa	.85
18	Mark Grace	.05
19	Frank Thomas	.75
20	Ray Durham	.05
21	Sean Casey	.10
22	Greg Vaughn	.05
23	Barry Larkin	.05
24	Manny Ramirez	.75
25	Jim Thome	.50
26	Jaret Wright	.05
27	Kenny Lofton	.05
28	Larry Walker	.05
29	Todd Helton	.65
30	Vinny Castilla	.05
31	Tony Clark	.05
32	Juan Encarnacion	.05
33	Dean Palmer	.05
34	Mark Kotsay	.05
35	Alex Gonzalez	.05
36	Shane Reynolds	.05
37	Ken Caminiti	.05
38	Jeff Bagwell	.75
39	Craig Biggio	.05
40	Carlos Febles	.35
41	Carlos Beltran	.35
42	Jeremy Giambi	.05
43	Raul Mondesi	.05
44	Adrian Beltre	.10
45	Kevin Brown	.05
46	Jeromy Burnitz	.05
47	Jeff Cirillo	.05
48	Corey Koskie	.05
49	Todd Walker	.05
50	Vladimir Guerrero	.75
51	Michael Barrett	.05
52	Mike Piazza	1.00
53	Robin Ventura	.05
54	Edgardo Alfonzo	.05
55	Derek Jeter	2.00
56	Roger Clemens	.90
57	Tino Martinez	.05
58	Orlando Hernandez	.05
59	Chuck Knoblauch	.05
60	Bernie Williams	.05
61	Eric Chavez	.10
62	Ben Grieve	.05

63	Jason Giambi	.40
64	Scott Rolen	.60
65	Curt Schilling	.25
66	Bobby Abreu	.10
67	Jason Kendall	.05
68	Kevin Young	.05
69	Mark McGwire	1.50
70	J.D. Drew	.60
71	Eric Davis	.05
72	Tony Gwynn	.85
73	Trevor Hoffman	.05
74	Barry Bonds	2.00
75	Robb Nen	.05
76	Ken Griffey Jr.	1.00
77	Alex Rodriguez	1.50
78	Jay Buhner	.05
79	Carlos Guillen	.05
80	Jose Canseco	.40
81	Bobby Smith	.05
82	Juan Gonzalez	.40
83	Ivan Rodriguez	.65
84	Rafael Palmeiro	.65
85	Rick Helling	.05
86	Jose Cruz Jr.	.05
87	David Wells	.05
88	Carlos Delgado	.20
89	Nolan Ryan	1.50
90	George Brett	.90
91	Robin Yount	.50
92	Paul Molitor	.50
93	Dave Winfield	.50
94	Steve Garvey	.25
95	Ozzie Smith	.85
96	Ted Williams	1.50
97	Don Mattingly	.90
98	Mickey Mantle	2.50
99	Harmon Killebrew	.25
100	Rollie Fingers	.10
101	Kirk Gibson	.05
102	Bucky Dent	.05
103	Willie Mays	1.00
104	Babe Ruth	1.50
105	Gary Carter	.50
106	Reggie Jackson	.85
107	Frank Robinson	.25
108	Ernie Banks	.50
109	Eddie Murray	.50
110	Mike Schmidt	.90

Gold/Platinum

This is a 110-card parallel to the base set. Cards have a gold-tone front and are sequentially numbered to 250 sets. A one-of-one Platinum parallel to the base set also is randomly seeded.

	NM/M
Common Gold:	1.00
Gold Stars:	15X
Platinum 1/1: Values Undetermined	

Distant Replay

This 15-card set recounts the most memorable plays from the 1998 season. Card fronts have a black-and-white photo of the player and along the bottom of the photo a date of the memorable play and brief description are given. These are seeded 1:8 packs. A parallel version, Level 2, is also randomly seeded, limited to 100 sequentially numbered sets.

	NM/M
Complete Set (15):	30.00

		NM/M
Common Player:		1.00
Inserted 1:8		
Level 2:		6X
Production 100 Sets		
1	Ken Griffey Jr.	2.50
2	Mark McGwire	3.00
3	Cal Ripken Jr.	4.00
4	Greg Maddux	2.00
5	Nomar Garciaparra	2.00
6	Roger Clemens	2.25
7	Alex Rodriguez	3.00
8	Frank Thomas	1.50
9	Mike Piazza	2.50
10	Chipper Jones	2.00
11	Juan Gonzalez	1.00
12	Tony Gwynn	2.00
13	Barry Bonds	4.00
14	Ivan Rodriguez	1.00
15	Derek Jeter	4.00

INKredible

INKredible is an autographed insert set that consists of both current players and retired stars. Card fronts have a small photo in the upper left portion of the featured player and a large signing area. These are seeded 1:23 packs.

		NM/M
Common Player:		4.00
Inserted 1:23		
CBe	Carlos Beltran	30.00
GB	George Brett/SP	80.00
PB	Pat Burrell	10.00
SC	Sean Casey	10.00
TC	Tony Clark	4.00
BD	Bucky Dent	8.00
DE	Darin Erstad	15.00
RF	Rollie Fingers	8.00
SG	Steve Garvey	10.00
KG	Kirk Gibson	10.00
RG	Rusty Greer	4.00
JR	Ken Griffey Jr.	80.00
TG	Tony Gwynn	30.00
CJ	Chipper Jones	40.00
GK	Gabe Kapler	5.00
HK	Harmon Killebrew	30.00
FL	Fred Lynn	10.00
DM	Don Mattingly	50.00
PM	Paul Molitor	20.00
EM	Eddie Murray/SP	50.00
PO	Paul O'Neill	15.00
AP	Angel Pena	4.00
MR	Manny Ramirez	30.00
IR	Ivan Rodriguez	25.00
NR	Nolan Ryan	150.00
OZ	Ozzie Smith	30.00
DWe	David Wells	15.00
BW	Bernie Williams	40.00
DW	Dave Winfield	20.00
RY	Robin Yount	35.00

INKredible Level 2

A parallel to INKredible autographed inserts, these are hand-numbered to the featured player's jersey number.

		NM/M
Common Player:		10.00
Limited to player's jersey #.		
CBe	Carlos Beltran/36	60.00
PB	Pat Burrell/76	50.00
SC	Sean Casey/21	40.00
TC	Tony Clark/17	20.00
BD	Bucky Dent/20	25.00
DE	Darin Erstad/17	50.00
RF	Rollie Fingers/34	25.00
KG	Kirk Gibson/23	30.00
RG	Rusty Greer/29	25.00
JR	Ken Griffey Jr./24	200.00
TG	Tony Gwynn/19	150.00
GK	Gabe Kapler/23	40.00
FL	Fred Lynn/19	30.00
DM	Don Mattingly/23	200.00
EM	Eddie Murray/33	80.00
PO	Paul O'Neill/21	50.00
AP	Angel Pena/36	10.00
MR	Manny Ramirez/24	80.00
NR	Nolan Ryan/34	400.00
DWe	David Wells/33	25.00
BW	Bernie Williams/51	60.00
DW	Dave Winfield/31	60.00
RY	Robin Yount/19	90.00

Old/New School

This 30-card insert set captures 15 Old School players and 15 New School players. Each card is sequentially numbered to 1,000. A parallel version is also randomly seeded and is limited to 50 sequentially numbered sets. Old School cards are basically black-and-white with color graphic highlights on front and back. New School cards have multiple computer-enhanced color photos and silver-foil highlights.

		NM/M
Complete Set (30):		35.00
Common Player:		.40
Production 1,000 Sets		
Level 2:		5X
Production 50 Sets		
1	Ken Griffey Jr.	2.50
2	Alex Rodriguez	3.00
3	Frank Thomas	1.50
4	Cal Ripken Jr.	4.00
5	Chipper Jones	2.00
6	Craig Biggio	.40
7	Greg Maddux	2.00
8	Jeff Bagwell	1.50
9	Juan Gonzalez	.75
10	Mark McGwire	3.00
11	Mike Piazza	2.50
12	Mo Vaughn	.40
13	Roger Clemens	2.25
14	Sammy Sosa	2.00
15	Tony Gwynn	2.00
16	Gabe Kapler	.40
17	J.D. Drew	1.00
18	Pat Burrell	1.00
19	Roy Halladay	.40
20	Jeff Weaver	.40
21	Troy Glaus	1.00
22	Vladimir Guerrero	1.50
23	Michael Barrett	.40
24	Carlos Beltran	.40
25	Scott Rolen	1.00
26	Nomar Garciaparra	2.00
27	Warren Morris	.40
28	Alex Gonzalez	.40
29	Kyle Farnsworth	.40
30	Derek Jeter	4.00

Piece of History 500 Club

Each one of these inserts features a piece of game-used bat swung by Ted Williams embedded into each card. A total of 350 of these were issued. Williams also autographed nine of the 500 Club Piece of History cards.

		NM/M
TW	Ted Williams/350	250.00

Throwback Attack

These inserts have a "Retro" look, borrowing heavily from 1959 Topps. Highlighting top players, the set features card fronts with a circular player photo on a bright orange background. At top in white is, "throwback attack." There is a white border. Backs have a ghosted image of the front photo and career highlights. Cards are numbered with a "T" prefix and are seeded 1:5 packs. A parallel version is also randomly seeded and limited to 500 numbered sets.

		NM/M
Complete Set (15):		20.00
Common Player:		.50
Inserted 1:5		
Level 2:		3X
Production 500 Sets		
1	Ken Griffey Jr.	2.00
2	Mark McGwire	2.50
3	Sammy Sosa	1.25
4	Roger Clemens	1.50
5	J.D. Drew	.75
6	Alex Rodriguez	2.50
7	Greg Maddux	1.25
8	Mike Piazza	2.00
9	Juan Gonzalez	.50
10	Mo Vaughn	.50
11	Cal Ripken Jr.	3.00
12	Frank Thomas	1.00
13	Nomar Garciaparra	1.25
14	Vladimir Guerrero	1.00
15	Tony Gwynn	1.25

Lunchbox

Lunchboxes were the packaging for UD Retro. Each lunchbox contains 24 six-card packs and features 16 different current or retired baseball legends including Babe Ruth.

		NM/M
Complete Set (17):		140.00
Common Lunchbox:		7.50
One dual-player per case.		
	Roger Clemens	7.50
	Ken Griffey Jr.	7.50
	Mickey Mantle	10.00
	Mark McGwire	10.00
	Mike Piazza	7.50
	Alex Rodriguez	7.50
	Babe Ruth	10.00
	Sammy Sosa	7.50
	Ted Williams	10.00
	Ken Griffey Jr., Mark McGwire	12.50
	Ken Griffey Jr., Babe Ruth	12.50
	Ken Griffey Jr., Ted Williams	12.50
	Mickey Mantle, Babe Ruth	15.00
	Mark McGwire, Mickey Mantle	15.00
	Mark McGwire, Babe Ruth	15.00
	Mark McGwire, Ted Williams	15.00

1999 Upper Deck Ultimate Victory

The 180-card base set includes two 30-card short-printed (1:4) subsets: McGwire Magic (151-180) and 1999 Rookie (121-150). The base cards have a silver foil border with the featured play-ers' last five seasons of statistics along with a brief career highlight. There are two parallels randomly inserted: Victory Collection and Ultimate Collection. Victory Collection is seeded 1:12 packs with a holographic, prismatic look. Ultimate Collection has a gold holographic, prismatic look and are serially numbered "xxx/100" on the card front.

		NM/M
Complete Set (180):		125.00
Common Player:		.10
Common 99 Rookie (121-150):		.50
Common McGwire Magic (151-180):		1.00
Victory (1-120): 3.5X		
Victory SP (121-180):		2X
Inserted 1:12		
Ultimate (1-120):		12X
Ultimate SP (121-180):		5X
Production 100 Sets		
Pack (5):		4.50
Wax Box (24):		75.00
1	Troy Glaus	.65
2	Tim Salmon	.10
3	Mo Vaughn	.10
4	Garret Anderson	.10
5	Darin Erstad	.30
6	Randy Johnson	.75
7	Matt Williams	.10
8	Travis Lee	.25
9	Jay Bell	.10
10	Steve Finley	.10
11	Luis Gonzalez	.10
12	Greg Maddux	1.00
13	Chipper Jones	1.00
14	Javy Lopez	.10
15	Tom Glavine	.35
16	John Smoltz	.10
17	Cal Ripken Jr.	3.00
18	Charles Johnson	.10
19	Albert Belle	.10
20	Mike Mussina	.40
21	Pedro Martinez	.75
22	Nomar Garciaparra	1.00
23	Jose Offerman	.10
24	Sammy Sosa	1.00
25	Mark Grace	.10
26	Kerry Wood	.35
27	Frank Thomas	.75
28	Ray Durham	.10
29	Paul Konerko	.20
30	Pete Harnisch	.10
31	Greg Vaughn	.10
32	Sean Casey	.20
33	Manny Ramirez	.75
34	Jim Thome	.65
35	Sandy Alomar	.10
36	Roberto Alomar	.30
37	Travis Fryman	.10
38	Kenny Lofton	.10
39	Omar Vizquel	.10
40	Larry Walker	.10
41	Todd Helton	.65
42	Vinny Castilla	.10
43	Tony Clark	.10
44	Juan Encarnacion	.10
45	Dean Palmer	.10
46	Damion Easley	.10
47	Mark Kotsay	.10
48	Cliff Floyd	.10
49	Jeff Bagwell	.75
50	Ken Caminiti	.10
51	Craig Biggio	.10
52	Moises Alou	.10
53	Johnny Damon	.35
54	Larry Sutton	.10
55	Kevin Brown	.10
56	Adrian Beltre	.25
57	Raul Mondesi	.10
58	Gary Sheffield	.50
59	Jeromy Burnitz	.10
60	Sean Berry	.10
61	Jeff Cirillo	.10
62	Brad Radke	.10
63	Todd Walker	.10
64	Matt Lawton	.10
65	Vladimir Guerrero	.75
66	Rondell White	.10
67	Dustin Hermanson	.10
68	Mike Piazza	2.00
69	Rickey Henderson	.75
70	Robin Ventura	.10
71	John Olerud	.10
72	Derek Jeter	3.00
73	Roger Clemens	1.25
74	Orlando Hernandez	.10
75	Paul O'Neill	.10
76	Bernie Williams	.10
77	Chuck Knoblauch	.10
78	Tino Martinez	.10
79	Jason Giambi	.50
80	Ben Grieve	.10
81	Matt Stairs	.10
82	Scott Rolen	.60
83	Ron Gant	.10
84	Bobby Abreu	.10
85	Curt Schilling	.35
86	Brian Giles	.10
87	Jason Kendall	.10
88	Kevin Young	.10
89	Mark McGwire	2.00
90	Fernando Tatis	.10
91	Ray Lankford	.10
92	Eric Davis	.10
93	Tony Gwynn	1.00
94	Reggie Sanders	.10
95	Wally Joyner	.10
96	Trevor Hoffman	.10
97	Robb Nen	.10
98	Barry Bonds	3.00
99	Jeff Kent	.10
100	J.T. Snow	.10
101	Ellis Burks	.10
102	Ken Griffey Jr.	1.50
103	Alex Rodriguez	2.00
104	Jay Buhner	.10
105	Edgar Martinez	.10
106	David Bell	.10
107	Bobby Smith	.10
108	Wade Boggs	1.00
109	Fred McGriff	.10
110	Rolando Arrojo	.10
111	Jose Canseco	.50
112	Ivan Rodriguez	.40
113	Juan Gonzalez	.40
114	Rafael Palmeiro	.65
115	Rusty Greer	.10
116	Todd Zeile	.10
117	Jose Cruz Jr.	.10
118	Carlos Delgado	.35
119	Shawn Green	.30
120	David Wells	.10
121	Eric Munson RC (99 Rookie)	2.50
122	Lance Berkman (99 Rookie)	2.00
123	Ed Yarnall (99 Rookie)	.50
124	Jacque Jones (99 Rookie)	1.00
125	Kyle Farnsworth (99 Rookie)	1.00
126	Ryan Rupe (99 Rookie)	1.00
127	Jeff Weaver RC (99 Rookie)	2.00
128	Gabe Kapler (99 Rookie)	.50
129	Alex Gonzalez (99 Rookie)	.50
130	Randy Wolf (99 Rookie)	1.00
131	Ben Davis (99 Rookie)	.50
132	Carlos Beltran (99 Rookie)	2.00
133	Jim Morris (99 Rookie)	2.00
134	Jeff Zimmerman (99 Rookie)	2.00
135	Bruce Aven (99 Rookie)	.50
136	Alfonso Soriano RC (99 Rookie)	50.00
137	Tim Hudson RC (99 Rookie)	10.00
138	Josh Beckett RC (99 Rookie)	50.00
139	Michael Barrett (99 Rookie)	.50
140	Eric Chavez (99 Rookie)	1.00
141	Pat Burrell RC (99 Rookie)	10.00
142	Kris Benson (99 Rookie)	1.00
143	J.D. Drew (99 Rookie)	2.00
144	Matt Clement (99 Rookie)	1.00
145	Rick Ankiel RC (99 Rookie)	25.00
146	Vernon Wells (99 Rookie)	1.00
147	Ruben Mateo (99 Rookie)	.50
148	Roy Halladay (99 Rookie)	.50
149	Joe McEwing (99 Rookie)	.50
150	Freddy Garcia RC (99 Rookie)	8.00
151	Mark McGwire (McGwire Magic)	1.00
152	Mark McGwire (McGwire Magic)	1.00
153	Mark McGwire (McGwire Magic)	1.00
154	Mark McGwire (McGwire Magic)	1.00
155	Mark McGwire (McGwire Magic)	1.00
156	Mark McGwire (McGwire Magic)	1.00
157	Mark McGwire (McGwire Magic)	1.00
158	Mark McGwire (McGwire Magic)	1.00
159	Mark McGwire (McGwire Magic)	1.00
160	Mark McGwire (McGwire Magic)	1.00
161	Mark McGwire (McGwire Magic)	1.00
162	Mark McGwire (McGwire Magic)	1.00
163	Mark McGwire (McGwire Magic)	1.00
164	Mark McGwire (McGwire Magic)	1.00
165	Mark McGwire (McGwire Magic)	1.00
166	Mark McGwire (McGwire Magic)	1.00
167	Mark McGwire (McGwire Magic)	1.00
168	Mark McGwire (McGwire Magic)	1.00
169	Mark McGwire (McGwire Magic)	1.00
170	Mark McGwire (McGwire Magic)	1.00
171	Mark McGwire (McGwire Magic)	1.00
172	Mark McGwire (McGwire Magic)	1.00
173	Mark McGwire (McGwire Magic)	1.00
174	Mark McGwire (McGwire Magic)	1.00
175	Mark McGwire (McGwire Magic)	1.00
176	Mark McGwire (McGwire Magic)	1.00
177	Mark McGwire (McGwire Magic)	1.00
178	Mark McGwire (McGwire Magic)	1.00
179	Mark McGwire (McGwire Magic)	1.00
180	Mark McGwire (McGwire Magic)	1.00

Victory Collection

This parallel of the base set features a prismatic foil design on front. The cards are found on average of one per 12 packs. A 1-of-1 edition also exists, but is not priced here due to rarity and demand variability.

	NM/M
Common Player (1-120, 151-180):	1.00
Common Player (121-150):	5.00
Stars (1-120):	3.5X
Stars (121-150):	2X

Ultimate Collection

This parallel insert set is individually serial numbered on front from within an edition of 100 cards each. Card fronts have silver holographic prismatic foil background and a silver-foil serial number. Backs are identical to the regular-issue cards.

	NM/M
Common Player (1-120, 151-180):	2.00
Common Player (121-150):	12.00
Stars (1-120):	12X
Stars (121-150):	5X

Bleacher Reachers

This 11-card set focuses on the hitters who were vying for the 1999 home run title. They have a horizontal format with a holographic foil card front. Card backs have a small photo along with three-year statistical totals. They are numbered with a "BR" prefix and were inserted 1:23 packs.

	NM/M
Complete Set (11):	20.00
Common Player:	.75

Inserted 1:23
1	Ken Griffey Jr.	2.50
2	Mark McGwire	3.00
3	Sammy Sosa	2.00
4	Barry Bonds	4.00
5	Nomar Garciaparra	2.00
6	Juan Gonzalez	.75
7	Jose Canseco	.75
8	Manny Ramirez	1.50
9	Mike Piazza	2.50
10	Jeff Bagwell	1.50
11	Alex Rodriguez	3.00

Fame-Used Memorabilia

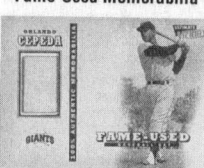

This four-card set has a piece of game-used bat embedded into each card, from either George Brett, Robin Yount, Nolan Ryan or Orlando Cepeda. Approximately 350 bat cards of each player were produced.

NM/M
Complete Set (4):		50.00
Common Player:		7.50
Production 350 Cards		
GB	George Brett	20.00
OC	Orlando Cepeda	7.50
NR	Nolan Ryan	25.00
RY	Robin Yount	10.00

Fame-Used Combo

This insert has a piece of game-used bat from each of the 1999 Hall of Fame inductees and is limited to 99 sequentially numbered singles.

NM/M
Edition of 99:		
HOF	Nolan Ryan, George Brett, Robin Yount, Orlando Cepeda	250.00

Frozen Ropes

This 10-card set spotlights baseball's top hitters and are seeded 1:23 packs.

NM/M
Complete Set (10):		15.00
Common Player:		.50
Inserted 1:23		
1	Ken Griffey Jr.	2.00
2	Mark McGwire	2.50
3	Sammy Sosa	1.50
4	Derek Jeter	3.00
5	Tony Gwynn	1.50
6	Nomar Garciaparra	1.50
7	Alex Rodriguez	2.50
8	Mike Piazza	2.00
9	Mo Vaughn	.50
10	Craig Biggio	.50

STATure

This 15-card set highlights players with outstanding statistical achievements. The featured stat for the player runs down the right side of the card. Fronts are printed on metallic foil with a textured pattern behind the player photo. Conventionally printed backs repeat the front design numbered with an "S" prefix. These were seeded 1:6 packs.

NM/M
Complete Set (15):		9.00
Common Player:		.30
Inserted 1:6		
1	Ken Griffey Jr.	.75
2	Mark McGwire	1.00
3	Sammy Sosa	.65
4	Nomar Garciaparra	.65
5	Roger Clemens	.65
6	Greg Maddux	.65
7	Alex Rodriguez	1.00
8	Derek Jeter	1.50
9	Juan Gonzalez	.30
10	Manny Ramirez	.50
11	Mike Piazza	.75
12	Tony Gwynn	.65
13	Chipper Jones	.75
14	Pedro Martinez	.50
15	Frank Thomas	.50

Tribute 1999

This four-card set is devoted to 1999's Hall of Fame inductees. Card fronts have a horizontal format over a holographic foil design. Card backs have the featured players' year-by-year statistics and are numbered with a "T" prefix.

NM/M
Complete Set (4):		5.00
Common Player:		1.00
Inserted 1:11		
1	Nolan Ryan	2.00
2	Robin Yount	1.50
3	George Brett	1.50
4	Orlando Cepeda	1.00

Ultimate Competitors

This 12-card set has a close-up photo, along with two miniature action photos in the foreground, all printed on silver foil. Backs repeat the front photos and have a few words about the player's competitive desire. These were seeded 1:23 packs and are numbered with a "U" prefix on the card back.

NM/M
Complete Set (12):		20.00
Common Player:		.60
Inserted 1:23		
1	Ken Griffey Jr.	3.00
2	Roger Clemens	2.50
3	Scott Rolen	1.00
4	Greg Maddux	2.00
5	Mark McGwire	4.00
6	Derek Jeter	5.00
7	Randy Johnson	1.50
8	Cal Ripken Jr.	5.00
9	Craig Biggio	.50
10	Kevin Brown	.50
11	Chipper Jones	2.00
12	Vladimir Guerrero	1.50

Ultimate Hit Men

This insert set spotlights the eight candidates who competed for the 1999 batting titles. Inserted on the average of 1:23 packs they were numbered with an "H" prefix on the card back.

NM/M
Complete Set (8):		15.00
Common Player:		1.00
Inserted 1:23		
1	Tony Gwynn	2.00
2	Cal Ripken Jr.	4.00
3	Wade Boggs	2.00
4	Larry Walker	1.00
5	Alex Rodriguez	3.00
6	Derek Jeter	4.00
7	Ivan Rodriguez	1.25
8	Ken Griffey Jr.	2.50

1999 Upper Deck Victory

This 470-card base set is printed on 20-point stock and has a white border with UV coating. The set consists of a number of subsets including, 30-card Mark McGwire Magic, 30 team checklist cards, 50 '99 rookies, 15 Power Trip, 20 Rookie Flashback, 15 Big Play Makers and 10 History in the Making. Twelve-card packs had an SRP of $.99.

NM/M
Complete Set (470):		30.00
Common Player:		.05
Pack (12):		.75
Wax Box (36):		20.00
1	Anaheim Angels (Team Checklist)	.05
2	Mark Harriger RC (99 Rookie)	.10
3	Mo Vaughn (Power Trip)	.05
4	Darin Erstad (Big Play Makers)	.10
5	Troy Glaus	.45
6	Tim Salmon	.05
7	Mo Vaughn	.05
8	Darin Erstad	.25
9	Garret Anderson	.05
10	Todd Greene	.05
11	Troy Percival	.05
12	Chuck Finley	.05
13	Jason Dickson	.05
14	Jim Edmonds	.05
15	Arizona Diamondbacks (Team Checklist)	.05
16	Randy Johnson	.50
17	Matt Williams	.05
18	Travis Lee	.15
19	Jay Bell	.05
20	Tony Womack	.05
21	Steve Finley	.05
22	Bernard Gilkey	.05
23	Tony Batista	.05
24	Todd Stottlemyre	.05
25	Omar Daal	.05
26	Atlanta Braves (Team Checklist)	.05
27	Bruce Chen (99 Rookie)	.05
28	George Lombard (99 Rookie)	.05
29	Chipper Jones (Power Trip)	.40
30	Chipper Jones (Big Play Makers)	.40
31	Greg Maddux	.65
32	Chipper Jones	.75
33	Javy Lopez	.05
34	Tom Glavine	.25
35	John Smoltz	.15
36	Andruw Jones	.50
37	Brian Jordan	.05
38	Walt Weiss	.05
39	Bret Boone	.05
40	Andres Galarraga	.05
41	Baltimore Orioles (Team Checklist)	.05
42	Ryan Minor (99 Rookie)	.05
43	Jerry Hairston Jr. (99 Rookie)	.05
44	Calvin Pickering (99 Rookie)	.05
45	Cal Ripken Jr. (History in the Making)	.75
46	Cal Ripken Jr.	1.50
47	Charles Johnson	.05
48	Albert Belle	.05
49	Delino DeShields	.05
50	Mike Mussina	.30
51	Scott Erickson	.05
52	Brady Anderson	.05
53	B.J. Surhoff	.05
54	Harold Baines	.05
55	Will Clark	.05
56	Boston Red Sox (Team Checklist)	.05
57	Shea Hillenbrand RC (99 Rookie)	.50
58	Trot Nixon (99 Rookie)	.10
59	Jin Ho Cho (99 Rookie)	.05
60	Nomar Garciaparra (Power Trip)	.35
61	Nomar Garciaparra (Big Play Makers)	.35
62	Pedro Martinez	.50
63	Nomar Garciaparra	.05
64	Jose Offerman	.05
65	Jason Varitek	.05
66	Darren Lewis	.05
67	Troy O'Leary	.05
68	Donnie Sadler	.05
69	John Valentin	.05
70	Tim Wakefield	.05
71	Bret Saberhagen	.05
72	Chicago Cubs (Team Checklist)	.05
73	Kyle Farnsworth RC (99 Rookie)	.10
74	Sammy Sosa (Power Trip)	.35
75	Sammy Sosa (Big Play Makers)	.35
76	Sammy Sosa (History in the Making)	.35
77	Kerry Wood (History in the Making)	.10
78	Sammy Sosa	.05
79	Mark Grace	.05
80	Kerry Wood	.25
81	Kevin Tapani	.05
82	Benito Santiago	.05
83	Gary Gaetti	.05
84	Mickey Morandini	.05
85	Glenallen Hill	.05
86	Henry Rodriguez	.05
87	Rod Beck	.05
88	Chicago White Sox (Team Checklist)	.05
89	Carlos Lee (99 Rookie)	.10
90	Mark Johnson (99 Rookie)	.05
91	Frank Thomas (Power Trip)	.30
92	Frank Thomas	.50
93	Jim Parque	.05
94	Mike Sirotka	.05
95	Mike Caruso	.05
96	Ray Durham	.05
97	Magglio Ordonez	.25
98	Paul Konerko	.15
99	Bob Howry	.05
100	Brian Simmons	.05
101	Jaime Navarro	.05
102	Cincinnati Reds (Team Checklist)	.05
103	Denny Neagle	.05
104	Pete Harnisch	.05
105	Greg Vaughn	.05
106	Brett Tomko	.05
107	Mike Cameron	.05
108	Sean Casey	.10
109	Aaron Boone	.05
110	Michael Tucker	.05
111	Dmitri Young	.05
112	Barry Larkin	.05
113	Cleveland Indians (Team Checklist)	.05
114	Russ Branyan (99 Rookie)	.05
115	Jim Thome (Power Trip)	.20
116	Manny Ramirez (Power Trip)	.25
117	Manny Ramirez	.50
118	Jim Thome	.40
119	David Justice	.05
120	Sandy Alomar	.05
121	Roberto Alomar	.20
122	Jaret Wright	.05
123	Bartolo Colon	.05
124	Travis Fryman	.05
125	Kenny Lofton	.05
126	Omar Vizquel	.05
127	Colorado Rockies (Team Checklist)	.05
128	Derrick Gibson (99 Rookie)	.05
129	Larry Walker (Big Play Makers)	.05
130	Larry Walker	.05
131	Dante Bichette	.05
132	Todd Helton	.45
133	Neifi Perez	.05
134	Vinny Castilla	.05
135	Darryl Kile	.05
136	Pedro Astacio	.05
137	Darryl Hamilton	.05
138	Mike Lansing	.05
139	Kirt Manwaring	.05
140	Detroit Tigers (Team Checklist)	.05
141	Jeff Weaver RC (99 Rookie)	.50
142	Gabe Kapler (99 Rookie)	.05
143	Tony Clark (Power Trip)	.05
144	Tony Clark	.05
145	Juan Encarnacion	.05
146	Dean Palmer	.05
147	Damion Easley	.05
148	Bobby Higginson	.05
149	Karim Garcia	.05
150	Justin Thompson	.05
151	Matt Anderson	.05
152	Willie Blair	.05
153	Brian Hunter	.05
154	Florida Marlins (Team Checklist)	.05
155	Alex Gonzalez (99 Rookie)	.05
156	Mark Kotsay	.05
157	Livan Hernandez	.05
158	Cliff Floyd	.05
159	Todd Dunwoody	.05
160	Alex Fernandez	.05
161	Mark Mantei	.05
162	Derrek Lee	.40
163	Kevin Orie	.05
164	Craig Counsell	.05
165	Rafael Medina	.05
166	Houston Astros (Team Checklist)	.05
167	Daryle Ward (99 Rookie)	.05
168	Mitch Meluskey (99 Rookie)	.05
169	Jeff Bagwell (Power Trip)	.50
170	Jeff Bagwell	.20
171	Ken Caminiti	.05
172	Craig Biggio	.05
173	Derek Bell	.05
174	Moises Alou	.05
175	Billy Wagner	.05
176	Shane Reynolds	.05
177	Carl Everett	.05
178	Scott Elarton	.05
179	Richard Hidalgo	.05
180	Kansas City Royals (Team Checklist)	.05
181	Carlos Beltran (99 Rookie)	.60
182	Carlos Febles (99 Rookie)	.05
183	Jeremy Giambi (99 Rookie)	.05
184	Johnny Damon	.30
185	Joe Randa	.05
186	Jeff King	.05
187	Hipolito Pichardo	.05
188	Kevin Appier	.05
189	Chad Kreuter	.05
190	Rey Sanchez	.05
191	Larry Sutton	.05
192	Jeff Montgomery	.05
193	Jermaine Dye	.05
194	Los Angeles Dodgers (Team Checklist)	.05
195	Adam Riggs (99 Rookie)	.05
196	Angel Pena (99 Rookie)	.05
197	Todd Hundley	.05
198	Kevin Brown	.05
199	Ismael Valdes	.05
200	Chan Ho Park	.05
201	Adrian Beltre	.15
202	Mark Grudzielanek	.05
203	Raul Mondesi	.05
204	Gary Sheffield	.35
205	Eric Karros	.05
206	Devon White	.05
207	Milwaukee Brewers (Team Checklist)	.05
208	Ron Belliard (99 Rookie)	.05
209	Rafael Roque (99 Rookie)	.05
210	Jeromy Burnitz	.05
211	Fernando Vina	.05
212	Scott Karl	.05
213	Jim Abbott	.05
214	Sean Berry	.05
215	Marquis Grissom	.05
216	Geoff Jenkins	.05
217	Jeff Cirillo	.05
218	Dave Nilsson	.05
219	Jose Valentin	.05
220	Minnesota Twins (Team Checklist)	.05
221	Corey Koskie (99 Rookie)	.05
222	Christian Guzman (99 Rookie)	.05
223	A.J. Pierzynski (99 Rookie)	.05
224	David Ortiz	.05
225	Brad Radke	.05
226	Todd Walker	.05
227	Matt Lawton	.05
228	Rick Aguilera	.05
229	Eric Milton	.05
230	Marty Cordova	.05
231	Torii Hunter	.05
232	Ron Coomer	.05
233	LaTroy Hawkins	.05
234	Montreal Expos (Team Checklist)	.05
235	Fernando Seguignol (99 Rookie)	.05
236	Michael Barrett (99 Rookie)	.05
237	Vladimir Guerrero (Big Play Makers)	.25
238	Vladimir Guerrero	.50
239	Brad Fullmer	.05
240	Rondell White	.05
241	Ugueth Urbina	.05
242	Dustin Hermanson	.05
243	Orlando Cabrera	.05
244	Wilton Guerrero	.05
245	Carl Pavano	.05
246	Javier Vasquez	.05
247	Chris Widger	.05
248	New York Mets (Team Checklist)	.05
249	Mike Kinkade (99 Rookie)	.05
250	Octavio Dotel (99 Rookie)	.05
251	Mike Piazza (Power Trip)	.40
252	Mike Piazza	.75
253	Rickey Henderson	.50
254	Edgardo Alfonzo	.05
255	Robin Ventura	.05
256	Al Leiter	.05
257	Brian McRae	.05
258	Rey Ordonez	.05
259	Bobby Bonilla	.05
260	Orel Hershiser	.05
261	John Olerud	.05
262	New York Yankees (Team Checklist)	.05
263	Ricky Ledee (99 Rookie)	.05
264	Bernie Williams (Big Play Makers)	.05
265	Derek Jeter (Big Play Makers)	.75
266	Scott Brosius (History in the Making)	.05
267	Derek Jeter	1.50
268	Roger Clemens	.65
269	Orlando Hernandez	.05
270	Scott Brosius	.05
271	Paul O'Neill	.05
272	Bernie Williams	.05
273	Chuck Knoblauch	.05
274	Tino Martinez	.05
275	Mariano Rivera	.10
276	Jorge Posada	.05
277	Oakland Athletics (Team Checklist)	.05
278	Eric Chavez (99 Rookie)	.15
279	Ben Grieve (History in the Making)	.05
280	Jason Giambi	.30
281	John Jaha	.05
282	Miguel Tejada	.15
283	Ben Grieve	.05
284	Matt Stairs	.05
285	Ryan Christenson	.05
286	A.J. Hinch	.05
287	Kenny Rogers	.05
288	Tom Candiotti	.05
289	Scott Spezio	.05
290	Philadelphia Phillies (Team Checklist)	.05
291	Pat Burrell RC (99 Rookie)	1.50
292	Marlon Anderson (99 Rookie)	.05
293	Scott Rolen (Big Play Makers)	.05
294	Scott Rolen	.40
295	Doug Glanville	.05
296	Rico Brogna	.05
297	Ron Gant	.05
298	Bobby Abreu	.05
299	Desi Relaford	.05
300	Curt Schilling	.25
301	Chad Ogea	.05
302	Kevin Jordan	.05
303	Carlton Loewer	.05
304	Pittsburgh Pirates (Team Checklist)	.05
305	Kris Benson (99 Rookie)	.05
306	Brian Giles	.05
307	Jason Kendall	.05
308	Jose Guillen	.05
309	Pat Meares	.05
310	Brant Brown	.05
311	Kevin Young	.05
312	Ed Sprague	.05
313	Francisco Cordova	.05
314	Aramis Ramirez	.05
315	Freddy Garcia	.05
316	Saint Louis Cardinals (Team Checklist)	.05
317	J.D. Drew (99 Rookie)	.40
318	Chad Hutchinson RC (99 Rookie)	.05
319	Mark McGwire (Power Trip)	.50
320	J.D. Drew (Power Trip)	.20
321	Mark McGwire (Big Play Makers)	.50
322	Mark McGwire (History in the Making)	.50
323	Mark McGwire	1.00
324	Fernando Tatis	.05
325	Edgar Renteria	.05
326	Ray Lankford	.05
327	Willie McGee	.05
328	Ricky Bottalico	.05
329	Eli Marrero	.05
330	Matt Morris	.05
331	Eric Davis	.05
332	Darren Bragg	.05
333	Padres (Team Checklist)	.05
334	Matt Clement (99 Rookie)	.05
335	Ben Davis (99 Rookie)	.05
336	Gary Matthews Jr. (99 Rookie)	.05
337	Tony Gwynn (Big Play Makers)	.35
338	Tony Gwynn (History in the Making)	.35
339	Tony Gwynn	.65
340	Reggie Sanders	.05
341	Ruben Rivera	.05
342	Wally Joyner	.05
343	Sterling Hitchcock	.05
344	Carlos Hernandez	.05
345	Andy Ashby	.05
346	Trevor Hoffman	.05
347	Chris Gomez	.05

#	Player	Price
348	Jim Leyritz	.05
349	San Francisco Giants (Team Checklist)	.05
350	Armando Rios (99 Rookie)	.05
351	Barry Bonds (Power Trip)	.75
352	Barry Bonds (Big Play Makers)	.75
353	Barry Bonds (History in the Making)	.75
354	Robb Nen	.05
355	Bill Mueller	.05
356	Barry Bonds	1.50
357	Jeff Kent	.05
358	J.T. Snow	.05
359	Ellis Burks	.05
360	F.P. Santangelo	.05
361	Marvin Benard	.05
362	Stan Javier	.05
363	Shawn Estes	.05
364	Seattle Mariners (Team Checklist)	.05
365	Carlos Guillen (99 Rookie)	.05
366	Ken Griffey Jr. (Power Trip)	.40
367	Alex Rodriguez (Power Trip)	.50
368	Ken Griffey Jr. (Big Play Makers)	.40
369	Alex Rodriguez (Big Play Makers)	.50
370	Ken Griffey Jr. (History in the Making)	.40
371	Alex Rodriguez (History in the Making)	.50
372	Ken Griffey Jr.	.75
373	Alex Rodriguez	1.00
374	Jay Buhner	.05
375	Edgar Martinez	.05
376	Jeff Fassero	.05
377	David Bell	.05
378	David Segui	.05
379	Russ Davis	.05
380	Dan Wilson	.05
381	Jamie Moyer	.05
382	Tampa Bay Devil Rays (Team Checklist)	.05
383	Roberto Hernandez	.05
384	Bobby Smith	.05
385	Wade Boggs	.65
386	Fred McGriff	.05
387	Rolando Arrojo	.05
388	Jose Canseco	.35
389	Wilson Alvarez	.05
390	Kevin Stocker	.05
391	Miguel Cairo	.05
392	Quinton McCracken	.05
393	Texas Rangers (Team Checklist)	.05
394	Ruben Mateo (99 Rookie)	.05
395	Cesar King (99 Rookie)	.05
396	Juan Gonzalez (Power Trip)	.15
397	Juan Gonzalez (Big Play Makers)	.15
398	Ivan Rodriguez	.40
399	Juan Gonzalez	.25
400	Rafael Palmeiro	.40
401	Rick Helling	.05
402	Aaron Sele	.05
403	John Wetteland	.05
404	Rusty Greer	.05
405	Todd Zeile	.05
406	Royce Clayton	.05
407	Tom Goodwin	.05
408	Toronto Blue Jays (Team Checklist)	.05
409	Kevin Witt (99 Rookie)	.05
410	Roy Halladay (99 Rookie)	.05
411	Jose Cruz Jr.	.05
412	Carlos Delgado	.30
413	Willie Greene	.05
414	Shawn Green	.25
415	Homer Bush	.05
416	Shannon Stewart	.05
417	David Wells	.05
418	Kelvim Escobar	.05
419	Joey Hamilton	.05
420	Alex Gonzalez	.05
421	Mark McGwire (McGwire Magic)	.20
422	Mark McGwire (McGwire Magic)	.20
423	Mark McGwire (McGwire Magic)	.20
424	Mark McGwire (McGwire Magic)	.20
425	Mark McGwire (McGwire Magic)	.20
426	Mark McGwire (McGwire Magic)	.20
427	Mark McGwire (McGwire Magic)	.20
428	Mark McGwire (McGwire Magic)	.20
429	Mark McGwire (McGwire Magic)	.20
430	Mark McGwire (McGwire Magic)	.20
431	Mark McGwire (McGwire Magic)	.20
432	Mark McGwire (McGwire Magic)	.20
433	Mark McGwire (McGwire Magic)	.20
434	Mark McGwire (McGwire Magic)	.20
435	Mark McGwire (McGwire Magic)	.20
436	Mark McGwire (McGwire Magic)	.20
437	Mark McGwire (McGwire Magic)	.20
438	Mark McGwire (McGwire Magic)	.20
439	Mark McGwire (McGwire Magic)	.20
440	Mark McGwire (McGwire Magic)	.20
441	Mark McGwire (McGwire Magic)	.20
442	Mark McGwire (McGwire Magic)	.20
443	Mark McGwire (McGwire Magic)	.20
444	Mark McGwire (McGwire Magic)	.20
445	Mark McGwire (McGwire Magic)	.20
446	Mark McGwire (McGwire Magic)	.20
447	Mark McGwire (McGwire Magic)	.20
448	Mark McGwire (McGwire Magic)	.20
449	Mark McGwire (McGwire Magic)	.20
450	Mark McGwire (McGwire Magic)	.20
451	Chipper Jones '93 (Rookie Flashback)	.40
452	Cal Ripken Jr. '81 (Rookie Flashback)	.75
453	Roger Clemens '84 (Rookie Flashback)	.40
454	Wade Boggs '82 (Rookie Flashback)	.35
455	Greg Maddux '86 (Rookie Flashback)	.35
456	Frank Thomas '90 (Rookie Flashback)	.30
457	Jeff Bagwell '91 (Rookie Flashback)	.25
458	Mike Piazza '92 (Rookie Flashback)	.45
459	Randy Johnson '88 (Rookie Flashback)	.25
460	Mo Vaughn '91 (Rookie Flashback)	.05
461	Mark McGwire '86 (Rookie Flashback)	.50
462	Rickey Henderson '79 (Rookie Flashback)	.25
463	Barry Bonds '86 (Rookie Flashback)	.75
464	Tony Gwynn '82 (Rookie Flashback)	.35
465	Ken Griffey Jr. '89 (Rookie Flashback)	.45
466	Alex Rodriguez '94 (Rookie Flashback)	.50
467	Sammy Sosa '89 (Rookie Flashback)	.35
468	Juan Gonzalez '89 (Rookie Flashback)	.15
469	Kevin Brown '86 (Rookie Flashback)	.05
470	Fred McGriff '86 (Rookie Flashback)	.05

2000 Upper Deck

Released in two 270-card series the base cards feature full-bleed fronts with gold foil etching and stamping. Card backs have complete year-by-year statistics.

	NM/M
Complete Set (540):	40.00
Complete Series I (270):	20.00
Complete Series II (270):	20.00
Common Player:	.15
Silver Stars:	5-10X
Rookies:	2-4X
Hobby Pack (10):	3.00
Hobby Box (24):	55.00

#	Player	Price
1	Rick Ankiel/SR	.25
2	Vernon Wells/SR	.50
3	Ryan Anderson/SR	.15
4	Ed Yarnall/SR	.15
5	Brian McNichol/SR	.15
6	Ben Petrick/SR	.15
7	Kip Wells/SR	.15
8	Eric Munson/SR	.15
9	Matt Riley/SR	.15
10	Peter Bergeron/SR	.15
11	Eric Gagne/SR	.25
12	Ramon Ortiz/SR	.25
13	Josh Beckett/SR	.50
14	Alfonso Soriano/SR	1.50
15	Jorge Toca/SR	.15
16	Buddy Carlyle/SR	.15
17	Chad Hermansen/SR	.15
18	Matt Perisho/SR	.15
19	Tomokazu Ohka/SR RC	.75
20	Jacque Jones/SR	.15
21	Josh Paul/SR	.15
22	Dermal Brown/SR	.15
23	Adam Kennedy/SR	.15
24	Chad Harville/SR	.15
25	Calvin Murray/SR	.15
26	Chad Meyers/SR	.15
27	Brian Cooper/SR	.15
28	Troy Glaus	.50
29	Ben Molina	.15
30	Troy Percival	.15
31	Ken Hill	.15
32	Chuck Finley	.15
33	Todd Greene	.15
34	Tim Salmon	.25
35	Gary DiSarcina	.15
36	Luis Gonzalez	.25
37	Tony Womack	.15
38	Omar Daal	.15
39	Randy Johnson	.50
40	Erubiel Durazo	.20
41	Jay Bell	.15
42	Steve Finley	.15
43	Travis Lee	.15
44	Greg Maddux	1.00
45	Bret Boone	.15
46	Brian Jordan	.15
47	Kevin Millwood	.25
48	Odalis Perez	.15
49	Javy Lopez	.25
50	John Smoltz	.25
51	Bruce Chen	.15
52	Albert Belle	.25
53	Jerry Hairston Jr.	.15
54	Will Clark	.40
55	Sidney Ponson	.15
56	Charles Johnson	.15
57	Cal Ripken Jr.	2.00
58	Ryan Minor	.15
59	Mike Mussina	.40
60	Tom Gordon	.15
61	Jose Offerman	.15
62	Trot Nixon	.15
63	Pedro Martinez	.75
64	John Valentin	.15
65	Jason Varitek	.15
66	Juan Pena	.15
67	Troy O'Leary	.15
68	Sammy Sosa	1.25
69	Henry Rodriguez	.15
70	Kyle Farnsworth	.15
71	Glenallen Hill	.15
72	Lance Johnson	.15
73	Mickey Morandini	.15
74	Jon Lieber	.15
75	Kevin Tapani	.15
76	Carlos Lee	.20
77	Ray Durham	.15
78	Jim Parque	.15
79	Bob Howry	.15
80	Magglio Ordonez	.25
81	Paul Konerko	.15
82	Mike Caruso	.15
83	Chris Singleton	.15
84	Sean Casey	.20
85	Barry Larkin	.25
86	Pokey Reese	.15
87	Eddie Taubensee	.15
88	Scott Williamson	.15
89	Jason LaRue	.15
90	Aaron Boone	.20
91	Jeffrey Hammonds	.15
92	Omar Vizquel	.20
93	Manny Ramirez	.50
94	Kenny Lofton	.20
95	Jaret Wright	.15
96	Einar Diaz	.15
97	Charles Nagy	.15
98	David Justice	.25
99	Richie Sexson	.25
100	Steve Karsay	.15
101	Todd Helton	.50
102	Dante Bichette	.15
103	Larry Walker	.25
104	Pedro Astacio	.15
105	Neifi Perez	.15
106	Brian Bohanon	.15
107	Edgard Clemente	.15
108	Dave Veres	.15
109	Gabe Kapler	.15
110	Juan Encarnacion	.15
111	Jeff Weaver	.15
112	Damion Easley	.15
113	Justin Thompson	.15
114	Brad Ausmus	.15
115	Frank Catalanotto	.15
116	Todd Jones	.15
117	Preston Wilson	.15
118	Cliff Floyd	.15
119	Mike Lowell	.15
120	Jorge Fabregas	.15
121	Alex Gonzalez	.15
122	Braden Looper	.15
123	Bruce Aven	.15
124	Richard Hidalgo	.15
125	Mitch Meluskey	.15
126	Jeff Bagwell	.50
127	Jose Lima	.15
128	Derek Bell	.15
129	Billy Wagner	.15
130	Shane Reynolds	.15
131	Moises Alou	.25
132	Carlos Beltran	.25
133	Carlos Febles	.15
134	Jermaine Dye	.15
135	Jeremy Giambi	.15
136	Joe Randa	.15
137	Jose Rosado	.15
138	Chad Kreuter	.15
139	Jose Vizcaino	.15
140	Adrian Beltre	.25
141	Kevin Brown	.25
142	Ismael Valdes	.15
143	Angel Pena	.15
144	Chan Ho Park	.15
145	Mark Grudzielanek	.15
146	Jeff Shaw	.15
147	Geoff Jenkins	.20
148	Jeromy Burnitz	.15
149	Hideo Nomo	.25
150	Ron Belliard	.15
151	Sean Berry	.15
152	Mark Loretta	.15
153	Steve Woodard	.15
154	Joe Mays	.15
155	Eric Milton	.15
156	Corey Koskie	.15
157	Ron Coomer	.15
158	Brad Radke	.15
159	Terry Steinbach	.15
160	Christian Guzman	.15
161	Vladimir Guerrero	.50
162	Wilton Guerrero	.15
163	Michael Barrett	.15
164	Chris Widger	.15
165	Fernando Seguignol	.15
166	Ugueth Urbina	.15
167	Dustin Hermanson	.15
168	Kenny Rogers	.15
169	Edgardo Alfonzo	.15
170	Orel Hershiser	.15
171	Robin Ventura	.20
172	Octavio Dotel	.15
173	Rickey Henderson	.25
174	Roger Cedeno	.15
175	John Olerud	.25
176	Derek Jeter	2.00
177	Tino Martinez	.25
178	Orlando Hernandez	.20
179	Chuck Knoblauch	.15
180	Bernie Williams	.40
181	Chili Davis	.15
182	David Cone	.20
183	Ricky Ledee	.15
184	Paul O'Neill	.25
185	Jason Giambi	.50
186	Eric Chavez	.25
187	Matt Stairs	.15
188	Miguel Tejada	.25
189	Olmedo Saenz	.15
190	Tim Hudson	.40
191	John Jaha	.15
192	Randy Velarde	.15
193	Rico Brogna	.15
194	Mike Lieberthal	.20
195	Marlon Anderson	.15
196	Bobby Abreu	.25
197	Ron Gant	.15
198	Randy Wolf	.15
199	Desi Relaford	.15
200	Doug Glanville	.15
201	Warren Morris	.15
202	Kris Benson	.15
203	Kevin Young	.15
204	Brian Giles	.25
205	Jason Schmidt	.15
206	Ed Sprague	.15
207	Francisco Cordova	.15
208	Mark McGwire	2.00
209	Jose Jimenez	.15
210	Fernando Tatis	.15
211	Kent Bottenfield	.15
212	Eli Marrero	.15
213	Edgar Renteria	.15
214	Joe McEwing	.15
215	J.D. Drew	.20
216	Tony Gwynn	.75
217	Gary Matthews Jr.	.15
218	Eric Owens	.15
219	Damian Jackson	.15
220	Reggie Sanders	.15
221	Trevor Hoffman	.15
222	Ben Davis	.15
223	Shawn Estes	.15
224	F.P. Santangelo	.15
225	Livan Hernandez	.15
226	Ellis Burks	.15
227	J.T. Snow	.15
228	Jeff Kent	.25
229	Robb Nen	.15
230	Marvin Benard	.15
231	Ken Griffey Jr.	1.00
232	John Halama	.15
233	Gil Meche	.15
234	David Bell	.15
235	Brian L. Hunter	.15
236	Jay Buhner	.15
237	Edgar Martinez	.25
238	Jose Mesa	.15
239	Wilson Alvarez	.15
240	Wade Boggs	.40
241	Fred McGriff	.15
242	Jose Canseco	.40
243	Kevin Stocker	.15
244	Roberto Hernandez	.15
245	Bubba Trammell	.15
246	John Flaherty	.15
247	Ivan Rodriguez	.40
248	Rusty Greer	.15
249	Rafael Palmeiro	.40
250	Jeff Zimmerman	.15
251	Royce Clayton	.15
252	Todd Zeile	.15
253	John Wetteland	.15
254	Ruben Mateo	.15
255	Kelvim Escobar	.15
256	David Wells	.15
257	Shawn Green	.40
258	Homer Bush	.15
259	Shannon Stewart	.15
260	Carlos Delgado	.50
261	Roy Halladay	.25
262	Fernando Tatis CL	.15
263	Jose Jimenez CL	.15
264	Tony Gwynn CL	.40
265	Wade Boggs CL	.25
266	Cal Ripken Jr. CL	1.00
267	David Cone CL	.15
268	Mark McGwire CL	.75
269	Pedro Martinez CL	.40
270	Nomar Garciaparra CL	.75
271	Nick Johnson/SR	.40
272	Mark Quinn/SR	.15
273	Roosevelt Brown/SR	.15
274	Adam Everett/SR	.15
275	Jason Marquis/SR	.15
276	Kazuhiro Sasaki/SR RC	1.50
277	Aaron Myette/SR	.15
278	Danys Baez/SR RC	.15
279	Travis Dawkins/SR	.15
280	Mark Mulder/SR	.25
281	Chris Haas/SR	.15
282	Milton Bradley/SR	.15
283	Brad Penny/SR	.15
284	Rafael Furcal/SR	.25
285	Luis Matos/SR RC	1.00
286	Victor Santos/SR	.15
287	Rico Washington/SR RC	.15
288	Rob Bell/SR	.15
289	Joe Crede/SR	.15
290	Pablo Ozuna/SR	.15
291	Wascar Serrano/SR RC	.15
292	Sang-Hoon Lee/SR RC	.25
293	Chris Wakeland/SR	.15
294	Luis Rivera/SR	.15
295	Mike Lamb/SR RC	.20
296	Wily Pena/SR	.20
297	Mike Meyers/SR RC	.15
298	Mo Vaughn	.20
299	Darin Erstad	.25
300	Garret Anderson	.25
301	Tim Belcher	.15
302	Scott Spiezio	.15
303	Kent Bottenfield	.15
304	Orlando Palmeiro	.15
305	Jason Dickson	.15
306	Matt Williams	.20
307	Brian Anderson	.15
308	Hanley Frias	.15
309	Todd Stottlemyre	.15
310	Matt Mantei	.15
311	David Dellucci	.15
312	Armando Reynoso	.15
313	Bernard Gilkey	.15
314	Chipper Jones	1.00
315	Tom Glavine	.25
316	Quilvio Veras	.15
317	Andruw Jones	.50
318	Bobby Bonilla	.15
319	Reggie Sanders	.15
320	Andres Galarraga	.20
321	George Lombard	.15
322	John Rocker	.15
323	Wally Joyner	.15
324	B.J. Surhoff	.15
325	Scott Erickson	.15
326	Delino DeShields	.15
327	Jeff Conine	.15
328	Mike Timlin	.15
329	Brady Anderson	.15
330	Mike Bordick	.15
331	Harold Baines	.15
332	Nomar Garciaparra	1.50
333	Bret Saberhagen	.15
334	Ramon Martinez	.15
335	Donnie Sadler	.15
336	Wilton Veras	.15
337	Mike Stanley	.15
338	Brian Rose	.15
339	Carl Everett	.15
340	Tim Wakefield	.15
341	Mark Grace	.25
342	Kerry Wood	.30
343	Eric Young	.15
344	Jose Nieves	.15
345	Ismael Valdes	.15
346	Joe Girardi	.15
347	Damon Buford	.15
348	Ricky Gutierrez	.15
349	Frank Thomas	.50
350	Brian Simmons	.15
351	James Baldwin	.15
352	Brook Fordyce	.15
353	Jose Valentin	.15
354	Mike Sirotka	.15
355	Greg Norton	.15
356	Dante Bichette	.15
357	Deion Sanders	.25
358	Ken Griffey Jr.	1.00
359	Denny Neagle	.15
360	Dmitri Young	.15
361	Pete Harnisch	.15
362	Michael Tucker	.15
363	Roberto Alomar	.40
364	Dave Roberts	.15
365	Jim Thome	.50
366	Bartolo Colon	.15
367	Travis Fryman	.20
368	Chuck Finley	.15
369	Russell Branyan	.15
370	Alex Ramirez	.15
371	Jeff Cirillo	.15
372	Jeffrey Hammonds	.15
373	Scott Karl	.15
374	Brent Mayne	.15
375	Tom Goodwin	.15
376	Jose Jimenez	.15
377	Rolando Arrojo	.15
378	Terry Shumpert	.15
379	Juan Gonzalez	.50
380	Bobby Higginson	.15
381	Tony Clark	.15
382	Dave Mlicki	.15
383	Deivi Cruz	.15
384	Brian Moehler	.15
385	Dean Palmer	.15
386	Luis Castillo	.15
387	Mike Redmond	.15
388	Alex Fernandez	.15
389	Brant Brown	.15
390	Dave Berg	.15
391	A.J. Burnett	.15
392	Mark Kotsay	.15
393	Craig Biggio	.20
394	Daryle Ward	.15
395	Lance Berkman	.25
396	Roger Cedeno	.15
397	Scott Elarton	.15
398	Octavio Dotel	.15
399	Ken Caminiti	.15
400	Johnny Damon	.25
401	Mike Sweeney	.15
402	Jeff Suppan	.15
403	Rey Sanchez	.15
404	Blake Stein	.15
405	Ricky Bottalico	.15
406	Jay Witasick	.15
407	Shawn Green	.40
408	Orel Hershiser	.15
409	Gary Sheffield	.40
410	Todd Hollandsworth	.15
411	Terry Adams	.15
412	Todd Hundley	.15
413	Eric Karros	.15
414	F.P. Santangelo	.15
415	Alex Cora	.15
416	Marquis Grissom	.15
417	Henry Blanco	.15
418	Jose Hernandez	.15
419	Kyle Peterson	.15
420	John Snyder RC	.15
421	Bob Wickman	.15
422	Jamey Wright	.15
423	Chad Allen	.15
424	Todd Walker	.15
425	J.C. Romero RC	.15
426	Butch Huskey	.15
427	Jacque Jones	.15
428	Matt Lawton	.15
429	Rondell White	.25
430	Jose Vidro	.15
431	Hideki Irabu	.15
432	Javier Vazquez	.15
433	Lee Stevens	.15
434	Mike Thurman	.15
435	Geoff Blum	.15
436	Mike Hampton	.15
437	Mike Piazza	1.00
438	Al Leiter	.15
439	Derek Bell	.15
440	Armando Benitez	.15
441	Rey Ordonez	.15
442	Todd Zeile	.15
443	Roger Clemens	1.25
444	Ramiro Mendoza	.15
445	Andy Pettitte	.25
446	Scott Brosius	.15
447	Mariano Rivera	.25
448	Jim Leyritz	.15
449	Jorge Posada	.25
450	Omar Olivares	.15
451	Ben Grieve	.15
452	A.J. Hinch	.15
453	Gil Heredia	.15
454	Kevin Appier	.15
455	Ryan Christenson	.15
456	Ramon Hernandez	.15
457	Scott Rolen	.50
458	Alex Arias	.15
459	Andy Ashby	.15
460		.15
461	Robert Person	.15
462	Paul Byrd	.15
463	Curt Schilling	.25
464	Mike Jackson	.15
465	Jason Kendall	.25
466	Pat Meares	.15
467	Bruce Aven	.15
468	Todd Ritchie	.15
469	Wil Cordero	.15
470	Aramis Ramirez	.15
471	Andy Benes	.15
472	Ray Lankford	.15
473	Fernando Vina	.15
474a	Jim Edmonds	.25
474b	Kevin Jordan (Should be #460).	.15
475	Craig Paquette	.15
476	Pat Hentgen	.15
477	Darryl Kile	.15
478	Sterling Hitchcock	.15
479	Ruben Rivera	.15
480	Ryan Klesko	.15
481	Phil Nevin	.15

482	Woody Williams	.15
483	Carlos Hernandez	.15
484	Brian Meadows	.15
485	Bret Boone	.25
486	Barry Bonds	1.50
487	Russ Ortiz	.15
488	Bobby Estalella	.15
489	Rich Aurilia	.15
490	Bill Mueller	.15
491	Joe Nathan	.15
492	Russ Davis	.15
493	John Olerud	.25
494	Alex Rodriguez	1.50
495	Fred Garcia	.15
496	Carlos Guillen	.15
497	Aaron Sele	.15
498	Brett Tomko	.15
499	Jamie Moyer	.15
500	Mike Cameron	.15
501	Vinny Castilla	.15
502	Gerald Williams	.15
503	Mike DiFelice	.15
504	Ryan Rupe	.15
505	Greg Vaughn	.15
506	Miguel Cairo	.15
507	Juan Guzman RC	.15
508	Jose Guillen	.15
509	Gabe Kapler	.15
510	Rick Helling	.15
511	David Segui	.15
512	Doug Davis	.15
513	Justin Thompson	.15
514	Chad Curtis	.15
515	Tony Batista	.15
516	Billy Koch	.15
517	Raul Mondesi	.20
518	Joey Hamilton	.15
519	Darrin Fletcher	.15
520	Brad Fullmer	.15
521	Jose Cruz Jr.	.15
522	Kevin Witt	.15
523	Mark McGwire (All-UD Team)	1.00
524	Roberto Alomar (All-UD Team)	.25
525	Chipper Jones (All-UD Team)	.50
526	Derek Jeter (All-UD Team)	1.00
527	Ken Griffey Jr. (All-UD Team)	.50
528	Sammy Sosa (All-UD Team)	.75
529	Manny Ramirez (All-UD Team)	.40
530	Ivan Rodriguez (All-UD Team)	.25
531	Pedro J. Martinez (All-UD Team)	.40
532	Mariano Rivera (Season Highlights Checklist)	.15
533	Sammy Sosa (Season Highlights Checklist)	.75
534	Cal Ripken Jr. (Season Highlights Checklist)	1.00
535	Vladimir Guerrero (Season Highlights Checklist)	.40
536	Tony Gwynn (Season Highlights Checklist)	.25
537	Mark McGwire (Season Highlights Checklist)	1.00
538	Bernie Williams (Season Highlights Checklist)	.25
539	Pedro J. Martinez (Season Highlights Checklist)	.40
540	Ken Griffey Jr. (Season Highlights Checklist)	.50

Exclusives

Labeled "UD Exclusives," these parallel sets were issued in two versions, silvers numbered to 100 each, and golds which were 1-of-1. Except for the appropriately colored foil highlights on front and dot-matrix serial number, the Exclusives are identical to the regular-issue cards. They were inserted exclusively into hobby packs. Because of their rarity and variable demand, the unique gold cards are not priced.

	NM/M
Common Silver Exclusive:	1.00
Silver Stars/Rookies:	8X

Cooperstown Calling

This insert set features players deemed by Upper Deck as future Hall of Famers. Card fronts feature silver holo-foil with gold foil stamping. Card backs are numbered with a "CC" prefix and are seeded 1:23 packs.

	NM/M
Complete Set (15):	25.00
Common Player:	.75
Inserted 1:23	
1 Roger Clemens	3.00
2 Cal Ripken Jr.	5.00
3 Ken Griffey Jr.	3.00
4 Mike Piazza	3.00
5 Tony Gwynn	2.00
6 Sammy Sosa	2.50
7 Jose Canseco	1.00
8 Larry Walker	.75
9 Barry Bonds	4.00
10 Greg Maddux	2.50
11 Derek Jeter	5.00
12 Mark McGwire	4.00
13 Randy Johnson	2.00
14 Frank Thomas	1.50
15 Jeff Bagwell	1.50

e-Card

Randomly inserted in series 2 packs, each e-card has an ID number stamped on the card front that can be entered on Upper Deck's website. Collectors then find out if that card "evolves" into a signature card, jersey card or a signed jersey card. They are seeded 1:9 packs and are numbered with an "E" prefix on the card back.

	NM/M
Complete Set (6):	10.00
Common Player:	1.00
Inserted 1:12	
1 Ken Griffey Jr.	2.00
2 Alex Rodriguez	3.00
3 Cal Ripken Jr.	3.00
4 Jeff Bagwell	1.00
5 Barry Bonds	3.00
6 Manny Ramirez	1.00

eVolve Jersey

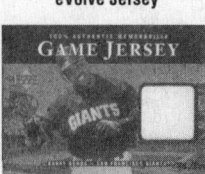

	NM/M
Common Player:	15.00
Production 300 Sets	
1 Ken Griffey Jr.	30.00
2 Alex Rodriguez	40.00
3 Cal Ripken Jr.	50.00
4 Jeff Bagwell	15.00
5 Barry Bonds	40.00
6 Manny Ramirez	20.00

eVolve Signed Jersey

	NM/M
Common Player:	80.00
Production 50 Sets	
1 Ken Griffey Jr.	150.00
2 Alex Rodriguez	150.00
3 Cal Ripken Jr.	200.00
4 Jeff Bagwell	60.00
5 Barry Bonds	150.00
6 Manny Ramirez	60.00

eVolve Signature

	NM/M
Common Player:	40.00
Production 200 Sets	
1 Ken Griffey Jr.	85.00
2 Alex Rodriguez	85.00
3 Cal Ripken Jr.	150.00
4 Jeff Bagwell	40.00
5 Barry Bonds	120.00
6 Manny Ramirez	40.00

Faces of the Game

Randomly inserted in Series 1 at a rate of 1:11 packs, card fronts feature a close-up photo of the featured player with bronze foil etching and stamping. Backs are numbered with an "F" prefix. Two parallel versions are available, Silvers are serially numbered to 100 and golds limited to one set.

	NM/M
Complete Set (20):	30.00
Common Player:	.75
Inserted 1:11	
Silver:	4-8X
Production 100 Sets	
1 Ken Griffey Jr.	2.50
2 Mark McGwire	3.00
3 Sammy Sosa	2.00
4 Alex Rodriguez	3.00
5 Manny Ramirez	1.00
6 Derek Jeter	4.00
7 Jeff Bagwell	1.00
8 Roger Clemens	2.00
9 Scott Rolen	.75
10 Tony Gwynn	1.50
11 Nomar Garciaparra	2.50
12 Randy Johnson	1.50
13 Greg Maddux	2.00
14 Mike Piazza	2.50
15 Frank Thomas	1.00
16 Cal Ripken Jr.	4.00
17 Ivan Rodriguez	.75
18 Mo Vaughn	.75
19 Chipper Jones	2.00
20 Sean Casey	.75

Five-Tool Talents

Randomly inserted in series 2 at a rate of 1:11 packs, this 15-card set spotlights players who have "five tools." Card fronts have

---

silver holo-foil throughout with silver foil stamping. Card backs are numbered with an "FT" prefix.

	NM/M
Complete Set (15):	15.00
Common Player:	.50
Inserted 1:11	
1 Vladimir Guerrero	1.50
2 Barry Bonds	3.00
3 Jason Kendall	.50
4 Derek Jeter	4.00
5 Ken Griffey Jr.	2.50
6 Andruw Jones	.75
7 Bernie Williams	.75
8 Jose Canseco	.75
9 Scott Rolen	.75
10 Shawn Green	.50
11 Nomar Garciaparra	2.50
12 Jeff Bagwell	1.00
13 Larry Walker	.75
14 Chipper Jones	2.00
15 Alex Rodriguez	3.00

Game Balls

These inserts feature a piece of game-used baseball embedded into the card from the featured player. Card backs are numbered with the featured player's initials and are found on the average of 1:287 series 2 packs.

	NM/M
Common Player:	10.00
JB Jeff Bagwell	10.00
RC Roger Clemens	30.00
KG Ken Griffey Jr.	25.00
VG Vladimir Guerrero	15.00
TG Tony Gwynn	25.00
DJ Derek Jeter	40.00
CJ Chipper Jones	20.00
GM Greg Maddux	20.00
MM Mark McGwire	50.00
AR Alex Rodriguez	30.00
BW Bernie Williams	10.00

Game Jersey

These have a piece of game-used jersey from the featured player embedded into the card. This regular version is found both in hobby and retail packs at a rate of 1:2,500 packs.

	NM/M
Common Player:	10.00
Inserted 1:2,500	
JC Jose Canseco	15.00
JG Juan Gonzalez	15.00
VG Vladimir Guerrero	20.00
TH Todd Helton	15.00
CJ Chipper Jones	25.00
GK Gabe Kapler	10.00
GM Greg Maddux	35.00
MR Manny Ramirez	20.00
CR Cal Ripken Jr.	60.00
GV Greg Vaughn	10.00

Game Jersey Series 2

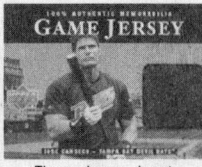

These jersey inserts are found in both hobby and retail packs and are seeded 1:287 packs.

	NM/M
Common Player:	10.00
AR Alex Rodriguez	30.00
TG Tony Gwynn	20.00
FT Frank Thomas	15.00
MW Matt Williams	15.00
JT Jim Thome	15.00
MV Mo Vaughn	10.00
TGl Tom Glavine	15.00
BG Ben Grieve	10.00
TrG Troy Glaus	15.00
RJ Randy Johnson	20.00

KM	Kevin Millwood	10.00
KG	Ken Griffey Jr.	25.00
AB	Albert Belle	10.00
DC	David Cone	10.00
MH	Mike Hampton	10.00
EC	Eric Chavez	10.00
EM	Edgar Martinez	15.00
PW	Preston Wilson	10.00
RV	Robin Ventura	10.00

Game Jersey Hobby

These game-used memorabilia inserts were found exclusively in series 1 packs at a rate of 1:288.

	NM/M
Common Player:	10.00
Inserted 1:288	
JB Jeff Bagwell	15.00
TG Troy Glaus	15.00
CY Tom Glavine	10.00
Jr. Ken Griffey Jr.	25.00
DJ Derek Jeter	40.00
PM Pedro J. Martinez	20.00
MP Mike Piazza	30.00
AR Alex Rodriguez	30.00
FT Frank Thomas	15.00
LW Larry Walker	10.00

Game Jersey Auto. Hobby Series 2

Found exclusively in series 2 packs these autographed game-used memorabilia inserts are found only in hobby packs at a rate of 1:287.

	NM/M
Common Player:	30.00
H-KG Ken Griffey Jr.	100.00
H-CR Cal Ripken Jr.	150.00
H-DJ Derek Jeter	150.00
H-IR Ivan Rodriguez	40.00
H-AR Alex Rodriguez	100.00
H-MR Manny Ramirez	50.00
H-JC Jose Canseco	30.00
H-BB Barry Bonds	180.00
H-SR Scott Rolen	40.00
H-PO Paul O'Neill	40.00
H-JK Jason Kendall	30.00
H-VG Vladimir Guerrero	50.00
H-JB Jeff Bagwell	40.00

Game Jersey Patch

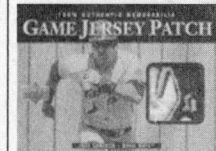

Inserted in Series 1 packs at a rate of 1:10,000, these memorabilia inserts have a piece of game-used uniform patch embedded. A 1-of-1 patch of each player was also issued, but cannot be priced due to rarity.

	NM/M
Common Player:	40.00
Inserted 1:10,000	
JB Jeff Bagwell	60.00
JC Jose Canseco	60.00
TG Troy Glaus	50.00
CY Tom Glavine	60.00
Jr. Ken Griffey Jr.	100.00
VG Vladimir Guerrero	100.00
TH Todd Helton	60.00
DJ Derek Jeter	150.00
CJ Chipper Jones	75.00
GK Gabe Kapler	40.00
GM Greg Maddux	60.00
PM Pedro J. Martinez	100.00
MP Mike Piazza	100.00
MR Manny Ramirez	80.00
CR Cal Ripken Jr.	200.00
AR Alex Rodriguez	125.00
FT Frank Thomas	80.00
GV Greg Vaughn	40.00
LW Larry Walker	50.00

Game Jersey Patch Series 2

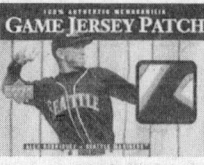

Inserted in Series 2 packs, these memorabilia inserts have a game-used uniform patch embedded and are seeded 1:7,500 packs. A limited one-of-one patch insert for each player is also randomly seeded and are not priced due to their limited nature.

	NM/M
Common Player:	50.00
JB Jeff Bagwell	75.00
BB Barry Bonds	200.00
JC Jose Canseco	75.00
TGl Troy Glaus	75.00
KG Ken Griffey Jr.	125.00
VG Vladimir Guerrero	100.00
TG Tony Gwynn	100.00
DJ Derek Jeter	150.00
RJ Randy Johnson	100.00
AJ Andruw Jones	80.00
CJ Chipper Jones	100.00
GM Greg Maddux	100.00
PM Pedro Martinez	100.00
MR Manny Ramirez	100.00
CR Cal Ripken Jr.	200.00
SR Scott Rolen	75.00
AR Alex Rodriguez	150.00
IR Ivan Rodriguez	90.00
FT Frank Thomas	100.00
MV Mo Vaughn	50.00
MW Matt Williams	50.00

Hit Brigade

Fifteen of the game's top hitters are featured on a full foiled front with bronze foil stamping. Card backs are numbered with an "H" prefix and are found in series 1 packs at a rate of 1:8. Two parallels are randomly inserted: Silvers are serial numbered to 100 and Golds are limited to one set.

	NM/M
Complete Set (15):	15.00
Common Player:	.50
Inserted 1:8	
Silver:	5-10X
Production 100 Sets	
1 Ken Griffey Jr.	2.00
2 Tony Gwynn	1.00
3 Alex Rodriguez	2.50
4 Derek Jeter	3.00
5 Mike Piazza	2.00
6 Sammy Sosa	1.50
7 Juan Gonzalez	.75
8 Scott Rolen	.50
9 Nomar Garciaparra	2.00
10 Barry Bonds	2.50
11 Craig Biggio	.50
12 Chipper Jones	1.50
13 Frank Thomas	.75
14 Larry Walker	.50
15 Mark McGwire	2.50

Hot Properties

This set spotlights rookies and prospects who have a bright future. Card fronts have a horizontal format on a holo-foiled stock with silver foil stamping. Card backs are numbered with an "HP" prefix and are found in series 2 packs at a rate of 1:11.

		NM/M
Complete Set (15):		10.00
Common Player:		.50
Inserted 1:11		
1	Carlos Beltran	1.00
2	Rick Ankiel	.50
3	Sean Casey	1.00
4	Preston Wilson	1.00
5	Vernon Wells	1.00
6	Pat Burrell	1.50
7	Eric Chavez	1.00
8	J.D. Drew	1.00
9	Alfonso Soriano	2.00
10	Gabe Kapler	.50
11	Rafael Furcal	1.00
12	Ruben Mateo	.50
13	Corey Koskie	.75
14	Kip Wells	.50
15	Ramon Ortiz	.75

The People's Choice

This 15-card set is printed on a full holo-foiled front with gold foil stamping. Card backs are numbered with a "PC" prefix and are seeded 1:23 packs.

		NM/M
Complete Set (15):		20.00
Common Player:		.75
Inserted 1:23		
1	Mark McGwire	3.00
2	Nomar Garciaparra	3.00
3	Derek Jeter	3.00
4	Shawn Green	.75
5	Manny Ramirez	1.00
6	Pedro Martinez	1.50
7	Ivan Rodriguez	.75
8	Alex Rodriguez	3.00
9	Juan Gonzalez	1.00
10	Ken Griffey Jr.	2.00
11	Sammy Sosa	2.50
12	Jeff Bagwell	1.00
13	Chipper Jones	2.00
14	Cal Ripken Jr.	4.00
15	Mike Piazza	2.00

Pennant Driven

This 10-card horizontal set has a holo-foiled card front with silver foil stamping. Card backs are numbered with a "PD" prefix and are seeded 1:4 packs.

		NM/M
Complete Set (10):		8.00
Common Player:		.50
Inserted 1:4		
1	Derek Jeter	2.00
2	Roberto Alomar	.50
3	Chipper Jones	1.50
4	Jeff Bagwell	.75
5	Roger Clemens	1.00
6	Nomar Garciaparra	1.50
7	Manny Ramirez	.75
8	Mike Piazza	1.50
9	Ivan Rodriguez	.75
10	Randy Johnson	.75

Piece of History-500 Club

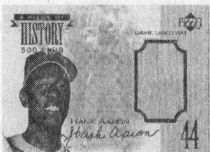

This card features a piece of a game-used Louisville Slugger once swung by Aaron. Approximately 350 cards were produced. Also randomly inserted are 44 autographed versions.

		NM/M
755HR Hank Aaron		300.00
HAAU Hank Aaron/Auto./44		1,200

Power Deck

Collectors need access to a CD-ROM in order to enjoy these interactive cards. Found exclusively in hobby packs cards 1-8 are seeded 1:23 packs and cards 9-11 are found 1:287 packs.

		NM/M
Complete Set (11):		60.00
Common Player:		2.50
Inserted 1:23		
1	Ken Griffey Jr.	5.00
2	Cal Ripken Jr.	7.50
3	Mark McGwire	6.00
4	Tony Gwynn	3.50
5	Roger Clemens	3.50
6	Alex Rodriguez	6.00
7	Sammy Sosa	3.50
8	Derek Jeter	7.50
9	Ken Griffey Jr.	25.00
10	Mark McGwire	30.00
11	Reggie Jackson	15.00

Power MARK

		NM/M
Complete Set (10):		25.00
Common McGwire:		3.00
Inserted 1:23		
Silver:		5-10X
Production 100 Sets		
1-10	Mark McGwire	3.00

Power Rally

This 15-card set highlights the top hitters and are numbered with an "P" prefix on the card back. They are found 1:11 packs. Two parallel version are also seeded: Coppers are limited to 100 serial numbered sets and Golds are limited to one set.

		NM/M
Complete Set (15):		20.00
Common Player:		.75
Inserted 1:11		
Silver:		4-8X
Production 100 Sets		
1	Ken Griffey Jr.	2.50
2	Mark McGwire	3.00
3	Sammy Sosa	2.00
4	Jose Canseco	.75
5	Juan Gonzalez	1.00
6	Bernie Williams	.75
7	Jeff Bagwell	1.00
8	Chipper Jones	2.00
9	Vladimir Guerrero	1.50

10	Mo Vaughn	.75
11	Derek Jeter	4.00
12	Mike Piazza	2.50
13	Barry Bonds	3.00
14	Alex Rodriguez	3.00
15	Nomar Garciaparra	2.50

Prime Performers

This 10-card set has a horizontal format on a full holo foiled front, with silver foil etching and stamping. Card backs are numbered with a "PP" prefix and found 1:8 packs.

		NM/M
Complete Set (10):		10.00
Common Player:		.50
Inserted 1:8		
1	Manny Ramirez	.75
2	Pedro Martinez	1.00
3	Carlos Delgado	.50
4	Ken Griffey Jr.	2.00
5	Derek Jeter	3.00
6	Chipper Jones	1.50
7	Sean Casey	.50
8	Shawn Green	.50
9	Sammy Sosa	1.50
10	Alex Rodriguez	2.50

STATitude

This 30-card set spotlights the most statistically dominant players on a horizontal format with silver foil stamping. Card backs are numbered with an "S" prefix and are inserted 1:4. Two parallel versions are randomly inserted: Coppers are limited to 100 serial numbered sets and Golds are limited to one set.

		NM/M
Complete Set (30):		25.00
Common Player:		.40
Inserted 1:4		
Silver:		5-10X
Production 100 Sets		
1	Mo Vaughn	.40
2	Matt Williams	.40
3	Travis Lee	.40
4	Chipper Jones	1.50
5	Greg Maddux	1.50
6	Gabe Kapler	.40
7	Cal Ripken Jr.	2.00
8	Nomar Garciaparra	2.00
9	Sammy Sosa	1.50
10	Frank Thomas	.75
11	Manny Ramirez	.75
12	Larry Walker	.50
13	Ivan Rodriguez	.50
14	Jeff Bagwell	.50
15	Craig Biggio	.50
16	Vladimir Guerrero	1.00
17	Mike Piazza	2.00
18	Bernie Williams	.50
19	Derek Jeter	3.00
20	Jose Canseco	.50
21	Eric Chavez	.50
22	Scott Rolen	.50
23	Mark McGwire	2.50
24	Tony Gwynn	1.00
25	Barry Bonds	2.50
26	Ken Griffey Jr.	2.00
27	Alex Rodriguez	2.50
28	J.D. Drew	.50
29	Juan Gonzalez	.50
30	Roger Clemens	1.50

2K Plus

This 12-card set showcases the talents of baseball's next millennium. They are numbered with an "2K" prefix on the card back and are seeded 1:23 packs. Two parallel versions are also randomly inserted: Coppers are limited to 100 serial numbered sets and Golds are limited on one set produced.

		NM/M
Complete Set (12):		15.00
Common Player:		.50
Inserted 1:23		
Silver:		5-10X

---

are full foiled with silver etching. Card backs have the player's past five years of statistics, a brief career note and small photo.

		NM/M
Complete Set (120):		25.00
Common Player:		.15
Common Diamond Debut:		.50
Pack (6):		1.50
Wax Box (24):		30.00
1	Darin Erstad	.25
2	Tim Salmon	.25
3	Mo Vaughn	.20
4	Matt Williams	.25
5	Travis Lee	.15
6	Randy Johnson	.75
7	Tom Glavine	.40
8	Chipper Jones	1.50
9	Greg Maddux	1.50
10	Andruw Jones	.50
11	Brian Jordan	.15
12	Cal Ripken Jr.	2.50
13	Albert Belle	.20
14	Mike Mussina	.50
15	Nomar Garciaparra	2.00
16	Troy O'Leary	.15
17	Pedro J. Martinez	1.00
18	Sammy Sosa	1.50
19	Henry Rodriguez	.15
20	Frank Thomas	.75
21	Magglio Ordonez	.40
22	Greg Vaughn	.15
23	Barry Larkin	.25
24	Sean Casey	.25
25	Jim Thome	.75
26	Kenny Lofton	.25
27	Roberto Alomar	.50
28	Manny Ramirez	.75
29	Larry Walker	.25
30	Todd Helton	.75
31	Gabe Kapler	.15
32	Tony Clark	.25
33	Dean Palmer	.15
34	Cliff Floyd	.15
35	Alex Gonzalez	.15
36	Moises Alou	.25
37	Jeff Bagwell	.75
38	Craig Biggio	.25
39	Richard Hidalgo	.15
40	Carlos Beltran	.25
41	Johnny Damon	.25
42	Adrian Beltre	.25
43	Gary Sheffield	.40
44	Kevin Brown	.25
45	Jeromy Burnitz	.15
46	Jeff Cirillo	.15
47	Joe Mays	.15
48	Todd Walker	.15
49	Vladimir Guerrero	.75
50	Michael Barrett	.15
51	Rickey Henderson	.40
52	Mike Piazza	1.50
53	Robin Ventura	.25
54	John Olerud	.25
55	Edgardo Alfonzo	.15
56	Derek Jeter	2.00
57	Orlando Hernandez	.15
58	Tino Martinez	.25
59	Bernie Williams	.50
60	Roger Clemens	1.50
61	Eric Chavez	.25
62	Ben Grieve	.25
63	Jason Giambi	1.00
64	Scott Rolen	.50
65	Bobby Abreu	.25
66	Curt Schilling	.40
67	Mike Lieberthal	.15
68	Warren Morris	.15
69	Brian Giles	.25
70	Eric Owens	.15
71	Tony Gwynn	1.00
72	Reggie Sanders	.15
73	Barry Bonds	2.00
74	J.T. Snow	.15
75	Jeff Kent	.25
76	Ken Griffey Jr.	1.50
77	Alex Rodriguez	2.00
78	Edgar Martinez	.15
79	Jay Buhner	.15
80	Mark McGwire	2.00
81	J.D. Drew	.25
82	Eric Davis	.15
83	Fernando Tatis	.15
84	Wade Boggs	.50
85	Fred McGriff	.25
86	Juan Gonzalez	.75
87	Ivan Rodriguez	.50
88	Rafael Palmeiro	.50
89	Shawn Green	.40
90	Carlos Delgado	.60
91	Pat Burrell (Diamond Debut)	1.00
92	Eric Munson (Diamond Debut)	.50
93	Jorge Toca (Diamond Debut)	.50
94	Rick Ankiel (Diamond Debut)	.50
95	Tony Armas Jr. (Diamond Debut)	.75
96	Byung-Hyun Kim (Diamond Debut)	.75
97	Alfonso Soriano (Diamond Debut)	3.00
98	Mark Quinn (Diamond Debut)	.50

2K Plus (cont.)

1	Ken Griffey Jr.	2.00
2	J.D. Drew	.50
3	Derek Jeter	3.00
4	Nomar Garciaparra	3.00
5	Pat Burrell	.75
6	Ruben Mateo	.50
7	Carlos Beltran	.50
8	Vladimir Guerrero	1.00
9	Scott Rolen	1.00
10	Chipper Jones	2.00
11	Alex Rodriguez	3.00
12	Magglio Ordonez	.75

3,000 Hit Club Series 1

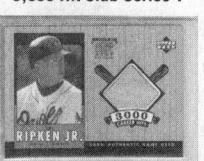

Game-used memorabilia from Orioles teammates Ripken and Murray were inserted in the cross-brand 3,000 Hit Club inserts in Series 1 UD.

		NM/M
CR-B	Cal Ripken Jr./Bat/350	25.00
CR-J	Cal Ripken Jr./Jsy/350	25.00
CR-JB	Cal Ripken Jr./Jsy/Bat/100	150.00
EM-B	Eddie Murray/Bat/350	10.00
EM-J	Eddie Murray/Jsy/350	8.00
EM-JB	Eddie Murray/Jsy/Bat/100	60.00

3,000 Hit Club Series 2

This cross-brand series spotlights Hank Aaron. The series includes a Jersey card (350 produced), Bat card (350 produced), Jersey/Bat combo (100 produced) and Autographed Jersey/Bat combo (44 produced).

		NM/M
HA-B	Hank Aaron/Bat/350	75.00
HA-JB	Hank Aaron/Bat/Jsy/100	150.00
HA-J	Hank Aaron/Jsy/350	75.00
HA-JBS	Hank Aaron/Auto. Bat/Jsy/44	1,000

2000 Upper Deck Black Diamond

The base set consists of 120-cards, including a 30 card Diamond Debut (91-120) subset that are seeded 1:4 packs. Card fronts

---

99	Ryan Rupe (Diamond Debut)	.50
100	Adam Kennedy (Diamond Debut)	.50
101	Jeff Weaver (Diamond Debut)	.75
102	Ramon Ortiz (Diamond Debut)	.75
103	Eugene Kingsale (Diamond Debut)	.50
104	Josh Beckett (Diamond Debut)	1.00
105	Eric Gagne (Diamond Debut)	1.00
106	Peter Bergeron (Diamond Debut)	.50
107	Erubiel Durazo (Diamond Debut)	.75
108	Chad Meyers (Diamond Debut)	.50
109	Kip Wells (Diamond Debut)	.50
110	Chad Harville (Diamond Debut)	.50
111	Matt Riley (Diamond Debut)	.50
112	Ben Petrick (Diamond Debut)	.50
113	Ed Yarnall (Diamond Debut)	.50
114	Calvin Murray (Diamond Debut)	.50
115	Vernon Wells (Diamond Debut)	1.00
116	A.J. Burnett (Diamond Debut)	.75
117	Jacque Jones (Diamond Debut)	.75
118	Francisco Cordero (Diamond Debut)	.50
119	Tomokazu Ohka **RC** (Diamond Debut)	1.50
120	Julio Ramirez (Diamond Debut)	.50

Reciprocal Cut

A parallel to the 120-card base set, the die-cut design can be used to differentiate them from base cards. Card backs are also numbered with an "R" prefix. Cards 1-90 are found 1:7 packs and Diamond Debuts (91-120) are seeded 1:12 packs.

	NM/M
Stars (1-90):	2-5X
Diamond Debuts	1-1.5X
1-90 inserted 1:7	
Diamond Debuts inserted 1:12	

Final Cut

A parallel to the 120-card base set the die-cut design can be used to distinguish them from base cards, the card backs are also numbered with an "F" prefix. Each card is serial numbered within an edition of 100 sets.

	NM/M
Stars (1-90):	5-10X
Diamond Debuts:	2-4X
Production 100 Sets	

A Piece of History Single

These memorabilia inserts have a piece of game-used bat embedded into the card front and are seeded 1:179 packs.

		NM/M
Common Player:		8.00
Inserted 1:179		
AB	Albert Belle	8.00
BB	Barry Bonds	40.00
JC	Jose Canseco	10.00
DE	Darin Erstad	8.00
JR	Ken Griffey Jr.	25.00
VG	Vladimir Guerrero	15.00
TG	Tony Gwynn	20.00
TH	Todd Helton	10.00
DJ	Derek Jeter	40.00
AJ	Andruw Jones	10.00
CJ	Chipper Jones	20.00
TL	Travis Lee	8.00
RM	Raul Mondesi	8.00
MP	Mike Piazza	25.00
CAL	Cal Ripken Jr.	50.00
AR	Alex Rodriguez	25.00
IR	Ivan Rodriguez	10.00
SR	Scott Rolen	10.00
MV	Mo Vaughn	25.00

A Piece of History Double

These memorabilia inserts have two pieces of game-used bat embedded into the card front and are a parallel to the single set. They are inserted at 1:1,079 packs.

		NM/M
Common Player:		10.00
Inserted 1:1079		
AB	Albert Belle	10.00
BB	Barry Bonds	75.00
JC	Jose Canseco	20.00
DE	Darin Erstad	15.00
JR	Ken Griffey Jr.	50.00
VG	Vladimir Guerrero	30.00
TG	Tony Gwynn	40.00
TH	Todd Helton	15.00
DJ	Derek Jeter	75.00
AJ	Andruw Jones	15.00
CJ	Chipper Jones	40.00
TL	Travis Lee	10.00
RM	Raul Mondesi	10.00
MP	Mike Piazza	50.00
CAL	Cal Ripken Jr.	80.00
AR	Alex Rodriguez	50.00
IR	Ivan Rodriguez	15.00
SR	Scott Rolen	15.00
MV	Mo Vaughn	10.00

Barrage

This 10-card set features a prismatic background with silver foil stamping. Card backs are numbered with a "B" prefix and are seeded 1:29 packs.

		NM/M
Complete Set (10):		15.00
Common Player:		1.00
Inserted 1:29		
1	Mark McGwire	3.00
2	Ken Griffey Jr.	2.00
3	Sammy Sosa	2.50
4	Jeff Bagwell	1.00
5	Juan Gonzalez	1.00
6	Alex Rodriguez	3.00
7	Manny Ramirez	1.00
8	Ivan Rodriguez	1.00
9	Chipper Jones	2.00
10	Mike Piazza	2.00

Constant Threat

A 10-card set spotlighting the top hitters in the game. Card backs are numbered with a "T" prefix and are seeded 1:29 packs.

		NM/M
Complete Set (10):		20.00
Common Player:		1.00
Inserted 1:29		
1	Ken Griffey Jr.	2.00
2	Vladimir Guerrero	1.00
3	Alex Rodriguez	3.00
4	Sammy Sosa	2.50
5	Juan Gonzalez	1.00
6	Derek Jeter	3.00
7	Nomar Garciaparra	3.00
8	Barry Bonds	4.00
9	Chipper Jones	2.00
10	Mike Piazza	2.00

Diamonation

This 10-card set has a holo-foil background with gold foil etching and stamping. Card backs are numbered with a "D" prefix and have an insertion ratio of 1:4 packs.

		NM/M
Complete Set (10):		6.00
Common Player:		.50
Inserted 1:4		
1	Ken Griffey Jr.	1.00
2	Randy Johnson	1.00
3	Mark McGwire	1.50
4	Manny Ramirez	.75
5	Scott Rolen	.75
6	Bernie Williams	.75
7	Roger Clemens	1.50
8	Mo Vaughn	.50
9	Frank Thomas	.75
10	Sean Casey	.50

Diamond Gallery

This 10-card set spotlights the featured player in a baseball diamond frame with a prismatic background. Gold foil etching and stamping is also used throughout. Card backs are numbered with a "G" prefix and are seeded 1:14 packs.

		NM/M
Complete Set (10):		20.00
Common Player:		1.50
Inserted 1:14		
1	Derek Jeter	3.00
2	Alex Rodriguez	3.00
3	Nomar Garciaparra	3.00
4	Cal Ripken Jr.	4.00
5	Sammy Sosa	2.50
6	Tony Gwynn	1.50
7	Mark McGwire	3.00
8	Roger Clemens	2.50
9	Greg Maddux	2.00
10	Pedro Martinez	1.50

DiamondMight

DiamondMight's have a horizontal format, utilizing holo-foil and gold foil stamping. Card backs are numbered with an "M" prefix and are seeded 1:14 packs.

		NM/M
Complete Set (10):		15.00
Common Player:		1.00
Inserted 1:14		
1	Ken Griffey Jr.	2.00
2	Mark McGwire	3.00
3	Sammy Sosa	2.50
4	Manny Ramirez	1.00
5	Jeff Bagwell	1.00
6	Frank Thomas	1.00
7	Mike Piazza	2.00
8	Juan Gonzalez	1.00
9	Barry Bonds	4.00
10	Alex Rodriguez	3.00

Diamonds in the Rough

This 10-card set has a horizontal format utilizing holo-foil and gold foil stamping. Card backs are numbered with an "R" prefix and seeded 1:9 packs.

		NM/M
Complete Set (10):		8.00
Common Player:		.75
Inserted 1:9		
1	Pat Burrell	2.00
2	Eric Munson	.75
3	Alfonso Soriano	3.00
4	Ruben Mateo	.75
5	A.J. Burnett	1.00
6	Ben Davis	.75
7	Lance Berkman	1.50
8	Ed Yarnall	.75
9	Rick Ankiel	1.00
10	Ryan Bradley	.75

500 Club Piece of History

These Reggie Jackson inserts are part of a cross brand insert series paying tribute to baseball's 500 home run club members. These have a piece of Jackson's game-used bat embedded. An autographed version signed to his jersey number (44) are also randomly inserted.

		NM/M
Reggie Jackson		165.00
Reggie Jackson/ Auto./44		500.00

2000 UD Rookie Edition

		NM/M
Complete Set (154):		200.00
Common Player:		.15
Common Rookie Gem (91-120):	4.00

Production 1,000
Rookie Jersey Gems (121-136): Inserted 1:24
USA Authentics (137-154): Inserted 1:96
Golds (1-90): 2-4X
Gold Gems (91-120): 1X
Gold Jerseys (121-136): 1-2X
Pack (6): 2.00
Box (24): 40.00

1	Troy Glaus	.75
2	Mo Vaughn	.40
3	Darin Erstad	.40
4	Jason Giambi	.40
5	Tim Hudson	.25
6	Ben Grieve	.25
7	Eric Chavez	.25
8	Tony Batista	.15
9	Carlos Delgado	.60
10	David Wells	.15
11	Greg Vaughn	.15
12	Fred McGriff	.25
13	Manny Ramirez	.75
14	Roberto Alomar	.60
15	Jim Thome	.40
16	Alex Rodriguez	2.50
17	Edgar Martinez	.15
18	John Olerud	.20
19	Albert Belle	.40
20	Mike Mussina	.40
21	Cal Ripken Jr.	2.50
22	Ivan Rodriguez	.75
23	Rafael Palmeiro	.40
24	Pedro J. Martinez	.75
25	Nomar Garciaparra	2.00
26	Carl Everett	.15
27	Jermaine Dye	.15
28	Mike Sweeney	.15
29	Juan Gonzalez	.75
30	Bobby Higginson	.15
31	Dean Palmer	.15
32	Jacque Jones	.15
33	Eric Milton	.15
34	Matt Lawton	.15
35	Magglio Ordonez	.25
36	Paul Konerko	.15
37	Frank Thomas	1.00
38	Ray Durham	.15
39	Roger Clemens	1.00
40	Derek Jeter	2.50
41	Bernie Williams	.50
42	Jose Canseco	.40
43	Craig Biggio	.25
44	Richard Hidalgo	.15
45	Jeff Bagwell	.75
46	Greg Maddux	1.50
47	Chipper Jones	1.50
48	Rafael Furcal	.25
49	Andruw Jones	.50
50	Geoff Jenkins	.25
51	Jeromy Burnitz	.15
52	Mark McGwire	3.00
53	Rick Ankiel	.50
54	Jim Edmonds	.25
55	Kerry Wood	.25
56	Sammy Sosa	2.00
57	Matt Williams	.25
58	Randy Johnson	.75
59	Steve Finley	.15
60	Curt Schilling	.15
61	Kevin Brown	.15
62	Gary Sheffield	.30
63	Shawn Green	.30
64	Jose Vidro	.15
65	Vladimir Guerrero	1.00
66	Jeff Kent	.15
67	Barry Bonds	1.00
68	Ryan Dempster	.15
69	Cliff Floyd	.15
70	Preston Wilson	.15
71	Mike Piazza	2.00
72	Al Leiter	.15
73	Edgardo Alfonzo	.25
74	Derek Bell	.15
75	Ryan Klesko	.15
76	Tony Gwynn	1.00
77	Bobby Abreu	.15
78	Pat Burrell	.50
79	Scott Rolen	.50
80	Mike Lieberthal	.15
81	Jason Kendall	.15
82	Brian Giles	.25
83	Ken Griffey Jr.	2.00
84	Pokey Reese	.15
85	Dmitri Young	.15
86	Sean Casey	.15
87	Jeff Cirillo	.15
88	Todd Helton	.75
89	Jeffrey Hammonds	.15
90	Larry Walker	.30
91	Barry Zito RC	15.00
92	Keith Ginter RC	6.00
93	Dane Sardinha RC	4.00
94	Kenny Kelly RC	4.00
95	Ryan Kohlmeier RC	4.00
96	Leo Estrella RC	4.00
97	Danys Baez RC	4.00
98	Paul Rigdon RC	4.00
99	Mike Lamb RC	4.00
100	Aaron McNeal RC	4.00
101	Juan Pierre RC	6.00
102	Rico Washington RC	4.00
103	Luis Matos RC	8.00
104	Adam Bernero RC	4.00
105	Wascar Serrano RC	4.00
106	Chris Richard RC	4.00
107	Justin Miller RC	4.00
108	Julio Zuleta RC	4.00
109	Alex Cabrera RC	4.00
110	Gene Stechschulte RC	4.00
111	Tony Mota RC	4.00
112	Tomokazu Ohka RC	4.00
113	Geraldo Guzman RC	4.00
114	Scott Downs RC	4.00
115	Timoniel Perez RC	4.00
116	Chad Durbin RC	4.00
117	Sun-Woo Kim RC	4.00
118	Tomas de la Rosa RC	4.00
119	Javier Cardona RC	4.00
120	Kazuhiro Sasaki RC	6.00
121	Brad Cresse RC (Rookie Jersey Gems)	5.00
122	Matt Wheatland RC (Rookie Jersey Gems)	5.00
123	Joe Torres RC (Rookie Jersey Gems)	5.00
124	Dave Krynzel RC (Rookie Jersey Gems)	5.00
125	Ben Diggins RC (Rookie Jersey Gems)	5.00
126	Sean Burnett RC (Rookie Jersey Gems)	8.00
127	David Espinosa RC (Rookie Jersey Gems)	5.00
128	Scott Heard RC (Rookie Jersey Gems)	5.00
129	Daylan Holt RC (Rookie Jersey Gems)	5.00
130	Koyie Hill RC (Rookie Jersey Gems)	5.00
131	Mark Buehrle RC (Rookie Jersey Gems)	15.00
132	Xavier Nady RC (Rookie Jersey Gems)	8.00
133	Mike Tonis RC (Rookie Jersey Gems)	5.00
134	Matt Ginter RC (Rookie Jersey Gems)	5.00
135	Lorenzo Barcelo RC (Rookie Jersey Gems)	5.00
136	Cory Vance RC (Rookie Jersey Gems)	5.00
137	Sean Burroughs RC (USA Authentics)	8.00
138	Todd Williams (USA Authentics)	5.00
139	Brad Wilkerson RC (USA Authentics)	5.00
140	Ben Sheets RC (USA Authentics)	20.00
141	Kurt Ainsworth RC (USA Authentics)	8.00
142	Anthony Sanders (USA Authentics)	5.00
143	Ryan Franklin (USA Authentics)	5.00
144	Shane Heams RC (USA Authentics)	5.00
145	Roy Oswalt RC (USA Authentics)	20.00
146	Jon Rauch RC (USA Authentics)	5.00
147	Brent Abernathy RC (USA Authentics)	5.00
148	Ernie Young (USA Authentics)	5.00
149	Chris George (USA Authentics)	5.00
150	Gookie Dawkins (USA Authentics)	5.00
151	Adam Everett (USA Authentics)	5.00
152	John Cotton RC (USA Authentics)	5.00
153	Pat Borders (USA Authentics)	5.00
154	Doug Mientkiewicz (USA Authentics)	5.00

Rookie Edition Authentics

		NM/M
Jeter Authentic Pinstripes		
APJ	Derek Jeter/Jsy/1,000	35.00
APB	Derek Jeter/Bat/1,000	35.00
APC	Derek Jeter/Cap/200	70.00
APG	Derek Jeter/Glv/200	80.00

Combos

Random game-used inserts. 25 produced of each combo bat. 100 produced of combo jersey.

		NM/M
JDM	Derek Jeter, Joe DiMaggio, Mickey Mantle/Bat	925.00
JWO	Derek Jeter, Bernie Williams, Paul O'Neill/Jsy	150.00

Rookie Editon Diamonation

		NM/M
Complete Set (9):		10.00
Common Player:		.50
Inserted 1:12		
1	Pedro J. Martinez	1.00
2	Derek Jeter	2.50
3	Jason Giambi	1.00

4	Todd Helton	.75
5	Nomar Garciaparra	2.50
6	Randy Johnson	1.00
7	Jeff Bagwell	.75
8	Cal Ripken Jr.	3.00
9	Ivan Rodriguez	.50

Gallery

		NM/M
Complete Set (6):		10.00
Common Player:		1.00
Inserted 1:20		
1	Sammy Sosa	2.00
2	Barry Bonds	3.00
3	Vladimir Guerrero	1.00
4	Cal Ripken Jr.	3.00
5	Mike Piazza	1.50
6	Mark McGwire	2.00

Might

		NM/M
Complete Set (9):		10.00
Common Player:		.50
Inserted 1:12		
1	Mark McGwire	2.50
2	Mike Piazza	1.50
3	Frank Thomas	.75
4	Ken Griffey Jr.	1.50
5	Sammy Sosa	2.00
6	Alex Rodriguez	2.50
7	Carlos Delgado	.50
8	Vladimir Guerrero	1.00
9	Barry Bonds	3.00

Skills

		NM/M
Complete Set (6):		8.00
Common Player:		.75
Inserted 1:20		
1	Alex Rodriguez	2.50
2	Chipper Jones	1.50
3	Ken Griffey Jr.	1.50
4	Pedro J. Martinez	1.00
5	Ivan Rodriguez	.75
6	Derek Jeter	2.50

Brooklyn Dodgers Master Collection

Following on the success of its Yankees Master Collection, UD produced a more limited edition set featuring the Brooklyn Dodgers. Only 250 numbered boxed sets were produced. Each set includes 15 base cards, 11 Legends of Flatbush memorabilia/autograph cards and a mystery pack containing a premium memorabilia/autograph card. The set concentrates on Dodgers of the 1950s, along with Zach Wheat. The set was issued in a laser-engraved wooden box.

	NM/M
Complete Unopened Set:	1,250
Complete Opened Set:	800.00

Brooklyn Dodgers Master Collection Base Set

Portrait and action photos are combined on a horizontal format for the base cards in the Dodgers Masters Collection. Cards are numbered on back with a "BD" prefix.

		NM/M
Complete Set (15):		230.00
Common Player:		10.00
1	Jackie Robinson	50.00
2	Duke Snider	25.00
3	Pee Wee Reese	25.00
4	Gil Hodges	25.00
5	Carl Furillo	15.00
6	Don Newcombe	10.00
7	Sandy Koufax	50.00
8	Roy Campanella	25.00
9	Jim Gilliam	10.00
10	Don Drysdale	20.00
11	Sandy Amoros	10.00
12	Joe Black	10.00
13	Carl Erskine	10.00
14	Johnny Podres	10.00
15	Zack Wheat	10.00

Brooklyn Dodgers Master Collection Legends

The "Legends of Flatbush" are remembered in this series of memorabilia cards inserted into each Dodgers Master Collection. Each card's number has a "LOF" prefix.

		NM/M
Complete Set (11):		800.00
Common Player:		20.00
1	Gil Hodges/Bat	35.00
2	Jackie Robinson/Bat	100.00
3	Pee Wee Reese/Bat	30.00
4	Jim Gilliam/Bat	20.00
5	Roy Campanella/Bat	50.00
6	Zack Wheat/Bat	20.00
7	Carl Furillo/Bat	40.00
8	Don Newcombe/ Bat/Auto.	45.00
9	Duke Snider/Bat/Auto.	80.00
10	Don Drysdale/Jsy	40.00
11	Sandy Koufax/ Jsy/Auto.	650.00

Brooklyn Dodgers Master Collection Mystery Pack

Each of the Master Collection sets included a sealed mystery pack containing a premium autograph/memorabilia card. Numbers produced are indicated where known.

NM/M

Values Undetermined

JR-BC	Jackie Robinson/ Bat/Cut Sig/5	3,500
PW-BC	Pee Wee Reese/ Bat/Cut Sig/8	325.00

2000 Upper Deck Gold Reserve

Gold Reserve is primarily a retail product that has virtually the same design as regular 2000 Upper Deck base cards. The set consists of 300-cards each with the Upper Deck logo and the featured player's last name stamped in gold foil. Above the player name "Gold Reserve" is stamped in gold foil. The Fantastic Finds subset (268-297) are serial stamped within an edition of 2,500 for each of the subset cards.

		NM/M
Complete Set (300):		75.00
Common Player:		.15
Common 268-297:		3.00
Production 2,500 Sets		
Pack (10):		2.00
Box (24):		40.00
1	Mo Vaughn	.20
2	Darin Erstad	.25
3	Garret Anderson	.25
4	Troy Glaus	.50
5	Troy Percival	.15
6	Kent Bottenfield	.15
7	Orlando Palmeiro	.15
8	Tim Salmon	.25
9	Jason Giambi	.75
10	Eric Chavez	.25
11	Matt Stairs	.15
12	Miguel Tejada	.40
13	Tim Hudson	.25
14	John Jaha	.15
15	Ben Grieve	.15
16	Kevin Appier	.15
17	David Wells	.15
18	Jose Cruz Jr.	.15
19	Homer Bush	.15
20	Shannon Stewart	.15
21	Carlos Delgado	.50
22	Roy Halladay	.25
23	Tony Batista	.15
24	Raul Mondesi	.25
25	Fred McGriff	.25
26	Jose Canseco	.40
27	Roberto Hernandez	.15
28	Vinny Castilla	.15
29	Gerald Williams	.15
30	Ryan Rupe	.15
31	Greg Vaughn	.15
32	Miguel Cairo	.15
33	Roberto Alomar	.40
34	Jim Thome	.50
35	Bartolo Colon	.15
36	Omar Vizquel	.25
37	Manny Ramirez	.50
38	Chuck Finley	.15
39	Travis Fryman	.25
40	Kenny Lofton	.25
41	Richie Sexson	.40
42	Charles Nagy	.15
43	John Halama	.15
44	David Bell	.15
45	Jay Buhner	.15
46	Edgar Martinez	.25
47	Alex Rodriguez	1.50
48	Fred Garcia	.15
49	Aaron Sele	.15
50	Jamie Moyer	.15
51	Mike Cameron	.15
52	Albert Belle	.20
53	Jerry Hairston Jr.	.15
54	Sidney Ponson	.15
55	Cal Ripken Jr.	2.00
56	Mike Mussina	.40
57	B.J. Surhoff	.15
58	Brady Anderson	.15
59	Mike Bordick	.15
60	Ivan Rodriguez	.40
61	Rusty Greer	.15
62	Rafael Palmeiro	.40
63	John Wetteland	.15
64	Ruben Mateo	.15
65	Gabe Kapler	.15
66	David Segui	.15
67	Justin Thompson	.15
68	Rick Helling	.15

69	Jose Offerman	.15
70	Trot Nixon	.15
71	Pedro Martinez	.75
72	Jason Varitek	.15
73	Troy O'Leary	.15
74	Nomar Garciaparra	1.50
75	Carl Everett	.15
76	Wilton Veras	.15
77	Tim Wakefield	.15
78	Ramon Martinez	.15
79	Johnny Damon	.25
80	Mike Sweeney	.15
81	Rey Sanchez	.15
82	Carlos Beltran	.25
83	Carlos Febles	.15
84	Jermaine Dye	.15
85	Joe Randa	.15
86	Jose Rosado	.15
87	Jeff Suppan	.15
88	Juan Encarnacion	.15
89	Damion Easley	.15
90	Brad Ausmus	.15
91	Todd Jones	.15
92	Juan Gonzalez	.50
93	Bobby Higginson	.15
94	Tony Clark	.15
95	Brian Moehler	.15
96	Dean Palmer	.15
97	Joe Mays	.15
98	Eric Milton	.15
99	Corey Koskie	.15
100	Ron Coomer	.15
101	Brad Radke	.15
102	Todd Walker	.15
103	Butch Huskey	.15
104	Jacque Jones	.15
105	Frank Thomas	.50
106	Mike Sirotka	.15
107	Carlos Lee	.15
108	Ray Durham	.15
109	Bob Howry	.15
110	Magglio Ordonez	.25
111	Paul Konerko	.15
112	Chris Singleton	.15
113	James Baldwin	.15
114	Derek Jeter	2.00
115	Tino Martinez	.25
116	Orlando Hernandez	.25
117	Chuck Knoblauch	.15
118	Bernie Williams	.50
119	David Cone	.25
120	Paul O'Neill	.25
121	Roger Clemens	1.25
122	Mariano Rivera	.25
123	Ricky Ledee	.15
124	Richard Hidalgo	.25
125	Jeff Bagwell	.50
126	Jose Lima	.15
127	Billy Wagner	.15
128	Shane Reynolds	.15
129	Moises Alou	.25
130	Craig Biggio	.25
131	Roger Cedeno	.15
132	Octavio Dotel	.15
133	Greg Maddux	1.00
134	Brian Jordan	.15
135	Kevin Millwood	.25
136	Javy Lopez	.25
137	Bruce Chen	.15
138	Chipper Jones	1.00
139	Tom Glavine	.40
140	Andruw Jones	.40
141	Andres Galarraga	.25
142	Reggie Sanders	.15
143	Geoff Jenkins	.25
144	Jeromy Burnitz	.15
145	Ron Belliard	.15
146	Mark Loretta	.15
147	Steve Woodard	.15
148	Marquis Grissom	.15
149	Bob Wickman	.15
150	Mark McGwire	1.50
151	Fernando Tatis	.15
152	Edgar Renteria	.15
153	J.D. Drew	.20
154	Ray Lankford	.15
155	Fernando Vina	.15
156	Pat Hentgen	.15
157	Jim Edmonds	.25
158	Mark Grace	.25
159	Kerry Wood	.40
160	Eric Young	.15
161	Ismael Valdes	.15
162	Sammy Sosa	1.25
163	Henry Rodriguez	.15
164	Kyle Farnsworth	.15
165	Glenallen Hill	.15
166	Jon Lieber	.15
167	Luis Gonzalez	.25
168	Tony Womack	.15
169	Omar Daal	.15
170	Randy Johnson	.75
171	Erubiel Durazo	.15
172	Jay Bell	.15
173	Steve Finley	.15
174	Travis Lee	.15
175	Matt Williams	.25
176	Matt Mantei	.15
177	Adrian Beltre	.25
178	Kevin Brown	.25
179	Chan Ho Park	.25
180	Mark Grudzielanek	.15
181	Jeff Shaw	.15
182	Shawn Green	.40
183	Gary Sheffield	.40
184	Todd Hundley	.15
185	Eric Karros	.25
186	Kevin Elster	.15

187	Vladimir Guerrero	.75
188	Michael Barrett	.15
189	Chris Widger	.15
190	Ugueth Urbina	.15
191	Dustin Hermanson	.15
192	Rondell White	.15
193	Jose Vidro	.15
194	Hideki Irabu	.15
195	Lee Stevens	.15
196	Livan Hernandez	.15
197	Ellis Burks	.15
198	J.T. Snow	.15
199	Jeff Kent	.25
200	Robb Nen	.15
201	Marvin Benard	.15
202	Barry Bonds	1.50
203	Russ Ortiz	.15
204	Rich Aurilia	.15
205	Joe Nathan	.15
206	Preston Wilson	.25
207	Cliff Floyd	.15
208	Mike Lowell	.15
209	Ryan Dempster	.15
210	Luis Castillo	.15
211	Alex Fernandez	.15
212	Mark Kotsay	.15
213	Brant Brown	.15
214	Edgardo Alfonzo	.15
215	Robin Ventura	.25
216	Rickey Henderson	.25
217	Mike Hampton	.15
218	Mike Piazza	1.00
219	Al Leiter	.15
220	Derek Bell	.15
221	Armando Benitez	.15
222	Rey Ordonez	.15
223	Todd Zeile	.15
224	Tony Gwynn	.75
225	Eric Owens	.15
226	Damian Jackson	.15
227	Trevor Hoffman	.15
228	Ben Davis	.15
229	Sterling Hitchcock	.15
230	Ruben Rivera	.15
231	Ryan Klesko	.15
232	Phil Nevin	.15
233	Mike Lieberthal	.15
234	Bobby Abreu	.25
235	Doug Glanville	.15
236	Rico Brogna	.15
237	Scott Rolen	.50
238	Andy Ashby	.15
239	Robert Person	.15
240	Curt Schilling	.25
241	Mike Jackson	.15
242	Warren Morris	.15
243	Kris Benson	.15
244	Kevin Young	.15
245	Brian Giles	.15
246	Jason Schmidt	.15
247	Jason Kendall	.25
248	Todd Ritchie	.15
249	Wil Cordero	.15
250	Aramis Ramirez	.15
251	Sean Casey	.25
252	Barry Larkin	.25
253	Pokey Reese	.15
254	Scott Williamson	.15
255	Aaron Boone	.25
256	Dante Bichette	.15
257	Ken Griffey Jr.	1.00
258	Denny Neagle	.15
259	Dmitri Young	.15
260	Todd Helton	.50
261	Larry Walker	.25
262	Pedro Astacio	.15
263	Neifi Perez	.15
264	Jeff Cirillo	.15
265	Jeffrey Hammonds	.15
266	Tom Goodwin	.15
267	Rolando Arrojo	.15
268	Rick Ankiel (Fantastic Finds)	3.00
269	Pat Burrell (Fantastic Finds)	4.00
270	Eric Munson (Fantastic Finds)	3.00
271	Rafael Furcal (Fantastic Finds)	3.00
272	Brad Penny (Fantastic Finds)	3.00
273	Adam Kennedy (Fantastic Finds)	3.00
274	Mike Lamb RC (Fantastic Finds)	3.00
275	Matt Riley (Fantastic Finds)	3.00
276	Eric Gagne (Fantastic Finds)	5.00
277	Kazuhiro Sasaki RC (Fantastic Finds)	6.00
278	Julio Lugo (Fantastic Finds)	3.00
279	Kip Wells (Fantastic Finds)	3.00
280	Danys Baez RC (Fantastic Finds)	3.00
281	Josh Beckett (Fantastic Finds)	4.00
282	Alfonso Soriano (Fantastic Finds)	4.00
283	Vernon Wells (Fantastic Finds)	4.00
284	Nick Johnson (Fantastic Finds)	3.00
285	Ramon Ortiz (Fantastic Finds)	3.00

286	Peter Bergeron (Fantastic Finds)	3.00
287	Wascar Serrano RC (Fantastic Finds)	3.00
288	Josh Paul (Fantastic Finds)	3.00
289	Mark Quinn (Fantastic Finds)	3.00
290	Jason Marquis (Fantastic Finds)	3.00
291	Rob Bell (Fantastic Finds)	3.00
292	Pablo Ozuna (Fantastic Finds)	3.00
293	Milton Bradley (Fantastic Finds)	3.00
294	Roosevelt Brown (Fantastic Finds)	3.00
295	Terrence Long (Fantastic Finds)	3.00
296	Chad Durbin RC (Fantastic Finds)	3.00
297	Matt LeCroy (Fantastic Finds)	3.00
298	Ken Griffey Jr. (Checklist)	.50
299	Mark McGwire (Checklist)	.75
300	Derek Jeter (Checklist)	1.00

Game-Used Ball

		NM/M
Common Player:		10.00
Inserted 1:480		
JB	Jeff Bagwell	25.00
BB	Barry Bonds	70.00
SC	Sean Casey	10.00
RC	Roger Clemens	35.00
NG	Nomar Garciaparra	40.00
SG	Shawn Green	10.00
KG	Ken Griffey Jr.	30.00
TG	Tony Gwynn	25.00
DJ	Derek Jeter	60.00
AJ	Andruw Jones	15.00
CJ	Chipper Jones	30.00
GM	Greg Maddux	30.00
MM	Mark McGwire	60.00
MP	Mike Piazza	30.00
MR	Manny Ramirez	15.00
IR	Ivan Rodriguez	15.00
SR	Scott Rolen	10.00
GS	Gary Sheffield	10.00
SS	Sammy Sosa	30.00
BW	Bernie Williams	10.00

Setting the Standard

This 15-card set spotlights the top hitters and are inserted 1:11 packs. Card fronts feature gold foil stamping and card backs are numbered with an "S" prefix.

		NM/M
Complete Set (15):		25.00
Common Player:		.50
Inserted 1:11		
1	Tony Gwynn	1.50
2	Manny Ramirez	1.00
3	Derek Jeter	3.00
4	Cal Ripken Jr.	4.00
5	Mo Vaughn	.50
6	Jose Canseco	.75
7	Barry Bonds	4.00
8	Nomar Garciaparra	3.00
9	Juan Gonzalez	1.00
10	Mark McGwire	3.00
11	Alex Rodriguez	3.00
12	Jeff Bagwell	1.00
13	Ken Griffey Jr.	2.00
14	Frank Thomas	1.00
15	Sammy Sosa	2.50

Solid Gold Gallery

This 12-card set features close-up shots of the featured player accentuated by gold foil

stamping. Card backs are numbered with a "G" prefix, these were seeded 1:13 packs.

		NM/M
Complete Set (12):		20.00
Common Player:		1.00
Inserted 1:13		
1	Ken Griffey Jr.	2.00
2	Alex Rodriguez	3.00
3	Mike Piazza	2.00
4	Sammy Sosa	2.50
5	Derek Jeter	3.00
6	Jeff Bagwell	1.00
7	Mark McGwire	3.00
8	Cal Ripken Jr.	4.00
9	Pedro Martinez	1.50
10	Chipper Jones	2.00
11	Ivan Rodriguez	1.00
12	Vladimir Guerrero	1.00

UD Authentics

		NM/M
Inserted 1:480		
CB	Carlos Beltran	40.00
JC	Jose Canseco	35.00
SG	Shawn Green	20.00
TG	Tony Gwynn	30.00
CJ	Chipper Jones	60.00
MR	Manny Ramirez	25.00
CR	Cal Ripken Jr.	100.00
AR	Alex Rodriguez	80.00
IR	Ivan Rodriguez	20.00

UD Authentics Gold

Values Undetermined

24-Karat Gems

This 15-card set features gold foil stamping on the front and are numbered on the back with a "K" prefix. They are found on the average of 1:7 packs.

		NM/M
Complete Set (15):		12.00
Common Player:		.50
Inserted 1:7		
1	Pedro Martinez	1.00
2	Scott Rolen	1.00
3	Jason Giambi	1.50
4	Jeromy Burnitz	1.00
5	Rafael Palmeiro	1.00
6	Rick Ankiel	.75
7	Carlos Beltran	.50
8	Derek Jeter	3.00
9	Jason Kendall	1.00
10	Chipper Jones	2.00

11	Carlos Delgado	1.00
12	Alex Rodriguez	3.00
13	Randy Johnson	1.50
14	Tony Gwynn	1.50
15	Shawn Green	.75

3,000 Hit Club

This on-going cross brand insert series features Al Kaline. Each card features a piece of Kaline's game-used bat, he also signed six cards.

		NM/M
AK-B	Al Kaline/Bat/400	20.00

2000 Upper Deck Hitter's Club

The 90-card base set includes only hitters and features past and current stars. The base set consists of 50 regular cards, 25 Why 3K?, and 15 Hitting the Show subset cards. Card backs of the 50 regular cards have complete year-by-year statistics.

		NM/M
Complete Set (90):		20.00
Common Player:		.15
Pack (5):		1.50
Wax Box (24):		25.00
1	Mo Vaughn	.20
2	Troy Glaus	.40
3	Jeff Bagwell	.50
4	Craig Biggio	.25
5	Jason Giambi	.75
6	Eric Chavez	.25
7	Carlos Delgado	.50
8	Chipper Jones	1.00
9	Andruw Jones	.50
10	Andres Galarraga	.20
11	Jeromy Burnitz	.15
12	Mark McGwire	1.50
13	Mark Grace	.25
14	Sammy Sosa	1.25
15	Jose Canseco	.40
16	Vinny Castilla	.15
17	Matt Williams	.25
18	Gary Sheffield	.25
19	Shawn Green	.25
20	Vladimir Guerrero	.50
21	Barry Bonds	1.50
22	Manny Ramirez	.50
23	Roberto Alomar	.40
24	Jim Thome	.50
25	Ken Griffey Jr.	1.00
26	Alex Rodriguez	1.50
27	Edgar Martinez	.15
28	Preston Wilson	.25
29	Mike Piazza	1.00
30	Robin Ventura	.25
31	Albert Belle	.20
32	Cal Ripken Jr.	2.00
33	Tony Gwynn	.75
34	Scott Rolen	.50
35	Bob Abreu	.25
36	Brian Giles	.25
37	Ivan Rodriguez	.40
38	Rafael Palmeiro	.40
39	Nomar Garciaparra	1.50
40	Sean Casey	.20
41	Larry Walker	.50
42	Todd Helton	.50
43	Carlos Beltran	.25
44	Dean Palmer	.15
45	Juan Gonzalez	.50
46	Corey Koskie	.15
47	Frank Thomas	.50
48	Magglio Ordonez	.25
49	Derek Jeter	2.00
50	Bernie Williams	.40
51	Paul Waner (Why 3k?)	.25
52	Honus Wagner (Why 3k?)	.50
53	Tris Speaker (Why 3k?)	.25
54	Nap Lajoie (Why 3k?)	.25
55	Eddie Collins (Why 3k?)	.25
56	Roberto Clemente (Why 3k?)	1.00
57	Ty Cobb (Why 3k?)	1.50
58	Cap Anson (Why 3k?)	.50
59	Robin Yount (Why 3k?)	.50
60	Carl Yastrzemski (Why 3k?)	.50
61	Dave Winfield (Why 3k?)	.25
62	Stan Musial (Why 3k?)	1.00
63	Eddie Murray (Why 3k?)	.40

64	Paul Molitor (Why 3k?)	.50
65	Willie Mays (Why 3k?)	1.50
66	Al Kaline (Why 3k?)	.50
67	Tony Gwynn (Why 3k?)	.75
68	Rod Carew (Why 3k?)	.40
69	Lou Brock (Why 3k?)	.25
70	George Brett (Why 3k?)	1.00
71	Wade Boggs (Why 3k?)	.25
72	Hank Aaron (Why 3k?)	1.50
73	Jorge Luis Toca (Hitting the Show)	.15
74	J.D. Drew (Hitting the Show)	.15
75	Pat Burrell (Hitting the Show)	.25
76	Vernon Wells (Hitting the Show)	.25
77	Julio Ramirez (Hitting the Show)	.15
78	Gabe Kapler (Hitting the Show)	.15
79	Erubiel Durazo (Hitting the Show)	.15
80	Lance Berkman (Hitting the Show)	.25
81	Peter Bergeron (Hitting the Show)	.15
82	Alfonso Soriano (Hitting the Show)	.75
83	Jacque Jones (Hitting the Show)	.15
84	Ben Petrick (Hitting the Show)	.15
85	Jerry Hairston Jr. (Hitting the Show)	.15
86	Kevin Witt (Hitting the Show)	.15
87	Dermal Brown (Hitting the Show)	.15
88	Chad Hermansen (Hitting the Show)	.15
89	Ruben Mateo (Hitting the Show)	.15
90	Checklist (Ken Griffey Jr.)	.50

Accolades

These inserts have a full foiled front with gold foil stamping. Card backs are numbered with an "A" prefix and are seeded 1:11 packs.

		NM/M
Complete Set (10):		12.00
Common Player:		.75
Inserted 1:11		
1	Robin Yount	1.00
2	Tony Gwynn	1.00
3	Sammy Sosa	2.00
4	Mike Piazza	1.50
5	Cal Ripken Jr.	3.00
6	Mark McGwire	2.50
7	Barry Bonds	2.50
8	Wade Boggs	.75
9	Ken Griffey Jr.	1.50
10	Willie Mays	2.00

Autographs

Former and current players are featured in this signature set, which are seeded 1:215 packs. Card backs are numbered with the featured player's initials.

		NM/M
Common Player:		15.00
Inserted 1:215		
HA	Hank Aaron #44	275.00
WB	Wade Boggs #12	30.00

GB	George Brett #5	80.00
Lou	Lou Brock #20	15.00
Rod	Rod Carew #29	15.00
TG	Tony Gwynn #19	40.00
Al	Al Kaline #6	30.00
WM	Willie Mays #24	150.00
PM	Paul Molitor #4	30.00
EM	Eddie Murray #33	25.00
Man	Stan Musial #6	75.00
Cal	Cal Ripken Jr. #8	150.00
DW	Dave Winfield #31	20.00
Yaz	Carl Yastrzemski #7	60.00
RY	Robin Yount #19	40.00

Epic Performances

This 10-card set (#EP2 was not issued) showcases some of baseball's top performances on a fully foiled card front with gold-foil stamping. Card backs are numbered with an "EP" prefix.

		NM/M
Complete Set (10):		12.00
Common Player:		1.00
Inserted 1:3		
1	Mark McGwire	2.50
3	Sammy Sosa	2.00
4	Ken Griffey Jr.	1.50
5	Carl Yastrzemski	1.00
6	Tony Gwynn	1.00
7	Nomar Garciaparra	2.50
8	Cal Ripken Jr.	3.00
9	George Brett	1.50
10	Hank Aaron	2.00
11	Wade Boggs	1.00

Eternals

These inserts were printed on a fully foiled front with "Eternals" printed a number of times in the background. The player name and Upper Deck logo are stamped in gold foil at bottom. Card backs are numbered with an "E" prefix.

		NM/M
Complete Set (10):		20.00
Common Player:		1.00
Inserted 1:23		
1	Cal Ripken Jr.	4.00
2	Mark McGwire	3.00
3	Ken Griffey Jr.	2.00
4	Nomar Garciaparra	3.00
5	Tony Gwynn	1.50
6	Derek Jeter	3.00
7	Jose Canseco	1.00
8	Mike Piazza	2.00
9	Alex Rodriguez	3.00
10	Barry Bonds	4.00

Generations of Excellence

This 10-card insert set features two players who are linked either by team or position. Gold-foil stamping is used throughout. Card backs are numbered with a "GE" prefix.

		NM/M
Complete Set (10):		15.00
Common Card:		1.00
Inserted 1:6		
1	Cal Ripken Jr., Eddie Murray	3.00
2	Vladimir Guerrero, Roberto Clemente	2.00

3	George Brett, Robin Yount	2.00
4	Barry Bonds, Willie Mays	3.00
5	Chipper Jones, Hank Aaron	2.00
6	Mark McGwire, Sammy Sosa	2.00
7	Tony Gwynn, Wade Boggs	1.00
8	Rickey Henderson, Lou Brock	1.00
9	Derek Jeter, Nomar Garciaparra	3.00
10	Alex Rodriguez, Ken Griffey Jr.	2.50

On Target

This 10-card set is printed on a full foiled front with silver foil stamping. Card backs are numbered with an "OT" prefix and are seeded 1:23 packs.

		NM/M
Complete Set (10):		12.00
Common Player:		.50
Inserted 1:23		
1	Nomar Garciaparra	3.00
2	Sean Casey	1.00
3	Alex Rodriguez	3.00
4	Troy Glaus	1.00
5	Ivan Rodriguez	1.00
6	Chipper Jones	2.00
7	Manny Ramirez	1.00
8	Derek Jeter	3.00
9	Vladimir Guerrero	1.00
10	Scott Rolen	1.00

The Hitters' Club

These inserts are seeded 1:95 packs and are numbered on the back with an "HC" prefix.

		NM/M
Complete Set (10):		60.00
Common Player:		3.00
1	Rod Carew	5.00
2	Alex Rodriguez	15.00
3	Willie Mays	10.00
4	George Brett	10.00
5	Tony Gwynn	8.00
6	Stan Musial	8.00
7	Frank Thomas	5.00
8	Wade Boggs	3.00
9	Larry Walker	3.00
10	Nomar Garciaparra	15.00

3,000 Hit Club

Upper Deck's cross brand series pays tribute to players who have reached 3,000 hits. Hitter's Club features Wade Boggs and Tony Gwynn inserts with Bat, Bat and Cap and Autographed versions randomly inserted.

		NM/M
Common Player:		25.00

WB	Wade Boggs/Bat/350	25.00
WB	Wade Boggs/Bat & Cap/50	65.00
TG	Tony Gwynn/Bat/350	25.00
TG	Tony Gwynn/Bat & Cap/50	100.00
TG	Tony Gwynn AU/19	550.00
GB	Tony Gwynn, Wade Boggs/Bat/99	85.00

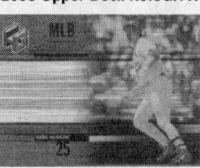

2000 Upper Deck HoloGrFX

The base set consists of 90-cards on a horizontal format. The cards have a holo-foil front utilizing HoloGrFX technology.

		NM/M
Complete Set (90):		20.00
Common Player:		.15
Pack (4):		1.50
Wax Box (32):		25.00
1	Mo Vaughn	.20
2	Troy Glaus	.50
3	Daryle Ward	.15
4	Jeff Bagwell	.50
5	Craig Biggio	.25
6	Jose Lima	.15
7	Jason Giambi	.75
8	Eric Chavez	.25
9	Tim Hudson	.25
10	Raul Mondesi	.25
11	Carlos Delgado	.50
12	David Wells	.15
13	Chipper Jones	1.00
14	Greg Maddux	1.00
15	Andruw Jones	.50
16	Brian Jordan	.15
17	Jeromy Burnitz	.15
18	Ron Belliard	.15
19	Mark McGwire	1.50
20	Fernando Tatis	.15
21	J.D. Drew	.25
22	Sammy Sosa	1.00
23	Mark Grace	.40
24	Greg Vaughn	.15
25	Jose Canseco	.40
26	Vinny Castilla	.15
27	Fred McGriff	.25
28	Matt Williams	.25
29	Randy Johnson	.75
30	Erubiel Durazo	.25
31	Shawn Green	.25
32	Gary Sheffield	.40
33	Kevin Brown	.25
34	Vladimir Guerrero	.50
35	Michael Barrett	.15
36	Russ Ortiz	.15
37	Barry Bonds	1.50
38	Jeff Kent	.25
39	Kenny Lofton	.25
40	Manny Ramirez	.50
41	Roberto Alomar	.40
42	Richie Sexson	.25
43	Edgar Martinez	.15
44	Alex Rodriguez	1.50
45	Fred Garcia	.15
46	Preston Wilson	.15
47	Alex Gonzalez	.15
48	Mike Hampton	.15
49	Mike Piazza	1.00
50	Robin Ventura	.25
51	Edgardo Alfonzo	.15
52	Albert Belle	.15
53	Cal Ripken Jr.	2.00
54	B.J. Surhoff	.15
55	Tony Gwynn	.75
56	Trevor Hoffman	.15
57	Mike Lieberthal	.15
58	Scott Rolen	.50
59	Bob Abreu	.25
60	Curt Schilling	.40
61	Jason Kendall	.25
62	Brian Giles	.25
63	Kris Benson	.15
64	Rafael Palmeiro	.40
65	Ivan Rodriguez	.50
66	Gabe Kapler	.40
67	Nomar Garciaparra	1.50
68	Pedro Martinez	.75
69	Troy O'Leary	.15
70	Barry Larkin	.25
71	Dante Bichette	.15
72	Sean Casey	.15
73	Ken Griffey Jr.	1.00
74	Jeff Cirillo	.15
75	Todd Helton	.25
76	Larry Walker	.25
77	Carlos Beltran	.15
78	Jermaine Dye	.15
79	Juan Gonzalez	.50
80	Juan Encarnacion	.15
81	Dean Palmer	.15
82	Corey Koskie	.15
83	Eric Milton	.15
84	Frank Thomas	.15
85	Magglio Ordonez	.25
86	Carlos Lee	.15

87	Derek Jeter	2.00
88	Tino Martinez	.25
89	Bernie Williams	.50
90	Roger Clemens	1.50

A Piece of the Series

This inserts have a piece of game-used base from a 1999 World Series game embedded. These were inserted at a rate of 1:215 packs.

		NM/M
Common Player:		5.00
Inserted 1:215		
1	Derek Jeter	40.00
2	Chipper Jones	20.00
3	Roger Clemens	30.00
4	Greg Maddux	30.00
5	Bernie Williams	10.00
6	Andruw Jones	10.00
7	Tino Martinez	8.00
8	Brian Jordan	5.00
9	Mariano Rivera	8.00
11	Paul O'Neill	8.00
12	Tom Glavine	10.00

A Piece of Series Autograph

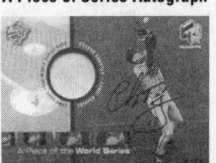

This is an autographed parallel of the Piece of Series insert set that is limited to 25 sets.

		NM/M
Common Player:		40.00
Production 25 Sets		
PSA1	Derek Jeter	300.00
PSA2	Chipper Jones	125.00
PSA3	Roger Clemens	220.00
PSA4	Greg Maddux	220.00
PSA6	Andruw Jones	85.00
PSA7	Tino Martinez	65.00
PSA8	Brian Jordan	40.00
PSA11	Paul O'Neill	75.00
PSA12	Tom Glavine	100.00

Bomb Squad

This set highlights top home run hitters in a horizontal format with complete holo-foiled fronts. Card backs are numbered with a "BS" prefix.

		NM/M
Complete Set (6):		15.00
Common Player:		2.00
Inserted 1:34		
1	Ken Griffey Jr.	2.00
2	Mark McGwire	3.00
3	Chipper Jones	2.00
4	Alex Rodriguez	3.00
5	Sammy Sosa	2.50
6	Barry Bonds	4.00

Future Fame

This six-card set has a horizontal format that is completely holo-foiled with silver foil stamping. Card backs are numbered with an "FF" prefix and seeded 1:34 packs.

		NM/M
Complete Set (6):		10.00
Common Player:		2.00
Inserted 1:34		
1	Cal Ripken Jr.	4.00
2	Mark McGwire	3.00

3	Greg Maddux	2.00
4	Tony Gwynn	1.50
5	Ken Griffey Jr.	2.00
6	Roger Clemens	2.50

Longball Legacy

This 15-card set spotlights the top home run hitters on a horizontal format and completely holo-foiled. Card backs are numbered with an "LL" prefix and seeded 1:6 packs.

		NM/M
Complete Set (15):		15.00
Common Player:		.50
Inserted 1:6		
1	Mike Piazza	2.00
2	Ivan Rodriguez	.75
3	Jeff Bagwell	1.00
4	Alex Rodriguez	3.00
5	Jose Canseco	.75
6	Mark McGwire	3.00
7	Scott Rolen	.75
8	Carlos Delgado	.75
9	Mo Vaughn	.50
10	Manny Ramirez	1.00
11	Matt Williams	.50
12	Sammy Sosa	2.50
13	Ken Griffey Jr.	2.00
14	Nomar Garciaparra	3.00
15	Larry Walker	.50

Stars of the System

This 10-card set features some of baseball's top prospects on a horizontal format. The fronts are completely holo-foiled with silver foil stamping. Card backs are numbered with an "SS" prefix and seeded 1:8 packs.

		NM/M
Complete Set (10):		8.00
Common Player:		.75
Inserted 1:8		
1	Rick Ankiel	.75
2	Alfonso Soriano	2.00
3	Vernon Wells	1.00
4	Ben Petrick	.75
5	Francisco Cordero	.75
6	Matt Riley	.75
7	A.J. Burnett	1.00
8	Pat Burrell	1.50
9	Ed Yarnall	.75
10	Dermal Brown	.75

StarView

This eight-card set features top stars on a horizontal format. Card backs are numbered with an "SV" prefix and inserted 1:11 packs.

		NM/M
Complete Set (8):		15.00
Common Player:		2.00
Inserted 1:11		
1	Ken Griffey Jr.	2.00
2	Nomar Garciaparra	3.00
3	Chipper Jones	3.00
4	Mark McGwire	3.00
5	Sammy Sosa	2.50
6	Derek Jeter	4.00
7	Mike Piazza	2.00
8	Alex Rodriguez	3.00

3,000 Hit Club

Upper Deck pays tribute to members of the 3,000 Hit Club with this cross-brand insert series. Robin Yount and George Brett are featured on a game-used bat card (350 produced), game-used jersey card (350

produced), a bat combo of both players (99 produced) and an autographed combo (10 produced).

		NM/M
Common Card:		20.00
RY	Robin Yount/Bat/350	20.00
RYJ	Robin Yount/Jsy/350	20.00
GB	George Brett/Bat/350	35.00
GBJ	George Brett/Jsy/350	35.00
BY	George Brett, Robin Yount/Bat/99	120.00
BYJ	George Brett, Robin Yount/Jsy/99	120.00

2000 UD Ionix

The base set consists of 90 cards, including a 30-card Futuristics subset that were seeded 1:4 packs. A Reciprocal parallel to the base set are also randomly inserted. The cards can distinguished by a holo-foiled front and the number on the back has an "R" prefix. Reciprocals 1-60 are found 1:4 packs, while Futuristics Reciprocals are found on the average of 1:11 packs.

		NM/M
Complete Set (90):		50.00
Common Player:		.15
Common Futuristic:		1.00
Inserted 1:4		
Reciprocal (1-60):		1.5-2X
Reciprocal (61-90):		1-1.5X
Inserted 1:4		
Future Recip. 1:11		
Pack (4):		2.00
Wax Box (24):		35.00
1	Mo Vaughn	.20
2	Troy Glaus	.75
3	Jeff Bagwell	.75
4	Craig Biggio	.40
5	Jose Lima	.15
6	Jason Giambi	1.00
7	Tim Hudson	.40
8	Shawn Green	.50
9	Carlos Delgado	.75
10	Chipper Jones	1.50
11	Andruw Jones	.75
12	Greg Maddux	1.50
13	Jeromy Burnitz	.15
14	Mark McGwire	2.00
15	J.D. Drew	.25
16	Sammy Sosa	2.00
17	Jose Canseco	.50
18	Fred McGriff	.40
19	Randy Johnson	.75
20	Matt Williams	.25
21	Kevin Brown	.40
22	Gary Sheffield	.40
23	Vladimir Guerrero	.75
24	Barry Bonds	2.50
25	Jim Thome	.75
26	Manny Ramirez	.75
27	Roberto Alomar	.50
28	Kenny Lofton	.25
29	Ken Griffey Jr.	1.50
30	Alex Rodriguez	2.50
31	Alex Gonzalez	.15
32	Preston Wilson	.15
33	Mike Piazza	1.50
34	Robin Ventura	.25
35	Cal Ripken Jr.	2.50
36	Albert Belle	.20
37	Tony Gwynn	1.00
38	Scott Rolen	.75
39	Curt Schilling	.50
40	Brian Giles	.25
41	Juan Gonzalez	.75
42	Ivan Rodriguez	.75
43	Rafael Palmeiro	.60
44	Pedro J. Martinez	1.00
45	Nomar Garciaparra	.25
46	Sean Casey	.25
47	Aaron Boone	.25
48	Barry Larkin	.40
49	Larry Walker	.25
50	Vinny Castilla	.20
51	Carlos Beltran	.25
52	Gabe Kapler	.15
53	Dean Palmer	.15
54	Eric Milton	.15
55	Corey Koskie	.15
56	Frank Thomas	.75
57	Magglio Ordonez	.40
58	Roger Clemens	2.00
59	Bernie Williams	.75
60	Derek Jeter	2.50
61	Josh Beckett (Futuristics)	1.50
62	Eric Munson (Futuristics)	1.00
63	Rick Ankiel (Futuristics)	1.00
64	Matt Riley (Futuristics)	1.00
65	Robert Ramsay (Futuristics)	1.00
66	Vernon Wells (Futuristics)	2.00
67	Eric Gagne (Futuristics)	1.50
68	Robert Fick (Futuristics)	1.50
69	Mark Quinn (Futuristics)	1.00
70	Kip Wells (Futuristics)	1.00
71	Peter Bergeron (Futuristics)	1.00
72	Ed Yarnall (Futuristics)	1.00
73	Jorge Luis Toca (Futuristics)	1.00
74	Alfonso Soriano (Futuristics)	4.00
75	Calvin Murray (Futuristics)	1.00
76	Ramon Ortiz (Futuristics)	1.50
77	Chad Meyers (Futuristics)	1.00
78	Jason LaRue (Futuristics)	1.00
79	Pat Burrell (Futuristics)	2.00
80	Chad Hermansen (Futuristics)	1.00
81	Lance Berkman (Futuristics)	1.50
82	Erubiel Durazo (Futuristics)	1.50
83	Juan Pena (Futuristics)	1.00
84	Adam Kennedy (Futuristics)	1.00
85	Ben Petrick (Futuristics)	1.00
86	Kevin Barker (Futuristics)	1.00
87	Bruce Chen (Futuristics)	1.00
88	Jerry Hairston Jr. (Futuristics)	1.00
89	A.J. Burnett (Futuristics)	1.00
90	Gary Matthews Jr. (Futuristics)	1.00

Atomic

This 15-card insert set has a horizontal format on a holo-foil front. Card backs are numbered with an "A" prefix and are found 1:8 packs.

		NM/M
Complete Set (15):		25.00
Common Player:		1.00
Inserted 1:8		
1	Pedro J. Martinez	1.50
2	Mark McGwire	3.00
3	Ken Griffey Jr.	2.00
4	Jeff Bagwell	1.00
5	Greg Maddux	2.00
6	Derek Jeter	3.00
7	Cal Ripken Jr.	4.00
8	Manny Ramirez	1.00
9	Randy Johnson	1.50
10	Nomar Garciaparra	3.00
11	Tony Gwynn	1.50
12	Bernie Williams	1.00
13	Mike Piazza	2.00
14	Roger Clemens	3.00
15	Alex Rodriguez	3.00

Awesome Powers

The title of this insert set is a takeoff from the Austin Powers movie that was popular at the time of this release. The cards have a holo-foil front with a "groovin" '70s backdrop. Card backs are numbered with an "AP" prefix.

		NM/M
Complete Set (15):		50.00
Common Player:		1.00
Inserted 1:23		
1	Ken Griffey Jr.	4.00
2	Mike Piazza	4.00
3	Carlos Beltran	2.00
4	Mark McGwire	6.00
5	Chipper Jones	4.00
6	Scott Rolen	2.00
7	Cal Ripken Jr.	8.00
8	Alex Rodriguez	6.00
9	Larry Walker	1.00
10	Sammy Sosa	5.00
11	Barry Bonds	6.00
12	Nomar Garciaparra	6.00
13	Jose Canseco	1.50
14	Manny Ramirez	2.00
15	Jeff Bagwell	2.00

BIOrhythm

This 15-card set has a holo-foil front and are seeded 1:11 packs. Card backs have a brief career note and are numbered with a "B" prefix.

		NM/M
Complete Set (15):		25.00
Common Player:		.50
Inserted 1:11		
1	Randy Johnson	1.50
2	Derek Jeter	3.00
3	Sammy Sosa	2.50
4	Jose Lima	.50
5	Chipper Jones	2.00
6	Barry Bonds	4.00
7	Ken Griffey Jr.	2.00
8	Nomar Garciaparra	3.00
9	Frank Thomas	1.00
10	Pedro Martinez	1.50
11	Larry Walker	.50
12	Greg Maddux	2.00
13	Alex Rodriguez	3.00
14	Mark McGwire	3.00
15	Cal Ripken Jr.	4.00

Pyrotechnics

This 15-card set has a holo-foiled front with an insertion ratio of 1:72 packs. Card backs are numbered with a "P" prefix.

		NM/M
Complete Set (15):		125.00
Common Player:		5.00
Inserted 1:72		
1	Roger Clemens	12.00
2	Chipper Jones	10.00
3	Alex Rodriguez	15.00
4	Jeff Bagwell	5.00
5	Mark McGwire	15.00
6	Pedro Martinez	6.00
7	Manny Ramirez	5.00
8	Cal Ripken Jr.	20.00
9	Mike Piazza	15.00
10	Derek Jeter	15.00
11	Ken Griffey Jr.	10.00
12	Frank Thomas	5.00
13	Sammy Sosa	12.00
14	Nomar Garciaparra	15.00
15	Greg Maddux	10.00

Shockwave

Baseball's top hitters are spotlighted on a holo-foil front. They are found on the average of 1:4 packs and are numbered on the card back with an "S" prefix.

		NM/M
Complete Set (15):		15.00
Common Player:		.50
Inserted 1:4		
1	Mark McGwire	2.00
2	Sammy Sosa	2.00
3	Manny Ramirez	1.00
4	Ken Griffey Jr.	1.50
5	Vladimir Guerrero	1.00
6	Barry Bonds	2.50
7	Albert Belle	.50
8	Ivan Rodriguez	.50
9	Chipper Jones	1.50
10	Mo Vaughn	.50
11	Jose Canseco	.75
12	Jeff Bagwell	1.00
13	Matt Williams	.50
14	Alex Rodriguez	2.50
15	Carlos Delgado	.75

UD Authentics

These autographed inserts have a horizontal format and are found on the average of 1:144 packs.

		NM/M
Common Player:		10.00
Inserted 1:144		
CBE	Carlos Beltran	30.00
AB	Adrian Beltre	15.00
PB	Pat Burrell	15.00
JC	Jose Canseco	25.00
SC	Sean Casey	15.00
BD	Ben Davis	10.00
SG	Shawn Green	20.00
JR	Ken Griffey Jr.	100.00
VG	Vladimir Guerrero	30.00
DJ	Derek Jeter	100.00
GK	Gabe Kapler	10.00
RM	Ruben Mateo	10.00
RB	Joe McEwing	10.00
MR	Manny Ramirez	35.00
SR	Scott Rolen	30.00
MW	Matt Williams	15.00

Warp Zone

This 15-card set has a holo-foiled front with an insertion ratio of 1:288 packs. Card backs are numbered with a "WZ" prefix.

		NM/M
Complete Set (15):		250.00
Common Player:		8.00
Inserted 1:288		
1	Cal Ripken Jr.	30.00
2	Barry Bonds	30.00
3	Ken Griffey Jr.	20.00
4	Nomar Garciaparra	25.00
5	Chipper Jones	20.00
6	Ivan Rodriguez	8.00
7	Greg Maddux	20.00
8	Derek Jeter	25.00
9	Mike Piazza	20.00
10	Sammy Sosa	20.00
11	Roger Clemens	20.00
12	Alex Rodriguez	25.00
13	Vladimir Guerrero	10.00
14	Pedro Martinez	10.00
15	Mark McGwire	25.00

3,000 Hit Club

Upper Deck's cross-brand insert series paying tribute to baseball's 3,000 Hit Club members spotlights Roberto Clemente in UD Ionix. Three versions were randomly inserted: A game-used bat card, bat/cut signature card and a cut signature card.

		NM/M
RC1	Roberto Clemente/Bat/350	125.00

2000 Upper Deck Legends

The 135-card base set consists of 90 regular player cards, 30 20th Century Legends (1:5) and 15 Generation Y2K (1:9). The base cards have a full foiled front with silver foil stamping. Card backs have complete year-by-year statistics.

		NM/M
Complete Set (135):		80.00
Common Player:		.15
Common Y2K:		.75
Inserted 1:9		
Common 20th Century Legend		1.00
Inserted 1:5		
Pack (7):		5.00
Box (24):		90.00
1	Darin Erstad	.25
2	Troy Glaus	.75
3	Mo Vaughn	.25
4	Craig Biggio	.25
5	Jeff Bagwell	.75
6	Reggie Jackson	1.00
7	Tim Hudson	.25
8	Jason Giambi	1.00
9	Hank Aaron	2.00
10	Greg Maddux	1.50
11	Chipper Jones	1.50
12	Andres Galarraga	.25
13	Robin Yount	.50
14	Jeromy Burnitz	.15
15	Paul Molitor	.50
16	David Wells	.15
17	Carlos Delgado	.75
18	Ernie Banks	.75
19	Sammy Sosa	2.00
20	Kerry Wood	.40
21	Stan Musial	.75
22	Bob Gibson	.40
23	Mark McGwire	2.00
24	Fernando Tatis	.15
25	Randy Johnson	1.00
26	Matt Williams	.40
27	Jackie Robinson	2.00
28	Sandy Koufax	1.50
29	Shawn Green	.40
30	Kevin Brown	.40
31	Gary Sheffield	.40
32	Greg Vaughn	.15
33	Jose Canseco	.50
34	Gary Carter	.25
35	Vladimir Guerrero	.75
36	Willie Mays	2.00
37	Barry Bonds	2.00
38	Jeff Kent	.25
39	Bob Feller	.40
40	Roberto Alomar	.40

41	Jim Thome	.75
42	Manny Ramirez	.75
43	Alex Rodriguez	2.00
44	Preston Wilson	.15
45	Tom Seaver	.75
46	Robin Ventura	.15
47	Mike Piazza	1.50
48	Mike Hampton	.15
49	Brooks Robinson	.75
50	Frank Robinson	.75
51	Cal Ripken Jr.	2.50
52	Albert Belle	.20
53	Eddie Murray	.40
54	Tony Gwynn	1.00
55	Roberto Clemente	1.50
56	Willie Stargell	.25
57	Brian Giles	.25
58	Jason Kendall	.25
59	Mike Schmidt	1.00
60	Bob Abreu	.25
61	Scott Rolen	.50
62	Curt Schilling	.40
63	Johnny Bench	1.00
64	Sean Casey	.15
65	Barry Larkin	.25
66	Ken Griffey Jr.	1.50
67	George Brett	1.50
68	Carlos Beltran	.15
69	Nolan Ryan	3.00
70	Ivan Rodriguez	.75
71	Rafael Palmeiro	.40
72	Larry Walker	.25
73	Todd Helton	.75
74	Jeff Cirillo	.15
75	Carl Everett	.15
76	Nomar Garciaparra	2.00
77	Pedro Martinez	1.00
78	Harmon Killebrew	.50
79	Corey Koskie	.15
80	Ty Cobb	2.00
81	Dean Palmer	.15
82	Juan Gonzalez	.75
83	Carlton Fisk	.15
84	Frank Thomas	.75
85	Magglio Ordonez	.25
86	Lou Gehrig	2.00
87	Babe Ruth	3.00
88	Derek Jeter	2.50
89	Roger Clemens	1.50
90	Bernie Williams	.50
91	Rick Ankiel (Generation Y2K)	.75
92	Kip Wells (Generation Y2K)	.75
93	Pat Burrell (Generation Y2K)	1.50
94	Mark Quinn (Generation Y2K)	.75
95	Ruben Mateo (Generation Y2K)	.75
96	Adam Kennedy (Generation Y2K)	.75
97	Brad Penny (Generation Y2K)	.75
98	Kazuhiro Sasaki RC (Generation Y2K)	2.00
99	Peter Bergeron (Generation Y2K)	.75
100	Rafael Furcal (Generation Y2K)	1.00
101	Eric Munson (Generation Y2K)	.75
102	Nick Johnson (Generation Y2K)	1.00
103	Rob Bell (Generation Y2K)	.75
104	Vernon Wells (Generation Y2K)	1.00
105	Ben Petrick (Generation Y2K)	.75
106	Babe Ruth (20th Century Legends)	8.00
107	Mark McGwire (20th Century Legends)	6.00
108	Nolan Ryan (20th Century Legends)	8.00
109	Hank Aaron (20th Century Legends)	5.00
110	Barry Bonds (20th Century Legends)	6.00
111	Nomar Garciaparra (20th Century Legends)	5.00
112	Roger Clemens (20th Century Legends)	5.00
113	Johnny Bench (20th Century Legends)	2.50
114	Alex Rodriguez (20th Century Legends)	6.00
115	Cal Ripken Jr. (20th Century Legends)	8.00
116	Willie Mays (20th Century Legends)	6.00
117	Mike Piazza (20th Century Legends)	4.00
118	Reggie Jackson (20th Century Legends)	2.00
119	Tony Gwynn (20th Century Legends)	3.00
120	Cy Young (20th Century Legends)	2.00
121	George Brett (20th Century Legends)	4.00
122	Greg Maddux (20th Century Legends)	4.00
123	Yogi Berra (20th Century Legends)	2.00
124	Sammy Sosa (20th Century Legends)	5.00
125	Randy Johnson (20th Century Legends)	2.50
126	Bob Gibson (20th Century Legends)	2.00
127	Lou Gehrig (20th Century Legends)	6.00
128	Ken Griffey Jr. (20th Century Legends)	4.00
129	Derek Jeter (20th Century Legends)	6.00
130	Mike Schmidt (20th Century Legends)	3.00
131	Pedro Martinez (20th Century Legends)	2.50
132	Jackie Robinson (20th Century Legends)	5.00
133	Jose Canseco (20th Century Legends)	1.00
134	Ty Cobb (20th Century Legends)	5.00
135	Stan Musial (20th Century Legends)	3.00

Gold

Gold graphic enhancements are featured on this parallel edition. On back, a dot-matrix printed "1/1" attests to the status of these cards as unique specimens. Because only one of each card was produced, attaching values can be problematic. Values shown here represent specimens offered at auction shortly after the cards were issued.

		NM/M
	Common Player:	75.00
10	Greg Maddux	340.00
13	Robin Yount	450.00
15	Paul Molitor	450.00
31	Gary Sheffield	175.00
36	Willie Mays	1,175
53	Eddie Murray	1,000
82	Juan Gonzalez	230.00
87	Babe Ruth	2,025
89	Roger Clemens	250.00
107	Mark McGwire (20th Century Legends)	1,580
119	Tony Gwynn (20th Century Legends)	190.00
126	Bob Gibson (20th Century Legends)	275.00
130	Mike Schmidt (20th Century Legends)	900.00

Commemorative Collection

A metallized photo background on front distinguishes these 1-of-100 inserts from their base-card parallels. Backs have an ink-jetted serial number from within each card's edition of 100.

Stars (1-90):	4-8X
Y2K:	1-2X
20th Century Legends:	2-3X
Production 100 Sets	

Defining Moments

This 10-card set highlights the featured player's greatest baseball moment with a date stamped in gold foil on the front and a description of the moment on the back. Card backs are numbered with a "DM" prefix and seeded 1:12 packs.

		NM/M
	Complete Set (10):	20.00
	Common Player:	1.00
	Inserted 1:12	
1	Reggie Jackson	1.50
2	Hank Aaron	3.00
3	Babe Ruth	4.00
4	Cal Ripken Jr.	4.00
5	Carlton Fisk	1.00
6	Ken Griffey Jr.	2.00
7	Nolan Ryan	4.00
8	Roger Clemens	2.50
9	Willie Mays	3.00
10	Mark McGwire	3.00

Eternal Glory

This six-card set has a full holo-foiled front with gold foil stamping. Card backs are numbered with an "EG" prefix and are inserted 1:24 packs.

		NM/M
	Complete Set (7):	15.00
	Common Player:	2.00
	Inserted 1:24	
1	Nolan Ryan	4.00
2	Ken Griffey Jr.	2.00
4	Sammy Sosa	2.50
5	Derek Jeter	4.00
6	Willie Mays	3.00
7	Roger Clemens	3.00

Legendary Jerseys

This game-used memorabilia insert set has a swatch of game-used jersey embedded and were inserted 1:48 packs.

		NM/M
	Common Player:	8.00
	Inserted 1:48	
HA	Hank Aaron	40.00
JB	Jeff Bagwell	10.00
JB	Johnny Bench	20.00
WB	Wade Boggs	10.00
BaB	Barry Bonds	40.00
BoB	Bobby Bonds	8.00
GB	George Brett	30.00
LB	Lou Brock	8.00
JC	Jose Canseco	10.00
RC	Roger Clemens	30.00
DC	Dave Concepcion	8.00
DD	Don Drysdale	25.00
RF	Rollie Fingers	8.00
LG	Lou Gehrig/Pants	250.00
BG	Bob Gibson/Pants	20.00
KG	Ken Griffey Jr.	35.00
TG	Tony Gwynn	20.00
RJ	Reggie Jackson	10.00
DJ	Derek Jeter	40.00
RaJ	Randy Johnson	20.00
CJ	Chipper Jones	20.00
SK	Sandy Koufax	250.00
SK	Sandy Koufax/Auto./32	1,200
GM	Greg Maddux	30.00
MM	Mickey Mantle	150.00
RM	Roger Maris/Pants	60.00
EM	Eddie Mathews	25.00
WM	Willie Mays/SP/29	675.00
BM	Bill Mazeroski	8.00
WMc	Willie McCovey	10.00
TM	Thurman Munson	30.00
DM	Dale Murphy	10.00
SM	Stan Musial/SP/28	650.00
JP	Jim Palmer	8.00
GP	Gaylord Perry	8.00
MR	Manny Ramirez	10.00
CR	Cal Ripken Jr.	40.00
BR	Brooks Robinson	20.00
FR	Frank Robinson	10.00
AR	Alex Rodriguez	35.00
NR	Nolan Ryan	40.00
MS	Mike Schmidt	25.00
TS	Tom Seaver	20.00
OS	Ozzie Smith	20.00
WS	Willie Stargell	8.00
FT	Frank Thomas	10.00
JT	Joe Torre	8.00
EW	Earl Weaver	8.00
MW	Matt Williams	8.00
MW	Maury Wills	8.00
DW	Dave Winfield	10.00

Legendary Signatures

These autographed inserts are signed in blue Sharpie on the bottom panel. A Gold parallel version is also randomly seeded which has gold-foil stamping and is individually numbered to 50.

		NM/M
	Common Player:	8.00
	Inserted 1:23	
	Golds:	1-2X
	Production 50 Sets	
HA	Hank Aaron/SP/94	300.00
JB	Johnny Bench	30.00
BB	Bobby Bonds	8.00
LB	Lou Brock	8.00
GB	George Brett	60.00
JC	Jose Canseco	20.00
GC	Gary Carter	10.00
SC	Sean Casey	8.00
RC	Roger Clemens	80.00
DC	Dave Concepcion	8.00
AD	Andre Dawson	10.00
KG	Ken Griffey Jr.	85.00
VG	Vladimir Guerrero	30.00
TG	Tony Gwynn	40.00
RJ	Reggie Jackson	20.00
DJ	Derek Jeter SP/61	400.00
RaJ	Randy Johnson	50.00
CJ	Chipper Jones	50.00
HK	Harmon Killebrew	25.00
FL	Fred Lynn	8.00
DM	Dale Murphy	15.00
SM	Stan Musial	50.00
PN	Phil Niekro	8.00
JP	Jim Palmer	10.00
MP	Mike Piazza	120.00
MR	Manny Ramirez/SP/141	60.00
CR	Cal Ripken Jr.	120.00
AR	Alex Rodriguez	85.00
IR	Ivan Rodriguez	25.00
NR	Nolan Ryan	85.00
MS	Mike Schmidt	50.00
TS	Tom Seaver	30.00
OS	Ozzie Smith	40.00
WS	Willie Stargell	60.00
FT	Frank Thomas	30.00
AT	Alan Trammell	10.00
BW	Matt Williams	8.00

Ones for the Ages

This seven-card set has a holo-foiled front with gold foil etching and stamping. The player image is in a classic picture framed design. Card backs are numbered with an "O" prefix and are seeded 1:24 packs.

		NM/M
	Complete Set (7):	15.00
	Inserted 1:24	
O1	Ty Cobb	2.50
O2	Cal Ripken Jr.	4.00
O3	Babe Ruth	4.00
O4	Jackie Robinson	2.50
O5	Mark McGwire	3.00
O6	Alex Rodriguez	3.00
O7	Mike Piazza	4.00

Reflections in Time

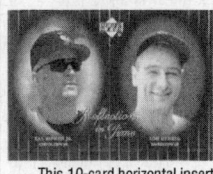

This 10-card horizontal insert set features two players, past and present, linked by significant events or statistics. Card fronts are completely holo-foiled with gold foil stamping. Card backs are numbered with an "R" prefix and inserted 1:12 packs.

		NM/M
	Complete Set (10):	25.00
	Common Player:	2.00
	Inserted 1:12	
1	Ken Griffey Jr., Hank Aaron	3.00
2	Sammy Sosa, Roberto Clemente	3.00
3	Roger Clemens, Nolan Ryan	4.00
4	Ivan Rodriguez, Johnny Bench	2.00
5	Alex Rodriguez, Ernie Banks	3.00
6	Tony Gwynn, Stan Musial	2.00
7	Barry Bonds, Willie Mays	4.00
8	Cal Ripken Jr., Lou Gehrig	4.00
9	Chipper Jones, Mike Schmidt	2.50
10	Mark McGwire, Babe Ruth	4.00

UD Millennium Team

This nine-card set has a complete holo-foiled front with silver foil stamping. The set is Upper Deck's selections for the all-time 20th century team and are inserted 1:4 packs. Card backs are numbered with an "UD" prefix.

		NM/M
	Complete Set (10):	15.00
	Common Player:	1.50
	Inserted 1:4	
1	Mark McGwire	2.00
2	Jackie Robinson	2.00
3	Mike Schmidt	1.50
4	Cal Ripken Jr.	3.00
5	Babe Ruth	3.00
7	Willie Mays	2.00
8	Johnny Bench	1.50
9	Nolan Ryan	3.00
10	Ken Griffey Jr.	1.50

3,000 Hit Club

Upper Deck's continuing series pays tribute to Carl Yastrzemski and Paul Molitor. The series includes 350 Bat cards, 350 Jersey cards, 100 Bat/Jersey combo cards and eight autographed Bat/Jersey combo cards from Yastrzemski and 350 Bat cards from Molitor.

		NM/M
CY	Carl Yastrzemski/Bat/350	30.00
CY	Carl Yastrzemski/Jsy/350	30.00
CY	Carl Yastrzemski/Bat/Jsy/100	80.00

2000 Upper Deck MVP

The base set consists of 220-cards with a white bordered design and bronze foil stamping. Card backs have a maximum of 10 year-by-year statistics.

		NM/M
	Complete Set (220):	20.00
	Common Player:	.10
	Pack (10):	1.25
	Wax Box (28):	25.00
1	Garret Anderson	.25
2	Mo Vaughn	.15
3	Tim Salmon	.20
4	Ramon Ortiz	.10
5	Darin Erstad	.25
6	Troy Glaus	.50
7	Troy Percival	.10
8	Jeff Bagwell	.50
9	Ken Caminiti	.10
10	Daryle Ward	.10
11	Craig Biggio	.25
12	Jose Lima	.10
13	Moises Alou	.20
14	Octavio Dotel	.10
15	Ben Grieve	.10
16	Jason Giambi	.50
17	Tim Hudson	.20
18	Eric Chavez	.10
19	Matt Stairs	.10
20	Miguel Tejada	.25
21	John Jaha	.10
22	Chipper Jones	1.00
23	Kevin Millwood	.20
24	Brian Jordan	.10
25	Andruw Jones	.25
26	Andres Galarraga	.20
27	Greg Maddux	1.00
28	Reggie Sanders	.10
29	Javy Lopez	.20
30	Jeromy Burnitz	.10
31	Kevin Barker	.10
32	Jose Hernandez	.10
33	Ron Belliard	.10
34	Henry Blanco	.10
35	Marquis Grissom	.10
36	Geoff Jenkins	.10
37	Carlos Delgado	.50
38	Raul Mondesi	.20
39	Roy Halladay	.10
40	Tony Batista	.10
41	David Wells	.10
42	Shannon Stewart	.10
43	Vernon Wells	.20
44	Sammy Sosa	1.00
45	Ismael Valdes	.10
46	Joe Girardi	.10
47	Mark Grace	.20
48	Henry Rodriguez	.10
49	Kerry Wood	.20
50	Eric Young	.10
51	Mark McGwire	2.00
52	Daryle Kile	.10
53	Fernando Vina	.10
54	Ray Lankford	.10
55	J.D. Drew	.20
56	Fernando Tatis	.10
57	Rick Ankiel	.10
58	Matt Williams	.10
59	Erubiel Durazo	.15
60	Tony Womack	.10
61	Jay Bell	.10
62	Randy Johnson	.75
63	Steve Finley	.10
64	Matt Mantei	.10
65	Luis Gonzalez	.10
66	Gary Sheffield	.25
67	Eric Gagne	.10
68	Adrian Beltre	.20
69	Mark Grudzielanek	.10
70	Kevin Brown	.20
71	Chan Ho Park	.10
72	Shawn Green	.40
73	Vinny Castilla	.10
74	Fred McGriff	.20
75	Wilson Alvarez	.10
76	Greg Vaughn	.10
77	Gerald Williams	.10
78	Ryan Rupe	.10
79	Jose Canseco	.25
80	Vladimir Guerrero	.50
81	Dustin Hermanson	.10
82	Michael Barrett	.10
83	Rondell White	.10
84	Tony Armas Jr.	.10
85	Wilton Guerrero	.10

86	Jose Vidro	.10
87	Barry Bonds	1.50
88	Russ Ortiz	.10
89	Ellis Burks	.10
90	Jeff Kent	.20
91	Russ Davis	.10
92	J.T. Snow	.10
93	Roberto Alomar	.40
94	Manny Ramirez	.50
95	Chuck Finley	.10
96	Kenny Lofton	.20
97	Jim Thome	.50
98	Bartolo Colon	.20
99	Omar Vizquel	.20
100	Richie Sexson	.25
101	Mike Cameron	.10
102	Brett Tomko	.10
103	Edgar Martinez	.20
104	Alex Rodriguez	1.50
105	John Olerud	.20
106	Fred Garcia	.10
107	Kazuhiro Sasaki RC	1.00
108	Preston Wilson	.20
109	Luis Castillo	.10
110	A.J. Burnett	.10
111	Mike Lowell	.10
112	Cliff Floyd	.10
113	Brad Penny	.10
114	Alex Gonzalez	.10
115	Mike Piazza	1.00
116	Derek Bell	.10
117	Edgardo Alfonzo	.20
118	Rickey Henderson	.20
119	Todd Zeile	.10
120	Mike Hampton	.10
121	Al Leiter	.20
122	Robin Ventura	.20
123	Cal Ripken Jr.	1.50
124	Mike Mussina	.40
125	B.J. Surhoff	.10
126	Jerry Hairston Jr.	.10
127	Brady Anderson	.10
128	Albert Belle	.20
129	Sidney Ponson	.10
130	Tony Gwynn	.75
131	Ryan Klesko	.10
132	Sterling Hitchcock	.10
133	Eric Owens	.10
134	Trevor Hoffman	.10
135	Al Martin	.10
136	Bret Boone	.25
137	Brian Giles	.10
138	Chad Hermansen	.10
139	Kevin Young	.10
140	Kris Benson	.10
141	Warren Morris	.10
142	Jason Kendall	.20
143	Wil Cordero	.10
144	Scott Rolen	.50
145	Curt Schilling	.40
146	Doug Glanville	.10
147	Mike Lieberthal	.10
148	Mike Jackson	.10
149	Rico Brogna	.10
150	Andy Ashby	.10
151	Bob Abreu	.20
152	Sean Casey	.20
153	Pete Harnisch	.10
154	Dante Bichette	.10
155	Pokey Reese	.10
156	Aaron Boone	.20
157	Ken Griffey Jr.	1.00
158	Barry Larkin	.25
159	Scott Williamson	.10
160	Carlos Beltran	.20
161	Jermaine Dye	.10
162	Jose Rosado	.10
163	Joe Randa	.10
164	Johnny Damon	.20
165	Mike Sweeney	.10
166	Mark Quinn	.10
167	Ivan Rodriguez	.40
168	Rusty Greer	.10
169	Ruben Mateo	.10
170	Doug Davis	.10
171	Gabe Kapler	.10
172	Justin Thompson	.10
173	Rafael Palmeiro	.40
174	Larry Walker	.20
175	Neifi Perez	.10
176	Rolando Arrojo	.10
177	Jeffrey Hammonds	.10
178	Todd Helton	.50
179	Pedro Astacio	.10
180	Jeff Cirillo	.10
181	Pedro Martinez	.75
182	Carl Everett	.10
183	Troy O'Leary	.10
184	Nomar Garciaparra	1.25
185	Jose Offerman	.10
186	Bret Saberhagen	.10
187	Trot Nixon	.10
188	Jason Varitek	.10
189	Todd Walker	.10
190	Eric Milton	.10
191	Chad Allen	.10
192	Jacque Jones	.10
193	Brad Radke	.10
194	Corey Koskie	.10
195	Joe Mays	.10
196	Juan Gonzalez	.50
197	Jeff Weaver	.10
198	Juan Encarnacion	.10
199	Deivi Cruz	.10
200	Damion Easley	.10
201	Tony Clark	.10
202	Dean Palmer	.10
203	Frank Thomas	.50

204	Carlos Lee	.10
205	Mike Sirotka	.10
206	Kip Wells	.10
207	Magglio Ordonez	.20
208	Paul Konerko	.20
209	Chris Singleton	.10
210	Derek Jeter	1.50
211	Tino Martinez	.25
212	Mariano Rivera	.20
213	Roger Clemens	.75
214	Nick Johnson	.25
215	Paul O'Neill	.20
216	Bernie Williams	.40
217	David Cone	.10
218	Checklist (Ken Griffey Jr.)	.50
219	Checklist (Sammy Sosa)	.50
220	Checklist (Mark McGwire)	.75

Silver

A parallel to the 220-card base set. These 1:2 pack inserts can be distinguished from the base cards by the silver foil stamping and a silver foiled facsimile signature of the featured player on the card bottom.

Stars:	1-2X
Inserted 1:2	

Gold

A parallel to the base set, these can be distinguished from base cards with gold script stamping. Each card is also serial numbered on the card front within an edition of 50 sets.

Stars:	10-20X
Production 50 Sets	

Super

A parallel to the 220-card base set, these inserts can be distinguished from the base cards by the holo-foil stamping used on the Upper Deck logo and the featured player's facsimile signature on the card bottom. The card fronts are also serial numbered within an edition of 25 sets.

Stars:	15-30X
Production 25 Sets	

2000 Upper Deck MVP All-Star Game

	NM/M
Complete Set (30):	25.00
Common Player:	.25

AS1	Mo Vaughn	.25
AS2	Jeff Bagwell	.75
AS3	Jason Giambi	.75
AS4	Chipper Jones	1.50
AS5	Greg Maddux	1.00
AS6	Tony Batista	.25
AS7	Sammy Sosa	2.00
AS8	Mark McGwire	2.50
AS9	Randy Johnson	.75
AS10	Shawn Green	.50
AS11	Greg Vaughn	.25
AS12	Vladimir Guerrero	.75
AS13	Barry Bonds	2.50
AS14	Manny Ramirez	.75
AS15	Alex Rodriguez	2.50
AS16	Preston Wilson	.25
AS17	Mike Piazza	1.50
AS18	Cal Ripken Jr.	3.00
AS19	Tony Gwynn	1.00
AS20	Scott Rolen	.75
AS21	Ken Griffey Jr.	1.50
AS22	Carlos Beltran	.25
AS23	Ivan Rodriguez	.60
AS24	Larry Walker	.25
AS25	Nomar Garciaparra	2.00
AS26	Pedro Martinez	.75
AS27	Juan Gonzalez	.75
AS28	Frank Thomas	.75
AS29	Derek Jeter	2.50
AS30	Bernie Williams	.50

Drawing Power

This seven-card set has a holo-foil front with silver foil stamping. Card backs are numbered with a "DP" prefix.

	NM/M
Complete Set (7):	12.00
Common Player:	1.00
Inserted 1:28	

1	Mark McGwire	3.00
2	Ken Griffey Jr.	2.00
3	Mike Piazza	2.00
4	Chipper Jones	2.00
5	Nomar Garciaparra	3.00
6	Sammy Sosa	2.50
7	Jose Canseco	1.00

Game-Used Souvenirs

These memorabilia inserts feature a game-used piece of glove embedded and are found exclusively in hobby packs at a rate of 1:130 packs.

	NM/M
Common Glove:	8.00
Inserted 1:130	

RA	Roberto Alomar	15.00
JB	Jeff Bagwell	20.00
AB	Albert Belle	8.00
BB	Barry Bonds	65.00
JC	Jose Canseco	15.00
WC	Will Clark	20.00
AF	Alex Fernandez	8.00
JG	Jason Giambi	15.00
TGI	Troy Glaus	15.00
AG	Alex Gonzalez	8.00
BG	Ben Grieve	8.00
KG	Ken Griffey Jr.	40.00
VG	Vladimir Guerrero	15.00
TG	Tony Gwynn	30.00
AJ	Andruw Jones	15.00
CJ	Chipper Jones	30.00
KL	Kenny Lofton	8.00
RM	Raul Mondesi	8.00
PO	Paul O'Neill	10.00
RP	Rafael Palmeiro	15.00
MR	Manny Ramirez	15.00
CR	Cal Ripken Jr.	65.00
AR	Alex Rodriguez	40.00
IR	Ivan Rodriguez	15.00
NR	Nolan Ryan	65.00
TS	Tim Salmon	8.00
LW	Larry Walker	8.00
BW	Bernie Williams	15.00
MW	Matt Williams	8.00

Game-Used Souvenirs - Bats

These memorabilia inserts have a piece of game-used bat embedded and are seeded exclusively in hobby packs at a rate of 1:130 packs.

	NM/M
Common Bat:	8.00

	NM/M
Inserted 1:130	
BB	Barry Bonds	40.00
JC	Jose Canseco	8.00
KG	Ken Griffey Jr.	20.00
VG	Vladimir Guerrero	10.00
TG	Tony Gwynn	15.00
CJ	Chipper Jones	15.00
MR	Manny Ramirez	10.00
AR	Alex Rodriguez	20.00
IR	Ivan Rodriguez	8.00
BW	Bernie Williams	10.00

Game Used Souvenirs - Bats Auto.

Production 25 Sets
Values Undetermined

Prolifics

This seven-card set features a full holo-foiled front with silver foil stamping and are seeded 1:28 packs. Card backs are numbered with a "P" prefix.

	NM/M
Complete Set (7):	10.00
Common Player:	.50
Inserted 1:28	

1	Manny Ramirez	1.00
2	Vladimir Guerrero	1.00
3	Derek Jeter	3.00
4	Pedro Martinez	1.50
5	Shawn Green	.50
6	Alex Rodriguez	3.00
7	Cal Ripken Jr.	4.00

ProSign

These autographed inserts are found exclusively in retail packs at a rate of 1:216.

	NM/M
Common Player:	5.00
Inserted 1:216 R	

RA	Rick Ankiel	10.00
MB	Michael Barrett	5.00
RB	Rob Bell	5.00
CB	Carlos Beltran	20.00
LB	Lance Berkman	25.00
RB	Rico Brogna	5.00
SC	Sean Casey	8.00
DD	Doug Davis	5.00
ED	Erubiel Durazo	8.00
RF	Robert Fick	8.00
NG	Nomar Garciaparra	65.00
AG	Alex Gonzalez	8.00
KG	Ken Griffey Jr.	60.00
TG	Tony Gwynn	40.00
TH	Tim Hudson	15.00
DJ	Derek Jeter	80.00
CJ	Chipper Jones	50.00
MM	Mike Meyers	5.00
EM	Eric Milton	8.00
JM	Jim Morris	8.00
WM	Warren Morris	5.00
TN	Trot Nixon	5.00
BP	Ben Petrick	5.00
AP	Adam Piatt	5.00
MP	Mike Piazza	60.00
MQ	Mark Quinn	5.00
MR	Manny Ramirez	25.00
RR	Rob Ramsay	5.00
MRe	Mike Redmond	5.00
MRi	Mariano Rivera	15.00
AR	Alex Rodriguez	65.00
MS	Mike Sweeney	8.00
BT	Bubba Trammell	5.00

JV	Jose Vidro	8.00
DW	Daryle Ward	5.00
KW	Kip Wells	5.00
SW	Scott Williamson	5.00
PW	Preston Wilson	8.00
KW	Kevin Witt	5.00
TW	Tony Womack	8.00
EY	Ed Yarnall	5.00
JZ	Jeff Zimmerman	5.00

Pure Grit

These 1:6 pack inserts have a full holo-foiled front with silver foil stamping. Card backs are numbered with a "G" prefix.

	NM/M
Complete Set (10):	10.00
Common Player:	.50
Inserted 1:6	

1	Derek Jeter	2.00
2	Kevin Brown	.50
3	Craig Biggio	.50
4	Ivan Rodriguez	.75
5	Scott Rolen	.75
6	Carlos Beltran	.50
7	Ken Griffey Jr.	1.50
8	Cal Ripken Jr.	2.50
9	Nomar Garciaparra	2.00
10	Randy Johnson	1.00

Scout's Choice

This ten-card set spotlights some of the best prospects in 2000. The inserts have a full holo-foiled front with silver foil stamping. Card backs are numbered with an "SC" prefix and are seeded 1:14 packs.

	NM/M
Complete Set (10):	8.00
Common Player:	.50
Inserted 1:14	

1	Rick Ankiel	.50
2	Vernon Wells	1.00
3	Pat Burrell	1.50
4	Travis Dawkins	.50
5	Eric Munson	.50
6	Nick Johnson	1.00
7	Dermal.Brown	.50
8	Alfonso Soriano	2.00
9	Ben Petrick	.50
10	Adam Everett	.50

Second Season Standouts

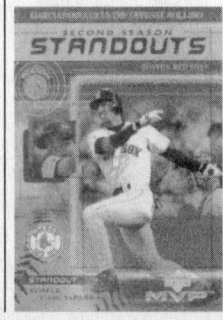

This 10-card set has a full holo-foiled card front with silver foil stamping. Card backs are numbered with an "SS" prefix and inserted 1:6 packs.

	NM/M
Complete Set (10):	6.00
Common Player:	.25
Inserted 1:6	

1	Pedro Martinez	1.00
2	Mariano Rivera	.40
3	Orlando Hernandez	.25
4	Ken Caminiti	.25
5	Bernie Williams	.50
6	Jim Thome	.75
7	Nomar Garciaparra	2.00
8	Edgardo Alfonzo	.25
9	Derek Jeter	2.50
10	Kevin Millwood	.40

3,000 Hit Club

Upper Deck used this cross-brand insert series to salute the players who accomplished 3,000 hits in their career. Stan Musial is featured and offers a game-used memorabilia bat, jersey, jersey/bat combo and combo autograph versions.

		NM/M
Common Player:		
SM	Stan Musial/Jsy/350	30.00
SM	Stan Musial/Bat/350	30.00
SM	Stan Musial/Jsy/Bat/100	80.00

2000 UD N.Y. Yankees Master Collection

The most popular franchise in sports history was the subject of this Master Collection limited to 500 numbered sets. Issued in a serially-numbered mahogany box with pewter team-logo inlay, each set includes 25 cards honoring the Yankees' World Championships between 1923-1999. There is also a "Team of the Century" card set with 10 game-used bat cards and a special Gehrig commemorative. Each set also includes a Mystery Pack containing one of 14 autographed memorabilia cards. Retail price at time of issue was around $6,000. Because unopened sets may contain one of the better "Mystery Pack" cards, they maintain a significant premium.

	NM/M
Complete Boxed Set, Unopened:	3,250
Complete Boxed Set, Opened:	1,100
N.Y. Yankees Master Collection Wood Box	100.00

Mystery Cards

Each Master Collection set contains one foil-pack Mystery Card ranging from autographed player memorabilia-cards to cut signatures. The Gehrig, Mantle

Martin, Munson and Ruth cards are each uniquely numbered on back with the player's initials or initials plus "C" (for cut signature) as a prefix. The Berra, Ford, Jackson and Jeter cards are not "numbered," but are identified by player initials and type of memorabilia. The number issued of each card is shown in parentheses. Some cards remain unpriced due to rarity.

		NM/M
Unopened Mystery Pack:		600.00
BM	Billy Martin/Bat-Cut/2	
	(8/05 Auction)	615.00
BR	Babe Ruth/Bat-Cut/3	9,500
BR-C	Babe Ruth/Bat-Cut/3	7,500
DJ-B	Derek Jeter/	
	Bat-Auto./100	450.00
DJ-J	Derek Jeter/	
	Jsy-Auto./100	500.00
LG-C	Lou Gehrig/Cut/3	3,000
MM	Mickey Mantle/	
	Bat-Cut/7	4,000
RJ-B	Reggie Jackson/	
	Bat-Auto./100	400.00
WF-J	Whitey Ford/	
	Jsy-Auto./100	450.00
YB-B	Yogi Berra/	
	Bat-Auto./80	450.00

Team of the Century

An 11-player "Team of the Century" card set within the Yankees Master Collection features game-used bat cards from 10 of the players and a special Lou Gehrig commemorative card (Upper Deck could not get a Gehrig gamer to cut up for the cards). Each card carries an individual serial number from an edition of 500 each.

		NM/M
Complete Set (11):		1,575
Common Player:		35.00
ATY1	Babe Ruth	400.00
ATY2	Mickey Mantle	550.00
ATY3	Reggie Jackson	135.00
ATY4	Don Mattingly	135.00
ATY5	Billy Martin	90.00
ATY6	Graig Nettles	55.00
ATY7	Derek Jeter	110.00
ATY8	Yogi Berra	135.00
ATY9	Thurman Munson	145.00
ATY10	Whitey Ford	110.00
ATY11	Lou Gehrig	35.00

Series Champions

Each of the Yankees' 25 World Series Championships between 1923-1999 is marked with one of these "base" cards in the Master Collection. Fronts of the 2-1/2" x 3-1/2" cards have black-and-white or color poses or action photos highlighted with holographic foil. Backs have a portrait photo, a World Series summary and the player's career and Series stats. Each card is serially numbered within an edition of 500.

		NM/M
Complete Set (25):		480.00
Common Player:		12.50
NYY1	Babe Ruth/1923	50.00
NYY2	Lou Gehrig/1927	35.00
NYY3	Tony Lazzeri/1928	12.50
NYY4	Babe Ruth/1932	50.00
NYY5	Lou Gehrig/1936	35.00
NYY6	Lefty Gomez/1937	25.00
NYY7	Bill Dickey/1938	25.00
NYY8	Bill Dickey/1939	25.00
NYY9	Tommy Henrich/1941	17.50
NYY10	Spud Chandler/1943	12.50
NYY11	Tommy Henrich/1947	17.50
NYY12	Phil Rizzuto/1949	25.00
NYY13	Whitey Ford/1950	25.00
NYY14	Yogi Berra/1951	30.00
NYY15	Casey Stengel/1952	17.50
NYY16	Billy Martin/1953	17.50
NYY17	Don Larsen/1956	22.00
NYY18	Elston Howard/1958	12.50
NYY19	Roger Maris/1961	30.00
NYY20	Mickey Mantle/1962	50.00
NYY21	Reggie Jackson/1977	30.00
NYY22	Bucky Dent/1978	15.00
NYY23	Derek Jeter/1996	25.00
NYY24	Derek Jeter/1998	25.00
NYY25	Derek Jeter/1999	25.00

2000 Upper Deck Opening Day 2K

As part of a multi-manufacturer promotion, UD issued eight cards of an "Opening Day 2K" set. Packages containing some of the 32 cards in the issue were distributed by MLB teams early in the season. The cards were also available exclusively as inserts in Upper Deck Victory and Hitters Club packs sold at K-Mart stores early in the season. The Upper Deck OD2K cards have gold-foil graphic highlights on front. Backs have a monochromatic version of the front photo and are numbered with an "OD" prefix.

		NM/M
Complete Set (8):		6.00
Common Player:		.50
17	Ken Griffey Jr.	1.50
18	Sammy Sosa	1.00
19	Pedro Martinez	.75
20	Manny Ramirez	.65
21	Shawn Green	.65
22	Carlos Beltran	.40
23	Juan Gonzalez	.50
24	Jeromy Burnitz	.50

2000 Upper Deck Ovation

The base set consists of 90-cards, including a 20-card World Premiere subset and 10-card Superstar Spotlight subset. World Premiere's are found 1:3 packs and Superstar Spotlight's 1:6 packs. Card fronts are embossed, intended to resemble the feel of a baseball and also has silver foil stamping.

	NM/M
Complete Set (90):	65.00
Common Player:	.25
Common World Prem. (61-80):	1.00

		NM/M
Inserted 1:3		
Common Super. Spot. (81-90):		1.50
Inserted 1:6		
Pack (5):		2.00
Wax Box (20):		30.00
1	Mo Vaughn	.25
2	Troy Glaus	.75
3	Jeff Bagwell	.75
4	Craig Biggio	.40
5	Mike Hampton	.25
6	Jason Giambi	.75
7	Tim Hudson	.40
8	Chipper Jones	1.50
9	Greg Maddux	1.50
10	Kevin Millwood	.40
11	Brian Jordan	.25
12	Jeromy Burnitz	.25
13	David Wells	.25
14	Carlos Delgado	.75
15	Sammy Sosa	2.50
16	Mark McGwire	3.00
17	Matt Williams	.25
18	Randy Johnson	.75
19	Erubiel Durazo	.40
20	Kevin Brown	.40
21	Shawn Green	.50
22	Gary Sheffield	.50
23	Jose Canseco	.50
24	Vladimir Guerrero	1.00
25	Barry Bonds	3.00
26	Manny Ramirez	.75
27	Roberto Alomar	.75
28	Richie Sexson	.40
29	Jim Thome	.75
30	Alex Rodriguez	2.50
31	Ken Griffey Jr.	1.50
32	Preston Wilson	.25
33	Mike Piazza	1.50
34	Al Leiter	.25
35	Robin Ventura	.25
36	Cal Ripken Jr.	3.00
37	Albert Belle	.25
38	Tony Gwynn	1.00
39	Brian Giles	.40
40	Jason Kendall	.40
41	Scott Rolen	.40
42	Bob Abreu	.40
43	Ken Griffey Jr.	1.50
44	Sean Casey	.25
45	Carlos Beltran	.40
46	Gabe Kapler	.25
47	Ivan Rodriguez	.75
48	Rafael Palmeiro	.50
49	Larry Walker	.40
50	Nomar Garciaparra	2.00
51	Pedro J. Martinez	1.00
52	Eric Milton	.25
53	Juan Gonzalez	.75
54	Tony Clark	.25
55	Frank Thomas	.75
56	Magglio Ordonez	.40
57	Roger Clemens	1.50
58	Derek Jeter	2.50
59	Bernie Williams	.50
60	Orlando Hernandez	.40
61	Rick Ankiel	
	(World Premiere)	1.00
62	Josh Beckett	
	(World Premiere)	1.50
63	Vernon Wells	
	(World Premiere)	1.50
64	Alfonso Soriano	
	(World Premiere)	3.00
65	Pat Burrell	
	(World Premiere)	2.00
66	Eric Munson	
	(World Premiere)	1.00
67	Chad Hutchinson	
	(World Premiere)	1.00
68	Eric Gagne	
	(World Premiere)	1.00
69	Peter Bergeron	
	(World Premiere)	1.00
70	Ryan Anderson (Supposed to have been withdrawn, all known cards have embossed UD racing mark.)	300.00
71	A.J. Burnett	
	(World Premiere)	1.00
72	Jorge Luis Toca	
	(World Premiere)	1.00
73	Matt Riley	
	(World Premiere)	1.00
74	Chad Hermansen	
	(World Premiere)	1.00
75	Doug Davis	
	(World Premiere)	1.00
76	Jim Morris	
	(World Premiere)	1.00
77	Ben Petrick	
	(World Premiere)	1.00
78	Mark Quinn	
	(World Premiere)	1.00
79	Ed Yarnall	
	(World Premiere)	1.00
80	Ramon Ortiz	
	(World Premiere)	1.00
81	Ken Griffey Jr.	
	(Superstar Spotlight)	3.00
82	Mark McGwire	
	(Superstar Spotlight)	5.00
83	Derek Jeter	
	(Superstar Spotlight)	5.00
84	Jeff Bagwell	
	(Superstar Spotlight)	1.50
85	Nomar Garciaparra	
	(Superstar Spotlight)	5.00
86	Sammy Sosa	
	(Superstar Spotlight)	4.00
87	Mike Piazza	
	(Superstar Spotlight)	3.00
88	Alex Rodriguez	
	(Superstar Spotlight)	5.00
89	Cal Ripken Jr.	
	(Superstar Spotlight)	6.00
90	Pedro Martinez	
	(Superstar Spotlight)	2.00

Standing Ovation

A parallel to the 120-card base set, these are identical to the base cards besides the holographic silver stamping on the card front and the backs serially numbered to 50.

Stars (1-60):	8-15X
World Prem. (61-80):	2-3X
Super. Spot. (81-90):	3-5X
Production 50 Sets	

A Piece of History

These memorabilia inserts feature a piece of game-used bat embedded and are limited to 400 sets produced.

		NM/M
Common Player:		5.00
Production 400 Sets		
JB	Jeff Bagwell	10.00
CB	Carlos Beltran	10.00
SC	Sean Casey	5.00
KG	Ken Griffey Jr.	25.00
DJ	Derek Jeter	35.00
TG	Tony Gwynn	15.00
AJ	Andruw Jones	10.00
CJ	Chipper Jones	20.00
RP	Rafael Palmeiro	10.00
MP	Mike Piazza	20.00
MR	Manny Ramirez	10.00
CR	Cal Ripken Jr.	35.00
AR	Alex Rodriguez	25.00
SR	Scott Rolen	15.00
SS	Sammy Sosa	25.00
FT	Frank Thomas	10.00

A Piece of History - Signed

Values Undetermined

Center Stage

Ten of baseball's top performers are highlighted on a card that features gold foil stamping and etching. Card backs are numbered with an "CS" prefix and are seeded 1:9 packs. Two parallels to this insert set are randomly inserted: Golds are found 1:39 packs and Rainbows are seeded 1:99 packs.

		NM/M
Complete Set (10):		20.00
Common Player:		1.00
Inserted 1:9		

86

86	Sammy Sosa	

(continued into Standing Ovation above)

Curtain Calls

This 20-card set features gold foil stamping and highlights some memorable playoff moments. Card backs are numbered with a "CC" prefix.

		NM/M
Complete Set (20):		15.00
Common Player:		.50
Inserted 1:3		
1	David Cone	.50
2	Mark McGwire	2.00
3	Sammy Sosa	.50
4	Eric Milton	.50
5	Bernie Williams	.75
6	Tony Gwynn	1.00
7	Nomar Garciaparra	2.00
8	Manny Ramirez	1.00
9	Wade Boggs	.50
10	Randy Johnson	1.00
11	Cal Ripken Jr.	3.00
12	Pedro J. Martinez	1.00
13	Alex Rodriguez	2.00
14	Fernando Tatis	.50
15	Vladimir Guerrero	1.00
16	Robin Ventura	.50
17	Larry Walker	.50
18	Carlos Beltran	.50
19	Jose Canseco	.75
20	Ken Griffey Jr.	1.50

Diamond Futures

This 10-card set highlights some of baseball's top prospects on a full foiled front with silver foil stamping. Card backs are numbered with a "DM" prefix.

		NM/M
Complete Set (10):		8.00
Common Player:		.50
Inserted 1:6		
1	J.D. Drew	1.00
2	Alfonso Soriano	2.50
3	Preston Wilson	1.00
4	Erubiel Durazo	.75
5	Rick Ankiel	.50
6	Octavio Dotel	.50
7	A.J. Burnett	.75
8	Carlos Beltran	.75
9	Vernon Wells	1.00
10	Troy Glaus	2.00

Lead Performers

Upper Deck chose 10 players for this set who are thought of as leaders on and off the field. Card fronts have silver foil stamping and card backs are numbered with an "LP" prefix.

Gold:	2X
Inserted 1:39	
Rainbow:	3-4X
Inserted 1:99	
1	Jeff Bagwell	1.00
2	Ken Griffey Jr.	2.00
3	Nomar Garciaparra	3.00
4	Mike Piazza	3.00
5	Mark McGwire	3.00
6	Alex Rodriguez	3.00
7	Cal Ripken Jr.	4.00
8	Derek Jeter	3.00
9	Chipper Jones	2.00
10	Sammy Sosa	2.50

	NM/M
Complete Set (10):	20.00
Common Player:	1.00
Inserted 1:19	
1	Mark McGwire	3.00
2	Derek Jeter	3.00
3	Vladimir Guerrero	1.00
4	Mike Piazza	2.00
5	Cal Ripken Jr.	4.00
6	Sammy Sosa	2.50
7	Jeff Bagwell	1.00
8	Nomar Garciaparra	3.00
9	Chipper Jones	2.00
10	Ken Griffey Jr.	2.00

Super Signatures

This two-card insert set features Ken Griffey Jr. and Mike Piazza. Spotlighting the autographs of Griffey and Piazza, Super Signatures is issued in three versions: Silver, numbered to 100; Gold, numbered to 50; and Rainbow, numbered to 10.

		NM/M
Common Card:		
KG	Ken Griffey/Gold/50	180.00
KG	Ken Griffey/Silver/100	100.00
MP	Mike Piazza/Gold/50	180.00
MP	Mike Piazza/Silver/100	150.00

Superstar Theatre

This 20-card set is printed on a full foiled card front enhanced by silver foil stamping and etching. Card backs are numbered with an "ST" prefix.

		NM/M
Complete Set (20):		20.00
Common Player:		.50
Inserted 1:19		
1	Ivan Rodriguez	1.00
2	Brian Giles	.50
3	Bernie Williams	1.00
4	Greg Maddux	2.00
5	Frank Thomas	1.00
6	Sean Casey	.50
7	Mo Vaughn	.50
8	Carlos Delgado	1.00
9	Tony Gwynn	1.50
10	Pedro Martinez	1.50
11	Scott Rolen	1.00
12	Mark McGwire	3.00
13	Manny Ramirez	1.00
14	Rafael Palmeiro	.75
15	Jose Canseco	.75
16	Randy Johnson	1.50
17	Gary Sheffield	.75
18	Larry Walker	.50
19	Barry Bonds	4.00
20	Roger Clemens	3.00

3,000 Hit Club

Upper Deck's cross brand insert series pays tribute to members of the elite 3,000 Hit Club. Ovation features Willie Mays in the series, which has four versions: Bat card, 300 produced; Jersey card, 350 produced; Bat/Jersey combo, 50 produced; and Bat/Jersey autograph, 24 produced.

		NM/M
1	Willie Mays/Jsy/350	40.00
2	Willie Mays/Bat/300	40.00
3	Willie Mays/Jsy/Bat/50	180.00
4	Willie Mays/Jsy/Bat/Auto./24	675.00

2000 Upper Deck PowerDeck

		NM/M
Complete Set (12):		50.00
Common Card:		3.00
Pack (1):		4.00
Box:		40.00
1	Sammy Sosa	6.00
2	Ken Griffey Jr.	6.00
3	Mark McGwire	8.00
4	Derek Jeter	6.00
5	Alex Rodriguez	8.00
6	Nomar Garciaparra	6.00
7	Mike Piazza	5.00
8	Cal Ripken Jr.	8.00
9	Ivan Rodriguez	3.00
10	Chipper Jones	5.00
11	Pedro Martinez	3.00
12	Manny Ramirez	3.00

Magical Moments

		NM/M
Inserted 1:10 H		
KG	Ken Griffey Jr.	6.00
CR	Cal Ripken Jr.	10.00

Magical Moments Autograph

		NM/M
Each signed 50 cards.		
KG	Ken Griffey Jr.	180.00
CR	Cal Ripken Jr.	275.00

Power Trio

		NM/M
Complete Set (3):		15.00
Common Player:		5.00
Inserted 1:7		
PT1	Derek Jeter	6.00
PT2	Ken Griffey Jr.	5.00
PT3	Mark McGwire	6.00

2000 Upper Deck Pros and Prospects

The 132-card base set consists of 90 regular player cards, a 30-card Prospective Superstars subset and a 12-card Pro-Fame subset. Prospective Superstars are serially numbered to 1,350 and Pro-Fame are serially numbered to 1,000. Card fronts have a white-bordered design with silver foil stamping. Both subsets are serially numbered on the card front.

		NM/M
Complete Set (132):		300.00
Common Player (1-90):		.15
Common (91-120):		5.00
Production 1,350 Sets		
Common (121-132):		4.00
Production 1,000 Sets		
Pack (5):		2.50
Box (24):		40.00
1	Darin Erstad	.40
2	Troy Glaus	.75

3	Mo Vaughn	.20
4	Jason Giambi	.75
5	Tim Hudson	.25
6	Ben Grieve	.15
7	Eric Chavez	.25
8	Shannon Stewart	.15
9	Raul Mondesi	.25
10	Carlos Delgado	.75
11	Jose Canseco	.40
12	Fred McGriff	.25
13	Greg Vaughn	.15
14	Manny Ramirez	.75
15	Roberto Alomar	.50
16	Jim Thome	.75
17	Alex Rodriguez	2.50
18	Fred Garcia	.15
19	John Olerud	.25
20	Cal Ripken Jr.	2.50
21	Albert Belle	.20
22	Mike Mussina	.40
23	Ivan Rodriguez	.50
24	Rafael Palmeiro	.50
25	Ruben Mateo	.15
26	Gabe Kapler	.15
27	Pedro Martinez	1.00
28	Nomar Garciaparra	2.00
29	Carl Everett	.15
30	Carlos Beltran	.25
31	Jermaine Dye	.15
32	Johnny Damon	.25
33	Juan Gonzalez	.75
34	Juan Encarnacion	.15
35	Dean Palmer	.15
36	Jacque Jones	.15
37	Matt Lawton	.15
38	Frank Thomas	.75
39	Paul Konerko	.15
40	Magglio Ordonez	.25
41	Derek Jeter	2.00
42	Bernie Williams	.50
43	Mariano Rivera	.25
44	Roger Clemens	1.50
45	Jeff Bagwell	.75
46	Craig Biggio	.25
47	Richard Hidalgo	.25
48	Chipper Jones	1.50
49	Andres Galarraga	.25
50	Andruw Jones	.50
51	Greg Maddux	1.50
52	Jeromy Burnitz	.15
53	Geoff Jenkins	.25
54	Mark McGwire	2.00
55	Jim Edmonds	.25
56	Fernando Tatis	.15
57	J.D. Drew	.15
58	Sammy Sosa	2.00
59	Kerry Wood	.50
60	Randy Johnson	.75
61	Matt Williams	.25
62	Erubiel Durazo	.25
63	Shawn Green	.25
64	Kevin Brown	.25
65	Gary Sheffield	.25
66	Adrian Beltre	.25
67	Vladimir Guerrero	.75
68	Jose Vidro	.15
69	Barry Bonds	2.00
70	Jeff Kent	.25
71	Preston Wilson	.15
72	Ryan Dempster	.15
73	Mike Lowell	.15
74	Mike Piazza	1.50
75	Robin Ventura	.25
76	Edgardo Alfonzo	.15
77	Derek Bell	.15
78	Tony Gwynn	1.00
79	Matt Clement	.15
80	Scott Rolen	.75
81	Bobby Abreu	.25
82	Curt Schilling	.40
83	Brian Giles	.25
84	Jason Kendall	.25
85	Kris Benson	.15
86	Ken Griffey Jr.	1.50
87	Sean Casey	.25
88	Pokey Reese	.15
89	Larry Walker	.25
90	Todd Helton	.75
91	Rick Ankiel (Prospective Superstars)	5.00
92	Milton Bradley (Prospective Superstars)	5.00
93	Vernon Wells (Prospective Superstars)	6.00
94	Rafael Furcal (Prospective Superstars)	6.00
95	Kazuhiro Sasaki RC (Prospective Superstars)	8.00
96	Joe Torres RC (Prospective Superstars)	5.00
97	Adam Kennedy (Prospective Superstars)	5.00
98	Adam Piatt (Prospective Superstars)	5.00
99	Matt Wheatland RC (Prospective Superstars)	5.00
100	Alex Cabrera RC (Prospective Superstars)	5.00
101	Barry Zito RC (Prospective Superstars)	25.00
102	Mike Lamb RC (Prospective Superstars)	5.00
103	Scott Heard RC (Prospective Superstars)	5.00
104	Danys Baez RC (Prospective Superstars)	8.00
105	Matt Riley (Prospective Superstars)	5.00

106	Mark Mulder (Prospective Superstars)	6.00
107	Wilfredo Rodriguez RC (Prospective Superstars)	5.00
108	Luis Matos RC (Prospective Superstars)	10.00
109	Alfonso Soriano (Prospective Superstars)	8.00
110	Pat Burrell (Prospective Superstars)	6.00
111	Mike Tonis RC (Prospective Superstars)	5.00
112	Aaron McNeal RC (Prospective Superstars)	5.00
113	Dave Krynzel RC (Prospective Superstars)	8.00
114	Josh Beckett (Prospective Superstars)	8.00
115	Sean Burnett RC (Prospective Superstars)	8.00
116	Eric Munson (Prospective Superstars)	5.00
117	Scott Downs RC (Prospective Superstars)	5.00
118	Brian Tollberg RC (Prospective Superstars)	5.00
119	Nick Johnson (Prospective Superstars)	5.00
120	Leo Estrella RC (Prospective Superstars)	5.00
121	Ken Griffey Jr. (Pro Fame)	8.00
122	Frank Thomas (Pro Fame)	4.00
123	Cal Ripken Jr. (Pro Fame)	15.00
124	Ivan Rodriguez (Pro Fame)	4.00
125	Derek Jeter (Pro Fame)	12.00
126	Mark McGwire (Pro Fame)	12.00
127	Pedro Martinez (Pro Fame)	5.00
128	Chipper Jones (Pro Fame)	8.00
129	Sammy Sosa (Pro Fame)	10.00
130	Alex Rodriguez (Pro Fame)	10.00
131	Vladimir Guerrero (Pro Fame)	4.00
132	Jeff Bagwell (Pro Fame)	4.00

Future Forces

This 10-card set highlights top prospects on a card front featuring gold foil stamping and etching. Card backs are numbered with an "F" prefix.

		NM/M
Complete Set (10):		5.00
Common Player:		.50
Inserted 1:6		
1	Pat Burrell	2.00
2	Brad Penny	.50
3	Rick Ankiel	.50
4	Adam Kennedy	.50
5	Eric Munson	.50
6	Rafael Furcal	.75
7	Mark Mulder	.75
8	Vernon Wells	.75
9	Matt Riley	.50
10	Nick Johnson	.75

ProMotion

This 10-card set spotlights some of baseball's best all-around talents using gold foil stamping. Card backs are numbered with a "P" prefix and are seeded 1:6 packs.

		NM/M
Complete Set (10):		15.00
Common Player:		.75
Inserted 1:6		
1	Derek Jeter	3.00
2	Mike Piazza	1.50
3	Mark McGwire	2.50
4	Ivan Rodriguez	.75
5	Kerry Wood	.75
6	Nomar Garciaparra	2.00
7	Sammy Sosa	2.00
8	Alex Rodriguez	2.50
9	Ken Griffey Jr.	1.50
10	Vladimir Guerrero	1.00

Rare Breed

Baseball's top performers are spotlighted in this 12-card set on a full foiled silver front with gold foil stamping. Card backs are numbered with an "R" prefix and are inserted 1:12 packs.

		NM/M
Complete Set (12):		15.00
Common Player:		.50
Inserted 1:12		
1	Mark McGwire	3.00
2	Frank Thomas	1.00
3	Mike Piazza	2.00
4	Barry Bonds	4.00
5	Manny Ramirez	1.00
6	Ken Griffey Jr.	2.00
7	Nomar Garciaparra	3.00
8	Randy Johnson	1.50
9	Vladimir Guerrero	1.00
10	Jeff Bagwell	1.00
11	Rick Ankiel	.50
12	Alex Rodriguez	3.00

Signed Game-Worn Jerseys

Each of these Game Jersey cards has a piece of jersey swatch and autograph from the featured player. A Level 2 "Gold" version is limited to the player's corresponding uniform number.

		NM/M
Common Player:		25.00
Inserted 1:96		
BB	Barry Bonds	200.00
JC	Jose Canseco	40.00
JD	J.D. Drew	25.00
TG	Tom Glavine	40.00
LG	Luis Gonzalez	25.00
KG	Ken Griffey Jr.	100.00
TG	Tony Gwynn	50.00
DJ	Derek Jeter/SP	350.00
RJ	Randy Johnson	80.00
CJ	Chipper Jones	50.00
KL	Kenny Lofton	25.00
CR	Cal Ripken Jr.	140.00
AR	Alex Rodriguez	120.00
IR	Ivan Rodriguez	40.00
SR	Scott Rolen	50.00
GS	Gary Sheffield	40.00
FT	Frank Thomas	40.00
MV	Mo Vaughn	25.00
RV	Robin Ventura	25.00
MW	Matt Williams	25.00
PW	Preston Wilson	25.00

The Best in the Bigs

This 10-card set spotlights baseball's best performers on a white bordered design with gold foil stamping. Card backs are numbered with a "B" prefix.

		NM/M
Complete Set (10):		15.00
Common Player:		1.00
Inserted 1:12		
1	Sammy Sosa	2.50
2	Tony Gwynn	1.50
3	Pedro Martinez	1.50
4	Mark McGwire	3.00
5	Chipper Jones	2.00
6	Derek Jeter	3.00
7	Ken Griffey Jr.	2.00
8	Cal Ripken Jr.	4.00
9	Greg Maddux	2.00
10	Ivan Rodriguez	1.00

3,000 Hit Club

Upper Deck's continuing series features Lou Brock and Rod Carew. The series features 350 numbered bat cards, 350 numbered jersey cards and 100 numbered bat/jersey combos. Each player also signed the bat/jersey combos to their jersey number, as Brock signed 20 and Carew 29.

		NM/M
Lou Brock/Bat/350		20.00
Lou Brock/Jsy/350		20.00
Lou Brock/Bat/Jsy/100		40.00
Rod Carew/Bat/350		20.00
Rod Carew/Jsy/350		20.00
Rod Carew/Bat/Jsy/100		40.00

2000 Upper Deck Rookie Update

		NM/M
Common Player:		.25
Common Rookie:		5.00
Pack (4):		4.50
Box (15):		50.00
SP Authentic Update		
(136-164) Production 1,700		
136	Barry Zito RC (Future Watch)	25.00
137	Aaron McNeal RC (Future Watch)	5.00
138	Teofilo Perez (Future Watch)	5.00
139	Sun-Woo Kim RC (Future Watch)	5.00
140	Xavier Nady RC (Future Watch)	15.00
141	Matt Wheatland RC (Future Watch)	5.00
142	Brent Abernathy RC (Future Watch)	5.00
143	Cory Vance RC (Future Watch)	5.00
144	Scott Heard RC (Future Watch)	5.00
145	Mike Meyers RC (Future Watch)	5.00
146	Ben Diggins RC (Future Watch)	5.00
147	Luis Matos RC (Future Watch)	5.00
148	Ben Sheets RC (Future Watch)	15.00

149	Kurt Ainsworth RC (Future Watch)	5.00
150	Dave Krynzel RC (Future Watch)	5.00
151	Alex Cabrera RC (Future Watch)	5.00
152	Mike Tonis RC (Future Watch)	5.00
153	Dane Sardinha RC (Future Watch)	5.00
154	Keith Ginter RC (Future Watch)	5.00
155	David Espinosa RC (Future Watch)	5.00
156	Joe Torres RC (Future Watch)	5.00
157	Daylan Holt RC (Future Watch)	5.00
158	Koyie Hill RC (Future Watch)	5.00
159	Brad Wilkerson RC (Future Watch)	8.00
160	Juan Pierre RC (Future Watch)	10.00
161	Matt Ginter RC (Future Watch)	5.00
162	Dane Artman RC (Future Watch)	5.00
163	Jon Rauch RC (Future Watch)	5.00
164	Sean Burnett RC (Future Watch)	5.00
166	Darin Erstad	.25
167	Ben Grieve	.25
168	David Wells	.25
169	Fred McGriff	.25
170	Bob Wickman	.25
171	Al Martin	.25
172	Melvin Mora	.25
173	Ricky Ledee	.25
174	Dante Bichette	.25
175	Mike Sweeney	.25
176	Bobby Higginson	.25
177	Matt Lawton	.25
178	Charles Johnson	.25
179	David Justice	.50
180	Richard Hidalgo	.40
181	B.J. Surhoff	.25
182	Richie Sexson	.50
183	Jim Edmonds	.50
184	Rondell White	.50
185	Curt Schilling	.50
186	Tom Goodwin	.25
187	Jose Vidro	.25
188	Ellis Burks	.25
189	Henry Rodriguez	.25
190	Mike Bordick	.25
191	Eric Owens	.25
192	Travis Lee	.25
193	Kevin Young	.25
194	Aaron Boone	.40
195	Todd Hollandsworth	.25
SPx Update		
(121-135, 182-196) 1,600		
(136-151) Production 1,500		
Common Autograph		10.00
121	Brad Wilkerson RC	15.00
122	Roy Oswalt RC	50.00
123	Wascar Serrano RC	5.00
124	Sean Burnett RC	10.00
125	Alex Cabrera RC	5.00
126	Timoniel Perez RC	5.00
127	Juan Pierre RC	15.00
128	Daylan Holt RC	5.00
129	Tomokazu Ohka RC	5.00
130	Kazuhiro Sasaki RC	10.00
131	Kurt Ainsworth RC	10.00
132	Brent Abernathy RC	5.00
133	Danys Baez RC	5.00
134	Brad Cresse RC	5.00
135	Ryan Franklin RC	5.00
136	Mike Lamb RC	5.00
137	David Espinosa RC	5.00
138	Matt Wheatland RC	5.00
139	Xavier Nady RC	20.00
140	Scott Heard RC	5.00
141	Pascual Coco RC	5.00
142	Justin Miller RC	5.00
143	Dave Krynzel RC	5.00
144	Dane Sardinha RC	5.00
145	Ben Sheets RC	25.00
146	Leo Estrella RC	10.00
147	Ben Diggins RC	10.00
148	Barry Zito RC	40.00
149	Joe Torres RC	10.00
150	Mike Meyers RC	10.00
151	Kris Wilson RC	10.00
152	Darin Erstad	.50
153	Richard Hidalgo	.50
154	Eric Chavez	.50
155	B.J. Surhoff	.75
156	Richie Sexson	.75
157	Raul Mondesi	.50
158	Rondell White	.75
159	Jim Edmonds	.75
160	Curt Schilling	.75
161	Tom Goodwin	.25
162	Fred McGriff	.75
163	Jose Vidro	.25
164	Ellis Burks	.25
165	David Segui	.25
166	Aaron Sele	.25
167	Henry Rodriguez	.25
168	Mike Bordick	.25
169	Mike Mussina	1.00
170	Ryan Klesko	.25
171	Kevin Young	.25
172	Travis Lee	.25

173	Aaron Boone	.50
174	Jermaine Dye	.25
175	Ricky Ledee	.25
176	Jeffrey Hammonds	.25
177	Carl Everett	.25
178	Matt Lawton	.25
179	Bobby Higginson	.25
180	Charles Johnson	.25
181	David Justice	.75
182	Joey Nation RC	4.00
183	Rico Washington RC	4.00
184	Luis Matos RC	10.00
185	Chris Wakeland RC	4.00
186	Sun-Woo Kim RC	4.00
187	Keith Ginter RC	5.00
188	Geraldo Guzman RC	4.00
189	Jay Spurgeon RC	4.00
190	Jace Brewer RC	4.00
191	Juan Guzman RC	4.00
192	Ross Gload RC	4.00
193	Paxton Crawford RC	4.00
194	Ryan Kohlmeier RC	4.00
195	Julio Zuleta RC	4.00
196	Matt Ginter RC	4.00

UD Pros & Prospects Update
(133-162) Production 1,600

133	Dane Artman RC	5.00
134	Juan Pierre RC	8.00
135	Jace Brewer RC	5.00
136	Sun-Woo Kim RC	6.00
137	Jon Rauch RC	6.00
138	Juan Guzman RC	5.00
139	Daylan Holt RC	5.00
140	Rico Washington RC	5.00
141	Ben Diggins RC	5.00
142	Mike Meyers RC	5.00
143	Chris Wakeland RC	5.00
144	Cory Vance RC	5.00
145	Keith Ginter RC	8.00
146	Koyie Hill RC	8.00
147	Julio Zuleta RC	5.00
148	Geraldo Guzman RC	5.00
149	Jay Spurgeon RC	5.00
150	Ross Gload RC	5.00
151	Ben Sheets RC	15.00
152	Josh Kalinowski RC	6.00
153	Kurt Ainsworth RC	5.00
154	Paxton Crawford RC	5.00
155	Xavier Nady RC	8.00
156	Brad Wilkerson RC	10.00
157	Kris Wilson RC	5.00
158	Paul Rigdon RC	5.00
159	Ryan Kohlmeier RC	5.00
160	Dane Sardinha RC	5.00
161	Javier Cardona RC	5.00
162	Brad Cresse RC	5.00
163	Ron Gant	.25
164	Mark Mulder	.50
165	David Wells	.25
166	Jason Tyner	.25
167	David Segui	.25
168	Al Martin	.25
169	Melvin Mora	.25
170	Ricky Ledee	.25
171	Rolando Arrojo	.25
172	Mike Sweeney	.25
173	Bobby Higginson	.25
174	Eric Milton	.25
175	Charles Johnson	.25
176	David Justice	.50
177	Moises Alou	.50
178	Andy Ashby	.25
179	Richie Sexson	.75
180	Will Clark	.75
181	Rondell White	.40
182	Curt Schilling	.75
183	Tom Goodwin	.25
184	Lee Stevens	.25
185	Ellis Burks	.25
186	Henry Rodriguez	.25
187	Mike Bordick	.25
188	Ryan Klesko	.50
189	Travis Lee	.25
190	Kevin Young	.25
191	Barry Larkin	.75
192	Jeff Cirillo	.25

Winning Materials

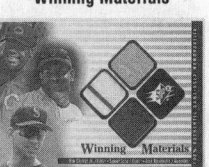

	NM/M
Common Card:	10.00
Inserted 1:15	
NG-PM	Nomar Garciaparra,
	Pedro Martinez	40.00
DJ-AR	Derek Jeter,
	Alex Rodriguez	40.00
DJ-NG	Derek Jeter,
	Nomar Garciaparra	40.00
MM-KG	Mark McGwire,
	Ken Griffey Jr.	40.00
MM-SS	Mark McGwire,
	Sammy Sosa	40.00
MM-RA	Mark McGwire,
	Rick Ankiel	30.00
KG-SS	Ken Griffey Jr.,
	Sammy Sosa	25.00
RC-PM	Roger Clemens,
	Pedro Martinez	30.00

CR-TG	Cal Ripken Jr.,
	Tony Gwynn	40.00
JC-BB	Jose Canseco,
	Barry Bonds	30.00
FT-MO	Frank Thomas,
	Magglio Ordonez	10.00
JB-CB	Jeff Bagwell,
	Craig Biggio	10.00
MP-RV	Mike Piazza,
	Robin Ventura	25.00
IR-RP	Ivan Rodriguez,
	Rafael Palmeiro	10.00
J-G-R	Derek Jeter,
	Nomar Garciaparra,
	Alex Rodriguez	75.00
G-S-R	Ken Griffey Jr.,
	Sammy Sosa,
	Alex Rodriguez	40.00

Winning Materials Gold

	NM/M
Common Player:	5.00
JC	John Cotton	5.00
BS	Ben Sheets	15.00
SB	Sean Burroughs	8.00
MN	Mike Neill	5.00
DM	Doug Mientkiewicz	8.00
EY	Ernie Young	5.00
GD	Travis Dawkins,
	Mike Kinkade	5.00
BS	Sean Burroughs,
	Ben Sheets	15.00
AE	Brent Abernathy,
	Adam Everett	5.00
EY	Brad Wilkerson,
	Ernie Young	8.00

2000 Upper Deck Ultimate Victory

	NM/M
Complete Set (120):	200.00
Common Player:	.15
Common Ultimate Rookie	
(91-120):	4.00
Varying Production Levels	
Pack (5):	1.50
Box (24):	25.00
1	Mo Vaughn	.20
2	Darin Erstad	.40
3	Troy Glaus	.75
4	Adam Kennedy	.15
5	Jason Giambi	.75
6	Ben Grieve	.15
7	Terrence Long	.15
8	Tim Hudson	.25
9	David Wells	.15
10	Carlos Delgado	.75
11	Shannon Stewart	.15
12	Greg Vaughn	.15
13	Gerald Williams	.15
14	Manny Ramirez	.75
15	Roberto Alomar	.60
16	Jim Thome	.75
17	Edgar Martinez	.25
18	Alex Rodriguez	2.50
19	Matt Riley	.15
20	Cal Ripken Jr.	2.50
21	Mike Mussina	.50
22	Albert Belle	.20
23	Ivan Rodriguez	.75
24	Rafael Palmeiro	.50
25	Nomar Garciaparra	2.00
26	Pedro Martinez	1.00
27	Carl Everett	.15
28	Tomokazu Ohka RC	.40
29	Jermaine Dye	.15
30	Johnny Damon	.25
31	Dean Palmer	.15
32	Juan Gonzalez	.75
33	Eric Milton	.15
34	Matt Lawton	.15
35	Frank Thomas	.75
36	Paul Konerko	.15
37	Magglio Ordonez	.25
38	Jon Garland	.15
39	Derek Jeter	2.50
40	Roger Clemens	1.50
41	Bernie Williams	.50
42	Nick Johnson	.15
43	Julio Lugo	.15
44	Jeff Bagwell	.75
45	Richard Hidalgo	.15
46	Chipper Jones	1.50
47	Greg Maddux	1.50
48	Andruw Jones	.50
49	Andres Galarraga	.25
50	Rafael Furcal	.50
51	Jeromy Burnitz	.15

52	Geoff Jenkins	.25
53	Mark McGwire	2.00
54	Jim Edmonds	.25
55	Rick Ankiel	.25
56	Sammy Sosa	2.00
57	Julio Zuleta RC	.25
58	Kerry Wood	.40
59	Randy Johnson	.75
60	Matt Williams	.15
61	Steve Finley	.15
62	Gary Sheffield	.40
63	Kevin Brown	.25
64	Shawn Green	.25
65	Milton Bradley	.15
66	Vladimir Guerrero	.75
67	Jose Vidro	.15
68	Barry Bonds	2.00
69	Jeff Kent	.25
70	Preston Wilson	.15
71	Mike Lowell	.15
72	Mike Piazza	2.00
73	Robin Ventura	.25
74	Edgardo Alfonzo	.15
75	Jay Payton	.15
76	Tony Gwynn	1.00
77	Adam Eaton	.15
78	Phil Nevin	.15
79	Scott Rolen	.75
80	Bob Abreu	.25
81	Pat Burrell	.50
82	Brian Giles	.25
83	Jason Kendall	.25
84	Kris Benson	.15
85	Gookie Dawkins	.15
86	Ken Griffey Jr.	1.50
87	Barry Larkin	.40
88	Larry Walker	.25
89	Todd Helton	.75
90	Ben Petrick	.15
91	Alex Cabrera 3,500 RC (Ultimate Rookie 2000)	6.00
92	Matt Wheatland 1,000 RC (Ultimate Rookie 2000)	4.00
93	Joe Torres 1,000 RC (Ultimate Rookie 2000)	4.00
94	Xavier Nady 1,000 RC (Ultimate Rookie 2000)	12.00
95	Kenny Kelly 3,500 RC (Ultimate Rookie 2000)	4.00
96	Matt Ginter 3,500 RC (Ultimate Rookie 2000)	6.00
97	Ben Diggins 1,000 RC (Ultimate Rookie 2000)	8.00
98	Danys Baez 3,500 RC (Ultimate Rookie 2000)	6.00
99	Daylan Holt 2,500 RC (Ultimate Rookie 2000)	4.00
100	Kazuhiro Sasaki 3,500 RC (Ultimate Rookie 2000)	5.00
101	Dane Artman 2,500 RC (Ultimate Rookie 2000)	4.00
102	Mike Tonis 1,000 RC (Ultimate Rookie 2000)	4.00
103	Timoniel Perez 2,500 RC (Ultimate Rookie 2000)	6.00
104	Barry Zito 2,500 RC (Ultimate Rookie 2000)	20.00
105	Koyie Hill 2,500 RC (Ultimate Rookie 2000)	4.00
106	Brad Wilkerson 2,500 RC (Ultimate Rookie 2000)	8.00
107	Juan Pierre 3,500 RC (Ultimate Rookie 2000)	8.00
108	Aaron McNeal 3,500 RC (Ultimate Rookie 2000)	4.00
109	Jay Spurgeon 3,500 RC (Ultimate Rookie 2000)	4.00
110	Sean Burnett 1,000 RC (Ultimate Rookie 2000)	8.00
111	Luis Matos 3,500 RC (Ultimate Rookie 2000)	8.00
112	Dave Krynzel 1,000 RC (Ultimate Rookie 2000)	6.00
113	Scott Heard 1,000 RC (Ultimate Rookie 2000)	4.00
114	Ben Sheets 2,500 RC (Ultimate Rookie 2000)	15.00
115	Dane Sardinha 1,000 RC (Ultimate Rookie 2000)	4.00
116	David Espinosa 1,000 RC (Ultimate Rookie 2000)	4.00
117	Leo Estrella 3,500 RC (Ultimate Rookie 2000)	4.00
118	Kurt Ainsworth 2,500 RC (Ultimate Rookie 2000)	4.00
119	Jon Rauch 2,500 RC (Ultimate Rookie 2000)	6.00
120	Ryan Franklin 2,500 (Ultimate Rookie 2000)	4.00

Collection

Parallel 25 Stars:	20-40X
Rookies (91-120):	2-4X
Production 25 Sets	
Parallel 100 Stars:	4-8X
Rookies (91-120):	1-2X
Production 100 Sets	
Parallel 250 Stars:	2-4X
Rookies (91-120):	1-2X
Production 250 Sets	

Diamond Dignitaries

	NM/M
Complete Set (10):	20.00
Common Player:	1.00
Inserted 1:23	
1	Ken Griffey Jr.	2.00
2	Nomar Garciaparra	3.00

3	Chipper Jones	2.00
4	Ivan Rodriguez	1.00
5	Mark McGwire	3.00
6	Cal Ripken Jr.	4.00
7	Vladimir Guerrero	1.00
8	Alex Rodriguez	3.00
9	Sammy Sosa	2.50
10	Derek Jeter	3.00

HOF Game Jersey

	NM/M
Common Card:	8.00
SA	Sparky Anderson	8.00
CF	Carlton Fisk	10.00
TP	Tony Perez	8.00

HOF Game Jersey Combo

| | NM/M |
| UV-C | Sparky Anderson, Carlton Fisk, Tony Perez | 40.00 |

Lasting Impressions

	NM/M
Complete Set (10):	15.00
Common Player:	1.00
Inserted 1:11	
1	Barry Bonds	3.00
2	Mike Piazza	2.00
3	Manny Ramirez	1.00
4	Pedro J. Martinez	1.50
5	Mark McGwire	2.00
6	Ken Griffey Jr.	2.00
7	Ivan Rodriguez	1.00
8	Jeff Bagwell	1.00
9	Randy Johnson	1.50
10	Alex Rodriguez	3.00

Starstruck

	NM/M
Complete Set (10):	20.00
Common Player:	1.00
Inserted 1:11	
1	Alex Rodriguez	3.00
2	Frank Thomas	1.00
3	Derek Jeter	3.00
4	Mark McGwire	3.00
5	Nomar Garciaparra	3.00
6	Chipper Jones	2.00
7	Cal Ripken Jr.	4.00
8	Sammy Sosa	2.00
9	Vladimir Guerrero	1.00
10	Ken Griffey Jr.	2.00

2000 Upper Deck Victory

Victory offers no inserts just your standard 440-card base set that features a white bordered design, with two player images on the card front. The base set includes three subsets: Rookie 2000 (331-370); Big Play Makers (371-390) and JUNIOR Circuit (391-440).

	NM/M
Complete Set (440):	20.00
Complete Factory Set (466):	25.00

Common Player:	.10
Common Griffey (391-440):	.50
Common USA (441-466):	.40
Pack (12):	1.00
Wax Box (36):	25.00
1	Mo Vaughn	.15
2	Garret Anderson	.20
3	Tim Salmon	.20
4	Troy Percival	.10
5	Orlando Palmeiro	.10
6	Darin Erstad	.20
7	Ramon Ortiz	.10
8	Ben Molina	.10
9	Troy Glaus	.40
10	Jim Edmonds	.10
11	Mo Vaughn, Troy Percival	.15
12	Craig Biggio	.25
13	Roger Cedeno	.10
14	Shane Reynolds	.10
15	Jeff Bagwell	.50
16	Octavio Dotel	.10
17	Moises Alou	.10
18	Jose Lima	.10
19	Ken Caminiti	.15
20	Richard Hidalgo	.10
21	Billy Wagner	.10
22	Lance Berkman	.20
23	Jeff Bagwell, Jose Lima	.15
24	Jason Giambi	.50
25	Randy Velarde	.10
26	Miguel Tejada	.25
27	Matt Stairs	.10
28	A.J. Hinch	.10
29	Olmedo Saenz	.10
30	Ben Grieve	.10
31	Ryan Christenson	.10
32	Eric Chavez	.20
33	Tim Hudson	.20
34	John Jaha	.10
35	Jason Giambi, Matt Stairs	.25
36	Raul Mondesi	.10
37	Tony Batista	.10
38	David Wells	.10
39	Homer Bush	.10
40	Carlos Delgado	.40
41	Billy Koch	.10
42	Darrin Fletcher	.10
43	Tony Fernandez	.10
44	Shannon Stewart	.10
45	Roy Halladay	.20
46	Chris Carpenter	.10
47	Carlos Delgado, David Wells	.20
48	Chipper Jones	1.00
49	Greg Maddux	1.00
50	Andruw Jones	.40
51	Andres Galarraga	.20
52	Tom Glavine	.20
53	Brian Jordan	.10
54	John Smoltz	.15
55	John Rocker	.10
56	Javy Lopez	.15
57	Eddie Perez	.10
58	Kevin Millwood	.20
59	Chipper Jones, Greg Maddux	.50
60	Jeromy Burnitz	.10
61	Steve Woodard	.10
62	Ron Belliard	.10
63	Geoff Jenkins	.20
64	Bob Wickman	.10
65	Marquis Grissom	.10
66	Henry Blanco	.10
67	Mark Loretta	.10
68	Alex Ochoa	.10
69	Marquis Grissom, Jeromy Burnitz	.10
70	Mark McGwire	1.50
71	Edgar Renteria	.10
72	Dave Veres	.10
73	Eli Marrero	.10
74	Fernando Tatis	.10
75	J.D. Drew	.20
76	Ray Lankford	.10
77	Daryle Kile	.10
78	Kent Bottenfield	.10
79	Joe McEwing	.10
80	Mark McGwire, Ray Lankford	.75
81	Sammy Sosa	1.25
82	Jose Nieves	.10
83	Jon Lieber	.10
84	Henry Rodriguez	.10
85	Mark Grace	.20
86	Eric Young	.10
87	Kerry Wood	.20
88	Ismael Valdes	.10
89	Glenallen Hill	.10

90	Sammy Sosa, Mark Grace	.60
91	Greg Vaughn	.10
92	Fred McGriff	.20
93	Ryan Rupe	.10
94	Bubba Trammell	.10
95	Miguel Cairo	.10
96	Roberto Hernandez	.10
97	Jose Canseco	.40
98	Wilson Alvarez	.10
99	John Flaherty	.10
100	Vinny Castilla	.15
101	Jose Canseco, Roberto Hernandez	.25
102	Randy Johnson	.50
103	Matt Williams	.15
104	Matt Mantei	.10
105	Steve Finley	.10
106	Luis Gonzalez	.20
107	Travis Lee	.10
108	Omar Daal	.10
109	Jay Bell	.10
110	Erubiel Durazo	.10
111	Tony Womack	.10
112	Todd Stottlemyre	.10
113	Randy Johnson, Matt Williams	.25
114	Gary Sheffield	.25
115	Adrian Beltre	.10
116	Kevin Brown	.20
117	Todd Hundley	.10
118	Eric Karros	.10
119	Shawn Green	.40
120	Chan Ho Park	.10
121	Mark Grudzielanek	.10
122	Todd Hollandsworth	.10
123	Jeff Shaw	.10
124	Darren Dreifort	.10
125	Gary Sheffield, Kevin Brown	.15
126	Vladimir Guerrero	.50
127	Michael Barrett	.10
128	Dustin Hermanson	.10
129	Jose Vidro	.10
130	Chris Widger	.10
131	Mike Thurman	.10
132	Wilton Guerrero	.10
133	Brad Fullmer	.10
134	Rondell White	.20
135	Ugueth Urbina	.10
136	Vladimir Guerrero, Rondell White	.40
137	Barry Bonds	1.50
138	Russ Ortiz	.10
139	J.T. Snow	.10
140	Joe Nathan	.10
141	Rich Aurilia	.10
142	Jeff Kent	.20
143	Armando Rios	.10
144	Ellis Burks	.10
145	Robb Nen	.10
146	Marvin Benard	.10
147	Barry Bonds, Russ Ortiz	.75
148	Manny Ramirez	.50
149	Bartolo Colon	.10
150	Kenny Lofton	.20
151	Sandy Alomar Jr.	.10
152	Travis Fryman	.15
153	Omar Vizquel	.15
154	Roberto Alomar	.40
155	Richie Sexson	.25
156	David Justice	.20
157	Jim Thome	.50
158	Manny Ramirez, Roberto Alomar	.25
159	Ken Griffey Jr.	1.00
160	Edgar Martinez	.15
161	Fred Garcia	.10
162	Alex Rodriguez	1.50
163	John Halama	.10
164	Russ Davis	.10
165	David Bell	.10
166	Gil Meche	.10
167	Jamie Moyer	.10
168	John Olerud	.10
169	Ken Griffey Jr., Fred Garcia	.50
170	Preston Wilson	.20
171	Antonio Alfonseca	.10
172	A.J. Burnett	.10
173	Luis Castillo	.10
174	Mike Lowell	.10
175	Alex Fernandez	.10
176	Mike Redmond	.10
177	Alex Gonzalez	.10
178	Vladimir Nunez	.10
179	Mark Kotsay	.10
180	Preston Wilson, Luis Castillo	.10
181	Mike Piazza	1.00
182	Darryl Hamilton	.10
183	Al Leiter	.20
184	Robin Ventura	.20
185	Rickey Henderson	.20
186	Rey Ordonez	.10
187	Edgardo Alfonzo	.10
188	Derek Bell	.10
189	Mike Hampton	.10
190	Armando Benitez	.10
191	Mike Piazza, Rickey Henderson	.50
192	Cal Ripken Jr.	1.50
193	B.J. Surhoff	.10
194	Mike Mussina	.20
195	Albert Belle	.10
196	Jerry Hairston Jr.	.10
197	Will Clark	.20
198	Sidney Ponson	.10
199	Brady Anderson	.10

#	Player	Price
200	Scott Erickson	.10
201	Ryan Minor	.10
202	Cal Ripken Jr., Albert Belle	.75
203	Tony Gwynn	.75
204	Bret Boone	.20
205	Ryan Klesko	.10
206	Ben Davis	.10
207	Matt Clement	.10
208	Eric Owens	.10
209	Trevor Hoffman	.10
210	Sterling Hitchcock	.10
211	Phil Nevin	.10
212	Tony Gwynn, Trevor Hoffman	.40
213	Scott Rolen	.50
214	Bob Abreu	.20
215	Curt Schilling	.25
216	Rico Brogna	.10
217	Robert Person	.10
218	Doug Glanville	.10
219	Mike Lieberthal	.10
220	Andy Ashby	.10
221	Randy Wolf	.10
222	Bob Abreu, Curt Schilling	.20
223	Brian Giles	.20
224	Jason Kendall	.20
225	Kris Benson	.10
226	Warren Morris	.10
227	Kevin Young	.10
228	Al Martin	.10
229	Wil Cordero	.10
230	Bruce Aven	.10
231	Todd Ritchie	.10
232	Jason Kendall, Brian Giles	.10
233	Ivan Rodriguez	.50
234	Rusty Greer	.10
235	Ruben Mateo	.10
236	Justin Thompson	.10
237	Rafael Palmeiro	.25
238	Chad Curtis	.10
239	Royce Clayton	.10
240	Gabe Kapler	.10
241	Jeff Zimmerman	.10
242	John Wetteland	.10
243	Ivan Rodriguez, Rafael Palmeiro	.25
244	Nomar Garciaparra	1.25
245	Pedro Martinez	.75
246	Jose Offerman	.10
247	Jason Varitek	.10
248	Troy O'Leary	.10
249	John Valentin	.10
250	Trot Nixon	.10
251	Carl Everett	.10
252	Wilton Veras	.10
253	Bret Saberhagen	.10
254	Nomar Garciaparra, Pedro J. Martinez	.60
255	Sean Casey	.10
256	Barry Larkin	.25
257	Pokey Reese	.10
258	Pete Harnisch	.10
259	Aaron Boone	.20
260	Dante Bichette	.10
261	Scott Williamson	.10
262	Steve Parris	.10
263	Dmitri Young	.10
264	Mike Cameron	.10
265	Sean Casey, Scott Williamson	.10
266	Larry Walker	.25
267	Rolando Arrojo	.10
268	Pedro Astacio	.10
269	Todd Helton	.50
270	Jeff Cirillo	.10
271	Neifi Perez	.10
272	Brian Bohanon	.10
273	Jeffrey Hammonds	.10
274	Tom Goodwin	.10
275	Larry Walker, Todd Helton	.25
276	Carlos Beltran	.15
277	Jermaine Dye	.10
278	Mike Sweeney	.10
279	Joe Randa	.10
280	Jose Rosado	.10
281	Carlos Febles	.10
282	Jeff Suppan	.10
283	Johnny Damon	.20
284	Jeremy Giambi	.10
285	Mike Sweeney, Carlos Beltran	.10
286	Tony Clark	.10
287	Damion Easley	.10
288	Jeff Weaver	.10
289	Dean Palmer	.10
290	Juan Gonzalez	.50
291	Juan Encarnacion	.10
292	Todd Jones	.10
293	Karim Garcia	.10
294	Deivi Cruz	.10
295	Dean Palmer, Juan Encarnacion	.10
296	Corey Koskie	.10
297	Brad Radke	.10
298	Doug Mientkiewicz	.10
299	Ron Coomer	.10
300	Joe Mays	.10
301	Eric Milton	.10
302	Jacque Jones	.10
303	Chad Allen	.10
304	Cristian Guzman	.10
305	Jason Ryan	.10
306	Todd Walker	.10
307	Corey Koskie, Eric Milton	.10
308	Frank Thomas	.50
309	Paul Konerko	.10
310	Mike Sirotka	.10
311	Jim Parque	.10

#	Player	Price
312	Magglio Ordonez	.25
313	Bob Howry	.10
314	Carlos Lee	.10
315	Ray Durham	.10
316	Chris Singleton	.10
317	Brook Fordyce	.10
318	Frank Thomas, Magglio Ordonez	.25
319	Derek Jeter	1.50
320	Roger Clemens	1.00
321	Paul O'Neill	.20
322	Bernie Williams	.40
323	Mariano Rivera	.20
324	Tino Martinez	.20
325	David Cone	.20
326	Chuck Knoblauch	.10
327	Darryl Strawberry	.20
328	Orlando Hernandez	.10
329	Ricky Ledee	.10
330	Derek Jeter, Bernie Williams	.75
331	Pat Burrell (Rookie 2000)	.50
332	Alfonso Soriano (Rookie 2000)	.75
333	Josh Beckett (Rookie 2000)	.25
334	Matt Riley (Rookie 2000)	.15
335	Brian Cooper (Rookie 2000)	.10
336	Eric Munson (Rookie 2000)	.20
337	Vernon Wells (Rookie 2000)	.25
338	Juan Pena (Rookie 2000)	.10
339	Mark DeRosa (Rookie 2000)	.10
340	Kip Wells (Rookie 2000)	.10
341	Roosevelt Brown (Rookie 2000)	.10
342	Jason LaRue (Rookie 2000)	.10
343	Ben Petrick (Rookie 2000)	.10
344	Mark Quinn (Rookie 2000)	.10
345	Julio Ramirez (Rookie 2000)	.10
346	Rod Barajas (Rookie 2000)	.10
347	Robert Fick (Rookie 2000)	.10
348	David Newhan (Rookie 2000)	.10
349	Eric Gagne (Rookie 2000)	.15
350	Jorge Toca (Rookie 2000)	.10
351	Mitch Meluskey (Rookie 2000)	.10
352	Ed Yarnall (Rookie 2000)	.10
353	Chad Hermansen (Rookie 2000)	.10
354	Peter Bergeron (Rookie 2000)	.10
355	Dermal Brown (Rookie 2000)	.10
356	Adam Kennedy (Rookie 2000)	.10
357	Kevin Barker (Rookie 2000)	.10
358	Francisco Cordero (Rookie 2000)	.10
359	Travis Dawkins (Rookie 2000)	.10
360	Jeff Williams (Rookie 2000)	.10
361	Chad Hutchinson (Rookie 2000)	.10
362	D'Angelo Jimenez (Rookie 2000)	.10
363	Derrick Gibson (Rookie 2000)	.10
364	Calvin Murray (Rookie 2000)	.10
365	Doug Davis (Rookie 2000)	.10
366	Rob Ramsay RC (Rookie 2000)	.20
367	Mark Redman (Rookie 2000)	.10
368	Rick Ankiel (Rookie 2000)	.10
369	Domingo Guzman (Rookie 2000)	.10
370	Eugene Kingsale (Rookie 2000)	.10
371	Nomar Garciaparra (Big Play Makers)	.75
372	Ken Griffey Jr. (Big Play Makers)	.50
373	Randy Johnson (Big Play Makers)	.25
374	Jeff Bagwell (Big Play Makers)	.25
375	Ivan Rodriguez (Big Play Makers)	.25
376	Derek Jeter (Big Play Makers)	.75
377	Carlos Beltran (Big Play Makers)	.10
378	Vladimir Guerrero (Big Play Makers)	.40
379	Sammy Sosa (Big Play Makers)	.60
380	Barry Bonds (Big Play Makers)	.75
381	Pedro Martinez (Big Play Makers)	.40
382	Chipper Jones (Big Play Makers)	.50
383	Mo Vaughn (Big Play Makers)	.10
384	Mike Piazza (Big Play Makers)	.50

#	Player	Price
385	Alex Rodriguez (Big Play Makers)	.75
386	Manny Ramirez (Big Play Makers)	.25
387	Mark McGwire (Big Play Makers)	.75
388	Tony Gwynn (Big Play Makers)	.40
389	Sean Casey (Big Play Makers)	.10
390	Cal Ripken Jr. (Big Play Makers)	.75
391-440	Ken Griffey Jr.	.40
441	Tommy Lasorda	.50
442	Sean Burroughs	.75
443	Rick Krivda	.40
444	Ben Sheets RC	1.50
445	Pat Borders	.40
446	Brent Abernathy RC	.75
447	Tim Young	.40
448	Adam Everett	.50
449	Anthony Sanders	.40
450	Ernie Young	.40
451	Brad Wilkerson RC	1.50
452	Kurt Ainsworth	1.00
453	Ryan Franklin	.40
454	Todd Williams	.40
455	Jon Rauch RC	.50
456	Roy Oswalt RC	5.00
457	Shane Heams	.50
458	Chris George	.50
459	Bobby Seay	.40
460	Mike Kinkade	.40
461	Marcus Jensen	.40
462	Travis Dawkins	.50
463	Doug Mientkiewicz	.40
464	John Cotton	.40
465	Mike Neill	.40
466	Team Photo USA	2.50

2000 Upper Deck Yankees Legends Sample

This promo card was issued to preview the Yankees Legends set. With silver-foil graphics on front, it is identical in design to the base cards in the regularly issued version. Back has a "SAMPLE" overprint across the stats.

		NM/M
NY7	Mickey Mantle	5.00

2000 Upper Deck Yankees Legends

		NM/M
Complete Set (90):		20.00
Common Player:		.15
Pack (5):		6.00
Box (24):		100.00
1	Babe Ruth	2.00
2	Mickey Mantle	2.00
3	Lou Gehrig	2.00
4	Joe DiMaggio	2.00
5	Yogi Berra	.75
6	Don Mattingly	1.00
7	Reggie Jackson	.75
8	Dave Winfield	.75
9	Bill Skowron	.15
10	Willie Randolph	.15
11	Phil Rizzuto	.50
12	Tony Kubek	.15
13	Thurman Munson	1.00
14	Roger Maris	1.00
15	Billy Martin	.40
16	Elston Howard	.15
17	Graig Nettles	.15

#	Player	Price
18	Whitey Ford	.50
19	Earl Combes	.15
20	Tony Lazzeri	.15
21	Bob Meusel	.15
22	Joe Gordon	.15
23	Jerry Coleman	.15
24	Joe Torre	.50
25	Bucky Dent	.40
26	Don Larsen	.40
27	Bobby Richardson	.15
28	Ron Guidry	.15
29	Bobby Murcer	.15
30	Tommy Henrich	.15
31	Hank Bauer	.15
32	Joe Pepitone	.15
33	Clete Boyer	.15
34	Chris Chambliss	.15
35	Tommy John	.15
36	Goose Gossage	.15
37	Red Ruffing	.15
38	Charlie Keller	.15
39	Billy Gardner	.15
40	Hector Lopez	.15
41	Cliff Johnson	.15
42	Oscar Gamble	.15
43	Allie Reynolds	.15
44	Mickey Rivers	.15
45	Bill Dickey	.40
46	Dave Righetti	.15
47	Mel Stottlemyre	.15
48	Waite Hoyt	.15
49	Lefty Gomez	.15
50	Wade Boggs	.50
51	Billy Martin (Magic Numbers)	.25
52	Babe Ruth (Magic Numbers)	1.00
53	Lou Gehrig (Magic Numbers)	1.00
54	Joe DiMaggio (Magic Numbers)	1.00
55	Mickey Mantle (Magic Numbers)	1.00
56	Yogi Berra (Magic Numbers)	.40
57	Bill Dickey (Magic Numbers)	.25
58	Roger Maris (Magic Numbers)	.50
59	Phil Rizzuto (Magic Numbers)	.25
60	Thurman Munson (Magic Numbers)	.50
61	Whitey Ford (Magic Numbers)	.25
62	Don Mattingly (Magic Numbers)	.50
63	Elston Howard (Magic Numbers)	.15
64	Casey Stengel (Magic Numbers)	.15
65	Reggie Jackson (Magic Numbers)	.50
66	Babe Ruth/1923 (The Championship Years)	1.00
67	Lou Gehrig/1927 (The Championship Years)	1.00
68	Tony Lazzeri/1928 (The Championship Years)	.15
69	Babe Ruth/1932 (The Championship Years)	1.00
70	Lou Gehrig/1936 (The Championship Years)	1.00
71	Lefty Gomez/1937 (The Championship Years)	.15
72	Bill Dickey/1938 (The Championship Years)	.25
73	Tommy Henrich/1939 (The Championship Years)	.15
74	Joe DiMaggio/1941 (The Championship Years)	.50
75	Spud Chandler/1943 (The Championship Years)	.15
76	Tommy Henrich/1947 (The Championship Years)	.15
77	Phil Rizzuto/1949 (The Championship Years)	.25
78	Whitey Ford/1950 (The Championship Years)	.25
79	Yogi Berra/1951 (The Championship Years)	.40
80	Casey Stengel/1952 (The Championship Years)	.15
81	Billy Martin/1953 (The Championship Years)	.25
82	Don Larsen/1956 (The Championship Years)	.25
83	Elston Howard/1958 (The Championship Years)	.15
84	Roger Maris/1961 (The Championship Years)	.50
85	Mickey Mantle/1962 (The Championship Years)	1.00
86	Reggie Jackson/1977 (The Championship Years)	.50
87	Bucky Dent/1978 (The Championship Years)	.15
88	Wade Boggs/1996 (The Championship Years)	.25
89	Joe Torre/1998 (The Championship Years)	.25
90	Joe Torre/1999 (The Championship Years)	.25

DiMaggio Memorabilia

		NM/M
YLB-JD	Joe DiMaggio/Bat	125.00

YLG-JD	Joe DiMaggio/ Gold Bat/56	200.00
YLC-JD	Joe DiMaggio/ Bat, Cut Sig./5	650.00

Legendary Lumber

		NM/M
Common Player:		5.00
Inserted 1:23		
HB	Hank Bauer	8.00
YB	Yogi Berra	20.00
PB	Paul Blair	5.00
CB	Clete Boyer	5.00
CC	Chris Chambliss	8.00
JC	Joe Collins	5.00
BD	Bucky Dent	8.00
JD	Joe DiMaggio	140.00
OG	Oscar Gamble	5.00
BG	Billy Gardner	5.00
TH	Tommy Henrich	5.00
RH	Ralph Houk	8.00
EH	Elston Howard	8.00
RJ	Reggie Jackson	20.00
TJ	Tommy John	8.00
CJ	Cliff Johnson	5.00
CK	Charlie Keller	5.00
TK	Tony Kubek	8.00
HL	Hector Lopez	5.00
MM	Mickey Mantle	165.00
RM	Roger Maris	70.00
DM	Don Mattingly	45.00
TM	Thurman Munson	35.00
BM	Bobby Murcer	8.00
GN	Graig Nettles	10.00
JP	Joe Pepitone	6.00
WR	Willie Randolph	6.00
MR	Mickey Rivers	5.00
BR	Babe Ruth	185.00
MS	Moose Skowron	6.00
DW	Dave Winfield	15.00

Leg. Lumber/Sign. Cut

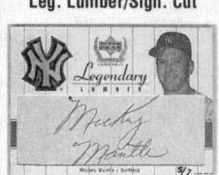

		NM/M
MM-LC	Mickey Mantle/7	4,000

Legendary Pinstripes

		NM/M
Common Player:		20.00
Inserted 1:144		
BD	Bucky Dent	20.00
WF	Whitey Ford	50.00
LG	Lou Gehrig	300.00
GG	Goose Gossage	20.00
RG	Ron Guidry	20.00
TH	Tommy Henrich	20.00
EH	Elston Howard	20.00
RJ	Reggie Jackson	40.00
HL	Hector Lopez	20.00
MM	Mickey Mantle	250.00
RM	Roger Maris	75.00
BM	Billy Martin	40.00
DM	Don Mattingly	60.00
TM	Thurman Munson	75.00
JP	Joe Pepitone	20.00
AR	Allie Reynolds	20.00
BR	Bobby Richardson	20.00
PR	Phil Rizzuto	40.00
DW	Dave Winfield	40.00

Auto. Legend. Pinstripe

		NM/M
Common Player:		30.00
BD	Bucky Dent	30.00
WF	Whitey Ford	60.00
GG	Goose Gossage	30.00
RG	Ron Guidry	35.00
TH	Tommy Henrich	30.00
GM	Gil MacDougald	30.00
DM	Don Mattingly	150.00
JP	Joe Pepitone	30.00
PR	Phil Rizzuto	60.00
DW	Dave Winfield	35.00

Monument Park

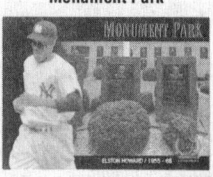

		NM/M
Complete Set (6):		20.00
Common Player:		3.00
Inserted 1:23		
1	Lou Gehrig	6.00
2	Babe Ruth	6.00
3	Mickey Mantle	6.00
4	Joe DiMaggio	6.00
5	Thurman Munson	3.00
6	Elston Howard	1.50

Murderer's Row

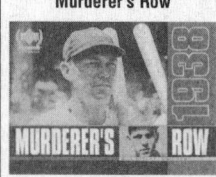

		NM/M
Complete Set (10):		17.50
Common Player:		1.50
Inserted 1:11		
1	Tony Lazzeri	1.50
2	Babe Ruth	6.00
3	Bob Meusel	1.50
4	Lou Gehrig	6.00
5	Joe Dugan	1.50
6	Bill Dickey	1.50
7	Waite Hoyt	1.50
8	Red Ruffing	1.50
9	Earl Combes	1.50
10	Lefty Gomez	1.50

Pride of the Pinstripes

		NM/M
Complete Set (6):		17.50
Common Player:		2.50
Inserted 1:23		
1	Babe Ruth	6.00
2	Mickey Mantle	5.00
3	Joe DiMaggio	5.00
4	Lou Gehrig	5.00
5	Reggie Jackson	2.50
6	Yogi Berra	2.50

The Golden Years

		NM/M
Complete Set (10):		20.00
Common Player:		1.50

Inserted 1:11
1	Joe DiMaggio	6.00
2	Phil Rizzuto	2.50
3	Yogi Berra	3.00
4	Billy Martin	2.50
5	Whitey Ford	2.50
6	Roger Maris	5.00
7	Mickey Mantle	7.50
8	Elston Howard	1.50
9	Tommy Henrich	1.50
10	Joe Gordon	1.50

The New Dynasty

	NM/M
Complete Set (10):	15.00
Common Player:	1.50

Inserted 1:11
1	Reggie Jackson	3.50
2	Graig Nettles	1.50
3	Don Mattingly	6.50
4	Goose Gossage	1.50
5	Dave Winfield	3.00
6	Chris Chambliss	1.50
7	Thurman Munson	4.00
8	Willie Randolph	1.50
9	Ron Guidry	2.50
10	Bucky Dent	2.50

22kt Gold Ken Griffey Jr. Rookie Card

A 22-karat gold embossed card replicating in all important details the 1989 Upper Deck Ken Griffey Jr. rookie card was issued by UD. The card was accompanied by a commemorative collectors' sheet describing the original rookie card and the gold version. The gold card was offered to members of UD's Collectors Club for $24.

	NM/M
1	Ken Griffey Jr.	24.00

2001 Upper Deck

	NM/M
Complete Set (450):	125.00
Complete Series 1 (270):	25.00
Complete Series 2 (180):	100.00
Common Player:	.15
Series 1 Pack (10):	2.00
Series 1 Box (24):	35.00
Series 2 Pack (10):	6.00
Series 2 Box (24):	120.00
1	Jeff DaVanon (Star Rookie)	.25
2	Aubrey Huff (Star Rookie)	.25
3	Pascual Coco (Star Rookie)	.25
4	Barry Zito (Star Rookie)	.75
5	Augie Ojeda (Star Rookie)	.25
6	Chris Richard (Star Rookie)	.25
7	Josh Phelps (Star Rookie)	.25
8	Kevin Nicholson (Star Rookie)	.25

9	Juan Guzman (Star Rookie)	.25
10	Brandon Kolb (Star Rookie)	.25
11	Johan Santana (Star Rookie)	4.00
12	Josh Kalinowski (Star Rookie)	.25
13	Tike Redman (Star Rookie)	.25
14	Ivanon Coffie (Star Rookie)	.25
15	Chad Durbin (Star Rookie)	.25
16	Derrick Turnbow (Star Rookie)	.25
17	Scott Downs (Star Rookie)	.25
18	Jason Grilli (Star Rookie)	.25
19	Mark Buehrle (Star Rookie)	.25
20	Paxton Crawford (Star Rookie)	.25
21	Bronson Arroyo (Star Rookie)	.25
22	Tomas de la Rosa (Star Rookie)	.25
23	Paul Rigdon (Star Rookie)	.25
24	Rob Ramsay (Star Rookie)	.25
25	Damian Rolls (Star Rookie)	.25
26	Jason Conti (Star Rookie)	.25
27	John Parrish (Star Rookie)	.25
28	Geraldo Guzman (Star Rookie)	.25
29	Tony Mota (Star Rookie)	.25
30	Luis Rivas (Star Rookie)	.25
31	Brian Tollberg (Star Rookie)	.25
32	Adam Bernero (Star Rookie)	.25
33	Michael Cuddyer (Star Rookie)	.25
34	Josue Espada (Star Rookie)	.25
35	Joe Lawrence (Star Rookie)	.25
36	Chad Moeller (Star Rookie)	.25
37	Nick Bierbrodt (Star Rookie)	.25
38	Dewayne Wise (Star Rookie)	.25
39	Javier Cardona (Star Rookie)	.25
40	Hiram Bocachica (Star Rookie)	.25
41	Giuseppe Chiaramonte (Star Rookie)	.25
42	Alex Cabrera (Star Rookie)	.25
43	Jimmy Rollins (Star Rookie)	1.00
44	Pat Flury RC (Star Rookie)	.25
45	Leo Estrella (Star Rookie)	.25
46	Darin Erstad	.40
47	Seth Etherton	.15
48	Troy Glaus	.40
49	Brian Cooper	.15
50	Tim Salmon	.25
51	Adam Kennedy	.15
52	Bengie Molina	.15
53	Jason Giambi	.50
54	Miguel Tejada	.40
55	Tim Hudson	.25
56	Eric Chavez	.25
57	Terrence Long	.15
58	Jason Isringhausen	.15
59	Ramon Hernandez	.15
60	Raul Mondesi	.25
61	David Wells	.15
62	Shannon Stewart	.15
63	Tony Batista	.15
64	Brad Fullmer	.15
65	Chris Carpenter	.15
66	Homer Bush	.15
67	Gerald Williams	.15
68	Miguel Cairo	.15
69	Ryan Rupe	.15
70	Greg Vaughn	.15
71	John Flaherty	.15
72	Dan Wheeler	.15
73	Fred McGriff	.25
74	Roberto Alomar	.40
75	Bartolo Colon	.25
76	Kenny Lofton	.25
77	David Segui	.15
78	Omar Vizquel	.25
79	Russ Branyan	.15
80	Chuck Finley	.15
81	Manny Ramirez	.50
82	Alex Rodriguez	1.50
83	John Halama	.15
84	Mike Cameron	.15
85	David Bell	.15
86	Jay Buhner	.15
87	Aaron Sele	.15
88	Rickey Henderson	.40
89	Brook Fordyce	.15
90	Cal Ripken Jr.	2.00
91	Mike Mussina	.40
92	Delino DeShields	.15
93	Melvin Mora	.15
94	Sidney Ponson	.15
95	Brady Anderson	.15
96	Ivan Rodriguez	.50
97	Ricky Ledee	.15
98	Rick Helling	.15

99	Ruben Mateo	.15
100	Luis Alicea	.15
101	John Wetteland	.15
102	Mike Lamb	.15
103	Carl Everett	.15
104	Troy O'Leary	.15
105	Wilton Veras	.15
106	Pedro Martinez	.75
107	Rolando Arrojo	.15
108	Scott Hatteberg	.15
109	Jason Varitek	.15
110	Jose Offerman	.15
111	Carlos Beltran	.50
112	Johnny Damon	.50
113	Mark Quinn	.15
114	Rey Sanchez	.15
115	Mac Suzuki	.15
116	Jermaine Dye	.25
117	Chris Fussell	.15
118	Jeff Weaver	.15
119	Dean Palmer	.15
120	Robert Fick	.15
121	Brian Moehler	.15
122	Damion Easley	.15
123	Juan Encarnacion	.15
124	Tony Clark	.15
125	Cristian Guzman	.15
126	Matt LeCroy	.15
127	Eric Milton	.15
128	Jay Canizaro	.15
129	David Ortiz	.75
130	Brad Radke	.15
131	Jacque Jones	.15
132	Magglio Ordonez	.40
133	Carlos Lee	.25
134	Mike Sirotka	.15
135	Ray Durham	.15
136	Paul Konerko	.25
137	Charles Johnson	.15
138	James Baldwin	.15
139	Jeff Abbott	.15
140	Roger Clemens	1.50
141	Derek Jeter	2.00
142	David Justice	.25
143	Ramiro Mendoza	.15
144	Chuck Knoblauch	.15
145	Orlando Hernandez	.25
146	Alfonso Soriano	.75
147	Jeff Bagwell	.50
148	Julio Lugo	.15
149	Mitch Meluskey	.15
150	Jose Lima	.15
151	Richard Hidalgo	.15
152	Moises Alou	.25
153	Scott Elarton	.15
154	Andruw Jones	.40
155	Quilvio Veras	.15
156	Greg Maddux	1.00
157	Brian Jordan	.15
158	Andres Galarraga	.20
159	Kevin Millwood	.25
160	Rafael Furcal	.25
161	Jeromy Burnitz	.15
162	Jimmy Haynes	.15
163	Mark Loretta	.15
164	Ron Belliard	.15
165	Richie Sexson	.15
166	Kevin Barker	.15
167	Jeff D'Amico	.15
168	Rick Ankiel	.50
169	Mark McGwire	1.50
170	J.D. Drew	.25
171	Eli Marrero	.15
172	Darryl Kile	.15
173	Edgar Renteria	.15
174	Will Clark	.40
175	Eric Young	.15
176	Mark Grace	.40
177	Jon Lieber	.15
178	Damon Buford	.15
179	Kerry Wood	.40
180	Rondell White	.15
181	Joe Girardi	.15
182	Curt Schilling	.40
183	Randy Johnson	.75
184	Steve Finley	.15
185	Kelly Stinnett	.15
186	Jay Bell	.15
187	Matt Mantei	.15
188	Luis Gonzalez	.25
189	Shawn Green	.25
190	Todd Hundley	.15
191	Chan Ho Park	.40
192	Adrian Beltre	.40
193	Mark Grudzielanek	.15
194	Gary Sheffield	.40
195	Tom Goodwin	.15
196	Lee Stevens	.15
197	Javier Vazquez	.15
198	Milton Bradley	.15
199	Vladimir Guerrero	.75
200	Carl Pavano	.15
201	Orlando Cabrera	.15
202	Tony Armas Jr.	.15
203	Jeff Kent	.25
204	Calvin Murray	.15
205	Ellis Burks	.15
206	Barry Bonds	2.00
207	Russ Ortiz	.15
208	Marvin Benard	.15
209	Joe Nathan	.15
210	Preston Wilson	.15
211	Cliff Floyd	.15
212	Mike Lowell	.15
213	Ryan Dempster	.15
214	Brad Penny	.15
215	Mike Redmond	.15
216	Luis Castillo	.15

217	Derek Bell	.15
218	Mike Hampton	.25
219	Todd Zeile	.15
220	Robin Ventura	.25
221	Mike Piazza	1.00
222	Al Leiter	.25
223	Edgardo Alfonzo	.15
224	Mike Bordick	.15
225	Phil Nevin	.15
226	Ryan Klesko	.25
227	Adam Eaton	.25
228	Eric Owens	.15
229	Tony Gwynn	.75
230	Matt Clement	.15
231	Wiki Gonzalez	.15
232	Robert Person	.15
233	Doug Glanville	.15
234	Scott Rolen	.50
235	Mike Lieberthal	.15
236	Randy Wolf	.15
237	Bobby Abreu	.40
238	Pat Burrell	.40
239	Bruce Chen	.15
240	Kevin Young	.15
241	Todd Ritchie	.15
242	Adrian Brown	.15
243	Chad Hermansen	.15
244	Warren Morris	.15
245	Kris Benson	.15
246	Jason Kendall	.25
247	Pokey Reese	.15
248	Rob Bell	.15
249	Ken Griffey Jr.	1.00
250	Sean Casey	.15
251	Aaron Boone	.15
252	Pete Harnisch	.15
253	Barry Larkin	.40
254	Dmitri Young	.15
255	Todd Hollandsworth	.15
256	Pedro Astacio	.15
257	Todd Helton	.50
258	Terry Shumpert	.15
259	Neifi Perez	.15
260	Jeffrey Hammonds	.15
261	Ben Petrick	.15
262	Mark McGwire	.75
263	Derek Jeter	1.00
264	Sammy Sosa	.75
265	Cal Ripken Jr.	1.00
266	Pedro J. Martinez	.40
267	Barry Bonds	1.00
268	Fred McGriff	.20
269	Randy Johnson	.40
270	Darin Erstad	.25
271	Ichiro Suzuki RC (Star Rookie)	10.00
272	Wilson Betemit RC (Star Rookie)	.50
273	Corey Patterson (Star Rookie)	.25
274	Sean Douglass RC (Star Rookie)	.25
275	Mike Penney RC (Star Rookie)	.25
276	Nate Teut RC (Star Rookie)	.25
277	Ricardo Rodriguez RC (Star Rookie)	.25
278	Brandon Duckworth RC (Star Rookie)	.50
279	Rafael Soriano RC (Star Rookie)	.75
280	Juan Diaz RC (Star Rookie)	.25
281	Horacio Ramirez RC (Star Rookie)	.50
282	Tsuyoshi Shinjo RC (Star Rookie)	.50
283	Keith Ginter (Star Rookie)	.25
284	Esix Snead RC (Star Rookie)	.25
285	Erick Almonte RC (Star Rookie)	.25
286	Travis Hafner RC (Star Rookie)	2.00
287	Jason Smith RC (Star Rookie)	.25
288	Jackson Melian RC (Star Rookie)	.25
289	Tyler Walker RC (Star Rookie)	.25
290	Jason Standridge RC (Star Rookie)	.25
291	Juan Uribe RC (Star Rookie)	.50
292	Adrian Hernandez RC (Star Rookie)	.25
293	Jason Michaels RC (Star Rookie)	.25
294	Jason Hart (Star Rookie)	.15
295	Albert Pujols RC (Star Rookie)	40.00
296	Morgan Ensberg RC (Star Rookie)	.50
297	Brandon Inge (Star Rookie)	.25
298	Jesus Colome (Star Rookie)	.25
299	Kyle Kessel RC (Star Rookie)	.25
300	Timo Perez (Star Rookie)	.25
301	Mo Vaughn	.25
302	Ismael Valdes	.15
303	Glenallen Hill	.15
304	Garret Anderson	.40
305	Johnny Damon	.25
306	Jose Ortiz	.15
307	Mark Mulder	.25

308	Adam Piatt	.15
309	Gil Heredia	.15
310	Mike Sirotka	.15
311	Carlos Delgado	.50
312	Alex Gonzalez	.15
313	Jose Cruz Jr.	.15
314	Darrin Fletcher	.15
315	Ben Grieve	.15
316	Vinny Castilla	.15
317	Wilson Alvarez	.15
318	Brent Abernathy	.15
319	Ellis Burks	.15
320	Jim Thome	.75
321	Juan Gonzalez	.50
322	Ed Taubensee	.15
323	Travis Fryman	.15
324	John Olerud	.25
325	Edgar Martinez	.25
326	Fred Garcia	.25
327	Bret Boone	.25
328	Kazuhiro Sasaki	.25
329	Albert Belle	.15
330	Mike Bordick	.15
331	David Segui	.15
332	Pat Hentgen	.15
333	Alex Rodriguez	1.50
334	Andres Galarraga	.25
335	Gabe Kapler	.15
336	Ken Caminiti	.15
337	Rafael Palmeiro	.50
338	Manny Ramirez	.50
339	David Cone	.15
340	Nomar Garciaparra	.75
341	Trot Nixon	.15
342	Derek Lowe	.15
343	Roberto Hernandez	.15
344	Mike Sweeney	.25
345	Carlos Febles	.15
346	Jeff Suppan	.15
347	Roger Cedeno	.15
348	Bobby Higginson	.15
349	Deivi Cruz	.15
350	Mitch Meluskey	.15
351	Matt Lawton	.15
352	Mark Redman	.15
353	Jay Canizaro	.15
354	Corey Koskie	.15
355	Matt Kinney	.15
356	Frank Thomas	.50
357	Sandy Alomar Jr.	.15
358	David Wells	.15
359	Jim Parque	.15
360	Chris Singleton	.15
361	Tino Martinez	.25
362	Paul O'Neill	.25
363	Mike Mussina	.40
364	Bernie Williams	.50
365	Andy Pettitte	.40
366	Mariano Rivera	.40
367	Brad Ausmus	.15
368	Craig Biggio	.40
369	Lance Berkman	.50
370	Shane Reynolds	.15
371	Chipper Jones	1.00
372	Tom Glavine	.40
373	B.J. Surhoff	.15
374	John Smoltz	.40
375	Rico Brogna	.15
376	Geoff Jenkins	.15
377	Jose Hernandez	.15
378	Tyler Houston	.15
379	Henry Blanco	.15
380	Jeffrey Hammonds	.15
381	Jim Edmonds	.25
382	Fernando Vina	.15
383	Andy Benes	.15
384	Ray Lankford	.15
385	Dustin Hermanson	.15
386	Todd Hundley	.15
387	Sammy Sosa	.75
388	Tom Gordon	.15
389	Bill Mueller	.15
390	Ron Coomer	.15
391	Matt Stairs	.15
392	Mark Grace	.40
393	Matt Williams	.25
394	Todd Stottlemyre	.15
395	Tony Womack	.15
396	Erubiel Durazo	.15
397	Reggie Sanders	.15
398	Andy Ashby	.15
399	Eric Karros	.15
400	Kevin Brown	.25
401	Darren Dreifort	.15
402	Fernando Tatis	.15
403	Jose Vidro	.15
404	Peter Bergeron	.15
405	Geoff Blum	.15
406	J.T. Snow	.15
407	Livan Hernandez	.15
408	Robb Nen	.15
409	Bobby Estalella	.15
410	Rich Aurilia	.15
411	Eric Davis	.15
412	Charles Johnson	.15
413	Alex Gonzalez	.15
414	A.J. Burnett	.15
415	Antonio Alfonseca	.15
416	Derrek Lee	.50
417	Jay Payton	.15
418	Kevin Appier	.15
419	Steve Trachsel	.15
420	Rey Ordonez	.15
421	Darryl Hamilton	.15
422	Ben Davis	.15
423	Damian Jackson	.15
424	Mark Kotsay	.15
425	Trevor Hoffman	.15

426	Travis Lee	.15
427	Omar Daal	.15
428	Paul Byrd	.15
429	Reggie Taylor	.15
430	Brian Giles	.25
431	Derek Bell	.15
432	Francisco Cordova	.15
433	Pat Meares	.15
434	Scott Williamson	.15
435	Jason LaRue	.15
436	Michael Tucker	.15
437	Wilton Guerrero	.15
438	Mike Hampton	.15
439	Ron Gant	.15
440	Jeff Cirillo	.15
441	Denny Neagle	.15
442	Larry Walker	.40
443	Juan Pierre	.15
444	Todd Walker	.15
445	Jason Giambi	.40
446	Jeff Kent	.25
447	Mariano Rivera	.40
448	Edgar Martinez	.15
449	Troy Glaus	.25
450	Alex Rodriguez	.75

Exclusives

Silver Stars:	8-15X
Production 100 Sets	
Gold Stars:	15-30X
Production 25 Sets	

All-Star Heroes Base Cards

	NM/M
Quantity Produced Listed	
DJ	Derek Jeter/2000	20.00
MP	Mike Piazza/1996	10.00

All-Star Heroes Bat Cards

		NM/M
Common Player:		10.00
RoC	Roberto Clemente/1961	75.00
KG	Ken Griffey Jr./1992	20.00
TP	Tony Perez/1967	10.00
CR	Cal Ripken Jr./1991	40.00
AR	Alex Rodriguez/1998	20.00
BR	Babe Ruth/1933	175.00

All-Star Heroes Jersey Cards

		NM/M
Common Player:		10.00
RC	Roger Clemens/1986	20.00
JD	Joe DiMaggio/36	300.00
TG	Tony Gwynn/1994	10.00
RJ	Randy Johnson/1993	10.00
ASH-MM	Mickey Mantle/54	400.00
ASH-SS	Sammy Sosa/2000	10.00

All-Star Salute

		NM/M
Common Player:		10.00
Inserted 1:288		
HA	Hank Aaron/Bat	40.00
HA	Hank Aaron/Jsy	40.00
LA	Luis Aparicio/Jsy	15.00
JB	Johnny Bench/Bat	20.00
JB	Johnny Bench/Jsy	20.00
LB	Lou Brock/Bat	15.00
RC	Roberto Clemente/Jsy	100.00
RJ	Reggie Jackson/Jsy	20.00
TM	Thurman Munson/Jsy	35.00
BR	Brooks Robinson/Bat	20.00
FR	Frank Robinson/Jsy	20.00
TS	Tom Seaver/Jsy	20.00

Big League Beat

	NM/M
Complete Set (20):	15.00
Common Player:	.50
Inserted 1:3	
1	Barry Bonds	2.00
2	Nomar Garciaparra	.75
3	Mark McGwire	1.50
4	Roger Clemens	1.25

Ramirez helps Tribe turn back Bucs

Bases-Loaded Bomber   RBI Champion

		NM/M
5	Chipper Jones	1.00
6	Jeff Bagwell	.50
7	Sammy Sosa	1.00
8	Cal Ripken Jr.	2.00
9	Randy Johnson	.75
10	Carlos Delgado	.50
11	Manny Ramirez	.50
12	Derek Jeter	2.00
13	Tony Gwynn	.75
14	Pedro J. Martinez	.75
15	Jose Canseco	.50
16	Frank Thomas	.75
17	Alex Rodriguez	1.50
18	Bernie Williams	.50
19	Greg Maddux	1.00
20	Rafael Palmeiro	.50

Big League Challenge Jerseys

		NM/M
	Common Player:	5.00
	Inserted 1:288	
BB	Barry Bonds	40.00
JC	Jose Canseco	8.00
JE	Jim Edmonds	8.00
TF	Steve Finley	5.00
TG	Troy Glaus	8.00
TH	Todd Helton	10.00
RH	Richard Hidalgo	5.00
RP	Rafael Palmeiro	10.00
MP	Mike Piazza	20.00
GS	Gary Sheffield	8.00
FT	Frank Thomas	10.00

Classic Midsummer Moments

PEDRO MARTINEZ MIDSUMMER CLASSIC MOMENTS RED SOX

		NM/M
	Complete Set (20):	25.00
	Common Player:	.50
	Inserted 1:12	
CM1	Joe DiMaggio/1936	3.00
CM2	Joe DiMaggio/1951	3.00
CM3	Mickey Mantle/1952	4.00
CM4	Mickey Mantle/1968	4.00
CM5	Roger Clemens/1986	2.50
CM6	Mark McGwire/1987	2.50
CM7	Cal Ripken Jr./1991	1.50
CM8	Ken Griffey Jr./1992	1.50
CM9	Randy Johnson/1993	1.00
CM10	Tony Gwynn/1994	1.00
CM11	Fred McGriff/1994	.50
CM12	Hideo Nomo/1995	.75
CM13	Jeff Conine/1995	.50
CM14	Mike Piazza/1996	1.50
CM15	Sandy Alomar Jr./1997	.50
CM16	Alex Rodriguez/1998	.75
CM17	Roberto Alomar/1998	.75
CM18	Pedro Martinez/1999	.50
CM19	Andres Galarraga/2000	.50
CM20	Derek Jeter/2000	2.50

2001 Upper Deck Joe DiMaggio Bat Cards - Hawaii

Joe DiMaggio

Three special Joe DiMaggio bat-piece cards were created by Upper Deck for distribution at the 2001 Hawaii trade show. Most cards have a photo of the player

on left-front with a small piece of game-used bat, either the "NY" logo or the surrounding area. These cards are numbered on back within an edition of 450 pieces. An even more limited card has both a bat piece and a cut-signature autograph on front, along with a small photo portrait. On back, these cards are numbered within an edition of just five.

		NM/M
KY-JD1	Joe DiMaggio (Bat Piece/Auto.)	2,250
KY-JD2	Joe DiMaggio (Bat piece.)	125.00

2001 Upper Deck e-Card

e-Card 33X884977

		NM/M
	Complete Set (6):	10.00
	Common Player:	1.00
	Inserted 1:12	
1	Andruw Jones	1.00
2	Alex Rodriguez	3.00
3	Frank Thomas	1.50
4	Todd Helton	1.50
5	Troy Glaus	1.00
6	Barry Bonds	4.00

Game Jersey

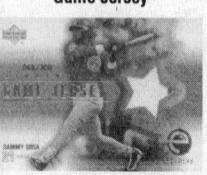

GAME JERSEY

Because of the addition of Suzuki and Sosa cards after the initial checklist was promulgated by Upper Deck, and the possibility that cards on the initial list may have been deleted, the accuracy of this list cannot be verified. Card numbers have an "EJ-" prefix. Production was reported as 300 of each card.

		NM/M
	Common Player:	10.00
BB	Barry Bonds	30.00
TG	Troy Glaus	8.00
TH	Todd Helton	10.00
AJ	Andruw Jones	10.00
AR	Alex Rodriguez	25.00
SS	Sammy Sosa	15.00
IS	Ichiro Suzuki	50.00
FT	Frank Thomas	15.00

Game Jersey Autograph

Because of the addition of Suzuki and Sosa cards after the initial checklist was promulgated by Upper Deck, and the possibility that cards on the initial list may have been deleted, the accuracy of this list cannot be verified. Cards have an "ESJ-" prefix. The edition is limited to 50 numbered cards each.

		NM/M
	Common Player:	50.00
BB	Barry Bonds	150.00
TG	Troy Glaus	40.00
TH	Todd Helton	50.00
AJ	Andruw Jones	25.00
AR	Alex Rodriguez	120.00
SS	Sammy Sosa	100.00
IS	Ichiro Suzuki	300.00
FT	Frank Thomas	75.00

Evolve Signature

Because of the addition of Suzuki and Sosa cards after the initial checklist was promulgated by Upper Deck, and the possibility that cards on the initial list may have been deleted, the accuracy of this list cannot be verified. Cards

102/200

have an "ES-" prefix to their number. Production was reported as 200 of each card.

		NM/M
	Common Player:	35.00
BB	Barry Bonds	150.00
TG	Troy Glaus	30.00
TH	Todd Helton	30.00
AJ	Andruw Jones	25.00
AR	Alex Rodriguez	100.00
SS	Sammy Sosa	80.00
IS	Ichiro Suzuki	250.00
FT	Frank Thomas	40.00

Game Jersey

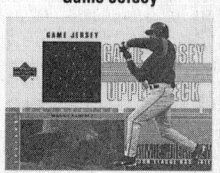

GAME JERSEY

		NM/M
	Common Player:	8.00
	Inserted 1:288	
KG	Ken Griffey Jr.	30.00
TG	Tony Gwynn	20.00
TH	Todd Helton	12.00
TiH	Tim Hudson	10.00
DJ	Derek Jeter	50.00
AJ	Andruw Jones	8.00
SK	Sandy Koufax	100.00
PO	Paul O'Neill	10.00
MR	Manny Ramirez	10.00
CR	Cal Ripken Jr.	60.00
AR	Alex Rodriguez	40.00
IR	Ivan Rodriguez	10.00
NRa	Nolan Ryan	65.00
NRr	Nolan Ryan	65.00
FT	Fernando Tatis	8.00
RV	Robin Ventura	8.00
BW	Bernie Williams	10.00
MW	Matt Williams	8.00

Game Jersey Autograph

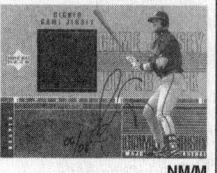

		NM/M
	Print runs listed.	
KG	Ken Griffey/30	150.00
RA	Rick Ankiel/66	40.00
SK	Sandy Koufax/32	900.00
NRa	Nolan Ryan/Mets/30	150.00
NRr	Nolan Ryan/Angels/30	150.00

Game Jersey Auto. Series 2

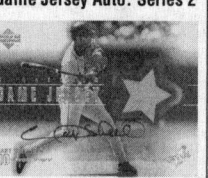

GAME JERSEY

		NM/M
	Common Player:	30.00
	Inserted 1:288 H	
JB	Johnny Bench	50.00
BB	Barry Bonds	150.00
JC	Jose Canseco	30.00
RC	Roger Clemens	100.00
TG	Troy Glaus	30.00
KG	Ken Griffey Jr.	100.00
AJ	Andruw Jones	30.00
CJ	Chipper Jones	50.00
CR	Cal Ripken Jr./SP	200.00
AR	Alex Rodriguez	100.00
IR	Ivan Rodriguez/SP	75.00
NR	Nolan Ryan	150.00
GS	Gary Sheffield	30.00
SS	Sammy Sosa/SP	100.00

Game Jersey Hobby Autograph

		NM/M
	Common Player:	15.00
	Inserted 1:288	
RA	Rick Ankiel	40.00
JB	Jeff Bagwell	40.00
BB	Barry Bonds	150.00
JC	Jose Canseco	40.00
SC	Sean Casey	20.00

		NM/M
JD	J.D. Drew	30.00
JG	Jason Giambi	30.00
SG	Shawn Green	20.00
KG	Ken Griffey Jr.	100.00
MH	Mike Hampton	20.00
RJ	Randy Johnson	75.00
JL	Javy Lopez	20.00
GM	Greg Maddux	125.00
RP	Rafael Palmeiro	40.00
AR	Alex Rodriguez	125.00
NRm	Nolan Ryan	125.00
NRa	Nolan Ryan	125.00
FT	Frank Thomas	50.00

Game Jersey Combo

COMBO GAME JERSEY

		NM/M
	Production 50 Sets	
BB-KG	Barry Bonds, Ken Griffey Jr.	100.00
IR-RP	Ivan Rodriguez, Rafael Palmeiro	25.00
DJ-AR	Derek Jeter, Alex Rodriguez	100.00
MM-KG	Mickey Mantle, Ken Griffey Jr.	250.00
TG-CR	Tony Gwynn, Cal Ripken Jr.	100.00
NR-AR	Nolan Ryan Astros/ Rangers	100.00
NR-MA	Nolan Ryan Mets/ Astros	100.00
RJ-GM	Randy Johnson, Greg Maddux	50.00
VG-MR	Vladimir Guerrero, Manny Ramirez	40.00
BB-JC	Barry Bonds, Jose Canseco	80.00
FT-JB	Frank Thomas, Jeff Bagwell	40.00
AJ-KG	Andruw Jones, Ken Griffey Jr.	60.00

Game Jersey Combo Autograph

Production 10 Sets
Values Undetermined

Game Jersey Patch

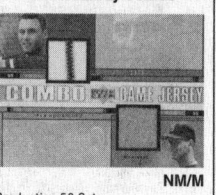

		NM/M
	Common Player:	40.00
	Production 25 Sets	
RA	Rick Ankiel	40.00
JB	Jeff Bagwell	50.00
BB	Barry Bonds	125.00
JC	Jose Canseco	50.00
JG	Jason Giambi	50.00
KG	Ken Griffey Jr.	75.00
TG	Tony Gwynn	75.00
DJ	Derek Jeter	125.00
RP	Rafael Palmeiro	50.00
CR	Cal Ripken Jr.	150.00
AR	Alex Rodriguez	100.00
IR	Ivan Rodriguez	50.00
NRa	Nolan Ryan	150.00
NRr	Nolan Ryan	150.00
FT	Frank Thomas	60.00

Game Jersey Patch Gold

		NM/M
	Production 25 Sets	
BB	Barry Bonds	100.00
JC	Jose Canseco	40.00
JG	Jason Giambi	50.00
KG	Ken Griffey Jr.	120.00
TG	Tony Gwynn	60.00
DJ	Derek Jeter	150.00
CR	Cal Ripken Jr.	150.00

		NM/M
NRa	Nolan Ryan	150.00
NRr	Nolan Ryan	150.00
FT	Frank Thomas	75.00

Game Jersey Patch Autograph

		NM/M
	Print runs listed.	
RA	Rick Ankiel /66	75.00
KG	Ken Griffey Jr /30	400.00

Game-Used Ball

GAME USED BALL 25

		NM/M
	Common Player:	8.00
	Production 100 Sets	
RA	Rick Ankiel	15.00
JB	Jeff Bagwell	15.00
BB	Barry Bonds	30.00
JG	Jason Giambi	10.00
SG	Shawn Green	8.00
KG	Ken Griffey Jr.	30.00
ToG	Tony Gwynn	20.00
DJ	Derek Jeter	40.00
RJ	Randy Johnson	10.00
AJ	Andruw Jones	10.00
MM	Mark McGwire	25.00
AR	Alex Rodriguez	30.00
IR	Ivan Rodriguez	10.00
SS	Sammy Sosa	15.00

Game-Used Ball Series 2

GAME USED BALL

		NM/M
	Common Player:	5.00
	Inserted 1:288	
JB	Jeff Bagwell	10.00
BB	Barry Bonds	30.00
RC	Roger Clemens	15.00
NG	Nomar Garciaparra	10.00
KG	Ken Griffey Jr.	20.00
VG	Vladimir Guerrero	10.00
DJ	Derek Jeter	30.00
AJ	Andruw Jones	8.00
CJ	Chipper Jones	15.00
JK	Jeff Kent	5.00
MM	Mark McGwire	20.00
MP	Mike Piazza	20.00
CR	Cal Ripken Jr.	25.00
MR	Mariano Rivera	10.00
AR	Alex Rodriguez	20.00
GS	Gary Sheffield	8.00
SS	Sammy Sosa	15.00
BW	Bernie Williams	8.00

Game-Used Ball Autographs

		NM/M
	Production 25 Sets	
RA	Rick Ankiel	40.00
JB	Jeff Bagwell	60.00
BB	Barry Bonds	150.00
JG	Jason Giambi	40.00
KG	Ken Griffey Jr.	90.00
SG	Shawn Green	40.00
TH	Todd Helton	40.00
RJ	Randy Johnson	75.00
AR	Alex Rodriguez	80.00

Home Run Explosion

		NM/M
	Complete Set (15):	20.00
	Common Player:	.50
	Inserted 1:12	
1	Mark McGwire	2.50
2	Chipper Jones	2.00
3	Jeff Bagwell	1.00
4	Carlos Delgado	1.00
5	Barry Bonds	3.00
6	Troy Glaus	2.00
7	Sammy Sosa	2.50

		NM/M
8	Alex Rodriguez	3.00
9	Mike Piazza	2.00
10	Vladimir Guerrero	1.50
11	Ken Griffey Jr.	2.00
12	Frank Thomas	1.00
13	Ivan Rodriguez	1.00
14	Jason Giambi	1.00
15	Carl Everett	.50

Home Run Derby Heroes

		NM/M
	Complete Set (10):	25.00
	Common Player:	1.00
	Inserted 1:36	
HD1	Mark McGwire/1999	2.50
HD2	Sammy Sosa/2000	3.00
HD3	Frank Thomas/1996	2.00
HD4	Cal Ripken Jr./1991	5.00
HD5	Tino Martinez/1997	1.00
HD6	Ken Griffey Jr./1999	3.00
HD7	Barry Bonds/1996	3.00
HD8	Albert Belle/1995	1.00
HD9	Mark McGwire/1992	2.00
HD10	Juan Gonzalez/1993	2.00

Midseason Superstar Summit

ALL-STAR GAME

		NM/M
	Complete Set (15):	25.00
	Common Player:	.75
	Inserted 1:24	
MS1	Derek Jeter	5.00
MS2	Sammy Sosa	3.00
MS3	Jeff Bagwell	1.50
MS4	Tony Gwynn	1.50
MS5	Alex Rodriguez	4.00
MS6	Greg Maddux	2.50
MS7	Jason Giambi	1.50
MS8	Mark McGwire	4.00
MS9	Barry Bonds	5.00
MS10	Ken Griffey Jr.	3.00
MS11	Carlos Delgado	1.00
MS12	Troy Glaus	1.00
MS13	Todd Helton	1.50
MS14	Manny Ramirez	1.50
MS15	Jeff Kent	.75

Most Wanted

MOST WANTED

		NM/M
	Complete Set (15):	20.00
	Common Player:	.75
	Inserted 1:14 Series 1	
MW1	Mark McGwire	2.50
MW2	Cal Ripken Jr.	3.00
MW3	Ivan Rodriguez	.75
MW4	Pedro Martinez	1.00
MW5	Sammy Sosa	1.00
MW6	Tony Gwynn	1.00
MW7	Vladimir Guerrero	1.00
MW8	Derek Jeter	3.00
MW9	Mike Piazza	2.00
MW10	Chipper Jones	1.50
MW11	Alex Rodriguez	2.50
MW12	Barry Bonds	2.50
MW13	Jeff Bagwell	1.00
MW14	Frank Thomas	1.00
MW15	Nomar Garciaparra	1.00

Rookie Roundup

		NM/M
Complete Set (10):		5.00
Common Player:		.50
Inserted 1:6		
1	Rick Ankiel	1.00
2	Adam Kennedy	.50
3	Mike Lamb	.50
4	Adam Eaton	.50
5	Rafael Furcal	1.00
6	Pat Burrell	1.50
7	Adam Piatt	.50
8	Eric Munson	.50
9	Brad Penny	.50
10	Mark Mulder	.75

2001 Upper Deck Subway Series Heroes - Hawaii

These cards were created for the Kit Young Hawaii trade show and were distributed on a one-per-day basis and as a complete set in a special engraved plexiglass frame measuring 8-1/2" x 6-7/8". Cards have black-and-white portrait or action photos. On a photo of a 1956 World Series scoreboard is a genuine autograph. Backs have career highlights, an authentication message, logos and are numbered from within an edition of 450 of each card.

		NM/M
Complete Set in Frame:		110.00
Complete Card Set (4):		75.00
Common Player:		20.00
KY-SS1	Don Larsen	20.00
KY-SS2	Whitey Ford	35.00
KY-SS3	Johnny Podres	20.00
KY-SS4	Duke Snider	35.00

Subway Series Jersey Cards

		NM/M
Common Player:		5.00
Inserted 1:144		
SS-EA	Edgardo Alfonzo	5.00
SS-RC	Roger Clemens	40.00
SS-JF	John Franco	5.00
SS-OH	Orlando Hernandez	8.00
SS-AL	Al Leiter	5.00
SS-PO	Paul O'Neill	10.00
SS-JP	Jay Payton	5.00
SS-TP	Timo Perez	5.00
SS-AP	Andy Pettitte	15.00
SS-BW	Bernie Williams	15.00

Superstar Summit

		NM/M
Complete Set (15):		25.00
Common Player:		1.00
Inserted 1:12		
1	Derek Jeter	4.00
2	Randy Johnson	1.50
3	Barry Bonds	4.00
4	Frank Thomas	1.00
5	Cal Ripken Jr.	4.00
6	Pedro J. Martinez	1.50
7	Ivan Rodriguez	1.00
8	Mike Piazza	2.00
9	Mark McGwire	3.00
10	Manny Ramirez	1.50
11	Ken Griffey Jr.	2.00
12	Sammy Sosa	2.50
13	Alex Rodriguez	3.00
14	Chipper Jones	2.00
15	Nomar Garciaparra	2.50

The Franchise

		NM/M
Complete Set (10):		25.00
Common Player:		1.50
Inserted 1:36		
F1	Frank Thomas	1.50
F2	Mark McGwire	5.00
F3	Ken Griffey Jr.	3.00
F4	Manny Ramirez	1.50
F5	Alex Rodriguez	5.00
F6	Greg Maddux	3.00
F7	Sammy Sosa	4.00
F8	Derek Jeter	6.00
F9	Mike Piazza	3.00
F10	Vladimir Guerrero	2.00

The People's Choice

		NM/M
Complete Set (15):		35.00
Common Player:		1.50
Inserted 1:24		
PC1	Alex Rodriguez	5.00
PC2	Ken Griffey Jr.	3.00
PC3	Mark McGwire	5.00
PC4	Todd Helton	1.50
PC5	Manny Ramirez	1.50
PC6	Mike Piazza	3.00
PC7	Vladimir Guerrero	2.00
PC8	Randy Johnson	2.00
PC9	Cal Ripken Jr.	6.00
PC10	Andruw Jones	1.50
PC11	Sammy Sosa	4.00
PC12	Derek Jeter	6.00
PC13	Pedro Martinez	2.00
PC14	Frank Thomas	1.50
PC15	Nomar Garciaparra	4.00

UD Game-Worn Patch

		NM/M
Common Player:		60.00
P-JB	Johnny Bench	120.00
P-BB	Barry Bonds	150.00
P-KG	Ken Griffey Jr.	100.00
P-CJ	Chipper Jones	60.00
P-CR	Cal Ripken Jr.	150.00
P-AR	Alex Rodriguez	125.00
P-IR	Ivan Rodriguez	60.00
P-NR	Nolan Ryan	150.00
P-SS	Sammy Sosa	100.00

2001 Upper Deck Cincinnati Reds Team Set

This boxed set has 20 player cards in standard 2-1/2" x 3-1/2" format and a 3-1/2" x 5" checklist/team history card. Cards have borderless action photos on front with an Upper Deck Collectibles logo at top-left. At bottom are the team and player name, position and uniform number. Backs have a smaller version of the front photo, to, some biographical and career notes and 1999-2000 stats. Cards are numbered with a "CR" prefix.

		NM/M
Complete Set (21):		7.50
Common Player:		.50
1	Ken Griffey Jr.	3.00
2	Dmitri Young	.50
3	Michael Tucker	.50
4	Aaron Boone	.75
5	Barry Larkin	1.00
6	Pokey Reese	.50
7	Sean Casey	1.00
8	Jason LaRue	.50
9	Scott Williamson	.50
10	Pete Harnisch	.50
11	Danny Graves	.50
12	Rob Bell	.50
13	Gookie Dawkins	.50
14	Kelly Stinnett	.50
15	Leo Estrella	.50
16	Wilton Guerrero	.50
17	Elmer Dessens	.65
18	Seth Etherton	.65
19	Donnie Sadler	.50
20	Scott Sullivan	.50
21	Checklist	.50

2001 Upper Deck Decade

		NM/M
Complete Set (180):		25.00
Common Player:		.15
Pack (5):		1.50
Box (24):		30.00
1	Nolan Ryan	3.00
2	Don Baylor	.15
3	Bobby Grich	.15
4	Reggie Jackson	.50
5	Jim "Catfish" Hunter	.25
6	Gene Tenace	.15
7	Rollie Fingers	.25
8	Sal Bando	.15
9	Bert Campaneris	.15
10	John Mayberry	.15
11	Rico Carty	.15
12	Gaylord Perry	.25
13	Andre Thornton	.15
14	Buddy Bell	.15
15	Dennis Eckersley	.25
16	Ruppert Jones	.15
17	Brooks Robinson	.75
18	Tommy Davis	.15
19	Eddie Murray	.25
20	Boog Powell	.15
21	Al Oliver	.15
22	Jeff Burroughs	.15
23	Mike Hargrove	.15
24	Dwight Evans	.15
25	Fred Lynn	.15
26	Rico Petrocelli	.15
27	Carlton Fisk	.50
28	Luis Aparicio	.15
29	Amos Otis	.15
30	Hal McRae	.15
31	Jason Thompson	.15
32	Al Kaline	.75
33	Jim Perry	.15
34	Bert Blyleven	.15
35	Harmon Killebrew	1.00
36	Wilbur Wood	.15
37	Jim Kaat	.15
38	Ron Guidry	.15
39	Thurman Munson	1.00
40	Graig Nettles	.15
41	Bobby Murcer	.15
42	Chris Chambliss	.15
43	Roy White	.15
44	J.R. Richard	.15
45	Jose Cruz	.15
46	Hank Aaron	2.00
47	Phil Niekro	.15
48	Bob Horner	.15
49	Darryl Evans	.15
50	Gorman Thomas	.15
51	Don Money	.15
52	Robin Yount	.75
53	Joe Torre	.25
54	Tim McCarver	.15
55	Lou Brock	.40
56	Keith Hernandez	.15
57	Bill Madlock	.15
58	Ron Santo	.15
59	Billy Williams	.15
60	Ferguson Jenkins	.25
61	Steve Garvey	.15
62	Bill Russell	.15
63	Maury Wills	.25
64	Ron Cey	.15
65	Manny Mota	.15
66	Ron Fairly	.15
67	Steve Rogers	.15
68	Gary Carter	.15
69	Andre Dawson	.25
70	Bobby Bonds	.25
71	Jack Clark	.15
72	Willie McCovey	.15
73	Tom Seaver	1.00
74	Bud Harrelson	.15
75	Dave Kingman	.15
76	Jerry Koosman	.15
77	Jon Matlack	.15
78	Randy Jones	.15
79	Ozzie Smith	1.00
80	Garry Maddox	.15
81	Mike Schmidt	1.00
82	Greg Luzinski	.15
83	Tug McGraw	.15
84	Willie Stargell	.75
85	Dave Parker	.15
86	Roberto Clemente	2.00
87	Johnny Bench	1.50
88	Joe Morgan	.40
89	George Foster	.15
90	Ken Griffey Sr.	.15
91	Carlton Fisk 1972 (1970s Rookie Flashbacks)	.50
92	Andre Dawson 1977 (1970s Rookie Flashbacks)	.25
93	Fred Lynn 1975 (1970s Rookie Flashbacks)	.25
94	Eddie Murray 1977 (1970s Rookie Flashbacks)	.25
95	Bob Horner 1978 (1970s Rookie Flashbacks)	.15
96	Jon Matlack 1972 (1970s Rookie Flashbacks)	.15
97	Mike Hargrove 1974 (1970s Rookie Flashbacks)	.15
98	Robin Yount 1974 (1970s Rookie Flashbacks)	.50
99	Mike Schmidt 1972 (1970s Rookie Flashbacks)	.50
100	Gary Carter 1974 (1970s Rookie Flashbacks)	.15
101	Ozzie Smith 1978 (1970s Rookie Flashbacks)	.50
102	Paul Molitor 1978 (1970s Rookie Flashbacks)	.50
103	Dennis Eckersley 1975 (1970s Rookie Flashbacks)	.25
104	Dale Murphy 1976 (1970s Rookie Flashbacks)	.15
105	Bert Blyleven 1970 (1970s Rookie Flashbacks)	.15
106	Thurman Munson 1970 (1970s Rookie Flashbacks)	.75
107	Dave Parker 1973 (1970s Rookie Flashbacks)	.15
108	Jack Clark 1975 (1970s Rookie Flashbacks)	.15
109	Keith Hernandez 1974 (1970s Rookie Flashbacks)	.15
110	Ron Cey 1971 (1970s Rookie Flashbacks)	.15
111	Billy Williams 1970 (Decade Dateline)	.75
112	Tom Seaver 1970 (Decade Dateline)	.75
113	Reggie Jackson 1971 (Decade Dateline)	.75
114	Barry Bonds 1971 (Decade Dateline)	.15
115	Willie Stargell 1971 (Decade Dateline)	.40
116	Harmon Killebrew 1971 (Decade Dateline)	.50
117	Roberto Clemente 1972 (Decade Dateline)	1.00
118	Wilbur Wood 1972 (Decade Dateline)	.15
119	Billy Williams 1972 (Decade Dateline)	.15
120	Nolan Ryan 1973 (Decade Dateline)	1.50
121	Ron Blomberg 1973 (Decade Dateline)	.15
122	Hank Aaron 1974 (Decade Dateline)	1.00
123	Lou Brock 1974 (Decade Dateline)	.25
124	Al Kaline 1974 (Decade Dateline)	.40
125	Brooks Robinson 1975 (Decade Dateline)	.40
126	Bill Madlock 1975 (Decade Dateline)	.15
127	Rennie Stennett 1975 (Decade Dateline)	.15
128	Carlton Fisk 1975 (Decade Dateline)	.40
129	Chris Chambliss 1976 (Decade Dateline)	.15
130	Ruppert Jones 1977 (Decade Dateline)	.15
131	Ron Fairly 1977 (Decade Dateline)	.15
132	George Foster 1977 (Decade Dateline)	.15
133	Reggie Jackson 1977 (Decade Dateline)	.75
134	Ron Guidry 1978 (Decade Dateline)	.15
135	Gaylord Perry 1978 (Decade Dateline)	.15
136	Bucky Dent 1978 (Decade Dateline)	.15
137	Dave Kingman 1979 (Decade Dateline)	.15
138	Lou Brock 1979 (Decade Dateline)	.15
139	Thurman Munson 1979 (Decade Dateline)	.75
140	Willie Stargell 1979 (Decade Dateline)	.40
141	Johnny Bench 1970 NL MVP (1970s Award Winners)	.75
142	Boog Powell 1970 AL MVP (1970s Award Winners)	.15
143	Jim Perry 1970 AL CY (1970s Award Winners)	.15
144	Joe Torre 1971 NL MVP (1970s Award Winners)	.15
145	Chris Chambliss 1971 AL ROY (1970s Award Winners)	.15
146	Ferguson Jenkins 1971 NL CY (1970s Award Winners)	.15
147	Carlton Fisk 1972 AL ROY (1970s Award Winners)	.40
148	Gaylord Perry 1972 AL CY (1970s Award Winners)	.15
149	Johnny Bench 1972 NL MVP (1970s Award Winners)	.75
150	Reggie Jackson 1973 AL MVP (1970s Award Winners)	.75
151	Tom Seaver 1973 NL CY (1970s Award Winners)	.75
152	Thurman Munson 1973 AL GG (1970s Award Winners)	.75
153	Steve Garvey 1974 NL MVP (1970s Award Winners)	.15
154	Jim "Catfish" Hunter 1974 AL CY (1970s Award Winners)	.15
155	Mike Hargrove 1974 AL ROY (1970s Award Winners)	.15
156	Joe Morgan 1975 NL MVP (1970s Award Winners)	.75
157	Fred Lynn 1975 AL MVP & ROY (1970s Award Winners)	.75
158	Tom Seaver 1975 NL CY (1970s Award Winners)	.75
159	Thurman Munson 1976 AL MVP (1970s Award Winners)	.75
160	Randy Jones 1976 NL CY (1970s Award Winners)	.15
161	Joe Morgan 1976 NL ROY (1970s Award Winners)	.15
162	George Foster 1977 NL MVP (1970s Award Winners)	.15
163	Eddie Murray 1977 AL ROY (1970s Award Winners)	.15
164	Andre Dawson 1977 AL ROY (1970s Award Winners)	.25
165	Gaylord Perry 1978 NL CY (1970s Award Winners)	.15
166	Ron Guidry 1978 AL CY (1970s Award Winners)	.15
167	Dave Parker 1978 NL MVP (1970s Award Winners)	.15
168	Don Baylor 1979 AL MVP (1970s Award Winners)	.15
169	Bruce Sutter 1979 NL CY (1970s Award Winners)	.30
170	Willie Stargell 1979 NL co-MVP (1970s Award Winners)	.40
171	Brooks Robinson 1970 (1970s World Series Highlights)	.50
172	Roberto Clemente 1971 (1970s World Series Highlights)	1.00
173	Gene Tenace 1972 (1970s World Series Highlights)	.15
174	Reggie Jackson 1973 (1970s World Series Highlights)	.15
175	Rollie Fingers 1974 (1970s World Series Highlights)	.15
176	Carlton Fisk 1975 (1970s World Series Highlights)	.15
177	Johnny Bench 1976 (1970s World Series Highlights)	.15
178	Reggie Jackson 1977 (1970s World Series Highlights)	.75
179	Bucky Dent 1978 (1970s World Series Highlights)	.15
180	Willie Stargell 1979 (1970s World Series Highlights)	.15

Bellbottomed Bashers

		NM/M
Complete Set (10):		12.00
Common Player:		1.00
Inserted 1:18		
BB1	Reggie Jackson	2.00
BB2	Gorman Thomas	1.00
BB3	Willie McCovey	1.50
BB4	Willie Stargell	1.50
BB5	Mike Schmidt	3.00
BB6	George Foster	1.00
BB7	Johnny Bench	2.50
BB8	Dave Kingman	1.00
BB9	Graig Nettles	1.00
BB10	Steve Garvey	1.00

Decade Dynasties

		NM/M
Complete Set (10):		15.00
Common Player:		1.00
Inserted 1:14		
D1	Boog Powell	1.00
D2	Johnny Bench	3.00
D3	Willie Stargell	1.50
D4	Jim "Catfish" Hunter	1.00
D5	Steve Garvey	1.00
D6	Carlton Fisk	2.00
D7	Mike Schmidt	4.00
D8	Hal McRae	1.00
D9	Tom Seaver	3.00
D10	Reggie Jackson	2.50

Game-Used Bat

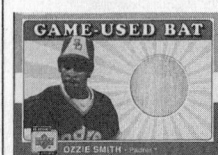

		NM/M
Common Player:		5.00
Inserted 1:24 H		
HA	Hank Aaron	40.00
DB	Don Baylor	5.00
BB	Bobby Bonds	5.00
GC	Gary Carter	8.00
JaC	Jack Clark	5.00
RC	Roberto Clemente/243	100.00
DC	Dave Concepcion	5.00
JoC	Jose Cruz	5.00
TD	Tommy Davis	5.00
AD	Andre Dawson	8.00
DaE	Darryl Evans	5.00
DwE	Dwight Evans	5.00
CF	Carlton Fisk	10.00
GF	George Foster	5.00
SG	Steve Garvey	5.00
BG	Bobby Grich	5.00
KG	Ken Griffey Sr.	5.00
BH	Bud Harrelson/290	5.00
KH	Keith Hernandez/243	20.00
RH	Ron Hunt	5.00
ReJ	Reggie Jackson	15.00
RaJ	Randy Jones	5.00
GL	Greg Luzinski	5.00
FL	Fred Lynn	5.00
GM	Garry Maddox	5.00
BiM	Bill Madlock	5.00
TiM	Tim McCarver	5.00
TuM	Tug McGraw/97	25.00
HM	Hal McRae	5.00
RM	Rick Monday	5.00
WM	Willie Montanez	5.00
JM	Joe Morgan	5.00
BoM	Bobby Murcer	20.00
EM	Eddie Murray	10.00
GN	Graig Nettles/219	15.00
AO	Al Oliver	5.00
DP	Dave Parker	5.00
BP	Boog Powell	5.00
WR	Willie Randolph	5.00
BR	Bill Russell	5.00
NR	Nolan Ryan	50.00
RS	Ron Santo	5.00
ToS	Tom Seaver/121	20.00
OS	Ozzie Smith	15.00
RW	Roy White	5.00
MW	Maury Wills	5.00
DW	Dave Winfield	8.00

Game-Used Bat Combo

	NM/M
Common Card:	20.00
Inserted 1:336	

NYY	Reggie Jackson, Graig Nettles, Chris Chambliss, Roy White	40.00
LA	Steve Garvey, Ron Cey, Bill Russell, Rick Monday	25.00
NYM	Tom Seaver, Bud Harrelson, Ron Hunt, Tug McGraw	50.00
CIN	Johnny Bench, George Foster, Ken Griffey Sr., Joe Morgan	50.00
ROY	Andre Dawson, Fred Lynn, Carlton Fisk, Eddie Murray	40.00
MVPN	Johnny Bench, Steve Garvey, Willie Stargell, George Foster	50.00
BAT	Keith Hernandez, Bill Madlock, Fred Lynn, Dave Parker	20.00
GGA	Carlton Fisk, Graig Nettles, Bobby Grich, Fred Lynn	25.00
GGN	Johnny Bench, Roberto Clemente, Dave Concepcion, Garry Maddox	100.00
WS72	Reggie Jackson, Bert Campaneris, Dave Concepcion, Johnny Bench/97	80.00
WS73	Reggie Jackson, Bert Campaneris, Tom Seaver, Bud Harrelson	40.00
WS74	Reggie Jackson, Bert Campaneris, Steve Garvey, Ron Cey	40.00
WS75	Carlton Fisk, Fred Lynn, George Foster, Joe Morgan	40.00
WS76	Chris Chambliss, Graig Nettles, Johnny Bench, Ken Griffey Sr./97	80.00
WS77	Reggie Jackson, Graig Nettles, Steve Garvey, Ron Cey	40.00
WS78	Graig Nettles, Chris Chambliss, Bill Russell, Ron Cey/238	50.00
ASMV	Bill Madlock, Joe Morgan, Steve Garvey, Dave Parker	40.00
RY	Chris Chambliss, Reggie Jackson, Roy White, Hal McRae/238	40.00
RD	George Foster, Joe Morgan, Ron Cey, Bill Russell	25.00

Game-Used Jersey

		NM/M
Common Player:		8.00
Inserted 1:168		
HA	Hank Aaron	40.00
LA	Luis Aparicio	8.00
JB	Johnny Bench	15.00
RC	Roberto Clemente	100.00
WD	Willie Davis	8.00
RF	Rollie Fingers	8.00
CF	Carlton Fisk	10.00
RG	Ron Guidry	8.00
BH	Burt Hooton	8.00
CH	Jim "Catfish" Hunter	10.00
RJ	Reggie Jackson	15.00
JKa	Jim Kaat	8.00
JKo	Jerry Koosman	8.00
BM	Bill Madlock	8.00
JM	Jon Matlack	8.00
TM	Tug McGraw	8.00
BM	Bobby Murcer	15.00
JP	Jim Perry	8.00
LP	Lou Piniella	10.00
WR	Willie Randolph	8.00
NR	Nolan Ryan/50	75.00
TS	Tom Seaver	20.00
WS	Willie Stargell	10.00
MW	Maury Wills	8.00

Game-Used Jersey Autograph

		NM/M
Common Autograph:		20.00
Inserted 1:168 H		
HA	Hank Aaron/97	250.00
LA	Luis Aparicio	30.00
SB	Sal Bando	20.00
JB	Johnny Bench	70.00
RF	Rollie Fingers	25.00

CF	Carlton Fisk/243	40.00
KG	Ken Griffey Sr.	20.00
RG	Ron Guidry	30.00
BH	Burt Hooton	20.00
RJ	Reggie Jackson/291	65.00
JKa	Jim Kaat	25.00
JKo	Jerry Koosman	20.00
BM	Bill Madlock	20.00
TM	Tug McGraw	20.00
BM	Bobby Murcer	50.00
RP	Rico Petrocelli	25.00
NR	Nolan Ryan/291	125.00
MW	Maury Wills	20.00

Game-Used Patch

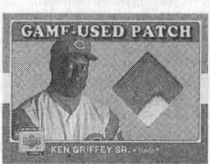

Inserted 1:7,500
No pricing due to scarcity.

The Arms Race

		NM/M
Complete Set (10):		10.00
Common Player:		.50
Inserted 1:14		
AR1	Nolan Ryan	4.00
AR2	Ferguson Jenkins	1.00
AR3	Jim "Catfish" Hunter	1.00
AR4	Tom Seaver	2.00
AR5	Randy Jones	.50
AR6	J.R. Richard	.50
AR7	Rollie Fingers	1.00
AR8	Gaylord Perry	.75
AR9	Ron Guidry	.75
AR10	Phil Niekro	.75

70s Disco Era Dandies

		NM/M
Complete Set (6):		5.00
Common Player:		.50
Inserted 1:23		
DE1	Mike Schmidt	2.00
DE2	Johnny Bench	1.00
DE3	Lou Brock	.50
DE4	Reggie Jackson	2.00
DE5	Willie Stargell	.50
DE6	Tom Seaver	1.00

70s Super Powers

		NM/M
Complete Set (6):		12.00
Common Player:		1.50
Inserted 1:24		
SP1	Reggie Jackson	3.00
SP2	Joe Morgan	1.50
SP3	Willie Stargell	2.00

SP4	Willie McCovey	1.50
SP5	Mike Schmidt	4.00
SP6	Nolan Ryan	5.00

2001 Upper Deck Evolution

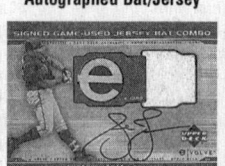

		NM/M
Complete Set (120):		125.00
Common Player:		.15
Common SP (91-120):		3.00
Production 2,250		
Pack (5):		2.00
Box (24):		40.00
1	Darin Erstad	.25
2	Troy Glaus	.50
3	Jason Giambi	.50
4	Tim Hudson	.40
5	Jermaine Dye	.15
6	Barry Zito	.40
7	Carlos Delgado	.50
8	Shannon Stewart	.15
9	Jose Cruz Jr.	.15
10	Greg Vaughn	.15
11	Juan Gonzalez	.50
12	Roberto Alomar	.50
13	Omar Vizquel	.25
14	Jim Thome	.50
15	Edgar Martinez	.25
16	John Olerud	.25
17	Kazuhiro Sasaki	.15
18	Cal Ripken Jr.	2.00
19	Alex Rodriguez	1.50
20	Ivan Rodriguez	.50
21	Rafael Palmeiro	.50
22	Pedro Martinez	.75
23	Nomar Garciaparra	.75
24	Manny Ramirez	.50
25	Carl Everett	.15
26	Mark Quinn	.15
27	Mike Sweeney	.15
28	Neifi Perez	.15
29	Tony Clark	.15
30	Eric Milton	.15
31	Doug Mientkiewicz	.15
32	Corey Koskie	.15
33	Frank Thomas	.50
34	David Wells	.15
35	Magglio Ordonez	.40
36	Derek Jeter	2.00
37	Mike Mussina	.40
38	Bernie Williams	.50
39	Roger Clemens	1.50
40	David Justice	.25
41	Jeff Bagwell	.50
42	Richard Hidalgo	.25
43	Wade Miller	.15
44	Chipper Jones	1.00
45	Greg Maddux	1.50
46	Andruw Jones	.50
47	Rafael Furcal	.40
48	Geoff Jenkins	.25
49	Jeromy Burnitz	.15
50	Ben Sheets	.25
51	Richie Sexson	.40
52	Mark McGwire	1.50
53	Jim Edmonds	.40
54	Darryl Kile	.15
55	J.D. Drew	.40
56	Sammy Sosa	1.00
57	Kerry Wood	.50
58	Randy Johnson	.75
59	Luis Gonzalez	.25
60	Matt Williams	.25
61	Kevin Brown	.25
62	Gary Sheffield	.40
63	Shawn Green	.40
64	Chan Ho Park	.15
65	Vladimir Guerrero	.75
66	Jose Vidro	.15

67	Fernando Tatis	.15
68	Barry Bonds	2.00
69	Jeff Kent	.25
70	Russ Ortiz	.15
71	Preston Wilson	.15
72	Ryan Dempster	.15
73	Charles Johnson	.15
74	Mike Piazza	1.00
75	Edgardo Alfonzo	.15
76	Robin Ventura	.25
77	Jay Payton	.15
78	Tony Gwynn	.75
79	Phil Nevin	.25
80	Pat Burrell	.40
81	Scott Rolen	.50
82	Bob Abreu	.40
83	Brian Giles	.25
84	Jason Kendall	.25
85	Ken Griffey Jr.	1.00
86	Barry Larkin	.40
87	Sean Casey	.25
88	Todd Helton	.50
89	Larry Walker	.25
90	Mike Hampton	.15
91	Ichiro Suzuki RC	20.00
92	Albert Pujols RC	40.00
93	Wilson Betemit RC	3.00
94	Jay Gibbons RC	3.00
95	Juan Uribe RC	4.00
96	Morgan Ensberg RC	3.00
97	Christian Parker RC	3.00
98	Tsuyoshi Shinjo RC	3.00
99	Jack Wilson RC	4.00
100	Donaldo Mendez RC	3.00
101	Ryan Freel RC	4.00
102	Juan Diaz RC	3.00
103	Horacio Ramirez RC	3.00
104	Ricardo Rodriguez RC	3.00
105	Erick Almonte RC	3.00
106	Josh Towers RC	3.00
107	Adrian Hernandez RC	3.00
108	Brandon Duckworth RC	3.00
109	Travis Hafner RC	8.00
110	Martin Vargas RC	3.00
111	Kris Keller RC	3.00
112	Brian Lawrence RC	3.00
113	Esix Snead RC	3.00
114	Wilken Ruan RC	3.00
115	Jose Mieses RC	3.00
116	Johnny Estrada RC	4.00
117	Elpidio Guzman RC	3.00
118	Sean Douglass RC	3.00
119	Billy Sylvester RC	3.00
120	Bret Prinz RC	3.00

Autographed Bat/Jersey

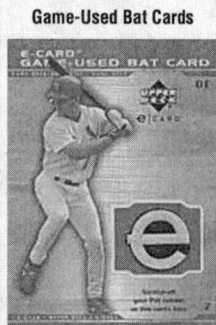

		NM/M
Common Player:		20.00
RB	Russell Branyan	20.00
PB	Pat Burrell	20.00
CD	Carlos Delgado	30.00
JD	J.D. Drew	25.00
JaG	Jason Giambi	30.00
SG	Shawn Green	25.00
KG	Ken Griffey Jr.	100.00
AJ	Andruw Jones	30.00
CJ	Chipper Jones	75.00
JK	Jason Kendall	20.00
CR	Cal Ripken Jr.	150.00
AR	Alex Rodriguez	150.00
GS	Gary Sheffield	30.00
SS	Sammy Sosa	80.00
IS	Ichiro Suzuki	300.00

Game-Used Bat Cards

		NM/M
Common Player:		5.00
Winners Evolve Into Bat/Jrsy Auto.		
Inserted 1:120		
RB	Russell Branyan	5.00
PB	Pat Burrell	5.00
CD	Carlos Delgado	5.00
JD	J.D. Drew	5.00
JaG	Jason Giambi	5.00
KG	Ken Griffey Jr.	20.00
AJ	Andruw Jones	5.00
JK	Jason Kendall	5.00
AR	Alex Rodriguez	15.00
GS	Gary Sheffield	6.00

Game-Used Jersey Cards

		NM/M
Common Player:		5.00
Inserted 1:120		
RB	Russell Branyan	5.00
PB	Pat Burrell	5.00
JD	J.D. Drew	5.00
JaG	Jason Giambi	5.00
BG	Brian Giles	5.00
TG	Troy Glaus	5.00
SG	Shawn Green	5.00
KG	Ken Griffey Jr.	20.00
AJ	Andruw Jones	5.00
CJ	Chipper Jones	10.00
JK	Jason Kendall	5.00
CR	Cal Ripken Jr.	30.00
AR	Alex Rodriguez	15.00
GS	Gary Sheffield	8.00
SS	Sammy Sosa	15.00

Ichiro Suzuki All-Star Game

		NM/M
Random Inserts		
51B	Ichiro Suzuki/Bronze	8.00
51S	Ichiro Suzuki/ Silver/2001	20.00
51G	Ichiro Suzuki/Gold/51	120.00

UD Classics

		NM/M
Complete Set (15):		15.00
Common Player:		.50
Prices for unscratched cards.		
Winners Evolve Into Game Jersey.		
Inserted 1:4		
EC1	Ken Griffey Jr.	3.00
EC2	Gary Sheffield	.75
EC3	Randy Johnson	1.50
EC4	Sammy Sosa	3.00
EC5	Carlos Delgado	1.00
EC6	Ichiro Suzuki	3.00
EC7	Andruw Jones	1.00
EC8	Chipper Jones	2.00
EC9	Kazuhiro Sasaki	.50
EC10	Shawn Green	.75
EC11	Alex Rodriguez	3.00
EC12	Brian Giles	.75
EC13	J.D. Drew	1.00
EC14	Pat Burrell	1.00
EC15	Ivan Rodriguez	1.00

UD Classics Jersey

		NM/M
Common Player:		1.00
Prices for unscratched cards.		
Winners evolve into Game Jersey.		

2001 Upper Deck Gold Glove

		NM/M
Common Player:		.25
Common SP (91-129):		4.00
Production 1,000		
Common SP (130-135):		8.00
Production 500		
Pack (4):		8.00
Box (20):		140.00
1	Troy Glaus	.50
2	Darin Erstad	.50

3	Jason Giambi	.75
4	Tim Hudson	.50
5	Jermaine Dye	.25
6	Raul Mondesi	.25
7	Carlos Delgado	.50
8	Shannon Stewart	.25
9	Greg Vaughn	.25
10	Aubrey Huff	.25
11	Juan Gonzalez	.50
12	Roberto Alomar	1.00
13	Omar Vizquel	.25
14	Jim Thome	1.00
15	John Olerud	.50
16	Edgar Martinez	.50
17	Kazuhiro Sasaki	.25
18	Aaron Sele	.25
19	Cal Ripken Jr.	4.00
20	Chris Richard	.25
21	Ivan Rodriguez	.75
22	Rafael Palmeiro	.75
23	Alex Rodriguez	3.00
24	Pedro Martinez	1.50
25	Nomar Garciaparra	1.00
26	Manny Ramirez	1.00
27	Neifi Perez	.25
28	Mike Sweeney	.25
29	Bobby Higginson	.25
30	Dean Palmer	.25
31	Tony Clark	.25
32	Doug Mientkiewicz	.25
33	Brad Radke	.25
34	Joe Mays	.25
35	Frank Thomas	1.00
36	Magglio Ordonez	.50
37	Carlos Lee	.40
38	Bernie Williams	.75
39	Mike Mussina	.75
40	Derek Jeter	4.00
41	Roger Clemens	2.50
42	Craig Biggio	.75
43	Jeff Bagwell	.75
44	Lance Berkman	.50
45	Andruw Jones	.50
46	Greg Maddux	2.00
47	Chipper Jones	2.00
48	Geoff Jenkins	.40
49	Ben Sheets	.25
50	Jeromy Burnitz	.25
51	Jim Edmonds	.50
52	Mark McGwire	2.00
53	Mike Matheny	.25
54	J.D. Drew	.50
55	Sammy Sosa	1.00
56	Kerry Wood	.50
57	Fred McGriff	.40
58	Randy Johnson	1.50
59	Steve Finley	.25
60	Mark Grace	.50
61	Matt Williams	.40
62	Luis Gonzalez	.40
63	Shawn Green	.40
64	Kevin Brown	.40
65	Gary Sheffield	.50
66	Vladimir Guerrero	1.00
67	Tony Armas Jr.	.25
68	Barry Bonds	4.00
69	J.T. Snow	.25
70	Jeff Kent	.40
71	Charles Johnson	.25
72	Preston Wilson	.25
73	Cliff Floyd	.25
74	Robin Ventura	.25
75	Mike Piazza	2.00
76	Edgardo Alfonzo	.25
77	Tony Gwynn	1.50
78	Ryan Klesko	.50
79	Scott Rolen	1.00
80	Mike Lieberthal	.25
81	Pat Burrell	.50
82	Jason Kendall	.25
83	Brian Giles	.25
84	Ken Griffey Jr.	2.50
85	Barry Larkin	.50
86	Pokey Reese	.25
87	Larry Walker	.40
88	Mike Hampton	.25
89	Juan Pierre	.25
90	Todd Helton	1.00
91	Mike Penney RC	4.00
92	Wilkin Ruan RC	4.00
93	Greg Miller RC	4.00
94	Johnny Estrada RC	4.00
95	Tsuyoshi Shinjo RC	4.00
96	Josh Towers RC	4.00
97	Horacio Ramirez RC	4.00
98	Ryan Freel RC	6.00
99	Morgan Ensberg RC	4.00
100	Adrian Hernandez RC	4.00
101	Juan Uribe RC	6.00
102	Jose Mieses RC	4.00
103	Jack Wilson RC	6.00
104	Cesar Crespo RC	4.00
105	Bud Smith RC	4.00
106	Erick Almonte RC	4.00
107	Elpidio Guzman RC	4.00
108	Brandon Duckworth RC	4.00
109	Juan Diaz RC	4.00
110	Kris Keller RC	4.00
111	Jason Michaels RC	4.00
112	Bret Prinz RC	4.00
113	Henry Mateo RC	4.00
114	Ricardo Rodriguez RC	4.00
115	Travis Hafner RC	10.00
116	Nate Teut RC	4.00
117	Alexis Gomez RC	4.00
118	Billy Sylvester RC	4.00
119	Adam Pettyjohn RC	4.00
120	Josh Fogg RC	4.00

121	Juan Cruz RC	4.00
122	Carlos Valderrama RC	4.00
123	Jay Gibbons RC	4.00
124	Donaldo Mendez RC	4.00
125	William Ortega RC	4.00
126	Sean Douglass RC	4.00
127	Christian Parker RC	4.00
128	Grant Balfour RC	4.00
129	Joe Kennedy RC	4.00
130	Albert Pujols RC	120.00
131	Wilson Betemit RC	10.00
132	Mark Teixeira RC	25.00
133	Mark Prior RC	6.00
134	Dewon Brazelton RC	4.00
135	Ichiro Suzuki RC	40.00

Limited

Stars (1-90):	4-8X
Rookies (91-135):	.75-1.5X
Production 100 Sets	

Finite

Stars (1-90):	15-25X
Rookies (91-135):	3-5X
Production 25 Sets	

Batting Gloves

		NM/M
	Common Player:	5.00
	Inserted 1:20	
BA	Bobby Abreu	8.00
BA	Brady Anderson	5.00
TB	Tony Batista	5.00
BB	Barry Bonds	30.00
MC	Marty Cordova	5.00
JC	Jose Cruz	5.00
RF	Rafael Furcal	5.00
AG	Andres Galarraga	5.00
JG	Juan Gonzalez	5.00
KGR	Ken Griffey Jr./Reds	20.00
KGM	Ken Griffey Jr.	20.00
CJ	Chipper Jones	10.00
EM	Edgar Martinez	5.00
PO	Paul O'Neill	8.00
RP	Rafael Palmeiro	10.00
NP	Neifi Perez	5.00
MR	Manny Ramirez	8.00
ARR	Alex Rodriguez/Rangers	20.00
ARM	Alex Rodriguez/M's	20.00
HR	Henry Rodriguez	5.00
IR	Ivan Rodriguez	8.00
GS	Gary Sheffield	8.00
SS	Sammy Sosa	10.00
FT	Fernando Tatis	5.00
MT	Miguel Tejada	6.00

Fielder's Gloves

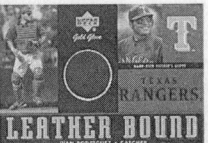

		NM/M
	Common Player:	6.00
	Inserted 1:60	
GA	Garret Anderson/100	8.00
CB	Craig Biggio	10.00
JBi	Johnny Blanchard	10.00
BB	Barry Bonds	50.00
KC	Ken Caminiti	6.00
RCa	Roy Campanella	125.00
GC	Gary Carter	10.00
RCe	Roger Cedeno	6.00
JD	Johnny Damon	20.00
LD	Leon Day/100	150.00
OD	Octavio Dotel	6.00
JE	Jim Edmonds	10.00
DE	Dock Ellis	10.00
AF	Alex Fernandez	6.00
CF	Cliff Floyd	6.00
NF	Nellie Fox	40.00
RF	Rafael Furcal	6.00
AG	Alex Gonzalez	6.00
BG	Ben Grieve	6.00
KG	Ken Griffey Jr.	30.00
MG	Marquis Grissom	6.00
LG	Lefty Grove	100.00
THe	Todd Helton	10.00
OH	Orlando Hernandez	6.00
THo	Todd Hollandsworth	6.00
HI	Hideki Irabu	6.00
JI	Jason Isringhausen	6.00
RJ	Reggie Jackson	20.00
CJ	Chipper Jones	25.00
JKa	Jim Kaat	10.00
JKe	Jason Kendall	6.00
RK	Ryan Klesko	6.00
HK	Harvey Kuenn	20.00
CL	Carlos Lee	10.00
KL	Kenny Lofton	6.00
JL	Javy Lopez	6.00
GL	Greg Luzinski	10.00
EM	Edgar Martinez	10.00
PM	Pedro Martinez	15.00
JO	John Olerud	6.00
PO	Paul O'Neill	10.00
RP	Rafael Palmeiro	8.00
CP	Chan Ho Park	8.00
MP	Mike Piazza	25.00
MR	Manny Ramirez	15.00
FR	Frank Robinson	25.00
AR	Alex Rodriguez	25.00
IR	Ivan Rodriguez	8.00
TS	Tim Salmon	6.00
AS	Aaron Sele	6.00
GS	Gary Sheffield	10.00
OS	Ozzie Smith	40.00
SS	Sammy Sosa	20.00
I	Ichiro Suzuki	250.00
FT	Frank Thomas	15.00
OV	Omar Vizquel	10.00
DW	Dave Winfield	20.00
MY	Masato Yoshii	6.00

Fielder's Gloves Autograph

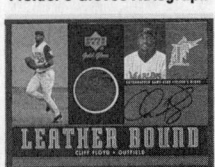

		NM/M
	Inserted 1:240	
JD	Johnny Damon	50.00
CF	Cliff Floyd	15.00
RF	Rafael Furcal	20.00
RP	Ken Griffey Jr./49	150.00
RJ	Reggie Jackson/68	60.00
JK	Jim Kaat	25.00
JK	Jason Kendall	15.00
RK	Ryan Klesko	15.00
KL	Kenny Lofton	15.00
JL	Javy Lopez	15.00
GL	Greg Luzinski	20.00
EM	Edgar Martinez	50.00
JO	John Olerud	15.00
PO	Paul O'Neill	50.00
FR	Frank Robinson	50.00
IR	Ivan Rodriguez	40.00
OS	Ozzie Smith	85.00
FT	Frank Thomas	60.00
DW	Dave Winfield	50.00

Game-Used Ball

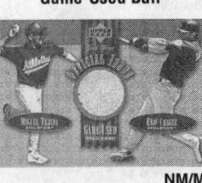

		NM/M
	Common Player:	5.00
	Inserted 1:20	
GC	Ken Griffey Jr., Sean Casey	15.00
RR	Alex Rodriguez, Ivan Rodriguez	15.00
SW	Sammy Sosa, Rondell White	10.00
MP	Mark McGwire, Albert Pujols	50.00
RE	Manny Ramirez, Carl Everett	15.00
GE	Troy Glaus, Darin Erstad	8.00
GT	Jason Giambi, Miguel Tejada	8.00
IO	Ichiro Suzuki, John Olerud	40.00
RP	Ivan Rodriguez, Rafael Palmeiro	8.00
GV	Vladimir Guerrero, Jose Vidro	10.00
PS	Mike Piazza, Tsuyoshi Shinjo	20.00
JJ	Chipper Jones, Andruw Jones	15.00
RB	Scott Rolen, Pat Burrell	5.00
WF	Preston Wilson, Cliff Floyd	5.00
JF	Andruw Jones, Rafael Furcal	8.00
BB	Jeff Bagwell, Lance Berkman	10.00
PE	Albert Pujols, Jim Edmonds	30.00
JB	Geoff Jenkins, Jeromy Burnitz	5.00
KG	Jason Kendall, Brian Giles	5.00
BK	Barry Bonds, Jeff Kent	25.00
NK	Phil Nevin, Ryan Klesko	5.00
SG	Gary Sheffield, Shawn Green	5.00
GG	Luis Gonzalez, Mark Grace	8.00
HW	Todd Helton, Larry Walker	8.00
WP	Larry Walker, Juan Pierre	5.00
AG	Roberto Alomar, Juan Gonzalez	8.00
VM	Greg Vaughn, Fred McGriff	5.00
RB	Cal Ripken Jr., Tony Batista	30.00
DM	Carlos Delgado, Raul Mondesi	5.00
MG	Doug Mientkiewicz, Cristian Guzman	5.00
TO	Frank Thomas, Magglio Ordonez	10.00
HC	Bobby Higginson, Tony Clark	5.00
SB	Mike Sweeney, Carlos Beltran	5.00
MO	Edgar Martinez, John Olerud	8.00
EA	Darin Erstad, Garret Anderson	5.00
TC	Miguel Tejada, Eric Chavez	8.00
PR	Rafael Palmeiro, Alex Rodriguez	15.00
BA	Pat Burrell, Bobby Abreu	8.00
FJ	Cliff Floyd, Charles Johnson	5.00
VP	Robin Ventura, Mike Piazza	15.00
WS	Kerry Wood, Sammy Sosa	15.00
DP	J.D. Drew, Albert Pujols	40.00
BH	Lance Berkman, Richard Hidalgo	8.00
BS	Jeromy Burnitz, Richie Sexson	5.00
LG	Barry Larkin, Ken Griffey Jr.	15.00
GR	Brian Giles, Aramis Ramirez	5.00
JG	Randy Johnson, Luis Gonzalez	10.00
GB	Shawn Green, Adrian Beltre	8.00
KA	Jeff Kent, Rich Aurilia	5.00
GK	Tony Gwynn, Ryan Klesko	10.00
MJ	Greg Maddux, Chipper Jones	20.00
HH	Mike Hampton, Todd Helton	8.00
SV	Tsuyoshi Shinjo, Robin Ventura	5.00
GJ	Cristian Guzman, Jacque Jones	5.00
CJ	Roger Clemens, Derek Jeter	50.00

Jerseys

		NM/M
	Inserted 1:20	
LA	Luis Aparicio	5.00
JB	Jeff Bagwell	8.00
BB	Barry Bonds	25.00
GC	Gary Carter	5.00
CC	Cesar Cedeno	5.00
DE	Darin Erstad	5.00
CF	Carlton Fisk	8.00
MG	Mark Grace	8.00
SG	Shawn Green	5.00
KG	Ken Griffey Jr.	20.00
RG	Ron Guidry	5.00
AJ	Andruw Jones	5.00
JK	Jim Kaat	5.00
GM	Greg Maddux	15.00
MM	Mickey Mantle	150.00
RM	Roger Maris	75.00
DM	Don Mattingly	30.00
TM	Thurman Munson	60.00
MM	Mike Mussina	10.00
RP	Rafael Palmeiro	10.00
BR	Bobby Richardson	8.00
CR	Cal Ripken Jr.	35.00
IR	Ivan Rodriguez	10.00
OS	Ozzie Smith	15.00
IS	Ichiro Suzuki	65.00
OV	Omar Vizquel	10.00
BW	Bernie Williams	8.00

2001 Upper Deck Hall of Famers

		NM/M
Complete Set (90):		25.00
Common Player:		.15
Hobby Pack (5):		4.00
Box (24):		80.00
1	Reggie Jackson	.75
2	Hank Aaron	1.50
3	Eddie Mathews	.75
4	Warren Spahn	.40
5	Robin Yount	.40
6	Lou Brock	.25
7	Dizzy Dean	.15
8	Bob Gibson	.40
9	Stan Musial	.75
10	Enos Slaughter	.15
11	Rogers Hornsby	.40
12	Ernie Banks	.50
13	Ferguson Jenkins	.15
14	Roy Campanella	.75
15	Pee Wee Reese	.15
16	Jackie Robinson	1.50
17	Juan Marichal	.15
18	Christy Mathewson	.15
19	Willie Mays	1.50
20	Hoyt Wilhelm	.15
21	Buck Leonard	.15
22	Bob Feller	.40
23	Cy Young	.40
24	Satchel Paige	.40
25	Tom Seaver	.50
26	Brooks Robinson	.75
27	Mike Schmidt	.75
28	Roberto Clemente	1.50
29	Ralph Kiner	.15
30	Willie Stargell	.75
31	Honus Wagner	.75
32	Josh Gibson	.40
33	Nolan Ryan	1.50
34	Carlton Fisk	.15
35	Jimmie Foxx	.75
36	Johnny Bench	.75
37	Joe Morgan	.40
38	George Brett	.75
39	Walter Johnson	.40
40	Cool Papa Bell	.15
41	Ty Cobb	1.00
42	Al Kaline	.15
43	Harmon Killebrew	.15
44	Luis Aparicio	.15
45	Yogi Berra	.75
46	Joe DiMaggio	1.50
47	Whitey Ford	.25
48	Lou Gehrig	2.00
49	Mickey Mantle	2.00
50	Babe Ruth	2.00
51	Josh Gibson (Origins of the Game)	.15
52	Honus Wagner (Origins of the Game)	.20
53	Hoyt Wilhelm (Origins of the Game)	.15
54	Cy Young (Origins of the Game)	.20
55	Walter Johnson (Origins of the Game)	.20
56	Satchel Paige (Origins of the Game)	.25
57	Rogers Hornsby (Origins of the Game)	.20
58	Christy Mathewson (Origins of the Game)	.15
59	Tris Speaker (Origins of the Game)	.20
60	Nap Lajoie (Origins of the Game)	.15
61	Mickey Mantle (The National Pastime)	1.00
62	Jackie Robinson (The National Pastime)	.75
63	Nolan Ryan (The National Pastime)	.75
64	Josh Gibson (The National Pastime)	.20
65	Yogi Berra (The National Pastime)	.40
66	Brooks Robinson (The National Pastime)	.40
67	Stan Musial (The National Pastime)	.40
68	Mike Schmidt (The National Pastime)	.40
69	Joe DiMaggio (The National Pastime)	1.00
70	Ernie Banks (The National Pastime)	.25
71	Willie Stargell (The National Pastime)	.25
72	Johnny Bench (The National Pastime)	.40
73	Willie Mays (The National Pastime)	.75
74	Satchel Paige (The National Pastime)	.25
75	Bob Gibson (The National Pastime)	.20
76	Harmon Killebrew (The National Pastime)	.15
77	Al Kaline (The National Pastime)	.15
78	Carlton Fisk (The National Pastime)	.15
79	Tom Seaver (The National Pastime)	.25
80	Reggie Jackson (The National Pastime)	.40
81	Bob Gibson (The Hall of Records)	.20
82	Nolan Ryan (The Hall of Records)	.75
83	Walter Johnson (The Hall of Records)	.20
84	Stan Musial (The Hall of Records)	.40
85	Josh Gibson (The Hall of Records)	.20
86	Cy Young (The Hall of Records)	.20
87	Joe DiMaggio (The Hall of Records)	1.00
88	Hoyt Wilhelm (The Hall of Records)	.15
89	Lou Brock (The Hall of Records)	.15
90	Mickey Mantle (The Hall of Records)	1.00

Coop. Coll. Game Bat

		NM/M
	Common Player:	5.00
	Inserted 1:24	
HA	Hank Aaron	30.00
LA	Luis Aparicio	5.00
EB	Ernie Banks	15.00
JB	Johnny Bench	15.00
YB	Yogi Berra	10.00
JBo	Jim Bottomley	5.00
GB	George Brett	20.00
RC	Roy Campanella	30.00
OC	Orlando Cepeda	5.00
RC	Roberto Clemente/SP/409	120.00
JD	Joe DiMaggio	100.00
CF	Carlton Fisk	10.00
RF	Rollie Fingers	5.00
JF	Jimmie Foxx	50.00
HG	Hank Greenberg	40.00
RH	Rogers Hornsby	5.00
RJ	Reggie Jackson	15.00
GK	George Kell	5.00
RK	Ralph Kiner	10.00
MM	Mickey Mantle	125.00
WM	Willie Mays	30.00
JM	Johnny Mize	10.00
JMo	Joe Morgan	5.00
MO	Mel Ott	50.00
JP	Jim Palmer/SP/372	50.00
TP	Tony Perez	5.00
BR	Brooks Robinson	10.00
FR	Frank Robinson	10.00
JR	Jackie Robinson/SP/371	175.00
BR	Babe Ruth	200.00
NR	Nolan Ryan	50.00
RS	Red Schoendienst	5.00
ES	Enos Slaughter	5.00
DS	Duke Snider	10.00
WS	Willie Stargell	10.00
BW	Billy Williams	5.00
EW	Early Wynn	5.00
RY	Robin Yount	15.00

Coop. Coll. Game Jersey

		NM/M
	Common Player:	10.00
	Inserted 1:168	
LA	Luis Aparicio	10.00
OC	Orlando Cepeda	15.00
RC	Roberto Clemente	100.00
JD	Joe DiMaggio	100.00
DD	Don Drysdale/SP/49	200.00
LG	Lou Gehrig/SP/194	250.00
MM	Mickey Mantle/SP/216	250.00
WM	Willie Mays	80.00
JM	Joe Morgan	10.00
TP	Tony Perez	10.00
PW	Pee Wee Reese	15.00
BR	Brooks Robinson	20.00
FR	Frank Robinson	15.00
NR	Nolan Ryan	30.00
TS	Tom Seaver	15.00
DS	Duke Snider/SP/267	50.00
WS	Willie Stargell	15.00
DSu	Don Sutton	10.00

Coop. Coll. Jersey Auto.

		NM/M
	Common Autograph:	40.00
	Inserted 1:504	
LA	Luis Aparicio	40.00
OC	Orlando Cepeda	40.00
RJ	Reggie Jackson	75.00
EB	Ernie Banks	90.00
JM	Joe Morgan	40.00
TP	Tony Perez	40.00
GB	George Brett	125.00
BR	Brooks Robinson	80.00
FR	Frank Robinson	60.00
NR	Nolan Ryan	175.00
TS	Tom Seaver	75.00
DS	Duke Snider	65.00
WS	Willie Stargell	85.00
DSu	Don Sutton	40.00

Hall of Fame Gallery

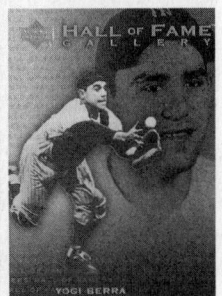

		NM/M
Complete Set (15):		25.00
Common Player:		1.00
	Inserted 1:6	
1	Reggie Jackson	1.50
2	Tom Seaver	1.50
3	Bob Gibson	1.50
4	Jackie Robinson	3.00
5	Joe DiMaggio	3.00
6	Ernie Banks	1.50
7	Mickey Mantle	4.00
8	Willie Mays	3.00
9	Cy Young	1.50
10	Nolan Ryan	4.00
11	Johnny Bench	1.50
12	Yogi Berra	1.50
13	Satchel Paige	1.00
14	George Brett	2.00
15	Stan Musial	2.00

Mantle Pinstripes Excl.

	NM/M
Complete Set (56):	75.00
Common Mantle:	2.00
One Pack/Box	

Mantle Pinstripe Memor.

		NM/M
Print Runs Listed		
MMB	Mickey Mantle/ Bat/100	100.00
MMCJ	Mickey Mantle, Joe DiMaggio/Jsy/50	300.00
MMJ	Mickey Mantle/ Jsy/100	125.00

The Class of '36

		NM/M
Complete Set (5):		8.00
Common Player:		1.50
Inserted 1:17		
1	Ty Cobb	2.00
2	Babe Ruth	5.00
3	Christy Mathewson	1.50
4	Walter Johnson	1.50
5	Honus Wagner	1.50

The Endless Summer

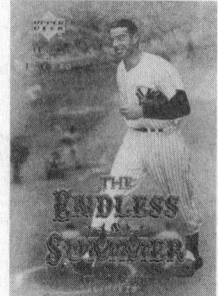

		NM/M
Complete Set (11):		15.00
Common Player:		1.00
Inserted 1:8		
1	Mickey Mantle	4.00
2	Yogi Berra	1.00
3	Mike Schmidt	2.50
4	Jackie Robinson	2.50
5	Johnny Bench	1.50
6	Tom Seaver	1.50
7	Ernie Banks	1.50
8	Harmon Killebrew	1.00
9	Joe DiMaggio	3.00
10	Willie Mays	3.00
11	Brooks Robinson	1.00

20th Century Showcase

		NM/M
Complete Set (11):		15.00
Common Player:		1.00
Inserted 1:8		
1	Cy Young	1.00
2	Joe DiMaggio	3.00
3	Harmon Killebrew	1.00
4	Stan Musial	2.00
5	Mickey Mantle	4.00
6	Satchel Paige	1.00
7	Nolan Ryan	4.00
8	Bob Gibson	1.00
9	Ernie Banks	1.50
10	Mike Schmidt	2.00
11	Willie Mays	3.00

2001 Upper Deck Legends

	NM/M
Complete Set (90):	20.00

		NM/M
Common Player:		.20
Pack (5):		4.00
Box (24):		80.00
1	Darin Erstad	.40
2	Troy Glaus	.75
3	Nolan Ryan	3.00
4	Reggie Jackson	.75
5	Jim "Catfish" Hunter	.20
6	Jason Giambi	.50
7	Tim Hudson	.30
8	Miguel Tejada	.30
9	Carlos Delgado	.50
10	Shannon Stewart	.20
11	Greg Vaughn	.20
12	Larry Doby	.20
13	Jim Thome	.40
14	Juan Gonzalez	.75
15	Roberto Alomar	.50
16	Edgar Martinez	.40
17	John Olerud	.40
18	Eddie Murray	.40
19	Cal Ripken Jr.	2.50
20	Alex Rodriguez	2.00
21	Ivan Rodriguez	.75
22	Rafael Palmeiro	.40
23	Jimmie Foxx	.50
24	Cy Young	.50
25	Manny Ramirez	.75
26	Pedro Martinez	1.00
27	Nomar Garciaparra	2.00
28	George Brett	1.00
29	Mike Sweeney	.20
30	Jermaine Dye	.20
31	Ty Cobb	1.50
32	Dean Palmer	.20
33	Harmon Killebrew	.50
34	Matt Lawton	.20
35	Luis Aparicio	.20
36	Frank Thomas	.75
37	Magglio Ordonez	.20
38	David Wells	.20
39	Mickey Mantle	3.00
40	Joe DiMaggio	3.00
41	Roger Maris	.75
42	Babe Ruth	3.00
43	Derek Jeter	2.50
44	Roger Clemens	1.00
45	Bernie Williams	.50
46	Jeff Bagwell	.75
47	Richard Hidalgo	.40
48	Warren Spahn	.40
49	Greg Maddux	1.50
50	Chipper Jones	1.50
51	Andruw Jones	.50
52	Robin Yount	.50
53	Jeromy Burnitz	.20
54	Jeffrey Hammonds	.20
55	Ozzie Smith	.50
56	Stan Musial	1.00
57	Mark McGwire	2.50
58	Jim Edmonds	.30
59	Sammy Sosa	1.50
60	Ernie Banks	.50
61	Kerry Wood	.20
62	Randy Johnson	.75
63	Luis Gonzalez	.40
64	Don Drysdale	.50
65	Jackie Robinson	2.00
66	Gary Sheffield	.20
67	Kevin Brown	.20
68	Vladimir Guerrero	1.00
69	Willie Mays	1.50
70	Mel Ott	.20
71	Jeff Kent	.20
72	Barry Bonds	1.00
73	Preston Wilson	.20
74	Ryan Dempster	.20
75	Tom Seaver	.40
76	Mike Piazza	2.00
77	Robin Ventura	.20
78	Dave Winfield	.40
79	Tony Gwynn	1.00
80	Bob Abreu	.20
81	Scott Rolen	.40
82	Mike Schmidt	.75
83	Roberto Clemente	1.50
84	Brian Giles	.20
85	Ken Griffey Jr.	2.00
86	Frank Robinson	.40
87	Johnny Bench	.75
88	Todd Helton	.75
89	Larry Walker	.40
90	Mike Hampton	.20

Fiorentino Collection

	NM/M
Complete Set (14):	40.00
Common Player:	1.50

		NM/M
Inserted 1:12		
F1	Babe Ruth	6.00
F2	Satchel Paige	1.50
F3	Joe DiMaggio	5.00
F4	Willie Mays	4.00
F5	Ty Cobb	3.00
F6	Nolan Ryan	5.00
F7	Lou Gehrig	5.00
F8	Jackie Robinson	4.00
F9	Hank Aaron	4.00
F10	Roberto Clemente	4.00
F11	Stan Musial	3.00
F12	Johnny Bench	2.00
F13	Honus Wagner	1.50
F14	Reggie Jackson	1.50

Legendary Cuts

		NM/M
Most not priced due to scarcity.		
C-TC	Ty Cobb/3	3,150
C-BRu	Babe Ruth/7	6,000

Legendary Game Jerseys

		NM/M
Common Player:		5.00
Inserted 1:24		
HA	Hank Aaron	40.00
JB	Jeff Bagwell	8.00
EB	Ernie Banks	15.00
YB	Yogi Berra	10.00
BB	Barry Bonds	25.00
JC	Jose Canseco	10.00
RCl	Roger Clemens	25.00
RoC	Roberto Clemente/195	170.00
JD	Joe DiMaggio/245	175.00
KG	Ken Griffey Jr.	15.00
TG	Tony Gwynn	10.00
RJa	Reggie Jackson	10.00
RJo	Randy Johnson	10.00
CJ	Chipper Jones	10.00
GM	Greg Maddux	15.00
MM	Mickey Mantle/245	200.00
RM	Roger Maris/343	65.00
PM	Pedro Martinez	10.00
WM	Willie Mays	30.00
SM	Stan Musial/490	30.00
MP	Mike Piazza	20.00
MR	Manny Ramirez	8.00
CR	Cal Ripken Jr.	30.00
AR	Alex Rodriguez	20.00
IR	Ivan Rodriguez	8.00
NR	Nolan Ryan	50.00
KS	Kazuhiro Sasaki	5.00
TS	Tom Seaver	15.00
GS	Gary Sheffield	5.00
OS	Ozzie Smith	15.00
SS	Sammy Sosa	15.00
DW	Dave Winfield	5.00
RY	Robin Yount	12.00

Legendary Jerseys Auto.

	NM/M
Inserted 1:288	
EB	Ernie Banks	75.00
RC	Roger Clemens/211	80.00
KG	Ken Griffey Jr.	80.00
RJ	Reggie Jackson/224	60.00
SM	Stan Musial/266	100.00

		NM/M
AR	Alex Rodriguez	100.00
NR	Nolan Ryan	125.00
TS	Tom Seaver	60.00
OS	Ozzie Smith	60.00
SS	Sammy Sosa/91	100.00

Legendary Jerseys Gold

	NM/M
Common Player:	20.00
Production 25 Sets	
RCl	Roger Clemens	30.00
RoC	Roberto Clemente	150.00
KG	Ken Griffey Jr.	40.00
RJ	Reggie Jackson	40.00
WM	Willie Mays	100.00
AR	Alex Rodriguez	40.00
NR	Nolan Ryan	50.00
SS	Sammy Sosa	30.00
DW	Dave Winfield	20.00

Legendary Jerseys Gold Auto.

No pricing due to scarcity.
Production 25 Sets

Legendary Lumber

		NM/M
Common Player:		5.00
Inserted 1:24		
HA	Hank Aaron	30.00
LA	Luis Aparicio	5.00
EB	Ernie Banks/80	50.00
JB	Johnny Bench	15.00
BB	Barry Bonds	25.00
RCa	Roy Campanella/335	40.00
JC	Jose Canseco	8.00
RCl	Roger Clemens	15.00
RoC	Roberto Clemente/170	120.00
JD	Joe DiMaggio	85.00
JF	Jimmie Foxx/351	50.00
KG	Ken Griffey Jr.	15.00
TG	Tony Gwynn	10.00
RJ	Reggie Jackson	10.00
RJ	Randy Johnson	10.00
AJ	Andruw Jones	8.00
CJ	Chipper Jones	10.00
MM	Mickey Mantle	150.00
RM	Roger Maris	40.00
WM	Willie Mays	30.00
EM	Eddie Murray	8.00
MO	Mel Ott/355	40.00
MP	Mike Piazza	15.00
AP	Albert Pujols	45.00
MR	Manny Ramirez	8.00
FR	Frank Robinson	8.00
CR	Cal Ripken Jr.	40.00
AR	Alex Rodriguez	15.00
IR	Ivan Rodriguez	8.00

GS	Gary Sheffield	5.00
OS	Ozzie Smith	10.00
SS	Sammy Sosa	10.00

Legendary Lumber Auto.

		NM/M
Common Player:		25.00
Inserted 1:288		
LA	Luis Aparicio	25.00
EB	Ernie Banks	65.00
RC	Roger Clemens/227	75.00
KG	Ken Griffey Jr.	80.00
TG	Tony Gwynn	50.00
RJ	Reggie Jackson/211	80.00
EM	Eddie Murray	30.00
AR	Alex Rodriguez	100.00
SS	Sammy Sosa/66	100.00

Legendary Lumber Gold

		NM/M
Common Player:		15.00
Production 25 Sets		
RC	Roger Clemens	30.00
RC	Roberto Clemente	150.00
KG	Ken Griffey Jr.	40.00
RJ	Reggie Jackson	30.00
WM	Willie Mays	100.00
AR	Alex Rodriguez	40.00
GS	Gary Sheffield	15.00
SS	Sammy Sosa	30.00

Legendary Lumber Gold Auto.

No pricing due to scarcity.
Production 25 Sets

Reflections

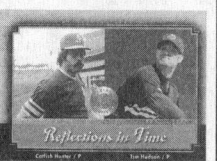

		NM/M
Complete Set (10):		25.00
Common Card:		1.00
Inserted 1:18		
R1	Bernie Williams, Mickey Mantle	6.00
R2	Pedro Martinez, Cy Young	2.00
R3	Barry Bonds, Willie Mays	5.00
R4	Scott Rolen, Mike Schmidt	3.00
R5	Mark McGwire, Stan Musial	4.00
R6	Ken Griffey Jr., Frank Robinson	3.00
R7	Sammy Sosa, Andre Dawson	3.00
R8	Kevin Brown, Don Drysdale	1.50
R9	Jason Giambi, Reggie Jackson	1.50
R10	Tim Hudson, Jim "Catfish" Hunter	1.00

2001 Upper Deck Legends of New York

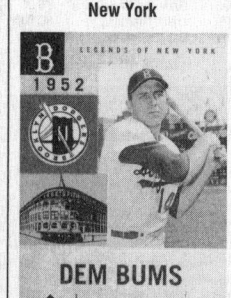

The greatest players, teams and events of 20th Century Major League baseball in New York City are featured in this specialty set.

The 200-card base set is comprised of a number of different subsets. The front of each card in the base set has an area of flocking in team colors.

		NM/M
Complete Set (200):		40.00
Common Player:		.20
Pack (5):		2.50
Box (24):		50.00
1	Billy Herman	.20
2	Carl Erskine	.20
3	Burleigh Grimes	.20
4	Don Newcombe	.20
5	Gil Hodges	.75
6	Pee Wee Reese	.75
7	Jackie Robinson	2.00
8	Duke Snider	1.00
9	Jim Gilliam	.20
10	Roy Campanella	1.50
11	Carl Furillo	.75
12	Casey Stengel	.75
13	Casey Stengel	.40
14	Billy Herman	.20
15	Jackie Robinson	1.00
16	Jackie Robinson	1.00
17	Gil Hodges	.40
18	Carl Furillo	.50
19	Roy Campanella	.50
20	Don Newcombe	.40
21	Duke Snider	.75
22	Casey Stengel	.40
23	Burleigh Grimes	.50
24	Pee Wee Reese	.50
25	Jackie Robinson	1.00
26	Jackie Robinson	1.00
27	Carl Erskine	.20
28	Roy Campanella	.50
29	Duke Snider	.75
30	Rube Marquard	.20
31	Ross Youngs	.20
32	Bobby Thomson	.20
33	Christy Mathewson	1.00
34	Carl Hubbell	.20
35	Hoyt Wilhelm	.20
36	Johnny Mize	.40
37	John McGraw	.50
38	Monte Irvin	.50
39	Travis Jackson	.20
40	Mel Ott	1.00
41	Dusty Rhodes	.20
42	Leo Durocher	.20
43	John McGraw	.20
44	Christy Mathewson	.20
45	The Polo Grounds	.20
46	Travis Jackson	.20
47	Mel Ott	.20
48	Johnny Mize	.20
49	Leo Durocher	.30
50	Bobby Thomson	.20
51	Monte Irvin	.20
52	Bobby Thomson	.20
53	Christy Mathewson	.50
54	Christy Mathewson	.50
55	Christy Mathewson	.50
56	John McGraw	.20
57	John McGraw	.20
58	John McGraw	.20
59	Travis Jackson	.20
60	Mel Ott	.50
61	Mel Ott	.50
62	Carl Hubbell	.20
63	Bobby Thomson	.20
64	Monte Irvin	.20
65	Al Weis	.20
66	Donn Clendenon	.20
67	Ed Kranepool	.20
68	Gary Carter	.20
69	Tommie Agee	.20
70	Jon Matlack	.20
71	Ken Boswell	.20
72	Len Dykstra	.20
73	Nolan Ryan	3.00
74	Ray Sadecki	.20
75	Ron Darling	.20
76	Ron Swoboda	.20
77	Dwight Gooden	.20
78	Tom Seaver	1.00
79	Wayne Garrett	.20
80	Casey Stengel	.50
81	Tom Seaver	.50
82	Tommie Agee	.50
83	Tom Seaver	.50
84	Yogi Berra	.50
85	Yogi Berra	.50
86	Tom Seaver	.50
87	Dwight Gooden	.20
88	Gary Carter	.20
89	Ron Darling	.20
90	Tommie Agee	.20
91	Tom Seaver	.50
92	Gary Carter	.20
93	Len Dykstra	.20
94	Babe Ruth	3.00
95	Bill Dickey	.50
96	Rich "Goose" Gossage	.20
97	Casey Stengel	.50
98	Jim "Catfish" Hunter	.20
99	Charlie Keller	.20
100	Chris Chambliss	.20
101	Don Larsen	.40
102	Dave Winfield	.75
103	Don Mattingly	2.00
104	Elston Howard	.20
105	Frankie Crosetti	.20
106	Hank Bauer	.20

07	Joe DiMaggio	3.00
08	Graig Nettles	.20
09	Lefty Gomez	.20
10	Phil Rizzuto	1.00
11	Lou Gehrig	2.00
12	Lou Piniella	.20
13	Mickey Mantle	3.00
14	Red Rolfe	.20
15	Reggie Jackson	1.00
16	Roger Maris	1.50
17	Ray White	.20
18	Thurman Munson	1.50
19	Tom Tresh	.20
20	Tommy Henrich	.20
21	Waite Hoyt	.20
22	Willie Randolph	.20
23	Whitey Ford	.75
24	Yogi Berra	1.00
25	Babe Ruth	1.50
26	Babe Ruth	1.50
27	Lou Gehrig	1.25
28	Babe Ruth	1.50
29	Joe DiMaggio	1.50
30	Joe DiMaggio	1.50
31	Mickey Mantle	1.50
32	Roger Marris	.75
33	Mickey Mantle	1.50
34	Reggie Jackson	.75
35	Babe Ruth	1.50
36	Babe Ruth	1.50
37	Babe Ruth	1.50
38	Lefty Gomez	.20
39	Lou Gehrig	1.25
140	Lou Gehrig	1.25
141	Joe DiMaggio	1.50
142	Joe DiMaggio	1.50
143	Casey Stengel	.40
144	Mickey Mantle	1.50
145	Yogi Berra	.50
146	Mickey Mantle	1.50
147	Elston Howard	.40
148	Whitey Ford	.50
149	Reggie Jackson	.50
150	Reggie Jackson	.50
151	John McGraw, Babe Ruth	1.00
152	Babe Ruth, John McGraw	1.00
153	Lou Gehrig, Mel Ott	.75
154	Joe DiMaggio, Mel Ott	1.00
155	Joe DiMaggio, Billy Herman	1.00
156	Joe DiMaggio, Jackie Robinson	1.50
157	Mickey Mantle, Bobby Thomson	1.00
158	Yogi Berra, Pee Wee Reese	.75
159	Roy Campanella, Mickey Mantle	1.00
160	Don Larsen, Duke Snider	.50
161	Christy Mathewson	.75
162	Christy Mathewson	.50
163	Rube Marquard	.20
164	Christy Mathewson	.50
165	John McGraw	.20
166	Burleigh Grimes	.20
167	Babe Ruth	1.50
168	Burleigh Grimes	.20
169	Babe Ruth	1.50
170	John McGraw	.40
171	Lou Gehrig	1.25
172	Babe Ruth	1.50
173	Babe Ruth	1.50
174	Carl Hubbell	.20
175	Joe DiMaggio	1.50
176	Lou Gehrig	1.25
177	Leo Durocher	.40
178	Mel Ott	.50
179	Joe DiMaggio	1.50
180	Jackie Robinson	1.00
181	Babe Ruth	1.50
182	Bobby Thomson	.20
183	Joe DiMaggio	1.50
184	Mickey Mantle	1.50
185	Monte Irvin	.20
186	Roy Campanella	.50
187	Duke Snider	.50
188	Dusty Rhodes	.20
189	Yogi Berra	.50
190	Mickey Mantle	1.50
191	Mickey Mantle	1.50
192	Casey Stengel	.40
193	Tom Seaver	.50
194	Mickey Mantle	1.50
195	Tommie Agee	.20
196	Tom Seaver	.50
197	Chris Chambliss	.20
198	Reggie Jackson	.50
199	Reggie Jackson	.50
200	Gary Carter	.20

Bat Cards

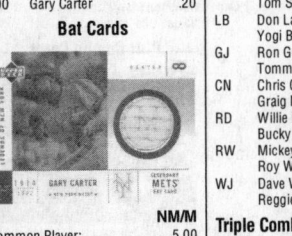

NM/M
Common Player: 5.00
Inserted 1:24
DODGERS
JG Jim Gilliam 10.00
BH Billy Herman 8.00
DN Don Newcombe/67 40.00

GIANTS
BTh Bobby Thomson . 25.00

METS
KB Ken Boswell 5.00
GC Gary Carter 15.00
LD Len Dykstra 5.00
WG Wayne Garrett 8.00
EK Ed Kranepool 10.00
JM J.C. Martin 8.00
NR Nolan Ryan 40.00
TS Tom Seaver 20.00
RSw Ron Swoboda 8.00
AW Al Weis 5.00

YANKEES
HB Hank Bauer 10.00
YB Yogi Berra 20.00
CC Chris Chambliss/130 15.00
BD Bill Dickey 15.00
TH Tommy Henrich 8.00
EH Elston Howard 15.00
RJ Reggie Jackson 15.00
CK Charlie Keller 8.00
MM Mickey Mantle/134 200.00
RM Roger Maris/60 85.00
DM Don Mattingly 30.00
TM Thurman Munson 25.00
LP Lou Piniella 10.00
MR Mickey Rivers 5.00
BR Babe Ruth/107 250.00
TT Tom Tresh 5.00
DW Dave Winfield 10.00

Autographs

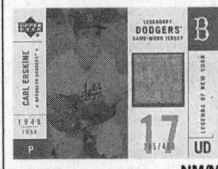

Common Autograph:
DODGERS
DN Don Newcombe 30.00
METS
GC Gary Carter 40.00
DC Donn Clendenon 30.00
NR Nolan Ryan/129 200.00
TS Tom Seaver/89 100.00
YANKEES
YB Yogi Berra 85.00
CC Chris Chambliss 30.00
RJ Reggie Jackson/123 75.00
DM Don Mattingly 100.00
MR Mickey Rivers 25.00
RW Roy White 25.00

Signatures

NM/M
Most not priced due to scarcity.
LC-JD Joe DiMaggio 1,000
(38 Issued)

Combination Signatures

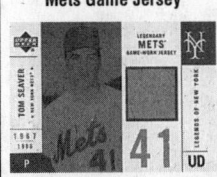

NM/M
Common Card: 75.00
NP Don Newcombe, Johnny Podres 85.00
WM Dave Winfield, Don Mattingly 200.00
RS Nolan Ryan, Tom Seaver 400.00
LB Don Larsen, Yogi Berra 150.00
GJ Ron Guidry, Tommy John 60.00
CN Chris Chambliss, Graig Nettles 60.00
RD Willie Randolph, Bucky Dent 60.00
RW Mickey Rivers, Roy White 60.00
WJ Dave Winfield, Reggie Jackson 150.00

Triple Combination Signatures
NM/M
Production 25 Sets
S-NPE Don Newcombe, Johnny Podres, Carl Erskine 175.00

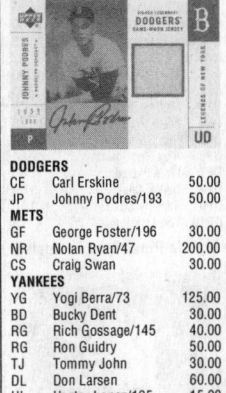

S-WMN Dave Winfield, Don Mattingly, Graig Nettles 175.00
S-RSS Nolan Ryan, Tom Seaver, Ron Swoboda 450.00
S-LBP Don Larsen, Yogi Berra, Joe Pepitone 125.00
S-GJG Ron Guidry, Tommy John, Rich "Goose" Gossage 100.00
S-CND Chris Chambliss, Graig Nettles, Bucky Dent 100.00
S-LRG Sparky Lyle, Dave Righetti, Rich "Goose" Gossage 100.00

Dodgers Game Jersey

Common Player: 5.00
Gold Edition of 400: 1.25X
HB Hank Behrman 5.00
CD Chuck Dressen 5.00
CE Carl Erskine 10.00
SJ Spider Jurgenson 5.00
JR Jackie Robinson/126 120.00

Giants Game Jersey

Complete Set (1):
CM Christy Mathewson/63 350.00

Mets Game Jersey

NM/M
Common Player: 5.00
Gold Edition of 400: 1.25X
RD Ron Darling 5.00
JM Jon Matlack 5.00
RS Ray Sadecki 5.00
TS Tom Seaver 15.00
CS Casey Stengel 8.00
JT Joe Torre 5.00

Yankees Game Jersey

NM/M
Common Player: 5.00
Gold Edition of 400: 1.25X
HB Hank Bauer 8.00
FC Frank Crosetti 10.00
TH Tommy Henrich 10.00
EH Elston Howard 10.00
CH Jim "Catfish" Hunter 10.00
DM Duke Maas 5.00
MM Mickey Mantle/63 250.00
LM Lindy McDaniel 5.00
TM Thurman Munson 30.00
GN Graig Nettles 10.00
PN Phil Niekro 10.00
JP Joe Pepitone 5.00
WR Willie Randolph 8.00
RR Red Rolfe 5.00
BT Bob Turley 8.00
DW Dave Winfield 15.00

Signed Game Jersey
NM/M
Common Autograph: 15.00

DODGERS
CE Carl Erskine 50.00
JP Johnny Podres/193 50.00
METS
GF George Foster/196 30.00
NR Nolan Ryan/47 200.00
CS Craig Swan 30.00
YANKEES
YB Yogi Berra/73 125.00
BD Bucky Dent 30.00
RG Rich Gossage/145 40.00
RG Ron Guidry 50.00
TJ Tommy John 30.00
DL Don Larsen 60.00
HL Hector Lopez/195 15.00
SL Sparky Lyle 30.00
DM Don Mattingly/72 125.00
PN Phil Niekro/195 40.00
GN Graig Nettles 30.00
JP Joe Pepitone 30.00
WR Willie Randolph 30.00

Ebbets Field G-U Base

Complete Set (1):
JR Jackie Robinson/100 50.00
JR Jackie Robinson/Silver/50 60.00
JR Jackie Robinson/Gold/25 75.00

Ebbets Field Seat
NM/M
Complete Set (1):
JR Jackie Robinson 50.00

Shea Stadium G-U Base
NM/M
Quantity produced listed.
TS Tom Seaver/100 25.00
TS Tom Seaver/Silver/50 40.00
TS Tom Seaver/Gold/25 50.00

United We Stand

Images from the aftermath of the 9/11/01 terrorist attack on New York's World Trade Center are featured in this insert series found in the UD Legends of New York issue. Red, white and blue stars and stripes are the background on card backs for a message from Upper Deck concerning relief efforts.

NM/M
Complete Set (15): 10.00
Common Card: 1.00
Inserted 1:12
USA1-15 United We Stand 1.00

Yankee Stadium Seat
Complete Set (1):

2001 Upper Deck Los Angeles Dodgers Team Set

This boxed set has 20 player cards in standard 2-1/2" x 3-1/2" format and a 3-1/2" x 5" checklist. Cards have borderless action photos on front with an Upper Deck Collectibles logo at top-left. At bottom are the team and player name, position and uniform number. Backs have a smaller version of the front photo, some biographical and career notes and 1999-2000 stats. Cards are numbered with an "LA" prefix.

NM/M
Complete Set (21): 10.00
Common Player: .50
1 Gary Sheffield 1.00
2 Shawn Green 1.00
3 Kevin Brown .50
4 Adrian Beltre .75
5 Eric Karros .50
6 Darren Dreifort .50
7 Chan Ho Park .50
8 Alex Cora .50
9 Mark Grudzielanek .50
10 Paul LoDuca .75
11 Dave Hansen .50
12 Tom Goodwin .50
13 Ramon Martinez .50
14 Luke Prokopec .50
15 Chad Kreuter .50
16 Jeff Shaw .50
17 Eric Gagne .75
18 Andy Ashby .50
19 F.P. Santangelo .50
20 Mike Fetters .50
21 Checklist .50

2001 Upper Deck MVP

NM/M
Complete Set (330): 35.00
Common Player: .10
Pack (8): 1.50
Box (24): 30.00
1 Mo Vaughn .10
2 Troy Percival .10
3 Adam Kennedy .10
4 Darin Erstad .25
5 Tim Salmon .10
6 Bengie Molina .10
7 Troy Glaus .40
8 Garret Anderson .10
9 Ismael Valdes .10
10 Glenallen Hill .10
11 Tim Hudson .25
12 Eric Chavez .20
13 Johnny Damon .20
14 Barry Zito .25
15 Jason Giambi .40
16 Terrence Long .10
17 Jason Hart .10
18 Jose Ortiz .10
19 Miguel Tejada .25
20 Jason Isringhausen .10
21 Adam Piatt .10

22	Jeremy Giambi	.10
23	Tony Batista	.10
24	Darrin Fletcher	.10
25	Mike Sirotka	.10
26	Carlos Delgado	.40
27	Billy Koch	.10
28	Shannon Stewart	.10
29	Raul Mondesi	.15
30	Brad Fullmer	.10
31	Jose Cruz Jr.	.10
32	Kelvim Escobar	.10
33	Greg Vaughn	.10
34	Aubrey Huff	.10
35	Albie Lopez	.10
36	Gerald Williams	.10
37	Ben Grieve	.10
38	John Flaherty	.10
39	Fred McGriff	.15
40	Ryan Rupe	.10
41	Travis Harper	.10
42	Steve Cox	.10
43	Roberto Alomar	.40
44	Jim Thome	.50
45	Russell Branyan	.10
46	Bartolo Colon	.20
47	Omar Vizquel	.15
48	Travis Fryman	.15
49	Kenny Lofton	.15
50	Chuck Finley	.10
51	Ellis Burks	.10
52	Eddie Taubensee	.10
53	Juan Gonzalez	.40
54	Edgar Martinez	.20
55	Aaron Sele	.10
56	John Olerud	.20
57	Jay Buhner	.10
58	Mike Cameron	.10
59	John Halama	.10
60	Ichiro Suzuki RC	8.00
61	David Bell	.10
62	Freddy Garcia	.10
63	Carlos Guillen	.10
64	Bret Boone	.20
65	Al Martin	.10
66	Cal Ripken Jr.	1.50
67	Delino DeShields	.10
68	Chris Richard	.10
69	Sean Douglass RC	.25
70	Melvin Mora	.10
71	Luis Matos	.10
72	Sidney Ponson	.10
73	Mike Bordick	.10
74	Brady Anderson	.10
75	David Segui	.10
76	Jeff Conine	.10
77	Alex Rodriguez	1.25
78	Gabe Kapler	.10
79	Ivan Rodriguez	.40
80	Rick Helling	.10
81	Kenny Rogers	.10
82	Andres Galarraga	.15
83	Rusty Greer	.10
84	Justin Thompson	.10
85	Ken Caminiti	.10
86	Rafael Palmeiro	.40
87	Ruben Mateo	.10
88	Travis Hafner RC	1.00
89	Manny Ramirez	.40
90	Pedro Martinez	.50
91	Carl Everett	.10
92	Dante Bichette	.10
93	Derek Lowe	.10
94	Jason Varitek	.10
95	Nomar Garciaparra	1.25
96	David Cone	.10
97	Tomokazu Ohka	.10
98	Troy O'Leary	.10
99	Trot Nixon	.10
100	Jermaine Dye	.10
101	Joe Randa	.10
102	Jeff Suppan	.10
103	Roberto Hernandez	.10
104	Mike Sweeney	.10
105	Mac Suzuki	.10
106	Carlos Febles	.10
107	Jose Rosado	.10
108	Mark Quinn	.10
109	Carlos Beltran	.20
110	Dean Palmer	.10
111	Mitch Meluskey	.10
112	Bobby Higginson	.10
113	Brandon Inge	.10
114	Tony Clark	.10
115	Brian Moehler	.10
116	Juan Encarnacion	.10
117	Damion Easley	.10
118	Roger Cedeno	.10
119	Jeff Weaver	.10
120	Matt Lawton	.10
121	Jay Canizaro	.10
122	Eric Milton	.10
123	Corey Koskie	.10
124	Mark Redman	.10
125	Jacque Jones	.10
126	Brad Radke	.10
127	Cristian Guzman	.10
128	Joe Mays	.10
129	Denny Hocking	.10
130	Frank Thomas	.40
131	David Wells	.10
132	Ray Durham	.10
133	Paul Konerko	.10
134	Joe Crede	.10
135	Jim Parque	.10
136	Carlos Lee	.10
137	Magglio Ordonez	.25
138	Sandy Alomar Jr.	.10
139	Chris Singleton	.10

#	Player	Price
140	Jose Valentin	.10
141	Roger Clemens	1.00
142	Derek Jeter	1.50
143	Orlando Hernandez	.15
144	Tino Martinez	.10
145	Bernie Williams	.40
146	Jorge Posada	.25
147	Mariano Rivera	.20
148	David Justice	.20
149	Paul O'Neill	.15
150	Mike Mussina	.25
151	Christian Parker RC	.10
152	Andy Pettitte	.25
153	Alfonso Soriano	.50
154	Jeff Bagwell	.40
155	Morgan Ensberg RC	.25
156	Daryle Ward	.10
157	Craig Biggio	.20
158	Richard Hidalgo	.10
159	Shane Reynolds	.10
160	Scott Elarton	.10
161	Julio Lugo	.10
162	Moises Alou	.20
163	Lance Berkman	.20
164	Chipper Jones	.75
165	Greg Maddux	1.00
166	Javy Lopez	.15
167	Andruw Jones	.40
168	Rafael Furcal	.25
169	Brian Jordan	.10
170	Wes Helms	.10
171	Tom Glavine	.25
172	B.J. Surhoff	.10
173	John Smoltz	.10
174	Quilvio Veras	.10
175	Rico Brogna	.10
176	Jeromy Burnitz	.10
177	Jeff D'Amico	.10
178	Geoff Jenkins	.20
179	Henry Blanco	.10
180	Mark Loretta	.10
181	Richie Sexson	.25
182	Jimmy Haynes	.10
183	Jeffrey Hammonds	.10
184	Ron Belliard	.10
185	Tyler Houston	.10
186	Mark McGwire	1.00
187	Rick Ankiel	.25
188	Darryl Kile	.10
189	Jim Edmonds	.25
190	Mike Matheny	.10
191	Edgar Renteria	.10
192	Ray Lankford	.10
193	Garrett Stephenson	.10
194	J.D. Drew	.20
195	Fernando Vina	.10
196	Dustin Hermanson	.10
197	Sammy Sosa	1.00
198	Corey Patterson	.25
199	Jon Lieber	.10
200	Kerry Wood	.40
201	Todd Hundley	.10
202	Kevin Tapani	.10
203	Rondell White	.10
204	Eric Young	.10
205	Matt Stairs	.10
206	Bill Mueller	.10
207	Randy Johnson	.50
208	Mark Grace	.25
209	Jay Bell	.10
210	Curt Schilling	.25
211	Erubiel Durazo	.10
212	Luis Gonzalez	.20
213	Steve Finley	.10
214	Matt Williams	.20
215	Reggie Sanders	.10
216	Tony Womack	.10
217	Gary Sheffield	.25
218	Kevin Brown	.15
219	Adrian Beltre	.10
220	Shawn Green	.20
221	Darren Dreifort	.10
222	Chan Ho Park	.15
223	Eric Karros	.15
224	Alex Cora	.10
225	Mark Grudzielanek	.10
226	Andy Ashby	.10
227	Vladimir Guerrero	.75
228	Tony Armas Jr.	.10
229	Fernando Tatis	.10
230	Jose Vidro	.10
231	Javier Vazquez	.10
232	Lee Stevens	.10
233	Milton Bradley	.10
234	Carl Pavano	.10
235	Peter Bergeron	.10
236	Wilton Guerrero	.10
237	Ugueth Urbina	.10
238	Barry Bonds	1.50
239	Livan Hernandez	.10
240	Jeff Kent	.15
241	Pedro Feliz	.10
242	Bobby Estalella	.10
243	J.T. Snow	.10
244	Shawn Estes	.10
245	Robb Nen	.10
246	Rich Aurilia	.10
247	Russ Ortiz	.10
248	Preston Wilson	.10
249	Brad Penny	.10
250	Cliff Floyd	.10
251	A.J. Burnett	.10
252	Mike Lowell	.10
253	Luis Castillo	.10
254	Ryan Dempster	.10
255	Derrek Lee	.10
256	Charles Johnson	.10
257	Pablo Ozuna	.10
258	Antonio Alfonseca	.10
259	Mike Piazza	1.00
260	Robin Ventura	.10
261	Al Leiter	.15
262	Timoniel Perez	.10
263	Edgardo Alfonzo	.10
264	Jay Payton	.10
265	Tsuyoshi Shinjo RC	.25
266	Todd Zeile	.10
267	Armando Benitez	.10
268	Glendon Rusch	.10
269	Rey Ordonez	.10
270	Kevin Appier	.10
271	Tony Gwynn	.50
272	Phil Nevin	.10
273	Mark Kotsay	.10
274	Ryan Klesko	.20
275	Adam Eaton	.10
276	Mike Darr	.10
277	Damian Jackson	.10
278	Woody Williams	.10
279	Chris Gomez	.10
280	Trevor Hoffman	.10
281	Xavier Nady	.15
282	Scott Rolen	.40
283	Bruce Chen	.10
284	Pat Burrell	.30
285	Mike Lieberthal	.10
286	Brandon Duckworth RC	.20
287	Travis Lee	.10
288	Bobby Abreu	.10
289	Jimmy Rollins	.25
290	Robert Person	.10
291	Randy Wolf	.10
292	Jason Kendall	.10
293	Derek Bell	.10
294	Brian Giles	.25
295	Kris Benson	.10
296	John Vander Wal	.10
297	Todd Ritchie	.10
298	Warren Morris	.10
299	Kevin Young	.10
300	Francisco Cordova	.10
301	Aramis Ramirez	.10
302	Ken Griffey Jr.	1.00
303	Pete Harnisch	.10
304	Aaron Boone	.10
305	Sean Casey	.20
306	Jackson Melian RC	.40
307	Rob Bell	.10
308	Barry Larkin	.25
309	Dmitri Young	.10
310	Danny Graves	.10
311	Pokey Reese	.10
312	Leo Estrella	.10
313	Todd Helton	.40
314	Mike Hampton	.15
315	Juan Pierre	.10
316	Brent Mayne	.10
317	Larry Walker	.25
318	Denny Neagle	.10
319	Jeff Cirillo	.10
320	Pedro Astacio	.10
321	Todd Hollandsworth	.10
322	Neifi Perez	.10
323	Ron Gant	.10
324	Todd Walker	.10
325	Alex Rodriguez CL	.50
326	Ken Griffey Jr. CL	.50
327	Mark McGwire CL	.50
328	Pedro Martinez CL	.25
329	Derek Jeter CL	.75
330	Mike Piazza CL	.40

Authentic Griffey

Inserted 1:288

Code	Card	Price
AGS	Ken Griffey Jr./Auto.	125.00
AGJ	Ken Griffey Jr./Jersey	15.00
AGC	Ken Griffey Jr./Cap	40.00
AGB	Ken Griffey Jr./Bat	15.00
AGU	Ken Griffey Jr./Uniform	15.00
AGGS	Ken Griffey/Gold Auto./30	250.00
AGGJ	Ken Griffey Jr./Gold Jsy/30	75.00
AGGC	Ken Griffey Jr./Gold Cap/30	75.00
AGGB	Ken Griffey/Gold Bat/30	75.00
CGR	Ken Griffey Jr., Alex Rodriguez/100	35.00
CGS	Ken Griffey Jr., Sammy Sosa/100	35.00
CGT	Ken Griffey Jr., Frank Thomas/100	25.00

Drawing Power

NM/M
Complete Set (10): 10.00
Common Player: .75
Inserted 1:12

Code	Player	Price
DP1	Mark McGwire	2.00
DP2	Vladimir Guerrero	1.00
DP3	Manny Ramirez	.75
DP4	Frank Thomas	.75
DP5	Ken Griffey Jr.	1.50
DP6	Alex Rodriguez	2.50
DP7	Mike Piazza	1.50
DP8	Derek Jeter	3.00
DP9	Sammy Sosa	2.00
DP10	Todd Helton	.75

Mantle Pinstripes Exclusive

NM/M
Complete Set (56): 75.00
Common Mantle: 2.00
One Pack/Box

Mantle Pinstripes Excl. Memorabilia

NM/M
Print Runs Listed

Code	Card	Price
MMCJ3	Mickey Mantle, Ken Griffey Jr./50	200.00
MMJ3	Mickey Mantle/Jsy/100	125.00

Souvenirs Batting Gloves

NM/M
Common Player: 8.00
Inserted 1:96 H

Code	Player	Price
BB	Barry Bonds	20.00
TrG	Troy Glaus	40.00
JG	Juan Gonzalez	10.00
KG	Ken Griffey Jr.	8.00
ToG	Tony Gwynn/200	20.00
CJ	Jose Canseco	30.00
JL	Javy Lopez	15.00
GM	Greg Maddux/95	8.00
EM	Edgar Martinez	60.00
FM	Fred McGriff	8.00
RP	Rafael Palmeiro	8.00
CR	Cal Ripken Jr.	15.00
AR	Alex Rodriguez	50.00
IR	Ivan Rodriguez	20.00
SS	Sammy Sosa	10.00
MT	Miguel Tejada	15.00
FT	Frank Thomas	8.00
MV	Mo Vaughn	10.00

Souvenirs Batting Gloves Autographs

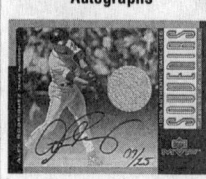

NM/M
Production 25 Sets

Code	Player	Price
KG	Ken Griffey Jr.	120.00
ToG	Tony Gwynn	60.00
CR	Cal Ripken Jr.	200.00
AR	Alex Rodriguez	120.00
IR	Ivan Rodriguez	50.00
SS	Sammy Sosa	100.00
FT	Frank Thomas	80.00

Souvenirs Two-Player Bat Combo

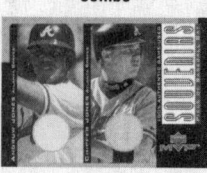

NM/M
Common Combo: 10.00
Inserted 1:144

Code	Players	Price
TS	Frank Thomas, Sammy Sosa	20.00
RR	Alex Rodriguez, Ivan Rodriguez	25.00
TG	Jim Thome, Ken Griffey Jr.	25.00
GS	Ken Griffey Jr., Sammy Sosa	25.00
WA	Kerry Wood, Rick Ankiel	10.00
3K	Tony Gwynn, Cal Ripken Jr.	40.00
DV	Carlos Delgado, Jose Vidro	10.00
JJ	Andruw Jones, Chipper Jones	20.00
HR	Jose Canseco, Ken Griffey Jr.	20.00
JF	Chipper Jones, Rafael Furcal	15.00
OW	Paul O'Neill, Bernie Williams	10.00
TO	Frank Thomas, Magglio Ordonez	15.00
RM	Alex Rodriguez, Edgar Martinez	20.00
RP	Ivan Rodriguez, Rafael Palmeiro	15.00

Souvenirs Two-Player Bat Autograph

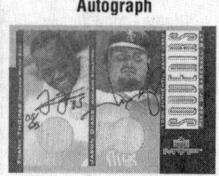

NM/M
Production 25 Sets

Code	Players	Price
RG	Alex Rodriguez, Ken Griffey Jr.	180.00
SG	Sammy Sosa, Ken Griffey Jr.	150.00
RR	Alex Rodriguez, Ivan Rodriguez	150.00
JG	Chipper Jones, Troy Glaus	125.00
TS	Frank Thomas, Sammy Sosa	125.00
GD	Jason Giambi, Carlos Delgado	50.00
3K	Cal Ripken Jr., Tony Gwynn	180.00
TG	Frank Thomas, Jason Giambi	75.00
HH	Todd Helton, Mike Hampton	40.00

Souvenirs Three Player Bat Combo

No pricing due to scarcity.
Production 25 Sets

Super Tools

NM/M
Complete Set (20): 20.00
Common Player: .50
Inserted 1:6

Code	Player	Price
ST1	Ken Griffey Jr.	1.50
ST2	Carlos Delgado	.75
ST3	Alex Rodriguez	2.50
ST4	Troy Glaus	.75
ST5	Jeff Bagwell	.75
ST6	Ichiro Suzuki	3.00
ST7	Derek Jeter	3.00
ST8	Jim Edmonds	.50
ST9	Vladimir Guerrero	.75
ST10	Jason Giambi	.75
ST11	Todd Helton	.75
ST12	Cal Ripken Jr.	3.00
ST13	Barry Bonds	3.00
ST14	Nomar Garciaparra	2.00
ST15	Randy Johnson	1.00
ST16	Jermaine Dye	.50
ST17	Andruw Jones	.75
ST18	Ivan Rodriguez	.75
ST19	Sammy Sosa	2.00
ST20	Pedro Martinez	1.00

2001 Upper Deck Ovation

NM/M
Complete Set (90): 100.00
Common Player: .20
Common WP (61-90): 3.00
WP Production 2,000
Pack (5): 5.00
Box (20): 80.00

#	Player	Price
1	Troy Glaus	.50
2	Darin Erstad	.40
3	Jason Giambi	.50
4	Tim Hudson	.40
5	Eric Chavez	.30
6	Carlos Delgado	.50
7	David Wells	.20
8	Greg Vaughn	.20
9	Omar Vizquel	.20
10	Jim Thome	.50
11	Roberto Alomar	.40
12	John Olerud	.30
13	Edgar Martinez	.20
14	Cal Ripken Jr.	2.00
15	Alex Rodriguez	1.50
16	Ivan Rodriguez	.50
17	Manny Ramirez	.50
18	Nomar Garciaparra	1.50
19	Pedro Martinez	.75
20	Jermaine Dye	.20
21	Juan Gonzalez	.50
22	Matt Lawton	.20
23	Frank Thomas	.75
24	Magglio Ordonez	.40
25	Bernie Williams	.40
26	Derek Jeter	2.00
27	Roger Clemens	1.50
28	Jeff Bagwell	1.00
29	Richard Hidalgo	.20
30	Chipper Jones	1.00
31	Greg Maddux	1.00
32	Andruw Jones	.50
33	Jeromy Burnitz	.20
34	Mark McGwire	1.50
35	Jim Edmonds	.40
36	Sammy Sosa	1.50
37	Kerry Wood	.50
38	Randy Johnson	.75
39	Steve Finley	.20
40	Gary Sheffield	.40
41	Kevin Brown	.40
42	Shawn Green	.40
43	Vladimir Guerrero	.75
44	Jose Vidro	.20
45	Barry Bonds	2.00
46	Jeff Kent	.30
47	Preston Wilson	.20
48	Luis Castillo	.20
49	Mike Piazza	1.00
50	Edgardo Alfonzo	.20
51	Tony Gwynn	.75
52	Ryan Klesko	.30
53	Scott Rolen	.50
54	Bob Abreu	.30
55	Jason Kendall	.20
56	Brian Giles	.30
57	Ken Griffey Jr.	1.00
58	Barry Larkin	.40
59	Todd Helton	.50
60	Mike Hampton	.20
61	Corey Patterson (World Premiere)	3.00
62	Timoniel Perez (World Premiere)	3.00
63	Toby Hall (World Premiere)	3.00
64	Brandon Inge (World Premiere)	3.00
65	Joe Crede (World Premiere)	3.00
66	Xavier Nady (World Premiere)	3.00
67	Adam Pettyjohn RC (World Premiere)	3.00
68	Keith Ginter (World Premiere)	3.00
69	Brian Cole (World Premiere)	3.00
70	Tyler Walker RC (World Premiere)	3.00
71	Juan Uribe RC (World Premiere)	5.00
72	Alex Hernandez (World Premiere)	3.00
73	Leo Estrella (World Premiere)	3.00
74	Joey Nation (World Premiere)	3.00
75	Aubrey Huff (World Premiere)	3.00
76	Ichiro Suzuki RC (World Premiere)	75.00
77	Jay Spurgeon (World Premiere)	3.00
78	Sun-Woo Kim (World Premiere)	3.00
79	Pedro Feliz (World Premiere)	3.00
80	Pablo Ozuna (World Premiere)	3.00
81	Hiram Bocachica (World Premiere)	3.00
82	Brad Wilkerson (World Premiere)	3.00
83	Rocky Biddle (World Premiere)	3.00
84	Aaron McNeal (World Premiere)	3.00
85	Adam Bernero (World Premiere)	3.00
86	Danys Baez (World Premiere)	3.00
87	Dee Brown (World Premiere)	3.00
88	Jimmy Rollins (World Premiere)	5.00
89	Jason Hart (World Premiere)	3.00
90	Ross Gload (World Premiere)	3.00

A Piece of History

NM/M
Common Player: 5.00
Inserted 1:40

Code	Player	Price
RA	Rick Ankiel	6.00
JB	Johnny Bench	15.00
BB	Barry Bonds	30.00
KB	Kevin Brown	5.00
JC	Jose Canseco	8.00
RC	Roger Clemens	15.00
DC	David Cone	5.00
CD	Carlos Delgado	8.00
JD	Joe DiMaggio	100.00
DD	Don Drysdale/SP	25.00
DE	Darin Erstad	5.00
RF	Rollie Fingers/SP	8.00
CF	Carlton Fisk	10.00
RF	Rafael Furcal	5.00
TrG	Troy Glaus	8.00
TG	Tom Glavine	8.00
SG	Shawn Green	5.00
KG	Ken Griffey Jr.	15.00
KGs	Ken Griffey Sr.	5.00
MH	Mike Hampton	5.00
RJ	Randy Johnson	10.00
AJ	Andruw Jones	8.00
CJ	Chipper Jones	15.00
GM	Greg Maddux	15.00
MM	Mickey Mantle	125.00
JP	Jim Palmer	10.00
CR	Cal Ripken Jr.	30.00
BR	Brooks Robinson	15.00
AR	Alex Rodriguez	15.00
IR	Ivan Rodriguez	8.00
NR	Nolan Ryan/SP	120.00
TS	Tom Seaver	8.00
GS	Gary Sheffield	5.00
OS	Ozzie Smith/SP	20.00
SS	Sammy Sosa	15.00
FT	Frank Thomas	8.00
BW	Bernie Williams	5.00
MW	Matt Williams	5.00
EW	Early Wynn	5.00

A Piece of History Autograph

Common Player:
Values Undetermined

POH Combo Cards

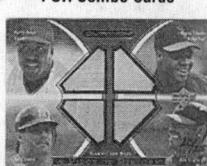

Production 25 Sets
Values Undetermined

Curtain Calls

NM/M
Complete Set (10): 10.00

Common Player: .50
Inserted 1:7

1	Sammy Sosa	2.00
2	Darin Erstad	.50
3	Barry Bonds	2.50
4	Todd Helton	.75
5	Mike Piazza	1.50
6	Ken Griffey Jr.	1.50
7	Nomar Garciaparra	2.00
8	Carlos Delgado	.75
9	Jason Giambi	.75
10	Alex Rodriguez	2.00

DiMaggio Pinstripes Exclusive

NM/M
Complete Set (56): 60.00
Common DiMaggio: 1.50
One Pack/Box

DiMaggio Pinstripes Memorabilia

NM/M
Print Runs Listed: 150.00
JDB	Joe DiMaggio/Bat/100	75.00
JDCJ	Joe DiMaggio, Mickey Mantle/Jsy/50	300.00
JDJ	Joe DiMaggio/Jsy/100	100.00

Lead Performers

NM/M
Complete Set (11): 15.00
Common Player: 1.00
Inserted 1:12

1	Mark McGwire	3.00
2	Derek Jeter	4.00
3	Alex Rodriguez	3.00
4	Frank Thomas	1.00
5	Sammy Sosa	2.50
6	Mike Piazza	1.50
7	Vladimir Guerrero	1.50
8	Pedro Martinez	1.50
9	Carlos Delgado	1.00
10	Ken Griffey Jr.	2.00
11	Jeff Bagwell	1.00

Superstar Theatre

NM/M
Complete Set (11): 20.00

Common Player: 1.00
Inserted 1:12

1	Nomar Garciaparra	2.50
2	Ken Griffey Jr.	2.00
3	Frank Thomas	1.00
4	Derek Jeter	4.00
5	Mike Piazza	2.00
6	Sammy Sosa	2.50
7	Barry Bonds	4.00
8	Alex Rodriguez	3.00
9	Todd Helton	1.00
10	Mark McGwire	3.00
11	Jason Giambi	1.00

2001 Upper Deck Pros & Prospects

NM/M
Complete Set (141):
Common Player: .15
Common (91-135): 4.00
Production 1,250
Common (136-141): 8.00
Production 500
Pack (5): 6.00
Box (24): 120.00

1	Troy Glaus	.50
2	Darin Erstad	.25
3	Tim Hudson	.40
4	Jason Giambi	.50
5	Jermaine Dye	.15
6	Barry Zito	.15
7	Carlos Delgado	.50
8	Shannon Stewart	.15
9	Raul Mondesi	.15
10	Greg Vaughn	.15
11	Ben Grieve	.15
12	Roberto Alomar	.40
13	Juan Gonzalez	.50
14	Jim Thome	.50
15	C.C. Sabathia	.40
16	Edgar Martinez	.25
17	Kazuhiro Sasaki	.15
18	Aaron Sele	.15
19	John Olerud	.25
20	Cal Ripken Jr.	2.00
21	Rafael Palmeiro	.50
22	Ivan Rodriguez	.75
23	Alex Rodriguez	1.50
24	Manny Ramirez	.50
25	Pedro Martinez	.75
26	Carl Everett	.15
27	Nomar Garciaparra	.75
28	Neifi Perez	.15
29	Mike Sweeney	.15
30	Bobby Higginson	.15
31	Tony Clark	.15
32	Doug Mientkiewicz	.15
33	Cristian Guzman	.15
34	Brad Radke	.15
35	Magglio Ordonez	.40
36	Carlos Lee	.25
37	Frank Thomas	.50
38	Roger Clemens	1.50
39	Bernie Williams	.50
40	Derek Jeter	2.00
41	Tino Martinez	.25
42	Wade Miller	.15
43	Jeff Bagwell	.50
44	Lance Berkman	.50
45	Richard Hidalgo	.15
46	Greg Maddux	1.00
47	Andruw Jones	.50
48	Chipper Jones	1.00
49	Rafael Furcal	.25
50	Jeromy Burnitz	.15
51	Geoff Jenkins	.25
52	Ben Sheets	.25
53	Mark McGwire	1.50

54	Jim Edmonds	.40
55	J.D. Drew	.25
56	Fred McGriff	.25
57	Sammy Sosa	1.00
58	Kerry Wood	.50
59	Randy Johnson	.75
60	Luis Gonzalez	.25
61	Curt Schilling	.40
62	Kevin Brown	.25
63	Shawn Green	.25
64	Gary Sheffield	.40
65	Vladimir Guerrero	.75
66	Jose Vidro	.15
67	Barry Bonds	2.00
68	Jeff Kent	.40
69	Rich Aurilia	.15
70	Preston Wilson	.15
71	Charles Johnson	.15
72	Cliff Floyd	.15
73	Mike Piazza	1.00
74	Al Leiter	.15
75	Matt Lawton	.15
76	Tony Gwynn	.75
77	Ryan Klesko	.25
78	Phil Nevin	.15
79	Scott Rolen	.50
80	Pat Burrell	.40
81	Jimmy Rollins	.75
82	Jason Kendall	.25
83	Brian Giles	.25
84	Aramis Ramirez	.25
85	Ken Griffey Jr.	1.00
86	Barry Larkin	.40
87	Sean Casey	.25
88	Larry Walker	.25
89	Todd Helton	.50
90	Mike Hampton	.15
91	Juan Cruz **RC**	4.00
92	Brian Lawrence **RC**	4.00
93	Brandon Lyon **RC**	4.00
94	Adrian Hernandez **RC**	4.00
95	Jose Mieses **RC**	4.00
96	Juan Uribe **RC**	4.00
97	Morgan Ensberg **RC**	4.00
98	Wilson Betemit **RC**	8.00
99	Ryan Freel **RC**	6.00
100	Jack Wilson **RC**	6.00
101	Cesar Crespo **RC**	4.00
102	Bret Prinz **RC**	4.00
103	Horacio Ramirez **RC**	4.00
104	Elpidio Guzman **RC**	4.00
105	Josh Towers **RC**	4.00
106	Brandon Duckworth **RC**	4.00
107	Esix Snead **RC**	4.00
108	Billy Sylvester **RC**	4.00
109	Alexis Gomez **RC**	4.00
110	Johnny Estrada **RC**	4.00
111	Joe Kennedy **RC**	4.00
112	Travis Hafner **RC**	10.00
113	Martin Vargas **RC**	4.00
114	Jay Gibbons **RC**	4.00
115	Andres Torres **RC**	4.00
116	Sean Douglass **RC**	4.00
117	Juan Diaz **RC**	4.00
118	Greg Miller **RC**	4.00
119	Carlos Valderrama **RC**	4.00
120	William Ortega **RC**	4.00
121	Josh Fogg **RC**	4.00
122	Wilken Ruan **RC**	4.00
123	Kris Keller **RC**	4.00
124	Erick Almonte **RC**	4.00
125	Ricardo Rodriguez **RC**	4.00
126	Grant Balfour **RC**	4.00
127	Nick Maness **RC**	4.00
128	Jeremy Owens **RC**	4.00
129	Doug Nickle **RC**	4.00
130	Bert Snow **RC**	4.00
131	Jason Smith **RC**	4.00
132	Henry Mateo **RC**	4.00
133	Mike Penney **RC**	4.00
134	Bud Smith **RC**	4.00
135	Junior Spivey **RC**	4.00
136	Ichiro Suzuki **RC**	75.00
137	Albert Pujols **RC**	180.00
138	Mark Teixeira **RC**	100.00
139	Dewon Brazelton **RC**	8.00
140	Mark Prior **RC**	12.00
141	Tsuyoshi Shinjo **RC**	8.00

Bats

NM/M
Common Card: 4.00
Inserted 1:24
Golds: 3-5X
Production 25 Sets

WI	Bernie Williams, Ichiro Suzuki	35.00
RG	Manny Ramirez, Juan Gonzalez	8.00
RP	Ivan Rodriguez, Mike Piazza	10.00
BT	Jeff Bagwell, Frank Thomas	8.00
GBo	Ken Griffey Jr., Barry Bonds	25.00
SG	Sammy Sosa, Luis Gonzalez	12.00

KA	Jeff Kent, Roberto Alomar	4.00
RF	Alex Rodriguez, Rafael Furcal	15.00
PT	Rafael Palmeiro, Jim Thome	10.00
JP	Chipper Jones, Albert Pujols	40.00
GBu	Shawn Green, Jeromy Burnitz	4.00
JL	Andruw Jones, Kenny Lofton	4.00
MJ	Greg Maddux, Randy Johnson	15.00

Legends Bats

NM/M
Common Card: 15.00
Inserted 1:216
Gold: 3-5X
Production 25 Sets

RF	Manny Ramirez, Carlton Fisk	15.00
BY	Jeromy Burnitz, Robin Yount	15.00
WJ	Bernie Williams, Reggie Jackson	15.00
RG	Cal Ripken Jr., Tony Gwynn	50.00

Franchise Building Blocks

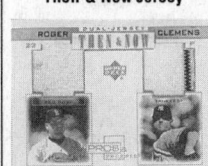

NM/M
Complete Set (30): 25.00
Common Player: .50
Inserted 1:6

F1	Darin Erstad, Elpidio Guzman	.50
F2	Jason Giambi, Jason Hart	1.00
F3	Carlos Delgado, Vernon Wells	.75
F4	Greg Vaughn, Aubrey Huff	.75
F5	Jim Thome, C.C. Sabathia	1.00
F6	Edgar Martinez, Ichiro Suzuki	3.00
F7	Cal Ripken Jr., Josh Towers	3.00
F8	Ivan Rodriguez, Carlos Pena	1.00
F9	Nomar Garciaparra, Dernell Stenson	2.00
F10	Mike Sweeney, Dee Brown	.50
F11	Bobby Higginson, Brandon Inge	.50
F12	Brad Radke, Adam Johnson	.50
F13	Frank Thomas, Joe Crede	1.00
F14	Derek Jeter, Nick Johnson	3.00
F15	Jeff Bagwell, Morgan Ensberg	1.00
F16	Chipper Jones, Wilson Betemit	1.50
F17	Jeromy Burnitz, Ben Sheets	.50
F18	Mark McGwire, Albert Pujols	3.00
F19	Sammy Sosa, Corey Patterson	2.00
F20	Luis Gonzalez, Jack Cust	.50
F21	Kevin Brown, Luke Prokopec	.50
F22	Vladimir Guerrero, Wilken Ruan	1.00
F23	Barry Bonds, Carlos Valderrama	3.00
F24	Preston Wilson, Abraham Nunez	1.00
F25	Mike Piazza, Alex Escobar	1.50
F26	Tony Gwynn, Xavier Nady	1.00
F27	Scott Rolen, Jimmy Rollins	1.00
F28	Jason Kendall, Jack Wilson	1.00
F29	Ken Griffey Jr., Adam Dunn	1.50
F30	Todd Helton, Juan Uribe	1.00

Ichiro World Tour

NM/M
Complete Set (15): 25.00
Common Ichiro: 2.00

Inserted 1:12
| WT1-15 | Ichiro Suzuki | 2.00 |

Specialty Jersey

NM/M
Common Player: 4.00
Inserted 1:24
Golds: 3-5X
Production 25 Sets

RA	Roberto Alomar	6.00
BB	Barry Bonds	25.00
JE	Jim Edmonds	6.00
JG	Juan Gonzalez	6.00
SG	Shawn Green	4.00
TG	Tony Gwynn	10.00
RJ	Randy Johnson	10.00
CR	Cal Ripken Jr.	30.00
AR	Alex Rodriguez	15.00
SR	Scott Rolen	4.00
SS	Sammy Sosa	10.00
I	Ichiro	60.00
JT	Jim Thome	8.00
LW	Larry Walker	4.00

Then & Now Jersey

NM/M
Common Player: 4.00
Inserted 1:24
Golds: 3-5X
Production 25 Sets

RA	Rick Ankiel	4.00
BB	Barry Bonds	30.00
KB	Kevin Brown	6.00
RC	Roger Clemens	20.00
JE	Jim Edmonds	6.00
FG	Freddy Garcia	4.00
JGi	Jason Giambi	8.00
JGo	Juan Gonzalez	8.00
KG	Ken Griffey Jr.	20.00
RJ	Randy Johnson	10.00
GM	Greg Maddux	20.00
PM	Pedro Martinez	10.00
XN	Xavier Nady	4.00
PN	Phil Nevin	4.00
MP	Mike Piazza	15.00
MR	Manny Ramirez	8.00
AR	Alex Rodriguez	15.00
CS	Curt Schilling	6.00
GS	Gary Sheffield	6.00
RV	Robin Ventura	4.00

Now Combo Jersey

NM/M
Complete Set (1):
| NR | Nolan Ryan | 100.00 |

2001 Upper Deck Prospect Premieres

NM/M
Complete Set (90): 100.00
Common Player: .25
Common Auto. SP (91-102): 10.00
Auto. Production 1,000
Pack (4): 8.00
Box (18): 125.00

1	Jeff Mathis **RC**	.50
2	Jake Woods **RC**	.50
3	Dallas McPherson **RC**	.50
4	Steven Shell **RC**	.25
5	Ryan Budde **RC**	.25
6	Kirk Saarloos **RC**	.40
7	Ryan Stegall **RC**	.25
8	Bobby Crosby **RC**	.50
9	J.T. Stotts **RC**	.25
10	Neal Cotts **RC**	.50
11	Jeremy Bonderman **RC**	.50
12	Brandon League **RC**	.40
13	Tyrell Godwin **RC**	.25
14	Gabe Gross **RC**	.50
15	Chris Neylan **RC**	.25
16	Michael Rouse **RC**	.25
17	Macay McBride **RC**	.25
18	Josh Burrus **RC**	.25
19	Adam Stern **RC**	.25
20	Richard Lewis **RC**	.40
21	Cole Barthel **RC**	.25
22	Mike Jones **RC**	.25
23	J.J. Hardy **RC**	.75
24	Brad Nelson **RC**	.75
25	Justin Pope **RC**	.25
26	Dan Haren **RC**	2.00
27	Andy Sisco **RC**	.50
28	Ryan Theriot **RC**	2.50
29	Ricky Nolasco **RC**	2.00
30	Jon Switzer **RC**	.25
31	Justin Wechsler **RC**	.25
32	Mike Gosling **RC**	.25
33	Scott Hairston **RC**	1.00
34	Brian Pilkington **RC**	.25
35	Kole Strayhorn **RC**	.25
36	David Taylor **RC**	.25
37	Donald Levinski **RC**	.25
38	Mike Hinckley **RC**	.50
39	Nick Long **RC**	.25
40	Brad Hennessey **RC**	.25
41	Noah Lowry **RC**	.75
42	Josh Cram **RC**	.25
43	Jesse Foppert **RC**	.50
44	Julian Benavidez **RC**	.25
45	Daniel Denham **RC**	.25
46	Travis Foley **RC**	.40
47	Mike Conroy **RC**	.25
48	Jake Dittler **RC**	.25
49	Rene Rivera **RC**	.25
50	John Cole **RC**	.25
51	Lazaro Abreu **RC**	.25
52	David Wright **RC**	25.00
53	Aaron Heilman **RC**	.40
54	Lenny DiNardo **RC**	.40
55	Alhaji Turay **RC**	.40
56	Chris Smith **RC**	.25
57	Rommie Lewis **RC**	.25
58	Bryan Bass **RC**	.25
59	David Crouthers **RC**	.25
60	Josh Barfield **RC**	.50
61	Jake Peavy **RC**	4.00
62	Ryan Howard **RC**	30.00
63	Gavin Floyd **RC**	1.50
64	Mike Floyd **RC**	.25
65	Stefan Bailie **RC**	.25
66	Jon DeVries **RC**	.25
67	Steve Kelly **RC**	.25
68	Alan Moye **RC**	.25
69	Justin Gillman **RC**	.25
70	Jayson Nix **RC**	.50
71	John Draper **RC**	.25
72	Kenny Baugh **RC**	.25
73	Michael Woods **RC**	.25
74	Preston Larrison **RC**	.25
75	Matt Coenen **RC**	.25
76	Scott Tyler **RC**	.50
77	Jose Morales **RC**	.25
78	Corwin Malone **RC**	.50
79	Dennis Ulacia **RC**	.40
80	Andy Gonzalez **RC**	.25
81	Kris Honel **RC**	.50
82	Wyatt Allen **RC**	.25
83	Ryan Wing **RC**	.25
84	Sean Henn **RC**	.40
85	John-Ford Griffin **RC**	.50
86	Bronson Sardinha **RC**	.50
87	Jon Skaggs **RC**	.25
88	Shelley Duncan **RC**	.25
89	Jason Arnold **RC**	.50
90	Aaron Rifkin **RC**	.25
91	Colt Griffin **RC**	10.00
92	J.D. Martin **RC**	10.00
93	Justin Wayne **RC**	10.00
94	John VanBenschoten **RC**	10.00
95	Chris Burke **RC**	10.00
96	Casey Kotchman **RC**	10.00
97	Michael Garciaparra **RC**	10.00
98	Jake Gautreau **RC**	10.00
99	Jerome Williams **RC**	10.00
100	Greg Nash **RC**	10.00
101	Joe Borchard **RC**	10.00
102	Mark Prior **RC**	15.00

Heroes of Baseball Bat

NM/M
Common Player: 4.00
Inserted 1:18

DB	Don Baylor	4.00
WB	Wade Boggs	8.00

JD Heroes of Baseball

BB	Bill Buckner	4.00
GC	Gary Carter	8.00
DE	Dwight Evans	4.00
SG	Steve Garvey	4.00
KiG	Kirk Gibson	4.00
KeG	Ken Griffey Sr.	4.00
RJ	Reggie Jackson	10.00
DL	Davey Lopes	4.00
FL	Fred Lynn	4.00
BM	Bill Madlock	4.00
TM	Tim McCarver	4.00
JM	Joe Morgan	4.00
MM	Manny Mota	4.00
EM	Eddie Murray	8.00
AO	Al Oliver	4.00
DP	Dave Parker	4.00
TP	Tony Perez	4.00
KP	Kirby Puckett	15.00
OS	Ozzie Smith	10.00
DW	Dave Winfield	8.00

HOB Bat Autograph

Production 25 Sets
Values Undetermined

Dual Combo Jersey

NM/M
Common Duo: 8.00
Inserted 1:144

BH	Bryan Bass, J.J. Hardy	10.00
DG	Shelley Duncan, Tyrell Godwin	8.00
GS	Steve Garvey, Reggie Smith	10.00
HB	Aaron Heilman, Jeremy Bonderman	10.00
JJ	Michael Jordan, Michael Jordan	100.00
SG	Jon Switzer, Mike Gosling	8.00
WP	Dave Winfield, Kirby Puckett	20.00

Dual Combo Jersey Auto.

Values Undetermined

Triple Combo Jersey

NM/M
Common Card:
Inserted 1:144

BKH	Bobby Crosby, Michael Garciaparra, Bronson Sardinha	15.00
BBC	Chris Burke, Bryan Bass, Bubba Crosby	10.00
GGH	Jake Gautreau, Tyrell Godwin, Aaron Heilman	8.00
GMS	Colt Griffin, J.D. Martin, Jon Switzer	8.00
GKB	Gabe Gross, Casey Kotchman, Kenny Baugh	10.00
JMD	Michael Jordan, Mickey Mantle, Joe DiMaggio	350.00
JPW	Michael Jordan, Kirby Puckett, Dave Winfield	40.00
MMD	Roger Maris, Mickey Mantle, Joe DiMaggio	700.00
VPJ	John VanBenschoten, Mark Prior, Mike Jones	25.00

Triple Combo Jersey Auto.

Values Undetermined

MJ Grandslam Bat

NM/M
Common MJ: 25.00

MJ1-4	Michael Jordan	25.00
MJ5	Michael Jordan (White Sox)	40.00

"Tribute to 42"

NM/M
Inserted 1:750

42-B	Jackie Robinson/Bat	40.00
42-J	Jackie Robinson/Jsy	60.00
42-C	Jackie Robinson/Cut	500.00
42-B	Jackie Robinson/Bat/42	100.00
42-J	Jackie Robinson/Jsy/42	100.00

2001 UD Reserve

NM/M
Complete Set (210):
Common Player:
Common SP (181-210): 3.00
Production 2,500
Pack (5): 3.00
Box (24): 60.00

#	Player	Value
1	Darin Erstad	.25
2	Tim Salmon	.25
3	Bengie Molina	.15
4	Troy Glaus	.50
5	Glenallen Hill	.15
6	Garret Anderson	.25
7	Jason Giambi	.50
8	Johnny Damon	.40
9	Eric Chavez	.25
10	Tim Hudson	.25
11	Miguel Tejada	.40
12	Barry Zito	.25
13	Jose Ortiz	.15
14	Tony Batista	.15
15	Carlos Delgado	.50
16	Shannon Stewart	.15
17	Raul Mondesi	.25
18	Ben Grieve	.15
19	Aubrey Huff	.15
20	Greg Vaughn	.15
21	Fred McGriff	.25
22	Gerald Williams	.15
23	Bartolo Colon	.25
24	Roberto Alomar	.40
25	Jim Thome	.50
26	Omar Vizquel	.25
27	Juan Gonzalez	.50
28	Ellis Burks	.15
29	Edgar Martinez	.25
30	Aaron Sele	.15
31	Jay Buhner	.15
32	Mike Cameron	.15
33	Kazuhiro Sasaki	.15
34	John Olerud	.25
35	Cal Ripken Jr.	2.00
36	Brady Anderson	.15
37	Pat Hentgen	.15
38	Chris Richard	.15
39	Jerry Hairston Jr.	.15
40	Mike Bordick	.15
41	Ivan Rodriguez	.50
42	Rick Helling	.15
43	Rafael Palmeiro	.50
44	Alex Rodriguez	1.50
45	Andres Galarraga	.25
46	Rusty Greer	.15
47	Ruben Mateo	.15
48	Ken Caminiti	.15
49	Nomar Garciaparra	.75
50	Pedro Martinez	.75
51	Manny Ramirez	.50
52	Carl Everett	.15
53	Dante Bichette	.15
54	Hideo Nomo	.40
55	Mike Sweeney	.15
56	Carlos Beltran	.50
57	Jeff Suppan	.15
58	Jermaine Dye	.25
59	Mark Quinn	.15
60	Joe Randa	.15
61	Bobby Higginson	.15
62	Tony Clark	.15
63	Brian Moehler	.15
64	Dean Palmer	.15
65	Brandon Inge	.15
66	Damion Easley	.15
67	Brad Radke	.15
68	Corey Koskie	.15
69	Cristian Guzman	.15
70	Eric Milton	.15
71	Jacque Jones	.15
72	Matt Lawton	.15
73	Frank Thomas	.50
74	David Wells	.15
75	Magglio Ordonez	.40
76	Paul Konerko	.25
77	Sandy Alomar Jr.	.15
78	Ray Durham	.15
79	Roger Clemens	1.50
80	Bernie Williams	.50
81	Derek Jeter	2.00
82	David Justice	.25
83	Paul O'Neill	.25
84	Mike Mussina	.40
85	Jorge Posada	.40
86	Jeff Bagwell	.50
87	Richard Hidalgo	.15
88	Craig Biggio	.25
89	Scott Elarton	.15
90	Moises Alou	.25
91	Greg Maddux	1.00
92	Rafael Furcal	.25
93	Andruw Jones	.50
94	Tom Glavine	.40
95	Chipper Jones	1.00
96	Javy Lopez	.25
97	Richie Sexson	.40
98	Jeromy Burnitz	.15
99	Jeff D'Amico	.15
100	Jeffrey Hammonds	.15
101	Geoff Jenkins	.25
102	Ben Sheets	.25
103	Mark McGwire	1.50
104	Rick Ankiel	.40
105	Darryl Kile	.15
106	Edgar Renteria	.25
107	Jim Edmonds	.25
108	J.D. Drew	.25
109	Sammy Sosa	1.00
110	Corey Patterson	.25
111	Kerry Wood	.50
112	Todd Hundley	.15
113	Rondell White	.15
114	Matt Stairs	.15
115	Randy Johnson	.75
116	Mark Grace	.40
117	Steve Finley	.15
118	Luis Gonzalez	.25
119	Matt Williams	.25
120	Curt Schilling	.40
121	Gary Sheffield	.40
122	Kevin Brown	.25
123	Shawn Green	.25
124	Eric Karros	.15
125	Chan Ho Park	.25
126	Adrian Beltre	.25
127	Vladimir Guerrero	.75
128	Fernando Tatis	.15
129	Lee Stevens	.15
130	Jose Vidro	.15
131	Peter Bergeron	.15
132	Michael Barrett	.15
133	Jeff Kent	.25
134	Russ Ortiz	.15
135	Barry Bonds	2.00
136	J.T. Snow	.15
137	Livan Hernandez	.15
138	Rich Aurilia	.15
139	Preston Wilson	.15
140	Mike Lowell	.25
141	Ryan Dempster	.15
142	Charles Johnson	.15
143	Matt Clement	.15
144	Luis Castillo	.15
145	Mike Piazza	1.00
146	Al Leiter	.15
147	Robin Ventura	.25
148	Jay Payton	.15
149	Todd Zeile	.15
150	Edgardo Alfonzo	.15
151	Tony Gwynn	.75
152	Ryan Klesko	.25
153	Phil Nevin	.15
154	Mark Kotsay	.15
155	Trevor Hoffman	.15
156	Damian Jackson	.15
157	Scott Rolen	.50
158	Mike Lieberthal	.15
159	Bruce Chen	.15
160	Bobby Abreu	.40
161	Pat Burrell	.40
162	Travis Lee	.15
163	Jason Kendall	.15
164	Derek Bell	.15
165	Kris Benson	.15
166	Kevin Young	.15
167	Brian Giles	.25
168	Pat Meares	.15
169	Sean Casey	.25
170	Pokey Reese	.15
171	Pete Harnisch	.15
172	Barry Larkin	.25
173	Ken Griffey Jr.	1.00
174	Dmitri Young	.15
175	Mike Hampton	.15
176	Todd Helton	.50
177	Jeff Cirillo	.15
178	Denny Neagle	.15
179	Larry Walker	.25
180	Todd Hollandsworth	.15
181	Ichiro Suzuki RC (Rookie Reserve)	30.00
182	Wilson Betemit RC (Rookie Reserve)	6.00
183	Adrian Hernandez RC (Rookie Reserve)	3.00
184	Travis Hafner RC (Rookie Reserve)	8.00
185	Sean Douglass RC (Rookie Reserve)	3.00
186	Juan Diaz RC (Rookie Reserve)	3.00
187	Horacio Ramirez RC (Rookie Reserve)	5.00
188	Morgan Ensberg RC (Rookie Reserve)	3.00
189	Brandon Duckworth RC (Rookie Reserve)	3.00
190	Jack Wilson RC (Rookie Reserve)	8.00
191	Erick Almonte RC (Rookie Reserve)	3.00
192	Ricardo Rodriguez RC (Rookie Reserve)	3.00
193	Elpidio Guzman RC (Rookie Reserve)	3.00
194	Juan Uribe RC (Rookie Reserve)	5.00
195	Ryan Freel RC (Rookie Reserve)	6.00
196	Christian Parker RC (Rookie Reserve)	3.00
197	Jackson Melian RC (Rookie Reserve)	3.00
198	Jose Mieses RC (Rookie Reserve)	3.00
199	Andres Torres RC (Rookie Reserve)	3.00
200	Jason Smith RC (Rookie Reserve)	3.00
201	Johnny Estrada RC (Rookie Reserve)	5.00
202	Cesar Crespo RC (Rookie Reserve)	3.00
203	Carlos Valderrama RC (Rookie Reserve)	3.00
204	Albert Pujols RC (Rookie Reserve)	100.00
205	Wilken Ruan RC (Rookie Reserve)	3.00
206	Josh Fogg RC (Rookie Reserve)	4.00
207	Bert Snow RC (Rookie Reserve)	3.00
208	Brian Lawrence RC (Rookie Reserve)	5.00
209	Esix Snead RC (Rookie Reserve)	4.00
210	Tsuyoshi Shinjo RC (Rookie Reserve)	4.00

Big Game Reserve

NM/M
Complete Set (10): 15.00
Common Player: 1.00
Inserted 1:24

BG1	Alex Rodriguez	3.00
BG2	Ken Griffey Jr.	2.00
BG3	Mark McGwire	3.00
BG4	Derek Jeter	4.00
BG5	Sammy Sosa	2.50
BG6	Pedro Martinez	1.50
BG7	Jason Giambi	1.00
BG8	Todd Helton	1.00
BG9	Carlos Delgado	1.00
BG10	Mike Piazza	2.00

G-U Reserve Base/Ball Duo

NM/M
Inserted 1:240

JR	Derek Jeter, Alex Rodriguez	50.00
JP	Derek Jeter, Mike Piazza	60.00
MP	Mark McGwire, Mike Piazza	100.00
MJ	Mark McGwire, Derek Jeter	100.00
RM	Alex Rodriguez, Mark McGwire	100.00
CR	Roger Clemens, Alex Rodriguez	40.00
ST	Sammy Sosa, Frank Thomas	40.00
GD	Vladimir Guerrero, Carlos Delgado	20.00
BH	Barry Bonds, Todd Helton	35.00
MG	Mark McGwire, Ken Griffey Jr.	35.00
GS	Ken Griffey Jr., Sammy Sosa	35.00
GJ	Ken Griffey Jr., Derek Jeter	35.00
JN	Chipper Jones, Nomar Garciaparra	20.00
NJ	Nomar Garciaparra, Derek Jeter	35.00
GR	Nomar Garciaparra, Alex Rodriguez	30.00

G-U Reserve Base/Ball Trio

NM/M
Inserted 1:480

JRG	Derek Jeter, Alex Rodriguez, Nomar Garciaparra	50.00
SGM	Sammy Sosa, Ken Griffey Jr., Mark McGwire	65.00
PRS	Mike Piazza, Alex Rodriguez, Sammy Sosa	40.00
GSG	Ken Griffey Jr., Sammy Sosa, Vladimir Guerrero	30.00
THM	Frank Thomas, Todd Helton, Mark McGwire	65.00
CMJ	Roger Clemens, Pedro Martinez, Derek Jeter	45.00
BSH	Barry Bonds, Gary Sheffield, Todd Helton	40.00
GPJ	Vladimir Guerrero, Mike Piazza, Chipper Jones	30.00
MJR	Mark McGwire, Derek Jeter, Alex Rodriguez	75.00
JGS	Derek Jeter, Ken Griffey Jr., Sammy Sosa	45.00

G-U Reserve Base/Ball Quad

NM/M
Production 50 Sets

SGRM	Sammy Sosa, Ken Griffey Jr., Alex Rodriguez, Mark McGwire	175.00
GPJG	Vladimir Guerrero, Mike Piazza, Chipper Jones, Nomar Garciaparra	65.00
THMJ	Frank Thomas, Todd Helton, Mark McGwire, Derek Jeter	90.00
GBJE	Ken Griffey Jr., Barry Bonds, Andruw Jones, Jim Edmonds	75.00
PMJR	Mike Piazza, Mark McGwire, Derek Jeter, Alex Rodriguez	150.00

Jerseys Duo

NM/M
Common Duo: 10.00
Inserted 1:240

HG	Tim Hudson, Jason Giambi	10.00
BK	Barry Bonds, Jeff Kent	20.00
JJ	Andruw Jones, Chipper Jones	20.00
GE	Troy Glaus, Darin Erstad	10.00
WO	David Wells, Magglio Ordonez	10.00
WE	Bernie Williams, Jim Edmonds	10.00
DG	Carlos Delgado, Jason Giambi	10.00
GK	Jason Giambi, Jeff Kent	10.00
JW	Randy Johnson, David Wells	15.00
JG	Chipper Jones, Troy Glaus	15.00
SB	Gary Sheffield, Barry Bonds	20.00
HE	Todd Helton, Darin Erstad	10.00
RB	Alex Rodriguez, Tony Batista	20.00
GW	Brian Giles, Bernie Williams	10.00
SG	Sammy Sosa, Troy Glaus	15.00

Jerseys Trio

NM/M
Common Trio: 20.00
Inserted 1:480

GHD	Jason Giambi, Todd Helton, Carlos Delgado	20.00
RSS	Alex Rodriguez, Sammy Sosa, Barry Sheffield	40.00
WEJ	Bernie Williams, Jim Edmonds, Andruw Jones	20.00
HJW	Tim Hudson, Randy Johnson, David Wells	20.00
SOD	Sammy Sosa, Magglio Ordonez, Carlos Delgado	30.00
GGR	Jason Giambi, Troy Glaus, Alex Rodriguez	30.00
BWD	Tony Batista, Bernie Williams, Carlos Delgado	20.00
BSH	Barry Bonds, Gary Sheffield, Todd Helton	30.00
WSH	David Wells, Sammy Sosa, Todd Helton	30.00
EKE	Darin Erstad, Jeff Kent, Jim Edmonds	20.00

Jerseys Quad

NM/M
Common Quad: 20.00
Production 50 Sets

DRGS	Carlos Delgado, Alex Rodriguez, Troy Glaus, Sammy Sosa	40.00
GWBG	Jason Giambi, Bernie Williams, Barry Bonds, Brian Giles	50.00
HKEJ	Todd Helton, Jeff Kent, Jim Edmonds, Chipper Jones	30.00
HKEJ	Jason Giambi, Magglio Ordonez, Darin Erstad, Tony Batista	20.00
JRSB	Andruw Jones, Alex Rodriguez, Sammy Sosa, Barry Bonds	100.00

The New Order

NM/M
Complete Set (10): 15.00
Common Player: .75

Inserted 1:24

		NM/M
NO1	Vladimir Guerrero	1.50
NO2	Andruw Jones	1.00
NO3	Corey Patterson	.75
NO4	Derek Jeter	4.00
NO5	Alex Rodriguez	3.00
NO6	Pat Burrell	.75
NO7	Ichiro Suzuki	5.00
NO8	Barry Zito	.75
NO9	Rafael Furcal	.75
NO10	Troy Glaus	1.00

UD Royalty

NM/M
Complete Set (10): 15.00
Common Player: 1.00
Inserted 1:24

R1	Ken Griffey Jr.	2.00
R2	Derek Jeter	4.00
R3	Alex Rodriguez	3.00
R4	Sammy Sosa	2.50
R5	Mark McGwire	3.00
R6	Mike Piazza	2.00
R7	Vladimir Guerrero	1.50
R8	Chipper Jones	2.00
R9	Frank Thomas	1.00
R10	Nomar Garciaparra	3.00

2001 Upper Deck Rookie Update

NM/M
Common Player: .25
Common Rookie:
Pack (4): 15.00
Box (18): 250.00
Sweet Spot
Common SP (121-150): 3.00
Production 1,500

91	Garret Anderson	.50
92	Jermaine Dye	.25
93	Shannon Stewart	.25
94	Ben Grieve	.25
95	Juan Gonzalez	.50
96	Bret Boone	.50
97	Tony Batista	.25
98	Rafael Palmeiro	1.00
99	Carl Everett	.25
100	Mike Sweeney	.25
101	Tony Clark	.25
102	Doug Mientkiewicz	.25
103	Jose Canseco	.50
104	Mike Mussina	.75
105	Lance Berkman	.50
106	Andruw Jones	.50
107	Geoff Jenkins	.40
108	Matt Morris	.25
109	Fred McGriff	.40
110	Luis Gonzalez	.50
111	Kevin Brown	.25
112	Tony Armas Jr.	.25
113	John Vander Wal	.25
114	Cliff Floyd	.25
115	Matt Lawton	.25
116	Phil Nevin	.25
117	Pat Burrell	.50
118	Aramis Ramirez	.50
119	Sean Casey	.40
120	Larry Walker	.40
121	Albert Pujols RC	150.00
122	Johnny Estrada RC	4.00
123	Wilson Betemit RC	3.00
124	Adrian Hernandez RC	3.00
125	Morgan Ensberg RC	3.00
126	Horacio Ramirez RC	3.00
127	Josh Towers RC	3.00
128	Juan Uribe RC	3.00
129	Wilken Ruan RC	3.00
130	Andres Torres RC	3.00

131	Brian Lawrence RC	3.00
132	Ryan Freel RC	5.00
133	Brandon Duckworth RC	3.00
134	Juan Diaz RC	3.00
135	Rafael Soriano RC	4.00
136	Ricardo Rodriguez RC	3.00
137	Bud Smith RC	3.00
138	Mark Teixeira RC	40.00
139	Mark Prior RC	6.00
140	Jackson Melian RC	3.00
141	Dewon Brazelton RC	3.00
142	Greg Miller RC	3.00
143	Billy Sylvester RC	3.00
144	Elpidio Guzman RC	3.00
145	Jack Wilson RC	5.00
146	Jose Mieses RC	3.00
147	Brandon Lyon RC	3.00
148	Tsuyoshi Shinjo RC	3.00
149	Juan Cruz RC	3.00
150	Jay Gibbons RC	3.00

SPx
Common (181-205) 3.00
Production 1,500
Cards (206-210) Autographed

151	Garret Anderson	.50
152	Jermaine Dye	.25
153	Shannon Stewart	.25
154	Toby Hall	.25
155	C.C. Sabathia	.50
156	Bret Boone	.25
157	Tony Batista	.25
158	Gabe Kapler	.25
159	Carl Everett	.25
160	Mike Sweeney	.25
161	Dean Palmer	.25
162	Doug Mientkiewicz	.25
163	Carlos Lee	.50
164	Mike Mussina	.75
165	Lance Berkman	.75
166	Ken Caminiti	.25
167	Ben Sheets	.40
168	Matt Morris	.25
169	Fred McGriff	.40
170	Curt Schilling	.75
171	Paul LoDuca	.25
172	Javier Vazquez	.25
173	Rich Aurilia	.25
174	A.J. Burnett	.25
175	Al Leiter	.40
176	Mark Kotsay	.25
177	Jimmy Rollins	.75
178	Aramis Ramirez	.50
179	Aaron Boone	.25
180	Jeff Cirillo	.25
181	Johnny Estrada RC	3.00
182	Dave Williams RC	3.00
183	Donaldo Mendez RC	3.00
184	Junior Spivey RC	3.00
185	Jay Gibbons RC	3.00
186	Kyle Lohse RC	5.00
187	Willie Harris RC	3.00
188	Juan Cruz RC	3.00
189	Joe Kennedy RC	3.00
190	Duaner Sanchez RC	3.00
191	Jorge Julio RC	3.00
192	Cesar Crespo RC	3.00
193	Casey Fossum RC	3.00
194	Brian Roberts RC	10.00
195	Troy Mattes RC	3.00
196	Rob Mackowiak RC	3.00
197	Tsuyoshi Shinjo RC	3.00
198	Nick Punto RC	3.00
199	Wilmy Caceres RC	3.00
200	Jeremy Affeldt RC	3.00
201	Bret Prinz RC	3.00
202	Delvin James RC	3.00
203	Luis Pineda RC	3.00
204	Matt White RC	3.00
205	Brandon Knight RC	3.00
206	Albert Pujols RC	500.00
207	Mark Teixeira RC	150.00
208	Mark Prior RC	15.00
209	Dewon Brazelton RC	8.00
210	Bud Smith RC	8.00

SP Authentic
Common (211-240): 4.00
Production 1,500

181	Garret Anderson	.50
182	Jermaine Dye	.25
183	Shannon Stewart	.25
184	Ben Grieve	.25
185	Ellis Burks	.25
186	John Olerud	.25
187	Tony Batista	.25
188	Ruben Sierra	.25
189	Carl Everett	.25
190	Neifi Perez	.25
191	Tony Clark	.25
192	Doug Mientkiewicz	.25
193	Carlos Lee	.50
194	Jorge Posada	.50
195	Ken Caminiti	.25
196	Ben Sheets	.25
197	Matt Morris	.25
198	Fred McGriff	.40
199	Mark Grace	.50
200	Paul LoDuca	.25
201	Tony Armas, Jr.	.25
202	Andres Galarraga	.40
203	Matt Lawton	.25
204	Ryan Klesko	.40
205	Jimmy Rollins	.25
206	Aramis Ramirez	.50
207	Aaron Boone	.25
208	Jose Ortiz	.25
210	Mark Prior	6.00
211	Mark Prior RC	6.00

212	Mark Teixeira RC	80.00
213	Bud Smith RC	4.00
214	Wilmy Caceres RC	4.00
215	Dave Williams RC	4.00
216	Delvin James RC	4.00
217	Endy Chavez RC	4.00
218	Doug Nickle RC	4.00
219	Bret Prinz RC	4.00
220	Troy Mattes RC	4.00
221	Duaner Sanchez RC	4.00
222	Dewon Brazelton RC	4.00
223	Brian Bowles RC	4.00
224	Donaldo Mendez RC	4.00
225	Jorge Julio RC	4.00
226	Matt White RC	4.00
227	Casey Fossum RC	4.00
228	Mike Rivera RC	4.00
229	Joe Kennedy RC	4.00
230	Kyle Lohse RC	6.00
231	Juan Cruz RC	4.00
232	Jeremy Affeldt RC	4.00
233	Brandon Lyon RC	4.00
234	Brian Roberts RC	10.00
235	Willie Harris RC	4.00
236	Pedro Santana RC	4.00
237	Rafael Soriano RC	6.00
238	Steve Green RC	4.00
239	Junior Spivey RC	4.00
240	Rob Mackowiak RC	4.00

Ichiro ROY

019/100

NM/M
Complete Set (51): 35.00
Common Ichiro: 1.00

1-50	Ichiro Suzuki	1.00
51	Checklist (Ichiro Suzuki)	1.00

Ichiro ROY Game Jersey

NM/M
Numbers 1-12 Production 100 50.00
Numbers 13-17 Production 50 75.00
Numbers 18-19
Production 25 150.00

J-I1-12	Ichiro Suzuki	50.00
J-I13-17	Ichiro Suzuki	75.00
J-I18-19	Ichiro Suzuki	150.00

Ichiro ROY Game-Used Bat

014/180

NM/M
Numbers 1-12 Production 100 50.00
Numbers 13-17 Production 50 75.00
Numbers 18-19
Production 25 150.00

B-I1-12	Ichiro Suzuki	50.00
B-I13-17	Ichiro Suzuki	75.00
B-I18-19	Ichiro Suzuki	150.00

SP Chirography

NM/M
Common Autograph: 15.00
Production 250
Silver: .75-1.5X
Production 100
Gold: No Pricing
Production 25 Sets

LB	Lance Berkman/100	20.00
KG	Ken Griffey Jr./250	90.00
TG	Tony Gwynn/250	30.00
TG	Tony Gwynn/100	30.00
MS	Doug Mientkiewicz/100	10.00
JP	Jorge Posada/250	25.00
JP	Jorge Posada/100	25.00
CR	Cal Ripken Jr.	100.00
MS	Mike Sweeney/100	10.00

SP Chirography - Ichiro

074/100

Available only as a redemption in UD Rookie Update. Three versions were produced, an un-numbered autographed card, a Silver parallel autograph numbered to 100 and a Gold autograph parallel numbered to 25.

	NM/M
Ichiro (Unnumbered)	300.00
Ichiro Silver/100	500.00

USA Touch of Gold

NM/M
Common Autograph: 8.00
Production 500 Sets

BA	Brent Abernathy	8.00
KU	Kurt Ainsworth	10.00
PB	Pat Borders	8.00
SB	Sean Burroughs	8.00
JC	John Cotton	8.00
TD	Gookie Dawkins	8.00
AE	Adam Everett	8.00
RF	Ryan Franklin	8.00
CG	Chris George	8.00
SH	Shane Heams	8.00
MJ	Marcus Jensen	8.00
MK	Mike Kinkade	8.00
RK	Rick Krivda	8.00
DM	Doug Mientkiewicz	10.00
MN	Mike Neill	8.00
RO	Roy Oswalt	20.00
JR	Jon Rauch	8.00
AS	Anthony Sanders	8.00
BSe	Bobby Seay	8.00
BSh	Ben Sheets	12.00
BW	Brad Wilkerson	8.00
TW	Todd Williams	8.00
EY	Ernie Young	8.00
TY	Tim Young	8.00

Materials 2-Player

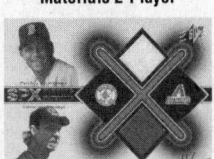

11/25

NM/M
Common Card: 10.00
Inserted 1:15

BB-LG	Barry Bonds, Luis Gonzalez	20.00
JG-BB	Jason Giambi, Barry Bonds	20.00
IR-AR	Ivan Rodriguez, Alex Rodriguez	20.00
AP-JE	Albert Pujols, Jim Edmonds	30.00
GS-SG	Gary Sheffield, Shawn Green	10.00
MP-EA	Mike Piazza, Edgardo Alfonzo	15.00
LW-TH	Larry Walker, Todd Helton	10.00
MR-JG	Manny Ramirez, Juan Gonzalez	15.00
TG-CR	Tony Gwynn, Cal Ripken Jr.	30.00
SR-BA	Scott Rolen, Bobby Abreu	10.00
JB-CB	Jeff Bagwell, Craig Biggio	10.00
KG-SC	Ken Griffey Jr., Sean Casey	20.00
EM-JM	Eric Milton, Joe Mays	10.00
HN-MY	Hideo Nomo, Masato Yoshii	10.00
TS-HN	Tsuyoshi Shinjo, Hideo Nomo	10.00
CS-RJ	Curt Schilling, Randy Johnson	15.00
AS-KS	Aaron Sele, Kazuhiro Sasaki	10.00
PM-RJ	Pedro Martinez, Randy Johnson	15.00
BW-MR	Bernie Williams, Mariano Rivera	15.00
TG-X2	Tony Gwynn	15.00
CR-X2	Cal Ripken Jr.	30.00
JB-RY	Jeremy Burnitz, Robin Yount	15.00
CR-EM	Cal Ripken Jr., Eddie Murray	30.00
TG-DW	Tony Gwynn, Dave Winfield	15.00
FT-MO	Frank Thomas, Magglio Ordonez	15.00
PM-GM	Pedro Martinez, Greg Maddux	15.00
BW-RJ	Bernie Williams, Reggie Jackson	15.00
SS-EB	Sammy Sosa, Ernie Banks	15.00
CP-FV	Chan Ho Park, Fernando Valenzuela	10.00

Materials 3-Player Jersey

NM/M
Common Card: 10.00
Inserted 1:15

KBA	Jeff Kent, Barry Bonds, Rich Aurilia	20.00
JAF	Chipper Jones, Andruw Jones, Rafael Furcal	15.00
GZH	Jason Giambi, Barry Zito, Tim Hudson	15.00
SKB	Gary Sheffield, Eric Karros, Kevin Brown	10.00
SSM	Aaron Sele, Ichiro Suzuki, Edgar Martinez	40.00
HDG	Todd Helton, Carlos Delgado, Jason Giambi	15.00
VRF	Omar Vizquel, Alex Rodriguez, Rafael Furcal	25.00
SYN	Kazuhiro Sasaki, Masato Yoshii, Hideo Nomo	20.00
BTD	Jeff Bagwell, Frank Thomas, Carlos Delgado	15.00
BGG	Barry Bonds, Luis Gonzalez, Ken Griffey Jr.	25.00
RPK	Ivan Rodriguez, Mike Piazza, Jason Kendall	20.00
PPV	Jay Payton, Mike Piazza, Robin Ventura	15.00
CHN	Roger Clemens, Tim Hudson, Hideo Nomo	20.00
PWO	Andy Pettitte, Bernie Williams, Paul O'Neill	20.00
TDK	Frank Thomas, Ray Durham, Paul Konerko	15.00
SJC	Curt Schilling, Randy Johnson, Roger Clemens	20.00
DEA	J.D. Drew, Jim Edmonds, Bobby Abreu	15.00
DOP	Carlos Delgado, Magglio Ordonez, Albert Pujols	35.00
TGA	Jim Thome, Juan Gonzalez, Roberto Alomar	15.00
GWS	Luis Gonzalez, Matt Williams, Curt Schilling	20.00
MGJ	Greg Maddux, Tom Glavine, Andruw Jones	20.00

2001 Upper Deck Sweet Spot

NM/M
Complete Set (90): 200.00
Common Player: .25
Common Sweet Beginnings: 5.00
(61-90) Production 1,000
Pack (4): 15.00
Box (18): 250.00

1	Troy Glaus	.50
2	Darin Erstad	.50
3	Jason Giambi	.50
4	Tim Hudson	.50
5	Ben Grieve	.25
6	Carlos Delgado	.50
7	David Wells	.25
8	Greg Vaughn	.25
9	Roberto Alomar	.50
10	Jim Thome	.75
11	John Olerud	.50
12	Edgar Martinez	.40
13	Cal Ripken Jr.	3.00
14	Albert Belle	.50
15	Ivan Rodriguez	.75
16	Alex Rodriguez	2.50
17	Pedro Martinez	1.00
18	Nomar Garciaparra	.75
19	Manny Ramirez	.75
20	Jermaine Dye	.40
21	Juan Gonzalez	.50
22	Dean Palmer	.25
23	Matt Lawton	.25
24	Eric Milton	.25
25	Frank Thomas	.75
26	Magglio Ordonez	.50
27	Derek Jeter	3.00
28	Bernie Williams	.50
29	Roger Clemens	2.00
30	Jeff Bagwell	.75
31	Richard Hidalgo	.25
32	Chipper Jones	1.50
33	Greg Maddux	2.00
34	Richie Sexson	.50
35	Jeromy Burnitz	.25
36	Mark McGwire	2.00
37	Jim Edmonds	.50
38	Sammy Sosa	1.00
39	Randy Johnson	1.00
40	Steve Finley	.25
41	Gary Sheffield	.50
42	Shawn Green	.50
43	Vladimir Guerrero	1.00
44	Jose Vidro	.25
45	Barry Bonds	3.00
46	Jeff Kent	.40
47	Preston Wilson	.25
48	Luis Castillo	.25
49	Mike Piazza	1.50
50	Edgardo Alfonzo	.25
51	Tony Gwynn	1.00
52	Ryan Klesko	.40
53	Scott Rolen	.75
54	Bob Abreu	.50
55	Jason Kendall	.40
56	Brian Giles	.40
57	Ken Griffey Jr.	2.00
58	Barry Larkin	.50
59	Todd Helton	.75
60	Mike Hampton	.25
61	Corey Patterson (Sweet Beginnings)	5.00
62	Ichiro Suzuki RC (Sweet Beginnings)	100.00
63	Jason Grilli (Sweet Beginnings)	5.00
64	Brian Cole (Sweet Beginnings)	5.00
65	Juan Pierre (Sweet Beginnings)	5.00
66	Matt Ginter (Sweet Beginnings)	5.00
67	Jimmy Rollins (Sweet Beginnings)	10.00
68	Jason Smith RC (Sweet Beginnings)	5.00
69	Israel Alcantara (Sweet Beginnings)	5.00
70	Adam Pettyjohn RC (Sweet Beginnings)	5.00
71	Luke Prokopec (Sweet Beginnings)	5.00
72	Barry Zito (Sweet Beginnings)	8.00
73	Keith Ginter (Sweet Beginnings)	5.00
74	Sun-Woo Kim (Sweet Beginnings)	5.00
75	Ross Gload (Sweet Beginnings)	5.00
76	Matt Wise (Sweet Beginnings)	5.00
77	Aubrey Huff (Sweet Beginnings)	5.00
78	Ryan Franklin (Sweet Beginnings)	5.00
79	Brandon Inge (Sweet Beginnings)	5.00
80	Wes Helms (Sweet Beginnings)	5.00
81	Junior Spivey RC (Sweet Beginnings)	5.00
82	Ryan Vogelsong (Sweet Beginnings)	5.00
83	John Parrish (Sweet Beginnings)	5.00
84	Joe Crede (Sweet Beginnings)	5.00
85	Damian Rolls (Sweet Beginnings)	5.00
86	Esix Snead RC (Sweet Beginnings)	5.00
87	Rocky Biddle (Sweet Beginnings)	5.00
88	Brady Clark (Sweet Beginnings)	5.00
89	Timoniel Perez (Sweet Beginnings)	5.00
90	Jay Spurgeon (Sweet Beginnings)	5.00

Big League Challenge

		NM/M
Complete Set (20):		20.00
Common Player:		.50
Inserted 1:6		
1	Mark McGwire	2.50
2	Richard Hidalgo	.50
3	Alex Rodriguez	2.50
4	Shawn Green	.75
5	Frank Thomas	1.00
6	Chipper Jones	1.50
7	Rafael Palmeiro	1.00
8	Troy Glaus	1.00
9	Mike Piazza	1.50
10	Andruw Jones	1.00
11	Todd Helton	1.00
12	Jason Giambi	1.00
13	Sammy Sosa	2.00
14	Carlos Delgado	1.00
15	Barry Bonds	3.00
16	Jose Canseco	.75
17	Jim Edmonds	.75
18	Manny Ramirez	1.00
19	Gary Sheffield	.75
20	Nomar Garciaparra	2.00

DiMaggio Pinstripes Excl.

		NM/M
Complete Set (56):		60.00
Common DiMaggio:		1.50
One Pack/Box		

DiMaggio Pinstripes Memor.

		NM/M
Print Runs Listed:		150.00
JDB	Joe DiMaggio/Bat/50	80.00
JDCJ	Joe DiMaggio, Lou Gehrig/Jsy/50	600.00
JDJ	Joe DiMaggio/Jsy/100	100.00

Game Jerseys

		NM/M
Common Player:		5.00
Inserted 1:18		
BB	Barry Bonds	15.00
JC	Jose Canseco	6.00
RC	Roger Clemens	12.00
RC	Roberto Clemente	125.00
JD	Joe DiMaggio	80.00
KG	Ken Griffey Jr.	20.00
RJ	Randy Johnson	10.00
AJ	Andruw Jones	5.00
CJ	Chipper Jones	10.00
MM	Mickey Mantle	150.00
WM	Willie Mays	100.00
SM	Stan Musial	65.00
CR	Cal Ripken Jr.	25.00
AR	Alex Rodriguez	20.00

IR	Ivan Rodriguez	8.00
NR	Nolan Ryan	40.00
DS	Duke Snider	10.00
SS	Sammy Sosa	10.00
IS	Ichiro Suzuki	100.00
FT	Frank Thomas	10.00

S.S. Game-Used Bases Tier 1

		NM/M
Common Card:		5.00
BH	Barry Bonds, Todd Helton	15.00
MG	Mark McGwire, Ken Griffey Jr.	25.00
JG	Chipper Jones, Nomar Garciaparra	15.00
GD	Vladimir Guerrero, Carlos Delgado	8.00
ST	Sammy Sosa, Frank Thomas	10.00
SR	Gary Sheffield, Alex Rodriguez	15.00
GR	Tony Gwynn, Ivan Rodriguez	10.00
PJ	Mike Piazza, Derek Jeter	25.00
HG	Jeffrey Hammonds, Troy Glaus	5.00
JGi	Randy Johnson, Jason Giambi	8.00
BD	Jeff Bagwell, Jermaine Dye	5.00
RR	Scott Rolen, Cal Ripken Jr.	25.00
GR	Ken Griffey Jr., Manny Ramirez	15.00
RJ	Alex Rodriguez, Derek Jeter	25.00
MP	Mark McGwire, Timoniel Perez	20.00
CP	Roger Clemens, Mike Piazza	15.00

S.S. Game-Used Bases Tier 2

		NM/M
Common Card:		15.00
Production 50 Sets		
BHK	Barry Bonds, Todd Helton, Jeff Kent	30.00
MGE	Mark McGwire, Ken Griffey Jr., Bobby Edmonds	80.00
JGJ	Chipper Jones, Nomar Garciaparra, Andruw Jones	30.00
GDM	Vladimir Guerrero, Carlos Delgado, Raul Mondesi	15.00
STO	Sammy Sosa, Frank Thomas, Magglio Ordonez	25.00
SRM	Gary Sheffield, Alex Rodriguez, Edgar Martinez	30.00
GRP	Tony Gwynn, Ivan Rodriguez, Rafael Palmeiro	20.00
PJW	Mike Piazza, Derek Jeter, Bernie Williams	40.00
HGH	Jeffrey Hammonds, Troy Glaus, Todd Helton	15.00
JGC	Randy Johnson, Jason Giambi, Eric Chavez	20.00
BDH	Jeff Bagwell, Jermaine Dye, Richard Hidalgo	15.00
RRB	Scott Rolen, Cal Ripken Jr., Albert Belle	40.00
GRT	Ken Griffey Jr., Manny Ramirez, Jim Thome	30.00

Game-Used Bat

		NM/M
Common Player:		5.00
Inserted 1:18		
HA	Hank Aaron	60.00
RA	Rick Ankiel	6.00
BB	Barry Bonds	15.00
JC	Jose Canseco	6.00
TC	Ty Cobb	150.00
JD	Joe DiMaggio	80.00
KG	Ken Griffey Jr.	15.00
RJ	Reggie Jackson	10.00
AJ	Andruw Jones	5.00
MM	Mickey Mantle	140.00
WM	Willie Mays	75.00
SM	Stan Musial	50.00

CR	Cal Ripken Jr.	30.00
AR	Alex Rodriguez	20.00
IR	Ivan Rodriguez	8.00
NR	Nolan Ryan	65.00
GS	Gary Sheffield	8.00
SS	Sammy Sosa	10.00
FT	Frank Thomas	10.00

Players Party

		NM/M
Complete Set (10):		10.00
Common Player:		.75
Inserted 1:12		
1	Derek Jeter	3.00
2	Randy Johnson	1.00
3	Frank Thomas	1.00
4	Nomar Garciaparra	2.00
5	Ken Griffey Jr.	1.50
6	Carlos Delgado	.75
7	Mike Piazza	1.50
8	Barry Bonds	3.00
9	Sammy Sosa	2.00
10	Pedro Martinez	1.00

Signatures

		NM/M
Common Player:		15.00
RAI	Roberto Alomar	30.00
RAn	Rick Ankiel	30.00
JB	Jeff Bagwell/SP/214	80.00
DB	Dusty Baker	25.00
DB	Don Baylor	15.00
BB	Buddy Bell	15.00
AB	Albert Belle	15.00
MB	Milton Bradley	15.00
PB	Pat Burrell	15.00
JC	Jose Canseco	25.00
CB	Chris Chambliss	20.00
RC	Roger Clemens	80.00
CD	Carlos Delgado	20.00
JD	Joe DiMaggio/SP/150	600.00
DE	Darin Erstad	15.00
RF	Rafael Furcal	15.00
JG	Joe Garagiola	40.00
JG	Jason Giambi	20.00
TGI	Troy Glaus	20.00
SG	Shawn Green	20.00
KG	Ken Griffey/SP/100	200.00
TGw	Tony Gwynn	50.00
AH	Art Howe	15.00
TH	Tim Hudson	15.00
DJ	Davey Johnson	15.00
RJ	Randy Johnson	75.00
AJ	Andruw Jones	20.00
CJ	Chipper Jones	80.00
ML	Mike Lamb	15.00
TL	Tony LaRussa	20.00
DL	Davey Lopes	15.00
BM	Bill Madlock	15.00
MM	Mickey Mantle/SP/10	3,500
WM	Willie Mays	200.00
HM	Hal McRae	15.00
SM	Stan Musial	120.00
PO	Paul O'Neill	50.00
LP	Lou Piniella	30.00
JR	Jim Rice	30.00
AR	Alex Rodriguez/SP/154	200.00
IR	Ivan Rodriguez/SP/150	100.00
BR	Babe Ruth/SP/1 (8/03 auction)	12,000
NR	Nolan Ryan	150.00
GS	Gary Sheffield	30.00
SS	Sammy Sosa/SP/148	100.00
FT	Frank Thomas	75.00
AT	Alan Trammell	20.00
BV	Bobby Valentine	15.00
RV	Robin Ventura	15.00
MW	Matt Williams	20.00

2001 Upper Deck Texas Rangers Team Set

This set was produced for sale by the team, retailing for about $15 at souvenir outlets. Standard-size cards have game-action pho-tos on front. Backs repeat part of the photo and have personal data, stats and logos. Card numbers carry a "TR" prefix.

		NM/M
Complete Set (20):		15.00
Common Player:		.50
1	Alex Rodriguez	3.00
2	Rafael Palmeiro	1.50
3	Ivan Rodriguez	1.50
4	Andres Galarraga	.50
5	Ken Caminiti	.50
6	Ruben Mateo	.50
7	Rusty Greer	.50
8	Rick Helling	.50
9	Gabe Kapler	.50
10	Kenny Rogers	.50
11	Randy Velarde	.50
12	Doug Davis	.50
13	Bill Haselman	.50
14	Tim Crabtree	.50
15	Darren Oliver	.50
16	Jeff Zimmerman	.50
17	Ricky Ledee	.50
18	Mark Petkovsek	.50
19	Frank Catalanotto	.50
20	Nolan Ryan	5.00

2001 Upper Deck Ultimate Collection

		NM/M
Common Player:		1.00
Common SP (91-100):		5.00
Production 1,000		
Common SP (101-110):		5.00
Production 750		
Common (111-120):		15.00
Production 250		
Pack (4):		160.00
Box (4):		575.00
1	Troy Glaus	2.50
2	Darin Erstad	1.50
3	Jason Giambi	3.00
4	Barry Zito	2.00
5	Tim Hudson	2.00
6	Miguel Tejada	1.50
7	Carlos Delgado	2.50
8	Shannon Stewart	1.00
9	Greg Vaughn	1.00
10	Toby Hall	1.00
11	Roberto Alomar	2.00
12	Juan Gonzalez	2.50
13	Jim Thome	3.00
14	Edgar Martinez	1.50
15	Freddy Garcia	1.50
16	Bret Boone	1.50
17	Kazuhiro Sasaki	1.00
18	Cal Ripken Jr.	10.00
19	Tim Raines	1.00
20	Alex Rodriguez	8.00
21	Ivan Rodriguez	2.50
22	Rafael Palmeiro	2.50
23	Pedro Martinez	3.00
24	Nomar Garciaparra	6.00
25	Manny Ramirez	2.50
26	Hideo Nomo	2.00
27	Mike Sweeney	1.00
28	Carlos Beltran	1.50
29	Tony Clark	1.00
30	Dean Palmer	1.00
31	Doug Mientkiewicz	1.00
32	Cristian Guzman	1.00
33	Corey Koskie	1.00
34	Frank Thomas	3.00
35	Magglio Ordonez	1.50
36	Jose Canseco	2.00
37	Roger Clemens	6.00

38	Derek Jeter	10.00
39	Bernie Williams	2.00
40	Mike Mussina	2.00
41	Tino Martinez	1.00
42	Jeff Bagwell	2.50
43	Lance Berkman	2.00
44	Roy Oswalt	1.50
45	Chipper Jones	5.00
46	Greg Maddux	5.00
47	Andruw Jones	2.50
48	Tom Glavine	2.00
49	Richie Sexson	2.00
50	Jeromy Burnitz	1.00
51	Ben Sheets	1.00
52	Mark McGwire	8.00
53	Matt Morris	1.00
54	Jim Edmonds	2.00
55	J.D. Drew	1.50
56	Sammy Sosa	6.00
57	Fred McGriff	1.00
58	Kerry Wood	2.50
59	Randy Johnson	3.00
60	Luis Gonzalez	2.00
61	Curt Schilling	2.00
62	Shawn Green	1.50
63	Kevin Brown	1.50
64	Gary Sheffield	2.00
65	Vladimir Guerrero	3.00
66	Barry Bonds	10.00
67	Jeff Kent	1.50
68	Rich Aurilia	1.00
69	Cliff Floyd	1.00
70	Charles Johnson	1.00
71	Josh Beckett	2.00
72	Mike Piazza	5.00
73	Edgardo Alfonzo	1.00
74	Robin Ventura	1.00
75	Tony Gwynn	2.50
76	Ryan Klesko	1.50
77	Phil Nevin	1.00
78	Scott Rolen	2.50
79	Bobby Abreu	1.00
80	Jimmy Rollins	1.50
81	Brian Giles	1.50
82	Jason Kendall	1.00
83	Aramis Ramirez	1.00
84	Ken Griffey Jr.	6.00
85	Adam Dunn	2.00
86	Sean Casey	1.50
87	Barry Larkin	2.00
88	Larry Walker	1.50
89	Mike Hampton	1.00
90	Todd Helton	2.50
91	Ken Harvey	5.00
92	William Ortega RC	5.00
93	Juan Diaz RC	5.00
94	Greg Miller RC	5.00
95	Brandon Berger RC	5.00
96	Brandon Lyon RC	5.00
97	Jay Gibbons RC	5.00
98	Rob Mackowiak RC	5.00
99	Erick Almonte RC	5.00
100	Jason Middlebrook RC	5.00
101	Johnny Estrada RC	8.00
102	Juan Uribe RC	8.00
103	Travis Hafner RC	20.00
104	Morgan Ensberg RC	5.00
105	Mike Rivera RC	5.00
106	Josh Towers RC	5.00
107	Adrian Hernandez RC	5.00
108	Rafael Soriano RC	8.00
109	Jackson Melian RC	5.00
110	Wilken Ruan RC	5.00
111	Albert Pujols RC	500.00
112	Tsuyoshi Shinjo RC	15.00
113	Brandon Duckworth RC	15.00
114	Juan Cruz RC	15.00
115	Dewon Brazelton RC	15.00
116	Mark Prior/Auto. RC	20.00
117	Mark Teixeira/Auto. RC	200.00
118	Wilson Betemit/Auto. RC	25.00
119	Bud Smith/Auto. RC	15.00
120	Ichiro Suzuki/Auto. RC	1,800

Ichiro

		NM/M
Pricing not available for all Ichiro's.		
B-IA	Ichiro Suzuki/Bat/Away	65.00
B-IH	Ichiro Suzuki/Bat/Home	65.00
B-IS	Ichiro Suzuki/Bat/50	80.00
B-IG	Ichiro Suzuki/Bat/200	90.00
SB-I	Ichiro Suzuki/Bat/Auto./50	675.00
J-IA	Ichiro Suzuki/Jsy/Away	50.00
J-IH	Ichiro Suzuki/Jsy/Home	50.00
J-IS	Ichiro Suzuki/Jsy/250	75.00
J-IG	Ichiro Suzuki/Jsy/200	85.00
SJ-I	Ichiro Suzuki/Jsy/Auto./50	675.00
UB-I	Ichiro Suzuki/Base	25.00
UB-IC	Ichiro Suzuki/Base/150	80.00
UB-IS	Ichiro Suzuki/Base/50	100.00
BB-I	Ichiro Suzuki/Ball	50.00
BB-IC	Ichiro Suzuki/Ball/150	85.00
BB-IS	Ichiro Suzuki/Ball/50	100.00

SBB-I	Ichiro Suzuki/Ball/Auto./25	675.00
C-I	Ichiro Suzuki/Glv/75	180.00
BG-I	Ichiro Suzuki/Bat/Glv/75	180.00

Game Jersey

		NM/M
Common Player:		8.00
Inserted 1:2		
RA	Roberto Alomar	10.00
JB	Jeff Bagwell	10.00
BB	Barry Bonds	20.00
JC	Jose Canseco	10.00
RC	Roger Clemens	20.00
CD	Carlos Delgado	10.00
DE	Darin Erstad	8.00
JaG	Jason Giambi	10.00
JG	Juan Gonzalez	10.00
LG	Luis Gonzalez	8.00
SG	Shawn Green	8.00
KG	Ken Griffey Jr.	25.00
TG	Tony Gwynn	15.00
TH	Todd Helton	10.00
RJ	Randy Johnson	10.00
AJ	Andruw Jones	8.00
CJ	Chipper Jones	15.00
GM	Greg Maddux	25.00
MO	Magglio Ordonez	8.00
MP	Mike Piazza	20.00
AP	Albert Pujols	60.00
CR	Cal Ripken Jr.	40.00
AR	Alex Rodriguez	30.00
IR	Ivan Rodriguez	10.00
SR	Scott Rolen	8.00
GS	Gary Sheffield	10.00
SS	Sammy Sosa	20.00
FT	Frank Thomas	15.00
LW	Larry Walker	10.00
BW	Bernie Williams	10.00

Magic Numbers

		NM/M
Common Player:		10.00
Production 150		
Coppers #'d to 24 not priced.		
Silvers #'d to 20 not priced.		
Golds #'d to 15 not priced.		
RA	Roberto Alomar	20.00
JB	Jeff Bagwell	20.00
BB	Barry Bonds	50.00
JC	Jose Canseco	15.00
RC	Roger Clemens	25.00
CD	Carlos Delgado	15.00
DE	Darin Erstad	10.00
JaG	Jason Giambi	20.00
JG	Juan Gonzalez	15.00
LG	Luis Gonzalez	15.00
SG	Shawn Green	10.00
KG	Ken Griffey Jr.	40.00
TG	Tony Gwynn	25.00
TH	Todd Helton	15.00
RJ	Randy Johnson	15.00
AJ	Andruw Jones	10.00
CJ	Chipper Jones	15.00
GM	Greg Maddux	40.00
MO	Magglio Ordonez	15.00
MP	Mike Piazza	30.00
AP	Albert Pujols	75.00
CR	Cal Ripken Jr.	90.00
AR	Alex Rodriguez	40.00
IR	Ivan Rodriguez	15.00
SR	Scott Rolen	15.00
GS	Gary Sheffield	10.00
SS	Sammy Sosa	40.00
FT	Frank Thomas	15.00
LW	Larry Walker	10.00
BW	Bernie Williams	10.00

Ultimate Signatures

		NM/M
Common Autograph:		15.00
Inserted 1:4		
Silvers #'d to 24 not priced.		
Golds #'d to 15 not priced.		
RA	Roberto Alomar	

(High-value listing)

Code	Player	Price
B	Ernie Banks	50.00
aB	Barry Bonds	200.00
RC	Roger Clemens	100.00
CD	Carlos Delgado	25.00
CF	Carlton Fisk	40.00
aG	Jason Giambi	25.00
TGl	Tom Glavine	40.00
LG	Luis Gonzalez	25.00
JG	Ken Griffey Jr.	100.00
TG	Tony Gwynn	60.00
RK	Ryan Klesko	20.00
SK	Sandy Koufax	275.00
EM	Edgar Martinez	30.00
TP	Tony Perez	20.00
KP	Kirby Puckett	50.00
CR	Cal Ripken Jr.	125.00
AR	Alex Rodriguez	80.00
IR	Ivan Rodriguez	50.00
TS	Tom Seaver	40.00
GS	Gary Sheffield	30.00
DS	Duke Snider	35.00
SS	Sammy Sosa	120.00
FT	Frank Thomas	40.00
JT	Jim Thome	50.00
RY	Robin Yount	60.00

2001 Upper Deck Victory

	NM/M
Complete Set (660):	50.00
Common Player:	.15

No.	Player	Price
1	Troy Glaus	.50
2	Scott Spiezio	.15
3	Gary DiSarcina	.15
4	Darin Erstad	.20
5	Tim Salmon	.20
6	Troy Percival	.15
7	Ramon Ortiz	.15
8	Orlando Palmeiro	.15
9	Tim Belcher	.15
10	Mo Vaughn	.15
11	Bengie Molina	.15
12	Benji Gil	.15
13	Scott Schoeneweis	.15
14	Garret Anderson	.15
15	Matt Wise	.15
16	Adam Kennedy	.15
17	Jarrod Washburn	.15
18	Darin Erstad, Troy Percival	.15
19	Jason Giambi	.20
20	Tim Hudson	.20
21	Ramon Hernandez	.15
22	Eric Chavez	.15
23	Gil Heredia	.15
24	Jason Isringhausen	.15
25	Jeremy Giambi	.15
26	Miguel Tejada	.15
27	Barry Zito	.50
28	Terrence Long	.15
29	Ryan Christenson	.15
30	Mark Mulder	.15
31	Olmedo Saenz	.15
32	Adam Piatt	.15
33	Ben Grieve	.20
34	Omar Olivares	.15
35	John Jaha	.15
36	Jason Giambi, Tim Hudson	.15
37	Carlos Delgado	.40
38	Esteban Loaiza	.15
39	Brad Fullmer	.15
40	David Wells	.15
41	Chris Woodward	.15
42	Billy Koch	.15
43	Shannon Stewart	.15
44	Chris Carpenter	.15
45	Steve Parris	.15
46	Darrin Fletcher	.15
47	Joey Hamilton	.15
48	Jose Cruz Jr.	.15
49	Vernon Wells	.15
50	Raul Mondesi	.15
51	Kelvim Escobar	.15
52	Tony Batista	.15
53	Alex Gonzalez	.15
54	Carlos Delgado, David Wells	.20
55	Greg Vaughn	.15
56	Albie Lopez	.15
57	Randy Winn	.15
58	Ryan Rupe	.15
59	Steve Cox	.15
60	Vinny Castilla	.15
61	Jose Guillen	.15
62	Wilson Alvarez	.15
63	Bryan Rekar	.15
64	Gerald Williams	.15
65	Esteban Yan	.15
66	Felix Martinez	.15
67	Fred McGriff	.20
68	John Flaherty	.15
69	Jason Tyner	.15
70	Russ Johnson	.15
71	Roberto Hernandez	.15
72	Greg Vaughn, Albie Lopez	.15
73	Eddie Taubensee	.15
74	Bob Wickman	.15
75	Ellis Burks	.15
76	Kenny Lofton	.20
77	Einar Diaz	.15
78	Travis Fryman	.15
79	Omar Vizquel	.15
80	Jason Bere	.15
81	Bartolo Colon	.15
82	Jim Thome	.20
83	Roberto Alomar	.40
84	Chuck Finley	.15
85	Steve Woodard	.15
86	Russ Branyan	.15
87	Dave Burba	.15
88	Jaret Wright	.15
89	Jacob Cruz	.15
90	Steve Karsay	.15
91	Manny Ramirez, Bartolo Colon	.20
92	Raul Ibanez	.15
93	Freddy Garcia	.15
94	Edgar Martinez	.15
95	Jay Buhner	.15
96	Jamie Moyer	.15
97	John Olerud	.20
98	Aaron Sele	.15
99	Kazuhiro Sasaki	.20
100	Mike Cameron	.15
101	John Halama	.15
102	David Bell	.15
103	Gil Meche	.15
104	Carlos Guillen	.15
105	Mark McLemore	.15
106	Stan Javier	.15
107	Al Martin	.15
108	Dan Wilson	.15
109	Alex Rodriguez, Kazuhiro Sasaki	.50
110	Cal Ripken Jr.	1.50
111	Delino DeShields	.15
112	Sidney Ponson	.15
113	Albert Belle	.15
114	Jose Mercedes	.15
115	Scott Erickson	.15
116	Jerry Hairston Jr.	.15
117	Brook Fordyce	.15
118	Luis Matos	.15
119	Eugene Kingsale	.15
120	Jeff Conine	.15
121	Chris Richard	.15
122	Fernando Lunar	.15
123	John Parrish	.15
124	Brady Anderson	.15
125	Ryan Kohlmeier	.15
126	Melvin Mora	.15
127	Albert Belle, Jose Mercedes	.15
128	Ivan Rodriguez	.50
129	Justin Thompson	.15
130	Kenny Rogers	.15
131	Rafael Palmeiro	.30
132	Rusty Greer	.15
133	Gabe Kapler	.15
134	John Wetteland	.15
135	Mike Lamb	.15
136	Doug Davis	.15
137	Ruben Mateo	.15
138	Alex Rodriguez	1.25
139	Chad Curtis	.15
140	Rick Helling	.15
141	Ryan Glynn	.15
142	Andres Galarraga	.25
143	Ricky Ledee	.15
144	Frank Catalanotto	.15
145	Rafael Palmeiro, Rick Helling	.20
146	Pedro Martinez	.60
147	Wilton Veras	.15
148	Manny Ramirez	.50
149	Rolando Arrojo	.15
150	Nomar Garciaparra	1.00
151	Darren Lewis	.15
152	Troy O'Leary	.15
153	Tomokazu Ohka	.15
154	Carl Everett	.15
155	Jason Varitek	.15
156	Frank Castillo	.15
157	Pete Schourek	.15
158	Jose Offerman	.15
159	Derek Lowe	.15
160	John Valentin	.15
161	Dante Bichette	.15
162	Trot Nixon	.15
163	Nomar Garciaparra, Pedro Martinez	.25
164	Jermaine Dye	.15
165	Jose Rosado	.15
166	Mike Sweeney	.15
167	Rey Sanchez	.15
168	Jeff Suppan	.15
169	Chad Durbin	.15
170	Carlos Beltran	.15
171	Brian Meadows	.15
172	Todd Dunwoody	.15
173	Johnny Damon	.15
174	Blake Stein	.15
175	Carlos Febles	.15
176	Joe Randa	.15
177	Makoto Suzuki	.15
178	Makoto Suzuki	.15
179	Mark Quinn	.15
180	Gregg Zaun	.15
181	Mike Sweeney, Jeff Suppan	.15
182	Juan Gonzalez	.50
183	Dean Palmer	.15
184	Wendell Magee	.15
185	Todd Jones	.15
186	Bobby Higginson	.15
187	Brian Moehler	.20
188	Juan Encarnacion	.15
189	Tony Clark	.15
190	Rich Becker	.15
191	Roger Cedeno	.15
192	Mitch Meluskey	.15
193	Shane Halter	.15
194	Jeff Weaver	.15
195	Deivi Cruz	.15
196	Damion Easley	.15
197	Robert Fick	.15
198	Matt Anderson	.15
199	Bobby Higginson, Brian Moehler	.15
200	Brad Radke	.15
201	Mark Redman	.15
202	Corey Koskie	.15
203	Matt Lawton	.15
204	Eric Milton	.15
205	Chad Moeller	.15
206	Jacque Jones	.15
207	Matt Kinney	.15
208	Jay Canizaro	.15
209	Torii Hunter	.15
210	Ron Coomer	.15
211	Chad Allen	.15
212	Denny Hocking	.15
213	Cristian Guzman	.15
214	LaTroy Hawkins	.15
215	Joe Mays	.15
216	David Ortiz	.15
217	Matt Lawton, Eric Milton	.15
218	Frank Thomas	.60
219	Jose Valentin	.15
220	Mike Sirotka	.15
221	Kip Wells	.15
222	Magglio Ordonez	.25
223	Herbert Perry	.15
224	James Baldwin	.15
225	Jon Garland	.15
226	Sandy Alomar	.15
227	Chris Singleton	.15
228	Keith Foulke	.15
229	Paul Konerko	.15
230	Jim Parque	.15
231	Greg Norton	.15
232	Carlos Lee	.15
233	Cal Eldred	.15
234	Ray Durham	.15
235	Jeff Abbott	.15
236	Frank Thomas, Mike Sirotka	.20
237	Derek Jeter	1.50
238	Glenallen Hill	.15
239	Roger Clemens	1.00
240	Bernie Williams	.40
241	David Justice	.25
242	Luis Sojo	.15
243	Orlando Hernandez	.20
244	Mike Mussina	.25
245	Jorge Posada	.20
246	Andy Pettitte	.20
247	Paul O'Neill	.20
248	Scott Brosius	.15
249	Alfonso Soriano	.50
250	Mariano Rivera	.20
251	Chuck Knoblauch	.20
252	Ramiro Mendoza	.15
253	Tino Martinez	.15
254	David Cone	.15
255	Derek Jeter, Andy Pettitte	.40
256	Jeff Bagwell	.50
257	Lance Berkman	.15
258	Craig Biggio	.20
259	Scott Elarton	.15
260	Bill Spiers	.15
261	Moises Alou	.15
262	Billy Wagner	.15
263	Shane Reynolds	.15
264	Tony Eusebio	.15
265	Julio Lugo	.15
266	Jose Lima	.15
267	Octavio Dotel	.15
268	Brad Ausmus	.15
269	Daryle Ward	.15
270	Glen Barker	.15
271	Wade Miller	.15
272	Richard Hidalgo	.25
273	Chris Truby	.15
274	Jeff Bagwell, Scott Elarton	.25
275	Greg Maddux	.75
276	Chipper Jones	.75
277	Tom Glavine	.15
278	Brian Jordan	.15
279	Andruw Jones	.40
280	Kevin Millwood	.15
281	Rico Brogna	.15
282	George Lombard	.15
283	Reggie Sanders	.15
284	John Rocker	.15
285	Rafael Furcal	.25
286	John Smoltz	.15
287	Javy Lopez	.15
288	Walt Weiss	.15
289	Quilvio Veras	.15
290	Eddie Perez	.15
291	B.J. Surhoff	.15
292	Chipper Jones, Tom Glavine	.25
293	Jeromy Burnitz	.15
294	Charlie Hayes	.15
295	Jeff D'Amico	.15
296	Jose Hernandez	.15
297	Richie Sexson	.15
298	Tyler Houston	.15
299	Paul Rigdon	.15
300	Jamey Wright	.15
301	Mark Loretta	.15
302	Geoff Jenkins	.20
303	Luis Lopez	.15
304	John Snyder	.15
305	Henry Blanco	.15
306	Curtis Leskanic	.15
307	Ron Belliard	.15
308	Jimmy Haynes	.15
309	Marquis Grissom	.15
310	Geoff Jenkins, Jeff D'Amico	.15
311	Mark McGwire	1.00
312	Rick Ankiel	.20
313	Dave Veres	.15
314	Carlos Hernandez	.15
315	Jim Edmonds	.20
316	Andy Benes	.15
317	Garrett Stephenson	.15
318	Ray Lankford	.15
319	Dustin Hermanson	.15
320	Steve Kline	.15
321	Mike Matheny	.15
322	Edgar Renteria	.15
323	J.D. Drew	.20
324	Craig Paquette	.15
325	Darryl Kile	.15
326	Fernando Vina	.15
327	Eric Davis	.15
328	Placido Polanco	.15
329	Jim Edmonds, Darryl Kile	.15
330	Sammy Sosa	1.00
331	Rick Aguilera	.15
332	Willie Greene	.15
333	Kerry Wood	.20
334	Todd Hundley	.15
335	Rondell White	.20
336	Julio Zuleta	.15
337	Jon Lieber	.15
338	Joe Girardi	.15
339	Damon Buford	.15
340	Kevin Tapani	.15
341	Ricky Gutierrez	.15
342	Bill Mueller	.15
343	Ruben Quevedo	.15
344	Eric Young	.15
345	Gary Matthews Jr.	.15
346	Daniel Garibay	.15
347	Sammy Sosa, Jon Lieber	.50
348	Randy Johnson	.50
349	Matt Williams	.20
350	Kelly Stinnett	.15
351	Brian Anderson	.15
352	Steve Finley	.15
353	Curt Schilling	.20
354	Erubiel Durazo	.15
355	Todd Stottlemyre	.15
356	Mark Grace	.20
357	Luis Gonzalez	.20
358	Danny Bautista	.15
359	Matt Mantei	.15
360	Tony Womack	.15
361	Armando Reynoso	.15
362	Greg Colbrunn	.15
363	Jay Bell	.15
364	Mike Darr	.15
365	Byung-Hyun Kim	.15
—	Luis Gonzalez, Randy Johnson	.20
366	Gary Sheffield	.20
367	Eric Karros	.15
368	Jeff Shaw	.15
369	Jim Leyritz	.15
370	Kevin Brown	.20
371	Alex Cora	.15
372	Andy Ashby	.15
373	Eric Gagne	.15
374	Chan Ho Park	.15
375	Shawn Green	.20
376	Kevin Elster	.15
377	Mark Grudzielanek	.15
378	Darren Dreifort	.15
379	Dave Hansen	.15
380	Bruce Aven	.15
381	Adrian Beltre	.20
382	Tom Goodwin	.15
383	Gary Sheffield, Chan Ho Park	.15
384	Vladimir Guerrero	.60
385	Ugueth Urbina	.15
386	Michael Barrett	.15
387	Geoff Blum	.15
388	Fernando Tatis	.15
389	Carl Pavano	.30
390	Jose Vidro	.15
391	Orlando Cabrera	.15
392	Terry Jones	.15
393	Mike Thurman	.15
394	Lee Stevens	.15
395	Tony Armas Jr.	.15
396	Wilton Guerrero	.15
397	Peter Bergeron	.15
398	Milton Bradley	.15
399	Javier Vazquez	.15
400	Fernando Seguignol	.15
401	Vladimir Guerrero, Dustin Hermanson	.25
402	Barry Bonds	.60
403	Russ Ortiz	.15
404	Calvin Murray	.15
405	Armando Rios	.15
406	Livan Hernandez	.15
407	Jeff Kent	.20
408	Bobby Estalella	.15
409	Felipe Crespo	.15
410	Shawn Estes	.15
411	J.T. Snow	.15
412	Marvin Benard	.15
413	Joe Nathan	.15
414	Robb Nen	.15
415	Shawon Dunston	.15
416	Mark Gardner	.15
417	Kirk Rueter	.15
418	Rich Aurilia	.15
419	Doug Mirabelli	.15
420	Russ Davis	.15
421	Barry Bonds, Livan Hernandez	.30
422	Cliff Floyd	.15
423	Luis Castillo	.15
424	Antonio Alfonseca	.15
425	Preston Wilson	.15
426	Ryan Dempster	.15
427	Jesus Sanchez	.15
428	Derrek Lee	.15
429	Brad Penny	.15
430	Mark Kotsay	.15
431	Alex Fernandez	.15
432	Mike Lowell	.15
433	Chuck Smith	.15
434	Alex Gonzalez	.15
435	Dave Berg	.15
436	A.J. Burnett	.15
437	Charles Johnson	.15
438	Reid Cornelius	.15
439	Mike Redmond	.15
440	Preston Wilson, Ryan Dempster	.15
441	Mike Piazza	.75
442	Kevin Appier	.15
443	Jay Payton	.15
444	Steve Trachsel	.15
445	Al Leiter	.20
446	Joe McEwing	.15
447	Armando Benitez	.15
448	Edgardo Alfonzo	.15
449	Glendon Rusch	.15
450	Mike Bordick	.15
451	Lenny Harris	.15
452	Matt Franco	.15
453	Darryl Hamilton	.15
454	Bobby J. Jones	.15
455	Robin Ventura	.15
456	Todd Zeile	.15
457	John Franco	.15
458	Mike Piazza, Al Leiter	.40
459	Tony Gwynn	.75
460	John Mabry	.15
461	Trevor Hoffman	.15
462	Phil Nevin	.15
463	Ryan Klesko	.15
464	Wiki Gonzalez	.15
465	Matt Clement	.15
466	Alex Arias	.15
467	Woody Williams	.15
468	Ruben Rivera	.15
469	Sterling Hitchcock	.15
470	Ben Davis	.15
471	Bubba Trammell	.15
472	Jay Witasick	.15
473	Eric Owens	.15
474	Damian Jackson	.15
475	Adam Eaton	.15
476	Mike Darr	.15
477	Phil Nevin, Trevor Hoffman	.15
478	Scott Rolen	.25
479	Robert Person	.15
480	Mike Lieberthal	.15
481	Reggie Taylor	.15
482	Paul Byrd	.15
483	Bruce Chen	.15
484	Pat Burrell	.25
485	Kevin Jordan	.15
486	Bobby Abreu	.15
487	Randy Wolf	.15
488	Kevin Sefcik	.15
489	Brian Hunter	.15
490	Doug Glanville	.15
491	Kent Bottenfield	.15
492	Travis Lee	.15
493	Jeff Brantley	.15
494	Omar Daal	.15
495	Bobby Abreu, Randy Wolf	.15
496	Jason Kendall	.15
497	Adrian Brown	.15
498	Warren Morris	.15
499	Brian Giles	.20
500	Jimmy Anderson	.15
501	John Vander Wal	.15
502	Mike Williams	.15
503	Aramis Ramirez	.15
504	Pat Meares	.15
505	Jason Schmidt	.15
506	Todd Ritchie	.15
507	Abraham Nunez	.15
508	Jose Silva	.15
509	Francisco Cordova	.15
510	Kevin Young	.15
511	Derek Bell	.15
512	Kris Benson	.15
513	Brian Giles, Jose Silva	.15
514	Ken Griffey Jr.	1.00
515	Scott Williamson	.15
516	Dmitri Young	.15
517	Sean Casey	.15
518	Barry Larkin	.25
519	Juan Castro	.15
520	Danny Graves	.15
521	Aaron Boone	.15
522	Pokey Reese	.15
523	Elmer Dessens	.15
524	Michael Tucker	.15
525	Benito Santiago	.15
526	Pete Harnisch	.15
527	Alex Ochoa	.15
528	Gookie Dawkins	.15
529	Seth Etherton	.15
530	Rob Bell	.15
531	Ken Griffey Jr., Steve Parris	.50
532	Todd Helton	.50
533	Jose Jimenez	.15
534	Todd Walker	.15
535	Ron Gant	.15
536	Neifi Perez	.15
537	Butch Huskey	.15
538	Pedro Astacio	.15
539	Juan Pierre	.15
540	Jeff Cirillo	.15
541	Ben Petrick	.15
542	Brian Bohanon	.15
543	Larry Walker	.25
544	Masato Yoshii	.15
545	Denny Neagle	.15
546	Brent Mayne	.15
547	Mike Hampton	.20
548	Todd Hollandsworth	.15
549	Brian Rose	.15
550	Todd Helton, Pedro Astacio	.20
551	Jason Hart	.15
552	Joe Crede	.15
553	Timoniel Perez	.15
554	Brady Clark	.15
555	Adam Pettyjohn RC	.15
556	Jason Grilli	.15
557	Paxton Crawford	.15
558	Jay Spurgeon	.15
559	Hector Ortiz	.15
560	Vernon Wells	.15
561	Aubrey Huff	.15
562	Xavier Nady	.25
563	Billy McMillon	.15
564	Ichiro Suzuki RC	8.00
565	Tomas de la Rosa	.15
566	Matt Ginter	.15
567	Sun-Woo Kim	.15
568	Nick Johnson	.15
569	Pablo Ozuna	.15
570	Tike Redman	.15
571	Brian Cole	.15
572	Ross Gload	.15
573	Dee Brown	.15
574	Tony McKnight	.15
575	Allen Levrault	.15
576	Lesli Brea	.15
577	Adam Bernero	.15
578	Tom Davey	.15
579	Morgan Burkhart	.15
580	Britt Reames	.15
581	Dave Coggin	.15
582	Trey Moore	.15
583	Matt Kinney	.15
584	Pedro Feliz	.15
585	Brandon Inge	.15
586	Alex Hernandez	.15
587	Toby Hall	.15
588	Grant Roberts	.15
589	Brian Sikorski	.15
590	Aaron Myette	.15
591	Derek Jeter (Big Play Makers)	1.00
592	Ivan Rodriguez (Big Play Makers)	.40
593	Alex Rodriguez (Big Play Makers)	.75
594	Carlos Delgado (Big Play Makers)	.30
595	Mark McGwire (Big Play Makers)	.75
596	Troy Glaus (Big Play Makers)	.40
597	Sammy Sosa (Big Play Makers)	.75
598	Vladimir Guerrero (Big Play Makers)	.50
599	Manny Ramirez (Big Play Makers)	.40
600	Pedro J. Martinez (Big Play Makers)	.50
601	Chipper Jones (Big Play Makers)	.75
602	Jason Giambi (Big Play Makers)	.20
603	Frank Thomas (Big Play Makers)	.50
604	Ken Griffey Jr. (Big Play Makers)	.75
605	Nomar Garciaparra (Big Play Makers)	.75
606	Randy Johnson (Big Play Makers)	.40
607	Mike Piazza (Big Play Makers)	.75
608	Barry Bonds (Big Play Makers)	.50
609	Todd Helton (Big Play Makers)	.40
610	Jeff Bagwell (Big Play Makers)	.40
611	Ken Griffey Jr. (Victory's Best)	.75
612	Carlos Delgado (Victory's Best)	.40
613	Jeff Bagwell (Victory's Best)	.40

614 Jason Giambi (Victory's Best) .20
615 Cal Ripken Jr. (Victory's Best) 1.00
616 Brian Giles (Victory's Best) .15
617 Bernie Williams (Victory's Best) .30
618 Greg Maddux (Victory's Best) .75
619 Troy Glaus (Victory's Best) .40
620 Greg Vaughn (Victory's Best) .15
621 Sammy Sosa (Victory's Best) .75
622 Pat Burrell (Victory's Best) .20
623 Ivan Rodriguez (Victory's Best) .40
624 Chipper Jones (Victory's Best) .75
625 Barry Bonds (Victory's Best) .50
626 Roger Clemens (Victory's Best) .50
627 Jim Edmonds (Victory's Best) .15
628 Nomar Garciaparra (Victory's Best) .75
629 Frank Thomas (Victory's Best) .50
630 Mike Piazza (Victory's Best) .75
631 Randy Johnson (Victory's Best) .40
632 Andruw Jones (Victory's Best) .30
633 David Wells (Victory's Best) .15
634 Manny Ramirez (Victory's Best) .40
635 Preston Wilson (Victory's Best) .15
636 Todd Helton (Victory's Best) .40
637 Kerry Wood (Victory's Best) .15
638 Albert Belle (Victory's Best) .15
639 Juan Gonzalez (Victory's Best) .40
640 Vladimir Guerrero (Victory's Best) .50
641 Gary Sheffield (Victory's Best) .15
642 Larry Walker (Victory's Best) .15
643 Magglio Ordonez (Victory's Best) .15
644 Jermaine Dye (Victory's Best) .15
645 Scott Rolen (Victory's Best) .20
646 Tony Gwynn (Victory's Best) .50
647 Shawn Green (Victory's Best) .15
648 Roberto Alomar (Victory's Best) .30
649 Eric Milton (Victory's Best) .15
650 Mark McGwire (Victory's Best) .75
651 Tim Hudson (Victory's Best) .15
652 Jose Canseco (Victory's Best) .20
653 Tom Glavine (Victory's Best) .20
654 Derek Jeter (Victory's Best) 1.00
655 Alex Rodriguez (Victory's Best) .75
656 Darin Erstad (Victory's Best) .15
657 Jason Kendall (Victory's Best) .15
658 Pedro Martinez (Victory's Best) .50
659 Richie Sexson (Victory's Best) .15
660 Rafael Palmeiro (Victory's Best) .20

2001 Upper Deck Vintage Sample

Styled shamelessly after the 1963 Topps set, this retro-look UD issue was previewed with a sample card. Virtually identical in format to the issued version, the promo has stats on back only through 1999 and is overprinted with a large diagonal "SAMPLE."

NM/M
30 Ken Griffey Jr. 4.00

2001 Upper Deck Vintage

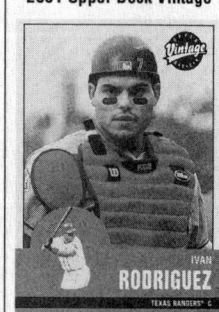

NM/M
Complete Set (400): 30.00
Common Player: .10
Pack (10): 2.00
Box (24): 40.00
1 Darin Erstad .25
2 Seth Etherton .10
3 Troy Glaus .50
4 Bengie Molina .10
5 Mo Vaughn .20
6 Tim Salmon .25
7 Ramon Ortiz .10
8 Adam Kennedy .10
9 Garret Anderson .25
10 Troy Percival .10
11 2000 Angels Lineup .10
12 Jason Giambi .50
13 Tim Hudson .25
14 Adam Piatt .10
15 Miguel Tejada .25
16 Mark Mulder .25
17 Eric Chavez .25
18 Ramon Hernandez .10
19 Terrence Long .10
20 Jason Isringhausen .10
21 Barry Zito .50
22 Ben Grieve .10
23 2000 Athletics Lineup .10
24 David Wells .10
25 Raul Mondesi .20
26 Darrin Fletcher .10
27 Shannon Stewart .10
28 Kelvim Escobar .10
29 Tony Batista .10
30 Carlos Delgado .50
31 Brad Fullmer .10
32 Billy Koch .10
33 Jose Cruz Jr. .10
34 2000 Blue Jays Lineup .10
35 Greg Vaughn .10
36 Roberto Hernandez .10
37 Vinny Castilla .10
38 Gerald Williams .10
39 Aubrey Huff .10
40 Bryan Rekar .10
41 Albie Lopez .10
42 Fred McGriff .25
43 Miguel Cairo .10
44 Ryan Rupe .10
45 2000 Devil Rays Lineup .10
46 Jim Thome .50
47 Roberto Alomar .50
48 Bartolo Colon .25
49 Omar Vizquel .20
50 Travis Fryman .20
51 Manny Ramirez .50
52 Dave Burba .10
53 Chuck Finley .10
54 Russ Branyan .10
55 Kenny Lofton .25
56 2000 Indians Lineup .10
57 Alex Rodriguez 1.50
58 Jay Buhner .10
59 Aaron Sele .10
60 Kazuhiro Sasaki .20
61 Edgar Martinez .20
62 John Halama .10
63 Mike Cameron .10
64 Fred Garcia .10
65 John Olerud .20
66 Jamie Moyer .10
67 Gil Meche .10
68 2000 Mariners Lineup .10
69 Cal Ripken Jr. 2.00
70 Sidney Ponson .10
71 Chris Richard .10
72 Jose Mercedes .10
73 Albert Belle .15
74 Mike Mussina .50
75 Brady Anderson .15
76 Delino DeShields .10
77 Melvin Mora .10
78 Luis Matos .10
79 Brook Fordyce .10

80 2000 Orioles Lineup .10
81 Rafael Palmeiro .50
82 Rick Helling .10
83 Ruben Mateo .10
84 Rusty Greer .10
85 Ivan Rodriguez .50
86 Doug Davis .10
87 Gabe Kapler .15
88 Mike Lamb .10
89 Alex Rodriguez 1.50
90 Kenny Rogers .10
91 2000 Rangers Lineup .10
92 Nomar Garciaparra .50
93 Trot Nixon .10
94 Tomokazu Ohka .10
95 Pedro Martinez .75
96 Dante Bichette .10
97 Jason Varitek .10
98 Rolando Arrojo .10
99 Carl Everett .10
100 Derek Lowe .10
101 Troy O'Leary .10
102 Tim Wakefield .10
103 2000 Red Sox Lineup .10
104 Mike Sweeney .10
105 Carlos Febles .10
106 Joe Randa .10
107 Jeff Suppan .10
108 Mac Suzuki .10
109 Jermaine Dye .10
110 Carlos Beltran .25
111 Mark Quinn .10
112 Johnny Damon .20
113 2000 Royals Lineup .10
114 Tony Clark .10
115 Dean Palmer .10
116 Brian Moehler .10
117 Brad Ausmus .10
118 Juan Gonzalez .50
119 Juan Encarnacion .10
120 Jeff Weaver .10
121 Bobby Higginson .10
122 Todd Jones .10
123 Deivi Cruz .10
124 2000 Tigers Lineup .10
125 Corey Koskie .10
126 Matt Lawton .10
127 Mark Redman .10
128 David Ortiz .10
129 Jay Canizaro .10
130 Eric Milton .10
131 Jacque Jones .10
132 J.C. Romero .10
133 Ron Coomer .10
134 Brad Radke .10
135 2000 Twins Lineup .10
136 Carlos Lee .10
137 Frank Thomas .75
138 Mike Sirotka .10
139 Charles Johnson .10
140 James Baldwin .10
141 Magglio Ordonez .25
142 Jon Garland .10
143 Paul Konerko .10
144 Ray Durham .10
145 Keith Foulke .10
146 Chris Singleton .10
147 2000 White Sox Lineup .10
148 Bernie Williams .50
149 Orlando Hernandez .15
150 David Justice .25
151 Andy Pettitte .25
152 Mariano Rivera .25
153 Derek Jeter 2.00
154 Jorge Posada .25
155 Jose Canseco .50
156 Glenallen Hill .10
157 Paul O'Neill .25
158 Denny Neagle .10
159 Chuck Knoblauch .10
160 Roger Clemens 1.50
161 2000 Yankees Lineup .10
162 Jeff Bagwell .50
163 Moises Alou .20
164 Lance Berkman .40
165 Shane Reynolds .10
166 Ken Caminiti .10
167 Craig Biggio .25
168 Jose Lima .10
169 Octavio Dotel .10
170 Richard Hidalgo .20
171 Scott Elarton .10
172 2000 Astros Lineup .10
173 Rafael Furcal .25
174 Greg Maddux 1.00
175 Quilvio Veras .10
176 Chipper Jones 1.00
177 Andres Galarraga .25
178 Brian Jordan .10
179 Tom Glavine .25
180 Kevin Millwood .25
181 Javier Lopez .25
182 B.J. Surhoff .10
183 Andruw Jones .50
184 Andy Ashby .10
185 2000 Braves Lineup .10
186 Richie Sexson .40
187 Jeff D'Amico .10
188 Ron Belliard .10
189 Jeromy Burnitz .10
190 Jimmy Haynes .10
191 Marquis Grissom .10
192 Jose Hernandez .10
193 Geoff Jenkins .10
194 Jamey Wright .10
195 Mark Loretta .10
196 2000 Brewers Lineup .10
197 Rick Ankiel .25

198 Mark McGwire 1.50
199 Fernando Vina .10
200 David Renteria .10
201 Darryl Kile .10
202 Jim Edmonds .25
203 Ray Lankford .10
204 Garrett Stephenson .10
205 Fernando Tatis .10
206 Will Clark .40
207 J.D. Drew .15
208 2000 Cardinals Lineup .10
209 Mark Grace .25
210 Eric Young .10
211 Sammy Sosa 1.00
212 Jon Lieber .10
213 Joe Girardi .10
214 Kevin Tapani .10
215 Ricky Gutierrez .10
216 Kerry Wood .50
217 Rondell White .10
218 Damon Buford .10
219 2000 Cubs Lineup .10
220 Luis Gonzalez .25
221 Randy Johnson .75
222 Jay Bell .10
223 Erubiel Durazo .10
224 Matt Williams .25
225 Steve Finley .10
226 Curt Schilling .40
227 Todd Stottlemyre .10
228 Tony Womack .10
229 Brian Anderson .10
230 2000 Diamondbacks Lineup .10
231 Gary Sheffield .40
232 Adrian Beltre .25
233 Todd Hundley .10
234 Chan Ho Park .10
235 Shawn Green .25
236 Kevin Brown .25
237 Tom Goodwin .10
238 Mark Grudzielanek .10
239 Ismael Valdes .10
240 Eric Karros .10
241 2000 Dodgers Lineup .10
242 Jose Vidro .10
243 Javier Vazquez .20
244 Orlando Cabrera .10
245 Peter Bergeron .10
246 Vladimir Guerrero .75
247 Dustin Hermanson .10
248 Tony Armas Jr. .10
249 Lee Stevens .10
250 Milton Bradley .10
251 Carl Pavano .10
252 2000 Expos Lineup .10
253 Ellis Burks .10
254 Robb Nen .10
255 J.T. Snow .10
256 Barry Bonds 2.00
257 Shawn Estes .10
258 Jeff Kent .20
259 Kirk Rueter .10
260 Bill Mueller .10
261 Livan Hernandez .10
262 Rich Aurilia .10
263 2000 Giants Lineup .10
264 Ryan Dempster .10
265 Cliff Floyd .10
266 Mike Lowell .10
267 A.J. Burnett .10
268 Preston Wilson .10
269 Luis Castillo .10
270 Henry Rodriguez .10
271 Antonio Alfonseca .10
272 Derek Lee .10
273 Mark Kotsay .10
274 Brad Penny .10
275 2000 Marlins Lineup .10
276 Mike Piazza 1.00
277 Jay Payton .10
278 Al Leiter .15
279 Mike Bordick .10
280 Armando Benitez .10
281 Todd Zeile .10
282 Mike Hampton .20
283 Edgardo Alfonzo .10
284 Derek Bell .10
285 Robin Ventura .20
286 2000 Mets Lineup .10
287 Tony Gwynn .75
288 Trevor Hoffman .10
289 Ryan Klesko .20
290 Phil Nevin .10
291 Matt Clement .10
292 Ben Davis .10
293 Ruben Rivera .10
294 Bret Boone .25
295 Adam Eaton .10
296 Eric Owens .10
297 2000 Padres Lineup .10
298 Bob Abreu .20
299 Mike Lieberthal .10
300 Robert Person .10
301 Scott Rolen .50
302 Randy Wolf .10
303 Bruce Chen .10
304 Travis Lee .10
305 Kent Bottenfield .10
306 Pat Burrell .50
307 Doug Glanville .10
308 2000 Phillies Lineup .10
309 Brian Giles .25
310 Todd Ritchie .10
311 Warren Morris .10
312 John Vander Wal .10
313 Kris Benson .10
314 Jason Kendall .10

315 Kevin Young .10
316 Francisco Cordova .10
317 Jimmy Anderson .10
318 2000 Pirates Lineup .10
319 Ken Griffey Jr. 1.00
320 Pokey Reese .10
321 Chris Stynes .10
322 Barry Larkin .40
323 Steve Parris .10
324 Michael Tucker .10
325 Dmitri Young .10
326 Pete Harnisch .10
327 Adam Graves .10
328 Aaron Boone .10
329 Sean Casey .10
330 2000 Reds Lineup .10
331 Todd Helton .50
332 Pedro Astacio .10
333 Larry Walker .25
334 Ben Petrick .10
335 Brian Bohanon .10
336 Juan Pierre .10
337 Jeffrey Hammonds .10
338 Jeff Cirillo .10
339 Todd Hollandsworth .10
340 2000 Rockies Lineup .10
341 Matt Wise, Keith Luuloa, Derrick Turnbow (Vintage Rookies) .10
342 Jason Hart, Jose Ortiz, Mario Encarnacion (Vintage Rookies) .10
343 Vernon Wells, Pascual Coco, Josh Phelps (Vintage Rookies) .25
344 Travis Harper, Kenny Kelley, Toby Hall (Vintage Rookies) .10
345 Danys Baez, Tim Drew, Martin Vargas RC (Vintage Rookies) .10
346 Ichiro Suzuki RC, Ryan Franklin, Ryan Christianson (Vintage Rookies) 10.00
347 Jay Spurgeon, Lesli Brea, Carlos Casimiro (Vintage Rookies) .10
348 B.J. Waszgis, Brian Sikorski, Joaquin Benoit (Vintage Rookies) .10
349 Sun-Woo Kim, Paxton Crawford, Steve Lomasney (Vintage Rookies) .10
350 Kris Wilson, Orber Moreno, Dee Brown (Vintage Rookies) .10
351 Mark Johnson, Brandon Inge, Adam Bernero (Vintage Rookies) .10
352 Danny Ardoin, Matt Kinney, Jason Ryan (Vintage Rookies) .10
353 Rocky Biddle, Joe Crede, Aaron Myette (Vintage Rookies) .10
354 Nick Johnson, D'Angelo Jimenez, Willi Mo Pena (Vintage Rookies) .10
355 Tony McKnight, Aaron McNeal, Keith Ginter (Vintage Rookies) .10
356 Mark DeRosa, Jason Marquis, Wes Helms (Vintage Rookies) .10
357 Allen Levrault, Horacio Estrada, Santiago Perez (Vintage Rookies) .10
358 Luis Saturria, Gene Stechschulte, Britt Reames (Vintage Rookies) .10
359 Joey Nation, Corey Patterson, Cole Liniak (Vintage Rookies) .25
360 Alex Cabrera, Geraldo Guzman, Nelson Figueroa (Vintage Rookies) .10
361 Hiram Bocachica, Mike Judd, Luke Prokopec (Vintage Rookies) .10
362 Tomas de la Rosa, Yohanny Valera, Talmadge Nunnari (Vintage Rookies) .10
363 Ryan Vogelsong, Juan Melo, Chad Zerbe (Vintage Rookies) .10
364 Jason Grilli, Pablo Ozuna, Ramon Castro (Vintage Rookies) .10
365 Timoniel Perez, Grant Roberts, Brian Cole (Vintage Rookies) .10
366 Tom Davey, Xavier Nady, Dave Maurer (Vintage Rookies) .50
367 Jimmy Rollins, Mark Brownson, Reggie Taylor (Vintage Rookies) .25
368 Alex Hernandez, Adam Hyzdu, Tike Redman (Vintage Rookies) .10

369 Brady Clark, John Riedling, Mike Bell (Vintage Rookies) .10
370 Giovanni Carrara, Josh Kalinowski, Elvis Pena (Vintage Rookies) .10
371 Jim Edmonds (Postseason Scrapbook) .10
372 Edgar Martinez (Postseason Scrapbook) .10
373 Rickey Henderson (Postseason Scrapbook) .10
374 Barry Zito (Postseason Scrapbook) .25
375 Tino Martinez (Postseason Scrapbook) .10
376 J.T. Snow (Postseason Scrapbook) .10
377 Bobby Jones (Postseason Scrapbook) .10
378 Alex Rodriguez (Postseason Scrapbook) 1.00
379 Mike Hampton (Postseason Scrapbook) .10
380 Roger Clemens (Postseason Scrapbook) .50
381 Jay Payton (Postseason Scrapbook) .10
382 John Olerud (Postseason Scrapbook) .10
383 David Justice (Postseason Scrapbook) .10
384 Mike Piazza (Postseason Scrapbook) .75
385 Yankees Celebrate (Postseason Scrapbook) .10
386 Jose Vizcaino (Postseason Scrapbook) .10
387 Roger Clemens (Postseason Scrapbook) .75
388 Todd Zeile (Postseason Scrapbook) .10
389 Derek Jeter (Postseason Scrapbook) 1.25
390 Yankees Celebrate (Postseason Scrapbook) .50
391 Nomar Garciaparra - AL Batting (Big League Leaders) .75
392 Todd Helton - NL Batting (Big League Leaders) .25
393 Troy Glaus - AL HR (Big League Leaders) .25
394 Sammy Sosa - NL HR (Big League Leaders) .50
395 Edgar Martinez - AL RBI (Big League Leaders) .10
396 Todd Helton - NL RBI (Big League Leaders) .10
397 Pedro Martinez - AL ERA (Big League Leaders) .40
398 Kevin Brown - NL ERA (Big League Leaders) .10
399 David Wells, Tim Hudson - AL Wins (Big League Leaders) .10
400 Tom Glavine - NL Wins (Big League Leaders) .10

All-Star Tributes

ALL-STAR TRIBUTES

NM/M
Complete Set (10): 20.00
Common Player: 1.00
Inserted 1:23
1 Derek Jeter 4.00
2 Mike Piazza 2.00
3 Carlos Delgado 1.00
4 Pedro Martinez 1.50
5 Vladimir Guerrero 1.50
6 Mark McGwire 3.00
7 Alex Rodriguez 3.00
8 Barry Bonds 4.00
9 Chipper Jones 2.00
10 Sammy Sosa 2.50

"Fantasy Outfield" Combo Jersey

NM/M
Production 25 Cards
FO-CJ Joe DiMaggio, Mickey Mantle, Ken Griffey Jr. 1,000

Glory Days

NM/M
Complete Set (15): 15.00
Common Player: .50
Inserted 1:15
1 Jermaine Dye .50

GLORY DAYS — JIM EDMONDS — cardinals' outfield

2	Chipper Jones	2.00
3	Todd Helton	1.00
4	Magglio Ordonez	.75
5	Tony Gwynn	1.50
6	Jim Edmonds	.75
7	Rafael Palmeiro	1.00
8	Barry Bonds	4.00
9	Carl Everett	.50
10	Mike Piazza	2.00
11	Brian Giles	.50
12	Tony Batista	.50
13	Jeff Bagwell	1.00
14	Ken Griffey Jr.	2.00
15	Troy Glaus	1.00

Mantle Pinstripes Exclusive
NM/M
Complete Set (56): 75.00
Common Mantle: 2.00
One Pack/Box

Mantle Pinstripes Memorabilia
NM/M
Print Runs Listed:

MMB	Mickey Mantle/Bat/100	100.00
MMCJ	Mickey Mantle, Roger Maris/Jsy/50	300.00
MMJ	Mickey Mantle, Jsy/100	125.00

Matinee Idols

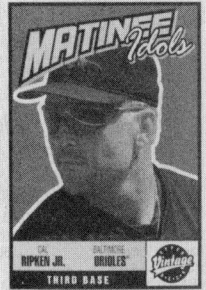

CAL RIPKEN JR. BALTIMORE ORIOLES — THIRD BASE

NM/M
Complete Set (20): 10.00
Common Player: .50
Inserted 1:4

1	Ken Griffey Jr.	1.00
2	Derek Jeter	2.00
3	Barry Bonds	2.00
4	Chipper Jones	1.00
5	Mike Piazza	1.00
6	Todd Helton	.50
7	Randy Johnson	.75
8	Alex Rodriguez	1.50
9	Sammy Sosa	1.50
10	Cal Ripken Jr.	2.00
11	Nomar Garciaparra	1.50
12	Carlos Delgado	.50
13	Jason Giambi	.50
14	Ivan Rodriguez	.50
15	Vladimir Guerrero	.75
16	Gary Sheffield	.50
17	Frank Thomas	.50
18	Jeff Bagwell	.50
19	Pedro Martinez	.75
20	Mark McGwire	1.50

Retro Rules

mark mcgwire • 1b — RETRO RULES

NM/M
Complete Set (15): 20.00
Common Player: .50
Inserted 1:15

1	Nomar Garciaparra	3.00
2	Frank Thomas	1.00
3	Jeff Bagwell	1.00
4	Sammy Sosa	2.50
5	Derek Jeter	4.00
6	David Wells	.50
7	Vladimir Guerrero	1.50
8	Jim Thome	1.00
9	Mark McGwire	3.00
10	Todd Helton	1.00
11	Tony Gwynn	1.50
12	Bernie Williams	.75
13	Cal Ripken Jr.	4.00
14	Brian Giles	.75
15	Jason Giambi	1.50

Timeless Teams Bat

GENE TENACE — TIMELESS TEAMS

NM/M
Common Player: 8.00
Inserted 1:72

NYY-JD	Joe DiMaggio	150.00
NYY-TH	Tommy Henrich	8.00
NYY-CK	Charlie Keller	8.00
NYY-BD	Bill Dickey	20.00
BK-JR	Jackie Robinson	90.00
BK-RC	Roy Campanella	50.00
BK-GH	Gil Hodges	25.00
BK-DN	Don Newcombe	8.00
LA-SG	Steve Garvey	8.00
LA-RC	Ron Cey	8.00
LA-BR	Bill Russell	8.00
LA-DB	Dusty Baker	8.00
BA-BP	Boog Powell	8.00
BA-BR	Brooks Robinson	25.00
BA-FR	Frank Robinson	20.00
BA-MB	Mark Belanger	8.00
PI-RC	Roberto Clemente	100.00
PI-WS	Willie Stargell	20.00
PI-MS	Manny Sanguillen	8.00
PI-AO	Al Oliver	8.00
OA-RJ	Reggie Jackson	20.00
OA-SB	Sal Bando	8.00
OA-GT	Gene Tenace	8.00
OA-JR	Joe Rudi	8.00
CI2-JB	Johnny Bench	25.00
CI2-TP	Tony Perez	15.00
CI2-JM	Joe Morgan	8.00
CI2-KG	Ken Griffey Sr.	8.00
NYM-NR	Nolan Ryan	40.00
NYM-RS	Ron Swoboda	8.00
NYM-EK	Ed Kranepool	8.00
NYM-TA	Tommie Agee	8.00

Timeless Teams Combo Bat

TIMELESS TEAMS

NM/M
Common Card: 75.00
Production 100 Sets

NYY41	Joe DiMaggio, Tommy Henrich, Bill Dickey, Charlie Keller	200.00
BKN55	Jackie Robinson, Roy Campanella, Gil Hodges, Don Newcombe	175.00
BAL70	Frank Robinson, Brooks Robinson, Mark Belanger, Boog Powell	120.00
LA81	Steve Garvey, Ron Cey, Dusty Baker, Bill Russell	75.00
PIT71	Roberto Clemente, Willie Stargell, Bill Mazeroski, Al Oliver	200.00
OAK72	Reggie Jackson, Sal Bando, Gene Tenace, Joe Rudi	80.00
CIN75	Johnny Bench, Tony Perez, Joe Morgan, Ken Griffey Sr.	120.00
NYM69	Nolan Ryan, Ron Swoboda, Ed Kranepool, Tommie Agee	200.00

"Timeless Teams" Jersey
NM/M
Common Player: 15.00
Inserted 1:288

NYY-MM	Mickey Mantle	160.00
NYY-RM	Roger Maris	50.00
NYY-BR	Bobby Richardson	15.00
CI-DC	Dave Concepcion	15.00

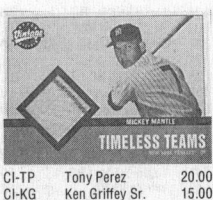

Mickey Mantle — TIMELESS TEAMS

CI-TP	Tony Perez	20.00
CI-KG	Ken Griffey Sr.	15.00
CI-JM	Joe Morgan	20.00

"Timeless Teams" Combo Jersey

TIMELESS TEAMS

NM/M
Production 100 Sets

NYY61	Mickey Mantle, Roger Maris, Bobby Richardson	250.00
CIN75	Dave Concepcion, Tony Perez, Ken Griffey Sr.	120.00

2001 Upper Deck/Coca-Cola Cal Ripken, Jr. Tribute

To commemorate his final season Upper Deck produced for Coca-Cola a set of eight cards featuring highlights from the Iron Man's career. Cards #1-4 were given away in a cello pack to fans at the September 21 and October 1 O's games at Camden Yards. Cards #5-8 were given away at games on September 22-23 and October 2-3. Also in each cello pack was a Coke coupon card. Fronts have borderless color photos with UD logo and Ripken's name in gold foil. A special Ripken Tribute logo appears at lower-left. Backs repeat the front photo, have a large uniform number 8 in the background and present various sets of stats. The Coke logo appears among those on back.

NM/M
Complete Set (8): 10.00
Common Card: 1.50

1	Cal Ripken, Jr. (Rookie of the Year)	1.50
2	Cal Ripken, Jr. (1991 AL MVP)	1.50
3	Cal Ripken, Jr. (1991 Gold Glove)	1.50
4	Cal Ripken, Jr. (The "Iron Man")	1.50
5	Cal Ripken, Jr. (400th HR)	1.50
6	Cal Ripken, Jr. (3,000 Hit)	1.50
7	Cal Ripken, Jr. (2001 All-Star MVP)	1.50
8	Cal Ripken, Jr. (Retirement Announcement)	1.50
	Coupon Card	.25

2001 Upper Deck/Ritz-Oreo

In conjunction with its sponsorship of the 2001 All-Star Game in Seattle, Ritz-Oreo issued a pair of cards distributed in product packages. In standard 2-1/2" x 3-1/2" format, one card is bordered in red and pictures Griffey batting; a blue bordered card has a picture of him throwing. Backs have biographical data - "Height: 150 Oreos / Weight: 27,060 Ritz," recent stats, a quote and logos of all

---

parties involved. The cards were also available with a pair of Fleer Derek Jeter cards in a mail-in offer.

NM/M
Complete Set (2): 3.00

(1)	Ken Griffey Jr./Btg	2.00
(2)	Ken Griffey Jr./Throwing	2.00

2001 Upper Deck/Twizzlers Big League Challenge

Each specially marked 16-oz. package of Twizzlers candy contained one card from this set. The 2-1/2" x 3-1/2" cards have on front a photo from the Big League Challenge event, with UD and Twizzlers logos and the player's 2000 home run total. Backs repeat the Big League Challenge logo and have career highlights.

NM/M
Complete Set (10): 7.50
Common Player: .50

1	Jason Giambi	1.00
2	Carlos Delgado	.50
3	Troy Glaus	1.00
4	Jim Edmonds	.50
5	Richard Hidalgo	.50
6	Gary Sheffield	.50
7	Todd Helton	.75
8	Jose Canseco	.75
9	Frank Thomas	1.00
10	Barry Bonds	1.50

2002 Upper Deck

JASON GIAMBI — OAKLAND ATHLETICS

NM/M
Complete Set (745): 150.00
Complete Series I (500): 100.00
Complete Series II (245): 50.00
Common Player: .15
Series 1 Hobby Pack (8): 4.00
Series 1 Hobby Box (24): 75.00
Series 2 Hobby Pack (8): 1.25
Series 2 Hobby Box (24): 25.00

1	Mark Prior (Star Rookie)	4.00
2	Mark Teixeira (Star Rookie)	1.50
3	Brian Roberts (Star Rookie)	.25
4	Jason Romano (Star Rookie)	.25
5	Dennis Stark RC (Star Rookie)	.50
6	Oscar Salazar (Star Rookie)	.50
7	John Patterson (Star Rookie)	.25
8	Shane Loux (Star Rookie)	.25
9	Marcus Giles (Star Rookie)	.40
10	Juan Cruz (Star Rookie)	.25
11	Jorge Julio (Star Rookie)	.25
12	Adam Dunn (Star Rookie)	.50
13	Delvin James (Star Rookie)	.25
14	Jeremy Affeldt (Star Rookie)	.25
15	Tim Raines Jr. (Star Rookie)	.25
16	Luke Hudson (Star Rookie)	.25
17	Todd Sears (Star Rookie)	.25
18	George Perez (Star Rookie)	.25
19	Wilmy Caceres (Star Rookie)	.25
20	Abraham Nunez (Star Rookie)	.25
21	Mike Amrhein (Star Rookie)	.25
22	Carlos Hernandez (Star Rookie)	.25
23	Scott Hodges (Star Rookie)	.25
24	Brandon Knight (Star Rookie)	.25
25	Geoff Goetz (Star Rookie)	.25
26	Carlos Garcia (Star Rookie)	.25
27	Luis Pineda (Star Rookie)	.25
28	Chris Gissell (Star Rookie)	.25
29	Jae Weong (Star Rookie)	.25
30	Paul Phillips (Star Rookie)	.25
31	Cory Aldridge (Star Rookie)	.25
32	Aaron Cook RC (Star Rookie)	.50
33	Rendy Espina (Star Rookie)	.25
34	Jason Phillips (Star Rookie)	.25
35	Carlos Silva (Star Rookie)	.25
36	Ryan Mills (Star Rookie)	.25
37	Pedro Santana (Star Rookie)	.25
38	John Grabow (Star Rookie)	.25
39	Cody Ransom (Star Rookie)	.15
40	Orlando Woodlands (Star Rookie)	.25
41	Bud Smith (Star Rookie)	.25
42	Junior Guerrero (Star Rookie)	.25
43	David Brous (Star Rookie)	.25
44	Steve Green (Star Rookie)	.25
45	Brian Rogers (Star Rookie)	.25
46	Juan Figueroa (Star Rookie)	.25
47	Nick Punto (Star Rookie)	.25
48	Junior Herndon (Star Rookie)	.25
49	Justin Kaye (Star Rookie)	.25
50	Jason Karnuth (Star Rookie)	.25
51	Troy Glaus	.40
52	Bengie Molina	.15
53	Ramon Ortiz	.15
54	Adam Kennedy	.15
55	Jarrod Washburn	.15
56	Troy Percival	.15
57	David Eckstein	.15
58	Ben Weber	.15
59	Larry Barnes	.15
60	Ismael Valdes	.15
61	Benji Gil	.15
62	Scott Schoeneweis	.15
63	Pat Rapp	.15
64	Jason Giambi	.50
65	Mark Mulder	.25
66	Ron Gant	.15
67	Johnny Damon	.25
68	Adam Piatt	.15
69	Jermaine Dye	.25
70	Jason Hart	.15
71	Eric Chavez	.40
72	Jim Mecir	.15
73	Barry Zito	.40
74	Jason Isringhausen	.15
75	Jeremy Giambi	.15
76	Olmedo Saenz	.15
77	Terrence Long	.15
78	Ramon Hernandez	.15
79	Chris Carpenter	.15
80	Raul Mondesi	.15
81	Carlos Delgado	.50
82	Billy Koch	.15
83	Vernon Wells	.15
84	Darrin Fletcher	.15
85	Homer Bush	.15
86	Pasqual Coco	.15
87	Shannon Stewart	.15
88	Chris Woodward	.15
89	Joe Lawrence	.15
90	Esteban Loaiza	.15
91	Cesar Izturis	.15
92	Kelvim Escobar	.15
93	Greg Vaughn	.15
94	Brent Abernathy	.15
95	Tanyon Sturtze	.15
96	Steve Cox	.15
97	Aubrey Huff	.15
98	Jesus Colome	.15
99	Ben Grieve	.15
100	Esteban Yan	.15
101	Joe Kennedy	.15
102	Felix Martinez	.15
103	Nick Bierbrodt	.15
104	Damian Rolls	.15
105	Russ Johnson	.15
106	Toby Hall	.15
107	Roberto Alomar	.40
108	Bartolo Colon	.25
109	John Rocker	.15
110	Juan Gonzalez	.50
111	Einar Diaz	.15
112	Chuck Finley	.15
113	Kenny Lofton	.25
114	Danys Baez	.15
115	Travis Fryman	.25
116	C.C. Sabathia	.25
117	Paul Shuey	.15
118	Marty Cordova	.15
119	Ellis Burks	.15
120	Bob Wickman	.15
121	Edgar Martinez	.25
122	Freddy Garcia	.15
123	Ichiro Suzuki	1.50
124	John Olerud	.25
125	Gil Meche	.15
126	Dan Wilson	.15
127	Aaron Sele	.15
128	Kazuhiro Sasaki	.15
129	Mark McLemore	.15
130	Carlos Guillen	.15
131	Al Martin	.15
132	David Bell	.15
133	Jay Buhner	.25
134	Stan Javier	.15
135	Tony Batista	.15
136	Jason Johnson	.15
137	Brook Fordyce	.15
138	Mike Kinkade	.15
139	Willis Roberts	.15
140	David Segui	.15
141	Josh Towers	.15
142	Jeff Conine	.15
143	Chris Richard	.15
144	Pat Hentgen	.15
145	Melvin Mora	.15
146	Jerry Hairston Jr.	.15
147	Calvin Maduro	.15
148	Brady Anderson	.15
149	Alex Rodriguez	1.50
150	Kenny Rogers	.15
151	Chad Curtis	.15
152	Ricky Ledee	.15
153	Rafael Palmeiro	.50
154	Rob Bell	.15
155	Rick Helling	.15
156	Doug Davis	.15
157	Mike Lamb	.15
158	Gabe Kapler	.15
159	Jeff Zimmerman	.15
160	Bill Haselman	.15
161	Tim Crabtree	.15
162	Carlos Pena	.15
163	Nomar Garciaparra	1.00
164	Shea Hillenbrand	.15
165	Hideo Nomo	.40
166	Manny Ramirez	.50
167	Jose Offerman	.15
168	Scott Hatteberg	.15
169	Trot Nixon	.25
170	Darren Lewis	.15
171	Derek Lowe	.25
172	Troy O'Leary	.15
173	Tim Wakefield	.15
174	Chris Stynes	.15
175	John Valentin	.15
176	David Cone	.15
177	Neifi Perez	.15
178	Brent Mayne	.15
179	Dan Reichert	.15
180	A.J. Hinch	.15
181	Chris George	.15
182	Mike Sweeney	.15
183	Jeff Suppan	.15
184	Roberto Hernandez	.15
185	Joe Randa	.15
186	Paul Byrd	.15
187	Luis Ordaz	.15
188	Kris Wilson	.15
189	Dee Brown	.15
190	Tony Clark	.15
191	Matt Anderson	.15
192	Robert Fick	.15
193	Juan Encarnacion	.15
194	Dean Palmer	.15
195	Victor Santos	.15
196	Damion Easley	.15
197	Jose Lima	.15
198	Deivi Cruz	.15
199	Roger Cedeno	.15
200	Jose Macias	.15
201	Jeff Weaver	.15
202	Brandon Inge	.15
203	Brian Moehler	.15
204	Brad Radke	.15
205	Doug Mientkiewicz	.15
206	Cristian Guzman	.15
207	Corey Koskie	.15
208	LaTroy Hawkins	.15
209	J.C. Romero	.15
210	Chad Allen	.15
211	Torii Hunter	.25
212	Travis Miller	.15
213	Joe Mays	.15
214	Todd Jones	.15
215	David Ortiz	.40

#	Player	Price
216	Brian Buchanan	.15
217	A.J. Pierzynski	.15
218	Carlos Lee	.15
219	Gary Glover	.15
220	Jose Valentin	.15
221	Aaron Rowand	.15
222	Sandy Alomar Jr.	.15
223	Herbert Perry	.15
224	Jon Garland	.15
225	Mark Buehrle	.15
226	Chris Singleton	.15
227	Kip Wells	.15
228	Ray Durham	.15
229	Joe Crede	.15
230	Keith Foulke	.15
231	Royce Clayton	.15
232	Andy Pettitte	.40
233	Derek Jeter	2.00
234	Jorge Posada	.50
235	Roger Clemens	1.50
236	Paul O'Neill	.25
237	Nick Johnson	.15
238	Gerald Williams	.15
239	Mariano Rivera	.25
240	Alfonso Soriano	.50
241	Ramiro Mendoza	.15
242	Mike Mussina	.50
243	Luis Sojo	.15
244	Scott Brosius	.15
245	David Justice	.25
246	Wade Miller	.15
247	Brad Ausmus	.15
248	Jeff Bagwell	.50
249	Daryle Ward	.15
250	Shane Reynolds	.15
251	Chris Truby	.15
252	Billy Wagner	.15
253	Craig Biggio	.25
254	Moises Alou	.25
255	Vinny Castilla	.15
256	Tim Redding	.15
257	Roy Oswalt	.40
258	Julio Lugo	.15
259	Chipper Jones	.75
260	Greg Maddux	1.00
261	Ken Caminiti	.15
262	Kevin Millwood	.25
263	Keith Lockhart	.15
264	Rey Sanchez	.15
265	Jason Marquis	.15
266	Brian Jordan	.15
267	Steve Karsay	.15
268	Wes Helms	.15
269	B.J. Surhoff	.15
270	Wilson Betemit	.15
271	John Smoltz	.25
272	Rafael Furcal	.25
273	Jeromy Burnitz	.15
274	Jimmy Haynes	.15
275	Mark Loretta	.15
276	Jose Hernandez	.15
277	Paul Rigdon	.15
278	Alex Sanchez	.15
279	Chad Fox	.15
280	Devon White	.15
281	Tyler Houston	.15
282	Ronnie Belliard	.15
283	Luis Lopez	.15
284	Ben Sheets	.40
285	Curtis Leskanic	.15
286	Henry Blanco	.15
287	Mark McGwire	2.00
288	Edgar Renteria	.25
289	Matt Morris	.25
290	Gene Stechschulte	.15
291	Dustin Hermanson	.15
292	Eli Marrero	.15
293	Albert Pujols	1.50
294	Luis Saturria	.15
295	Bobby Bonilla	.15
296	Garrett Stephenson	.15
297	Jim Edmonds	.40
298	Rick Ankiel	.25
299	Placido Polanco	.15
300	Dave Veres	.15
301	Sammy Sosa	1.50
302	Eric Young	.15
303	Kerry Wood	.75
304	Jon Lieber	.15
305	Joe Girardi	.15
306	Fred McGriff	.25
307	Jeff Fassero	.15
308	Julio Zuleta	.15
309	Kevin Tapani	.15
310	Rondell White	.15
311	Julian Tavarez	.15
312	Tom Gordon	.15
313	Corey Patterson	.25
314	Bill Mueller	.15
315	Randy Johnson	.75
316	Chad Moeller	.15
317	Tony Womack	.15
318	Erubiel Durazo	.15
319	Luis Gonzalez	.25
320	Brian Anderson	.15
321	Reggie Sanders	.15
322	Greg Colbrunn	.15
323	Robert Ellis	.15
324	Jack Cust	.15
325	Bret Prinz	.15
326	Steve Finley	.15
327	Byung-Hyun Kim	.15
328	Albie Lopez	.15
329	Gary Sheffield	.40
330	Mark Grudzielanek	.15
331	Paul LoDuca	.15
332	Tom Goodwin	.15
333	Andy Ashby	.15
334	Hiram Bocachica	.15
335	Dave Hansen	.15
336	Kevin Brown	.25
337	Marquis Grissom	.15
338	Terry Adams	.15
339	Chan Ho Park	.15
340	Adrian Beltre	.25
341	Luke Prokopec	.15
342	Jeff Shaw	.15
343	Vladimir Guerrero	.75
344	Orlando Cabrera	.15
345	Tony Armas Jr.	.15
346	Michael Barrett	.15
347	Geoff Blum	.15
348	Ryan Minor	.15
349	Peter Bergeron	.15
350	Graeme Lloyd	.15
351	Jose Vidro	.15
352	Javier Vazquez	.15
353	Matt Blank	.15
354	Masato Yoshii	.15
355	Carl Pavano	.15
356	Barry Bonds	2.00
357	Shawon Dunston	.15
358	Livan Hernandez	.15
359	Felix Rodriguez	.15
360	Pedro Feliz	.15
361	Calvin Murray	.15
362	Robb Nen	.15
363	Marvin Benard	.15
364	Russ Ortiz	.15
365	Jason Schmidt	.25
366	Rich Aurilia	.15
367	John Vander Wal	.15
368	Benito Santiago	.15
369	Ryan Dempster	.15
370	Charles Johnson	.15
371	Alex Gonzalez	.15
372	Luis Castillo	.15
373	Mike Lowell	.25
374	Antonio Alfonseca	.15
375	A.J. Burnett	.15
376	Brad Penny	.15
377	Jason Grilli	.15
378	Derrek Lee	.25
379	Matt Clement	.15
380	Eric Owens	.15
381	Vladimir Nunez	.15
382	Cliff Floyd	.15
383	Mike Piazza	1.25
384	Lenny Harris	.15
385	Glendon Rusch	.15
386	Todd Zeile	.15
387	Al Leiter	.25
388	Armando Benitez	.15
389	Alex Escobar	.15
390	Kevin Appier	.15
391	Matt Lawton	.15
392	Bruce Chen	.15
393	John Franco	.15
394	Tsuyoshi Shinjo	.15
395	Rey Ordonez	.15
396	Joe McEwing	.15
397	Ryan Klesko	.15
398	Brian Lawrence	.15
399	Kevin Walker	.15
400	Phil Nevin	.15
401	Bubba Trammell	.15
402	Wiki Gonzalez	.15
403	D'Angelo Jimenez	.15
404	Rickey Henderson	.40
405	Mike Darr	.15
406	Trevor Hoffman	.15
407	Damian Jackson	.15
408	Santiago Perez	.15
409	Cesar Crespo	.15
410	Robert Person	.15
411	Travis Lee	.15
412	Scott Rolen	.75
413	Turk Wendell	.15
414	Randy Wolf	.15
415	Kevin Jordan	.15
416	Jose Mesa	.15
417	Mike Lieberthal	.15
418	Bobby Abreu	.25
419	Tomas Perez	.15
420	Doug Glanville	.15
421	Reggie Taylor	.15
422	Jimmy Rollins	.40
423	Brian Giles	.25
424	Rob Mackowiak	.15
425	Bronson Arroyo	.15
426	Kevin Young	.15
427	Jack Wilson	.15
428	Adam Brown	.15
429	Chad Hermansen	.15
430	Jimmy Anderson	.15
431	Aramis Ramirez	.25
432	Todd Ritchie	.15
433	Pat Meares	.15
434	Warren Morris	.15
435	Derek Bell	.15
436	Ken Griffey Jr.	1.00
437	Elmer Dessens	.15
438	Ruben Mateo	.15
439	Jason LaRue	.15
440	Sean Casey	.25
441	Pete Harnisch	.15
442	Danny Graves	.15
443	Aaron Boone	.15
444	Dmitri Young	.15
445	Brandon Larson	.15
446	Pokey Reese	.15
447	Todd Walker	.15
448	Juan Castro	.15
449	Todd Helton	.50
450	Ben Petrick	.15
451	Juan Pierre	.15
452	Jeff Cirillo	.15
453	Jose Uribe	.15
454	Brian Bohanon	.15
455	Terry Shumpert	.15
456	Mike Hampton	.15
457	Shawn Chacon	.15
458	Adam Melhuse	.15
459	Greg Norton	.15
460	Gabe White	.15
461	Ichiro Suzuki (World Stage)	1.50
462	Carlos Delgado (World Stage)	.40
463	Manny Ramirez (World Stage)	.50
464	Miguel Tejada (World Stage)	.25
465	Tsuyoshi Shinjo (World Stage)	.15
466	Bernie Williams (World Stage)	.40
467	Juan Gonzalez (World Stage)	.50
468	Andruw Jones (World Stage)	.40
469	Ivan Rodriguez (World Stage)	.50
470	Larry Walker (World Stage)	.25
471	Hideo Nomo (World Stage)	.25
472	Albert Pujols (World Stage)	1.00
473	Pedro Martinez (World Stage)	.75
474	Vladimir Guerrero (World Stage)	.75
475	Tony Batista (World Stage)	.15
476	Kazuhiro Sasaki (World Stage)	.15
477	Richard Hidalgo (World Stage)	.15
478	Carlos Lee (World Stage)	.15
479	Roberto Alomar (World Stage)	.40
480	Rafael Palmeiro (World Stage)	.50
481	Ken Griffey Jr. (Griffey Gallery)	.50
482	Ken Griffey Jr. (Griffey Gallery)	.50
483	Ken Griffey Jr. (Griffey Gallery)	.50
484	Ken Griffey Jr. (Griffey Gallery)	.50
485	Ken Griffey Jr. (Griffey Gallery)	.50
486	Ken Griffey Jr. (Griffey Gallery)	.50
487	Ken Griffey Jr. (Griffey Gallery)	.50
488	Ken Griffey Jr. (Griffey Gallery)	.50
489	Ken Griffey Jr. (Griffey Gallery)	.50
490	Ken Griffey Jr. (Griffey Gallery)	.50
491	Barry Bonds (Season Highlights Checklist)	.75
492	Hideo Nomo (Season Highlights Checklist)	.15
493	Ichiro Suzuki (Season Highlights Checklist)	.50
494	Cal Ripken Jr. (Season Highlights Checklist)	.75
495	Tony Gwynn (Season Highlights Checklist)	.40
496	Randy Johnson (Season Highlights Checklist)	.40
497	A.J. Burnett (Season Highlights Checklist)	.15
498	Rickey Henderson (Season Highlights Checklist)	.15
499	Albert Pujols (Season Highlights Checklist)	.75
500	Luis Gonzalez (Season Highlights Checklist)	.25
501	Brandon Puffer RC	.50
502	Rodrigo Rosario RC	.50
503	Tom Shearn RC	.50
504	Reed Johnson RC	.50
505	Chris Baker RC	.50
506	John Ennis RC	.50
507	Luis Martinez RC	.50
508	So Taguchi RC	.75
509	Scotty Layfield RC	.50
510	Francis Beltran RC	.50
511	Brandon Backe RC	.50
512	Doug DeVore RC	.50
513	Jeremy Ward RC	.50
514	Jose Vaverde RC	.50
515	P.J. Bevis RC	.50
516	Victor Alvarez RC	.50
517	Kazuhisa Ishii RC	.50
518	Jorge Nunez RC	.50
519	Eric Good RC	.50
520	Ron Calloway RC	.50
521	Valentino Pasucci RC	.25
522	Nelson Castro RC	.50
523	Deivis Santos RC	.25
524	Luis Ugueto RC	.50
525	Matt Thornton RC	.25
526	Hansel Izquierdo RC	.75
527	Tyler Yates RC	.50
528	Mark Corey RC	.50
529	Jaime Cerda RC	.50
530	Satoru Komiyama RC	.50
531	Steve Bechler RC	.50
532	Ben Howard RC	.50
533	Anderson Machado RC	.50
534	Jorge Padilla RC	.50
535	Eric Junge RC	.50
536	Adrian Burnside RC	.50
537	Mike Gonzalez RC	.50
538	Josh Hancock RC	.50
539	Colin Young RC	.50
540	Rene Reyes RC	.50
541	Cam Esslinger RC	.50
542	Tim Kalita RC	.50
543	Kevin Frederick RC	.50
544	Kyle Kane RC	.50
545	Edwin Almonte RC	.50
546	Aaron Sele	.15
547	Garret Anderson	.25
548	Darin Erstad	.25
549	Brad Fullmer	.15
550	Kevin Appier	.15
551	Tim Salmon	.25
552	David Justice	.15
553	Billy Koch	.15
554	Scott Hatteberg	.15
555	Tim Hudson	.15
556	Miguel Tejada	.25
557	Carlos Pena	.15
558	Mike Sirotka	.15
559	Jose Cruz Jr.	.15
560	Josh Phelps	.15
561	Brandon Lyon	.15
562	Luke Prokopec	.15
563	Felipe Lopez	.15
564	Jason Standridge	.15
565	Chris Gomez	.15
566	John Flaherty	.15
567	Jason Tyner	.15
568	Bobby Smith	.15
569	Wilson Alvarez	.15
570	Matt Lawton	.15
571	Omar Vizquel	.25
572	Jim Thome	.75
573	Brady Anderson	.15
574	Alex Escobar	.15
575	Russell Branyan	.15
576	Bret Boone	.25
577	Ben Davis	.15
578	Mike Cameron	.15
579	Jamie Moyer	.15
580	Ruben Sierra	.15
581	Jeff Cirillo	.15
582	Marty Cordova	.15
583	Mike Bordick	.15
584	Brian Roberts	.15
585	Luis Matos	.15
586	Geronimo Gil	.15
587	Jay Gibbons	.15
588	Carl Everett	.15
589	Ivan Rodriguez	.50
590	Chan Ho Park	.15
591	Juan Gonzalez	.50
592	Hank Blalock	.40
593	Todd Van Poppel	.15
594	Pedro J. Martinez	.75
595	Jason Varitek	.15
596	Tony Clark	.15
597	Johnny Damon	.25
598	Dustin Hermanson	.15
599	John Burkett	.15
600	Carlos Beltran	.40
601	Mark Quinn	.15
602	Chuck Knoblauch	.15
603	Michael Tucker	.15
604	Carlos Febles	.15
605	Jose Rosado	.15
606	Dmitri Young	.15
607	Bobby Higginson	.15
608	Craig Paquette	.15
609	Mitch Meluskey	.15
610	Wendell Magee	.15
611	Mike Rivera	.15
612	Jacque Jones	.15
613	Luis Rivas	.15
614	Eric Milton	.15
615	Eddie Guardado	.15
616	Matt LeCroy	.15
617	Mike Jackson	.15
618	Magglio Ordonez	.25
619	Frank Thomas	.50
620	Rocky Biddle	.15
621	Paul Konerko	.25
622	Todd Ritchie	.15
623	Jon Rauch	.15
624	John Vander Wal	.15
625	Rondell White	.15
626	Jason Giambi	.50
627	Robin Ventura	.25
628	David Wells	.15
629	Bernie Williams	.50
630	Lance Berkman	.25
631	Richard Hidalgo	.15
632	Gregg Zaun	.15
633	Jose Vizcaino	.15
634	Octavio Dotel	.15
635	Morgan Ensberg	.15
636	Andruw Jones	.50
637	Tom Glavine	.40
638	Gary Sheffield	.40
639	Vinny Castilla	.15
640	Javy Lopez	.25
641	Albie Lopez	.15
642	Geoff Jenkins	.15
643	Jeffrey Hammonds	.15
644	Alex Ochoa	.15
645	Richie Sexson	.25
646	Eric Young	.15
647	Glendon Rusch	.15
648	Tino Martinez	.25
649	Fernando Vina	.15
650	J.D. Drew	.25
651	Woody Williams	.15
652	Darryl Kile	.15
653	Jason Isringhausen	.15
654	Moises Alou	.15
655	Alex Gonzalez	.15
656	Delino DeShields	.15
657	Todd Hundley	.15
658	Chris Stynes	.15
659	Jason Bere	.15
660	Curt Schilling	.40
661	Craig Counsell	.15
662	Mark Grace	.40
663	Matt Williams	.25
664	Jay Bell	.15
665	Rick Helling	.15
666	Shawn Green	.40
667	Eric Karros	.15
668	Hideo Nomo	.40
669	Omar Daal	.15
670	Brian Jordan	.15
671	Cesar Izturis	.15
672	Fernando Tatis	.15
673	Lee Stevens	.15
674	Tomokazu Ohka	.15
675	Brian Schneider	.15
676	Brad Wilkerson	.15
677	Bruce Chen	.15
678	Tsuyoshi Shinjo	.15
679	Jeff Kent	.25
680	Kirk Rueter	.15
681	J.T. Snow	.15
682	David Bell	.15
683	Reggie Sanders	.15
684	Preston Wilson	.15
685	Vic Darensbourg	.15
686	Josh Beckett	.40
687	Pablo Ozuna	.15
688	Mike Redmond	.15
689	Scott Strickland	.15
690	Mo Vaughn	.25
691	Roberto Alomar	.50
692	Edgardo Alfonzo	.15
693	Shawn Estes	.15
694	Roger Cedeno	.15
695	Jeromy Burnitz	.15
696	Ray Lankford	.15
697	Mark Kotsay	.15
698	Kevin Jarvis	.15
699	Bobby Jones	.15
700	Sean Burroughs	.15
701	Ramon Vazquez	.15
702	Pat Burrell	.40
703	Marlon Byrd	.15
704	Brandon Duckworth	.15
705	Marlon Anderson	.15
706	Vicente Padilla	.15
707	Kip Wells	.15
708	Jason Kendall	.15
709	Pokey Reese	.15
710	Pat Meares	.15
711	Kris Benson	.15
712	Armando Rios	.15
713	Mike Williams	.15
714	Barry Larkin	.40
715	Adam Dunn	.40
716	Juan Encarnacion	.15
717	Scott Williamson	.15
718	Wilton Guerrero	.15
719	Chris Reitsma	.15
720	Larry Walker	.25
721	Denny Neagle	.15
722	Todd Zeile	.15
723	Jose Ortiz	.15
724	Jason Jennings	.15
725	Tony Eusebio	.15
726	Ichiro Suzuki	1.00
727	Barry Bonds	1.50
728	Randy Johnson	.50
729	Albert Pujols	1.00
730	Roger Clemens	.50
731	Sammy Sosa	.50
732	Alex Rodriguez	.50
733	Chipper Jones	.40
734	Rickey Henderson	.25
735	Mariners Team Photo	.15
736	Luis Gonzalez	.25
737	Derek Jeter	1.50
738	Ichiro Suzuki	1.50
739	Barry Bonds	1.50
740	Curt Schilling	.25
741	Shawn Green	.25
742	Jason Giambi	.50
743	Roberto Alomar	.25
744	Larry Walker	.15
745	Mark McGwire	.75

AL Centennial Bats

		NM/M
	Inserted 1:144	
JD	Joe DiMaggio	125.00
MM	Mickey Mantle	150.00
BR	Babe Ruth	150.00

AL Centennial Jerseys

		NM/M
	Common Player:	10.00
	Inserted 1:144	
PM	Pedro Martinez	10.00
CR	Cal Ripken Jr.	40.00
AR	Alex Rodriguez	15.00
IR	Ivan Rodriguez	10.00
NR	Nolan Ryan	40.00
FT	Frank Thomas	10.00

AL Centennial G-U Jerseys Autograph

No Pricing
Production 25 Sets

All-Star Salute Game Jerseys

		NM/M
	Common Player:	10.00
	Inserted 1:288	
SA	Sparky Anderson	10.00
LB	Lou Boudreau	10.00
DE	Dennis Eckersley	10.00
NF	Nellie Fox	15.00
KG	Ken Griffey Jr.	25.00
AR	Alex Rodriguez	25.00
DS	Don Sutton	10.00
IS	Ichiro Suzuki	40.00

Big Fly Zone

		NM/M
	Complete Set (10):	15.00
	Common Player:	.50
	Inserted 1:14	
Z1	Mark McGwire	4.00
Z2	Ken Griffey Jr.	3.00
Z3	Manny Ramirez	1.00
Z4	Sammy Sosa	1.00
Z5	Todd Helton	1.00
Z6	Barry Bonds	4.00
Z7	Luis Gonzalez	1.00
Z8	Alex Rodriguez	4.00
Z9	Carlos Delgado	1.00
Z10	Chipper Jones	1.50

Breakout Performers

		NM/M
	Complete Set (10):	10.00
	Common Player:	.50
	Inserted 1:14	
BP1	Ichiro Suzuki	3.00
BP2	Albert Pujols	4.00
BP3	Doug Mientkiewicz	1.00
BP4	Lance Berkman	1.00
BP5	Tsuyoshi Shinjo	1.00
BP6	Ben Sheets	1.00
BP7	Jimmy Rollins	.75
BP8	J.D. Drew	.75
BP9	Bret Boone	.50
BP10	Alfonso Soriano	.50

Championship Caliber

		NM/M
	Complete Set (6):	10.00
	Common Player:	1.00
	Inserted 1:23	
CC1	Derek Jeter	5.00
CC2	Roberto Alomar	1.00
CC3	Chipper Jones	2.00
CC4	Gary Sheffield	1.00
CC5	Roger Clemens	3.00
CC6	Greg Maddux	2.50

Championship Caliber Swatches

		NM/M
	Common Player:	8.00
	Inserted 1:288	
RA	Roberto Alomar/SP	20.00
KB	Kevin Brown/SP	10.00
CF	Cliff Floyd	10.00
ChJ	Charles Johnson	8.00
RJ	Randy Johnson	10.00
CJo	Chipper Jones/SP	25.00
BL	Barry Larkin	8.00
GM	Greg Maddux/SP	40.00

TM Tino Martinez 8.00
JO John Olerud 8.00
AP Andy Pettitte 10.00
JP Jorge Posada 10.00
CS Curt Schilling 10.00
BW Bernie Williams 10.00

Chasing History

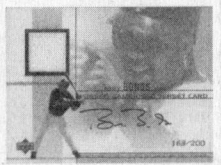

		NM/M
Complete Set (15):		12.00
Common Player:		.50
Inserted 1:11		
CH1	Sammy Sosa	2.00
CH2	Ken Griffey Jr.	1.50
CH3	Roger Clemens	2.00
CH4	Barry Bonds	3.00
CH5	Rafael Palmeiro	1.00
CH6	Andres Galarraga	.50
CH7	Juan Gonzalez	1.00
CH8	Roberto Alomar	1.00
CH9	Randy Johnson	1.00
CH10	Jeff Bagwell	1.00
CH11	Fred McGriff	.50
CH12	Matt Williams	.50
CH13	Greg Maddux	1.50
CH14	Robb Nen	.50
CH15	Kenny Lofton	.50

Combo Bat

		NM/M
Inserted 1:288		
CB-RG	Alex Rodriguez, Ken Griffey Jr.	30.00
CB-DM	Joe DiMaggio, Mickey Mantle	200.00

Combo Jersey

		NM/M
Common Duo:		10.00
Inserted 1:288		
RS	Alex Rodriguez, Sammy Sosa	30.00
RM	Nolan Ryan, Pedro Martinez	40.00
RC	Nolan Ryan, Roger Clemens	50.00
BS	Barry Bonds, Sammy Sosa	40.00
HK	Shigetoshi Hasegawa, Byung-Hun Kim	10.00

First Timers Jerseys

		NM/M
Common Player:		8.00
Inserted 1:288		
RB	Russell Branyan	8.00
OD	Omar Daal	8.00
FG	Freddy Garcia	8.00
ML	Matt Lawton	8.00
JM	Joe Mays	8.00
EM	Eric Milton	8.00
CP	Corey Patterson	10.00
AP	Albert Pujols	50.00
SS	Shannon Stewart	8.00

First Timers Jerseys Autograph

No Pricing
Production 25 Sets

Game Jerseys

		NM/M
Common Player:		8.00
Production 350 Sets		
Golds:		.75-1.5X
Production 100		
TB	Tony Batista	8.00
AB	Adrian Beltre	8.00
JC	Jeff Cirillo	8.00
KG	Ken Griffey Jr.	20.00
TH	Tim Hudson	10.00
MP	Mike Piazza	15.00
SR	Scott Rolen	15.00
CS	Curt Schilling	15.00
SS	Sammy Sosa	25.00
FT	Frank Thomas	12.00
PW	Preston Wilson	8.00

Game Jersey Autograph

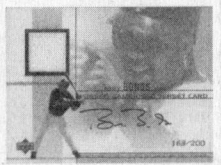

		NM/M
Common Player:		20.00
Production 200 Sets		
BB	Barry Bonds	200.00
CD	Carlos Delgado	25.00
RF	Rafael Furcal	20.00
JGi	Jason Giambi	35.00
KG	Ken Griffey Jr.	125.00
AJ	Andruw Jones	35.00
AP	Albert Pujols	125.00
CR	Cal Ripken Jr.	200.00
NR	Nolan Ryan	140.00
GS	Gary Sheffield	20.00
IS	Ichiro Suzuki	300.00
PW	Preston Wilson	20.00

Game-Used Base

		NM/M
Common Player:		5.00
Inserted 1:288		
BB	Barry Bonds	20.00
RC	Roger Clemens	20.00
CD	Carlos Delgado	5.00
JG	Jason Giambi	10.00
TG	Troy Glaus	8.00
JG	Juan Gonzalez	10.00
LG	Luis Gonzalez	5.00
SG	Shawn Green	5.00
KG	Ken Griffey Jr.	15.00
DJ	Derek Jeter	25.00
AJ	Andruw Jones	8.00
CJ	Chipper Jones	10.00
MM	Mark McGwire	40.00
MP	Mike Piazza	15.00
CR	Cal Ripken Jr.	40.00
AR	Alex Rodriguez	15.00
IR	Ivan Rodriguez	8.00
KS	Kazuhiro Sasaki	5.00
SS	Sammy Sosa	20.00
IS	Ichiro Suzuki	50.00

Game-Used Base Autograph

Complete Set (1):
Production 25

Game-Used Base Combo

		NM/M
Common Combo:		40.00
Inserted 1:288		
RG	Alex Rodriguez, Ken Griffey Jr.	40.00
MJ	Mark McGwire, Derek Jeter	60.00

Game-Worn Gems

		NM/M
Common Player:		5.00
Inserted 1:48		
Golds:		1-2X
Production 100 Sets		
RA	Roberto Alomar	8.00
EC	Eric Chavez	5.00
CD	Carlos Delgado	5.00
DE	Darin Erstad/SP	8.00
FG	Freddy Garcia/SP	8.00
TG	Tom Glavine	8.00
JG	Juan Gonzalez	8.00
LG	Luis Gonzalez/SP	10.00
MH	Mike Hampton/SP	8.00
CJ	Chipper Jones	10.00
JK	Jason Kendall	5.00
RK	Ryan Klesko/SP	5.00
GM	Greg Maddux	15.00
EM	Edgar Martinez	6.00
PM	Pedro Martinez/SP	15.00
TM	Tino Martinez	8.00
JM	Joe Mays	5.00
EM	Eric Milton	5.00
PN	Phil Nevin	5.00
HN	Hideo Nomo/SP	20.00
JO	John Olerud/SP	5.00
RP	Robert Person	5.00
CR	Cal Ripken Jr.	40.00
IR	Ivan Rodriguez	10.00
SR	Scott Rolen	15.00
CS	Curt Schilling	10.00
AS	Aaron Sele	5.00
GS	Gary Sheffield/SP	8.00
FT	Frank Thomas	10.00
OV	Omar Vizquel/SP	10.00
RY	Robin Yount	10.00

Double Game-Worn Gems

		NM/M
Common Card:		8.00
Production 450 Sets		
Golds:		1-2X
Production 100 Sets		
NK	Phil Nevin, Ryan Klesko	8.00
VB	Omar Vizquel, Russell Branyan	10.00
DH	Jermaine Dye, Tim Hudson	10.00
TO	Frank Thomas, Magglio Ordonez	15.00
MI	Edgar Martinez, Ichiro Suzuki/150	80.00
GS	Luis Gonzalez, Curt Schilling	15.00
AP	Roberto Alomar, Mike Piazza	20.00
PL	Robert Person, Mike Lieberthal	8.00
MM	Kevin Millwood, Greg Maddux	20.00
KG	Jason Kendall, Brian Giles	10.00
DF	Carlos Delgado, Shannon Stewart	10.00
PN	Chan Ho Park, Hideo Nomo	30.00

Global Swatch Jerseys

		NM/M
Common Player:		5.00
Inserted 1:144		
CD	Carlos Delgado	8.00
SH	Shigetoshi Hasegawa	5.00
BK	Byung-Hun Kim	5.00
HN	Hideo Nomo	35.00
CP	Chan Ho Park	5.00
MR	Manny Ramirez	10.00
KS	Kazuhiro Sasaki	5.00
TS	Tsuyoshi Shinjo	5.00
IS	Ichiro Suzuki	50.00
MY	Masato Yoshii	5.00

Global Swatch Jerseys Autograph

No Pricing
Production 25 Sets

McGwire Memorabilia

		NM/M
Common Card:		
AM-J	Mark McGwire/Jsy/70	75.00
AM-B	Mark McGwire/Bat/70	75.00
MMc	Mark McGwire/500 HR Club Bat/350	300.00
MM-SS	Mark McGwire, Sammy Sosa/25 (Combo Jersey)	200.00
MM-KG	Mark McGwire, Ken Griffey Jr./25 (Combo Jersey)	250.00
MM-JG	Mark McGwire, Jason Giambi/25 (Combo Jersey)	200.00

Patch Numbers

Complete Set (3)
No Pricing

Return of the Ace

		NM/M
Complete Set (15):		15.00
Common Player:		1.00
Inserted 1:11		
RA1	Randy Johnson	2.00
RA2	Greg Maddux	3.00
RA3	Pedro Martinez	2.00
RA4	Freddy Garcia	1.00
RA5	Matt Morris	1.00
RA6	Mark Mulder	1.00
RA7	Wade Miller	1.00
RA8	Kevin Brown	1.00
RA9	Roger Clemens	4.00
RA10	Jon Lieber	1.00
RA11	C.C. Sabathia	1.00
RA12	Tim Hudson	1.50
RA13	Curt Schilling	2.00
RA14	Al Leiter	1.00
RA15	Mike Mussina	1.50

Sons of Summer Game Jerseys

		NM/M
Common Player:		10.00
Inserted 1:288		
RA	Roberto Alomar	10.00
JB	Jeff Bagwell	10.00
RC	Roger Clemens	15.00
JG	Juan Gonzalez	10.00
GM	Greg Maddux	15.00
PM	Pedro Martinez/SP	15.00
MP	Mike Piazza	15.00
AR	Alex Rodriguez	15.00

Superstar Summit

Inserted 1:11		
SS1	Alex Rodriguez	4.00
SS2	Jason Giambi	1.00
SS3	Vladimir Guerrero	1.50
SS4	Randy Johnson	1.50
SS5	Chipper Jones	1.50
SS6	Ichiro Suzuki	3.00
SS7	Sammy Sosa	2.50
SS8	Greg Maddux	2.00
SS9	Ken Griffey Jr.	2.50
SS10	Todd Helton	4.00
SS11	Barry Bonds	4.00
SS12	Derek Jeter	4.00
SS13	Mike Piazza	3.00
SS14	Ivan Rodriguez	1.00
SS15	Frank Thomas	1.00

The People's Choice Game Jerseys

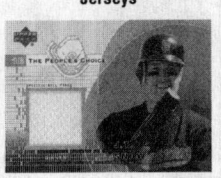

		NM/M
Common Player:		5.00
Inserted 1:24		
Golds:		1-2X
Production 100 Sets		
JBa	Jeff Bagwell	10.00
EB	Ellis Burks/SP	10.00
JBu	Jeromy Burnitz	5.00
OD	Omar Daal	5.00
CD	Carlos Delgado	8.00
RF	Rafael Furcal	6.00
AG	Andres Galarraga/SP	10.00
BG	Brian Giles	5.00
JG	Juan Gonzalez	10.00
KG	Ken Griffey Jr.	20.00
TG	Tony Gwynn	12.00
SH	Sterling Hitchcock	5.00
HI	Hideki Irabu	5.00
CJ	Charles Johnson	5.00
DL	Derek Lowe	5.00
GM	Greg Maddux	15.00
TM	Tino Martinez	10.00
JN	Jeff Nelson	5.00
RO	Rey Ordonez	5.00
RP	Rafael Palmeiro/SP	15.00
RP	Robert Person/SP	10.00
AP	Andy Pettitte	10.00
MP	Mike Piazza	15.00
TR	Tim Raines	5.00
MRa	Manny Ramirez	10.00
MRi	Mariano Rivera	10.00
AR	Alex Rodriguez	15.00
TS	Tim Salmon	6.00
CS	Curt Schilling	10.00
TSh	Tsuyoshi Shinjo	5.00
JS	J.T. Snow	5.00
SS	Sammy Sosa	20.00
MS	Mike Stanton	5.00
FT	Frank Thomas	10.00
RV	Robin Ventura	6.00
OV	Omar Vizquel	5.00
DW	David Wells	6.00
BW	Bernie Williams	10.00
MW	Matt Williams/SP	10.00

UD Patch Logo

		NM/M
Complete Set (6):		15.00
Common Player:		1.50
Inserted 1:23		
SS1	Sammy Sosa	3.00
SS2	Alex Rodriguez	4.00
SS3	Mark McGwire	4.00
SS4	Barry Bonds	4.00
SS5	Mike Piazza	4.00
SS6	Ken Griffey Jr.	2.50

		NM/M
Common Player:		60.00
Inserted 1:2,500		
Prices for Stripes & Numbers identical.		
BB	Barry Bonds	125.00
JG	Jason Giambi	60.00
KG	Ken Griffey Jr.	100.00
PM	Pedro Martinez	80.00
CR	Cal Ripken Jr.	150.00
AR	Alex Rodriguez	125.00
SS	Sammy Sosa	100.00

Superstar Summit II

	NM/M
Complete Set (15):	25.00
Common Player:	1.00

UD Patch Numbers

Complete Set (7):
Common Player:

UD Patch Stripes

Complete Set (7):
Common Player:

Patch Stripes Autograph

Complete Set (2):
Common Player:

Yankees Dynasty Combo Base

		NM/M
Common Combo:		50.00
JW	Derek Jeter, Bernie Williams	60.00
CJ	Roger Clemens, Derek Jeter	75.00

Yankees Dynasty Jerseys

		NM/M
Common Combo:		20.00
Inserted 1:288		
PR	Andy Pettitte, Mariano Rivera	25.00
BT	Wade Boggs, Joe Torre	25.00
CP	Roger Clemens, Jorge Posada	50.00
DM	Joe DiMaggio, Mickey Mantle	300.00
RK	Willie Randolph, Chuck Knoblauch	20.00
BJ	Scott Brosius, David Justice	20.00
OM	Paul O'Neill, Tino Martinez	25.00
WO	Bernie Williams, Paul O'Neill	25.00
WG	David Wells, Dwight Gooden	25.00
GC	Joe Girardi, David Cone	25.00
KR	Chuck Knoblauch, Tim Raines	25.00

2001 All-Star HR Derby Jerseys

		NM/M
Common Player:		10.00
Inserted 1:288		
Golds:		1-2X
Production 100 Sets		
BrB	Bret Boone	10.00
JG	Jason Giambi	15.00
TH	Todd Helton	15.00
AR	Alex Rodriguez	20.00
SS	Sammy Sosa	25.00

2001's Greatest Hits

		NM/M
Complete Set (10):		20.00
Common Player:		1.00
Inserted 1:14		
GH1	Barry Bonds	4.00
GH2	Ichiro Suzuki	3.00
GH3	Albert Pujols	3.00
GH4	Mike Piazza	2.50
GH5	Alex Rodriguez	3.00
GH6	Mark McGwire	3.00
GH7	Manny Ramirez	3.00
GH8	Ken Griffey Jr.	2.00
GH9	Sammy Sosa	3.00
GH10	Derek Jeter	3.00

2002 UD Authentics

Kazuhisa Ishii

	NM/M
Complete Set (200):	50.00
Common Player:	.25

Reversed Negatives:		1-2.5X
Inserted 1:9		
Pack (5):		2.50
Box (18):		35.00
1	Brad Fullmer	.25
2	Garret Anderson	.40
3	Darin Erstad	.40
4	Jarrod Washburn	.25
5	Troy Glaus	.50
6	Barry Zito	.40
7	David Justice	.40
8	Eric Chavez	.40
9	Tim Hudson	.40
10	Miguel Tejada	.40
11	Jermaine Dye	.25
12	Mark Mulder	.40
13	Carlos Delgado	.50
14	Jose Cruz Jr.	.25
15	Shannon Stewart	.25
16	Raul Mondesi	.25
17	Tanyon Sturtze	.25
18	Toby Hall	.25
19	Greg Vaughn	.25
20	Aubrey Huff	.25
21	Ben Grieve	.25
22	Brent Abernathy	.25
23	Jim Thome	.75
24	C.C. Sabathia	.25
25	Matt Lawton	.25
26	Omar Vizquel	.25
27	Ellis Burks	.25
28	Russ Branyan	.25
29	Bartolo Colon	.25
30	Ichiro Suzuki	1.50
31	John Olerud	.40
32	Freddy Garcia	.25
33	Mike Cameron	.25
34	Jeff Cirillo	.25
35	Kazuhiro Sasaki	.25
36	Edgar Martinez	.25
37	Bret Boone	.25
38	Jeff Conine	.25
39	Melvin Mora	.25
40	Jason Johnson	.25
41	Chris Richard	.25
42	Tony Batista	.25
43	Ivan Rodriguez	.50
44	Gabe Kapler	.25
45	Rafael Palmeiro	.25
46	Alex Rodriguez	1.50
47	Juan Gonzalez	.50
48	Carl Everett	.25
49	Nomar Garciaparra	1.50
50	Trot Nixon	.25
51	Manny Ramirez	.50
52	Pedro J. Martinez	.75
53	Johnny Damon	.40
54	Shea Hillenbrand	.25
55	Mike Sweeney	.25
56	Mark Quinn	.25
57	Joe Randa	.25
58	Carlos Beltran	.40
59	Chuck Knoblauch	.25
60	Robert Fick	.25
61	Jeff Weaver	.25
62	Bobby Higginson	.25
63	Dean Palmer	.25
64	Dmitri Young	.25
65	Corey Koskie	.25
66	Doug Mientkiewicz	.25
67	Joe Mays	.25
68	Torii Hunter	.40
69	Cristian Guzman	.25
70	Jacque Jones	.25
71	Magglio Ordonez	.40
72	Paul Konerko	.25
73	Carlos Lee	.25
74	Mark Buehrle	.25
75	Jose Canseco	.50
76	Frank Thomas	.50
77	Roger Clemens	1.50
78	Derek Jeter	2.00
79	Jason Giambi	.50
80	Rondell White	.25
81	Bernie Williams	.50
82	Jorge Posada	.50
83	Mike Mussina	.50
84	Alfonso Soriano	.75
85	Wade Miller	.25
86	Jeff Bagwell	.50
87	Craig Biggio	.40
88	Roy Oswalt	.40
89	Lance Berkman	.40
90	Daryle Ward	.25
91	Chipper Jones	.75
92	Greg Maddux	1.00
93	Marcus Giles	.25
94	Gary Sheffield	.50
95	Tom Glavine	.50
96	Andruw Jones	.50
97	Rafael Furcal	.25
98	Richie Sexson	.40
99	Ben Sheets	.40
100	Jose Hernandez	.25
101	Geoff Jenkins	.40
102	Jeffrey Hammonds	.25
103	Edgar Renteria	.40
104	Matt Morris	.40
105	Tino Martinez	.25
106	Jim Edmonds	.40
107	Albert Pujols	1.50
108	J.D. Drew	.40
109	Fernando Vina	.25
110	Darryl Kile	.25
111	Sammy Sosa	1.50
112	Fred McGriff	.40
113	Kerry Wood	.75
114	Moises Alou	.40

116	Jon Lieber	.25
117	Mark Grace	.50
118	Randy Johnson	.75
119	Curt Schilling	.50
120	Luis Gonzalez	.40
121	Steve Finley	.25
122	Matt Bradley	.40
123	Shawn Green	.40
124	Kevin Brown	.40
125	Adrian Beltre	.40
126	Paul LoDuca	.25
127	Hideo Nomo	.50
128	Brian Jordan	.25
129	Vladimir Guerrero	.75
130	Javier Vazquez	.25
131	Jose Vidro	.25
132	Orlando Cabrera	.25
133	Jeff Kent	.25
134	Rich Aurilia	.25
135	Russ Ortiz	.25
136	Barry Bonds	2.00
137	Preston Wilson	.25
138	Ryan Dempster	.25
139	Cliff Floyd	.25
140	Josh Beckett	.40
141	Mike Lowell	.40
142	Mike Piazza	1.00
143	Roberto Alomar	.50
144	Al Leiter	.40
145	Edgardo Alfonzo	.25
146	Roger Cedeno	.25
147	Jeromy Burnitz	.25
148	Phil Nevin	.25
149	Mark Kotsay	.25
150	Ryan Klesko	.25
151	Trevor Hoffman	.25
152	Bobby Abreu	.40
153	Scott Rolen	.75
154	Jimmy Rollins	.40
155	Robert Person	.25
156	Pat Burrell	.25
157	Randy Wolf	.25
158	Brian Giles	.40
159	Aramis Ramirez	.50
160	Kris Benson	.25
161	Jason Kendall	.25
162	Ken Griffey Jr.	1.00
163	Sean Casey	.40
164	Adam Dunn	.50
165	Barry Larkin	.50
166	Todd Helton	.25
167	Mike Hampton	.25
168	Larry Walker	.25
169	Juan Pierre	.25
170	Juan Uribe	.25
171	So Taguchi RC	.50
172	Brendan Donnelly RC	.75
173	Chris Baker RC	.50
174	John Ennis RC	.75
175	Francis Beltran RC	.50
176	Danny Wright RC	.50
177	Brandon Backe RC	.75
178	Mark Corey RC	.75
179	Kazuhisa Ishii RC	.50
180	Ron Calloway RC	.50
181	Kevin Frederick RC	.75
182	Jaime Cerda RC	.75
183	Doug DeVore RC	.50
184	Brandon Puffer RC	.50
185	Andy Pratt RC	.50
186	Adrian Burnside RC	.50
187	Josh Hancock RC	.75
188	Jorge Nunez RC	.50
189	Tyler Yates RC	.50
190	Kyle Kane RC	.75
191	Jose Valverde RC	1.00
192	Matt Thornton RC	.50
193	Ben Howard RC	.50
194	Reed Johnson RC	1.00
195	Rene Reyes RC	.50
196	Jeremy Ward RC	.50
197	Steve Bechler RC	.50
198	Cam Esslinger RC	.50
199	Michael Crudale RC	.50
200	Todd Donovan RC	.50

Retro UD Jerseys

NM/M

Common Player: 5.00
Inserted 1:16
Golds: 1-2X
Production 275 Sets
Reverse Neg.: 1-2X
Production 350 Sets

JB	Jeff Bagwell	8.00
KB	Kevin Brown	5.00
EC	Eric Chavez	5.00
RC	Roger Clemens/SP	20.00
CD	Carlos Delgado	8.00
JD	J.D. Drew	5.00
JE	Jim Edmonds	5.00
DE	Darin Erstad	5.00
RF	Rafael Furcal	5.00
JG	Jason Giambi	8.00
TG	Tom Glavine	10.00
LG	Luis Gonzalez	5.00
KG	Ken Griffey Jr.	20.00
TH	Todd Helton	10.00
RJ	Randy Johnson	8.00
AJ	Andruw Jones	8.00
CJ	Chipper Jones	15.00
GM	Greg Maddux	15.00
MP	Mike Piazza	15.00
MR	Manny Ramirez	10.00
AR	Alex Rodriguez	15.00
IR	Ivan Rodriguez	8.00
SS	Sammy Sosa/SP	20.00
MS	Mike Sweeney	5.00
FT	Frank Thomas	10.00

BW	Bernie Williams	10.00
BZ	Barry Zito	5.00

UD Heroes of Baseball

JC	Jose Canseco	8.00
RC	Roger Clemens	15.00
DC	David Cone	5.00
AG	Andres Galarraga	5.00
TG	Tom Glavine	10.00
JG	Juan Gonzalez	8.00
MG	Mark Grace	8.00
KG	Ken Griffey Jr.	20.00
RH	Rickey Henderson	10.00
RJ	Randy Johnson	10.00
DJ	David Justice	5.00
BL	Barry Larkin/SP	15.00
AL	Al Leiter	5.00
GM	Greg Maddux	15.00
EM	Edgar Martinez	8.00
FM	Fred McGriff	5.00
JO	John Olerud	5.00
PO	Paul O'Neill	5.00
RP	Rafael Palmeiro	8.00
CS	Curt Schilling	8.00
GS	Gary Sheffield	8.00
SS	Sammy Sosa	15.00
RV	Robin Ventura	5.00
LW	Larry Walker	5.00
MW	Matt Williams	5.00

NM/M

Complete Set (30): 150.00
Ichiro: 8.00
Griffey Jr.: 6.00
Alex Rodriguez: 8.00
Production 1,989 Sets
HB-I1-10 Ichiro Suzuki 8.00
HB-R1-10 Alex Rodriguez 8.00

Signed UD Heroes of Baseball

NM/M

Random Inserts:

G	Ken Griffey Jr./185	125.00
R	Alex Rodriguez/185	90.00
I	Ichiro Suzuki/125	400.00

Retro UD Star Rookie Jerseys

NM/M

Common Player: 5.00
Inserted 1:16
Golds: 1-2X
Production 275 Sets

CB	Craig Biggio	8.00
PB	Pat Burrell	8.00
BG	Brian Giles	5.00
JG	Juan Gonzalez	8.00
LG	Luis Gonzalez	8.00
SG	Shawn Green	8.00
KG	Ken Griffey Jr.	20.00
RJ	Randy Johnson	10.00
CJ	Chipper Jones	10.00
DJ	David Justice	5.00
RK	Ryan Klesko	5.00
KL	Kenny Lofton	5.00
PM	Pedro J. Martinez	15.00
HN	Hideo Nomo	15.00
JO	John Olerud	8.00
MO	Magglio Ordonez	8.00
RP	Robert Person	5.00
AP	Albert Pujols	25.00
MR	Manny Ramirez/SP	15.00
AR	Alex Rodriguez	20.00
IR	Ivan Rodriguez	10.00
KS	Kazuhiro Sasaki	5.00
GS	Gary Sheffield	8.00
SS	Sammy Sosa/SP	20.00
I	Ichiro Suzuki	40.00
JT	Jim Thome	12.00
LW	Larry Walker	5.00

Signed Retro UD Star Rookie Jerseys

NM/M

Production 40 Sets

KG	Ken Griffey Jr.	100.00
AR	Alex Rodriguez	150.00
JT	Jim Thome	75.00

Reverse Negative Retro UD Jerseys

Complete Set (29):
Common Player:

Stars of '89 Jerseys

NM/M

Common Player: 5.00
Inserted 1:16

RA	Roberto Alomar	8.00
KB	Kevin Brown	5.00
EB	Ellis Burks	5.00

25	Jim Thome	.75
26	Omar Vizquel	.25
27	Ricky Gutierrez	.15
28	C.C. Sabathia	.15
29	Ellis Burks	.15
30	Matt Lawton	.15
31	Milton Bradley	.15
32	Edgar Martinez	.15
33	Ichiro Suzuki	1.50
34	Bret Boone	.15
35	Freddy Garcia	.25
36	Mike Cameron	.15
37	John Olerud	.15
38	Kazuhiro Sasaki	.15
39	Jeff Cirillo	.15
40	Jeff Conine	.15
41	Marty Cordova	.15
42	Tony Batista	.15
43	Jerry Hairston Jr.	.15
44	Jason Johnson	.15
45	David Segui	.15
46	Alex Rodriguez	2.00
47	Rafael Palmeiro	.50
48	Carl Everett	.15
49	Chan Ho Park	.15
50	Ivan Rodriguez	.50
51	Juan Gonzalez	.50
52	Hank Blalock	.25
53	Manny Ramirez	.50
54	Pedro J. Martinez	.75
55	Tony Clark	.15
56	Nomar Garciaparra	1.25
57	Johnny Damon	.25
58	Trot Nixon	.15
59	Rickey Henderson	.50
60	Mike Sweeney	.15
61	Neifi Perez	.15
62	Joe Randa	.15
63	Carlos Beltran	.25
64	Chuck Knoblauch	.15
65	Michael Tucker	.15
66	Dean Palmer	.15
67	Bobby Higginson	.15
68	Dmitri Young	.15
69	Randall Simon	.15
70	Mitch Meluskey	.15
71	Damion Easley	.15
72	Joe Mays	.15
73	Doug Mientkiewicz	.15
74	Corey Koskie	.15
75	Brad Radke	.15
76	Cristian Guzman	.15
77	Torii Hunter	.25
78	Eric Milton	.15
79	Frank Thomas	.50
80	Paul Konerko	.25
81	Mark Buehrle	.15
82	Magglio Ordonez	.25
83	Carlos Lee	.15
84	Joe Crede	.15
85	Derek Jeter	2.00
86	Bernie Williams	.50
87	Mike Mussina	.50
88	Jorge Posada	.25
89	Roger Clemens	1.50
90	Jason Giambi	.50
91	Alfonso Soriano	.75
92	Rondell White	.15
93	Jeff Bagwell	.50
94	Lance Berkman	.40
95	Roy Oswalt	.25
96	Richard Hidalgo	.15
97	Wade Miller	.15
98	Craig Biggio	.25
99	Greg Maddux	.75
100	Chipper Jones	.75
101	Gary Sheffield	.40
102	Rafael Furcal	.15
103	Andruw Jones	.50
104	Vinny Castilla	.15
105	Marcus Giles	.15
106	Tom Glavine	.25
107	Richie Sexson	.40
108	Geoff Jenkins	.15
109	Glendon Rusch	.15
110	Eric Young	.15
111	Ben Sheets	.25
112	Alex Sanchez	.15
113	Albert Pujols	1.50
114	J.D. Drew	.25
115	Matt Morris	.25
116	Jim Edmonds	.25
117	Tino Martinez	.15
118	Scott Rolen	.75
119	Edgar Renteria	.15
120	Sammy Sosa	1.50
121	Kerry Wood	.25
122	Moises Alou	.15
123	Jon Lieber	.15
124	Fred McGriff	.25
125	Juan Cruz	.15
126	Alex Gonzalez	.15
127	Corey Patterson	.15
128	Randy Johnson	.75
129	Luis Gonzalez	.25
130	Steve Finley	.15
131	Matt Williams	.15
132	Curt Schilling	.50
133	Mark Grace	.40
134	Craig Counsell	.15
135	Shawn Green	.25
136	Kevin Brown	.15
137	Hideo Nomo	.40
138	Paul LoDuca	.15
139	Brian Jordan	.15
140	Eric Karros	.15
141	Adrian Beltre	.25
142	Vladimir Guerrero	.75

1989 Flashbacks

NM/M

Complete Set (12): 30.00
Common Player: 1.50
Production 4,225 Sets

F1	Ken Griffey Jr.	8.00
F2	Gary Sheffield	1.50
F3	Randy Johnson	3.00
F4	Roger Clemens	4.00
F5	Greg Maddux	5.00
F6	Mark Grace	2.00
F7	Barry Bonds	5.00
F8	Roberto Alomar	3.00
F9	Sammy Sosa	5.00
F10	Rafael Palmeiro	2.00
F11	Edgar Martinez	1.50
F12	Jose Canseco	2.00

2002 Upper Deck Ballpark Idols

NM/M

Complete Set (245): 125.00
Common Player: .15
Common (201-245): 3.00
Production 1,750
Pack (5): 2.00
Box (24 + Bobber): 50.00

1	Troy Glaus	.40
2	Kevin Appier	.15
3	Darin Erstad	.25
4	Garret Anderson	.25
5	Brad Fullmer	.15
6	Tim Salmon	.25
7	Eric Chavez	.25
8	Tim Hudson	.25
9	David Justice	.25
10	Barry Zito	.25
11	Miguel Tejada	.25
12	Mark Mulder	.40
13	Jermaine Dye	.25
14	Carlos Delgado	.40
15	Jose Cruz Jr.	.15
16	Brandon Lyon	.15
17	Shannon Stewart	.15
18	Eric Hinske	.15
19	Chris Carpenter	.15
20	Greg Vaughn	.15
21	Tanyon Sturtze	.15
22	Jason Tyner	.15
23	Toby Hall	.15
24	Ben Grieve	.15

143	Fernando Tatis	.15
144	Javier Vazquez	.15
145	Orlando Cabrera	.15
146	Tony Armas Jr.	.15
147	Jose Vidro	.15
148	Barry Bonds	2.00
149	Rich Aurilia	.15
150	Tsuyoshi Shinjo	.15
151	Jeff Kent	.15
152	Russ Ortiz	.15
153	Jason Schmidt	.25
154	Reggie Sanders	.15
155	Preston Wilson	.15
156	Luis Castillo	.15
157	Charles Johnson	.15
158	Josh Beckett	.40
159	Derrek Lee	.25
160	Mike Lowell	.25
161	Mike Piazza	1.00
162	Roberto Alomar	.40
163	Al Leiter	.25
164	Mo Vaughn	.25
165	Jeromy Burnitz	.25
166	Edgardo Alfonzo	.15
167	Roger Cedeno	.15
168	Ryan Klesko	.25
169	Brian Lawrence	.15
170	Sean Burroughs	.15
171	Phil Nevin	.15
172	Ramon Vazquez	.15
173	Mark Kotsay	.15
174	Marlon Anderson	.15
175	Mike Lieberthal	.15
176	Bobby Abreu	.25
177	Pat Burrell	.40
178	Robert Person	.15
179	Brandon Duckworth	.15
180	Jimmy Rollins	.25
181	Brian Giles	.15
182	Pokey Reese	.15
183	Kris Benson	.15
184	Aramis Ramirez	.25
185	Jason Kendall	.15
186	Kip Wells	.15
187	Ken Griffey Jr.	1.00
188	Adam Dunn	.50
189	Barry Larkin	.40
190	Sean Casey	.25
191	Austin Kearns	.25
192	Aaron Boone	.15
193	Todd Helton	.50
194	Juan Pierre	.15
195	Mike Hampton	.15
196	Jose Ortiz	.15
197	Larry Walker	.25
198	Juan Uribe	.15
199	Ichiro Suzuki (Checklist)	.75
200	Jason Giambi (Checklist)	.25
201	Franklyn German RC	3.00
202	Rodrigo Rosario RC	3.00
203	Brandon Puffer RC	3.00
204	Kirk Saarloos RC	3.00
205	Chris Baker RC	3.00
206	John Ennis RC	3.00
207	Luis Martinez RC	3.00
208	So Taguchi RC	3.00
209	Michael Crudale RC	3.00
210	Francis Beltran RC	3.00
211	Brandon Backe RC	3.00
212	Felix Escalona RC	3.00
213	Jose Valverde RC	4.00
214	Doug DeVore RC	3.00
215	Kazuhisa Ishii RC	3.00
216	Victor Alvarez RC	3.00
217	Ron Calloway RC	3.00
218	Eric Good RC	3.00
219	Jorge Nunez	3.00
220	Deivis Santos	3.00
221	Nelson Castro RC	3.00
222	Matt Thornton RC	3.00
223	Jason Simontacchi RC	3.00
224	Hansel Izquierdo RC	3.00
225	Tyler Yates RC	4.00
226	Jaime Cerda RC	3.00
227	Satoru Komiyama RC	3.00
228	Steve Bechler RC	3.00
229	Ben Howard RC	3.00
230	Todd Donovan RC	3.00
231	Jorge Padilla RC	3.00
232	Eric Junge RC	3.00
233	Anderson Machado RC	3.00
234	Adrian Burnside RC	3.00
235	Mike Gonzalez RC	3.00
236	Josh Hancock RC	3.00
237	Anastacio Martinez RC	3.00
238	Chris Booker RC	3.00
239	Rene Reyes RC	3.00
240	Cam Esslinger RC	3.00
241	Oliver Perez RC	3.00
242	Tim Kalita RC	3.00
243	Kevin Frederick RC	3.00
244	Mitch Wylie RC	3.00
245	Edwin Almonte RC	3.00

Bronze

Stars (1-200): 5-10X
SP's (201-245): .75-1.5X
Production 100 Sets

Gold

No pricing due to scarcity.
Production 25 Sets

Bobbers

NM/M

Inserted 1:Box

Roberto Alomar	10.00
Jeff Bagwell	15.00

Josh Beckett	10.00
Barry Bonds	30.00
Sean Burroughs	8.00
Roger Clemens	20.00
Joe DiMaggio/555/Away	40.00
Joe DiMaggio/361/Home	50.00
Nomar Garciaparra	20.00
Jason Giambi	10.00
Luis Gonzalez	8.00
Ken Griffey Jr.	15.00
Vladimir Guerrero	15.00
Kazuhisa Ishii	8.00
Derek Jeter/SP/Away	40.00
Randy Johnson/D'backs	15.00
Randy Johnson/Expos	15.00
Chipper Jones	15.00
Greg Maddux	20.00
Mickey Mantle/777/Away	50.00
Mickey Mantle/536/Home	60.00
Mark McGwire/Cards	35.00
Mike Piazza/Mets	20.00
Mark Prior	15.00
Albert Pujols	25.00
Alex Rodriguez	20.00
Ivan Rodriguez	8.00
Curt Schilling/D'backs	10.00
Sammy Sosa/Cubs/Away	25.00
Ichiro Suzuki/SP/Away	30.00
Frank Thomas	10.00
Jim Thome	15.00

Bobbers Autograph

NM/M

Common Autograph
Inserted 1:14 boxes
Josh Beckett 60.00

Bobbers Gold

NM/M

Amount produced listed.

Joe DiMaggio/56/Away	100.00
Joe DiMaggio/41/Home	125.00
Mickey Mantle/77/Away	140.00
Mickey Mantle/61/Home	125.00

Field Garb Jerseys

NM/M

Common Player: 4.00
Inserted 1:72

TB	Tony Batista	4.00
BG	Brian Giles	4.00
RJ	Randy Johnson	10.00
JK	Jeff Kent	4.00
TM	Tino Martinez	4.00
JO	John Olerud	4.00
AR	Alex Rodriguez	12.00
IR	Ivan Rodriguez	6.00
MS	Mike Sweeney	4.00
RV	Robin Ventura	4.00
LW	Larry Walker	4.00
BZ	Barry Zito	6.00

Figure Heads

NM/M

Complete Set (10): 20.00
Common Player: 1.00
Inserted 1:12

F1	Ichiro Suzuki	3.00
F2	Sammy Sosa	2.50
F3	Alex Rodriguez	4.00
F4	Jason Giambi	1.00
F5	Barry Bonds	4.00
F6	Chipper Jones	1.50
F7	Mike Piazza	2.00
F8	Derek Jeter	4.00
F9	Nomar Garciaparra	2.50
F10	Ken Griffey Jr.	2.00

Player's Club Jerseys

NM/M

Common Player: 6.00
Inserted 1:72

KB	Kevin Brown	6.00
DE	Darin Erstad	8.00
RF	Rafael Furcal	6.00
TH	Tim Hudson	6.00
AJ	Andruw Jones	8.00
JK	Jason Kendall	6.00
MM	Mark McGwire/SP	70.00
PN	Phil Nevin	6.00
HN	Hideo Nomo	20.00
MO	Magglio Ordonez	6.00
CS	Curt Schilling	6.00
IS	Ichiro Suzuki/SP	40.00
JT	Jim Thome	12.00

Playmakers 2002

NM/M

Complete Set (20): 25.00

Common Player: .75
Inserted 1:6

P1	Ken Griffey Jr.	2.00
P2	Alex Rodriguez	4.00
P3	Sammy Sosa	2.50
P4	Derek Jeter	4.00
P5	Mike Piazza	2.00
P6	Jason Giambi	1.00
P7	Barry Bonds	4.00
P8	Frank Thomas	1.00
P9	Randy Johnson	1.50
P10	Chipper Jones	1.50
P11	Jeff Bagwell	1.00
P12	Vladimir Guerrero	1.50
P13	Albert Pujols	3.00
P14	Nomar Garciaparra	2.50
P15	Ichiro Suzuki	3.00
P16	Troy Glaus	1.00
P17	Ivan Rodriguez	1.00
P18	Carlos Delgado	.75
P19	Greg Maddux	2.00
P20	Todd Helton	1.00

Uniform Sluggers

NM/M
Common Player: 5.00
Inserted 1:72

JB	Jeff Bagwell	8.00
JGi	Jason Giambi	8.00
JGo	Juan Gonzalez	8.00
SG	Shawn Green	5.00
KG	Ken Griffey Jr./SP	25.00
TH	Todd Helton	8.00
CJ	Chipper Jones	10.00
MM	Mickey Mantle/SP	100.00
MP	Mike Piazza	15.00
AR	Alex Rodriguez	12.00
BW	Bernie Williams	5.00

2002 Upper Deck Collectors Club

As one of the membership benefits of its Collector's Club, persons opting for the MLB option received an exclusive 20-card set. Typical UD quality with UV coating on front and back, silver-foil highlights on front and a hologram on back, the cards are standard 2-1/2" x 3-1/2". Fronts have game-action photos bordered in blue. Backs have a portrait photo, biographical data, career highlights and recent stats. Cards are numbered with an "MLB" prefix.

NM/M
Complete Set (20): 15.00
Common Player: .25

1	Alex Rodriguez	2.00
2	Barry Bonds	1.00
3	Ken Griffey Jr.	2.00
4	Sammy Sosa	1.00
5	Jason Giambi	.50
6	Ichiro	3.00
7	Chipper Jones	1.50
8	Derek Jeter	1.50
9	Nomar Garciaparra	1.00
10	Greg Maddux	.75
11	Mike Piazza	1.50
12	Frank Thomas	1.00
13	Albert Pujols	1.50
14	Randy Johnson	.50
15	Pedro Martinez	.50
16	Todd Helton	.25
17	Vladimir Guerrero	.60
18	Jeff Bagwell	.60
19	Roger Clemens	.75
20	Shawn Green	.25

2002 Upper Deck Collectors Club Memorabilia

Besides the 20-card base set benefit of joining Upper Deck's Collectors Club, one of six game-

used memorabilia cards was also included. The cards are horizontal in format with a color action photo on front. Backs have a statement of authenticity.

NM/M
Complete Set (6): 50.00
Common Player: 10.00

AR-B	Alex Rodriguez/Bat	10.00
AR-J	Alex Rodriguez/Jsy	10.00
JR-B	Ken Griffey Jr./Bat	10.00
JR-J	Ken Griffey Jr./Jsy	10.00
SS-B	Sammy Sosa/Bat	15.00
SS-J	Sammy Sosa/Jsy	15.00

2002 Upper Deck Diamond Connection

NM/M
Complete Set (550):
Common Player: .15
Common Rk (91-200): 4.00
Common Jersey (201-270): 4.00
Production 1,500
Common Jersey (271-320): 5.00
Production 775
Common Jersey (321-353): 5.00
Production 200
Common Jersey (354-368): 6.00
Production 150
Common Bat (369-438): 5.00
Production 100
Common Bat (439-488): 5.00
Production 775
Common Bat (489-521): 5.00
Production 200
Common Bat (522-536): 10.00
Production 150
Production 100
Pack (5): 4.00
Box (14): 50.00

1	Troy Glaus	.50
2	Darin Erstad	.40
3	Barry Zito	.40
4	Eric Chavez	.40
5	Tim Hudson	.40
6	Miguel Tejada	.40
7	Carlos Delgado	.40
8	Shannon Stewart	.15
9	Greg Vaughn	.15
10	Jim Thome	.75
11	C.C. Sabathia	.15
12	Ichiro Suzuki	1.50
13	Edgar Martinez	.25
14	Bret Boone	.25
15	Freddy Garcia	.15
16	Jeff Conine	.15
17	Alex Rodriguez	2.00
18	Rafael Palmeiro	.50
19	Ivan Rodriguez	.50
20	Juan Gonzalez	.50
21	Pedro J. Martinez	.75
22	Nomar Garciaparra	1.50
23	Manny Ramirez	.50
24	Carlos Beltran	.25
25	Mike Sweeney	.15
26	Dmitri Young	.15
27	Bobby Higginson	.15
28	Corey Koskie	.15
29	Cristian Guzman	.15
30	Doug Mientkiewicz	.15
31	Torii Hunter	.25
32	Frank Thomas	.50
33	Mark Buehrle	.15
34	Carlos Lee	.15
35	Magglio Ordonez	.40
36	Roger Clemens	1.50
37	Bernie Williams	.50
38	Jason Giambi	.75
39	Derek Jeter	2.00
40	Mike Mussina	.50
41	Jeff Bagwell	.50
42	Richard Hidalgo	.15
43	Lance Berkman	.40
44	Roy Oswalt	.40
45	Chipper Jones	.75
46	Gary Sheffield	.40
47	Andruw Jones	.50
48	Greg Maddux	1.00
49	Geoff Jenkins	.15
50	Ben Sheets	.25
51	Richie Sexson	.40
52	Albert Pujols	1.50
53	Matt Morris	.25
54	J.D. Drew	.40
55	Tino Martinez	.25
56	Sammy Sosa	1.50
57	Kerry Wood	.75
58	Moises Alou	.25
59	Fred McGriff	.25
60	Randy Johnson	.75
61	Luis Gonzalez	.25
62	Curt Schilling	.50
63	Kevin Brown	.25
64	Shawn Green	.40
65	Paul LoDuca	.15
66	Vladimir Guerrero	.75
67	Jose Vidro	.15
68	Barry Bonds	2.00
69	Jeff Kent	.25
70	Rich Aurilia	.15
71	Preston Wilson	.15
72	Josh Beckett	.40
73	Cliff Floyd	.25
74	Mike Piazza	1.00
75	Mo Vaughn	.25
76	Roberto Alomar	.40
77	Jeromy Burnitz	.15
78	Phil Nevin	.15
79	Sean Burroughs	.25
80	Scott Rolen	.75
81	Bobby Abreu	.25
82	Pat Burrell	.40
83	Brian Giles	.40
84	Jason Kendall	.15
85	Ken Griffey Jr.	1.00
86	Adam Dunn	.50
87	Aaron Boone	.15
88	Larry Walker	.25
89	Todd Helton	.50
90	Mike Hampton	.15
91	Brandon Puffer RC	4.00
92	Rodrigo Rosario RC	4.00
93	Tom Shearn RC	4.00
94	Morgan Ensberg RC	4.00
95	Jason Lane RC	4.00
96	Franklyn German RC	4.00
97	Carlos Pena	4.00
98	Joe Orloski RC	4.00
99	Reed Johnson RC	6.00
100	Chris Baker RC	4.00
101	Corey Thurman RC	4.00
102	Gustavo Chacin RC	4.00
103	Eric Hinske	4.00
104	John Foster RC	4.00
105	John Ennis RC	4.00
106	Kevin Gryboski RC	4.00
107	Jung Bong RC	4.00
108	Travis Wilson RC	4.00
109	Luis Martinez RC	4.00
110	Brian Mallette RC	4.00
111	Takahito Nomura RC	4.00
112	Bill Hall RC	4.00
113	Jeff Deardorff RC	4.00
114	Cristian Guerrero RC	4.00
115	Scotty Layfield RC	4.00
116	Michael Crudale RC	4.00
117	So Taguchi RC	6.00
118	Jeremy Lambert RC	4.00
119	Jimmy Journell RC	4.00
120	Francis Beltran RC	4.00
121	Mark Prior	6.00
122	Ben Christensen	4.00
123	Jorge Sosa RC	4.00
124	Brandon Backe RC	4.00
125	Steve Kent RC	4.00
126	Felix Escalona RC	4.00
127	P.J. Bevis RC	4.00
128	Jose Valverde RC	4.00
129	Doug DeVore RC	4.00
130	Jeremy Ward RC	4.00
131	Mike Koplove RC	4.00
132	Luis Terrero RC	4.00
133	John Patterson RC	4.00
134	Victor Alvarez RC	4.00
135	Kirk Saarloos RC	4.00
136	Kazuhisa Ishii RC	8.00
137	Steve Colyer RC	4.00
138	Cesar Izturis RC	4.00
139	Ron Calloway RC	4.00
140	Eric Good RC	4.00
141	Jorge Nunez RC	4.00
142	Ron Chiavacci RC	4.00
143	Donnie Bridges RC	4.00
144	Nelson Castro RC	4.00
145	Deivis Santos RC	4.00
146	Kurt Ainsworth RC	4.00
147	Arturo McDowell RC	4.00
148	Allan Simpson RC	4.00
149	Matt Thornton RC	4.00
150	Luis Ugueto RC	4.00
151	J.J. Putz RC	4.00
152	Hansel Izquierdo RC	4.00
153	Oliver Perez RC	4.00
154	Jaime Cerda RC	4.00
155	Mark Corey RC	4.00
156	Tyler Yates RC	6.00
157	Satoru Komiyama RC	4.00
158	Adam Walker RC	4.00
159	Steve Bechler RC	6.00
160	Erik Bedard RC	4.00
161	Todd Donovan RC	4.00
162	Clifford Bartosh RC	4.00
163	Ben Howard RC	4.00
164	Andy Shibilo RC	4.00
165	Dennis Tankersley	4.00
166	Mike Bynum	4.00
167	Anderson Machado RC	4.00
168	Peter Zamora RC	4.00
169	Eric Junge RC	4.00
170	Elio Serrano RC	4.00
171	Jorge Padilla RC	4.00
172	Marlon Byrd	4.00
173	Adrian Burnside RC	4.00
174	Mike Gonzalez RC	4.00
175	J.R. House	4.00
176	Hank Blalock	6.00
177	Travis Hughes RC	4.00
178	Mark Teixeira	8.00
179	Josh Hancock RC	4.00
180	Anastacio Martinez RC	4.00
181	Jorge de la Rosa RC	4.00
182	Ben Broussard	4.00
183	Austin Kearns	4.00
184	Corky Miller	4.00
185	Colin Young RC	4.00
186	Cam Esslinger RC	4.00
187	Rene Reyes RC	4.00
188	Aaron Cook RC	4.00
189	Alexis Gomez	4.00
190	Nate Field RC	4.00
191	Miguel Asencio RC	4.00
192	Brandon Berger	4.00
193	Fernando Rodney	4.00
194	Andy Van Hekken	4.00
195	Kevin Frederick RC	4.00
196	Todd Sears	4.00
197	Edwin Almonte RC	4.00
198	Kyle Kane RC	4.00
199	Mitch Wylie RC	4.00
200	Mike Porzio	4.00
201	Darin Erstad	4.00
202	Tim Salmon	6.00
203	Jeff Bagwell	10.00
204	Lance Berkman	8.00
205	Eric Chavez	6.00
206	Tim Hudson	6.00
207	Carlos Delgado	6.00
208	Chipper Jones	8.00
209	Gary Sheffield	6.00
210	Greg Maddux	15.00
211	Tom Glavine	6.00
212	Mike Mussina	10.00
213	J.D. Drew	6.00
214	Rick Ankiel	6.00
215	Sammy Sosa	15.00
216	Mike Lieberthal	6.00
217	Fred McGriff	8.00
218	David Wells	4.00
219	Curt Schilling	10.00
220	Luis Gonzalez	6.00
221	Mark Grace	10.00
222	Kevin Brown	4.00
223	Hideo Nomo	20.00
224	Jose Vidro	4.00
225	Jeff Kent	6.00
226	Rich Aurilia	4.00
227	Kenny Lofton	4.00
228	C.C. Sabathia	4.00
229	Edgar Martinez	8.00
230	Freddy Garcia	4.00
231	Cliff Floyd	4.00
232	Preston Wilson	4.00
233	Mike Piazza	10.00
234	Roberto Alomar	8.00
235	Trevor Hoffman	4.00
236	Ryan Klesko	5.00
237	Sean Burroughs	4.00
238	Scott Rolen	10.00
239	Pat Burrell	8.00
240	Edgardo Alfonzo	4.00
241	Brian Giles	8.00
242	Jason Kendall	5.00
243	Alex Rodriguez	15.00
244	Juan Gonzalez	8.00
245	Ivan Rodriguez	8.00
246	Rafael Palmeiro	8.00
247	Ken Griffey Jr.	12.00
248	Adam Dunn	8.00
249	Barry Larkin	5.00
250	Manny Ramirez	10.00
251	Pedro Martinez	10.00
252	Todd Helton	8.00
253	Larry Walker	6.00
254	Randy Johnson	10.00
255	Mike Sweeney	6.00
256	Carlos Beltran	6.00
257	Dmitri Young	4.00
258	Joe Mays	4.00
259	Doug Mientkiewicz	4.00
260	Corey Koskie	4.00
261	Magglio Ordonez	8.00
262	Frank Thomas	8.00
263	Ray Durham	4.00
264	Jason Giambi	10.00
265	Bernie Williams	8.00
266	Roger Clemens	15.00
267	Mariano Rivera	8.00
268	Robin Ventura	6.00
269	Andy Pettitte	6.00
270	Jorge Posada	8.00
271	Mike Piazza	8.00
272	Alex Rodriguez	15.00
273	Ken Griffey Jr.	15.00
274	Jason Giambi	10.00
275	Frank Thomas	8.00
276	Greg Maddux	15.00
277	Sammy Sosa	15.00
278	Roger Clemens	15.00
279	Jeff Bagwell	10.00
280	Todd Helton	8.00
281	Ichiro Suzuki	40.00
282	Randy Johnson	10.00
283	Jim Thome	15.00
284	Ivan Rodriguez	8.00
285	Darin Erstad	6.00
286	Eric Chavez	8.00
287	Barry Zito	10.00
288	Carlos Delgado	8.00
289	Omar Vizquel	6.00
290	Edgar Martinez	8.00
291	Manny Ramirez	8.00
292	Mike Sweeney	6.00
293	Tom Glavine	8.00
294	Joe Mays	5.00
295	Eric Milton	6.00
296	Magglio Ordonez	8.00
297	Bernie Williams	8.00
298	Trevor Hoffman	6.00
299	Andruw Jones	8.00
300	Aubrey Huff	5.00
301	Jim Edmonds	8.00
302	Kerry Wood	10.00
303	Luis Gonzalez	8.00
304	Shawn Green	6.00
305	Jose Vidro	5.00
306	Jeff Kent	5.00
307	Edgardo Alfonzo	5.00
308	Preston Wilson	4.00
309	Roberto Alomar	10.00
310	Jeromy Burnitz	5.00
311	Phil Nevin	5.00
312	Ryan Klesko	5.00
313	Bobby Abreu	6.00
314	Scott Rolen	12.00
315	Kazuhiro Sasaki	5.00
316	Jason Kendall	5.00
317	Sean Casey	5.00
318	Larry Walker	5.00
319	Mike Hampton	5.00
320	Juan Gonzalez	8.00
321	Darin Erstad	8.00
322	Tim Hudson	8.00
323	Carlos Delgado	8.00
324	Greg Vaughn	5.00
325	Jim Thome	15.00
326	Ichiro Suzuki	40.00
327	Rafael Palmeiro	8.00
328	Alex Rodriguez	15.00
329	Juan Gonzalez	8.00
330	Manny Ramirez	10.00
331	Carlos Beltran	6.00
332	Eric Milton	5.00
333	Frank Thomas	15.00
334	Roger Clemens	15.00
335	Jason Giambi	10.00
336	Lance Berkman	8.00
337	Greg Maddux	15.00
338	Chipper Jones	10.00
339	Sean Casey	5.00
340	Jim Edmonds	8.00
341	Kerry Wood	10.00
342	Sammy Sosa	15.00
343	Luis Gonzalez	8.00
344	Shawn Green	6.00
345	Jeff Kent	5.00
346	Preston Wilson	5.00
347	Roberto Alomar	8.00
348	Phil Nevin	5.00
349	Scott Rolen	12.00
350	Mike Sweeney	5.00
351	Ken Griffey Jr.	15.00
352	Todd Helton	8.00
353	Larry Walker	5.00
354	Alex Rodriguez	15.00
355	Pedro J. Martinez	10.00
356	Frank Thomas	10.00
357	Jason Giambi	10.00
358	Bernie Williams	10.00
359	Jeff Bagwell	8.00
360	Chipper Jones	10.00
361	Sammy Sosa	20.00
362	Randy Johnson	10.00
363	Shawn Green	6.00
364	Mike Piazza	15.00
365	Ichiro Suzuki	50.00
366	Ken Griffey Jr.	15.00
367	Larry Walker	5.00
368	Jim Edmonds	8.00
369	Darin Erstad	8.00
370	Tim Salmon	8.00
371	Mark Kotsay	6.00
372	Craig Biggio	8.00
373	Eric Chavez	10.00
374	David Justice	5.00
375	Carlos Delgado	8.00
376	Chipper Jones	15.00
377	Gary Sheffield	6.00
378	Greg Maddux	10.00
379	Eric Karros	5.00
380	Fred McGriff	8.00
381	J.D. Drew	5.00
382	Rick Ankiel	5.00
383	Sammy Sosa	15.00
384	Moises Alou	5.00
385	Ben Grieve	5.00
386	Greg Vaughn	5.00
387	Jay Payton	5.00
388	Luis Gonzalez	5.00
389	Ray Durham	5.00
390	Shawn Green	8.00
391	Hideo Nomo	20.00
392	Jose Vidro	5.00
393	Jeff Kent	5.00
394	Adrian Beltre	5.00
395	Jim Thome	15.00
396	Bobby Abreu	5.00
397	Edgar Martinez	10.00
398	Carl Everett	5.00
399	Luis Castillo	5.00
400	Preston Wilson	5.00
401	Jermaine Dye	8.00
402	Roberto Alomar	8.00
403	Todd Hundley	5.00
404	Ryan Klesko	5.00
405	Phil Nevin	5.00
406	Scott Rolen	10.00
407	Rafael Furcal	5.00
408	Miguel Tejada	8.00
409	Brian Giles	6.00
410	Jason Kendall	5.00
411	Alex Rodriguez	15.00
412	Juan Gonzalez	8.00
413	Ivan Rodriguez	8.00
414	Rafael Palmeiro	8.00
415	Ken Griffey Jr.	15.00
416	Edgardo Alfonzo	5.00
417	Barry Larkin	5.00
418	Manny Ramirez	8.00
419	Pedro J. Martinez	12.00
420	Todd Helton	8.00
421	Larry Walker	8.00
422	Garret Anderson	6.00
423	Mike Sweeney	5.00
424	Carlos Beltran	5.00
425	Javier Lopez	5.00
426	J.T. Snow	5.00
427	Doug Mientkiewicz	5.00
428	John Olerud	5.00
429	Magglio Ordonez	5.00
430	Frank Thomas	10.00
431	Kenny Lofton	5.00
432	Al Leiter	5.00
433	Bernie Williams	8.00
434	Roger Clemens	15.00
435	Tom Glavine	8.00
436	Robin Ventura	5.00
437	Chan Ho Park	5.00
438	Jorge Posada	5.00
439	Charles Johnson	5.00
440	Alex Rodriguez	20.00
441	Ken Griffey Jr.	15.00
442	Mark Kotsay	5.00
443	Frank Thomas	10.00
444	Greg Maddux	20.00
445	Sammy Sosa	15.00
446	Tom Glavine	10.00
447	Chipper Jones	15.00
448	Todd Helton	8.00
449	Jeff Cirillo	5.00
450	Steve Finley	5.00
451	Jim Thome	15.00
452	Ivan Rodriguez	8.00
453	Darin Erstad	8.00
454	Eric Chavez	8.00
455	Miguel Tejada	8.00
456	Carlos Delgado	8.00
457	Omar Vizquel	5.00
458	Edgar Martinez	10.00
459	Johnny Damon	5.00
460	Russell Branyan	5.00
461	Kenny Lofton	5.00
462	Jermaine Dye	5.00
463	Ellis Burks	5.00
464	Magglio Ordonez	5.00
465	Bernie Williams	10.00
466	Tim Salmon	5.00
467	Andruw Jones	8.00
468	Jeffrey Hammonds	5.00
469	Jim Edmonds	10.00
470	Kerry Wood	15.00
471	Luis Gonzalez	5.00
472	Shawn Green	8.00
473	Jose Vidro	5.00
474	Jeff Kent	5.00
475	Javier Lopez	5.00
476	Preston Wilson	5.00
477	Roberto Alomar	10.00
478	Robin Ventura	5.00
479	Phil Nevin	5.00
480	Ryan Klesko	5.00
481	Bobby Abreu	6.00
482	Scott Rolen	10.00
483	Brian Giles	5.00
484	Jason Kendall	5.00
485	Tsuyoshi Shinjo	5.00
486	Larry Walker	5.00
487	Mike Lieberthal	5.00
488	Juan Gonzalez	8.00
489	Darin Erstad	8.00
490	Tom Glavine	10.00
491	Carlos Delgado	6.00
492	Greg Vaughn	5.00
493	Jim Thome	15.00
494	Mark Grace	15.00
495	Rafael Palmeiro	8.00
496	Alex Rodriguez	20.00
497	Juan Gonzalez	8.00
498	Miguel Tejada	8.00
499	Carlos Beltran	5.00
500	Andruw Jones	8.00
501	Frank Thomas	10.00
502	Andres Galarraga	5.00
503	Gary Sheffield	8.00
504	Craig Biggio	8.00
505	Greg Maddux	20.00
506	Chipper Jones	20.00
507	Pat Burrell	10.00
508	Jim Edmonds	8.00
509	Kerry Wood	15.00
510	Sammy Sosa	20.00
511	Luis Gonzalez	8.00
512	Shawn Green	8.00
513	Edgardo Alfonzo	5.00
514	Preston Wilson	5.00
515	Roberto Alomar	10.00
516	Phil Nevin	5.00
517	Scott Rolen	15.00
518	Brian Giles	5.00

519	Jorge Posada	10.00
520	Todd Helton	12.00
521	Larry Walker	8.00
522	Alex Rodriguez	25.00
523	Pedro J. Martinez	20.00
524	Frank Thomas	12.00
525	Jason Giambi	15.00
526	Bernie Williams	10.00
527	J.D. Drew	10.00
528	Chipper Jones	20.00
529	Sammy Sosa	25.00
530	Randy Johnson	15.00
531	Shawn Green	10.00
532	Kevin Brown	10.00
533	Brian Giles	10.00
534	Ken Griffey Jr.	20.00
535	Larry Walker	10.00
536	Jim Edmonds	10.00
537	Sean Casey/Jsy/775	8.00
538	Ichiro Suzuki/Jsy/775	40.00
539	Pat Burrell/Jsy/200	6.00
540	Adam Dunn/Jsy/200	20.00
541	Lance Berkman/Jsy/200	10.00
542	Cliff Floyd/Jsy/775	8.00
543	Roger Clemens/Jsy/100	25.00
544	Kerry Wood/Bat/775	15.00
545	Andruw Jones/Bat/775	10.00
546	Manny Ramirez/Bat/200	10.00
547	Jorge Posada/Bat/200	10.00
548	Fred McGriff/Bat/200	8.00
549	Mike Sweeney/Bat/150	6.00
550	Todd Helton/Bat/100	12.00

Great Connections

NM/M
Production 50 Sets

GC-GR	Jason Giambi, Babe Ruth	350.00
GC-MD	Mickey Mantle, Joe DiMaggio	350.00
GC-MR	Mark McGwire, Babe Ruth	350.00
GC-MS	Mark McGwire, Sammy Sosa	200.00
GC-RR	Alex Rodriguez, Nolan Ryan	150.00
GC-IG	Ichiro Suzuki, Ken Griffey Jr.	150.00

Mem. Signatures Bat

NM/M
Varying quantities produced.

JD	Joe DiMaggio/20	600.00
JG	Jason Giambi/49	60.00
KG	Ken Griffey Jr./49	150.00
MMc	Mark McGwire/49	300.00
JM	Joe Morgan/99	35.00
KP	Kirby Puckett/145	75.00
CR	Cal Ripken Jr/145	150.00
AR	Alex Rodriguez/145	100.00
NR	Nolan Ryan/99	150.00
SS	Sammy Sosa/99	150.00
IS	Ichiro Suzuki/99	250.00

Mem. Signatures Jsy

NM/M
Varying quantities produced.
Gold: .75-1X
Production 150

EB	Ernie Banks/150	80.00
JD	Joe DiMaggio/20	550.00
KG	Ken Griffey Jr./49	150.00
SK	Sandy Koufax/150	300.00
MMc	Mark McGwire/49	300.00
JM	Joe Morgan/99	35.00
CR	Cal Ripken Jr/145	150.00
AR	Alex Rodriguez/145	100.00
NR	Nolan Ryan/99	150.00
SS	Sammy Sosa/99	200.00
IS	Ichiro Suzuki/99	250.00

2002 Upper Deck Employees Mark McGwire Jersey-Bat Card

To thank its employees for "dedication and commitment to excellence," UD created this special game-used jersey-bat card in an edition of 350 serially numbered pieces. The 3-1/2" x 2-1/2" horizontal cards have action and portrait photos of Big Mac on front. Near the center is a laser-cut Cardinals logo cut from a McGwire bat, superimposed on a swatch of jersey. The serial number is in gold foil below. Back has another portrait photo and a message from UD CEO Richard McWilliam.

NM/M

UDC-MM	Mark McGwire	125.00

2002 Upper Deck Honor Roll

NM/M
Complete Set (100): 25.00
Common Player: .15
Pack (5): 2.00
Box (24): 30.00

1	Randy Johnson	.50
2	Mike Piazza	.75
3	Albert Pujols	1.00
4	Roberto Alomar	.25
5	Chipper Jones	.50
6	Rich Aurilia	.15
7	Barry Bonds	1.00
8	Ken Griffey Jr.	.75
9	Sammy Sosa	.75
10	Roger Clemens	.75
11	Ivan Rodriguez	.40
12	Jason Giambi	.40
13	Bret Boone	.15
14	Troy Glaus	.25
15	Alex Rodriguez	.75
16	Manny Ramirez	.40
17	Bernie Williams	.25
18	Ichiro Suzuki	.75
19	Matt Thornton	.25
20	Chris Baker RC	.25
21	Tyler Yates RC	.50
22	Jorge Nunez RC	.50
23	Rene Reyes RC	.50
24	Ben Howard RC	.50
25	Ron Calloway RC	.40
26	Danny Wright	.15
27	Reed Johnson RC	.50
28-31	Randy Johnson	.50
32-35	Mike Piazza	.50
36-39	Albert Pujols	.75
40-43	Roberto Alomar	.50
44-47	Chipper Jones	.50
48-51	Rich Aurilia	.15
52-55	Barry Bonds	1.00
56-59	Ken Griffey Jr.	.75
60-63	Sammy Sosa	.50
64-67	Roger Clemens	.75
68-71	Ivan Rodriguez	.25
72-75	Jason Giambi	.25
76-79	Bret Boone	.15
80-83	Troy Glaus	.20
84-87	Alex Rodriguez	.50
88-91	Manny Ramirez	.25
92-95	Bernie Williams	.25
96-99	Ichiro Suzuki	1.00
100	Checklist (Original nine players.) (Nine team names.))	.25

Silver

Stars: 4-8X
Production 100 Sets

Batting Glove

NM/M
Numbered to 250

NR	Nolan Ryan/99	150.00
SS	Sammy Sosa/99	200.00
IS	Ichiro Suzuki/99	250.00
BB	Bret Boone/89	20.00
JG	Jason Giambi	20.00
KG	Ken Griffey Jr.	40.00
AR	Alex Rodriguez	25.00
IR1	Ivan Rodriguez	20.00
IR2	Ivan Rodriguez	20.00
SS	Sammy Sosa	30.00
I	Ichiro Suzuki/46	150.00

Game Jersey

NM/M
Common Player: 10.00
Inserted 1:90
Golds: 2-3X
Production 99 Sets
Each player has multiple versions.

BB	Bret Boone/SP/45	10.00
RC	Roger Clemens	20.00
JG	Jason Giambi/SP	15.00
KG	Ken Griffey Jr.	25.00
CJ	Chipper Jones	15.00
AR	Alex Rodriguez	15.00
IR	Ivan Rodriguez	10.00
SS	Sammy Sosa/SP	25.00
I	Ichiro Suzuki/SP	40.00

Star Swatches Game Jersey

NM/M
Common Player: 10.00
Inserted 1:90
Golds: 2-5X
Production 24

BB	Bret Boone/45	10.00
RC	Roger Clemens/29	40.00
JG	Jason Giambi	10.00
KG	Ken Griffey Jr./SP	25.00
CJ	Chipper Jones	15.00
AR	Alex Rodriguez	15.00
IR	Ivan Rodriguez	10.00
SS	Sammy Sosa	20.00
I	Ichiro Suzuki/SP	40.00

Time Capsule Game Jersey

NM/M
Common Player: 8.00
Inserted 1:90
Golds: 2-3X
Production 99 Sets

BB	Bret Boone	8.00
RC	Roger Clemens	20.00
JG	Jason Giambi/52	15.00
CJ	Chipper Jones	10.00
AR	Alex Rodriguez	15.00
IR	Ivan Rodriguez/SP	15.00
SS	Sammy Sosa	20.00
I	Ichiro Suzuki	40.00

Stitch of Nine Game Jersey

NM/M
Common Player: 10.00
Inserted 1:90
Golds: 2-5X
Production 24 Sets

BB	Bret Boone/45	10.00
RC	Roger Clemens	20.00
JG	Jason Giambi/SP	15.00
KG	Ken Griffey Jr.	15.00
CJ	Chipper Jones	10.00
AR	Alex Rodriguez	15.00
IR	Ivan Rodriguez	10.00
SS	Sammy Sosa	20.00
I	Ichiro Suzuki/85	40.00

Game-Used Bat

NM/M
Common Player: 10.00
Numbered to 99.
Each player has multiple versions.

BB	Bret Boone	10.00
RC	Roger Clemens	30.00
JG	Jason Giambi	15.00
KG	Ken Griffey Jr.	40.00
CJ	Chipper Jones	20.00
AR	Alex Rodriguez	20.00
IR	Ivan Rodriguez	15.00
SS	Sammy Sosa	30.00
I	Ichiro Suzuki	40.00

2002 Upper Deck MVP

NM/M
Complete Set (300): 20.00
Common Player: .10
Pack (8): 1.50
Box (24): 25.00

1	Darin Erstad	.20
2	Ramon Ortiz	.10
3	Garret Anderson	.20
4	Jarrod Washburn	.10
5	Troy Glaus	.20
6	Brendan Donnelly RC	.10
7	Troy Percival	.10
8	Tim Salmon	.15
9	Aaron Sele	.10
10	Brad Fullmer	.10
11	Scott Hatteberg	.10
12	Barry Zito	.20
13	Tim Hudson	.20
14	Miguel Tejada	.25
15	Jermaine Dye	.10
16	Mark Mulder	.20
17	Eric Chavez	.15
18	Terrence Long	.10
19	Carlos Pena	.20
20	David Justice	.20
21	Jeremy Giambi	.10
22	Shannon Stewart	.10
23	Raul Mondesi	.10
24	Chris Carpenter	.10
25	Carlos Delgado	.20
26	Mike Sirotka	.10
27	Reed Johnson RC	.40
28	Darrin Fletcher	.10
29	Jose Cruz Jr.	.10
30	Vernon Wells	.20
31	Tanyon Sturtze	.10
32	Toby Hall	.10
33	Brent Abernathy	.10
34	Ben Grieve	.10
35	Joe Kennedy	.10
36	Dewon Brazelton	.10
37	Aubrey Huff	.10
38	Steve Cox	.10
39	Greg Vaughn	.10
40	Brady Anderson	.10
41	Chuck Finley	.10
42	Jim Thome	.40
43	Russell Branyan	.10
44	C.C. Sabathia	.10
45	Matt Lawton	.10
46	Omar Vizquel	.10
47	Bartolo Colon	.15
48	Alex Escobar	.10
49	Ellis Burks	.10
50	Bret Boone	.20
51	John Olerud	.20
52	Jeff Cirillo	.10
53	Ichiro Suzuki	1.00
54	Kazuhiro Sasaki	.20
55	Freddy Garcia	.10
56	Edgar Martinez	.15
57	Matt Thornton	.10
58	Mike Cameron	.10
59	Carlos Guillen	.10
60	Jeff Conine	.10
61	Tony Batista	.10
62	Jason Johnson	.10
63	Melvin Mora	.10
64	Brian Roberts	.10
65	Josh Towers	.10
66	Steve Bechler RC	.10
67	Jerry Hairston Jr.	.10
68	Chris Richard	.10
69	Alex Rodriguez	1.00
70	Chan Ho Park	.10
71	Ivan Rodriguez	.25
72	Jeff Zimmerman	.10
73	Mark Teixeira	.20
74	Gabe Kapler	.10
75	Frank Catalanotto	.10
76	Rafael Palmeiro	.25
77	Doug Davis	.10
78	Carl Everett	.10
79	Pedro J. Martinez	.40
80	Nomar Garciaparra	.75
81	Tony Clark	.10
82	Trot Nixon	.10
83	Manny Ramirez	.25
84	Josh Hancock RC	.10
85	Johnny Damon	.10
86	Jose Offerman	.10
87	Rich Garces	.10
88	Shea Hillenbrand	.10
89	Carlos Beltran	.20
90	Mike Sweeney	.10
91	Jeff Suppan	.10
92	Joe Randa	.10
93	Chuck Knoblauch	.10
94	Mark Quinn	.10
95	Neifi Perez	.10
96	Carlos Febles	.10
97	Miguel Asencio RC	.10
98	Michael Tucker	.10
99	Dean Palmer	.10
100	Jose Lima	.10
101	Craig Paquette	.10
102	Dmitri Young	.10
103	Bobby Higginson	.10
104	Jeff Weaver	.10
105	Matt Anderson	.10
106	Damion Easley	.10
107	Eric Milton	.10
108	Doug Mientkiewicz	.10
109	Cristian Guzman	.10
110	Brad Radke	.10
111	Torii Hunter	.20
112	Corey Koskie	.10
113	Joe Mays	.10
114	Jacque Jones	.10
115	David Ortiz	.20
116	Kevin Frederick RC	.10
117	Magglio Ordonez	.20
118	Ray Durham	.10
119	Mark Buehrle	.10
120	Jon Garland	.10
121	Paul Konerko	.10
122	Todd Ritchie	.10
123	Frank Thomas	.40
124	Edwin Almonte RC	.10
125	Carlos Lee	.10
126	Kenny Lofton	.15
127	Roger Clemens	.75
128	Derek Jeter	1.00
129	Jorge Posada	.20
130	Bernie Williams	.25
131	Mike Mussina	.25
132	Alfonso Soriano	.50
133	Robin Ventura	.15
134	John Vander Wal	.10
135	Jason Giambi	.25
136	Mariano Rivera	.20
137	Rondell White	.10
138	Jeff Bagwell	.25
139	Wade Miller	.10
140	Richard Hidalgo	.10
141	Julio Lugo	.10
142	Roy Oswalt	.20
143	Rodrigo Rosario RC	.10
144	Lance Berkman	.20
145	Craig Biggio	.20
146	Shane Reynolds	.10
147	John Smoltz	.20
148	Chipper Jones	.40
149	Gary Sheffield	.20
150	Rafael Furcal	.10
151	Greg Maddux	.50
152	Tom Glavine	.20
153	Andruw Jones	.20
154	John Ennis RC	.10
155	Vinny Castilla	.10
156	Marcus Giles	.10
157	Javy Lopez	.20
158	Richie Sexson	.10
159	Geoff Jenkins	.20
160	Jeffrey Hammonds	.10
161	Alex Ochoa	.10
162	Ben Sheets	.20
163	Jose Hernandez	.10
164	Eric Young	.10
165	Luis Montanez	.10
166	Albert Pujols	.75
167	Darryl Kile	.10
168	So Taguchi RC	.50
169	Jim Edmonds	.20
170	Fernando Vina	.10
171	Matt Morris	.10
172	J.D. Drew	.20
173	Bud Smith	.10
174	Edgar Renteria	.10
175	Placido Polanco	.10
176	Tino Martinez	.20
177	Sammy Sosa	.75
178	Moises Alou	.10
179	Kerry Wood	.40
180	Delino DeShields	.10
181	Alex Gonzalez	.10
182	Jon Lieber	.10
183	Fred McGriff	.15
184	Corey Patterson	.15
185	Mark Prior	.50
186	Tom Gordon	.10
187	Francis Beltran RC	.10
188	Randy Johnson	.40
189	Luis Gonzalez	.20
190	Matt Williams	.10
191	Mark Grace	.25
192	Curt Schilling	.25
193	Doug DeVore RC	.10
194	Erubiel Durazo	.10
195	Steve Finley	.15
196	Craig Counsell	.10
197	Shawn Green	.20
198	Kevin Brown	.10
199	Paul LoDuca	.10
200	Brian Jordan	.15
201	Andy Ashby	.10
202	Darren Dreifort	.10
203	Adrian Beltre	.10
204	Victor Alvarez RC	.10
205	Eric Karros	.10
206	Hideo Nomo	.20
207	Vladimir Guerrero	.40
208	Javier Vazquez	.10
209	Michael Barrett	.10
210	Jose Vidro	.10
211	Brad Wilkerson	.10
212	Tony Armas Jr.	.10
213	Eric Good RC	.10
214	Orlando Cabrera	.10
215	Lee Stevens	.10
216	Jeff Kent	.20
217	Rich Aurilia	.10
218	Robb Nen	.10
219	Calvin Murray	.10
220	Russ Ortiz	.10
221	Deivis Santos	.10
222	Marvin Benard	.10
223	Jason Schmidt	.10
224	Reggie Sanders	.10
225	Barry Bonds	1.00
226	Brad Penny	.10
227	Cliff Floyd	.10
228	Mike Lowell	.20
229	Derrek Lee	.10
230	Ryan Dempster	.10
231	Josh Beckett	.20
232	Hansel Izquierdo RC	.10
233	Preston Wilson	.10
234	A.J. Burnett	.10
235	Charles Johnson	.10
236	Mike Piazza	.50
237	Al Leiter	.10
238	Jay Payton	.10
239	Roger Cedeno	.10
240	Jeromy Burnitz	.10
241	Roberto Alomar	.20
242	Mo Vaughn	.20
243	Shawn Estes	.10
244	Armando Benitez	.10
245	Tyler Yates RC	.10
246	Phil Nevin	.10
247	D'Angelo Jimenez	.10
248	Ramon Vazquez	.10
249	Bubba Trammell	.10
250	Trevor Hoffman	.10
251	Ben Howard RC	.10
252	Mark Kotsay	.10
253	Ray Lankford	.10
254	Ryan Klesko	.20
255	Scott Rolen	.40
256	Robert Person	.10
257	Jimmy Rollins	.20
258	Pat Burrell	.20
259	Anderson Machado RC	.10
260	Randy Wolf	.10
261	Travis Lee	.10
262	Mike Lieberthal	.10
263	Doug Glanville	.10
264	Bobby Abreu	.20
265	Brian Giles	.20
266	Kris Benson	.10
267	Aramis Ramirez	.10
268	Kevin Young	.10
269	Jack Wilson	.10
270	Mike Williams	.10
271	Jimmy Anderson	.10
272	Jason Kendall	.20
273	Pokey Reese	.10
274	Robert Mackowiak	.10
275	Sean Casey	.20
276	Juan Encarnacion	.10
277	Austin Kearns	.10
278	Danny Graves	.10
279	Ken Griffey Jr.	.50
280	Barry Larkin	.20

281	Todd Walker	.10
282	Elmer Dessens	.10
283	Aaron Boone	.10
284	Adam Dunn	.40
285	Larry Walker	.15
286	Rene Reyes RC	.20
287	Juan Uribe	.10
288	Mike Hampton	.10
289	Todd Helton	.40
290	Juan Pierre	.10
291	Denny Neagle	.10
292	Jose Ortiz	.10
293	Todd Zeile	.10
294	Ben Petrick	.10
295	Checklist 1-50 (Ken Griffey Jr.)	.25
296	Checklist 51-100 (Derek Jeter)	.50
297	Checklist 101-150 (Sammy Sosa)	.30
298	Checklist 151-200 (Ichiro Suzuki)	.50
299	Checklist 201-250 (Barry Bonds)	.50
300	Checklist 251-300 (Alex Rodriguez)	.40

Silver
Stars: 5-10X
Production 100 Sets

Gold
No Pricing
Production 25 Sets

Ichiro - A Season to Remember

Complete Set (10): 15.00
Ichiro's (1-10): 2.00
Inserted 1:10
I1-10 Ichiro Suzuki 2.50

Ichiro - A Season to Remember Bat
No Pricing
Production 25

- A Season to Remember Jersey
Complete Set (1):

Souvenirs Bats
NM/M
Common Player: 8.00
Inserted 1:144

RA	Roberto Alomar	20.00
CD	Carlos Delgado	8.00
BG	Brian Giles	8.00
LG	Luis Gonzalez	8.00
SG	Shawn Green	8.00
KG	Ken Griffey Jr.	25.00
TH	Todd Helton	15.00
DJ	David Justice	8.00
JK	Jeff Kent	8.00
RK	Ryan Klesko	8.00
GM	Greg Maddux	20.00
EM	Edgar Martinez	10.00
DM	Doug Mientkiewicz	8.00
MO	Magglio Ordonez	8.00
RP	Rafael Palmeiro/97	18.00
MP	Mike Piazza/97	25.00
AR	Alex Rodriguez	15.00
IR	Ivan Rodriguez	10.00
SR	Scott Rolen	10.00
GS	Gary Sheffield	8.00
SS	Sammy Sosa	20.00
MS	Mike Sweeney	8.00
FT	Frank Thomas/97	25.00
JT	Jim Thome	10.00
GV	Greg Vaughn	8.00
LW	Larry Walker	8.00
BW	Bernie Williams	8.00

Souvenirs Jerseys
NM/M
Common Player: 5.00
Inserted 1:48

RA	Roberto Alomar	10.00
GA	Garret Anderson	10.00
JB	Jeff Bagwell	10.00
AB	Adrian Beltre	8.00
JB	Jeromy Burnitz	5.00
RC	Roger Clemens	15.00
CD	Carlos Delgado	8.00
DE	Darin Erstad	8.00
RF	Rafael Furcal	8.00
JG	Juan Gonzalez	10.00
THo	Trevor Hoffman	5.00
THu	Tim Hudson	8.00
JK	Jeff Kent	8.00
PK	Paul Konerko/SP	10.00
MK	Mark Kotsay	5.00
KL	Kenny Lofton	8.00
EM	Edgar Martinez	10.00
JP	Jay Payton/SP	10.00
MP	Mike Piazza	15.00
AR	Alex Rodriguez	15.00
IR	Ivan Rodriguez	10.00
SR	Scott Rolen	10.00
TS	Tim Salmon	10.00
FT	Frank Thomas	15.00
JT	Jim Thome/SP	15.00
RV	Robin Ventura	8.00
OV	Omar Vizquel	8.00
PW	Preston Wilson	5.00
TZ	Todd Zeile	5.00

Souvenirs Bat/Jersey Combos
NM/M
Common Card: 10.00
Inserted 1:144
Gold: No Pricing
Production 25 Sets

EA	Edgardo Alfonzo	10.00
RA	Roberto Alomar	15.00
JB	Jeff Bagwell	20.00
AB	Adrian Beltre	15.00
CD	Carlos Delgado	15.00
DE	Darin Erstad	20.00
JG	Jason Giambi	20.00
BG	Brian Giles	15.00
LG	Luis Gonzalez	15.00
SG	Shawn Green	15.00
KG	Ken Griffey Jr.	40.00
TH	Todd Helton	20.00
RJ	Randy Johnson	25.00
CJ	Chipper Jones	20.00
JK	Jeff Kent	15.00
MO	Magglio Ordonez	15.00
RP	Rafael Palmeiro	20.00
MP	Mike Piazza	15.00
AR	Alex Rodriguez	25.00
IR	Ivan Rodriguez	15.00
SR	Scott Rolen	15.00
SS	Sammy Sosa	15.00
JT	Jim Thome	25.00
RV	Robin Ventura	10.00
OV	Omar Vizquel/97	20.00
BW	Bernie Williams/97	25.00
TZ	Todd Zeile	10.00

2002 Upper Deck National Convention

A multi-sport set of 15 cards was specially produced as a giveaway for attendees at the 2002 National Sports Collectors Convention in Chicago. VIP admissions received the complete set, regular show-goers received a three-card cello pack. The baseball cards follow the format of UD's regular 2002 issue and feature a distinguishing line of type on front and special numbering on back. Only the baseball players from the set are listed here.

NM/M
Complete Baseball Set (5): 10.00
Common Player: 2.00

N1	Mark McGwire	3.00
N2	Sammy Sosa	3.00
N3	Jason Giambi	2.00
N4	Ichiro	3.00
N5	Ken Griffey Jr.	3.00

2002 Upper Deck Ovation
NM/M
Complete Set (120): 120.00
Common Player: .25
Common (61-89, 120): 3.00
Production 2,002
Pack (5): 1.50
Box (24): 30.00

1	Troy Glaus	.40
2	David Justice	.40
3	Tim Hudson	.40
4	Jermaine Dye	.25
5	Carlos Delgado	.40
6	Greg Vaughn	.25
7	Jim Thome	.75
8	C.C. Sabathia	.25
9	Ichiro Suzuki	1.50
10	Edgar Martinez	.40
11	Chris Richard	.25
12	Rafael Palmeiro	.40
13	Alex Rodriguez	2.00
14	Ivan Rodriguez	.40
15	Nomar Garciaparra	1.50
16	Manny Ramirez	.75
17	Pedro J. Martinez	.75
18	Mike Sweeney	.25
19	Dmitri Young	.25
20	Doug Mientkiewicz	.25
21	Brad Radke	.25
22	Cristian Guzman	.25
23	Frank Thomas	.50
24	Magglio Ordonez	.40
25	Bernie Williams	.50
26	Derek Jeter	2.00
27	Jason Giambi	.50
28	Roger Clemens	.75
29	Jeff Bagwell	.50
30	Lance Berkman	.40
31	Chipper Jones	.40
32	Gary Sheffield	.40
33	Greg Maddux	1.00
34	Richie Sexson	.40
35	Albert Pujols	1.50
36	Tino Martinez	.25
37	J.D. Drew	.40
38	Sammy Sosa	1.50
39	Moises Alou	.40
40	Randy Johnson	.75
41	Luis Gonzalez	.40
42	Shawn Green	.25
43	Kevin Brown	.25
44	Vladimir Guerrero	.75
45	Barry Bonds	2.00
46	Jeff Kent	.40
47	Cliff Floyd	.25
48	Josh Beckett	.50
49	Mike Piazza	1.00
50	Mo Vaughn	.25
51	Jeromy Burnitz	.25
52	Roberto Alomar	.40
53	Phil Nevin	.25
54	Scott Rolen	.75
55	Jimmy Rollins	.50
56	Brian Giles	.25
57	Ken Griffey Jr.	1.00
58	Sean Casey	.40
59	Larry Walker	.40
60	Todd Helton	.50
61	Rodrigo Rosario RC	3.00
62	Reed Johnson RC	8.00
63	John Ennis RC	3.00
64	Luis Martinez RC	3.00
65	So Taguchi RC	3.00
66	Brandon Backe RC	3.00
67	Doug DeVore RC	3.00
68	Victor Alvarez RC	3.00
69	Kazuhisa Ishii RC	3.00
70	Eric Good RC	3.00
71	Deivis Santos RC	3.00
72	Matt Thornton RC	3.00
73	Hansel Izquierdo RC	3.00
74	Tyler Yates RC	3.00
75	Jaime Cerda RC	3.00
76	Satoru Komiyama RC	3.00
77	Steve Bechler RC	3.00
78	Ben Howard RC	3.00
79	Jorge Padilla RC	3.00
80	Eric Junge RC	3.00
81	Anderson Machado RC	3.00
82	Adrian Burnside RC	3.00
83	Josh Hancock RC	3.00
84	Anastacio Martinez RC	3.00
85	Rene Reyes RC	3.00
86	Nate Field RC	3.00
87	Tim Kalita RC	3.00
88	Kevin Frederick RC	3.00
89	Edwin Almonte RC	3.00
90-94	Ichiro Suzuki	.75
95-99	Ken Griffey Jr.	.75
100-104	Jason Giambi	.75
105-109	Sammy Sosa	.75
110-114	Alex Rodriguez	.75
115-119	Mark McGwire	.75
120	Alex Rodriguez, Ken Griffey Jr., Mark McGwire, Sammy Sosa, Jason Giambi, Ichiro Suzuki	15.00

Silver
(1-60): 1-30X
(61-89, 120): .5-1X
(90-119): 2-4X

Gold
(1-60) Print Run 25-50: 8-15X
(1-60) P/R 51-75: 4-8X
(1-60) P/R 76-90: 3-5X
(61-120) 25 of each produced
Print runs based on stats.

Authentic McGwire
NM/M
Varying quantities produced.

AM-B	Mark McGwire/Bat/70	100.00
AM-BG	Mark McGwire/Bat/50	100.00
AM-J	Mark McGwire/Jsy/70	100.00
AM-JG	Mark McGwire/Jsy/50	100.00

Diamond Futures Jersey
NM/M
Common Player: 5.00
Inserted 1:72
Golds production 25 No Pricing.

LB	Lance Berkman	8.00
RB	Russell Branyan	5.00
PB	Pat Burrell	8.00
FG	Freddy Garcia	5.00
TH	Tim Hudson	6.00
JK	Jason Kendall	8.00
JP	Jorge Posada	10.00
IR	Ivan Rodriguez	10.00
JR	Jimmy Rollins	5.00
KS	Kazuhiro Sasaki	5.00
JV	Jose Vidro	5.00
BZ	Barry Zito	8.00

Lead Performer Jersey
NM/M
Common Player: 5.00
Inserted 1:72
Golds: No Pricng
Production 25 Sets

JB	Jeff Bagwell	8.00
CD	Carlos Delgado	6.00
JGi	Jason Giambi	6.00
JG	Juan Gonzalez	5.00
LG	Luis Gonzalez	5.00
KG	Ken Griffey Jr./SP	20.00
MP	Mike Piazza	15.00
AR	Alex Rodriguez	15.00
IR	Ivan Rodriguez	6.00
SS	Sammy Sosa/SP	12.00
IS	Ichiro Suzuki	30.00
FT	Frank Thomas	8.00

Spokesman Spotlight

No Pricng
Production 25 Sets

Swatches Jersey

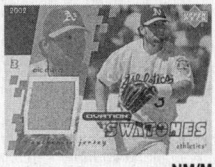

NM/M
Common Player: 5.00
Inserted 1:72
Golds: 25 sets produced, No Pricing.

RA	Roberto Alomar/SP	20.00
EB	Ellis Burks	5.00
JB	Jeromy Burnitz	5.00
EC	Eric Chavez	6.00
CD	Carlos Delgado	5.00
DE	Darin Erstad	5.00
MG	Mark Grace	10.00
CJ	Chipper Jones	12.00
GM	Greg Maddux	10.00
PM	Pedro J. Martinez	10.00
AR	Alex Rodriguez	15.00
BW	Bernie Williams	10.00

2002 Upper Deck Piece of History

NM/M
Complete Set (132): 200.00
Common Player: .15
Common SP (91-132): 5.00
Production 625
Pack (5): 2.00
Box (24): 40.00

1	Troy Glaus	.40
2	Darin Erstad	.25
3	Reggie Jackson	.40
4	Miguel Tejada	.25
5	Tim Hudson	.25
6	Jim "Catfish" Hunter	.25
7	Joe Carter	.15
8	Carlos Delgado	.25
9	Greg Vaughn	.15
10	Early Wynn	.15
11	Omar Vizquel	.15
12	Jim Thome	.25
13	Ichiro Suzuki	1.50
14	Edgar Martinez	.25
15	Freddy Garcia	.15
16	Cal Ripken Jr/SP	15.00
17	Jeff Conine	.15
18	Juan Gonzalez	.50
19	Nolan Ryan/SP	15.00
20	Alex Rodriguez/SP	10.00
21	Rafael Palmeiro	.50
22	Ivan Rodriguez	.50
23	Carlton Fisk	.25
24	Wade Boggs	.30
25	Pedro J. Martinez	.75
26	Nomar Garciaparra	1.50
27	Manny Ramirez	.50
28	Mike Sweeney	.15
29	Bobby Higginson	.15
30	Kirby Puckett	.75
31	Doug Mientkiewicz	.15
32	Corey Koskie	.15
33	Joe Mays	.15
34	Frank Thomas	.50
35	Magglio Ordonez	.25
36	Jason Giambi/SP	5.00
37	Derek Jeter/SP	15.00
38	Mickey Mantle/SP	15.00
39	Joe DiMaggio	2.00
40	Roger Maris	1.00
41	Roger Clemens	1.50
42	Bernie Williams	.50
43	Jeff Bagwell	.50
44	Lance Berkman	.25
45	Eddie Mathews	.50
46	Andruw Jones	.40
47	Phil Niekro	.25
48	Gary Sheffield	.25
49	Chipper Jones	.75
50	Greg Maddux	1.00
51	Robin Yount	.50
52	Richie Sexson	.25
53	Jim Edmonds	.25
54	J.D. Drew	.25
55	Albert Pujols	1.50
56	Andre Dawson	.25
57	Billy Williams	.15
58	Ernie Banks	.50
59	Sammy Sosa/SP	10.00
60	Randy Johnson	.75
61	Curt Schilling	.50
62	Luis Gonzalez	.25
63	Kirk Gibson	.15
64	Steve Garvey	.15
65	Sandy Koufax/SP	15.00
66	Shawn Green	.25
67	Hideo Nomo	.25
68	Kevin Brown	.15
69	Vladimir Guerrero	.25
70	Tim Raines	.15
71	Gaylord Perry	.15
72	Mel Ott	.25
73	Willie McCovey	.15
74	Barry Bonds/SP	10.00
75	Jeff Kent	.15
76	Cliff Floyd	.15
77	Dwight Gooden	.15
78	Tom Seaver	.50
79	Mike Piazza	1.00
80	Roberto Alomar	.25
81	Dave Winfield	.25
82	Tony Gwynn	.75
83	Scott Rolen	.75
84	Bill Mazeroski	.15
85	Willie Stargell	.25
86	Brian Giles	.15
87	Ken Griffey Jr./SP	10.00
88	Sean Casey	.25
89	Todd Helton	.50
90	Larry Walker	.25
91	Brendan Donnelly RC	5.00
92	Tom Shearn RC	5.00
93	Brandon Puffer RC	5.00
94	Corey Thurman RC	5.00
95	Reed Johnson RC	8.00
96	Gustavo Chacin RC	5.00
97	Chris Baker RC	5.00
98	John Ennis RC	5.00
99	So Taguchi RC	5.00
100	Michael Crudale RC	5.00
101	Francis Beltran RC	5.00
102	Jose Valverde RC	8.00
103	Doug DeVore RC	5.00
104	Jeremy Ward RC	5.00
105	P.J. Bevis RC	5.00
106	Steve Kent RC	5.00
107	Brandon Backe RC	5.00
108	Jorge Nunez RC	5.00
109	Kazuhisa Ishii RC	5.00
110	Ron Calloway RC	5.00
111	Valentino Pasucci RC	5.00
112	J.J. Putz RC	5.00
113	Matt Thornton RC	5.00
114	Allan Simpson RC	5.00
115	Jaime Cerda RC	5.00
116	Mark Corey RC	5.00
117	Tyler Yates RC	5.00
118	Steve Bechler RC	5.00
119	Ben Howard RC	5.00
120	Clifford Bartosh RC	5.00
121	Todd Donovan RC	5.00
122	Eric Junge RC	5.00
123	Adrian Burnside RC	5.00
124	Andy Pratt RC	5.00
125	Josh Hancock RC	5.00
126	Rene Reyes RC	5.00
127	Cam Esslinger RC	5.00
128	Colin Young RC	5.00
129	Kevin Frederick RC	5.00
130	Kyle Kane RC	5.00
131	Mitch Wylie RC	5.00
132	Danny Wright RC	5.00

Batting Champs

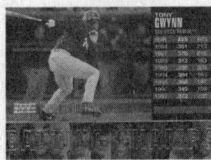

NM/M
Complete Set (10): 18.00
Common Player: 1.50
Inserted 1:30

B1	Tony Gwynn	2.00
B2	Frank Thomas	2.00
B3	Billy Williams	1.50
B4	Edgar Martinez	1.50
B5	Bernie Williams	1.50
B6	Mickey Mantle	6.00
B7	Larry Walker	1.50
B8	Gary Sheffield	1.50
B9	Wade Boggs	1.50
B10	Alex Rodriguez	4.00

Batting Champ Jerseys
NM/M
Common Player: 5.00
Inserted 1:96

WB	Wade Boggs	10.00
AG	Andres Galarraga	5.00
TG	Tony Gwynn	15.00
MM	Mickey Mantle/50	200.00
EM	Edgar Martinez	10.00
JO	John Olerud	8.00
PO	Paul O'Neil	5.00
TR	Tim Raines	8.00
AR	Alex Rodriguez	15.00
GS	Gary Sheffield/SP	8.00
FT	Frank Thomas	10.00
LW	Larry Walker/SP	8.00
BeW	Bernie Williams	10.00

Champ Jerseys Auto.
Complete Set (5):

ERA Leaders

NM/M
Complete Set (10): 18.00
Common Player: 1.00
Inserted 1:30

E1	Greg Maddux	3.00
E2	Pedro J. Martinez	2.00
E3	Freddy Garcia	1.00
E4	Randy Johnson	2.00
E5	Tom Seaver	1.00
E6	Early Wynn	1.00
E7	Dwight Gooden	1.00
E8	Kevin Brown	1.00
E9	Roger Clemens	3.00
E10	Nolan Ryan	6.00

ERA Leaders Jerseys
NM/M
Common Player: 8.00
Inserted 1:96

KB	Kevin Brown	8.00
RC	Roger Clemens	15.00
FG	Freddy Garcia	8.00
DG	Dwight Gooden	8.00
CH	"Catfish" Hunter/SP	15.00
RJ	Randy Johnson	15.00
SK	Sandy Koufax/SP	100.00
GM	Greg Maddux	15.00
PM	Pedro Martinez	15.00
PN	Phil Niekro	8.00
NR	Nolan Ryan/SP	50.00
TS	Tom Seaver	15.00

ERA Leaders Jerseys Autographs
NM/M
Production 24 Sets

RC	Roger Clemens	200.00
SK	Sandy Koufax	750.00

Hitting for the Cycle

		NM/M
Complete Set (20):		35.00
Common Player:		1.00
Inserted 1:15		
H1	Alex Rodriguez	4.00
H2	Andre Dawson	1.00
H3	Cal Ripken Jr.	6.00
H4	Carlton Fisk	1.50
H5	Dante Bichette	1.00
H6	Dave Winfield	1.50
H7	Eric Chavez	1.00
H8	Robin Yount	2.00
H9	Jason Kendall	1.00
H10	Jay Buhner	1.00
H11	Jeff Kent	1.00
H12	Joe DiMaggio	6.00
H13	John Olerud	1.00
H14	Kirby Puckett	3.00
H15	Luis Gonzalez	1.50
H16	Mark Grace	1.50
H17	Mickey Mantle	6.00
H18	Miguel Tejada	1.00
H19	Rondell White	1.00
H20	Todd Helton	2.00

Hitting for the Cycle Bats

		NM/M
Inserted 1:576		
DB	Dante Bichette	10.00
JB	Jay Buhner	10.00
EC	Eric Chavez	10.00
AD	Andre Dawson	10.00
CF	Carlton Fisk	25.00
LG	Luis Gonzalez	10.00
MM	Mickey Mantle/50	200.00
CR	Cal Ripken Jr./SP	75.00
AR	Alex Rodriguez	25.00
DW	Dave Winfield	15.00

Hitting for the Cycle Bats Auto.

No Pricing
Production 10 Sets

Tape Measure Heroes

		NM/M
Complete Set (30):		50.00
Common Player:		1.00
Inserted 1:10		
TM1	Joe Carter	1.00
TM2	Cal Ripken Jr.	6.00
TM3	Mike Piazza	4.00
TM4	Shawn Green	1.25
TM5	Mark McGwire	5.00
TM6	Reggie Jackson	1.50
TM7	Mickey Mantle	6.00
TM8	Manny Ramirez	2.00
TM9	Mo Vaughn	1.00
TM10	Jeff Bagwell	2.00
TM11	Sammy Sosa	3.00
TM12	Tony Gwynn	2.00
TM13	Bill Mazeroski	1.00
TM14	Jose Canseco	1.50
TM15	Brian Giles	1.00
TM16	Kirk Gibson	1.00
TM17	Kirby Puckett	3.00
TM18	Wade Boggs	1.50
TM19	Albert Pujols	3.00
TM20	David Justice	1.00
TM21	Steve Garvey	1.50
TM22	Luis Gonzalez	1.50
TM23	Derek Jeter	6.00
TM24	Robin Yount	2.00
TM25	Barry Bonds	3.00
TM26	Alex Rodriguez	4.00
TM27	Willie Stargell	1.50
TM28	Carlton Fisk	1.50
TM29	Carlos Delgado	1.50
TM30	Ken Griffey Jr.	5.00

Tape Measure Heroes Jerseys

	NM/M
Common Player:	5.00
Inserted 1:96	

JB	Jeff Bagwell	12.00
WB	Wade Boggs	15.00
JCa	Jose Canseco	10.00
JoC	Joe Carter	5.00
CD	Carlos Delgado	8.00
CF	Carlton Fisk	10.00
SGa	Steve Garvey	5.00
KGi	Kirk Gibson	8.00
BG	Brian Giles	5.00
SGr	Shawn Green	8.00
KGr	Ken Griffey Jr./90	40.00
MMa	Mickey Mantle/50	200.00
RM	Roger Maris/50	100.00
BM	Bill Mazeroski	10.00
MP	Mike Piazza	15.00
MR	Manny Ramirez	10.00
CR	Cal Ripken Jr.	30.00
AR	Alex Rodriguez	15.00
SS	Sammy Sosa	15.00
WS	Willie Stargell	15.00
RY	Robin Yount/SP	25.00

The MVP Club

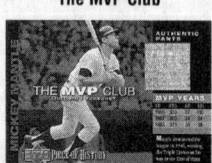

		NM/M
Complete Set (14):		30.00
Common Player:		1.00
Inserted 1:22		
M1	Jason Giambi	2.00
M2	Sammy Sosa	3.00
M3	Cal Ripken Jr.	6.00
M4	Robin Yount	2.00
M5	Ken Griffey Jr.	5.00
M6	Kirk Gibson	1.00
M7	Mickey Mantle	6.00
M8	Barry Bonds	3.00
M9	Frank Thomas	2.00
M10	Reggie Jackson	2.00
M11	Jeff Bagwell	2.00
M12	Roger Clemens	3.00
M13	Steve Garvey	1.00
M14	Chipper Jones	3.00

MVP Club Jerseys

		NM/M
Common Player:		8.00
Inserted 1:96		
JB	Jeff Bagwell	10.00
RC	Roger Clemens	15.00
SG	Steve Garvey	8.00
JGi	Jason Giambi	10.00
KGi	Kirk Gibson	10.00
JGo	Juan Gonzalez	10.00
KGr	Ken Griffey Jr.	15.00
RJ	Reggie Jackson	15.00
CJ	Chipper Jones	15.00
JK	Jeff Kent	8.00
BL	Barry Larkin/SP	25.00
MM	Mickey Mantle/50	200.00
RM	Roger Maris/50	100.00
CR	Cal Ripken Jr.	35.00
IR	Ivan Rodriguez	10.00
SS	Sammy Sosa	15.00
FT	Frank Thomas	10.00
RY	Robin Yount/SP	25.00

MVP Club Jerseys Auto.

No Pricing
Production 10 Sets

The 500 Home Run Club

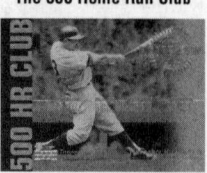

		NM/M
Complete Set (9):		25.00
Common Player:		1.50
Inserted 1:9		
HR1	Harmon Killebrew	3.00
HR2	Jimmie Foxx	3.00
HR3	Reggie Jackson	3.00
HR4	Mickey Mantle	8.00
HR5	Ernie Banks	3.00
HR6	Eddie Mathews	3.00
HR7	Mark McGwire	6.00
HR8	Willie McCovey	1.50
HR9	Mel Ott	3.00

HR Club Jerseys

		NM/M
Inserted 1:336		
HA	Hank Aaron	50.00
EB	Ernie Banks/SP	40.00
JF	Jimmie Foxx	40.00
RJ	Reggie Jackson	25.00
MM	Mickey Mantle/50	200.00
EM	Eddie Mathews	30.00
WM	Willie McCovey	20.00
MO	Mel Ott	40.00

HR Club Jerseys Auto.

No Pricing
Production 10 Sets

300 Game Winners

		NM/M
Complete Set (6):		12.00
Common Player:		1.00
Inserted 1:50		
GW1	Nolan Ryan	6.00
GW2	Tom Seaver	3.00
GW3	Cy Young	3.00
GW4	Gaylord Perry	1.00
GW5	Early Wynn	1.00
GW6	Phil Niekro	1.00

300 Game Winners Jerseys

		NM/M
Common Player:		15.00
Inserted 1:576		
PN	Phil Niekro	10.00
GP	Gaylord Perry	10.00
NR	Nolan Ryan/SP	50.00
TS	Tom Seaver/SP	20.00

2002 Upper Deck Prospect Premieres

		NM/M
Complete Set (109):		
Common Player (1-60):		.40
Common Jersey (61-85):		5.00
Inserted 1:18		
Common Auto. (86-97):		10.00
Inserted 1:18		
Pack (4):		8.00
Box (18):		120.00
1	Josh Rupe RC	.40
2	Blair Johnson RC	.40
3	Jason Pridie RC	.75
4	Tim Gilhooly RC	.40
5	Kennard Jones RC	.40
6	Darrell Rasner RC	.40
7	Adam Donachie RC	.75
8	Josh Murray RC	.40
9	Brian Dopirak RC	1.00
10	Jason Cooper RC	.50
11	Zach Hammes RC	.40
12	Jon Lester RC	15.00
13	Kevin Jepsen RC	.40
14	Curtis Granderson RC	4.00
15	David Bush RC	.75
16	Joel Guzman RC	.50
17a	Matt Pender RC (Black, photo is Curtis Granderson.)	.40
17b	Matt Pender (White, correct photo.)	2.00
18	Derick Grigsby RC	.40
19	Jeremy Reed RC	.40
20	Jonathan Broxton RC	1.00
21	Jesse Crain RC	.40
22	Justin Jones RC	.50
23	Brian Slocum RC	.40
24	Brian McCann RC	5.00
25	Francisco Liriano RC	8.00
26	Fred Lewis RC	1.00
27	Steve Stanley RC	.40
28	Chris Snyder RC	.40
29	Daniel Cevette RC	.40
30	Kiel Fisher RC	.40
31	Brandon Wheeder RC	.40
32	Pat Osborn RC	.40
33	Taber Lee RC	.40
34	Dan Ortmeyer RC	.75
35	Josh Johnson RC	4.00
36	Val Majewski RC	.75
37	Larry Broadway RC	.50
38	Joey Gomes RC	1.00
39	Eric Thomas RC	.40
40	James Loney RC	3.00
41	Charlie Morton RC	.40
42	Mark McLemore RC	.40
43	Matt Craig RC	.40
44	Ryan Rodriguez RC	.40
45	Rich Hill RC	.75
46	Bob Malek RC	.40
47	Justin Maureau RC	.40
48	Randy Braun RC	.40
49	Brian Grant RC	.50
50	Tyler Davidson RC	.50
51	Travis Hanson RC	.50
52	Kyle Boyer RC	.40
53	James Holcomb RC	.40
54	Ryan Williams RC	.40
55	Ben Crockett RC	.40
56	Adam Greenberg RC	.75
57	John Baker RC	.40
58	Matt Carson RC	.40
59	Jonathan George RC	.40
60	David Jensen RC	.40
61	Nick Swisher RC	10.00
62	Brent Cleven RC	5.00
63	Royce Ring RC	5.00
64	Mike Nixon RC	5.00
65	Ricky Barrett RC	5.00
66	Russ Adams RC	5.00
67	Joe Mauer RC	35.00
68	Jeff Francoeur RC	12.00
69	Joseph Blanton RC	8.00
70	Micah Schilling RC	5.00
71	John McCurdy RC	5.00
72	Sergio Santos RC	5.00
73	Josh Womack RC	5.00
74	Jared Doyle RC	5.00
75	Ben Fritz RC	5.00
76	Greg Miller RC	5.00
77	Luke Hagerty RC	5.00
78	Matt Whitney RC	5.00
79	Dan Meyer RC	5.00
80	Bill Murphy RC	5.00
81	Zach Segovia RC	5.00
82	Steve Obenchain RC	5.00
83	Matt Clanton RC	5.00
84	Mark Teahen RC	8.00
85	Kyle Pawelczyk RC	5.00
86	Khalil Greene/ Auto. RC	10.00
87	Joe Saunders/ Auto. RC	12.00
88	Jeremy Hermida/ Auto. RC	12.00
89	Drew Meyer/Auto. RC	10.00
90	Jeff Francis/Auto. RC	12.00
91	Scott Moore/Auto. RC	10.00
92	Prince Fielder/ Auto. RC	140.00
93	Zack Greinke/Auto. RC	75.00
94	Chris Gruler/Auto. RC	10.00
95	Scott Kazmir/Auto. RC	25.00
96	B.J. Upton/Auto. RC	30.00
97	Clint Everts/Auto. RC	10.00
98	Cal Ripken Jr.	1.00
99	Cal Ripken Jr.	1.00
100-104	Cal Ripken Jr.	1.00
105-109	Joe DiMaggio	1.00

Heroes of Baseball

	NM/M
Complete Ripken Set (10):	15.00
Common Ripken:	2.00
Complete Morgan Set (10):	4.00
Common Morgan:	.50
Complete Stargell Set (10):	5.00
Common Stargell:	.50
Complete Seaver Set (10):	10.00
Common Seaver:	1.25
Complete Mantle Set (10):	15.00
Common Mantle:	2.00
Complete DiMaggio Set (10):	12.00
Common DiMaggio:	1.50
Complete Gwynn Set (10):	10.00
Common Gwynn:	1.25
Complete McGwire Set (10):	12.00
Common McGwire:	1.50
Complete Ozzie Smith (10):	8.00
Common Ozzie:	1.00

Sets include Headers
Inserted 1:1

Heroes of Baseball Quads

		NM/M
Common Quad:		10.00
Production 85 Sets		
1	Joe DiMaggio, Tony Gwynn	15.00
2	Joe DiMaggio, Tony Gwynn, Cal Ripken Jr.	20.00
3	Joe DiMaggio, Mickey Mantle, Willie Stargell	20.00
4	Tony Gwynn, Ozzie Smith, Willie Stargell	10.00
5	Tony Gwynn, Willie Stargell, Joe DiMaggio	15.00
6	Tony Gwynn, Willie Stargell, Cal Ripken Jr., Ozzie Smith	15.00
7	Mickey Mantle, Mark McGwire, Joe Morgan, Tom Seaver	20.00
8	Mickey Mantle, Tom Seaver	20.00
9	Mark McGwire, Joe Morgan	20.00
10	Mark McGwire, Cal Ripken Jr., Tony Gwynn, Joe DiMaggio	25.00
11	Mark McGwire, Tom Seaver, Joe Morgan, Ozzie Smith	15.00
12	Joe Morgan, Tony Gwynn	10.00
13	Joe Morgan, Joe DiMaggio, Mickey Mantle, Cal Ripken Jr.	25.00
14	Joe Morgan, Joe DiMaggio, Willie Stargell, Tony Gwynn	15.00
15	Ozzie Smith, Joe DiMaggio, Ozzie Smith, Willie Stargell	15.00
16	Ozzie Smith, Mark McGwire, Willie Stargell, Tony Gwynn	15.00
17	Ozzie Smith, Tom Seaver, Mark McGwire	15.00
18	Cal Ripken Jr., Mickey Mantle, Joe DiMaggio, Joe Morgan	20.00
19	Cal Ripken Jr., Mark McGwire, Cal Ripken Jr.	20.00
20	Tom Seaver, Joe DiMaggio, Tom Seaver, Joe DiMaggio	15.00
21	Tom Seaver, Joe Morgan, Ozzie Smith, Willie Stargell	10.00
22	Tom Seaver, Cal Ripken Jr., Mark McGwire, Mickey Mantle	20.00
23	Willie Stargell, Ozzie Smith	10.00
24	Willie Stargell, Ozzie Smith, Tom Seaver, Joe Morgan	10.00

Future Gems Quads

		NM/M
Common Card:		4.00
Inserted 1:Box		
1	David Bush, Matt Craig, Blair Johnson, Brian McCann	4.00
2	Jason Cooper, Jonathan George, Larry Broadway, Joel Guzman	4.00
3	Matt Craig, Josh Murray, Brian McCann, Jason Pridie	4.00
4	Jesse Crain, Brian Grant, Curtis Granderson, Joey Gomes	4.00
5	Tyler Davidson, Val Majewski, Kennard Jones, Daniel Cevette	4.00
6	Joe DiMaggio, Jon Lester, Mac, Mark McLemore	4.00
7	Jonathan George, Jeremy Reed, Adam Donachie, Matt Carson	4.00
8	Jonathan George, Eric Thomas, Joel Guzman, Kiel Fisher	4.00
9	Tim Gilhooly, Brandon Wheeder, Brian Slocum,	4.00
10	Brian Grant, Rich Hill, Joey Gomes, Joe DiMaggio	4.00
11	Derick Grigsby, Bob Malek, James Loney, Fred Lewis	4.00
12	Zach Hammes, James Holcomb, Cal Ripken Jr., Kennard Jones	4.00
13	Rich Hill, Mark McGwire, Brian Grant, Matt Carson	4.00
14	James Holcomb, David Jensen, Kennard Jones, Ryan Williams	4.00
15	David Jensen, Francisco Liriano, Ryan Williams, Travis Hanson	4.00
16	Blair Johnson, Jesse Crain, Adam Greenberg, Curtis Granderson	4.00
17	Jon Lester, Jonathan George, Adam Donachie, Mark McLemore	4.00
18	Francisco Liriano, Mark McGwire, Travis Hanson, Taber Lee	4.00
19	Val Majewski, Charlie Morton, Daniel Cevette, Joey Gomes	4.00
20	Bob Malek, Zach Hammes, Fred Lewis, Cal Ripken Jr.	4.00
21	Justin Maureau, Joe DiMaggio, Chris Snyder, Mark McGwire	4.00
22	Mark McGwire, Bob Malek, Joe DiMaggio, Kyle Boyer	4.00
23	Charlie Morton, David Bush, Joey Gomes, Blair Johnson	4.00
24	Josh Murray, Mark McGwire, Jason Pridie, Joe DiMaggio	4.00
25	Matt Pender, Mark McGwire, Mark McLemore, Ryan Rodriguez	4.00
26	Jason Pridie, Josh Murray, Matt Craig, Brian McCann	4.00
27	Jeremy Reed, Blair Johnson, Matt Carson, Adam Greenberg	4.00
28	Cal Ripken Jr., Jason Cooper, Matt Carson, Larry Broadway	4.00
29	Ryan Rodriguez, Eric Thomas, Pat Osborn, Randy Braun	4.00
30	Josh Rupe, Tyler Davidson, John Baker, Kennard Jones	4.00
31	Eric Thomas, Derick Grigsby, Randy Braun, James Loney	4.00
32	Eric Thomas, Matt Pender, Kiel Fisher, Mark McLemore	4.00
33	Brandon Wheeder, Rich Hill, Brian Dopirak, Brian Grant	4.00

2002 Upper Deck Rookie Debut

	NM/M
Common Player:	.10
Pack (5):	1.50
Box (24):	30.00

Honor Roll
Common Honor Roll
Rk (131-190): .25

Golds (131-190): 5-10X
Production 50
101	Curt Schilling	.40
102	Geronimo Gil	.10
103	Cliff Floyd	.10
104	Derek Lowe	.10
105	Hee Seop Choi	.10
106	Mark Prior	.50
107	Joe Borchard	.10
108	Austin Kearns	.40
109	Adam Dunn	.50
110	Brandon Phillips	.10
111	Carlos Pena	.10
112	Andy Van Hekken	.10
113	Juan Encarnacion	.10
114	Lance Berkman	.25
115	Torii Hunter	.25
116	Bartolo Colon	.10
117	Raul Mondesi	.20
118	Alfonso Soriano	.75
119	Miguel Tejada	.40
120	Ray Durham	.10
121	Eric Chavez	.20
122	Brett Myers	.10
123	Marlon Byrd	.10
124	Sean Burroughs	.10
125	Kenny Lofton	.10
126	Scott Rolen	.50
127	Carl Crawford	.10
128	Josh Phelps	.10
129	Eric Hinske	.10
130	Orlando Hudson	.10
131	Barry Wesson	.40
132	Jose Valverde RC	.25
133	Kevin Gryboski RC	.25
134	Trey Hodges RC	.25
135	Howie Clark RC	.25
136	Josh Hancock RC	.25
137	Freddy Sanchez RC	.25
138	Francis Beltran RC	.10
139	Mike Mahoney	.10
140	Brian Tallet	.10
141	Jason Davis RC	.50
142	Carl Sadler RC	.25
143	Jason Beverlin RC	.25
144	Josh Bard RC	.25
145	Aaron Cook RC	.25
146	Eric Eckenstahler RC	.25
147	Tim Kalita RC	.25
148	Franklyn German RC	.25
149	Hansel Izquierdo RC	.25
150	Brandon Puffer RC	.25
151	Rodrigo Rosario RC	.25
152	Kirk Saarloos RC	.25
153	Jeriome Robertson RC	.25
154	Jeremy Hill RC	.25
155	Wes Obermueller RC	.25
156	Aaron Guiel RC	.25
157	Kazuhisa Ishii RC	.50
158	David Ross	.10
159	Jayson Durocher RC	.25
160	Luis Martinez RC	.25
161	Shane Nance RC	.25
162	Eric Good RC	.25
163	Jamey Carroll RC	.25
164	Jaime Cerda RC	.25
165	Satoru Komiyama RC	.25
166	Adam Walker RC	.25
167	Nate Field RC	.25
168	Cody McKay RC	.25
169	Jose Flores RC	.25
170	Eric Junge RC	.25
171	Jorge Padilla RC	.25
172	Oliver Perez RC	1.00
173	Julius Matos RC	.25
174	Wilbert Nieves RC	.25
175	Clay Condrey RC	.25
176	Mike Crudale RC	.25
177	Jason Simontacchi RC	.25
178	So Taguchi RC	.50
179	Jose Rodriguez	.10
180	Jorge Sosa RC	.25
181	Felix Escalona RC	.25
182	Lance Carter RC	.25
183	Travis Hughes	.10
184	Reynaldo Garcia RC	.25
185	Mike Smith	.10
186	Corey Thurman RC	.25
187	Ken Huckaby RC	.25
188	Reed Johnson RC	.50
189	Kevin Cash RC	.25
190	Scott Wiggins RC	.25

Ovation
Common SP (151-180): 3.00
Production 2,002
Golds (151-180): 2-4X
Production 50
121	Curt Schilling	.50
122	Cliff Floyd	.15
123	Derek Lowe	.15
124	Hee Seop Choi	.25
125	Mark Prior	.75
126	Joe Borchard	.15
127	Austin Kearns	.50
128	Adam Dunn	.75
129	Jay Payton	.15
130	Carlos Pena	.15
131	Andy Van Hekken	.15
132	Andres Torres	.15
133	Ben Diggins	.15
134	Torii Hunter	.40
135	Bartolo Colon	.15
136	Raul Mondesi	.25
137	Alfonso Soriano	1.00
138	Miguel Tejada	.75
139	Ray Durham	.15
140	Eric Chavez	.40
141	Marlon Byrd	.15

142	Brett Myers	.15
143	Sean Burroughs	.15
144	Kenny Lofton	.15
145	Scott Rolen	.75
146	Carl Crawford	.15
147	Jayson Werth	.15
148	Josh Phelps	.15
149	Eric Hinske	.15
150	Orlando Hudson	.15
151	Jose Valverde RC	5.00
152	Trey Hodges RC	3.00
153	Joey Dawley	3.00
154	Travis Driskill RC	3.00
155	Howie Clark RC	3.00
156	Jorge De La Rosa RC	3.00
157	Freddy Sanchez RC	3.00
158	Earl Snyder RC	5.00
159	Cliff Lee RC	15.00
160	Josh Bard RC	3.00
161	Aaron Cook RC	3.00
162	Franklyn German RC	3.00
163	Brandon Puffer RC	3.00
164	Kirk Saarloos RC	3.00
165	Jeriome Robertson RC	3.00
166	Miguel Asencio RC	3.00
167	Shawn Sedlacek	3.00
168	Jayson Durocher RC	3.00
169	Shane Nance RC	3.00
170	Jamey Carroll RC	5.00
171	Oliver Perez RC	5.00
172	Wilbert Nieves RC	3.00
173	Clay Condrey RC	5.00
174	Chris Snelling RC	3.00
175	Mike Crudale RC	3.00
176	Jason Simontacchi RC	3.00
177	Felix Escalona RC	3.00
178	Lance Carter RC	3.00
179	Scott Wiggins RC	3.00
180	Kevin Cash RC	3.00

Victory
Common Rk (606-660): .20
551	John Lackey	.25
552	Francisco Rodriguez	.50
553	Cliff Floyd	.10
554	Derek Lowe	.10
555	Mark Bellhorn	.10
556	Matt Clement	.10
557	Hee Seop Choi	.25
558	Joe Borchard	.10
559	Ryan Dempster	.10
560	Russell Branyan	.10
561	Brandon Larson	.10
562	Coco Crisp	.10
563	Karim Garcia	.10
564	Brandon Phillips	.10
565	Jay Payton	.10
566	Gabe Kapler	.10
567	Carlos Pena	.10
568	George Lombard	.10
569	Andy Van Hekken	.10
570	Andres Torres	.10
571	Justin Wayne	.10
572	Juan Encarnacion	.10
573	Abraham Nunez	.10
574	Peter Munro	.10
575	Jason Lane	.10
576	Dave Roberts	.10
577	Eric Gagne	.10
578	Alex Sanchez	.10
579	Jim Rushford RC	.10
580	Ben Diggins	.10
581	Eddie Guardado	.10
582	Bartolo Colon	.20
583	Endy Chavez	.10
584	Raul Mondesi	.10
585	Jeff Weaver	.10
586	Marcus Thames	.10
587	Ted Lilly	.10
588	Ray Durham	.10
589	Jeremy Giambi	.10
590	Vicente Padilla	.10
591	Brett Myers	.10
592	Josh Fogg	.10
593	Tony Alvarez	.10
594	Jake Peavy	.10
595	Dennis Tankersley	.10
596	Sean Burroughs	.10
597	Kenny Lofton	.10
598	Scott Rolen	.50
599	Chuck Finley	.10
600	Carl Crawford	.10
601	Kevin Mench	.10
602	Juan Gonzalez	.50
603	Jayson Werth	.20
604	Eric Hinske	.10
605	Josh Phelps	.10
606	Jose Valverde RC	.20
607	John Ennis RC	.20
608	Trey Hodges RC	.20
609	Kevin Gryboski RC	.20
610	Travis Driskill RC	.20
611	Howie Clark RC	.20
612	Freddy Sanchez RC	.20
613	Josh Hancock RC	.20
614	Jorge De La Rosa RC	.20
615	Mike Mahoney	.10
616	Jason Davis RC	.20
617	Josh Bard RC	.50
618	Jason Beverlin RC	.20
619	Carl Sadler RC	.20
620	Earl Snyder RC	.50
621	Aaron Cook RC	.20
622	Eric Eckenstahler RC	.20
623	Franklyn German RC	.20
624	Kirk Saarloos RC	.50
625	Rodrigo Rosario RC	.20
626	Jeriome Robertson RC	.20
627	Brandon Puffer RC	.20

628	Miguel Asencio RC	.20
629	Aaron Guiel RC	.30
630	Ryan Bukvich RC	.20
631	Jeremy Hill RC	.20
632	Kazuhisa Ishii RC	.75
633	Jayson Durocher RC	.20
634	Shane Nance RC	.20
635	Eric Good RC	.20
636	Jamey Carroll RC	.50
637	Jaime Cerda RC	.20
638	Nate Field RC	.20
639	Cody McKay RC	.20
640	Jose Flores RC	.20
641	Jorge Padilla RC	.20
642	Anderson Machado RC	.20
643	Eric Junge RC	.20
644	Oliver Perez RC	.75
645	Julius Matos RC	.20
646	Ben Howard RC	.20
647	Julio Mateo RC	.20
648	Matt Thornton	.10
649	Chris Snelling RC	.50
650	Jason Simontacchi RC	.50
651	So Taguchi RC	.40
652	Mike Crudale RC	.20
653	Mike Coolbaugh	.10
654	Felix Escalona RC	.20
655	Jorge Sosa RC	.20
656	Lance Carter RC	.20
657	Reynaldo Garcia RC	.20
658	Kevin Cash RC	.40
659	Ken Huckaby RC	.20
660	Scott Wiggins RC	.20

Climbing the Ladder
Common Player: .25
Production 25 Sets, Not Priced

Elite Company
Common Player: .25
Production 25, Not Priced

Making Their Marks
Common Player: .25
Production 25 Sets, Not Priced

Solid Contact

Common Player: 4.00
Inserted 1:24
BA	Bobby Abreu	4.00
EA	Edgardo Alfonzo	4.00
RA	Roberto Alomar	10.00
MA	Moises Alou	6.00
JC	Jose Cruz Jr.	6.00
CD	Carlos Delgado/SP	8.00
JE	Jim Edmonds	4.00
CE	Carl Everett	4.00
JG	Jason Giambi/50	15.00
BG	Brian Giles	4.00
KG	Ken Griffey Jr.	15.00
TH	Todd Helton	8.00
JK	Jason Kendall	4.00
BL	Barry Larkin	10.00
EM	Edgar Martinez	8.00
FM	Fred McGriff	6.00
DM	Doug Mientkiewicz	6.00
JO	John Olerud	6.00
MO	Magglio Ordonez	6.00
JP	Jorge Posada	10.00
AR	Alex Rodriguez	15.00
IR	Ivan Rodriguez	6.00
GS	Gary Sheffield	6.00
SS	Sammy Sosa	15.00
TA	Fernando Tatis	4.00
FT	Frank Thomas	8.00
JT	Jim Thome	12.00
OV	Omar Vizquel	6.00
BW	Bernie Williams	8.00
MW	Matt Williams	4.00

2002 Upper Deck Rookie Update

Common Player: .25
Pack (5): 3.00
Box (15): 35.00
SP Authentic
Common SP (201-230): 5.00

Production 1,999
171	Erubiel Durazo	.25
172	Junior Spivey	.25
173	Geronimo Gil	.25
174	Cliff Floyd	.25
175	Brandon Larsen	.25
176	Aaron Boone	.25
177	Shawn Estes	.25
178	Austin Kearns	.75
179	Joe Borchard	.25
180	Russell Branyan	.25
181	Jay Payton	.25
182	Andres Torres	.25
183	Andy Van Hekken	.25
184	Alex Sanchez	.25
185	Endy Chavez	.25
186	Bartolo Colon	.25
187	Raul Mondesi	.40
188	Robin Ventura	.25
189	Mike Mussina	.75
190	Jorge Posada	.75
191	Ted Lilly	.25
192	Ray Durham	.25
193	Brett Myers	.25
194	Marlon Byrd	.25
195	Vicente Padilla	.25
196	Josh Fogg	.25
197	Kenny Lofton	.25
198	Scott Rolen	1.00
199	Jason Lane	.25
200	Josh Phelps	.25

Diamond Connection
Common SP (601-630): 4.00
Production 1,999
571	Erubiel Durazo	.25
572	Geronimo Gil	.25
573	Shea Hillenbrand	.50
574	Cliff Floyd	.25
575	Corey Patterson	.50
576	Joe Borchard	.25
577	Austin Kearns	.75
578	Ryan Dempster	.25
579	Brandon Larsen	.25
580	Luis Castillo	.25
581	Juan Encarnacion	.25
582	Chin-Feng Chen	.25
583	Hideo Nomo	.75
584	Bartolo Colon	.40
585	Raul Mondesi	.25
586	Eric Munson	.25
587	Alfonso Soriano	1.00
588	Ted Lilly	.25
589	Ray Durham	.25
590	Brett Myers	.25
591	Brandon Phillips	.25
592	Kenny Lofton	.25
593	Scott Rolen	.50
594	Jim Edmonds	.50
595	Carl Crawford	.50
596	Hank Blalock	.50
597	Kevin Mench	.25
598	Josh Phelps	.25
599	Orlando Hudson	.25
600	Eric Hinske	.25
601	Mike Mahoney	5.00
602	Jason Davis RC	4.00
603	Trey Hodges RC	4.00
604	Josh Bard RC	4.00
605	Jeriome Robertson RC	4.00
606	Jose Diaz	4.00
607	Jorge Nunez	4.00
608	Danny Mota	4.00
609	David Ross	4.00
610	Jayson Durocher RC	4.00
611	Freddy Sanchez RC	4.00
612	Julius Matos RC	4.00
613	Wilbert Nieves RC	4.00
614	Brian Kozlowski	4.00
615	Jason Simontacchi RC	4.00
616	Mike Coolbaugh	4.00
617	Travis Driskill RC	4.00
618	Howie Clark RC	4.00
619	Earl Snyder RC	4.00
620	Carl Sadler RC	4.00
621	Jason Beverlin RC	4.00
622	Terry Pearson	4.00
623	Eric Eckenstahler RC	4.00
624	Shawn Sedlacek	4.00
625	Aaron Guiel RC	4.00
626	Ryan Bukvich RC	4.00
627	Julio Mateo RC	4.00
628	Chris Snelling RC	4.00
629	Lance Carter RC	4.00
630	Scott Wiggins RC	4.00

Star Tributes

Common Player: 5.00
Inserted 1:15
JB	Josh Beckett	8.00
LB	Lance Berkman	6.00
RC	Roger Clemens	15.00
CD	Carlos Delgado	5.00
JD	Joe DiMaggio/SP	75.00
AD	Adam Dunn	8.00
JG	Jason Giambi	10.00
TG	Tom Glavine	8.00
LG	Luis Gonzalez/SP	8.00
SG	Shawn Green	5.00
KG	Ken Griffey Jr.	12.00
KI	Kazuhisa Ishii	8.00
RJ	Randy Johnson	10.00
CJ	Chipper Jones	10.00
PM	Pedro J. Martinez	8.00
MM	Mark McGwire/SP	50.00
RP	Rafael Palmeiro	8.00
MPi	Mike Piazza	10.00
MPr	Mark Prior	5.00
AR	Alex Rodriguez	10.00
IR	Ivan Rodriguez	8.00
KS	Kazuhiro Sasaki	5.00
CS	Curt Schilling	5.00
TS	Tsuyoshi Shinjo	5.00
AS	Alfonso Soriano	10.00
SS	Sammy Sosa	12.00
MS	Mike Sweeney	5.00
FT	Frank Thomas	8.00

Signed Star Tributes
Production 50 Sets
Copper & Silver: No Pricing

245	Freddy Sanchez RC	10.00
246	Miguel Asencio RC	10.00
247	Juan Brito	10.00
248	Franklyn German RC	10.00
249	Chris Snelling RC	10.00
250	Ken Huckaby RC	10.00

Production 25
Gold: No Pricing
Production 5
SS-MM Mark McGwire 350.00

USA Future Watch Swatches

Common Player: 5.00
Inserted 1:15
Red: 1.5-2X
Production 50
Copper: No Pricing
Production 25
Gold: No Pricing
Production 5
AA	Abe Alvarez	5.00
MA	Michael Aubrey	5.00
KB	Kyle Bakker	5.00
CC	Chad Cordero	5.00
SC	Shane Costa	5.00
SF	Sam Fuld	8.00
AH	Aaron Hill	5.00
PH	Philip Humber	5.00
CJ	Conor Jackson	5.00
GJ	Grant Johnson	5.00
MJ	Mark Jurich	5.00
WL	Wes Littleton	5.00
EP	Eric Patterson	5.00
DP	Dustin Pedroia	5.00
LP	Landon Powell	5.00
CQ	Carlos Quentin	10.00
CS	Clint Sammons	5.00
KS	Kyle Sleeth	6.00
HS	Huston Street	5.00
BS	Brad Sullivan	5.00
RW	Rickie Weeks	10.00
BZ	Bob Zimmermann	5.00

2002 Upper Deck Sweet Spot

Complete Set (175): .25
Common Player: .25
Common (91-130): 4.00
Production 1,300
Common Auto. (131-145): 10.00
Production 750 or 100
Common Game Faces
(146-175): 3.00
Inserted 1:24
Parallel (146-175): 1.5-3X
Production 100
Pack (4): 8.00
Box (12): 90.00
1	Troy Glaus	.50
2	Darin Erstad	.50
3	Tim Hudson	.50
4	Eric Chavez	.50
5	Barry Zito	.50
6	Miguel Tejada	.50
7	Carlos Delgado	.50
8	Eric Hinske	.25
9	Ben Grieve	.25
10	Jim Thome	1.00
11	C.C. Sabathia	.25
12	Omar Vizquel	.40
13	Ichiro Suzuki	2.00
14	Edgar Martinez	.40
15	Bret Boone	.25
16	Freddy Garcia	.25
17	Tony Batista	.25
18	Geronimo Gil	.25
19	Alex Rodriguez	2.50
20	Rafael Palmeiro	.75
21	Ivan Rodriguez	.75
22	Hank Blalock	.50
23	Juan Gonzalez	.75
24	Nomar Garciaparra	2.00
25	Pedro J. Martinez	1.00
26	Manny Ramirez	1.00
27	Mike Sweeney	.25
28	Carlos Beltran	.50
29	Dmitri Young	.25
30	Torii Hunter	.50
31	Eric Milton	.25
32	Corey Koskie	.25
33	Frank Thomas	.75
34	Mark Buehrle	.25
35	Magglio Ordonez	.25

Column 4 (continued) — SPx
Common SPx Auto.(221-250): 10.00
Production 825
191	Tom Glavine	.75
192	Cliff Floyd	.25
193	Mark Prior	.25
194	Corey Patterson	.50
195	Paul Konerko	.50
196	Adam Dunn	.75
197	Joe Borchard	.25
198	Carlos Pena	.25
199	Juan Encarnacion	.25
200	Luis Castillo	.25
201	Torii Hunter	.50
202	Hee Seop Choi	.50
203	Bartolo Colon	.40
204	Raul Mondesi	.40
205	Jeff Weaver	.25
206	Eric Munson	.25
207	Alfonso Soriano	1.00
208	Ray Durham	.25
209	Eric Chavez	.50
210	Brett Myers	.25
211	Jeremy Giambi	.25
212	Vicente Padilla	.25
213	Felipe Lopez	.25
214	Sean Burroughs	.25
215	Kenny Lofton	.25
216	Scott Rolen	.50
217	Carl Crawford	.25
218	Juan Gonzalez	.75
219	Orlando Hudson	.25
220	Eric Hinske	.25
221	Adam Walker RC	10.00
222	Aaron Cook RC	12.00
223	Cam Esslinger RC	10.00
224	Kirk Saarloos RC	10.00
225	Jose Diaz	10.00
226	David Ross	10.00
227	Jayson Durocher RC	10.00
228	Brian Mallette	10.00
229	Aaron Guiel RC	10.00
230	Jorge Nunez	10.00
231	Satoru Komiyama RC	10.00
232	Tyler Yates RC	10.00
233	Peter Zamora RC	10.00
234	Mike Gonzalez RC	10.00
235	Oliver Perez RC	15.00
236	Julius Matos RC	10.00
237	Andy Shibilo	10.00
238	Jason Simontacchi RC	10.00
239	Ron Chiavacci	10.00
240	Deivis Santos	10.00
241	Travis Driskill RC	10.00
242	Jorge De La Rosa RC	15.00
243	Anastacio Martinez RC	10.00
244	Earl Snyder RC	10.00

36	Roger Clemens	2.00
37	Derek Jeter	3.00
38	Jason Giambi	.75
39	Alfonso Soriano	1.00
40	Bernie Williams	.50
41	Jeff Bagwell	.75
42	Roy Oswalt	.50
43	Lance Berkman	.50
44	Greg Maddux	1.50
45	Chipper Jones	1.00
46	Gary Sheffield	.75
47	Andruw Jones	.75
48	Richie Sexson	.50
49	Ben Sheets	.50
50	Albert Pujols	2.00
51	Matt Morris	.40
52	J.D. Drew	.50
53	Sammy Sosa	2.00
54	Kerry Wood	1.00
55	Mark Prior	1.00
56	Moises Alou	.50
57	Corey Patterson	.50
58	Randy Johnson	1.00
59	Luis Gonzalez	.40
60	Curt Schilling	.75
61	Shawn Green	.50
62	Kevin Brown	.40
63	Paul LoDuca	.25
64	Adrian Beltre	.50
65	Vladimir Guerrero	1.00
66	Jose Vidro	.25
67	Javier Vazquez	.25
68	Barry Bonds	3.00
69	Jeff Kent	.40
70	Rich Aurilia	.25
71	Mike Lowell	.40
72	Josh Beckett	.50
73	Brad Penny	.25
74	Roberto Alomar	.50
75	Mike Piazza	1.50
76	Jeromy Burnitz	.25
77	Mo Vaughn	.25
78	Phil Nevin	.25
79	Sean Burroughs	.25
80	Jeremy Giambi	.25
81	Bobby Abreu	.50
82	Jimmy Rollins	.50
83	Pat Burrell	.50
84	Brian Giles	.50
85	Aramis Ramirez	.50
86	Ken Griffey Jr.	1.50
87	Adam Dunn	.75
88	Austin Kearns	.75
89	Todd Helton	.75
90	Larry Walker	.50
91	Earl Snyder RC	4.00
92	Jorge Padilla RC	4.00
93	Felix Escalona RC	4.00
94	John Foster RC	4.00
95	Brandon Puffer RC	4.00
96	Steve Bechler RC	4.00
97	Hansel Izquierdo RC	4.00
98	Chris Baker RC	4.00
99	Jeremy Ward RC	4.00
100	Kevin Frederick RC	4.00
101	Josh Hancock RC	4.00
102	Allan Simpson RC	4.00
103	Mitch Wylie RC	4.00
104	Mark Corey RC	4.00
105	Victor Alvarez RC	4.00
106	Todd Donovan RC	4.00
107	Nelson Castro RC	4.00
108	Chris Booker RC	4.00
109	Corey Thurman RC	4.00
110	Kirk Saarloos RC	4.00
111	Michael Crudale RC	4.00
112	Jason Simontacchi RC	4.00
113	Ron Calloway RC	4.00
114	Brandon Backe RC	4.00
115	Tom Shearn RC	4.00
116	Oliver Perez RC	6.00
117	Kyle Kane RC	4.00
118	Francis Beltran RC	4.00
119	So Taguchi RC	4.00
120	Doug DeVore RC	4.00
121	Juan Brito RC	4.00
122	Clifford Bartosh RC	4.00
123	Eric Junge RC	4.00
,124	Joe Orloski RC	4.00
125	Scotty Layfield RC	4.00
126	Jorge Sosa RC	4.00
127	Satoru Komiyama RC	4.00
128	Edwin Almonte RC	4.00
129	Takahito Nomura RC	4.00
130	John Ennis RC	4.00
131	Kazuhisa Ishii/ Auto./100 RC	15.00
132	Ben Howard/ Auto./100 RC	10.00
133	Aaron Cook/ Auto./750 RC	15.00
134	Anderson Machado/ Auto./750 RC	10.00
135	Luis Ugueto/ Auto./750 RC	10.00
136	Tyler Yates/ Auto./750 RC	10.00
137	Rodrigo Rosario/ Auto./750 RC	10.00
138	Jaime Cerda/ Auto./750 RC	10.00
139	Luis Martinez/ Auto./750 RC	10.00
140	Rene Reyes/ Auto./750 RC	10.00
141	Eric Good/Auto./750 RC	10.00
142	Matt Thornton/ Auto./100	15.00
143	Steve Kent/ Auto./750 RC	10.00
144	Jose Valverde/ Auto./750 RC	15.00
145	Adrian Burnside/ Auto./750 RC	10.00
146	Barry Bonds	10.00
147	Ken Griffey Jr.	10.00
148	Alex Rodriguez	12.00
149	Jason Giambi	4.00
150	Chipper Jones	5.00
151	Nomar Garciaparra	8.00
152	Mike Piazza	8.00
153	Sammy Sosa	8.00
154	Derek Jeter	15.00
155	Jeff Bagwell	4.00
156	Albert Pujols	15.00
157	Ichiro Suzuki	10.00
158	Randy Johnson	5.00
159	Frank Thomas	4.00
160	Greg Maddux	8.00
161	Jim Thome	5.00
162	Scott Rolen	6.00
163	Shawn Green	3.00
164	Vladimir Guerrero	6.00
165	Troy Glaus	3.00
166	Carlos Delgado	4.00
167	Luis Gonzalez	3.00
168	Roger Clemens	8.00
169	Todd Helton	4.00
170	Eric Chavez	3.00
171	Rafael Palmeiro	4.00
172	Pedro J. Martinez	3.00
173	Lance Berkman	3.00
174	Josh Beckett	4.00
175	Sean Burroughs	3.00

Bat Barrels

Common Player:
100 Total Produced

Legendary Signatures

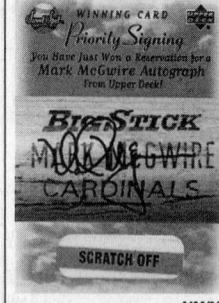

		NM/M
Common Autograph:		20.00
Inserted 1:72		
LA	Luis Aparicio/485	25.00
RF	Rollie Fingers/866	20.00
SG	Steve Garvey/871	20.00
KH	Keith Hernandez/906	20.00
FJ	Ferguson Jenkins/857	20.00
AK	Al Kaline/835	40.00
SK	Sandy Koufax/485	200.00
FL	Fred Lynn/853	20.00
MM	Mark McGwire/90	200.00
PM	Paul Molitor/852	*30.00
GP	Gaylord Perry/921	25.00
BP	Boog Powell/944	20.00
CR	Cal Ripken Jr./194	175.00
BR	Brooks Robinson	35.00
AT	Alan Trammell/843	25.00

McGwire Priority Signing Redem.

		NM/M
100 Redemptions Produced		
MM	Mark McGwire	200.00

Signatures

		NM/M
Common Autograph:		15.00
Inserted 1:72		
LB	Lance Berkman/291	30.00
HB	Hank Blalock/291	20.00
BB	Barry Bonds/380	150.00
JB	Jeromy Burnitz/291	15.00
SB	Sean Burroughs/291	15.00
RC	Roger Clemens/194	100.00
CD	Carlos Delgado/291	20.00
AD	Adam Dunn/291	15.00
FG	Freddy Garcia/145	30.00
JG	Jason Giambi/291	25.00
BG	Brian Giles/291	20.00
TG	Tom Glavine/291	40.00
LG	Luis Gonzalez/291	20.00
KG	Ken Griffey Jr./291	125.00
AJ	Andruw Jones/291	25.00
RO	Roy Oswalt/291	20.00
MPr	Mark Prior/291	50.00
AR	Alex Rodriguez/291	150.00
SR	Scott Rolen/291	40.00
SS	Sammy Sosa/145	100.00
MS	Mike Sweeney/291	15.00
IS	Ichiro Suzuki/145	400.00
FT	Frank Thomas/291	60.00
JT	Jim Thome/291	50.00
BZ	Barry Zito/291	30.00

Sweet Swatches

SWEET SPOT SWATCHES

		NM/M
Common Player:		5.00
Inserted 1:12		
JBa	Jeff Bagwell	8.00
JBe	Josh Beckett	6.00
SB	Sean Burroughs	5.00
EC	Eric Chavez	5.00
JE	Jim Edmonds	5.00
DE	Darin Erstad	5.00
JGi	Jason Giambi	8.00
BG	Brian Giles	6.00
JGo	Juan Gonzalez	6.00
LG	Luis Gonzalez	6.00
SG	Shawn Green	5.00
KG	Ken Griffey Jr.	15.00
KI	Kazuhisa Ishii	5.00
CJ	Chipper Jones	8.00
GM	Greg Maddux	12.00
PM	Pedro J. Martinez	5.00
MP	Mike Piazza	10.00
AR	Alex Rodriguez	15.00
IR	Ivan Rodriguez	6.00
SR	Scott Rolen	6.00
SS	Sammy Sosa	10.00
IS	Ichiro Suzuki	40.00
FT	Frank Thomas	8.00
OV	Omar Vizquel	5.00
BW	Bernie Williams	8.00

USA Jerseys

		NM/M
Common Player:		5.00
Inserted 1:12		
BA	Brent Abernathy	5.00
TB	Taggert Bozied	5.00
DB	Dewon Brazelton	5.00
AE	Adam Everett	5.00
DG	Danny Graves	5.00
JG	Jake Gautreau	5.00
JK	Josh Karp	5.00
AK	Adam Kennedy	5.00
JM	Joe Mauer	25.00
DM	Doug Mientkiewicz	6.00
EM	Eric Munson	5.00
XN	Xavier Nady	5.00
RO	Roy Oswalt	8.00
MP	Mark Prior	8.00
JR	Jon Rauch	5.00
MT	Mark Teixeira	10.00
JW	Justin Wayne	5.00

2002 Upper Deck Sweet Spot Classics

	NM/M
Complete Set (90):	40.00
Common Player:	.40
Pack (4):	20.00

Box (12):		200.00
1	Mickey Mantle	4.00
2	Joe DiMaggio	3.00
3	Babe Ruth	3.00
4	Ty Cobb	1.50
5	Nolan Ryan	3.00
6	Sandy Koufax	2.00
7	Cy Young	1.00
8	Roberto Clemente	2.00
9	Lefty Grove	.50
10	Lou Gehrig	2.50
11	Walter Johnson	1.00
12	Honus Wagner	1.50
13	Christy Mathewson	.75
14	Jackie Robinson	1.50
15	Joe Morgan	.50
16	Reggie Jackson	.75
17	Eddie Collins	.40
18	Cal Ripken Jr.	3.00
19	Hank Greenberg	.40
20	Harmon Killebrew	.75
21	Johnny Bench	1.00
22	Ernie Banks	1.00
23	Willie McCovey	.40
24	Mel Ott	.40
25	Tom Seaver	1.00
26	Tony Gwynn	.75
27	Dave Winfield	.50
28	Willie Stargell	.40
29	Mark McGwire	2.00
30	Al Kaline	.75
31	Jimmie Foxx	.40
32	Satchel Paige	1.50
33	Eddie Murray	.40
34	Lou Boudreau	.40
35	"Shoeless" Joe Jackson	1.50
36	Luke Appling	.40
37	Ralph Kiner	.40
38	Robin Yount	.75
39	Paul Molitor	.75
40	Juan Marichal	.40
41	Brooks Robinson	.75
42	Wade Boggs	.50
43	Kirby Puckett	1.00
44	Yogi Berra	1.00
45	George Sisler	.40
46	Buck Leonard	.40
47	Billy Williams	.40
48	Duke Snider	.75
49	Don Drysdale	.60
50	Bill Mazeroski	.40
51	Tony Oliva	.40
52	Luis Aparicio	.40
53	Carlton Fisk	.40
54	Kirk Gibson	.40
55	Jim "Catfish" Hunter	.40
56	Joe Carter	.40
57	Gaylord Perry	.40
58	Don Mattingly	2.00
59	Eddie Mathews	1.25
60	Ferguson Jenkins	.40
61	Roy Campanella	1.00
62	Orlando Cepeda	.40
63	Tony Perez	.40
64	Dave Parker	.40
65	Richie Ashburn	.40
66	Andre Dawson	.40
67	Dwight Evans	.40
68	Rollie Fingers	.40
69	Dale Murphy	.40
70	Ron Santo	.40
71	Steve Garvey	.40
72	Monte Irvin	.40
73	Alan Trammell	.40
74	Ryne Sandberg	1.00
75	Gary Carter	.40
76	Fred Lynn	.40
77	Maury Wills	.40
78	Ozzie Smith	1.00
79	Bobby Bonds	.40
80	Mickey Cochrane	.60
81	Dizzy Dean	.60
82	Graig Nettles	.40
83	Keith Hernandez	.40
84	Boog Powell	.40
85	Jack Clark	.40
86	Dave Stewart	.40
87	Tommy Lasorda	.40
88	Dennis Eckersley	.40
89	Ken Griffey Sr.	.40
90	Bucky Dent	.40

Bat Barrels

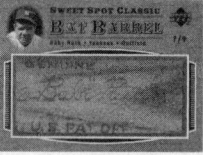

Values undetermined due to scarcity.

Game Jersey

		NM/M
Common Player:		5.00
Inserted 1:8		
WB	Wade Boggs	12.00
GC	Gary Carter	10.00
JC	Joe Carter	5.00
JD	Joe DiMaggio/53	180.00
RF	Rollie Fingers	5.00
SG	Steve Garvey	5.00
TG	Tony Gwynn	15.00
RJ	Reggie Jackson	15.00
SK	Sandy Koufax/SP	125.00
BM	Bill Madlock	5.00
MM	Mickey Mantle/53	250.00
JMa	Juan Marichal	10.00
DM	Don Mattingly	25.00
PM	Paul Molitor	15.00
EM	Eddie Murray	10.00
GN	Graig Nettles	8.00
DP	Dave Parker	5.00
CR	Cal Ripken Jr.	25.00
NR	Nolan Ryan	45.00
RS	Ryne Sandberg	15.00
TS	Tom Seaver	15.00
OS	Ozzie Smith	15.00
DSn	Duke Snider/53	80.00
WS	Willie Stargell	5.00
DSt	Dave Stewart	15.00
BW	Billy Williams	8.00
RY	Robin Yount	15.00

Game Jersey Gold

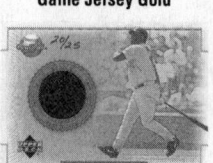

The game-jersey cards in Sweet Spot Classics were paralleled in a special Gold Edition, with each player's swatch cards numbered within an edition of 25 each.
No Pricing
Production 25 Sets

Game-Used Bats

		NM/M
Common Player:		5.00
Inserted 1:8		
JB	Johnny Bench	15.00
YB	Yogi Berra	15.00
WB	Wade Boggs	12.00
BBo	Bob Boone	5.00
BBu	Bill Buckner	5.00
GC	Gary Carter	10.00
RC	Roberto Clemente	50.00
BD	Bucky Dent	8.00
JD	Joe DiMaggio/40	180.00
DE	Dwight Evans	8.00
SG	Steve Garvey	8.00
HG	Hank Greenberg/SP	40.00
KG	Ken Griffey Sr.	5.00
TG	Tony Gwynn	15.00
RJ	Reggie Jackson	10.00
FJ	Ferguson Jenkins	5.00
AK	Al Kaline	15.00
FL	Fred Lynn	5.00
BM	Bill Madlock	5.00
DM	Don Mattingly	25.00
PM	Paul Molitor	15.00
TM	Thurman Munson	35.00
GN	Graig Nettles	5.00
DP	Dave Parker	5.00
KP	Kirby Puckett	15.00
CR	Cal Ripken Jr.	25.00
BR	Brooks Robinson	15.00
NR	Nolan Ryan	40.00
BW	Billy Williams	8.00
DW	Dave Winfield	10.00

Game-Used Bats Gold

Each of the Game-Used Bats cards in Sweet Spot Classics can also be found in a Gold Edition, numbered to just 25 for each player.

		NM/M
Common Player:		15.00
JB	Johnny Bench	50.00
YB	Yogi Berra	75.00
WB	Wade Boggs	30.00
BBo	Bob Boone	15.00
BBu	Bill Buckner	15.00
GC	Gary Carter	15.00
RC	Roberto Clemente	120.00
BD	Bucky Dent	20.00
JD	Joe DiMaggio	150.00
DE	Dwight Evans	15.00
SG	Steve Garvey	15.00
HG	Hank Greenberg	100.00
KG	Ken Griffey Sr.	15.00
TG	Tony Gwynn	40.00
RJ	Reggie Jackson	40.00
FJ	Ferguson Jenkins	25.00
AK	Al Kaline	30.00
FL	Fred Lynn	15.00
BM	Bill Madlock	15.00
DM	Don Mattingly	75.00
PM	Paul Molitor	40.00
TM	Thurman Munson	50.00
GN	Graig Nettles	15.00
DP	Dave Parker	15.00
KP	Kirby Puckett	60.00
CR	Cal Ripken Jr.	60.00
BR	Brooks Robinson	40.00
NR	Nolan Ryan	80.00
BW	Billy Williams	40.00
DW	Dave Winfield	25.00

Signatures

		NM/M
Common Autograph:		20.00
Inserted 1:24		
EB	Ernie Banks	60.00
JB	Johnny Bench	60.00
YB	Yogi Berra/100	75.00
AD	Andre Dawson/100	80.00
BD	Bucky Dent	15.00
DeE	Dennis Eckersley	40.00
RF	Rollie Fingers	25.00
CF	Carlton Fisk/100	125.00
SG	Steve Garvey	50.00
KG	Kirk Gibson/SP	50.00
KH	Keith Hernandez	15.00
RJ	Reggie Jackson/SP	100.00
FJ	Ferguson Jenkins	25.00
AK	Al Kaline	40.00
SK	Sandy Koufax/SP	275.00
TL	Tommy Lasorda	35.00
FL	Fred Lynn	25.00
DoM	Don Mattingly	100.00
BM	Bill Mazeroski	30.00
WM	Willie McCovey/SP	60.00
PM	Paul Molitor	20.00
JM	Joe Morgan	20.00
DaM	Dale Murphy	30.00
GP	Gaylord Perry	25.00
BP	Boog Powell	25.00
KP	Kirby Puckett	180.00
CR	Cal Ripken Jr.	180.00
BR	Brooks Robinson	60.00
NR	Nolan Ryan/74	300.00
TS	Tom Seaver	50.00
OS	Ozzie Smith/137	200.00
DaS	Dave Stewart	25.00
AT	Alan Trammell	15.00
DW	Dave Winfield/70	125.00

Signatures Gold

Each of the Sweet Spot Signatures autographed ball-panel cards was also made in a Gold Edition numbered to just 25 of each player.

No Pricing
Production 25 Sets

2002 UD Sweet Spot Classics Classic Signatures - Hawaii

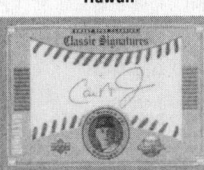

As part of its participation in the Hawaii hobby trade conference in March, 2002, Upper Deck foil-packed 400 specially marked pieces of its Classic Signatures insert card for distribution to retailers. The ultra-thick cards with an actual autographed piece of baseball displayed are overprinted "HAWAII XVII" in the lower-right corner. Numbers in parentheses are the reported production for that player.

		NM/M
Common Player:		50.00
AD	Andre Dawson (10)	200.00
AK	Al Kaline (25)	80.00
AT	Alan Trammell (25)	60.00
BD	Bucky Dent (25)	50.00
BP	Boog Powell (25)	60.00
BR	Brooks Robinson (25)	150.00
CF	Carlton Fisk (25)	200.00
CR	Cal Ripken Jr. (10)	600.00
DaM	Dale Murphy (10)	400.00
DaS	Dave Stewart (25)	50.00
DeE	Dennis Eckersley (25)	75.00
EB	Ernie Banks (10)	150.00
FJ	Ferguson Jenkins (25)	50.00
FL	Fred Lynn (25)	75.00
GP	Gaylord Perry (25)	75.00
KH	Keith Hernandez (20)	65.00
PM	Paul Molitor (25)	75.00
RF	Rollie Fingers (25)	60.00
SG	Steve Garvey (25)	75.00
SK	Sandy Koufax (5)	800.00

UD-Plus

		NM/M
Common Player:		2.00
Production 1,125 Sets		
1 two-card pack per Series 2 H pack		
Comp. Set can be exchanged for Jsy cards.		
Redemption deadline 5-16-03.		
UD1	Darin Erstad	3.00
UD2	Troy Glaus	3.00
UD3	Tim Hudson	3.00
UD4	Jermaine Dye	2.00
UD5	Barry Zito	2.00
UD6	Carlos Delgado	3.00
UD7	Shannon Stewart	2.00
UD8	Greg Vaughn	2.00
UD9	Jim Thome	5.00
UD10	C.C. Sabathia	2.00
UD11	Ichiro Suzuki	10.00
UD12	Edgar Martinez	2.00
UD13	Bret Boone	2.00
UD14	Freddy Garcia	2.00
UD15	Matt Thornton	2.00
UD16	Jeff Conine	2.00
UD17	Steve Bechler	2.00
UD18	Rafael Palmeiro	4.00
UD19	Juan Gonzalez	4.00
UD20	Alex Rodriguez	10.00
UD21	Ivan Rodriguez	4.00
UD22	Carl Everett	2.00
UD23	Manny Ramirez	4.00
UD24	Nomar Garciaparra	10.00
UD25	Pedro J. Martinez	4.00
UD26	Mike Sweeney	2.00
UD27	Chuck Knoblauch	2.00
UD28	Dmitri Young	2.00
UD29	Bobby Higginson	2.00

UD30	Dean Palmer	2.00
UD31	Doug Mientkiewicz	2.00
UD32	Corey Koskie	2.00
UD33	Brad Radke	2.00
UD34	Cristian Guzman	2.00
UD35	Frank Thomas	4.00
UD36	Magglio Ordonez	3.00
UD37	Carlos Lee	2.00
UD38	Roger Clemens	10.00
UD39	Bernie Williams	3.00
UD40	Derek Jeter	15.00
UD41	Jason Giambi	4.00
UD42	Mike Mussina	3.00
UD43	Jeff Bagwell	4.00
UD44	Lance Berkman	3.00
UD45	Wade Miller	2.00
UD46	Greg Maddux	8.00
UD47	Chipper Jones	5.00
UD48	Andruw Jones	4.00
UD49	Gary Sheffield	3.00
UD50	Richie Sexson	2.00
UD51	Albert Pujols	10.00
UD52	J.D. Drew	3.00
UD53	Matt Morris	2.00
UD54	Jim Edmonds	3.00
UD55	So Taguchi	2.00
UD56	Sammy Sosa	10.00
UD57	Fred McGriff	3.00
UD58	Kerry Wood	5.00
UD59	Moises Alou	3.00
UD60	Randy Johnson	5.00
UD61	Luis Gonzalez	3.00
UD62	Mark Grace	3.00
UD63	Curt Schilling	4.00
UD64	Matt Williams	2.00
UD65	Kevin Brown	2.00
UD66	Brian Jordan	2.00
UD67	Shawn Green	3.00
UD68	Hideo Nomo	3.00
UD69	Kazuhisa Ishii	4.00
UD70	Vladimir Guerrero	4.00
UD71	Jose Vidro	2.00
UD72	Eric Good	2.00
UD73	Barry Bonds	15.00
UD74	Jeff Kent	3.00
UD75	Rich Aurilia	2.00
UD76	Deivis Santos	2.00
UD77	Preston Wilson	2.00
UD78	Cliff Floyd	2.00
UD79	Josh Beckett	4.00
UD80	Hansel Izquierdo	2.00
UD81	Mike Piazza	10.00
UD82	Roberto Alomar	3.00
UD83	Mo Vaughn	3.00
UD84	Jeromy Burnitz	2.00
UD85	Phil Nevin	2.00
UD86	Ryan Klesko	3.00
UD87	Bobby Abreu	3.00
UD88	Scott Rolen	5.00
UD89	Jimmy Rollins	2.50
UD90	Jason Kendall	2.00
UD91	Brian Giles	3.00
UD92	Aramis Ramirez	2.00
UD93	Ken Griffey Jr.	10.00
UD94	Sean Casey	2.00
UD95	Barry Larkin	3.00
UD96	Adam Dunn	4.00
UD97	Todd Helton	4.00
UD98	Larry Walker	3.00
UD99	Mike Hampton	2.00
UD100	Rene Reyes	2.00

UD-Plus Memorabila Moments Jerseys

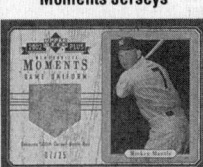

		NM/M
Common DiMaggio (1-5):		125.00
Common Mantle: (1-5):		200.00
MM-JD1-5	Joe DiMaggio	125.00
MM-MM1	Mickey Mantle/25 (Pants)	200.00
MM-MM2-5	Mickey Mantle	200.00

UD-Plus Pinstripe Immortals

Complete Set (10):		
Common Player:		

2002 Upper Deck Ultimate Collection

		NM/M
Complete Set (120):		
Common Player (1-60):		2.00
Production 799		
Common Player (61-110, 114-120):		8.00
Production 550		
Common (111-113):		15.00
Production 330		
Pack (4):		100.00
Box (4):		350.00
1	Troy Glaus	2.50
2	Luis Gonzalez	2.00
3	Curt Schilling	2.50
4	Randy Johnson	4.00
5	Andruw Jones	2.50
6	Greg Maddux	6.00
7	Chipper Jones	5.00
8	Gary Sheffield	2.00
9	Cal Ripken Jr.	12.00
10	Manny Ramirez	3.00
11	Pedro J. Martinez	4.00
12	Nomar Garciaparra	8.00
13	Sammy Sosa	6.00
14	Kerry Wood	4.00
15	Mark Prior	4.00
16	Magglio Ordonez	2.00
17	Frank Thomas	3.00
18	Adam Dunn	3.00
19	Ken Griffey Jr.	8.00
20	Jim Thome	4.00
21	Larry Walker	2.00
22	Todd Helton	3.00
23	Nolan Ryan	12.00
24	Jeff Bagwell	3.00
25	Roy Oswalt	2.00
26	Lance Berkman	2.00
27	Mike Sweeney	2.00
28	Shawn Green	2.00
29	Hideo Nomo	2.00
30	Torii Hunter	2.00
31	Vladimir Guerrero	5.00
32	Tom Seaver	4.00
33	Mike Piazza	8.00
34	Roberto Alomar	2.00
35	Derek Jeter	12.00
36	Alfonso Soriano	5.00
37	Jason Giambi	4.00
38	Roger Clemens	8.00
39	Mike Mussina	2.50
40	Bernie Williams	2.50
41	Joe DiMaggio	10.00
42	Mickey Mantle	15.00
43	Miguel Tejada	3.00
44	Eric Chavez	2.00
45	Barry Zito	2.00
46	Pat Burrell	2.50
47	Jason Kendall	2.00
48	Brian Giles	2.00
49	Barry Bonds	15.00
50	Ichiro Suzuki	8.00
51	Stan Musial	8.00
52	J.D. Drew	2.00
53	Scott Rolen	5.00
54	Albert Pujols	10.00
55	Mark McGwire	10.00
56	Alex Rodriguez	10.00
57	Ivan Rodriguez	3.00
58	Juan Gonzalez	2.50
59	Rafael Palmeiro	3.00
60	Carlos Delgado	2.50
61	Jose Valverde RC	10.00
62	Doug DeVore RC	8.00
63	John Ennis RC	8.00
64	Joey Dawley	8.00
65	Trey Hodges RC	8.00
66	Mike Mahoney RC	8.00
67	Aaron Cook RC	10.00
68	Rene Reyes RC	8.00
69	Mark Corey	8.00
70	Hansel Izquierdo RC	8.00
71	Brandon Puffer RC	8.00
72	Jeriome Robertson RC	8.00
73	Jose Diaz	8.00
74	David Ross	8.00
75	Jayson Durocher RC	8.00
76	Eric Good RC	8.00
77	Satoru Komiyama RC	8.00
78	Tyler Yates RC	8.00
79	Eric Junge RC	8.00
80	Anderson Machado RC	8.00
81	Adrian Burnside RC	8.00
82	Ben Howard RC	8.00
83	Clay Condrey RC	8.00
84	Nelson Castro RC	8.00
85	So Taguchi RC	8.00
86	Mike Crudale RC	8.00
87	Scotty Layfield RC	8.00
88	Steve Bechler RC	8.00
89	Travis Driskill RC	8.00
90	Howie Clark RC	8.00
91	Josh Hancock RC	8.00
92	Jorge De La Rosa RC	15.00
93	Anastacio Martinez RC	8.00
94	Brian Tallet RC	8.00
95	Carl Sadler RC	8.00
96	Cliff Lee RC	25.00
97	Josh Bard RC	8.00
98	Wes Obermueller RC	8.00
99	Juan Brito	8.00
100	Aaron Guiel RC	8.00
101	Jeremy Hill RC	8.00
102	Kevin Frederick RC	8.00
103	Nate Field RC	8.00
104	Julio Mateo RC	8.00
105	Chris Snelling RC	10.00
106	Felix Escalona RC	8.00

107	Reynaldo Garcia RC	8.00
108	Mike Smith RC	8.00
109	Ken Huckaby RC	8.00
110	Kevin Cash RC	8.00
111	Kazuhisa Ishii/Auto. RC	20.00
112	Freddy Sanchez/ Auto. RC	15.00
113	Jason Simontacchi/ Auto. RC	15.00
114	Jorge Padilla/Auto. RC	15.00
115	Kirk Saarloos/Auto.	15.00
116	Rodrigo Rosario/ Auto. RC	15.00
117	Oliver Perez/Auto. RC	15.00
118	Miguel Asencio/ Auto. RC	15.00
119	Franklyn German/ Auto. RC	15.00
120	Jaime Cerda/Auto. RC	15.00

Double Barrel

		NM/M
Quantity Produced Listed		
DB-RI	Ivan Rodriguez, Alex Rodriguez/5	2,225
DB-RR	Cal Ripken Jr., Alex Rodriguez/9	1,625
DB-TO	Magglio Ordonez, Frank Thomas/4	950.00

Jerseys Tier 1

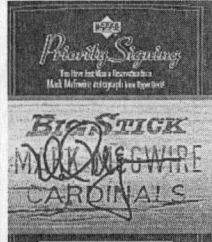

		NM/M
Common Player:		10.00
Production 99 Sets		
Golds:		.75-1.5X
Production 50 Sets		
RC	Roger Clemens	20.00
JD	Joe DiMaggio	100.00
AD	Adam Dunn	15.00
JG	Jason Giambi	15.00
KG	Ken Griffey Jr.	20.00
KI	Kazuhisa Ishii	10.00
RJ	Randy Johnson	15.00
AJ	Andruw Jones	10.00
CJ	Chipper Jones	15.00
MM	Mickey Mantle	125.00
PM	Pedro J. Martinez	15.00
MC	Mark McGwire	60.00
MP	Mike Piazza	15.00
PR	Mark Prior	10.00
MR	Manny Ramirez	10.00
CR	Cal Ripken Jr.	40.00
AR	Alex Rodriguez	20.00
IR	Ivan Rodriguez	10.00
AS	Alfonso Soriano	15.00
SS	Sammy Sosa	15.00
IS	Ichiro Suzuki	30.00

Jerseys Tier 2

		NM/M
Same price as Tier 1.		
Production 99 Sets		
Golds:		1.5-2X
Production 25 Sets		
JF-RC	Roger Clemens	20.00
JF-JD	Joe DiMaggio	100.00
JF-AD	Adam Dunn	15.00
JF-JG	Jason Giambi	15.00
JF-KG	Ken Griffey Jr.	20.00
JF-KI	Kazuhisa Ishii	10.00
JF-RJ	Randy Johnson	15.00
JF-AJ	Andruw Jones	15.00
JF-CJ	Chipper Jones	15.00
JF-MM	Mickey Mantle	125.00
JF-PM	Pedro J. Martinez	15.00
JF-MC	Mark McGwire	60.00
JF-MP	Mike Piazza	15.00
JF-PR	Mark Prior	20.00
JF-MR	Manny Ramirez	15.00
JF-CR	Cal Ripken Jr.	40.00
JF-AR	Alex Rodriguez	25.00
JF-IR	Ivan Rodriguez	15.00
JF-AS	Alfonso Soriano	20.00
JF-SS	Sammy Sosa	25.00
JF-IS	Ichiro Suzuki	45.00

Jerseys Tier 3

		NM/M
Common Player:		.4-.6X Tier 1 Price
Stars:		
Production 199 Sets		
JP-RC	Roger Clemens	15.00
JP-AD	Adam Dunn	10.00
JP-JG	Jason Giambi	10.00
JP-KG	Ken Griffey Jr.	15.00
JP-KI	Kazuhisa Ishii	8.00
JP-RJ	Randy Johnson	12.00
JP-AJ	Andruw Jones	8.00
JP-CJ	Chipper Jones	12.00
JP-MM	Mickey Mantle	75.00
JP-PM	Pedro J. Martinez	10.00
JP-MC	Mark McGwire	40.00
JP-MP	Mike Piazza	15.00
JP-PR	Mark Prior	8.00
JP-MR	Manny Ramirez	8.00
JP-CR	Cal Ripken Jr.	30.00
JP-AR	Alex Rodriguez	15.00
JP-IR	Ivan Rodriguez	8.00
JP-AS	Alfonso Soriano	12.00
JP-SS	Sammy Sosa	20.00
JP-IS	Ichiro Suzuki	30.00
JP-BW	Bernie Williams	8.00

Jerseys Tier 4

		NM/M
Common Player:		8.00
Stars:		.4-.6X Tier 1 Price
Production 199 Sets		
JR-RC	Roger Clemens	15.00
JR-AD	Adam Dunn	10.00
JR-JG	Jason Giambi	10.00
JR-KG	Ken Griffey Jr.	15.00
JR-KI	Kazuhisa Ishii	8.00
JR-RJ	Randy Johnson	10.00
JR-AJ	Andruw Jones	8.00
JR-CJ	Chipper Jones	10.00
JR-MM	Mickey Mantle	75.00
JR-PM	Pedro J. Martinez	10.00
JR-MC	Mark McGwire	40.00
JR-MP	Mike Piazza	15.00
JR-PR	Mark Prior	10.00
JR-MR	Manny Ramirez	8.00
JR-CR	Cal Ripken Jr.	25.00
JR-AR	Alex Rodriguez	15.00
JR-IR	Ivan Rodriguez	8.00
JR-AS	Alfonso Soriano	15.00
JR-SS	Sammy Sosa	20.00
JR-IS	Ichiro Suzuki	30.00
JR-BW	Bernie Williams	8.00

Mark McGwire Signing Redem.

		NM/M
Exchange Card 1:500 Packs:		
1-MM	Mark McGwire	200.00

Signatures Tier 1

		NM/M
Common Autograph:		20.00
Quantity Produced Listed		
Golds:		No Pricing
Production 25 Sets		
RA1	Roberto Alomar/155	30.00
LB1	Lance Berkman/179	25.00
PB1	Pat Burrell/95	25.00
RC1	Roger Clemens/320	80.00
CD1	Carlos Delgado/95	25.00
JD1	J.D. Drew/220	25.00
AD1	Adam Dunn/125	45.00
JG1	Jason Giambi/295	25.00
BG1	Brian Giles/220	20.00
LG1	Luis Gonzalez/199	20.00
KG1	Ken Griffey Jr./195	100.00
JK1	Jason Kendall/220	20.00
MP1	Mark Prior/160	20.00
CR1	Cal Ripken Jr./75	165.00
AR1	Alex Rodriguez/329	100.00
SR1	Scott Rolen/160	30.00
GS1	Gary Sheffield/95	20.00
JT1	Jim Thome/95	50.00
BZ1	Barry Zito/199	25.00

Signatures Tier 2

		NM/M
Quantity produced listed		
Golds:		No Pricing
Production 10 Sets		
JB2	Jeff Bagwell/51	40.00
LB2	Lance Berkman/85	40.00
JG2	Jason Giambi/50	40.00
LG2	Luis Gonzalez/70	25.00
KG2	Ken Griffey Jr./30	150.00
TG2	Tony Gwynn/51	75.00
TH2	Todd Helton/51	50.00
AJ2	Andruw Jones/51	40.00
MP2	Mark Prior/60	25.00
KP2	Kirby Puckett/75	75.00
AR2	Alex Rodriguez/75	100.00
SR2	Scott Rolen/60	50.00
DS2	Duke Snider/51	60.00
FT2	Frank Thomas/51	65.00
KW2	Kerry Wood/51	25.00
BZ2	Barry Zito/70	35.00

Signed Excellence

		NM/M
Quantity Produced Listed		
Golds:		No Pricing
Production One Set		
I1	Ichiro Suzuki/56	375.00
I2	Ichiro Suzuki/51	375.00
I5	Ichiro Suzuki/Btg	250.00
I6	Ichiro Suzuki/ Throwing	250.00
MM1	Mark McGwire/70	200.00
MM2	Mark McGwire/65	200.00
MM3	Mark McGwire/49	200.00
MM5	Mark McGwire/ Standing	150.00
MM6	Mark McGwire/Waving	150.00
MM7	Mark McGwire/Fldg	150.00
SS1	Sammy Sosa/66	100.00
SS2	Sammy Sosa/64	100.00
SS3	Sammy Sosa/64	100.00
SS5	Sammy Sosa/Running	100.00
SS6	Sammy Sosa/ Holding Bat	100.00
SS7	Sammy Sosa/150	100.00

Excellence Gold

Complete Set (5):	
Common Player:	

Patch

		NM/M
Common Player:		15.00
Production 100 Sets		
LG	Luis Gonzalez	15.00
SG	Shawn Green	15.00
TH	Todd Helton	25.00
KI	Kazuhisa Ishii	15.00
CJ	Chipper Jones	40.00
MM	Mark McGwire	75.00
MP	Mark Prior	20.00
IR	Ivan Rodriguez	20.00
SS	Sammy Sosa	50.00
IS	Ichiro Suzuki	150.00

Double Patches

		NM/M
Production 100 Sets		
Golds:		.75-1.5X
Production 50 Sets		
DE	J.D. Drew, Jim Edmonds	60.00
GC	Jason Giambi, Roger Clemens	80.00

IG	Ken Griffey Jr., Ichiro Suzuki	125.00
JS	Randy Johnson, Curt Schilling	60.00
MG	Tom Glavine, Greg Maddux	75.00
MS	Sammy Sosa, Mark McGwire	150.00
PA	Mike Piazza, Roberto Alomar	80.00
RG	Alex Rodriguez, Juan Gonzalez	80.00
RM	Manny Ramirez, Pedro J. Martinez	50.00

2002 Upper Deck Victory

VLADIMIR GUERRERO

	NM/M
Complete Set (550):	40.00
Common Player:	.10
Pack (10):	1.00
Box (36):	25.00

1 Troy Glaus .30
2 Tim Salmon .20
3 Troy Percival .10
4 Darin Erstad .25
5 Adam Kennedy .10
6 Scott Spiezio .10
7 Ramon Ortiz .10
8 Ismael Valdes .10
9 Jarrod Washburn .10
10 Garret Anderson .10
11 David Eckstein .10
12 Mo Vaughn .25
13 Benji Gil .10
14 Bengie Molina .10
15 Scott Schoeneweis .10
16 Troy Glaus, Ramon Ortiz .20
17 David Justice .25
18 Jermaine Dye .25
19 Eric Chavez .25
20 Jeremy Giambi .10
21 Terrence Long .10
22 Miguel Tejada .20
23 Johnny Damon .10
24 Jason Hart .10
25 Adam Piatt .10
26 Billy Koch .10
27 Ramon Hernandez .10
28 Eric Byrnes .10
29 Olmedo Saenz .10
30 Barry Zito .20
31 Tim Hudson .25
32 Mark Mulder .20
33 Jason Giambi, Mark Mulder .25
34 Carlos Delgado .40
35 Shannon Stewart .10
36 Vernon Wells .10
37 Homer Bush .10
38 Brad Fullmer .10
39 Jose Cruz .10
40 Felipe Lopez .10
41 Raul Mondesi .20
42 Esteban Loaiza .10
43 Darrin Fletcher .10
44 Mike Sirotka .10
45 Luke Prokopec .10
46 Chris Carpenter .10
47 Roy Halladay .10
48 Kelvim Escobar .10
49 Carlos Delgado, Billy Koch .20
50 Nick Bierbrodt .10
51 Greg Vaughn .10
52 Ben Grieve .10
53 Damian Rolls .10
54 Russ Johnson .10
55 Brent Abernathy .10
56 Steve Cox .10
57 Aubrey Huff .10
58 Randy Winn .10
59 Jason Tyner .10
60 Tanyon Sturtze .10
61 Joe Kennedy .10
62 Jared Sandberg .10
63 Esteban Yan .10
64 Ryan Rupe .10
65 Toby Hall .10
66 Greg Vaughn, Tanyon Sturtze .10
67 Matt Lawton .10
68 Juan Gonzalez .40
69 Jim Thome .25
70 Einar Diaz .10
71 Ellis Burks .10
72 Kenny Lofton .10
73 Omar Vizquel .10
74 Russell Branyan .10
75 Brady Anderson .10
76 John Rocker .10
77 Travis Fryman .10
78 Wil Cordero .10
79 Chuck Finley .10
80 C.C. Sabathia .10
81 Bartolo Colon .10
82 Bob Wickman .10
83 Roberto Alomar, C.C. Sabathia .20
84 Ichiro Suzuki 1.50
85 Edgar Martinez .10
86 Aaron Sele .10
87 Carlos Guillen .10
88 Bret Boone .10
89 John Olerud .20
90 Jamie Moyer .10
91 Ben Davis .10
92 Dan Wilson .10
93 Jeff Cirillo .10
94 John Halama .10
95 Freddy Garcia .10
96 Kazuhiro Sasaki .10
97 Mike Cameron .10
98 Paul Abbott .10
99 Mark McLemore .10
100 Ichiro Suzuki, Freddy Garcia .50
101 Jeff Conine .10
102 David Segui .10
103 Marty Cordova .10
104 Tony Batista .10
105 Chris Richard .10
106 Willis Roberts .10
107 Melvin Mora .10
108 Mike Bordick .10
109 Jay Gibbons .10
110 Jamie Kinkade .10
111 Brian Roberts .10
112 Jerry Hairston Jr. .10
113 Jason Johnson .10
114 Josh Towers .10
115 Calvin Maduro .10
116 Sidney Ponson .10
117 Jeff Conine, Jason Johnson .10
118 Alex Rodriguez 1.00
119 Ivan Rodriguez .40
120 Frank Catalanotto .10
121 Mike Lamb .10
122 Ruben Sierra .10
123 Rusty Greer .10
124 Rafael Palmeiro .20
125 Gabe Kapler .15
126 Carl Everett .10
127 Kenny Rogers .10
128 Carl Everett .10
129 Rick Helling .10
130 Ricky Ledee .10
131 Michael Young .10
132 Doug Davis .10
133 Jeff Zimmerman .10
134 Alex Rodriguez, Rick Helling .10
135 Manny Ramirez .40
136 Nomar Garciaparra 1.00
137 Jason Varitek .10
138 Dante Bichette .10
139 Tony Clark .10
140 Scott Hatteberg .10
141 Trot Nixon .10
142 Hideo Nomo .25
143 Dustin Hermanson .10
144 Chris Stynes .10
145 Jose Offerman .10
146 Pedro Martinez .50
147 Shea Hillenbrand .10
148 Tim Wakefield .10
149 Troy O'Leary .10
150 Ugueth Urbina .10
151 Manny Ramirez, Hideo Nomo .25
152 Carlos Beltran .10
153 Dee Brown .10
154 Mike Sweeney .10
155 Luis Alicea .10
156 Raul Ibanez .10
157 Mark Quinn .10
158 Joe Randa .10
159 Roberto Hernandez .10
160 Neifi Perez .10
161 Carlos Febles .10
162 Jeff Suppan .10
163 Dave McCarty .10
164 Blake Stein .10
165 Chad Durbin .10
166 Paul Byrd .10
167 Carlos Beltran, Jeff Suppan .10
168 Craig Paquette .10
169 Dean Palmer .10
170 Shane Halter .10
171 Bobby Higginson .10
172 Robert Fick .10
173 Jose Macias .10
174 Deivi Cruz .10
175 Damion Easley .10
176 Brandon Inge .10
177 Mark Redman .10
178 Dmitri Young .10
179 Steve Sparks .10
180 Jeff Weaver .10
181 Victor Santos .10
182 Jose Lima .10
183 Matt Anderson .10
184 Roger Cedeno, Steve Sparks .10
185 Doug Mientkiewicz .10
186 Cristian Guzman .10
187 Torii Hunter .10
188 Matt LeCroy .10
189 Corey Koskie .10
190 Jacque Jones .10
191 Luis Rivas .10
192 David Ortiz .10
193 A.J. Pierzynski .10
194 Brian Buchanan .10
195 Joe Mays .10
196 Brad Radke .10
197 Denny Hocking .10
198 Eric Milton .10
199 LaTroy Hawkins .10
200 Doug Mientkiewicz, Joe Mays .10
201 Magglio Ordonez .20
202 Jose Valentin .10
203 Chris Singleton .10
204 Aaron Rowand .10
205 Paul Konerko .10
206 Carlos Lee .10
207 Ray Durham .10
208 Keith Foulke .10
209 Todd Ritchie .10
210 Royce Clayton .10
211 Jose Canseco .20
212 Frank Thomas .40
213 David Wells .10
214 Mark Buehrle .10
215 Jon Garland .10
216 Magglio Ordonez, Mark Buehrle .15
217 Derek Jeter 1.50
218 Bernie Williams .30
219 Rondell White .10
220 Jorge Posada .20
221 Alfonso Soriano .50
222 Ramiro Mendoza .10
223 Jason Giambi .75
224 John Vander Wal .10
225 Steve Karsay .10
226 Nick Johnson .10
227 Mariano Rivera .20
228 Orlando Hernandez .10
229 Andy Pettitte .10
230 Robin Ventura .10
231 Roger Clemens .50
232 Mike Mussina .40
233 Derek Jeter, Roger Clemens .50
234 Moises Alou .20
235 Lance Berkman .20
236 Craig Biggio .20
237 Octavio Dotel .10
238 Jeff Bagwell .40
239 Richard Hidalgo .10
240 Morgan Ensberg .10
241 Julio Lugo .10
242 Daryle Ward .10
243 Roy Oswalt .20
244 Billy Wagner .10
245 Brad Ausmus .10
246 Jose Vizcaino .10
247 Wade Miller .10
248 Shane Reynolds .10
249 Jeff Bagwell, Wade Miller .20
250 Chipper Jones .75
251 Brian Jordan .10
252 B.J. Surhoff .10
253 Rafael Furcal .10
254 Julio Franco .10
255 Javy Lopez .10
256 John Burkett .10
257 Andruw Jones .20
258 Marcus Giles .10
259 Wes Helms .10
260 Greg Maddux .75
261 John Smoltz .10
262 Tom Glavine .20
263 Vinny Castilla .10
264 Kevin Millwood .10
265 Jason Marquis .10
266 Chipper Jones, Greg Maddux .40
267 Tyler Houston .10
268 Mark Loretta .10
269 Richie Sexson .20
270 Jeromy Burnitz .10
271 Jimmy Haynes .10
272 Geoff Jenkins .20
273 Ron Belliard .10
274 Jose Hernandez .10
275 Jeffrey Hammonds .10
276 Curtis Leskanic .10
277 Devon White .10
278 Ben Sheets .20
279 Henry Blanco .10
280 Jamey Wright .10
281 Allen Levrault .10
282 Jeff D'Amico .10
283 Richie Sexson, Jimmy Haynes .10
284 Albert Pujols .75
285 Jason Isringhausen .10
286 J.D. Drew .25
287 Placido Polanco .10
288 Jim Edmonds .20
289 Fernando Vina .10
290 Edgar Renteria .10
291 Mike Matheny .10
292 Bud Smith .10
293 Mike Defelice .10
294 Woody Williams .10
295 Eli Marrero .10
296 Matt Morris .10
297 Darryl Kile .10
298 Kerry Robinson .10
299 Luis Saturria .10
300 Albert Pujols, Matt Morris .40
301 Sammy Sosa .75
302 Michael Tucker .10
303 Bill Mueller .10
304 Ricky Gutierrez .10
305 Fred McGriff .20
306 Eric Young .10
307 Corey Patterson .10
308 Alex Gonzalez .10
309 Ron Coomer .10
310 Kerry Wood .20
311 Delino DeShields .10
312 Jon Lieber .10
313 Tom Gordon .10
314 Todd Hundley .10
315 Jason Bere .10
316 Kevin Tapani .10
317 Sammy Sosa, Jon Lieber .40
318 Steve Finley .10
319 Luis Gonzalez .25
320 Mark Grace .25
321 Craig Counsell .10
322 Matt Williams .20
323 Tony Womack .10
324 Junior Spivey .10
325 David Dellucci .10
326 Jay Bell .10
327 Curt Schilling .25
328 Randy Johnson .40
329 Danny Bautista .10
330 Miguel Batista .10
331 Erubiel Durazo .10
332 Brian Anderson .10
333 Byung-Hyun Kim .10
334 Luis Gonzalez, Curt Schilling .20
335 Paul LoDuca .10
336 Gary Sheffield .20
337 Shawn Green .25
338 Adrian Beltre .20
339 Darren Dreifort .10
340 Mark Grudzielanek .10
341 Eric Karros .10
342 Cesar Izturis .10
343 Tom Goodwin .10
344 Marquis Grissom .10
345 Kevin Brown .20
346 James Baldwin .10
347 Terry Adams .10
348 Alex Cora .10
349 Andy Ashby .10
350 Chan Ho Park .20
351 Shawn Green, Chan Ho Park .20
352 Jose Vidro .10
353 Vladimir Guerrero .40
354 Orlando Cabrera .10
355 Fernando Tatis .10
356 Michael Barrett .10
357 Lee Stevens .10
358 Geoff Blum .10
359 Brad Wilkerson .10
360 Peter Bergeron .10
361 Javier Vazquez .10
362 Tony Armas Jr. .10
363 Tomokazu Ohka .10
364 Scott Strickland .10
365 Vladimir Guerrero, Javier Vazquez .20
366 Barry Bonds .75
367 Rich Aurilia .10
368 Jeff Kent .10
369 Andres Galarraga .10
370 Desi Relaford .10
371 Shawon Dunston .10
372 Benito Santiago .10
373 Tsuyoshi Shinjo .10
374 Calvin Murray .10
375 Marvin Benard .10
376 J.T. Snow .10
377 Livan Hernandez .10
378 Russ Ortiz .10
379 Robb Nen .10
380 Jason Schmidt .10
381 Barry Bonds, Russ Ortiz .30
382 Cliff Floyd .10
383 Antonio Alfonseca .10
384 Mike Redmond .10
385 Mike Lowell .10
386 Derek Lee .10
387 Preston Wilson .10
388 Luis Castillo .10
389 Charles Johnson .10
390 Eric Owens .10
391 Alex Gonzalez .10
392 Josh Beckett .10
393 Brad Penny .10
394 Ryan Dempster .10
395 Matt Clement .10
396 A.J. Burnett .10
397 Cliff Floyd, Ryan Dempster .10
398 Mike Piazza 1.00
399 Joe McEwing .10
400 Todd Zeile .10
401 Jay Payton .10
402 Roger Cedeno .10
403 Rey Ordonez .10
404 Edgardo Alfonzo .10
405 Roberto Alomar .30
406 Glendon Rusch .10
407 Timo Perez .10
408 Al Leiter .15
409 Lenny Harris .10
410 Shawn Estes .10
411 Armando Benitez .10
412 Kevin Appier .10
413 Bruce Chen .10
414 Mike Piazza, Al Leiter .40
415 Phil Nevin .10
416 Ryan Klesko .10
417 Mark Kotsay .10
418 Ray Lankford .10
419 Mike Darr .10
420 D'Angelo Jimenez .10
421 Bubba Trammell .10
422 Adam Eaton .10
423 Ramon Vazquez .10
424 Cesar Crespo .10
425 Trevor Hoffman .10
426 Kevin Jarvis .10
427 Wiki Gonzalez .10
428 Damian Jackson .10
429 Brian Lawrence .10
430 Phil Nevin, Trevor Hoffman .10
431 Scott Rolen .25
432 Marlon Anderson .10
433 Bobby Abreu .10
434 Jimmy Rollins .20
435 Doug Glanville .10
436 Travis Lee .10
437 Brandon Duckworth .10
438 Pat Burrell .25
439 Kevin Jordan .10
440 Robert Person .10
441 Johnny Estrada .10
442 Randy Wolf .10
443 Jose Mesa .10
444 Mike Lieberthal .10
445 Bobby Abreu, Robert Person .10
446 Brian Giles .20
447 Jason Kendall .10
448 Aramis Ramirez .10
449 Rob Mackowiak .10
450 Abraham Nunez .10
451 Pat Meares .10
452 Craig Wilson .10
453 Jack Wilson .10
454 Gary Matthews Jr. .10
455 Kevin Young .10
456 Derek Bell .10
457 Kip Wells .10
458 Jimmy Anderson .10
459 Kris Benson .10
460 Brian Giles, Todd Ritchie .10
461 Sean Casey .20
462 Wilton Guerrero .10
463 Jason LaRue .10
464 Juan Encarnacion .10
465 Todd Walker .10
466 Aaron Boone .10
467 Pete Harnisch .10
468 Ken Griffey Jr. 1.00
469 Adam Dunn .40
470 Barry Larkin .20
471 Kelly Stinnett .10
472 Pokey Reese .10
473 Brady Clark .10
474 Scott Williamson .10
475 Danny Graves .10
476 Ken Griffey Jr., Elmer Dessens .10
477 Larry Walker .25
478 Todd Helton .40
479 Juan Pierre .10
480 Juan Uribe .10
481 Mario Encarnacion .10
482 Jose Ortiz .10
483 Todd Hollandsworth .10
484 Alex Ochoa .10
485 Mike Hampton .10
486 Terry Shumpert .10
487 Denny Neagle .10
488 Jose Jimenez .10
489 Jason Jennings .10
490 Todd Helton, Mike Hampton .20
491 Tim Redding .10
492 Mark Teixeira 2.00
493 Alex Cintron .10
494 Tim Raines Jr. .10
495 Juan Cruz .20
496 Joe Crede .10
497 Steve Green .10
498 Mike Rivera .10
499 Mark Prior 1.00
500 Ken Harvey .10
501 Tim Spooneybarger .10
502 Adam Everett .10
503 Jason Standridge .10
504 Nick Neugebauer .10
505 Adam Johnson .10
506 Sean Douglass .10
507 Brandon Berger .10
508 Alex Escobar .10
509 Doug Nickle .10
510 Jason Middlebrook .10
511 Dewon Brazelton .10
512 Yorvit Torrealba .10
513 Henry Mateo .10
514 Dennis Tankersley .10
515 Marlon Byrd .75
516 Andy Barkett .10
517 Orlando Hudson .10
518 Josh Fogg .10
519 Ryan Drese .10
520 Mike MacDougal .10
521 Luis Pineda .10
522 Jack Cust .10
523 Kurt Ainsworth .10
524 Bart Miadich .10
525 Dernell Stenson .10
526 Carlos Zambrano .10
527 Austin Kearns .50
528 Larry Barnes .10
529 Mike Cuddyer .1
530 Carlos Pena .75
531 Derek Jeter 1.00
532 Ken Griffey Jr. .75
533 Manny Ramirez .25
534 Luis Gonzalez .20
535 Sammy Sosa .50
536 Roger Clemens .40
537 Phil Nevin .10
538 Mike Piazza .75
539 Alex Rodriguez .75
540 Jason Giambi .50
541 Randy Johnson .50
542 Albert Pujols .5
543 Jeff Bagwell .25
544 Shawn Green .15
545 Carlos Delgado .15
546 Pedro Martinez .25
547 Todd Helton .25
548 Roberto Alomar .20
549 Barry Bonds .40
550 Ichiro Suzuki 1.00

Gold

RANDY JOHNSON

Stars: 3-6X
Inserted 1:2

2002 Upper Deck Vintage

RED SOX
manny ramirez • outfield

	NM/M
Complete Set (300):	30.00
Common Player:	.10
Pack (10):	1.00
Box (24):	35.00

1 Darin Erstad .20
2 Mo Vaughn .20
3 Ramon Ortiz .10
4 Garret Anderson .25
5 Troy Glaus .40
6 Troy Percival .10
7 Tim Salmon .20
8 Wilmy Caceres, Elpidio Guzman .10
9 2001 Anaheim Angels .10
10 Jason Giambi .50
11 Mark Mulder .25
12 Jermaine Dye .10
13 Miguel Tejada .40
14 Tim Hudson .25
15 Eric Chavez .25
16 Barry Zito .10
17 Oscar Salazar, Juan Pena .10
18 2001 Oakland Athletics .10
19 Carlos Delgado .40
20 Raul Mondesi .15
21 Chris Carpenter .10
22 Jose Cruz Jr. .10
23 Alex Gonzalez .10
24 Brad Fullmer .10
25 Shannon Stewart .10
26 Brandon Lyon, Vernon Wells .10
27 2001 Toronto Blue Jays .10
28 Greg Vaughn .10
29 Toby Hall .10
30 Ben Grieve .10
31 Aubrey Huff .10
32 Tanyon Sturtze .10
33 Brent Abernathy .10
34 Dewon Brazelton, Delvin James .10
35 2001 Tampa Bay Devil Rays .10
36 Roberto Alomar .10
37 Juan Gonzalez .25
38 Bartolo Colon .10
39 C.C. Sabathia .10
40 Jim Thome .25
41 Omar Vizquel .10

#	Player	Price
42	Russell Branyan	.10
43	Ryan Drese, Roy Smith	.10
44	2001 Cleveland Indians	.10
45	Edgar Martinez	.20
46	Bret Boone	.20
47	Freddy Garcia	.10
48	John Olerud	.25
49	Kazuhiro Sasaki	.10
50	Ichiro Suzuki	1.50
51	Mike Cameron	.10
52	Rafael Soriano, Dennis Stark	.10
53	2001 Seattle Mariners	.10
54	Tony Batista	.10
55	Jeff Conine	.10
56	Jason Johnson	.10
57	Jay Gibbons	.10
58	Chris Richard	.10
59	Josh Towers	.10
60	Jerry Hairston Jr.	.10
61	Sean Douglass, Tim Raines Jr.	.10
62	2001 Baltimore Orioles	.10
63	Alex Rodriguez	1.50
64	Ruben Sierra	.10
65	Ivan Rodriguez	.50
66	Gabe Kapler	.20
67	Rafael Palmeiro	.50
68	Frank Catalanotto	.10
69	Mark Teixeira, Carlos Pena	.40
70	2001 Texas Rangers	.10
71	Nomar Garciaparra	1.00
72	Pedro Martinez	.75
73	Trot Nixon	.10
74	Dante Bichette	.10
75	Manny Ramirez	.50
76	Carl Everett	.10
77	Hideo Nomo	.40
78	Dernell Stenson, Juan Diaz	.10
79	2001 Boston Red Sox	.10
80	Mike Sweeney	.10
81	Carlos Febles	.10
82	Dee Brown	.10
83	Neifi Perez	.10
84	Mark Quinn	.10
85	Carlos Beltran	.25
86	Joe Randa	.10
87	Ken Harvey, Mike MacDougal	.10
88	2001 Kansas City Royals	.10
89	Dean Palmer	.10
90	Jeff Weaver	.10
91	Jose Lima	.10
92	Tony Clark	.10
93	Damion Easley	.10
94	Bobby Higginson	.10
95	Robert Fick	.10
96	Pedro Santana, Mike Rivera	.10
97	2001 Detroit Tigers	.10
98	Doug Mientkiewicz	.10
99	David Ortiz	.25
100	Joe Mays	.10
101	Corey Koskie	.10
102	Eric Milton	.10
103	Cristian Guzman	.10
104	Brad Radke	.10
105	Adam Johnson, Juan Rincon	.10
106	2001 Minnesota Twins	.10
107	Frank Thomas	.50
108	Carlos Lee	.10
109	Mark Buehrle	.10
110	Jose Canseco	.25
111	Magglio Ordonez	.25
112	Jon Garland	.10
113	Ray Durham	.10
114	Joe Crede, Josh Fogg	.10
115	2001 Chicago White Sox	.10
116	Derek Jeter	2.00
117	Roger Clemens	1.50
118	Alfonso Soriano	.75
119	Paul O'Neill	.25
120	Jorge Posada	.25
121	Bernie Williams	.40
122	Mariano Rivera	.25
123	Tino Martinez	.20
124	Mike Mussina	.50
125	Nick Johnson, Erick Almonte	.10
126	2001 New York Yankees	.10
127	Jeff Bagwell	.50
128	Wade Miller	.10
129	Lance Berkman	.25
130	Moises Alou	.25
131	Craig Biggio	.20
132	Roy Oswalt	.20
133	Richard Hidalgo	.15
134	Morgan Ensberg, Tim Redding	.10
135	2001 Houston Astros	.10
136	Greg Maddux	1.00
137	Chipper Jones	.75
138	Brian Jordan	.10
139	Marcus Giles	.10
140	Andruw Jones	.40
141	Tom Glavine	.40
142	Rafael Furcal	.25
143	Wilson Betemit, Horacio Ramirez	.10
144	2001 Atlanta Braves	.10
145	Jeromy Burnitz	.10
146	Ben Sheets	.25
147	Geoff Jenkins	.20
148	Devon White	.10
149	Jimmy Haynes	.10
150	Richie Sexson	.40
151	Jose Hernandez	.10
152	Jose Mieses, Alex Sanchez	.10
153	2001 Milwaukee Brewers	.10
154	Mark McGwire	2.00
155	Albert Pujols	1.50
156	Matt Morris	.20
157	J.D. Drew	.25
158	Jim Edmonds	.25
159	Bud Smith	.10
160	Darryl Kile	.10
161	William Ortega, Luis Saturria	.10
162	2001 St. Louis Cardinals	.10
163	Sammy Sosa	1.00
164	Jon Lieber	.10
165	Eric Young	.10
166	Kerry Wood	.10
167	Fred McGriff	.25
168	Corey Patterson	.25
169	Rondell White	.15
170	Juan Cruz, Mark Prior	1.00
171	2001 Chicago Cubs	.10
172	Luis Gonzalez	.25
173	Randy Johnson	.75
174	Matt Williams	.20
175	Mark Grace	.25
176	Steve Finley	.10
177	Reggie Sanders	.10
178	Curt Schilling	.40
179	Alex Cintron, Jack Cust	.10
180	2001 Arizona Diamondbacks	.10
181	Gary Sheffield	.25
182	Paul LoDuca	.25
183	Chan Ho Park	.10
184	Shawn Green	.25
185	Eric Karros	.15
186	Adrian Beltre	.25
187	Kevin Brown	.25
188	Ricardo Rodriguez, Carlos Garcia	.10
189	2001 Los Angeles Dodgers	.10
190	Vladimir Guerrero	.75
191	Javier Vazquez	.10
192	Jose Vidro	.10
193	Fernando Tatis	.10
194	Orlando Cabrera	.10
195	Lee Stevens	.10
196	Tony Armas Jr.	.10
197	Donnie Bridges, Henry Mateo	.10
198	2001 Montreal Expos	.10
199	Barry Bonds	2.00
200	Rich Aurilia	.10
201	Russ Ortiz	.10
202	Jeff Kent	.20
203	Jason Schmidt	.25
204	John Vander Wal	.10
205	Robb Nen	.10
206	Yorvit Torrealba, Kurt Ainsworth	.10
207	2001 San Francisco Giants	.10
208	Preston Wilson	.10
209	Brad Penny	.10
210	Cliff Floyd	.10
211	Luis Castillo	.10
212	Ryan Dempster	.10
213	Charles Johnson	.10
214	A.J. Burnett	.10
215	Abraham Nunez, Josh Beckett	.20
216	2001 Florida Marlins	.10
217	Mike Piazza	1.00
218	Al Leiter	.20
219	Edgardo Alfonzo	.10
220	Tsuyoshi Shinjo	.10
221	Matt Lawton	.10
222	Robin Ventura	.15
223	Jay Payton	.10
224	Alex Escobar, Jae Weong Seo	.10
225	2001 New York Mets	.10
226	Ryan Klesko	.20
227	D'Angelo Jimenez	.10
228	Trevor Hoffman	.10
229	Phil Nevin	.10
230	Mark Kotsay	.10
231	Brian Lawrence	.10
232	Bubba Trammell	.10
233	Jason Middlebrook, Xavier Nady	.10
234	2001 San Diego Padres	.10
235	Scott Rolen	.75
236	Jimmy Rollins	.10
237	Mike Lieberthal	.10
238	Bobby Abreu	.25
239	Brandon Duckworth	.10
240	Robert Person	.10
241	Pat Burrell	.20
242	Nick Punto, Carlos Silva	.10
243	2001 Philadelphia Phillies	.10
244	Brian Giles	.20
245	Jack Wilson	.10
246	Kris Benson	.10
247	Jason Kendall	.10
248	Aramis Ramirez	.25
249	Todd Ritchie	.10
250	Robert Mackowiak	.10
251	John Grabow, Humberto Cota	.10
252	2001 Pittsburgh Pirates	.10
253	Ken Griffey Jr.	1.00
254	Barry Larkin	.25
255	Sean Casey	.25
256	Aaron Boone	.10
257	Dmitri Young	.10
258	Pokey Reese	.10
259	Adam Dunn	.50
260	David Espinosa, Dane Sardinha	.10
261	2001 Cincinnati Reds	.10
262	Todd Helton	.50
263	Mike Hampton	.10
264	Juan Pierre	.10
265	Larry Walker	.25
266	Juan Uribe	.10
267	Jose Ortiz	.10
268	Jeff Cirillo	.10
269	Jason Jennings, Luke Hudson	.10
270	2001 Colorado Rockies	.10
271	Ichiro Suzuki, Jason Giambi, Roberto Alomar (League Leaders)	.75
272	Larry Walker, Todd Helton, Moises Alou (League Leaders)	.10
273	Alex Rodriguez, Jim Thome, Rafael Palmeiro (League Leaders)	.75
274a	Barry Bonds, Sammy Sosa, Juan Gonzalez (League Leaders) (No player names.)	1.00
274b	Barry Bonds, Sammy Sosa, Juan Gonzalez (League Leaders) (Player names added.)	3.00
275	Roger Clemens, Mark Mulder, Jamie Moyer (League Leaders)	.50
276	Curt Schilling, Matt Morris, Randy Johnson (League Leaders)	.10
277	Freddy Garcia, Mike Mussina, Joe Mays (League Leaders)	.10
278	Randy Johnson, Curt Schilling, John Burkett (League Leaders)	.10
279	Mariano Rivera, Kazuhiro Sasaki, Keith Foulke (League Leaders)	.10
280	Robb Nen, Armando Benitez, Trevor Hoffman (League Leaders)	.10
281	Jason Giambi	.25
282	Jorge Posada	.15
283	Jim Thome	.25
284	Edgar Martinez	.10
285	Andruw Jones	.20
286	Chipper Jones	.50
287	Matt Williams	.10
288	Curt Schilling	.20
289	Derek Jeter	1.00
290	Mike Mussina	.25
291	Bret Boone	.10
292	Alfonso Soriano	.40
293	Randy Johnson	.25
294	Tom Glavine	.10
295	Curt Schilling	.20
296	Randy Johnson	.40
297	Derek Jeter	1.00
298	Tino Martinez	.10
299	Curt Schilling	.20
300	Luis Gonzalez	.20

Day at the Park

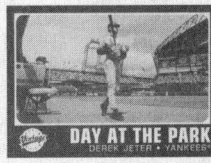

		NM/M
Complete Set (6):		15.00
Inserted 1:23		
DP1	Ichiro Suzuki	3.00
DP2	Derek Jeter	5.00
DP3	Alex Rodriguez	4.00
DP4	Mark McGwire	4.00
DP5	Barry Bonds	5.00
DP6	Sammy Sosa	3.00

Night-Gamers

		NM/M
Complete Set (12):		10.00
Common Player:		.50
Inserted 1:11		
NG1	Todd Helton	.75
NG2	Manny Ramirez	.75
NG3	Ivan Rodriguez	.50
NG4	Albert Pujols	2.50
NG5	Greg Maddux	1.50
NG6	Carlos Delgado	.50
NG7	Frank Thomas	.75
NG8	Derek Jeter	3.00
NG9	Troy Glaus	.50
NG10	Jeff Bagwell	.75
NG11	Juan Gonzalez	.75
NG12	Randy Johnson	1.00

Sandlot Stars

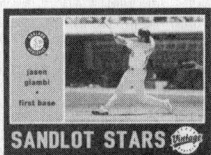

		NM/M
Complete Set (12):		15.00
Common Player:		.75
Inserted 1:11		
SS1	Ken Griffey Jr.	1.50
SS2	Derek Jeter	3.00
SS3	Ichiro Suzuki	2.00
SS4	Nomar Garciaparra	2.00
SS5	Sammy Sosa	2.00
SS6	Chipper Jones	1.00
SS7	Jason Giambi	.75
SS8	Alex Rodriguez	2.50
SS9	Mark McGwire	2.50
SS10	Barry Bonds	3.00
SS11	Mike Piazza	2.00
SS12	Vladimir Guerrero	1.00

Special Collection Jerseys

		NM/M
Common Player:		8.00
Inserted 1:144		
StB	Stan Bahnsen	8.00
SaB	Sal Bando	10.00
BC	Bert Campaneris	10.00
AD	Andre Dawson	15.00
RF	Rollie Fingers	15.00
MG	Mark Grace	15.00
MH	Mike Hegan	8.00
CH	"Catfish" Hunter	20.00
RJ	Reggie Jackson	15.00
FJ	Ferguson Jenkins	15.00
PL	Paul Linblad	8.00
JR	Joe Rudi	10.00
RS	Ryne Sandberg	50.00
SS	Sammy Sosa	25.00
BW	Billy Williams	10.00

Timeless Teams Bat

		NM/M
Inserted 1:288		
SEA	Ichiro Suzuki, Edgar Martinez, John Olerud, Bret Boone	75.00
NYY	Mariano Rivera, Bernie Williams, Paul O'Neill, Jorge Posada	40.00
ATL	Tom Glavine, Greg Maddux, Chipper Jones, Andruw Jones	40.00
CLE	Juan Gonzalez, Jim Thome, Roberto Alomar, Kenny Lofton	30.00
OAK	Jose Canseco, Ricky Henderson, Dave Parker, Don Baylor	30.00
OF	Mickey Mantle, Joe DiMaggio, Reggie Jackson, Babe Ruth	300.00
1B	Willie McCovey, Frank Thomas, Hank Greenberg, Eddie Murray	30.00
OF	Ken Griffey Jr., Barry Bonds, Ricky Henderson, Tony Gwynn	50.00

Timeless Teams Combos

		NM/M
Inserted 1:288		
NYY00	Roger Clemens, Mariano Rivera, Bernie Williams	40.00
ATL96	Greg Maddux, Chipper Jones, Andruw Jones	40.00
OAK74	Rollie Fingers, Jim "Catfish" Hunter, Reggie Jackson	40.00
HOF36	Ty Cobb, Babe Ruth, Honus Wagner (Pants)	1,500

Timeless Teams Jerseys

		NM/M
Common Player:		10.00
Inserted 1:144		
JB	Johnny Bench	20.00
DE	Dwight Evans	15.00
RF	Rollie Fingers	15.00
CH	"Catfish" Hunter	15.00
RJ	Reggie Jackson	15.00
AJ	Andruw Jones	15.00
CJ	Chipper Jones	15.00
FL	Fred Lynn	15.00
EMa	Edgar Martinez	15.00
WM	Willie McCovey	15.00
EMu	Eddie Murray	15.00
KS	Kazuhiro Sasaki	10.00

Vintage Aces Jerseys

		NM/M
Common Player:		8.00
Inserted 1:144		
JD	John Denny	8.00
TH	Tim Hudson	10.00
FJ	Ferguson Jenkins	10.00
RJ	Randy Johnson	20.00
GM	Greg Maddux	25.00
JM	Juan Marichal	15.00
MMa	Mike Marshall	8.00
PM	Pedro Martinez	20.00
MMu	Mike Mussina	25.00
HN	Hideo Nomo	20.00
NR	Nolan Ryan	100.00
JS	Johnny Sain	20.00
MT	Mike Torrez	8.00

Vintage Signature Combos

		NM/M
Production 100 Sets		
FB	Carlton Fisk, Johnny Bench	100.00
JM	Reggie Jackson, Willie McCovey	80.00
SD	Ryne Sandberg, Andre Dawson	100.00
BR	Sal Bando, Joe Rudi	40.00
EL	Fred Lynn, Dwight Evans	60.00
AT	Roberto Alomar, Jim Thome	75.00
BB	Yogi Berra, Johnny Bench	100.00
GR	Ken Griffey Jr., Alex Rodriguez	300.00
JO	Edgar Martinez, John Olerud	60.00

2002 Upper Deck World Series Heroes

		NM/M
Complete Set (180):		20.00
Common Player:		.15
Common RC (91-135):		1.50
Common (136-180):		1.00
Inserted 1:10		
Pack (5):		.75
Box (24):		40.00
1	Jim "Catfish" Hunter	.15
2	Jimmie Foxx	.50
3	Mark McGwire	2.00
4	Rollie Fingers	.25
5	Rickey Henderson	.40
6	Joe Carter	.15
7	John Olerud	.15
8	Roberto Alomar	.50
9	Pat Hentgen	.15
10	Devon White	.15
11	Eddie Mathews	.50
12	Greg Maddux	1.00
13	Chipper Jones	.75
14	Tom Glavine	.25
15	Andruw Jones	.50
16	David Justice	.25
17	Fred McGriff	.15
18	Ryan Klesko	.15
19	John Smoltz	.25
20	Javy Lopez	.25
21	Marquis Grissom	.15
22	Robin Yount	.75
23	Ozzie Smith	.50
24	Frankie Frisch	.15
25	Stan Musial	1.00
26	Randy Johnson	.75
27	Luis Gonzalez	.25
28	Matt Williams	.15
29	Steve Finley	.15
30	Sandy Koufax	1.50
31	Duke Snider	.50
32	Kirk Gibson	.15
33	Steve Garvey	.15
34	Jackie Robinson	1.50
35	Don Drysdale	.50
36	Juan Marichal	.50
37	Mel Ott	.50
38	Orlando Cepeda	.15
39	Jim Thome	.75
40	Manny Ramirez	.50
41	Omar Vizquel	.15
42	Lou Boudreau	.15
43	Gary Sheffield	.25
44	Moises Alou	.15
45	Livan Hernandez	.15
46	Edgar Renteria	.15
47	Al Leiter	.15
48	Tom Seaver	.75
49	Gary Carter	.15
50	Mike Piazza	1.00
51	Nolan Ryan	2.00
52	Robin Ventura	.15
53	Mike Hampton	.15
54	Jesse Orosco	.15
55	Cal Ripken Jr.	2.00
56	Brooks Robinson	.75
57	Tony Gwynn	.75
58	Kevin Brown	.15
59	Curt Schilling	.50
60	Cy Young	.50
61	Honus Wagner	.75
62	Willie Stargell	.40
63	Wade Boggs	.40
64	Carlton Fisk	.40
65	Ken Griffey Sr.	.15
66	Joe Morgan	.15
67	Johnny Bench	1.00
68	Barry Larkin	.40
69	Jose Rijo	.15
70	Ty Cobb	1.50
71	Kirby Puckett	1.00
72	Chuck Knoblauch	.15
73	Harmon Killebrew	.50
74	Mickey Mantle	2.50
75	Joe DiMaggio	2.00
76	Don Larsen	.40
77	Thurman Munson	.75
78	Roger Maris	1.50
79	Phil Rizzuto	.50
80	Babe Ruth	2.50
81	Lou Gehrig	2.00
82	Billy Martin	.40
83	Derek Jeter	2.00
84	Roger Clemens	1.50
85	Tino Martinez	.15
86	Bernie Williams	.50
87	Andy Pettitte	.40
88	Mariano Rivera	.25
89	David Wells	.15
90	Jorge Posada	.25
91	Rodrigo Rosario RC	1.50
92	Brandon Puffer RC	1.50
93	Franklyn German RC	1.50
94	Reed Johnson RC	2.50
95	Chris Baker RC	1.50
96	John Ennis RC	1.50
97	Luis Martinez RC	1.50
98	Takaki Nomura RC	1.50
99	So Taguchi RC	1.50
100	Michael Crudale RC	1.50
101	Francis Beltran RC	1.50
102	Steve Kent RC	1.50
103	Jorge Sosa RC	1.50
104	Felix Escalona RC	1.50
105	Jose Valverde RC	2.50
106	Doug DeVore RC	1.50
107	Kazuhisa Ishii RC	1.50
108	Victor Alvarez RC	1.50
109	Eric Good RC	1.50
110	Jorge Nunez RC	1.50
111	Ron Calloway RC	1.50
112	Nelson Castro RC	1.50
113	Matt Thornton RC	1.50
114	Luis Ugueto RC	1.50
115	Hansel Izquierdo RC	1.50
116	Jaime Cerda RC	1.50
117	Mark Corey RC	1.50
118	Tyler Yates RC	1.50
119	Satoru Komiyama RC	1.50
120	Steve Bechler RC	1.50
121	Ben Howard RC	1.50
122	Anderson Machado RC	1.50
123	Jorge Padilla RC	1.50
124	Eric Junge RC	1.50
125	Adrian Burnside RC	1.50
126	Mike Gonzalez RC	1.50
127	Anastacio Martinez RC	1.50
128	Josh Hancock RC	1.50
129	Rene Reyes RC	1.50
130	Aaron Cook RC	1.50
131	Cam Esslinger RC	1.50
132	Juan Brito RC	1.50
133	Miguel Ascencio RC	1.50
134	Kevin Frederick RC	1.50
135	Edwin Almonte RC	1.50
136	Troy Glaus	1.00
137	Darin Erstad	.50
138	Jeff Bagwell	1.50
139	Lance Berkman	1.50
140	Tim Hudson	1.25
141	Eric Chavez	1.25
142	Barry Zito	1.50

143	Carlos Delgado	1.00
144	Richie Sexson	1.50
145	Albert Pujols	4.00
146	Sammy Sosa	4.00
147	Kerry Wood	2.00
148	Greg Vaughn	1.00
149	Shawn Green	1.00
150	Vladimir Guerrero	2.50
151	Barry Bonds	6.00
152	C.C. Sabathia	1.00
153	Ichiro Suzuki	5.00
154	Freddy Garcia	1.00
155	Edgar Martinez	1.00
156	Josh Beckett	1.00
157	Cliff Floyd	1.00
158	Mo Vaughn	1.00
159	Jeromy Burnitz	1.00
160	Sean Burroughs	1.00
161	Phil Nevin	1.00
162	Scott Rolen	2.00
163	Brian Giles	1.25
164	Alex Rodriguez	5.00
165	Ivan Rodriguez	1.50
166	Juan Gonzalez	1.25
167	Rafael Palmeiro	1.50
168	Nomar Garciaparra	4.00
169	Pedro J. Martinez	2.00
170	Ken Griffey Jr.	4.00
171	Adam Dunn	1.50
172	Todd Helton	1.50
173	Mike Sweeney	1.00
174	Carlos Beltran	1.00
175	Dmitri Young	1.00
176	Doug Mientkiewicz	1.00
177	Torii Hunter	1.00
178	Frank Thomas	1.50
179	Magglio Ordonez	1.00
180	Jason Giambi	1.50

Base
NM/M

Complete Set (1):
DJ	Derek Jeter	35.00

Bats
NM/M

Common Player: 15.00
Inserted 1:288
JD	Joe DiMaggio/SP	100.00
MM	Mickey Mantle	125.00
KP	Kirby Puckett	25.00
ES	Enos Slaughter	15.00

Jerseys
NM/M

Common Player: 10.00
Inserted 1:288
JC	Joe Carter	10.00
CF	Carlton Fisk	15.00
DL	Don Larsen	20.00
BM	Bill Mazeroski	15.00

Jerseys Autograph
No Pricing
Production 25 Sets

Matchups Memorabilia

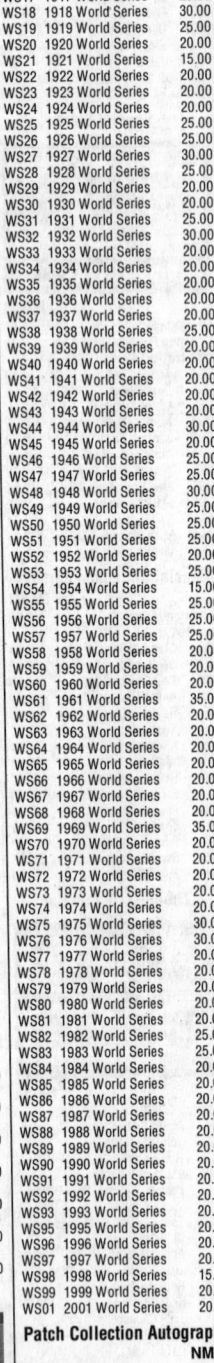

NM/M

Common Card: 8.00
Inserted 1:24
MU00	Mike Piazza, Roger Clemens	15.00
MU00a	Andy Pettitte, Mike Piazza	15.00
MU00b	Al Leiter, Derek Jeter	10.00
MU00d	Edgardo Alfonzo, Mariano Rivera	8.00
MU00e	John Franco, Derek Jeter	10.00
MU00c	Robin Ventura, Roger Clemens	8.00
MU01	Mariano Rivera, Luis Gonzalez	8.00
MU01a	Paul O'Neill, Curt Schilling	8.00
MU01b	Bernie Williams, Randy Johnson	8.00
MU01c	David Justice, Curt Schilling	8.00
MU01d	Randy Johnson, Bernie Williams	8.00
MU01e	Curt Schilling, Tino Martinez	8.00
MU01f	Roger Clemens, Luis Gonzalez	15.00
MU01g	Paul O'Neill, Byung-Hyun Kim	10.00
MU01h	Luis Gonzalez, Mariano Rivera/97	12.00
MU03	Honus Wagner, Cy Young	100.00
MU09	Ty Cobb, Honus Wagner/SP	125.00
MU30	Jimmie Foxx	25.00
MU36	Joe DiMaggio, Mel Ott/SP	80.00

MU49	Duke Snider, Joe DiMaggio	25.00
MU53	Jackie Robinson, Billy Martin	25.00
MU55	Mickey Mantle, Jackie Robinson	110.00
MU56	Don Larsen, Duke Snider	25.00
MU56a	Don Larsen, Jackie Robinson	20.00
MU57	Eddie Mathews, Yogi Berra	15.00
MU58	Yogi Berra, Eddie Mathews	15.00
MU62	Roger Maris, Juan Marichal	40.00
MU63	Sandy Koufax, Mickey Mantle	100.00
MU66	Don Drysdale, Brooks Robinson/SP	40.00
MU69	Nolan Ryan, Brooks Robinson	50.00
MU72	Joe Morgan, Jim "Catfish" Hunter	8.00
MU72a	Rollie Fingers, Johnny Bench	10.00
MU73	Tom Seaver, "Catfish" Hunter	15.00
MU74	Jim "Catfish" Hunter, Steve Garvey	8.00
MU74a	Davey Lopes, Jim "Catfish" Hunter	8.00
MU76	Ken Griffey Sr., Thurman Munson	12.00
MU76a	Thurman Munson, Johnny Bench	20.00
MU78	Thurman Munson, Steve Garvey	15.00
MU78a	Bill Russell, Thurman Munson	12.00
MU81	Steve Garvey, Dave Winfield	8.00
MU82	Robin Yount, Ozzie Smith	15.00
MU83	Cal Ripken Jr., Joe Morgan	25.00
MU84	Jack Morris, Tony Gwynn	12.00
MU86	Jesse Orosco, Roger Clemens	15.00
MU87	Ozzie Smith, Kirby Puckett	15.00
MU88	Mark McGwire, Kirk Gibson/SP	60.00
MU90	Barry Larkin, Mark McGwire/SP	20.00
MU91	Tom Glavine, Kirby Puckett	15.00
MU93	Joe Carter, Curt Schilling	8.00
MU95	Dennis Martinez, David Justice	8.00
MU96	Andruw Jones, Andy Pettitte	8.00
MU96a	Tim Raines, Tom Glavine	10.00
MU96b	Kenny Rogers, Chipper Jones	8.00
MU95a	Kenny Lofton, John Smoltz	8.00
MU97	Jim Thome, Kevin Brown	10.00
MU98	Tony Gwynn, Bernie Williams	10.00
MU98a	Trevor Hoffman, Bernie Williams/SP	8.00
MU99	Jorge Posada, Greg Maddux	15.00
MU99a	Greg Maddux, Derek Jeter	15.00
MU99b	Paul O'Neill, John Smoltz	8.00
MU99c	Chipper Jones, Mariano Rivera	15.00

Patch Collection

NM/M

Common Patch: 15.00
Inserted 1:Hobby Box
WS03	1903 World Series	25.00
WS05	1905 World Series	25.00
WS06	1906 World Series	20.00
WS07	1907 World Series	20.00
WS08	1908 World Series	25.00
WS09	1909 World Series	20.00
WS10	1910 World Series	20.00
WS11	1911 World Series	20.00
WS12	1912 World Series	30.00
WS13	1913 World Series	20.00
WS14	1914 World Series	25.00
WS15	1915 World Series	20.00
WS16	1916 World Series	25.00
WS17	1917 World Series	20.00
WS18	1918 World Series	30.00
WS19	1919 World Series	25.00
WS20	1920 World Series	20.00
WS21	1921 World Series	15.00
WS22	1922 World Series	20.00
WS23	1923 World Series	20.00
WS24	1924 World Series	25.00
WS25	1925 World Series	20.00
WS26	1926 World Series	25.00
WS27	1927 World Series	30.00
WS28	1928 World Series	25.00
WS29	1929 World Series	20.00
WS30	1930 World Series	20.00
WS31	1931 World Series	25.00
WS32	1932 World Series	30.00
WS33	1933 World Series	20.00
WS34	1934 World Series	20.00
WS35	1935 World Series	20.00
WS36	1936 World Series	20.00
WS37	1937 World Series	20.00
WS38	1938 World Series	20.00
WS39	1939 World Series	20.00
WS40	1940 World Series	20.00
WS41	1941 World Series	20.00
WS42	1942 World Series	20.00
WS43	1943 World Series	20.00
WS44	1944 World Series	30.00
WS45	1945 World Series	20.00
WS46	1946 World Series	20.00
WS47	1947 World Series	25.00
WS48	1948 World Series	30.00
WS49	1949 World Series	25.00
WS50	1950 World Series	25.00
WS51	1951 World Series	25.00
WS52	1952 World Series	25.00
WS53	1953 World Series	25.00
WS54	1954 World Series	15.00
WS55	1955 World Series	25.00
WS56	1956 World Series	25.00
WS57	1957 World Series	25.00
WS58	1958 World Series	20.00
WS59	1959 World Series	20.00
WS60	1960 World Series	20.00
WS61	1961 World Series	35.00
WS62	1962 World Series	20.00
WS63	1963 World Series	20.00
WS64	1964 World Series	20.00
WS65	1965 World Series	20.00
WS66	1966 World Series	20.00
WS67	1967 World Series	20.00
WS68	1968 World Series	20.00
WS69	1969 World Series	35.00
WS70	1970 World Series	20.00
WS71	1971 World Series	20.00
WS72	1972 World Series	20.00
WS73	1973 World Series	20.00
WS74	1974 World Series	20.00
WS75	1975 World Series	30.00
WS76	1976 World Series	20.00
WS77	1977 World Series	20.00
WS78	1978 World Series	20.00
WS79	1979 World Series	20.00
WS80	1980 World Series	20.00
WS81	1981 World Series	20.00
WS82	1982 World Series	25.00
WS83	1983 World Series	25.00
WS84	1984 World Series	20.00
WS85	1985 World Series	20.00
WS86	1986 World Series	20.00
WS87	1987 World Series	20.00
WS88	1988 World Series	20.00
WS89	1989 World Series	20.00
WS90	1990 World Series	20.00
WS91	1991 World Series	20.00
WS92	1992 World Series	20.00
WS93	1993 World Series	20.00
WS95	1995 World Series	20.00
WS96	1996 World Series	20.00
WS97	1997 World Series	15.00
WS98	1998 World Series	20.00
WS99	1999 World Series	20.00
WS01	2001 World Series	20.00

Patch Collection Autographs
NM/M

Inserted 1:336
WS93	Joe Carter	40.00
WS99	Roger Clemens	100.00
WS74	Rollie Fingers	30.00
WS75	Carlton Fisk	60.00
WS81	Steve Garvey	35.00
WS65	Sandy Koufax	250.00
WS56	Don Larsen	60.00
WS89	Mark McGwire	275.00
WS76	Joe Morgan	40.00
WS91	Kirby Puckett	60.00
WS83	Cal Ripken Jr.	175.00
WS70	Brooks Robinson	80.00
WS69	Nolan Ryan	200.00
WS73	Tom Seaver	60.00
WS55	Duke Snider	75.00
WS82	Ozzie Smith	90.00

2002 Upper Deck 40-Man
NM/M

Complete Set (1182): 250.00
Common Player: .15
Silvers: 1-30X
Inserted 1:4
Rainbows: 5-10X
Production 40 Sets
Hobby Pack (10): 1.75
Hobby Box (24): 30.00

1	Darin Erstad	.40
2	Kevin Appier	.15
3	Scott Schoeneweis	.15
4	Bengie Molina	.15
5	Troy Glaus	.50
6	Adam Kennedy	.15
7	Aaron Sele	.15
8	Garret Anderson	.25
9	Ramon Ortiz	.15
10	Dennis Cook	.15
11	Scott Spiezio	.15
12	Orlando Palmeiro	.15
13	Troy Percival	.15
14	David Eckstein	.15
15	Jarrod Washburn	.40
16	Nathan Haynes	.15
17	Benji Gil	.15
18	Alfredo Amezaga	.15
19	Ben Weber	.15
20	Al Levine	.15
21	Brad Fullmer	.15
22	Elpidio Guzman	.15
23	Tim Salmon	.25
24	Jose Nieves	.15
25	Shawn Wooten	.15
26	Lou Pote	.15
27	Mickey Callaway	.15
28	Steve Green	.15
29	John Lackey	.15
30	Mark Lukasiewicz	.15
31	Jorge Fabregas	.15
32	Jeff Da Vanon	.15
33	Elvin Nina	.15
34	Donne Wall	.15
35	Eric Chavez	.50
36	Jermaine Dye	.15
37	Scott Hatteberg	.15
38	Mark Mulder	.50
39	Ramon Hernandez	.15
40	Jim Mecir	.15
41	Barry Zito	.50
42	Greg Myers	.15
43	David Justice	.50
44	Mike Magnante	.15
45	Terrence Long	.15
46	Tim Hudson	.50
47	Olmedo Saenz	.15
48	Billy Koch	.15
49	Carlos Pena	.50
50	Mike Venafro	.15
51	Mark Ellis	.15
52	Randy Velarde	.15
53	Jeremy Giambi	.15
54	Mike Colangelo	.15
55	Mike Holtz	.15
56	Chad Bradford	.15
57	Miguel Tejada	.50
58	Mike Fyhrie	.15
59	Eric Hiljus	.15
60	Juan Pena	.15
61	Mario Valdez	.15
62	Franklyn German RC	.50
63	Carlos Delgado	.50
64	Orlando Hudson	.50
65	Chris Carpenter	.15
66	Kelvim Escobar	.15
67	Felipe Lopez	.15
68	Brandon Lyon	.15
69	Jose Cruz Jr.	.15
70	Luke Prokopec	.15
71	Darrin Fletcher	.15
72	Bob File	.15
73	Felix Heredia	.15
74	Mike Sirotka	.15
75	Shannon Stewart	.15
76	Joe Lawrence	.15
77	Chris Woodward	.15
78	Dan Plesac	.15
79	Pedro Borbon	.15
80	Roy Halladay	.40
81	Raul Mondesi	.40
82	Steve Parris	.15
83	Homer Bush	.15
84	Esteban Loaiza	.15
85	Vernon Wells	.15
86	Justin Miller	.15
87	Scott Eyre	.15
88	Dave Berg	.15
89	Gustavo Chacin RC	.15
90	Joe Orloski RC	.15
91	Corey Thurman RC	.15
92	Tom Wilson	.15
93	Eric Hinske	.50
94	Chris Baker RC	.40
95	Reed Johnson RC	.40
96	Greg Vaughn	.15
97	Toby Hall	.15
98	Brent Abernathy	.15

99	Bobby Smith	.15
100	Tanyon Sturtze	.15
101	Chris Gomez	.15
102	Joe Kennedy	.15
103	Ben Grieve	.15
104	Aubrey Huff	.15
105	Jesus Colome	.15
106	Felix Escalona RC	.40
107	Paul Wilson	.15
108	Ryan Rupe	.15
109	Jason Tyner	.15
110	Esteban Yan	.15
111	Russ Johnson	.15
112	Randy Winn	.15
113	Wilson Alvarez	.15
114	Wilmy Caceres	.15
115	Steve Cox	.15
116	Dewon Brazelton	.15
117	Doug Creek	.15
118	Jason Conti	.15
119	John Flaherty	.15
120	Delvin James	.15
121	Steve Kent RC	.15
122	Kevin McGlinchy	.15
123	Travis Phelps	.15
124	Bobby Seay	.15
125	Travis Harper	.15
126	Victor Zambrano	.15
127	Jace Brewer	.15
128	Jason Smith	.15
129	Ramon Soler	.15
130	Brandon Backe RC	.50
131	Jorge Sosa RC	.25
132	Jim Thome	.75
133	Brady Anderson	.15
134	C.C. Sabathia	.15
135	Einar Diaz	.15
136	Ricky Gutierrez	.15
137	Danys Baez	.15
138	Bob Wickman	.15
139	Milton Bradley	.15
140	Bartolo Colon	.40
141	Jolbert Cabrera	.15
142	Eddie Taubensee	.15
143	Ellis Burks	.15
144	Omar Vizquel	.40
145	Eddie Perez	.15
146	Jaret Wright	.15
147	Chuck Finley	.15
148	Paul Shuey	.15
149	Travis Fryman	.15
150	Wil Cordero	.15
151	Ricardo Rincon	.15
152	Victor Martinez	.15
153	Charles Nagy	.15
154	Alex Escobar	.15
155	Russell Branyan	.15
156	Matt Lawton	.15
157	Ryan Drese	.15
158	Jerrod Riggan	.15
159	David Riske	.15
160	Jake Westbrook	.15
161	Mark Wohlers	.15
162	John McDonald	.15
163	Ichiro Suzuki	1.50
164	Freddy Garcia	.15
165	Edgar Martinez	.15
166	Ben Davis	.15
167	Shigetoshi Hasegawa	.15
168	Carlos Guillen	.15
169	Ruben Sierra	.15
170	Joel Pineiro	.15
171	Norm Charlton	.15
172	Bret Boone	.15
173	Jamie Moyer	.15
174	Jeff Nelson	.15
175	Kazuhiro Sasaki	.50
176	Jeff Cirillo	.15
177	Mark McLemore	.15
178	Paul Abbott	.15
179	Mike Cameron	.15
180	Dan Wilson	.15
181	John Olerud	.50
182	Arthur Rhodes	.15
183	Desi Relaford	.15
184	John Halama	.15
185	Antonio Perez	.15
186	Ryan Anderson	.15
187	James Baldwin	.15
188	Ryan Franklin	.15
189	Justin Kaye	.15
190	J.J. Putz RC	.40
191	Allan Simpson RC	.40
192	Matt Thornton	.15
193	Luis Ugueto RC	.40
194	Chris Richard	.15
195	Sidney Ponson	.15
196	Brook Fordyce	.15
197	Luis Matos	.15
198	Josh Towers	.15
199	David Segui	.15
200	Chris Brock	.15
201	Tony Batista	.15
202	Erik Bedard	.15
203	Marty Cordova	.15
204	Jerry Hairston Jr.	.15
205	Jason Johnson	.15
206	Buddy Groom	.15
207	Mike Bordick	.15
208	Melvin Mora	.15
209	Calvin Maduro	.15
210	Jeff Conine	.15
211	Luis Rivera	.15
212	Jay Gibbons	.15
213	B.J. Ryan	.15
214	Sean Douglass	.15
215	Rodrigo Lopez	.15
216	Rick Bauer	.15

217	Scott Erickson	.15
218	Jorge Julio	.15
219	Willis Roberts	.15
220	John Stephens	.15
221	Geronimo Gil	.15
222	Chris Singleton	.15
223	Mike Paradis	.15
224	John Parrish	.15
225	Steve Bechler RC	.50
226	Mike Moriarty RC	.15
227	Luis Garcia	.15
228	Alex Rodriguez	1.50
229	Mark Teixeira	.50
230	Chan Ho Park	.15
231	Todd Van Poppel	.15
232	Mike Young	.15
233	Kenny Rogers	.15
234	Rusty Greer	.15
235	Rafael Palmeiro	.50
236	Francisco Cordero	.15
237	John Rocker	.15
238	Dave Burba	.15
239	Travis Hafner	.15
240	Kevin Mench	.15
241	Carl Everett	.15
242	Ivan Rodriguez	.50
243	Jeff Zimmerman	.15
244	Juan Gonzalez	.50
245	Herbert Perry	.15
246	Rob Bell	.15
247	Doug Davis	.15
248	Frank Catalanotto	.15
249	Jay Powell	.15
250	Gabe Kapler	.15
251	Joaquin Benoit	.15
252	Jovanny Cedeno	.15
253	Hideki Irabu	.15
254	Dan Miceli	.15
255	Danny Kolb	.15
256	Colby Lewis	.15
257	Rich Rodriguez	.15
258	Ismael Valdes	.15
259	Bill Haselman	.15
260	Jason Hart	.15
261	Rudy Seanez	.15
262	Travis Hughes RC	.40
263	Hank Blalock	.50
264	Steve Woodard	.15
265	Nomar Garciaparra	1.50
266	Pedro J. Martinez	.75
267	Frank Castillo	.15
268	Johnny Damon	.15
269	Doug Mirabelli	.15
270	Derek Lowe	.40
271	Shea Hillenbrand	.50
272	Paxton Crawford	.15
273	Tony Clark	.15
274	Dustin Hermanson	.15
275	Trot Nixon	.15
276	John Burkett	.15
277	Rich Garces	.15
278	Josh Hancock RC	.15
279	Michael Coleman	.15
280	Darren Oliver	.15
281	Jason Varitek	.15
282	Jose Offerman	.15
283	Tim Wakefield	.15
284	Rolando Arrojo	.15
285	Rickey Henderson	.50
286	Ugueth Urbina	.15
287	Casey Fossum	.15
288	Manny Ramirez	.50
289	Sun-Woo Kim	.15
290	Juan Diaz	.15
291	Willie Banks	.15
292	Jorge De La Rosa RC	.75
293	Juan Pena	.15
294	Jeff Wallace	.15
295	Calvin Pickering	.15
296	Anastacio Martinez RC	.40
297	Carlos Baerga	.15
298	Rey Sanchez	.15
299	Mike Sweeney	.15
300	Jeff Suppan	.15
301	Brent Mayne	.15
302	Chad Durbin	.15
303	Dan Reichert	.15
304	Raul Ibanez	.15
305	Joe Randa	.15
306	Chris George	.15
307	Michael Tucker	.15
308	Paul Byrd	.15
309	Kris Wilson	.15
310	Luis Alicea	.15
311	Neifi Perez	.15
312	Brian Shouse	.15
313	Chuck Knoblauch	.15
314	Dave McCarty	.15
315	Blake Stein	.15
316	Alexis Gomez	.15
317	Mark Quinn	.15
318	A.J. Hinch	.15
319	Carlos Febles	.15
320	Roberto Hernandez	.15
321	Brandon Berger	.15
322	Jeff Austin RC	.40
323	Corey Bailey	.15
324	Tony Cogan	.15
325	Nate Field RC	.40
326	Jason Grimsley	.15
327	Darrell May	.15
328	Donnie Sadler	.15
329	Carlos Beltran	.15
330	Miguel Asencio RC	.15
331	Jeff Weaver	.15
332	Bobby Higginson	.15
333	Mike Rivera	.15
334	Matt Anderson	.15

No.	Player	Price
335	Craig Paquette	.15
336	Jose Lima	.15
337	Juan Acevedo	.15
338	Danny Patterson	.15
339	Andres Torres	.15
340	Dean Palmer	.15
341	Randall Simon	.15
342	Craig Monroe	.15
343	Damion Easley	.15
344	Robert Fick	.15
345	Steve Sparks	.15
346	Dmitri Young	.15
347	Nate Cornejo	.15
348	Matt Miller	.15
349	Wendell Magee	.15
350	Shane Halter	.15
351	Brian Moehler	.15
352	Mitch Meluskey	.15
353	Jose Macias	.15
354	Mark Redman	.15
355	Jeff Farnsworth	.15
356	Kris Keller	.15
357	Adam Pettyjohn	.15
358	Fernando Rodney	.15
359	Andy Van Hekken	.15
360	Damian Jackson	.15
361	Jose Paniagua	.15
362	Jacob Cruz	.15
363	Doug Mientkiewicz	.15
364	Torii Hunter	.15
365	Brad Radke	.15
366	Denny Hocking	.15
367	Mike Jackson	.15
368	Eddie Guardado	.15
369	Jacque Jones	.15
370	Joe Mays	.15
371	Matt Kinney	.15
372	Kyle Lohse	.15
373	David Ortiz	.15
374	Luis Rivas	.15
375	Jay Canizaro	.15
376	Dustan Mohr	.15
377	LaTroy Hawkins	.15
378	Warren Morris	.15
379	A.J. Pierzynski	.15
380	Eric Milton	.15
381	Bob Wells	.15
382	Cristian Guzman	.15
383	Brian Buchanan	.15
384	Bobby Kielty	.15
385	Corey Koskie	.15
386	J.C. Romero	.15
387	Jack Cressend	.15
388	Mike Duvall	.15
389	Tony Fiore	.15
390	Tom Prince	.15
391	Todd Sears	.15
392	Kevin Frederick RC	.40
393	Frank Thomas	.50
394	Mark Buehrle	.15
395	Jon Garland	.15
396	Jeff Liefer	.15
397	Magglio Ordonez	.50
398	Rocky Biddle	.15
399	Lorenzo Barcelo	.15
400	Ray Durham	.15
401	Bob Howry	.15
402	Aaron Rowand	.15
403	Keith Foulke	.15
404	Paul Konerko	.50
405	Sandy Alomar Jr.	.15
406	Mark Johnson	.15
407	Carlos Lee	.15
408	Jose Valentin	.15
409	Jon Rauch	.15
410	Royce Clayton	.15
411	Kenny Lofton	.40
412	Tony Graffanino	.15
413	Todd Ritchie	.15
414	Antonio Osuna	.15
415	Gary Glover	.15
416	Mike Porzio	.15
417	Danny Wright	.15
418	Kelly Wunsch	.15
419	Miguel Olivo	.15
420	Edwin Almonte RC	.15
421	Kyle Kane RC	.50
422	Mitch Wylie RC	.50
423	Derek Jeter	2.00
424	Jason Giambi	.50
425	Roger Clemens	1.50
426	Enrique Wilson	.15
427	David Wells	.15
428	Mike Mussina	.50
429	Bernie Williams	.50
430	Mike Stanton	.15
431	Sterling Hitchcock	.15
432	Alex Graman	.15
433	Robin Ventura	.50
434	Mariano Rivera	.50
435	Jay Tessmer	.15
436	Andy Pettitte	.50
437	John Vander Wal	.15
438	Adrian Hernandez	.15
439	Alberto Castillo	.15
440	Steve Karsay	.15
441	Alfonso Soriano	.75
442	Rondell White	.15
443	Nick Johnson	.50
444	Jorge Posada	.50
445	Ramiro Mendoza	.15
446	Gerald Williams	.15
447	Orlando Hernandez	.15
448	Randy Choate	.15
449	Randy Keisler	.15
450	Ted Lilly	.15
451	Christian Parker	.15
452	Ron Coomer	.15
453	Marcus Thames	.15
454	Drew Henson	.50
455	Jeff Bagwell	.50
456	Wade Miller	.15
457	Lance Berkman	.50
458	Julio Lugo	.15
459	Roy Oswalt	.40
460	Nelson Cruz	.15
461	Morgan Ensberg	.15
462	Geoff Blum	.15
463	Ryan Jamison RC	.50
464	Billy Wagner	.15
465	Dave Mlicki	.15
466	Brad Ausmus	.15
467	Jose Vizcaino	.15
468	Craig Biggio	.50
469	Shane Reynolds	.15
470	Gregg Zaun	.15
471	Octavio Dotel	.15
472	Carlos Hernandez	.15
473	Richard Hidalgo	.15
474	Daryle Ward	.15
475	Orlando Merced	.15
476	John Buck	.15
477	Adam Everett	.15
478	Doug Brocail	.15
479	Brad Lidge	.15
480	Scott Linebrink	.15
481	T.J. Mathews	.15
482	Greg Miller	.15
483	Hipolito Pichardo	.15
484	Brandon Puffer RC	.15
485	Ricky Stone	.15
486	Jason Lane	.15
487	Brian L. Hunter	.15
488	Rodrigo Rosario RC	.50
489	Tom Shearn RC	.50
490	Gary Sheffield	.40
491	Tom Glavine	.40
492	Mike Remlinger	.15
493	Henry Blanco	.15
494	Vinny Castilla	.15
495	Chris Hammond	.15
496	Kevin Millwood	.50
497	Darren Holmes	.15
498	Cory Aldridge	.15
499	Tim Spooneybarger	.15
500	Rafael Furcal	.15
501	Albie Lopez	.15
502	Javy Lopez	.40
503	Greg Maddux	1.00
504	Andruw Jones	.50
505	Steve Torrealba	.15
506	George Lombard	.15
507	B.J. Surhoff	.15
508	Marcus Giles	.15
509	Derrick Lewis	.15
510	Wes Helms	.15
511	John Smoltz	.50
512	Chipper Jones	.75
513	Jason Marquis	.15
514	Mark DeRosa	.15
515	Jung Bong	.15
516	Kevin Gryboski RC	.15
517	Damian Moss	.15
518	Horacio Ramirez	.15
519	Scott Sobkowiak	.15
520	Billy Sylvester	.15
521	Nick Green	.15
522	Travis Wilson	.15
523	Ryan Langerhans	.15
524	John Ennis RC	.50
525	John Foster RC	.15
526	Keith Lockhart	.15
527	Julio Franco	.15
528	Richie Sexson	.15
529	Jeffrey Hammonds	.15
530	Ben Sheets	.50
531	Mike DeJean	.15
532	Mark Loretta	.15
533	Alex Ochoa	.15
534	Jamey Wright	.15
535	Jose Hernandez	.15
536	Glendon Rusch	.15
537	Geoff Jenkins	.50
538	Luis S. Lopez	.15
539	Curtis Leskanic	.15
540	Chad Fox	.15
541	Tyler Houston	.15
542	Nick Neugebauer	.15
543	Paul Rigdon	.15
544	Bill Hall	.15
545	Luis Vizcaino	.15
546	Lenny Harris	.15
547	Alex Sanchez	.15
548	Raul Casanova	.15
549	Eric Young	.15
550	Jeff Deardorff RC	.15
551	Nelson Figueroa	.15
552	Ron Belliard	.15
553	Mike Buddie	.15
554	Jose Cabrera	.15
555	J.M. Gold	.15
556	Ray King	.15
557	Jose Mieses	.15
558	Takahito Nomura RC	.15
559	Ruben Quevedo	.15
560	Jackson Melian	.15
561	Cristian Guerrero	.15
562	Paul Bako	.15
563	Luis Martinez RC	.50
564	Brian Mallette RC	.50
565	Matt Morris	.50
566	Tino Martinez	.40
567	Fernando Vina	.15
568	Gene Stechschulte	.15
569	Andy Benes	.15
570	Andy Benes	.15
571	Placido Polanco	.15
572	Luis Garcia	.15
573	Jim Edmonds	.50
574	Bud Smith	.15
575	Mike Matheny	.15
576	Garrett Stephenson	.15
577	Miguel Cairo	.15
578	Darryl Kile	.15
579	Mike Timlin	.15
580	Rick Ankiel	.50
581	Jason Isringhausen	.15
582	Albert Pujols	1.50
583	Eli Marrero	.15
584	Steve Kline	.15
585	J.D. Drew	.50
586	Mike DiFelice	.15
587	Dave Veres	.15
588	Kerry Robinson	.15
589	Edgar Renteria	.15
590	Woody Williams	.15
591	Chance Caple	.15
592	Michael Crudale RC	.15
593	Luther Hackman	.15
594	Josh Pearce	.15
595	Kevin Joseph	.15
596	Jimmy Journell	.15
597	Jeremy Lambert RC	.40
598	Mike Matthews	.15
599	Les Walrond	.15
600	Keith McDonald	.15
601	William Ortega	.15
602	Scotty Layfield RC	.50
603	So Taguchi RC	.50
604	Eduardo Perez	.15
605	Sammy Sosa	1.50
606	Kerry Wood	.75
607	Kyle Farnsworth	.15
608	Alex Gonzalez	.15
609	Tom Gordon	.15
610	Carlos Zambrano	.15
611	Roosevelt Brown	.15
612	Bill Mueller	.15
613	Mark Prior	1.50
614	Darren Lewis	.15
615	Joe Girardi	.15
616	Fred McGriff	.50
617	Jon Lieber	.15
618	Robert Machado	.15
619	Corey Patterson	.50
620	Joe Borowski	.15
621	Todd Hundley	.15
622	Jason Bere	.15
623	Moises Alou	.40
624	Jeff Fassero	.15
625	Jesus Sanchez	.15
626	Chris Stynes	.15
627	Delino DeShields	.15
628	Augie Ojeda	.15
629	Juan Cruz	.15
630	Ben Christensen	.15
631	Mike Meyers	.15
632	Will Ohman	.15
633	Steve Smyth	.15
634	Mark Bellhorn	.15
635	Nate Frese	.15
636	David Kelton	.15
637	Francis Beltran RC	.40
638	Antonio Alfonseca	.15
639	Donovan Osborne	.15
640	Shawn Sonnier	.15
641	Matt Clement	.15
642	Luis Gonzalez	.25
643	Brian Anderson	.15
644	Randy Johnson	.75
645	Mark Grace	.50
646	Danny Bautista	.15
647	Junior Spivey	.15
648	Jay Bell	.15
649	Miguel Batista	.15
650	Tony Womack	.15
651	Byung-Hyun Kim	.15
652	Steve Finley	.40
653	Rick Helling	.15
654	Curt Schilling	.50
655	Erubiel Durazo	.15
656	Chris Donnels	.15
657	Greg Colbrunn	.15
658	Mike Morgan	.15
659	Jose Guillen	.15
660	Matt Williams	.50
661	Craig Counsell	.15
662	Greg Swindell	.15
663	Rod Barajas	.15
664	David Dellucci	.15
665	Todd Stottlemyre	.15
666	P.J. Bevis RC	.15
667	Mike Koplove	.15
668	Mike Myers	.15
669	John Patterson	.15
670	Bret Prinz	.15
671	Jeremy Ward RC	.50
672	Danny Klassen	.15
673	Luis Terrero	.15
674	Jose Valverde RC	.50
675	Doug DeVore RC	.50
676	Quinton McCracken	.15
677	Paul LoDuca	.15
678	Mark Grudzielanek	.15
679	Kevin Brown	.50
680	Paul Quantrill	.15
681	Shawn Green	.50
682	Hideo Nomo	.50
683	Eric Gagne	.15
684	Giovanni Carrara	.15
685	Marquis Grissom	.15
686	Hiram Bocachica	.15
687	Guillermo Mota	.15
688	Alex Cora	.15
689	Odalis Perez	.15
690	Brian Jordan	.15
691	Andy Ashby	.15
692	Eric Karros	.40
693	Chad Krueter	.15
694	Dave Roberts	.15
695	Omar Daal	.15
696	Dave Hansen	.15
697	Adrian Beltre	.50
698	Terry Mulholland	.15
699	Cesar Izturis	.15
700	Steve Colyer	.15
701	Carlos Garcia	.15
702	Ricardo Rodriguez	.15
703	Darren Dreifort	.15
704	Jeff Reboulet	.15
705	Victor Alvarez RC	.50
706	Kazuhisa Ishii	.50
707	Jose Vidro	.15
708	Henry Mateo	.15
709	Tony Armas Jr.	.15
710	Carl Pavano	.15
711	Peter Bergeron	.15
712	Bruce Chen	.15
713	Orlando Cabrera	.15
714	Britt Reames	.15
715	Masato Yoshii	.15
716	Fernando Tatis	.15
717	Graeme Lloyd	.15
718	Scott Stewart	.15
719	Lou Collier	.15
720	Michael Barrett	.15
721	Vladimir Guerrero	.75
722	Troy Mattes	.15
723	Brian Schneider	.15
724	Lee Stevens	.15
725	Javier Vazquez	.15
726	Brad Wilkerson	.15
727	Zach Day	.15
728	Ed Vosberg	.15
729	Tomokazu Ohka	.15
730	Mike Mordecai	.15
731	Donnie Bridges	.15
732	Ron Chiavacci	.15
733	T.J. Tucker	.15
734	Scott Hodges	.15
735	Valentino Pascucci	.15
736	Andres Galarraga	.15
737	Scott Downs	.15
738	Eric Good RC	.15
739	Ron Calloway RC	.50
740	Jorge Nunez RC	.15
741	Henry Rodriguez	.15
742	Jeff Kent	.15
743	Russ Ortiz	.15
744	Felix Rodriguez	.15
745	Benito Santiago	.15
746	Tsuyoshi Shinjo	.50
747	Tim Worrell	.15
748	Marvin Benard	.15
749	Kurt Ainsworth	.15
750	Edwards Guzman	.15
751	J.T. Snow	.15
752	Jason Christiansen	.15
753	Robb Nen	.15
754	Barry Bonds	2.00
755	Shawon Dunston	.15
756	Chad Zerbe	.15
757	Ramon E. Martinez	.15
758	Calvin Murray	.15
759	Pedro Feliz	.15
760	Jason Schmidt	.15
761	Damon Minor	.15
762	Reggie Sanders	.15
763	Rich Aurilia	.15
764	Kirk Rueter	.15
765	David Bell	.15
766	Yorvit Torrealba	.15
767	Livan Hernandez	.15
768	Felix Diaz	.15
769	Aaron Fultz	.15
770	Ryan Jensen	.15
771	Arturo McDowell	.15
772	Carlos Valderrama	.15
773	Nelson Castro RC	.50
774	Jay Witasick	.15
775	Deivis Santos	.15
776	Josh Beckett	.50
777	Charles Johnson	.15
778	Derrek Lee	.15
779	A.J. Burnett	.15
780	Vic Darensbourg	.15
781	Cliff Floyd	.50
782	Jose Cueto	.15
783	Nate Teut	.15
784	Alex Gonzalez	.15
785	Brad Penny	.15
786	Kevin Olsen	.15
787	Mike Lowell	.15
788	Mike Redmond	.15
789	Braden Looper	.15
790	Eric Owens	.15
791	Andy Fox	.15
792	Vladimir Nunez	.15
793	Luis Castillo	.15
794	Ryan Dempster	.15
795	Armando Almanza	.15
796	Preston Wilson	.15
797	Pablo Ozuna	.15
798	Gary Knotts	.15
799	Ramon Castro	.15
800	Benito Baez	.15
801	Michael Tejera	.15
802	Claudio Vargas	.15
803	Chip Ambres	.15
804	Hansel Izquierdo RC	.50
805	Tim Raines	.15
806	Marty Malloy	.15
807	Julian Tavarez	.15
808	Roberto Alomar	.50
809	Al Leiter	.50
810	Jeromy Burnitz	.15
811	John Franco	.15
812	Edgardo Alfonzo	.15
813	Mike Piazza	1.00
814	Shawn Estes	.15
815	Joe McEwing	.15
816	David Weathers	.15
817	Pedro Astacio	.15
818	Timoniel Perez	.15
819	Grant Roberts	.15
820	Rey Ordonez	.15
821	Steve Trachsel	.15
822	Roger Cedeno	.15
823	Mark Johnson	.15
824	Armando Benitez	.15
825	Vance Wilson	.15
826	Jay Payton	.15
827	Mo Vaughn	.50
828	Scott Strickland	.15
829	Mark Guthrie	.15
830	Jeff D'Amico	.15
831	Mark Corey RC	.50
832	Kane Davis	.15
833	Jae Weong Seo	.15
834	Pat Strange	.15
835	Adam Walker RC	.15
836	Tyler Walker	.15
837	Gary Matthews Jr.	.15
838	Jaime Cerda RC	.25
839	Satoru Komiyama RC	.15
840	Tyler Yates RC	.50
841	John Valentin	.15
842	Ryan Klesko	.40
843	Wiki Gonzalez	.15
844	Trevor Hoffman	.15
845	Sean Burroughs	.40
846	Alan Embree	.15
847	Dennis Tankersley	.15
848	D'Angelo Jimenez	.15
849	Kevin Jarvis	.15
850	Mark Kotsay	.15
851	Phil Nevin	.25
852	Jeremy Fikac	.15
853	Brett Tomko	.15
854	Brian Lawrence	.15
855	Steve Reed	.15
856	Bubba Trammell	.15
857	Tom Davey	.15
858	Ramon Vazquez	.15
859	Tom Lampkin	.15
860	Bobby Jones	.15
861	Ray Lankford	.15
862	Mark Sweeney	.15
863	Adam Eaton	.15
864	Trenidad Hubbard	.15
865	Jason Boyd	.15
866	Javier Cardona	.15
867	Clifford Bartosh RC	.50
868	Mike Bynum	.15
869	Eric Cyr RC	.50
870	Jose Nunez	.15
871	Ron Gant	.15
872	Deivi Cruz	.15
873	Ben Howard RC	.50
874	Todd Donovan RC	.25
875	Andy Shibilo RC	.15
876	Scott Rolen	.75
877	Jose Mesa	.15
878	Rheal Cormier	.15
879	Travis Lee	.15
880	Mike Lieberthal	.15
881	Brandon Duckworth	.15
882	David Coggin	.15
883	Bobby Abreu	.50
884	Turk Wendell	.15
885	Marlon Byrd	.15
886	Jason Michaels	.15
887	Robert Person	.15
888	Tomas Perez	.15
889	Jimmy Rollins	.50
890	Vicente Padilla	.15
891	Pat Burrell	.50
892	Dave Hollins	.15
893	Randy Wolf	.15
894	Jose Santiago	.15
895	Doug Glanville	.15
896	Cliff Politte	.15
897	Marlon Anderson	.15
898	Ricky Bottalico	.15
899	Terry Adams	.15
900	Brad Baisley	.15
901	Hector Mercado	.15
902	Elio Serrano	.50
903	Todd Pratt	.15
904	Peter Zamora RC	.15
905	Nick Punto	.15
906	Ricky Ledee	.15
907	Eric Junge RC	.50
908	Anderson Machado RC	.50
909	Jorge Padilla	.15
910	John Mabry	.15
911	Brian Giles	.15
912	Jason Kendall	.40
913	Jack Wilson	.15
914	Kris Benson	.15
915	Aramis Ramirez	.15
916	Mike Fetters	.15
917	Adrian Brown	.15
918	Pokey Reese	.15
919	Dave Williams	.15
920	Mike Benjamin	.15
921	Kip Wells	.15
922	Mike Williams	.15
923	Pat Meares	.15
924	Ron Villone	.15
925	Armando Rios	.15
926	Jimmy Anderson	.15
927	Robert Mackowiak	.15
928	Kevin Young	.15
929	Brian Boehringer	.15
930	Joe Beimel	.15
931	Chad Hermansen	.15
932	Scott Sauerbeck	.15
933	Josh Fogg	.15
934	Mike Gonzalez RC	.15
935	Mike Lincoln	.15
936	Sean Lowe	.15
937	Matt Guerrier	.15
938	Ryan Vogelsong	.15
939	J.R. House	.15
940	Craig Wilson	.15
941	Tony Alvarez	.15
942	J.J. Davis	.15
943	Abraham Nunez	.15
944	Adrian Burnside RC	.15
945	Ken Griffey Jr.	1.00
946	Jimmy Haynes	.15
947	Juan Castro	.15
948	Jose Rijo	.15
949	Corky Miller	.15
950	Elmer Dessens	.15
951	Aaron Boone	.15
952	Juan Encarnacion	.15
953	Chris Reitsma	.15
954	Wilton Guerrero	.15
955	Danny Graves	.15
956	Jim Brower	.15
957	Barry Larkin	.50
958	Todd Walker	.15
959	Gabe White	.15
960	Adam Dunn	.50
961	Jason LaRue	.15
962	Reggie Taylor	.15
963	Sean Casey	.40
964	Scott Williamson	.15
965	Austin Kearns	.50
966	Kelly Stinnett	.15
967	Jose Acevedo	.15
968	Gookie Dawkins	.15
969	Brady Clark	.15
970	Scott Sullivan	.15
971	Ricardo Aramboles	.15
972	Lance Davis	.15
973	Seth Etherton	.15
974	Luke Hudson	.15
975	Joey Hamilton	.15
976	Luis Pineda	.15
977	John Riedling	.15
978	Jose Silva	.15
979	Dane Sardinha	.15
980	Ben Broussard	.15
981	David Espinosa	.15
982	Ruben Mateo	.15
983	Larry Walker	.50
984	Juan Uribe	.15
985	Mike Hampton	.15
986	Aaron Cook RC	.50
987	Jose Ortiz	.15
988	Todd Jones	.15
989	Todd Helton	.50
990	Shawn Chacon	.15
991	Jason Jennings	.15
992	Todd Zeile	.15
993	Ben Petrick	.15
994	Denny Neagle	.15
995	Jose Jimenez	.15
996	Juan Pierre	.15
997	Todd Hollandsworth	.15
998	Kent Mercker	.15
999	Greg Norton	.15
1000	Terry Shumpert	.15
1001	Mark Little	.15
1002	Gary Bennett	.15
1003	Dennys Reyes	.15
1004	Justin Speier	.15
1005	John Thomson	.15
1006	Rick White	.15
1007	Colin Young RC	.40
1008	Cam Esslinger RC	.50
1009	Rene Reyes RC	.50
1010	Mike James	.15
1011	Morgan Ensberg	.15
1012	Adam Everett	.15
1013	Rodrigo Rosario	.15
1014	Carlos Pena	.15
1015	Eric Hinske	.50
1016	Orlando Hudson	.15
1017	Reed Johnson	.15
1018	Jung Bong	.15
1019	Bill Hall	.15
1020	Mark Prior	1.50
1021	Francis Beltran	.15
1022	David Kelton	.15
1023	Felix Escalona	.15
1024	Jorge Sosa	.15
1025	Dewon Brazelton	.15
1026	Jose Valverde	.15
1027	Luis Terrero	.15
1028	Kazuhisa Ishii	1.00
1029	Cesar Izturis	.15
1030	Ryan Jensen	.15
1031	Matt Thornton	.15
1032	Hansel Izquierdo	.15
1033	Jaime Cerda	.15
1034	Erik Bedard	.15
1035	Sean Burroughs	.15
1036	Ben Howard	.15
1037	Ramon Vazquez	.15
1038	Marlon Byrd	.15
1039	Josh Fogg	.15
1040	Hank Blalock	.50
1041	Mark Teixeira	.50
1042	Kevin Mench	.15

No.	Player	Price
1043	Dane Sardinha	.15
1044	Austin Kearns	.50
1045	Anastacio Martinez	.15
1046	Eric Munson	.15
1047	Jon Rauch	.15
1048	Nick Johnson	.50
1049	Alex Graman	.15
1050	Drew Henson	.50
1051	Darin Erstad	.50
1052	Garret Anderson	.15
1053	Craig Biggio	.50
1054	Lance Berkman	.50
1055	Jeff Bagwell	.50
1056	Shannon Stewart	.15
1057	Chipper Jones	.75
1058	J.D. Drew	.50
1059	Moises Alou	.15
1060	Mark Grace	.50
1061	Jose Vidro Expos	.15
1062	Vladimir Guerrero	.75
1063	Matt Lawton	.15
1064	Ichiro Suzuki	1.50
1065	Edgar Martinez	.50
1066	John Olerud	.50
1067	Jeff Cirillo	.15
1068	Mike Lowell	.15
1069	Mike Piazza	1.00
1070	Roberto Alomar	.15
1071	Bobby Abreu	.15
1072	Jason Kendall	.15
1073	Brian Giles	.50
1074	Rafael Palmeiro	.50
1075	Ivan Rodriguez	.50
1076	Alex Rodriguez	1.50
1077	Juan Gonzalez	.50
1078	Nomar Garciaparra	1.50
1079	Manny Ramirez	.50
1080	Sean Casey	.25
1081	Barry Larkin	.25
1082	Larry Walker	.40
1083	Carlos Beltran	.15
1084	Corey Koskie	.15
1085	Magglio Ordonez	.25
1086	Frank Thomas	.50
1087	Kenny Lofton	.25
1088	Derek Jeter	2.00
1089	Bernie Williams	.50
1090	Jason Giambi	.50
1091	Troy Glaus	.50
1092	Jeff Bagwell	.50
1093	Lance Berkman	.50
1094	David Justice	.25
1095	Eric Chavez	.25
1096	Carlos Delgado	.40
1097	Gary Sheffield	.40
1098	Chipper Jones	.75
1099	Andruw Jones	.40
1100	Richie Sexson	.40
1101	Albert Pujols	1.50
1102	Sammy Sosa	1.50
1103	Fred McGriff	.40
1104	Greg Vaughn	.15
1105	Matt Williams	.15
1106	Luis Gonzalez	.40
1107	Shawn Green	.40
1108	Andres Galarraga	.15
1109	Vladimir Guerrero	.75
1110	Barry Bonds	2.00
1111	Rich Aurilia	.15
1112	Ellis Burks	.15
1113	Jim Thome	.50
1114	Bret Boone	.15
1115	Cliff Floyd	.15
1116	Mike Piazza	1.00
1117	Jeromy Burnitz	.15
1118	Phil Nevin	.15
1119	Brian Giles	.50
1120	Rafael Palmeiro	.50
1121	Juan Gonzalez	.50
1122	Alex Rodriguez	1.50
1123	Manny Ramirez	.50
1124	Ken Griffey Jr.	1.00
1125	Larry Walker	.40
1126	Todd Helton	.50
1127	Mike Sweeney	.15
1128	Frank Thomas	.50
1129	Paul Konerko	.40
1130	Jason Giambi	.50
1131	Aaron Sele	.15
1132	Roy Oswalt	.40
1133	Wade Miller	.15
1134	Tim Hudson	.40
1135	Barry Zito	.15
1136	Mark Mulder	.25
1137	Greg Maddux	1.00
1138	Tom Glavine	.40
1139	Ben Sheets	.40
1140	Darryl Kile	.15
1141	Matt Morris	.15
1142	Kerry Wood	.40
1143	Jon Lieber	.15
1144	Juan Cruz	.15
1145	Randy Johnson	.75
1146	Curt Schilling	.50
1147	Kevin Brown	.15
1148	Javier Vazquez	.15
1149	Russ Ortiz	.15
1150	C.C. Sabathia	.15
1151	Bartolo Colon	.15
1152	Freddy Garcia	.15
1153	Jamie Moyer	.15
1154	Josh Beckett	.75
1155	Brad Penny	.15
1156	Al Leiter	.15
1157	Brandon Duckworth	.15
1158	Robert Person	.15
1159	Kris Benson	.15
1160	Chan Ho Park	.15
1161	Pedro J. Martinez	.75
1162	Mike Hampton	.15
1163	Jeff Weaver	.15
1164	Joe Mays	.15
1165	Brad Radke	.15
1166	Eric Milton	.15
1167	Roger Clemens	1.00
1168	Mike Mussina	.50
1169	Andy Pettitte	.50
1170	David Wells	.15
1171	Ken Griffey Jr.	1.00
1172	Ichiro Suzuki	1.00
1173	Jason Giambi	.50
1174	Alex Rodriguez	1.00
1175	Sammy Sosa	.75
1176	Nomar Garciaparra	1.00
1177	Barry Bonds	1.00
1178	Mike Piazza	.75
1179	Derek Jeter	1.50
1180	Randy Johnson	.40
1181	Jeff Bagwell	.40
1182	Albert Pujols	1.00

Gargantuan Gear

		NM/M
Common Player:		3.00
Gold:		2X
Production 100 Sets		
G-JB	James Baldwin	3.00
G-BC	Bruce Chen	3.00
G-JD	Jermaine Dye/SP	5.00
G-JG	Juan Gonzalez	6.00
G-BG	Ben Grieve	3.00
G-KG	Ken Griffey Jr.	10.00
G-TH	Tim Hudson	6.00
G-AJ	Andruw Jones	6.00
G-JK	Jeff Kent	6.00
G-ML	Mike Lieberthal	3.00
G-TM	Tino Martinez	3.00
G-JO	John Olerud	3.00
G-MO	Magglio Ordonez	5.00
G-MP	Mike Piazza	15.00
G-JP	Jorge Posada	8.00
G-AP	Andy Pettitte	6.00
G-BR	Brad Radke	3.00
G-AR	Alex Rodriguez	15.00
G-SR	Scott Rolen	10.00
G-CS	Curt Schilling	8.00
G-AS	Aaron Sele	3.00
G-IS	Ichiro Suzuki/SP	30.00
G-BW	Bernie Williams	8.00
G-DY	Dmitri Young	3.00
G-TZ	Todd Zeile	3.00

Looming Large Jerseys

		NM/M
Common Player:		8.00
Production 250 Sets		
Gold:		2X
Production 40 Sets		
LBa	Jeff Bagwell	10.00
LB	Lance Berkman	10.00
JBu	John Burkett	8.00
SC	Sean Casey	10.00
TC	Tony Clark	8.00
RC	Roger Clemens	20.00
JC	Jeff Cirillo	8.00
JD	J.D. Drew	10.00
CE	Carl Everett	8.00
CF	Chuck Finley	8.00
TF	Travis Fryman	8.00
JGi	Jason Giambi	10.00
BG	Brian Giles	10.00
TG	Tom Glavine	10.00
JGo	Juan Gonzalez	10.00
KG	Ken Griffey Jr.	20.00
TH	Todd Helton	15.00
RJ	Randy Johnson	15.00
DK	Darryl Kile	8.00
AL	Al Leiter	8.00
ML	Mike Lieberthal	8.00
KL	Kenny Lofton	8.00
GM	Greg Maddux	15.00
EM	Edgar Martinez	8.00
FM	Fred McGriff	10.00
MO	Magglio Ordonez	8.00
HN	Hideo Nomo	50.00
RP	Rafael Palmeiro	10.00
JP	Jorge Posada	10.00
SR	Shane Reynolds	8.00
AR	Alex Rodriguez	8.00
JR	Jimmy Rollins	8.00
KS	Kazuhiro Sasaki	8.00
CS	Curt Schilling	8.00
JS	J.T. Snow	8.00
SS	Sammy Sosa	20.00
FT	Frank Thomas	10.00
IV	Ismael Valdes	8.00
RV	Randy Velarde	8.00
RV	Ron Villone	8.00
BZ	Barry Zito	8.00

Lumber Yard

		NM/M
Common Player:		10.00
Inserted 1:168		
LY1	Chipper Jones	15.00
LY2	Joe DiMaggio	40.00
LY3	Albert Pujols	20.00
LY4	Mark McGwire	30.00
LY5	Sammy Sosa	15.00
LY6	Vladimir Guerrero	15.00
LY7	Barry Bonds	25.00
LY8	Mickey Mantle	50.00
LY9	Mike Piazza	15.00
LY10	Alex Rodriguez	15.00
LY11	Nomar Garciaparra	15.00
LY12	Ken Griffey Jr.	20.00
LY13	Frank Thomas	15.00
LY14	Jason Giambi	15.00
LY15	Derek Jeter	25.00
LY16	Luis Gonzalez	15.00
LY17	Jeff Bagwell	10.00
LY18	Todd Helton	10.00

Mark McGwire Flashbacks

Mark McGwire Flashbacks

	NM/M
Complete Set (40):	120.00
Common McGwire:	4.00
Inserted 1:24	
MM1-40 Mark McGwire	4.00

Super Swatches

		NM/M
Common Player:		5.00
Production 250 Sets		
Gold:		1-2X
Production 40 Sets		
EA	Edgardo Alfonso	5.00
RA	Rich Aurilia	5.00
JB	Jeff Bagwell	15.00
SC	Sean Casey	8.00
CD	Carlos Delgado	8.00
RD	Ray Durham	5.00
DE	Darin Erstad	8.00
JG	Juan Gonzalez	8.00
MG	Mark Grace	8.00
SG	Shawn Green	8.00
KG	Ken Griffey Jr.	20.00
TG	Tony Gwynn	15.00
MH	Mike Hampton	5.00
TH	Trevor Hoffman	5.00
CJ	Chipper Jones	10.00
DJ	David Justice	8.00
KL	Kenny Lofton	5.00
JM	Joe Mays	5.00
EM	Eric Milton	5.00
MM	Matt Morris	5.00
HN	Hideo Nomo	20.00
JP	Jorge Posada	10.00
MR	Manny Ramirez	12.00
MR	Mariano Rivera	10.00
AR	Alex Rodriguez	15.00
IR	Ivan Rodriguez	10.00
KS	Kazuhiro Sasaki	10.00
CS	Curt Schilling	10.00
BS	Ben Sheets	8.00
SS	Sammy Sosa	20.00
IS	Ichiro Suzuki	40.00
MS	Mike Sweeney	5.00
FT	Frank Thomas	10.00
GV	Greg Vaughn	5.00
JV	Jose Vidro	5.00
DW	David Wells	5.00
MY	Masato Yoshii	5.00

2002 Upper Deck/Twizzlers

Specially marked packages of Twizzlers candy contained one of 10 cards in a set comprised of portrait and action cards of each of five athletes. Only a single baseball player was included in the set and listed here. Fronts are bordered in white with vignetted photos. Blue-bordered backs have a few sentences about the player along with Twizzlers and UD logos.

		NM/M
3	Nomar Garciaparra/ Action	2.00
4	Nomar Garciaparra/ Portrait	2.00

2003 Upper Deck

	NM/M
Complete Set (540):	75.00
Common Player:	.15
Common RC (501-529):	.50
Series 1 or 2 Pack (8):	2.50
Series 1 or 2 Box (24):	45.00

No.	Player	Price
1	John Lackey	.15
2	Alex Cintron	.15
3	Jose Leon	.15
4	Bobby Hill	.15
5	Brandon Larson	.15
6	Raul Gonzalez	.15
7	Ben Broussard	.15
8	Earl Snyder	.15
9	Ramon Santiago	.15
10	Jason Lane	.15
11	Keith Ginter	.15
12	Kirk Saarloos	.15
13	Juan Brito	.15
14	Runelvys Hernandez	.15
15	Shawn Sedlacek	.15
16	Jayson Durocher	.15
17	Kevin Frederick	.15
18	Zach Day	.15
19	Marcus Thames	.15
20	Esteban German	.15
21	Brett Myers	.15
22	Oliver Perez	.25
23	Dennis Tankersley	.15
24	Julius Matos	.15
25	Jake Peavy	.15
26	Eric Cyr	.15
27	Mike Crudale	.15
28	Josh Pearce	.15
29	Carl Crawford	.15
30	Tim Salmon	.25
31	Troy Glaus	.50
32	Adam Kennedy	.15
33	David Eckstein	.15
34	Bengie Molina	.15
35	Jarrod Washburn	.15
36	Ramon Ortiz	.15
37	Eric Chavez	.40
38	Miguel Tejada	.50
39	Adam Piatt	.15
40	Jermaine Dye	.15
41	Olmedo Saenz	.15
42	Tim Hudson	.25
43	Barry Zito	.25
44	Billy Koch	.15
45	Shannon Stewart	.15
46	Kelvim Escobar	.15
47	Jose Cruz Jr.	.15
48	Vernon Wells	.25
49	Roy Halladay	.25
50	Esteban Loaiza	.15
51	Eric Hinske	.15
52	Steve Cox	.15
53	Brent Abernathy	.15
54	Ben Grieve	.15
55	Aubrey Huff	.15
56	Jared Sandberg	.15
57	Paul Wilson	.15
58	Tanyon Sturtze	.15
59	Jim Thome	.60
60	Omar Vizquel	.25
61	C.C. Sabathia	.15
62	Chris Magruder	.15
63	Ricky Gutierrez	.15
64	Einar Diaz	.15
65	Danys Baez	.15
66	Ichiro Suzuki	2.00
67	Ruben Sierra	.15
68	Carlos Guillen	.15
69	Mike McLemore	.15
70	Dan Wilson	.15
71	Jamie Moyer	.15
72	Joel Pineiro	.15
73	Edgar Martinez	.25
74	Tony Batista	.15
75	Jay Gibbons	.15
76	Chris Singleton	.15
77	Melvin Mora	.15
78	Geronimo Gil	.15
79	Rodrigo Lopez	.15
80	Jorge Julio	.15
82	Rafael Palmeiro	.50
83	Juan Gonzalez	.50
84	Mike Young	.15
85	Hideki Irabu	.15
86	Chan Ho Park	.15
87	Kevin Mench	.15
88	Doug Davis	.15
89	Pedro Martinez	.50
90	Shea Hillenbrand	.15
91	Derek Lowe	.15
92	Jason Varitek	.25
93	Tony Clark	.15
94	John Burkett	.15
95	Frank Castillo	.15
96	Nomar Garciaparra	2.00
97	Rickey Henderson	.40
98	Mike Sweeney	.15
99	Carlos Febles	.15
100	Mark Quinn	.15
101	Raul Ibanez	.15
102	A.J. Hinch	.15
103	Paul Byrd	.15
104	Chuck Knoblauch	.15
105	Dmitri Young	.15
106	Randall Simon	.15
107	Brandon Inge	.15
108	Damion Easley	.15
109	Carlos Pena	.15
110	George Lombard	.15
111	Juan Acevedo	.15
112	Torii Hunter	.25
113	Doug Mientkiewicz	.15
114	David Ortiz	.50
115	Eric Milton	.15
116	Eddie Guardado	.15
117	Cristian Guzman	.15
118	Corey Koskie	.15
119	Magglio Ordonez	.25
120	Mark Buehrle	.15
121	Todd Ritchie	.15
122	Jose Valentin	.15
123	Paul Konerko	.25
124	Carlos Lee	.15
125	Jon Garland	.15
126	Jason Giambi	.40
127	Derek Jeter	2.00
128	Roger Clemens	1.50
129	Raul Mondesi	.15
130	Jorge Posada	.25
131	Rondell White	.15
132	Robin Ventura	.25
133	Mike Mussina	.50
134	Jeff Bagwell	.50
135	Craig Biggio	.25
136	Morgan Ensberg	.15
137	Richard Hidalgo	.15
138	Brad Ausmus	.15
139	Roy Oswalt	.25
140	Carlos Hernandez	.15
141	Shane Reynolds	.15
142	Gary Sheffield	.25
143	Andruw Jones	.50
144	Tom Glavine	.40
145	Rafael Furcal	.15
146	Javy Lopez	.25
147	Vinny Castilla	.15
148	Marcus Giles	.15
149	Kevin Millwood	.15
150	Jason Marquis	.15
151	Ruben Quevedo	.15
152	Ben Sheets	.15
153	Geoff Jenkins	.15
154	Jose Hernandez	.15
155	Glendon Rusch	.15
156	Jeffrey Hammonds	.15
157	Alex Sanchez	.15
158	Jim Edmonds	.25
159	Tino Martinez	.25
160	Albert Pujols	1.50
161	Eli Marrero	.15
162	Woody Williams	.15
163	Fernando Vina	.15
164	Jason Isringhausen	.15
165	Jason Simontacchi	.15
166	Kerry Robinson	.15
167	Sammy Sosa	1.25
168	Juan Cruz	.15
169	Fred McGriff	.25
170	Antonio Alfonseca	.15
171	Jon Lieber	.15
172	Mark Prior	.50
173	Moises Alou	.15
174	Matt Clement	.15
175	Mark Bellhorn	.15
176	Randy Johnson	.75
177	Luis Gonzalez	.15
178	Tony Womack	.15
179	Mark Grace	.30
180	Junior Spivey	.15
181	Byung-Hyun Kim	.15
182	Danny Bautista	.15
183	Brian Anderson	.15
184	Shawn Green	.25
185	Brian Jordan	.15
186	Eric Karros	.15
187	Andy Ashby	.15
188	Cesar Izturis	.15
189	Dave Roberts	.15
190	Eric Gagne	.40
191	Kazuhisa Ishii	.15
192	Adrian Beltre	.25
193	Vladimir Guerrero	.75
194	Tony Armas Jr.	.15
195	Bartolo Colon	.15
196	Troy O'Leary	.15
197	Tomokazu Ohka	.15
198	Brad Wilkerson	.15
199	Orlando Cabrera	.15
200	Barry Bonds	2.00
201	David Bell	.15
202	Tsuyoshi Shinjo	.15
203	Benito Santiago	.15
204	Livan Hernandez	.15
205	Jason Schmidt	.40
206	Kirk Reuter	.15
207	Ramon E. Martinez	.15
208	Mike Lowell	.25
209	Luis Castillo	.15
210	Derrek Lee	.25
211	Andy Fox	.15
212	Eric Owens	.15
213	Charles Johnson	.15
214	Brad Penny	.15
215	A.J. Burnett	.15
216	Edgardo Alfonzo	.15
217	Roberto Alomar	.50
218	Rey Ordonez	.15
219	Al Leiter	.15
220	Roger Cedeno	.15
221	Timoniel Perez	.15
222	Jeromy Burnitz	.15
223	Pedro Astacio	.15
224	Joe McEwing	.15
225	Ryan Klesko	.15
226	Ramon Vazquez	.15
227	Mark Kotsay	.15
228	Bubba Trammell	.15
229	Wiki Gonzalez	.15
230	Trevor Hoffman	.15
231	Ron Gant	.15
232	Bobby Abreu	.25
233	Marlon Anderson	.15
234	Jeremy Giambi	.15
235	Jimmy Rollins	.15
236	Mike Lieberthal	.15
237	Vicente Padilla	.15
238	Randy Wolf	.15
239	Pokey Reese	.15
240	Brian Giles	.25
241	Jack Wilson	.15
242	Mike Williams	.15
243	Kip Wells	.15
244	Robert Mackowiak	.15
245	Craig Wilson	.15
246	Adam Dunn	.60
247	Sean Casey	.15
248	Todd Walker	.15
249	Corky Miller	.15
250	Ryan Dempster	.15
251	Reggie Taylor	.15
252	Aaron Boone	.15
253	Larry Walker	.30
254	Jose Ortiz	.15
255	Todd Zeile	.15
256	Bobby Estalella	.15
257	Juan Pierre	.15
258	Terry Shumpert	.15
259	Mike Hampton	.15
260	Denny Stark	.15
261	Shawn Green	.25
262	Derek Lowe	.15
263	Barry Bonds	1.00
264	Mike Cameron	.15
265	Luis Castillo	.15
266	Vladimir Guerrero	.40
267	Jason Giambi	.25
268	Eric Gagne	.25
269	Magglio Ordonez	.20
270	Jim Thome	.25
271	Garret Anderson	.15
272	Tony Percival	.15
273	Brad Fullmer	.15
274	Scott Spezio	.15
275	Darin Erstad	.40
276	Francisco Rodriguez	.15
277	Kevin Appier	.15
278	Shawn Wooten	.15
279	Eric Owens	.15
280	Scott Hatteberg	.15
281	Terrence Long	.15
282	Mark Mulder	.25
283	Ramon Hernandez	.15
284	Ted Lilly	.15
285	Erubiel Durazo	.15
286	Mark Ellis	.15
287	Carlos Delgado	.15
288	Orlando Hudson	.15
289	Chris Woodward	.15
290	Mark Hendrickson	.15
291	Josh Phelps	.15
292	Ken Huckaby	.15
293	Justin Miller	.15
294	Travis Lee	.15
295	Jorge Sosa	.15
296	Joe Kennedy	.15
297	Carl Crawford	.15
298	Toby Hall	.15
299	Rey Ordonez	.15
300	Brandon Phillips	.15
301	Matt Lawton	.15
302	Ellis Burks	.15
303	Bill Selby	.15
304	Travis Hafner	.15
305	Milton Bradley	.15
306	Karim Garcia	.15
307	Cliff Lee	.15
308	Jeff Cirillo	.15
309	John Olerud	.15
310	Kazuhiro Sasaki	.15
311	Freddy Garcia	.15
312	Bret Boone	.15
313	Mike Cameron	.15
314	Ben Davis	.15
315	Randy Winn	.15
316	Gary Matthews Jr.	.15
317	Jeff Conine	.15

#	Player	Price
318	Sidney Ponson	.15
319	Jerry Hairston	.15
320	David Segui	.15
321	Scott Erickson	.15
322	Marty Cordova	.15
323	Hank Blalock	.50
324	Herbert Perry	.15
325	Alex Rodriguez	2.00
326	Carl Everett	.15
327	Einar Diaz	.15
328	Ugueth Urbina	.15
329	Mark Teixeira	.40
330	Manny Ramirez	.75
331	Johnny Damon	.50
332	Trot Nixon	.15
333	Tim Wakefield	.15
334	Casey Fossum	.15
335	Todd Walker	.15
336	Jeremy Giambi	.15
337	Bill Mueller	.15
338	Ramiro Mendoza	.15
339	Carlos Beltran	.50
340	Jason Grimsley	.15
341	Brent Mayne	.15
342	Angel Berroa	.15
343	Albie Lopez	.15
344	Michael Tucker	.15
345	Bobby Higginson	.15
346	Shane Halter	.15
347	Jeremy Bonderman	2.00
348	Eric Munson	.15
349	Andy Van Hekken	.15
350	Matt Anderson	.15
351	Jacque Jones	.15
352	A.J. Pierzynski	.15
353	Joe Mays	.15
354	Brad Radke	.15
355	Dustan Mohr	.15
356	Bobby Kielty	.15
357	Michael Cuddyer	.15
358	Luis Rivas	.15
359	Frank Thomas	.75
360	Joe Borchard	.15
361	D'Angelo Jimenez	.15
362	Bartolo Colon	.25
363	Joe Crede	.15
364	Miguel Olivo	.15
365	Billy Koch	.15
366	Bernie Williams	.50
367	Nick Johnson	.15
368	Andy Pettitte	.40
369	Mariano Rivera	.15
370	Alfonso Soriano	.75
371	David Wells	.15
372	Drew Henson	.15
373	Juan Rivera	.15
374	Steve Karsay	.15
375	Jeff Kent	.25
376	Lance Berkman	.50
377	Octavio Dotel	.15
378	Julio Lugo	.15
379	Jason Lane	.15
380	Wade Miller	.15
381	Billy Wagner	.15
382	Brad Ausmus	.15
383	Mike Hampton	.15
384	Chipper Jones	.75
385	John Smoltz	.25
386	Greg Maddux	1.25
387	Javy Lopez	.25
388	Robert Fick	.15
389	Mark DeRosa	.15
390	Russ Ortiz	.15
391	Julio Franco	.15
392	Richie Sexson	.50
393	Eric Young	.15
394	Robert Machado	.15
395	Mike DeJean	.15
396	Todd Ritchie	.15
397	Royce Clayton	.15
398	Nick Neugebauer	.15
399	J.D. Drew	.25
400	Edgar Renteria	.25
401	Scott Rolen	.75
402	Matt Morris	.25
403	Garrett Stephenson	.15
404	Eduardo Perez	.15
405	Mike Matheny	.15
406	Miguel Cairo	.15
407	Brett Tomko	.15
408	Bobby Hill	.15
409	Troy O'Leary	.15
410	Corey Patterson	.40
411	Kerry Wood	.75
412	Eric Karros	.15
413	Hee Seop Choi	.15
414	Alex Gonzalez	.15
415	Matt Clement	.15
416	Mark Grudzielanek	.15
417	Curt Schilling	.50
418	Steve Finley	.15
419	Craig Counsell	.15
420	Matt Williams	.15
421	Quinton McCracken	.15
422	Chad Moeller	.15
423	Lyle Overbay	.15
424	Miguel Batista	.15
425	Paul LoDuca	.25
426	Kevin Brown	.25
427	Hideo Nomo	.40
428	Fred McGriff	.25
429	Joe Thurston	.15
430	Odalis Perez	.15
431	Darren Dreifort	.15
432	Todd Hundley	.15
433	Dave Roberts	.15
434	Jose Vidro	.15
435	Javier Vazquez	.15
436	Michael Barrett	.15
437	Fernando Tatis	.15
438	Peter Bergeron	.15
439	Endy Chavez	.15
440	Orlando Hernandez	.15
441	Marvin Bernard	.15
442	Rich Aurilia	.15
443	Pedro Feliz	.15
444	Robb Nen	.15
445	Ray Durham	.15
446	Marquis Grissom	.15
447	Damian Moss	.15
448	Edgardo Alfonzo	.15
449	Juan Pierre	.15
450	Braden Looper	.15
451	Alex Gonzalez	.15
452	Justin Wayne	.15
453	Josh Beckett	.25
454	Juan Encarnacion	.15
455	Ivan Rodriguez	.50
456	Todd Hollandsworth	.15
457	Cliff Floyd	.15
458	Rey Sanchez	.15
459	Mike Piazza	1.50
460	Mo Vaughn	.15
461	Armando Benitez	.15
462	Tsuyoshi Shinjo	.15
463	Tom Glavine	.40
464	David Cone	.15
465	Phil Nevin	.15
466	Sean Burroughs	.15
467	Jake Peavy	.15
468	Brian Lawrence	.15
469	Mark Loretta	.15
470	Dennis Tankersley	.15
471	Jesse Orosco	.15
472	Jim Thome	.75
473	Kevin Millwood	.40
474	David Bell	.15
475	Pat Burrell	.40
476	Brandon Duckworth	.15
477	Jose Mesa	.15
478	Marlon Byrd	.15
479	Reggie Sanders	.15
480	Jason Kendall	.25
481	Aramis Ramirez	.40
482	Kris Benson	.15
483	Matt Stairs	.15
484	Kevin Young	.15
485	Kenny Lofton	.25
486	Austin Kearns	.40
487	Barry Larkin	.25
488	Jason LaRue	.15
489	Ken Griffey Jr.	1.25
490	Danny Graves	.15
491	Russell Branyan	.15
492	Reggie Taylor	.15
493	Jimmy Haynes	.15
494	Charles Johnson	.15
495	Todd Helton	.75
496	Juan Uribe	.15
497	Preston Wilson	.15
498	Chris Stynes	.15
499	Jason Jennings	.15
500	Jay Payton	.15
501	Hideki Matsui RC	5.00
502	Jose Contreras RC	1.00
503	Brandon Webb RC	3.00
504	Robby Hammock RC	.50
505	Matt Kata RC	.50
506	Tim Olson RC	.50
507	Michael Hessman RC	.50
508	Jon Leicester RC	.50
509	Todd Wellemeyer RC	.50
510	David Sanders RC	.50
511	Josh Stewart RC	.50
512	Luis Ayala RC	.50
513	Clint Barmes RC	1.00
514	Josh Willingham RC	1.00
515	Alejandro Machado RC	.50
516	Felix Sanchez RC	.50
517	Willie Eyre RC	.50
518	Brent Hoard RC	.50
519	Lew Ford RC	.50
520	Terrmel Sledge RC	.50
521	Jeremy Griffiths	.15
522	Phil Seibel RC	.50
523	Craig Brazell RC	.50
524	Prentice Redman RC	.50
525	Jeff Duncan RC	.50
526	Shane Bazzell RC	.75
527	Bernie Castro RC	.50
528	Rett Johnson RC	.50
529	Bobby Madritsch RC	.50
530	Rocco Baldelli	.40
531	Alex Rodriguez	1.00
532	Eric Chavez	.25
533	Miguel Tejada	.25
534	Ichiro Suzuki	.75
535	Sammy Sosa	.75
536	Barry Zito	.25
537	Darin Erstad	.25
538	Alfonso Soriano	.50
539	Troy Glaus	.25
540	Nomar Garciaparra	.75

Gold

Gold (541-600): 2-3X
One gold set per hobby case

AL All-Star Swatch

NM/M
Common Player: 5.00
Inserted 1:144 Retail

MC	Mike Cameron	5.00
RD	Ray Durham	5.00
CE	Carl Everett	5.00
CF	Chuck Finley	5.00

TF	Travis Fryman	6.00
JG	Juan Gonzalez	8.00
JM	Joe Mays	5.00
MO	Magglio Ordonez	8.00
AP	Andy Pettitte	8.00
JP	Jorge Posada	8.00
MR	Mariano Rivera	10.00
AS	Aaron Sele	5.00
MS	Mike Sweeney	5.00

Big League Breakdown

NM/M
Complete Set (15): 20.00
Common Player: .50
Inserted 1:8

BL1	Troy Glaus	.75
BL2	Miguel Tejada	.75
BL3	Chipper Jones	1.50
BL4	Torii Hunter	.50
BL5	Nomar Garciaparra	3.00
BL6	Sammy Sosa	2.50
BL7	Todd Helton	1.00
BL8	Lance Berkman	.75
BL9	Shawn Green	.50
BL10	Vladimir Guerrero	1.50
BL11	Jason Giambi	.50
BL12	Derek Jeter	4.00
BL13	Barry Bonds	4.00
BL14	Ichiro Suzuki	3.00
BL15	Alex Rodriguez	4.00

Game Jersey Autograph

NM/M
Golds: 1.5-2X
Production 25 or 75

RC	Roger Clemens/350	100.00
JG	Jason Giambi/350	40.00
KG	Ken Griffey Jr./350	110.00
MM	Mark McGwire/150	350.00
CR	Cal Ripken Jr/350	150.00
AR	Alex Rodriguez/350	120.00
SS	Sammy Sosa/150	140.00

Game Swatches Hobby

NM/M
Common Player: 5.00
Inserted 1:8

SB	Sean Burroughs/SP	8.00
CD	Carlos Delgado/SP	8.00
GM	Greg Maddux	15.00
MM	Mike Mussina	10.00
MO	Magglio Ordonez	10.00
CP	Carlos Pena	5.00
MP	Mike Piazza/SP	15.00
AR	Alex Rodriguez	15.00
CC	C.C. Sabathia	10.00
CS	Curt Schilling/100	10.00
SS	Sammy Sosa	15.00
BW	Bernie Williams	10.00

Game Swatches Retail

NM/M
Common Player: 5.00
Inserted 1:72

RC	Roger Clemens	15.00
JD	J.D. Drew	5.00
AD	Adam Dunn	8.00
JE	Jim Edmonds	8.00
DE	Darin Erstad	8.00
JG	Jason Giambi	8.00
KG	Ken Griffey Jr.	12.00
TH	Tim Hudson	6.00
RJ	Randy Johnson	8.00
JK	Jeff Kent	5.00
EM	Edgar Martinez	6.00
IR	Ivan Rodriguez	6.00
FT	Frank Thomas	8.00

Leading Swatches

NM/M
Common Player: 4.00
Inserted 1:24
Golds: 1-2X
Production 100 Sets

BA	Bobby Abreu	5.00
GA	Garret Anderson	6.00
JB	Jeff Bagwell	6.00
JB1	Jeff Bagwell	6.00
TB	Tony Batista	4.00
AB	Adrian Beltre	6.00
LB	Lance Berkman	6.00
PB	Pat Burrell	6.00
PB1	Pat Burrell	6.00
EC	Eric Chavez	6.00
RC	Roger Clemens	10.00
RC1	Roger Clemens	10.00
CD	Carlos Delgado	6.00
JD	J.D. Drew	4.00
AD	Adam Dunn	8.00
AD1	Adam Dunn	8.00
JE	Jim Edmonds	4.00
JG	Jason Giambi	6.00
JG1	Jason Giambi	6.00
BG	Brian Giles	4.00
TG	Troy Glaus	4.00
GO	Juan Gonzalez	6.00
SG	Shawn Green	4.00
SG1	Shawn Green	4.00
KG	Ken Griffey Jr.	12.00
KG1	Ken Griffey Jr.	12.00
VG	Vladimir Guerrero	8.00
THe	Todd Helton	6.00
THu	Tim Hudson	4.00
TH1	Tim Hudson	4.00
KI	Kazuhisa Ishii	4.00
RJ	Randy Johnson	8.00
RJ1	Randy Johnson	8.00
AJ	Andruw Jones	6.00
AJ1	Andruw Jones	6.00
CJ	Chipper Jones	8.00
KE	Jason Kendall	4.00
JL	Javy Lopez	4.00
GM	Greg Maddux	10.00
GM1	Greg Maddux	10.00
PM	Pedro J. Martinez	8.00
HM	Hideki Matsui	40.00
HM1	Hideki Matsui	50.00
HN	Hideo Nomo	8.00
RO	Roy Oswalt	4.00
RO1	Roy Oswalt	4.00
RP	Rafael Palmeiro	6.00
RP1	Rafael Palmeiro	6.00
CP	Corey Patterson	6.00
JP	Jay Payton	4.00
TP	Troy Percival	4.00
AP	Andy Pettitte	6.00
MP	Mike Piazza	10.00
MP1	Mike Piazza	10.00
AR	Alex Rodriguez	10.00
AR1	Alex Rodriguez	10.00
IR	Ivan Rodriguez	8.00
SR	Scott Rolen	8.00
KS	Kazuhisa Sasaki	4.00
CS	Curt Schilling	4.00
AS	Aaron Sele	4.00
JS	J.T. Snow	4.00
AS	Alfonso Soriano	8.00
AS1	Alfonso Soriano	8.00
SS	Sammy Sosa	12.00
SS1	Sammy Sosa	12.00
MS	Mike Stanton	4.00
IS	Ichiro Suzuki	25.00
IS1	Ichiro Suzuki	25.00
MS	Mike Sweeney	4.00
MT	Miguel Tejada	6.00
MT1	Miguel Tejada	6.00
JT	Jim Thome	8.00
JT1	Jim Thome	8.00
OV	Omar Vizquel	4.00
LW	Larry Walker	4.00
BW	Bernie Williams	6.00
BW1	Bernie Williams	6.00
KW	Kerry Wood	6.00
BZ	Barry Zito	6.00

Lineup Time Jerseys

NM/M
Common Player: 6.00
Inserted 1:96

RC	Roger Clemens/SP	20.00
CD	Carlos Delgado	8.00
JD	J.D. Drew	6.00
SG	Shawn Green	8.00
TH	Todd Helton	8.00
RJ	Randy Johnson/SP	15.00
GM	Greg Maddux	10.00
IS	Ichiro Suzuki	40.00
JT	Jim Thome	10.00
BW	Bernie Williams	10.00

Magical Performances

NM/M
Common Player: 8.00
Inserted 1:96
Golds: 1-2X
Production 50 Sets

MP1	Hideki Matsui	20.00
MP2	Ken Griffey Jr.	15.00
MP3	Ichiro Suzuki	15.00
MP4	Ken Griffey Jr.	15.00
MP5	Hideo Nomo	8.00
MP6	Mickey Mantle	40.00
MP7	Ken Griffey Jr.	15.00
MP8	Barry Bonds	20.00
MP9	Mickey Mantle	40.00
MP10	Tom Seaver	8.00
MP11	Mike Piazza	15.00
MP12	Roger Clemens	12.00
MP13	Nolan Ryan	30.00
MP14	Nomar Garciaparra	15.00
MP15	Ernie Banks	15.00
MP16	Stan Musial	25.00
MP17	Mickey Mantle	40.00
MP18	Nolan Ryan	30.00
MP19	Nolan Ryan	30.00
MP20	Mickey Mantle	40.00
MP21	Ichiro Suzuki	15.00
MP22	Nolan Ryan	30.00
MP23	Tom Seaver	8.00
MP24	Ken Griffey Jr.	15.00
MP25	Hideo Nomo	8.00
MP26	Ken Griffey Jr.	15.00
MP27	Mark McGwire	30.00
MP28	Barry Bonds	20.00
MP29	Barry Bonds	20.00
MP30	Nolan Ryan	30.00
MP31	Mark McGwire	30.00
MP32	Nolan Ryan	30.00
MP33	Sammy Sosa	15.00
MP34	Ichiro Suzuki	15.00
MP35	Barry Bonds	20.00
MP36	Derek Jeter	20.00
MP37	Roger Clemens	15.00
MP38	Jason Giambi	8.00
MP39	Mickey Mantle	40.00
MP40	Ted Williams	40.00
MP41	Ted Williams	40.00
MP42	Ted Williams	40.00

Mark of Greatness

NM/M
400 Total cards produced.

MoG	Mark McGwire	350.00
MoG	Mark McGwire/Silver/70	400.00

Masters with the Leather

NM/M
Complete Set (12): 20.00
Common Player: -.75
Inserted 1:12

L1	Darin Erstad	.75
L2	Andruw Jones	1.50
L3	Greg Maddux	3.00
L4	Nomar Garciaparra	3.00
L5	Torii Hunter	1.00
L6	Roberto Alomar	1.00
L7	Derek Jeter	5.00
L8	Eric Chavez	1.00
L9	Ichiro Suzuki	3.00
L10	Jim Edmonds	1.00
L11	Scott Rolen	1.50
L12	Alex Rodriguez	4.00

Matsui Mania

Complete Set (18):
Common Player:

Mid-Summer Stars

MID-SUMMER STARS SWATCHES

NM/M
Common Player: 5.00
Inserted 1:72

RC	Roger Clemens	12.00
CD	Carlos Delgado	8.00
JE	Jim Edmonds	8.00
DE	Darin Erstad	8.00
FG	Freddy Garcia	8.00
TG	Tom Glavine	8.00
JG	Juan Gonzalez	8.00
SG	Shawn Green/SP	15.00
RJ	Randy Johnson	10.00
AJ	Andruw Jones	6.00
EM	Edgar Martinez	10.00
HN	Hideo Nomo	20.00
MP	Mike Piazza	15.00
MR	Manny Ramirez	8.00
AR	Alex Rodriguez	15.00
KS	Kazuhiro Sasaki	8.00
CS	Curt Schilling	10.00
SS	Sammy Sosa	15.00
IS	Ichiro Suzuki/SP	40.00
FT	Frank Thomas	8.00
RV	Robin Ventura	8.00
DW	David Wells	5.00
BZ	Barry Zito	8.00

National Pride

NM/M
Common Player: 3.00
Inserted 1:24

AA	Abe Alvarez	3.00
MA	Michael Aubrey	15.00
KB	Kyle Bakker	5.00
SB	Sean Burroughs	5.00
CC	Chad Cordero	3.00
SC	Shane Costa	5.00
RF	Robert Fick	3.00
SF	Sam Fuld	3.00
AH	Aaron Hill	8.00
BH	Bobby Hill	3.00
BH1	Bobby Hill	3.00
AJ	A.J. Hinch	3.00
PH	Phillip Humber	5.00
CJ	Conor Jackson	8.00
JJe	Jason Jennings	3.00
GJ	Grant Johnson	4.00
JJ	Jacque Jones	8.00
JJ1	Jacque Jones	8.00
MJ	Mark Jurich	3.00
AK	Austin Kearns	12.00
AK1	Austin Kearns	12.00
WL	Wes Littleton	3.00
EM	Eric Milton	5.00
EM1	Eric Milton	5.00
RO	Roy Oswalt	6.00
RO1	Roy Oswalt	6.00
EP	Eric Patterson	3.00
DP	Dustin Pedroia	3.00
LP	Landon Powell	3.00
MP	Mark Prior	15.00
MP1	Mark Prior	15.00
CQ	Carlos Quentin	5.00
KSa	Kirk Saarloos	3.00
KSa1	Kirk Saarloos	3.00
CS	Clint Sammons	5.00
KSI	Kyle Sleeth	5.00
HS	Huston Street	5.00
BS	Brad Sullivan	3.00
BS1	Brad Sullivan	3.00
RW	Rickie Weeks	10.00
RW1	Rickie Weeks	10.00
BZ	Bob Zimmermann	3.00

NL All-Star Swatch

NM/M
Common Player: 5.00
Inserted 1:72

SC	Sean Casey	5.00
CF	Cliff Floyd	5.00
TGI	Tom Glavine	8.00
TGw	Tony Gwynn	12.00
MH	Mike Hampton	5.00
TH	Trevor Hoffman	5.00
RK	Ryan Klesko	5.00
AL	Al Leiter	5.00
FM	Fred McGriff	5.00
MM	Matt Morris	8.00
CS	Curt Schilling	8.00
JV	Jose Vidro	5.00

Patch Logo

NM/M
Quantity produced listed

JB	Jeff Bagwell/41	60.00
KG	Ken Griffey Jr./50	100.00
TH	Todd Helton/50	50.00
KI	Kazuhisa Ishii/54	40.00
RJ	Randy Johnson/50	75.00
CJ	Chipper Jones/52	80.00
GM	Greg Maddux/50	100.00
MP	Mike Piazza/61	120.00
SS	Sammy Sosa/60	100.00
FT	Frank Thomas/52	60.00
BW	Bernie Williams/42	50.00

Patch Number

NM/M
Quantity produced listed

JG	Jason Giambi/68	40.00
KG	Ken Griffey Jr./97	70.00
KI	Kazuhisa Ishii/63	40.00
RJ	Randy Johnson/90	75.00
MG	Mark McGwire/60	180.00
AR	Alex Rodriguez/56	90.00
SS	Sammy Sosa/100	60.00
FT	Frank Thomas/91	60.00
BW	Bernie Williams/66	50.00

Patch Stripes

NM/M
Quantity produced listed

JB	Jeff Bagwell/73	60.00
JG	Jason Giambi/66	40.00
KG	Ken Griffey Jr./82	75.00
KI	Kazuhisa Ishii/58	40.00
RJ	Randy Johnson/58	65.00
CJ	Chipper Jones/58	60.00
MG	Mark McGwire/63	180.00
AR	Alex Rodriguez/63	80.00
SS	Sammy Sosa/63	100.00
IS	Ichiro Suzuki/63	180.00
FT	Frank Thomas/58	60.00
BW	Bernie Williams/58	50.00

Piece of the Action

NM/M
Common Player: 5.00
Inserted 1:288
Cards are not serial numbered.
Print runs provided by Upper Deck.

BA	Bobby Abreu/125	5.00
GA	Garret Anderson/150	5.00
AB	Adrian Beltre/100	10.00
BB	Barry Bonds/125	30.00
KB	Kevin Brown/100	5.00
PB	Pat Burrell/150	8.00
DE	Darin Erstad/125	5.00
FG	Freddy Garcia/100	5.00
BG	Brian Giles/100	5.00
TG	Troy Glaus/150	5.00
JG	Juan Gonzalez/100	8.00
LG	Luis Gonzalez/100	8.00
SG	Shawn Green/175	5.00
VG	Vladimir Guerrero/50	10.00
THe	Todd Helton/100	10.00
THo	Trevor Hoffman/150	5.00
DJ	Derek Jeter/65	40.00
RJ	Randy Johnson/100	10.00

CJ	Chipper Jones/62	15.00
JK	Jason Kendall/100	5.00
KE	Jeff Kent/150	5.00
RK	Ryan Klesko/75	6.00
EM	Edgar Martinez/125	5.00
PM	Pedro Martinez/150	10.00
PN	Phil Nevin/75	5.00
HN	Hideo Nomo/100	20.00
RP	Rafael Palmeiro/150	5.00
Ara	Aramis Ramirez/100	8.00
MP	Mike Piazza/150	15.00
ARo	Alex Rodriguez/100	15.00
KS	Kazuhiro Sasaki/100	5.00
CS	Curt Schilling/100	10.00
RS	Richie Sexson/160	8.00
GS	Gary Sheffield/125	6.00
SS	Sammy Sosa/85	20.00
FT	Frank Thomas/150	8.00
JT	Jim Thome/100	10.00
JV	Jose Vidro/100	5.00
LW	Larry Walker/150	5.00
BW	Bernie Williams/125	6.00

Slammin' Sammy Tribute Jersey

NM/M

384 Total produced.

SST	Sammy Sosa	175.00
SST	Sammy Sosa/Gold/25	290.00
SST	Sammy Sosa/Silver/66	240.00

Star-Spangled Swatches

NM/M

Common Player: 4.00
Inserted 1:72

MA	Michael Aubrey	8.00
KB	Kyle Bakker	4.00
CC	Chad Cordero	4.00
SC	Shane Costa	6.00
AH	Aaron Hill	4.00
PH	Philip Humber	6.00
CJ	Conor Jackson	8.00
GJ	Grant Johnson	4.00
EP	Eric Patterson	8.00
DP	Dustin Pedroia	10.00
LP	Landon Powell	6.00
CQ	Carlos Quentin	8.00
KS	Kyle Sleeth	6.00
HS	Huston Street	10.00
BS	Brad Sullivan	4.00
RW	Rickie Weeks	10.00

Superior Sluggers

NM/M

Complete Set (18): 30.00
Common Player: 1.00
Inserted 1:8

S1	Troy Glaus	1.00
S2	Chipper Jones	1.50
S3	Manny Ramirez	1.50
S4	Ken Griffey Jr.	2.50
S5	Jim Thome	1.50
S6	Todd Helton	1.00
S7	Lance Berkman	1.00
S8	Derek Jeter	4.00
S9	Vladimir Guerrero	1.50
S10	Mike Piazza	2.50
S11	Hideki Matsui	3.00
S12	Barry Bonds	4.00
S13	Mickey Mantle	5.00
S14	Alex Rodriguez	3.00
S15	Ted Williams	3.00
S16	Carlos Delgado	1.00
S17	Frank Thomas	1.50
S18	Adam Dunn	1.50

Super Patch Logos

Common Player:
Inserted 1:7,500
No Pricing

Super Patch Numbers

Common Player:
Inserted 1:7,500
No Pricing

Super Patch Stripes

Common Player:
Inserted 1:7,500
No Pricing

Superstar Scrapbooks

No pricing due to scarcity.
Production 24 Sets
Silvers: No Pricing
Production Six Sets
Golds: No Pricing
Production One Set

Superstar Slam Jerseys

UD Superstar Slam

NM/M

Common Player: 4.00
Inserted 1:48

JB	Jeff Bagwell	8.00
JG	Jason Giambi	6.00
JGo	Juan Gonzalez	6.00
LG	Luis Gonzalez	6.00
KG	Ken Griffey Jr.	15.00
CJ	Chipper Jones	10.00
MP	Mike Piazza	10.00
AR	Alex Rodriguez	15.00
SS	Sammy Sosa	15.00
FT	Frank Thomas	8.00

The Chase for 755

NM/M

Complete Set (15): 15.00
Common Player: .75
Inserted 1:8

C1	Troy Glaus	.75
C2	Andruw Jones	1.00
C3	Manny Ramirez	1.25
C4	Sammy Sosa	2.50
C5	Ken Griffey Jr.	3.00
C6	Adam Dunn	1.25
C7	Todd Helton	1.00
C8	Lance Berkman	.75
C9	Jeff Bagwell	1.00
C10	Shawn Green	.75
C11	Vladimir Guerrero	1.50
C12	Barry Bonds	4.00
C13	Alex Rodriguez	3.00
C14	Juan Gonzalez	.75
C15	Carlos Delgado	.75

Triple Game Jersey

NM/M

Quantity Produced Listed
Golds: 1.5-2X
Production 50, 25 or 10

ARZ	Randy Johnson, Curt Schilling, Luis Gonzalez/150	40.00
CIN	Ken Griffey Jr., Sean Casey, Adam Dunn/150	40.00
HOU	Jeff Bagwell, Lance Berkman, Craig Biggio/150	40.00
TEX	Rafael Palmeiro, Alex Rodriguez, Juan Gonzalez/150	40.00
ATL	Chipper Jones, Greg Maddux, Gary Sheffield/75	65.00
CHC	Sammy Sosa, Moises Alou, Kerry Wood/75	50.00
NYM	Mike Piazza, Roberto Alomar, Mo Vaughn/75	40.00
SEA	Ichiro Suzuki, Freddy Garcia, Bret Boone/75	40.00

500 HR Club

NM/M

Production 350 Cards

SS	Sammy Sosa/350	150.00
SS	Sammy Sosa Auto./21	2,300

2003 UD Authentics

TED WILLIAMS

		NM/M
	Complete Set (130):	
	Common Player:	.25
	Common Rk Hype (101-130):	4.00
	Production 999	
	Pack (4):	10.00
	Box (10 + Framed Auto.):	170.00
1	Pee Wee Reese	.25
2	Richie Ashburn	.25
3	Derek Jeter	2.50
4	Alex Rodriguez	2.00
5	Jose Vidro	.25
6	Miguel Tejada	.50
7	Nomar Garciaparra	2.00
8	Pat Burrell	.50
9	Albert Pujols	2.00
10	Jeff Bagwell	.75
11	Stan Musial	1.00
12	Mickey Mantle	3.00
13	J.D. Drew	.75
14	Ivan Rodriguez	.75
15	Joe Morgan	.75
16	Ted Williams	2.00
17	Travis Hafner	.50
18	Chipper Jones	1.50
19	Hideo Nomo	.50
20	Gary Sheffield	.50
21	Jacque Jones	.25
22	Alfonso Soriano	1.50
23	Roberto Alomar	.50
24	Jeff Kent	.40
25	Omar Vizquel	.40
26	Ernie Banks	1.00
27	Shawn Green	.50
28	Tim Hudson	.50
29	Jim Edmonds	.50
30	Brandon Larson	.25
31	Doug Mientkiewicz	.25
32	Darin Erstad	.50
33	Bobby Hill	.25
34	Todd Helton	.75
35	Kazuhisa Ishii	.25
36	Lance Berkman	.75
37	Eric Hinske	.25
38	Jason Bartlett	.25
39	Bob Feller	.50
40	Luis Gonzalez	.40
41	Sammy Sosa	2.00
42	Mike Piazza	1.50
43	Roger Clemens	2.00
44	Jose Cruz Jr.	.25
45	Mark Prior	1.50
46	Mark Teixeira	.40
47	Phil Nevin	.25
48	Lyle Overbay	.25
49	Manny Ramirez	.75
50	Brian Giles	.40
51	Preston Wilson	.25
52	Jermaine Dye	.25
53	Troy Glaus	.50
54	Frank Thomas	.75
55	Jim Thome	.75
56	Barry Bonds	2.50
57	Carlos Delgado	.50
58	Jason Giambi	1.00
59	Joe Mays	.25
60	Andruw Jones	.75
61	Billy Williams	.75
62	Vladimir Guerrero	.75
63	Scott Rolen	.75
64	Juan Marichal	.25
65	Austin Kearns	.50
66	Kerry Wood	.75
67	Bret Boone	.25
68	Shea Hillenbrand	.25
69	Mike Sweeney	.25
70	Rocco Baldelli	.25
71	Ken Griffey Jr.	1.50
72	Cliff Floyd	.25
73	Greg Maddux	1.50
74	Mike Hampton	.25
75	Larry Walker	.40
76	Nolan Ryan	3.00
77	Rollie Fingers	.50
78	Mike Mussina	.75
79	Matt Morris	.25
80	Robin Roberts	.25
81	Barry Zito	.50
82	Curt Schilling	.50
83	Ken Harvey	.25
84	Troy Percival	.25
85	Tom Seaver	.50
86	Mariano Rivera	.40
87	Raul Mondesi	.25
88	Adam Dunn	.50
89	Roy Oswalt	.25
90	Pedro J. Martinez	1.00
91	Andy Pettitte	.50
92	Tom Glavine	.50
93	Torii Hunter	.50
94	Joe Thurston	.25
95	Runelvys Hernandez	.25
96	Randy Johnson	1.00
97	Bernie Williams	.75
98	Ichiro Suzuki	1.50
99	C.C. Sabathia	.25
100	Bobby Abreu	.40
101	Jose Contreras RC	6.00
102	Hideki Matsui RC	15.00
103	Chris Capuano RC	4.00
104	Willie Eyre RC	4.00
105	Lew Ford RC	4.00
106	Shane Bazzell RC	4.00
107	Guillermo Quiroz RC	4.00
108	Fernando Cabrera RC	4.00
109	Francisco Cruceta RC	4.00
110	Jhonny Peralta RC	4.00
111	Bobby Madritsch RC	4.00
112	Diegomar Markwell RC	4.00
113	Matt Bruback RC	4.00
114	Matt Kata RC	4.00
115	Rob Hammock RC	4.00
116	Brandon Webb RC	12.00
117	Jon Leicester RC	4.00
118	Josh Willingham RC	8.00
119	Prentice Redman RC	4.00
120	Jeff Duncan RC	4.00
121	Craig Brazell RC	4.00
122	Jeremy Griffiths RC	4.00
123	Phil Seibel RC	4.00
124	Luis Ayala RC	4.00
125	Miguel Ojeda RC	4.00
126	Jeremy Wedel RC	4.00
127	Josh Hall RC	4.00
128	Oscar Villarreal RC	4.00
129	Clint Barmes RC	6.00
130	Nook Logan RC	4.00

Rookie Hype Gold

Cards (101-130): 1-2X
Production 50

Cut Signatures

Common Player:

Framed Autograph

NM/M

Common Framed Autograph: 40.00
Inserted 1:Box

Lance Berkman/150	50.00
Lance Berkman/100	70.00
Hank Blalock/325	45.00
Hank Blalock/300	45.00
Hank Blalock/200	45.00
Hank Blalock/175	45.00
Pat Burrell/330	40.00
Pat Burrell/240	40.00
Pat Burrell/100	40.00
Gary Carter/225	50.00
Gary Carter/75	60.00
Jose Contreras/350	50.00
Jose Contreras/120	50.00
Carlton Fisk/250	50.00
Carlton Fisk/125	75.00
Carlton Fisk/70	80.00
Nomar Garciaparra/250	100.00
Nomar Garciaparra/150	100.00
Nomar Garciaparra/75	120.00
Jason Giambi/350	40.00
Jason Giambi/300	40.00
Jason Giambi/200	40.00
Jason Giambi/150	40.00
Jason Giambi/100	40.00
Jason Giambi/75	40.00
Bob Gibson/200	50.00
Bob Gibson/50	120.00
Bob Gibson/45	120.00
Troy Glaus/350	40.00
Troy Glaus/200	40.00
Troy Glaus/100	50.00
Tom Glavine/275	50.00
Tom Glavine/150	50.00
Tom Glavine/47	75.00
Ken Griffey Jr/325	90.00
Ken Griffey Jr/200	90.00
Ken Griffey Jr/75	100.00
Ken Griffey Jr./30	120.00
Vladimir Guerrero/150	60.00
Vladimir Guerrero/27	125.00
Drew Henson/350	40.00
Drew Henson/300	40.00
Drew Henson/250	40.00
Drew Henson/100	40.00
Chipper Jones/350	75.00
Chipper Jones/200	75.00
Chipper Jones/100	90.00
Austin Kearns/325	40.00
Austin Kearns/300	40.00
Austin Kearns/200	40.00
Austin Kearns/175	40.00
Austin Kearns/28	80.00
Hideki Matsui/75	300.00
Hideki Matsui/55	300.00
Mark Prior/300	60.00
Mark Prior/250	60.00
Mark Prior/175	60.00
Mark Prior/100	60.00
Cal Ripken Jr/125	175.00
Cal Ripken Jr./50	200.00
Phil Rizzuto/350	60.00
Phil Rizzuto/200	60.00
Phil Rizzuto/100	75.00
Scott Rolen/300	50.00
Scott Rolen/100	65.00
Scott Rolen/27	120.00
Nolan Ryan/150	125.00
Nolan Ryan/100	180.00
Nolan Ryan/50	200.00
Nolan Ryan/34	240.00
Tom Seaver/100	75.00
Tom Seaver/50	100.00
Tom Seaver/41	100.00
Ozzie Smith/150	85.00
Ozzie Smith/50	120.00
Duke Snider/150	60.00
Duke Snider/100	100.00
Ichiro Suzuki/75	300.00
Ichiro Suzuki/51	350.00
Mark Teixeira/325	60.00
Mark Teixeira/200	60.00
Mark Teixeira/175	60.00
Mark Teixeira/150	60.00

Star Quality

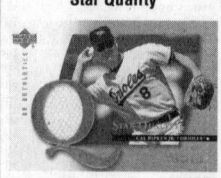

NM/M

Common Player: 4.00
Production 350 unless noted.
Golds: 1-2X
Production 350, 25 or 10
No Pricing for #'d to 25 or less.

RA	Roberto Alomar	6.00
JB	Jeff Bagwell	8.00
JO	Josh Beckett	5.00
LB	Lance Berkman	5.00
RC	Roger Clemens	15.00
RC1	Roger Clemens	15.00
CD	Carlos Delgado	5.00
JD	J.D. Drew	4.00
AD	Adam Dunn	6.00
JG	Jason Giambi	5.00
TR	Troy Glaus	5.00
TG	Tom Glavine	5.00
SG	Shawn Green	4.00
KG	Ken Griffey Jr./250	12.00
VG	Vladimir Guerrero	6.00
TH	Todd Helton	6.00
EH	Eric Hinske	4.00
CJ	Chipper Jones	8.00
AK	Austin Kearns	4.00
JK	Jeff Kent	4.00
MM	Mickey Mantle/250	100.00
HM	Hideki Matsui/250	25.00
PM	Paul Molitor/250	8.00
MU	Mike Mussina	8.00
HN	Hideo Nomo	8.00
RO	Roy Oswalt	4.00
RP	Rafael Palmeiro	6.00
MP	Mark Prior	10.00
AP	Albert Pujols	20.00
AP1	Albert Pujols	20.00
CR	Cal Ripken Jr./250	25.00
NR	Nolan Ryan/130	50.00
TS	Tom Seaver	8.00
GS	Gary Sheffield	5.00
AS	Alfonso Soriano	10.00
SS	Sammy Sosa/250	12.00
CS	Casey Stengel	15.00
JT	Jim Thome	8.00
BW	Bernie Williams	8.00
TW	Ted Williams/250	65.00
KW	Kerry Wood	8.00

Threads of Time

NM/M

Common Player: 4.00
Production 350, unless noted.
Golds: 1-2X
Production 350, 25 or 10
No Pricing for #'d to 25 or less.

JB	Johnny Bench	10.00
GC	Gary Carter	8.00
RC	Roger Clemens	15.00
TC	Ty Cobb	100.00
DD	Don Drysdale	15.00
DE	Dennis Eckersley	4.00
RF	Rollie Fingers	8.00
LG	Lou Gehrig/250	140.00
JG	Jason Giambi/250	6.00
JU	Juan Gonzalez	6.00
KG	Ken Griffey Jr./250	12.00
VG	Vladimir Guerrero	6.00
RJ	Randy Johnson	8.00
CJ	Chipper Jones	8.00
HK	Harmon Killebrew	12.00
GM	Greg Maddux	8.00
MM	Mickey Mantle/250	100.00
RM	Roger Maris	40.00
PM	Pedro J. Martinez	8.00
DM	Don Mattingly	20.00
HN	Hideo Nomo	8.00
AP	Andy Pettitte	8.00
MP	Mike Piazza	10.00
AP	Albert Pujols	20.00
CR	Cal Ripken Jr.	25.00
FR	Frank Robinson	8.00
AR	Alex Rodriguez	12.00
IR	Ivan Rodriguez	8.00
NR	Nolan Ryan	8.00
RS	Ryne Sandberg	12.00
TS	Tom Seaver	8.00
OS	Ozzie Smith	8.00
SS	Sammy Sosa/250	12.00
IS	Ichiro Suzuki/250	30.00
FT	Frank Thomas	8.00
JT	Jim Thome	8.00
HW	Honus Wagner	75.00
TW	Ted Williams/250	65.00
MW	Maury Wills	4.00
DW	Dave Winfield/250	8.00

2003 Upper Deck Gary Carter Hawaii Autograph

Participants in the card com pany's golf outing at the SCD Ha waii Trade Conference receive this specially produced card o Gary Carter, long known for his re fusal to sign cards except for spe cific charitable causes. The car has the Hawaii show logo on front along with a gold-foil notation o his Hall of Fame election. Back has a statement of authenticity.

NM/M

GC	Gary Carter	25.00

2003 Upper Deck Classic Portraits

NM/M

Complete Set (232): .15
Common Player: .15
Common SP (101-145): 2.00
Inserted 1:4
Common SP (145-190): 3.00
Production 2,003
Common Royalty (191-232): 2.00
Production 1,200
Pack (5): 3.00
Box (18 + Bust): 75.00

1	Ken Griffey Jr.	1.00
2	Randy Johnson	1.00
3	Rafael Furcal	.25
4	Omar Vizquel	.25
5	Shawn Green	.40
6	Roy Oswalt	.40
7	Hideo Nomo	.40
8	Jason Giambi	.40
9	Barry Bonds	2.50
10	Mike Piazza	1.50
11	Ichiro Suzuki	2.00
12	Carlos Delgado	.40
13	Preston Wilson	.15
14	Lance Berkman	.25
15	Magglio Ordonez	.25
16	Kerry Wood	.75
17	Ivan Rodriguez	.75
18	Chipper Jones	1.00
19	Adam Dunn	.75
20	C.C. Sabathia	.25
21	Mike MacDougal	.15
22	Torii Hunter	.40
23	Jim Thome	.75
24	Hank Blalock	.40
25	Johnny Damon	.50
26	Troy Glaus	.40
27	Manny Ramirez	.75
28	Mark Prior	1.00
29	Brent Mayne	.15
30	Derek Jeter	2.50
31	Tim Hudson	.40
32	Mike Cameron	.15
33	Mark Teixeira	.40
34	Shannon Stewart	.15
35	Tim Salmon	.40
36	Luis Gonzalez	.25
37	Jason Johnson	.15
38	Shea Hillenbrand	.15
39	Bartolo Colon	.15
40	Austin Kearns	.25
41	Vladimir Guerrero	1.00
42	Tom Glavine	.40
43	Andres Galarraga	.25
44	Kazuhiro Sasaki	.15
45	Juan Gonzalez	.75
46	Vernon Wells	.25

#	Player	Price
47	Jeff Bagwell	.75
48	Mike Sweeney	.15
49	Carlos Beltran	.50
50	Dave Roberts	.15
51	Todd Helton	.75
52	Carlos Pena	.15
53	Darin Erstad	.25
54	Gary Sheffield	.40
55	Lyle Overbay	.15
56	Sammy Sosa	1.50
57	Mike Mussina	.50
58	Matt Morris	.25
59	Roberto Alomar	.50
60	Larry Walker	.25
61	Jacque Jones	.15
62	Josh Beckett	.40
63	Richie Sexson	.50
64	Derek Lowe	.15
65	Pedro J. Martinez	1.00
66	Moises Alou	.25
67	Craig Biggio	.25
68	Curt Schilling	.75
69	Jesse Foppert	.15
70	Nomar Garciaparra	1.50
71	Barry Zito	.40
72	Alfonso Soriano	.75
73	Miguel Tejada	.50
74	Rafael Palmeiro	.50
75	Albert Pujols	2.00
76	Mariano Rivera	.25
77	Bobby Abreu	.25
78	Alex Rodriguez	2.00
79	Andruw Jones	.50
80	Frank Thomas	.75
81	Greg Maddux	1.50
82	Jim Edmonds	.40
83	Bernie Williams	.50
84	Roger Clemens	2.00
85	Eric Chavez	.25
86	Scott Rolen	1.00
87	Jorge Posada	.50
88	Bret Boone	.25
89	Ben Sheets	.25
90	John Olerud	.15
91	J.D. Drew	.25
92	Aaron Boone	.15
93	Corey Koskie	.15
94	Sean Casey	.25
95	Jose Cruz Jr.	.15
96	Pat Burrell	.40
97	Jose Guillen	.15
98	Mark Mulder	.25
99	Garret Anderson	.25
100	Kazuhisa Ishii	.15
101	Dave Matranga RC	2.00
102	Colin Porter RC	2.00
103	Jason Gilfillan RC	2.00
104	Carlos Mendez RC	2.00
105	Jason Shiell RC	2.00
106	Kevin Tolar RC	2.00
107	Terrmel Sledge RC	3.00
108	Craig Brazell RC	4.00
109	Bernie Castro RC	2.00
110	Tim Olson RC	3.00
111	Kevin Ohme RC	2.00
112	Pedro Liriano RC	2.00
113	Joe Borowski RC	2.00
114	Edgar Gonzalez RC	3.00
115	Joe Thurston	2.00
116	Bobby Hill	2.00
117	Michel Hernandez RC	2.00
118	Arnie Munoz RC	2.00
119	David Sanders RC	2.00
120	Willie Eyre RC	3.00
121	Brent Hoard RC	2.00
122	Lew Ford RC	4.00
123	Beau Kemp RC	2.00
124	Jonathan Pridie RC	2.00
125	Mike Ryan RC	4.00
126	Richard Fischer RC	2.00
127	Luis Ayala RC	2.00
128	Mike Neu RC	2.00
129	Joe Valentine RC	2.00
130	Nate Bland RC	2.00
131	Shane Bazzell RC	2.00
132	Jason Roach RC	2.00
133	Diegomar Markwell RC	2.00
134	Francisco Rosario RC	2.00
135	Guillermo Quiroz RC	4.00
136	Jerome Williams	2.00
137	Fernando Cabrera RC	2.00
138	Francisco Cruceta RC	2.00
139	Jhonny Peralta	4.00
140	Rett Johnson RC	2.00
141	Aaron Looper RC	2.00
142	Bobby Madritsch RC	2.00
143	Dan Haren	3.00
144	Jose Castillo	2.00
145	Chris Waters RC	2.00
146	Hideki Matsui RC	10.00
147	Jose Contreras RC	4.00
148	Felix Sanchez RC	3.00
149	Jon Leicester RC	3.00
150	Todd Wellemeyer RC	3.00
151	Matt Bruback RC	3.00
152	Chris Capuano RC	3.00
153	Oscar Villarreal RC	3.00
154	Matt Kata RC	3.00
155	Robby Hammock RC	3.00
156	Gerald Laird	3.00
157	Brandon Webb RC	8.00
158	Tommy Whiteman RC	3.00
159	Andrew Brown RC	3.00
160	Alfredo Gonzalez RC	3.00
161	Carlos Rivera RC	3.00
162	Rick Roberts RC	3.00
163	Dontrelle Willis RC	3.00
164	Josh Willingham RC	5.00

#	Player	Price
165	Prentice Redman RC	3.00
166	Jeff Duncan RC	4.00
167	Jose Reyes	3.00
168	Jeremy Griffiths	3.00
169	Phil Seibel RC	3.00
170	Heath Bell RC	3.00
171	Anthony Ferrari RC	3.00
172	Mike Nicolas RC	3.00
173	Cory Stewart RC	3.00
174	Miguel Ojeda RC	5.00
175	Rickie Weeks RC	8.00
176	Delmon Young RC	8.00
177	Tommy Phelps	3.00
178	Josh Hall RC	4.00
179	Ryan Cameron RC	3.00
180	Garrett Atkins	3.00
181	Clint Barmes RC	4.00
182	Michael Hessman RC	3.00
183	Chin-Hui Tsao	3.00
184	Rocco Baldelli	3.00
185	Bo Hart RC	3.00
186	Wilfredo Ledezma RC	3.00
187	Miguel Cabrera	5.00
188	Ian Ferguson RC	3.00
189	Micheal Nakamura RC	3.00
190	Alejandro Machado RC	3.00
191	Mickey Mantle	12.00
192	Ted Williams	10.00
193	Mark Prior	6.00
194	Stan Musial	10.00
195	Phil Rizzuto	3.00
196	Nolan Ryan	12.00
197	Tom Seaver	4.00
198	Robin Yount	5.00
199	Yogi Berra	3.00
200	Ernie Banks	8.00
201	Willie McCovey	3.00
202	Ralph Kiner	3.00
203	Ken Griffey Jr.	4.00
204	Sammy Sosa	5.00
205	Derek Jeter	8.00
206	Nomar Garciaparra	6.00
207	Alex Rodriguez	6.00
208	Ichiro Suzuki	4.00
209	Mike Piazza	4.00
210	Jackie Robinson	6.00
211	Roberto Clemente	4.00
212	Babe Ruth	12.00
213	Duke Snider	3.00
214	Greg Maddux	4.00
215	Juan Marichal	3.00
216	Joe Morgan	2.00
217	Rollie Fingers	2.00
218	Warren Spahn	4.00
219	Pee Wee Reese	2.00
220	Troy Glaus	2.00
221	Jason Giambi	2.00
222	Roger Clemens	6.00
223	Pedro J. Martinez	3.00
224	Chipper Jones	4.00
225	Randy Johnson	3.00
226	Jim Thome	3.00
227	Barry Bonds	8.00
228	Hideo Nomo	2.00
229	Whitey Ford	3.00
230	Bob Gibson	4.00
231	Alfonso Soriano	4.00
232	Richie Ashburn	3.00

Gold

No pricing due to scarcity.
Production 25 Sets

Bust Signature

	NM/M
Complete Set (17):	
Common Player:	

	NG	Nomar Garciaparra	80.00
	HM	Hideki Matsui	180.00

Stitches Jersey

		NM/M
Common Player:		4.00
Production 299 Sets		
Golds:		No Pricing
Production 25 Sets		
JB	Jeff Bagwell	6.00
RB	Rocco Baldelli	4.00
HB	Hank Blalock	4.00
HC	Hee Seop Choi	4.00
RC	Roger Clemens	15.00
JD	J.D. Drew	4.00
AD	Adam Dunn	8.00
JE	Jim Edmonds	4.00
RF	Rafael Furcal	4.00
JG	Jason Giambi	6.00
TG	Troy Glaus	4.00
SG	Shawn Green	4.00
KG	Ken Griffey Jr.	10.00
VG	Vladimir Guerrero	6.00
TH	Torii Hunter	6.00
RJ	Randy Johnson	6.00
AJ	Andruw Jones	6.00
CJ	Chipper Jones	8.00
JK	Jeff Kent	4.00
ML	Mike Lowell	4.00
GM	Greg Maddux	10.00
PM	Pedro J. Martinez	8.00
HM	Hideki Matsui	40.00
MM	Matt Morris	4.00
HN	Hideo Nomo	4.00
MO	Magglio Ordonez	4.00
RO	Roy Oswalt	4.00
CP	Corey Patterson	4.00
AP	Andy Pettitte	6.00
MI	Mike Piazza	8.00
MP	Mark Prior	8.00
AL	Albert Pujols	15.00
AR	Alex Rodriguez	10.00
IR	Ivan Rodriguez	6.00
CS	Curt Schilling	8.00
GS	Gary Sheffield	6.00
AS	Alfonso Soriano	6.00
SS	Sammy Sosa	15.00
IS	Ichiro Suzuki	25.00
JT	Jim Thome	5.00
DW	Dontrelle Willis	4.00
KW	Kerry Wood	4.00

Stitches Patch

	NM/M
Common Player:	10.00
Production 99 Sets	
Golds:	No Pricing
Production 10 Sets	
JB	Jeff Bagwell	15.00
RB	Rocco Baldelli	10.00
HB	Hank Blalock	10.00
HC	Hee Seop Choi	10.00
RC	Roger Clemens	25.00
JD	J.D. Drew	10.00
AD	Adam Dunn	15.00
JE	Jim Edmonds	10.00
RF	Rafael Furcal	10.00
JG	Jason Giambi	15.00
TG	Troy Glaus	15.00
SG	Shawn Green	10.00
KG	Ken Griffey Jr.	30.00
VG	Vladimir Guerrero	15.00
TH	Torii Hunter	15.00
RJ	Randy Johnson	20.00
AJ	Andruw Jones	10.00
CJ	Chipper Jones	25.00
JK	Jeff Kent	10.00
ML	Mike Lowell	10.00
GM	Greg Maddux	25.00
PM	Pedro J. Martinez	20.00
HM	Hideki Matsui	60.00
MM	Matt Morris	10.00
HN	Hideo Nomo	20.00
MO	Magglio Ordonez	15.00
RO	Roy Oswalt	15.00
CP	Corey Patterson	10.00
AP	Andy Pettitte	15.00
MI	Mike Piazza	30.00
MP	Mark Prior	30.00
AL	Albert Pujols	40.00
AR	Alex Rodriguez	50.00
IR	Ivan Rodriguez	15.00
CS	Curt Schilling	20.00
GS	Gary Sheffield	15.00
AS	Alfonso Soriano	20.00
SS	Sammy Sosa	25.00
IS	Ichiro Suzuki	120.00
JT	Jim Thome	20.00
DW	Dontrelle Willis	10.00
KW	Kerry Wood	15.00

Signs of Success

		NM/M
Common Player:		6.00
MI	Milton Bradley/220	6.00
DB	Dewon Brazelton/299	6.00
JB	John Buck/98	8.00

MB	Mark Buehrle/220	10.00
BR	Brandon Claussen/121	6.00
BC	Brad Cresse/121	10.00
JD	Johnny Damon/297	30.00
BD	Ben Diggins/299	8.00
AG	Alex Graman/215	10.00
KG	Ken Griffey Jr./299	90.00
TG	Tony Gwynn/49	80.00
DH	Drew Henson/246	8.00
BH	Ben Howard/299	6.00
HI	Hansel Izquierdo/299	8.00
JJ	Jimmy Journell/98	8.00
DK	David Kelton/102	8.00
KL	Kenny Lofton/296	10.00
CM	Corwin Malone/103	8.00
BP	Brandon Phillips/131	12.00
SR	Scott Rolen/100	20.00
CC	C.C. Sabathia/106	25.00
MT	Mark Teixeira/280	30.00
TH	Mark Thornton/298	6.00
AH	Andy Van Hekken/299	8.00
JU	Justin Wayne/299	8.00
JW	Jayson Werth/299	20.00
JE	Jerome Williams/103	8.00

Bronze Bust

		NM/M
Common Player:		
YB	Yogi Berra	25.00
RC	Roberto Clemente	60.00
NG	Nomar Garciaparra	40.00
JG	Jason Giambi	25.00
BG	Bob Gibson	25.00
KG	Ken Griffey Jr./300	45.00
MM	Mickey Mantle	70.00
HM	Hideki Matsui	30.00
SM	Stan Musial	30.00
BRS	Babe Ruth/Sox/300	60.00
BRY	Babe Ruth/Yanks	60.00
NRA	Nolan Ryan/Astros	50.00
NRA	Nolan Ryan/Astros/300	50.00
NRM	Nolan Ryan/Mets	50.00
TSM	Tom Seaver/Mets	25.00
TSR	Tom Seaver/Reds/300	25.00
TSR	Tom Seaver/Reds	25.00
DS	Duke Snider	25.00
SS	Sammy Sosa/300	40.00
IS	Ichiro Suzuki/300	50.00
TW	Ted Williams	50.00

Bronze Bust Autograph

		NM/M
Some not priced due to scarcity.		
YB	Yogi Berra	100.00
NG	Nomar Garciaparra/106	125.00
BG	Bob Gibson	60.00
KG	Ken Griffey Jr.	100.00
HM	Hideki Matsui	250.00
SM	Stan Musial/62	120.00
DS	Duke Snider	90.00
IS	Ichiro Suzuki/62	275.00

Marble Bust

		NM/M
Common Player:		
YB	Yogi Berra/125	40.00
YB	Yogi Berra/250	25.00
RC	Roberto Clemente/250	70.00
NG	Nomar Garciaparra/250	40.00
JG	Jason Giambi	25.00
BG	Bob Gibson/125	30.00
BG	Bob Gibson/250	25.00
KG	Ken Griffey Jr./250	40.00
MM	Mickey Mantle/80	80.00
MM	Mickey Mantle/125	80.00
HM	Hideki Matsui/250	40.00
SM	Stan Musial/250	30.00
BRS	Babe Ruth/Sox/250	60.00
BRY	Babe Ruth/Yanks/125	75.00
BRY	Babe Ruth/Yanks/250	65.00
NRA	Nolan Ryan/Astros/125	60.00
NRA	Nolan Ryan/Astros/250	50.00
NRM	Nolan Ryan/Mets/250	50.00
TSM	Tom Seaver/Mets/125	40.00
TSM	Tom Seaver/Mets/250	30.00
TSR	Tom Seaver/Reds/125	30.00
TSR	Tom Seaver/Reds/250	30.00
DS	Duke Snider/125	40.00
DS	Duke Snider/250	40.00
SS	Sammy Sosa/250	40.00
TW	Ted Williams/125	65.00
TW	Ted Williams/250	40.00

Marble Autograph

No pricing due to scarcity.

Pewter Bust

		NM/M
Common Player:		
YB	Yogi Berra/75	40.00
YB	Yogi Berra/100	40.00
RC	Roberto Clemente/100	100.00
NG	Nomar Garciaparra/100	60.00
JG	Jason Giambi/100	40.00
BG	Bob Gibson/75	40.00

BG	Bob Gibson/100	40.00
KG	Ken Griffey Jr./100	70.00
MM	Mickey Mantle/75	125.00
MM	Mickey Mantle/100	125.00
HM	Hideki Matsui/100	60.00
SM	Stan Musial/100	60.00
BRS	Babe Ruth/Sox/100	80.00
BRY	Babe Ruth/Yanks/100	90.00
BRY	Babe Ruth/Yanks/75	90.00
NRA	Nolan Ryan/Astros/75	80.00
NRA	Nolan Ryan/Astros/100	80.00
NRM	Nolan Ryan/Mets/100	80.00
NRM	Nolan Ryan/Mets/100	80.00
TSM	Tom Seaver/Mets/75	40.00
TSM	Tom Seaver/Mets/100	40.00
TSR	Tom Seaver/Reds/100	40.00
TSR	Tom Seaver/Reds/75	40.00
DS	Duke Snider/75	40.00
DS	Duke Snider/100	40.00
SS	Sammy Sosa/100	60.00
IS	Ichiro Suzuki/100	65.00
TW	Ted Williams/75	100.00
TW	Ted Williams/100	100.00

Pewter Autograph Bust

No pricing due to scarcity.

2003 Upper Deck Roger Clemens 300 Wins

To commemorate The Rocket's milestone, fans at Yankee Stadium on August 28 received this cello-wrapped set. Backs repeat the front format and have a line of stats and a career highlight.

		NM/M
Complete Set (6):		15.00
Common Card:		3.00
1	Roger Clemens (1999 post-season wins)	3.00
2	Roger Clemens (2000 post-season wins)	3.00
3	Roger Clemens (Sixth Cy Young)	3.00
4	Roger Clemens (4,000 Ks)	3.00
5	Roger Clemens (300th win)	3.00
--	Header Card	3.00

2003 Upper Deck Finite

	NM/M
Complete Set (380):	
Common Player (1-100):	1.00
Production 1,999	
Common (101-150):	1.00
Production 1,599	
Common (151-180):	2.00
Production 499	
Common (181-200):	2.50
Production 299	
Common (201-300):	1.50
Production 1,299	
Common (301-330):	3.00
Production 599	
Common (331-360):	3.00
Production 299	
Common (361-380):	5.00

Production 150		
Pack (3):		9.00
Box (10):		80.00
1	Darin Erstad	1.00
2	Garret Anderson	1.50
3	Tim Salmon	1.00
4	Troy Glaus	1.50
5	Luis Gonzalez	1.00
6	Randy Johnson	2.00
7	Curt Schilling	1.50
8	Andruw Jones	1.50
9	Gary Sheffield	1.50
10	Rafael Furcal	1.00
11	Greg Maddux	3.00
12	Chipper Jones	2.50
13	Tony Batista	1.00
14	Jay Gibbons	1.00
15	Johnny Damon	1.00
16	Derek Lowe	1.00
17	Nomar Garciaparra	3.00
18	Pedro J. Martinez	2.00
19	Manny Ramirez	1.50
20	Mark Prior	2.00
21	Kerry Wood	1.50
22	Corey Patterson	1.00
23	Sammy Sosa	3.00
24	Moises Alou	1.00
25	Magglio Ordonez	1.00
26	Frank Thomas	1.50
27	Paul Konerko	1.00
28	Bartolo Colon	1.00
29	Adam Dunn	1.00
30	Austin Kearns	1.00
31	Aaron Boone	1.00
32	Ken Griffey Jr.	2.50
33	Omar Vizquel	1.00
34	C.C. Sabathia	1.00
35	Brandon Phillips	1.00
36	Larry Walker	1.00
37	Preston Wilson	1.00
38	Todd Helton	1.50
39	Eric Munson	1.00
40	Ivan Rodriguez	1.50
41	Josh Beckett	1.50
42	Roy Oswalt	1.00
43	Craig Biggio	1.50
44	Jeff Bagwell	1.50
45	Dontrelle Willis	1.00
46	Carlos Beltran	1.00
47	Brent Mayne	1.00
48	Hideo Nomo	1.00
49	Rickey Henderson	1.00
50	Adrian Beltre	1.00
51	Miguel Cabrera	2.00
52	Kazuhisa Ishii	1.00
53	Richie Sexson	1.00
54	Torii Hunter	1.00
55	Jacque Jones	1.00
56	A.J. Pierzynski	1.00
57	Jose Vidro	1.00
58	Vladimir Guerrero	2.00
59	Tom Glavine	1.00
60	Jose Reyes	1.00
61	Mike Piazza	2.50
62	Jorge Posada	1.50
63	Mike Mussina	1.50
64	Robin Ventura	1.00
65	Mariano Rivera	1.50
66	Roger Clemens	3.00
67	Jason Giambi	2.00
68	Bernie Williams	1.50
69	Alfonso Soriano	2.00
70	Derek Jeter	5.00
71	Miguel Tejada	1.50
72	Eric Chavez	1.00
73	Tim Hudson	1.00
74	Barry Zito	1.00
75	Pat Burrell	1.00
76	Jim Thome	2.00
77	Bobby Abreu	1.00
78	Brian Giles	1.00
79	Reggie Sanders	1.00
80	Ryan Klesko	1.00
81	Edgardo Alfonzo	1.00
82	Rich Aurilia	1.00
83	Barry Bonds	5.00
84	Mike Cameron	1.00
85	Kazuhiro Sasaki	1.00
86	Bret Boone	1.00
87	Ichiro Suzuki	3.00
88	J.D. Drew	1.00
89	Jim Edmonds	1.50
90	Scott Rolen	2.00
91	Matt Morris	1.00
92	Tino Martinez	1.00
93	Albert Pujols	3.00
94	Rocco Baldelli	1.50
95	Hank Blalock	1.50

#	Player	Price
96	Alex Rodriguez	3.00
97	Rafael Palmeiro	1.50
98	Eric Hinske	1.00
99	Orlando Hudson	1.00
100	Carlos Delgado	1.50
101	Albert Pujols	3.00
102	Alex Rodriguez	3.00
103	Alfonso Soriano	2.00
104	Andruw Jones	1.50
105	Barry Zito	1.50
106	Bernie Williams	1.50
107	Carlos Delgado	1.50
108	Chipper Jones	2.50
109	Curt Schilling	1.50
110	Doug Mientkiewicz	1.00
111	Frank Thomas	1.50
112	Garret Anderson	1.50
113	Gary Sheffield	1.50
114	Greg Maddux	3.00
115	Hank Blalock	1.00
116	Hideki Matsui	4.00
117	Hideo Nomo	1.00
118	Ichiro Suzuki	3.00
119	Ivan Rodriguez	1.50
120	Jason Giambi	2.00
121	Jeff Bagwell	1.50
122	Jeff Kent	1.00
123	Jerome Williams	1.00
124	Jeromy Burnitz	1.00
125	Jim Thome	2.00
126	Jose Cruz Jr.	1.00
127	Ken Griffey Jr.	2.50
128	Kerry Wood	1.50
129	Lance Berkman	1.00
130	Luis Gonzalez	1.00
131	Manny Ramirez	1.50
132	Mark Prior	2.00
133	Miguel Cabrera	2.00
134	Miguel Tejada	1.50
135	Mike Piazza	2.50
136	Pat Burrell	1.00
137	Pedro J. Martinez	2.00
138	Rafael Furcal	1.00
139	Randy Johnson	2.00
140	Rich Harden	1.00
141	Rickey Henderson	1.50
142	Roberto Alomar	1.50
143	Roger Clemens	3.00
144	Sammy Sosa	3.00
145	Shawn Green	1.00
146	Todd Helton	1.50
147	Tom Glavine	1.00
148	Torii Hunter	1.00
149	Troy Glaus	1.00
150	Vladimir Guerrero	2.00
151	Adam Dunn	2.00
152	Albert Pujols	6.00
153	Alex Rodriguez	6.00
154	Alfonso Soriano	3.00
155	Andruw Jones	2.50
156	Barry Bonds	8.00
157	Carlos Delgado	2.50
158	Chipper Jones	3.00
159	Derek Jeter	8.00
160	Gary Sheffield	2.50
161	Hank Blalock	2.50
162	Hideki Matsui	6.00
163	Ichiro Suzuki	4.00
164	J.D. Drew	2.00
165	Jason Giambi	3.00
166	Jeff Bagwell	3.00
167	Jeff Kent	2.00
168	Jim Edmonds	2.00
169	Jim Thome	3.00
170	Ken Griffey Jr.	5.00
171	Luis Gonzalez	2.00
172	Magglio Ordonez	2.00
173	Manny Ramirez	2.50
174	Mike Lowell	2.00
175	Mike Piazza	4.00
176	Nomar Garciaparra	6.00
177	Rafael Palmeiro	2.50
178	Shawn Green	2.00
179	Troy Glaus	2.00
180	Vladimir Guerrero	3.00
181	Albert Pujols	8.00
182	Alex Rodriguez	8.00
183	Alfonso Soriano	4.00
184	Bernie Williams	2.50
185	Chipper Jones	4.00
186	Derek Jeter	10.00
187	Hideki Matsui	8.00
188	Ichiro Suzuki	6.00
189	Jim Thome	3.00
190	Joe DiMaggio	8.00
191	Ken Griffey Jr.	6.00
192	Mickey Mantle	12.00
193	Mike Piazza	5.00
194	Pedro J. Martinez	4.00
195	Randy Johnson	4.00
196	Roger Clemens	6.00
197	Sammy Sosa	4.00
198	Ted Williams	8.00
199	Troy Glaus	2.50
200	Vladimir Guerrero	3.00
201	Aaron Looper RC	2.00
202	Alejandro Machado RC	2.00
203	Alfredo Gonzalez RC	2.00
204	Andrew Brown RC	2.00
205	Anthony Ferrari RC	1.50
206	Aquilino Lopez RC	2.00
207	Beau Kemp RC	2.00
208	Bernie Castro RC	1.50
209	Bobby Madritsch RC	2.00
210	Brandon Villafuerte RC	1.50
211	Brent Hoard RC	2.00
212	Brian Stokes RC	1.50
213	Carlos Mendez RC	1.50

#	Player	Price
214	Chris Capuano RC	2.00
215	Chris Waters RC	1.50
216	Clint Barmes RC	3.00
217	Colin Porter RC	1.50
218	Cory Stewart	1.50
219	Craig Brazell RC	1.50
220	D.J. Carrasco RC	1.50
221	Daniel Cabrera RC	1.50
222	Dave Matranga RC	1.50
223	David Sanders	1.50
224	Diegomar Markwell	1.50
225	Edgar Gonzalez RC	2.00
226	Felix Sanchez	1.50
227	Fernando Cabrera RC	2.00
228	Francisco Cruceta RC	2.00
229	Francisco Rosario RC	2.00
230	Garrett Atkins RC	1.50
231	Gerald Laird	1.50
232	Guillermo Quiroz RC	2.00
233	Heath Bell RC	1.50
234	Delmon Young RC	8.00
235	Jason Shiell RC	2.00
236	Jeremy Bonderman	5.00
237	Jeremy Griffiths	1.50
238	Jeremy Guthrie	1.50
239	Jeremy Wedel RC	2.00
240	Carlos Rivera	1.50
241	Joe Valentine	1.50
242	Jon Leicester	1.50
243	Jonathan Pridie	1.50
244	Jorge Cordova	1.50
245	Jose Castillo	1.50
246	Josh Hall	2.00
247	Josh Stewart RC	1.50
248	Josh Willingham RC	4.00
249	Julio Manon RC	1.50
250	Kevin Correia RC	1.50
251	Kevin Ohme RC	2.00
252	Kevin Tolar	1.50
253	Luis De Los Santos	1.50
254	Jermaine Clark	1.50
255	Mark Malaska RC	2.00
256	Juan Dominguez	1.50
257	Michael Hessman RC	1.50
258	Micheal Nakamura RC	2.00
259	Miguel Ojeda RC	1.50
260	Mike Gallo	1.50
261	Edwin Jackson RC	4.00
262	Mike Ryan RC	1.50
263	Nate Bland RC	1.50
264	Nate Robertson	2.00
265	Nook Logan RC	2.00
266	Phil Seibel RC	1.50
267	Prentice Redman RC	2.00
268	Rafael Betancourt	1.50
269	Rett Johnson RC	2.00
270	Richard Fischer	1.50
271	Rick Roberts RC	1.50
272	Roger Deago	1.50
273	Ryan Cameron RC	1.50
274	Shane Bazzell	2.00
275	Erasmo Ramirez	1.50
276	Terrmel Sledge RC	2.00
277	Tim Olson RC	2.00
278	Tommy Phelps	1.50
279	Tommy Whiteman	1.50
280	Willie Eyre RC	1.50
281	Alex Prieto RC	2.00
282	Michel Hernandez RC	1.50
283	Greg Jones RC	1.50
284	Victor Martinez	2.50
285	Tom Gregorio RC	2.00
286	Marcus Thames RC	1.50
287	Jorge DePaula RC	2.00
288	Aaron Miles RC	2.00
289	Reynaldo Garcia	1.50
290	Brian Sweeney RC	1.50
291	Pete LaForest RC	2.00
292	Pete Zoccolillo RC	1.50
293	Danny Garcia RC	1.50
294	Jonny Gomes	3.00
295	Rosman Garcia RC	1.50
296	Mike Edwards	1.50
297	Marlon Byrd	1.50
298	Khalil Greene	1.50
299	Jose Valverde	1.50
300	Drew Henson	1.50
301	Chris Bootcheck	3.00
302	Matt Belisle	3.00
303	Kevin Gregg	3.00
304	Bobby Jenks	3.00
305	Jason Young	3.00
306	Laynce Nix	3.00
307	Robb Quinlan	3.00
308	Chase Utley	3.00
309	Humberto Quintero RC	4.00
310	Tim Raines Jr.	3.00
311	Stephen Smitherman	3.00
312	Jason Anderson	3.00
313	Joe Dawley	3.00
314	Chad Cordero RC	3.00
315	Victor Alvarez	3.00
316	Jimmy Gobble	3.00
317	Jared Fernandez	3.00
318	Eric Bruntlett	3.00
319	Neal Cotts	3.00
320	Ryan Madson	3.00
321	Rocco Baldelli	3.00
322	Graham Koonce RC	3.00
323	Bobby Crosby	3.00
324	Mike Wood	3.00
325	Jesse Garcia	3.00
326	Noah Lowry	6.00
327	Edwin Almonte	3.00
328	Justin Morneau	3.00
329	Steve Colyer	3.00
330	Vinnie Chulk	3.00
331	Brian Schmack	3.00

#	Player	Price
332	Stephen Randolph RC	3.00
333	Pedro Feliciano	3.00
334	Koyie Hill	3.00
335	Geoff Geary RC	3.00
336	Jon Switzer	3.00
337	Xavier Nady	3.00
338	Rich Harden	4.00
339	Dontrelle Willis	4.00
340	Angel Berroa	3.00
341	Jerome Williams	3.00
342	Brandon Claussen	3.00
343	Kurt Ainsworth	3.00
344	Horacio Ramirez	3.00
345	Hee Seop Choi	3.00
346	Billy Traber	3.00
347	Brandon Phillips	3.00
348	Jody Gerut	3.00
349	Mark Teixeira	4.00
350	Javier Lopez	3.00
351	Miguel Cabrera	5.00
352	Brad Lidge	3.00
353	Mike MacDougal	3.00
354	Ken Harvey	3.00
355	Chien-Ming Wang RC	15.00
356	Aaron Heilman	3.00
357	Jason Phillips	3.00
358	Jason Bay	3.00
359	Arnie Munoz	3.00
360	Ian Ferguson RC	3.00
361	Ryan Wagner RC	5.00
362	Rickie Weeks RC	15.00
363	Chad Gaudin RC	5.00
364	Jason Gilfillan RC	5.00
365	Jason Roach	3.00
366	Jhonny Peralta	6.00
367	Mike Neu RC	5.00
368	Jose Contreras RC	8.00
369	Wilfredo Ledezma RC	5.00
370	Lew Ford RC	5.00
371	Luis Ayala RC	5.00
372	Bo Hart RC	5.00
373	Brandon Webb RC	15.00
374	Dan Haren	15.00
375	Hideki Matsui RC	40.00
376	Jeff Duncan RC	8.00
377	Matt Kata RC	5.00
378	Oscar Villarreal RC	5.00
379	Rob Hammock RC	5.00
380	Todd Wellemeyer RC	5.00

Game Face (193-217):
Common Rookie: 5.00
Production 299

#	Player	Price
193	Aaron Looper RC	5.00
194	Alex Prieto RC	5.00
195	Bo Hart RC	5.00
196	Chad Gaudin RC	8.00
197	Colin Porter RC	5.00
198	D.J. Carrasco RC	5.00
199	Dan Haren	10.00
200	Delmon Young RC	15.00
201	Dontrelle Willis	8.00
202	Jon Switzer	5.00
203	Edwin Jackson RC	8.00
204	Fernando Cabrera RC	5.00
205	Garrett Atkins RC	5.00
206	Jeremy Bonderman	5.00
207	Kevin Ohme RC	5.00
208	Khalil Greene	5.00
209	Luis Ayala RC	5.00
210	Matt Kata RC	5.00
211	Noah Lowry	5.00
212	Rich Harden	5.00
213	Rickie Weeks RC	10.00
214	Rosman Garcia RC	5.00
215	Ryan Wagner RC	5.00
216	Tom Gregorio RC	5.00
217	Wilfredo Ledezma RC	5.00

SP Authentic (190-239):
Common SP Authentic Rookie: 4.00
Production 699

#	Player	Price
190	Aaron Looper	4.00
191	Alex Prieto	4.00
192	Alfredo Gonzalez RC	4.00
193	Andrew Brown RC	4.00
194	Anthony Ferrari	4.00
195	Aquilino Lopez RC	4.00
196	Beau Kemp RC	4.00
197	Bo Hart RC	4.00
198	Chad Gaudin RC	6.00
199	Colin Porter RC	4.00
200	D.J. Carrasco RC	4.00
201	Dan Haren	20.00
202	Danny Garcia RC	4.00
203	Jon Switzer	4.00
204	Edwin Jackson RC	4.00
205	Fernando Cabrera RC	4.00
206	Garrett Atkins	4.00
207	Gerald Laird	4.00
208	Greg Jones RC	4.00
209	Ian Ferguson RC	4.00
210	Jason Roach	4.00
211	Jason Shiell RC	4.00
212	Jeremy Bonderman	6.00
213	Jeremy Wedel RC	4.00
214	Jhonny Peralta	4.00
215	Delmon Young RC	15.00
216	Jorge DePaula RC	4.00
217	Josh Hall RC	4.00
218	Julio Manon RC	4.00
219	Kevin Correia RC	4.00
220	Kevin Ohme RC	4.00
221	Kevin Tolar	4.00
222	Luis Ayala RC	4.00
223	Luis De Los Santos	4.00
224	Chad Cordero RC	4.00
225	Mark Malaska RC	4.00
226	Khalil Greene	4.00
227	Micheal Nakamura RC	4.00

#	Player	Price
228	Michel Hernandez RC	4.00
229	Miguel Ojeda RC	4.00
230	Mike Neu RC	4.00
231	Nate Bland RC	4.00
232	Pete LaForest RC	4.00
233	Rickie Weeks RC	15.00
234	Rosman Garcia RC	4.00
235	Ryan Wagner RC	4.00
236	Lance Niekro	4.00
237	Tom Gregorio RC	4.00
238	Tommy Phelps	4.00
239	Wilfredo Ledezma RC	4.00

SPX (179-193, 381-387):

#	Player	Price
179	Chad Gaudin/150 RC	8.00
180	Chris Capuano/150 RC	8.00
181	Danny Garcia/150 RC	8.00
182	Delmon Young/150 RC	20.00
183	Edwin Jackson/150 RC	15.00
184	Greg Jones/150 RC	8.00
185	Jeremy Bonderman/150	10.00
186	Jorge DePaula/150 RC	8.00
187	Khalil Greene/150	8.00
188	Chad Cordero/150 RC	8.00
189	Miguel Cabrera/150	12.00
190	Rich Harden/150	10.00
191	Rickie Weeks/150 RC	20.00
192	Rosman Garcia/150 RC	8.00
193	Tom Gregorio/150 RC	8.00
381	Andrew Brown/Jsy/Auto./355 RC	15.00
382	Delmon Young/Jsy/Auto./355 RC	75.00
383	Colin Porter/Jsy/Auto./355 RC	15.00
385	Rickie Weeks/Jsy/Auto./355 RC	50.00
386	Dave Matranga/Jsy/Auto./355 RC	15.00
387	Bo Hart/Jsy/Auto./355 RC	15.00

UD Authentics (131-140):
Common Authentics: 5.00
Production 150

#	Player	Price
131	Dan Haren	10.00
132	Delmon Young RC	10.00
133	Dontrelle Willis	5.00
134	Edwin Jackson RC	5.00
135	Jeremy Bonderman	6.00
136	Khalil Greene	5.00
137	Rich Harden	5.00
138	Rickie Weeks RC	10.00
139	Rosman Garcia RC	5.00
140	Ryan Wagner RC	5.00

Gold

	Price
Gold (1-150):	1-2X
Gold (151-180):	1X
Production 199	
Gold (181-200):	1-2X
Production 99	

Elements Jersey

	NM/M
Common Player:	4.00
JB	Jeff Bagwell	8.00
RB	Rocco Baldelli	4.00
HB	Hank Blalock	6.00
HC	Hee Seop Choi	4.00
CJ	J.D. Drew	4.00
AD	Adam Dunn	5.00
JE	Jim Edmonds	5.00
SG	Shawn Green	4.00
KG	Ken Griffey Jr./SP	15.00
TH	Torii Hunter	6.00
CJ	Chipper Jones	4.00
JK	Jeff Kent	4.00
ML	Mike Lowell	4.00
GM	Greg Maddux	8.00
HM	Hideki Matsui	25.00

Code	Player	NM/M
MM	Matt Morris	5.00
RO	Roy Oswalt	5.00
CP	Corey Patterson	4.00
AP	Andy Pettitte	6.00
MI	Mike Piazza	8.00
MP	Mark Prior	6.00
AL	Albert Pujols	15.00
AR	Alex Rodriguez	10.00
AS	Alfonso Soriano	6.00
IS	Ichiro Suzuki	15.00
JT	Jim Thome	10.00
RW	Rickie Weeks/SP	6.00
DW	Dontrelle Willis	6.00
KW	Kerry Wood	6.00
DY	Delmon Young/SP	10.00

Elements Patch

No pricing due to scarcity.
Production 25 Sets
Patch Gold: No Pricing
Production 10 Sets

First Class Jersey

	NM/M
Common Player:	4.00
RC	Roger Clemens	6.00
JD	Joe DiMaggio/SP	80.00
TG	Troy Glaus	5.00
LG	Luis Gonzalez	4.00
KG	Ken Griffey Jr.	12.00
VG	Vladimir Guerrero	6.00
RJ	Randy Johnson	8.00
CJ	Chipper Jones	4.00
MM	Mickey Mantle/SP	100.00
PM	Pedro J. Martinez	8.00
HM	Hideki Matsui	25.00
MP	Mike Piazza	8.00
AP	Albert Pujols	20.00
AR	Alex Rodriguez	10.00
AS	Alfonso Soriano	6.00
SS	Sammy Sosa	10.00
IS	Ichiro Suzuki	15.00
JT	Jim Thome	10.00
BW	Bernie Williams	6.00
TW	Ted Williams/SP	75.00

Signatures

	NM/M
Common Auto:	6.00
Varying quantities produced	
EA	Erick Almonte/355	6.00
SZ	Shane Bazzell/250	6.00
MC	Miguel Cabrera/100	50.00
RC	Roger Clemens/50	75.00
WE	Willie Eyre/200	6.00
NG	Nomar Garciaparra/50	50.00
RK	Rob Hammock/200	6.00
RN	Rich Harden/150	15.00
BH	Bo Hart/150	8.00
HM	Hideki Matsui/99	150.00
MP	Mark Prior/75	10.00
JR	Jose Reyes/100	25.00
SR	Scott Rolen/100	30.00
CS	C.C. Sabathia/50	25.00
DS	David Sanders/150	6.00
PS	Phil Seibel/200	6.00
IS	Ichiro Suzuki/25	350.00
MT	Mark Teixeira/200	35.00
BW	Brandon Webb/150	20.00
JW	Jerome Williams/150	8.00
DW	Dontrelle Willis/50	10.00
DY	Delmon Young/50	25.00

SPX Jersey Autograph

	NM/M
Production 355	
DW	Dontrelle Willis	20.00

Code	Player	Price
KG	Khalil Greene	10.00
RH	Rich Harden	15.00

Stars and Stripes

	NM/M
Common Player:	2.00
Production 299 Sets	
USA-1	Justin Orenduff	2.00
USA-2	Micah Owings	2.00
USA-3	Steven Register	2.00
USA-4	Huston Street	5.00
USA-5	Justin Verlander	8.00
USA-6	Jered Weaver	8.00
USA-7	Matt Campbell	4.00
USA-8	Stephen Head	2.00
USA-9	Mark Romanczuk	2.00
USA-10	Jeff Clement	2.00
USA-11	Mike Nickeas	2.00
USA-12	Tyler Greene	2.00
USA-13	Paul Janish	2.00
USA-14	Jeff Larish	2.00
USA-15	Eric Patterson	2.00
USA-16	Dustin Pedroia	8.00
USA-17	Michael Griffin	2.00
USA-18	Brent Lillibridge	2.00
USA-19	Danny Putnam	2.00
USA-20	Seth Smith	3.00

Stars and Stripes Jersey

	NM/M
Common Player:	4.00
J1	Justin Orenduff	4.00
J2	Micah Owings	4.00
J3	Steven Register	4.00
J4	Huston Street	8.00
J5	Justin Verlander	8.00
J6	Jered Weaver	8.00
J7	Matt Campbell	6.00
J8	Stephen Head	4.00
J9	Mark Romanczuk	4.00
J10	Jeff Clement	4.00
J11	Mike Nickeas	4.00
J12	Tyler Greene	4.00
J13	Paul Janish	4.00
J14	Jeff Larish	4.00
J15	Eric Patterson	4.00
J16	Dustin Pedroia	10.00
J17	Michael Griffin	4.00
J18	Brent Lillibridge	4.00
J19	Danny Putnam	4.00
J20	Seth Smith	6.00

2003 Upper Deck First Pitch

	NM/M
Complete Set (300):	50.00
Common Player:	.10
Common SP (271-300):	1.00
Inserted 1:4	
Pack (5):	1.00
Box (36):	25.00
1	John Lackey	.10
2	Alex Cintron	.10
3	Jose Leon	.10
4	Bobby Hill	.10
5	Brandon Larson	.10
6	Raul Gonzalez	.10
7	Ben Broussard	.10
8	Earl Snyder	.10
9	Ramon Santiago	.10
10	Jason Lane	.10
11	Rob Hammock RC	.50
12	Kirk Saarloos	.10
13	Juan Brito	.10
14	Runelvys Hernandez	.10
15	Shawn Sedlacek	.10
16	Jayson Durocher	.10

#	Player	
17	Kevin Frederick	.10
18	Zach Day	.10
19	Marco Scutaro	.10
20	Marcus Thames	.10
21	Esteban German	.10
22	Brett Myers	.10
23	Oliver Perez	.10
24	Dennis Tankersley	.10
25	Julius Matos	.10
26	Jake Peavy	.10
27	Eric Cyr	.10
28	Mike Crudale	.10
29	Josh Pearce	.10
30	Carl Crawford	.10
31	Tim Salmon	.25
32	Troy Glaus	.50
33	Adam Kennedy	.10
34	David Eckstein	.10
35	Bengie Molina	.10
36	Jarrod Washburn	.10
37	Ramon Ortiz	.10
38	Eric Chavez	.25
39	Miguel Tejada	.25
40	Adam Piatt	.10
41	Jermaine Dye	.10
42	Olmedo Saenz	.10
43	Tim Hudson	.20
44	Barry Zito	.25
45	Billy Koch	.10
46	Shannon Stewart	.10
47	Kelvim Escobar	.10
48	Jose Cruz Jr.	.10
49	Vernon Wells	.25
50	Roy Halladay	.10
51	Esteban Loaiza	.10
52	Eric Hinske	.10
53	Steve Cox	.10
54	Brent Abernathy	.10
55	Ben Grieve	.10
56	Aubrey Huff	.10
57	Jared Sandberg	.10
58	Paul Wilson	.10
59	Tanyon Sturtze	.10
60	Jim Thome	.50
61	Omar Vizquel	.20
62	C.C. Sabathia	.10
63	Chris Magruder	.10
64	Ricky Gutierrez	.10
65	Einar Diaz	.10
66	Danys Baez	.10
67	Ichiro Suzuki	.75
68	Ruben Sierra	.10
69	Carlos Guillen	.10
70	Mark McLemore	.10
71	Dan Wilson	.10
72	Jamie Moyer	.10
73	Joel Pineiro	.10
74	Edgar Martinez	.10
75	Tony Batista	.10
76	Jay Gibbons	.10
77	Chris Singleton	.10
78	Melvin Mora	.10
79	Geronimo Gil	.10
80	Rodrigo Lopez	.10
81	Jorge Julio	.10
82	Rafael Palmeiro	.40
83	Juan Gonzalez	.40
84	Mike Young	.10
85	Hideki Irabu	.10
86	Chan Ho Park	.10
87	Kevin Mench	.10
88	Doug Davis	.10
89	Pedro J. Martinez	.75
90	Shea Hillenbrand	.10
91	Derek Lowe	.10
92	Jason Varitek	.10
93	Tony Clark	.10
94	John Burkett	.10
95	Frank Castillo	.10
96	Nomar Garciaparra	1.00
97	Rickey Henderson	.25
98	Mike Sweeney	.10
99	Carlos Febles	.10
100	Mark Quinn	.10
101	Raul Ibanez	.10
102	A.J. Hinch	.10
103	Paul Byrd	.10
104	Chuck Knoblauch	.10
105	Dmitri Young	.10
106	Randall Simon	.10
107	Brandon Inge	.10
108	Damion Easley	.10
109	Carlos Pena	.10
110	George Lombard	.10
111	Juan Acevedo	.10
112	Torii Hunter	.25
113	Doug Mientkiewicz	.10
114	David Ortiz	.10
115	Eric Milton	.10
116	Eddie Guardado	.10
117	Cristian Guzman	.10
118	Corey Koskie	.10
119	Magglio Ordonez	.25
120	Mark Buehrle	.10
121	Todd Ritchie	.10
122	Jose Valentin	.10
123	Paul Konerko	.10
124	Carlos Lee	.10
125	Jon Garland	.10
126	Jason Giambi	.75
127	Derek Jeter	1.50
128	Roger Clemens	1.00
129	Raul Mondesi	.25
130	Jorge Posada	.25
131	Rondell White	.10
132	Robin Ventura	.20
133	Mike Mussina	.40
134	Jeff Bagwell	.50
135	Craig Biggio	.20
136	Morgan Ensberg	.10
137	Richard Hidalgo	.10
138	Brad Ausmus	.10
139	Roy Oswalt	.20
140	Carlos Hernandez	.10
141	Shane Reynolds	.10
142	Gary Sheffield	.25
143	Andruw Jones	.25
144	Tom Glavine	.25
145	Rafael Furcal	.20
146	Javy Lopez	.10
147	Vinny Castilla	.10
148	Marcus Giles	.10
149	Kevin Millwood	.20
150	Jason Marquis	.10
151	Ruben Quevedo	.10
152	Ben Sheets	.10
153	Geoff Jenkins	.10
154	Jose Hernandez	.10
155	Glendon Rusch	.10
156	Jeffrey Hammonds	.10
157	Alex Sanchez	.10
158	Jim Edmonds	.25
159	Tino Martinez	.10
160	Albert Pujols	.75
161	Eli Marrero	.10
162	Woody Williams	.10
163	Fernando Vina	.10
164	Jason Isringhausen	.10
165	Jason Simontacchi	.10
166	Kerry Robinson	.10
167	Sammy Sosa	.75
168	Juan Cruz	.10
169	Fred McGriff	.20
170	Antonio Alfonseca	.10
171	Jon Lieber	.10
172	Mark Prior	.50
173	Moises Alou	.20
174	Matt Clement	.10
175	Mark Bellhorn	.10
176	Randy Johnson	.50
177	Luis Gonzalez	.20
178	Tony Womack	.10
179	Mark Grace	.25
180	Junior Spivey	.10
181	Byung-Hyun Kim	.10
182	Danny Bautista	.10
183	Brian Anderson	.10
184	Shawn Green	.25
185	Brian Jordan	.10
186	Eric Karros	.10
187	Andy Ashby	.10
188	Cesar Izturis	.10
189	Dave Roberts	.10
190	Eric Gagne	.10
191	Kazuhisa Ishii	.10
192	Adrian Beltre	.10
193	Vladimir Guerrero	.50
194	Tony Armas Jr.	.10
195	Bartolo Colon	.10
196	Troy O'Leary	.10
197	Tomokazu Ohka	.10
198	Brad Wilkerson	.10
199	Orlando Cabrera	.10
200	Barry Bonds	1.50
201	David Bell	.10
202	Tsuyoshi Shinjo	.10
203	Benito Santiago	.10
204	Livan Hernandez	.10
205	Jason Schmidt	.10
206	Kirk Rueter	.10
207	Ramon E. Martinez	.10
208	Mike Lowell	.10
209	Luis Castillo	.10
210	Derek Lee	.10
211	Andy Fox	.10
212	Eric Owens	.10
213	Charles Johnson	.10
214	Brad Penny	.10
215	A.J. Burnett	.10
216	Edgardo Alfonzo	.10
217	Roberto Alomar	.40
218	Rey Ordonez	.10
219	Al Leiter	.10
220	Roger Cedeno	.10
221	Timoniel Perez	.10
222	Jeromy Burnitz	.10
223	Pedro Astacio	.10
224	Joe McEwing	.10
225	Ryan Klesko	.20
226	Ramon Vazquez	.10
227	Mark Kotsay	.10
228	Bubba Trammell	.10
229	Wiki Gonzalez	.10
230	Trevor Hoffman	.10
231	Ron Gant	.10
232	Bobby Abreu	.20
233	Marlon Anderson	.10
234	Jeremy Giambi	.10
235	Jimmy Rollins	.20
236	Mike Lieberthal	.10
237	Vicente Padilla	.10
238	Randy Wolf	.10
239	Pokey Reese	.10
240	Brian Giles	.10
241	Jack Wilson	.10
242	Mike Williams	.10
243	Kip Wells	.10
244	Robert Mackowiak	.10
245	Craig Wilson	.10
246	Adam Dunn	.50
247	Sean Casey	.10
248	Todd Walker	.10
249	Corky Miller	.10
250	Ryan Dempster	.10
251	Reggie Taylor	.10
252	Aaron Boone	.10
253	Larry Walker	.10
254	Jose Ortiz	.10
255	Todd Zeile	.10
256	Bobby Estalella	.10
257	Juan Pierre	.10
258	Terry Shumpert	.10
259	Mike Hampton	.10
260	Denny Stark	.10
261	Shawn Green	.20
262	Derek Lowe	.10
263	Barry Bonds	.50
264	Mike Cameron	.10
265	Luis Castillo	.10
266	Vladimir Guerrero	.40
267	Jason Giambi	.40
268	Eric Gagne	.10
269	Magglio Ordonez	.20
270	Jim Thome	.25
271	Hideki Matsui RC	20.00
272	Jose Contreras RC	4.00
273	Robert Madritsch	1.00
274	Shane Bazzell RC	1.50
275	Felix Sanchez RC	2.00
276	Todd Wellemeyer RC	2.00
277	Lew Ford RC	2.00
278	Jeremy Griffiths	1.00
279	Oscar Villarreal RC	1.00
280	Brandon Webb RC	4.00
281	Delvis Lantigua	3.00
282	Josh Willingham RC	1.00
283	Mike Nicolas RC	1.00
284	Mike Hampton	1.00
285	Jim Thome	2.00
286	Bartolo Colon	1.00
287	Orlando Hernandez	1.00
288	Jeremy Giambi	1.00
289	Jeff Kent	1.50
290	Tom Glavine	1.50
291	Cliff Floyd	1.00
292	Tsuyoshi Shinjo	1.00
293	Jose Cruz Jr.	1.00
294	Edgardo Alfonzo	1.00
295	Andres Galarraga	1.00
296	Troy O'Leary	1.00
297	Eric Karros	1.00
298	Ivan Rodriguez	1.00
299	Fred McGriff	1.50
300	Preston Wilson	1.00

Signature Stars

Print runs listed:

		NM/M
NM	Nomar Garciaparra/100	100.00
JG	Jason Giambi/100	30.00
KG	Ken Griffey Jr./100	75.00
KGS	Ken Griffey Sr./800	6.00
SS	Sammy Sosa/50	175.00
IS	Ichiro Suzuki/50	375.00

2003 Upper Deck Game Face Promo

This card introduces UD's Game Face brand for '03. Back has a large diagonal "SAMPLE" overprint.

		NM/M
30	Ken Griffey Jr.	2.00

2003 Upper Deck Game Face

	NM/M
Complete Set (192):	
Common Player:	.25
Common Base SP:	1.00
Inserted 1:4	
Common SP (121-150):	2.00
Inserted 1:8	
Common SP (151-192):	3.00
Inserted 1:16	
Pack (4):	4.00
Box (24):	75.00

#	Player	
1	Darin Erstad	.50
2	Garret Anderson	.50
3	Tim Salmon	.50
4	Jarrod Washburn	.25
5	Troy Glaus/SP	1.50
6	Luis Gonzalez	.50

AUSTIN KEARNS

#	Player	
7	Junior Spivey	.25
8	Randy Johnson/SP	2.00
9	Curt Schilling/SP	1.50
10	Andruw Jones	.75
11	Gary Sheffield	.25
12	Rafael Furcal	.25
13	Greg Maddux/SP	3.00
14	Chipper Jones/SP	3.00
15	Tony Batista	.25
16	Rodrigo Lopez	.25
17	Jay Gibbons	.25
18	Shea Hillenbrand	.25
19	Johnny Damon	.25
20	Derek Lowe	.25
21	Nomar Garciaparra	2.50
22	Pedro J. Martinez/SP	2.00
23	Manny Ramirez/SP	1.50
24	Mark Prior	1.00
25	Kerry Wood	.75
26	Corey Patterson	.25
27	Sammy Sosa	2.00
28	Magglio Ordonez	.50
29	Frank Thomas	1.00
30	Paul Konerko	.25
31	Adam Dunn	1.00
32	Austin Kearns	1.00
33	Aaron Boone	.25
34	Ken Griffey Jr./SP	3.00
35	Omar Vizquel	.40
36	C.C. Sabathia	.25
37	Karim Garcia/SP	1.00
38	Larry Walker	.40
39	Preston Wilson	.25
40	Jay Payton	.25
41	Todd Helton/SP	1.50
42	Carlos Pena	.25
43	Eric Munson	.25
44	Mike Lowell	.25
45	Josh Beckett	.25
46	A.J. Burnett	.25
47	Roy Oswalt	.50
48	Craig Biggio	.50
49	Jeff Bagwell/SP	1.50
50	Lance Berkman/SP	1.25
51	Mike Sweeney	1.25
52	Carlos Beltran	.25
53	Hideo Nomo	.75
54	Odalis Perez	.25
55	Adrian Beltre	.25
56	Shawn Green/SP	1.00
57	Kazuhisa Ishii/SP	1.00
58	Ben Sheets	.50
59	Richie Sexson	.50
60	Torii Hunter	.50
61	Jacque Jones	.25
62	Eric Milton	.25
63	Corey Koskie	.25
64	A.J. Pierzynski	.25
65	Jose Vidro	.25
66	Bartolo Colon	.25
67	Vladimir Guerrero/SP	1.50
68	Tom Glavine	.50
69	Mike Piazza/SP	3.00
70	Roberto Alomar/SP	1.50
71	Jorge Posada	.50
72	Mike Mussina	.75
73	Robin Ventura	.25
74	Raul Mondesi	.50
75	Roger Clemens/SP	3.00
76	Jason Giambi/SP	2.00
77	Bernie Williams/SP	1.50
78	Alfonso Soriano/SP	2.00
79	Derek Jeter/SP	6.00
80	Miguel Tejada	.75
81	Eric Chavez	.50
82	Tim Hudson	.50
83	Barry Zito	.50
84	Mark Mulder	.50
85	Pat Burrell	1.00
86	Jim Thome	1.00
87	Bobby Abreu	.50
88	Brian Giles	.50
89	Jason Kendall	.40
90	Aramis Ramirez	.25
91	Ryan Klesko	.25
92	Phil Nevin	.25
93	Sean Burroughs	.25
94	J.T. Snow	.25
95	Rich Aurilia	.25
96	Benito Santiago	.25
97	Barry Bonds/SP	6.00
98	Edgar Martinez	.25
99	John Olerud	.50
100	Bret Boone	.25
101	Ichiro Suzuki/SP	3.00
102	J.D. Drew	.50
103	Jim Edmonds	.50
104	Scott Rolen	1.00
105	Matt Morris	.50
106	Tino Martinez	.25
107	Albert Pujols/SP	2.00
108	Aubrey Huff	.25
109	Carl Crawford	.25
110	Rafael Palmeiro	.75
111	Hank Blalock	.50
112	Alex Rodriguez/SP	5.00
113	Kevin Mench/SP	2.00
114	Juan Gonzalez/SP	1.50
115	Shannon Stewart	.25
116	Vernon Wells	.25
117	Josh Phelps	.25
118	Eric Hinske	.25
119	Orlando Hudson	.25
120	Carlos Delgado/SP	2.00
121	David Sanders RC	2.00
122	Rob Hammock RC	2.00
123	Rett Johnson RC	2.00
124	Mike Nicolas RC	2.00
125	Terrmel Sledge RC	3.00
126	Ryan Cameron RC	2.00
127	Prentice Redman RC	2.00
128	Clint Barmes RC	4.00
129	Brent Hoard RC	2.00
130	Willie Eyre RC	2.00
131	Phil Seibel RC	2.00
132	Chris Capuano RC	3.00
133	Bobby Madritsch RC	2.00
134	Shane Bazzell RC	2.00
135	Jeremy Griffiths	2.00
136	Jon Leicester RC	2.00
137	Brandon Webb RC	5.00
138	Todd Wellemeyer RC	2.00
139	Jose Contreras RC	4.00
140	Felix Sanchez RC	2.00
141	Arnie Munoz RC	2.00
142	Delvis Lantigua RC	2.00
143	Francisco Cruceta RC	2.00
144	Josh Willingham RC	3.00
145	Oscar Villarreal RC	2.00
146	Ian Ferguson RC	2.00
147	Pedro Liriano	2.00
148	Lew Ford RC	2.00
149	Jeff Duncan RC	2.00
150	Richard Fischer RC	2.00
151	Troy Glaus	3.00
152	Randy Johnson	5.00
153	Hideki Matsui	15.00
154	Chipper Jones	6.00
155	Nomar Garciaparra	8.00
156	Pedro J. Martinez	5.00
157	Ted Williams	15.00
158	Sammy Sosa	8.00
159	Ken Griffey Jr.	8.00
160	Vladimir Guerrero	5.00
161	Mike Piazza	8.00
162	Mickey Mantle	30.00
163	Alfonso Soriano	6.00
164	Derek Jeter	15.00
165	Roger Clemens	8.00
166	Jason Giambi	8.00
167	Barry Bonds	15.00
168	Ichiro Suzuki	8.00
169	Albert Pujols	8.00
170	Mark McGwire	15.00
171	Alex Rodriguez	10.00
172	Ken Griffey Jr., Roy Oswalt	
173	Barry Zito, Troy Glaus	3.00
174	Tim Hudson, Ichiro Suzuki	8.00
175	Alex Rodriguez, Mark Mulder	10.00
176	Tom Glavine, Vladimir Guerrero	4.00
177	Mike Piazza, Greg Maddux	6.00
178	Mark McGwire, Sammy Sosa	10.00
179	Lance Berkman, Mark Prior	4.00
180	Albert Pujols, Kerry Wood	6.00
181	Randy Johnson, Jeff Bagwell	4.00
182	Derek Jeter, Curt Schilling	10.00
183	Barry Bonds, Hideo Nomo	10.00
184	Todd Helton, Kazuhisa Ishii	4.00
185	Freddy Garcia, Eric Chavez	3.00
186	Al Leiter, Chipper Jones	6.00
187	Ted Williams, Nomar Garciaparra	10.00
188	Pedro J. Martinez, Hideki Matsui	15.00
189	Derek Lowe, Bernie Williams	3.00
190	Roger Clemens, Mike Piazza	10.00
191	Mike Mussina, Manny Ramirez	4.00
192	Jason Giambi, Mickey Mantle	20.00

Autograph

	NM/M
Common Player:	
Inserted 1:576	
Golds:	No Pricing
Production 25	

LB	Lance Berkman/SP	50.00
JG	Jason Giambi	40.00
KG	Ken Griffey Jr.	125.00
TH	Todd Helton/SP	45.00
HM	Hideki Matsui/SP	250.00
MM	Mark McGwire/SP	350.00
MP	Mark Prior/SP	40.00
SS	Sammy Sosa	120.00
IS	Ichiro Suzuki/SP	300.00
BZ	Barry Zito	40.00

Gear

GAME FACE GEAR

	NM/M
Common Player:	4.00
Inserted 1:8	
Patches:	3-5X
Production 100 Sets	

BA	Bobby Abreu	4.00
EA	Edgardo Alfonzo	4.00
JB	Jeff Bagwell	8.00
CB	Carlos Beltran	6.00
LB	Lance Berkman	4.00
AB	Aaron Boone	8.00
PB	Pat Burrell	4.00
EC	Eric Chavez	4.00
RC	Roger Clemens	15.00
CD	Carlos Delgado	4.00
DR	J.D. Drew	4.00
DR2	J.D. Drew	4.00
AD	Adam Dunn	8.00
JE	Jim Edmonds	4.00
DE	Darin Erstad	4.00
DE2	Darin Erstad	4.00
JG	Jason Giambi	6.00
BG	Brian Giles	4.00
TG	Tom Glavine	6.00
GO	Juan Gonzalez	6.00
LG	Luis Gonzalez	4.00
LG2	Luis Gonzalez	4.00
SG	Shawn Green	4.00
TH	Todd Helton	8.00
TI	Tim Hudson	4.00
HU	Torii Hunter	4.00
KI	Kazuhisa Ishii	4.00
RJ	Randy Johnson	8.00
AJ	Andruw Jones	6.00
CJ	Chipper Jones	8.00
JJ	Jacque Jones	4.00
AK	Austin Kearns	4.00
JK	Jason Kendall	4.00
KE	Jeff Kent	6.00
RK	Ryan Klesko	4.00
ML	Mike Lowell	4.00
GM	Greg Maddux	10.00
GM2	Greg Maddux	10.00
EM	Edgar Martinez	6.00
PM	Pedro J. Martinez	8.00
MM	Mike Mussina	8.00
HN	Hideo Nomo	8.00
MO	Magglio Ordonez	4.00
RO	Roy Oswalt	4.00
RP	Rafael Palmeiro	4.00
MiP	Mike Piazza	10.00
JP	Jorge Posada	8.00
MaP	Mark Prior	8.00
MR	Manny Ramirez	8.00
AR	Alex Rodriguez	10.00
AR2	Alex Rodriguez	10.00
IR	Ivan Rodriguez	8.00
SR	Scott Rolen	8.00
CS	Curt Schilling	8.00
RS	Richie Sexson	6.00
AS	Alfonso Soriano	10.00
SS	Sammy Sosa	10.00
IS	Ichiro Suzuki/SP	50.00
MS	Mike Sweeney	4.00
MT	Miguel Tejada	6.00
FT	Frank Thomas	8.00
JT	Jim Thome	8.00
JV	Jose Vidro	4.00
OV	Omar Vizquel	4.00
LW	Larry Walker	4.00
BW	Bernie Williams	4.00
PW	Preston Wilson	4.00
KW	Kerry Wood	8.00
BZ	Barry Zito	4.00
BZ2	Barry Zito	4.00

Patch

GAME FACE PATCH

Common Player:
Production 100 Sets

2003 Upper Deck Honor Roll

	NM/M
Complete Set (161):	
Common Player:	.20
Common Even # SP (2-60):	1.00
Inserted 1:6	
Common SP (131-161):	3.00
Production 2,500	
Pack (5):	1.50

Box (24):		30.00
1	Derek Jeter	2.00
2	Derek Jeter/SP	5.00
3	Alex Rodriguez	1.50
4	Alex Rodriguez/SP	5.00
5	Roger Clemens	1.50
6	Roger Clemens/SP	4.00
7	Mike Piazza	1.00
8	Mike Piazza/SP	3.00
9	Jeff Bagwell	.50
10	Jeff Bagwell/SP	1.50
11	Vladimir Guerrero	.75
12	Vladimir Guerrero/SP	2.00
13	Ken Griffey Jr.	1.50
14	Ken Griffey Jr./SP	3.00
15	Greg Maddux	1.50
16	Greg Maddux/SP	3.00
17	Chipper Jones	.75
18	Chipper Jones/SP	2.00
19	Randy Johnson	.75
20	Randy Johnson/SP	2.00
21	Miguel Tejada	.50
22	Miguel Tejada/SP	1.50
23	Nomar Garciaparra	1.50
24	Nomar Garciaparra/SP	4.00
25	Ichiro Suzuki	1.50
26	Ichiro Suzuki/SP	4.00
27	Sammy Sosa	1.00
28	Sammy Sosa/SP	3.00
29	Albert Pujols	2.00
30	Albert Pujols/SP	5.00
31	Alfonso Soriano	.75
32	Alfonso Soriano/SP	2.00
33	Barry Bonds	2.00
34	Barry Bonds/SP	6.00
35	Jeff Kent	.30
36	Jeff Kent/SP	1.00
37	Jim Thome	.50
38	Jim Thome/SP	1.50
39	Pedro J. Martinez	.75
40	Pedro J. Martinez/SP	2.00
41	Todd Helton	.50
42	Todd Helton/SP	1.50
43	Troy Glaus	.50
44	Troy Glaus/SP	1.50
45	Mark Prior	.75
46	Mark Prior/SP	2.00
47	Tom Glavine	.40
48	Tom Glavine/SP	1.50
49	Pat Burrell	.40
50	Pat Burrell/SP	1.00
51	Barry Zito	.40
52	Barry Zito/SP	1.00
53	Bernie Williams	.50
54	Bernie Williams/SP	1.50
55	Curt Schilling	.50
56	Curt Schilling/SP	1.50
57	Darin Erstad	.30
58	Darin Erstad/SP	1.00
59	Carlos Delgado	.50
60	Carlos Delgado/SP	1.50
61	Gary Sheffield	.40
62	Gary Sheffield/SP	.40
63	Frank Thomas	.50
64	Frank Thomas	.50
65	Lance Berkman	.40
66	Lance Berkman	.40
67	Shawn Green	.40
68	Shawn Green	.40
69	Hideo Nomo	.40
70	Hideo Nomo	.40
71	Torii Hunter	.40
72	Torii Hunter	.40
73	Roberto Alomar	.50
74	Roberto Alomar	.50
75	Andruw Jones	.50
76	Andruw Jones	.50
77	Scott Rolen	.75
78	Scott Rolen	.75
79	Eric Chavez	.40
80	Eric Chavez	.40
81	Rafael Palmeiro	.50
82	Rafael Palmeiro	.50
83	Bobby Abreu	.20
84	Bobby Abreu	.20
85	Craig Biggio	.20
86	Craig Biggio	.20
87	Rafael Furcal	.20
88	Rafael Furcal	.20
89	Jose Vidro	.20
90	Jose Vidro	.20
91	Luis Gonzalez	.20
92	Luis Gonzalez	.20
93	Roy Oswalt	.20
94	Roy Oswalt	.20
95	Cliff Floyd	.20
96	Cliff Floyd	.20
97	Larry Walker	.20

98	Larry Walker	.20
99	Jim Edmonds	.30
100	Jim Edmonds	.30
101	Adam Dunn	.40
102	Adam Dunn	.40
103	J.D. Drew	.20
104	J.D. Drew	.20
105	Josh Beckett	.20
106	Josh Beckett	.20
107	Brian Giles	.20
108	Brian Giles	.20
109	Magglio Ordonez	.40
110	Magglio Ordonez	.40
111	Edgardo Alfonzo	.20
112	Edgardo Alfonzo	.20
113	Bartolo Colon	.20
114	Bartolo Colon	.20
115	Roy Halladay	.20
116	Roy Halladay	.20
117	Joe Thurston	.20
118	Joe Thurston	.20
119	Brandon Phillips	.20
120	Brandon Phillips	.20
121	Kazuhisa Ishii	.20
122	Kazuhisa Ishii	.20
123	Mike Mussina	.40
124	Mike Mussina	.40
125	Tim Hudson	.40
126	Tim Hudson	.40
127	Mariano Rivera	.20
128	Mariano Rivera	.20
129	Travis Hafner	.20
130	Travis Hafner	.20
131	Hideki Matsui RC	20.00
132	Jose Contreras RC	5.00
133	Jason Anderson	3.00
134	Willie Eyre RC	3.00
135	Shane Bazzell RC	3.00
136	Guillermo Quiroz RC	5.00
137	Francisco Cruceta RC	3.00
138	Jhonny Peralta	4.00
139	Aaron Looper RC	3.00
140	Bobby Madritsch RC	3.00
141	Michael Hessman RC	3.00
142	Todd Wellemeyer RC	3.00
143	Matt Bruback RC	3.00
144	Chris Capuano RC	4.00
145	Oscar Villarreal RC	3.00
146	Prentice Redman RC	3.00
147	Jeff Duncan RC	5.00
148	Phil Seibel RC	3.00
149	Arnaldo Munoz	3.00
150	David Sanders RC	3.00
151	Rick Roberts RC	3.00
152	Termmel Sledge RC	4.00
153	Franklin Perez	3.00
154	Jeremy Wedel RC	3.00
155	Ian Ferguson RC	3.00
156	Josh Hall RC	4.00
157	Rocco Baldelli	5.00
158	Alejandro Machado RC	3.00
159	Jorge Cordova RC	3.00
160	Wilfredo Ledezma RC	3.00
161	Luis Ayala RC	3.00

Silver

Even # SP's (2-60):	1-2X
Non-SP's (1-130):	4-8X
SP's (132-161):	.5-1X
Production 150 Sets	

Gold

Production 25 Sets:
No pricing due to scarcity.

Dean's List

		NM/M
Common Player:		4.00
Inserted 1:24		
RC	Roger Clemens	10.00
RC1	Roger Clemens	10.00
JG1	Jason Giambi	4.00
JG1	Jason Giambi	4.00
TG	Troy Glaus	4.00
TG1	Troy Glaus	4.00
NG	Shawn Green	4.00
NG1	Shawn Green	4.00
VG	Vladimir Guerrero	6.00
VG	Vladimir Guerrero	6.00
KG	Ken Griffey Jr.	10.00
KG1	Ken Griffey Jr.	10.00
CJ	Chipper Jones	8.00
CJ1	Chipper Jones	8.00
HM	Hideki Matsui	20.00
HM1	Hideki Matsui	20.00
HN	Hideo Nomo	10.00
HN1	Hideo Nomo	10.00
MP	Mike Piazza	10.00
MP1	Mike Piazza	10.00
MA	Mark Prior	8.00
MA1	Mark Prior	8.00
AP	Albert Pujols	15.00
AP1	Albert Pujols	15.00
AR	Alex Rodriguez	10.00
AR1	Alex Rodriguez	10.00
SS	Sammy Sosa	10.00
IS	Ichiro Suzuki	20.00
IS1	Ichiro Suzuki	20.00

Grade A Batting Gloves

		NM/M
Most not priced due to scarcity.		
Inserted 1:960		
RA	Roberto Alomar/65	20.00
CD	Carlos Delgado/65	15.00
TG	Troy Glaus/60	15.00
JG	Juan Gonzalez/65	15.00
RM	Raul Mondesi/65	10.00
RP	Rafael Palmeiro/65	20.00
MR	Manny Ramirez/69	20.00
AR	Alex Rodriguez/67	25.00
IR	Ivan Rodriguez/70	20.00
MT	Miguel Tejada/70	10.00
FT	Frank Thomas/70	20.00

Leather of Distinction

		NM/M
Most not priced due to scarcity.		
Inserted 1:960		
KG	Ken Griffey Jr./70	30.00
RP	Rafael Palmeiro/70	20.00
MP	Mike Piazza/50	40.00
MR	Manny Ramirez/70	20.00
AR	Alex Rodriguez/70	25.00
IR	Ivan Rodriguez/69	20.00
TS	Tim Salmon/70	10.00
GS	Gary Sheffield/70	10.00
FT	Frank Thomas/70	20.00
OV	Omar Vizquel/65	10.00

2003 Upper Deck Magazine

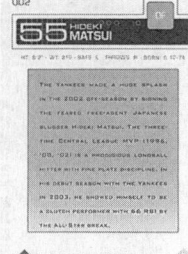

Three baseball players were included in a nine-card sheet inserted into a special-edition collectors' magazine produced by Upper Deck in November 2003. Cards are in standard 2-1/2" x 3-1/2" format perforated on two, three, or four sides, depending on their placement on the panel. Fronts have game-action photos with player name, position and uniform number. Backs have personal data and a career summary. Only the baseball players are listed here.

		NM/M
Complete Magazine:		12.00
Common Player:		1.00
UD2	Hideki Matsui	1.00
UD4	Ichiro	1.50
UD7	Mickey Mantle	2.00

2003 Upper Deck Hideki Matsui Hawaii

The first licensed card of Yankees Japanese import slugger Hideki Matsui was distributed to attendees at the 2003 Hawaii Trade Conference. The card features silver-foil accents on front.

		NM/M
HM	Hideki Matsui	75.00

2003 Upper Deck MVP

		NM/M
Complete Set (220):		20.00
Complete Factory Set (330):		30.00
Common Player:		.10
Pack (8):		1.50
Box (24):		25.00
1	Troy Glaus	.40
2	Darin Erstad	.25
3	Jarrod Washburn	.10
4	Francisco Rodriguez	.10
5	Garret Anderson	.20
6	Tim Salmon	.20
7	Adam Kennedy	.10
8	Randy Johnson	.50
9	Luis Gonzalez	.20
10	Curt Schilling	.50
11	Junior Spivey	.10
12	Craig Counsell	.10
13	Mark Grace	.25
14	Steve Finley	.10
15	Javy Lopez	.10
16	Rafael Furcal	.10
17	John Smoltz	.15
18	Greg Maddux	.75
19	Chipper Jones	.50
20	Gary Sheffield	.20
21	Andruw Jones	.20
22	Tony Batista	.10
23	Geronimo Gil	.10
24	Jay Gibbons	.10
25	Rodrigo Lopez	.10
26	Chris Singleton	.10
27	Melvin Mora	.10
28	Jeff Conine	.10
29	Nomar Garciaparra	1.00
30	Pedro J. Martinez	.50
31	Manny Ramirez	.50
32	Shea Hillenbrand	.10
33	Johnny Damon	.40
34	Jason Varitek	.25
35	Derek Lowe	.10
36	Trot Nixon	.10
37	Sammy Sosa	.75
38	Kerry Wood	.50
39	Mark Prior	.50
40	Moises Alou	.20
41	Corey Patterson	.25
42	Hee Seop Choi	.10
43	Mark Bellhorn	.10
44	Frank Thomas	.40
45	Mark Buehrle	.10
46	Magglio Ordonez	.20
47	Carlos Lee	.20
48	Paul Konerko	.20
49	Joe Borchard	.10
50	Joe Crede	.10
51	Ken Griffey Jr.	.75
52	Adam Dunn	.40
53	Austin Kearns	.10
54	Aaron Boone	.10
55	Sean Casey	.10
56	Danny Graves	.10
57	Russell Branyan	.10
58	Matt Lawton	.10
59	C.C. Sabathia	.10
60	Omar Vizquel	.20
61	Brandon Phillips	.10
62	Karim Garcia	.10
63	Ellis Burks	.10
64	Cliff Lee	.10
65	Todd Helton	.40
66	Larry Walker	.20
67	Jay Payton	.10
68	Brent Butler	.10
69	Juan Uribe	.10
70	Jason Jennings	.10
71	Denny Stark	.10
72	Dmitri Young	.10
73	Carlos Pena	.10
74	Andres Torres	.10
75	Andy Van Hekken	.10
76	George Lombard	.10
77	Eric Munson	.10
78	Bobby Higginson	.10
79	Luis Castillo	.10
80	A.J. Burnett	.10
81	Juan Encarnacion	.10
82	Ivan Rodriguez	.40
83	Mike Lowell	.10
84	Josh Beckett	.25
85	Brad Penny	.10
86	Craig Biggio	.20
87	Jeff Kent	.25
88	Morgan Ensberg	.10
89	Daryle Ward	.10
90	Jeff Bagwell	.40
91	Roy Oswalt	.20

92	Lance Berkman	.25
93	Mike Sweeney	.10
94	Carlos Beltran	.40
95	Raul Ibanez	.10
96	Carlos Febles	.10
97	Joe Randa	.10
98	Shawn Green	.25
99	Kevin Brown	.15
100	Paul LoDuca	.10
101	Adrian Beltre	.25
102	Eric Gagne	.20
103	Kazuhisa Ishii	.10
104	Odalis Perez	.10
105	Brian Jordan	.10
106	Geoff Jenkins	.10
107	Richie Sexson	.25
108	Ben Sheets	.20
109	Alex Sanchez	.10
110	Eric Young	.10
111	Jose Hernandez	.10
112	Torii Hunter	.25
113	Eric Milton	.10
114	Corey Koskie	.10
115	Doug Mientkiewicz	.10
116	A.J. Pierzynski	.10
117	Jacque Jones	.10
118	Cristian Guzman	.10
119	Bartolo Colon	.10
120	Brad Wilkerson	.10
121	Michael Barrett	.10
122	Vladimir Guerrero	.50
123	Jose Vidro	.10
124	Javier Vazquez	.10
125	Endy Chavez	.10
126	Roberto Alomar	.25
127	Mike Piazza	1.00
128	Jeromy Burnitz	.10
129	Mo Vaughn	.15
130	Tom Glavine	.25
131	Al Leiter	.15
132	Armando Benitez	.10
133	Timoniel Perez	.10
134	Roger Clemens	1.00
135	Derek Jeter	1.50
136	Jason Giambi	.25
137	Alfonso Soriano	.50
138	Bernie Williams	.25
139	Mike Mussina	.25
140	Jorge Posada	.20
141	Hideki Matsui RC	4.00
142	Robin Ventura	.10
143	David Wells	.10
144	Nick Johnson	.10
145	Tim Hudson	.20
146	Eric Chavez	.20
147	Barry Zito	.25
148	Miguel Tejada	.40
149	Jermaine Dye	.10
150	Mark Mulder	.20
151	Terrence Long	.10
152	Scott Hatteberg	.10
153	Marlon Byrd	.10
154	Jim Thome	.40
155	Marlon Anderson	.10
156	Vicente Padilla	.10
157	Bobby Abreu	.20
158	Jimmy Rollins	.25
159	Pat Burrell	.40
160	Brian Giles	.20
161	Aramis Ramirez	.20
162	Jason Kendall	.20
163	Josh Fogg	.10
164	Kip Wells	.10
165	Pokey Reese	.10
166	Kris Benson	.10
167	Ryan Klesko	.20
168	Brian Lawrence	.10
169	Mark Kotsay	.10
170	Jake Peavy	.20
171	Phil Nevin	.10
172	Sean Burroughs	.10
173	Trevor Hoffman	.20
174	Jason Schmidt	.20
175	Kirk Rueter	.10
176	Barry Bonds	1.50
177	Pedro Feliz	.10
178	Rich Aurilia	.10
179	Benito Santiago	.10
180	J.T. Snow	.10
181	Robb Nen	.10
182	Ichiro Suzuki	1.00
183	Edgar Martinez	.20
184	Bret Boone	.10
185	Freddy Garcia	.10
186	John Olerud	.10
187	Mike Cameron	.10
188	Joel Pineiro	.10
189	Albert Pujols	1.25
190	Matt Morris	.10
191	J.D. Drew	.20
192	Scott Rolen	.50
193	Tino Martinez	.20
194	Jim Edmonds	.30
195	Edgar Renteria	.20
196	Fernando Vina	.10
197	Jason Isringhausen	.10
198	Ben Grieve	.10
199	Carl Crawford	.20
200	Dewon Brazelton	.10
201	Aubrey Huff	.10
202	Jared Sandberg	.10
203	Steve Cox	.10
204	Carl Everett	.20
205	Kevin Mench	.10
206	Alex Rodriguez	1.00
207	Rafael Palmeiro	.40
208	Michael Young	.10
209	Hank Blalock	.40

210	Juan Gonzalez	.25
211	Carlos Delgado	.25
212	Eric Hinske	.10
213	Josh Phelps	.10
214	Mark Hendrickson	.10
215	Roy Halladay	.20
216	Orlando Hudson	.10
217	Shannon Stewart	.10
218	Vernon Wells	.20
219	Ichiro Suzuki	.40
220	Jason Giambi	.25
221	Scott Spiezio	.10
222	Rich Fischer	.10
223	Bengie Molina	.10
224	David Eckstein	.10
225	Brandon Webb RC	2.00
226	Oscar Villarreal	.10
227	Rob Hammock RC	.40
228	Matt Kata RC	.40
229	Lyle Overbay	.10
230	Chris Capuano RC	.50
231	Horacio Ramirez	.10
232	Shane Reynolds	.10
233	Russ Ortiz	.10
234	Mike Hampton	.10
235	Mike Hessman	.10
236	Byung-Hyun Kim	.10
237	Freddy Sanchez	.10
238	Jason Shiell	.10
239	Ryan Cameron	.10
240	Todd Wellemeyer RC	.40
241	Joe Borowski	.10
242	Alex Gonzalez	.10
243	Jon Leicester	.10
244	David Sanders	.10
245	Roberto Alomar	.25
246	Barry Larkin	.20
247	Jhonny Peralta	.20
248	Zach Sorensen	.10
249	Jason Davis	.10
250	Coco Crisp	.10
251	Greg Vaughn	.10
252	Preston Wilson	.10
253	Denny Neagle	.10
254	Clint Barmes RC	.50
255	Jeremy Bonderman	.25
256	Wilfredo Ledezma RC	.10
257	Dontrelle Willis	.25
258	Alex Gonzalez	.10
259	Tommy Phelps	.10
260	Kirk Saarloos	.10
261	Colin Porter RC	.10
262	Nate Bland	.10
263	Jason Gilfillan	.10
264	Mike MacDougal	.10
265	Ken Harvey	.10
266	Brent Mayne	.10
267	Miguel Cabrera	.40
268	Hideo Nomo	.20
269	Dave Roberts	.10
270	Fred McGriff	.20
271	Joe Thurston	.10
272	Royce Clayton	.10
273	Micheal Nakamura	.10
274	Brad Radke	.10
275	Joe Mays	.10
276	Lew Ford RC	1.00
277	Michael Cuddyer	.10
278	Luis Ayala	.10
279	Julio Manon	.10
280	Anthony Ferrari	.10
281	Livan Hernandez	.10
282	Jae Weong Seo	.10
283	Jose Reyes	.40
284	Tony Clark	.10
285	Ty Wigginton	.10
286	Cliff Floyd	.10
287	Jeremy Griffiths	.10
288	Jason Roach	.10
289	Jeff Duncan	.10
290	Phil Seibel	.10
291	Prentice Redman RC	.25
292	Jose Contreras RC	1.00
293	Ruben Sierra	.10
294	Andy Pettitte	.25
295	Aaron Boone	.10
296	Mariano Rivera	.10
297	Michel Hernandez	.10
298	Mike Neu	.10
299	Erubiel Durazo	.10
300	Billy McMillon	.10
301	Rich Harden	.10
302	David Bell	.10
303	Kevin Millwood	.10
304	Mike Lieberthal	.10
305	Jeremy Wedel	.10
306	Kenny Lofton	.10
307	Reggie Sanders	.10
308	Randall Simon	.10
309	Xavier Nady	.10
310	Rod Beck	.10
311	Miguel Ojeda	.10
312	Mark Loretta	.10
313	Edgardo Alfonzo	.10
314	Andres Galarraga	.10
315	Jose Cruz Jr.	.10
316	Jesse Foppert	.10
317	Kurt Ainsworth	.10
318	Dan Wilson	.10
319	Ben Davis	.10
320	Rocco Baldelli	.20
321	Al Martin	.10
322	Runelvys Hernandez	.10
323	Dan Haren	.40
324	Bo Hart RC	.20
325	Einar Diaz	.10
326	Mike Lamb	.10
327	Aquilino Lopez	.10

328	Reed Johnson	.10
329	Diegomar Markwell	.10
330	Hideki Matsui	.75

Gold

Stars (1-220):	6-12X
Production 150 Sets	
Black Stars:	10-20X
Production 50 Sets	
Silver Stars:	1-2X
Inserted 1:2	

Base-to-Base

NM/M

Inserted 1:488

CP	Roger Clemens, Mike Piazza	25.00
IG	Ichiro Suzuki, Ken Griffey Jr.	40.00
IJ	Ichiro Suzuki, Derek Jeter	45.00
JW	Derek Jeter, Bernie Williams	25.00
MB	Mark McGwire, Barry Bonds	60.00
RJ	Alex Rodriguez, Derek Jeter	40.00

Covering the Bases

NM/M

Common Player: 4.00
Inserted 1:125

BB	Barry Bonds	15.00
CD	Carlos Delgado	4.00
JD	J.D. Drew	4.00
DE	Darin Erstad	6.00
TG	Troy Glaus	6.00
LG	Luis Gonzalez	4.00
SG	Shawn Green	6.00
DJ	Derek Jeter	15.00
MP	Mike Piazza	12.00
AR	Alex Rodriguez	12.00
IR	Ivan Rodriguez	4.00
IS	Ichiro Suzuki	15.00
MT	Miguel Tejada	6.00
FT	Frank Thomas	8.00
JT	Jim Thome	12.00

Covering the Plate Bat

NM/M

Common Player: 6.00
Inserted 1:160

RA	Roberto Alomar	15.00
RF	Rafael Furcal	8.00
VG	Vladimir Guerrero	8.00
FM	Fred McGriff	6.00
MM	Mark McGwire	60.00
JT	Jim Thome	12.00

Dual Aces

NM/M

Common Card: 8.00
Inserted 1:488

BS	Kevin Brown, Curt Schilling	10.00
CJ	Roger Clemens, Randy Johnson	20.00
CL	Roger Clemens, Al Leiter	15.00
ML	Matt Morris, Al Leiter	8.00
SJ	Curt Schilling, Randy Johnson	12.00
SM	Curt Schilling, Andy Pettitte	10.00

Express Delivery

NM/M

Complete Set (15): 10.00

Common Player:		.50
Inserted 1:12		
ED1	Randy Johnson	2.00
ED2	Curt Schilling	1.00
ED3	Pedro J. Martinez	2.00
ED4	Kerry Wood	1.00
ED5	Mark Prior	1.50
ED6	A.J. Burnett	.50
ED7	Josh Beckett	.50
ED8	Roy Oswalt	.75
ED9	Hideo Nomo	.75
ED10	Ben Sheets	.50
ED11	Bartolo Colon	.50
ED12	Roger Clemens	2.50
ED13	Mike Mussina	.75
ED14	Tim Hudson	.75
ED15	Matt Morris	.50

MVP Celebration

NM/M

Common Player: 1.50
#'d to yr. MVP was won

MVP1	Yogi Berra	4.00
MVP2	Mickey Mantle	15.00
MVP3	Mickey Mantle	15.00
MVP4	Mickey Mantle	15.00
MVP5	Roger Clemens	5.00
MVP6	Rickey Henderson	4.00
MVP7	Frank Thomas	4.00
MVP8	Mo Vaughn	1.50
MVP9	Juan Gonzalez	3.00
MVP10	Ken Griffey Jr.	6.00
MVP11	Juan Gonzalez	3.00
MVP12	Ivan Rodriguez	2.00
MVP13	Jason Giambi	4.00
MVP14	Ichiro Suzuki	6.00
MVP15	Miguel Tejada	2.00
MVP16	Barry Bonds	8.00
MVP17	Barry Bonds	8.00
MVP18	Barry Bonds	8.00
MVP19	Jeff Bagwell	4.00
MVP20	Barry Larkin	1.50
MVP21	Larry Walker	1.50
MVP22	Sammy Sosa	6.00
MVP23	Chipper Jones	5.00
MVP24	Jeff Kent	1.50
MVP25	Barry Bonds	8.00
MVP26	Barry Bonds	8.00
MVP27	Ken Griffey Sr.	1.50
MVP28	Roger Clemens	5.00
MVP29	Ken Griffey Jr.	6.00
MVP30	Fred McGriff	1.50
MVP31	Jeff Conine	1.50
MVP32	Mike Piazza	6.00
MVP33	Sandy Alomar Jr.	1.50
MVP34	Roberto Alomar	2.50
MVP35	Pedro J. Martinez	4.00
MVP36	Derek Jeter	8.00
MVP37	Rickey Henderson	4.00
MVP38	Roberto Alomar	2.50
MVP39	Bernie Williams	3.00
MVP40	Marquis Grissom	1.50
MVP41	David Wells	1.50
MVP42	Orlando Hernandez	1.50
MVP43	David Justice	1.50
MVP44	Andy Pettitte	2.00
MVP45	Adam Kennedy	1.50
MVP46	John Smoltz	1.50
MVP47	Curt Schilling	2.00
MVP48	Javy Lopez	1.50
MVP49	Livan Hernandez	1.50
MVP50	Sterling Hitchcock	1.50
MVP51	Mike Hampton	1.50
MVP52	Craig Counsell	1.50
MVP53	Benito Santiago	1.50
MVP54	Tom Glavine	2.00
MVP55	Livan Hernandez	1.50
MVP56	Mariano Rivera	1.50
MVP57	Derek Jeter	8.00
MVP58	Randy Johnson	4.00
MVP59	Curt Schilling	2.50
MVP60	Troy Glaus	3.00
MVP61	Yogi Berra	4.00
MVP62	Yogi Berra	4.00
MVP63	Mickey Mantle	15.00
MVP64	Mickey Mantle	15.00
MVP65	Ken Griffey Sr.	1.50
MVP66	Rickey Henderson	4.00
MVP67	Roberto Alomar	2.50
MVP68	Bernie Williams	3.00
MVP69	Livan Hernandez	1.50
MVP70	Sammy Sosa	6.00
MVP71	Sterling Hitchcock	1.50
MVP72	David Wells	1.50
MVP73	Mariano Rivera	1.50
MVP74	Chipper Jones	5.00
MVP75	Ivan Rodriguez	2.00
MVP76	Derek Jeter	8.00
MVP77	Jason Giambi	4.00
MVP78	Jeff Kent	1.50
MVP79	Mike Hampton	1.50
MVP80	Randy Johnson	4.00
MVP81	Curt Schilling	2.50
MVP82	Barry Bonds	8.00
MVP83	Ichiro Suzuki	6.00
MVP84	Ichiro Suzuki	6.00
MVP85	Adam Kennedy	1.50
MVP86	Benito Santiago	1.50
MVP87	Troy Glaus	3.00
MVP88	Troy Glaus	3.00
MVP89	Miguel Tejada	2.00
MVP90	Barry Bonds	8.00

Prosign

Common Autograph:
Production 25 Sets
No Pricing

Pro View

NM/M

Complete Set (45):		65.00
Common Player:		.75
Inserted 2:Box		
Golds:		2-3X
PV1	Troy Glaus	1.50
PV2	Darin Erstad	1.00
PV3	Randy Johnson	2.00
PV4	Curt Schilling	1.50
PV5	Luis Gonzalez	.75
PV6	Chipper Jones	2.00
PV7	Andruw Jones	1.00
PV8	Greg Maddux	3.00
PV9	Pedro J. Martinez	2.00
PV10	Manny Ramirez	2.00
PV11	Sammy Sosa	3.00
PV12	Mark Prior	1.50
PV13	Magglio Ordonez	1.50
PV14	Frank Thomas	1.50
PV15	Ken Griffey Jr.	3.00
PV16	Adam Dunn	1.50
PV17	Jim Thome	1.50
PV18	Todd Helton	1.00
PV19	Jeff Bagwell	1.50
PV20	Lance Berkman	1.00
PV21	Shawn Green	.75
PV22	Hideo Nomo	1.50
PV23	Vladimir Guerrero	2.00
PV24	Roberto Alomar	1.00
PV25	Mike Piazza	4.00
PV26	Jason Giambi	1.00
PV27	Roger Clemens	3.00
PV28	Alfonso Soriano	2.00
PV29	Derek Jeter	6.00
PV30	Miguel Tejada	1.50
PV31	Eric Chavez	.75
PV32	Barry Zito	1.00
PV33	Pat Burrell	1.50
PV34	Brian Giles	.75
PV35	Barry Bonds	6.00
PV36	Ichiro Suzuki	3.00
PV37	Albert Pujols	5.00
PV38	Scott Rolen	1.50
PV39	J.D. Drew	.75
PV40	Mark McGwire	5.00
PV41	Alex Rodriguez	5.00
PV42	Rafael Palmeiro	1.00
PV43	Juan Gonzalez	1.50
PV44	Eric Hinske	.75
PV45	Carlos Delgado	.75

SportsNut Fantasy

NM/M

Complete Set (90): 45.00
Common Player: .40
Inserted 1:12
Prices for unscratched cards.

SN1	Troy Glaus	1.00
SN2	Darin Erstad	.50
SN3	Luis Gonzalez	.50
SN4	Andruw Jones	.75
SN5	Chipper Jones	2.00
SN6	Gary Sheffield	.50
SN7	Jay Gibbons	.40
SN8	Manny Ramirez	1.50
SN9	Shea Hillenbrand	.40
SN10	Johnny Damon	.40
SN11	Nomar Garciaparra	2.50
SN12	Sammy Sosa	2.00
SN13	Magglio Ordonez	.75
SN14	Frank Thomas	.75
SN15	Ken Griffey Jr.	1.50
SN16	Adam Dunn	1.00
SN17	Matt Lawton	.40
SN18	Larry Walker	.40
SN19	Todd Helton	.75
SN20	Carlos Pena	.40
SN21	Mike Lowell	.40
SN22	Jeff Bagwell	1.00
SN23	Lance Berkman	.75
SN24	Mike Sweeney	.50
SN25	Carlos Beltran	.40
SN26	Shawn Green	.75
SN27	Richie Sexson	.40
SN28	Torii Hunter	.40
SN29	Jacque Jones	.40
SN30	Vladimir Guerrero	1.50
SN31	Jose Vidro	.40
SN32	Roberto Alomar	.50
SN33	Mike Piazza	2.00
SN34	Alfonso Soriano	1.50
SN35	Derek Jeter	3.00
SN36	Jason Giambi	2.00
SN37	Bernie Williams	.75
SN38	Eric Chavez	.75
SN39	Miguel Tejada	.75
SN40	Jim Thome	1.00
SN41	Pat Burrell	1.00
SN42	Bobby Abreu	.50
SN43	Brian Giles	.50
SN44	Jason Kendall	.40
SN45	Ryan Klesko	.40
SN46	Phil Nevin	.40
SN47	Barry Bonds	4.00
SN48	Rich Aurilia	.40
SN49	Ichiro Suzuki	2.00
SN50	Bret Boone	.40
SN51	J.D. Drew	.40
SN52	Jim Edmonds	.75
SN53	Albert Pujols	1.50
SN54	Scott Rolen	1.00
SN55	Ben Grieve	.40
SN56	Alex Rodriguez	3.00
SN57	Rafael Palmeiro	.75
SN58	Juan Gonzalez	.50
SN59	Carlos Delgado	.40
SN60	Josh Phelps	.40
SN61	Jarrod Washburn	.40
SN62	Randy Johnson	1.00
SN63	Curt Schilling	.75
SN64	Greg Maddux	1.50
SN65	Mike Hampton	.40
SN66	Rodrigo Lopez	.40
SN67	Pedro J. Martinez	1.50
SN68	Derek Lowe	.40
SN69	Mark Prior	1.00
SN70	Kerry Wood	.75
SN71	Mark Buehrle	.40
SN72	Roy Oswalt	.50
SN73	Wade Miller	.40
SN74	Odalis Perez	.40
SN75	Hideo Nomo	.50
SN76	Ben Sheets	.40
SN77	Eric Milton	.40
SN78	Bartolo Colon	.40
SN79	Tom Glavine	.40
SN80	Al Leiter	.40
SN81	Roger Clemens	2.00
SN82	Mike Mussina	.75
SN83	Tim Hudson	.75
SN84	Barry Zito	.75
SN85	Mark Mulder	.50
SN86	Vicente Padilla	.40
SN87	Jason Schmidt	.40
SN88	Freddy Garcia	.40
SN89	Matt Morris	.40
SN90	Roy Halladay	.40

Talk of the Town

NM/M

Complete Set (15): 20.00
Common Player: .75
Inserted 1:12

TT1	Hideki Matsui	3.00
TT2	Chipper Jones	1.00
TT3	Manny Ramirez	1.50
TT4	Sammy Sosa	2.00
TT5	Ken Griffey Jr.	2.00
TT6	Lance Berkman	.75
TT7	Shawn Green	.75
TT8	Vladimir Guerrero	1.50
TT9	Mike Piazza	2.50
TT10	Jason Giambi	.75
TT11	Alfonso Soriano	1.50
TT12	Ichiro Suzuki	2.50
TT13	Albert Pujols	3.00
TT14	Alex Rodriguez	3.00
TT15	Eric Hinske	.75

Three Bagger

NM/M

Inserted 1:488

BMP	Barry Bonds, Mark McGwire, Mike Piazza	80.00
GIB	Ken Griffey Jr., Ichiro Suzuki, Barry Bonds	60.00
GTD	Troy Glaus, Frank Thomas, Carlos Delgado	10.00
IBJ	Ichiro Suzuki, Barry Bonds, Derek Jeter	80.00
JWP	Derek Jeter, Bernie Williams, Jorge Posada	35.00
SCB	Curt Schilling, Roger Clemens, Kevin Brown	20.00

Total Bases

NM/M

Production 150 Sets

BB	Barry Bonds	20.00
RC	Roger Clemens	20.00
TG	Troy Glaus	8.00
KG	Ken Griffey Jr.	15.00
DJ	Derek Jeter	20.00
MM	Mark McGwire	25.00
MP	Mike Piazza	15.00
AR	Alex Rodriguez	15.00
IS	Ichiro Suzuki	30.00

Promo

NM/M

SAMPLE Ichiro 6.00

2003 Upper Deck Patch Collection

NM/M

Complete Set (161):		
Common Player:		.25
Common SP Patch (121-161):		4.00
All-Star & HOF Patches (121-150):		
Inserted 1:40		
Rookie Patches (151-161):		
Inserted 1:20		
Pack (5):		4.75
Box (20):		80.00
1	Darin Erstad	.40
2	Troy Glaus	.75
3	Robby Hammock RC	.25
4	Luis Gonzalez	.50
5	Randy Johnson/SP	3.00
6	Curt Schilling/SP	2.50
7	Oscar Villarreal RC	.25
8	Gary Sheffield	.50
9	Mike Hampton	.25
10	Greg Maddux	1.50
11	Chipper Jones	1.50
12	Tony Batista	.25
13	Rodrigo Lopez	.25
14	Jay Gibbons	.25
15	Shea Hillenbrand	.25
16	Johnny Damon	.25
17	Derek Lowe	.25
18	Nomar Garciaparra	1.00
19	Pedro J. Martinez	1.00
20	Manny Ramirez	.75
21	Mark Prior	.75
22	Kerry Wood	.50
23	Corey Patterson	.25
24	Sammy Sosa	1.50
25	Troy O'Leary	.25
26	Frank Thomas	.75
27	Magglio Ordonez	.40
28	Bartolo Colon	.25
29	Austin Kearns	.25
30	Aaron Boone	.25
31	Ken Griffey Jr.	1.50
32	Adam Dunn	.75
33	C.C. Sabathia	.25
34	Karim Garcia	.25
35	Larry Walker	.40
36	Preston Wilson	.25
37	Jason Jennings	.25
38	Todd Helton	.75
39	Carlos Pena	.25
40	Eric Munson	.25
41	Ivan Rodriguez	.50
42	Josh Beckett	.25
43	A.J. Burnett	.25
44	Roy Oswalt	.25
45	Craig Biggio	.40
46	Jeff Bagwell	.75
47	Lance Berkman	.50
48	Jeff Kent	.40
49	Carlos Beltran	.25
50	Mike Sweeney	.25
51	Hideo Nomo	.50
52	Adrian Beltre	.25
53	Shawn Green	.25
54	Kazuhisa Ishii	.25
55	Ben Sheets	.25
56	Richie Sexson	.50
57	Torii Hunter	.50
58	Doug Mientkiewicz	.25
59	Eric Milton	.25
60	Corey Koskie	.25
61	Joe Mays	.25
62	Jose Vidro	.25
63	Vladimir Guerrero	.75
64	Luis Ayala RC	.25
65	Cliff Floyd	.25
66	Tom Glavine	.50
67	Mike Piazza	2.00
68	Roberto Alomar	.50
69	Al Leiter	.25
70	Mike Mussina	.50
71	Mariano Rivera	.40
72	Drew Henson	.25
73	Roger Clemens	1.50
74	Jason Giambi	1.00
75	Bernie Williams	.50
76	Alfonso Soriano	.50
77	Derek Jeter	3.00
78	Miguel Tejada	.50
79	Jermaine Dye	.25
80	Tim Hudson	.50
81	Barry Zito	.50
82	Mark Mulder	.40
83	Pat Burrell	.50
84	Jim Thome	.75
85	Bobby Abreu	.40
86	Kevin Millwood	.25
87	Jason Kendall	.40
88	Brian Giles	.40
89	Phil Nevin	.25
90	Sean Burroughs	.25
91	Oliver Perez	.25
92	Jose Cruz Jr.	.25
93	Rich Aurilia	.25
94	Edgardo Alfonzo	.25
95	Barry Bonds	3.00
96	J.T. Snow	.25
97	Mike Cameron	.25
98	John Olerud	.50
99	Bret Boone	.25
100	Ichiro Suzuki	1.50
101	J.D. Drew	.40
102	Jim Edmonds	.50
103	Scott Rolen	.75
104	Matt Morris	.40
105	Tino Martinez	.25
106	Albert Pujols	1.50
107	Rocco Baldelli	.25
108	Carl Crawford	.25
109	Mark Teixeira	.50
110	Rafael Palmeiro	.50
111	Hank Blalock	.50
112	Alex Rodriguez	2.50
113	Kevin Mench	.25
114	Juan Gonzalez	.75
115	Shannon Stewart	.25
116	Vernon Wells	.40
117	Josh Phelps	.25
118	Eric Hinske	.25
119	Orlando Hudson	.25
120	Carlos Delgado	.50
121	Alex Rodriguez	10.00
122	Nomar Garciaparra	10.00
123	Miguel Tejada	4.00
124	Jim Thome	8.00
125	Alfonso Soriano	6.00
126	Vladimir Guerrero	6.00
127	Derek Jeter	15.00
128	Mike Piazza	8.00
129	Ichiro Suzuki	12.00
130	Pedro J. Martinez	4.00
131	Luis Gonzalez	4.00
132	Adam Dunn	6.00
133	Shawn Green	4.00
134	Barry Zito	4.00
135	Torii Hunter	5.00
136	Ted Williams	20.00
137	Mickey Mantle	25.00
138	Ernie Banks	10.00
139	Yogi Berra	8.00
140	Rollie Fingers	4.00
141	Jim "Catfish" Hunter	8.00
142	Juan Marichal	8.00
143	Eddie Mathews	10.00
144	Willie McCovey	10.00
145	Joe Morgan	5.00
146	Stan Musial	12.00
147	Pee Wee Reese	10.00
148	Phil Rizzuto	6.00
149	Nolan Ryan	20.00

150	Tom Seaver	8.00
151	Hideki Matsui RC	15.00
152	Jose Contreras RC	5.00
153	Lew Ford RC	5.00
154	Jeremy Griffiths	4.00
155	Guillermo Quiroz RC	4.00
156	Ryan Cameron RC	4.00
157	Jon Leicester RC	4.00
158	Josh Willingham RC	8.00
159	Shane Bazzell RC	4.00
160	Willie Eyre RC	4.00
161	Prentice Redman RC	4.00

All-Star Game History Patches

		NM/M
Common Patch:		8.00
Inserted 2:Box		
1	1933 All-Star Game	12.00
2	1934 All-Star Game	15.00
3	1935 All-Star Game	15.00
4	1936 All-Star Game	10.00
5	1937 All-Star Game	10.00
6	1938 All-Star Game	10.00
7	1939 All-Star Game	15.00
8	1940 All-Star Game	15.00
9	1941 All-Star Game	10.00
10	1942 All-Star Game	15.00
11	1943 All-Star Game	12.00
12	1944 All-Star Game	12.00
13	1946 All-Star Game	15.00
14	1947 All-Star Game	15.00
15	1948 All-Star Game	15.00
16	1949 All-Star Game	15.00
17	1950 All-Star Game	12.00
18	1951 All-Star Game	12.00
19	1952 All-Star Game	15.00
20	1953 All-Star Game	12.00
21	1954 All-Star Game	12.00
22	1955 All-Star Game	10.00
23	1956 All-Star Game	12.00
24	1957 All-Star Game	15.00
25	1958 All-Star Game	12.00
26	1959 All-Star Game	15.00
27	1959 All-Star Game	15.00
28	1960 All-Star Game	10.00
29	1960 All-Star Game	15.00
30	1961 All-Star Game	10.00
31	1961 All-Star Game	15.00
32	1962 All-Star Game	8.00
33	1962 All-Star Game	12.00
34	1963 All-Star Game	15.00
35	1964 All-Star Game	15.00
36	1965 All-Star Game	15.00
37	1966 All-Star Game	15.00
38	1967 All-Star Game	12.00
39	1968 All-Star Game	8.00
40	1969 All-Star Game	10.00
41	1970 All-Star Game	15.00
42	1971 All-Star Game	10.00
43	1972 All-Star Game	10.00
44	1973 All-Star Game	10.00
45	1974 All-Star Game	10.00
46	1975 All-Star Game	10.00
47	1976 All-Star Game	15.00
48	1977 All-Star Game	12.00
49	1978 All-Star Game	10.00
50	1979 All-Star Game	8.00
51	1980 All-Star Game	8.00
52	1981 All-Star Game	8.00
53	1982 All-Star Game	10.00
54	1983 All-Star Game	10.00
55	1984 All-Star Game	10.00
56	1985 All-Star Game	10.00
57	1986 All-Star Game	10.00
58	1987 All-Star Game	8.00
59	1988 All-Star Game	8.00
60	1989 All-Star Game	8.00
61	1990 All-Star Game	15.00
62	1991 All-Star Game	8.00
63	1992 All-Star Game	8.00
64	1993 All-Star Game	10.00
65	1994 All-Star Game	15.00
66	1995 All-Star Game	10.00
67	1996 All-Star Game	12.00
68	1997 All-Star Game	10.00
69	1998 All-Star Game	8.00
70	1999 All-Star Game	15.00
71	2000 All-Star Game	10.00
72	2001 All-Star Game	10.00
73	2002 All-Star Game	12.00

MVPs Patches

		NM/M
Common Player:		5.00
Inserted 1:20		
1	Derek Jeter	15.00
2	Randy Johnson	8.00
3	Curt Schilling	6.00
4	Troy Glaus	5.00

5	Ted Williams	15.00
6	Ted Williams	15.00
7	Mickey Mantle	20.00
8	Mickey Mantle	20.00
9	Phil Rizzuto	5.00
10	Roger Clemens	10.00
11	Ken Griffey Jr.	10.00
12	Jason Giambi	5.00
13	Ichiro Suzuki	15.00
14	Roger Clemens	10.00
15	Yogi Berra	6.00
16	Sammy Sosa	10.00
17	Derek Jeter	15.00
18	Mike Piazza	10.00
19	Barry Bonds	15.00
20	Stan Musial	12.00
21	Joe Morgan	5.00

Signature Patches

P. JUAN MARICHAL 27

		NM/M
Common Autograph:		25.00
Inserted 1:320		
JB	Jeff Bagwell	50.00
LB	Lance Berkman	50.00
RC	Roger Clemens	160.00
AD	Adam Dunn	60.00
FG	Freddy Garcia	30.00
JG	Jason Giambi	40.00
LG	Luis Gonzalez	40.00
KG	Ken Griffey Jr.	100.00
DH	Drew Henson	40.00
EH	Eric Hinske	25.00
TP	Troy Percival	25.00
SR	Scott Rolen	50.00
CS	Curt Schilling	50.00
GS	Gary Sheffield	50.00
IS	Ichiro Suzuki	300.00
MT	Miguel Tejada	50.00
BZ	Barry Zito	40.00

2003 Upper Deck Play Ball Promos

BARRY ZITO

Each April 2003 newsstand issue of Tuff Stuff magazine included a Play Ball promo card inside its poly bag. The cards differ from the issued version only in the appearance on front of a silver-foil "UD PROMO" notation. It is not known how many different players cards were used in the promotion.

	NM/M
Common Player:	.25
Stars:	1.5-2.5X

2003 Upper Deck Play Ball Sample

MARK McGWIRE

This promo card differs from the issued version in its card number and in the appearance on back of a large overprinted typewriter-style "SAMPLE."

		NM/M
1	Mark McGwire	2.00

2003 Upper Deck Play Ball

ROBIN YOUNT

		NM/M
Complete Set (104):		
Common Player:		.25
Common Summer of '41		
(74-88):		4.00
Inserted 1:24		
Common Ted Williams		
(89-103):		10.00
Inserted 1:24		
Pack (5):		2.50
Box (24):		40.00
1	Troy Glaus	.40
2	Darin Erstad	.25
3	Randy Johnson	.75
4	Luis Gonzalez	.40
5	Curt Schilling	.75
6	Tom Glavine	.75
7	Chipper Jones	.75
8	Greg Maddux	1.00
9	Andruw Jones	.40
10	Pedro J. Martinez	.75
11	Manny Ramirez	.75
12	Nomar Garciaparra	1.00
13	Billy Williams	.25
14	Sammy Sosa	1.00
15	Kerry Wood	.75
16	Mark Prior	.75
17	Ernie Banks	1.00
18	Frank Thomas	.75
19	Joe Morgan	.25
20	Ken Griffey Jr.	1.25
21	Adam Dunn	.50
22	Jim Thome	.75
23	Todd Helton	.50
24	Larry Walker	.40
25	Lance Berkman	.40
26	Roy Oswalt	.40
27	Jeff Bagwell	.50
28	Nolan Ryan	2.00
29	Mike Sweeney	.40
30	Shawn Green	.40
31	Hideo Nomo	.40
32	Kazuhisa Ishii	.25
33	Richie Sexson	.40
34	Robin Yount	.75
35	Harmon Killebrew	.75
36	Torii Hunter	.50
37	Vladimir Guerrero	.75
38	Roberto Alomar	.50
39	Mike Piazza	1.00
40	Tom Seaver	.75
41	Phil Rizzuto	.50
42	Yogi Berra	.75
43	Mike Mussina	.50
44	Roger Clemens	1.50
45	Derek Jeter	2.00
46	Jason Giambi	.25
47	Bernie Williams	.40
48	Alfonso Soriano	.75
49	Jim "Catfish" Hunter	.25
50	Barry Zito	.40
51	Eric Chavez	.40
52	Tim Hudson	.40
53	Rollie Fingers	.25
54	Miguel Tejada	.50
55	Pat Burrell	.40
56	Brian Giles	.40
57	Willie Stargell	.50
58	Phil Nevin	.25
59	Orlando Cepeda	.25
60	Barry Bonds	2.00
61	Jeff Kent	.40
62	Willie McCovey	.25
63	Ichiro Suzuki	1.50
64	Stan Musial	1.50
65	Albert Pujols	2.00
66	J.D. Drew	.40
67	Scott Rolen	.50
68	Mark McGwire	1.00
69	Alex Rodriguez	1.00
70	Juan Gonzalez	.40
71	Ivan Rodriguez	.50
72	Rafael Palmeiro	.50
73	Carlos Delgado	.40
74	Ted Williams	15.00
75	Hank Greenberg	6.00
76	Joe DiMaggio	15.00
77	Lefty Gomez	6.00

78	Tommy Henrich	4.00
79	Pee Wee Reese	5.00
80	Mel Ott	6.00
81	Carl Hubbell	6.00
82	Jimmie Foxx	8.00
83	Joe Cronin	4.00
84	Charlie Gehringer	5.00
85	Frank Hayes	5.00
86	Babe Dahlgren	4.00
87	Dolph Camilli	4.00
88	Johnny Vander Meer	4.00
89-103	Ted Williams	5.00
104	Hideki Matsui RC	5.00

Red Back

	NM/M
Stars (1-73):	1.5-2X
SP's (74-103):	1-1.5X
Matsui Red #104:	10.00
Inserted 1:2	

BuyBacks

No Pricing

Game-Used Memorabilia Tier 1

SAMMY SOSA
Outfield   Cubs

		NM/M
Common Player:		5.00
Inserted 1:82		
Golds: Not Priced		
Production 25 Sets		
RC1	Roger Clemens	20.00
CD1	Carlos Delgado	5.00
DR1	J.D. Drew	5.00
AD1	Adam Dunn	10.00
JG1	Jason Giambi	5.00
LG1	Luis Gonzalez	5.00
KG1	Ken Griffey Jr.	15.00
TH1	Tommy Henrich	5.00
KI1	Kazuhisa Ishii	5.00
CJ1	Chipper Jones	10.00
MM1	Mark McGwire	50.00
RP1	Rafael Palmeiro	5.00
MP1	Mike Piazza	10.00
PR1	Mark Prior	8.00
IR1	Ivan Rodriguez	8.00
CS1	Curt Schilling	8.00
AS1	Alfonso Soriano	8.00
SS1	Sammy Sosa	10.00
IS1	Ichiro Suzuki	30.00
MS1	Mike Sweeney	5.00
BW1	Bernie Williams	5.00

Game-Used Memorabilia Tier 2

		NM/M
Common Player:		5.00
Production 150 Sets		
JB2	Jeff Bagwell	10.00
LB2	Lance Berkman	5.00
JD2	Joe DiMaggio	100.00
DE2	Darin Erstad	5.00
JG2	Jason Giambi	5.00
SG2	Shawn Green	5.00
KG2	Ken Griffey Jr.	15.00
RJ2	Randy Johnson	8.00
AJ2	Andruw Jones	8.00
CJ2	Chipper Jones	15.00
GM2	Greg Maddux	15.00
PM2	Pedro J. Martinez	10.00
MM2	Mark McGwire	60.00
MP2	Mike Piazza	10.00
MR2	Manny Ramirez	10.00
AR2	Alex Rodriguez	15.00
CS2	Curt Schilling	10.00
SS2	Sammy Sosa	15.00
IS2	Ichiro Suzuki	50.00
JT2	Jim Thome	10.00
KW2	Kerry Wood	10.00

Game-Used Memorabilia Auto.

		NM/M
Common Player:		
Production 50 except A-Rod.		
JB2	Jeff Bagwell	75.00
LB2	Lance Berkman	75.00
JG2	Jason Giambi	50.00
KG2	Ken Griffey Jr.	125.00
AJ2	Andruw Jones	50.00
MM2	Mark McGwire	350.00
AR2	Alex Rodriguez/285	150.00
CS2	Curt Schilling	75.00
SS2	Sammy Sosa	180.00

Game-Used Memorabilia

MARK McGWIRE
10/50

IS2	Ichiro Suzuki	375.00
JT2	Jim Thome	75.00
KW2	Kerry Wood	75.00

Mini

RICHIE SEXSON

		NM/M
Complete Set (73):		40.00
Common Player:		.50
Inserted 1:2		
1	Troy Glaus	.50
2	Darin Erstad	.50
3	Randy Johnson	1.00
4	Luis Gonzalez	.50
5	Curt Schilling	.75
6	Tom Glavine	.75
7	Chipper Jones	1.00
8	Greg Maddux	1.50
9	Andruw Jones	.50
10	Pedro J. Martinez	1.00
11	Manny Ramirez	1.00
12	Nomar Garciaparra	2.00
13	Billy Williams	.50
14	Sammy Sosa	2.00
15	Kerry Wood	1.00
16	Mark Prior	1.00
17	Ernie Banks	1.50
18	Frank Thomas	1.50
19	Joe Morgan	.50
20	Ken Griffey Jr.	2.00
21	Adam Dunn	1.00
22	Jim Thome	1.00
23	Todd Helton	.75
24	Larry Walker	.50
25	Lance Berkman	.75
26	Roy Oswalt	.50
27	Jeff Bagwell	.75
28	Nolan Ryan	3.00
29	Mike Sweeney	.50
30	Shawn Green	.50
31	Hideo Nomo	.75
32	Kazuhisa Ishii	.50
33	Richie Sexson	.50
34	Robin Yount	1.00
35	Harmon Killebrew	1.00
36	Torii Hunter	.75
37	Vladimir Guerrero	1.00
38	Roberto Alomar	.75
39	Mike Piazza	2.00
40	Tom Seaver	1.00
41	Phil Rizzuto	.75
42	Yogi Berra	1.50
43	Mike Mussina	.75
44	Roger Clemens	2.00
45	Derek Jeter	3.00
46	Jason Giambi	.75
47	Bernie Williams	.75
48	Alfonso Soriano	1.00
49	Jim "Catfish" Hunter	.50
50	Barry Zito	.50
51	Eric Chavez	.50
52	Tim Hudson	.50
53	Rollie Fingers	.50
54	Miguel Tejada	1.00
55	Pat Burrell	1.00
56	Brian Giles	.75
57	Willie Stargell	.75
58	Phil Nevin	.50
59	Orlando Cepeda	.50
60	Barry Bonds	3.00
61	Jeff Kent	.50
62	Willie McCovey	.75
63	Ichiro Suzuki	2.50
64	Stan Musial	2.00
65	Albert Pujols	3.00
66	J.D. Drew	.75
67	Scott Rolen	1.00
68	Mark McGwire	2.00
69	Alex Rodriguez	2.50
70	Juan Gonzalez	.75
71	Ivan Rodriguez	1.00

72	Rafael Palmeiro	.75
73	Carlos Delgado	.50

Original Artwork Redemption
89 Total Redemption Cards

Reprint Series Original 1941

		NM/M
Complete Set (25):		15.00
Common Player:		.75
Inserted 1:2		
R1	Ted Williams	2.50
R2	Hank Greenberg	.75
R3	Joe DiMaggio	2.50
R4	Lefty Gomez	.75
R5	Tommy Henrich	.75
R6	Pee Wee Reese	.75
R7	Mel Ott	1.00
R8	Carl Hubbell	.75
R9	Jimmie Foxx	1.00
R10	Joe Cronin	.75
R11	Charley Gehringer	.75
R12	Frank Hayes	.75
R13	Babe Dahlgren	.75
R14	Dolph Camilli	.75
R15	Johnny Vander Meer	.75
R16	Bucky Walters	.75
R17	Red Ruffing	.75
R18	Charlie Keller	.75
R19	Bob Johnson	.75
R20	Emil "Dutch" Leonard	.75
R21	Barney McCosky	.75
R22	Soupy Campbell	.75
R23	Roy Weatherly	.75
R24	Bobby Doerr	.75
R25	Bill Dickey	.75

Yankee Clipper: 1941 Streak

THE YANKEE CLIPPER: 1941 STREAK

JOE DiMAGGIO

		NM/M
Complete Set (56):		250.00
Common DiMaggio (1-41):		5.00
Inserted 1:12		
Common DiMaggio (42-56):		8.00
Inserted 1:24		
S-1-41	Joe DiMaggio	5.00
S-42-56	Joe DiMaggio	8.00

2003 Upper Deck Play Ball Hawaii

JASON GIAMBI

To introduce its retro-styled Play Ball brand, Upper Deck created a special promo set for the SCD Hawaii Trade Conference. Each of the special cards has a whimsical tropical artwork background and the trade show logo on front. Three of the cards, with appropriate authentication on back, were seeded in the promo packs in an autographed version, with the McGwire card reported as much scarcer than the Sosa and Giambi autographs.

		NM/M
Complete Set (10):		30.00
Common Player:		5.00
KY1	"Slammin" Sammy Sosa	
SS	"Slammin" Sammy	
	Sosa/Auto.	125.00
KY2	Ken "The Kid" Griffey Jr.	6.00
KY3	Jason Giambi	3.00
JG	Jason Giambi/Auto.	35.00
KY4	Ichiro	10.00
KY5	Mark "Big Mac"	
	McGwire	7.50
MM	Mark "Big Mac"	
	McGwire/Auto.	250.00
KY6	Troy Glaus	2.00
KY7	Derek Jeter	6.50
KY8	Barry Bonds	6.50
KY9	Alex "A-Rod" Rodriguez	6.00
KY10	Nomar Garciaparra	6.00

2003 Upper Deck Prospect Premieres

	NM/M
Complete Set (90):	30.00

Common Player:	.25
Pack (4):	7.00
Box (18):	100.00

#	Player	Price
1	Bryan Opdyke RC	.25
2	Gabriel Sosa RC	.25
3	Tila Reynolds RC	.25
4	Aaron Hill RC	.50
5	Aaron Marsden RC	.25
6	Abe Alvarez RC	.75
7	Adam Jones RC	2.00
8	Adam Miller RC	.50
9	Andre Ethier RC	3.00
10	Tony Gwynn Jr. RC	.75
11	Brad Snyder RC	.50
12	Brad Sullivan RC	.75
13	Brian Anderson RC	.50
14	Brian Buscher RC	.25
15	Brian Snyder RC	.75
16	Carlos Quentin RC	2.00
17	Chad Billingsley RC	2.00
18	Fraser Dizard RC	.25
19	Chris Durbin RC	.50
20	Chris Ray RC	.50
21	Conor Jackson RC	.75
22	Kory Casto RC	.50
23	Craig Whitaker RC	.75
24	Daniel Moore RC	.25
25	Daric Barton RC	.75
26	Darin Downs RC	.50
27	David Murphy RC	.75
28	Dustin Majewski RC	.50
29	Edgardo Baez RC	.25
30	Jake Fox RC	.25
31	Jake Stevens RC	.50
32	Jamie D'Antona RC	.75
33	James Houser RC	.50
34	Jarrod Saltalamacchia RC	.75
35	Jason Hirsh RC	.75
36	Javi Herrera RC	.25
37	Jeff Allison RC	.75
38	John Hudgins RC	.25
39	Jo Jo Reyes RC	.50
40	Justin James RC	.50
41	Kurt Isenberg RC	.50
42	Kyle Boyer RC	.75
43	Lastings Milledge RC	2.00
44	Luis Atilano RC	.50
45	Matt Murton RC	.75
46	Matt Moses RC	.75
47	Matt Harrison RC	.50
48	Michael Bourn RC	1.00
49	Miguel Vega RC	1.00
50	Mitch Maier RC	1.00
51	Omar Quintanilla RC	.50
52	Ryan Sweeney RC	1.00
53	Scott Baker RC	.75
54	Sean Rodriguez RC	.75
55	Steve Lerud RC	.25
56	Thomas Pauly RC	.25
57	Tom Gorzelanny RC	1.00
58	Tim Moss RC	.50
59	Robbie Wooley RC	.50
60	Trey Webb RC	.25
61	Wes Littleton RC	.50
62	Beau Vaughan RC	.25
63	Willy Jo Ronda RC	.50
64	Chris Lubanski RC	.75
65	Ian Stewart RC	2.00
66	John Danks RC	1.00
67	Kyle Sleeth RC	.75
68	Michael Aubrey RC	.75
69	Kevin Kouzmanoff RC	1.00
70	Ryan Harvey RC	1.00
71	Tim Stauffer RC	.75
72	Tony Richie RC	.75
73	Brandon Wood RC	2.00
74	David Aardsma RC	.50
75	David Shinskie RC	.50
76	Dennis Dove RC	.25
77	Eric Sultemeier RC	.25
78	Jay Sborz RC	.25
79	Jimmy Barthmaier RC	.25
80	Josh Whitesell RC	.25
81	Josh Anderson RC	.50
82	Kenny Lewis RC	.50
83	Mateo Miramontes RC	.25
84	Nick Markakis RC	4.00
85	Paul Bacot RC	.50
86	Peter Stonard RC	.25
87	Reggie Willits RC	1.00
88	Shane Costa RC	.50
89	Billy Sadler RC	.25
90	Delmon Young RC	3.00

Star Rookie Signature

	NM/M
Common Autograph:	5.00
Inserted 1:9	

#	Player	Price
P1	Bryan Opdyke	5.00
P2	Gabriel Sosa	5.00
P3	Tila Reynolds	5.00
P4	Aaron Hill	10.00
P5	Aaron Marsden	5.00
P6	Abe Alvarez	5.00
P7	Adam Jones	75.00
P8	Adam Miller	20.00
P9	Andre Ethier	50.00
P10	Tony Gwynn Jr.	20.00
P11	Brad Snyder	15.00
P12	Brad Sullivan	10.00
P13	Brian Anderson	10.00
P14	Brian Buscher	5.00
P15	Brian Snyder	5.00
P16	Carlos Quentin	30.00
P17	Chad Billingsley	40.00
P19	Chris Durbin	5.00
P20	Chris Ray	8.00
P21	Conor Jackson	10.00
P22	Kory Casto	5.00
P23	Craig Whitaker	5.00
P24	Daniel Moore	5.00
P25	Daric Barton	15.00
P26	Darin Downs	8.00
P27	David Murphy	12.00
P28	Edgardo Baez	8.00
P29		
P30	Jake Fox	15.00
P31	Jake Stevens	10.00
P32	Jamie D'Antona	8.00
P33	James Houser	8.00
P34	Jarrod Saltalamacchia	20.00
P35	Jason Hirsh	15.00
P36	Javi Herrera	8.00
P37	Jeff Allison	8.00
P38	John Hudgins	8.00
P39	Jo Jo Reyes	10.00
P40	Justin James	8.00
P41	Kurt Isenberg	8.00
P42	Kyle Boyer	8.00
P43	Lastings Milledge	25.00
P44	Luis Atilano	8.00
P45	Matt Murton	8.00
P46	Matt Moses	15.00
P48	Michael Bourn	15.00
P49	Miguel Vega	8.00
P50	Mitch Maier	10.00
P51	Omar Quintanilla	8.00
P52	Ryan Sweeney	15.00
P53	Scott Baker	15.00
P55	Steve Lerud	15.00
P56	Thomas Pauly	8.00
P57	Tom Gorzelanny	15.00
P58	Tim Moss	8.00
P60	Trey Webb	8.00
P61	Wes Littleton	8.00
P62	Beau Vaughan	8.00
P63	Willy Jo Ronda	8.00
P64	Chris Lubanski	15.00
P65	Ian Stewart	40.00
P66	John Danks	20.00
P67	Kyle Sleeth	12.00
P68	Michael Aubrey	15.00
P70	Ryan Harvey	15.00
P71	Tim Stauffer	10.00

Star Rookie Jersey

	NM/M
Common Player:	4.00
Inserted 1:18	

#	Player	Price
P72	Tony Richie	4.00
P73	Brandon Wood	6.00
P74	David Aardsma	4.00
P75	David Shinskie	4.00
P76	Dennis Dove	4.00
P77	Eric Sultemeier	4.00
P78	Jay Sborz	4.00
P79	Jimmy Barthmaier	4.00
P80	Josh Whitesell	4.00
P81	Josh Anderson	4.00
P82	Kenny Lewis	4.00
P83	Mateo Miramontes	4.00
P84	Nicholas Markakis	15.00
P85	Paul Bacot	4.00
P86	Peter Stonard	4.00
P87	Reggie Willits	8.00
P88	Shane Costa	4.00
P89	Billy Sadler	4.00
P91	Kyle Sleeth	6.00
P92	Ian Stewart	15.00
P93	Fraser Dizard	6.00
P94	Abe Alvarez	6.00
P95	Adam Jones	15.00
P96	Brian Anderson	4.00
P97	Chris Durbin	4.00
P98	Craig Whitaker	4.00
P99	Jake Fox	4.00
P100	Kurt Isenberg	4.00
P101	Luis Atilano	4.00
P102	Miguel Vega	4.00
P103	Mitch Maier	4.00
P104	Ryan Sweeney	8.00
P105	Scott Baker	4.00
P106	Sean Rodriguez	8.00
P108	Trey Webb	4.00
P109	Willy Jo Ronda	6.00
P110	John Danks	8.00
P111	Michael Aubrey	8.00
P112	Lastings Milledge	10.00
P113	Chris Lubanski	6.00

2003 Upper Deck SportsFest Star Rookies

Persons who opened a box of Upper Deck product at the company's booth during the June 27-29 show in Chicago received this cellophane wrapped set of six Star Rookies.

	NM/M
Complete Set (6):	6.00
Common Player:	.25
AM	Alejandro Machado	.25
HB	Hank Blalock	.50
HC	Hee Seop Choi	.25
HM	Hideki Matsui	5.00
RB	Rocco Baldelli	1.50
RH	Runelvys Hernandez	.25

2003 Upper Deck Standing O!

	NM/M
Complete Set (126):	30.00
Common Player:	.15
Common SP (85-126):	.75
Inserted 1:4	
Pack (4):	1.50
Box (24):	25.00

#	Player	Price
1	Darin Erstad	.25
2	Troy Glaus	.40
3	Tim Salmon	.25
4	Luis Gonzalez	.25
5	Randy Johnson	.40
6	Curt Schilling	.40
7	Andruw Jones	.25
8	Greg Maddux	.75
9	Chipper Jones	.25
10	Gary Sheffield	.25
11	Rodrigo Lopez	.15
12	Geronimo Gil	.15
13	Nomar Garciaparra	1.00
14	Pedro J. Martinez	1.00
15	Manny Ramirez	.40
16	Mark Prior	.50
17	Kerry Wood	.25
18	Sammy Sosa	.75
19	Magglio Ordonez	.25
20	Frank Thomas	.40
21	Adam Dunn	.40
22	Ken Griffey Jr.	.75
23	Sean Casey	.15
24	Omar Vizquel	.15
25	C.C. Sabathia	.15
26	Larry Walker	.25
27	Todd Helton	.40
28	Ivan Rodriguez	.40
29	Josh Beckett	.15
30	Roy Oswalt	.25
31	Jeff Kent	.25
32	Jeff Bagwell	.40
33	Lance Berkman	.25
34	Mike Sweeney	.15
35	Carlos Beltran	.25
36	Hideo Nomo	.40
37	Shawn Green	.25
38	Kazuhisa Ishii	.15
39	Geoff Jenkins	.15
40	Richie Sexson	.25
41	Torii Hunter	.15
42	Jacque Jones	.15
43	Jose Vidro	.15
44	Vladimir Guerrero	.50
45	Cliff Floyd	.15
46	Al Leiter	.15
47	Mike Piazza	1.00
48	Tom Glavine	.25
49	Roberto Alomar	.25
50	Roger Clemens	.75
51	Jason Giambi	.50
52	Bernie Williams	.25
53	Alfonso Soriano	1.00
54	Derek Jeter	1.50
55	Miguel Tejada	.25
56	Eric Chavez	.25
57	Barry Zito	.25
58	Pat Burrell	.25
59	Jim Thome	.40
60	Brian Giles	.25
61	Jason Kendall	.25
62	Ryan Klesko	.25
63	Phil Nevin	.15
64	Sean Burroughs	.15
65	Jason Schmidt	.15
66	Rich Aurilia	.15
67	Barry Bonds	1.50
68	Randy Winn	.15
69	Freddy Garcia	.15
70	Ichiro Suzuki	.75
71	J.D. Drew	.15
72	Jim Edmonds	.25
73	Scott Rolen	.40
74	Matt Morris	.25
75	Albert Pujols	.75
76	Tino Martinez	.15
77	Rey Ordonez	.15
78	Carl Crawford	.25
79	Rafael Palmeiro	.25
80	Kevin Mench	.15
81	Alex Rodriguez	1.25
82	Juan Gonzalez	.40
83	Carlos Delgado	.25
84	Eric Hinske	.15
85	Richard Fischer RC	.75
86	Brandon Webb RC	2.00
87	Rob Hammock RC	.75
88	Matt Kata RC	.75
89	Tim Olson RC	.75
90	Oscar Villarreal RC	.75
91	Michael Hessman RC	.75
92	Daniel Cabrera RC	.75
93	Jon Leicester RC	.75
94	Todd Wellemeyer RC	1.00
95	Felix Sanchez RC	.75
96	David Sanders RC	.75
97	Josh Stewart RC	.75
98	Arnie Munoz RC	.75
99	Ryan Cameron RC	.75
100	Clint Barmes RC	1.50
101	Josh Willingham RC	1.50
103	Willie Eyre RC	.75
104	Brent Hoard RC	.75
105	Termel Sledge RC	1.00
106	Phil Seibel RC	.75
107	Craig Brazell RC	.75
108	Jeff Duncan RC	.75
110	Bernie Castro RC	.75
111	Mike Nicolas RC	.75
112	Rett Johnson RC	.75
113	Bobby Madritsch RC	.75
114	Luis Ayala RC	.75
115	Hideki Matsui RC	10.00
116	Jose Contreras RC	1.50
117	Lew Ford RC	.75
118	Jeremy Griffiths RC	.75
119	Guillermo Quiroz RC	1.00
120	Alejandro Machado RC	.75
121	Francisco Cruceta RC	.75
122	Prentice Redman RC	.75
123	Shane Bazzell RC	.75
124	Jason Anderson RC	.75
125	Ian Ferguson RC	.75
126	Nook Logan RC	.75

Die-Cut Disc

Stars (1-84)	1-2X
Inserted 1:1	
SP's (85-126)	1.5-3X
Inserted 1:48	

Starring Role Jersey

	NM/M
Not Priced yet, not enough market info.	
Inserted 1:240	
SR-RC	Roger Clemens	20.00
SR-JG	Jason Giambi	10.00
SR-LG	Luis Gonzalez	8.00
SR-SG	Shawn Green	5.00
SR-RJ	Randy Johnson	10.00
SR-MC	Mark McGwire/SP	40.00
SR-AR	Alex Rodriguez	20.00

2003 Upper Deck Sweet Spot

	NM/M
Complete Set (232):	
Common Player:	.25
Common SP:	1.00
Inserted 1:4	
Common SP (131-190):	3.00
Production 2,003	
Common SP (191-232):	4.00
Production 1,430 unless noted.	
Pack (4):	9.00
Box (12):	90.00

#	Player	Price
1	Darin Erstad	.50
2	Garret Anderson	.50
3	Tim Salmon	.50
4	Troy Glaus	.75
5	Luis Gonzalez	.50
6	Randy Johnson	1.00
7	Curt Schilling	.50
8	Lyle Overbay	.25
9	Andruw Jones/SP	2.00
10	Gary Sheffield/SP	1.50
11	Rafael Furcal/SP	1.00
12	Greg Maddux/SP	4.00
13	Chipper Jones/SP	4.00
14	Tony Batista	.25
15	Rodrigo Lopez	.25
16	Jay Gibbons	.25
17	Jason Johnson	.25
18	Byung-Hyun Kim/SP	1.00
19	Johnny Damon/SP	2.50
20	Derek Lowe/SP	1.00
21	Nomar Garciaparra/SP	.75
22	Pedro Martinez/SP	3.00
23	Manny Ramirez/SP	2.50
24	Mark Prior	1.00
25	Kerry Wood	1.00
26	Corey Patterson	.50
27	Sammy Sosa	2.00
28	Moises Alou	.40
29	Magglio Ordonez	.40
30	Frank Thomas	.75
31	Paul Konerko	.25
32	Roberto Alomar	.50
33	Adam Dunn	.75
34	Austin Kearns	.50
35	Ryan Wagner RC	.25
36	Ken Griffey Jr.	1.50
37	Sean Casey	.25
38	Omar Vizquel	.40
39	C.C. Sabathia	.25
40	Jason Davis	.25
41	Travis Hafner	.25
42	Brandon Phillips	.25
43	Larry Walker	.40
44	Preston Wilson	.25
45	Jay Payton	.25
46	Todd Helton	.75
47	Carlos Pena	.25
48	Eric Munson	.25
49	Ivan Rodriguez	.75
50	Josh Beckett	.50
51	Alex Gonzalez	.25
52	Roy Oswalt	.40
53	Craig Biggio	.40
54	Jeff Bagwell	.75
55	Lance Berkman	.50
56	Mike Sweeney	.25
57	Carlos Beltran	.75
58	Brent Mayne	.25
59	Mike MacDougal	.25
60	Hideo Nomo	.50
61	Dave Roberts	.25
62	Adrian Beltre	.50
63	Shawn Green	.50
64	Kazuhisa Ishii	.25
65	Rickey Henderson	.50
66	Richie Sexson	.50
67	Torii Hunter	.25
68	Jacque Jones	.25
69	Joe Mays	.25
70	Corey Koskie	.25
71	A.J. Pierzynski	.25
72	Jose Vidro	.25
73	Vladimir Guerrero	.50
74	Tom Glavine	.50
75	Mike Piazza	1.50
76	Jose Reyes	.50
77	Jae Weong Seo	.25
78	Jorge Posada/SP	2.00
79	Mike Mussina/SP	2.00
80	Robin Ventura/SP	1.00
81	Mariano Rivera/SP	1.50
82	Roger Clemens/SP	6.00
83	Jason Giambi/SP	1.50
84	Bernie Williams/SP	2.00
85	Alfonso Soriano/SP	3.00
86	Derek Jeter/SP	2.50
87	Miguel Tejada	.75
88	Eric Chavez	.50
89	Tim Hudson	.50
90	Barry Zito	.50
91	Mark Mulder	.50
92	Erubiel Durazo	.25
93	Pat Burrell	.50
94	Jim Thome	.75
95	Bobby Abreu	.50
96	Brian Giles	.40
97	Reggie Sanders	.25
98	Jose Hernandez	.25
99	Ryan Klesko	.25
100	Sean Burroughs	.25
101	Edgardo Alfonzo/SP	1.00
102	Rich Aurilia/SP	1.00
103	Jose Cruz Jr./SP	1.00
104	Barry Bonds/SP	6.00
105	Andres Galarraga/SP	1.00
106	Mike Cameron	.25
107	Kazuhiro Sasaki	.25
108	Bret Boone	.40
109	Ichiro Suzuki	2.00
110	John Olerud	.40
111	J.D. Drew/SP	1.50
112	Jim Edmonds/SP	2.00
113	Scott Rolen/SP	3.00
114	Matt Morris/SP	1.00
115	Tino Martinez/SP	1.00
116	Albert Pujols/SP	6.00
117	Jared Sandberg	.25
118	Carl Crawford	.25
119	Rafael Palmeiro	.50
120	Hank Blalock	.50
121	Alex Rodriguez	2.50
122	Kevin Mench	.25
123	Juan Gonzalez	.75
124	Mark Teixeira	.25
125	Shannon Stewart	.25
126	Vernon Wells	.50
127	Josh Phelps	.25
128	Eric Hinske	.25
129	Orlando Hudson	.25
130	Carlos Delgado	.75
131	Jason Shiell RC	3.00
132	Kevin Tolar RC	3.00
133	Nate Bland RC	3.00
134	Brent Hoard RC	3.00
135	Jonathan Pridie RC	3.00
136	Mike Ryan RC	4.00
137	Francisco Rosario RC	3.00
138	Runelvys Hernandez	3.00
139	Guillermo Quiroz RC	4.00
140	Chin-Hui Tsao	3.00
141	Rett Johnson RC	3.00
142	Colin Porter RC	3.00
143	Jose Castillo RC	3.00
144	Chris Waters RC	3.00
145	Jeremy Guthrie RC	3.00
146	Pedro Liriano	3.00
147	Joe Borowski	3.00
148	Felix Sanchez RC	3.00
149	Todd Wellemeyer RC	3.00
150	Gerald Laird	3.00
151	Brandon Webb RC	8.00
152	Tommy Whiteman RC	3.00
153	Carlos Rivera	3.00
154	Rick Roberts RC	3.00
155	Termel Sledge RC	3.00
156	Jeff Duncan RC	3.00
157	Craig Brazell RC	3.00
158	Bernie Castro RC	3.00
159	Cory Stewart RC	3.00
160	Brandon Villafuerte RC	3.00
161	Tommy Phelps	3.00
162	Josh Hall RC	3.00
163	Ryan Cameron RC	3.00
164	Garrett Atkins RC	3.00
165	Brian Stokes RC	3.00
166	Rafael Betancourt RC	3.00
167	Jaime Cerda	3.00
168	Danny Carrasco RC	3.00
169	Ian Ferguson RC	3.00
170	Jorge Cordova RC	3.00
171	Eric Munson RC	3.00
172	Nook Logan RC	3.00
173	Jeremy Bonderman	5.00
174	Kyle Snyder	5.00
175	Rich Harden	5.00
176	Kevin Ohme RC	3.00
177	Roger Deago RC	3.00
178	Marlon Byrd	5.00
179	Dontrelle Willis	5.00
180	Bobby Hill	3.00
181	Jesse Foppert	3.00
182	Andrew Good	3.00
183	Chase Utley	5.00
184	Bo Hart RC	5.00
185	Dan Haren	4.00
186	Tim Olson RC	3.00
187	Joe Thurston	3.00
188	Jason Anderson	3.00
189	Jason Gilfillan RC	3.00
190	Rickie Weeks RC	10.00
191	Hideki Matsui/500 RC	25.00

#	Player	Price	Code
192	Jose Contreras RC	8.00	TS
193	Willie Eyre RC	4.00	TS
194	Matt Bruback RC	4.00	CS
195	Heath Bell RC	8.00	CS
196	Lew Ford RC	5.00	GS
197	Jeremy Griffiths RC	5.00	GS
198	Oscar Villarreal/500 RC	5.00	SS
199	Francisco Cruceta RC	5.00	IS
200	Fernando Cabrera RC	5.00	IS
201	Jhonny Peralta RC	4.00	MT
202	Shane Bazzell RC	4.00	MT
203	Bobby Madritsch/500 RC	6.00	JT
204	Phil Seibel RC	4.00	BW
205	Josh Willingham RC	8.00	BW
206	Robby Hammock/500 RC	5.00	RW
207	Alejandro Machado RC	5.00	JW
208	David Sanders RC	4.00	JW
209	Mike Neu/500 RC	5.00	
210	Andrew Brown RC	4.00	DW
211	Nathan Robertson RC	6.00	DW
212	Miguel Ojeda RC	4.00	
213	Beau Kemp RC	4.00	
214	Aaron Looper RC	4.00	
215	Alfredo Gonzalez RC	5.00	
216	Richard Fischer/500 RC	5.00	
218	Jeremy Wedel RC	6.00	
219	Prentice Redman RC	4.00	
220	Michel Hernandez RC	6.00	
221	Rocco Baldelli/500	5.00	
222	Luis Ayala RC	5.00	
223	Arnie Munoz RC	4.00	
224	Wilfredo Ledezma RC	4.00	
225	Chris Capuano RC	8.00	
226	Aquilino Lopez RC	4.00	
227	Joe Valentine/500 RC	5.00	
228	Matt Kata/1,200 RC	5.00	
229	Diegomar Markwell/1,200 RC	4.00	
230	Clint Barmes/1,200 RC	8.00	
231	Mike Nicolas/500 RC	4.00	
232	Jon Leicester/1,200 RC	5.00	

Autographs Black Ink

Common Player: NM/M
Red & Blue Ink variations exist.
Reds not priced due to scarcity.
Mirror Parallel: No Pricing
Production 25

Code	Player	Price
HB	Hank Blalock	20.00
HB	Hank Blalock/Blue/40	25.00
PB	Pat Burrell	20.00
PB	Pat Burrell/Blue/40	25.00
RC	Roger Clemens/73	125.00
RC	Roger Clemens/Blue/40	150.00
JC	Jose Contreras	40.00
JC	Jose Contreras/Blue/40	50.00
AD	Adam Dunn	30.00
AD	Adam Dunn/Blue/40	40.00
NG	Nomar Garciaparra	40.00
NG	Nomar Garciaparra/Blue/40	50.00
JG	Jason Giambi	20.00
JG	Jason Giambi/Blue/40	30.00
TR	Troy Glaus	25.00
TR	Troy Glaus/Blue/40	40.00
GL	Tom Glavine	30.00
GL	Tom Glavine/Blue/40	50.00
KG	Ken Griffey Jr.	75.00
KG	Ken Griffey Jr./Blue/40	100.00
KGs	Ken Griffey Sr.	15.00
KGs	Ken Griffey Sr./Blue/40	20.00
VG	Vladimir Guerrero	50.00
VG	Vladimir Guerrero/Blue/40	65.00
TG	Tony Gwynn	40.00
HA	Travis Hafner	15.00
HA	Travis Hafner/Blue/40	25.00
BH	Bo Hart	10.00
BH	Bo Hart/Blue/40	15.00
TH	Todd Helton/45	75.00
TH	Todd Helton/Blue/40	75.00
DH	Drew Henson	15.00
DH	Drew Henson/Blue/40	25.00
KI	Kazuhisa Ishii	15.00
KI	Kazuhisa Ishii/Blue/40	20.00
AK	Austin Kearns	20.00
AK	Austin Kearns/Blue/40	25.00
HM	Hideki Matsui	300.00
HM	Hideki Matsui/Blue/40	375.00
RO	Roy Oswalt	25.00
RO	Roy Oswalt/Blue/40	35.00
LO	Lyle Overbay	15.00
LO	Lyle Overbay/Blue/40	20.00
BP	Brandon Phillips	15.00
BP	Brandon Phillips/Blue/40	20.00
MP	Mark Prior	15.00
MP	Mark Prior/Blue/40	20.00
JR	Jose Reyes	30.00
JR	Jose Reyes/Blue/40	60.00
CR	Cal Ripken Jr.	165.00
CR	Cal Ripken Jr./Blue/40	220.00
NR	Nolan Ryan	120.00
NR	Nolan Ryan/Blue/40	165.00
TS	Tim Salmon	25.00
TS	Tim Salmon/Blue/40	30.00
CS	Curt Schilling	25.00
CS	Curt Schilling/Blue/40	75.00
GS	Gary Sheffield	30.00
GS	Gary Sheffield/Blue/40	40.00
SS	Sammy Sosa/Blue/40	120.00
IS	Ichiro Suzuki/Blue/40	400.00
IS	Ichiro Suzuki/Red/35	400.00
MT	Mark Teixeira	50.00
MT	Mark Teixeira/Blue/40	60.00
JT	Jim Thome	50.00
JT	Jim Thome/Blue/40	60.00
BW	Brandon Webb	40.00
BW	Brandon Webb/Blue/40	75.00
RW	Rickie Weeks	40.00
JW	Jerome Williams	15.00
JW	Jerome Williams/Blue/40	20.00
DW	Dontrelle Willis	15.00
DW	Dontrelle Willis/Blue/40	40.00

Game-Used Barrel

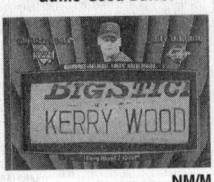

NM/M
Quantity produced listed
No Pricing due to scarcity.

Code	Player	Price
KW-BB	Kerry Wood/2 (2/04 Auction)	1,000

Barrel Autographs

NM/M
Quantity produced listed

Code	Player	Price
HB	Hank Blalock/420	25.00
PB	Pat Burrell/345	25.00
RC	Roger Clemens/49	100.00
AD	Adam Dunn/345	40.00
TR	Troy Glaus/345	40.00
TG	Tom Glavine/345	50.00
KG	Ken Griffey Jr./295	125.00
HM	Hideki Matsui/124	200.00
CR	Cal Ripken Jr./149	180.00
NR	Nolan Ryan/445	150.00
JT	Jim Thome/345	65.00

Patch

NM/M
Common Player: 4.00
Inserted 1:6
Logo Patch Parallel: 1-2X
Production 75 Sets

Code	Player	Price
JB1	Jeff Bagwell	6.00
LB1	Lance Berkman	5.00
BB1	Barry Bonds	15.00
PB1	Pat Burrell	5.00
RC1	Roger Clemens	12.00
CD1	Carlos Delgado	4.00
AD1	Adam Dunn	5.00
JE1	Jim Edmonds	4.00
DE1	Darin Erstad	4.00
NG1	Nomar Garciaparra	10.00
JG1	Jason Giambi	5.00
TG1	Troy Glaus	5.00
TO1	Tom Glavine	5.00
LG1	Luis Gonzalez	5.00
SG1	Shawn Green	5.00
KG1	Ken Griffey Jr.	8.00
VG1	Vladimir Guerrero	6.00
TH1	Torii Hunter	5.00
KI1	Kazuhisa Ishii	4.00
DJ1	Derek Jeter	15.00
RJ1	Randy Johnson	8.00
AJ1	Andruw Jones	5.00
CJ1	Chipper Jones	10.00
JK1	Jeff Kent	4.00
GM1	Greg Maddux	10.00
PM1	Pedro J. Martinez	10.00
HN1	Hideo Nomo	5.00
MO1	Magglio Ordonez	4.00
CP1	Corey Patterson	6.00
MP1	Mike Piazza	10.00
MA1	Mark Prior	4.00
AP1	Albert Pujols	15.00
AR1	Alex Rodriguez	10.00
CS1	Curt Schilling	6.00
GS1	Gary Sheffield	6.00
AS1	Alfonso Soriano	8.00
SS1	Sammy Sosa	10.00
IS1	Ichiro Suzuki	10.00
MT1	Miguel Tejada	6.00
JT1	Jim Thome	6.00
BW1	Bernie Williams	5.00
BZ1	Barry Zito	4.00

Game-Used Patch

Production 25 or 10
No pricing due to scarcity.

Swatches

NM/M
Common Player: 4.00
Inserted 1:24
Tier 2: 1-2X
Production 75

Code	Player	Price
RA	Roberto Alomar	4.00
PB	Pat Burrell	6.00
RC	Roger Clemens	10.00
NM	Nomar Garciaparra	15.00
NG1	Nomar Garciaparra	4.00
JG	Jason Giambi	8.00
TG	Troy Glaus	4.00
TG1	Troy Glaus	5.00
TO	Tom Glavine	4.00
LG	Luis Gonzalez	4.00
KG	Ken Griffey Jr.	10.00
VG	Vladimir Guerrero	6.00
TH	Torii Hunter	5.00
RJ	Randy Johnson	6.00
AJ	Andruw Jones	4.00
CJ	Chipper Jones	8.00
AK	Austin Kearns	6.00
GM	Greg Maddux	10.00
MM	Mickey Mantle	120.00
HM	Hideki Matsui	45.00
HM1	Hideki Matsui	4.00
RO	Roy Oswalt	4.00
RO1	Roy Oswalt	4.00
MP	Mike Piazza	10.00
MA	Mark Prior	4.00
AP	Albert Pujols	15.00
AR	Alex Rodriguez	10.00
CS	Curt Schilling	5.00
GS	Gary Sheffield	6.00
AS	Alfonso Soriano	10.00
AS1	Alfonso Soriano	4.00
SS	Sammy Sosa	12.00
IS	Ichiro Suzuki	20.00
MT	Miguel Tejada	4.00
FT	Frank Thomas	6.00
JT	Jim Thome	8.00
BW	Bernie Williams	4.00
TW	Ted Williams	60.00
BZ	Barry Zito	4.00

2003 Upper Deck Sweet Spot Classic

NM/M
Complete Set (150):
Common Player: .40
Common Ted Williams (91-120): 5.00
Production 1,941
Common Yankee Heritage (121-150): 2.00
Production 1,500
Pack (4): 12.00
Box (12): 120.00

#	Player	Price
1	Al Hrabosky	.40
2	Al Lopez	.40
3	Andre Dawson	.75
4	Bill Buckner	.40
5	Billy Williams	.50
6	Bob Feller	.75
7	Bob Lemon	.40
8	Bobby Doerr	.40
9	Cecil Cooper	.40
10	Cal Ripken Jr.	2.50
11	Carlton Fisk	.60
12	Jim "Catfish" Hunter	.40
13	Chris Chambliss	.40
14	Dale Murphy	.75
15	Gaylord Perry	.40
16	Dave Kingman	.40
17	Dave Parker	.40
18	Dave Stewart	.40
19	David Cone	.40
20	Dennis Eckersley	.60
21	Don Baylor	.40
22	Don Sutton	.40
23	Duke Snider	1.00
24	Dwight Evans	.40
25	Dwight Gooden	.40
26	Earl Weaver	.40
27	Early Wynn	.40
28	Eddie Mathews	1.50
29	Enos Slaughter	.40
30	Ernie Banks	1.50
31	Fred Lynn	.40
32	Fred Stanley	.40
33	Gary Carter	.75
34	George Foster	.40
35	Hal Newhouser	.40
36	George Kell	.40
37	Harmon Killebrew	1.50
38	Hoyt Wilhelm	.40
39	Jack Morris	.40
40	Jim Bunning	.40
41	Jim Gilliam	.40
42	Jim Leyritz	.40
43	Jimmy Key	.40
44	Joe Carter	.40
45	Joe Morgan	.40
46	John Montefusco	.40
47	Johnny Bench	2.00
48	Johnny Podres	.40
49	Jose Canseco	.75
50	Juan Marichal	.40
51	Keith Hernandez	.40
52	Ken Griffey Sr.	.40
53	Kirby Puckett	1.50
54	Kirk Gibson	.40
55	Larry Doby	.40
56	Lee May	.40
57	Lee Mazzilli	.40
58	Lou Boudreau	.40
59	Mark McGwire	3.00
60	Maury Wills	.40
61	Mike Pagliarulo	.40
62	Monte Irvin	.75
63	Nolan Ryan	3.00
64	Orlando Cepeda	.40
65	Ozzie Smith	1.50
66	Paul O'Neill	.40
67	Pee Wee Reese	.40
68	Phil Niekro	.40
69	Ralph Kiner	.40
70	Red Schoendienst	.40
71	Richie Ashburn	.40
72	Rick Ferrell	.40
73	Robin Roberts	.40
74	Robin Yount	1.50
75	Hideki Matsui/1,999 RC	10.00
75	Hideki Matsui/Red/500	25.00
75	Hideki Matsui/Blue/250	30.00
75	Hideki Matsui/Silver/25	200.00
76	Rollie Fingers	.40
77	Ron Cey	.40
78	Tom Seaver	1.00
79	Sparky Anderson	.40
80	Stan Musial	2.00
81	Steve Garvey	.40
82	Ted Williams	3.00
83	Tommy Lasorda	.40
84	Tony Gwynn	1.00
85	Tony Perez	.40
86	Vida Blue	.40
87	Warren Spahn	.75
88	Bob Gibson	1.00
89	Willie McCovey	.40
90	Willie Stargell	.75
91-120	Ted Williams	5.00
121	Babe Ruth	8.00
122	Bucky Dent	2.00
123	Casey Stengel	3.00
124	Dave Righetti	2.00
125	Dave Winfield	3.00
126	Dick Tidrow	2.00
127	Dock Ellis	2.00
128	Don Mattingly	8.00
129	Hank Bauer	2.00
130	Jim Bouton	2.00
131	Jim Kaat	2.00
132	Joe DiMaggio	6.00
133	Joe Torre	2.00
134	Lou Piniella	2.00
135	Mel Stottlemyre	2.00
136	Mickey Mantle	15.00
137	Mickey Rivers	2.00
138	Phil Rizzuto	2.00
139	Ralph Branca	2.00
140	Ralph Houk	2.00
141	Roger Maris	6.00
142	Ron Guidry	2.00
143	Ruben Amaro Jr.	2.00
144	Sparky Lyle	2.00
145	Thurman Munson	5.00
146	Tommy Henrich	2.00
147	Tommy John	2.00
148	Tony Kubek	2.00
149	Whitey Ford	4.00
150	Yogi Berra	4.00

Game Jersey

NM/M
Common Player: 5.00
Inserted 1:16

Code	Player	Price
EB	Ernie Banks	15.00
JB	Johnny Bench	15.00
JC	Jose Canseco	6.00
GC	Gary Carter	6.00
RC	Ron Cey	5.00
CC	Cecil Cooper	6.00
AD	Andre Dawson	6.00
RF	Rollie Fingers	6.00
CF	Carlton Fisk	8.00
GF	George Foster	5.00
SG	Steve Garvey	5.00
JG	Jim Gilliam	6.00
TG	Tony Gwynn	8.00
HK	Harmon Killebrew	12.00
FL	Fred Lynn	5.00
LM	Lee May	5.00
MM	Mark McGwire	20.00
JM	Joe Morgan	6.00
DM	Dale Murphy	6.00
SM	Stan Musial	25.00
DP	Dave Parker	5.00
JP	Johnny Podres	5.00
KP	Kirby Puckett	12.00
CR	Cal Ripken Jr.	20.00
NR	Nolan Ryan	30.00
OS	Ozzie Smith	12.00
DS	Duke Snider	12.00
WS	Willie Stargell/SP	20.00
TW	Ted Williams/SP	100.00
RY	Robin Yount	10.00

Greats Autograph

NM/M
Common Autograph:
Blue, Black and Red ink variations exist.
Listings without notations are blue ink.

Code	Player	Price
EB	Ernie Banks/Black/73	80.00
DB	Don Baylor	25.00
DB	Don Baylor/Black/50	35.00
JB	Johnny Bench/Black/73	100.00
BB	Bill Buckner	20.00
BB	Bill Buckner/Black/85	25.00
GC	Gary Carter/Black/173	40.00
JC	Joe Carter/Black/173	35.00
OC	Orlando Cepeda	20.00
OC	Orlando Cepeda/Black/34	35.00
AD	Andre Dawson	30.00
AD	Andre Dawson/Black/75	30.00
DEc	Dennis Eckersley	25.00
DE	Dwight Evans	20.00
DE	Dwight Evans/Black/100	30.00
RF	Rollie Fingers/Black/73	30.00
RF	Rollie Fingers/Red/25	90.00
GF	George Foster/Black/173	35.00
SG	Steve Garvey/Black/174	30.00
GC	Kirk Gibson/Black/173	30.00
KG	Ken Griffey Sr.	20.00
KG	Ken Griffey Sr./Black/100	25.00
TG	Tony Gwynn	45.00
TG	Tony Gwynn/Black/101	60.00
KH	Keith Hernandez/Black/173	40.00
KH	Keith Hernandez/Red/25	110.00
AH	Al Hrabosky	25.00
AH	Al Hrabosky/Black/100	35.00
HK	Harmon Killebrew/Black/73	80.00
MM	Mark McGwire/Black/73	425.00
JoM	Joe Morgan/Black/169	40.00
JMo	Jack Morris/Black/123	40.00
DM	Dale Murphy	30.00
PN	Phil Niekro/Black/173	30.00
PN	Phil Niekro/Red/25	75.00
DP	Dave Parker/Black/113	30.00
TP	Tony Perez/Black/51	65.00
JP	Johnny Podres/Black/173	30.00
JP	Johnny Podres/Red/25	80.00
KP	Kirby Puckett	45.00
KP	Kirby Puckett/Black/174	60.00
CR	Cal Ripken Jr.	150.00
CR	Cal Ripken Jr/Black/38	250.00
RR	Robin Roberts/Black/173	35.00
TS	Tom Seaver/Black/74	80.00
TS	Tom Seaver/Red/25	135.00
SN	Duke Snider	50.00
SN	Duke Snider/Black/100	50.00
DSt	Dave Stewart	15.00
DSu	Don Sutton/Black/123	40.00
AT	Alan Trammell/Black/173	35.00
BW	Billy Williams/Black/173	35.00
TW	Ted Williams/9	3,650
MW	Maury Wills/Black/173	100.00
RY	Robin Roberts/Black/73	100.00
RY	Robin Yount/Red/25	200.00

Patch Logo

NM/M
Common Player: 5.00
Note: some are actual game-used patches.

Code	Player	Price
EB1	Ernie Banks	12.00
JB1	Johnny Bench	12.00
JB2	Johnny Bench/150	40.00
JB3	Johnny Bench/150	35.00
YB1	Yogi Berra	12.00
YB2	Yogi Berra/350	25.00
YB3	Yogi Berra/150	35.00
JD1	Joe DiMaggio	20.00
JD2	Joe DiMaggio/50	85.00
JD3	Joe DiMaggio/150	40.00
JD4	Joe DiMaggio/150	30.00
CF1	Carlton Fisk	8.00
CF2	Carlton Fisk/150	10.00
GF1	George Foster/350	10.00
GF2	George Foster	5.00
SG1	Steve Garvey	5.00
SG2	Steve Garvey/350	10.00
SG3	Steve Garvey/150	30.00
SG4	Steve Garvey/50	25.00
SG5	Steve Garvey/50	25.00
KG1	Kirk Gibson	5.00
KG2	Kirk Gibson/350	12.00
TG1	Tony Gwynn	8.00
TG2	Tony Gwynn/150	50.00
TG3	Tony Gwynn/150	25.00
CH1	Catfish Hunter	10.00
CH2	Catfish Hunter	5.00
CH4	Catfish Hunter/50	30.00
FL1	Fred Lynn	5.00
FL2	Fred Lynn/350	10.00
FL3	Fred Lynn/150	15.00
FL4	Fred Lynn/50	20.00
MM1	Mickey Mantle	35.00
MM2	Mickey Mantle/150	85.00
MM3	Mickey Mantle/150	85.00
MM4	Mickey Mantle/150	75.00
RM1	Roger Maris	15.00
RM2	Roger Maris/350	25.00
RM3	Roger Maris/150	40.00
RM4	Roger Maris/150	60.00
HM1	Hideki Matsui	25.00
MC1	Mark McGwire	20.00
MC2	Mark McGwire/350	50.00
JM1	Joe Morgan	6.00
JM2	Joe Morgan/350	8.00
JM3	Joe Morgan/150	15.00
JM4	Joe Morgan/150	30.00
JM5	Joe Morgan/150	15.00
KP1	Kirby Puckett	10.00
KP2	Kirby Puckett/40	100.00
CR1	Cal Ripken Jr.	25.00
CR2	Cal Ripken Jr/75	100.00
CR3	Cal Ripken Jr./150	50.00
BR1	Babe Ruth/350	40.00
BR2	Babe Ruth	30.00
BR3	Babe Ruth/150	50.00
NR1	Nolan Ryan	25.00
NR2	Nolan Ryan/350	40.00
NR3	Nolan Ryan/100	100.00
NR4	Nolan Ryan/105	100.00
OS1	Ozzie Smith	10.00
OS2	Ozzie Smith/350	20.00
OS3	Ozzie Smith/150	60.00
OS4	Ozzie Smith/100	40.00
OS5	Ozzie Smith/100	35.00
DS1	Duke Snider	8.00
DS2	Duke Snider/150	25.00
DS3	Duke Snider/150	15.00
DS5	Duke Snider/150	20.00
DS6	Duke Snider/150	20.00
WS1	Willie Stargell	5.00
WS2	Willie Stargell/137	50.00

WS3	Willie Stargell/150	25.00
WS4	Willie Stargell/50	40.00
BW1	Billy Williams	6.00
TW1	Ted Williams	20.00
TW2	Ted Williams/350	40.00
RY1	Robin Yount	8.00
RY2	Robin Yount/150	40.00
RY3	Robin Yount/350	20.00

Pinstripes

		NM/M
	Common Player:	5.00
	Inserted 1:40	
YB	Yogi Berra	15.00
JB	Jim Bouton	5.00
DE	Bucky Dent	8.00
JD	Joe DiMaggio	100.00
DG	Dwight Gooden	5.00
MM	Mickey Mantle	140.00
DM	Don Mattingly	25.00
TM	Thurman Munson	30.00
DR	Dave Righetti	5.00
PR	Phil Rizzuto	15.00
BR	Babe Ruth	250.00
CS	Casey Stengel	12.00

Yankee Greats Auto.

		NM/M
	Common Autograph:	
RA	Ruben Amaro Sr.	25.00
RA	Ruben Amaro Sr./Black/100	30.00
RA	Ruben Amaro Sr./Red/25	60.00
HB	Hank Bauer	30.00
HB	Hank Bauer/Black/75	40.00
YB	Yogi Berra/73	100.00
JB	Jim Bouton	25.00
JB	Jim Bouton/Black/100	30.00
RB	Ralph Branca	25.00
RB	Ralph Branca/Black/100	30.00
JC	Jose Canseco/Black/73	90.00
JC	Jose Canseco/Red/25	150.00
CC	Chris Chambliss	30.00
CC	Chris Chambliss/Black/101	35.00
CC	Chris Chambliss/Red/25	75.00
DC	David Cone/Black/74	75.00
DC	David Cone/Red/25	110.00
BD	Bucky Dent	20.00
JD	Joe DiMaggio/5	2,325
DE	Dock Ellis/Black/174	25.00
DE	Dock Ellis/Red/25	65.00
DG	Dwight Gooden/Black/74	70.00
GU	Ron Guidry	35.00
GU	Ron Guidry/Black/100	45.00
TH	Tommy Henrich	35.00
TH	Tommy Henrich/Black/100	40.00
TH	Tommy Henrich/Red/25	125.00
RH	Ralph Houk	25.00
RH	Ralph Houk/Black/100	30.00
TJ	Tommy John	30.00
TJ	Tommy John/Black/100	35.00
JKa	Jim Kaat	20.00
JKa	Jim Kaat/Black/25	25.00
JKe	Jimmy Key	30.00
JKe	Jimmy Key/Black/100	50.00
DK	Dave Kingman	25.00
DK	Dave Kingman/Black/100	30.00
TK	Tony Kubek/Black/123	15.00
JL	Jim Leyritz	25.00
JL	Jim Leyritz/Black/35	35.00
JL	Jim Leyritz/Red/25	65.00
SL	Sparky Lyle	30.00
SL	Sparky Lyle/Black/100	40.00
MM	Mickey Mantle/Blue/7	2,850
DM	Don Mattingly/Black/74	100.00
DM	Don Mattingly/Red/25	340.00
LM	Lee Mazzilli	20.00
JM	John Montefusco	20.00
JM	John Montefusco/Black/100	25.00
JM	John Montefusco/Red/25	50.00
PO	Paul O'Neill	40.00
PO	Paul O'Neill/Black/100	65.00
PO	Paul O'Neill/Red/25	100.00
MP	Mike Pagliarulo	20.00
MP	Mike Pagliarulo/Black/99	35.00
MP	Mike Pagliarulo/Red/25	60.00
LP	Lou Piniella	40.00

LP	Lou Piniella/Black/100	45.00
DR	Dave Righetti/Black/173	40.00
DR	Dave Righetti/Red/25	85.00
MR	Mickey Rivers/Black/73	40.00
PR	Phil Rizzuto/Black/173	55.00
FS	Fred Stanley	25.00
FS	Fred Stanley/Black/101	25.00
MS	Mel Stottlemyre/Black/73	85.00
DT	Dick Tidrow	20.00
DT	Dick Tidrow/Black/101	25.00
DT	Dick Tidrow/Red/25	70.00
JT	Joe Torre/Black/73	60.00
JT	Joe Torre/Red/25	140.00
DW	Dave Winfield/Black/25	165.00

2003 Upper Deck Ultimate Collection

	NM/M
Complete Set (181):	
Common Player (1-84):	2.00
Production 850	
Common (85-117):	3.00
Production 625	
Common (118-140):	3.00
Production 399	
Common (141-158):	4.00
Production 250	
Common (159-168):	6.00
Production 100	
Common (169-174):	25.00
Common (175-180):	10.00
169-180 Production 250	
Pack (4):	90.00
Box (4):	300.00

#	Player	Price
1	Ichiro Suzuki	8.00
2	Ken Griffey Jr.	6.00
3	Sammy Sosa	6.00
4	Jason Giambi	2.00
5	Mike Piazza	5.00
6	Derek Jeter	10.00
7	Randy Johnson	4.00
8	Barry Bonds	10.00
9	Carlos Delgado	3.00
10	Mark Prior	3.00
11	Vladimir Guerrero	4.00
12	Alfonso Soriano	4.00
13	Jim Thome	4.00
14	Pedro J. Martinez	4.00
15	Nomar Garciaparra	5.00
16	Chipper Jones	4.00
17	Rocco Baldelli	2.00
18	Dontrelle Willis	2.00
19	Garret Anderson	2.00
20	Jeff Bagwell	2.00
21	Jim Edmonds	2.50
22	Rickey Henderson	3.00
23	Torii Hunter	2.00
24	Tom Glavine	2.50
25	Hideo Nomo	2.50
26	Luis Gonzalez	2.50
27	Alex Rodriguez	8.00
28	Albert Pujols	10.00
29	Manny Ramirez	4.00
30	Rafael Palmeiro	3.00
31	Bernie Williams	3.00
32	Curt Schilling	3.00
33	Roger Clemens	8.00
34	Andruw Jones	2.00
35	J.D. Drew	3.00
36	Kerry Wood	3.00
37	Scott Rolen	3.00
38	Darin Erstad	2.00
39	Joe DiMaggio	8.00
40	Magglio Ordonez	3.00
41	Todd Helton	3.00
42	Barry Zito	2.00
43	Mickey Mantle	10.00
44	Miguel Tejada	3.00
45	Troy Glaus	2.00
46	Kazuhisa Ishii	3.00
47	Adam Dunn	3.00
48	Ted Williams	8.00
49	Mike Mussina	3.00
50	Ivan Rodriguez	3.00
51	Jacque Jones	2.00
52	Stan Musial	6.00
53	Mariano Rivera	2.50
54	Larry Walker	2.50
55	Aaron Boone	2.00
56	Hank Blalock	2.50
57	Rich Harden	2.00
58	Lance Berkman	2.00
59	Eric Chavez	2.00
60	Carlos Beltran	3.00
61	Roy Oswalt	2.00
62	Moises Alou	2.00
63	Nolan Ryan	10.00
64	Jeff Kent	2.00
65	Roberto Alomar	2.00
66	Runelvys Hernandez	2.00
67	Roy Halladay	3.00
68	Tim Hudson	2.50
69	Tom Seaver	4.00
70	Edgardo Alfonzo	2.00
71	Andy Pettitte	2.00
72	Preston Wilson	2.00
73	Frank Thomas	3.00
74	Jerome Williams	2.00
75	Shawn Green	2.50
76	David Wells	2.00
77	John Smoltz	2.00
78	Jorge Posada	3.00
79	Marlon Byrd	2.00
80	Austin Kearns	2.00
81	Bret Boone	2.00
82	Rafael Furcal	2.50
83	Jay Gibbons	2.00
84	Shane Reynolds	2.00
85	Nate Bland RC	3.00
86	Willie Eyre RC	3.00
87	Jeremy Guthrie RC	3.00
88	Jeremy Wedel RC	3.00
89	Jhonny Peralta RC	4.00
90	Luis Ayala RC	3.00
91	Michael Hessman RC	3.00
92	Micheal Nakamura RC	3.00
93	Nook Logan RC	3.00
94	Rett Johnson RC	5.00
95	Josh Hall RC	3.00
96	Julio Manon RC	3.00
97	Heath Bell RC	3.00
98	Ian Ferguson RC	3.00
99	Jason Gilfillan RC	3.00
100	Jason Roach RC	3.00
101	Jason Shiell RC	3.00
102	Terrmel Sledge RC	5.00
103	Phil Seibel RC	3.00
104	Jeff Duncan RC	6.00
105	Mike Neu RC	3.00
106	Colin Porter RC	3.00
107	Dave Matranga RC	3.00
108	Aaron Looper RC	3.00
109	Jeremy Bonderman RC	5.00
110	Miguel Ojeda RC	3.00
111	Chad Cordero RC	3.00
112	Shane Bazell RC	4.00
113	Tim Olson RC	5.00
114	Michel Hernandez RC	3.00
115	Chien-Ming Wang RC	15.00
116	Josh Stewart RC	3.00
117	Clint Barmes RC	8.00
118	Craig Brazell RC	8.00
119	Josh Willingham RC	8.00
120	Brent Hoard RC	3.00
121	Francisco Rosario RC	3.00
122	Rick Roberts RC	3.00
123	Geoff Geary RC	3.00
124	Edgar Gonzalez RC	3.00
125	Kevin Correia RC	3.00
126	Ryan Cameron RC	3.00
127	Beau Kemp RC	3.00
128	Tommy Phelps RC	3.00
129	Mark Malaska RC	3.00
130	Kevin Ohme RC	3.00
131	Humberto Quintero RC	3.00
132	Aquilino Lopez RC	3.00
133	Andrew Brown RC	3.00
134	Wilfredo Ledezma RC	3.00
135	Luis De Los Santos RC	3.00
136	Garrett Atkins RC	3.00
137	Fernando Cabrera RC	3.00
138	D.J. Carrasco RC	3.00
139	Alfredo Gonzalez RC	3.00
140	Alex Prieto RC	3.00
141	Matt Kata RC	5.00
142	Chris Capuano RC	4.00
143	Bobby Madritsch RC	4.00
144	Greg Jones RC	4.00
145	Pete Zoccolillo RC	4.00
146	Chad Gaudin RC	5.00
147	Rosman Garcia RC	4.00
148	Gerald Laird RC	4.00
149	Danny Garcia RC	4.00
150	Stephen Randolph RC	4.00
151	Pete LaForest RC	4.00
152	Brian Sweeney RC	4.00
153	Aaron Miles RC	4.00
154	Jorge DePaula RC	4.00
155	Graham Koonce RC	4.00
156	Tom Gregorio RC	4.00
157	Javier Lopez	4.00
158	Oscar Villarreal RC	4.00
159	Prentice Redman RC	6.00
160	Francisco Cruceta RC	6.00
161	Guillermo Quiroz RC	6.00
162	Jeremy Griffiths RC	4.00
163	Lew Ford RC	6.00
164	Rob Hammock RC	6.00
165	Todd Wellemeyer RC	6.00
166	Ryan Wagner RC	6.00
167	Edwin Jackson RC	10.00
168	Dan Haren RC	15.00
169	Hideki Matsui/Auto. RC	175.00
170	Jose Contreras/Auto.	30.00
171	Delmon Young/Auto. RC	50.00
172	Rickie Weeks/Auto. RC	50.00
173	Brandon Webb/Auto. RC	50.00
174	Bo Hart/Auto. RC	10.00
175	Rocco Baldelli/Auto.	10.00
176	Jose Reyes/Auto.	25.00
177	Dontrelle Willis/Auto.	15.00
178	Bobby Hill/Auto.	10.00
179	Jae Weong Seo/Auto.	10.00
180	Jesse Foppert/Auto.	10.00
CL	Checklist	2.00

Gold

Stars (1-184):	1.5-3X
(85-117):	1-2X
Production 50	
(118-140):	1-2X
Production 35	
(141-158):	1-2X
Production 25	
(159-168):	No Pricing
Production 10	
(169-180):	No Pricing
Production 25	

Buybacks

	NM/M
Production 1-75	
Hank Blalock/35	40.00
Hank Blalock 03 40M/25	40.00
Hank Blalock 03 GF/25	40.00
Hank Blalock 03 Patch/25	40.00
Hank Blalock 03 SPA/20	40.00
Hank Blalock 03 SPA/25	40.00
Hank Blalock 03 VIN/25	40.00
Luis Gonzalez 03 40M HR/25	40.00
Luis Gonzalez 03 SPA/25	40.00
Luis Gonzalez 03 VIN/25	40.00
Ken Griffey Jr. 02-3 SUP/75	80.00
Ken Griffey Jr. 02-3 SUP Spok/50	80.00
Ken Griffey Jr. 03 40M/50	80.00
Ken Griffey Jr. 03 40M/50	80.00
Ken Griffey Jr. 03 40M/50	80.00
Ken Griffey Jr. 03 40M/50	80.00
Ken Griffey Jr. 03 40M T40/50	80.00
Ken Griffey Jr. 03 GF/50	80.00
Ken Griffey Jr. 03 HON/50	80.00
Ken Griffey Jr. 03 HON SP/30	100.00
Ken Griffey Jr. 03 Patch/75	80.00
Ken Griffey Jr. 03 PB/75	80.00
Ken Griffey Jr. 03 SPA/50	80.00
Ken Griffey Jr. 03 SPA/75	80.00
Ken Griffey Jr. 03 SPx/75	80.00
Ken Griffey Jr. 03 SWS/75	80.00
Ken Griffey Jr. 03 UDA/75	80.00
Ken Griffey Jr. 03 VIN/50	80.00
Torii Hunter 03 Patch/25	40.00
Torii Hunter 03 PB/50	30.00
Torii Hunter 03 VIN/25	40.00
Austin Kearns 03 40M/33	30.00
Hideki Matsui 03 40M/20	250.00
Hideki Matsui 03 40M Flag/20	250.00
Hideki Matsui 03 GF/18	250.00
Hideki Matsui 03 PB/17	250.00
Hideki Matsui 03 UD/25	250.00
Hideki Matsui 03 VIN/25	250.00
Stan Musial 02 SPLC/30	75.00
Stan Musial 02 WSH/25	75.00
Stan Musial 03 PB/50	60.00
Stan Musial 03 SWSC/37	75.00
Stan Musial 03 VIN/50	60.00
Sammy Sosa 02-3 SUP/25	120.00
Sammy Sosa 03 PB/25	120.00
Sammy Sosa 03 SPA/25	120.00
Sammy Sosa 03 VIN/25	120.00
Mark Teixeira 03 40M/50	40.00
Mark Teixeira 03 Patch/50	40.00
Mark Teixeira 03 SPA RA/25	50.00
Mark Teixeira 03 SWS/23	50.00
Mark Teixeira 03 UD/25	50.00
Mark Teixeira 03 VIN/25	50.00

Double Barrel

	NM/M
No pricing due to scarcity.	
DB-AE Darin Erstad, Garret Anderson/3 (3/04 Auction)	645.00
DB-GS Tom Seaver, Tom Glavine/2 (3/04 Auction)	700.00

Game Jersey Tier 1

		NM/M
	Common Player:	8.00
	Production 99 Sets	
	Copper:	No Pricing
	Production 10 Sets	
	Gold:	.75-2X
	No pricing production of 20 or less.	
RB	Rocco Baldelli	8.00
PB	Pat Burrell	8.00
RC	Roger Clemens	20.00
CD	Carlos Delgado	10.00
AD	Adam Dunn	8.00
JE	Jim Edmonds	8.00
RF	Rafael Furcal	8.00
JG	Jason Giambi	8.00
TR	Troy Glaus	8.00
TG	Tom Glavine	10.00
SG	Shawn Green	8.00
KG	Ken Griffey Jr.	20.00
VG	Vladimir Guerrero	10.00
TH	Torii Hunter	8.00
KI	Kazuhisa Ishii	8.00
RJ	Randy Johnson	12.00
AJ	Andruw Jones	10.00
CJ	Chipper Jones	15.00
GM	Greg Maddux	15.00
HM	Hideki Matsui	50.00
MM	Mike Mussina	15.00
HN	Hideo Nomo	15.00
MI	Mike Piazza	15.00
MP	Mark Prior	15.00
AP	Albert Pujols	25.00
MR	Manny Ramirez	12.00
JR	Jose Reyes	10.00
AR	Alex Rodriguez	15.00
CS	Curt Schilling	10.00
GS	Gary Sheffield	10.00
AS	Alfonso Soriano	8.00
SS	Sammy Sosa	25.00
IS	Ichiro Suzuki	50.00
MT	Miguel Tejada	10.00
FT	Frank Thomas	15.00
JT	Jim Thome	15.00
RW	Rickie Weeks	15.00
BW	Bernie Williams	15.00
DW	Dontrelle Willis	10.00
KW	Kerry Wood	10.00
DY	Delmon Young	15.00
BZ	Barry Zito	10.00

Game Jersey Tier 2

Tier 2:	1X Tier 1 Price
Production 75 Sets	

Dual Jersey

		NM/M
	Common Duo:	10.00
	Production 50 Sets	
	Gold:	1-1.25X
	Production 25 Sets	
AH	Alfonso Soriano, Hideki Matsui	40.00
AI	Albert Pujols, Ichiro Suzuki	50.00
BK	Jeff Kent, Jeff Bagwell	15.00
CA	Chipper Jones, Andruw Jones	15.00
CJ	Carlos Delgado, Jason Giambi	15.00
DE	Jim Edmonds, J.D. Drew	10.00
DG	Carlos Delgado, Vladimir Guerrero	15.00
DM	Mickey Mantle, Joe DiMaggio	250.00
DC	Carlos Delgado, Rafael Palmeiro	15.00
DW	Joe DiMaggio, Ted Williams	150.00
GB	Shawn Green, Kevin Brown	10.00
GD	Adam Dunn, Ken Griffey Jr.	25.00
GE	Darin Erstad, Troy Glaus	10.00
GP	Rafael Palmeiro, Ken Griffey Jr.	25.00
GR	Alex Rodriguez, Nomar Garciaparra	25.00
GS	Vladimir Guerrero, Sammy Sosa	25.00
HJ	Torii Hunter, Jacque Jones	10.00
HZ	Roy Halladay, Barry Zito	10.00
IG	Ken Griffey Jr., Ichiro Suzuki	50.00
IN	Ichiro Suzuki, Hideo Nomo	50.00
IS	Sammy Sosa, Ichiro Suzuki	45.00
JF	Andruw Jones, Rafael Furcal	15.00
JM	Mike Piazza, Jorge Posada	20.00
MC	Greg Maddux, Roger Clemens	30.00
MW	Ted Williams, Mickey Mantle	250.00
NI	Hideo Nomo, Kazuhisa Ishii	30.00
NM	Hideki Matsui, Hideo Nomo	60.00
PC	Roger Clemens, Pedro J. Martinez	25.00
PM	Mike Mussina, Andy Pettitte	15.00
PS	Sammy Sosa, Mark Prior	30.00
RM	Pedro J. Martinez, Manny Ramirez	15.00
RP	Rafael Palmeiro, Alex Rodriguez	20.00
SA	Albert Pujols, Scott Rolen	40.00
SB	Alfonso Soriano, Bernie Williams	15.00
SJ	Randy Johnson, Curt Schilling	20.00
SM	Greg Maddux, John Smoltz	25.00
TB	Mark Teixeira, Hank Blalock	15.00
TH	Todd Helton, Jim Thome	15.00
TR	Alex Rodriguez, Miguel Tejada	20.00
WL	Mike Lowell, Dontrelle Willis	15.00
YW	Delmon Young, Rickie Weeks	35.00

Game-Used Patch

		NM/M
	Common Player:	15.00
	Production 99 Sets	
	Copper:	1-1.5X
	Production 35 Sets	
	Gold:	1-1.5X
	Production 20 Sets	
RB	Rocco Baldelli	15.00
PB	Pat Burrell	15.00
RC	Roger Clemens	40.00
CD	Carlos Delgado	15.00
AD	Adam Dunn	20.00
JE	Jim Edmonds	15.00
RF	Rafael Furcal	15.00
JG	Jason Giambi	15.00
TR	Troy Glaus	15.00
TG	Tom Glavine	25.00
SG	Shawn Green	15.00
KG	Ken Griffey Jr.	45.00
VG	Vladimir Guerrero	30.00
RH	Roy Halladay	25.00
TH	Torii Hunter	20.00
KI	Kazuhisa Ishii	15.00
RJ	Randy Johnson	25.00
AJ	Andruw Jones	15.00
CJ	Chipper Jones	30.00
GM	Greg Maddux	40.00
HM	Hideki Matsui	85.00
MM	Mike Mussina	25.00
HN	Hideo Nomo	40.00
MI	Mike Piazza	35.00
MP	Mark Prior	15.00
AP	Albert Pujols	50.00
MR	Manny Ramirez	30.00
JR	Jose Reyes	30.00
AR	Alex Rodriguez	50.00
CS	Curt Schilling	25.00
AS	Alfonso Soriano/42	25.00
SS	Sammy Sosa	35.00
IS	Ichiro Suzuki	75.00
MT	Miguel Tejada	25.00
FT	Frank Thomas	25.00
JT	Jim Thome	30.00
RW	Rickie Weeks	25.00
BW	Bernie Williams	15.00
DW	Dontrelle Willis	15.00
KW	Kerry Wood	15.00
DY	Delmon Young	15.00
BZ	Barry Zito	15.00

Dual Patch

NM/M

Common Duo:		20.00

Production 99 unless noted.

Gold:		.75-1.25X

Production 35

AI	Ichiro Suzuki,	
	Albert Pujols	100.00
AM	Andy Pettitte,	
	Mike Mussina	25.00
BK	Jeff Bagwell, Jeff Kent	25.00
CA	Andruw Jones,	
	Chipper Jones	30.00
CV	Carlos Delgado,	
	Vladimir Guerrero	35.00
DE	Jim Edmonds,	
	J.D. Drew	25.00
DG	Carlos Delgado,	
	Jason Giambi	25.00
DP	Carlos Delgado,	
	Rafael Palmeiro/35	40.00
GB	Shawn Green,	
	Kevin Brown	20.00
GD	Adam Dunn,	
	Ken Griffey Jr.	45.00
GE	Darin Erstad,	
	Troy Glaus	30.00
GP	Ken Griffey Jr.,	
	Rafael Palmeiro/35	50.00
GR	Alex Rodriguez,	
	Nomar Garciaparra	75.00
GS	Vladimir Guerrero,	
	Sammy Sosa	40.00
HJ	Torii Hunter,	
	Jacque Jones/83	20.00
HZ	Roy Halladay,	
	Barry Zito	35.00
IG	Ken Griffey Jr.,	
	Ichiro Suzuki	90.00
IN	Ichiro Suzuki,	
	Hideo Nomo	140.00
IS	Sammy Sosa,	
	Ichiro Suzuki	90.00
JF	Rafael Furcal,	
	Andruw Jones	25.00
JG	John Smoltz,	
	Greg Maddux	40.00
MC	Greg Maddux,	
	Roger Clemens/75	60.00
NI	Hideo Nomo,	
	Kazuhisa Ishii/63	65.00
NM	Hideki Matsui,	
	Hideo Nomo/35	180.00
PM	Mike Piazza,	
	Jorge Posada/73	35.00
PR	Roger Clemens,	
	Pedro Martinez/35	60.00
PS	Sammy Sosa,	
	Mark Prior	40.00
RM	Pedro J. Martinez,	
	Manny Ramirez	40.00
RP	Rafael Palmeiro,	
	Alex Rodriguez/35	40.00
SA	Albert Pujols,	
	Scott Rolen	75.00
SJ	Randy Johnson,	
	Curt Schilling	40.00
SM	Alfonso Soriano,	
	Hideki Matsui	80.00
TB	Mark Teixeira,	
	Hank Blalock	40.00
TH	Jim Thome,	
	Todd Helton	35.00
TR	Alex Rodriguez,	
	Miguel Tejada	50.00
WL	Mike Lowell,	
	Dontrelle Willis/85	35.00
YW	Delmon Young,	
	Rickie Weeks/28	75.00

Ultimate Signature Tier 1

NM/M

Common Player:		15.00
AP1	Albert Pujols/40	200.00
AP2	Albert Pujols/35	200.00
AR1	Alex Rodriguez/	
	75 EXCH	125.00
AR2	Alex Rodriguez/	
	60 EXCH	125.00
BG1	Bob Gibson/299	20.00
BG2	Bob Gibson/199	20.00
CD1	Carlos Delgado/150	20.00
CR1	Cal Ripken Jr./85	150.00
CR2	Cal Ripken Jr./85	150.00
CY1	Carl Yastrzemski/199	65.00
DY1	Delmon Young/300	20.00
DY2	Delmon Young/300	20.00
EG1	Eric Gagne/350	15.00
GC1	Gary Carter/199	20.00
GM1	Greg Maddux/250	60.00
GM2	Greg Maddux/140	80.00
HM1	Hideki Matsui/250	250.00
HM2	Hideki Matsui/240	250.00
IS1	Ichiro Suzuki/199	300.00
IS2	Ichiro Suzuki/99	350.00
JG1	Jason Giambi/35	30.00
JG2	Jason Giambi/35	30.00

KG1	Ken Griffey Jr./350	75.00
KG2	Ken Griffey Jr./350	75.00
KW1	Kerry Wood/170	20.00
KW2	Kerry Wood/85	20.00
MP1	Mark Prior/299	20.00
MP2	Mark Prior/225	20.00
NG1	Nomar Garciaparra/	
	125 EXCH	50.00
NG2	Nomar Garciaparra/180	50.00
NR1	Nolan Ryan/85	100.00
NR2	Nolan Ryan/75	100.00
OS1	Ozzie Smith/199	50.00
RC1	Roger Clemens/70	100.00
RC2	Roger Clemens/30	100.00
RJ1	Randy Johnson/75	75.00
RJ2	Randy Johnson/85	85.00
RS1	Ryne Sandberg/240	50.00
RS2	Ryne Sandberg/200	50.00
RW1	Rickie Weeks/300	30.00
RW2	Rickie Weeks/300	30.00
TS1	Tom Seaver/75	50.00
TS2	Tom Seaver/60	50.00
VG1	Vladimir Guerrero/75	50.00
VG2	Vladimir Guerrero/50	50.00

Ultimate Signatures Tier 2

NM/M

Production 25 Sets

GC	Gary Carter	50.00
RC	Roger Clemens	200.00
CD	Carlos Delgado	40.00
EG	Eric Gagne	25.00
NG	Nomar Garciaparra	60.00
JG	Jason Giambi	50.00
BG	Bob Gibson	60.00
KG	Ken Griffey Jr.	120.00
VG	Vladimir Guerrero	80.00
RJ	Randy Johnson	100.00
GM	Greg Maddux	200.00
HM	Hideki Matsui	380.00
MP	Mark Prior	20.00
AP	Albert Pujols	250.00
CR	Cal Ripken Jr.	250.00
AR	Alex Rodriguez	200.00
NR	Nolan Ryan	165.00
RS	Ryne Sandberg	120.00
TS	Tom Seaver	65.00
OS	Ozzie Smith	100.00
IS	Ichiro Suzuki	400.00
RW	Rickie Weeks	50.00
KW	Kerry Wood	25.00
CY	Carl Yastrzemski	125.00
DY	Delmon Young	25.00

2003 Upper Deck Victory

ADRIAN BELTRE

NM/M

Complete Set (200):		40.00
Common Player (1-100):		.10
Common (101-200):		.40
Cards (101-128): Inserted 1:4		
(129-168): 1:5		
(169-188): 1:10		
(189-200): 1:20		
Pack (6):		.75
Box (36):		20.00
1	Troy Glaus	.40
2	Garret Anderson	.20
3	Tim Salmon	.20
4	Darin Erstad	.20
5	Luis Gonzalez	.20
6	Curt Schilling	.25
7	Randy Johnson	.50
8	Junior Spivey	.10
9	Andruw Jones	.25
10	Greg Maddux	.75
11	Chipper Jones	.75
12	Gary Sheffield	.20
13	John Smoltz	.10
14	Geronimo Gil	.10
15	Tony Batista	.10
16	Trot Nixon	.10
17	Manny Ramirez	.40
18	Pedro J. Martinez	.50
19	Nomar Garciaparra	1.00
20	Derek Lowe	.10
21	Shea Hillenbrand	.10
22	Sammy Sosa	.75
23	Kerry Wood	.25
24	Mark Prior	.40
25	Magglio Ordonez	.20
26	Frank Thomas	.40
27	Mark Buehrle	.10
28	Paul Konerko	.20
29	Adam Dunn	.20
30	Ken Griffey Jr.	.75
31	Austin Kearns	.25
32	Matt Lawton	.10
33	Larry Walker	.20

34	Todd Helton	.25
35	Jeff Bagwell	.40
36	Roy Oswalt	.20
37	Lance Berkman	.25
38	Mike Sweeney	.10
39	Carlos Beltran	.10
40	Kazuhisa Ishii	.10
41	Shawn Green	.20
42	Hideo Nomo	.25
43	Adrian Beltre	.20
44	Richie Sexson	.25
45	Ben Sheets	.20
46	Torii Hunter	.25
47	Jacque Jones	.10
48	Corey Koskie	.10
49	Vladimir Guerrero	.50
50	Jose Vidro	.10
51	Mo Vaughn	.20
52	Mike Piazza	1.00
53	Roberto Alomar	.25
54	Derek Jeter	1.50
55	Alfonso Soriano	.75
56	Jason Giambi	.75
57	Roger Clemens	.75
58	Mike Mussina	.25
59	Bernie Williams	.25
60	Jorge Posada	.20
61	Nick Johnson	.10
62	Hideki Matsui RC	4.00
63	Eric Chavez	.20
64	Barry Zito	.20
65	Miguel Tejada	.25
66	Tim Hudson	.20
67	Pat Burrell	.40
68	Bobby Abreu	.20
69	Jimmy Rollins	.20
70	Brett Myers	.10
71	Jim Thome	.40
72	Jason Kendall	.10
73	Brian Giles	.20
74	Aramis Ramirez	.10
75	Sean Burroughs	.10
76	Ryan Klesko	.20
77	Phil Nevin	.10
78	Barry Bonds	1.50
79	J.T. Snow	.10
80	Rich Aurilia	.10
81	Ichiro Suzuki	1.00
82	Edgar Martinez	.10
83	Freddy Garcia	.10
84	Jim Edmonds	.20
85	J.D. Drew	.10
86	Scott Rolen	.40
87	Albert Pujols	.50
88	Mark McGwire	1.25
89	Matt Morris	.20
90	Ben Grieve	.10
91	Carl Crawford	.10
92	Alex Rodriguez	1.25
93	Carl Everett	.10
94	Juan Gonzalez	.25
95	Rafael Palmeiro	.20
96	Hank Blalock	.20
97	Carlos Delgado	.20
98	Josh Phelps	.10
99	Eric Hinske	.10
100	Shannon Stewart	.10
101	Albert Pujols	1.00
102	Alex Rodriguez	2.50
103	Alfonso Soriano	1.00
104	Barry Bonds	3.00
105	Bernie Williams	.50
106	Brian Giles	.50
107	Chipper Jones	.75
108	Darin Erstad	.50
109	Derek Jeter	3.00
110	Eric Chavez	.50
111	Miguel Tejada	.50
112	Ichiro Suzuki	1.50
113	Rafael Palmeiro	.40
114	Jason Giambi	1.50
115	Jeff Bagwell	.75
116	Jim Thome	.75
117	Ken Griffey Jr.	1.50
118	Lance Berkman	.50
119	Luis Gonzalez	.40
120	Manny Ramirez	.75
121	Mike Piazza	2.00
122	J.D. Drew	.40
123	Sammy Sosa	1.50
124	Scott Rolen	.75
125	Shawn Green	.50
126	Todd Helton	.50
127	Troy Glaus	.75
128	Vladimir Guerrero	1.00
129	Albert Pujols	1.00
130	Brian Giles	.50
131	Carlos Delgado	.50
132	Curt Schilling	.50
133	Derek Jeter	3.00
134	Frank Thomas	.75
135	Greg Maddux	1.50
136	Jeff Bagwell	.75
137	Jim Thome	.75
138	Jorge Posada	.50
139	Kazuhisa Ishii	.40
140	Larry Walker	.40
141	Luis Gonzalez	.40
142	Miguel Tejada	.50
143	Pat Burrell	.75
144	Pedro J. Martinez	1.00
145	Rafael Palmeiro	.50
146	Roger Clemens	1.50
147	Tim Hudson	.50
148	Troy Glaus	.75
149	Alfonso Soriano	1.00
150	Andruw Jones	.50
151	Barry Zito	.50

152	Darin Erstad	.50
153	Eric Chavez	.50
154	Alex Rodriguez	2.50
155	J.D. Drew	.40
156	Jason Giambi	1.50
157	Jason Kendall	.40
158	Ken Griffey Jr.	1.50
159	Lance Berkman	.50
160	Mike Mussina	.50
161	Mike Piazza	2.00
162	Nomar Garciaparra	2.00
163	Randy Johnson	1.00
164	Roberto Alomar	.50
165	Scott Rolen	.75
166	Shawn Green	.50
167	Torii Hunter	.50
168	Vladimir Guerrero	1.00
169	Alex Rodriguez	2.50
170	Andruw Jones	.50
171	Bernie Williams	.50
172	Ichiro Suzuki	1.50
173	Miguel Tejada	.50
174	Nomar Garciaparra	2.00
175	Pedro J. Martinez	1.00
176	Randy Johnson	1.00
177	Todd Helton	.50
178	Vladimir Guerrero	1.00
179	Barry Bonds	3.00
180	Carlos Delgado	.50
181	Chipper Jones	1.50
182	Frank Thomas	.75
183	Lance Berkman	.50
184	Larry Walker	.40
185	Manny Ramirez	.75
186	Mike Piazza	2.00
187	Sammy Sosa	1.50
188	Shawn Green	.50
189	Chipper Jones	1.50
190	Curt Schilling	.50
191	Derek Jeter	3.00
192	Ken Griffey Jr.	1.50
193	Sammy Sosa	1.50
194	Vladimir Guerrero	1.00
195	Alex Rodriguez	2.50
196	Barry Bonds	3.00
197	Greg Maddux	1.50
198	Ichiro Suzuki	1.50
199	Jason Giambi	1.50
200	Mike Piazza	2.00

Parallels

Tier 1 Green:		1-2X
Inserted 1:1		
Tier 2 Orange:		2-4X
Inserted 1:8		
Tier 3 Blue:		3-6X
Production 650		
Tier 4 Purple:		10-25X
Production 50 Sets		
Tier 5 Red:		No Pricing
Production 25 Sets		

2003 Upper Deck Vintage

TORII HUNTER

NM/M

Complete Set (280):		
Common Player:		.15
Common SP (223-232):		1.50
Inserted 1:7		
Common SP (233-247):		.50
Inserted 1:5		
Common 3D SP (248-277):		6.00
Inserted 1:48		
Pack (8):		2.00
Box (24):		45.00
1	Troy Glaus	.25
2	Darin Erstad	.25
3	Garret Anderson	.25
4	Jarrod Washburn	.15
5	Nolan Ryan	2.00
6	Tim Salmon	.25
7	Troy Percival	.15
8	Alex Ochoa/SP	4.00
9	Daryle Ward	.15
10	Jeff Bagwell	.50
11	Roy Oswalt	.25
12	Lance Berkman	.40
13	Craig Biggio	.25
14	Richard Hidalgo	.15
15	Tim Hudson	.25
16	Eric Chavez	.25
17	Barry Zito	.25
18	Miguel Tejada	.50
19	Mark Mulder	.25
20	Rollie Fingers	.50
21	Jim "Catfish" Hunter	.25
22	Jermaine Dye	.25
23	Ray Durham/SP	4.00
24	Carlos Delgado	.25

25	Eric Hinske	.15
26	Josh Phelps	.15
27	Shannon Stewart	.15
28	Vernon Wells	.25
29	John Smoltz	.25
30	Greg Maddux	1.00
31	Chipper Jones	.25
32	Gary Sheffield	.25
33	Andruw Jones	.40
34	Tom Glavine	.25
35	Rafael Furcal	.15
36	Phil Niekro	.50
37	Eddie Mathews	.50
38	Robin Yount	.50
39	Richie Sexson	.25
40	Ben Sheets	.15
41	Geoff Jenkins	.15
42	Alex Sanchez	.15
43	Jason Isringhausen	.15
44	Albert Pujols	1.50
45	Matt Morris	.15
46	J.D. Drew	.25
47	Jim Edmonds	.25
48	Stan Musial	1.00
49	Red Schoendienst	.50
50	Edgar Renteria	.25
51	Mark McGwire/SP	10.00
52	Scott Rolen/SP	5.00
53	Mark Bellhorn	.15
54	Kerry Wood	.50
55	Mark Prior	.50
56	Moises Alou	.25
57	Corey Patterson	.15
58	Ernie Banks	.75
59	Hee Seop Choi	.15
60	Billy Williams	.15
61	Sammy Sosa/SP	8.00
62	Ben Grieve	.15
63	Jared Sandberg	.15
64	Carl Crawford	.15
65	Randy Johnson	.75
66	Luis Gonzalez	.25
67	Steve Finley	.15
68	Junior Spivey	.15
69	Erubiel Durazo	.15
70	Curt Schilling/SP	8.00
71	Al Lopez	.15
72	Pee Wee Reese	.15
73	Eric Gagne	.25
74	Shawn Green	.25
75	Kevin Brown	.15
76	Paul LoDuca	.25
77	Adrian Beltre	.25
78	Hideo Nomo	.40
79	Eric Karros	.15
80	Odalis Perez	.15
81	Kazuhisa Ishii/SP	5.00
82	Tommy Lasorda	.15
83	Fernando Tatis	.15
84	Vladimir Guerrero	.75
85	Jose Vidro	.15
86	Javier Vazquez	.15
87	Brad Wilkerson	.15
88	Bartolo Colon/SP	4.00
89	Monte Irvin	.15
90	Robb Nen	.15
91	Reggie Sanders	.15
92	Jeff Kent	.25
93	Rich Aurilia	.15
94	Orlando Cepeda	.15
95	Juan Marichal	.25
96	Willie McCovey	.25
97	David Bell	.15
98	Barry Bonds/SP	10.00
99	Kenny Lofton/SP	4.00
100	Jim Thome	.50
101	C.C. Sabathia	.25
102	Omar Vizquel	.25
103	Lou Boudreau	.25
104	Larry Doby	.25
105	Bob Lemon	.15
106	John Olerud	.25
107	Edgar Martinez	.15
108	Bret Boone	.15
109	Freddy Garcia	.15
110	Mike Cameron	.15
111	Kazuhiro Sasaki	.15
112	Ichiro Suzuki/SP	8.00
113	Mike Lowell	.15
114	Josh Beckett	.25
115	A.J. Burnett	.15
116	Juan Pierre	.15
117	Derrek Lee	.15
118	Luis Castillo	.15
119	Juan Encarnacion/SP	4.00
120	Roberto Alomar	.40
121	Edgardo Alfonzo	.15
122	Jeromy Burnitz	.15
123	Mo Vaughn	.25
124	Tom Seaver	.50
125	Al Leiter	.15
126	Mike Piazza/SP	8.00
127	Tony Batista	.15
128	Geronimo Gil	.15
129	Chris Singleton	.15
130	Rodrigo Lopez	.15
131	Jay Gibbons	.15
132	Melvin Mora	.15
133	Earl Weaver	.15
134	Trevor Hoffman	.15
135	Phil Nevin	.15
136	Sean Burroughs	.15
137	Ryan Klesko	.15
138	Mark Kotsay	.15
139	Mike Lieberthal	.15
140	Bobby Abreu	.25
141	Jimmy Rollins	.25
142	Pat Burrell	.40

143	Vicente Padilla	.15
144	Richie Ashburn	.15
145	Jeremy Giambi/SP	4.00
146	Josh Fogg	.15
147	Brian Giles	.25
148	Aramis Ramirez	.25
149	Jason Kendall	.15
150	Ralph Kiner	.15
151	Willie Stargell	.25
152	Kevin Mench	.15
153	Rafael Palmeiro	.25
154	Ivan Rodriguez	.25
155	Hank Blalock	.25
156	Juan Gonzalez	.25
157	Carl Everett	.15
158	Alex Rodriguez/SP	10.00
159	Nomar Garciaparra	1.25
160	Derek Lowe	.15
161	Manny Ramirez	.25
162	Shea Hillenbrand	.25
163	Bobby Doerr	.15
164	Johnny Damon	.40
165	Jason Varitek	.25
166	Pedro Martinez/SP	8.00
167	Cliff Floyd/SP	4.00
168	Ken Griffey Jr.	1.25
169	Adam Dunn	.50
170	Austin Kearns	.15
171	Aaron Boone	.15
172	Joe Morgan	.25
173	Sean Casey	.15
174	Todd Walker	.15
175	Ryan Dempster/SP	4.00
176	Shawn Estes/SP	4.00
177	Gabe Kapler/SP	4.00
178	Jason Jennings	.15
179	Todd Helton	.40
180	Larry Walker	.25
181	Preston Wilson	.15
182	Jay Payton/SP	4.00
183	Mike Sweeney	.15
184	Carlos Beltran	.25
185	Paul Byrd	.15
186	Raul Ibanez	.15
187	Rick Ferrell	.15
188	Early Wynn	.15
189	Dmitri Young	.15
190	Jim Bunning	.15
191	George Kell	.15
192	Hal Newhouser	.15
193	Bobby Higginson	.15
194	Carlos Pena/SP	4.00
195	Sparky Anderson	.15
196	Torii Hunter	.15
197	Eric Milton	.15
198	Corey Koskie	.15
199	Jacque Jones	.15
200	Harmon Killebrew	.50
201	Doug Mientkiewicz	.15
202	Frank Thomas	.50
203	Mark Buehrle	.15
204	Magglio Ordonez	.25
205	Paul Konerko	.15
206	Joe Borchard	.15
207	Hoyt Wilhelm	.15
208	Carlos Lee	.15
209	Roger Clemens	1.50
210	Nick Johnson	.15
211	Jason Giambi	.25
212	Alfonso Soriano	.25
213	Bernie Williams	.40
214	Robin Ventura	.15
215	Jorge Posada	.25
216	Mike Mussina	.40
217	Yogi Berra	.50
218	Phil Rizzuto	.40
219	Mariano Rivera	.25
220	Derek Jeter/SP	12.00
221	Jeff Weaver/SP	4.00
222	Raul Mondesi/SP	4.00
223	Freddy Sanchez,	
	Josh Hancock	2.00
224	Joe Borchard,	
	Miguel Olivo	2.00
225	Brandon Phillips,	
	Josh Bard	1.50
226	Andy Van Hekken,	
	Andres Torres	1.50
227	Jason Lane,	
	Jeriome Robertson	1.50
228	Chin-Feng Chen,	
	Joe Thurston	1.50
229	Endy Chavez,	
	Jamey Carroll	1.50
230	Drew Henson,	
	Alex Graman	2.50
231	Dewon Brazelton,	
	Lance Carter	1.50
232	Jayson Werth,	
	Kevin Cash	1.50
233	Randy Johnson,	
	Curt Schilling, Barry Zito	1.50
234	Pedro J. Martinez,	
	Randy Johnson,	
	Derek Lowe	1.00
235	Randy Johnson,	
	Curt Schilling,	
	Pedro J. Martinez	1.00
236	John Smoltz, Eric Gagne,	
	Mike Williams	
237	Randy Johnson,	
	Bartolo Colon,	
	A.J. Burnett	1.00
238	Alfonso Soriano,	
	Ichiro Suzuki,	
	Vladimir Guerrero	.50
239	Alex Rodriguez, Jim Thome,	
	Sammy Sosa	1.50

240	Barry Bonds, Manny Ramirez, Mike Sweeney	2.00
241	Alfonso Soriano, Alex Rodriguez, Derek Jeter	2.00
242	Alex Rodriguez, Magglio Ordonez, Miguel Tejada	2.00
243	Luis Castillo, Juan Pierre, Dave Roberts	.50
244	Nomar Garciaparra, Garret Anderson, Alfonso Soriano	1.00
245	Johnny Damon, Jimmy Rollins, Kenny Lofton	.50
246	Barry Bonds, Jim Thome, Manny Ramirez	2.00
247	Barry Bonds, Brian Giles, Manny Ramirez	2.00
248	Troy Glaus	10.00
249	Luis Gonzalez	6.00
250	Chipper Jones	15.00
251	Nomar Garciaparra	15.00
252	Manny Ramirez	10.00
253	Sammy Sosa	15.00
254	Frank Thomas	10.00
255	Magglio Ordonez	6.00
256	Adam Dunn	10.00
257	Ken Griffey Jr.	15.00
258	Jim Thome	10.00
259	Todd Helton	8.00
260	Larry Walker	6.00
261	Lance Berkman	6.00
262	Jeff Bagwell	10.00
263	Mike Sweeney	6.00
264	Shawn Green	6.00
265	Vladimir Guerrero	12.00
266	Mike Piazza	15.00
267	Jason Giambi	15.00
268	Pat Burrell	20.00
269	Barry Bonds	15.00
270	Mark McGwire	20.00
271	Alex Rodriguez	15.00
272	Carlos Delgado	6.00
273	Richie Sexson	6.00
274	Andruw Jones	8.00
275	Derek Jeter	20.00
276	Juan Gonzalez	8.00
277	Albert Pujols	12.00
278	Jason Giambi/CL	.75
279	Sammy Sosa/CL	.75
280	Ichiro Suzuki/CL	.75

All Caps

		NM/M
Common Player:		8.00
Production 250 Sets		
JB	Jeff Bagwell	15.00
LB	Lance Berkman	8.00
DE	Darin Erstad	8.00
RF	Rafael Furcal	8.00
JG	Juan Gonzalez	10.00
LG	Luis Gonzalez	8.00
TG	Tony Gwynn	25.00
TH	Tim Hudson	10.00
GM	Greg Maddux	30.00
RP	Rafael Palmeiro	10.00
CP	Chan Ho Park	8.00
MP	Mike Piazza	35.00
KS	Kazuhiro Sasaki	8.00
MV	Mo Vaughn	8.00
RV	Robin Ventura	8.00

Capping the Action

		NM/M
Common Player:		10.00
Quantity produced listed		
RA	Roberto Alomar/101	20.00
CD	Carlos Delgado/91	10.00
JG	Juan Gonzalez/99	20.00
SG	Shawn Green/125	20.00
KG	Ken Griffey Jr./99	40.00
TH	Todd Helton/99	20.00
PM	Pedro Martinez/125	25.00
MM	Mike Mussina/109	40.00
HM	Hideo Nomo/117	45.00
RP	Rafael Palmeiro/125	20.00
AR	Alex Rodriguez/110	25.00
IR	Ivan Rodriguez/125	15.00
SR	Scott Rolen/109	15.00
AS	Alfonso Soriano/109	20.00
SS	Sammy Sosa/125	40.00

Crackin the Lumber

		NM/M
Production 25		
Golds:		No Pricing
Production 5		
JG	Jason Giambi	25.00
IS	Ichiro Suzuki	125.00

Crowning Glory

No pricing due to scarcity.
Production 25 Sets

Dropping the Hammer

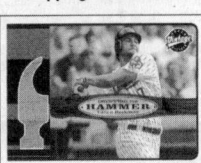

		NM/M
Common Player:		6.00
Inserted 1:130		
Golds:		1.5-2X
Production 100 Sets		
BA	Bobby Abreu	8.00
RA	Roberto Alomar	10.00
LB	Lance Berkman	8.00
RF	Rafael Furcal	6.00
JG	Jason Giambi	6.00
SG	Shawn Green	6.00
KG	Ken Griffey Jr.	15.00
TH	Todd Helton	8.00
AJ	Andruw Jones	8.00
DJ	David Justice	8.00
KL	Kenny Lofton	6.00
FM	Fred McGriff	8.00
MO	Magglio Ordonez	6.00
RP	Rafael Palmeiro	6.00
MP	Mike Piazza	15.00
AR	Alex Rodriguez	15.00
SS	Sammy Sosa	20.00
TA	Fernando Tatis	6.00
MT	Miguel Tejada	8.00
FT	Frank Thomas	10.00
JT	Jim Thome	10.00
RV	Robin Ventura	6.00
OV	Omar Vizquel	6.00
LW	Larry Walker	8.00
PW	Preston Wilson	6.00

Men with Hats

		NM/M
Common Player:		8.00
Inserted 1:285		
VC	Vinny Castilla	8.00
EC	Eric Chavez	10.00
JD	Johnny Damon	15.00
AD	Adam Dunn	15.00
JG	Jason Giambi	8.00
TH	Todd Helton	10.00
HU	Tim Hudson	10.00
AJ	Andruw Jones	10.00
JK	Jason Kendall	8.00
KL	Kenny Lofton	8.00
AR	Alex Rodriguez	20.00
MT	Miguel Tejada	12.00
FT	Frank Thomas	12.00
TW	Todd Walker	8.00
BW	Bernie Williams	10.00

Slugfest

		NM/M
Common Player:		8.00
Production 200 Sets		
Golds:		1.5-2.5X
Production 50 Sets		
CD	Carlos Delgado	8.00
SG	Shawn Green	8.00
AJ	Andruw Jones	8.00
RP	Rafael Palmeiro	8.00
MP	Mike Piazza	20.00
AR	Alex Rodriguez	15.00
FT	Frank Thomas	10.00
JT	Jim Thome	10.00
LW	Larry Walker	8.00
BW	Bernie Williams	10.00

Timeless Teams Bat

		NM/M
Common Card:		20.00
Production 175 Sets		
BLAR	Pat Burrell, Mike Lieberthal, Bobby Abreu, Jimmy Rollins	25.00
CTDJ	Eric Chavez, Miguel Tejada, Jermaine Dye, David Justice	25.00
DEMR	J.D. Drew, Jim Edmonds, Tino Martinez, Scott Rolen	40.00

DGCL	Adam Dunn, Ken Griffey Jr., Sean Casey, Barry Larkin	40.00
GNBL	Shawn Green, Hideo Nomo, Adrian Beltre, Paul LoDuca	40.00
GPMS	Jason Giambi, Jorge Posada, Raul Mondesi, Alfonso Soriano	30.00
GWVS	Jason Giambi, Bernie Williams, Robin Ventura, Alfonso Soriano	30.00
HWPZ	Todd Helton, Larry Walker, Juan Pierre, Todd Zeile	25.00
IMBC	Ichiro Suzuki, Edgar Martinez, Bret Boone, Mike Cameron	90.00
JGSW	Randy Johnson, Luis Gonzalez, Curt Schilling, Matt Williams	40.00
JJSF	Chipper Jones, Andruw Jones, Gary Sheffield, Rafael Furcal	40.00
KNKB	Ryan Klesko, Phil Nevin, Mark Kotsay, Sean Burroughs	20.00
MGLJ	Greg Maddux, Tom Glavine, Javy Lopez, Chipper Jones	40.00
OTLK	Magglio Ordonez, Frank Thomas, Carlos Lee, Paul Konerko	30.00
PVAA	Mike Piazza, Mo Vaughn, Roberto Alomar, Edgardo Alfonzo	40.00
RGRP	Alex Rodriguez, Juan Gonzalez, Ivan Rodriguez, Rafael Palmeiro	40.00
RMHN	Manny Ramirez, Pedro J. Martinez, Shea Hillenbrand, Trot Nixon	30.00
SMAP	Sammy Sosa, Fred McGriff, Moises Alou, Corey Patterson	40.00

UD Giants

		NM/M
Complete Set (42):		45.00
Common Player:		.75
Inserted 1:Box		
RA	Roberto Alomar	1.00
JB	Jeff Bagwell	1.00
LB	Lance Berkman	1.00
BB	Barry Bonds	4.00
PB	Pat Burrell	1.00
RC	Roger Clemens	4.00
CD	Carlos Delgado	.75
JD	J.D. Drew	.75
AD	Adam Dunn	1.50
NG	Nomar Garciaparra	.75
JG	Jason Giambi	1.00
BG	Brian Giles	.75
JG	Juan Gonzalez	1.00
LG	Luis Gonzalez	.75
SG	Shawn Green	.75
KG	Ken Griffey Jr.	3.00
VG	Vladimir Guerrero	1.50
TH	Todd Helton	1.50
KI	Kazuhisa Ishii	.75
RJ	Randy Johnson	1.50
AJ	Andruw Jones	1.00
CJ	Chipper Jones	2.50
GM	Greg Maddux	2.50
PM	Pedro J. Martinez	1.50
MM	Mike Mussina	1.00
HN	Hideo Nomo	1.00
MO	Magglio Ordonez	1.00
RP	Rafael Palmeiro	1.00
MP	Mike Piazza	2.50
PR	Mark Prior	1.00
AP	Albert Pujols	2.50
MR	Manny Ramirez	1.50
AR	Alex Rodriguez	4.00
IR	Ivan Rodriguez	1.00
SR	Scott Rolen	1.50
CS	Curt Schilling	1.50
SS	Sammy Sosa	2.50
IS	Ichiro Suzuki	3.00
FT	Frank Thomas	1.50
JT	Jim Thome	1.50

BW	Bernie Williams	1.00
KW	Kerry Wood	1.50

Vintage Hitmen

		NM/M
Production 150 Sets		
Golds: No Pricing		
Production 10 Sets		
JG	Jason Giambi	10.00
KG	Ken Griffey Jr.	30.00
MM	Mark McGwire	60.00
IS	Ichiro Suzuki	60.00

Vintage Hitmen Double Signed

		NM/M
Production 75		
Gold: Not Priced		
Production 5		
MS	Mark McGwire, Sammy Sosa	600.00

2003 UD Yankees Signature Series

		NM/M
Complete Set (90):		65.00
Common Player:		.50
Pack (3):		17.00
Box (10):		140.00
1	Al Downing	.50
2	Allen Gettel	.50
3	Art Ditmar	.50
4	Babe Ruth	6.00
5	Bill Virdon	.50
6	Billy Martin	2.00
7	Bob Cerv	.50
8	Bob Turley	.50
9	Bobby Cox	.75
10	Bobby Richardson	1.00
11	Bobby Shantz	.50
12	Bucky Dent	.75
13	Bud Metheny	.50
14	Casey Stengel	2.00
15	Charlie Hayes	.50
16	Charlie Silvera	.50
17	Chris Chambliss	.50
18	Danny Cater	.50
19	Dave Kingman	.75
20	Dave Righetti	.75
21	Dave Winfield	2.00
22	David Cone	.75
23	Dick Tidrow	.50
24	Doc Medich	.50
25	Dock Ellis	.50
26	Don Gullett	.50
27	Don Mattingly	5.00
28	Dwight Gooden	.75
29	Eddie Robinson	.50
30	Felipe Alou	.50
31	Fred Sanford	.50
32	Fred Stanley	.50
33	Gene Michael	.50
34	Hank Bauer	.50
35	Hector Lopez	.50
36	Horace Clarke	.50
37	Jake Gibbs	.50
38	Jerry Coleman	.50
39	Jerry Lumpe	.50
40	Jim Bouton	.75
41	Jim Kaat	1.00
42	Jim Mason	.50
43	Jimmy Key	.50
44	Joe DiMaggio	5.00
45	Joe Torre	1.00
46	John Montefusco	.50
47	Johnny Blanchard	.50
48	Johnny Callison	.50
49	Lew Burdette	.50
50	Johnny Kucks	.50
51	Steve Balboni	.50
52	Ken Singleton	.50
53	Lee Mazzilli	.50
54	Lou Gehrig	5.00
55	Lou Piniella	1.00
56	Luis Tiant	.50
57	Marius Russo	.50
58	Mel Stottlemyre	.50
59	Mickey Mantle	6.00
60	Mike Pagliarulo	.50
61	Mike Torrez	.50
62	Miller Huggins	.50
63	Norm Siebern	.50
64	Paul O'Neill	.50
65	Phil Niekro	.50
66	Phil Rizzuto	3.00
67	Ralph Branca	.50
68	Ralph Houk	.50
69	Ralph Terry	.50
70	Randy Gumpert	.50
71	Roger Maris	5.00

72	Ron Blomberg	.50
73	Ron Guidry	1.00
74	Ruben Amaro	.50
75	Ryne Duren	.50
76	Sam McDowell	.50
77	Sparky Lyle	.50
78	Thurman Munson	3.00
79	Tom Sturdivant	.50
80	Tom Tresh	.50
81	Tommy Byrne	.50
82	Tommy Henrich	.50
83	Tommy John	.75
84	Tony Kubek	.75
85	Tony Lazzeri	.50
86	Virgil Trucks	.50
87	Wade Boggs	1.00
88	Whitey Ford	3.00
89	Willie Randolph	.75
90	Yogi Berra	3.00

Monumental Cuts

		NM/M
30 total cards produced:		
MC-LG	Lou Gehrig/1 (6/03 Auction)	17,600
MC-MM	Mickey Mantle/1 (1/04 Auction)	10,000
MC-BM	Billy Martin/9	825.00
MC-TM	Thurman Munson/1 (3/04 Auction)	2,605
MC-BR	Babe Ruth/1 (4/04 Auction)	12,600

Pinstripe Excell. Dual

		NM/M
Common Dual Autograph:		20.00
Production 125 Sets		
AA	Felipe Alou, Ruben Amaro	50.00
BA	Hank Bauer, Felipe Alou	50.00
BP	Wade Boggs, Mike Pagliarulo	60.00
BT	Jim Bouton, Ralph Terry	50.00
CK	Chris Chambliss, Dave Kingman	60.00
DC	Bucky Dent, Chris Chambliss	50.00
DR	Bucky Dent, Willie Randolph	80.00
DS	Ryne Duren, Tom Sturdivant	35.00
FB	Whitey Ford, Yogi Berra	150.00
GB	Jake Gibbs, Johnny Blanchard	40.00
GM	Ron Guidry, John Montefusco	80.00
GR	Ron Guidry, Willie Randolph	80.00
JK	Tommy John, Jim Kaat	60.00
LG	Sparky Lyle, Ron Guidry	75.00
LM	Jerry Lumpe, Jim Mason	25.00
MC	John Montefusco, Chris Chambliss	60.00
MK	Gene Michael, Tony Kubek	60.00
ML	Sam McDowell, Sparky Lyle	50.00
MR	Don Mattingly, Dave Righetti	150.00
NT	Phil Niekro, Luis Tiant	50.00
RB	Bobby Richardson, Hank Bauer	75.00
RC	Bobby Richardson, Jerry Coleman	50.00
SC	Ken Singleton, Jerry Coleman	60.00
ST	Tom Sturdivant, Bob Turley	40.00
TK	Luis Tiant, Jim Kaat	60.00
TM	Mike Torrez, Lee Mazzilli	50.00
BRi	Hank Bauer, Phil Rizzuto	75.00
BRu	Tommy Byrne, Marius Russo	30.00

Pride of New York Auto.

Common Autograph:		8.00
Inserted 1:1		
JA	Jason Alexander/SP	600.00
FA	Felipe Alou	15.00
RA	Ruben Amaro	8.00
SB	Steve Balboni	8.00
HB	Hank Bauer	10.00
YB	Yogi Berra	85.00
BL	Johnny Blanchard	15.00
RBI	Ron Blomberg	10.00
WB	Wade Boggs	40.00
JB	Jim Bouton	10.00
RBr	Ralph Branca	10.00
LB	Lew Burdette	10.00
TB	Tommy Byrne	10.00
CAS	Johnny Callison	8.00
TC	Tom Carroll	8.00
CAL	Brian Cashman/SP	250.00
DC	Danny Cater	8.00
CE	Bob Cerv	8.00
CC	Chris Chambliss	12.00
HC	Horace Clarke	8.00
JC	Jerry Coleman	10.00
CO	David Cone	25.00
CX	Bobby Cox	12.00
DE	Bucky Dent	12.00
DI	Art Ditmar	10.00
AD	Al Downing	8.00
BD	Brian Doyle	8.00
RD	Ryne Duren	10.00
EL	Dock Ellis	10.00
WF	Whitey Ford	50.00
AG	Allen Gettel	8.00
JG	Jake Gibbs	8.00
GO	Dwight Gooden	15.00
JO	John Goodman	300.00
RaG	Ron Guidry	15.00
DG	Don Gullett	8.00
RoG	Randy Gumpert	8.00
CH	Charlie Hayes	10.00
TH	Tommy Henrich	30.00
RH	Ralph Houk	12.00
TJ	Tommy John	15.00
JK	Jim Kaat	15.00
KE	Jimmy Key	15.00
DK	Dave Kingman	15.00
TK	Tony Kubek	25.00
KU	Johnny Kucks	10.00
HL	Hector Lopez	8.00
JL	Jerry Lumpe	8.00
SL	Sparky Lyle	10.00
JM	Jim Mason	8.00
MA	Don Mattingly	80.00
LM	Lee Mazzilli	10.00
SM	Sam McDowell	8.00
DM	Doc Medich	8.00
GM	Gene Michael	10.00
MO	John Montefusco	8.00
PN	Phil Niekro	15.00
PO	Paul O'Neill/SP	35.00
MP	Mike Pagliarulo	8.00
LP	Lou Piniella/SP	20.00
WR	Willie Randolph/SP	15.00
HR	Hal Reniff	10.00
BR	Bobby Richardson	10.00
DR	Dave Righetti	15.00
PR	Phil Rizzuto	40.00
ER	Eddie Robinson	8.00
MR	Marius Russo	10.00
FS	Fred Sanford	10.00
BS	Bobby Shantz	10.00
NS	Norm Siebern	10.00
CS	Charlie Silvera	10.00
KS	Ken Singleton	10.00
ST	Fred Stanley	10.00
MS	Mel Stottlemyre	15.00
TS	Tom Sturdivant	10.00
RT	Ralph Terry	10.00
LT	Luis Tiant	10.00
DT	Dick Tidrow	10.00
JT	Joe Torre	35.00
MT	Mike Torrez	10.00
TT	Tom Tresh	10.00
VT	Virgil Trucks	10.00
BT	Bob Turley	12.00
BV	Bill Virdon	8.00
DW	Dave Winfield/SP	75.00
JW	Jim Wynn	8.00
DZ	Don Zimmer	40.00

Yankees Forever Triple

		NM/M
Common Triple Auto.:		
Production 50 Sets		
ALB	Felipe Alou, Hector Lopez, Hank Bauer	120.00
AOM	Felipe Alou, Paul O'Neill, Lee Mazzilli	150.00
BSB	Yogi Berra, Bobby Shantz, Hank Bauer	200.00
DFB	Al Downing, Whitey Ford, Yogi Berra	240.00
DRC	Bucky Dent, Willie Randolph, Chris Chambliss	125.00
EMG	Dock Ellis, Doc Medich, Don Gullett	125.00
FKB	Whitey Ford, Johnny Kucks, Jim Bouton	150.00
GCK	Dwight Gooden, David Cone, Jimmy Key	150.00
GRJ	Ron Guidry, Dave Righetti, Tommy John	150.00
HMC	Ralph Houk, Gene Michael, Bobby Cox	150.00
HRB	Tommy Henrich, Phil Rizzuto, Ralph Branca	150.00

Code	Players	Price
JKL	Tommy John, Jim Kaat, Sparky Lyle	120.00
KCC	Dave Kingman, Chris Chambliss, Danny Cater	120.00
KGT	Jim Kaat, Don Gullett, Mike Torrez	120.00
KJB	Jim Kaat, Tommy John, Jim Bouton	120.00
MTT	John Montefusco, Mike Torrez, Dick Tidrow	120.00
OBK	Paul O'Neill, Wade Boggs, Jimmy Key	175.00
PTV	Lou Piniella, Joe Torre, Bill Virdon	150.00
RBC	Phil Rizzuto, Yogi Berra, Jerry Coleman	220.00
RKD	Phil Rizzuto, Tony Kubek, Bucky Dent	150.00
RRC	Bobby Richardson, Willie Randolph, Jerry Coleman	150.00
RSB	Marius Russo, Tom Sturdivant, Tommy Byrne	120.00
SSB	Fred Stanley, Charlie Silvera, Johnny Blanchard	120.00
STE	Mel Stottlemyre, Luis Tiant, Dock Ellis	120.00
TCO	Joe Torre, David Cone, Paul O'Neill	175.00
TLN	Luis Tiant, Sparky Lyle, Phil Niekro	120.00
TMT	Luis Tiant, Sam McDowell, Ralph Terry	120.00
WHM	Dave Winfield, Tommy Henrich, Lee Mazzilli	160.00
WMG	Dave Winfield, Don Mattingly, Ron Guidry	300.00
WPC	Dave Winfield, Lou Piniella, Chris Chambliss	100.00

2003 Upper Deck Yankees 100th Anniversary

		NM/M
Complete Set (30):		15.00
Common Player:		.50
1	Babe Ruth	2.00
2	Tony Lazzeri	.50
3	Lou Gehrig	1.50
4	Lou Gehrig	1.50
5	Red Rolfe	.50
6	Lou Gehrig	1.50
7	Bill Dickey	.50
8	Joe DiMaggio	1.50
9	Charlie Keller	.50
10	Frank Crosetti	.50
11	Phil Rizzuto	.50
12	Joe DiMaggio	1.50
13	Joe DiMaggio	1.50
14	Phil Rizzuto	.50
15	Mickey Mantle	2.00
16	Yogi Berra	.75
17	Yogi Berra	.75
18	Mickey Mantle	2.00
19	Whitey Ford	.50
20	Mickey Mantle	2.00
21	Thurman Munson	.75
22	Thurman Munson	.75
23	Bernie Williams	.50
24	Jorge Posada	.50
25	Mariano Rivera	.50
26	Derek Jeter	1.50
27	Hideki Matsui	1.00
28	Hideki Matsui	1.00
29	Roger Clemens	1.50
30	Yankee Stadium	.50

2003 Upper Deck 40-Man Sample

A different front photo and a large black "SAMPLE" on back distinguish the promo card for UD's large set.

		NM/M
KG	Ken Griffey Jr.	3.00

2003 Upper Deck 40-Man

	NM/M
Complete Set (990):	200.00
Common Player:	.25
Common Rk (877-960):	.40
Pack (10):	2.00
Box (24):	35.00

#	Player	Price
1	Troy Glaus	.50
2	Darin Erstad	.40
3	Garret Anderson	.50
4	Aaron Sele	.25
5	Adam Kennedy	.25
6	Scott Spiezio	.25
7	Troy Percival	.25
8	David Eckstein	.25
9	Ramon Ortiz	.25
10	Bengie Molina	.25
11	Tim Salmon	.50
12	John Lackey	.25
13	Brad Fullmer	.25
14	Jarrod Washburn	.25
15	Shawn Wooten	.25
16	Kevin Appier	.25
17	Ben Weber	.25
18	Eric Owens	.25
19	Matt Wise	.25
20	Francisco Rodriguez	.25
21	Scot Shields	.25
22	Jose Molina	.25
23	Scott Schoeneweis	.25
24	Derrick Turnbow	.25
25	Benji Gil	.25
26	Julio Ramirez	.25
27	Mickey Callaway	.25
28	Barry Zito	.50
29	Tim Hudson	.50
30	Mark Mulder	.50
31	Eric Chavez	.40
32	Miguel Tejada	.50
33	Terrence Long	.25
34	Jermaine Dye	.25
35	Erubiel Durazo	.25
36	Scott Hatteberg	.25
37	Chris Singleton	.25
38	Keith Foulke	.25
39	John Halama	.25
40	Mark Ellis	.25
41	Ted Lilly	.25
42	Jim Mecir	.25
43	Adam Piatt	.25
44	Freddie Bynum	.25
45	Adam Morrissey	.25
46	Jeremy Fikac	.25
47	Ricardo Rincon	.25
48	Ramon Hernandez	.25
49	Micah Bowie	.25
50	Chad Bradford	.25
51	Eric Byrnes	.25
52	Ron Gant	.25
53	Jose Flores	.25
54	Mark Johnson	.25
55	Carlos Delgado	.75
56	Orlando Hudson	.25
57	Kelvim Escobar	.25
58	Eric Hinske	.25
59	Doug Creek	.25
60	Josh Phelps	.25
61	Shannon Stewart	.25
62	Roy Halladay	.40
63	Vernon Wells	.40
64	Mark Henrickson	.25
65	Mike Bordick	.25
66	Jayson Werth	.25
67	Chris Woodward	.25
68	Ken Huckaby	.25
69	Frank Catalanotto	.25
70	Jason Kershner	.25
71	Greg Myers	.25
72	Tanyon Sturtze	.25
73	Trever Miller	.25
74	Pete Walker	.25
75	Alexis Rios	.25
76	Tom Wilson	.25
77	Dave Berg	.25
78	Doug Linton	.25
79	Cliff Politte	.25
80	Damion Easley	.25
81	Toby Hall	.25
82	George Lombard	.25
83	Ben Grieve	.25
84	Aubrey Huff	.25
85	Jesus Colome	.25
86	Dewon Brazelton	.25
87	Rey Ordonez	.25
88	Al Martin	.25
89	Carl Crawford	.25
90	Travis Lee	.25
91	Marlon Anderson	.25
92	Javier Valentin	.25
93	Joe Kennedy	.25
94	Jorge Sosa	.25
95	Travis Harper	.25
96	Bobby Seay	.25
97	Seth McClung	.25
98	Delvin James	.25
99	Victor Zambrano	.25
100	Terry Shumpert	.25
101	Josh Hamilton	.50
102	Jared Sandberg	.25
103	Steve Parris	.25
104	C.C. Sabathia	.25
105	Omar Vizquel	.40
106	Milton Bradley	.25
107	Ellis Burks	.25
108	Danys Baez	.25
109	Jason Davis	.25
110	Terry Mulholland	.25
111	Matt Lawton	.25
112	Alex Escobar	.25
113	Mark Wohlers	.25
114	Josh Bard	.25
115	Bill Selby	.25
116	Brandon Phillips	.25
117	Jason Bere	.25
118	Casey Blake	.25
119	Travis Hafner	.25
120	Brian Anderson	.25
121	David Riske	.25
122	Karim Garcia	.25
123	Ricardo Rodriguez	.25
124	Carl Sadler	.25
125	Jose Santiago	.25
126	Tim Laker	.25
127	John McDonald	.25
128	Jake Westbrook	.25
129	Ichiro Suzuki	1.00
130	Freddy Garcia	.25
131	Edgar Martinez	.40
132	Ben Davis	.25
133	Shigetoshi Hasegawa	.25
134	Carlos Guillen	.25
135	Randy Winn	.25
136	John Mabry	.25
137	Matt Thornton	.25
138	Bret Boone	.40
139	Jamie Moyer	.25
140	Giovanni Carrara	.25
141	Kazuhiro Sasaki	.25
142	Jeff Cirillo	.25
143	Mark McLemore	.25
144	Pat Borders	.25
145	Mike Cameron	.25
146	Dan Wilson	.25
147	John Olerud	.40
148	Arthur Rhodes	.25
149	Rafael Soriano	.25
150	Greg Colbrunn	.25
151	Ryan Franklin	.25
152	Joel Pineiro	.25
153	Jeff Nelson	.25
154	Jerry Hairston	.25
155	Rick Helling	.25
156	Gary Matthews Jr.	.25
157	Jeff Conine	.25
158	Sidney Ponson	.25
159	Tony Batista	.25
160	Jay Gibbons	.40
161	Marty Cordova	.25
162	Geronimo Gil	.25
163	Deivi Cruz	.25
164	B.J. Ryan	.25
165	Jason Johnson	.25
166	Buddy Groom	.25
167	Pat Hentgen	.25
168	Omar Daal	.25
169	Willis Roberts	.25
170	Scott Erickson	.25
171	David Segui	.25
172	Brook Fordyce	.25
173	Rodrigo Lopez	.25
174	Jose Leon	.25
175	Jose Morban	.25
176	Melvin Mora	.25
177	B.J. Surhoff	.25
178	Jorge Julio	.25
179	Alex Rodriguez	2.00
180	Mark Teixeira	.40
181	Chan Ho Park	.25
182	Todd Van Poppel	.25
183	Todd Greene	.25
184	Ismael Valdes	.25
185	Rusty Greer	.25
186	Rafael Palmeiro	.50
187	Francisco Cordero	.25
188	Einar Diaz	.25
189	Doug Glanville	.25
190	Michael Young	.25
191	Kevin Mench	.25
192	Carl Everett	.25
193	Herbert Perry	.25
194	Jeff Zimmerman	.25
195	Juan Gonzalez	.50
196	Ugueth Urbina	.25
197	Jermaine Clark	.25
198	John Thomson	.25
199	Hank Blalock	.50
200	Jay Powell	.25
201	Mike Lamb	.25
202	Aaron Fultz	.25
203	Esteban Yan	.25
204	Nomar Garciaparra	2.00
205	Pedro J. Martinez	.75
206	John Burkett	.25
207	Johnny Damon	.40
208	Doug Mirabelli	.25
209	Derek Lowe	.25
210	Shea Hillenbrand	.25
211	Brandon Lyon	.25
212	Trot Nixon	.25
213	Jason Varitek	.25
214	Tim Wakefield	.25
215	Manny Ramirez	.75
216	Todd Walker	.25
217	Jeremy Giambi	.25
218	Ramiro Mendoza	.25
219	Bill Mueller	.25
220	David Ortiz	.25
221	Mike Timlin	.25
222	Alan Embree	.25
223	Bob Howry	.25
224	Chad Fox	.25
225	Damian Jackson	.25
226	Casey Fossum	.25
227	Steve Woodard	.25
228	Freddy Sanchez	.25
229	Mike Sweeney	.25
230	Desi Relaford	.25
231	Brent Mayne	.25
232	Angel Berroa	.25
233	Albie Lopez	.25
234	Raul Ibanez	.25
235	Joe Randa	.25
236	Chris George	.25
237	Michael Tucker	.25
238	Mendy Lopez	.25
239	Kris Wilson	.25
240	Jason Grimsley	.25
241	Carlos Febles	.25
242	Runelvys Hernandez	.25
243	Mike MacDougal	.25
244	Carlos Beltran	.40
245	Brandon Berger	.25
246	Darrell May	.25
247	Miguel Asencio	.25
248	Ryan Bukvich	.25
249	Dee Brown	.25
250	Jeremy Hill	.25
251	Jeremy Affeldt	.25
252	Ken Harvey	.25
253	Bobby Higginson	.25
254	Matt Anderson	.25
255	Dmitri Young	.25
256	Gene Kingsdale	.25
257	Craig Paquette	.25
258	Adam Bernero	.25
259	Andres Torres	.25
260	Carlos Pena	.25
261	Dean Palmer	.25
262	Eric Munson	.25
263	Omar Infante	.25
264	Shane Halter	.25
265	Jeremy Bonderman	2.00
266	Steve Sparks	.25
267	Gary Knotts	.25
268	Mike Maroth	.25
269	Nate Cornejo	.25
270	Matt Roney	.25
271	Franklyn German	.25
272	Matt Walbeck	.25
273	Brandon Inge	.25
274	Hiram Bocachica	.25
275	Chris Spurling	.25
276	Craig Monroe	.25
277	Ramon Santiago	.25
278	Doug Mientkiewicz	.25
279	Torii Hunter	.50
280	Brad Radke	.25
281	Denny Hocking	.25
282	Tom Prince	.25
283	Eddie Guardado	.25
284	Jacque Jones	.25
285	Joe Mays	.25
286	Mike Fetters	.25
287	LaTroy Hawkins	.25
288	A.J. Pierzynski	.25
289	Eric Milton	.25
290	Cristian Guzman	.25
291	Bobby Kielty	.25
292	Corey Koskie	.25
293	J.C. Romero	.25
294	Mike Cuddyer	.25
295	Luis Rivas	.25
296	Matt LeCroy	.25
297	Tony Fiore	.25
298	Dustan Mohr	.25
299	Chris Gomez	.25
300	Johan Santana	.25
301	Kyle Lohse	.25
302	Frank Thomas	.75
303	Mark Buehrle	.25
304	Jon Garland	.25
305	Magglio Ordonez	.50
306	Paul Konerko	.25
307	Sandy Alomar Jr.	.25
308	Carlos Lee	.25
309	Jon Rauch	.25
310	Esteban Loaiza	.25
311	Gary Glover	.25
312	Kelly Wunsch	.25
313	Tony Graffanino	.25
314	Aaron Rowand	.25
315	Armando Rios	.25
316	Jose Valentin	.25
317	D'Angelo Jimenez	.25
318	Joe Crede	.25
319	Miguel Olivo	.25
320	Rick White	.25
321	Billy Koch	.25
322	Tom Gordon	.25
323	Bartolo Colon	.25
324	Josh Paul	.25
325	Joe Borchard	.25
326	Damaso Marte	.25
327	Derek Jeter	2.00
328	Jason Giambi	.75
329	Roger Clemens	2.00
330	Enrique Wilson	.25
331	Dave Wells	.25
332	Mike Mussina	.25
333	Bernie Williams	.50
334	Todd Zeile	.25
335	Sterling Hitchcock	.25
336	Juan Acevedo	.25
337	Robin Ventura	.25
338	Mariano Rivera	.40
339	John Flaherty	.25
340	Andy Pettitte	.50
341	Antonio Osuna	.25
342	Erick Almonte	.25
343	Chris Hammond	.25
344	Steve Karsay	.25
345	Alfonso Soriano	1.00
346	Bubba Trammell	.25
347	Nick Johnson	.25
348	Jorge Posada	.50
349	Jeff Weaver	.25
350	Raul Mondesi	.25
351	Randy Choate	.25
352	Drew Henson	.25
353	Jeff Bagwell	.75
354	Wade Miller	.25
355	Lance Berkman	.40
356	Julio Lugo	.25
357	Roy Oswalt	.40
358	Bruce Chen	.25
359	Morgan Ensberg	.25
360	Geoff Blum	.25
361	Brian Moehler	.25
362	Billy Wagner	.40
363	Peter Munro	.25
364	Brad Ausmus	.25
365	Jose Vizcaino	.25
366	Craig Biggio	.40
367	Tim Redding	.25
368	Gregg Zaun	.25
369	Octavio Dotel	.25
370	Carlos Hernandez	.25
371	Richard Hidalgo	.25
372	Jeriome Robertson	.25
373	Orlando Merced	.25
374	John Buck	.25
375	Adam Everett	.25
376	Raul Chavez	.25
377	Brad Lidge	.25
378	Jeff Kent	.40
379	Scott Linebrink	.25
380	Greg Miller	.25
381	Kirk Saarloos	.25
382	Brandon Puffer	.25
383	Ricky Stone	.25
384	Jason Lane	.25
385	Brian L. Hunter	.25
386	Rodrigo Rosario	.25
387	Horacio Ramirez	.25
388	Gary Sheffield	.50
389	Mike Hampton	.25
390	Robert Fick	.25
391	Henry Blanco	.25
392	Vinny Castilla	.25
393	Joe Dawley	.25
394	Jung Bong	.25
395	Rafael Furcal	.25
396	Javy Lopez	.25
397	Greg Maddux	1.25
398	Andruw Jones	.50
399	John Smoltz	.40
400	Chipper Jones	1.00
401	Mark DeRosa	.25
402	Shane Reynolds	.25
403	Kevin Gryboski	.25
404	Russ Ortiz	.25
405	Roberto Hernandez	.25
406	Ray King	.25
407	Matt Franco	.25
408	Marcus Giles	.25
409	Trey Hodges	.25
410	Darren Holmes	.25
411	Julio Franco	.25
412	Darren Bragg	.25
413	Richie Sexson	.50
414	Jeffrey Hammonds	.25
415	Ben Sheets	.25
416	Mike DeJean	.25
417	Royce Clayton	.25
418	Wes Helms	.25
419	Valerio de los Santos	.25
420	Brady Clark	.25
421	Glendon Rusch	.25
422	Geoff Jenkins	.40
423	John Foster	.25
424	Curtis Leskanic	.25
425	Todd Ritchie	.25
426	Enrique Cruz	.25
427	Wayne Franklin	.25
428	Matt Ford	.25
429	Matt Kinney	.25
430	Scott Podsednik	2.00
431	Luis Vizcaino	.25
432	Shane Nance	.25
433	Alex Sanchez	.25
434	John Vander Wal	.25
435	Eric Young	.25
436	Eddie Perez	.25
437	Jason Conti	.25
438	Matt Morris	.25
439	Tino Martinez	.25
440	Fernando Vina	.25
441	Cal Eldred	.25
442	Kiko Calero	.25
443	Jimmy Journell	.25
444	Jim Edmonds	.40
445	Jeff Fassero	.25
446	Mike Matheny	.25
447	Garrett Stephenson	.25
448	Brett Tomko	.25
449	So Taguchi	.25
450	Eduardo Perez	.25
451	Lance Painter	.25
452	Jason Isringhausen	.25
453	Albert Pujols	2.00
454	Eli Marrero	.25
455	Jason Simontacchi	.25
456	J.D. Drew	.75
457	Scott Rolen	.75
458	Orlando Palmeiro	.25
459	Dustin Hermanson	.25
460	Edgar Renteria	.25
461	Woody Williams	.25
462	Chris Carpenter	.25
463	Sammy Sosa	1.50
464	Kerry Wood	.75
465	Kyle Farnsworth	.25
466	Alex Gonzalez	.25
467	Eric Karros	.25
468	Troy O'Leary	.25
469	Mark Grudzielanek	.25
470	Alan Benes	.25
471	Mark Prior	1.50
472	Paul Bako	.25
473	Shawn Estes	.25
474	Matt Clement	.25
475	Ramon Martinez	.25
476	Tom Goodwin	.25
477	Corey Patterson	.25
478	Moises Alou	.40
479	Juan Cruz	.25
480	Bobby Hill	.25
481	Mark Bellhorn	.25
482	Mark Guthrie	.25
483	Mike Remlinger	.25
484	Lenny Harris	.25
485	Antonio Alfonseca	.25
486	Dave Veres	.25
487	Hee Seop Choi	.40
488	Luis Gonzalez	.25
489	Lyle Overbay	.25
490	Randy Johnson	.75
491	Mark Grace	.25
492	Danny Bautista	.25
493	Junior Spivey	.25
494	Matt Williams	.25
495	Miguel Batista	.25
496	Tony Womack	.25
497	Byung-Hyun Kim	.25
498	Steve Finley	.25
499	Craig Counsell	.25
500	Curt Schilling	.75
501	Elmer Dessens	.25
502	Rod Barajas	.25
503	David Dellucci	.25
504	Mike Koplove	.25
505	Mike Myers	.25
506	Matt Mantei	.25
507	Stephen Randolph RC	.25
508	Chad Moeller	.25
509	Carlos Baerga	.25
510	Andrew Good	.25
511	Quinton McCracken	.25
512	Jason Romano	.25
513	Jolbert Cabrera	.25
514	Darren Dreifort	.25
515	Kevin Brown	.40
516	Paul Quantrill	.25
517	Shawn Green	.40
518	Hideo Nomo	.40
519	Eric Gagne	.25
520	Troy Brohawn	.25
521	Kazuhisa Ishii	.25
522	Guillermo Mota	.25
523	Alex Cora	.25
524	Odalis Perez	.25
525	Brian Jordan	.25
526	Andy Ashby	.25
527	Fred McGriff	.40
528	Adrian Beltre	.40
529	Daryle Ward	.25
530	Todd Hundley	.25
531	David Ross	.25
532	Paul Shuey	.25
533	Paul LoDuca	.25
534	Dave Roberts	.25
535	Mike Kinkade	.25
536	Cesar Izturis	.25
537	Ron Coomer	.25
538	Jose Vidro	.25
539	Henry Mateo	.25
540	Tony Armas Jr.	.25
541	Joey Eischen	.25
542	Orlando Cabrera	.25
543	Jose Macias	.25
544	Fernando Tatis	.25
545	Jeff Liefer	.25
546	Michael Barrett	.25
547	Vladimir Guerrero	.75
548	Javier Vazquez	.25
549	Brad Wilkerson	.25
550	Zach Day	.25
551	Tomokazu Ohka	.25
552	Livan Hernandez	.25
553	Endy Chavez	.25
554	Dan Smith	.25
555	Scott Stewart	.25
556	T.J. Tucker	.25
557	Jamey Carroll	.25
558	Ron Calloway	.25
559	Brian Schneider	.25
560	Orlando Hernandez	.25
561	Wil Cordero	.25
562	Rocky Biddle	.25
563	Edgardo Alfonso	.25
564	Andres Galarraga	.25
565	Felix Rodriguez	.25
566	Benito Santiago	.25
567	Jose Cruz	.25
568	Tim Worrell	.25
569	Marvin Benard	.25
570	Kurt Ainsworth	.25

#	Player	Price	#	Player	Price	#	Player	Price	#	Player	Price
571	Jim Brower	.25	689	Jason Kendall	.40	807	Odalis Perez	.25	925	Andrew Brown RC	.40
572	J.T. Snow	.25	690	Matt Stairs	.25	808	Mike Piazza	.50	926	Alfredo Gonzalez RC	.40
573	Scott Eyre	.25	691	Kris Benson	.25	809	Mike Remlinger	.25	927	Carlos Rivera RC	.40
574	Robb Nen	.25	692	Julian Tavarez	.25	810	Scott Rolen	.40	928	Rick Roberts RC	.40
575	Barry Bonds	2.50	693	Reggie Sanders	.25	811	Jimmy Rollins	.25	929	Terrmel Sledge RC	.40
576	Ray Durham	.25	694	Jeff D'Amico	.25	812	Benito Santiago	.25	930	Josh Willingham RC	.40
577	Marquis Grissom	.25	695	Pokey Reese	.25	813	Curt Schilling	.50	931	Prentice Redman RC	.50
578	Pedro Feliz	.25	696	Kenny Lofton	.25	814	Richie Sexson	.40	932	Jeff Duncan RC	1.50
579	Jason Schmidt	.25	697	Mike Williams	.25	815	John Smoltz	.25	933	Craig Brazell RC	1.00
580	Rich Aurilia	.25	698	David Williams	.25	816	Sammy Sosa	.40	934	Jeremy Griffiths RC	.40
581	Kirk Rueter	.25	699	Kevin Young	.25	817	Junior Spivey	.25	935	Phil Seibel RC	.40
582	Chad Zerbe	.25	700	Brian Boehringer	.25	818	Jose Vidro	.25	936	Heath Bell RC	.40
583	Damian Moss	.25	701	Scott Sauerbeck	.25	819	Mike Williams	.25	937	Bernie Castro RC	.40
584	Neifi Perez	.25	702	Josh Fogg	.25	820	Luis Castillo	.25	938	Mike Nicolas RC	.40
585	Joe Nathan	.25	703	Joe Beimel	.25	821	Jason Giambi	.40	939	Cory Stewart RC	.40
586	Ruben Rivera	.25	704	Dennys Reyes	.25	822	Luis Gonzalez	.25	940	Shane Victorino RC	.40
587	Yorvit Torrealba	.25	705	Jeff Suppan	.25	823	Sammy Sosa	.75	941	Brandon Villafuerte RC	.40
588	Josh Beckett	.50	706	Solomon Torres	.25	824	Ken Griffey Jr.	.75	942	Jeremy Wedel RC	.40
589	Todd Hollandsworth	.25	707	Kip Wells	.25	825	Ken Griffey Jr.	.75	943	Tommy Phelps	.25
590	Derrek Lee	.25	708	Craig Wilson	.25	826	Tino Martinez	.25	944	Josh Hall RC	.75
591	A.J. Burnett	.25	709	Jack Wilson	.25	827	Barry Bonds	1.00	945	Ryan Cameron RC	.40
592	Juan Pierre	.25	710	Robert Mackowiak	.25	828	Frank Thomas	.40	946	Garrett Atkins RC	.40
593	Mark Redman	.25	711	Abraham Nunez	.25	829	Ken Griffey Jr.	.75	947	Clint Barmes RC	.75
594	Blaine Neal	.25	712	Randall Simon	.25	830	Barry Bonds	1.00	948	Michael Hessman RC	.40
595	Mike Mordecai	.25	713	Josias Manzanillo	.25	831	Tim Salmon	.25	949	Brian Stokes RC	.40
596	Alex Gonzalez	.25	714	Ken Griffey Jr.	1.00	832	Troy Glaus	.25	950	Rocco Baldelli	1.00
597	Brad Penny	.25	715	Jimmy Haynes	.25	833	Robb Nen	.25	951	Hector Luna	.25
598	Tim Spooneybarger	.25	716	Felipe Lopez	.25	834	Jeff Kent	.25	952	Jaime Cerda	.25
599	Mike Lowell	.25	717	Jimmy Anderson	.25	835	Scott Spiezio	.25	953	D.J. Carrasco RC	.40
600	Mike Redmond	.25	718	Ryan Dempster	.25	836	Darin Erstad	.25	954	Ian Ferguson RC	.40
601	Braden Looper	.25	719	Russell Branyan	.25	837	Randy Johnson	.25	955	Tim Olson RC	.75
602	Ivan Rodriguez	.50	720	Aaron Boone	.25	838	Chipper Jones	.50	956	Alejandro Machado RC	.40
603	Andy Fox	.25	721	Luke Prokopec	.25	839	Greg Maddux	.50	957	Jorge Cordova RC	.40
604	Vladimir Nunez	.25	722	Felix Heredia	.25	840	Nomar Garciaparra	.75	958	Wilfredo Ledezma RC	.40
605	Luis Castillo	.25	723	Scott Sullivan	.25	841	Manny Ramirez	.40	959	Nathan Robertson RC	.40
606	Juan Encarnacion	.25	724	Danny Graves	.25	842	Pedro J. Martinez	.40	960	Nook Logan RC	.40
607	Armando Almanza	.25	725	Kent Mercker	.25	843	Sammy Sosa	.75	961	Anaheim Angels	.25
608	Gerald Williams	.25	726	Barry Larkin	.40	844	Ken Griffey Jr.	.75	962	Baltimore Orioles	.25
609	Carl Pavano	.25	727	Jason LaRue	.25	845	Jim Thome	.40	963	Boston Red Sox	.25
610	Michael Tejera	.25	728	Gabe White	.25	846	Vladimir Guerrero	.40	964	Chicago White Sox	.25
611	Ramon Castro	.25	729	Adam Dunn	.50	847	Mike Piazza	.50	965	Cleveland Indians	.25
612	Brian Banks	.25	730	Brandon Larson	.25	848	Derek Jeter	1.00	966	Detroit Tigers	.25
613	Roberto Alomar	.50	731	Reggie Taylor	.25	849	Jason Giambi	.40	967	Kansas City Royals	.25
614	Al Leiter	.25	732	Sean Casey	.25	850	Roger Clemens	1.00	968	Minnesota Twins	.25
615	Jeromy Burnitz	.25	733	Scott Williamson	.25	851	Alfonso Soriano	.40	969	New York Yankees	.25
616	John Franco	.25	734	Austin Kearns	.50	852	Hideki Matsui	4.00	970	Oakland Athletics	.25
617	Tom Glavine	.40	735	Kelly Stinnett	.25	853	Barry Bonds	1.00	971	Seattle Mariners	.25
618	Mike Piazza	1.00	736	Ruben Mateo	.25	854	Ichiro Suzuki	.50	972	Tampa Bay Devil Rays	.25
619	Cliff Floyd	.25	737	Wily Mo Pena	.25	855	Albert Pujols	.75	973	Texas Rangers	.25
620	Joe McEwing	.25	738	Larry Walker	.40	856	Alex Rodriguez	.40	974	Toronto Blue Jays	.25
621	David Weathers	.25	439	Juan Uribe	.25	857	Darin Erstad	.25	975	Arizona Diamondbacks	.25
622	Pedro Astacio	.25	740	Denny Neagle	.25	858	Troy Glaus	.25	976	Atlanta Braves	.25
623	Timoniel Perez	.25	741	Darren Oliver	.25	859	Curt Schilling	.25	977	Chicago Cubs	.25
624	Jason Phillips	.25	742	Charles Johnson	.25	860	Luis Gonzalez	.25	978	Cincinnati Reds	.25
625	Ty Wigginton	.25	743	Todd Jones	.25	861	Tom Glavine	.25	979	Colorado Rockies	.25
626	Steve Trachsel	.25	744	Todd Helton	.75	862	Andruw Jones	.40	980	Florida Marlins	.25
627	Roger Cedeno	.25	745	Shawn Chacon	.25	863	Gary Sheffield	.25	981	Houston Astros	.25
628	Tsuyoshi Shinjo	.25	746	Jason Jennings	.25	864	Frank Thomas	.40	982	Los Angeles Dodgers	.25
629	Armando Benitez	.25	747	Preston Wilson	.25	865	Mark Prior	1.00	983	Milwaukee Brewers	.25
630	Vance Wilson	.25	748	Chris Richard	.25	866	Ivan Rodriguez	.40	984	Montreal Expos	.25
631	Mike Stanton	.25	749	Chris Stynes	.25	867	Jeff Bagwell	.25	985	New York Mets	.25
632	Mo Vaughn	.25	750	Jose Jimenez	.25	868	Lance Berkman	.25	986	Philadelphia Phillies	.25
633	Scott Strickland	.25	751	Gabe Kapler	.25	869	Shawn Green	.25	987	Pittsburgh Pirates	.25
634	Rey Sanchez	.25	752	Jay Payton	.25	870	Hideo Nomo	.25	988	San Diego Padres	.25
635	Jay Bell	.25	753	Aaron Cook	.25	871	Torii Hunter	.25	989	San Francisco Giants	.25
636	David Cone	.25	754	Greg Norton	.25	872	Bernie Williams	.25	990	St. Louis Cardinals	.25
637	Jae Weong So	.25	755	Scott Elarton	.25	873	Barry Zito	.25			
638	Ryan Klesko	.40	756	Brian Fuentes	.25	874	Pat Burrell	.25			
639	Wiki Gonzalez	.25	757	Jose Hernandez	.25	875	Carlos Delgado	.25			
640	Trevor Hoffman	.25	758	Nelson Cruz	.25	876	Miguel Tejada	.25			
641	Sean Burroughs	.25	759	Justin Speier	.25	877	Hideki Matsui RC	4.00			
642	Mike Bynum	.25	760	Javier Lopez	.40	878	Jose Contreras RC	2.00			
643	Clay Condrey	.25	761	Garret Anderson	.25	879	Jason Anderson	.40			
644	Gary Bennett	.25	762	Tony Batista	.25	880	Jason Shiell RC	.40			
645	Kevin Jarvis	.25	763	Mark Buehrle	.25	881	Kevin Tolar RC	.40			
646	Mark Kotsay	.25	764	Johnny Damon	.40	882	Michel Hernandez RC	.40			
647	Phil Nevin	.25	765	Freddy Garcia	.25	883	Arnie Munoz RC	.40			
648	Dave Hansen	.25	766	Nomar Garciaparra	.75	884	David Sanders RC	.40			
649	Keith Lockhart	.25	767	Jason Giambi	.50	885	Willie Eyre RC	.40			
650	Brian Lawrence	.25	768	Roy Halladay	.25	886	Brent Hoard RC	.40			
651	Jay Witasick	.25	769	Shea Hillenbrand	.25	887	Lew Ford RC	2.00			
652	Rondell White	.25	770	Torii Hunter	.25	888	Beau Kemp RC	.75			
653	Jaret Wright	.25	771	Derek Jeter	1.00	889	Jonathan Pridie RC	.40			
654	Luther Hackman	.25	772	Paul Konerko	.25	890	Mike Ryan RC	.40			
655	Jake Peavy	.25	773	Derek Lowe	.25	891	Richard Fischer RC	.40			
656	Brian Buchanan	.25	774	Pedro J. Martinez	.50	892	Luis Ayala RC	.40			
657	Mark Loretta	.25	775	A.J. Pierzynski	.25	893	Mike Neu RC	.40			
658	Oliver Perez	.25	776	Jorge Posada	.40	894	Joe Valentine RC	.40			
659	Adam Eaton	.25	777	Manny Ramirez	.25	895	Nate Bland RC	.40			
660	Xavier Nady	.25	778	Mariano Rivera	.25	896	Shane Bazzell RC	.75			
661	Jesse Orosco	.25	779	Jason Giambi	1.00	897	Aquilino Lopez RC	.40			
662	Ramon Vazquez	.25	780	Kazuhiro Sasaki	.50	898	Diegomar Markwell RC	.40			
663	Jim Thome	.75	781	Alfonso Soriano	.50	899	Francisco Rosario RC	.40			
664	Jose Mesa	.25	782	Ichiro Suzuki	.75	900	Guillermo Quiroz RC	.75			
665	Rheal Cormier	.25	783	Mike Sweeney	.25	901	Luis De Los Santos RC	.40			
666	David Bell	.25	784	Miguel Tejada	.25	902	Fernando Cabrera RC	.40			
667	Mike Lieberthal	.25	785	Ugueth Urbina	.25	903	Francisco Cruceta RC	.40			
668	Brandon Duckworth	.25	786	Robin Ventura	.25	904	Jhonny Peralta	.50			
669	David Coggin	.25	787	Omar Vizquel	.25	905	Rett Johnson RC	.40			
670	Bobby Abreu	.40	788	Randy Winn	.25	906	Aaron Looper RC	.40			
671	Turk Wendell	.25	789	Barry Zito	.25	907	Bobby Madritsch RC	.40			
672	Marlon Byrd	.25	790	Lance Berkman	.25	908	Luis Matos	.40			
673	Jason Michaels	.25	791	Barry Bonds	1.00	909	Jose Castillo RC	.40			
674	Kevin Millwood	.40	792	Adam Dunn	.40	910	Chris Waters RC	.40			
675	Tomas Perez	.25	793	Tom Glavine	.25	911	Jeremy Guthrie RC	.75			
676	Jimmy Rollins	.50	794	Luis Gonzalez	.25	912	Pedro Liriano RC	.40			
677	Vicente Padilla	.25	795	Shawn Green	.25	913	Joe Borowski	.25			
678	Pat Burrell	.50	796	Vladimir Guerrero	.40	914	Felix Sanchez RC	.40			
679	Tyler Houston	.25	797	Todd Helton	.40	915	Jon Leicester RC	.40			
680	Hector Mercado	.25	798	Trevor Hoffman	.25	916	Todd Wellemeyer RC	.75			
681	Carlos Silva	.25	799	Randy Johnson	.50	917	Matt Bruback RC	.40			
682	Nick Punto	.25	800	Andruw Jones	.40	918	Chris Capuano RC	.50			
683	Ricky Ledee	.25	801	Byung-Hyun Kim	.25	919	Oscar Villarreal RC	.40			
684	Randy Wolf	.25	802	Mike Lowell	.25	920	Matt Kata RC	.75			
685	Todd Pratt	.25	803	Eric Gagne	.25	921	Robby Hammock RC	.75			
686	Placido Polanco	.25	804	Matt Morris	.25	922	Gerald Laird	.40			
687	Chase Utley	1.00	805	Robb Nen	.25	923	Brandon Webb RC	3.00			
688	Brian Giles	.25	806	Vicente Padilla	.25	924	Tommy Whiteman RC	.40			

Rainbow

Stars (1-990):	10-20X
Rookies:	4-8X
Production 40 Sets	

Red, White & Blue

Stars (1-990):	1-30X
Rookies:	1-2X
#'s 1-752 Inserted 1:6	
#'s 877-960 1:36	

Endorsements

NM/M

Inserted 1:500
Some not priced due to scarcity.

RA	Rick Ankiel	20.00
DB	Dewon Brazelton/50	15.00
BD	Ben Diggins	15.00
AG	Alex Graman/50	15.00
KGS	Ken Griffey Sr.	15.00
HI	Hansel Izquierdo/50	15.00
JL	Jon Lieber	15.00
CM	Corwin Malone/50	15.00
TO	Tomokazu Ohka	20.00

Vintage Update

NM/M

Complete Set (61):		15.00
Common Player:		.40
Inserted 1:Pack		
281	Tom Glavine	1.00
282	Josh Stewart	.40
283	Aquilino Lopez	.40
284	Horacio Ramirez	.40
285	Brandon Phillips	.40
286	Kirk Saarloos	.40
287	Runelvys Hernandez	.40
288	Hideki Matsui	5.00
289	Jeremy Bonderman	3.00
290	Russ Ortiz	.40
291	Ken Harvey	.40
292	Edgardo Alfonzo	.40
293	Oscar Villarreal	.40
294	Marlon Byrd	.40
295	Josh Bard	.40
296	David Cone	.40
297	Mike Neu	.40
298	Cliff Floyd	.40
299	Travis Lee	.40
300	Jeff Kent	.50
301	Ron Calloway	.40
302	Bartolo Colon	.40
303	Jose Contreras	1.50
304	Mark Teixeira	1.00
305	Ivan Rodriguez	1.00
306	Jim Thome	.40
307	Shane Reynolds	.40
308	Luis Ayala	.40
309	Lyle Overbay	.40
310	Travis Hafner	.40
311	Wilfredo Ledezma	.40
312	Rocco Baldelli	1.50
313	Jason Anderson	.40
314	Kenny Lofton	.75
315	Brandon Larson	.40
316	Ty Wigginton	.40
317	Fred McGriff	.40
318	Antonio Osuna	.40
319	Corey Patterson	.40
320	Erubiel Durazo	.40
321	Mike MacDougal	.40
322	Sammy Sosa	2.00
323	Mike Hampton	.40
324	Ramiro Mendoza	.40
325	Kevin Millwood	.75
326	Dave Roberts	.40
327	Todd Zeile	.40
328	Reggie Sanders	.40
329	Billy Koch	.40
330	Mike Stanton	.40
331	Orlando Hernandez	.40
332	Tony Clark	.40
333	Chris Hammond	.40
334	Michael Cuddyer	.40
335	Sandy Alomar	.40
336	Jose Cruz Jr.	.40
337	Omar Daal	.40
338	Robert Fick	.40
339	Daryle Ward	.40
340	David Bell	.40
341	Checklist	.40

2003 Upper Deck/Post MVP Action

Half a dozen former MVPs are featured in this cereal-box insert set. Cards have 3-D game-action sequences on front. Backs have another (regular) player photo along with personal data and stats. The cards were issued two per cello pack in special two-box packages of Post cereals.

NM/M

Complete Set (6):		4.00
Common Player:		.50
1	Barry Bonds	.75
2	Miguel Tejada	.50
3	Ichiro	1.00
4	Ken Griffey Jr.	.75
5	Jason Giambi	.50
6	Sammy Sosa	.75

2003 Upper Deck/Post Redemption

This set of 31 cards was only available via a mail-in redemption offer. Collectors who assembled all six CD-Roms six CD-Roms from Post cereal boxes could find a coded number to order the set. Fronts are white-bordered with an action photo and player name, position and team logo. Backs have a portrait photo, uniform number, personal data, 2002 and career stats, a UD hologram and logos of the sponsors and licensors. Cards are printed on extra-thick stock.

NM/M

Complete Set (31):		15.00
Common Player:		.50
1	Troy Percival	.50
2	Curt Schilling	.65
3	John Smoltz	.50
4	Tony Batista	.50
5	Pedro Martinez	.75
6	Sammy Sosa	1.00
7	Paul Konerko	.50
8	Ken Griffey Jr.	1.00
9	Jim Thome	.50
10	Larry Walker	.50
11	Bobby Higginson	.50
12	Luis Castillo	.50
13	Craig Biggio	.50
14	Mike Sweeney	.50
15	Shawn Green	.60
16	Richie Sexson	.50
17	Torii Hunter	.60
18	Vladimir Guerrero	.75
19	Mike Piazza	1.50
20	Jason Giambi	.60
21	Miguel Tejada	.60
22	Pat Burrell	.50
23	Brian Giles	.50
24	Trevor Hoffman	.50
25	Barry Bonds	2.00
26	Ichiro	2.00
27	Albert Pujols	2.00
28	Randy Winn	.50
29	Alex Rodriguez	1.50
30	Carlos Delgado	.50
31	Troy Glaus	.75

2003 Upper Deck/SSS Puerto Rico

To commemorate the historic "home" games of the Montreal Expos at San Juan, P.R., the SSS Group health care plan sponsored an uncut sheet featuring Latin players from the Expos and among the five teams which visited the island during the season. Sheets measure 7-1/2" x 10-1/2". Individual cards are UV-coated, silver-foil highlighted and feature color poses or action photos. Back of the sheet has a ghost-image action photo of Jose Vidro overprinted with advertising for the sponsor. Licensor logos also appear.

NM/M

Uncut Sheet:		10.00
Complete Set (9):		10.00
Common Player:		1.00
(1)	Roberto Alomar	1.00
(2)	Juan Gonzalez	1.50
(3)	Alex Rodriguez	3.00
(4)	Ivan Rodriguez	1.50
(5)	Sammy Sosa	3.00
(6)	Jose Vidro	1.00
(7)	Javier Vazquez	1.00
(8)	Javy Lopez	1.00
(9)	Sponsor's Logo	.10

2004 Upper Deck

DEREK LOWE B

NM/M

Complete Set (540):		75.00
Common Player:		.15
Hobby Pack:		2.00
Hobby Box (24):		40.00
1	Dontrelle Willis	.40
2	Edgar Gonzalez	.15
3	Jose Reyes	.50
4	Jae Weong Seo	.15
5	Miguel Cabrera	.25
6	Jesse Foppert	.15
7	Mike Neu	.15
8	Micheal Nakamura	.15
9	Luis Ayala	.15
10	Jared Sandberg	.15
11	Jhonny Peralta	.15
12	Wilfredo Ledezma	.15
13	Jason Roach	.15
14	Kirk Saarloos	.15
15	Cliff Lee	.15
16	Bobby Hill	.15
17	Lyle Overbay	.15

No.	Player	Price
18	Josh Hall	.15
19	Joe Thurston	.15
20	Matt Kata	.15
21	Jeremy Bonderman	.15
22	Julio Manon	.15
23	Rodrigo Rosario	.15
24	Robby Hammock	.15
25	David Sanders	.15
26	Miguel Ojeda	.15
27	Mark Teixeira	.25
28	Franklyn German	.15
29	Ken Harvey	.15
30	Xavier Nady	.15
31	Tim Salmon	.25
32	Troy Glaus	.40
33	Adam Kennedy	.15
34	David Eckstein	.15
35	Bengie Molina	.15
36	Jarrod Washburn	.15
37	Ramon Ortiz	.15
38	Eric Chavez	.25
39	Miguel Tejada	.25
40	Chris Singleton	.15
41	Jermaine Dye	.15
42	John Halama	.15
43	Tim Hudson	.40
44	Barry Zito	.40
45	Ted Lilly	.15
46	Bobby Kielty	.15
47	Kelvim Escobar	.15
48	Josh Phelps	.15
49	Vernon Wells	.25
50	Roy Halladay	.25
51	Orlando Hudson	.15
52	Eric Hinske	.15
53	Brandon Backe	.15
54	Dewon Brazelton	.15
55	Ben Grieve	.15
56	Aubrey Huff	.15
57	Toby Hall	.15
58	Rocco Baldelli	.40
59	Al Martin	.15
60	Brandon Phillips	.15
61	Omar Vizquel	.25
62	C.C. Sabathia	.15
63	Milton Bradley	.15
64	Ricky Gutierrez	.15
65	Matt Lawton	.15
66	Danys Baez	.15
67	Ichiro Suzuki	1.00
68	Randy Winn	.15
69	Carlos Guillen	.15
70	Mark McLemore	.15
71	Dan Wilson	.15
72	Jamie Moyer	.15
73	Joel Pineiro	.15
74	Edgar Martinez	.25
75	Tony Batista	.15
76	Jay Gibbons	.15
77	Jeff Conine	.15
78	Melvin Mora	.15
79	Geronimo Gil	.15
80	Rodrigo Lopez	.15
81	Jorge Julio	.15
82	Rafael Palmeiro	.50
83	Juan Gonzalez	.40
84	Mike Young	.15
85	Alex Rodriguez	1.50
86	Einar Diaz	.15
87	Kevin Mench	.15
88	Hank Blalock	.40
89	Pedro J. Martinez	.75
90	Byung-Hyun Kim	.15
91	Derek Lowe	.25
92	Jason Varitek	.15
93	Manny Ramirez	.50
94	John Burkett	.15
95	Todd Walker	.15
96	Nomar Garciaparra	1.50
97	Trot Nixon	.15
98	Mike Sweeney	.15
99	Carlos Febles	.15
100	Mike MacDougal	.15
101	Raul Ibanez	.15
102	Jason Grimsley	.15
103	Chris George	.15
104	Brent Mayne	.15
105	Dmitri Young	.15
106	Eric Munson	.15
107	A.J. Hinch	.15
108	Andres Torres	.15
109	Bobby Higginson	.15
110	Shane Halter	.15
111	Matt Walbeck	.15
112	Torii Hunter	.40
113	Doug Mientkiewicz	.15
114	Lew Ford	.15
115	Eric Milton	.15
116	Eddie Guardado	.15
117	Cristian Guzman	.15
118	Corey Koskie	.15
119	Magglio Ordonez	.40
120	Mark Buehrle	.15
121	Billy Koch	.15
122	Jose Valentin	.15
123	Paul Konerko	.15
124	Carlos Lee	.25
125	Jon Garland	.15
126	Jason Giambi	.75
127	Derek Jeter	1.50
128	Roger Clemens	1.50
129	Andy Pettitte	.40
130	Jorge Posada	.40
131	David Wells	.15
132	Hideki Matsui	1.50
133	Mike Mussina	.50
134	Jeff Bagwell	.50
135	Craig Biggio	.25
136	Morgan Ensberg	.15
137	Richard Hidalgo	.15
138	Brad Ausmus	.15
139	Roy Oswalt	.25
140	Billy Wagner	.25
141	Octavio Dotel	.15
142	Gary Sheffield	.40
143	Andruw Jones	.40
144	John Smoltz	.25
145	Rafael Furcal	.25
146	Javy Lopez	.25
147	Shane Reynolds	.15
148	Horacio Ramirez	.15
149	Mike Hampton	.15
150	Jung Bong	.15
151	Ruben Quevedo	.15
152	Ben Sheets	.15
153	Geoff Jenkins	.25
154	Royce Clayton	.15
155	Glendon Rusch	.15
156	John Vander Wal	.15
157	Scott Podsednik	.40
158	Jim Edmonds	.40
159	Tino Martinez	.15
160	Albert Pujols	1.50
161	Matt Morris	.15
162	Woody Williams	.15
163	Edgar Renteria	.15
164	Jason Isringhausen	.15
165	Jason Simontacchi	.15
166	Kerry Robinson	.15
167	Sammy Sosa	1.25
168	Joe Borowski	.15
169	Tony Womack	.15
170	Antonio Alfonseca	.15
171	Corey Patterson	.15
172	Mark Prior	1.00
173	Moises Alou	.25
174	Matt Clement	.15
175	Randall Simon	.15
176	Randy Johnson	.75
177	Luis Gonzalez	.25
178	Craig Counsell	.15
179	Miguel Batista	.15
180	Steve Finley	.15
181	Brandon Webb	.15
182	Danny Bautista	.15
183	Oscar Villarreal	.15
184	Shawn Green	.25
185	Brian Jordan	.15
186	Fred McGriff	.25
187	Andy Ashby	.15
188	Rickey Henderson	.50
189	Dave Roberts	.15
190	Eric Gagne	.15
191	Kazuhisa Ishii	.15
192	Adrian Beltre	.15
193	Vladimir Guerrero	.75
194	Livan Hernandez	.15
195	Ron Calloway	.15
196	Sun-Woo Kim	.15
197	Wil Cordero	.15
198	Brad Wilkerson	.15
199	Orlando Cabrera	.15
200	Barry Bonds	2.00
201	Ray Durham	.15
202	Andres Galarraga	.15
203	Benito Santiago	.15
204	Jose Cruz Jr.	.15
205	Jason Schmidt	.15
206	Kirk Rueter	.15
207	Felix Rodriguez	.15
208	Mike Lowell	.15
209	Luis Castillo	.25
210	Derrek Lee	.25
211	Andy Fox	.15
212	Tommy Phelps	.15
213	Todd Hollandsworth	.15
214	Brad Penny	.15
215	Juan Pierre	.15
216	Mike Piazza	1.00
217	Jae Weong Seo	.15
218	Ty Wigginton	.15
219	Al Leiter	.15
220	Roger Cedeno	.15
221	Timoniel Perez	.15
222	Aaron Heilman	.15
223	Pedro Astacio	.15
224	Joe McEwing	.15
225	Ryan Klesko	.15
226	Brian Giles	.25
227	Mark Kotsay	.15
228	Brian Lawrence	.15
229	Rod Beck	.15
230	Trevor Hoffman	.15
231	Sean Burroughs	.15
232	Bobby Abreu	.25
233	Jim Thome	.50
234	David Bell	.15
235	Jimmy Rollins	.25
236	Mike Lieberthal	.15
237	Vicente Padilla	.15
238	Randy Wolf	.15
239	Reggie Sanders	.15
240	Jason Kendall	.15
241	Jack Wilson	.15
242	Jose Hernandez	.15
243	Kip Wells	.15
244	Carlos Rivera	.15
245	Craig Wilson	.15
246	Adam Dunn	.40
247	Sean Casey	.15
248	Danny Graves	.15
249	Ryan Dempster	.15
250	Barry Larkin	.40
251	Reggie Taylor	.15
252	Wily Mo Pena	.15
253	Larry Walker	.25
254	Mark Sweeney	.15
255	Preston Wilson	.15
256	Jason Jennings	.15
257	Charles Johnson	.15
258	Jay Payton	.15
259	Chris Stynes	.15
260	Juan Uribe	.15
261	Hideki Matsui	1.00
262	Barry Bonds	1.00
263	Dontrelle Willis	.25
264	Kevin Millwood	.15
265	Billy Wagner	.15
266	Rocco Baldelli	.25
267	Roger Clemens	.75
268	Rafael Palmeiro	.25
269	Miguel Cabrera	.25
270	Jose Contreras	.15
271	Aaron Sele	.15
272	Bartolo Colon	.25
273	Darin Erstad	.25
274	Francisco Rodriguez	.15
275	Garret Anderson	.40
276	Jose Guillen	.15
277	Troy Percival	.15
278	Alex Cintron	.15
279	Casey Fossum	.15
280	Elmer Dessens	.15
281	Jose Valverde	.15
282	Matt Mantei	.15
283	Richie Sexson	.40
284	Roberto Alomar	.40
285	Shea Hillenbrand	.15
286	Chipper Jones	.75
287	Greg Maddux	1.00
288	J.D. Drew	.25
289	Marcus Giles	.15
290	Mike Hessman	.15
291	John Thomson	.15
292	Russ Ortiz	.15
293	Adam Loewen	.15
294	Jack Cust	.15
295	Jerry Hairston	.15
296	Kurt Ainsworth	.15
297	Luis Matos	.15
298	Marty Cordova	.15
299	Sidney Ponson	.15
300	Bill Mueller	.15
301	Curt Schilling	.50
302	David Ortiz	.50
303	Johnny Damon	.25
304	Keith Foulke	.15
305	Pokey Reese	.15
306	Scott Williamson	.15
307	Tim Wakefield	.15
308	Alex Gonzalez	.15
309	Aramis Ramirez	.40
310	Carlos Zambrano	.40
311	Juan Cruz	.15
312	Kerry Wood	.75
313	Kyle Farnsworth	.15
314	Aaron Rowand	.15
315	Esteban Loaiza	.15
316	Frank Thomas	.50
317	Joe Borchard	.15
318	Joe Crede	.15
319	Miguel Olivo	.15
320	Willie Harris	.15
321	Aaron Harang	.15
322	Austin Kearns	.25
323	Brandon Claussen	.15
324	Brandon Larson	.15
325	Ryan Freel	.15
326	Ken Griffey Jr.	1.00
327	Ryan Wagner	.15
328	Alex Escobar	.15
329	Coco Crisp	.15
330	David Riske	.15
331	Jody Gerut	.15
332	Josh Bard	.15
333	Travis Hafner	.25
334	Chin-Hui Tsao	.15
335	Denny Stark	.15
336	Jeromy Burnitz	.15
337	Shawn Chacon	.15
338	Todd Helton	.50
339	Vinny Castilla	.15
340	Alex Sanchez	.15
341	Carlos Pena	.15
342	Fernando Vina	.15
343	Jason Johnson	.15
344	Matt Anderson	.15
345	Mike Maroth	.15
346	Rondell White	.15
347	A.J. Burnett	.15
348	Alex Gonzalez	.15
349	Armando Benitez	.15
350	Carl Pavano	.15
351	Hee Seop Choi	.15
352	Ivan Rodriguez	.50
353	Josh Beckett	.50
354	Josh Willingham	.15
355	Adam Everett	.15
356	Brandon Duckworth	.15
357	Jason Lane	.15
358	Jeff Kent	.25
359	Jeriome Robertson	.15
360	Lance Berkman	.25
361	Wade Miller	.15
362	Aaron Guiel	.15
363	Angel Berroa	.15
364	Carlos Beltran	.50
365	David DeJesus	.15
366	Desi Relaford	.15
367	Joe Randa	.15
368	Runelvys Hernandez	.15
369	Edwin Jackson	.15
370	Hideo Nomo	.40
371	Jeff Weaver	.15
372	Juan Encarnacion	.15
373	Odalis Perez	.15
374	Paul LoDuca	.15
375	Robin Ventura	.15
376	Bill Hall	.15
377	Chad Moeller	.15
378	Chris Capuano	.15
379	Junior Spivey	.15
380	Rickie Weeks	.25
381	Wes Helms	.15
382	Brad Radke	.15
383	Jacque Jones	.15
384	Joe Mays	.15
385	Joe Nathan	.15
386	Johan Santana	.15
387	Nick Punto	.15
388	Shannon Stewart	.15
389	Carl Everett	.15
390	Claudio Vargas	.15
391	Jose Vidro	.15
392	Nick Johnson	.15
393	Rocky Biddle	.15
394	Tony Armas	.15
395	Braden Looper	.15
396	Cliff Floyd	.15
397	Jason Phillips	.15
398	Mike Cameron	.15
399	Tom Glavine	.40
400	Kenny Lofton	.25
401	Alfonso Soriano	.50
402	Bernie Williams	.40
403	Javier Vazquez	.15
404	Jon Lieber	.15
405	Jose Contreras	.15
406	Kevin Brown	.15
407	Mariano Rivera	.25
408	Arthur Rhodes	.15
409	Eric Byrnes	.15
410	Erubiel Durazo	.15
411	Graham Koonce	.15
412	Marco Scutaro	.15
413	Mark Mulder	.15
414	Mark Redman	.15
415	Rich Harden	.15
416	Brett Myers	.15
417	Chase Utley	.40
418	Kevin Millwood	.15
419	Marlon Byrd	.15
420	Pat Burrell	.15
421	Placido Polanco	.15
422	Tim Worrell	.15
423	Jason Bay	.15
424	Josh Fogg	.15
425	Kris Benson	.15
426	Mike Gonzalez	.15
427	Oliver Perez	.15
428	Tike Redman	.15
429	Adam Eaton	.15
430	Ismael Valdez	.15
431	Jake Peavy	.15
432	Khalil Greene	.15
433	Mark Loretta	.15
434	Phil Nevin	.15
435	Ramon Hernandez	.15
436	A.J. Pierzynski	.15
437	Edgardo Alfonzo	.15
438	J.T. Snow	.15
439	Jerome Williams	.15
440	Marquis Grissom	.15
441	Robb Nen	.15
442	Bret Boone	.25
443	Freddy Garcia	.15
444	Gil Meche	.15
445	John Olerud	.25
446	Rich Aurilia	.15
447	Shigetoshi Hasegawa	.15
448	Bo Hart	.15
449	Dan Haren	.15
450	Jason Marquis	.15
451	Marlon Anderson	.15
452	Scott Rolen	.75
453	So Taguchi	.15
454	Carl Crawford	.15
455	Delmon Young	.25
456	Geoff Blum	.15
457	Jesus Colome	.15
458	Jonny Gomes	.15
459	Lance Carter	.15
460	Robert Fick	.15
461	Chan Ho Park	.15
462	Francisco Cordero	.15
463	Jeff Nelson	.15
464	Jeff Zimmerman	.15
465	Kenny Rogers	.15
466	Aquilino Lopez	.15
467	Carlos Delgado	.50
468	Frank Catalanotto	.15
469	Reed Johnson	.15
470	Pat Hentgen	.15
471	Curt Schilling	.25
472	Gary Sheffield	.25
473	Javier Vazquez	.25
474	Kazuo Matsui	1.00
475	Kevin Brown	.25
476	Rafael Palmeiro	.25
477	Richie Sexson	.25
478	Roger Clemens	.25
479	Vladimir Guerrero	.50
480	Alex Rodriguez	1.00
481	Jake Woods	.15
482	Tim Bittner	.15
483	Brandon Medders	.15
484	Casey Daigle	.25
485	Jerry Gil	.15
486	Mike Gosling	.25
487	Jose Capellan	1.00
488	Odalis Perez	.25
489	Roman Colon	.25
490	David Crouthers	.25
491	Eddy Rodriguez	.25
492	Franklyn Gracesqui	.25
493	Jamie Brown	.25
494	Jerome Gamble	.25
495	Tim Hamulack	.25
496	Carlos Vasquez	.25
497	Renyel Pinto	.50
498	Ronny Cedeno	.25
499	Enemencio Pacheco	.25
500	Ryan Meaux	.25
501	Ryan Wing	.25
502	Shingo Takatsu	1.00
503	William Bergolla	.25
504	Ivan Ochoa	.25
505	Mariano Gomez	.25
506	Justin Hampson	.25
507	Justin Huisman	.25
508	Scott Dohmann	.25
509	Donnie Kelly	.50
510	Chris Aguila	.25
511	Lincoln Holdzkom RC	.25
512	Freddy Guzman	.25
513	Hector Gimenez	.25
514	Jorge Vasquez	.25
515	Jason Frasor	.25
516	Chris Saenz	.50
517	Dennis Sarfate	.25
518	Colby Miller	.25
519	Jason Bartlett	.25
520	Chad Bentz	.25
521	Josh Labandeira	.25
522	Shawn Hill	.25
523	Kazuo Matsui RC	1.00
524	Carlos Hines	.25
525	Michael Vento	2.00
526	Scott Proctor	.50
527	Sean Henn	.25
528	David Aardsma	.25
529	Ian Snell	.50
530	Mike Johnson	.25
531	Akinori Otsuka	.75
532	Rusty Tucker	.25
533	Justin Knoedler	.25
534	Merkin Valdez	1.00
535	Greg Dobbs	.25
536	Justin Leone	.25
537	Shawn Camp	.25
538	Edwin Moreno	.25
539	Angel Chavez	.25
540	Jesse Harper	.25

Reflections Update Set (50): 30.00

No.	Player	Price
341	Shingo Takatsu	.75
342	Franklyn Gracesqui	.75
343	Angel Chavez	.75
344	Jorge Sequea	.75
345	David Aardsma	.75
346	Ramon Ramirez RC	.75
347	Lino Urdaneta	.75
348	Orlando Rodriguez	.75
349	Jason Szuminski	.75
350	Luis Gonzalez	.75
351	John Gall	1.00
352	Kevin Cave	.75
353	Chris Oxspring	.75
354	Freddy Guzman	.75
355	Jeff Bennett	.75
356	Jorge Vasquez	.75
357	Merkin Valdez	.75
358	Tim Hamulack	.75
359	Hector Gimenez	.75
360	Jerry Gil	.75
361	Ryan Wing	.75
362	Shawn Hill	.75
363	Jason Bartlett	.75
364	Renyel Pinto	.75
365	Carlos Vasquez	.75
366	Mike Vento	.75
367	Casey Daigle	.75
368	Chad Bentz	.75
369	Chris Saenz	.75
370	Shawn Camp	.75
371	Carlos Hines	.75
372	Edwin Moreno	.75
373	Mike Wuertz	.75
374	Aarom Baldiris RC	.75
376	Akinori Otsuka	.75
377	Jose Capellan	.75
378	Justin Germano	.75
379	Justin Knoedler	.75
380	Mariano Gomez	.75
381	Fernando Nieve	.75
382	Scott Proctor	.75
383	Roman Colon	.75
385	Eddy Rodriguez	.75
386	Enemencio Pacheco	.75
387	William Bergolla	.75
388	Ivan Ochoa	.75
389	Rusty Tucker	.75
390	Roberto Novoa	.75

SPGU Patch Edition Update Set (50): 85.00

No.	Player	Price
121	Richie Sexson	3.00
122	Javier Vazquez	2.00
123	Alex Rodriguez	8.00
124	Javy Lopez	3.00
125	Miguel Tejada	3.00
126	Bartolo Colon	2.00
127	Ivan Rodriguez	4.00
128	Rafael Palmeiro	3.00
129	Kevin Brown	3.00
130	Gary Sheffield	3.00
131	Greg Maddux	5.00
132	Curt Schilling	4.00
133	Roger Clemens	8.00
134	Alfonso Soriano	3.00
135	Vladimir Guerrero	4.00
136	Carlos Vasquez	2.00
137	Roman Colon	2.00
138	William Bergolla	2.00
139	Jason Bartlett	2.00
140	Casey Daigle	2.00
141	Ryan Wing	2.00
142	Chris Saenz	2.00
143	Edwin Moreno	2.00
144	Shawn Hill	2.00
145	Eddy Rodriguez	2.00
146	Justin Knoedler	2.00
147	Renyel Pinto	2.00
148	Kevin Cave	2.00
149	Carlos Hines	2.00
150	Merkin Valdez RC	2.00
151	Tim Hamulack RC	2.00
152	Hector Gimenez RC	2.00
153	Mike Vento RC	2.00
154	Scott Proctor RC	3.00
155	Rusty Tucker RC	2.00
156	Akinori Otsuka RC	3.00
157	Ronny Cedeno RC	2.00
158	Jose Capellan RC	2.00
159	Justin Germano	2.00
160	Shingo Takatsu RC	2.00
161	Fernando Nieve	2.00
162	Mike Wuertz	2.00
163	Jerry Gil	2.00
164	Jorge Vasquez	2.00
165	Chad Bentz	2.00
166	Luis Gonzalez	2.00
167	Ivan Ochoa	2.00
168	Onil Joseph	2.00
169	Enemencio Pacheco	2.00
170	Kazuo Matsui RC	2.00

Play Ball Update Set (50): 20.00

No.	Player	Price
183	Kazuo Matsui RC	1.00
184	Jerry Gil	.50
185	Jose Capellan RC	.50
186	Tim Hamulack	.50
187	Renyel Pinto	.50
188	Carlos Vasquez	.50
189	Enemencio Pacheco	.50
190	Ronny Cedeno	.50
191	Mariano Gomez	.50
192	Carlos Hines	.50
193	Michael Vento	.50
194	David Aardsma	.50
195	Hector Gimenez	.50
196	Fernando Nieve	.50
197	Chris Saenz	.50
198	Shawn Hill	.50
199	Angel Chavez	.50
200	Scott Proctor	.50
201	William Bergolla	.50
202	Justin Germano	.50
203	Onil Joseph	.50
204	Rusty Tucker	.50
205	Justin Knoedler	.50
206	Casey Daigle	.50
207	Edwin Moreno	.50
208	Chad Bentz	.50
209	Ryan Wing	.50
210	Shawn Camp	.50
211	Eddy Rodriguez	.50
212	Roman Colon	.50
213	Jason Bartlett	.50
214	Jorge Vasquez	.50
215	Ivan Ochoa	.50
216	Akinori Otsuka	.50
217	Merkin Valdez RC	.50
218	Shingo Takatsu RC	.50
219	Chris Oxspring	.50
220	Kevin Cave	.50
221	Ramon Ramirez	.50
222	Orlando Rodriguez	.50
223	Lino Urdaneta	.50
224	Franklyn Gracesqui	.50
225	Mike Wuertz	.50
226	Jorge Sequea	.50
227	Luis Gonzalez	.50
228	Jason Szuminski	.50
229	John Gall	.50
230	Freddy Guzman	.50
231	Jeff Bennett	.50
232	Roberto Novoa	.50

Vintage Update Set (50): 10.00

No.	Player	Price
451	Alex Rodriguez	1.50
452	Javy Lopez	.50
453	Alfonso Soriano	.50
454	Vladimir Guerrero	.50
455	Rafael Palmeiro	.50
456	Gary Sheffield	.50
457	Curt Schilling	.50
458	Miguel Tejada	.50
459	Kevin Brown	.40
460	Richie Sexson	.50
461	Roger Clemens	1.50
462	Javier Vazquez	.25
463	Bartolo Colon	.25
464	Ivan Rodriguez	.50
465	Greg Maddux	1.00
466	Jamie Brown	.25
467	David Crouthers	.25
468	Jason Frasor	.25
469	Greg Dobbs	.25
470	Jesse Harper	.25
471	Nick Regilio RC	.25
472	Ryan Wing	.25
473	Akinori Otsuka RC	1.00
474	Shingo Takatsu RC	1.00
475	Kazuo Matsui RC	1.00
476	Michael Vento RC	1.00
477	Mike Gosling	.25
478	Justin Huisman	.25
479	Justin Hampson	.25
480	Dennis Sarfate	.25

481	Ian Snell RC	.50
482	Tim Bausher RC	.25
483	Donnie Kelly	.25
484	Jerome Gamble	.25
485	Mike Rouse	.50
486	Merkin Valdez RC	.75
487	Lincoln Holdzkom RC	.25
488	Justin Leone RC	.25
489	Sean Henn	.25
490	Brandon Medders RC	.25
491	Mike Johnston RC	.25
492	Tim Bittner	.25
493	Mike Wuertz	.25
494	Chad Bentz	.50
495	Ryan Meaux RC	.25
496	Chris Aguila RC	.25
497	Jake Woods RC	.25
498	Scott Dohmann RC	.25
499	Colby Miller	.25
500	Josh Labandeira	.25

2004 Upper Deck Glossy

NM/M
Complete Factory Set (590): 85.00
Glossy: 1-2X
Issued only in factory sets.

Authentic Stars Jersey

NM/M
Common Player: 4.00
Inserted 1:48
Golds: 1-2X
Production 100 Sets

BA	Bobby Abreu	6.00
RO	Roberto Alomar	6.00
JB	Jeff Bagwell	6.00
RB	Rocco Baldelli	4.00
JH	Josh Beckett	5.00
HB	Hank Blalock	5.00
EC	Eric Chavez	4.00
RC	Roger Clemens	15.00
CD	Carlos Delgado	4.00
JD	J.D. Drew	4.00
DE	Darin Erstad	4.00
JG	Jason Giambi	8.00
TG	Troy Glaus	5.00
TL	Tom Glavine	6.00
VG	Vladimir Guerrero	8.00
SG	Shawn Green	5.00
KG	Ken Griffey Jr.	15.00
TH	Todd Helton	8.00
TO	Torii Hunter	6.00
RJ	Randy Johnson	8.00
AJ	Andruw Jones	6.00
CJ	Chipper Jones	8.00
JK	Jeff Kent	4.00
GM	Greg Maddux	10.00
PM	Pedro J. Martinez	6.00
TM	Tino Martinez	6.00
HM	Hideki Matsui	35.00
PN	Phil Nevin	4.00
MI	Mike Piazza	10.00
MP	Mark Prior	8.00
AP	Albert Pujols	15.00
AR	Alex Rodriguez	12.00
IR	Ivan Rodriguez	6.00
CS	Curt Schilling	5.00
AS	Alfonso Soriano	10.00
SS	Sammy Sosa	12.00
IS	Ichiro Suzuki	30.00
MT	Mark Teixeira	10.00
FT	Frank Thomas	8.00
LW	Larry Walker	4.00
BW	Bernie Williams	6.00
BZ	Barry Zito	6.00

Awesome Honors

NM/M
Complete Set (10): 15.00

1	Albert Pujols	5.00
2	Alex Rodriguez	5.00
3	Angel Berroa	5.00
4	Dontrelle Willis	1.00
5	Eric Gagne	1.50
6	Garret Anderson	1.00
7	Ivan Rodriguez	1.50
8	Josh Beckett	1.50
9	Mariano Rivera	1.00
10	Roy Halladay	.75

Awesome Honors Jersey

NM/M
Golds: 1.5-2X
Production 165

GA	Garret Anderson	4.00
JB	Josh Beckett	6.00
BB	Bret Boone	4.00
MC	Mike Cameron	4.00

LC	Luis Castillo	4.00
EC	Eric Chavez	4.00
JE	Jim Edmonds	4.00
EG	Eric Gagne	4.00
EG1	Eric Gagne	4.00
JG	Jason Giambi	4.00
VG	Vladimir Guerrero	8.00
RH	Roy Halladay	10.00
MH	Mike Hampton	4.00
TH	Todd Helton	6.00
HU	Torii Hunter	5.00
AJ	Andruw Jones	6.00
DL	Derrek Lee	5.00
EM	Edgar Martinez	5.00
BM	Bengie Molina	4.00
JM	Jamie Moyer	4.00
MU	Mike Mussina	5.00
JO	John Olerud	5.00
MO	Magglio Ordonez	5.00
AP	Albert Pujols	10.00
AP2	Albert Pujols	10.00
MR	Mariano Rivera	5.00
AR	Alex Rodriguez	10.00
AR3	Alex Rodriguez	10.00
IR	Ivan Rodriguez	8.00
SR	Scott Rolen	8.00
JS	John Smoltz	5.00
AS	Alfonso Soriano	8.00
IS	Ichiro Suzuki	20.00
JT	Jim Thome	8.00
DW	Dontrelle Willis	6.00

Famous Quotes

NM/M
Complete Set (20): 30.00

Q-1	Al Lopez	.75
Q-2	Bob Feller	1.00
Q-3	Bob Gibson	1.50
Q-4	Brooks Robinson	1.50
Q-5	Cal Ripken Jr.	5.00
Q-6	Carl Yastrzemski	2.00
Q-7	Earl Weaver	.75
Q-8	Eddie Mathews	2.00
Q-9	Ernie Banks	2.00
Q-10	Greg Maddux	2.00
Q-11	Joe DiMaggio	3.00
Q-12	Mickey Mantle	6.00
Q-13	Nolan Ryan	6.00
Q-14	Stan Musial	3.00
Q-15	Ted Williams	5.00
Q-16	Tom Seaver	2.00
Q-17	Tommy Lasorda	.75
Q-18	Warren Spahn	2.00
Q-19	Whitey Ford	1.50
Q-20	Yogi Berra	2.00

First Pitch

NM/M
Common Player: 5.00
Inserted 1:72

SP7	LeBron James	20.00
SP8	Mr. Hockey	5.00
SP10	Ernie Banks	10.00
SP11	General Tommy Franks	5.00
SP12	Ben Affleck	10.00
SP13	Halle Berry	10.00
SP14	George H.W. Bush	10.00
SP15	George W. Bush	5.00

Game Winners

NM/M
Common Player: 5.00
Golds: 1-1.5X
Production 50 Sets

GW-BA	Bobby Abreu	8.00
GW-JB	Jeff Bagwell	8.00
GW-HB	Hank Blalock	8.00
GW-MC	Miguel Cabrera	8.00
GW-JE	Jim Edmonds	5.00
GW-DE	Darin Erstad	5.00
GW-RF	Rafael Furcal (Gold parallel only.)	
GW-JG	Jason Giambi	8.00
GW-TG	Troy Glaus	5.00
GW-AG	Alex Gonzalez	5.00
GW-SG	Shawn Green	5.00
GW-VG	Vladimir Guerrero	8.00
GW-TH	Todd Helton	8.00
GW-RH	Ramon Hernandez	5.00
GW-HU	Torii Hunter	5.00
GW-DJ	Derek Jeter	25.00
GW-AJ	Andruw Jones	8.00
GW-CJ	Chipper Jones	8.00
GW-RK	Ryan Klesko	5.00
GW-ML	Mike Lowell	5.00
GW-HM	Hideki Matsui	25.00
GW-TN	Trot Nixon (Gold parallel only.)	5.00
GW-MO	Magglio Ordonez	5.00
GW-CP	Corey Patterson	5.00
GW-MP	Mike Piazza	10.00
GW-JP	Jorge Posada	8.00
GW-AP	Albert Pujols	15.00
GW-IR	Ivan Rodriguez	8.00
GW-SR	Scott Rolen	10.00
GW-GS	Gary Sheffield	5.00
GW-AS	Alfonso Soriano	8.00
GW-MT	Mark Teixeira	5.00
GW-TE	Miguel Tejada	5.00
GW-JT	Jim Thome	10.00
GW-BW	Bernie Williams	8.00

Going Deep Bat

NM/M
Common Player: 6.00
Inserted 1:288
Some not priced yet due to scarcity.
Golds: 1-2X
Production 50 Sets

BA	Bobby Abreu/SP/110	6.00
RO	Roberto Alomar	8.00
SC	Sandy Alomar Jr./SP/95	6.00
GA	Garret Anderson	4.00
RA	Rich Aurilia/SP/102	6.00
JB	Jeff Bagwell/SP/92	10.00
RB	Rocco Baldelli/SP	15.00
CB	Craig Biggio/SP/89	8.00
JE	Jim Edmonds/SP	8.00
DE	Darin Erstad	6.00
RF	Rafael Furcal/SP	6.00
TG	Troy Glaus/SP/113	8.00
SG	Shawn Green/SP/100	8.00
KG	Ken Griffey Jr./SP	30.00
RH	Rickey Henderson/SP/77	10.00
TH	Torii Hunter/SP/115	8.00
CJ	Chipper Jones/SP/69	15.00
JL	Javy Lopez/SP/77	8.00
HM	Hideki Matsui/SP/70	45.00
DM	Doug Mientkiewicz/SP/123	4.00
HN	Hideo Nomo	15.00
MO	Magglio Ordonez	6.00
PO	Jay Payton/SP/100	6.00
MP	Mike Piazza	15.00
JP	Jorge Posada	8.00
AP	Albert Pujols	20.00
SR	Scott Rolen/SP/77	10.00
CS	Curt Schilling/SP/57	10.00
AS	Alfonso Soriano/SP/53	10.00
JT	Jim Thome	10.00
OV	Omar Vizquel/SP/115	6.00
BW	Bernie Williams/SP/56	8.00
KW	Kerry Wood/SP/108	10.00

Headliners Jersey

NM/M
Common Player: 5.00
Inserted 1:48
Golds: 1-2X
Production 100 Sets

TB	Tony Batista	4.00
JB	Josh Beckett	8.00
LB	Lance Berkman	8.00
MB	Mark Buehrle	4.00
LC	Luis Castillo	4.00
JD	Joe DiMaggio/SP/153	90.00
AD	Adam Dunn	6.00
JE	Jim Edmonds	6.00
RF	Robert Fick	4.00
TG	Tom Glavine	6.00
LG	Luis Gonzalez	4.00
SG	Shawn Green	4.00
KG	Ken Griffey Jr.	15.00
VG	Vladimir Guerrero/SP/153	10.00
RH	Roy Halladay	8.00
JH	Jose Hernandez	4.00
TH	Trevor Hoffman	4.00
BK	Byung-Hyun Kim	4.00
RK	Ryan Klesko	4.00
PK	Paul Konerko	4.00
ML	Mike Lowell	4.00
GM	Greg Maddux	12.00
MM	Mickey Mantle/SP/97	125.00
PM	Pedro J. Martinez	8.00
HM	Hideki Matsui	35.00
MY	Matt Morris	4.00
MU	Mike Mussina	8.00
MO	Magglio Ordonez	4.00
RO	Roy Oswalt	4.00
MR	Manny Ramirez	6.00
MA	Mariano Rivera	6.00
JR	Jimmy Rollins	6.00
BS	Benito Santiago	4.00
CS	Curt Schilling	6.00
JS	Junior Spivey	4.00
IS	Ichiro Suzuki/SP/153	30.00
MS	Mike Sweeney	4.00
MT	Miguel Tejada	6.00
JT	Jim Thome	8.00
JV	Jose Vidro	4.00
TW	Ted Williams/SP/153	75.00

Magical Performances

NM/M
Common Player: 6.00
Inserted 1:96
Golds: 1-1.5X
Production 50 Sets

MP1	Mickey Mantle	35.00
MP2	Mickey Mantle	35.00
MP3	Joe DiMaggio	25.00
MP4	Joe DiMaggio	25.00
MP5	Derek Jeter	25.00
MP6	Derek Jeter	25.00
MP7	Roger Clemens	20.00
MP8	Roger Clemens	20.00
MP9	Alfonso Soriano	10.00
MP10	Andy Pettitte	8.00
MP11	Hideki Matsui	30.00
MP12	Mike Mussina	10.00
MP13	Jorge Posada	10.00
MP14	Jason Giambi	10.00
MP15	David Wells	6.00
MP16	Mariano Rivera	10.00
MP17	Yogi Berra	15.00
MP18	Phil Rizzuto	10.00
MP19	Whitey Ford	10.00
MP20	Jose Contreras	8.00
MP21	Jim "Catfish" Hunter	6.00
MP22	Mickey Mantle	35.00
MP23	Mickey Mantle	35.00
MP24	Joe DiMaggio	25.00
MP25	Joe DiMaggio	25.00
MP26	Derek Jeter	25.00
MP27	Derek Jeter	25.00
MP28	Roger Clemens	20.00
MP29	Roger Clemens	20.00
MP30	Alfonso Soriano	10.00
MP31	Andy Pettitte	8.00
MP32	Hideki Matsui	30.00
MP33	Mike Mussina	10.00
MP34	Jorge Posada	10.00
MP35	Jason Giambi	10.00
MP36	David Wells	6.00
MP37	Mariano Rivera	10.00
MP38	Yogi Berra	15.00
MP39	Phil Rizzuto	10.00
MP40	Whitey Ford	10.00
MP41	Jose Contreras	10.00
MP42	Jim "Catfish" Hunter	6.00

Matsui Chronicles

NM/M
Complete Set (60): 35.00
Common Matsui: 1.00
HM1-60 Hideki Matsui 1.00

National Pride

NM/M
Complete Set (20): 25.00
Common Player: 1.00
Inserted 1:6

USA1	Justin Orenduff	1.00
USA2	Micah Owings	2.00
USA3	Steven Register	2.00
USA4	Huston Street	1.00
USA5	Justin Verlander	2.00
USA6	Jered Weaver	1.00
USA7	Matt Campbell	1.00
USA8	Stephen Head	1.00
USA9	Mark Romanczuk	1.00
USA10	Jeff Clement	6.00
USA11	Mike Nickeas	2.00
USA12	Tyler Greene	1.00
USA13	Paul Janish	2.00
USA14	Jeff Larish	1.00
USA15	Eric Patterson	1.00
USA16	Dustin Pedroia	1.00
USA17	Michael Griffin	1.00
USA18	Brent Lillibridge	1.00
USA19	Danny Putnam	1.00
USA20	Seth Smith	1.00

National Pride Jersey

NM/M
Common Player: 4.00
Inserted 1:24

USA1	Justin Orenduff	4.00
USA2	Micah Owings	4.00
USA3	Steven Register	4.00
USA4	Huston Street	4.00
USA5	Justin Verlander	10.00
USA6	Jered Weaver	6.00
USA7	Matt Campbell	4.00
USA8	Stephen Head	4.00
USA9	Mark Romanczuk	4.00
USA10	Jeff Clement	4.00
USA11	Mike Nickeas	4.00
USA12	Tyler Greene	4.00
USA13	Paul Janish	4.00
USA14	Jeff Larish	4.00
USA15	Eric Patterson	4.00
USA16	Dustin Pedroia	12.00
USA17	Michael Griffin	4.00
USA18	Brent Lillibridge	4.00
USA19	Danny Putnam	4.00
USA20	Seth Smith	6.00
USA21	Justin Orenduff	4.00
USA22	Micah Owings	4.00
USA23	Steven Register	4.00
USA24	Huston Street	6.00
USA25	Justin Verlander	10.00
USA26	Jered Weaver	8.00
USA27	Matt Campbell	6.00
USA28	Stephen Head	4.00
USA29	Mark Romanczuk	4.00
USA30	Jeff Clement	4.00
USA31	Mike Nickeas	4.00
USA32	Tyler Greene	4.00
USA33	Paul Janish	4.00
USA34	Jeff Larish	4.00
USA35	Eric Patterson	4.00
USA36	Dustin Pedroia	12.00
USA37	Michael Griffin	4.00
USA38	Brent Lillibridge	4.00
USA39	Danny Putnam	4.00
USA40	Seth Smith	6.00
USA41	Delmon Young	8.00
USA42	Rickie Weeks	8.00

Series 2

TB	Thad Bosley	4.00
BB	Brian Bruney	4.00
CB	Chris Burke	4.00
JC	Jesse Crain	4.00
DU	Justin Duchscherer	6.00
JD	J.D. Durbin	4.00
JG	John Grabow	4.00
GG	Gabe Gross	4.00
JH	J.J. Hardy	6.00
GK	Graham Koonce	4.00
GL	Gerald Laird	4.00
ML	Mike Lamb	4.00
JL	Justin Leone	4.00
JM	Joe Mauer	15.00
HR	Horacio Ramirez	4.00
JR	Jeremy Reed	6.00
RR	Royce Ring	4.00
ER	Eddie Rodriguez	4.00
MR	Mike Rouse	4.00
GS	Grady Sizemore	10.00
JS	Jason Stanford	4.00
JB	John Van Benschoten	4.00
TW	Todd Williams	4.00
EY	Ernie Young	4.00

National Pride Pants

NM/M

CB	Chris Burke	4.00
JC	Jesse Crain	4.00
DU	Justin Duchscherer	6.00
GK	Graham Koonce	4.00
JL	Justin Leone	8.00
RM	Ryan Madson	4.00
JM	Joe Mauer	15.00
HR	Horacio Ramirez	4.00
RR	Royce Ring	4.00
ER	Eddie Rodriguez	4.00
MR	Mike Rouse	4.00
GS	Grady Sizemore	10.00
JS	Jason Stanford	4.00
JB	John Van Benschoten	4.00

Peak Performers

NM/M
Golds: 1.5X-2X
Production 165

PP-JB	Jeff Bagwell	8.00
PP-BE	Josh Beckett	5.00
PP-LB	Lance Berkman	5.00
PP-CB	Craig Biggio	5.00
PP-HB	Hank Blalock	5.00
PP-PB	Pat Burrell	4.00
PP-LC	Luis Castillo	4.00
PP-CD	Carlos Delgado	6.00
PP-RF	Rafael Furcal	4.00
PP-EG	Eric Gagne	4.00
PP-SG	Shawn Green	5.00
PP-KG	Ken Griffey Jr.	15.00
PP-VG	Vladimir Guerrero	8.00
PP-TH	Todd Helton	8.00
PP-PL	Paul LoDuca	4.00
PP-PM	Pedro J. Martinez	8.00
PP-HM	Hideki Matsui	25.00
PP-MM	Mike Mussina	8.00
PP-HN	Hideo Nomo	8.00
PP-MO	Magglio Ordonez	5.00
PP-RP	Rafael Palmeiro	6.00
PP-PE	Andy Pettitte	6.00
PP-BP	Brandon Phillips	4.00
PP-MP	Mark Prior	8.00
PP-AP	Albert Pujols	15.00
PP-JR	Jose Reyes	5.00
PP-IR	Ivan Rodriguez	8.00
PP-SR	Scott Rolen	8.00
PP-SA	C.C. Sabathia	8.00
PP-CS	Curt Schilling	8.00
PP-AS	Alfonso Soriano	8.00
PP-IS	Ichiro Suzuki	20.00
PP-MT	Miguel Tejada	5.00
PP-FT	Frank Thomas	8.00
PP-JT	Jim Thome	8.00
PP-DV	Omar Vizquel	4.00
PP-VW	Vernon Wells	4.00
PP-KW	Kerry Wood	4.00

Signature Stars Black Ink

Some not priced due to lack of info.
Inserted 1:288

RA	Rich Aurilia/479	8.00
AG	Andres Galarraga/248	10.00
NG	Nomar Garciaparra/69	75.00
VG	Vladimir Guerrero/68	40.00
RH	Rich Harden/163	8.00
AH	Aaron Heilman/49	8.00
TH	Torii Hunter/374	10.00
KI	Kazuhisa Ishii/58	10.00
BK	Billy Koch/429	8.00
HM	Hideki Matsui/25	325.00
MU	Mike Mussina/68	50.00
MO	Magglio Ordonez/377	15.00
JRa	Joe Randa/69	4.00
CR	Cal Ripken Jr./69	200.00
DR	Dave Roberts/278	8.00
NR	Nolan Ryan/69	120.00

Series 2

BB	Bret Boone/43	10.00
DB	Dewon Brazelton/96	5.00
JC	Jose Canseco/160	15.00
EC	Eric Chavez/60	10.00
EG	Eric Gagne/160	10.00
KG	Ken Griffey Jr./450	90.00
RH	Rich Harden/65	12.00
DR	Dave Roberts/450	5.00
NR	Nolan Ryan/95	10.00
DS	Darryl Strawberry/160	10.00
MT	Mark Teixeira/200	30.00
JV	Javier Vazquez/60	15.00
BW	Brandon Webb/60	15.00
RW	Rickie Weeks/65	15.00
DW	Dontrelle Willis/160	15.00

Signature Stars Gold Ink

Gold Ink: 1-2X Black Ink
Production 99 Sets

Signature Stars Blue Ink

NM/M
No Pricing
Production 25 Sets
Matsui #'d to 324.
HM Hideki Matsui/324 180.00

Signature Stars Red Ink

No Pricing
Production 10 Sets

SPGU Patch Edition Update Patch

		NM/M
Production 20 unless noted.

BA	Bobby Abreu	40.00
GA	Garret Anderson	40.00
RB	Rocco Baldelli	30.00
LB	Lance Berkman	40.00
HB	Hank Blalock	40.00
BB	Bret Boone	30.00
BC	Bartolo Colon	25.00
JE	Jim Edmonds	35.00
EG	Eric Gagne	75.00
TG	Troy Glaus	35.00
VG	Vladimir Guerrero	50.00
TH	Torii Hunter	25.00
JJ	Jacque Jones	25.00
AK	Austin Kearns	30.00
JK	Jeff Kent	25.00
RK	Ryan Klesko	25.00
EM	Edgar Martinez	50.00
KM	Kevin Millwood	30.00
MM	Mark Mulder	40.00
HN	Hideo Nomo	35.00
RO	Roy Oswalt	35.00
CP	Corey Patterson	30.00
JR	Jose Reyes	30.00
RS	Richie Sexson	40.00
MS	Mike Sweeney	25.00
BW	Brandon Webb	25.00
VW	Vernon Wells/21	25.00
KW	Kerry Wood	50.00

Super Patches Logos
No pricing due to scarcity.
Inserted 1:7,500
Series 2

Super Patches Numbers
No pricing due to scarcity.
Inserted 1:7,500
Series 2

Super Patches Stripes
No pricing due to scarcity.
Inserted 1:7,500
Series 2

Super Sluggers

		NM/M
Complete Set (30):		15.00
Common Player:		.50
Inserted 1:1 Retail

SL-1	Albert Pujols	2.00
SL-2	Alex Rodriguez	2.00
SL-3	Alfonso Soriano	.75
SL-4	Andruw Jones	.75
SL-5	Bret Boone	.50
SL-6	Carlos Delgado	.50
SL-7	Edgar Renteria	.50
SL-8	Eric Chavez	.50
SL-9	Frank Thomas	.75
SL-10	Garret Anderson	.50
SL-11	Gary Sheffield	.50
SL-12	Jason Giambi	.50
SL-13	Javy Lopez	.50
SL-14	Jeff Bagwell	.50
SL-15	Jim Edmonds	.50
SL-16	Jim Thome	1.00
SL-17	Jorge Posada	.50
SL-18	Lance Berkman	.50
SL-19	Magglio Ordonez	.50
SL-20	Manny Ramirez	.75
SL-21	Mike Lowell	.50
SL-22	Nomar Garciaparra	1.50
SL-23	Preston Wilson	.50
SL-24	Rafael Palmeiro	.75
SL-25	Richie Sexson	.50
SL-26	Sammy Sosa	2.00
SL-27	Shawn Green	.50
SL-28	Todd Helton	.75
SL-29	Vernon Wells	.50
SL-30	Vladimir Guerrero	1.00

Twenty-Five Salute

		NM/M
Common Player:		6.00
Inserted 1:12

S1	Barry Bonds	3.00
S2	Troy Glaus	.75
S3	Andruw Jones	.75
S4	Jay Gibbons	.75
S5	Jeremy Giambi	.75
S6	Jason Giambi	1.00
S7	Jim Thome	1.00
S8	Rafael Palmeiro	1.00
S9	Carlos Delgado	1.00
S10	Dmitri Young	.75

500 HR Club

		NM/M
Production 350

RP	Rafael Palmeiro	180.00

2003 Update

		NM/M
Complete Set (60):		10.00

7	Andruw Jones	.50
8	Chipper Jones	.75
9	Gary Sheffield	.40
10	Jay Gibbons	.25
11	Miguel Tejada	.40
12	Tony Batista	.15
13	Nomar Garciaparra	1.25
14	Manny Ramirez	.50
15	Pedro J. Martinez	.75
16	Mark Prior	1.00
17	Kerry Wood	.75
18	Sammy Sosa	1.25
19	Bartolo Colon	.25
20	Magglio Ordonez	.25
21	Frank Thomas	.50
22	Adam Dunn	.40
23	Austin Kearns	.25
24	Ken Griffey Jr.	1.00
25	Brandon Phillips	.15
26	Milton Bradley	.15
27	Jody Gerut	.15
28	Todd Helton	.50
29	Larry Walker	.25
30	Preston Wilson	.15
31	Jeremy Bonderman	.15
32	Carlos Pena	.15
33	Dmitri Young	.15
34	Dontrelle Willis	.40
35	Miguel Cabrera	.50
36	Mike Lowell	.25
37	Jeff Bagwell	.50
38	Roy Oswalt	.25
39	Lance Berkman	.25
40	Carlos Beltran	.40
41	Mike Sweeney	.15
42	Rondell White	.15
43	Hideo Nomo	.40
44	Kevin Brown	.25
45	Shawn Green	.25
46	Ben Sheets	.25
47	Geoff Jenkins	.25
48	Richie Sexson	.40
49	Jacque Jones	.15
50	Johan Santana	.15
51	Torii Hunter	.25
52	Javier Vazquez	.15
53	Jose Vidro	.15
54	Vladimir Guerrero	.50
55	Cliff Floyd	.15
56	Mike Piazza	1.00
57	Jose Reyes	.50
58	Derek Jeter	2.00
59	Jason Giambi	.50
60	Alfonso Soriano	.50
61	Eric Chavez	.25
62	Barry Zito	.25
63	Tim Hudson	.25
64	Bobby Abreu	.25
65	Jim Thome	.75
66	Kevin Millwood	.15
67	Roger Clemens	1.50
68	Jason Kendall	.15
69	Reggie Sanders	.15
70	Phil Nevin	.15
71	Ryan Klesko	.25
72	Brian Giles	.25
73	A.J. Pierzynski	.15
74	Jason Schmidt	.25
75	Sidney Ponson	.15
76	Edgar Martinez	.25
77	Ichiro Suzuki	1.00
78	Bret Boone	.25
79	Albert Pujols	1.50
80	Scott Rolen	.75
81	Jim Edmonds	.25
82	Aubrey Huff	.15
83	Delmon Young	.40
84	Rocco Baldelli	.25
85	Alex Rodriguez	1.50
86	Mark Teixeira	.25
87	Rafael Palmeiro	.25
88	Carlos Delgado	.50
89	Vernon Wells	.25
90	Roy Halladay	.25
91	Brandon Medders RC	2.00
92	Colby Miller RC	4.00
93	David Crouthers RC	2.00
94	Dennis Sarfate RC	3.00
95	Donald Kelly RC	2.00
96	Alec Zumwalt RC	2.00
97	Frank Brooks RC	2.00
98	Greg Dobbs RC	2.00
99	Ian Snell RC	3.00
100	Jake Woods RC	2.00
101	Jamie Brown RC	2.00
102	Jason Frasor RC	2.00
103	Jerome Gamble RC	2.00
104	Jesse Harper RC	2.00
105	Josh Labandeira RC	2.00
106	Justin Hampson RC	2.00
107	Justin Huisman RC	2.00
108	Justin Leone RC	2.00
109	Chris Aguila RC	2.00
110	Lincoln Holdzkom RC	2.00
111	Mike Bumatay RC	2.00
112	Mike Gosling RC	2.00
113	Mike Johnston RC	2.00
114	Mike Rouse RC	2.00
115	Nick Regilio RC	2.00
116	Ryan Meaux RC	2.00
117	Scott Dohmann RC	2.00
118	Sean Henn RC	2.00
119	Tim Bausher RC	2.00
120	Tim Bittner RC	2.00

2004 Upper Deck Diamond Collection

		NM/M
Complete Set (120):		60.00
Common Player:		.15
Common (91-120):		2.00
Inserted 1:6
Pack (6): 2.00
Box (24): 40.00

1	Garret Anderson	.25
2	Darin Erstad	.25
3	Troy Glaus	.40
4	Curt Schilling	.50
5	Brandon Webb	.15
6	Randy Johnson	.75

Common Player: .15
One set per hobby box.

541	Bo Hart	.15
542	Dan Haren	.50
543	Ryan Wagner	.15
544	Rich Harden	.25
545	Dontrelle Willis	.25
546	Jerome Williams	.25
547	Bobby Crosby	.25
548	Greg Jones	.15
549	Todd Linden	.25
550	Byung-Hyun Kim	.15
551	Rickie Weeks	2.00
552	Jason Roach	.25
553	Oscar Villarreal	.25
554	Justin Duchscherer	.15
555	Chris Capuano	.15
556	Josh Hall	.15
557	Luis Matos	.15
558	Miguel Ojeda	.15
559	Kevin Ohme	.15
560	Julio Manon	.15
561	Kevin Correia	.15
562	Delmon Young	2.00
563	Aaron Boone	.15
564	Aaron Looper	.15
565	Mike Neu	.15
566	Aquilino Lopez	.15
567	Jhonny Peralta	.25
568	Duaner Sanchez	.15
569	Stephen Randolph	.15
570	Nate Bland	.15
571	Chin-Hui Tsao	.15
572	Michel Hernandez	.15
573	Rocco Baldelli	.15
574	Robb Quinlan	.15
575	Aaron Heilman	.15
576	Jae Weong Seo	.15
577	Joe Borowski	.15
578	Chris Bootcheck	.15
579	Michael Ryan	.15
580	Mark Malaska	.15
581	Jose Guillen	.25
582	Josh Towers	.15
583	Tom Gregorio	.15
584	Edwin Jackson	.15
585	Jason Anderson	.15
586	Jose Reyes	1.00
587	Miguel Cabrera	1.00
588	Nate Bump	.15
589	Jeromy Burnitz	.15
590	David Ross	.15
591	Chase Utley	1.50
592	Brandon Webb	1.00
593	Masao Kida	.15
594	Jimmy Journell	.15
595	Eric Young	.15
596	Tony Womack	.15
597	Amaury Telemaco	.15
598	Rickey Henderson	.50
599	Esteban Loaiza	.15
600	Sidney Ponson	.15

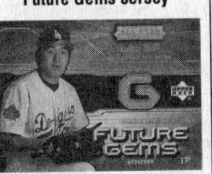

1-90 inserted 1:6		
91-120 inserted 1:48		

Gold Honors

Gold (1-90):	5-10X
Gold (91-120):	1-2X
Production 50 Sets

II-Star Promo e-Card

		NM/M
Common Player:		1.00
Inserted 1:12

CD	Carlos Delgado	1.00
NG	Nomar Garciaparra	2.50
VG	Vladimir Guerrero	1.50
TH	Todd Helton	1.00
AP	Albert Pujols	3.00
AS	Alfonso Soriano	1.00
SS	Sammy Sosa	2.50
IS	Ichiro Suzuki	2.50
AR	Alex Rodriguez	3.00

Class of 2004 Autograph

		NM/M
Quantity produced listed

MC	Miguel Cabrera/50	40.00
KG	Ken Griffey Jr./100	75.00
VG	Vladimir Guerrero/100	40.00
RH	Rich Harden/100	15.00
HM	Hideki Matsui/100	250.00
MP	Mark Prior/100	20.00
JR	Jose Reyes/100	30.00
DW	Dontrelle Willis/100	20.00
BZ	Barry Zito/100	25.00

Dean's List Jersey

		NM/M
Common Player:		4.00
Inserted 1:72

BA	Jeff Bagwell	8.00
HB	Hank Blalock	6.00
JG	Jason Giambi	6.00
GL	Troy Glaus	6.00
LG	Luis Gonzalez	4.00
SG	Shawn Green	4.00
KG	Ken Griffey Jr.	10.00
VG	Vladimir Guerrero	8.00
GM	Greg Maddux	10.00
HM	Hideki Matsui	20.00
HN	Hideo Nomo	8.00
PI	Mike Piazza	8.00
MP	Mark Prior	4.00
AP	Albert Pujols	15.00
AR	Alex Rodriguez	10.00
AS	Alfonso Soriano	8.00
SS	Sammy Sosa	10.00
IS	Ichiro Suzuki	20.00
JT	Jim Thome	6.00
DW	Dontrelle Willis	6.00

Future Gems Jersey

		NM/M
Common Player:		4.00
Inserted 1:72

BA	Josh Bard	4.00
JB	Josh Beckett	8.00
SB	Sean Burroughs	4.00
MC	Mike Cameron	4.00
AE	Adam Eaton	4.00
WE	Willie Eyre	4.00
LF	Lew Ford	4.00
GU	Jeremy Guthrie	4.00
TH	Travis Hafner	6.00
RH	Roy Halladay	6.00
AH	Aaron Heilman	4.00
IS	Kazuhisa Ishii	4.00
JJ	Jason Jennings	4.00
KA	Matt Kata	4.00
MK	Mark Kotsay	4.00
JL	Jon Leicester	4.00
EM	Eric Milton	4.00
JR	Jose Reyes	8.00
RR	Rick Roberts	4.00
PS	Phil Seibel	4.00
BS	Ben Sheets	6.00
MT	Mark Teixeira	4.00
TW	Todd Wellemeyer	4.00
WI	Josh Willingham	4.00

Silver Honors

Silver (1-90):	2-4X
Silver (91-120):	.75-1X

Pick The All-Star MVP

		NM/M
Common Player:		.50
Inserted 1:1

BA	Bobby Abreu	.50
GA	Garret Anderson	.50
JB	Jeff Bagwell	.50
BE	Josh Beckett	.50
CB	Carlos Beltran	.50
HB	Hank Blalock	.50
BO	Bret Boone	.50
OC	Orlando Cabrera	.50
EC	Eric Chavez	.50
BC	Bartolo Colon	.50
JD	Johnny Damon	.50
CD	Carlos Delgado	.50
AD	Adam Dunn	.50
JE	Jim Edmonds	.50
RF	Rafael Furcal	.50
NG	Nomar Garciaparra	1.50
JG	Jason Giambi	.75
MG	Marcus Giles	.50
TG	Troy Glaus	.50
SG	Shawn Green	.50
KG	Ken Griffey Jr.	1.00
VG	Vladimir Guerrero	.75
RH	Roy Halladay	.50
TH	Todd Helton	.50
HU	Tim Hudson	.50
TH	Torii Hunter	.50
DJ	Derek Jeter	2.50
RJ	Randy Johnson	.75
AJ	Andruw Jones	.50
CJ	Chipper Jones	.75
JJ	Jacque Jones	.50
AK	Austin Kearns	.50
JK	Jeff Kent	.50
JL	Javy Lopez	.50
ML	Mike Lowell	.50
PM	Pedro J. Martinez	.75
HM	Hideki Matsui	1.50
MM	Mark Mulder	.75
MU	Mike Mussina	.75
MO	Magglio Ordonez	.50
RP	Rafael Palmeiro	.75
PI	Mike Piazza	1.00
JP	Jorge Posada	.50
MP	Mark Prior	1.00
AP	Albert Pujols	2.00
MR	Manny Ramirez	.75
ER	Edgar Renteria	.50
AR	Alex Rodriguez	2.00
IR	Ivan Rodriguez	.75
SR	Scott Rolen	.75
CS	Curt Schilling	.75
JS	Jason Schmidt	.50
RS	Richie Sexson	.50
GS	Gary Sheffield	.50
AS	Alfonso Soriano	.50
SS	Sammy Sosa	1.50
IS	Ichiro Suzuki	1.50
MS	Mike Sweeney	.50
MT	Mark Teixeira	.50
TE	Miguel Tejada	.50
FT	Frank Thomas	.75
JT	Jim Thome	.75
JV	Jason Varitek	.50
VI	Jose Vidro	.50
VW	Vernon Wells	.50
DW	Dontrelle Willis	.50
PW	Preston Wilson	.50
KW	Kerry Wood	1.00
BZ	Barry Zito	.50

Premium Stars

Complete Set (15):		
Common Player:		

2004 UD Diamond Collection Pro Sigs

		NM/M
Complete Set (1-240):		
Common Player (1-90):		.15
Common SP (91-150):		2.00
Inserted 1:6
Common Auto. (151-240):		5.00
Inserted 1:24
Pack (6): 2.00
Box (24): 40.00

1	Alfonso Soriano	.50
2	Josh Beckett	.50
3	Kerry Wood	.75
4	Brandon Webb	.15
5	Shannon Stewart	.25
6	Larry Walker	.25
7	Tim Hudson	.25
8	Carlos Lee	.25

9	Austin Kearns	.25
10	Vernon Wells	.25
11	Jeff Bagwell	.50
12	Hideo Nomo	.40
13	Jerome Williams	.15
14	Kevin Brown	.25
15	Jose Vidro	.15
16	Rocco Baldelli	.25
17	Frank Thomas	.50
18	Albert Pujols	1.50
19	Bartolo Colon	.25
20	C.C. Sabathia	.15
21	Andruw Jones	.25
22	Reggie Sanders	.15
23	Carlos Beltran	.40
24	Curt Schilling	.50
25	Miguel Tejada	.40
26	Barry Zito	.40
27	Pedro Martinez	.75
28	Sean Burroughs	.25
29	Sammy Sosa	1.50
30	Eric Chavez	.25
31	Roy Halladay	.25
32	Todd Helton	.50
33	Mark Prior	1.00
34	Mike Mussina	.25
35	Alex Rodriguez	2.00
36	Ivan Rodriguez	.25
37	Mike Piazza	1.00
38	Angel Berroa	.15
39	Orlando Cabrera	.25
40	Jim Thome	.75
41	Brian Giles	.25
42	Ichiro Suzuki	1.00
43	Edgar Renteria	.25
44	Eric Gagne	.25
45	Gary Sheffield	.40
46	Torii Hunter	.25
47	Roger Clemens	1.50
48	Scott Rolen	.75
49	Johan Santana	.15
50	Jacque Jones	.15
51	Hank Blalock	.40
52	Rafael Palmeiro	.50
53	Dmitri Young	.15
54	Ryan Klesko	.25
55	Mark Teixeira	.25
56	Nomar Garciaparra	1.50
57	Jose Reyes	.25
58	Vladimir Guerrero	.75
59	Mike Sweeney	.15
60	Jorge Posada	.25
61	Derek Jeter	2.00
62	Milton Bradley	.15
63	Bobby Abreu	.25
64	Greg Maddux	1.00
65	Adam Dunn	.50
66	Troy Glaus	.40
67	Luis Gonzalez	.25
68	Shawn Green	.25
69	Bret Boone	.25
70	Mark Mulder	.25
71	Lance Berkman	.25
72	Preston Wilson	.15
73	Phil Nevin	.15
74	Chipper Jones	.75
75	Garret Anderson	.40
76	Jason Giambi	.75
77	Magglio Ordonez	.25
78	Jeff Kent	.25
79	Richie Sexson	.40
80	Mike Lowell	.25
81	Ben Sheets	.25
82	Randy Johnson	.75
83	Dontrelle Willis	.25
84	Javier Vazquez	.25
85	Geoff Jenkins	.25
86	Manny Ramirez	.50
87	Jim Edmonds	.40
88	Roy Oswalt	.25
89	Edgar Martinez	.25
90	Carlos Delgado	.40
91	Chris Saenz RC	2.00
92	Justin Leone RC	2.00
93	Shawn Hill RC	2.00
94	Chad Bentz RC	4.00
95	Jesse Harper RC	2.00
96	David Crouthers RC	2.00
97	Justin Germano RC	2.00
98	Tim Bausher RC	2.00
99	Greg Dobbs RC	2.00
100	Enemencio Pacheco RC	2.00
101	Dennis Sarfate RC	2.00
102	Edwin Moreno RC	2.00
103	Colby Miller RC	4.00
104	Mike Rouse RC	2.00
105	Fernando Nieve RC	2.00
106	Tim Hamulack RC	2.00
107	Jason Frasor RC	2.00
108	Jose Capellan RC	2.00
109	Jamie Brown RC	2.00
110	Mariano Gomez RC	2.00
111	Mike Vento RC	2.00
112	Josh Labandeira RC	2.00
113	Mike Gosling RC	2.00
114	Shingo Takatsu RC	2.00
115	Justin Hampson RC	2.00
116	Tim Bittner RC	2.00
117	Jerry Gil RC	2.00
118	Carlos Vasquez RC	5.00
119	Lincoln Holdzkom RC	2.00
120	Mike Johnston RC	2.00
121	William Bergolla RC	2.00
122	Luis Gonzalez RC	2.00
123	Ivan Ochoa RC	2.00
124	Roman Colon RC	2.00
125	Renyel Pinto RC	2.00
126	Donnie Kelly RC	2.00

No.	Player	Price
127	Chris Oxspring RC	2.00
128	Sean Henn	2.00
129	Ryan Meaux RC	2.00
130	Shawn Camp RC	2.00
131	Brandon Medders RC	2.00
132	Rusty Tucker RC	2.00
133	Kazuo Matsui RC	4.00
134	Jorge Sequea RC	2.00
135	Hector Gimenez RC	2.00
136	Casey Daigle RC	2.00
137	Ian Snell RC	3.00
138	Scott Dohmann RC	2.00
139	Ronny Cedeno RC	2.00
140	Jorge Vasquez RC	2.00
141	David Aardsma	2.00
142	Carlos Hines RC	2.00
143	Scott Proctor RC	3.00
144	Jerome Gamble RC	2.00
145	Jason Bartlett RC	5.00
146	Akinori Otsuka RC	4.00
147	Merkin Valdez RC	2.00
148	Jake Woods	2.00
149	Chris Aguila RC	2.00
150	John Gall RC	2.00
151	Aaron Miles	10.00
152	Aquilino Lopez	10.00
153	Bill Hall	10.00
154	Billy Traber	15.00
155	Brad Lidge	12.00
156	Brady Clark	10.00
157	Brandon Duckworth	8.00
158	Brett Tomko	6.00
159	Brian Fuentes	6.00
161	Brooks Kieschnick	8.00
162	Carlos Rivera	6.00
163	Chad Cordero	6.00
164	Chad Tracy	10.00
165	Claudio Vargas	5.00
166	D.J. Carrasco	5.00
167	Damian Rolls	6.00
168	David Sanders	5.00
170	Derrick Turnbow	5.00
171	Desi Relaford	5.00
172	Doug Davis	5.00
173	Dustan Mohr	6.00
176	Frank Catalanotto	8.00
178	Franklyn German	5.00
179	Ron Belliard	5.00
180	Geoff Geary	5.00
181	Greg Colbrunn	5.00
182	Henry Mateo	5.00
183	Brent Mayne	5.00
184	Horacio Ramirez	5.00
185	J.C. Romero	5.00
186	J.J. Putz	8.00
187	Ferdin Tejeda	8.00
188	Jaime Cerda	8.00
189	Jason Michaels	5.00
190	Jason Simontacchi	5.00
191	Jay Witasick	5.00
192	Joe Valentine	5.00
193	Joey Eischen	5.00
194	Johnny Estrada	8.00
195	Jon Garland	5.00
196	Jon Switzer	5.00
197	Jorge Julio	5.00
198	Jorge Sosa	8.00
199	Jose Castillo	8.00
200	Jose Macias	5.00
201	Josh Bard	5.00
202	Juan Cruz	5.00
203	Juan Rivera	5.00
204	Ken Griffey Jr.	150.00
205	Kevin Hooper	5.00
206	Kiko Calero RC	5.00
207	Chad Gaudin	5.00
208	Luis Rivas	5.00
209	Mark Corey	5.00
210	Matt Ford	8.00
211	Matt Herges	5.00
212	Miguel Cairo	5.00
213	Fernando Cabrera	5.00
214	Mike MacDougal	5.00
215	Mike Neu	8.00
216	Lew Ford	5.00
217	Mike Wood	8.00
218	Nate Robertson	5.00
219	Nick Punto	5.00
221	Oscar Villarreal	5.00
222	Ramon Vazquez	5.00
223	Randall Simon	5.00
225	Ricky Stone	5.00
229	Ryan Drese	5.00
230	Ryan Ludwick	5.00
231	Scot Shields	5.00
232	Shane Nance	5.00
233	Steve Colyer	5.00
234	Tony Armas	5.00
235	Bobby Hammock	5.00
236	Travis Hafner	8.00
237	Victor Martinez	5.00
238	Wilfredo Ledezma	5.00
239	Willie Bloomquist	5.00
240	Yorvit Torrealba	8.00

Silver
Silver (1-90): 2-3X
Overall odds for parallel 1:6.

Gold
Gold (1-90): 3-6X
Overall odds for parallel 1:6.

Blue Ink Autograph
No Pricing
Production 25 Sets

Red Signature
No Pricing
Production 10 Sets

Hall of Famers
No Pricing

2004 Upper Deck Etchings

	NM/M
Complete Set (150):	
Common Player:	.15
Common SP (91-120):	4.00
Production 2,004	
Common SP Black Auto. (121-150):	8.00
Production 700	
Blue Auto. (121-150):	.75-1.5X
Production 200	
Red Auto. (121-150):	No Pricing
Production 25	
Pack (5):	12.00
Box (12):	120.00

No.	Player	Price
1	Albert Pujols	1.50
2	Torii Hunter	.40
3	Jim Edmonds	.40
4	Alex Rodriguez	1.50
5	Rafael Palmeiro	.50
6	Ken Griffey Jr.	1.00
7	Adam Dunn	.50
8	Andruw Jones	.50
9	Carlos Lee	.15
10	Mike Piazza	1.00
11	Jeff Bagwell	.50
12	Hideki Matsui	1.50
13	Gary Sheffield	.40
14	Edgar Renteria	.40
15	Shawn Green	.25
16	Kerry Wood	.75
17	Ivan Rodriguez	.50
18	Josh Beckett	.40
19	Scott Rolen	.75
20	Brian Giles	.25
21	Derrek Lee	.25
22	Mike Lowell	.25
23	Mike Mussina	.40
24	Sammy Sosa	1.50
25	Brandon Webb	.15
26	Jacque Jones	.15
27	Randy Johnson	1.00
28	Luis Gonzalez	.25
29	Eric Chavez	.25
30	Carlos Delgado	.40
31	Phil Nevin	.15
32	Ichiro Suzuki	1.50
33	Roy Oswalt	.25
34	Tim Hudson	.25
35	Juan Gonzalez	.25
36	Frank Thomas	.50
37	Mark Mulder	.40
38	Mark Teixeira	.40
39	Miguel Tejada	.40
40	Jeff Kent	.25
41	Andy Pettitte	.40
42	Barry Zito	.40
43	Roy Halladay	.25
44	Rocco Baldelli	.25
45	Derek Jeter	2.00
46	Corey Patterson	.40
47	Javy Lopez	.40
48	A.J. Burnett	.25
49	Chipper Jones	.75
50	Curt Schilling	.50
51	Todd Helton	.50
52	Pedro J. Martinez	.75
53	Hideo Nomo	.40
54	Jose Reyes	.50
55	Vernon Wells	.15
56	Geoff Jenkins	.15
57	Troy Glaus	.15
58	Greg Maddux	1.00
59	Jason Schmidt	.40
60	Preston Wilson	.15
61	Miguel Cabrera	.75
62	Hank Blalock	.50
63	Rafael Furcal	.15
64	Vladimir Guerrero	.75
65	Lance Berkman	.15
66	Javier Vazquez	.15
67	Bret Boone	.15
68	Mark Prior	1.00
69	Magglio Ordonez	.25
70	Dontrelle Willis	.25
71	Richie Sexson	.25
72	Alfonso Soriano	.75
73	Edwin Jackson	.15
74	Jose Vidro	.15
75	Jason Giambi	.50
76	Kevin Brown	.25
77	Orlando Cabrera	.15
78	Nomar Garciaparra	1.00
79	Bobby Abreu	.25
80	Manny Ramirez	.50
81	J.D. Drew	.15
82	Roger Clemens	1.50
83	Pat Burrell	.15
84	Ryan Klesko	.15
85	Garret Anderson	.15
86	Johan Santana	.15
87	Kevin Millwood	.25
88	Austin Kearns	.25
89	Jim Thome	.75
90	Carlos Beltran	.25
91	Kazuo Matsui RC	6.00
92	Jamie Brown RC	4.00
93	Brandon Medders RC	4.00
94	Carlos Vasquez RC	4.00
95	Chris Aguila RC	4.00
96	David Aardsma RC	4.00
97	Justin Leone RC	4.00
98	Mike Johnston RC	4.00
99	Tim Bittner RC	4.00
100	Mike Rouse RC	4.00
101	Dennis Sarfate RC	4.00
102	Jason Frasor RC	4.00
103	Jorge Vasquez RC	4.00
104	Mike Gosling RC	4.00
105	Jake Woods RC	4.00
106	Akinori Otsuka RC	6.00
107	Lincoln Holdzkom RC	4.00
108	Jesse Harper RC	4.00
109	Edwin Moreno RC	4.00
110	Shingo Takatsu RC	6.00
111	Ryan Meaux RC	4.00
112	Donnie Kelly RC	4.00
113	Jerome Gamble RC	4.00
114	Josh Labandeira RC	4.00
115	Ian Snell RC	4.00
116	Mike Wuertz RC	4.00
117	Greg Dobbs RC	4.00
118	Sean Henn	4.00
119	David Crouthers RC	4.00
120	Hector Gimenez RC	4.00
121	Renyel Pinto RC	8.00
122	Tim Hamulack RC	8.00
123	Chris Saenz RC	8.00
124	Carlos Hines RC	8.00
125	Justin Knoedler RC	8.00
126	Onil Joseph RC	8.00
127	Ryan Wing	8.00
128	Scott Proctor RC	8.00
129	Rusty Tucker RC	8.00
130	Fernando Nieve RC	8.00
131	Chad Bentz RC	8.00
132	Jerry Gil RC	8.00
133	Mariano Gomez RC	8.00
134	Justin Germano RC	8.00
135	Jason Bartlett RC	12.00
136	Ronald Belisario RC	8.00
137	Enemencio Pacheco	8.00
138	Justin Hampson RC	8.00
139	Michael Vento RC	8.00
140	Merkin Valdez RC	10.00
141	Casey Daigle RC	8.00
142	Eddy Rodriguez RC	8.00
143	William Bergolla RC	8.00
144	Jose Capellan RC	8.00
145	Ronny Cedeno RC	8.00
146	Franklyn Gracesqui RC	8.00
147	Roman Colon RC	8.00
148	Roberto Novoa RC	8.00
149	Ivan Ochoa RC	8.00
150	Shawn Hill RC	8.00

Combo Etchings

	NM/M
Production 5-115	
Gold Foil:	.75-1.5X
Production 1-50	
Silver Foil:	.75-1X
Production 4-50	
No Pricing 15 or less.	

	Player	Price
JB	Josh Beckett/25	60.00
MC	Miguel Cabrera/23	50.00
KG	Ken Griffey Jr./100	80.00
KG1	Ken Griffey Jr./90	80.00
KG2	Ken Griffey Jr./90	80.00
VG	Vladimir Guerrero/60	65.00
DJ1	Derek Jeter/25	200.00
MR	Manny Ramirez/60	65.00
MR1	Manny Ramirez/60	65.00
CR	Cal Ripken Jr./15	250.00
CR1	Cal Ripken Jr./15	250.00
AR	Alex Rodriguez/15	200.00
AR1	Alex Rodriguez/15	200.00
AR2	Alex Rodriguez/115	150.00
KW	Kerry Wood/20	40.00
KW1	Kerry Wood/20	40.00
KW2	Kerry Wood/30	40.00

Dual Etchings

NM/M
Production 150 Sets

	Player	Price
RJ	Alex Rodriguez, Derek Jeter	60.00
WP	Kerry Wood, Mark Prior	25.00
RP	Jose Reyes, Mike Piazza	30.00
PG	Albert Pujols, Vladimir Guerrero	30.00
MM	Hideki Matsui, Kazuo Matsui	40.00
MW	Mickey Mantle, Ted Williams	180.00

Master Etchings
No Pricing
Production One Set

Star Etchings

NM/M
Quantity produced listed

	Player	Price
BA	Bobby Abreu/50	10.00
GA	Garret Anderson/50	10.00
JB	Josh Beckett/50	15.00
CB	Carlos Beltran/50	15.00
HB	Hank Blalock/50	15.00
BB	Bret Boone/50	5.00
MC	Miguel Cabrera/50	30.00
EC	Eric Chavez/50	10.00
JD	J.D. Drew/50	10.00
AD	Adam Dunn/50	25.00
NG	Nomar Garciaparra/15	60.00
KG	Ken Griffey Jr./50	85.00
KG1	Ken Griffey Jr./50	85.00
VG	Vladimir Guerrero/15	80.00
RH	Roy Halladay/50	40.00
TH	Tim Hudson/50	25.00
GJ	Geoff Jenkins/50	10.00
DL	Derrek Lee/50	25.00
JL	Javy Lopez/50	10.00
ML	Mike Lowell/50	15.00
MU	Mark Mulder/50	8.00
MO	Magglio Ordonez/50	15.00
RO	Roy Oswalt/50	25.00
PR	Mark Prior/50	10.00
JS	Jason Schmidt/50	10.00
MT	Mark Teixeira/50	40.00
TE	Miguel Tejada/50	15.00
BW	Brandon Webb/50	15.00
VW	Vernon Wells/50	15.00
DW	Dontrelle Willis/50	12.00
KW	Kerry Wood/50	15.00

Triple Etchings

NM/M
Production 50 Sets

	Players	Price
RJM	Alex Rodriguez, Derek Jeter, Hideki Matsui	125.00
PER	Albert Pujols, Jim Edmonds, Scott Rolen	90.00
SRG	Curt Schilling, Manny Ramirez, Nomar Garciaparra	40.00
SBT	Alfonso Soriano, Hank Blalock, Mark Teixeira	40.00
WPS	Kerry Wood, Mark Prior, Sammy Sosa	50.00
DMW	Joe DiMaggio, Mickey Mantle, Ted Williams	400.00

Etched in Time Black Ink

NM/M
Quantity produced listed
Common Autograph: 6.00

	Player	Price
AA	Alfredo Amezaga/375	6.00
SA	Sparky Anderson/375	15.00
TA	Tony Armas/375	6.00
BA	Dusty Baker/150	15.00
JB	Jason Bay/375	15.00
BE	Carlos Beltran/150	20.00
AB	Angel Berroa/1,325	6.00
HB	Hank Blalock/375	10.00
GB	Geoff Blum/375	6.00
BB	Bert Blyleven/375	8.00
CB	Chris Bootcheck/375	6.00
DB	Dewon Brazelton/375	6.00
MB	Marlon Byrd/1,025	8.00
EB	Eric Byrnes/Redemp.	8.00
MC	Miguel Cabrera/375	15.00
CA	Chris Capuano/375	8.00
EC	Eric Chavez/375	15.00
AC	Alex Cintron/375	8.00
WC	Will Clark/150	20.00
CC	Brandon Claussen/375	8.00
CC	Chad Cordero/375	6.00
BC	Bobby Crosby/1,325	10.00
AD	Andre Dawson/375	10.00
BD	Brandon Duckworth/375	8.00
ME	Morgan Ensberg/1,325	8.00
DE	Dwight Evans/375	15.00
AE	Adam Everett/375	6.00
WE	Willie Eyre/375	6.00
KF	Kyle Farnsworth/1,325	8.00
PF	Pedro Feliz/375	8.00
RF	Rollie Fingers/375	10.00
JF	Josh Fogg/375	8.00
LF	Lew Ford/375	8.00
NG	Nomar Garciaparra/100	50.00
CG	Chad Gaudin/375	8.00
BG	Brian Giles/375	10.00
MG	Marcus Giles/375	10.00
GO	Jonny Gomes/325	8.00
AG	Adrian Gonzalez/325	20.00
DG	Dwight Gooden/375	10.00
KG	Ken Griffey Jr./1,625	60.00
GR	Ken Griffey Sr./375	15.00
TG	Tony Gwynn/150	40.00
SH	Scott Hairston/375	8.00
RH	Rob Hammock/325	8.00
AH	Aaron Harang/375	12.00
HE	Rich Harden/375	8.00
RI	Ramon Hernandez/325	8.00
EJ	Raul Ibanez/375	8.00
DJ	Edwin Jackson/325	8.00
JJ	Derek Jeter/375	100.00
KA	Jacque Jones/375	6.00
MK	Al Kaline/375	25.00
AK	Matt Kata/325	8.00
BK	Adam Kennedy/375	6.00
	Bobby Kielty/1,325	6.00
HK	Harmon Killebrew/Redemp.	35.00
DK	Dave Kingman/375	8.00
GK	Graham Koonce/375	8.00
LA	Adam LaRoche/1,325	8.00
CS	Carlos Lee/325	10.00
LE	Cliff Lee/1,325	12.00
TL	Ted Lilly/325	8.00
AL	Adam Loewen/375	8.00
ML	Mike Lowell/375	10.00
LM	Luis Matos/325	8.00
DM	Don Mattingly/150	50.00
MA	Joe Mauer/375	30.00
JM	Justin Miller/325	8.00
MO	Jack Morris/375	10.00
MM	Mark Mulder/375	8.00
MU	Dale Murphy/375	20.00
MN	Mike Neu/325	6.00
LN	Laynce Nix/Redemp.	8.00
RO	Roy Oswalt/375	12.00
LO	Lyle Overbay/1,325	8.00
PA	Jim Palmer/375	15.00
CP	Corey Patterson/375	8.00
BP	Brad Penny/375	8.00
JP	Jason Phillips/375	8.00
PO	Boog Powell/375	15.00
MP	Mark Prior/100	10.00
JR	Jose Reyes/325	25.00
JI	Jim Rice/375	10.00
CR	Cal Ripken Jr./100	120.00
BR	Brooks Robinson/375	25.00
RS	Ryne Sandberg/375	50.00
SO	Ron Santo/375	25.00
SS	Steve Sax/375	10.00
MS	Mike Scioscia/375	10.00
BS	Ben Sheets/375	15.00
TS	Terrmel Sledge/325	6.00
DS	Darryl Strawberry/150	15.00
MT	Mark Teixeira/325	25.00
LT	Luis Tiant/375	10.00
AT	Alan Trammell/375	15.00
CU	Chase Utley/375	30.00
RW	Ryan Wagner/1,325	8.00
WK	Rickie Weeks/Redemp.	15.00
JW	Jerome Williams/1,325	8.00
WI	Josh Willingham/1,325	10.00
RA	Randy Winn/375	8.00
KW	Kerry Wood/150	10.00
DY	Delmon Young/375	10.00
MY	Michael Young/1,325	15.00
CZ	Carlos Zambrano/375	10.00

Etched in Time Red Ink
No Pricing
Production 25 Sets

Etched in Time Blue Ink

NM/M
Quantity produced listed
Common Autograph: 6.00

	Player	Price
AA	Alfredo Amezaga/375	6.00
SA	Sparky Anderson/375	15.00
TA	Tony Armas/375	6.00
JB	Jason Bay/375	15.00
BE	Carlos Beltran/375	20.00
AB	Angel Berroa/1,325	6.00
HB	Hank Blalock/375	10.00
GB	Geoff Blum/375	6.00
BB	Bert Blyleven/375	8.00
CB	Chris Bootcheck/375	8.00
DB	Dewon Brazelton/375	8.00
MB	Marlon Byrd/375	12.00
EB	Eric Byrnes/Redemp.	8.00
MC	Miguel Cabrera/375	25.00
CA	Chris Capuano/375	8.00
EC	Eric Chavez/375	10.00
AC	Alex Cintron/375	10.00
WC	Will Clark/375	20.00
CL	Brandon Claussen/100	8.00
CC	Chad Cordero/100	6.00
BC	Bobby Crosby/150	6.00
BD	Andre Dawson/250	10.00
BD	Brandon Duckworth/100	8.00
ME	Morgan Ensberg/150	8.00
DE	Dwight Evans/250	15.00
AE	Adam Everett/150	8.00
WE	Willie Eyre/150	6.00
KF	Kyle Farnsworth/150	8.00
PF	Pedro Feliz/150	6.00
RF	Rollie Fingers/250	10.00
JF	Josh Fogg/150	8.00
LF	Lew Ford/250	8.00
NG	Nomar Garciaparra/50	85.00
CG	Chad Gaudin/100	6.00
BG	Brian Giles/250	6.00
MG	Marcus Giles/150	10.00
GO	Jonny Gomes/150	8.00
AG	Adrian Gonzalez/150	20.00
DG	Dwight Gooden/250	15.00
KG	Ken Griffey Jr./150	75.00
GR	Ken Griffey Sr./250	50.00
VG	Vladimir Guerrero/50	50.00
TG	Tony Gwynn/50	50.00
SH	Scott Hairston/100	8.00
RH	Rob Hammock/150	8.00
AH	Aaron Harang/100	10.00
HE	Rich Harden/150	8.00
HE	Ramon Hernandez/150	8.00
RI	Raul Ibanez/150	12.00
EJ	Edwin Jackson/100	8.00
DJ	Derek Jeter/50	120.00
JJ	Jacque Jones/250	10.00
KA	Al Kaline/250	25.00
MK	Matt Kata/150	8.00
AK	Adam Kennedy/100	8.00
BK	Bobby Kielty/150	8.00
DK	Dave Kingman/250	8.00
GK	Graham Koonce/250	8.00
LA	Adam LaRoche/150	8.00
LE	Cliff Lee/150	15.00
TL	Ted Lilly/150	8.00
ML	Mike Lowell/250	10.00
LM	Luis Matos/150	8.00
DM	Don Mattingly/250	60.00
MA	Joe Mauer/250	30.00
JM	Justin Miller/150	8.00
MO	Jack Morris/250	10.00
MM	Mark Mulder/250	10.00
MU	Dale Murphy/250	25.00
MN	Mike Neu/150	8.00
RO	Roy Oswalt/150	15.00
LO	Lyle Overbay/150	8.00
PA	Jim Palmer/250	15.00
CP	Corey Patterson/250	10.00
BP	Brad Penny/100	8.00
JP	Jason Phillips/250	8.00
LP	Lou Piniella/150	15.00
PO	Boog Powell/250	15.00
MP	Mark Prior/50	10.00
JR	Jose Reyes/325	10.00
JI	Jim Rice/250	10.00
CR	Cal Ripken Jr./50	150.00
BR	Brooks Robinson/250	25.00
RS	Ryne Sandberg/50	60.00
SO	Ron Santo/250	25.00
SS	Steve Sax/250	10.00
MS	Mike Scioscia/250	10.00
BS	Ben Sheets/250	15.00
TS	Terrmel Sledge/150	6.00
MT	Mark Teixeira/150	30.00
LT	Luis Tiant/250	10.00
AT	Alan Trammell/150	15.00
CU	Chase Utley/100	40.00
RW	Ryan Wagner/150	8.00
JW	Jerome Williams/150	8.00
WI	Josh Willingham/150	6.00
RA	Randy Winn/150	8.00
KW	Kerry Wood/50	10.00
DY	Delmon Young/250	15.00
MY	Michael Young/150	15.00
CZ	Carlos Zambrano/250	15.00

Game Bat Blue

NM/M
Quantity produced listed
Common Autograph: 6.00

	Player	Price
AA	Alfredo Amezaga/100	8.00
SA	Sparky Anderson/250	15.00
TA	Tony Armas/150	6.00
JB	Jason Bay/250	15.00
HB	Hank Blalock/250	15.00
GB	Geoff Blum/250	6.00
BB	Bert Blyleven/250	8.00
CB	Chris Bootcheck/100	8.00
DB	Dewon Brazelton/250	8.00
MB	Marlon Byrd/150	12.00
EB	Eric Byrnes/Redemp.	8.00
MC	Miguel Cabrera/150	25.00
CA	Chris Capuano/150	8.00
EC	Eric Chavez/150	15.00
WC	Will Clark/150	20.00
CL	Brandon Claussen/100	8.00
CD	Chad Cordero/100	6.00
BD	Bobby Crosby/150	8.00
AD	Andre Dawson/250	15.00
BD	Brandon Duckworth/100	8.00
ME	Morgan Ensberg/150	8.00
DE	Dwight Evans/250	15.00
AE	Adam Everett/150	8.00
WE	Willie Eyre/150	8.00
KF	Kyle Farnsworth/150	8.00
PF	Pedro Feliz/150	8.00
RF	Rollie Fingers/250	10.00
JF	Josh Fogg/150	8.00
LF	Lew Ford/250	8.00
NG	Nomar Garciaparra/50	85.00
JG	Jason Giambi	6.00

Common Player:

Purple:		1X
Production 250		
Red:		1X
Production 150		
Green:		1-2X
Production 50		

	Player	Price
BA	Bobby Abreu	6.00
RA	Roberto Alomar	6.00
GA	Garret Anderson	6.00
CB	Carlos Beltran	6.00
AB	Adrian Beltre	6.00
LB	Lance Berkman	4.00
HB	Hank Blalock	4.00
BB	Bret Boone	4.00
SC	Sean Casey	4.00
EC	Eric Chavez	6.25
JC	Jose Cruz Jr.	4.00
CD	Carlos Delgado	6.00
JD	J.D. Drew	4.00
AD	Adam Dunn	6.00
JE	Jim Edmonds	4.00
CF	Cliff Floyd	4.00
RF	Rafael Furcal	4.00
NG	Nomar Garciaparra	6.00
JG	Jason Giambi	6.00
BG	Brian Giles	6.00
TG	Troy Glaus	6.00
LG	Luis Gonzalez	6.00
SG	Shawn Green	6.00
KG	Ken Griffey Jr.	12.00
VG	Vladimir Guerrero	8.00
TH	Todd Helton	8.00

2004 Upper Deck Etchings (Autographs)

Code	Player	Price
HU	Torii Hunter	6.00
GJ	Geoff Jenkins	6.00
DJ	Derek Jeter	20.00
RJ	Randy Johnson	8.00
AJ	Andruw Jones	8.00
CJ	Chipper Jones	8.00
JL	Javy Lopez	6.00
ML	Mike Lowell	6.00
KM	Kazuo Matsui	4.00
MO	Magglio Ordonez	4.00
RP	Rafael Palmeiro	8.00
JP	Jay Payton	4.00
PI	Mike Piazza	10.00
AP	Albert Pujols	15.00
MR	Manny Ramirez	8.00
JR	Jose Reyes	6.00
AR	Alex Rodriguez	15.00
IR	Ivan Rodriguez	8.00
SR	Scott Rolen	6.00
TS	Tim Salmon	6.00
CS	Curt Schilling	6.00
GS	Gary Sheffield	6.00
AS	Alfonso Soriano	8.00
SS	Sammy Sosa	8.00
IS	Ichiro Suzuki	15.00
MT	Mark Teixeira	6.00
TE	Miguel Tejada	8.00
FT	Frank Thomas	8.00
JT	Jim Thome	8.00
OV	Omar Vizquel	4.00
LW	Larry Walker	4.00
VW	Vernon Wells	4.00
BW	Bernie Williams	6.00
KW	Kerry Wood	6.00

2004 Upper Deck First Pitch

NM/M
Complete Set (300): 40.00
Common Player: .10
Common SP (271-300): 1.00
Inserted 1:4
Pack (5):
Box (36): 25.00

#	Player	Price
1	Dontrelle Willis	.50
2	Edgar Gonzalez	.25
3	Jose Reyes	.50
4	Jae Weong Seo	.25
5	Miguel Cabrera	.75
6	Jesse Foppert	.25
7	Mike Neu	.25
8	Micheal Nakamura	.25
9	Luis Ayala	.25
10	Jared Sandberg	.25
11	Jhonny Peralta	.25
12	Wilfredo Ledezma	.25
13	Jason Roach	.25
14	Kirk Saarloos	.25
15	Cliff Lee	.25
16	Bobby Hill	.25
17	Lyle Overbay	.25
18	Josh Hall	.25
19	Joe Thurston	.25
20	Matt Kata	.25
21	Jeremy Bonderman	.25
22	Julio Manon	.25
23	Rodrigo Rosario	.25
24	Robby Hammock	.25
25	David Sanders	.25
26	Miguel Ojeda	.25
27	Mark Teixeira	.50
28	Franklyn German	.25
29	Ken Harvey	.25
30	Xavier Nady	.25
31	Tim Salmon	.25
32	Troy Glaus	.25
33	Adam Kennedy	.10
34	David Eckstein	.10
35	Bengie Molina	.10
36	Jarrod Washburn	.10
37	Ramon Ortiz	.10
38	Eric Chavez	.25
39	Miguel Tejada	.25
40	Chris Singleton	.10
41	Jermaine Dye	.10
42	John Halama	.10
43	Tim Hudson	.25
44	Barry Zito	.25
45	Ted Lilly	.10
46	Bobby Kielty	.10
47	Kelvim Escobar	.10
48	Josh Phelps	.10
49	Vernon Wells	.20
50	Roy Halladay	.20
51	Orlando Hudson	.10
52	Eric Hinske	.10
53	Brandon Backe	.10
54	Dewon Brazelton	.10
55	Ben Grieve	.10
56	Aubrey Huff	.10
57	Toby Hall	.10
58	Rocco Baldelli	.50
59	Al Martin	.10
60	Brandon Phillips	.10
61	Omar Vizquel	.10
62	C.C. Sabathia	.10
63	Milton Bradley	.10
64	Ricky Gutierrez	.10
65	Matt Lawton	.10
66	Danys Baez	.10
67	Ichiro Suzuki	1.00
68	Randy Winn	.10
69	Carlos Guillen	.10
70	Mark McLemore	.10
71	Dan Wilson	.10
72	Jamie Moyer	.10
73	Joel Pineiro	.10
74	Edgar Martinez	.20
75	Tony Batista	.10
76	Jay Gibbons	.10
77	Jeff Conine	.10
78	Melvin Mora	.10
79	Geronimo Gil	.10
80	Rodrigo Lopez	.10
81	Jorge Julio	.10
82	Rafael Palmeiro	.40
83	Juan Gonzalez	.40
84	Mike Young	.10
85	Alex Rodriguez	1.00
86	Einar Diaz	.10
87	Kevin Mench	.10
88	Hank Blalock	.25
89	Pedro J. Martinez	.50
90	Byung-Hyun Kim	.10
91	Derek Lowe	.20
92	Jason Varitek	.10
93	Manny Ramirez	.40
94	John Burkett	.10
95	Todd Walker	.10
96	Nomar Garciaparra	1.00
97	Trot Nixon	.10
98	Mike Sweeney	.10
99	Carlos Febles	.10
100	Mike MacDougal	.10
101	Raul Ibanez	.10
102	Jason Grimsley	.10
103	Chris George	.10
104	Brent Mayne	.10
105	Dmitri Young	.10
106	Eric Munson	.10
107	A.J. Hinch	.10
108	Andres Torres	.10
109	Bobby Higginson	.10
110	Shane Halter	.10
111	Matt Walbeck	.10
112	Torii Hunter	.25
113	Doug Mientkiewicz	.10
114	Lew Ford	.10
115	Eric Milton	.10
116	Eddie Guardado	.10
117	Cristian Guzman	.10
118	Corey Koskie	.10
119	Magglio Ordonez	.25
120	Mark Buehrle	.10
121	Billy Koch	.10
122	Jose Valentin	.10
123	Paul Konerko	.10
124	Carlos Lee	.10
125	Jon Garland	.10
126	Jason Giambi	.50
127	Derek Jeter	1.50
128	Roger Clemens	1.00
129	Andy Pettitte	.25
130	Jorge Posada	.25
131	David Wells	.10
132	Hideki Matsui	1.25
133	Mike Mussina	.40
134	Jeff Bagwell	.40
135	Craig Biggio	.20
136	Morgan Ensberg	.10
137	Richard Hidalgo	.10
138	Brad Ausmus	.10
139	Roy Oswalt	.10
140	Billy Wagner	.20
141	Octavio Dotel	.10
142	Gary Sheffield	.25
143	Andruw Jones	.40
144	John Smoltz	.20
145	Rafael Furcal	.10
146	Javy Lopez	.25
147	Shane Reynolds	.10
148	Horacio Ramirez	.10
149	Mike Hampton	.10
150	Jung Bong	.10
151	Ruben Quevedo	.10
152	Ben Sheets	.20
153	Geoff Jenkins	.20
154	Royce Clayton	.10
155	Glendon Rusch	.10
156	John Vander Wal	.10
157	Scott Podsednik	.25
158	Jim Edmonds	.25
159	Tino Martinez	.20
160	Albert Pujols	1.00
161	Matt Morris	.10
162	Woody Williams	.10
163	Edgar Renteria	.10
164	Jason Isringhausen	.10
165	Jason Simontacchi	.10
166	Kerry Robinson	.10
167	Sammy Sosa	1.00
168	Joe Borowski	.10
169	Tony Womack	.10
170	Antonio Alfonseca	.10
171	Corey Patterson	.10
172	Mark Prior	.75
173	Moises Alou	.20
174	Matt Clement	.10
175	Randall Simon	.10
176	Randy Johnson	.50
177	Luis Gonzalez	.10
178	Craig Counsell	.10
179	Miguel Batista	.10
180	Steve Finley	.10
181	Brandon Webb	.10
182	Danny Bautista	.10
183	Oscar Villarreal	.10
184	Shawn Green	.10
185	Brian Jordan	.10
186	Fred McGriff	.20
187	Andy Ashby	.10
188	Rickey Henderson	.25
189	Dave Roberts	.10
190	Eric Gagne	.20
191	Kazuhisa Ishii	.10
192	Adrian Beltre	.10
193	Vladimir Guerrero	.50
194	Livan Hernandez	.10
195	Ron Calloway	.10
196	Sun-Woo Kim	.10
197	Wil Cordero	.10
198	Brad Wilkerson	.10
199	Orlando Cabrera	.10
200	Sidney Ponson	.10
201	Ray Durham	.10
202	Andres Galarraga	.10
203	Benito Santiago	.10
204	Jose Cruz Jr.	.10
205	Jason Schmidt	.10
206	Kirk Rueter	.10
207	Felix Rodriguez	.10
208	Mike Lowell	.10
209	Luis Castillo	.10
210	Derrek Lee	.10
211	Andy Fox	.10
212	Tommy Phelps	.10
213	Todd Hollandsworth	.10
214	Brad Penny	.10
215	Juan Pierre	.10
216	Mike Piazza	.75
217	Jae Weong Seo	.10
218	Ty Wigginton	.10
219	Al Leiter	.10
220	Roger Cedeno	.10
221	Timoniel Perez	.10
222	Aaron Heilman	.10
223	Pedro Astacio	.10
224	Joe McEwing	.10
225	Ryan Klesko	.20
226	Brian Giles	.20
227	Mark Kotsay	.10
228	Brian Lawrence	.10
229	Rod Beck	.10
230	Trevor Hoffman	.10
231	Sean Burroughs	.10
232	Bobby Abreu	.20
233	Jim Thome	.50
234	David Bell	.10
235	Jimmy Rollins	.20
236	Mike Lieberthal	.10
237	Vicente Padilla	.10
238	Randy Wolf	.10
239	Reggie Sanders	.10
240	Jason Kendall	.10
241	Jack Wilson	.10
242	Jose Hernandez	.10
243	Kip Wells	.10
244	Carlos Rivera	.10
245	Craig Wilson	.10
246	Adam Dunn	.25
247	Sean Casey	.10
248	Danny Graves	.10
249	Ryan Dempster	.10
250	Barry Larkin	.25
251	Reggie Taylor	.10
252	Wily Mo Pena	.10
253	Larry Walker	.20
254	Mark Sweeney	.10
255	Preston Wilson	.10
256	Jason Jennings	.10
257	Charles Johnson	.10
258	Jay Payton	.10
259	Chris Stynes	.10
260	Juan Uribe	.10
261	Hideki Matsui/CL	.50
262	Josh Beckett/CL	.20
263	Dontrelle Willis/CL	.20
264	Kevin Millwood/CL	.20
265	Billy Wagner/CL	.10
266	Rocco Baldelli/CL	.25
267	Roger Clemens/CL	.50
268	Rafael Palmeiro/CL	.25
269	Miguel Cabrera/CL	.25
270	Jose Contreras/CL	.10
271	Rickie Weeks	3.00
272	Delmon Young	4.00
273	Chien-Ming Wang	1.00
274	Rich Harden	1.00
275	Edwin Jackson	1.00
276	Dan Haren	1.00
277	Todd Wellemeyer	1.00
278	Prentice Redman	1.00
279	Ryan Wagner	1.50
280	Aaron Looper	1.00
281	Rick Roberts	1.00
282	Josh Willingham	1.00
283	David Crouthers	1.00
284	Chris Capuano	1.00
285	Mike Gosling	1.00
286	Brian Sweeney	1.00
287	Donald Kelly RC	1.00
288	Ryan Meaux RC	1.50
289	Colin Porter	1.00
290	Jerome Gamble RC	1.50
291	Colby Miller RC	1.50
292	Ian Ferguson	1.00
293	Tim Bittner RC	1.00
294	Jason Frasor RC	1.00
295	Brandon Medders RC	1.00
296	Mike Johnston RC	1.00
297	Tim Bausher RC	1.00
298	Justin Leone RC	1.00
299	Sean Henn	1.00
300	Michel Hernandez	1.00

First and Foremost

NM/M
Complete Set (14): 40.00
Common Player: 3.00
Inserted 1:Blaster Box

Code	Player	Price
EB	Ernie Banks	5.00
GH	George H.W. Bush	5.00
GW	George W. Bush	5.00
JC	Jose Contreras	3.00
WF	Whitey Ford	4.00
RH	Rich Harden	3.00
DH	Dan Haren	3.00
HR	Horacio Ramirez	3.00
MS	Mike Schmidt	5.00
LT	Luis Tiant	3.00
RW	Ryan Wagner	3.00
BW	Brandon Webb	3.00
JW	Jerome Williams	3.00
DW	Dontrelle Willis	3.00

2004 Upper Deck Holiday Greeting Card

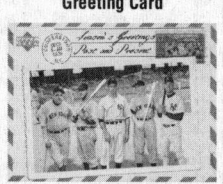

Continuing its tradition of producing a hobby-related greeting card for its customers, UD in 2004 issued a postcard-sized (6-1/4" x 4-5/8") card featuring a composite black-and-white photo of Yankees greats. The red-and-green design on front includes a replica of the 1939 Baseball Centennial stamp and a Cooperstown postmark.

NM/M
HH04 Babe Ruth, Lou Gehrig, Joe DiMaggio, Mickey Mantle, Derek Jeter

2004 Upper Deck Japan Series Souvenir Sheet

It was reported that 200,000 of these 7-1/2" x 10-1/2" souvenir sheets were produced to commemorate the 2004 season opening series in Japan between the Yankees and Devil Rays. Sheets were distributed at the exhibition games played between the MLB and Japanese teams. Some were reportedly given to youngsters at the ESPN Zone in New York City as well. Fronts picture three Yankees, three Devil Rays and a pair of Japanese players. On back is a large ghosted image of Hideki Matsui over which is printed in Japanese addresses and phone numbers of UD outlets. The sheets are not perforated.

NM/M
Uncut Sheet: 15.00

2004 UD Legends Timeless Teams

NM/M
Complete Set (300): 40.00
Common Player: .15
Pack (5): 5.00
Box (18): 75.00

#	Player	Price
1	Bob Gibson	.50
2	Lou Brock	.50
3	Ray Washburn	.15
4	Tim McCarver	.15
5	Harmon Killebrew	1.00
6	Jim Kaat	.25
7	Jim Perry	.15
8	Jim "Mudcat" Grant	.15
9	Boog Powell	.15
10	Brooks Robinson	.50
11	Frank Robinson	.50
12	Jim Palmer	.25
13	Carl Yastrzemski	1.00
14	Jim Lonborg	.15
15	George Scott	.15
16	Sparky Lyle	.15
17	Rico Petrocelli	.15
18	Bob Gibson	.15
19	Julian Javier	.15
20	Lou Brock	.15
21	Orlando Cepeda	.15
22	Ray Washburn	.15
23	Steve Carlton	.50
24	Tim McCarver	.15
25	Al Kaline	.50
26	Bill Freehan	.15
27	Denny McLain	.15
28	Dick McAuliffe	.15
29	Jim Northrup	.15
30	John Hiller	.15
31	Mickey Lolich	.15
32	Mickey Stanley	.15
33	Willie Horton	.15
34	Bob Gibson	.50
35	Julian Javier	.15
36	Lou Brock	.50
37	Orlando Cepeda	.25
38	Steve Carlton	.50
39	Boog Powell	.15
40	Brooks Robinson	.50
41	Davey Johnson	.15
42	Merv Rettenmund	.15
43	Eddie Watt	.15
44	Frank Robinson	.50
45	Jim Palmer	.25
46	Mike Cuellar	.15
47	Paul Blair	.15
48	Pete Richert	.15
49	Ellie Hendricks	.15
50	Billy Williams	.25
51	Randy Hundley	.15
52	Ernie Banks	1.00
53	Fergie Jenkins	.25
54	Jim Hickman	.15
55	Ken Holtzman	.15
56	Ron Santo	.15
57	Ed Kranepool	.15
58	Jerry Koosman	.15
59	Nolan Ryan	2.00
60	Tom Seaver	.50
61	Boog Powell	.15
62	Brooks Robinson	.50
63	Davey Johnson	.15
64	Merv Rettenmund	.15
65	Eddie Watt	.15
66	Frank Robinson	.50
67	Jim Palmer	.25
68	Mike Cuellar	.15
69	Paul Blair	.15
70	Pete Richert	.15
71	Ellie Hendricks	.15
72	Al Kaline	.50
73	Bill Freehan	.15
74	Dick McAuliffe	.15
75	Jim Northrup	.15
76	John Hiller	.15
77	Mickey Lolich	.15
78	Mickey Stanley	.15
79	Willie Horton	.15
80	Bert Campaneris	.15
81	Blue Moon Odom	.15
82	Sal Bando	.15
83	Joe Rudi	.15
84	Ken Holtzman	.15
85	Bill North	.15
86	Blue Moon Odom	.15
87	Gene Tenace	.15
88	Manny Trillo	.15
89	Dick Green	.15
90	Rollie Fingers	.25
91	Sal Bando	.15
92	Vida Blue	.15
93	Bill Buckner	.15
94	Davey Lopes	.15
95	Don Sutton	.25
96	Al Downing	.15
97	Ron Cey	.15
98	Steve Garvey	.15
99	Tommy John	.15
100	Bert Campaneris	.15
101	Bill North	.15
102	Joe Rudi	.15
103	Sal Bando	.15
104	Vida Blue	.15
105	Carl Yastrzemski	.75
106	Carlton Fisk	.25
107	Cecil Cooper	.15
108	Dwight Evans	.15
109	Fred Lynn	.15
110	Jim Rice	.25
111	Luis Tiant	.15
112	Rick Burleson	.15
113	Rico Petrocelli	.15
114	Pedro Borbon	.15
115	Dave Concepcion	.15
116	Don Gullett	.15
117	George Foster	.15
118	Joe Morgan	.25
119	Johnny Bench	.50
120	Rawly Eastwick	.15
121	Sparky Anderson	.15
122	Tony Perez	.25
123	Billy Williams	.15
124	Gene Tenace	.15
125	Jim Perry	.15
126	Vida Blue	.15
127	Pedro Borbon	.15
128	Dave Concepcion	.15
129	Don Gullett	.15
130	George Foster	.15
131	Joe Morgan	.25
132	Johnny Bench	.15
133	Ken Griffey Sr.	.15
134	Rawly Eastwick	.15
135	Tony Perez	.25
136	Bill Russell	.15
137	Burt Hooton	.15
138	Davey Lopes	.15
139	Don Sutton	.15
140	Dusty Baker	.15
141	Steve Yeager	.15
142	Ron Cey	.15
143	Steve Garvey	.15
144	Tommy John	.15
145	Bucky Dent	.15
146	Chris Chambliss	.15
147	Ed Figueroa	.15
148	Graig Nettles	.15
149	Lou Piniella	.15
150	Roy White	.15
151	Don Gullett	.15
152	Sparky Lyle	.15
153	Brian Doyle	.15
154	Bucky Dent	.15
155	Chris Chambliss	.15
156	Ed Figueroa	.15
157	Graig Nettles	.15
158	Lou Piniella	.25
159	Roy White	.15
160	Rich "Goose" Gossage	.15
161	Sparky Lyle	.15
162	Bobby Grich	.15
163	Brian Downing	.15
164	Dan Ford	.15
165	Nolan Ryan	2.00
166	Dave Concepcion	.15
167	George Foster	.15
168	Johnny Bench	.50
169	Ray Knight	.15
170	Tom Seaver	.50
171	Bert Blyleven	.15
172	Bill Madlock	.15
173	Dave Parker	.25
174	Phil Garner	.15
175	Bill Russell	.15
176	Steve Yeager	.15
177	Don Sutton	.25
178	Dusty Baker	.25
179	Jerry Reuss	.15
180	Mickey Hatcher	.15
181	Pedro Guerrero	.15
182	Ron Cey	.15
183	Steve Garvey	.15
184	Rudy May	.15
185	Brian Doyle	.15
186	Bucky Dent	.15
187	Jim Kaat	.15
188	Lou Piniella	.15
189	Luis Tiant	.15
190	Bake McBride	.15
191	Bob Boone	.15
192	Dickie Noles	.15
193	Manny Trillo	.15
194	Mike Schmidt	1.00
195	Sparky Lyle	.15
196	Steve Carlton	.50
197	Steve Yeager	.15
198	Burt Hooton	.15
199	Dusty Baker	.15
200	Jerry Reuss	.15
201	Mike Scioscia	.15
202	Pedro Guerrero	.15
203	Ron Cey	.15
204	Steve Garvey	.15
205	Alejandro Pena	.15
206	Steve Sax	.15
207	Cecil Cooper	.15
208	Gorman Thomas	.15
209	Paul Molitor	.50
210	Robin Yount	.25
211	Rollie Fingers	.25
212	Don Money	.15
213	Rudy May	.15
214	Bucky Dent	.15
215	Dave Winfield	.15
216	Lou Piniella	.15
217	Rich "Goose" Gossage	.15
218	Tommy John	.15
219	Tommy John	.15

#	Player	Price
220	Cecil Cooper	.15
221	Gorman Thomas	.15
222	Paul Molitor	.50
223	Robin Yount	1.00
224	Don Money	.15
225	Cal Ripken Jr.	2.00
226	Dan Ford	.15
227	Jim Palmer	.25
228	John Shelby	.15
229	Alan Trammell	.25
230	Chet Lemon	.15
231	Howard Johnson	.15
232	Jack Morris	.15
233	Kirk Gibson	.25
234	Lou Whitaker	.15
235	Sparky Anderson	.15
236	Dave Winfield	.50
237	Don Mattingly	1.00
238	Ken Griffey Sr.	.15
239	Phil Niekro	.15
240	Yogi Berra	.75
241	Bill Buckner	.15
242	Bruce Hurst	.15
243	Dave Henderson	.15
244	Dwight Evans	.15
245	Jim Rice	.15
246	Tom Seaver	.50
247	Wade Boggs	.50
248	Bob Boone	.15
249	Bobby Grich	.15
250	Brian Downing	.15
251	Don Sutton	.25
252	Terry Forster	.15
253	Rick Burleson	.15
254	Wally Joyner	.15
255	Darryl Strawberry	.15
256	Dwight Gooden	.15
257	Gary Carter	.15
258	Jesse Orosco	.15
259	Keith Hernandez	.15
260	Lenny Dykstra	.15
261	Mookie Wilson	.15
262	Ray Knight	.15
263	Wally Backman	.15
264	Sid Fernandez	.15
265	Alan Trammell	.25
266	Dan Petry	.15
267	Chet Lemon	.15
268	Sparky Anderson	.15
269	Jack Morris	.15
270	Kirk Gibson	.15
271	Lou Whitaker	.15
272	Bert Blyleven	.15
273	Kent Hrbek	.15
274	Kirby Puckett	.75
275	Alejandro Pena	.15
276	Jesse Orosco	.15
277	John Shelby	.15
278	Kirk Gibson	.15
279	Mickey Hatcher	.15
280	Mike Scioscia	.15
281	Steve Sax	.15
282	Darryl Strawberry	.15
283	Dwight Gooden	.15
284	Gary Carter	.15
285	Howard Johnson	.15
286	Keith Hernandez	.15
287	Lenny Dykstra	.15
288	Mookie Wilson	.15
289	Wally Backman	.15
290	Sid Fernandez	.15
291	Jack Morris	.15
292	Kent Hrbek	.15
293	Kirby Puckett	.75
294	Dave Winfield	.50
295	Jack Morris	.15
296	Joe Carter	.15
297	Don Mattingly	1.00
298	Paul O'Neill	.15
299	Jack McDowell	.15
300	Wade Boggs	.50

Gold
No Pricing
Production Five Sets

Autographs

		NM/M
Common Autograph:		10.00
Golds:		No Pricing
Production Five Sets		
Platinum:		No Pricing
Production One Set		
2	Lou Brock MM/SP/75	20.00
3	Ray Washburn	10.00
4	Tim McCarver	15.00
5	Harmon Killebrew	40.00
6	Jim Kaat	10.00

#	Player	Price
7	Jim Perry	12.00
9	Boog Powell	10.00
10	Brooks Robinson	35.00
12	Jim Palmer/SP	20.00
13	Carl Yastrzemski/SP/25	80.00
14	Jim Lonborg	10.00
15	George Scott	10.00
16	Sparky Lyle	10.00
17	Rico Petrocelli	10.00
18	Bob Gibson/SP/35	40.00
19	Julian Javier	10.00
20	Lou Brock/SP/60	20.00
21	Orlando Cepeda/SP/50	20.00
22	Ray Washburn	10.00
24	Tim McCarver	12.00
25	Al Kaline	25.00
26	Bill Freehan	10.00
27	Denny McLain	20.00
28	Dick McAuliffe	10.00
29	Jim Northrup	15.00
30	John Hiller	10.00
31	Mickey Lolich	15.00
32	Mickey Stanley	10.00
33	Willie Horton	10.00
35	Julian Javier	10.00
36	Lou Brock/SP/50	20.00
38	Steve Carlton/SP/35	30.00
39	Boog Powell	10.00
40	Brooks Robinson/SP/100	40.00
41	Davey Johnson	10.00
42	Merv Rettenmund	10.00
43	Eddie Watt	10.00
46	Mike Cuellar	10.00
47	Paul Blair	10.00
48	Pete Richert	10.00
49	Ellie Hendricks	10.00
50	Billy Williams/SP/75	25.00
51	Randy Hundley	10.00
53	Fergie Jenkins	15.00
54	Jim Hickman	20.00
55	Ken Holtzman	15.00
56	Ron Santo	25.00
57	Ed Kranepool	10.00
58	Jerry Koosman	15.00
59	Nolan Ryan/SP/50	175.00
60	Tom Seaver/SP/50	50.00
61	Boog Powell	12.00
62	Brooks Robinson/SP/35	50.00
63	Davey Johnson	10.00
64	Merv Rettenmund	10.00
65	Eddie Watt	10.00
66	Frank Robinson/SP/50	30.00
67	Jim Palmer/SP/75	30.00
68	Mike Cuellar	12.00
69	Paul Blair	10.00
70	Pete Richert	10.00
71	Ellie Hendricks	10.00
72	Al Kaline	25.00
73	Bill Freehan	10.00
74	Dick McAuliffe	15.00
75	Jim Northrup	15.00
76	John Hiller	10.00
77	Mickey Lolich	15.00
78	Mickey Stanley	10.00
79	Willie Horton	12.00
80	Bert Campaneris	10.00
81	Blue Moon Odom	15.00
82	Sal Bando/Exch.	10.00
83	Joe Rudi	10.00
84	Ken Holtzman	10.00
85	Bill North	10.00
86	Blue Moon Odom	15.00
87	Gene Tenace	10.00
88	Manny Trillo	15.00
89	Dick Green	10.00
90	Rollie Fingers	15.00
91	Sal Bando	10.00
92	Blue Moon	10.00
93	Bill Buckner	15.00
94	Davey Lopes	10.00
95	Don Sutton	15.00
96	Al Downing MM	10.00
100	Bert Campaneris	10.00
101	Bill North	10.00
102	Joe Rudi	10.00
103	Sal Bando	10.00
104	Vida Blue/SP/100	15.00
105	Carl Yastrzemski/SP/50	60.00
106	Carlton Fisk/SP/100	30.00
107	Cecil Cooper/SP/75	15.00
108	Dwight Evans/SP/75	15.00
109	Fred Lynn	10.00
110	Jim Rice/SP/100/Exch.	20.00
111	Luis Tiant/Exch.	10.00
112	Rick Burleson	10.00
113	Rico Petrocelli	10.00
114	Pedro Borbon	10.00
115	Dave Concepcion/Exch.	10.00
116	Don Gullett	10.00
117	George Foster/SP/50	15.00
119	Johnny Bench/SP/85	50.00
120	Rawly Eastwick	10.00
121	Sparky Anderson	10.00
122	Tony Perez	30.00
123	Billy Williams/SP/50	10.00
124	Gene Tenace	10.00
125	Jim Perry	10.00
126	Vida Blue/SP/75	20.00
127	Pedro Borbon	10.00
128	Dave Concepcion/Exch.	10.00
129	Don Gullett	15.00
132	Ken Griffey Sr.	10.00
133	Ken Griffey Sr.	10.00
134	Rawly Eastwick	10.00
135	Tony Perez	30.00
136	Bill Russell	10.00
137	Burt Hooton	10.00
138	Davey Lopes	10.00

#	Player	Price
139	Don Sutton	15.00
140	Dusty Baker/Exch.	15.00
141	Steve Yeager/SP/75/Exch.	10.00
144	Tommy John/SP/35	15.00
145	Bucky Dent/SP/75	15.00
146	Chris Chambliss	15.00
147	Ed Figueroa	10.00
148	Graig Nettles	15.00
150	Roy White	15.00
151	Don Gullett	15.00
152	Sparky Lyle	15.00
153	Brian Doyle	15.00
155	Chris Chambliss	15.00
156	Ed Figueroa	10.00
157	Graig Nettles	15.00
159	Roy White	10.00
160	Rich "Goose" Gossage	15.00
161	Sparky Lyle	15.00
162	Bobby Grich	10.00
163	Brian Downing	10.00
164	Dan Ford	10.00
166	Dave Concepcion/SP/75/Exch.	10.00
169	Ray Knight	10.00
171	Bert Blyleven	15.00
172	Bill Madlock	10.00
173	Dave Parker	12.00
174	Phil Garner	10.00
175	Bill Russell	10.00
176	Steve Yeager	10.00
177	Don Sutton/SP/50	25.00
178	Dusty Baker	10.00
179	Jerry Reuss	10.00
180	Mickey Hatcher	10.00
181	Pedro Guerrero	10.00
182	Ron Cey/SP/50	15.00
183	Steve Garvey/SP/50	15.00
184	Rudy May	10.00
185	Brian Doyle	10.00
186	Bucky Dent/SP/60	15.00
187	Jim Kaat	10.00
188	Lou Piniella/SP/50	15.00
189	Luis Tiant	10.00
190	Tommy John/SP/50	10.00
191	Bake McBride	10.00
192	Bob Boone	10.00
193	Dickie Noles	10.00
194	Manny Trillo	10.00
195	Mike Schmidt/SP/50	75.00
196	Sparky Lyle	10.00
197	Steve Carlton/SP/50	20.00
198	Steve Yeager	10.00
199	Burt Hooton	10.00
200	Dusty Baker/Exch.	15.00
201	Jerry Reuss	10.00
202	Mike Scioscia	10.00
203	Pedro Guerrero	10.00
204	Ron Cey/SP/75	10.00
205	Steve Garvey/SP/75	15.00
206	Alejandro Pena	10.00
207	Steve Sax/SP/100	10.00
208	Cecil Cooper/SP/85	15.00
209	Gorman Thomas/Exch.	10.00
212	Rollie Fingers	10.00
213	Don Money	10.00
214	Rudy May	10.00
216	Dave Winfield/SP/50	30.00
217	Lou Piniella/SP/75	15.00
218	Rich "Goose" Gossage	15.00
219	Tommy John/SP/75	10.00
220	Cecil Cooper	10.00
221	Gorman Thomas/Exch.	10.00
222	Paul Molitor/SP/50	45.00
223	Robin Yount/SP/50	75.00
224	Don Money	10.00
225	Cal Ripken Jr./SP/50	180.00
226	Dan Ford	10.00
228	John Shelby	10.00
229	Alan Trammell	15.00
230	Chet Lemon	10.00
231	Howard Johnson	15.00
232	Jack Morris/SP/35	15.00
233	Kirk Gibson	15.00
234	Lou Whitaker/SP/100	15.00
235	Sparky Anderson	10.00
237	Don Mattingly/SP/50	60.00
238	Ken Griffey Sr.	15.00
239	Phil Niekro	15.00
240	Yogi Berra/SP/47	50.00
241	Bill Buckner	10.00
242	Bruce Hurst	15.00
243	Dave Henderson	10.00
245	Jim Rice/SP/75/Exch.	20.00
247	Wade Boggs/SP/50	30.00
248	Bob Boone	10.00
249	Bobby Grich	10.00
250	Brian Downing	10.00
251	Don Sutton/SP/75	15.00
252	Terry Forster	10.00
253	Rick Burleson	10.00
254	Wally Joyner	10.00
255	Darryl Strawberry	15.00
256	Dwight Gooden	15.00
257	Gary Carter/SP/75	20.00
258	Jesse Orosco	10.00
259	Keith Hernandez	15.00
260	Lenny Dykstra	15.00
261	Mookie Wilson	10.00
262	Ray Knight	10.00
263	Wally Backman	10.00
264	Sid Fernandez/Exch.	10.00
265	Alan Trammell	15.00
266	Dan Petry	10.00
267	Chet Lemon	10.00
268	Sparky Anderson	10.00
270	Kirk Gibson	15.00
271	Lou Whitaker/SP/50	20.00

#	Player	Price
272	Bert Blyleven	10.00
273	Kent Hrbek	15.00
275	Alejandro Pena	10.00
276	Jesse Orosco	10.00
277	John Shelby	10.00
278	Kirk Gibson/SP/50	20.00
279	Mickey Hatcher	10.00
280	Mike Scioscia	10.00
281	Steve Sax	10.00
282	Darryl Strawberry	15.00
283	Dwight Gooden	10.00
284	Gary Carter/SP/50	20.00
285	Howard Johnson	10.00
286	Keith Hernandez	15.00
287	Lenny Dykstra	10.00
288	Mookie Wilson	10.00
289	Wally Backman	10.00
290	Sid Fernandez/Exch.	10.00
291	Jack Morris/SP/50	15.00
292	Kent Hrbek	15.00
293	Kirby Puckett/SP/50	50.00
294	Dave Winfield/SP/35	35.00
295	Jack Morris/SP/75	15.00
298	Paul O'Neill	40.00
299	Jack McDowell	10.00
300	Wade Boggs/SP/75	25.00

Legendary Combo Signs.
No Pricing

Legendary Combo Cuts
No Pricing

Legendary Sign. Dual
NM/M
Quantity produced listed

	Players	Price
BC	Lou Brock, Orlando Cepeda/75	40.00
BJ	Lou Brock, Julian Javier/150	25.00
BM	Wade Boggs, Don Mattingly/50	140.00
BO	Vida Blue, Blue Moon Odom/150	25.00
BW	Ernie Banks, Billy Williams/25	100.00
CB	Steve Carlton, Bret Boone/150	50.00
CG	Ron Cey, Steve Garvey/150	40.00
CH	Gary Carter, Keith Hernandez/150	30.00
CM	Dave Concepcion, Joe Morgan/75 Exch	35.00
DD	Bucky Dent, Brian Doyle/150	25.00
FR	Fred Lynn, Jim Rice/50	40.00
GA	Kirk Gibson, Sparky Anderson/150	40.00
GB	Bob Gibson, Lou Brock/50	75.00
GC	Dwight Gooden, Gary Carter/150	30.00
GL	Rich "Goose" Gossage, Sparky Lyle/150 Exch	25.00
HJ	Ken Holtzman, Fergie Jenkins/150	40.00
HK	Keith Hernandez, Ray Knight/150	30.00
JH	Fergie Jenkins, Randy Hundley/150	40.00
JS	Tommy John, Don Sutton/150	25.00
KH	Al Kaline, Willie Horton/150	40.00
KK	Harmon Killebrew, Jim Kaat/150	50.00
LM	Mickey Lolich, Denny McLain/75	60.00
MB	Joe Morgan, Johnny Bench/25	80.00
MF	Denny McLain, Bill Freehan/150	40.00
NC	Graig Nettles, Chris Chambliss/150	30.00
OM	Paul O'Neill, Don Mattingly/75	140.00
PC	Jim Palmer, Mike Cuellar/150	30.00
PF	Tony Perez, George Foster/150	40.00
PH	Kirby Puckett, Kent Hrbek/150	65.00
PN	Lou Piniella, Graig Nettles/150	30.00
PR	Jim Palmer, Merv Rettenmund/150	35.00
RL	Bill Russell, Davey Lopes/150	30.00
RR	Brooks Robinson, Frank Robinson/50	70.00
RS	Nolan Ryan, Tom Seaver/25	250.00
SD	Steve Garvey, Davey Lopes/150	25.00
SG	Darryl Strawberry, Dwight Gooden/150	40.00
SY	Don Sutton, Steve Yeager/150	30.00
TF	Luis Tiant, Carlton Fisk/50	45.00
TM	Gorman Thomas, Paul Molitor/150 Exch	35.00
WB	Mookie Wilson, Bill Buckner/150	30.00
WT	Lou Whitaker, Alan Trammell/75	75.00
YM	Robin Yount, Paul Molitor/50	120.00
YP	Carl Yastrzemski, Rico Petrocelli/50	75.00

Legendary Sign. Triple
NM/M
Quantity produced listed

	Players	Price
BCM	Johnny Bench, Dave Concepcion, Joe Morgan/25 Exch	100.00
BOM	Wade Boggs, Paul O'Neill, Don Mattingly/50	150.00
BRB	Sal Bando, Joe Rudi, Vida Blue/75	50.00
BSW	Ernie Banks, Ron Santo, Billy Williams/5	140.00
CDK	Gary Carter, Lenny Dykstra, Ray Knight/75	75.00
CND	Chris Chambliss, Graig Nettles, Bucky Dent/50	50.00
ERL	Dwight Evans, Jim Rice, Fred Lynn/50	125.00
GBC	Steve Garvey, Dusty Baker, Ron Cey/50	
GBM	Bob Gibson, Lou Brock, Tim McCarver/25	175.00
GDR	Bobby Grich, Al Downing, Nolan Ryan/25	175.00
GHS	Kirk Gibson, Mickey Hatcher, Mike Scioscia/5	
GMP	Phil Garner, Bill Madlock, Dave Parker/50	75.00
HHS	Jim Hickman, Ken Holtzman, Ron Santo/75	60.00
HSJ	Burt Hooton, Don Sutton, Tommy John/50	50.00
JHH	Fergie Jenkins, Randy Hundley, Ken Holtzman/75	50.00
KKP	Harmon Killebrew, Jim Kaat, Jim Perry/50	65.00
KPG	Jim Kaat, Jim Perry, Jim "Mudcat" Grant/75 Exch	40.00
KSR	Jerry Koosman, Tom Seaver, Nolan Ryan/25	250.00
MHP	Jack Morris, Kent Hrbek, Kirby Puckett/100	100.00
MLF	Denny McLain, Mickey Lolich, Bill Freehan/50	75.00
NKH	Jim Northrup, Al Kaline, Willie Horton/65	65.00
PBH	Kirby Puckett, Bert Blyleven, Kent Hrbek/90	90.00
PCR	Jim Palmer, Mike Cuellar, Pete Richert/75	45.00
PPW	Jim Palmer, Boog Powell, Earl Weaver/50	60.00
RPR	Frank Robinson, Boog Powell, Brooks Robinson/50	80.00
RWP	Cal Ripken Jr., Earl Weaver, Jim Palmer/25	250.00
SCB	Mike Schmidt, Steve Carlton, Bob Boone/50	125.00
SGS	Steve Sax, Pedro Guerrero, Mike Scioscia/75	60.00
TWA	Alan Trammell, Lou Whitaker, Sparky Anderson/75	75.00
YCT	Robin Yount, Cecil Cooper, Gorman Thomas/50 Exch	120.00
YFT	Carl Yastrzemski, Carlton Fisk, Luis Tiant/25	140.00
YMT	Robin Yount, Paul Molitor, Gorman Thomas/75 Exch	140.00

Team Terrific GU Brand Logo
NM/M
Quantity produced listed

	Team	Price
BO	Baltimore Orioles/35	90.00
BR	Boston Red Sox/35	
CR	Cincinnati Reds/35	80.00
LD	Los Angeles Dodgers/35	
MB	Milwaukee Brewers/41	50.00
NM	New York Mets/35	50.00
OA	Oakland A's/39	
SC	St. Louis Cardinals/35	75.00

Team Terrific GU Hat Logo
NM/M
Quantity produced listed

	Team	Price
BO	Baltimore Orioles/50	90.00
BR	Boston Red Sox/50	80.00
CR	Cincinnati Reds/50	80.00
LD	Los Angeles Dodgers/50	
MB	Milwaukee Brewers/82	40.00
NM	New York Mets/50	50.00
OA	Oakland A's/50	40.00
SC	St. Louis Cardinals/50	75.00

Team Terrific GU League
No Pricing
Production 15 Sets

Team Terrific GU Stats
No Pricing
Production 1-5

Team Terrific GU Team Logo
NM/M
Quantity produced listed

	Team	Price
BO	Baltimore Orioles/85	60.00
BR	Boston Red Sox/85	50.00
CR	Cincinnati Reds/85	75.00
LD	Los Angeles Dodgers/85	
MB	Milwaukee Brewers/100	30.00
NM	New York Mets/85	30.00
OA	Oakland A's/100	
SC	St. Louis Cardinals/100	50.00

2004 Upper Deck National Trading Card Day

As part of its participation in NTCD on April 3, Upper Deck issued a 15-card foil pack with four baseball player cards, two each football and hockey, three basketball and four golf, plus a header. Only the baseball players are listed here. Fronts have action photos on a ghosted background; backs have recent stats, a photo detail and biographical data. The NTCD logo appears on front in silver foil.

	NM/M
Unopened Pack:	4.00
Common Player:	.25
UD-2 Hideki Matsui	.50
UD-3 Ichiro	.50
UD-5 Ken Griffey Jr.	.25
UD-12 Sammy Sosa	.25

2004 Upper Deck National VIP

Persons purchasing a VIP admission package at the 2004 National Sports Collectors Convention in Cleveland received a cello-wrapped pack of five UV-coated cards with silver-foil stamping on front. Only one baseball player was included.

	NM/M
Complete Set (5):	12.00
VIP3 Derek Jeter	3.00

2004 Upper Deck Play Ball Promos

Each July 2004 newsstand issue of Tuff Stuff magazine included a Play Ball promo card inside its poly bag. The cards differ from the issued version only in the appearance on front of a silver-foil

"UD PROMO" notation. It is not known how many different players cards were used in the promotion.
Common Player:
Stars: 1.5-2.5X

2004 Upper Deck Play Ball

NM/M
Complete Set (183):
Common Player: .15
Common SP (133-162): 3.00
Production 2,004
Common Classic Combo
(163-183): 2.00
Production 1,999
Pack (5): 3.00
Box (24): 65.00

1	Hideo Nomo	.25
2	Curt Schilling	.50
3	Barry Zito	.40
4	Nomar Garciaparra	1.50
5	Yogi Berra	.50
6	Randy Johnson	.75
7	Jason Giambi	.75
8	Sammy Sosa	1.25
9	David Ortiz	.40
10	Derek Jeter	2.00
11	Warren Spahn	.50
12	Mark Prior	1.00
13	Roger Clemens	1.50
14	Mike Piazza	1.00
15	Nolan Ryan	2.00
16	Joe DiMaggio	1.50
17	Alfonso Soriano	.75
18	Brandon Webb	.25
19	Shawn Green	.25
20	Bob Feller	.25
21	Mike Schmidt	.75
22	Mark Teixeira	.25
23	Pedro J. Martinez	.75
24	Vladimir Guerrero	.75
25	Rafael Furcal	.25
26	Derek Lee	.25
27	Carlos Delgado	.50
28	Mickey Mantle	3.00
29	Dontrelle Willis	.25
30	Ted Williams	1.50
31	Vernon Wells	.25
32	Alex Rodriguez	1.50
33	Brooks Robinson	.50
34	Tom Seaver	.50
35	Ernie Banks	.50
36	Bob Gibson	.50
37	Jim Thome	.75
38	Mike Mussina	.50
39	Eric Chavez	.25
40	Roy Halladay	.25
41	Eric Gagne	.40
42	Jose Reyes	.40
43	Jeff Bagwell	.50
44	Rich Harden	.15
45	Jeff Kent	.25
46	Lance Berkman	.25
47	Adam Dunn	.40
48	Richie Sexson	.40
49	Andruw Jones	.50
50	Ichiro Suzuki	1.25
51	Edgar Renteria	.25
52	Rocco Baldelli	.25
53	Jim Edmonds	.25
54	Magglio Ordonez	.25
55	Austin Kearns	.25
56	Garret Anderson	.40
57	Manny Ramirez	.50
58	Roy Oswalt	.25
59	Gary Sheffield	.40
60	Mark Mulder	.25
61	Ben Sheets	.25
62	Scott Rolen	.75
63	Greg Maddux	1.00
64	Jose Contreras	.15
65	Miguel Cabrera	.50
66	Hank Blalock	.40
67	Miguel Tejada	.40
68	Albert Pujols	1.50
69	Hideki Matsui	1.50
70	Mike Lowell	.25
71	Tim Hudson	.25
72	Bret Boone	.25
73	Ivan Rodriguez	.50
74	Josh Beckett	.50
75	Todd Helton	.50
76	Brian Giles	.25
77	Orlando Cabrera	.15
78	Carlos Beltran	.40
79	Jason Schmidt	.25
80	Kerry Wood	.75

81	Preston Wilson	.15
82	Troy Glaus	.40
83	Kevin Brown	.25
84	Rafael Palmeiro	.50
85	Chipper Jones	1.00
86	Reggie Sanders	.15
87	Cliff Floyd	.15
88	Corey Patterson	.25
89	Kevin Millwood	.25
90	Aaron Boone	.15
91	Darin Erstad	.25
92	Richard Hidalgo	.15
93	Dmitri Young	.15
94	Jeremy Bonderman	.15
95	Larry Walker	.25
96	Edgar Martinez	.25
97	Jerome Williams	.15
98	Luis Gonzalez	.25
99	Roberto Alomar	.40
100	Jerry Hairston Jr.	.15
101	Luis Matos	.15
102	Andy Pettitte	.40
103	Frank Thomas	.50
104	Rondell White	.25
105	Jody Gerut	.15
106	Bartolo Colon	.25
107	Johnny Damon	.25
108	Ryan Klesko	.25
109	Geoff Jenkins	.25
110	Jorge Posada	.40
111	Melvin Mora	.15
112	Bernie Williams	.40
113	Shannon Stewart	.15
114	Bobby Abreu	.25
115	Jose Guillen	.25
116	Brandon Phillips	.15
117	Jose Vidro	.15
118	Mike Sweeney	.15
119	Jacque Jones	.15
120	Josh Phelps	.15
121	Milton Bradley	.15
122	Torii Hunter	.25
123	Carl Crawford	.15
124	Javier Vazquez	.25
125	Juan Gonzalez	.50
126	Travis Hafner	.15
127	Ken Griffey Jr.	1.00
128	Phil Nevin	.15
129	Trot Nixon	.15
130	Carlos Lee	.15
131	Javy Lopez	.25
132	Jay Gibbons	.15
133	Brandon Medders RC	3.00
134	Colby Miller RC	3.00
135	David Crouthers	3.00
136	Dennis Sarfate RC	5.00
137	Donald Kelly RC	3.00
138	Frank Brooks RC	3.00
139	Chris Aguila RC	3.00
140	Greg Dobbs RC	3.00
141	Ian Snell RC	5.00
142	Jake Woods	3.00
143	Jamie Brown RC	3.00
144	Jason Frasor RC	4.00
145	Jerome Gamble RC	4.00
146	Jesse Harper RC	5.00
147	Josh Labandeira RC	4.00
148	Justin Hampson RC	4.00
149	Justin Huisman RC	4.00
150	Justin Leone RC	5.00
151	Lincoln Holdzkom RC	3.00
152	Mike Bumatay RC	5.00
153	Mike Gosling	5.00
154	Mike Johnston RC	3.00
155	Mike Rouse	3.00
156	Nick Regilio RC	5.00
157	Ryan Meaux RC	3.00
158	Scott Dohmann RC	3.00
159	Sean Henn	3.00
160	Tim Bausher RC	3.00
161	Tim Bittner RC	3.00
162	Alec Zumwalt RC	3.00
163	Aaron Boone, Bret Boone, Geoff Jenkins, Mark Prior, Barry Zito	2.00
164	Albert Pujols, Edgar Renteria, Alex Rodriguez	5.00
165	Alfonso Soriano, Sammy Sosa	4.00
166	Bobby Abreu, Jim Thome	2.00
167	Bret Boone, John Olerud, Ichiro Suzuki	4.00
168	Derek Jeter, Alfonso Soriano	6.00
169	Eric Chavez, Miguel Tejada	2.00
170	Garret Anderson, Jim Edmonds, Troy Glaus	2.00
171	Hank Blalock, Alex Rodriguez, Mark Teixeira, Michael Young, Rafael Palmeiro	5.00
172	Alex Rodriguez, Mark Teixeira, Michael Young, Rafael Palmeiro	5.00
173	Ivan Rodriguez, Dontrelle Willis	2.00
174	Jason Giambi, Derek Jeter	6.00
175	Joe DiMaggio, Mickey Mantle	8.00
176	Joe DiMaggio, Mickey Mantle, Ted Williams	8.00
177	Joe DiMaggio, Ted Williams	6.00
178	Nomar Garciaparra, Alfonso Soriano	4.00

179	Nomar Garciaparra, Jason Giambi	4.00
180	Paul LoDuca, Hideo Nomo	2.00
181	Rafael Palmeiro, Alex Rodriguez, Michael Young	4.00
182	Ralph Kiner, Ted Williams	5.00
183	Aaron Boone, Derek Jeter	6.00

Blue
Blue (1-132): 2-3X
Inserted 1:6

Die-Cut
Die-Cut (1-132): 3-6X
Production 175

Green
No Pricing
Production 15 Sets

Purple
No Pricing
Production One Set

Apparel Collection

NM/M
Common Player: 4.00
Inserted 1:24

JB	Jeff Bagwell	6.00
RB	Rocco Baldelli	8.00
BE	Josh Beckett	6.00
LB	Lance Berkman	4.00
CD	Carlos Delgado	6.00
JD	Joe DiMaggio/SP/150	75.00
AD	Adam Dunn	6.00
RF	Rafael Furcal	5.00
JG	Jason Giambi	6.00
TG	Troy Glaus	5.00
KG	Ken Griffey Jr.	15.00
RH	Roy Halladay	5.00
RH	Rich Harden/SP	8.00
BH	Bo Hart	4.00
TH	Torii Hunter	5.00
DJ	Derek Jeter	15.00
RJ	Randy Johnson	8.00
CJ	Chipper Jones	8.00
ML	Mike Lowell	5.00
MM	Mickey Mantle/SP/150	100.00
PM	Pedro J. Martinez	8.00
HM	Hideki Matsui	20.00
MU	Mike Mussina	6.00
HN	Hideo Nomo	6.00
RO	Roy Oswalt	4.00
RP	Rafael Palmeiro	5.00
PI	Mike Piazza	10.00
JP	Jorge Posada	8.00
MP	Mark Prior	8.00
AP	Albert Pujols	10.00
MR	Manny Ramirez	6.00
AR	Alex Rodriguez	8.00
CS	Curt Schilling	6.00
AS	Alfonso Soriano	4.00
SS	Sammy Sosa	10.00
IS	Ichiro Suzuki	15.00
JT	Jim Thome	8.00
BW	Bernie Williams	5.00
TW	Ted Williams/SP/150	70.00
DW	Dontrelle Willis	5.00
KW	Kerry Wood	5.00
BZ	Barry Zito	5.00

Artist's Touch

NM/M
Common Player: 4.00
Production 250
Parallel: 1-2X
Production 50

RB	Rocco Baldelli	8.00
JB	Josh Beckett	8.00
LB	Lance Berkman	5.00
CD	Carlos Delgado	8.00
RF	Rafael Furcal	5.00
JG	Jason Giambi	5.00
TG	Troy Glaus	6.00
KG	Ken Griffey Jr.	15.00
HA	Roy Halladay	5.00
BH	Bo Hart	4.00
TH	Torii Hunter	5.00
DJ	Derek Jeter	15.00
RJ	Randy Johnson	8.00
CJ	Chipper Jones	8.00
PM	Pedro J. Martinez	8.00
HM	Hideki Matsui	20.00
MM	Mike Mussina	8.00
HN	Hideo Nomo	8.00
RO	Roy Oswalt	4.00
RP	Rafael Palmeiro	5.00
PI	Mike Piazza	10.00
JP	Jorge Posada	8.00
MP	Mark Prior	10.00
AP	Albert Pujols	10.00
MR	Manny Ramirez/50	15.00
AR	Alex Rodriguez	10.00
AS	Alfonso Soriano	5.00
SS	Sammy Sosa	15.00

IS	Ichiro Suzuki	20.00
JT	Jim Thome	10.00
BW	Bernie Williams	6.00
DW	Dontrelle Willis	5.00
KW	Kerry Wood	8.00
BZ	Barry Zito	6.00

Home Run Heroics

NM/M
Common Player: 2.00
Inserted 1:24

EB	Ernie Banks	4.00
HB	Hank Blalock	3.00
AB	Aaron Boone	2.00
MC	Miguel Cabrera	4.00
CD	Carlos Delgado	3.00
JD	Joe DiMaggio	8.00
JD1	Joe DiMaggio	8.00
JG	Jason Giambi	3.00
SG	Shawn Green	2.00
KG	Ken Griffey Jr.	6.00
KG1	Ken Griffey Jr.	6.00
RH	Rickey Henderson	4.00
RJ	Randy Johnson	3.00
HK	Harmon Killebrew	4.00
MM	Mickey Mantle	15.00
MM1	Mickey Mantle	15.00
MM2	Mickey Mantle	15.00
EM	Eddie Mathews	4.00
HM	Hideki Matsui	6.00
HM1	Hideki Matsui	6.00
WM	Willie McCovey	2.00
BM	Bill Mueller	2.00
SM	Stan Musial	5.00
RP	Rafael Palmeiro	3.00
CR	Cal Ripken Jr.	10.00
CR1	Cal Ripken Jr.	10.00
AR	Alex Rodriguez	6.00
AR1	Alex Rodriguez	6.00
FR	Frank Robinson	3.00
MS	Mike Schmidt	5.00
RS	Red Schoendienst	2.00
AS	Alfonso Soriano	4.00
SS	Sammy Sosa	6.00
SS1	Sammy Sosa	6.00
SS2	Sammy Sosa	6.00
SS3	Sammy Sosa	6.00
TW	Ted Williams	10.00
TW1	Ted Williams	10.00
TW2	Ted Williams	10.00
TW3	Ted Williams	10.00

Rookie Signature Portfolio

NM/M
Common Player: 5.00
Inserted 1:30

CA	Chris Aguila	6.00
TB	Tim Bausher	8.00
BI	Tim Bittner	8.00
FB	Frank Brooks	8.00
JB	Jamie Brown	5.00
MB	Mike Bumatay	8.00
DC	David Crouthers	8.00
GD	Greg Dobbs	6.00
SD	Scott Dohmann	8.00
JF	Jason Frasor	8.00
JG	Jerome Gamble	8.00
MG	Mike Gosling	8.00
JH	Justin Hampson	6.00
JH	Jesse Harper	8.00
SH	Sean Henn	15.00
LH	Lincoln Holdzkom	5.00
HU	Justin Huisman	5.00
MJ	Mike Johnston	10.00
DK	Donald Kelly	5.00
JL	Josh Labandeira	8.00
LE	Justin Leone	10.00
RM	Ryan Meaux	5.00
BM	Brandon Medders	5.00
CM	Colby Miller	5.00
NR	Nick Regilio	5.00
MR	Mike Rouse	6.00
DS	Dennis Sarfate	5.00
IS	Ian Snell	20.00
JW	Jake Woods	5.00
AZ	Alec Zumwalt	8.00

Signature Portfolio

NM/M
Production 100
Parallel: No Pricing
Production 25 or 10

KG	Ken Griffey Jr.	100.00
HM	Hideki Matsui	250.00
CR	Cal Ripken Jr.	120.00
TS	Tom Seaver	40.00
CY	Carl Yastrzemski	50.00
BZ	Barry Zito	30.00

Tools of the Stars

NM/M
Common Player: 6.00
Inserted 1:48
Level 1 Parallel: 1-1.5X
Production 250
Level 2 Parallel: No Pricing
Production 25

JB	Josh Beckett	6.00
CD	Carlos Delgado	6.00
KG	Ken Griffey Jr./SP	15.00
DJ	Derek Jeter	15.00
CJ	Chipper Jones	8.00
HM	Hideki Matsui	15.00
HN	Hideo Nomo	6.00
PI	Mike Piazza	10.00
AP	Albert Pujols	15.00
AR	Alex Rodriguez	10.00
AS	Alfonso Soriano	6.00
IS	Ichiro Suzuki	15.00
JT	Jim Thome	8.00
KW	Kerry Wood	6.00

2004 Upper Deck Power Up

NM/M
Complete Set (100): 20.00
Common Player: .15
Pack (9): 1.50
Box (24): 25.00

1	Austin Kearns	.25
2	Rafael Furcal	.25
3	Larry Walker	.25
4	Jeremy Bonderman	.15
5	Scott Rolen	.50
6	Nomar Garciaparra	1.00
7	Jody Gerut	.15
8	Troy Glaus	.25
9	Roy Halladay	.25
10	Barry Zito	.25
11	Gary Sheffield	.40
12	Ichiro Suzuki	1.00
13	Juan Gonzalez	.25
14	Jim Edmonds	.25
15	Hank Blalock	.40
16	Roy Oswalt	.25
17	Magglio Ordonez	.25
18	Garret Anderson	.40
19	Mark Teixeira	.25
20	Mike Sweeney	.15
21	Reggie Sanders	.15
22	Rafael Palmeiro	.40
23	Orlando Cabrera	.15
24	Edgar Renteria	.25
25	Ryan Klesko	.25
26	Torii Hunter	.25
27	Bret Boone	.25
28	Roberto Alomar	.25
29	Frank Thomas	.50
30	Chipper Jones	.50
31	Eric Chavez	.25
32	Miguel Tejada	.40
33	Carlos Beltran	.40
34	Geoff Jenkins	.25
35	Hideki Matsui	1.00
36	Jason Kendall	.15
37	Adam Dunn	.40
38	Jay Gibbons	.15
39	Ivan Rodriguez	.50
40	Sidney Ponson	.15
41	Albert Pujols	1.00
42	Bartolo Colon	.25
43	Lance Berkman	.25
44	Brandon Webb	.15
45	Shannon Stewart	.15
46	Josh Beckett	.50
47	Jason Schmidt	.25
48	Luis Gonzalez	.25
49	Jacque Jones	.15
50	Andruw Jones	.40
51	Todd Helton	.50
52	Javier Vazquez	.25
53	Alfonso Soriano	.50
54	Manny Ramirez	.50
55	Bobby Abreu	.25
56	Rocco Baldelli	.25
57	Kerry Wood	.50
58	Derek Jeter	1.50
59	Phil Nevin	.15
60	Jeff Bagwell	.40
61	Sammy Sosa	.50
62	Tom Glavine	.25
63	Miguel Cabrera	.50
64	Shawn Green	.25
65	Mark Prior	1.00
66	Jose Reyes	.25
67	Curt Schilling	.40
68	Hideo Nomo	.25
69	Mike Lowell	.25
70	Randy Johnson	.50
71	Edgar Martinez	.25
72	Dontrelle Willis	.25
73	Milton Bradley	.15
74	Preston Wilson	.15
75	Mike Piazza	.40
76	Mike Mussina	.40
77	Darin Erstad	.25
78	Greg Maddux	.50
79	Tim Hudson	.25
80	Kevin Millwood	.25
81	Dmitri Young	.15
82	Ben Sheets	.25
83	Alex Rodriguez	1.00
84	Johan Santana	.25
85	Jeff Kent	.25
86	Pedro Martinez	.50
87	Carlos Delgado	.40
88	Jim Thome	.50
89	Aubrey Huff	.25
90	Ken Griffey Jr.	1.00
91	Kevin Brown	.25
92	Tony Batista	.15
93	Richie Sexson	.25
94	Cliff Floyd	.15
95	Jose Vidro	.15
96	Brian Giles	.25
97	Jorge Posada	.40
98	Vernon Wells	.25
99	Vladimir Guerrero	.50
100	Jason Giambi	.50

Rare
Stars: 3-4X
Inserted 1:6

Super Rare
Stars: 5-10X
Inserted 1:96

Ultra Rare
Stars: 4-6X
Inserted 1:24

Mega Rare
No Pricing
Inserted 1:240

Shining Through

NM/M

1	Hideo Nomo	.25
2	Mark Prior	1.00
3	Scott Rolen	.75
4	Luis Gonzalez	.40
5	Miguel Tejada	.40
6	Richie Sexson	.40
7	Jim Edmonds	.40
8	Carlos Beltran	.40
9	Manny Ramirez	.50
10	Torii Hunter	.40
11	Garret Anderson	.40
12	Eric Chavez	.40
13	Juan Gonzalez	.40
14	Albert Pujols	1.50
15	Tim Hudson	.40
16	Roy Halladay	.40
17	Roy Oswalt	.25
18	Andruw Jones	.50
19	Gary Sheffield	.40
20	Magglio Ordonez	.40
21	Jason Giambi	.75
22	Brian Giles	.40
23	Barry Zito	.40
24	Todd Helton	.50
25	Randy Johnson	.75
26	Pedro Martinez	.75
27	Vernon Wells	.40
28	Lance Berkman	.40
29	Mike Mussina	.50
30	Carlos Delgado	.50
31	Ivan Rodriguez	.50
32	Kevin Brown	.40
33	Kerry Wood	.75
34	Mark Teixeira	.50
35	Hideki Matsui	.75
36	Troy Glaus	.40
37	Mike Piazza	1.00
38	Nomar Garciaparra	1.50

39	Vladimir Guerrero	.75
40	Derek Jeter	2.00
41	Jason Schmidt	.40
42	Alex Rodriguez/Yanks	
43	Jeff Bagwell	.50
44	Shawn Green	.40
45	Sammy Sosa	1.50
46	Josh Beckett	.75
47	Bret Boone	.40
48	Ichiro Suzuki	1.00
49	Jeff Kent	.40
50	Rafael Palmeiro	.50
51	Curt Schilling	.50
52	Greg Maddux	1.00
53	Mike Lowell	.40
54	Dontrelle Willis	.40
55	Alfonso Soriano	.50
56	Preston Wilson	.25
57	Jorge Posada	.40
58	Frank Thomas	.50
59	Jim Thome	.75
60	Ken Griffey Jr.	1.00
61	Rocco Baldelli	.40
63	Jose Vidro	.25
63	Austin Kearns	.25
64	Cliff Floyd	.25
65	Phil Nevin	.25
66	Darin Erstad	.25
67	Johan Santana	.25
68	Chipper Jones	.75
69	Brandon Webb	.25
70	Hank Blalock	.40
71	Adam Dunn	.40
72	Javier Vazquez	.25
73	Jacque Jones	.25
74	Bobby Abreu	.40
75	Edgar Renteria	.40
76	Roger Clemens	1.50
77	Rafael Furcal	.40
78	Mike Sweeney	.25
79	Geoff Jenkins	.25
80	Orlando Cabrera	.25
81	Ben Sheets	.40
82	Shannon Stewart	.25
83	Ryan Klesko	.25
84	Edgar Martinez	.40
85	Kevin Millwood	.40
86	Bartolo Colon	.40
87	Larry Walker	.25
88	Tom Glavine	.50
89	Miguel Cabrera	.75
90	Jose Reyes	.40

Stickers

POWER UP YOUR POINTS!
SCRATCH OFF

		NM/M
1	Hideo Nomo	.50
2	Mark Prior	2.00
3	Scott Rolen	1.50
4	Luis Gonzalez	.50
5	Miguel Tejada	.75
6	Richie Sexson	.75
7	Jim Edmonds	.75
8	Carlos Beltran	.75
9	Manny Ramirez	1.00
10	Torii Hunter	.75
11	Garret Anderson	.75
12	Eric Chavez	.75
13	Juan Gonzalez	.75
14	Albert Pujols	3.00
15	Tim Hudson	.75
16	Roy Halladay	.75
17	Roy Oswalt	.50
18	Andruw Jones	1.00
19	Gary Sheffield	.75
20	Magglio Ordonez	.75
21	Jason Giambi	1.50
22	Brian Giles	.75
23	Barry Zito	.75
24	Todd Helton	1.00
25	Randy Johnson	1.50
26	Pedro Martinez	1.50
27	Vernon Wells	.75
28	Lance Berkman	.75
29	Mike Mussina	.75
30	Carlos Delgado	.75
31	Ivan Rodriguez	1.00
32	Kevin Brown	.75
33	Kerry Wood	1.50
34	Mark Teixeira	.75
35	Hideki Matsui	2.50
36	Troy Glaus	.75
37	Mike Piazza	2.00
38	Nomar Garciaparra	1.50
39	Vladimir Guerrero	1.50
40	Derek Jeter	4.00
41	Jason Schmidt	.50
42	Alex Rodriguez	3.00

43	Jeff Bagwell	1.00
44	Shawn Green	.75
45	Sammy Sosa	2.50
46	Josh Beckett	1.00
47	Bret Boone	.50
48	Ichiro Suzuki	2.00
49	Jeff Kent	.75
50	Rafael Palmeiro	1.00
51	Curt Schilling	1.00
52	Greg Maddux	2.00
53	Mike Lowell	.75
54	Dontrelle Willis	.75
55	Alfonso Soriano	1.00
56	Preston Wilson	.50
57	Jorge Posada	.75
58	Frank Thomas	1.00
59	Jim Thome	1.50
60	Ken Griffey Jr.	2.00
61	Rocco Baldelli	.50
62	Jose Vidro	.50
63	Austin Kearns	.50
64	Phil Nevin	.50
65	Darin Erstad	.50
66	Johan Santana	.50
67	Chipper Jones	1.50
68	Brandon Webb	.50
69	Hank Blalock	.75
70	Adam Dunn	.75
71	Javier Vazquez	.75
72	Jacque Jones	.75
73	Bobby Abreu	.75
74	Edgar Renteria	.75
75	Rafael Furcal	.75
76	Mike Sweeney	.50
77	Geoff Jenkins	.50
78	Shannon Stewart	.50
79	Ryan Klesko	.75
80	Edgar Martinez	.75
81	Kevin Millwood	.75
82	Bartolo Colon	.75
83	Tom Glavine	.75
84	Miguel Cabrera	1.50
85	Jose Reyes	.75
86	Padres/Astros/A's/ Angels/Cubs/D-Rays	
87	Pirates/M's/Expos/ Twins/Reds/Phils	.50
88	Royals/O's/W.Sox/ Dodgers/Marlins/Yanks	.50
89	Giants/Mets/Cards/ Indians/Braves/Rangers	
90	Tigers/R.Sox/Rockies/ D-Backs/Brewers/Jay	.50

2004 Upper Deck R Class

3B hankBLALOCK

		NM/M
Complete Set (180):		50.00
Common Player:		.10
Pack (6):		2.50
Box (24):		50.00
1	Adam Dunn	.50
2	Jose Vidro	.10
3	Vladimir Guerrero	.75
4	Hideo Nomo	.25
5	Eric Chavez	.50
6	Carlos Delgado	.40
7	Javy Lopez	.25
8	Javier Vazquez	.25
9	Miguel Cabrera	.75
10	Manny Ramirez	.50
11	Scott Rolen	.50
12	Rafael Furcal	.10
13	Jim Thome	.75
14	Edgar Renteria	.25
15	Jason Kendall	.10
16	Alfonso Soriano	.50
17	Troy Glaus	.40
18	Vernon Wells	.10
19	Todd Helton	.50
20	Mark Mulder	.10
21	Albert Pujols	2.00
22	Andy Pettitte	.25
23	Kevin Millwood	.10
24	Bret Boone	.10
25	Ken Griffey Jr.	1.00
26	Kevin Brown	.25
27	J.D. Drew	.25
28	Corey Patterson	.40
29	Jason Giambi	.40
30	Jason Schmidt	.25
31	Jose Reyes	.25
32	Torii Hunter	.25
33	Brian Giles	.25
34	Garret Anderson	.25
35	Mark Teixeira	.40
36	Sammy Sosa	1.50
37	Rocco Baldelli	.25
38	Jeff Bagwell	.50

39	Rafael Palmeiro	.50
40	Derek Lee	.25
41	Randy Johnson	.75
42	Roger Clemens	1.50
43	Austin Kearns	.10
44	Dontrelle Willis	.10
45	Lance Berkman	.25
46	Juan Gonzalez	.40
47	Ichiro Suzuki	1.50
48	Pat Burrell	.40
49	Miguel Tejada	.40
50	Mike Piazza	1.00
51	Mark Prior	.75
52	C.C. Sabathia	.25
53	Jacque Jones	.10
54	Carlos Beltran	.75
55	Mike Mussina	.25
56	Mike Lowell	.25
57	Phil Nevin	.25
58	Andruw Jones	.40
59	Barry Zito	.25
60	Magglio Ordonez	.25
61	Carlos Lee	.25
62	Nomar Garciaparra	1.00
63	Kerry Wood	.75
64	Luis Gonzalez	.20
65	Derek Jeter	2.00
66	Preston Wilson	.10
67	Greg Maddux	1.00
68	Pedro J. Martinez	.75
69	Richie Sexson	.25
70	Hank Blalock	.50
71	Chipper Jones	.75
72	Ivan Rodriguez	.50
73	Roy Halladay	.25
74	Tim Hudson	.25
75	Ryan Klesko	.25
76	Hideki Matsui	1.50
77	Josh Beckett	.40
78	Brandon Webb	.25
79	Alex Rodriguez	2.00
80	Jim Edmonds	.40
81	Jeff Kent	.25
82	Bobby Abreu	.25
83	Curt Schilling	.25
84	Roy Oswalt	.25
85	Orlando Cabrera	.75
86	Johan Santana	.50
87	Geoff Jenkins	.10
88	Gary Sheffield	.40
89	Shawn Green	.25
90	Frank Thomas	.25
91	Tim Hamulack RC	.25
92	Shingo Takatsu RC	.25
93	Justin Huisman	.25
94	Sean Henn	.50
95	Jamie Brown	.25
96	Dennis Sarfate RC	.25
97	Lincoln Holdzkom RC	.25
98	Roman Colon RC	.25
99	Scott Dohmann RC	.25
100	Ivan Ochoa	.25
101	Akinori Otsuka RC	.50
102	Fernando Nieve RC	.25
103	Mike Johnston RC	.25
104	Mariano Gomez RC	.25
105	Justin Leone RC	.25
106	Evan Rust RC	.25
107	Mike Rouse	.25
108	Ian Snell RC	.25
109	Jason Bartlett	.50
110	Ryan Wing	.25
111	Nick Regilio RC	.25
112	Merkin Valdez RC	.50
113	Josh Labandeira RC	.25
114	David Aardsma	.75
115	Justin Knoedler RC	.25
116	Shawn Hill RC	.25
117	Casey Daigle RC	.25
118	Donnie Kelly RC	.25
119	Justin Germano RC	.25
120	Eddy Rodriguez RC	.25
121	Onil Joseph RC	.25
122	Mike Wuertz	.25
123	Roberto Novoa RC	.25
124	Jerome Gamble RC	.50
125	Justin Hampson RC	.25
126	Ronald Belisario RC	.25
127	Tim Bausher RC	.25
128	Chris Saenz RC	.25
129	Hector Gimenez RC	.25
130	Ronny Cedeno RC	.25
131	Jason Frasor RC	.25
132	Kazuo Matsui RC	.50
133	Mike Gosling	.25
134	Jerry Gil RC	.25
135	Orlando Rodriguez RC	.25
136	Jorge Vasquez RC	.50
137	Chris Aguila RC	.25
138	Tim Bittner RC	.25
139	Jake Woods RC	.25
140	Enemencio Pacheco RC	.25
141	David Crouthers RC	.25
142	Jose Capellan RC	.50
143	Chad Bentz RC	.25
144	Michael Vento RC	.75
145	Scott Proctor RC	.50
146	Edwin Moreno RC	.25
147	Brandon Medders RC	.25
148	Renyel Pinto RC	.25
149	Rusty Tucker RC	.25
150	Ryan Meaux RC	.25
151	William Bergolla RC	.25
152	Angel Chavez RC	.25
153	Colby Miller RC	.25
154	John Gall RC	.25
155	Carlos Hines RC	.25
156	Carlos Vasquez RC	.50

157	Justin Lehr RC	.25
158	Kevin Cave RC	.25
159	Jeff Bennett RC	.25
160	Greg Dobbs RC	.25
161	Jorge Sequea RC	.25
162	Chris Oxspring RC	.25
163	Franklyn Gracesqui RC	.25
164	Shawn Camp RC	.25
165	Lino Urdaneta RC	.25
166	Luis Gonzalez	.25
167	Ramon Ramirez RC	.50
168	Freddy Guzman RC	.25
169	Chris Shelton RC	.50
170	Andres Blanco	.25
171	Aarom Baldiris RC	.25
172	Kazuhito Tadano RC	.50
173	Brian Dallimore RC	.25
174	Eduardo Villacis	.25
175	Frank Francisco RC	.25
176	Edwin Jackson	.25
177	Bobby Crosby	.50
178	Joe Mauer	.50
179	Rickie Weeks	.50
180	Delmon Young	.50

First Class Black Ink Auto

		NM/M
Inserted 1:2,880		
SA	Sandy Alomar	20.00
PB	Pat Burrell	30.00
MC	Miguel Cabrera	40.00
CD	Carlos Delgado	30.00
EG	Eric Gagne	50.00
KG	Ken Griffey Jr.	80.00
TH	Trevor Hoffman	30.00
BL	Barry Larkin	40.00
PL	Paul LoDuca	30.00
EM	Edgar Martinez	40.00
MP	Mark Prior	40.00
HR	Horacio Ramirez	20.00
DW	Dontrelle Willis	30.00

First Class Blue Ink Auto

No Pricing
Production Three Sets

Jersey

		NM/M
Common Player:		4.00
Inserted 1:12		
RA	Roberto Alomar	6.00
BA	Jeff Bagwell	8.00
RB	Rocco Baldelli	4.00
JB	Josh Beckett	8.00
HB	Hank Blalock	8.00
BB	Bret Boone	4.00
KB	Kevin Brown	4.00
EC	Eric Chavez	4.00
RC	Roger Clemens	12.00
CD	Carlos Delgado	4.00
JG	Jason Giambi	6.00
GL	Troy Glaus	4.00
TG	Tom Glavine	6.00
KG	Ken Griffey Jr.	12.00
VG	Vladimir Guerrero	8.00
TH	Todd Helton	8.00
HU	Torii Hunter	4.00
DJ	Derek Jeter	15.00
RJ	Randy Johnson	8.00
AJ	Andruw Jones	6.00
CJ	Chipper Jones	8.00
EM	Edgar Martinez	4.00
PM	Pedro J. Martinez	8.00
HM	Hideki Matsui	20.00
KM	Kazuo Matsui	10.00
HN	Hideo Nomo	4.00
PI	Mike Piazza	10.00
MP	Mark Prior	6.00
AP	Albert Pujols	15.00
MR	Manny Ramirez	8.00
RI	Mariano Rivera	8.00
IR	Ivan Rodriguez	8.00
SR	Scott Rolen	8.00
CS	Curt Schilling	8.00
GS	Gary Sheffield	6.00
AS	Alfonso Soriano	4.00
SS	Sammy Sosa	10.00
IS	Ichiro Suzuki	25.00
MT	Miguel Tejada	6.00
BW	Bernie Williams	6.00
DW	Dontrelle Willis	4.00
KW	Kerry Wood	8.00

Taking Over!

		NM/M
Common Player:		3.00
1-20 production 650		
21-30 production 150		
TO-1	Richie Sexson, Lyle Overbay	3.00
TO-2	Jason Phillips, Mike Piazza	6.00
TO-3	Barry Larkin, William Bergolla	4.00
TO-4	Jason Dubois, Moises Alou	3.00
TO-5	Nook Logan, Alex Sanchez	3.00
TO-6	Merkin Valdez, Robb Nen	4.00
TO-7	Troy Percival, Francisco Rodriguez	3.00
TO-8	Carlos Beltran, David DeJesus	3.00
TO-9	Alex Rodriguez, Michael Young	6.00
TO-10	Alexis Rios, Vernon Wells	3.00

TO-11	Matt Lawton, Grady Sizemore	3.00
TO-12	Danny Graves, Ryan Wagner	3.00
TO-13	Miguel Cabrera, Jeff Conine	4.00
TO-14	Josh Willingham, Ramon Castro	3.00
TO-15	Junior Spivey, Rickie Weeks	3.00
TO-16	Guillermo Quiroz, Greg Myers	3.00
TO-17	Scott Hatteberg, Graham Koonce	3.00
TO-18	Rene Reyes, Larry Walker	3.00
TO-19	Khalil Greene, Ramon Vazquez	4.00
TO-20	Billy Wagner, Octavio Dotel	3.00
TO-21	Joe Mauer, A.J. Pierzynski	8.00
TO-22	Javier Vazquez, Roger Clemens	10.00
TO-23	Curt Schilling, Brandon Webb	3.00
TO-24	Delmon Young, Cirilo Cruz Jr.	8.00
TO-25	Vladimir Guerrero, Tim Salmon	8.00
TO-26	Gary Sheffield, J.D. Drew	8.00
TO-27	Miguel Tejada, Bobby Crosby	8.00
TO-28	Edwin Jackson, Kevin Brown	3.00
TO-29	Kazuo Matsui, Jose Reyes	10.00
TO-30	Wily Mo Pena, Ken Griffey Jr.	10.00

2004 Upper Deck Reflections Sample

		NM/M
S38	Ichiro	3.00

2004 Upper Deck Reflections

		NM/M
Complete Set (340):		
Common (1-100):		.50
Common SP (101-130):		4.00
Production 1,250		
Common Jersey (131-214):		4.00
Common Jersey (215-298):		4.00
Production 100 (215-298):		
Common Auto. (299-340):		15.00
Production 35		
Pack (4):		8.00
Box (8):		50.00
1	Adam Dunn	1.00
2	Albert Pujols	3.00
3	Alex Rodriguez	3.00
4	Alfonso Soriano	1.00
5	Andruw Jones	1.00
6	Austin Kearns	.50
7	Rafael Furcal	.50
8	Barry Zito	.75
9	Bartolo Colon	.50
10	Ben Sheets	.50
11	Bernie Williams	.75
12	Bobby Abreu	.50
13	Brandon Webb	.50
14	Bret Boone	.50
15	Brian Giles	.50
16	Carlos Beltran	.50
17	Carlos Delgado	.75
18	Carlos Lee	.50
19	Chipper Jones	1.50

20	Corey Patterson	.50
21	Curt Schilling	.75
22	Delmon Young	.50
23	Derek Jeter	4.00
24	Dmitri Young	.50
25	Dontrelle Willis	.50
26	Edgar Martinez	.50
27	Edgar Renteria	.50
28	Eric Chavez	.50
29	Eric Gagne	.75
30	Frank Thomas	1.50
31	Garret Anderson	.50
32	Gary Sheffield	.50
33	Geoff Jenkins	.50
34	Greg Maddux	2.00
35	Hank Blalock	.75
36	Hideki Matsui	3.00
37	Hideo Nomo	.75
38	Ichiro Suzuki	2.50
39	Ivan Rodriguez	1.00
40	Jacque Jones	.50
41	Jason Giambi	1.50
42	Jason Schmidt	.75
43	Javy Lopez	.50
44	Jay Gibbons	.50
45	Jeff Bagwell	1.00
46	Jeff Kent	.50
47	Jeremy Bonderman	.50
48	Jim Edmonds	.75
49	Jim Thome	1.00
50	Johnny Damon	.50
51	Jorge Posada	.75
52	Jose Contreras	.50
53	Jose Reyes	.75
54	Jose Vidro	.50
55	Josh Beckett	1.00
56	Juan Gonzalez	1.00
57	Ken Griffey Jr.	2.50
58	Kerry Wood	1.50
59	Kevin Brown	.50
60	Kevin Millwood	.50
61	Lance Berkman	.50
62	Larry Walker	.50
63	Luis Gonzalez	.50
64	Magglio Ordonez	.50
65	Manny Ramirez	1.00
66	Mark Mulder	.50
67	Mark Prior	2.00
68	Mark Teixeira	.50
69	Miguel Cabrera	1.50
70	Miguel Tejada	.75
71	Mike Lowell	.75
72	Mike Mussina	.75
73	Mike Piazza	2.00
74	Mike Sweeney	.50
75	Milton Bradley	.50
76	Nomar Garciaparra	2.00
77	Orlando Cabrera	.50
78	Pedro Martinez	1.50
79	Phil Nevin	.50
80	Preston Wilson	.50
81	Rafael Palmeiro	1.00
82	Randy Johnson	1.50
83	Rich Harden	.50
84	Richie Sexson	.75
85	Rickie Weeks	.50
86	Rocco Baldelli	.75
87	Roy Halladay	.75
88	Roy Oswalt	.75
89	Ryan Klesko	.50
90	Sammy Sosa	2.50
91	Scott Rolen	1.50
92	Shannon Stewart	.50
93	Shawn Green	.50
94	Tim Hudson	.75
95	Todd Helton	1.00
96	Torii Hunter	.75
97	Trot Nixon	.50
98	Troy Glaus	.50
99	Vernon Wells	.50
100	Vladimir Guerrero	1.50
101	Brandon Medders RC	4.00
102	Colby Miller RC	6.00
103	David Crouthers RC	4.00
104	Dennis Sarfate RC	4.00
105	Donnie Kelly RC	4.00
106	Alec Zumwalt RC	4.00
107	Chris Aguila RC	4.00
108	Greg Dobbs RC	4.00
109	Ian Snell RC	4.00
110	Jake Woods RC	4.00
111	Jamie Brown RC	4.00
112	Jason Frasor RC	4.00
113	Jerome Gamble RC	4.00
114	Jesse Harper RC	4.00
115	Josh Labandeira RC	5.00
116	Justin Hampson RC	4.00
117	Justin Huisman RC	4.00
118	Justin Leone RC	6.00
119	Kazuo Matsui RC	4.00
120	Lincoln Holdzkom RC	4.00
121	Mike Bumatay RC	4.00
122	Mike Gosling RC	4.00
123	Mike Johnston RC	4.00
124	Mike Rouse RC	4.00
125	Nick Regilio RC	4.00
126	Ryan Meaux RC	4.00
127	Scott Dohmann RC	4.00
128	Sean Henn RC	4.00
129	Tim Bausher RC	4.00
130	Tim Bittner RC	4.00
131	Adam Dunn	6.00
132	Andruw Jones	6.00
133	Austin Kearns	4.00
134	Bartolo Colon	4.00
135	Ben Sheets	5.00
136	Bernie Williams	5.00
137	Bobby Abreu	4.00

#	Player	Price
138	Brian Giles	4.00
139	Carlos Lee	4.00
140	Chipper Jones	8.00
141	Corey Patterson	4.00
142	Darin Erstad	4.00
143	Edgar Martinez	4.00
144	Vladimir Guerrero	8.00
145	Eric Gagne	4.00
146	Frank Thomas	8.00
147	Garret Anderson	4.00
148	Roger Clemens	12.00
149	Greg Maddux	8.00
150	Jacque Jones	4.00
151	Randy Johnson	8.00
152	Javy Lopez	4.00
153	Mike Piazza	8.00
154	Albert Pujols	15.00
155	Jim Edmonds	4.00
156	Eric Milton	4.00
157	Jorge Posada	6.00
158	J.D. Drew	4.00
159	Jose Vidro	4.00
160	Kevin Millwood	4.00
161	Larry Walker	4.00
162	Luis Gonzalez	4.00
163	Mike Sweeney	4.00
164	Kerry Wood	4.00
165	Mike Cameron	4.00
166	Phil Nevin	4.00
167	Rocco Baldelli	4.00
168	Ryan Klesko	4.00
169	Shannon Stewart	4.00
170	Torii Hunter	6.00
171	Trot Nixon	4.00
172	Vernon Wells	4.00
173	Alfonso Soriano	6.00
174	Andruw Jones	6.00
175	Barry Zito	4.00
176	Brandon Webb	4.00
177	Bret Boone	4.00
178	Scott Rolen	6.00
179	Carlos Delgado	4.00
180	Curt Schilling	8.00
181	Dontrelle Willis	4.00
182	Eric Chavez	4.00
183	Frank Thomas	8.00
184	Gary Sheffield	4.00
185	Greg Maddux	8.00
186	Hank Blalock	4.00
187	Hideki Matsui	15.00
188	Hideo Nomo	4.00
189	Ichiro Suzuki	15.00
190	Ivan Rodriguez	6.00
191	Jason Giambi	4.00
192	Rafael Furcal	4.00
193	Jeff Bagwell	6.00
194	Jeff Kent	4.00
195	Jim Thome	4.00
196	Jose Reyes	8.00
197	Josh Beckett	6.00
198	Juan Gonzalez	4.00
199	Ken Griffey Jr.	15.00
200	Kevin Brown	4.00
201	Lance Berkman	4.00
202	Magglio Ordonez	5.00
203	Mark Mulder	4.00
204	Mark Teixeira	6.00
205	Miguel Tejada	4.00
206	Mike Mussina	6.00
207	Preston Wilson	4.00
208	Rafael Palmeiro	6.00
209	Alex Rodriguez	15.00
210	Richie Sexson	4.00
211	Roy Halladay	6.00
212	Roy Oswalt	4.00
213	Tim Hudson	5.00
214	Troy Glaus	4.00
215	Adam Dunn	8.00
216	Austin Kearns	4.00
217	Bartolo Colon	4.00
218	Ben Sheets	4.00
219	Bernie Williams	6.00
220	Bobby Abreu	5.00
221	Bret Boone	4.00
222	Todd Helton	6.00
223	Chipper Jones	8.00
224	Corey Patterson	4.00
225	Darin Erstad	4.00
226	Dontrelle Willis	4.00
227	Edgar Martinez	4.00
228	Eric Gagne	4.00
229	Garret Anderson	4.00
230	Roger Clemens	20.00
231	Hank Blalock	4.00
232	Jacque Jones	4.00
233	Jeff Bagwell	8.00
234	Jeff Kent	4.00
235	Jeremy Bonderman	4.00
236	Jim Edmonds	4.00
237	Jorge Posada	8.00
238	J.D. Drew	4.00
239	Jose Reyes	10.00
240	Jose Vidro	4.00
241	Kevin Millwood	4.00
242	Luis Gonzalez	4.00
243	Mike Sweeney	4.00
244	Jason Giambi	6.00
245	Manny Ramirez	8.00
246	Phil Nevin	4.00
247	Preston Wilson	4.00
248	Alex Rodriguez	20.00
249	Richie Sexson	4.00
250	Rocco Baldelli	4.00
251	Ryan Klesko	4.00
252	Sammy Sosa	8.00
253	Torii Hunter	6.00
254	Mike Lowell	6.00
255	Troy Glaus	4.00
256	Vernon Wells	6.00

#	Player	Price
257	Albert Pujols	20.00
258	Alex Rodriguez	20.00
259	Alfonso Soriano	8.00
260	Roger Clemens	20.00
261	Barry Zito	4.00
262	Brandon Webb	6.00
263	Carlos Delgado	6.00
264	Curt Schilling	8.00
265	Derek Jeter	25.00
266	Eric Chavez	4.00
267	Gary Sheffield	8.00
268	Hideki Matsui	25.00
269	Hideo Nomo	10.00
270	Ichiro Suzuki	25.00
271	Ivan Rodriguez	8.00
272	Jason Giambi	6.00
273	Jim Thome	6.00
274	Josh Beckett	10.00
275	Juan Gonzalez	8.00
276	Ken Griffey Jr.	20.00
277	Kerry Wood	4.00
278	Kevin Brown	4.00
279	Lance Berkman	8.00
280	Magglio Ordonez	8.00
281	Manny Ramirez	8.00
282	Mark Mulder	4.00
283	Mark Prior	6.00
284	Mark Teixeira	8.00
285	Miguel Tejada	6.00
286	Mike Mussina	8.00
287	Mike Piazza	10.00
288	Pedro Martinez	10.00
289	Rafael Palmeiro	8.00
290	Randy Johnson	10.00
291	Roy Halladay	6.00
292	Roy Oswalt	6.00
293	Sammy Sosa	10.00
294	Scott Rolen	8.00
295	Shawn Green	6.00
296	Tim Hudson	6.00
297	Todd Helton	8.00
298	Vladimir Guerrero	10.00
299	Bret Boone	10.00
300	Alex Rodriguez	200.00
301	Dontrelle Willis	30.00
302	Barry Larkin	30.00
303	Barry Zito	25.00
304	Eric Chavez	20.00
305	Bernie Williams	85.00
306	Brandon Webb	20.00
307	Cal Ripken Jr.	175.00
308	Carl Yastrzemski	65.00
309	Carlos Delgado	25.00
310	Shawn Green	25.00
311	Eric Gagne	15.00
312	Frank Thomas	40.00
313	Carlos Lee	20.00
314	Garret Anderson	20.00
315	Hideki Matsui	300.00
316	Jim Edmonds	40.00
317	Jeff Bagwell	40.00
318	Luis Gonzalez	20.00
319	Mike Mussina	40.00
320	John Smoltz	60.00
321	Jose Reyes	40.00
322	Josh Beckett	50.00
323	Juan Gonzalez	25.00
324	Ken Griffey Jr.	140.00
325	Rich Harden	20.00
326	Pat Burrell	25.00
327	Mark Teixeira	25.00
328	Roy Oswalt	30.00
329	Miguel Tejada	40.00
330	Mike Hampton	15.00
331	Mike Piazza	175.00
332	Nolan Ryan	120.00
333	Orlando Hernandez	25.00
334	Paul Lo Duca	25.00
335	Roberto Alomar	25.00
336	Rocco Baldelli	20.00
337	Trevor Hoffman	25.00
338	Tom Glavine	50.00
339	Tom Seaver	60.00
340	Mark Prior	25.00

Black

Black (1-100):		No Pricing
Production One Set		
Black Auto. (101-130):		No Pricing
Production One Set		
Black Jersey (173-214):		No Pricing
Production One Set		
Black Jersey (257-298):		No Pricing
Production One Set		
Black Jsy Auto. (299-340):		No Pricing
Production One Set		

Blue

Blue (1-100):		2-4X
Production 250		
Blue (215-256):		1-2X
Production 15		

Gold

Gold (1-100):		5-10X
Production 15		
Gold Auto. (101-130):		2X
Production 250		
Gold Auto. Parallel (101-130):		2X
Production 125		
Gold Jersey (131-172):		1.5-3X
Production 15		
Gold Jersey (257-298):		No Pricing
Production 5		
Gold Jsy Auto. (299-340):		1X
Production 15		

Red

Red (1-100):		4-6X
Production 50		
Red Jersey (131-214):		1.5-2X
Production 50		
Red (215-256):		1-1.5X
Production 50		

2004 Upper Deck Rivals: Yankees vs Red Sox

	NM/M
Complete Sealed Set (32):	25.00
Common Player (1-30):	.50
1 Alex Rodriguez	2.00
2 Bobby Doerr	.75
3 Don Mattingly	1.50
4 Dwight Evans	.50
5 Fred Lynn	.50
6 Jason Giambi	.50
7 Jim Rice	.50
8 Lou Gehrig	2.00
9 Luis Tiant	.50
10 Manny Ramirez	1.00
11 Mike Mussina	.75
12 Pedro Martinez	1.00
13 Phil Rizzuto	.75
14 Whitey Ford	.75
15 Yogi Berra	1.00
16 Tim Wakefield	.50
17 Billy Martin	.75
18 Mike Torrez, Bucky Dent	.50
19 Nomar Garciaparra, Derek Jeter	2.00
20 Gary Sheffield, Curt Schilling	1.00
21 Joe DiMaggio, Dick Newsome	1.50
22 Joe DiMaggio, Lefty Grove	1.50
23 Joe DiMaggio, Ted Williams	1.50
24 Jorge Posada, Jason Varitek	.50
25 Mickey Mantle, Carl Yastrzemski	2.00
26 Tracy Stallard, Roger Maris	1.00
27 Carlton Fisk, Thurman Munson	1.00
28 Babe Ruth	2.00
29 Roger Clemens	1.50
30 Wade Boggs	.50

Commemorative

	NM/M
Complete Set (5):	10.00
One oversized card per set.	
Babe Ruth	4.00
Ted Williams	3.00
Derek Jeter	3.00
Nomar Garciaparra	2.00
Mickey Mantle	5.00

"What If"

	NM/M
Common Player:	4.00
Production 2,150 Sets	
1 Aaron Boone	4.00
2 Alex Rodriguez	10.00
3 Babe Ruth	10.00
4 Babe Ruth	10.00
5 Billy Martin	4.00
6 Bucky Dent	4.00
7 Carl Yastrzemski	8.00
8 Carlton Fisk	5.00
9 Derek Jeter	10.00
10 Hideki Matsui	8.00
11 Joe DiMaggio	8.00
12 Joe Torre	4.00
13 Mickey Mantle	15.00
14 Pedro Martinez	6.00
15 Pee Wee Reese	4.00
16 Roger Clemens	8.00
17 Roger Maris	8.00
18 Ted Williams	8.00
19 Ted Williams	8.00
20 Carl Yastrzemski	8.00

What If Auto.

No Pricing

2004 Upper Deck Sweet Spot

	NM/M
Complete Set (262):	
Common Player:	.25
Common (91-170):	3.00
Common SP (171-230):	1.50
Production 399	
Common SP (231-250):	1.50
Production 299	
Common SP (251-260):	3.00
Production 199	
Pack (4):	10.00
Box (12):	100.00
1 Albert Pujols	3.00
2 Alex Rodriguez	3.00
3 Alfonso Soriano	1.00
4 Andruw Jones	.50
5 Andy Pettitte	.50
6 Aubrey Huff	.25
7 Austin Kearns	.50
8 Barry Zito	.50
9 Bobby Abreu	.50
10 Brandon Webb	.25
11 Bret Boone	.25
12 Brian Giles	.25
13 C.C. Sabathia	.25
14 Carlos Beltran	1.00
15 Carlos Delgado	.50
16 Chipper Jones	1.00
17 Cliff Floyd	.25
18 Curt Schilling	1.00
19 Delmon Young	.50
20 Derek Jeter	3.00
21 Dontrelle Willis	.25
22 Edgar Martinez	.50
23 Edgar Renteria	.50
24 Eric Chavez	.50
25 Eric Gagne	.50
26 Frank Thomas	.75

#	Player	Price
27	Garret Anderson	.50
28	Gary Sheffield	.75
29	Geoff Jenkins	.25
30	Greg Maddux	1.50
31	Hank Blalock	.75
32	Hideo Nomo	.50
33	Ichiro Suzuki	2.00
34	Ivan Rodriguez	.75
35	Jacque Jones	.25
36	Jason Giambi	.50
37	Jason Schmidt	.50
38	Javier Vazquez	.50
39	Javy Lopez	.50
40	Jeff Bagwell	.75
41	Jim Edmonds	.50
42	Jim Thome	.75
43	Joe Mauer	.50
44	John Smoltz	.50
45	Jose Cruz Jr.	.50
46	Jose Reyes	.50
47	Jose Vidro	.25
48	Josh Beckett	.50
49	Ken Griffey Jr.	1.50
50	Kerry Wood	1.00
51	Kevin Brown	.25
52	Larry Walker	.25
53	Magglio Ordonez	.25
54	Manny Ramirez	.75
55	Mark Mulder	.50
56	Mark Prior	1.00
57	Mark Teixeira	.50
58	Miguel Cabrera	1.00
59	Miguel Tejada	.50
60	Mike Lowell	.40
61	Mike Mussina	.75
62	Mike Piazza	1.50
63	Nomar Garciaparra	1.50
64	Orlando Cabrera	.40
65	Pat Burrell	.25
66	Pedro J. Martinez	1.00
67	Phil Nevin	.25
68	Preston Wilson	.25
69	Rafael Furcal	.25
70	Rafael Palmeiro	.75
71	Randy Johnson	1.00
72	Craig Wilson	.25
73	Rich Harden	.25
74	Richie Sexson	.50
75	Rickie Weeks	.50
76	Rocco Baldelli	.50
77	Roger Clemens	2.50
78	Roy Halladay	.50
79	Roy Oswalt	.50
80	Ryan Klesko	.25
81	Sammy Sosa	2.00
82	Scott Podsednik	.25
83	Scott Rolen	1.00
84	Shawn Green	.40
85	Tim Hudson	.40
86	Todd Helton	.75
87	Torii Hunter	.40
88	Troy Glaus	.25
89	Vernon Wells	.25
90	Vladimir Guerrero	1.00
91	Aarom Baldiris RC	3.00
92	Akinori Otsuka RC	5.00
93	Andres Blanco RC	5.00
94	Angel Chavez RC	3.00
95	Brian Dallimore RC	3.00
96	Carlos Hines RC	3.00
97	Carlos Vasquez RC	3.00
98	Casey Daigle RC	3.00
99	Chad Bentz RC	3.00
100	Chris Aguila RC	3.00
101	Chris Oxspring RC	3.00
102	Chris Saenz RC	3.00
103	Chris Shelton RC	3.00
104	Colby Miller RC	5.00
105	David Crouthers RC	3.00
106	David Aardsma RC	5.00
107	Dennis Sarfate RC	3.00
108	Donnie Kelly RC	3.00
109	Eddy Rodriguez RC	3.00
110	Eduardo Villacis RC	3.00
111	Edwin Moreno RC	3.00
112	Enemencio Pacheco RC	3.00
113	Fernando Nieve RC	3.00
114	Franklyn Gracesqui RC	3.00
115	Freddy Guzman RC	3.00
116	Greg Dobbs RC	3.00
117	Hector Gimenez RC	3.00
118	Ian Snell RC	5.00
119	Ivan Ochoa RC	3.00
120	Jake Woods RC	3.00
121	Jamie Brown RC	3.00
122	Jason Bartlett RC	5.00
123	Jason Frasor RC	3.00
124	Jeff Bennett RC	3.00
125	Jerome Gamble RC	3.00
126	Jerry Gil RC	3.00
127	Brandon Medders RC	3.00
128	Ryan Meaux RC	3.00
129	John Gall RC	3.00
130	Jorge Sequea RC	3.00
131	Jorge Vasquez RC	5.00
132	Jose Capellan RC	3.00
133	Josh Labandeira RC	3.00
134	Justin Germano RC	3.00
135	Justin Hampson RC	3.00
136	Justin Huisman RC	3.00
137	Justin Knoedler RC	3.00
138	Justin Leone RC	3.00
139	Kazuhito Tadano RC	5.00
140	Kazuo Matsui RC	5.00
141	Kevin Cave RC	5.00
142	Lincoln Holdzkom RC	3.00
143	Lino Urdaneta RC	3.00
144	Luis A. Gonzalez RC	5.00

#	Player	Price
145	Mariano Gomez RC	5.00
146	Merkin Valdez RC	5.00
147	Michael Vento RC	5.00
148	Mike Wuertz RC	5.00
149	Mike Gosling	5.00
150	Mike Johnston RC	3.00
151	Mike Rouse	5.00
152	Nick Regilio RC	5.00
153	Onil Joseph RC	3.00
154	Orlando Rodriguez RC	5.00
155	Ramon Ramirez RC	5.00
156	Renyel Pinto RC	5.00
157	Roberto Novoa RC	5.00
158	Roman Colon RC	3.00
159	Ronald Belisario RC	5.00
160	Ronny Cedeno RC	8.00
161	Rusty Tucker RC	3.00
162	Ryan Wing	3.00
163	Scott Dohmann RC	3.00
164	Scott Proctor RC	5.00
165	Sean Henn	5.00
166	Shawn Camp RC	5.00
167	Shawn Hill RC	5.00
168	Shingo Takatsu RC	8.00
169	Tim Hamulack RC	3.00
170	William Bergolla RC	5.00
171	Adam Dunn	2.00
172	Albert Pujols	8.00
173	Alex Rodriguez	8.00
174	Alfonso Soriano	2.00
175	Andruw Jones	2.00
176	Bret Boone	1.50
177	Brian Giles	1.50
178	Carlos Delgado	2.00
179	Derrek Lee	2.00
180	Eric Chavez	1.50
181	Frank Thomas	4.00
182	Garret Anderson	1.50
183	Gary Sheffield	2.00
184	Hank Blalock	2.00
185	Jason Giambi	1.50
186	Javy Lopez	1.50
187	Jeff Bagwell	2.00
188	Jim Edmonds	2.00
189	Jim Thome	2.00
190	Ken Griffey Jr.	4.00
191	Lance Berkman	2.00
192	Magglio Ordonez	1.50
193	Manny Ramirez	3.00
194	Mike Lowell	1.50
195	Mike Piazza	3.00
196	Preston Wilson	1.50
197	Rafael Palmeiro	2.00
198	Richie Sexson	1.50
199	Sammy Sosa	5.00
200	Scott Rolen	4.00
201	Shawn Green	1.50
202	Todd Helton	2.00
203	Troy Glaus	1.50
204	Vernon Wells	1.50
205	Vladimir Guerrero	3.00
206	Garret Anderson, Vladimir Guerrero	3.00
207	Luis Gonzalez, Richie Sexson	2.00
208	Andruw Jones, Chipper Jones	3.00
209	Javy Lopez, Miguel Tejada	2.00
210	Manny Ramirez, David Ortiz	5.00
211	Derrek Lee, Sammy Sosa	5.00
212	Frank Thomas, Magglio Ordonez	2.00
213	Austin Kearns, Ken Griffey Jr.	4.00
214	Preston Wilson, Todd Helton	2.00
215	Delmon Young, Ivan Rodriguez	2.00
216	Miguel Cabrera, Mike Lowell	3.00
217	Jeff Bagwell, Lance Berkman	
218	Lyle Overbay, Geoff Jenkins	1.50
219	Adrian Beltre, Shawn Green	2.00
220	Jacque Jones, Torii Hunter	1.50
221	Jose Vidro, N. Johnson	1.50
222	Kazuo Matsui, Mike Piazza	5.00
223	Alex Rodriguez, Jason Giambi	6.00
224	Eric Chavez, Jermaine Dye	1.50
225	Jim Thome, Pat Burrell	2.00
226	Brian Giles, Phil Nevin	1.50
227	Bret Boone, Ichiro Suzuki	6.00
228	Albert Pujols, Scott Rolen	8.00
229	Hank Blalock, Mark Teixeira	3.00
230	Carlos Delgado, Vernon Wells	2.00
231	Albert Pujols	8.00
232	Alex Rodriguez	8.00
233	Chipper Jones	3.00
234	Craig Biggio	1.50
235	Curt Schilling	2.00
236	Derek Jeter	8.00
237	Ivan Rodriguez	2.00
238	Jeff Bagwell	2.00
239	Jim Edmonds	2.00
240	Jim Thome	2.00
241	Josh Beckett	

242	Kerry Wood	3.00
243	Kevin Brown	1.50
244	Mark Prior	2.00
245	Miguel Tejada	2.00
246	Mike Mussina	2.00
247	Nomar Garciaparra	4.00
248	Pedro J. Martinez	3.00
249	Randy Johnson	3.00
250	Roger Clemens	6.00
251	Alex Rodriguez, Derek Jeter	12.00
252	Alfonso Soriano, Hank Blalock	4.00
253	Bobby Abreu, Pat Burrell	3.00
254	Edgar Renteria, Scott Rolen	4.00
255	Garret Anderson, Vladimir Guerrero	4.00
256	Jeff Bagwell, Jeff Kent	3.00
257	Jose Reyes, Kazuo Matsui	4.00
258	K. Greene, S. Burroughs	4.00
259	Marcus Giles, Rafael Furcal	3.00
260	Manny Ramirez, Johnny Damon	6.00
261	Tim Bausher RC	3.00
262	Tim Bittner RC	5.00

Limited
No Pricing
Production 10 Sets

Sweet Impressions Plates
No Pricing
Production One Set

Wood
Stars (1-90): 3-6X
SP's (91-262): .75-1.5X
Production 99 Sets

Diamond Champs Jersey
NM/M
Common Player: 5.00
Production 150 Sets

GA	Garret Anderson	5.00
JB	Josh Beckett	8.00
RC	Roger Clemens	12.00
EG	Eric Gagne	8.00
KG	Ken Griffey Jr.	12.00
RH	Roy Halladay	5.00
DJ	Derek Jeter	20.00
RJ	Randy Johnson	10.00
CJ	Chipper Jones	8.00
GM	Greg Maddux	10.00
PM	Pedro J. Martinez	8.00
PE	Andy Pettitte	5.00
MP	Mike Piazza	10.00
AP	Albert Pujols	20.00
AR	Alex Rodriguez/Yanks	15.00
IR	Ivan Rodriguez	8.00
CS	Curt Schilling	10.00
IS	Ichiro Suzuki	30.00
MT	Miguel Tejada	6.00
BZ	Barry Zito	5.00

Home Run Heroes Jersey
NM/M
Common Player: 5.00
Production 199 Sets

GA	Garret Anderson	5.00
JB	Jeff Bagwell	8.00
CB	Carlos Beltran	8.00
AB	Adrian Beltre	8.00
LB	Lance Berkman	5.00
HB	Hank Blalock	8.00
BB	Bret Boone	5.00
PB	Pat Burrell	5.00
MC	Miguel Cabrera	10.00
EC	Eric Chavez	5.00
CD	Carlos Delgado	5.00
JD	J.D. Drew	5.00
AD	Adam Dunn	8.00
JE	Jim Edmonds	8.00
JG	Jason Giambi	5.00
BG	Brian Giles	5.00
TG	Troy Glaus	5.00
LG	Luis Gonzalez	5.00
SG	Shawn Green	5.00
KG	Ken Griffey Jr./Bat Up	12.00
KG1	Ken Griffey Jr./Swing	12.00
VG	Vladimir Guerrero	10.00
HA	Travis Hafner	5.00
TH	Todd Helton	8.00
DJ	Derek Jeter	20.00
AJ	Andruw Jones	6.00
CJ	Chipper Jones	5.00
JK	Jeff Kent	5.00
DL	Derek Lee	5.00
ML	Mike Lowell	5.00
HM	Hideki Matsui	25.00
JM	Joe Mauer	15.00
FM	Fred McGriff	5.00
MO	Magglio Ordonez	5.00
DO	David Ortiz	15.00
RP	Rafael Palmeiro	8.00
MP	Mike Piazza	10.00
JP	Jorge Posada	5.00
AP	Albert Pujols	20.00
MR	Manny Ramirez	8.00
AR	Alex Rodriguez/ Yanks/Bat Up	15.00
AR1	Alex Rodriguez/ Yanks/Swing	15.00
IR	Ivan Rodriguez	8.00
SR	Scott Rolen	5.00
RS	Richie Sexson	5.00
GS	Gary Sheffield	8.00
AS	Alfonso Soriano	8.00
SS	Sammy Sosa	12.00
MT	Mark Teixeira	6.00
TE	Miguel Tejada	6.00
FT	Frank Thomas	8.00
JT	Jim Thome	10.00
VW	Vernon Wells	5.00
BW	Bernie Williams	8.00
PW	Preston Wilson	5.00

Marquee Attractions Jersey
NM/M
Common Player: 5.00
Production 199 Sets

HB	Hank Blalock	5.00
MC	Miguel Cabrera	10.00
EC	Eric Chavez	5.00
RC	Roger Clemens	12.00
CD	Carlos Delgado	5.00
EG	Eric Gagne	5.00
BG	Brian Giles	5.00
KG	Ken Griffey Jr.	12.00
VG	Vladimir Guerrero	10.00
TH	Todd Helton	8.00
HU	Torii Hunter	5.00
DJ	Derek Jeter	20.00
RJ	Randy Johnson	10.00
AJ	Andruw Jones	6.00
PI	Mike Piazza	10.00
MP	Mark Prior	5.00
AP	Albert Pujols	20.00
AR	Alex Rodriguez	15.00
IR	Ivan Rodriguez	8.00
CS	Curt Schilling	10.00
JS	Jason Schmidt	5.00
BS	Ben Sheets	5.00
IS	Ichiro Suzuki	30.00
MS	Mike Sweeney	5.00
MT	Miguel Tejada	8.00
FT	Frank Thomas	8.00
JT	Jim Thome	10.00

Signatures

NM/M
Common Player: 10.00
Black Stitch: No Pricing
Production One Set

GA	Garret Anderson	15.00
RB	Rocco Baldelli	10.00
BE	Josh Beckett	40.00
CB	Carlos Beltran	15.00
AB	Angel Berroa	10.00
HB	Hank Blalock	15.00
BB	Bret Boone	10.00
PB	Pat Burrell	15.00
SB	Sean Burroughs	10.00
MC	Miguel Cabrera	40.00
EC	Eric Chavez	12.00
WC	Will Clark	25.00
RC	Roger Clemens	150.00
JD	J.D. Drew	15.00
AD	Adam Dunn	20.00
NG	Nomar Garciaparra	50.00
BG	Brian Giles	10.00
MG	Marcus Giles	10.00
GL	Tom Glavine	40.00
JG	Juan Gonzalez	20.00
LG	Luis Gonzalez	15.00
KG	Ken Griffey Jr.	75.00
VG	Vladimir Guerrero	50.00
TG	Tony Gwynn	40.00
HA	Roy Halladay	35.00
RH	Rich Harden	15.00
TH	Todd Helton	40.00
HI	Richard Hidalgo	10.00
HO	Trevor Hoffman	20.00
TI	Tim Hudson	20.00
HU	Torii Hunter	20.00
GJ	Geoff Jenkins	10.00
DJ	Derek Jeter	160.00
JJ	Jacque Jones	10.00
AK	Austin Kearns	15.00
RK	Ryan Klesko	10.00
CL	Carlos Lee	15.00
DL	Derek Lee	20.00
ML	Mike Lieberthal	10.00
EL	Esteban Loaiza	10.00
LO	Mike Lowell	20.00
MA	Mike Marshall/SP/34	15.00
EM	Edgar Martinez	50.00
DM	Don Mattingly	60.00
JM	Joe Mauer	35.00
MU	Mark Mulder	10.00
MM	Mark Mussina	40.00
RO	Roy Oswalt	20.00
CP	Corey Patterson	15.00
OP	Odalis Perez	10.00
PI	Mike Piazza	150.00
SP	Scott Podsednik	10.00
MP	Mark Prior	15.00
AP	Albert Pujols	220.00
MR	Manny Ramirez	60.00
JR	Jose Reyes	40.00
CR	Cal Ripken Jr.	180.00
IR	Ivan Rodriguez	20.00
SR	Scott Rolen	20.00
NR	Nolan Ryan	150.00
RS	Ryne Sandberg	75.00
SA	Johan Santana	40.00
JS	Jason Schmidt	15.00
TS	Tom Seaver	50.00
BS	Ben Sheets	15.00
GS	Gary Sheffield	20.00
SM	John Smoltz	50.00
IS	Ichiro Suzuki	250.00
MT	Mark Teixeira	30.00
TE	Miguel Tejada	25.00
FT	Frank Thomas	50.00
JV	Javier Vazquez	15.00
WA	Billy Wagner	15.00
BW	Brandon Webb	15.00
WE	Rickie Weeks	15.00
VW	Vernon Wells/30	25.00
RW	Randy Wolf	12.00
KW	Kerry Wood	15.00
DY	Delmon Young	15.00
CZ	Carlos Zambrano	15.00

Signatures Red-Blue Stitch
NM/M
Quantity produced listed

GA	Garret Anderson/45	20.00
RB	Rocco Baldelli/35	20.00
BE	Josh Beckett/45	30.00
CB	Carlos Beltran/45	25.00
AB	Angel Berroa/45	20.00
HB	Hank Blalock/45	20.00
BB	Bret Boone/45	20.00
PB	Pat Burrell/35	20.00
SB	Sean Burroughs/45	15.00
MC	Miguel Cabrera/45	40.00
EC	Eric Chavez/45	20.00
RC	Roger Clemens/30	175.00
JD	J.D. Drew/40	25.00
AD	Adam Dunn/45	25.00
NG	Nomar Garciaparra/45	60.00
BG	Brian Giles/45	15.00
MG	Marcus Giles/45	20.00
GL	Tom Glavine/45	60.00
JG	Juan Gonzalez/45	25.00
LG	Luis Gonzalez/45	25.00
KG	Ken Griffey Jr./44	100.00
VG	Vladimir Guerrero/45	75.00
TG	Tony Gwynn/45	60.00
HA	Roy Halladay/35	60.00
RH	Rich Harden/45	20.00
TH	Todd Helton/45	40.00
HI	Richard Hidalgo/45	15.00
HO	Trevor Hoffman/45	20.00
TI	Tim Hudson/45	25.00
HU	Torii Hunter/45	25.00
EJ	Edwin Jackson/45	15.00
GJ	Geoff Jenkins/45	15.00
DJ	Derek Jeter/35	275.00
JJ	Jacque Jones/45	15.00
AK	Austin Kearns/45	20.00
RK	Ryan Klesko/45	15.00
CL	Carlos Lee/45	20.00
DL	Derek Lee/45	25.00
ML	Mike Lieberthal/45	15.00
EL	Esteban Loaiza/45	15.00
LO	Mike Lowell/35	30.00
EM	Edgar Martinez/30	50.00
DM	Don Mattingly/45	85.00
JM	Joe Mauer/45	60.00
MU	Mark Mulder/45	15.00
RO	Roy Oswalt/45	25.00
CP	Corey Patterson/45	20.00
OP	Odalis Perez/45	15.00
SP	Scott Podsednik/45	15.00
MP	Mark Prior/45	20.00
AP	Albert Pujols/45	250.00
MR	Manny Ramirez/40	80.00
JR	Jose Reyes/45	50.00
CR	Cal Ripken Jr./35	250.00
IR	Ivan Rodriguez/45	50.00
NR	Nolan Ryan/40	170.00
RS	Ryne Sandberg/80	80.00
SA	Johan Santana/45	65.00
JS	Jason Schmidt/45	15.00
TS	Tom Seaver/55	75.00
BS	Ben Sheets/55	15.00
GS	Gary Sheffield/45	50.00
SM	John Smoltz/40	80.00
IS	Ichiro Suzuki/25	500.00
MT	Mark Teixeira/25	50.00
TE	Miguel Tejada/25	40.00
FT	Frank Thomas/25	75.00
JV	Javier Vazquez/45	20.00
WA	Billy Wagner/45	20.00
BW	Brandon Webb/45	20.00
WE	Rickie Weeks/45	20.00
VW	Vernon Wells/29	20.00
DW	Dontrelle Willis/45	15.00
RW	Randy Wolf/45	20.00
KW	Kerry Wood/45	20.00
DY	Delmon Young/45	20.00
CZ	Carlos Zambrano/30	25.00

Signatures Barrel
NM/M
Cards not serial numbered, quantity produced provided by Upper Deck.

GA	Garret Anderson/74	15.00
RB	Rocco Baldelli/19	15.00
BE	Josh Beckett/65	50.00
CB	Carlos Beltran/55	25.00
AB	Angel Berroa/64	15.00
HB	Hank Blalock/64	15.00
BB	Bret Boone/64	15.00
SB	Sean Burroughs/45	15.00
MC	Miguel Cabrera/64	40.00
EC	Eric Chavez/74	20.00
AD	Adam Dunn/74	30.00
NG	Nomar Garciaparra/38	75.00
BG	Brian Giles/64	15.00
MG	Marcus Giles/64	15.00
GL	Tom Glavine/64	50.00
KG	Ken Griffey Jr./64	125.00
VG	Vladimir Guerrero/38	75.00
HA	Roy Halladay/64	50.00
RH	Rich Harden/64	20.00
TH	Todd Helton/38	40.00
HI	Richard Hidalgo/64	15.00
HO	Trevor Hoffman/68	25.00
TI	Tim Hudson/64	30.00
HU	Torii Hunter/64	25.00
EJ	Edwin Jackson/64 Exch	15.00
GJ	Geoff Jenkins/64	15.00
DJ	Derek Jeter/53	275.00
JJ	Jacque Jones/64	15.00
AK	Austin Kearns/64	20.00
RK	Ryan Klesko/64	15.00
CL	Carlos Lee/64	25.00
DL	Derek Lee/64	50.00
EL	Esteban Loaiza/64	15.00
LO	Mike Lowell/64	30.00
EM	Edgar Martinez/64	40.00
DM	Don Mattingly/38	125.00
JM	Joe Mauer/72	50.00
MU	Mark Mulder/64	15.00
MM	Mike Mussina/64	40.00
RO	Roy Oswalt/64	30.00
CP	Corey Patterson/ 74 Exch	20.00
OP	Odalis Perez/64	15.00
PI	Mike Piazza/38	150.00
SP	Scott Podsednik/64	15.00
MP	Mark Prior/64	15.00
AP	Albert Pujols/64	250.00
MR	Manny Ramirez/63	25.00
JR	Jose Reyes/49	50.00
CR	Cal Ripken Jr./38	220.00
AR	Alex Rodriguez/28	300.00
IR	Ivan Rodriguez/64	15.00
NR	Nolan Ryan/38	180.00
SA	Johan Santana/64	15.00
JS	Jason Schmidt/64	15.00
TS	Tom Seaver/38	75.00
BS	Ben Sheets/64	25.00
GS	Gary Sheffield/38	60.00
IS	Ichiro Suzuki/64	500.00
MT	Mark Teixeira/64	50.00
TE	Miguel Tejada/64	50.00
JV	Javier Vazquez/64	20.00
WA	Billy Wagner/64	20.00
BW	Brandon Webb/64	30.00
WE	Rickie Weeks/64	25.00
VW	Vernon Wells/33	20.00
DW	Dontrelle Willis/64	15.00
RW	Randy Wolf/64	15.00
KW	Kerry Wood/64	20.00
DY	Delmon Young/74	20.00
CZ	Carlos Zambrano/38	20.00

Signatures Dual
No Pricing
Production 10 Sets

Signatures Glove
NM/M
Production 5-25

GA	Garret Anderson/25	30.00
RB	Rocco Baldelli/25	30.00
BE	Josh Beckett/25	50.00
CB	Carlos Beltran/25	40.00
AB	Angel Berroa/25	15.00
HB	Hank Blalock/25	20.00
BB	Bret Boone/25	15.00
PB	Pat Burrell/15	20.00
SB	Sean Burroughs/25	15.00
MC	Miguel Cabrera/25	100.00
EC	Eric Chavez/25	20.00
WC	Will Clark/25	100.00
AD	Adam Dunn/25	60.00
NG	Nomar Garciaparra/25	100.00
BG	Brian Giles/25	15.00
MG	Marcus Giles/25	15.00
GL	Tom Glavine/25	65.00
JG	Juan Gonzalez/25	25.00
LG	Luis Gonzalez/25	30.00
KG	Ken Griffey Jr./25	200.00
VG	Vladimir Guerrero/25	70.00
TG	Tony Gwynn/25	80.00
HA	Roy Halladay/24	80.00
RH	Rich Harden/25	20.00
TH	Todd Helton/25	50.00
HI	Richard Hidalgo/15	15.00
HO	Trevor Hoffman/15	30.00
TI	Tim Hudson/25	20.00
HU	Torii Hunter/25	40.00
EJ	Edwin Jackson/25	20.00
GJ	Geoff Jenkins/25	20.00
JJ	Jacque Jones/25	20.00
AK	Austin Kearns/25	25.00
CL	Carlos Lee/25	40.00
DL	Derek Lee/25	40.00
ML	Mike Lieberthal/25	15.00
EL	Esteban Loaiza/25	15.00
MA	Mike Marshall/25	50.00
EM	Edgar Martinez/25	75.00
DM	Don Mattingly/25	180.00
JM	Joe Mauer/25	75.00
MU	Mark Mulder/25	20.00
MM	Mike Mussina/25	75.00
RO	Roy Oswalt/25	50.00
CP	Corey Patterson/25	15.00
OP	Odalis Perez/25	15.00
SP	Scott Podsednik/25	20.00
MP	Mark Prior/25	20.00
AP	Albert Pujols/25	300.00
MR	Manny Ramirez/25	120.00
JR	Jose Reyes/25	75.00
CR	Cal Ripken Jr./25	275.00
IR	Ivan Rodriguez/25	50.00
NR	Nolan Ryan/25	250.00
RS	Ryne Sandberg/20	125.00
SA	Johan Santana/25	20.00
JS	Jason Schmidt/25	20.00
BS	Ben Sheets/25	20.00
GS	Gary Sheffield/20	25.00
MT	Mark Teixeira/25	75.00
TE	Miguel Tejada/25	40.00
JV	Javier Vazquez/25	25.00
WA	Billy Wagner/25	40.00
BW	Brandon Webb/25	25.00
WE	Rickie Weeks/25	25.00
DW	Dontrelle Willis/25	25.00
KW	Kerry Wood/25	25.00
DY	Delmon Young/25	25.00

Signatures Historical Ball
No Pricing
Production One Set

Sweet Sticks

NM/M
Common Player: 4.00
Production 199 Sets

BA	Bobby Abreu	6.00
MA	Moises Alou	6.00
GA	Garret Anderson	6.00
JB	Jeff Bagwell	8.00
BE	Carlos Beltran	4.00
AB	Adrian Beltre	4.00
LB	Lance Berkman	4.00
CB	Craig Biggio	6.00
HB	Hank Blalock	4.00
BB	Bret Boone	4.00
PB	Pat Burrell	4.00
MC	Miguel Cabrera	8.00
EC	Eric Chavez	6.00
RC	Roger Clemens	15.00
CD	Carlos Delgado	6.00
JD	J.D. Drew	6.00
AD	Adam Dunn	6.00
JE	Jim Edmonds	6.00
RF	Rafael Furcal	6.00
NG	Nomar Garciaparra	12.00
JG	Jason Giambi	6.00
BG	Brian Giles	4.00
MG	Marcus Giles	4.00
TG	Troy Glaus	4.00
GL	Tom Glavine	8.00
LG	Luis Gonzalez	4.00
SG	Shawn Green	4.00
KG	Ken Griffey Jr.	15.00
VG	Vladimir Guerrero	8.00
TH	Todd Helton	8.00
DJ	Derek Jeter	25.00
RJ	Randy Johnson	8.00
CJ	Chipper Jones	10.00
AJ	Andruw Jones	6.00
JK	Jeff Kent	4.00
DL	Derek Lee	4.00
ML	Mike Lowell	4.00
GM	Greg Maddux	10.00
HM	Hideki Matsui	35.00
KM	Kazuo Matsui	8.00
MO	Magglio Ordonez	4.00
RP	Rafael Palmeiro	6.00
MP	Mike Piazza	10.00
PR	Mark Prior	8.00
AP	Albert Pujols	20.00
MR	Manny Ramirez	8.00
ER	Edgar Renteria	6.00
JR	Jose Reyes	6.00
CR	Cal Ripken Jr.	30.00
AR	Alex Rodriguez	15.00
IR	Ivan Rodriguez	6.00
SR	Scott Rolen	10.00
CS	Curt Schilling	6.00
RS	Richie Sexson	6.00
GS	Gary Sheffield	6.00
AS	Alfonso Soriano	6.00

Sweet Sticks Dual
NM/M
Common Duo: 10.00
Production 100 Sets

BT	Hank Blalock, Mark Teixeira	10.00
CL	Miguel Cabrera, Mike Lowell	10.00
JC	Randy Johnson, Roger Clemens	25.00
JG	Derek Jeter, Nomar Garciaparra	25.00
JM	Jose Reyes, Kazuo Matsui	25.00
MM	Hideki Matsui, Kazuo Matsui	40.00
PR	Albert Pujols, Scott Rolen	40.00
RG	Manny Ramirez, Nomar Garciaparra	15.00
RJ	Alex Rodriguez, Derek Jeter	50.00
RP	Ivan Rodriguez, Mike Piazza	15.00
TB	Jim Thome, Pat Burrell	20.00
WP	Kerry Wood, Mark Prior	10.00

Sweet Sticks Triple
NM/M
Production 50 Sets

GPS	Ken Griffey Jr., Rafael Palmeiro, Sammy Sosa	40.00
JJD	Andruw Jones, Chipper Jones, J.D. Drew	25.00
JSG	Derek Jeter, Ichiro Suzuki, Ken Griffey Jr.	120.00
MWP	Greg Maddux, Kerry Wood, Mark Prior	35.00
RJG	Alex Rodriguez, Derek Jeter, Jason Giambi	65.00

Sweet Sticks Quad
NM/M
Production 25 Sets

PRSG	Albert Pujols, Alex Rodriguez, Ichiro Suzuki, Ken Griffey Jr.	125.00
RGDM	Babe Ruth, Lou Gehrig, Joe DiMaggio, Mickey Mantle	1,200

Sweet Threads

NM/M
Common Player: 4.00
Patch: 1.5-2.5X
Production 85 Sets

JB	Jeff Bagwell	8.00
CB	Carlos Beltran	4.00
LB	Lance Berkman	4.00
HB	Hank Blalock	8.00
BB	Bret Boone	4.00
MC	Miguel Cabrera	8.00
EC	Eric Chavez	4.00
BC	Bartolo Colon	4.00
CD	Carlos Delgado	4.00
JG	Jason Giambi	4.00
BG	Brian Giles	4.00
TG	Troy Glaus	4.00
SG	Shawn Green	4.00
VG	Vladimir Guerrero	8.00
RH	Rich Harden	4.00
HE	Todd Helton	8.00
TH	Tim Hudson	4.00
ML	Mike Lowell	4.00
EM	Edgar Martinez	4.00
KM	Kazuo Matsui/SP	15.00
JM	Joe Mauer	8.00
MM	Mark Mulder	8.00
HN	Hideo Nomo	8.00
MO	Magglio Ordonez	4.00
RO	Roy Oswalt	4.00
MP	Mark Prior	4.00
MR	Manny Ramirez	8.00
JR	Jose Reyes	4.00
SS	Sammy Sosa	10.00
JS	Jason Schmidt	6.00
RS	Richie Sexson	6.00
GS	Gary Sheffield	6.00
AS	Alfonso Soriano	6.00
MT	Mark Teixeira	6.00
FT	Frank Thomas	8.00
JT	Jim Thome	8.00
RW	Rickie Weeks	4.00
VW	Vernon Wells	4.00
DW	Dontrelle Willis	4.00
PW	Preston Wilson	4.00
KW	Kerry Wood	8.00
DY	Delmon Young	8.00

Sweet Threads Dual

NM/M

Common Duo: 5.00
Production 150 Sets
Patch: 1.5-2X
Production 60 Sets

BP	Angel Berroa, Scott Podsednik	4.00
BT	Hank Blalock, Mark Teixeira	10.00
CK	Curt Schilling, Kevin Brown	10.00
CS	Roger Clemens, Sammy Sosa	20.00
DT	Carlos Delgado, Jim Thome	8.00
GH	Eric Gagne, Roy Halladay	8.00
HG	Tim Hudson, Vladimir Guerrero	10.00
JC	Randy Johnson, Roger Clemens	25.00
JH	Andruw Jones, Torii Hunter	8.00
JJ	Andruw Jones, Chipper Jones	10.00
MM	Hideki Matsui, Kazuo Matsui	50.00
MP	Joe Mauer, Mark Prior	10.00
PC	Andy Pettitte, Roger Clemens	20.00
PP	Jorge Posada, Mike Piazza	15.00
PS	Albert Pujols, Ichiro Suzuki	50.00
PW	Albert Pujols, Kerry Wood	15.00
RJ	Alex Rodriguez, Derek Jeter	50.00
RM	Jose Reyes, Kazuo Matsui	15.00
SB	Alfonso Soriano, Bret Boone	8.00
SM	Gary Sheffield, Pedro J. Martinez	12.00
WP	Kerry Wood, Mark Prior	10.00
YW	Delmon Young, Rickie Weeks	8.00

Sweet Threads Triple

NM/M

Common Trio: 10.00
Production 99 Sets
Triple Patch: 2X
No pricing 15 or less.

AGG	Garret Anderson, Troy Glaus, Vladimir Guerrero	20.00
BKE	Jeff Bagwell, Jeff Kent, Morgan Ensberg	15.00
BLR	Adrian Beltre, Mike Lowell, Scott Rolen	20.00
BMS	Bret Boone, Edgar Martinez, Ichiro Suzuki	50.00
BWC	Josh Beckett, Kerry Wood, Roger Clemens	30.00
CMM	Bobby Crosby, Joe Mauer, Kazuo Matsui	30.00
DHW	Carlos Delgado, Roy Halladay, Vernon Wells	15.00
DKG	Adam Dunn, Austin Kearns, Ken Griffey Jr.	20.00
DMJ	Joe DiMaggio, Mickey Mantle, Derek Jeter	220.00
DMW	Joe DiMaggio, Mickey Mantle, Ted Williams	250.00
DRN	Johnny Damon, Manny Ramirez, Trot Nixon	40.00
FRP	Keith Foulke, Mariano Rivera, Troy Percival	25.00
GPS	Ken Griffey Jr., Rafael Palmeiro, Sammy Sosa	35.00
JJD	Andruw Jones, Chipper Jones, J.D. Drew	20.00
JTG	Derek Jeter, Miguel Tejada, Nomar Garciaparra	40.00
JWH	Edwin Jackson, Jerome Williams, Rich Harden	10.00
KVG	Jeff Kent, Jose Vidro, Marcus Giles	10.00
LTO	Carlos Lee, Frank Thomas, Magglio Ordonez	20.00
LTP	Javy Lopez, Miguel Tejada, Rafael Palmeiro	20.00
MCF	Kazuo Matsui, Miguel Cabrera, Rafael Furcal	20.00
MMH	Mike Mussina, Pedro J. Martinez, Tim Hudson	25.00
MSH	Joe Mauer, Johan Santana, Torii Hunter	35.00
MWP	Greg Maddux, Kerry Wood, Mark Prior	25.00
PAS	Corey Patterson, Moises Alou, Sammy Sosa	30.00
PCO	Andy Pettitte, Roger Clemens, Roy Oswalt	25.00
PRR	Albert Pujols, Edgar Renteria, Scott Rolen	40.00
PTH	Albert Pujols, Jim Thome, Todd Helton	30.00
RCB	Alex Rodriguez, Eric Chavez, Hank Blalock	30.00
RGJ	Alex Rodriguez, Ken Griffey Jr., Randy Johnson	35.00
RGW	Jose Reyes, Khalil Greene, Rickie Weeks	25.00
RJG	Alex Rodriguez, Derek Jeter, Jason Giambi	60.00
RMP	Jose Reyes, Kazuo Matsui, Mike Piazza	25.00
SBK	Alfonso Soriano, Bret Boone, Jeff Kent	20.00
SBP	Jason Schmidt, Josh Beckett, Mark Prior	15.00
SBT	Alfonso Soriano, Hank Blalock, Mark Teixeira	20.00
SLM	Curt Schilling, Derek Lowe, Pedro J. Martinez	40.00
VBM	Javier Vazquez, Kevin Brown, Mike Mussina	30.00
WBP	Brandon Webb, Josh Beckett, Mark Prior	15.00
WGS	Billy Wagner, Eric Gagne, John Smoltz	20.00
WRC	Kerry Wood, Nolan Ryan, Roger Clemens	60.00
YCW	Delmon Young, Miguel Cabrera, Rickie Weeks	15.00
ZMH	Barry Zito, Mark Mulder, Tim Hudson	10.00

Sweet Threads Quad

NM/M

Common Quad: 20.00
Production 99 Sets
Quad Patch: No Pricing
Production 1-15

BADH	Carlos Beltran, Garret Anderson, Johnny Damon, Torii Hunter	30.00
BBGS	Angel Berroa, Carlos Beltran, Alex Gonzalez, Mike Sweeney	20.00
BPJC	Josh Beckett, Mark Prior, Randy Johnson, Roger Clemens	30.00
BWRC	Josh Beckett, Kerry Wood, Nolan Ryan, Roger Clemens	50.00
CAGG	Bartolo Colon, Garret Anderson, Troy Glaus, Vladimir Guerrero	25.00
DHHW	Carlos Delgado, Eric Hinske, Roy Halladay, Vernon Wells	20.00
DOGP	Carlos Delgado, David Ortiz, Jason Giambi, Rafael Palmeiro	20.00
GNKB	Brian Giles, Phil Nevin, Ryan Klesko, Sean Burroughs	25.00
GNLG	Eric Gagne, Hideo Nomo, Paul LoDuca, Shawn Green	30.00
JBGB	Chipper Jones, Lance Berkman, Luis Gonzalez, Pat Burrell	25.00
JEGW	Andruw Jones, Jim Edmonds, Ken Griffey Jr., Preston Wilson	35.00
JJDF	Andruw Jones, Chipper Jones, J.D. Drew, Rafael Furcal	25.00
JMSH	Jacque Jones, Joe Mauer, Shannon Stewart, Torii Hunter	35.00
JRMT	Derek Jeter, Edgar Renteria, Kazuo Matsui, Miguel Tejada	40.00
KGCS	Austin Kearns, Brian Giles, Miguel Cabrera, Sammy Sosa	25.00
LMRS	Carlos Lee, Hideki Matsui, Manny Ramirez, Shannon Stewart	75.00
LTOK	Carlos Lee, Frank Thomas, Magglio Ordonez, Paul Konerko	25.00
LTPP	Javy Lopez, Miguel Tejada, Raffy, Sidney Ponson	25.00
MMMH	Mark Mulder, Mike Mussina, Pedro J. Martinez, Roy Halladay	25.00
MTTS	Edgar Martinez, Jim Thome, Mark Teixeira, Mike Sweeney	20.00
NSGH	Phil Nevin, Richie Sexson, Shawn Green, Todd Helton	20.00
PBBC	Andy Pettitte, Craig Biggio, Jeff Bagwell, Roger Clemens	40.00
PLBT	Albert Pujols, Lee, Jeff Bagwell, Jim Thome	40.00
PRER	Albert Pujols, Edgar Renteria, Jim Edmonds, Scott Rolen	70.00
PWPS	Corey Patterson, Kerry Wood, Mark Prior, Sammy Sosa	30.00
RCBG	Alex Rodriguez, Eric Chavez, Hank Blalock, Troy Glaus	30.00
RJDM	Alex Rodriguez, Derek Jeter, Joe DiMaggio, Mickey Mantle	275.00
RLPM	Ivan Rodriguez, Javy Lopez, Jorge Posada, Joe Mauer	40.00
RMPG	Jose Reyes, Kazuo Matsui, Mike Piazza, Tom Glavine	30.00
SBKV	Alfonso Soriano, Bret Boone, Jeff Kent, Jose Vidro	20.00
SBMM	Curt Schilling, Kevin Brown, Mike Mussina, Pedro J. Martinez	40.00
SDRM	Curt Schilling, Johnny Damon, Manny Ramirez, Pedro J. Martinez	60.00
SSOG	Gary Sheffield, Ichiro Suzuki, Magglio Ordonez, Vladimir Guerrero	50.00
VCBM	Javier Vazquez, Jose Contreras, Kevin Brown, Mike Mussina	25.00
WATM	Billy Wagner, Bobby Abreu, Jim Thome, Kevin Millwood	30.00
WBCL	Dontrelle Willis, Josh Beckett, Miguel Cabrera, Mike Lowell	20.00
WGJS	Brandon Webb, Luis Gonzalez, Randy Johnson, Richie Sexson	25.00
ZMHH	Barry Zito, Mark Mulder, Rich Harden, Tim Hudson	35.00

2004 Upper Deck Sweet Spot Classic

NM/M

Complete Set (161):
Common Player (1-90): .40
Common (91-161): 2.00
Production 1,910-1,999
Pack (4): 15.00
Box (12): 150.00

1	Al Kaline	1.00
2	Andre Dawson	.40
3	Bert Blyleven	.40
4	Bill Dickey	.40
5	Bill Mazeroski	.40
6	Billy Martin	.40
7	Bob Feller	.50
8	Bob Gibson	1.00
9	Bob Lemon	.40
10	George Kell	.40
11	Bobby Doerr	.40
12	Brooks Robinson	1.00
13	Cal Ripken Jr.	4.00
14	Carl Hubbell	.40
15	Carl Yastrzemski	1.50
16	Charlie Keller	.40
17	Chuck Dressen	.40
18	Cy Young	1.00
19	Dave Winfield	.75
20	Dizzy Dean	.75
21	Don Drysdale	.75
22	Don Larsen	.75
23	Don Mattingly	2.50
24	Don Newcombe	.40
25	Duke Snider	.75
26	Early Wynn	.40
27	Eddie Mathews	1.00
28	Elston Howard	.40
29	Frank Robinson	.75
30	Gary Carter	.40
31	Gil Hodges	.40
32	Gil McDougald	.40
33	Hank Greenberg	.75
34	Harmon Killebrew	1.50
35	Harry Caray	.40
36	Honus Wagner	1.00
37	Hoyt Wilhelm	.40
38	Jackie Robinson	2.00
39	Jim Bunning	.40
40	Jim Palmer	.75
41	Jimmie Foxx	1.00
42	Jimmy Wynn	.40
43	Joe DiMaggio	3.00
44	Joe Torre	.40
45	Johnny Mize	.40
46	Juan Marichal	.75
47	Larry Doby	.40
48	Lefty Gomez	.40
49	Lefty Grove	.40
50	Leo Durocher	.40
51	Lou Boudreau	.40
52	Lou Brock	.50
53	Lou Gehrig	3.00
54	Luis Aparicio	.40
55	Maury Wills	.40
56	Mel Allen	.40
57	Mel Ott	.40
58	Mickey Cochrane	.40
59	Mickey Mantle	4.00
60	Mike Schmidt	2.00
61	Monte Irvin	.40
62	Nolan Ryan	4.00
63	Pee Wee Reese	.40
64	Phil Rizzuto	.50
65	Ralph Kiner	.40
66	Richie Ashburn	.40
67	Rick Ferrell	.40
68	Roberto Clemente	2.50
69	Robin Roberts	.40
70	Robin Yount	1.00
71	Rogers Hornsby	.75
72	Rollie Fingers	.75
73	Roy Campanella	.75
74	Ryne Sandberg	1.50
75	Satchel Paige	.75
76	Shoeless Joe Jackson	2.00
77	Stan Musial	2.00
78	Ted Williams	3.00
79	Thurman Munson	.75
80	Tom Seaver	1.50
81	Tommy Henrich	.40
82	Tommy Henrich	.40
83	Tony Perez	.40
84	Tris Speaker	.40
85	Vida Blue	.40
86	Wade Boggs	.50
87	Walter Johnson	.75
88	Warren Spahn	1.00
89	Whitey Ford	.75
90	Willie McCovey	.40
91	Andre Dawson	2.50
92	Andre Dawson	2.50
93	Ernie Banks	4.00
94	Bob Lemon	2.00
95	Cal Ripken Jr.	8.00
96	Cal Ripken Jr.	8.00
97	Carl Yastrzemski	3.00
98	Carlton Fisk	2.50
99	Cy Young	4.00
100	Don Larsen	2.50
101	Don Newcombe	2.00
102	Don Newcombe	2.00
103	Dwight Evans	2.00
104	Elston Howard	2.50
105	Frank Robinson	3.00
106	Frank Robinson	3.00
107	Frank Robinson	3.00
108	Gil McDougald	2.00
109	Hank Greenberg	4.00
110	Harmon Killebrew	4.00
111	Hoyt Wilhelm	2.00
112	Hoyt Wilhelm	2.00
113	Jackie Robinson	5.00
114	Jackie Robinson	5.00
115	Jackie Robinson	5.00
116	Jackie Robinson	5.00
117	Jim Bunning	2.00
118	Joe DiMaggio	6.00
119	Joe Morgan	2.00
120	Johnny Mize	2.50
121	Johnny Mize	2.50
122	Juan Marichal	3.00
123	Ken Griffey Sr.	2.00
124	Larry Doby	2.50
125	Lefty Gomez	2.00
126	Lou Boudreau	2.00
127	Lou Gehrig	6.00
128	Lou Gehrig	6.00
129	Mark McGwire	6.00
130	Mark McGwire	6.00
131	Maury Wills	2.00
132	Mel Ott	3.00
133	Mike Schmidt	5.00
134	Nolan Ryan	8.00
135	Nolan Ryan	8.00
136	Pee Wee Reese	2.00
137	Nolan Ryan	8.00
138	Richie Ashburn	2.50
139	Roberto Clemente	8.00
140	Roberto Clemente	8.00
141	Robin Roberts	2.00
142	Robin Yount	3.00
143	Roger Clemens	5.00
144	Rollie Fingers	2.00
145	Rollie Fingers	2.00
146	Roy Campanella	3.00
147	Ryne Sandberg	4.00
148	Satchel Paige	5.00
149	Stan Musial	5.00
150	Stan Musial	5.00
151	Stan Musial	5.00
152	Ted Williams	6.00
153	Ted Williams	6.00
154	Tom Seaver	3.00
155	Tom Seaver	3.00
156	Tom Seaver	3.00
157	Wade Boggs	2.50
158	Warren Spahn	3.00
159	Warren Spahn	3.00
160	Joe DiMaggio	6.00
161	Yogi Berra	4.00

Game-Used Patch

NM/M

Some not priced due to scarcity.
Holofoil: No Pricing
Production 10

BB	Bert Blyleven/113	25.00
WB	Wade Boggs/90	30.00
AD	Andre Dawson/100	20.00
TG	Tony Gwynn/100	35.00
CK	Charlie Keller/55	30.00
ML	Mickey Lolich/115	15.00
DM	Don Mattingly/176	45.00
GM	Gil McDougald/31	25.00
TM	Thurman Munson/100	30.00
FR	Frank Robinson/50	30.00
NR	Nolan Ryan/96	65.00
TS	Tom Seaver/94	30.00
MW	Maury Wills/78	25.00
CY	Carl Yastrzemski/20	65.00
RY	Robin Yount/100	30.00

Jersey

NM/M

Common Player: 5.00
Production 275 Sets
Holofoils: 1.5-2X
Production 50

SA	Sparky Anderson	6.00
SB	Sal Bando	5.00
RB	Ron Blomberg	5.00
BB	Bert Blyleven	5.00
WB	Wade Boggs	8.00
WB1	Wade Boggs	8.00
JB	Jim Bunning	5.00
GC	Gary Carter	6.00
RC	Roberto Clemente	65.00
AD	Andre Dawson	5.00
AD1	Andre Dawson	5.00
JD	Joe DiMaggio	70.00
CD	Chuck Dressen	5.00
KG	Ken Griffey Sr.	5.00
TG	Tony Gwynn	10.00
EH	Elston Howard	8.00
CK	Charlie Keller	15.00
ML	Mickey Lolich	6.00
MM	Mickey Mantle	125.00
JM	Juan Marichal	8.00
RM	Roger Maris	45.00
BM	Billy Martin	8.00
EM	Eddie Mathews	10.00
DM	Don Mattingly	20.00
GM	Gil McDougald	8.00
JO	Johnny Mize	10.00
TM	Thurman Munson	20.00
SM	Stan Musial	25.00
JP	Jim Palmer	8.00
CR	Cal Ripken Jr.	20.00
PR	Phil Rizzuto	15.00
FR	Frank Robinson	8.00
JR	Jackie Robinson	40.00
NR	Nolan Ryan	25.00
TS	Tom Seaver	15.00
OS	Ozzie Smith	10.00
JT	Joe Torre	8.00
TW	Ted Williams	70.00
MW	Maury Wills	5.00
CY	Carl Yastrzemski	15.00
RY	Robin Yount	10.00

Logo Patch

NM/M

Common Level 1: 5.00
Production 300
Level 2: 1X
Production 230
Level 3: 1X
Production 200
Level 4: 1-1.5X
Production 150
Level 5: 1-1.5X
Production 125
Level 6: 1-2X
Production 75
Level 7: 1.5-2.5X
Production 50
Level 8: No Pricing
Production 25

AL	Mel Allen	5.00
LA	Luis Aparicio	5.00
RA	Richie Ashburn	5.00
WB	Wade Boggs	8.00
LB	Lou Boudreau	5.00
BR	Lou Brock	5.00
JB	Jim Bunning	5.00
CA	Roy Campanella	5.00
GC	Gary Carter	5.00
HC	Harry Caray	10.00
RC	Roberto Clemente	25.00
TC	Ty Cobb	12.00
CO	Mickey Cochrane	5.00
AD	Andre Dawson	8.00
DD	Dizzy Dean	5.00
BD	Bill Dickey	5.00
JD	Joe DiMaggio	15.00
LD	Larry Doby	5.00
DO	Bobby Doerr	6.00
DR	Don Drysdale	6.00
DU	Leo Durocher	5.00
BF	Bob Feller	5.00
RF	Rick Ferrell	5.00
FI	Rollie Fingers	6.00
WF	Whitey Ford	8.00
JF	Jimmie Foxx	8.00
FF	Frankie Frisch	5.00
GE	Lou Gehrig	15.00
CG	Charlie Gehringer	8.00
BG	Bob Gibson	8.00
LG	Lefty Gomez	5.00
HG	Hank Greenberg	10.00
GR	Lefty Grove	6.00
TH	Tommy Henrich	5.00
GH	Gil Hodges	8.00
RH	Rogers Hornsby	8.00
CH	Carl Hubbell	5.00
IR	Monte Irvin	5.00
JJ	Shoeless Joe Jackson	20.00
FJ	Ferguson Jenkins	6.00
WJ	Walter Johnson	8.00
AK	Al Kaline	15.00
HK	Harmon Killebrew	8.00
RK	Ralph Kiner	8.00
DL	Don Larsen	6.00
TL	Tommy Lasorda	6.00
BL	Bob Lemon	5.00
ML	Mickey Lolich	5.00
MI	Mickey Mantle	40.00
MA	Juan Marichal	8.00
BM	Billy Martin	8.00
EM	Eddie Mathews	8.00
CM	Christy Mathewson	10.00
DM	Don Mattingly	20.00
WM	Willie McCovey	8.00
JM	Johnny Mize	6.00
TM	Thurman Munson	10.00
SM	Stan Musial	10.00
DN	Don Newcombe	5.00
MO	Mel Ott	6.00
SP	Satchel Paige	10.00
JP	Jim Palmer	8.00
TP	Tony Perez	5.00
GP	Gaylord Perry	5.00
PR	Pee Wee Reese	6.00
CR	Cal Ripken Jr.	30.00
RI	Phil Rizzuto	5.00
RR	Robin Roberts	6.00
RO	Brooks Robinson	12.00
FR	Frank Robinson	8.00
JR	Jackie Robinson	12.00
RU	Babe Ruth	20.00
NR	Nolan Ryan	25.00
RS	Ryne Sandberg	20.00
MS	Mike Schmidt	15.00
TS	Tom Seaver	15.00
SK	Bill "Moose" Skowron	5.00
ES	Enos Slaughter	5.00
DS	Duke Snider	8.00
WS	Warren Spahn	10.00
TR	Tris Speaker	8.00
JT	Joe Torre	5.00
HW	Honus Wagner	10.00
WI	Hoyt Wilhelm	5.00
TW	Ted Williams	20.00
MW	Maury Wills	5.00
DW	Dave Winfield	6.00
EW	Early Wynn	5.00
YA	Carl Yastrzemski	12.00
CY	Cy Young	10.00

Signature Black Ink

NM/M

Common Autograph: 15.00

2	Preacher Roe/225	25.00
4	Bob Feller/65	45.00
5	Bob Gibson/50	50.00
6	Harry Kalas/100	45.00
7	Bobby Doerr/100	25.00
8	Cal Ripken Jr./50	165.00
9	Carl Yastrzemski/35	110.00
10	Carlton Fisk/100	45.00
11	Chuck Tanner/150	15.00
12	Cito Gaston/150	15.00
13	Danny Ozark/150	15.00

14	Dave Winfield/80	50.00
15	Davey Johnson/175	15.00
16	Ernie Harwell/100	50.00
17	Dick Williams/150	15.00
18	Don Mattingly/40	100.00
19	Don Newcombe/40	35.00
20	Duke Snider/35	60.00
21	Steve Carlton/150	35.00
22	Felipe Alou/175	20.00
23	Frank Robinson/65	40.00
24	Gary Carter/100	35.00
25	Gene Mauch/225	15.00
26	George Bamberger/225	15.00
28	Gus Suhr/100	30.00
30	Harmon Killebrew/50	100.00
31	Jack McKeon/225	20.00
32	Jim Bunning/100	25.00
33	Jimmy Piersall/212	15.00
34	Johnny Bench/50	75.00
36	Juan Marichal/40	40.00
37	Lou Brock/50	50.00
38	George Kell/40	50.00
39	Maury Wills/40	30.00
41	Mike Schmidt/40	100.00
42	Nolan Ryan/50	135.00
43	Ozzie Smith/65	75.00
44	Eddie Mayo/140	15.00
45	Phil Rizzuto/50	50.00
46	Ralph Kiner/40	45.00
47	Lonny Frey/114	15.00
48	Bill Mazeroski/50	40.00
49	Robin Roberts/40	40.00
50	Robin Yount/40	75.00
52	Roger Craig/175	15.00
55	Tony Perez/40	70.00
56	Sparky Anderson/175	20.00
57	Stan Musial/40	100.00
58	Ted Radcliffe/225	25.00
60	Tom Seaver/25	70.00
61	Tony Gwynn/65	50.00
62	Tony LaRussa/275	15.00
63	Tony Oliva/150	15.00
64	Tony Pena/150	15.00
66	Whitey Ford/45	65.00
67	Yogi Berra/65	75.00

Signature Blue Ink

NM/M

Common Autograph: 15.00
Some not priced due to scarcity.

2	Preacher Roe/150	25.00
4	Bob Feller/50	45.00
5	Bob Gibson/50	60.00
6	Harry Kalas/50	50.00
7	Bobby Doerr/50	30.00
8	Cal Ripken Jr./25	200.00
10	Carlton Fisk/50	50.00
11	Chuck Tanner/125	15.00
12	Cito Gaston/125	15.00
13	Danny Ozark/125	15.00
14	Dave Winfield/35	60.00
15	Davey Johnson/150	15.00
16	Ernie Harwell/50	15.00
17	Dick Williams/125	15.00
21	Steve Carlton/100	35.00
22	Felipe Alou/150	20.00
23	Frank Robinson/50	40.00
24	Gary Carter/75	35.00
25	Gene Mauch/150	15.00
26	George Bamberger/150	15.00
28	Gus Suhr/85	30.00
31	Jack McKeon/150	25.00
32	Jim Bunning/65	60.00
33	Jimmy Piersall/128	15.00
35	Johnny Bench/20	90.00
38	George Kell/25	50.00
39	Maury Wills/25	25.00
41	Mike Schmidt/25	80.00
42	Nolan Ryan/25	175.00
43	Ozzie Smith/50	75.00
44	Eddie Mayo/50	20.00
45	Phil Rizzuto/25	50.00
47	Lonny Frey/75	15.00
48	Bill Mazeroski/25	40.00
49	Robin Roberts/25	40.00
50	Robin Yount/25	75.00
52	Roger Craig/150	15.00
56	Sparky Anderson/150	25.00
57	Stan Musial/25	120.00
58	Ted Radcliffe/150	50.00
62	Tony LaRussa/145	15.00
63	Tony Oliva/125	15.00
64	Tony Pena/115	15.00
67	Yogi Berra/50	75.00

Signature Holofoil

NM/M

Many not priced due to scarcity.

SSA-4	Bob Feller/25	70.00
SSA-5	Bob Gibson/25	60.00
SSA-11	Chuck Tanner/100	15.00
SSA-12	Cito Gaston/100	15.00
SSA-13	Danny Ozark/100	15.00
SSA-17	Dick Williams/100	15.00
SSA-22	Felipe Alou/50	45.00
SSA-24	Gary Carter/50	45.00
SSA-45	Phil Rizzuto/25	60.00
SSA-49	Robin Roberts/25	50.00
SSA-50	Robin Yount/50	75.00
SSA-52	Roger Craig/50	20.00
SSA-56	Sparky Anderson/50	30.00
SSA-57	Stan Musial/50	120.00
SSA-62	Tony LaRussa/50	15.00
SSA-63	Tony Oliva/100	25.00
SSA-64	Tony Pena/100	15.00

Signature Red Ink

NM/M

Many not priced due to scarcity.

SSA-14	Dave Winfield/25	65.00
SSA-25	Gene Mauch/25	25.00
SSA-26	George Bamberger/25	30.00

Wood Barrel Auto.

NM/M

Varying quantities produced
Some not priced due to scarcity.

HB	Harold Baines/200	35.00
JB	Johnny Bench/50	120.00
WB	Wade Boggs/200	60.00
SM	Stan Musial/25	185.00
CR	Cal Ripken Jr./25	300.00
NR	Nolan Ryan/25	100.00
RS	Ron Santo/203	45.00
TS	Tom Seaver/25	140.00
BW	Billy Williams/200	60.00

2004 Upper Deck Ultimate Collection

NM/M

Complete Set (222):		
Common Player (1-126):	2.00
Production 675	
Common (127-168):	4.00
Production 525	
Common (169-194):	6.00
Production 299	
Common (195-209, 222)	8.00
Production 199	
Common (210-221):	15.00
Production 75	
Pack (4):	80.00
Box (4):	275.00
1	Al Kaline	4.00
2	Billy Williams	2.00
3	Bob Feller	4.00
4	Bob Gibson	4.00
5	Bob Lemon	2.00
6	Bobby Doerr	2.00
7	Brooks Robinson	3.00
8	Cal Ripken Jr.	10.00
9	Jim "Catfish" Hunter	2.00
10	Eddie Mathews	4.00
11	Enos Slaughter	2.00
12	Ernie Banks	4.00
13	Fergie Jenkins	2.00
14	Gaylord Perry	2.00
15	Harmon Killebrew	4.00
16	Jim Bunning	2.00
17	Joe DiMaggio	6.00
18	Joe Morgan	2.00
19	Juan Marichal	2.00
20	Lou Brock	2.00
21	Luis Aparicio	2.00
22	Mickey Mantle	12.00
23	Mike Schmidt	6.00
24	Monte Irvin	2.00
25	Nolan Ryan	8.00
26	Pee Wee Reese	2.00
27	Phil Niekro	2.00
28	Phil Rizzuto	2.00
29	Ralph Kiner	3.00
30	Richie Ashburn	3.00
31	Robin Roberts	3.00
32	Robin Yount	5.00
33	Rod Carew	2.00
34	Rollie Fingers	2.00
35	Stan Musial	6.00
36	Ted Williams	8.00
37	Tom Seaver	4.00
38	Warren Spahn	4.00
39	Whitey Ford	3.00
40	Willie McCovey	3.00
41	Willie Stargell	3.00
42	Yogi Berra	4.00
43	Adrian Beltre	2.00
44	Albert Pujols	6.00
45	Alex Rodriguez	6.00
46	Alfonso Soriano	3.00
47	Andruw Jones	2.00
48	Andy Pettitte	3.00
49	Aubrey Huff	2.00
50	Barry Larkin	2.00
51	Ben Sheets	2.00
52	Bernie Williams	3.00
53	Bobby Abreu	2.00
54	Brad Penny	2.00
55	Bret Boone	2.00
56	Brian Giles	2.00
57	Carlos Beltran	2.00
58	Carlos Delgado	2.00
59	Carlos Guillen	2.00
60	Carlos Lee	2.00

61	Carlos Zambrano	2.00
62	Chipper Jones	4.00
63	Craig Biggio	2.00
64	Craig Wilson	2.00
65	Curt Schilling	4.00
66	David Ortiz	4.00
67	Derek Jeter	10.00
68	Eric Chavez	2.00
69	Eric Gagne	3.00
70	Frank Thomas	3.00
71	Garret Anderson	2.00
72	Gary Sheffield	3.00
73	Greg Maddux	5.00
74	Hank Blalock	3.00
75	Hideki Matsui	6.00
76	Ichiro Suzuki	8.00
77	Ivan Rodriguez	3.00
78	J.D. Drew	2.00
79	Jake Peavy	2.00
80	Jason Schmidt	2.00
81	Jeff Bagwell	3.00
82	Jeff Kent	2.00
83	Jim Thome	4.00
84	Joe Mauer	2.00
85	Johan Santana	3.00
86	Jose Reyes	3.00
87	Jose Vidro	2.00
88	Ken Griffey Jr.	5.00
89	Kerry Wood	4.00
90	Larry Walker	2.00
91	Luis Gonzalez	2.00
92	Lyle Overbay	2.00
93	Magglio Ordonez	2.00
94	Manny Ramirez	4.00
95	Mark Mulder	2.00
96	Mark Prior	3.00
97	Mark Teixeira	2.00
98	Melvin Mora	2.00
99	Michael Young	2.00
100	Miguel Cabrera	4.00
101	Miguel Tejada	3.00
102	Mike Lowell	2.00
103	Mike Piazza	6.00
104	Mike Sweeney	2.00
105	Nomar Garciaparra	6.00
106	Oliver Perez	2.00
107	Pedro J. Martinez	4.00
108	Preston Wilson	2.00
109	Rafael Palmeiro	4.00
110	Randy Johnson	4.00
111	Roger Clemens	10.00
112	Roy Halladay	2.00
113	Roy Oswalt	2.00
114	Sammy Sosa	6.00
115	Scott Podsednik	2.00
116	Scott Rolen	4.00
117	Shawn Green	2.00
118	Tim Hudson	2.00
119	Todd Helton	3.00
120	Tom Glavine	3.00
121	Torii Hunter	2.00
122	Travis Hafner	2.00
123	Troy Glaus	2.00
124	Vernon Wells	2.00
125	Victor Martinez	2.00
126	Vladimir Guerrero	4.00
127	Aarom Baldiris **RC**	4.00
128	Alfredo Simon **RC**	4.00
129	Andres Blanco **RC**	4.00
130	Jeff Bajenaru **RC**	4.00
131	Bartolome Fortunato **RC**	4.00
132	Brandon Medders **RC**	4.00
133	Brian Dallimore **RC**	4.00
134	Carlos Hines **RC**	4.00
135	Carlos Vasquez **RC**	4.00
136	Casey Daigle **RC**	4.00
137	Chad Bentz **RC**	4.00
138	Chris Aguila **RC**	4.00
139	Chris Saenz **RC**	4.00
140	Chris Shelton **RC**	4.00
141	Colby Miller **RC**	6.00
142	David Crouthers **RC**	4.00
143	David Aardsma **RC**	4.00
144	Dennis Sarfate **RC**	4.00
145	Donnie Kelly **RC**	4.00
146	Eddy Rodriguez **RC**	8.00
147	Eduardo Villacis **RC**	4.00
148	Edwardo Sierra **RC**	6.00
149	Edwin Moreno **RC**	6.00
150	Kyle Denney **RC**	4.00
151	Evan Rust **RC**	4.00
152	Fernando Nieve **RC**	4.00
153	Frank Francisco **RC**	4.00
154	Franklyn Gracesqui **RC**	4.00
155	Freddy Guzman **RC**	4.00
156	Greg Dobbs **RC**	4.00
157	Hector Gimenez **RC**	4.00
158	Jason Alfaro **RC**	4.00
159	Andy Green **RC**	4.00
160	Jason Bartlett **RC**	8.00
161	Jason Frasor **RC**	4.00
162	Jeff Bennett **RC**	4.00
163	Jerome Gamble **RC**	4.00
164	Jerry Gil **RC**	4.00
165	Joe Hietpas **RC**	4.00
166	Jorge Sequea **RC**	4.00
167	Jorge Vasquez **RC**	4.00
168	Josh Labandeira **RC**	6.00
169	Justin Germano **RC**	6.00
170	Justin Hampson **RC**	6.00
171	Chris Young **RC**	10.00
172	Justin Knoedler **RC**	6.00
173	Justin Lehr **RC**	6.00
174	Justin Leone **RC**	6.00
175	Kazuhito Tadano **RC**	8.00
176	Kevin Cave **RC**	6.00
177	Lincoln Holdzkom **RC**	6.00
178		

179	Mike Rose **RC**	6.00
180	Luis Gonzalez **RC**	6.00
181	Mariano Gomez **RC**	6.00
182	Rene Rivera **RC**	6.00
183	Mike Wuertz **RC**	8.00
184	Mike Gosling **RC**	6.00
185	Mike Johnston **RC**	6.00
186	Mike Rouse **RC**	6.00
187	Nick Regilio **RC**	6.00
188	Onil Joseph **RC**	6.00
189	Orlando Rodriguez **RC**	6.00
190	Phil Stockman **RC**	6.00
191	Renyel Pinto **RC**	6.00
192	Roberto Novoa **RC**	6.00
193	Roman Colon **RC**	6.00
194	Ronald Belisario **RC**	6.00
195	Ronny Cedeno **RC**	8.00
196	Ryan Meaux **RC**	8.00
197	Ryan Wing **RC**	6.00
198	Scott Dohmann **RC**	8.00
199	Joey Gathright **RC**	8.00
200	Shawn Camp **RC**	8.00
201	Shawn Hill **RC**	8.00
202	Steve Andrade **RC**	8.00
203	Tim Bausher **RC**	8.00
204	Tim Bittner **RC**	8.00
205	Brad Halsey **RC**	10.00
206	William Bergolla **RC**	8.00
207	Kameron Loe **RC**	8.00
208	Jesse Crain **RC**	10.00
209	Scott Kazmir **RC**	15.00
210	Akinori Otsuka/Auto. **RC**	40.00
211	Chris Oxspring/Auto. **RC**	15.00
212	Ian Snell/Auto. **RC**	20.00
213	John Gall/Auto. **RC**	15.00
214	Jose Capellan/Auto. **RC**	15.00
215	Yadier Molina/Auto. **RC**	40.00
216	Merkin Valdez/Auto. **RC**	15.00
217	Ramon Ramirez/Auto. **RC**	15.00
218	Rusty Tucker/Auto. **RC**	15.00
219	Scott Proctor/Auto. **RC**	15.00
220	Sean Henn/Auto.	15.00
221	Shingo Takatsu/Auto. **RC**	25.00
222	Kazuo Matsui **RC**	20.00

Gold

Gold (1-194):	1-2X
Production 50	
Gold (195-209):	No Pricing
Production 25	
Gold 210-221 Production 15	

Platinum

Platinum (1-126) No Pricing	
Production 10	
Platinum (210-221):	No Pricing
Production One	

Rainbow

Rainbows:	No Pricing
Production One Set	

Achievement Material

NM/M

Common Player:

EB	Ernie Banks/58	25.00
JB	Johnny Bench/68	15.00
YB	Yogi Berra/51	20.00
GB	George Brett/80	25.00
CA	Roy Campanella/51	25.00
RC	Rod Carew/77	15.00
SC	Steve Carlton/72	10.00
OC	Orlando Cepeda/58	10.00
CL	Roger Clemens/86	25.00
RC	Roberto Clemente/66	100.00
JD	Joe DiMaggio/39	100.00
DD	Don Drysdale/62	15.00
BG	Bob Gibson/68	15.00
KG	Ken Griffey Jr./97	25.00
DJ	Derek Jeter/96	40.00
RJ	Randy Johnson/99	15.00
HK	Harmon Killebrew/69	15.00
GM	Greg Maddux/92	20.00
MA	Mickey Mantle/56	200.00
RM	Roger Maris/61	80.00
PM	Pedro J. Martinez/99	15.00
DM	Don Mattingly/85	20.00
MC	Willie McCovey/59	15.00
TM	Thurman Munson/70	15.00
EM	Eddie Murray/77	15.00
JP	Jim Palmer/73	15.00
MP	Mike Piazza/93	20.00
CR	Cal Ripken Jr./82	50.00
BR	Brooks Robinson/64	15.00
FR	Frank Robinson/66	15.00
JR	Jackie Robinson/47	65.00
RS	Ryne Sandberg/84	40.00
MS	Mike Schmidt/80	25.00
TS	Tom Seaver/69	15.00
SS	Sammy Sosa/98	20.00
TW	Ted Williams/42	100.00
CY	Carl Yastrzemski/67	25.00
RY	Robin Yount/82	25.00

All-Stars Signatures

NM/M

Most not priced.

RC	Rod Carew/18	40.00
SM	Stan Musial/24	75.00
BR	Brooks Robinson/15	60.00
CY	Carl Yastrzemski/18	80.00

Bat Barrel Signatures

No Pricing
Production 1-5

Dual Legendary Materials

NM/M

Common Player:
Production 50 Sets

BM	Willie McCovey, Ernie Banks	40.00
BR	Roger Maris, Babe Ruth	300.00
CB	Yogi Berra, Roy Campanella	35.00
CM	Roberto Clemente, Thurman Munson	100.00
CS	Duke Snider, Roy Campanella	40.00
DM	Mickey Mantle, Joe DiMaggio	200.00
DW	Joe DiMaggio, Ted Williams	150.00
FD	Don Drysdale, Bob Feller	25.00
MB	Yogi Berra, Thurman Munson	50.00
MC	Mickey Mantle, Roberto Clemente	180.00
MM	Mickey Mantle, Roger Maris	220.00
MW	Mickey Mantle, Ted Williams	200.00
RB	Ernie Banks, Jackie Robinson	75.00
RC	Jackie Robinson, Roy Campanella	75.00
RD	Joe DiMaggio, Babe Ruth	275.00
RM	Babe Ruth, Mickey Mantle	400.00
RP	Jackie Robinson, Satchel Paige	100.00
RW	Roberto Clemente, Willie McCovey	100.00
WM	Eddie Mathews, Ted Williams	125.00

Dual Materials

NM/M

Common Player:
Production 60 Sets

BC	Brooks Robinson, Cal Ripken Jr.	50.00
BM	Yogi Berra, Thurman Munson	40.00
BP	Johnny Bench, Mike Piazza	25.00
BS	Mike Schmidt, George Brett	40.00
CK	Harmon Killebrew, Rod Carew	30.00
CM	Willie McCovey, Will Clark	30.00
ER	Ryne Sandberg, Ernie Banks	60.00
GS	Sammy Sosa, Ken Griffey Jr.	40.00
JC	Randy Johnson, Roger Clemens	50.00
JM	Derek Jeter, Don Mattingly	150.00
MB	Johnny Bench, Thurman Munson	40.00
MC	Don Mattingly, Will Clark	40.00
MP	Mark Prior, Joe Mauer	25.00
MR	Bill Mazeroski, Jackie Robinson	60.00
MT	Kazuo Matsui, Shingo Takatsu	30.00
MY	Robin Yount, Paul Molitor	50.00
PR	Manny Ramirez, Albert Pujols	50.00
RC	Nolan Ryan, Roger Clemens	60.00
RP	Mike Piazza, Ivan Rodriguez	20.00
RR	Brooks Robinson, Frank Robinson	25.00
RT	Thurman Munson, Roy Campanella	30.00
SG	Ken Griffey Jr., Ichiro Suzuki	60.00
SP	Mark Prior, Ben Sheets	10.00
SR	Duke Snider, Pee Wee Reese	30.00
SS	Sammy Sosa, Ryne Sandberg	50.00
TS	Jim Thome, Mike Schmidt	35.00
WM	Don Mattingly, Dave Winfield	40.00
WP	Mark Prior, Kerry Wood	20.00
WR	Kerry Wood, Nolan Ryan	50.00
YR	Manny Ramirez, Carl Yastrzemski	35.00

Dual Materials Signature

NM/M

Production 25 Sets

AB	Luis Aparicio, Ernie Banks	100.00
BB	Wade Boggs, Hank Blalock	80.00
BC	Brooks Robinson, Cal Ripken Jr.	250.00
BF	Carlton Fisk, Johnny Bench	100.00

BG	Carlos Beltran, Ken Griffey Jr.	150.00
BJ	Derek Jeter, Yogi Berra	200.00
BM	Brian Giles, Marcus Giles	35.00
BP	Johnny Bench, Mike Piazza	160.00
BR	Jim Bunning, Robin Roberts	40.00
BT	Hank Blalock, Mark Teixeira	60.00
CB	Hank Blalock, Eric Chavez	50.00
CC	Steve Carlton, Roger Clemens	150.00
CJ	Roger Clemens, Randy Johnson	300.00
CK	Harmon Killebrew, Rod Carew	80.00
CL	Miguel Cabrera, Mike Lowell	75.00
CM	Miguel Cabrera, Carlos Beltran	125.00
DD	Derek Jeter, Don Mattingly	300.00
DG	Gaylord Perry, Don Sutton	50.00
DJ	Jim Rice, Dave Parker	80.00
DS	Ryne Sandberg, Andre Dawson	125.00
DW	Andre Dawson, Billy Williams	50.00
ER	Ryne Sandberg, Ernie Banks	160.00
FC	Bob Feller, Rocky Colavito	75.00
FR	Bob Feller, Nolan Ryan	180.00
GB	Brooks Robinson, George Brett	140.00
GC	Ron Guidry, Steve Carlton	50.00
GG	Ken Griffey Sr., Ken Griffey Jr.	150.00
GM	Mike Schmidt, George Brett	150.00
GP	Rafael Palmeiro, Ken Griffey Jr.	150.00
GR	Greg Maddux, Roger Clemens	300.00
GS	John Smoltz, Eric Gagne	75.00
IV	Ivan Rodriguez, Victor Martinez	65.00
JB	Ernie Banks, Fergie Jenkins	100.00
JC	Randy Johnson, Steve Carlton	125.00
JD	Johnny Podres, Don Sutton	50.00
JG	Randy Johnson, Ken Griffey Jr.	200.00
JM	Chipper Jones, Dale Murphy	150.00
JP	Jim Palmer, Fergie Jenkins	50.00
JR	Cal Ripken Jr., Derek Jeter	500.00
KG	Ken Griffey Jr., Harmon Killebrew	150.00
KN	Kerry Wood, Nolan Ryan	175.00
KT	Scott Kazmir, Shingo Takatsu	75.00
LB	Yogi Berra, Don Larsen	180.00
MB	Johnny Bench, Joe Morgan	80.00
MC	Don Mattingly, Will Clark	125.00
MH	Mark Mulder, Tim Hudson	50.00
MP	Mark Prior, Joe Mauer	80.00
MS	Bill Mazeroski, Ryne Sandberg	50.00
MW	Will Clark, Mark Grace	75.00
MY	Robin Yount, Paul Molitor	150.00
NR	Roger Clemens, Nolan Ryan	300.00
OR	Manny Ramirez, David Ortiz	200.00
OS	Stan Musial, Ozzie Smith	150.00
PC	Will Clark, Rafael Palmeiro	100.00
PN	Phil Niekro, Gaylord Perry	50.00
PS	Johnny Podres, Duke Snider	60.00
RB	Rod Carew, Bill Mazeroski	75.00
RC	Eric Chavez, Brooks Robinson	60.00
RM	Eddie Murray, Cal Ripken Jr.	275.00
RP	Brooks Robinson, Jim Palmer	65.00
RR	Brooks Robinson, Frank Robinson	75.00
RS	Robin Roberts, Steve Carlton	60.00
RT	Miguel Tejada, Cal Ripken Jr.	200.00
SC	Mike Schmidt, Steve Carlton	150.00
SF	Ben Sheets, Bob Feller	50.00

Code	Player	NM/M
SG	Eric Gagne, Bruce Sutter	75.00
SO	Ben Sheets, Roy Oswalt	50.00
SP	Mark Prior, Ben Sheets	80.00
SR	Brooks Robinson, Mike Schmidt	150.00
SS	Tom Seaver, Ben Sheets	75.00
TB	Tony Gwynn, Brian Giles	75.00
TC	Mark Teixeira, Miguel Cabrera	75.00
WM	Dave Winfield, Don Mattingly	150.00
WO	Orlando Cepeda, Willie McCovey	75.00
WW	Will Clark, Willie McCovey	75.00
YR	Carl Yastrzemski, Manny Ramirez	160.00

Game Materials
Common Player: 8.00
Production 99 Sets

Code	Player	NM/M
EB	Ernie Banks	15.00
JB	Johnny Bench	10.00
WB	Wade Boggs	8.00
GB	George Brett	20.00
LB	Lou Brock	8.00
RC	Rod Carew	8.00
SC	Steve Carlton	8.00
WC	Will Clark	8.00
CL	Roger Clemens	20.00
TC	Ty Cobb	100.00
DD	Don Drysdale	8.00
BF	Bob Feller	8.00
CF	Carlton Fisk	10.00
BG	Bob Gibson	10.00
KG	Ken Griffey Jr.	20.00
TG	Tony Gwynn	10.00
DJ	Derek Jeter	30.00
RJ	Randy Johnson	15.00
AK	Al Kaline	15.00
HK	Harmon Killebrew	10.00
MA	Juan Marichal	8.00
RM	Roger Maris	8.00
ED	Eddie Mathews	15.00
DM	Don Mattingly	25.00
BM	Bill Mazeroski	8.00
WM	Willie McCovey	8.00
PM	Paul Molitor	10.00
TM	Thurman Munson	15.00
EM	Eddie Murray	15.00
SM	Stan Musial	25.00
JP	Jim Palmer	8.00
PI	Mike Piazza	15.00
MP	Mark Prior	10.00
AP	Albert Pujols	25.00
CR	Cal Ripken Jr.	40.00
BR	Brooks Robinson	10.00
FR	Frank Robinson	8.00
JR	Jackie Robinson	40.00
RS	Ryne Sandberg	25.00
MS	Mike Schmidt	15.00
TS	Tom Seaver	10.00
OS	Ozzie Smith	15.00
DS	Duke Snider	8.00
WS	Warren Spahn	15.00
WSt	Willie Stargell	8.00
IS	Ichiro Suzuki	60.00
DW	Dave Winfield	8.00
KW	Kerry Wood	10.00
CY	Carl Yastrzemski	20.00
RY	Robin Yount	20.00

Game Patch
Common Player:
Production 75 unless noted.
5 Color +: 1.5X

Code	Player	NM/M
BA	Jeff Bagwell	25.00
BE	Josh Beckett	15.00
CB	Carlos Beltran	25.00
JB	Johnny Bench	50.00
YB	Yogi Berra	50.00
HB	Hank Blalock	15.00
WB	Wade Boggs	20.00
GB	George Brett	50.00
LB	Lou Brock	40.00
BU	Jim Bunning/66	30.00
CA	Miguel Cabrera	30.00
RC	Rod Carew	30.00
RO	Rod Carew	30.00
GC	Gary Carter	30.00
EC	Eric Chavez	15.00
WC	Will Clark	30.00
WC1	Will Clark	30.00
RC	Roger Clemens	40.00
RB	Roberto Clemente	200.00
CO1	Rocky Colavito	80.00
JD	Joe DiMaggio	180.00
BF	Bob Feller	40.00
NF	Nellie Fox/55	125.00
GL	Troy Glaus	20.00
KG	Ken Griffey Jr.	60.00
VG	Vladimir Guerrero	30.00
RG	Ron Guidry	30.00
TG	Tony Gwynn	30.00
TH	Todd Helton	30.00
CH	Jim "Catfish" Hunter	30.00
DJ	Derek Jeter	40.00
RJ	Randy Johnson	25.00
RJ1	Randy Johnson	25.00
CJ	Chipper Jones	30.00
HK	Harmon Killebrew	40.00
GM	Greg Maddux	50.00
GM1	Greg Maddux	35.00
MA	Juan Marichal	25.00
PE	Pedro J. Martinez	25.00
HM	Hideki Matsui/44	80.00
KM	Kazuo Matsui	50.00
DM	Don Mattingly	60.00
JM	Joe Mauer	30.00
BM	Bill Mazeroski/55	60.00
WM	Willie McCovey	35.00
PM	Paul Molitor	30.00
MO	Joe Morgan	20.00
TM	Thurman Munson	40.00
MU	Eddie Murray	40.00
SM	Stan Musial	75.00
RP	Rafael Palmeiro	25.00
JP	Jim Palmer	25.00
PI	Mike Piazza	30.00
PO	Johnny Podres	40.00
MP	Mark Prior	20.00
AP	Albert Pujols	50.00
MR	Manny Ramirez	25.00
CR	Cal Ripken Jr.	60.00
BR	Brooks Robinson	40.00
IR	Ivan Rodriguez	25.00
NR	Nolan Ryan	50.00
NR1	Nolan Ryan/51	50.00
NR2	Nolan Ryan	50.00
RS	Ryne Sandberg	50.00
CS	Curt Schilling	25.00
MS	Mike Schmidt	40.00
TS	Tom Seaver	50.00
BS	Ben Sheets	25.00
GS	Gary Sheffield	25.00
OS	Ozzie Smith	40.00
AS	Alfonso Soriano	25.00
SS	Sammy Sosa	35.00
SP	Warren Spahn/62	60.00
WS	Willie Stargell	30.00
IS	Ichiro Suzuki	120.00
MT	Mark Teixeira	15.00
TE	Miguel Tejada	15.00
JT	Jim Thome	35.00
BW	Bernie Williams	20.00
WI	Billy Williams	20.00
DW	Dave Winfield	35.00
KW	Kerry Wood	25.00
CY	Carl Yastrzemski	50.00
RY	Robin Yount	40.00

Dual Game Patch
Production 25 Sets

Code	Player	NM/M
BB	Carlos Beltran, Jeff Bagwell	40.00
BC	Josh Beckett, Miguel Cabrera	40.00
BG	Lou Brock, Tony Gwynn	75.00
BS	Mike Schmidt, George Brett	100.00
BT	Hank Blalock, Mark Teixeira	40.00
CG	Rod Carew, Tony Gwynn	50.00
CP	Mike Piazza, Gary Carter	50.00
CR	Eric Chavez, Scott Rolen	50.00
FB	Johnny Bench, Carlton Fisk	50.00
FR	Nolan Ryan, Bob Feller	100.00
GC	Will Clark, Mark Grace	40.00
GG	Ken Griffey Sr., Ken Griffey Jr.	75.00
GM	Stan Musial, Bob Gibson	60.00
GS	Mark Grace, Ryne Sandberg	100.00
HF	Rollie Fingers, Jim "Catfish" Hunter	30.00
JC	Roger Clemens, Randy Johnson	75.00
JJ	Chipper Jones, Andruw Jones	40.00
JM	Derek Jeter, Hideki Matsui	125.00
KC	Rod Carew, Harmon Killebrew	60.00
KM	Willie McCovey, Harmon Killebrew	50.00
KS	Sammy Sosa, Ken Griffey Jr.	75.00
LS	Fred Lynn, Ichiro Suzuki	100.00
MG	Greg Maddux, Tom Glavine	50.00
MJ	Chipper Jones, Eddie Mathews	75.00
MM	Kazuo Matsui, Hideki Matsui	120.00
MY	Robin Yount, Paul Molitor	60.00
PC	Will Clark, Rafael Palmeiro	40.00
PR	Scott Rolen, Albert Pujols	100.00
RC	Roger Clemens, Nolan Ryan	100.00
RM	Cal Ripken Jr., Eddie Murray	150.00
RP	Cal Ripken Jr., Jim Palmer	125.00
RR	Jackie Robinson, Pee Wee Reese	150.00
RS	Nolan Ryan, Tom Seaver	100.00
RT	Cal Ripken Jr., Miguel Tejada	75.00
SB	Jim Bunning, Mike Schmidt	75.00
SM	Pedro J. Martinez, Curt Schilling	60.00
ST	Mike Schmidt, Jim Thome	75.00
WM	Don Mattingly, Dave Winfield	75.00
WP	Mark Prior, Kerry Wood	50.00
WS	Billy Williams, Sammy Sosa	60.00
YR	Carl Yastrzemski, Jim Rice	75.00

Game Patch Signatures
Common Player:
Production 30 Sets

Code	Player	NM/M
EB	Ernie Banks	75.00
CB	Carlos Beltran	65.00
JB	Johnny Bench	65.00
HB	Hank Blalock	50.00
WB	Wade Boggs	65.00
GB	George Brett	100.00
MC	Miguel Cabrera	65.00
RC	Rod Carew	65.00
EC	Eric Chavez	40.00
WC	Will Clark	60.00
AD	Andre Dawson	40.00
BG	Bob Gibson	75.00
KG	Ken Griffey Jr.	125.00
TG	Tony Gwynn	65.00
DJ	Derek Jeter	200.00
RJ	Randy Johnson	125.00
AK	Al Kaline	75.00
HK	Harmon Killebrew	75.00
GM	Greg Maddux	150.00
MA	Juan Marichal	50.00
DM	Don Mattingly	100.00
JM	Joe Mauer	60.00
WM	Willie McCovey	50.00
PM	Paul Molitor	50.00
MU	Mark Mulder	40.00
EM	Eddie Murray	80.00
SM	Stan Musial	120.00
RO	Roy Oswalt	50.00
JP	Jim Palmer	50.00
PI	Mike Piazza	125.00
MP	Mark Prior	60.00
JR	Jim Rice	50.00
CR	Cal Ripken Jr.	200.00
BR	Brooks Robinson	50.00
FR	Frank Robinson	50.00
NR	Nolan Ryan	150.00
RS	Ryne Sandberg	150.00
MS	Mike Schmidt	125.00
SC	Red Schoendienst	40.00
TS	Tom Seaver	75.00
BS	Ben Sheets	50.00
OS	Ozzie Smith	75.00
MT	Mark Teixeira	50.00
KW	Kerry Wood	75.00
CY	Carl Yastrzemski	100.00
RY	Robin Yount	80.00

Stat Patch
Quantity produced listed
5+ Color Patch: 1.5X

Code	Player	NM/M
JB	Jeff Bagwell/47	25.00
CB	Carlos Beltran/29	35.00
CB1	Carlos Beltran/41	30.00
BE	Johnny Bench/45	30.00
HB	Hank Blalock/29	20.00
GB	George Brett/20	50.00
GB1	George Brett/30	75.00
WC	Will Clark/35	50.00
CL1	Roger Clemens/24	50.00
DD	Don Drysdale/25	50.00
EG	Eric Gagne/55	25.00
VG	Vladimir Guerrero/44	25.00
VG1	Vladimir Guerrero/40	25.00
TG	Tony Gwynn/56	40.00
TG1	Tony Gwynn/25	40.00
DJ	Derek Jeter/32	60.00
DJ1	Derek Jeter/24	60.00
RJ	Randy Johnson/20	50.00
CJ	Chipper Jones/45	25.00
HK	Harmon Killebrew/49	50.00
GM1	Greg Maddux/20	40.00
GM2	Greg Maddux/17	50.00
JM	Juan Marichal/26	30.00
MA	Pedro Martinez/35	25.00
HM	Hideki Matsui/31	120.00
DM	Don Mattingly/35	75.00
PM	Paul Molitor/39	75.00
TM	Thurman Munson/20	75.00
PN	Phil Niekro/23	30.00
PN1	Phil Niekro/23	30.00
RP	Rafael Palmeiro/47	25.00
JP1	Jim Palmer/23	70.00
PI	Mike Piazza/40	70.00
AP	Albert Pujols/43	45.00
AP1	Albert Pujols/51	50.00
MR	Manny Ramirez/45	25.00
JR1	Jim Rice/46	25.00
CR	Cal Ripken/34	100.00
CR1	Cal Ripken/47	75.00
IR	Ivan Rodriguez/35	30.00
IR1	Ivan Rodriguez/25	30.00
SR	Scott Rolen/31	35.00
RS	Ryne Sandberg/40	65.00
RS1	Ryne Sandberg/19	65.00
MS	Mike Schmidt/48	65.00
TS	Tom Seaver/25	75.00
JS	John Smoltz/24	25.00
JS1	John Smoltz/55	25.00
AS	Alfonso Soriano/39	20.00
AS1	Alfonso Soriano/45	20.00
SS1	Sammy Sosa/66	20.00
WS	Willie Stargell/48	50.00
IS	Ichiro Suzuki/56	120.00
MT	Miguel Tejada/34	25.00
JT	Jim Thome/52	25.00
CY	Carl Yastrzemski/44	50.00
RY	Robin Yount/49	50.00
DW	Dave Winfield/37	25.00

Super Patch
No Pricing
Production 4-20

Gold Glove Sign. Materials
No Pricing
Production 1-16

Legendary Materials
Common Player: 10.00
Production 50 Sets

Code	Player	NM/M
EB	Ernie Banks	20.00
CB	Roy Campanella	15.00
YB	Yogi Berra	20.00
RC	Roberto Clemente	100.00
TC	Ty Cobb	100.00
JD	Joe DiMaggio	100.00
DD	Don Drysdale	15.00
BF	Bob Feller	10.00
MM	Mickey Mantle	200.00
RM	Roger Maris	60.00
EM	Eddie Mathews	20.00
WM	Willie McCovey	15.00
TM	Thurman Munson	25.00
SM	Stan Musial	40.00
SP	Satchel Paige	50.00
JR	Jackie Robinson	60.00
RR	Babe Ruth	250.00
DS	Duke Snider	15.00
TW	Ted Williams	80.00

Logo Patch Signatures
No Pricing
Production One Set

Game Jersey Sign.
Quantity produced listed

Code	Player	NM/M
EB	Ernie Banks/19	85.00
GB	George Brett/21	100.00
TG	Tony Gwynn/20	70.00
HK	Harmon Killebrew/21	75.00
CR	Cal Ripken Jr./21	200.00
BR	Brooks Robinson/23	50.00
MS	Mike Schmidt/18	100.00
CY	Carl Yastrzemski/23	85.00
RY	Robin Yount/20	85.00

Materials Signatures
Production 50 Sets

Code	Player	NM/M
BA	Bobby Abreu	25.00
JE	Jeff Bagwell	50.00
EB	Ernie Banks	75.00
BE	Josh Beckett	25.00
CB	Carlos Beltran	60.00
JB	Johnny Bench	60.00
HB	Hank Blalock	30.00
WB	Wade Boggs	50.00
WB1	Wade Boggs	50.00
GB	George Brett	80.00
LB	Lou Brock	40.00
LB1	Lou Brock	40.00
BU	Jim Bunning	30.00
CA	Miguel Cabrera	40.00
RC	Rod Carew	40.00
RC1	Rod Carew	40.00
SC	Steve Carlton	35.00
SC1	Steve Carlton	35.00
GC	Gary Carter	30.00
GC1	Gary Carter	30.00
JC	Joe Carter	30.00
OC	Orlando Cepeda	35.00
OC1	Orlando Cepeda	35.00
EC	Eric Chavez	30.00
WC	Will Clark	40.00
WC1	Will Clark	40.00
WC2	Will Clark	40.00
WC3	Will Clark	40.00
CL	Roger Clemens	125.00
CL1	Roger Clemens	125.00
CL2	Roger Clemens	125.00
CO	Rocky Colavito	75.00
CO1	Rocky Colavito	75.00
AD	Andre Dawson	30.00
AD1	Andre Dawson	30.00
DE	Dennis Eckersley	30.00
DE1	Dennis Eckersley	30.00
BF	Bob Feller	30.00
RF	Rollie Fingers	30.00
RF1	Rollie Fingers	30.00
CF	Carlton Fisk	40.00
CF1	Carlton Fisk	40.00
EG	Eric Gagne	30.00
NG	Nomar Garciaparra	125.00
NG1	Nomar Garciaparra	125.00
BG	Bob Gibson	50.00
MG	Mark Grace	40.00
KG	Ken Griffey Jr.	100.00
KG1	Ken Griffey Jr.	100.00
VG	Vladimir Guerrero	65.00
RG	Ron Guidry	30.00
TG	Tony Gwynn	50.00
HE	Todd Helton	40.00
TH	Tim Hudson	30.00
FJ	Fergie Jenkins	30.00
DJ	Derek Jeter	150.00
RJ	Randy Johnson	100.00
RJ1	Randy Johnson	100.00
CJ	Chipper Jones	50.00
AK	Al Kaline	50.00
HK	Harmon Killebrew	60.00
DL	Don Larsen	30.00
ML	Mike Lowell	20.00
GM	Greg Maddux	100.00
GM1	Greg Maddux	100.00
JU	Juan Marichal	30.00
DO	Don Mattingly	80.00
JM	Joe Mauer	40.00
JM1	Joe Mauer	40.00
BM	Bill Mazeroski	40.00
MC	Willie McCovey	40.00
PM	Paul Molitor	50.00
PM1	Paul Molitor	50.00
PM2	Paul Molitor	50.00
MO	Joe Morgan	30.00
MU	Mark Mulder	30.00
DM	Dale Murphy	40.00
EM	Eddie Murray	80.00
EM1	Eddie Murray	80.00
RO	Roy Oswalt	25.00
RP	Rafael Palmeiro	50.00
JP	Jim Palmer	30.00
TP	Tony Perez	30.00
GP	Gaylord Perry	25.00
GP1	Gaylord Perry	25.00
PI	Mike Piazza	100.00
PI1	Mike Piazza	100.00
PO	Johnny Podres	30.00
MP	Mark Prior	60.00
MP1	Mark Prior	60.00
MR	Manny Ramirez	75.00
JR	Jim Rice	30.00
CR	Cal Ripken Jr.	180.00
RR	Robin Roberts	30.00
BR	Brooks Robinson	40.00
FR	Frank Robinson	35.00
FR1	Frank Robinson	35.00
IR	Ivan Rodriguez	50.00
SR	Scott Rolen	50.00
NR	Nolan Ryan	120.00
NR1	Nolan Ryan	120.00
NR2	Nolan Ryan	120.00
NR3	Nolan Ryan	120.00
SA	Ryne Sandberg	100.00
MS	Mike Schmidt	75.00
RS	Red Schoendienst	30.00
TS	Tom Seaver	50.00
TS1	Tom Seaver	50.00
BS	Ben Sheets	30.00
BS1	Ben Sheets	30.00
OS	Ozzie Smith	60.00
JS	John Smoltz	50.00
SN	Duke Snider	40.00
SN1	Duke Snider	40.00
AS	Alfonso Soriano	40.00
DS	Don Sutton	40.00
MT	Miguel Tejada	40.00
TE	Miguel Tejada	40.00
TE1	Miguel Tejada/34	40.00
FT	Frank Thomas	60.00
RW	Rickie Weeks	30.00
RW1	Rickie Weeks	30.00
BW	Billy Williams	40.00
DW	Dave Winfield	40.00
DW1	Dave Winfield	40.00
KW	Kerry Wood	50.00
CY	Carl Yastrzemski	75.00
DY	Delmon Young	30.00
DY1	Delmon Young	30.00
RY	Robin Yount	60.00

Quadruple Materials
No Pricing
Production 15 Sets

Signature Numbers Patch
Quantity produced listed

Code	Player	NM/M
WB	Wade Boggs/26	65.00
LB	Lou Brock/20	50.00
MC	Miguel Cabrera/24	60.00
BF	Bob Feller/19	50.00
EG	Eric Gagne/38	50.00
KG	Ken Griffey Jr./30	120.00
VG	Vladimir Guerrero/27	80.00
DM	Don Mattingly/23	100.00
WM	Willie McCovey/44	60.00
RO	Roy Oswalt/44	30.00
PI	Mike Piazza/31	120.00
MP	Mark Prior/22	20.00
RS	Ryne Sandberg/23	125.00
MS	Mike Schmidt/100	100.00
MT	Mark Teixeira/23	40.00
BW	Billy Williams/26	40.00
DW	Dave Winfield/31	50.00
RY	Robin Yount/19	100.00

Signatures
Common Player: 20.00
Production 25 unless noted.
Gold: 1-1.5X
Production 10-25
No pricing 25 or less.
Platinum: No Pricing
Production One Set

Code	Player	NM/M
LA1	Luis Aparicio	20.00
JB	Johnny Bench	50.00
YB	Yogi Berra	50.00
WB	Wade Boggs	50.00
MC1	Miguel Cabrera	50.00
CW	Rod Carew	40.00
CA1	Steve Carlton	40.00
CL	Roger Clemens	125.00
BF1	Bob Feller	35.00
RF1	Rollie Fingers	25.00
WF	Whitey Ford	50.00
NG	Nomar Garciaparra	100.00
GI	Bob Gibson	40.00
VG	Vladimir Guerrero	50.00
RJ	Randy Johnson	100.00
AK1	Al Kaline	50.00
HK1	Harmon Killebrew	60.00
RK1	Ralph Kiner	40.00
GM	Greg Maddux	80.00
WI	Willie McCovey	40.00
MO	Joe Morgan	25.00
EM	Eddie Murray	75.00
MU	Stan Musial	75.00
JP1	Jim Palmer	30.00
PI	Mike Piazza	100.00
MP	Mark Prior	20.00
KP	Kirby Puckett	65.00
CR	Cal Ripken Jr.	160.00
RR1	Robin Roberts	30.00
BR1	Brooks Robinson	50.00
RY	Ryne Sandberg	75.00
TS	Tom Seaver	50.00
OS	Ozzie Smith	60.00
SN	Duke Snider	40.00
DW	Dave Winfield	35.00
CY	Carl Yastrzemski	75.00

Signatures Tier B
Common Player:

Code	Player	NM/M
BA	Bobby Abreu/25	30.00
LA	Luis Aparicio/25	25.00
CB	Carlos Beltran/25	50.00
BI	Craig Biggio/25	40.00
HB	Hank Blalock/25	35.00
BL	Bert Blyleven/25	20.00
JB	Jim Bunning/99	20.00
MC	Miguel Cabrera/99	30.00
SC	Sean Casey/99	20.00
OC	Orlando Cepeda/25	25.00
EC	Eric Chavez/25	20.00
WC	Will Clark/25	40.00
RC	Rocky Colavito/99	50.00
DC	David Cone/99	20.00
CC	Carl Crawford/99	10.00
AD	Andre Dawson/25	25.00
BD	Bobby Doerr/99	25.00
DE	Dennis Eckersley/25	35.00
BF	Bob Feller/25	30.00
RF	Rollie Fingers/25	25.00
GF	George Foster/25	20.00
EG	Eric Gagne/25	50.00
BG	Brian Giles/99	10.00
MG	Marcus Giles/99	10.00
DG	Dwight Gooden/99	20.00
RG	Rich "Goose" Gossage/99	10.00
GR	Mark Grace/99	30.00
KG	Ken Griffey Sr./69	15.00
RG	Ron Guidry/25	25.00
TH	Travis Hafner/99	20.00
KH	Keith Hernandez/25	15.00
FH	Frank Howard/99	15.00
MI	Monte Irvin/25	25.00
JK	Jim Kaat/99	20.00
AK	Al Kaline/25	60.00
GK	George Kell/99	25.00
HK	Harmon Killebrew/25	60.00
RK	Ralph Kiner/25	40.00
ML	Mike Lowell/99	10.00
SL	Sparky Lyle/99	15.00
FL	Fred Lynn/25	20.00
VM	Victor Martinez/99	20.00
JM	Joe Mauer/99	25.00
BM	Bill Mazeroski/25	50.00
MM	Mark Mulder/99	20.00
DM	Dale Murphy/99	30.00
GN	Graig Nettles/99	15.00
DN	Don Newcombe/25	20.00
RO	Roy Oswalt/99	20.00
AO	Akinori Otsuka/99	40.00
JP	Jim Palmer/99	20.00
DP	Dave Parker/25	20.00
CP	Corey Patterson/99	20.00
TP	Tony Perez/25	35.00
GP	Gaylord Perry/25	25.00
PO	Johnny Podres/99	25.00
RR	Robin Roberts/99	25.00
BR	Brooks Robinson/25	50.00
AR	Al Rosen/99	20.00
SA	Ron Santo/99	25.00
JS	Jason Schmidt/99	20.00
RS	Red Schoendienst/99	30.00
BS	Ben Sheets/99	25.00
SM	John Smoltz/99	25.00
SU	Bruce Sutter/99	25.00
ST	Shingo Takatsu/99	20.00
MT	Mark Teixeira/99	40.00
LT	Luis Tiant/99	10.00
RW	Rickie Weeks/99	20.00
BW	Billy Williams/25	30.00
WM	Maury Wills/25	20.00
DY	Delmon Young/99	20.00

Signatures Duals
Production 25 Sets

Code	Player	NM/M
BB	Wade Boggs, Hank Blalock	80.00
BC	Miguel Cabrera, Carlos Beltran	120.00
BG	Carlos Beltran, Ken Griffey Jr.	175.00
BR	Jim Bunning, Robin Roberts	75.00
BS	George Brett, Mike Schmidt	150.00

Code	Player	NM/M
BT	Hank Blalock, Mark Teixeira	70.00
CB	Hank Blalock, Eric Chavez	50.00
CJ	Roger Clemens, Randy Johnson	300.00
CL	Mike Lowell, Miguel Cabrera	50.00
CR	Eric Chavez, Brooks Robinson	65.00
DW	Billy Williams, Andre Dawson	40.00
EF	Rollie Fingers, Dennis Eckersley	50.00
FR	Bob Feller, Nolan Ryan	160.00
GC	Will Clark, Mark Grace	65.00
GG	Marcus Giles, Brian Giles	40.00
GK	Ken Griffey Jr., Harmon Killebrew	150.00
GS	John Smoltz, Eric Gagne	85.00
IC	Monte Irvin, Orlando Cepeda	50.00
JC	Steve Carlton, Randy Johnson	125.00
JM	Derek Jeter, Don Mattingly	300.00
JP	Jim Palmer, Fergie Jenkins	50.00
JT	Fergie Jenkins, Luis Tiant	50.00
KG	Ken Griffey Sr., Ken Griffey Jr.	175.00
KK	Al Kaline, Harmon Killebrew	80.00
MC	Don Mattingly, Will Clark	125.00
MH	Mark Mulder, Tim Hudson	40.00
MP	Joe Mauer, Mark Prior	60.00
NR	Roger Clemens, Nolan Ryan	400.00
NS	Don Sutton, Don Newcombe	40.00
PC	Rafael Palmeiro, Will Clark	120.00
PN	Phil Niekro, Gaylord Perry	40.00
PR	Jim Rice, Dave Parker	60.00
PS	Ben Sheets, Mark Prior	60.00
RC	Steve Carlton, Robin Roberts	40.00
RJ	Derek Jeter, Cal Ripken Jr.	500.00
RP	Brooks Robinson, Jim Palmer	75.00
SF	Ben Sheets, Bob Feller	40.00
SG	Eric Gagne, Bruce Sutter	60.00
SO	Ben Sheets, Roy Oswalt	40.00
SP	Don Sutton, Gaylord Perry	40.00
TC	Mark Teixeira, Miguel Cabrera	80.00
VM	Miguel Cabrera, Vladimir Guerrero	100.00
WS	Billy Williams, Ron Santo	60.00

Signatures Triple
No Pricing
Production 20 Sets

Signatures Quadruple
No Pricing
Production 10 Sets

Signatures Six
No Pricing
Production Five Sets

Signatures Eight
No Pricing
Production One Set

2004 Upper Deck USA

#	Player	NM/M
	Complete Factory Set (204):	50.00
	Complete Set (200):	25.00
	Common Player:	.15
1	Jim Abbott	.25
2	Brent Abernathy	.15
3	Kurt Ainsworth	.15
4	Abe Alvarez	.15
5	Matt Anderson	.15
6	Jeff Austin	.15
7	Justin Wayne	.15
8	Scott Bankhead	.15
9	Josh Bard	.15
10	Michael Barrett	.15
11	Mark Bellhorn	.25
12	Buddy Bell	.25
13	Andy Benes	.25
14	Kris Benson	.25
15	Peter Bergeron	.15
16	Rocky Biddle	.15
17	Casey Blake	.25
18	Willie Bloomquist	.25
19	Jeremy Bonderman	.25
20	Jeff Weaver	.25
21	Joe Borchard	.25
22	Rickie Weeks	.50
23	Rob Bowen	.15
24	Milton Bradley	.15
25	Dan Wheeler	.15
26	Ben Broussard	.15
27	Brian Bruney	.15
28	Mark Budzinski	.15
29	Kirk Bullinger	.15
30	Chris Burke	.15
31	Sean Burnett	.15
32	Jeremy Burnitz	.25
33	Pat Burrell	.50
34	Sean Burroughs	.50
35	Paul Byrd	.15
36	Chris Capuano	.25
37	Scott Cassidy	.15
38	Will Clark	.75
39	Chad Cordero	.25
40	Carl Crawford	.25
41	Bobby Crosby	.75
42	Brad Wilkerson	.15
43	Michael Cuddyer	.25
44	Ben Davis	.15
45	Gookie Dawkins	.15
46	Rod Dedeaux	.15
47	R.A. Dickey	.15
48	Ben Diggins	.15
49	Lenny DiNardo	.15
50	Ryan Drese	.15
51	Tim Drew	.15
52	Todd Williams	.15
53	Justin Duchscherer	.15
54	J.D. Durbin	.15
55	Scott Elarton	.15
56	Adam Everett	.15
57	Dan Wilson	.15
58	Steve Finley	.25
59	Casey Fossum	.15
60	Terry Francona	.15
61	Ryan Franklin	.15
62	Ryan Freel	.15
63	John Van Benschoten	.15
64	Nomar Garciaparra	1.00
65	Chris George	.15
66	Jody Gerut	.15
67	Jason Giambi	.40
68	Matt Ginter	.15
69	Troy Glaus	.50
70	Tom Goodwin	.15
71	Mike Gosling	.15
72	Danny Graves	.15
73	Shawn Green	.50
74	Khalil Greene	.75
75	Todd Greene	.15
76	Seth Greisinger	.15
77	Gabe Gross	.25
78	Jeffrey Hammonds	.15
79	Aaron Heilman	.15
80	Paul Wilson	.15
81	Todd Helton	.75
82	Dustin Hermanson	.15
83	Bobby Hill	.15
84	Koyie Hill	.15
85	A.J. Hinch	.15
86	Matt Holliday	.50
87	Ted Wood	.15
88	Ken Huckaby	.15
89	Orlando Hudson	.15
90	Ernie Young	.15
91	Jason Jennings	.25
92	Charles Johnson	.15
93	Jacque Jones	.15
94	Matt Kata	.15
95	Austin Kearns	.25
96	Adam Kennedy	.25
97	Brooks Kieschnick	.25
98	Jesse Crain	.15
99	Scott Kazmir	1.00
100	Billy Koch	.25
101	Paul Konerko	.25
102	Graham Koonce	.15
103	Casey Kotchman	.50
104	Chris Snyder	.50
105	Nick Swisher	.50
106	Gerald Laird	.15
107	Barry Larkin	.50
108	Mike Lamb	.15
109	Tommy Lasorda	.25
110	Matt LeCroy	.15
111	Travis Lee	.25
112	Justin Leone	.15
113	John Vander Wal	.15
114	Braden Looper	.15
115	Shane Loux	.15
116	Ryan Ludwick	1.00
117	Jason Varitek	.40
118	Ryan Madson	.15
119	Dave Magadan	.15
120	Tino Martinez	.25
121	Joe Mauer	.50
122	David McCarty	.15
123	Robin Ventura	.25
124	Jack McDowell	.15
125	Todd Walker	.15
126	Mark McGwire	1.50
127	Gil Meche	.15
128	Doug Mientkiewicz	.15
129	Matt Morris	.25
130	Warren Morris	.15
131	Mark Mulder	.25
132	Calvin Murray	.15
133	Eric Munson	.25
134	Mike Mussina	.50
135	Xavier Nady	.15
136	Shane Nance	.15
137	Mike Neill	.15
138	Augie Ojeda	.15
139	John Olerud	.15
140	Gregg Olson	.15
141	Roy Oswalt	.50
142	Jim Parque	.15
143	John Patterson	.15
144	Brad Penny	.15
145	Jay Powell	.15
146	Mark Prior	.75
147	Horacio Ramirez	.15
148	Jon Rauch	.15
149	Jeremy Reed	.25
150	Bob Watson	.15
151	Matt Riley	.15
152	Brian Roberts	.15
153	Dave Roberts	.15
154	Frank Robinson	.15
155	J.C. Romero	.15
156	David Ross	.15
157	Cory Vance	.15
158	Kirk Saarloos	.15
159	Anthony Sanders	.15
160	Dane Sardinha	.15
161	Bobby Seay	.15
162	Phil Seibel	.15
163	Aaron Sele	.15
164	Ben Sheets	.50
165	Paul Shuey	.50
166	Grady Sizemore	.50
167	Reggie Smith	.50
168	John Smoltz	.50
169	Zach Sorensen	.15
170	Scott Spezio	.25
171	Ed Sprague	.15
172	Jason Stanford	.15
173	Dave Stewart	.15
174	Scott Stewart	.15
175	B.J. Surhoff	.15
176	Bill Swift	.15
177	Mike Tonis	.15
178	Jason Tyner	.15
179	Michael Tucker	.15
180	B.J. Upton	.75
181	Eric Valent	.15
182	Ron Villone	.15
183	2000: Team USA Shocks Cuba	.15
184	1984: Abbott halts Japan	.15
185	1996: Berman's Boys Take Third	.15
186	1984: Team USA Takes Second	.15
187	2000: Home Run Heroics	.15
188	1999: Neill's Hit Boosts Team USA	.15
189	1996: High Five for Team USA	.15
190	1992: Garciaparra Makes the Roster	.50
191	2003: USA Rolls to Record	.15
192	1995: Juniors Are Golden In Boston	.15
193	1999: The Streak Goes On	.15
194	1998: Perfect Finish in St. Louis	.15
195	1999: McGwire's Number Retired	1.00
196	2000: Filled with Firsts	.15
197	Red, White and Blue Cardinal	.15
198	2000: Quick Start for Neill	.15
199	1999: Jensen Goes Deep vs. Cuba	.15
200	2000: Mauer on the Mark	.25

Team USA Jersey

Code	Player	NM/M
	Common Player:	4.00
	Inserted 1:Factory Set	
KA	Kurt Ainsworth	4.00
BB	Brian Bruney	4.00
CB	Chris Burke	4.00
SB	Sean Burroughs	4.00
JD	Justin Duchscherer	4.00
AE	Adam Everett	4.00
JG	Jason Giambi	6.00
GG	Gabe Gross	4.00
DH	Dustin Hermanson	4.00
MH	Matt Holliday	15.00
GK	Graham Koonce	4.00
GL	Gerald Laird	4.00
JL	Justin Leone	4.00
JM	Joe Mauer	20.00
DM	Doug Mientkiewicz	4.00
EM	Eric Munson	4.00
XN	Xavier Nady	4.00
RO	Roy Oswalt	6.00
MP	Mark Prior	6.00
HR	Horacio Ramirez	4.00
JR	Jon Rauch	4.00
RE	Jeremy Reed	4.00
FR	Frank Robinson	8.00
MR	Mike Rouse	4.00
BS	Ben Sheets	6.00
GS	Grady Sizemore	10.00
DS	Dave Stewart	4.00
JV	John Van Benschoten	4.00
JW	Jeff Weaver	4.00
BW	Brad Wilkerson	4.00

Team USA Signature Black Ink

Code	Player	NM/M
	Common Autograph:	5.00
	Signatures Inserted 3:Factory Set	
ABB	Jim Abbott/180	20.00
ABE	Brent Abernathy/360	5.00
AIN	Kurt Ainsworth/360	8.00
ALV	Abe Alvarez/360	5.00
AND	Matt Anderson/360	5.00
AUS	Jeff Austin/360	5.00
BANK	Scott Bankhead/360	5.00
BARD	Josh Bard/350	5.00
BARR	Michael Barrett/360	5.00
BELL	Buddy Bell/81	15.00
BEN	Andy Benes/145	5.00
BENS	Kris Benson/180	8.00
BERG	Peter Bergeron/360	5.00
BLA	Casey Blake/180	10.00
BLO	Willie Bloomquist/175	8.00
BON	Jeremy Bonderman/150	8.00
BOR	Joe Borchard/350	8.00
BRAD	Milton Bradley/360	8.00
BRO	Ben Broussard/210	8.00
BRU	Brian Bruney/160	5.00
BUD	Mark Budzinski/360	5.00
BULL	Kirk Bullinger/360	5.00
BURK	Chris Burke/350	8.00
BU	Sean Burnett/180	5.00
BURN	Jeremy Burnitz/360	10.00
BUR	Pat Burrell/360	8.00
BURR	Sean Burroughs/360	8.00
BYRD	Paul Byrd/360	5.00
CAP	Chris Capuano/150	8.00
CASS	Scott Cassidy/360	5.00
CLA	Will Clark/60	75.00
COR	Chad Cordero/360	5.00
CR	Jesse Crain/180	10.00
CRA	Carl Crawford/360	35.00
CUD	Michael Cuddyer/370	8.00
DAV	Ben Davis/344	5.00
DED	Rod Dedeaux/29	10.00
DIC	R.A. Dickey/180	8.00
DIG	Ben Diggins/180	8.00
DIN	Lenny DiNardo/150	8.00
DRE	Ryan Drese/180	8.00
DREW	Tim Drew/360	8.00
DUCH	Justin Duchscherer/210	10.00
DUR	J.D. Durbin/180	5.00
ELAR	Scott Elarton/180	5.00
EVER	Adam Everett/360	5.00
FIN	Steve Finley/360	10.00
FOSS	Casey Fossum/360	5.00
FRAN	Terry Francona/150	40.00
FRA	Ryan Franklin/360	5.00
FRE	Ryan Freel/360	5.00
GEO	Chris George/360	5.00
GER	Jody Gerut/360	5.00
GIAM	Jason Giambi/60	30.00
GIN	Matt Ginter/179	5.00
GLA	Troy Glaus/120	25.00
GOS	Mike Gosling/150	8.00
DRA	Danny Graves/360	5.00
GR	Shawn Green/150	20.00
GRE	Khalil Greene/180	8.00
GREE	Todd Greene/360	5.00
GREI	Seth Greisinger/360	5.00
GRO	Gabe Gross/150	8.00
HAM	Jeffrey Hammonds/150	8.00
HEIL	Aaron Heilman/350	5.00
HELT	Todd Helton/71	40.00
HERM	Dustin Hermanson/150	8.00
HI	Bobby Hill/360	5.00
HILL	Koyie Hill/150	5.00
HIN	A.J. Hinch/360	5.00
HUCK	Ken Huckaby/360	5.00
HUD	Orlando Hudson/360	10.00
JENN	Jason Jennings/350	8.00
JON	Jacque Jones/150	10.00
KATA	Matt Kata/350	5.00
KAZ	Scott Kazmir/360	15.00
KENN	Adam Kennedy/150	8.00
KIES	Brooks Kieschnick/360	8.00
KOCH	Billy Koch/71	10.00
KON	Paul Konerko/179	15.00
KOO	Graham Koonce/360	5.00
KOTC	Casey Kotchman/150	8.00
LAMB	Mike Lamb/360	5.00
LAR	Barry Larkin/60	40.00
LEC	Matt LeCroy/360	5.00
LEE	Travis Lee/360	8.00
LEO	Justin Leone/360	10.00
LOO	Braden Looper/360	5.00
LOUX	Shane Loux/360	5.00
MAD	Ryan Madson/360	8.00
MAG	Dave Magadan/360	8.00
MART	Tino Martinez/360	25.00
MAU	Joe Mauer/360	75.00
MCC	David McCarty/360	5.00
MCDO	Jack McDowell/360	20.00
MEC	Gil Meche/360	5.00
MIE	Doug Mientkiewicz/300	10.00
MOR	Matt Morris/360	5.00
MORR	Warren Morris/360	5.00
MUL	Mark Mulder/180	8.00
MUN	Eric Munson/510	5.00
MURR	Calvin Murray/360	5.00
MUSS	Mike Mussina/60	50.00
NADY	Xavier Nady/360	5.00
NAN	Shane Nance/150	5.00
NEI	Mike Neill/360	5.00
OJE	Augie Ojeda/119	5.00
OLE	John Olerud/180	15.00
OLS	Gregg Olson/180	5.00
OSW	Roy Oswalt/360	15.00
PARQ	Jim Parque/360	5.00
PATT	John Patterson/210	5.00
PEN	Brad Penny/360	5.00
POW	Jay Powell/180	5.00
PRI	Mark Prior/350	10.00
RAU	Jon Rauch/359	5.00
REED	Jeremy Reed/180	5.00
RIL	Matt Riley/360	5.00
ROB	Brian Roberts/60	20.00
ROBE	Dave Roberts/360	5.00
ROM	J.C. Romero/360	5.00
ROSS	David Ross/360	5.00
SAAR	Kirk Saarloos/360	5.00
SAND	Anthony Sanders/360	5.00
SAR	Dane Sardinha/110	8.00
SEAY	Bobby Seay/360	5.00
SEI	Phil Seibel/360	5.00
SELE	Aaron Sele/360	10.00
SHE	Ben Sheets/143	15.00
SHU	Paul Shuey/360	5.00
SIZE	Grady Sizemore/160	35.00
SMI	Reggie Smith/360	10.00
SMO	John Smoltz/360	35.00
SNY	Chris Snyder/360	5.00
SPI	Scott Spiezio/360	10.00
SPR	Ed Sprague/360	5.00
STE	Dave Stewart/180	15.00
STEW	Scott Stewart/360	5.00
SUR	B.J. Surhoff/60	10.00
SWIF	Bill Swift/360	5.00
SWI	Nick Swisher/360	5.00
TON	Mike Tonis/360	5.00
TUCK	Michael Tucker/150	10.00
TYN	Jason Tyner/360	5.00
VAL	Eric Valent/360	5.00
VANB	John Van Benschoten/180	10.00
VAN	Cory Vance/360	5.00
VAND	John Vander Wal/360	5.00
VAR	Jason Varitek/360	40.00
VENT	Robin Ventura/360	15.00
VILL	Ron Villone/359	5.00
WALK	Todd Walker/60	8.00
WAT	Bob Watson/360	5.00
WAY	Justin Wayne/150	8.00
WEA	Jeff Weaver/360	5.00
WEEK	Rickie Weeks/360	15.00
WHEE	Dan Wheeler/360	5.00
WILL	Todd Williams/360	5.00
WI	Dan Wilson/360	10.00
WIL	Paul Wilson/360	5.00
WOOD	Ted Wood/330	5.00
YOUN	Ernie Young/350	5.00

Team USA Signature Blue Ink

Code	Player	NM/M
	Common Autograph:	8.00
ABB	Jim Abbott/60	30.00
ABE	Brent Abernathy/120	8.00
AIN	Kurt Ainsworth/120	8.00
ALV	Abe Alvarez/120	10.00
AND	Matt Anderson/110	8.00
AUS	Jeff Austin/120	8.00
BANK	Scott Bankhead/120	8.00
BARD	Josh Bard/100	8.00
BARR	Michael Barrett/120	8.00
BELL	Buddy Bell/29	25.00
BEN	Andy Benes/100	8.00
BENS	Kris Benson/60	10.00
BERG	Peter Bergeron/120	8.00
BLA	Casey Blake/80	20.00
BLO	Willie Bloomquist/51	10.00
BON	Jeremy Bonderman/90	8.00
BOR	Joe Borchard/100	8.00
BOW	Rob Bowen/510	5.00
BRAD	Milton Bradley/150	15.00
BRO	Ben Broussard/150	8.00
BRU	Brian Bruney/60	8.00
BUD	Mark Budzinski/120	8.00
BULL	Kirk Bullinger/120	8.00
BURK	Chris Burke/71	10.00
BU	Sean Burnett/60	8.00
BURN	Jeremy Burnitz/15	15.00
BUR	Pat Burrell/80	15.00
BURR	Sean Burroughs/142	8.00
BYRD	Paul Byrd/120	8.00
CAP	Chris Capuano/90	8.00
CASS	Scott Cassidy/120	8.00
CLA	Will Clark/30	80.00
COR	Chad Cordero/120	8.00
CR	Jesse Crain/60	8.00
CUD	Michael Cuddyer/89	20.00
DAV	Ben Davis/100	8.00
DED	Rod Dedeaux/25	10.00
DIC	R.A. Dickey/60	8.00
DIG	Ben Diggins/60	8.00
DIN	Lenny DiNardo/120	8.00
DRE	Ryan Drese/60	8.00
DREW	Tim Drew/120	8.00
DUCH	Justin Duchscherer/110	10.00
DUR	J.D. Durbin/60	8.00
ELAR	Scott Elarton/60	10.00
EVER	Adam Everett/120	8.00
FIN	Steve Finley/120	15.00
FOSS	Casey Fossum/100	8.00
FRAN	Terry Francona/40	40.00
FRA	Ryan Franklin/120	8.00
FRE	Ryan Freel/110	8.00
GAR	Nomar Garciaparra/60	60.00
GEO	Chris George/120	8.00
GER	Jody Gerut/100	8.00
GIAM	Jason Giambi/40	40.00
GIN	Matt Ginter/42	8.00
GLA	Troy Glaus/30	30.00
GOS	Mike Gosling/60	8.00
DRA	Danny Graves/120	8.00
GR	Shawn Green/90	20.00
GRE	Khalil Greene/60	15.00
GREE	Todd Greene/120	8.00
GREI	Seth Greisinger/120	8.00
GRO	Gabe Gross/60	8.00
HAM	Jeffrey Hammonds/90	8.00
HEIL	Aaron Heilman/90	8.00
HELT	Todd Helton/50	50.00
HERM	Dustin Hermanson/90	8.00
HI	Bobby Hill/120	8.00
HILL	Koyie Hill/90	8.00
HIN	A.J. Hinch/120	8.00
HUCK	Ken Huckaby/120	8.00
HUD	Orlando Hudson/110	10.00
JENN	Jason Jennings/120	8.00
JON	Jacque Jones/60	20.00
KATA	Matt Kata/75	8.00
KAZ	Scott Kazmir/110	15.00
KEAR	Austin Kearns/110	20.00
KENN	Adam Kennedy/90	8.00
KIES	Brooks Kieschnick/120	8.00
KOCH	Billy Koch/18	12.00
KON	Paul Konerko/52	25.00
KOO	Graham Koonce/120	8.00
KOTC	Casey Kotchman/60	30.00
LAMB	Mike Lamb/120	8.00
LAR	Barry Larkin/20	60.00
LAS	Tommy Lasorda/30	60.00
LEC	Matt LeCroy/120	8.00
LEE	Travis Lee/120	8.00
LEO	Justin Leone/60	8.00
LOO	Braden Looper/120	8.00
LOUX	Shane Loux/110	8.00
LUD	Ryan Ludwick/45	25.00
MAD	Ryan Madson/110	8.00
MAG	Dave Magadan/120	8.00
MART	Tino Martinez/30	30.00
MAU	Joe Mauer/120	85.00
MCC	David McCarty/120	8.00
MCDO	Jack McDowell/30	20.00
MEC	Gil Meche/120	8.00
MIE	Doug Mientkiewicz/120	10.00
MOR	Matt Morris/90	10.00
MORR	Warren Morris/120	8.00
MUL	Mark Mulder/110	10.00
MURR	Calvin Murray/120	8.00
MUSS	Mike Mussina/30	40.00
NADY	Xavier Nady/120	8.00
NAN	Shane Nance/60	8.00
NEI	Mike Neill/110	8.00
OJE	Augie Ojeda/119	8.00
OLE	John Olerud/120	15.00
OLS	Gregg Olson/60	8.00
OSW	Roy Oswalt/100	15.00
PARQ	Jim Parque/120	8.00
PATT	John Patterson/120	8.00
PEN	Brad Penny/110	8.00
POW	Jay Powell/60	10.00
PRI	Mark Prior/108	12.00
RAM	Horacio Ramirez/90	8.00
RAU	Jon Rauch/90	8.00
REED	Jeremy Reed/45	15.00
ROBE	Dave Roberts/90	8.00
ROBI	Frank Robinson/30	100.00
ROM	J.C. Romero/120	8.00
ROSS	David Ross/120	8.00
SAAR	Kirk Saarloos/120	8.00
SAND	Anthony Sanders/120	8.00
SAR	Dane Sardinha/110	8.00
SEAY	Bobby Seay/120	8.00
SEI	Phil Seibel/90	8.00
SELE	Aaron Sele/120	10.00
SHU	Paul Shuey/120	8.00
SIZE	Grady Sizemore/120	35.00
SMI	Reggie Smith/120	10.00
SMO	John Smoltz/120	40.00
SNY	Chris Snyder/120	8.00
SOR	Zach Sorensen/450	5.00
SPI	Scott Spiezio/120	8.00
SPR	Ed Sprague/120	8.00
STAN	Jason Stanford/450	5.00
STE	Dave Stewart/90	10.00
STEW	Scott Stewart/119	8.00
SWIF	Bill Swift/120	8.00
SWI	Nick Swisher/110	20.00
TON	Mike Tonis/100	8.00
TUCK	Michael Tucker/90	8.00
TYN	Jason Tyner/120	8.00
UPT	B.J. Upton/30	30.00
VAL	Eric Valent/120	8.00
VANB	John Van Benschoten/60	20.00
VAN	Cory Vance/120	8.00
VAND	John Vander Wal/120	8.00
VENT	Robin Ventura/100	40.00
VILL	Ron Villone/120	8.00
WAT	Bob Watson/100	8.00
WAY	Justin Wayne/60	10.00
WEA	Jeff Weaver/120	10.00
WEEK	Rickie Weeks/120	15.00
WHEE	Dan Wheeler/120	8.00
WILL	Todd Williams/90	8.00
WI	Dan Wilson/120	10.00
WIL	Paul Wilson/120	8.00
WOOD	Ted Wood/120	8.00
YOUN	Ernie Young/130	12.00

Team USA Signature Red Ink

Code	Player	NM/M
	Common Autograph:	10.00
	Some not priced due to scarcity:	
ABE	Brent Abernathy/20	15.00
AIN	Kurt Ainsworth/20	15.00
AND	Matt Anderson/30	15.00
AUS	Jeff Austin/20	15.00
BARD	Josh Bard/50	15.00
BARR	Michael Barrett/20	15.00
BEN	Andy Benes/20	15.00
BLO	Willie Bloomquist/25	25.00
BOR	Joe Borchard/50	10.00
BRAD	Milton Bradley/25	25.00
BRO	Ben Broussard/40	15.00
BRU	Brian Bruney/20	15.00
BURK	Chris Burke/25	25.00
BURN	Jeremy Burnitz/20	25.00
BUR	Pat Burrell/29	25.00
BYRD	Paul Byrd/20	15.00
CRO	Bobby Crosby/60	15.00
CUD	Michael Cuddyer/40	25.00
DAV	Ben Davis/50	15.00
DIN	Lenny DiNardo/40	15.00
EVER	Adam Everett/20	15.00
FIN	Steve Finley/20	25.00
FOSS	Casey Fossum/42	15.00
FRE	Ryan Freel/15	15.00

GAR	Nomar Garciaparra/30	125.00
GER	Jody Gerut/50	10.00
GLA	Troy Glaus/20	50.00
GOS	Mike Gosling/40	10.00
HEIL	Aaron Heilman/50	10.00
HIN	A.J. Hinch/20	15.00
HUD	Orlando Hudson/30	25.00
JENN	Jason Jennings/50	15.00
JON	Jacque Jones/40	20.00
KATA	Matt Kata/50	15.00
KAZ	Scott Kazmir/30	30.00
KEAR	Austin Kearns/30	30.00
KON	Paul Konerko/23	35.00
KOO	Graham Koonce/20	15.00
KOTC	Casey Kotchman/40	20.00
LEC	Matt LeCroy/20	15.00
LEE	Travis Lee/20	15.00
LEO	Justin Leone/40	20.00
LOUX	Shane Loux/30	15.00
LUD	Ryan Ludwick/50	35.00
MAD	Ryan Madson/30	15.00
MART	Tino Martinez/20	40.00
MAU	Joe Mauer/20	120.00
MCC	David McCarty/20	15.00
MIE	Doug Mientkiewicz/20	15.00
NADY	Xavier Nady/20	15.00
NAN	Shane Nance/40	10.00
NEI	Mike Neill/30	15.00
OSW	Roy Oswalt/50	20.00
PARQ	Jim Parque/20	15.00
PATT	John Patterson/20	15.00
PEN	Brad Penny/30	15.00
PRI	Mark Prior/48	15.00
RAU	Jon Rauch/53	10.00
REED	Jeremy Reed/25	15.00
ROM	J.C. Romero/20	15.00
SAR	Dane Sardinha/30	15.00
SIZE	Grady Sizemore/30	40.00
SMO	John Smoltz/20	65.00
SOR	Zach Sorensen/50	10.00
SPR	Ed Sprague/20	15.00
STAN	Jason Stanford/50	10.00
STE	Dave Stewart/30	25.00
SWI	Nick Swisher/30	40.00
TON	Mike Tonis/50	10.00
UPT	B.J. Upton/20	60.00
VAR	Jason Varitek/30	70.00
VENT	Robin Ventura/20	25.00
WAT	Bob Watson/30	10.00
WAY	Justin Wayne/40	10.00
WEA	Jeff Weaver/20	15.00
WEEK	Rickie Weeks/20	25.00
WILL	Todd Williams/50	10.00
WIL	Paul Wilson/30	15.00
WOOD	Ted Wood/30	15.00
YOUN	Ernie Young/50	10.00

Team USA Signature Green Ink

No Pricing
Production 1-3

2004 Upper Deck Vintage

ROGER CLEMENS
HOUSTON ASTROS® - PITCHER

	NM/M
Complete Set (450):	
Common Player:	.15
Common SP (301-315):	.50
Inserted 1:5	
Common SP (316-325):	.40
Inserted 1:7	
Common SP (326-350):	.40
Inserted 1:5	
Common 3D SP (351-440):	2.00
Inserted 1:12	
Old Judge (441-450) found in bonus packs	
Pack (8):	2.50
Box (24 + 1 Bonus Pack):	50.00
1	Albert Pujols	1.50
2	Carlos Delgado	.50
3	Todd Helton	.50
4	Nomar Garciaparra	1.50
5	Vladimir Guerrero	.75
6	Alfonso Soriano	.75
7	Alex Rodriguez	1.50
8	Jason Giambi	.75
9	Derek Jeter	2.00
10	Pedro J. Martinez	.75
11	Ivan Rodriguez	.50
12	Mark Prior	1.00
13	Marquis Grissom	.15
14	Barry Zito	.25
15	Alex Cintron	.15
16	Wade Miller	.15
17	Eric Chavez	.25
18	Matt Clement	.15
19	Orlando Cabrera	.15
20	Odalis Perez	.15

21	Lance Berkman	.25
22	Keith Foulke	.15
23	Shawn Green	.25
24	Byung-Hyun Kim	.15
25	Geoff Jenkins	.15
26	Torii Hunter	.40
27	Richard Hidalgo	.25
28	Edgar Martinez	.25
29	Placido Polanco	.15
30	Brad Lidge	.15
31	Alex Escobar	.15
32	Garret Anderson	.25
33	Larry Walker	.25
34	Ken Griffey Jr.	1.00
35	Junior Spivey	.15
36	Carlos Beltran	.25
37	Bartolo Colon	.15
38	Ichiro Suzuki	1.00
39	Ramon Ortiz	.15
40	Roy Oswalt	.25
41	Mike Piazza	1.00
42	Benito Santiago	.15
43	Mike Mussina	.50
44	Jeff Kent	.25
45	Curt Schilling	.50
46	Adam Dunn	.40
47	Mike Sweeney	.15
48	Chipper Jones	1.00
49	Frank Thomas	.50
50	Kerry Wood	.50
51	Rod Beck	.15
52	Brian Giles	.25
53	Hank Blalock	.25
54	Andruw Jones	.50
55	Dmitri Young	.15
56	Juan Pierre	.15
57	Jacque Jones	.15
58	Phil Nevin	.15
59	Rocco Baldelli	.25
60	Greg Maddux	1.00
61	Eric Gagne	.15
62	Tim Hudson	.25
63	Brian Lawrence	.15
64	Sammy Sosa	1.00
65	Corey Koskie	.15
66	Bobby Abreu	.25
67	Preston Wilson	.15
68	Jay Gibbons	.15
69	Dontrelle Willis	.25
70	Richie Sexson	.40
71	Kevin Millwood	.25
72	Randy Johnson	.75
73	Jack Cust	.15
74	Randy Wolf	.15
75	Johan Santana	.25
76	Magglio Ordonez	.25
77	Sean Casey	.15
78	Billy Wagner	.25
79	Javier Vazquez	.15
80	Jorge Posada	.40
81	Jason Schmidt	.15
82	Bret Boone	.25
83	Jeff Bagwell	.50
84	Rickie Weeks	.25
85	Troy Percival	.15
86	Jose Vidro	.15
87	Freddy Garcia	.15
88	Manny Ramirez	.50
89	John Smoltz	.25
90	Moises Alou	.25
91	Ugueth Urbina	.15
92	Bobby Hill	.15
93	Marcus Giles	.15
94	Aramis Ramirez	.25
95	Brad Wilkerson	.15
96	Ray Durham	.15
97	David Wells	.15
98	Paul LoDuca	.15
99	Danny Graves	.15
100	Jason Kendall	.25
101	Carlos Lee	.25
102	Rafael Furcal	.25
103	Mike Lowell	.25
104	Kevin Brown	.25
105	Vicente Padilla	.15
106	Miguel Tejada	.40
107	Bernie Williams	.40
108	Octavio Dotel	.15
109	Steve Finley	.15
110	Lyle Overbay	.15
111	Delmon Young	.25
112	Bo Hart	.15
113	Jason Lane	.15
114	Matt Roney	.15
115	Brian Roberts	.15
116	Tom Glavine	.25
117	Rich Aurilia	.15
118	Adam Kennedy	.15
119	Hee Seop Choi	.15
120	Trot Nixon	.15
121	Gary Sheffield	.40
122	Jay Payton	.15
123	Brad Penny	.15
124	Garrett Atkins	.15
125	Aubrey Huff	.25
126	Juan Gonzalez	.40
127	Jason Jennings	.15
128	Luis Gonzalez	.25
129	Vinny Castilla	.15
130	Esteban Loaiza	.15
131	Erubiel Durazo	.15
132	Eric Hinske	.15
133	Scott Rolen	.25
134	Craig Biggio	.25
135	Tim Wakefield	.15
136	Darin Erstad	.25
137	Denny Stark	.15
138	Ben Sheets	.25

139	Hideo Nomo	.40
140	Derrek Lee	.25
141	Matt Mantei	.15
142	Reggie Sanders	.15
143	Jose Guillen	.15
144	Joe Mays	.15
145	Jimmy Rollins	.25
146	Juan Encarnacion	.15
147	Joe Crede	.15
148	Aaron Guiel	.15
149	Mark Mulder	.25
150	Travis Lee	.15
151	Josh Phelps	.15
152	Michael Young	.15
153	Paul Konerko	.15
154	John Lackey	.15
155	Damian Moss	.15
156	Javy Lopez	.25
157	Joe Borowski	.15
158	Jose Cruz Jr.	1.50
159	Ramon Hernandez	.15
160	Raul Ibanez	.15
161	Adrian Beltre	.15
162	Bobby Higginson	.15
163	Jorge Julio	.15
164	Miguel Batista	.15
165	Luis Castillo	.15
166	Aaron Harang	.15
167	Ken Harvey	.15
168	Rocky Biddle	.15
169	Mariano Rivera	.25
170	Matt Morris	.15
171	Laynce Nix	.25
172	Mike Maroth	.15
173	Francisco Rodriguez	.25
174	Livan Hernandez	.15
175	Aaron Heilman	.15
176	Nick Johnson	.15
177	Woody Williams	.15
178	Joe Kennedy	.15
179	Jesse Foppert	.15
180	Ryan Franklin	.15
181	Endy Chavez	.15
182	Chin-Hui Tsao	.15
183	Todd Walker	.15
184	Edgardo Alfonzo	.15
185	Edgar Renteria	.15
186	Matt LeCroy	.15
187	Carl Everett	.15
188	Jeff Conine	.15
189	Jason Varitek	.15
190	Russ Ortiz	.15
191	Melvin Mora	.15
192	Mark Buehrle	.15
193	Bill Mueller	.15
194	Miguel Cabrera	.25
195	Carlos Zambrano	.15
196	Jose Valverde	.15
197	Danys Baez	.15
198	Mike MacDougal	.15
199	Zach Day	.15
200	Roy Halladay	.25
201	Jerome Williams	.15
202	Josh Fogg	.15
203	Mark Kotsay	.15
204	Pat Burrell	.40
205	A.J. Pierzynski	.15
206	Fred McGriff	.25
207	Brandon Larson	.15
208	Robb Quinlan	.15
209	David Ortiz	.15
210	A.J. Burnett	.15
211	John Vander Wal	.15
212	Jim Thome	.75
213	Matt Kata	.15
214	Kip Wells	.15
215	Scott Podsednik	.40
216	Rickey Henderson	.25
217	Travis Hafner	.15
218	Tony Batista	.15
219	Robert Fick	.15
220	Derek Lowe	.25
221	Ryan Klesko	.15
222	Joe Beimel	.15
223	Doug Mientkiewicz	.15
224	Angel Berroa	.15
225	Adam Eaton	.15
226	C.C. Sabathia	.15
227	Wilfredo Ledezma	.15
228	Jason Johnson	.15
229	Ryan Wagner	.25
230	Al Leiter	.15
231	Joel Pineiro	.15
232	Jason Isringhausen	.15
233	John Olerud	.25
234	Ron Calloway	.15
235	Jose Reyes	.40
236	J.D. Drew	.15
237	Jared Sandberg	.15
238	Gil Meche	.15
239	Jose Contreras	.15
240	Eric Milton	.15
241	Jason L. Phillips	.15
242	Luis Ayala	.15
243	Bobby Kielty	.15
244	Jose Lima	.15
245	Brooks Kieschnick	.15
246	Xavier Nady	.15
247	Dan Haren	.15
248	Victor Zambrano	.15
249	Kelvim Escobar	.15
250	Oliver Perez	.15
251	Jamie Moyer	.15
252	Orlando Hudson	.15
253	Danny Kolb	.15
254	Jake Peavy	.25
255	Kris Benson	.15
256	Roger Clemens	1.50

257	Jim Edmonds	.40
258	Rafael Palmeiro	.50
259	Jae Weong Seo	.15
260	Chase Utley	.40
261	Rich Harden	.15
262	Mark Teixeira	.25
263	Johnny Damon	.25
264	Luis Matos	.15
265	Shigetoshi Hasegawa	.15
266	Alfredo Amezaga	.15
267	Tim Worrell	.15
268	Kazuhisa Ishii	.15
269	Miguel Ojeda	.15
270	Kazuhiro Sasaki	.15
271	Hideki Matsui	2.00
272	Troy Glaus	.40
273	Michael Tucker	.15
274	Lew Ford	.15
275	Brian Jordan	.15
276	David Eckstein	.15
277	Robby Hammock	.15
278	Corey Patterson	.25
279	Wes Helms	.15
280	Jermaine Dye	.15
281	Cliff Floyd	.15
282	Dustan Mohr	.15
283	Kevin Mench	.15
284	Ellis Burks	.15
285	Jerry Hairston Jr.	.15
286	Tim Salmon	.25
287	Omar Vizquel	.25
288	Andy Pettitte	.40
289	Guillermo Mota	.15
290	Tino Martinez	.25
291	Lance Carter	.15
292	Francisco Cordero	.15
293	Robb Nen	.15
294	Mike Cameron	.15
295	Jhonny Peralta	.15
296	Braden Looper	.15
297	Jarrod Washburn	.15
298	Mark Prior	.50
299	Alfonso Soriano	.25
300	Rocco Baldelli	.25
301	Pedro J. Martinez	1.50
302	Mark Prior	2.00
303	Barry Zito	.75
304	Roger Clemens	2.50
305	Randy Johnson	1.50
306	Roy Halladay	.50
307	Hideo Nomo	.75
308	Roy Oswalt	.50
309	Kerry Wood	1.00
310	Dontrelle Willis	.75
311	Mark Mulder	.50
312	Brandon Webb	.50
313	Mike Mussina	.75
314	Curt Schilling	.75
315	Tim Hudson	.75
316	Dontrelle Willis	.75
317	Juan Pierre	.40
318	Hideki Matsui	4.00
319	Andy Pettitte	.75
320	Mike Mussina	.75
321	Roger Clemens	2.50
322	Alex Gonzalez	.40
323	Brad Penny	.40
324	Ivan Rodriguez	.75
325	Josh Beckett	1.00
326	Aaron Boone	.40
327	Jeff Suppan	.40
328	Shea Hillenbrand	.40
329	Jeromy Burnitz	.40
330	Sidney Ponson	.40
331	Rondell White	.50
332	Shannon Stewart	.40
333	Armando Benitez	.40
334	Roberto Alomar	1.00
335	Raul Mondesi	.50
336	Morgan Ensberg	.40
337	Milton Bradley	.50
338	Brandon Webb	.50
339	Marlon Byrd	.40
340	Carlos Pena	.40
341	Brandon Phillips	.40
342	Josh Beckett	1.00
343	Eric Munson	.40
344	Brett Myers	.40
345	Austin Kearns	1.00
346	Jody Gerut	.40
347	Vernon Wells	.40
348	Jeff Duncan	.40
349	Sean Burroughs	.40
350	Jeremy Bonderman	.40
351	Hideki Matsui	15.00
352	Jason Giambi	8.00
353	Alfonso Soriano	8.00
354	Derek Jeter	15.00
355	Aaron Boone	3.00
356	Jorge Posada	5.00
357	Bernie Williams	5.00
358	Manny Ramirez	12.00
359	Nomar Garciaparra	12.00
360	Johnny Damon	3.00
361	Jason Varitek	2.50
362	Carlos Delgado	5.00
363	Vernon Wells	4.00
364	Jay Gibbons	4.00
365	Tony Batista	2.00
366	Rocco Baldelli	5.00
367	Aubrey Huff	4.00
368	Carlos Beltran	4.00
369	Mike Sweeney	3.00
370	Magglio Ordonez	6.00
371	Frank Thomas	6.00
372	Carlos Lee	4.00
373	Roberto Alomar	4.00
374	Jacque Jones	2.00

375	Torii Hunter	4.00
376	Milton Bradley	2.00
377	Travis Hafner	2.00
378	Jody Gerut	2.00
379	Dmitri Young	2.00
380	Carlos Pena	2.00
381	Ichiro Suzuki	10.00
382	Bret Boone	3.00
383	Edgar Martinez	3.00
384	Eric Chavez	3.00
385	Miguel Tejada	3.00
386	Erubiel Durazo	2.00
387	Jose Guillen	2.00
388	Garret Anderson	3.00
389	Troy Glaus	4.00
390	Alex Rodriguez	10.00
391	Rafael Palmeiro	5.00
392	Hank Blalock	4.00
393	Mark Teixeira	4.00
394	Gary Sheffield	4.00
395	Andruw Jones	5.00
396	Chipper Jones	8.00
397	Javy Lopez	3.00
398	Marcus Giles	2.00
399	Rafael Furcal	3.00
400	Jim Thome	5.00
401	Bobby Abreu	3.00
402	Pat Burrell	4.00
403	Mike Lowell	3.00
404	Ivan Rodriguez	5.00
405	Derek Lee	3.00
406	Miguel Cabrera	5.00
407	Vladimir Guerrero	6.00
408	Orlando Cabrera	2.00
409	Jose Vidro	2.00
410	Mike Piazza	8.00
411	Cliff Floyd	3.00
412	Albert Pujols	15.00
413	Scott Rolen	6.00
414	Jim Edmonds	4.00
415	Edgar Renteria	3.00
416	Lance Berkman	3.00
417	Jeff Bagwell	5.00
418	Jeff Kent	3.00
419	Richard Hidalgo	2.00
420	Morgan Ensberg	2.00
421	Sammy Sosa	10.00
422	Moises Alou	3.00
423	Ken Griffey Jr.	10.00
424	Adam Dunn	4.00
425	Austin Kearns	4.00
426	Richie Sexson	4.00
427	Geoff Jenkins	3.00
428	Brian Giles	3.00
429	Reggie Sanders	2.00
430	Rich Aurilia	2.00
431	Jose Cruz Jr.	2.00
432	Shawn Green	3.00
433	Jeromy Burnitz	2.00
434	Luis Gonzalez	3.00
435	Todd Helton	5.00
436	Preston Wilson	2.00
437	Larry Walker	3.00
438	Ryan Klesko	2.00
439	Phil Nevin	2.00
440	Sean Burroughs	2.00
441	Sammy Sosa	3.00
442	Albert Pujols	4.00
443	Magglio Ordonez	.50
444	Vladimir Guerrero	1.50
445	Todd Helton	1.00
446	Jason Giambi	1.50
447	Ichiro Suzuki	3.00
448	Alex Rodriguez	3.00
449	Carlos Delgado	.75
450	Manny Ramirez	1.00

Black & White

Cards (1-300):	1-2X
Inserted 1:6	
SP's (301-325):	1-2X
Inserted 1:24	
SP's (326-350):	1-2X
Inserted 1:20	
B/W Color Variations:	6-10X
Inserted 1:48	

Old Judge

HIDEKI MATSUI, OF
NEW YORK YANKEES

THE UPPER DECK COMPANY, LLC

	NM/M
Complete Set (20):	15.00
Common Player:	.40
Inserted 3:bonus pack.	
Blue Back:	1-2X
Inserted 1:4 bonus packs.	
Red Back:	2-3X
Inserted 1:12 bonus packs.	
11	Randy Johnson	1.50
12	Pedro J. Martinez	1.50

13	Mark Prior	2.00
14	Barry Zito	.50
15	Roy Oswalt	.40
16	Roy Halladay	.50
17	Curt Schilling	.75
18	Mike Mussina	.75
19	Kevin Brown	.40
20	Roger Clemens	2.50
21	Eric Gagne	.50
22	Mariano Rivera	.50
23	Mike Piazza	2.00
24	Jorge Posada	.75
25	Jeff Kent	.50
26	Alfonso Soriano	1.00
27	Scott Rolen	1.00
28	Eric Chavez	.50
29	Edgar Renteria	.40
30	Hideki Matsui	4.00

Stellar Signatures

		NM/M
Inserted 1:600		
HM	Hideki Matsui	300.00
MP	Mike Piazza	150.00
AR	Alex Rodriguez	100.00
TS	Tom Seaver	50.00
IS	Ichiro Suzuki	200.00
CY	C. Yastrzemski/125	75.00
BZ	Barry Zito	40.00

Stellar Stat Men

		NM/M
Common Player:		4.00
Inserted 1:24		
1	Jose Reyes	6.00
2	Bo Hart	8.00
3	Hideki Matsui	30.00
4	Dontrelle Willis	6.00
5	Rocco Baldelli	6.00
6	Ichiro Suzuki	20.00
7	Mike Lowell	6.00
8	Derek Jeter	20.00
9	Ken Griffey Jr.	15.00
10	Sammy Sosa	12.00
11	Kerry Wood	10.00
12	Chipper Jones	8.00
13	Alfonso Soriano	8.00
14	Khalil Greene	6.00
15	Jim Thome	8.00
16	Rafael Furcal	5.00
17	Andrew Brown	4.00
18	Mark Prior	10.00
19	Barry Zito	6.00
20	Al Leiter	4.00
21	Carlos Delgado	6.00
22	Pedro J. Martinez	6.00
23	Alex Rodriguez	10.00
24	Lance Berkman	5.00
25	Jeff Bagwell	6.00
26	Bernie Williams	6.00
27	Hideo Nomo	8.00
28	Randy Johnson	8.00
29	Curt Schilling	8.00
30	Mike Piazza	10.00
31	Albert Pujols	12.00
32	Joe DiMaggio	100.00
33	Ted Williams	60.00
34	Mickey Mantle	100.00
35	Mike Mussina	5.00
36	Rich Harden	5.00
37	Roy Oswalt	4.00
38	Torii Hunter	5.00
39	Jorge Posada	6.00
40	Troy Glaus	5.00
41	Manny Ramirez	6.00
42	Roy Halladay	5.00

Timeless Teams

		NM/M
Common Quad:		15.00
Inserted 1:400		
Production 175 Sets		
1	Derek Jeter, Jason Giambi, Alfonso Soriano, Hideki Matsui	90.00
2	Randy Johnson, Luis Gonzalez, Steve Finley, Curt Schilling	20.00
4	Johnny Damon, Manny Ramirez, Nomar Garciaparra, Trot Nixon	35.00
5	Alex Rodriguez, Rafael Palmeiro, Mark Teixeira, Hank Blalock	35.00
6	Roberto Alomar, Frank Thomas, Magglio Ordonez, Carl Everett	20.00
7	Shannon Stewart, Torii Hunter, Jacque Jones, Doug Mientkiewicz	15.00
8	Jim Edmonds, Scott Nolen, J.D. Drew, Albert Pujols	

9	Bret Boone, John Olerud, Mike Cameron, Ichiro Suzuki,	45.00
10	Jeff Bagwell, Craig Biggio, Jeff Kent, Lance Berkman	20.00
11	Tim Salmon, Garret Anderson, Darin Erstad, Troy Glaus	15.00
12	Bernie Williams, Alfonso Soriano, Jorge Posada, Hideki Matsui	85.00
13	Carlos Beltran, Michael Tucker, Mike Sweeney, Brent Mayne	15.00
14	Jim Thome, Mike Lieberthal, Bobby Abreu, Marlon Byrd	30.00
15	Ivan Rodriguez, Juan Encarnacion, Mike Lowell, Miguel Cabrera	25.00
16	Sammy Sosa, Kerry Wood, Moises Alou, Corey Patterson	50.00
17	Andres Galarraga, Edgardo Alfonzo, Jose Cruz Jr., Rich Aurilia	15.00
18	Derek Jeter, Bernie Williams, Alfonso Soriano, Hideki Matsui	90.00

2004 Upper Deck Yankees Classics Promos

Each of the cards in Yankees Classics was issued in a foil-over-printed version with "UD PROMO" across the front. Cards were inserted into specially marked card shop and newsstand issues of Tuff Stuff magazine.

	NM/M
Common Player:	.50
Stars:	1.5X

2004 Upper Deck Yankees Classics

	NM/M
Complete Set (90):	20.00
Common Player:	.25
Pack (5):	6.00
Box (24):	120.00
1 Bill "Moose" Skowron	.50
2 Bob Cerv	.25
3 Bobby Murcer	.50
4 Bobby Richardson	.25
5 Brian Doyle	.25
6 Bucky Dent	.25
7 Chris Chambliss	.25
8 Clete Boyer	.25
9 Dave Kingman	.25
10 Dave Righetti	.25
11 Dave Winfield	.50
12 David Cone	.25
13 Red Ruffing	.25
14 Dock Ellis	.25
15 Don Baylor	.25
16 Don Larsen	.75
17 Don Mattingly	1.50
18 Dwight Gooden	.40
19 Ed Figueroa	.25
20 Joe Torre	.50
21 Darryl Strawberry	.40
22 Horace Clarke	.25
23 Gaylord Perry	.25
24 Phil Linz	.25
25 Gil McDougald	.25
26 Rich "Goose" Gossage	.25
27 Graig Nettles	.25
28 Hank Bauer	.25
29 Jack Clark	.25
30 Don Gullett	.25
31 Jim Abbott	.25
32 Jim Bouton	.25
33 Jim Kaat	.40
34 Jim Leyritz	.25
35 Jim Wynn	.25
36 Jimmy Key	.25
37 Joe Niekro	.25
38 Joe Pepitone	.25
39 John Wetteland	.25
40 Ken Griffey Sr.	.25
41 Felipe Alou	.25
42 Kevin Maas	.25
43 Lindy McDaniel	.25
44 Lou Piniella	.50
45 Luis Tiant	.25
46 Mel Stottlemyre	.25
47 Mickey Rivers	.25
48 Oscar Gamble	.25
49 Pat Dobson	.25
50 Paul O'Neill	.50
51 Phil Niekro	.25
52 Phil Rizzuto	.75
53 Doc Medich	.25
54 Rick Cerone	.25
55 Ron Blomberg	.25
56 Ron Guidry	.25
57 Roy White	.25
58 Rudy May	.25
59 Sam McDowell	.25
60 Sparky Lyle	.25
61 Steve Balboni	.25
62 Steve Sax	.25
63 Jerry Coleman	.25
64 Tom Tresh	.25
65 Tommy John	.25
66 Tony Kubek	.50
67 Wade Boggs	.50
68 Whitey Ford	.75
69 Willie Randolph	.25
70 Yogi Berra	1.00
71 Babe Ruth	3.00
72 Bill Dickey	.50
73 Billy Martin	.50
74 Bob Meusel	.25
75 Casey Stengel	.50
76 Elston Howard	.25
77 Jim "Catfish" Hunter	.25
78 Joe DiMaggio	2.00
79 Lefty Gomez	.50
80 Lou Gehrig	2.00
81 Mickey Mantle	3.00
82 Miller Huggins	.25
83 Roger Maris	1.50
84 Thurman Munson	.75
85 Tony Lazzeri	.75
86 Yankee Stadium	.50
87 Times Square	.50
88 Central Park	.50
89 Empire State Building	.50
90 Statue of Liberty	.50

Bronze
Bronze: 4-8X
Production 99 Sets

Silver
Silver: No Pricing

Gold
Gold: 8-15X
Production 30 Sets

Classic Cuts
No Pricing
Production One Set

Scripts Triple Auto.
No Pricing
Production 20 Sets

Scripts (Single Auto)

	NM/M
Common Autograph:	10.00
Inserted 1:8	
AU-1 Bill "Moose" Skowron	15.00
AU-2 Bob Cerv	15.00
AU-3 Bobby Murcer/SP	60.00
AU-4 Bobby Richardson	15.00
AU-5 Brian Doyle	10.00
AU-6 Bucky Dent	10.00
AU-7 Chris Chambliss	12.00
AU-8 Clete Boyer	15.00
AU-9 Dave Kingman	10.00
AU-10 Dave Righetti	10.00
AU-11 Dave Winfield/SP	60.00
AU-12 David Cone	10.00
AU-13 Dock Ellis	10.00
AU-14 Dock Ellis	10.00
AU-15 Don Baylor/SP	25.00
AU-16 Don Larsen/SP	40.00
AU-17 Don Mattingly/SP	85.00
AU-18 Dwight Gooden	15.00
AU-19 Ed Figueroa	10.00
AU-20 Joe Torre/SP	125.00
AU-21 Darryl Strawberry	20.00
AU-22 Gaylord Perry	20.00
AU-23 Gaylord Perry	20.00
AU-24 Phil Linz	10.00
AU-25 Gil McDougald	15.00
AU-26 Rich "Goose" Gossage	20.00
AU-27 Graig Nettles	15.00
AU-28 Hank Bauer	15.00
AU-29 Jack Clark	15.00
AU-31 Jim Abbott	15.00
AU-32 Jim Bouton	15.00
AU-33 Jim Kaat	15.00
AU-34 Jim Leyritz/SP	25.00
AU-35 Jim Wynn	10.00
AU-36 Jimmy Key	10.00
AU-37 Joe Niekro	10.00
AU-38 Joe Pepitone	15.00
AU-39 John Wetteland/SP	15.00
AU-40 Ken Griffey Sr.	12.00
AU-42 Kevin Maas	10.00
AU-43 Lindy McDaniel	10.00
AU-44 Lou Piniella/SP	35.00
AU-45 Luis Tiant	20.00
AU-46 Mel Stottlemyre	15.00
AU-47 Mickey Rivers	15.00
AU-48 Oscar Gamble	15.00
AU-49 Pat Dobson	15.00
AU-50 Paul O'Neill/SP	40.00
AU-51 Phil Niekro	15.00
AU-52 Phil Rizzuto/SP	75.00
AU-53 Doc Medich	10.00
AU-54 Rick Cerone	10.00
AU-55 Ron Blomberg	10.00
AU-56 Ron Guidry	25.00
AU-57 Roy White	12.00
AU-58 Rudy May	10.00
AU-59 Sam McDowell	10.00
AU-60 Sparky Lyle	12.00
AU-61 Steve Balboni	10.00
AU-62 Steve Sax	15.00
AU-63 Jerry Coleman	15.00
AU-64 Tom Tresh	15.00
AU-65 Tommy John	15.00
AU-66 Tony Kubek/SP	400.00
AU-67 Wade Boggs/SP	60.00
AU-68 Whitey Ford/SP	60.00
AU-69 Willie Randolph/SP	25.00
AU-70 Yogi Berra/SP	75.00

Scripts (Dual Auto.)

		NM/M
Production 100 Sets		
SC	Bill "Moose" Skowron, Bob Cerv	50.00
MP	Bobby Murcer, Lou Piniella	65.00
CB	Chris Chambliss, Ron Blomberg	50.00
BN	Clete Boyer, Graig Nettles	50.00
RC	Dave Righetti, Rick Cerone	60.00
ED	Dock Ellis, Pat Dobson	70.00
BG	Don Baylor, Ken Griffey Sr.	65.00
MW	Don Mattingly, Dave Winfield	150.00
FG	Ed Figueroa, Ron Guidry	60.00
MB	Bobby Murcer, Hank Bauer	75.00
GL	Rich "Goose" Gossage, Sparky Lyle	50.00
NB	Graig Nettles, Wade Boggs	80.00
KJ	Jim Kaat, Tommy John	60.00
KA	Jimmy Key, Jim Abbott	50.00
PS	Joe Pepitone, Bill "Moose" Skowron	50.00
MM	Kevin Maas, Don Mattingly	100.00
RW	Mickey Rivers, Roy White	50.00
OL	Paul O'Neill, Jim Leyritz	75.00
RM	Phil Rizzuto, Gil McDougald	100.00
SD	Steve Sax, Brian Doyle	40.00
KR	Tony Kubek, Bobby Richardson	100.00
FL	Whitey Ford, Don Larsen	125.00
BL	Yogi Berra, Don Larsen	150.00
BH	Yogi Berra, Joe Torre	100.00
BF	Yogi Berra, Whitey Ford	150.00
WM	Bobby Murcer, Roy White	75.00
DN	Bucky Dent, Graig Nettles	50.00
CN	Chris Chambliss, Graig Nettles	50.00
CL	David Cone, Don Larsen	100.00
MC	Don Mattingly, Jack Clark	85.00
BM	Don Mattingly, Wade Boggs	150.00
SG	Darryl Strawberry, Dwight Gooden	75.00
CG	David Cone, Dwight Gooden	70.00

Scripts (Triple Auto.)
No Pricing
Production 20 Sets

Scripts (Quad Auto.)
No Pricing
Production 10 Sets

Mitchell & Ness Pennant

		NM/M
Inserted 1:Box		
Cards:		.3X
P2	1927 World Series/96	25.00
P3	1928 World Series/96	25.00
P4	1932 World Series/96	25.00
P6	1937 World Series/96	25.00
P8	1939 World Series/96	25.00
P10	1943 World Series/97	25.00
P11	1947 World Series/97	25.00
P13	1950 World Series/97	25.00
P15	1952 World Series/97	25.00
P17	1956 World Series/97	25.00
P18	1958 World Series/97	25.00
P23	1996 World Series/99	25.00
P24	1998 World Series/99	25.00
P25	1999 World Series/99	25.00
P26	2000 World Series/100	25.00
MM57	Mickey Mantle - 1957 MVP/97	30.00
MM62	Mickey Mantle - 1962 MVP/98	30.00

Mitchell & Ness Pennant Card

		NM/M
Inserted 1:Box		
P2	1927 World Series/ 1927	5.00
P3	1928 World Series/ 1,928	5.00
P4	1932 World Series/ 1,932	5.00
P5	1936 World Series/36	10.00
P6	1937 World Series/ 1,937	5.00
P7	1938 World Series/38	10.00
P8	1939 World Series/ 1,939	5.00
P9	1941 World Series/41	5.00
P10	1943 World Series/1,943	5.00
P11	1947 World Series/1 ,947	5.00
P12	1949 World Series/49	10.00
P13	1950 World Series/ 1,950	5.00
P14	1951 World Series/51	10.00
P15	1952 World Series/ 1,952	5.00
P16	1953 World Series/53	10.00
P17	1956 World Series/ 1,956	5.00
P18	1958 World Series/ 1,958	5.00
P19	1961 World Series/61	10.00
P20	1962 World Series/62	10.00
P21	1977 World Series/77	8.00
P22	1978 World Series/78	8.00
P23	1996 World Series/ 1,996	5.00
P24	1998 World Series/ 1,998	5.00
P25	1999 World Series/ 1,999	5.00
P26	2000 World Series/ 2,000	5.00
MM57	Mickey Mantle - 1957 MVP/1,957	8.00
MM62	Mickey Mantle - 1962 MVP/1,962	8.00

Mitchell & Ness Jersey Redemption

		NM/M
Inserted 1:384		
Production 40-99		
MNJ1	Babe Ruth/40	350.00
MNJ2	Bill Dickey/75	120.00
MNJ3	Billy Martin/99	150.00
MNJ4	Bobby Murcer/99	100.00
MNJ5	Bucky Dent/92	100.00
MNJ6	Casey Stengel/65	120.00
MNJ7	"Catfish" Hunter/92	120.00
MNJ8	Chris Chambliss/99	80.00
MNJ9	Don Larsen/75	120.00
MNJ10	Don Mattingly/92	150.00
MNJ11	Elston Howard/88	120.00
MNJ12	Rich "Goose" Gossage/92	100.00
MNJ13	Graig Nettles/99	100.00
MNJ14	Joe DiMaggio/55	200.00
MNJ15	Lefty Gomez/81	120.00
MNJ16	Lou Gehrig/40	200.00
MNJ17	Lou Piniella/92	120.00
MNJ18	Mickey Mantle/50	275.00
MNJ19	Bill "Moose" Skowron/85	125.00
MNJ20	Phil Rizzuto/40	150.00
MNJ21	Roy White/50	100.00
MNJ22	Roger Maris/92	200.00
MNJ23	Ron Guidry/99	100.00
MNJ24	Sparky Lyle/99	100.00
MNJ25	Thurman Munson/91	200.00
MNJ26	Tony Kubek/75	150.00
MNJ27	Tony Lazzeri/79	120.00
MNJ28	Whitey Ford/43	180.00
MNJ29	Willie Randolph/92	100.00
MNJ30	Yogi Berra/50	200.00

2004 Upper Deck/Gravity Games Cleveland Indians

In conjunction with the Gravity Games held September 15-19 in Cleveland, Upper Deck created this team set. Cards were distributed in team-logoed foil packs containing four player cards and a header card. Fronts are bordered in red with game action photos. Backs have a close-up from the front photo, personal data, career highlights, 2003 and lifetime stats.

	NM/M
Complete Set (12):	7.50
Common Player:	.50
1 C.C. Sabathia	.65
2 Travis Hafner	.75
3 Casey Blake	.75
4 Matt Lawton	.50
5 Jason Davis	.50
6 Ben Broussard	.50
7 Omar Vizquel	.50
8 Cliff Lee	.50
9 Ronnie Belliard	.50
10 Jody Gerut	.75
11 Victor Martinez	1.00
12 Coco Crisp	1.00
--- Header Card	.05

2004 Upper Deck/Sunkist

Photos of six former major leaguers in their Little League days are featured on this set. Five million of the cards were inserted into bags of oranges to help promote the fruit company's sponsorship of the youth program.

	NM/M
Complete Set (6):	6.00
Common Player:	.50
1 Rollie Fingers	1.00
2 Gary Carter	2.00
3 Mark McGwire	3.00
4 Mickey Morandini	.50
5 Paul O'Neill	.50
6 Dave Steib	.50

2005 Upper Deck

	NM/M
Complete Set (500):	75.00
Common Player:	.15
Common (211-250):	.50
Hobby Pack (8):	3.00
Hobby Box (24):	65.00
1 Casey Kotchman	.15
2 Chone Figgins	.15
3 David Eckstein	.15
4 Jarrod Washburn	.15
5 Robb Quinlan	.15
6 Troy Glaus	.25
7 Vladimir Guerrero	.75
8 Brandon Webb	.15
9 Danny Bautista	.15
10 Luis Gonzalez	.15
11 Matt Kata	.15
12 Randy Johnson	.75
13 Robby Hammock	.15
14 Shea Hillenbrand	.15
15 Adam LaRoche	.15
16 Andruw Jones	.25
17 Horacio Ramirez	.15
18 John Smoltz	.25
19 Johnny Estrada	.15
20 Mike Hampton	.15
21 Rafael Furcal	.15
22 Brian Roberts	.15
23 Javy Lopez	.25
24 Jay Gibbons	.15
25 Jorge Julio	.15
26 Melvin Mora	.15
27 Miguel Tejada	.25
28 Rafael Palmeiro	.50
29 Derek Lowe	.25
30 Jason Varitek	.25
31 Kevin Youkilis	.15
32 Manny Ramirez	.75
33 Curt Schilling	.75
34 Pedro Martinez	.75
35 Trot Nixon	.15
36 Corey Patterson	.25
37 Derek Lee	.25
38 LaTroy Hawkins	.15
39 Mark Prior	.75
40 Matt Clement	.15
41 Moises Alou	.25
42 Sammy Sosa	1.50
43 Aaron Rowand	.15
44 Carlos Lee	.15
45 Jose Valentin	.15
46 Juan Uribe	.15
47 Magglio Ordonez	.25
48 Mark Buehrle	.15
49 Paul Konerko	.25
50 Adam Dunn	.50
51 Barry Larkin	.25
52 D'Angelo Jimenez	.15
53 Danny Graves	.15
54 Paul Wilson	.15
55 Sean Casey	.25
56 Wily Mo Pena	.25
57 Ben Broussard	.15
58 C.C. Sabathia	.15
59 Casey Blake	.15
60 Cliff Lee	.15
61 Matt Lawton	.15
62 Omar Vizquel	.15
63 Victor Martinez	.15
64 Charles Johnson	.15
65 Joe Kennedy	.15
66 Jeromy Burnitz	.15
67 Matt Holliday	.50
68 Preston Wilson	.15
69 Royce Clayton	.15
70 Shawn Estes	.15
71 Bobby Higginson	.15
72 Brandon Inge	.15
73 Carlos Guillen	.15
74 Dmitri Young	.15
75 Eric Munson	.15
76 Jeremy Bonderman	.15
77 Ugueth Urbina	.15
78 Josh Beckett	.40
79 Dontrelle Willis	.50
80 Jeff Conine	.15
81 Juan Pierre	.15
82 Luis Castillo	.15
83 Miguel Cabrera	.75
84 Mike Lowell	.25
85 Andy Pettitte	.25
86 Brad Lidge	.25
87 Carlos Beltran	.50
88 Craig Biggio	.25
89 Jeff Bagwell	.50
90 Roger Clemens	1.50

91 Roy Oswalt .25
92 Benito Santiago .15
93 Jeremy Affeldt .15
94 Juan Gonzalez .25
95 Ken Harvey .15
96 Mike MacDougal .15
97 Mike Sweeney .15
98 Zack Greinke .15
99 Adrian Beltre .40
100 Alex Cora .15
101 Cesar Izturis .15
102 Eric Gagne .40
103 Kazuhisa Ishii .15
104 Milton Bradley .15
105 Shawn Green .25
106 Danny Kolb .15
107 Ben Sheets .25
108 Brooks Kieschnick .15
109 Craig Counsell .15
110 Geoff Jenkins .15
111 Lyle Overbay .15
112 Scott Podsednik .15
113 Corey Koskie .15
114 Johan Santana .40
115 Joe Mauer .25
116 Justin Morneau .25
117 Lew Ford .15
118 Matt LeCroy .15
119 Torii Hunter .25
120 Brad Wilkerson .15
121 Chad Cordero .15
122 Livan Hernandez .15
123 Jose Vidro .15
124 Terrmel Sledge .15
125 Tony Batista .15
126 Zach Day .15
127 Al Leiter .15
128 Jae Weong Seo .15
129 Jose Reyes .40
130 Kazuo Matsui .15
131 Mike Piazza 1.00
132 Todd Zeile .15
133 Cliff Floyd .15
134 Alex Rodriguez 2.00
135 Derek Jeter 2.00
136 Gary Sheffield .40
137 Hideki Matsui 1.50
138 Jason Giambi .25
139 Jorge Posada .25
140 Mike Mussina .40
141 Barry Zito .25
142 Bobby Crosby .25
143 Octavio Dotel .15
144 Eric Chavez .25
145 Jermaine Dye .15
146 Mark Kotsay .15
147 Tim Hudson .25
148 Billy Wagner .15
149 Bobby Abreu .25
150 David Bell .15
151 Jim Thome .50
152 Jimmy Rollins .25
153 Mike Lieberthal .15
154 Randy Wolf .15
155 Craig Wilson .15
156 Daryle Ward .15
157 Jack Wilson .15
158 Jason Kendall .15
159 Kip Wells .15
160 Oliver Perez .15
161 Robert Mackowiak .15
162 Brian Giles .25
163 Brian Lawrence .15
164 David Wells .15
165 Jay Payton .15
166 Ryan Klesko .15
167 Sean Burroughs .15
168 Trevor Hoffman .15
169 Brett Tomko .15
170 J.T. Snow .15
171 Jason Schmidt .25
172 Kirk Rueter .15
173 A.J. Pierzynski .15
174 Pedro Feliz .15
175 Ray Durham .15
176 Eddie Guardado .15
177 Edgar Martinez .15
178 Ichiro Suzuki 1.50
179 Jamie Moyer .15
180 Joel Pineiro .15
181 Randy Winn .15
182 Raul Ibanez .15
183 Albert Pujols 2.00
184 Edgar Renteria .25
185 Jason Isringhausen .15
186 Jim Edmonds .40
187 Matt Morris .15
188 Reggie Sanders .15
189 Tony Womack .15
190 Aubrey Huff .15
191 Danys Baez .15
192 Carl Crawford .15
193 Jose Cruz Jr. .15
194 Rocco Baldelli .15
195 Tino Martinez .15
196 Dewon Brazelton .15
197 Alfonso Soriano .75
198 Brad Fullmer .15
199 Gerald Laird .15
200 Hank Blalock .50
201 Laynce Nix .15
202 Mark Teixeira .25
203 Mike Young .25
204 Alexis Rios .15
205 Eric Hinske .15
206 Miguel Batista .15
207 Orlando Hudson .15
208 Roy Halladay .15

209 Ted Lilly .15
210 Vernon Wells .15
211 Aarom Baldiris .50
212 B.J. Upton 1.00
213 Dallas McPherson .50
214 Brian Dallimore .50
215 Chris Oxspring .50
216 Chris Shelton .50
217 David Wright 1.50
218 Edwardo Sierra .50
219 Fernando Nieve .50
220 Frank Francisco .50
221 Jeff Bennett .50
222 Justin Lehr .50
223 John Gall .50
224 Jorge Sequea .50
225 Justin Germano .50
226 Kazuhito Tadano .50
227 Kevin Cave .50
228 Joe Blanton .50
229 Luis Gonzalez .50
230 Mike Wuertz .50
231 Mike Rouse .50
232 Nick Regilio .50
233 Orlando Rodriguez .50
234 Phil Stockman .50
235 Ramon Ramirez .50
236 Roberto Novoa .50
237 Dioner Navarro .50
238 Tim Bausher .50
239 Logan Kensing .50
240 Andy Green .50
241 Brad Halsey .50
242 Charles Thomas .50
243 George Sherrill .50
244 Jesse Crain .50
245 Jimmy Serrano .50
246 Joe Horgan .50
247 Chris Young RC 1.50
248 Joey Gathright .50
249 Gavin Floyd .50
250 Ryan Howard 1.00
251 Lance Cormier .15
252 Matt Treanor .15
253 Jeff Francis .15
254 Nick Swisher .15
255 Scott Atchison .15
256 Travis Blackley .15
257 Travis Smith .15
258 Yadier Molina .15
259 Jeff Keppinger .15
260 Scott Kazmir 1.00
261 Garret Anderson, Vladimir Guerrero .40
262 Luis Gonzalez, Randy Johnson .40
263 Andruw Jones, Chipper Jones .40
264 Miguel Tejada, Rafael Palmeiro .40
265 Curt Schilling, Manny Ramirez .50
266 Mark Prior, Sammy Sosa .75
267 Frank Thomas, Magglio Ordonez .25
268 Barry Larkin, Ken Griffey Jr. .75
269 C.C. Sabathia, Victor Martinez .15
270 Jeromy Burnitz, Todd Helton .25
271 Dmitri Young, Ivan Rodriguez .40
272 Josh Beckett, Miguel Cabrera .40
273 Jeff Bagwell, Roger Clemens .75
274 Ken Harvey, Mike Sweeney .15
275 Adrian Beltre, Eric Gagne .25
276 Ben Sheets, Geoff Jenkins .15
277 Joe Mauer, Torii Hunter .15
278 Jose Vidro, Livan Hernandez .15
279 Kazuo Matsui, Mike Piazza .50
280 Alex Rodriguez, Derek Jeter 1.00
281 Eric Chavez, Tim Hudson .15
282 Bobby Abreu, Jim Thome .40
283 Craig Wilson, Jason Kendall .15
284 Brian Giles, Phil Nevin .15
285 A.J. Pierzynski, Jason Schmidt .15
286 Bret Boone, Ichiro Suzuki .75
287 Albert Pujols, Scott Rolen .75
288 Aubrey Huff, Tino Martinez .15
289 Hank Blalock, Mark Teixeira .15
290 Carlos Delgado, Roy Halladay .15
291 Vladimir Guerrero .40
292 Curt Schilling .25
293 Mark Prior .40
294 Josh Beckett .15
295 Roger Clemens .50
296 Derek Jeter .75
297 Eric Chavez .15
298 Jim Thome .25
299 Albert Pujols .75
300 Hank Blalock .25
301 Bartolo Colon .15
302 Darin Erstad .15
303 Garret Anderson .15
304 Orlando Cabrera .15
305 Steve Finley .15
306 Javier Vazquez .15

307 Russ Ortiz .15
308 Chipper Jones .75
309 Marcus Giles .15
310 Raul Mondesi .15
311 B.J. Ryan .15
312 Luis Matos .15
313 Sidney Ponson .15
314 Bill Mueller .15
315 David Ortiz .75
316 Johnny Damon .75
317 Keith Foulke .15
318 Mark Bellhorn .15
319 Wade Miller .15
320 Aramis Ramirez .40
321 Carlos Zambrano .40
322 Greg Maddux 1.25
323 Kerry Wood .50
324 Nomar Garciaparra 1.00
325 Todd Walker .15
326 Frank Thomas .50
327 Freddy Garcia .15
328 Joe Crede .15
329 Jose Contreras .15
330 Orlando Hernandez .15
331 Shingo Takatsu .15
332 Austin Kearns .15
333 Eric Milton .15
334 Ken Griffey Jr. 1.00
335 Aaron Boone .15
336 David Riske .15
337 Jake Westbrook .15
338 Kevin Millwood .15
339 Travis Hafner .25
340 Aaron Miles .15
341 Jeff Baker .15
342 Todd Helton .50
343 Garrett Atkins .15
344 Carlos Pena .15
345 Ivan Rodriguez .50
346 Rondell White .15
347 Troy Percival .15
348 A.J. Burnett .25
349 Carlos Delgado .40
350 Guillermo Mota .15
351 Paul LoDuca .15
352 Jason Lane .15
353 Lance Berkman .25
354 Angel Berroa .15
355 David DeJesus .15
356 Ruben Gotay .15
357 Jose Lima .15
358 Brad Penny .15
359 J.D. Drew .25
360 Jayson Werth .15
361 Jeff Kent .25
362 Odalis Perez .15
363 Brady Clark .15
364 Junior Spivey .15
365 Rickie Weeks .25
366 Jacque Jones .15
367 Joe Nathan .15
368 Nick Punto .15
369 Shannon Stewart .15
370 Doug Mientkiewicz .15
371 Kris Benson .15
372 Tom Glavine .25
373 Victor Zambrano .15
374 Bernie Williams .40
375 Carl Pavano .15
376 Jaret Wright .15
377 Kevin Brown .15
378 Mariano Rivera .40
379 Dan Haren .15
380 Eric Byrnes .15
381 Erubiel Durazo .15
382 Rich Harden .25
383 Brett Myers .15
384 Chase Utley .50
385 Marlon Byrd .15
386 Pat Burrell .25
387 Placido Polanco .15
388 Freddy Sanchez .15
389 Jason Bay .25
390 Josh Fogg .15
391 Adam Eaton .15
392 Jake Peavy .40
393 Khalil Greene .40
394 Mark Loretta .15
395 Phil Nevin .15
396 Ramon Hernandez .15
397 Woody Williams .15
398 Armando Benitez .15
399 Edgardo Alfonzo .15
400 Marquis Grissom .15
401 Mike Matheny .15
402 Richie Sexson .40
403 Bret Boone .15
404 Gil Meche .15
405 Chris Carpenter .40
406 Jeff Suppan .15
407 Larry Walker .40
408 Mark Grudzielanek .15
409 Mark Mulder .25
410 Scott Rolen .75
411 Josh Phelps .15
412 Jonny Gomes .15
413 Francisco Cordero .15
414 Kenny Rogers .15
415 Richard Hidalgo .15
416 David Bush .15
417 Frank Catalanotto .15
418 Gabe Gross .15
419 Guillermo Quiroz .15
420 Reed Johnson .15
421 Cristian Guzman .15
422 Esteban Loaiza .15
423 Jose Guillen .25
424 Nick Johnson .15

425 Vinny Castilla .15
426 Peter Orr RC .50
427 Tadahito Iguchi RC 1.00
428 Jeff Baker .15
429 Marcos Carvajal RC .50
430 Justin Verlander RC 3.00
431 Luke Scott RC 1.00
432 Willy Taveras .50
433 Ambiorix Burgos RC .50
434 Andy Sisco .15
435 Denny Bautista .15
436 Mark Teahen .15
437 Ervin Santana .40
438 Dennis Houlton RC .50
439 Philip Humber RC 1.00
440 Steve Schmoll RC .50
441 J.J. Hardy .15
442 Ambiorix Concepcion RC .50
443 Dae-Sung Koo RC .50
444 Andy Phillips .15
445 Dan Meyer .15
446 Huston Street .50
447 Keiichi Yabu RC .50
448 Jeff Niemann RC .50
449 Jeremy Reed .15
450 Tony Blanco .15
451 Albert Pujols .75
452 Alex Rodriguez .75
453 Curt Schilling .40
454 Derek Jeter .75
455 Greg Maddux .50
456 Ichiro Suzuki .50
457 Ivan Rodriguez .25
458 Jeff Bagwell .25
459 Jim Thome .25
460 Ken Griffey Jr. .50
461 Manny Ramirez .40
462 Mike Mussina .25
463 Mike Piazza .40
464 Pedro Martinez .40
465 Rafael Palmeiro .25
466 Randy Johnson .40
467 Roger Clemens .75
468 Sammy Sosa .50
469 Todd Helton .25
470 Vladimir Guerrero .40
471 Vladimir Guerrero .40
472 Shawn Green .15
473 John Smoltz .25
474 Miguel Tejada .25
475 Curt Schilling .25
476 Mark Prior .40
477 Frank Thomas .25
478 Ken Griffey Jr. .50
479 C.C. Sabathia .15
480 Todd Helton .25
481 Ivan Rodriguez .25
482 Miguel Cabrera .40
483 Roger Clemens .50
484 Mike Sweeney .15
485 Eric Gagne .15
486 Ben Sheets .15
487 Johan Santana .15
488 Mike Piazza .40
489 Derek Jeter .50
490 Eric Chavez .15
491 Jim Thome .25
492 Craig Wilson .15
493 Jake Peavy .15
494 Jason Schmidt .15
495 Ichiro Suzuki .50
496 Albert Pujols .50
497 Carl Crawford .15
498 Mark Teixeira .25
499 Vernon Wells .15
500 Jose Vidro .15

Emerald

Stars (301-500): 10-20X
Production 25 Sets
Exclusive to Series 2.

Blue

Stars (301-500): 4-6X
Production 150 Sets
Exclusive to Series 2.

Gold

Stars (301-500): 4-8X
Production 99 Sets
Exclusive to Series 2.

Platinum

No Pricing
Production Five Sets
Exclusive to Series 2.

American Flag

No Pricing
Production 15 Sets

Retro

Retro: 2-3X
One retro box per hobby case.

Lasting Impressions

No Pricing
Production One Set
One press plate per color.

Plates

No Pricing
Production one set per color.

Diamond Images - Wingfield Collection

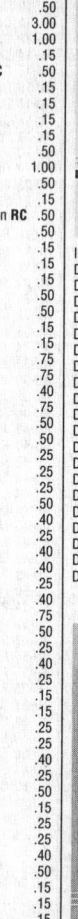

NM/M
Complete Set (20): 45.00
Common Player: 2.00

Inserted 1:9
DI-1 Eddie Mathews 3.00
DI-2 Ernie Banks 3.00
DI-3 Joe DiMaggio 6.00
DI-4 Mickey Mantle 8.00
DI-5 Pee Wee Reese 2.00
DI-6 Phil Rizzuto 2.00
DI-7 Stan Musial 3.00
DI-8 Ted Williams 6.00
DI-9 Bob Feller 2.00
DI-10 Whitey Ford 2.00
DI-11 Willie Stargell 2.00
DI-12 Yogi Berra 2.00
DI-13 Roy Campanella 2.00
DI-14 Franklin D. Roosevelt 2.00
DI-15 Harry S. Truman 2.00
DI-16 Dwight D. Eisenhower 2.00
DI-17 John F. Kennedy 2.00
DI-18 Lyndon B. Johnson 2.00
DI-19 Richard Nixon 2.00
DI-20 Thurman Munson 3.00

Hall of Fame Plaques

NM/M
Complete Set (10): 40.00
Common Player: 3.00
Inserted 1:36
SP-16 Ernie Banks 4.00
SP-17 Yogi Berra 4.00
SP-18 Whitey Ford 3.00
SP-19 Bob Gibson 3.00
SP-20 Willie McCovey 3.00
SP-21 Stan Musial 6.00
SP-22 Nolan Ryan 12.00
SP-23 Mike Schmidt 8.00
SP-24 Tom Seaver 4.00
SP-25 Robin Yount 4.00

Game Jersey

NM/M
Common Jersey: 5.00
Inserted 1:8
JB Jeff Bagwell/SP 8.00
CB Carlos Beltran/SP 8.00
AB Adrian Beltre 5.00
LB Lance Berkman 5.00
HB Hank Blalock 5.00
MC Miguel Cabrera 8.00
EC Eric Chavez 5.00
EG Eric Gagne 5.00
TG Troy Glaus 5.00
KG Ken Griffey Jr./SP 15.00
VG Vladimir Guerrero 8.00
HE Todd Helton 8.00
TH Tim Hudson 5.00
HU Torii Hunter 5.00
DJ Derek Jeter 25.00
RJ Randy Johnson/SP 10.00
CJ Chipper Jones 8.00
JK Jeff Kent 5.00
GM Greg Maddux/SP 10.00
PM Pedro Martinez 8.00
MM Mark Mulder 5.00
DO David Ortiz/SP 10.00
PI Mike Piazza 8.00
MP Mark Prior 8.00
AP Albert Pujols 20.00
MR Manny Ramirez/SP 10.00
IR Ivan Rodriguez 8.00
SR Scott Rolen 8.00
JS Johan Santana/SP 10.00
CS Curt Schilling 8.00
SM John Smoltz 8.00
AS Alfonso Soriano 8.00
SS Sammy Sosa 10.00
MT Mark Teixeira/SP 8.00
TE Miguel Tejada 8.00
FT Frank Thomas 8.00

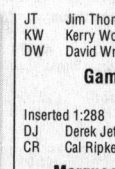

JT Jim Thome/SP 8.00
KW Kerry Wood 8.00
DW David Wright 10.00

Game Patch

NM/M
Inserted 1:288
DJ Derek Jeter 75.00
CR Cal Ripken Jr. 75.00

Marquee Attractions

NM/M
Common Player: 4.00
Inserted 1:12
GA Garret Anderson 4.00
JB Jeff Bagwell 8.00
BE Josh Beckett 4.00
KB Kevin Brown 4.00
MC Miguel Cabrera 8.00
RC Roger Clemens 15.00
CD Carlos Delgado 4.00
AD Adam Dunn 4.00
EG Eric Gagne 6.00
JG Jason Giambi 4.00
BG Brian Giles 4.00
SG Shawn Green 4.00
KG Ken Griffey Jr. 12.00
VG Vladimir Guerrero 8.00
TH Todd Helton 8.00
HO Trevor Hoffman 4.00
DJ Derek Jeter 20.00
RJ Randy Johnson 10.00
AJ Andruw Jones 6.00
CJ Chipper Jones 8.00
GM Greg Maddux 10.00
PM Pedro Martinez 10.00
HM Hideki Matsui 30.00
KM Kazuo Matsui 8.00
JM Joe Mauer 8.00
HN Hideo Nomo 10.00
RO Roy Oswalt 4.00
PE Andy Pettitte 6.00
PI Mike Piazza 10.00
MP Mark Prior 6.00
AP Albert Pujols 15.00
IR Ivan Rodriguez 8.00
CS Curt Schilling 8.00
JS Jason Schmidt 6.00
SS Sammy Sosa 12.00
IS Ichiro Suzuki 25.00
MT Miguel Tejada 6.00
JT Jim Thome 8.00
BW Billy Wagner 4.00
DW Dontrelle Willis 4.00
PW Preston Wilson 4.00
KW Kerry Wood 8.00

Matinee Idols

NM/M
Common Player: 4.00
Inserted 1:12 Hobby
JB Jeff Bagwell 8.00
RB Rocco Baldelli 4.00
BE Josh Beckett 6.00
HB Hank Blalock 8.00
BB Bret Boone/SP 8.00
PB Pat Burrell 8.00
SB Sean Burroughs 4.00
EC Eric Chavez 4.00
RC Roger Clemens 15.00
CD Carlos Delgado 6.00
JE Jim Edmonds 6.00
JG Jason Giambi 4.00
TG Troy Glaus 4.00
KG Ken Griffey Jr. 12.00
VG Vladimir Guerrero 8.00
RH Roy Halladay 4.00
TH Todd Helton 4.00
HU Torii Hunter 4.00
DJ Derek Jeter 20.00
RJ Randy Johnson 8.00
CJ Chipper Jones 8.00
ML Mike Lowell 4.00
MM Mike Mussina 6.00
PI Mike Piazza 10.00
MP Mark Prior 6.00
CR Cal Ripken Jr. 25.00
SR Scott Rolen 8.00

		NM/M
NR	Nolan Ryan	25.00
CS	Curt Schilling	8.00
TS	Tom Seaver	8.00
GS	Gary Sheffield	6.00
SS	Sammy Sosa	12.00
MT	Mark Teixeira	6.00
JT	Jim Thome	8.00
BW	Billy Wagner	4.00
RW	Rickie Weeks	4.00
VW	Vernon Wells	4.00
DW	Dontrelle Willis	4.00
KW	Kerry Wood	8.00
BZ	Barry Zito	4.00

Milestone Materials

		NM/M
	Common Jersey:	5.00
BA	Jeff Bagwell	8.00
JB	Jason Bay	5.00
CB	Carlos Beltran	8.00
BC	Bobby Crosby	5.00
EG	Eric Gagne	5.00
KG	Ken Griffey Jr.	15.00
VG	Vladimir Guerrero	8.00
RJ	Randy Johnson	8.00
GM	Greg Maddux	10.00
DO	David Ortiz	8.00
RP	Rafael Palmeiro	8.00
JP	Jake Peavy	8.00
AP	Albert Pujols	20.00
MR	Manny Ramirez	8.00
JS	Johan Santana	8.00
CS	Curt Schilling	8.00
MT	Mark Teixeira	5.00
TE	Miguel Tejada	8.00
JT	Jim Thome	8.00

Origins

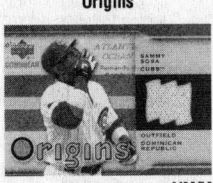

		NM/M
	Common Player:	4.00
	Inserted 1:12 Hobby	
	Inserted 1:24 Retail	
GA	Garret Anderson	4.00
CB	Carlos Beltran	10.00
AB	Adrian Beltre	6.00
LB	Lance Berkman	4.00
MC	Miguel Cabrera	8.00
RF	Rafael Furcal	4.00
EG	Eric Gagne	6.00
BG	Brian Giles	4.00
JG	Juan Gonzalez	8.00
LG	Luis Gonzalez	4.00
VG	Vladimir Guerrero	8.00
TH	Tim Hudson	4.00
AJ	Andruw Jones	6.00
JK	Jeff Kent	4.00
JL	Javy Lopez	4.00
GM	Greg Maddux	10.00
PM	Pedro Martinez	10.00
HM	Hideki Matsui	30.00
KM	Kazuo Matsui	8.00
MM	Mark Mulder	4.00
HN	Hideo Nomo	10.00
MO	Magglio Ordonez	4.00
RP	Rafael Palmeiro	8.00
PE	Jake Peavy	4.00
JP	Jorge Posada	4.00
AP	Albert Pujols	15.00
MR	Manny Ramirez	8.00
JR	Jose Reyes	4.00
IR	Ivan Rodriguez	8.00
JS	Jason Schmidt	4.00
RS	Richie Sexson	4.00
AS	Alfonso Soriano	8.00
SS	Sammy Sosa	12.00
IS	Ichiro Suzuki	25.00
MT	Miguel Tejada	6.00
BU	B.J. Upton	8.00
JV	Javier Vazquez	4.00
PW	Preston Wilson	4.00

Rewind to 1997 Jersey

		NM/M
	Common Jersey:	8.00
	Inserted 1:288	
JB	Jeff Bagwell	25.00
WC	Will Clark	20.00

KG	Ken Griffey Jr.	40.00
VG	Vladimir Guerrero	25.00
TG	Tony Gwynn	30.00
DJ	Derek Jeter	40.00
RJ	Randy Johnson	25.00
AJ	Andruw Jones	20.00
CJ	Chipper Jones	30.00
GM	Greg Maddux	40.00
PM	Pedro Martinez	25.00
MP	Mike Piazza	30.00
MR	Manny Ramirez	30.00
CR	Cal Ripken Jr.	40.00
IR	Ivan Rodriguez	20.00
SR	Scott Rolen	25.00
CS	Curt Schilling	20.00
JS	John Smoltz	25.00
FT	Frank Thomas	25.00
JT	Jim Thome	25.00

Signature Sensations

No Pricing
Production 15 Sets
Die-Cut: No Pricing
Production 10 Sets

Signature Stars

		NM/M
	Common Player:	
	Inserted 1:288 Hobby	
CB	Carlos Beltran/SP	40.00
HB	Hank Blalock	25.00
MC	Miguel Cabrera	35.00
BC	Bobby Crosby	30.00
LF	Lew Ford	10.00
KG	Ken Griffey Jr.	80.00
JL	Javy Lopez	15.00
JM	Joe Mauer	20.00
OP	Odalis Perez	15.00
CR	Cal Ripken Jr./SP	180.00
BS	Ben Sheets	15.00
DW	Dontrelle Willis	20.00
KW	Kerry Wood	25.00
DY	Delmon Young	20.00

Signature Stars Retail

Inserted 1:480 Retail

Super Patch - Names

No Pricing
Cards are not serial numbered.

Super Patch - Numbers

No Pricing
Cards are not serial numbered.

Super Patch - Logos

No Pricing
Cards are not serial numbered.

World Series Heroes

		NM/M
	Complete Set (45):	20.00
	Common Player:	.25
	Inserted 1:1 Retail	
WS-1	Garret Anderson	.50
WS-2	Troy Glaus	.50
WS-3	Vladimir Guerrero	1.00
WS-4	Andruw Jones	.50
WS-5	Chipper Jones	1.00
WS-6	Curt Schilling	1.00
WS-7	Keith Foulke	.25
WS-8	Manny Ramirez	1.00
WS-9	Nomar Garciaparra	1.50
WS-10	Pedro Martinez	1.00
WS-11	Kerry Wood	1.00
WS-12	Mark Prior	1.00
WS-13	Sammy Sosa	2.00
WS-14	Frank Thomas	.75
WS-15	Magglio Ordonez	.25
WS-16	Dontrelle Willis	.50
WS-17	Josh Beckett	.50
WS-18	Hideki Matsui	.75
WS-19	Jeff Bagwell	.75
WS-20	Lance Berkman	.50
WS-21	Roger Clemens	2.00
WS-22	Eric Gagne	.50
WS-23	Torii Hunter	.50
WS-24	Mike Piazza	1.50
WS-25	Alex Rodriguez	2.00
WS-26	Derek Jeter	2.00
WS-27	Gary Sheffield	.50
WS-28	Hideki Matsui	1.50
WS-29	Jason Giambi	.50
WS-30	Jorge Posada	.50
WS-31	Kevin Brown	.25
WS-32	Mariano Rivera	.50
WS-33	Mike Mussina	.50
WS-34	Eric Chavez	.25
WS-35	Mark Mulder	.25
WS-36	Tim Hudson	.25
WS-37	Billy Wagner	.25
WS-38	Jim Thome	.75
WS-39	Brian Giles	.25
WS-40	Jason Schmidt	.25
WS-41	Albert Pujols	2.00
WS-42	Scott Rolen	.75
WS-43	Alfonso Soriano	.75
WS-44	Hank Blalock	.75
WS-45	Mark Teixeira	.50

2004 Update Set

		NM/M
	Complete Set (50):	10.00
	Common Player:	.15
	Inserted 1:Hobby Box	
541	Alex Rodriguez	1.50
542	Roger Clemens	1.50
543	Andy Pettitte	.25
544	Vladimir Guerrero	.75
545	David Wells	.15
546	Derek Lee	.15
547	Carlos Beltran	.50
548	Orlando Cabrera	.15
549	Paul LoDuca	.15
550	Dave Roberts	.15
551	Guillermo Mota	.15
552	Steve Finley	.15
553	Juan Encarnacion	.15
554	Larry Walker	.50
555	Ty Wigginton	.15
556	Doug Mientkiewicz	.15
557	Roberto Alomar	.40
558	B.J. Upton	.50
559	Brad Penny	.15
560	Hee Seop Choi	.15
561	David Wright	1.00
562	Nomar Garciaparra	1.00
563	Felix Rodriguez	.15
564	Victor Zambrano	.15
565	Kris Benson	.15
566	Aarom Baldiris	.15
567	Joey Gathright	.15
568	Charles Thomas	.15
569	Brian Dallimore	.15
570	Chris Oxspring	.15
571	Chris Shelton	.15
572	Dioner Navarro	.15
573	Edwardo Sierra	.15
574	Fernando Nieve	.15
575	Frank Francisco	.15
576	Jeff Bennett	.15
577	Justin Lehr	.15
578	John Gall	.15
579	Jorge Sequea	.15
580	Justin Germano	.15
581	Kazuhito Tadano	.15
582	Kevin Cave	.15
583	Jesse Crain	.15
584	Luis Gonzalez	.15
585	Mike Wuertz	.15
586	Orlando Rodriguez	.15
587	Phil Stockman	.15
588	Ramon Ramirez	.15
589	Roberto Novoa	.15
590	Scott Kazmir	.50

2004 Update - Authentic Stars

		NM/M
	Common Player:	8.00
	1:12 '04 Update Sets	
	Production 75 Sets	
CB	Carlos Beltran	15.00
LB	Lance Berkman	8.00
JE	Jim Edmonds	8.00
RF	Rafael Furcal	8.00
HA	Roy Halladay	8.00
RH	Rich Harden	8.00
HU	Tim Hudson	8.00
DJ	Derek Jeter	35.00
AK	Austin Kearns	8.00
HN	Hideo Nomo	20.00
MO	Magglio Ordonez	8.00
OS	Roy Oswalt	8.00
RP	Rafael Palmeiro	12.00
MR	Manny Ramirez	15.00
JR	Jose Reyes	8.00
SR	Scott Rolen	15.00
TE	Miguel Tejada	8.00
JT	Jim Thome	12.00
WE	Brandon Webb	8.00
VW	Vernon Wells	8.00
PW	Preston Wilson	8.00
KW	Kerry Wood	8.00

2004 Update - Awesome Honors

		NM/M
	Common Player:	8.00
	1:12 '04 Update Set	
	Production 75 Sets	
BE	Adrian Beltre	10.00
AB	Angel Berroa	8.00
KB	Kevin Brown	8.00
MC	Miguel Cabrera	15.00
RC	Roger Clemens	20.00
EG	Eric Gagne	12.00
BG	Brian Giles	8.00
DL	Derek Lee	8.00
KM	Kazuo Matsui	20.00
JM	Joe Mauer	10.00
PE	Andy Pettitte	10.00
SP	Scott Podsednik	8.00
AP	Albert Pujols	25.00
IR	Ivan Rodriguez	12.00
SC	Curt Schilling	12.00
RS	Richie Sexson	8.00
GS	Gary Sheffield	8.00
AS	Alfonso Soriano	15.00
VA	Javier Vazquez	8.00

4,000 Strikeout Autographs

Production 50 Sets
Quad Signature: No Pricing
Production 10

4,000-Strikeout Commemorative

	NM/M
Production 4,000	
Steve Carlton, Nolan Ryan, Roger Clemens, Randy Johnson	12.00

2005 UD All-Star Classics

		NM/M
	Complete Set (100):	25.00
	Common Player:	.15
	Pack (8):	3.00
	Box (24):	60.00
1	Albert Pujols	2.00
2	Alex Rodriguez	1.50
3	Alfonso Soriano	.75
4	Barry Zito	.25
5	Bobby Abreu	.40
6	Carlos Beltran	.50
7	Carlos Delgado	.40
8	Chipper Jones	.75
9	Curt Schilling	.75
10	David Ortiz	.75
11	Derek Jeter	2.00
12	Edgar Renteria	.25
13	Eric Gagne	.25
14	Frank Thomas	.50
15	Gary Sheffield	.40
16	Greg Maddux	1.00
17	Hank Blalock	.40
18	Hideki Matsui	1.50
19	Ichiro Suzuki	1.50
20	Ivan Rodriguez	.50
21	Jason Schmidt	.25
22	Jason Varitek	.25
23	Jeff Kent	.25
24	Jim Thome	.75
25	Jorge Posada	.25
26	Ken Griffey Jr.	1.00
27	Kerry Wood	.75
28	Lance Berkman	.25
29	Manny Ramirez	.75
30	Mariano Rivera	.40
31	Mark Mulder	.25
32	Mark Prior	.75
33	Miguel Cabrera	.75
34	Miguel Tejada	.50
35	Mike Piazza	.75
36	Nomar Garciaparra	1.00
37	Pedro Martinez	.75
38	Randy Johnson	.75
39	Richie Sexson	.25
40	Roger Clemens	2.00
41	Roy Halladay	.25
42	Sammy Sosa	1.50
43	Scott Rolen	.75
44	Sean Casey	.25
45	Tim Hudson	.25
46	Todd Helton	.50
47	Tom Glavine	.40
48	Torii Hunter	.25
49	Troy Glaus	.25
50	Vladimir Guerrero	.75
51	Adrian Beltre	.25
52	Alexis Rios	.15
53	Aubrey Huff	.15
54	Brandon Webb	.25
55	Dallas McPherson	.25
56	David Wright	.75
57	Edwin Jackson	.25
58	Grady Sizemore	.40
59	Tadahito Iguchi RC	1.00
60	Jake Peavy	.40
61	Jake Westbrook	.15
62	Jason Bay	.25
63	Jeff Francis	.15
64	Jeremy Reed	.15
65	Joe Mauer	.40
66	Johan Santana	.50
67	Jose Capellan	.15
68	Jose Reyes	.25
69	Justin Morneau	.40
70	Mark Teixeira	.25
71	Oliver Perez	.25
72	Rich Harden	.25
73	Rickie Weeks	.75
74	Ryan Howard	.75
75	Scott Kazmir	.15
76	Al Kaline	.75
77	Bill Mazeroski	.50
78	Bob Feller	.50
79	Bob Gibson	.75
80	Brooks Robinson	.75
81	Cal Ripken Jr.	3.00
82	Carlton Fisk	.25
83	Eddie Murray	.50
84	Gaylord Perry	.50
85	Harmon Killebrew	.75
86	Jim Palmer	.25
87	Joe DiMaggio	1.50
88	Joe Morgan	.25
89	Johnny Bench	.75
90	Juan Marichal	.25
91	Lou Brock	.50
92	Mike Schmidt	1.00
93	Nolan Ryan	2.00
94	Ozzie Smith	.75
95	Phil Niekro	.25
96	Robin Yount	.50
97	Rollie Fingers	.25
98	Tom Seaver	.50
99	Willie McCovey	.50
100	Yogi Berra	.75

Gold

Stars (1-100): 4-8X
Production 499 Sets

Box Scores

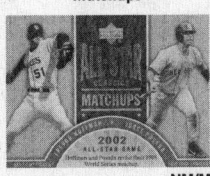

		NM/M
	Complete Set (20):	50.00
	Common Player:	1.50
	Inserted 1:24	
1	Juan Marichal	2.00
2	Brooks Robinson	3.00
3	Tony Perez	1.50
4	Willie McCovey	3.00
5	Harmon Killebrew	3.00
6	Johnny Bench	3.00
7	Joe Morgan	1.50
8	Lou Brock	3.00
9	Jim Palmer	1.50
10	Mike Schmidt	5.00
11	Ozzie Smith	3.00
12	Roger Clemens	6.00
13	Cal Ripken Jr.	4.00
14	Ken Griffey Jr.	4.00
15	Alex Rodriguez	5.00
16	Derek Jeter	4.00
17	Johnny Damon	3.00
18	Garret Anderson	1.50
19	Alfonso Soriano	2.00

Matchups

		NM/M
	Complete Set (20):	40.00
	Common Player:	1.50
	Inserted 1:24	
1	Hank Blalock	2.00
2	Curt Schilling	3.00
3	Manny Ramirez	3.00
4	Ken Griffey Jr.	4.00
5	Brooks Robinson	3.00
6	Harmon Killebrew	3.00
7	Carl Yastrzemski	4.00
8	Cal Ripken Jr.	4.00
9	Trevor Hoffman	1.50
10	Eric Gagne	1.50
11	Alfonso Soriano	2.00
12	David Ortiz	3.00
13	Andruw Jones	3.00
14	Garret Anderson	1.50
15	Magglio Ordonez	1.50
16	Derek Jeter	3.00
17	Chipper Jones	3.00
18	Roberto Alomar	2.00
19	Mike Piazza	3.00
20	Alex Rodriguez	5.00

Midsummer Classics

		NM/M
	Complete Set (20):	40.00
	Common Player:	1.50
	Inserted 1:24	
1	Derek Jeter	6.00
2	Pedro Martinez	2.00
3	Mike Piazza	3.00
4	Randy Johnson	2.00
5	Gary Sheffield	2.00
6	Albert Pujols	6.00
7	David Ortiz	3.00
8	Manny Ramirez	3.00
9	Garret Anderson	1.50
10	Andruw Jones	1.50
11	Todd Helton	2.00
12	Paul Konerko	1.50
13	Alfonso Soriano	2.00
14	Magglio Ordonez	1.50
15	Cal Ripken Jr.	8.00
16	Ken Griffey Jr.	3.00
17	Harmon Killebrew	3.00
18	Mike Schmidt	5.00
19	Frank Thomas	5.00
20	Alex Rodriguez	2.00

Midsummer Swatches

		NM/M
	Common Player:	4.00
	Inserted 1:12	
	Patches:	No Pricing
	Production 25 Sets	
MA	Moises Alou/Jsy	6.00
JB	Jeff Bagwell/Jsy	8.00
CB	Carlos Beltran/Jsy	8.00
CI	Craig Biggio/Jsy	6.00
BB	Bret Boone/Jsy	6.00
CD	Carlos Delgado/Jsy	6.00
JE	Jim Edmonds/Jsy	6.00
KF	Keith Foulke/Jsy	6.00
RF	Rafael Furcal/Jsy	4.00
EG	Eric Gagne/Jsy	8.00
SG	Shawn Green/Jsy	4.00
KG	Ken Griffey Jr./Jsy	25.00
TH	Todd Helton/Jsy	8.00
TI	Torii Hunter/Jsy	8.00
AJ	Andruw Jones/Pants	4.00
CJ	Chipper Jones/Jsy	8.00
JK	Jeff Kent/Jsy	4.00
RK	Ryan Klesko	4.00
ML	Matt Lawton/Jsy	4.00
PL	Paul LoDuca/Jsy	4.00
JL	Javy Lopez/Jsy	4.00
PM	Pedro Martinez/Jsy	8.00
VM	Victor Martinez/Jsy	4.00
DO	David Ortiz/Pants	4.00
RP	Rafael Palmeiro/Jsy	4.00
MP	Mike Piazza/Jsy	15.00
ER	Edgar Renteria/Jsy	4.00
CR	Cal Ripken Jr./Pants	35.00
CC	C.C. Sabathia/Jsy	4.00
SC	Jason Schmidt/Jsy	4.00
BS	Ben Sheets/Jsy	4.00
GS	Gary Sheffield/Jsy	4.00
JS	John Smoltz/Jsy	10.00
SS	Sammy Sosa/Jsy	10.00
IS	Ichiro Suzuki/Jsy	30.00
MS	Mike Sweeney/Jsy	4.00
MT	Miguel Tejada/Jsy	8.00
FT	Frank Thomas/Jsy	8.00

JT	Jim Thome/Jsy	8.00
OM	Omar Vizquel/Jsy	6.00
WE	David Wells/Jsy	4.00
DW	Dontrelle Willis/Jsy	8.00

MVP's

		NM/M
Complete Set (20):		45.00
Common Player:		1.00
Inserted 1:24		
1	Alfonso Soriano	2.00
2	Ken Griffey Sr.	4.00
3	Brooks Robinson	3.00
4	Cal Ripken Jr.	8.00
5	Cal Ripken Jr.	8.00
6	Derek Jeter	6.00
7	Carl Yastrzemski	4.00
8	Garret Anderson	1.50
9	Jeff Conine	1.00
10	Joe Morgan	1.50
11	Juan Marichal	2.00
12	Julio Franco	1.00
13	Ken Griffey Jr.	4.00
14	Mike Piazza	3.00
15	Pedro Martinez	3.00
16	Roberto Alomar	2.00
17	Roger Clemens	6.00
18	Sandy Alomar Jr.	1.00
19	Tony Perez	1.50
20	Willie McCovey	2.00

Perennial All-Stars

		NM/M
Complete Set (20):		40.00
Common Player:		2.00
Inserted 1:24		
1	Albert Pujols	6.00
2	Alex Rodriguez	5.00
3	Alfonso Soriano	3.00
4	Curt Schilling	3.00
5	Derek Jeter	6.00
6	Eric Gagne	2.00
7	Greg Maddux	4.00
8	Ichiro Suzuki	4.00
9	Ivan Rodriguez	2.00
10	Jim Thome	4.00
11	Ken Griffey Jr.	4.00
12	Mariano Rivera	2.00
13	Miguel Tejada	3.00
14	Mike Piazza	3.00
15	Randy Johnson	4.00
16	Roger Clemens	6.00
17	Sammy Sosa	3.00
18	Scott Rolen	3.00
19	Todd Helton	2.00
20	Vladimir Guerrero	2.00

2005 Upper Deck Artifacts Promos

Each of the first 100 cards in Upper Deck Artifacts was issued in a foil-overprinted version with "UD PROMO" across the front. Cards were inserted into specially marked card shop and newsstand issues of Tuff Stuff magazine.

	NM/M
Common Player:	.50
Stars:	1.5X

2005 Upper Deck Artifacts

	NM/M
Complete Set (200):	
Common Player (1-100):	.25
Common (101-150):	2.00
Production 1,350	

Common (151-200):		2.00
Production 1,999		
Pack (4):		10.00
Box (10):		90.00
1	Adam Dunn	.75
2	Adrian Beltre	.75
3	Albert Pujols	3.00
4	Alex Rodriguez	2.50
5	Alfonso Soriano	1.00
6	Andruw Jones	.50
7	Andy Pettitte	.50
8	Aramis Ramirez	.50
9	Aubrey Huff	.25
10	Barry Larkin	.50
11	Ben Sheets	.50
12	Bernie Williams	.50
13	Bobby Abreu	.50
14	Brad Penny	.25
15	Bret Boone	.25
16	Brian Giles	.25
17	Carl Crawford	.50
18	Carl Pavano	.25
19	Carlos Beltran	.75
20	Carlos Delgado	.75
21	Carlos Guillen	.25
22	Carlos Lee	.50
23	Carlos Zambrano	.50
24	Chipper Jones	1.00
25	Craig Biggio	.50
26	Craig Wilson	.25
27	Curt Schilling	1.00
28	David Ortiz	1.00
29	Derek Jeter	3.00
30	Eric Chavez	.50
31	Eric Gagne	.50
32	Frank Thomas	.75
33	Garret Anderson	.50
34	Gary Sheffield	.50
35	Greg Maddux	1.50
36	Hank Blalock	.75
37	Hideki Matsui	2.00
38	Ichiro Suzuki	2.50
39	Ivan Rodriguez	.75
40	J.D. Drew	.50
41	Jake Peavy	.50
42	Jason Kendall	.25
43	Jason Schmidt	.50
44	Jeff Bagwell	.75
45	Jeff Kent	.50
46	Jim Edmonds	.50
47	Jim Thome	1.00
48	Joe Mauer	.75
49	Johan Santana	.75
50	John Smoltz	.50
51	Jose Reyes	.50
52	Jose Vidro	.25
53	Josh Beckett	.50
54	Ken Griffey Jr.	1.50
55	Kerry Wood	1.00
56	Kevin Brown	.25
57	Lance Berkman	.50
58	Larry Walker	.50
59	Livan Hernandez	.25
60	Luis Gonzalez	.25
61	Lyle Overbay	.25
62	Magglio Ordonez	.25
63	Manny Ramirez	1.00
64	Mark Mulder	.50
65	Mark Prior	1.00
66	Mark Teixeira	.50
67	Melvin Mora	.25
68	Michael Young	.25
69	Miguel Cabrera	1.00
70	Miguel Tejada	.75
71	Mike Lowell	.25
72	Mike Mussina	.50
73	Mike Piazza	1.50
74	Mike Sweeney	.25
75	Nomar Garciaparra	2.00
76	Oliver Perez	.25
77	Paul Konerko	.50
78	Pedro Martinez	1.00
79	Preston Wilson	.25
80	Rafael Furcal	.25
81	Rafael Palmeiro	.75
82	Randy Johnson	1.00
83	Richie Sexson	.50
84	Roger Clemens	3.00
85	Roy Halladay	.50
86	Roy Oswalt	.50
87	Sammy Sosa	2.00
88	Scott Podsednik	.25
89	Scott Rolen	1.00
90	Shawn Green	.25
91	Steve Finley	.25
92	Tim Hudson	.50
93	Todd Helton	.75
94	Tom Glavine	.50
95	Torii Hunter	.25
96	Travis Hafner	.25
97	Troy Glaus	.50
98	Vernon Wells	.25
99	Victor Martinez	.50
100	Vladimir Guerrero	1.00
101	Aaron Rowand	2.00
102	Adam LaRoche	2.00
103	Adrian Gonzalez	2.00
104	Alexis Rios	2.00
105	Angel Guzman	2.00
106	B.J. Upton	3.00
107	Bobby Crosby	3.00
108	Bobby Madritsch	2.00
109	Brandon Claussen	2.00
110	Bucky Jacobsen	2.00
111	Casey Kotchman	2.00
112	Chad Cordero	2.00
113	Chase Utley	4.00
114	Chris Burke	4.00
115	Dallas McPherson	4.00
116	Daniel Cabrera	2.00
117	David DeJesus	2.00
118	David Wright	6.00
119	Eddy Rodriguez	2.00
120	Edwin Jackson	2.00
121	Gabe Gross	2.00
122	Garrett Atkins	2.00
123	Gavin Floyd	2.00
124	Gerald Laird	2.00
125	Guillermo Quiroz	2.00
126	J.D. Closser	2.00
127	Jason Bay	4.00
128	Jason Dubois	2.00
129	Jason Lane	2.00
130	Jayson Werth	2.00
131	Jeff Francis	2.00
132	Jesse Crain	2.00
133	Joe Blanton	2.00
134	Joe Mauer	4.00
135	Jose Capellan	2.00
136	Kevin Youkilis	2.00
137	Khalil Greene	3.00
138	Laynce Nix	2.00
139	Nick Swisher	2.00
140	Oliver Perez	2.00
141	Rickie Weeks	2.00
142	Robb Quinlan	2.00
143	Roman Colon	2.00
144	Ryan Howard	4.00
145	Ryan Wagner	2.00
146	Scott Kazmir	4.00
147	Scott Proctor	2.00
148	Wily Mo Pena	2.00
149	Yhency Brazoban	2.00
150	Zack Greinke	2.00
151	Al Kaline	5.00
152	Babe Ruth	8.00
153	Billy Williams	4.00
154	Bob Feller	3.00
155	Bob Gibson	4.00
156	Bob Lemon	2.00
157	Bobby Doerr	2.00
158	Brooks Robinson	4.00
159	Cal Ripken Jr.	10.00
160	Christy Mathewson	4.00
161	Cy Young	5.00
162	Dizzy Dean	5.00
163	Don Drysdale	4.00
164	Eddie Mathews	4.00
165	Enos Slaughter	2.00
166	Ernie Banks	5.00
167	Fergie Jenkins	2.00
168	George Sisler	2.00
169	Harmon Killebrew	5.00
170	Honus Wagner	5.00
171	Jackie Robinson	5.00
172	Jimmie Foxx	4.00
173	Joe DiMaggio	6.00
174	Joe Morgan	2.00
175	Juan Marichal	2.00
176	Lou Brock	2.00
177	Lou Gehrig	6.00
178	Luis Aparicio	2.00
179	Mel Ott	4.00
180	Mickey Cochrane	4.00
181	Mickey Mantle	10.00
182	Mike Schmidt	6.00
183	Nolan Ryan	8.00
184	Pee Wee Reese	4.00
185	Phil Rizzuto	2.00
186	Ralph Kiner	2.00
187	Rogers Hornsby	3.00
188	Roy Campanella	3.00
189	Satchel Paige	4.00
190	Stan Musial	5.00
191	Rick Ferrell	2.00
192	Thurman Munson	4.00
193	Tom Seaver	4.00
194	Ty Cobb	6.00
195	Walter Johnson	5.00
196	Warren Spahn	4.00
197	Whitey Ford	4.00
198	Willie McCovey	3.00
199	Willie Stargell	3.00
200	Yogi Berra	3.00

Rainbow Blue

Blue (1-100):	3-5X
Blue (101-200):	1-2X
Production 100 Sets	

Rainbow Gold

Gold (1-100):	6-10X
Gold (101-200):	2-3X
Production 25 Sets	

Rainbow Platinum

No Pricing
Production One Set

Rainbow Red

Red (1-100):	4-8X
Red (101-200):	1.5-3X
Production 50 Sets	

AL/NL Artifacts

		NM/M
Common Player:		4.00
Production 325 unless noted.		
Rainbow:		.75-1.5X
Production 99 Sets		
BA	Bobby Abreu/Jsy	6.00
JB	Jason Bay/Jsy	6.00
CB	Carlos Beltran/Jsy	8.00
AB	Adrian Beltre/Jsy	6.00
BE	Johnny Bench/Jsy	10.00
YB	Yogi Berra/Pants	15.00
HB	Hank Blalock/Jsy	8.00
BB	Bert Blyleven/Jsy	4.00
WB	Wade Boggs/Jsy	8.00
GB	George Brett/Jsy	15.00
MC	Miguel Cabrera/Jsy	10.00
RCA	Rod Carew/Jsy	8.00
CA	Steve Carlton/Jsy	6.00
SC	Sean Casey/Jsy	4.00
OC	Orlando Cepeda/Jsy/185	8.00
EC	Eric Chavez/Jsy	4.00
WC	Will Clark/Jsy/100	10.00
CN	Roger Clemens/Jsy	15.00
BC	Bobby Crosby/Jsy	6.00
AD	Andre Dawson/Jsy	8.00
BD	Bobby Doerr/Bat	6.00
BF	Bob Feller/Pants	10.00
EG	Eric Gagne/Jsy	8.00
BG	Bob Gibson/Pants	10.00
GI	Brian Giles/Jsy	4.00
MG	Marcus Giles/Jsy	4.00
DG	Dwight Gooden/Pants	6.00
MK	Mark Grace/Jsy/175	4.00
KG	Ken Griffey Jr./Jsy	15.00
GR	Ken Griffey Sr./Jsy	4.00
TG	Tony Gwynn/Jsy	10.00
TH	Travis Hafner/Jsy	4.00
RH	Rich Harden/Jsy	4.00
KHN	Keith Hernandez/Bat	4.00
KHA	Kent Hrbek/Jsy	4.00
AH	Aubrey Huff/Jsy	4.00
DJ	Derek Jeter/Jsy	20.00
RJ	Randy Johnson/Jsy	10.00
JK	Jim Kaat/Jsy	6.00
AK	Al Kaline/Jsy	10.00
GK	George Kell/Bat	6.00
HK	Harmon Killebrew/Jsy	10.00
RK	Ralph Kiner/Bat	6.00
DK	Dave Kingman/Bat	4.00
CK	Casey Kotchman/Jsy	4.00
DL	Derrek Lee/Jsy	4.00
ML	Mike Lowell/Jsy	4.00
SL	Sparky Lyle/Pants	4.00
FL	Fred Lynn/Bat	4.00
GM	Greg Maddux/Jsy/275	12.00
VM	Victor Martinez/Jsy	6.00
MA	Don Mattingly/Jsy	20.00
JM	Joe Mauer/Jsy	10.00
WM	Willie McCovey/Jsy	8.00
DMA	Dallas McPherson/Jsy	8.00
PM	Paul Molitor/Jsy	8.00
MM	Mark Mulder/Jsy	6.00
DMN	Dale Murphy/Jsy/150	4.00
RO	Roy Oswalt/Jsy	4.00
AO	Akinori Otsuka/Jsy	4.00
JPA	Jim Palmer/Jsy	8.00
LN	Laynce Nix/Jsy	4.00
DO	David Ortiz/Jsy	10.00
RO	Roy Oswalt/Jsy	4.00
AO	Akinori Otsuka/Jsy	4.00
CP	Corey Patterson/Jsy	4.00
JPN	Jake Peavy/Jsy	4.00
RP	Rico Petrocelli/Pants	8.00
SP	Scott Podsednik/Jsy	4.00
BPA	Boog Powell/Jsy	6.00
MP	Mark Prior/Jsy	8.00
AP	Albert Pujols/Jsy	25.00
JRN	Jose Reyes/Jsy/250	8.00
JRA	Jim Rice/Jsy	8.00
CR	Cal Ripken Jr./Jsy	25.00
BR	Brooks Robinson/Jsy	8.00
FR	Frank Robinson/Jsy	8.00
SR	Scott Rolen/Jsy	10.00
NR	Nolan Ryan/Jsy	25.00
JSA	Johan Santana/Jsy	10.00
JSN	Jason Schmidt/Jsy	8.00
MS	Mike Schmidt/Jsy	15.00
TS	Tom Seaver/Jsy	8.00
BS	Ben Sheets/Jsy	8.00
SM	John Smoltz/Jsy	8.00
SU	Bruce Sutter/Jsy	8.00
ST	Shingo Takatsu/Jsy	8.00
MT	Mark Teixeira/Jsy	8.00
BU	B.J. Upton/Jsy	6.00
RW	Rickie Weeks/Jsy	6.00
MW	Maury Wills/Jsy	6.00

KW	Kerry Wood/Jsy	8.00
DW	David Wright/Jsy	10.00
CY	Carl Yastrzemski/Jsy	15.00
MY	Michael Young/Jsy	6.00
RY	Robin Yount/Jsy	15.00
CZ	Carlos Zambrano/Jsy	6.00

AL/NL Artifacts Signatures

		NM/M
Production 30 Sets		
Rare Artifacts:		No Pricing
Production One Set		
BA	Bobby Abreu/ Jsy/Redemp.	20.00
JB	Jason Bay/Jsy	30.00
CB	Carlos Beltran/ Jsy/Redemp.	25.00
AB	Adrian Beltre/Jsy	20.00
BE	Johnny Bench/Jsy	65.00
YB	Yogi Berra/Pants	60.00
HB	Hank Blalock/Jsy	15.00
BB	Bert Blyleven/Jsy	30.00
WB	Wade Boggs/Jsy	50.00
GB	George Brett/Jsy	120.00
MC	Miguel Cabrera/Jsy	40.00
RCA	Rod Carew/Jsy	40.00
SC	Sean Casey/Jsy	20.00
CA	Steve Carlton/Jsy	40.00
OC	Orlando Cepeda/Jsy	35.00
EC	Eric Chavez/Jsy	20.00
WC	Will Clark/Jsy	50.00
RCN	Roger Clemens/ Jsy/Redemp.	100.00
BC	Bobby Crosby/ Jsy/Redemp.	20.00
AD	Andre Dawson/Jsy	30.00
BD	Bobby Doerr/Bat	35.00
BF	Bob Feller/Pants	40.00
EG	Eric Gagne/ Jsy/Redemp.	50.00
BG	Bob Gibson/Pants	50.00
GI	Brian Giles/Jsy	20.00
MG	Marcus Giles/Jsy	20.00
DG	Dwight Gooden/Pants	30.00
MK	Mark Grace/Jsy	40.00
KL	Khalil Greene/Jsy	20.00
KG	Ken Griffey Jr./Jsy	120.00
GR	Ken Griffey Sr./Jsy	25.00
TG	Tony Gwynn/Jsy	90.00
TH	Travis Hafner/Jsy	20.00
RH	Rich Harden/Jsy	20.00
KHN	Keith Hernandez/Bat	20.00
KHA	Kent Hrbek/Jsy	30.00
AH	Aubrey Huff/Jsy	20.00
DJ	Derek Jeter/Jsy	200.00
JK	Jim Kaat/Jsy	25.00
AK	Al Kaline/Jsy	50.00
GK	George Kell/Bat	30.00
HK	Harmon Killebrew/Jsy	60.00
RK	Ralph Kiner/Bat	50.00
DK	Dave Kingman/Bat	20.00
CK	Casey Kotchman/Jsy	20.00
DL	Derrek Lee/Jsy	40.00
ML	Mike Lowell/Jsy	20.00
SL	Sparky Lyle/Pants	20.00
FL	Fred Lynn/Bat	25.00
GM	Greg Maddux/ Jsy/Redemp.	150.00
VM	Victor Martinez/Jsy	30.00
MA	Don Mattingly/Jsy	100.00
JM	Joe Mauer/Jsy/Redemp.	40.00
BM	Bill Mazeroski/ Jsy/Redemp.	30.00
WM	Willie McCovey/Jsy	50.00
DMA	Dallas McPherson/ Jsy/Redemp.	20.00
PM	Paul Molitor/Jsy	40.00
MM	Mark Mulder/Jsy	15.00
DMN	Dale Murphy/Jsy	35.00
GN	Graig Nettles/Jsy	35.00
PN	Phil Niekro/Jsy	25.00
LN	Laynce Nix/Jsy	20.00
DO	David Ortiz/Jsy	50.00
RO	Roy Oswalt/Jsy	25.00
AO	Akinori Otsuka/Jsy	40.00
JPA	Jim Palmer/Jsy	40.00
CP	Corey Patterson/ Jsy/Redemp.	20.00
JPN	Jake Peavy/Jsy	30.00
BPN	Brad Penny/Jsy	20.00
RP	Rico Petrocelli/Jsy	25.00
SP	Scott Podsednik/Jsy	20.00
MP	Mark Prior/Jsy	20.00
AP	Albert Pujols/ Jsy/Redemp.	220.00
JRN	Jose Reyes/ Jsy/Redemp.	30.00
JRA	Jim Rice/Jsy	40.00
CR	Cal Ripken Jr./Jsy	200.00
BR	Brooks Robinson/Jsy	50.00
FR	Frank Robinson/Jsy	40.00
SR	Scott Rolen/ Jsy/Redemp.	75.00
NR	Nolan Ryan/Jsy	125.00
JSA	Johan Santana/ Jsy/Redemp.	65.00
JSN	Jason Schmidt/Jsy	15.00
MS	Mike Schmidt/Jsy	60.00
TS	Tom Seaver/Jsy	50.00
BS	Ben Sheets/ Jsy/Redemp.	30.00
SM	John Smoltz/ Jsy/Redemp.	75.00
SU	Bruce Sutter/Jsy	20.00
ST	Shingo Takatsu/Jsy	20.00
MT	Mark Teixeira/Jsy	50.00
BU	B.J. Upton/Jsy	20.00
RW	Rickie Weeks/Jsy	20.00

MW	Maury Wills/Jsy	25.00
KW	Kerry Wood/Jsy	25.00
DW	David Wright/Jsy	35.00
CY	Carl Yastrzemski/Jsy	85.00
MY	Michael Young/ Jsy/Redemp.	25.00
RY	Robin Yount/Jsy	75.00
CZ	Carlos Zambrano/Jsy	25.00

Autofacts

		NM/M
Production 15-699		
Rainbow:		No Pricing
Production One Set		
JB	Jason Bay/599	15.00
AB	Adrian Beltre/ 75 Redemp.	25.00
BE	Johnny Bench/15	75.00
HB	Hank Blalock/25	25.00
GB	George Brett/15	140.00
MI	Miguel Cabrera/25	40.00
OC	Orlando Cepeda/25	35.00
EC	Eric Chavez/25	20.00
RC	Rocky Colavito/75	75.00
BC	Bobby Crosby/ 350 Redemp.	25.00
AD	Andre Dawson/25	30.00
BF	Bob Feller/25	40.00
SF	Sid Fernandez/599	10.00
LD1	Lenny Dykstra Mets/599	10.00
LD2	Lenny Dykstra Phils/599	10.00
FR	Bill Freehan/ 599 Redemp.	10.00
GI	Marcus Giles/350	12.00
DG1	Dwight Gooden Mets/350	15.00
DG2	Dwight Gooden Yanks/350	15.00
GR	Khalil Greene/599	15.00
JR	Ken Griffey Jr./699	75.00
KG1	Ken Griffey Sr. Reds/699	10.00
KG2	Ken Griffey Sr. Yanks/699	10.00
TH	Travis Hafner/599	15.00
RH	Rich Harden/599	20.00
KH1	Keith Hernandez Mets/350	15.00
KH2	Keith Hernandez Cards/350	15.00
HO	Ken Holtzman/599	10.00
BH	Burt Hooton/599	8.00
HR	Kent Hrbek/599	15.00
AH	Aubrey Huff/350	8.00
DJ	Derek Jeter/350	150.00
JK1	Jim Kaat Cards/458	15.00
JK2	Jim Kaat Twins/458	15.00
AK	Al Kaline/15	80.00
DK	Dave Kingman/75	25.00
CK	Casey Kotchman/599	10.00
EK	Ed Kranepool/	12.00
JL	Jim Lonborg/599	15.00
ML	Mike Lowell/75	15.00
SL1	Sparky Lyle Sox/599	8.00
SL2	Sparky Lyle Yanks/599	8.00
FL	Fred Lynn/25	15.00
VM	Victor Martinez/599	15.00
JM	Joe Mauer/25 Redemp.	40.00
MC	Dallas McPherson/ 599 Redemp.	10.00
DM	Dale Murphy/75	25.00
GN	Graig Nettles/75	25.00
PN1	Phil Niekro Braves/75	20.00
PN2	Phil Niekro Yanks/75	20.00
LN	Laynce Nix/599	10.00
RO	Roy Oswalt/350	15.00
AO	Akinori Otsuka/599	25.00
JP	Jim Palmer/25	35.00
CP	Corey Patterson/ 75 Redemp.	25.00
JA	Jake Peavy/75	30.00
BP	Brad Penny/599	15.00
OP	Oliver Perez/350	15.00
PE	Jim Perry/599	10.00
RP	Rico Petrocelli/599	15.00
SP	Scott Podsednik/75	15.00
PO	Boog Powell/350	15.00
MP	Mark Prior/15	50.00
CR	Cal Ripken Jr./15	200.00
BR	Brooks Robinson/25	50.00
NR	Nolan Ryan/15	175.00
JS	Johan Santana/ 350 Redemp.	40.00
BS	Ben Sheets/75 Redemp.	20.00
SU	Bruce Sutter/350	12.00
ST	Shingo Takatsu/599	20.00
MT	Mark Teixeira/25	40.00
LT	Luis Tiant/75	20.00
BU	B.J. Upton/599	15.00
RW	Rickie Weeks/75	15.00
KW	Kerry Wood/15	50.00
DW	David Wright/599	50.00
MY	Michael Young/ 599 Redemp.	12.00

Dual Artifacts

NM/M

Production 99 Sets
Rainbow: 1-2X
Production 25 Sets

- AB Bobby Abreu/Jsy, Carlos Beltran/Jsy 15.00
- AD Adrian Beltre/Jsy, Dallas McPherson/Jsy 15.00
- AG Bobby Abreu/Jsy, Ken Griffey Jr./Jsy 15.00
- BB George Brett/Jsy, Wade Boggs/Jsy 20.00
- BC Adrian Beltre/Jsy, Eric Chavez/Jsy 8.00
- BD Bob Gibson/Pants, Dwight Gooden/Pants 8.00
- BE Bobby Crosby/Jsy, Eric Chavez/Jsy 10.00
- BJ Brooks Robinson/Jsy, Jim Palmer/Jsy 20.00
- BK Jason Bay/Jsy, Ralph Kiner/Bat 10.00
- BM Brian Giles/Jsy, Marcus Giles/Jsy 8.00
- BN Hank Blalock/Jsy, Laynce Nix/Jsy 8.00
- BP Carlos Beltran/Jsy, Corey Patterson/Jsy 12.00
- BR Ernie Banks/Pants, Frank Robinson/Jsy 20.00
- BS Ben Sheets/Jsy, Scott Podsednik/Jsy 8.00
- BY Hank Blalock/Jsy, Michael Young/Jsy 8.00
- CB Jason Bay/Jsy, Bobby Crosby/Jsy 8.00
- CC Miguel Cabrera/Jsy, Orlando Cepeda/Jsy 12.00
- CG Dwight Gooden/Pants, Gary Carter/Jsy 10.00
- CH Sean Casey/Jsy, Travis Hafner/Jsy 8.00
- CK Harmon Killebrew/Jsy, Rod Carew/Jsy 25.00
- CL Miguel Cabrera/Jsy, Mike Lowell/Jsy 10.00
- CM Will Clark/Jsy, Willie McCovey/Jsy/56 25.00
- CN Eric Chavez/Jsy, Graig Nettles/Jsy 8.00
- CO Roger Clemens/Jsy, Roy Oswalt/Jsy 15.00
- CR Bobby Crosby/Jsy, Cal Ripken Jr./Jsy 40.00
- DC Andre Dawson/Jsy, Orlando Cepeda/Jsy 10.00
- DK Bobby Doerr/Bat, George Kell/Bat 10.00
- FB Carlton Fisk/Jsy, Johnny Bench/Jsy 20.00
- FW Bob Feller/Pants, Kerry Wood/Jsy 15.00
- GB Brian Giles/Jsy, Jason Bay/Jsy 8.00
- GC Ken Griffey Jr./Jsy, Sean Casey/Jsy 15.00
- GG Ken Griffey Sr./Jsy, Ken Griffey Jr./Jsy 15.00
- GK Ken Griffey Jr./Jsy, Ralph Kiner/Bat 20.00
- GL Eric Gagne/Jsy, Sparky Lyle/Pants 10.00
- GS Dwight Gooden/Pants, Tom Seaver/Jsy 15.00
- HC Bobby Crosby/Jsy, Rich Harden/Jsy 8.00
- HG Keith Hernandez/Bat, Mark Grace/Jsy 10.00
- HH Aubrey Huff/Jsy, Travis Hafner/Jsy 8.00
- HM Travis Hafner/Jsy, Victor Martinez/Jsy 8.00
- HU Aubrey Huff/Jsy, B.J. Upton/Jsy 10.00
- HW Harmon Killebrew/Jsy, Willie McCovey/Jsy/44 25.00
- JG Derek Jeter/Jsy, Khalil Greene/Jsy 35.00
- JJ Joe Mauer/Jsy, Johan Santana/Jsy 15.00
- JR Jim Rice/Jsy, Rico Petrocelli/Pants 8.00
- JW Derek Jeter/Jsy, Maury Wills/Jsy 35.00
- JY Johnny Bench/Jsy, Yogi Berra/Pants 25.00
- KB Jim Kaat/Jsy, Bert Blyleven/Jsy 10.00
- KC Jim Kaat/Jsy, Steve Carlton/Jsy 10.00
- KD Keith Hernandez/Bat, Don Mattingly/Jsy 20.00
- KK Al Kaline/Jsy, Ralph Kiner/Bat 15.00
- KM Al Kaline/Jsy, Dale Murphy/Jsy 15.00
- KN Jim Kaat/Jsy, Phil Niekro/Jsy 10.00
- LC Derrek Lee/Jsy, Sean Casey/Jsy 10.00
- LG Derrek Lee/Jsy, Mark Grace/Jsy 10.00
- LP Fred Lynn/Bat, Rico Petrocelli/Pants 10.00
- LR Fred Lynn/Bat, Jim Rice/Jsy 10.00
- MC Don Mattingly/Jsy, Will Clark/Jsy 20.00
- MD Bill Mazeroski/Jsy, Bobby Doerr/Bat 10.00
- MH Mark Mulder/Jsy, Rich Harden/Jsy 10.00
- MK Bill Mazeroski/Jsy, Ralph Kiner/Bat 20.00
- MM Joe Mauer/Jsy, Victor Martinez/Jsy 8.00
- MS Dale Murphy/Jsy, Mike Schmidt/Jsy 20.00
- MW Paul Molitor/Jsy, Rickie Weeks/Jsy 15.00
- NL Graig Nettles/Jsy, Sparky Lyle/Pants 15.00
- NT Laynce Nix/Jsy, Mark Teixeira/Jsy 10.00
- NY Laynce Nix/Jsy, Michael Young/Jsy 10.00
- OF David Ortiz/Jsy, Carlton Fisk/Jsy 20.00
- OG Akinori Otsuka/Jsy, Khalil Greene/Jsy 15.00
- OP Akinori Otsuka/Jsy, Jake Peavy/Jsy 15.00
- OT Akinori Otsuka/Jsy, Shingo Takatsu/Jsy 20.00
- PD Andre Dawson/Jsy, Corey Patterson/Jsy 15.00
- PG Brad Penny/Jsy, Eric Gagne/Jsy 10.00
- PH Jake Peavy/Jsy, Rich Harden/Jsy 12.00
- PP Boog Powell/Jsy, Jim Palmer/Jsy 15.00
- PR Boog Powell/Jsy, Brooks Robinson/Jsy 20.00
- PS Brad Penny/Jsy, Jason Schmidt/Jsy 8.00
- RB Ernie Banks/Pants, Cal Ripken Jr./Jsy 40.00
- RC Nolan Ryan/Jsy, Steve Carlton/Jsy 30.00
- RJ Jose Reyes/Jsy, Rickie Weeks/Jsy 10.00
- RP Frank Robinson/Jsy, Boog Powell/Jsy 25.00
- RR Frank Robinson/Jsy, Brooks Robinson/Jsy 25.00
- RW David Wright/Jsy, Scott Rolen/Jsy 15.00
- SB Bert Blyleven/Jsy, Johan Santana/Jsy 15.00
- SC Johan Santana/Jsy, Roger Clemens/Jsy 20.00
- SF Ben Sheets/Jsy, Bob Feller/Pants 15.00
- SG Bruce Sutter/Jsy, Eric Gagne/Jsy 15.00
- SM Jason Schmidt/Jsy, Mark Mulder/Jsy 10.00
- SO Ben Sheets/Jsy, Roy Oswalt/Jsy 10.00
- SP Ben Sheets/Jsy, Brad Penny/Jsy 10.00
- TH Mark Teixeira/Jsy, Travis Hafner/Jsy 10.00
- TL Shingo Takatsu/Jsy, Sparky Lyle/Pants 10.00
- TY Mark Teixeira/Jsy, Michael Young/Jsy 10.00
- UJ B.J. Upton/Jsy, Derek Jeter/Jsy 30.00
- WL David Wright/Jsy, Mike Lowell/Jsy 10.00
- WR David Wright/Jsy, Jose Reyes/Jsy 10.00
- YM Robin Yount/Jsy, Paul Molitor/Jsy 25.00
- YP Carl Yastrzemski/Jsy, Rico Petrocelli/Pants 15.00
- ZM Carlos Zambrano/Jsy, Greg Maddux/Jsy 15.00
- ZP Carlos Zambrano/Jsy, Mark Prior/Jsy 10.00
- ZW Carlos Zambrano/Jsy, Kerry Wood/Jsy 20.00

Dual Artifacts Bat
NM/M
Production 25 Sets

- BC Josh Beckett, Miguel Cabrera 20.00
- BW Josh Beckett, Kerry Wood 20.00
- DR Carlos Delgado, Manny Ramirez 20.00
- GC Ken Griffey Jr., Miguel Cabrera 30.00
- GS Ken Griffey Sr., Ichiro Suzuki 80.00
- JP Derek Jeter, Mike Piazza 50.00
- JR Derek Jeter, Manny Ramirez 50.00
- RG Manny Ramirez, Vladimir Guerrero 20.00
- RJ Cal Ripken Jr., Derek Jeter 100.00
- RT Cal Ripken Jr., Miguel Tejada 60.00
- SG Ichiro Suzuki, Vladimir Guerrero 60.00
- WP Kerry Wood, Mark Prior 25.00

Dual Artifacts Signatures
No Pricing
Production 10 Sets

MLB Apparel

NM/M
Rainbow: 1-2X
Production 99 Sets

- BA Bobby Abreu/Jsy 6.00
- GA Garret Anderson/Jsy 6.00
- JB Jason Bay/Jsy 6.00
- CB Carlos Beltran/Jsy 8.00
- AB Adrian Beltre/Jsy 6.00
- BE Johnny Bench/Jsy 10.00
- YB Yogi Berra/Pants 15.00
- HB Hank Blalock/Jsy 8.00
- BB Bert Blyleven/Jsy/150 8.00
- WB Wade Boggs/Jsy 8.00
- BO Bret Boone/Jsy 4.00
- GB George Brett/Jsy 15.00
- MI Miguel Cabrera/Jsy 10.00
- RC Rod Carew/Jsy 8.00
- CA Steve Carlton/Jsy 6.00
- SC Sean Casey/Jsy 4.00
- OC Orlando Cepeda/Jsy 8.00
- EC Eric Chavez/Jsy 4.00
- WC Will Clark/Jsy/100 10.00
- CL Roger Clemens/Jsy 15.00
- BC Bobby Crosby/Jsy 6.00
- AD Andre Dawson/Jsy 6.00
- BF Bob Feller/Jsy 10.00
- CF Carlton Fisk R. Sox/Jsy/175 10.00
- CF1 Carlton Fisk W. Sox/Jsy/175 10.00
- EG Eric Gagne/Jsy 8.00
- BG Bob Gibson/Pants 10.00
- GI Brian Giles/Jsy 4.00
- GS Marcus Giles/Jsy 4.00
- DG Dwight Gooden/Pants 6.00
- MK Mark Grace/Jsy/175 4.00
- KL Khalil Greene/Jsy 8.00
- KG Ken Griffey Jr./Jsy 15.00
- GR Ken Griffey Sr./Jsy 8.00
- TG Tony Gwynn/Jsy 10.00
- TH Travis Hafner/Jsy 4.00
- RH Rich Harden/Jsy 8.00
- KH Kent Hrbek/Jsy 4.00
- HU Tim Hudson/Jsy 6.00
- AH Aubrey Huff/Jsy 4.00
- TO Torii Hunter/Jsy 4.00
- DJ Derek Jeter/Jsy 20.00
- JJ Jacque Jones/Jsy 4.00
- JK Jim Kaat/Jsy 6.00
- AK Al Kaline/Jsy 8.00
- HK Harmon Killebrew/Jsy 10.00
- CK Casey Kotchman/Jsy 4.00
- DL Derrek Lee/Jsy 4.00
- ML Mike Lowell/Jsy 4.00
- SL Sparky Lyle/Pants 6.00
- VM Victor Martinez/Jsy 6.00
- MA Don Mattingly/Jsy 20.00
- JM Joe Mauer/Jsy 10.00
- BM Bill Mazeroski/Jsy/100 12.00
- WM Willie McCovey/Jsy 8.00
- MC Dallas McPherson/Jsy 8.00
- PM Paul Molitor/Jsy 6.00
- MM Mark Mulder/Jsy 6.00
- DM Dale Murphy/Jsy/150 8.00
- GN Graig Nettles/Jsy 4.00
- PN Phil Niekro/Jsy 4.00
- LN Laynce Nix/Jsy 4.00
- DO David Ortiz/Jsy 10.00
- RO Roy Oswalt/Jsy 4.00
- AO Akinori Otsuka/Jsy 4.00
- PA Jim Palmer/Jsy 8.00
- CP Corey Patterson/Jsy 6.00
- JP Jake Peavy/Jsy 6.00
- PE Brad Penny/Jsy 4.00
- RP Rico Petrocelli/Pants 4.00
- SP Scott Podsednik/Jsy 4.00
- MP Mark Prior/Jsy 6.00
- RE Jose Reyes/Jsy 8.00
- JR Jim Rice/Jsy 8.00
- CR Cal Ripken Jr./Jsy 25.00
- BR Brooks Robinson/Jsy 8.00
- FR Frank Robinson/Jsy 8.00
- SR Scott Rolen/Jsy 10.00
- NR Nolan Ryan/Jsy 25.00
- SA Johan Santana/Jsy 10.00
- JS Jason Schmidt/Jsy 6.00
- MS Mike Schmidt/Jsy 15.00
- TS Tom Seaver/Jsy/300 8.00
- BS Ben Sheets/Jsy 8.00
- SM John Smoltz/Jsy 8.00
- SU Bruce Sutter/Jsy 6.00
- ST Shingo Takatsu/Jsy 6.00
- MT Mark Teixeira/Jsy 8.00
- BU B.J. Upton/Jsy 6.00
- JV Jose Vidro/Jsy 4.00
- RW Rickie Weeks/Jsy 6.00
- MW Maury Wills/Jsy 6.00
- KW Kerry Wood/Jsy 8.00
- DW David Wright/Jsy 10.00
- CY Carl Yastrzemski/Jsy 15.00
- MY Michael Young/Jsy 6.00
- RY Robin Yount/Jsy 15.00
- CZ Carlos Zambrano/Jsy 6.00

MLB Apparel Autographs
NM/M
Production 30 Sets
Rare: No Pricing
Production One Set

- BA Bobby Abreu/Jsy/Redemp. 25.00
- GA Garret Anderson/Jsy 20.00
- JB Jason Bay/Jsy 30.00
- CB Carlos Beltran/Jsy/Redemp. 20.00
- AB Adrian Beltre/Jsy 25.00
- BE Johnny Bench/Jsy 65.00
- YB Yogi Berra/Pants 60.00
- HB Hank Blalock/Jsy 25.00
- BB Bert Blyleven/Jsy 30.00
- WB Wade Boggs/Jsy 50.00
- BO Bret Boone/Jsy 20.00
- GB George Brett/Jsy 100.00
- MI Miguel Cabrera/Jsy 40.00
- RC Rod Carew/Jsy 40.00
- CA Steve Carlton/Jsy 30.00
- GC Gary Carter/Jsy 30.00
- SC Sean Casey/Jsy 20.00
- OC Orlando Cepeda/Jsy 35.00
- EC Eric Chavez/Jsy/Redemp. 20.00
- WC Will Clark/Jsy 50.00
- CL Roger Clemens/Jsy/Redemp. 120.00
- BC Bobby Crosby/Jsy/Redemp. 20.00
- AD Andre Dawson/Jsy 20.00
- BF Bob Feller/Pants 40.00
- CF Carlton Fisk R. Sox/Jsy 40.00
- CF1 Carlton Fisk W. Sox/Jsy 40.00
- EG Eric Gagne/Jsy 30.00
- BG Bob Gibson/Pants 50.00
- GI Brian Giles/Jsy 20.00
- GS Marcus Giles/Jsy 20.00
- DG Dwight Gooden/Pants 30.00
- MK Mark Grace/Jsy 40.00
- KL Khalil Greene/Jsy 10.00
- KG Ken Griffey Jr./Jsy 120.00
- GR Ken Griffey Sr./Jsy 25.00
- TG Tony Gwynn/Jsy 80.00
- TH Travis Hafner/Jsy 20.00
- RH Rich Harden/Jsy 15.00
- KH Kent Hrbek/Jsy 20.00
- HU Tim Hudson/Jsy 30.00
- AH Aubrey Huff/Jsy 20.00
- TO Torii Hunter/Jsy 20.00
- DJ Derek Jeter/Jsy 200.00
- JJ Jacque Jones/Jsy 20.00
- JK Jim Kaat/Jsy 25.00
- AK Al Kaline/Jsy 50.00
- HK Harmon Killebrew/Jsy 60.00
- CK Casey Kotchman/Jsy 15.00
- DL Derrek Lee/Jsy 40.00
- ML Mike Lowell/Jsy 20.00
- SL Sparky Lyle/Pants 20.00
- VM Victor Martinez/Jsy 25.00
- MA Don Mattingly/Jsy 150.00
- JM Joe Mauer/Jsy/Redemp. 40.00
- BM Bill Mazeroski/Jsy 30.00
- WM Willie McCovey/Jsy 50.00
- MC Dallas McPherson/Jsy/Redemp. 15.00
- PM Paul Molitor/Jsy 40.00
- MM Mark Mulder/Jsy 10.00
- DM Dale Murphy/Jsy 35.00
- GN Graig Nettles/Jsy 35.00
- PN Phil Niekro/Jsy 25.00
- LN Laynce Nix/Jsy 20.00
- DO David Ortiz/Jsy 50.00
- RO Roy Oswalt/Jsy 25.00
- AO Akinori Otsuka/Jsy 20.00
- PA Jim Palmer/Jsy 40.00
- CP Corey Patterson/Jsy/Redemp. 20.00
- JP Jake Peavy/Jsy 40.00
- PE Brad Penny/Jsy 20.00
- RP Rico Petrocelli/Pants 25.00
- SP Scott Podsednik/Jsy 25.00
- BP Boog Powell/Jsy 25.00
- MP Mark Prior/Jsy 20.00
- RE Jose Reyes/Jsy/Redemp. 40.00
- JR Jim Rice/Jsy 30.00
- CR Cal Ripken Jr./Jsy 200.00
- BR Brooks Robinson/Jsy 50.00
- FR Frank Robinson/Jsy 50.00
- SR Scott Rolen/Jsy/Redemp. 40.00
- NR Nolan Ryan/Jsy 125.00
- SA Johan Santana/Jsy/Redemp. 50.00
- JS Jason Schmidt/Jsy 15.00
- MS Mike Schmidt/Jsy 60.00
- TS Tom Seaver/Jsy 50.00
- BS Ben Sheets/Jsy/Redemp. 25.00
- SM John Smoltz/Jsy 75.00
- SU Bruce Sutter/Jsy 20.00
- ST Shingo Takatsu/Jsy 25.00
- MT Mark Teixeira/Jsy 40.00
- BU B.J. Upton/Jsy 25.00
- JV Jose Vidro/Jsy 15.00
- RW Rickie Weeks/Jsy 25.00
- MW Maury Wills/Jsy 25.00
- KW Kerry Wood/Jsy 25.00
- DW David Wright/Jsy 80.00
- CY Carl Yastrzemski/Jsy 85.00
- MY Michael Young/Jsy/Redemp. 25.00
- RY Robin Yount/Jsy 75.00
- CZ Carlos Zambrano/Jsy 25.00

Patches
NM/M
Production 50 unless noted.

- BA Bobby Abreu 15.00
- GA Garret Anderson 15.00
- JB Jason Bay 20.00
- CB Carlos Beltran 20.00
- AB Adrian Beltre 20.00
- BE Johnny Bench 25.00
- BB Bert Blyleven 20.00
- WB Wade Boggs 20.00
- BO Bret Boone 12.00
- GB George Brett 40.00
- MI Miguel Cabrera 25.00
- RC Rod Carew 25.00
- CA Steve Carlton/30 25.00
- GC Gary Carter 30.00
- SC Sean Casey 12.00
- EC Eric Chavez 15.00
- WC Will Clark/20 50.00
- CL Roger Clemens 25.00
- BC Bobby Crosby 20.00
- AD Andre Dawson 20.00
- EG Eric Gagne 20.00
- GI Brian Giles 12.00
- GS Marcus Giles 12.00
- DG Dwight Gooden 20.00
- MK Mark Grace 35.00
- KL Khalil Greene 25.00
- KG Ken Griffey Jr. 40.00
- GR Ken Griffey Sr. 12.00
- TG Tony Gwynn 25.00
- TH Travis Hafner 20.00
- RH Rich Harden 20.00
- KH Kent Hrbek 35.00
- HU Tim Hudson 20.00
- AH Aubrey Huff 15.00
- TO Torii Hunter 15.00
- DJ Derek Jeter 65.00
- RJ Randy Johnson 25.00
- JJ Jacque Jones 15.00
- JK Jim Kaat 20.00
- HK Harmon Killebrew 40.00
- CK Casey Kotchman 15.00
- DL Derrek Lee 15.00
- ML Mike Lowell 12.00
- GM Greg Maddux 35.00
- VM Victor Martinez 15.00
- MA Don Mattingly 30.00
- JM Joe Mauer 30.00
- WM Willie McCovey 25.00
- MC Dallas McPherson 20.00
- MM Mark Mulder 20.00
- DM Dale Murphy 20.00
- GN Graig Nettles 20.00
- PN Phil Niekro 20.00
- LN Laynce Nix 12.00
- DO David Ortiz 20.00
- RO Roy Oswalt 15.00
- AO Akinori Otsuka 25.00
- PA Jim Palmer 20.00
- CP Corey Patterson 25.00
- JP Jake Peavy 20.00
- PE Brad Penny 12.00
- SP Scott Podsednik 12.00
- BP Boog Powell 20.00
- MP Mark Prior 20.00
- RE Jose Reyes 20.00
- CR Cal Ripken Jr. 60.00
- BR Brooks Robinson/35 40.00
- FR Frank Robinson 20.00
- SR Scott Rolen 20.00
- NR Nolan Ryan 50.00
- SA Johan Santana 25.00
- JS Jason Schmidt 25.00
- MS Mike Schmidt 30.00
- BS Ben Sheets 30.00
- SM John Smoltz 30.00
- SU Bruce Sutter 15.00
- ST Shingo Takatsu 20.00
- MT Mark Teixeira 20.00
- BU B.J. Upton 20.00
- JV Jose Vidro 12.00
- RW Rickie Weeks 20.00
- MW Maury Wills/20 20.00
- KW Kerry Wood 25.00
- DW David Wright 35.00
- CY Carl Yastrzemski 40.00
- MY Michael Young 20.00
- RY Robin Yount 30.00
- CZ Carlos Zambrano 25.00

Signature Patches

No Pricing
Production 10 unless noted.

2005 Upper Deck Baseball Heroes

NM/M

- Complete Set (200):
- Common (1-100): 2.00
- Common (101-200): 2.00
- Production 575
- Tin (8): 50.00
- 1-5 Bob Feller 3.00
- 6-10 Brooks Robinson 3.00
- 11-15 Cal Ripken Jr. 8.00
- 16-20 Carl Yastrzemski 5.00
- 21-25 Don Mattingly 6.00
- 26-30 Tom Seaver 4.00
- 31-35 Harmon Killebrew 3.00
- 36-40 Jim Palmer 2.00
- 41-45 Mike Schmidt 6.00
- 46-50 Ozzie Smith 4.00
- 51-55 Paul Molitor 4.00
- 56-60 Al Kaline 3.00
- 61-65 Robin Yount 4.00
- 66-70 Ryne Sandberg 4.00
- 71-75 Stan Musial 4.00
- 76-80 Steve Carlton 2.00
- 81-85 Tony Gwynn 3.00
- 86-90 Wade Boggs 3.00
- 91-95 Will Clark 3.00
- 96-100 Yogi Berra 4.00
- 101-105 Babe Ruth 8.00
- 106-110 Roger Maris 6.00
- 111-115 Don Drysdale 2.00
- 116-120 Eddie Mathews 4.00
- 121-125 Honus Wagner 5.00
- 126-130 Jackie Robinson 5.00
- 131-135 Jimmie Foxx 4.00
- 136-140 Joe DiMaggio 6.00
- 141-145 Johnny Mize 3.00
- 146-150 Lefty Grove 3.00
- 151-155 Lou Gehrig 6.00
- 156-160 Mel Ott 4.00
- 161-165 Mickey Mantle 12.00
- 166-170 Roberto Clemente 8.00
- 171-175 Rogers Hornsby 6.00
- 176-180 Roy Campanella 3.00
- 181-185 Satchel Paige 6.00
- 186-190 Ted Williams 8.00
- 191-195 Thurman Munson 6.00
- 196-200 Ty Cobb 5.00

Emerald
- Emerald (1-100): 1-1.5X
- Emerald (101-200): 1-1.5X
- Production 199 Sets

Red
- Red (1-200): 1-2X
- Production 75 Sets

Blue
- No Pricing
- Production 10 Sets

Gold
- No Pricing
- Production One Set

Baseball Heroes Jersey
- Common Jeter:
- Production 75 Sets

Baseball Heroes Jeter
NM/M
- Complete Set (9): 25.00
- Common Jeter: 3.00
- Inserted 1:6
- 91-100 Derek Jeter 3.00

Baseball Heroes Jeter Jersey
- Common Jeter:
- Production 75 Sets

Baseball Heroes Jeter Signature
- No Pricing
- Production Two Sets

Memorabilia
- No Pricing
- Production 10 Sets

Memorabilia Emerald
NM/M
- Production 99 Sets
- Blue: 1X
- Production 99 Sets
- Bronze: 1-1.5X
- Production 50 Sets

Gold:		No Pricing
Production One Set		
Red:		1X
Production 99 Sets		
Silver:		No Pricing
Production 15 Sets		
1-5	Bob Feller	10.00
6-10	Brooks Robinson	10.00
11-15	Cal Ripken Jr.	25.00
16-20	Carl Yastrzemski	15.00
21-25	Don Mattingly	20.00
26-30	Tom Seaver	10.00
31-35	Harmon Killebrew	10.00
36-40	Jim Palmer	8.00
41-45	Steve Carlton	20.00
46-50	Ozzie Smith	20.00
51-55	Paul Molitor	10.00
56-60	Al Kaline	12.00
61-65	Robin Yount	15.00
66-70	Ryne Sandberg	15.00
71-75	Stan Musial	20.00
76-80	Steve Carlton	10.00
81-85	Tony Gwynn	20.00
86-90	Wade Boggs	10.00
91-95	Will Clark	10.00
96-100	Yogi Berra	15.00

Signature Cuts
No Pricing
Production 1-10

Signature Emerald
		NM/M
Production 99 Sets		
Blue:		1-1.5X
Production 20 Sets		
Red:		1X
Production 49 Sets		
Gold:		No Pricing
Production One Set		
Patches:		No Pricing
Production Five Sets		
1-5	Bob Feller	35.00
6-10	Brooks Robinson	35.00
11-15	Cal Ripken Jr.	125.00
16-20	Carl Yastrzemski	65.00
21-25	Don Mattingly	60.00
26-30	Tom Seaver	50.00
31-35	Harmon Killebrew	40.00
36-40	Jim Palmer	25.00
41-45	Steve Carlton	50.00
46-50	Ozzie Smith	50.00
51-55	Paul Molitor	30.00
56-60	Al Kaline	40.00
61-65	Robin Yount	40.00
66-70	Ryne Sandberg	50.00
71-75	Stan Musial	75.00
76-80	Steve Carlton	25.00
81-85	Tony Gwynn	40.00
86-90	Wade Boggs	35.00
91-95	Will Clark	30.00
96-100	Yogi Berra	60.00

Signature Memorabilia
No Pricing
Production 15 Sets

2005 Upper Deck Classics Promos

Each of the first 100 cards in Upper Deck Classics was issued in a silver foil-overprinted version with "UD PROMO" across the front. Cards were inserted into specially marked card shop and newsstand issues of Tuff Stuff magazine.

Common Player:	
Stars:	1.5X

2005 Upper Deck Classics

Complete Set (130):		50.00
Common Player:		.15
Common SP (101-130):		1.00
Inserted 1:4		
Pack (8):		3.00
Hobby Box (28):		60.00
1	Al Kaline	.50
2	Al Lopez	.15
3	Allie Reynolds	.15
4	Babe Herman	.15
5	Bill Mazeroski	.15
6	Bill Russell	.15
7	Billy Herman	.15
8	Billy Williams	.25
9	Bob Feller	.50
10	Bob Gibson	.75
11	Bob Lemon	.15
12	Bobby Doerr	.15
13	Boog Powell	.15
14	Ken Hubbs	.15
15	Brooks Robinson	.75
16	Buck Leonard	.15
17	Cal Ripken Jr.	2.00
18	Carl Hubbell	.15
19	Jim "Catfish" Hunter	.25
20	Johnny Hopp	.15
21	Charlie Gehringer	.15
22	Curt Flood	.15
23	Jimmie Foxx	.75
24	Dave McNally	.15
25	Davey Lopes	.15
26	Don Drysdale	.50
27	Don Sutton	.50
28	Earl Weaver	.15
29	Early Wynn	.15
30	Edd Roush	.15
31	Eddie Mathews	.75
32	Enos Slaughter	.15
33	Fergie Jenkins	.50
34	Frank Howard	.15
35	Leon Wagner	.15
36	Frank Crosetti	.15
37	Gaylord Perry	.15
38	George Bell	.15
39	George Kell	.15
40	Graig Nettles	.15
41	Hal Newhouser	.15
42	Harmon Killebrew	.75
43	Harvey Kuenn	.15
44	Howard Johnson	.15
45	Hoyt Wilhelm	.15
46	Jack Clark	.15
47	Jack Morris	.15
48	Jim Bunning	.15
49	Jim Palmer	.50
50	Joe Adcock	.15
51	Joe Carter	.15
52	Casey Stengel	.50
53	Joe Morgan	.50
54	Joe Sewell	.15
55	"Smoky" Joe Wood	.15
56	Johnny Bench	.75
57	Johnny Mize	.15
58	Jose Canseco	.50
59	Juan Marichal	.15
60	Keith Hernandez	.15
61	Ken Griffey Sr.	.15
62	Kent Hrbek	.15
63	Kevin Mitchell	.15
64	Kirk Gibson	.25
65	Larry Doby	.15
66	Lou Boudreau	.15
67	Lou Brock	.50
68	Luis Aparicio	.15
69	Luke Appling	.15
70	Monte Irvin	.50
71	Nellie Fox	.15
72	Norm Cash	.15
73	Orlando Cepeda	.25
74	Pedro Guerrero	.15
75	Pee Wee Reese	.15
76	Phil Niekro	.50
77	Phil Rizzuto	.50
78	Ralph Kiner	.15
79	Ray Dandridge	.15
80	Red Schoendienst	.15
81	Richie Ashburn	.15
82	Rick Ferrell	.15
83	Robin Roberts	.50
84	Rollie Fingers	.15
85	Ron Cey	.15
86	Sparky Anderson	.15
87	Stan Coveleski	.15
88	Ted Kluszewski	.15
89	Ted Lyons	.15
90	Tom Seaver	.50
91	Tommie Agee	.15
92	Tommy Lasorda	.15
93	Tony Perez	.25
94	Vada Pinson	.15
95	Waite Hoyt	.15
96	Warren Spahn	.75
97	Willie McCovey	.50
98	Lyman Bostock	.15
99	Willie Stargell	.50
100	Yogi Berra	.75
101	Andre Dawson	1.00
102	Andy Van Slyke	1.00
103	Bret Saberhagen	1.00
104	Carl Yastrzemski	2.50
105	Carlton Fisk	1.50
106	Dale Murphy	1.50
107	Darryl Strawberry	1.00
108	David Cone	1.00
109	Dennis Eckersley	1.50
110	Don Mattingly	2.50

111	Dwight Gooden	1.00
112	Eddie Murray	1.50
113	Eric Davis	1.00
114	Fred Lynn	1.00
115	George Brett	3.00
116	Jim Rice	1.00
117	John Kruk	1.50
118	Lenny Dykstra	1.00
119	Mickey Mantle	4.00
120	Mike Schmidt	3.00
121	Nolan Ryan	3.00
122	Ozzie Smith	2.00
123	Paul Molitor	2.00
124	Robin Yount	2.00
125	Ryne Sandberg	2.00
126	Steve Carlton	1.50
127	Ted Williams	3.00
128	Tony Gwynn	2.00
129	Wade Boggs	2.00
130	Will Clark	2.00

Silver
Silver (1-100):		2-3X
Silver (101-130):		1-2X
Production 399 Sets		

Gold
Gold (1-100):		2-4X
Gold (101-130):		1-2X
Production 199 Sets		

Platinum
Platinum (1-100):		5-10X
Platinum (101-130):		3-5X
Production 25 Sets		

Classic Counterparts

		NM/M
Common Duo:		2.00
Production 1,999 Sets		
CC	Will Clark, Jack Clark	2.00
CG	David Cone, Dwight Gooden	2.00
DS	Darryl Strawberry, Lenny Dykstra	2.00
GB	Wade Boggs, Tony Gwynn	4.00
GP	Ken Griffey Sr., Tony Perez	2.00
KD	John Kruk, Lenny Dykstra	2.00
KH	John Kruk, Kent Hrbek	2.00
LR	Jim Rice, Fred Lynn	2.00
MC	Kevin Mitchell, Will Clark	2.00
MH	Don Mattingly, Keith Hernandez	6.00
MY	Robin Yount, Paul Molitor	5.00
NC	Ron Cey, Graig Nettles	2.00
PH	Boog Powell, Frank Howard	2.00
RC	Steve Carlton, Nolan Ryan	8.00
RL	Bill Russell, Davey Lopes	2.00
RS	Tom Seaver, Nolan Ryan	8.00
SD	Darryl Strawberry, Eric Davis	2.00
SG	Dwight Gooden, Darryl Strawberry	2.00
SR	Cal Ripken Jr., Mike Schmidt	10.00
VC	Andy Van Slyke, Jack Clark	2.00

Classic Counterparts Materials
		NM/M
CC	Jack Clark, Will Clark	8.00
CG	David Cone, Dwight Gooden	8.00
DS	Darryl Strawberry, Lenny Dykstra	8.00
GB	Wade Boggs, Tony Gwynn	20.00
GP	Ken Griffey Sr., Tony Perez	8.00
KD	John Kruk, Lenny Dykstra	15.00
KH	John Kruk, Kent Hrbek	8.00
LR	Jim Rice, Fred Lynn	8.00
MC	Kevin Mitchell, Will Clark	8.00
MH	Don Mattingly, Keith Hernandez	15.00
MY	Robin Yount, Paul Molitor	15.00
NC	Graig Nettles, Ron Cey	8.00
PH	Boog Powell, Frank Howard	10.00
RC	Steve Carlton, Nolan Ryan	40.00
RL	Bill Russell, Davey Lopes	8.00
RS	Tom Seaver, Nolan Ryan	50.00
SD	Darryl Strawberry, Eric Davis	10.00

SG	Dwight Gooden, Darryl Strawberry	8.00
SR	Cal Ripken Jr., Mike Schmidt	50.00
VC	Andy Van Slyke, Jack Clark	10.00

Classic Counterparts Sign.
		NM/M
DS	Darryl Strawberry, Lenny Dykstra	20.00
GP	Ken Griffey Sr., Tony Perez	30.00
KD	John Kruk, Lenny Dykstra	40.00
KH	John Kruk, Kent Hrbek	40.00
LR	Jim Rice, Fred Lynn	40.00
NC	Graig Nettles, Ron Cey	35.00
RL	Bill Russell, Davey Lopes	25.00

Classic Cuts
		NM/M
Quantity produced listed		
FC	Frankie Crosetti/84	100.00
BH	Babe Herman/50	150.00
CH	Carl Hubbell/25	150.00
TL	Ted Lyons/83	120.00

Classic Fantasy Team
No Pricing
Inserted 1:448

Classic Materials

		NM/M
Common Player:		5.00
WB	Wade Boggs	5.00
GB	George Brett	10.00
CA	Jose Canseco	10.00
JO	Joe Carter	5.00
RC	Ron Cey	5.00
JC	Jack Clark	5.00
WC	Will Clark	8.00
DC	David Cone	5.00
ED	Eric Davis	10.00
AD	Andre Dawson	8.00
AD1	Andre Dawson	8.00
LD	Lenny Dykstra	5.00
DE	Dennis Eckersley	8.00
FI	Carlton Fisk	8.00
GI	Kirk Gibson	8.00
DG	Dwight Gooden	5.00
GG	Rich "Goose" Gossage	5.00
KG	Ken Griffey Jr.	5.00
PG	Pedro Guerrero	5.00
TG	Tony Gwynn	10.00
KH	Keith Hernandez	5.00
FH	Frank Howard	5.00
HR	Kent Hrbek	8.00
DL	Davey Lopes	5.00
FL	Fred Lynn	5.00
MA	Don Mattingly	15.00
PM	Paul Molitor	10.00
PM1	Paul Molitor/SP	10.00
JM	Jack Morris	8.00
DM	Dale Murphy	8.00
GN	Graig Nettles	5.00
BP	Boog Powell/SP	8.00
JR	Jim Rice	5.00
CR	Cal Ripken Jr.	25.00
BR	Bill Russell	5.00
NR	Nolan Ryan	20.00
RS	Ryne Sandberg	15.00
MS	Mike Schmidt	15.00
DS	Darryl Strawberry	5.00
AV	Andy Van Slyke	20.00
CY	Carl Yastrzemski	20.00
RY	Robin Yount	10.00

Classic Moments

Breaks the Streak
9.6.95
CAL RIPKEN JR.

		NM/M
Common Player:		2.00
Production 1,999 Sets		
WB	Wade Boggs	4.00
SC	Steve Carlton	2.00
CA	Joe Carter	2.00
JC	Jack Clark	2.00
LD	Lenny Dykstra	2.00
FI	Carlton Fisk	3.00
KG	Kirk Gibson	2.00
TG	Tony Gwynn	4.00
WJ	Wally Joyner	2.00
KM	Kevin Mitchell	2.00
PM	Paul Molitor	4.00
JM	Jack Morris	2.00
GP	Gaylord Perry	2.00
CR	Cal Ripken Jr.	8.00
NR	Nolan Ryan	8.00
BS	Bret Saberhagen	2.00
RS	Ryne Sandberg	5.00
MS	Mike Schmidt	6.00
DS	Don Sutton	2.00
RY	Robin Yount	5.00

Classic Moments Materials
		NM/M
Common Player:		5.00
WB	Wade Boggs	10.00
SC	Steve Carlton	8.00
CA	Joe Carter	5.00
JC	Jack Clark	5.00
LD	Lenny Dykstra	5.00
FI	Carlton Fisk	8.00
KG	Kirk Gibson	5.00
TG	Tony Gwynn	10.00
WJ	Wally Joyner	5.00
KM	Kevin Mitchell	5.00
PM	Paul Molitor	10.00
JM	Jack Morris	5.00
GP	Gaylord Perry	5.00
CR	Cal Ripken Jr.	25.00
NR	Nolan Ryan	20.00
RS	Ryne Sandberg	15.00
MS	Mike Schmidt	15.00
DS	Don Sutton	5.00
RY	Robin Yount	12.00

Classic Moments Signatures
		NM/M
Common Autograph:		10.00
SC	Steve Carlton	20.00
JC	Jack Clark	20.00
LD	Lenny Dykstra	15.00
FI	Carlton Fisk	40.00
KG	Kirk Gibson	25.00
TG	Tony Gwynn	40.00
WJ	Wally Joyner	20.00
KM	Kevin Mitchell	10.00
PM	Paul Molitor	25.00
JM	Jack Morris	15.00
GP	Gaylord Perry	15.00
BS	Bret Saberhagen	15.00
MS	Mike Schmidt	60.00
DS	Don Sutton	15.00
RY	Robin Yount	40.00

Classic Seasons

1987
ANDRE DAWSON

		NM/M
Common Player:		2.00
Production 1,999 Sets		
BE	George Bell	2.00
JC	Jose Canseco	3.00
CL	Jack Clark	2.00
WC	Will Clark	3.00
DC	David Cone	2.00
ED	Eric Davis	2.00
AD	Andre Dawson	2.00
KG	Kirk Gibson	2.00
DG	Dwight Gooden	2.00
FL	Fred Lynn	2.00
MA	Don Mattingly	6.00
KM	Kevin Mitchell	2.00
DM	Dale Murphy	3.00
JR	Jim Rice	2.00
CR	Cal Ripken Jr.	10.00
NR	Nolan Ryan	8.00
BS	Bret Saberhagen	2.00
RS	Ryne Sandberg	5.00
MS	Mike Schmidt	6.00
CY	Carl Yastrzemski	6.00

Classic Seasons Materials
		NM/M
Common Player:		5.00
BE	George Bell	5.00
JC	Jose Canseco	10.00
CL	Jack Clark	5.00
WC	Will Clark	8.00

DC	David Cone	5.00
ED	Eric Davis/SP	8.00
AD	Andre Dawson	5.00
KG	Kirk Gibson	5.00
DG	Dwight Gooden	5.00
FL	Fred Lynn	5.00
MA	Don Mattingly	15.00
KM	Kevin Mitchell	5.00
DM	Dale Murphy	8.00
JR	Jim Rice	5.00
CR	Cal Ripken Jr.	25.00
NR	Nolan Ryan	20.00
RS	Ryne Sandberg	15.00
MS	Mike Schmidt	15.00
CY	Carl Yastrzemski	20.00

Classic Seasons Signatures
		NM/M
Common Auto.:		10.00
BE	George Bell	15.00
JC	Jose Canseco	40.00
CL	Jack Clark	15.00
WC	Will Clark	40.00
DC	David Cone	15.00
ED	Eric Davis	20.00
AD	Andre Dawson	25.00
KG	Kirk Gibson	25.00
DG	Dwight Gooden	12.00
FL	Fred Lynn	15.00
MA	Don Mattingly	60.00
KM	Kevin Mitchell	10.00
DM	Dale Murphy	20.00
BS	Bret Saberhagen	15.00
MS	Mike Schmidt	60.00

League Leaders

LEAGUE LEADERS
Frank Howard

		NM/M
Common Player:		2.00
Production 999 Sets		
GB	George Bell	2.00
WB	Wade Boggs	4.00
JC	Jack Clark	2.00
WC	Will Clark	3.00
AD	Andre Dawson	3.00
LD	Lenny Dykstra	2.00
DE	Dennis Eckersley	3.00
DG	Dwight Gooden	2.00
GG	Rich "Goose" Gossage	2.00
PG	Pedro Guerrero	2.00
TG	Tony Gwynn	4.00
KH	Keith Hernandez	2.00
FH	Frank Howard	2.00
HJ	Howard Johnson	2.00
MA	Don Mattingly	2.00
KM	Kevin Mitchell	2.00
PM	Paul Molitor	4.00
DM	Dale Murphy	3.00
JR	Jim Rice	2.00
AV	Andy Van Slyke	2.00

League Leaders Materials
		NM/M
Common Player:		5.00
GB	George Bell	5.00
WB	Wade Boggs	10.00
JC	Jack Clark	5.00
WC	Will Clark	8.00
AD	Andre Dawson	8.00
LD	Lenny Dykstra	5.00
DE	Dennis Eckersley	8.00
DG	Dwight Gooden	5.00
GG	Rich "Goose" Gossage	5.00
PG	Pedro Guerrero	5.00
TG	Tony Gwynn/SP	10.00
KH	Keith Hernandez	5.00
FH	Frank Howard	8.00
HJ	Howard Johnson	5.00
MA	Don Mattingly	15.00
KM	Kevin Mitchell	5.00
PM	Paul Molitor	10.00
DM	Dale Murphy	8.00
JR	Jim Rice	5.00
AV	Andy Van Slyke	20.00

League Leaders Signatures
		NM/M
Common Auto.:		10.00
GB	George Bell	15.00
JC	Jack Clark	15.00
WC	Will Clark	40.00
AD	Andre Dawson	20.00
LD	Lenny Dykstra	15.00
DE	Dennis Eckersley	15.00
DG	Dwight Gooden	15.00
GG	Rich "Goose" Gossage	10.00
PG	Pedro Guerrero	10.00
KH	Keith Hernandez	15.00
FH	Frank Howard	15.00

HJ	Howard Johnson	15.00
MA	Don Mattingly	60.00
KM	Kevin Mitchell	10.00
PM	Paul Molitor	25.00
DM	Dale Murphy	20.00
JR	Jim Rice	15.00

Post Season Performers

NM/M
Common Player:		2.00
Production 999 Sets		
JO	Jose Canseco	3.00
CA	Joe Carter	2.00
JC	Jack Clark	2.00
WC	Will Clark	3.00
DC	David Cone	2.00
ED	Eric Davis	2.00
LD	Lenny Dykstra	2.00
CF	Carlton Fisk	3.00
DG	Dwight Gooden	2.00
PG	Pedro Guerrero	2.00
KH	Kent Hrbek	2.00
JK	John Kruk	3.00
KM	Kevin Mitchell	2.00
PM	Paul Molitor	4.00
JM	Jack Morris	2.00
CR	Cal Ripken Jr.	10.00
BR	Brooks Robinson	4.00
BS	Bret Saberhagen	2.00
MS	Mike Schmidt	6.00
DS	Darryl Strawberry	2.00

Post Season Performers Materials

NM/M
Common Player:		5.00
JO	Jose Canseco	10.00
CA	Joe Carter	5.00
JC	Jack Clark/SP	5.00
WC	Will Clark	8.00
DC	David Cone	8.00
ED	Eric Davis/SP	10.00
LD	Lenny Dykstra/SP	5.00
CF	Carlton Fisk	8.00
DG	Dwight Gooden	5.00
PG	Pedro Guerrero	5.00
KH	Kent Hrbek	8.00
JK	John Kruk/SP	15.00
KM	Kevin Mitchell	5.00
PM	Paul Molitor/SP	10.00
JM	Jack Morris	5.00
CR	Cal Ripken Jr./SP	25.00
BR	Brooks Robinson	10.00
MS	Mike Schmidt	15.00
DS	Darryl Strawberry	5.00

Post Season Performers Signatures

NM/M
Common Auto.:		10.00
JO	Jose Canseco	40.00
JC	Jack Clark	15.00
WC	Will Clark	40.00
DC	David Cone	15.00
ED	Eric Davis	20.00
LD	Lenny Dykstra	15.00
CF	Carlton Fisk	40.00
DG	Dwight Gooden	12.00
PG	Pedro Guerrero	10.00
KH	Kent Hrbek	20.00
JK	John Kruk	30.00
KM	Kevin Mitchell	10.00
PM	Paul Molitor	25.00
JM	Jack Morris	20.00
BR	Brooks Robinson	25.00
BS	Bret Saberhagen	15.00
MS	Mike Schmidt	60.00
SS	Darryl Strawberry	60.00

2005 Upper Deck Classics Pirates All-Stars

An All-Star Game logo was added to UD Classics cards of seven Pirates All-Stars and the cards were given away at PNC Park one per game between September 19-22 and September 30-October 2.

NM/M
Complete Set (7):		20.00
Common Player:		2.00
PP1	Ralph Kiner	4.00
PP2	Bill Mazeroski	5.00
PP3	Roberto Clemente	7.50
PP4	Willie Stargell	4.00
PP5	Tony Pena	2.00

PP6	Andy Van Slyke	2.00
PP7	Jason Bay	2.00

2005 Upper Deck ESPN

NM/M
Complete Set (90):		20.00
Common Player:		.15
Pack (9):		3.00
Box (24):		60.00
1	Garret Anderson	.25
2	Troy Glaus	.25
3	Vladimir Guerrero	.75
4	Luis Gonzalez	.25
5	Randy Johnson	.75
6	Andruw Jones	.40
7	Chipper Jones	.75
8	J.D. Drew	.25
9	John Smoltz	.25
10	Miguel Tejada	.50
11	Rafael Palmeiro	.50
12	Curt Schilling	.75
13	David Ortiz	.75
14	Manny Ramirez	.75
15	Pedro J. Martinez	.75
16	Carlos Zambrano	.25
17	Greg Maddux	1.00
18	Kerry Wood	.75
19	Mark Prior	.75
20	Nomar Garciaparra	1.50
21	Sammy Sosa	1.50
22	Carlos Lee	.25
23	Frank Thomas	.50
24	Magglio Ordonez	.25
25	Paul Konerko	.25
26	Adam Dunn	.50
27	Ken Griffey Jr.	1.00
28	Travis Hafner	.15
29	Victor Martinez	.25
30	Todd Helton	.50
31	Ivan Rodriguez	.50
32	Carl Pavano	.15
33	Josh Beckett	.25
34	Miguel Cabrera	.75
35	Mike Lowell	.15
36	Carlos Beltran	.25
37	Craig Biggio	.25
38	Jeff Bagwell	.25
39	Lance Berkman	.25
40	Roger Clemens	2.00
41	Roy Oswalt	.25
42	Mike Sweeney	.15
43	Adrian Beltre	.25
44	Brad Penny	.15
45	Eric Gagne	.40
46	Shawn Green	.25
47	Steve Finley	.15
48	Ben Sheets	.15
49	Scott Podsednik	.15
50	Joe Mauer	.25
51	Johan Santana	.50
52	Torii Hunter	.25
53	Jose Vidro	.15
54	Livan Hernandez	.15
55	Jose Reyes	.25
56	Mike Piazza	1.00
57	Tom Glavine	.25
58	Alex Rodriguez	1.50
59	Bernie Williams	.25
60	Derek Jeter	2.00
61	Gary Sheffield	.50
62	Hideki Matsui	1.50
63	Kevin Brown	.15
64	Mike Mussina	.25
65	Eric Chavez	.25
66	Mark Mulder	.25
67	Tim Hudson	.25
68	Bobby Abreu	.25
69	Jim Thome	.75
70	Craig Wilson	.15

71	Jason Kendall	.15
72	Oliver Perez	.15
73	Brian Giles	.15
74	Jake Peavy	.15
75	Jason Schmidt	.25
76	Bret Boone	.15
77	Ichiro Suzuki	1.50
78	Albert Pujols	2.00
79	Jim Edmonds	.25
80	Larry Walker	.40
81	Scott Rolen	.75
82	Aubrey Huff	.15
83	Carl Crawford	.15
84	Alfonso Soriano	.75
85	Hank Blalock	.50
86	Mark Teixeira	.50
87	Michael Young	.25
88	Carlos Delgado	.40
89	Roy Halladay	.25
90	Vernon Wells	.25

Award Winners

NM/M
Inserted 1:5		
25th Anniv.:		4X-8X
Production 25 Sets		
AW-1	Gary Sheffield	1.00
AW-2	Greg Maddux	2.00
AW-3	Mike Piazza	2.00
AW-4	Jeff Bagwell	1.00
AW-5	Kenny Rogers	.50
AW-6	Cal Ripken Jr.	4.00
AW-7	Greg Maddux	2.00
AW-8	Hideo Nomo	.75
AW-9	Javier Lopez	.50
AW-10	Jim Edmonds	.75
AW-11	Ken Griffey Jr.	2.00
AW-12	Larry Walker	.50
AW-13	Nomar Garciaparra	2.50
AW-14	Roger Clemens	4.00
AW-15	David Wells	.50
AW-16	Sammy Sosa	2.50
AW-17	Pedro J. Martinez	1.50
AW-18	Andres Galarraga	.50
AW-19	Derek Jeter	4.00
AW-20	Alfonso Soriano	1.50

Ink

Inserted 1:480

Sports Center Swatches

NM/M
Common Player:		4.00
Inserted 1:12		
GA	Garret Anderson	4.00
RB	Rocco Baldelli	4.00
CB	Carlos Beltran	8.00
AB	Adrian Beltre	8.00
LB	Lance Berkman	4.00
BI	Craig Biggio	4.00
HB	Hank Blalock	8.00
BB	Bret Boone	4.00
MG	Miguel Cabrera	8.00
EC	Eric Chavez	4.00
BC	Bartolo Colon	4.00
CC	Carl Crawford	4.00
JD	J.D. Drew	4.00
AD	Adam Dunn	8.00
JE	Jim Edmonds	6.00
EG	Eric Gagne	6.00
TG	Troy Glaus	6.00
KG	Ken Griffey Jr.	15.00
TH	Tim Hudson	4.00
AH	Aubrey Huff	4.00
DJ	Derek Jeter	20.00
JK	Jeff Kent	4.00
PK	Paul Konerko	4.00
DL	Derek Lee	4.00
LO	Derek Lowe	4.00
MM	Mark Mulder	6.00
CP	Corey Patterson	6.00
AP	Albert Pujols	20.00
IR	Ivan Rodriguez	8.00
SA	Johan Santana	6.00
JS	Jason Schmidt	6.00
BS	Ben Sheets	6.00
AS	Alfonso Soriano	8.00

IS	Ichiro Suzuki	25.00
MS	Mike Sweeney	4.00
MT	Mark Teixeira	6.00
JT	Jim Thome	10.00
BU	B.J. Upton	6.00
VW	Vernon Wells	4.00
DW	David Wright/SP	15.00
MY	Mike Young/SP	10.00

Sports Century

NM/M
Inserted 1:5		
25th Anniv.:		4-8X
Production 25 Sets		
SC-1	Babe Ruth	4.00
SC-2	Jackie Robinson	2.00
SC-4	Ty Cobb	2.00
SC-5	Joe DiMaggio	3.00
SC-6	Lou Gehrig	3.00
SC-7	Mickey Mantle	5.00
SC-8	Walter Johnson	1.00
SC-9	Stan Musial	2.00
SC-10	Satchel Paige	1.00
SC-11	Bob Gibson	1.00
SC-12	Roberto Clemente	3.00
SC-13	Cy Young	1.00
SC-14	Honus Wagner	2.00
SC-15	Rogers Hornsby	1.00

Sports Century Signatures
Inserted 1:480

The Magazine Covers

NM/M
Inserted 1:5		
25th Anniv.:		4-8X
Production 25 Sets		
MC-1	Roger Clemens	4.00
MC-2	Derek Jeter	4.00
MC-3	Randy Johnson, Pedro J. Martinez	1.50
MC-4	Nomar Garciaparra	1.50
MC-5	Manny Ramirez	1.50
MC-6	Ken Griffey Jr.	2.00
MC-7	Mike Piazza	2.00
MC-8	Ichiro Suzuki	3.00
MC-9	Vladimir Guerrero	1.50
MC-10	Randy Johnson	1.50
MC-11	A.J. Pierzynski, Doug Mientkiewicz, Jacque Jones, Torii Hunter	.50
MC-12	Jason Giambi	.50
MC-13	Jeff Kent	.50
MC-14	Albert Pujols	4.00
MC-15	Kazuo Matsui	.50
MC-16	Miguel Cabrera	1.50
MC-17	Alex Rodriguez	3.00
MC-18	Ivan Rodriguez	1.00
MC-19	Eric Gagne	1.00
MC-20	Jim Edmonds, Albert Pujols, Scott Rolen	.75

This Day in Baseball History

NM/M
Inserted 1:5		
25th Anniv.:		4-8X
Production 25 Sets		
BH-1	Cal Ripken Jr.	4.00
BH-2	Nolan Ryan	4.00
BH-3	Nolan Ryan	4.00
BH-4	Roger Clemens	2.00
BH-5	Thurman Munson	2.00
BH-6	Mickey Mantle	5.00
BH-7	Ernie Banks	1.00
BH-8	Roy Campanella	1.00
BH-9	Yogi Berra	2.00
BH-10	Mickey Mantle	5.00

NM/M
BH-11	Jackie Robinson	3.00
BH-12	Joe DiMaggio	3.00
BH-13	Bob Feller	1.00
BH-14	Lou Gehrig	3.00
BH-15	Ty Cobb	2.00
BH-16	Babe Ruth	4.00
BH-17	Walter Johnson	1.00
BH-18	Rogers Hornsby	1.00
BH-19	George Sisler	1.00
BH-20	Cy Young	1.00

Web Gems

NM/M
Inserted 1:5		
25th Anniv.:		4-8X
Production 25 Sets		
WG-1	Adrian Beltre	.75
WG-2	Alex Rodriguez	3.00
WG-3	Andruw Jones	.75
WG-4	Bernie Williams	.75
WG-5	Bret Boone	.50
WG-6	Cesar Izturis	.50
WG-7	Darin Erstad	.50
WG-8	Derek Jeter	4.00
WG-9	Derrek Lee	.75
WG-10	Eric Chavez	.75
WG-11	Greg Maddux	2.00
WG-12	Ichiro Suzuki	3.00
WG-13	Ivan Rodriguez	1.00
WG-14	Jim Edmonds	.75
WG-15	Ken Griffey Jr.	2.00
WG-16	Larry Walker	.75
WG-17	Miguel Tejada	.75
WG-18	Mike Mussina	.75
WG-19	Nomar Garciaparra	2.50
WG-20	Scott Rolen	1.50
WG-21	Steve Finley	.50
WG-22	Todd Helton	.50
WG-23	Torii Hunter	.50
WG-24	Vernon Wells	.50
WG-25	Vladimir Guerrero	1.50

2005 Upper Deck First Pitch

NM/M
Complete Set (330):		
Common (1-330):		.10
Common (301-330):		1.00
Inserted 1:4		
Common (321-330):		2.00
Inserted 1:36		
Pack (5):		1.00
Box (36):		30.00
1	Casey Kotchman	.10
2	Chone Figgins	.10
3	David Eckstein	.10
4	Jarrod Washburn	.10
5	Robb Quinlan	.10
6	Troy Glaus	.10
7	Vladimir Guerrero	.50
8	Brandon Webb	.10
9	Danny Bautista	.10
10	Luis Gonzalez	.25
11	Matt Kata	.10
12	Randy Johnson	.50
13	Robby Hammock	.10
14	Shea Hillenbrand	.10
15	Adam LaRoche	.10
16	Andruw Jones	.10

17	Horacio Ramirez	.10
18	John Smoltz	.25
19	Johnny Estrada	.10
20	Mike Hampton	.10
21	Rafael Furcal	.10
22	Brian Roberts	.10
23	Javy Lopez	.25
24	Jay Gibbons	.10
25	Jorge Julio	.10
26	Melvin Mora	.10
27	Miguel Tejada	.40
28	Rafael Palmeiro	.40
29	Derek Lowe	.10
30	Jason Varitek	.25
31	Kevin Youkilis	.10
32	Manny Ramirez	.50
33	Curt Schilling	.50
34	Pedro J. Martinez	.50
35	Trot Nixon	.10
36	Corey Patterson	.25
37	Derrek Lee	.25
38	LaTroy Hawkins	.10
39	Mark Prior	.50
40	Matt Clement	.10
41	Moises Alou	.25
42	Sammy Sosa	1.00
43	Aaron Rowand	.10
44	Carlos Lee	.10
45	Jose Valentin	.10
46	Juan Uribe	.10
47	Magglio Ordonez	.10
48	Mark Buehrle	.10
49	Paul Konerko	.10
50	Adam Dunn	.40
51	Barry Larkin	.25
52	D'Angelo Jimenez	.10
53	Danny Graves	.10
54	Paul Wilson	.10
55	Sean Casey	.10
56	Wily Mo Pena	.10
57	Ben Broussard	.10
58	C.C. Sabathia	.10
59	Casey Blake	.10
60	Cliff Lee	.10
61	Matt Lawton	.10
62	Omar Vizquel	.10
63	Victor Martinez	.25
64	Charles Johnson	.10
65	Joe Kennedy	.10
66	Jeromy Burnitz	.10
67	Matt Holliday	.25
68	Preston Wilson	.10
69	Royce Clayton	.10
70	Shawn Estes	.10
71	Bobby Higginson	.10
72	Brandon Inge	.10
73	Carlos Guillen	.10
74	Dmitri Young	.10
75	Eric Munson	.10
76	Jeremy Bonderman	.10
77	Ugueth Urbina	.10
78	Josh Beckett	.25
79	Dontrelle Willis	.25
80	Jeff Conine	.10
81	Juan Pierre	.10
82	Luis Castillo	.10
83	Miguel Cabrera	.50
84	Mike Lowell	.10
85	Andy Pettitte	.25
86	Brad Lidge	.10
87	Carlos Beltran	.40
88	Craig Biggio	.25
89	Jeff Bagwell	.40
90	Roger Clemens	1.50
91	Roy Oswalt	.10
92	Benito Santiago	.10
93	Jeremy Affeldt	.10
94	Juan Gonzalez	.10
95	Ken Harvey	.10
96	Mike MacDougal	.10
97	Mike Sweeney	.10
98	Zack Greinke	.10
99	Adrian Beltre	.25
100	Alex Cora	.10
101	Cesar Izturis	.10
102	Eric Gagne	.25
103	Kazuhisa Ishii	.10
104	Milton Bradley	.10
105	Shawn Green	.25
106	Danny Kolb	.10
107	Ben Sheets	.25
108	Brooks Kieschnick	.10
109	Craig Counsell	.10
110	Geoff Jenkins	.10
111	Lyle Overbay	.10
112	Scott Podsednik	.10
113	Corey Koskie	.10
114	Johan Santana	.50
115	Joe Mauer	.25
116	Justin Morneau	.10
117	Lew Ford	.10
118	Matt LeCroy	.10
119	Torii Hunter	.25
120	Brad Wilkerson	.10
121	Chad Cordero	.10
122	Livan Hernandez	.10
123	Jose Vidro	.10
124	Termmel Sledge	.10
125	Tony Batista	.10
126	Zach Day	.10
127	Al Leiter	.10
128	Jae Weong Seo	.10
129	Jose Reyes	.25
130	Kazuo Matsui	.10
131	Mike Piazza	.75
132	Todd Zeile	.10
133	Cliff Floyd	.10
134	Alex Rodriguez	1.50

No.	Player	Price
135	Derek Jeter	1.50
136	Gary Sheffield	.40
137	Hideki Matsui	1.00
138	Jason Giambi	.25
139	Jorge Posada	.25
140	Mike Mussina	.25
141	Barry Zito	.25
142	Bobby Crosby	.25
143	Octavio Dotel	.25
144	Eric Chavez	.25
145	Jermaine Dye	.10
146	Mark Kotsay	.10
147	Tim Hudson	.25
148	Billy Wagner	.25
149	Bobby Abreu	.25
150	David Bell	.10
151	Jim Thome	.50
152	Jimmy Rollins	.20
153	Mike Lieberthal	.10
154	Randy Wolf	.10
155	Craig Wilson	.10
156	Daryle Ward	.10
157	Jack Wilson	.10
158	Jason Kendall	.10
159	Kip Wells	.10
160	Oliver Perez	.25
161	Robert Mackowiak	.10
162	Brian Giles	.10
163	Brian Lawrence	.10
164	David Wells	.10
165	Jay Payton	.10
166	Ryan Klesko	.10
167	Sean Burroughs	.10
168	Trevor Hoffman	.10
169	Brett Tomko	.10
170	J.T. Snow	.10
171	Jason Schmidt	.25
172	Kirk Rueter	.10
173	A.J. Pierzynski	.10
174	Pedro Feliz	.10
175	Ray Durham	.10
176	Eddie Guardado	.10
177	Edgar Martinez	.10
178	Ichiro Suzuki	1.00
179	Jamie Moyer	.10
180	Joel Pineiro	.10
181	Randy Winn	.10
182	Raul Ibanez	.10
183	Albert Pujols	1.50
184	Edgar Renteria	.25
185	Jason Isringhausen	.10
186	Jim Edmonds	.25
187	Matt Morris	.10
188	Reggie Sanders	.10
189	Tony Womack	.10
190	Aubrey Huff	.10
191	Danys Baez	.10
192	Carl Crawford	.25
193	Jose Cruz Jr.	.10
194	Rocco Baldelli	.10
195	Tino Martinez	.10
196	Dewon Brazelton	.10
197	Alfonso Soriano	.50
198	Brad Fullmer	.10
199	Gerald Laird	.10
200	Hank Blalock	.50
201	Laynce Nix	.10
202	Mark Teixeira	.40
203	Mike Young	.25
204	Alexis Rios	.10
205	Eric Hinske	.10
206	Miguel Batista	.10
207	Orlando Hudson	.10
208	Roy Halladay	.10
209	Ted Lilly	.10
210	Vernon Wells	.10
211	Aarom Baldiris	.10
212	B.J. Upton	.25
213	Dallas McPherson	.25
214	Brian Dallimore	.10
215	Chris Oxspring	.10
216	Chris Shelton	.10
217	David Wright	.75
218	Edwardo Sierra	.10
219	Fernando Nieve	.10
220	Frank Francisco	.10
221	Jeff Bennett	.10
222	Justin Lehr	.10
223	John Gall	.10
224	Jorge Sequea	.10
225	Justin Germano	.10
226	Kazuhito Tadano	.10
227	Kevin Cave	.10
228	Joe Blanton	.10
229	Luis Gonzalez	.10
230	Mike Wuertz	.10
231	Mike Rouse	.10
232	Nick Regilio	.10
233	Orlando Rodriguez	.10
235	Ramon Ramirez	.10
236	Roberto Novoa	.10
237	Dioner Navarro	.10
238	Tim Bausher	.10
239	Logan Kensing	.10
240	Andy Green	.10
241	Brad Halsey	.10
242	Charles Thomas	.10
243	George Sherrill	.10
244	Jesse Crain	.10
245	Jimmy Serrano	.10
246	Joe Horgan	.10
247	Chris Young	.10
248	Joey Gathright	.10
249	Gavin Floyd	.50
250	Ryan Howard	.50
251	Lance Cormier	.10
252	Matt Treanor	.10
253	Jeff Francis	.10
254	Nick Swisher	.10
255	Scott Atchison	.10
256	Travis Blackley	.10
257	Travis Smith	.10
258	Yadier Molina	.10
259	Jeff Keppinger	.10
260	Scott Kazmir	.50
261	Garret Anderson, Vladimir Guerrero	.25
262	Luis Gonzalez, Randy Johnson	.25
263	Chipper Jones, Andruw Jones	.25
264	Miguel Tejada, Rafael Palmeiro	.25
265	Manny Ramirez, Curt Schilling	.25
266	Mark Prior, Sammy Sosa	.50
267	Frank Thomas, Magglio Ordonez	.25
268	Barry Larkin, Ken Griffey Jr.	.50
269	C.C. Sabathia, Victor Martinez	.10
270	Jeromy Burnitz, Todd Helton	.25
271	Ivan Rodriguez, Dmitri Young	.25
272	Josh Beckett, Miguel Cabrera	.25
273	Jeff Bagwell, Roger Clemens	.50
274	Mike Sweeney, Ken Harvey	.10
275	Eric Gagne, Adrian Beltre	.25
276	Ben Sheets, Geoff Jenkins	.10
277	Torii Hunter, Joe Mauer	.10
278	Jose Vidro, Livan Hernandez	.10
279	Mike Piazza, Kazuo Matsui	.25
280	Alex Rodriguez, Derek Jeter	.75
281	Eric Chavez, Tim Hudson	.10
282	Bobby Abreu, Jim Thome	.25
283	Jason Kendall, Craig Wilson	.10
284	Phil Nevin, Brian Giles	.10
285	Jason Schmidt, A.J. Pierzynski	.10
286	Bret Boone, Ichiro Suzuki	.50
287	Albert Pujols, Scott Rolen	.75
288	Aubrey Huff, Tino Martinez	.10
289	Hank Blalock, Mark Teixeira	.25
290	Roy Halladay, Carlos Delgado	.10
291	Vladimir Guerrero	.50
292	Curt Schilling	.50
293	Mark Prior	.50
294	Josh Beckett	.25
295	Roger Clemens	1.00
296	Derek Jeter	1.00
297	Eric Chavez	.10
298	Jim Thome	.50
299	Albert Pujols	1.00
300	Hank Blalock	.25
301	Guillermo Quiroz	1.00
302	Jeff Bajenaru	1.00
303	Bartolome Fortunato	1.00
304	Jason Alfaro	1.00
305	Mike Rose	1.00
306	Joe Hietpas	1.00
307	Kyle Denney	1.00
308	Rene Rivera	1.00
309	Kameron Loe	1.00
310	Rickie Weeks	1.50
311	Gustavo Chacin	1.00
312	Chris Burke	1.00
313	Yhency Brazoban	1.00
314	Brandon League	1.00
315	Jose Capellan	1.00
316	Russ Adams	1.00
317	Adrian Gonzalez	1.00
318	Jason Dubois	1.00
319	Abe Alvarez	1.00
320	Eric Crozier	1.00
321	Bengie Molina, Bartolo Colon	2.00
322	C.C. Sabathia, Victor Martinez	2.00
323	Jake Peavy, Ramon Hernandez	2.00
324	A.J. Pierzynski, Jason Schmidt	3.00
325	Joe Mauer, Johan Santana	3.00
326	Mark Prior, Michael Barrett	3.00
327	Jorge Posada, Mike Mussina	3.00
328	Roger Clemens, Brad Ausmus	4.00
329	Roy Halladay, Guillermo Quiroz	2.00
330	Mike Piazza, Tom Glavine	3.00

Fabric

Common Player:
Inserted 1:180

		NM/M
JB	Jeff Bagwell	8.00
BE	Josh Beckett	5.00
BB	Bret Boone	5.00
EC	Eric Chavez	5.00
JE	Jim Edmonds	5.00
EG	Eric Gagne	8.00

		Price
TG	Troy Glaus	5.00
KG	Ken Griffey Jr./SP	20.00
TH	Torii Hunter	5.00
DJ	Derek Jeter	20.00
AJ	Andruw Jones	5.00
CJ	Chipper Jones	8.00
MM	Mark Mulder	5.00
MO	Magglio Ordonez	5.00
SR	Scott Rolen	8.00
CS	Curt Schilling	8.00
GS	Gary Sheffield/SP	8.00
AS	Alfonso Soriano	8.00
SS	Sammy Sosa	10.00
IS	Ichiro Suzuki/SP	25.00

Jumbos

		NM/M
	Common Player:	1.00
FP-1	Shingo Takatsu	1.00
FP-2	Jeff Francis	1.00
FP-3	Jesse Crain	1.00
FP-4	Jose Capellan	1.00
FP-5	Zack Greinke	1.00
FP-6	Scott Proctor	1.00
FP-7	Scott Kazmir	3.00
FP-8	Gavin Floyd	1.00
FP-9	Joe Blanton	1.00
FP-10	Akinori Otsuka	1.00

Signature Stars

Inserted 1:720

2005 UD Hall of Fame

		NM/M
Complete Set (100):		
Common Player:		3.00
Production 550 Sets		
Tin (4):		125.00
1	Al Kaline	4.00
2	Al Lopez	3.00
3	Bill Mazeroski	3.00
4	Billy Williams	4.00
5	Bob Feller	4.00
6	Bob Gibson	4.00
7	Bob Lemon	3.00
8	Bobby Doerr	3.00
9	Brooks Robinson	5.00
10	Buck Leonard	4.00
11	Carl Yastrzemski	5.00
12	Carlton Fisk	4.00
13	Casey Stengel	4.00
14	Jim "Catfish" Hunter	3.00
15	Dave Winfield	4.00
16	Dennis Eckersley	3.00
17	Dizzy Dean	4.00
18	Don Drysdale	4.00
19	Don Sutton	3.00
20	Duke Snider	4.00
21	Early Wynn	3.00
22	Eddie Mathews	5.00
23	Eddie Murray	4.00
24	Enos Slaughter	3.00
25	Ernie Banks	5.00
26	Fergie Jenkins	4.00
27	Frank Robinson	4.00
28	Gary Carter	3.00
29	Gaylord Perry	3.00
30	George Brett	8.00
31	George Kell	3.00
32	George Sisler	3.00
33	Hal Newhouser	3.00
34	Harmon Killebrew	5.00
35	Hoyt Wilhelm	3.00
36	Jackie Robinson	5.00
37	Jim Bunning	3.00
38	Jim Palmer	4.00
39	Jimmie Foxx	5.00
40	Joe Morgan	4.00
41	Johnny Bench	5.00
42	Johnny Mize	4.00
43	Juan Marichal	4.00
44	Kirby Puckett	4.00
45	Larry Doby	3.00
46	Lefty Grove	4.00
47	Lou Boudreau	3.00
48	Lou Brock	4.00
49	Luis Aparicio	3.00
50	Mel Ott	4.00
51	Mickey Cochrane	4.00
52	Monte Irvin	3.00
53	Orlando Cepeda	3.00
54	Ozzie Smith	5.00
55	Paul Molitor	4.00
56	Pee Wee Reese	3.00
57	Phil Niekro	3.00
58	Phil Rizzuto	3.00
59	Pie Traynor	3.00
60	Ralph Kiner	3.00
61	Red Schoendienst	3.00
62	Richie Ashburn	3.00
63	Rick Ferrell	3.00
64	Robin Roberts	3.00
65	Robin Yount	5.00
66	Rod Carew	5.00
67	Rogers Hornsby	4.00
68	Rollie Fingers	4.00
69	Roy Campanella	4.00
70	Steve Carlton	3.00
71	Tony Perez	3.00
72	Warren Spahn	4.00
73	Whitey Ford	4.00
74	Willie McCovey	4.00
75	Willie Stargell	4.00
76	Yogi Berra	5.00
77	Babe Ruth	8.00
78	Honus Wagner	4.00
79	Lou Gehrig	6.00
80	Mickey Mantle	15.00
81	Ty Cobb	6.00
82	Ryne Sandberg	4.00
83	Satchel Paige	5.00
84	Wade Boggs	4.00
85	Reggie Jackson	4.00
86	Babe Ruth	8.00
87	Christy Mathewson	4.00
88	Cy Young	4.00
89	Honus Wagner	5.00
90	Joe DiMaggio	6.00
91	Lou Gehrig	6.00
92	Mickey Mantle	15.00
93	Mike Schmidt	6.00
94	Nolan Ryan	8.00
95	Satchel Paige	5.00
96	Stan Musial	6.00
97	Ted Williams	6.00
98	Tony Gwynn	4.00
99	Ty Cobb	6.00
100	Walter Johnson	4.00

Green

Green (1-100):	1X
Production 200 Sets	

Silver

Silver (1-100):	1-1.5X
Production 99 Sets	

Gold

Gold (1-100):	1.5-2X
Production 25 Sets	

Rainbow

No Pricing
Production One Set

Class of Cooperstown

		NM/M
Production 50 Sets		
Gold:		No Pricing
Production Five Sets		
Silver:		No Pricing
Production 15 Sets		
Rainbow:		No Pricing
Production One Set		
LA1	Luis Aparicio	4.00
LA2	Luis Aparicio	4.00
EB1	Ernie Banks	6.00
EB2	Ernie Banks	6.00
BE1	Johnny Bench	6.00
BE2	Johnny Bench	6.00
YB1	Yogi Berra	5.00
YB2	Yogi Berra	5.00
GB1	George Brett	10.00
GB2	George Brett	10.00
GB3	George Brett	10.00
LB1	Lou Brock	4.00
JB1	Jim Bunning	3.00
JB2	Jim Bunning	3.00
RC1	Rod Carew	4.00
RC2	Rod Carew	4.00
SC1	Steve Carlton	4.00
SC2	Steve Carlton	4.00
SC3	Steve Carlton	4.00
SC4	Steve Carlton	4.00
GC1	Gary Carter	4.00
GC2	Gary Carter	4.00
OC1	Orlando Cepeda	4.00
BD1	Bobby Doerr	4.00
BD2	Bobby Doerr	4.00
DE1	Dennis Eckersley	4.00
BF1	Bob Feller	4.00
BF2	Bob Feller	4.00
RF1	Rollie Fingers	4.00
CF1	Carlton Fisk	4.00
CF2	Carlton Fisk	4.00
WF1	Whitey Ford	5.00
WF2	Whitey Ford	5.00
BG1	Bob Gibson	5.00
BG2	Bob Gibson	5.00
MI1	Monte Irvin	3.00
MI2	Monte Irvin	4.00
RJ1	Reggie Jackson	5.00
RJ2	Reggie Jackson	5.00
RJ3	Reggie Jackson	5.00
FJ1	Fergie Jenkins	4.00
AK1	Al Kaline	6.00
AK2	Al Kaline	6.00
AK3	Al Kaline	6.00
GK1	George Kell	4.00
HK1	Harmon Killebrew	6.00
HK2	Harmon Killebrew	6.00
HK3	Harmon Killebrew	6.00
HK4	Harmon Killebrew	6.00
RK1	Ralph Kiner	4.00
RK2	Ralph Kiner	4.00
MA1	Juan Marichal	4.00
MA2	Juan Marichal	4.00
BM1	Bill Mazeroski	4.00
WM1	Willie McCovey	5.00
WM2	Willie McCovey	5.00
PM1	Paul Molitor	5.00
PM2	Paul Molitor	5.00
PM3	Paul Molitor	5.00
JM1	Joe Morgan	4.00
JM2	Joe Morgan	4.00
EM1	Eddie Murray	4.00
SM1	Stan Musial	6.00
SM2	Stan Musial	6.00
PN1	Phil Niekro	4.00
JP1	Jim Palmer	4.00
JP2	Jim Palmer	4.00
TP1	Tony Perez	4.00
GP1	Gaylord Perry	4.00
GP2	Gaylord Perry	4.00
KP1	Kirby Puckett	5.00
RR1	Robin Roberts	4.00
BR1	Brooks Robinson	5.00
BR2	Brooks Robinson	5.00
BR3	Brooks Robinson	5.00
FR1	Frank Robinson	5.00
FR2	Frank Robinson	5.00
NR1	Nolan Ryan	10.00
NR2	Nolan Ryan	10.00
NR3	Nolan Ryan	10.00
NR4	Nolan Ryan	10.00
MS1	Mike Schmidt	6.00
MS2	Mike Schmidt	6.00
MS3	Mike Schmidt	6.00
RS1	Red Schoendienst	4.00
TS1	Tom Seaver	4.00
TS2	Tom Seaver	5.00
OS1	Ozzie Smith	5.00
OS2	Ozzie Smith	6.00
SN1	Duke Snider	4.00
DS1	Don Sutton	4.00
BW1	Billy Williams	4.00
BW2	Billy Williams	4.00
BW3	Billy Williams	4.00
DW1	Dave Winfield	4.00
DW2	Dave Winfield	4.00
CY1	Carl Yastrzemski	6.00
CY2	Carl Yastrzemski	6.00
RY1	Robin Yount	6.00
RY2	Robin Yount	6.00

Class of Cooperstown Autograph

		NM/M
Production 25 Sets		
Gold:		No Pricing
Production Five Sets		
Silver:		No Pricing
Production 15 Sets		
Rainbow:		No Pricing
Material Gold:		No Pricing
Production Five Sets		
Material Silver:		No Pricing
Production 15 Sets		
Patch Gold:		No Pricing
Production Five Sets		
Patch Silver:		No Pricing
Production 10 Sets		
LA1	Luis Aparicio	20.00
LA2	Luis Aparicio	20.00
EB1	Ernie Banks	50.00
EB2	Ernie Banks	50.00
BE1	Johnny Bench	40.00
BE2	Johnny Bench	40.00
YB1	Yogi Berra	60.00
YB2	Yogi Berra	60.00
GB1	George Brett	60.00
GB2	George Brett	60.00
GB3	George Brett	60.00
LB1	Lou Brock	35.00
JB1	Jim Bunning	25.00
JB2	Jim Bunning	25.00
RC1	Rod Carew	30.00
RC2	Rod Carew	30.00
SC1	Steve Carlton	20.00
SC2	Steve Carlton	20.00
GC1	Gary Carter	25.00
GC2	Gary Carter	25.00
OC1	Orlando Cepeda	25.00
BD1	Bobby Doerr	15.00
BD2	Bobby Doerr	15.00
DE1	Dennis Eckersley	20.00
BF1	Bob Feller	30.00
BF2	Bob Feller	30.00
RF1	Rollie Fingers	20.00
CF1	Carlton Fisk	30.00
CF2	Carlton Fisk	30.00
WF1	Whitey Ford	50.00
WF2	Whitey Ford	50.00
BG1	Bob Gibson	35.00
BG2	Bob Gibson	35.00
MI1	Monte Irvin	25.00
MI2	Monte Irvin	25.00
RJ1	Reggie Jackson	40.00
RJ2	Reggie Jackson	40.00
RJ3	Reggie Jackson	40.00
FJ1	Fergie Jenkins	20.00
AK1	Al Kaline	40.00
AK2	Al Kaline	40.00
AK3	Al Kaline	40.00
GK1	George Kell	20.00
HK1	Harmon Killebrew	40.00
HK2	Harmon Killebrew	40.00
HK3	Harmon Killebrew	40.00
HK4	Harmon Killebrew	40.00
RK1	Ralph Kiner	40.00
RK2	Ralph Kiner	40.00
MA1	Juan Marichal	25.00
MA2	Juan Marichal	25.00
BM1	Bill Mazeroski	40.00
WM1	Willie McCovey	40.00
WM2	Willie McCovey	40.00
PM1	Paul Molitor	30.00
PM2	Paul Molitor	30.00
PM3	Paul Molitor	30.00
JM1	Joe Morgan	25.00
JM2	Joe Morgan	25.00
EM1	Eddie Murray	25.00
PN1	Phil Niekro	20.00
JP1	Jim Palmer	20.00
JP2	Jim Palmer	20.00
TP1	Tony Perez	20.00
GP1	Gaylord Perry	20.00
GP2	Gaylord Perry	20.00
KP1	Kirby Puckett	40.00
RR1	Robin Roberts	25.00
BR1	Brooks Robinson	30.00
BR2	Brooks Robinson	30.00
BR3	Brooks Robinson	30.00
FR1	Frank Robinson	20.00
FR2	Frank Robinson	20.00
NR1	Nolan Ryan	90.00
NR2	Nolan Ryan	90.00
NR3	Nolan Ryan	90.00
NR4	Nolan Ryan	90.00
MS1	Mike Schmidt	50.00
MS2	Mike Schmidt	50.00
MS3	Mike Schmidt	50.00
RS1	Red Schoendienst	35.00
TS1	Tom Seaver	40.00
TS2	Tom Seaver	40.00
OS1	Ozzie Smith	40.00
OS2	Ozzie Smith	40.00
SN1	Duke Snider	40.00
DS1	Don Sutton	20.00
BW1	Billy Williams	20.00
BW2	Billy Williams	20.00
BW3	Billy Williams	20.00
DW1	Dave Winfield	30.00
DW2	Dave Winfield	30.00
CY1	Carl Yastrzemski	50.00
CY2	Carl Yastrzemski	50.00
RY1	Robin Yount	40.00
RY2	Robin Yount	40.00

Class of Cooperstown Calling

		NM/M
Production 50 Sets		
Gold:		No Pricing
Production Five Sets		
Green:		.75-1.5X
Production 25 Sets		
Silver:		No Pricing
Production 15 Sets		
Rainbow:		No Pricing
Production One Set		
LA1	Luis Aparicio	4.00
LA2	Luis Aparicio	4.00
EB1	Ernie Banks	6.00
BE1	Johnny Bench	6.00
YB1	Yogi Berra	5.00
WB1	Wade Boggs	5.00
WB2	Wade Boggs	5.00
WB3	Wade Boggs	5.00
GB1	George Brett	10.00
GB2	George Brett	10.00
LB1	Lou Brock	4.00
LB2	Lou Brock	4.00
JB1	Jim Bunning	4.00
RC1	Rod Carew	4.00
RC2	Rod Carew	4.00
SC1	Steve Carlton	4.00
SC2	Steve Carlton	4.00
GC1	Gary Carter	4.00
GC2	Gary Carter	4.00
GC3	Gary Carter	4.00
OC1	Orlando Cepeda	4.00
OC2	Orlando Cepeda	4.00
BD1	Bobby Doerr	4.00
BD2	Bobby Doerr	4.00
DE1	Dennis Eckersley	4.00
DE2	Dennis Eckersley	4.00
BF1	Bob Feller	4.00
BF2	Bob Feller	4.00
RF1	Rollie Fingers	4.00
RF2	Rollie Fingers	4.00
CF1	Carlton Fisk	4.00
CF2	Carlton Fisk	4.00
WF1	Whitey Ford	5.00
BG1	Bob Gibson	5.00
MI1	Monte Irvin	4.00

(continued)

Code	Player	Price
RJ1	Reggie Jackson	5.00
RJ2	Reggie Jackson	5.00
RJ3	Reggie Jackson	5.00
FJ1	Fergie Jenkins	4.00
FJ2	Fergie Jenkins	4.00
AK1	Al Kaline	6.00
AK2	Al Kaline	6.00
GK1	George Kell	4.00
HK1	Harmon Killebrew	6.00
HK2	Harmon Killebrew	6.00
RK1	Ralph Kiner	4.00
JM1	Juan Marichal	4.00
BM1	Bill Mazeroski	4.00
WM1	Willie McCovey	5.00
PM1	Paul Molitor	5.00
PM2	Paul Molitor	5.00
PM3	Paul Molitor	5.00
MO1	Joe Morgan	4.00
MO2	Joe Morgan	4.00
EM1	Eddie Murray	4.00
EM2	Eddie Murray	4.00
SM1	Stan Musial	6.00
SM2	Stan Musial	6.00
PN1	Phil Niekro	4.00
PN2	Phil Niekro	4.00
JP1	Jim Palmer	4.00
JP2	Jim Palmer	4.00
TP1	Tony Perez	4.00
TP2	Tony Perez	4.00
GP1	Gaylord Perry	4.00
GP2	Gaylord Perry	4.00
KP1	Kirby Puckett	5.00
KP2	Kirby Puckett	5.00
RR1	Robin Roberts	4.00
BR1	Brooks Robinson	5.00
BR2	Brooks Robinson	5.00
BR3	Brooks Robinson	5.00
FR1	Frank Robinson	5.00
NR1	Nolan Ryan	10.00
NR2	Nolan Ryan	10.00
NR3	Nolan Ryan	10.00
NR4	Nolan Ryan	10.00
SA1	Ryne Sandberg	6.00
SA2	Ryne Sandberg	6.00
SA3	Ryne Sandberg	6.00
MS1	Mike Schmidt	6.00
MS2	Mike Schmidt	6.00
MS3	Mike Schmidt	6.00
RS1	Red Schoendienst	4.00
TS1	Tom Seaver	5.00
OS1	Ozzie Smith	6.00
OS2	Ozzie Smith	6.00
OS3	Ozzie Smith	6.00
SN1	Duke Snider	5.00
DS1	Don Sutton	4.00
DS2	Don Sutton	4.00
DS3	Don Sutton	4.00
BW1	Billy Williams	4.00
BW2	Billy Williams	4.00
DW1	Dave Winfield	4.00
CY1	Carl Yastrzemski	6.00
CY2	Carl Yastrzemski	6.00
RY1	Robin Yount	6.00
RY2	Robin Yount	6.00
RY3	Robin Yount	6.00

Class of Cooperstown Calling Auto.

	NM/M
Production 25 Sets	
Gold:	No Pricing
Production Five Sets	
Silver:	No Pricing
Production 15 Sets	
Rainbow:	No Pricing
Production One Set	
Material Gold:	No Pricing
Production Five Sets	
Material Silver:	No Pricing
Production 15 Sets	
Patch Gold:	No Pricing
Production Two Sets	
Patch Silver:	No Pricing
Production 10 Sets	

Code	Player	Price
LA1	Luis Aparicio	20.00
LA2	Luis Aparicio	20.00
EB1	Ernie Banks	50.00
BE1	Johnny Bench	40.00
YB1	Yogi Berra	60.00
WB1	Wade Boggs	35.00
WB2	Wade Boggs	35.00
WB3	Wade Boggs	35.00
GB1	George Brett	60.00
GB2	George Brett	60.00
LB1	Lou Brock	35.00
LB2	Lou Brock	35.00
JB1	Jim Bunning	25.00
RC1	Rod Carew	30.00
RC2	Rod Carew	30.00
SC1	Steve Carlton	20.00
SC2	Steve Carlton	20.00
GC1	Gary Carter	25.00
GC2	Gary Carter	25.00
GC3	Gary Carter	25.00
OC1	Orlando Cepeda	25.00
OC2	Orlando Cepeda	25.00
BD1	Bobby Doerr	15.00
BD2	Bobby Doerr	15.00
DE1	Dennis Eckersley	20.00
DE2	Dennis Eckersley	20.00
BF1	Bob Feller	30.00
BF2	Bob Feller	30.00
RF1	Rollie Fingers	20.00
RF2	Rollie Fingers	20.00
CF1	Carlton Fisk	30.00
CF2	Carlton Fisk	30.00
WF1	Whitey Ford	50.00
BG1	Bob Gibson	35.00
MI1	Monte Irvin	25.00
RJ1	Reggie Jackson	40.00
RJ2	Reggie Jackson	40.00
RJ3	Reggie Jackson	40.00
FJ1	Fergie Jenkins	20.00
FJ2	Fergie Jenkins	20.00
AK1	Al Kaline	40.00
AK2	Al Kaline	40.00
GK1	George Kell	20.00
HK1	Harmon Killebrew	40.00
HK2	Harmon Killebrew	40.00
RK1	Ralph Kiner	40.00
JM1	Juan Marichal	25.00
BM1	Bill Mazeroski	40.00
WM1	Willie McCovey	40.00
PM1	Paul Molitor	30.00
PM2	Paul Molitor	30.00
PM3	Paul Molitor	30.00
MO1	Joe Morgan	25.00
MO2	Joe Morgan	25.00
EM1	Eddie Murray	50.00
EM2	Eddie Murray	50.00
SM1	Stan Musial	60.00
SM2	Stan Musial	60.00
PN1	Phil Niekro	20.00
PN2	Phil Niekro	20.00
JP1	Jim Palmer	20.00
JP2	Jim Palmer	20.00
TP1	Tony Perez	20.00
TP2	Tony Perez	20.00
GP1	Gaylord Perry	20.00
GP2	Gaylord Perry	20.00
KP1	Kirby Puckett	40.00
KP2	Kirby Puckett	40.00
RR1	Robin Roberts	40.00
BR1	Brooks Robinson	30.00
BR2	Brooks Robinson	30.00
BR3	Brooks Robinson	30.00
FR1	Frank Robinson	20.00
NR1	Nolan Ryan	90.00
NR2	Nolan Ryan	90.00
NR3	Nolan Ryan	90.00
NR4	Nolan Ryan	90.00
SA1	Ryne Sandberg	60.00
SA2	Ryne Sandberg	60.00
SA3	Ryne Sandberg	60.00
MS1	Mike Schmidt	50.00
MS2	Mike Schmidt	50.00
MS3	Mike Schmidt	50.00
RS1	Red Schoendienst	35.00
TS1	Tom Seaver	40.00
OS1	Ozzie Smith	40.00
OS2	Ozzie Smith	40.00
OS3	Ozzie Smith	40.00
SN1	Duke Snider	40.00
DS1	Don Sutton	20.00
DS2	Don Sutton	20.00
DS3	Don Sutton	20.00
BW1	Billy Williams	20.00
BW2	Billy Williams	20.00
DW1	Dave Winfield	30.00
CY1	Carl Yastrzemski	50.00
CY2	Carl Yastrzemski	50.00
RY1	Robin Yount	40.00
RY2	Robin Yount	40.00
RY3	Robin Yount	40.00

Cooperstown Cuts

(Christy Mathewson cut signature)

	NM/M
Production 1-20	
JM Johnny Mize/20	180.00

Cooperstown Cuts Memorabilia

No Pricing
Production 1-20

Essential Enshrinement

	NM/M
Production 50 Sets	
Gold:	No Pricing
Production Five Sets	
Silver:	No Pricing
Production 15 Sets	
Rainbow:	No Pricing
Production One Set	

Code	Player	Price
LA1	Luis Aparicio	4.00
EB1	Ernie Banks	6.00
BE1	Johnny Bench	6.00
BE2	Johnny Bench	6.00
YB1	Yogi Berra	5.00
YB2	Yogi Berra	5.00
WB1	Wade Boggs	5.00
WB2	Wade Boggs	5.00
WB3	Wade Boggs	5.00
GB1	George Brett	10.00
GB2	George Brett	10.00
GB3	George Brett	10.00
LB1	Lou Brock	4.00
LB2	Lou Brock	4.00
JB1	Jim Bunning	4.00
RC1	Rod Carew	4.00
RC2	Rod Carew	4.00
SC1	Steve Carlton	4.00
GC2	Gary Carter	4.00
OC1	Orlando Cepeda	4.00
BD1	Bobby Doerr	4.00
BD2	Bobby Doerr	4.00
DE1	Dennis Eckersley	4.00
BF1	Bob Feller	4.00
BF2	Bob Feller	4.00
RF1	Rollie Fingers	4.00
CF1	Carlton Fisk	4.00
CF2	Carlton Fisk	4.00
WF1	Whitey Ford	5.00
WF2	Whitey Ford	5.00
BG1	Bob Gibson	5.00
BG2	Bob Gibson	5.00
MI1	Monte Irvin	4.00
RJ1	Reggie Jackson	5.00
RJ2	Reggie Jackson	5.00
RJ3	Reggie Jackson	5.00
FJ1	Fergie Jenkins	4.00
FJ2	Fergie Jenkins	4.00
AK1	Al Kaline	6.00
AK2	Al Kaline	6.00
GK1	George Kell	4.00
HK1	Harmon Killebrew	6.00
HK2	Harmon Killebrew	6.00
JM1	Juan Marichal	4.00
BM1	Bill Mazeroski	4.00
WM1	Willie McCovey	5.00
PM1	Paul Molitor	5.00
PM2	Paul Molitor	5.00
PM3	Paul Molitor	5.00
MO1	Joe Morgan	4.00
MO2	Joe Morgan	4.00
MO3	Joe Morgan	4.00
EM1	Eddie Murray	4.00
EM2	Eddie Murray	4.00
SM1	Stan Musial	6.00
SM2	Stan Musial	6.00
PN1	Phil Niekro	4.00
PN2	Phil Niekro	4.00
JP1	Jim Palmer	4.00
JP2	Jim Palmer	4.00
TP1	Tony Perez	4.00
GP1	Gaylord Perry	4.00
GP2	Gaylord Perry	4.00
KP1	Kirby Puckett	5.00
KP2	Kirby Puckett	5.00
RR1	Robin Roberts	4.00
BR1	Brooks Robinson	5.00
BR2	Brooks Robinson	5.00
BR3	Brooks Robinson	5.00
FR1	Frank Robinson	5.00
FR2	Frank Robinson	5.00
NR1	Nolan Ryan	10.00
NR2	Nolan Ryan	10.00
NR3	Nolan Ryan	10.00
NR4	Nolan Ryan	10.00
SA1	Ryne Sandberg	6.00
SA2	Ryne Sandberg	6.00
SA3	Ryne Sandberg	6.00
MS1	Mike Schmidt	6.00
MS2	Mike Schmidt	6.00
RS1	Red Schoendienst	4.00
TS1	Tom Seaver	5.00
OS1	Ozzie Smith	6.00
OS2	Ozzie Smith	6.00
SN1	Duke Snider	5.00
SN2	Duke Snider	5.00
DS1	Don Sutton	4.00
DS2	Don Sutton	4.00
BW1	Billy Williams	4.00
BW2	Billy Williams	4.00
DW1	Dave Winfield	4.00
CY1	Carl Yastrzemski	6.00
CY2	Carl Yastrzemski	6.00
CY3	Carl Yastrzemski	6.00
RY1	Robin Yount	6.00
RY2	Robin Yount	6.00
RY3	Robin Yount	6.00

Essential Enshrinement Autograph

	NM/M
Production 25 Sets	
Gold:	No Pricing
Production Five Sets	
Silver:	No Pricing
Production 15 Sets	
Rainbow:	No Pricing
Production One Set	
Material Gold:	No Pricing
Production Five Sets	
Material Silver:	No Pricing
Production 15 Sets	
Patch Gold:	No Pricing
Production Five Sets	
Patch Silver:	No Pricing
Production 10 Sets	

Code	Player	Price
LA1	Luis Aparicio	20.00
EB1	Ernie Banks	50.00
BE1	Johnny Bench	40.00
BE2	Johnny Bench	40.00
YB1	Yogi Berra	60.00
YB2	Yogi Berra	60.00
WB1	Wade Boggs	35.00
WB2	Wade Boggs	35.00
WB3	Wade Boggs	35.00
GB1	George Brett	60.00
GB2	George Brett	60.00
GB3	George Brett	60.00
LB1	Lou Brock	35.00
LB2	Lou Brock	35.00
JB1	Jim Bunning	25.00
RC1	Rod Carew	30.00
RC2	Rod Carew	30.00
SC1	Steve Carlton	20.00
SC2	Steve Carlton	20.00
GC1	Gary Carter	25.00
GC2	Gary Carter	25.00
OC1	Orlando Cepeda	25.00
BD1	Bobby Doerr	15.00
BD2	Bobby Doerr	15.00
DE1	Dennis Eckersley	20.00
BF1	Bob Feller	30.00
BF2	Bob Feller	30.00
RF1	Rollie Fingers	20.00
CF1	Carlton Fisk	30.00
CF2	Carlton Fisk	30.00
WF1	Whitey Ford	50.00
WF2	Whitey Ford	50.00
BG1	Bob Gibson	35.00
BG2	Bob Gibson	35.00
MI1	Monte Irvin	25.00
RJ1	Reggie Jackson	40.00
RJ2	Reggie Jackson	40.00
RJ3	Reggie Jackson	40.00
FJ1	Fergie Jenkins	20.00
FJ2	Fergie Jenkins	20.00
AK1	Al Kaline	40.00
AK2	Al Kaline	40.00
GK1	George Kell	20.00
HK1	Harmon Killebrew	40.00
HK2	Harmon Killebrew	40.00
RK1	Ralph Kiner	40.00
JM1	Juan Marichal	25.00
BM1	Bill Mazeroski	40.00
WM1	Willie McCovey	40.00
PM1	Paul Molitor	30.00
PM2	Paul Molitor	30.00
PM3	Paul Molitor	30.00
MO1	Joe Morgan	25.00
MO2	Joe Morgan	25.00
MO3	Joe Morgan	25.00
EM1	Eddie Murray	50.00
EM2	Eddie Murray	50.00
SM1	Stan Musial	60.00
SM2	Stan Musial	60.00
PN1	Phil Niekro	20.00
PN2	Phil Niekro	20.00
JP1	Jim Palmer	20.00
JP2	Jim Palmer	20.00
TP1	Tony Perez	20.00
GP1	Gaylord Perry	20.00
GP2	Gaylord Perry	20.00
KP1	Kirby Puckett	40.00
KP2	Kirby Puckett	40.00
RR1	Robin Roberts	25.00
BR1	Brooks Robinson	30.00
BR2	Brooks Robinson	30.00
BR3	Brooks Robinson	30.00
FR1	Frank Robinson	20.00
FR2	Frank Robinson	20.00
NR1	Nolan Ryan	90.00
NR2	Nolan Ryan	90.00
NR3	Nolan Ryan	90.00
NR4	Nolan Ryan	90.00
SA1	Ryne Sandberg	60.00
SA2	Ryne Sandberg	60.00
SA3	Ryne Sandberg	60.00
MS1	Mike Schmidt	50.00
MS2	Mike Schmidt	50.00
RS1	Red Schoendienst	35.00
TS1	Tom Seaver	40.00
OS1	Ozzie Smith	40.00
OS2	Ozzie Smith	40.00
SN1	Duke Snider	40.00
SN2	Duke Snider	40.00
DS1	Don Sutton	20.00
DS2	Don Sutton	20.00
BW1	Billy Williams	20.00
BW2	Billy Williams	20.00
DW1	Dave Winfield	30.00
CY1	Carl Yastrzemski	50.00
CY2	Carl Yastrzemski	50.00
CY3	Carl Yastrzemski	50.00
RY1	Robin Yount	40.00
RY2	Robin Yount	40.00
RY3	Robin Yount	40.00

(continued — Mel Ott etc.)

Code	Player	Price
MO1	Mel Ott	40.00
MO2	Mel Ott	40.00
SP1	Satchel Paige	50.00
SP2	Satchel Paige	50.00
SP3	Satchel Paige	50.00
JR1	Jackie Robinson	60.00
JR2	Jackie Robinson	60.00
JR3	Jackie Robinson	60.00
BR1	Babe Ruth	250.00
BR2	Babe Ruth	250.00
BR3	Babe Ruth	250.00
GS1	George Sisler	40.00
GS2	George Sisler	40.00
TW1	Ted Williams	85.00
TW2	Ted Williams	85.00
TW3	Ted Williams	85.00

Hall of Fame Seasons

	NM/M
Production 50 Sets	
Gold:	No Pricing
Production Five Sets	
Silver:	No Pricing
Production 15 Sets	
Rainbow:	No Pricing
Production One Set	

Code	Player	Price
LA1	Luis Aparicio	4.00
EB1	Ernie Banks	6.00
BE1	Johnny Bench	6.00
BE2	Johnny Bench	6.00
YB1	Yogi Berra	5.00
YB2	Yogi Berra	5.00
WB1	Wade Boggs	5.00
WB2	Wade Boggs	5.00
WB3	Wade Boggs	5.00
GB1	George Brett	10.00
GB2	George Brett	10.00
LB1	Lou Brock	4.00
LB2	Lou Brock	4.00
JB1	Jim Bunning	4.00
RC1	Rod Carew	4.00
RC2	Rod Carew	4.00
GC1	Gary Carter	4.00
SC1	Steve Carlton	4.00
SC2	Steve Carlton	4.00
SC3	Steve Carlton	4.00
OC1	Orlando Cepeda	4.00
BD1	Bobby Doerr	4.00
DE1	Dennis Eckersley	4.00
DE2	Dennis Eckersley	4.00
DE3	Dennis Eckersley	4.00
BF1	Bob Feller	4.00
BF2	Bob Feller	4.00
RF1	Rollie Fingers	4.00
CF1	Carlton Fisk	4.00
CF2	Carlton Fisk	4.00
WF1	Whitey Ford	5.00
WF2	Whitey Ford	5.00
BG1	Bob Gibson	5.00
BG2	Bob Gibson	5.00
MI1	Monte Irvin	4.00
RJ1	Reggie Jackson	5.00
RJ2	Reggie Jackson	5.00
RJ3	Reggie Jackson	5.00
FJ1	Fergie Jenkins	4.00
FJ2	Fergie Jenkins	4.00
AK1	Al Kaline	6.00
AK2	Al Kaline	6.00
GK1	George Kell	4.00
HK1	Harmon Killebrew	6.00
HK2	Harmon Killebrew	6.00
RK1	Ralph Kiner	4.00
JM1	Juan Marichal	4.00
BM1	Bill Mazeroski	4.00
WM1	Willie McCovey	5.00
PM1	Paul Molitor	5.00
PM2	Paul Molitor	5.00
PM3	Paul Molitor	5.00
MO1	Joe Morgan	4.00
MO2	Joe Morgan	4.00
MO3	Joe Morgan	4.00
EM1	Eddie Murray	4.00
EM2	Eddie Murray	4.00
SM1	Stan Musial	6.00
SM2	Stan Musial	6.00
PN1	Phil Niekro	4.00
PN2	Phil Niekro	4.00
JP1	Jim Palmer	4.00
JP2	Jim Palmer	4.00
JP3	Jim Palmer	4.00
TP1	Tony Perez	4.00
GP1	Gaylord Perry	4.00
GP2	Gaylord Perry	4.00
KP1	Kirby Puckett	5.00
KP2	Kirby Puckett	5.00
RR1	Robin Roberts	4.00
BR1	Brooks Robinson	5.00
BR2	Brooks Robinson	5.00
BR3	Brooks Robinson	5.00
FR1	Frank Robinson	5.00
FR2	Frank Robinson	5.00
NR1	Nolan Ryan	10.00
NR2	Nolan Ryan	10.00
NR3	Nolan Ryan	10.00
NR4	Nolan Ryan	10.00
SA1	Ryne Sandberg	6.00
SA2	Ryne Sandberg	6.00
SA3	Ryne Sandberg	6.00
MS1	Mike Schmidt	6.00
MS2	Mike Schmidt	6.00
RS1	Red Schoendienst	4.00
TS1	Tom Seaver	5.00
OS1	Ozzie Smith	6.00
OS2	Ozzie Smith	6.00
SN1	Duke Snider	5.00
SN2	Duke Snider	5.00
DS1	Don Sutton	4.00
DS2	Don Sutton	4.00
BW1	Billy Williams	4.00
BW2	Billy Williams	4.00
DW1	Dave Winfield	4.00
CY1	Carl Yastrzemski	6.00
CY2	Carl Yastrzemski	6.00
RY1	Robin Yount	6.00
RY2	Robin Yount	6.00

Hall of Fame Seasons Autograph

	NM/M
Production 25 Sets	
Gold:	No Pricing
Production Five Sets	
Silver:	No Pricing
Production 15 Sets	
Rainbow:	No Pricing
Production One Set	
Material Gold:	No Pricing
Production Five Sets	
Material Silver:	No Pricing
Production 15 Sets	
Patch Gold:	No Pricing
Production Five Sets	
Patch Silver:	No Pricing
Production 10 Sets	

Code	Player	Price
LA1	Luis Aparicio	20.00
EB1	Ernie Banks	50.00
BE1	Johnny Bench	40.00
BE2	Johnny Bench	40.00
YB1	Yogi Berra	60.00
YB2	Yogi Berra	60.00
WB1	Wade Boggs	35.00
WB2	Wade Boggs	35.00
WB3	Wade Boggs	35.00
GB1	George Brett	60.00
GB2	George Brett	60.00
LB1	Lou Brock	35.00
LB2	Lou Brock	35.00
JB1	Jim Bunning	25.00
RC1	Rod Carew	30.00
RC2	Rod Carew	30.00
GC1	Gary Carter	25.00
SC1	Steve Carlton	20.00
SC2	Steve Carlton	20.00
SC3	Steve Carlton	20.00
OC1	Orlando Cepeda	25.00
BD1	Bobby Doerr	15.00
DE1	Dennis Eckersley	20.00
DE2	Dennis Eckersley	20.00
DE3	Dennis Eckersley	20.00
BF1	Bob Feller	30.00
BF2	Bob Feller	30.00
RF1	Rollie Fingers	30.00
CF1	Carlton Fisk	30.00
CF2	Carlton Fisk	30.00
WF1	Whitey Ford	50.00
WF2	Whitey Ford	50.00
BG1	Bob Gibson	35.00
BG2	Bob Gibson	35.00
MI1	Monte Irvin	25.00
RJ1	Reggie Jackson	40.00
RJ2	Reggie Jackson	40.00
RJ3	Reggie Jackson	40.00
FJ1	Fergie Jenkins	20.00
FJ2	Fergie Jenkins	20.00
AK1	Al Kaline	40.00
AK2	Al Kaline	40.00
AK3	Al Kaline	40.00
GK1	George Kell	20.00
HK1	Harmon Killebrew	40.00
HK2	Harmon Killebrew	40.00
HK3	Harmon Killebrew	40.00
RK1	Ralph Kiner	40.00
JM1	Juan Marichal	25.00
BM1	Bill Mazeroski	40.00
WM1	Willie McCovey	40.00
PM1	Paul Molitor	30.00
PM2	Paul Molitor	30.00
PM3	Paul Molitor	30.00
MO1	Joe Morgan	25.00
MO2	Joe Morgan	25.00
EM1	Eddie Murray	50.00
EM2	Eddie Murray	50.00
SM1	Stan Musial	60.00
SM2	Stan Musial	60.00
PN1	Phil Niekro	20.00
PN2	Phil Niekro	20.00
JP1	Jim Palmer	20.00
JP2	Jim Palmer	20.00
JP3	Jim Palmer	20.00
TP1	Tony Perez	20.00
GP1	Gaylord Perry	20.00
GP2	Gaylord Perry	20.00
KP1	Kirby Puckett	40.00
KP2	Kirby Puckett	40.00
RR1	Robin Roberts	25.00
BR1	Brooks Robinson	30.00
BR2	Brooks Robinson	30.00
BR3	Brooks Robinson	30.00
FR1	Frank Robinson	20.00
FR2	Frank Robinson	20.00
NR1	Nolan Ryan	90.00
NR2	Nolan Ryan	90.00
NR3	Nolan Ryan	90.00
NR4	Nolan Ryan	90.00
SA1	Ryne Sandberg	60.00
SA2	Ryne Sandberg	60.00
MS1	Mike Schmidt	50.00
MS2	Mike Schmidt	50.00
MS3	Mike Schmidt	50.00
RS1	Red Schoendienst	35.00
TS1	Tom Seaver	40.00
OS1	Ozzie Smith	40.00
OS2	Ozzie Smith	40.00

Hall of Fame Materials

	NM/M
Production 25 Sets	
Gold:	No Pricing
Production Five Sets	
Silver:	No Pricing
Production 15 Sets	
Rainbow:	No Pricing
Production One Set	
Green:	No Pricing
Production 10 Sets	

Code	Player	Price
RC1	Roberto Clemente	120.00
RC2	Roberto Clemente	120.00
RC3	Roberto Clemente	120.00
TC1	Ty Cobb	100.00
TC2	Ty Cobb	100.00
TC3	Ty Cobb	100.00
MC1	Mickey Cochrane	40.00
DD1	Dizzy Dean	80.00
DD2	Dizzy Dean	80.00
JD1	Joe DiMaggio	90.00
JD2	Joe DiMaggio	90.00
JD3	Joe DiMaggio	90.00
JF1	Jimmie Foxx	60.00
JF2	Jimmie Foxx	60.00
LG1	Lou Gehrig	180.00
LG2	Lou Gehrig	180.00
LG3	Lou Gehrig	180.00
RH1	Rogers Hornsby	80.00
MM1	Mickey Mantle	250.00
MM2	Mickey Mantle	250.00
MM3	Mickey Mantle	250.00
JM1	Johnny Mize	30.00
JM2	Johnny Mize	30.00
JM3	Johnny Mize	30.00

SN1	Duke Snider	40.00
DS1	Don Sutton	20.00
DS2	Don Sutton	20.00
BW1	Billy Williams	20.00
BW2	Billy Williams	20.00
DW1	Dave Winfield	30.00
CY1	Carl Yastrzemski	50.00
CY2	Carl Yastrzemski	50.00
RY1	Robin Yount	40.00
RY2	Robin Yount	40.00

Hall Worthy

NM/M

Production 50 Sets
Gold: No Pricing
Production Five Sets
Silver: No Pricing
Production 15 Sets
Rainbow: No Pricing
Production One Set

LA1	Luis Aparicio	4.00
EB1	Ernie Banks	6.00
BE1	Johnny Bench	6.00
BE2	Johnny Bench	6.00
YB1	Yogi Berra	5.00
WB1	Wade Boggs	5.00
WB2	Wade Boggs	5.00
WB3	Wade Boggs	5.00
GB1	George Brett	10.00
GB2	George Brett	10.00
GB3	George Brett	10.00
LB1	Lou Brock	4.00
LB2	Lou Brock	4.00
JB1	Jim Bunning	4.00
RC1	Rod Carew	4.00
RC2	Rod Carew	4.00
SC1	Steve Carlton	4.00
SC2	Steve Carlton	4.00
GC1	Gary Carter	4.00
GC2	Gary Carter	4.00
OC1	Orlando Cepeda	4.00
OC2	Orlando Cepeda	4.00
BD1	Bobby Doerr	4.00
DE1	Dennis Eckersley	4.00
DE2	Dennis Eckersley	4.00
DE3	Dennis Eckersley	4.00
DE4	Dennis Eckersley	4.00
BF1	Bob Feller	4.00
BF2	Bob Feller	4.00
RF1	Rollie Fingers	4.00
RF2	Rollie Fingers	4.00
CF1	Carlton Fisk	4.00
CF2	Carlton Fisk	4.00
WF1	Whitey Ford	5.00
BG1	Bob Gibson	5.00
MI1	Monte Irvin	4.00
RJ1	Reggie Jackson	5.00
RJ2	Reggie Jackson	5.00
RJ3	Reggie Jackson	5.00
RJ4	Reggie Jackson	5.00
FJ1	Fergie Jenkins	4.00
FJ2	Fergie Jenkins	4.00
FJ3	Fergie Jenkins	4.00
AK1	Al Kaline	4.00
AK2	Al Kaline	4.00
GK1	George Kell	4.00
HK1	Harmon Killebrew	6.00
HK2	Harmon Killebrew	6.00
RK1	Ralph Kiner	4.00
JM1	Juan Marichal	4.00
BM1	Bill Mazeroski	4.00
WM1	Willie McCovey	5.00
PM1	Paul Molitor	5.00
PM2	Paul Molitor	5.00
MO1	Joe Morgan	4.00
MO2	Joe Morgan	4.00
EM1	Eddie Murray	4.00
EM2	Eddie Murray	4.00
EM3	Eddie Murray	4.00
SM1	Stan Musial	6.00
PN1	Phil Niekro	4.00
PN2	Phil Niekro	4.00
JP1	Jim Palmer	4.00
JP2	Jim Palmer	4.00
TP1	Tony Perez	4.00
TP2	Tony Perez	4.00
GP1	Gaylord Perry	4.00
GP2	Gaylord Perry	4.00
KP1	Kirby Puckett	5.00
RR1	Robin Roberts	4.00
BR1	Brooks Robinson	5.00
BR2	Brooks Robinson	5.00
FR1	Frank Robinson	5.00
FR2	Frank Robinson	5.00
NR1	Nolan Ryan	10.00
NR2	Nolan Ryan	10.00
NR3	Nolan Ryan	10.00
NR4	Nolan Ryan	10.00
SA1	Ryne Sandberg	6.00
SA2	Ryne Sandberg	6.00
SA3	Ryne Sandberg	6.00
MS1	Mike Schmidt	6.00
MS2	Mike Schmidt	6.00
MS3	Mike Schmidt	6.00
RS1	Red Schoendienst	4.00
TS1	Tom Seaver	5.00
TS2	Tom Seaver	5.00
OS1	Ozzie Smith	6.00
OS2	Ozzie Smith	6.00
SN1	Duke Snider	5.00
SN2	Duke Snider	5.00
DS1	Don Sutton	4.00
DS2	Don Sutton	4.00
DS3	Don Sutton	4.00
BW1	Billy Williams	4.00
DW1	Dave Winfield	4.00
CY1	Carl Yastrzemski	6.00
CY2	Carl Yastrzemski	6.00
RY1	Robin Yount	6.00
RY2	Robin Yount	6.00

Hall Worthy Autograph

NM/M

Production 25 Sets
Gold: No Pricing
Production Five Sets
Silver: No Pricing
Production 15 Sets
Rainbow: No Pricing
Production One Set
Material Gold: No Pricing
Production Five Sets
Material Silver: No Pricing
Production 15 Sets
Patch Gold: No Pricing
Production Five Sets
Patch Silver: No Pricing
Production 10 Sets

LA1	Luis Aparicio	20.00
EB1	Ernie Banks	50.00
BE1	Johnny Bench	40.00
BE2	Johnny Bench	40.00
YB1	Yogi Berra	60.00
WB1	Wade Boggs	35.00
WB2	Wade Boggs	35.00
WB3	Wade Boggs	35.00
GB1	George Brett	60.00
GB2	George Brett	60.00
GB3	George Brett	60.00
LB1	Lou Brock	35.00
LB2	Lou Brock	35.00
JB1	Jim Bunning	25.00
RC1	Rod Carew	30.00
RC2	Rod Carew	30.00
SC1	Steve Carlton	20.00
SC2	Steve Carlton	20.00
GC1	Gary Carter	25.00
GC2	Gary Carter	25.00
OC1	Orlando Cepeda	25.00
OC2	Orlando Cepeda	25.00
BD1	Bobby Doerr	15.00
DE1	Dennis Eckersley	20.00
DE2	Dennis Eckersley	20.00
DE3	Dennis Eckersley	20.00
DE4	Dennis Eckersley	20.00
BF1	Bob Feller	30.00
BF2	Bob Feller	30.00
RF1	Rollie Fingers	20.00
RF2	Rollie Fingers	20.00
CF1	Carlton Fisk	30.00
CF2	Carlton Fisk	30.00
WF1	Whitey Ford	50.00
BG1	Bob Gibson	35.00
MI1	Monte Irvin	25.00
RJ1	Reggie Jackson	40.00
RJ2	Reggie Jackson	40.00
RJ3	Reggie Jackson	40.00
RJ4	Reggie Jackson	40.00
FJ1	Fergie Jenkins	20.00
FJ2	Fergie Jenkins	20.00
FJ3	Fergie Jenkins	20.00
AK1	Al Kaline	40.00
AK2	Al Kaline	40.00
GK1	George Kell	20.00
HK1	Harmon Killebrew	40.00
HK2	Harmon Killebrew	40.00
RK1	Ralph Kiner	40.00
JM1	Juan Marichal	25.00
BM1	Bill Mazeroski	40.00
WM1	Willie McCovey	40.00
PM1	Paul Molitor	30.00
PM2	Paul Molitor	30.00
MO1	Joe Morgan	25.00
MO2	Joe Morgan	25.00
EM1	Eddie Murray	50.00
EM2	Eddie Murray	50.00
EM3	Eddie Murray	50.00
SM1	Stan Musial	60.00
PN1	Phil Niekro	20.00
PN2	Phil Niekro	20.00
JP1	Jim Palmer	20.00
JP2	Jim Palmer	20.00
TP1	Tony Perez	20.00
TP2	Tony Perez	20.00
GP1	Gaylord Perry	20.00
GP2	Gaylord Perry	20.00
KP1	Kirby Puckett	40.00
RR1	Robin Roberts	25.00
BR1	Brooks Robinson	30.00
BR2	Brooks Robinson	30.00
FR1	Frank Robinson	20.00
FR2	Frank Robinson	20.00
NR1	Nolan Ryan	90.00
NR2	Nolan Ryan	90.00
NR3	Nolan Ryan	90.00
NR4	Nolan Ryan	90.00
SA1	Ryne Sandberg	60.00
SA2	Ryne Sandberg	60.00
SA3	Ryne Sandberg	60.00
MS1	Mike Schmidt	50.00
MS2	Mike Schmidt	50.00
MS3	Mike Schmidt	50.00
RS1	Red Schoendienst	35.00
TS1	Tom Seaver	40.00
TS2	Tom Seaver	40.00
OS1	Ozzie Smith	40.00
OS2	Ozzie Smith	40.00
SN1	Duke Snider	40.00
SN2	Duke Snider	40.00
DS1	Don Sutton	20.00
DS2	Don Sutton	20.00
DS3	Don Sutton	20.00
BW1	Billy Williams	20.00
DW1	Dave Winfield	30.00
CY1	Carl Yastrzemski	50.00
CY2	Carl Yastrzemski	50.00
RY1	Robin Yount	40.00
RY2	Robin Yount	40.00

Signs of Cooperstown Duals

NM/M

Production 50 Sets
Gold: No Pricing
Production Five Sets
Silver: No Pricing
Production 15 Sets
Rainbow: No Pricing
Production One Set

AB	Ernie Banks, Luis Aparicio	6.00
AS	Luis Aparicio, Ozzie Smith	8.00
BC	Steve Carlton, Jim Bunning	4.00
BF	Frank Robinson, Brooks Robinson	5.00
BG	George Brett, Brooks Robinson	10.00
BM	Lou Brock, Stan Musial	8.00
BR	Jim Bunning, Robin Roberts	4.00
BS	Ernie Banks, Ryne Sandberg	10.00
CM	Orlando Cepeda, Willie McCovey	4.00
CS	Tom Seaver, Gary Carter	4.00
DB	Wade Boggs, Bobby Doerr	4.00
EF	Dennis Eckersley, Rollie Fingers	4.00
FB	Johnny Bench, Carlton Fisk	6.00
FC	Bob Feller, Steve Carlton	4.00
FP	Bob Feller, Gaylord Perry	4.00
GC	Bob Gibson, Steve Carlton	4.00
GF	Bob Gibson, Whitey Ford	5.00
IM	Monte Irvin, Willie McCovey	5.00
JJ	Joe Morgan, Johnny Bench	6.00
JM	Reggie Jackson, Willie McCovey	5.00
JW	Reggie Jackson, Dave Winfield	5.00
JY	Yogi Berra, Johnny Bench	6.00
KK	Al Kaline, George Kell	6.00
KP	Kirby Puckett, Harmon Killebrew	6.00
LO	Lou Brock, Ozzie Smith	8.00
MK	Bill Mazeroski, Ralph Kiner	75.00
MP	Joe Morgan, Tony Perez	4.00
MY	Robin Yount, Paul Molitor	6.00
NS	Steve Carlton, Nolan Ryan	10.00
PM	Gaylord Perry, Juan Marichal	4.00
PN	Gaylord Perry, Phil Niekro	4.00
PR	Rod Carew, Paul Molitor	5.00
RC	Rod Carew, Nolan Ryan	10.00
RP	Jim Palmer, Brooks Robinson	5.00
RS	Tom Seaver, Nolan Ryan	10.00
RW	Ryne Sandberg, Wade Boggs	10.00
SB	George Brett, Mike Schmidt	10.00
SC	Mike Schmidt, Steve Carlton	10.00
SK	Ralph Kiner, Duke Snider	5.00
SM	Ozzie Smith, Stan Musial	8.00
SP	Gaylord Perry, Don Sutton	4.00
SR	Mike Schmidt, Brooks Robinson	10.00
SS	Red Schoendienst, Ozzie Smith	8.00
SW	Billy Williams, Ryne Sandberg	10.00
WB	Billy Williams, Ernie Banks	6.00
WJ	Billy Williams, Fergie Jenkins	4.00
WS	Ozzie Smith, Dave Winfield	6.00
WY	Yogi Berra, Whitey Ford	6.00
YF	Carlton Fisk, Carl Yastrzemski	6.00
YJ	Reggie Jackson, Carl Yastrzemski	6.00

Signs of Cooperstown Duals Auto.

NM/M

Production 20 Sets
Gold: No Pricing
Production Five Sets
Silver: No Pricing
Production 10 Sets
Rainbow: No Pricing
Production One Set

AB	Ernie Banks, Luis Aparicio	80.00
AS	Luis Aparicio, Ozzie Smith	60.00
BC	Steve Carlton, Jim Bunning	35.00
BF	Frank Robinson, Brooks Robinson	60.00
BG	George Brett, Brooks Robinson	90.00
BM	Lou Brock, Stan Musial	100.00
BR	Jim Bunning, Robin Roberts	60.00
BS	Ernie Banks, Ryne Sandberg	120.00
CM	Orlando Cepeda, Willie McCovey	50.00
CS	Tom Seaver, Gary Carter	80.00
DB	Wade Boggs, Bobby Doerr	50.00
EF	Dennis Eckersley, Rollie Fingers	35.00
FB	Johnny Bench, Carlton Fisk	75.00
FC	Bob Feller, Steve Carlton	40.00
FP	Bob Feller, Gaylord Perry	40.00
GC	Bob Gibson, Steve Carlton	60.00
GF	Bob Gibson, Whitey Ford	75.00
IM	Monte Irvin, Willie McCovey	60.00
JJ	Joe Morgan, Johnny Bench	80.00
JM	Reggie Jackson, Willie McCovey	100.00
JW	Reggie Jackson, Dave Winfield	80.00
JY	Yogi Berra, Johnny Bench	150.00
KK	Al Kaline, George Kell	85.00
KP	Kirby Puckett, Harmon Killebrew	80.00
LO	Lou Brock, Ozzie Smith	65.00
MK	Bill Mazeroski, Ralph Kiner	75.00
MP	Joe Morgan, Tony Perez	50.00
MY	Robin Yount, Paul Molitor	85.00
NS	Steve Carlton, Nolan Ryan	150.00
PM	Gaylord Perry, Juan Marichal	40.00
PN	Gaylord Perry, Phil Niekro	40.00
PR	Rod Carew, Paul Molitor	50.00
RC	Rod Carew, Nolan Ryan	150.00
RP	Jim Palmer, Brooks Robinson	50.00
RS	Tom Seaver, Nolan Ryan	180.00
RW	Ryne Sandberg, Wade Boggs	100.00
SB	George Brett, Mike Schmidt	140.00
SC	Mike Schmidt, Steve Carlton	85.00
SK	Ralph Kiner, Duke Snider	65.00
SM	Ozzie Smith, Stan Musial	120.00
SP	Gaylord Perry, Don Sutton	40.00
SR	Mike Schmidt, Brooks Robinson	75.00
SS	Red Schoendienst, Ozzie Smith	65.00
SW	Billy Williams, Ryne Sandberg	90.00
WB	Billy Williams, Ernie Banks	90.00
WJ	Billy Williams, Fergie Jenkins	50.00
WS	Ozzie Smith, Dave Winfield	75.00
WY	Yogi Berra, Whitey Ford	100.00
YF	Carlton Fisk, Carl Yastrzemski	100.00
YJ	Reggie Jackson, Carl Yastrzemski	100.00

Signs of Cooperstown Triples

NM/M

Production 50 Sets
Gold: No Pricing
Production Five Sets
Silver: No Pricing
Production 15 Sets
Rainbow: No Pricing
Production One Set

ASY	Robin Yount, Luis Aparicio, Ozzie Smith	8.00
BFJ	Jim Palmer, Frank Robinson, Brooks Robinson	5.00
BSB	George Brett, Mike Schmidt, Wade Boggs	10.00
BSY	Ernie Banks, Robin Yount, Ozzie Smith	8.00
CMI	Monte Irvin, Orlando Cepeda, Willie McCovey	5.00
DFY	Carlton Fisk, Carl Yastrzemski, Bobby Doerr	8.00
DYB	Carl Yastrzemski, Wade Boggs, Bobby Doerr	8.00
FPE	Bob Feller, Dennis Eckersley, Gaylord Perry	4.00
FRC	Bob Feller, Steve Carlton, Nolan Ryan	10.00
FSE	Dennis Eckersley, Rollie Fingers, Don Sutton	4.00
GCE	Bob Gibson, Dennis Eckersley, Steve Carlton	4.00
GSM	Bob Gibson, Stan Musial, Ozzie Smith	8.00
JFB	Yogi Berra, Reggie Jackson, Whitey Ford	5.00
JPR	Nolan Ryan, Gaylord Perry, Fergie Jenkins	5.00
KKB	Al Kaline, George Kell, Jim Bunning	5.00
KPC	Rod Carew, Kirby Puckett, Harmon Killebrew	6.00
KSR	Ralph Kiner, Duke Snider, Frank Robinson	5.00
KWR	Al Kaline, Frank Robinson, Dave Winfield	6.00
MBP	Johnny Bench, Tony Perez, Joe Morgan	6.00
MCM	Orlando Cepeda, Willie McCovey, Juan Marichal	5.00
MMS	Joe Morgan, Red Schoendienst, Bill Mazeroski	4.00
MRJ	Eddie Murray, Reggie Jackson, Frank Robinson	5.00
MSC	Rod Carew, Joe Morgan, Ryne Sandberg	6.00
MYF	Robin Yount, Paul Molitor, Rollie Fingers	6.00
PMC	Rod Carew, Kirby Puckett, Paul Molitor	6.00
RAP	Jim Palmer, Luis Aparicio, Brooks Robinson	5.00
RBC	Steve Carlton, Jim Bunning, Robin Roberts	5.00
RBS	George Brett, Mike Schmidt, Brooks Robinson	10.00
RSR	Robin Roberts, Don Sutton, Nolan Ryan	10.00
SRC	Mike Schmidt, Steve Carlton, Robin Roberts	8.00
WBI	Billy Williams, Monte Irvin, Lou Brock	4.00
WBJ	Billy Williams, Ernie Banks, Fergie Jenkins	6.00
WJB	Reggie Jackson, Wade Boggs, Dave Winfield	6.00
WSP	Dave Winfield, Ozzie Smith, Gaylord Perry	6.00
YKM	Ralph Kiner, Carl Yastrzemski, Stan Musial	8.00

Signs of Cooperstown Triple Auto.

NM/M

Production 20 Sets 75.00
Gold: No Pricing
Production Five Sets
Silver: No Pricing
Production 10 Sets
Rainbow: No Pricing
Production One Set

ASY	Robin Yount, Luis Aparicio, Ozzie Smith	140.00
BFJ	Jim Palmer, Frank Robinson, Brooks Robinson	80.00
BSB	George Brett, Mike Schmidt, Wade Boggs	185.00
BSY	Ernie Banks, Robin Yount, Ozzie Smith	150.00
CMI	Monte Irvin, Orlando Cepeda, Willie McCovey	75.00
DFY	Carlton Fisk, Carl Yastrzemski, Bobby Doerr	125.00
DYB	Carl Yastrzemski, Wade Boggs, Bobby Doerr	125.00
FRC	Bob Feller, Steve Carlton, Nolan Ryan	200.00
GSM	Bob Gibson, Ozzie Smith, Stan Musial	185.00
JFB	Yogi Berra, Reggie Jackson, Whitey Ford	185.00
JPR	Nolan Ryan, Gaylord Perry, Fergie Jenkins	150.00
KPC	Rod Carew, Kirby Puckett, Harmon Killebrew	120.00
KSR	Ralph Kiner, Duke Snider, Frank Robinson	120.00
MBP	Joe Morgan, Tony Perez, Johnny Bench	160.00
MCM	Orlando Cepeda, Willie McCovey, Juan Marichal	100.00
MSC	Joe Morgan, Rod Carew, Ryne Sandberg	125.00
MYF	Robin Yount, Paul Molitor, Rollie Fingers	125.00
PMC	Rod Carew, Kirby Puckett, Paul Molitor	100.00
RAP	Jim Palmer, Luis Aparicio, Brooks Robinson	80.00
RBC	Steve Carlton, Jim Bunning, Robin Roberts	85.00
RBS	George Brett, Mike Schmidt, Brooks Robinson	200.00
SRC	Mike Schmidt, Steve Carlton, Robin Roberts	150.00
WJB	Reggie Jackson, Wade Boggs, Dave Winfield	120.00
WSP	Dave Winfield, Ozzie Smith, Gaylord Perry	120.00
YKM	Ralph Kiner, Carl Yastrzemski, Stan Musial	140.00

Signs of Cooperstown Quads

NM/M

Production 50 Sets
Gold: No Pricing
Production Five Sets
Silver: No Pricing
Production 15 Sets
Rainbow: No Pricing
Production One Set

BMYC	George Brett, Rod Carew, Robin Yount, Paul Molitor	10.00
BSAY	Ernie Banks, Robin Yount, Luis Aparicio, Ozzie Smith	8.00
FCBB	Yogi Berra, Johnny Bench, Carlton Fisk, Gary Carter	6.00
FGRC	Bob Feller, Bob Gibson, Steve Carlton, Nolan Ryan	10.00
KCPM	Tony Perez, Orlando Cepeda, Harmon Killebrew, Willie McCovey	6.00
KYBM	Al Kaline, Lou Brock, Carl Yastrzemski, Stan Musial	8.00
MBKM	Ernie Banks, Eddie Murray, Harmon Killebrew, Willie McCovey	8.00
MDMC	Bill Mazeroski, Rod Carew, Joe Morgan, Bobby Doerr	8.00
MRKS	Eddie Murray, Mike Schmidt, Frank Robinson, Harmon Killebrew	10.00
RBKS	George Brett, Mike Schmidt, Brooks Robinson, George Kell	10.00
SPNS	Tom Seaver, Phil Niekro, Don Sutton, Gaylord Perry	6.00
SPSF	Tom Seaver, Jim Palmer, Whitey Ford, Don Sutton	6.00
SRCS	Tom Seaver, Steve Carlton, Don Sutton, Nolan Ryan	10.00
WYKM	Billy Williams, Ralph Kiner, Carl Yastrzemski, Stan Musial	8.00
YWMM	Eddie Murray, Carl Yastrzemski, Stan Musial, Dave Winfield	8.00

Signs of Cooperstown Quads Auto.

No Pricing
Production 10 Sets
Gold: No Pricing
Production Five Sets
Rainbow: No Pricing
Production One Set

2005 UD Mini Jersey Collection

NM/M

Complete Set (100): 15.00
Common Player: .15
Pack (3 + Mini Jersey): 6.00
Box (18): 90.00

1	Garret Anderson	.25
2	Vladimir Guerrero	.75
3	Luis Gonzalez	.25
4	Shawn Green	.25
5	Troy Glaus	.25
6	Andruw Jones	.50
7	Chipper Jones	.75
8	John Smoltz	.40
9	Tim Hudson	.40
10	Miguel Tejada	.40
11	Sammy Sosa	1.00

DAVID ORTIZ

#	Player	
12	Curt Schilling	.75
13	David Ortiz	.75
14	Johnny Damon	.75
15	Manny Ramirez	.75
16	Greg Maddux	1.00
17	Kerry Wood	.50
18	Mark Prior	.75
19	Nomar Garciaparra	1.00
20	Frank Thomas	.50
21	Adam Dunn	.25
22	Ken Griffey Jr.	1.50
23	Travis Hafner	.25
24	Victor Martinez	.15
25	Todd Helton	.50
26	Ivan Rodriguez	.50
27	Magglio Ordonez	.15
28	Carlos Delgado	.40
29	Miguel Cabrera	.75
30	Jeff Bagwell	.50
31	Lance Berkman	.25
32	Roger Clemens	2.00
33	Roy Oswalt	.25
34	Mike Sweeney	.15
35	Eric Gagne	.15
36	J.D. Drew	.15
37	Ben Sheets	.40
38	Johan Santana	.50
39	Torii Hunter	.15
40	Carlos Beltran	.50
41	Mike Piazza	1.00
42	Pedro Martinez	.75
43	Alex Rodriguez	1.50
44	Derek Jeter	2.00
45	Hideki Matsui	1.50
46	Mike Mussina	.40
47	Randy Johnson	.75
48	Bobby Crosby	.40
49	Eric Chavez	.40
50	Bobby Abreu	.40
51	Jim Thome	.50
52	Jason Bay	.15
53	Oliver Perez	.15
54	Jake Peavy	.40
55	Khalil Greene	.40
56	Jason Schmidt	.15
57	Moises Alou	.40
58	Adrian Beltre	.40
59	Ichiro Suzuki	1.50
60	Albert Pujols	2.00
61	Jim Edmonds	.40
62	Mark Mulder	.40
63	Scott Rolen	.75
64	Aubrey Huff	.15
65	Alfonso Soriano	.50
66	Hank Blalock	.40
67	Mark Teixeira	.50
68	Roy Halladay	.40
69	Jose Vidro	.15
70	Livan Hernandez	.15
71	Atlanta Braves	.15
72	Chicago Cubs	.15
73	Chicago White Sox	.15
74	Cincinnati Reds	.15
75	Cleveland Indians	.15
76	Houston Astros	.15
77	L.A. Angels of Anaheim	.15
78	Los Angeles Dodgers	.15
79	New York Yankees	.15
80	Oakland Athletics	.15
81	Philadelphia Phillies	.15
82	Pittsburgh Pirates	.15
83	San Diego Padres	.15
84	San Francisco Giants	.15
85	Texas Rangers	.15
86	Cal Ripken Jr.	2.00
87	Derek Jeter	2.00
88	Hank Blalock	.40
89	Hideo Nomo	.40
90	Joe DiMaggio	1.00
91	Joe Morgan	.50
92	Ken Griffey Jr.	1.50
93	Larry Doby	.50
94	Pedro J. Martinez	.75
95	Randy Johnson	.75
96	Rick Ferrell	.15
97	Roger Clemens	2.00
98	Stan Musial	1.00
99	Ted Williams	1.50
100	Torii Hunter	.15

Mini Jerseys
NM/M
1	Vladimir Guerrero	5.00
2	Chipper Jones	5.00
3	Curt Schilling	5.00
4	Johnny Damon	5.00
5	Manny Ramirez	5.00
6	Kerry Wood	5.00
7	Nomar Garciaparra	5.00
8	Ken Griffey Jr.	5.00
9	Miguel Cabrera	5.00
10	Roger Clemens	10.00
11	Eric Gagne	5.00
12	Johan Santana	5.00
13	Carlos Beltran	5.00
14	Mike Piazza	5.00
15	Pedro Martinez	5.00
16	Alex Rodriguez	5.00
17	Derek Jeter	15.00
18	Hideki Matsui	8.00
19	Randy Johnson	5.00
20	Jim Thome	5.00
21	Ichiro Suzuki	8.00
22	Albert Pujols	5.00

Mini Jersey Autograph
NM/M
Inserted 1:480
1	Ken Griffey Jr.	150.00
2	David Wright	50.00
5	Adrian Beltre	50.00

Replica Flannel Jerseys
NM/M
Inserted 1:18
1	Ted Williams	20.00
2	Jackie Robinson	15.00
3	Satchel Paige	15.00
4	Ty Cobb	15.00
5	Babe Ruth	30.00
6	Joe DiMaggio	20.00
7	Lou Gehrig	25.00
8	Mickey Mantle	30.00
9	Roberto Clemente	20.00

2005 Upper Deck MVP
NM/M
Complete Set (90): 20.00
Common Player: .10
Pack (6): 1.50
Box (24): 30.00
1	Adam Dunn	.40
2	Adrian Beltre	.40
3	Albert Pujols	1.50
4	Alex Rodriguez	1.50
5	Alfonso Soriano	.50
6	Andruw Jones	.40
7	Aubrey Huff	.10
8	Barry Zito	.25
9	Ben Sheets	.25
10	Bobby Abreu	.25
11	Bobby Crosby	.25
12	Bret Boone	.10
13	Brian Giles	.10
14	Carlos Beltran	.40
15	Carlos Delgado	.25
16	Carlos Lee	.25
17	Chipper Jones	.40
18	Craig Biggio	.25
19	Curt Schilling	.40
20	Dallas McPherson	.10
21	David Ortiz	.50
22	David Wright	.50
23	Derek Jeter	1.50
24	Derek Lowe	.10
25	Eric Chavez	.25
26	Eric Gagne	.25
27	Frank Thomas	.40
28	Garret Anderson	.25
29	Gary Sheffield	.40
30	Greg Maddux	1.00
31	Hank Blalock	.25
32	Hideki Matsui	1.00
33	Ichiro Suzuki	1.00
34	Ivan Rodriguez	.40
35	J.D. Drew	.10
36	Jake Peavy	.25
37	Jason Bay	.10
38	Jason Giambi	.25
39	Jason Schmidt	.25
40	Jeff Bagwell	.40
41	Jeff Kent	.25
42	Jim Edmonds	.25
43	Jim Thome	.40
44	Joe Mauer	.25
45	Johan Santana	.25
46	John Smoltz	.25
47	Johnny Damon	.50
48	Jorge Posada	.25
49	Jose Vidro	.10
50	Josh Beckett	.25
51	Kazuo Matsui	.10
52	Ken Griffey Jr.	1.00
53	Kerry Wood	.25
54	Khalil Greene	.25
55	Lance Berkman	.25
56	Livan Hernandez	.10
57	Luis Gonzalez	.10
58	Magglio Ordonez	.10
59	Manny Ramirez	.25
60	Mark Mulder	.25
61	Mark Prior	.50
62	Mark Teixeira	.25
63	Miguel Cabrera	.50
64	Miguel Tejada	.25
65	Mike Mussina	.25
66	Mike Piazza	.50
67	Mike Sweeney	.10
68	Moises Alou	.25
69	Nomar Garciaparra	.75
70	Oliver Perez	.10
71	Paul Konerko	.25
72	Pedro Martinez	.50
73	Rafael Palmeiro	.50
74	Randy Johnson	.50
75	Richie Sexson	.25
76	Roger Clemens	1.50
77	Roy Halladay	.25
78	Roy Oswalt	.25
79	Sammy Sosa	.75
80	Scott Rolen	.50
81	Shawn Green	.10
82	Steve Finley	.10
83	Tim Hudson	.25
84	Todd Helton	.40
85	Tom Glavine	.25
86	Torii Hunter	.25
87	Travis Hafner	.10
88	Troy Glaus	.25
89	Victor Martinez	.25
90	Vladimir Guerrero	.50

All-Star Signatures
No Pricing
Inserted 1:480

Batter Up!
NM/M
Common Player: .25
Inserted 1:1
BU-1	Al Kaline	.50
BU-2	Bill Mazeroski	.25
BU-3	Billy Williams	.25
BU-4	Bob Feller	.50
BU-5	Bob Gibson	.25
BU-6	Bob Lemon	.25
BU-7	Brooks Robinson	.50
BU-8	Carlton Fisk	.25
BU-9	Jim "Catfish" Hunter	.25
BU-10	Dennis Eckersley	.25
BU-11	Eddie Mathews	.75
BU-12	Eddie Murray	.50
BU-13	Fergie Jenkins	.25
BU-14	Gaylord Perry	.25
BU-15	Harmon Killebrew	.75
BU-16	Jim Bunning	.25
BU-17	Jim Palmer	.50
BU-18	Joe DiMaggio	1.50
BU-19	Joe Morgan	.25
BU-20	Johnny Bench	.75
BU-21	Juan Marichal	.50
BU-22	Lou Brock	.50
BU-23	Luis Aparicio	.25
BU-24	Mike Schmidt	1.50
BU-25	Monte Irvin	.50
BU-26	Nolan Ryan	2.00
BU-27	Orlando Cepeda	.25
BU-28	Ozzie Smith	.25
BU-29	Pee Wee Reese	.25
BU-30	Phil Niekro	.25
BU-31	Phil Rizzuto	.50
BU-32	Ralph Kiner	.25
BU-33	Richie Ashburn	.25
BU-34	Robin Roberts	.25
BU-35	Robin Yount	.75
BU-36	Rollie Fingers	.25
BU-37	Tom Seaver	.75
BU-38	Tony Perez	.25
BU-39	Warren Spahn	.75
BU-40	Willie McCovey	.50
BU-41	Willie Stargell	.50
BU-42	Yogi Berra	.75

Jersey
NM/M
Common Jersey: 4.00
Inserted 1:24
CB	Carlos Beltran	6.00
AB	Adrian Beltre	4.00
HB	Hank Blalock	4.00
SB	Sean Burroughs	4.00
MC	Miguel Cabrera	6.00
EC	Eric Chavez	4.00
EG	Eric Gagne	4.00
KG	Ken Griffey Jr.	10.00
VG	Vladimir Guerrero	6.00
TH	Todd Helton	6.00
DJ	Derek Jeter	15.00
RJ	Randy Johnson	6.00
CJ	Chipper Jones	6.00
GM	Greg Maddux	8.00
PI	Mike Piazza	8.00
MP	Mark Prior	6.00
AP	Albert Pujols	15.00
MR	Manny Ramirez	6.00
IR	Ivan Rodriguez	6.00
SR	Scott Rolen	6.00
JS	Johan Santana	6.00
CS	Curt Schilling	6.00
AS	Alfonso Soriano	6.00
SS	Sammy Sosa	8.00
MT	Mark Teixeira	6.00
TE	Miguel Tejada	6.00
JT	Jim Thome	6.00
KW	Kerry Wood	4.00

2005 UD Origins Promos

UD PROMO — DAVID DeJESUS

Each of the cards in UD Origins was issued in a foil-overprinted version with "UD PROMO" across the front. Cards were inserted into specially marked card shop and newsstand issues of Tuff Stuff magazine.
NM/M
Common Player: .50
Stars: 1.5X

2005 UD Origins

BOB GIBSON

NM/M
Complete Set (200): ...
Common Player: .50
Tin (20): 50.00
1	Jim Edmonds	.75
2	Jason Schmidt	.75
3	J.D. Drew	.75
4	Luis Gonzalez	.50
5	Nomar Garciaparra	2.00
6	Jake Peavy	.50
7	Rafael Furcal	.50
8	Craig Biggio	.75
9	Ken Griffey Jr.	3.00
10	Mike Piazza	2.00
11	Jose Vidro	.50
12	Ivan Rodriguez	.50
13	Carl Crawford	.50
14	Roger Clemens	4.00
15	Kerry Wood	1.00
16	Vernon Wells	.50
17	Carlos Guillen	.50
18	Tim Hudson	.75
19	Carl Pavano	.50
20	Carlos Beltran	1.00
21	Pedro Martinez	1.50
22	Hideki Matsui	3.00
23	Frank Thomas	1.00
24	Curt Schilling	1.50
25	Manny Ramirez	1.50
26	Alex Rodriguez	4.00
27	Aubrey Huff	.50
28	David Ortiz	1.50
29	Mark Prior	1.00
30	Albert Pujols	4.00
31	Miguel Cabrera	1.50
32	Brad Penny	.50
33	Carlos Delgado	.75
34	Aramis Ramirez	1.00
35	Josh Beckett	.75
36	Rafael Palmeiro	1.00
37	Bret Boone	.50
38	Lance Berkman	.75
39	Carlos Zambrano	.75
40	Adam Dunn	1.00
41	Livan Hernandez	.50
42	Mike Mussina	.75
43	Ben Sheets	.50
44	Derek Jeter	4.00
45	Kazuo Matsui	.50
46	Bobby Abreu	.75
47	Jeff Bagwell	1.00
48	Travis Hafner	.50
49	Torii Hunter	.50
50	Kevin Brown	.50
51	Alfonso Soriano	1.50
52	Jim Thome	1.00
53	John Smoltz	.75
54	Mike Sweeney	.50
55	Andy Pettitte	.75
56	Chipper Jones	1.50
57	Randy Johnson	1.50
58	Steve Finley	.50
59	Larry Walker	.75
60	Troy Glaus	.75
61	Greg Maddux	2.50
62	Shawn Green	.50
63	Roy Halladay	.75
64	Jeff Kent	.50
65	Scott Podsednik	.50
66	Miguel Tejada	1.00
67	Lyle Overbay	.50
68	Bernie Williams	.75
69	Todd Helton	1.00
70	Melvin Mora	.50
71	Magglio Ordonez	.50
72	Carlos Lee	.75
73	Roy Oswalt	.75
74	Victor Martinez	.50
75	Scott Rolen	1.50
76	Eric Chavez	.50
77	Paul Konerko	.50
78	Jose Reyes	.50
79	Barry Larkin	.75
80	Johnny Damon	1.00
81	Eric Gagne	.75
82	Andruw Jones	1.00
83	Gary Sheffield	1.00
84	Richie Sexson	.75
85	Sammy Sosa	2.50
86	Mark Teixeira	1.00
87	Vladimir Guerrero	1.50
88	Michael Young	.50
89	Johan Santana	1.00
90	Adrian Beltre	.75
91	Tom Glavine	.75
92	Hank Blalock	.75
93	Preston Wilson	.50
94	Jason Kendall	.50
95	Mike Lowell	.50
96	Craig Wilson	.50
97	Ichiro Suzuki	3.00
98	Mark Mulder	.75
99	Garret Anderson	.50
100	Brian Giles	.50
101	Robin Yount	3.00
102	Ernie Banks	3.00
103	Mike Schmidt	5.00
104	Enos Slaughter	1.00
105	Red Schoendienst	1.00
106	Hoyt Wilhelm	1.00
107	Lou Brock	2.00
108	Rollie Fingers	1.00
109	Gaylord Perry	1.00
110	Bobby Doerr	1.00
111	Larry Doby	1.00
112	Al Lopez	1.00
113	Joe Morgan	1.50
114	Luis Aparicio	1.00
115	Willie McCovey	2.00
116	Bob Lemon	1.00
117	Early Wynn	1.00
118	Bob Feller	2.00
119	Cal Ripken Jr.	8.00
120	George Kell	1.00
121	Juan Marichal	1.50
122	Monte Irvin	1.50
123	Harmon Killebrew	3.00
124	Lou Boudreau	1.00
125	Mickey Mantle	8.00
126	Richie Ashburn	1.00
127	Pee Wee Reese	1.50
128	Whitey Ford	2.00
129	Tom Seaver	2.00
130	Phil Rizzuto	2.00
131	Yogi Berra	3.00
132	Warren Spahn	2.00
133	Billy Williams	1.50
134	Jim Bunning	1.00
135	Ralph Kiner	1.00
136	Ted Williams	6.00
137	Rick Ferrell	1.00
138	Robin Roberts	1.00
139	Brooks Robinson	3.00
140	Hal Newhouser	1.00
141	Jim "Catfish" Hunter	1.00
142	Phil Niekro	1.00
143	Fergie Jenkins	1.00
144	Al Kaline	3.00
145	Stan Musial	4.00
146	Joe DiMaggio	6.00
147	Willie Stargell	2.00
148	Nolan Ryan	6.00
149	Babe Ruth	6.00
150	Bob Gibson	2.00
151	David DeJesus	.50
152	Chris Burke	.50
153	Chad Cordero	.50
154	Kevin Youkilis	.50
155	Bucky Jacobsen	.50
156	B.J. Upton	.50
157	Aaron Rowand	.50
158	Jose Capellan	.50
159	David Wright	2.00
160	Jason Bay	.50
161	Edwin Jackson	.50
162	Scott Kazmir	.50
163	J.D. Closser	.50
164	Chase Utley	1.00
165	Nick Swisher	.50
166	Casey Kotchman	.50
167	Bobby Crosby	.50
168	Zack Greinke	.50
169	Gavin Floyd	.50
170	Jeff Francis	.50
171	Dallas McPherson	.50
172	Gabe Gross	.50
173	Brandon Claussen	.50
174	Wily Mo Pena	.50
175	Robb Quinlan	.50
176	Oliver Perez	.50
177	Guillermo Quiroz	.50
178	Ryan Howard	1.00
179	Gerald Laird	.50
180	Jayson Werth	.50
181	Bobby Madritsch	.50
182	Laynce Nix	.50
183	Eddy Rodriguez	.50
184	Rickie Weeks	1.00
185	Scott Proctor	.50
186	Adam LaRoche	.50
187	Yhency Brazoban	.50
188	Adrian Gonzalez	.50
189	Jason Lane	.50
190	Ryan Wagner	.50
191	Roman Colon	.50
192	Alexis Rios	.50
193	Joe Mauer	1.00
194	Garrett Atkins	.50
195	Daniel Cabrera	.50
196	Khalil Greene	2.00
197	Joe Blanton	.50
198	Jason Dubois	.50
199	Angel Guzman	.50
200	Jesse Crain	.50

Black
No Pricing
Production One Set

Blue
Stars (1-200): 2-4X
Production 50 Sets

Gold
No Pricing
Production 20 Sets

Red
Stars (1-200): 2-3X
Production 99 Sets

Origins Materials Jersey

MIGUEL CABRERA OF

NM/M
Inserted 2:Tin
Old Judge: 1X
JB	Jeff Bagwell	8.00
CB	Carlos Beltran	5.00
AB	Adrian Beltre	5.00
LB	Lance Berkman	5.00
HB	Hank Blalock	5.00
MC	Miguel Cabrera	8.00
EC	Eric Chavez	5.00
JD	J.D. Drew	5.00
GL	Troy Glaus	5.00
KG	Ken Griffey Jr.	10.00
VG	Vladimir Guerrero	8.00
TG	Tony Gwynn/SP	10.00
HE	Todd Helton	5.00
TH	Tim Hudson	5.00
HU	Torii Hunter	5.00
DJ	Derek Jeter	15.00
RJ	Randy Johnson	8.00
AJ	Andruw Jones	5.00
CJ	Chipper Jones	8.00
GM	Greg Maddux	10.00
HM	Hideki Matsui	8.00
KM	Hideki Matsui	5.00
DO	David Ortiz	8.00
PI	Mike Piazza	8.00
MP	Mark Prior	8.00
AP	Albert Pujols	15.00
MR	Manny Ramirez	8.00
CR	Cal Ripken Jr./SP	25.00
IR	Ivan Rodriguez	8.00
SR	Scott Rolen	5.00
NR	Nolan Ryan/SP	30.00
CS	Curt Schilling	5.00
BS	Ben Sheets	5.00
GS	Gary Sheffield	5.00
AS	Alfonso Soriano	5.00
SS	Sammy Sosa	8.00
IS	Ichiro Suzuki	10.00
MT	Mark Teixeira	8.00
TE	Miguel Tejada	8.00
FT	Frank Thomas	8.00
JT	Jim Thome	8.00
KW	Kerry Wood	8.00

Origins Nostalgic Signs
NM/M
One sign per tin.
CB	Carlos Beltran	8.00
AB	Adrian Beltre	5.00
HB	Hank Blalock	5.00
MC	Miguel Cabrera	8.00
EC	Eric Chavez	5.00
RC	Roger Clemens	15.00
TC	Ty Cobb	20.00
JD	Joe DiMaggio	20.00
LG	Lou Gehrig	15.00
KG	Ken Griffey Jr.	12.00
VG	Vladimir Guerrero	8.00
TH	Todd Helton	5.00
DJ	Derek Jeter	15.00
RJ	Randy Johnson	8.00
WJ	Walter Johnson	15.00
CJ	Chipper Jones	8.00
PM	Pedro Martinez	8.00
HM	Hideki Matsui	20.00
DO	David Ortiz	8.00
SP	Satchel Paige	12.00
MP	Mike Piazza	10.00
MPR	Mark Prior	8.00
AP	Albert Pujols	20.00
MR	Manny Ramirez	8.00
CR	Cal Ripken Jr.	25.00
JR	Jackie Robinson	12.00
AR	Alex Rodriguez	12.00
IR	Ivan Rodriguez	8.00
SR	Scott Rolen	8.00
BR	Babe Ruth	20.00

NR	Nolan Ryan	20.00
JS	Johan Santana	8.00
CS	Curt Schilling	10.00
AS	Alfonso Soriano	8.00
SS	Sammy Sosa	10.00
IS	Ichiro Suzuki	12.00
MT	Miguel Tejada	8.00
FT	Frank Thomas	8.00
JT	Jim Thome	8.00
HW	Honus Wagner	10.00
TW	Ted Williams	25.00

Origins Old Judge

		NM/M
Common Player:		.50
Blue:		2-3X
Red:		1-2X
Gold:		No Pricing
1	Jake Peavy	1.00
2	Derek Jeter	5.00
3	Adrian Beltre	1.00
4	Hank Blalock	1.00
5	Preston Wilson	.50
6	Randy Johnson	2.00
7	Pedro Martinez	2.00
8	Michael Young	1.00
9	Steve Finley	.50
10	Shawn Green	.75
11	Carlos Beltran	1.50
12	Bernie Williams	.50
13	Brian Giles	.50
14	Kevin Brown	.50
15	Barry Larkin	1.00
16	Troy Glaus	.50
17	Bret Boone	.50
18	Jason Kendall	.50
19	Johnny Damon	1.50
20	Josh Beckett	1.00
21	Carl Pavano	.50
22	Chipper Jones	2.00
23	Ivan Rodriguez	1.50
24	Kerry Wood	1.50
25	Ken Griffey Jr.	3.00
26	Greg Maddux	3.00
27	Kazuo Matsui	.50
28	Albert Pujols	4.00
29	Victor Martinez	.50
30	Johan Santana	1.50
31	Bobby Abreu	.75
32	Paul Konerko	.75
33	Gary Sheffield	.50
34	Jose Vidro	.50
35	Alex Rodriguez	4.00
36	Alfonso Soriano	1.50
37	Mark Teixeira	1.50
38	Nomar Garciaparra	2.50
39	Sammy Sosa	3.00
40	Garret Anderson	1.00
41	Eric Chavez	1.00
42	Magglio Ordonez	.50
43	Larry Walker	1.00
44	Brad Penny	.50
45	Jeff Bagwell	1.50
46	Craig Biggio	.75
47	Torii Hunter	.75
48	Mike Lowell	.50
49	Ben Sheets	1.00
50	Miguel Tejada	1.50
51	Jim Edmonds	1.00
52	Mark Mulder	1.00
53	Curt Schilling	1.50
54	Roger Clemens	5.00
55	Jason Schmidt	.50
56	Rafael Furcal	.50
57	Scott Rolen	2.00
58	Carlos Zambrano	.75
59	Mike Sweeney	.50
60	Vladimir Guerrero	2.00
61	Miguel Cabrera	2.00
62	Lance Berkman	.50
63	Lyle Overbay	.50
64	Livan Hernandez	.50
65	Aramis Ramirez	1.00
66	Ichiro Suzuki	4.00
67	Roy Oswalt	.50
68	Carl Crawford	.50
69	Craig Wilson	.50
70	Carlos Lee	.75
71	J.D. Drew	.50
72	Rafael Palmeiro	1.50
73	Jeff Kent	.50
74	Adam Dunn	1.50
75	Andy Pettitte	1.00
76	Luis Gonzalez	.50
77	Frank Thomas	1.50
78	John Smoltz	1.00
79	Hideki Matsui	3.00
80	Tom Glavine	.50
81	Jose Reyes	1.50
82	Jim Thome	1.50
83	Mark Prior	2.00
84	Roy Halladay	.75
85	Carlos Delgado	1.00
86	Melvin Mora	.50
87	David Ortiz	2.00
88	Travis Hafner	.50
89	Carlos Guillen	.50
90	Tim Hudson	.50
91	Vernon Wells	.50
92	Andruw Jones	1.50
93	Mike Mussina	1.00
94	Mike Piazza	3.00
95	Richie Sexson	.50
96	Aubrey Huff	.50
97	Scott Podsednik	.50
98	Eric Gagne	.50
99	Manny Ramirez	2.00
100	Todd Helton	1.50
101	Joe Morgan	1.00
102	Billy Williams	1.00
103	Pee Wee Reese	1.00
104	Lou Boudreau	1.00
105	Richie Ashburn	1.00
106	Jim Bunning	1.00
107	Hal Newhouser	1.00
108	Rick Ferrell	1.00
109	Ted Williams	5.00
110	Ralph Kiner	1.00
111	Warren Spahn	2.50
112	George Kell	.50
113	Willie Stargell	2.00
114	Jim "Catfish" Hunter	.50
115	Tom Seaver	2.00
116	Cal Ripken Jr.	8.00
117	Al Lopez	.50
118	Ernie Banks	3.00
119	Lou Brock	2.00
120	Robin Yount	3.00
121	Nolan Ryan	6.00
122	Larry Doby	1.00
123	Al Kaline	2.00
124	Willie McCovey	2.00
125	Stan Musial	3.00
126	Phil Niekro	1.00
127	Babe Ruth	6.00
128	Rollie Fingers	1.00
129	Juan Marichal	1.00
130	Early Wynn	1.00
131	Luis Aparicio	1.00
132	Brooks Robinson	3.00
133	Mike Schmidt	5.00
134	Gaylord Perry	1.00
135	Bob Lemon	1.00
136	Monte Irvin	1.50
137	Mickey Mantle	8.00
138	Phil Rizzuto	1.50
139	Robin Roberts	1.50
140	Bobby Doerr	1.00
141	Bob Gibson	2.00
142	Enos Slaughter	1.00
143	Yogi Berra	3.00
144	Whitey Ford	2.00
145	Red Schoendienst	1.00
146	Joe DiMaggio	5.00
147	Harmon Killebrew	2.00
148	Hoyt Wilhelm	1.00
149	Fergie Jenkins	1.00
150	Bob Feller	1.50
151	Scott Proctor	.50
152	Adam LaRoche	.50
153	Ryan Howard	1.00
154	Laynce Nix	.50
155	Garrett Atkins	.50
156	Chris Burke	.50
157	Oliver Perez	.50
158	Wily Mo Pena	.50
159	B.J. Upton	.50
160	Gavin Floyd	.50
161	Jesse Crain	.50
162	Khalil Greene	3.00
163	Eddy Rodriguez	.50
164	Edwin Jackson	.50
165	Scott Kazmir	.50
166	Ryan Wagner	.50
167	Nick Swisher	.50
168	Joe Blanton	.50
169	Alexis Rios	.50
170	Chad Cordero	.50
171	Jason Dubois	.50
172	Chase Utley	1.00
173	David DeJesus	.50
174	Zack Greinke	.50
175	Bobby Crosby	.50
176	Angel Guzman	.50
177	Adrian Gonzalez	.50
178	Guillermo Quiroz	.50
179	Gerald Laird	.50
180	Rickie Weeks	1.00
181	Jayson Werth	.50
182	Buck Jacobsen	.50
183	J.D. Closser	.50
184	Jason Bay	.50
185	Roman Colon	.50
186	Casey Kotchman	.50
187	Yhency Brazoban	.50
188	Bobby Madritsch	.50
189	Gabe Gross	.50
190	Brandon Claussen	.50
191	Aaron Rowand	.50
192	Jeff Francis	.50
193	David Wright	2.00
194	Jose Capellan	.50
195	Jason Lane	.50
196	Daniel Cabrera	.50
197	Joe Mauer	1.00
198	Kevin Youkilis	.50
199	Dallas McPherson	.50
200	Robb Quinlan	.50

Origins Old Judge Autographs

		NM/M
Common Auto.:		10.00
Bronze:		No Pricing
JB	Jason Bay	15.00
AB	Adrian Beltre	12.00
MC	Miguel Cabrera	25.00
CC	Carl Crawford	15.00
BC	Bobby Crosby	10.00
BD	Bobby Doerr	15.00
BF	Bob Feller	25.00
MG	Marcus Giles Exch	10.00
DG	Dwight Gooden	15.00
GR	Khalil Greene	12.00
KG	Ken Griffey Jr.	75.00
RG	Ron Guidry	15.00
TG	Tony Gwynn	50.00
TH	Travis Hafner	15.00
RH	Rich Harden	15.00
KH	Keith Hernandez	15.00
FH	Frank Howard	20.00
HO	Ryan Howard	75.00
AH	Aubrey Huff	8.00
DJ	Derek Jeter	150.00
SK	Scott Kazmir	20.00
DK	Dave Kingman	15.00
CK	Casey Kotchman	15.00
SL	Sparky Lyle	12.00
VM	Victor Martinez	15.00
MA	Don Mattingly	65.00
DM	Dallas McPherson	10.00
PM	Paul Molitor	40.00
OS	Roy Oswalt	15.00
AO	Akinori Otsuka	10.00
JP	Jim Palmer	15.00
PE	Jake Peavy	25.00
OP	Oliver Perez	10.00
CR	Cal Ripken Jr./25	180.00
BR	Brooks Robinson	30.00
RO	Al Rosen	15.00
JS	Johan Santana Exch	35.00
RS	Ron Santo	25.00
MS	Mike Schmidt	75.00
BS	Ben Sheets	12.00
ST	Shingo Takatsu	15.00
MT	Mark Teixeira	30.00
BU	B.J. Upton	15.00
CU	Chase Utley	25.00
RW	Rickie Weeks	15.00
DW	David Wright	60.00
RY	Robin Yount	50.00
CZ	Carlos Zambrano	15.00

Origins Old Judge Materials Jersey

FRANK THOMAS

		NM/M
Common Jersey:		5.00
JB	Jeff Bagwell	8.00
CB	Carlos Beltran	5.00
AB	Adrian Beltre	5.00
LB	Lance Berkman	5.00
HB	Hank Blalock	5.00
MC	Miguel Cabrera	8.00
EC	Eric Chavez	5.00
JD	J.D. Drew	5.00
GL	Troy Glaus	5.00
KG	Ken Griffey Jr.	10.00
VG	Vladimir Guerrero	8.00
TG	Tony Gwynn/SP	10.00
HE	Todd Helton	5.00
TH	Tim Hudson	5.00
HU	Torii Hunter	5.00
DJ	Derek Jeter	15.00
RJ	Randy Johnson	8.00
AJ	Andruw Jones	5.00
CJ	Chipper Jones	8.00
GM	Greg Maddux	10.00
HM	Hideki Matsui	15.00
KM	Kazuo Matsui	5.00
DO	David Ortiz	8.00
PI	Mike Piazza	8.00
MP	Mark Prior	8.00
AP	Albert Pujols	15.00
MR	Manny Ramirez	8.00
CR	Cal Ripken Jr./SP	25.00
SR	Scott Rolen	8.00
NR	Nolan Ryan/SP	30.00
CS	Curt Schilling	8.00
BS	Ben Sheets	5.00
GS	Gary Sheffield	5.00
AS	Alfonso Soriano	8.00
SS	Sammy Sosa	8.00
IS	Ichiro Suzuki	20.00
MT	Mark Teixeira	8.00
TE	Miguel Tejada	8.00
FT	Frank Thomas	8.00
JT	Jim Thome	8.00
KW	Kerry Wood	8.00

Origins Signatures

		NM/M
Common Auto.:		10.00
Bronze:		No Pricing
Production Five Sets		
JB1	Jason Bay	15.00
AB1	Adrian Beltre	10.00
MC1	Miguel Cabrera	25.00
CC1	Carl Crawford	12.00
BC1	Bobby Crosby	10.00
BD1	Bobby Doerr	15.00
BF1	Bob Feller	25.00
MG1	Marcus Giles	10.00
DG1	Dwight Gooden	15.00
GR1	Khalil Greene	10.00
KG1	Ken Griffey Jr.	75.00
RG1	Ron Guidry	15.00
TG1	Tony Gwynn	50.00
TH1	Travis Hafner	15.00
RH1	Rich Harden	15.00
KH1	Keith Hernandez	15.00
FH1	Frank Howard	20.00
HO1	Ryan Howard	75.00
AH1	Aubrey Huff	8.00
DJ1	Derek Jeter	150.00
SK1	Scott Kazmir	20.00
DK1	Dave Kingman	15.00
CK1	Casey Kotchman	10.00
SL1	Sparky Lyle	12.00
VM1	Victor Martinez	15.00
MA1	Don Mattingly	65.00
DM1	Dallas McPherson	10.00
PM1	Paul Molitor	40.00
OS1	Roy Oswalt	15.00
AO1	Akinori Otsuka	10.00
JP1	Jim Palmer	15.00
PE1	Jake Peavy	25.00
OP1	Oliver Perez	10.00
CR1	Cal Ripken Jr./25	180.00
BR1	Brooks Robinson	30.00
RO1	Al Rosen	15.00
JS1	Johan Santana Exch	35.00
RS1	Ron Santo	25.00
MS1	Mike Schmidt	75.00
BS1	Ben Sheets	12.00
ST1	Shingo Takatsu	15.00
MT1	Mark Teixeira	25.00
BU1	B.J. Upton	15.00
CU1	Chase Utley	15.00
RW1	Rickie Weeks	15.00
DW1	David Wright	60.00
RY1	Robin Yount	50.00
CZ1	Carlos Zambrano	15.00

Origins Tins

		NM/M
Common Tin:		5.00
TC	Ty Cobb	5.00
DJ	Derek Jeter	10.00
WJ	Walter Johnson	5.00
HW	Honus Wagner	5.00

2005 UD Past Time Pennants

PAUL MOLITOR

		NM/M
Complete Set (90):		20.00
Common Player:		.20
Pack (5):		4.00
Box (20):		70.00
1	Al Kaline	.50
2	Al Rosen	.20
3	Bert Blyleven	.20
4	Bill Mazeroski	.20
5	Billy Williams	.50
6	Bob Feller	.50
7	Bob Gibson	.75
8	Bob Lemon	.20
9	Bobby Doerr	.40
10	Brooks Robinson	.75
11	Bruce Sutter	.30
12	Bucky Dent	.20
13	Cal Ripken Jr.	2.00
14	Carl Yastrzemski	.75
15	Carlton Fisk	.40
16	Jim "Catfish" Hunter	.40
17	Dale Murphy	.40
18	Dave Parker	.20
19	Don Larsen	.20
20	Don Mattingly	1.00
21	Don Newcombe	.20
22	Duke Snider	.50
23	Early Wynn	.20
24	Eddie Mathews	.75
25	Eddie Murray	.50
26	Enos Slaughter	.20
27	Ernie Banks	.75
28	Fergie Jenkins	.20
29	Frank Howard	.20
30	Frank Robinson	.50
31	Fred Lynn	.20
32	Gary Carter	.20
33	Gaylord Perry	.20
34	George Brett	1.50
35	George Kell	.20
36	Rich "Goose" Gossage	.20
37	Graig Nettles	.20
38	Harmon Killebrew	.75
39	Jack Morris	.20
40	Jim Bunning	.20
41	Felipe Alou	.20
42	Jim Palmer	.40
43	Jim Rice	.20
44	Joe DiMaggio	1.50
45	Joe Morgan	.20
46	Johnny Bench	.75
47	Johnny Podres	.20
48	Juan Marichal	.20
49	Keith Hernandez	.20
50	Kirby Puckett	.75
51	Larry Doby	.20
52	Lou Brock	.40
53	Luis Aparicio	.20
54	Luis Tiant	.20
55	Maury 4illis	.20
56	Mickey Mantle	2.00
57	Mike Schmidt	1.50
58	Monte Irvin	.20
59	Nolan Ryan	1.50
60	Orlando Cepeda	.20
61	Ozzie Smith	.75
62	Paul Molitor	.50
63	Pee Wee Reese	.20
64	Phil Niekro	.20
65	Phil Rizzuto	.50
66	Ralph Kiner	.20
67	Richie Ashburn	.20
68	Rico Petrocelli	.20
69	Robin Roberts	.20
70	Robin Yount	.75
71	Rocky Colavito	.20
72	Rod Carew	.40
73	Rollie Fingers	.20
74	Ron Guidry	.20
75	Ron Santo	.20
76	Tony Gwynn	.75
77	Sparky Lyle	.20
78	Stan Musial	1.00
79	Steve Carlton	.40
80	Rick Ferrell	.20
81	Tom Seaver	.75
82	Tommy John	.20
83	Tony Perez	.20
84	Wade Boggs	.50
85	Warren Spahn	.75
86	Whitey Ford	.40
87	Will Clark	.50
88	Willie McCovey	.50
89	Willie Stargell	.40
90	Yogi Berra	.75

Silver
Gold: 3-5X
Production 100 Sets

Gold
Gold: 4-8X
Production 50 Sets

Mitchell & Ness Jersey Redemption
Total Production
Per Player 36-37

Mitchell & Ness Pennants

		NM/M
Common Pennant:		15.00
Inserted 1:Hobby Box		
1903	1903 Boston Americans/100	20.00
1905	1095 New York Giants/100	20.00
1906	1906 Chicago White Sox/100	20.00
1907	1907 Detroit Tigers/100	20.00
1908	1908 Chicago Cubs/105	25.00
1909	1909 Pittsburgh Pirates/125	20.00
1910	1910 Philadelphia A's/125	20.00
1912	1912 Boston Red Sox/125	20.00
1914	1914 Boston Braves/125	20.00
1915	1915 Philadelphia Phillies/125	20.00
1916	1916 Brooklyn Robins/125	20.00
1917	1917 New York Giants/200	20.00
1918	1918 Boston Red Sox/200	20.00
1919	1919 Chicago White Sox/200	20.00
1920	1920 Cleveland Indians/200	15.00
1921	1921 New York Yankees/200	25.00
1922	1922 New York Giants/200	20.00
1924	1924 Washington Senators/200	20.00
1925	1925 Pittsburgh Pirates/200	15.00
1926	1926 Saint Louis Cardinals/200	20.00
1927	1927 New York Yankees/500	25.00
1928	1928 New York Yankees/500	25.00
1929	1929 Chicago Cubs/337	20.00
1930	1930 Philadelphia A's/337	15.00
1931	1931 Saint Louis Cardinals/337	20.00
1932	1932 Chicago Cubs/337	20.00
1934	1934 Detroit Tigers/337	15.00
1935	1935 Chicago Cubs/337	20.00
1936	1936 New York Yankees/337	25.00
1937	1937 New York Giants/337	20.00
1938	1938 New York Yankees/337	25.00
1939	1939 Cincinnati Reds/337	15.00
1940	1940 Cincinnati Reds/337	15.00
1941	1941 Brooklyn Dodgers/337	25.00
1942	1942 Saint Louis Cardinals/337	20.00
1943	1943 New York Yankees/500	20.00
1944	1944 Saint Louis Browns/337	15.00
1945	1945 Chicago Cubs/337	20.00
1946	1946 Boston Red Sox/337	20.00
1947	1947 Brooklyn Dodgers/337	25.00
1948	1948 Boston Braves/337	15.00
1949	1949 New York Yankees/337	20.00
1950	1950 Philadelphia Phillies/337	20.00
1951	1951 New York Giants/337	15.00
1952	1952 Brooklyn Dodgers/500	20.00
1953	1953 New York Yankees/337	25.00
1954	1954 Cleveland Indians/337	15.00
1955	1955 Brooklyn Dodgers/337	25.00
1956	1956 Brooklyn Dodgers/500	25.00
1957	1957 Milwaukee Braves/337	20.00
1958	1958 New York Yankees/500	25.00
1959	1959 Los Angeles Dodgers/337	20.00
1960	1960 Pittsburgh Pirates/337	15.00
1961	1961 Cincinnati Reds/337	15.00
1962	1962 San Francisco Giants/337	20.00
1963	1963 Los Angeles Dodgers/337	20.00
1964	1964 Saint Louis Cardinals/337	20.00
1965	1965 Minnesota Twins/337	15.00
1966	1966 Baltimore Orioles/337	20.00
1967	1967 Boston Red Sox/337	20.00
1968	1968 Detroit Tigers/337	15.00
1969	1969 New York Mets/337	20.00
1970	1970 Baltimore Orioles/337	20.00
1971	1971 Pittsburgh Pirates/337	15.00
1972	1972 Oakland A's/337	20.00
1973	1973 Oakland A's/337	20.00
1974	1974 Los Angeles Dodgers/337	20.00
1977	1977 New York Yankees/337	25.00
1978	1978 Los Angeles Dodgers/337	20.00
1979	1979 Pittsburgh Pirates/337	15.00
1980	1980 Philadelphia Phillies/337	20.00
1981	1981 Los Angeles Dodgers/337	20.00
1982	1982 Milwaukee Brewers/337	20.00
1983	1983 Baltimore Orioles/337	20.00
1984	1984 San Diego Padres/337	15.00
1985	1985 Kansas City Royals/337	15.00
1986	1986 Boston Red Sox/337	25.00
1988	1988 Los Angeles Dodgers/337	20.00
1975B	1975 Boston Red Sox/337	20.00
1975C	1975 Cincinnati Reds/337	20.00

Mitchell & Ness Penn Autograph

		NM/M
Production 86-87		
JB	Johnny Bench/87	80.00
SC	Steve Carlton/87	60.00
RF	Rollie Fingers/87	60.00
CF	Carlton Fisk/87	60.00
SG	Steve Garvey/40	40.00
AK	Al Kaline/87	75.00
PM	Paul Molitor/87	75.00
GN	Graig Nettles/87	40.00
DN	Don Newcombe/87	40.00
BR	Brooks Robinson/87	75.00
TS	Tom Seaver/87	80.00
CY	Carl Yastrzemski/86	80.00

Signatures Bronze

SP's Production 3-25

		NM/M
FA	Felipe Alou	15.00
RB	Rick Burleson	10.00
DC	David Cone	15.00
LD	Lenny Dykstra	12.00
SF	Sid Fernandez	10.00
BF	Bill Freehan	15.00
DG	Dwight Gooden	15.00
KG	Ken Griffey Sr.	10.00
GU	Don Gullett	8.00
PG	Pedro Guerrero	10.00
HO	Ken Holtzman	10.00
BH	Burt Hooton	10.00
WH	Willie Horton EXCH	12.00
FH	Frank Howard	15.00
HR	Kent Hrbek	15.00
RH	Randy Hundley	10.00
TJ	Tommy John	15.00
WJ	Wally Joyner	15.00
DK	Dave Kingman	10.00
KN	Ray Knight	10.00
SL	Sparky Lyle	10.00
BM	Bill Madlock	10.00
BO	Bobby Murcer	25.00
RP	Rico Petrocelli	12.00
BP	Boog Powell	25.00
AR	Al Rosen	15.00
SS	Steve Sax	10.00
SC	Mike Scioscia EXCH	15.00
WI	Mookie Wilson	15.00

Signatures Silver

		NM/M
FA	Felipe Alou	10.00
LA	Luis Aparicio	20.00
BB	Bert Blyleven	15.00
BR	Lou Brock	30.00
JB	Jim Bunning/Exch.	15.00
RB	Rick Burleson	10.00
ST	Steve Carlton	35.00
GC	Gary Carter	20.00
OC	Orlando Cepeda	20.00
CC	Chris Chambliss	15.00
WC	Will Clark	40.00
RC	Rocky Colavito	65.00
DC	David Cone	15.00
DE	Bucky Dent	12.00
BD	Bobby Doerr	15.00
LD	Lenny Dykstra	10.00
CE	Carl Erskine/Exch.	12.00
EV	Dwight Evans	30.00
FE	Bob Feller	30.00
SF	Sid Fernandez	10.00
RF	Rollie Fingers	20.00
BF	Bill Freehan	10.00
DG	Dwight Gooden	15.00
GG	Rich "Goose" Gossage	15.00
KG	Ken Griffey Sr.	10.00
GU	Don Gullett	8.00
PG	Pedro Guerrero	10.00
KH	Keith Hernandez	15.00
HO	Ken Holtzman	10.00
BH	Burt Hooton	10.00
WH	Willie Horton/Exch.	10.00
FH	Frank Howard	15.00
HR	Kent Hrbek	15.00
RH	Randy Hundley	10.00
MI	Monte Irvin	25.00
FJ	Fergie Jenkins	20.00
TJ	Tommy Jones	15.00
WJ	Wally Joyner	15.00
AK	Al Kaline	50.00
GK	George Kell	15.00
HK	Harmon Killebrew	50.00
RK	Ralph Kiner	40.00
DK	Dave Kingman	15.00
KN	Ray Knight	10.00
DL	Don Larsen/Exch.	30.00
SL	Sparky Lyle	10.00
FL	Fred Lynn	15.00
BM	Bill Madlock	10.00
JU	Juan Marichal/Exch.	20.00
MA	Bill Mazeroski	30.00
PM	Paul Molitor	40.00
MO	Joe Morgan	20.00
JM	Jack Morris	15.00
BO	Bobby Murcer	30.00
MU	Dale Murphy	25.00
GN	Graig Nettles	20.00
DN	Don Newcombe	15.00
JP	Jim Palmer	30.00
DP	Dave Parker	15.00
TP	Tony Perez/Exch.	40.00
GP	Gaylord Perry	15.00
RP	Rico Petrocelli	15.00
PO	Johnny Podres	25.00
BP	Boog Powell	20.00
JR	Jim Rice	20.00
RO	Brooks Robinson	60.00
AR	Al Rosen	15.00
RS	Ron Santo	25.00
SS	Steve Sax	10.00
SC	Mike Scioscia/Exch.	20.00
BS	Bill "Moose" Skowron	15.00
SU	Bruce Sutter	15.00
LT	Luis Tiant	15.00
BW	Billy Williams/Exch.	15.00
MW	Maury Wills	20.00

Signatures Gold

NM/M

Many not priced due to scarcity.

FA	Felipe Alou	20.00
RB	Rick Burleson	15.00
LD	Lenny Dykstra	20.00
SF	Sid Fernandez	15.00
BF	Bill Freehan	15.00
KG	Ken Griffey Sr.	15.00
PG	Pedro Guerrero	15.00
GU	Don Gullett	10.00
HO	Ken Holtzman	15.00
BH	Burt Hooton	15.00
WH	Willie Horton/Exch.	15.00
HR	Kent Hrbek	20.00
RH	Randy Hundley	10.00
DK	Dave Kingman	15.00
KN	Ray Knight	15.00
SL	Sparky Lyle	15.00
BM	Bill Madlock	15.00
BO	Bobby Murcer	35.00
RP	Rico Petrocelli	15.00

Signatures Dual

Production 15-24

2005 Upper Deck Portraits

		NM/M
Complete Set (100):		25.00
Common Player:		.25
Box (7 Cards + 8x10):		100.00
1	Dallas McPherson	.25
2	Steve Finley	.25
3	Vladimir Guerrero	.75
4	Troy Glaus	.25
5	Andruw Jones	.50
6	Chipper Jones	.75
7	John Smoltz	.50
8	Marcus Giles	.25
9	Tim Hudson	.50
10	Cal Ripken Jr.	3.00
11	Miguel Tejada	.50
12	Curt Schilling	.75
13	David Ortiz	.75
14	Edgar Renteria	.25
15	Jason Varitek	.50
16	Jim Rice	.50
17	Johnny Damon	.75
18	Matt Clement	.25
19	Wade Boggs	.75
20	Aramis Ramirez	.50
21	Carlos Zambrano	.25
22	Corey Patterson	.25
23	Fergie Jenkins	.25
24	Greg Maddux	1.50
25	Kerry Wood	.50
26	Mark Prior	.75
27	Nomar Garciaparra	.75
28	Ryne Sandberg	1.50
29	Frank Thomas	.50
30	Adam Dunn	.50
31	Barry Larkin	.50
32	Ken Griffey Jr.	1.50
33	Sean Casey	.25
34	Travis Hafner	.25
35	Victor Martinez	.25
36	Todd Helton	.50
37	Ivan Rodriguez	.50
38	Magglio Ordonez	.25
39	Josh Beckett	.25
40	Miguel Cabrera	.75
41	Mike Lowell	.25
42	Craig Biggio	.50
43	Jeff Bagwell	.50
44	Roger Clemens	2.00
45	Roy Oswalt	.50
46	Bo Jackson	.50
47	Prince Fielder	5.00
48	Eric Gagne	.25
49	J.D. Drew	.25
50	Ben Sheets	.50
51	Robin Yount	.75
52	Jacque Jones	.25
53	Joe Mauer	.50
54	Johan Santana	.75
55	Justin Morneau	.25
56	Torii Hunter	.25
57	Dontrelle Willis	.50
58	David Wright	1.00
59	Gary Carter	.25
60	Jose Reyes	.40
61	Keith Hernandez	.25
62	Mike Piazza	1.00
63	Pedro Martinez	.75
64	Tom Glavine	.50
65	Carl Pavano	.25
66	Derek Jeter	2.00
67	Don Mattingly	1.00
68	Mike Mussina	.50
69	Randy Johnson	.75
70	Bobby Crosby	.25
71	Eric Chavez	.25
72	Rich Harden	.25
73	Bobby Abreu	.50
74	Mike Schmidt	1.00
75	Jason Bay	.25
76	Oliver Perez	.25
77	Brian Giles	.25
78	Jake Peavy	.50
79	Khalil Greene	.25
80	Tony Gwynn	.75
81	Jason Schmidt	.25
82	Will Clark	.50
83	Adrian Beltre	.25
84	Justin Verlander	2.00
85	Albert Pujols	2.00
86	Jim Edmonds	.50
87	Mark Mulder	.50
88	Scott Rolen	.75
89	Aubrey Huff	.25
90	B.J. Upton	.25
91	Carl Crawford	.25
92	Tadahito Iguchi	4.00
93	Scott Kazmir	.25
94	Alfonso Soriano	.75
95	Hank Blalock	.25
96	Mark Teixeira	.50
97	Michael Young	.25
98	Nolan Ryan	2.00
99	Roy Halladay	.50
100	Jose Vidro	.25

Emerald Jersey

		NM/M
Common Player:		4.00
Production 99 Sets		
Blue:		1-1.5X
Production 25 Sets		
Gold:		1-2X
Production 15 Sets		
1	Dallas McPherson	4.00
2	Steve Finley	4.00
3	Vladimir Guerrero	8.00
4	Troy Glaus	4.00
5	Andruw Jones	6.00
6	Chipper Jones	8.00
7	John Smoltz	6.00
8	Marcus Giles	4.00
9	Tim Hudson	6.00
10	Cal Ripken Jr.	25.00
11	Miguel Tejada	8.00
12	Curt Schilling	8.00
13	David Ortiz	8.00
14	Edgar Renteria	4.00
15	Jason Varitek	8.00
16	Jim Rice	8.00
17	Johnny Damon	6.00
18	Matt Clement	4.00
19	Wade Boggs	8.00
20	Aramis Ramirez	6.00
21	Carlos Zambrano	6.00
22	Corey Patterson	4.00
23	Fergie Jenkins	6.00
24	Greg Maddux	10.00
25	Kerry Wood	6.00
26	Mark Prior	8.00
27	Nomar Garciaparra	8.00
28	Ryne Sandberg	12.00
29	Frank Thomas	6.00
30	Adam Dunn	6.00
31	Barry Larkin	4.00
32	Ken Griffey Jr.	15.00
33	Sean Casey	4.00
34	Travis Hafner	4.00
35	Victor Martinez	6.00
36	Todd Helton	6.00
37	Ivan Rodriguez	6.00
38	Magglio Ordonez	4.00
39	Josh Beckett	4.00
40	Miguel Cabrera	8.00
41	Mike Lowell	4.00
42	Craig Biggio	6.00
43	Jeff Bagwell	8.00
44	Roger Clemens	15.00
45	Roy Oswalt	4.00
46	Bo Jackson	10.00
47	Eric Gagne	4.00
48	J.D. Drew	4.00
49	Ben Sheets	4.00
50	Robin Yount	15.00
51	Jacque Jones	4.00
52	Joe Mauer	6.00
53	Johan Santana	6.00
54	Justin Morneau	4.00
55	Torii Hunter	6.00
56	Dontrelle Willis	6.00
57	David Wright	10.00
58	Gary Carter	6.00
59	Jose Reyes	6.00
60	Keith Hernandez	4.00
62	Mike Piazza	8.00
63	Pedro Martinez	8.00
64	Tom Glavine	6.00
65	Carl Pavano	4.00
66	Derek Jeter	15.00
67	Don Mattingly	15.00
68	Mike Mussina	6.00
69	Randy Johnson	8.00
70	Bobby Crosby	4.00
71	Eric Chavez	4.00
72	Rich Harden	4.00
73	Bobby Abreu	6.00
74	Mike Schmidt	10.00
75	Jason Bay	4.00
76	Oliver Perez	4.00
77	Brian Giles	4.00
78	Jake Peavy	6.00
79	Khalil Greene	6.00
80	Tony Gwynn	8.00
81	Jason Schmidt	4.00
82	Will Clark	8.00
83	Adrian Beltre	6.00
84	Justin Verlander	2.00
85	Albert Pujols	15.00
86	Jim Edmonds	6.00
87	Mark Mulder	6.00
88	Scott Rolen	6.00
89	Aubrey Huff	4.00
90	B.J. Upton	6.00
91	Carl Crawford	4.00
92	Tadahito Iguchi	15.00
93	Scott Kazmir	6.00
94	Alfonso Soriano	6.00
95	Hank Blalock	6.00
96	Mark Teixeira	6.00
97	Michael Young	6.00
98	Nolan Ryan	15.00
99	Roy Halladay	6.00
100	Jose Vidro	4.00

Jersey Auto. Platinum

No Pricing
Production 10 Sets

Scrapbook Materials

		NM/M
Complete Set (59):		
Common Player:		
BA	Bobby Abreu	4.00
JB	Jeff Bagwell	6.00
BE	Josh Beckett	4.00
AB	Adrian Beltre	4.00
BI	Craig Biggio	6.00
CA	Miguel Cabrera	8.00
WC	Will Clark	6.00
CL	Matt Clement	4.00
BC	Bobby Crosby	4.00
JE	Jim Edmonds	6.00
SF	Steve Finley	4.00
BG	Brian Giles	4.00
GK	Khalil Greene	6.00
KG	Ken Griffey Jr.	15.00
TG	Tony Gwynn	8.00
RH	Roy Halladay	4.00
TH	Todd Helton	6.00
KH	Keith Hernandez	4.00
HU	Torii Hunter	4.00
BJ	Bo Jackson	10.00
DJ	Derek Jeter	20.00
AJ	Andruw Jones	6.00
CJ	Chipper Jones	8.00
JJ	Jacque Jones	4.00
SK	Scott Kazmir	4.00
BL	Barry Larkin	6.00
ML	Mike Lowell	4.00
VM	Victor Martinez	4.00
MA	Don Mattingly	15.00
JM	Joe Mauer	6.00
MC	Dallas McPherson	4.00
MO	Justin Morneau	4.00
DM	Dale Murphy	6.00
MM	Mike Mussina	6.00
OR	Magglio Ordonez	4.00
DO	David Ortiz	8.00
PA	Corey Patterson	4.00
CP	Carl Pavano	4.00
JP	Jake Peavy	6.00
OP	Oliver Perez	4.00
MP	Mark Prior	6.00
AP	Albert Pujols	15.00
JR	Jim Rice	6.00
CR	Cal Ripken Jr.	20.00
NR	Nolan Ryan	15.00
RS	Ryne Sandberg	6.00
SA	Johan Santana	6.00
JS	Jason Schmidt	4.00
MS	Mike Schmidt	10.00
SM	John Smoltz	6.00
MT	Mark Teixeira	6.00
FT	Frank Thomas	6.00
BU	B.J. Upton	4.00
JV	Jose Vidro	4.00
WI	Dontrelle Willis	6.00
DW	David Wright	10.00
CZ	Carlos Zambrano	6.00

Scrapbook Moments

		NM/M
Common Player:		1.00
Production 250 Sets		
BA	Bobby Abreu	1.50
JB	Jeff Bagwell	1.50
BE	Josh Beckett	1.50
AB	Adrian Beltre	1.50
BI	Craig Biggio	1.50
CA	Miguel Cabrera	2.00
WC	Will Clark	1.50
RC	Roger Clemens	6.00
CL	Matt Clement	1.00
BC	Bobby Crosby	1.00
JE	Jim Edmonds	1.50
PF	Prince Fielder	6.00
SF	Steve Finley	1.00
BG	Brian Giles	1.00
GR	Khalil Greene	1.50
KG	Ken Griffey Jr.	4.00
TG	Tony Gwynn	2.00
RH	Roy Halladay	1.00
TH	Todd Helton	1.50
KH	Keith Hernandez	1.00
HU	Torii Hunter	1.00
BJ	Bo Jackson	2.00
DJ	Derek Jeter	6.00
AJ	Andruw Jones	1.50
CJ	Chipper Jones	2.00
JJ	Jacque Jones	1.00
SK	Scott Kazmir	1.50
BL	Barry Larkin	1.50
ML	Mike Lowell	1.00
VM	Victor Martinez	1.00
MA	Don Mattingly	1.50
JM	Joe Mauer	1.50
MC	Dallas McPherson	1.00
MO	Justin Morneau	1.00
DM	Dale Murphy	2.00
MM	Mike Mussina	1.50
OR	Magglio Ordonez	1.00
DO	David Ortiz	2.00
PA	Corey Patterson	1.00
CP	Carl Pavano	1.00
JP	Jake Peavy	1.50
OP	Oliver Perez	1.00
MP	Mark Prior	2.00
AP	Albert Pujols	6.00
JR	Jim Rice	1.50
CR	Cal Ripken Jr.	8.00
NR	Nolan Ryan	6.00
RS	Ryne Sandberg	4.00
SA	Johan Santana	1.00
JS	Jason Schmidt	1.00
MS	Mike Schmidt	4.00
SM	John Smoltz	1.50
MT	Mark Teixeira	1.50
FT	Frank Thomas	1.50
BU	B.J. Upton	1.00
VE	Justin Verlander	2.00
JV	Jose Vidro	1.00
WI	Dontrelle Willis	1.50
DW	David Wright	3.00
CZ	Carlos Zambrano	1.50

Scrapbook Signatures

No Pricing
Production 20 Sets

Signature Portraits 8x10

		NM/M
Common Player:		
DB	Dusty Baker/100	25.00
JB	Jason Bay	25.00
HB	Hank Blalock	25.00
WB	Wade Boggs/40	50.00
CA	Miguel Cabrera	40.00
JD	Johnny Damon/99	50.00
GR	Khalil Greene	25.00
VG	Vladimir Guerrero/40	75.00
KH	Keith Hernandez	20.00
DJ	Derek Jeter/150	200.00
SK	Scott Kazmir	25.00
VM	Victor Martinez	25.00
MA	Don Mattingly	65.00
JM	Joe Mauer	30.00
DM	Dale Murphy	30.00
SM	Stan Musial/40	80.00
JN	Jeff Niemann	25.00
RO	Roy Oswalt	30.00
PI	Mike Piazza/35	125.00
MP	Mark Prior/50	40.00
CR	Cal Ripken Jr./50	160.00
BR	Brooks Robinson	50.00
NR	Nolan Ryan/25	140.00
RS	Ryne Sandberg/99	100.00
MS	Mike Schmidt	50.00
BS	Ben Sheets	25.00
OS	Ozzie Smith	50.00
DS	Duke Snider/150	60.00
MT	Mark Teixeira	35.00
BU	B.J. Upton	20.00
VE	Justin Verlander	40.00
DW	David Wright	80.00

Sig. Portraits Cuts 8x10 Card

No Pricing
Production 1-25

Signature Portraits Dual 8x10

		NM/M
Production 25-99		
BT	Mark Teixeira, Hank Blalock 99	50.00
HS	Rich Harden, Ben Sheets 99	40.00
NV	Justin Verlander, Jeff Niemann 99	50.00
SH	Tim Hudson, John Smoltz 75	75.00
WP	Kerry Wood, Mark Prior 99	85.00
WR	David Wright, Jose Reyes 99	140.00

Sig. Portraits Dual Cuts 8x10

No Pricing
Production 1-2

Sign. Portraits Triple 8x10

No Pricing
Production 15 Sets

Signature Portraits Quad 8x10

No Pricing
Production Five Sets

2005 Upper Deck Pros & Prospects

		NM/M
Complete Set (200):		
Common Player (1-100):		.15
Common SP (101-150):		3.00
Production 999		
Common SP (151-175):		4.00
Production 499		
Common SP (176-200):		5.00
Production 199		
Pack (6):		2.75
Box (24):		60.00
1	Adam Dunn	.40
2	Aramis Ramirez	.40
3	Bobby Abreu	.25
4	Mike Lowell	.15
5	Josh Beckett	.25
6	Derek Jeter	1.50
7	Alex Rodriguez	1.25
8	Andruw Jones	.25
9	Brian Giles	.15
10	Ivan Rodriguez	.40
11	Aubrey Huff	.15
12	Jake Peavy	.25
13	Hank Blalock	.25
14	Curt Schilling	.50
15	Carlos Zambrano	.40
16	Mike Mussina	.40
17	Travis Hafner	.15
18	Scott Rolen	.50
19	Luis Gonzalez	.25
20	Torii Hunter	.25
21	Greg Maddux	1.00
22	J.D. Drew	.25
23	Kevin Brown	.15
24	Carl Pavano	.25
25	David Ortiz	.50
26	Jose Reyes	.40
27	Johan Santana	.40
28	Todd Helton	.25
29	Jason Kendall	.15
30	Pedro Martinez	.50
31	Carlos Beltran	.50
32	Ben Sheets	.25
33	Garret Anderson	.25
34	Carl Crawford	.25
35	Jason Schmidt	.15

#	Player	Price
36	Johnny Damon	.50
37	Richie Sexson	.25
38	Brad Penny	.15
39	Carlos Delgado	.40
40	Gary Sheffield	.40
41	John Smoltz	.25
42	Eric Chavez	.25
43	Carlos Guillen	.15
44	Jeff Kent	.25
45	Miguel Tejada	.40
46	Shawn Green	.25
47	Vernon Wells	.15
48	Albert Pujols	1.50
49	Alfonso Soriano	.50
50	Eric Gagne	.40
51	Mark Prior	.50
52	Rafael Furcal	.25
53	Preston Wilson	.15
54	Barry Larkin	.50
55	Randy Johnson	.50
56	Craig Wilson	.15
57	Victor Martinez	.15
58	Jim Thome	.25
59	Paul Konerko	.15
60	Jeff Bagwell	.40
61	Lyle Overbay	.15
62	Miguel Cabrera	.50
63	Melvin Mora	.15
64	Scott Podsednik	.25
65	Mark Mulder	.25
66	Mark Teixeira	.40
67	Tom Glavine	.25
68	Frank Thomas	.40
69	Livan Hernandez	.15
70	Kazuo Matsui	.15
71	Jose Vidro	.15
72	Ichiro Suzuki	1.25
73	Roger Clemens	1.50
74	Manny Ramirez	.50
75	Michael Young	.15
76	Rafael Palmeiro	.40
77	Steve Finley	.15
78	Andy Pettitte	.25
79	Lance Berkman	.25
80	Adrian Beltre	.25
81	Carlos Lee	.25
82	Bret Boone	.15
83	Magglio Ordonez	.15
84	Sammy Sosa	1.00
85	Tim Hudson	.25
86	Vladimir Guerrero	.50
87	Carlos Beltran	.40
88	Kerry Wood	.50
89	Jim Edmonds	.25
90	Mike Sweeney	.15
91	Nomar Garciaparra	1.00
92	Mike Piazza	1.00
93	Roy Halladay	.25
94	Troy Glaus	.25
95	Bernie Williams	.25
96	Larry Walker	.25
97	Craig Biggio	.25
98	Roy Oswalt	.25
99	Ken Griffey Jr.	1.00
100	Hideki Matsui	1.00
101	Bucky Jacobsen	3.00
102	J.D. Closser	3.00
103	Antonio Perez	3.00
104	Chris Shelton	3.00
105	David Aardsma	3.00
106	Jake Woods	3.00
107	Jung Bong	3.00
108	Kazuhito Tadano	3.00
109	John Van Benschoten	3.00
110	Jesse Foppert	3.00
111	Joe Borchard	3.00
112	Brandon Phillips	3.00
113	J.D. Durbin	3.00
114	Brandon Claussen	3.00
115	Robb Quinlan	3.00
116	Aaron Harang	3.00
117	Chris Burke	3.00
118	Sergio Mitre	3.00
119	David DeJesus	3.00
120	Gustavo Chacin	3.00
121	Xavier Nady	3.00
122	Garrett Atkins	3.00
123	Jimmy Gobble	3.00
124	Yhency Brazoban	3.00
125	David Kelton	3.00
126	Dewon Brazelton	3.00
127	Koyie Hill	3.00
128	Roman Colon	3.00
129	Daniel Cabrera	3.00
130	Chris Bootcheck	3.00
131	Brad Halsey	3.00
132	Bobby Madritsch	3.00
133	Grady Sizemore	3.00
134	Akinori Otsuka	3.00
135	Wilfredo Ledezma	3.00
136	Russ Adams	3.00
137	Joe Crede	3.00
138	Chad Cordero	3.00
139	Willie Harris	3.00
140	Joey Gathright	3.00
141	Logan Kensing	3.00
142	Jon Leicester	3.00
143	Freddy Guzman	3.00
144	Jonny Gomes	3.00
145	Jeff Bajenaru	3.00
146	Andres Blanco	3.00
147	Jhonny Peralta	3.00
148	Jayson Werth	3.00
149	Bill Hall	3.00
150	Jason Davis	3.00
151	Gabe Gross	4.00
152	Abe Alvarez	4.00
153	Josh Willingham	4.00

#	Player	Price
154	Merkin Valdez	4.00
155	Jeff Niemann **RC**	5.00
156	Yadier Molina	4.00
157	Guillermo Quiroz	4.00
158	Ian Snell	4.00
159	Dan Meyer	4.00
160	Jason Lane	4.00
161	Adrian Gonzalez	4.00
162	Eddy Rodriguez	4.00
163	Jason Dubois	4.00
164	Juan Rincon	4.00
165	Ryan Wagner	4.00
166	Nick Swisher	4.00
167	Chad Tracy	4.00
168	Dioner Navarro	4.00
169	Gerald Laird	4.00
170	Alexis Rios	4.00
171	Aaron Rowand	4.00
172	Adam LaRoche	4.00
173	Kevin Youkilis	4.00
174	Philip Humber **RC**	6.00
175	Chin-Hui Tsao	4.00
176	Jeff Francis	5.00
177	Chase Utley	5.00
178	Gavin Floyd	5.00
179	David Wright	10.00
180	B.J. Upton	5.00
181	Laynce Nix	5.00
182	Joe Mauer	8.00
183	Justin Morneau	5.00
184	Zack Greinke	5.00
185	Jose Capellan	5.00
186	Khalil Greene	5.00
187	Oliver Perez	5.00
188	Joe Blanton	5.00
189	Wily Mo Pena	5.00
190	Dallas McPherson	6.00
191	Edwin Jackson	5.00
192	Casey Kotchman	5.00
193	Jesse Crain	5.00
194	Ryan Howard	6.00
195	Bobby Crosby	5.00
196	Jason Bay	5.00
197	Rickie Weeks	5.00
198	Scott Proctor	5.00
199	Dan Haren	5.00
200	Scott Kazmir	5.00

Gold

Gold (1-100):		4-8X
Production 125		
Gold (101-150):		1X
Production 150		
Gold (151-175):		1X
Production 99		
Gold (176-200):		No Pricing
Production 25		

Future Fabrics

		NM/M
Common Player:		4.00
Gold:		1-2X
Production 75 Sets		
MC	Miguel Cabrera	8.00
BC	Bobby Crosby	4.00
KG	Khalil Greene	4.00
RH	Rich Harden	4.00
EH	Eric Hinske	4.00
JJ	Jacque Jones	4.00
KE	Austin Kearns	4.00
AK	Adam Kennedy	4.00
CK	Casey Kotchman	4.00
VM	Victor Martinez	4.00
KM	Kazuo Matsui	4.00
JM	Joe Mauer	10.00
DM	Dallas McPherson	6.00
TN	Trot Nixon	4.00
SP	Sidney Ponson	4.00
JR	Jose Reyes	4.00
CS	C.C. Sabathia	8.00
SS	Shannon Stewart	4.00
BU	B.J. Upton	8.00
JW	Jayson Werth	8.00
DW	David Wright	15.00

Pro Material

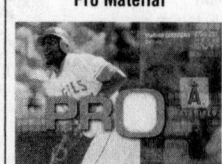

		NM/M
Common Player:		6.00
Gold:		1-2X
Production 50 Sets		
JB	Jeff Bagwell	6.00
CB	Carlos Beltran	6.00
AB	Adrian Beltre	6.00
HB	Hank Blalock	6.00
EC	Eric Chavez	6.00
KG	Ken Griffey Jr.	10.00
VG	Vladimir Guerrero	8.00
TH	Todd Helton	8.00
DJ	Derek Jeter	20.00
RJ	Randy Johnson	8.00
CJ	Chipper Jones	8.00
PJ	Mike Piazza	8.00
MP	Mark Prior	8.00
AP	Albert Pujols	15.00
MR	Manny Ramirez	8.00
SR	Scott Rolen	6.00
CS	Curt Schilling	8.00

SS	Sammy Sosa	8.00
IS	Ichiro Suzuki	25.00
MT	Miguel Tejada	8.00
JT	Jim Thome	8.00

Signs of Stardom

		NM/M
Common Autograph:		8.00
RB	Rocco Baldelli	10.00
JB	Josh Beckett	15.00
AB	Angel Berroa	8.00
HB	Hank Blalock	10.00
SB	Sean Burroughs	8.00
MC	Miguel Cabrera	30.00
CC	Chad Cordero	8.00
BC	Bobby Crosby	8.00
AE	Adam Eaton	8.00
FF	Frank Francisco	8.00
JF	Jason Frasor	8.00
GA	John Gall	8.00
MG	Marcus Giles	8.00
GR	Khalil Greene	8.00
RH	Rich Harden	12.00
MJ	Mike Johnston	8.00
SK	Scott Kazmir	12.00
JK	Jeff Keppinger	8.00
CK	Casey Kotchman	8.00
CL	Cliff Lee	15.00
JL	Justin Leone	8.00
MA	Joe Mauer	35.00
AO	Akinori Otsuka	10.00
LO	Lyle Overbay	10.00
CP	Corey Patterson	10.00
PE	Jake Peavy	30.00
OP	Oliver Perez	10.00
SP	Scott Podsednik	15.00
HR	Horacio Ramirez	8.00
JR	Jose Reyes	30.00
MR	Mike Rouse	8.00
BS	Ben Sheets	15.00
TS	Terrmel Sledge	10.00
KT	Kazuhito Tadano	10.00
ST	Shingo Takatsu	15.00
MT	Mark Teixeira	30.00
WA	Ryan Wagner	8.00
WE	Brandon Webb	10.00
RW	Rickie Weeks	15.00
JW	Jerome Williams	8.00
DW	Dontrelle Willis	10.00

Stardom Signatures

		NM/M
EB	Ernie Banks/240	50.00
BE	Josh Beckett/50	20.00
BL	Hank Blalock/50	20.00
JG	Jason Giambi/100	20.00
KG	Ken Griffey Jr./198	75.00
AK	Al Kaline/99	50.00
JM	Joe Morgan/194	25.00
KP	Kirby Puckett/156	60.00

2005 Upper Deck Pro Sigs.

MANNY RAMIREZ

		NM/M
Complete Set (132):		25.00
Common Player:		.10
Common Rookie (91-132):		.25
Inserted 1:1		
Pack (6):		2.00
Box (24):		40.00
1	Dallas McPherson	.25
2	Garret Anderson	.25
3	Steve Finley	.10
4	Vladimir Guerrero	.50
5	Luis Gonzalez	.10
6	Shawn Green	.25
7	Troy Glaus	.25
8	Andruw Jones	.40
9	Chipper Jones	.25
10	John Smoltz	.25
11	Tim Hudson	.25
12	Miguel Tejada	.40
13	Rafael Palmeiro	.25
14	Sammy Sosa	.75
15	Curt Schilling	.25
16	David Ortiz	.50
17	Johnny Damon	.50
18	Manny Ramirez	.50
19	Greg Maddux	1.00

#	Player	Price
20	Kerry Wood	.25
21	Mark Prior	.50
22	Nomar Garciaparra	.50
23	Frank Thomas	.40
24	Paul Konerko	.25
25	Adam Dunn	.40
26	Ken Griffey Jr.	1.00
27	Travis Hafner	.10
28	Victor Martinez	.10
29	Todd Helton	.40
30	Ivan Rodriguez	.25
31	Magglio Ordonez	.10
32	Carlos Delgado	.25
33	Josh Beckett	.25
34	Miguel Cabrera	.50
35	Craig Biggio	.25
36	Jeff Bagwell	.25
37	Lance Berkman	.25
38	Roger Clemens	1.50
39	Roy Oswalt	.25
40	Mike Sweeney	.10
41	Derek Lowe	.25
42	Eric Gagne	.25
43	J.D. Drew	.10
44	Jeff Kent	.10
45	Ben Sheets	.25
46	Bobby Crosby	.25
47	Joe Mauer	.25
48	Johan Santana	.25
49	Torii Hunter	.25
50	Carlos Beltran	.40
51	David Wright	1.00
52	Kazuo Matsui	.10
53	Mike Piazza	.50
54	Pedro Martinez	.50
55	Tom Glavine	.25
56	Alex Rodriguez	1.50
57	Derek Jeter	1.50
58	Gary Sheffield	.40
59	Hideki Matsui	1.00
60	Jason Giambi	.25
61	Jorge Posada	.25
62	Mike Mussina	.25
63	Randy Johnson	.50
64	Barry Zito	.25
65	Bobby Crosby	.25
66	Eric Chavez	.25
67	Bobby Abreu	.25
68	Jim Thome	.40
69	Jason Bay	.25
70	Oliver Perez	.25
71	Brian Giles	.10
72	Jake Peavy	.25
73	Khalil Greene	.25
74	Jason Schmidt	.10
75	Moises Alou	.25
76	Adrian Beltre	.25
77	Bret Boone	.10
78	Ichiro Suzuki	1.00
79	Richie Sexson	.25
80	Albert Pujols	1.50
81	Jim Edmonds	.25
82	Mark Mulder	.25
83	Scott Rolen	.50
84	Aubrey Huff	.10
85	Alfonso Soriano	.50
86	Hank Blalock	.25
87	Mark Teixeira	.25
88	Roy Halladay	.25
89	Jose Vidro	.25
90	Livan Hernandez	.10
91	Tony Pena **RC**	.25
92	Luis Hernandez **RC**	.25
93	Peter Orr **RC**	.25
94	Anibal Sanchez **RC**	.75
95	Luis Mendoza **RC**	.25
96	Stephen Drew **RC**	3.00
97	Russel Rohlicek **RC**	.25
98	Casey Rogowski **RC**	.25
99	Pedro Lopez **RC**	.25
100	Tadahito Iguchi **RC**	.50
101	Daylan Childress **RC**	.25
102	Juan Morillo **RC**	.50
103	Marcos Carvajal **RC**	.25
104	Ubaldo Jimenez **RC**	5.00
105	Justin Verlander **RC**	2.00
106	Chris Resop **RC**	.25
107	Yorman Bazardo **RC**	.25
108	Jared Gothreaux **RC**	.25
109	Luke Scott **RC**	1.00
110	Ambiorix Burgos **RC**	.25
111	Prince Fielder **RC**	5.00
112	Dennis Houlton **RC**	.25
113	Franquelis Osoria **RC**	.75
114	Norihiro Nakamura **RC**	1.00
115	Oscar Robles **RC**	.25
116	Steve Schmoll **RC**	.25
117	Luis Pena **RC**	.25
118	David Gassner **RC**	.25
119	Ambiorix Concepcion **RC**	.50
120	Dae-Sung Koo **RC**	.25
121	Matt Lindstrom **RC**	.25
122	Colter Bean **RC**	.25
123	Keiichi Yabu **RC**	.25
124	Philip Humber **RC**	1.00
125	Wladimir Balentien **RC**	1.00
126	Tony Giarratano **RC**	.25
127	Shane Costa **RC**	.25
128	Jeff Niemann **RC**	.75
129	Nick Masset **RC**	.25
130	Ismael Ramirez **RC**	.25
131	John Hattig Jr. **RC**	.25
132	Brandon McCarthy **RC**	.50

Silver

Silver:		1-30X
Inserted 1:5		

Gold

Gold:		2-4X
Production 350 Sets		

Signature Sensations

		NM/M
Inserted 1:24		
Silver:		1-2X
Production 50 Sets		
Gold:		No Pricing
Production Five Sets		
AA	Abe Alvarez	8.00
BA	Bronson Arroyo	15.00
GA	Garrett Atkins	5.00
DB	Denny Bautista	5.00
RB	Russell Branyan	5.00
MC	Miguel Cabrera	35.00
KC	Kiko Calero	5.00
CC	Chad Cordero	8.00
JC	Juan Cruz	5.00
BD	Brandon Duckworth	5.00
JE	Johnny Estrada	5.00
LF	Lew Ford/SP	5.00
TH	Travis Hafner	5.00
KH	Keith Hernandez/SP	20.00
OH	Orlando Hernandez	50.00
OI	Omar Infante	5.00
DJ	Derek Jeter/SP	150.00
JJ	Jorge Julio	5.00
AM	Aaron Miles	5.00
YM	Yadier Molina	15.00
RN	Roberto Novoa	5.00
NP	Nick Punto	5.00
HR	Horacio Ramirez/SP	5.00
AR	Aaron Rowand	25.00
CS	Cory Sullivan	8.00
JS	Jeff Suppan	5.00
BT	Brett Tomko	5.00
MV	Merkin Valdez	5.00
DW	David Wright	70.00

2005 Upper Deck Reflections Promos

Each of the first 100 cards in Upper Deck Reflections was issued in a foil-overprinted version with "UD PROMO" across the front. Cards were inserted into specially marked card shop and newsstand issues of Tuff Stuff magazine.

		NM/M
Common Player:		.50
Stars:		1.5X

2005 Upper Deck Reflections

		NM/M
Complete Set (200):		
Common (1-100):		.50
Common SP (101-150):		1.00
Inserted 1:2		
Common SP (151-200):		2.00
Inserted 1:2		
Pack (4):		8.00
Box (80):		80.00

#	Player	Price
1	Corey Patterson	.50
2	Curt Schilling	1.00
3	Todd Helton	.75
4	Johnny Damon	1.00
5	Alex Rodriguez	2.50
6	Vladimir Guerrero	.50
7	John Smoltz	.50
8	Ivan Rodriguez	.75
9	Roy Halladay	.50
10	Carlos Beltran	.75
11	Ichiro Suzuki	2.00
12	Jim Edmonds	.50
13	Andruw Jones	.50
14	Scott Podsednik	.50
15	Troy Glaus	.50
16	Miguel Cabrera	1.00
17	Adrian Beltre	.50
18	Ben Sheets	.50
19	Alfonso Soriano	1.00
20	Brian Giles	.50
21	Carl Crawford	.50
22	Frank Thomas	.75
23	Jeff Kent	.50
24	Eric Gagne	.50
25	Shawn Green	.50
26	Sammy Sosa	2.00
27	Carlos Lee	.50
28	Ken Griffey Jr.	2.00
29	Mike Lowell	.50
30	Magglio Ordonez	.50
31	Aubrey Huff	.50
32	Travis Hafner	.50
33	Albert Pujols	3.00
34	Vernon Wells	.50
35	Roy Oswalt	.50
36	Jose Guillen	.50
37	Jim Thome	.75
38	Bobby Abreu	.50
39	Bret Boone	.50
40	Mark Teixeira	.50
41	Garret Anderson	.50
42	Jose Reyes	.75
43	Bernie Williams	.50
44	Greg Maddux	1.50
45	Gary Sheffield	.50
46	Josh Beckett	.50
47	Chipper Jones	1.00
48	Hank Blalock	.50
49	C.C. Sabathia	.50
50	Manny Ramirez	1.00
51	Pedro Martinez	1.00
52	Michael Young	.50
53	Jacque Jones	.50
54	Marcus Giles	.50
55	Steve Finley	.50
56	Miguel Tejada	.75
57	Mike Sweeney	.50
58	Lance Berkman	.50
59	J.D. Drew	.50
60	Jeromy Burnitz	.50
61	Johan Santana	.75
62	Victor Martinez	.50
63	Carl Pavano	.50
64	Roger Clemens	3.00
65	Richie Sexson	.50
66	Tim Hudson	.50
67	Melvin Mora	.50
68	Angel Berroa	.50
69	Rafael Palmeiro	.50
70	Randy Johnson	1.00
71	Torii Hunter	.50
72	Luis Gonzalez	.50
73	Kazuo Matsui	.50
74	Hideki Matsui	2.00
75	Mark Prior	1.00
76	Jeff Bagwell	1.00
77	Eric Chavez	.50
78	Mark Loretta	.50
79	Adam Dunn	.75
80	Kerry Wood	1.00
81	Jose Vidro	.50
82	Jason Schmidt	.50
83	Carlos Delgado	.50
84	Scott Rolen	1.00
85	David Ortiz	.50
86	Edgar Renteria	.50
87	Nomar Garciaparra	1.50
88	Mike Piazza	1.50
89	Mark Mulder	.50
90	Tom Glavine	.50
91	Paul Konerko	.50
92	Larry Walker	.50
93	Derek Jeter	3.00
94	Jake Peavy	.50
95	Carlos Zambrano	.50
96	Russ Ortiz	.50
97	Barry Zito	.50
98	Austin Kearns	.50
99	Pedro Feliz	.50
100	Rich Harden	.50
101	Adam LaRoche	1.00
102	Brandon Claussen	1.00
103	Gavin Floyd	1.00
104	Daniel Cabrera	1.00
105	Joe Mauer	2.00
106	Khalil Greene	1.00
107	David Wright	3.00
108	Rickie Weeks	2.00
109	Robb Quinlan	1.00
110	Bucky Jacobsen	1.00
111	Ryan Howard	2.00
112	Jeff Francis	1.00
113	Jason Lane	1.00
114	Alexis Rios	1.00
115	Bobby Madritsch	1.00
116	Jesse Crain	1.00
117	Oliver Perez	1.00
118	Garrett Atkins	1.00

#	Player	Price
119	Casey Kotchman	2.00
120	B.J. Upton	1.00
121	Laynce Nix	1.00
122	Adrian Gonzalez	1.00
123	Joe Blanton	1.00
124	Gabe Gross	1.00
125	Scott Kazmir	2.00
126	Zack Greinke	1.00
127	Edwin Jackson	1.00
128	Jason Bay	1.00
129	J.D. Closser	1.00
130	Jason Dubois	1.00
131	Dallas McPherson	2.00
132	Chad Cordero	1.00
133	Angel Guzman	1.00
134	Jayson Werth	1.00
135	Ryan Wagner	1.00
136	Guillermo Quiroz	1.00
137	Scott Proctor	1.00
138	Chris Burke	1.00
139	Nick Swisher	1.00
140	David DeJesus	1.00
141	Yhency Brazoban	1.00
142	Bobby Crosby	1.00
143	Chase Utley	1.00
144	Wily Mo Pena	1.00
145	Roman Colon	1.00
146	Eddy Rodriguez	1.00
147	Gerald Laird	1.00
148	Jose Capellan	1.00
149	Aaron Rowand	1.00
150	Kevin Youkilis	1.00
151	Bob Feller	2.00
152	Robin Yount	4.00
153	Willie Stargell	2.00
154	Cal Ripken Jr.	8.00
155	Monte Irvin	2.00
156	Nolan Ryan	6.00
157	Bob Lemon	2.00
158	Richie Ashburn	2.00
159	Billy Williams	2.00
160	Luis Aparicio	2.00
161	Phil Niekro	2.00
162	Bobby Doerr	2.00
163	Mike Schmidt	6.00
164	Stan Musial	4.00
165	George Kell	2.00
166	Joe Morgan	2.00
167	Whitey Ford	3.00
168	Rick Ferrell	2.00
169	Jim "Catfish" Hunter	2.00
170	Red Schoendienst	2.00
171	Tom Seaver	4.00
172	Pee Wee Reese	2.00
173	Lou Boudreau	2.00
174	Hal Newhouser	2.00
175	Harmon Killebrew	3.00
176	Jim Bunning	2.00
177	Willie McCovey	3.00
178	Bob Gibson	3.00
179	Juan Marichal	2.00
180	Robin Roberts	2.00
181	Gaylord Perry	2.00
182	Brooks Robinson	4.00
183	Al Lopez	2.00
184	Joe DiMaggio	6.00
185	Al Kaline	3.00
186	Rollie Fingers	2.00
187	Mickey Mantle	10.00
188	Enos Slaughter	2.00
189	Ernie Banks	4.00
190	Eddie Mathews	3.00
191	Tommy Lasorda	2.00
192	Fergie Jenkins	2.00
193	Lou Brock	2.00
194	Larry Doby	2.00
195	Phil Rizzuto	3.00
196	Warren Spahn	4.00
197	Ralph Kiner	2.00
198	Hoyt Wilhelm	2.00
199	Early Wynn	2.00
200	Yogi Berra	4.00

Blue
Blue (1-100): 2-4X
Blue (101-200): 1-2.5X
Production 75 Sets

Emerald
Emerald (1-100): 4-8X
Emerald (101-200): 3-5X
Production 25 Sets

Platinum
Platinum (1-200): No Pricing
Production One Set

Purple
Purple (1-100): 2-4X
Purple (101-200): 1-2.5X
Production 99 Sets

Red
Red (1-100): 2-4X
Red (101-200): 1-2.5X
Production 99 Sets

Turquoise
Turquoise (1-100): 3-5X
Turquoise (101-200): 1.5-3X
Production 50 Sets

Cut From the Same Cloth
NM/M
Common Duo: 8.00
Production 225 Sets
Red: 1-1.5X
Production 99 Sets
Blue: 1-2X

Production 50 Sets
Platinum: No Pricing
Production One Set

AA	Albert Pujols, Adrian Beltre	20.00
AB	Carlos Beltran, Bobby Abreu	10.00
AG	Garret Anderson, Vladimir Guerrero	10.00
AH	Alfonso Soriano, Hank Blalock	10.00
AJ	Albert Pujols, Jim Thome	20.00
AM	Adrian Beltre, Miguel Cabrera	10.00
AT	Jim Thome, Bobby Abreu	10.00
AW	Albert Pujols, Will Clark	20.00
BB	Jeff Bagwell, Craig Biggio	10.00
BG	Carlos Beltran, Ken Griffey Jr.	15.00
BM	Paul Molitor, George Brett	20.00
BO	Josh Beckett, Roy Oswalt	8.00
BP	Johnny Bench, Mike Piazza	15.00
BR	Adrian Beltre, Scott Rolen	10.00
BS	George Brett, Mike Schmidt	25.00
BT	Mark Teixeira, Hank Blalock	
BW	Hank Blalock, David Wright	15.00
CB	Bobby Crosby, Jason Bay	8.00
CC	Bobby Crosby, Eric Chavez	8.00
CG	Bobby Crosby, Khalil Greene	8.00
CL	Miguel Cabrera, Mike Lowell	10.00
CP	Carl Crawford, Scott Podsednik	8.00
CR	Scott Rolen, Eric Chavez	10.00
CT	Miguel Tejada, Bobby Crosby	10.00
DM	Mike Schmidt, Dale Murphy	15.00
DR	Manny Ramirez, Johnny Damon	15.00
GI	Brian Giles, Marcus Giles	8.00
GS	Sammy Sosa, Ken Griffey Jr.	20.00
GV	Jose Guillen, Jose Vidro	8.00
HH	Tim Hudson, Rich Harden	8.00
HK	Kent Hrbek, Harmon Killebrew	20.00
JD	J.D. Drew, Chipper Jones	10.00
JH	Torii Hunter, Jacque Jones	8.00
JJ	Chipper Jones, Andruw Jones	10.00
JM	Don Mattingly, Derek Jeter	30.00
JR	Randy Johnson, Nolan Ryan	30.00
JS	Steve Carlton, Johan Santana	10.00
JT	Miguel Tejada, Derek Jeter	25.00
KH	Jason Kendall, Tim Hudson	8.00
KM	Dallas McPherson, Casey Kotchman	10.00
MB	Wade Boggs, Don Mattingly	20.00
MC	Don Mattingly, Will Clark	20.00
MH	Mark Mulder, Tim Hudson	8.00
MJ	Dale Murphy, Chipper Jones	15.00
MK	Harmon Killebrew, Justin Morneau	15.00
MM	Kazuo Matsui, Hideki Matsui	30.00
MS	Johan Santana, Joe Mauer	12.00
MW	Dallas McPherson, David Wright	20.00
MY	Robin Yount, Paul Molitor	20.00
OD	Johnny Damon, David Ortiz	15.00
OT	Shingo Takatsu, Akinori Otsuka	15.00
PB	Jim Bunning, Jim Palmer	10.00
PC	Miguel Cabrera, Albert Pujols	20.00
PG	Albert Pujols, Vladimir Guerrero	25.00
PP	Mike Piazza, Jorge Posada	15.00
PX	Albert Pujols, Scott Rolen	25.00
PS	Tom Seaver, Mark Prior	10.00
PT	Mark Teixeira, Albert Pujols	20.00
RJ	Cal Ripken Jr., Derek Jeter	40.00
RM	Ivan Rodriguez, Victor Martinez	8.00
RO	Manny Ramirez, David Ortiz	20.00
RP	Ivan Rodriguez, Mike Piazza	15.00
RR	Cal Ripken Jr., Brooks Robinson	35.00
RT	Miguel Tejada, Cal Ripken Jr.	30.00
RW	Scott Rolen, David Wright	15.00
SB	Ryne Sandberg, Wade Boggs	25.00
SM	Pedro J. Martinez, Curt Schilling	15.00
SO	Curt Schilling, David Ortiz	15.00
SP	Ben Sheets, Mark Prior	10.00
SR	Scott Rolen, Mike Schmidt	15.00
ST	Alfonso Soriano, Mark Teixeira	15.00
TC	Mark Teixeira, Miguel Cabrera	15.00
TH	Todd Helton, Jim Thome	10.00
TP	Rafael Palmeiro, Miguel Tejada	10.00
TR	Manny Ramirez, Jim Thome	12.00
TS	Jim Thome, Mike Schmidt	15.00
UJ	Derek Jeter, B.J. Upton	25.00
UK	B.J. Upton, Scott Kazmir	8.00
UW	B.J. Upton, David Wright	15.00
VJ	Jose Vidro, Nick Johnson	8.00
WB	Bernie Williams, Carlos Beltran	10.00
WJ	Bernie Williams, Derek Jeter	25.00
WM	Bernie Williams, Hideki Matsui	30.00
WP	Mark Prior, Kerry Wood	10.00
WR	Kerry Wood, Nolan Ryan	30.00
YR	Manny Ramirez, Carl Yastrzemski	20.00
ZM	Mark Mulder, Barry Zito	8.00
BD1	Carlos Beltran, Johnny Damon	10.00
BD2	Johnny Damon, Carlos Beltran	10.00
GG1	Ken Griffey Jr., Ken Griffey Sr.	15.00
GG2	Ken Griffey Sr., Ken Griffey Jr.	15.00

Cut From Same Cloth Patch
NM/M
Production 99 Sets

AM	Adrian Beltre, Miguel Cabrera	25.00
BR	Adrian Beltre, Scott Rolen	25.00
BS	George Brett, Mike Schmidt	40.00
BT	Mark Teixeira, Hank Blalock	20.00
CB	Jason Bay, Bobby Crosby	20.00
CG	Bobby Crosby, Khalil Greene	20.00
CP	Gary Carter, Mike Piazza	35.00
CR	Eric Chavez, Scott Rolen	25.00
DG	Ken Griffey Jr., Adam Dunn	40.00
GC	Miguel Cabrera, Ken Griffey Jr.	40.00
GI	Brian Giles, Marcus Giles	15.00
JM	Derek Jeter, Don Mattingly	60.00
JR	Cal Ripken Jr., Derek Jeter	80.00
KM	Dallas McPherson, Casey Kotchman	25.00
MJ	Chipper Jones, Dale Murphy	30.00
MP	Mike Piazza, Joe Mauer	30.00
MW	Dallas McPherson, David Wright	30.00
MY	Robin Yount, Paul Molitor	40.00
OB	Wade Boggs, David Ortiz	30.00
OT	Shingo Takatsu, Akinori Otsuka	30.00
PB	Albert Pujols, Adrian Beltre	40.00
PC	Albert Pujols, Miguel Cabrera	40.00
PR	Albert Pujols, Scott Rolen	40.00
RJ	Randy Johnson, Nolan Ryan	40.00
RP	Ivan Rodriguez, Mike Piazza	30.00
RR	Cal Ripken Jr., Brooks Robinson	50.00
RW	Nolan Ryan, Kerry Wood	40.00
SB	Ryne Sandberg, Wade Boggs	50.00
SP	Ben Sheets, Mark Prior	20.00
TC	Mark Teixeira, Miguel Cabrera	30.00
TO	Mark Teixeira, David Ortiz	25.00
UJ	Derek Jeter, B.J. Upton	40.00
UW	B.J. Upton, David Wright	25.00
WB	David Wright, Hank Blalock	30.00
WP	Mark Prior, Kerry Wood	30.00
WR	David Wright, Scott Rolen	30.00
YO	David Ortiz, Carl Yastrzemski	50.00
GG1	Ken Griffey Sr., Ken Griffey Jr.	40.00
GG2	Ken Griffey Jr., Ken Griffey Sr.	40.00

Cut From the Same Cloth Auto. Patch
NM/M
Production 25 Sets

BT	Mark Teixeira, Hank Blalock	120.00
DG	Ken Griffey Jr., Adam Dunn	240.00
GC	Miguel Cabrera, Ken Griffey Jr.	240.00
JR	Derek Jeter, Cal Ripken Jr.	500.00
MJ	Chipper Jones, Dale Murphy	140.00
PC	Albert Pujols, Miguel Cabrera	350.00
RP	Mike Piazza, Ivan Rodriguez	140.00
SB	Ryne Sandberg, Wade Boggs	160.00
TO	Mark Teixeira, David Ortiz	100.00
WB	David Wright, Hank Blalock	100.00
WR	David Wright, Scott Rolen	100.00

Dual Signature
NM/M
Red: 1-1.5X
Production 99 Sets
Blue: 1.5-2X
Production 35 Sets
Platinum: No Pricing
Production One Set

ABAR	Al Rosen, Adrian Beltre	30.00
ABDM	Adrian Beltre, Dallas McPherson	30.00
ABDW	David Wright, Adrian Beltre	40.00
ABEC	Adrian Beltre, Eric Chavez	30.00
ABJL	Adrian Beltre, Justin Leone	30.00
ABSR	Adrian Beltre, Scott Rolen	30.00
AHBU	Aubrey Huff, B.J. Upton	25.00
AHCC	Carl Crawford, Aubrey Huff	25.00
AKDM	Al Kaline, Dale Murphy	50.00
AOST	Akinori Otsuka, Shingo Takatsu	40.00
ARCC	Alexis Rios, Carl Crawford	20.00
ARKG	Alexis Rios, Ken Griffey Jr.	65.00
ARTH	Al Rosen, Travis Hafner	25.00
BAKY	Kevin Youkilis, Bronson Arroyo	50.00
BCCR	Bobby Crosby, Cal Ripken Jr.	160.00
BCDJ	Derek Jeter, Bobby Crosby	125.00
BCEC	Bobby Crosby, Eric Chavez	25.00
BCJB	Bobby Crosby, Jason Bay	35.00
BCKG	Khalil Greene, Bobby Crosby	35.00
BDWB	Bobby Doerr, Wade Boggs	50.00
BGMG	Brian Giles, Marcus Giles	25.00
BPFH	Frank Howard, Boog Powell	30.00
BRRS	Brooks Robinson, Ron Santo	40.00
BSJC	Ben Sheets, Jose Capellan	20.00
BSRW	Rickie Weeks, Ben Sheets	35.00
BSSK	Ben Sheets, Scott Kazmir	20.00
BUDJ	B.J. Upton, Derek Jeter	125.00
BURW	B.J. Upton, Rickie Weeks	30.00
BUSK	B.J. Upton, Scott Kazmir	25.00
BWKG	Billy Williams, Ken Griffey Jr.	80.00
CCNJ	Nick Johnson, Chad Cordero	25.00
CKDM	Casey Kotchman, Dallas McPherson	35.00
CKKH	Keith Hernandez, Casey Kotchman	20.00
CKMT	Casey Kotchman, Mark Teixeira	35.00
CTDM	Charles Thomas, Dale Murphy	30.00
CTJC	Charles Thomas, Jose Capellan	15.00
CTRH	Charles Thomas, Ryan Howard	50.00
CZJS	Johan Santana, Carlos Zambrano	60.00
CZLT	Carlos Zambrano, Luis Tiant	20.00
DGDB	Dwight Gooden, Dewon Brazelton	20.00
DGJB	Jim Bouton, Dwight Gooden	20.00
DGJS	Dwight Gooden, Johan Santana	50.00
DJDM	Derek Jeter, Don Mattingly	200.00
DJKG	Derek Jeter, Khalil Greene	140.00
DKFH	Frank Howard, Dave Kingman	25.00
DMDW	David Wright, Dallas McPherson	50.00
DMJB	Dale Murphy, Jason Bay	40.00
DMJL	Justin Leone, Dallas McPherson	20.00
DMKY	Dallas McPherson, Kevin Youkilis	20.00
DMMS	Dallas McPherson, Mike Schmidt	75.00
DMRH	Dallas McPherson, Ryan Howard	50.00
DOKY	David Ortiz, Kevin Youkilis	60.00
DWJL	Justin Leone, David Wright	40.00
DWKH	David Wright, Keith Hernandez	65.00
DWKY	David Wright, Kevin Youkilis	40.00
DWMS	David Wright, Mike Schmidt	100.00
DWSR	David Wright, Scott Rolen	65.00
ECSR	Scott Rolen, Eric Chavez	50.00
FHMT	Mark Teixeira, Frank Howard	40.00
FHNJ	Frank Howard, Nick Johnson	25.00
GPJP	Gaylord Perry, Jake Peavy	30.00
ISJC	Jose Capellan, Ian Snell	15.00
ISMV	Ian Snell, Merkin Valdez	15.00
ISSK	Ian Snell, Scott Kazmir	20.00
JBIS	Ian Snell, Joe Blanton	20.00
JBJP	Jim Bunning, Jim Palmer	30.00
JBMV	Merkin Valdez, Joe Blanton	15.00
JBRH	Joe Blanton, Rich Harden	20.00
JBSK	Scott Kazmir, Joe Blanton	20.00
JCMV	Merkin Valdez, Jose Capellan	15.00
JLRH	Justin Leone, Ryan Howard	50.00
JPJB	Jake Peavy, Joe Blanton	25.00
JPKG	Jake Peavy, Khalil Greene	50.00
JPRH	Jake Peavy, Rich Harden	40.00
JPSK	Jake Peavy, Scott Kazmir	30.00
JRDW	Jose Reyes, David Wright	75.00
JSMP	Johan Santana, Mark Prior	100.00
JSSC	Johan Santana, Steve Carlton	50.00
JSSK	Johan Santana, Scott Kazmir	40.00
JVMG	Marcus Giles, Jose Vidro	20.00
KGKG	Ken Griffey Sr., Ken Griffey Jr.	100.00
KGMC	Ken Griffey Jr., Miguel Cabrera	100.00
KYWB	Kevin Youkilis, Wade Boggs	50.00
MCRH	Ryan Howard, Miguel Cabrera	80.00
MGRW	Rickie Weeks, Marcus Giles	35.00
MTHB	Hank Blalock, Mark Teixeira	50.00
MTMC	Miguel Cabrera, Mark Teixeira	60.00
MTRH	Mark Teixeira, Ryan Howard	80.00
MVRH	Merkin Valdez, Rich Harden	20.00
PBKG	Pat Burrell, Ken Griffey Jr.	85.00
PBMC	Pat Burrell, Miguel Cabrera	40.00
RHDO	Ryan Howard, David Ortiz	80.00
RHRO	Roy Oswalt, Ryan Howard	40.00
RHSK	Rich Harden, Scott Kazmir	25.00
THVM	Victor Martinez, Travis Hafner	20.00
TOKH	Kent Hrbek, Tony Oliva	30.00
VMYM	Victor Martinez, Yadier Molina	20.00

Fabric Jersey
NM/M
Common Player:
Inserted 1:12

CB	Carlos Beltran	8.00
AB	Adrian Beltre	6.00
HB	Hank Blalock	6.00
WB	Wade Boggs/SP	6.00
GB	George Brett/SP	15.00
MC	Miguel Cabrera	8.00
EC	Eric Chavez	4.00
WC	Will Clark/SP	10.00
JD	Johnny Damon	8.00
KG	Ken Griffey Jr.	15.00
VG	Vladimir Guerrero	8.00
TH	Todd Helton	6.00
DJ	Derek Jeter/SP	20.00
RJ	Randy Johnson	8.00
CJ	Chipper Jones	8.00
GM	Greg Maddux	10.00
HM	Hideki Matsui	20.00
DM	Don Mattingly/SP	8.00
PM	Paul Molitor/SP	8.00
DO	David Ortiz	8.00
PI	Mike Piazza	10.00
MP	Mark Prior	8.00
AP	Albert Pujols	15.00
MR	Manny Ramirez	8.00
CR	Cal Ripken Jr./SP	25.00
IR	Ivan Rodriguez	8.00
SR	Scott Rolen	8.00
NR	Nolan Ryan/SP	25.00
JS	Johan Santana	8.00
CS	Curt Schilling	8.00
MS	Mike Schmidt/SP	15.00
AS	Alfonso Soriano	8.00
MT	Mark Teixeira	6.00
TE	Miguel Tejada	8.00
JT	Jim Thome	8.00
BW	Bernie Williams	6.00
KW	Kerry Wood	8.00
DW	David Wright	10.00
CY	Carl Yastrzemski/SP	25.00
RY	Robin Yount/SP	10.00

Fabric Reflections Patch
NM/M
Production 99 Sets

JB	Jason Bay	15.00
AB	Adrian Beltre	15.00
HB	Hank Blalock	15.00
WB	Wade Boggs	20.00
GB	George Brett	50.00
PB	Pat Burrell	15.00
CA	Miguel Cabrera	20.00
EC	Eric Chavez	10.00
BC	Bobby Crosby	10.00
MG	Marcus Giles	10.00
DG	Dwight Gooden	15.00
GR	Khalil Greene	15.00
KG	Ken Griffey Jr.	40.00
RH	Rich Harden	15.00
DJ	Derek Jeter	50.00
RJ	Randy Johnson	15.00
AJ	Andruw Jones	15.00
SK	Scott Kazmir	15.00
MA	Don Mattingly	30.00
MC	Dallas McPherson	10.00
PM	Paul Molitor	15.00
DM	Dale Murphy	15.00
DO	David Ortiz	15.00
RO	Roy Oswalt	10.00
JP	Jake Peavy	15.00
GP	Gaylord Perry	15.00
PI	Mike Piazza	10.00
MP	Mark Prior	10.00
AP	Albert Pujols	50.00
CR	Cal Ripken Jr.	60.00
SR	Scott Rolen	10.00
NR	Nolan Ryan	40.00
JS	Johan Santana	15.00
MS	Mike Schmidt	25.00
BS	Ben Sheets	15.00
ST	Shingo Takatsu	15.00
MT	Mark Teixeira	15.00
BU	B.J. Upton	10.00
DW	David Wright	20.00
RY	Robin Yount	30.00
CZ	Carlos Zambrano	15.00

Reflections Auto. Patch
NM/M
Production 50 Sets

JB	Jason Bay	25.00
AB	Adrian Beltre	30.00
HB	Hank Blalock	40.00
WB	Wade Boggs	60.00
PB	Pat Burrell	35.00
CA	Miguel Cabrera	40.00
EC	Eric Chavez	30.00
BC	Bobby Crosby	40.00
DG	Dwight Gooden	40.00
GR	Khalil Greene	40.00
KG	Ken Griffey Jr.	125.00
RH	Rich Harden	35.00
DJ	Derek Jeter	275.00
RJ	Randy Johnson	100.00
AJ	Andruw Jones	75.00
SK	Scott Kazmir	40.00
MA	Don Mattingly	50.00
MC	Dallas McPherson	30.00
PM	Paul Molitor	50.00
DM	Dale Murphy	50.00
DO	David Ortiz	75.00
RO	Roy Oswalt	50.00
JP	Jake Peavy	40.00
GP	Gaylord Perry	30.00

PI	Mike Piazza	120.00
MP	Mark Prior	20.00
AP	Albert Pujols	300.00
CR	Cal Ripken Jr.	225.00
SR	Scott Rolen	50.00
NR	Nolan Ryan	150.00
JS	Johan Santana	50.00
MS	Mike Schmidt	100.00
BS	Ben Sheets	30.00
ST	Shingo Takatsu	40.00
MT	Mark Teixeira	50.00
BU	B.J. Upton	35.00
DW	David Wright	100.00
RY	Robin Yount	75.00
CZ	Carlos Zambrano	40.00

Super Swatch

NM/M
Production 50 Sets
Red: 1-1.5X
Production 25 Sets
Blue: No Pricing
Production 10 Sets

BO	Bobby Abreu	15.00
RA	Roberto Alomar	15.00
MA	Moises Alou	10.00
GA	Garret Anderson	10.00
BA	Jeff Bagwell	15.00
RB	Rocco Baldelli	10.00
JB	Jason Bay	15.00
BE	Josh Beckett	15.00
CB	Carlos Beltran	15.00
AB	Adrian Beltre	8.00
LB	Lance Berkman	10.00
BI	Craig Biggio	10.00
HB	Hank Blalock	10.00
BB	Bret Boone	8.00
KB	Kevin Brown	8.00
MC	Miguel Cabrera	15.00
EC	Eric Chavez	10.00
CC	Carl Crawford	10.00
BC	Bobby Crosby	10.00
DA	Johnny Damon	20.00
CD	Carlos Delgado	15.00
JD	J.D. Drew	15.00
AD	Adam Dunn	15.00
JE	Jim Edmonds	10.00
KF	Keith Foulke	10.00
EG	Eric Gagne	10.00
JG	Jason Giambi	10.00
BG	Brian Giles	8.00
MG	Marcus Giles	8.00
TG	Tom Glavine	10.00
LG	Luis Gonzalez	10.00
SG	Shawn Green	10.00
GR	Khalil Greene	12.00
KG	Ken Griffey Jr.	40.00
VG	Vladimir Guerrero	15.00
HA	Roy Halladay	10.00
RH	Rich Harden	10.00
HE	Todd Helton	10.00
HO	Trevor Hoffman	10.00
TH	Tim Hudson	12.00
AH	Aubrey Huff	10.00
HU	Torii Hunter	10.00
DJ	Derek Jeter	40.00
RJ	Randy Johnson	15.00
AJ	Andruw Jones	15.00
CJ	Chipper Jones	15.00
JJ	Jacque Jones	8.00
SK	Scott Kazmir	8.00
JK	Jason Kendall	8.00
ML	Mike Lowell	8.00
GM	Greg Maddux	30.00
PM	Pedro Martinez	15.00
VM	Victor Martinez	8.00
HM	Hideki Matsui	50.00
KM	Kazuo Matsui	15.00
DM	Dallas McPherson	12.00
JM	Justin Morneau	20.00
MM	Mark Mulder	10.00
MU	Mike Mussina	15.00
HN	Hideo Nomo	40.00
MO	Magglio Ordonez	8.00
DO	David Ortiz	15.00
RO	Roy Oswalt	10.00
AO	Akinori Otsuka	15.00
RP	Rafael Palmeiro	15.00
CP	Corey Patterson	10.00
PI	Mike Piazza	20.00
SP	Scott Podsednik	10.00
JP	Jorge Posada	15.00
MP	Mark Prior	15.00
AP	Albert Pujols	40.00
MR	Manny Ramirez	20.00
ER	Edgar Renteria	10.00
JR	Jose Reyes	12.00
IR	Ivan Rodriguez	12.00
SR	Scott Rolen	15.00
CS	C.C. Sabathia	8.00
SA	Johan Santana	15.00
SC	Curt Schilling	15.00
JS	Jason Schmidt	12.00
RS	Richie Sexson	10.00
BS	Ben Sheets	10.00
GS	Gary Sheffield	15.00
AS	Alfonso Soriano	15.00
SS	Sammy Sosa	20.00
MS	Mike Sweeney	8.00
ST	Shingo Takatsu	15.00
MT	Mark Teixeira	15.00
TE	Miguel Tejada	15.00
JT	Jim Thome	15.00
JV	Jose Vidro	8.00
WA	Billy Wagner	10.00
VW	Vernon Wells	8.00
BW	Bernie Williams	10.00
KW	Kerry Wood	15.00
DW	David Wright	25.00
BZ	Barry Zito	10.00

2005 Upper Deck San Diego Padres

This cello-wrapped team set was a stadium giveaway at a promotional game.

NM/M
Complete Set (33): 7.00
Common Player: .25

1	Rod Beck	.25
2	Adam Eaton	.25
3	Trevor Hoffman	.40
4	Brian Lawrence	.25
5	Scott Linebrink	.25
6	Blaine Neal	.25
7	Akinori Otsuka	.50
8	Jake Peavy	.25
9	Ricky Stone	.25
10	David Wells	.25
11	Jay Witasick	.25
12	Ramon Hernandez	.25
13	Miguel Ojeda	.25
14	Rich Aurilia	.25
15	Sean Burroughs	.35
16	Brian Buchanan	.25
17	Khalil Greene	.40
18	Dave Hansen	.25
19	Mark Loretta	.25
20	Phil Nevin	.25
21	Brian Giles	.35
22	Ryan Klesko	.25
23	Terrence Long	.25
24	Xavier Nady	.25
25	Jay Payton	.25
26	Sterling Hitchcock	.25
27	Bruce Bochy	.25
28	Rob Picciolo	.25
29	Swinging Friar (Mascot)	.25
30	Davey Lopes	.25
31	Dave Magadan	.25
32	Tony Muser	.25
33	Darren Balsley	.25

2005 Upper Deck SportsFest Redemption

Six-card cello packs with individual cards serially numbered on front from an edition of 750 were available to persons redeeming wrappers from Upper Deck products purchased at SportsFest 2005 in Chicago.

NM/M
Complete Set (6): 5.00
Common Player: .50

MLB1	Ken Griffey Jr.	1.50
MLB2	Mark Prior	.75
MLB3	Derek Jeter	2.00
MLB4	Carlos Beltran	1.00
MLB5	Albert Pujols	2.00
MLB6	Curt Schilling	.50

2005 Upper Deck Sweet Spot

NM/M
Complete Set (90): 20.00
Common Player: .25
Pack (5): 12.00
Box (12): 120.00

1	Magglio Ordonez	.25
2	Craig Biggio	.50
3	Hank Blalock	.40
4	Nomar Garciaparra	.75

5	Ken Griffey Jr.	1.50
6	Khalil Greene	.40
7	Andruw Jones	.50
8	Ichiro Suzuki	1.50
9	Philip Humber RC	1.00
10	Vladimir Guerrero	.75
11	Carlos Delgado	.40
12	Jeff Niemann RC	1.50
13	Chipper Jones	.75
14	Jose Vidro	.25
15	Miguel Cabrera	.75
16	Albert Pujols	2.00
17	Tadahito Iguchi RC	1.00
18	Norihiro Nakamura RC	1.00
19	Jeff Bagwell	.50
20	Troy Glaus	.40
21	Scott Rolen	.25
22	Derek Lowe	.25
23	Mark Prior	.75
24	Bobby Abreu	.40
25	David Wright	.75
26	Barry Zito	.40
27	Livan Hernandez	.25
28	Mark Teixeira	.50
29	Manny Ramirez	.75
30	Paul Konerko	.40
31	Victor Martinez	.25
32	Greg Maddux	1.50
33	Jim Thome	.50
34	Miguel Tejada	.50
35	Ivan Rodriguez	.50
36	Carlos Beltran	.50
37	Steve Finley	.25
38	Torii Hunter	.25
39	Bobby Crosby	.25
40	Jorge Posada	.40
41	Ben Sheets	.40
42	Mike Piazza	1.00
43	Luis Gonzalez	.25
44	Joe Mauer	.50
45	Shawn Green	.25
46	Eric Gagne	.40
47	Kerry Wood	.25
48	Derek Jeter	2.00
49	Josh Beckett	.25
50	Alex Rodriguez	1.50
51	Aubrey Huff	.25
52	Eric Chavez	.40
53	Sammy Sosa	1.00
54	Roger Clemens	2.00
55	Mike Mussina	.50
56	Mike Sweeney	.25
57	Oliver Perez	.25
58	Tim Hudson	.25
59	Justin Verlander RC	2.50
60	Johan Santana	.50
61	Hideki Matsui	1.50
62	Mark Mulder	.40
63	Jake Peavy	.40
64	Adam Dunn	.50
65	Dallas McPherson	.25
66	Jeff Kent	.25
67	Pedro Martinez	.75
68	J.D. Drew	.25
69	Frank Thomas	.50
70	Kazuo Matsui	.25
71	Travis Hafner	.40
72	John Smoltz	.40
73	Jason Schmidt	.25
74	Carlos Lee	.25
75	Todd Helton	.50
76	David Ortiz	.75
77	Roy Oswalt	.25
78	Brian Giles	.25
79	Gary Sheffield	.50
80	Jason Bay	.40
81	Alfonso Soriano	.75
82	Randy Johnson	.75
83	Tom Glavine	.40
84	Richie Sexson	.25
85	Curt Schilling	.75
86	Adrian Beltre	.40
87	Jim Edmonds	.40
88	Roy Halladay	.40
89	Johnny Damon	.75
90	Lance Berkman	.40

Gold

NM/M
Gold (1-90): 1-2X
Production 599 Sets

Platinum

Platinum (1-90): 2-4X
Production 99 Sets

Plutonium

No Pricing
Production One Set

Majestic Materials

NM/M
Common Player:
Gold: 1-1.5X
Production 75 Sets
Platinum: No Pricing
Production 10 Sets
Plutonium: No Pricing
Production One Set
Patch: 2-3X
Production 35 Sets

BA	Bobby Abreu	4.00
MA	Moises Alou	6.00
JB	Jason Bay	4.00
BE	Josh Beckett	4.00
LB	Lance Berkman	4.00
CB	Craig Biggio	6.00
BB	Bret Boone	4.00
BC	Bobby Crosby	4.00
CD	Carlos Delgado	4.00
JD	J.D. Drew	4.00
AD	Adam Dunn	6.00
JE	Jim Edmonds	6.00
JG	Jason Giambi	6.00
BG	Brian Giles	4.00
TG	Troy Glaus	4.00
LG	Luis Gonzalez	4.00
SG	Shawn Green	4.00
KG	Khalil Greene	4.00
HA	Travis Hafner	4.00
RH	Roy Halladay	4.00
TH	Tim Hudson	4.00
HU	Torii Hunter	4.00
TI	Tadahito Iguchi	5.00
AJ	Andruw Jones	6.00
SK	Scott Kazmir	4.00
JK	Jeff Kent	4.00
VM	Victor Martinez	4.00
KM	Kazuo Matsui	4.00
JM	Joe Mauer	6.00
DM	Dallas McPherson	4.00
MM	Mark Mulder	4.00
MU	Mike Mussina	6.00
MO	Magglio Ordonez	4.00
RO	Roy Oswalt	4.00
JP	Jake Peavy	6.00
OP	Oliver Perez	4.00
AP	Andy Pettitte	6.00
PO	Jorge Posada	6.00
ER	Edgar Renteria	4.00
JR	Jose Reyes	4.00
JS	Jason Schmidt	4.00
RS	Richie Sexson	4.00
BS	Ben Sheets	4.00
GS	Gary Sheffield	6.00
ST	Shingo Takatsu	4.00
BU	B.J. Upton	4.00
JV	Jose Vidro	4.00
VW	Vernon Wells	4.00
DW	David Wright	10.00
BZ	Barry Zito	4.00

Majestic Materials Dual

NM/M
Production 25 Sets
Gold: No Pricing
Production Five Sets
Plutonium: No Pricing
Production One Set
Patch: No Pricing
Production Five Sets

BB	Craig Biggio, Jeff Bagwell	15.00
BP	Jason Bay, Oliver Perez	10.00
BS	Adrian Beltre, Richie Sexson	10.00
BT	Hank Blalock, Mark Teixeira	12.00
CC	Bobby Crosby, Eric Chavez	10.00
DG	Adam Dunn, Ken Griffey Jr.	25.00
DK	J.D. Drew, Jeff Kent	10.00
DR	Johnny Damon, Manny Ramirez	15.00
GG	Shawn Green, Troy Glaus	10.00
GR	Eric Gagne, Mariano Rivera	15.00
HM	Travis Hafner, Victor Martinez	10.00
JJ	Andruw Jones, Chipper Jones	15.00
MC	Don Mattingly, Will Clark	25.00
MW	Dallas McPherson, David Wright	15.00
PC	Albert Pujols, Miguel Cabrera	25.00
PG	Jake Peavy, Khalil Greene	12.00
PL	Albert Pujols, Derek Lee	25.00
RM	Jose Reyes, Kazuo Matsui	10.00
RO	Ivan Rodriguez, Magglio Ordonez	10.00
RT	Brian Roberts, Miguel Tejada	15.00
SH	John Smoltz, Tim Hudson	12.00
SM	Joe Mauer, Johan Santana	15.00
TI	Shingo Takatsu, Tadahito Iguchi	20.00
UK	B.J. Upton, Scott Kazmir	10.00
WC	David Wright, Miguel Cabrera	15.00

Majestic Materials Triple

NM/M
Production 25 Sets
Gold: No Pricing
Production Five Sets
Plutonium: No Pricing
Production One Set
Patch: No Pricing
Production Five Sets

BPO	Josh Beckett, Mark Prior, Roy Oswalt	15.00
BSB	George Brett, Mike Schmidt, Wade Boggs	30.00
BTH	Jeff Bagwell, Jim Thome, Todd Helton	20.00
HRG	Torii Hunter, Manny Ramirez, Vladimir Guerrero	20.00
JCG	Andruw Jones, Miguel Cabrera, Vladimir Guerrero	15.00
JRT	Derek Jeter, Edgar Renteria, Miguel Tejada	25.00
MMP	Greg Maddux, Pedro Martinez, Jake Peavy	25.00
MSG	Greg Maddux, John Smoltz, Tom Glavine	40.00
OGP	David Ortiz, Jason Giambi, Rafael Palmeiro	20.00
PBC	Albert Pujols, Carlos Beltran, Miguel Tejada	
RBW	Nolan Ryan, Josh Beckett, Kerry Wood	40.00
RGB	Cal Ripken Jr., Tony Gwynn, Wade Boggs	50.00
SSJ	Curt Schilling, Johan Santana, Randy Johnson	25.00
VPP	Jason Varitek, Jorge Posada, Mike Piazza	20.00
WRG	David Wright, Scott Rolen, Troy Glaus	25.00

Majestic Materials Quad

NM/M
Production 25 Sets
Gold: No Pricing
Production Five Sets
Plutonium: No Pricing
Production One Set
Patch: No Pricing
Production Five Sets

JJSH	Andruw Jones, Chipper Jones, John Smoltz, Tim Hudson	25.00
JSJP	Derek Jeter, Gary Sheffield, Randy Johnson, Jorge Posada	60.00
OVDR	David Ortiz, Jason Varitek, Johnny Damon, Manny Ramirez	40.00
PEWR	Albert Pujols, Jim Edmonds, Larry Walker, Scott Rolen	50.00
ZMWP	Carlos Zambrano, Greg Maddux, Kerry Wood, Mark Prior	30.00

Signatures Game Used Ball

No Pricing
Production One Set

Sign. Black Stitch Black Ink

No Pricing
Production One Set
Blue Ink: No Pricing
Production One Set
Red Ink: No Pricing
Production One Set

Sign. Red Stitch Black Ink

NM/M
Production 58-350

JB	Jason Bay/350	20.00
HB	Hank Blalock/175	15.00
WB	Wade Boggs/175	40.00
CA	Miguel Cabrera/175	40.00
SC	Steve Carlton/58	25.00
SE	Sean Casey/350	15.00
WC	Will Clark/175	25.00
RC	Roger Clemens/175	80.00
CC	Carl Crawford/350	15.00
BC	Bobby Crosby/350	10.00
DA	Andre Dawson/175	25.00
AD	Adam Dunn/175	20.00
GF	Gavin Floyd/350	15.00
NG	Nomar Garciaparra/175	50.00
MG	Marcus Giles/350	10.00
GR	Khalil Greene/350	10.00
KG	Ken Griffey Jr./175	75.00
RH	Rich Harden/350	15.00
KH	Keith Hernandez/350	15.00
HO	Ryan Howard/350	75.00
AH	Aubrey Huff/350	15.00
PH	Philip Humber/350	15.00
BJ	Bo Jackson/175	70.00
DJ	Derek Jeter/175	150.00
RJ	Randy Johnson/175	75.00
AJ	Andruw Jones/175	20.00
SK	Scott Kazmir/350	15.00
BL	Barry Larkin/175	25.00
EM	Edgar Martinez/175	25.00
MA	Don Mattingly/175	60.00
PM	Paul Molitor/175	25.00
MO	Justin Morneau/350	25.00
MM	Mark Mulder/350	10.00
JN	Jeff Niemann/350	15.00
RO	Roy Oswalt/350	25.00
LO	Lyle Overbay/350	10.00
JP	Jake Peavy/350	20.00
PI	Mike Piazza/350	80.00
MP	Mark Prior/175	25.00
AP	Albert Pujols/175	160.00
AR	Aramis Ramirez/350	25.00
RE	Jose Reyes/350	35.00
CR	Cal Ripken Jr./175	120.00
NR	Nolan Ryan/175	80.00
RS	Ryne Sandberg/175	65.00
MS	Mike Schmidt/175	75.00
MT	Mark Teixeira/175	40.00
BU	B.J. Upton/350	15.00
JV	Justin Verlander/350	35.00
DW	David Wright/350	60.00
RY	Robin Yount/175	50.00
CZ	Carlos Zambrano/350	15.00

Sign. Red Stitch Blue Ink

NM/M
Production 75-135

JB	Jason Bay	25.00
HB	Hank Blalock/75	15.00
WB	Wade Boggs/75	40.00
CA	Miguel Cabrera/75	25.00
SE	Sean Casey/135	10.00
WC	Will Clark/75	25.00
RC	Roger Clemens/75	120.00
CC	Carl Crawford/135	15.00
BC	Bobby Crosby/135	15.00
DA	Andre Dawson/75	20.00
AD	Adam Dunn/75	15.00
GF	Gavin Floyd/135	15.00
NG	Nomar Garciaparra/75	65.00
MG	Marcus Giles/135	10.00
GL	Tom Glavine/135	25.00
GR	Khalil Greene/135	10.00
KG	Ken Griffey Jr./75	80.00
HA	Travis Hafner/135	15.00
RH	Rich Harden/135	15.00
KH	Keith Hernandez/135	15.00
HO	Ryan Howard/135	75.00
AH	Aubrey Huff/135	15.00
PH	Philip Humber/135	10.00
BJ	Bo Jackson/75	75.00
DJ	Derek Jeter/75	150.00
RJ	Randy Johnson/75	85.00
AJ	Andruw Jones/75	20.00
SK	Scott Kazmir/135	15.00
BL	Barry Larkin/75	30.00
EM	Edgar Martinez/75	35.00
MA	Don Mattingly/75	70.00
PM	Paul Molitor/75	30.00
MO	Justin Morneau/135	30.00
MM	Mark Mulder/135	15.00
JN	Jeff Niemann/135	15.00
RO	Roy Oswalt/135	25.00
LO	Lyle Overbay/135	12.00
CP	Corey Patterson/135	15.00
JP	Jake Peavy/135	25.00
PI	Mike Piazza/75	80.00
MP	Mark Prior/75	25.00
AP	Albert Pujols/75	160.00
AR	Aramis Ramirez/135	25.00
RE	Jose Reyes/135	35.00
CR	Cal Ripken Jr./75	120.00
NR	Nolan Ryan/75	65.00
RS	Ryne Sandberg/75	65.00
MS	Mike Schmidt/75	50.00
MT	Mark Teixeira/75	40.00
BU	B.J. Upton/135	15.00
JV	Justin Verlander/135	35.00
DW	David Wright/135	60.00
RY	Robin Yount/75	50.00
CZ	Carlos Zambrano/135	15.00

Sign. Red Stitch Red Ink

NM/M
Production 15-35

JB	Jason Bay/35	25.00
SE	Sean Casey/35	20.00
CC	Carl Crawford/35	20.00
BC	Bobby Crosby	15.00
AD	Adam Dunn/15	60.00
GF	Gavin Floyd/35	10.00
MG	Marcus Giles/35	10.00
GL	Tom Glavine/35	40.00
GR	Khalil Greene/35	20.00
HA	Travis Hafner/35	20.00
RH	Rich Harden/35	20.00
KH	Keith Hernandez/35	25.00
HO	Ryan Howard/35	90.00
AH	Aubrey Huff/35	20.00
PH	Philip Humber/35	20.00
SK	Scott Kazmir/35	20.00
MO	Justin Morneau/35	30.00

MM	Mark Mulder/35	20.00
IN	Jeff Niemann/35	25.00
KO	Roy Oswalt/35	40.00
P	Lyle Overbay/35	15.00
P	Corey Patterson/35	15.00
P	Jake Peavy/35	30.00
AP	Albert Pujols/15	250.00
AR	Aramis Ramirez/35	40.00
R	Jose Reyes/35	40.00
BU	B.J. Upton/35	25.00
V	Justin Verlander/35	50.00
DW	David Wright/35	100.00
CZ	Carlos Zambrano/35	25.00

Signatures Dual Red Stitch
NM/M
Production 25 Sets

BJ	Bobby Crosby, Jason Bay	30.00
G	Bobby Crosby, Khalil Greene	15.00
DC	Adam Dunn, Sean Casey	50.00
FH	Gavin Floyd, Ryan Howard	120.00
GC	Ken Griffey Jr., Miguel Cabrera	120.00
GL	Khalil Greene, Mark Loretta	20.00
JC	Randy Johnson, Roger Clemens	120.00
JG	Andruw Jones, Ken Griffey Jr.	150.00
JM	Derek Jeter, Don Mattingly	300.00
LG	Barry Larkin, Ken Griffey Jr.	120.00
LR	Barry Larkin, Cal Ripken Jr.	160.00
NH	Jeff Niemann, Philip Humber	25.00
PB	Jason Bay, Oliver Perez	40.00
PC	Albert Pujols, Miguel Cabrera	300.00
PO	Jake Peavy, Roy Oswalt	50.00
RJ	Cal Ripken Jr., Derek Jeter	300.00
SB	Ryne Sandberg, Wade Boggs	125.00
SG	Nomar Garciaparra, Ryne Sandberg	100.00
SP	Ben Sheets, Jake Peavy	40.00
WC	David Wright, Miguel Cabrera	100.00
WR	David Wright, Jose Reyes	100.00

Red-Blue Stitch Black Ink
NM/M
Production 25-50

JB	Jason Bay/50	25.00
HB	Hank Blalock/25	15.00
WB	Wade Boggs/25	30.00
CA	Miguel Cabrera/25	65.00
SC	Steve Carlton/25	25.00
SE	Sean Casey/50	15.00
WC	Will Clark/25	25.00
CC	Roger Clemens/25	160.00
CC	Carl Crawford/50	15.00
BC	Bobby Crosby/25	10.00
DA	Andre Dawson/25	25.00
AD	Adam Dunn/25	40.00
GF	Gavin Floyd/50	15.00
NG	Nomar Garciaparra/25	65.00
MG	Marcus Giles/50	15.00
GR	Khalil Greene/50	10.00
KG	Ken Griffey Jr./25	120.00
RH	Rich Harden/50	15.00
KH	Keith Hernandez/50	20.00
HO	Ryan Howard/50	85.00
AH	Aubrey Huff/50	20.00
PH	Philip Humber/50	15.00
BJ	Bo Jackson/25	90.00
DJ	Derek Jeter/25	250.00
RJ	Randy Johnson/25	120.00
AJ	Andruw Jones/25	40.00
SK	Scott Kazmir/50	20.00
BL	Barry Larkin/25	40.00
EM	Edgar Martinez/25	40.00
MA	Don Mattingly/25	90.00
PM	Paul Molitor/25	40.00
MO	Justin Morneau/50	25.00
MM	Mark Mulder/50	12.00
JN	Jeff Niemann/50	20.00
RO	Roy Oswalt/50	25.00
JP	Jake Peavy/50	25.00
PI	Mike Piazza/50	100.00
MP	Mark Prior/25	40.00
AP	Albert Pujols/25	220.00
CR	Cal Ripken Jr./25	165.00
NR	Nolan Ryan/25	100.00
RS	Ryne Sandberg/25	80.00
JS	Johan Santana/25	50.00
MS	Mike Schmidt/25	75.00
MT	Mark Teixeira/25	50.00
BU	B.J. Upton/50	20.00
JV	Justin Verlander/50	40.00
DW	David Wright/50	100.00
RY	Robin Yount/25	65.00
CZ	Carlos Zambrano/50	20.00

Red-Blue Stitch Blue Ink
NM/M
Production 15-30
Red Ink: No Pricing
Production 5-10

JB	Jason Bay/30	25.00
SE	Sean Casey/30	20.00
CC	Carl Crawford/30	20.00
BC	Bobby Crosby/30	15.00
GF	Gavin Floyd/30	15.00
MG	Marcus Giles/30	15.00
GL	Tom Glavine/30	15.00
GR	Khalil Greene/30	15.00
HA	Travis Hafner/30	15.00
RH	Rich Harden/30	15.00
KH	Keith Hernandez/30	25.00
HO	Ryan Howard/30	90.00
PH	Philip Humber/30	20.00
SK	Scott Kazmir/30	20.00
MO	Justin Morneau/30	35.00
MM	Mark Mulder/30	25.00
JN	Jeff Niemann/30	25.00
RO	Roy Oswalt/30	30.00
LO	Lyle Overbay/30	15.00
JP	Jake Peavy/30	30.00
AR	Aramis Ramirez/30	15.00
BU	B.J. Upton/30	50.00
JV	Justin Verlander/30	25.00
DW	David Wright/30	120.00
CZ	Carlos Zambrano/30	25.00

Signature Game Used Barrel
No Pricing
Production 1-10

Signatures Barrel Black Ink
NM/M
Production 25-50

JB	Jason Bay/50	20.00
HB	Hank Blalock/50	20.00
CA	Miguel Cabrera/50	70.00
SC	Steve Carlton/25	25.00
SE	Sean Casey/50	15.00
WC	Will Clark/25	25.00
CC	Carl Crawford/50	15.00
BC	Bobby Crosby/50	15.00
DA	Andre Dawson/25	25.00
AD	Adam Dunn/25	40.00
GF	Gavin Floyd/50	15.00
NG	Nomar Garciaparra/25	80.00
MG	Marcus Giles/50	15.00
GL	Tom Glavine/50	30.00
GR	Khalil Greene/50	10.00
KG	Ken Griffey Jr./25	85.00
HA	Travis Hafner/50	15.00
RH	Rich Harden/50	15.00
KH	Keith Hernandez/50	20.00
HO	Ryan Howard/50	90.00
AH	Aubrey Huff/50	15.00
PH	Philip Humber/50	15.00
BJ	Bo Jackson/25	75.00
DJ	Derek Jeter/50	250.00
RJ	Randy Johnson/25	125.00
AJ	Andruw Jones/50	40.00
SK	Scott Kazmir/50	20.00
BL	Barry Larkin/50	40.00
MA	Don Mattingly/25	85.00
PM	Paul Molitor/25	40.00
MO	Justin Morneau/50	25.00
MM	Mark Mulder/50	15.00
JN	Jeff Niemann/50	20.00
RO	Roy Oswalt/50	35.00
LO	Lyle Overbay/50	15.00
JP	Jake Peavy/50	20.00
MP	Mark Prior/50	20.00
AP	Albert Pujols/25	220.00
AR	Aramis Ramirez/50	30.00
CR	Cal Ripken Jr./25	180.00
NR	Nolan Ryan/25	100.00
RS	Ryne Sandberg/25	75.00
MS	Mike Schmidt/25	70.00
MT	Mark Teixeira/25	40.00
BU	B.J. Upton/50	20.00
JV	Justin Verlander/50	40.00
DW	David Wright/50	100.00
RY	Robin Yount/25	90.00
CZ	Carlos Zambrano/50	20.00

Signatures Barrel Blue Ink
NM/M
Production 15-30

JB	Jason Bay/30	25.00
SE	Sean Casey/30	15.00
CC	Carl Crawford/30	20.00
BC	Bobby Crosby/30	10.00
AD	Adam Dunn/15	60.00
GF	Gavin Floyd/30	20.00
MG	Marcus Giles/30	15.00
GL	Tom Glavine/30	40.00
GR	Khalil Greene/30	20.00
HA	Travis Hafner/30	20.00
RH	Rich Harden/30	15.00
KH	Keith Hernandez/30	25.00
HO	Ryan Howard/30	90.00
AH	Aubrey Huff/30	20.00
PH	Philip Humber/30	15.00
SK	Scott Kazmir/30	20.00
MO	Justin Morneau/30	30.00
MM	Mark Mulder/30	15.00
JN	Jeff Niemann/30	25.00
RO	Roy Oswalt/30	40.00
LO	Lyle Overbay/30	15.00
CP	Corey Patterson/30	15.00
JP	Jake Peavy/30	30.00
AP	Albert Pujols/15	250.00
AR	Aramis Ramirez/30	40.00
BU	B.J. Upton/30	25.00
JV	Justin Verlander/30	50.00
DW	David Wright/30	100.00
CZ	Carlos Zambrano/30	20.00

Signatures Barrel Red Ink
No Pricing
Production 5-10

Signatures Dual Barrel
No Pricing
Production 15 Sets

Signatures Game Used Glove
No Pricing
Production 9-10

Signatures Glove Black Ink
NM/M
Production 15-30

JB	Jason Bay/30	40.00
SE	Sean Casey/30	20.00
CC	Carl Crawford/30	30.00
BC	Bobby Crosby/30	15.00
GF	Gavin Floyd/30	15.00
MG	Marcus Giles/30	10.00
GL	Tom Glavine/30	50.00
GR	Khalil Greene/30	10.00
HA	Travis Hafner/30	20.00
RH	Rich Harden/30	20.00
KH	Keith Hernandez/30	30.00
HO	Ryan Howard/30	100.00
AH	Aubrey Huff/30	20.00
PH	Philip Humber/30	20.00
SK	Scott Kazmir/30	20.00
MO	Justin Morneau/30	40.00
MM	Mark Mulder/30	20.00
JN	Jeff Niemann/30	30.00
RO	Roy Oswalt/30	30.00
LO	Lyle Overbay/30	20.00
CP	Corey Patterson/30	15.00
JP	Jake Peavy/30	40.00
AR	Aramis Ramirez/30	50.00
BU	B.J. Upton/30	25.00
JV	Justin Verlander/30	50.00
DW	David Wright/30	100.00
CZ	Carlos Zambrano/30	25.00

Signatures Glove Blue Ink
No Pricing
Production 5-10
Red Ink: No Pricing
Production 2-5

Signatures Dual Glove
No Pricing
Production 10 Sets

Sweet Threads

NM/M
Common Player: 4.00
Gold: 1-1.5X
Production 75 Sets
Platinum: No Pricing
Production 10 Sets
Plutonium: No Pricing
Production One Set
Patch: 2-4X
Production 35 Sets

JB	Jeff Bagwell	6.00
CB	Carlos Beltran	6.00
AB	Adrian Beltre	4.00
HB	Hank Blalock	4.00
WB	Wade Boggs	8.00
BG	George Brett	10.00
MC	Miguel Cabrera	8.00
EC	Eric Chavez	4.00
WC	Will Clark	6.00
BC	Bartolo Colon	4.00
JD	Johnny Damon	6.00
EG	Eric Gagne	4.00
TG	Tom Glavine	6.00
KG	Ken Griffey Jr.	12.00
VG	Vladimir Guerrero	8.00
GW	Tony Gwynn	8.00
TH	Todd Helton	6.00
HO	Trevor Hoffman	4.00
BJ	Bo Jackson	8.00
DJ	Derek Jeter	20.00
RJ	Randy Johnson	8.00
CJ	Chipper Jones	8.00
CL	Carlos Lee	4.00
GM	Greg Maddux	10.00
PM	Pedro Martinez	8.00
DM	Don Mattingly	10.00
DO	David Ortiz	8.00
RP	Rafael Palmeiro	8.00
PI	Mike Piazza	8.00
MP	Mark Prior	8.00
AP	Albert Pujols	15.00
MR	Manny Ramirez	8.00
CR	Cal Ripken Jr.	20.00
IR	Ivan Rodriguez	6.00
SR	Scott Rolen	4.00
NR	Nolan Ryan	12.00
RS	Ryne Sandberg	8.00
JS	Johan Santana	6.00
CS	Curt Schilling	6.00
MS	Mike Schmidt	10.00
SM	John Smoltz	6.00
AS	Alfonso Soriano	6.00
SS	Sammy Sosa	8.00
MT	Mark Teixeira	6.00
TE	Miguel Tejada	6.00
FT	Frank Thomas	6.00
JT	Jim Thome	6.00
JV	Jason Varitek	10.00
BW	Bernie Williams	6.00
KW	Kerry Wood	6.00

Sweet Threads Dual
NM/M
Production 25 Sets
Gold: No Pricing
Production Five Sets
Patch: No Pricing
Production Five Sets
Plutonium: No Pricing
Production One Set

BG	Carlos Beltran, Ken Griffey Jr.	25.00
BM	Carlos Beltran, Pedro Martinez	15.00
DC	Carlos Delgado, Miguel Cabrera	15.00
GC	Ken Griffey Jr., Miguel Cabrera	25.00
GM	Dallas McPherson, Vladimir Guerrero	15.00
JB	Bo Jackson, George Brett	25.00
JJ	Randy Johnson, Derek Jeter	40.00
JM	Derek Jeter, Don Mattingly	50.00
JS	Jim Thome, Mike Schmidt	30.00
MG	Greg Maddux, Tom Glavine	25.00
MJ	Mike Mussina, Randy Johnson	20.00
MP	Greg Maddux, Mark Prior	25.00
OR	David Ortiz, Manny Ramirez	20.00
PO	Andy Pettitte, Roy Oswalt	10.00
PR	Pedro Martinez, Randy Johnson	20.00
PS	Rafael Palmeiro, Sammy Sosa	20.00
PW	David Wright, Mike Piazza	30.00
RJ	Cal Ripken Jr., Derek Jeter	70.00
RP	Albert Pujols, Scott Rolen	30.00
RT	Cal Ripken Jr., Miguel Tejada	40.00
SB	Ryne Sandberg, Wade Boggs	30.00
SJ	Curt Schilling, Randy Johnson	20.00
SV	Curt Schilling, Jason Varitek	20.00
WP	Kerry Wood, Mark Prior	15.00

Sweet Threads Triple
NM/M
Production 25 Sets
Gold: No Pricing
Production Five Sets
Plutonium: No Pricing
Production One Set
Patch: No Pricing
Production Five Sets

BBB	Craig Biggio, Jeff Bagwell, Lance Berkman	20.00
BWP	Carlos Beltran, David Wright, Mike Piazza	25.00
GGG	Luis Gonzalez, Shawn Green, Troy Glaus	10.00
JMB	Randy Johnson, Mike Mussina, Kevin Brown	25.00
JWS	Derek Jeter, Bernie Williams, Gary Sheffield	50.00
KGD	Austin Kearns, Ken Griffey Jr., Adam Dunn	30.00
LOP	Brad Lidge, Roy Oswalt, Andy Pettitte	15.00
ODR	David Ortiz, Johnny Damon, Manny Ramirez	25.00
PER	Albert Pujols, Jim Edmonds, Scott Rolen	40.00
PWM	Mark Prior, Kerry Wood, Greg Maddux	30.00
RDN	Manny Ramirez, Johnny Damon, Trot Nixon	8.00
SBT	Alfonso Soriano, Hank Blalock, Mark Teixeira	20.00
SMJ	Curt Schilling, Pedro Martinez, Randy Johnson	20.00
TPS	Miguel Tejada, Rafael Palmeiro, Sammy Sosa	20.00

Sweet Threads Quad
NM/M
Production 25 Sets
Gold: No Pricing
Production Five Sets
Plutonium: No Pricing
Production One Set
Patch: No Pricing
Production Five Sets

BMCB	Adrian Beltre, Dallas McPherson, Eric Chavez, Hank Blalock	25.00
BRGG	Carlos Beltran, Manny Ramirez, Ken Griffey Jr., Vladimir Guerrero	40.00
POTH	Albert Pujols, David Ortiz, Jim Thome, Todd Helton	40.00
RBGB	Cal Ripken Jr., Brett George, Tony Gwynn, Wade Boggs	90.00
RVMP	Ivan Rodriguez, Jason Varitek, Joe Mauer, Jorge Posada	30.00

2005 Upper Deck Sweet Spot Classic

NM/M
Complete Set (100): 30.00
Common Player: .40
Pack (4): 12.00
Box (12): 120.00

1	Al Kaline	1.00
2	Al Rosen	.40
3	Babe Ruth	4.00
4	Bill Mazeroski	.40
5	Billy Williams	.40
6	Bob Feller	.75
7	Bob Gibson	.40
8	Bobby Doerr	.40
9	Brooks Robinson	1.00
10	Cal Ripken Jr.	4.00
11	Carl Yastrzemski	.40
12	Carlton Fisk	.40
13	Casey Stengel	.40
14	Christy Mathewson	2.00
15	Cy Young	1.50
16	Dale Murphy	.75
17	Dave Winfield	.75
18	Dennis Eckersley	.40
19	Dizzy Dean	1.00
20	Don Drysdale	.75
21	Don Mattingly	3.00
22	Don Newcombe	.40
23	Don Sutton	.40
24	Duke Snider	1.00
25	Dwight Evans	.40
26	Eddie Mathews	1.50
27	Eddie Murray	1.00
28	Enos Slaughter	.40
29	Ernie Banks	2.00
30	Frank Howard	.40
31	Frank Robinson	.75
32	Gary Carter	.40
33	Gaylord Perry	.40
34	George Brett	3.00
35	George Kell	.40
36	George Sisler	.40
37	Larry Doby	.40
38	Harmon Killebrew	1.50
39	Honus Wagner	2.00
40	Jackie Robinson	2.00
41	Jim Bunning	.40
42	Jim Palmer	.75
43	Jim Rice	.40
44	Jimmie Foxx	.40
45	Joe DiMaggio	3.00
46	Joe Morgan	.40
47	Johnny Bench	2.00
48	Johnny Mize	.40
49	Johnny Podres	.40
50	Juan Marichal	.40
51	Keith Hernandez	.40
52	Kirby Puckett	1.00
53	Lefty Grove	.40
54	Lou Brock	.75
55	Lou Gehrig	4.00
56	Luis Aparicio	.40
57	Fergie Jenkins	.40
58	Maury Wills	.40
59	Mel Ott	1.50
60	Mickey Cochrane	1.00
61	Mickey Mantle	4.00
62	Mike Schmidt	3.00
63	Monte Irvin	.75
64	Nolan Ryan	4.00
65	Orlando Cepeda	.40
66	Ozzie Smith	1.50
67	Paul Molitor	.40
68	Pee Wee Reese	.40
69	Phil Niekro	.40
70	Phil Rizzuto	.40
71	Ralph Kiner	.40
72	Richie Ashburn	.40
73	Roberto Clemente	4.00
74	Robin Roberts	.40
75	Robin Yount	2.00
76	Rocky Colavito	1.00
77	Rod Carew	.75
78	Rogers Hornsby	1.00
79	Rollie Fingers	.40
80	Roy Campanella	1.00
81	Bob Lemon	.40
82	Red Schoendienst	.40
83	Satchel Paige	2.00
84	Stan Musial	2.50
85	Steve Carlton	.75
86	Ted Williams	3.00
87	Thurman Munson	1.50
88	Tom Seaver	1.50
89	Tony Gwynn	1.50
90	Tony Perez	.40
91	Ty Cobb	2.00
92	Wade Boggs	1.00
93	Walter Johnson	1.50
94	Warren Spahn	1.50
95	Whitey Ford	.75
96	Will Clark	.75
97	Jim "Catfish" Hunter	.40
98	Willie McCovey	.75
99	Willie Stargell	1.00
100	Yogi Berra	1.50

Silver
Cards (1-100): 2-4X
Production 100 Sets

Gold

Cards (1-100): 4-8X
Production 50 Sets

Classic Materials

NM/M
Common Player: 6.00

BE	Johnny Bench	15.00
YB	Yogi Berra	20.00
WB	Wade Boggs	10.00
GB	George Brett	10.00
GB1	George Brett	10.00
LB	Lou Brock	8.00
JB	Jim Bunning	10.00
CP	Roy Campanella	12.00
CA	Rod Carew	8.00
SC	Steve Carlton	8.00
GC	Gary Carter	6.00
OC	Orlando Cepeda	8.00
WC	Will Clark	10.00
WC1	Will Clark	10.00
RC	Roberto Clemente	60.00
TC	Ty Cobb/SP	100.00
CO	Rocky Colavito	25.00
DC	David Cone	6.00
AD	Andre Dawson	6.00
JD	Joe DiMaggio	80.00
DD	Don Drysdale	8.00
BF	Bob Feller	12.00
CF	Carlton Fisk	8.00
LG	Lou Gehrig/SP	160.00
BG	Bob Gibson	10.00
MG	Mark Grace	8.00
RG	Ron Guidry	8.00
TG	Tony Gwynn	12.00
CH	Jim "Catfish" Hunter	8.00
FJ	Fergie Jenkins	8.00
AK	Al Kaline	8.00
HK	Harmon Killebrew	12.00
MM	Mickey Mantle/SP	120.00
MA	Juan Marichal	8.00
EM	Eddie Mathews	10.00
DM	Don Mattingly	15.00
DM1	Don Mattingly	15.00
BM	Bill Mazeroski	10.00
WI	Willie McCovey	10.00
PM	Paul Molitor	10.00

JM	Joe Morgan	6.00
JM1	Joe Morgan	6.00
TM	Thurman Munson/SP	25.00
MU	Dale Murphy	10.00
ED	Eddie Murray	8.00
ED1	Eddie Murray	8.00
SM	Stan Musial/SP	20.00
PN	Phil Niekro	6.00
SP	Satchel Paige/SP	50.00
JP	Jim Palmer	8.00
TP	Tony Perez	8.00
GP	Gaylord Perry	6.00
RE	Pee Wee Reese/SP	15.00
RI	Jim Rice	8.00
CR	Cal Ripken Jr.	20.00
CR1	Cal Ripken Jr.	20.00
PR	Phil Rizzuto	15.00
RR	Robin Roberts	10.00
RO	Brooks Robinson	10.00
FR	Frank Robinson	8.00
JR	Jackie Robinson	50.00
BR	Babe Ruth/SP	275.00
NR	Nolan Ryan	25.00
NR1	Nolan Ryan	25.00
MS	Mike Schmidt	15.00
MS1	Mike Schmidt	15.00
SD	Red Schoendienst	8.00
TS	Tom Seaver	10.00
OS	Ozzie Smith/SP	15.00
SN	Duke Snider	10.00
WS	Warren Spahn	15.00
DS	Don Sutton	6.00
DS1	Don Sutton	6.00
FV	Fernando Valenzuela	6.00
TW	Ted Williams/SP	75.00
MW	Maury Wills	6.00
MW1	Maury Wills	6.00
DW	Dave Winfield	6.00
DW1	Dave Winfield	6.00
EW	Early Wynn	10.00
CY	Carl Yastrzemski	15.00
RY	Robin Yount	12.00

Dual Signatures
No Pricing
Production 15 Sets

Patch
NM/M
Some not priced due to scarcity.

LA	Luis Aparicio/19	150.00
BE	Johnny Bench/32	100.00
WB	Wade Boggs/25	60.00
WB1	Wade Boggs/34	60.00
GB	George Brett/38	80.00
GB1	George Brett/50	80.00
LB	Lou Brock/34	90.00
SC	Steve Carlton/50	60.00
GC	Gary Carter/47	50.00
GC1	Gary Carter/34	50.00
OC	Orlando Cepeda/40	50.00
DC	David Cone/39	50.00
JD	Joe DiMaggio/38	250.00
CF	Carlton Fisk/50	70.00
RG	Ron Guidry/30	40.00
TG	Tony Gwynn/34	80.00
TG1	Tony Gwynn/30	80.00
FH	Frank Howard/34	85.00
FJ	Fergie Jenkins/34	
WI	Willie McCovey/50	60.00
JM	Joe Morgan/50	60.00
MU	Dale Murphy/34	80.00
ED	Eddie Murray/34	70.00
ED1	Eddie Murray/34	70.00
PN	Phil Niekro/44	50.00
TP	Tony Perez/34	75.00
GP	Gaylord Perry/34	50.00
PO	Johnny Podres/50	60.00
RI	Jim Rice/34	50.00
CR	Cal Ripken Jr./34	150.00
CR1	Cal Ripken Jr./34	150.00
RO	Brooks Robinson/50	85.00
RO1	Brooks Robinson/43	85.00
FR	Frank Robinson/34	80.00
JR	Jackie Robinson/12	250.00
SD	Red Schoendienst/42	60.00
TS	Tom Seaver/50	60.00
TS1	Tom Seaver/50	50.00
OS	Ozzie Smith/34	100.00
ST	Willie Stargell/50	65.00
BS	Bruce Sutter/50	50.00
DS	Don Sutton/34	60.00
DS1	Don Sutton/34	40.00
MW	Maury Wills/50	60.00
MW1	Maury Wills/47	60.00
DW1	Dave Winfield/50	75.00
CY	Carl Yastrzemski/35	100.00
RY	Robin Yount/34	75.00

Leather Signatures
No Pricing
Production 25 Sets

Signatures

NM/M
Common Autograph: 20.00
Inserted 1:12

Blue/Red Stitch:		1.5-2X
Production 40 Sets		
Black Stitch:		No Pricing
Production One Set		
LA	Luis Aparicio	25.00
HB	Harold Baines	20.00
EB	Ernie Banks	75.00
BE	Johnny Bench	60.00
YB	Yogi Berra/SP	60.00
WB	Wade Boggs	50.00
GB	George Brett	85.00
JB	Jim Bunning	20.00
JC	Jose Canseco	40.00
CA	Rod Carew	50.00
SC	Steve Carlton	40.00
GC	Gary Carter	25.00
OC	Orlando Cepeda	25.00
WC	Will Clark	50.00
RC	Rocky Colavito/SP	85.00
DC	David Cone	25.00
AD	Andre Dawson	20.00
BD	Bobby Doerr	25.00
DE	Dennis Eckersley	25.00
EV	Dwight Evans	20.00
BF	Bob Feller	40.00
RF	Rollie Fingers	20.00
CF	Carlton Fisk	40.00
WF	Whitey Ford	60.00
BG	Bob Gibson	40.00
MG	Mark Grace	40.00
TG	Tony Gwynn	50.00
EH	Ernie Harwell/SP	50.00
KH	Keith Hernandez	20.00
FH	Frank Howard	25.00
MI	Monte Irvin	25.00
BJ	Bo Jackson	75.00
DJ	David Justice	20.00
KA	Harry Kalas	25.00
AK	Al Kaline	40.00
GK	George Kell	25.00
HK	Harmon Killebrew	50.00
RK	Ralph Kiner/SP	50.00
MA	Juan Marichal	25.00
DM	Don Mattingly	80.00
BM	Bill Mazeroski	40.00
MC	Willie McCovey/SP	60.00
PM	Paul Molitor	40.00
JM	Joe Morgan/SP	35.00
MU	Dale Murphy	25.00
SM	Stan Musial	100.00
DN	Don Newcombe	25.00
PN	Phil Niekro	25.00
JP	Jim Palmer	25.00
TP	Tony Perez	25.00
GP	Gaylord Perry	25.00
PO	Johnny Podres	20.00
KP	Kirby Puckett/SP	50.00
JR	Jim Rice	25.00
CR	Cal Ripken Jr.	160.00
PR	Phil Rizzuto	50.00
RR	Robin Roberts	30.00
BR	Brooks Robinson	40.00
FR	Frank Robinson	40.00
AR	Al Rosen	20.00
NR	Nolan Ryan	125.00
RS	Ron Santo	35.00
MS	Mike Schmidt	80.00
RE	Red Schoendienst	30.00
TS	Tom Seaver	60.00
OS	Ozzie Smith	60.00
SN	Duke Snider	40.00
ST	Rusty Staub	20.00
SU	Bruce Sutter	20.00
DS	Don Sutton	20.00
LT	Luis Tiant	20.00
FV	Fernando Valenzuela	30.00
BW	Billy Williams	25.00
MW	Matt Williams	20.00
WI	Maury Wills	20.00
CY	Carl Yastrzemski	80.00
RY	Robin Yount/SP	75.00

Sweet Sticks Signatures
NM/M
Production 35 Sets

LA	Luis Aparicio	50.00
HB	Harold Baines	40.00
EB	Ernie Banks	125.00
BE	Johnny Bench	75.00
YB	Yogi Berra	80.00
WB	Wade Boggs	75.00
GB	George Brett	140.00
JB	Jim Bunning	40.00
JC	Jose Canseco	75.00
CA	Rod Carew	75.00
SC	Steve Carlton	50.00
GC	Gary Carter	40.00
OC	Orlando Cepeda	50.00
WC	Will Clark	65.00
RC	Rocky Colavito	120.00
DC	David Cone	50.00
AD	Andre Dawson	50.00
BD	Bobby Doerr	50.00
DE	Dennis Eckersley	50.00
EV	Dwight Evans	60.00
BF	Bob Feller	75.00
RF	Rollie Fingers	45.00
CF	Carlton Fisk	75.00
WF	Whitey Ford	85.00
BG	Bob Gibson	65.00
MG	Mark Grace	75.00
TG	Tony Gwynn	85.00
EH	Ernie Harwell	50.00
KH	Keith Hernandez	40.00
FH	Frank Howard	50.00
MI	Monte Irvin	50.00
BJ	Bo Jackson	140.00
DJ	David Justice	40.00

AK	Al Kaline	80.00
GK	George Kell	80.00
HK	Harmon Killebrew	80.00
RK	Ralph Kiner	75.00
MA	Juan Marichal	50.00
DM	Don Mattingly	125.00
BM	Bill Mazeroski	90.00
MC	Willie McCovey	85.00
PM	Paul Molitor	60.00
JM	Joe Morgan	50.00
MU	Dale Murphy	50.00
SM	Stan Musial	140.00
DN	Don Newcombe	50.00
PN	Phil Niekro	40.00
JP	Jim Palmer	50.00
TP	Tony Perez	40.00
GP	Gaylord Perry	40.00
PO	Johnny Podres	40.00
KP	Kirby Puckett	100.00
JR	Jim Rice	50.00
CR	Cal Ripken Jr.	240.00
RR	Robin Roberts	50.00
BR	Brooks Robinson	65.00
FR	Frank Robinson	60.00
AR	Al Rosen	50.00
NR	Nolan Ryan	150.00
RS	Ron Santo	65.00
MS	Mike Schmidt	125.00
RE	Red Schoendienst	50.00
TS	Tom Seaver	85.00
OS	Ozzie Smith	90.00
SN	Duke Snider	75.00
ST	Rusty Staub	40.00
SU	Bruce Sutter	30.00
DS	Don Sutton	40.00
LT	Luis Tiant	40.00
BW	Billy Williams	40.00
MW	Matt Williams	50.00
WI	Maury Wills	40.00
CY	Carl Yastrzemski	120.00
RY	Robin Yount	75.00

Wingfield Classic Collection
NM/M
Common Player: 4.00
Inserted 1:Box

1	Al Kaline	4.00
2	Pee Wee Reese	4.00
3	Stan Musial, Ted Williams	6.00
4	Bill Dickey	6.00
5	Frank Robinson	5.00
6	Billy Martin	4.00
7	Casey Stengel, Joe DiMaggio	6.00
8	Bob Feller, Dwight D. Eisenhower	4.00
9	Duke Snider	5.00
10	Carl Yastrzemski	8.00
11	Honus Wagner	6.00
12	Dwight D. Eisenhower, Clark Griffith	4.00
13	Mickey Mantle, Joe DiMaggio	15.00
14	Don Drysdale	4.00
15	Ted Williams	8.00
16	Al Kaline, Mickey Mantle	15.00
17	Ernie Banks	6.00
18	Lou Boudreau	4.00
19	George Sisler, Harmon Killebrew	6.00
20	Gil Hodges	4.00
21	Rogers Hornsby	6.00
22	Luis Aparicio	4.00
23	Jackie Robinson	10.00
24	Joe Morgan	4.00
25	Enos Slaughter	4.00
26	Joe DiMaggio	15.00
27	Mickey Mantle, Ted Kluszewski	15.00
28	John F. Kennedy	6.00
29	Johnny Bench	8.00
30	Juan Marichal	4.00
31	Larry Doby	4.00
32	Don Newcombe, Elston Howard	4.00
33	Harmon Killebrew, Dwight D. Eisenhower	6.00
34	Roger Maris, Mickey Mantle	20.00
35	Mickey Mantle, Stan Musial	15.00
36	Ted Williams, Mickey Mantle, Yogi Berra	15.00
37	Nellie Fox	6.00
38	Richie Ashburn	4.00
39	Roberto Clemente	15.00
40	Stan Musial, Robin Roberts	8.00
41	Tommy Heinrich, Joe DiMaggio	8.00
42	Roy Campanella	6.00
43	Rocky Colavito, Harmon Killebrew	6.00
44	Steve Carlton	6.00
45	Thurman Munson	6.00
46	Luis Aparicio, Ernie Banks	6.00
47	Gil Hodges, Yogi Berra, Dwight D. Eisenhower	6.00
48	Whitey Ford	6.00
49	Mickey Mantle, Yogi Berra, Joe DiMaggio	15.00
50	Yogi Berra	8.00

2005 Upper Deck The National Chicago Legends

These gold-foil enhanced cards were only available as an Upper Deck wrapper redemption on July 31 during the National Sports Collectors Convention in Chicago. On front cards have a serial number from within an edition of 750 each. Two of the six cards in the set were former Cubs.

NM/M
CL1	Ernie Banks	3.00
CL2	Ryne Sandberg	3.00

2005 Upper Deck The National Cubs/White Sox

These gold-foil enhanced cards were only available as an Upper Deck wrapper redemption on July 30 during the National Sports Collectors Convention in Chicago. On front cards have a serial number from within an edition of 750 each. Special autographed versions of each card, serially numbered to five each, were randomly distributed.

NM/M
Complete Set (6):		12.50
Common Player:		2.00
MLB1	Mark Prior	3.00
MLB2	Greg Maddux	4.00
MLB3	Derrek Lee	4.00
MLB4	Kerry Wood	3.00
MLB5	Tadahito Iguchi	2.00
MLB6	Paul Konerko	2.00

2005 UD Ultimate Collection
NM/M
Common (1-100): 1.50
Production 475
Common (101-237): 3.00
Production 275
Common (238-242): 50.00
Production 99
Pack (4): 85.00
Box (4): 300.00

1	A.J. Burnett	1.50
2	Adam Dunn	1.50
3	Adrian Beltre	2.00
4	Albert Pujols	8.00
5	Alex Rodriguez	8.00
6	Alfonso Soriano	3.00
7	Andruw Jones	2.00
8	Andy Pettitte	2.00
9	Aramis Ramirez	2.00
10	Aubrey Huff	1.50
11	Ben Sheets	2.00
12	Bobby Abreu	2.00
13	Bobby Crosby	1.50
14	Chris Carpenter	2.00
15	Brian Giles	1.50
16	Brian Roberts	1.50
17	Carl Crawford	2.00
18	Carlos Beltran	2.00
19	Carlos Delgado	2.00
20	Carlos Zambrano	2.00
21	Chipper Jones	3.00
22	Corey Patterson	1.50
23	Craig Biggio	2.00
24	Curt Schilling	3.00
25	Dallas McPherson	1.50
26	David Ortiz	3.00
27	David Wright	5.00
28	Delmon Young	2.00
29	Derek Jeter	8.00
30	Derrek Lee	3.00
31	Dontrelle Willis	2.00
32	Eric Chavez	2.00
33	Eric Gagne	2.00
34	Francisco Rodriguez	1.50
35	Gary Sheffield	2.00
36	Greg Maddux	5.00
37	Hank Blalock	1.50
38	Hideki Matsui	5.00
39	Ichiro Suzuki	8.00
40	Ivan Rodriguez	3.00
41	J.D. Drew	1.50
42	Jake Peavy	2.00
43	Jason Bay	2.00
44	Jason Schmidt	1.50
45	Jeff Bagwell	2.00
46	Jeff Kent	2.00
47	Jeremy Bonderman	2.00
48	Jim Edmonds	2.00
49	Jim Thome	2.00
50	Joe Mauer	2.00
51	Johan Santana	2.00
52	John Smoltz	2.00
53	Johnny Damon	3.00
54	Jose Reyes	2.00
55	Jose Vidro	1.50
56	Josh Beckett	1.50
57	Justin Morneau	2.00
58	Ken Griffey Jr.	5.00
59	Kerry Wood	2.00
60	Khalil Greene	1.50
61	Lance Berkman	2.00
62	Larry Walker	2.00
63	Luis Gonzalez	1.50
64	Manny Ramirez	3.00
65	Mark Buehrle	2.00
66	Mark Mulder	2.00
67	Mark Prior	3.00
68	Mark Teixeira	2.00
69	Michael Young	2.00
70	Miguel Cabrera	3.00
71	Miguel Tejada	2.00
72	Mike Mussina	2.00
73	Mike Piazza	4.00
74	Moises Alou	2.00
75	Nomar Garciaparra	4.00
76	Oliver Perez	1.50
77	Pat Burrell	2.00
78	Paul Konerko	2.00
79	Pedro Feliz	1.50
80	Pedro Martinez	3.00
81	Randy Johnson	3.00
82	Richie Sexson	2.00
83	Rickie Weeks	2.00
84	Roger Clemens	8.00
85	Roy Halladay	2.00
86	Roy Oswalt	2.00
87	Sammy Sosa	3.00
88	Scott Kazmir	1.50
89	Scott Rolen	2.00
90	Shawn Green	2.00
91	Tim Hudson	2.00
92	Todd Helton	2.00
93	Tom Glavine	3.00
94	Torii Hunter	2.00
95	Travis Hafner	2.00
96	Troy Glaus	2.00
97	Vernon Wells	1.50
98	Victor Martinez	2.00
99	Vladimir Guerrero	3.00
100	Zack Greinke	1.50
101	Al Kaline	4.00
102	Babe Ruth	10.00
103	Bo Jackson	5.00
104	Bob Gibson	5.00
105	Brooks Robinson	4.00
106	Cal Ripken Jr.	12.00
107	Carl Yastrzemski	5.00
108	Carlton Fisk	4.00
109	Jim "Catfish" Hunter	5.00
110	Christy Mathewson	5.00
111	Cy Young	5.00
112	Don Mattingly	6.00
113	Eddie Mathews	4.00
114	Eddie Murray	4.00
115	Gary Carter	3.00
116	Harmon Killebrew	4.00
117	Jim Palmer	4.00
118	Jimmie Foxx	4.00
119	Joe DiMaggio	8.00
120	Johnny Bench	4.00
121	Lefty Grove	4.00
122	Lou Gehrig	8.00
123	Mel Ott	3.00
124	Reggie Jackson	5.00
125	Mike Schmidt	5.00
126	Nolan Ryan	5.00
127	Ozzie Smith	5.00
128	Paul Molitor	4.00
129	Pee Wee Reese	3.00
130	Robin Yount	4.00
131	Ryne Sandberg	6.00
132	Ted Williams	8.00
133	Thurman Munson	5.00
134	Tom Seaver	4.00
135	Tony Gwynn	5.00
136	Wade Boggs	3.00
137	Walter Johnson	4.00
138	Warren Spahn	4.00
139	Will Clark	3.00
140	Willie McCovey	3.00
141	Willie Stargell	4.00
142	Yogi Berra	5.00
143	Ambiorix Burgos RC	4.00
144	Ambiorix Concepcion RC	4.00
145	Anibal Sanchez RC	6.00
146	Bill McCarthy RC	4.00
147	Brian Burres RC	4.00
148	Carlos Ruiz RC	4.00
149	Casey Rogowski RC	4.00
150	Chris Resop RC	4.00
151	Chris Roberson RC	4.00
152	Chris Seddon RC	4.00
153	Colter Bean RC	4.00
154	Dae-Sung Koo RC	4.00
155	Danny Rueckel RC	4.00
156	David Gassner RC	4.00
157	Ryan Howard RC	8.00
158	D.J. Houlton RC	4.00
159	Derek Wathan RC	4.00
160	Devon Lowery RC	4.00
161	Enrique Gonzalez RC	4.00
162	Erick Threets RC	4.00
163	Eude Brito RC	4.00
164	Francisco Butto RC	4.00
165	Franquelis Osoria RC	4.00
166	Garrett Jones RC	4.00
167	Geovany Soto RC	20.00
168	Ismael Ramirez RC	4.00
169	Jared Gothreaux RC	4.00
170	Jason Hammel RC	4.00
171	Jeff Housman RC	4.00
172	Jeff Miller RC	4.00
173	Jeff Francoeur RC	6.00
174	John Hattig Jr. RC	4.00
175	Jorge Campillo RC	4.00
176	Juan Morillo RC	4.00
177	Justin Wechsler RC	4.00
178	Keiichi Yabu RC	4.00
179	Kendry Morales RC	15.00
180	Luis Hernandez RC	4.00
181	Luis Mendoza RC	4.00
182	Luis Pena RC	4.00
183	Luis Rodriguez RC	4.00
184	Luke Scott RC	10.00
185	Marcos Carvajal RC	4.00
186	Mark Woodyard RC	4.00
187	Matt Smith RC	4.00
188	Matt Lindstrom RC	4.00
189	Miguel Negron RC	4.00
190	Mike Morse RC	4.00
191	Nate McLouth RC	4.00
192	Nick Masset RC	4.00
193	Paulino Reynoso RC	4.00
194	Pedro Lopez RC	4.00
195	Peter Orr RC	4.00
196	Randy Messenger RC	4.00
197	Randy Williams RC	4.00
198	Raul Tablado RC	4.00
199	Ronny Paulino RC	6.00
200	Russel Rohlicek RC	4.00
201	Russell Martin RC	8.00
202	Scott Baker RC	6.00
203	Scott Munter RC	4.00
204	Sean Thompson RC	4.00
205	Sean Tracey RC	4.00
206	Steve Schmoll RC	4.00
207	Tony Pena RC	4.00
208	Travis Bowyer RC	4.00
209	Ubaldo Jimenez RC	20.00
210	Wladimir Balentien RC	8.00
211	Yorman Bazardo RC	4.00
212	Yuniesky Betancourt RC	8.00
213	Adam Shabala RC	4.00
214	Brandon McCarthy RC	4.00
215	Chad Orvella RC	4.00
216	Jermaine Van Buren RC	4.00
217	Anthony Reyes RC	8.00
218	Dana Eveland RC	10.00
219	Brian Anderson RC	8.00
220	Hayden Penn RC	4.00
221	Chris Denorfia RC	4.00
222	Joel Peralta RC	4.00
223	Ryan Garko RC	8.00
224	Felix Hernandez RC	10.00
225	Mark McLemore RC	4.00
226	Melky Cabrera RC	8.00
227	Nelson Cruz RC	8.00
228	Norihiro Nakamura RC	6.00
229	Oscar Robles RC	4.00
230	Rick Short RC	4.00
231	Ryan Zimmerman RC	25.00
232	Ryan Speier RC	4.00
233	Ryan Spilborghs RC	8.00
234	Shane Costa RC	4.00
235	Zach Duke RC	8.00
236	Tony Giarratano RC	4.00
237	Jeff Niemann RC	10.00
238	Stephen Drew/Auto. RC	100.00
239	Justin Verlander/Auto. RC	200.00
240	Prince Fielder/Auto. RC	300.00
241	Philip Humber/Auto. RC	50.00
242	Tadahito Iguchi/Auto. RC	65.00

Silver
Silver (101-237): 1X-2X
Production 50 Sets

2005 UD Ultimate Signature Edition
NM/M
Complete Set (110):
Common (1-100): 2.00
Production 825
Common (101-110):
Production 225
Tin (3): 85.00

100	Vladimir Guerrero	4.00
101	Adrian Gonzalez	8.00
102	Ambiorix Burgos **RC**	8.00
103	Ambiorix Concepcion **RC**	8.00
104	Dan Meyer	8.00
105	Ervin Santana	15.00
106	Gavin Floyd	15.00
107	Joe Blanton	12.00
108	Eric Crozier	8.00
109	Mark Teahen	12.00
110	Ryan Howard	50.00

Platinum
Cards (101-110):
Production One Set

Immortal Inscriptions
NM/M
Production 10-99

Platinum:		No Pricing
Production One Set		
WB	Wade Boggs/75	80.00
JB	Jim Bunning/99	60.00
SC	Steve Carlton/99	40.00
WC	Will Clark/99	60.00
EG	Eric Gagne/99	20.00
KG	Ken Griffey Jr./99	200.00
TG	Tony Gwynn/50	140.00
DM	Don Mattingly/75	150.00
BR	Brooks Robinson/99	50.00
TS	Tom Seaver/25	90.00
OS	Ozzie Smith/75	80.00
FT	Frank Thomas/50	100.00

Signature Cuts
Production One Set

Signature Cy Young
NM/M
Production 1-250

CM	David Cone, Greg Maddux/35	150.00
EG	Eric Gagne, Dennis Eckersley/200	40.00
ES	Dennis Eckersley, Bruce Sutter/250	30.00
GF	Ron Guidry, Whitey Ford/250	65.00
GM	Bob Gibson, Denny McLain/175	40.00
LC	Sparky Lyle, Steve Carlton/250	30.00
MS	Tom Seaver, Denny McLain/250	50.00
NF	Don Newcombe, Whitey Ford	60.00
PC	Gaylord Perry, Steve Carlton/250	40.00
PS	Jim Palmer, Tom Seaver/100	75.00

Signature Decades

NM/M
Some not priced due to scarcity.

Platinum:		No Pricing
Production One Set		
LA	Luis Aparicio	20.00
LA1	Luis Aparicio	20.00
CB	Carlos Beltran/99	25.00
YB	Yogi Berra/25	80.00
WB	Wade Boggs/25	65.00
WB1	Wade Boggs/25	65.00
LB	Lou Brock/50	35.00
JB	Jim Bunning	20.00
MC	Miguel Cabrera	30.00
JC	Jose Canseco/99	40.00
SC	Steve Carlton	20.00
SC1	Steve Carlton	20.00
GC	Gary Carter/25	25.00
OC	Orlando Cepeda	15.00
WC	Will Clark/99	40.00
RC	Rocky Colavito	50.00
RC1	Rocky Colavito	50.00
AD	Andre Dawson	15.00
BD	Bobby Doerr	15.00
DE	Dennis Eckersley	25.00
BF	Bob Feller	25.00
RF	Rollie Fingers	15.00
KG	Ken Griffey Jr.	65.00
RG	Ron Guidry	25.00
KH	Keith Hernandez	10.00
KH1	Keith Hernandez	10.00
MI	Monte Irvin	20.00
BJ	Bo Jackson/50	60.00
FJ	Fergie Jenkins/50	20.00
DJ	Derek Jeter/99	160.00
AK	Al Kaline/99	30.00
GK	George Kell	15.00
HK	Harmon Killebrew/99	40.00
RK	Ralph Kiner/99	30.00
DL	Don Larsen/99	25.00
FL	Fred Lynn	15.00
JM	Juan Marichal/99	25.00
DM	Don Mattingly/25	85.00
BM	Bill Mazeroski/99	40.00
PM	Paul Molitor/99	25.00

(left index column)
1	Al Kaline	4.00
2	Babe Ruth	10.00
3	Billy Williams	2.00
4	Bob Feller	3.00
5	Bob Gibson	3.00
6	Brooks Robinson	3.00
7	Carlton Fisk	2.00
8	Cy Young	3.00
9	Dizzy Dean	3.00
10	Don Drysdale	2.00
11	Eddie Mathews	2.00
12	Enos Slaughter	2.00
13	Ernie Banks	5.00
14	Fergie Jenkins	2.00
15	Eddie Murray	4.00
16	Harmon Killebrew	4.00
17	Honus Wagner	3.00
18	Jackie Robinson	5.00
19	Jimmie Foxx	4.00
20	Joe DiMaggio	6.00
21	Joe Morgan	2.00
22	Juan Marichal	2.00
23	Larry Doby	2.00
24	Jim Palmer	2.00
25	Johnny Bench	4.00
26	Lou Brock	2.00
27	Lou Gehrig	6.00
28	Mel Ott	3.00
29	Mickey Cochrane	2.00
30	Mickey Mantle	12.00
31	Mike Schmidt	5.00
32	Nolan Ryan	8.00
33	Pee Wee Reese	2.00
34	Phil Rizzuto	3.00
35	Ralph Kiner	2.00
36	Robin Yount	3.00
37	Ozzie Smith	4.00
38	Roy Campanella	3.00
39	Satchel Paige	4.00
40	Stan Musial	5.00
41	Ted Williams	8.00
42	Thurman Munson	4.00
43	Tom Seaver	3.00
44	Ty Cobb	4.00
45	Walter Johnson	4.00
46	Warren Spahn	4.00
47	Whitey Ford	3.00
48	Willie McCovey	3.00
49	Willie Stargell	3.00
50	Yogi Berra	4.00
51	Adrian Beltre	8.00
52	Albert Pujols	6.00
53	Alex Rodriguez	3.00
54	Alfonso Soriano	2.00
55	Andruw Jones	2.00
56	B.J. Upton	2.00
57	Ben Sheets	2.00
58	Bret Boone	2.00
59	Brian Giles	2.00
60	Carlos Beltran	3.00
61	Carlos Delgado	2.00
62	Chipper Jones	4.00
63	Curt Schilling	2.00
64	David Ortiz	4.00
65	Derek Jeter	8.00
66	Eric Chavez	2.00
67	Frank Thomas	3.00
68	Gary Sheffield	2.00
69	Greg Maddux	5.00
70	Hank Blalock	2.00
71	Hideki Matsui	6.00
72	Ichiro Suzuki	6.00
73	Ivan Rodriguez	2.00
74	Jason Schmidt	2.00
75	Jeff Bagwell	3.00
76	Jim Thome	3.00
77	Johnny Damon	4.00
78	Jose Vidro	2.00
79	Ken Griffey Jr.	5.00
80	Kerry Wood	4.00
81	Manny Ramirez	4.00
82	Mark Prior	2.00
83	Mark Teixeira	2.00
84	Miguel Cabrera	3.00
85	Miguel Tejada	3.00
86	Mike Mussina	2.00
87	Mike Piazza	5.00
88	Mike Sweeney	2.00
89	Oliver Perez	2.00
90	Pedro Martinez	4.00
91	Rafael Palmeiro	3.00
92	Randy Johnson	4.00
93	Roger Clemens	8.00
94	Sammy Sosa	5.00
95	Scott Rolen	3.00
96	Tim Hudson	2.00
97	Todd Helton	2.00
98	Torii Hunter	2.00
99	Victor Martinez	2.00

MO	Joe Morgan/50	25.00
MU	Dale Murphy/25	25.00
DN	Don Newcombe/99	20.00
PN	Phil Niekro	20.00
DO	David Ortiz	40.00
RO	Roy Oswalt	15.00
JP	Jim Palmer	20.00
TP	Tony Perez	25.00
GP	Gaylord Perry	15.00
GP1	Gaylord Perry	15.00
JR	Jim Rice	20.00
BR	Brooks Robinson	30.00
FR	Frank Robinson/25	40.00
AR	Al Rosen	15.00
JS	Johan Santana	15.00
RS	Ron Santo	25.00
BS	Ben Sheets	15.00
SU	Don Sutton	15.00
MT	Mark Teixeira	25.00
LT	Luis Tiant	15.00
LT1	Luis Tiant	15.00
BU	B.J. Upton	15.00
RW	Rickie Weeks	20.00
BW	Billy Williams	20.00
MW	Maury Wills	15.00
RY	Robin Yount/25	70.00

Signature Hits
NM/M
Production 1-125

BM	Stan Musial, Lou Brock/35	125.00
MY	Robin Yount, Paul Molitor/125	75.00
WG	Dave Winfield, Tony Gwynn/35	90.00
YB	Wade Boggs, Carl Yastrzemski/35	100.00

Signature HRs
NM/M
Production 1-250

BS	Mike Schmidt, Ernie Banks/25	180.00
GM	Ken Griffey Jr., Willie McCovey/250	100.00
KM	Willie McCovey, Harmon Killebrew/35	75.00
RG	Frank Robinson, Ken Griffey Jr./250	85.00

Signature MVPs
NM/M
Production 1-250

BM	Don Mattingly, Yogi Berra/175	100.00
BS	Ernie Banks, Ryne Sandberg/25	200.00
CM	Stan Musial, Orlando Cepeda/100	75.00
DS	Ryne Sandberg, Andre Dawson/175	80.00
EF	Dennis Eckersley, Rollie Fingers/250	30.00
FC	George Foster, Rod Carew/125	40.00
GM	Joe Morgan, Ken Griffey Jr./250	75.00
HY	Robin Yount, Keith Hernandez/200	50.00
JR	Ivan Rodriguez, Chipper Jones/35	125.00
KC	Harmon Killebrew, Rod Carew/100	80.00
KM	Harmon Killebrew, Willie McCovey/35	80.00
LM	Fred Lynn, Joe Morgan/200	30.00
LW	Maury Wills, Barry Larkin/250	35.00
MB	Joe Morgan, Johnny Bench/100	60.00
MG	Denny McLain, Bob Gibson/175	40.00
MY	Robin Yount, Dale Murphy/175	60.00
PR	Dave Parker, Jim Rice/250	40.00
SF	Mike Schmidt, Rollie Fingers/175	60.00
SS	Mike Schmidt, Ryne Sandberg/75	140.00
TB	Frank Thomas, Jeff Bagwell/50	90.00
YC	Orlando Cepeda, Carl Yastrzemski/100	65.00
YS	Carl Yastrzemski, Jim Rice/100	75.00

Signature No-Hitters
NM/M
Production 1-250

BG	Bob Gibson, Jim Bunning/125	60.00
CL	Don Larsen, David Cone/250	40.00
FR	Nolan Ryan, Bob Feller/25	150.00
GP	Bob Gibson, Jim Palmer/125	50.00

Signature Numbers
NM/M
Production 1-49

Platinum:		No Pricing
Production One Set		
WB	Wade Boggs/26	40.00
MC	Miguel Cabrera/24	50.00

JC	Jose Canseco/33	50.00
CA	Rod Carew/29	35.00
SC	Steve Carlton/32	25.00
OC	Orlando Cepeda/30	25.00
WC	Will Clark/22	60.00
CL	Roger Clemens/22	200.00
RF	Rollie Fingers/34	20.00
CF	Carlton Fisk/27	40.00
EG	Eric Gagne/38	40.00
BG	Bob Gibson/45	25.00
GL	Tom Glavine/47	40.00
KG	Ken Griffey Jr./30	125.00
VG	Vladimir Guerrero/27	50.00
RG	Ron Guidry/49	60.00
TG	Tony Gwynn/19	80.00
MI	Monte Irvin/30	30.00
FJ	Fergie Jenkins/31	20.00
RJ	Randy Johnson/41	75.00
MA	Juan Marichal/27	40.00
DM	Don Mattingly/23	125.00
WM	Willie McCovey/44	80.00
EM	Eddie Murray/33	120.00
DO	David Ortiz/34	50.00
RO	Roy Oswalt/44	25.00
JP	Jim Palmer/22	30.00
PI	Mike Piazza/31	100.00
MP	Mark Prior/22	60.00
KP	Kirby Puckett/34	85.00
FR	Frank Robinson/20	75.00
SR	Scott Rolen/27	20.00
NR	Nolan Ryan/34	120.00
TS	Tom Seaver/41	75.00
JS	John Smoltz/29	60.00
FT	Frank Thomas/35	80.00
BW	Billy Williams/26	30.00
DW	Dave Winfield/31	35.00
KW	Kerry Wood/34	40.00
RY	Robin Yount/19	75.00

Signature ROYs
NM/M
Production 1-250

CM	Willie McCovey, Orlando Cepeda/75	65.00
CS	Rod Carew, Tom Seaver/25	100.00
DM	Andre Dawson, Eddie Murray/25	70.00
FB	Carlton Fisk, Johnny Bench/35	80.00
FL	Fred Lynn/125, Carlton Fisk/125	60.00
GR	Nomar Garciaparra, Scott Rolen/200	85.00
GS	Dwight Gooden, Tom Seaver/100	60.00
JG	Derek Jeter, Nomar Garciaparra/75	185.00
RA	Frank Robinson, Luis Aparicio/125	50.00
RJ	Derek Jeter, Cal Ripken Jr./75	300.00
SG	Dwight Gooden, Darryl Strawberry/250	40.00
WD	Andre Dawson, Billy Williams/250	30.00

Signature Supremacy
NM/M
Production 15-99

LA	Luis Aparicio/50	40.00
JB	Jeff Bagwell	75.00
CB	Carlos Beltran/50	30.00
BE	Johnny Bench/25	60.00
YB	Yogi Berra/25	60.00
HB	Hank Blalock/50	25.00
WB	Wade Boggs/25	60.00
LB	Lou Brock/25	40.00
BU	Jim Bunning/99	25.00
MC	Miguel Cabrera/99	40.00
JC	Jose Canseco/25	60.00
CA	Rod Carew/25	35.00
SC	Steve Carlton/99	20.00
OC	Orlando Cepeda/99	20.00
EC	Eric Chavez/99	15.00
WC	Will Clark/50	40.00
AD	Andre Dawson/99	20.00
BD	Bobby Doerr/99	20.00
BF	Bob Feller/99	25.00
RF	Rollie Fingers/99	15.00
CF	Carlton Fisk/25	40.00
EG	Eric Gagne/25	25.00
KG	Ken Griffey Jr./99	80.00
RG	Ron Guidry/99	20.00
TH	Tim Hudson/99	25.00
MI	Monte Irvin/99	20.00
DJ	Derek Jeter/50	200.00
AK	Al Kaline/50	60.00
GK	George Kell/99	25.00
HK	Harmon Killebrew/50	40.00
RK	Ralph Kiner/25	40.00
JU	Juan Marichal/25	50.00
MA	Don Mattingly/25	80.00
BM	Bill Mazeroski/50	25.00
PM	Paul Molitor/50	40.00
JM	Joe Morgan/25	30.00
MM	Mark Mulder/99	15.00
DM	Dale Murphy/99	25.00
MU	Stan Musial/25	125.00
DN	Don Newcombe/99	20.00
DO	David Ortiz/99	40.00
RO	Roy Oswalt/99	15.00
JP	Jim Palmer/99	20.00
TP	Tony Perez/25	30.00
MP	Mark Prior/25	60.00
JR	Jim Rice/99	15.00
RR	Robin Roberts/99	30.00
BR	Brooks Robinson/99	30.00

FR	Frank Robinson/25	40.00
SR	Scott Rolen/25	50.00
AR	Al Rosen/99	25.00
SA	Ryne Sandberg/25	85.00
JS	Johan Santana/99	20.00
RS	Ron Santo	25.00
MS	Mike Schmidt/25	100.00
TS	Tom Seaver/25	50.00
BS	Ben Sheets/99	20.00
OS	Ozzie Smith/25	50.00
SM	John Smoltz/50	5.00
AS	Alfonso Soriano/25	40.00
MT	Mark Teixeira/99	25.00
FT	Frank Thomas/25	80.00
BW	Billy Williams/99	25.00
DW	Dave Winfield/25	40.00
CY	Carl Yastrzemski/25	100.00
RY	Robin Yount/25	75.00

Signs of October
NM/M
Production 1-250

BW	Mookie Wilson, Bill Buckner/250	40.00
CS	John Smoltz, Joe Carter/250	50.00
EG	Kirk Gibson, Dennis Eckersley/200	40.00
FM	Carlton Fisk, Joe Morgan/50	50.00
GB	Bob Gibson, Lou Brock/70	70.00
GG	Ron Guidry, Steve Garvey/250	30.00
GL	Mickey Lolich, Bob Gibson/100	40.00
JG	Derek Jeter, Tony Gwynn/250	185.00
LB	Yogi Berra, Don Larsen/250	85.00
MP	Jack Morris, Kirby Puckett/100	85.00
PS	Ozzie Smith, Kirby Puckett/35	125.00
RR	Frank Robinson, Brooks Robinson/250	65.00
SB	George Brett, Ozzie Smith	150.00
SY	Ozzie Smith, Robin Yount/100	85.00
TG	Kirk Gibson, Alan Trammell/250	40.00

2005 Upper Deck Trilogy

NM/M
Complete Set (100): 40.00
Common Player: .50
Pack (5): 20.00
Box (9): 170.00

1	A.J. Burnett	.50
2	Adam Dunn	1.00
3	Adrian Beltre	.50
4	Albert Pujols	4.00
5	Alex Rodriguez	3.00
6	Alfonso Soriano	1.00
7	Andruw Jones	1.00
8	Aramis Ramirez	.50
9	Ben Sheets	.75
10	Bobby Abreu	.50
11	Bobby Crosby	.50
12	Ryan Zimmerman **RC**	15.00
13	Brian Giles	.50
14	Brian Roberts	.50
15	Carl Crawford	.50
16	Carlos Beltran	1.00
17	Carlos Delgado	.75
18	Carlos Zambrano	.75
19	Chipper Jones	1.00
20	Corey Patterson	.50
21	Craig Biggio	.50
22	Curt Schilling	1.50
23	Dallas McPherson	.50
24	David Ortiz	1.50
25	David Wright	2.00
26	Delmon Young	1.00
27	Derek Jeter	4.00
28	Derek Lee	1.00
29	Dontrelle Willis	1.00
30	Eric Chavez	.50
31	Eric Gagne	.50
32	Francisco Rodriguez	.50
33	Gary Sheffield	1.00
34	Greg Maddux	2.00
35	Hank Blalock	.50
36	Hideki Matsui	2.50
37	Ichiro Suzuki	3.00
38	Ivan Rodriguez	1.00
39	J.D. Drew	.50

40	Jake Peavy	.75
41	Jason Bay	.50
42	Jason Schmidt	.50
43	Jeff Bagwell	1.00
44	Jeff Kent	.75
45	Jeff Niemann **RC**	2.00
46	Jeremy Bonderman	.50
47	Jim Edmonds	.75
48	Jim Thome	1.00
49	Joe Mauer	.75
50	Johan Santana	1.00
51	John Smoltz	.75
52	Johnny Damon	1.00
53	Jose Reyes	.75
54	Jose Vidro	.50
55	Josh Beckett	.50
56	Justin Morneau	.50
57	Justin Verlander **RC**	10.00
58	Ken Griffey Jr.	3.00
59	Kendry Morales **RC**	8.00
60	Kerry Wood	.75
61	Khalil Greene	.75
62	Lance Berkman	.75
63	Luis Gonzalez	.50
64	Manny Ramirez	1.50
65	Mark Buehrle	.75
66	Mark Mulder	.50
67	Mark Prior	1.00
68	Mark Teixeira	1.00
69	Michael Young	.75
70	Miguel Cabrera	1.50
71	Miguel Tejada	1.00
72	Mike Mussina	.75
73	Mike Piazza	1.50
74	Nomar Garciaparra	1.00
75	Pat Burrell	.50
76	Paul Konerko	.75
77	Pedro Martinez	1.50
78	Philip Humber **RC**	2.00
79	Prince Fielder	8.00
80	Randy Johnson	1.50
81	Richie Sexson	.75
82	Rickie Weeks	.50
83	Roger Clemens	4.00
84	Roy Halladay	.75
85	Roy Oswalt	.75
86	Sammy Sosa	1.50
87	Scott Kazmir	.50
88	Scott Rolen	1.00
89	Stephen Drew **RC**	8.00
90	Tadahito Iguchi **RC**	2.00
91	Tim Hudson	.75
92	Todd Helton	1.00
93	Tom Glavine	.75
94	Torii Hunter	.75
95	Travis Hafner	.75
96	Troy Glaus	.75
97	Vernon Wells	.50
98	Victor Martinez	.50
99	Vladimir Guerrero	1.50
100	Zack Greinke	.50

Generations
Complete Set (6):
Common Player:

Generation Future Lumber
Silver
NM/M
Production 100 Sets

Gold:		1X
Production 60 Sets		
RC	Robinson Cano	20.00
CA	Jorge Cantu	6.00
GF	Gavin Floyd	4.00
BH	Brad Halsey	4.00
JJ	J.J. Hardy	4.00
RH	Ryan Howard	50.00
LN	Laynce Nix	4.00
JP	Jhonny Peralta	6.00
JR	Jeremy Reed	4.00
AR	Alexis Rios	6.00
RI	Juan Rivera	4.00
BJ	B.J. Upton	6.00
JW	Jayson Werth	4.00
YO	Kevin Youkilis	6.00

Generation Future Materials
Silver

NM/M
Common Player: 4.00
Production 120 Sets

Gold:		1X
Production 75 Sets		
BA	Bronson Arroyo	6.00
GA	Garrett Atkins	4.00
JE	Jeff Baker	4.00

CL	Clint Barmes	4.00
JB	Jason Bartlett	4.00
BL	Joe Blanton	4.00
DB	Dewon Brazelton	4.00
YB	Yhency Brazoban	4.00
CB	Chris Burke	6.00
DC	Daniel Cabrera	4.00
RC	Robinson Cano	20.00
CA	Jorge Cantu	6.00
GC	Gustavo Chacin	4.00
JD	J.D. Closser	4.00
DD	David DeJesus	4.00
DU	Jason Dubois	4.00
GF	Gavin Floyd	4.00
JF	Jeff Francis	4.00
AG	Adrian Gonzalez	8.00
BH	Brad Halsey	4.00
JJ	J.J. Hardy	4.00
DH	Danny Haren	4.00
AH	Aaron Hill	4.00
HO	Dennis Houlton	4.00
RH	Ryan Howard	20.00
TI	Tadahito Iguchi	6.00
EJ	Edwin Jackson	4.00
DK	Dae-Sung Koo	4.00
KO	Casey Kotchman	4.00
JL	Jason Lane	4.00
DM	Dallas McPherson	4.00
AM	Aaron Miles	4.00
YM	Yadier Molina	4.00
MY	Brett Myers	4.00
XN	Xavier Nady	4.00
LN	Laynce Nix	4.00
JP	Jhonny Peralta	4.00
RQ	Robb Quinlan	4.00
JR	Jeremy Reed	4.00
AR	Alexis Rios	6.00
RI	Juan Rivera	4.00
ES	Ervin Santana	6.00
SS	Steve Schmoll	4.00
LS	Luke Scott	4.00
SI	Grady Sizemore	10.00
HS	Huston Street	6.00
NS	Nick Swisher	8.00
WT	Willy Taveras	4.00
MT	Mark Teahen	4.00
TH	Charles Thomas	4.00
CT	Chad Tracy	4.00
BJ	B.J. Upton	4.00
CU	Chase Utley	10.00
WA	Ryan Wagner	4.00
RW	Rickie Weeks	8.00
JW	Jayson Werth	8.00
KY	Keiichi Yabu	4.00
YO	Kevin Youkilis	6.00

Generations Future Sig. Silver

Common Player: 8.00 NM/M
Production 50-199
Bronze: 1-1.5X
Production 35 Sets
Gold: No Pricing
Production 15 Sets

GA	Garrett Atkins/199	8.00
JB	Jason Bartlett/199	8.00
BE	Colter Bean/199	8.00
BL	Joe Blanton/99	10.00
YB	Yhency Brazoban/199	10.00
AB	Ambiorix Burgos/199	8.00
CB	Chris Burke/199	15.00
DC	Daniel Cabrera/199	8.00
JO	Jose Capellan/199	8.00
JD	J.D. Closser/99	8.00
AC	Ambiorix Concepcion/199	8.00
DD	David DeJesus/99	12.00
SD	Stephen Drew/75	50.00
DU	Jason Dubois/99	10.00
PF	Prince Fielder/75	50.00
GF	Gavin Floyd/99	10.00
JF	Jeff Francis/99	12.00
AG	Adrian Gonzalez/99	25.00
JG	Jared Gothreaux/199	8.00
GG	Gabe Gross/99	8.00
JJ	J.J. Hardy/199	15.00
JH	John Hattig Jr./199	8.00
FH	Felix Hernandez/60	50.00
HO	Dennis Houlton/199	10.00
RH	Ryan Howard/99	40.00
PH	Philip Humber/75	15.00
TI	Tadahito Iguchi/75	40.00
EJ	Edwin Jackson/99	8.00
KO	Casey Kotchman/99	10.00
JL	Jason Lane/99	8.00
ML	Matt Lindstrom/199	8.00
PL	Pedro Lopez/189	10.00
RM	Russell Martin/199	15.00
KM	Kendry Morales/199	30.00
JN	Jeff Niemann/75	20.00
PO	Peter Orr/199	15.00
TP	Tony Pena/199	8.00
RQ	Robb Quinlan/199	8.00
AR	Alexis Rios/99	15.00
CR	Casey Rogowski/199	8.00
RR	Russel Rohlicek/199	8.00
SS	Steve Schmoll/199	8.00
LS	Luke Scott/99	10.00
TS	Tim Stauffer/199	8.00
NS	Nick Swisher/199	15.00
MT	Mark Teahen/199	8.00
TH	Charles Thomas/199	8.00
BJ	B.J. Upton/50	20.00
CU	Chase Utley/50	25.00
JV	Justin Verlander/99	60.00
RW	Rickie Weeks/50	20.00
JW	Jayson Werth/99	25.00
KY	Keiichi Yabu/199	15.00
YO	Kevin Youkilis/99	25.00
DY	Delmon Young/50	20.00
RZ	Ryan Zimmerman/150	50.00

Generations of Lumber Triple

Production 85 Sets NM/M 10.00

ARU	B.J. Upton, Jimmy Rollins, Luis Aparicio	15.00
BCU	Wade Boggs, B.J. Upton, Carl Crawford	50.00
BHH	Travis Hafner, Ryan Howard, Harold Baines	15.00
BMY	Bill Mueller, Wade Boggs, Kevin Youkilis	15.00
CCC	Will Clark, Jack Clark, Orlando Cepeda	12.00
DAR	Bobby Abreu, Eric Davis, Alex Rios	10.00
EDY	Kevin Youkilis, Dwight Evans, Johnny Damon	15.00
GDP	Ken Griffey Jr., Wily Mo Pena, Adam Dunn	25.00
GGC	Miguel Cabrera, Ken Griffey Jr., Tony Gwynn	25.00
HDH	Ryan Howard, Adam Dunn, Frank Howard	15.00
HOH	Frank Howard, Ryan Howard, David Ortiz	15.00
JGU	Bo Jackson, Ken Griffey Jr., B.J. Upton	25.00
JHR	Alex Rios, Bo Jackson, Torii Hunter	15.00
JSP	Bo Jackson, Gary Sheffield, Wily Mo Pena	15.00
KBH	Pat Burrell, John Kruk, Ryan Howard	15.00
LJU	Barry Larkin, Derek Jeter, B.J. Upton	30.00
LYU	B.J. Upton, Barry Larkin, Michael Young	12.00
MDW	Jayson Werth, Dale Murphy, Adam Dunn	15.00
MMJ	Don Mattingly, Derek Jeter, Bobby Murcer	50.00
MOH	Ryan Howard, David Ortiz, Eddie Murray	20.00
NBW	Adrian Beltre, David Wright, Graig Nettles	15.00
OAR	Bobby Abreu, Tony Oliva, Alex Rios	10.00
PDP	Wily Mo Pena, Eric Davis, Tony Perez	10.00
PGP	Tony Perez, Ken Griffey Jr., Wily Mo Pena	25.00
RJC	Cal Ripken Jr., Derek Jeter, Bobby Crosby	50.00
ROY	David Ortiz, Jim Rice, Kevin Youkilis	20.00
RRT	Brooks Robinson, Cal Ripken Jr., Miguel Tejada	40.00
SBW	Mike Schmidt, Adrian Beltre, David Wright	20.00
SDW	Duke Snider, Jayson Werth, J.D. Drew	20.00
SMR	Aramis Ramirez, Bill Madlock, Ron Santo	20.00
SSP	Ron Santo, Ryne Sandberg, Corey Patterson	35.00

Generations of Materials Triple

Common Trio: 10.00 NM/M
Production 50 Sets

AAD	Aramis Ramirez, Al Rosen, Dallas McPherson	15.00
AFB	Luis Aparicio, Rafael Furcal, Jason Bartlett	15.00
API	Tadahito Iguchi, Scott Podsednik, Luis Aparicio	25.00
ARU	Jimmy Rollins, Luis Aparicio, B.J. Upton	20.00
BCU	B.J. Upton, Carl Crawford, Wade Boggs	15.00
BHH	Ryan Howard, Harold Baines, Travis Hafner	15.00
BLS	Craig Biggio, Jason Lane, Luke Scott	15.00
BMY	Kevin Youkilis, Wade Boggs, Bill Mueller	15.00
CCC	Will Clark, Jack Clark, Orlando Cepeda	15.00
CCK	Sean Casey, Will Clark, Casey Kotchman	15.00
CMG	Justin Morneau, Adrian Gonzalez, Will Clark	15.00
CTG	Will Clark, Adrian Gonzalez, Mark Teixeira	15.00
DAR	Alex Rios, Eric Davis, Bobby Abreu	10.00
DBS	Lenny Dykstra, Jason Bay, Nick Swisher	10.00
DGL	Jason Lane, Ken Griffey Jr., Andre Dawson	25.00
DHL	Lenny Dykstra, Torii Hunter, Jason Lane	10.00
DPD	Jason Dubois, Corey Patterson, Andre Dawson	10.00
DPT	Lenny Dykstra, Scott Podsednik, Willy Taveras	15.00
EDY	Kevin Youkilis, Johnny Damon, Dwight Evans	20.00
GAS	Bobby Abreu, Tony Gwynn, Nick Swisher	15.00
GDP	Wily Mo Pena, Adam Dunn, Ken Griffey Jr.	25.00
GGC	Ken Griffey Jr., Tony Gwynn, Miguel Cabrera	25.00
GMY	Kevin Youkilis, Mike Greenwell, Bill Mueller	15.00
GWJ	Dwight Gooden, Dontrelle Willis, Edwin Jackson	15.00
HDH	Frank Howard, Adam Dunn, Ryan Howard	15.00
HOH	Ryan Howard, David Ortiz, Frank Howard	20.00
JGU	B.J. Upton, Bo Jackson, Ken Griffey Jr.	25.00
JHR	Bo Jackson, Torii Hunter, Alex Rios	20.00
JMK	Casey Kotchman, Wally Joyner, Dallas McPherson	10.00
JSP	Bo Jackson, Gary Sheffield, Wily Mo Pena	15.00
KBH	Pat Burrell, John Kruk, Ryan Howard	15.00
KBU	John Kruk, Pat Burrell, Chase Utley	25.00
LJU	B.J. Upton, Barry Larkin, Derek Jeter	35.00
LYU	Barry Larkin, Michael Young, B.J. Upton	35.00
MBS	Nick Swisher, Pat Burrell, Dale Murphy	15.00
MCG	Don Mattingly, Sean Casey, Adrian Gonzalez	30.00
MDW	Adam Dunn, Jayson Werth, Dale Murphy	20.00
MMJ	Don Mattingly, Derek Jeter, Bobby Murcer	60.00
MOH	Ryan Howard, David Ortiz, Eddie Murray	20.00
NBW	Adrian Beltre, David Wright, Graig Nettles	20.00
OAR	Bobby Abreu, Tony Oliva, Alex Rios	15.00
PDP	Wily Mo Pena, Eric Davis, Tony Perez	10.00
PGD	Tony Perez, Brian Giles, Jason Dubois	10.00
PGP	Wily Mo Pena, Ken Griffey Jr., Tony Perez	30.00
RBT	Brooks Robinson, Adrian Beltre, Mark Teahen	20.00
RCD	Carl Crawford, David DeJesus, Tim Raines	10.00
RJC	Derek Jeter, Cal Ripken Jr., Bobby Crosby	50.00
ROY	Jim Rice, David Ortiz, Kevin Youkilis	25.00
RRM	Brooks Robinson, Cal Ripken Jr., Melvin Mora	50.00
RRT	Miguel Tejada, Cal Ripken Jr., Brooks Robinson	50.00
SBM	Dallas McPherson, Adrian Beltre, Mike Schmidt	20.00
SBW	Mike Schmidt, Adrian Beltre, David Wright	20.00
SDW	Duke Snider, Jayson Werth, J.D. Drew	20.00
SGU	Ryne Sandberg, Chase Utley, Marcus Giles	35.00
SRU	Chase Utley, Mike Schmidt, Jimmy Rollins	40.00
SRW	Ryne Sandberg, Brian Roberts, Rickie Weeks	20.00
VGB	Jason Bay, Brian Giles, Andy Van Slyke	10.00
VPD	Andy Van Slyke, Corey Patterson, David DeJesus	15.00
WBI	Tadahito Iguchi, Frank White, Craig Biggio	20.00
WCT	Willie Wilson, Willy Taveras, Carl Crawford	15.00

Generations of Signatures

Production 35 Sets NM/M

AYU	B.J. Upton, Luis Aparicio, Michael Young	40.00
BPN	Jake Peavy, Jeff Niemann, Jim Bunning	50.00
CTG	Will Clark, Mark Teixeira, Adrian Gonzalez	60.00
DBU	Chase Utley, Craig Biggio, Bobby Doerr	50.00
DGL	Ken Griffey Jr., Jason Lane	100.00
DGU	Marcus Giles, Chase Utley, Bobby Doerr	50.00
DLB	Bobby Doerr, Mark Loretta, Chris Burke	30.00
FPH	Rich Harden, Mark Prior, Bob Feller	50.00
GDP	Ken Griffey Jr., Adam Dunn, Wily Mo Pena	100.00
HDG	Adam Dunn, Frank Howard, Gabe Gross	40.00
JHR	Torii Hunter, Bo Jackson, Alex Rios	85.00
JKM	Casey Kotchman, Kendry Morales, Wally Joyner	50.00
LJU	Barry Larkin, Derek Jeter, B.J. Upton	250.00
MBV	Justin Verlander, Jack Morris, Jeremy Bonderman	90.00
MMJ	Derek Jeter, Don Mattingly, Bobby Murcer	260.00
NBW	David Wright, Graig Nettles, Adrian Beltre	75.00
OHM	Tony Oliva, Kent Hrbek, Justin Morneau	50.00
PBF	Gaylord Perry, Jeremy Bonderman, Gavin Floyd	35.00
PGP	Tony Perez, Ken Griffey Jr., Wily Mo Pena	100.00
PPH	Philip Humber, Jim Palmer, Jake Peavy	50.00
PPS	Jake Peavy, Tim Stauffer, Gaylord Perry	40.00
RCD	Tim Raines, David DeJesus, Carl Crawford	40.00
RJC	Bobby Crosby, Cal Ripken Jr., Derek Jeter	400.00
RRM	Cal Ripken Jr., Melvin Mora, Brooks Robinson	180.00
RSH	Nolan Ryan, John Smoltz, Philip Humber	165.00
SBT	Mark Teahen, Adrian Beltre, Ron Santo	50.00
SBW	Adrian Beltre, Mike Schmidt, David Wright	100.00
SGH	J.J. Hardy, Ozzie Smith, Khalil Greene	70.00
SMR	Ron Santo, Bill Madlock, Aramis Ramirez	50.00
SRW	Brian Roberts, Ryne Sandberg, Rickie Weeks	75.00
VGB	Jason Bay, Brian Giles, Andy Van Slyke	65.00

Generations Past Lumber

Common Player: 4.00 NM/M
Production 115 unless noted.
Gold: 1-1.5X
Production 25-75

LA	Luis Aparicio	8.00
HB	Harold Baines	8.00
DB	Dusty Baker	6.00
JB	Johnny Bench	8.00
WB	Wade Boggs	8.00
BB	Bill Buckner	6.00
CA	Rod Carew	8.00
SC	Steve Carlton	6.00
GC	Gary Carter	6.00
OC	Orlando Cepeda	6.00
CY	Ron Cey	4.00
JC	Jack Clark	8.00
WC	Will Clark	8.00
TC	Ty Cobb/99	10.00
MC	Mickey Cochrane/99	25.00
ED	Eric Davis	4.00
AD	Andre Dawson	6.00
JD	Joe DiMaggio/99	65.00
BD	Bobby Doerr	4.00
LD	Lenny Dykstra	4.00
DE	Dwight Evans	4.00
CF	Carlton Fisk	6.00
GF	George Foster	4.00
JF	Jimmie Foxx/99	50.00
FR	Bill Freehan	4.00
LG	Lou Gehrig/99	140.00
DG	Dwight Gooden	4.00
GR	Lefty Grove/99	40.00
TG	Tony Gwynn	10.00
KH	Keith Hernandez	6.00
RH	Rogers Hornsby/99	40.00
FH	Frank Howard	6.00
BJ	Bo Jackson	10.00
RJ	Reggie Jackson	10.00
JO	Wally Joyner	4.00
GK	George Kell	8.00
JK	John Kruk	6.00
BL	Barry Larkin	8.00
DL	Davey Lopes	4.00
BM	Bill Madlock	4.00
MA	Don Mattingly	25.00
FM	Fred McGriff	6.00
JM	Johnny Mize	4.00
TM	Thurman Munson	4.00
MU	Bobby Murcer	4.00
DM	Dale Murphy	8.00
MY	Eddie Murray	8.00
SM	Stan Musial	20.00
GN	Graig Nettles	6.00
TO	Tony Oliva	6.00
MO	Mel Ott	25.00
TP	Tony Perez	6.00
GP	Gaylord Perry	6.00
RP	Rico Petrocelli	6.00
BP	Boog Powell	4.00
TR	Tim Raines	6.00
RI	Jim Rice	6.00
CR	Cal Ripken Jr.	25.00
RO	Brooks Robinson	10.00
AR	Al Rosen	10.00
NR	Nolan Ryan	25.00
SA	Ryne Sandberg	15.00
RS	Ron Santo	10.00
MS	Mike Schmidt	15.00
SI	George Sisler	20.00
SK	Bill "Moose" Skowron	20.00
OS	Ozzie Smith	20.00
SN	Duke Snider	10.00
DS	Darryl Strawberry	8.00
AT	Alan Trammell	8.00
AV	Andy Van Slyke	4.00
FW	Frank White	4.00
WW	Willie Wilson	4.00
YA	Carl Yastrzemski	25.00

Generation Past Material Silver

Common Player: 4.00 NM/M
Production 99 unless noted.
Gold: 1-1.5X
Production 25 Sets

LA	Luis Aparicio	8.00
HB	Harold Baines	6.00
DB	Dusty Baker	6.00
JB	Johnny Bench	10.00
WB	Wade Boggs	8.00
BU	Jim Bunning	6.00
RC	Roy Campanella	20.00
CA	Rod Carew	8.00
SC	Steve Carlton	6.00
GC	Gary Carter	6.00
OC	Orlando Cepeda	6.00
CY	Ron Cey	4.00
JC	Jack Clark	4.00
WC	Will Clark	4.00
DC	David Cone	4.00
ED	Eric Davis	4.00
AD	Andre Dawson	6.00
DD	Dizzy Dean/75	40.00
JD	Joe DiMaggio/75	85.00
DR	Don Drysdale	10.00
LD	Lenny Dykstra	4.00
BF	Bob Feller	10.00
CF	Carlton Fisk	6.00
LG	Lou Gehrig/75	150.00
DG	Dwight Gooden	4.00
RG	Ron Guidry	4.00
TG	Tony Gwynn	10.00
KH	Keith Hernandez	4.00
RH	Rogers Hornsby/75	65.00
HR	Kent Hrbek	8.00
BJ	Bo Jackson	10.00
RJ	Reggie Jackson	10.00
JO	Wally Joyner	6.00
JK	John Kruk	6.00
BL	Barry Larkin	6.00
DL	Davey Lopes	4.00
BM	Bill Madlock	4.00
EM	Eddie Mathews/75	20.00
CM	Christy Mathewson/75	80.00
MA	Don Mattingly	25.00
JM	Johnny Mize	15.00
JA	Jack Morris	8.00
TM	Thurman Munson	20.00
MU	Bobby Murcer	4.00
DM	Dale Murphy	8.00
MY	Eddie Murray	8.00
SM	Stan Musial	20.00
GN	Graig Nettles	6.00
TO	Tony Oliva	6.00
MO	Mel Ott/75	30.00
SP	Satchel Paige/75	50.00
JP	Jim Palmer	6.00
TP	Tony Perez	6.00
GP	Gaylord Perry	6.00
RP	Rico Petrocelli	4.00
BP	Boog Powell	4.00
TR	Tim Raines	4.00
RI	Jim Rice	6.00
CR	Cal Ripken Jr.	25.00
RO	Brooks Robinson	10.00
AR	Al Rosen	10.00
NR	Nolan Ryan	25.00
SA	Ryne Sandberg	15.00
MS	Mike Schmidt	15.00
AV	Andy Van Slyke	4.00
OS	Ozzie Smith	15.00
SN	Duke Snider	10.00
DS	Darryl Strawberry	4.00
FW	Frank White	4.00
WW	Willie Wilson	4.00
YA	Carl Yastrzemski	15.00

Generations Past Auto. Silver

Common Player: 10.00 NM/M
Production 24-99.
Bronze: 1-1.5X
Production 10 or 35.
No pricing for prod. of 10.
Gold: No Pricing
Production 5-15

LA	Luis Aparicio/50	20.00
HB	Harold Baines/199	15.00
DB	Dusty Baker/25	20.00
WB	Wade Boggs/50	35.00
BB	Bill Buckner/50	15.00
BU	Jim Bunning/99	15.00
CA	Rod Carew/25	35.00
SC	Steve Carlton/25	20.00
CY	Ron Cey/199	15.00
JC	Jack Clark/199	10.00
WC	Will Clark/25	40.00
DC	David Cone/99	15.00
ED	Eric Davis/199	15.00
AD	Andre Dawson/99	20.00
BD	Bobby Doerr/199	15.00
LD	Lenny Dykstra/199	15.00
DE	Dwight Evans/50	25.00
BF	Bob Feller/99	25.00
GF	George Foster/199	10.00
FR	Bill Freehan/199	15.00
RG	Ron Guidry/199	15.00
KH	Keith Hernandez/199	15.00
FH	Frank Howard/199	15.00
HR	Kent Hrbek/199	15.00
BJ	Bo Jackson/50	50.00
RJ	Reggie Jackson/25	50.00
JO	Wally Joyner/199	15.00
GK	George Kell/199	15.00
JK	John Kruk/199	20.00
BL	Barry Larkin/99	25.00
DL	Davey Lopes/199	10.00
BM	Bill Madlock/199	15.00
MA	Don Mattingly/25	75.00
FM	Fred McGriff/199	25.00
JA	Jack Morris/199	15.00
MU	Bobby Murcer/199	25.00
DM	Dale Murphy/99	25.00
SM	Stan Musial/25	80.00
GN	Graig Nettles/199	15.00
TO	Tony Oliva/99	15.00
JP	Jim Palmer/50	20.00
TP	Tony Perez/25	30.00
GP	Gaylord Perry/199	15.00
BP	Boog Powell/199	15.00
TR	Tim Raines/199	15.00
RI	Jim Rice/99	15.00
RO	Brooks Robinson/50	30.00
AR	Al Rosen/199	15.00
NR	Nolan Ryan/25	100.00
SA	Ryne Sandberg/50	60.00
RS	Ron Santo/199	15.00
MS	Mike Schmidt/50	60.00
SK	Bill Skowron/25	15.00
OS	Ozzie Smith/25	50.00
DS	Darryl Strawberry/99	15.00
AT	Alan Trammell/50	20.00
AV	Andy Van Slyke/199	20.00
FW	Frank White/199	15.00
WW	Willie Wilson/199	15.00

Generation Present Lumber Silvr

Common Player: 4.00 NM/M
Production 115 Sets
Gold: 1X
Production 75 Sets

BA	Bobby Abreu	4.00
GA	Garret Anderson	4.00
JE	Jeff Bagwell	6.00
CB	Carlos Beltran	6.00
AB	Adrian Beltre	4.00
LB	Lance Berkman	6.00
BI	Craig Biggio	6.00
HB	Hank Blalock	4.00
BO	Jeremy Bonderman	4.00
PB	Pat Burrell	4.00
AJ	A.J. Burnett	4.00
MC	Miguel Cabrera	8.00
SC	Sean Casey	4.00
EC	Eric Chavez	4.00
RC	Roger Clemens	12.00
CC	Carl Crawford	6.00
BC	Bobby Crosby	4.00
DA	Johnny Damon	6.00
CD	Carlos Delgado	6.00
JD	J.D. Drew	4.00
AD	Adam Dunn	6.00
RF	Rafael Furcal	4.00
JG	Jason Giambi	6.00
BG	Brian Giles	4.00
MG	Marcus Giles	4.00
TG	Troy Glaus	4.00
GR	Khalil Greene	6.00
HA	Travis Hafner	6.00
TH	Todd Helton	6.00
AH	Aubrey Huff	4.00
HU	Torii Hunter	6.00
DJ	Derek Jeter	20.00
RJ	Randy Johnson	8.00
JO	Andruw Jones	6.00
CJ	Chipper Jones	8.00

JK	Jeff Kent	4.00
DL	Derrek Lee	8.00
ML	Mark Loretta	4.00
GM	Greg Maddux	15.00
PM	Pedro Martinez	8.00
VM	Victor Martinez	4.00
JM	Joe Mauer	10.00
BM	Bill Mueller	4.00
DO	David Ortiz	8.00
PA	Corey Patterson	4.00
WM	Wily Mo Pena	4.00
PI	Mike Piazza	8.00
SP	Scott Podsednik	4.00
MP	Mark Prior	4.00
AP	Albert Pujols	20.00
AR	Aramis Ramirez	4.00
MR	Manny Ramirez	8.00
RE	Jose Reyes	6.00
BR	Brian Roberts	4.00
IR	Ivan Rodriguez	6.00
SR	Scott Rolen	6.00
JR	Jimmy Rollins	4.00
CS	Curt Schilling	8.00
GS	Gary Sheffield	6.00
SM	John Smoltz	6.00
AS	Alfonso Soriano	6.00
SS	Sammy Sosa	8.00
MT	Mark Teixeira	8.00
TE	Miguel Tejada	6.00
FT	Frank Thomas	6.00
JT	Jim Thome	6.00
JV	Jason Varitek	8.00
VI	Jose Vidro	4.00
BW	Bernie Williams	6.00
WI	Dontrelle Willis	4.00
KW	Kerry Wood	4.00
DW	David Wright	10.00
MY	Michael Young	4.00
CZ	Carlos Zambrano	4.00

Generations Present Materials Silver

NM/M
Common Player: 4.00
Production 99 Sets
Gold: 1-1.5X
Production 25 Sets

BA	Bobby Abreu	4.00
GA	Garret Anderson	4.00
JE	Jeff Bagwell	6.00
JB	Jason Bay	4.00
CB	Carlos Beltran	6.00
AB	Adrian Beltre	4.00
LB	Lance Berkman	4.00
BI	Craig Biggio	6.00
HB	Hank Blalock	4.00
BO	Jeremy Bonderman	4.00
PB	Pat Burrell	4.00
AJ	A.J. Burnett	4.00
MC	Miguel Cabrera	8.00
SC	Sean Casey	4.00
EC	Eric Chavez	4.00
RC	Roger Clemens	12.00
CC	Carl Crawford	4.00
BC	Bobby Crosby	4.00
DA	Johnny Damon	8.00
CD	Carlos Delgado	4.00
JD	J.D. Drew	4.00
AD	Adam Dunn	6.00
RF	Rafael Furcal	4.00
JG	Jason Giambi	6.00
BG	Brian Giles	4.00
MG	Marcus Giles	4.00
TG	Troy Glaus	4.00
KG	Khalil Greene	4.00
ZG	Zack Greinke	4.00
KG1	Ken Griffey Jr.	20.00
KG2	Ken Griffey Jr.	20.00
KG3	Ken Griffey Jr.	20.00
VG	Vladimir Guerrero	8.00
HA	Travis Hafner	4.00
RH	Rich Harden	4.00
TH	Todd Helton	6.00
AH	Aubrey Huff	4.00
HU	Torii Hunter	4.00
DJ	Derek Jeter	20.00
RJ	Randy Johnson	8.00
JO	Andruw Jones	4.00
CJ	Chipper Jones	8.00
SK	Scott Kazmir	4.00
JK	Jeff Kent	4.00
DL	Derrek Lee	8.00
BL	Brad Lidge	4.00
ML	Mark Loretta	4.00
GM	Greg Maddux	15.00
PM	Pedro Martinez	8.00
VM	Victor Martinez	4.00
JM	Joe Mauer	8.00
ME	Melvin Mora	4.00
MO	Justin Morneau	6.00
BM	Bill Mueller	4.00
MM	Mark Mulder	4.00
DO	David Ortiz	8.00
RO	Roy Oswalt	4.00
PA	Corey Patterson	4.00
JP	Jake Peavy	4.00
WM	Wily Mo Pena	4.00
PI	Mike Piazza	8.00
SP	Scott Podsednik	4.00
MP	Mark Prior	4.00
AP	Albert Pujols	20.00
AR	Aramis Ramirez	4.00
MR	Manny Ramirez	8.00
RE	Jose Reyes	6.00
BR	Brian Roberts	4.00
IR	Ivan Rodriguez	6.00
SR	Scott Rolen	6.00
JR	Jimmy Rollins	4.00
JS	Johan Santana	6.00
CS	Curt Schilling	8.00
BS	Ben Sheets	4.00
GS	Gary Sheffield	6.00
SM	John Smoltz	6.00
AS	Alfonso Soriano	6.00
SS	Sammy Sosa	8.00
MT	Mark Teixeira	8.00
TE	Miguel Tejada	6.00
FT	Frank Thomas	6.00
JT	Jim Thome	6.00
JV	Jason Varitek	8.00
VI	Jose Vidro	4.00
BW	Bernie Williams	6.00
WI	Dontrelle Willis	4.00
KW	Kerry Wood	4.00
DW	David Wright	10.00
MY	Michael Young	4.00
CZ	Carlos Zambrano	4.00

Generations Present Signatures

NM/M
Common Player: 10.00
Production 25-199.
Bronze: 1-1.5X
Production 10 or 35.
No pricing for prod. of 10.
Gold: No Pricing
Production 5-15.

GA	Garret Anderson/25	15.00
JB	Jason Bay/199	15.00
BI	Craig Biggio/25	35.00
JB	Jeremy Bonderman/199	15.00
MC	Miguel Cabrera/25	40.00
SC	Sean Casey/50	15.00
CC	Carl Crawford/99	15.00
BC	Bobby Crosby/99	15.00
AD	Adam Dunn/95	25.00
RF	Rafael Furcal/99	15.00
BG	Brian Giles/99	12.00
MG	Marcus Giles/199	10.00
GR	Khalil Greene/135	10.00
ZG	Zack Greinke/199	25.00
KG1	Ken Griffey Jr./199	75.00
KG2	Ken Griffey Jr./199	75.00
KG3	Ken Griffey Jr./199	75.00
HA	Travis Hafner/199	15.00
RH	Rich Harden/199	15.00
AH	Aubrey Huff/199	15.00
HU	Torii Hunter/25	25.00
DJ	Derek Jeter/99	150.00
DL	Derrek Lee/25	40.00
BL	Brad Lidge/99	25.00
ML	Mark Loretta/199	15.00
VM	Victor Martinez/99	15.00
JM	Joe Mauer/25	40.00
ME	Melvin Mora/199	10.00
MO	Justin Morneau/99	20.00
MM	Mark Mulder/99	15.00
DO	David Ortiz/25	50.00
RO	Roy Oswalt/25	30.00
JP	Jake Peavy/99	15.00
WM	Wily Mo Pena/199	15.00
SP	Scott Podsednik/99	20.00
MP	Mark Prior/25	20.00
AR	Aramis Ramirez/99	15.00
BR	Brian Roberts/99	15.00
BS	Ben Sheets/99	15.00
GS	Gary Sheffield/25	35.00
SM	John Smoltz/25	50.00
MT	Mark Teixeira/25	50.00
TE	Miguel Tejada/25	40.00
FT	Frank Thomas/25	50.00
VI	Jose Vidro/99	10.00
WI	Dontrelle Willis/25	15.00
DW	David Wright/135	50.00
MY	Michael Young/199	15.00

Signature Dual Material

NM/M
Common Player: 20.00
Production 75 Sets

HB	Harold Baines	25.00
AB	Adrian Beltre	25.00
BI	Craig Biggio	40.00
WB	Wade Boggs	50.00
MC	Miguel Cabrera	50.00
SC	Sean Casey	25.00
OC	Orlando Cepeda	40.00
JC	Jack Clark	20.00
WC	Will Clark	50.00
CC	Carl Crawford	20.00
BC	Bobby Crosby	30.00
ED	Eric Davis	35.00
AD	Andre Dawson	30.00
DU	Adam Dunn	40.00
LD	Lenny Dykstra	20.00
BG	Brian Giles	20.00
GI	Marcus Giles	20.00
KG	Ken Griffey Jr.	150.00
TG	Tony Gwynn	60.00
TH	Travis Hafner	30.00
FH	Frank Howard	30.00
RH	Ryan Howard	75.00
AH	Aubrey Huff	20.00
HU	Torii Hunter	30.00
DJ	Derek Jeter	300.00
WJ	Wally Joyner	40.00
BL	Barry Larkin	40.00
MA	Bill Madlock	25.00
VM	Victor Martinez	25.00
DM	Don Mattingly	90.00
BM	Bobby Murcer	35.00
GN	Graig Nettles	30.00
TO	Tony Oliva	25.00
DO	David Ortiz	75.00
CP	Corey Patterson	20.00
WP	Wily Mo Pena	25.00
TP	Tony Perez	40.00
SP	Scott Podsednik	50.00
AP	Albert Pujols	250.00
TR	Tim Raines	30.00
RA	Aramis Ramirez	35.00
RE	Jose Reyes	40.00
RI	Jim Rice	35.00
CR	Cal Ripken Jr.	150.00
BR	Brooks Robinson	50.00
RS	Ryne Sandberg	80.00
MS	Mike Schmidt	75.00
MT	Mark Teixeira	60.00
MI	Miguel Tejada	50.00
BU	B.J. Upton	25.00
AV	Andy Van Slyke	30.00
JV	Jose Vidro	20.00
JW	Jayson Werth	20.00
DW	David Wright	80.00
KY	Kevin Youkilis	20.00

2005 Upper Deck Update

NM/M
Complete Update Set (186):
Common Player (1-100): .15
Common Rookie (101-177): 3.00
Production 599
Common Rk Auto. (178-186): 10.00
Production 75
Pack (5): 5.00
Box (24): 100.00

1	A.J. Burnett	.15
2	Adam Dunn	.50
3	Adrian Beltre	.25
4	Albert Pujols	2.00
5	Alex Rodriguez	2.00
6	Alfonso Soriano	.50
7	Andruw Jones	.50
8	Aramis Ramirez	.25
9	Barry Zito	.25
10	Bartolo Colon	.25
11	Ben Sheets	.25
12	Bobby Abreu	.25
13	Bobby Crosby	.25
14	Michael Cuddyer	.25
15	Brian Giles	.15
16	Brian Roberts	.15
17	Carl Crawford	.15
18	Carlos Beltran	.25
19	Carlos Delgado	.40
20	Carlos Lee	.15
21	Carlos Zambrano	.25
22	Chase Utley	.25
23	Chipper Jones	.75
24	Chris Carpenter	.25
25	Craig Biggio	.25
26	Curt Schilling	.25
27	David Ortiz	.75
28	David Wright	.75
29	Derek Jeter	2.00
30	Derrek Lee	.50
31	Dontrelle Willis	.25
32	Eric Chavez	.25
33	Eric Gagne	.25
34	Francisco Rodriguez	.15
35	Gary Sheffield	.40
36	Greg Maddux	1.00
37	Hank Blalock	.25
38	Hideki Matsui	1.50
39	Ichiro Suzuki	.50
40	Ivan Rodriguez	.50
41	J.D. Drew	.15
42	Jake Peavy	.25
43	Jason Bay	.25
44	Jason Schmidt	.25
45	Jeff Bagwell	.40
46	Jeff Kent	.25
47	Jeremy Bonderman	.15
48	Jim Edmonds	.40
49	Jim Thome	.50
50	Joe Mauer	.50
51	Johan Santana	.50
52	John Smoltz	.25
53	Johnny Damon	.75
54	Jose Reyes	.25
55	Jose Vidro	.15
56	Josh Beckett	.25
57	Justin Morneau	.25
58	Ken Griffey Jr.	1.50
59	Kenny Rogers	.15
60	Kerry Wood	.25
61	Khalil Greene	.25
62	Lance Berkman	.25
63	Livan Hernandez	.15
64	Luis Gonzalez	.15
65	Manny Ramirez	.75
66	Mark Buehrle	.15
67	Mark Mulder	.25
68	Mark Prior	.50
69	Mark Teixeira	.50
70	Michael Young	.25
71	Miguel Cabrera	.75
72	Miguel Tejada	.25
73	Mike Mussina	.40
74	Mike Piazza	.75
75	Moises Alou	.25
76	Morgan Ensberg	.25
77	Nomar Garciaparra	.50
78	Pat Burrell	.25
79	Paul Konerko	.75
80	Pedro Martinez	.75
81	Randy Johnson	.25
82	Rich Harden	.25
83	Richie Sexson	.25
84	Rickie Weeks	.25
85	Robinson Cano	.25
86	Roger Clemens	2.00
87	Roy Halladay	.25
88	Roy Oswalt	.25
89	Sammy Sosa	.75
90	Scott Kazmir	.15
91	Scott Rolen	.25
92	Shawn Green	.25
93	Tim Hudson	.25
94	Todd Helton	.50
95	Tom Glavine	.25
96	Torii Hunter	.25
97		.25
98		.15
99	Vernon Wells	.15
100	Vladimir Guerrero	.75
101	Adam Shabala RC	3.00
102	Ambiorix Burgos RC	3.00
103	Anibal Sanchez RC	5.00
104	Bill McCarthy RC	3.00
105	Brandon McCarthy RC	4.00
106	Brian Burres RC	3.00
107	Carlos Ruiz RC	4.00
108	Casey Rogowski RC	3.00
109	Chad Orvella RC	3.00
110	Chris Resop RC	3.00
111	Chris Roberson RC	3.00
112	Chris Seddon RC	3.00
113	Colter Bean RC	3.00
114	Dae-Sung Koo RC	3.00
115	David Gassner RC	3.00
116	Brian Anderson	3.00
117	D.J. Houlton RC	3.00
118	Derek Wathan RC	3.00
119	Devon Lowery RC	3.00
120	Enrique Gonzalez RC	3.00
121	Eude Brito RC	3.00
122	Francisco Butto RC	3.00
123	Franquelis Osoria RC	3.00
124	Garrett Jones RC	6.00
125	Geovany Soto RC	10.00
126	Hayden Penn RC	3.00
127	Ismael Ramirez RC	3.00
128	Jared Gothreaux RC	3.00
129	Jason Hammel RC	3.00
130	Jeff Miller RC	3.00
131	Joel Peralta RC	3.00
132	John Hattig Jr. RC	3.00
133	Jorge Campillo RC	3.00
134	Juan Morillo RC	3.00
135	Ryan Garko RC	5.00
136	Keiichi Yabu RC	3.00
137	Luis Hernandez RC	5.00
138	Luis Pena RC	3.00
139	Luis Rodriguez RC	3.00
140	Luke Scott RC	5.00
141	Marcos Carvajal RC	3.00
142	Mark Woodyard RC	3.00
143	Matt Smith RC	3.00
144	Matt Lindstrom RC	5.00
145	Miguel Negron RC	3.00
146	Mike Morse RC	3.00
147	Nate McLouth RC	5.00
148	Nelson Cruz RC	15.00
149	Nick Masset RC	3.00
150	Oscar Robles RC	3.00
151	Paulino Reynoso RC	3.00
152	Pedro Lopez RC	4.00
153	Peter Orr RC	3.00
154	Randy Messenger RC	3.00
155	Randy Williams RC	3.00
156	Raul Tablado RC	3.00
157	Ronny Paulino RC	3.00
158	Russel Rohlicek RC	3.00
159	Russell Martin RC	8.00
160	Scott Baker RC	3.00
161	Scott Munter RC	3.00
162	Sean Thompson RC	3.00
163	Sean Tracey RC	3.00
164	Shane Costa RC	3.00
165	Steve Schmoll RC	3.00
166	Tony Giarratano RC	3.00
167	Tony Pena RC	3.00
168	Travis Bowyer RC	3.00
169	Ubaldo Jimenez RC	15.00
170	Wladimir Balentien RC	3.00
171	Yorman Bazardo RC	3.00
172	Yuniesky Betancourt RC	3.00
173	Chris Denorfia RC	3.00
174	Dana Eveland RC	5.00
175	Jermaine Van Buren RC	3.00
176	Mark McLemore RC	3.00
177	Ryan Spilborghs RC	3.00
178	Ambiorix Concepcion RC	5.00
179	Jeff Niemann RC	20.00
180	Justin Verlander RC	80.00
181	Kendry Morales RC	25.00
182	Philip Humber RC	15.00
183	Prince Fielder RC	125.00
184	Stephen Drew RC	40.00
185	Tadahito Iguchi RC	20.00
186	Ryan Zimmerman RC	85.00

Common Artifacts RC (201-285): 3.00
Production 799

201	Adam Shabala RC	3.00
202	Ambiorix Burgos RC	3.00
203	Ambiorix Concepcion RC	3.00
204	Anibal Sanchez RC	5.00
205	Bill McCarthy RC	3.00
206	Brandon McCarthy RC	3.00
207	Brian Burres RC	3.00
208	Carlos Ruiz RC	4.00
209	Casey Rogowski RC	3.00
210	Chad Orvella RC	3.00
211	Chris Resop RC	3.00
212	Chris Roberson RC	3.00
213	Chris Seddon RC	3.00
214	Colter Bean RC	3.00
215	Dae-Sung Koo RC	3.00
216	David Gassner RC	3.00
217	Brian Anderson	3.00
218	D.J. Houlton RC	3.00
219	Derek Wathan RC	3.00
220	Devon Lowery RC	3.00
221	Enrique Gonzalez RC	3.00
222	Eude Brito RC	3.00
223	Francisco Butto RC	3.00
224	Franquelis Osoria RC	3.00
225	Garrett Jones RC	5.00
226	Geovany Soto RC	8.00
227	Hayden Penn RC	3.00
228	Ismael Ramirez RC	3.00
229	Jared Gothreaux RC	3.00
230	Jason Hammel RC	3.00
231	Jeff Miller RC	3.00
232	Jeff Niemann RC	5.00
233	Joel Peralta RC	3.00
234	John Hattig Jr. RC	3.00
235	Jorge Campillo RC	3.00
236	Juan Morillo RC	3.00
237	Justin Verlander RC	10.00
238	Ryan Garko RC	5.00
239	Keiichi Yabu RC	3.00
240	Kendry Morales RC	8.00
241	Luis Hernandez RC	3.00
242	Luis Pena RC	3.00
243	Luis Rodriguez RC	3.00
244	Luke Scott RC	5.00
245	Marcos Carvajal RC	3.00
246	Mark Woodyard RC	3.00
247	Matt Smith RC	3.00
248	Matt Lindstrom RC	3.00
249	Miguel Negron RC	3.00
250	Mike Morse RC	3.00
251	Nate McLouth RC	5.00
252	Nelson Cruz RC	10.00
253	Nick Masset RC	3.00
254	Oscar Robles RC	3.00
255	Paulino Reynoso RC	3.00
256	Pedro Lopez RC	3.00
257	Peter Orr RC	3.00
258	Philip Humber RC	3.00
259	Prince Fielder RC	15.00
260	Randy Messenger RC	3.00
261	Randy Williams RC	3.00
262	Raul Tablado RC	3.00
263	Ronny Paulino RC	3.00
264	Russel Rohlicek RC	3.00
265	Russell Martin RC	8.00
266	Scott Baker RC	5.00
267	Scott Munter RC	3.00
268	Sean Thompson RC	3.00
269	Sean Tracey RC	3.00
270	Shane Costa RC	3.00
271	Stephen Drew RC	8.00
272	Steve Schmoll RC	3.00
273	Tadahito Iguchi RC	5.00
274	Tony Giarratano RC	3.00
275	Tony Pena RC	3.00
276	Travis Bowyer RC	3.00
277	Ubaldo Jimenez RC	10.00
278	Wladimir Balentien RC	3.00
279	Yorman Bazardo RC	4.00
280	Yuniesky Betancourt RC	5.00
281	Ryan Zimmerman RC	8.00
282	Chris Denorfia RC	3.00
283	Dana Eveland RC	3.00
284	Jermaine Van Buren RC	3.00
285	Mark McLemore RC	3.00

Common Reflections RC (201-286): 1.00

201	Adam Shabala RC	1.00
202	Ambiorix Burgos RC	1.00
203	Ambiorix Concepcion RC	1.00
204	Anibal Sanchez RC	1.00
205	Bill McCarthy RC	1.00
206	Brandon McCarthy RC	1.00
207	Brian Burres RC	1.00
208	Carlos Ruiz RC	1.50
209	Casey Rogowski RC	1.00
210	Chad Orvella RC	1.00
211	Chris Resop RC	1.50
212	Chris Roberson RC	1.00
213	Chris Seddon RC	1.00
214	Colter Bean RC	1.00
215	Dae-Sung Koo RC	1.00
216	Yuniesky Betancourt RC	2.00
217	David Gassner RC	1.00
218	Brian Anderson	1.00
219	Dennis Houlton RC	1.00
220	Derek Wathan RC	1.00
221	Devon Lowery RC	1.00
222	Enrique Gonzalez RC	1.00
223	Ryan Zimmerman RC	8.00
224	Eude Brito RC	1.00
225	Francisco Butto RC	1.00
226	Franquelis Osoria RC	1.00
227	Garrett Jones RC	3.00
228	Geovany Soto RC	6.00
229	Hayden Penn RC	1.00
230	Ismael Ramirez RC	1.00
231	Jared Gothreaux RC	1.00
232	Jason Hammel RC	1.00
233	Chris Denorfia RC	1.00
234	Jeff Miller RC	.75
235	Jeff Niemann RC	1.50
236	Dana Eveland RC	1.00
237	Joel Peralta RC	.75
238	John Hattig Jr. RC	1.00
239	Jorge Campillo RC	1.00
240	Juan Morillo RC	1.00
241	Justin Verlander RC	5.00
242	Ryan Garko RC	1.00
243	Keiichi Yabu RC	1.00
244	Kendry Morales RC	2.50
245	Luis Hernandez RC	.75
246	Jermaine Van Buren RC	.75
247	Luis Pena RC	.75
248	Luis Rodriguez RC	.75
249	Luke Scott RC	1.50
250	Marcos Carvajal RC	.75
251	Mark Woodyard RC	1.00
252	Matt Smith RC	1.00
253	Matt Lindstrom RC	1.50
254	Miguel Negron RC	1.00
255	Mike Morse RC	1.00
256	Nate McLouth RC	2.00
257	Nelson Cruz RC	4.00
258	Nick Masset RC	.75
259	Mark McLemore RC	1.00
260	Oscar Robles RC	1.00
261	Paulino Reynoso RC	1.00
262	Pedro Lopez RC	1.00
263	Peter Orr RC	1.00
264	Philip Humber RC	1.50

234	Jeff Miller RC	1.00
235	Jeff Niemann RC	1.00
236	Dana Eveland RC	1.00
237	Joel Peralta RC	1.00
238	John Hattig Jr. RC	1.00
239	Jorge Campillo RC	1.00
240	Juan Morillo RC	1.00
241	Justin Verlander RC	8.00
242	Ryan Garko RC	3.00
243	Keiichi Yabu RC	1.00
244	Kendry Morales RC	5.00
245	Luis Hernandez RC	1.00
246	Jermaine Van Buren RC	1.00
247	Luis Pena RC	1.00
248	Luis Rodriguez RC	1.00
249	Luke Scott RC	3.00
250	Marcos Carvajal RC	1.00
251	Mark Woodyard RC	1.00
252	Matt Smith RC	1.00
253	Matt Lindstrom RC	1.00
254	Miguel Negron RC	1.00
255	Mike Morse RC	1.00
256	Nate McLouth RC	1.00
257	Nelson Cruz RC	6.00
258	Nick Masset RC	1.00
259	Mark McLemore RC	1.00
260	Oscar Robles RC	1.00
261	Paulino Reynoso RC	1.00
262	Pedro Lopez RC	1.00
263	Peter Orr RC	1.00
264	Philip Humber RC	2.00
265	Prince Fielder RC	10.00
266	Randy Messenger RC	1.00
267	Randy Williams RC	1.00
268	Raul Tablado RC	1.00
269	Ronny Paulino RC	1.00
270	Russel Rohlicek RC	1.00
271	Russell Martin RC	3.00
272	Scott Baker RC	2.00
273	Scott Munter RC	1.00
274	Sean Thompson RC	1.00
275	Sean Tracey RC	1.00
276	Shane Costa RC	1.00
277	Stephen Drew RC	5.00
278	Steve Schmoll RC	1.00
279	Ryan Spilborghs RC	2.00
280	Tadahito Iguchi RC	2.00
281	Tony Giarratano RC	1.00
282	Tony Pena RC	1.00
283	Travis Bowyer RC	1.00
284	Ubaldo Jimenez RC	8.00
285	Wladimir Balentien RC	2.50
286	Yorman Bazardo RC	1.00

Common Origins RC (201-286): .75

201	Adam Shabala RC	.75
202	Ambiorix Burgos RC	.75
203	Ambiorix Concepcion RC	.75
204	Anibal Sanchez RC	1.00
205	Bill McCarthy RC	.75
206	Brandon McCarthy RC	.75
207	Brian Burres RC	.75
208	Carlos Ruiz RC	1.00
209	Casey Rogowski RC	.75
210	Chad Orvella RC	.75
211	Chris Resop RC	1.00
212	Chris Roberson RC	.75
213	Chris Seddon RC	.75
214	Colter Bean RC	.75
215	Dae-Sung Koo RC	.75
216	Yuniesky Betancourt RC	1.50
217	David Gassner RC	.75
218	Brian Anderson	.75
219	Dennis Houlton RC	.75
220	Derek Wathan RC	.75
221	Devon Lowery RC	.75
222	Enrique Gonzalez RC	.75
223	Ryan Zimmerman RC	5.00
224	Eude Brito RC	.75
225	Francisco Butto RC	.75
226	Franquelis Osoria RC	.75
227	Garrett Jones RC	2.00
228	Geovany Soto RC	4.00
229	Hayden Penn RC	.75
230	Ismael Ramirez RC	.75
231	Jared Gothreaux RC	.75
232	Jason Hammel RC	.75
233	Chris Denorfia RC	.75
234	Jeff Miller RC	.75
235	Jeff Niemann RC	1.50
236	Dana Eveland RC	1.00
237	Joel Peralta RC	.75
238	John Hattig Jr. RC	.75
239	Jorge Campillo RC	1.00
240	Juan Morillo RC	1.00
241	Justin Verlander RC	5.00
242	Ryan Garko RC	1.00
243	Keiichi Yabu RC	1.00
244	Kendry Morales RC	2.50
245	Luis Hernandez RC	.75
246	Jermaine Van Buren RC	.75
247	Luis Pena RC	.75
248	Luis Rodriguez RC	.75
249	Luke Scott RC	1.50
250	Marcos Carvajal RC	.75
251	Mark Woodyard RC	1.00
252	Matt Smith RC	1.00
253	Matt Lindstrom RC	1.50
254	Miguel Negron RC	1.00
255	Mike Morse RC	1.00
256	Nate McLouth RC	2.00
257	Nelson Cruz RC	4.00
258	Nick Masset RC	.75
259	Mark McLemore RC	1.00
260	Oscar Robles RC	.75
261	Paulino Reynoso RC	1.00
262	Pedro Lopez RC	1.00
263	Peter Orr RC	1.00
264	Philip Humber RC	1.50

#	Player	Price
265	Prince Fielder	8.00
266	Randy Messenger RC	.75
267	Randy Williams RC	1.00
268	Raul Tablado RC	.75
269	Ronny Paulino RC	1.00
270	Russel Rohlicek RC	.75
271	Russell Martin RC	2.50
272	Scott Baker RC	2.00
273	Ryan Spilborghs RC	1.00
274	Scott Munter RC	.75
275	Sean Thompson RC	1.00
276	Sean Tracey RC	1.00
277	Shane Costa RC	1.00
278	Stephen Drew RC	4.00
279	Steve Schmoll RC	1.00
280	Tadahito Iguchi RC	1.50
281	Tony Giarratano RC	.75
282	Tony Pena RC	.75
283	Travis Bowyer RC	1.00
284	Ubaldo Jimenez RC	5.00
285	Wladimir Balentien RC	2.00
286	Yorman Bazardo RC	1.00

Common SP Authentic Auto. (101-186): 8.00
Production 185

#	Player	Price
101	Adam Shabala RC	8.00
102	Ambiorix Burgos RC	8.00
103	Ambiorix Concepcion RC	8.00
104	Anibal Sanchez RC	15.00
106	Brandon McCarthy RC	10.00
107	Brian Burres RC	8.00
108	Carlos Ruiz RC	15.00
109	Casey Rogowski RC	10.00
110	Chad Orvella RC	8.00
111	Chris Resop RC	8.00
112	Chris Roberson RC	8.00
113	Chris Seddon RC	8.00
114	Colter Bean RC	8.00
116	David Gassner RC	8.00
117	Brian Anderson	8.00
120	Devon Lowery RC	8.00
121	Enrique Gonzalez RC	8.00
122	Eude Brito RC	8.00
123	Francisco Butto RC	8.00
124	Franquelis Osoria RC	8.00
125	Garrett Jones RC	25.00
126	Geovany Soto RC	40.00
127	Hayden Penn RC	8.00
128	Ismael Ramirez RC	8.00
129	Jared Gothreaux RC	800
130	Jason Hammel RC	8.00
131	Jeff Miller RC	8.00
132	Jeff Niemann RC	25.00
133	Joel Peralta RC	8.00
134	John Hattig Jr. RC	8.00
135	Jorge Campillo RC	10.00
136	Juan Morillo RC	8.00
137	Justin Verlander RC	100.00
138	Ryan Garko RC	12.00
139	Keiichi Yabu RC	12.00
140	Kendry Morales RC	35.00
141	Luis Hernandez RC	10.00
143	Luis Rodriguez RC	10.00
144	Luke Scott RC	30.00
145	Marcos Carvajal RC	8.00
146	Mark Woodyard RC	8.00
147	Matt Smith RC	8.00
148	Matt Lindstrom RC	15.00
149	Miguel Negron RC	8.00
150	Mike Morse RC	8.00
151	Nate McLouth RC	20.00
152	Nelson Cruz RC	85.00
153	Nick Masset RC	8.00
155	Paulino Reynoso RC	8.00
156	Pedro Lopez RC	8.00
157	Peter Orr RC	8.00
158	Philip Humber RC	15.00
159	Prince Fielder	200.00
160	Randy Messenger RC	8.00
162	Raul Tablado RC	8.00
163	Ronny Paulino RC	10.00
164	Russel Rohlicek RC	8.00
165	Russell Martin RC	30.00
166	Scott Baker RC	15.00
167	Scott Munter RC	8.00
168	Sean Thompson RC	8.00
169	Sean Tracey RC	8.00
170	Shane Costa RC	8.00
171	Stephen Drew RC	40.00
172	Steve Schmoll RC	8.00
173	Tadahito Iguchi RC	30.00
174	Tony Giarratano RC	10.00
175	Tony Pena RC	8.00
176	Travis Bowyer RC	8.00
177	Ubaldo Jimenez RC	200.00
178	Wladimir Balentien RC	20.00
179	Yorman Bazardo RC	10.00
181	Ryan Zimmerman RC	100.00
182	Chris Denorfia RC	8.00
184	Jermaine Van Buren RC	10.00
185	Mark McLemore RC	8.00

Common SPx Auto. (101-179): 8.00
Production 185

#	Player	Price
101	Adam Shabala RC	8.00
102	Ambiorix Burgos RC	80.00
103	Ambiorix Concepcion RC	8.00
104	Anibal Sanchez RC	15.00
106	Brandon McCarthy RC	8.00
107	Brian Burres RC	80.00
108	Carlos Ruiz RC	15.00
109	Casey Rogowski RC	10.00
110	Chad Orvella RC	8.00
111	Chris Resop RC	8.00
112	Chris Roberson RC	10.00
113	Chris Seddon RC	8.00
114	Colter Bean RC	10.00
115	David Gassner RC	8.00
116	Brian Anderson RC	85.00
118	Devon Lowery RC	8.00
119	Enrique Gonzalez RC	8.00
120	Eude Brito RC	8.00
121	Francisco Butto RC	8.00
122	Franquelis Osoria RC	8.00
123	Garrett Jones RC	20.00
124	Geovany Soto RC	40.00
125	Hayden Penn RC	10.00
126	Ismael Ramirez RC	8.00
127	Jared Gothreaux RC	8.00
128	Jason Hammel RC	8.00
129	Jeff Miller RC	8.00
130	Jeff Niemann RC	20.00
131	Joel Peralta RC	8.00
132	John Hattig Jr. RC	8.00
133	Jorge Campillo RC	10.00
134	Juan Morillo RC	8.00
135	Justin Verlander RC	100.00
136	Ryan Garko RC	15.00
137	Kendry Morales RC	35.00
138	Luis Hernandez RC	8.00
140	Luis Rodriguez RC	80.00
141	Mark Woodyard RC	8.00
142	Matt Smith RC	8.00
143	Matt Lindstrom RC	15.00
144	Miguel Negron RC	10.00
145	Mike Morse RC	10.00
146	Nate McLouth RC	15.00
147	Nelson Cruz RC	60.00
148	Nick Masset RC	8.00
150	Paulino Reynoso RC	8.00
151	Pedro Lopez RC	8.00
152	Philip Humber RC	10.00
153	Prince Fielder	150.00
155	Randy Messenger RC	8.00
156	Raul Tablado RC	8.00
157	Ronny Paulino RC	10.00
158	Russel Rohlicek RC	8.00
159	Russell Martin RC	30.00
160	Scott Baker RC	20.00
161	Scott Munter RC	8.00
162	Sean Thompson RC	80.00
163	Sean Tracey RC	8.00
164	Shane Costa RC	10.00
165	Stephen Drew RC	40.00
166	Tony Giarratano RC	8.00
167	Tony Pena RC	8.00
168	Travis Bowyer RC	8.00
170	Ubaldo Jimenez RC	180.00
171	Wladimir Balentien RC	20.00
172	Yorman Bazardo RC	8.00
173	Ryan Zimmerman RC	85.00
174	Chris Denorfia RC	8.00
177	Jermaine Van Buren RC	8.00
178	Mark McLemore RC	8.00
179	Russell Martin RC	8.00

Common Sweet Spot RC (91-174): .75

#	Player	Price
91	Adam Shabala RC	.75
92	Ambiorix Burgos RC	.75
93	Ambiorix Concepcion RC	1.00
94	Anibal Sanchez RC	1.00
95	Bill McCarthy RC	.75
96	Brandon McCarthy RC	1.00
97	Brian Burres RC	.75
98	Carlos Ruiz RC	1.00
99	Casey Rogowski RC	1.00
100	Chad Orvella RC	.75
101	Chris Resop RC	1.00
102	Chris Roberson RC	.75
103	Chris Seddon RC	.75
104	Colter Bean RC	.75
105	Dae-Sung Koo RC	.75
106	Ryan Zimmerman RC	5.00
107	David Gassner RC	1.00
108	Brian Anderson	1.00
109	D.J. Houlton RC	1.00
110	Derek Wathan RC	.75
111	Devon Lowery RC	.75
112	Enrique Gonzalez RC	.75
113	Chris Denorfia RC	1.00
114	Eude Brito RC	.75
115	Francisco Butto RC	1.00
116	Franquelis Osoria RC	1.00
117	Garrett Jones RC	2.00
118	Geovany Soto RC	3.00
119	Hayden Penn RC	1.00
120	Ismael Ramirez RC	.75
121	Jared Gothreaux RC	.75
122	Jason Hammel RC	.75
123	Dana Eveland RC	.75
124	Jeff Miller RC	.75
125	Jermaine Van Buren RC	.75
126	Joel Peralta RC	.75
127	John Hattig Jr. RC	1.00
128	Jorge Campillo RC	1.00
129	Juan Morillo RC	.75
130	Ryan Garko RC	1.50
131	Keiichi Yabu RC	.75
132	Kendry Morales RC	2.50
133	Luis Hernandez RC	.75
134	Mark McLemore RC	.75
135	Luis Pena RC	.75
136	Luis Rodriguez RC	.75
137	Luke Scott RC	2.00
138	Marcos Carvajal RC	1.00
139	Mark Woodyard RC	.75
140	Matt Smith RC	.75
141	Matt Lindstrom RC	1.50
142	Miguel Negron RC	1.00
143	Mike Morse RC	1.00
144	Nate McLouth RC	2.00
145	Nelson Cruz RC	4.00
146	Nick Masset RC	.75
147	Ryan Spilborghs RC	1.00
148	Oscar Robles RC	.75
149	Paulino Reynoso RC	.75
150	Pedro Lopez RC	1.00
151	Peter Orr RC	.75
152	Prince Fielder	8.00
153	Randy Messenger RC	.75
154	Randy Williams RC	1.00
155	Raul Tablado RC	.75
156	Ronny Paulino RC	1.00
157	Russel Rohlicek RC	.75
158	Russell Martin RC	2.00
159	Scott Baker RC	1.50
160	Scott Munter RC	.75
161	Sean Thompson RC	1.00
162	Sean Tracey RC	1.00
163	Shane Costa RC	1.00
164	Stephen Drew RC	4.00
165	Steve Schmoll RC	.75
166	Ryan Speier RC	1.00
167	Tadahito Iguchi RC	1.50
168	Tony Giarratano RC	1.00
169	Tony Pena RC	.75
170	Travis Bowyer RC	.75
171	Ubaldo Jimenez RC	6.00
172	Wladimir Balentien RC	1.50
173	Yorman Bazardo RC	.75
174	Yuniesky Betancourt RC	1.50

Common Ultimate Signature Ed. (111-193): 8.00
Production 125

#	Player	Price
111	Adam Shabala RC	8.00
112	Anibal Sanchez RC	12.00
114	Brandon McCarthy RC	10.00
115	Brian Burres RC	10.00
116	Carlos Ruiz RC	15.00
117	Casey Rogowski RC	8.00
118	Chad Orvella RC	8.00
119	Chris Resop RC	8.00
120	Chris Roberson RC	8.00
121	Chris Seddon RC	8.00
122	Colter Bean RC	8.00
124	David Gassner RC	8.00
125	Brian Anderson	8.00
128	Devon Lowery RC	8.00
129	Enrique Gonzalez RC	8.00
130	Eude Brito RC	8.00
131	Francisco Butto RC	8.00
132	Franquelis Osoria RC	8.00
133	Garrett Jones RC	20.00
134	Geovany Soto RC	40.00
135	Hayden Penn RC	10.00
136	Ismael Ramirez RC	8.00
137	Jared Gothreaux RC	8.00
138	Jason Hammel RC	8.00
139	Jeff Miller RC	8.00
140	Jeff Niemann RC	25.00
141	Joel Peralta RC	8.00
142	John Hattig Jr. RC	8.00
143	Jorge Campillo RC	10.00
144	Juan Morillo RC	8.00
145	Justin Verlander RC	80.00
146	Ryan Garko RC	15.00
147	Keiichi Yabu RC	10.00
148	Kendry Morales RC	35.00
149	Luis Hernandez RC	8.00
151	Luis Rodriguez RC	8.00
152	Luke Scott RC	25.00
153	Marcos Carvajal RC	8.00
154	Mark Woodyard RC	8.00
155	Matt Smith RC	8.00
156	Matt Lindstrom RC	15.00
157	Miguel Negron RC	8.00
158	Mike Morse RC	10.00
159	Nate McLouth RC	15.00
160	Nelson Cruz RC	60.00
161	Nick Masset RC	8.00
162	Mark McLemore RC	8.00
164	Paulino Reynoso RC	8.00
165	Pedro Lopez RC	8.00
166	Peter Orr RC	8.00
167	Philip Humber RC	15.00
168	Prince Fielder	150.00
169	Randy Messenger RC	8.00
171	Raul Tablado RC	8.00
172	Ronny Paulino RC	10.00
173	Russel Rohlicek RC	8.00
174	Russell Martin RC	30.00
175	Scott Baker RC	20.00
176	Scott Munter RC	8.00
177	Sean Thompson RC	8.00
178	Sean Tracey RC	8.00
179	Shane Costa RC	8.00
180	Stephen Drew RC	30.00
181	Steve Schmoll RC	6.00
182	Tadahito Iguchi RC	15.00
183	Tony Giarratano RC	8.00
184	Tony Pena RC	8.00
185	Travis Bowyer RC	8.00
186	Ubaldo Jimenez RC	180.00
187	Wladimir Balentien RC	15.00
188	Yorman Bazardo RC	10.00
190	Ryan Zimmerman RC	75.00
191	Chris Denorfia RC	8.00
192	Ryan Speier RC	8.00
193	Jermaine Van Buren RC	8.00

Silver
Silver (101-177): 1X
Production 450
Silver (178-186): No Pricing
Production 25 Sets

Gold
Gold (101-177): 1-1.5X
Production 150
Gold (178-186): No Pricing
Production 10 Sets

Platinum
Platinum (101-177): No Pricing
Production 25
Platinum (178-186): No Pricing
Production One Set

Artifacts Blue
Blue (201-285): 1-1.5X
Production 100

Artifacts Gold
Gold (201-285): No Pricing
Production 25 Sets

Artifacts Red
Red (201-285): 1-2X
Production 50

Artifacts Platinum
No Pricing
Production One Set

Generations Triple Signatures
No Pricing
Production 10 Sets

Link to Future Dual Autographs

		NM/M
	Common Duo:	15.00
	Production 35 Sets	
BR	Wladimir Balentien, Jeremy Reed	15.00
BW	Dontrelle Willis, Yorman Bazardo	10.00
CD	David DeJesus, Shane Costa	15.00
DD	J.D. Drew, Stephen Drew	40.00
DJ	Stephen Drew, Derek Jeter	180.00
FO	Prince Fielder, Lyle Overbay	50.00
FT	Prince Fielder, Mark Teixeira	75.00
FW	Prince Fielder, Rickie Weeks	50.00
GO	Roy Oswalt, Jared Gothreaux	25.00
HF	Luis Hernandez, Rafael Furcal	20.00
HG	Tom Glavine, Philip Humber	40.00
MB	Jason Bay, Nate McLouth	25.00
MK	Casey Kotchman, Kendry Morales	25.00
NK	Scott Kazmir, Jeff Niemann	30.00
NW	Vernon Wells, Miguel Negron	25.00
OB	Yhency Brazoban, Franquelis Osoria	15.00
OG	Peter Orr, Marcus Giles	15.00
PV	Javier Vazquez, Tony Pena	15.00
RH	Roy Halladay, Ismael Ramirez	40.00
SK	Chris Seddon, Scott Kazmir	20.00
SL	Jason Lane, Luke Scott	30.00
VB	Justin Verlander, Jeremy Bonderman	50.00
VC	Roger Clemens, Justin Verlander	85.00
ZC	Ryan Zimmerman, Chad Cordero	50.00

Link to the Past Dual Autographs

		NM/M
	Common Duo:	20.00
	Production 25 Sets	
BC	Steve Carlton, Eude Brito	30.00
BM	Juan Marichal, Brian Burres	30.00
CS	Darryl Strawberry, Ambiorix Concepcion	20.00
GT	Alan Trammell, Tony Giarratano	20.00
HG	Dwight Gooden, Philip Humber	20.00
HS	Philip Humber, Tom Seaver	50.00
IA	Luis Aparicio, Tadahito Iguchi	30.00
IC	Tadahito Iguchi, Rod Carew	40.00
JH	Kent Hrbek, Garrett Jones	30.00
JJ	Jack Morris, Justin Verlander	50.00
MC	Rod Carew, Kendry Morales	40.00
MJ	Kendry Morales, Wally Joyner	30.00
MV	Andy Van Slyke, Nate McLouth	40.00
NB	Miguel Negron, George Bell	40.00
NR	Nolan Ryan, Jeff Niemann	150.00
PP	Jim Palmer, Hayden Penn	40.00
RD	Lenny Dykstra, Chris Roberson	20.00
TP	Gaylord Perry, Sean Thompson	20.00
VM	Justin Verlander, Denny McLain	50.00

Origins Blue
Blue (201-286): 2-4X
Production 50 Sets

Origins Gold
Gold (201-286): No Pricing
Production 20 Sets

Origins Black
No Pricing
Production One Set

Origins Red
Red (201-286): 2-3X
Production 99 Sets

Origins Old Judge
Old Judge (201-286): 1X
Inserted 1:2
Blue: 2-3X
Production 50 Sets
Red: 1-2X
Production 99 Sets
Gold: No Pricing
Production 20 Sets
Black: No Pricing
Production One Set

Quad Signatures
No Pricing
Production Five Sets

Reflections Blue
Blue (201-286): 2-4X
Production 75 Sets

Reflections Emerald
Emerald (201-286): 3-6X
Production 25 Sets

Reflections Purple
Purple (201-286): 1.5-3X
Production 99 Sets

Reflections Platinum
No Pricing
Production One Set

Reflections Red
Red (201-286): 1.5-3X
Production 99 Sets

Reflections Turquoise
Turquoise (201-286): 2-4X
Production 50 Sets

SP Authentic Gold
Gold (101-186): No Pricing
Production 10

SPx Silver
Silver (101-179): No Pricing
Production 10

Sweet Spot Gold
Gold (91-174): 1.5-2X
Production 399

Sweet Spot Platinum
Platinum (91-174): 2-3X
Production 99

Sweet Spot Plutonium
No Pricing
Production One Set

Ultimate Signature Ed. Platinum

No Pricing
Production One Set

2006 Upper Deck

	NM/M
Complete Series 1 (500):	150.00
Complete Series 2 (500):	100.00
Complete Update (250):	
Common Player:	.15
Common Update SP:	4.00
Inserted 1:2 Update	
Series 1 Pack (8):	3.00
Series 1 Box (24):	60.00
Series 2 Pack (6):	3.00
Series 2 Box (24):	60.00
Update Pack (8):	3.00
Update Box (24):	60.00

#	Player	Price
1	Adam Kennedy	.15
2	Bartolo Colon	.25
3	Bengie Molina	.15
4	Casey Kotchman	.25
5	Chone Figgins	.25
6	Dallas McPherson	.25
7	Darin Erstad	.15
8	Ervin Santana	.25
9	Francisco Rodriguez	.25
10	Garret Anderson	.15
11	Jarrod Washburn	.15
12	John Lackey	.25
13	Juan Rivera	.15
14	Orlando Cabrera	.25
15	Paul Byrd	.15
16	Steve Finley	.15
17	Vladimir Guerrero	.25
18	Alex Cintron	.15
19	Brandon Lyon	.15
20	Brandon Webb	.50
21	Chad Tracy	.15
22	Chris Snyder	.15
23	Claudio Vargas	.15
24	Conor Jackson RC	.50
25	Craig Counsell	.15
26	Javier Vazquez	.25
27	Jose Valverde	.15
28	Luis Gonzalez	.25
29	Royce Clayton	.15
30	Russ Ortiz	.15
31	Shawn Green	.15
32	Dustin Nippert RC	.15
33	Tony Clark	.15
34	Troy Glaus	.25
35	Adam LaRoche	.15
36	Andruw Jones	.25
37	Craig Hansen RC	.15
38	Chipper Jones	.75
39	Horacio Ramirez	.15
40	Jeff Francoeur	.50
41	John Smoltz	.25
42	Joey Devine RC	.15
43	Johnny Estrada	.15
44	Anthony Lerew RC	.15
45	Julio Franco	.15
46	Kyle Farnsworth	.15
47	Marcus Giles	.15
48	Mike Hampton	.15
49	Rafael Furcal	.25
50	Chuck James RC	.40
51	Tim Hudson	.25
52	B.J. Ryan	.15
53	Bernie Castro	.15
54	Brian Roberts	.25
55	Walter Young	.15
56	Daniel Cabrera	.15
57	Eric Byrnes	.15
58	Alejandro Freire RC	.50
59	Erik Bedard	.25
60	Javy Lopez	.25
61	Jay Gibbons	.15
62	Jorge Julio	.15
63	Luis Matos	.15
64	Melvin Mora	.25
65	Miguel Tejada	.40
66	Rafael Palmeiro	.25
67	Rodrigo Lopez	.15
68	Sammy Sosa	.75
69	Alejandro Machado	.15
70	Bill Mueller	.15
71	Bronson Arroyo	.15
72	Curt Schilling	.75
73	David Ortiz	.75
74	David Wells	.15
75	Edgar Renteria	.25
76	Ryan Jorgensen RC	.15
77	Jason Varitek	.50
78	Johnny Damon	.75
79	Keith Foulke	.15
80	Kevin Youkilis	.25
81	Manny Ramirez	.75
82	Matt Clement	.15
83	Hanley Ramirez RC	1.50
84	Tim Wakefield	.15
85	Trot Nixon	.15
86	Wade Miller	.15
87	Aramis Ramirez	.40
88	Carlos Zambrano	.25
89	Corey Patterson	.15
90	Derrek Lee	.25
91	Geovany Soto RC	1.00
92	Greg Maddux	.75
93	Jeromy Burnitz	.15
94	Jerry Hairston	.15
95	Kerry Wood	.25
96	Mark Prior	.25
97	Matt Murton	.25
98	Michael Barrett	.15

#	Player	Value
99	Neifi Perez	.15
100	Nomar Garciaparra	.50
101	Rich Hill	.25
102	Ryan Dempster	.15
103	Todd Walker	.15
104	A.J. Pierzynski	.15
105	Aaron Rowand	.15
106	Bobby Jenks	.15
107	Carl Everett	.15
108	Dustin Hermanson	.15
109	Frank Thomas	.40
110	Freddy Garcia	.15
111	Jermaine Dye	.25
112	Joe Crede	.15
113	Jon Garland	.15
114	Jose Contreras	.25
115	Juan Uribe	.15
116	Mark Buehrle	.25
117	Orlando Hernandez	.15
118	Paul Konerko	.40
119	Scott Podsednik	.15
120	Tadahito Iguchi	.25
121	Aaron Harang	.25
122	Adam Dunn	.50
123	Austin Kearns	.25
124	Brandon Claussen	.15
125	Chris Denorfia RC	.15
126	Edwin Encarnacion	.15
127	Miguel Perez RC	.15
128	Felipe Lopez	.15
129	Jason LaRue	.15
130	Ken Griffey Jr.	1.50
131	Chris Booker	.15
132	Luke Hudson	.15
133	Jason Bergmann RC	.50
134	Ryan Freel	.15
135	Sean Casey	.15
136	Wily Mo Pena	.15
137	Aaron Boone	.15
138	Ben Broussard	.15
139	Ryan Garko RC	.25
140	C.C. Sabathia	.40
141	Casey Blake	.15
142	Cliff Lee	.15
143	Coco Crisp	.15
144	David Riske	.15
145	Grady Sizemore	.50
146	Jake Westbrook	.15
147	Jhonny Peralta	.15
148	Josh Bard	.15
149	Kevin Millwood	.25
150	Ronnie Belliard	.15
151	Scott Elarton	.15
152	Travis Hafner	.25
153	Victor Martinez	.25
154	Aaron Cook	.15
155	Aaron Miles	.15
156	Brad Hawpe	.25
157	Mike Esposito	.15
158	Chin-Hui Tsao	.15
159	Clint Barmes	.15
160	Cory Sullivan	.15
161	Garrett Atkins	.25
162	J.D. Closser	.15
163	Jason Jennings	.15
164	Jeff Baker	.15
165	Jeff Francis	.15
166	Luis Gonzalez	.15
167	Matt Holliday	.50
168	Todd Helton	.50
169	Brandon Inge	.15
170	Carlos Guillen	.40
171	Carlos Pena	.40
172	Chris Shelton	.15
173	Craig Monroe	.15
174	Curtis Granderson	.50
175	Dmitri Young	.15
176	Ivan Rodriguez	.40
177	Jason Johnson	.15
178	Jeremy Bonderman	.15
179	Magglio Ordonez	.25
180	Mark Woodyard RC	.15
181	Nook Logan	.15
182	Omar Infante	.15
183	Placido Polanco	.15
184	Chris Heintz RC	.50
185	A.J. Burnett	.25
186	Alex Gonzalez	.15
187	Josh Johnson RC	.15
188	Carlos Delgado	.40
189	Dontrelle Willis	.25
190	Josh Wilson RC	.15
191	Jason Vargas	.15
192	Jeff Conine	.15
193	Jeremy Hermida RC	.15
194	Josh Beckett	.50
195	Juan Encarnacion	.15
196	Juan Pierre	.15
197	Luis Castillo	.15
198	Miguel Cabrera	.75
199	Mike Lowell	.40
200	Paul LoDuca	.15
201	Todd Jones	.15
202	Adam Everett	.15
203	Andy Pettitte	.50
204	Brad Ausmus	.15
205	Brad Lidge	.15
206	Brandon Backe	.15
207	Charlton Jimerson	.15
208	Chris Burke	.15
209	Craig Biggio	.25
210	Daniel Wheeler	.15
211	Jason Lane	.15
212	Jeff Bagwell	.50
213	Lance Berkman	.50
214	Luke Scott	.15
215	Morgan Ensberg	.25
216	Roger Clemens	2.00
217	Roy Oswalt	.25
218	Willy Taveras	.15
219	Andres Blanco	.15
220	Angel Berroa	.15
221	Ruben Gotay	.15
222	David DeJesus	.15
223	Emil Brown	.15
224	J.P. Howell	.15
225	Jeremy Affeldt	.15
226	Jimmy Gobble	.15
227	John Buck	.15
228	Jose Lima	.15
229	Mark Teahen	.15
230	Matt Stairs	.15
231	Mike MacDougal	.15
232	Mike Sweeney	.15
233	Runelvys Hernandez	.15
234	Terrence Long	.15
235	Zack Greinke	.25
236	Ron Flores RC	.50
237	Brad Penny	.15
238	Cesar Izturis	.15
239	D.J. Houlton	.15
240	Derek Lowe	.15
241	Eric Gagne	.25
242	Hee Seop Choi	.15
243	J.D. Drew	.25
244	Jason Phillips	.15
245	Jason Repko	.15
246	Jayson Werth	.15
247	Jeff Kent	.25
248	Jeff Weaver	.15
249	Milton Bradley	.15
250	Odalis Perez	.15
251	Hong-Chih Kuo	.25
252	Oscar Robles	.15
253	Ben Sheets	.25
254	Bill Hall	.15
255	Brady Clark	.15
256	Carlos Lee	.15
257	Chris Capuano	.15
258	Nelson Cruz RC	.50
259	Derrick Turnbow	.15
260	Doug Davis	.15
261	Geoff Jenkins	.15
262	J.J. Hardy	.15
263	Lyle Overbay	.15
264	Prince Fielder RC	1.00
265	Rickie Weeks	.25
266	Russell Branyan	.15
267	Tomokazu Ohka	.15
268	Jonah Bayliss RC	.75
269	Brad Radke	.15
270	Carlos Silva	.15
271	Francisco Liriano RC	.50
272	Jacque Jones	.15
273	Joe Mauer	.25
274	Travis Bower	.15
275	Joe Nathan	.15
276	Johan Santana	.50
277	Justin Morneau	.40
278	Kyle Lohse	.15
279	Lew Ford	.15
280	Matthew LeCroy	.15
281	Michael Cuddyer	.15
282	Nick Punto	.15
283	Scott Baker	.15
284	Shannon Stewart	.15
285	Torii Hunter	.25
286	Braden Looper	.15
287	Carlos Beltran	.50
288	Cliff Floyd	.15
289	David Wright	.75
290	Doug Mientkiewicz	.15
291	Anderson Hernandez RC	.15
292	Jose Reyes	.75
293	Kazuo Matsui	.15
294	Kris Benson	.15
295	Miguel Cairo	.15
296	Mike Cameron	.15
297	Robert Andino RC	.50
298	Mike Piazza	.75
299	Pedro Martinez	.75
300	Tom Glavine	.50
301	Victor Diaz	.15
302	Tim Hamulack	.15
303	Alex Rodriguez	2.00
304	Bernie Williams	.25
305	Carl Pavano	.15
306	Chien-Ming Wang	.50
307	Derek Jeter	2.00
308	Gary Sheffield	.40
309	Hideki Matsui	1.00
310	Jason Giambi	.40
311	Jorge Posada	.25
312	Kevin Brown	.15
313	Mariano Rivera	.40
314	Matt Lawton	.15
315	Mike Mussina	.25
316	Randy Johnson	.75
317	Robinson Cano	.25
318	Michael Vento	.15
319	Tino Martinez	.25
320	Tony Womack	.15
321	Barry Zito	.25
322	Bobby Crosby	.15
323	Bobby Kielty	.15
324	Dan Johnson	.15
325	Danny Haren	.40
326	Eric Chavez	.25
327	Erubiel Durazo	.15
328	Huston Street	.25
329	Jason Kendall	.15
330	Jay Payton	.15
331	Joe Blanton	.15
332	Joe Kennedy	.15
333	Kirk Saarloos	.15
334	Mark Kotsay	.15
335	Nick Swisher	.25
336	Rich Harden	.25
337	Scott Hatteberg	.15
338	Billy Wagner	.25
339	Bobby Abreu	.50
340	Brett Myers	.15
341	Chase Utley	.75
342	Danny Sandoval RC	.50
343	David Bell	.15
344	Gavin Floyd	.15
345	Jim Thome	.50
346	Jimmy Rollins	.75
347	Jon Lieber	.15
348	Kenny Lofton	.15
349	Mike Lieberthal	.15
350	Pat Burrell	.25
351	Randy Wolf	.15
352	Ryan Howard	.75
353	Vicente Padilla	.15
354	Bryan Bullington	.15
355	J.J. Furmaniak RC	.15
356	Craig Wilson	.15
357	Matt Capps RC	.25
358	Tom Gorzelanny RC	.25
359	Jack Wilson	.15
360	Jason Bay	.25
361	Jose Mesa	.15
362	Josh Fogg	.15
363	Kip Wells	.15
364	Steve Stemle RC	.50
365	Oliver Perez	.15
366	Robert Mackowiak	.15
367	Ronny Paulino RC	.15
368	Tike Redman	.15
369	Zach Duke	.25
370	Adam Eaton	.15
371	Scott Feldman RC	.50
372	Brian Giles	.25
373	Brian Lawrence	.15
374	Damian Jackson	.15
375	Dave Roberts	.15
376	Jake Peavy	.50
377	Joe Randa	.15
378	Khalil Greene	.15
379	Mark Loretta	.25
380	Ramon Hernandez	.15
381	Robert Fick	.15
382	Ryan Klesko	.15
383	Trevor Hoffman	.15
384	Woody Williams	.15
385	Xavier Nady	.15
386	Armando Benitez	.15
387	Brad Hennessey	.15
388	Brian Myrow RC	.50
389	Edgardo Alfonzo	.15
390	J.T. Snow	.15
391	Jeremy Accardo RC	.15
392	Jason Schmidt	.25
393	Lance Niekro	.15
394	Matt Cain	.25
395	Daniel Ortmeier RC	.15
396	Moises Alou	.15
397	Doug Clark	.15
398	Omar Vizquel	.15
399	Pedro Feliz	.15
400	Randy Winn	.15
401	Ray Durham	.15
402	Adrian Beltre	.40
403	Eddie Guardado	.15
404	Felix Hernandez	.50
405	Gil Meche	.15
406	Ichiro Suzuki	1.50
407	Jamie Moyer	.15
408	Jeff Nelson	.15
409	Jeremy Reed	.15
410	Joel Pineiro	.15
411	Jaime Bubela RC	.15
412	Raul Ibanez	.15
413	Richie Sexson	.25
414	Ryan Franklin	.15
415	Willie Bloomquist	.15
416	Yorvit Torrealba	.15
417	Yuniesky Betancourt	.15
418	Jeff Harris RC	.25
419	Albert Pujols	2.00
420	Chris Carpenter	.25
421	David Eckstein	.15
422	Jason Isringhausen	.15
423	Jason Marquis	.15
424	Adam Wainwright RC	1.50
425	Jim Edmonds	.25
426	Ryan Theriot RC	1.00
427	Chris Duncan	.15
428	Mark Grudzielanek	.15
429	Mark Mulder	.25
430	Matt Morris	.15
431	Reggie Sanders	.15
432	Scott Rolen	.50
433	Tyler Johnson RC	.15
434	Yadier Molina	.15
435	Alex Gonzalez	.15
436	Aubrey Huff	.15
437	Tim Corcoran RC	.40
438	Carl Crawford	.25
439	Casey Fossum	.15
440	Danys Baez	.15
441	Edwin Jackson	.15
442	Joey Gathright	.15
443	Jonny Gomes	.25
444	Jorge Cantu	.15
445	Julio Lugo	.15
446	Nick Green	.15
447	Rocco Baldelli	.15
448	Scott Kazmir	.25
449	Seth McClung	.15
450	Toby Hall	.15
451	Travis Lee	.15
452	Craig Breslow RC	.25
453	Alfonso Soriano	.50
454	Chris Young	.40
455	David Dellucci	.15
456	Francisco Cordero	.15
457	Gary Matthews	.15
458	Hank Blalock	.25
459	Juan Dominguez	.15
460	Josh Rupe	.15
461	Kenny Rogers	.15
462	Kevin Mench	.15
463	Laynce Nix	.15
464	Mark Teixeira	.50
465	Michael Young	.25
466	Richard Hidalgo	.15
467	Jason Botts RC	.15
468	Aaron Hill	.15
469	Alex Rios	.40
470	Corey Koskie	.15
471	Chris Demaria RC	.50
472	Eric Hinske	.15
473	Frank Catalanotto	.15
474	John-Ford Griffin RC	.15
475	Gustavo Chacin	.15
476	Josh Towers	.15
477	Miguel Batista	.15
478	Orlando Hudson	.15
479	Reed Johnson	.15
480	Roy Halladay	.40
481	Shaun Marcum RC	.50
482	Shea Hillenbrand	.15
483	Ted Lilly	.15
484	Vernon Wells	.25
485	Brad Wilkerson	.15
486	Darrell Rasner RC	.15
487	Chad Cordero	.15
488	Cristian Guzman	.15
489	Esteban Loaiza	.15
490	John Patterson	.15
491	Jose Guillen	.15
492	Jose Vidro	.15
493	Livan Hernandez	.15
494	Marlon Byrd	.15
495	Nick Johnson	.15
496	Preston Wilson	.15
497	Ryan Church	.15
498	Ryan Zimmerman RC	1.00
499	Tony Armas	.15
500	Vinny Castilla	.15
501	Andy Green	.15
502	Damion Easley	.15
503	Eric Byrnes	.25
504	Jason Grimsley	.15
505	Jeff DaVanon	.15
506	Johnny Estrada	.15
507	Luis Vizcaino	.15
508	Miguel Batista	.15
509	Orlando Hernandez	.15
510	Orlando Hudson	.15
511	Terry Mulholland	.15
512	Chris Reitsma	.15
513	Edgar Renteria	.25
514	John Thomson	.15
515	Jorge Sosa	.15
516	Oscar Villarreal	.15
517	Peter Orr	.15
518	Ryan Langerhans	.15
519	Todd Pratt	.15
520	Wilson Betemit	.15
521	Brian Jordan	.15
522	Lance Cormier	.15
523	Matt Diaz	.15
524	Mike Remlinger	.15
525	Bruce Chen	.15
526	Chris Gomez	.15
527	Chris Ray	.15
528	Corey Patterson	.15
529	David Newhan	.15
530	Ed Rogers RC	.25
531	John Halama	.15
532	Kris Benson	.15
533	LaTroy Hawkins	.15
534	Raul Chavez	.15
535	Alex Cora	.15
536	Alex Gonzalez	.15
537	Coco Crisp	.15
538	David Riske	.15
539	Doug Mirabelli	.15
540	Josh Beckett	.50
541	J.T. Snow	.15
542	Mike Timlin	.15
543	Julian Tavarez	.15
544	Rudy Seanez	.15
545	Wily Mo Pena	.15
546	Bob Howry	.15
547	Glendon Rusch	.15
548	Henry Blanco	.15
549	Jacque Jones	.15
550	Jerome Williams	.15
551	John Mabry	.15
552	Juan Pierre	.15
553	Scott Eyre	.15
554	Scott Williamson	.15
555	Wade Miller	.15
556	Will Ohman	.15
557	Alex Cintron	.15
558	Robert Mackowiak	.15
559	Brandon McCarthy	.15
560	Chris Widger	.15
561	Cliff Politte	.15
562	Javier Vazquez	.15
563	Jim Thome	.75
564	Matt Thornton	.15
565	Neal Cotts	.15
566	Pablo Ozuna	.15
567	Ross Gload	.15
568	Brandon Phillips	.15
569	Bronson Arroyo	.15
570	Dave Williams	.15
571	David Ross	.15
572	David Weathers	.15
573	Eric Milton	.15
574	Javier Valentin	.15
575	Kent Mercker	.15
576	Matt Belisle	.15
577	Paul Wilson	.15
578	Rich Aurilia	.15
579	Rick White	.15
580	Scott Hatteberg	.15
581	Todd Coffey	.15
582	Bob Wickman	.15
583	Danny Graves	.15
584	Eduardo Perez	.15
585	Guillermo Mota	.15
586	Jason Davis	.15
587	Jason Johnson	.15
588	Jason Michaels	.15
589	Rafael Betancourt	.15
590	Ramon Vazquez	.15
591	Scott Sauerbeck	.15
592	Todd Hollandsworth	.15
593	Brian Fuentes	.15
594	Danny Ardoin	.15
595	David Cortes	.15
596	Eli Marrero	.15
597	Jamey Carroll	.15
598	Jason Smith	.15
599	Josh Fogg	.15
600	Miguel Ojeda	.15
601	Mike DeJean	.15
602	Ray King	.15
603	Omar Quintanilla RC	.25
604	Zach Day	.15
605	Fernando Rodney	.15
606	Kenny Rogers	.15
607	Mike Maroth	.15
608	Nate Robertson	.15
609	Todd Jones	.15
610	Vance Wilson	.15
611	Bobby Seay	.15
612	Chris Spurling	.15
613	Raul Colon	.15
614	Jason Grilli	.15
615	Marcus Thames	.15
616	Ramon Santiago	.15
617	Alfredo Amezaga	.15
618	Brian Moehler	.15
619	Chris Aguila	.15
620	Franklyn German	.15
621	Joe Borowski	.15
622	Logan Kensing RC	.25
623	Matt Treanor	.15
624	Miguel Olivo	.15
625	Sergio Mitre	.15
626	Todd Wellemeyer	.25
627	Wes Helms	.15
628	Chad Qualls	.15
629	Eric Bruntlett	.15
630	Mike Gallo	.15
631	Mike Lamb	.15
632	Orlando Palmeiro	.15
633	Russ Springer	.15
634	Dan Wheeler	.15
635	Eric Munson	.15
636	Trever Miller	.15
637	Ambiorix Burgos	.15
638	Andrew Sisco	.15
639	Denny Bautista	.15
640	Doug Mientkiewicz	.15
641	Elmer Dessens	.15
642	Esteban German	.15
643	Joe Nelson RC	.25
644	Mark Grudzielanek	.15
645	Mark Redman	.15
646	Mike Wood	.15
647	Paul Bako	.15
648	Reggie Sanders	.15
649	Scott Elarton	.15
650	Shane Costa	.15
651	Tony Graffanino	.15
652	Jason Bulger RC	.25
653	Chris Bootcheck RC	.25
654	Esteban Yan	.15
655	Hector Carrasco	.15
656	J.C. Romero	.15
657	Jeff Weaver	.15
658	Jose Molina	.15
659	Kelvim Escobar	.15
660	Maicer Izturis	.15
661	Robb Quinlan	.15
662	Scot Shields	.15
663	Tim Salmon	.15
664	Bill Mueller	.15
665	Brett Tomko	.15
666	Dioner Navarro	.15
667	Jae Weong Seo	.15
668	Jose Cruz	.15
669	Kenny Lofton	.15
670	Lance Carter	.15
671	Nomar Garciaparra	.75
672	Olmedo Saenz	.15
673	Rafael Furcal	.40
674	Ramon Martinez	.15
675	Ricky Ledee	.15
676	Sandy Alomar	.15
677	Yhency Brazoban	.15
678	Corey Koskie	.15
679	Dan Kolb	.15
680	Gabe Gross	.15
681	Jeff Cirillo	.15
682	Matt Wise	.15
683	Rick Helling	.15
684	Chad Moeller	.15
685	David Bush	.15
686	Jorge De La Rosa	.15
687	Justin Lehr	.15
688	Jason Bartlett	.15
689	Jason Bartlett	.15
690	Jesse Crain	.15
691	Juan Rincon	.15
692	Luis Castillo	.15
693	Mike Redmond	.15
694	Rondell White	.15
695	Tony Batista	.15
696	Juan Castro	.15
697	Luis Rodriguez	.15
698	Matt Guerrier	.15
699	Willie Eyre RC	.25
700	Aaron Heilman	.15
701	Billy Wagner	.25
702	Carlos Delgado	.50
703	Chad Bradford	.15
704	Chris Woodward	.15
705	Darren Oliver	.15
706	Duaner Sanchez	.15
707	Endy Chavez	.15
708	Jorge Julio	.15
709	Jose Valentin	.15
710	Julio Franco	.15
711	Paul LoDuca	.15
712	Ramon Castro	.15
713	Steve Trachsel	.15
714	Victor Zambrano	.15
715	Xavier Nady	.15
716	Andy Phillips	.15
717	Bubba Crosby	.15
718	Jaret Wright	.15
719	Kelly Stinnett	.15
720	Kyle Farnsworth	.15
721	Mike Meyers	.15
722	Octavio Dotel	.15
723	Ron Villone	.15
724	Scott Proctor	.15
725	Shawn Chacon	.15
726	Tanyon Sturtze	.15
727	Adam Melhuse	.15
728	Brad Halsey	.15
729	Esteban Loaiza	.15
730	Frank Thomas	.50
731	Jay Witasick	.15
732	Justin Duchscherer	.15
733	Kiko Calero	.15
734	Marco Scutaro	.15
735	Mark Ellis	.15
736	Milton Bradley	.15
737	Aaron Fultz	.15
738	Aaron Rowand	.25
739	Geoff Geary	.15
740	Arthur Rhodes	.15
741	Chris Coste RC	.40
742	Rheal Cormier	.15
743	Ryan Franklin	.15
744	Ryan Madson	.15
745	Sal Fasano	.15
746	Tom Gordon	.15
747	Abraham Nunez	.15
748	David Dellucci	.15
749	Julio Santana	.15
750	Shane Victorino	.25
751	Damaso Marte	.15
752	Freddy Sanchez	.15
753	Humberto Cota	.15
754	Jeromy Burnitz	.15
755	Joe Randa	.15
756	Jose Castillo	.15
757	Mike Gonzalez	.15
758	Ryan Doumit	.15
759	Sean Burnett	.15
760	Sean Casey	.15
761	Ian Snell	.15
762	John Grabow	.15
763	Jose Hernandez	.15
764	Roberto Hernandez	.15
765	Ryan Vogelsong	.15
766	Victor Sanchez	.15
767	Adrian Gonzalez	.40
768	Alan Embree	.15
769	Brian Sweeney RC	.25
770	Chan Ho Park	.15
771	Clay Hensley	.15
772	Dewon Brazelton	.15
773	Doug Brocail	.15
774	Eric Young	.15
775	Geoff Blum	.15
776	Josh Bard	.15
777	Mark Bellhorn	.15
778	Mike Cameron	.15
779	Mike Piazza	.75
780	Rob Bowen	.15
781	Scott Cassidy	.15
782	Scott Linebrink	.15
783	Shawn Estes	.15
784	Termel Sledge	.15
785	Vinny Castilla	.15
786	Jeff Fassero	.15
787	Jose Vizcaino	.15
788	Mark Sweeney	.15
789	Matt Morris	.15
790	Steve Finley	.15
791	Tim Worrell	.15
792	Jamey Wright	.15
793	Jason Ellison	.15
794	Noah Lowry	.15
795	Steve Kline	.15
796	Todd Greene	.15
797	Carl Everett	.15
798	George Sherrill	.15
799	J.J. Putz	.15
800	Jake Woods	.15
801	Jose Lopez	.15
802	Julio Mateo	.15
803	Mike Morse	.15
804	Rafael Soriano	.15
805	Roberto Petagine	.15
806	Aaron Miles	.15
807	Braden Looper	.15

#	Player	
808	Gary Bennett	.15
809	Hector Luna	.15
810	Jeff Suppan	.15
811	John Rodriguez	.15
812	John Hancock	.15
813	Juan Encarnacion	.15
814	Larry Bigbie	.15
815	Scott Spiezio	.15
816	Sidney Ponson	.15
817	So Taguchi	.15
818	Brian Meadows	.15
819	Damon Hollins	.15
820	Dan Miceli	.15
821	Doug Waechter	.15
822	Jason Childers	.25
823	Josh Paul	.15
824	Julio Lugo	.15
825	Mark Hendrickson	.15
826	Sean Burroughs	.15
827	Shawn Camp	.15
828	Travis Harper	.15
829	Ty Wigginton	.15
830	Adam Eaton	.15
831	Adrian Brown	.15
832	Akinori Otsuka	.15
833	Antonio Alfonseca	.15
834	Brad Wilkerson	.15
835	D'Angelo Jimenez	.15
836	Gerald Laird	.15
837	Joaquin Benoit	.15
838	Kameron Loe	.15
839	Kevin Millwood	.15
840	Mark DeRosa	.15
841	Phil Nevin	.15
842	Rod Barajas	.15
843	Vicente Padilla	.15
844	A.J. Burnett	.25
845	Bengie Molina	.15
846	Gregg Zaun	.15
847	John McDonald	.15
848	Lyle Overbay	.15
849	Russ Adams	.15
850	Troy Glaus	.25
851	Vinnie Chulk	.15
852	B.J. Ryan	.15
853	Justin Speier	.15
854	Pete Walker	.15
855	Scott Downs	.15
856	Scott Schoeneweis	.15
857	Alfonso Soriano	.75
858	Brian Schneider	.15
859	Daryle Ward	.15
860	Felix Rodriguez	.15
861	Gary Majewski	.15
862	Joey Eischen	.15
863	Jon Rauch	.15
864	Marlon Anderson	.15
865	Matthew LeCroy	.15
866	Mike Stanton	.15
867	Ramon Ortiz	.15
868	Robert Fick	.15
869	Royce Clayton	.15
870	Ryan Drese	.15
871	Vladimir Guerrero	.50
872	Craig Biggio	.25
873	Barry Zito	.15
874	Vernon Wells	.25
875	Chipper Jones	.50
876	Prince Fielder	.75
877	Albert Pujols	1.00
878	Greg Maddux	.75
879	Carl Crawford	.25
880	Brandon Webb	.40
881	J.D. Drew	.25
882	Jason Schmidt	.15
883	Victor Martinez	.25
884	Ichiro Suzuki	.75
885	Miguel Cabrera	.40
886	David Wright	.50
887	Alfonso Soriano	.40
888	Miguel Tejada	.40
889	Khalil Greene	.15
890	Ryan Howard	1.00
891	Jason Bay	.25
892	Mark Teixeira	.25
893	Manny Ramirez	.40
894	Ken Griffey Jr.	.75
895	Todd Helton	.25
896	Angel Berroa	.15
897	Ivan Rodriguez	.25
898	Johan Santana	.25
899	Paul Konerko	.25
900	Derek Jeter	1.00
901	Macay McBride RC	.25
902	Tony Pena RC	.25
903	Peter Moylan RC	.50
904	Aaron Rakers RC	.50
905	Chris Britton RC	.50
906	Nick Markakis RC	1.00
907	Sendy Rleal RC	.25
908	Val Majewski RC	.25
909	Jermaine Van Buren RC	.25
910	Jonathan Papelbon RC	2.00
911	Angel Pagan RC	.50
912	David Aardsma RC	.25
913	Sean Marshall RC	.25
914	Brian Anderson RC	.25
915	Freddie Bynum RC	.25
916	Fausto Carmona RC	.50
917	Kelly Stoppach RC	.25
918	Choo Freeman RC	.25
919	Ryan Shealy RC	.25
920	Joel Zumaya RC	.75
921	Jordan Tata RC	.25
922	Justin Verlander RC	1.00
923	Carlos Martinez RC	.25
924	Chris Resop RC	.25
925	Dan Uggla RC	1.00

#	Player	
926	Eric Reed RC	.25
927	Hanley Ramirez RC	2.00
928	Yusmeiro Petit RC	.50
929	Josh Willingham RC	.75
930	Mike Jacobs RC	.50
931	Reggie Abercrombie RC	.25
932	Ricky Nolasco RC	.25
933	Scott Olsen RC	.25
934	Fernando Nieve RC	.25
935	Taylor Buchholz RC	.25
936	Cody Ross RC	.25
937	James Loney RC	.75
938	Takashi Saito RC	1.00
939	Tim Hamulack RC	.25
940	Chris Demaria RC	.50
941	Jose Capellan RC	.25
942	David Gassner RC	.25
943	Jason Kubel RC	.75
944	Brian Bannister RC	.50
945	Mike Thompson RC	.25
946	Cole Hamels RC	4.00
947	Paul Maholm RC	.50
948	John Van Benschoten RC	.25
949	Nate McLouth RC	.50
950	Ben Johnson RC	.25
951	Josh Barfield RC	.50
952	Travis Ishikawa RC	.25
953	Jack Taschner RC	.25
954	Kenji Johjima RC	.75
955	Skip Schumaker RC	.25
956	Ruddy Lugo RC	.25
957	Jason Hammel RC	.25
958	Chris Roberson RC	.25
959	Fabio Castro RC	.50
960	Ian Kinsler RC	.50
961	John Koronka RC	.25
962	Brandon Watson RC	.15
963	Jon Lester RC	5.00
964	Ben Hendrickson RC	.25
965	Martin Prado RC	1.00
966	Erick Aybar RC	.50
967	Bobby Livingston RC	.25
968	Ryan Spilborghs RC	.25
969	Tommy Murphy RC	.25
970	Howie Kendrick RC	2.00
971	Casey Janssen RC	1.00
972	Michael O'Connor RC	.50
973	Conor Jackson RC	.50
974	Jeremy Hermida RC	.50
975	Renyel Pinto RC	.25
976	Prince Fielder RC	1.50
977	Kevin Frandsen RC	.50
978	Ty Taubenheim RC	.50
979	Rich Hill RC	.50
980	Jonathan Broxton RC	.50
981	Jamie Shields RC	.50
982	Carlos Villanueva RC	.50
983	Boone Logan RC	.25
984	Brian Wilson RC	.50
985	Andre Ethier RC	3.00
986	Michael Napoli RC	1.00
987	Agustin Montero RC	.25
988	Jack Hannahan RC	.25
989	Boof Bonser RC	.25
990	Carlos Ruiz RC	.50
991	Jason Botts RC	.50
992	Kendry Morales RC	1.00
993	Alay Soler RC	.25
994	Santiago Ramirez RC	.25
995	Saul Rivera RC	.25
996	Anthony Reyes RC	.25
997	Matthew Kemp RC	2.50
998	Jae-Kuk Ryu RC	.50
999	Lastings Milledge RC	1.00
1000	Jered Weaver RC	3.00
1001	Stephen Drew RC	1.00
1002	Carlos Quentin RC	.50
1003	Livan Hernandez	.15
1004	Chris Young RC	.50
1005	Alberto Callaspo/SP RC	6.00
1006	Enrique Gonzalez RC	.25
1007	Tony Pena RC	.25
1008	Bob Melvin	.15
1009	Fernando Tatis RC	.25
1010	Willy Aybar RC	.25
1011	Ken Ray RC	.25
1012	Scott Thorman RC	.50
1013	Eric Hinske/SP	.75
1014	Kevin Barry RC	.50
1015	Bobby Cox	.15
1016	Phil Stockman RC	.25
1017	Brayan Pena RC	.25
1018	Adam Loewen RC	.25
1019	Brandon Fahey RC	.50
1020	Jim Hoey RC	.25
1021	Kurt Birkins/SP RC	5.00
1022	Jim Johnson RC	.75
1023	Sam Perlozzo	.15
1024	Cory Morris RC	.50
1025	Hayden Penn RC	.25
1026	Javy Lopez	.15
1027	Dustin Pedroia RC	.50
1028	Kason Gabbard RC	.50
1029	David Pauley RC	.25
1030	Kyle Snyder RC	.25
1031	Terry Francona	.15
1032	Craig Breslow RC	.50
1033	Bryan Corey RC	.25
1034	Manny Delcarmen RC	.50
1035	Carlos Marmol RC	.50
1036	Buck Coats RC	.25
1037	Ryan O'Malley/SP RC	4.00
1038	Angel Guzman RC	.25
1039	Ronny Cedeno RC	.50
1040	Juan Mateo RC	.50
1041	Cesar Izturis	.15
1042	Les Walrond RC	.25
1043	Geovany Soto RC	.50

#	Player	
1044	Sean Tracey RC	.25
1045	Ozzie Guillen/SP	5.00
1046	Royce Clayton	.15
1047	Norris Hopper RC	.50
1048	Bill Bray RC	.50
1049	Jerry Narron	.15
1050	Brendan Harris RC	.15
1051	Brian Shackelford RC	.25
1052	Jeremy Sowers RC	.50
1053	Joe Inglett RC	.25
1054	Brian Slocum RC	.25
1055	Andrew Brown RC	.50
1056	Rafael Perez RC	.50
1057	Edward Mujica RC	.25
1058	Andy Marte RC	.25
1059	Shin-Soo Choo RC	1.50
1060	Jeremy Guthrie RC	.25
1061	Franklin Gutierrez/SP RC	6.00
1062	Kazuo Matsui	.15
1063	Chris Iannetta RC	.50
1064	Manny Corpas RC	.25
1065	Clint Hurdle	.15
1066	Ramon Ramirez RC	.25
1067	Sean Casey	.15
1068	Zach Miner RC	.25
1069	Brent Clevlen/SP RC	4.00
1070	Bob Wickman	.15
1071	Jim Leyland	.15
1072	Alexis Gomez RC	.25
1073	Anibal Sanchez RC	.50
1074	Taylor Tankersley RC	.50
1075	Eric Wedge	.15
1076	Jonah Bayliss RC	.50
1077	Paul Hoover/SP RC	4.00
1078	Eddie Guardado	.15
1079	Cody Ross RC	.25
1080	Aubrey Huff	.15
1081	Jason Hirsh RC	.25
1082	Brandon League	.15
1083	Matt Albers RC	.50
1084	Chris Sampson RC	.50
1085	Phil Garner	.15
1086	J.R. House RC	.25
1087	Ryan Shealy RC	.25
1088	Stephen Andrade RC	.25
1089	Bob Keppel RC	.25
1090	Buddy Bell	.15
1091	Justin Huber RC	.25
1092	Paul Phillips RC	.25
1093	Greg Jones/SP RC	4.00
1094	Jeff Mathis RC	.50
1095	Dustin Moseley RC	.50
1096	Joe Saunders RC	.50
1097	Reggie Willits RC	.75
1098	Mike Scioscia	.15
1099	Greg Maddux	1.50
1100	Wilson Betemit	.15
1101	Chad Billingsley/SP RC	8.00
1102	Russell Martin RC	.75
1103	Grady Little	.15
1104	David Bell	.15
1105	Kevin Mench	.15
1106	Laynce Nix	.15
1107	Chris Barnwell RC	.50
1108	Tony Gwynn Jr. RC	.50
1109	Corey Hart RC	.50
1110	Zach Jackson RC	.25
1111	Francisco Cordero	.15
1112	Joe Winklesas RC	.25
1113	Ned Yost	.15
1114	Matt Garza RC	.50
1115	Chris Heintz	.15
1116	Pat Neshek RC	4.00
1117	Josh Rabe/SP RC	10.00
1118	Mike Rivera	.15
1119	Ron Gardenhire	.15
1120	Shawn Green	.15
1121	Oliver Perez	.15
1122	Heath Bell	.15
1123	Bartolome Fortunato RC	.15
1124	Anderson Garcia RC	.25
1125	John Maine/SP	8.00
1126	Henry Owens RC	.25
1127	Mike Pelfrey RC	3.00
1128	Royce Ring RC	.25
1129	Willie Randolph	.15
1130	Bobby Abreu	.15
1131	Craig Wilson	.15
1132	T.J. Beam RC	.25
1133	Colter Bean/SP RC	4.00
1134	Melky Cabrera RC	.50
1135	Mitch Jones RC	.50
1136	Jeffrey Karstens RC	1.00
1137	Wilbert Nieves RC	.50
1138	Kevin Reese RC	.50
1139	Kevin Thompson RC	.50
1140	Jose Veras RC	.15
1141	Joe Torre	.15
1142	Jeremy Brown RC	.25
1143	Santiago Casilla RC	.25
1144	Shane Komine RC	1.00
1145	Mike Rouse RC	.25
1146	Jason Windsor RC	.75
1147	Ken Macha	.15
1148	Jamie Moyer	.15
1149	Phil Nevin/SP	4.00
1150	Eude Brito RC	.50
1151	Fabio Castro	.15
1152	Jeff Conine	.15
1153	Scott Mathieson RC	.50
1154	Brian Sanches RC	.25
1155	Matt Smith RC	.25
1156	Joe Thurston RC	.25
1157	Marlon Anderson/SP	4.00
1158	Xavier Nady	.15
1159	Shawn Chacon	.15
1160	Rajai Davis RC	.75
1161	Yurendell de Caster RC	.50

#	Player	
1162	Marty McLeary RC	.25
1163	Chris Duffy	.15
1164	Joshua Sharpless RC	1.00
1165	Jim Tracy	.15
1166	David Wells	.15
1167	Russell Branyan	.15
1168	Todd Walker	.15
1169	Paul McAnulty RC	.25
1170	Bruce Bochy	.15
1171	Shea Hillenbrand	.15
1172	Eliezer Alfonzo RC	.50
1173	Justin Knoedler/SP RC	4.00
1174	Jonathan Sanchez RC	.25
1175	Travis Smith RC	.25
1176	Cha Sueng Baek	.15
1177	T.J. Bohn RC	.25
1178	Emiliano Fruto RC	.50
1179	Sean Green RC	.50
1180	Jon Huber RC	.25
1181	Adam Jones/SP RC	8.00
1182	Mark Lowe RC	.25
1183	Eric O'Flaherty RC	.50
1184	Preston Wilson	.15
1185	Mike Hargrove	.15
1186	Jeff Weaver	.15
1187	Ronnie Belliard	.15
1188	John Gall RC	.15
1189	Josh Kinney/SP RC	6.00
1190	Tony LaRussa	.15
1191	Scott Dunn RC	.25
1192	B.J. Upton	.40
1193	Jon Switzer RC	.15
1194	Benjamin Zobrist RC	.50
1195	Joe Maddon	.15
1196	Carlos Lee	.40
1197	Matt Stairs	.15
1198	Nick Massett RC	.25
1199	Nelson Cruz RC	1.50
1200	Francisco Rosario RC	.25
1201	Wes Littleton RC	.25
1202	Drew Meyer RC	.25
1203	John Rheinecker RC	.25
1204	Robinson Tejeda	.15
1205	Jeremy Accardo/SP	.25
1206	Luis Figueroa RC	.50
1207	John Hattig Jr. RC	.25
1208	Dustin McGowan RC	.50
1209	Ryan Roberts RC	.50
1210	Davis Romero RC	.25
1211	Ty Taubenheim	.15
1212	John Gibbons	.15
1213	Shawn Hill/SP RC	6.00
1214	Brandon Harper RC	.25
1215	Travis Hughes RC	.25
1216	Chris Schroder RC	.25
1217	Austin Kearns	.15
1218	Felipe Lopez	.15
1219	Roy Corcoran RC	.25
1220	Melvin Dorta RC	.25
1221	Brandon Webb/SP	6.00
1222	Andruw Jones/SP	4.00
1223	Miguel Tejada/SP	8.00
1224	David Ortiz/SP	8.00
1225	Derek Lee/SP	6.00
1226	Jim Thome/SP	6.00
1227	Ken Griffey Jr./SP	8.00
1228	Travis Hafner/SP	6.00
1229	Todd Helton/SP	6.00
1230	Magglio Ordonez/SP	4.00
1231	Miguel Cabrera/SP	6.00
1232	Lance Berkman/SP	6.00
1233	Mike Sweeney/SP	4.00
1234	Vladimir Guerrero/SP	8.00
1235	Nomar Garciaparra/SP	8.00
1236	Prince Fielder/SP	8.00
1237	Johan Santana/SP	8.00
1238	Pedro Martinez/SP	6.00
1239	Derek Jeter/SP	10.00
1240	Barry Zito/SP	4.00
1241	Ryan Howard/SP	10.00
1242	Jason Bay/SP	6.00
1243	Trevor Hoffman/SP	4.00
1244	Jason Schmidt/SP	4.00
1245	Ichiro Suzuki/SP	8.00
1246	Albert Pujols/SP	10.00
1247	Carl Crawford/SP	4.00
1248	Mark Teixeira/SP	6.00
1249	Vernon Wells/SP	5.00
1250	Alfonso Soriano/SP	4.00

All-Upper Deck Team

		NM/M
2:Series 1 Fat pack		.75
UD-1	Ken Griffey Jr.	3.00
UD-2	Derek Jeter	4.00
UD-3	Albert Pujols	4.00
UD-4	Alex Rodriguez	4.00
UD-5	Vladimir Guerrero	1.50
UD-6	Roger Clemens	3.00
UD-7	Derek Lee	1.00
UD-8	David Ortiz	1.50
UD-9	Miguel Cabrera	1.50
UD-10	Bobby Abreu	1.00
UD-11	Mark Teixeira	1.00
UD-12	Johan Santana	1.50
UD-13	Hideki Matsui	2.50
UD-14	Ichiro Suzuki	3.00
UD-15	Andruw Jones	1.00
UD-16	Eric Chavez	.75
UD-17	Roy Oswalt	1.00
UD-18	Curt Schilling	1.50
UD-19	Randy Johnson	1.50
UD-20	Ivan Rodriguez	1.00
UD-21	Chipper Jones	2.00
UD-22	Mark Prior	.75
UD-23	Jason Bay	.75
UD-24	Pedro Martinez	1.50
UD-25	David Wright	3.00
UD-26	Carlos Beltran	1.50
UD-27	Jim Edmonds	.75
UD-28	Chris Carpenter	1.00
UD-29	Roy Halladay	1.00
UD-30	Jake Peavy	1.00
UD-31	Paul Konerko	1.00
UD-32	Travis Hafner	1.00
UD-33	Barry Zito	1.00
UD-34	Miguel Tejada	1.00
UD-35	Josh Beckett	1.50
UD-36	Todd Helton	1.00
UD-37	Dontrelle Willis	.75
UD-38	Manny Ramirez	1.50
UD-39	Mariano Rivera	1.00
UD-40	Jeff Kent	.75

Amazing Greats

		NM/M
Complete Set:		25.00
Common Player:		.50
BA	Bobby Abreu	.75
JB	Jeff Bagwell	.75
CB	Carlos Beltran	1.00
AB	Adrian Beltre	.50
MC	Miguel Cabrera	1.00
RC	Roger Clemens	3.00
CC	Carl Crawford	.75
JD	Johnny Damon	1.00
JE	Jim Edmonds	.50
RF	Rafael Furcal	.50
EG	Eric Gagne	.50
JG	Jason Giambi	.75
TG	Tom Glavine	.75
KG	Ken Griffey Jr.	2.00
HE	Todd Helton	.75
TH	Tim Hudson	.50
DJ	Derek Jeter	3.00
RJ	Randy Johnson	1.00
AJ	Andruw Jones	1.00
CJ	Chipper Jones	1.00
JJ	Jacque Jones	.50
PK	Paul Konerko	.75
CL	Carlos Lee	.50
JL	Javy Lopez	.50
GM	Greg Maddux	2.00
PM	Pedro Martinez	1.00
DO	David Ortiz	1.00
RO	Roy Oswalt	.75
RP	Rafael Palmeiro	.75
CP	Corey Patterson	.50
MP	Mike Piazza	1.00
PR	Mark Prior	.75
AP	Albert Pujols	3.00
MR	Manny Ramirez	1.00
JR	Jose Reyes	.75
IR	Ivan Rodriguez	1.00
SR	Scott Rolen	1.00
JS	Johan Santana	1.00
CS	Curt Schilling	1.00
GS	Gary Sheffield	1.00
SM	John Smoltz	.50
AS	Alfonso Soriano	1.00
SS	Sammy Sosa	1.00
MT	Mark Teixeira	1.00
TE	Miguel Tejada	1.00
FT	Frank Thomas	1.50
JT	Jim Thome	1.00
DW	Dontrelle Willis	.75
KW	Kerry Wood	.50
WR	David Wright	1.50

Blue
Blue: 2-4X
Production 299 Sets

Gold

Gold: 2-4X
Production 299 Sets

Amazing Greats Material

		NM/M
Complete Set:		
Common Player:		
BA	Bobby Abreu	6.
JB	Jeff Bagwell	6.
CB	Carlos Beltran	4.
AB	Adrian Beltre	4.
MC	Miguel Cabrera	4.
RC	Roger Clemens	15.
CC	Carl Crawford	5.
JD	Johnny Damon	10.
JE	Jim Edmonds	5.
RF	Rafael Furcal	4.
EG	Eric Gagne	4.
JG	Jason Giambi	4.
KG	Ken Griffey Jr.	20.
HE	Todd Helton	6.
TH	Tim Hudson	4.
DJ	Derek Jeter	20.
RJ	Randy Johnson	8.
AJ	Andruw Jones	8.
CJ	Chipper Jones	8.
JJ	Jacque Jones	6.
PK	Paul Konerko	6.
CL	Carlos Lee	5.
JL	Javy Lopez	4.
GM	Greg Maddux	12.
PM	Pedro Martinez	8.
DO	David Ortiz	8.
RO	Roy Oswalt	8.
RP	Rafael Palmeiro	8.
CP	Corey Patterson	8.
MP	Mike Piazza	10.
PR	Mark Prior	8.
AP	Albert Pujols	20.
MR	Manny Ramirez	8.
JR	Jose Reyes	8.
IR	Ivan Rodriguez	8.
SR	Scott Rolen	5.
JS	Johan Santana	8.
CS	Curt Schilling	8.
GS	Gary Sheffield	8.
SM	John Smoltz	8.
AS	Alfonso Soriano	8.
SS	Sammy Sosa	10.
MT	Mark Teixeira	8.
TE	Miguel Tejada	10.
FT	Frank Thomas	6.
JT	Jim Thome	8.
DW	Dontrelle Willis	6.
KW	Kerry Wood	6.
WR	David Wright	15.

Diamond Collection Materials

		NM/M
Common Player:		4.0
AL	Moises Alou	6.0
JB	Jeff Bagwell	4.0
RB	Rocco Baldelli	4.0
OC	Orlando Cabrera	4.0
MC	Mike Cameron	4.0
EC	Eric Chavez	4.0
CO	Jose Contreras	4.0
JC	Jesse Crain	4.0
BC	Bobby Crosby	4.0
JD	Johnny Damon	10.0
AE	Adam Eaton	4.0
JE	Jim Edmonds	4.0
SF	Steve Finley	4.0
FG	Freddy Garcia	4.0
GO	Juan Gonzalez	4.0
KG	Ken Griffey Jr.	20.0
JG	Jose Guillen	4.0
MH	Mike Hampton	4.0
AH	Aubrey Huff	4.0
EJ	Edwin Jackson	4.0
DJ	Derek Jeter	20.0
NJ	Nick Johnson	4.0
RJ	Randy Johnson	8.0
JJ	Jacque Jones	4.0
SK	Scott Kazmir	4.0
KE	Austin Kearns	4.0
JK	Jason Kendall	4.0
AK	Adam Kennedy	4.0
CK	Casey Kotchman	4.0
LA	Matt Lawton	4.0
ML	Mike Lieberthal	4.0
PL	Paul LoDuca	4.0
KL	Kenny Lofton	4.0
LO	Mike Lowell	4.0
GM	Greg Maddux	12.00
MA	Kazuo Matsui	4.0
KM	Kevin Millwood	4.0
DO	David Ortiz	8.0

AO	Akinori Otsuka	4.00
CP	Carl Pavano	4.00
JP	Jorge Posada	6.00
BR	Brad Radke	4.00
IR	Ivan Rodriguez	6.00
CC	C.C. Sabathia	6.00
CS	Chris Shelton	4.00
JS	John Smoltz	8.00
SS	Shannon Stewart	4.00
JT	Jim Thome	8.00
JW	Jayson Werth	4.00
PW	Preston Wilson	4.00

Diamond Debut

NM/M

Common Player: 1.00
#'s 1-40 found in Series 1 packs
#'s 41-82 found in Series 2 packs
Inserted 1:4 Walmart packs.
Series 2 Common Player: .50

1	Tadahito Iguchi	1.00
2	Huston Street	.50
3	Norihiro Nakamura	.50
4	Chien-Ming Wang	3.00
5	Pedro Lopez	.50
6	Robinson Cano	2.00
7	Tim Stauffer	.50
8	Ervin Santana	1.00
9	Brandon McCarthy	.50
10	Hayden Penn	.50
11	Derek Jeter	5.00
12	Ken Griffey Jr.	3.00
13	Prince Fielder	3.00
14	Edwin Encarnacion	1.00
15	Scott Olsen	.50
16	Chris Resop	.50
17	Justin Verlander	2.00
18	Melky Cabrera	1.00
19	Jeff Francoeur	1.50
20	Yuniesky Betancourt	.50
21	Conor Jackson	1.00
22	Felix Hernandez	1.50
23	Anthony Reyes	.50
24	John-Ford Griffin	.50
25	Adam Wainwright	1.00
26	Ryan Garko	.50
27	Ryan Zimmerman	3.00
28	Tom Seaver	2.00
29	Johnny Bench	2.00
30	Reggie Jackson	2.00
31	Rod Carew	2.00
32	Nolan Ryan	4.00
33	Richie Ashburn	1.00
34	Yogi Berra	2.50
35	Lou Brock	2.00
36	Carlton Fisk	2.00
37	Joe Morgan	2.00
38	Bob Gibson	2.00
39	Willie McCovey	2.00
40	Harmon Killebrew	2.00
41	Takashi Saito	2.00
42	Kenji Johjima	3.00
43	Joel Zumaya	1.50
44	Dan Uggla	2.00
45	Taylor Buchholz	1.00
46	Josh Barfield	1.00
47	Brian Bannister	1.00
48	Nick Markakis	2.00
49	Carlos Martinez	1.00
50	Macay McBride	1.00
51	Brian Anderson	1.00
52	Freddie Bynum	1.00
53	Kelly Stoppach	1.00
54	Choo Freeman	1.00
55	Ryan Shealy	1.00
56	Chris Resop	1.00
57	Hanley Ramirez	2.50
58	Mike Jacobs	1.00
59	Cody Ross	1.00
60	Jose Capellan	1.00
61	David Gassner	1.00
62	Jason Kubel	1.00
63	Jered Weaver	3.00
64	Paul Maholm	1.00
65	Nate McLouth	1.00
66	Ben Johnson	1.00
67	Jack Taschner	1.00
68	Skip Schumaker	1.00
69	Brandon Watson	1.00
70	David Wright	3.00
71	David Ortiz	2.50
72	Alex Rodriguez	4.00
73	Johan Santana	2.00
74	Greg Maddux	3.00
75	Ichiro Suzuki	3.00
76	Albert Pujols	4.00
77	Hideki Matsui	3.00
78	Vladimir Guerrero	2.00
79	Pedro Martinez	2.00
80	Mike Schmidt	4.00
81	Al Kaline	3.00
82	Robin Yount	3.00

First Class Cuts

No Pricing
Production One Set

First Class Legends

NM/M

Gold: 1-2X
Production 699 Sets
Platinum: 2-3X
Production 99 Sets
Spectrum: No Pricing
Production One Set

1-20	Babe Ruth	3.00
21-40	Ty Cobb	2.00

FIRST CLASS LEGENDS

41-60	Honus Wagner	2.00
61-80	Christy Mathewson	1.00
81-100	Walter Johnson	1.00

Signature Sensations

NM/M

Inserted 1:288 Hobby

BA	Bronson Arroyo	15.00
GA	Garrett Atkins	8.00
SB	Scott Baker	15.00
KC	Kiko Calero	5.00
JE	Johnny Estrada	8.00
KG	Ken Griffey Jr.	100.00
TR	Travis Hafner	15.00
BH	Bobby Hill	5.00
JJ	Josh Johnson	10.00
AL	Al Leiter	15.00
AM	Aaron Miles	10.00
YM	Yadier Molina	15.00
NP	Nick Punto	8.00
AR	Aaron Rowand	15.00
CS	Cory Sullivan	8.00
JS	Jeff Suppan	8.00
JV	Joe Valentine	10.00
DY	Delmon Young	15.00

Star Attractions

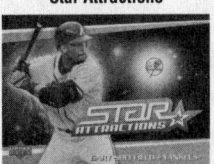

STAR ATTRACTIONS

NM/M

Gold: 1-2X
Production 699 Sets

BA	Bobby Abreu	.75
GA	Garret Anderson	.50
JB	Josh Beckett	.50
CB	Carlos Beltran	.75
AB	Adrian Beltre	.50
LB	Lance Berkman	.50
JC	Jose Contreras	.50
JD	Johnny Damon	1.00
CD	Carlos Delgado	.75
JE	Jim Edmonds	.75
EG	Eric Gagne	.50
JG	Jason Giambi	.75
SG	Shawn Green	.50
KG	Khalil Greene	.50
KG	Ken Griffey Jr.	2.00
GU	Jose Guillen	.50
RH	Rich Harden	.50
AH	Aubrey Huff	.50
TH	Torii Hunter	.50
TI	Tadahito Iguchi	.50
DJ	Derek Jeter	3.00
AJ	Andruw Jones	1.00
CJ	Chipper Jones	.50
JJ	Jacque Jones	.50
CL	Carlos Lee	.50
DL	Derrek Lee	1.00
JL	Javy Lopez	.50
GM	Greg Maddux	2.00
PM	Pedro Martinez	1.00
JM	Joe Mauer	1.50
MM	Mark Mulder	.50
MO	Magglio Ordonez	.50
DO	David Ortiz	1.00
AP	Andy Pettitte	.75
JP	Jorge Posada	.75
MP	Mark Prior	.75
PU	Albert Pujols	3.00
MR	Manny Ramirez	1.00
JR	Jose Reyes	.75
CS	Curt Schilling	1.00
JS	Jason Schmidt	.50
GS	Gary Sheffield	.75
JS	John Smoltz	.75
AS	Alfonso Soriano	.75
MT	Mark Teixeira	.75
FT	Frank Thomas	.75
DW	Dontrelle Willis	.50
KW	Kerry Wood	.50
WR	David Wright	1.50
BZ	Barry Zito	.50

Star Attractions Swatches

NM/M

Common Player: 4.00

BA	Bobby Abreu	6.00
GA	Garret Anderson	4.00
JB	Josh Beckett	6.00
CB	Carlos Beltran	6.00

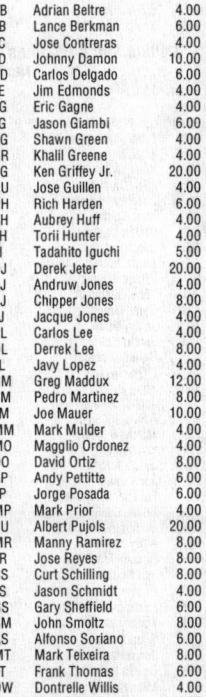

AB	Adrian Beltre	4.00
LB	Lance Berkman	6.00
JC	Jose Contreras	4.00
JD	Johnny Damon	10.00
CD	Carlos Delgado	6.00
JE	Jim Edmonds	4.00
EG	Eric Gagne	4.00
JG	Jason Giambi	6.00
SG	Shawn Green	4.00
GR	Khalil Greene	4.00
KG	Ken Griffey Jr.	20.00
GU	Jose Guillen	4.00
RH	Rich Harden	6.00
AH	Aubrey Huff	4.00
TH	Torii Hunter	4.00
TI	Tadahito Iguchi	5.00
DJ	Derek Jeter	20.00
AJ	Andruw Jones	4.00
CJ	Chipper Jones	8.00
JJ	Jacque Jones	4.00
CL	Carlos Lee	4.00
DL	Derrek Lee	8.00
JL	Javy Lopez	4.00
GM	Greg Maddux	12.00
PM	Pedro Martinez	8.00
JM	Joe Mauer	10.00
MM	Mark Mulder	4.00
MO	Magglio Ordonez	4.00
DO	David Ortiz	8.00
AP	Andy Pettitte	6.00
JP	Jorge Posada	6.00
MP	Mark Prior	4.00
PU	Albert Pujols	20.00
MR	Manny Ramirez	8.00
JR	Jose Reyes	8.00
CS	Curt Schilling	8.00
JS	Jason Schmidt	4.00
GS	Gary Sheffield	6.00
SM	John Smoltz	8.00
AS	Alfonso Soriano	6.00
MT	Mark Teixeira	8.00
FT	Frank Thomas	6.00
DW	Dontrelle Willis	4.00
KW	Kerry Wood	4.00
WR	David Wright	15.00
BZ	Barry Zito	4.00

Team Pride

TEAM PRIDE

NM/M

Gold: 1X-2X
Production 699 Sets

BA	Bobby Abreu	.75
GA	Garret Anderson	.50
JB	Jeff Bagwell	.75
RB	Rocco Baldelli	.50
SC	Sean Casey	.50
LC	Luis Castillo	.50
EC	Eric Chavez	.50
JD	Johnny Damon	1.00
CD	Carlos Delgado	.75
JE	Jim Edmonds	.75
ME	Morgan Ensberg	.50
KF	Keith Foulke	.50
EG	Eric Gagne	.50
LG	Luis Gonzalez	.50
GR	Khalil Greene	.50
KG	Ken Griffey Jr.	2.00
RH	Rich Harden	.50
TH	Trevor Hoffman	.50
AH	Aubrey Huff	.50
DJ	Derek Jeter	3.00
NJ	Nick Johnson	.50
AJ	Andruw Jones	1.00
CJ	Chipper Jones	1.00
RK	Ryan Klesko	.50
CK	Casey Kotchman	.50
ML	Mike Lieberthal	.50
LO	Mike Lowell	.50
GM	Greg Maddux	2.00
MA	Joe Mauer	1.50
JM	Jamie Moyer	.50
MO	Magglio Ordonez	.50
DO	David Ortiz	1.00
PE	Andy Pettitte	.75
JP	Jorge Posada	.50
MP	Mark Prior	.75
AP	Albert Pujols	3.00
JR	Jose Reyes	.50
IR	Ivan Rodriguez	.75
CC	C.C. Sabathia	1.50
CS	Curt Schilling	1.00
JS	John Smoltz	.75
MS	Mike Sweeney	.50
FT	Frank Thomas	.75
JT	Jim Thome	.75
VA	Jason Varitek	.75
JV	Jose Vidro	.75
BW	Bernie Williams	.50
DW	Dontrelle Willis	.50
KW	Kerry Wood	.50
MY	Michael Young	.50

Diamond Collection

NM/M

Gold: 1-2X
Production 699 Sets
Series 2

BA	Bobby Abreu	6.00
GA	Garrett Atkins	4.00

RB	Rocco Baldelli	.50
OC	Orlando Cabrera	.50
MC	Mike Cameron	.50
EC	Eric Chavez	.50
CO	Jose Contreras	.50
JC	Jesse Crain	.50
BC	Bobby Crosby	.50
JD	Johnny Damon	1.00
AE	Adam Eaton	.50
JE	Jim Edmonds	.50
SF	Steve Finley	.50
FG	Freddy Garcia	.50
GO	Juan Gonzalez	.50
KG	Ken Griffey Jr.	2.00
JG	Jose Guillen	.50
MH	Mike Hampton	.50
AH	Aubrey Huff	.50
EJ	Edwin Jackson	.50
DJ	Derek Jeter	3.00
NJ	Nick Johnson	.50
RJ	Randy Johnson	1.00
JJ	Jacque Jones	.50
SK	Scott Kazmir	.50
KE	Austin Kearns	.50
JK	Jason Kendall	.50
AK	Adam Kennedy	.50
CK	Casey Kotchman	.50
LA	Matt Lawton	.50
ML	Mike Lieberthal	.50
PL	Paul LoDuca	.50
KL	Kenny Lofton	.50
LO	Mike Lowell	.50
GM	Greg Maddux	2.00
MA	Kazuo Matsui	.50
KM	Kevin Millwood	.50
DO	David Ortiz	1.00
AO	Akinori Otsuka	.50
CP	Carl Pavano	.50
JP	Jorge Posada	.50
BR	Brad Radke	.50
IR	Ivan Rodriguez	.75
CC	C.C. Sabathia	1.00
CS	Chris Shelton	.50
JS	John Smoltz	.75
SS	Shannon Stewart	.50
JT	Jim Thome	.75
JW	Jayson Werth	1.50
PW	Preston Wilson	.50

Game Jersey

UD GAME

NM/M

Common Player: 4.00

JB	Jeff Bagwell	6.00
MC	Miguel Cabrera	8.00
EC	Eric Chavez	4.00
RC	Roger Clemens	15.00
JD	Johnny Damon	10.00
JE	Jim Edmonds	4.00
RF	Rafael Furcal	6.00
EG	Eric Gagne	4.00
JG	Jason Giambi	6.00
KG	Ken Griffey Jr.	20.00
VG	Vladimir Guerrero	8.00
RH	Roy Halladay	10.00
DJ	Derek Jeter	20.00
RJ	Randy Johnson	8.00
AJ	Andruw Jones	8.00
CJ	Chipper Jones	8.00
JJ	Jacque Jones	4.00
DL	Derrek Lee	8.00
GM	Greg Maddux	12.00
PM	Pedro Martinez	8.00
DO	David Ortiz	8.00
RP	Rafael Palmeiro	6.00
PE	Corey Patterson	4.00
JP	Jake Peavy	6.00
MP	Mike Piazza	8.00
JP	Jorge Posada	6.00
PR	Mark Prior	4.00
AP	Albert Pujols	20.00
MR	Manny Ramirez	6.00
BR	Brian Roberts	6.00
IR	Ivan Rodriguez	8.00
SR	Scott Rolen	8.00
SA	Johan Santana	8.00
CS	Curt Schilling	8.00
SM	John Smoltz	8.00
AS	Alfonso Soriano	8.00
MT	Mark Teixeira	8.00
TE	Miguel Tejada	6.00
FT	Frank Thomas	8.00
JT	Jim Thome	8.00
DW	Dontrelle Willis	4.00
WR	David Wright	15.00

Game Patch

NM/M

Inserted 1:288

JB	Jeff Bagwell	20.00
MC	Miguel Cabrera	25.00
RC	Roger Clemens	30.00
JD	Johnny Damon	25.00
JE	Jim Edmonds	20.00
RF	Rafael Furcal	15.00
KG	Ken Griffey Jr.	40.00
VG	Vladimir Guerrero	25.00
RH	Roy Halladay	25.00
DJ	Derek Jeter	50.00
RJ	Randy Johnson	20.00
AJ	Andruw Jones	20.00
DL	Derrek Lee	20.00
GM	Greg Maddux	30.00
PM	Pedro Martinez	25.00
RP	Rafael Palmeiro	15.00
JP	Jake Peavy	20.00
MP	Mike Piazza	20.00
PR	Mark Prior	15.00
AP	Albert Pujols	50.00
MR	Manny Ramirez	30.00
BR	Brian Roberts	15.00

JB	Josh Beckett	8.00
CB	Carlos Beltran	4.00
AB	Adrian Beltre	4.00
BI	Craig Biggio	6.00
HB	Hank Blalock	4.00
SC	Sean Casey	4.00
JD	Johnny Damon	10.00
CD	Carlos Delgado	6.00
AD	Adam Dunn	6.00
PF	Prince Fielder	15.00
TG	Tom Glavine	6.00
GR	Khalil Greene	4.00
KG	Ken Griffey Jr.	20.00
HA	Travis Hafner	6.00
TH	Todd Helton	6.00
RH	Ryan Howard	20.00
TI	Tadahito Iguchi	4.00
DJ	Derek Jeter	20.00
PK	Paul Konerko	6.00
CL	Carlos Lee	6.00
JL	Javy Lopez	4.00
VM	Victor Martinez	6.00
JM	Joe Mauer	10.00
MM	Mike Mussina	6.00
MO	Magglio Ordonez	6.00
RO	Roy Oswalt	6.00
AP	Andy Pettitte	6.00
MP	Mike Piazza	8.00
JR	Jose Reyes	8.00
GS	Gary Sheffield	6.00
SI	Grady Sizemore	8.00
JV	Jason Varitek	6.00
CW	Chien-Ming Wang	8.00
RW	Rickie Weeks	6.00
KW	Kerry Wood	6.00
MY	Michael Young	4.00
RZ	Ryan Zimmerman	10.00
BZ	Barry Zito	4.00

Team Pride Materials

NM/M

Common Player: 4.00

BA	Bobby Abreu	6.00
GA	Garret Anderson	4.00
JB	Jeff Bagwell	6.00
RB	Rocco Baldelli	4.00
SC	Sean Casey	4.00
LC	Luis Castillo	4.00
EC	Eric Chavez	4.00
JD	Johnny Damon	10.00
CD	Carlos Delgado	6.00
JE	Jim Edmonds	4.00
ME	Morgan Ensberg	4.00
KF	Keith Foulke	4.00
EG	Eric Gagne	4.00
LG	Luis Gonzalez	4.00
GR	Khalil Greene	4.00
KG	Ken Griffey Jr.	20.00
RH	Rich Harden	4.00
TH	Trevor Hoffman	4.00
AH	Aubrey Huff	4.00
DJ	Derek Jeter	20.00
NJ	Nick Johnson	4.00
AJ	Andruw Jones	8.00
CJ	Chipper Jones	8.00
RK	Ryan Klesko	4.00
CK	Casey Kotchman	4.00
ML	Mike Lieberthal	4.00
LO	Mike Lowell	4.00
GM	Greg Maddux	12.00
MA	Joe Mauer	10.00
JM	Jamie Moyer	4.00
DO	David Ortiz	8.00
PE	Andy Pettitte	6.00
JP	Jorge Posada	6.00
MP	Mark Prior	4.00
AP	Albert Pujols	20.00
JR	Jose Reyes	8.00
IR	Ivan Rodriguez	8.00
CC	C.C. Sabathia	8.00
CS	Curt Schilling	8.00
JS	John Smoltz	8.00
MS	Mike Sweeney	6.00
FT	Frank Thomas	8.00
JT	Jim Thome	8.00
VA	Jason Varitek	8.00
JV	Jose Vidro	4.00
BW	Bernie Williams	6.00
DW	Dontrelle Willis	4.00
KW	Kerry Wood	4.00
MY	Michael Young	4.00
BZ	Barry Zito	4.00

SR	Scott Rolen	20.00
JS	Johan Santana	25.00
SM	John Smoltz	25.00
TE	Miguel Tejada	20.00
FT	Frank Thomas	20.00
JT	Jim Thome	20.00
DW	Dontrelle Willis	15.00
WR	David Wright	40.00

Series 2: No Pricing

Silver Spectrum

No Pricing
Production 25 Sets

Printing Plates

No Pricing
Production one set per color.

Rookie Foil Gold

MAJEWSKI

Gold: 4-8X
Production 99 Sets
Platinum: No Pricing
Production 15 Sets

Rookie Foil Silver

TRAUBENHEIM

Silver: 2-4X
Production 399 Sets

Inaugural Images

INAUGURAL IMAGES

NM/M

Common Player:		.50
II-1	Sung-Heon Hong	.50
II-2	Yulieski Gourriel	.50
II-3	Tsuyoshi Nishioka	1.00
II-4	Miguel Cabrera	1.50
II-5	Yung-Chi Chen	.50
II-6	Omari Romero	.50
II-7	Ken Griffey Jr.	2.00
II-8	Bernie Williams	.75
II-9	Daniel Cabrera	.50
II-10	David Ortiz	1.50
II-11	Alex Rodriguez	3.00
II-12	Frederich Cepeda	.50
II-13	Derek Jeter	3.00
II-14	Jorge Cantu	.50
II-15	Alexi Ramirez	.50
II-16	Yoandy Garlobo	.50
II-17	Koji Uehara	.50
II-18	Nobuhiko Matsunaka	.50
II-19	Tomoya Satozaki	.50
II-20	Seung-Yeop Lee	.50
II-21	Yulieski Gourriel	.50
II-22	David Ortiz	.50
II-23	Ken Griffey Jr.	2.00
II-24	Jong Beom Lee	.50
II-25	Ichiro Suzuki	2.00
II-26	Yoandy Garlobo	.50
II-27	Daisuke Matsuzaka	15.00
II-28	Yadel Marti	.50

II-29	Chan Ho Park	.50
II-30	Daisuke Matsuzaka	15.00

INKredible

NM/M
Inserted 1:288

JB	Joe Blanton	10.00
CA	Miguel Cabrera	40.00
CO	Chad Cordero	10.00
JC	Jesse Crain	10.00
CC	Carl Crawford	20.00
NG	Nomar Garciaparra	60.00
KG	Ken Griffey Jr.	120.00
TH	Travis Hafner	20.00
JH	J.J. Hardy	10.00
TI	Tadahito Iguchi/SP 91	
DJ	Derek Jeter	125.00
SK	Scott Kazmir	20.00
CK	Casey Kotchman	10.00
VM	Victor Martinez	25.00
JM	Joe Mauer/SP 91	50.00
MO	Justin Morneau	25.00
BM	Brett Myers/SP 72	15.00
LO	Lyle Overbay/SP 91	15.00
JR	Jeremy Reed	15.00
RE	Jose Reyes/SP 91	40.00
AR	Alexis Rios	20.00
BR	Brian Roberts	20.00
MT	Mark Teixeira	25.00
JV	Justin Verlander/SP 91	40.00
WI	Dontrelle Willis	15.00
DW	David Wright/SP 91	60.00
KY	Kevin Youkilis	25.00
RZ	Ryan Zimmerman/SP 91	40.00

Player Highlights

MIGUEL TEJADA - BALTIMORE ORIOLES • 56
TEJADA EARNS ALL-STAR MVP

NM/M
Common Player: .50

PH-1	Andruw Jones	1.00
PH-2	Manny Ramirez	1.00
PH-3	Travis Hafner	1.00
PH-4	Johnny Damon	1.00
PH-5	Miguel Cabrera	1.00
PH-6	Chris Carpenter	.75
PH-7	Derrek Lee	1.00
PH-8	Jason Bay	.75
PH-9	Jason Varitek	1.00
PH-10	Ryan Howard	2.00
PH-11	Mark Teixeira	.75
PH-12	Carlos Delgado	.75
PH-13	Bartolo Colon	.50
PH-14	David Wright	2.00
PH-15	Miguel Tejada	.75
PH-16	Mike Piazza	1.00
PH-17	Paul Konerko	.75
PH-18	Jermaine Dye	.75
PH-19	Ichiro Suzuki	2.00
PH-20	Brad Wilkerson	.50
PH-21	Hideki Matsui	2.00
PH-22	Albert Pujols	3.00
PH-23	Chris Burke	.50
PH-24	Derek Jeter	3.00
PH-25	Brian Roberts	.75
PH-26	David Ortiz	1.50
PH-27	Alex Rodriguez	3.00
PH-28	Ken Griffey Jr.	2.00
PH-29	Prince Fielder	2.00
PH-30	Bobby Abreu	.75
PH-31	Vladimir Guerrero	1.00
PH-32	Tadahito Iguchi	1.00
PH-33	Jose Reyes	1.00
PH-34	Scott Podsednik	.75
PH-35	Gary Sheffield	.75

Run Producers

run producers
DEREK JETER

NM/M
Common Player: .50

RP-1	Ty Cobb	2.00
RP-2	Derrek Lee	1.00
RP-3	Andruw Jones	1.00
RP-4	David Ortiz	1.50
RP-5	Lou Gehrig	3.00
RP-6	Ken Griffey Jr.	2.00
RP-7	Albert Pujols	3.00
RP-8	Derek Jeter	3.00
RP-9	Manny Ramirez	1.00
RP-10	Alex Rodriguez	3.00
RP-11	Gary Sheffield	.75
RP-12	Miguel Cabrera	1.00
RP-13	Hideki Matsui	2.00
RP-14	Vladimir Guerrero	1.00
RP-15	David Wright	2.00
RP-16	Mike Schmidt	2.00
RP-17	Mark Teixeira	.75
RP-18	Babe Ruth	4.00
RP-19	Jimmie Foxx	2.00
RP-20	Honus Wagner	2.00

Speed to Burn

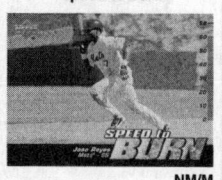

SPEED to BURN
Jose Reyes Mets • SS

NM/M
Common Player: .50

SB-1	Lou Brock	1.00
SB-3	Alfonso Soriano	1.50
SB-4	Carl Crawford	.75
SB-5	Chone Figgins	.50
SB-6	Ichiro Suzuki	2.00
SB-7	Jose Reyes	1.00
SB-8	Juan Pierre	.50
SB-9	Scott Podsednik	.75
SB-11	Alex Rodriguez	3.00
SB-12	David Wright	2.00
SB-14	Bobby Abreu	.75
SB-15	Brian Roberts	.75

All-Time Legends

NM/M
Common Player: 1.00

AT-1	Ty Cobb	3.00
AT-2	Lou Gehrig	4.00
AT-3	Babe Ruth	5.00
AT-4	Jimmie Foxx	3.00
AT-5	Honus Wagner	3.00
AT-6	Lou Brock	2.00
AT-8	Christy Mathewson	2.00
AT-9	Walter Johnson	2.00
AT-10	Mike Schmidt	3.00
AT-11	Al Kaline	2.00
AT-12	Robin Yount	2.00
AT-13	Johnny Bench	2.00
AT-14	Yogi Berra	2.00
AT-15	Rod Carew	1.00
AT-16	Bob Feller	1.00
AT-17	Carlton Fisk	1.00
AT-18	Bob Gibson	2.00
AT-19	Cy Young	2.00
AT-21	Jackie Robinson	3.00
AT-22	Harmon Killebrew	2.00
AT-23	Mickey Cochrane	1.00
AT-24	Eddie Mathews	2.00
AT-25	Bill Mazeroski	1.00
AT-26	Willie McCovey	2.00
AT-27	Eddie Murray	2.00
AT-28	Lefty Grove	1.00
AT-29	Jim Palmer	2.00
AT-30	Pee Wee Reese	1.00
AT-31	Phil Rizzuto	2.00
AT-32	Brooks Robinson	2.00
AT-33	Nolan Ryan	4.00
AT-34	Tom Seaver	2.00
AT-35	Ozzie Smith	2.00
AT-36	Roy Campanella	2.00
AT-37	Thurman Munson	3.00
AT-38	Mel Ott	2.00
AT-39	Satchel Paige	2.00
AT-40	Rogers Hornsby	2.00

World Baseball Classic Jersey

DAISUKE MATSUZAKA

NM/M
Inserted 1:24
Patch: No Pricing
Production Eight Sets

JB	Jason Bay	10.00
EB	Erik Bedard	8.00
CB	Carlos Beltran	15.00
MC	Miguel Cabrera	15.00
VC	Vinny Castilla	4.00
FC	Frederich Cepeda	15.00
TC	Tai-San Chang	200.00
RC	Roger Clemens	30.00
JD	Johnny Damon	15.00
CD	Carlos Delgado	10.00
ME	Michel Enriquez	20.00
MF	Maikel Folch	20.00
JF	Jeff Francis	4.00
FR	Jeff Francoeur	15.00
FG	Freddy Garcia	4.00
YG	Yulieski Gourriel	25.00
KG	Ken Griffey Jr.	25.00
JG	Jason Grilli	4.00
HS	Chia-Hsien Hseih	100.00
CH	Chin-Lung Hu	75.00
JH	Justin Huber	4.00
AI	Akinori Iwamura	40.00
AJ	Andruw Jones	15.00
MK	Munenori Kawasaki	50.00
PL	Pedro Lazo	20.00
CL	Carlos Lee	8.00
DL	Derrek Lee	10.00
JL	Jong Beom Lee	8.00
WL	Wei-Chu Lin	80.00
GL	Guangbiao Liu	10.00
VM	Victor Martinez	10.00
NM	Nobuhiko Matsunaka	60.00
DM	Daisuke Matsuzaka	100.00
YM	Yunieski Maya	15.00
JM	Justin Morneau	10.00
TN	Tsuyoshi Nishioka	25.00
MO	Michihiro Ogasawara	60.00
DO	David Ortiz	20.00
WP	Wei-Lun Pan	80.00
EP	Eduardo Paret	20.00
JP	Jin Man Park	15.00
OP	Oliver Perez	4.00
PE	Ariel Pestano	20.00
MP	Mike Piazza	25.00
AP	Albert Pujols	30.00
AR	Alex Rodriguez	25.00
IR	Ivan Rodriguez	10.00
JS	Johan Santana	15.00
MS	Min Han Son	10.00
AS	Alfonso Soriano	15.00
IS	Ichiro Suzuki	220.00
HT	Hitoshi Tamura	50.00
MT	Mark Teixeira	10.00
TE	Miguel Tejada	15.00
KU	Koji Uehara	40.00
JV	Jason Varitek	20.00
TW	Tsuyoshi Wada	25.00
WW	Wei Wang	15.00
SW	Shunsuke Watanabe	30.00
GY	Guogang Yang	10.00

Update Gold

Gold (1001-1250):	4-8X
Gold SP's:	.5-1X

Production 99 Sets

Update Inkredible

NM/M
Inserted 1:24 Retail

EA	Erick Aybar	10.00
BA	Brandon Backe	10.00
CB	Colter Bean	10.00
YB	Yuniesky Betancourt	10.00
EB	Eude Brito	15.00
BB	Ben Broussard	10.00
AB	Ambiorix Burgos	15.00
GC	Gustavo Chacin	8.00
BC	Brandon Claussen	10.00
CO	Chad Cordero/SP	15.00
CA	Carl Crawford	15.00
CC	Coco Crisp	15.00
CD	Chris Duffy	15.00
JD	Jermaine Dye	15.00
GF	Gavin Floyd	8.00
RF	Ryan Freel	15.00
RG	Ryan Garko	15.00
KG	Ken Griffey Jr./SP	125.00
AH	Aaron Harang	10.00
JH	John Hattig Jr.	10.00
MH	Matt Holliday	20.00
TI	Tadahito Iguchi/SP	30.00
CI	Cesar Izturis	5.00
DJ	Derek Jeter/SP	200.00
AJ	Adam Jones	30.00
JO	Jacque Jones	10.00
JJ	Jorge Julio/SP	10.00
CK	Casey Kotchman	10.00
CL	Cliff Lee	10.00
NL	Noah Lowry	15.00
BM	Brandon McCarthy/SP	15.00
ZM	Zach Miner	10.00
YM	Yadier Molina	20.00
MM	Matt Murton	15.00
LN	Leo Nunez	8.00
AP	Angel Pagan	10.00
PA	John Patterson	15.00
RP	Ronny Paulino	15.00
JP	Jhonny Peralta	15.00
PE	Joel Peralta	8.00
PI	Joel Pineiro	8.00
DR	Darrell Rasner	10.00
KR	Ken Ray	8.00
AR	Alex Rios/SP	30.00
JR	Juan Rivera/SP	20.00
BR	Brian Roberts	15.00
MR	Mike Rouse	15.00
RS	Ryan Shealy	15.00
NS	Nick Swisher	15.00
MT	Mark Teahen	15.00
MV	Michael Vento	8.00
BW	Brian Wilson	8.00
CW	C.J. Wilson	5.00
KY	Kevin Youkilis	15.00

Update Star Attractions

NM/M
Inserted 1:2 Retail
Silver: 2-3X
Production 99 Sets

BR	Brian Anderson	.50
EA	Erick Aybar	.50
WA	Willy Aybar	.50
JO	Josh Barfield	.50
BI	Chad Billingsley	.75
MC	Matt Cain	.75
RC	Ronny Cedeno	.50
SD	Stephen Drew	1.50
AE	Andre Ethier	1.00
PF	Prince Fielder	1.50
TG	Tony Gwynn Jr.	.75
CH	Cole Hamels	1.00
HI	Jason Hirsh	.50
HU	Justin Huber	.50
CO	Conor Jackson	.50
JA	Chuck James	.50
KJ	Kenji Johjima	1.50
JJ	Josh Johnson	.50
AJ	Adam Jones	.50
MK	Matthew Kemp	1.50
HK	Howie Kendrick	1.00
JK	Jason Kubel	.50
LE	Jon Lester	1.50
FL	Francisco Liriano	1.00
AL	Adam Loewen	.50
NM	Nicholas Markakis	1.00
AM	Andy Marte	.50
RM	Russell Martin	.50
MA	Jeff Mathis	.50
DM	Dustin McGowan	.50
LM	Lastings Milledge	1.00
KM	Kendry Morales	.50
SO	Scott Olsen	.50
PA	Jonathan Papelbon	1.00
DP	Dustin Pedroia	.50
PE	Mike Pelfrey	1.50
HP	Hayden Penn	.50
CQ	Carlos Quentin	.50
HR	Hanley Ramirez	1.50
AR	Anthony Reyes	.50
AN	Anibal Sanchez	.50
SW	Jeremy Sowers	.50
DU	Dan Uggla	.50
JV	Justin Verlander	2.00
CY	Chris Young	.50
AW	Adam Wainwright	.50
JW	Jered Weaver	1.00
RZ	Ryan Zimmerman	.50
JZ	Joel Zumaya	.50

2006 Upper Deck World Baseball Classic

NM/M
Complete Set (50): 20.00
Common Player: .25

1	Derek Jeter	1.50
2	Ken Griffey Jr.	1.00
3	Derrek Lee	1.50
4	Dontrelle Willis	.50
5	Alex Rodriguez	1.50
6	Jeff Francoeur	.25
7	Roger Clemens	1.50
8	Johnny Damon	.50
9	Chipper Jones	.50
10	Mark Teixeira	.50
11	Chase Utley	.50
12	Jake Peavy	.25
13	Michael Collins	.25
14	Justin Huber	.25
15	Jason Bay	.50
16	Jeff Francis	.25
17	Justin Morneau	.25
18	Guogang Yang	.25
19	Wei Wang	.25
20	Chia-Hsien Hseih	.25
21	Chin-Lung Hu	.25
22	Wei-Lun Pan	.25
23	Yung-Chi Chen	.25
24	Mike Piazza	.50
25	Albert Pujols	1.50
26	David Ortiz	.50
27	Jose Reyes	.50
28	Miguel Tejada	.50
29	Ichiro Suzuki	1.00
30	Nobuhiko Matsunaka	.25
31	Toshiaki Imae	.25
32	Kazuhiro Wada	.25
33	Shunsuke Watanabe	.25
34	Jung Bong	.25
35	Jong Beom Lee	.25
36	Seung-Yeop Lee	.25
37	Vinny Castilla	.25
38	Oliver Perez	.25
39	Jorge Cantu	.25
40	Andruw Jones	.50
41	Carlos Lee	.50
42	Carlos Beltran	.50
43	Carlos Delgado	.50
44	Ivan Rodriguez	.50
45	Bernie Williams	.50
46	Bobby Abreu	.50
47	Miguel Cabrera	.50
48	Johan Santana	.50
49	Victor Martinez	.50
50	Omar Vizquel	.50

2006 Upper Deck Artifacts

NM/M
Complete Set (100): 35.00
Common Player: .25

ARTIFACTS
D Justin Verlander 35
ROOKIE CARD

Pack (4):		8.00
Box (10):		70.00
1	Luis Gonzalez	.25
2	Conor Jackson RC	.50
3	Joey Devine RC	1.00
4	Andruw Jones	.50
5	Chipper Jones	1.00
6	John Smoltz	.50
7	Jeff Francoeur	.50
8	Brian Roberts	.25
9	Miguel Tejada	.75
10	Nick Markakis RC	.75
11	Curt Schilling	1.00
12	David Ortiz	1.00
13	Johnny Damon	.50
14	Manny Ramirez	1.00
15	Jonathan Papelbon RC	2.00
16	Aramis Ramirez	.50
17	Carlos Zambrano	.50
18	Derrek Lee	.75
19	Greg Maddux	2.00
20	Mark Prior	.50
21	Mark Buehrle	.50
22	Paul Konerko	.50
23	Adam Dunn	.75
24	Ken Griffey Jr.	2.00
25	Travis Hafner	.50
26	Victor Martinez	.50
27	Todd Helton	.75
28	Ivan Rodriguez	.75
29	Jeremy Bonderman	.25
30	Jeremy Hermida RC	.50
31	Carlos Delgado	.50
32	Dontrelle Willis	.50
33	Josh Beckett	.75
34	Miguel Cabrera	1.00
35	Craig Biggio	.50
36	Lance Berkman	.50
37	Roger Clemens	3.00
38	Roy Oswalt	.50
39	Josh Willingham RC	.50
40	Hanley Ramirez RC	2.00
41	Prince Fielder RC	2.00
42	Zack Greinke	.25
43	Francisco Rodriguez	.25
44	Vladimir Guerrero	.75
45	Tim Hamulack RC	.25
46	Jeff Kent	.50
47	Ben Sheets	.50
48	Rickie Weeks	.50
49	Francisco Liriano RC	2.00
50	Joe Mauer	.75
51	Johan Santana	1.00
52	Justin Morneau	.50
53	Torii Hunter	.50
54	Carlos Beltran	.75
55	David Wright	2.00
56	Jose Reyes	1.00
57	Mike Piazza	1.00
58	Pedro Martinez	.50
59	Alex Rodriguez	3.00
60	Derek Jeter	2.00
61	Hideki Matsui	2.00
62	Randy Johnson	1.00
63	Justin Verlander RC	3.00
64	Bobby Crosby	.25
65	Eric Chavez	.50
66	Brian Anderson RC	.25
67	Bobby Abreu	.50
68	Pat Burrell	.50
69	Jason Bay	.50
70	Oliver Perez	.25
71	Chuck James RC	.50
72	Brian Giles	.50
73	Jake Peavy	.50
74	Khalil Greene	.25
75	Jason Schmidt	.50
76	Kenji Johjima RC	.75
77	Jeremy Accardo RC	.50
78	Adrian Beltre	.50
79	Ichiro Suzuki	2.00
80	Jeff Harris RC	.50
81	Felix Hernandez	.75
82	Albert Pujols	3.00
83	Chris Carpenter	.75
84	Jim Edmonds	.50
85	Scott Rolen	.75
86	Mike Jacobs	.50
87	Carl Crawford	.50
88	Anderson Hernandez RC	.25
89	Scott Kazmir	.50
90	Josh Rupe RC	.50
91	Scott Feldman RC	.50
92	Alfonso Soriano	.75
93	Hank Blalock	.50
94	Mark Teixeira	.75
95	Michael Young	.50
96	Roy Halladay	.50
97	Vernon Wells	
98	Jason Bergmann RC	
99	Ryan Zimmerman RC	
100	Jose Vidro	

AL/NL Artifacts

245/325
REDS 39
NL ARTIFACTS

Common Player:	4.00
Production 325 Sets	
Red:	.75-1.5
Production 100-250	
Green:	.75-1.5
Production 150 Sets	

GA	Garrett Atkins	4.00
JB	Jeff Bagwell	8.00
SB	Scott Baker	4.00
RB	Rocco Baldelli	4.00
CL	Clint Barmes	4.00
JA	Jason Bay	6.00
HB	Hank Blalock	4.00
BL	Joe Blanton	4.00
JB	Jeremy Bonderman	4.00
BB	Ben Broussard	4.00
MB	Mark Buehrle	6.00
CB	Chris Burke	4.00
MC	Miguel Cabrera	8.00
MA	Matt Cain	4.00
JC	Jorge Cantu	4.00
CA	Chris Capuano	4.00
CC	Chris Carpenter	10.00
GC	Gustavo Chacin	4.00
EC	Eric Chavez	4.00
RC	Ryan Church	4.00
CH	Chad Cordero	4.00
CC	Carl Crawford	6.00
JC	Joe Crede	4.00
CO	Coco Crisp	6.00
ZD	Zachary Duke	4.00
AD	Adam Dunn/250	4.00
JE	Jim Edmonds	4.00
ME	Morgan Ensberg	4.00
PF	Prince Fielder	10.00
JF	Jeff Francoeur	8.00
EG	Eric Gagne	4.00
GA	Jon Garland	4.00
MG	Marcus Giles	4.00
JG	Jonny Gomes	4.00
KG	Ken Griffey Jr.	15.00
VG	Vladimir Guerrero	8.00
TH	Travis Hafner	8.00
BH	Bill Hall/235	4.00
AH	Aaron Harang	4.00
DH	Danny Haren	4.00
TH	Todd Helton	6.00
FH	Felix Hernandez	6.00
RH	Ramon Hernandez	4.00
TR	Trevor Hoffman	4.00
MH	Matt Holliday	8.00
RY	Ryan Howard	15.00
TI	Tadahito Iguchi	4.00
CO	Conor Jackson	4.00
DJ	Derek Jeter	25.00
DA	Dan Johnson	4.00
NJ	Nick Johnson	4.00
RJ	Randy Johnson/235	4.00
JG	Chipper Jones	8.00
SK	Scott Kazmir	4.00
LE	Carlos Lee	6.00
CL	Cliff Lee	4.00
DL	Derrek Lee	8.00
BL	Brad Lidge	4.00
FL	Felipe Lopez	4.00
ML	Mark Loretta	4.00
NL	Noah Lowry	4.00
PM	Pedro Martinez	8.00
VM	Victor Martinez	4.00
JM	Joe Mauer	10.00
BM	Brian McCann	8.00
BM	Brandon McCarthy	4.00
YM	Yadier Molina	4.00
JU	Justin Morneau	6.00
JN	Joe Nathan	4.00
DO	David Ortiz	10.00
RO	Roy Oswalt	6.00
JP	Jake Peavy	6.00
PE	Jhonny Peralta	6.00
JP	Joel Pineiro	4.00
SP	Scott Podsednik	4.00
MP	Mark Prior	4.00
AP	Albert Pujols/250	20.00
MR	Manny Ramirez	8.00
JR	Jose Reyes	8.00
IR	Ivan Rodriguez	6.00
ES	Ervin Santana	4.00
CS	Chris Shelton	4.00
GS	Grady Sizemore	10.00
JS	John Smoltz/250	8.00
AS	Alfonso Soriano	6.00

HS	Huston Street	4.00
NS	Nick Swisher	4.00
MT	Miguel Tejada	6.00
CU	Chase Utley	10.00
JV	Jason Varitek	8.00
RW	Rickie Weeks	6.00
JW	Jake Westbrook	4.00
DW	Dontrelle Willis	8.00
JW	Jack Wilson/200	4.00
WR	David Wright	20.00
DY	Dmitri Young	4.00
MY	Michael Young	4.00
RZ	Ryan Zimmerman	10.00

Awesome Artifacts
NM/M
Common Player: 10.00
Production 45 unless noted.

BA	Jeff Bagwell	12.00
HB	Harold Baines	10.00
SB	Scott Baker	10.00
RB	Rocco Baldelli	10.00
CB	Clint Barmes	10.00
JB	Jason Bay	12.00
HA	Hank Blalock	10.00
BL	Joe Blanton	10.00
MB	Mark Buehrle	10.00
BU	Chris Burke	10.00
MC	Miguel Cabrera	15.00
CA	Matt Cain	10.00
CH	Chris Carpenter	15.00
GC	Gustavo Chacin	10.00
EC	Eric Chavez	10.00
WC	Will Clark	12.00
CC	Carl Crawford	12.00
DD	Don Drysdale/25	25.00
ZD	Zachary Duke	10.00
AD	Adam Dunn	15.00
JE	Jim Edmonds	12.00
ME	Morgan Ensberg	10.00
PF	Prince Fielder	15.00
CF	Carlton Fisk	15.00
FG	Gavin Floyd	10.00
JF	Jeff Francoeur	20.00
EG	Eric Gagne	10.00
FG	Freddy Garcia/21	10.00
JG	Jon Garland	10.00
SG	Steve Garvey	10.00
JG	Jonny Gomes	10.00
KG	Ken Griffey Jr.	30.00
VG	Vladimir Guerrero	20.00
BH	Bill Hall	10.00
AH	Aaron Harang	10.00
DH	Danny Haren	10.00
TH	Todd Helton	10.00
FH	Felix Hernandez	15.00
TR	Trevor Hoffman	10.00
RH	Rogers Hornsby/25	100.00
RY	Ryan Howard	30.00
BO	Bo Jackson	15.00
CO	Conor Jackson	10.00
DJ	Derek Jeter	40.00
DJ	Dan Johnson	10.00
NJ	Nick Johnson	10.00
RA	Randy Johnson	15.00
CJ	Chipper Jones	15.00
JL	Jason Lane	10.00
DL	Don Larsen/25	25.00
CL	Cliff Lee	10.00
DL	Derek Lee	15.00
NL	Noah Lowry	10.00
PM	Pedro Martinez	15.00
EM	Eddie Mathews	40.00
BR	Brian McCann	15.00
BM	Brandon McCarthy	10.00
JM	Johnny Mize/25	20.00
YM	Yadier Molina	10.00
JU	Justin Morneau	15.00
DO	David Ortiz	25.00
RO	Roy Oswalt	10.00
SP	Satchel Paige	100.00
DP	Dave Parker	10.00
JP	Jake Peavy	10.00
JP	Jhonny Peralta	10.00
GP	Gaylord Perry	10.00
JP	Joel Pineiro	10.00
MP	Mark Prior	10.00
AP	Albert Pujols	40.00
MR	Manny Ramirez	15.00
CR	Cal Ripken Jr.	40.00
IR	Ivan Rodriguez	10.00
AR	Aaron Rowand	10.00
ES	Ervin Santana	10.00
RS	Ron Santo	15.00
JA	Jason Schmidt	10.00
CS	Chris Shelton	10.00
GS	Grady Sizemore	15.00
JS	John Smoltz	15.00
AS	Alfonso Soriano	15.00
AS	Huston Street	10.00
NS	Nick Swisher	10.00
MI	Miguel Tejada	15.00
FT	Frank Thomas	15.00
CU	Chase Utley	25.00
AV	Andy Van Slyke	10.00
JV	Jason Varitek	20.00
RW	Rickie Weeks	10.00
DW	Dave Wells	10.00
WE	Jake Westbrook	10.00
WI	Dontrelle Willis	12.00
JW	Jack Wilson	10.00
WR	David Wright	30.00
CY	Carl Yastrzemski/25	40.00
RZ	Ryan Zimmerman	15.00

Apparel
NM/M
Common Player: 10.00
Production 325 Sets

Gold: .75-1.5X
Silver: 1X
Rare Apparel: No Pricing
Production One Set

AT	Garrett Atkins	4.00
HB	Harold Baines	4.00
SB	Scott Baker	4.00
RB	Rocco Baldelli	4.00
BA	Clint Barmes	4.00
BY	Jason Bay	6.00
YB	Yuniesky Betancourt	4.00
JO	Joe Blanton	4.00
JE	Jeremy Bonderman	4.00
BB	Ben Broussard	4.00
CB	Chris Burke	4.00
MC	Miguel Cabrera	8.00
MA	Matt Cain	6.00
JU	Jorge Cantu	4.00
CS	Chris Capuano	4.00
CH	Chris Carpenter	8.00
GC	Gustavo Chacin	4.00
RC	Ryan Church	4.00
WC	Will Clark	8.00
CD	Chad Cordero	4.00
CA	Carl Crawford	6.00
CO	Coco Crisp	4.00
PF	Prince Fielder	10.00
CF	Carlton Fisk	8.00
GF	Gavin Floyd	4.00
GA	Jon Garland	4.00
SG	Steve Garvey	6.00
MG	Marcus Giles	4.00
JG	Jonny Gomes	4.00
GO	Adrian Gonzalez	6.00
GG	Rich "Goose" Gossage	
KG	Ken Griffey Jr.	15.00
AH	Aaron Harang	4.00
DH	Danny Haren	4.00
JH	Jeremy Hermida	4.00
FH	Felix Hernandez	8.00
RH	Ramon Hernandez	4.00
MH	Matt Holliday	4.00
HO	Ryan Howard	15.00
TI	Tadahito Iguchi	6.00
BO	Bo Jackson	10.00
CJ	Conor Jackson	4.00
DJ	Derek Jeter	25.00
DA	Dan Johnson	4.00
SK	Scott Kazmir	8.00
KE	Jason Kendall	4.00
CK	Casey Kotchman	4.00
JK	John Kruk	6.00
JL	Jason Lane	4.00
DO	Don Larsen	15.00
LE	Carlos Lee	6.00
CL	Cliff Lee	4.00
DL	Derek Lee	8.00
BL	Brad Lidge	4.00
FL	Felipe Lopez	4.00
ML	Mark Loretta	4.00
NL	Noah Lowry	4.00
BI	Bill Madlock	4.00
JM	Joe Mauer	8.00
BC	Brian McCann	4.00
BM	Brandon McCarthy	4.00
FM	Fred McGriff	6.00
MY	Yadier Molina	4.00
MO	Justin Morneau	8.00
JN	Joe Nathan	4.00
GN	Graig Nettles	4.00
OR	Magglio Ordonez	4.00
OR	Roy Oswalt	6.00
PE	Jake Peavy	6.00
JP	Jhonny Peralta	4.00
GP	Gaylord Perry	4.00
PI	Joel Pineiro	4.00
SP	Scott Podsednik	4.00
BP	Boog Powell	5.00
JR	Jose Reyes	6.00
RS	Ron Santo	15.00
MS	Mike Schmidt	10.00
SH	Chris Shelton	4.00
HS	Huston Street	4.00
NS	Nick Swisher	6.00
ST	So Taguchi	4.00
CU	Chase Utley	10.00
AV	Andy Van Slyke	4.00
RW	Rickie Weeks	6.00
JW	Jake Westbrook	4.00
DW	Dontrelle Willis	4.00
WR	David Wright	20.00
CY	Carl Yastrzemski	15.00
DY	Dmitri Young	4.00
MY	Michael Young	4.00
RZ	Ryan Zimmerman	10.00

Apparel Autographs
NM/M
Production 30 Sets

Patch Auto.: No Pricing
Production 10 Sets

AT	Garrett Atkins	10.00
HB	Harold Baines	15.00
SB	Scott Baker	15.00
BA	Clint Barmes	15.00
BY	Jason Bay	25.00
YB	Yuniesky Betancourt	15.00
JO	Joe Blanton	10.00
JE	Jeremy Bonderman	20.00
BB	Ben Broussard	15.00
CB	Chris Burke	15.00
MC	Miguel Cabrera	40.00
MA	Matt Cain	40.00
CS	Chris Capuano	15.00
CH	Chris Carpenter	50.00
GC	Gustavo Chacin	15.00
RC	Ryan Church	15.00
WC	Will Clark	40.00
CD	Chad Cordero	15.00
CA	Carl Crawford	25.00
CO	Coco Crisp	40.00
JD	Jermaine Dye	20.00
PF	Prince Fielder	50.00
CF	Carlton Fisk	40.00
SG	Steve Garvey	25.00
MG	Marcus Giles	10.00
JG	Jonny Gomes	15.00
GG	Rich "Goose" Gossage	25.00
KG	Ken Griffey Jr.	100.00
AH	Aaron Harang	15.00
DH	Danny Haren	20.00
JH	Jeremy Hermida	15.00
FH	Felix Hernandez	40.00
RH	Ramon Hernandez	15.00
HO	Ryan Howard	85.00
TI	Tadahito Iguchi	50.00
BO	Bo Jackson	50.00
CJ	Conor Jackson	15.00
DJ	Derek Jeter	200.00
DA	Dan Johnson	15.00
SK	Scott Kazmir	20.00
CK	Casey Kotchman	15.00
JK	John Kruk	20.00
DO	Don Larsen	25.00
LE	Carlos Lee	15.00
CL	Cliff Lee	25.00
DL	Derek Lee	40.00
BL	Brad Lidge	15.00
FL	Felipe Lopez	15.00
NL	Noah Lowry	15.00
BI	Bill Madlock	15.00
JM	Joe Mauer	50.00
BM	Brandon McCarthy	15.00
YM	Yadier Molina	40.00
MO	Justin Morneau	30.00
JN	Joe Nathan	25.00
GN	Graig Nettles	30.00
OR	Magglio Ordonez	35.00
RO	Roy Oswalt	25.00
PE	Jake Peavy	40.00
JP	Jhonny Peralta	15.00
GP	Gaylord Perry	25.00
PI	Joel Pineiro	15.00
SP	Scott Podsednik	30.00
BP	Boog Powell	25.00
JR	Jose Reyes	25.00
CR	Cal Ripken Jr.	180.00
AR	Aaron Rowand	20.00
RS	Ron Santo	75.00
MS	Mike Schmidt	60.00
SH	Chris Shelton	15.00
HS	Huston Street	20.00
NS	Nick Swisher	25.00
CU	Chase Utley	75.00
AV	Andy Van Slyke	25.00
RW	Rickie Weeks	25.00
JW	Jake Westbrook	10.00
DW	Dontrelle Willis	15.00
WR	David Wright	85.00
CY	Carl Yastrzemski	65.00
DY	Dmitri Young	15.00
MY	Michael Young	25.00
RZ	Ryan Zimmerman	40.00

Autofacts
NM/M
Production 5-800

JA	Jeremy Accardo/800	10.00
LA	Luis Aparicio/250	15.00
GA	Garrett Atkins/800	10.00
CB	Clint Barmes/800	10.00
JB	Jason Bay/200	20.00
GB	George Bell/715	20.00
BE	Jason Bergmann/800	10.00
BY	Clete Boyer/485	15.00
MC	Miguel Cabrera/250	30.00
MA	Matt Cain/700	10.00
CP	Jose Capellan/800	10.00
CA	Chris Capuano/800	10.00
CH	Chris Carpenter/51	40.00
JC	Joe Carter/400	15.00
GC	Gustavo Chacin/800	10.00
CC	Chris Chambliss/400	15.00
RC	Ryan Church/800	10.00
CK	Jack Clark/800	10.00
CO	Coco Crisp/600	25.00
ED	Eric Davis/487	1.00
AD	Andre Dawson/300	20.00
CD	Chris Demaria/800	10.00
DA	Chris Denorfia/659	10.00
DE	Joey Devine/150	10.00
JD	Jermaine Dye/652	15.00
LD	Lenny Dykstra/412	15.00
SF	Scott Feldman/800	10.00
PF	Prince Fielder/200	40.00
GF	George Foster/300	15.00
SG	Steve Garvey/300	15.00
MG	Marcus Giles/350	15.00
GO	Jonny Gomes/700	10.00
GF	Rich "Goose" Gossage/300	25.00
KG	Ken Griffey Jr./800	60.00
TH	Travis Hafner/400	15.00
TM	Tim Hamulack/742	10.00
AH	Aaron Harang/800	15.00
DH	Danny Haren/800	10.00
JE	Jeff Harris/800	10.00
FH	Felix Hernandez/300	15.00
KH	Kent Hrbek/239	15.00
TI	Tadahito Iguchi/700	30.00
BO	Bo Jackson/250	50.00
CJ	Conor Jackson/800	15.00
RJ	Reggie Jackson/200	50.00
DJ	Derek Jeter/100	150.00
AJ	Andruw Jones/150	25.00
IK	Ian Kinsler/800	30.00
JK	Jason Kubel/400	15.00
JL	Jason Lane/800	10.00
BL	Barry Larkin/300	35.00
CL	Cliff Lee/600	25.00
DL	Derrek Lee/300	30.00
BI	Bill Madlock/300	15.00
PM	Pedro Martinez/100	60.00
JM	Joe Mauer/400	40.00
AM	Aaron Miles/494	15.00
YM	Yadier Molina/800	20.00
JN	Joe Nathan/800	15.00
GN	Graig Nettles/300	20.00
TO	Tony Oliva/300	15.00
MO	Magglio Ordonez/437	15.00
JP	Jhonny Peralta/700	10.00
TP	Tony Perez/251	15.00
HR	Hanley Ramirez/500	25.00
RE	Chris Resop/800	10.00
JR	Jim Rice/200	25.00
CR	Cal Ripken Jr./100	100.00
BR	Brian Roberts/200	15.00
AR	Aaron Rowand/520	15.00
JS	Johan Santana/150	50.00
CS	Chris Shelton/350	15.00
HS	Huston Street/500	15.00
NS	Nick Swisher/700	15.00
WT	Willy Taveras/500	10.00
CU	Chase Utley/700	40.00
JV	Justin Verlander/700	40.00
RW	Rickie Weeks/91	25.00
JW	Jake Westbrook/650	15.00
WI	Dontrelle Willis/50	15.00
MW	Maury Wills/150	15.00
DW	David Wright/300	65.00
CY	Chris Young/700	10.00
DY	Dmitri Young/300	10.00
MY	Michael Young/600	20.00
CZ	Carlos Zambrano/200	15.00
RZ	Ryan Zimmerman/800	25.00

2006 Upper Deck Cardinals World Series
NM/M
Complete Set (25): 25.00
Complete Factory Set: 40.00
Common Player: .50

1	Ronnie Belliard	.50
2	Gary Bennett	.50
3	Chris Carpenter	3.00
4	Chris Duncan	1.00
5	David Eckstein	1.00
6	Jim Edmonds	3.00
7	Juan Encarnacion	1.00
8	Randy Flores	.50
9	Josh Hancock	.50
10	Tyler Johnson	.50
11	Josh Kinney	.50
12	Braden Looper	.50
13	Aaron Miles	.50
14	Yadier Molina	.50
15	Albert Pujols	5.00
16	Anthony Reyes	1.50
17	John Rodriguez	.50
18	Scott Rolen	3.00
19	Jeff Suppan	1.00
20	Scott Spiezio	.50
21	So Taguchi	.50
22	Brad Thompson	.50
23	Adam Wainwright	2.00
24	Jeff Weaver	.50
25	Preston Wilson	.50

Jumbo
NM/M
Jumbo Team Photo: 2.00

Memorable Moment
NM/M
Complete Set (9): 5.00

1	Albert Pujols	.50
2	Juan Encarnacion	.50
3	So Taguchi	.50
4	Jeff Suppan	.50
5	Albert Pujols	.50
6	Yadier Molina	.50
7	Anthony Reyes	.50
8	David Eckstein	1.00
9	Jeff Weaver	.50

Season Highlight
NM/M
Complete Set (15):

1	Scott Rolen	1.00
2	Mark Mulder	.50
3	Albert Pujols	2.00
4	Albert Pujols	2.00
5	Chris Carpenter	.50
6	Juan Encarnacion	.50
7	Adam Wainwright	.50
8	Yadier Molina	.50
9	So Taguchi	.50
10	Jeff Suppan	.50
11	Jim Edmonds	1.00
12	Chris Duncan	.50
13	Scott Spiezio	.50
14	Scott Rolen	1.00
15	Ronnie Belliard	.50

2006 Upper Deck Epic
NM/M
Complete Set (300):
Common Player: 2.00
Production 450 Sets
Pack (3): 35.00
Box (5): 150.00

1	Conor Jackson RC	
2	Brandon Webb	3.00
3	Craig Counsell	2.00
4	Luis Gonzalez	2.00
5	Miguel Batista	2.00
6	Orlando Hudson	2.00
7	Russ Ortiz	2.00
8	Shawn Green	2.00
9	Andruw Jones	3.00
10	Chipper Jones	3.00
11	Edgar Renteria	3.00
12	Jeff Francoeur	3.00
13	John Smoltz	3.00
14	Marcus Giles	2.00
15	Mike Hampton	2.00
16	Tim Hudson	3.00
17	Erik Bedard	2.00
18	Brian Roberts	2.00
19	Javy Lopez	2.00
20	Jay Gibbons	2.00
21	Jeff Conine	2.00
22	Melvin Mora	2.00
23	Miguel Tejada	4.00
24	Daniel Cabrera	2.00
25	Rodrigo Lopez	2.00
26	Ramon Hernandez	2.00
27	Bronson Arroyo	2.00
28	Curt Schilling	5.00
29	David Ortiz	5.00
30	David Wells	2.00
31	Jason Varitek	4.00
32	Josh Beckett	4.00
33	Kevin Youkilis	3.00
34	Manny Ramirez	5.00
35	Matt Clement	2.00
36	Mike Lowell	3.00
37	Tim Wakefield	2.00
38	Trot Nixon	2.00
39	Aramis Ramirez	3.00
40	Carlos Zambrano	2.00
41	Derrek Lee	4.00
42	Greg Maddux	10.00
43	Juan Pierre	3.00
44	Kerry Wood	3.00
45	Mark Prior	3.00
46	Michael Barrett	2.00
47	Ryan Dempster	2.00
48	Todd Walker	2.00
49	Wade Miller	2.00
50	A.J. Pierzynski	2.00
51	Brian Anderson RC	2.00
52	Frank Thomas	4.00
53	Javier Vazquez	2.00
54	Jim Thome	4.00
55	Joe Crede	2.00
56	Jon Garland	2.00
57	Juan Uribe	2.00
58	Mark Buehrle	3.00
59	Paul Konerko	3.00
60	Scott Podsednik	2.00
61	Tadahito Iguchi	3.00
62	Aaron Harang	2.00
63	Adam Dunn	4.00
64	Austin Kearns	2.00
65	Edwin Encarnacion	2.00
66	Eric Milton	2.00
67	Felipe Lopez	2.00
68	Jason LaRue	2.00
69	Ken Griffey Jr.	10.00
70	Wily Mo Pena	2.00
71	Aaron Boone	2.00
72	Ben Broussard	2.00
73	C.C. Sabathia	4.00
74	Casey Blake	2.00
75	Cliff Lee	2.00
76	Grady Sizemore	4.00
77	Jake Westbrook	2.00
78	Josh Bard	2.00
79	Travis Hafner	3.00
80	Victor Martinez	3.00
81	Chin-Hui Tsao	2.00
82	Clint Barmes	2.00
83	Garrett Atkins	2.00
84	Josh Wilson RC	2.00
85	Luis Gonzalez	2.00
86	Matt Holliday	4.00
87	Todd Helton	4.00
88	Brandon Inge	2.00
89	Carlos Guillen	3.00
90	Chris Shelton	2.00
91	Craig Monroe	2.00
92	Dmitri Young	2.00
93	Ivan Rodriguez	3.00
94	Jeremy Bonderman	3.00
95	Magglio Ordonez	3.00
96	Alberto Gonzalez RC	2.00
97	Brian Moehler	2.00
98	Dontrelle Willis	2.00
99	Jeremy Hermida RC	3.00
100	Jason Vargas	2.00
101	Miguel Cabrera	5.00
102	Adam Everett	2.00
103	Andy Pettitte	3.00
104	Brad Ausmus	2.00
105	Brad Lidge	2.00
106	Craig Biggio	3.00
107	Dan Wheeler	2.00
108	Jeff Bagwell	4.00
109	Lance Berkman	3.00
110	Morgan Ensberg	2.00
111	Preston Wilson	2.00
112	Roger Clemens	10.00
113	Roy Oswalt	3.00
114	David Gassner RC	2.00
115	Angel Berroa	2.00
116	Doug Mientkiewicz	2.00
117	Joe Mays	2.00
118	Mark Grudzielanek	2.00
119	Mike Sweeney	2.00
120	Reggie Sanders	2.00
121	Runelvys Hernandez	2.00
122	Scott Elarton	2.00
123	Brandon Watson RC	2.00
124	Zack Greinke	2.00
125	Brad Penny	2.00
126	Derek Lowe	2.00
127	Eric Gagne	2.00
128	J.D. Drew	3.00
129	Jayson Werth	2.00
130	Jeff Kent	3.00
131	Nomar Garciaparra	3.00
132	Olmedo Saenz	2.00
133	Rafael Furcal	2.00
134	Ben Sheets	3.00
135	Bill Hall	2.00
136	Carlos Lee	3.00
137	Geoff Jenkins	2.00
138	Prince Fielder RC	10.00
139	Rickie Weeks	3.00
140	Jose Capellan RC	2.00
141	Brad Radke	2.00
142	Joe Mauer	4.00
143	Joe Nathan	2.00
144	Johan Santana	5.00
145	Justin Morneau	5.00
146	Kyle Lohse	2.00
147	Lew Ford	2.00
148	Luis Castillo	2.00
149	Matthew LeCroy	2.00
150	Michael Cuddyer	2.00
151	Shannon Stewart	2.00
152	Torii Hunter	3.00
153	Billy Wagner	2.00
154	Carlos Beltran	5.00
155	Carlos Delgado	4.00
156	Cliff Floyd	2.00
157	David Wright	10.00
158	Jose Reyes	8.00
159	Kazuo Matsui	2.00
160	Mike Piazza	6.00
161	Paul LoDuca	2.00
162	Pedro Martinez	5.00
163	Tom Glavine	3.00
164	Victor Diaz	2.00
165	Alex Rodriguez	15.00
166	Bernie Williams	4.00
167	Carl Pavano	2.00
168	Chien-Ming Wang	5.00
169	Derek Jeter	15.00
170	Gary Sheffield	4.00
171	Hideki Matsui	8.00
172	Jason Giambi	3.00
173	Johnny Damon	4.00
174	Jorge Posada	4.00
175	Robinson Cano	4.00
176	Mariano Rivera	4.00
177	Mike Mussina	4.00
178	Randy Johnson	5.00
179	Miguel Cairo	2.00
180	Barry Zito	3.00
181	Bobby Crosby	2.00
182	Bobby Kielty	2.00
183	Eric Chavez	2.00
184	Josh Barfield RC	2.00
185	Esteban Loaiza	2.00
186	Huston Street	2.00
187	Jason Kendall	2.00
188	Nick Swisher	3.00
189	Aaron Rowand	2.00
190	Bobby Abreu	3.00
191	Chase Utley	5.00
192	Gavin Floyd	2.00
193	Jimmy Rollins	5.00
194	Mike Lieberthal	2.00
195	Pat Burrell	4.00
196	Ryan Howard	8.00
197	Craig Wilson	2.00
198	Jack Wilson	2.00
199	Jason Bay	4.00
200	Joe Randa	2.00
201	Josh Fogg	2.00
202	Kip Wells	2.00
203	Sean Casey	2.00
204	Zachary Duke	2.00
205	Brian Giles	2.00
206	Dave Roberts	2.00

#	Player	Price
207	Jake Peavy	4.00
208	Khalil Greene	2.00
209	Mike Cameron	2.00
210	Ryan Klesko	2.00
211	Trevor Hoffman	2.00
212	Vinny Castilla	2.00
213	Armando Benitez	2.00
214	Jason Schmidt	2.00
215	Matt Morris	2.00
216	Moises Alou	2.00
217	Omar Vizquel	2.00
218	Ray Durham	2.00
219	Adrian Beltre	3.00
220	Carl Everett	2.00
221	Kenji Johjima RC	4.00
222	Felix Hernandez	2.00
223	Ichiro Suzuki	10.00
224	Jamie Moyer	2.00
225	Jeremy Reed	2.00
226	Joel Pineiro	2.00
227	Raul Ibanez	2.00
228	Rickie Sexson	3.00
229	Albert Pujols	15.00
230	Chris Carpenter	5.00
231	David Eckstein	2.00
232	Jason Marquis	2.00
233	Jeff Suppan	2.00
234	Jim Edmonds	4.00
235	Yadier Molina	2.00
236	Mark Mulder	2.00
237	Scott Rolen	5.00
238	Alex Gonzalez	2.00
239	Aubrey Huff	2.00
240	Carl Crawford	3.00
241	Casey Fossum	2.00
242	Joey Gathright	2.00
243	Scott Kazmir	3.00
244	Toby Hall	2.00
245	Travis Lee	2.00
246	Adam Eaton	2.00
247	Francisco Cordero	2.00
248	Hank Blalock	3.00
249	Kevin Mench	2.00
250	Kevin Millwood	2.00
251	Laynce Nix	2.00
252	Mark Teixeira	4.00
253	Michael Young	3.00
254	A.J. Burnett	2.00
255	Alex Rios	3.00
256	B.J. Ryan	2.00
257	Corey Koskie	2.00
258	Josh Towers	2.00
259	Lyle Overbay	2.00
260	Reed Johnson	2.00
261	Roy Halladay	3.00
262	Russ Adams	2.00
263	Troy Glaus	3.00
264	Vernon Wells	3.00
265	Alfonso Soriano	4.00
266	John Patterson	2.00
267	Damian Jackson	2.00
268	Jose Guillen	2.00
269	Jose Vidro	2.00
270	Livan Hernandez	2.00
271	Adam Kennedy	2.00
272	Bartolo Colon	2.00
273	Bengie Molina	2.00
274	Casey Kotchman	2.00
275	Chone Figgins	3.00
276	Matt Cain RC	5.00
277	Darin Erstad	2.00
278	Edgardo Alfonzo	2.00
279	Francisco Rodriguez	2.00
280	Garret Anderson	2.00
281	Vladimir Guerrero	5.00
282	Chris Denorfia RC	2.00
283	Joey Devine RC	2.00
284	Justin Verlander RC	10.00
285	Scott Feldman RC	3.00
286	Jason Bergmann RC	2.00
287	Jeremy Accardo RC	2.00
288	Adam Wainwright RC	8.00
289	Hanley Ramirez RC	10.00
290	Josh Johnson RC	5.00
291	Ryan Zimmerman RC	15.00
292	Anderson Hernandez RC	4.00
293	Francisco Liriano RC	15.00
294	Josh Willingham RC	5.00
295	Hong-Chih Kuo RC	5.00
296	Steve Stemle RC	4.00
297	Jeff Harris RC	4.00
298	John Van Benschoten RC	4.00
299	Jonathan Papelbon RC	10.00
300	Jason Kubel RC	4.00

Awesome 8 Materials
Production 1-10

Epic Endorsements
NM/M
Production 10-45

	Player	Price
JB	Jason Bay/45	30.00
CB	Craig Biggio/30	60.00
WB	Wade Boggs/75	75.00
LB	Lou Brock/30	75.00
JI	Jim Bunning/30	30.00
MC1	Miguel Cabrera/30	50.00
MC2	Miguel Cabrera/30	50.00
RC	Rod Carew/30	40.00
SC1	Steve Carlton/27	35.00
SC2	Steve Carlton/27	35.00
EC	Eric Chavez/30	30.00
WC	Will Clark/23	50.00
AD	Adam Dunn/45	40.00
BF1	Bob Feller/45	40.00
BF2	Bob Feller/45	40.00
PF	Prince Fielder/45	50.00
CF	Carlton Fisk/30	50.00
SG	Steve Garvey/30	30.00
BG	Bob Gibson/30	60.00
KG1	Ken Griffey Jr./30	120.00
KG2	Ken Griffey Jr./30	120.00
KG3	Ken Griffey Jr./30	120.00
TG	Tony Gwynn/30	50.00
JH1	Jeremy Hermida/45	30.00
JH2	Jeremy Hermida/45	30.00
FH1	Felix Hernandez/30	40.00
FH2	Felix Hernandez/30	40.00
RH	Ryan Howard/45	100.00
BO	Bo Jackson/30	85.00
DJ1	Derek Jeter/30	180.00
DJ2	Derek Jeter/30	180.00
DJ3	Derek Jeter/30	180.00
AJ	Andruw Jones/30	40.00
LA	Don Larsen/30	40.00
FL	Fred Lynn/45	25.00
BM	Bill Mazeroski/30	60.00
PM1	Paul Molitor/30	40.00
PM2	Paul Molitor/30	40.00
TO	Tony Oliva/45	30.00
DO	David Ortiz/30	85.00
RO1	Roy Oswalt/45	40.00
RO2	Roy Oswalt/45	40.00
JP1	Jim Palmer/30	40.00
JP2	Jim Palmer/30	40.00
JA	Jake Peavy/45	25.00
TP	Tony Perez/45	40.00
AP	Albert Pujols/15	400.00
CR	Cal Ripken Jr./15	280.00
BN	Brian Roberts/45	30.00
BR1	Brooks Robinson/30	75.00
BR2	Brooks Robinson/30	75.00
FR	Frank Robinson/30	40.00
RS1	Ryne Sandberg/23	100.00
CS	Curt Schilling/15	75.00
TS	Tom Seaver/30	60.00
OS	Ozzie Smith/30	75.00
SM	John Smoltz/30	150.00
AS	Alfonso Soriano/45	30.00
DS	Don Sutton/30	30.00
CU	Chase Utley/45	50.00
BW	Billy Williams/45	25.00
DW1	Dontrelle Willis/30	40.00
DW2	Dontrelle Willis/30	40.00
MW	Maury Wills/45	25.00
WR	David Wright/25	100.00
RZ1	Ryan Zimmerman/30	50.00
RZ2	Ryan Zimmerman/30	50.00

Epic Events
NM/M
Common Player: 2.00
Production 675 Sets

	Player	Price
EE1	Ryan Howard	4.00
EE2	Tadahito Iguchi	2.00
EE3	Paul Konerko	2.00
EE4	Craig Biggio	2.00
EE5	Alex Rodriguez	6.00
EE6	Ichiro Suzuki	5.00
EE7	David Ortiz	4.00
EE8	Miguel Cabrera	3.00
EE9	Dontrelle Willis	2.00
EE10	Mark Teixeira	3.00
EE11	Hideki Matsui	5.00
EE12	Albert Pujols	8.00
EE13	Albert Pujols	8.00
EE14	Greg Maddux	5.00
EE15	Greg Maddux	5.00
EE16	Manny Ramirez	3.00
EE17	Mark Teixeira	3.00
EE18	Alex Rodriguez	6.00
EE19	Manny Ramirez	3.00
EE20	Randy Johnson	3.00
EE21	Jason Varitek	3.00
EE22	Vladimir Guerrero	3.00
EE23	Roger Clemens	8.00
EE24	Manny Ramirez	3.00
EE25	Curt Schilling	3.00
EE26	Johnny Damon	3.00
EE27	David Ortiz	4.00
EE28	David Wright	6.00
EE29	Ichiro Suzuki	5.00
EE30	Ichiro Suzuki	5.00
EE31	Adam Dunn	3.00
EE32	Adrian Beltre	2.00
EE33	Javy Lopez	2.00
EE34	Greg Maddux	3.00
EE35	Randy Johnson	3.00
EE36	Jim Thome	3.00
EE37	Adam Dunn	3.00
EE38	Bobby Abreu	3.00
EE39	Felix Hernandez	3.00
EE40	Greg Maddux	3.00
EE41	Ken Griffey Jr.	6.00
EE42	Randy Johnson	3.00
EE43	Johan Santana	3.00
EE44	Magglio Ordonez	3.00
EE45	Josh Beckett	4.00
EE46	Ivan Rodriguez	3.00
EE47	Alfonso Soriano	3.00
EE48	Eric Gagne	2.00
EE49	Hank Blalock	2.00
EE50	Roger Clemens	8.00
EE51	Derek Jeter	8.00
EE52	Derek Jeter	8.00
EE53	Barry Zito	2.00
EE54	Alex Rodriguez	6.00
EE55	Nomar Garciaparra	3.00
EE56	Torii Hunter	2.00
EE57	Ichiro Suzuki	5.00
EE58	Randy Johnson	3.00
EE59	Ichiro Suzuki	5.00
EE60	Albert Pujols	8.00
EE61	Albert Pujols	8.00
EE62	Ichiro Suzuki	5.00
EE63	Derek Jeter	8.00
EE64	Pedro Martinez	3.00
EE65	Chris Shelton	2.00
EE66	Ivan Rodriguez	3.00
EE67	Chipper Jones	3.00
EE68	Pedro Martinez	3.00
EE69	Ken Griffey Jr.	6.00
EE70	Jeff Bagwell	3.00
EE71	Nomar Garciaparra	3.00
EE72	Mark Prior	3.00
EE73	Kerry Wood	2.00
EE74	Andruw Jones	3.00
EE75	Derek Jeter	8.00
EE76	Cal Ripken Jr.	10.00
EE77	Ken Griffey Jr.	6.00
EE78	Ken Griffey Jr.	6.00
EE79	Mike Piazza	4.00
EE80	Nolan Ryan	6.00
EE81	Greg Maddux	5.00
EE82	Greg Maddux	5.00
EE83	Greg Maddux	8.00
EE84	Ozzie Smith	4.00
EE85	Tom Seaver	4.00
EE86	Thurman Munson	4.00
EE87	Reggie Jackson	3.00
EE88	Johnny Bench	5.00
EE89	Mike Schmidt	5.00
EE90	Carlton Fisk	2.00
EE91	Eddie Mathews	3.00
EE92	Roy Campanella	4.00
EE93	Jackie Robinson	6.00
EE94	Joe DiMaggio	6.00
EE95	Jimmie Foxx	5.00
EE96	Lou Gehrig	10.00
EE97	Babe Ruth	10.00
EE98	Ty Cobb	6.00
EE99	Honus Wagner	5.00
EE100	Cy Young	5.00

Four Barrel
No Pricing
Production One Set

Foursome Fabrics
NM/M
Production 5-50

	Players	Price
CMBF	Carlton Fisk, Thurman Munson, Johnny Bench, Gary Carter/25	70.00
GRSM	Roger Clemens, Nolan Ryan, Juan Marichal, Bob Gibson/30	60.00
MBSP	Albert Pujols, Lou Brock, Stan Musial, Ozzie Smith/30	100.00
PJGG	Ken Griffey Jr., Derek Jeter, Vladimir Guerrero, Albert Pujols/50	100.00
RCJP	Mark Prior, Nolan Ryan, Roger Clemens, Randy Johnson/50	50.00
WRRJ	Pee Wee Reese, Honus Wagner, Cal Ripken Jr., Derek Jeter/20	300.00
WYBS	Ted Williams, Wade Boggs, Curt Schilling, Carl Yastrzemski/50	85.00

Materials
NM/M
Production 10-185
No pricing production 15 or less.

Orange:		.75-1.5X
Production 5-185		
Red:		.75-1.5X
Production 10-185		
Light Purple:		.75-1.5X
Production 4-185		
Dark Purple:		.75-1.5X
Production 3-185		
Blue:		.75-1.5X
Production 3-99		
Teal:		.75-1.5X
Production 5-99		
Green:		1-1.5X
Production 3-75		
Dark Green:		1-2X
Production 3-50		
Grey:		1-2X
Production 3-40		
Gold:		1-1.25X
Production 1-25		
EB	Ernie Banks/155	15.00
JB1	Johnny Bench/155	10.00
JB2	Johnny Bench/155	10.00
WB1	Wade Boggs/185	10.00
WB2	Wade Boggs/185	10.00
LB1	Lou Brock/48	10.00
LB2	Lou Brock/48	10.00
RC1	Roger Clemens/155	20.00
RC2	Roger Clemens/155	20.00
RC3	Roger Clemens/155	20.00
CL1	Roberto Clemente/50	75.00
JD1	Joe DiMaggio/185	65.00
JD2	Joe DiMaggio/173	65.00
JD3	Joe DiMaggio/99	75.00
CF	Carlton Fisk/169	10.00
CF2	Carlton Fisk/185	10.00
WF	Whitey Ford/155	15.00
LG1	Lou Gehrig/15	165.00
LG2	Lou Gehrig/15	165.00
LG3	Lou Gehrig/15	165.00
BG	Bob Gibson/155	10.00
BG2	Bob Gibson/155	15.00
HG	Hank Greenberg/50	40.00
KG1	Ken Griffey Jr./175	15.00
KG2	Ken Griffey Jr./175	15.00
KG3	Ken Griffey Jr./175	15.00
VG	Vladimir Guerrero/145	8.00
VG2	Vladimir Guerrero/145	8.00
GH	Gil Hodges/39	15.00
RH	Rogers Hornsby/50	75.00
RE1	Reggie Jackson/52	12.00
RE2	Reggie Jackson/52	12.00
RE3	Reggie Jackson/52	12.00
DJ1	Derek Jeter/185	25.00
DJ2	Derek Jeter/185	25.00
DJ3	Derek Jeter/185	25.00
RJ1	Randy Johnson/145	10.00
RJ2	Randy Johnson/145	10.00
HK	Harmon Killebrew/155	15.00
JM	Juan Marichal/155	8.00
ED	Eddie Mathews/75	20.00
DM1	Don Mattingly/185	15.00
DM2	Don Mattingly/185	15.00
WM	Willie McCovey/155	15.00
WM2	Willie McCovey/155	15.00
WM3	Willie McCovey/155	15.00
PM1	Paul Molitor/155	10.00
PM2	Paul Molitor/155	10.00
JO	Joe Morgan/145	8.00
JO2	Joe Morgan/155	8.00
TH1	Thurman Munson/35	30.00
TH2	Thurman Munson/35	30.00
EM1	Eddie Murray/185	8.00
EM2	Eddie Murray/165	8.00
EM3	Eddie Murray/185	8.00
SM1	Stan Musial/50	25.00
SM2	Stan Musial/75	25.00
MP1	Mike Piazza/145	12.00
MP2	Mike Piazza/145	12.00
MA	Mark Prior/185	8.00
MA2	Mark Prior/185	8.00
KP1	Kirby Puckett/155	15.00
KP2	Kirby Puckett/155	15.00
AP1	Albert Pujols/185	20.00
AP2	Albert Pujols/185	20.00
AP3	Albert Pujols/185	20.00
PR1	Pee Wee Reese/145	15.00
PR2	Pee Wee Reese/145	15.00
CR1	Cal Ripken Jr./185	25.00
CR2	Cal Ripken Jr./177	25.00
CR3	Cal Ripken Jr./155	25.00
RO	Brooks Robinson/49	15.00
RO2	Brooks Robinson/99	15.00
FR1	Frank Robinson/130	10.00
FR2	Frank Robinson/130	10.00
BR1	Babe Ruth/15	250.00
BR2	Babe Ruth/15	250.00
NR1	Nolan Ryan/155	20.00
NR2	Nolan Ryan/155	20.00
NR3	Nolan Ryan/155	20.00
RS1	Ryne Sandberg/155	15.00
RS2	Ryne Sandberg/155	15.00
RS3	Ryne Sandberg/155	15.00
MS1	Mike Schmidt/185	15.00
MS2	Mike Schmidt/185	15.00
MS3	Mike Schmidt/185	15.00
TS	Tom Seaver/155	15.00
TS2	Tom Seaver/155	15.00
OS1	Ozzie Smith/155	15.00
OS2	Ozzie Smith/155	15.00
HW	Honus Wagner/16	200.00
TW1	Ted Williams/125	50.00
TW2	Ted Williams/125	50.00
CY1	Carl Yastrzemski/185	15.00
CY2	Carl Yastrzemski/185	15.00
CY3	Carl Yastrzemski/185	15.00
RY1	Robin Yount/155	10.00
RY2	Robin Yount/155	10.00

Materials Blue
No Pricing

Materials Dark Green
No Pricing

Materials Dark Purple
No Pricing

Materials Green
No Pricing

Materials Grey
No Pricing

Materials Gold
No Pricing

Materials Light Purple
No Pricing

Materials Orange
No Pricing

Materials Red
No Pricing

Materials Signatures
NM/M
Production Five Sets

Materials Teal
No Pricing

Swatch
NM/M
Common Player: 10.00
Production 50 Sets

	Player	Price
JB	Jason Bay	15.00
EC	Eric Chavez	10.00
RC	Roger Clemens	30.00
CF	Carlton Fisk	15.00
KG1	Ken Griffey Jr.	30.00
KG2	Ken Griffey Jr.	30.00
VG	Vladimir Guerrero	15.00
TG	Tony Gwynn	25.00
DJ1	Derek Jeter	50.00
DJ2	Derek Jeter	50.00
RJ	Randy Johnson	20.00
PM	Pedro J. Martinez	15.00
JM	Joe Morgan	10.00
DO	David Ortiz	25.00
RO	Roy Oswalt	10.00
JP	Jake Peavy	10.00
MP	Mark Prior	10.00
AP	Albert Pujols	40.00
MR	Manny Ramirez	15.00
JR	Jose Reyes	10.00
CR	Cal Ripken Jr.	40.00
IR	Ivan Rodriguez	12.00
SR	Scott Rolen	15.00
JS	Johan Santana	10.00
CS	Curt Schilling	15.00
MT	Mark Teixeira	12.00
MI	Miguel Tejada	10.00
DW	Dontrelle Willis	10.00
CY	Carl Yastrzemski	20.00
RZ	Ryan Zimmerman	20.00

Triple Materials
NM/M
Production 3-99

	Players	Price
BER	Eddie Murray, Brooks Robinson, Johnny Bench/60	35.00
BMR	Brooks Robinson, Wade Boggs, Paul Molitor/99	30.00
BSP	Ryne Sandberg, Ernie Banks, Mark Prior/99	40.00
CDG	Ken Griffey Jr., Ty Cobb, Joe DiMaggio/15	300.00
FJJ	Whitey Ford, Reggie Jackson, Derek Jeter/99	60.00
FMJ	Don Mattingly, Reggie Jackson, Whitey Ford/51	40.00
GJK	Randy Johnson, Roger Clemens, Bob Gibson/99	40.00
GMG	Eddie Murray, Hank Greenberg, Lou Gehrig/25	150.00
GPS	Tom Seaver, Bob Gibson, Mark Prior/99	30.00
GRM	Ken Griffey Jr., Willie McCovey, Frank Robinson/99	40.00
JGK	Vladimir Guerrero, Reggie Jackson, Harmon Killebrew/99	40.00
JKR	Harmon Killebrew, Frank Robinson, Reggie Jackson/99	40.00
JMM	Derek Jeter, Don Mattingly, Thurman Munson/25	125.00
JPG	Albert Pujols, Ken Griffey Jr., Derek Jeter/99	100.00
MBF	Carlton Fisk, Thurman Munson, Johnny Bench/99	40.00
MBG	Ken Griffey Jr., Joe Morgan, Ken Griffey Jr./99	50.00
MBP	Albert Pujols, Lou Brock, Stan Musial/24	90.00
MFM	Carlton Fisk, Eddie Murray, Thurman Munson/99	30.00
MMG	Steve Garvey, Eddie Murray, Don Mattingly/49	40.00
MPS	Tom Seaver, Mike Piazza, Eddie Murray/30	30.00
MSY	Ozzie Smith, Paul Molitor, Robin Yount/49	40.00
RBS	Cal Ripken Jr., Wade Boggs, Mike Schmidt/99	50.00
RCJ	Nolan Ryan, Roger Clemens, Randy Johnson/75	50.00
RJD	Reggie Jackson, Joe DiMaggio, Babe Ruth/99	300.00
RRM	Jackie Robinson, Frank Robinson, Willie McCovey/50	50.00
SMH	Ryne Sandberg, Rogers Hornsby, Joe Morgan/25	80.00
WSR	Honus Wagner, Pee Wee Reese, Ozzie Smith/99	100.00
YRJ	Cal Ripken Jr., Derek Jeter, Robin Yount/99	60.00
YWB	Ted Williams, Wade Boggs, Carl Yastrzemski/25	140.00

Pairings
NM/M
Production 5-99

	Players	Price
BB	Wade Boggs, Brooks Robinson/99	25.00
BM	Johnny Bench, Joe Morgan/99	20.00
BR	Bob Gibson, Nolan Ryan/99	30.00
BS	Lou Brock, Ozzie Smith/99	30.00
BS2	Wade Boggs, Ryne Sandberg/99	25.00
CJ	Roger Clemens, Randy Johnson/99	25.00
CR	Roger Clemens, Nolan Ryan/99	40.00
DG	Joe DiMaggio, Lou Gehrig/25	220.00
FB	Carlton Fisk, Johnny Bench/99	20.00
FP	Carlton Fisk, Mike Piazza/99	20.00
GB	Bob Gibson, Lou Brock/99	25.00
GC	Hank Greenberg, Ty Cobb/25	150.00
GG	Ken Griffey Jr., Vladimir Guerrero/99	40.00
GP	Ken Griffey Jr., Kirby Puckett/99	35.00
GR	Lou Gehrig, Cal Ripken Jr./45	180.00
JD	Derek Jeter, Joe DiMaggio/99	125.00
JG	Derek Jeter, Ken Griffey Jr./99	75.00
JJ	Reggie Jackson, Derek Jeter/99	40.00
JK	Reggie Jackson, Harmon Killebrew/99	30.00
JM	Derek Jeter, Don Mattingly/99	80.00
JS	Reggie Jackson, Mike Schmidt/99	30.00
KP	Harmon Killebrew, Kirby Puckett/99	30.00
MB	Thurman Munson, Johnny Bench/30	40.00
MM	Juan Marichal, Willie McCovey/99	25.00
MM2	Don Mattingly, Thurman Munson/30	75.00
MR	Eddie Mathews, Brooks Robinson/50	50.00
MS	Eddie Mathews, Mike Schmidt/50	40.00
MY	Paul Molitor, Robin Yount/99	25.00
PH	Albert Pujols, Rogers Hornsby/99	75.00
PM	Albert Pujols, Stan Musial/99	60.00
RJ	Pee Wee Reese, Derek Jeter/99	35.00
RM	Cal Ripken Jr., Eddie Murray/99	40.00
RR2	Brooks Robinson, Frank Robinson/99	25.00
RY	Frank Robinson, Carl Yastrzemski/99	40.00
SB	Ryne Sandberg, Ernie Banks/99	40.00
SM	Ryne Sandberg, Joe Morgan/99	30.00
SR	Tom Seaver, Nolan Ryan/99	40.00
SS	Ryne Sandberg, Ozzie Smith/99	35.00
WC	Honus Wagner, Roberto Clemente/25	225.00
WD	Ted Williams, Joe DiMaggio/45	200.00
WM	Ted Williams, Stan Musial/45	75.00
YW	Carl Yastrzemski, Ted Williams/50	100.00

2006 Upper Deck First Pitch
NM/M
Complete Set (220): 35.00
Common Player: .10
Pack (5): 1.50
Box (36): 40.00

#	Player	Price
1	Chad Tracy	.10
2	Conor Jackson RC	.40
3	Craig Counsell	.10
4	Javier Vazquez	.10
5	Luis Gonzalez	.10
6	Shawn Green	.25
7	Troy Glaus	.25
8	Joey Devine RC	.50
9	Andruw Jones	.40
10	Chipper Jones	.25
11	John Smoltz	.25
12	Marcus Giles	.10
13	Jeff Francoeur	.25
14	Tim Hudson	.25
15	Brian Roberts	.10
16	Erik Bedard	.10
17	Javy Lopez	.10
18	Melvin Mora	.10
19	Miguel Tejada	.40
20	Alejandro Freire RC	.25
21	Sammy Sosa	.75
22	Craig Hansen RC	.25
23	Curt Schilling	.50
24	David Ortiz	.50
25	Edgar Renteria	.25
26	Johnny Damon	.50
27	Manny Ramirez	.50
28	Matt Clement	.10
29	Trot Nixon	.25
30	Aramis Ramirez	.25
31	Carlos Zambrano	.25
32	Derek Lee	.50
33	Greg Maddux	.50
34	Jeromy Burnitz	.10
35	Kerry Wood	.25
36	Mark Prior	.40
37	Nomar Garciaparra	.50
38	Aaron Rowand	.25
39	Chris Demaria RC	.25
40	Jon Garland	.25
41	Mark Buehrle	.25

#	Player	Price
42	Paul Konerko	.25
43	Scott Podsednik	.25
44	Tadahito Iguchi	.25
45	Adam Dunn	.40
46	Austin Kearns	.10
47	Felipe Lopez	.10
48	Ken Griffey Jr.	1.00
49	Ryan Freel	.10
50	Sean Casey	.10
51	Wily Mo Pena	.10
52	C.C. Sabathia	.10
53	Cliff Lee	.10
54	Coco Crisp	.10
55	Grady Sizemore	.25
56	Jake Westbrook	.10
57	Travis Hafner	.25
58	Victor Martinez	.25
59	Aaron Miles	.10
60	Clint Barmes	.10
61	Garrett Atkins	.10
62	Jeff Baker	.10
63	Jeff Francis	.10
64	Matt Holliday	.25
65	Todd Helton	.40
66	Carlos Guillen	.10
67	Chris Shelton	.10
68	Dmitri Young	.10
69	Ivan Rodriguez	.40
70	Jeremy Bonderman	.10
71	Magglio Ordonez	.25
72	Placido Polanco	.10
73	A.J. Burnett	.10
74	Carlos Delgado	.40
75	Dontrelle Willis	.25
76	Josh Beckett	.25
77	Juan Pierre	.10
78	Ryan Jorgensen RC	.50
79	Miguel Cabrera	.10
80	Robert Andino RC	.50
81	Andy Pettitte	.25
82	Brad Lidge	.10
83	Craig Biggio	.25
84	Jeff Bagwell	.40
85	Lance Berkman	.25
86	Morgan Ensberg	.25
87	Roger Clemens	1.00
88	Roy Oswalt	.25
89	Angel Berroa	.10
90	David DeJesus	.10
91	Steve Stemle RC	.50
92	Jonah Bayliss RC	.50
93	Mike Sweeney	.10
94	Ryan Theriot RC	1.00
95	Zack Greinke	.10
96	Brad Penny	.10
97	Cesar Izturis	.10
98	Brian Myrow RC	.50
99	Eric Gagne	.25
100	J.D. Drew	.10
101	Jeff Kent	.25
102	Milton Bradley	.10
103	Odalis Perez	.10
104	Ben Sheets	.25
105	Brady Clark	.10
106	Carlos Lee	.25
107	Geoff Jenkins	.10
108	Lyle Overbay	.10
109	Prince Fielder RC	2.50
110	Rickie Weeks	.25
111	Jacque Jones	.10
112	Joe Mauer	.25
113	Joe Nathan	.10
114	Johan Santana	.50
115	Justin Morneau	.20
116	Chris Heintz RC	.50
117	Torii Hunter	.25
118	Carlos Beltran	.40
119	Cliff Floyd	.10
120	David Wright	.75
121	Jose Reyes	.40
122	Mike Cameron	.10
123	Mike Piazza	.50
124	Pedro Martinez	.50
125	Tom Glavine	.25
126	Alex Rodriguez	1.50
127	Derek Jeter	1.50
128	Gary Sheffield	.40
129	Hideki Matsui	.75
130	Jason Giambi	.25
131	Jorge Posada	.25
132	Mariano Rivera	.25
133	Mike Mussina	.25
134	Randy Johnson	.50
135	Barry Zito	.25
136	Bobby Crosby	.10
137	Danny Haren	.10
138	Eric Chavez	.25
139	Huston Street	.10
140	Ron Flores RC	.50
141	Nick Swisher	.10
142	Rich Harden	.25
143	Bobby Abreu	.25
144	Danny Sandoval RC	.50
145	Chase Utley	.25
146	Jim Thome	.40
147	Jimmy Rollins	.25
148	Pat Burrell	.25
149	Ryan Howard	.50
150	Craig Wilson	.10
151	Jack Wilson	.10
152	Jason Bay	.25
153	Matt Lawton	.10
154	Oliver Perez	.10
155	Robert Mackowiak	.10
156	Zachary Duke	.10
157	Brian Giles	.25
158	Jake Peavy	.25
159	Craig Breslow RC	.50
160	Khalil Greene	.10
161	Mark Loretta	.10
162	Ryan Klesko	.10
163	Trevor Hoffman	.10
164	J.T. Snow	.10
165	Jason Schmidt	.25
166	Marquis Grissom	.10
167	Moises Alou	.25
168	Omar Vizquel	.10
169	Pedro Feliz	.10
170	Jeremy Accardo RC	.50
171	Adrian Beltre	.25
172	Ichiro Suzuki	1.00
173	Felix Hernandez	.50
174	Jeff Harris RC	.25
175	Randy Winn	.10
176	Raul Ibanez	.10
177	Richie Sexson	.25
178	Albert Pujols	1.50
179	Chris Carpenter	.25
180	David Eckstein	.10
181	Jim Edmonds	.25
182	Larry Walker	.25
183	Matt Morris	.10
184	Reggie Sanders	.10
185	Scott Rolen	.40
186	Aubrey Huff	.10
187	Jonny Gomes	.10
188	Carl Crawford	.25
189	Tim Corcoran RC	.50
190	Julio Lugo	.10
191	Rocco Baldelli	.10
192	Scott Kazmir	.10
193	Alfonso Soriano	.40
194	Hank Blalock	.25
195	Kenny Rogers	.10
196	Scott Feldman RC	1.00
197	Laynce Nix	.10
198	Mark Teixeira	.50
199	Michael Young	.10
200	Aaron Hill	.10
201	Alex Rios	.10
202	Eric Hinske	.10
203	Gustavo Chacin	.10
204	Roy Halladay	.25
205	Shea Hillenbrand	.10
206	Vernon Wells	.25
207	Brad Wilkerson	.10
208	Chad Cordero	.10
209	Jose Guillen	.10
210	Jose Vidro	.10
211	Livan Hernandez	.10
212	Preston Wilson	.10
213	Jason Bergmann RC	.50
214	Bartolo Colon	.25
215	Chone Figgins	.10
216	Darin Erstad	.25
217	Francisco Rodriguez	.10
218	Garret Anderson	.25
219	Steve Finley	.10
220	Vladimir Guerrero	.50

Diamond Stars

NM/M
Complete Set (35): 30.00
Common Player: .50
Inserted 1:3

#	Player	Price
1	Luis Gonzalez	.50
2	Andruw Jones	1.00
3	John Smoltz	.75
4	Miguel Tejada	1.00
5	Johnny Damon	1.50
6	Manny Ramirez	1.50
7	Derek Lee	1.50
8	Mark Prior	1.00
9	Mark Buehrle	.50
10	Ken Griffey Jr.	3.00
11	Travis Hafner	.75
12	Todd Helton	1.00
13	Ivan Rodriguez	.75
14	Miguel Cabrera	1.50
15	Roger Clemens	4.00
16	Mike Sweeney	.50
17	Jeff Kent	.75
18	Carlos Lee	.50
19	Johan Santana	1.50
20	Torii Hunter	.50
21	Pedro Martinez	1.50
22	Alex Rodriguez	4.00
23	Derek Jeter	4.00
24	Eric Chavez	.75
25	Bobby Abreu	.75
26	Jason Bay	.75
27	Jake Peavy	.75
28	Moises Alou	.50
29	Ichiro Suzuki	3.00
30	Albert Pujols	4.00
31	Carl Crawford	.75
32	Mark Teixeira	1.50
33	Roy Halladay	.50
34	Jose Guillen	.50
35	Vladimir Guerrero	1.50

Goin' Deep

NM/M
Complete Set (35): 20.00
Common Player: .50
Inserted 1:3

#	Player	Price
1	Adam Dunn	1.00
2	Albert Pujols	4.00
3	Alex Rodriguez	4.00
4	Alfonso Soriano	1.00
5	Andruw Jones	1.00
6	Aramis Ramirez	.75
7	Bobby Abreu	.75
8	Brian Giles	.75
9	Carlos Delgado	.75
10	Carlos Lee	.50
11	Chipper Jones	1.50
12	David Ortiz	1.50
13	David Wright	2.00
14	Derrek Lee	1.00
15	Eric Chavez	.50
16	Gary Sheffield	.75
17	Hideki Matsui	2.50
18	Jeff Kent	.75
19	Jim Edmonds	.75
20	Ken Griffey Jr.	3.00
21	Luis Gonzalez	.50
22	Manny Ramirez	1.50
23	Mark Teixeira	1.00
24	Miguel Cabrera	1.50
25	Miguel Tejada	.50
26	Moises Alou	.50
27	Pat Burrell	.75
28	Paul Konerko	.75
29	Rafael Palmeiro	.75
30	Richie Sexson	.75
31	Todd Helton	1.00
32	Torii Hunter	.50
33	Travis Hafner	.75
34	Vernon Wells	.50
35	Vladimir Guerrero	1.50

Hot Stove Headlines

NM/M
Complete Set (20): 15.00
Common Player: .50
Inserted 1:3

#	Player	Price
1	Alex Rodriguez	3.00
2	Carlos Beltran	.75
3	Carlos Delgado	.50
4	Curt Schilling	1.00
5	Derrek Lee	.75
6	Greg Maddux	2.00
7	Hideki Matsui	2.00
8	Ichiro Suzuki	3.00
9	Ivan Rodriguez	.50
10	Jim Thome	.50
11	Johnny Damon	1.00
12	Ken Griffey Jr.	2.00
13	Manny Ramirez	1.00
14	Miguel Tejada	.75
15	Nomar Garciaparra	.75
16	Pedro Martinez	1.00
17	Randy Johnson	1.00
18	Roger Clemens	3.00
19	Scott Rolen	.75
20	Vladimir Guerrero	1.00

Signature Stars

NM/M
Common Player:

#	Player	Price
DR	J.D. Drew	15.00
JE	Johnny Estrada	10.00
RH	Rich Harden	15.00
PL	Paul LoDuca	15.00
VM	Victor Martinez	15.00
YM	Yadier Molina	10.00
GQ	Guillermo Quiroz	10.00
RI	Juan Rivera	10.00
IS	Ian Snell	15.00
RW	Ryan Wagner	10.00

2006 Upper Deck Frito Lay

NM/M
Complete Set (30): 25.00
Common Player: 1.00

#	Player	Price
1	Luis Gonzalez	1.00
2	Miguel Tejada	1.50
3	Chipper Jones	2.00
4	David Ortiz	2.00
5	Mark Prior	1.00
6	Paul Konerko	1.00
7	Ken Griffey Jr.	3.00
8	Travis Hafner	1.00
9	Todd Helton	1.00
10	Ivan Rodriguez	1.50
11	Dontrelle Willis	1.00
12	Mike Sweeney	1.00
13	Lance Berkman	1.00
14	Vladimir Guerrero	2.00
15	Jeff Kent	1.00
16	Ben Sheets	1.00
17	Torii Hunter	1.00
18	Pedro Martinez	1.50
19	Alex Rodriguez	4.00
20	Bobby Abreu	1.00
21	Eric Chavez	.75
22	Jason Bay	1.00
23	Ichiro Suzuki	2.50
24	Jake Peavy	1.50
25	Carl Crawford	1.00
26	Omar Vizquel	1.00
27	Mark Teixeira	2.00
28	Albert Pujols	4.00
29	Roy Halladay	1.00
30	Ryan Zimmerman	1.50

2006 Upper Deck Future Stars

NM/M
Complete Set (159):
Common Player (1-75): .25
Common Autograph (76-159): 5.00
Some SP Auto's not priced yet.
Pack (4): 4.00
Box (24): 80.00

#	Player	Price
1	Miguel Tejada	.75
2	Brian Roberts	.50
3	Brandon Webb	.50
4	Luis Gonzalez	.50
5	Andruw Jones	.75
6	Chipper Jones	1.00
7	John Smoltz	.75
8	Curt Schilling	1.00
9	Josh Beckett	1.00
10	David Ortiz	1.00
11	Manny Ramirez	1.00
12	Jim Thome	.75
13	Paul Konerko	.75
14	Jermaine Dye	.25
15	Derrek Lee	.75
16	Greg Maddux	2.00
17	Ken Griffey Jr.	2.00
18	Adam Dunn	.75
19	Felipe Lopez	.25
20	Travis Hafner	.50
21	Victor Martinez	.50
22	Grady Sizemore	.75
23	Todd Helton	.75
24	Matt Holliday	.75
25	Jeremy Bonderman	.25
26	Ivan Rodriguez	.75
27	Miguel Cabrera	1.00
28	Dontrelle Willis	.75
29	Roger Clemens	2.00
30	Roy Oswalt	.50
31	Lance Berkman	.75
32	Reggie Sanders	.25
33	Vladimir Guerrero	1.00
34	Chone Figgins	.50
35	Jeff Kent	.75
36	Eric Gagne	.25
37	Carlos Lee	.25
38	Rickie Weeks	.50
39	Johan Santana	1.00
40	Torii Hunter	.50
41	Alex Rodriguez	2.50
42	Derek Jeter	2.50
43	Randy Johnson	.75
44	Hideki Matsui	1.50
45	Johnny Damon	1.00
46	Pedro Martinez	1.00
47	David Wright	2.00
48	Carlos Beltran	.75
49	Rich Harden	.25
50	Eric Chavez	.25
51	Huston Street	.25
52	Ryan Howard	2.00
53	Bobby Abreu	.75
54	Chase Utley	1.00
55	Jason Bay	.75
56	Jake Peavy	.75
57	Brian Giles	.25
58	Trevor Hoffman	.25
59	Jason Schmidt	.25
60	Randy Winn	.25
61	Kenji Johjima RC	.75
62	Ichiro Suzuki	1.50
63	Felix Hernandez	.75
64	Albert Pujols	2.50
65	Chris Carpenter	.75
66	Jim Edmonds	.25
67	Carl Crawford	.50
68	Scott Kazmir	.50
69	Jonny Gomes	.25
70	Mark Teixeira	.75
71	Michael Young	.50
72	Vernon Wells	.50
73	Roy Halladay	.50
74	Nick Johnson	.25
75	Alfonso Soriano	.75
76	Adam Wainwright RC	25.00
77	Anderson Hernandez RC	5.00
78	Andre Ethier/SP RC	30.00
79	Colter Bean/SP RC	10.00
80	Ben Johnson RC	5.00
81	Boof Bonser/SP RC	8.00
82	Boone Logan RC	8.00
83	Brian Anderson RC	8.00
84	Brian Bannister RC	8.00
85	Chris Denorfia/SP RC	8.00
86	Chad Billingsley/SP RC	20.00
87	Cody Ross RC	5.00
88	Cole Hamels/SP RC	40.00
89	Conor Jackson RC	12.00
90	Dave Gassner/SP RC	8.00
91	Jordan Tata RC	10.00
92	Eric Reed RC	8.00
93	Fausto Carmona RC	12.00
94	Luis Figueroa/SP RC	8.00
95	Francisco Liriano/SP RC	20.00
96	Freddie Bynum RC	5.00
97	Hanley Ramirez/SP RC	8.00
98	Hong-Chih Kuo/SP RC	30.00
99	Ian Kinsler RC	20.00
100	Nelson Cruz/SP RC	20.00
101	Ruddy Lugo RC	5.00
102	Jason Kubel RC	12.00
103	Jeff Harris RC	5.00
104	Santiago Ramirez RC	5.00
105	Jered Weaver/SP RC	40.00
106	Jeremy Accardo/SP RC	8.00
107	Jeremy Hermida/SP RC	10.00
108	Joel Zumaya/SP RC	8.00
109	Joey Devine RC	8.00
110	John Koronka RC	5.00
111	Jonathan Papelbon RC	15.00
112	Jose Capellan RC	5.00
113	Josh Johnson RC	15.00
114	Josh Rupe/SP RC	10.00
115	Josh Willingham/SP RC	12.00
117	Josh Wilson RC	8.00
119	Kelly Shoppach RC	8.00
120	Kendry Morales RC	15.00
121	Sean Tracey RC	5.00
122	Macay McBride RC	5.00
123	Martin Prado/SP RC	8.00
124	Matt Cain RC	20.00
125	Russell Martin RC	12.00
126	Tim Hamulack/SP RC	8.00
127	Mike Jacobs RC	10.00
128	Ben Hendrickson RC	5.00
129	Jack Taschner RC	5.00
130	Nate McLouth RC	5.00
131	Jeremy Sowers/SP RC	15.00
132	Paul Maholm RC	5.00
134	Jason Bergmann RC	8.00
135	Rich Hill/SP RC	10.00
137	Scott Dunn RC	5.00
138	Ryan Zimmerman RC	40.00
139	Anibal Sanchez RC	10.00
140	Sean Marshall RC	10.00
141	Takashi Saito/SP RC	15.00
142	Taylor Buchholz RC	10.00
143	Carlos Quentin/SP RC	15.00
144	Matt Garza RC	15.00
145	Wilbert Nieves RC	8.00
146	Jamie Shields RC	15.00
147	Jon Lester/SP RC	40.00
149	Aaron Rakers RC	5.00
150	Bobby Livingston RC	8.00
151	Brendan Harris RC	5.00
152	Alay Soler/SP RC	8.00
153	Chris Britton RC	8.00
154	Howie Kendrick/SP RC	25.00
155	Jermaine Van Buren RC	8.00
156	Choo Freeman/SP RC	8.00
157	Matt Capps RC	12.00
158	Peter Moylan RC	5.00
159	Ty Taubenheim RC	8.00

Black
Black (1-75): 8-15X
Production 50 Sets

Blue
Blue (1-75): 4-8X
Production 99 Sets

Gold
Gold (1-75): 15-25X
Production 25 Sets

Green
Green (1-75): 2-4X
Production 499 Sets

Purple
Purple (1-75): 1-2X
Production 1,799 Sets

Red
Red (1-75): 3-5X
Production 299 Sets

Rookie Signatures Red Ink
Red Ink (76-159): 1.5-2X
Production 35 Sets

Future Stars

NM/M
Common Player: 1.00
Black: 8-15X
Production 50 Sets
Blue: 4-8X
Production 99 Sets
Gold: 15-25X
Production 25 Sets
Green: 2-4X
Production 499 Sets
Purple: 1-2X
Production 1,799 Sets
Red: 3-5X
Production 299 Sets

#	Player	Price
1	Adam Loewen	1.00
2	Nan Wang	2.00
3	Yi Feng	1.50
4	Chien-Ming Chang	2.00
5	Yung-Chi Chen	1.00
6	Chin-Lung Hu	1.50
7	Yadel Marti	1.00
8	Frederich Cepeda	1.00
9	Pedro Luis Lazo	1.00
10	Joey Devine	8.00
11	Osmany Urrutia	1.00
12	Yoandy Garlobo	1.00
13	Nobuhiko Matsunaka	1.00
14	Daisuke Matsuzaka	5.00
15	Tsuyoshi Nishioka	2.00
16	Tomoya Satozaki	1.00
17	Koji Uehara	1.00
17	Shunsuke Watanabe	2.00
18	Jong Beom Lee	1.00
19	Sidney de Jong	1.00
20	Shairon Martis	1.00
21	Len Pecota	1.00
22	Dicky Gonzalez	1.00
23	Nicholas Dempsey	1.00
24	Jason Kubel	1.00
25	Chase Utley	2.00

Clear Patch to History Triple Sign

NM/M

#	Players	Price
BSJ	Andruw Jones, Alfonso Soriano, Jason Bay	40.00
CPO	Chris Carpenter, Roy Oswalt, Jake Peavy	30.00
CUK	Carl Crawford, Scott Kazmir, B.J. Upton	30.00
DRR	Jose Reyes, Stephen Drew, Hanley Ramirez	50.00
GEH	Andre Ethier, Jeremy Hermida, Tony Gwynn Jr.	40.00
JVW	Josh Johnson, Justin Verlander, Jered Weaver	50.00
KTZ	Ryan Zimmerman, Howie Kendrick, Troy Tulowitzki	40.00
MKW	Kendry Morales, Howie Kendrick, Jered Weaver	40.00
MML	Justin Morneau, Joe Mauer, Francisco Liriano	75.00
MOH	Travis Hafner, Justin Morneau, Lyle Overbay	40.00
NHP	Trevor Hoffman, Joe Nathan, Jonathan Papelbon	30.00
PSO	Ben Sheets, Roy Oswalt, Jake Peavy	40.00
PVW	Justin Verlander, Jonathan Papelbon, Jered Weaver	50.00
SBH	Chad Billingsley, Alay Soler, Cole Hamels	40.00
SHL	Francisco Liriano, Jeremy Sowers, Cole Hamels	40.00
TZU	Ryan Zimmerman, B.J. Upton, Troy Tulowitzki	50.00
URB	Craig Biggio, Brian Roberts, Chase Utley	50.00
VBZ	Jeremy Bonderman, Justin Verlander, Joel Zumaya	50.00

2006 Upper Deck Ovation

NM/M
Complete Set (126):
Common (1-84): .25
Common SP (85-126): 5.00
Production 999
Pack (5): 3.00
Box (18): 40.00

#	Player	Price
1	Vladimir Guerrero	.75
2	Bartolo Colon	.25
3	Chone Figgins	.40
4	Lance Berkman	.40
5	Roy Oswalt	.40
6	Craig Biggio	.40
7	Rich Harden	.25
8	Eric Chavez	.25
9	Huston Street	.25
10	Vernon Wells	.40
11	Roy Halladay	.40
12	Troy Glaus	.40
13	Andruw Jones	.40
14	Chipper Jones	.75
15	John Smoltz	.40
16	Carlos Lee	.40
17	Rickie Weeks	.40
18	J.J. Hardy	.25
19	Albert Pujols	2.00
20	Chris Carpenter	.50
21	Scott Rolen	.50
22	Derrek Lee	.50
23	Mark Prior	.50
24	Aramis Ramirez	.40
25	Carl Crawford	.40
26	Scott Kazmir	.40
27	Luis Gonzalez	.50
28	Brandon Webb	.50
29	Chad Tracy	.40
30	Jeff Kent	.40
31	J.D. Drew	.40
32	Jason Schmidt	.40
33	Randy Winn	.40
34	Travis Hafner	.50
35	Victor Martinez	.40
36	Grady Sizemore	.40
37	Ichiro Suzuki	1.50
38	Felix Hernandez	.75
39	Adrian Beltre	.40
40	Miguel Cabrera	.75
41	Dontrelle Willis	.25
42	David Wright	1.50
43	Jose Reyes	.75
44	Pedro Martinez	.75
45	Carlos Beltran	.50
46	Alfonso Soriano	.75
47	Livan Hernandez	.25
48	Jose Guillen	.25
49	Miguel Tejada	.50

50	Brian Roberts	.40
51	Melvin Mora	.25
52	Jake Peavy	.40
53	Brian Giles	.25
54	Khalil Greene	.25
55	Bobby Abreu	.40
56	Ryan Howard	1.00
57	Chase Utley	.75
58	Jason Bay	.40
59	Sean Casey	.25
60	Mark Teixeira	.50
61	Michael Young	.40
62	Hank Blalock	.40
63	Manny Ramirez	.75
64	David Ortiz	.75
65	Josh Beckett	.75
66	Jason Varitek	.50
67	Ken Griffey Jr.	1.50
68	Adam Dunn	.50
69	Todd Helton	.50
70	Garrett Atkins	.40
71	Reggie Sanders	.25
72	Mike Sweeney	.25
73	Chris Shelton	.25
74	Ivan Rodriguez	.50
75	Johan Santana	.75
76	Torii Hunter	.40
77	Justin Morneau	.50
78	Jim Thome	.50
79	Paul Konerko	.40
80	Scott Podsednik	.25
81	Derek Jeter	2.00
82	Hideki Matsui	1.50
83	Johnny Damon	.75
84	Alex Rodriguez	2.00
85	Conor Jackson RC	8.00
86	Joey Devine RC	5.00
87	Jonathan Papelbon RC	8.00
88	Freddie Bynum RC	5.00
89	Chris Denorfia RC	5.00
90	Ryan Shealy RC	5.00
91	Josh Wilson RC	5.00
92	Brian Anderson RC	5.00
93	Justin Verlander RC	15.00
94	Jeremy Hermida RC	5.00
95	Mike Jacobs RC	8.00
96	Josh Johnson RC	8.00
97	Hanley Ramirez RC	15.00
98	Josh Willingham RC	8.00
99	Cole Hamels RC	12.00
100	Hong-Chih Kuo RC	10.00
101	Cody Ross RC	5.00
102	Jose Capellan RC	5.00
103	Prince Fielder RC	10.00
104	Dave Gassner RC	5.00
105	Jason Kubel RC	8.00
106	Francisco Liriano RC	10.00
107	Anderson Hernandez RC	5.00
108	Boof Bonser RC	5.00
109	Jered Weaver RC	10.00
110	Ben Johnson RC	5.00
111	Jeff Harris RC	5.00
112	Stephen Drew RC	10.00
113	Matt Cain RC	8.00
114	Skip Schumaker RC	5.00
115	Adam Wainwright RC	12.00
116	Jeremy Sowers RC	5.00
117	Jason Bergmann RC	5.00
118	Chad Billingsley RC	10.00
119	Ryan Zimmerman RC	10.00
120	Macay McBride RC	5.00
121	Aaron Rakers RC	5.00
122	Alay Soler RC	8.00
123	Melky Cabrera RC	8.00
124	Tim Hamulack RC	5.00
125	Andre Ethier RC	15.00
126	Kenji Johjima RC	6.00

Gold

Gold (1-84): 4-8X
Production 499 Sets

Gold Autographs

NM/M
Production 99 Sets

85	Conor Jackson	15.00
86	Joey Devine	15.00
87	Jonathan Papelbon	30.00
88	Freddie Bynum	15.00
89	Chris Denorfia	10.00
90	Ryan Shealy	10.00
92	Brian Anderson	10.00
93	Justin Verlander	50.00
94	Jeremy Hermida	15.00
95	Mike Jacobs	15.00
96	Josh Johnson	15.00
97	Hanley Ramirez	40.00
98	Josh Willingham	15.00
99	Cole Hamels	50.00
100	Cody Ross	20.00
101	Jose Capellan	15.00
104	Dave Gassner	10.00
105	Jason Kubel	15.00
106	Francisco Liriano	35.00
107	Anderson Hernandez	10.00
108	Boof Bonser	10.00
109	Jered Weaver	40.00
110	Ben Johnson	10.00
111	Jeff Harris	10.00
112	Stephen Drew	25.00
113	Matt Cain	20.00
114	Skip Schumaker	15.00
115	Adam Wainwright	25.00
116	Jeremy Sowers	10.00
117	Jason Bergmann	10.00
118	Chad Billingsley	10.00
119	Ryan Zimmerman	50.00
120	Macay McBride	10.00
121	Aaron Rakers	10.00
122	Alay Soler	10.00
123	Melky Cabrera	15.00
124	Tim Hamulack	10.00
125	Andre Ethier	40.00

Apparel

NM/M
Common Player: 4.00

BA	Jason Bay	6.00
LB	Lance Berkman	4.00
JB	Jeremy Bonderman	4.00
AJ	A.J. Burnett	4.00
EC	Eric Chavez	4.00
CC	Carl Crawford	6.00
JE	Jim Edmonds	4.00
PF	Prince Fielder	10.00
CF	Chone Figgins	4.00
JF	Jeff Francoeur	4.00
JG	Jonny Gomes	4.00
KG	Khalil Greene	4.00
GR	Ken Griffey Jr.	20.00
VG	Vladimir Guerrero	8.00
HA	Travis Hafner	4.00
JH	J.J. Hardy	4.00
HE	Todd Helton	6.00
FH	Felix Hernandez	8.00
TH	Trevor Hoffman	4.00
RH	Ryan Howard	20.00
HU	Torii Hunter	4.00
DJ	Derek Jeter	25.00
JK	Jeff Kent	4.00
KR	Ryan Klesko	4.00
CL	Carlos Lee	4.00
VM	Victor Martinez	6.00
JM	Joe Mauer	10.00
TN	Trot Nixon	4.00
DO	David Ortiz	8.00
RO	Roy Oswalt	6.00
AO	Akinori Otsuka	4.00
MP	Mark Prior	4.00
AP	Albert Pujols	25.00
MR	Manny Ramirez	8.00
SR	Scott Rolen	6.00
CS	Chris Shelton	4.00
GS	Grady Sizemore	8.00
HS	Huston Street	6.00
MT	Mark Teixeira	8.00
VW	Vernon Wells	400
DW	David Wright	10.00
RZ	Ryan Zimmerman/SP	15.00

Center Stage

NM/M
Common Player: 1.00

JB	Josh Beckett	3.00
DC	Daniel Cabrera	1.00
CA	Miguel Cabrera	3.00
JC	Jose Contreras	1.00
AC	Aaron Cook	1.00
BC	Bobby Crosby	1.00
MC	Michael Cuddyer	1.00
DD	David DeJesus	1.00
SD	Stephen Drew	2.00
JF	Jason Frasor	1.00
KG	Ken Griffey Jr.	5.00
VG	Vladimir Guerrero	3.00
FH	Felix Hernandez	2.00
RH	Runelvys Hernandez	1.00
DJ	Derek Jeter	8.00
DL	Derrek Lee	2.00
YM	Yadier Molina	1.00
MP	Mark Prior	2.00
AP	Albert Pujols	8.00
FS	Freddy Sanchez	1.00
CS	Chris Shelton	1.00
IS	Ian Snell	1.00
MT	Mark Teixeira	2.00
CW	Chien-Ming Wang	10.00
DW	David Wright	4.00

Center Stage Signatures

No Pricing
Production 25 Sets

Curtain Calls

NM/M
Common Player: 1.00

DC	Daniel Cabrera	1.00
EC	Eric Chavez	1.00
JC	Jose Contreras	1.00
BC	Bobby Crosby	1.00
DD	David DeJesus	1.00
KG1	Ken Griffey Jr.	4.00
KG2	Ken Griffey Jr.	4.00
RH	Rich Harden	1.00
RH	Runelvys Hernandez	1.00
YM	Yadier Molina	1.00
TO	Tomokazu Ohka	1.00
MP	Mark Prior	2.00
HR	Horacio Ramirez	1.00
FS	Freddy Sanchez	1.00
CS	Chris Shelton	1.00
MT	Miguel Tejada	2.00
CW	Chien-Ming Wang	10.00
JE	Jered Weaver	2.00
JW	Josh Willingham	1.00
MY	Michael Young	1.00

Curtain Calls Signatures

No Pricing
Production 25 Sets

Ovation Nation

NM/M
Common Player: 2.00

JB	Jason Bay	3.00
DC	Daniel Cabrera	2.00
MC	Miguel Cabrera	4.00
FC	Frederich Cepeda	2.00
YG	Yoandy Garlobo	2.00
KG	Ken Griffey Jr.	8.00
DJ	Derek Jeter	8.00
AJ	Andruw Jones	3.00
SL	Seung-Yeop Lee	4.00
DM	Daisuke Matsuzaka	15.00
NM	Nobuhiko Matsunaka	4.00
AP	Albert Pujols	8.00
JS	Johan Santana	3.00
JA	Jae Weong Seo	2.00
MT	Miguel Tejada	3.00

Ovation Nation Signatures

No Pricing
Production 25 Sets

Spotlight Signatures

NM/M
Common Autograph: 10.00

JB	Josh Beckett/SP	40.00
DC	Daniel Cabrera	15.00
CA	Miguel Cabrera	25.00
SC	Shawn Camp	8.00
EC	Eric Chavez/SP	15.00
JC	Jose Contreras	15.00
AC	Aaron Cook	6.00
LC	Lance Cormier	8.00
BC	Bobby Crosby	10.00
MC	Michael Cuddyer/SP	15.00
DD	David DeJesus	15.00
JD	Jorge De La Rosa	8.00
JF	Jason Frasor	15.00
FG	Franklyn German	8.00
MG	Mike Gonzalez	10.00
AG	Andy Green	6.00
KG1	Ken Griffey Jr.	75.00
KG2	Ken Griffey Jr.	75.00
HA	Rich Harden/SP	15.00
RH	Runelvys Hernandez	10.00
EJ	Edwin Jackson	15.00
YM	Yadier Molina	15.00
FN	Fernando Nieve	15.00
TO	Tomokazu Ohka	20.00
MP	Mark Prior	20.00
RH	Horacio Ramirez/SP	15.00
DR	David Ross	15.00
KS	Kirk Saarloos	10.00
FS	Freddy Sanchez	20.00
CS1	Chris Shelton	10.00
CS2	Chris Shelton	10.00
TE	Miguel Tejada/SP	20.00
MT	Matt Thornton	10.00
TR	Matt Treanor	10.00
RW	Ryan Wagner	10.00
CW	Chien-Ming Wang	100.00
JW	Josh Willingham/SP	15.00
MW	Mike Wuertz	10.00
MY	Michael Young	15.00

Superstar Theatre

NM/M
Common Player: 1.00

BA	Jason Bay	2.00
JB	Josh Beckett	1.00
DC	Daniel Cabrera	1.00
MC	Miguel Cabrera	3.00
CC	Chris Carpenter	2.00
JC	Jose Contreras	1.00
BC	Bobby Crosby	1.00
DD	David DeJesus	1.00
KG1	Ken Griffey Jr.	6.00
KG2	Ken Griffey Jr.	6.00
TH	Travis Hafner	2.00
RH	Rich Harden	1.00
DJ	Derek Jeter	8.00
AJ	Andruw Jones	2.00
DL	Derrek Lee	3.00
PM	Pedro Martinez	3.00
HM	Hideki Matsui	4.00
YM	Yadier Molina	1.00
TO	Tomokazu Ohka	1.00
DO	David Ortiz	3.00
MP	Mark Prior	2.00
AP	Albert Pujols	8.00
MR	Manny Ramirez	3.00
AR	Alex Rodriguez	6.00
CS	Chris Shelton	1.00
IS	Ichiro Suzuki	6.00
TE	Mark Teixeira	2.00
MT	Miguel Tejada	2.00
CW	Chien-Ming Wang	10.00
MY	Michael Young	2.00

Superstar Theatre Signatures

No Pricing
Production 25 Sets

2006 Upper Deck Special FX

NM/M
Complete Set (1025):
Common Player: .25
Common RC (901-1025): .50
Pack (4): 5.00
Box (16): 75.00

1	Adam Kennedy	.25
2	Bartolo Colon	.25
3	Bengie Molina	.25
4	Casey Kotchman	.25
5	Chone Figgins	.50
6	Dallas McPherson	.25
7	Darin Erstad	.25
8	Ervin Santana	.50
9	Francisco Rodriguez	.25
10	Garret Anderson	.25
11	Jarrod Washburn	.25
12	John Lackey	.50
13	Juan Rivera	.25
14	Orlando Cabrera	.50
15	Paul Byrd	.25
16	Steve Finley	.25
17	Vladimir Guerrero	1.00
18	Alex Cintron	.25
19	Brandon Lyon	.25
20	Brandon Webb	.75
21	Chad Tracy	.25
22	Chris Snyder	.25
23	Claudio Vargas	.25
24	Conor Jackson	.50
25	Craig Counsell	.25
26	Javier Vazquez	.25
27	Jose Valverde	.25
28	Luis Gonzalez	.25
29	Royce Clayton	.25
30	Russ Ortiz	.25
31	Shawn Green	.25
32	Dustin Nippert	.25
33	Tony Clark	.25
34	Troy Glaus	.50
35	Adam LaRoche	.25
36	Andruw Jones	.50
37	Craig Hansen	.25
38	Chipper Jones	1.00
39	Horacio Ramirez	.25
40	Jeff Francoeur	.75
41	John Smoltz	.75
42	Joey Devine	.25
43	Johnny Estrada	.25
44	Anthony Lerew	.25
45	Julio Franco	.25
46	Kyle Farnsworth	.25
47	Marcus Giles	.25
48	Mike Hampton	.25
49	Rafael Furcal	.50
50	Chuck James	.25
51	Tim Hudson	.50
52	B.J. Ryan	.25
53	Bernie Castro	.25
54	Brian Roberts	.50
55	Walter Young	.25
56	Daniel Cabrera	.25
57	Eric Byrnes	.25
58	Alejandro Freire	.25
59	Erik Bedard	.50
60	Javy Lopez	.25
61	Jay Gibbons	.25
62	Jorge Julio	.25
63	Luis Matos	.25
64	Melvin Mora	.25
65	Miguel Tejada	.75
66	Rafael Palmeiro	.25
67	Rodrigo Lopez	.25
68	Sammy Sosa	.75
69	Alejandro Machado	.25
70	Bill Mueller	.25
71	Bronson Arroyo	.25
72	Curt Schilling	.75
73	David Ortiz	1.00
74	David Wells	.25
75	Edgar Renteria	.25
76	Ryan Jorgensen	.25
77	Jason Varitek	.75
78	Johnny Damon	1.00
79	Keith Foulke	.25
80	Kevin Youkilis	.50
81	Manny Ramirez	1.00
82	Matt Clement	.25
83	Hanley Ramirez	1.00
84	Tim Wakefield	.75
85	Trot Nixon	.25
86	Wade Miller	.25
87	Aramis Ramirez	.50
88	Carlos Zambrano	.25
89	Corey Patterson	.25
90	Derrek Lee	.75
91	Geovany Soto	.50
92	Greg Maddux	2.00
93	Jeromy Burnitz	.25
94	Jerry Hairston Jr.	.25
95	Kerry Wood	.50
96	Mark Prior	.50
97	Matt Murton	.25
98	Michael Barrett	.25
99	Neifi Perez	.25
100	Nomar Garciaparra	.75
101	Rich Hill	.50
102	Ryan Dempster	.25
103	Todd Walker	.25
104	A.J. Pierzynski	.25
105	Aaron Rowand	.25
106	Bobby Jenks	.25
107	Carl Everett	.25
108	Dustin Hermanson	.25
109	Frank Thomas	1.00
110	Freddy Garcia	.25
111	Jermaine Dye	.25
112	Joe Crede	.50
113	Jon Garland	.25
114	Jose Contreras	.25
115	Juan Uribe	.25
116	Mark Buehrle	.25
117	Orlando Hernandez	.25
118	Paul Konerko	.75
119	Scott Podsednik	.25
120	Tadahito Iguchi	.25
121	Aaron Harang	.25
122	Adam Dunn	.75
123	Austin Kearns	.25
124	Brandon Claussen	.25
125	Chris Denorfia	.25
126	Edwin Encarnacion	.25
127	Manuel Perez	.25
128	Felipe Lopez	.25
129	Jason LaRue	.25
130	Ken Griffey Jr.	2.00
131	Chris Booker	.25
132	Luke Hudson	.25
133	Jason Bergmann	.25
134	Ryan Freel	.25
135	Sean Casey	.50
136	Wily Mo Pena	.25
137	Aaron Boone	.25
138	Ben Broussard	.25
139	Ryan Garko	.25
140	C.C. Sabathia	.75
141	Casey Blake	.25
142	Cliff Lee	.25
143	Coco Crisp	.25
144	David Riske	.25
145	Grady Sizemore	.75
146	Jake Westbrook	.25
147	Jhonny Peralta	.25
148	Josh Bard	.25
149	Kevin Millwood	.25
150	Ronnie Belliard	.25
151	Scott Elarton	.25
152	Travis Hafner	.50
153	Victor Martinez	.50
154	Aaron Cook	.25
155	Aaron Miles	.25
156	Brad Hawpe	.25
157	Mike Esposito	.25
158	Chin-Hui Tsao	.25
159	Clint Barmes	.25
160	Cory Sullivan	.25
161	Garrett Atkins	.50
162	J.D. Closser	.25
163	Jason Jennings	.25
164	Jeff Baker	.25
165	Jeff Francis	.25
166	Luis Gonzalez	.25
167	Matt Holliday	.75
168	Todd Helton	.75
169	Brandon Inge	.25
170	Carlos Guillen	.50
171	Carlos Pena	.50
172	Chris Shelton	.25
173	Craig Monroe	.25
174	Curtis Granderson	.75
175	Dmitri Young	.25
176	Ivan Rodriguez	.75
177	Jason Johnson	.25
178	Jeremy Bonderman	.50
179	Magglio Ordonez	.50
180	Mark Woodyard	.25
181	Nook Logan	.25
182	Omar Infante	.25
183	Placido Polanco	.25
184	Chris Heintz	.25
185	A.J. Burnett	.50
186	Alex Gonzalez	.25
187	Josh Johnson	.25
188	Carlos Delgado	.75
189	Dontrelle Willis	.50
190	Josh Wilson	.25
191	Jason Vargas	.25
192	Jeff Conine	.25
193	Jeremy Hermida	.25
194	Josh Beckett	.75
195	Juan Encarnacion	.25
196	Juan Pierre	.25
197	Luis Castillo	.25
198	Miguel Cabrera	1.00
199	Mike Lowell	.50
200	Paul LoDuca	.25
201	Todd Jones	.25
202	Adam Everett	.25
203	Andy Pettitte	.50
204	Brad Ausmus	.25
205	Brad Lidge	.25
206	Brandon Backe	.25
207	Charlton Jimerson	.25
208	Chris Burke	.25
209	Craig Biggio	.50
210	Dan Wheeler	.25
211	Jason Lane	.25
212	Jeff Bagwell	.50
213	Lance Berkman	.75
214	Luke Scott	.25
215	Morgan Ensberg	.25
216	Roger Clemens	2.50
217	Roy Oswalt	.50
218	Willy Taveras	.25
219	Andres Blanco	.25
220	Angel Berroa	.25
221	Ruben Gotay	.25
222	David DeJesus	.25
223	Emil Brown	.25
224	J.P. Howell	.25
225	Jeremy Affeldt	.25
226	Jimmy Gobble	.25
227	John Buck	.25
228	Jose Lima	.25
229	Mark Teahen	.25
230	Matt Stairs	.25
231	Mike MacDougal	.25
232	Mike Sweeney	.25
233	Runelvys Hernandez	.25
234	Terrence Long	.25
235	Zack Greinke	.50
236	Ron Flores	.25
237	Brad Penny	.25
238	Cesar Izturis	.25
239	D.J. Houlton	.25
240	Derek Lowe	.25
241	Eric Gagne	.25
242	Hee Seop Choi	.25
243	J.D. Drew	.50
244	Jason Phillips	.25
245	Jason Repko	.25
246	Jayson Werth	.25
247	Jeff Kent	.25
248	Jeff Weaver	.25
249	Milton Bradley	.25
250	Odalis Perez	.25
251	Hong-Chih Kuo	.25
252	Oscar Robles	.25
253	Ben Sheets	.50
254	Bill Hall	.25
255	Brady Clark	.25
256	Carlos Lee	.50
257	Chris Capuano	.25
258	Nelson Cruz	.25
259	Derrick Turnbow	.25
260	Doug Davis	.25
261	Geoff Jenkins	.25
262	J.J. Hardy	.25
263	Lyle Overbay	.25
264	Prince Fielder	.75
265	Rickie Weeks	.25
266	Russell Branyan	.25
267	Tomokazu Ohka	.25
268	Jonah Bayliss	.25
269	Brad Radke	.25
270	Carlos Silva	.25
271	Francisco Liriano	.50
272	Jacque Jones	.25
273	Joe Mauer	.50
274	Travis Bowyer	.25
275	Joe Nathan	.25
276	Johan Santana	1.00
277	Justin Morneau	.50
278	Kyle Lohse	.25
279	Lew Ford	.25
280	Matthew LeCroy	.25
281	Michael Cuddyer	.25
282	Nick Punto	.25
283	Scott Baker	.25
284	Shannon Stewart	.25
285	Torii Hunter	.50
286	Braden Looper	.25
287	Carlos Beltran	.75
288	Cliff Floyd	.25
289	David Wright	1.50
290	Doug Mientkiewicz	.25
291	Anderson Hernandez	.25
292	Jose Reyes	1.00
293	Kazuo Matsui	.25
294	Kris Benson	.25
295	Miguel Cairo	.25
296	Mike Cameron	.25
297	Robert Andino	.25
298	Mike Piazza	1.00
299	Pedro Martinez	1.00
300	Tom Glavine	.50
301	Victor Diaz	.25
302	Tim Hamulack	.25
303	Alex Rodriguez	2.50
304	Bernie Williams	.50
305	Carl Pavano	.25
306	Chien-Ming Wang	1.00
307	Derek Jeter	2.50
308	Gary Sheffield	.50
309	Hideki Matsui	1.50
310	Jason Giambi	.75
311	Jorge Posada	.50
312	Kevin Brown	.25
313	Mariano Rivera	.50
314	Matt Lawton	.25
315	Mike Mussina	.50
316	Randy Johnson	1.00
317	Robinson Cano	.50
318	Michael Vento	.25
319	Tino Martinez	.50
320	Tony Womack	.25
321	Barry Zito	.50
322	Bobby Crosby	.25
323	Bobby Kielty	.25
324	Dan Johnson	.25
325	Dan Haren	.25
326	Eric Chavez	.50
327	Erubiel Durazo	.25
328	Huston Street	.50
329	Jason Kendall	.25
330	Jay Payton	.25
331	Joe Blanton	.25
332	Joe Kennedy	.25
333	Kirk Saarloos	.25
334	Mark Kotsay	.25
335	Nick Swisher	.50
336	Rich Harden	.25
337	Scott Hatteberg	.25
338	Billy Wagner	.25
339	Bobby Abreu	.50
340	Brett Myers	.25
341	Chase Utley	1.00
342	Danny Sandoval	.25
343	David Bell	.25
344	Gavin Floyd	.25
345	Jim Thome	.75

#	Player	Price
346	Jimmy Rollins	.75
347	Jon Lieber	.25
348	Kenny Lofton	.25
349	Mike Lieberthal	.25
350	Pat Burrell	.50
351	Randy Wolf	.25
352	Ryan Howard	1.50
353	Vicente Padilla	.25
354	Bryan Bullington	.25
355	J.J. Furmaniak	.25
356	Craig Wilson	.25
357	Matt Capps	.25
358	Tom Gorzelanny	.25
359	Jack Wilson	.25
360	Jason Bay	.50
361	Jose Mesa	.25
362	Josh Fogg	.25
363	Kip Wells	.25
364	Steve Stemle	.25
365	Oliver Perez	.25
366	Robert Mackowiak	.25
367	Ronny Paulino	.25
368	Tike Redman	.25
369	Zach Duke	.25
370	Adam Eaton	.25
371	Scott Feldman	.25
372	Brian Giles	.25
373	Brian Lawrence	.25
374	Damian Jackson	.25
375	Dave Roberts	.25
376	Jake Peavy	.50
377	Joe Randa	.25
378	Khalil Greene	.25
379	Mark Loretta	.25
380	Ramon Hernandez	.25
381	Robert Fick	.25
382	Ryan Klesko	.25
383	Trevor Hoffman	.25
384	Woody Williams	.25
385	Xavier Nady	.25
386	Armando Benitez	.25
387	Brad Hennessey	.25
388	Brian Myrow	.25
389	Edgardo Alfonzo	.25
390	J.T. Snow	.25
391	Jeremy Accardo	.25
392	Jason Schmidt	.50
393	Lance Niekro	.25
394	Matt Cain	.25
395	Daniel Ortmeier	.25
396	Moises Alou	.50
397	Doug Clark	.25
398	Omar Vizquel	.25
399	Pedro Feliz	.25
400	Randy Winn	.25
401	Ray Durham	.25
402	Adrian Beltre	.50
403	Eddie Guardado	.25
404	Felix Hernandez	.50
405	Gil Meche	.25
406	Ichiro Suzuki	1.50
407	Jamie Moyer	.25
408	Jeff Nelson	.25
409	Jeremy Reed	.25
410	Joel Pineiro	.25
411	Jaime Bubela	.25
412	Raul Ibanez	.25
413	Richie Sexson	.50
414	Ryan Franklin	.25
415	Willie Bloomquist	.25
416	Yorvit Torrealba	.25
417	Yuniesky Betancourt	.25
418	Jeff Harris	.25
419	Albert Pujols	2.50
420	Chris Carpenter	.75
421	David Eckstein	.50
422	Jason Isringhausen	.25
423	Jason Marquis	.25
424	Adam Wainwright	.50
425	Jim Edmonds	.50
426	Ryan Theriot	.50
427	Tim Duncan	.25
428	Mark Grudzielanek	.25
429	Mark Mulder	.50
430	Matt Morris	.25
431	Reggie Sanders	.25
432	Scott Rolen	1.00
433	Tyler Johnson	.25
434	Yadier Molina	.25
435	Alex Gonzalez	.25
436	Aubrey Huff	.25
437	Tim Corcoran	.25
438	Carl Crawford	.50
439	Casey Fossum	.25
440	Danys Baez	.25
441	Edwin Jackson	.25
442	Joey Gathright	.25
443	Jonny Gomes	.25
444	Jorge Cantu	.25
445	Julio Lugo	.25
446	Nick Green	.25
447	Rocco Baldelli	.25
448	Scott Kazmir	.50
449	Seth McClung	.25
450	Toby Hall	.25
451	Travis Lee	.25
452	Craig Breslow	.25
453	Alfonso Soriano	1.00
454	Chris Young	.50
455	David Dellucci	.25
456	Francisco Cordero	.25
457	Gary Matthews	.25
458	Hank Blalock	.50
459	Juan Dominguez	.25
460	Josh Rupe	.25
461	Kenny Rogers	.25
462	Kevin Mench	.25
463	Laynce Nix	.25
464	Mark Teixeira	.75
465	Michael Young	.50
466	Richard Hidalgo	.25
467	Jason Botts	.25
468	Aaron Hill	.25
469	Alex Rios	.50
470	Corey Koskie	.25
471	Chris Demaria	.25
472	Eric Hinske	.25
473	Frank Catalanotto	.25
474	John-Ford Griffin	.25
475	Gustavo Chacin	.25
476	Josh Towers	.25
477	Miguel Batista	.25
478	Orlando Hudson	.25
479	Reed Johnson	.25
480	Roy Halladay	.50
481	Shaun Marcum	.25
482	Shea Hillenbrand	.25
483	Ted Lilly	.25
484	Vernon Wells	.50
485	Brad Wilkerson	.25
486	Darrell Rasner	.25
487	Chad Cordero	.25
488	Cristian Guzman	.25
489	Esteban Loaiza	.25
490	John Patterson	.25
491	Jose Guillen	.25
492	Jose Vidro	.25
493	Livan Hernandez	.25
494	Marlon Byrd	.25
495	Nick Johnson	.25
496	Preston Wilson	.25
497	Ryan Church	.25
498	Ryan Zimmerman	.50
499	Tony Armas	.25
500	Vinny Castilla	.25
501	Andy Green	.25
502	Damion Easley	.25
503	Eric Byrnes	.50
504	Jason Grimsley	.25
505	Jeff DaVanon	.25
506	Johnny Estrada	.25
507	Luis Vizcaino	.25
508	Miguel Batista	.25
509	Orlando Hernandez	.25
510	Orlando Hudson	.25
511	Terry Mulholland	.25
512	Chris Reitsma	.25
513	Edgar Renteria	.25
514	John Thomson	.25
515	Jorge Sosa	.25
516	Oscar Villarreal	.25
517	Peter Orr	.25
518	Ryan Langerhans	.25
519	Todd Pratt	.25
520	Wilson Betemit	.25
521	Brian Jordan	.25
522	Lance Cormier	.25
523	Matt Diaz	.25
524	Mike Remlinger	.25
525	Bruce Chen	.25
526	Chris Gomez	.25
527	Chris Ray	.25
528	Corey Patterson	.25
529	David Newhan	.25
530	Ed Rogers	.25
531	John Halama	.25
532	Kris Benson	.25
533	LaTroy Hawkins	.25
534	Raul Chavez	.25
535	Alex Cora	.25
536	Alex Gonzalez	.25
537	Coco Crisp	.25
538	David Riske	.25
539	Doug Mirabelli	.25
540	Josh Beckett	.75
541	J.T. Snow	.25
542	Mike Timlin	.25
543	Julian Tavarez	.25
544	Rudy Seanez	.25
545	Wily Mo Pena	.25
546	Bob Howry	.25
547	Glendon Rusch	.25
548	Henry Blanco	.25
549	Jacque Jones	.25
550	Jerome Williams	.25
551	John Mabry	.25
552	Juan Pierre	.25
553	Scott Eyre	.25
554	Scott Williamson	.25
555	Wade Miller	.25
556	Will Ohman	.25
557	Alex Cintron	.25
558	Robert Mackowiak	.25
559	Brandon McCarthy	.25
560	Chris Widger	.25
561	Cliff Politte	.25
562	Javier Vazquez	.25
563	Jim Thome	.75
564	Matt Thornton	.25
565	Neal Cotts	.25
566	Pablo Ozuna	.25
567	Ross Gload	.25
568	Brandon Phillips	.50
569	Bronson Arroyo	.25
570	Dave Williams	.25
571	David Ross	.25
572	David Weathers	.25
573	Eric Milton	.25
574	Javier Valentin	.25
575	Kent Mercker	.25
576	Matt Belisle	.25
577	Paul Wilson	.25
578	Rich Aurilia	.25
579	Rick White	.25
580	Scott Hatteberg	.25
581	Todd Coffey	.25
582	Bob Wickman	.25
583	Danny Graves	.25
584	Eduardo Perez	.25
585	Guillermo Mota	.25
586	Jason Davis	.25
587	Jason Johnson	.25
588	Jason Michaels	.25
589	Rafael Betancourt	.25
590	Ramon Vazquez	.25
591	Scott Sauerbeck	.25
592	Todd Hollandsworth	.25
593	Brian Fuentes	.25
594	Danny Ardoin	.25
595	David Cortes	.25
596	Eli Marrero	.25
597	Jamey Carroll	.25
598	Jason Smith	.25
599	Josh Fogg	.25
600	Miguel Ojeda	.25
601	Mike DeJean	.25
602	Ray King	.25
603	Omar Quintanilla	.25
604	Zach Day	.25
605	Fernando Rodney	.25
606	Kenny Rogers	.25
607	Mike Maroth	.25
608	Nate Robertson	.25
609	Todd Jones	.25
610	Vance Wilson	.25
611	Bobby Seay	.25
612	Chris Spurling	.25
613	Ramon Colon	.25
614	Jason Grilli	.25
615	Marcus Thames	.25
616	Ramon Santiago	.25
617	Alfredo Amezaga	.25
618	Brian Moehler	.25
619	Chris Aguila	.25
620	Franklyn German	.25
621	Joe Borowski	.25
622	Logan Kensing	.25
623	Matt Treanor	.25
624	Miguel Olivo	.25
625	Sergio Mitre	.25
626	Todd Wellemeyer	.25
627	Wes Helms	.25
628	Chad Qualls	.25
629	Eric Bruntlett	.25
630	Mike Gallo	.25
631	Mike Lamb	.25
632	Orlando Palmeiro	.25
633	Russ Springer	.25
634	Dan Wheeler	.25
635	Eric Munson	.25
636	Preston Wilson	.25
637	Trever Miller	.25
638	Ambiorix Burgos	.25
639	Andrew Sisco	.25
640	Denny Bautista	.25
641	Doug Mientkiewicz	.25
642	Elmer Dessens	.25
643	Esteban German	.25
644	Joe Nelson	.25
645	Mark Grudzielanek	.25
646	Mark Redman	.25
647	Mike Wood	.25
648	Paul Bako	.25
649	Reggie Sanders	.25
650	Scott Elarton	.25
651	Shane Costa	.25
652	Tony Graffanino	.25
653	Jason Bulger	.25
654	Chris Bootcheck	.25
655	Esteban Yan	.25
656	Hector Carrasco	.25
657	J.C. Romero	.25
658	Jeff Weaver	.25
659	Jose Molina	.25
660	Kelvim Escobar	.25
661	Maicer Izturis	.25
662	Robb Quinlan	.25
663	Scot Shields	.25
664	Tim Salmon	.25
665	Bill Mueller	.25
666	Brett Tomko	.25
667	Dioner Navarro	.25
668	Jae Weong Seo	.25
669	Jose Cruz	.25
670	Kenny Lofton	.25
671	Lance Carter	.25
672	Nomar Garciaparra	1.00
673	Olmedo Saenz	.25
674	Rafael Furcal	.25
675	Ramon Martinez	.25
676	Ricky Ledee	.25
677	Sandy Alomar	.25
678	Yhency Brazoban	.25
679	Corey Koskie	.25
680	Danny Kolb	.25
681	Gabe Gross	.25
682	Jeff Cirillo	.25
683	Matt Wise	.25
684	Rick Helling	.25
685	Chad Moeller	.25
686	David Bush	.25
687	Jorge De La Rosa	.25
688	Justin Lehr	.25
689	Jason Bartlett	.25
690	Jesse Crain	.25
691	Juan Rincon	.25
692	Luis Castillo	.25
693	Mike Redmond	.25
694	Rondell White	.25
695	Tony Batista	.25
696	Juan Castro	.25
697	Luis Rodriguez	.25
698	Matt Guerrier	.25
699	Willie Eyre	.25
700	Aaron Heilman	.25
701	Billy Wagner	.25
702	Carlos Delgado	.75
703	Chad Bradford	.25
704	Chris Woodward	.25
705	Darren Oliver	.25
706	Duaner Sanchez	.25
707	Endy Chavez	.25
708	Jorge Julio	.25
709	Jose Valentin	.25
710	Julio Franco	.25
711	Paul LoDuca	.25
712	Ramon Castro	.25
713	Steve Trachsel	.25
714	Victor Zambrano	.25
715	Xavier Nady	.25
716	Andy Phillips	.25
717	Bubba Crosby	.25
718	Jaret Wright	.25
719	Kelly Stinnett	.25
720	Kyle Farnsworth	.25
721	Mike Meyers	.25
722	Octavio Dotel	.25
723	Ron Villone	.25
724	Scott Proctor	.25
725	Shawn Chacon	.25
726	Tanyon Sturtze	.25
727	Adam Melhuse	.25
728	Brad Halsey	.25
729	Esteban Loaiza	.25
730	Frank Thomas	1.00
731	Jay Witasick	.25
732	Justin Duchscherer	.25
733	Kiko Calero	.25
734	Marco Scutaro	.25
735	Mark Ellis	.25
736	Milton Bradley	.25
737	Aaron Fultz	.25
738	Aaron Rowand	.25
739	Geoff Geary	.25
740	Arthur Rhodes	.25
741	Chris Coste	.25
742	Rheal Cormier	.25
743	Ryan Franklin	.25
744	Ryan Madson	.25
745	Sal Fasano	.25
746	Tom Gordon	.25
747	Abraham Nunez	.25
748	David Dellucci	.25
749	Julio Santana	.25
750	Shane Victorino	.25
751	Damaso Marte	.25
752	Freddy Sanchez	.25
753	Humberto Cota	.25
754	Jeromy Burnitz	.25
755	Joe Randa	.25
756	Jose Castillo	.25
757	Mike Gonzalez	.25
758	Ryan Doumit	.25
759	Sean Burnett	.25
760	Sean Casey	.25
761	Ian Snell	.25
762	John Grabow	.25
763	Jose Hernandez	.25
764	Roberto Hernandez	.25
765	Ryan Vogelsong	.25
766	Victor Sanchez	.25
767	Adrian Gonzalez	.50
768	Alan Embree	.25
769	Brian Sweeney	.25
770	Chan Ho Park	.25
771	Clay Hensley	.25
772	Dewon Brazelton	.25
773	Doug Brocail	.25
774	Eric Young	.25
775	Geoff Blum	.25
776	Josh Bard	.25
777	Mark Bellhorn	.25
778	Mike Cameron	.25
779	Mike Piazza	1.00
780	Rob Bowen	.25
781	Scott Cassidy	.25
782	Scott Linebrink	.25
783	Shawn Estes	.25
784	Termel Sledge	.25
785	Vinny Castilla	.25
786	Jeff Fassero	.25
787	Mike Vizcaino	.25
788	Mark Sweeney	.25
789	Matt Morris	.25
790	Steve Finley	.25
791	Tim Worrell	.25
792	Jamey Wright	.25
793	Jason Ellison	.25
794	Noah Lowry	.25
795	Steve Kline	.25
796	Todd Greene	.25
797	Carl Everett	.25
798	George Sherrill	.25
799	J.J. Putz	.25
800	Jake Woods	.25
801	Jose Lopez	.25
802	Julio Mateo	.25
803	Mike Morse	.25
804	Rafael Soriano	.25
805	Roberto Petagine	.25
806	Aaron Miles	.25
807	Braden Looper	.25
808	Gary Bennett	.25
809	Hector Luna	.25
810	Jeff Suppan	.25
811	John Rodriguez	.25
812	Josh Hancock	.25
813	Juan Encarnacion	.25
814	Larry Bigbie	.25
815	Scott Spiezio	.25
816	Sidney Ponson	.25
817	So Taguchi	.25
818	Brian Meadows	.25
819	Damon Hollins	.25
820	Dan Miceli	.25
821	Doug Waechter	.25
822	Jason Childers	.25
823	Josh Paul	.25
824	Julio Lugo	.25
825	Mark Hendrickson	.25
826	Sean Burroughs	.25
827	Shawn Camp	.25
828	Travis Harper	.25
829	Ty Wigginton	.25
830	Adam Eaton	.25
831	Adrian Brown	.25
832	Akinori Otsuka	.25
833	Antonio Alfonseca	.25
834	Brad Wilkerson	.25
835	D'Angelo Jimenez	.25
836	Gerald Laird	.25
837	Joaquin Benoit	.25
838	Kameron Loe	.25
839	Kevin Millwood	.25
840	Mark DeRosa	.25
841	Phil Nevin	.25
842	Rod Barajas	.25
843	Vicente Padilla	.25
844	A.J. Burnett	.25
845	Bengie Molina	.25
846	Gregg Zaun	.25
847	John McDonald	.25
848	Lyle Overbay	.25
849	Russ Adams	.25
850	Troy Glaus	.50
851	Vinnie Chulk	.25
852	B.J. Ryan	.25
853	Justin Speier	.25
854	Pete Walker	.25
855	Scott Downs	.25
856	Scott Schoeneweis	.25
857	Alfonso Soriano	1.00
858	Brian Schneider	.25
859	Daryle Ward	.25
860	Felix Rodriguez	.25
861	Gary Majewski	.25
862	Joey Eischen	.25
863	Jon Rauch	.25
864	Marlon Anderson	.25
865	Matthew LeCroy	.25
866	Mike Stanton	.25
867	Ramon Ortiz	.25
868	Robert Fick	.25
869	Royce Clayton	.25
870	Ryan Drese	.25
871	Vladimir Guerrero	.50
872	Craig Biggio	.25
873	Barry Zito	.25
874	Vernon Wells	.25
875	Chipper Jones	.50
876	Prince Fielder	.50
877	Albert Pujols	1.50
878	Greg Maddux	1.00
879	Carl Crawford	.25
880	Brandon Webb	.25
881	J.D. Drew	.25
882	Jason Schmidt	.25
883	Victor Martinez	.25
884	Ichiro Suzuki	.75
885	Miguel Cabrera	.50
886	David Wright	.75
887	Alfonso Soriano	.25
888	Miguel Tejada	.25
889	Khalil Greene	.25
890	Ryan Howard	1.00
891	Jason Bay	.25
892	Mark Teixeira	.50
893	Manny Ramirez	.25
894	Ken Griffey Jr.	1.00
895	Todd Helton	.50
896	Angel Berroa	.25
897	Ivan Rodriguez	.50
898	Johan Santana	.50
899	Paul Konerko	.50
900	Derek Jeter	1.50
901	Macay McBride RC	.50
902	Tony Pena RC	.50
903	Peter Moylan RC	.50
904	Aaron Rakers RC	.50
905	Chris Britton RC	.50
906	Nick Markakis RC	1.00
907	Sendy Rleal RC	.50
908	Val Majewski RC	.50
909	Jermaine Van Buren RC	.50
910	Jonathan Papelbon RC	1.00
911	Angel Pagan RC	.50
912	David Aardsma RC	.50
913	Sean Marshall RC	.50
914	Brian Anderson RC	.50
915	Freddie Bynum RC	.50
916	Fausto Carmona RC	.50
917	Kelly Shoppach RC	.50
918	Choo Freeman RC	.50
919	Ryan Shealy RC	.50
920	Joel Zumaya RC	.75
921	Jordan Tata RC	.50
922	Justin Verlander RC	2.00
923	Carlos Martinez RC	.50
924	Chris Resop RC	.50
925	Dan Uggla RC	2.00
926	Eric Reed RC	.50
927	Hanley Ramirez RC	2.50
928	Yusmeiro Petit RC	.50
929	Josh Willingham RC	.75
930	Mike Jacobs RC	.75
931	Reggie Abercrombie RC	.50
932	Ricky Nolasco RC	1.00
933	Scott Olsen RC	.50
934	Fernando Nieve RC	.50
935	Taylor Buchholz RC	.50
936	Cody Ross RC	.50
937	James Loney RC	.75
938	Takashi Saito RC	1.00
939	Tim Hamulack RC	.50
940	Chris Demaria RC	.50
941	Jose Capellan RC	.50
942	Dave Gassner RC	.50
943	Jason Kubel RC	.50
944	Brian Bannister RC	.50
945	Mike Thompson RC	.50
946	Cole Hamels RC	2.00
947	Paul Maholm RC	.50
948	John Van Benschoten RC	.50
949	Nate McLouth RC	.50
950	Ben Johnson RC	.50
951	Josh Barfield RC	.50
952	Travis Ishikawa RC	.50
953	Jack Taschner RC	.50
954	Kenji Johjima RC	1.00
955	Skip Schumaker RC	.50
956	Ruddy Lugo RC	.50
957	Jason Hammel RC	.50
958	Chris Roberson RC	.50
959	Fabio Castro RC	.50
960	Ian Kinsler RC	1.00
961	John Koronka RC	.50
962	Brandon Watson RC	.50
963	Jon Lester RC	4.00
964	Ben Hendrickson RC	.50
965	Martin Prado RC	1.50
966	Erick Aybar RC	.50
967	Bobby Livingston RC	.50
968	Ryan Spilborghs RC	.75
969	Tommy Murphy RC	.50
970	Howie Kendrick RC	1.50
971	Casey Janssen RC	.50
972	Michael O'Connor RC	.50
973	Conor Jackson RC	1.00
974	Jeremy Hermida RC	.50
975	Renyel Pinto RC	.50
976	Prince Fielder RC	2.00
977	Kevin Frandsen RC	.50
978	Ty Taubenheim RC	.50
979	Rich Hill RC	.75
980	Jonathan Broxton RC	.75
981	Jamie Shields RC	1.00
982	Carlos Villanueva RC	.75
983	Boone Logan RC	.50
984	Brian Wilson RC	.75
985	Andre Ethier RC	2.00
986	Michael Napoli RC	1.00
987	Agustin Montero RC	.50
988	Jack Hannahan RC	.50
989	Boof Bonser RC	.50
990	Carlos Ruiz RC	.75
991	Jason Botts RC	.25
992	Kendry Morales RC	1.50
993	Alay Soler RC	.50
994	Santiago Ramirez RC	.50
995	Saul Rivera RC	.50
996	Anthony Reyes RC	.50
997	Matthew Kemp RC	1.50
998	Jae-Kuk Ryu RC	.50
999	Lastings Milledge RC	1.00
1000	Jered Weaver RC	2.00
1001	Jeremy Sowers RC	.50
1002	Chad Billingsley RC	1.00
1003	Stephen Drew RC	2.00
1004	Tony Gwynn Jr. RC	.50
1005	Melky Cabrera RC	1.00
1006	Eliezer Alfonzo RC	.50
1007	Dana Eveland RC	.50
1008	Luis Figueroa RC	.50
1009	Emiliano Fruto RC	.50
1010	Clay Hensley RC	.50
1011	Zach Jackson RC	.50
1012	Bobby Keppel RC	.50
1013	Carlos Marmol RC	1.00
1014	Russell Martin RC	1.00
1015	Leo Nunez RC	.50
1016	Ken Ray RC	.50
1017	Mike Rouse RC	.50
1018	Kevin Thompson RC	.50
1019	C.J. Wilson RC	.50
1020	Steve Andrade RC	.50
1021	Ed Rogers RC	.50
1022	Joe Nelson RC	.50
1023	Omar Quintanilla RC	.50
1024	Chris Bootcheck RC	.50
1025	Jason Childers RC	.50

Blue

Blue (1-900):	1-1.5X
Blue RC:	1X
Inserted 1:4	

Green

Green (1-900):	2-3X
Green RC:	1-2X
Production 99 Sets	

Purple

Purple (1-900):	2-3X
Purple RC:	1-2X
Production 150 Sets	

Red

Red (1-900):	3-4X
Red RC:	2-3X
Production 50 Sets	

Materials

		NM/M
	Common Player:	5.00
JB	Jason Bay	8.00
LB	Lance Berkman	5.00
MC	Miguel Cabrera	10.00
MA	Matt Cain	10.00

CA	Chris Carpenter	8.00
CC	Carl Crawford	5.00
CR	Coco Crisp	8.00
AD	Adam Dunn	8.00
PF	Prince Fielder	10.00
RF	Rafael Furcal	5.00
JG	Jason Giambi	8.00
TG	Troy Glaus	5.00
KG	Ken Griffey Jr.	15.00
VG	Vladimir Guerrero	8.00
TH	Travis Hafner	8.00
HA	Roy Halladay	8.00
CH	Cole Hamels	15.00
JH	Jeremy Hermida	5.00
FH	Felix Hernandez	10.00
RH	Ryan Howard	20.00
DJ	Derek Jeter	20.00
KJ	Kenji Johjima	15.00
AJ	Andruw Jones	8.00
SK	Scott Kazmir	5.00
IK	Ian Kinsler	8.00
DL	Derek Lee	10.00
FL	Francisco Liriano	10.00
PM	Pedro Martinez	8.00
VM	Victor Martinez	5.00
JM	Joe Mauer	10.00
LM	Lastings Milledge	10.00
KM	Kendry Morales	5.00
DO	David Ortiz	15.00
JP	Jonathan Papelbon	15.00
AP	Albert Pujols	20.00
HR	Hanley Ramirez	5.00
JR	Jose Reyes	15.00
JS	Johan Santana	10.00
GS	Grady Sizemore	10.00
AS	Alfonso Soriano	10.00
MT	Mark Teixeira	8.00
TE	Miguel Tejada	8.00
JT	Jim Thome	10.00
CU	Chase Utley	15.00
JV	Justin Verlander	15.00
WE	Jered Weaver	10.00
RW	Rickie Weeks	8.00
JW	Josh Willingham	5.00
RZ	Ryan Zimmerman	10.00

Player Highlights

REYES SCORES KEY RUN FOR METS

NM/M

	Common Player:	.50
1	Andruw Jones	1.00
2	Manny Ramirez	1.00
3	Travis Hafner	.75
4	Johnny Damon	1.00
5	Miguel Cabrera	1.00
6	Chris Carpenter	1.00
7	Derek Lee	1.00
8	Jason Bay	.75
9	Jason Varitek	1.00
10	Ryan Howard	3.00
11	Mark Teixeira	1.00
12	Carlos Delgado	.75
13	Bartolo Colon	.50
14	David Wright	2.00
15	Miguel Tejada	.75
16	Mike Piazza	1.50
17	Paul Konerko	.75
18	Jermaine Dye	.50
19	Ichiro Suzuki	2.00
20	Brad Wilkerson	.50
21	Hideki Matsui	2.00
22	Albert Pujols	3.00
23	Chris Burke	.50
24	Derek Jeter	3.00
25	Brian Roberts	.50
26	David Ortiz	1.00
27	Alex Rodriguez	2.00
28	Ken Griffey Jr.	2.00
29	Prince Fielder	.75
30	Bobby Abreu	.75
31	Vladimir Guerrero	1.00
32	Tadahito Iguchi	.50
33	Jose Reyes	.75
34	Scott Podsednik	.50
35	Gary Sheffield	.75

Run Producers

NM/M

	Common Player:	1.00
1	Ty Cobb	3.00
2	Derrek Lee	1.50
3	Andruw Jones	1.50
4	David Ortiz	1.50
5	Lou Gehrig	4.00
6	Ken Griffey Jr.	4.00
7	Albert Pujols	5.00
8	Derek Jeter	5.00
9	Manny Ramirez	1.50
10	Alex Rodriguez	5.00
11	Gary Sheffield	1.00
12	Miguel Cabrera	1.50
13	Hideki Matsui	3.00
14	Vladimir Guerrero	1.50
15	David Wright	3.00
16	Mike Schmidt	1.50
17	Mark Teixeira	1.00
18	Babe Ruth	5.00
19	Jimmie Foxx	3.00
20	Honus Wagner	3.00

Special Endorsements

NM/M

	Common Player:	5.00
	Inserted 1:16	
RA	Reggie Abercrombie	5.00
AC	Jeremy Accardo	5.00
BA	Brian Anderson	5.00
AN	Robert Andino	5.00
BR	Brian Bannister	12.00
JB	Jason Bay	15.00
BW	Craig Breslow	8.00
CB	Chris Britton	5.00
TB	Taylor Buchholz	10.00
FB	Freddie Bynum	8.00
MI	Miguel Cabrera	20.00
MC	Matt Cain	15.00
JC	Jose Capellan/SP	8.00
CM	Matt Capps	5.00
FC	Fausto Carmona	10.00
TC	Tim Corcoran	5.00
DE	Chris Denorfia	8.00
JD	Joey Devine	8.00
AE	Andre Ethier	15.00
EV	Dana Eveland	12.00
RF	Ron Flores	5.00
KF	Kevin Frandsen	8.00
DG	Dave Gassner	8.00
KG	Ken Griffey Jr.	60.00
TH	Travis Hafner	15.00
CH	Cole Hamels	40.00
BH	Brendan Harris	5.00
HA	Jeff Harris	5.00
HG	Keith Hattig	8.00
HE	Jeremy Hermida	15.00
AH	Anderson Hernandez/SP	5.00
JU	Justin Huber	8.00
JA	Conor Jackson	15.00
MJ	Mike Jacobs	10.00
DJ	Derek Jeter	200.00
BJ	Ben Johnson	8.00
JJ	Josh Johnson	5.00
KE	Howie Kendrick	15.00
IK	Ian Kinsler	15.00
KO	John Koronka	8.00
JK	Jason Kubel	8.00
HK	Hong-Chih Kuo	40.00
FL	Francisco Liriano	20.00
BL	Boone Logan	5.00
RL	Ruddy Lugo	5.00
PM	Paul Maholm	8.00
SM	Sean Marshall	10.00
NI	Nick Massett	8.00
MM	Macay McBride	8.00
NM	Nate McLouth	15.00
KM	Kendry Morales	8.00
PE	Peter Moylan	8.00
FN	Fernando Nieve	5.00
WN	Wilbert Nieves	8.00
JP	Jonathan Papelbon	30.00
AA	Aaron Rakers	5.00
HR	Hanley Ramirez	30.00
RE	Chris Resop	8.00
RB	Chris Roberson	8.00
CR	Cody Ross	8.00
RC	Carlos Ruiz	8.00
RU	Josh Rupe	8.00
TS	Takashi Saito	25.00
RS	Ryan Shealy	10.00
JS	James Shields	20.00
KS	Kelly Shoppach	8.00
MS	Matt Smith	8.00
GS	Geovany Soto	35.00
DU	Dan Uggla	20.00
CU	Chase Utley	30.00
JV	John Van Benschoten	5.00
VE	Justin Verlander/SP	30.00
AW	Adam Wainwright	20.00
JW	Jered Weaver	15.00
RW	Rickie Weeks	15.00
WI	Josh Willingham	15.00
DW	Dontrelle Willis	15.00
JO	Josh Wilson	8.00
RZ	Ryan Zimmerman/SP	30.00
JZ	Joel Zumaya	15.00

Star Attractions

NM/M

	Common Player:	.50
	Inserted 1:8	
BA	Bobby Abreu	.75
JB	Josh Beckett	.50
CB	Carlos Beltran	1.00
LB	Lance Berkman	.75
JC	Jose Contreras	.50
JD	Johnny Damon	1.50
CD	Carlos Delgado	.75
JE	Jim Edmonds	.75
JG	Jason Giambi	1.00
KG	Ken Griffey Jr.	3.00
RH	Rich Harden	.50
DJ	Derek Jeter	4.00
AJ	Andruw Jones	1.00
CJ	Chipper Jones	1.50
DL	Derrek Lee	1.50
GM	Greg Maddux	3.00
PM	Pedro Martinez	1.50
JM	Joe Mauer	1.00
MO	Magglio Ordonez	1.50
DO	David Ortiz	1.50
PU	Albert Pujols	4.00
MR	Manny Ramirez	1.50
JR	Jose Reyes	1.50
CS	Curt Schilling	1.50
JS	Jason Schmidt	.50
SM	John Smoltz	.75
AS	Alfonso Soriano	1.50
MT	Mark Teixeira	1.00
DW	Dontrelle Willis	.50
WR	David Wright	2.50

WBC Counterparts

NM/M

	Common Duo:	1.00
	Inserted 1:6	
1	Yulieski Gourriel, Daisuke Matsushita	5.00
2	Ken Griffey Jr., Yoandy Garlobo	3.00
3	Ken Griffey Jr., Ichiro Suzuki	3.00
4	Derek Jeter, Chin-Lung Hu	4.00
5	Frederich Cepeda, Jong Beom Lee	1.00
6	Nobuhiko Matsunaka, Seung-Yeop Lee	2.00
7	Tsuyoshi Nishioka, Guangbiao Liu	1.00
8	Ichiro Suzuki, Osmany Urrutia	2.50
9	Daisuke Matsuzaka, Roger Clemens	8.00
10	Yadel Marti, Chan Ho Park	1.00
11	Koji Uehara, Jae Weong Seo	1.00
12	Shunsuke Watanabe, Bartolo Colon	2.00
13	Daisuke Matsuzaka, Johan Santana	5.00
14	Pedro Luis Lazo, Freddy Garcia	1.00
15	Koji Uehara, Roger Clemens	3.00

2006 Upper Deck Sweet Spot

NM/M

Complete Set (184):	
Common Player:	.25
Common Auto. (101-184):	15.00
Production 45-275	
Pack (5):	10.00
Box (12):	100.00

1	Bartolo Colon	.25
2	Garret Anderson	.25
3	Francisco Rodriguez	.25
4	Dallas McPherson	.25
5	Andy Pettitte	.40
6	Lance Berkman	.50
7	Willy Taveras	.25
8	Bobby Crosby	.25
9	Dan Haren	.50
10	Nick Swisher	.50
11	Vernon Wells	.50
12	Orlando Hudson	.25
13	Roy Halladay	.50
14	Andruw Jones	.50
15	Chipper Jones	.75
16	Jeff Francoeur	.50
17	John Smoltz	.50
18	Carlos Lee	.50
19	Rickie Weeks	.25
20	Bill Hall	.25
21	Jim Edmonds	.40
22	David Eckstein	.25
23	Mark Mulder	.25
24	Aramis Ramirez	.50
25	Greg Maddux	1.50
26	Nomar Garciaparra	.50
27	Carlos Zambrano	.50
28	Scott Kazmir	.25
29	Jorge Cantu	.25
30	Carl Crawford	.50
31	Luis Gonzalez	.25
32	Troy Glaus	.40
33	Shawn Green	.25
34	Jeff Kent	.40
35	Milton Bradley	.25
36	Cesar Izturis	.25
37	Omar Vizquel	.25
38	Moises Alou	.50
39	Randy Winn	.25
40	Jason Schmidt	.40
41	Coco Crisp	.25
42	C.C. Sabathia	.25
43	Cliff Lee	.25
44	Ichiro Suzuki	1.50
45	Richie Sexson	.25
46	Jeremy Reed	.25
47	Carlos Delgado	.50
48	Miguel Cabrera	.75
49	Luis Castillo	.25
50	Carlos Beltran	.50
51	Tom Glavine	.50
52	David Wright	1.50
53	Cliff Floyd	.25
54	Chad Cordero	.25
55	Jose Vidro	.25
56	Jose Guillen	.25
57	Nick Johnson	.25
58	Miguel Tejada	.50
59	Melvin Mora	.25
60	Javy Lopez	.25
61	Khalil Greene	.25
62	Brian Giles	.25
63	Trevor Hoffman	.25
64	Bobby Abreu	.50
65	Jimmy Rollins	.25
66	Pat Burrell	.40
67	Billy Wagner	.25
68	Jack Wilson	.25
69	Zach Duke	.25
70	Craig Wilson	.25
71	Mark Teixeira	.50
72	Hank Blalock	.40
73	David Dellucci	.25
74	Manny Ramirez	.75
75	Johnny Damon	.50
76	Jason Varitek	.50
77	Trot Nixon	.25
78	Adam Dunn	.50
79	Felipe Lopez	.25
80	Brandon Claussen	.25
81	Sean Casey	.25
82	Todd Helton	.50
83	Clint Barmes	.25
84	Matt Holliday	.50
85	Mike Sweeney	.25
86	Zack Greinke	.25
87	David DeJesus	.25
88	Ivan Rodriguez	.50
89	Jeremy Bonderman	.25
90	Magglio Ordonez	.50
91	Torii Hunter	.50
92	Joe Nathan	.25
93	Michael Cuddyer	.25
94	Paul Konerko	.50
95	Jermaine Dye	.25
96	Jon Garland	.25
97	Alex Rodriguez	2.00
98	Hideki Matsui	1.50
99	Jason Giambi	.50
100	Mariano Rivera	.40
101	Adrian Beltre/99	25.00
102	Matt Cain/99 RC	30.00
103	Craig Biggio/99	35.00
104	Eric Chavez/99	15.00
105	J.D. Drew/99	15.00
106	Eric Gagne/99	15.00
107	Tim Hudson/99	20.00
108	Tom Glavine/275	40.00
109	David Ortiz/99	75.00
110	Scott Rolen/275	30.00
111	Johan Santana/99	50.00
112	Curt Schilling/96	75.00
113	John Smoltz/99	60.00
114	Alfonso Soriano/99	50.00
115	Kerry Wood/99	20.00
116	Edwin Jackson/99	50.00
117	Felix Hernandez/125	50.00
118	Prince Fielder/99 RC	50.00
119	Vladimir Guerrero/86	50.00
120	Roger Clemens/99	35.00
121	Albert Pujols/45	250.00
122	Chris Carpenter/99	50.00
123	Derrek Lee/99	40.00
124	Dontrelle Willis/99	20.00
125	Roy Oswalt/99	25.00
126	Ryan Garko/275 RC	20.00
127	Tadahito Iguchi/275	25.00
128	Mark Loretta/275	15.00
129	Joe Mauer/275	50.00
130	Victor Martinez/275	25.00
131	Wily Mo Pena/275	15.00
132	Oliver Perez/274	10.00
133	Corey Patterson/275	15.00
134	Ben Sheets/275	15.00
135	Michael Young/275	15.00
136	Jonny Gomes/275	15.00
137	Derek Jeter/99	150.00
138	Ken Griffey Jr./99	75.00
139	Ryan Zimmerman/275 RC	40.00
140	Scott Baker/275 RC	20.00
141	Huston Street/275	20.00
142	Jason Bay/275	25.00
143	Ryan Howard/275	75.00
145	Travis Hafner/275	20.00
146	Brian Myrow/275 RC	15.00
147	Scott Podsednik/275	25.00
148	Brian Roberts/275	25.00
149	Grady Sizemore/135	35.00
150	Chris Demaria/275 RC	15.00
151	Jonah Bayliss/275 RC	15.00
152	Geovany Soto/275 RC	30.00
153	Lyle Overbay/275	15.00
154	Joey Devine/275 RC	15.00
155	Alejandro Freire/275 RC	15.00
156	Conor Jackson/275 RC	25.00
157	Danny Sandoval/275 RC	15.00
158	Chase Utley/275	60.00
159	Jeff Harris/275 RC	15.00
160	Ron Flores/275 RC	15.00
161	Scott Feldman/275 RC	15.00
162	Yadier Molina/275	25.00
163	Tim Corcoran/275 RC	15.00
164	Craig Hansen/275 RC	15.00
165	Jason Bergmann/275 RC	15.00
166	Craig Breslow/275 RC	15.00
167	Jhonny Peralta/275	15.00
168	Jeremy Hermida/275 RC	15.00
169	Scott Kazmir/275	15.00
170	Bobby Crosby/99	15.00
171	Rich Harden/275	15.00
172	Casey Kotchman/275	15.00
173	Tim Hamulack/275 RC	15.00
174	Justin Morneau/275	30.00
175	Jake Peavy/275	15.00
176	Yuniesky Betancourt/275	20.00
177	Jeremy Accardo/275 RC	15.00
178	Jorge Cantu/200	20.00
179	Marlon Byrd/275	20.00
180	Ryan Jorgensen/275 RC	15.00
181	Chris Denorfia/275 RC	15.00
182	Steve Stemle/275	15.00
183	Robert Andino/275 RC	15.00
184	Chris Heintz/275 RC	15.00

Sign. Bat Barrel Black Ink

NM/M

Production 13-25

107	Tim Hudson/25	50.00
110	Scott Rolen/25	50.00
111	Johan Santana/25	60.00
115	Kerry Wood/25	30.00
117	Felix Hernandez/25	60.00
118	Prince Fielder/25	60.00
119	Vladimir Guerrero/25	75.00
121	Albert Pujols/25	275.00
125	Roy Oswalt/25	40.00
127	Tadahito Iguchi/25	30.00
131	Wily Mo Pena/25	20.00
139	Ryan Zimmerman/25	75.00
143	Ryan Howard/25	80.00
151	Jonah Bayliss/25	20.00
153	Lyle Overbay/25	20.00
154	Joey Devine/25	20.00
160	Ron Flores/25	20.00
167	Jhonny Peralta/25	20.00
174	Justin Morneau/25	50.00
178	Jorge Cantu/25	40.00
182	Steve Stemle/25	15.00

Sign. Bat Barrel Blue Ink

No Pricing
Production Three to Five Sets

Sign. Black Stitch Black Ink

No Pricing
Production One Set
Blue Ink: No Pricing
Production One Set

Sig. Glove Leather Black Ink

No Pricing
Production 5-15
Blue Ink: No Pricing
Production 5-15

Sign. Red Stitch Blue Ink

NM/M

Production 15-150

101	Adrian Beltre/25	25.00
102	Matt Cain/150	30.00
103	Craig Biggio/25	50.00
106	Eric Gagne/25	25.00
107	Tim Hudson/25	30.00
109	David Ortiz/25	80.00
110	Scott Rolen/150	25.00
111	Johan Santana/25	50.00
112	Curt Schilling/25	50.00
113	John Smoltz/25	75.00
116	Edwin Jackson/150	20.00
118	Prince Fielder/25	25.00
119	Vladimir Guerrero/25	60.00
122	Chris Carpenter/25	25.00
123	Derek Lee/25	40.00
124	Dontrelle Willis/25	25.00
125	Roy Oswalt/25	30.00
126	Ryan Garko/25	20.00
127	Tadahito Iguchi/150	25.00
128	Mark Loretta/114	25.00
129	Joe Mauer/150	50.00
130	Victor Martinez/25	25.00
131	Wily Mo Pena/150	15.00
132	Oliver Perez/135	10.00
133	Corey Patterson/150	15.00
134	Ben Sheets/150	20.00
135	Michael Young/150	25.00
136	Jonny Gomes/150	15.00
137	Derek Jeter/50	200.00
138	Ken Griffey Jr./150	100.00
139	Ryan Zimmerman/150	40.00
140	Scott Baker/150	20.00
141	Huston Street/150	25.00
142	Jason Bay/150	25.00
143	Ryan Howard/150	75.00
144	Mike Piazza/100	100.00
145	Travis Hafner/150	15.00
146	Brian Myrow/150	15.00
147	Scott Podsednik/150	25.00
148	Brian Roberts/150	25.00
149	Grady Sizemore/75	40.00
150	Chris Demaria/150	15.00
151	Jonah Bayliss/150	15.00
152	Geovany Soto/150	40.00
153	Lyle Overbay/150	20.00
154	Joey Devine/150	15.00
155	Alejandro Freire/150	15.00
156	Conor Jackson/150	25.00
157	Danny Sandoval/150	15.00
158	Chase Utley/150	60.00
159	Jeff Harris/150	15.00
160	Ron Flores/150	15.00
161	Scott Feldman/150	15.00
162	Yadier Molina/135	30.00
163	Tim Corcoran/150	15.00
164	Craig Hansen/150	15.00
165	Jason Bergmann/150	15.00
166	Craig Breslow/150	15.00
167	Jhonny Peralta/120	20.00
168	Jeremy Hermida/150	25.00
169	Scott Kazmir/150	20.00
170	Bobby Crosby/25	15.00
171	Rich Harden/150	15.00
172	Casey Kotchman/150	15.00
173	Tim Hamulack/150	15.00
174	Justin Morneau/150	35.00
175	Jake Peavy/150	15.00
176	Yuniesky Betancourt/150	20.00
177	Jeremy Accardo/150	15.00
178	Jorge Cantu/150	30.00
179	Marlon Byrd/40	20.00
180	Ryan Jorgensen/150	15.00
181	Chris Denorfia/150	15.00
182	Steve Stemle/150	15.00
183	Robert Andino/150	15.00
184	Chris Heintz/150	15.00

Red-Blue Stitch Black Ink

NM/M

Production 25-99

101	Adrian Beltre/50	30.00
102	Matt Cain/99	40.00
103	Craig Biggio/50	50.00
105	J.D. Drew/50	30.00
106	Eric Gagne/50	25.00
107	Tim Hudson/50	40.00
108	Tom Glavine/99	50.00
109	David Ortiz/50	75.00
110	Scott Rolen/99	40.00
111	Johan Santana/50	50.00
112	Curt Schilling/45	50.00
113	John Smoltz/50	80.00
114	Alfonso Soriano/50	80.00
115	Kerry Wood/49	30.00
116	Edwin Jackson/60	50.00
117	Felix Hernandez/60	50.00
118	Prince Fielder/50	50.00
119	Vladimir Guerrero/50	80.00
120	Roger Clemens/50	80.00
121	Albert Pujols/25	250.00
122	Chris Carpenter/25	50.00
123	Derek Lee/50	30.00
124	Dontrelle Willis/50	20.00
125	Roy Oswalt/50	30.00
126	Ryan Garko/99	20.00
127	Tadahito Iguchi/99	15.00
128	Mark Loretta/99	15.00
129	Joe Mauer/50	50.00
130	Victor Martinez/99	25.00
131	Wily Mo Pena/99	15.00
132	Oliver Perez/99	10.00
133	Corey Patterson/99	15.00
134	Ben Sheets/99	25.00
135	Michael Young/99	25.00
136	Jonny Gomes/99	15.00
137	Derek Jeter/50	175.00
138	Ken Griffey Jr./99	100.00
139	Ryan Zimmerman/99	50.00
140	Scott Baker/99	

#	Player	Price
141	Huston Street/99	25.00
142	Jason Myrow/99	25.00
143	Ryan Howard/99	75.00
145	Travis Hafner/99	25.00
146	Brian Myrow/99	15.00
147	Scott Podsednik/99	30.00
148	Brian Roberts/99	25.00
149	Grady Sizemore/50	40.00
150	Chris Demaria/99	15.00
151	Jonah Bayliss/99	15.00
152	Geovany Soto/99	40.00
153	Lyle Overbay/99	20.00
154	Joey Devine/99	15.00
155	Alejandro Freire/99	15.00
156	Conor Jackson/99	15.00
157	Danny Sandoval/99	15.00
158	Chase Utley/99	60.00
159	Jeff Harris/99	15.00
160	Ron Flores/99	15.00
161	Scott Feldman/99	15.00
162	Yadier Molina/99	30.00
163	Tim Corcoran/99	15.00
164	Craig Hansen/99	15.00
165	Jason Bergmann/99	15.00
166	Craig Breslow/99	15.00
167	Jhonny Peralta/90	15.00
168	Jeremy Hermida/99	20.00
169	Scott Kazmir/99	25.00
170	Bobby Crosby/50	15.00
171	Rich Harden/99	20.00
172	Casey Kotchman/99	15.00
173	Tim Hamulack/99	15.00
174	Justin Morneau/99	35.00
175	Jake Peavy/99	25.00
176	Yuniesky Betancourt/99	25.00
177	Jeremy Accardo/99	15.00
178	Jorge Cantu/99	30.00
179	Marlon Byrd/99	25.00
180	Ryan Jorgensen/99	15.00
181	Chris Denorfia/99	15.00
182	Steve Stemle/99	15.00
183	Robert Andino/91	15.00
184	Chris Heintz/99	15.00

Red-Blue Stitch Blue Ink

NM/M

Production 10-50

#	Player	Price
102	Matt Cain/40	30.00
110	Scott Rolen/50	40.00
116	Edwin Jackson/50	20.00
127	Tadahito Iguchi/50	40.00
128	Mark Loretta/50	25.00
129	Joe Mauer/50	40.00
130	Victor Martinez/50	30.00
131	Wily Mo Pena/50	15.00
132	Oliver Perez/30	15.00
133	Corey Patterson/50	15.00
134	Ben Sheets/50	20.00
136	Jonny Gomes/50	15.00
138	Ken Griffey Jr./50	125.00
139	Ryan Zimmerman/50	50.00
140	Scott Baker/50	20.00
141	Huston Street/50	30.00
142	Jason Bay/50	25.00
143	Ryan Howard/50	75.00
144	Mike Piazza/50	120.00
145	Travis Hafner/50	20.00
146	Brian Myrow/50	15.00
147	Scott Podsednik/50	25.00
148	Brian Roberts/50	25.00
149	Grady Sizemore/25	40.00
150	Chris Demaria/50	15.00
151	Jonah Bayliss/50	15.00
152	Geovany Soto/50	25.00
153	Lyle Overbay/50	15.00
154	Joey Devine/50	15.00
155	Alejandro Freire/50	15.00
156	Conor Jackson/50	15.00
157	Danny Sandoval/50	15.00
158	Chase Utley/50	65.00
159	Jeff Harris/50	15.00
160	Ron Flores/50	15.00
161	Scott Feldman/50	15.00
162	Yadier Molina/30	30.00
163	Tim Corcoran/50	15.00
164	Craig Hansen/50	15.00
165	Jason Bergmann/50	15.00
166	Craig Breslow/50	15.00
167	Jhonny Peralta/50	20.00
168	Jeremy Hermida/50	20.00
170	Bobby Crosby/50	15.00
171	Rich Harden/50	20.00
172	Casey Kotchman/50	15.00
173	Tim Hamulack/50	15.00
174	Justin Morneau/50	30.00
175	Jake Peavy/49	30.00
176	Jeremy Accardo/50	15.00
180	Ryan Jorgensen/50	15.00
181	Chris Denorfia/50	15.00
182	Steve Stemle/50	15.00
183	Robert Andino/50	15.00
184	Chris Heintz/50	15.00

Super Sweet Swatch

NM/M

Production 299 Sets
Gold: 1-2X
Production 75 Sets
Platinum: 1.5-3X
Production 45 Sets

Code	Player	Price
BA	Bobby Abreu	8.00
GA	Garret Anderson	5.00
AT	Garrett Atkins	5.00
JB	Jeff Bagwell	8.00
BE	Josh Beckett	8.00
LB	Lance Berkman	8.00
RB	Rocco Baldelli	5.00
CB	Craig Biggio	6.00
HB	Hank Blalock	6.00
MI	Miguel Cabrera	12.00
MA	Matt Cain	10.00
EC	Eric Chavez	5.00
BC	Brandon Claussen	5.00
MC	Matt Clement	5.00
CR	Bobby Crosby/136	5.00
CD	Carlos Delgado	8.00
ZD	Zachary Duke	5.00
AD	Adam Dunn	8.00
DY	Jermaine Dye	5.00
AE	Adam Eaton	5.00
ED	Jim Edmonds	8.00
JE	Johnny Estrada	5.00
PF	Prince Fielder	15.00
FR	Jeff Francoeur	8.00
EG	Eric Gagne	5.00
FG	Freddy Garcia	5.00
JG	Jason Giambi	8.00
BG	Brian Giles	5.00
MG	Marcus Giles	5.00
TG	Troy Glaus/160	5.00
GL	Tom Glavine	8.00
KG	Ken Griffey Jr.	25.00
VG	Vladimir Guerrero	10.00
HA	Travis Hafner	8.00
HY	Roy Halladay	10.00
HT	Todd Helton/232	8.00
FH	Felix Hernandez	10.00
HE	Ramon Hernandez	5.00
HO	Trevor Hoffman	5.00
RH	Ryan Howard	20.00
TH	Tim Hudson	8.00
HU	Torii Hunter	5.00
DJ	Derek Jeter	30.00
NJ	Nick Johnson	5.00
AJ	Andruw Jones	5.00
CJ	Chipper Jones	10.00
JJ	Jacque Jones	5.00
SK	Scott Kazmir	5.00
RK	Ryan Klesko	5.00
KO	Paul Konerko	8.00
DL	Derek Lee	10.00
ML	Mark Loretta	5.00
NL	Noah Lowry	5.00
PM	Pedro Martinez	15.00
VM	Victor Martinez	8.00
JM	Joe Mauer	10.00
JU	Justin Morneau	8.00
MM	Mark Mulder	5.00
TN	Trot Nixon	5.00
RO	David Ortiz	8.00
RO	Roy Oswalt	5.00
JA	Jay Payton	5.00
PE	Jake Peavy	8.00
AN	Andy Pettitte	5.00
PI	Mike Piazza	10.00
JP	Jorge Posada	10.00
MP	Mark Prior	5.00
AP	Albert Pujols	30.00
MR	Manny Ramirez	10.00
JR	Jose Reyes	10.00
IR	Ivan Rodriguez/193	10.00
SR	Scott Rolen	8.00
SA	Johan Santana	10.00
CS	Curt Schilling	5.00
JS	Jason Schmidt	5.00
RS	Richie Sexson	5.00
BS	Ben Sheets	5.00
GS	Gary Sheffield	10.00
GR	Grady Sizemore	20.00
JO	John Smoltz	5.00
ST	Huston Street	5.00
MS	Mike Sweeney	5.00
NS	Nick Swisher	5.00
TX	Mark Teixeira	10.00
MT	Miguel Tejada	10.00
FT	Frank Thomas	15.00
JV	Jason Varitek	5.00
RW	Rickie Weeks	5.00
WE	David Wells	5.00
VW	Vernon Wells	8.00
BW	Bernie Williams	5.00
DW	Dontrelle Willis	8.00
JW	Jack Wilson	5.00
KW	Kerry Wood	5.00
RZ	Ryan Zimmerman	10.00
BZ	Barry Zito	5.00

2006 UD Sweet Spot Update

NM/M
Complete Set (182):
Common Player (1-100): .25
Common Auto. (101-184): 10.00
Production 98-499
Pack (5): 10.00
Box (12): 100.00

#	Player	Price
1	Luis Gonzalez	.25
2	Chad Tracy	.25
3	Brandon Webb	.50
4	Andruw Jones	.50
5	Chipper Jones	1.00
6	John Smoltz	.50
7	Tim Hudson	.50
8	Miguel Tejada	.50
9	Brian Roberts	.50
10	Ramon Hernandez	.25
11	Curt Schilling	.75
12	David Ortiz	1.00
13	Manny Ramirez	1.00
14	Jason Varitek	1.00
15	Josh Beckett	.75
16	Greg Maddux	2.00
17	Derrek Lee	.75
18	Mark Prior	.50
19	Aramis Ramirez	.50
20	Jim Thome	.75
21	Paul Konerko	.50
22	Scott Podsednik	.25
23	Jose Contreras	.25
24	Ken Griffey Jr.	2.00
25	Adam Dunn	.75
26	Felipe Lopez	.25
27	Travis Hafner	.50
28	Victor Martinez	.50
29	Grady Sizemore	.75
30	Jhonny Peralta	.25
31	Todd Helton	.50
32	Garrett Atkins	.50
33	Clint Barmes	.25
34	Ivan Rodriguez	.75
35	Chris Shelton	.50
36	Jeremy Bonderman	.50
37	Miguel Cabrera	1.00
38	Dontrelle Willis	.50
39	Lance Berkman	.50
40	Morgan Ensberg	.25
41	Roy Oswalt	.50
42	Reggie Sanders	.25
43	Mike Sweeney	.25
44	Vladimir Guerrero	1.00
45	Bartolo Colon	.50
46	Chone Figgins	.50
47	Nomar Garciaparra	.50
48	Jeff Kent	.50
49	J.D. Drew	.50
50	Carlos Lee	.50
51	Ben Sheets	.50
52	Rickie Weeks	.50
53	Johan Santana	1.00
54	Torii Hunter	.50
55	Joe Mauer	.75
56	Pedro Martinez	.75
57	David Wright	2.00
58	Carlos Beltran	.75
59	Carlos Delgado	.50
60	Jose Reyes	1.00
61	Derek Jeter	3.00
62	Alex Rodriguez	2.50
63	Randy Johnson	1.00
64	Hideki Matsui	2.00
65	Gary Sheffield	.75
66	Rich Harden	.50
67	Eric Chavez	.25
68	Huston Street	.25
69	Bobby Crosby	.25
70	Bobby Abreu	.50
71	Ryan Howard	2.00
72	Chase Utley	1.50
73	Pat Burrell	.50
74	Jason Bay	.50
75	Sean Casey	.25
76	Mike Piazza	1.50
77	Jake Peavy	.25
78	Brian Giles	.25
79	Milton Bradley	.25
80	Omar Vizquel	.25
81	Jason Schmidt	.25
82	Ichiro Suzuki	2.00
83	Felix Hernandez	.50
84	Kenji Johjima	.50
85	Albert Pujols	3.00
86	Chris Carpenter	.75
87	Scott Rolen	.50
88	Jim Edmonds	.50
89	Carl Crawford	.50
90	Jonny Gomes	.25
91	Scott Kazmir	.50
92	Mark Teixeira	.50
93	Michael Young	.50
94	Phil Nevin	.25
95	Vernon Wells	.50
96	Roy Halladay	.50
97	Troy Glaus	.50
98	Alfonso Soriano	1.00
99	Nick Johnson	.25
100	Jose Vidro	.25
101	Adam Wainwright/100 RC	40.00
102	Anderson Hernandez/100 RC	15.00
103	Andre Ethier/150 RC	30.00
104	Jason Botts/100 RC	10.00
105	Ben Johnson/400 RC	10.00
106	Boof Bonser/100 RC	10.00
107	Boone Logan/200 RC	10.00
108	Brian Anderson/200 RC	10.00
109	Brian Bannister/100 RC	10.00
110	Chris Denorfia/100 RC	10.00
111	Agustin Montero/100 RC	10.00
112	Cody Ross/100 RC	10.00
113	Cole Hamels/399 RC	35.00
114	Conor Jackson/400 RC	35.00
115	Dan Uggla/125 RC	35.00
116	Dave Gassner/100 RC	10.00
117	C.J. Wilson/150 RC	10.00
118	Eric Reed/150 RC	10.00
119	Fausto Carmona/99 RC	15.00
120	Fernando Nieve/100 RC	10.00
121	Francisco Liriano/499 RC	25.00
122	Freddie Bynum/100 RC	10.00
123	Hanley Ramirez/400 RC	40.00
124	Hong-Chih Kuo/100 RC	40.00
125	Ian Kinsler/100 RC	40.00
126	Carlos Marmol/100 RC	25.00
127	Bobby Keppel/200 RC	10.00
128	Jason Kubel/100 RC	15.00
129	Jeff Harris/100 RC	10.00
130	Alay Soler/100 RC	10.00
131	Jered Weaver/100 RC	30.00
132	Carlos Quentin/100 RC	25.00
133	Jeremy Hermida/100 RC	10.00
134	Joel Zumaya/100 RC	15.00
135	Joey Devine/100 RC	15.00
136	Jon Koronka/98 RC	10.00
137	Jonathan Papelbon/399 RC	25.00
138	Jose Capellan/240 RC	10.00
139	Josh Johnson/100 RC	15.00
140	Josh Rupe/100 RC	10.00
141	Josh Willingham/100 RC	15.00
143	Justin Verlander/100 RC	40.00
144	Kelly Shoppach/100 RC	10.00
145	Kendry Morales/100 RC	25.00
146	Kevin Thompson/100 RC	10.00
147	Macay McBride/100 RC	10.00
148	Martin Prado/100 RC	20.00
149	Matt Cain/150 RC	30.00
150	Clay Hensley/100 RC	10.00
151	Ty Taubenheim/100 RC	10.00
152	Mike Jacobs/200 RC	15.00
153	Saul Rivera/100 RC	10.00
154	Mike Thompson/100 RC	10.00
155	Nate McLouth/100 RC	10.00
156	Michael Vento/100 RC	15.00
157	Paul Maholm/200 RC	15.00
159	Reggie Abercrombie/100 RC	10.00
160	Mike Rouse/100 RC	10.00
161	Ken Ray/100 RC	10.00
162	Ron Flores/100 RC	10.00
163	Ryan Zimmerman/100 RC	40.00
164	Erick Aybar/100 RC	20.00
165	Sean Marshall/150 RC	15.00
166	Takashi Saito/100 RC	10.00
167	Taylor Buchholz/100 RC	15.00
168	Matt Murton/100 RC	10.00
169	Luis Figueroa/100 RC	15.00
170	Wilbert Nieves/100 RC	10.00
171	James Shields/100 RC	20.00
172	Jon Lester/399 RC	50.00
173	Craig Hansen/100 RC	10.00
174	Aaron Rakers/100 RC	10.00
175	Bobby Livingston/100 RC	10.00
176	Brendan Harris/100 RC	10.00
177	Zach Jackson/100 RC	10.00
178	Chris Britton/100 RC	10.00
179	Howie Kendrick/399 RC	25.00
180	Zach Miner/100 RC	10.00
181	Kevin Frandsen/100 RC	10.00
182	Matt Capps/100 RC	15.00
183	Peter Moylan/100 RC	10.00
184	Melky Cabrera/100 RC	15.00

Sig. Red/Blue Stitch Red Ink

NM/M

Production 40-225

#	Player	Price
101	Adam Wainwright/50	40.00
103	Andre Ethier/50	40.00
105	Ben Johnson/100	10.00
106	Boof Bonser/50	10.00
107	Boone Logan/50	10.00
108	Brian Anderson/100	10.00
109	Brian Bannister/100	10.00
110	Chris Denorfia/50	10.00
112	Cody Ross/50	10.00
113	Cole Hamels/225	40.00
114	Conor Jackson/100	30.00
115	Dan Uggla/50	40.00
116	Dave Gassner/50	10.00
117	C.J. Wilson/50	10.00
118	Eric Reed/100	10.00
119	Fausto Carmona/50	10.00
120	Fernando Nieve/50	10.00
121	Francisco Liriano/175	30.00
122	Freddie Bynum/50	10.00
123	Hanley Ramirez/50	60.00
124	Hong-Chih Kuo/50	10.00
125	Ian Kinsler/45	50.00
126	Carlos Marmol/50	30.00
127	Bobby Keppel/50	10.00
128	Jason Kubel/50	10.00
130	Alay Soler/50	15.00
131	Jered Weaver/50	30.00
132	Carlos Quentin/50	30.00
133	Jeremy Hermida/50	20.00
134	Joel Zumaya/50	40.00
135	Joey Devine/50	15.00
136	Jon Koronka/50	10.00
137	Jonathan Papelbon/175	30.00
138	Jose Capellan/50	10.00
139	Josh Johnson/50	10.00
140	Josh Rupe/50	10.00
141	Josh Willingham/50	20.00
143	Justin Verlander/50	15.00
144	Kelly Shoppach/50	15.00
146	Kevin Thompson/50	15.00
147	Macay McBride/50	15.00
150	Clay Hensley/49	10.00
151	Ty Taubenheim/50	20.00
152	Mike Jacobs/100	15.00
153	Saul Rivera/50	15.00
154	Mike Thompson/50	15.00
155	Nate McLouth/50	20.00
156	Michael Vento/50	15.00
159	Reggie Abercrombie/50	15.00
160	Mike Rouse/50	15.00
161	Ken Ray/50	15.00
162	Ron Flores/50	15.00
163	Ryan Zimmerman/50	50.00
165	Sean Kazmir/50	15.00
167	Taylor Buchholz/50	15.00
168	Matt Murton/50	15.00
169	Luis Figueroa/50	15.00
170	Wilbert Nieves/50	15.00
171	James Shields/50	20.00
172	Jon Lester/175	50.00
174	Aaron Rakers/50	10.00
175	Bobby Livingston/50	15.00
177	Zach Jackson/50	15.00
178	Chris Britton/50	10.00
179	Howie Kendrick/175	25.00
181	Kevin Frandsen/50	10.00
182	Matt Capps/50	10.00
183	Peter Moylan/50	10.00

Veteran Red Stitch Blue Ink

NM/M

Production 30-525

Code	Player	Price
AG	Tony Gwynn Jr./425	20.00
AH	Aaron Harang/425	15.00
AP	Albert Pujols/30	250.00
AZ	Aramis Ramirez/225	25.00
BJ	B.J. Upton/193	15.00
BR	Brian Roberts/300	15.00
CC	Carl Crawford/425	20.00
CU	Chase Utley/425	60.00
DJ	Derek Jeter/75	200.00
DW	Dontrelle Willis/125	15.00
HS	Huston Street/200	15.00
JB	Jason Bay/425	20.00
JM	Joe Mauer/57	50.00
JN	Joe Nathan/200	20.00
JS	Jeremy Sowers/425	15.00
JT	Jim Thome/75	20.00
KG	Ken Griffey Jr./359	80.00
KG2	Ken Griffey Jr./358	80.00
KY	Kevin Youkilis/425	25.00
LO	Lyle Overbay/525	15.00
MC	Miguel Cabrera/525	30.00
MO	Justin Morneau/425	25.00
RC	Roger Clemens/30	100.00
SD	Stephen Drew/425	20.00
SK	Scott Kazmir/522	20.00
SM	John Smoltz/507	35.00
SP	Scott Podsednik/247	15.00
SS	Mark Mulder/300	15.00
TH	Travis Hafner/525	25.00
TI	Tadahito Iguchi/525	15.00
VM	Victor Martinez/71	20.00

Veteran Red/Blue Stitch Red Ink

NM/M

Production 10-299

Code	Player	Price
AG	Tony Gwynn Jr./299	25.00
AH	Aaron Harang/299	15.00
AZ	Aramis Ramirez/99	30.00
BJ	B.J. Upton/299	20.00
BR	Brian Roberts/100	20.00
CC	Carl Crawford/299	20.00
CU	Chase Utley/299	60.00
DW	Dontrelle Willis/35	25.00
HS	Huston Street/100	15.00
JB	Jason Bay/299	25.00
JN	Joe Nathan/100	20.00
JS	Jeremy Sowers/299	15.00
KG	Ken Griffey Jr./38	120.00
KG2	Ken Griffey Jr./37	120.00
KY	Kevin Youkilis/299	30.00
LO	Lyle Overbay/299	15.00
MC	Miguel Cabrera/299	30.00
MO	Justin Morneau/299	30.00
SD	Stephen Drew/299	25.00
SK	Scott Kazmir/296	25.00
SP	Scott Podsednik/199	15.00
SS	Mark Mulder/298	15.00
TH	Travis Hafner/299	20.00
TI	Tadahito Iguchi/299	30.00
VM	Victor Martinez/61	20.00

Signatures Black Stitch/Ink

No Pricing
Production One Set

Sweet Beginnings Swatches

NM/M

Code	Player	Price
	Common Player:	5.00
AB	Adrian Beltre	5.00
AI	Akinori Iwamura	5.00
AJ	Andruw Jones	8.00
AP	Ariel Pestano	5.00
AR	Alex Rios	8.00
AS	Alfonso Soriano	10.00
BA	Bobby Abreu	5.00
BB	Brian Bannister	5.00
BI	Chad Billingsley	5.00
BW	Bernie Williams	10.00
CA	Miguel Cabrera	10.00
CB	Carlos Beltran	8.00
CD	Carlos Delgado	8.00
CH	Chin-Lung Hu	10.00
CJ	Conor Jackson	5.00
CL	Carlos Lee	5.00
CM	Matt Cain	10.00
CU	Chris Duncan	8.00
CZ	Carlos Zambrano	8.00
DL	Derrek Lee	8.00
DO	David Ortiz	12.00
EB	Erik Bedard	8.00
EP	Eduardo Paret	8.00
FA	Fausto Carmona	5.00
FC	Frederich Cepeda	8.00
FL	Francisco Liriano/SP	20.00
GY	Guogang Yang	5.00
HA	Cole Hamels	15.00
HC	Hee Seop Choi	8.00
HT	Hitoshi Tamura	15.00
IK	Ian Kinsler	10.00
IR	Ivan Rodriguez	15.00
IS	Ichiro Suzuki	100.00
JB	Jason Bay	10.00
JD	Johnny Damon	10.00
JF	Jeff Francis	5.00
JH	Jeremy Hermida	8.00
JL	Jong Beom Lee	8.00
JM	Justin Morneau	15.00
JP	Jin Man Park	8.00
JS	Johan Santana	15.00
JV	Jason Varitek	15.00
JZ	Joel Zumaya	8.00
KE	Matthew Kemp	15.00
KG	Ken Griffey Jr.	20.00
KJ	Kenji Johjima/SP	15.00
KU	Koji Uehara	10.00
LO	Javy Lopez	8.00
MA	Moises Alou	8.00
MC	Michael Collins	8.00
ME	Michel Enriquez	8.00
MF	Maikel Folch	5.00
MJ	Mike Jacobs	8.00
MK	Munenori Kawasaki	25.00
MN	Michael Napoli	8.00
MO	Michihiro Ogasawara	20.00
MP	Mike Piazza	15.00
MS	Min Han Son	8.00
MT	Miguel Tejada	8.00
NM	Nobuhiko Matsunaka	25.00
NS	Naoyuki Shimizu	20.00
OU	Osmany Urrutia	10.00
PF	Prince Fielder/SP	20.00
PL	Pedro Luis Lazo	8.00
PU	Albert Pujols	25.00
RO	Alex Rodriguez	20.00
SH	Jamie Shields	10.00
SW	Shunsuke Watanabe	8.00
TN	Tsuyoshi Nishioka	20.00
TW	Tsuyoshi Wada	20.00
VE	Justin Verlander	15.00
VM	Victor Martinez	8.00
VO	Vicyohandry Odelin	5.00
WI	Josh Willingham	8.00
WL	Wei-Chu Lin	40.00
YG	Yulieski Gourriel	15.00
YM	Yuniesky Maya	10.00

Dual Signatures

NM/M

Production 1-55

Code	Players	Price
BN	Taylor Buchholz, Fernando Nieve/55	25.00
CK	Scott Kazmir, Carl Crawford/55	40.00
CU	Carl Crawford, B.J. Upton/45	40.00
CW	Chris Carpenter, Dontrelle Willis/35	40.00
CZ	Miguel Cabrera, Ryan Zimmerman/35	50.00
EG	Andre Ethier, Tony Gwynn Jr./35	40.00
GG	Vladimir Guerrero, Ken Griffey Jr./35	150.00
GT	Ken Griffey Jr., Jim Thome/35	150.00
HD	Dan Uggla, Howie Kendrick/55	40.00
HK	Jeremy Hermida, Jason Kubel/55	30.00
HW	Jeremy Hermida, Josh Willingham/55	30.00
KR	Brian Roberts, Howie Kendrick/35	40.00
KU	B.J. Upton, Scott Kazmir/35	35.00
KW	Scott Kazmir, Dontrelle Willis/35	30.00
LN	Francisco Liriano, Joe Nathan/35	50.00
MM	Joe Mauer, Justin Morneau/35	60.00
MO	Justin Morneau, Lyle Overbay/35	40.00
PO	Jake Peavy, Roy Oswalt/35	40.00
PZ	Jonathan Papelbon, Joel Zumaya/35	90.00
RO	Alex Rios, Lyle Overbay/35	30.00
RR	Jose Reyes, Hanley Ramirez/60	60.00
SN	Huston Street, Joe Nathan/35	30.00
TI	Jim Thome, Tadahito Iguchi/35	100.00

TJ	Jeremy Sowers, Travis Hafner/35	30.00
UD	Stephen Drew, B.J. Upton/35	75.00
UH	Cole Hamels, Chase Utley/35	90.00
UU	Chase Utley, Dan Uggla/35	50.00
UW	Dan Uggla, Josh Willingham/55	30.00
ZU	Ryan Zimmerman, B.J. Upton/35	40.00

Spokesmen Signatures
No Pricing
Production Five Sets

Sweet Beginnings Patch
NM/M
Common Player:

AB	Adrian Beltre	30.00
AE	Andre Ethier	50.00
AJ	Andruw Jones	20.00
AP	Ariel Pestano	20.00
AS	Alfonso Soriano	40.00
BA	Bobby Abreu	30.00
BB	Brian Bannister	20.00
BI	Chad Billingsley	20.00
BW	Bernie Williams	30.00
CA	Miguel Cabrera	50.00
CB	Carlos Beltran	30.00
CD	Carlos Delgado	30.00
CJ	Conor Jackson	20.00
CL	Carlos Lee	20.00
CM	Matt Cain	30.00
CU	Chris Duncan	30.00
CZ	Carlos Zambrano	30.00
DL	Derrek Lee	30.00
DO	David Ortiz	50.00
DU	Dan Uggla	25.00
EB	Erik Bedard	20.00
EP	Eduardo Paret	20.00
FA	Fausto Carmona	20.00
FC	Frederich Cepeda	20.00
FL	Francisco Liriano	30.00
HA	Cole Hamels	40.00
HK	Hong-Chih Kuo	100.00
JB	Jason Bay	40.00
JD	Johnny Damon	40.00
JF	Jeff Francis	20.00
JH	Jeremy Hermida	20.00
JJ	Josh Johnson	20.00
JO	Josh Barfield	20.00
JS	Johan Santana	40.00
JV	Jason Varitek	40.00
JZ	Joel Zumaya	50.00
KE	Matthew Kemp	50.00
KJ	Kenji Johjima	40.00
KU	Koji Uehara	80.00
LE	Jon Lester	60.00
LO	Javy Lopez	20.00
MC	Michael Collins	30.00
ME	Michel Enriquez	30.00
MF	Maikel Folch	30.00
MJ	Mike Jacobs	20.00
MK	Munenori Kawasaki	150.00
MN	Michael Napoli	30.00
MO	Michihiro Ogasawara	100.00
MP	Mike Piazza	75.00
MS	Min Han Son/SP	80.00
NI	Nick Markakis	40.00
NM	Nobuhiko Matsunaka	65.00
NS	Naoyuki Shimizu	80.00
OU	Osmany Urrutia	30.00
PA	Jonathan Papelbon	40.00
PE	Mike Pelfrey	50.00
PL	Pedro Luis Lazo	30.00
PU	Albert Pujols	150.00
RN	Ricky Nolasco	25.00
RZ	Ryan Zimmerman	40.00
TW	Tsuyoshi Wada	150.00
VE	Justin Verlander	40.00
VM	Victor Martinez	40.00
VO	Vicyohandry Odelin	30.00
WE	Jered Weaver	40.00
WI	Josh Willingham	30.00
YG	Yulieski Gourriel	50.00
YM	Yuneiski Maya	25.00
RM	Russell Martin	40.00

Signatures Barrels Black Ink
NM/M
Production 34-70
Blue Ink: No Pricing
Production 9-20
Silver Ink: No Pricing
Production One Set

101	Adam Wainwright/35	50.00
103	Andre Ethier/35	50.00
105	Ben Johnson/35	20.00
106	Boof Bonser/35	20.00
107	Boone Logan/35	20.00
108	Brian Anderson/35	20.00
109	Brian Bannister/35	20.00
110	Chris Denorfia/35	20.00
112	Cody Ross/35	20.00
113	Cole Hamels/70	50.00
114	Conor Jackson/35	20.00
115	Dan Uggla/35	35.00
116	Dave Gassner/35	20.00
117	C.J. Wilson/35	15.00
118	Eric Reed/35	20.00
119	Fausto Carmona/35	20.00
120	Fernando Nieve/35	15.00
121	Francisco Liriano/70	80.00
122	Freddie Bynum/35	15.00
123	Hanley Ramirez/35	40.00
124	Hong-Chih Kuo/35	80.00
125	Ian Kinsler/35	50.00
126	Carlos Marmol/35	30.00
127	Bobby Keppel/35	15.00
128	Jason Kubel/35	20.00
130	Alay Soler/35	20.00
132	Carlos Quentin/35	30.00
133	Jeremy Hermida/35	25.00
134	Joel Zumaya/35	20.00
135	Joey Devine/35	15.00
136	John Koronka/35	15.00
137	Jonathan Papelbon/70	30.00
138	Jose Capellan/35	15.00
139	Josh Johnson/35	25.00
141	Josh Willingham/35	20.00
143	Justin Verlander/35	50.00
144	Kelly Shoppach/35	20.00
146	Kevin Thompson/35	20.00
147	Macay McBride/35	15.00
149	Matt Cain/35	40.00
150	Clay Hensley/35	15.00
151	Ty Taubenheim/35	20.00
152	Mike Jacobs/35	20.00
153	Saul Rivera/35	15.00
154	Mike Thompson/35	20.00
155	Nate McLouth/35	20.00
156	Michael Vento/35	20.00
157	Paul Maholm/35	20.00
159	Reggie Abercrombie/35	20.00
160	Mike Rouse/35	15.00
161	Ken Ray/35	15.00
162	Ron Flores/35	15.00
163	Ryan Zimmerman/35	50.00
164	Erick Aybar/35	25.00
165	Sean Marshall/35	15.00
167	Taylor Buchholz/35	15.00
168	Matt Murton/35	20.00
169	Luis Figueroa/34	20.00
170	Wilbert Nieves/30	15.00
171	Jamie Shields/35	35.00
172	Jon Lester/37	60.00
174	Aaron Rakers/35	15.00
175	Bobby Livingston/35	15.00
176	Brendan Harris/35	15.00
177	Zach Jackson/35	15.00
178	Chris Britton/35	15.00
179	Howie Kendrick/70	40.00
181	Kevin Frandsen/35	15.00
182	Matt Capps/35	15.00
183	Peter Moylan/35	15.00

Signatures Leather Black Ink
NM/M
Production 20-40
Blue Ink: No Pricing
Production 5-10
Silver Ink: No Pricing
Production One Set

113	Cole Hamels/40	60.00
121	Francisco Liriano/40	60.00
137	Jonathan Papelbon/40	75.00
172	Jon Lester/40	60.00
179	Howie Kendrick/40	50.00

Veterans Barrels Black Ink
NM/M
Production 10-35
Blue Ink: No Pricing
Production 1-20
Silver Ink: No Pricing
Production One Set

AG	Tony Gwynn Jr./35	30.00
AH	Aaron Harang/35	35.00
AZ	Aramis Ramirez/35	30.00
BJ	B.J. Upton/35	35.00
BR	Brian Roberts/35	25.00
CC	Carl Crawford/35	30.00
CU	Chase Utley/35	75.00
HS	Huston Street/35	30.00
JB	Jason Bay/35	30.00
JN	Joe Nathan/35	30.00
JS	Jeremy Sowers/35	35.00
KG	Ken Griffey Jr./28	100.00
KG2	Ken Griffey Jr./27	100.00
KY	Kevin Youkilis/35	40.00
LO	Lyle Overbay/35	25.00
MC	Miguel Cabrera/35	50.00
MO	Justin Morneau/35	35.00
SD	Stephen Drew/35	60.00
SK	Scott Kazmir/33	30.00
SM	John Smoltz/35	50.00
SO	Scott Podsednik/35	25.00
SS	Mark Mulder/35	25.00
TH	Travis Hafner/35	40.00
TI	Tadahito Iguchi/35	60.00
VM	Victor Martinez/35	30.00

Veteran Lether Black Ink
NM/M
Production 5-20
Blue Ink: No Pricing
Production 1-5
Silver Ink: No Pricing
Production One Set

2006 UD Ultimate Collection
NM/M
Complete Set (290):
Common Player (1-100): 1.50
Common RC Auto. (101-175): 10.00
Production 180 unless noted.
Common (191-290): 2.00
Production 799
Pack (4): 75.00
Box (4): 250.00

1	Babe Ruth	8.00
2	Chad Tracy	1.50
3	Brandon Webb	2.00
4	Andruw Jones	3.00
5	Chipper Jones	4.00
6	John Smoltz	2.00
7	Eddie Mathews	4.00
8	Miguel Tejada	3.00
9	Brian Roberts	2.00
10	Mickey Cochrane	2.00
11	Curt Schilling	3.00
12	David Ortiz	4.00
13	Manny Ramirez	4.00
14	Johnny Bench	4.00
15	Cy Young	5.00
16	Greg Maddux	5.00
17	Derek Lee	3.00
18	Yogi Berra	4.00
19	Walter Johnson	2.00
20	Jim Thome	3.00
21	Paul Konerko	2.00
22	Lou Gehrig	6.00
23	Jose Contreras	1.50
24	Ken Griffey Jr.	5.00
25	Adam Dunn	3.00
26	Reggie Jackson	3.00
27	Travis Hafner	2.00
28	Victor Martinez	2.00
29	Grady Sizemore	4.00
30	Casey Stengel	3.00
31	Todd Helton	3.00
32	Nolan Ryan	8.00
33	Clint Barmes	1.50
34	Ivan Rodriguez	3.00
35	Chris Shelton	1.50
36	Ty Cobb	5.00
37	Miguel Cabrera	4.00
38	Dontrelle Willis	1.50
39	Lance Berkman	2.00
40	Tom Seaver	4.00
41	Roy Oswalt	2.00
42	Christy Mathewson	3.00
43	Luis Aparicio	1.50
44	Vladimir Guerrero	4.00
45	Bartolo Colon	1.50
46	Roy Campanella	2.00
47	George Sisler	1.50
48	Jeff Kent	1.50
49	J.D. Drew	2.00
50	Carlos Lee	2.00
51	Willie Stargell	3.00
52	Rickie Weeks	1.50
53	Johan Santana	4.00
54	Torii Hunter	2.00
55	Joe Mauer	2.00
56	Pedro Martinez	4.00
57	David Wright	5.00
58	Carlos Beltran	3.00
59	Jimmie Foxx	3.00
60	Jose Reyes	4.00
61	Derek Jeter	8.00
62	Alex Rodriguez	6.00
63	Randy Johnson	4.00
64	Hideki Matsui	5.00
65	Thurman Munson	4.00
66	Rich Harden	1.50
67	Eric Chavez	1.50
68	Don Drysdale	3.00
69	Bobby Crosby	1.50
70	Pee Wee Reese	1.50
71	Ryan Howard	6.00
72	Chase Utley	4.00
73	Jackie Robinson	5.00
74	Jason Bay	3.00
75	Honus Wagner	4.00
76	Lefty Grove	3.00
77	Jake Peavy	2.00
78	Brian Giles	1.50
79	Eddie Murray	3.00
80	Omar Vizquel	1.50
81	Jason Schmidt	2.00
82	Ichiro Suzuki	5.00
83	Felix Hernandez	3.00
84	Kenji Johjima RC	5.00
85	Albert Pujols	8.00
86	Chris Carpenter	2.00
87	Brooks Robinson	3.00
88	Dizzy Dean	3.00
89	Carl Crawford	2.00
90	Rogers Hornsby	3.00
91	Scott Kazmir	2.00
92	Mark Teixeira	3.00
93	Michael Young	2.00
94	Johnny Mize	1.50
95	Vernon Wells	3.00
96	Roy Halladay	2.00
97	Mel Ott	1.50
98	Alfonso Soriano	3.00
99	Joe Morgan	3.00
100	Satchel Paige	4.00
101	Adam Wainwright RC	30.00
102	Josh Anderson Hernandez RC	10.00
103	Andre Ethier RC	30.00
104	Ben Johnson RC	10.00
105	Boof Bonser RC	10.00
106	Boone Logan RC	10.00
107	Brian Anderson RC	10.00
108	Brian Bannister RC	15.00
109	Chris Demaria RC	10.00
110	Chris Denorfia RC	10.00
111	Cody Ross RC	10.00
112	Cole Hamels RC	50.00
113	Conor Jackson RC	15.00
114	Dan Uggla RC	40.00
115	Dave Gassner RC	10.00
116	Eric Reed RC	10.00
117	Fausto Carmona RC	25.00
118	Fernando Nieve RC	10.00
119	Francisco Liriano RC	40.00
120	Freddie Bynum RC	10.00
121	Hanley Ramirez RC	50.00
122	Hong-Chih Kuo RC	30.00
123	Ian Kinsler RC	40.00
124	Jason Hammel RC	10.00
125	Jason Kubel RC	10.00
126	Jeff Harris RC	10.00
127	Jered Weaver/150 RC	40.00
128	Jeremy Accardo RC	10.00
129	Jeremy Hermida RC	10.00
130	Joel Zumaya RC	10.00
131	Joey Devine RC	10.00
132	John Koronka RC	10.00
133	John Van Benschoten RC	10.00
134	Jonathan Papelbon RC	30.00
135	Jose Capellan RC	10.00
136	Josh Johnson RC	15.00
137	Josh Rupe RC	10.00
138	Josh Willingham RC	15.00
139	Josh Wilson RC	10.00
140	Justin Verlander RC	50.00
141	Kelly Shoppach RC	10.00
142	Kendry Morales RC	20.00
143	Macay McBride RC	10.00
144	Martin Prado RC	10.00
145	Matt Cain RC	30.00
146	Mike Jacobs RC	15.00
147	Mike Thompson RC	10.00
148	Nate McLouth RC	10.00
149	Paul Maholm RC	10.00
150	Prince Fielder RC	75.00
151	Reggie Abercrombie RC	10.00
152	Rich Hill RC	15.00
153	Ron Flores RC	10.00
154	Ruddy Lugo RC	10.00
155	Ryan Zimmerman RC	50.00
156	Sean Marshall RC	15.00
157	Takashi Saito RC	20.00
158	Taylor Buchholz RC	15.00
159	Tony Pena RC	10.00
160	Wilbert Nieves RC	10.00
161	Jamie Shields RC	20.00
162	Jon Lester RC	50.00
163	Craig Hansen RC	15.00
164	Aaron Rakers RC	10.00
165	Yusmeiro Petit RC	10.00
166	Bobby Livingston RC	10.00
167	Brendan Harris RC	10.00
168	Carlos Ruiz RC	15.00
169	Chris Britton RC	10.00
170	Howie Kendrick RC	30.00
172	Jermaine Van Buren RC	10.00
173	Kevin Frandsen RC	15.00
174	Matt Capps RC	15.00
175	Peter Moylan RC	10.00
191	Richie Ashburn/799	4.00
192	Lou Brock	4.00
193	Lou Boudreau	2.00
194	Orlando Cepeda	2.00
195	Bobby Doerr	2.00
196	Dennis Eckersley	2.00
197	Bob Feller	3.00
198	Rollie Fingers	2.00
199	Carlton Fisk	4.00
200	Bob Gibson	4.00
201	Jim "Catfish" Hunter	3.00
202	Fergie Jenkins	3.00
203	Al Kaline	5.00
204	Harmon Killebrew	5.00
205	Ralph Kiner	3.00
206	Buck Leonard	2.00
207	Juan Marichal	2.00
208	Bill Mazeroski	4.00
209	Willie McCovey	4.00
210	Jim Palmer	2.00
211	Tony Perez	2.00
212	Gaylord Perry	2.00
213	Phil Rizzuto	4.00
214	Robin Roberts	2.00
215	Mike Schmidt	6.00
216	Enos Slaughter	2.00
217	Ozzie Smith	5.00
218	Billy Williams	2.00
219	Robin Yount	4.00
220	Carlos Quentin RC	4.00
221	Jeff Francoeur	2.00
222	Brian McCann	2.00
223	Nick Markakis RC	6.00
224	Josh Beckett	2.00
225	Jason Varitek	4.00
226	Mark Prior	4.00
227	Aramis Ramirez	3.00
228	Jermaine Dye	2.00
229	Tadahito Iguchi	2.00
230	Bobby Jenks	2.00
231	C.C. Sabathia	2.00
232	Jeff Francis	2.00
233	Matt Holliday	2.00
234	Magglio Ordonez	2.00
235	Kenny Rogers	2.00
236	Roger Clemens	8.00
237	Andy Pettitte	4.00
238	Craig Biggio	3.00
239	Chone Figgins	2.00
240	John Lackey	2.00
241	Nomar Garciaparra	4.00
242	Prince Fielder	6.00
243	Ben Sheets	2.00
244	Bill Hall	2.00
245	Justin Morneau	4.00
246	Joe Nathan	2.00
247	Carlos Delgado	2.00
248	Shawn Green	2.00
249	Billy Wagner	2.00
250	Jason Giambi	4.00
251	Mike Mussina	4.00
252	Mariano Rivera	4.00
253	Robinson Cano	4.00
254	Bobby Abreu	3.00
255	Huston Street	2.00
256	Frank Thomas	4.00
257	Danny Haren	2.00
258	Jason Kendall	2.00
259	Nick Swisher	3.00
260	Pat Burrell	3.00
261	Tom Gordon	2.00
262	Freddy Sanchez	2.00
263	Trevor Hoffman	2.00
264	Khalil Greene	2.00
265	Adrian Gonzalez	2.00
266	Moises Alou	2.00
267	Matt Morris	2.00
268	Pedro Feliz	2.00
269	Richie Sexson	3.00
270	Hoyt Wilhelm	2.00
271	Adrian Beltre	2.00
272	Jim Edmonds	3.00
273	Scott Rolen	4.00
274	Jason Isringhausen	2.00
275	Jorge Cantu	2.00
276	Hank Blalock	2.00
277	Kevin Millwood	2.00
278	Alex Rios	2.00
279	Troy Glaus	3.00
280	B.J. Ryan	2.00
281	Nick Johnson	2.00
282	Chad Cordero	2.00
283	Austin Kearns	2.00
284	Ricky Nolasco RC	2.00
285	Travis Ishikawa RC	2.00
286	Lastings Milledge RC	3.00
287	James Loney RC	4.00
288	Red Schoendienst	3.00
289	Warren Spahn	2.00
290	Early Wynn RC	2.00

Printing Plates
No Pricing
Production one set per color.

Ensemble Materials 3
Production 25 Sets
Patch: No Pricing
Production 20 Sets

Ensemble Materials 4
Production 20 Sets
Patch: No Pricing
Production 15 Sets

Ensemble Signature 3
NM/M
Production 50 Sets
Triple 15:
Production 15 Sets
Triple 1 of 1: No Pricing

AHW	Josh Willingham, Reggie Abercrombie, Jeremy Hermida	40.00
BBB	Jeff Bagwell, Craig Biggio, Lance Berkman	100.00
BBW	Taylor Buchholz, Adam Wainwright, Brian Bannister	50.00
BDD	George Bell, Eric Davis, Andre Dawson	50.00
BHR	Roy Halladay, A.J. Burnett, Alex Rios	40.00
BKM	Ralph Kiner, Bill Mazeroski, Jason Bay	85.00
BNO	Taylor Buchholz, Roy Oswalt, Fernando Nieve	30.00
BSH	A.J. Burnett, Rich Harden, Ben Sheets	40.00
BUK	Craig Biggio, Chase Utley, Ian Kinsler	75.00
BWC	Matt Cain, Brian Bannister, Adam Wainwright	40.00
BWV	Justin Verlander, Boof Bonser, Jered Weaver	85.00
CBP	Oliver Perez, Jason Bay, Sean Casey	30.00
CBS	Ron Cey, Dusty Baker, Don Sutton	50.00
CBZ	Boof Bonser, Joel Zumaya, Matt Cain	50.00
CDV	Jack Clark, Eric Davis, Andy Van Slyke	50.00
CHK	Jason Kubel, Melky Cabrera, Jeremy Hermida	50.00
CHO	Chris Carpenter, Roy Oswalt, Rich Harden	60.00
CKH	Rich Harden, Bobby Crosby, Jason Kendall	40.00
CKS	Carl Crawford, Scott Kazmir, Jamie Shields	50.00
CLH	Cole Hamels, Fausto Carmona, Francisco Liriano	80.00
CMH	Victor Martinez, Travis Hafner, Fausto Carmona	60.00
CNS	Graig Nettles, Ron Cey, Ron Santo	50.00
CPC	Carl Crawford, Coco Crisp, Scott Podsednik	40.00
CSS	John Smoltz, Roger Clemens, Curt Schilling	200.00
CWW	Josh Willingham, Dontrelle Willis, Miguel Cabrera	50.00
CZC	Miguel Cabrera, Eric Chavez, Ryan Zimmerman	60.00
DJH	Hanley Ramirez, Derek Jeter, Jose Reyes	200.00

DPA	Scott Podsednik, Jermaine Dye, Brian Anderson	40.00
DPI	Jermaine Dye, Scott Podsednik, Tadahito Iguchi	60.00
FGC	David Cone, Dwight Gooden, Sid Fernandez	75.00
FJM	Prince Fielder, Conor Jackson, Kendry Morales	40.00
FWL	Rickie Weeks, Prince Fielder, Carlos Lee	40.00
GCN	Graig Nettles, Rich "Goose" Gossage, Chris Chambliss	50.00
GCS	Bret Saberhagen, Dwight Gooden, David Cone	30.00
GJB	Derek Jeter, Ken Griffey Jr., Jason Bay	250.00
GJP	Derek Jeter, Albert Pujols, Ken Griffey Jr.	500.00
GLK	Dave Gassner, Jason Kubel, Francisco Liriano	50.00
GPN	Joe Nathan, Eric Gagne, Jonathan Papelbon	50.00
GRS	Alex Rios, Alfonso Soriano, Vladimir Guerrero	90.00
HBS	Rich Harden, Nick Swisher, Joe Blanton	40.00
HKP	Boog Powell, John Kruk, Kent Hrbek	40.00
HMK	Mark Mulder, Scott Kazmir, Cole Hamels	60.00
HNP	Jonathan Papelbon, Trevor Hoffman, Joe Nathan	75.00
HOT	David Ortiz, Travis Hafner, Mark Teixeira	100.00
HWU	Josh Willingham, Jeremy Hermida, Dan Uggla	30.00
IKU	Dan Uggla, Ian Kinsler, Tadahito Iguchi	85.00
JCN	Melky Cabrera, Wilbert Nieves, Derek Jeter	150.00
JGS	Ken Griffey Jr., Andruw Jones, Alfonso Soriano	120.00
JRR	Derek Jeter, Jose Reyes, Hanley Ramirez	200.00
JWV	Jered Weaver, Justin Verlander, Josh Johnson	75.00
KGJ	John Kruk, Mark Grace, Wally Joyner	80.00
KLB	Francisco Liriano, Boof Bonser, Jason Kubel	50.00
KUU	Ian Kinsler, Dan Uggla, Chase Utley	65.00
KWM	Josh Willingham, Victor Martinez, Jason Kendall	30.00
LGB	Francisco Liriano, Boof Bonser, Dave Gassner	40.00
LHC	Cole Hamels, Fausto Carmona, Francisco Liriano	50.00
LPO	Derrek Lee, David Ortiz, Albert Pujols	250.00
MCN	Ron Cey, Graig Nettles, Bill Madlock	50.00
MMK	Jason Kendall, Joe Mauer, Victor Martinez	40.00
MNL	Joe Mauer, Francisco Liriano, Joe Nathan	50.00
MWC	Chris Carpenter, Mark Mulder, Adam Wainwright	75.00
MWP	Josh Willingham, Russell Martin, Ronny Paulino	30.00
NLP	Jonathan Papelbon, Brad Lidge, Joe Nathan	50.00
OBL	Brad Lidge, Roy Oswalt, Taylor Buchholz	40.00
PCL	Oliver Perez, Francisco Liriano, Fausto Carmona	50.00
PHL	Cole Hamels, Francisco Liriano, Oliver Perez	65.00
PSO	Roy Oswalt, Jake Peavy, Ben Sheets	40.00
PVW	Justin Verlander, Jered Weaver, Jonathan Papelbon	90.00
RHW	Jeremy Hermida, Josh Willingham, Cody Ross	30.00
RMM	Victor Martinez, Joe Mauer, Ivan Rodriguez	65.00
RRB	Jose Reyes, Yuniesky Betancourt, Hanley Ramirez	60.00
SGM	Greg Maddux, John Smoltz, Tom Glavine	180.00
SJF	Prince Fielder, Mike Jacobs, Chris Shelton	30.00
SKM	Russell Martin, Takashi Saito, Hong-Chih Kuo	200.00
SWB	Taylor Buchholz, Jamie Shields, Jered Weaver	60.00

Code	Player	NM/M
TGB	Frank Thomas, Ken Griffey Jr., Jeff Bagwell	150.00
TKY	Michael Young, Mark Teixeira, Ian Kinsler	75.00
UHC	Jeremy Hermida, Dan Uggla, Miguel Cabrera	75.00
URC	Miguel Cabrera, Dan Uggla, Hanley Ramirez	40.00
URW	Hanley Ramirez, Dan Uggla, Josh Willingham	35.00
VBZ	Justin Verlander, Jeremy Bonderman, Joel Zumaya	120.00
VWL	Jered Weaver, Francisco Liriano, Justin Verlander	120.00
WJC	Josh Johnson, Jered Weaver, Matt Cain	70.00
WJO	Scott Olsen, Josh Johnson, Dontrelle Willis	40.00
WSV	Justin Verlander, Jered Weaver, Jamie Shields	65.00
ZBC	Joel Zumaya, Matt Cain, Boof Bonser	60.00
ZHZ	Carlos Zambrano, Felix Hernandez, Joel Zumaya	60.00

Ensemble Signatures 4
No Pricing
Production 25 Sets

Ensemble Signatures 5
No Pricing
Production 15 Sets

Ensemble Signatures 6
No Pricing
Production 10 Sets

Ensemble Signatures 8
Production One Set

Game Materials

NM/M
Common Player: 8.00
Production 50 Sets

Code	Player	NM/M
AB	A.J. Burnett	8.00
AD	Adam Dunn	10.00
AJ	Andruw Jones	8.00
AP	Albert Pujols	30.00
AR	Alex Rios	8.00
AS	Alfonso Soriano	10.00
BA	Brian Bannister	8.00
BG	Brian Giles	8.00
BM	Bill Mazeroski	15.00
BO	Jeremy Bonderman	10.00
BR	Brian Roberts	8.00
CC	Melky Cabrera	15.00
CC	Carl Crawford	10.00
CH	Chris Carpenter	15.00
CJ	Conor Jackson	10.00
CL	Carlos Lee	10.00
CR	Coco Crisp	10.00
CS	Chris Shelton	8.00
CU	Chase Utley	20.00
CZ	Carlos Zambrano	10.00
DJ	Derek Jeter	30.00
DJ2	Derek Jeter	30.00
DL	Derek Lee	30.00
DU	Dan Uggla	10.00
DW	Dontrelle Willis	10.00
FH	Felix Hernandez	12.00
FL	Francisco Liriano	15.00
GA	Garrett Atkins	8.00
GP	Gaylord Perry	10.00
HA	Cole Hamels	15.00
HB	Hank Blalock	10.00
HC	Craig Hansen	15.00
HO	Trevor Hoffman	10.00
HR	Hanley Ramirez	15.00
HT	Tim Hudson	10.00
HU	Torii Hunter	10.00
HY	Roy Halladay	10.00
IK	Ian Kinsler	10.00
IR	Ivan Rodriguez	10.00
JB	Jason Bay	12.00
JD	Jermaine Dye	10.00
JH	Jeremy Hermida	8.00
JJ	Josh Johnson	8.00
JK	Jason Kendall	8.00
JM	Joe Mauer	10.00
JN	Joe Nathan	10.00
JP	Jake Peavy	10.00
JR	Jose Reyes	15.00
JS	Johan Santana	12.00
JV	Justin Verlander	15.00
JW	Jered Weaver	15.00
JZ	Joel Zumaya	15.00
KG	Ken Griffey Jr.	25.00
KG2	Ken Griffey Jr.	25.00
KH	Khalil Greene	8.00
KJ	Kenji Johjima	20.00
KM	Kendry Morales	8.00
KU	Jason Kubel	10.00
KY	Kevin Youkilis	10.00
LA	Luis Aparicio	10.00
LM	Lastings Milledge	10.00
LY	Fred Lynn	8.00
MA	Matt Cain	15.00
MC	Miguel Cabrera	15.00
MG	Marcus Giles	8.00
MH	Matt Holliday	15.00
ML	Mark Loretta	8.00
MM	Melvin Mora	8.00
MO	Justin Morneau	12.00
MS	Mike Schmidt	20.00
MT	Mark Teixeira	12.00
MU	Mark Mulder	10.00
MY	Michael Young	10.00
NS	Nick Swisher	10.00
PA	Jonathan Papelbon	20.00
PF	Prince Fielder	10.00
PM	Paul Molitor	15.00
RC	Cal Ripken Jr.	40.00
RH	Rich Harden	10.00
RO	Roy Oswalt	10.00
RW	Rickie Weeks	10.00
RZ	Ryan Zimmerman	15.00
SK	Scott Kazmir	10.00
SP	Scott Podsednik	10.00
TE	Miguel Tejada	12.00
TG	Tony Gwynn	15.00
TH	Travis Hafner	10.00
TI	Tadahito Iguchi	10.00
TP	Tony Perez	10.00
VM	Victor Martinez	10.00
WC	Will Clark	15.00
WI	Josh Willingham	8.00
YB	Yuniesky Betancourt	8.00

Legendary Materials

NM/M
Production 5-55

Code	Player	NM/M
AR	Al Rosen/55	15.00
BD	Bill Dickey/55	30.00
BD2	Bill Dickey/55	30.00
BG	Bob Gibson/25	20.00
BM	Bill Mazeroski/25	20.00
BO	Bo Jackson/55	20.00
BO2	Bo Jackson/55	20.00
CF	Carlton Fisk/55	10.00
CF2	Carlton Fisk/55	15.00
CW	Rod Carew/55	10.00
CW2	Rod Carew/55	10.00
CY	Carl Yastrzemski/25	20.00
CY2	Carl Yastrzemski/25	20.00
GP	Gaylord Perry/55	10.00
GP2	Gaylord Perry/55	10.00
JB	Johnny Bench/55	20.00
JO	Joe Morgan/55	10.00
JO2	Joe Morgan/55	10.00
JU	Juan Marichal/55	10.00
KI	Kirk Gibson/55	10.00
KP	Kirby Puckett/55	20.00
KP2	Kirby Puckett/55	15.00
MA	Don Mattingly/55	25.00
MA2	Don Mattingly/55	25.00
MW	Maury Wills/41	10.00
NR	Nolan Ryan/55	35.00
NR2	Nolan Ryan/25	40.00
NR3	Nolan Ryan/25	40.00
OS	Ozzie Smith/55	20.00
OS2	Ozzie Smith/55	20.00
PM	Paul Molitor/55	10.00
PM2	Paul Molitor/55	10.00
PN	Phil Niekro/55	10.00
PN2	Phil Niekro/55	10.00
RJ	Reggie Jackson/25	20.00
RJ2	Reggie Jackson/35	15.00
RK	Ralph Kiner/25	10.00
RO	Brooks Robinson/35	15.00
RO2	Brooks Robinson/35	15.00
RS	Ryne Sandberg/35	25.00
RY	Robin Yount/25	15.00
RY2	Robin Yount/25	15.00
SC	Steve Carlton/55	10.00
SC2	Steve Carlton/47	10.00
SU	Don Sutton/55	10.00
SU2	Don Sutton/55	10.00
TG	Tony Gwynn/55	20.00
TG2	Tony Gwynn/55	15.00
TP	Tony Perez/55	15.00
TP2	Tony Perez/55	15.00
WB	Wade Boggs/55	15.00
WB2	Wade Boggs/55	15.00
WC	Will Clark/45	15.00
WC2	Will Clark/45	15.00

Legendary Ensemble Signatures
No Pricing
Production 25 Sets

Maximum Materials
Production 25 Sets
Patch: No Pricing
Production 15 Sets

Numbers Materials

NM/M
Production 35 Sets

Code	Player	NM/M
AB	A.J. Burnett	10.00
AD	Adam Dunn	12.00
AJ	Andruw Jones	15.00
AP	Albert Pujols	40.00
AR	Alex Rios	10.00
AS	Alfonso Soriano	15.00
BA	Brian Bannister	10.00
BG	Brian Giles	10.00
BM	Bill Mazeroski	15.00
BO	Jeremy Bonderman	15.00
BR	Brian Roberts	10.00
CC	Melky Cabrera	15.00
CC	Carl Crawford	15.00
CJ	Conor Jackson	15.00
CL	Carlos Lee	10.00
CS	Chris Shelton	10.00
CU	Chase Utley	20.00
CZ	Carlos Zambrano	15.00
DJ	Derek Jeter	40.00
DJ2	Derek Jeter	40.00
DL	Derek Lee	15.00
DU	Dan Uggla	15.00
DW	Dontrelle Willis	15.00
FH	Felix Hernandez	15.00
FL	Francisco Liriano	20.00
GA	Garrett Atkins	10.00
GP	Gaylord Perry	15.00
HA	Cole Hamels	25.00
HB	Hank Blalock	10.00
HC	Craig Hansen	20.00
HO	Trevor Hoffman	10.00
HR	Hanley Ramirez	20.00
HT	Tim Hudson	10.00
HU	Torii Hunter	10.00
HY	Roy Halladay	10.00
IK	Ian Kinsler	10.00
IR	Ivan Rodriguez	15.00
JB	Jason Bay	15.00
JD	Jermaine Dye	10.00
JH	Jeremy Hermida	10.00
JJ	Josh Johnson	12.00
JK	Jason Kendall	10.00
JM	Joe Mauer	15.00
JN	Joe Nathan	10.00
JP	Jake Peavy	15.00
JR	Jose Reyes	20.00
JS	Johan Santana	20.00
JV	Justin Verlander	20.00
JW	Jered Weaver	20.00
JZ	Joel Zumaya	20.00
KG	Ken Griffey Jr.	35.00
KG2	Ken Griffey Jr.	35.00
KH	Khalil Greene	10.00
KJ	Kenji Johjima	30.00
KM	Kendry Morales	10.00
KU	Jason Kubel	10.00
KY	Kevin Youkilis	15.00
LA	Luis Aparicio	10.00
LM	Lastings Milledge	15.00
LY	Fred Lynn	10.00
MA	Matt Cain	15.00
MC	Miguel Cabrera	15.00
MG	Marcus Giles	10.00
MH	Matt Holliday	10.00
ML	Mark Loretta	10.00
MM	Melvin Mora	10.00
MO	Justin Morneau	15.00
MS	Mike Schmidt	25.00
MT	Mark Teixeira	15.00
MU	Mark Mulder	15.00
MY	Michael Young	20.00
NS	Nick Swisher	20.00
PF	Prince Fielder	20.00
PM	Paul Molitor	20.00
RC	Cal Ripken Jr.	75.00
RH	Rich Harden	20.00
RI	Jim Rice/31	20.00
RO	Roy Oswalt	25.00
RW	Rickie Weeks	20.00
RZ	Ryan Zimmerman	40.00
SK	Scott Kazmir	20.00
SP	Scott Podsednik	15.00
TE	Miguel Tejada	15.00
TG	Tony Gwynn	30.00
TH	Travis Hafner	20.00
TI	Tadahito Iguchi	30.00
VM	Victor Martinez	15.00
WC	Will Clark	20.00
WI	Josh Willingham	15.00
YB	Yuniesky Betancourt	15.00

Ultimate Patch

NM/M
Production 50 unless noted.
Patch Signature: No Pricing
Production 10 Sets

Code	Player	NM/M
AB	A.J. Burnett	15.00
AD	Adam Dunn	20.00
AJ	Andruw Jones	20.00
AP	Albert Pujols	60.00
AR	Alex Rios	15.00
AS	Alfonso Soriano	25.00
BA	Brian Bannister	15.00
BG	Brian Giles	15.00
BO	Jeremy Bonderman	25.00
BR	Brian Roberts	15.00
CA	Melky Cabrera	25.00
CC	Carl Crawford	25.00
CH	Chris Carpenter	20.00
CJ	Conor Jackson	15.00
CL	Carlos Lee	15.00
CR	Coco Crisp	20.00
CS	Chris Shelton	15.00
CU	Chase Utley	35.00
CZ	Carlos Zambrano	20.00
DJ	Derek Jeter	50.00
DJ2	Derek Jeter	50.00
DL	Derek Lee	20.00
DU	Dan Uggla	20.00
DW	Dontrelle Willis	20.00
FH	Felix Hernandez	20.00
FL	Francisco Liriano	25.00
GA	Garrett Atkins	20.00
GP	Gaylord Perry/27	20.00
HA	Cole Hamels	25.00
HB	Hank Blalock	15.00
HO	Trevor Hoffman	15.00
HR	Hanley Ramirez	25.00
HT	Tim Hudson	15.00
HU	Torii Hunter	15.00
HY	Roy Halladay	15.00
IR	Ivan Rodriguez	20.00
JB	Jason Bay	20.00
JD	Jermaine Dye	15.00
JH	Jeremy Hermida	20.00
JJ	Josh Johnson	20.00
JK	Jason Kendall	15.00
JM	Joe Mauer	25.00
JN	Joe Nathan	15.00
JP	Jake Peavy	15.00
JS	Jose Reyes	30.00
JS	Johan Santana	25.00
JV	Justin Verlander	40.00
JW	Jered Weaver	25.00
JZ	Joel Zumaya/47	30.00
KG	Ken Griffey Jr.	50.00
KG2	Ken Griffey Jr.	50.00
KH	Khalil Greene	15.00
KJ	Kenji Johjima	35.00
KM	Kendry Morales	15.00
KU	Jason Kubel	15.00
LA	Luis Aparicio	20.00
LM	Lastings Milledge	30.00
LY	Fred Lynn	15.00
MA	Matt Cain	25.00
MC	Miguel Cabrera	25.00
MG	Marcus Giles	15.00
MH	Matt Holliday	30.00
ML	Mark Loretta/40	15.00
MM	Melvin Mora	15.00
MO	Justin Morneau	30.00
MS	Mike Schmidt	30.00
MT	Mark Teixeira	25.00
MU	Mark Mulder	15.00
MY	Michael Young	20.00
NS	Nick Swisher	20.00
PF	Prince Fielder	20.00
PM	Paul Molitor	20.00
RC	Cal Ripken Jr.	75.00
RH	Rich Harden	20.00
RI	Jim Rice	20.00
RO	Roy Oswalt	25.00
RW	Rickie Weeks	20.00
RZ	Ryan Zimmerman	40.00
SK	Scott Kazmir	20.00
SP	Scott Podsednik	15.00
TE	Miguel Tejada	15.00
TG	Tony Gwynn	30.00
TH	Travis Hafner	20.00
TI	Tadahito Iguchi	30.00
VM	Victor Martinez	15.00
WC	Will Clark	20.00
WI	Josh Willingham	15.00
YB	Yuniesky Betancourt	15.00

Tandem Materials

NM/M
Production 25 Sets
Signature: No Pricing
Production 15 Sets
Signature Patch: No Pricing
Production Five Sets
Signature Logo: No Pricing
Production One Set

Code	Players	NM/M
AA	Alfonso Soriano, Alex Rios	20.00
AH	Garrett Atkins, Matt Holliday	10.00
BH	Felix Hernandez, Yuniesky Betancourt	20.00
BM	Brian Bannister, Lastings Milledge	20.00
BR	Yuniesky Betancourt, Hanley Ramirez	25.00
BV	Justin Verlander, Jeremy Bonderman	40.00
CL	Coco Crisp, Mark Loretta	20.00
CP	Carl Crawford, Scott Podsednik	20.00
CS	Cole Hamels, Scott Kazmir	25.00
CW	Dontrelle Willis, Chris Carpenter	15.00
CZ	Miguel Cabrera, Ryan Zimmerman	20.00
FP	Tony Perez, Prince Fielder	15.00
FW	Prince Fielder, Rickie Weeks	15.00
GP	Ken Griffey Jr., Albert Pujols	50.00
HB	Matt Holliday, Jason Bay	20.00
HF	Prince Fielder, Travis Hafner	15.00
HG	Trevor Hoffman, Brian Giles	10.00
HJ	Andruw Jones, Torii Hunter	15.00
HK	Jeremy Hermida, Jason Kubel	10.00
HM	Travis Hafner, Victor Martinez	10.00
HN	Trevor Hoffman, Joe Nathan	10.00
HO	Roy Oswalt, Rich Harden	15.00
HP	Trevor Hoffman, Jonathan Papelbon	25.00
HR	Hanley Ramirez, Jeremy Hermida	15.00
HW	Jeremy Hermida, Josh Willingham	10.00
ID	Jermaine Dye, Tadahito Iguchi	15.00
JB	Bill Mazeroski, Jason Bay	20.00
JG	Derek Jeter, Ken Griffey Jr.	40.00
JR	Derek Jeter, Cal Ripken Jr.	60.00
KB	Brian Giles, Khalil Greene	10.00
KM	Joe Mauer, Jason Kendall	15.00
KU	Ian Kinsler, Dan Uggla	10.00
KY	Ian Kinsler, Michael Young	10.00
LF	Prince Fielder, Carlos Lee	15.00
MH	Livan Hernandez, Kendry Morales	10.00
MM	Joe Mauer, Victor Martinez	15.00
MP	Tony Perez, Kendry Morales	15.00
MR	Melvin Mora, Brian Roberts	10.00
MW	Rickie Weeks, Paul Molitor	20.00
NJ	Joe Mauer, Joe Nathan	20.00
NM	Joe Mauer, Joe Nathan	15.00
PO	Roy Oswalt, Jake Peavy	15.00
PP	Jake Peavy, Gaylord Perry	15.00
SH	Rich Harden, Nick Swisher	15.00
TY	Michael Young, Mark Teixeira	15.00
VM	Justin Verlander, Jack Morris	20.00
WM	Josh Willingham, Joe Mauer	20.00
YL	Kevin Youkilis, Mark Loretta	15.00
ZJ	Josh Johnson, Joel Zumaya	20.00
ZZ	Joel Zumaya, Carlos Zambrano	20.00

Tri-Marks Signatures
No Pricing
Production 15 Sets

Game Materials Signatures

NM/M
Production 35 Sets

Code	Player	NM/M
AB	A.J. Burnett	25.00
AD	Adam Dunn	25.00
AJ	Andruw Jones	25.00
AP	Albert Pujols	250.00
AR	Alex Rios	25.00
AS	Alfonso Soriano	40.00
BA	Brian Bannister	15.00
BG	Brian Giles	15.00
BM	Bill Mazeroski	40.00
BO	Jeremy Bonderman	20.00
BR	Brian Roberts	20.00
CA	Melky Cabrera	20.00
CC	Carl Crawford	25.00
CH	Chris Carpenter	40.00
CJ	Conor Jackson	15.00
CL	Carlos Lee	25.00
CR	Coco Crisp	25.00
CS	Chris Shelton	25.00
CU	Chase Utley	60.00
CZ	Carlos Zambrano	20.00
DJ	Derek Jeter	250.00
DJ2	Derek Jeter	250.00
DL	Derek Lee	25.00
DU	Dan Uggla	30.00
DW	Dontrelle Willis	20.00
FH	Felix Hernandez	40.00
FL	Francisco Liriano	50.00
GA	Garrett Atkins	15.00
GP	Gaylord Perry	25.00
HA	Cole Hamels	60.00
HB	Hank Blalock	15.00
HC	Craig Hansen	15.00
HO	Trevor Hoffman	20.00
HR	Hanley Ramirez	60.00
HT	Tim Hudson	25.00
HU	Torii Hunter	40.00
HY	Roy Halladay	30.00
IK	Ian Kinsler	30.00
IR	Ivan Rodriguez	25.00
JB	Jason Bay	25.00
JD	Jermaine Dye	20.00
JH	Jeremy Hermida	20.00
JJ	Josh Johnson	35.00
JK	Jason Kendall	20.00
JM	Joe Mauer	50.00
JN	Joe Nathan	20.00
JP	Jake Peavy	30.00
JR	Jose Reyes	40.00
JS	Johan Santana	40.00
JV	Justin Verlander	60.00
JW	Jered Weaver	40.00
JZ	Joel Zumaya	20.00
KG	Ken Griffey Jr.	120.00
KG2	Ken Griffey Jr.	120.00
KH	Khalil Greene	15.00
KM	Kendry Morales	30.00
KU	Jason Kubel	25.00
KY	Kevin Youkilis	25.00
LA	Luis Aparicio	25.00
LY	Fred Lynn	25.00
MA	Matt Cain	40.00
MC	Miguel Cabrera	50.00
MG	Marcus Giles	15.00
MH	Matt Holliday	40.00
ML	Mark Loretta	25.00
MM	Melvin Mora	25.00
MO	Justin Morneau	40.00
MS	Mike Schmidt	50.00
MT	Mark Teixeira	40.00
MU	Mark Mulder	25.00
MY	Michael Young	30.00
NS	Nick Swisher	25.00
PA	Jonathan Papelbon	30.00
PM	Paul Molitor	35.00
RC	Cal Ripken Jr.	150.00
RH	Rich Harden	20.00
RI	Jim Rice	30.00
RO	Roy Oswalt	30.00
RW	Rickie Weeks	25.00
RZ	Ryan Zimmerman	50.00
SK	Scott Kazmir	25.00
SP	Scott Podsednik	25.00
TE	Miguel Tejada	30.00
TG	Tony Gwynn	60.00
TH	Travis Hafner	25.00
TI	Tadahito Iguchi	25.00
TP	Tony Perez	30.00
VM	Victor Martinez	25.00
WC	Will Clark	35.00
WI	Josh Willingham	25.00
YB	Yuniesky Betancourt	25.00

Numbers Patch

NM/M
Production 35 unless noted.

Code	Player	NM/M
AB	A.J. Burnett	15.00
AD	Adam Dunn	25.00
AJ	Andruw Jones	20.00
AP	Albert Pujols	80.00
AR	Alex Rios	20.00
AS	Alfonso Soriano	25.00
BA	Brian Bannister	15.00
BG	Brian Giles	15.00
BO	Jeremy Bonderman	15.00
BR	Brian Roberts	15.00
CC	Carl Crawford	20.00
CH	Chris Carpenter	25.00
CJ	Conor Jackson	15.00
CL	Carlos Lee	15.00
CR	Coco Crisp	15.00
CS	Chris Shelton	20.00
CU	Chase Utley	40.00
CZ	Carlos Zambrano	15.00
DJ	Derek Jeter	65.00
DJ2	Derek Jeter	65.00
DL	Derek Lee	25.00
DU	Dan Uggla	25.00
DW	Dontrelle Willis	15.00
FH	Felix Hernandez	25.00
FL	Francisco Liriano	30.00
GA	Garrett Atkins	15.00
HA	Cole Hamels	40.00
HB	Hank Blalock	15.00
HO	Trevor Hoffman	20.00
HR	Hanley Ramirez	30.00
HT	Tim Hudson	15.00
HU	Torii Hunter	20.00
HY	Roy Halladay	30.00
IK	Ian Kinsler	20.00
IR	Ivan Rodriguez	20.00
JB	Jason Bay	25.00
JD	Jermaine Dye	20.00
JH	Jeremy Hermida	20.00
JJ	Josh Johnson	20.00
JK	Jason Kendall	15.00
JM	Joe Mauer	40.00
JN	Joe Nathan	20.00
JP	Jake Peavy	20.00
JR	Jose Reyes	40.00
JS	Johan Santana	30.00
JV	Justin Verlander	40.00
JW	Jered Weaver	30.00
JZ	Joel Zumaya	25.00
KG	Ken Griffey Jr.	50.00
KG2	Ken Griffey Jr.	50.00
KH	Khalil Greene	15.00
KJ	Kenji Johjima	25.00
KM	Kendry Morales	25.00
KU	Jason Kubel	25.00
KY	Kevin Youkilis	25.00
LA	Luis Aparicio	15.00
LM	Lastings Milledge	20.00
LY	Fred Lynn	20.00
MA	Matt Cain	30.00
MC	Miguel Cabrera	30.00
MG	Marcus Giles	15.00
MH	Matt Holliday	40.00
ML	Mark Loretta	15.00
MM	Melvin Mora	15.00
MO	Justin Morneau	25.00
MS	Mike Schmidt	50.00
MT	Mark Teixeira	25.00
MU	Mark Mulder	15.00
MY	Michael Young	20.00
NS	Nick Swisher	20.00
PF	Prince Fielder	25.00
PM	Paul Molitor	30.00
RC	Cal Ripken Jr.	100.00
RH	Rich Harden	25.00
RI	Jim Rice	25.00
RO	Roy Oswalt	20.00
RW	Rickie Weeks	20.00
RZ	Ryan Zimmerman	25.00
SK	Scott Kazmir	20.00
SP	Scott Podsednik	20.00
TE	Miguel Tejada	25.00
TG	Tony Gwynn	30.00
TH	Travis Hafner	25.00
TI	Tadahito Iguchi	25.00
VM	Victor Martinez	25.00
WC	Will Clark	25.00
WI	Josh Willingham	25.00
YB	Yuniesky Betancourt	15.00

Signature Patch
No Pricing
Production 10 Sets

Tandem Patch

NM/M
Production 35 Sets

Code	Players	NM/M
AA	Alfonso Soriano, Alex Rios	15.00

2006 UD Ultimate Collection (insert)

Code	Players	Price
AH	Garrett Atkins, Matt Holliday	15.00
AJ	Luis Aparicio, Derek Jeter	40.00
BH	Felix Hernandez, Yuniesky Betancourt	20.00
BM	Brian Bannister, Lastings Milledge	15.00
BR	Yuniesky Betancourt, Hanley Ramirez	20.00
BV	Justin Verlander, Jeremy Bonderman	40.00
CH	Melky Cabrera, Jeremy Hermida	20.00
CL	Coco Crisp, Mark Loretta	15.00
CM	Lastings Milledge, Melky Cabrera	25.00
CO	Roy Oswalt, Roger Clemens	50.00
CP	Carl Crawford, Scott Podsednik	15.00
CR	Miguel Cabrera, Hanley Ramirez	20.00
CS	Cole Hamels, Scott Kazmir	50.00
CV	Justin Verlander, Matt Cain	40.00
CW	Dontrelle Willis, Chris Carpenter	30.00
CZ	Miguel Cabrera, Ryan Zimmerman	25.00
DH	Hanley Ramirez, Derek Jeter	60.00
FW	Prince Fielder, Rickie Weeks	25.00
GD	Adam Dunn, Ken Griffey Jr.	40.00
GG	Tony Gwynn, Brian Giles	30.00
GP	Ken Griffey Jr., Albert Pujols	80.00
GR	Ken Griffey Jr., Alex Rios	40.00
GT	Ken Griffey Jr., Frank Thomas	50.00
HB	Matt Holliday, Jason Bay	20.00
HF	Prince Fielder, Travis Hafner	25.00
HG	Trevor Hoffman, Brian Giles	15.00
HJ	Andruw Jones, Torii Hunter	25.00
HK	Jeremy Hermida, Jason Kubel	15.00
HM	Travis Hafner, Victor Martinez	15.00
HN	Trevor Hoffman, Joe Nathan	15.00
HO	Roy Oswalt, Rich Harden	20.00
HP	Trevor Hoffman, Jonathan Papelbon	30.00
HR	Hanley Ramirez, Jeremy Hermida	25.00
HW	Jeremy Hermida, Josh Willingham	15.00
ID	Jermaine Dye, Tadahito Iguchi	25.00
JC	Derek Jeter, Melky Cabrera	65.00
JG	Derek Jeter, Ken Griffey Jr.	80.00
JJ	Derek Jeter, Reggie Jackson	60.00
JK	Kendry Morales, Jered Weaver	30.00
JM	Kenji Johjima, Victor Martinez	30.00
JR	Derek Jeter, Cal Ripken Jr.	100.00
KB	Brian Giles, Khalil Greene	20.00
KC	Scott Kazmir, Carl Crawford	15.00
KM	Joe Mauer, Jason Kendall	25.00
KU	Ian Kinsler, Dan Uggla	20.00
KY	Ian Kinsler, Michael Young	15.00
LC	Fred Lynn, Coco Crisp	20.00
LF	Prince Fielder, Carlos Lee	15.00
LH	Francisco Liriano, Cole Hamels	40.00
MF	Kendry Morales, Prince Fielder	20.00
MH	Livan Hernandez, Kendry Morales	15.00
ML	Francisco Liriano, Joe Mauer	35.00
MM	Joe Mauer, Victor Martinez	25.00
MR	Melvin Mora, Brian Roberts	15.00
MW	Rickie Weeks, Paul Molitor	20.00
NJ	Joe Mauer, Joe Nathan	20.00
NL	Joe Nathan, Francisco Liriano	
NM	Joe Mauer, Joe Nathan	30.00
NP	Joe Nathan, Jonathan Papelbon	30.00
PC	Matt Cain, Gaylord Perry	30.00
PH	Jonathan Papelbon, Craig Hansen	50.00
PO	Roy Oswalt, Jake Peavy	20.00
PP	Jake Peavy, Gaylord Perry	15.00
RC	Coco Crisp, Alex Rios	15.00
RM	Lastings Milledge, Jose Reyes	30.00
RR	Jose Reyes, Hanley Ramirez	40.00
RS	Mike Schmidt, Cal Ripken Jr.	75.00
RU	Hanley Ramirez, Dan Uggla	25.00
RV	Ivan Rodriguez, Justin Verlander	35.00
SH	Rich Harden, Nick Swisher	15.00
SJ	Conor Jackson, Chris Shelton	25.00
SZ	Ryan Zimmerman, Mike Schmidt	30.00
TY	Michael Young, Mark Teixeira	20.00
UK	Chase Utley, Ian Kinsler	40.00
UM	Chase Utley, Joe Morgan	40.00
UR	Brian Roberts, Dan Uggla	15.00
VM	Justin Verlander, Jack Morris	40.00
VZ	Justin Verlander, Joel Zumaya	40.00
WM	Josh Willingham, Joe Mauer	25.00
WR	Hanley Ramirez, Josh Willingham	25.00
WV	Justin Verlander, Jered Weaver	40.00
YL	Kevin Youkilis, Mark Loretta	20.00
ZA	Garrett Atkins, Ryan Zimmerman	30.00
ZC	Ryan Zimmerman, Miguel Cabrera	30.00
ZJ	Josh Johnson, Joel Zumaya	20.00
ZZ	Joel Zumaya, Carlos Zambrano	15.00

2007 Upper Deck

NM/M

		Price
	Complete Set (1020):	
	Common Player:	.15
	Rookie Redemption:	75.00
	Hobby Pack (15):	5.00
	Hobby Box (16):	70.00

#	Player	Price
1	Doug Slaten RC	.50
2	Miguel Montero (RC)	.25
3	Brian Burres (RC)	.25
4	Devern Hansack RC	.50
5	David Murphy (RC)	.25
6	Jose Reyes RC	.50
7	Scott Moore (RC)	.25
8	Josh Fields (RC)	.50
9	Chris Stewart (RC)	.50
10	Jerry Owens (RC)	.25
11	Ryan Sweeney (RC)	.25
12	Kevin Kouzmanoff (RC)	.50
13	Jeff Baker (RC)	.25
14	Justin Hampson (RC)	.25
15	Jeff Salazar (RC)	.25
16	Alvin Colina RC	.50
17	Troy Tulowitzki (RC)	1.00
18	Andrew Miller RC	1.00
19	Mike Rabelo (RC)	.50
20	Jose Diaz (RC)	.25
21	Angel Sanchez (RC)	.50
22	Ryan Braun (RC)	1.00
23	Delwyn Young (RC)	.25
24	Drew Anderson (RC)	.25
25	Dennis Sarfate (RC)	.25
26	Vinny Rottino (RC)	.25
27	Glen Perkins (RC)	.25
28	Alexi Casilla RC	1.00
29	Philip Humber (RC)	.50
30	Andy Cannizaro RC	.50
31	Jeremy Brown	.25
32	Sean Henn (RC)	.25
33	Brian Rogers	.15
34	Carlos Maldonado (RC)	.25
35	Juan Morillo (RC)	.25
36	Fred Lewis (RC)	.25
37	Patrick Misch (RC)	.25
38	Billy Sadler (RC)	.25
39	Ryan Feierabend (RC)	.25
40	Cesar Jimenez RC	.75
41	Oswaldo Navarro RC	.50
42	Travis Chick (RC)	.25
43	Delmon Young (RC)	1.00
44	Shawn Riggans (RC)	.25
45	Brian Stokes (RC)	.25
46	Juan Salas (RC)	.25
47	Joaquin Arias (RC)	.25
48	Adam Lind (RC)	.50
49	Beltran Perez (RC)	.25
50	Brett Campbell RC	.50
51	Brian Roberts	.25
52	Miguel Tejada	.50
53	Brandon Fahey	.15
54	Jay Gibbons	.15
55	Corey Patterson	.15
56	Nicholas Markakis	.50
57	Ramon Hernandez	.15
58	Kris Benson	.15
59	Adam Loewen	.15
60	Erik Bedard	.25
61	Chris Ray	.15
62	Chris Britton	.15
63	Daniel Cabrera	.15
64	Sendy Rleal	.15
65	Manny Ramirez	.75
66	David Ortiz	.75
67	Gabe Kapler	.15
68	Alex Cora	.15
69	Dustin Pedroia	.15
70	Trot Nixon	.15
71	Doug Mirabelli	.15
72	Mark Loretta	.15
73	Curt Schilling	.75
74	Jonathan Papelbon	.50
75	Tim Wakefield	.15
76	Jon Lester	.25
77	Craig Hansen	.15
78	Keith Foulke	.15
79	Jermaine Dye	.15
80	Jim Thome	.50
81	Tadahito Iguchi	.15
82	Robert Mackowiak	.15
83	Brian Anderson	.15
84	Juan Uribe	.15
85	A.J. Pierzynski	.15
86	Alex Cintron	.15
87	Jon Garland	.15
88	Jose Contreras	.15
89	Neal Cotts	.15
90	Bobby Jenks	.15
91	Mike MacDougal	.15
92	Javier Vazquez	.15
93	Travis Hafner	.40
94	Jhonny Peralta	.25
95	Ryan Garko	.15
96	Victor Martinez	.25
97	Hector Luna	.15
98	Casey Blake	.15
99	Jason Michaels	.15
100	Shin-Soo Choo	.15
101	C.C. Sabathia	.25
102	Paul Byrd	.15
103	Jeremy Sowers	.15
104	Cliff Lee	.15
105	Rafael Betancourt	.15
106	Francisco Cruceta	.15
107	Sean Casey	.15
108	Brandon Inge	.15
109	Placido Polanco	.15
110	Omar Infante	.15
111	Ivan Rodriguez	.50
112	Maggilo Ordonez	.25
113	Craig Monroe	.15
114	Marcus Thames	.15
115	Justin Verlander	.50
116	Todd Jones	.15
117	Kenny Rogers	.15
118	Joel Zumaya	.25
119	Jeremy Bonderman	.50
120	Nate Robertson	.15
121	Mark Teahen	.15
122	Ryan Shealy	.25
123	Mitch Maier (RC)	.25
124	Doug Mientkiewicz	.15
125	Mark Grudzielanek	.15
126	Shane Costa	.15
127	John Buck	.15
128	Reggie Sanders	.15
129	Mike Sweeney	.15
130	Mark Redman	.15
131	Todd Wellemeyer	.15
132	Scott Elarton	.15
133	Ambiorix Burgos	.15
134	Joe Nelson	.15
135	Howie Kendrick	.40
136	Chone Figgins	.15
137	Orlando Cabrera	.25
138	Maicer Izturis	.15
139	Jose Molina	.15
140	Vladimir Guerrero	.75
141	Darin Erstad	.15
142	Juan Rivera	.15
143	Jered Weaver	.40
144	John Lackey	.25
145	Joe Saunders	.15
146	Bartolo Colon	.15
147	Scot Shields	.15
148	Francisco Rodriguez	.25
149	Justin Morneau	.50
150	Jason Bartlett	.15
151	Luis Castillo	.15
152	Nick Punto	.15
153	Shannon Stewart	.15
154	Michael Cuddyer	.15
155	Jason Kubel	.15
156	Joe Mauer	.50
157	Francisco Liriano	.25
158	Joe Nathan	.25
159	Dennys Reyes	.15
160	Brad Radke	.15
161	Boof Bonser	.15
162	Juan Rincon	.15
163	Derek Jeter	2.00
164	Jason Giambi	.50
165	Robinson Cano	.50
166	Andy Phillips	.15
167	Bobby Abreu	.40
168	Gary Sheffield	.25
169	Bernie Williams	.40
170	Melky Cabrera	.25
171	Mike Mussina	.50
172	Chien-Ming Wang	.50
173	Mariano Rivera	.50
174	Scott Proctor	.15
175	Jaret Wright	.15
176	Kyle Farnsworth	.15
177	Eric Chavez	.15
178	Bobby Crosby	.15
179	Frank Thomas	.50
180	Dan Johnson	.15
181	Marco Scutaro	.15
182	Nick Swisher	.40
183	Milton Bradley	.25
184	Jay Payton	.15
185	Joe Blanton	.15
186	Barry Zito	.15
187	Rich Harden	.25
188	Esteban Loaiza	.15
189	Huston Street	.15
190	Chad Gaudin	.15
191	Richie Sexson	.15
192	Yuniesky Betancourt	.15
193	Willie Bloomquist	.15
194	Ben Broussard	.15
195	Kenji Johjima	.25
196	Ichiro Suzuki	1.00
197	Raul Ibanez	.15
198	Chris Snelling/SP	.15
199	Felix Hernandez	.50
200	Cha Sueng Baek	.15
201	Joel Pineiro	.15
202	Julio Mateo	.15
203	J.J. Putz	.15
204	Rafael Soriano	.15
205	Jorge Cantu	.15
206	B.J. Upton	.25
207	Ty Wigginton	.15
208	Greg Norton	.15
209	Dioner Navarro	.15
210	Carl Crawford	.40
211	Jonny Gomes	.15
212	Damon Hollins	.15
213	Scott Kazmir	.25
214	Casey Fossum	.15
215	Ruddy Lugo	.15
216	James Shields	.15
217	Tyler Walker	.15
218	Shawn Camp	.15
219	Mark Teixeira	.50
220	Hank Blalock	.25
221	Ian Kinsler	.25
222	Jerry Hairston Jr.	.15
223	Gerald Laird	.15
224	Carlos Lee	.40
225	Gary Matthews	.15
226	Mark DeRosa	.15
227	Kip Wells	.15
228	Akinori Otsuka	.15
229	Vicente Padilla	.15
230	John Koronka	.15
231	Kevin Millwood	.25
232	Wes Littleton	.15
233	Troy Glaus	.40
234	Lyle Overbay	.25
235	Aaron Hill	.15
236	John McDonald	.15
237	Bengie Molina	.15
238	Vernon Wells	.25
239	Reed Johnson	.15
240	Frank Catalanotto	.15
241	Roy Halladay	.40
242	B.J. Ryan	.15
243	Gustavo Chacin	.15
244	Scott Downs	.15
245	Casey Janssen	.15
246	Justin Speier	.15
247	Stephen Drew	.40
248	Conor Jackson	.25
249	Orlando Hudson	.15
250	Chad Tracy	.15
251	Johnny Estrada	.15
252	Luis Gonzalez	.15
253	Eric Byrnes	.15
254	Carlos Quentin	.15
255	Brandon Webb	.25
256	Claudio Vargas	.15
257	Juan Cruz	.15
258	Jorge Julio	.15
259	Luis Vizcaino	.15
260	Livan Hernandez	.15
261	Chipper Jones	.75
262	Edgar Renteria	.25
263	Adam LaRoche	.25
264	Willy Aybar	.15
265	Brian McCann	.40
266	Ryan Langerhans	.15
267	Jeff Francoeur	.40
268	Matt Diaz	.15
269	Tim Hudson	.25
270	John Smoltz	.40
271	Oscar Villarreal	.15
272	Horacio Ramirez	.15
273	Bob Wickman	.15
274	Chad Paronto	.15
275	Ryan Theriot	.15
276	Cesar Izturis	.15
277	Ronny Cedeno	.15
278	Michael Barrett	.25
279	Michael Barrett	.15
280	Juan Pierre	.15
281	Jacque Jones	.15
282	Matt Murton	.25
283	Carlos Zambrano	.25
284	Mark Prior	.25
285	Rich Hill	.40
286	Sean Marshall	.15
287	Ryan Dempster	.15
288	Ryan O'Malley	.15
289	Scott Hatteberg	.15
290	Brandon Phillips	.15
291	Edwin Encarnacion	.15
292	Rich Aurilia	.15
293	David Ross	.15
294	Ken Griffey Jr.	1.00
295	Ryan Freel	.15
296	Chris Denorfia	.15
297	Bronson Arroyo	.15
298	Aaron Harang	.15
299	Brandon Claussen	.15
300	Todd Coffey	.15
301	David Weathers	.15
302	Eric Milton	.15
303	Todd Helton	.50
304	Clint Barmes	.15
305	Kazuo Matsui	.15
306	Jamey Carroll	.15
307	Yorvit Torrealba	.15
308	Matt Holliday	.50
309	Choo Freeman	.15
310	Brad Hawpe	.25
311	Jason Jennings	.15
312	Jeff Francis	.15
313	Josh Fogg	.15
314	Aaron Cook	.15
315	Ubaldo Jimenez	.15
316	Manny Corpas	.15
317	Miguel Cabrera	.75
318	Dan Uggla	.25
319	Hanley Ramirez	.50
320	Wes Helms	.15
321	Miguel Olivo	.15
322	Jeremy Hermida	.25
323	Cody Ross	.15
324	Josh Willingham	.15
325	Dontrelle Willis	.25
326	Anibal Sanchez	.15
327	Josh Johnson	.15
328	Jose Garcia	.15
329	Joe Borowski	.15
330	Taylor Tankersley	.15
331	Lance Berkman	.50
332	Craig Biggio	.40
333	Aubrey Huff	.15
334	Adam Everett	.15
335	Brad Ausmus	.15
336	Willy Taveras	.25
337	Luke Scott	.15
338	Chris Burke	.15
339	Roger Clemens	1.50
340	Andy Pettitte	.15
341	Brandon Backe	.15
342	Hector Gimenez	.15
343	Brad Lidge	.15
344	Dan Wheeler	.15
345	Nomar Garciaparra	.75
346	Rafael Furcal	.25
347	Wilson Betemit	.15
348	Julio Lugo	.15
349	Russell Martin	.25
350	Andre Ethier	.25
351	Matthew Kemp	.25
352	Kenny Lofton	.15
353	Brad Penny	.15
354	Derek Lowe	.25
355	Chad Billingsley	.25
356	Greg Maddux	1.00
357	Takashi Saito	.15
358	Jonathan Broxton	.25
359	Prince Fielder	1.00
360	Rickie Weeks	.40
361	Bill Hall	.15
362	J.J. Hardy	.15
363	Jeff Cirillo	.15
364	Tony Gwynn Jr.	.15
365	Corey Hart	.15
366	Laynce Nix	.15
367	Doug Davis	.15
368	Ben Sheets	.40
369	Chris Capuano	.15
370	David Bush	.15
371	Derrick Turnbow	.15
372	Francisco Cordero	.15
373	Jose Reyes	1.00
374	Carlos Delgado	.50
375	Julio Franco	.15
376	Jose Valentin	.15
377	Paul LoDuca	.15
378	Carlos Beltran	.50
379	Shawn Green	.15
380	Lastings Milledge	.25
381	Endy Chavez	.15
382	Pedro Martinez	.75
383	John Maine	.15
384	Orlando Hernandez	.15
385	Steve Trachsel	.15
386	Billy Wagner	.15
387	Ryan Howard	1.50
388	Chase Utley	.75
389	Jimmy Rollins	.50
390	Chris Coste	.15
391	Jeff Conine	.15
392	Aaron Rowand	.15
393	Shane Victorino	.15
394	David Dellucci	.15
395	Cole Hamels	.40
396	Jamie Moyer	.15
397	Ryan Madson	.15
398	Brett Myers	.25
399	Tom Gordon	.15
400	Geoff Geary	.15
401	Freddy Sanchez	.15
402	Xavier Nady	.15
403	Jose Castillo	.15
404	Joe Randa	.15
405	Jason Bay	.40
406	Chris Duffy	.15
407	Jose Bautista	.15
408	Ronny Paulino	.15
409	Ian Snell	.15
410	Zachary Duke	.15
411	Tom Gorzelanny	.15
412	Shane Youman	.15
413	Mike Gonzalez	.15
414	Matt Capps	.15
415	Adrian Gonzalez	.50
416	Josh Barfield	.15
417	Todd Walker	.15
418	Khalil Greene	.15
419	Mike Piazza	.75
420	Dave Roberts	.15
421	Mike Cameron	.15
422	Geoff Blum	.15
423	Jake Peavy	.40
424	Chris Young	.25
425	Woody Williams	.15
426	Clay Hensley	.15
427	Cla Meredith	.15
428	Trevor Hoffman	.25
429	Shea Hillenbrand	.15
430	Pedro Feliz	.15
431	Ray Durham	.15
432	Mark Sweeney	.15
433	Eliezer Alfonso	.15
434	Moises Alou	.25
435	Steve Finley	.15
436	Todd Linden	.15
437	Jason Schmidt	.25
438	Matt Cain	.25
439	Noah Lowry	.15
440	Brad Hennessey	.15
441	Armando Benitez	.15
442	Jonathan Sanchez	.15
443	Albert Pujols	2.00
444	Ronnie Belliard	.15
445	David Eckstein	.15
446	Aaron Miles	.15
447	Yadier Molina	.15
448	Jim Edmonds	.25
449	Chris Duncan	.15
450	Juan Encarnacion	.15
451	Chris Carpenter	.50
452	Jeff Suppan	.15
453	Jason Marquis	.15
454	Jeff Weaver	.15
455	Jason Isringhausen	.15
456	Braden Looper	.15
457	Ryan Zimmerman	.40
458	Nick Johnson	.15
459	Felipe Lopez	.25
460	Brian Schneider	.15
461	Alfonso Soriano	.75
462	Austin Kearns	.15
463	Ryan Church	.15
464	Alex Escobar	.15
465	Ramon Ortiz	.15
466	Tony Armas	.15
467	Michael O'Connor	.15
468	Chad Cordero	.15
469	Jon Rauch	.15
470	Pedro Astacio	.15
471	Miguel Tejada	.25
472	David Ortiz	.50
473	Jermaine Dye	.25
474	Travis Hafner	.25
475	Maggilo Ordonez	.25
476	Mark Teahen	.15
477	Vladimir Guerrero	.50
478	Justin Morneau	.50
479	Derek Jeter	1.00
480	Nick Swisher	.25
481	Ichiro Suzuki	.50
482	Scott Kazmir	.25
483	Mark Teixeira	.25
484	Vernon Wells	.25
485	Brandon Webb	.25
486	Andruw Jones	.25
487	Carlos Zambrano	.25
488	Adam Dunn	.25
489	Matt Holliday	.50
490	Miguel Cabrera	.50
491	Lance Berkman	.25
492	Nomar Garciaparra	.25
493	Prince Fielder	1.00
494	Carlos Beltran	.40
495	Ryan Howard	1.00
496	Jason Bay	.25
497	Adrian Gonzalez	.50
498	Matt Cain	.25
499	Albert Pujols	1.00
500	Ryan Zimmerman	.50
501	Daisuke Matsuzaka/Suit RC	20.00
502	Kei Igawa RC	2.00
503	Akinori Iwamura RC	2.00
521	Randy Johnson	.25
522	Brandon Lyon	.15
523	Robby Hammock	.15
524	Micah Owings (RC)	.25
525	Doug Davis	.15
526	Brian Barden RC	.50
527	Alberto Callaspo	.15
528	Stephen Drew	.25
529	Chris Young	.25
530	Edgar Gonzalez	.15
531	Brandon Medders	.15

#	Player	Price
532	Tony Pena	.15
533	Jose Valverde	.15
534	Chris Snyder	.15
535	Tony Clark	.15
536	Scott Hairston	.15
537	Jeff DaVanon	.15
538	Randy Johnson	.40
539	Mark Redman	.15
540	Andruw Jones	.50
541	Rafael Soriano	.15
542	Scott Thorman	.15
543	Chipper Jones	.75
544	Mike Gonzalez	.15
545	Lance Cormier	.15
546	Kyle Davies	.15
547	Mike Hampton	.15
548	Chuck James	.15
549	Macay McBride	.15
550	Tanyon Sturtze	.15
551	Tyler Yates	.15
552	Peter Orr	.15
553	Craig Wilson	.15
554	Chris Woodward	.15
555	Chipper Jones	.40
556	Chad Bradford	.15
557	John Parrish	.15
558	Jeremy Guthrie	.15
559	Steve Trachsel	.15
560	Scott Williamson	.15
561	Jaret Wright	.15
562	Paul Bako	.15
563	Chris Gomez	.15
564	Melvin Mora	.15
565	Freddie Bynum	.15
566	Aubrey Huff	.15
567	Jay Payton	.15
568	Miguel Tejada	.50
569	Kurt Birkins	.15
570	Danys Baez	.15
571	Brian Roberts	.25
572	Josh Beckett	.50
573	Matt Clement	.15
574	Hideki Okajima RC	1.00
575	Javier Lopez	.15
576	Joel Pineiro	.15
577	J.C. Romero	.15
578	Kyle Snyder	.15
579	Julian Tavarez	.15
580	Mike Timlin	.15
581	Jason Varitek	.50
582	Mike Lowell	.25
583	Kevin Youkilis	.25
584	Coco Crisp	.15
585	J.D. Drew	.25
586	Eric Hinske	.15
587	Wily Mo Pena	.15
588	Julio Lugo	.15
589	David Ortiz	.75
590	Manny Ramirez	.75
591	Daisuke Matsuzaka	2.00
592	Scott Eyre	.15
593	Angel Guzman	.15
594	Bob Howry	.15
595	Ted Lilly	.15
596	Juan Mateo	.15
597	Wade Miller	.15
598	Carlos Zambrano	.25
599	Will Ohman	.15
600	Mike Wuertz	.15
601	Henry Blanco	.15
602	Aramis Ramirez	.40
603	Cliff Floyd	.15
604	Kerry Wood	.25
605	Alfonso Soriano	.75
606	Daryle Ward	.15
607	Jason Marquis	.15
608	Mark DeRosa	.15
609	Neal Cotts	.15
610	Derrek Lee	.50
611	Aramis Ramirez	.25
612	David Aardsma	.15
613	Mark Buehrle	.25
614	Nick Massett	.15
615	Andrew Sisco	.15
616	Matt Thornton	.15
617	Toby Hall	.15
618	Joe Crede	.15
619	Paul Konerko	.25
620	Darin Erstad	.15
621	Pablo Ozuna	.15
622	Scott Podsednik	.15
623	Jim Thome	.50
624	Jermaine Dye	.15
625	Jim Thome	.25
626	Adam Dunn	.50
627	Bill Bray	.15
628	Alex Gonzalez	.15
629	Josh Hamilton (RC)	2.00
630	Matt Belisle	.15
631	Rheal Cormier	.15
632	Kyle Lohse	.15
633	Eric Milton	.15
634	Kirk Saarloos	.15
635	Mike Stanton	.15
636	Javier Valentin	.15
637	Juan Castro	.15
638	Jeff Conine	.15
639	Jon Coutlangus (RC)	.50
640	Ken Griffey Jr.	1.50
641	Ken Griffey Jr.	.75
642	Fernando Cabrera	.15
643	Fausto Carmona	.25
644	Jason Davis	.15
645	Aaron Fultz	.15
646	Roberto Hernandez	.15
647	Jake Westbrook	.15
648	Kelly Stoppach	.15
649	Josh Barfield	.25

#	Player	Price
651	Andy Marte	.15
652	Joe Inglett	.15
653	David Dellucci	.15
654	Joe Borowski	.15
655	Franklin Gutierrez	.15
656	Trot Nixon	.15
657	Grady Sizemore	.50
658	Mike Rouse	.15
659	Travis Hafner	.40
660	Victor Martinez	.40
661	C.C. Sabathia	.40
662	Grady Sizemore	.25
663	Jeremy Affeldt	.15
664	Taylor Buchholz	.15
665	Brian Fuentes	.15
666	LaTroy Hawkins	.15
667	Byung-Hyun Kim	.15
668	Brian Lawrence	.15
669	Rodrigo Lopez	.15
670	Jeff Francis	.15
671	Chris Iannetta	.15
672	Garrett Atkins	.25
673	Todd Helton	.50
674	Steve Finley	.15
675	John Mabry	.15
676	Willy Taveras	.15
677	Jason Hirsh	.15
678	Ramon Ramirez	.15
679	Matt Holliday	.75
680	Todd Helton	.25
681	Roman Colon	.15
682	Chad Durbin	.15
683	Jason Grilli	.15
684	Wilfredo Ledezma	.15
685	Mike Maroth	.15
686	Jose Mesa	.15
687	Justin Verlander	.50
688	Fernando Rodney	.15
689	Vance Wilson	.15
690	Carlos Guillen	.15
691	Neifi Perez	.15
692	Curtis Granderson	.15
693	Gary Sheffield	.50
694	Justin Verlander	.25
695	Kevin Gregg	.15
696	Logan Kensing	.15
697	Randy Messenger	.15
698	Sergio Mitre	.15
699	Ricky Nolasco	.15
700	Scott Olsen	.25
701	Renyel Pinto	.15
702	Matt Treanor	.15
703	Alfredo Amezaga	.15
704	Aaron Boone	.15
705	Mike Jacobs	.15
706	Miguel Cabrera	.75
707	Joe Borchard	.15
708	Jorge Julio	.15
709	Rick Vanden Hurk RC	.75
710	Lee Gardner (RC)	.15
711	Matt Lindstrom (RC)	.50
712	Henry Owens	.15
713	Hanley Ramirez	.50
714	Alejandro De Aza RC	.50
715	Hanley Ramirez	.25
716	Dave Borkowski	.15
717	Jason Jennings	.15
718	Trever Miller	.15
719	Roy Oswalt	.40
720	Wandy Rodriguez	.15
721	Humberto Quintero	.15
722	Morgan Ensberg	.15
723	Mike Lamb	.15
724	Mark Loretta	.15
725	Jason Lane	.15
726	Carlos Lee	.40
727	Orlando Palmeiro	.15
728	Woody Williams	.15
729	Chad Qualls	.15
730	Lance Berkman	.40
731	Rick White	.15
732	Chris Sampson	.15
733	Carlos Lee	.15
734	Jorge De La Rosa	.15
735	Octavio Dotel	.15
736	Jimmy Gobble	.15
737	Zack Greinke	.15
738	Luke Hudson	.15
739	Gil Meche	.15
740	Joel Peralta	.15
741	Odalis Perez	.15
742	David Riske	.15
743	Jason LaRue	.15
744	Tony Pena	.15
745	Esteban German	.15
746	Ross Gload	.15
747	Emil Brown	.15
748	David DeJesus	.15
749	Brandon Duckworth	.15
750	Alex Gordon RC	1.00
751	Jered Weaver	.50
752	Vladimir Guerrero	.75
753	Hector Carrasco	.15
754	Kelvim Escobar	.15
755	Darren Oliver	.15
756	Dustin Moseley	.15
757	Ervin Santana	.15
758	Mike Napoli	.15
759	Shea Hillenbrand	.15
760	Casey Kotchman	.15
761	Reggie Willits	.15
762	Robb Quinlan	.15
763	Garret Anderson	.15
764	Gary Mathews	.15
765	Justin Speier	.15
766	Shawn Chacon	.15
767	Joe Beimel	.15
768	Yhency Brazoban	.15

#	Player	Price
769	Elmer Dessens	.15
770	Mark Hendrickson	.15
771	Hong-Chih Kuo	.25
772	Jason Schmidt	.25
773	Brett Tomko	.15
774	Randy Wolf	.15
775	Mike Lieberthal	.15
776	Marlon Anderson	.15
777	Jeff Kent	.25
778	Ramon Martinez	.15
779	Olmedo Saenz	.15
780	Luis Gonzalez	.25
781	Juan Pierre	.15
782	Jason Repko	.15
783	Nomar Garciaparra	.75
784	Wilson Valdez	.15
785	Jason Schmidt	.15
786	Greg Aquino	.15
787	Brian Shouse	.15
788	Jeff Suppan	.15
789	Carlos Villanueva	.15
790	Matt Wise	.15
791	Johnny Estrada	.15
792	Craig Counsell	.15
793	Tony Graffanino	.15
794	Corey Koskie	.15
795	Claudio Vargas	.15
796	Brady Clark	.15
797	Gabe Gross	.15
798	Geoff Jenkins	.15
799	Kevin Mench	.15
800	Bill Hall	.15
801	Sidney Ponson	.15
802	Jesse Crain	.15
803	Matt Guerrier	.15
804	Pat Neshek	.15
805	Ramon Ortiz	.15
806	Johan Santana	.75
807	Carlos Silva	.15
808	Mike Redmond	.15
809	Jeff Cirillo	.15
810	Luis Rodriguez	.15
811	Lew Ford	.15
812	Torii Hunter	.40
813	Jason Tyner	.15
814	Rondell White	.15
815	Justin Morneau	.50
816	Joe Mauer	.40
817	Johan Santana	.40
818	David Newhan	.15
819	Aaron Sele	.15
820	Ambiorix Burgos	.15
821	Pedro Feliciano	.15
822	Tom Glavine	.50
823	Aaron Heilman	.15
824	Guillermo Mota	.15
825	Jose Reyes	1.00
826	Oliver Perez	.15
827	Duaner Sanchez	.15
828	Scott Schoeneweis	.15
829	Ramon Castro	.15
830	Damion Easley	.15
831	David Wright	1.50
832	Moises Alou	.25
833	Carlos Beltran	.50
834	Dave Williams	.15
835	David Wright	.75
836	Brian Bruney	.15
837	Mike Myers	.15
838	Carl Pavano	.15
839	Andy Pettitte	.40
840	Luis Vizcaino	.15
841	Jorge Posada	.40
842	Mariano Cairo	.15
843	Doug Mientkiewicz	.15
844	Derek Jeter	2.00
845	Alex Rodriguez	.75
846	Johnny Damon	.75
847	Hideki Matsui	1.00
848	Josh Phelps	.15
849	Phil Hughes (RC)	4.00
850	Roger Clemens	2.00
851	Jason Giambi	.25
852	Kiko Calero	.15
853	Justin Duchscherer	.15
854	Alan Embree	.15
855	Todd Walker	.15
856	Rich Harden	.15
857	Danny Haren	.40
858	Joe Kennedy	.15
859	Jason Kendall	.15
860	Adam Melhuse	.15
861	Mark Ellis	.15
862	Mark Kotsay	.15
863	Shannon Stewart	.15
864	Mike Piazza	.75
865	Mike Piazza	.40
866	Antonio Alfonseca	.15
867	Carlos Ruiz	.15
868	Adam Eaton	.15
869	Freddy Garcia	.15
870	Jon Lieber	.15
871	Matt Smith	.15
872	Rod Barajas	.15
873	Wes Helms	.15
874	Abraham Nunez	.15
875	Jayson Werth	.15
876	Pat Burrell	.25
877	Greg Dobbs	.15
878	Joseph Bisenius RC	.15
879	Michael Bourn (RC)	.50
880	Chase Utley	.75
881	Chase Utley	.15
882	Ryan Howard	1.50
883	Chase Utley	.15
884	Tony Armas	.15
885	Shawn Chacon	.15
886	John Grabow	.15
887	Paul Maholm	.15

#	Player	Price
888	Damaso Marte	.15
889	Salomon Torres	.15
890	Humberto Cota	.15
891	Ryan Doumit	.15
892	Adam LaRoche	.25
893	Jack Wilson	.15
894	Nate McLouth	.15
895	Brad Eldred	.15
896	Jonah Bayliss	.15
897	Juan Perez RC	.50
898	Jason Bay	.40
899	Adam LaRoche	.15
900	Doug Brocail	.15
901	Scott Cassidy	.15
902	Scott Linebrink	.15
903	Greg Maddux	1.50
904	Jake Peavy	.40
905	Mike Thompson	.15
906	David Wells	.15
907	Josh Bard	.15
908	Rob Bowen	.15
909	Marcus Giles	.15
910	Russell Branyan	.15
911	Jose Cruz	.15
912	Termmel Sledge	.15
913	Trevor Hoffman	.25
914	Brian Giles	.25
915	Trevor Hoffman	.15
916	Vinnie Chulk	.15
917	Kevin Correia	.15
918	Tim Lincecum RC	25.00
919	Matt Morris	.15
920	Russ Ortiz	.15
921	Barry Zito	.25
922	Bengie Molina	.15
923	Rich Aurilia	.15
924	Omar Vizquel	.25
925	Jason Ellison	.15
926	Ryan Klesko	.15
927	Dave Roberts	.15
928	Randy Winn	.15
929	Barry Zito	.15
930	Miguel Batista	.15
931	Horacio Ramirez	.15
932	Chris Reitsma	.15
933	George Sherrill	.15
934	Jarrod Washburn	.15
935	Jeff Weaver	.15
936	Jake Woods	.15
937	Adrian Beltre	.25
938	Jose Lopez	.15
939	Ichiro Suzuki	1.50
940	Jose Vidro	.15
941	Jose Guillen	.15
942	Sean White RC	.15
943	Brandon Morrow RC	1.00
944	Felix Hernandez	.50
945	Felix Hernandez	.25
946	Randy Flores	.15
947	Ryan Franklin	.15
948	Kelvin Jimenez RC	.50
949	Tyler Johnson	.15
950	Mark Mulder	.15
951	Anthony Reyes	.15
952	Russ Springer	.15
953	Brad Thompson	.15
954	Adam Wainwright	.15
955	Kip Wells	.15
956	Gary Bennett	.15
957	Adam Kennedy	.15
958	Scott Rolen	.75
959	Scott Spiezio	.15
960	So Taguchi	.15
961	Preston Wilson	.15
962	Skip Schumaker	.15
963	Albert Pujols	2.00
964	Chris Carpenter	.15
965	Chris Carpenter	.25
966	Edwin Jackson	.15
967	Jae-Kuk Ryu	.15
968	Jae Weong Seo	.15
969	Jon Switzer	.15
970	Josh Paul	.15
971	Benjamin Zobrist	.15
972	Rocco Baldelli	.15
973	Scott Kazmir	.25
974	Carl Crawford	.25
975	Delmon Young	.50
976	Bruce Chen	.15
977	Joaquin Benoit	.15
978	Scott Feldman	.15
979	Eric Gagne	.15
980	Kameron Loe	.15
981	Brandon McCarthy	.15
982	Robinson Tejeda	.15
983	C.J. Wilson	.15
984	Mark Teixeira	.50
985	Michael Young	.25
986	Kenny Lofton	.25
987	Brad Wilkerson	.15
988	Nelson Cruz	.15
989	Sammy Sosa	.75
990	Michael Young	.15
991	Vernon Wells	.40
992	Matt Stairs	.15
993	Jeremy Accardo	.15
994	A.J. Burnett	.15
995	Jason Frasor	.15
996	Roy Halladay	.40
997	Shaun Marcum	.15
998	Tomokazu Ohka	.15
999	Josh Towers	.15
1000	Gregg Zaun	.15
1001	Royce Clayton	.15
1002	Jason Smith	.15
1003	Alex Rios	.25
1004	Frank Thomas	.15
1005	Roy Halladay	.25

#	Player	Price
1006	Jesus Flores RC	.50
1007	Dmitri Young	.15
1008	Ray King	.15
1009	Micah Bowie	.15
1010	Shawn Hill	.15
1011	John Patterson	.15
1012	Levale Speigner RC	.50
1013	Ryan Wagner	.15
1014	Jerome Williams	.15
1015	Ryan Zimmerman	.50
1016	Cristian Guzman	.15
1017	Nook Logan	.15
1018	Chris Snelling	.15
1019	Ronnie Belliard	.15
1020	Nick Johnson	.15

Gold
Gold: 8-15X
Production 75 Sets

Printing Plates
No Pricing
Production one set per color.

1989 Reprints

Jackie Robinson

	Player	NM/M
	Common Player:	1.00
AK	Al Kaline	2.00
BF	Bob Feller	1.00
BR	Babe Ruth	5.00
CA	Rod Carew	1.00
CF	Carlton Fisk	1.00
CM	Christy Mathewson	1.00
CS	Casey Stengel	1.00
CY	Cy Young	1.00
DR	Don Drysdale	1.00
FR	Frank Robinson	1.00
GE	Lou Gehrig	3.00
HW	Honus Wagner	2.00
JB	Johnny Bench	1.50
JF	Jimmie Foxx	2.00
JR	Jackie Robinson	2.00
LG	Lefty Grove	1.00
LJ	LeBron James	3.00
MJ	Michael Jordan	5.00
MO	Mel Ott	1.00
RB	Reggie Bush	2.00
RC	Roy Campanella	1.00
RH	Rogers Hornsby	1.00
RJ	Reggie Jackson	1.50
RO	Brooks Robinson	1.50
SC	Sidney Crosby	4.00
SM	Stan Musial	1.50
SP	Satchel Paige	3.00
TC	Ty Cobb	3.00
TM	Thurman Munson	2.00
WJ	Walter Johnson	2.00

Ripken Jr. and Tony Gwynn Road to the Hall
No Pricing

Cal Ripken Jr. Chronicles

		NM/M
	Common Ripken:	8.00
1-50	Cal Ripken Jr.	8.00

Cal Ripken Jr./Lou Gehrig Iron Man

		NM/M
	Common Ripken/Gehrig:	20.00
	Autograph:	No Pricing
	Production One	
1-50	Cal Ripken Jr., Lou Gehrig	20.00

Cooperstown Calling

	Player	NM/M
	Common Player:	1.00
AJ	Andruw Jones	1.50
AP	Albert Pujols	5.00
AR	Alex Rodriguez	5.00
AS	Alfonso Soriano	2.00
BI	Craig Biggio	1.00
BW	Billy Wagner	1.00
CA	Chris Carpenter	1.50
CB	Carlos Beltran	1.50
CC	Carl Crawford	1.00
CD	Carlos Delgado	1.50
CJ	Chipper Jones	2.00
CR	Cal Ripken Jr.	5.00
CS	Curt Schilling	2.00
DJ	Derek Jeter	5.00
DO	David Ortiz	2.00
FT	Frank Thomas	1.50
GM	Greg Maddux	3.00
GS	Gary Sheffield	1.00
HA	Travis Hafner	1.00
HE	Todd Helton	1.50
HO	Ryan Howard	4.00
IR	Ivan Rodriguez	1.50
IS	Ichiro Suzuki	3.00
JD	Johnny Damon	2.00
JG	Jason Giambi	1.50
JK	Jeff Kent	1.00
JM	Justin Morneau	2.00
JS	Johan Santana	2.00
JT	Jim Thome	1.50
KG	Ken Griffey Jr.	4.00
MC	Miguel Cabrera	2.00
MM	Mike Mussina	1.50
MP	Mike Piazza	3.00
MR	Manny Ramirez	2.00
MT	Mark Teixeira	1.50
OV	Omar Vizquel	1.00
PE	Andy Pettitte	1.00
PM	Pedro Martinez	2.00
RH	Roy Halladay	1.50
RI	Mariano Rivera	1.50
RJ	Randy Johnson	2.00
RO	Roy Oswalt	1.00
SI	Grady Sizemore	2.00
SM	John Smoltz	1.50
SR	Scott Rolen	1.00
SS	Sammy Sosa	2.00
TE	Miguel Tejada	1.00
TG	Tom Glavine	1.00
TH	Trevor Hoffman	1.00
VG	Vladimir Guerrero	2.00

Cooperstown Calling Autograph
No Pricing

Ken Griffey Jr. Chronicles

		NM/M
	Common Griffey:	5.00
1-50	Ken Griffey Jr.	5.00

MVP Predictors

Alfonso Soriano

	Player	NM/M
	Common Predictor:	3.00
1	Miguel Tejada	4.00
2	David Ortiz	4.00
3	Manny Ramirez	8.00
4	Jermaine Dye	4.00
5	Jim Thome	6.00
6	Paul Konerko	5.00
7	Travis Hafner	4.00
8	Grady Sizemore	6.00
9	Victor Martinez	4.00
10	Magglio Ordonez	3.00
11	Justin Verlander	8.00
12	Vladimir Guerrero	8.00
13	Jered Weaver	4.00
14	Justin Morneau	4.00
15	Joe Mauer	6.00
16	Johan Santana	8.00
17	Alex Rodriguez	25.00
18	Derek Jeter	15.00
19	Jason Giambi	4.00
20	Johnny Damon	6.00
21	Bobby Abreu	4.00
23	Frank Thomas	5.00
24	Eric Chavez	3.00
25	Ichiro Suzuki	8.00
26	Adrian Beltre	3.00
27	Carl Crawford	4.00
28	Scott Kazmir	4.00
29	Mark Teixeira	6.00
30	Michael Young	5.00
31	Carlos Lee	4.00
32	Vernon Wells	4.00
33	Roy Halladay	4.00
34	Troy Glaus	4.00
35	Stephen Drew	3.00

#	Player	Price
36	Chipper Jones	5.00
37	Andruw Jones	5.00
38	Adam LaRoche	4.00
39	Derrek Lee	8.00
40	Aramis Ramirez	6.00
41	Adam Dunn	4.00
42	Ken Griffey Jr.	10.00
43	Matt Holliday	8.00
44	Garrett Atkins	5.00
45	Miguel Cabrera	6.00
46	Hanley Ramirez	4.00
47	Dan Uggla	3.00
48	Lance Berkman	5.00
49	Roy Oswalt	4.00
50	Nomar Garciaparra	4.00
51	J.D. Drew	4.00
52	Rafael Furcal	4.00
53	Prince Fielder	10.00
54	Bill Hall	5.00
55	Jose Reyes	8.00
56	Carlos Beltran	8.00
57	Carlos Delgado	5.00
58	David Wright	10.00
60	Chase Utley	8.00
61	Ryan Howard	10.00
62	Jimmy Rollins	15.00
63	Jason Bay	5.00
64	Freddy Sanchez	3.00
65	Adrian Gonzalez	4.00
66	Albert Pujols	15.00
67	Scott Rolen	6.00
68	Chris Carpenter	5.00
69	Alfonso Soriano	8.00
70	Ryan Zimmerman	4.00

Playoff Predictors

NM/M

Common Predictor: 3.00

#	Team	Price
1	Arizona Diamondbacks	5.00
2	Atlanta Braves	5.00
3	Baltimore Orioles	3.00
4	Boston Red Sox	25.00
5	Chicago Cubs	5.00
6	Chicago White Sox	5.00
7	Cincinnati Reds	3.00
8	Cleveland Indians	5.00
9	Colorado Rockies	5.00
10	Detroit Tigers	5.00
11	Florida Marlins	3.00
12	Houston Astros	5.00
13	Kansas City Royals	3.00
14	Los Angeles Angels	5.00
15	Los Angeles Dodgers	5.00
16	Milwaukee Brewers	5.00
17	Minnesota Twins	5.00
18	New York Mets	5.00
19	New York Yankees	15.00
20	Oakland Athletics	5.00
21	Philadelphia Phillies	5.00
22	Pittsburgh Pirates	3.00
23	San Diego Padres	5.00
24	San Francisco Giants	5.00
25	Seattle Mariners	5.00
26	St. Louis Cardinals	5.00
27	Tampa Bay Devil Rays	3.00
28	Texas Rangers	5.00
29	Toronto Blue Jays	5.00
30	Washington Nationals	3.00

Star Power

NM/M

Inserted 2:1 Fat Packs

	Player	Price
AJ	Andruw Jones	1.50
AP	Albert Pujols	5.00
AR	Alex Rodriguez	5.00
BR	Brian Roberts	1.00
BZ	Barry Zito	.75
CA	Chris Carpenter	1.50
CB	Carlos Beltran	1.50
CC	Carl Crawford	1.00
CJ	Chipper Jones	2.00
CS	Curt Schilling	1.50
CU	Chase Utley	1.50
CZ	Carlos Zambrano	1.00
DA	Johnny Damon	1.50
DJ	Derek Jeter	5.00
DO	David Ortiz	2.00
DW	Dontrelle Willis	.75
FS	Freddy Sanchez	.75
FT	Frank Thomas	1.50
HA	Roy Halladay	1.00
HO	Trevor Hoffman	.75
IS	Ichiro Suzuki	3.00
JB	Jason Bay	1.00
JD	Jermaine Dye	.75
JM	Joe Mauer	1.00
JP	Jake Peavy	1.00
JR	Jose Reyes	2.00
JS	Johan Santana	1.50
JT	Jim Thome	1.50
JU	Justin Morneau	1.50
JV	Justin Verlander	1.50
KG	Ken Griffey Jr.	4.00
KR	Kenny Rogers	.75
LB	Lance Berkman	1.00
MA	Matt Cain	1.00
MC	Miguel Cabrera	2.00
MH	Matt Holliday	1.00
MO	Magglio Ordonez	.75
MR	Manny Ramirez	1.50
MT	Mark Teixeira	1.00
MY	Michael Young	1.00
NG	Nomar Garciaparra	1.50
NS	Nick Swisher	1.00
PF	Prince Fielder	1.50
RH	Ryan Howard	3.00
RO	Roy Oswalt	1.00
RZ	Ryan Zimmerman	1.00

Star Signings

	Player	Price
SM	John Smoltz	1.00
TH	Travis Hafner	1.00
VG	Vladimir Guerrero	1.50
WR	David Wright	2.00

NM/M

Common Auto.: 5.00

	Player	Price
AB	Ambiorix Burgos	8.00
AC	Aaron Cook	5.00
AH	Aubrey Huff/SP	15.00
AR	Alex Rios	20.00
BA	Bobby Abreu	35.00
BL	Joe Blanton	8.00
BO	Jeremy Bonderman	25.00
BR	Brandon Backe	8.00
CJ	Conor Jackson	15.00
CO	Chad Cordero	10.00
CP	Corey Patterson	10.00
CS	Chris Shelton	8.00
CY	Chris Young/SP	20.00
DH	Danny Haren	10.00
DJ	Derek Jeter	150.00
DU	Chris Duffy	10.00
GA	Garrett Atkins	10.00
GC	Gustavo Chacin	8.00
HS	Huston Street	15.00
HU	Torii Hunter	15.00
IS	Ian Snell/SP	15.00
JA	Jeremy Accardo	8.00
JB	Jason Bergmann/SP	8.00
JD	Joey Devine	8.00
JG	Jonny Gomes	8.00
JJ	Jorge Julio	8.00
JK	Jason Kubel	8.00
JM	Justin Morneau	25.00
JN	Joe Nathan	15.00
JS	Jason Bay	15.00
KW	Jake Westbrook	10.00
KF	Keith Foulke	10.00
KG	Ken Griffey Jr.	75.00
KM	Kevin Mench	10.00
KS	Kirk Saarloos	8.00
KY	Kevin Youkilis	20.00
LN	Laynce Nix/SP	8.00
LO	Lyle Overbay	10.00
MH	Matt Holliday	25.00
MK	Mark Kotsay	10.00
MM	Melvin Mora	15.00
NM	Nate McLouth/SP	15.00
RC	Ryan Church	15.00
RG	Ryan Garko	15.00
RI	Juan Rivera/SP	8.00
RJ	Reed Johnson	10.00
RU	Carlos Ruiz	10.00
SC	Sean Casey/SP	10.00
SD	Stephen Drew	20.00
SP	Scott Podsednik/SP	20.00
TI	Tadahito Iguchi	20.00
VE	Justin Verlander	30.00
WM	Wily Mo Pena	15.00
XN	Xavier Nady	15.00
YB	Yuniesky Betancourt	20.00

Common Player: 10.00

	Player	Price
AC	Alberto Callaspo	10.00
AG	Alex Gordon	40.00
AI	Akinori Iwamura/SP	30.00
AS	Angel Sanchez	10.00
BA	Jeff Baker	10.00
BB	Brian Burres	10.00
BE	Josh Beckett/SP	40.00
BO	Ben Broussard	10.00
BU	B.J. Upton/SP	40.00
CB	Craig Biggio/SP	40.00
CC	Carl Crawford/SP	20.00
CR	Cal Ripken Jr./SP	125.00
DJ	Derek Jeter	140.00
DY	Delmon Young/SP	20.00
ED	Elijah Dukes	15.00
FH	Felix Hernandez	30.00
IK	Ian Kinsler/SP	15.00
IS	Ian Snell	15.00
JD	J.D. Drew/SP	15.00
KG	Ken Griffey Jr./SP	75.00
KI	Kei Igawa/SP	50.00
NC	Nelson Cruz	15.00
OP	Oliver Perez/SP	15.00
RA	Chris Ray	15.00
SA	Juan Salas	10.00
SH	Sean Henn	10.00
YO	Chris Young	20.00
ZS	Zack Segovia	15.00

Game Materials

NM/M

Common Player: 4.00

Patch: 2-4X

	Player	Price
AJ	Andruw Jones	4.00
AP	Albert Pujols	20.00
BE	Josh Beckett	6.00
BR	Brian Roberts	6.00
BS	Ben Sheets	4.00
CA	Chris Carpenter	8.00
CB	Carlos Beltran	6.00
CC	Carl Crawford	6.00
CD	Carlos Delgado	6.00
CL	Carlos Lee	6.00
CP	Corey Patterson	4.00
CS	C.C. Sabathia	8.00
DJ	Derek Jeter	20.00
DO	David Ortiz	10.00
DW	Dontrelle Willis	4.00
EC	Eric Chavez	4.00
FH	Felix Hernandez	8.00
HU	Torii Hunter	6.00
IR	Ivan Rodriguez	6.00
JB	Jason Bay	6.00
JG	Jason Giambi	6.00
JM	Joe Mauer	6.00
JR	Jose Reyes	10.00
JS	Johan Santana	8.00
JU	Juan Uribe	4.00
JV	Justin Verlander	10.00
KG	Ken Griffey Jr.	15.00
MC	Miguel Cabrera	8.00
MH	Matt Holliday	8.00
MM	Melvin Mora	4.00
MO	Justin Morneau	8.00
MR	Manny Ramirez	8.00
MS	Mike Sweeney	4.00
MT	Miguel Tejada	6.00
MU	Mike Mussina	4.00
OR	Magglio Ordonez	4.00
PF	Prince Fielder	10.00
RH	Roy Halladay	6.00
RZ	Ryan Zimmerman	8.00
SR	Scott Rolen	6.00
TH	Tim Hudson	4.00
VM	Victor Martinez	4.00

Series 2:

	Player	Price
AB	A.J. Burnett	4.00
AP	Albert Pujols	20.00
AR	Alex Rios	4.00
BA	Bobby Abreu	5.00
BC	Bartolo Colon	4.00
BJ	Bobby Jenks	4.00
CC	Carl Crawford	4.00
CJ	Chipper Jones	10.00
CS	Curt Schilling	8.00
CU	Chase Utley	10.00
DJ	Derek Jeter	20.00
EB	Erik Bedard	6.00
EN	Juan Encarnacion	4.00
FR	Jeff Francoeur/SP	8.00
GS	Gary Sheffield	8.00
HB	Hank Blalock	4.00
HO	Trevor Hoffman	4.00
JD	Johnny Damon	8.00
JE	Jim Edmonds	5.00
JF	Jeff Francis	4.00
JS	John Smoltz	10.00
JT	Jim Thome	8.00
JV	Jose Vidro	4.00
KG	Ken Griffey Jr.	15.00
LB	Lance Berkman	8.00
LG	Luis Gonzalez	4.00
MR	Manny Ramirez	8.00
MT	Mark Teixeira	4.00
RB	Rocco Baldelli	4.00
RJ	Randy Johnson	8.00
RN	Ricky Nolasco	4.00
RO	Roy Oswalt	8.00
RW	Rickie Weeks	4.00
SD	Stephen Drew	4.00
SK	Scott Kazmir	4.00
SR	Scott Rolen	8.00
TG	Tom Glavine	8.00
TH	Todd Helton	8.00
TN	Trot Nixon	4.00
VG	Vladimir Guerrero	8.00
ZD	Zachary Duke	4.00

2007 Upper Deck Cal Ripken Box Set

NM/M

Complete Set (45): 35.00
Common Ripken: 1.00
1-45 Cal Ripken Jr. 1.00

1989 Rookie Reprint Signatures

No Pricing
Production Five Sets

1989 Rookie Reprints

Joakim Soria

NM/M

Common Player: 1.00

	Player	Price
AG	Alex Gordon	3.00
AI	Akinori Iwamura	3.00
AS	Angel Sanchez	1.00
BN	Jared Burton	1.00
BU	Jamie Burke	1.00
CA	Cesar Jimenez	1.00
CB	Carlos Beltran	1.00
CC	Carl Crawford	1.00
CD	Carlos Delgado	1.00
CL	Carlos Lee	1.00
CP	Corey Patterson	4.00
CS	C.C. Sabathia	8.00
DJ	Derek Jeter	20.00
DO	David Ortiz	10.00
DW	Dontrelle Willis	4.00
EC	Eric Chavez	4.00
FH	Felix Hernandez	8.00
HU	Torii Hunter	6.00
IR	Ivan Rodriguez	6.00
JB	Jason Bay	6.00
JG	Jason Giambi	6.00
JM	Joe Mauer	6.00
JR	Jose Reyes	10.00
JS	Johan Santana	8.00
JU	Juan Uribe	4.00
JV	Justin Verlander	10.00
KG	Ken Griffey Jr.	15.00
MC	Miguel Cabrera	8.00
MH	Matt Holliday	8.00
MM	Melvin Mora	4.00
MO	Justin Morneau	8.00
MR	Manny Ramirez	8.00
MS	Mike Sweeney	4.00
MT	Miguel Tejada	6.00
MU	Mike Mussina	4.00
OR	Magglio Ordonez	4.00
PF	Prince Fielder	10.00
RH	Roy Halladay	6.00
RZ	Ryan Zimmerman	8.00
SR	Scott Rolen	6.00
TH	Tim Hudson	4.00
VM	Victor Martinez	4.00

(continued)

	Player	Price
DK	Donald Kelly	1.00
DM	Daisuke Matsuzaka	10.00
DY	Delmon Young	2.00
ED	Elijah Dukes	1.00
GM	Gustavo Molina	1.00
HG	Hector Gimenez	1.00
JA	Joaquin Arias	1.00
JB	Jeff Baker	1.00
JD	John Danks	1.00
JF	Jesus Flores	1.00
JG	Jose Garcia	1.00
JH	Josh Hamilton	2.00
JM	Jay Marshall	1.00
JP	Juan Perez	1.00
KC	Kevin Cameron	1.00
KI	Kei Igawa	1.00
KK	Kevin Kouzmanoff	2.00
KO	Kory Casto	1.00
MB	Michael Bourn	1.00
MC	Matt Chico	1.00
MM	Miguel Montero	1.00
MO	Micah Owings	1.00
MR	Mike Rabelo	1.00
RB	Ryan Braun	1.00
SA	Juan Salas	1.00
SH	Sean Henn	1.00
SL	Doug Slaten	1.00
SO	Joakim Soria	1.00
ST	Brian Stokes	1.00
TB	Travis Buck	1.00
TT	Troy Tulowitzki	2.00
ZS	Zack Segovia	1.00

MVP Potential

NM/M

Common Player: 1.00

#	Player	Price
1	Stephen Drew	1.00
2	Brian McCann	1.00
3	Adam LaRoche	1.00
4	Brian Roberts	1.00
5	Manny Ramirez	2.00
6	David Ortiz	2.00
7	J.D. Drew	1.00
8	Alfonso Soriano	1.00
9	Aramis Ramirez	1.50
10	Derrek Lee	1.50
11	Jermaine Dye	1.00
12	Paul Konerko	1.00
13	Jim Thome	1.00
14	Adam Dunn	1.50
15	Travis Hafner	1.00
16	Victor Martinez	1.00
17	Grady Sizemore	2.00
18	Garrett Atkins	1.00
19	Matt Holliday	1.00
20	Magglio Ordonez	1.00
21	Miguel Cabrera	2.00
22	Hanley Ramirez	2.00
23	Dan Uggla	1.00
24	Lance Berkman	1.50
25	Carlos Lee	1.00
26	Jered Weaver	1.50
27	Nomar Garciaparra	1.50
28	Rafael Furcal	1.00
29	Prince Fielder	2.00
30	Joe Mauer	1.50
31	Johan Santana	2.00
32	David Wright	3.00
33	Jose Reyes	3.00
34	Carlos Beltran	2.00
35	Robinson Cano	1.50
36	Derek Jeter	5.00
37	Bobby Abreu	1.00
38	Johnny Damon	2.00
39	Nick Swisher	1.00
40	Chase Utley	2.00
41	Jason Bay	2.00
42	Adrian Gonzalez	1.00
43	Adrian Beltre	1.00
44	Scott Rolen	1.50
45	Carl Crawford	1.50
46	Mark Teixeira	1.50
47	Michael Young	1.00
48	Vernon Wells	1.00
49	Roy Halladay	1.00
50	Ryan Zimmerman	2.00

Rookie of the Year Predictor

Lee Gardner

NM/M

Common Player: 3.00

#	Player	Price
1	Doug Slaten	3.00
2	Miguel Montero	3.00
3	Kory Casto	3.00
4	Jesus Flores	3.00
5	John Danks	3.00
6	Daisuke Matsuzaka	60.00
7	Chris Stewart	3.00
9	Jose Reyes	3.00
10	Kevin Cameron	3.00

Ticket to Stardom

NM/M

Common Player: 2.00

	Player	Price
AG	Alex Gordon	2.00
AI	Akinori Iwamura	2.00
AS	Angel Sanchez	2.00
BN	Jared Burton	2.00
BU	Jamie Burke	2.00
CH	Matt Chico	2.00
CJ	Cesar Jimenez	2.00
CS	Chris Stewart	2.00
DA	John Danks	2.00
DK	Donald Kelly	2.00
DM	Daisuke Matsuzaka	2.00
DS	Doug Slaten	2.00
DY	Delmon Young	2.00
ED	Elijah Dukes	2.00
GM	Gustavo Molina	2.00
HG	Hector Gimenez	2.00
JA	Joaquin Arias	2.00
JB	Jeff Baker	2.00
JF	Jesus Flores	2.00
JG	Jose Garcia	2.00
JH	Josh Hamilton	4.00
JM	Jay Marshall	2.00
JP	Juan Perez	2.00
KC	Kevin Cameron	2.00
KI	Kei Igawa	2.00
KK	Kevin Kouzmanoff	2.00
KO	Kory Casto	2.00
MB	Michael Bourn	2.00
MM	Miguel Montero	2.00
MO	Micah Owings	2.00
MR	Mike Rabelo	2.00
RB	Ryan Braun	2.00
SA	Juan Salas	2.00
SH	Sean Henn	2.00
SO	Joakim Soria	2.00
ST	Brian Stokes	2.00
TB	Travis Buck	2.00
TT	Troy Tulowitzki	4.00
ZS	Zack Segovia	2.00

Ticket to Stardom Autograph

No Pricing

#	Player	Price
13	Kevin Kouzmanoff	5.00
14	Jeff Baker	3.00
15	Donald Kelly	3.00
16	Troy Tulowitzki	8.00
18	Cesar Jimenez	3.00
20	Jose Garcia	3.00
21	Micah Owings	3.00
22	Josh Hamilton	6.00
24	Jamie Burke	3.00
25	Mike Rabelo	3.00
26	Elijah Dukes	3.00
27	Travis Buck	3.00
28	Kei Igawa	5.00
29	Sean Henn	3.00
32	Michael Bourn	3.00
33	Alex Gordon	20.00
35	Matt Chico	3.00
38	Gustavo Molina	3.00
39	Jared Burton	3.00
40	Jay Marshall	3.00
42	Akinori Iwamura	8.00
43	Delmon Young	3.00
44	Juan Salas	3.00
45	Zack Segovia	3.00
46	Brian Stokes	3.00
47	Joaquin Arias	3.00
48	Hector Gimenez	3.00
49	Ryan Braun	3.00
50	Juan Perez	3.00

2007 UD SP Rookie Edition

NM/M

Complete Set (284):
Common Player (1-100): .25
Common RC (101-142): .50
Common SP (143-234): 1.00
Inserted 1:2
Common (235-284): .25
Pack (8): 5.00
Box (14): 65.00

#	Player	Price
1	Chipper Jones	.75
2	Andruw Jones	.50
3	Jeff Francoeur	.50
4	Stephen Drew	.25
5	Randy Johnson	.75
6	Brandon Webb	.50
7	Alfonso Soriano	.75
8	Derrek Lee	.50
9	Aramis Ramirez	.50
10	Carlos Zambrano	.40
11	Ken Griffey Jr.	1.50
12	Adam Dunn	.50
13	Bronson Arroyo	.25
14	Todd Helton	.50
15	Jeff Francis	.25
16	Matt Holliday	.50
17	Hanley Ramirez	.50
18	Dontrelle Willis	.25
19	Miguel Cabrera	.50
20	Lance Berkman	.40
21	Roy Oswalt	.50
22	Carlos Lee	.25
23	Nomar Garciaparra	.75
24	Jason Schmidt	.25
25	Juan Pierre	.40
26	Rafael Furcal	.25
27	Rickie Weeks	.25
28	Prince Fielder	.75
29	Ben Sheets	.25
30	David Wright	1.00
31	Jose Reyes	.75
32	Pedro Martinez	.75
33	Carlos Beltran	.50
34	Cole Hamels	.50
35	Jimmy Rollins	.50
36	Ryan Howard	1.00
37	Jason Bay	.40
38	Freddy Sanchez	.25
39	Zachary Duke	.25
40	Jake Peavy	.40
41	Greg Maddux	1.50
42	Trevor Hoffman	.25
43	Matt Cain	.25
44	Barry Zito	.25
45	Omar Vizquel	.25
46	Albert Pujols	2.00
47	Chris Carpenter	.50
48	Jim Edmonds	.40
49	Scott Rolen	.50
50	Ryan Zimmerman	.50
51	Felipe Lopez	.25
52	Austin Kearns	.25
53	Miguel Tejada	.50
54	Erik Bedard	.40
55	Chris Ray	.25
56	David Ortiz	.75
57	Curt Schilling	.50
58	Manny Ramirez	.50
59	Jonathan Papelbon	.50
60	Jim Thome	.50
61	Paul Konerko	.50
62	Bobby Jenks	.25
63	Grady Sizemore	.75
64	Victor Martinez	.40
65	C.C. Sabathia	.40
66	Ivan Rodriguez	.50
67	Justin Verlander	.50
68	Joel Zumaya	.50
69	Jeremy Bonderman	.40
70	Gil Meche	.25
71	Mike Sweeney	.25
72	Mark Teahen	.25
73	Vladimir Guerrero	.75
74	Howie Kendrick	.25
75	Francisco Rodriguez	.50
76	Johan Santana	.75
77	Justin Morneau	.50
78	Joe Mauer	.50
79	Joe Nathan	.40
80	Alex Rodriguez	2.00
81	Derek Jeter	2.00
82	Johnny Damon	.75
83	Mariano Rivera	.50
84	Rich Harden	.25
85	Mike Piazza	.75
86	Nick Swisher	.40
87	Ichiro Suzuki	1.50
88	Felix Hernandez	.50
89	Kenji Johjima	.50
90	Richie Sexson	.40
91	Carl Crawford	.40
92	Scott Kazmir	.50
93	B.J. Upton	.40
94	Michael Young	.40
95	Mark Teixeira	.50
96	Eric Gagne	.25
97	Hank Blalock	.25
98	Vernon Wells	.40
99	Roy Halladay	.40
100	Frank Thomas	.50
101	Joaquin Arias (RC)	.50
102	Jeff Baker (RC)	.50
103	Brian Barden RC	.50
104	Michael Bourn RC	.50
105	Kevin Slowey (RC)	1.00
106	Chase Wright RC	.50
107	Kory Casto (RC)	.50
108	Matt Chico (RC)	.50
109	Matt DeSalvo (RC)	.50
110	Homer Bailey (RC)	1.00
111	Ryan Braun (RC)	3.00
112	Felix Pie (RC)	1.00
113	Jesus Flores (RC)	.50
114	Ryan Sweeney (RC)	.50
115	Ryan Braun RC	.50
116	Alex Gordon RC	1.00
117	Josh Hamilton (RC)	1.50
118	Sean Henn RC	.50
119	Kei Igawa RC	1.00
120	Akinori Iwamura RC	1.00
121	Andy LaRoche (RC)	1.00
122	Kevin Kouzmanoff (RC)	1.00
123	Matt Lindstrom (RC)	.50
124	Tim Lincecum RC	6.00
125	Daisuke Matsuzaka RC	3.00
126	Gustavo Molina RC	.50
127	Miguel Montero RC	.50
128	Brandon Morrow RC	1.00
129	Hideki Okajima RC	.50
130	Adam Lind RC	.75
131	Mike Rabelo RC	.50
132	Micah Owings (RC)	.50
133	Brandon Wood (RC)	.50
134	Alexi Casilla RC	1.00
135	Joe Smith RC	.50
136	Hunter Pence RC	2.00
137	Glen Perkins (RC)	.50
138	Chris Stewart RC	.50
139	Troy Tulowitzki (RC)	2.00
140	Billy Butler (RC)	1.00
141	Delmon Young (RC)	1.00
142	Phil Hughes (RC)	1.00
143	Joaquin Arias	1.00
144	Jeff Baker	1.00
145	Brian Barden	1.00
146	Michael Bourn	1.00
147	Kevin Slowey	1.00
148	Chase Wright	1.00
149	Kory Casto	1.00
150	Matt Chico	1.00

Base Set (continued)

No.	Name	Price
151	Shawn Riggans	1.00
152	Juan Salas	1.00
153	Ryan Braun	5.00
154	Felix Pie	1.00
155	Jesus Flores	1.00
156	Ryan Sweeney	1.00
157	Ryan Braun	1.00
158	Alex Gordon	2.00
159	Josh Hamilton	2.00
160	Sean Henn	1.00
161	Kei Igawa	1.00
162	Akinori Iwamura	1.00
163	Andy LaRoche	1.00
164	Kevin Kouzmanoff	1.00
165	Matt Lindstrom	1.00
166	Tim Lincecum	8.00
167	Daisuke Matsuzaka	4.00
168	Gustavo Molina	1.00
169	Miguel Montero	1.00
170	Brandon Morrow	2.00
171	Hideki Okajima	1.00
172	Adam Lind	1.00
173	Mike Rabelo	1.00
174	Micah Owings	1.00
175	Brandon Wood	1.00
176	Alexi Casilla	1.00
177	Joe Smith	1.00
178	Hunter Pence	2.50
179	Glen Perkins	1.00
180	Chris Stewart	1.00
181	Troy Tulowitzki	3.00
182	Billy Butler	2.00
183	Delmon Young	2.00
184	Phil Hughes	4.00
185	Joaquin Arias	1.00
186	Jeff Baker	1.00
187	Mark Reynolds	1.50
188	Joseph Bisenius	1.00
189	Michael Bourn	1.00
190	Zack Segovia	1.00
191	Kevin Slowey	2.00
192	Chase Wright	1.00
193	Rocky Cherry	1.00
194	Danny Putnam	1.00
195	Kory Casto	1.00
196	Matt Chico	1.00
197	John Danks	1.00
198	Homer Bailey	1.00
199	Ryan Braun	6.00
200	Felix Pie	1.00
201	Jesus Flores	1.00
202	Andy Gonzalez	1.00
203	Ryan Sweeney	1.00
204	Jarrod Saltalamacchia	1.00
205	Alex Gordon	2.00
206	Josh Hamilton	2.50
207	Sean Henn	1.00
208	Kei Igawa	1.00
209	Akinori Iwamura	1.00
210	Andy LaRoche	1.00
211	Rick Vanden Hurk	1.00
212	Kevin Kouzmanoff	1.00
213	Matt Lindstrom	1.00
214	Tim Lincecum	8.00
215	Daisuke Matsuzaka	4.00
216	Gustavo Molina	1.00
217	Miguel Montero	1.00
218	Brandon Morrow	1.00
219	Hideki Okajima	1.00
220	Adam Lind	1.00
221	Mike Rabelo	1.00
222	Brian Burres	1.00
223	Micah Owings	1.00
224	Brandon Wood	1.00
225	Alexi Casilla	1.00
226	Joe Smith	1.00
227	Hunter Pence	2.50
228	Glen Perkins	1.00
229	Chris Stewart	1.00
230	Ben Francisco	1.00
231	Troy Tulowitzki	2.00
232	Billy Butler	2.00
233	Delmon Young	2.00
234	Phil Hughes	4.00
235	Joaquin Arias	.50
236	Jeff Baker	.50
237	Mark Reynolds	1.00
238	Joseph Bisenius	.50
239	Michael Bourn	.50
240	Zack Segovia	.50
241	Travis Buck	.50
242	Chase Wright	1.00
243	Rocky Cherry	.50
244	Danny Putnam	.50
245	Kory Casto	.50
246	Matt Chico	.50
247	John Danks	.50
248	Juan Salas	.50
249	Ryan Braun	4.00
250	Felix Pie	.50
251	Jesus Flores	.50
252	Andy Gonzalez	.50
253	Ryan Sweeney	.50
254	Jarrod Saltalamacchia	1.00
255	Alex Gordon	.50
256	Josh Hamilton	1.50
257	Sean Henn	.50
258	Kei Igawa	.50
259	Akinori Iwamura	1.00
260	Andy LaRoche	.50
261	Rick Vanden Hurk	.50
262	Kevin Kouzmanoff	.50
263	Matt Lindstrom	.50
264	Tim Lincecum	6.00
265	Daisuke Matsuzaka	3.00
266	Gustavo Molina	.50
267	Miguel Montero	.50
268	Brandon Morrow	1.00
269	Hideki Okajima	1.00
270	Adam Lind	.50
271	Mike Rabelo	.50
272	Brian Burres	.50
273	Micah Owings	.50
274	Brandon Wood	.50
275	Alexi Casilla	1.00
276	Joe Smith	.50
277	Hunter Pence	2.00
278	Glen Perkins	.50
279	Chris Stewart	.50
280	Ben Francisco	.50
281	Troy Tulowitzki	2.00
282	Billy Butler	1.00
283	Delmon Young	1.00
284	Phil Hughes	1.00

Autographs

NM/M

Common Autograph: 8.00

No.	Name	Price
101	Joaquin Arias	8.00
102	Jeff Baker	8.00
103	Brian Barden	8.00
104	Michael Bourn	8.00
105	Kevin Slowey	10.00
106	Chase Wright	8.00
107	Kory Casto	8.00
108	Matt Chico	8.00
109	Matt DeSalvo	8.00
110	Homer Bailey	10.00
111	Ryan Braun	75.00
112	Felix Pie	15.00
113	Jesus Flores	10.00
114	Ryan Sweeney	8.00
115	Ryan Braun	10.00
116	Alex Gordon/SP	15.00
117	Josh Hamilton	50.00
118	Sean Henn	8.00
120	Andy LaRoche	10.00
121	Kevin Kouzmanoff	10.00
122	Matt Lindstrom	8.00
123	Tim Lincecum/SP	120.00
124	Daisuke Matsuzaka/SP	80.00
125	Gustavo Molina	8.00
126	Miguel Montero	8.00
127	Brandon Morrow	15.00
128	Adam Lind	10.00
129	Mike Rabelo	8.00
130	Micah Owings	12.00
131	Brandon Wood	15.00
132	Alexi Casilla	10.00
133	Joe Smith	10.00
134	Hunter Pence/SP	30.00
135	Glen Perkins	8.00
136	Chris Stewart	8.00
137	Troy Tulowitzki/SP	20.00
138	Billy Butler	20.00
139	Phil Hughes/SP	50.00
140	Joaquin Arias	8.00
141	Jeff Baker	8.00
142	Brian Barden	8.00
143	Michael Bourn	10.00
144	Jeff Baker	8.00
145	Brian Barden	8.00
146	Michael Bourn	10.00
147	Kevin Slowey	10.00
148	Chase Wright	10.00
149	Kory Casto	8.00
150	Matt Chico	8.00
151	Shawn Riggans	8.00
152	Juan Salas	8.00
153	Ryan Braun	75.00
154	Felix Pie	15.00
155	Jesus Flores	15.00
156	Ryan Sweeney	8.00
157	Ryan Braun	10.00
158	Alex Gordon/SP	15.00
159	Josh Hamilton	50.00
160	Sean Henn	8.00
163	Andy LaRoche	15.00
164	Kevin Kouzmanoff	15.00
165	Matt Lindstrom	12.00
166	Tim Lincecum/SP	120.00
167	Daisuke Matsuzaka/SP	80.00
168	Gustavo Molina	10.00
169	Miguel Montero	8.00
170	Brandon Morrow	15.00
172	Adam Lind	10.00
173	Mike Rabelo	8.00
174	Micah Owings	10.00
175	Brandon Wood	15.00
176	Alexi Casilla	10.00
177	Joe Smith	10.00
178	Hunter Pence	25.00
179	Glen Perkins	8.00
180	Chris Stewart	8.00
181	Troy Tulowitzki	25.00
182	Billy Butler	20.00
184	Phil Hughes/SP	50.00
185	Joaquin Arias	8.00
186	Jeff Baker	8.00
188	Joseph Bisenius	8.00
189	Michael Bourn	8.00
190	Zack Segovia	8.00
191	Kevin Slowey	15.00
192	Chase Wright	10.00
193	Rocky Cherry	10.00
194	Danny Putnam	8.00
195	Kory Casto	8.00
196	Matt Chico	8.00
197	John Danks	8.00
198	Homer Bailey	15.00
199	Ryan Braun	75.00
200	Felix Pie	15.00
201	Jesus Flores	15.00
202	Andy Gonzalez	8.00
203	Ryan Sweeney	8.00
204	Jarrod Saltalamacchia	10.00
205	Alex Gordon/SP	15.00
206	Josh Hamilton/SP	50.00
207	Sean Henn	8.00
210	Andy LaRoche	15.00
211	Rick Vanden Hurk	8.00
212	Kevin Kouzmanoff	15.00
213	Matt Lindstrom	12.00
214	Tim Lincecum/SP	120.00
215	Daisuke Matsuzaka/SP	80.00
216	Gustavo Molina	15.00
217	Miguel Montero	8.00
218	Brandon Morrow	15.00
220	Adam Lind	10.00
221	Mike Rabelo	10.00
222	Brian Burres	8.00
223	Micah Owings	10.00
224	Brandon Wood/SP	15.00
225	Alexi Casilla	8.00
226	Joe Smith	10.00
227	Hunter Pence/SP	25.00
228	Glen Perkins	8.00
229	Chris Stewart	8.00
230	Ben Francisco	8.00
231	Troy Tulowitzki/SP	25.00
232	Billy Butler/SP	20.00
234	Phil Hughes/SP	50.00
235	Joaquin Arias	8.00
236	Jeff Baker	8.00
238	Joseph Bisenius	8.00
239	Michael Bourn	10.00
240	Zack Segovia	10.00
242	Chase Wright	10.00
243	Rocky Cherry	10.00
244	Danny Putnam	8.00
245	Kory Casto	8.00
246	Matt Chico	8.00
247	John Danks	8.00
248	Juan Salas	8.00
249	Ryan Braun/SP	75.00
250	Felix Pie	15.00
251	Jesus Flores	15.00
252	Andy Gonzalez	8.00
253	Ryan Sweeney	8.00
254	Jarrod Saltalamacchia/SP	15.00
255	Alex Gordon/SP	15.00
256	Josh Hamilton	50.00
257	Sean Henn	8.00
260	Andy LaRoche	12.00
261	Rick Vanden Hurk	8.00
262	Kevin Kouzmanoff	15.00
263	Matt Lindstrom	8.00
264	Tim Lincecum/SP	120.00
265	Daisuke Matsuzaka/SP	80.00
266	Gustavo Molina	15.00
267	Miguel Montero	8.00
268	Brandon Morrow	8.00
270	Adam Lind	10.00
271	Mike Rabelo	8.00
272	Brian Burres	8.00
273	Micah Owings	15.00
274	Brandon Wood	15.00
275	Alexi Casilla	10.00
276	Joe Smith	10.00
277	Hunter Pence/SP	25.00
278	Glen Perkins	8.00
279	Chris Stewart	8.00
280	Ben Francisco	8.00
281	Troy Tulowitzki/SP	25.00
282	Billy Butler/SP	20.00
284	Phil Hughes/SP	50.00

2007 Upper Deck Artifacts

NM/M

	Price
Complete Set (100):	35.00
Common Player:	.25
Pack (4):	10.00
Box (10):	90.00

No.	Name	Price
1	Miguel Tejada	.50
2	David Ortiz	1.00
3	Manny Ramirez	1.00
4	Curt Schilling	.75
5	Jim Thome	.75
6	Paul Konerko	.50
7	Jermaine Dye	.50
8	Travis Hafner	.50
9	Victor Martinez	.50
10	Grady Sizemore	.50
11	Ivan Rodriguez	.75
12	Maggio Ordonez	.50
13	Justin Verlander	.75
14	Mark Teahen	.25
15	Vladimir Guerrero	1.00
16	Jered Weaver	.75
17	Justin Morneau	.75
18	Joe Mauer	.75
19	Torii Hunter	.50
20	Johan Santana	1.00
21	Derek Jeter	3.00
22	Alex Rodriguez	3.00
23	Johnny Damon	.75
24	Huston Street	.25
25	Nick Swisher	.50
26	Ichiro Suzuki	2.00
27	Richie Sexson	.50
28	Carl Crawford	.50
29	Scott Kazmir	.50
30	Michael Young	.50
31	Mark Teixeira	.75
32	Vernon Wells	.50
33	Roy Halladay	.50
34	Brandon Webb	.50
35	Stephen Drew	.50
36	Chipper Jones	1.00
37	Andruw Jones	.75
38	Derrek Lee	.75
39	Aramis Ramirez	.50
40	Ken Griffey Jr.	2.00
41	Adam Dunn	.50
42	Todd Helton	.75
43	Matt Holliday	.75
44	Miguel Cabrera	1.00
45	Hanley Ramirez	1.00
46	Dontrelle Willis	.50
47	Lance Berkman	.50
48	Roy Oswalt	.50
49	Craig Biggio	.50
50	Nomar Garciaparra	1.00
51	Derek Lowe	.25
52	Prince Fielder	1.00
53	Rickie Weeks	.25
54	Jose Reyes	2.00
55	David Wright	2.00
56	Carlos Beltran	.75
57	Ryan Howard	2.00
58	Chase Utley	1.00
59	Jimmy Rollins	.75
60	Jason Bay	.50
61	Freddy Sanchez	.25
62	Trevor Hoffman	.50
63	Adrian Gonzalez	.50
64	Omar Vizquel	.25
65	Matt Cain	.50
66	Albert Pujols	3.00
67	Jim Edmonds	.50
68	Chris Carpenter	.50
69	David Eckstein	.25
70	Ryan Zimmerman	.75
71	Alexi Casilla RC	.50
72	Andrew Miller RC	.50
73	Andy Cannizaro RC	1.00
74	Brian Stokes RC	.50
75	Carlos Maldonado (RC)	.50
76	Cesar Jimenez RC	.50
77	Daisuke Matsuzaka RC	3.00
78	Delmon Young (RC)	.50
79	Delwyn Young (RC)	.50
80	Fred Lewis (RC)	1.00
81	Glen Perkins (RC)	.50
82	Jeff Baker (RC)	.50
83	Jeff Fiorentino (RC)	.50
84	Jeff Salazar (RC)	.50
85	Jerry Owens (RC)	.50
86	Josh Fields (RC)	.50
87	Juan Perez RC	.50
88	Juan Salas (RC)	.50
89	Justin Hampson (RC)	.50
90	Kevin Kouzmanoff (RC)	.50
91	Michael Bourn (RC)	.50
92	Miguel Montero (RC)	.50
93	Mike Rabelo (RC)	.50
94	Oswaldo Navarro RC	.50
95	Philip Humber RC	.50
96	Ryan Braun RC	.50
97	Ryan Sweeney (RC)	.50
98	Sean Henn (RC)	.50
99	Jose Reyes RC	1.00
100	Troy Tulowitzki (RC)	1.00

Antiquity Artifacts

NM/M

Production 199 Sets
Patch: 1.5-3X
Production 50 Sets

Code	Name	Price
AB	Adrian Beltre	6.00
AJ	Andruw Jones	6.00
AL	Adam LaRoche	4.00
AP	Albert Pujols	20.00
AR	Aramis Ramirez	6.00
AT	Garrett Atkins	4.00
BA	Bobby Abreu	6.00
BC	Bartolo Colon	4.00
BE	Carlos Beltran	6.00
BG	Brian Giles	4.00
BO	Jeremy Bonderman	4.00
BR	Brian Roberts	6.00
BU	B.J. Upton	6.00
BW	Billy Wagner	4.00
BZ	Barry Zito	4.00
CA	Miguel Cabrera	8.00
CB	Craig Biggio	6.00
CC	Carl Crawford	6.00
CF	Chone Figgins	4.00
CH	Chris Carpenter	4.00
CJ	Chipper Jones	8.00
CL	Carlos Lee	6.00
CR	Cal Ripken Jr.	25.00
CS	Curt Schilling	6.00
CU	Chase Utley	10.00
DJ	Derek Jeter	20.00
DO	David Ortiz	10.00
DR	J.D. Drew	4.00
DU	Dan Uggla	4.00
DW	Dontrelle Willis	4.00
EC	Eric Chavez	4.00
ED	Jim Edmonds	6.00
FG	Freddy Garcia	4.00
FH	Felix Hernandez	6.00
FL	Francisco Liriano	6.00
FT	Frank Thomas	8.00
GA	Garret Anderson	4.00
GJ	Geoff Jenkins	4.00
GM	Greg Maddux	10.00
GR	Ken Griffey Jr.	20.00
GS	Grady Sizemore	8.00
HA	Rich Harden	4.00
HB	Hank Blalock	4.00
HO	Trevor Hoffman	6.00
HR	Hanley Ramirez	8.00
HS	Huston Street	4.00
HU	Torii Hunter	6.00
IR	Ivan Rodriguez	6.00
JA	Jason Bay	6.00
JC	Jorge Cantu	4.00
JD	Jermaine Dye	4.00
JE	Johnny Estrada	4.00
JF	Jeff Francoeur	6.00
JG	Jason Giambi	6.00
JJ	Josh Johnson	6.00
JK	Jeff Kent	6.00
JM	Joe Mauer	8.00
JP	Jake Peavy	6.00
JR	Jimmy Rollins	6.00
JS	Jason Schmidt	4.00
JT	Jim Thome	8.00
JV	Justin Verlander	6.00
JZ	Joel Zumaya	4.00
KG	Khalil Greene	4.00
LB	Lance Berkman	6.00
LG	Luis Gonzalez	4.00
MO	Justin Morneau	8.00
MR	Manny Ramirez	8.00
MT	Mark Teixeira	4.00
MY	Michael Young	6.00
NS	Nick Swisher	4.00
OR	Magglio Ordonez	4.00
PA	Jonathan Papelbon	6.00
PB	Pat Burrell	4.00
PE	Jhonny Peralta	4.00
PF	Prince Fielder	6.00
PK	Paul Konerko	6.00
PM	Pedro Martinez	8.00
PO	Jorge Posada	8.00
RC	Roger Clemens	10.00
RE	Jose Reyes	10.00
RH	Roy Halladay	8.00
RJ	Randy Johnson	8.00
RO	Roy Oswalt	6.00
RW	Rickie Weeks	4.00
RZ	Ryan Zimmerman	6.00
SA	Johan Santana	8.00
SK	Scott Kazmir	4.00
SM	John Smoltz	6.00
SR	Scott Rolen	6.00
TE	Miguel Tejada	6.00
TG	Tom Glavine	6.00
TH	Todd Helton	8.00
TI	Tim Hudson	6.00
VA	Jason Varitek	6.00
VG	Vladimir Guerrero	8.00
VM	Victor Martinez	6.00
VW	Vernon Wells	4.00

Bat Knobs

Production One Set

Autofacts

NM/M

Common Auto.: 10.00

Code	Name	Price
AD	Adam Dunn	20.00
AK	Austin Kearns	10.00
AL	Adam LaRoche	10.00
AM	Andrew Miller	12.00
AS	Angel Sanchez	10.00
BC	Bobby Crosby	10.00
BE	Josh Beckett	35.00
BO	Jeremy Bonderman/SP	12.00
BT	Jason Bartlett	10.00
BU	Ambiorix Burgos/SP	10.00
CJ	Cesar Jimenez	10.00
CL	Carlos Lee/SP	15.00
CR	Cal Ripken Jr.	125.00
CY	Chris Young	15.00
CZ	Carlos Zambrano	15.00
DJ	Derek Jeter	140.00
DO	David Ortiz/SP	50.00
DW	Dontrelle Willis	15.00
DY	Delmon Young/SP	15.00
EC	Eric Chavez	15.00
GA	Garrett Atkins	10.00
HA	Rich Harden	10.00
HG	Hector Gimenez	10.00
HK	Hong-Chih Kuo	15.00
HR	Hanley Ramirez	25.00
IK	Ian Kinsler	20.00
JA	Joaquin Arias	10.00
JB	Jason Bay	15.00
JC	Jesse Crain	10.00
JE	Johnny Estrada	15.00
JG	Jonny Gomes	15.00
JJ	Josh Johnson	10.00
JW	Jered Weaver	15.00
JZ	Joel Zumaya/SP	10.00
KE	Howie Kendrick	15.00
KG	Ken Griffey Jr.	75.00
KM	Kendry Morales	15.00
KN	Jon Knott	15.00
KW	Kerry Wood	15.00
MJ	Mike Jacobs	10.00
MM	Miguel Montero	10.00
PA	Jonathan Papelbon	15.00
PE	Jhonny Peralta	15.00
PH	Philip Humber	10.00
RA	Chris Ray	10.00
RC	Roger Clemens	80.00
RH	Rich Hill	10.00
RW	Rickie Weeks	10.00
SB	Scott Baker	15.00
SD	Stephen Drew	15.00
SK	Scott Kazmir	15.00
SR	Scott Rolen/SP	20.00
TI	Tadahito Iguchi	15.00
TT	Troy Tulowitzki	20.00
UP	B.J. Upton	15.00
VE	Justin Verlander	15.00
VG	Vladimir Guerrero/SP	40.00
VM	Victor Martinez	15.00
WI	Josh Willingham	10.00
YB	Yuniesky Betancourt	15.00
ZG	Zack Greinke	25.00
ZS	Zack Segovia	10.00

Awesome Artifacts

NM/M

Production 50 Sets

Code	Name	Price
AD	Adam Dunn	15.00
AG	Adrian Gonzalez	15.00
AP	Albert Pujols	30.00
AR	Aramis Ramirez	15.00
AS	Alfonso Soriano	15.00
BA	Bobby Abreu	10.00
BC	Bartolo Colon	8.00
BG	Brian Giles	8.00
BI	Craig Biggio	15.00
BR	Brian Roberts	10.00
BW	Billy Wagner	10.00
BZ	Barry Zito	10.00
CA	Carl Crawford	10.00
CB	Carlos Beltran	10.00
CC	Carl Crawford	10.00
CD	Carlos Delgado	10.00
CF	Chone Figgins	8.00
CJ	Chipper Jones	20.00
CL	Carlos Lee	15.00
CR	Cal Ripken Jr.	30.00
CS	Curt Schilling	15.00
CU	Chase Utley	30.00
DJ	Derek Jeter	30.00
DO	David Ortiz	15.00
DU	Dan Uggla	10.00
DW	Dontrelle Willis	8.00
EC	Eric Chavez	8.00
FG	Freddy Garcia	8.00
FH	Felix Hernandez	15.00
FL	Francisco Liriano	15.00
FT	Frank Thomas	20.00
GA	Garret Anderson	8.00
GM	Greg Maddux	20.00
GR	Khalil Greene	8.00
GS	Grady Sizemore	15.00
HA	Roy Halladay	15.00
HB	Hank Blalock	8.00
HE	Todd Helton	10.00
HR	Hanley Ramirez	20.00
HS	Huston Street	8.00
HU	Torii Hunter	10.00
IK	Ian Kinsler	15.00
IR	Ivan Rodriguez	10.00
JA	Jason Bay	10.00
JB	Jeremy Bonderman	8.00
JC	Jorge Cantu	10.00
JD	Jermaine Dye	10.00
JE	Jim Edmonds	8.00
JF	Jeff Francoeur	10.00
JG	Jason Giambi	10.00
JH	Johnny Damon	10.00
JJ	Josh Johnson	10.00
JK	Jeff Kent	10.00
JM	Joe Mauer	15.00
JO	Josh Barfield	8.00
JP	Jake Peavy	10.00
JR	Jimmy Rollins	12.00
JS	Jason Schmidt	8.00
JT	Jim Thome	10.00
JV	Justin Verlander	15.00
JW	Jered Weaver	15.00
JZ	Joel Zumaya	10.00
KG	Ken Griffey Jr.	30.00
KM	Kendry Morales	12.00
MC	Miguel Cabrera	15.00
MO	Justin Morneau	15.00
MR	Manny Ramirez	15.00
MT	Mark Teixeira	10.00
MY	Michael Young	10.00
OR	Magglio Ordonez	10.00
OS	Roy Oswalt	10.00
PA	Jonathan Papelbon	10.00
PB	Pat Burrell	8.00
PE	Jhonny Peralta	10.00
PF	Prince Fielder	15.00
PO	Jorge Posada	20.00
RC	Robinson Cano	15.00
RE	Jose Reyes	30.00
RF	Rafael Furcal	10.00
RH	Rich Harden	8.00

RJ	Randy Johnson	20.00
RO	Roger Clemens	25.00
RW	Rickie Weeks	10.00
RZ	Ryan Zimmerman	15.00
SK	Scott Kazmir	10.00
SM	John Smoltz	10.00
SR	Scott Rolen	10.00
TG	Tom Glavine	10.00
TH	Trevor Hoffman	10.00
TI	Tim Hudson	10.00
TR	Travis Hafner	10.00
VA	Jason Varitek	10.00
VG	Vladimir Guerrero	15.00
VM	Victor Martinez	10.00
VW	Vernon Wells	8.00

Divisional Artifacts

NM/M

Common Player:
Production 199 Sets
Gold: 1X
Production 130 Sets

AA	Aaron Rowand	6.00
AD	Adam Dunn	4.00
AJ	Andruw Jones	4.00
AL	Adam LaRoche	400
AR	Aramis Ramirez	10.00
BA	Bobby Abreu	4.00
BC	Bartolo Colon	4.00
BE	Carlos Beltran	4.00
BG	Brian Giles	4.00
BO	Jeremy Bonderman	4.00
BR	Brian Roberts	4.00
BW	Billy Wagner	4.00
BZ	Barry Zito	4.00
CA	Robinson Cano	10.00
CB	Craig Biggio	6.00
CC	Carl Crawford	6.00
CD	Carlos Delgado/178	6.00
CH	Chris Carpenter	8.00
CJ	Chipper Jones	8.00
CL	Carlos Lee	6.00
CR	Cal Ripken Jr.	25.00
CS	Curt Schilling	6.00
CU	Chase Utley	10.00
DJ	Derek Jeter	25.00
DO	David Ortiz	8.00
DU	Dan Uggla	8.00
DW	Dontrelle Willis	4.00
EC	Eric Chavez	4.00
FG	Freddy Garcia	4.00
FH	Felix Hernandez	6.00
FL	Francisco Liriano	8.00
FT	Frank Thomas	8.00
GA	Garret Anderson	4.00
GM	Greg Maddux	10.00
GR	Ken Griffey Jr.	15.00
GS	Grady Sizemore	8.00
HA	Rich Harden	4.00
HB	Hank Blalock	4.00
HO	Trevor Hoffman	4.00
HR	Hanley Ramirez	6.00
HU	Torii Hunter	6.00
IK	Ian Kinsler	4.00
IR	Ivan Rodriguez	4.00
JA	Jason Bay	4.00
JC	Jorge Cantu	4.00
JD	Jermaine Dye	4.00
JE	Jim Edmonds	4.00
JF	Jeff Francoeur	4.00
JG	Jason Giambi	4.00
JJ	Josh Johnson	4.00
JK	Jeff Kent	4.00
JM	Joe Mauer	10.00
JN	Joe Nathan	4.00
JO	Josh Barfield	4.00
JP	Jake Peavy	6.00
JR	Jimmy Rollins	8.00
JS	Jason Schmidt	4.00
JT	Jim Thome	6.00
JV	Justin Verlander	10.00
JW	Jered Weaver	8.00
JZ	Joel Zumaya	4.00
KG	Khalil Greene	4.00
KM	Kendry Morales	4.00
LB	Lance Berkman	6.00
MC	Miguel Cabrera	4.00
ME	Melky Cabrera	4.00
MO	Justin Morneau	8.00
MR	Manny Ramirez	8.00
MT	Mark Teixeira	8.00
MY	Michael Young	4.00
NS	Nick Swisher	4.00
OR	Magglio Ordonez	4.00
PA	Jonathan Papelbon	4.00
PB	Pat Burrell	4.00
PE	Jhonny Peralta	4.00
PF	Prince Fielder	6.00
PK	Paul Konerko	6.00
PO	Jorge Posada	6.00
RC	Roger Clemens	8.00
RE	Jose Reyes	8.00
RH	Roy Halladay	8.00
RJ	Randy Johnson	8.00
RO	Roy Oswalt	6.00
RW	Rickie Weeks	8.00
RZ	Ryan Zimmerman	8.00

SK	Scott Kazmir	4.00
SM	John Smoltz	8.00
SR	Scott Rolen	4.00
TG	Tom Glavine	8.00
TH	Todd Helton	8.00
TI	Tim Hudson	4.00
TR	Travis Hafner/117	4.00
VA	Jason Varitek	6.00
VG	Vladimir Guerrero	8.00
VM	Victor Martinez	8.00
VW	Vernon Wells	4.00

Apparel

NM/M

Production 199 unless noted.
Rare Apparel: No Pricing
Production One Set
Gold: 1X
Production 130 Sets

AB	Adrian Beltre	6.00
AD	Adam Dunn	8.00
AJ	Andruw Jones/25	10.00
AL	Adam LaRoche	4.00
AP	Albert Pujols	20.00
AR	Aramis Ramirez	10.00
AT	Garrett Atkins	4.00
BA	Bobby Abreu	4.00
BA	Bartolo Colon	4.00
BG	Brian Giles	4.00
BI	Craig Biggio	6.00
BO	Jeremy Bonderman	10.00
BR	Brian Roberts	4.00
BU	B.J. Upton	4.00
BW	Billy Wagner	4.00
BZ	Barry Zito	4.00
CB	Carlos Beltran	4.00
CC	Carl Crawford	6.00
CH	Cole Hamels	10.00
CJ	Chipper Jones	8.00
CL	Carlos Lee	6.00
CR	Cal Ripken Jr.	25.00
CS	Curt Schilling	8.00
CU	Chase Utley	10.00
DJ	Derek Jeter	25.00
DO	David Ortiz	8.00
DU	Dan Uggla	6.00
DW	Dontrelle Willis	4.00
DY	Jermaine Dye	4.00
EC	Eric Chavez	4.00
ES	Johnny Estrada	4.00
FG	Freddy Garcia	4.00
FH	Felix Hernandez	6.00
FL	Francisco Liriano	4.00
FT	Frank Thomas	8.00
GA	Garret Anderson	4.00
GJ	Geoff Jenkins	4.00
GM	Greg Maddux	10.00
GR	Khalil Greene	4.00
GS	Grady Sizemore	8.00
HA	Roy Halladay	8.00
HB	Hank Blalock	4.00
HE	Todd Helton	8.00
HO	Trevor Hoffman	4.00
HR	Hanley Ramirez	8.00
HU	Torii Hunter	8.00
IR	Ivan Rodriguez	8.00
JB	Jason Bay	4.00
JC	Jorge Cantu	4.00
JD	J.D. Drew	6.00
JE	Jim Edmonds	6.00
JF	Jeff Francoeur	4.00
JG	Jason Giambi	8.00
JJ	Josh Johnson	4.00
JK	Jeff Kent	4.00
JM	Joe Mauer	10.00
JN	Joe Nathan	4.00
JO	Johnny Damon	6.00
JP	Jake Peavy	6.00
JR	Jimmy Rollins	8.00
JS	Jason Schmidt	4.00
JT	Jim Thome	6.00
JV	Justin Verlander	10.00
JZ	Joel Zumaya	4.00
KG	Ken Griffey Jr.	15.00
LB	Lance Berkman	6.00
LG	Luis Gonzalez	4.00
MC	Miguel Cabrera/67	10.00
MO	Justin Morneau	8.00
MR	Manny Ramirez	8.00
MT	Mark Teixeira	8.00
MY	Michael Young	4.00
OR	Magglio Ordonez	4.00
PA	Jonathan Papelbon	4.00
PB	Pat Burrell	4.00
PE	Jhonny Peralta	4.00
PF	Prince Fielder	10.00
PM	Pedro Martinez	6.00
PO	Jorge Posada	6.00

RC	Roger Clemens	10.00
RE	Jose Reyes	10.00
RH	Rich Harden	4.00
RI	Mariano Rivera	10.00
RJ	Randy Johnson	8.00
RO	Roy Oswalt	6.00
RW	Rickie Weeks	6.00
RZ	Ryan Zimmerman	10.00
SA	Johan Santana	8.00
SK	Scott Kazmir/31	4.00
SM	John Smoltz	8.00
SR	Scott Rolen	4.00
TG	Tom Glavine	6.00
TH	Tim Hudson	4.00
TR	Travis Hafner	4.00
VA	Jason Varitek	4.00
VG	Vladimir Guerrero/99	8.00
VM	Victor Martinez	4.00
VW	Vernon Wells	4.00

Divisional Artifacts Auto.

NM/M

Production 25 unless noted.

BO	Jeremy Bonderman	20.00
BR	Brian Roberts	30.00
CB	Craig Biggio	40.00
CC	Carl Crawford/55	20.00
CL	Carlos Lee	25.00
CR	Cal Ripken Jr.	180.00
CS	Curt Schilling	40.00
DO	David Ortiz	50.00
DW	Dontrelle Willis/55	20.00
EC	Eric Chavez	15.00
FH	Felix Hernandez/55	50.00
FT	Frank Thomas	75.00
GA	Garret Anderson/55	15.00
HA	Rich Harden	15.00
HR	Hanley Ramirez/55	25.00
IK	Ian Kinsler	20.00
JA	Jason Bay	20.00
JD	Jermaine Dye	20.00
JJ	Josh Johnson/55	15.00
JM	Joe Mauer	40.00
JP	Jake Peavy	30.00
JT	Jim Thome	50.00
JZ	Joel Zumaya	15.00
KM	Khalil Greene	15.00
KM	Kendry Morales/55	25.00
MC	Miguel Cabrera	35.00
MO	Justin Morneau	40.00
MY	Michael Young	15.00
PA	Jonathan Papelbon	20.00
PE	Jhonny Peralta	20.00
PM	Pedro Martinez	80.00
RC	Roger Clemens	120.00
RH	Roy Halladay	50.00
RW	Rickie Weeks	15.00
SK	Scott Kazmir	20.00
TI	Tim Hudson	25.00
VG	Vladimir Guerrero	50.00
VM	Victor Martinez	25.00

Apparel Autograph

NM/M

Production 25 unless noted.

AL	Adam LaRoche	15.00
AT	Garrett Atkins/55	15.00
BI	Craig Biggio	40.00
BO	Jeremy Bonderman	15.00
BR	Brian Roberts	30.00
BU	B.J. Upton	25.00
CC	Carl Crawford/55	20.00
CH	Cole Hamels	40.00
CL	Carlos Lee	25.00
CR	Cal Ripken Jr.	180.00
CS	Curt Schilling	40.00
DO	David Ortiz	50.00
DW	Dontrelle Willis	15.00
EC	Eric Chavez	15.00
ES	Johnny Estrada	15.00
FH	Felix Hernandez/23	50.00
FT	Frank Thomas	50.00
GA	Garret Anderson/55	15.00
GR	Khalil Greene/55	15.00
HA	Roy Halladay	50.00
HR	Hanley Ramirez	30.00
JB	Jason Bay/55	20.00
JJ	Josh Johnson	15.00
JP	Jake Peavy	30.00
JT	Jim Thome	50.00
JZ	Joel Zumaya	15.00
MC	Miguel Cabrera	35.00
MO	Justin Morneau	40.00
PA	Jonathan Papelbon	30.00
PE	Jhonny Peralta	20.00
PM	Pedro Martinez	25.00
RC	Roger Clemens	120.00
RH	Rich Harden	20.00
OW	Rickie Weeks	15.00
SK	Scott Kazmir	15.00
VG	Vladimir Guerrero	50.00
VW	Victor Martinez	20.00

2007 UD Black

NM/M

Common Jersey Auto. (1-42): 15.00
Production 16-75
Common RC Auto. (43-72): 25.00
Production 99
Pack (1): 80.00
Box (2): 150.00

1	Brandon Webb/75	25.00
2	Tim Hudson/75	25.00
3	Cal Ripken Jr./75	150.00
4	Nicholas Markakis/35	25.00
5	David Ortiz/52	100.00
6	Jonathan Papelbon/75	25.00
7	Coco Crisp/43	25.00
8	Derrek Lee/62	30.00
10	Adam Dunn/75	40.00
11	Ken Griffey Jr./75	80.00
12	Travis Hafner/52	40.00
13	Victor Martinez/75	30.00
14	Garrett Atkins/75	15.00
15	Justin Verlander/75	40.00
16	Jeremy Bonderman/75	15.00
17	Curtis Granderson/75	40.00
18	Hanley Ramirez/75	40.00
19	Dan Uggla/74	15.00
20	Lance Berkman/75	25.00
21	Mark Teahen/75	15.00
22	John Lackey/75	20.00
23	Howie Kendrick/75	25.00
25	Prince Fielder/75	50.00
26	Torii Hunter/75	25.00
27	Justin Morneau/75	40.00
28	John Maine/75	20.00
30	Dan Haren/75	25.00
31	Eric Chavez/64	15.00
32	Cole Hamels/75	30.00
33	Jason Bay/75	25.00
34	Adrian Gonzalez/75	25.00
35	Chris Young/75	20.00
36	Matt Cain/75	30.00
37	Felix Hernandez/75	50.00
38	Chris Duncan/75	20.00
39	B.J. Upton/75	30.00
40	Ian Kinsler/75	40.00
41	Roy Halladay/75	40.00
42	Chad Cordero/72	15.00
43	Adam Lind (RC)	25.00
44	Akinori Iwamura RC	40.00
45	Alex Gordon RC	40.00
46	Andy LaRoche (RC)	20.00
47	Billy Butler (RC)	50.00
48	David Murphy (RC)	30.00
49	Brandon Wood (RC)	30.00
50	Carlos Gomez RC	20.00
51	Chase Headley (RC)	20.00
52	Curtis Thigpen (RC)	20.00
53	Joba Chamberlain RC	80.00
54	Delmon Young (RC)	40.00
55	Felix Pie (RC)	20.00
56	Homer Bailey (RC)	20.00
57	Hunter Pence (RC)	40.00
58	Josh Hamilton (RC)	100.00
59	Kei Igawa RC	40.00
60	Kevin Slowey (RC)	30.00
61	Kurt Suzuki (RC)	30.00
62	Mark Reynolds RC	50.00
63	Daisuke Matsuzaka RC	150.00
64	Justin Upton RC	85.00
65	Phil Hughes (RC)	85.00
66	Ryan Braun (RC)	125.00
67	Ryan Sweeney (RC)	25.00
68	Sean Gallagher (RC)	25.00
69	Tim Lincecum RC	200.00
70	Travis Buck (RC)	25.00
71	Troy Tulowitzki (RC)	40.00
72	Yovani Gallardo (RC)	50.00

Printing Plates
No Pricing
Production one set per color.

Natural Pearl
No Pricing
Production One Set

Gold
No Pricing
Production 10 Sets

Pure White Pack Autographs
Production One Set

August - Auto. Patch
NM/M
Production 25 unless noted.
Gold: No Pricing
Production Five Sets
Pearl: No Pricing
Production One Set

BS	Ben Sheets	30.00
BU	B.J. Upton	40.00
CC	Carl Crawford	40.00
CD	Chris Duncan	20.00
CG	Curtis Granderson	40.00
CH	Cole Hamels	40.00
CO	Chad Cordero	40.00
DL	Derrek Lee	40.00
DW	Dontrelle Willis	20.00
FH	Felix Hernandez	80.00
FT	Frank Thomas	125.00
GA	Garrett Atkins	20.00
GR	Khalil Greene	20.00
HR	Hanley Ramirez	75.00
JM	Justin Morneau	50.00
MH	Matt Holliday	60.00
PK	Paul Konerko	40.00
RH	Roy Halladay	75.00
TH	Travis Hafner	30.00
VM	Victor Martinez	30.00

Exclusive - Eight Autos
Production Three Sets
Gold: No Pricing
Production Two Sets

Game Day - Box Score Autos
NM/M
Production 50 Sets
Gold: No Pricing
Production 10 Sets

AE	Andre Ethier	25.00
AG	Adrian Gonzalez	25.00
AH	Aaron Harang	20.00
AI	Akinori Iwamura	35.00
AL	Adam LaRoche	15.00
AM	Andrew Miller	30.00
AR	Aaron Rowand	20.00
BA	Bronson Arroyo	15.00
BB	Billy Butler	30.00
BP	Brandon Phillips	20.00
BS	Ben Sheets	20.00
CC	Coco Crisp	20.00
CG	Curtis Granderson	40.00
CH	Cole Hamels	30.00
DH	Danny Haren	20.00
DW	Dontrelle Willis	20.00
FC	Fausto Carmona	25.00
FL	Fred Lewis	15.00
GO	Alex Gordon	40.00
JB	Joe Blanton	15.00
JM	John Maine	20.00
JN	Joe Nathan	15.00
JV	Justin Verlander	35.00
KG	Ken Griffey Jr.	80.00
KI	Kei Igawa	30.00
KJ	Kelly Johnson	15.00
LI	Francisco Liriano	25.00
MC	Matt Cain	20.00
MM	Melvin Mora	15.00
PH	Phil Hughes	60.00
RB	Ryan Braun	50.00
RZ	Ryan Zimmerman	25.00
TB	Travis Buck	15.00
TH	Tim Hudson	30.00

Game Day - Lineup Card Autos
NM/M
Production 50 Sets
Gold: No Pricing
Production 10 Sets

AE	Andre Ethier	25.00
AG	Alberto Gonzalez	25.00
AH	Aaron Harang	20.00
AI	Akinori Iwamura	35.00
AL	Adam LaRoche	15.00
AM	Andre Miller	30.00
AR	Aaron Rowand	20.00
BA	Bronson Arroyo	15.00
BB	Billy Butler	30.00
BP	Brandon Phillips	20.00
BS	Ben Sheets	20.00
CC	Coco Crisp	20.00
CG	Curtis Granderson	40.00
CH	Cole Hamels	30.00
DH	Danny Haren	20.00
20	Dontrelle Willis	20.00
FC	Fausto Carmona	25.00
FL	Fred Lewis	15.00
GO	Alex Gordon	40.00
JB	Joe Blanton	15.00
JM	John Maine	20.00
JN	Joe Nathan	15.00
JV	Justin Verlander	35.00
KG	Ken Griffey Jr.	80.00
KI	Kei Igawa	30.00
KJ	Kelly Johnson	15.00
LI	Francisco Liriano	25.00
MC	Matt Cain	20.00
MM	Melvin Mora	15.00
PH	Phil Hughes	60.00
RB	Ryan Braun	50.00
RZ	Ryan Zimmerman	25.00
TB	Travis Buck	15.00
TH	Tim Hudson	30.00

Game Day - Ticket Autos.
NM/M
Production 50 unless noted.
Gold: No Pricing
Production 10 Sets

AE	Andre Ethier	30.00
AG	Alberto Gonzalez	20.00
AH	Aaron Harang	20.00
AI	Akinori Iwamura	25.00
AL	Adam LaRoche	15.00
AM	Andre Miller	20.00
AR	Aaron Rowand	20.00
BA	Bronson Arroyo	15.00
BB	Billy Butler	30.00
BP	Brandon Phillips	20.00
BS	Ben Sheets	20.00
CC	Coco Crisp	20.00
CG	Curtis Granderson	40.00
CH	Cole Hamels	40.00
DH	Danny Haren	20.00
DW	Dontrelle Willis	20.00
FC	Fausto Carmona	15.00
FL	Fred Lewis	15.00
GO	Alex Gordon	40.00
JB	Joe Blanton	15.00
JN	Joe Nathan	15.00
JV	Justin Verlander	35.00
KG	Ken Griffey Jr./15	80.00
KI	Kei Igawa	15.00
KJ	Kelly Johnson	15.00
LI	Francisco Liriano	25.00
MC	Matt Cain	25.00
MM	Melvin Mora	15.00
PH	Phil Hughes	60.00
RB	Ryan Braun	60.00
TB	Travis Buck	15.00
TH	Tim Hudson	15.00

Illustrious - Dual Autos.
NM/M
Production 25 unless noted.
Gold: No Pricing

AE	Andre Ethier	25.00
AG	Adrian Gonzalez	25.00

Production 15 Sets

BB	Joe Blanton, Dallas Braden	15.00
BH	Chase Headley, Ryan Braun	50.00
CK	Austin Kearns, Chad Cordero	15.00
CL	Matt Cain, Tim Lincecum	85.00
GB	Alex Gordon, Billy Butler	25.00
GL	Adam LaRoche, Tom Gorzelanny	15.00
HB	Matt Holliday, Jeff Baker	35.00
HC	Aaron Harang, Jon Coutlangus	15.00
HG	Rich Hill, Sean Gallagher	15.00
HP	Josh Hamilton, Brandon Phillips	20.00
KW	Howie Kendrick, Brandon Wood	15.00
LL	Adam LaRoche, Andy LaRoche	15.00
MF	Victor Martinez, Ben Francisco	15.00
MM	Melvin Mora, Nicholas Markakis	30.00
PS	Kevin Slowey, Cal Ripken Jr.	
SM	John Maine, Ben Sheets	25.00
YI	Delmon Young, Akinori Iwamura	30.00

Illustrious - Dual Materials Auto.
NM/M
Production 50 unless noted.
Patch: No Pricing
Production 15 Sets

CI	Akinori Iwamura, Eric Chavez	20.00
CK	Carl Crawford, Scott Kazmir	30.00
CP	Coco Crisp, Jonathan Papelbon	30.00
GB	Alex Gordon, Ryan Braun	75.00
GC	Coco Crisp, Curtis Granderson	30.00
GY	Adrian Gonzalez, Chris Young	30.00
HH	Danny Haren, Rich Harden	20.00
HM	John Maine, Aaron Harang	20.00
HW	Dontrelle Willis, Jeremy Hermida	20.00
LC	Matt Cain, Tim Lincecum	85.00
LK	John Lackey, Howie Kendrick	25.00
LP	Carlos Lee, Hunter Pence	25.00
MM	Victor Martinez, Russell Martin	25.00
NH	Torii Hunter, Joe Nathan	25.00
NM	Melvin Mora, Nicholas Markakis	30.00
RG	Brian Giles, Aaron Rowand	20.00
SB	Huston Street, Joe Blanton	20.00
UW	Josh Willingham, Dan Uggla	20.00
UY	B.J. Upton, Delmon Young	20.00
ZB	Jeremy Bonderman, Joel Zumaya	20.00

Lustrous - Autos.
NM/M
Production 50 unless noted.
Gold: No Pricing
Production 10 Sets

AG	Alex Gordon	15.00
BB	Billy Butler	25.00
BU	B.J. Upton	20.00
CC	Carl Crawford	20.00
CH	Cole Hamels	30.00
DL	Derrek Lee	25.00
DU	Dan Uggla	20.00
DW	Dontrelle Willis	15.00
GA	Garrett Atkins	10.00
GR	Khalil Greene	10.00
HA	Josh Hamilton	35.00
HP	Hunter Pence	25.00
HR	Hanley Ramirez	30.00
HS	Huston Street	15.00
IK	Ian Kinsler	20.00
JB	Jason Bay	20.00
JH	Jeremy Hermida	15.00
JL	Jon Lester	40.00
JN	Joe Nathan	20.00
JV	Justin Verlander	40.00
KE	Howie Kendrick	15.00
KG	Ken Griffey Jr.	80.00
KI	Kei Igawa	20.00
MO	Justin Morneau	25.00
PA	Jonathan Papelbon	25.00
PF	Prince Fielder	50.00
PH	Phil Hughes	60.00
PK	Paul Konerko	20.00
RO	Roy Oswalt	25.00

RT	Ryan Theriot	25.00
RZ	Ryan Zimmerman	25.00
TH	Torii Hunter	20.00
JW	Vernon Wells	20.00

Lustrous - Materials Auto.
NM/M
Production 32-50
Gold: No Pricing
Production 10 Sets

AD	Adam Dunn/35	25.00
AE	Andre Ethier/50	30.00
BO	Jeremy Bonderman/46	15.00
BU	B.J. Upton/48	20.00
CC	Carl Crawford/43	20.00
CL	Carlos Lee/46	20.00
CR	Cal Ripken Jr./50	140.00
DH	Danny Haren/50	20.00
DJ	Derek Jeter/50	150.00
DL	Derek Lee/46	25.00
DU	Dan Uggla/46	20.00
DW	Dontrelle Willis/45	15.00
FH	Felix Hernandez/32	40.00
GR	Khalil Greene/37	10.00
HR	Hanley Ramirez/33	30.00
HS	Huston Street/32	10.00
IK	Ian Kinsler/50	20.00
JB	Jason Bay/48	25.00
JH	Jeremy Hermida/49	15.00
JM	Joe Mauer/50	40.00
JN	Joe Nathan/34	10.00
JV	Justin Verlander/37	40.00
KE	Howie Kendrick/41	10.00
KG	Ken Griffey Jr./50	80.00
KM	Kendry Morales/50	25.00
MC	Matt Cain/50	25.00
MM	Melvin Mora/46	15.00
NM	Nick Markakis/50	25.00
PA	Jonathan Papelbon/48	25.00
PF	Prince Fielder/49	50.00
RZ	Ryan Zimmerman/44	30.00
SD	Stephen Drew/45	25.00
TH	Torii Hunter/50	20.00
VW	Vernon Wells/50	20.00

Bat Barrels - Auto
NM/M
Production 50 Sets
Gold: No Pricing
Production 10 Sets

AD	Adam Dunn	40.00
AE	Andre Ethier	25.00
AI	Akinori Iwamura	50.00
AL	Andy LaRoche	15.00
BO	Jeremy Bonderman	15.00
BU	B.J. Upton	20.00
CC	Carl Crawford	20.00
CL	Carlos Lee	20.00
DY	Delmon Young	20.00
GA	Garrett Atkins	15.00
HK	Howie Kendrick	20.00
HR	Hanley Ramirez	40.00
HU	Torii Hunter	25.00
IK	Ian Kinsler	20.00
JB	Jason Bay	20.00
JH	Josh Hamilton	40.00
JM	Joe Mauer	40.00
KG	Ken Griffey Jr.	75.00
KJ	Kelly Johnson	15.00
MO	Justin Morneau	35.00
MT	Mark Teixeira	30.00
RB	Ryan Braun	75.00
TH	Travis Hafner	20.00
TT	Troy Tulowitzki	40.00

Pride of a Nation
NM/M
Production 75 Sets
Gold: No Pricing
Production 10 Sets

AH	Aaron Harang	15.00
AR	Aaron Rowand	15.00
BO	Jeremy Bonderman	15.00
BP	Brandon Phillips	20.00
CA	Carl Crawford	25.00
CC	Coco Crisp	25.00
CG	Curtis Granderson	40.00
CL	Carlos Lee	25.00
DH	Danny Haren	20.00
DL	Derek Lee	30.00
DU	Dan Uggla	25.00
DW	Dontrelle Willis	15.00
EC	Eric Chavez	15.00
FH	Felix Hernandez	75.00
FT	Frank Thomas	60.00
HR	Hanley Ramirez	50.00
JB	Jason Bay	25.00
JL	John Lackey	20.00
JM	John Maine	15.00
LB	Lance Berkman	40.00
MM	Melvin Mora	15.00
MO	Justin Morneau	40.00
PF	Prince Fielder	50.00
RO	Roy Oswalt	40.00
SK	Scott Kazmir	20.00
VM	Victor Martinez	20.00

Prodigious - Materials Auto.
NM/M
Production 50 Sets unless noted.
Gold: No Pricing
Production 10 Sets

AD	Adam Dunn	40.00
AE	Andre Ethier	30.00
AR	Aaron Rowand	15.00
BO	Jeremy Bonderman	15.00
BP	Brandon Phillips	25.00
BU	B.J. Upton	20.00
CC	Coco Crisp	20.00
CD	Chris Duncan	20.00
CH	Cole Hamels	30.00
CL	Cliff Lee	25.00
CR	Carl Crawford	20.00
CY	Chris Young	15.00
DH	Danny Haren	20.00
DU	Dan Uggla	20.00
DW	Dontrelle Willis	15.00
FH	Felix Hernandez	50.00
GA	Garrett Atkins	15.00
HA	Josh Hamilton	40.00
HK	Hong-Chih Kuo	25.00
HR	Hanley Ramirez	50.00
HS	Huston Street	25.00
IK	Ian Kinsler	20.00
JB	Joe Blanton	15.00
JH	Jeremy Hermida	15.00
JL	Jon Lester	40.00
JN	Joe Nathan	15.00
JS	Johan Santana	50.00
JV	Justin Verlander	35.00
JZ	Joel Zumaya	15.00
KE	Howie Kendrick	15.00
KW	Kerry Wood	20.00
MO	Justin Morneau	35.00
MT	Mark Teixeira	35.00
PA	Jonathan Papelbon	25.00
RI	Cal Ripken Jr.	125.00
RW	Rickie Weeks	20.00
SK	Scott Kazmir	15.00
SR	Scott Rolen	20.00
TG	Tom Glavine	50.00
VW	Vernon Wells	20.00

Prodigious Autos.
NM/M
Production 75 unless noted.
Gold: 1-1.5X
Production 25 Sets

AE	Andre Ethier	30.00
AG	Adrian Gonzalez	30.00
AH	Aaron Harang	20.00
AI	Akinori Iwamura	20.00
AR	Aaron Rowand/50	15.00
BB	Billy Butler	20.00
BP	Brandon Phillips/50	25.00
BS	Ben Sheets/50	20.00
BU	B.J. Upton	20.00
CA	Carl Crawford	20.00
CC	Coco Crisp/50	20.00
CG	Curtis Granderson/50	40.00
CH	Cole Hamels/50	30.00
CO	Chad Cordero/50	15.00
CR	Cal Ripken Jr.	150.00
CY	Chris Young/50	20.00
DH	Danny Haren	20.00
DU	Dan Uggla	20.00
DY	Delmon Young	20.00
FP	Felix Pie	20.00
GA	Garrett Atkins	20.00
GO	Alex Gordon	15.00
GP	Glen Perkins	15.00
HB	Homer Bailey	20.00
HK	Howie Kendrick/50	20.00
HP	Hunter Pence	20.00
HS	Huston Street/50	20.00
JB	Jeremy Bonderman	15.00
JE	Johnny Estrada	15.00
JH	Josh Hamilton/50	40.00
JL	John Lackey/50	15.00
JM	John Maine/50	15.00
JP	Jonathan Papelbon	25.00
JS	Joakim Soria	15.00
JV	Justin Verlander/50	35.00
JW	Josh Willingham/50	15.00
KI	Kei Igawa	20.00
KJ	Kelly Johnson/50	15.00
LE	Jon Lester	40.00
MC	Matt Cain	30.00
MH	Matt Holliday	35.00
MM	Melvin Mora/50	15.00
MO	Justin Morneau	35.00
NM	Nicholas Markakis	25.00
NS	Nick Swisher	25.00
PK	Paul Konerko/50	25.00
RB	Ryan Braun	50.00
RH	Rich Harden/50	15.00
RZ	Ryan Zimmerman	30.00
SK	Scott Kazmir	15.00
TH	Tim Hudson	25.00
TL	Tim Lincecum	75.00
VM	Victor Martinez/50	20.00
YG	Yovani Gallardo/50	30.00

Prominent Numbers Autos.
NM/M
Production 1-58
Gold: No Pricing
Production 10 Sets

AH	Aaron Harang/39	20.00
BL	Joe Blanton/55	15.00
CG	Curtis Granderson/28	40.00
CH	Cole Hamels/35	30.00
CY	Chris Young/32	20.00
DY	Delmon Young/26	20.00
FH	Felix Hernandez/34	40.00
GA	Garrett Atkins/27	15.00
HK	Howie Kendrick/47	20.00
JB	Jason Bay/38	20.00
JE	Johnny Estrada/33	15.00
JN	Joe Nathan/36	15.00
JP	Jonathan Papelbon/58	25.00
JV	Justin Verlander/35	40.00
JZ	Joel Zumaya/54	15.00
MA	John Maine/33	15.00
MB	Michael Bourn/45	20.00
RH	Rich Harden/40	20.00

Triptych - Triple Autos.
No Pricing
Production 15 Sets
Gold: No Pricing
Production Five Sets

Triptych - Triple Materials Auto.
NM/M
Production 25 Sets

DU	Dan Uggla	30.00
PF	Prince Fielder	40.00
TH	Torii Hunter	25.00

Upper Echelon - Quad Autos.
No Pricing
Production Five Sets
Gold: No Pricing
Production Three Sets

Upper Echelon - Quad Materials Auto.
Production 2-5
Patch: No Pricing
Production One Set

2007 Upper Deck Elements

NM/M

Complete Set (252):		.50
Common Player (1-126):		.25
Common RC (127-252):		5.00
Production 550		
Pack (3):		7.00
Box (15):		80.00
1	Stephen Drew	.50
2	Andruw Jones	1.00
3	Chipper Jones	1.00
4	Miguel Tejada	.75
5	David Ortiz	1.00
6	Manny Ramirez	.75
7	Derek Lee	.75
8	Alfonso Soriano	1.00
9	Jermaine Dye	.50
10	Jim Thome	.75
11	Ken Griffey Jr.	2.00
12	Adam Dunn	.75
13	Travis Hafner	.50
14	Grady Sizemore	1.00
15	Todd Helton	.75
16	Gary Sheffield	.75
17	Miguel Cabrera	1.00
18	Lance Berkman	.75
19	Mark Teahen	.25
20	Vladimir Guerrero	1.00
21	Jered Weaver	.50
22	Rafael Furcal	.50
23	Prince Fielder	1.00
24	Justin Morneau	.75
25	Johan Santana	1.00
26	David Wright	2.00
27	Jose Reyes	2.00
28	Derek Jeter	3.00
29	Alex Rodriguez	3.00
30	Nick Swisher	.50
31	Ryan Howard	2.00
32	Jason Bay	.50
33	Adrian Gonzalez	.50
34	Ray Durham	.25
35	Ichiro Suzuki	2.00
36	Albert Pujols	3.00
37	Scott Rolen	.50
38	Carl Crawford	.50
39	Mark Teixeira	.75
40	Michael Young	.50
41	Vernon Wells	.50
42	Ryan Zimmerman	.50
43	Stephen Drew	.50
44	Andruw Jones	1.00
45	Chipper Jones	1.00
46	Miguel Tejada	.75
47	David Ortiz	1.00
48	Manny Ramirez	1.00
49	Derek Lee	.50
50	Alfonso Soriano	1.00
51	Jermaine Dye	.50
52	Jim Thome	.75
53	Ken Griffey Jr.	2.00
54	Adam Dunn	.75
55	Travis Hafner	.50
56	Grady Sizemore	1.00
57	Todd Helton	.75
58	Gary Sheffield	.75
59	Miguel Cabrera	1.00
60	Lance Berkman	.50
61	Mark Teahen	.25
62	Vladimir Guerrero	1.00
63	Jered Weaver	.50
64	Rafael Furcal	.50
65	Prince Fielder	1.00
66	Justin Morneau	.75
67	Johan Santana	1.00
68	David Wright	2.00
69	Jose Reyes	2.00
70	Derek Jeter	3.00
71	Alex Rodriguez	3.00
72	Nick Swisher	.50
73	Ryan Howard	2.00
74	Jason Bay	.50
75	Adrian Gonzalez	.50
76	Ray Durham	.25
77	Ichiro Suzuki	2.00
78	Albert Pujols	3.00
79	Scott Rolen	.75
80	Carl Crawford	.50
81	Mark Teixeira	.50
82	Michael Young	.50
83	Vernon Wells	.50
84	Ryan Zimmerman	.50
85	Stephen Drew	.50
86	Andruw Jones	1.00
87	Chipper Jones	1.00
88	Miguel Tejada	1.00
89	David Ortiz	1.00
90	Manny Ramirez	1.00
91	Derek Lee	.75
92	Alfonso Soriano	1.00
93	Jermaine Dye	.50
94	Jim Thome	.75
95	Ken Griffey Jr.	2.00
96	Adam Dunn	.75
97	Travis Hafner	.50
98	Grady Sizemore	1.00
99	Todd Helton	.75
100	Gary Sheffield	.75
101	Miguel Cabrera	1.00
102	Lance Berkman	.75
103	Mark Teahen	.25
104	Vladimir Guerrero	1.00
105	Jered Weaver	.50
106	Rafael Furcal	.50
107	Prince Fielder	1.00
108	Justin Morneau	.75
109	Johan Santana	1.00
110	David Wright	2.00
111	Jose Reyes	2.00
112	Derek Jeter	3.00
113	Alex Rodriguez	3.00
114	Nick Swisher	.50
115	Ryan Howard	2.00
116	Jason Bay	.50
117	Adrian Gonzalez	.50
118	Ray Durham	.25
119	Ichiro Suzuki	2.00
120	Albert Pujols	3.00
121	Scott Rolen	.75
122	Carl Crawford	.50
123	Mark Teixeira	.50
124	Michael Young	.50
125	Vernon Wells	.50
126	Ryan Zimmerman	.50
127	Miguel Montero (RC)	5.00
128	Doug Slaten RC	5.00
129	Hunter Pence (RC)	8.00
130	Brian Burres (RC)	5.00
131	Daisuke Matsuzaka RC	10.00
132	Hideki Okajima RC	5.00
133	Devern Hansack RC	5.00
134	Felix Pie (RC)	5.00
135	Ryan Sweeney (RC)	5.00
136	Chris Stewart RC	5.00
137	Jarrod Saltalamacchia (RC)	5.00
138	John Danks (RC)	5.00
139	Travis Buck (RC)	5.00
140	Troy Tulowitzki (RC)	5.00
141	Chase Wright RC	5.00
142	Matt DeSalvo (RC)	5.00
143	Micah Owings (RC)	5.00
144	Jeff Baker (RC)	5.00
145	Andy LaRoche (RC)	5.00
146	Billy Butler (RC)	8.00
147	Jose Garcia RC	5.00
148	Angel Sanchez RC	5.00
149	Alex Gordon RC	6.00
150	Glen Perkins RC	5.00
151	Alexi Casilla RC	5.00
152	Joe Smith RC	5.00
153	Kei Igawa RC	5.00
154	Sean Henn RC	5.00
155	Phil Hughes (RC)	10.00
156	Michael Bourn (RC)	5.00
157	Josh Hamilton (RC)	10.00
158	Kevin Kouzmanoff (RC)	5.00
159	Tim Lincecum RC	30.00
160	Brandon Morrow RC	8.00
161	Brandon Wood (RC)	5.00
162	Akinori Iwamura RC	5.00
163	Delmon Young (RC)	5.00
164	Juan Salas (RC)	5.00
165	Elijah Dukes RC	5.00
166	Joaquin Arias (RC)	5.00
167	Adam Lind (RC)	8.00
168	Matt Chico (RC)	5.00
169	Miguel Montero (RC)	5.00
170	Doug Slaten RC	5.00
171	Hunter Pence (RC)	8.00
172	Brian Burres (RC)	5.00
173	Daisuke Matsuzaka RC	10.00
174	Hideki Okajima RC	5.00
175	Devern Hansack RC	5.00
176	Felix Pie (RC)	5.00
177	Ryan Sweeney (RC)	5.00
178	Chris Stewart RC	5.00
179	Jarrod Saltalamacchia (RC)	5.00
180	John Danks (RC)	5.00
181	Travis Buck (RC)	5.00
182	Troy Tulowitzki (RC)	5.00
183	Chase Wright RC	5.00
184	Matt DeSalvo (RC)	5.00
185	Micah Owings (RC)	5.00
186	Jeff Baker (RC)	5.00
187	Andy LaRoche (RC)	5.00
188	Billy Butler (RC)	8.00
189	Jose Garcia RC	5.00
190	Angel Sanchez RC	5.00
191	Alex Gordon RC	6.00
192	Glen Perkins (RC)	5.00
193	Alexi Casilla RC	5.00
194	Joe Smith RC	5.00
195	Kei Igawa RC	5.00
196	Sean Henn (RC)	5.00
197	Phil Hughes (RC)	10.00
198	Michael Bourn (RC)	5.00
199	Josh Hamilton (RC)	10.00
200	Kevin Kouzmanoff (RC)	5.00
201	Tim Lincecum RC	30.00
202	Brandon Morrow RC	8.00
203	Brandon Wood RC	5.00
204	Akinori Iwamura RC	5.00
205	Delmon Young (RC)	5.00
206	Juan Salas (RC)	5.00
207	Elijah Dukes RC	5.00
208	Joaquin Arias (RC)	5.00
209	Adam Lind (RC)	8.00
210	Matt Chico (RC)	5.00
211	Miguel Montero (RC)	5.00
212	Doug Slaten RC	5.00
213	Hunter Pence (RC)	8.00
214	Brian Burres (RC)	5.00
215	Daisuke Matsuzaka RC	10.00
216	Hideki Okajima (RC)	5.00
217	Devern Hansack RC	5.00
218	Felix Pie (RC)	5.00
219	Ryan Sweeney (RC)	5.00
220	Chris Stewart RC	5.00
221	Jarrod Saltalamacchia (RC)	5.00
222	John Danks (RC)	5.00
223	Travis Buck (RC)	5.00
224	Troy Tulowitzki (RC)	8.00
225	Chase Wright RC	5.00
226	Matt DeSalvo (RC)	5.00
227	Micah Owings (RC)	5.00
228	Jeff Baker (RC)	5.00
229	Andy LaRoche (RC)	5.00
230	Billy Butler (RC)	8.00
231	Jose Garcia RC	5.00
232	Angel Sanchez RC	5.00
233	Alex Gordon RC	6.00
234	Glen Perkins (RC)	5.00
235	Alexi Casilla RC	5.00
236	Joe Smith RC	5.00
237	Kei Igawa RC	5.00
238	Sean Henn (RC)	5.00
239	Phil Hughes (RC)	10.00
240	Michael Bourn (RC)	5.00
241	Josh Hamilton (RC)	10.00
242	Kevin Kouzmanoff (RC)	5.00
243	Tim Lincecum RC	30.00
244	Brandon Morrow (RC)	8.00
245	Brandon Wood (RC)	5.00
246	Akinori Iwamura RC	5.00
247	Delmon Young (RC)	5.00
248	Juan Salas (RC)	5.00
249	Elijah Dukes (RC)	5.00
250	Joaquin Arias (RC)	5.00
251	Adam Lind (RC)	8.00
252	Matt Chico (RC)	5.00

Printing Plates
Production one set per color.

Clear-Cut Elements
NM/M
Production 350 unless noted.
Gold: 1X
Production 49-199 Sets
Silver: 1.5X
Production 13-99 Sets

AH	Aaron Harang	15.00
AK	Austin Kearns/234	15.00
AS	Alfonso Soriano	40.00
BB	Brian Bannister	15.00
BR	Brian Roberts	20.00
CA	Matt Cain	15.00
CC	Chris Carpenter	25.00
CP	Corey Patterson	15.00
CR	Cal Ripken Jr.	100.00
CR	Carl Crawford	20.00
DJ	Derek Jeter	150.00
DW	Dontrelle Willis	15.00
FL	Francisco Liriano	20.00
GR	Ken Griffey Jr.	75.00
HR	Hanley Ramirez	30.00
JB	Jason Bay	20.00
JG	Jonny Gomes	10.00
JH	Jeremy Hermida	10.00
JP	Jake Peavy	15.00
JT	Jim Thome	25.00
JV	Justin Verlander	40.00
JZ	Joel Zumaya	10.00
KG	Khalil Greene	10.00
KW	Kerry Wood	15.00
MC	Miguel Cabrera	20.00
MG	Marcus Giles	10.00
MH	Matt Holliday	25.00
ML	Mark Loretta	10.00
MM	Melvin Mora	10.00
MT	Miguel Tejada	15.00
RH	Rich Harden	15.00
RJ	Reed Johnson	10.00
RZ	Ryan Zimmerman	20.00
SA	Johan Santana	30.00
SK	Scott Kazmir	15.00
SR	Scott Rolen	20.00
TH	Travis Hafner	15.00
VM	Victor Martinez	15.00

Dual Elements
NM/M
Production 50 unless noted.

BB	Craig Biggio	10.00
BB	Lance Berkman	10.00
BM	Josh Beckett	15.00
BM	Daisuke Matsuzaka	40.00
BS	Freddy Sanchez	10.00
BS	Jason Bay	10.00
CA	Carlos Beltran	10.00
CA	Alfonso Soriano	20.00
CB	Carl Crawford	10.00
CB	Rocco Baldelli	10.00
CM	Mark Mulder	15.00
CM	Chris Carpenter	15.00
DB	Carlos Delgado	10.00
DB	Carlos Beltran	10.00
DG	Ken Griffey Jr. /29	25.00
DG	Adam Dunn	25.00
DJ	Derek Jeter	40.00
DJ	Johnny Damon	20.00
GG	Brian Giles	10.00
GG	Marcus Giles	10.00
GJ	Ken Griffey Jr.	50.00
GJ	Derek Jeter	50.00
GM	Tom Glavine	15.00
GM	Pedro Martinez	15.00
GS	Vladimir Guerrero	15.00
GS	Alfonso Soriano	15.00
GT	Ken Griffey Jr.	30.00
GT	Frank Thomas	30.00
HB	Roy Halladay	10.00
HB	A.J. Burnett	10.00
HU	Chase Utley	25.00
HU	Cole Hamels	15.00
JJ	Andruw Jones	15.00
JJ	Chipper Jones	25.00
JR	Derek Jeter	50.00
JR	Jose Reyes	25.00
JT	Derek Jeter	30.00
JT	Miguel Tejada	15.00
LP	Jon Lester	30.00
LP	Jonathan Papelbon	20.00
MM	Victor Martinez	15.00
MM	Joe Mauer	25.00
MS	Greg Maddux	30.00
MS	John Smoltz	15.00
MT	Justin Morneau	20.00
MT	Joe Mauer	25.00
OR	Manny Ramirez	20.00
OR	David Ortiz	15.00
PG	Ken Griffey Jr.	50.00
PG	Albert Pujols	50.00
PZ	Jonathan Papelbon	15.00
PZ	Joel Zumaya	10.00
RH	Mariano Rivera	15.00
RH	Trevor Hoffman	15.00
RR	Jose Reyes	15.00
RR	Hanley Ramirez	25.00
RW	Vernon Wells	15.00
RW	Alex Rios	15.00
SB	Curt Schilling	20.00
SB	Josh Beckett	15.00
SH	Travis Hafner	15.00
SH	Grady Sizemore	15.00
SZ	Barry Zito	15.00
SZ	Johan Santana	20.00
TH	Jim Thome	15.00
TH	Travis Hafner	15.00
TK	Jim Thome	15.00
TK	Paul Konerko	15.00
TM	Mark Teixeira	20.00
TM	Justin Morneau	20.00
TR	Miguel Tejada	15.00
TR	Brian Roberts	15.00
TY	Michael Young	15.00
TY	Mark Teixeira	20.00
UU	Chase Utley	20.00
UU	Dan Uggla	15.00
VB	Jeremy Bonderman	10.00
VB	Justin Verlander	15.00
WH	Vernon Wells	15.00
WH	Torii Hunter	15.00
WJ	Randy Johnson	15.00
WJ	Brandon Webb	15.00
WS	Johan Santana	25.00
WS	Brandon Webb	15.00
ZR	Scott Rolen	20.00
ZR	Ryan Zimmerman	15.00

Elemental Autographs

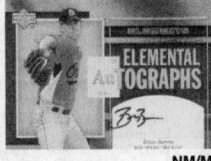

NM/M

Common Autograph:		8.00
AI	Akinori Iwamura	10.00
AL	Adam LaRoche	10.00
BA	Bronson Arroyo	8.00
BH	Bill Hall	8.00
BL	Joe Blanton	8.00
BN	Brendan Harris	8.00
BO	Jeremy Bonderman	8.00
BR	Jared Burton	8.00
BT	Jason Bartlett	10.00

BU	Brian Burres	8.00
BW	Brandon Wood	15.00
CB	Cha Sueng Baek	8.00
CO	Jon Coutlangus	10.00
CR	Cal Ripken Jr.	100.00
CU	Chase Utley	30.00
CW	Chase Wright	10.00
DB	Denny Bautista	8.00
DC	Daniel Cabrera	8.00
DJ	Derek Jeter	150.00
DU	Dan Uggla	15.00
DW	Dontrelle Willis	10.00
FP	Felix Pie	10.00
GA	Garrett Atkins	8.00
GC	Gustavo Chacin	10.00
GO	Alex Gordon	12.00
GP	Glen Perkins	8.00
HA	Rich Harden	10.00
HE	Sean Henn	8.00
HR	Hanley Ramirez	25.00
IK	Ian Kinsler	20.00
JA	Joaquin Arias	8.00
JB	Jason Bay	15.00
JC	Jesse Crain	8.00
JG	Jonny Gomes	8.00
JH	Josh Hamilton	30.00
JK	Jon Knott	10.00
JO	Josh Willingham	10.00
JP	Jake Peavy	20.00
JV	Justin Verlander	25.00
JW	Jayson Werth	20.00
KE	Howie Kendrick	10.00
KI	Kei Igawa	20.00
KM	Kendry Morales	20.00
KY	Kevin Youkilis	15.00
LA	Andy LaRoche	10.00
LI	Bobby Livingston	8.00
LS	Luke Scott	10.00
PA	Jonathan Papelbon	15.00
PE	Jhonny Peralta	10.00
RC	Roger Clemens	60.00
RH	Rich Hill	10.00
RL	Ruddy Lugo	8.00
RO	Scott Rolen	8.00
RT	Ryan Theriot	15.00
SD	Stephen Drew	20.00
SH	James Shields	15.00
SK	Scott Kazmir	15.00
SM	John Smoltz	25.00
SO	Jeremy Sowers	10.00
SS	Skip Schumaker	10.00
ST	Scott Thorman	8.00
TB	Travis Buck	10.00
TH	Travis Hafner	10.00
TI	Tadahito Iguchi	10.00
VG	Vladimir Guerrero	25.00
VM	Victor Martinez	15.00
WO	Jason Wood	8.00

Elemental Autographs Dual
Production 15 Sets

Elemental Autographs Triple
Production Five Sets

Elemental Autographs Quad
Production One Set

Essential Elements

NM/M
Common Player: 5.00
Patches: 2-4x

AB	Adrian Beltre	5.00
AD	Adam Dunn	8.00
AJ	Andruw Jones	5.00
AP	Andy Pettitte	8.00
AR	Aramis Ramirez	8.00
AS	Alfonso Soriano	8.00
BA	Bobby Abreu	5.00
BC	Bobby Crosby	5.00
BE	Carlos Beltran	5.00
BG	Brian Giles	5.00
BO	Jeremy Bonderman	5.00
BR	Brian Roberts	5.00
BU	B.J. Upton	5.00
BW	Billy Wagner	5.00
BZ	Barry Zito	5.00
CA	Miguel Cabrera	10.00
CB	Craig Biggio	8.00
CC	Carl Crawford	8.00
CH	Cole Hamels	10.00
CJ	Chipper Jones	8.00
CS	Curt Schilling	8.00
CU	Chase Utley	20.00
DA	Johnny Damon	5.00
DM	Daisuke Matsuzaka	20.00
DO	David Ortiz	8.00
DR	J.D. Drew	5.00
DU	Dan Uggla	8.00
DW	Dontrelle Willis	5.00
EC	Eric Chavez	5.00
ED	Jim Edmonds	5.00
FG	Freddy Garcia	5.00
FH	Felix Hernandez	8.00
FL	Francisco Liriano	5.00
FT	Frank Thomas	8.00
GA	Garret Anderson	5.00
GJ	Geoff Jenkins	5.00

GM	Greg Maddux	20.00
GS	Grady Sizemore	8.00
HA	Rich Harden	5.00
HB	Hank Blalock	5.00
HO	Trevor Hoffman	5.00
HS	Huston Street	5.00
HU	Torii Hunter	5.00
IR	Ivan Rodriguez	5.00
JA	Jason Bay	5.00
JB	Josh Beckett	5.00
JC	Jorge Cantu	5.00
JD	Jermaine Dye	5.00
JE	Johnny Estrada	5.00
JF	Jeff Francoeur	5.00
JG	Jason Giambi	5.00
JJ	Josh Johnson	5.00
JK	Jeff Kent	5.00
JM	Joe Mauer	10.00
JP	Jake Peavy	5.00
JR	Jimmy Rollins	8.00
JS	Johan Santana	10.00
JT	Jim Thome	8.00
JV	Justin Verlander	10.00
KG	Khalil Greene	5.00
LB	Lance Berkman	5.00
LG	Luis Gonzalez	5.00
MM	Mike Mussina	5.00
MO	Justin Morneau	10.00
MP	Mike Piazza	15.00
MR	Manny Ramirez	8.00
MT	Mark Teixeira	8.00
MY	Michael Young	5.00
OR	Magglio Ordonez	5.00
PA	Jonathan Papelbon	8.00
PB	Pat Burrell	5.00
PE	Jhonny Peralta	5.00
PO	Jorge Posada	8.00
PU	Albert Pujols	25.00
RE	Jose Reyes	8.00
RH	Roy Halladay	10.00
RI	Mariano Rivera	10.00
RJ	Randy Johnson	8.00
RO	Roy Oswalt	5.00
RW	Rickie Weeks	5.00
RZ	Ryan Zimmerman	8.00
SK	Scott Kazmir	5.00
SM	John Smoltz	5.00
SR	Scott Rolen	5.00
ST	Miguel Tejada	5.00
TH	Todd Helton	5.00
TI	Tim Hudson	5.00
TR	Travis Hafner	5.00
VG	Vladimir Guerrero	8.00
VM	Victor Martinez	5.00

Quad Elements
No Pricing Production 10 Sets

Triple Elements
Production 25 Sets

2007 UD Exquisite Rookie Signatures

NM/M
Common Player (1-100): 4.00
Production 99
Common RC Auto. (101-191): 15.00
Production 125-235
Box (Six Cards): 250.00

1	Ichiro Suzuki	15.00
2	Alex Rodriguez	20.00
3	David Wright	15.00
4	Ryan Howard	15.00
5	Ken Griffey Jr.	15.00
6	Derek Jeter	20.00
7	Vladimir Guerrero	8.00
8	Roger Clemens	10.00
9	Greg Maddux	10.00
10	Johan Santana	8.00
11	Nomar Garciaparra	4.00
12	Carlos Beltran	5.00
13	Carlos Delgado	5.00
14	Manny Ramirez	6.00
15	John Lackey	4.00
16	David Ortiz	8.00
17	Curt Schilling	6.00
18	Cal Ripken Jr.	20.00
19	Albert Pujols	20.00
20	Frank Thomas	5.00
21	Chris Carpenter	8.00
22	Prince Fielder	8.00
23	Justin Morneau	6.00
24	Joe Mauer	10.00
25	Torii Hunter	5.00
26	Jake Peavy	6.00
27	Roy Oswalt	5.00
28	Craig Biggio	8.00
29	Lance Berkman	4.00
30	Carlos Zambrano	4.00
31	Derrek Lee	5.00
32	Aramis Ramirez	5.00
33	Noah Lowry	4.00
34	Magglio Ordonez	4.00
35	Ivan Rodriguez	4.00
36	Johnny Damon	5.00
37	Justin Verlander	5.00
38	John Smoltz	5.00
39	Chipper Jones	8.00
40	Jeff Francoeur	5.00
41	Hanley Ramirez	8.00
42	Miguel Cabrera	8.00
43	Josh Beckett	8.00
44	Cole Hamels	6.00
45	Chase Utley	6.00
46	Grady Sizemore	8.00
47	Travis Hafner	5.00
48	Victor Martinez	5.00
49	Russell Martin	5.00
50	Jason Varitek	4.00
51	Hideki Matsui	10.00
52	Carl Crawford	5.00
53	Scott Kazmir	5.00
54	Miguel Tejada	5.00
55	Erik Bedard	5.00
56	Carlos Lee	5.00
57	Sammy Sosa	5.00
58	Mark Teixeira	6.00
59	Michael Young	4.00
60	Jim Thome	6.00
61	Paul Konerko	5.00
62	Jermaine Dye	5.00
63	Mark Teahen	4.00
64	Felix Hernandez	6.00
65	Andruw Jones	5.00
66	Pedro Martinez	8.00
67	Randy Johnson	6.00
68	Ryan Zimmerman	8.00
69	Matt Holliday	8.00
70	Todd Helton	5.00
71	Brian Bannister	4.00
72	Jeremy Bonderman	5.00
73	Adam Dunn	5.00
74	Aaron Harang	4.00
75	Jason Bay	5.00
76	Adam LaRoche	4.00
77	Freddy Sanchez	4.00
78	Dan Uggla	4.00
79	Joe Nathan	4.00
80	Brad Penny	4.00
81	Takashi Saito	4.00
82	Jimmy Rollins	8.00
83	Jose Reyes	10.00
84	Jered Weaver	6.00
85	Chien-Ming Wang	4.00
86	Jonathan Papelbon	8.00
87	Mariano Rivera	6.00
88	Eric Byrnes	4.00
89	Nicholas Markakis	6.00
90	Brian Roberts	4.00
91	Omar Vizquel	4.00
92	Vernon Wells	5.00
93	Danny Haren	5.00
94	Ben Sheets	4.00
95	B.J. Upton	6.00
96	Adrian Gonzalez	6.00
97	J.J. Hardy	4.00
98	Mike Piazza	8.00
99	Roy Halladay	8.00
100	Alfonso Soriano	8.00
101	Sean Henn / Auto./235 (RC)	15.00
102	Sean White / Auto./235 (RC)	15.00
103	Mike Schultz / Auto./235 (RC)	15.00
104	Michael Bourn / Auto./235 (RC)	20.00
105	Matt Chico / Auto./235 (RC)	15.00
106	Matt Lindstrom / Auto./235 (RC)	20.00
107	Connor Robertson / Auto./235 RC	15.00
108	Jay Marshall / Auto./235 RC	15.00
109	Jared Burton / Auto./235 RC	15.00
110	Juan Perez / Auto./235 RC	15.00
111	Scott Moore / Auto./235 (RC)	15.00
112	Brad Salmon / Auto./235 RC	15.00
113	Danny Putnam / Auto./235 (RC)	15.00
114	Kelvin Jimenez / Auto./235 (RC)	15.00
115	Dennis Dove / Auto./235 (RC)	15.00
116	Yoel Hernandez / Auto./235 (RC)	15.00
117	Devern Hansack / Auto./235 RC	15.00
118	Mike Rabelo / Auto./235 (RC)	15.00
119	Miguel Montero / Auto./235 RC	20.00
120	Kevin Cameron / Auto./235 (RC)	15.00
121	Joseph Bisenius / Auto./235 RC	15.00
122	Ryan Z. Braun / Auto./235 RC	15.00
123	Levale Speigner / Auto./235 RC	15.00
124	Lee Gardner / Auto./235 RC	15.00
125	Ryan Rowland-Smith / Auto./235 RC	15.00
126	Zack Segovia / Auto./235 (RC)	15.00
127	Rick Vanden Hurk / Auto./235 (RC)	15.00
128	Dallas Braden / Auto./235 RC	15.00
129	Rocky Cherry / Auto./235 RC	15.00
130	Andy Gonzalez / Auto./235 (RC)	15.00
131	Neal Musser / Auto./235 RC	15.00
132	Garrett Jones / Auto./235 (RC)	20.00
133	Ben Francisco / Auto./235 (RC)	15.00
134	Jon Coutlangus / Auto./235 RC	15.00
135	A.J. Murray / Auto./235 RC	15.00
136	Brett Carroll / Auto./235 RC	15.00
137	John Danks / Auto./235 RC	20.00
138	Kyle Kendrick / Auto./235 (RC)	15.00
139	Joaquin Arias / Auto./235 (RC)	15.00
140	Matt Brown / Auto./235 RC	15.00
141	Kurt Suzuki / Auto./150 (RC)	25.00
142	Curtis Thigpen / Auto./150 (RC)	15.00
143	Jerry Owens / Auto./150 (RC)	15.00
144	Billy Butler / Auto./150 (RC)	25.00
145	Kei Igawa / Auto./150 RC	20.00
146	Mike Fontenot / Auto./150 (RC)	15.00
147	Brandon Wood / Auto./150 (RC)	20.00
148	Alexi Casilla / Auto./150 RC	15.00
149	Jeff Baker / Auto./150 (RC)	15.00
150	Brian Barden / Auto./150 RC	15.00
151	Chris Stewart / Auto./150 RC	15.00
152	Jon Knott / Auto./150 (RC)	15.00
153	Chase Wright / Auto./150 RC	15.00
154	Chase Headley / Auto./150 (RC)	25.00
155	Jesse Litsch / Jsy Auto./199 RC	15.00
156	Tyler Clippard / Auto./150 RC	15.00
157	Matt DeSalvo / Auto./150 (RC)	15.00
158	Kory Casto / Auto./150 (RC)	15.00
159	Jarrod Saltalamacchia / Jsy Auto./199 (RC)	15.00
160	Glen Perkins / Auto./150 (RC)	15.00
161	Ryan Braun / Jsy Auto./199 (RC)	80.00
162	Justin Upton / Jsy Auto./199 RC	60.00
163	Tim Lincecum / Jsy Auto./199 RC	150.00
164	Fred Lewis / Auto./150 (RC)	15.00
165	Alex Gordon / Jsy Auto./199 RC	25.00
166	Akinori Iwamura / Jsy Auto./199 RC	20.00
167	Delmon Young / Jsy Auto./199 (RC)	20.00
168	Troy Tulowitzki / Jsy Auto./199 (RC)	40.00
169	Daisuke Matsuzaka / Jsy Auto./199 RC	150.00
170	Josh Hamilton / Jsy Auto./199 (RC)	80.00
171	Kevin Kouzmanoff / Jsy Auto./199 (RC)	20.00
172	Hunter Pence / Jsy Auto./199 (RC)	30.00
173	Felix Pie / Jsy Auto./199 (RC)	15.00
174	Andrew Miller / Jsy Auto./199 RC	20.00
175	Yovani Gallardo / Jsy Auto./199 (RC)	50.00
176	Ryan Sweeney / Jsy Auto./199 (RC)	15.00
177	Josh Fields / Jsy Auto./199 (RC)	15.00
178	Mark Reynolds / Jsy Auto./199 RC	30.00
180	Homer Bailey / Auto./150 (RC)	20.00
182	Joba Chamberlain / Auto./150 RC	50.00
184	Travis Metcalf / Jsy Auto./125 RC	15.00
185	Kevin Slowey / Jsy Auto./199 (RC)	25.00
186	Phil Hughes / Auto./150 (RC)	75.00
187	Micah Owings / Auto./150 (RC)	15.00
188	Joe Smith / Auto./150 RC	15.00
189	Joakim Soria / Jsy Auto./199 RC	15.00
190	Adam Lind / Jsy Auto./199 (RC)	20.00
191	Andy LaRoche / Jsy Auto./199 (RC)	20.00
192	Brandon Morrow / Jsy Auto./199 RC	20.00
193	Carlos Gomez / Jsy Auto./125 RC	20.00
194	Yunel Escobar / Auto./150 (RC)	30.00

Gold
Gold (1-100): 1-1.5X
Production 75
Gold RC (101-191): 1-1.5X
Production 25-99

Gold Spectrum Patch
Production One Set

Silver Spectrum
Production One Set

Rookie Team Autos.
No Pricing
Production 8 Sets
Silver Spectrum: No Pricing
Production One Set

College Ties Auto.
NM/M
Production 25 unless noted.
Gold: No Pricing
Production 2 Sets
Silver Spectrum: No Pricing
Production One Set

CT	Bobby Crosby, Troy Tulowitzki	40.00
DE	Andre Ethier, Chris Duffy	20.00
EB	Andre Ethier, Travis Buck	20.00
GG	Jeremy Guthrie, Ryan Garko	25.00
GH	Aaron Harang, Tony Gwynn Jr.	20.00
KO	Lyle Overbay, Kevin Kouzmanoff	25.00
RS	Kurt Suzuki, Aaron Rowand	30.00
TF	Ryan Theriot, Mike Fontenot	40.00

Common Ground Sign.
NM/M
Production 25 Sets
Gold: No Pricing
Production 2 Sets
Silver Spectrum: No Pricing
Production One Set

BL	Homer Bailey, Tim Lincecum	60.00
BR	Ryan Braun, Mark Reynolds	60.00
BT	Tom Gorzelanny, Brian Bannister	20.00
GB	Alex Gordon, Billy Butler	25.00
LB	Fred Lewis, Michael Bourn	20.00
MB	Jay Marshall, Dallas Braden	20.00
MF	Jesus Flores, Gustavo Molina	20.00
PG	Felix Pie, Carlos Gomez	20.00
SB	Nick Swisher, Travis Buck	20.00

Derek Jeter All Rookie Team
Production 2 Sets
Silver Spectrum: No Pricing
Production One Set

Rookie Team Autos
NM/M
Production 20 Sets
Copper Spectrum: No Pricing
Production 5 Sets
Silver Spectrum: No Pricing
Production 15 Sets

JB	Jeff Baker	10.00
RB	Ryan Braun	60.00
TB	Travis Buck	15.00
MC	Matt Chico	10.00
TC	Tyler Clippard	10.00
DA	John Danks	15.00
JD	J.D. Durbin	10.00
MF	Mike Fontenot	15.00
AG	Alex Gordon	20.00
JH	Josh Hamilton	35.00
HA	Justin Hampson	10.00
SH	Sean Henn	10.00
AI	Akinori Iwamura	15.00
KE	Kyle Kendrick	10.00
KK	Kevin Kouzmanoff	15.00
FL	Fred Lewis	15.00
TL	Tim Lincecum	85.00
JL	Jesse Litsch	10.00
AL	Adam Lind	15.00
AM	Andrew Miller	10.00
FP	Felix Pie	15.00
MR	Mark Reynolds	30.00
SA	Juan Salas	15.00
KS	Kevin Slowey	20.00
DY	Delmon Young	20.00

Common Numbers
NM/M
Production 2-60
Silver: No Pricing
Production 2 Sets
Gold: No Pricing
Production One Set

BB	Jeremy Bonderman, Jason Bay/38	20.00
BC	Matt Chico, Ryan Z. Braun/47	15.00
CP	Manny Corpas, Glen Perkins/60	15.00
FR	Josh Fields, Mark Reynolds/27	25.00
GH	Philip Humber, Yovani Gallardo/49	30.00
GS	Jose Garcia, Kevin Slowey/59	20.00
LT	Jim Thome, Derrek Lee/25	40.00
MS	Andrew Miller, Joakim Soria/48	20.00
VG	Sean Gallagher, Jamie Vermilyea/36	15.00
VT	Frank Thomas, Justin Verlander/35	100.00

Draft Choice Autos.
NM/M
Production 20 Sets
Copper: No Pricing
Production One Set
Gold: No Pricing
Production 5 Sets
Silver: No Pricing
Production 15 Sets

AG	Alex Gordon	20.00
AM	Andrew Miller	15.00
DY	Delmon Young	15.00
HB	Homer Bailey	15.00
JH	Josh Hamilton	30.00
KS	Kevin Slowey	20.00
TL	Tim Lincecum	75.00

Draft Duals Autos.
NM/M
Production 25 Sets
Gold: No Pricing
Production 2 Sets
Silver: No Pricing
Production One Set

BP	Homer Bailey, Glen Perkins	20.00
GB	Alex Gordon, Ryan Braun	80.00
GT	Ryan Theriot, Curtis Granderson	40.00
GY	Ken Griffey Jr., Delmon Young	100.00
HS	Kevin Slowey, Chase Headley	30.00
MB	Hank Blalock, Justin Morneau	25.00
MS	Nick Swisher, Nick Markakis	25.00
PG	Yovani Gallardo, Hunter Pence	40.00
ZB	Ryan Zimmerman, Ryan Braun	50.00
ZG	Alex Gordon, Ryan Zimmerman	40.00

Dual Signatures
NM/M
Production 35 Sets
Gold: No Pricing
Production 5-25
Silver: No Pricing
Production 1-10

AC	Andrew Miller, Cameron Maybin	20.00
AD	Alexi Casilla, Don Kelly	15.00
AJ	Aaron Harang, Jeff Keppinger	15.00
AM	Joaquin Arias, Travis Metcalf	15.00
BB	Ryan Z. Braun, Ryan Braun	60.00
BC	Jared Burton, Jon Coutlangus	15.00
BG	Jason Bay, Tom Gorzelanny	15.00
BH	Ramon Hernandez, Brian Burres	15.00
BI	Akinori Iwamura, Ryan Braun	60.00
BJ	Johnny Estrada, Bill Hall	15.00
50	Hong-Chih Kuo, Chad Billingsley	20.00
BL	Homer Bailey, Tim Lincecum	75.00
BR	Brian Barden, Mark Reynolds	15.00
BW	Brandon Wood, Billy Butler	25.00
CC	Curtis Granderson, Cameron Maybin	40.00
CD	Matt Chico, Matt DeSalvo	

Code	Player	Price
CH	Phil Hughes, Joba Chamberlain	80.00
CJ	Garrett Jones, Alexi Casilla	20.00
CK	Cesar Jimenez, Kelvin Jimenez	15.00
CY	Carl Crawford, Delmon Young	20.00
DH	J.D. Durbin, Yoel Hernadez	15.00
DM	Doug Slaten, Mike Schultz	15.00
DO	Micah Owings, Stephen Drew	25.00
DW	Chase Wright, Matt DeSalvo	15.00
FE	Mark Ellis, Mike Fontenot	15.00
FL	Carlos Lee, Prince Fielder	40.00
GB	Alex Gordon, Ryan Braun	60.00
GC	Sean Gallagher, Rocky Cherry	15.00
GG	Jose Garcia, Lee Gardner	15.00
GJ	Andruw Jones, Vladimir Guerrero	40.00
GK	Casey Kotchman, Adrian Gonzalez	25.00
GL	Jose Garcia, Matt Lindstrom	15.00
GM	Gustavo Molina, Miguel Montero	15.00
GP	Felix Pie, Carlos Gomez	15.00
GV	Lee Gardner, Rick Vanden Hurk	15.00
HA	Aaron Harang, Homer Bailey	25.00
HB	Joseph Bisenius, Yoel Hernandez	15.00
HC	Sean Henn, Tyler Clippard	15.00
HD	Sean Henn, Matt DeSalvo	15.00
HE	Ramon Hernandez, Johnny Estrada	15.00
HG	Josh Hamilton, Curtis Granderson	50.00
HH	Justin Hampson, Chase Headley	15.00
HK	Hong-Chih Kuo, Phil Hughes	75.00
HL	Phil Hughes, Tim Lincecum	150.00
HM	Cole Hamels, Andrew Miller	40.00
HP	Homer Bailey, Phil Hughes	50.00
IC	Kei Igawa, Tyler Clippard	20.00
IH	Kei Igawa, Phil Hughes	50.00
JE	Kelly Johnson, Yunel Escobar	25.00
JJ	Juan Salas, James Shields	20.00
KB	Hank Blalock, Ian Kinsler	25.00
KH	Kevin Kouzmanoff, Chase Headley	20.00
KK	Casey Kotchman, Howie Kendrick	30.00
KW	Howie Kendrick, Brandon Wood	30.00
LA	Andy LaRoche, Tony Abreu	25.00
LB	Fred Lewis, Michael Bourn	20.00
LE	Kelvim Escobar, John Lackey	15.00
LH	Jon Lester, Devern Hansack	40.00
LO	Roy Oswalt, Tim Lincecum	60.00
LP	Carlos Lee, Hunter Pence	25.00
LS	Jesse Litsch, Kevin Slowey	15.00
ME	Brian McCann, Yunel Escobar	30.00
MH	Josh Hamilton, Nick Markakis	40.00
MM	Brian McCann, Russell Martin	30.00
MO	Micah Owings, Andrew Miller	25.00
MS	John Maine, Joe Smith	15.00
NT	Nick Swisher, Travis Buck	20.00
OC	Micah Owings, Matt Chico	20.00
PH	Josh Hamilton, Hunter Pence	50.00
PM	Corey Patterson, Nick Markakis	40.00
PO	Jerry Owens, Felix Pie	15.00
RB	Ryan Braun, Mark Reynolds	50.00
RM	Jay Marshall, Connor Robertson	15.00
RO	Micah Owings, Mark Reynolds	25.00
RU	Hanley Ramirez, Dan Uggla	30.00
RZ	Aramis Ramirez, Carlos Zambrano	50.00
SA	Jeremy Accardo, Joakim Soria	15.00

Code	Player	Price
SB	Ryan Z. Braun, Joakim Soria	15.00
SG	Joe Smith, Carlos Gomez	15.00
SM	Kurt Suzuki, Gustavo Molina	15.00
SO	Ryan Sweeney, Jerry Owens	15.00
SR	Mike Rabelo, Chris Stewart	15.00
SS	Joe Smith, Kevin Slowey	15.00
ST	Sean Henn, Tyler Clippard	15.00
TB	Jeff Baker, Troy Tulowitzki	30.00
TE	Ryan Theriot, Yunel Escobar	25.00
TF	Ryan Theriot, Mike Fontenot	30.00
TJ	Curtis Thigpen, Garrett Jones	20.00
TL	Curtis Thigpen, Adam Lind	15.00
TR	Travis Hafner, Ryan Garko	25.00
TT	Frank Thomas, Jim Thome	100.00
TV	Travis Hafner, Victor Martinez	25.00
VL	Matt Lindstrom, Rick Vanden Hurk	15.00
VM	Justin Verlander, Andrew Miller	40.00
WI	Kei Igawa, Chase Wright	20.00
YT	Yovani Gallardo, Tim Lincecum	60.00
ZB	Ryan Zimmerman, Ryan Braun	50.00
ZG	Alex Gordon, Ryan Zimmerman	40.00

Exquisite Endorsements
NM/M
Production 50 Sets
Gold: No Pricing
Production 15 Sets
Silver: No Pricing
Production One Set

Code	Player	Price
AC	Alexi Casilla	10.00
AE	Andre Ethier	15.00
AL	Adam Lind	10.00
BH	Brendan Harris	10.00
BO	Jeremy Bonderman	10.00
CP	Corey Patterson	10.00
DH	Danny Haren	10.00
DL	Derrek Lee	20.00
DM	David Murphy	10.00
DU	Dan Uggla	15.00
FL	Fred Lewis	10.00
FP	Felix Pie	10.00
GP	Glen Perkins	10.00
HB	Homer Bailey	10.00
HP	Hunter Pence	15.00
HR	Hanley Ramirez	25.00
JB	Jason Bay	15.00
JF	Josh Fields	10.00
JL	Jon Lester	25.00
JP	Jonathan Papelbon	20.00
JS	James Shields	15.00
JV	Justin Verlander	30.00
KI	Kei Igawa	15.00
KS	Kevin Slowey	15.00
LG	Luis Gonzalez	10.00
MH	Matt Holliday	35.00
MO	Micah Owings	10.00
NS	Nick Swisher	15.00
PF	Prince Fielder	40.00
RB	Ryan Braun	60.00
RM	Russell Martin	10.00
RS	Ryan Sweeney	15.00
RT	Ryan Theriot	15.00
RZ	Ryan Zimmerman	25.00
SM	Joe Smith	10.00
TH	Travis Hafner	10.00
TL	Tim Lincecum	75.00
TT	Troy Tulowitzki	30.00
VM	Victor Martinez	20.00
YE	Yunel Escobar	15.00

Ensemble Triple Autos.
NM/M
Production 35 unless noted.
Gold: No Pricing
Production 3 Sets
Silver: No Pricing
Production One Set

Code	Player	Price
BGL	Alex Gordon, Andy LaRoche, Ryan Braun	75.00
BLG	Fred Lewis, Michael Bourn, Carlos Gomez	20.00
BTY	Delmon Young, Troy Tulowitzki, Ryan Braun	75.00
BWL	Adam Lind, Brandon Wood, Billy Butler	40.00
CSP	Glen Perkins, Joakim Soria, Joba Chamberlain	40.00
FCE	Alexi Casilla, Mike Fontenot, Yunel Escobar	30.00
GFC	Sean Gallagher, Rocky Cherry, Mike Fontenot	25.00
GIB	Alex Gordon, Akinori Iwamura, Ryan Braun	80.00

Code	Player	Price
IGR	Alex Gordon, Akinori Iwamura, Mark Reynolds	30.00
KHH	Justin Hampson, Kevin Kouzmanoff, Chase Headley	25.00
LHB	Homer Bailey, Phil Hughes, Tim Lincecum	150.00
LLT	Curtis Thigpen, Adam Lind, Jesse Litsch	30.00
MKI	Andrew Miller, Kei Igawa, Kyle Kendrick	25.00
PHY	Josh Hamilton, Delmon Young, Hunter Pence	50.00
SHG	Justin Hampson, Sean Gallagher, Joakim Soria	20.00
SMA	David Murphy, Jarrod Saltalamacchia, Joaquin Arias	20.00
UBB	Travis Buck, Billy Butler, Justin Upton	50.00

Ensemble Quad Autos.
No Pricing
Production 15 Sets
Gold: No Pricing
Production One Set
Silver: No Pricing
Production 4 Sets

First Signs Autos.
No Pricing
Production 20 Sets
Silver Spectrum: No Pricing
Production 15 Sets
Gold: No Pricing
Production 5 Sets
Silver Ink: No Pricing
Production One Set

Futures Autographs
No Pricing
Production 20 Sets
Gold: No Pricing
Production One Set
Silver: No Pricing
Production 5 Sets

Debut Signatures
NM/M
Production 20 Sets
Silver Spectrum: No Pricing
Production 15 Sets
Gold: No Pricing
Production 5 Sets
Silver Ink: No Pricing
Production One Set

Code	Player	Price
TA	Tony Abreu	10.00
JA	Joaquin Arias	10.00
HB	Homer Bailey	15.00
JE	Jeff Baker	10.00
BB	Brian Bannister	15.00
BA	Brian Barden	10.00
JB	Joseph Bisenius	10.00
BO	Michael Bourn	15.00
DB	Dallas Braden	15.00
RB	Ryan Braun	80.00
BR	Ryan Z. Braun	15.00
MB	Matt Brown	10.00
JB	Jared Burton	10.00
BU	Billy Butler	25.00
KC	Kevin Cameron	10.00
AC	Alexi Casilla	10.00
JC	Joba Chamberlain	50.00
RC	Rocky Cherry	15.00
MC	Matt Chico	10.00
TC	Tyler Clippard	10.00
CC	Jon Coutlangus	10.00
CC	Carl Crawford	20.00
JD	John Danks	25.00
MD	Matt DeSalvo	10.00
DD	Dennis Dove	10.00
JD	J.D. Durbin	10.00
YE	Yunel Escobar	15.00
JF	Josh Fields	10.00
MF	Mike Fontenot	10.00
BF	Ben Francisco	10.00
YG	Yovani Gallardo	40.00
JG	Jose Garcia	10.00
LG	Lee Gardner	10.00
CG	Carlos Gomez	10.00
AG	Alex Gordon	15.00
TH	Travis Hafner	15.00
HA	Cole Hamels	30.00
JH	Josh Hamilton	30.00
JU	Justin Hampson	10.00
DH	Devern Hansack	10.00
CH	Chase Headley	10.00
HE	Sean Henn	10.00
YH	Yoel Hernandez	10.00
PH	Phil Hughes	80.00
KI	Kei Igawa	15.00
AI	Akinori Iwamura	15.00
CJ	Cesar Jimenez	10.00
GJ	Garrett Jones	10.00
DK	Don Kelly	10.00
JK	Jon Knott	10.00
KK	Kevin Kouzmanoff	10.00
FL	Fred Lewis	10.00
TL	Tim Lincecum	100.00
AL	Adam Lind	15.00
ML	Matt Lindstrom	10.00
JL	Jesse Litsch	10.00
JM	Jay Marshall	10.00
VM	Victor Martinez	20.00
TM	Travis Metcalf	10.00

Code	Player	Price
AM	Andrew Miller	10.00
GM	Gustavo Molina	10.00
MO	Justin Morneau	30.00
NM	Neal Musser	10.00
RO	Roy Oswalt	15.00
JO	Jerry Owens	10.00
OW	Micah Owings	10.00
HP	Hunter Pence	15.00
GP	Glen Perkins	10.00
BP	Brandon Phillips	20.00
FP	Felix Pie	10.00
DP	Danny Putnam	10.00
HR	Hanley Ramirez	40.00
MR	Mark Reynolds	30.00
RI	Shawn Riggans	10.00
CR	Connor Robertson	10.00
RR	Ryan Rowland-Smith	10.00
JS	Juan Salas	10.00
SA	Jarrod Saltalamacchia	10.00
BS	Brad Salmon	10.00
LS	Luke Scott	15.00
SB	James Shields	15.00
KS	Kevin Slowey	20.00
SM	Joe Smith	10.00
SO	Joakim Soria	15.00
CS	Chris Stewart	10.00
ST	Brian Stokes	10.00
SU	Kurt Suzuki	15.00
RS	Ryan Sweeney	10.00
CT	Curtis Thigpen	10.00
TT	Troy Tulowitzki	40.00
RV	Rick Vanden Hurk	15.00
JV	Justin Verlander	40.00
JW	Josh Willingham	15.00
BW	Brandon Wood	15.00
CW	Chase Wright	10.00
DY	Delmon Young	15.00
CZ	Carlos Zambrano	15.00
RZ	Ryan Zimmerman	30.00

Imagery Autographs
NM/M
Production 25 Sets
Gold: No Pricing
Production 10 Sets
Silver: No Pricing
Production One Set

Code	Player	Price
AC	Alexi Casilla	10.00
AG	Alex Gordon	15.00
AL	Adam Lind	20.00
BB	Billy Butler	25.00
BH	Bill Hall	10.00
BO	Michael Bourn	15.00
BR	Ryan Z. Braun	10.00
BS	Brian Stokes	10.00
CG	Chris Gomez	15.00
CH	Chase Headley	20.00
CT	Curtis Thigpen	10.00
CW	Chase Wright	10.00
CZ	Carlos Zambrano	15.00
DD	Dennis Dove	15.00
DH	Devern Hansack	10.00
DM	David Murphy	10.00
FL	Fred Lewis	15.00
FP	Felix Pie	15.00
GJ	Garrett Jones	15.00
GM	Gustavo Molina	10.00
GP	Glen Perkins	10.00
HA	Justin Hampson	10.00
HB	Homer Bailey	20.00
HP	Hunter Pence	20.00
HR	Hanley Ramirez	40.00
JB	Jason Bay	20.00
JF	Josh Fields	15.00
JH	Josh Hamilton	30.00
JL	Jesse Litsch	15.00
JO	Jerry Owens	10.00
JS	James Shields	15.00
JU	Justin Upton	60.00
JW	Josh Willingham	15.00
KE	Kyle Kendrick	15.00
KI	Kei Igawa	15.00
KK	Kevin Kouzmanoff	15.00
KS	Kevin Slowey	20.00
LA	Andy LaRoche	15.00
MB	Matt Brown	10.00
MD	Matt DeSalvo	10.00
MF	Mike Fontenot	15.00
MH	Matt Holliday	40.00
MO	Micah Owings	15.00
MR	Mark Reynolds	30.00
NM	Nick Markakis	30.00
RB	Ryan Braun	80.00
RC	Rocky Cherry	15.00
RM	Russell Martin	15.00
RS	Ryan Sweeney	15.00
RV	Rick Vanden Hurk	15.00
RZ	Ryan Zimmerman	30.00
SA	Jarrod Saltalamacchia	15.00
SG	Sean Gallagher	10.00
SH	Sean Henn	10.00
SM	Joe Smith	10.00
TA	Tony Abreu	10.00
TB	Travis Buck	15.00
TC	Tyler Clippard	10.00
TH	Travis Hafner	15.00
TM	Travis Metcalf	10.00
VM	Victor Martinez	20.00
YE	Yunel Escobar	15.00
YG	Yovani Gallardo	40.00
YH	Yoel Hernandez	15.00
ZS	Zack Segovia	10.00

Phenoms Autographs
NM/M
Production 20 Sets
Gold: No Pricing
Production 15 Sets

Silver Spectrum:	No Pricing	
Production 15 Sets		
Silver Ink:	No Pricing	
Production One Set		
AG	Alex Gordon	20.00
AI	Akinori Iwamura	20.00
AL	Adam Lind	20.00
BB	Brian Bannister	15.00
CT	Curtis Thigpen	15.00
FL	Fred Lewis	15.00
FP	Felix Pie	20.00
HB	Homer Bailey	20.00
JD	John Danks	20.00
JS	James Shields	20.00
KK	Kevin Kouzmanoff	22.00
KS	Kevin Slowey	20.00
MC	Matt Chico	15.00
MR	Mark Reynolds	30.00
NM	Nick Markakis	30.00
PH	Phil Hughes	80.00
RB	Ryan Braun	80.00
SU	Kurt Suzuki	15.00
TL	Tim Lincecum	100.00
TT	Troy Tulowitzki	40.00

Reflections Autos
NM/M
Common Dual Auto.: Production 40 unless noted
Gold: No Pricing
Production 5-20
Silver Ink: No Pricing
Production 5-20
Silver Spectrum: No Pricing
Production 1-10

Code	Player	Price
AB	Alex Gordon, Billy Butler	40.00
AC	Joaquin Arias, Alexi Casilla	15.00
AH	Aaron Harang, Homer Bailey	20.00
AJ	Jeremy Sowers, Andrew Miller	15.00
BA	Matt Brown, Tony Abreu	15.00
BB	Boof Bonser, Brian Bannister	15.00
BD	John Danks, Brian Bannister	15.00
BG	Alex Gordon, Ryan Braun	50.00
BH	Travis Hafner, Josh Barfield	20.00
BJ	Jared Burton, Brad Salmon	15.00
BL	Fred Lewis, Michael Bourn	20.00
BS	Joseph Bisenius, Zack Segovia	15.00
BT	Mark Teahen, Brian Bannister	15.00
BV	Jeremy Bonderman, Justin Verlander	30.00
BW	Brandon Wood, Matt Brown	15.00
CG	Carl Crawford, Carlos Gomez	25.00
CH	Justin Hampson, Kevin Cameron	15.00
CK	Curtis Thigpen, Kurt Suzuki	15.00
CS	Joakim Soria, Rocky Cherry	15.00
DC	Matt Chico, Matt DeSalvo	15.00
DH	J.D. Durbin, Yoel Hernandez	15.00
DO	Micah Owings, John Danks	15.00
DS	J.D. Durbin, Zack Segovia	15.00
EC	Alexi Casilla, Yunel Escobar	15.00
EL	Fred Lewis, Andre Ethier	20.00
EP	Mark Ellis, Danny Putnam	15.00
FM	Josh Fields, Travis Metcalf	15.00
FO	David Ortiz, Prince Fielder	40.00
FY	Yovani Gallardo, Felix Hernandez	40.00
GA	Alexi Casilla, Glen Perkins	15.00
GB	Jeremy Guthrie, Brian Burres	15.00
GC	Sean Gallagher, Rocky Cherry	15.00
GG	Jeremy Guthrie, Tom Gorzelanny	15.00
GK	Alex Gordon, Kevin Kouzmanoff	15.00
GL	Matt Lindstrom, Lee Gardner	15.00
GM	Gustavo Molina, Miguel Montero	15.00
GV	Jose Garcia, Rick Vanden Hurk	15.00
HB	Homer Bailey, Phil Hughes	50.00
HC	Justin Hampson, Jon Coutlangus	15.00
HD	Huston Street, Dallas Braden	15.00
HG	Rich Hill, Sean Gallagher	15.00

Code	Player	Price
HH	Sean Henn, Phil Hughes	50.00
HK	Kevin Kouzmanoff, Chase Headley	20.00
HM	Cole Hamels, Andrew Miller	30.00
HP	Josh Hamilton, Hunter Pence	40.00
HT	Homer Bailey, Tim Lincecum	60.00
HW	Josh Willingham, Jeremy Hermida	15.00
IM	Andrew Miller, Kei Igawa	15.00
JC	Chad Billingsley, James Shields	20.00
JD	Kelvin Jimenez, Dennis Dove	15.00
JE	Kelly Johnson, Yunel Escobar	15.00
JJ	Josh Fields, Jerry Owens	15.00
JK	Jarrod Saltalamacchia, Kurt Suzuki	25.00
JL	Reed Johnson, Adam Lind	15.00
JM	John Danks, Matt Chico	15.00
KC	Cesar Jimenez, Kelvin Jimenez	15.00
KG	Kurt Suzuki, Gustavo Molina	15.00
LA	Andy LaRoche, Tony Abreu	15.00
LB	Jeff Baker, Adam Lind	15.00
LH	Jon Lester, Cole Hamels	60.00
LL	Adam Lind, Jesse Litsch	25.00
LO	Fred Lewis, Jerry Owens	15.00
MA	Mark Ellis, Alexi Casilla	15.00
MB	Jay Marshall, Dallas Braden	15.00
MG	Jeremy Guthrie, Nick Markakis	40.00
MJ	Matt Holliday, Jason Bay	40.00
MK	Nick Markakis, Jon Knott	25.00
MM	Brian McCann, Russell Martin	25.00
MR	Jay Marshall, Connor Robertson	15.00
MS	Kurt Suzuki, Russell Martin	20.00
NR	Ryan Z. Braun, Neal Musser	15.00
OB	Micah Owings, Homer Bailey	20.00
PB	Danny Putnam, Travis Buck	15.00
PC	Matt Chico, Glen Perkins	15.00
PD	Glen Perkins, Matt DeSalvo	15.00
PG	Felix Pie, Carlos Gomez	15.00
PO	Jerry Owens, Felix Pie	15.00
RB	Ryan Braun, Mark Reynolds	60.00
RC	Ryan Braun, Chase Headley	60.00
RM	Gustavo Molina, Mike Rabelo	15.00
RR	Ryan Z. Braun, Ryan Braun	50.00
SB	Ryan Z. Braun, Joakim Soria	15.00
SG	Ben Sheets, Yovani Gallardo	40.00
SH	Justin Hampson, Joe Smith	15.00
SM	David Murphy, Jarrod Saltalamacchia	15.00
SP	Glen Perkins, Kevin Slowey	15.00
SR	Kurt Suzuki, Shawn Riggans	15.00
SS	Joe Smith, Kevin Slowey	20.00
ST	Sean Henn, Tyler Clippard	15.00
TJ	Curtis Thigpen, Garrett Jones	20.00
TR	Curtis Thigpen, Shawn Riggans	15.00
TS	Mark Teahen, Angel Sanchez	15.00
VG	Lee Gardner, Rick Vanden Hurk	15.00
WD	John Danks, Chase Wright	15.00
WH	Bill Hall, Josh Willingham	15.00
ZY	Zack Segovia, Yoel Hernandez	15.00

Retro Rookie Duals
No Pricing
Production 5-15
Gold: No Pricing
Production 2 Sets
Silver: No Pricing
Production One Set

Rookie Biography Autos.
NM/M
Production 20 Sets

Blue: No Pricing
Production One Set
Gold: No Pricing
Production 15 Sets
Silver Spectrum: No Pricing
Production 10 Sets
Silver Ink: No Pricing
Production One Set

AC	Alexi Casilla	15.00
AG	Alex Gordon	20.00
AI	Akinori Iwamura	20.00
AL	Adam Lind	20.00
AM	Andrew Miller	15.00
AS	Anibal Sanchez	15.00
BA	Brian Barden	15.00
BB	Billy Butler	30.00
BF	Ben Francisco	15.00
BH	Bill Hall	15.00
BI	Joseph Bisenius	15.00
BS	Ben Sheets	15.00
BU	Jamie Burke	15.00
BW	Brandon Wood	15.00
CC	Chris Carpenter	25.00
CG	Carlos Gomez	15.00
CH	Chase Headley	20.00
CJ	Cesar Jimenez	15.00
CO	Manny Corpas	15.00
CS	Chris Stewart	15.00
CT	Curtis Thigpen	15.00
CW	Chase Wright	15.00
DA	John Danks	15.00
DB	Dallas Braden	15.00
DD	Dennis Dove	15.00
DH	Danny Haren	20.00
DK	Don Kelly	15.00
DL	Derrek Lee	30.00
DS	Doug Slaten	15.00
DY	Delmon Young	15.00
FL	Fred Lewis	15.00
FP	Felix Pie	15.00
FT	Frank Thomas	60.00
GJ	Garrett Jones	20.00
GO	Tom Gorzelanny	15.00
GP	Glen Perkins	15.00
HA	Devern Hansack	15.00
HB	Homer Bailey	20.00
HG	Hector Gimenez	15.00
HP	Hunter Pence	20.00
JA	Joaquin Arias	15.00
JB	Jeff Baker	15.00
JC	Jon Coutlangus	15.00
JD	J.D. Durbin	15.00
JF	Josh Fields	15.00
JG	Jose Garcia	15.00
JH	Justin Hampson	15.00
JK	Jon Knott	15.00
JL	Jesse Litsch	15.00
JM	Jay Marshall	15.00
JO	Jerry Owens	15.00
JS	Jarrod Saltalamacchia	15.00
JT	Jim Thome	30.00
JV	Justin Verlander	40.00
JW	Josh Willingham	20.00
KI	Kei Igawa	20.00
KJ	Kelvin Jimenez	15.00
KK	Kevin Kouzmanoff	15.00
KS	Kevin Slowey	20.00
LA	Andy LaRoche	15.00
LG	Lee Gardner	15.00
LS	Levale Speigner	15.00
MA	Nick Markakis	40.00
MB	Michael Bourn	20.00
MC	Matt Chico	15.00
MD	Matt DeSalvo	15.00
MF	Mike Fontenot	15.00
ML	Matt Lindstrom	15.00
MM	Miguel Montero	15.00
MO	Micah Owings	15.00
MR	Mark Reynolds	30.00
NM	Neal Musser	15.00
PH	Phil Hughes	80.00
RA	Mike Rabelo	15.00
RB	Ryan Braun	80.00
RC	Rocky Cherry	15.00
RO	Connor Robertson	15.00
RR	Ryan Rowland-Smith	15.00
RS	Ryan Sweeney	15.00
RV	Rick Vanden Hurk	15.00
SA	Brad Salmon	15.00
SG	Sean Gallagher	15.00
SH	Sean Henn	15.00
SM	Joe Smith	15.00
SO	Joakim Soria	15.00
SR	Shawn Riggans	15.00
SU	Kurt Suzuki	15.00
SW	Sean White	15.00
TA	Tony Abreu	15.00
TB	Travis Buck	15.00
TC	Tyler Clippard	15.00
TG	Tom Glavine	50.00
TL	Tim Lincecum	100.00
TT	Troy Tulowitzki	40.00
VM	Victor Martinez	25.00
YE	Yunel Escobar	30.00
YH	Yoel Hernandez	15.00
ZS	Zack Segovia	15.00

Rookie Heroes Autographs
NM/M
Production 25 Sets
Gold: 1-1.5X
Production 15 Sets
Silver Spectrum: 1-2X
Production 10 Sets
Silver Ink: No Pricing
Production One Set

AI1-5	Akinori Iwamura	20.00
AM1-5	Andrew Miller	10.00
BB1-5	Billy Butler	25.00
CG1-5	Carlos Gomez	15.00
FL1-5	Fred Lewis	15.00
FP1-5	Felix Pie	15.00
HB1-5	Homer Bailey	15.00
HP1-5	Hunter Pence	20.00
JD1-5	John Danks	15.00
JS1-5	Jarrod Saltalamacchia	15.00
KE1-5	Kyle Kendrick	15.00
KK1-5	Kevin Kouzmanoff	10.00
KS1-5	Kevin Slowey	15.00
MR1-5	Mark Reynolds	25.00
RB1-5	Ryan Braun	60.00
SO1-5	Joakim Soria	15.00
TB1-5	Travis Buck	15.00
TL1-5	Tim Lincecum	85.00
TT1-5	Troy Tulowitzki	40.00
YE1-5	Yunel Escobar	30.00

Signature Materials
NM/M
Production 85 unless noted
Gold: 1-1.5X
Production 15-50
Gold Spectrum: No Pricing
Production One Set
Silver Spectrum: No Pricing
Production 10-25

AD	Adam Dunn	25.00
AG	Adrian Gonzalez	25.00
AH	Aaron Harang	15.00
AR	Aramis Ramirez	20.00
BH	Bill Hall	10.00
BL	Joe Blanton	10.00
BO	Jeremy Bonderman	10.00
BR	Brian Roberts	20.00
BS	Ben Sheets	20.00
BU	B.J. Upton	20.00
CC	Carl Crawford	20.00
CH	Cole Hamels	40.00
CL	Carlos Lee	20.00
CR	Cal Ripken Jr.	125.00
CZ	Carlos Zambrano	20.00
DH	Danny Haren	20.00
DL	Derrek Lee	25.00
DU	Dan Uggla	15.00
DW	Dontrelle Willis	15.00
FH	Felix Hernandez	40.00
FT	Frank Thomas	60.00
HA	Travis Hafner	15.00
HK	Howie Kendrick	20.00
HR	Hanley Ramirez	40.00
HS	Huston Street	15.00
IK	Ian Kinsler	20.00
JB	Jason Bay	20.00
JM	John Maine	15.00
JO	Josh Barfield	10.00
JP	Jonathan Papelbon	25.00
JV	Justin Verlander	35.00
JW	Josh Willingham	15.00
LS	Luke Scott	15.00
MC	Matt Cain	20.00
MO	Justin Morneau	20.00
MT	Mark Teixeira	25.00
NM	Nick Markakis	25.00
NS	Nick Swisher	15.00
PF	Prince Fielder	40.00
RH	Rich Harden	15.00
RM	Russell Martin	15.00
RW	Rickie Weeks	20.00
RZ	Ryan Zimmerman	25.00
SD	Stephen Drew	20.00
TH	Torii Hunter	20.00
VM	Victor Martinez	20.00

Future Autographs
No Pricing
Production 20 Sets
Gold: No Pricing
Production 15 Sets
Silver: No Pricing
Production One Set

All Rookie Team Autos.
Production 3 Sets
Silver: No Pricing
Production One Set

Generation Sign.
NM/M
Production 20 Sets
Gold: No Pricing
Production 15 Sets
Silver: No Pricing
Production One Set

AC	Alexi Casilla	10.00
AG	Alex Gordon	20.00
AM	Andrew Miller	10.00
BB	Brian Bannister	15.00
BF	Ben Francisco	10.00
CH	Chase Headley	15.00
CT	Curtis Thigpen	10.00
DD	Dennis Dove	10.00
DH	Devern Hansack	10.00
DP	Danny Putnam	10.00
FL	Fred Lewis	15.00
FP	Felix Pie	10.00
HB	Homer Bailey	15.00
HP	Hunter Pence	20.00
HR	Hanley Ramirez	40.00
JA	Joaquin Arias	10.00
JD	J.D. Durbin	10.00
JF	Josh Fields	10.00
JH	Justin Hampson	10.00
JS	Joakim Soria	15.00
JV	Justin Verlander	40.00
JW	Josh Willingham	20.00
KI	Kei Igawa	20.00
KK	Kevin Kouzmanoff	15.00
KS	Kevin Slowey	20.00
MF	Mike Fontenot	15.00
MR	Mark Reynolds	30.00
RB	Ryan Braun	80.00
RS	Ryan Sweeney	15.00
RT	Ryan Theriot	20.00
RV	Rick Vanden Hurk	15.00
SG	Sean Gallagher	15.00
SM	Joe Smith	10.00
SU	Kurt Suzuki	15.00
TL	Tim Lincecum	120.00
YE	Yunel Escobar	30.00
YH	Yoel Hernandez	10.00
ZS	Zack Segovia	10.00

2007 Upper Deck First Edition

NM/M
Complete Set (300): 35.00
Common Player: .10
Pack (10): 1.00
Box (36): 30.00

1	Doug Slaten RC	.25
2	Miguel Montero (RC)	.50
3	Brian Burres (RC)	.25
4	Devern Hansack RC	.50
5	David Murphy (RC)	.25
6	Jose Reyes RC	.25
7	Scott Moore (RC)	.25
8	Josh Fields (RC)	.25
9	Chris Stewart RC	.25
10	Jerry Owens (RC)	.25
11	Ryan Sweeney (RC)	.25
12	Kevin Kouzmanoff (RC)	.40
13	Jeff Baker (RC)	.25
14	Justin Hampson (RC)	.25
15	Jeff Salazar (RC)	.25
16	Alvin Colina RC	.25
17	Troy Tulowitzki (RC)	.50
18	Andrew Miller RC	.50
19	Mike Rabelo RC	.25
20	Jose Diaz (RC)	.25
21	Angel Sanchez RC	.25
22	Ryan Braun (RC)	.75
23	Delwyn Young (RC)	.25
24	Drew Anderson (RC)	.25
25	Dennis Sarfate (RC)	.25
26	Vinny Rottino (RC)	.25
27	Glen Perkins (RC)	.25
28	Alexi Casilla (RC)	.25
29	Philip Humber (RC)	.25
30	Andy Cannizaro RC	.25
31	Jeremy Brown	.10
32	Sean Henn (RC)	.25
33	Brian Rogers (RC)	.25
34	Carlos Maldonado (RC)	.25
35	Juan Morillo (RC)	.25
36	Fred Lewis (RC)	.25
37	Patrick Misch (RC)	.25
38	Billy Sadler (RC)	.25
39	Ryan Feierabend (RC)	.25
40	Cesar Jimenez RC	.25
41	Oswaldo Navarro RC	.25
42	Travis Chick (RC)	.25
43	Delmon Young (RC)	.50
44	Shawn Riggans (RC)	.25
45	Brian Stokes (RC)	.25
46	Juan Salas (RC)	.25
47	Joaquin Arias (RC)	.25
48	Adam Lind (RC)	.50
49	Beltran Perez (RC)	.25
50	Brett Campbell RC	.25
51	Miguel Tejada	.40
52	Brandon Fahey	.10
53	Jay Gibbons	.10
54	Nicholas Markakis	.25
55	Kris Benson	.10
56	Erik Bedard	.25
57	Chris Ray	.10
58	Chris Britton	.10
59	Manny Ramirez	.50
60	David Ortiz	.50
61	Alex Cora	.10
62	Trot Nixon	.10
63	Doug Mirabelli	.10
64	Curt Schilling	.50
65	Jonathan Papelbon	.50
66	Craig Hansen	.10
67	Jermaine Dye	.25
68	Jim Thome	.40
69	Robert Mackowiak	.10
70	Brian Anderson	.10
71	A.J. Pierzynski	.10
72	Alex Cintron	.10
73	Jose Contreras	.10
74	Bobby Jenks	.10
75	Mike MacDougal	.10
76	Travis Hafner	.40
77	Ryan Garko	.10
78	Victor Martinez	.25
79	Casey Blake	.10
80	Shin-Soo Choo	.10
81	Paul Byrd	.10
82	Jeremy Sowers	.10
83	Cliff Lee	.10
84	Sean Casey	.10
85	Brandon Inge	.10
86	Omar Infante	.10
87	Magglio Ordonez	.25
88	Marcus Thames	.10
89	Justin Verlander	.50
90	Todd Jones	.10
91	Joel Zumaya	.10
92	Nate Robertson	.10
93	Mark Teahen	.10
94	Ryan Shealy	.10
95	Mark Grudzielanek	.10
96	Shane Costa	.10
97	Reggie Sanders	.10
98	Mark Redman	.10
99	Todd Wellemeyer	.10
100	Ambiorix Burgos	.10
101	Joe Nelson	.10
102	Orlando Cabrera	.25
103	Maicer Izturis	.10
104	Vladimir Guerrero	.50
105	Juan Rivera	.10
106	Jered Weaver	.40
107	Joe Saunders	.10
108	Bartolo Colon	.10
109	Francisco Rodriguez	.10
110	Justin Morneau	.50
111	Luis Castillo	.10
112	Michael Cuddyer	.10
113	Joe Mauer	.40
114	Francisco Liriano	.25
115	Joe Nathan	.10
116	Brad Radke	.10
117	Juan Rincon	.10
118	Derek Jeter	1.50
119	Jason Giambi	.40
120	Bobby Abreu	.40
121	Gary Sheffield	.25
122	Melky Cabrera	.25
123	Chien-Ming Wang	.40
124	Mariano Rivera	.40
125	Jaret Wright	.10
126	Kyle Farnsworth	.10
127	Frank Thomas	.50
128	Dan Johnson	.10
129	Marco Scutaro	.10
130	Jay Payton	.10
131	Joe Blanton	.10
132	Rich Harden	.25
133	Esteban Loaiza	.10
134	Chad Gaudin	.10
135	Yuniesky Betancourt	.10
136	Willie Bloomquist	.10
137	Ichiro Suzuki	1.00
138	Raul Ibanez	.10
139	Chris Snelling	.10
140	Cha Seung Baek	.10
141	Julio Mateo	.10
142	Rafael Soriano	.10
143	Jorge Cantu	.10
144	B.J. Upton	.10
145	Dioner Navarro	.10
146	Carl Crawford	.40
147	Damon Hollins	.10
148	Casey Fossum	.10
149	Ruddy Lugo	.10
150	Tyler Walker	.10
151	Shawn Camp	.10
152	Ian Kinsler	.25
153	Jerry Hairston Jr.	.10
154	Gerald Laird	.10
155	Mark DeRosa	.10
156	Kip Wells	.10
157	Vicente Padilla	.10
158	John Koronka	.10
159	Wes Littleton	.10
160	Lyle Overbay	.10
161	Aaron Hill	.10
162	John McDonald	.10
163	Vernon Wells	.25
164	Frank Catalanotto	.10
165	Roy Halladay	.25
166	B.J. Ryan	.10
167	Casey Janssen	.10
168	Stephen Drew	.50
169	Conor Jackson	.10
170	Chad Tracy	.10
171	Johnny Estrada	.10
172	Eric Byrnes	.10
173	Carlos Quentin	.10
174	Brandon Webb	.25
175	Jorge Julio	.10
176	Luis Vizcaino	.10
177	Chipper Jones	.50
178	Adam LaRoche	.25
179	Brian McCann	.25
180	Ryan Langerhans	.10
181	Matt Diaz	.10
182	John Smoltz	.25
183	Oscar Villarreal	.10
184	Chad Paronto	.10
185	Derrek Lee	.40
186	Ryan Theriot	.10
187	Ronny Cedeno	.10
188	Juan Pierre	.10
189	Matt Murton	.10
190	Carlos Zambrano	.25
191	Mark Prior	.25
192	Ryan Dempster	.10
193	Ryan O'Malley	.10
194	Brandon Phillips	.10
195	Rich Aurilia	.10
196	Ken Griffey Jr.	1.00
197	Ryan Freel	.10
198	Aaron Harang	.10
199	Brandon Claussen	.10
200	David Weathers	.10
201	Eric Milton	.10
202	Kazuo Matsui	.10
203	Jamey Carroll	.10
204	Matt Holliday	.25
205	Brad Hawpe	.10
206	Jason Jennings	.10
207	Josh Fogg	.10
208	Aaron Cook	.10
209	Miguel Cabrera	.50
210	Dan Uggla	.25
211	Hanley Ramirez	.40
212	Jeremy Hermida	.10
213	Cody Ross	.10
214	Josh Willingham	.10
215	Anibal Sanchez	.10
216	Jose Garcia	.10
217	Taylor Tankersley	.10
218	Lance Berkman	.40
219	Craig Biggio	.25
220	Brad Ausmus	.10
221	Willy Taveras	.10
222	Chris Burke	.10
223	Roger Clemens	1.00
224	Brandon Backe	.10
225	Brad Lidge	.10
226	Dan Wheeler	.10
227	Wilson Betemit	.10
228	Julio Lugo	.10
229	Russell Martin	.25
230	Kenny Lofton	.10
231	Brad Penny	.10
232	Chad Billingsley	.25
233	Greg Maddux	1.00
234	Jonathan Broxton	.10
235	Rickie Weeks	.25
236	Bill Hall	.25
237	Tony Gwynn Jr.	.10
238	Corey Hart	.10
239	Laynce Nix	.10
240	Ben Sheets	.25
241	David Bush	.10
242	Francisco Cordero	.10
243	Jose Reyes	.50
244	Carlos Delgado	.40
245	Paul LoDuca	.10
246	Carlos Beltran	.40
247	Lastings Milledge	.25
248	Pedro Martinez	.50
249	John Maine	.10
250	Steve Trachsel	.10
251	Ryan Howard	1.00
252	Jimmy Rollins	.25
253	Chris Coste	.10
254	Jeff Conine	.10
255	David Dellucci	.10
256	Cole Hamels	.25
257	Ryan Madson	.10
258	Brett Myers	.10
259	Freddy Sanchez	.25
260	Xavier Nady	.10
261	Jose Castillo	.10
262	Jason Bay	.25
263	Jose Bautista	.10
264	Ronny Paulino	.10
265	Zachary Duke	.10
266	Shane Youman	.10
267	Matt Capps	.10
268	Adrian Gonzalez	.25
269	Josh Barfield	.10
270	Mike Piazza	.75
271	Dave Roberts	.10
272	Geoff Blum	.10
273	Chris Young	.10
274	Woody Williams	.10
275	Cla Meredith	.10
276	Trevor Hoffman	.25
277	Ray Durham	.10
278	Mark Sweeney	.10
279	Eliezer Alfonzo	.10
280	Todd Linden	.10
281	Jason Schmidt	.10
282	Noah Lowry	.10
283	Brad Hennessey	.10
284	Jonathan Sanchez	.10
285	Albert Pujols	1.50
286	David Eckstein	.10
287	Jim Edmonds	.25
288	Chris Duncan	.10
289	Juan Encarnacion	.10
290	Jeff Suppan	.10
291	Jeff Weaver	.10
292	Braden Looper	.10
293	Ryan Zimmerman	.25
294	Nick Johnson	.10
295	Alfonso Soriano	.50
296	Austin Kearns	.10
297	Alex Escobar	.10
298	Tony Armas	.10
299	Chad Cordero	.10
300	Jon Rauch	.10

Printing Plates
No Pricing
Production one set per color.

Aces
NM/M
Common Player: .50
Inserted 1:6

BW	Brandon Webb	.50
CC	Chris Carpenter	.75
CS	Curt Schilling	.75
CZ	Carlos Zambrano	.50
DW	Dontrelle Willis	.50
FH	Felix Hernandez	.75
JS	Johan Santana	.75
JV	Justin Verlander	.75
PM	Pedro Martinez	.75
RC	Roger Clemens	2.00
RH	Roy Halladay	.50
SA	C.C. Sabathia	.50
SM	John Smoltz	.75
RJ	Randy Johnson	.75
SK	Scott Kazmir	.50

Foundations

NM/M
Common Player: .50
Inserted 1:6

AL	Adam Lind	1.00
AM	Andrew Miller	3.00
DM	David Murphy	1.00
DY	Delmon Young	1.00
FL	Fred Lewis	.50
GP	Glen Perkins	.50
JA	Joaquin Arias	.50
JF	Josh Fields	.50
JO	Jerry Owens	.50
JS	Jeff Salazar	.50
MM	Mitch Maier	.50
MO	Miguel Montero	.50
PH	Philip Humber	.50
RB	Ryan Braun	.50
RS	Ryan Sweeney	.50
SM	Scott Moore	.50
SR	Shawn Riggans	.50
TC	Travis Chick	.50
TT	Troy Tulowitzki	1.00
UJ	Ubaldo Jimenez	.50

Leading Off

NM/M
Common Player: .50
Inserted 1:6

AS	Alfonso Soriano	1.00
BR	Brian Roberts	.50
CF	Chone Figgins	.50
DR	Dave Roberts	.50
FR	Ryan Freel	.50
GS	Grady Sizemore	1.00
HR	Hanley Ramirez	.75
IS	Ichiro Suzuki	2.00
JD	Johnny Damon	.50
JP	Juan Pierre	.50
JR	Jose Reyes	2.00
RF	Rafael Furcal	.50
RO	Jimmy Rollins	.75
SP	Scott Podsednik	.50
WT	Willy Taveras	.50

Momentum Swing

NM/M
Common Player: .50
Inserted 1:6

AD	Adam Dunn	.75
AJ	Andruw Jones	1.00
AP	Albert Pujols	2.50
AR	Alex Rodriguez	2.50
AS	Alfonso Soriano	1.00
CB	Carlos Beltran	1.00
CD	Carlos Delgado	.75
DL	Derrek Lee	.75
DO	David Ortiz	1.00
JB	Jason Bay	.75
JD	Jermaine Dye	.75
JG	Jason Giambi	.75
JM	Justin Morneau	1.00
JT	Jim Thome	.75
LB	Lance Berkman	1.00
MC	Miguel Cabrera	1.00
MT	Mark Teixeira	.75
RH	Ryan Howard	2.00
TH	Travis Hafner	.75
VG	Vladimir Guerrero	1.00

Pennant Chasers

NM/M
Common Player: .25
Inserted 1:4

AR	Aramis Ramirez	.75
CC	Carl Crawford	.75
CG	Carlos Guillen	.50
CJ	Chipper Jones	1.00
CU	Chase Utley	1.00
DA	Johnny Damon	1.00
DU	Dan Uggla	.75
DW	David Wright	1.50
FS	Freddy Sanchez	.75
JM	Joe Mauer	.75
JR	Juan Rivera	.25
KG	Ken Griffey Jr.	2.00
MH	Matt Holliday	.75
MR	Manny Ramirez	1.00
MT	Miguel Tejada	.50
MY	Michael Young	.50
NG	Nomar Garciaparra	.75
NS	Nick Swisher	.25
OH	Orlando Hudson	.25
PF	Prince Fielder	.75
PK	Paul Konerko	.50
RD	Ray Durham	.25
RI	Raul Ibanez	.50
RO	Roy Oswalt	.50
RZ	Ryan Zimmerman	.75
SR	Scott Rolen	.75
TE	Mark Teahen	.25
TH	Trevor Hoffman	.25
VM	Victor Martinez	.50
VW	Vernon Wells	.50

2007 Upper Deck Future Stars

NM/M
Common Player (1-100): .25
Common RC Auto. (101-189): 8.00
Pack (4): 4.00
Box (24): 75.00

1	Brandon Webb	.50
2	Conor Jackson	.25
3	Stephen Drew	.40
4	Chipper Jones	.75
5	Andruw Jones	.40
6	Jeff Francoeur	.50
7	John Smoltz	.50
8	Miguel Tejada	.50
9	Nicholas Markakis	.50
10	Brian Roberts	.40
11	David Ortiz	.75
12	Manny Ramirez	.75
13	Josh Beckett	.75
14	Curt Schilling	.75
15	Derrek Lee	.50
16	Aramis Ramirez	.50
17	Carlos Zambrano	.50
18	Alfonso Soriano	.75
19	Jim Thome	.50
20	Paul Konerko	.50
21	Jon Garland	.25
22	Ken Griffey Jr.	1.50
23	Adam Dunn	.50
24	Aaron Harang	.25
25	Travis Hafner	.40
26	Victor Martinez	.50
27	Grady Sizemore	.75
28	C.C. Sabathia	.50
29	Todd Helton	.50
30	Matt Holliday	.50
31	Garrett Atkins	.40
32	Ivan Rodriguez	.50
33	Magglio Ordonez	.40
34	Gary Sheffield	.50
35	Justin Verlander	.50
36	Miguel Cabrera	.75
37	Hanley Ramirez	.75
38	Dontrelle Willis	.25
39	Lance Berkman	.50
40	Roy Oswalt	.50
41	Carlos Lee	.25
42	Gil Meche	.25
43	Emil Brown	.25
44	Mark Teahen	.25
45	Vladimir Guerrero	.75
46	Jered Weaver	.40
47	Howie Kendrick	.25
48	Juan Pierre	.25
49	Nomar Garciaparra	.75
50	Rafael Furcal	.40
51	Jeff Kent	.40
52	Prince Fielder	1.00
53	Ben Sheets	.40
54	Rickie Weeks	.40
55	Justin Morneau	.50
56	Joe Mauer	.50
57	Torii Hunter	.40
58	Johan Santana	.75
59	Jose Reyes	.75
60	David Wright	1.00
61	Carlos Delgado	.50
62	Carlos Beltran	.50
63	Derek Jeter	2.00
64	Alex Rodriguez	2.00
65	Johnny Damon	.50
66	Jason Giambi	.50
67	Bobby Abreu	.50
68	Mike Piazza	.75
69	Nick Swisher	.40
70	Eric Chavez	.25
71	Ryan Howard	1.00
72	Chase Utley	.75
73	Jimmy Rollins	.50
74	Jason Bay	.40
75	Freddy Sanchez	.25
76	Zachary Duke	.25
77	Greg Maddux	1.00
78	Adrian Gonzalez	.40
79	Jake Peavy	.40
80	Ray Durham	.25
81	Barry Zito	.25
82	Matt Cain	.25
83	Ichiro Suzuki	1.50
84	Felix Hernandez	.50
85	Richie Sexson	.40
86	Albert Pujols	2.00
87	Scott Rolen	.75
88	Chris Carpenter	.50
89	Chris Duncan	.25
90	Carl Crawford	.40
91	Rocco Baldelli	.25
92	Scott Kazmir	.25
93	Michael Young	.25
94	Mark Teixeira	.50
95	Ian Kinsler	.25
96	Troy Glaus	.40
97	Vernon Wells	.40
98	Roy Halladay	.40
99	Ryan Zimmerman	.50
100	Nick Johnson	.25
101	Zack Segovia (RC)	8.00
102	Joaquin Arias (RC)	8.00
104	Travis Buck (RC)	10.00
105	Mike Schultz RC	8.00
107	Sean Henn RC	8.00
108	Ryan Braun RC	10.00
109	Rick Vanden Hurk RC	10.00
110	Carlos Gomez/SP RC	15.00
111	Mike Rabelo RC	8.00
112	Felix Pie RC	15.00
113	Miguel Montero (RC)	8.00
114	Michael Bourn (RC)	8.00
115	Micah Owings/SP RC	15.00
116	Matt Lindstrom (RC)	15.00
117	Matt Chico (RC)	8.00
118	Levale Speigner RC	8.00
119	Lee Gardner (RC)	8.00
120	Kory Casto (RC)	8.00
121	Kevin Kouzmanoff (RC)	15.00
122	Kevin Cameron RC	8.00
123	Tyler Clippard (RC)	10.00
124	Juan Perez RC	8.00
125	Josh Hamilton/SP RC	40.00
127	Joseph Bisenius RC	8.00
128	Jose Garcia RC	8.00
129	Jon Knott RC	8.00
130	Jon Coutlangus (RC)	8.00
131	John Danks RC	12.00
132	Joe Smith RC	8.00
133	Matt Brown RC	8.00
134	Joakim Soria RC	20.00
135	Jesus Flores RC	8.00
136	Jeff Baker (RC)	8.00
137	Jay Marshall RC	10.00
138	Jared Burton RC	10.00
139	Jamie Vermilyea RC	8.00
140	Jamie Burke (RC)	8.00
141	Ryan Rowland-Smith (RC)	8.00
142	Connor Robertson (RC)	8.00
143	Hector Gimenez (RC)	8.00
144	Gustavo Molina RC	8.00
145	Glen Perkins (RC)	8.00
146	Joba Chamberlain/SP RC	60.00
147	Doug Slaten RC	8.00
148	Ryan Braun (RC)	70.00
149	Delmon Young/SP (RC)	20.00
150	Garrett Jones (RC)	15.00
152	Cesar Jimenez RC	8.00
153	Brian Stokes (RC)	8.00
154	Brian Burres (RC)	10.00
155	Brian Barden/SP RC	8.00
156	Kyle Kendrick RC	15.00
157	Andrew Miller RC	10.00
158	Alexi Casilla RC	10.00
159	Alex Gordon/SP RC	20.00
159	A.J. Murray RC	8.00
162	Adam Lind (RC)	12.00
163	Chase Wright RC	8.00
164	Dallas Braden RC	12.00
165	Rocky Cherry RC	10.00
166	Andy Gonzalez RC	8.00
167	Neal Musser RC	8.00
168	Mark Reynolds RC	25.00
169	Dennis Dove (RC)	10.00
170	Justin Hampson (RC)	8.00
171	Phil Hughes/SP (RC)	60.00
172	Kelvin Jimenez RC	8.00
173	Hunter Pence/SP (RC)	25.00
174	Brad Salmon RC	8.00
175	Ryan Sweeney (RC)	10.00
176	Brandon Wood (RC)	12.00
177	Billy Butler/SP (RC)	25.00
178	Ben Francisco (RC)	8.00
180	Yoel Hernandez (RC)	8.00
181	Tim Lincecum/SP RC	120.00
182	Danny Putnam (RC)	8.00
183	Jarrod Saltalamacchia/SP (RC)	12.00
184	Andy LaRoche/SP (RC)	15.00
185	Matt DeSalvo (RC)	10.00
186	Fred Lewis (RC)	10.00
187	Anthony Lerew (RC)	8.00
188	Jesse Litsch (RC)	10.00
189	Daisuke Matsuzaka/SP RC	100.00

Gold

Gold (1-100, 189): 3-6X
Production 99 Sets

Red

Red (1-100, 189): 2-4X
Production 199 Sets

All-Star Futures

NM/M
Common Player: 2.00
Production 500 Sets

AD	Alejandro De Aza	2.00
AG	Alex Gordon	8.00
AI	Akinori Iwamura	3.00
AL	Adam Lind	2.00
AM	Andrew Miller	4.00
BA	Jeff Baker	2.00
BI	Billy Butler	5.00
BM	Brandon Morrow	3.00
BU	B.J. Upton	3.00
BW	Brandon Wood	2.00
CA	Alexi Casilla	2.00
CG	Carlos Gomez	3.00
CW	Chase Wright	2.00
CY	Chris Young	3.00
DM	Daisuke Matsuzaka	8.00
DP	Danny Putnam	2.00
DY	Delmon Young	4.00
FL	Fred Lewis	2.00
FP	Felix Pie	3.00
GP	Glen Perkins	2.00
HA	Josh Hamilton	2.00
HK	Howie Kendrick	3.00
HP	Hunter Pence	8.00
IK	Ian Kinsler	3.00
JA	Joaquin Arias	2.00
JD	John Danks	2.00
JS	Jarrod Saltalamacchia	2.00
JV	Justin Verlander	3.00
KC	Kory Casto	2.00
KI	Kei Igawa	2.00
KK	Kevin Kouzmanoff	2.00
LA	Andy LaRoche	3.00
MA	Matt Chico	3.00
MB	Michael Bourn	2.00
MC	Matt Cain	2.00
MI	Miguel Montero	2.00
ML	Matt Lindstrom	2.00
MO	Micah Owings	2.00
PF	Prince Fielder	3.00
PH	Phil Hughes	6.00
RB	Ryan Braun	10.00
RS	Ryan Sweeney	2.00
RZ	Ryan Zimmerman	4.00
SD	Stephen Drew	3.00
SM	Joe Smith	2.00
SO	Joakim Soria	2.00
TB	Travis Buck	2.00
TL	Tim Lincecum	8.00
TP	Tony Pena	2.00
TT	Troy Tulowitzki	4.00

Clear Path to History Triple Auto.

NM/M
Some not priced due to scarcity.

CCH	Eric Chavez, Bobby Crosby, Rich Harden	15.00
CWR	Miguel Cabrera, Dontrelle Willis, Hanley Ramirez	60.00
DMY	Chris Young, Stephen Drew, Miguel Montero	25.00
FEG	Luis Gonzalez, Andre Ethier, Rafael Furcal	30.00
GKW	Vladimir Guerrero, Howie Kendrick, Jered Weaver/SP	100.00
GPC	Vladimir Guerrero, Albert Pujols, Miguel Cabrera/SP	200.00
HAT	Garrett Atkins, Matt Holliday, Troy Tulowitzki	75.00
HMS	Travis Hafner, Victor Martinez, Jeremy Sowers	40.00
KUC	Carl Crawford, Scott Kazmir, B.J. Upton	40.00
KUK	Ian Kinsler, Dan Uggla, Howie Kendrick	25.00
MPM	Melvin Mora, Corey Patterson, Nick Markakis	25.00
VZR	Justin Verlander, Ryan Zimmerman, Hanley Ramirez	40.00

Cy Young Futures

NM/M
Common Player: 2.00
Production 500 Sets

AL	Anthony Lerew	2.00
AM	Andrew Miller	4.00
BM	Brandon Morrow	3.00
CH	Cole Hamels	4.00
CW	Chase Wright	2.00
DM	Daisuke Matsuzaka	8.00
GP	Glen Perkins	2.00
JD	John Danks	2.00
JG	Jose Garcia	2.00
JL	Jon Lester	4.00
JS	Jeremy Sowers	2.00
JV	Justin Verlander	3.00
JZ	Joel Zumaya	2.00
KI	Kei Igawa	2.00
MA	Matt Chico	2.00
MC	Matt Cain	2.00
MO	Micah Owings	2.00
PH	Phil Hughes	6.00
RV	Rick Vanden Hurk	2.00
SH	Sean Henn	2.00
SK	Scott Kazmir	3.00
SM	Joe Smith	2.00
TC	Tyler Clippard	2.00
TL	Tim Lincecum	8.00
ZS	Zack Segovia	2.00

MVP Futures

NM/M
Common Player: 2.00
Production 500 Sets

AD	Alejandro De Aza	2.00
AG	Alex Gordon	8.00
AI	Akinori Iwamura	3.00
AL	Adam Lind	2.00
BA	Jeff Baker	2.00
BI	Billy Butler	5.00
BM	Brandon Morrow	3.00
BU	B.J. Upton	3.00
BW	Brandon Wood	2.00
CA	Alexi Casilla	2.00
CG	Carlos Gomez	3.00
CW	Chase Wright	2.00
CY	Chris Young	3.00
DM	Daisuke Matsuzaka	8.00
DP	Danny Putnam	2.00
DY	Delmon Young	4.00
FP	Felix Pie	3.00
HP	Hunter Pence	8.00
IK	Ian Kinsler	3.00
JA	Joaquin Arias	2.00
JB	Jeff Baker	2.00
JH	Josh Hamilton	2.00
JS	Jarrod Saltalamacchia	2.00
JV	Justin Verlander	

Rookie Dated Debuts

NM/M
Common Player: 2.00
Production 999 Sets
Autographs: No Pricing
Production 10 Sets

AC	Alexi Casilla	2.00
AD	Alejandro De Aza	2.00
AG	Alex Gordon	5.00
AI	Akinori Iwamura	2.00
AL	Adam Lind	2.00
BA	Jeff Baker	2.00
BB	Brian Barden	2.00
BI	Joseph Bisenius	2.00
BM	Brandon Morrow	2.00
BW	Brandon Wood	2.00
CA	Kory Casto	2.00
CG	Carlos Gomez	3.00
CR	Cal Ripken Jr.	10.00
CW	Chase Wright	2.00
DA	John Danks	2.00
DJ	Derek Jeter	10.00
DM	Daisuke Matsuzaka	8.00
DY	Delmon Young	3.00
ED	Elijah Dukes	2.00
FL	Fred Lewis	2.00
FP	Felix Pie	2.00
GM	Gustavo Molina	2.00
GP	Glen Perkins	2.00
HO	Hideki Okajima	3.00
HP	Hunter Pence	6.00
JA	Joaquin Arias	2.00
JC	Jon Coutlangus	2.00
JF	Jesus Flores	2.00
JH	Josh Hamilton	2.00
JM	Jay Marshall	2.00
JP	Juan Perez	2.00
JS	Joakim Soria	2.00
KC	Kevin Cameron	2.00
KG	Ken Griffey Jr.	8.00
KI	Kei Igawa	2.00
KK	Kevin Kouzmanoff	2.00
LA	Andy LaRoche	3.00
LG	Lee Gardner	2.00
MB	Michael Bourn	2.00
MC	Matt Chico	2.00
MM	Miguel Montero	2.00
MO	Micah Owings	2.00
MR	Mike Rabelo	2.00
PH	Phil Rollins	5.00
RS	Ryan Sweeney	2.00
SA	Jarrod Saltalamacchia	2.00
SM	Joe Smith	2.00
TB	Travis Buck	2.00
TL	Tim Lincecum	5.00
TT	Troy Tulowitzki	4.00

Two for the Bigs

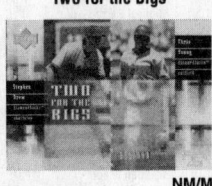

NM/M
Common Duo: 2.00
Production 999 Sets
Autographs: No Pricing
Production 10 Sets

AS	Joaquin Arias, Chris Stewart	2.00
BB	Michael Bourn, Joseph Bisenius	2.00
BD	Travis Buck, Elijah Dukes	2.00
BG	Ryan Braun, Alex Gordon	8.00
BS	Ryan Braun, Joakim Soria	8.00
BT	Jeff Baker, Troy Tulowitzki	4.00
CF	Kory Casto, Jesus Flores	2.00
CP	Alexi Casilla, Matt Chico	2.00
CS	Matt Chico, Levale Speigner	2.00
DG	Alejandro De Aza, Lee Gardner	2.00
DK	Daisuke Matsuzaka, Kei Igawa	6.00
DM	John Danks, Gustavo Molina	2.00
DT	Stephen Drew, Troy Tulowitzki	4.00
DV	Alejandro De Aza, Rick Vanden Hurk	2.00
DW	Chase Wright, Matt DeSalvo	2.00
DY	Chris Young, Stephen Drew	3.00
GB	Alex Gordon, Billy Butler	5.00
GF	Hector Gimenez, Jesus Flores	2.00
GI	Alex Gordon, Akinori Iwamura	5.00
GL	Alex Gordon, Andy LaRoche	5.00
GM	Alex Gordon, Daisuke Matsuzaka	8.00
GP	Hector Gimenez, Hunter Pence	4.00
HB	Josh Hamilton, Jared Burton	2.00
HD	Josh Hamilton, Alejandro De Aza	2.00
HL	Phil Hughes, Tim Lincecum	8.00
HP	Josh Hamilton, Hunter Pence	4.00
II	Akinori Iwamura, Kei Igawa	3.00
KC	Kevin Kouzmanoff, Kevin Cameron	2.00
LG	Matt Lindstrom, Lee Gardner	2.00
LV	Adam Lind	2.00
MG	Hector Gimenez, Miguel Montero	2.00
MI	Daisuke Matsuzaka, Akinori Iwamura	5.00
MO	Daisuke Matsuzaka, Hideki Okajima	5.00
MR	Gustavo Molina, Mike Rabelo	2.00
MW	Brandon Morrow, Sean White	2.00
OL	Micah Owings, Tim Lincecum	4.00
OM	Micah Owings, Miguel Montero	2.00
PB	Danny Putnam, Travis Buck	2.00
PD	Hunter Pence, Alejandro De Aza	4.00
PH	Josh Hamilton, Felix Pie	2.00
PP	Felix Pie, Hunter Pence	4.00
RS	Mike Rabelo, Chris Stewart	2.00
SM	Jarrod Saltalamacchia, Miguel Montero	2.00
ST	Jarrod Saltalamacchia, Troy Tulowitzki	4.00
SW	Joe Smith, Chase Wright	2.00
TB	Travis Buck, Billy Butler	3.00
WH	Chase Wright, Phil Hughes	4.00
YD	Delmon Young, Elijah Dukes	2.00
YM	Delmon Young, Daisuke Matsuzaka	5.00

All-Star Futures Auto.

NM/M
Common Auto.: 8.00

AG	Alex Gordon/SP	20.00
AI	Akinori Iwamura/SP	15.00
AL	Adam Lind	8.00
AM	Andrew Miller	10.00
BA	Jeff Baker	8.00
BI	Billy Butler	25.00
BU	B.J. Upton	10.00
BW	Brandon Wood	15.00
CA	Alexi Casilla	8.00
CG	Carlos Gomez	10.00
CW	Chase Wright	8.00
CY	Chris Young	15.00
DM	Daisuke Matsuzaka/SP	100.00
DP	Danny Putnam	8.00
DY	Delmon Young/SP	10.00
FL	Fred Lewis	10.00
FP	Felix Pie	15.00
GP	Glen Perkins	8.00
HA	Josh Hamilton	25.00
HK	Howie Kendrick	15.00
HP	Hunter Pence	20.00
IK	Ian Kinsler	20.00
JA	Joaquin Arias	8.00
JD	John Danks	10.00
JS	Jarrod Saltalamacchia	10.00
JV	Justin Verlander/SP	40.00
KC	Kory Casto	8.00
KI	Kei Igawa/SP	10.00
KK	Kevin Kouzmanoff	10.00
LA	Andy LaRoche	10.00
MA	Matt Chico	8.00
MC	Matt Cain	15.00
MI	Miguel Montero	8.00
ML	Matt Lindstrom	10.00
MO	Micah Owings	10.00
PF	Prince Fielder/SP	50.00
PH	Phil Hughes/SP	60.00
RB	Ryan Braun	60.00
RS	Ryan Sweeney	8.00
RZ	Ryan Zimmerman/SP	20.00
SD	Stephen Drew/SP	15.00
SM	Joe Smith	

SO	Joakim Soria	15.00
TB	Travis Buck	10.00
TL	Tim Lincecum	85.00
TP	Tony Pena	8.00
TT	Troy Tulowitzki	25.00

Cy Young Futures Auto.

		NM/M
Common Auto.:		8.00
AL	Anthony Lerew	8.00
AM	Andrew Miller	8.00
CW	Chase Wright	8.00
DM	Daisuke Matsuzaka/SP	80.00
GP	Glen Perkins	8.00
JD	John Danks	10.00
JG	Jose Garcia	8.00
JZ	Joel Zumaya	8.00
MA	Matt Chico	8.00
MC	Matt Cain	15.00
MO	Micah Owings	8.00
PH	Phil Hughes/SP	60.00
RV	Rick Vanden Hurk	10.00
SH	Sean Henn	8.00
SM	Joe Smith	8.00
TC	Tyler Clippard	8.00
TL	Tim Lincecum	80.00
ZS	Zack Segovia	8.00

MVP Futures Auto.

		NM/M
Common Auto.:		8.00
AG	Alex Gordon/SP	15.00
AL	Adam Lind	8.00
DM	Daisuke Matsuzaka/SP	80.00
FP	Felix Pie	15.00
HP	Hunter Pence	20.00
IK	Ian Kinsler	20.00
JA	Joaquin Arias	8.00
JB	Jeff Baker	8.00
JH	Josh Hamilton	25.00
JS	Jarrod Saltalamacchia	8.00
KK	Kevin Kouzmanoff	10.00
LA	Andy LaRoche	8.00
MB	Michael Bourn	10.00
MM	Miguel Montero	8.00
PF	Prince Fielder	50.00
RB	Ryan Braun	60.00
RS	Ryan Sweeney	8.00
TB	Travis Buck	10.00

2007 Upper Deck Goudey

		NM/M
Complete Set (288):		
Common Player (1-200):		.15
Common SP (201-240):		1.50
Inserted 1:6		
Common Heads Up (241-288):		2.00
Inserted 1:10		
Hobby Pack (8):		4.00
Hobby Box (24):		80.00
1	A.J. Burnett	.25
2	Aaron Boone	.15
3	Aaron Rowand	.25
4	Adam Dunn	.50
5	Adrian Beltre	.25
6	Albert Pujols	2.00
7	Ivan Rodriguez	.50
8	Alfonso Soriano	.75
9	Andruw Jones	.50
10	Andy Pettitte	.50
11	Aramis Ramirez	.40
12	B.J. Upton	.25
13	Barry Zito	.25
14	Bartolo Colon	.15
15	Ben Sheets	.25
16	Bobby Abreu	.25
17	Bobby Crosby	.15
18	Brian Giles	.15
19	Brian Roberts	.25
20	C.C. Sabathia	.40
21	Carlos Beltran	.75

22	Carlos Delgado	.50
23	Carlos Lee	.25
24	Carlos Zambrano	.25
25	Chad Cordero	.15
26	Chad Tracy	.15
27	Chipper Jones	.75
28	Craig Biggio	.25
29	Curt Schilling	.50
30	Danny Haren	.25
31	Darin Erstad	.15
32	David Ortiz	.75
33	Billy Wagner	.15
34	Derek Jeter	2.00
35	Derek Lee	.50
36	Dontrelle Willis	.25
37	Edgar Renteria	.25
38	Eric Chavez	.25
39	Felix Hernandez	.25
40	Garret Anderson	.25
41	Garrett Atkins	.25
42	Gary Sheffield	.50
43	Grady Sizemore	.75
44	Greg Maddux	1.50
45	Hank Blalock	.25
46	Hanley Ramirez	.75
47	J.D. Drew	.25
48	Jacque Jones	.15
49	Jake Peavy	.40
50	Jake Westbrook	.15
51	Jason Bay	.25
52	Jason Giambi	.50
53	Jason Schmidt	.25
54	Jason Varitek	.40
55	Troy Tulowitzki	.40
56	Jeff Francoeur	.40
57	Jeff Kent	.25
58	Jeremy Bonderman	.25
59	Jim Edmonds	.25
60	Jim Thome	.50
61	Jimmy Rollins	.50
62	Joe Mauer	.25
63	Johan Santana	.75
64	John Smoltz	.40
65	Johnny Damon	.25
66	Jose Reyes	.75
67	Josh Beckett	.40
68	Justin Morneau	.40
69	Ken Griffey Jr.	1.50
70	Kerry Wood	.15
71	Khalil Greene	.25
72	Lance Berkman	.25
73	Livan Hernandez	.15
74	Manny Ramirez	.75
75	Mark Mulder	.25
76	Chase Utley	.75
77	Mark Teixeira	.50
78	Miguel Tejada	.40
79	Miguel Cabrera	.75
80	Mike Piazza	.75
81	Pat Burrell	.25
82	Paul LoDuca	.15
83	Pedro Martinez	.75
84	Prince Fielder	1.00
85	Rafael Furcal	.25
86	Randy Johnson	.75
87	Richie Sexson	.25
88	Robinson Cano	.75
89	Roy Halladay	.40
90	Roy Oswalt	.40
91	Scott Rolen	.50
92	Tim Hudson	.25
93	Todd Helton	.50
94	Tom Glavine	.50
95	Torii Hunter	.40
96	Travis Hafner	.40
97	Trevor Hoffman	.40
98	Vernon Wells	.40
99	Vladimir Guerrero	.75
100	Zachary Duke	.15
101	Alex Rodriguez	2.00
102	Ryan Howard	1.00
103	Michael Barrett	.15
104	Ichiro Suzuki	1.50
105	Hideki Matsui	1.50
106	Jered Weaver	.40
107	Dan Uggla	.25
108	Ryan Freel	.15
109	Bill Hall	.15
110	Ray Durham	.15
111	Morgan Ensberg	.15
112	Shawn Green	.25
113	Brandon Webb	.40
114	Frank Thomas	.75
115	Corey Patterson	.15
116	Edwin Encarnacion	.25
117	Mike Cameron	.15
118	Matt Holliday	.40
119	Jhonny Peralta	.25
120	Nick Swisher	.25
121	Brad Penny	.15
122	Kenji Johjima	.25
123	Francisco Rodriguez	.25
124	Mark Teahen	.15
125	Jonathan Papelbon	.50
126	Carlos Guillen	.15
127	Freddy Sanchez	.15
128	Chien-Ming Wang	.75
129	Andre Ethier	.15
130	Matt Cain	.25
131	Austin Kearns	.15
132	Ramon Hernandez	.15
133	Chris Carpenter	.25
134	Michael Cuddyer	.15
135	Stephen Drew	.25
136	David Wright	.75
137	David DeJesus	.15
138	Gary Matthews	.15
139	Brandon Phillips	.15

140	Josh Barfield	.15
141	Alex Gordon	1.00
142	Scott Kazmir	.15
143	Luis Gonzalez	.15
144	Mike Sweeney	.15
145	Luis Castillo	.15
146	Huston Street	.15
147	Phil Hughes	1.00
148	Adrian Gonzalez	.25
149	Raul Ibanez	.15
150	Joe Crede	.15
151	Mark Loretta	.15
152	Adam LaRoche	.25
153	Troy Glaus	.40
154	Conor Jackson	.15
155	Michael Young	.25
156	Scott Podsednik	.15
157	David Eckstein	.15
158	Mike Jacobs	.15
159	Nomar Garciaparra	.75
160	Mariano Rivera	.50
161	Pedro Feliz	.15
162	Josh Hamilton	.15
163	Ryan Langerhans	.15
164	Willy Taveras	.15
165	Carl Crawford	.25
166	Melvin Mora	.15
167	Francisco Liriano	.25
168	Orlando Cabrera	.25
169	Chris Duncan	.15
170	Johnny Estrada	.15
171	Ryan Zimmerman	.50
172	Rickie Weeks	.25
173	Paul Konerko	.40
174	Jack Wilson	.15
175	Jorge Posada	.40
176	Magglio Ordonez	.25
177	Nick Johnson	.15
178	Geoff Jenkins	.15
179	Reggie Sanders	.15
180	Moises Alou	.25
181	Glen Perkins	.15
182	Brad Lidge	.15
183	Kevin Kouzmanoff	.15
184	Jorge Cantu	.15
185	Carlos Quentin	.15
186	Rich Harden	.15
187	Jose Vidro	.15
188	Aaron Harang	.15
189	Noah Lowry	.15
190	Jermaine Dye	.25
191	Victor Martinez	.25
192	Chone Figgins	.25
193	Aubrey Huff	.15
194	Jason Isringhausen	.15
195	Brian McCann	.40
196	Juan Pierre	.15
197	Delmon Young	.50
198	Felipe Lopez	.15
199	Brad Hawpe	.15
200	Justin Verlander	.40
201	Mike Schmidt	3.00
202	Nolan Ryan	4.00
203	Cal Ripken Jr.	4.00
204	Harmon Killebrew	3.00
205	Reggie Jackson	2.00
206	Johnny Bench	2.00
207	Carlton Fisk	2.00
208	Yogi Berra	3.00
209	Al Kaline	3.00
210	Alan Trammell	1.50
211	Bill Mazeroski	2.00
212	Bob Gibson	2.00
213	Brooks Robinson	2.00
214	Carl Yastrzemski	3.00
215	Don Mattingly	3.00
216	Fergie Jenkins	1.50
217	Jim Rice	1.50
218	Lou Brock	2.00
219	Rod Carew	2.00
220	Stan Musial	3.00
221	Tom Seaver	3.00
222	Tony Gwynn	3.00
223	Wade Boggs	2.00
224	Alex Rodriguez	4.00
225	David Wright	3.00
226	Ryan Howard	3.00
227	Ichiro Suzuki	3.00
228	Ken Griffey Jr.	3.00
229	Daisuke Matsuzaka	4.00
230	Kei Igawa	1.50
231	Akinori Iwamura	1.50
232	Derek Jeter	4.00
233	Albert Pujols	4.00
234	Greg Maddux	3.00
235	David Ortiz	3.00
236	Manny Ramirez	3.00
237	Johan Santana	2.00
238	Pedro Martinez	2.00
239	Roger Clemens	4.00
240	Vladimir Guerrero	2.00
241	Ken Griffey Jr.	5.00
242	Derek Jeter	5.00
243	Ichiro Suzuki	5.00
244	Cal Ripken Jr.	5.00
245	Daisuke Matsuzaka	5.00
246	Kei Igawa	2.00
247	Joe Mauer	2.00
248	Babe Ruth	5.00
249	Johnny Bench	3.00
250	Reggie Jackson	3.00
251	Carlton Fisk	3.00
252	Albert Pujols	5.00
253	Nolan Ryan	5.00
254	Ryan Howard	4.00
255	Mike Schmidt	4.00
256	Brooks Robinson	4.00
257	Harmon Killebrew	4.00

258	Alex Rodriguez	5.00
259	David Ortiz	4.00
260	David Wright	4.00
261	Al Kaline	4.00
262	Justin Verlander	3.00
263	Chase Utley	4.00
264	Justin Morneau	3.00
265	Ken Griffey Jr.	4.00
266	Derek Jeter	5.00
267	Ichiro Suzuki	4.00
268	Cal Ripken Jr.	5.00
269	Daisuke Matsuzaka	5.00
270	Kei Igawa	2.00
271	Joe Mauer	2.00
272	Babe Ruth	5.00
273	Johnny Bench	3.00
274	Reggie Jackson	3.00
275	Carlton Fisk	3.00
276	Albert Pujols	5.00
277	Nolan Ryan	5.00
278	Ryan Howard	4.00
279	Mike Schmidt	4.00
280	Brooks Robinson	4.00
281	Harmon Killebrew	4.00
282	Alex Rodriguez	5.00
283	David Ortiz	4.00
284	David Wright	4.00
285	Al Kaline	4.00
286	Justin Verlander	3.00
287	Chase Utley	4.00
288	Justin Morneau	3.00

1933 Goudey Originals

Inserted 2:Case
See 1933 Goudey Pricing

1934-36 Diamond Stars

No Pricing	
Production 15 Sets	
Autographs:	No Pricing
Production One Set	

1941 Double Play

No Pricing	
Production 15 Sets	
Autographs:	No Pricing
Production One Set	

Graphs

		NM/M
Common Autograph:		5.00
AC	Alberto Callaspo	5.00
AH	Aaron Harang	10.00
AK	Al Kaline/SP	150.00
AM	Andy Marte	5.00
AR	Aaron Rowand	8.00
BA	Brian Anderson	5.00
BB	Brian Bannister	8.00
BE	Johnny Bench/SP	150.00
BO	Boof Bonser	2.00
BU	B.J. Upton	5.00
CC	Carl Crawford	10.00
CF	Carlton Fisk/SP	50.00
CL	Cliff Lee	15.00
CO	Coco Crisp	5.00
CR	Cal Ripken Jr./SP	150.00
CY	Chris Young	8.00
DJ	Derek Jeter	150.00
FH	Felix Hernandez	30.00
GA	Garrett Atkins	5.00
GP	Glen Perkins	5.00
HA	Bill Hall	5.00
HI	Rich Hill	5.00
HR	Hanley Ramirez	25.00
JB	Jason Bay	10.00
JW	Jered Weaver	15.00
JZ	Joel Zumaya	8.00
KG	Ken Griffey Jr./SP	100.00
KJ	Kelly Johnson	8.00
KK	Kevin Kouzmanoff	8.00
LS	Luke Scott	8.00
MO	Justin Morneau	25.00
MS	Mike Schmidt/SP	80.00
RA	Reggie Abercrombie	5.00
RT	Ryan Theriot	20.00
RZ	Ryan Zimmerman	20.00
SA	Anibal Sanchez	5.00
SK	Scott Kazmir	8.00
TB	Taylor Buchholz	5.00
VM	Victor Martinez	15.00
YB	Yogi Berra/SP	75.00

Sports Royalty

		NM/M
Common Player:		2.00
AI	Akinori Iwamura	5.00
AP	Albert Pujols	8.00
AS	Alfonso Soriano	3.50
CC	Chris Carpenter	2.00
CR	Cal Ripken Jr.	15.00
DJ	Derek Jeter	20.00

SPORT ROYALTY

JOHAN SANTANA

DM	Daisuke Matsuzaka	8.00
DO	David Ortiz	4.00
DS	Dean Smith	3.00
ES	Emmitt Smith	5.00
GH	Gordie Howe	10.00
GM	Greg Maddux	5.00
HI	Martina Hingis	4.00
HR	Hanley Ramirez	3.00
JM	Justin Morneau	3.00
JN	Joe Namath	5.00
JV	Justin Verlander	2.00
JW	John Wooden	2.00
KB	Kobe Bryant	4.00
KD	Kevin Durant	4.00
KG	Ken Griffey Jr.	8.00
KH	Katie Hoff	2.00
KI	Kei Igawa	2.00
LE	Jeanette Lee	2.00
LJ	LeBron James	10.00
LT	LaDainian Tomlinson	8.00
MH	Mia Hamm	5.00
MJ	Michael Jordan	15.00
NR	Nolan Ryan	15.00
PI	Mike Piazza	4.00
PM	Peyton Manning	8.00
RH	Roy Halladay	2.00
RJ	Randy Johnson	3.00
RL	Ryan Lochte	2.00
SA	Johan Santana	3.00
SC	Sidney Crosby	15.00
TH	Trevor Hoffman	2.00
TW	Tiger Woods	20.00
VG	Vladimir Guerrero	3.00

Immortals Memorabilia

Inserted 1:288

Sports Royalty Auto.

		NM/M
Common Autograph:		15.00
AI	Akinori Iwamura	15.00
CR	Cal Ripken Jr.	250.00
DJ	Derek Jeter	175.00
DM	Daisuke Matsuzaka	100.00
DO	David Ortiz	60.00
GH	Gordie Howe	100.00
GM	Greg Maddux	160.00
HI	Martina Hingis	100.00
HR	Hanley Ramirez	30.00
JM	Justin Morneau	25.00
JV	Justin Verlander	60.00
JW	John Wooden	125.00
KG	Ken Griffey Jr.	100.00
KH	Katie Hoff	75.00
KI	Kei Igawa	20.00
LE	Jeanette Lee	150.00
LJ	LeBron James	300.00
LT	LaDainian Tomlinson	100.00
MH	Mia Hamm	125.00
RH	Roy Halladay	75.00
RL	Ryan Lochte	65.00
SC	Sidney Crosby	250.00
VG	Vladimir Guerrero	120.00

Memorabilia

BOBBY CROSBY

		NM/M
Common Player:		4.00
1	A.J. Burnett	4.00
2	Aaron Rowand	4.00
3	Adam Dunn	8.00
4	Adrian Beltre	4.00
5	Albert Pujols	20.00
6	Ivan Rodriguez	6.00
7	Alfonso Soriano	15.00
8	Andruw Jones	6.00
9	Andy Pettitte	8.00
10	Aramis Ramirez	8.00
11	B.J. Upton	6.00
12	Barry Zito	6.00
13	Bartolo Colon/SP	6.00
14	Ben Sheets	6.00
15	Bobby Abreu/SP	6.00
16	Bobby Crosby	4.00

18	Brian Giles	4.00
19	Brian Roberts	6.00
20	C.C. Sabathia	8.00
21	Carlos Beltran	8.00
22	Carlos Delgado	6.00
23	Carlos Lee	6.00
24	Carlos Zambrano	6.00
26	Chad Tracy	4.00
27	Chipper Jones	8.00
28	Craig Biggio	8.00
29	Curt Schilling	8.00
31	Darin Erstad	4.00
32	David Ortiz	10.00
33	Billy Wagner	6.00
34	Derek Jeter	20.00
35	Derrek Lee	8.00
36	Dontrelle Willis	6.00
37	Edgar Renteria	4.00
38	Eric Chavez	6.00
39	Felix Hernandez	8.00
40	Garret Anderson	4.00
41	Garrett Atkins	4.00
42	Gary Sheffield	8.00
43	Grady Sizemore	8.00
44	Greg Maddux	15.00
45	Hank Blalock	4.00
46	Hanley Ramirez	10.00
47	J.D. Drew	4.00
49	Jake Peavy	6.00
50	Jake Westbrook	4.00
51	Jason Bay	8.00
52	Jason Giambi	8.00
54	Jason Varitek	10.00
56	Jeff Francoeur	10.00
57	Jeff Kent	6.00
58	Jeremy Bonderman	6.00
59	Jim Edmonds	6.00
60	Jim Thome	6.00
61	Jimmy Rollins	8.00
62	Joe Mauer	8.00
63	Johan Santana	8.00
64	John Smoltz	8.00
66	Jose Reyes	20.00
67	Josh Beckett	8.00
68	Justin Morneau	8.00
69	Ken Griffey Jr.	15.00
70	Kerry Wood	6.00
71	Khalil Greene	6.00
72	Lance Berkman	6.00
73	Livan Hernandez	4.00
74	Manny Ramirez	8.00
75	Mark Mulder	4.00
76	Chase Utley	15.00
77	Mark Teixeira	8.00
78	Miguel Tejada	8.00
79	Miguel Cabrera	8.00
80	Mike Piazza	10.00
81	Pat Burrell	6.00
82	Paul LoDuca	4.00
83	Pedro Martinez	8.00
84	Prince Fielder	10.00
85	Rafael Furcal	6.00
86	Randy Johnson	8.00
87	Richie Sexson	6.00
88	Robinson Cano	8.00
89	Roy Halladay	8.00
90	Roy Oswalt	8.00
91	Scott Rolen	8.00
92	Tim Hudson	6.00
93	Todd Helton	8.00
94	Tom Glavine	8.00
95	Torii Hunter	6.00
96	Travis Hafner	6.00
97	Trevor Hoffman	6.00
98	Vernon Wells	6.00
99	Vladimir Guerrero	8.00
100	Zachary Duke	4.00

2007 UD Masterpieces

		NM/M
Complete Set (90):		50.00
Common Player (1-90):		.50
Pack (4):		8.00
Box (18):		120.00
1	Babe Ruth	4.00
2	Babe Ruth	4.00
3	Bobby Thomson	.50
4	Bill Mazeroski	1.00
5	Carlton Fisk	1.00
6	Kirk Gibson	1.00
7	Don Larsen	2.00
8	Lou Gehrig	3.00
9	Roger Maris	3.00
10	Cal Ripken Jr.	4.00
11	Bucky Dent	.50
12	Ryan Howard	3.00
13	Brooks Robinson	2.00
14	David Ortiz	4.00

15	Hideki Matsui	3.00
16	Roger Clemens	4.00
17	Sandy Koufax	5.00
18	Reggie Jackson	2.00
19	Ozzie Smith	3.00
20	Ty Cobb	3.00
21	Walter Johnson	2.00
22	Babe Ruth	4.00
23	Roy Campanella	2.00
24	Jackie Robinson	3.00
25	Carl Yastrzemski	4.00
26	Sandy Koufax	5.00
27	Daisuke Matsuzaka RC	4.00
28	Kei Igawa RC	1.00
29	Ken Griffey Jr.	3.00
30	Derek Jeter	4.00
31	David Ortiz	2.00
32	Vladimir Guerrero	2.00
33	Chase Utley	2.00
34	Troy Tulowitzki (RC)	2.00
35	Joe Mauer	1.00
36	Travis Hafner	1.00
37	Miguel Cabrera	2.00
38	Albert Pujols	4.00
39	Frank Thomas	2.00
40	Mike Piazza	2.00
41	Josh Hamilton	.50
42	Cal Ripken Jr., Tony Gwynn	3.00
43	Ichiro Suzuki	3.00
44	Hideki Matsui	3.00
45	Ken Griffey Jr.	4.00
46	Michael Jordan	4.00
47	John F. Kennedy	2.00
48	Randy Johnson	2.00
49	Albert Pujols	4.00
50	Carlos Beltran	1.50
51	Delmon Young	1.00
52	Johan Santana	2.00
53	Cal Ripken Jr.	4.00
54	Yogi Berra, Jackie Robinson	3.00
55	Cal Ripken Jr.	3.00
56	Hanley Ramirez	2.00
57	Victor Martinez	1.00
58	Cole Hamels	2.00
59	Bobby Doerr	1.00
60	Bruce Sutter	.50
61	Jason Bay	1.00
62	Luis Aparicio	.50
63	Stephen Drew	1.00
64	Jered Weaver	1.00
65	Alex Gordon RC	1.50
66	Howie Kendrick	.50
67	Ryan Zimmerman	1.00
68	Akinori Iwamura RC	1.00
69	Chien-Ming Wang	2.00
70	David Wright	2.00
71	Ryan Howard	3.00
72	Alex Rodriguez	4.00
73	Justin Morneau	1.50
74	Andrew Miller RC	1.00
75	Richard Nixon	1.00
76	Bill Clinton	1.00
77	Phil Hughes (RC)	3.00
78	Tom Glavine	2.00
79	Chipper Jones	2.00
80	Craig Biggio	1.00
81	Chris Chambliss	.50
82	Tim Lincecum RC	5.00
83	Billy Butler (RC)	1.00
84	Andy LaRoche (RC)	1.00
85	1969 New York Mets	1.00
86	2004 Boston Red Sox	2.00
87	Roberto Clemente	3.00
88	Chase Utley	2.00
89	Reggie Jackson	2.00
90	Curt Schilling	2.00

Printing Plates
No Pricing
Production one set per color.

Artist's Proof
Production One Set

Black Linen
Black Linen (1-90): 4-6X
Production 99 Sets

Blue Steel
Blue Steel (1-90): 4-8X
Production 50 Sets

Bronze
Production One Set

Celestial Blue
Production One Set

Deep Blue
Black Linen (1-90): 4-6X
Production 75 Sets

Green Linen
Green (1-90): 2-3X

Hades
Hades (1-90): 4-8X
Production 50 Sets

Ionised
Production One Set

Persian Blue Linen
Production One Set

Pinot Red
Pinot Red (1-90): 4-6X
Production 75 Sets

Red Linen
Production One Set

Rusted
Rusted (1-90): 4-8X
Production 50 Sets

Black
Black (1-90): 4-6X
Production 99 Sets

Urban Gray
Production One Set

5x7 Box Topper

		NM/M
Common Player:		5.00
Inserted 1:Box		
1	Cal Ripken Jr.	15.00
2	Ken Griffey Jr.	10.00
3	Derek Jeter	15.00
4	Sandy Koufax	15.00
5	Babe Ruth	15.00
6	Lou Gehrig	15.00
7	Travis Hafner	5.00
8	Victor Martinez	5.00
9	Jered Weaver	5.00
10	Phil Hughes	5.00
11	Bobby Doerr	5.00
12	Billy Butler	5.00
13	Andy LaRoche	5.00
14	Josh Hamilton	5.00
15	Reggie Jackson	8.00
16	Hanley Ramirez	8.00
17	Don Larsen	5.00
18	Ken Griffey Jr.	10.00
19	Jason Bay	5.00
20	Daisuke Matsuzaka	15.00

5x7 Box Topper Autograph

		NM/M
Inserted 1:Case		
2	Ken Griffey Jr.	85.00
3	Derek Jeter	150.00
7	Travis Hafner	25.00
8	Victor Martinez	25.00
9	Jered Weaver	30.00
10	Phil Hughes	60.00
11	Bobby Doerr	50.00
12	Billy Butler	40.00
13	Andy LaRoche	20.00
14	Josh Hamilton	30.00
15	Reggie Jackson	50.00
16	Hanley Ramirez	35.00
17	Don Larsen	65.00
18	Ken Griffey Jr.	85.00
19	Jason Bay	20.00
20	Daisuke Matsuzaka	80.00

Captured on Canvas

		NM/M
Common Player:		4.00
Bronze:		No Pricing
Forest Green:		No Pricing
Production One Set		
AB	Adrian Beltre	4.00
AD	Adam Dunn	8.00
AI	Akinori Iwamura	6.00
AJ	Andruw Jones	6.00
AP	Albert Pujols	25.00
BA	Bobby Abreu	6.00
BC	Bobby Crosby	4.00
BE	Carlos Beltran	4.00
BG	Brian Giles	4.00
BL	Brad Lidge	4.00
BO	Jeremy Bonderman	4.00
BR	Brian Roberts	6.00
BS	Ben Sheets	4.00
CA	Chris Carpenter	8.00
CB	Craig Biggio	6.00
CC	Carl Crawford	6.00
CF	Carlton Fisk	8.00
CJ	Chipper Jones	10.00
CL	Carlos Lee	6.00
CR	Coco Crisp	4.00
CS	C.C. Sabathia	6.00
CU	Chase Utley	15.00
CY	Carl Yastrzemski	10.00
DJ	Derek Jeter	25.00
DL	Derrek Lee	8.00
DM	Don Mattingly	20.00
DO	David Ortiz	15.00
DR	J.D. Drew	4.00
DW	Dontrelle Willis	6.00
EB	Erik Bedard	6.00
EC	Eric Chavez	6.00
EG	Eric Gagne	4.00
FH	Felix Hernandez	8.00
FL	Francisco Liriano	6.00
GA	Garrett Atkins	6.00
GL	Tom Glavine	8.00
GR	Khalil Greene	6.00
GS	Grady Sizemore	10.00
HA	Roy Halladay	6.00
HB	Hank Blalock	6.00
HE	Todd Helton	8.00
HR	Hanley Ramirez	10.00
HS	Huston Street	4.00
IR	Ivan Rodriguez	8.00
JA	Jason Bay	8.00
JB	Josh Beckett	8.00
JH	J.J. Hardy	6.00
JK	Jason Kendall	4.00
JM	Joe Mauer	8.00
JN	Joe Nathan	6.00
JP	Jake Peavy	8.00
JR	Jose Reyes	15.00
JS	John Smoltz	8.00
JV	Jason Varitek	6.00
JW	Jered Weaver	6.00
KG	Ken Griffey Jr.	20.00
LB	Lance Berkman	6.00
MA	Daisuke Matsuzaka	15.00
MC	Miguel Cabrera	8.00
MG	Marcus Giles	4.00
MH	Matt Holliday	6.00
MO	Magglio Ordonez	6.00
MR	Mariano Rivera	8.00
MT	Miguel Tejada	8.00
MY	Michael Young	6.00
PA	Jonathan Papelbon	6.00
RA	Manny Ramirez	8.00
RB	Rocco Baldelli	4.00
RC	Roger Clemens	10.00
RH	Rich Harden	4.00
RI	Cal Ripken Jr.	20.00
RJ	Randy Johnson	8.00
RO	Roy Oswalt	6.00
RW	Rickie Weeks	6.00
RZ	Ryan Zimmerman	8.00
SA	Johan Santana	8.00
SC	Curt Schilling	8.00
SH	Gary Sheffield	8.00
SK	Scott Kazmir	6.00
SR	Scott Rolen	6.00
TE	Mark Teixeira	8.00
TG	Tony Gwynn	10.00
TH	Tim Hudson	6.00
TR	Travis Hafner	6.00
VG	Vladimir Guerrero	8.00
VM	Victor Martinez	8.00
WC	Will Clark	8.00

Stroke of Genius Signatures

		NM/M
Common Autograph:		10.00
Parallel:		No Pricing
Production One Set		
AG	Adrian Gonzalez	15.00
AK	Al Kaline	30.00
AL	Andy LaRoche	15.00
BA	Bronson Arroyo	15.00
BB	Billy Butler	25.00
BO	Boof Bonser	10.00
BR	Brooks Robinson	40.00
BS	Ben Sheets	15.00
BU	B.J. Upton	15.00
CD	Chris Duffy	10.00
CF	Chone Figgins	15.00
CH	Cole Hamels	40.00
CQ	Carlos Quentin	15.00
CR	Cal Ripken Jr.	125.00
DH	Danny Haren	15.00
DJ	Derek Jeter	150.00
DO	David Ortiz	50.00
DU	Dan Uggla	10.00
DW	Dontrelle Willis	10.00
EC	Eric Chavez	10.00
GO	Alex Gordon	50.00
GP	Glen Perkins	10.00
HA	Justin Hampson	10.00
HI	Rich Hill	10.00
HK	Howie Kendrick	15.00
HP	Hunter Pence	20.00
HR	Hanley Ramirez	25.00
HS	Huston Street	10.00
HU	Torii Hunter	15.00
IK	Ian Kinsler	20.00
JA	Jason Bay	15.00
JB	Jeff Baker	10.00
JH	Josh Hamilton	15.00
JP	Jonathan Papelbon	20.00
JT	Jim Thome	30.00
JU	Justin Morneau	10.00
JV	Justin Verlander	30.00
JW	Jered Weaver	10.00
JZ	Joel Zumaya	10.00
KE	Austin Kearns	10.00
KG	Ken Griffey Jr.	80.00
KK	Kevin Kouzmanoff	15.00
LE	Cliff Lee	10.00
LI	Adam Lind	10.00
MB	Michael Bourn	15.00
MC	Matt Cain	15.00
MO	Micah Owings	15.00
MS	Mike Schmidt	50.00
PS	Phil Hughes	60.00
RA	Aramis Ramirez	10.00
RC	Roger Clemens	75.00
RH	Rich Harden	10.00
RO	Roy Oswalt	15.00
RZ	Ryan Zimmerman	25.00
SD	Stephen Drew	15.00
SH	Sean Henn	10.00
SK	Scott Kazmir	15.00
SO	Jeremy Sowers	10.00
TI	Tim Hudson	10.00
TL	Tim Lincecum	75.00
TR	Travis Hafner	15.00
TT	Troy Tulowitzki	25.00
VM	Victor Martinez	20.00
XN	Xavier Nady	10.00

2007 Upper Deck Premier

		NM/M
Common Player (1-200):		4.00
Production 99 Sets		
Common RC (201-244):		4.00
Production 199 Sets		
Box (1):		250.00
1	Roy Campanella	15.00
2	Ty Cobb	12.00
3	Mickey Cochrane	4.00
4	Dizzy Dean	8.00
5	Don Drysdale	8.00
6	Jimmie Foxx	8.00
7	Lou Gehrig	15.00
8	Lefty Grove	4.00
9	Rogers Hornsby	8.00
10	Walter Johnson	8.00
11	Eddie Mathews	10.00
12	Christy Mathewson	10.00
13	Johnny Mize	8.00
14	Thurman Munson	10.00
15	Mel Ott	8.00
16	Satchel Paige	10.00
17	Jackie Robinson	8.00
18	Babe Ruth	20.00
19	George Sisler	4.00
20	Honus Wagner	10.00
21	Cy Young	10.00
22	Luis Aparicio	4.00
23	Johnny Bench	10.00
24	Yogi Berra	10.00
25	Rod Carew	8.00
26	Orlando Cepeda	6.00
27	Bob Feller	8.00
28	Carlton Fisk	8.00
29	Bob Gibson	8.00
30	Jim "Catfish" Hunter	6.00
31	Reggie Jackson	8.00
32	Al Kaline	8.00
33	Harmon Killebrew	8.00
34	Buck Leonard	6.00
35	Juan Marichal	4.00
36	Bill Mazeroski	6.00
37	Willie McCovey	6.00
38	Joe Morgan	6.00
39	Eddie Murray	6.00
40	Jim Palmer	6.00
41	Tony Perez	6.00
42	Pee Wee Reese	4.00
43	Brooks Robinson	8.00
44	Nolan Ryan	20.00
45	Mike Schmidt	10.00
46	Tom Seaver	8.00
47	Enos Slaughter	4.00
48	Willie Stargell	6.00
49	Early Wynn	4.00
50	Robin Yount	8.00
51	Tony Gwynn	8.00
52	Cal Ripken Jr.	10.00
53	Ernie Banks	10.00
54	Wade Boggs	8.00
55	Steve Carlton	8.00
56	Will Clark	8.00
57	Fergie Jenkins	4.00
58	Bo Jackson	10.00
59	Don Mattingly	15.00
60	Stan Musial	10.00
61	Frank Robinson	8.00
62	Ryne Sandberg	8.00
63	Ozzie Smith	10.00
64	Carl Yastrzemski	10.00
65	Dave Winfield	8.00
66	Paul Molitor	8.00
67	Jason Bay	6.00
68	Freddy Sanchez	4.00
69	Josh Beckett	6.00
70	Carlos Beltran	8.00
71	Craig Biggio	6.00
72	Matt Holliday	8.00
73	A.J. Burnett	4.00
74	Miguel Cabrera	8.00
75	Dontrelle Willis	6.00
76	Chris Carpenter	8.00
77	Roger Clemens	15.00
78	Johnny Damon	6.00
79	Jermaine Dye	6.00
80	Jim Thome	8.00
81	Vladimir Guerrero	8.00
82	Travis Hafner	6.00
83	Victor Martinez	6.00
84	Trevor Hoffman	6.00
85	Derek Jeter	20.00
86	Ken Griffey Jr.	15.00
87	Randy Johnson	8.00
88	Andruw Jones	6.00
89	Derrek Lee	6.00
90	Greg Maddux	10.00
91	Magglio Ordonez	6.00
92	David Ortiz	10.00
93	Jake Peavy	6.00
94	Roy Oswalt	6.00
95	Mike Piazza	10.00
96	Jose Reyes	15.00
97	Ivan Rodriguez	8.00
98	Johan Santana	8.00
99	Scott Rolen	8.00
100	Curt Schilling	6.00
101	John Smoltz	8.00
102	Alfonso Soriano	8.00
103	Miguel Tejada	6.00
104	Frank Thomas	8.00
105	Chase Utley	10.00
106	Joe Mauer	8.00
107	Alex Rodriguez	20.00
108	Alex Rios	6.00
109	Justin Verlander	8.00
110	Ryan Howard	15.00
111	Jered Weaver	6.00
112	Francisco Liriano	6.00
113	David Wright	10.00
114	Felix Hernandez	8.00
115	Jeremy Sowers	4.00
116	Cole Hamels	8.00
117	B.J. Upton	8.00
118	Chien-Ming Wang	35.00
119	Justin Morneau	8.00
120	Jonny Gomes	6.00
121	Adrian Gonzalez	6.00
122	Bill Hall	4.00
123	Rich Harden	4.00
124	Rich Hill	6.00
125	Tadahito Iguchi	8.00
126	Scott Kazmir	6.00
127	Howie Kendrick	6.00
128	Dan Uggla	4.00
129	Hanley Ramirez	8.00
130	Josh Willingham	4.00
131	Nicholas Markakis	8.00
132	Grady Sizemore	8.00
133	Ian Kinsler	8.00
134	Jonathan Papelbon	8.00
135	Ryan Zimmerman	8.00
136	Stephen Drew	6.00
137	Adam Wainwright	4.00
138	Joel Zumaya	6.00
139	Prince Fielder	10.00
140	Carl Crawford	6.00
141	Huston Street	4.00
142	Matt Cain	8.00
143	Andre Ethier	4.00
144	Brian McCann	4.00
145	Josh Barfield	4.00
146	Anibal Sanchez	4.00
147	Brian Roberts	4.00
148	Brandon Webb	6.00
149	Chipper Jones	10.00
150	Tim Hudson	6.00
151	Adam LaRoche	4.00
152	Jeff Francoeur	6.00
153	Marcus Giles	4.00
154	Jason Varitek	6.00
155	Coco Crisp	4.00
156	Manny Ramirez	8.00
157	Trot Nixon	4.00
158	Carlos Zambrano	6.00
159	Mark Prior	6.00
160	Aramis Ramirez	6.00
161	Mark Buehrle	4.00
162	Paul Konerko	6.00
163	Adam Dunn	6.00
164	C.C. Sabathia	6.00
165	Todd Helton	8.00
166	Garrett Atkins	6.00
167	Jeremy Bonderman	6.00
168	Curtis Granderson	6.00
169	Sean Casey	4.00
170	Lance Berkman	6.00
171	Brad Lidge	4.00
172	Reggie Sanders	4.00
173	Brad Penny	4.00
174	Nomar Garciaparra	8.00
175	Jeff Kent	4.00
176	Chone Figgins	4.00
177	Ben Sheets	6.00
178	Rickie Weeks	6.00
179	Joe Nathan	4.00
180	Torii Hunter	8.00
181	Carlos Delgado	8.00
182	Tom Glavine	6.00
183	Paul LoDuca	4.00
184	Mariano Rivera	8.00
185	Robinson Cano	8.00
186	Bobby Abreu	6.00
187	Hideki Matsui	10.00
188	Barry Zito	6.00
189	Eric Chavez	4.00
190	Jimmy Rollins	8.00
191	Khalil Greene	4.00
192	Brian Giles	4.00
193	Jason Schmidt	4.00
194	Ichiro Suzuki	30.00
195	David Eckstein	4.00
196	Jim Edmonds	6.00
197	Mark Teixeira	8.00
198	Michael Young	6.00
199	Vernon Wells	6.00
200	Roy Halladay	8.00
201	Delmon Young (RC)	8.00
202	Andrew Miller RC	4.00
203	Troy Tulowitzki (RC)	6.00
204	Jeff Fiorentino (RC)	4.00
205	David Murphy (RC)	4.00
206	Jeff Baker (RC)	4.00
207	Kevin Hooper (RC)	4.00
208	Kevin Kouzmanoff (RC)	4.00
209	Adam Lind (RC)	4.00
210	Mike Rabelo RC	4.00
212	Mitch Maier RC	4.00
213	Ryan Braun (RC)	4.00
214	Vinny Rottino (RC)	4.00
215	Drew Anderson (RC)	4.00
216	Alexi Casilla RC	4.00
217	Glen Perkins (RC)	4.00
218	Cesar Jimenez RC	4.00
219	Tim Gradoville RC	4.00
220	Shane Youman (RC)	4.00
221	Billy Sadler (RC)	4.00
222	Patrick Misch (RC)	4.00
223	Juan Salas (RC)	4.00
224	Beltran Perez (RC)	4.00
225	Hector Gimenez (RC)	4.00
226	Philip Humber (RC)	4.00
227	Eric Stults RC	4.00
228	Dennis Sarfate (RC)	4.00
229	Andy Cannizaro (RC)	4.00
230	Juan Morillo (RC)	4.00
231	Fred Lewis (RC)	4.00
232	Ryan Sweeney (RC)	4.00
233	Chris Narveson (RC)	4.00
234	Michael Bourn (RC)	4.00
235	Joaquin Arias (RC)	4.00
236	Carlos Maldonado (RC)	4.00
237	Alvin Colina RC	4.00
238	Jon Knott (RC)	4.00
239	Justin Hampson (RC)	4.00
240	Jeff Salazar (RC)	4.00
241	Josh Fields (RC)	4.00
242	Delwyn Young (RC)	4.00
243	Daisuke Matsuzaka RC	20.00
244	Kei Igawa RC	6.00

Bronze
Bronze (201-244): 1X
Production 75 Sets

Printing Plates
Production one set per color.

Gold
Gold (201-244): 1-1.5X
Production 49 Sets

Platinum
Production One Set

Silver
Silver (201-244): 1X
Production 99 Sets

Autograph Parallel
No Pricing
Production 25 Sets

Emerging Stars Dual Auto

		NM/M
Production 50 Sets		
Bronze:		1-1.5X
Production 25 Sets		
Gold:		No Pricing
Production 10 Sets		
Platinum:		No Pricing
Production One Set		
BU	Josh Barfield, Dan Uggla	20.00
BV	Jeremy Bonderman, Justin Verlander	40.00
CA	Carlos Rios, Carl Crawford	30.00
FJ	Felix Hernandez, Jered Weaver	50.00
GB	Josh Barfield, Adrian Gonzalez	25.00
GC	Carl Crawford, Jonny Gomes	25.00
HP	Philip Humber, Mike Pelfrey	25.00
HS	Huston Street, Rich Harden	20.00
HV	Rich Harden, Justin Verlander	40.00
IK	Tadahito Iguchi, Ian Kinsler	25.00
KL	Francisco Liriano, Scott Kazmir	35.00
KS	Scott Kazmir, Jeremy Sowers	20.00
LH	Jon Lester, Craig Hansen	40.00
MB	Jeremy Brown, Joe Mauer	40.00
MG	Justin Morneau, Adrian Gonzalez	40.00
MH	Andrew Miller, Cole Hamels	50.00
MZ	Andrew Miller, Joel Zumaya	20.00
PH	Jonathan Papelbon, Craig Hansen	20.00
PW	Jonathan Papelbon, Adam Wainwright	
QD	Carlos Quentin, Stephen Drew	30.00
RB	Rickie Weeks, Bill Hall	20.00
RD	Jose Reyes, Stephen Drew	60.00
RR	Hanley Ramirez, Jose Reyes	75.00

RY	Alex Rios, Delmon Young	40.00
SH	Jeremy Sowers, Cole Hamels	25.00
SJ	Anibal Sanchez, Josh Johnson	20.00
SW	Adam Wainwright, Huston Street	30.00
TD	Stephen Drew, Troy Tulowitzki	30.00
TR	Troy Tulowitzki, Hanley Ramirez	30.00
UG	Jonny Gomes, B.J. Upton	25.00
UR	Dan Uggla, Hanley Ramirez	30.00
UU	Chase Utley, Dan Uggla	50.00
VH	Felix Hernandez, Justin Verlander	75.00
VM	Justin Verlander, Andrew Miller	75.00
WE	Josh Willingham, Andre Ethier	25.00
WK	Jered Weaver, Howie Kendrick	40.00
WL	Jered Weaver, Francisco Liriano	50.00
YT	Delmon Young, Troy Tulowitzki	40.00
ZW	Joel Zumaya, Adam Wainwright	30.00

Emerging Stars Triple Auto

NM/M
Production 50 Sets
Bronze: 1-1.5X
Production 25 Sets
Gold: No Pricing
Production 10 Sets
Platinum: No Pricing
Production One Set

ELS	James Loney, Andre Ethier, Takashi Saito	75.00
HHL	Cole Hamels, Rich Hill, Francisco Liriano	75.00
HQE	Carlos Quentin, Matt Holliday, Andre Ethier	75.00
KUK	Howie Kendrick, Dan Uggla, Ian Kinsler	40.00
LBG	Matt Garza, Francisco Liriano, Boof Bonser	40.00
MHL	Francisco Liriano, Cole Hamels, Andrew Miller	80.00
MKL	Jason Kubel, Francisco Liriano, Justin Morneau	40.00
MSK	Scott Kazmir, Jeremy Sowers, Andrew Miller	30.00
MVB	Andrew Miller, Justin Verlander, Jeremy Bonderman	100.00
MYE	Andre Ethier, Nicholas Markakis, Delmon Young	70.00
PSW	Adam Wainwright, Huston Street, Jonathan Papelbon	50.00
QEY	Carlos Quentin, Delmon Young, Andre Ethier	40.00
RRD	Hanley Ramirez, Stephen Drew, Jose Reyes	75.00
SHK	Scott Kazmir, Jeremy Sowers, Cole Hamels	50.00
TDR	Troy Tulowitzki, Stephen Drew, Hanley Ramirez	50.00
THA	Matt Holliday, Garrett Atkins, Troy Tulowitzki	50.00
UKW	Howie Kendrick, Chase Utley, Rickie Weeks	50.00
UUW	Rickie Weeks, Chase Utley, Dan Uggla	40.00
UYK	B.J. Upton, Scott Kazmir, Delmon Young	40.00
VMZ	Justin Verlander, Joel Zumaya, Andrew Miller	40.00
WHV	Jered Weaver, Justin Verlander, Felix Hernandez	50.00
WZS	Adam Wainwright, Joel Zumaya, Takashi Saito	40.00
YER	Alex Rios, Delmon Young, Andre Ethier	40.00

Hallmarks Autographs

NM/M
Production 5-57
Gold: No Pricing
Production 25 Sets
Platinum: No Pricing
Production One Set

LA	Luis Aparicio/57	25.00
MS	Mike Schmidt/48	40.00
OS	Ozzie Smith/57	50.00
PM	Paul Molitor/39	25.00
RJ	Reggie Jackson/47	50.00
RS	Ryne Sandberg/40	60.00
RY	Robin Yount/46	40.00
SC	Steve Carlton/27	35.00
WF	Whitey Ford/25	50.00
WM	Willie McCovey/45	30.00

Insignias Autographs

NM/M
Production 50 Sets
Gold: 1-1.5X
Production 25 Sets
Platinum: No Pricing
Production One Set

AK	Al Kaline	35.00
AM	Andrew Miller	15.00
BU	B.J. Upton	25.00
CR	Cal Ripken Jr.	100.00
DJ	Derek Jeter	150.00
DL	Derrek Lee	30.00
DM	Don Mattingly	60.00
DY	Delmon Young	15.00
EB	Ernie Banks	50.00
FH	Felix Hernandez	50.00
JM	Joe Mauer	50.00
JP	Jake Peavy	30.00
JR	Jose Reyes	50.00
JT	Jim Thome	50.00
JW	Jered Weaver	50.00
KG	Ken Griffey Jr.	90.00
MO	Justin Morneau	30.00
OS	Ozzie Smith	50.00
PA	Jim Palmer	20.00
TG	Tony Gwynn	40.00
TT	Troy Tulowitzki	25.00
WC	Will Clark	25.00

Noteworthy Autographs

NM/M
Production 1-86 15.00
Gold: No Pricing
Production 25 Sets
Platinum: No Pricing
Production One Set

AD	Andre Dawson/50	50.00
AK	Al Kaline/50	50.00
AS	Alfonso Soriano/35	35.00
BA	Jeff Bagwell/75	75.00
BE	Josh Beckett/50	40.00
BJ	Bo Jackson/35	75.00
BR	Brooks Robinson/35	40.00
CB	Craig Biggio/65	45.00
CC	Chris Carpenter/50	40.00
DB	Dusty Baker/25	30.00
DE	Dennis Eckersley/75	15.00
DS	Don Sutton/35	15.00
FJ	Fergie Jenkins/74	15.00
FR	Frank Robinson/31	40.00
GS	Gary Sheffield/86	35.00
JB	Jim Bunning/54	30.00
JC	Jack Clark/75	15.00
JM	Juan Marichal/65	25.00
JP	Jim Palmer/65	20.00
JS	Johan Santana/65	50.00
KW	Kerry Wood/35	20.00
LA	Luis Aparicio/35	15.00
MM	Mark Mulder/35	15.00
MO	Justin Morneau/50	15.00
MT	Miguel Tejada/50	25.00
PE	Jake Peavy/55	30.00
PM	Paul Molitor/40	25.00
RS	Ryne Sandberg/45	50.00
TG	Tom Glavine/47	60.00
TH	Torii Hunter/26	30.00
WB	Wade Boggs/65	25.00
AP	Albert Pujols/49	200.00
BF	Bob Feller/62	30.00
CF	Carlton Fisk/37	40.00
CR	Cal Ripken Jr./34	125.00
DJ	Derek Jeter/44	150.00
DM	Don Mattingly/35	75.00
HR	Hanley Ramirez/51	30.00
JB	Johnny Bench/45	50.00
JM	Joe Mauer/36	40.00
JT	Jim Thome/52	40.00
JZ	Joel Zumaya/62	15.00
KG	Ken Griffey Jr./56	75.00
RY	Robin Yount/29	50.00
TG	Tony Gwynn/56	40.00

Preeminence

NM/M
Production 50 Sets
Gold: 1-1.5X
Production 25 Sets
Platinum: No Pricing
Production One Set

AP	Albert Pujols	200.00
BJ	Bo Jackson	60.00
BR	Brooks Robinson	25.00
CC	Chris Carpenter	25.00
CR	Cal Ripken Jr.	120.00
CY	Carl Yastrzemski	50.00
DJ	Derek Jeter	150.00
GM	Greg Maddux	100.00
JB	Johnny Bench	50.00
JM	Joe Mauer	40.00
JT	Jim Thome	40.00
JV	Justin Verlander	50.00
KG	Ken Griffey Jr.	75.00
MS	Mike Schmidt	50.00
NR	Nolan Ryan	90.00
RC	Roger Clemens	100.00
RJ	Reggie Jackson	50.00
RS	Ryne Sandberg	60.00
SM	Stan Musial	50.00
TG	Tony Gwynn	40.00
VG	Vladimir Guerrero	50.00

Foursomes

No Pricing
Production 15 Sets

Octographs

No Pricing
Production Five Sets

Pairings

NM/M
Production 25 Sets

AK	Andruw Jones, Ken Griffey Jr.	100.00
BD	Dave Winfield, Bo Jackson	75.00
BF	Johnny Bench, Carlton Fisk	75.00
BJ	Yogi Berra, Derek Jeter	250.00
BM	Don Mattingly, Wade Boggs	120.00
BU	Chase Utley, Craig Biggio	75.00
CG	Chris Carpenter, Bob Gibson	50.00
CO	Chris Carpenter, Roy Oswalt	60.00
CR	Craig Biggio, Ryne Sandberg	100.00
ER	Ernie Banks, Ryne Sandberg	150.00
GF	Bob Feller, Roy Oswalt	125.00
GO	Bob Feller, Bob Gibson	50.00
GR	Cal Ripken Jr., Ken Griffey Jr.	250.00
JG	Ken Griffey Jr., Derek Jeter	250.00
JW	Dave Winfield, Reggie Jackson	75.00
MC	Don Mattingly, Will Clark	80.00
MG	Tony Gwynn, Stan Musial	125.00
MM	Joe Mauer, Victor Martinez	50.00
MR	Frank Robinson, Eddie Murray	75.00
OY	Carl Yastrzemski, David Ortiz	125.00
PG	Albert Pujols, Ken Griffey Jr.	250.00
RG	Tony Gwynn, Cal Ripken Jr.	200.00
RJ	Cal Ripken Jr., Derek Jeter	250.00
RN	Roger Clemens, Nolan Ryan	275.00
RP	Ivan Rodriguez, Mike Piazza	75.00
RR	Cal Ripken Jr., Brooks Robinson	180.00
SA	Luis Aparicio, Ozzie Smith	75.00
SB	Brooks Robinson, Scott Rolen	60.00
SG	Alfonso Soriano, Vladimir Guerrero	80.00
SM	Ryne Sandberg, Joe Morgan	75.00
TM	Willie McCovey, Jim Thome	60.00
WC	Dontrelle Willis, Miguel Cabrera	50.00
YM	Paul Molitor, Robin Yount	80.00

Patches Dual

NM/M
Production 75 unless noted.
Platinum: No Pricing
Production 5-10
Masterpiece: No Pricing
Production One Set
Gold: .75-1X
Production 6-58
No pricing prod. 25 or less.

AD	Adam Dunn	20.00
AP	Albert Pujols	60.00
AS	Alfonso Soriano	20.00
BU	B.J. Upton	20.00
CH	Cole Hamels	25.00
CR	Cal Ripken Jr.	50.00
CU	Chase Utley	25.00
DJ	Derek Jeter	40.00
DJ2	Derek Jeter	40.00
DM	Don Mattingly	35.00
ED	Jim Edmonds	20.00
FL	Francisco Liriano	15.00
GM	Greg Maddux	30.00
IR	Ivan Rodriguez	20.00
JB	Johnny Bench	30.00
JG	Jason Giambi	15.00
JM	Joe Mauer	20.00
JO	Randy Johnson	20.00
JP	Jake Peavy	15.00
JR	Jose Reyes	20.00
JT	Jim Thome	20.00
JT2	Jim Thome	20.00
JV	Justin Verlander/42	25.00
JW	Jered Weaver	20.00
KG	Ken Griffey Jr.	40.00
KG2	Ken Griffey Jr.	40.00
KM	Kendry Morales	15.00
LB	Lance Berkman	15.00
MC	Miguel Cabrera	20.00
MR	Manny Ramirez	25.00
MS	Mike Schmidt	35.00
MT	Mark Teixeira	20.00
NR	Nolan Ryan	50.00
PF	Prince Fielder	20.00
PM	Pedro Martinez	30.00
RJ	Reggie Jackson	25.00
RS	Ryne Sandberg	40.00
RZ	Ryan Zimmerman	25.00
SA	Johan Santana	25.00
TE	Miguel Tejada	20.00
TG	Tony Gwynn	25.00
TO	Tom Glavine	30.00
VG	Vladimir Guerrero	25.00
VG2	Vladimir Guerrero	25.00

Patches Triple

NM/M
Production 1-99
Gold: .75-1X
Production 1-57
No pricing prod. 25 or less.
Platinum: No Pricing
Production Five Sets
Masterpiece: No Pricing
Production One Set

AJ	Andruw Jones/97	30.00
CC	Chris Carpenter/97	30.00
CD	Carlos Delgado/94	25.00
CJ	Chipper Jones/95	40.00
CL	Carlos Lee/99	20.00
CR	Cal Ripken Jr./82	60.00
CS	Curt Schilling/90	30.00
EM	Eddie Murray/77	30.00
FR	Frank Robinson/56	25.00
FT	Frank Thomas/90	30.00
GM	Greg Maddux/87	40.00
JT	Jim Thome/91	25.00
KG	Ken Griffey Jr./89	50.00
MR	Manny Ramirez/94	25.00
OS	Ozzie Smith/56	50.00
RJ	Randy Johnson/89	30.00
RO	Roy Halladay/95	25.00
TE	Miguel Tejada/98	20.00
TG	Tony Gwynn/82	40.00
TS	Tom Seaver/67	35.00
VG	Vladimir Guerrero/97	30.00
WB	Wade Boggs/82	30.00
JT2	Jim Thome/91	20.00
KG2	Ken Griffey Jr./89	50.00

Penmanship Autographs

NM/M
Production 1-98
Masterpiece: No Pricing
Production One Set

AK	Al Kaline/53	30.00
BF	Bob Feller/36	25.00
BJ	Bo Jackson/86	40.00
BR	Brooks Robinson/57	30.00
CB	Craig Biggio/88	50.00
CC	Chris Carpenter/97	40.00
CF	Carlton Fisk/72	25.00
CR	Cal Ripken Jr./82	100.00
CR2	Cal Ripken Jr./82	100.00
CY	Carl Yastrzemski/61	60.00
DJ	Derek Jeter/96	150.00
DJ2	Derek Jeter/96	150.00
DL	Derrek Lee/97	25.00
DM	Don Mattingly/83	50.00
DM2	Don Mattingly/83	50.00
EB	Ernie Banks/54	60.00
GM	Greg Maddux/87	80.00
IR	Ivan Rodriguez/91	40.00
JB	Johnny Bench/68	50.00
JI	Jim Palmer/65	25.00
JS	John Smoltz/88	75.00
JT	Jim Thome/91	40.00
KG	Ken Griffey Jr./89	75.00
KG2	Ken Griffey Jr./89	75.00
LA	Luis Aparicio/56	25.00
MS	Mike Schmidt/73	50.00
NR	Nolan Ryan/68	100.00
OZ	Ozzie Smith/78	50.00
PM	Paul Molitor/78	35.00
PM2	Paul Molitor/78	35.00
RA	Randy Johnson/89	25.00
RC	Roger Clemens/84	100.00
RJ	Reggie Jackson/68	65.00
RS	Ryne Sandberg/82	50.00
RY	Robin Yount/74	45.00
SC	Steve Carlton/87	25.00
SM	Stan Musial/42	40.00
SR	Scott Rolen/97	35.00
TE	Miguel Tejada/98	25.00
TG	Tony Gwynn/82	40.00
TG2	Tony Gwynn	30.00
TP	Tony Perez/65	30.00
VG	Vladimir Guerrero/97	60.00
WB	Wade Boggs/82	35.00
WC	Will Clark/86	25.00
WF	Whitey Ford/50	50.00
WM	Willie McCovey/59	50.00
YB	Yogi Berra/47	50.00

Remnants Triple

NM/M
Production 75 Sets
Gold: .75-1.5X
Production 6-60
No pricing prod. 25 or less.
Platinum: No Pricing
Production 10 Sets
Masterpiece: No Pricing
Production One Set

AP	Albert Pujols	30.00
AP2	Albert Pujols	30.00
AS	Alfonso Soriano	15.00
BM	Bill Mazeroski	20.00
BR	Babe Ruth	400.00
CA	Roy Campanella	35.00
CF	Carlton Fisk	15.00
CJ	Chipper Jones	25.00
CL	Roger Clemens	25.00
CR	Cal Ripken Jr.	30.00
CS	Curt Schilling	15.00
CU	Chase Utley	25.00
CY	Carl Yastrzemski	25.00
DJ	Derek Jeter	30.00
DJ2	Derek Jeter	30.00
DM	Don Mattingly	40.00
DO	David Ortiz	25.00
EM	Eddie Mathews	30.00
FR	Frank Robinson	20.00
HO	Rogers Hornsby	80.00
JB	Johnny Bench	20.00
JD	Joe DiMaggio	125.00
JO	Jose Reyes	30.00
JR	Jackie Robinson	75.00
JT	Jim Thome	20.00
KG	Ken Griffey Jr.	25.00
KG2	Ken Griffey Jr.	25.00
MO	Mel Ott	50.00
MR	Manny Ramirez	15.00
MS	Mike Schmidt	25.00
NR	Nolan Ryan	40.00
PM	Paul Molitor	15.00
PR	Pee Wee Reese	25.00
RC	Roberto Clemente	75.00
RJ	Reggie Jackson	30.00
RO	Brooks Robinson	15.00
RS	Ryne Sandberg	25.00
RY	Robin Yount	25.00
SM	Stan Musial	30.00
TG	Tony Gwynn	20.00
TM	Thurman Munson	35.00
VG	Vladimir Guerrero	15.00

Remnants Quad

NM/M
Production 1-96
Gold: .75-1.5X
Production 2-57
No pricing prod. 25 or less.
Platinum: No Pricing
Production Five Sets
Masterpiece: No Pricing
Production One Set

AK	Al Kaline/53	35.00
BM	Bill Mazeroski/56	30.00
CL	Roberto Clemente/55	120.00
CR	Cal Ripken Jr./82	50.00
DJ	Derek Jeter/96	50.00
DM	Don Mattingly/83	25.00
EM	Eddie Mathews/52	40.00
HK	Harmon Killebrew/55	40.00
JB	Johnny Bench/68	25.00
JD	Joe DiMaggio/36	125.00
JF	Jimmie Foxx/27	100.00
JR	Jackie Robinson/47	100.00
JT	Jim Thome/91	15.00
KG	Ken Griffey Jr./89	25.00
LG	Lou Gehrig/25	400.00
MI	Johnny Mize/36	40.00
MS	Mike Schmidt/73	30.00
NR	Nolan Ryan/68	60.00
RC	Roger Clemens/84	30.00
RJ	Reggie Jackson/68	25.00
RN	Brooks Robinson/57	25.00
RO	Roy Campanella/48	25.00
SM	Stan Musial/42	40.00
TM	Thurman Munson/70	40.00

Six

Production 10 Sets

Stitchings

NM/M
Production 50 Sets
Stitchings 35: 1X
Production 35 Sets

1	Babe Ruth	40.00
2	Babe Ruth	40.00
3	Babe Ruth	40.00
4	Ty Cobb	25.00
5	Ty Cobb	25.00
6	Lou Gehrig	30.00
7	Lou Gehrig	30.00
8	Joe DiMaggio	30.00
9	Joe DiMaggio	30.00
12	Roberto Clemente	30.00
13	Roberto Clemente	30.00
14	Jackie Robinson	30.00
15	Jackie Robinson	30.00
16	Cy Young	15.00
17	Cy Young	15.00
18	Nolan Ryan	30.00
19	Nolan Ryan	30.00
20	Reggie Jackson	15.00
21	Reggie Jackson	15.00
22	Ken Griffey Jr.	25.00
23	Ken Griffey Jr.	25.00
24	Derek Jeter	30.00
25	Derek Jeter	30.00
26	Jimmie Foxx	20.00
27	Jimmie Foxx	20.00
28	Rogers Hornsby	20.00
29	Walter Johnson	25.00
30	Walter Johnson	25.00
31	Ernie Banks	25.00
32	Ernie Banks	25.00
33	Ernie Banks	25.00
34	Christy Mathewson	15.00
35	Johnny Mize	20.00
36	Thurman Munson	25.00
37	Thurman Munson	25.00
38	Mel Ott	15.00
39	Satchel Paige	20.00
40	George Sisler	15.00
41	Casey Stengel	15.00
42	Honus Wagner	25.00
43	Honus Wagner	25.00
44	Roy Campanella	20.00
45	Mickey Cochrane	15.00
46	Dizzy Dean	15.00
47	Don Drysdale	15.00
48	Lefty Grove	15.00
49	Roger Clemens	25.00
50	Roger Clemens	25.00
51	Cal Ripken Jr.	40.00
52	Cal Ripken Jr.	40.00
53	Tony Gwynn	20.00
54	Tony Gwynn	20.00
55	Johnny Bench	20.00
56	Yogi Berra	20.00
57	Carlton Fisk	15.00
58	Joe Morgan	15.00
59	Brooks Robinson	15.00
60	Mike Schmidt	25.00
61	Willie Stargell	20.00
62	Tom Seaver	20.00
63	Ozzie Smith	25.00
64	Albert Pujols	30.00
65	Albert Pujols	30.00
66	Ryan Howard	25.00
67	David Ortiz	20.00
68	Randy Johnson	25.00
69	Greg Maddux	20.00
70	Greg Maddux	20.00
71	Johan Santana	20.00
72	Al Kaline	15.00
73	Ryne Sandberg	20.00
74	Robin Yount	20.00
75	Frank Robinson	15.00
76	Frank Robinson	15.00
78	Stan Musial	30.00
79	Carl Yastrzemski	20.00
80	Don Mattingly	30.00
81	Ichiro Suzuki	30.00
82	Yogi Berra	15.00
83	Carlton Fisk, Johnny Bench	20.00
84	Johnny Bench, Thurman Munson	25.00
85	Babe Ruth, Lou Gehrig	35.00
86	Yogi Berra, Whitey Ford	20.00
87	Yogi Berra, Don Larsen	20.00
88	Dennis Eckersley, Kirk Gibson	15.00
90	Pee Wee Reese, Jackie Robinson	20.00
91	Jackie Robinson, Satchel Paige	25.00
92	Lou Gehrig, Cal Ripken Jr.	30.00
93	George Sisler, Ichiro Suzuki	30.00
94	Steve Carlton, Roger Clemens, Randy Johnson, Nolan Ryan	40.00
95	Dave Concepcion, Tony Perez, Johnny Bench, Joe Morgan	25.00
96	Babe Ruth, Jimmie Foxx, Mel Ott, Eddie Mathews	40.00
97	Roger Clemens, Greg Maddux, Tom Seaver, Nolan Ryan	40.00
98	Roberto Clemente, Tony Gwynn, Stan Musial, Cal Ripken Jr.	40.00
DM	Daisuke Matsuzaka	60.00
KI	Kei Igawa	25.00
MI	Daisuke Matsuzaka, Kei Igawa	50.00

Stitchings Cuts

Production One Set

Trios Autographs

No Pricing
Production 20 Sets

Rare Patches Dual

NM/M
Production 50 Sets
Gold: 1-1.5X
Production 25 Sets
Platinum: No Pricing
Production 10 Sets
Masterpiece: No Pricing
Production One Set

BM	Joe Mauer, Johnny Bench	40.00
BR	Brian Roberts, Robinson Cano	25.00
BS	Anibal Sanchez, A.J. Burnett	25.00
CP	Jake Peavy, Chris Carpenter	25.00
CW	Miguel Cabrera, Dontrelle Willis	30.00
DB	Carlos Beltran, Carlos Delgado	30.00
DT	Miguel Tejada, Stephen Drew	25.00
ER	Scott Rolen, Jim Edmonds	40.00
FM	Justin Morneau, Prince Fielder	30.00
FW	Prince Fielder, Rickie Weeks	30.00
GP	Albert Pujols, Ken Griffey Jr.	75.00
HR	Trevor Hoffman, Mariano Rivera	40.00
HS	Jeremy Sowers, Cole Hamels	

JG	Ken Griffey Jr., Derek Jeter	75.00
MJ	Andruw Jones, Chipper Jones	40.00
MG	Tom Glavine, Greg Maddux	70.00
MH	Travis Hafner, Victor Martinez	25.00
MJ	Derek Jeter, Don Mattingly	80.00
OT	Jim Thome, David Ortiz	35.00
PO	Roy Oswalt, Jake Peavy	25.00
PS	Curt Schilling, Jonathan Papelbon	50.00
RC	Roger Clemens, Nolan Ryan	80.00
RD	Derek Jeter, Reggie Jackson	50.00
RG	Cal Ripken Jr., Tony Gwynn	75.00
RJ	Roy Halladay, Johan Santana	40.00
RU	Jimmy Rollins, Chase Utley	50.00
SG	Alfonso Soriano, Vladimir Guerrero	40.00
SH	Johan Santana, Felix Hernandez	40.00
SM	Joe Morgan, Ryne Sandberg	50.00
TR	Miguel Tejada, Jose Reyes	40.00
TT	Jim Thome, Frank Thomas	40.00
UC	Carl Crawford, B.J. Upton	40.00
WJ	Josh Johnson, Dontrelle Willis	20.00
WL	Francisco Liriano, Jered Weaver	30.00
YM	Robin Yount, Paul Molitor	40.00
ZU	Ryan Zimmerman, B.J. Upton	30.00

Rare Patches Triple
NM/M

Production 25 Sets
Gold: No Pricing
Production 10 Sets
Platinum: No Pricing
Production Five Sets
Masterpiece: No Pricing
Production One Set

CRM	Nolan Ryan, Greg Maddux, Roger Clemens	125.00
MRM	Ivan Rodriguez, Victor Martinez, Joe Mauer	40.00
POG	Albert Pujols, David Ortiz, Vladimir Guerrero	80.00
RGM	Cal Ripken Jr., Tony Gwynn, Paul Molitor	100.00
SHK	Scott Kazmir, Jeremy Sowers, Cole Hamels	30.00
UWR	Chase Utley, Rickie Weeks, Brian Roberts	30.00
WLV	Francisco Liriano, Justin Verlander, Jered Weaver	50.00

Rare Remnants Quad
No Pricing
Production 25 Sets
Gold: No Pricing
Production 10 Sets
Platinum: No Pricing
Production Five Sets
Masterpiece: No Pricing
Production One Set

Rare Remnants Triple
NM/M

Production 50 Sets
Gold: 1-1.5X
Production 25 Sets
Platinum: No Pricing
Production 10 Sets
Masterpiece: No Pricing
Production One Set

BMP	Tony Perez, Joe Morgan, Johnny Bench	30.00
BZV	Jeremy Bonderman, Justin Verlander, Joel Zumaya	25.00
CBF	Brooks Robinson, Frank Robinson, Cal Ripken Jr.	50.00
CFY	Jimmie Foxx, Joe Cronin, Carl Yastrzemski	60.00
CMK	Ralph Kiner, Bill Mazeroski, Roberto Clemente	100.00
CPR	Chris Carpenter, Albert Pujols, Scott Rolen	40.00
DMP	Jorge Posada, Thurman Munson, Bill Dickey	50.00
DMR	Pedro Martinez, Carlos Delgado, Jose Reyes	40.00
DRB	Jose Reyes, Carlos Delgado, Carlos Beltran	40.00
FBM	Carlton Fisk, Thurman Munson, Johnny Bench	35.00
FGG	Hank Greenberg, Lou Gehrig, Jimmie Foxx	180.00

FMT	Justin Morneau, Mark Teixeira, Prince Fielder	25.00
GGJ	Andruw Jones, Ken Griffey Jr., Vladimir Guerrero	40.00
JCM	Greg Maddux, Randy Johnson, Roger Clemens	40.00
JJR	Derek Jeter, Randy Johnson, Mariano Rivera	50.00
JMM	Thurman Munson, Don Mattingly, Reggie Jackson	75.00
KUC	B.J. Upton, Carl Crawford, Scott Kazmir	25.00
KVJ	Joe Mauer, Victor Martinez, Kenji Johjima	25.00
LMS	Joe Mauer, Francisco Liriano, Johan Santana	25.00
LSH	Francisco Liriano, Jeremy Sowers, Cole Hamels	25.00
OPS	Jake Peavy, Roy Oswalt, Ben Sheets	20.00
OTB	Lance Berkman, David Ortiz, Jim Thome	25.00
PJG	Derek Jeter, Ken Griffey Jr., Albert Pujols	50.00
PMH	Albert Pujols, Stan Musial, Rogers Hornsby	80.00
RCD	Nolan Ryan, Don Drysdale, Roger Clemens	50.00
RDG	Lou Gehrig, Joe DiMaggio, Babe Ruth	475.00
RFS	Bruce Sutter, Rollie Fingers, Mariano Rivera	25.00
RRR	Nolan Ryan	60.00
RWH	Nolan Ryan, Felix Hernandez, Jered Weaver	25.00
RYS	Robin Yount, Cal Ripken Jr., Ozzie Smith	40.00
SGA	Vladimir Guerrero, Bobby Abreu, Alfonso Soriano	25.00
SHM	Joe Morgan, Rogers Hornsby, Ryne Sandberg	50.00
SJZ	Randy Johnson, Barry Zito, Johan Santana	25.00
SRB	Brooks Robinson, Wade Boggs, Mike Schmidt	40.00
TJY	Miguel Tejada, Derek Jeter, Michael Young	30.00
TTH	Mark Teixeira, Jim Thome, Todd Helton	20.00
VWJ	Josh Johnson, Justin Verlander, Jered Weaver	25.00
YBM	Paul Molitor, Wade Boggs, Robin Yount	25.00

World Series Ticket
Production One

Patches Dual Auto.
NM/M

Production 25 Sets

AD	Adam Dunn	40.00
BR	Brooks Robinson	50.00
BU	B.J. Upton	40.00
CH	Cole Hamels	50.00
CR	Cal Ripken Jr.	180.00
DJ	Derek Jeter	200.00
DM	Don Mattingly	140.00
FL	Francisco Liriano	40.00
IR	Ivan Rodriguez	50.00
JB	Johnny Bench	60.00
KM	Kendry Morales	30.00
NR	Nolan Ryan	150.00
RJ	Reggie Jackson	75.00
RS	Ryne Sandberg	75.00

Patches Triple Auto.
No Pricing
Production 15 Sets

Penmanship Auto. Jersey Number
NM/M

Production 1-58

AM	Andrew Miller/50	15.00
CF	Carlton Fisk/27	40.00
CH	Cole Hamels/35	50.00
CZ	Carlos Zambrano/38	15.00
DL	Derek Lee/25	35.00
DW	Dontrelle Willis/35	15.00
DY	Delmon Young/35	15.00
FH	Felix Hernandez/34	50.00
FL	Francisco Liriano/47	30.00
GM	Greg Maddux/36	100.00
JG	Jonny Gomes/31	15.00
JP	Jake Peavy/44	40.00
JS	John Smoltz/29	65.00
JV	Justin Verlander/35	50.00
JW	Jered Weaver/56	25.00
JZ	Joel Zumaya/54	15.00
MO	Justin Morneau/33	30.00
NR	Nolan Ryan/34	100.00
NS	Nick Swisher/33	20.00
PA	Jonathan Papelbon/58	25.00
PH	Philip Humber/49	15.00
RA	Randy Johnson/41	50.00
RO	Roy Oswalt/45	25.00
SA	John Santana/57	40.00
SC	Steve Carlton/32	25.00
SR	Scott Rolen/27	40.00
VG	Vladimir Guerrero/27	50.00
VM	Victor Martinez/41	25.00
WB	Wade Boggs/26	40.00
WM	Willie McCovey/44	40.00

Remnants Triple Autograph
No Pricing
Production 25 Sets

Remnants Quad Autograph
Production 15 Sets

Stitchings Autograph
No Pricing
Production 25 Sets

2007 Upper Deck Spectrum

NM/M

#		
	Complete Set (149):	
	Common Player (1-100):	.25
	Common Auto. (101-149):	8.00
	Pack (5):	5.00
	Box (20):	80.00
1	Miguel Tejada	.50
2	Brian Roberts	.40
3	Melvin Mora	.25
4	David Ortiz	1.00
5	Manny Ramirez	.75
6	Jason Varitek	.50
7	Curt Schilling	.75
8	Jim Thome	.50
9	Paul Konerko	.40
10	Jermaine Dye	.40
11	Travis Hafner	.50
12	Victor Martinez	.50
13	Grady Sizemore	.50
14	C.C. Sabathia	.50
15	Ivan Rodriguez	.50
16	Magglio Ordonez	.40
17	Carlos Guillen	.25
18	Justin Verlander	.50
19	Shane Costa	.25
20	Emil Brown	.25
21	Mark Teahen	.25
22	Vladimir Guerrero	.50
23	Jered Weaver	.50
24	Juan Rivera	.25
25	Justin Morneau	.75
26	Joe Mauer	.75
27	Torii Hunter	.40
28	Johan Santana	.75
29	Derek Jeter	2.00
30	Alex Rodriguez	2.00
31	Johnny Damon	.75
32	Jason Giambi	.50
33	Frank Thomas	.50
34	Nick Swisher	.40
35	Eric Chavez	.25
36	Ichiro Suzuki	1.50
37	Raul Ibanez	.25
38	Richie Sexson	.40
39	Carl Crawford	.40
40	Rocco Baldelli	.40
41	Scott Kazmir	.40
42	Michael Young	.40
43	Mark Teixeira	.50
44	Carlos Lee	.40
45	Gary Matthews	.25
46	Vernon Wells	.50
47	Roy Halladay	.50
48	Lyle Overbay	.25
49	Brandon Webb	.50
50	Conor Jackson	.25
51	Stephen Drew	.50
52	Chipper Jones	.75
53	Andruw Jones	.50
54	Adam LaRoche	.25
55	John Smoltz	.50
56	Derek Lee	.50
57	Aramis Ramirez	.50
58	Carlos Zambrano	.50
59	Ken Griffey Jr.	1.50
60	Adam Dunn	.40
61	Aaron Harang	.40
62	Todd Helton	.50
63	Matt Holliday	.50
64	Garrett Atkins	.40
65	Miguel Cabrera	.75
66	Hanley Ramirez	.50
67	Dontrelle Willis	.25
68	Lance Berkman	.50
69	Roy Oswalt	.50
70	Roger Clemens	1.50
71	J.D. Drew	.40
72	Nomar Garciaparra	.75
73	Rafael Furcal	.40
74	Jeff Kent	.40
75	Prince Fielder	1.00
76	Bill Hall	.25
77	Rickie Weeks	.40
78	Jose Reyes	.75
79	David Wright	1.00
80	Carlos Delgado	.50
81	Carlos Beltran	.50
82	Ryan Howard	1.00
83	Chase Utley	.75

#		
84	Jimmy Rollins	.75
85	Jason Bay	.40
86	Freddy Sanchez	.25
87	Zachary Duke	.25
88	Trevor Hoffman	.25
89	Adrian Gonzalez	.50
90	Mike Piazza	.75
91	Ray Durham	.25
92	Omar Vizquel	.25
93	Jason Schmidt	.40
94	Albert Pujols	2.00
95	Scott Rolen	.75
96	Jim Edmonds	.50
97	Chris Carpenter	.50
98	Alfonso Soriano	.75
99	Ryan Zimmerman	.75
100	Nick Johnson	.25
101	Adam Lind (RC)	10.00
102	Alexi Casilla/SP RC	10.00
103	Andrew Miller RC	8.00
104	Andy Cannizaro RC	8.00
105	Angel Sanchez/SP RC	10.00
106	Brian Stokes (RC)	8.00
107	Carlos Maldonado (RC)	8.00
108	Cesar Jimenez RC	8.00
109	Chris Stewart RC	8.00
111	David Murphy (RC)	10.00
112	Delmon Young/SP (RC)	15.00
113	Delwyn Young (RC)	8.00
114	Dennis Sarfate (RC)	8.00
116	Drew Anderson (RC)	8.00
117	Fred Lewis (RC)	10.00
118	Glen Perkins (RC)	8.00
119	Hector Gimenez (RC)	8.00
120	Jeff Baker (RC)	8.00
121	Jeff Fiorentino (RC)	8.00
122	Jeff Salazar (RC)	8.00
124	Joaquin Arias (RC)	8.00
125	Jon Knott (RC)	8.00
128	Juan Morillo RC	8.00
129	Juan Perez RC	8.00
130	Juan Salas (RC)	8.00
131	Justin Hampson (RC)	8.00
132	Kevin Hooper/SP (RC)	12.00
133	Kevin Kouzmanoff (RC)	10.00
134	Michael Bourn (RC)	15.00
135	Miguel Montero (RC)	8.00
136	Mike Rabelo/SP RC	10.00
137	Mitch Maier (RC)	8.00
138	Oswaldo Navarro/SP RC	10.00
139	Patrick Misch (RC)	8.00
140	Philip Humber (RC)	10.00
141	Ryan Braun (RC)	10.00
143	Ryan Sweeney (RC)	8.00
144	Scott Moore (RC)	8.00
145	Sean Henn/SP (RC)	10.00
146	Shawn Riggans (RC)	8.00
148	Troy Tulowitzki (RC)	25.00
149	Ubaldo Jimenez (RC)	40.00

Gold
Stars (1-100): 5-10X
Production 99 Sets

Red
Stars (1-100): 5-10X
Production 99 Sets

Jersey Number
Jersey # (25-57): 5-10X
No pricing production 1-24.
Cards are #'d to jersey number.

Grand Slamarama
NM/M

	Common Player:	10.00
AD	Adam Dunn	15.00
AP	Albert Pujols	50.00
AR	Alex Rodriguez	40.00
BA	Bobby Abreu	15.00
BG	Brian Giles	10.00
CD	Carlos Delgado	20.00
CJ	Chipper Jones	30.00
DA	Johnny Damon	25.00
DO	David Ortiz	30.00
DW	David Wright	40.00
HA	Travis Hafner	15.00
JD	Jermaine Dye	15.00
JM	Justin Morneau	20.00
JT	Jim Thome	20.00
KG	Ken Griffey Jr.	40.00
MR	Manny Ramirez	25.00
NG	Nomar Garciaparra	15.00
RH	Ryan Howard	40.00
RS	Richie Sexson	20.00
VG	Vladimir Guerrero	20.00

Ripken Road to the Hall

NM/M

	Common Ripken:	8.00

	Production 99 Sets	
	Autographs:	No Pricing
	Production Five Sets	
CR1-100	Cal Ripken Jr.	8.00

Rookie Retrospectrum

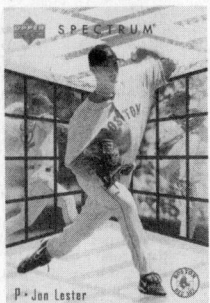

NM/M

	Common Player:	.50
	Red:	2-4X
	Production 99 Sets	
AE	Andre Ethier	.50
AW	Adam Wainwright	1.00
BA	Josh Barfield	.50
BB	Boof Bonser	.50
BO	Jason Botts	.50
CA	Matt Capps	.50
CB	Chad Billingsley	.50
CD	Chris Demaria	.50
CF	Choo Freeman	.50
CH	Clay Hensley	.50
CQ	Carlos Quentin	.50
DE	Chris Denorfia	.50
DU	Dan Uggla	.50
FC	Fausto Carmona	.50
FL	Francisco Liriano	1.00
HA	Cole Hamels	1.00
HK	Howie Kendrick	1.00
HR	Hanley Ramirez	1.00
JA	Jeremy Accardo	.50
JB	Jason Bergmann	.50
JC	Jose Capellan	.50
JD	Joey Devine	.50
JH	Jeremy Hermida	.50
JK	Jason Kubel	.50
JL	Jon Lester	1.00
JP	Jonathan Papelbon	1.00
JV	Justin Verlander	1.00
JW	Jered Weaver	1.00
JZ	Joel Zumaya	1.00
KM	Kendry Morales	1.00
LM	Lastings Milledge	1.00
MA	Nicholas Markakis	1.00
MC	Matt Cain	1.00
ME	Melky Cabrera	1.00
MG	Matt Garza	1.00
MJ	Mike Jacobs	.50
MM	Matt Murton	.50
NM	Nate McLouth	.50
PF	Prince Fielder	1.00
RA	Reggie Abercrombie	.50
RG	Ryan Garko	.50
RM	Russell Martin	.50
RP	Ronny Paulino	.50
RS	Ryan Shealy	.50
RZ	Ryan Zimmerman	1.00
SD	Stephen Drew	1.00
TB	Taylor Buchholz	.50
TG	Tony Gwynn Jr.	.50
TS	Takashi Saito	.50
WI	Josh Willingham	.50

Season Retrospectrum
NM/M

	Common Player:	.50
	Red:	2-4X
	Production 99 Sets	
AH	Aaron Harang	.50
AP	Albert Pujols	4.00
AR	Aramis Ramirez	1.00
AS	Alfonso Soriano	1.50
BA	Bobby Abreu	1.50
BH	Bill Hall	.50
BL	Joe Blanton	.50
CA	Miguel Cabrera	1.50
CB	Carlos Beltran	1.00
CC	Chris Carpenter	1.00
CD	Carlos Delgado	1.00
CO	Jose Contreras	1.50
CU	Chase Utley	1.50
CW	Chien-Ming Wang	1.50
CY	Chris Young	1.50
CZ	Carlos Zambrano	1.50
DJ	Derek Jeter	4.00
DO	David Ortiz	1.50
FS	Freddy Sanchez	1.00
FT	Frank Thomas	1.00
GM	Greg Maddux	2.50
GS	Grady Sizemore	1.50
HO	Trevor Hoffman	.50
HR	Hanley Ramirez	1.00
JB	Jason Bay	1.00
JC	Joe Crede	.50
JD	Johnny Damon	1.50
JM	Joe Mauer	1.50
JR	Jose Reyes	1.50
JS	Jeff Suppan	.50
JT	Jim Thome	1.50
KG	Ken Griffey Jr.	3.00

MC	Michael Cuddyer	.50
MH	Matt Holliday	.50
ML	Mark Loretta	.50
MO	Justin Morneau	1.50
MY	Michael Young	1.00
NG	Nomar Garciaparra	1.50
OR	Magglio Ordonez	.50
OV	Omar Vizquel	.50
RC	Roger Clemens	3.00
RF	Rafael Furcal	.50
RH	Ryan Howard	3.00
SA	Johan Santana	1.50
SK	Scott Kazmir	.50
TH	Travis Hafner	1.00
TI	Tadahito Iguchi	.50
VG	Vladimir Guerrero	1.50
VW	Vernon Wells	.50
WT	Willy Taveras	.50

Shining Star Signatures
NM/M

Production 15-99

AD	Adam Dunn/99	25.00
AG	Adrian Gonzalez/99	25.00
AP	Albert Pujols/50	180.00
AR	Alex Rios/99	15.00
BH	Bill Hall/99	10.00
CJ	Conor Jackson/54	15.00
CZ	Carlos Zambrano/99	15.00
DJ	Derek Jeter/54	200.00
DL	Derek Lee/99	30.00
DO	David Ortiz/99	60.00
GA	Garrett Atkins/99	15.00
HR	Hanley Ramirez/99	25.00
JB	Jason Bay/99	15.00
JM	Joe Mauer/99	40.00
JR	Jose Reyes/99	25.00
JS	Johan Santana/99	50.00
KG	Ken Griffey Jr./99	70.00
KY	Kevin Youkilis/99	15.00
MH	Matt Holliday/99	30.00
MO	Justin Morneau/99	25.00
RI	Juan Rivera/99	10.00
TH	Travis Hafner/72	15.00

Aligning the Stars

NM/M

Production 99 Sets

BPO	David Ortiz, Lance Berkman, Albert Pujols	30.00
CJM	Roger Clemens, Greg Maddux, Randy Johnson	30.00
CRR	Scott Rolen, Aramis Ramirez, Miguel Cabrera	25.00
DBF	Lance Berkman, Prince Fielder, Carlos Delgado	15.00
GRS	Manny Ramirez, Gary Sheffield, Ken Griffey Jr.	35.00
HRW	Trevor Hoffman, Mariano Rivera, Billy Wagner	20.00
HTT	Travis Hafner, Frank Thomas, Jim Thome	20.00
JDB	Andruw Jones, Carlos Beltran, Adam Dunn	25.00
JGC	Jason Giambi, Derek Jeter, Robinson Cano	60.00
JTY	Derek Jeter, Miguel Tejada, Michael Young	30.00
LHP	Albert Pujols, Derek Lee, Todd Helton	30.00
LVP	Francisco Liriano, Justin Verlander, Jonathan Papelbon	30.00
MKT	Mark Teixeira, Justin Morneau, Paul Konerko	20.00
MOW	Pedro Martinez, Roy Oswalt, Dontrelle Willis	20.00
RFR	Jose Reyes, Jimmy Rollins, Rafael Furcal	20.00
RMM	Ivan Rodriguez, Victor Martinez, Joe Mauer	20.00
RSV	Jason Varitek, Curt Schilling, Manny Ramirez	30.00
SBA	Carlos Beltran, Alfonso Soriano, Bobby Abreu	25.00
SCF	Carl Crawford, Grady Sizemore, Chone Figgins	20.00
SHS	Johan Santana, Roy Halladay, C.C. Sabathia	20.00
WGD	Vladimir Guerrero, Vernon Wells, Johnny Damon	20.00

Super Swatches
NM/M

Production 50 Sets

AD	Adam Dunn	10.00
AJ	Andruw Jones	15.00

Code	Player	Price
AP	Albert Pujols	35.00
AR	Aramis Ramirez	10.00
BA	Bobby Abreu	10.00
BC	Bobby Crosby	10.00
BE	Josh Beckett	15.00
BU	B.J. Upton	15.00
BZ	Barry Zito	10.00
CB	Carlos Beltran	8.00
CC	Carl Crawford	10.00
CD	Carlos Delgado	10.00
CJ	Chipper Jones	15.00
CL	Roger Clemens	25.00
CS	Curt Schilling	15.00
CU	Chase Utley	20.00
DA	Johnny Damon	15.00
DJ	Derek Jeter	35.00
DL	Derrek Lee	10.00
DO	David Ortiz	25.00
FT	Frank Thomas	15.00
GS	Gary Sheffield	15.00
HA	Travis Hafner	10.00
HR	Hanley Ramirez	15.00
JB	Jeremy Bonderman	10.00
JD	J.D. Drew	10.00
JR	Jose Reyes	25.00
JS	Johan Santana	15.00
JT	Jim Thome	15.00
JV	Jason Varitek	15.00
JW	Jered Weaver	15.00
KG	Ken Griffey Jr.	30.00
KJ	Kenji Johjima	10.00
LB	Lance Berkman	10.00
MT	Miguel Tejada	10.00
PE	Andy Pettitte	10.00
PF	Prince Fielder	10.00
PK	Paul Konerko	10.00
RB	Rocco Baldelli	10.00
RC	Robinson Cano	20.00
RH	Roy Halladay	15.00
RJ	Randy Johnson	15.00
RS	Richie Sexson	10.00
SR	Scott Rolen	15.00
TH	Todd Helton	10.00
VE	Justin Verlander	15.00
VG	Vladimir Guerrero	15.00
VW	Vernon Wells	10.00

Spectrum Swatches

NM/M
Production 199 Sets
Gold: 1X
Production 75 Sets
Patch: 2-3X
Production 50 Sets

Code	Player	Price
AB	Adrian Beltre	4.00
AG	Adrian Gonzalez	6.00
AH	Aaron Hill	4.00
AK	Austin Kearns	4.00
AP	Albert Pujols	25.00
AR	Aaron Rowand	4.00
AS	Alfonso Soriano	10.00
BA	Bobby Abreu	4.00
BC	Bartolo Colon	4.00
BG	Brian Giles	4.00
BI	Brandon Inge	4.00
BJ	B.J. Upton	6.00
BL	Joe Blanton	4.00
BR	B.J. Ryan	4.00
BS	Ben Sheets	4.00
BW	Billy Wagner	6.00
CA	Jorge Cantu	4.00
CB	Clint Barmes	4.00
CC	Chad Cordero	4.00
CD	Chris Duffy	4.00
CG	Carlos Guillen	4.00
CK	Casey Kotchman	4.00
CO	Coco Crisp	6.00
CR	Bobby Crosby	4.00
CS	C.C. Sabathia	8.00
CU	Chase Utley	15.00
CY	Chris Young	6.00
CZ	Carlos Zambrano	8.00
DA	Johnny Damon	10.00
DC	Daniel Cabrera	6.00
DH	Danny Haren	6.00
DJ	Derek Jeter	25.00
DL	Derrek Lee	6.00
DM	Dallas McPherson	4.00
DO	David Ortiz	15.00
DU	Dan Uggla	6.00
DW	Dontrelle Willis	6.00
ES	Johnny Estrada	4.00
FG	Freddy Garcia	4.00
FL	Francisco Liriano	6.00
FS	Freddy Sanchez	4.00
GA	Garrett Atkins	4.00
GC	Gustavo Chacin	4.00
GR	Curtis Granderson	8.00
GS	Grady Sizemore	10.00
HR	Hanley Ramirez	8.00
HS	Huston Street	6.00
HU	Aubrey Huff	4.00
IS	Ian Snell	4.00
JB	Jeremy Bonderman	10.00
JC	Joe Crede	6.00
JD	J.D. Drew	6.00
JE	Jermaine Dye	6.00
JF	Jeff Francoeur	8.00
JH	J.J. Hardy	6.00
JM	Joe Mauer	10.00
JN	Joe Nathan	6.00
JP	Jake Peavy	8.00
JR	Jose Reyes	8.00
JT	Jim Thome	8.00
JU	Justin Duchscherer	4.00
JW	Jake Westbrook	4.00
KG	Ken Griffey Jr.	25.00
KH	Khalil Greene	6.00
LN	Laynce Nix	4.00
MA	Matt Cain	8.00
MB	Mark Buehrle	4.00
MC	Mike Cameron	4.00
ME	Morgan Ensberg	4.00
MH	Matt Holliday	8.00
MI	Michael Cuddyer	6.00
MM	Melvin Mora	4.00
MO	Justin Morneau	10.00
MT	Miguel Tejada	8.00
NL	Noah Lowry	4.00
NS	Nick Swisher	6.00
OR	Magglio Ordonez	6.00
PA	Jonathan Papelbon	15.00
PE	Jhonny Peralta	6.00
PF	Prince Fielder	10.00
PL	Paul LoDuca	4.00
RA	Aramis Ramirez	8.00
RF	Rafael Furcal	8.00
RH	Rich Harden	8.00
RJ	Reed Johnson	4.00
RO	Brian Roberts	6.00
RQ	Robb Quinlan	4.00
RW	Rickie Weeks	8.00
RZ	Ryan Zimmerman	15.00
SC	Sean Casey	4.00
SK	Scott Kazmir	8.00
TH	Torii Hunter	8.00
TI	Tadahito Iguchi	6.00
TN	Trot Nixon	6.00
VM	Victor Martinez	6.00
WT	Willy Taveras	6.00
YM	Yadier Molina	6.00
ZD	Zachary Duke	6.00
ZG	Zack Greinke	6.00

Rookie Retrospectrum Signatures

NM/M
Production 199 unless noted.

Code	Player	Price
BB	Boof Bonser	8.00
BO	Jason Botts	8.00
CA	Matt Capps/134	10.00
CD	Chris Demaria	8.00
CF	Choo Freeman	8.00
CH	Clay Hensley	8.00
CQ	Carlos Quentin	20.00
DU	Dan Uggla	15.00
FC	Fausto Carmona/158	8.00
FL	Francisco Liriano	25.00
HA	Cole Hamels/90	35.00
HK	Howie Kendrick	20.00
HR	Hanley Ramirez	25.00
JA	Jeremy Accardo/32	10.00
JC	Jose Capellan	6.00
JD	Joey Devine	8.00
JH	Jeremy Hermida	10.00
JK	Jason Kubel	8.00
JL	Jon Lester	25.00
JP	Jonathan Papelbon	20.00
JW	Jered Weaver/99	40.00
JZ	Joel Zumaya	15.00
KM	Kendry Morales	15.00
MG	Matt Garza	20.00
MJ	Mike Jacobs	12.00
MM	Matt Murton	10.00
RA	Reggie Abercrombie	8.00
RG	Ryan Garko	10.00
RM	Russell Martin	10.00
RS	Ryan Shealy	10.00
RZ	Ryan Zimmerman	30.00
SD	Stephen Drew	25.00
TB	Taylor Buchholz	10.00
TS	Takashi Saito	10.00
WI	Josh Willingham	15.00

Retrospectrum Signatures

Production 25 unless noted.

Code	Player	Price
AS	Alfonso Soriano	40.00
BA	Bobby Abreu	40.00
BH	Bill Hall	10.00
BL	Joe Blanton	10.00
CA	Miguel Cabrera	50.00
CU	Chase Utley	65.00
CZ	Carlos Zambrano	15.00
DJ	Derek Jeter	180.00
DO	David Ortiz	80.00
FT	Frank Thomas	75.00
GM	Greg Maddux	150.00
HO	Trevor Hoffman	25.00
HR	Hanley Ramirez	35.00
JB	Jason Bay	25.00
JM	Joe Mauer	50.00
KG	Ken Griffey Jr.	120.00
MH	Matt Holliday	25.00
ML	Mark Loretta	15.00
MO	Justin Morneau	30.00
RC	Roger Clemens	100.00
RF	Rafael Furcal	30.00
SA	Johan Santana	50.00
SK	Scott Kazmir	25.00
TH	Travis Hafner	20.00
TI	Tadahito Iguchi	10.00
VG	Vladimir Guerrero	50.00

Rookie Signatures Gold Die-Cut

NM/M
Production 50 Sets

No.	Player	Price
101	Adam Lind	20.00
103	Andrew Miller	15.00
104	Andy Cannizaro	15.00
105	Angel Sanchez	15.00
106	Brian Stokes	15.00
109	Chris Stewart	15.00
111	David Murphy	20.00
112	Delmon Young	20.00
113	Delwyn Young	15.00
114	Dennis Sarfate	15.00
116	Drew Anderson	15.00
117	Fred Lewis	15.00
118	Glen Perkins	15.00
120	Jeff Baker	15.00
121	Jeff Fiorentino	15.00
122	Jeff Salazar	15.00
125	Jon Knott	15.00
128	Juan Morillo	15.00
131	Justin Hampson	15.00
132	Kevin Hooper	40.00
133	Kevin Kouzmanoff	15.00
136	Michael Bourn	15.00
137	Mitch Maier	15.00
139	Patrick Misch	15.00
140	Philip Humber	15.00
141	Ryan Braun	15.00
143	Ryan Sweeney	15.00
144	Scott Moore	15.00
145	Sean Henn	15.00
146	Shawn Riggans	15.00
148	Troy Tulowitzki	35.00
149	Ubaldo Jimenez	40.00

Signature Patch

NM/M
Production 6-25

Code	Player	Price
AG	Adrian Gonzalez/25	40.00
AS	Alfonso Soriano/25	50.00
BA	Bobby Abreu/25	50.00
BJ	B.J. Upton/25	30.00
BS	Ben Sheets/25	25.00
CR	Bobby Crosby/25	15.00
CZ	Carlos Zambrano/25	25.00
DJ	Derek Jeter/25	200.00
DL	Derrek Lee/25	40.00
DO	David Ortiz/25	75.00
DU	Dan Uggla/25	35.00
DW	Dontrelle Willis/25	20.00
GA	Garrett Atkins/25	15.00

2007 UD Sweet Spot

NM/M
Common Player (1-100): 2.00
Production 850
Common RC Auto. (101-142): 8.00
Tin (6): 100.00

No.	Player	Price
1	Adam Dunn	3.00
2	Adrian Beltre	2.00
3	Albert Pujols	10.00
4	Alex Rios	3.00
5	Alex Rodriguez	10.00
6	Alfonso Soriano	4.00
7	Andruw Jones	3.00
8	Aramis Ramirez	3.00
9	B.J. Upton	3.00
10	Barry Zito	2.00
11	Bartolo Colon	2.00
12	Ben Sheets	2.00
13	Bill Hall	2.00
14	Brad Penny	2.00
15	Brandon Webb	3.00
16	C.C. Sabathia	3.00
17	Carl Crawford	2.00
18	Carlos Beltran	2.00
19	Carlos Guillen	2.00
20	Carlos Lee	3.00
21	Chase Utley	5.00
22	Chien-Ming Wang	4.00
23	Chipper Jones	4.00
24	Chris Carpenter	3.00
25	Cole Hamels	4.00
26	Craig Biggio	3.00
27	Curt Schilling	3.00
28	Danny Haren	3.00
29	David Ortiz	5.00
30	David Wright	5.00
31	Delmon Young	3.00
32	Derek Jeter	10.00
33	Derrek Lee	3.00
34	Dontrelle Willis	2.00
35	Felix Hernandez	4.00
36	Frank Thomas	4.00
37	Gil Meche	2.00
38	Grady Sizemore	5.00
39	Greg Maddux	6.00
40	Ian Kinsler	2.00
41	Ichiro Suzuki	6.00
42	Ivan Rodriguez	3.00
43	Jake Peavy	3.00
44	Jason Bay	3.00
45	Jason Varitek	3.00
46	Jeff Kent	3.00
47	Jermaine Dye	2.00
48	Jim Edmonds	2.00
49	Jim Thome	3.00
50	Jimmy Rollins	5.00
51	Joe Mauer	3.00
52	Johan Santana	4.00
53	John Smoltz	3.00
54	Jonathan Papelbon	4.00
55	Jorge Posada	3.00
56	Jose Reyes	4.00
57	Josh Beckett	3.00
58	Justin Morneau	3.00
59	Justin Verlander	3.00
60	Ken Griffey Jr.	8.00
61	Kenji Johjima	2.00
62	Lance Berkman	3.00
63	Magglio Ordonez	3.00
64	Manny Ramirez	4.00
65	Mariano Rivera	3.00
66	Mark Buehrle	2.00
67	Mark Teixeira	3.00
68	Matt Holliday	4.00
69	Matt Morris	2.00
70	Melvin Mora	2.00
71	Michael Young	2.00
72	Miguel Cabrera	4.00
73	Miguel Tejada	3.00
74	Mike Lowell	3.00
75	Mike Mussina	4.00
76	Mike Piazza	4.00
77	Nick Swisher	2.00
78	Orlando Hudson	2.00
79	Paul Konerko	3.00
80	Paul LoDuca	2.00
81	Pedro Martinez	4.00
82	Prince Fielder	4.00
83	Randy Johnson	4.00
84	Rickie Weeks	2.00
85	Roger Clemens	6.00
86	Roy Halladay	3.00
87	Roy Oswalt	3.00
88	Russell Martin	6.00
89	Ryan Howard	6.00
90	Ryan Zimmerman	6.00
91	Sammy Sosa	3.00
92	Scott Rolen	3.00
93	Shawn Green	2.00
94	Todd Helton	3.00
95	Tom Glavine	3.00
96	Torii Hunter	2.00
97	Travis Hafner	2.00
98	Vernon Wells	3.00
99	Victor Martinez	3.00
100	Vladimir Guerrero	4.00
101	Adam Lind (RC)	10.00
102	Akinori Iwamura/SP RC	25.00
103	Alex Gordon RC	15.00
104	Alexi Casilla RC	10.00
105	Andy LaRoche (RC)	10.00
106	Billy Butler (RC)	25.00
107	Ryan Rowland-Smith RC	10.00
108	Brandon Wood (RC)	15.00
109	Brian Burres (RC)	10.00
110	Chase Wright RC	15.00
111	Chris Stewart RC	10.00
112	Daisuke Matsuzaka/SP RC	120.00
113	Delmon Young/SP (RC)	20.00
114	Andrew Sonnanstine RC	15.00
115	Andrew Miller RC	15.00
116	Fred Lewis (RC)	15.00
117	Glen Perkins/SP (RC)	15.00
118	David Murphy (RC)	15.00
119	Hunter Pence (RC)	20.00
120	Jarrod Saltalamacchia (RC)	15.00
121	Jeff Baker/SP (RC)	15.00
122	Jesus Flores/SP RC	20.00
123	Joakim Soria/SP RC	15.00
124	Joe Smith RC	15.00
125	Jon Knott (RC)	10.00
126	Josh Hamilton (RC)	40.00
127	Justin Hampson (RC)	10.00
128	Kei Igawa/SP RC	10.00
129	Kevin Cameron RC	8.00
130	Matt Chico (RC)	8.00
131	Matt DeSalvo (RC)	10.00
132	Micah Owings/SP (RC)	15.00
133	Michael Bourn (RC)	15.00
134	Miguel Montero (RC)	10.00
135	Phil Hughes/SP (RC)	50.00
136	Rick Vanden Hurk RC	15.00
137	Tim Lincecum RC	100.00
138	Travis Buck (RC)	15.00
139	Troy Tulowitzki/SP (RC)	30.00
140	Sean Henn (RC)	8.00
141	Zach Segovia (RC)	8.00
142	Mark Buysner/SP	20.00

Dual Signatures Red Stitch Blue Ink

No Pricing
Production 5-15

Signatures Red Stitch Blue Ink

NM/M
Common Auto.: 4.00

Code	Player	Price
AG	Adrian Gonzalez/350	25.00
AK	Austin Kearns/350	20.00
AL	Adam LaRoche/350	20.00
BB	Boof Bonser/299	10.00
BR	Brian Bruney/299	10.00
BW	Brandon Wood/350	10.00
CB	Chad Billingsley/299	25.00
CC	Chris Capuano/299	10.00
CJ	Conor Jackson/299	15.00
CL	Cliff Lee/299	20.00
CQ	Carlos Quentin/299	15.00
CY	Chris Young/350	15.00
DC	Daniel Cabrera/299	10.00
DH	Danny Haren/299	20.00
DR	Darrell Rasner/299	10.00
EA	Erick Aybar/299	15.00
GP	Glen Perkins/350	10.00
HK	Howie Kendrick/350	15.00
HP	Hunter Pence/350	25.00
JH	Josh Hamilton/350	40.00
JK	Jason Kubel/299	15.00
JN	Joe Nathan/299	15.00
JW	Josh Willingham/299	10.00
KA	Jeff Karstens/299	10.00
KS	Kurt Suzuki/299	15.00
LI	Adam Lind/299	10.00
LO	Lyle Overbay/299	10.00
MC	Matt Cain/299	20.00
RH	Rich Hill/299	10.00
RM	Russell Martin/299	15.00
SE	Sergio Mitre/299	10.00
TB	Travis Buck/299	15.00
YG	Chris B. Young/299	15.00
AD	Adam Dunn/299	20.00
AI	Akinori Iwamura/99	15.00
AM	Andrew Miller/99	15.00
AX	Alex Gordon/99	15.00
BP	Brandon Phillips/99	15.00
CA	Carl Crawford/99	15.00
CH	Cole Hamels/99	30.00
CK	Casey Kotchman/99	15.00
DY	Delmon Young/99	15.00
FH	Felix Hernandez/99	35.00
FP	Felix Pie/99	15.00
HA	Travis Hafner/99	15.00
HS	Huston Street/99	10.00
JL	Jon Lester/99	30.00
JP	Jonathan Papelbon/99	20.00
JS	Jeremy Sowers/99	15.00
JV	Jason Varitek/99	40.00
MH	Matt Holliday/99	40.00
MM	Melvin Mora/99	20.00
PH	Phil Hughes/99	60.00
PK	Paul Konerko/99	25.00
RC	Roger Clemens/99	60.00
RI	Rich Harden/99	10.00
RW	Rickie Weeks/99	15.00
RZ	Ryan Zimmerman/99	20.00
SK	Scott Kazmir/99	15.00
TG	Tom Glavine/99	40.00
TH	Torii Hunter/99	15.00
TL	Tim Lincecum/99	75.00
VE	Justin Verlander/99	45.00
VM	Victor Martinez/99	20.00

Sweet Swatch Memorabilia

NM/M
Common Player: 4.00
Patch: 2-4X
Production 25 Sets

Code	Player	Price
AD	Adam Dunn	8.00
AJ	Andruw Jones	6.00
AP	Albert Pujols	15.00
AS	Alfonso Soriano	8.00
AT	Garrett Atkins	4.00
BA	Bobby Abreu	6.00
BE	Josh Beckett	6.00
BG	Brian Giles	4.00
BI	Craig Biggio	6.00
BO	Jeremy Bonderman	4.00
BR	Brian Roberts	6.00
BU	B.J. Upton	6.00
BW	Billy Wagner	6.00
CA	Chris Carpenter	6.00
CB	Carlos Beltran	4.00
CC	Carl Crawford	4.00
CH	Cole Hamels	8.00
CJ	Chipper Jones	8.00
CL	Carlos Lee	6.00
CS	Curt Schilling	4.00
CU	Chase Utley	15.00
DJ	Derek Jeter	20.00
DM	Daisuke Matsuzaka	15.00
DO	David Ortiz	10.00
DW	Dontrelle Willis	4.00
EB	Erik Bedard	6.00
EC	Eric Chavez	4.00
FG	Freddy Garcia	4.00
FH	Felix Hernandez	8.00
FL	Francisco Liriano	8.00
FT	Frank Thomas	8.00
GA	Garret Anderson	4.00
GM	Greg Maddux	8.00
GS	Grady Sizemore	8.00
HA	Roy Halladay	10.00
HB	Hank Blalock	4.00
HE	Todd Helton	6.00
HO	Trevor Hoffman	4.00
HR	Hanley Ramirez	8.00
HS	Huston Street	4.00
HU	Torii Hunter	6.00
IK	Ian Kinsler	4.00
IR	Ivan Rodriguez	6.00
JB	Jason Bay	6.00
JD	Jermaine Dye	4.00
JE	Jim Edmonds	4.00
JF	Jeff Francoeur	8.00
JG	Jason Giambi	6.00
JK	Jeff Kent	4.00
JM	Joe Mauer	10.00
JN	Joe Nathan	4.00
JP	Jake Peavy	6.00
JR	Jimmy Rollins	10.00
JS	Jason Schmidt	4.00
JT	Jim Thome	8.00
JV	Jason Varitek	6.00
JW	Jered Weaver	6.00
JZ	Joel Zumaya	4.00
KG	Ken Griffey Jr.	15.00
KM	Kendry Morales	6.00
LB	Lance Berkman	4.00
LG	Luis Gonzalez	4.00
MC	Miguel Cabrera	8.00
MM	Mike Mussina	8.00
MO	Justin Morneau	8.00
MR	Manny Ramirez	6.00
MT	Mark Teixeira	6.00
MY	Michael Young	6.00
OR	Magglio Ordonez	6.00
OS	Roy Oswalt	6.00
PA	Jonathan Papelbon	8.00
PB	Pat Burrell	4.00
PE	Jhonny Peralta	4.00
PF	Prince Fielder	8.00
PM	Pedro Martinez	8.00
PO	Jorge Posada	8.00
RC	Robinson Cano	8.00
RE	Jose Reyes	10.00
RH	Rich Harden	4.00
RI	Mariano Rivera	8.00
RJ	Randy Johnson	8.00
RO	Roger Clemens	10.00
RW	Rickie Weeks	4.00
RZ	Ryan Zimmerman	6.00
SA	Johan Santana	6.00
SD	Stephen Drew	6.00
SK	Scott Kazmir	6.00
SM	John Smoltz	6.00
SR	Scott Rolen	6.00
TE	Miguel Tejada	6.00
TG	Tom Glavine	6.00
TH	Tim Hudson	6.00
TR	Travis Hafner	4.00
VE	Justin Verlander	8.00
VG	Vladimir Guerrero	8.00
VM	Victor Martinez	8.00
VW	Vernon Wells	4.00

Dual Signatures Black Glove Gold Ink

No Pricing
Production 5-10
Silver Ink: No Pricing
Production One Set
Leather Black Ink: No Pricing
Production 5-15

Dual Signatures Gold Stitch Gold Ink

No Pricing
Production 5-10
Silver Ink: No Pricing
Production Five Sets

Signatures Bat Barrel Blue Ink

NM/M
Production 1-99
Silver Ink: 1-1.5X
Production 25 or 15
Gold Ink: No Pricing
Production One Set
Red Ink: No Pricing
Production Five Sets
No pricing production under 25.

Code	Player	Price
AK	Austin Kearns/25	15.00
AL	Adam LaRoche/25	15.00
BB	Boof Bonser/26	10.00
BR	Brian Bruney/99	10.00
CB	Chad Billingsley/58	30.00
CC	Chris Capuano/39	10.00
CL	Cliff Lee/31	25.00
CY	Chris Young/32	15.00
DC	Daniel Cabrera/35	10.00
DR	Darrell Rasner/27	10.00
EA	Erick Aybar/23	20.00
GP	Glen Perkins/60	10.00
HK	Howie Kendrick/47	20.00
JH	Josh Hamilton/33	50.00
JN	Joe Nathan/36	20.00
KS	Kurt Suzuki/99	20.00
LI	Adam Lind/99	15.00
RH	Rich Hill/51	10.00
RM	Russell Martin/55	20.00
SE	Sergio Mitre/99	10.00
AD	Adam Dunn/44	25.00
AM	Andrew Miller/48	15.00
BP	Brandon Phillips/99	15.00
CH	Cole Hamels/35	35.00
CK	Casey Kotchman/99	15.00
FH	Felix Hernandez/34	50.00
FP	Felix Pie/99	20.00
HA	Travis Hafner/48	20.00
JL	Jon Lester/31	25.00
JP	Jonathan Papelbon/58	25.00
JS	Jeremy Sowers/45	15.00
JV	Jason Varitek/33	50.00
PH	Phil Hughes/65	50.00
PK	Paul Konerko/25	25.00
RI	Rich Harden/40	15.00
TG	Tom Glavine/47	40.00
TH	Torii Hunter/48	20.00
TL	Tim Lincecum/55	80.00
VE	Justin Verlander/35	50.00
VM	Victor Martinez/41	30.00

Sign. Black Bat Barrel Silver Ink

Production 10 or 15
Gold Ink: No Pricing
Production One Set
Red Ink: No Pricing
Production Five Sets

Signatures Glove Black Ink

		NM/M
Production 25 or 75
Silver Ink: 1-1.5X
Production 25 or 10
Green Ink: No Pricing
Production One Set
No pricing product. under 25.

		NM/M
AG	Adrian Gonzalez/75	25.00
AK	Austin Kearns/75	15.00
AL	Adam LaRoche/75	15.00
BB	Boof Bonser/75	15.00
BR	Brian Bruney/75	15.00
BW	Brandon Wood/75	20.00
CB	Chad Billingsley/75	30.00
CC	Chris Capuano/75	15.00
CJ	Conor Jackson/75	15.00
CL	Cliff Lee/75	25.00
CQ	Carlos Quentin/75	15.00
CY	Chris Young/75	20.00
DC	Daniel Cabrera/75	10.00
DH	Dan Haren/75	30.00
DR	Darrell Rasner/75	10.00
EA	Erick Aybar/75	20.00
GP	Glen Perkins/75	15.00
HK	Howie Kendrick/75	20.00
HP	Hunter Pence/75	15.00
JH	Josh Hamilton/75	40.00
JK	Jason Kubel/75	15.00
JN	Joe Nathan/75	20.00
JW	Josh Willingham/75	15.00
KA	Jeff Karstens/75	15.00
KS	Kurt Suzuki/75	20.00
LO	Lyle Overbay/75	15.00
MC	Matt Cain/75	25.00
RH	Rich Hill/75	15.00
RM	Russell Martin/75	20.00
SE	Sergio Mitre/75	15.00
TB	Travis Buck/75	15.00
YG	Chris B. Young/75	15.00
AD	Adam Dunn/25	30.00
AI	Akinori Iwamura/25	20.00
AM	Andrew Miller/25	20.00
AX	Alex Gordon/25	20.00
BP	Brandon Phillips/25	30.00
CA	Carl Crawford/25	25.00
CH	Cole Hamels/25	40.00
CK	Casey Kotchman/25	15.00
DY	Delmon Young/25	25.00
FH	Felix Hernandez/25	50.00
FP	Felix Pie/25	20.00
HA	Travis Hafner/25	15.00
HS	Huston Street/25	20.00
JL	Jon Lester/25	50.00
JP	Jonathan Papelbon/25	25.00
JS	Jeremy Sowers/25	15.00
JV	Jason Varitek/25	60.00
MH	Matt Holliday/25	60.00
MM	Melvin Mora/25	15.00
PH	Phil Hughes/25	60.00
PK	Paul Konerko/25	40.00
RC	Roger Clemens/25	80.00
RI	Rich Harden/25	20.00
RW	Rickie Weeks/25	20.00
RZ	Ryan Zimmerman/25	30.00
SK	Scott Kazmir/25	20.00
TG	Tom Glavine/25	50.00
TH	Torii Hunter/25	25.00
TL	Tim Lincecum/25	120.00
VE	Justin Verlander/25	50.00
VM	Victor Martinez/25	25.00

Signatures Gold Stitch Gold Ink

		NM/M
Production 25 or 99
Red/Blue Stitch Red Ink: No Pricing
Production 5 or 15

AG	Adrian Gonzalez/99	25.00
AK	Austin Kearns/99	20.00
AL	Adam LaRoche/99	20.00
BB	Boof Bonser/99	10.00
BR	Brian Bruney/99	10.00
BW	Brandon Wood/99	15.00
CB	Chad Billingsley/99	25.00
CC	Chris Capuano/99	10.00
CJ	Conor Jackson/99	10.00
CL	Cliff Lee/99	20.00
CQ	Carlos Quentin/99	15.00
CY	Chris Young/99	15.00
DC	Daniel Cabrera/99	10.00
DH	Dan Haren/99	30.00
DR	Darrell Rasner/99	15.00
EA	Erick Aybar/99	20.00
GP	Glen Perkins/99	15.00
HK	Howie Kendrick/99	15.00
HP	Hunter Pence/99	25.00
JH	Josh Hamilton/99	40.00
JK	Jason Kubel/99	20.00
JN	Joe Nathan/99	20.00
JW	Josh Willingham/99	20.00
KA	Jeff Karstens/99	15.00
KS	Kurt Suzuki/99	20.00
LI	Adam Lind/99	15.00
LO	Lyle Overbay/99	15.00
MC	Matt Cain/99	25.00
RH	Rich Hill/99	15.00
RM	Russell Martin/99	20.00
SE	Sergio Mitre/99	15.00

Signatures Silver Stitch Silver Ink

		NM/M
Production 1-99
No pricing product. under 25

AK	Austin Kearns/25	20.00
AL	Adam LaRoche/25	20.00
BB	Boof Bonser/26	10.00
BR	Brian Bruney/49	10.00
CB	Chad Billingsley/58	25.00
CC	Chris Capuano/39	15.00
CL	Cliff Lee/31	25.00
CY	Chris Young/32	15.00
DC	Daniel Cabrera/35	15.00
DR	Darrell Rasner/27	15.00
EA	Erick Aybar/32	20.00
GP	Glen Perkins/60	15.00
HK	Howie Kendrick/47	15.00
JH	Josh Hamilton/33	40.00
JN	Joe Nathan/36	20.00
KS	Kurt Suzuki/99	20.00
AI	Adam Lind/99	20.00
RH	Rich Hill/51	15.00
RM	Russell Martin/55	20.00
SE	Sergio Mitre/10	15.00
YG	Chris B. Young/24	20.00
AD	Adam Dunn/44	25.00
AM	Andrew Miller/48	15.00
BP	Brandon Phillips/99	15.00
CH	Cole Hamels/35	35.00
CK	Casey Kotchman/99	10.00
FH	Felix Hernandez/34	50.00
FP	Felix Pie/99	20.00
HA	Travis Hafner/48	15.00
JL	Jon Lester/31	40.00
JP	Jonathan Papelbon/58	25.00
JS	Jeremy Sowers/43	10.00
JV	Jason Varitek/33	50.00
PH	Phil Hughes/65	50.00
PK	Paul Konerko/36	40.00
RI	Rich Harden/40	15.00
TG	Tom Glavine/47	50.00
TH	Torii Hunter/48	20.00
TL	Tim Lincecum/35	85.00
VE	Justin Verlander/35	25.00
VM	Victor Martinez/41	25.00

Signatures Black Glove Silver Ink

		NM/M
Production 10 or 25
Gold Ink: No Pricing
Production Five Sets
Metallic Blue Ink: No Pricing
Production One Set
No pricing product. under 25.

AG	Adrian Gonzalez/25	30.00
AK	Austin Kearns/25	20.00
AL	Adam LaRoche/25	20.00
BB	Boof Bonser/25	10.00
BR	Brian Bruney/25	20.00
BW	Brandon Wood/25	20.00
CB	Chad Billingsley/25	25.00
CC	Chris Capuano/25	15.00
CJ	Conor Jackson/25	15.00
CL	Cliff Lee/25	25.00
CQ	Carlos Quentin/25	15.00
CY	Chris Young/25	15.00
DC	Daniel Cabrera/25	15.00
DH	Danny Haren/25	35.00
DR	Darrell Rasner/25	10.00
EA	Erick Aybar/25	15.00
GP	Glen Perkins/25	15.00
HP	Hunter Pence/25	25.00
JH	Josh Hamilton/25	50.00
JK	Jason Kubel/25	20.00
JN	Joe Nathan/25	20.00
JW	Josh Willingham/25	20.00
KA	Jeff Karstens/25	15.00
KS	Kurt Suzuki/25	20.00
LO	Lyle Overbay/25	15.00
MC	Matt Cain/25	30.00
RH	Rich Hill/25	15.00
RM	Russell Martin/25	20.00
SE	Sergio Mitre/25	15.00
TB	Travis Buck/25	15.00
YG	Chris B. Young/25	15.00

2007 UD Sweet Spot Classic

	NM/M
Common Player:	2.00
Production 575 Sets
Tin (5):	100.00
1	Phil Niekro	2.00
2	Fred McGriff	3.00
3	Bob Horner	2.00
4	Earl Weaver	2.00
5	Boog Powell	2.00
6	Eddie Murray	4.00
7	Fred Lynn	2.00
8	Dwight Evans	2.00
9	Jim Rice	3.00
10	Carlton Fisk	4.00
11	Luis Tiant	2.00
12	Robin Yount	4.00
13	Bobby Doerr	3.00
14	Ryne Sandberg	5.00
15	Billy Williams	3.00
16	Andre Dawson	3.00
17	Mark Grace	3.00
18	Ron Santo	3.00
19	Shawon Dunston	2.00
20	Harold Baines	2.00
21	Carlton Fisk	4.00
22	Sparky Anderson	2.00
23	George Foster	2.00
24	Dave Parker	2.00
25	Ken Griffey Jr.	2.00
26	Dave Concepcion	2.00
27	Rafael Palmeiro	3.00
28	Al Rosen	2.00
29	Kirk Gibson	2.00
30	Alan Trammell	3.00
31	Jack Morris	2.00
32	Willie Horton	2.00
33	J.R. Richard	2.00
34	Jose Cruz	2.00
35	Willie Wilson	2.00
36	Bo Jackson	4.00
37	Nolan Ryan	8.00
38	Don Baylor	2.00
39	Maury Wills	2.00
40	Tommy John	2.00
41	Ron Cey	2.00
42	Davey Lopes	2.00
43	Tommy Lasorda	2.00
44	Burt Hooton	2.00
45	Reggie Smith	2.00
46	Rollie Fingers	2.00
47	Cecil Cooper	2.00
48	Paul Molitor	4.00
49	Vern Stephens	2.00
50	Tony Oliva	2.00
51	Andres Galarraga	2.00
52	Tim Raines	2.00
53	Dennis Martinez	2.00
54	Lee Mazzilli	2.00
55	Rusty Staub	2.00
56	David Cone	2.00
57	Reggie Jackson	4.00
58	Ron Guidry	2.00
59	Tino Martinez	3.00
60	Don Mattingly	6.00
61	Chris Chambliss	2.00
62	Sparky Lyle	2.00
63	Rich "Goose" Gossage	2.00
64	Dave Righetti	2.00
65	Phil Garner	2.00
66	Bill Madlock	2.00
67	Kent Hrbek	2.00
68	Al Oliver	2.00
69	John Kruk	2.00
70	Greg Luzinski	2.00
71	Dick Allen	2.00
72	Richie Ashburn	3.00
73	Gary Matthews	2.00
74	Mike Schmidt	5.00
75	Waite Hoyt	2.00
76	Bruce Sutter	2.00
77	Roger Maris	6.00
78	Joe Torre	3.00
79	Kevin Mitchell	2.00
80	John Montefusco	2.00
81	Rick Reuschel	2.00
82	Will Clark	3.00
83	Jack Clark	2.00
84	Matt Williams	2.00
85	Steve Garvey	2.00
86	Dave Winfield	3.00
87	Jay Buhner	2.00
88	Edgar Martinez	2.00

91	Carney Lansford	2.00
92	Sal Bando	2.00
93	Dave Stewart	2.00
94	Dennis Eckersley	3.00
95	Jose Canseco	3.00
96	Dennis Eckersley	3.00
97	Roberto Alomar	3.00
98	George Bell	2.00
99	Joe Carter	2.00
100	Frank Howard	2.00
101	Brooks Robinson	4.00
102	Frank Robinson	4.00
103	Jim Palmer	3.00
104	Cal Ripken Jr.	8.00
105	Warren Spahn	4.00
106	Cy Young	2.00
107	Waite Hoyt	2.00
108	Carl Yastrzemski	4.00
109	Johnny Pesky	3.00
110	Wade Boggs	3.00
111	Jackie Robinson	8.00
112	Roy Campanella	4.00
113	Pee Wee Reese	4.00
114	Don Newcombe	2.00
115	Rod Carew	4.00
116	Ernie Banks	4.00
117	Fergie Jenkins	2.00
118	Al Lopez	2.00
119	Luis Aparicio	2.00
120	Toby Harrah	2.00
121	Joe Morgan	3.00
122	Johnny Bench	4.00
123	Tony Perez	3.00
124	Ted Kluszewski	2.00
125	Bob Feller	3.00
126	Bob Lemon	2.00
127	Larry Doby	3.00
128	Lou Boudreau	2.00
129	George Kell	2.00
130	Hal Newhouser	2.00
131	Al Kaline	4.00
132	Ty Cobb	5.00
133	Denny McLain	2.00
134	Buck Leonard	3.00
135	Dean Chance	2.00
136	Don Drysdale	3.00
137	Don Sutton	3.00
138	Eddie Mathews	4.00
139	Paul Molitor	4.00
140	Kirby Puckett	5.00
141	Rod Carew	3.00
142	Harmon Killebrew	4.00
143	Monte Irvin	3.00
144	Mel Ott	3.00
145	Christy Mathewson	5.00
146	Hoyt Wilhelm	2.00
147	Tom Seaver	4.00
148	Joe McCarthy	2.00
149	Joe DiMaggio	5.00
150	Lou Gehrig	6.00
151	Babe Ruth	8.00
152	Casey Stengel	3.00
153	Phil Rizzuto	4.00
154	Thurman Munson	5.00
155	Johnny Mize	2.00
156	Yogi Berra	4.00
157	Roger Maris	5.00
158	Don Larsen	3.00
159	Bill "Moose" Skowron	2.00
160	Lou Piniella	3.00
161	Joe Pepitone	2.00
162	Ray Dandridge	2.00
163	Rollie Fingers	2.00
164	Reggie Jackson	4.00
165	Mickey Cochrane	3.00
166	Jimmie Foxx	4.00
167	Lefty Grove	3.00
168	Gus Zernial	2.00
169	Jim Bunning	2.00
170	Steve Carlton	3.00
171	Robin Roberts	3.00
172	Ralph Kiner	3.00
173	Willie Stargell	4.00
174	Roberto Clemente	6.00
175	Bill Mazeroski	2.00
176	Honus Wagner	5.00
177	Pie Traynor	3.00
178	Elroy Face	2.00
179	Dick Groat	2.00
180	Tony Gwynn	4.00
181	Willie McCovey	3.00
182	Gaylord Perry	2.00
183	Juan Marichal	3.00
184	Orlando Cepeda	3.00
185	Satchel Paige	3.00
186	George Sisler	3.00
187	Rogers Hornsby	3.00
188	Stan Musial	4.00
189	Dizzy Dean	4.00
190	Bob Gibson	4.00
191	Red Schoendienst	2.00
192	Lou Brock	3.00
193	Enos Slaughter	2.00
194	Nolan Ryan	8.00
195	Mickey Vernon	2.00
196	Walter Johnson	4.00
197	Rick Ferrell	2.00
198	Roy Sievers	2.00
199	Judy Johnson	2.00

Ripken Immortal Membership

Production One Set

Classic Memorabilia

	NM/M
Common Player:	5.00
Patch:	2-4X
Production 55 Sets

AD	Andre Dawson	8.00
AK	Al Kaline	10.00
AO	Al Oliver	8.00
BE	Johnny Bench	15.00
BJ	Bo Jackson	15.00
BM	Bill Madlock	5.00
BO	Wade Boggs	8.00
BR	Babe Ruth/SP	200.00
BS	Bruce Sutter	5.00
CL	Roberto Clemente	40.00
CM	Christy Mathewson/SP	125.00
CR	Cal Ripken Jr.	20.00
CS	Casey Stengel	10.00
CY	Carl Yastrzemski	10.00
DD	Dizzy Dean	30.00
DE	Dennis Eckersley	5.00
DM	Don Mattingly	15.00
DP	Dave Parker	5.00
DR	Don Drysdale	5.00
DS	Don Sutton	5.00
DW	Dave Winfield	10.00
ED	Eddie Murray	8.00
EM	Eddie Mathews	15.00
EV	Dwight Evans	5.00
EW	Early Wynn	8.00
FG	Fred McGriff	5.00
FI	Rollie Fingers	5.00
FR	Frank Robinson	10.00
GF	George Foster	5.00
GG	Rich "Goose" Gossage	8.00
GK	Kirk Gibson	5.00
GP	Gaylord Perry	5.00
GW	Tony Gwynn	10.00
HB	Harold Baines/SP	8.00
HK	Harmon Killebrew/SP	10.00
JB	Jim Bunning	8.00
JD	Joe DiMaggio	60.00
JI	Jim Rice	8.00
JM	Jack Morris	5.00
JP	Jim Palmer	8.00
JU	Juan Marichal	8.00
KG	Ken Griffey Jr.	25.00
KH	Kent Hrbek	5.00
KP	Kirby Puckett	15.00
LA	Luis Aparicio	5.00
LB	Lou Brock	8.00
LG	Lou Gehrig	150.00
MA	Don Mattingly	15.00
ME	Eddie Murray	8.00
MG	Mark Grace	5.00
MO	Mel Ott	20.00
MP	Paul Molitor	10.00
MR	Edgar Martinez	5.00
MS	Mike Schmidt	15.00
MW	Maury Wills	5.00
NR	Nolan Ryan	20.00
PA	Dave Parker	5.00
PE	Tony Perez	5.00
PM	Paul Molitor	5.00
PN	Phil Niekro	5.00
PR	Pee Wee Reese/SP	25.00
RF	Rollie Fingers	5.00
RG	Ron Guidry	5.00
RH	Rogers Hornsby	25.00
RK	Ralph Kiner	10.00
RM	Roger Maris	25.00
RO	Roy Campanella	15.00
RS	Ron Santo	10.00
RY	Nolan Ryan	20.00
SC	Red Schoendienst	8.00
SG	Steve Garvey	8.00
ST	Steve Carlton	8.00
SU	Bruce Sutter	5.00
TG	Tony Gwynn	10.00
TM	Thurman Munson	20.00
TO	Tony Oliva	5.00
TP	Tony Perez	5.00
TR	Tim Raines	5.00
WB	Wade Boggs	8.00
WC	Will Clark	5.00
WM	Willie McCovey	8.00
WS	Willie Stargell	8.00
YO	Robin Yount	10.00
CF1	Carlton Fisk	8.00
CF2	Carlton Fisk	8.00
FR1	Frank Robinson	10.00
MI1	Johnny Mize	10.00
MI2	Johnny Mize	10.00
RC1	Rod Carew	8.00
RC2	Rod Carew	8.00
RJ1	Reggie Jackson	10.00
RJ2	Reggie Jackson	10.00
RJ3	Reggie Jackson	10.00

Legendary Lettermen

	NM/M
Represents total cards produced
| LL1 | Babe Ruth/100 | |

LL2	Ty Cobb/100	75.00
LL3	Christy Mathewson/90	50.00
LL4	Jackie Robinson/80	60.00
LL5	Roy Campanella/100	50.00
LL6	Lou Gehrig/90	150.00
LL7	Mel Ott/75	25.00
LL8	Jimmie Foxx/100	50.00
LL9	Satchel Paige/125	40.00
LL10	Don Drysdale/200	30.00
LL11	Rogers Hornsby/175	60.00
LL12	Honus Wagner/150	50.00
LL13	Babe Ruth/105	150.00
LL14	Dizzy Dean/100	50.00
LL15	Ty Cobb/60	75.00
LL16	Walter Johnson/105	50.00
LL17	Walter Johnson/80	50.00
LL18	Cal Ripken Jr./200	100.00
LL19	Sandy Koufax/150	250.00
LL20	Thurman Munson/150	50.00
LL21	Thurman Munson/70	40.00
LL22	Cal Ripken Jr./175	
LL23	Tony Gwynn/125	50.00
LL24	Nolan Ryan/80	50.00
LL25	Nolan Ryan/165	50.00
LL26	Jackie Robinson/70	60.00
LL27	Carlton Fisk/80	50.00
LL28	Carl Yastrzemski/165	60.00
LL29	Johnny Bench/125	50.00
LL30	Ryne Sandberg/200	100.00
LL31	Don Mattingly/135	75.00
LL32	Ernie Banks/165	40.00
LL33	Bill Mazeroski/135	50.00
LL34	Ernie Banks/150	40.00
LL35	Bob Gibson/150	40.00
LL36	Mike Schmidt/175	60.00
LL37	Al Kaline/150	40.00
LL38	Reggie Jackson/175	50.00
LL39	Stan Musial/150	50.00
LL40	Bo Jackson/175	50.00
LL41	Bo Jackson/105	50.00
LL42	Stan Musial/150	50.00

Dual Sig Red Stitch-Blue Ink

		NM/M
Production 50 Sets
Black Stitch Red Ink: No Pricing
Production One Set
Gold Stitch Black Ink: No Pricing
Production 15 Sets

AG	Luis Aparicio, Ozzie Guillen	30.00
BC	Cal Ripken Jr., Brooks Robinson	140.00
BF	Carlton Fisk, Johnny Bench	75.00
BG	Harold Baines, Ozzie Guillen	50.00
BR	Robin Roberts, Jim Bunning	60.00
CG	Tony Gwynn, Rod Carew	90.00
CO	Tony Oliva, Rod Carew	40.00
FE	Dennis Eckersley, Rollie Fingers	50.00
FG	Elroy Face, Dick Groat	50.00
FM	Mike Schmidt, Frank Robinson	80.00
FR	Carlton Fisk, Jim Rice	50.00
GR	Bob Gibson, J.R. Richard	50.00
GS	Steve Garvey, Reggie Smith	30.00
GW	Tony Gwynn, Dave Winfield	
HK	Al Kaline, Willie Horton	80.00
JS	Reggie Smith, Reggie Jackson	50.00
KM	Ralph Kiner, Bill Mazeroski	75.00
LT	Tim Raines, Lou Brock	40.00
MC	Jack Clark, Willie McCovey	75.00
MG	Juan Marichal, Bob Gibson	60.00
MK	Stan Musial, Al Kaline	125.00
MM	Don Mattingly, Tino Martinez	80.00
MR	Edgar Martinez, Harold Reynolds	50.00
OH	Tony Oliva, Kent Hrbek	40.00
RG	Tony Gwynn, Cal Ripken Jr.	160.00
RR	Nolan Ryan, J.R. Richard	150.00
RS	Cal Ripken Jr., Mike Schmidt	180.00
SB	Ron Santo, Ernie Banks	125.00
SC	Mike Schmidt, Steve Carlton	80.00
SD	Ryne Sandberg, Shawon Dunston	80.00
SF	Rollie Fingers, Bruce Sutter	60.00
SS	Ron Santo, Ryne Sandberg	125.00
SV	Mickey Vernon, Roy Sievers	30.00
WC	Cal Ripken Jr., Wade Boggs	125.00
YP	Carl Yastrzemski, Johnny Pesky	100.00

Immortal Signatures

Common Player

Signatures Sepia Black Ink

	NM/M
Production 16-199

	Red Ink	No Pricing
	Production 15 Sets	
CF	Carlton Fisk/124	30.00
CY	Carl Yastrzemski/124	50.00
DM	Don Mattingly/124	50.00
DS	Duke Snider/30	75.00
JM	Juan Marichal/124	30.00
JR	Jim Rice/85	30.00
MU	Dale Murphy/183	25.00
NR	Nolan Ryan/123	80.00
OS	Ozzie Smith/183	50.00
RS	Ryne Sandberg/199	50.00
TG	Tony Gwynn/199	50.00

Signatures Sepia Blue Ink
NM/M
Production 15-199

AK	Al Kaline/199	30.00
BW	Billy Williams/199	20.00
CF	Carlton Fisk/78	20.00
CY	Carl Yastrzemski/90	60.00
DM	Don Mattingly/78	60.00
DS	Duke Snider/199	40.00
EM	Edgar Martinez/74	40.00
JM	Juan Marichal/84	25.00
JR	Jim Rice/75	25.00
LM	Lee Mazzilli/199	15.00
MU	Dale Murphy/75	25.00
NR	Nolan Ryan/80	80.00
OS	Ozzie Smith/199	50.00
RC	Rocky Colavito/199	20.00
TG	Tony Gwynn/199	50.00
WC	Will Clark/199	25.00

Signatures Black Ink
NM/M
Common Signature: 15.00
Production 175 unless noted.

AG	Andres Galarraga	20.00
AK	Al Kaline	20.00
AO	Al Oliver	15.00
BJ	Bo Jackson	50.00
BM	Bill Mazeroski	40.00
BO	Wade Boggs	40.00
BS	Bruce Sutter/75	25.00
CF	Carlton Fisk/75	35.00
DA	Dick Allen	20.00
DL	Don Larsen	20.00
DM	Don Mattingly/75	60.00
EC	Dennis Eckersley	20.00
EM	Edgar Martinez	30.00
FM	Fred McGriff	20.00
GP	Gaylord Perry	20.00
HB	Harold Baines	15.00
JB	Johnny Bench/75	60.00
JK	John Kruk	20.00
MO	Jack Morris	20.00
MS	Mike Schmidt/75	75.00
NR	Nolan Ryan/75	80.00
OG	Ozzie Guillen	20.00
RA	Roberto Alomar	25.00
RI	Jim Rice	20.00
RJ	Reggie Jackson/75	60.00
RS	Ryne Sandberg/75	40.00
SA	Ron Santo	30.00
SM	Reggie Smith	20.00
TG	Tony Gwynn/75	60.00
TM	Tino Martinez	35.00
TP	Tony Perez	20.00
TR	Tim Raines	20.00
WB	Wade Boggs	40.00
WD	Willie Davis/75	25.00
WM	Willie McCovey/75	50.00
YB	Yogi Berra/75	80.00
BR	Brooks Robinson	30.00
BW	Billy Williams	20.00
CL	Carney Lansford	20.00
CO	Dave Concepcion	25.00
CY	Carl Yastrzemski	50.00
DG	Dick Groat	20.00
DS	Don Sutton	20.00
DW	Dave Winfield	30.00
EB	Ernie Banks	60.00
EF	Elroy Face	20.00
EV	Dwight Evans	20.00
FL	Fred Lynn	15.00
FR	Frank Robinson/35	40.00
GI	Bob Gibson	40.00
JI	Jim Bunning	20.00
JP	Johnny Pesky	20.00
JR	Jim Rice	20.00
KG	Ken Griffey Sr.	15.00
KO	Sandy Koufax	350.00
LA	Luis Aparicio	20.00
LB	Lou Brock/75	40.00
MA	Juan Marichal	20.00
MG	Mark Grace	30.00
MU	Stan Musial/75	80.00
MV	Mickey Vernon	20.00
OS	Ozzie Smith/75	60.00
PN	Phil Niekro	20.00
RC	Rod Carew	30.00
RF	Rollie Fingers	40.00
RK	Ralph Kiner/75	40.00
RR	Robin Roberts	20.00
RY	Robin Yount	40.00
SC	Steve Carlton	30.00
SD	Shawon Dunston	25.00
SG	Steve Garvey	25.00
SK	Bill "Moose" Skowron	20.00
TH	Toby Harrah	15.00
TO	Tony Oliva	20.00
WH	Willie Horton	20.00

Signatures Blue Ink
NM/M
Common Signature: 20.00
Production 125 unless noted.

AG	Andres Galarraga	20.00
AK	Al Kaline	30.00
AO	Al Oliver	20.00
BJ	Bo Jackson	50.00
BM	Bill Mazeroski	40.00
BO	Wade Boggs	50.00
BS	Bruce Sutter/25	25.00
CF	Carlton Fisk/35	40.00
DA	Dick Allen	20.00
DL	Don Larsen	30.00
DM	Don Mattingly/35	60.00
EC	Dennis Eckersley	20.00
EM	Edgar Martinez	30.00
FM	Fred McGriff	30.00
GP	Gaylord Perry	25.00
HB	Harold Baines	20.00
JB	Johnny Bench/35	60.00
JK	John Kruk	20.00
MO	Jack Morris	20.00
MS	Mike Schmidt/35	75.00
NR	Nolan Ryan/35	120.00
OG	Ozzie Guillen	20.00
RA	Roberto Alomar	25.00
RI	Jim Rice	20.00
RJ	Reggie Jackson/35	60.00
RS	Ryne Sandberg/35	60.00
SA	Ron Santo	30.00
SM	Reggie Smith	20.00
TG	Tony Gwynn/35	60.00
TM	Tino Martinez	40.00
TP	Tony Perez	25.00
TR	Tim Raines	20.00
WB	Wade Boggs/35	50.00
WD	Willie Davis/35	25.00
WM	Willie McCovey/35	60.00
YB	Yogi Berra/35	80.00
BR	Brooks Robinson	30.00
BW	Billy Williams	20.00
CL	Carney Lansford	15.00
CO	Dave Concepcion	20.00
CY	Carl Yastrzemski	60.00
DG	Dick Groat	25.00
DS	Don Sutton	20.00
DW	Dave Winfield	25.00
EB	Ernie Banks	60.00
EF	Elroy Face	30.00
EV	Dwight Evans	20.00
FL	Fred Lynn	15.00
FR	Frank Robinson/75	40.00
GI	Bob Gibson	30.00
JI	Jim Bunning	20.00
JP	Johnny Pesky	25.00
JR	Jim Rice	20.00
KG	Ken Griffey Sr.	20.00
KO	Sandy Koufax	300.00
LA	Luis Aparicio	20.00
LB	Lou Brock/35	40.00
MA	Juan Marichal	30.00
MG	Mark Grace	25.00
MU	Stan Musial/35	80.00
MV	Mickey Vernon	20.00
OS	Ozzie Smith/35	60.00
PN	Phil Niekro	15.00
RC	Rod Carew	30.00
RF	Rollie Fingers	20.00
RK	Ralph Kiner/35	40.00
RR	Robin Roberts	20.00
RY	Robin Yount	40.00
SC	Steve Carlton	25.00
SD	Shawon Dunston	25.00
SG	Steve Garvey	25.00
SK	Bill "Moose" Skowron	20.00
TH	Toby Harrah	15.00
TO	Tony Oliva	20.00
WH	Willie Horton	20.00

Signatures Barrel Black Ink
NM/M
Production 50 or 15
Barrel Blue Ink: 1X
Production 25 or 75
No pricing for production 15 or 25.

AG	Andres Galarraga/50	25.00
AK	Al Kaline/50	50.00
AO	Al Oliver/50	25.00
BJ	Bo Jackson/50	60.00
BM	Bill Mazeroski/50	50.00
DL	Don Larsen/50	50.00
EC	Dennis Eckersley/50	30.00
EM	Edgar Martinez/50	40.00
FM	Fred McGriff/50	30.00
GP	Gaylord Perry/50	25.00
HB	Harold Baines/50	25.00
JK	John Kruk/50	20.00
MO	Jack Morris/50	20.00
OG	Ozzie Guillen/50	25.00
RA	Roberto Alomar/50	25.00
RI	Jim Rice/50	30.00
SA	Ron Santo/50	30.00
SM	Reggie Smith/50	25.00
TM	Tino Martinez/50	30.00
TP	Tony Perez/50	30.00
TR	Tim Raines/50	30.00
EV	Dwight Evans/50	20.00
JI	Jim Bunning/50	25.00
KG	Ken Griffey Sr./50	20.00
LA	Luis Aparicio/50	20.00
MA	Juan Marichal/50	20.00
WH	Willie Horton/50	20.00

Sig. Black Barrel Silver Ink
NM/M
Production 3-47
Gold Ink: No Pricing
Production One Set

EC	Dennis Eckersley/43	30.00
FM	Fred McGriff/27	40.00
GP	Gaylord Perry/36	20.00
JK	John Kruk/29	30.00
MO	Jack Morris/47	25.00
TM	Tino Martinez/24	50.00
TP	Tony Perez/24	40.00
EV	Dwight Evans/24	35.00
KG	Ken Griffey Sr./25	20.00
WH	Willie Horton/23	35.00

Sig Black Leather Silver Ink
NM/M
Production 3-47
Green Ink: No Pricing
Production One Set

BS	Bruce Sutter/42	30.00
CF	Carlton Fisk/27	30.00
EC	Dennis Eckersley/43	30.00
FM	Fred McGriff/27	40.00
GP	Gaylord Perry/36	25.00
JK	John Kruk/29	30.00
MO	Jack Morris/47	25.00
NR	Nolan Ryan/30	140.00
RJ	Reggie Jackson/44	60.00
TM	Tino Martinez/24	50.00
TP	Tony Perez/24	40.00
TR	Tim Raines/30	20.00
WM	Willie McCovey/44	60.00
BW	Billy Williams/26	25.00
DG	Dick Groat/24	50.00
DW	Dave Winfield/31	30.00
EF	Elroy Face/26	20.00
EV	Dwight Evans/24	35.00
GI	Bob Gibson/45	50.00
KG	Ken Griffey Sr./30	25.00
KO	Sandy Koufax/32	350.00
MA	Juan Marichal/27	35.00
PN	Phil Niekro/35	35.00
RC	Rod Carew/29	30.00
RF	Rollie Fingers/34	20.00
RR	Robin Roberts/36	40.00
SC	Steve Carlton/32	30.00
WH	Willie Horton/23	35.00

Sig. Gold Stitch Black Ink
NM/M
Production 25 or 99
Blue Ink: 1-1.5X
Production 15 or 50

AG	Andres Galarraga/99	20.00
AK	Al Kaline/99	40.00
AO	Al Oliver/99	15.00
BJ	Bo Jackson/99	60.00
BM	Bill Mazeroski/99	40.00
BO	Wade Boggs/25	40.00
CF	Carlton Fisk/25	40.00
DA	Dick Allen/99	20.00
DL	Don Larsen/99	30.00
DM	Don Mattingly/25	75.00
EC	Dennis Eckersley/99	30.00
EM	Edgar Martinez/99	40.00
FM	Fred McGriff/99	40.00
GP	Gaylord Perry/99	20.00
HB	Harold Baines/99	20.00
JK	John Kruk/99	25.00
MO	Jack Morris/99	15.00
MS	Mike Schmidt/99	80.00
OG	Ozzie Guillen/99	20.00
RA	Roberto Alomar/99	30.00
RI	Jim Rice/99	20.00
RS	Ryne Sandberg/25	80.00
SA	Ron Santo/99	40.00
SM	Reggie Smith/99	20.00
TG	Tony Gwynn/99	75.00
TM	Tino Martinez/99	30.00
TP	Tony Perez/99	20.00
TR	Tim Raines/99	15.00
WB	Wade Boggs/25	50.00
WD	Willie Davis/25	30.00
WM	Willie McCovey/25	60.00
YB	Yogi Berra/25	80.00
BR	Brooks Robinson/99	35.00
BW	Billy Williams/99	25.00
CL	Carney Lansford/99	20.00
CO	Dave Concepcion/99	25.00
CY	Carl Yastrzemski/99	65.00
DG	Dick Groat/99	20.00
DS	Don Sutton/99	20.00
DW	Dave Winfield/99	30.00
EB	Ernie Banks/99	65.00
EF	Elroy Face/99	25.00
EV	Dwight Evans/99	20.00
FL	Fred Lynn/99	20.00
FR	Frank Robinson/25	50.00
GI	Bob Gibson/99	40.00
JI	Jim Bunning/99	25.00
JP	Johnny Pesky/99	30.00
JR	Jim Rice/99	25.00
KG	Ken Griffey Sr./99	25.00
KO	Sandy Koufax/99	300.00
LA	Luis Aparicio/99	20.00
LB	Lou Brock/25	40.00
MA	Juan Marichal/99	25.00
MG	Mark Grace/99	30.00
MU	Stan Musial/99	100.00
MV	Mickey Vernon/99	20.00
OS	Ozzie Smith/25	75.00
PN	Phil Niekro/99	20.00
RC	Rod Carew/99	35.00
RF	Rollie Fingers/34	20.00
RK	Ralph Kiner/25	60.00
RR	Robin Roberts/99	40.00
RY	Robin Yount/99	40.00
SC	Steve Carlton/99	30.00
SD	Shawon Dunston/99	20.00
SG	Steve Garvey/99	20.00
SK	"Moose" Skowron/99	20.00
TH	Toby Harrah/99	15.00
TO	Tony Oliva/99	20.00
WH	Willie Horton/99	20.00

Signatures Leather Blue Ink
NM/M
Production 75 unless noted.
Gold Ink: 1-1.5X
Production 15 or 50

AG	Andres Galarraga	25.00
AK	Al Kaline	50.00
AO	Al Oliver	25.00
BJ	Bo Jackson	75.00
BM	Bill Mazeroski	50.00
BO	Wade Boggs	40.00
CF	Carlton Fisk/25	40.00
DA	Dick Allen	20.00
DL	Don Larsen	30.00
DM	Don Mattingly/75	75.00
EC	Dennis Eckersley	30.00
EM	Edgar Martinez	50.00
FM	Fred McGriff	40.00
GP	Gaylord Perry	20.00
HB	Harold Baines	20.00
JK	John Kruk	20.00
MO	Jack Morris	20.00
MS	Mike Schmidt/25	80.00
OG	Ozzie Guillen	20.00
RA	Roberto Alomar	50.00
RI	Jim Rice	25.00
RS	Ryne Sandberg/25	80.00
SA	Ron Santo	50.00
SM	Reggie Smith	20.00
TG	Tony Gwynn/25	75.00
TM	Tino Martinez	30.00
TP	Tony Perez	20.00
TR	Tim Raines	20.00
WB	Wade Boggs/25	40.00
WD	Willie Davis/25	30.00
WM	Willie McCovey/25	60.00
YB	Yogi Berra/25	80.00
BR	Brooks Robinson/25	60.00
BW	Billy Williams/25	25.00
CL	Carney Lansford/25	20.00
CO	Dave Concepcion/25	20.00
CY	Carl Yastrzemski/25	80.00
DG	Dick Groat/25	25.00
DS	Don Sutton/25	20.00
DW	Dave Winfield/25	40.00
EB	Ernie Banks/25	80.00
EF	Elroy Face/25	30.00
EV	Dwight Evans	25.00
FL	Fred Lynn/25	25.00
FR	Frank Robinson/25	50.00
GI	Bob Gibson	25.00
JI	Jim Bunning	25.00
JP	Johnny Pesky/25	35.00
JR	Jim Rice/25	25.00
KG	Ken Griffey Sr.	15.00
KO	Sandy Koufax/25	350.00
LA	Luis Aparicio	30.00
LB	Lou Brock/25	40.00
MA	Juan Marichal	35.00
MG	Mark Grace/25	40.00
MU	Stan Musial/25	100.00
MV	Mickey Vernon/25	30.00
OS	Ozzie Smith/25	80.00
PN	Phil Niekro/25	25.00
RC	Rod Carew/25	50.00
RF	Rollie Fingers/25	30.00
RK	Ralph Kiner/25	50.00
RR	Robin Roberts/25	40.00
RY	Robin Yount/25	60.00
SC	Steve Carlton/25	25.00
SD	Shawon Dunston/25	25.00
SG	Steve Garvey/25	30.00
SK	"Moose" Skowron/25	30.00
TH	Toby Harrah/25	20.00
TO	Tony Oliva/25	30.00
WH	Willie Horton/25	20.00

Sig. Silver Stitch Blue Ink
NM/M
Production 3-47
Black Ink: No Pricing
Production 15 or 25

BS	Bruce Sutter/42	30.00
CF	Carlton Fisk/27	40.00
EC	Dennis Eckersley/43	30.00
FM	Fred McGriff/27	40.00
GP	Gaylord Perry/36	25.00
JK	John Kruk/29	30.00
MO	Jack Morris/47	25.00
NR	Nolan Ryan/30	140.00
RJ	Reggie Jackson/44	60.00
TM	Tino Martinez/24	50.00
TP	Tony Perez/24	40.00
TR	Tim Raines/30	40.00
WB	Wade Boggs/26	50.00
WM	Willie McCovey/44	60.00
BW	Billy Williams/26	25.00
DG	Dick Groat/24	20.00
DW	Dave Winfield/31	40.00
EF	Elroy Face/26	25.00
EV	Dwight Evans/24	35.00
GI	Bob Gibson/45	50.00
KG	Ken Griffey Sr./30	25.00
KO	Sandy Koufax/32	350.00
MA	Juan Marichal/27	40.00
PN	Phil Niekro/35	35.00
RC	Rod Carew/29	40.00
RF	Rollie Fingers/34	20.00
RR	Robin Roberts/36	40.00
SC	Steve Carlton/32	30.00
SD	Shawon Dunston/99	20.00
SG	Steve Garvey/99	20.00
SK	"Moose" Skowron/99	20.00
TH	Toby Harrah/99	15.00
TO	Tony Oliva/99	20.00
WH	Willie Horton/99	20.00

2007 UD Ultimate Collection
NM/M
Common Player (1-100): 1.50
Production 450
Common RC Auto. (101-141): 10.00
Production 289-299
Pack (4): 75.00

	Box (4):	250.00
1	Chipper Jones	4.00
2	Andruw Jones	2.00
3	Tim Hudson	2.00
4	Stephen Drew	2.00
5	Randy Johnson	3.00
6	Brandon Webb	2.00
7	Alfonso Soriano	3.00
8	Derrek Lee	2.00
9	Aramis Ramirez	2.00
10	Carlos Zambrano	2.00
11	Ken Griffey Jr.	6.00
12	Adam Dunn	2.00
13	Ryan Freel	1.50
14	Todd Helton	2.00
15	Garrett Atkins	1.50
16	Matt Holliday	2.00
17	Hanley Ramirez	3.00
18	Dontrelle Willis	1.50
19	Miguel Cabrera	3.00
20	Lance Berkman	2.00
21	Roy Oswalt	2.00
22	Carlos Lee	2.00
23	Nomar Garciaparra	3.00
24	Jason Schmidt	1.50
25	Juan Pierre	1.50
26	Russell Martin	2.00
27	Rickie Weeks	1.50
28	Prince Fielder	3.00
29	Ben Sheets	1.50
30	David Wright	5.00
31	Jose Reyes	4.00
32	Pedro Martinez	2.00
33	Carlos Beltran	2.00
34	Brett Myers	1.50
35	Jimmy Rollins	3.00
36	Ryan Howard	6.00
37	Jason Bay	2.00
38	Freddy Sanchez	1.50
39	Ian Snell	1.50
40	Jake Peavy	1.50
41	Greg Maddux	3.00
42	Brian Giles	1.50
43	Matt Cain	1.50
44	Barry Zito	1.50
45	Ray Durham	1.50
46	Albert Pujols	8.00
47	Chris Carpenter	2.00
48	Chris Duncan	1.50
49	Scott Rolen	2.00
50	Ryan Zimmerman	3.00
51	Chad Cordero	1.50
52	Ryan Church	1.50
53	Miguel Tejada	2.00
54	Erik Bedard	2.00
55	Brian Roberts	1.50
56	David Ortiz	4.00
57	Josh Beckett	2.00
58	Manny Ramirez	3.00
59	Daisuke Matsuzaka RC	15.00
60	Jim Thome	2.00
61	Paul Konerko	2.00
62	Jermaine Dye	1.50
63	Grady Sizemore	3.00
64	Victor Martinez	2.00
65	C.C. Sabathia	2.00
66	Ivan Rodriguez	2.00
67	Justin Verlander	2.00
68	Gary Sheffield	2.00
69	Jeremy Bonderman	2.00
70	Gil Meche	1.50
71	Mike Sweeney	1.50
72	Mark Teahen	1.50
73	Vladimir Guerrero	3.00
74	Howie Kendrick	1.50
75	Francisco Rodriguez	1.50
76	Johan Santana	2.00
77	Justin Morneau	2.00
78	Joe Mauer	3.00
79	Michael Cuddyer	1.50
80	Alex Rodriguez	8.00
81	Derek Jeter	8.00
82	Johnny Damon	3.00
83	Roger Clemens	6.00
84	Rich Harden	1.50
85	Mike Piazza	3.00
86	Huston Street	1.50
87	Ichiro Suzuki	6.00
88	Felix Hernandez	2.00
89	Kenji Johjima	1.50
90	Adrian Beltre	1.50
91	Carl Crawford	1.50
92	Scott Kazmir	1.50
93	B.J. Upton	1.50
94	Michael Young	1.50
95	Mark Teixeira	2.00
96	Sammy Sosa	3.00
97	Hank Blalock	1.50
98	Vernon Wells	2.00
99	Roy Halladay	3.00
100	Frank Thomas	3.00
101	Adam Lind (RC)	10.00
102	Akinori Iwamura RC	15.00
103	Andrew Miller RC	10.00
104	Michael Bourn (RC)	10.00
105	Kory Casto (RC)	10.00
106	Ryan Braun (RC)	80.00
107	Sean Gallagher (RC)	10.00
108	Billy Butler (RC)	30.00
109	Alexi Casilla RC	10.00
110	Chris Stewart RC	10.00
111	Matt DeSalvo (RC)	10.00
112	Chase Headley (RC)	15.00
113	Delmon Young (RC)	10.00
114	Homer Bailey (RC)	15.00
115	Kurt Suzuki (RC)	15.00
116	Alex Gordon RC	15.00
117	Josh Hamilton (RC)	40.00
118	Fred Lewis (RC)	10.00
119	Glen Perkins (RC)	10.00
120	Hector Gimenez (RC)	10.00
121	Phil Hughes (RC)	50.00
122	Jeff Baker (RC)	10.00
123	Adam LaRoche (RC)	-15.00
124	Tim Lincecum RC	120.00
125	Joaquin Arias (RC)	10.00
126	Daisuke Matsuzaka RC	100.00
127	Micah Owings (RC)	10.00
128	Hunter Pence (RC)	25.00
129	Matt Chico (RC)	10.00
130	Kei Igawa (RC)	15.00
131	Kevin Kouzmanoff (RC)	15.00
132	Miguel Montero (RC)	10.00
133	Mike Rabelo RC	10.00
134	Felix Pie (RC)	15.00
135	Curtis Thigpen (RC)	10.00
136	Ryan Braun RC	10.00
137	Ryan Sweeney (RC)	10.00
138	Brandon Wood (RC)	10.00
139	Troy Tulowitzki (RC)	40.00
140	Justin Upton RC	60.00
141	Joba Chamberlain RC	50.00

America's Pastime Signature
NM/M

AD	Adam Dunn	15.00
AE	Andre Ethier	10.00
AG	Adrian Gonzalez	10.00
AJ	A.J. Burnett	10.00
AK	Al Kaline	30.00
AL	Adam LaRoche	10.00
AP	Albert Pujols	150.00
AV	Andy Van Slyke	15.00
BB	Boof Bonser	10.00
BE	Johnny Bench	30.00
BJ	B.J. Upton	15.00
BM	Bill Mazeroski	25.00
CB	Chad Billingsley	15.00
CC	Chad Cordero	10.00
CH	Cole Hamels	30.00
CK	Casey Kotchman	10.00
CQ	Carlos Quentin	10.00
CR	Craig Biggio	50.00
CT	Curtis Thigpen	10.00
CW	Chien-Ming Wang	40.00
CY	Chris Young	10.00
DH	Danny Haren	15.00
DJ	Derek Jeter	125.00
DM	Don Mattingly	50.00
DS	Don Sutton	15.00
DU	Dan Uggla	15.00
DY	Delmon Young	15.00
EB	Ernie Banks	50.00
FH	Felix Hernandez	25.00
FR	Frank Robinson	25.00
GA	Garrett Atkins	10.00
GP	Gaylord Perry	10.00
GR	Khalil Greene	10.00
GW	Tony Gwynn	50.00
HA	Travis Hafner	15.00
HB	Homer Bailey	15.00
HE	Chase Headley	10.00
HO	Howie Kendrick	10.00
HR	Hanley Ramirez	20.00
HS	Huston Street	10.00
HU	Torii Hunter	15.00
IK	Ian Kinsler	20.00
JB	Jason Bay	10.00
JE	Jeremy Bonderman	10.00
JI	Jim Rice	20.00
JL	James Loney	20.00
JM	Jack Morris	20.00
JN	Joe Nathan	10.00
JO	Joe Blanton	10.00
JT	Jim Thome	20.00
JV	Justin Verlander	30.00
JZ	Joel Zumaya	10.00
KI	Kei Igawa	10.00
KJ	Kelly Johnson	10.00
KM	Kendry Morales	10.00
LA	Andy LaRoche	15.00
LE	Jon Lester	25.00
LY	John Lackey	10.00
MA	Daisuke Matsuzaka	100.00
MB	Matt Brown	10.00
MC	Matt Cain	15.00
MH	Matt Holliday	40.00
MM	Melvin Mora	10.00
MS	Mike Schmidt	40.00
MT	Mark Teixeira	25.00
NM	Nicholas Markakis	20.00
NW	Nick Swisher	15.00
OS	Ozzie Smith	50.00
PA	Jim Palmer	25.00
PB	Jonathan Papelbon	25.00
PK	Paul Konerko	15.00
RA	Aramis Ramirez	15.00
RB	Ryan Braun	50.00
RF	Rafael Furcal	10.00
RG	Ryan Garko	10.00
RH	Rich Harden	10.00
RI	Rich Hill	10.00
RT	Ryan Theriot	10.00
RW	Rickie Weeks	10.00
RZ	Ryan Zimmerman	20.00
SD	Stephen Drew	15.00
SG	Sean Gallagher	10.00
SK	Scott Kazmir	15.00
SM	Stan Musial	75.00
SO	Joakim Soria	10.00
TG	Tom Glavine	50.00
TP	Tony Perez	15.00
TR	Tim Raines	20.00
TU	Troy Tulowitzki	40.00

M	Victor Martinez	15.00
W	Vernon Wells	15.00
VC	Will Clark	15.00
VI	Josh Willingham	10.00
	Willie McCovey	60.00
N	Xavier Nady	10.00

America's Ultimate Pastime Materials

		NM/M
Production 75 unless noted.		
Patch:		2X
Production 5-50		
No pricing 25 or less.		
Gold:		No Pricing
Production 25 Sets		
B	Adrian Beltre	8.00
J	Andruw Jones	5.00
P	Andy Pettitte	10.00
S	Alfonso Soriano	10.00
A	Bobby Abreu	8.00
G	Josh Beckett	5.00
G	Brian Giles	5.00
J	Jeff Bagwell	8.00
R	Brian Roberts	5.00
	Ben Sheets	5.00
W	Brandon Webb	8.00
C	Chris Carpenter	8.00
B	Carlos Beltran	5.00
C	Carl Crawford	5.00
F	Carlton Fisk	10.00
J	Chipper Jones	10.00
L	Carlos Lee	5.00
R	Cal Ripken Jr.	25.00
S	Curt Schilling	8.00
U	Chase Utley	10.00
J	Derek Jeter	25.00
L	Derek Lee	8.00
O	David Ortiz	8.00
W	Dontrelle Willis	5.00
H	Felix Hernandez	10.00
L	Francisco Liriano	10.00
L	Francisco Rodriguez/64	5.00
A	Garrett Atkins	5.00
S	Greg Maddux	15.00
S	Gary Sheffield	8.00
W	Tony Gwynn	10.00
H	Rich Harden	5.00
B	Hank Blalock	5.00
R	Hanley Ramirez	5.00
A	Jason Bay	8.00
B	Jeremy Bonderman	5.00
E	Jim Edmonds	5.00
G	Jason Giambi	5.00
N	Justin Morneau	5.00
N	Joe Nathan	5.00
O	Randy Johnson	10.00
P	Jonathan Papelbon	8.00
R	Jim Rice	5.00
S	Johan Santana	10.00
T	Jim Thome	10.00
V	Justin Verlander	8.00
W	Josh Willingham	5.00
G	Ken Griffey Jr.	12.00
P	Kirby Puckett	25.00
Y	Kevin Youkilis	5.00
B	Lance Berkman	5.00
B	Lou Brock/25	15.00
A	Joe Mauer	8.00
C	Matt Cain	8.00
H	Matt Holliday	10.00
I	Miguel Cabrera	10.00
M	Mike Mussina	10.00
R	Manny Ramirez	10.00
S	Mike Schmidt	20.00
T	Miguel Tejada	5.00
Y	Michael Young	8.00
Z	Pedro Martinez	10.00
R	Nolan Ryan	25.00
R	Magglio Ordonez	5.00
S	Ozzie Smith	15.00
E	Jake Peavy	10.00
F	Prince Fielder	10.00
M	Paul Molitor	10.00
U	Albert Pujols	25.00
B	Rocco Baldelli	5.00
C	Roger Clemens	15.00
E	Jose Reyes	5.00
H	Roy Halladay	10.00
O	Reggie Jackson	15.00
O	Roy Oswalt	5.00
W	Ryne Sandberg	15.00
W	Rickie Weeks	5.00
Z	Ryan Zimmerman	8.00
C	Steve Carlton	8.00
E	Richie Sexson	5.00
I	Grady Sizemore	8.00
K	Scott Kazmir	5.00
M	John Smoltz	10.00
E	Mark Teixeira	8.00
G	Troy Glaus	5.00
R	Todd Helton	8.00
R	Travis Hafner	5.00
A	Jason Varitek	8.00
G	Vladimir Guerrero	10.00
M	Victor Martinez	5.00
C	Will Clark	8.00
F2	Carlton Fisk	10.00
W2	Tony Gwynn	15.00
R2	Manny Ramirez	8.00
E2	Jose Reyes	15.00
I2	Grady Sizemore	8.00
F2	Travis Hafner	8.00
G	Vladimir Guerrero	8.00

The Ultimate Card

Production One Set

Ultimate Iron Man Signature

Production Eight Sets

The Ultimate Logo

Production One Set

The Ultimate Patch

Production 25 unless noted.

The Ultimate Six Signatures

Production 10 Sets

Ultimate Champions Signatures

Production 4-10

Ultimate Ensemble Dual Patches

No Pricing
Production 25 Sets

Ultimate Ensemble Triple Patch

Production 15 Sets

Ultimate Ensemble Quad Patch

Production 10 Sets

Ultimate Ensemble Dual Swatch

		NM/M
Production 75 sets unless noted.		
BD	J.D. Drew, Jason Bay	10.00
BH	Jeremy Bonderman, Rich Harden	10.00
BZ	Wade Boggs, Ryan Zimmerman	10.00
CG	Vladimir Guerrero, Miguel Cabrera	15.00
CJ	Curt Schilling, Josh Beckett	15.00
CR	Roger Clemens, Nolan Ryan	25.00
CW	Matt Cain, Jered Weaver	10.00
FT	Mark Teixeira, Prince Fielder	10.00
GD	Ken Griffey Jr., Adam Dunn	20.00
GM	Tom Glavine, Pedro Martinez	10.00
GP	Tony Gwynn, Jake Peavy	15.00
GR	Tony Gwynn, Cal Ripken Jr.	30.00
HH	Todd Helton, Matt Holliday	10.00
HJ	Felix Hernandez, Kenji Johjima	10.00
HR	J.J. Hardy, Jose Reyes	10.00
HW	Vernon Wells, Roy Halladay	10.00
IK	Paul Konerko, Tadahito Iguchi	10.00
JJ	Andruw Jones, Chipper Jones	10.00
JR	Derek Jeter, Mariano Rivera	25.00
JV	Victor Martinez, Joe Mauer	10.00
KY	Scott Kazmir, Delmon Young	10.00
LS	Derek Lee, Alfonso Soriano	10.00
MB	Mike Schmidt, Brooks Robinson	25.00
MC	Michael Cuddyer, Justin Morneau	10.00
MM	Justin Morneau, Joe Mauer	10.00
NR	Mariano Rivera, Joe Nathan	10.00
OB	Lance Berkman, Roy Oswalt	10.00
PC	Chris Carpenter, Albert Pujols	20.00
PO	David Ortiz, Albert Pujols	20.00
RB	Ivan Rodriguez, Johnny Bench	15.00
SB	Carlos Beltran, Grady Sizemore	15.00
SC	Alfonso Soriano, Carl Crawford/52	10.00
SL	Johan Santana, Francisco Liriano	10.00
SP	John Smoltz, Jake Peavy	10.00
SR	Cal Ripken Jr., Ryne Sandberg/63	50.00
SW	Johan Santana, Brandon Webb	10.00
TR	Cal Ripken Jr., Miguel Tejada	20.00
WU	Rickie Weeks, Chase Utley	15.00
YR	Michael Young, Jose Reyes	15.00

Ultimate Ensemble Triple Swatch

		NM/M
Production 50 Sets		
BCG	Troy Glaus, Eric Chavez, Hank Blalock	15.00

CBG	Tony Gwynn, Will Clark, Wade Boggs	20.00
CRS	Nolan Ryan, Don Sutton, Steve Carlton	20.00
CSK	Johan Santana, Scott Kazmir, Steve Carlton	15.00
FHS	Ben Sheets, J.J. Hardy, Prince Fielder	10.00
GRR	Khalil Greene, Jose Reyes, Hanley Ramirez	10.00
HTP	Mike Piazza, Frank Thomas, Travis Hafner	15.00
LPD	Barry Larkin, Tony Perez, Adam Dunn	15.00
LRS	Ozzie Smith, Barry Larkin, Cal Ripken Jr.	25.00
MCS	Roger Clemens, Pedro Martinez, Don Sutton	25.00
MJG	Ken Griffey Jr., Chipper Jones, Joe Mauer	25.00
MMP	Jorge Posada, Victor Martinez, Joe Mauer	15.00
MSB	Curt Schilling, Josh Beckett, Daisuke Matsuzaka	65.00
MSU	Ryne Sandberg, Bill Mazeroski, Chase Utley	25.00
OCZ	Chris Carpenter, Roy Oswalt, Carlos Zambrano	15.00
ODH	Jermaine Dye, Travis Hafner, David Ortiz	15.00
OMT	David Ortiz, Mark Teixeira, Justin Morneau	15.00
OPR	David Ortiz, Albert Pujols, Jose Reyes	25.00
PJL	Andruw Jones, Derek Lee, Albert Pujols	25.00
RDB	Carlos Delgado, Carlos Beltran, Ivan Rodriguez	15.00
RJG	Ken Griffey Jr., Cal Ripken Jr., Derek Jeter	50.00
RPJ	Kirby Puckett, Jim Rice, Reggie Jackson	60.00
RPS	Manny Ramirez, Alfonso Soriano, Albert Pujols	25.00
RSB	Wade Boggs, Mike Schmidt, Brooks Robinson	40.00
SHS	Roy Halladay, Josh Beckett, Johan Santana	
UWG	Marcus Giles, Rickie Weeks, Chase Utley	20.00
YBO	Wade Boggs, David Ortiz, Carl Yastrzemski	25.00
YJT	Derek Jeter, Miguel Tejada, Michael Young	25.00
YTS	Sammy Sosa, Michael Young, Mark Teixeira	20.00
ZAJ	Chipper Jones, Garrett Atkins, Ryan Zimmerman	15.00

Ultimate Ensemble Quad Swatch

No Pricing
Production 25 unless noted.

Ultimate Futures Signatures

Production 25 unless noted.

Ultimate Legendary Signatures

Production 25 Sets

Ultimate Numbers Match Signature

		NM/M
Production 2-48		
AR	Garrett Atkins, Mark Reynolds/27	15.00
BW	Jeremy Bonderman, Chase Wright/38	15.00
BZ	Carlos Zambrano, Jason Bay/38	25.00
FG	Vladimir Guerrero, Carlton Fisk/27	75.00
HH	Travis Hafner, Torii Hunter/48	25.00
HR	Nolan Ryan, Felix Hernandez/34	100.00
HV	Justin Verlander, Cole Hamels/35	50.00
HW	Chien-Ming Wang, Rich Harden/40	180.00
JD	Adam Dunn, Reggie Jackson/44	50.00
WH	Dontrelle Willis, Cole Hamels/35	50.00

Ultimate Numbers Materials

		NM/M
Production 1-75		
No pricing 25 or less.		
AB	A.J. Burnett/34	8.00
AD	Adam Dunn/44	10.00
AJ	Andruw Jones/25	10.00
AN	Andy Pettitte/46	10.00
BA	Bobby Abreu/53	8.00
BE	Adrian Beltre/29	8.00
BZ	Barry Zito/75	8.00
CC	Chris Carpenter/29	10.00
CF	Carlton Fisk/27	10.00
CL	Carlos Lee/45	8.00
CS	Curt Schilling/38	10.00

CU	Chase Utley/26	15.00
DL	Derek Lee/25	10.00
DO	David Ortiz/34	15.00
DY	Delmon Young/26	8.00
FH	Felix Hernandez/34	10.00
FL	Francisco Liriano/47	8.00
GA	Garrett Atkins/27	8.00
GL	Troy Glaus/25	8.00
GP	Gaylord Perry/36	10.00
HA	Roy Halladay/32	8.00
HF	Travis Hafner/48	8.00
HU	Torii Hunter/48	8.00
JE	Jeremy Bonderman/38	8.00
JH	Josh Hamilton/33	15.00
JS	Johan Santana/57	10.00
JH	Jim Thome/25	10.00
JV	Jason Varitek/33	20.00
MO	Magglio Ordonez/30	8.00
NR	Nolan Ryan/34	40.00
OS	Roy Oswalt/44	10.00
PF	Prince Fielder/28	10.00
RC	Rod Carew/29	10.00
RH	Rich Harden/40	8.00
RJ	Randy Johnson/51	10.00
SA	C.C. Sabathia/52	8.00
SC	Steve Carlton/32	10.00
SR	Scott Rolen/27	10.00
TG	Tom Glavine/47	15.00
TR	Tim Raines/30	8.00
TV	Trevor Hoffman/51	8.00
VG	Vladimir Guerrero/27	10.00
VM	Victor Martinez/41	8.00
WI	Dontrelle Willis/35	8.00
CF2	Carlton Fisk/72	10.00
DL2	Derek Lee/25	10.00
DO2	David Ortiz/25	15.00

Ultimate Star Materials

		NM/M
Common Player:		5.00
Patch Autograph:		No Pricing
Production Five Sets		
Autographs:		No Pricing
Production 15 Sets		
AD	Adam Dunn	8.00
AG	Alex Gordon	5.00
AK	Austin Kearns	5.00
AP	Albert Pujols	20.00
BG	Brian Giles	5.00
BI	Craig Biggio	5.00
BO	Jeremy Bonderman	5.00
BS	Ben Sheets	5.00
BU	B.J. Upton	8.00
CA	Chris Carpenter	8.00
CF	Carlton Fisk	8.00
CL	Carlos Lee	5.00
CR	Cal Ripken Jr.	20.00
CY	Carl Yastrzemski	15.00
CZ	Carlos Zambrano	5.00
DH	Danny Haren	5.00
DJ	Derek Jeter	20.00
DL	Derek Lee	5.00
DM	Don Mattingly	15.00
DO	David Ortiz	8.00
DW	Dontrelle Willis	5.00
EC	Eric Chavez	5.00
FH	Felix Hernandez	8.00
FL	Francisco Liriano	8.00
FR	Francisco Rodriguez	8.00
FT	Frank Thomas	10.00
GA	Garrett Atkins	5.00
GR	Khalil Greene	5.00
GW	Tony Gwynn	10.00
HA	Roy Halladay	10.00
HP	Hunter Pence	8.00
HR	Hanley Ramirez	10.00
HS	Huston Street	5.00
HU	Torii Hunter	5.00
JA	Jason Bay	5.00
JB	Josh Beckett	5.00
JL	Jeremy Hermida	5.00
JL	John Lackey	5.00
JM	Joe Mauer	10.00
JN	Joe Nathan	5.00
JP	Jonathan Papelbon	8.00
JR	Jim Rice	8.00
JS	John Smoltz	8.00
JT	Jim Thome	8.00
JU	Justin Morneau	5.00
KG	Ken Griffey Jr.	15.00
MC	Matt Cain	8.00
MC	Miguel Cabrera	10.00
MS	Matt Holliday	10.00
MS	Mike Schmidt	15.00
MT	Mark Teixeira	8.00
MY	Michael Young	5.00
NM	Nicholas Markakis	5.00
NR	Nolan Ryan	20.00
NS	Nick Swisher	5.00
OR	Roy Oswalt	5.00
OS	Ozzie Smith	15.00
PA	Jim Palmer	8.00
PE	Jake Peavy	8.00
PF	Prince Fielder	8.00
PK	Paul Konerko	5.00
PM	Paul Molitor	5.00
RA	Roberto Alomar	5.00
RC	Roger Clemens	15.00
RF	Rollie Fingers	8.00
RH	Rich Harden	8.00
RJ	Randy Johnson	10.00
RO	Rod Carew	10.00
RW	Rickie Weeks	5.00
RY	Robin Yount	8.00
RZ	Ryan Zimmerman	8.00
SK	Scott Kazmir	5.00
TG	Tom Glavine	8.00
TH	Travis Hafner	5.00
RI	Cal Ripken Jr.	30.00

TI	Tim Hudson	5.00
TT	Troy Tulowitzki	10.00
VM	Victor Martinez	5.00
VW	Vernon Wells	5.00
WB	Wade Boggs	10.00
WI	Josh Willingham	5.00
AG2	Alex Gordon	5.00
AK2	Austin Kearns	5.00
CL2	Carlos Lee	5.00
CR2	Cal Ripken Jr.	20.00
DJ2	Derek Jeter	20.00
DW2	Dontrelle Willis	5.00
FH2	Felix Hernandez	8.00
GA2	Garrett Atkins	5.00
JT2	Jim Thome	8.00
JU2	Justin Morneau	8.00
MA2	Matt Cain	8.00
MH2	Matt Holliday	10.00
MT2	Mark Teixeira	8.00
MY2	Michael Young	5.00
PE2	Jake Peavy	8.00
PM2	Paul Molitor	5.00
RZ2	Ryan Zimmerman	10.00
TH2	Travis Hafner	5.00

Ultimate Team Marks

		NM/M
Production 60 sets unless noted.		
CL	Carlos Lee/57	20.00
CY	Carl Yastrzemski/58	50.00
DJ	Derek Jeter	140.00
DL	Derek Lee/58	25.00
DO	David Ortiz	50.00
DW	Dontrelle Willis/56	10.00
FH	Felix Hernandez	30.00
JM	Joe Mauer	40.00
MO	Justin Morneau	25.00
MT	Mark Teixeira	20.00
PF	Prince Fielder	40.00
VM	Victor Martinez	15.00
VW	Vernon Wells	10.00

Ultimate Team Materials

		NM/M
Production 50 unless noted.		
Patch:		No Pricing
Production 19-25		
Autographs:		No Pricing
Production 1-10		
AD	Adam Dunn	8.00
AK	Austin Kearns	5.00
AN	Garret Anderson	5.00
AP	Albert Pujols	20.00
BE	Josh Beckett	10.00
BG	Brian Giles	5.00
BS	Ben Sheets	5.00
BU	B.J. Upton	8.00
CA	Rod Carew	10.00
CF	Carlton Fisk	8.00
CH	Chris Carpenter	8.00
CL	Carlos Lee	5.00
CR	Bobby Crosby	5.00
CY	Carl Yastrzemski	15.00
DH	Danny Haren	5.00
DJ	Derek Jeter	25.00
DL	Derek Lee	5.00
DM	Don Mattingly	15.00
DO	David Ortiz	10.00
DW	Dontrelle Willis	5.00
EC	Eric Chavez	5.00
FH	Felix Hernandez	8.00
FJ	Fergie Jenkins	8.00
FL	Francisco Liriano	10.00
FR	Francisco Rodriguez	5.00
FT	Frank Thomas	8.00
GA	Garrett Atkins	5.00
GR	Khalil Greene	5.00
GW	Tony Gwynn	8.00
HA	Rich Harden	5.00
HP	Hunter Pence	15.00
HR	Hanley Ramirez	10.00
HS	Huston Street	5.00
HU	Tim Hudson	5.00
JA	Jason Bay	5.00
JE	Jeremy Bonderman	5.00
JG	Jonny Gomes	5.00
JH	Jeremy Hermida	5.00
JI	Jim Palmer	8.00
JL	John Lackey	5.00
JM	Joe Mauer	10.00
JN	Joe Nathan	5.00
JP	Jake Peavy	8.00
JR	Jim Rice	8.00
JS	John Smoltz	8.00
JT	Jim Thome	8.00
KG	Ken Griffey Jr.	15.00
KM	Kendry Morales	5.00
MA	Daisuke Matsuzaka	60.00
MC	Matt Cain	8.00
MH	Matt Holliday	10.00
MI	Miguel Cabrera	10.00
MO	Justin Morneau	8.00
MS	Mike Schmidt	10.00
MT	Mark Teixeira	8.00
MY	Michael Young	5.00
NM	Nicholas Markakis	5.00
NR	Nolan Ryan	25.00
OS	Ozzie Smith	15.00
PA	Jonathan Papelbon	10.00
PF	Prince Fielder	8.00
PK	Paul Konerko	5.00
PN	Phil Niekro	8.00
RA	Roberto Alomar	8.00
RC	Roger Clemens	15.00
RF	Rollie Fingers	8.00
RH	Roy Halladay	8.00
RI	Cal Ripken Jr.	30.00

RJ	Randy Johnson	10.00
RO	Roy Oswalt	8.00
RS	Ryne Sandberg	15.00
RW	Rickie Weeks	8.00
RY	Robin Yount/25	15.00
RZ	Ryan Zimmerman	8.00
SK	Scott Kazmir	5.00
TG	Tom Glavine	10.00
TH	Torii Hunter	8.00
TR	Travis Hafner	8.00
TT	Troy Tulowitzki	8.00
VM	Victor Martinez	8.00
WI	Josh Willingham	5.00
DW2	Dontrelle Willis	5.00
EC2	Eric Chavez	5.00
GA2	Garrett Atkins	5.00
HS2	Huston Street	5.00
KG2	Ken Griffey Jr.	15.00
MH2	Matt Holliday	10.00
MI2	Miguel Cabrera	10.00
MO2	Justin Morneau	8.00
OS2	Ozzie Smith	15.00
RI2	Cal Ripken Jr.	30.00
RZ2	Ryan Zimmerman	8.00
SK2	Scott Kazmir	8.00
TR2	Travis Hafner	8.00
WI2	Josh Willingham	5.00

Ultimate Write of Passage

		NM/M
Production 60 Sets		
BH	Jeff Baker/Auto., Matt Holliday	10.00
BR	Ryan Braun/Auto., Scott Rolen	75.00
GR	Alex Gordon/Auto., Alex Rodriguez	30.00
HS	Cole Hamels/Auto., Johan Santana	40.00
IC	Kei Igawa/Auto.	20.00
IR	Akinori Iwamura/Auto., Aramis Ramirez	20.00
KB	Howie Kendrick/Auto., Craig Biggio	10.00
KJ	Kevin Kouzmanoff/Auto., Chipper Jones	10.00
LZ	Tim Lincecum/Auto., Barry Zito	75.00
MS	Andrew Miller/Auto., C.C. Sabathia	15.00
PG	Hunter Pence/Auto., Ken Griffey Jr.	25.00
PK	Glen Perkins/Auto., Scott Kazmir	10.00
QC	Carlos Quentin/Auto., Carl Crawford	10.00
RF	Hanley Ramirez/Auto., Rafael Furcal	25.00
SD	Ryan Sweeney/Auto., Jermaine Dye	
SS	Jeremy Sowers/Auto., C.C. Sabathia	
TD	Curtis Thigpen/Auto., Carlos Delgado	10.00
TJ	Troy Tulowitzki/Auto., Derek Jeter	40.00
UU	B.J. Upton/ Auto., Chase Utley	15.00
YG	Delmon Young/Auto., Vladimir Guerrero	15.00

Ultimate Collection Jersey Parallel

		NM/M
Production 50 Sets		
Patch:		No Pricing
Production 25 Sets		
1	Chipper Jones	10.00
2	Andruw Jones	8.00
3	Tim Hudson	8.00
4	Stephen Drew	8.00
5	Randy Johnson	10.00
6	Brandon Webb	8.00
7	Alfonso Soriano	8.00
8	Derek Lee	8.00
9	Aramis Ramirez	8.00
10	Carlos Zambrano	10.00
11	Ken Griffey Jr.	15.00
12	Adam Dunn	8.00
13	Ryan Freel	5.00
14	Todd Helton	8.00
15	Garrett Atkins	5.00
16	Matt Holliday	10.00
17	Hanley Ramirez	10.00
18	Dontrelle Willis	5.00
19	Miguel Cabrera	8.00
20	Lance Berkman	8.00
21	Roy Oswalt	5.00
22	Carlos Lee	8.00
24	Jason Schmidt	8.00
25	Juan Pierre	5.00
26	Russell Martin	8.00
27	Rickie Weeks	5.00
28	Prince Fielder	10.00
29	Ben Sheets	8.00
31	Jose Reyes	8.00
32	Pedro Martinez	8.00
33	Carlos Beltran	5.00
34	Brett Myers	8.00
35	Jimmy Rollins	15.00
37	Jason Bay	8.00
38	Freddy Sanchez	5.00
39	Ian Snell	5.00
40	Jake Peavy	8.00
41	Greg Maddux	15.00
42	Brian Giles	8.00
43	Matt Cain	8.00
44	Barry Zito	8.00

#	Player	Price
45	Ray Durham	5.00
46	Albert Pujols	20.00
47	Chris Carpenter	8.00
48	Chris Duncan	5.00
49	Scott Rolen	8.00
50	Ryan Zimmerman	8.00
51	Chad Cordero	5.00
52	Ryan Church	5.00
53	Miguel Tejada	5.00
54	Erik Bedard	15.00
55	Brian Roberts	5.00
56	David Ortiz	8.00
57	Josh Beckett	5.00
58	Manny Ramirez	8.00
59	Daisuke Matsuzaka	20.00
60	Jim Thome	8.00
61	Paul Konerko	5.00
62	Jermaine Dye	5.00
63	Grady Sizemore	8.00
64	Victor Martinez	8.00
65	C.C. Sabathia	8.00
66	Ivan Rodriguez	8.00
67	Justin Verlander	10.00
68	Gary Sheffield	8.00
69	Jeremy Bonderman	5.00
70	Gil Meche	5.00
71	Mike Sweeney	5.00
72	Mark Teahen	5.00
73	Vladimir Guerrero	8.00
74	Howie Kendrick	8.00
75	Francisco Rodriguez	5.00
76	Johan Santana	10.00
77	Justin Morneau	8.00
78	Joe Mauer	10.00
79	Michael Cuddyer	5.00
80	Derek Jeter	25.00
81	Derek Jeter	25.00
83	Roger Clemens	15.00
84	Rich Harden	5.00
85	Mike Piazza	15.00
86	Huston Street	5.00
87	Felix Hernandez	10.00
88	Felix Hernandez	10.00
89	Kenji Johjima	5.00
90	Adrian Beltre	5.00
91	Carl Crawford	5.00
92	Scott Kazmir	5.00
93	B.J. Upton	5.00
94	Michael Young	5.00
95	Mark Teixeira	8.00
97	Hank Blalock	5.00
98	Vernon Wells	5.00
99	Vernon Wells	8.00
100	Frank Thomas	10.00

2008 Upper Deck

	NM/M
Complete Series 1 Set (400):	50.00
Complete Series 2 Set (399):	40.00
Common Player:	.15
Hobby Pack (20):	5.00
Hobby Box (16):	70.00

#	Player	Price
1	Joe Saunders	.15
2	Kelvim Escobar	.15
3	Jered Weaver	.25
4	Justin Speier	.15
5	Scot Shields	.15
6	Mike Napoli	.15
7	Orlando Cabrera	.25
8	Casey Kotchman	.15
9	Vladimir Guerrero	.75
10	Garret Anderson	.15
11	Roy Oswalt	.50
12	Wandy Rodriguez	.15
13	Woody Williams	.15
14	Chad Qualls	.15
15	Brian Moehler	.15
16	Mark Loretta	.15
17	Brad Ausmus	.15
18	Ty Wigginton	.15
19	Carlos Lee	.50
20	Hunter Pence	.50
21	Danny Haren	.25
22	Lenny DiNardo	.15
23	Chad Gaudin	.15
24	Huston Street	.15
25	Andrew Brown	.15
26	Mike Piazza	.50
27	Jack Cust	.15
28	Mark Ellis	.15
29	Shannon Stewart	.15
30	Travis Buck	.15
31	Shaun Marcum	.15
32	A.J. Burnett	.15
33	Jesse Litsch	.15
34	Casey Janssen	.15
35	Jeremy Accardo	.15
36	Gregg Zaun	.15
37	Aaron Hill	.25
38	Frank Thomas	.50
39	Matt Stairs	.15
40	Vernon Wells	.25
41	Tim Hudson	.25
42	Chuck James	.15
43	Buddy Carlyle	.15
44	Rafael Soriano	.15
45	Peter Moylan	.15
46	Brian McCann	.25
47	Edgar Renteria	.15
48	Mark Teixeira	.50
49	Willie Harris	.15
50	Andruw Jones	.50
51	Ben Sheets	.25
52	David Bush	.15
53	Yovani Gallardo	.50
54	Francisco Cordero	.15
55	Matt Wise	.15
56	Johnny Estrada	.15
57	Prince Fielder	1.00
58	J.J. Hardy	.15
59	Corey Hart	.15
60	Geoff Jenkins	.15
61	Adam Wainwright	.15
62	Joel Pineiro	.15
63	Brad Thompson	.15
64	Jason Isringhausen	.15
65	Troy Percival	.15
66	Yadier Molina	.15
67	Albert Pujols	2.00
68	David Eckstein	.15
69	Jim Edmonds	.25
70	Rick Ankiel	.25
71	Ted Lilly	.15
72	Rich Hill	.25
73	Jason Marquis	.15
74	Carlos Marmol	.15
75	Ryan Dempster	.15
76	Jason Kendall	.15
77	Aramis Ramirez	.50
78	Ryan Theriot	.15
79	Alfonso Soriano	.50
80	Jacque Jones	.15
81	James Shields	.25
82	Andrew Sonnanstine	.15
83	Scott Dohmann	.15
84	Al Reyes	.15
85	Dioner Navarro	.15
86	B.J. Upton	.50
87	Carlos Pena	.25
88	Brendan Harris	.15
89	Josh Wilson	.15
90	Jonny Gomes	.15
91	Brandon Webb	.25
92	Micah Owings	.15
93	Livan Hernandez	.15
94	Doug Slaten	.15
95	Brandon Lyon	.15
96	Miguel Montero	.15
97	Stephen Drew	.25
98	Mark Reynolds	.15
99	Conor Jackson	.15
100	Chris B. Young	.25
101	Chad Billingsley	.25
102	Derek Lowe	.15
103	Mark Hendrickson	.15
104	Takashi Saito	.15
105	Rudy Seanez	.15
106	Russell Martin	.50
107	Jeff Kent	.25
108	Nomar Garciaparra	.25
109	Matthew Kemp	.50
110	Juan Pierre	.15
111	Matt Cain	.25
112	Barry Zito	.15
113	Kevin Correia	.15
114	Brad Hennessey	.15
115	Jack Taschner	.15
116	Bengie Molina	.15
117	Ryan Klesko	.15
118	Omar Vizquel	.15
119	Dave Roberts	.15
120	Rajai Davis	.15
121	Fausto Carmona	.25
122	Jake Westbrook	.15
123	Cliff Lee	.15
124	Rafael Betancourt	.15
125	Joe Borowski	.15
126	Victor Martinez	.25
127	Travis Hafner	.25
128	Ryan Garko	.25
129	Kenny Lofton	.25
130	Franklin Gutierrez	.15
131	Felix Hernandez	.50
132	Jeff Weaver	.15
133	J.J. Putz	.15
134	Brandon Morrow	.15
135	Sean Green	.15
136	Kenji Johjima	.15
137	Jose Vidro	.15
138	Richie Sexson	.15
139	Ichiro Suzuki	1.50
140	Ben Broussard	.15
141	Sergio Mitre	.15
142	Scott Olsen	.15
143	Rick Vanden Hurk	.15
144	Justin Miller	.15
145	Lee Gardner	.15
146	Miguel Olivo	.15
147	Hanley Ramirez	.75
148	Mike Jacobs	.15
149	Josh Willingham	.15
150	Alfredo Amezaga	.15
151	John Maine	.25
152	Tom Glavine	.25
153	Orlando Hernandez	.15
154	Billy Wagner	.15
155	Aaron Heilman	.15
156	David Wright	1.00
157	Luis Castillo	.15
158	Shawn Green	.15
159	Damion Easley	.15
160	Carlos Delgado	.50
161	Shawn Hill	.15
162	Mike Bacsik	.15
163	John Lannan	.15
164	Chad Cordero	.15
165	Jon Rauch	.15
166	Jesus Flores	.15
167	Dmitri Young	.15
168	Cristian Guzman	.15
169	Austin Kearns	.15
170	Nook Logan	.15
171	Erik Bedard	.25
172	Daniel Cabrera	.15
173	Chris Ray	.15
174	Danys Baez	.15
175	Chad Bradford	.15
176	Ramon Hernandez	.15
177	Miguel Tejada	.50
178	Freddie Bynum	.15
179	Corey Patterson	.15
180	Aubrey Huff	.15
181	Chris Young	.25
182	Greg Maddux	1.50
183	Clay Hensley	.15
184	Kevin Cameron	.15
185	Doug Brocail	.15
186	Josh Bard	.15
187	Kevin Kouzmanoff	.25
188	Geoff Blum	.15
189	Milton Bradley	.15
190	Brian Giles	.15
191	Jamie Moyer	.15
192	Kyle Kendrick	.15
193	Kyle Lohse	.15
194	Antonio Alfonseca	.15
195	Ryan Madson	.15
196	Chris Coste	.15
197	Chase Utley	.75
198	Tadahito Iguchi	.15
199	Aaron Rowand	.15
200	Shane Victorino	.25
201	Paul Maholm	.15
202	Ian Snell	.15
203	Shane Youman	.15
204	Damaso Marte	.15
205	Shawn Chacon	.15
206	Ronny Paulino	.15
207	Jack Wilson	.15
208	Adam LaRoche	.25
209	Ryan Doumit	.15
210	Xavier Nady	.15
211	Kevin Millwood	.15
212	Brandon McCarthy	.15
213	Joaquin Benoit	.15
214	Wes Littleton	.15
215	Mike Wood	.15
216	Gerald Laird	.15
217	Hank Blalock	.25
218	Ian Kinsler	.25
219	Marlon Byrd	.15
220	Brad Wilkerson	.15
221	Tim Wakefield	.15
222	Daisuke Matsuzaka	1.00
223	Julian Tavarez	.15
224	Hideki Okajima	.15
225	Manny Delcarmen	.15
226	Doug Mirabelli	.15
227	Dustin Pedroia	.25
228	Mike Lowell	.25
229	Manny Ramirez	.75
230	Coco Crisp	.15
231	Bronson Arroyo	.15
232	Matt Belisle	.15
233	Jared Burton	.15
234	David Weathers	.15
235	Mike Gosling	.15
236	David Ross	.15
237	Jeff Keppinger	.15
238	Edwin Encarnacion	.25
239	Ken Griffey Jr.	1.50
240	Adam Dunn	.25
241	Jeff Francis	.25
242	Jason Hirsh	.15
243	Josh Fogg	.15
244	Manny Corpas	.15
245	Jeremy Affeldt	.15
246	Yorvit Torrealba	.15
247	Todd Helton	.50
248	Kazuo Matsui	.15
249	Brad Hawpe	.25
250	Willy Taveras	.15
251	Brian Bannister	.15
252	Zack Greinke	.15
253	Kyle Davies	.15
254	David Riske	.15
255	Joel Peralta	.15
256	Joe Buck	.15
257	Mark Grudzielanek	.15
258	Ross Gload	.15
259	Billy Butler	.25
260	David DeJesus	.15
261	Jeremy Bonderman	.25
262	Chad Durbin	.15
263	Andrew Miller	.25
264	Bobby Seay	.15
265	Todd Jones	.15
266	Brandon Inge	.15
267	Sean Casey	.15
268	Placido Polanco	.15
269	Gary Sheffield	.50
270	Magglio Ordonez	.25
271	Matt Garza	.25
272	Boof Bonser	.15
273	Scott Baker	.15
274	Joe Nathan	.15
275	Dennys Reyes	.15
276	Joe Mauer	.50
277	Michael Cuddyer	.15
278	Jason Bartlett	.15
279	Torii Hunter	.50
280	Jason Tyner	.15
281	Matt Bacsik	.15
282	Jon Garland	.15
283	Jose Contreras	.15
284	Matt Thornton	.15
285	Ryan Bukvich	.15
286	Juan Uribe	.15
287	Jim Thome	.50
288	Scott Podsednik	.15
289	Jerry Owens	.15
290	Jermaine Dye	.25
291	Andy Pettitte	.50
292	Phil Hughes	.50
293	Mike Mussina	.25
294	Joba Chamberlain	.50
295	Brian Bruney	.15
296	Jorge Posada	.25
297	Derek Jeter	2.00
298	Jason Giambi	.15
299	Johnny Damon	.50
300	Melky Cabrera	.25
301	Jonathan Albaladejo RC	.15
302	Josh Anderson (RC)	.25
303	Wladimir Balentien (RC)	.25
304	Josh Banks (RC)	.25
305	Daric Barton (RC)	.25
306	Jerry Blevins RC	.50
307	Emilio Bonifacio RC	.50
308	Lance Broadway RC	.50
309	Clay Buchholz (RC)	.50
310	Billy Buckner (RC)	.25
311	Jeff Clement (RC)	.25
312	Willie Collazo RC	.15
313	Ross Detwiler RC	.50
314	Sam Fuld RC	1.00
315	Harvey Garcia (RC)	.50
316	Alberto Gonzalez (RC)	.50
317	Ryan Hanigan RC	.50
318	Kevin Hart (RC)	.50
319	Luke Hochevar RC	1.50
320	Chin-Lung Hu (RC)	.50
321	Rob Johnson (RC)	.25
322	Radhames Liz RC	.50
323	Ian Kennedy RC	1.00
324	Joe Koshansky (RC)	.50
325	Donny Lucy (RC)	.25
326	Justin Maxwell RC	.50
327	Jonathan Meloan RC	.50
328	Luis Mendoza (RC)	.25
329	Jose Morales (RC)	.50
330	Nyjer Morgan (RC)	.50
331	Carlos Muniz RC	.50
332	Bill Murphy (RC)	.25
333	Josh Newman RC	.50
334	Ross Ohlendorf RC	.50
335	Troy Patton (RC)	.50
336	Felipe Paulino RC	.50
337	Steve Pearce RC	1.50
338	Heath Phillips RC	.50
339	Justin Ruggiano RC	.50
340	Clint Sammons (RC)	.50
341	Bronson Sardinha (RC)	.50
342	Chris Seddon (RC)	.25
343	Seth Smith (RC)	.50
344	Mitch Stetter RC	.50
345	David Davidson RC	.50
346	Rich Thompson (RC)	.25
347	J.R. Towles RC	.75
348	Eugenio Velez RC	.75
349	Joey Votto (RC)	1.00
350	Bill White RC	.50
351	Vladimir Guerrero	.75
352	Lance Berkman	.50
353	Danny Haren	.15
354	Frank Thomas	.50
355	Chipper Jones	.75
356	Prince Fielder	1.00
357	Albert Pujols	2.00
358	Alfonso Soriano	.75
359	B.J. Upton	.25
360	Eric Byrnes	.15
361	Russell Martin	.50
362	Tim Lincecum	.50
363	Grady Sizemore	.50
364	Ichiro Suzuki	1.50
365	Hanley Ramirez	.75
366	David Wright	1.00
367	Ryan Zimmerman	.50
368	Nicholas Markakis	.50
369	Jake Peavy	.50
370	Ryan Howard	1.00
371	Freddy Sanchez	.15
372	Michael Young	.25
373	David Ortiz	.75
374	Ken Griffey Jr.	1.50
375	Matt Holliday	.50
376	Brian Bannister	.15
377	Magglio Ordonez	.25
378	Johan Santana	.50
379	Jim Thome	.50
380	Alex Rodriguez	2.00
381	Alex Rodriguez	2.00
382	Brandon Webb	.25
383	Chone Figgins	.15
384	Clay Buchholz	.50
385	Curtis Granderson	.50
386	Frank Thomas	.50
387	Fred Lewis	.15
388	Garret Anderson	.15
389	J.R. Towles	.15
390	Jake Peavy	.50
391	Jim Thome	.50
392	Jimmy Rollins	.75
393	Johan Santana	.75
394	Justin Verlander	.50
395	Mark Buehrle	.15
396	Matt Holliday	.50
397	Jarrod Saltalamacchia	.15
398	Sammy Sosa	.50
399	Tom Glavine	.50
400	Trevor Hoffman	.15
401	Dan Haren	.25
402	Randy Johnson	.75
403	Chris Burke	.15
404	Orlando Hudson	.15
405	Justin Upton	.50
406	Eric Byrnes	.15
407	Doug Davis	.15
408	Chad Tracy	.15
409	Tom Glavine	.40
410	Kelly Johnson	.15
411	Chipper Jones	.75
412	Matt Diaz	.15
413	Jeff Francoeur	.25
414	Mark Kotsay	.15
415	John Smoltz	.40
416	Tyler Yates	.15
417	Yunel Escobar	.25
418	Mike Hampton	.15
419	Luke Scott	.15
420	Adam Jones	.15
421	Jeremy Guthrie	.15
422	Nick Markakis	.40
423	Jay Payton	.15
424	Brian Roberts	.25
425	Melvin Mora	.15
426	Adam Loewen	.15
427	Luis Hernandez	.15
428	Steve Trachsel	.15
429	Josh Beckett	.50
430	Jon Lester	.25
431	Curt Schilling	.50
432	Jonathan Papelbon	.40
433	Jason Varitek	.25
434	David Ortiz	.75
435	Jacoby Ellsbury	.50
436	Julio Lugo	.15
437	Sean Casey	.15
438	Kevin Youkilis	.25
439	J.D. Drew	.25
440	Alex Cora	.15
441	Derrek Lee	.50
442	Carlos Zambrano	.40
443	Sean Marshall	.15
444	Matt Murton	.15
445	Kerry Wood	.25
446	Felix Pie	.15
447	Mark DeRosa	.15
448	Ronny Cedeno	.15
449	Jon Lieber	.15
450	Geovany Soto	.50
451	Gavin Floyd	.15
452	Bobby Jenks	.15
453	Scott Linebrink	.15
454	Javier Vazquez	.15
455	A.J. Pierzynski	.15
456	Orlando Cabrera	.15
457	Joe Crede	.15
458	Josh Fields	.15
459	Paul Konerko	.25
460	Brian Anderson	.15
461	Nick Swisher	.15
462	Carlos Quentin	.15
463	Homer Bailey	.15
464	Francisco Cordero	.15
465	Aaron Harang	.15
466	Alex Gonzalez	.15
467	Brandon Phillips	.25
468	Ryan Freel	.15
469	Scott Hatteberg	.15
470	Juan Castro	.15
471	Norris Hopper	.15
472	Josh Barfield	.15
473	Casey Blake	.15
474	Paul Byrd	.15
475	Grady Sizemore	.50
476	Jason Michaels	.15
477	Jhonny Peralta	.15
478	Asdrubal Cabrera	.15
479	David Dellucci	.15
480	C.C. Sabathia	.40
481	Andy Marte	.15
482	Troy Tulowitzki	.40
483	Matt Holliday	.40
484	Garrett Atkins	.15
485	Aaron Cook	.15
486	Brian Fuentes	.15
487	Ryan Spilborghs	.15
488	Ubaldo Jimenez	.15
489	Jayson Nix	.15
490	Nate Robertson	.15
491	Kenny Rogers	.15
492	Justin Verlander	.40
493	Dontrelle Willis	.15
494	Joel Zumaya	.15
495	Ivan Rodriguez	.25
496	Miguel Cabrera	.25
497	Carlos Guillen	.15
498	Edgar Renteria	.15
499	Curtis Granderson	.50
500	Jacque Jones	.15
501	Marcus Thames	.15
502	Josh Johnson	.15
503	Jeremy Hermida	.15
504	Dan Uggla	.25
505	Mark Hendrickson	.15
506	Luis Gonzalez	.15
507	Dallas McPherson	.15
508	Cody Ross	.15
509	Matt Treanor	.15
510	Andrew Miller	.25
511	Jorge Cantu	.1
512	Kazuo Matsui	.1
513	Lance Berkman	.1
514	Darin Erstad	.1
515	Miguel Tejada	.4
516	Jose Valverde	.1
517	Geoff Blum	.1
518	Reggie Abercrombie	.1
519	Brandon Backe	.1
520	Michael Bourn	.1
521	Gil Meche	.1
522	Brett Tomko	.1
523	Miguel Olivo	.1
524	Shane Costa	.1
525	Joey Gathright	.1
526	Mark Teahen	.1
527	Alex Gordon	.4
528	Tony Pena	.1
529	Jose Guillen	.1
530	Torii Hunter	.1
531	Ervin Santana	.1
532	Francisco Rodriguez	.1
533	Howie Kendrick	.1
534	Reggie Willits	.1
535	John Lackey	.1
536	Gary Matthews	.1
537	Jon Garland	.1
538	Kendry Morales	.1
539	Chone Figgins	.1
540	Andruw Jones	.1
541	Jason Schmidt	.1
542	James Loney	.1
543	Andre Ethier	.1
544	Rafael Furcal	.1
545	Brad Penny	.1
546	Hong-Chih Kuo	.1
547	Jonathan Broxton	.1
548	Esteban Loaiza	.1
549	Delwyn Young	.1
550	Mike Cameron	.1
551	Ryan Braun	.75
552	Rickie Weeks	.25
553	Bill Hall	.1
554	Tony Gwynn	.1
555	Eric Gagne	.1
556	Jeff Suppan	.1
557	Chris Capuano	.1
558	Derrick Turnbow	.1
559	Jason Kendall	.1
560	Livan Hernandez	.1
561	Philip Humber	.1
562	Francisco Liriano	.1
563	Pat Neshek	.1
564	Adam Everett	.1
565	Brendan Harris	.1
566	Justin Morneau	.4
567	Craig Monroe	.1
568	Carlos Gomez	.1
569	Delmon Young	.1
570	Mike Lamb	.1
571	Oliver Perez	.1
572	Jose Reyes	.1
573	Moises Alou	.25
574	Carlos Beltran	.1
575	Endy Chavez	.1
576	Ryan Church	.1
577	Pedro Martinez	.50
578	Johan Santana	.50
579	Mike Pelfrey	.1
580	Brian Schneider	.1
581	Joe Smith	.1
582	Matt Wise	.1
583	Duaner Sanchez	.1
584	Ramon Castro	.1
585	Kei Igawa	.1
586	Mariano Rivera	.40
587	Chien-Ming Wang	.50
588	Wilson Betemit	.1
589	Robinson Cano	.40
590	Alex Rodriguez	2.00
591	Bobby Abreu	.40
592	Shelley Duncan	.1
593	Hideki Matsui	.75
594	Kyle Farnsworth	.1
595	Joe Blanton	.1
596	Bobby Crosby	.1
597	Eric Chavez	.1
598	Dan Johnson	.1
599	Rich Harden	.1
600	Justin Duchscherer	.1
601	Kurt Suzuki	.1
602	Chris Denorfia	.1
603	Emil Brown	.1
604	Ryan Howard	.50
605	Jimmy Rollins	.50
606	Pedro Feliz	.1
607	Adam Eaton	.1
608	Brad Lidge	.1
609	Brett Myers	.1
610	Pat Burrell	.1
611	So Taguchi	.1
612	Geoff Jenkins	.1
613	Tom Gordon	.1
614	Zach Duke	.1
615	Matt Morris	.1
616	Tom Gorzelanny	.1
617	Jason Bay	.1
618	Chris Duffy	.1
619	Freddy Sanchez	.1
620	Jose Bautista	.1
621	Nyjer Morgan	.1
622	Matt Capps	.1
623	Paul Maholm	.1
624	Tadahito Iguchi	.1
625	Adrian Gonzalez	.1
626	Jim Edmonds	.1
627	Jake Peavy	.1
628	Khalil Greene	.1

#	Player	Price
29	Trevor Hoffman	.15
30	Mark Prior	.15
31	Randy Wolf	.15
32	Michael Barrett	.15
33	Scott Hairston	.15
34	Tim Lincecum	.40
35	Noah Lowry	.15
36	Rich Aurilia	.15
37	Aaron Rowand	.25
38	Randy Winn	.15
39	Daniel Ortmeier	.15
40	Ray Durham	.15
41	Brian Wilson	.15
42	Adrian Beltre	.25
43	Jeremy Reed	.15
44	Jarrod Washburn	.15
45	Yuniesky Betancourt	.15
46	Jose Lopez	.15
47	Raul Ibanez	.15
48	Mike Morse	.15
49	Erik Bedard	.15
50	Brad Wilkerson	.15
51	Chris Carpenter	.25
52	Mark Mulder	.15
53	Juan Encarnacion	.15
54	Skip Schumaker	.15
55	Troy Glaus	.25
56	Anthony Reyes	.15
57	Cesar Izturis	.15
58	Adam Kennedy	.15
59	Chris Duncan	.15
60	Matt Clement	.15
61	Scott Kazmir	.25
62	Troy Percival	.15
63	Akinori Iwamura	.15
64	Carl Crawford	.40
65	Cliff Floyd	.15
66	Jason Bartlett	.15
67	Rocco Baldelli	.15
68	Matt Garza	.25
69	Edwin Jackson	.15
70	Vicente Padilla	.15
71	Josh Hamilton	.50
72	Jason Botts	.15
73	Milton Bradley	.15
74	Michael Young	.15
75	Eddie Guardado	.15
76	David Murphy	.15
77	Ramon Vazquez	.15
78	Ben Broussard	.15
79	C.J. Wilson	.15
80	Jason Jennings	.15
81	Gustavo Chacin	.15
82	B.J. Ryan	.15
83	David Eckstein	.15
84	Alex Rios	.25
85	John McDonald	.15
86	Rod Barajas	.15
87	Lyle Overbay	.15
88	Scott Rolen	.40
89	Reed Johnson	.15
90	Marco Scutaro	.15
91	Lastings Milledge	.15
92	Johnny Estrada	.15
93	Paul LoDuca	.15
94	Ryan Zimmerman	.15
95	Odalis Perez	.15
96	Wily Mo Pena	.15
97	Elijah Dukes	.15
98	Aaron Boone	.15
99	Ronnie Belliard	.15
700	Nick Johnson	.15
701	Randor Bierd RC	.50
702	Brian Barton RC	.50
703	Brian Bass (RC)	.25
704	Brian Bocock RC	.50
705	Gregor Blanco (RC)	.25
706	Callix Crabbe (RC)	.25
707	Johnny Cueto RC	1.00
707	Kosuke Fukudome RC	2.00
708	Kosuke Fukudome Japanese/SP	65.00
709	Scott Kazmir	.25
710	Steve Holm RC	.50
711	Fernando Hernandez RC	.50
712	Elliot Johnson (RC)	.50
713	Masahide Kobayashi RC	.50
714	Hiroki Kuroda RC	1.00
715	Blake DeWitt (RC)	.50
716	Kyle McClellan RC	.50
717	Evan Meek RC	.50
718	Denard Span (RC)	.15
719	Darren O'Day RC	.15
720	Alexei Ramirez RC	3.00
721	Alex Romero (RC)	.15
722	Clete Thomas RC	.50
723	Matt Tolbert RC	.50
724	Ramon Troncoso RC	.50
725	Matt Tupman RC	.50
726	Rico Washington (RC)	.15
727	Randy Wells RC	.50
728	Wesley Wright RC	.50
729	Yasuhiko Yabuta RC	1.00
730	Alex Rodriguez	1.00
731	Andruw Jones	.15
732	C.C. Sabathia	.25
733	Carlos Beltran	.25
734	David Wright	.25
735	Derek Lee	.25
736	Dustin Pedroia	.25
737	Grady Sizemore	.25
738	Greg Maddux	.50
739	Ichiro Suzuki	.50
740	Ivan Rodriguez	.15
741	Jake Peavy	.25
742	Jimmy Rollins	.25
743	Johan Santana	.25
744	Josh Beckett	.25

#	Player	Price
745	Kevin Youkilis	.25
746	Matt Holliday	.25
747	Mike Lowell	.15
748	Ryan Braun	.50
749	Torii Hunter	.15
750	Alex Rodriguez	1.00
751	Torii Hunter	.15
752	Miguel Tejada	.25
753	Huston Street	.15
754	Scott Rolen	.25
755	Tom Glavine	.25
756	Ryan Braun	.50
757	Troy Glaus	.25
758	Carlos Zambrano	.25
759	Carl Crawford	.25
760	Dan Haren	.15
761	Andruw Jones	.25
762	Barry Zito	.15
763	Victor Martinez	.15
764	Erik Bedard	.15
765	Josh Willingham	.15
766	Johan Santana	.25
767	Dmitri Young	.15
768	Brian Roberts	.15
769	Jim Edmonds	.15
770	Jimmy Rollins	.25
771	Jason Bay	.15
772	Josh Hamilton	.25
773	Josh Beckett	.25
774	Aaron Harang	.15
775	Troy Tulowitzki	.15
776	Jose Guillen	.15
777	Miguel Cabrera	.25
778	Joe Mauer	.15
779	Nick Swisher	.15
780	Derek Jeter	1.00
781	Brandon Webb	.25
782	Brian Roberts	.15
783	C.C. Sabathia	.25
784	Carl Crawford	.15
785	Curtis Granderson	.25
786	David Ortiz	.25
787	Ichiro Suzuki	.50
788	Jake Peavy	.25
789	Jimmy Rollins	.40
790	Joe Borowski	.15
791	Johan Santana	.40
792	John Lackey	.25
793	Jose Reyes	.40
794	Jose Valverde	.15
795	Josh Beckett	.25
796	Juan Pierre	.15
797	Magglio Ordonez	.15
798	Matt Holliday	.25
799	Prince Fielder	.40

Gold

Gold: 4-8X
Production 99 Sets

1969 O Pee Chee reprints

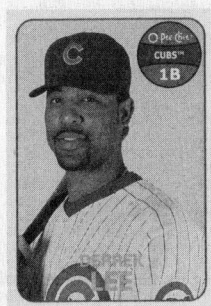

NM/M
Common Player: .25

Code	Player	Price
AG	Alex Gordon	.50
AP	Albert Pujols	2.00
AR	Alex Rodriguez	2.00
BP	Brad Penny	.25
BR	Babe Ruth	2.00
BU	B.J. Upton	.50
BW	Brandon Webb	.50
CD	Chris Duncan	.25
CJ	Chipper Jones	1.00
CL	Carlos Lee	.50
CP	Carlos Pena	.50
CU	Chase Utley	.75
CY	Chris Young	.25
DH	Danny Haren	.25
DJ	Derek Jeter	2.00
DL	Derrek Lee	.50
DM	Daisuke Matsuzaka	1.00
DO	David Ortiz	1.00
DW	David Wright	1.00
EB	Erik Bedard	.50
ER	Edgar Renteria	.25
GS	Gary Sheffield	.50
HP	Hunter Pence	.50
HR	Hanley Ramirez	.75
IS	Ichiro Suzuki	1.50
JB	Jason Bay	.50
JJ	J.J. Putz	.25
JM	Justin Morneau	.50
JP	Jake Peavy	.50
JR	Jose Reyes	.75
JS	Johan Santana	.75
JT	Jim Thome	.75
JW	Jered Weaver	.50
KG	Ken Griffey Jr.	1.50
MC	Miguel Cabrera	.75
MH	Matt Holliday	.50
MO	Magglio Ordonez	.75
MR	Manny Ramirez	.75
MT	Mark Teixeira	.50
NL	Noah Lowry	.25
PF	Prince Fielder	1.00
PH	Brandon Phillips	.50
RA	Aramis Ramirez	.50
RB	Ryan Braun	.75
RH	Ryan Howard	1.00
RM	Russell Martin	.50
RZ	Ryan Zimmerman	.50
TH	Todd Helton	.50
VG	Vladimir Guerrero	.75
VW	Vernon Wells	.25

1997 UD Jersey

NM/M
Common Jersey: 4.00
Patch: 2-4X

Code	Player	Price
AP	Albert Pujols	15.00
BC	Bobby Crosby	4.00
BG	Brian Giles	4.00
BR	B.J. Ryan	4.00
BS	Ben Sheets	6.00
CS	Curt Schilling	8.00
DL	Derek Lowe	4.00
DO	David Ortiz	10.00
GJ	Geoff Jenkins	4.00
HK	Hong-Chih Kuo	6.00
IR	Ivan Rodriguez	6.00
JB	Joe Blanton	4.00
JC	Joe Crede	4.00
JJ	Josh Johnson	4.00
JS	James Shields	6.00
JW	Jake Westbrook	4.00
LM	Lastings Milledge	6.00
MC	Miguel Cabrera	8.00
MO	Magglio Ordonez	6.00
NM	Nicholas Markakis	8.00
PE	Andy Pettitte	6.00
RB	Rocco Baldelli	4.00
TH	Todd Helton	6.00
VM	Victor Martinez	6.00
XN	Xavier Nady	4.00

Series 2

Code	Player	Price
CH	Cole Hamels	10.00
DO	David Ortiz	10.00
DU	Dan Uggla	8.00
JM	Justin Morneau	10.00
JP	Jonathan Papelbon	10.00
JV	Justin Verlander	8.00
JZ	Joel Zumaya	6.00
PF	Prince Fielder	10.00
PO	Jorge Posada	8.00
VG	Vladimir Guerrero	10.00

1998 UD Jersey

NM/M
Common Jersey: 4.00
Patch: 2-4X

Code	Player	Price
BH	Bill Hall	4.00
BS	Ben Sheets	6.00
CF	Chone Figgins	4.00
CZ	Carlos Zambrano	6.00
EG	Eric Gagne	4.00
FC	Fausto Carmona	6.00
FH	Felix Hernandez	8.00
GS	Grady Sizemore	8.00
HB	Hank Blalock	6.00
IS	Ian Snell	4.00
JE	Johnny Estrada	4.00
JJ	Jacque Jones	4.00
JK	Jason Kendall	4.00
JS	Johan Santana	8.00
KM	Kevin Millwood	4.00
MB	Mark Buehrle	4.00
MG	Marcus Giles	4.00
NM	Nicholas Markakis	8.00
PK	Paul Konerko	6.00
VM	Victor Martinez	8.00

Series 2

Code	Player	Price
AJ	Andruw Jones	4.00
CD	Chris Duncan	4.00
DJ	Derek Jeter	20.00
DL	Derrek Lee	10.00
GM	Greg Maddux	15.00
RM	Russell Martin	10.00
RO	Roy Oswalt	6.00
TH	Travis Hafner	6.00
VG	Vladimir Guerrero	10.00
VM	Victor Martinez	6.00

1999 UD Jersey

NM/M
Common Jersey: 4.00
Patch: 2-4X

Code	Player	Price
BR	Brian Roberts	4.00
CD	Chris Duffy	4.00
CJ	Chipper Jones	10.00
CS	C.C. Sabathia	8.00
DL	Derrek Lee	8.00
DW	David Wells	4.00
EB	Erik Bedard	8.00
FS	Freddy Sanchez	4.00
JB	Jason Bay	6.00
JD	Johnny Damon	6.00
JG	Jeremy Guthrie	4.00
JH	J.J. Hardy	6.00
JK	Jason Kubel	4.00
JP	Jorge Posada	6.00
KJ	Kenji Johjima	4.00
KM	Kendry Morales	6.00
MT	Mark Teixeira	8.00
RW	Rickie Weeks	6.00
TE	Miguel Tejada	6.00
TH	Travis Hafner	6.00

Series 2

Code	Player	Price
BU	B.J. Upton	8.00
BW	Brandon Webb	8.00
CA	Matt Cain	8.00
DO	David Ortiz	10.00
HR	Hanley Ramirez	10.00
JM	Joe Mauer	8.00
KG	Khalil Greene	4.00
MC	Miguel Cabrera	10.00
NM	Nick Markakis	10.00
TH	Torii Hunter	8.00

500 Home Run Club Bat

NM/M

Code	Player	Price
FT	Frank Thomas	80.00
JT	Jim Thome	50.00

All Rookie Team Signatures

NM/M
Common Auto.: 10.00

Code	Player	Price
AI	Akinori Iwamura	30.00
AL	Adam Lind	10.00
AM	Andrew Miller	25.00
BB	Billy Butler	15.00
BU	Brian Burres	10.00
DM	Daisuke Matsuzaka	300.00
HA	Justin Hampson	10.00
KC	Kevin Cameron	10.00
KK	Kyle Kendrick	20.00
MB	Michael Bourn	10.00
MF	Mike Fontenot	15.00
MO	Micah Owings	15.00
RB	Ryan Braun	40.00
SO	Joakim Soria	10.00

Autographs

NM/M
Common Auto.: 8.00

Code	Player	Price
CD	Chris Duffy	8.00
CS	Curt Schilling	25.00
JP	Joel Peralta	8.00
JS	Jorge Sosa	15.00
JV	John Van Benschoten	8.00
LS	Luke Scott	8.00
RH	Ramon Hernandez	15.00
SA	Kirk Saarloos	10.00
SF	Scott Feldman	10.00
SR	James Shields	15.00
SS	Saul Rivera	10.00
ZG	Zack Greinke	15.00

Derek Jeter Chronicles

NM/M
Common Jeter: 10.00
1-20 Derek Jeter 10.00

Derek Jeter OPC Reprints

NM/M
Common Jeter: 8.00
1-15 Derek Jeter 8.00

Diamond Collection

NM/M
Complete Set (20): 10.00
Common Player: .50

#	Player	Price
1	Adam LaRoche	.50
2	Brian McCann	1.00
3	Bronson Arroyo	.50
4	Chad Billingsley	1.00
5	Chin-Lung Hu	.50
6	Felix Pie	.50
7	Garrett Atkins	1.00
8	Homer Bailey	.50
9	Ian Kennedy	.50
10	James Shields	1.00
11	Jarrod Saltalamacchia	.50
12	Manny Corpas	.50
13	Mark Ellis	.50
14	Micah Owings	.50
15	Nick Swisher	1.00
16	Rich Hill	.50
17	Russell Martin	1.50
18	Ryan Theriot	1.00
19	Steve Pearce	1.00
20	Victor Martinez	1.00

Diamond Collection Autographs

No Pricing
Production Five Sets

Game Jersey

NM/M
Common Jersey: 4.00
Patch: 2-4X

Code	Player	Price
BR	Brian Roberts	6.00
CB	Carlos Beltran	10.00
CC	Coco Crisp	4.00
CG	Carlos Guillen	6.00
DC	Daniel Cabrera	4.00
DJ	Derek Jeter	20.00
DO	David Ortiz	10.00
DW	Dontrelle Willis	4.00
EG	Eric Gagne	4.00
GC	Gustavo Chacin	4.00
GJ	Geoff Jenkins	4.00
JB	Jason Bay	6.00
JD	Justin Duchscherer	4.00
JP	Jake Peavy	8.00
JS	Jeremy Sowers	4.00
JV	Jason Varitek	10.00
KM	Kazuo Matsui	6.00
ME	Morgan Ensberg	4.00
MM	Melvin Mora	4.00
MS	Mike Sweeney	4.00
MY	Michael Young	6.00
PA	Jonathan Papelbon	15.00
RH	Roy Halladay	6.00
TS	Takashi Saito	6.00

Series 2

Code	Player	Price
AP	Albert Pujols	20.00
BB	Boof Bonser	4.00
BM	Brandon McCarthy	4.00
BP	Brandon Phillips	6.00
BU	B.J. Upton	6.00
BZ	Barry Zito	4.00
CA	Matt Cain	6.00
CB	Chris Burke	4.00
CC	Chris Carpenter	6.00
CD	Chris Duncan	4.00
CJ	Conor Jackson	4.00
CL	Cliff Lee	4.00
CQ	Carlos Quentin	6.00
CU	Michael Cuddyer	4.00
DJ	Derek Jeter	20.00
DL	Derrek Lee	8.00
DO	David Ortiz	10.00
DW	David Wells	4.00
EC	Eric Chavez	4.00
ES	Ervin Santana	4.00
FH	Felix Hernandez	6.00
FL	Francisco Liriano	6.00
FR	Francisco Rodriguez	6.00
FS	Freddy Sanchez	4.00
GA	Garrett Atkins	6.00
GL	Troy Glaus	4.00
GM	Gil Meche	4.00
GO	Jonny Gomes	4.00
HR	Hanley Ramirez	8.00
IR	Ivan Rodriguez	6.00
JB	Jeremy Bonderman	4.00
JD	Jermaine Dye	4.00
JG	Jason Giambi	6.00
JH	Jeremy Hermida	4.00
JJ	Josh Johnson	4.00
JL	James Loney	6.00
JP	Jonathan Papelbon	10.00
JR	Jeremy Reed	4.00
JS	Jason Schmidt	4.00
JV	Justin Verlander	6.00
JW	Jered Weaver	6.00
KG	Khalil Greene	4.00
KJ	Kenji Johjima	4.00
KW	Kerry Wood	6.00
MC	Miguel Cabrera	8.00
ME	Melky Cabrera	4.00
MG	Marcus Giles	4.00
MJ	Mike Jacobs	4.00
MN	Mike Napoli	4.00
MP	Mark Prior	4.00
MY	Brett Myers	4.00
OL	Scott Olsen	4.00
PE	Mike Pelfrey	8.00
PF	Prince Fielder	8.00
PK	Paul Konerko	6.00
RC	Ryan Church	4.00
RD	Ray Durham	4.00
RF	Ryan Freel	4.00
RJ	Reed Johnson	4.00
RO	Robb Quinlan	4.00
RW	Rickie Weeks	4.00
RZ	Ryan Zimmerman	8.00
SK	Scott Kazmir	6.00
SO	Jeremy Sowers	4.00
TG	Tom Glavine	4.00
VW	Vernon Wells	4.00
WI	Dontrelle Willis	4.00
YM	Yadier Molina	4.00
ZD	Zach Duke	4.00

Hit Brigade

NM/M
Complete Set (15): 25.00
Common Player: 1.00

#	Player	Price
1	Albert Pujols	5.00
2	Alex Rodriguez	5.00
3	David Ortiz	2.50
4	David Wright	3.00
5	Derek Jeter	5.00
6	Derrek Lee	2.00
7	Freddy Sanchez	1.00
8	Hanley Ramirez	3.00
9	Ichiro Suzuki	3.00
10	Joe Mauer	1.00
11	Magglio Ordonez	1.00
12	Matt Holliday	1.50
13	Miguel Cabrera	2.00
14	Todd Helton	1.50
15	Vladimir Guerrero	2.00

Hot Commodities

NM/M
Common Player: .75

#	Player	Price
1	Miguel Tejada	.75
2	Daisuke Matsuzaka	3.00
3	David Ortiz	1.50
4	Manny Ramirez	1.00
5	Alex Rodriguez	3.00
6	Derek Jeter	3.00
7	Carl Crawford	.50
8	Alex Rios	.50
9	Jim Thome	.50
10	Grady Sizemore	.50
11	Travis Hafner	.50
12	Victor Martinez	.50
13	Justin Verlander	1.00
14	Magglio Ordonez	.50
15	Gary Sheffield	.75
16	Alex Gordon	.75
17	Justin Morneau	.50
18	Johan Santana	1.00
19	Vladimir Guerrero	.50
20	Danny Haren	.50
21	Ichiro Suzuki	2.00
22	Mark Teixeira	1.00
23	Chipper Jones	1.00
24	John Smoltz	.50
25	Miguel Cabrera	1.00
26	Hanley Ramirez	1.00
27	Jose Reyes	1.00
28	David Wright	2.00
29	Carlos Beltran	1.00
30	Ryan Howard	2.00
31	Chase Utley	1.00
32	Ryan Zimmerman	1.00
33	Aramis Ramirez	.75
34	Derrek Lee	.75
35	Alfonso Soriano	.75
36	Ken Griffey Jr.	2.00
37	Adam Dunn	1.00
38	Carlos Lee	.75
39	Lance Berkman	.75
40	Prince Fielder	1.50
41	Ryan Braun	1.50
42	Jason Bay	.75
43	Albert Pujols	3.00
44	Brandon Webb	.75
45	Matt Holliday	.75
46	Brad Penny	.50
47	Russell Martin	.75
48	Trevor Hoffman	.50
49	Jake Peavy	.75
50	Tim Lincecum	1.00

Inkredible

NM/M
Common Auto.: 10.00

Code	Player	Price
AL	Adam Lind	10.00
CP	Corey Patterson	10.00
CR	Cody Ross	10.00
DL	Derrek Lee	25.00

		NM/M
EA	Erick Aybar	10.00
JB	Josh Barfield	10.00
JH	Jason Hammel	10.00
JS	James Shields	15.00
LS	Luke Scott	10.00
MJ	Mike Jacobs	10.00
RC	Ryan Church	15.00
RL	Ruddy Lugo	10.00
RS	Ryan Shealy	10.00
SO	Jorge Sosa	15.00
TB	Taylor Buchholz	10.00

Milestone Memorabilia

		NM/M
Common Player:		8.00
GS	Gary Sheffield	10.00
KG	Ken Griffey Jr.	25.00
TG	Tom Glavine	15.00
TH	Trevor Hoffman	8.00

Mr. November

		NM/M
Common Jeter:		10.00
1-15	Derek Jeter	10.00

Presidential Predictors

		NM/M
Common Predictor:		4.00
1	Rudolph Giuliani	8.00
2	John Edwards	8.00
3	John McCain	10.00
4	Barack Obama	10.00
5	Mitt Romney	4.00
6	Fred Thompson	4.00
8	Al Gore	4.00
9	Wild Card	4.00

Presidential Running Mate Predictors

		NM/M
Common Predictor:		4.00
PP10	John McCain, Barack Obama	4.00
PP11	John McCain, Barack Obama	4.00
PP12	John McCain, Barack Obama	4.00
PP13	John McCain, Barack Obama	4.00
PP14	John McCain, Barack Obama	4.00
PP7B	Barack Obama, Hillary Clinton	4.00
PP7H	Barack Obama, Hillary Clinton	4.00
PP10A	John McCain, Hillary Clinton	4.00
PP11A	John McCain, Hillary Clinton	4.00

PP12A	John McCain, Hillary Clinton	4.00
PP13A	John McCain, Hillary Clinton	4.00
PP14A	John McCain, Hillary Clinton	4.00

Season Highlights Signatures

		NM/M
Common Auto.:		10.00
BB	Brian Bannister	15.00
BF	Ben Francisco	10.00
CS	Curt Schilling	30.00
FL	Fred Lewis	10.00
FT	Frank Thomas	100.00
JS	Jarrod Saltalamacchia	15.00
JW	Josh Willingham	8.00
KK	Kevin Kouzmanoff	10.00
MO	Micah Owings	15.00
MR	Mark Reynolds	8.00
MT	Miguel Tejada	20.00
PF	Prince Fielder	40.00
RS	Ryan Spilborghs	10.00

Signature Sensations

		NM/M
Common Auto.:		8.00
AM	Aaron Miles	20.00
BH	Brendan Harris	8.00
CB	Cha Sueng Baek	15.00
DL	Derrek Lee	25.00
JP	Joel Peralta	8.00
JS	James Shields	10.00
JV	John Van Benschoten	8.00
LS	Luke Scott	10.00
MC	Matt Cain	15.00
RA	Reggie Abercrombie	10.00
SM	Sean Marshall	15.00

Star Quest

		NM/M
Common Player:		.75
Blue:		1X
Rainbow:		2-3X
Red:		3-4X
1	Ichiro Suzuki	3.00
2	Ryan Braun	2.00
3	Prince Fielder	2.00
4	Ken Griffey Jr.	3.00
5	Vladimir Guerrero	1.50
6	Travis Hafner	.75
7	Matt Holliday	1.00
8	Ryan Howard	2.50
9	Derek Jeter	4.00
10	Chipper Jones	1.50
11	Carlos Lee	.75
12	Justin Morneau	1.00
13	Magglio Ordonez	1.00
14	David Ortiz	2.00
15	Jake Peavy	1.00
16	Albert Pujols	4.00
17	Hanley Ramirez	1.50
18	Manny Ramirez	1.50
19	Jose Reyes	2.00
20	Alex Rodriguez	4.00
21	Johan Santana	1.50
22	Grady Sizemore	1.50
23	Alfonso Soriano	1.50
24	Mark Teixeira	1.00
25	Frank Thomas	1.00
26	Jim Thome	1.00
27	Chase Utley	1.50
28	Brandon Webb	1.00
29	David Wright	2.50
30	Michael Young	.75
Series 2		
31	Adam Dunn	1.00
32	Albert Pujols	4.00
33	Alex Rodriguez	4.00
34	B.J. Upton	1.00
35	C.C. Sabathia	1.00
36	Carlos Beltran	1.00
37	Carlos Pena	1.00
38	Cole Hamels	1.50
39	Curtis Granderson	1.50
40	Daisuke Matsuzaka	2.00
41	David Ortiz	2.00
42	Derek Jeter	4.00
43	Derrek Lee	1.50
44	Eric Byrnes	.75
45	Felix Hernandez	1.50
46	Ichiro Suzuki	2.50
47	Jeff Francoeur	1.00
48	Jimmy Rollins	1.00
49	Joe Mauer	1.50
50	John Smoltz	1.00
51	Ken Griffey Jr.	3.00
52	Lance Berkman	1.00
53	Miguel Cabrera	1.50
54	Paul Konerko	1.00
55	Pedro Martinez	1.00
56	Randy Johnson	1.50
57	Russell Martin	1.00
58	Troy Tulowitzki	1.00
59	Vernon Wells	1.00
60	Vladimir Guerrero	1.00

The House that Ruth Built

		NM/M
Complete Set (25):		50.00
Common Ruth:		3.00
1-25	Babe Ruth	3.00

Superstar

		NM/M
Common Player:		1.00
Retail Jumbo Exclusive		

Cards have bronze foil.

Autograph:		No Pricing
Production Five Sets		
9	Vladimir Guerrero	2.00
48	Mark Teixeira	2.00
57	Prince Fielder	3.00
67	Albert Pujols	4.00
139	Ichiro Suzuki	5.00
147	Hanley Ramirez	2.00
156	David Wright	3.00
239	Ken Griffey Jr.	3.00
270	Magglio Ordonez	1.00
297	Derek Jeter	4.00

Superstar Scrapbook

		NM/M
Complete Set (10):		20.00
Common Player:		1.50
1	Albert Pujols	4.00
2	Alex Rodriguez	4.00
3	Chase Utley	2.00
4	Chipper Jones	2.00
5	David Ortiz	2.00
6	Derek Jeter	4.00
7	Ichiro Suzuki	2.00
8	Johan Santana	1.50
9	Jose Reyes	1.50
10	Ken Griffey Jr.	3.00
11	Manny Ramirez	1.50
12	Prince Fielder	1.50
13	Randy Johnson	1.50
14	Ryan Howard	2.00
15	Vladimir Guerrero	1.50

Star Attractions

		NM/M
Complete Set (10):		25.00
Common Player:		1.00
1	B.J. Upton	3.00
2	Carl Crawford	3.00
3	Chris Young	3.00
4	John Maine	2.00
5	Jonathan Papelbon	4.00
6	Nick Markakis	5.00
7	Prince Fielder	5.00
8	Takashi Saito	1.00
9	Tom Gorzelanny	1.00
10	Troy Tulowitzki	3.00

Star Attractions Autographs

No Pricing
Production Five Sets

USA National Team

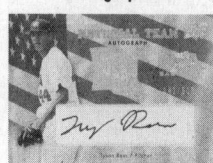

		NM/M
Complete Set (25):		25.00
Common Player:		1.00
1	Brett Hunter	1.00
2	Brian Matusz	1.50
3	Brett Wallace	2.00
4	Cody Satterwhite	1.00
5	Dan Espinosa	1.00
6	Eric Surkamp	1.00
7	Jordan Danks	1.50
8	Jeremy Hamilton	1.00
9	Joe Kelly	1.00
10	Jordy Mercer	1.00
11	Josh Romanski	1.00
12	Justin Smoak	2.50
13	Jacob Thompson	1.00
14	Logan Forsythe	1.50
15	Lance Lynn	1.00
16	Mike Minor	1.00
17	Pedro Alvarez	2.50
18	Petey Paramore	1.00
19	Ryan Berry	1.50
20	Ryan Flaherty	1.00
21	Roger Kieschnick	1.00
22	Seth Frankoff	1.00
23	Scott Gorgen	1.00
24	Tommy Medica	1.00
25	Tyson Ross	1.00

USA National Team Highlights

		NM/M
Complete Set (5):		5.00
1	Game 1	1.00
2	Game 2	1.00
3	Game 3	1.00

4	Game 4	1.00
5	Game 5	1.00

USA National Team Autographs

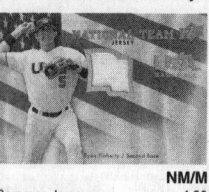

		NM/M
Common Auto.:		8.00
BH	Brett Hunter/297	8.00
BM	Brian Matusz/264	15.00
BW	Brett Wallace/183	25.00
CS	Cody Satterwhite/375	15.00
DE	Dan Espinosa/285	10.00
JD	Jordan Danks/311	10.00
JH	Jeremy Hamilton/375	8.00
JK	Joe Kelly/457	8.00
JM	Jordy Mercer/375	8.00
JR	Josh Romanski/375	8.00
JS	Justin Smoak/345	30.00
JT	Jacob Thompson/267	8.00
LF	Logan Forsythe/201	15.00
LL	Lance Lynn/425	10.00
MM	Mike Minor/375	8.00
PA	Pedro Alvarez/205	20.00
PP	Petey Paramore/237	10.00
RB	Ryan Berry/375	10.00
RF	Ryan Flaherty/244	10.00
RK	Roger Kieschnick/272	10.00
TM	Tommy Medica/487	8.00
TR	Tyson Ross/500	8.00

USA National Team Blue Autographs

		NM/M
Common Auto.:		8.00
BH	Brett Hunter/129	10.00
BM	Brian Matusz/50	25.00
BW	Brett Wallace/75	25.00
CS	Cody Satterwhite/131	20.00
DE	Dan Espinosa/75	15.00
ES	Eric Surkamp/117	8.00
JD	Jordan Danks/75	15.00
JH	Jeremy Hamilton/204	8.00
JK	Joe Kelly/125	8.00
JM	Jordy Mercer/175	10.00
JR	Josh Romanski/175	8.00
JS	Justin Smoak/60	30.00
JT	Jacob Thompson/105	10.00
LF	Logan Forsythe/75	15.00
MM	Mike Minor/175	10.00
PA	Pedro Alvarez/75	25.00
PP	Petey Paramore/175	15.00
RB	Ryan Berry/175	10.00
RF	Ryan Flaherty/75	15.00
RK	Roger Kieschnick/113	10.00
SF	Seth Frankoff/175	8.00
SG	Scott Gorgen/175	10.00
TM	Tommy Medica/175	10.00
TR	Tyson Ross/75	10.00

USA National Team Red Autographs

		NM/M
Common Auto.:		8.00
	Green Autos:	No Pricing
	Production 10 Sets	
BH	Brett Hunter/50	10.00
BM	Brian Matusz/50	25.00
BW	Brett Wallace/50	25.00
CS	Cody Satterwhite/50	20.00
DE	Dan Espinosa/50	15.00
JD	Jordan Danks/50	15.00
JH	Jeremy Hamilton/50	10.00
JK	Joe Kelly/50	8.00
JM	Jordy Mercer/50	10.00
JR	Josh Romanski/50	8.00
JS	Justin Smoak/50	30.00
JT	Jacob Thompson/30	15.00
LF	Logan Forsythe/50	15.00
LL	Lance Lynn/50	15.00
MM	Mike Minor/50	15.00
PA	Pedro Alvarez/50	25.00
PP	Petey Paramore/50	15.00
RB	Ryan Berry/50	10.00
RF	Ryan Flaherty/50	15.00
RK	Roger Kieschnick/50	10.00
SF	Seth Frankoff/50	10.00

SG	Scott Gorgen/50	10.00
TM	Tommy Medica/50	10.00
TR	Tyson Ross/50	10.00

USA National Team Jerseys

		NM/M
Common Jersey:		4.00
Patch:		1.5-2X
Production 99 Sets		
BH	Brett Hunter	4.00
BM	Brian Matusz	6.00
BW	Brett Wallace	6.00
CS	Cody Satterwhite	6.00
DE	Dan Espinosa	4.00
ES	Eric Surkamp	4.00
JD	Jordan Danks	4.00
JH	Jeremy Hamilton	4.00
JK	Joe Kelly	4.00
JM	Jordy Mercer	4.00
JR	Josh Romanski	4.00
JS	Justin Smoak	10.00
JT	Jacob Thompson	4.00
LF	Logan Forsythe	6.00
LL	Lance Lynn	4.00
MM	Mike Minor	4.00
PA	Pedro Alvarez	8.00
PP	Petey Paramore	4.00
RB	Ryan Berry	4.00
RF	Ryan Flaherty	4.00
RK	Roger Kieschnick	4.00
SF	Seth Frankoff	4.00
SG	Scott Gorgen	4.00
TM	Tommy Medica	4.00
TR	Tyson Ross	4.00

USA National Team Jersey Black Autos

		NM/M
Common Jersey Auto.:		10.00
Patch Autos:		1.5X
Production 99 Sets		
BH	Brett Hunter/99	15.00
BM	Brian Matusz/181	20.00
BW	Brett Wallace/199	25.00
CS	Cody Satterwhite/273	15.00
DE	Dan Espinosa/130	15.00
JD	Jordan Danks/99	15.00
JH	Jeremy Hamilton/271	10.00
JK	Joe Kelly/300	10.00
JM	Jordy Mercer/287	10.00
JR	Josh Romanski/311	10.00
JS	Justin Smoak/199	35.00
JT	Jacob Thompson/199	10.00
LF	Logan Forsythe/199	15.00
LL	Lance Lynn/149	15.00
MM	Mike Minor/359	15.00
PA	Pedro Alvarez/275	25.00
PP	Petey Paramore/199	15.00
RB	Ryan Berry/284	10.00
RF	Ryan Flaherty/149	10.00
RK	Roger Kieschnick/199	15.00
TM	Tommy Medica/400	10.00
TR	Tyson Ross/199	10.00

USA National Team Jersey Blue Autos

		NM/M
Common Blue Jsy Auto.:		8.00
Jersey Red Autos:		1-1.5X
Production 50 Sets		
Jersey Green Autos:		No Pricing
Production 10 Sets		
BH	Brett Hunter/150	15.00
BM	Brian Matusz/100	25.00
BW	Brett Wallace/50	30.00
CS	Cody Satterwhite/200	20.00
DE	Dan Espinosa/75	15.00
ES	Eric Surkamp/200	10.00
JD	Jordan Danks/75	15.00
JH	Jeremy Hamilton/200	10.00
JK	Joe Kelly/187	10.00
JM	Jordy Mercer/136	10.00
JR	Josh Romanski/123	10.00
JS	Justin Smoak/75	35.00
JT	Jacob Thompson/174	10.00
LF	Logan Forsythe/75	15.00
MM	Mike Minor/132	15.00
PA	Pedro Alvarez/89	30.00
PP	Petey Paramore/108	15.00
RB	Ryan Berry/192	10.00
RF	Ryan Flaherty/75	15.00
RK	Roger Kieschnick/99	15.00
SF	Seth Frankoff/69	10.00
SG	Scott Gorgen/247	10.00
TM	Tommy Medica/134	10.00
TR	Tyson Ross/292	10.00

USA Junior National Team

		NM/M
Complete Set (20):		15.00
Common USA Junior:		
1	Eric Hosmer	2.00
2	Garrison Lassiter	1.00
3	Harold Martinez	1.00
4	J.P. Ramirez	1.00
5	Jeff Malm	1.00
6	Jordan Swagerty	1.00

7	Kyle Buchanan	1.00
8	Kyle Skipworth	1.00
9	L.J. Hoes	1.50
10	Matt Purke	1.00
11	Mychal Givens	1.00
12	Nick Maronde	1.00
13	Riccio Torrez	1.00
14	Rob Grossman	1.00
15	Ryan Weber	1.00
16	T.J. House	1.00
17	Tim Melville	1.00
18	Tyler Hibbs	1.00
19	Tyler Stovall	1.50
20	Tyler Wilson	1.00

USA Junior National Team Autographs

		NM/M
Common Auto.:		8.00
EH	Eric Hosmer/238	20.00
GL	Garrison Lassiter/375	15.00
HI	Tyler Hibbs/375	10.00
HM	Harold Martinez/237	8.00
JM	Jeff Malm/375	10.00
JR	J.P. Ramirez/239	8.00
JS	Jordan Swagerty/350	8.00
KB	Kyle Buchanan/375	8.00
KS	Kyle Skipworth/177	15.00
LH	L.J. Hoes/158	8.00
MG	Mychal Givens/209	8.00
MP	Matt Purke/375	8.00
NM	Nick Maronde/166	10.00
RG	Rob Grossman/155	10.00
RT	Riccio Torrez/500	8.00
RW	Ryan Weber/375	10.00
TH	T.J. House/147	8.00
TM	Tim Melville/133	8.00
TS	Tyler Stovall/375	10.00
TW	Tyler Wilson/375	8.00

USA Junior National Team Blue Autos.

		NM/M
Common Auto.:		8.00
EH	Eric Hosmer/75	25.00
GL	Garrison Lassiter/175	15.00
HI	Tyler Hibbs/400	10.00
HM	Harold Martinez/275	8.00
JM	Jeff Malm/175	10.00
JR	J.P. Ramirez/90	15.00
JS	Jordan Swagerty/195	10.00
KB	Kyle Buchanan/175	10.00
KS	Kyle Skipworth/200	15.00
LH	L.J. Hoes/300	10.00
MG	Mychal Givens/309	8.00
MP	Matt Purke/390	8.00
NM	Nick Maronde/100	10.00
RG	Rob Grossman/175	8.00
RT	Riccio Torrez/400	8.00
RW	Ryan Weber/392	10.00
TH	T.J. House/75	10.00
TM	Tim Melville/330	10.00
TS	Tyler Stovall/186	10.00
TW	Tyler Wilson/75	8.00

USA Junior National Team Red Autos.

		NM/M
Production 50 unless noted.		8.00
Green Autos:		No Pricing
Production 10 Sets		
EH	Eric Hosmer	25.00
GL	Garrison Lassiter	15.00
HI	Tyler Hibbs/90	10.00
HM	Harold Martinez	10.00
JM	Jeff Malm	10.00
JR	J.P. Ramirez	15.00
JS	Jordan Swagerty	15.00
KB	Kyle Buchanan	10.00
KS	Kyle Skipworth	15.00
LH	L.J. Hoes	10.00
MG	Mychal Givens	15.00
MP	Matt Purke	15.00
NM	Nick Maronde/75	10.00
RG	Rob Grossman	10.00
RT	Riccio Torrez/100	10.00
RW	Ryan Weber/85	10.00
TH	T.J. House	10.00
TM	Tim Melville	10.00
TS	Tyler Stovall	10.00
TW	Tyler Wilson	10.00

USA Junior National Team Jerseys

		NM/M
Common Jersey:		4.00
Patch:		1.5-2X

Production 99 Sets
EH	Eric Hosmer	10.00
GL	Garrison Lassiter	6.00
HI	Tyler Hibbs	4.00
HM	Harold Martinez	4.00
JM	Jeff Malm	4.00
JR	J.P. Ramirez	6.00
JS	Jordan Swagerty	4.00
KB	Kyle Buchanan	4.00
KS	Kyle Skipworth	6.00
LH	L.J. Hoes	4.00
MG	Mychal Givens	4.00
MP	Matt Purke	4.00
NM	Nick Maronde	4.00
RG	Rob Grossman	4.00
RT	Riccio Torrez	4.00
RW	Ryan Weber	4.00
TH	T.J. House	4.00
TM	Tim Melville	4.00
TS	Tyler Stovall	4.00
TW	Tyler Wilson	4.00

USA Junior Nat. Team Jersey Black Autos.

NM/M
- Common Jersey Auto.: 8.00
- Patch Autos: 1-1.5X
- Production 99 Sets

EH	Eric Hosmer/100	30.00
GL	Garrison Lassiter/226	20.00
HI	Tyler Hibbs/222	10.00
HM	Harold Martinez/99	10.00
JM	Jeff Malm/258	10.00
JR	J.P. Ramirez/99	15.00
JS	Jordan Swagerty/199	10.00
KB	Kyle Buchanan/205	10.00
KS	Kyle Skipworth/99	20.00
LH	L.J. Hoes/150	10.00
MG	Mychal Givens/99	15.00
MP	Matt Purke/209	10.00
NM	Nick Maronde/99	10.00
RG	Rob Grossman/150	10.00
RT	Riccio Torrez/400	10.00
RW	Ryan Weber/222	10.00
TH	T.J. House/149	10.00
TM	Tim Melville/175	10.00
TS	Tyler Stovall/199	10.00
TW	Tyler Wilson/99	8.00

USA Junior Nat. Team Jersey Blue Autos.

NM/M
- Common Jersey Auto.: 8.00
- Jersey Red Autos: 1-1.25X
- Production 25-150
- Jersey Green Autos: No Pricing
- Production 10 Sets

EH	Eric Hosmer/121	30.00
GL	Garrison Lassiter/172	20.00
HI	Tyler Hibbs/392	10.00
HM	Harold Martinez/375	10.00
JM	Jeff Malm/107	10.00
JR	J.P. Ramirez/200	15.00
JS	Jordan Swagerty/173	10.00
KB	Kyle Buchanan/131	10.00
KS	Kyle Skipworth/300	20.00
LH	L.J. Hoes/340	10.00
MG	Mychal Givens/300	15.00
MP	Matt Purke/390	10.00
NM	Nick Maronde/50	15.00
RG	Rob Grossman/100	10.00
RT	Riccio Torrez/400	10.00
RW	Ryan Weber/400	10.00
TH	T.J. House/75	10.00
TM	Tim Melville/350	10.00
TS	Tyler Stovall/125	10.00
TW	Tyler Wilson/235	8.00

Yankee Stadium Legacy Collection

GAME 6688: 06/03/2008
YANKEES 3 - BLUE JAYS 9

NM/M
- Common Player: 2.50
- Common Ruth: 8.00
- Common DiMaggio: 6.00
- Common Maris: 5.00
- Common Jeter: 8.00
- Common A-Rod: 6.00
- Common Clemens: 4.00
- Common Mattingly: 5.00

2008 Upper Deck Yankee Stadium Box Set

NM/M
- Complete Set (100): 25.00

2008 UD A Piece of History

NM/M
- Common Player (1-100): .25

- Common RC (101-150):
- Common Historical Moments (151-200):
- Pack (8): 5.00
- Box (16): 75.00

1	Brandon Webb	.40
2	Dan Haren	.40
3	Justin Upton	.40
4	Chris B. Young	.40
5	Mark Teixeira	.40
6	Jeff Francoeur	.50
7	John Smoltz	.50
8	Tom Glavine	.50
9	Brian McCann	.50
10	Chipper Jones	1.00
11	Erik Bedard	.25
12	Nick Markakis	.50
13	Josh Beckett	.50
14	David Ortiz	.75
15	Manny Ramirez	.75
16	Dustin Pedroia	.40
17	Grady Sizemore	.50
18	Jonathan Papelbon	.50
19	Daisuke Matsuzaka	1.00
20	Curt Schilling	.50
21	Alfonso Soriano	.50
22	Aramis Ramirez	.40
23	Carlos Zambrano	.40
24	Nick Swisher	.25
25	Jim Thome	.40
26	Ken Griffey Jr.	1.50
27	Adam Dunn	.50
28	Aaron Harang	.25
29	Matt Holliday	.50
30	Troy Tulowitzki	.40
31	Todd Helton	.50
32	Magglio Ordonez	.40
33	Justin Verlander	.50
34	Miguel Cabrera	.75
35	Gary Sheffield	.50
36	Ivan Rodriguez	.50
37	Dontrelle Willis	.25
38	Hanley Ramirez	.50
39	Andrew Miller	.25
40	Lance Berkman	.50
41	Roy Oswalt	.40
42	Carlos Lee	.40
43	Hunter Pence	.40
44	Alex Gordon	.40
45	Mark Teahen	.25
46	Torii Hunter	.40
47	Vladimir Guerrero	.75
48	Victor Martinez	.25
49	Andruw Jones	.50
50	James Loney	.25
51	Russell Martin	.40
52	Jeff Kent	.50
53	Ryan Braun	.75
54	Prince Fielder	.50
55	Joe Mauer	.25
56	Justin Morneau	.40
57	Delmon Young	.25
58	Jose Reyes	.75
59	David Wright	.75
60	Carlos Beltran	.50
61	Johan Santana	.50
62	Pedro Martinez	.50
63	Alex Rodriguez	2.00
64	Derek Jeter	2.00
65	Hideki Matsui	1.00
66	Robinson Cano	.40
67	Joba Chamberlain	2.00
68	Phil Hughes	.40
69	Mariano Rivera	.50
70	Rich Harden	.25
71	Joe Blanton	.25
72	Cole Hamels	.50
73	Ryan Howard	.75
74	Jimmy Rollins	.75
75	Chase Utley	.75
76	Jason Bay	.40
77	Freddy Sanchez	.25
78	Jake Peavy	.40
79	Greg Maddux	1.50
80	Trevor Hoffman	.25
81	Barry Zito	.25
82	Tim Lincecum	.75
83	Travis Hafner	.40
84	C.C. Sabathia	.50
85	Felix Hernandez	.50
86	Ichiro Suzuki	1.50
87	Troy Glaus	.25
88	Albert Pujols	2.00
89	Chris Carpenter	.40
90	Scott Kazmir	.40
91	Carl Crawford	.25
92	B.J. Upton	.25
93	Michael Young	.25
94	Josh Hamilton	.50
95	Vernon Wells	.40
96	Alex Rios	.40
97	Scott Rolen	.40
98	Frank Thomas	.50
99	Chad Cordero	.25
100	Ryan Zimmerman	.40
101	Emilio Bonifacio RC	.50
102	Bill Murphy (RC)	.50
103	Billy Buckner (RC)	.50
104	Brandon Jones RC	1.00
105	Clint Sammons (RC)	.50
106	Clay Buchholz (RC)	1.00
107	Kevin Hart (RC)	.50
108	Lance Broadway RC	.50
109	Donny Lucy (RC)	.50
110	Heath Phillips RC	.50
111	Ryan Hanigan RC	.50
112	Joey Votto (RC)	2.00
113	Joe Koshansky (RC)	.50
114	Josh Newman RC	.50
115	Seth Smith (RC)	.50
116	Harvey Garcia (RC)	.50
117	Chris Seddon (RC)	.50
118	Josh Anderson (RC)	.50
119	Troy Patton RC	.50
120	Felipe Paulino RC	.50
121	J.R. Towles RC	.50
122	Luke Hochevar RC	.50
123	Chin-Lung Hu (RC)	1.00
124	Jonathan Meloan RC	.50
125	Sam Fuld RC	.50
126	Mitch Stetter RC	.50
127	Jose Morales (RC)	.50
128	Carlos Muniz RC	.50
129	Alberto Gonzalez (RC)	.50
130	Ian Kennedy RC	1.00
131	Ross Ohlendorf RC	.50
132	Jonathan Albaladejo RC	1.00
133	Daric Barton (RC)	1.00
134	Jerry Blevins RC	.50
135	David Davidson RC	.50
136	Nyjer Morgan (RC)	1.00
137	Steve Pearce RC	1.00
138	Colt Morton RC	.50
139	Eugenio Velez RC	.50
140	Erick Threets (RC)	.50
141	Bronson Sardinha (RC)	.50
142	Wladimir Balentien (RC)	.50
143	Jeff Clement (RC)	.50
144	Rob Johnson (RC)	.50
145	Jeff Ridgway RC	.50
146	Justin Ruggiano (RC)	.50
147	Luis Mendoza (RC)	.50
148	Bill White RC	.50
149	Ross Detwiler RC	.50
150	Justin Maxwell RC	.50
151	Fall of Berlin Wall	.50
152	Wright Bros. 1st Flight	.50
153	Signing of Dec. of Independence	.50
154	Columbus Discovers America	.50
155	First Space Shuttle launch	.50
156	Hawaii becomes 50th state	.50
157	Statue of Liberty given to U.S.	.50
158	Gettysburg Address	.50
159	Completion of Transcontinental Railroad	.50
160	Opening of Panama Canal	.50
161	U.S. enters World War I	.50
162	Treaty of Versailes	.50
163	Television invented	.50
164	Geneva Summit	.50
165	Woodstock	.50
166	Invention of Cotton Gin	.50
167	Eiffel Tower	.50
168	Suez Canal opens	.50
169	New York City Subway opens	.50
170	Polio Vaccine invented	.50
171	Bell X-1 Breaks Sound Barrier	.50
172	USS Enterprise Aircraft Carrier launched	.50
173	Hubble Telescope launches	.50
174	N.A.T.O. created	.50
175	Sputnik launched by Russia	.50
176	U.S.S.R. Crumbles	.50
177	Boston Tea Party	.50
178	Paul Revere's Ride	.50
179	Civil Rights Act Passes	.50
180	Hindenburg blows up	.50
181	Franklin discovers electricity	.50
182	Creation of the Internet	.50
183	1st World's Fair - 1851 London	.50
184	Pope John Paul II	.50
185	1st Heart Transplant	.50
186	California Gold Rush	.50
187	Creation of the personal computer	.50
188	Louisiana Purchase	.50
189	1st Dictionary published	.50
190	Steam Engine invented	.50
191	History of Nobel Prize	.50
192	Liberty Bell	.50
193	International Space Station	.50
194	Human Genome Project	.50
195	The Supreme Court	.50
196	Lewis and Clark	.50
197	Battle of the Alamo	.50
198	The creation of baseball	.50
199	Juan Ponce De Leon	.50
200	Jamestown - 1607	.50

Silver
- Silver (1-100): 2-3X
- Silver RC (101-150): 1-2X
- Silver (151-200): 2-3X

Red
- Red (1-100): 2-4X
- Red RC (101-150): 1-2X
- Red (151-200): 2-4X
- Production 149 Sets

Gold
- Gold (1-100): 3-5X
- Gold RC (101-150): 2-3X
- Gold (151-200): 3-5X
- Production 75 Sets

Blue
- Blue (1-100): 4-8X
- Blue RC (101-150): 3-4X
- Blue (151-200): 4-8X
- Production 25 Sets

A Piece of Hollywood Memor.

NM/M
Common Memorabilia: 10.00

1	Amanda Bynes/Costume	10.00
2	Mel Gibson/Shirt	10.00
3	Brad Pitt/Shirt	10.00
4	George Clooney/Jjt	15.00
5	Denzell Washington/Jkt	10.00
6	Jamie Foxx/Shirt	10.00
7	Kevin Costner/Shirt	10.00
8	Jack Nicholson/Shirt	15.00
9	Mike Myers/Pants	15.00
10	Dana Carvey/Jsy	15.00
11	Phillip Seymour Hoffman/Sweater	10.00
12	Jim Carrey/Shirt	10.00
13	Scarlett Johanson/T-Shirt	25.00
14	Demi Moore/Jacket	15.00
15	Christopher Reeves/Cape	30.00
16	Mel Gibson Shoe/SP	30.00
17	Denzell Washington/Hat/SP	25.00
18	Jim Carrey/Pants	10.00
19	George Clooney/Pants	15.00
20	Scarlett Johanson/Undershirt/SP	30.00
21	Phillip Seymour Hoffman/Jkt	10.00
22	Denzell Washington/Pants	10.00
23	Mel Gibson/Pants	10.00
24	Woody Harrelson/Jkt	10.00
25	Robin Williams/Shirt	15.00
26	Jennifer Garner/Pajamas	15.00
27	Tom Cruise/Shirt	25.00

Box Score Memories

NM/M
- Common Player: 2.00
- Production 699 Sets
- Blue: 2X
- Production 75 Sets
- Copper: 2X
- Production 99 Sets
- Red: 1.5-2X
- Production 149 Sets
- Silver: No Pricing
- Production 25 Sets

1	Chris B. Young	2.00
2	Stephen Drew	2.00
3	Chipper Jones	5.00
4	Mark Teixeira	3.00
5	Jeff Francoeur	2.00
6	David Ortiz	3.00
7	Dustin Pedroia	3.00
8	Manny Ramirez	3.00
9	Mike Lowell	2.00
10	Alfonso Soriano	3.00
11	Aramis Ramirez	2.00
12	Jim Thome	2.00
13	Ken Griffey Jr.	3.00
14	Adam Dunn	2.00
15	Grady Sizemore	3.00
16	Travis Hafner	2.00
17	Victor Martinez	2.00
18	Matt Holliday	3.00
19	Todd Helton	3.00
20	Troy Tulowitzki	2.00
21	Ivan Rodriguez	2.00
22	Miguel Cabrera	3.00
23	Magglio Ordonez	2.00
24	Hanley Ramirez	3.00
25	Hunter Pence	2.00
26	Lance Berkman	3.00
27	Carlos Lee	2.00
28	Alex Gordon	2.00
29	Vladimir Guerrero	3.00
30	Andruw Jones	2.00
31	Jeff Kent	2.00
32	Ryan Braun	4.00
33	Prince Fielder	3.00
34	Joe Mauer	2.00
35	Justin Morneau	2.00
36	David Wright	4.00
37	Carlos Beltran	3.00
38	Jose Reyes	3.00
39	Derek Jeter	8.00
40	Alex Gordon	8.00
41	Hideki Matsui	4.00
42	Bobby Abreu	2.00
43	Chase Utley	4.00
45	Jimmy Rollins	4.00
46	Jason Bay	4.00
47	Khalil Greene	2.00
49	Albert Pujols	20.00
50	Frank Thomas	8.00

Box Score Mem Jersey Auto. Blue

NM/M
Production 10-99

1	Chris B. Young/99	25.00
5	Jeff Francoeur/99	25.00
11	Aramis Ramirez/99	30.00
16	Travis Hafner/50	25.00
17	Victor Martinez/99	25.00
20	Troy Tulowitzki/99	25.00
24	Hanley Ramirez/40	40.00
46	Carlos Lee/99	30.00
46	Jason Bay/99	20.00

Box Score Mem. Jersey Red

NM/M
- Common Jersey: 4.00
- Gold: 1.5-2X
- Production 75 Sets
- Blue: No Pricing
- Production 25 Sets
- Patch: No Pricing
- Production 25 Sets
- Jersey Button: No Pricing
- Production Five Sets

1	Chris B. Young	6.00
2	Stephen Drew	6.00
3	Chipper Jones	10.00
4	Mark Teixeira	6.00
5	Jeff Francoeur	6.00
6	David Ortiz	10.00
7	Dustin Pedroia	8.00
8	Manny Ramirez	8.00
10	Alfonso Soriano	6.00
11	Aramis Ramirez	6.00
12	Jim Thome	8.00
16	Travis Hafner	6.00
17	Victor Martinez	4.00
18	Matt Holliday	8.00
19	Todd Helton	8.00
20	Troy Tulowitzki	6.00
21	Ivan Rodriguez	8.00
23	Magglio Ordonez	4.00
24	Hanley Ramirez	8.00
26	Lance Berkman	6.00
27	Carlos lee	6.00
28	Alex Gordon	6.00
29	Vladimir Guerrero	6.00
31	Jeff Kent	4.00
33	Prince Fielder	6.00
34	Joe Mauer	6.00
35	Justin Morneau	8.00
37	Carlos Beltran	6.00
38	Jose Reyes	8.00
39	Derek Jeter	20.00
42	Bobby Abreu	6.00
45	Jimmy Rollins	6.00
46	Jason Bay	4.00
47	Khalil Greene	6.00
49	Albert Pujols	20.00
50	Frank Thomas	8.00

Cut From the Same Cloth Jersey

NM/M
Common Dual Jersey: 6.00

BB	Jeremy Bonderman, Joe Blanton	6.00
BP	A.J. Burnett, Jake Peavy	8.00
BR	Carlos Beltran, Jose Reyes	10.00
BS	Mark Buehrle, Johan Santana	8.00
BV	Mark Buehrle, Justin Verlander	6.00
BZ	Ryan Zimmerman, Ryan Braun	15.00
CB	Carlos Beltran	10.00
CH	Trevor Hoffman, Chad Cordero	6.00
CS	Curt Schilling	4.00
DD	Johnny Damon	10.00
FT	Frank Thomas	10.00
GM	Greg Maddux	15.00
GO	Magglio Ordonez, Curtis Granderson	8.00
HH	Todd Helton, Matt Holliday	10.00
HJ	Andruw Jones, Matt Holliday	8.00
HL	Francisco Liriano, Cole Hamels	8.00
HM	Greg Maddux, Tim Hudson	15.00
HP	Dan Haren, Jake Peavy	8.00
HS	John Smoltz, Tim Hudson	10.00
HY	Michael Young, J.J. Hardy	6.00
HZ	Carlos Zambrano, Felix Hernandez	10.00
JB	Josh Beckett	8.00
JD	Jason Varitek, Daisuke Matsuzaka	20.00
JH	Andruw Jones, Torii Hunter	8.00
JS	Randy Johnson, Johan Santana	10.00
JT	Jim Thome	6.00
JY	Derek Jeter, Michael Young	25.00
JZ	Chipper Jones, Ryan Zimmerman	10.00
LF	Derek Lee, Prince Fielder	10.00
MA	Joe Mauer, Russell Martin	8.00
MJ	Mariano Rivera, Jonathan Papelbon	10.00
MK	Justin Morneau, Jason Kubel	6.00
MM	Victor Martinez, Joe Mauer	6.00
MS	Curt Schilling, Daisuke Matsuzaka	20.00
OF	David Ortiz, Prince Fielder	10.00
OG	Carlos Guillen, Magglio Ordonez	6.00
OP	David Ortiz, Albert Pujols	20.00
OR	Manny Ramirez, David Ortiz	15.00
OV	Jason Varitek, David Ortiz	15.00
PG	Vladimir Guerrero, Albert Pujols	15.00
PH	Roy Halladay, Jake Peavy	6.00
PM	Pedro Martinez	8.00
PO	Roy Oswalt, Jake Peavy	6.00
PS	Curt Schilling, Jonathan Papelbon	8.00
PV	Jason Varitek, Jorge Posada	10.00
RJ	Randy Johnson	8.00
RL	Derek Lee, Aramis Ramirez	10.00
RP	B.J. Ryan, Jonathan Papelbon	8.00
RR	Jose Reyes, Hanley Ramirez	10.00
RU	Jimmy Rollins, Chase Utley	15.00
SH	Travis Hafner, Grady Sizemore	8.00
SL	Johan Santana, Francisco Liriano	8.00
SM	Pedro Martinez, Curt Schilling	8.00
TR	Tim Hudson, Roy Halladay	6.00
UU	Chase Utley, Dan Uggla	8.00
VR	Manny Ramirez, Jason Varitek	15.00
WS	Dontrelle Willis, C.C. Sabathia	6.00

Cut From The Same Cloth

NM/M
- Common Duo: 2.00
- Silver: 1-2X
- Production 149 Sets
- Red: 1-2X
- Production 99 Sets
- Pewter: 1-2X
- Production 75 Sets
- Blue: 2-3X
- Production 25 Sets

(Dual Player cards)

Code	Players	Price
BB	Jeremy Bonderman, Joe Blanton	2.00
BP	A.J. Burnett, Jake Peavy	3.00
BR	Carlos Beltran, Jose Reyes	4.00
BS	Mark Buehrle, Johan Santana	3.00
BV	Mark Buehrle, Justin Verlander	2.00
BZ	Ryan Zimmerman, Ryan Braun	3.00
CB	Carlos Beltran	3.00
CH	Trevor Hoffman, Chad Cordero	2.00
CS	Curt Schilling	3.00
DD	Johnny Damon	3.00
FT	Frank Thomas	3.00
GD	Ken Griffey Jr., Adam Dunn	5.00
GM	Greg Maddux	5.00
GO	Magglio Ordonez, Curtis Granderson	3.00
GT	Ken Griffey Jr., Frank Thomas	5.00
HH	Todd Helton, Matt Holliday	3.00
HJ	Andruw Jones, Matt Holliday	3.00
HL	Francisco Liriano, Cole Hamels	3.00
HM	Greg Maddux, Tim Hudson	5.00
HP	Dan Haren, Jake Peavy	3.00
HS	John Smoltz, Tim Hudson	3.00
HY	Michael Young, J.J. Hardy	2.00
HZ	Carlos Zambrano, Felix Hernandez	3.00
JB	Josh Beckett	3.00
JD	Jason Varitek, Daisuke Matsuzaka	5.00
JH	Andruw Jones, Torii Hunter	2.00
JS	Randy Johnson, Johan Santana	3.00
JT	Jim Thome,	
JY	Derek Jeter, Michael Young	8.00
JZ	Chipper Jones, Ryan Zimmerman	4.00
KS	Johan Santana, Scott Kazmir	3.00
LF	Derek Lee, Prince Fielder	4.00
MA	Joe Mauer, Russell Martin	3.00
MJ	Mariano Rivera, Jonathan Papelbon	3.00
MK	Justin Morneau, Jason Kubel	2.00
MM	Victor Martinez, Joe Mauer	2.00
MS	Curt Schilling, Daisuke Matsuzaka	4.00
OF	David Ortiz, Prince Fielder	4.00
OG	Carlos Guillen, Magglio Ordonez	2.00
OP	David Ortiz, Albert Pujols	8.00
OR	Manny Ramirez, David Ortiz	4.00
OV	Jason Varitek, David Ortiz	4.00
PG	Vladimir Guerrero, Albert Pujols	8.00
PH	Roy Halladay, Jake Peavy	3.00
PM	Pedro Martinez	3.00
PO	Roy Oswalt, Jake Peavy	3.00
PS	Curt Schilling, Jonathan Papelbon	3.00
PV	Jason Varitek, Jorge Posada	3.00
RJ	Randy Johnson	3.00
RL	Derek Lee, Aramis Ramirez	3.00
RP	B.J. Ryan, Jonathan Papelbon	3.00
RR	Jose Reyes, Hanley Ramirez	4.00
RU	Jimmy Rollins, Chase Utley	4.00
SH	Travis Hafner, Grady Sizemore	3.00
SL	Johan Santana, Francisco Liriano	3.00
SM	Pedro Martinez, Curt Schilling	3.00
TR	Tim Hudson, Roy Halladay	3.00
UU	Chase Utley, Dan Uggla	3.00
VR	Manny Ramirez, Jason Varitek	3.00
WS	Dontrelle Willis, C.C. Sabathia	

Franchise History

NM/M

		Price
Common Player:		1.50
Red:		1-2X
Production 149 Sets		
Copper:		1-2X
Production 99 Sets		
Blue:		1-2X
Production 75 Sets		
Silver:		2-3X
Production 25 Sets		
1	Justin Upton	2.00
2	Randy Johnson	3.00
3	Mark Teixeira	2.00
4	John Smoltz	2.00
5	Chipper Jones	4.00
6	Jonathan Papelbon	3.00
7	Manny Ramirez	3.00
8	Daisuke Matsuzaka	5.00
9	Josh Beckett	2.00
10	David Ortiz	3.00
11	Alfonso Soriano	3.00
12	Jim Thome	2.00
13	Adam Dunn	2.00
14	Ken Griffey Jr.	5.00
15	C.C. Sabathia	2.00
16	Grady Sizemore	2.00
17	Travis Hafner	1.50
18	Matt Holliday	2.00
19	Troy Tulowitzki	1.50
20	Magglio Ordonez	1.50
21	Ivan Rodriguez	1.50
22	Miguel Cabrera	3.00
23	Hanley Ramirez	3.00
24	Hunter Pence	2.00
25	Lance Berkman	2.00
26	Vladimir Guerrero	3.00
27	Andruw Jones	1.50
28	Prince Fielder	2.00
29	Ryan Braun	3.00
30	Joe Mauer	1.50
31	Carlos Beltran	2.00
32	Pedro Martinez	2.00
33	Johan Santana	2.00
34	Jose Reyes	3.00
35	David Wright	4.00
36	Joba Chamberlain	6.00
37	Hideki Matsui	4.00
38	Alex Rodriguez	8.00
39	Derek Jeter	8.00
40	Jimmy Rollins	3.00
41	Ryan Howard	4.00
42	Chase Utley	3.00
43	Greg Maddux	5.00
44	Jake Peavy	2.00
45	Trevor Hoffman	1.50
46	Ichiro Suzuki	5.00
47	Felix Hernandez	2.00
48	Albert Pujols	8.00
49	Frank Thomas	3.00
50	Vernon Wells	1.50

Franchise History Jersey Auto.

NM/M

		Price
Production 5-99		
6	Jonathan Papelbon/99	25.00
17	Travis Hafner/50	20.00
19	Troy Tulowitzki/50	25.00
23	Hanley Ramirez/50	35.00
47	Felix Hernandez/75	30.00

Franchise History Red Jersey

NM/M

		Price
Common Jersey:		4.00
Gold Jersey:		1-1.5X
Production 49 Sets		
Blue Jersey:		1.5-2X
Production 25 Sets		
Patch:		No Pricing 1-2X
Production 25 Sets		
Jersey Button:		No Pricing
Production Five Sets		
1	Justin Upton	6.00
2	Randy Johnson	6.00
3	Mark Teixeira	6.00
4	John Smoltz	8.00
5	Chipper Jones	8.00
6	Jonathan Papelbon	6.00
7	Manny Ramirez	8.00
8	Daisuke Matsuzaka	15.00
9	Josh Beckett	6.00
10	David Ortiz	8.00
11	Alfonso Soriano	6.00
12	Jim Thome	6.00
13	Adam Dunn	6.00
14	Ken Griffey Jr.	15.00
15	C.C. Sabathia	6.00
16	Grady Sizemore	8.00
17	Travis Hafner	4.00
18	Matt Holliday	6.00
19	Troy Tulowitzki	4.00
20	Magglio Ordonez	4.00
21	Ivan Rodriguez	6.00
22	Miguel Cabrera	8.00
23	Hanley Ramirez	8.00
24	Hunter Pence	6.00
25	Lance Berkman	6.00
26	Vladimir Guerrero	8.00
27	Andruw Jones	4.00
28	Prince Fielder	8.00
29	Ryan Braun	10.00
30	Joe Mauer	6.00
31	Carlos Beltran	6.00
32	Pedro Martinez	6.00
33	Johan Santana	6.00
34	Jose Reyes	8.00
36	Joba Chamberlain	8.00
38	Alex Rodriguez	15.00
39	Derek Jeter	15.00
40	Jimmy Rollins	8.00
42	Chase Utley	8.00
43	Greg Maddux	10.00
44	Jake Peavy	6.00
45	Trevor Hoffman	4.00
47	Felix Hernandez	6.00
48	Albert Pujols	15.00
49	Frank Thomas	8.00
50	Vernon Wells	8.00

Franchise Members 3

NM/M

		Price
Common Trio:		2.00
Production 799 Sets		
Silver:		1-2X
Production 149 Sets		
Red:		1-2X
Production 99 Sets		
Pewter:		1-2X
Production 75 Sets		
Blue:		2-3X
Production 25 Sets		
1	Tom Glavine, John Smoltz, Tim Hudson	2.00
2	Curt Schilling, Josh Beckett, Daisuke Matsuzaka	4.00
3	Manny Ramirez, Jason Varitek, David Ortiz	4.00
4	Ken Griffey Jr., Frank Thomas, Jim Thome	5.00
5	Travis Hafner, Victor Martinez, Grady Sizemore	2.00
6	Carlos Lee, Matt Holliday, Jason Bay	2.00
7	Carlos Guillen, Magglio Ordonez, Miguel Cabrera	3.00
8	Dan Haren, Roy Oswalt, Jake Peavy	2.00
9	Vladimir Guerrero, Casey Kotchman, Jered Weaver	2.00
10	Joe Mauer, Brian McCann, Russell Martin	2.00
11	Prince Fielder, J.J. Hardy, Ryan Braun	3.00
12	Joe Nathan, Justin Morneau, Joe Mauer	2.00
13	Pedro Martinez, Billy Wagner, Johan Santana	3.00
14	Derek Jeter, Jose Reyes, Hanley Ramirez	6.00
15	Derek Jeter, Jason Giambi, Robinson Cano	6.00
16	Greg Maddux, Trevor Hoffman, Jake Peavy	4.00
17	Rich Harden, Justin Verlander, Felix Hernandez	2.00
18	Randy Johnson, Chris Carpenter, Cole Hamels	2.00
19	Troy Glaus, Albert Pujols, Chris Duncan	4.00
20	Vernon Wells, Roy Halladay, A.J. Burnett	2.00

Franchise Members 3 Jersey

NM/M

		Price
Production 99 Sets		
1	Tom Glavine, John Smoltz, Tim Hudson	20.00
2	Curt Schilling, Josh Beckett, Daisuke Matsuzaka	30.00
3	Manny Ramirez, Jason Varitek, David Ortiz	20.00
4	Travis Hafner, Victor Martinez, Grady Sizemore	10.00
6	Carlos Lee, Matt Holliday, Jason Bay	10.00
7	Carlos Guillen, Magglio Ordonez, Miguel Cabrera	10.00
8	Dan Haren, Roy Oswalt, Jake Peavy	10.00
9	Vladimir Guerrero, Casey Kotchman, Jered Weaver	10.00
10	Joe Mauer, Brian McCann, Russell Martin	10.00
11	Prince Fielder, J.J. Hardy, Ryan Braun	10.00
12	Joe Nathan, Justin Morneau, Joe Mauer	10.00
13	Pedro Martinez, Billy Wagner, Johan Santana	15.00
14	Derek Jeter, Jose Reyes, Hanley Ramirez	25.00
15	Derek Jeter, Jason Giambi, Robinson Cano	25.00
16	Greg Maddux, Trevor Hoffman, Jake Peavy	15.00
17	Rich Harden, Justin Verlander, Felix Hernandez	10.00
18	Randy Johnson, Chris Carpenter, Cole Hamels	10.00
19	Troy Glaus, Albert Pujols, Chris Duncan	15.00
20	Vernon Wells, Roy Halladay, A.J. Burnett	10.00

Franchise Members 4

NM/M

		Price
Common Quad:		2.00
Production 799 Sets		
Silver:		1-2X
Production 149 Sets		
Red:		1-2X
Production 99 Sets		
Pewter:		1-2X
Production 75 Sets		
Blue:		2-3X
Production 25 Sets		
1	Derek Jeter, Jason Giambi, Johnny Damon, Jorge Posada	5.00
2	Curt Schilling, Josh Beckett, Jonathan Papelbon, Daisuke Matsuzaka	5.00
3	Carlos Delgado, Carlos Beltran, Johan Santana, Jose Reyes	4.00
4	Chipper Jones, Mark Teixeira, Brian McCann, Jeff Francoeur	3.00
5	Rickie Weeks, Prince Fielder, J.J. Hardy, Ryan Braun	3.00
6	Ken Griffey Jr., Adam Dunn, Brandon Phillips, Aaron Harang	4.00
7	Jeremy Bonderman, Dontrelle Willis, Justin Verlander, Joel Zumaya	2.00
8	Frank Thomas, Jim Thome, Gary Sheffield, David Ortiz	3.00
9	Greg Maddux, Mark Prior, Jake Peavy, Chris Young	4.00
10	Randy Johnson, Dan Haren, Conor Jackson, Brandon Webb	3.00
11	Eric Chavez, Bobby Crosby, Huston Street, Rich Harden	2.00
12	Adrian Beltre, Erik Bedard, Felix Hernandez, Kenji Johjima	2.00
13	Garret Anderson, Vladimir Guerrero, Torii Hunter, Chone Figgins	3.00
14	Derek Jeter, Rafael Furcal, Jose Reyes, Jhonny Peralta	5.00
15	Ken Griffey Jr., Andruw Jones, Carlos Beltran, Jim Edmonds	4.00
16	Ivan Rodriguez, Jason Varitek, Jorge Posada, Joe Mauer	3.00
17	Josh Willingham, Hanley Ramirez, Jeremy Hermida, Dan Uggla	3.00
18	Johan Santana, Francisco Liriano, C.C. Sabathia, Cole Hamels	3.00
19	Derrek Lee, Lance Berkman, Conor Jackson, Prince Fielder	3.00
20	Andruw Jones, Jeff Kent, Rafael Furcal, Matt Kemp	2.00

Hair Cuts

Production One Set

Rookie Autographs

NM/M

		Price
Production 50-499		
Blue Autos:		1-1.5X
Production 15-50		
Gold Autos:		1-1.5X
Production 25-75		
Red Autos:		1-1.5X
Production 25-99		
Silver:		1.5-2X
Production 10-25		
No pricing production 20 or less.		
101	Emilio Bonifacio/499	10.00
102	Bill Murphy/499	8.00
103	Billy Buckner/149	8.00
104	Brandon Jones/499	8.00
105	Clint Sammons/499	8.00
106	Clay Buchholz/499	25.00
107	Kevin Hart/499	10.00
108	Lance Broadway/99	10.00
109	Ryan Hanigan/499	10.00
110	Joey Votto/50	20.00
111	Joe Koshansky/499	8.00
112	Josh Newman/499	10.00
113	Seth Smith/499	10.00
114	Harvey Garcia/499	8.00
115	Chris Seddon/499	8.00
116	Josh Anderson/499	10.00
117	Troy Patton/499	10.00
118	Felipe Paulino/499	8.00
119	J.R. Towles/499	8.00
120	Chin-Lung Hu/99	20.00
121	Jonathan Meloan/99	8.00
122	Jose Morales/499	8.00
123	Alberto Gonzalez/499	8.00
130	Ian Kennedy/199	15.00
131	Ross Ohlendorf/499	8.00
132	Jonathan Albaladejo/499	8.00
133	Daric Barton/99	10.00
134	Jerry Blevins/499	8.00
135	David Davidson/499	8.00
136	Nyjer Morgan/499	8.00
137	Steve Pearce/499	10.00
138	Colt Morton/499	10.00
139	Eugenio Velez/499	10.00
141	Bronson Sardinha/499	10.00
142	Wladimir Balentien/199	8.00
144	Rob Johnson/499	8.00
146	Justin Ruggiano/499	10.00
147	Luis Mendoza/499	10.00
148	Bill White/499	8.00
149	Ross Detwiler/499	10.00
150	Justin Maxwell/498	15.00

Stadium Scenes

NM/M

		Price
Common Player:		2.00
Production 699 Sets		
Red:		1-2X
Production 149 Sets		
Copper:		1-2X
Production 99 Sets		
Blue:		1-2X
Production 75 Sets		
Silver:		2-3X
Production 25 Sets		
1	Randy Johnson	3.00
2	Justin Upton	3.00
3	Mark Teixeira	2.00
4	Chipper Jones	3.00
5	John Smoltz	3.00
6	David Ortiz	3.00
7	Josh Beckett	3.00
8	Daisuke Matsuzaka	5.00
9	Manny Ramirez	3.00
10	Jonathan Papelbon	3.00
11	Alfonso Soriano	3.00
12	Kerry Wood	2.00
13	Derek Lee	3.00
14	Jim Thome	3.00
15	Ken Griffey Jr.	5.00
16	Adam Dunn	3.00
17	Grady Sizemore	3.00
18	Travis Hafner	3.00
19	Victor Martinez	2.00
20	C.C. Sabathia	3.00
21	Miguel Cabrera	3.00
22	Justin Verlander	3.00
23	Ivan Rodriguez	3.00
24	Magglio Ordonez	3.00
25	Lance Berkman	3.00
26	Roy Oswalt	2.00
27	Vladimir Guerrero	3.00
28	Andruw Jones	3.00
29	Rickie Weeks	2.00
30	Ryan Braun	4.00
31	Prince Fielder	3.00
32	Joe Mauer	3.00
33	Pedro Martinez	3.00
34	Jose Reyes	4.00
35	David Wright	5.00
36	Johan Santana	3.00
37	Derek Jeter	8.00
38	Alex Rodriguez	8.00
39	Hideki Matsui	5.00
40	Joba Chamberlain	6.00
41	Cole Hamels	4.00
42	Chase Utley	4.00
43	Ryan Howard	4.00
44	Jimmy Rollins	3.00
45	Jake Peavy	2.00
46	Greg Maddux	5.00
47	Felix Hernandez	2.00
48	Ichiro Suzuki	5.00
49	Albert Pujols	8.00
50	Frank Thomas	3.00

Stadium Scenes Jersey Auto

NM/M

		Price
Production 10-99		
4	Chipper Jones/25	70.00
10	Jonathan Papelbon/99	30.00
12	Kerry Wood/99	20.00
13	Derek Lee/25	30.00
16	Adam Dunn/25	30.00
18	Travis Hafner/50	20.00
19	Victor Martinez/99	20.00
29	Rickie Weeks/50	20.00
47	Felix Hernandez/75	30.00

Stadium Scenes Red Jersey

NM/M

		Price
Common Jersey:		4.00
Gold Jersey:		1X
Production 99 Sets		
Blue Jersey:		1-1.5X
Production 25 Sets		
Patch:		2-3X
Production 25 Sets		
Jersey Button:		No Pricing
Production 25 Sets		
1	Randy Johnson	6.00
2	Justin Upton	6.00
3	Mark Teixeira	8.00
4	Chipper Jones	8.00
5	John Smoltz	8.00
6	David Ortiz	8.00
7	Josh Beckett	6.00
8	Daisuke Matsuzaka	15.00
9	Manny Ramirez	8.00
10	Jonathan Papelbon	8.00
11	Alfonso Soriano	8.00
12	Kerry Wood	6.00
13	Derek Lee	6.00
14	Jim Thome	4.00
15	Ken Griffey Jr.	6.00
16	Adam Dunn	6.00
17	Grady Sizemore	8.00
18	Travis Hafner	4.00
19	Victor Martinez	4.00
20	C.C. Sabathia	4.00
21	Miguel Cabrera	6.00
22	Justin Verlander	6.00
23	Ivan Rodriguez	6.00
24	Magglio Ordonez	6.00

5	Lance Berkman	6.00
	Roy Oswalt	4.00
	Vladimir Guerrero	8.00
8	Andruw Jones	4.00
	Rickie Weeks	8.00
0	Ryan Braun	8.00
	Prince Fielder	8.00
	Joe Mauer	4.00
	Pedro Martinez	6.00
	Jose Reyes	8.00
	Johan Santana	6.00
	Derek Jeter	15.00
	Alex Rodriguez	15.00
	Joba Chamberlain	15.00
	Cole Hamels	6.00
	Chase Utley	6.00
	Jimmy Rollins	6.00
	Jake Peavy	6.00
	Greg Maddux	10.00
	Felix Hernandez	6.00
	Albert Pujols	15.00
0	Frank Thomas	8.00

Timeless Moments

Timeless Moments

	NM/M
Common Player:	2.00
Production 699 Sets	
Red:	1-2X
Production 149 Sets	
Copper:	1-2X
Production 99 Sets	
Blue:	1-2X
Production 75 Sets	
Silver:	1-2.5X
Production 25 Sets	

	Randy Johnson	3.00
	Dan Haren	2.00
	John Smoltz	3.00
	Chipper Jones	4.00
	Mark Teixeira	3.00
	David Ortiz	3.00
	Dustin Pedroia	3.00
	Josh Beckett	3.00
	Curt Schilling	3.00
0	Daisuke Matsuzaka	5.00
	Alfonso Soriano	3.00
2	Carlos Zambrano	3.00
3	Jim Thome	3.00
4	Ken Griffey Jr.	5.00
	Adam Dunn	2.00
6	Grady Sizemore	3.00
7	C.C. Sabathia	3.00
8	Troy Tulowitzki	3.00
9	Matt Holliday	3.00
	Justin Verlander	2.00
1	Ivan Rodriguez	2.00
2	Hanley Ramirez	3.00
3	Alex Gordon	2.00
4	Vladimir Guerrero	3.00
	Jeff Kent	2.00
6	Nomar Garciaparra	2.00
	Prince Fielder	3.00
8	Joe Mauer	2.00
9	Justin Morneau	2.00
0	Jose Reyes	3.00
1	David Wright	4.00
2	Pedro Martinez	3.00
3	Johan Santana	3.00
4	Joba Chamberlain	5.00
5	Derek Jeter	8.00
6	Alex Rodriguez	8.00
7	Hideki Matsui	4.00
8	Ryan Howard	4.00
9	Chase Utley	4.00
0	Jimmy Rollins	3.00
1	Cole Hamels	3.00
2	Jake Peavy	3.00
3	Greg Maddux	5.00
4	Phil Hughes	2.00
5	Felix Hernandez	2.00
6	Ichiro Suzuki	5.00
7	Albert Pujols	8.00
8	Chris Carpenter	2.00
9	Frank Thomas	3.00
50	Vernon Wells	2.00

Timeless Moments Jersey Auto.

	NM/M
Production 5-75	
	Dan Haren/50	20.00
4	Chipper Jones/25	70.00
18	Troy Tulowitzki/50	20.00
19	Matt Holliday/25	25.00
23	Hanley Ramirez/50	35.00
23	Alex Gordon/25	35.00
34	Joba Chamberlain/50	180.00
45	Phil Hughes/50	25.00
45	Felix Hernandez/75	30.00

Timeless Moments Jersey

Timeless Moments

	NM/M
Common Jersey:	4.00
Gold Jersey:	1-1.5X
Production 75 Sets	
Blue Jersey:	1-2X
Production 25 Sets	
Jersey Button:	No Pricing
Production Five Sets	
Patch:	2-3X
Production 25 Sets	

1	Randy Johnson	6.00
2	Dan Haren	4.00
3	John Smoltz	8.00
5	Mark Teixeira	6.00
7	David Ortiz	8.00
7	Dustin Pedroia	8.00
8	Josh Beckett	6.00
9	Curt Schilling	6.00
10	Daisuke Matsuzaka	15.00
11	Alfonso Soriano	8.00
12	Carlos Zambrano	6.00
13	Jim Thome	4.00
17	C.C. Sabathia	4.00
18	Troy Tulowitzki	4.00
19	Matt Holliday	6.00
20	Justin Verlander	6.00
21	Ivan Rodriguez	6.00
22	Hanley Ramirez	8.00
23	Alex Gordon	8.00
24	Vladimir Guerrero	8.00
25	Jeff Kent	4.00
27	Prince Fielder	8.00
28	Joe Mauer	4.00
29	Justin Morneau	4.00
30	Jose Reyes	8.00
32	Pedro Martinez	6.00
33	Johan Santana	6.00
34	Joba Chamberlain	20.00
35	Derek Jeter	15.00
36	Alex Rodriguez	15.00
39	Chase Utley	8.00
40	Jimmy Rollins	8.00
41	Cole Hamels	6.00
42	Jake Peavy	6.00
43	Greg Maddux	10.00
44	Phil Hughes	6.00
45	Felix Hernandez	6.00
47	Albert Pujols	15.00
48	Chris Carpenter	4.00
49	Frank Thomas	6.00
50	Vernon Wells	4.00

2008 UD Ballpark Collection

2008 UD Ballpark Collection

	NM/M
Common Player (1-100):	1.00
Common RC Auto. (101-150):	8.00
Common Dual Jsy (151-200):	8.00
Common Quad Jsy (201-250):	10.00
Common 6X memorabilia (251-295):	15.00
Common 8x memor. (296-340):	15.00
Pack (5):	50.00
Box (4):	180.00

1	Brandon Webb	2.00
2	Dan Haren	1.50
3	Chris B. Young	1.50
4	Randy Johnson	3.00
5	Mark Teixeira	2.00
6	John Smoltz	2.00
7	Tom Glavine	1.50
8	Brian McCann	1.50
9	Chipper Jones	5.00
10	Nick Markakis	2.00
11	Brian Roberts	1.50
12	Josh Beckett	2.50

13	David Ortiz	4.00
14	Manny Ramirez	3.00
15	Dustin Pedroia	3.00
16	Jonathan Papelbon	2.00
17	Daisuke Matsuzaka	5.00
18	Alfonso Soriano	2.00
19	Aramis Ramirez	2.00
20	Carlos Zambrano	1.00
21	Nick Swisher	1.00
22	Jim Thome	2.00
23	Ken Griffey Jr.	6.00
24	Adam Dunn	2.00
25	Grady Sizemore	2.50
26	Victor Martinez	2.00
27	Travis Hafner	1.50
28	C.C. Sabathia	2.50
29	Garrett Atkins	1.50
30	Matt Holliday	2.00
31	Troy Tulowitzki	1.50
32	Magglio Ordonez	1.50
33	Justin Verlander	2.00
34	Miguel Cabrera	3.00
35	Gary Sheffield	2.00
36	Ivan Rodriguez	2.00
37	Dontrelle Willis	1.00
38	Curtis Granderson	2.50
39	Hanley Ramirez	3.00
40	Dan Uggla	1.50
41	Lance Berkman	2.00
42	Roy Oswalt	2.00
43	Carlos Lee	2.00
44	Hunter Pence	2.00
45	Alex Gordon	2.00
46	Jose Guillen	1.00
47	Torii Hunter	1.50
48	Vladimir Guerrero	3.00
49	Andruw Jones	1.00
50	Matt Kemp	2.50
51	Russell Martin	2.00
52	Jeff Kent	1.50
53	Ryan Braun	4.00
54	Prince Fielder	3.00
55	Delmon Young	1.00
56	Joe Mauer	2.00
57	Justin Morneau	2.00
58	Jose Reyes	4.00
59	David Wright	5.00
60	Carlos Beltran	2.50
61	Johan Santana	3.00
62	Pedro Martinez	2.50
63	Alex Rodriguez	6.00
64	Derek Jeter	8.00
65	Hideki Matsui	3.00
66	Robinson Cano	2.00
67	Joba Chamberlain	5.00
68	Phil Hughes	3.00
69	Mariano Rivera	2.50
70	Eric Chavez	1.00
71	Bobby Crosby	1.00
72	Cole Hamels	2.50
73	Ryan Howard	3.00
74	Jimmy Rollins	2.50
75	Chase Utley	3.00
76	Jason Bay	1.50
77	Freddy Sanchez	1.00
78	Jake Peavy	2.00
79	Greg Maddux	5.00
80	Trevor Hoffman	1.00
81	Kosuke Fukudome RC	4.00
82	Barry Zito	1.00
83	Tim Lincecum	3.00
84	Erik Bedard	1.00
85	Felix Hernandez	2.00
86	Ichiro Suzuki	5.00
87	Troy Glaus	1.50
88	Albert Pujols	8.00
89	Chris Carpenter	1.50
90	Scott Kazmir	1.50
91	Carl Crawford	1.50
92	Michael Young	1.50
93	Hank Blalock	1.50
94	Roy Halladay	2.00
95	Vernon Wells	1.00
96	Alex Rios	2.00
97	Scott Rolen	2.00
98	Frank Thomas	3.00
99	Lastings Milledge	1.00
100	Ryan Zimmerman	2.00
101	Bobby Wilson/Auto. RC	10.00
102	Alex Romero/Auto. (RC)	8.00
104	Brandon Boggs/ Auto. (RC)	10.00
105	Brian Barton/Auto. RC	10.00
106	Brian Bass/Auto. (RC)	10.00
107	Brian Bixler/Auto. RC	8.00
108	Brian Bocock/Auto. RC	8.00
109	Burke Badenhop/ Auto. RC	8.00
110	Callix Crabbe/Auto. (RC)	8.00
111	Clayton Kershaw/ Auto. RC	35.00
112	Chin-Lung Hu/ Auto. (RC)	25.00
113	Clay Buchholz/ Auto. (RC)	20.00
114	Eider Torres/Auto. (RC)	10.00
115	Clete Thomas/Auto. RC	12.00
116	Colt Morton/Auto. RC	8.00
117	Daric Barton/Auto. RC	8.00
118	Cory Wade/Auto. (RC)	12.00
119	Elliot Johnson/Auto. (RC)	8.00
120	Evan Longoria/Auto. RC	75.00
121	Evan Meek/Auto. RC	10.00
122	German Duran/Auto. RC	8.00
124	Fernando Hernandez/ Auto. RC	8.00
125	Greg Smith/Auto. RC	8.00
126	Jay Bruce/Auto. (RC)	40.00

127	Wladimir Balentien/ Auto. (RC)	10.00
128	Hernan Iribarren/ Auto. (RC)	8.00
129	Jed Lowrie/Auto. (RC)	40.00
130	Ian Kennedy/Auto. RC	12.00
131	Jeff Clement/Auto. (RC)	10.00
132	Jesse Carlson/Auto. RC	15.00
133	Jonathan Herrera/ Auto. RC	8.00
134	Johnny Cueto/Auto. RC	20.00
135	Jonathan Albaladejo/ Auto. RC	8.00
136	Josh Newman/Auto. RC	8.00
137	Kevin Hart/Auto. (RC)	8.00
138	Justin Masterson/ Auto. RC	20.00
140	Luis Mendoza/ Auto. (RC)	8.00
141	Matt Tupman/Auto. RC	15.00
142	Max Scherzer/Auto. RC	30.00
143	Nick Blackburn/ Auto. RC	12.00
144	Nick Adenhart/ Auto. (RC)	12.00
145	Ramon Troncoso/ Auto. (RC)	10.00
146	Paul Janish/Auto. (RC)	10.00
147	Randor Bierd/Auto. RC	15.00
148	Robinzon Diaz/ Auto. (RC)	10.00
149	Steve Holm/Auto. RC	10.00
150	Wesley Wright/Auto. RC	10.00
151	David Ortiz, Jason Giambi	10.00
152	Jonathan Papelbon, Mariano Rivera	15.00
153	Johan Santana, Nolan Ryan	15.00
154	Jorge Posada, Mike Mussina	10.00
155	Jonathan Papelbon, Jason Varitek	10.00
156	Howie Kendrick, Dan Uggla	8.00
157	Kenji Johjima, Jason Varitek	10.00
158	Roy Oswalt, Carlos Lee	8.00
159	Albert Pujols, Derek Lee	15.00
160	Albert Pujols, Ozzie Smith	20.00
161	Carlos Zambrano, Alfonso Soriano	10.00
162	Trevor Hoffman, Tony Gwynn	10.00
163	Cole Hamels, Johan Santana	10.00
164	Kendry Morales, David Ortiz	10.00
165	Curt Schilling, Randy Johnson	10.00
166	B.J. Upton, Curtis Granderson	10.00
167	Chase Utley, Ryne Sandberg	15.00
168	Nick Markakis, Melvin Mora	10.00
169	Prince Fielder, Conor Jackson	10.00
170	Ben Sheets, Roy Halladay	8.00
171	Kerry Wood, Mark Mulder	8.00
172	Andruw Jones, Ken Griffey Jr.	15.00
173	Troy Tulowitzki, J.J. Hardy	8.00
174	Tim Lincecum, Matt Cain	10.00
175	Orlando Cabrera, Derek Jeter	15.00
176	Prince Fielder, Albert Pujols	15.00
177	Roy Halladay, Frank Thomas	10.00
178	Josh Beckett, Jason Varitek	10.00
179	Miguel Cabrera, Mike Schmidt	12.00
180	Chris Duncan, Albert Pujols	15.00
181	C.C. Sabathia, Dontrelle Willis	10.00
182	Matt Holliday, Manny Ramirez	10.00
183	Zack Greinke, Roy Halladay	8.00
184	Nick Markakis, Vladimir Guerrero	10.00
185	Ben Sheets, Roy Halladay	8.00
186	Albert Pujols, Vladimir Guerrero	15.00
187	Manny Ramirez, Johnny Damon	10.00
188	Johan Santana, Chris Carpenter	10.00
189	Ken Griffey Jr., Frank Thomas	15.00
190	Jonathan Papelbon, Curt Schilling	10.00
191	Jonathan Papelbon, Curt Schilling	10.00
192	Derek Jeter, Cal Ripken Jr.	25.00
193	Jason Varitek, Wade Boggs	10.00
194	Alfonso Soriano, Derek Lee	10.00

196	Kenji Johjima, Hong-Chih Kuo	10.00
197	Alfonso Soriano, Kerry Wood	10.00
198	Albert Pujols, Carlos Delgado	15.00
199	Derek Jeter, Don Mattingly	25.00
200	Johnny Damon, Derek Jeter	15.00
201	Matt Kemp, Prince Fielder, Ben Sheets, James Loney	10.00
202	Kevin Youkilis, Jason Giambi, David Ortiz, Derek Jeter	20.00
203	Troy Tulowitzki, Cal Ripken Jr., Derek Jeter, Khalil Greene	25.00
204	Robin Yount, Prince Fielder, Rickie Weeks, J.J. Hardy	15.00
205	Howie Kendrick, Casey Kotchman, Chone Figgins	10.00
206	Kenji Johjima, Jorge Posada, Jason Varitek, Ivan Rodriguez	10.00
207	Joe Nathan, Trevor Hoffman, Mariano Rivera, Eric Gagne	10.00
208	Brandon Inge, Carlos Guillen, Gary Sheffield, Ivan Rodriguez	10.00
209	Scott Kazmir, Randy Johnson, Francisco Liriano, Johan Santana	15.00
210	John Maine, Pedro Martinez, Billy Wagner, Johan Santana	15.00
211	Prince Fielder, Albert Pujols, Derek Lee, Conor Jackson	15.00
212	Jered Weaver, Justin Verlander, Josh Beckett, Zack Greinke	10.00
213	Chris Young, Trevor Hoffman, Jake Peavy, Greg Maddux	15.00
215	Khalil Greene, Tony Gwynn, Trevor Hoffman, Greg Maddux	15.00
216	Aaron Harang, Carlos Zambrano, Alfonso Soriano, Ken Griffey Jr.	15.00
217	Roy Halladay, Mike Mussina, John Smoltz, Greg Maddux	15.00
218	Manny Ramirez, Frank Thomas, Jim Thome, Ken Griffey Jr.	20.00
220	Albert Pujols, Manny Ramirez, Vladimir Guerrero, Johnny Damon	20.00
221	Jason Bay, Derek Lee, Alfonso Soriano, Ken Griffey Jr.	15.00
222	Pat Burrell, Geoff Jenkins, Cole Hamels, Brad Lidge	10.00
223	Alfonso Soriano, Derek Jeter, Derek Lee, Jason Giambi	20.00
224	Takashi Saito, Tadahito Iguchi, Akinori Iwamura, Kenji Johjima	10.00
225	Cole Hamels, C.C. Sabathia, Randy Johnson, Scott Kazmir	15.00
226	Albert Pujols, Rick Ankiel, Chris Carpenter, Ozzie Smith	25.00
227	Albert Pujols, David Ortiz, Mike Schmidt, Ken Griffey Jr.	25.00
228	Curtis Granderson, Rickie Weeks, Derek Jeter, Rafael Furcal	15.00
229	David Ortiz, Wade Boggs, Jason Varitek, Manny Ramirez	15.00
230	Jake Peavy, Khalil Greene, Derek Jeter, Andy Pettitte	15.00
231	David Ortiz, Manny Ramirez, Don Mattingly, Derek Jeter	25.00
232	Johan Santana, Carlos Delgado, Chipper Jones, John Smoltz	15.00
233	Brian Roberts, Melvin Mora, Jason Giambi, Derek Jeter	15.00
234	Chris Duncan, Albert Pujols, Aramis Ramirez, Derek Lee	15.00
235	Prince Fielder, Ben Sheets, Albert Pujols, Mark Mulder	15.00

237	Albert Pujols, Vladimir Guerrero, Manny Ramirez, Pat Burrell	15.00
238	Justin Verlander, Ivan Rodriguez, Derek Jeter, Andy Pettitte	15.00
239	Kenji Johjima, Jorge Posada, Jason Varitek, Ivan Rodriguez	10.00
240	Dan Uggla, Chase Utley, Rickie Weeks, Brian Roberts	12.00
241	Albert Pujols, Magglio Ordonez, Ivan Rodriguez, Mark Mulder	15.00
242	Nick Markakis, David Ortiz, Prince Fielder, Ken Griffey Jr.	15.00
243	Dan Uggla, Derek Jeter, Brian Roberts, Michael Young	15.00
244	David Ortiz, Vladimir Guerrero, Magglio Ordonez, Manny Ramirez	15.00
245	Chad Billingsley, James Loney, Randy Johnson, Conor Jackson	10.00
246	Josh Willingham, Magglio Ordonez, Manny Ramirez, Pat Burrell	10.00
247	Chien-Ming Wang, Mariano Rivera, Derek Jeter, Jason Giambi	25.00
248	B.J. Upton, Carl Crawford, Hanley Ramirez, Dan Uggla	12.00
249	Prince Fielder, Ken Griffey Jr., Albert Pujols, Derek Lee	20.00
251	Cole Hamels, Jake Peavy, Dan Haren, Ben Sheets, Chris Carpenter, Randy Johnson	15.00
252	Nick Markakis, Rocco Baldelli, Mark Teahen, Curtis Granderson, Manny Ramirez, Vladimir Guerrero	10.00
253	Scott Kazmir, Francisco Liriano, Mark Mulder, Barry Zito, Johan Santana, Randy Johnson	15.00
255	Howie Kendrick, John Lackey, Vladimir Guerrero, Victor Martinez, C.C. Sabathia, Travis Hafner	15.00
256	Adam LaRoche, Prince Fielder, Adrian Gonzalez, Carlos Delgado, Derek Lee, Albert Pujols	20.00
257	Josh Willingham, Tony Gwynn, Jason Bay, Matt Holliday, Carlos Lee, Ken Griffey Jr.	25.00
260	Moises Alou, Johan Santana, Carlos Delgado, Jason Giambi, Andy Pettitte, Derek Jeter	30.00
261	Frank Thomas, Jason Giambi, David Ortiz, Aubrey Huff, Casey Kotchman, Rod Carew	15.00
262	Jered Weaver, Howie Kendrick, Scott Kazmir, Khalil Greene, Zack Greinke, Rickie Weeks	15.00
263	Roy Halladay, Tom Glavine, Randy Johnson, John Smoltz, Andy Pettitte, Mike Mussina	20.00
265	Chris Duncan, Mark Mulder, Albert Pujols, Aramis Ramirez, Kerry Wood, Derek Lee	25.00
266	Jered Weaver, Howie Kendrick, Vladimir Guerrero, Takashi Saito, Rafael Furcal, Andruw Jones	15.00
267	Prince Fielder, Ben Sheets, Kerry Wood, Derrek Lee, Mark Mulder, Albert Pujols	20.00
268	Albert Pujols, David Ortiz, Vladimir Guerrero, Manny Ramirez, Derek Jeter, Ken Griffey Jr.	40.00
269	Moises Alou, Dan Uggla, Josh Willingham, Chipper Jones, Mark Teixeira, Carlos Delgado	15.00
270	Frank Thomas, Manny Ramirez, Vladimir Guerrero, Carlos Lee, Mike Schmidt, Albert Pujols	25.00

271 Kenji Johjima, Brian McCann, Joe Mauer, Jason Varitek, Jorge Posada, Ivan Rodriguez 15.00
272 Nick Markakis, Delmon Young, Josh Willingham, Pat Burrell, Magglio Ordonez, Manny Ramirez 15.00
273 Roy Oswalt, Josh Hamilton, Michael Young, Kevin Millwood, Mark Loretta, Miguel Tejada 15.00
274 Moises Alou, Cole Hamels, Pat Burrell, Cole Hamels, Carlos Delgado, Johan Santana 20.00
275 Akinori Iwamura, Dan Uggla, Chris Burke, Chase Utley, Rickie Weeks, Aaron Hill 15.00
276 Chad Tracy, Dan Haren, Randy Johnson, Aramis Ramirez, Derrek Lee, Kerry Wood 25.00
277 Chris Duncan, Mark Mulder, Albert Pujols, Brandon Inge, Magglio Ordonez, Ivan Rodriguez 20.00
278 Nick Markakis, David Ortiz, Geoff Jenkins, Prince Fielder, Ken Griffey Jr., Garret Anderson 20.00
280 Kendry Morales, Aramis Ramirez, David Ortiz, Magglio Ordonez, Vladimir Guerrero, Manny Ramirez 15.00
281 Kenji Johjima, Eric Chavez, Melvin Mora, Miguel Cabrera, Jorge Posada, Jason Varitek
282 Delmon Young, Mark Teahen, Grady Sizemore, Jason Bay, Mike Cameron, Ken Griffey Jr. 15.00
284 Joel Zumaya, Dontrelle Willis, Magglio Ordonez, Josh Beckett, Jonathan Papelbon, David Ortiz 15.00
285 Delmon Young, Francisco Liriano, Justin Morneau, Rickie Weeks, Mike Cameron, Prince Fielder 15.00
286 Carl Crawford, Scott Kazmir, Akinori Iwamura, Luis Gonzalez, Dan Uggla, Josh Johnson 15.00
287 Chris Duncan, J.D. Drew, Xavier Nady, Josh Hamilton, Rick Ankiel, Nick Markakis 15.00
288 Troy Tulowitzki, Aaron Rowand, Matt Cain, Jeff Francis, Chris Young, Jake Peavy 15.00
290 Chien-Ming Wang, Don Mattingly, Jorge Posada, Mariano Rivera, Jason Giambi, Derek Jeter 40.00
291 Jonathan Papelbon, Wade Boggs, J.D. Drew, Josh Beckett, Jason Varitek, Manny Ramirez 25.00
292 Troy Tulowitzki, Chad Billingsley, Rafael Furcal, Jeff Francis, Conor Jackson, Dan Haren 15.00
294 Dontrelle Willis, Miguel Cabrera, Magglio Ordonez, Carlos Guillen, Ivan Rodriguez, Gary Sheffield 20.00
295 Jered Weaver, Casey Kotchman, Chone Figgins, John Lackey, Garret Anderson, Vladimir Guerrero 15.00
297 Jonathan Papelbon, Mariano Rivera, Jorge Posada, Jason Giambi, Derek Jeter, David Ortiz, Jason Varitek, Manny Ramirez 40.00
298 Howie Kendrick, Grady Sizemore, Victor Martinez, C.C. Sabathia, Travis Hafner, John Lackey, Vladimir Guerrero, Kendry Morales 20.00
299 Adam LaRoche, Adrian Gonzalez, Carlos Delgado, Mark Teixeira, Derrek Lee, Prince Fielder, Lance Berkman, Albert Pujols 25.00
300 Chris Duncan, Mike Cameron, Carlos Beltran, Ken Griffey Jr.,
Josh Willingham, Carlos Lee, Matt Holliday, Jason Bay 20.00
301 Cole Hamels, Pat Burrell, Chipper Jones, John Smoltz, Josh Willingham, Josh Johnson, Carlos Delgado, Johan Santana 20.00
302 Ozzie Smith, Derek Jeter, Khalil Greene, Stephen Drew, Brian Roberts, Dan Uggla, Mark Loretta, Rickie Weeks 25.00
303 Moises Alou, Johnny Damon, Jason Giambi, Derek Jeter, Andy Pettitte, Carlos Delgado, Jose Reyes, Johan Santana 30.00
304 Justin Morneau, Jim Thome, Aubrey Huff, Richie Sexson, Frank Thomas, Jason Giambi, Casey Kotchman, David Ortiz 30.00
306 Chris Duncan, Prince Fielder, Alfonso Soriano, Lance Berkman, Derrek Lee, Carlos Lee, Albert Pujols, Ken Griffey Jr. 30.00
307 Randy Johnson, John Smoltz, Tom Glavine, Pedro Martinez, Mike Mussina, John Lackey, Andy Pettitte, Roy Halladay 25.00
308 Brian Roberts, Melvin Mora, Nick Markakis, Aubrey Huff, Johnny Damon, Derek Jeter, Jason Giambi, Jorge Posada 25.00
311 Tom Gorzelanny, Xavier Nady, Ben Sheets, Prince Fielder, Kerry Wood, Albert Pujols, Mark Mulder, Derrek Lee 25.00
312 Mark Teixeira, Vladimir Guerrero, David Ortiz, Ken Griffey Jr., Albert Pujols, Derek Jeter, Cal Ripken Jr., Manny Ramirez 40.00
314 Albert Pujols, Manny Ramirez, Aramis Ramirez, Carlos Lee, Frank Thomas, Jason Giambi, Pat Burrell, Vladimir Guerrero 30.00
317 Moises Alou, Delmon Young, Josh Willingham, Pat Burrell, Rocco Baldelli, Nick Markakis, Magglio Ordonez, Manny Ramirez 15.00
318 Hank Blalock, Mark Loretta, Miguel Tejada, Roy Oswalt, Carlos Lee, Josh Hamilton, Kevin Millwood, Michael Young 15.00
319 Moises Alou, Johan Santana, Carlos Delgado, Brad Lidge, Pat Burrell, Cole Hamels, Chase Utley, Billy Wagner 25.00
320 Dan Uggla, Chris Burke, Aaron Hill, Mark Loretta, Brian Roberts, Rickie Weeks, Robinson Cano, Chase Utley 15.00
321 Stephen Drew, Aramis Ramirez, Derrek Lee, Alfonso Soriano, Kerry Wood, Chris Burke, Chad Tracy, Randy Johnson 20.00
322 Chris Duncan, Chris Carpenter, Albert Pujols, Ivan Rodriguez, Brandon Inge, Joel Zumaya, Magglio Ordonez, Mark Mulder 25.00
323 Troy Tulowitzki, Garrett Atkins, Jeff Francis, Matt Holliday, Jason Varitek, Jonathan Papelbon, Manny Ramirez, David Ortiz 20.00
324 Nick Markakis, Garret Anderson, David Ortiz, Chad Tracy, Geoff Jenkins, Prince Fielder, Ken Griffey Jr., Eric Chavez 40.00
325 Lance Berkman, Casey Kotchman, Aubrey Huff, Justin Morneau, Carlos Delgado, Jason Giambi, Kevin Youkilis, James Loney 20.00
326 Michael Young, Chase Utley, Troy Tulowitzki, Akinori Iwamura, Aaron Hill, Khalil Greene, Dan Uggla, Derek Jeter 20.00
327 Johan Santana, Magglio Ordonez, Vladimir Guerrero, David Ortiz, Aramis Ramirez, Kendry Morales, Ivan Rodriguez, Manny Ramirez 20.00
329 Ken Griffey Jr., Mike Cameron, Chris Duncan, Jason Bay, Magglio Ordonez, Delmon Young, Grady Sizemore, Mark Teahen 30.00
330 James Loney, Adam LaRoche, Mark Teixeira, Aaron Boone, Casey Kotchman, Kevin Youkilis, Jason Giambi, Aubrey Huff 20.00
331 Miguel Cabrera, Magglio Ordonez, Dontrelle Willis, Joel Zumaya, Manny Ramirez, David Ortiz, Jonathan Papelbon, Josh Beckett 25.00
333 Carl Crawford, Scott Kazmir, Rocco Baldelli, B.J. Upton, Hanley Ramirez, Josh Johnson, Josh Willingham, Dan Uggla 15.00
334 Pat Burrell, Nick Markakis, Josh Willingham, Xavier Nady, J.D. Drew, Chris Duncan, Rick Ankiel, Josh Hamilton 20.00
335 Jake Peavy, Chris Young, Jeff Francis, Troy Tulowitzki, Randy Johnson, Chad Tracy, Matt Cain, Tim Lincecum 20.00
336 Derek Jeter, Mike Mussina, Mariano Rivera, Chien-Ming Wang, Andy Pettitte, Jason Giambi, Don Mattingly, Jorge Posada 50.00
337 David Ortiz, Manny Ramirez, Jonathan Papelbon, Josh Beckett, J.D. Drew, Jason Varitek, Kevin Youkilis, Wade Boggs 50.00
338 Ken Griffey Jr., Aaron Harang, Derrek Lee, Carlos Zambrano, Prince Fielder, Ben Sheets, Albert Pujols, Mark Mulder 25.00
339 Aaron Harang, Dan Haren, Roy Oswalt, Chad Billingsley, Josh Johnson, Zack Greinke, A.J. Burnett, Jered Weaver 15.00

Jersey Autographs

NM/M
Common Player: 8.00
Some not priced due to scarcity

#	Player	Price
1	Aaron Harang	10.00
2	Kevin Saito	30.00
3	Troy Tulowitzki	20.00
4	Adam LaRoche	15.00
5	Adrian Gonzalez	20.00
6	Andre Ethier	20.00
7	Joe Mauer	35.00
8	Justin Upton	25.00
9	Aramis Ramirez	30.00
10	Scott Baker	15.00
11	B.J. Upton	25.00
12	Bill Hall	8.00
13	Billy Wagner	50.00
14	Brandon Phillips	20.00
15	Brandon Webb	25.00
16	Brian McCann	20.00
18	Brian Roberts	15.00
19	Bronson Arroyo	20.00
20	Tim Lincecum	70.00
22	Mark Reynolds	15.00
23	Chad Billingsley	20.00
24	Chad Cordero	8.00
25	Chone Figgins	15.00
27	Chris B. Young	15.00
28	Tom Gorzelanny	8.00
29	Corey Hart	15.00
30	Dan Uggla	15.00
32	Derek Jeter	125.00
33	Edinson Volquez	25.00
35	Xavier Nady	15.00
38	Felix Pie	10.00
42	Garrett Atkins	10.00
43	Ken Griffey Jr.	70.00
44	Derek Jeter	125.00
45	Hanley Ramirez	25.00
46	Hong-Chih Kuo	40.00
48	Ian Kinsler	20.00
49	Derek Lowe	15.00
50	Alfonso Soriano	40.00
51	Jeff Baker	8.00
52	Jeff Francis	10.00
53	Jeff Francoeur	20.00
54	Jered Weaver	10.00
55	Ben Sheets	20.00
56	Jeremy Guthrie	15.00
59	Jeremy Hermida	15.00
60	Joakim Soria	15.00
61	Joe Blanton	10.00
62	Joe Nathan	20.00
63	Chien-Ming Wang	100.00
64	Chris Young	8.00
66	Jon Lester	30.00
67	Jonathan Papelbon	8.00
68	Cole Hamels	50.00
69	Josh Johnson	15.00
70	Josh Willingham	15.00
71	Kelly Johnson	15.00
72	Ken Griffey Jr.	70.00
73	Kevin Kouzmanoff	10.00
74	Kevin Youkilis	30.00
75	Derek Lee	25.00
76	James Shields	25.00
77	Jason Bay	15.00
78	Jason Varitek	35.00
81	Mark Teahen	10.00
83	Matt Cain	15.00
84	John Lackey	15.00
85	Matt Kemp	25.00
86	John Maine	10.00
88	Melvin Mora	15.00
91	Kerry Wood	25.00
92	Nick Markakis	25.00
93	Lance Berkman	20.00
94	Noah Lowry	10.00
95	Rickie Weeks	15.00
96	Prince Fielder	30.00
97	Roy Halladay	12.00
98	Tim Hudson	15.00
99	Grady Sizemore	40.00

Swatch Memorabilia Auto.

No pricing due to scarcity

Jersey Buttons

NM/M

Production 5-25	8.00
Laundry Tags:	No Pricing
Production 2-15	
MLB Logos:	No Pricing
Production 1-5	
6 Albert Pujols/25	125.00
32 Derek Jeter/25	100.00
44 Derek Jeter/25	100.00
55 Ben Sheets/25	25.00
68 Cole Hamels/25	50.00
77 Jason Bay/25	30.00
78 Jason Varitek/25	50.00
83 Matt Cain/20	25.00
97 Roy Halladay/25	35.00

2008 Upper Deck First Edition

NM/M

Complete Set (1-300):	20.00
Complete Update Set (301-500):	20.00
Common Player:	.15
Pack (10):	1.00
Box (36):	25.00
1 Joe Saunders	.15
2 Kelvim Escobar	.15
3 Jered Weaver	.25
4 Justin Speier	.15
5 Scot Shields	.15
6 Orlando Cabrera	.25
7 Casey Kotchman	.15
8 Vladimir Guerrero	.50
9 Garret Anderson	.25
10 Roy Oswalt	.40
11 Wandy Rodriguez	.15
12 Woody Williams	.15
13 Chad Qualls	.15
14 Mark Loretta	.15
15 Brad Ausmus	.15
16 Carlos Lee	.40
17 Hunter Pence	.40
18 Dan Haren	.25
19 Lenny DiNardo	.15
20 Chad Gaudin	.15
21 Huston Street	.15
22 Andrew Brown	.15
23 Mike Piazza	.50
24 Mark Ellis	.15
25 Shannon Stewart	.15
26 Shaun Marcum	.15
27 A.J. Burnett	.25
28 Casey Janssen	.15
29 Jeremy Accardo	.15
30 Aaron Hill	.15
31 Frank Thomas	.25
32 Matt Stairs	.15
33 Vernon Wells	.25
34 Tim Hudson	.25
35 Buddy Carlyle	.15
36 Rafael Soriano	.15
37 Brian McCann	.25
38 Edgar Renteria	.25
39 Mark Teixeira	.40
40 Willie Harris	.15
41 Andruw Jones	.15
42 Ben Sheets	.25
43 David Bush	.15
44 Yovani Gallardo	.40
45 Matt Wise	.15
46 Johnny Estrada	.15
47 Prince Fielder	.50
48 J.J. Hardy	.15
49 Corey Hart	.25
50 Adam Wainwright	.15
51 Joel Pineiro	.15
52 Jason Isringhausen	.15
53 Troy Percival	.15
54 Albert Pujols	1.50
55 David Eckstein	.15
56 Jim Edmonds	.15
57 Rick Ankiel	.25
58 Ted Lilly	.15
59 Rich Hill	.15
60 Jason Marquis	.15
61 Carlos Marmol	.15
62 Jason Kendall	.15
63 Aramis Ramirez	.40
64 Ryan Theriot	.15
65 Alfonso Soriano	.40
66 Jack Jones	.15
67 James Shields	.25
68 Andrew Sonnanstine	.15
69 Scott Dohmann	.15
70 Dioner Navarro	.15
71 B.J. Upton	.40
72 Carlos Pena	.40
73 Brendan Harris	.15
74 Josh Wilson	.15
75 Brandon Webb	.40
76 Micah Owings	.15
77 Doug Slaten	.15
78 Brandon Lyon	.15
79 Miguel Montero	.15
80 Stephen Drew	.25
81 Mark Reynolds	.15
82 Chris B. Young	.25
83 Chad Billingsley	.25
84 Derek Lowe	.25
85 Mark Hendrickson	.15
86 Takashi Saito	.15
87 Russell Martin	.25
88 Jeff Kent	.25
89 Matt Kemp	.40
90 Juan Pierre	.15
91 Matt Cain	.25
92 Barry Zito	.25
93 Kevin Correia	.15
94 Jack Taschner	.15
95 Bengie Molina	.15
96 Omar Vizquel	.15
97 Dave Roberts	.15
98 Rajai Davis	.15
99 Fausto Carmona	.15
100 Jake Westbrook	.15
101 Rafael Betancourt	.15
102 Joe Borowski	.15
103 Victor Martinez	.25
104 Travis Hafner	.25
105 Ryan Garko	.15
106 Kenny Lofton	.25
107 Franklin Gutierrez	.15
108 Felix Hernandez	.40
109 J.J. Putz	.15
110 Brandon Morrow	.15
111 Kenji Johjima	.15
112 Jose Vidro	.15
113 Richie Sexson	.15
114 Ichiro Suzuki	1.00
115 Ben Broussard	.15
116 Sergio Mitre	.15
117 Scott Olsen	.15
118 Rick Vanden Hurk	.15
119 Lee Gardner	.15
120 Miguel Olivo	.15
121 Hanley Ramirez	.75
122 Mike Jacobs	.15
123 Josh Willingham	.15
124 John Maine	.15
125 Tom Glavine	.40
126 Billy Wagner	.25
127 Aaron Heilman	.15
128 David Wright	1.00
129 Luis Castillo	.15
130 Shawn Green	.15
131 Damion Easley	.15
132 Carlos Delgado	.40
133 Shawn Hill	.15
134 John Lannan	.15
135 Chad Cordero	.15
136 Jon Rauch	.15
137 Jesus Flores	.15
138 Dmitri Young	.15
139 Cristian Guzman	.15
140 Austin Kearns	.15
141 Nook Logan	.15
142 Erik Bedard	.25
143 Daniel Cabrera	.15
144 Chris Ray	.15
145 Chad Bradford	.15
146 Ramon Hernandez	.15
147 Miguel Tejada	.40
148 Freddie Bynum	.15
149 Corey Patterson	.15
150 Chris Young	.25
151 Greg Maddux	1.00
152 Kevin Cameron	.15
153 Doug Brocail	.15
154 Kevin Kouzmanoff	.15
155 Geoff Blum	.15
156 Milton Bradley	.25
157 Brian Giles	.25
158 Jamie Moyer	.15
159 Kyle Kendrick	.15
160 Kyle Lohse	.15
161 Antonio Alfonseca	.15
162 Chris Coste	.15
163 Chase Utley	.50
164 Tadahito Iguchi	.15
165 Aaron Rowand	.15
166 Shane Victorino	.40
167 Ian Snell	.15
168 Shane Youman	.15
169 Shawn Chacon	.15
170 Ronny Paulino	.15
171 Jack Wilson	.15
172 Adam LaRoche	.25
173 Ryan Doumit	.15
174 Xavier Nady	.15
175 Kevin Millwood	.15
176 Brandon McCarthy	.15
177 Wes Littleton	.15
178 Mike Wood	.15
179 Hank Blalock	.25
180 Ian Kinsler	.40
181 Marlon Byrd	.15
182 Brad Wilkerson	.15
183 Tim Wakefield	.15
184 Daisuke Matsuzaka	1.00
185 Julian Tavarez	.15
186 Hideki Okajima	
187 Doug Mirabelli	
188 Dustin Pedroia	
189 Mike Lowell	
190 Manny Ramirez	
191 Coco Crisp	
192 Bronson Arroyo	
193 Matt Belisle	
194 Jared Burton	
195 Mike Gosling	
196 David Ross	
197 Edwin Encarnacion	
198 Ken Griffey Jr.	1.0
199 Adam Dunn	
200 Jeff Francis	
201 Jason Hirsh	
202 Manny Corpas	
203 Jeremy Affeldt	
204 Yorvit Torrealba	
205 Todd Helton	
206 Kazuo Matsui	
207 Brad Hawpe	
208 Willy Taveras	
209 Brian Bannister	
210 Zack Greinke	
211 Kyle Davies	
212 David Riske	
213 John Buck	
214 Mark Grudzielanek	
215 Billy Butler	
216 David DeJesus	
217 Jeremy Bonderman	
218 Chad Durbin	
219 Andrew Miller	
220 Todd Jones	
221 Brandon Inge	
222 Placido Polanco	
223 Gary Sheffield	
224 Magglio Ordonez	
225 Matt Garza	
226 Boof Bonser	
227 Joe Nathan	
228 Dennys Reyes	
229 Joe Mauer	
230 Michael Cuddyer	
231 Jason Bartlett	
232 Torii Hunter	
233 Jason Tyner	
234 Mark Buehrle	
235 Jon Garland	
236 Jose Contreras	
237 Matt Thornton	
238 Juan Uribe	
239 Jim Thome	
240 Jerry Owens	
241 Jermaine Dye	
242 Andy Pettitte	
243 Phil Hughes	
244 Mike Mussina	
245 Joba Chamberlain	.7
246 Brian Bruney	
247 Jorge Posada	
248 Derek Jeter	1.5
249 Jason Giambi	
250 Johnny Damon	
251 Jonathan Albaladejo RC	
252 Josh Anderson RC	
253 Wladimir Balentien (RC)	
254 Josh Banks (RC)	
255 Daric Barton (RC)	.5
256 Jerry Blevins RC	
257 Emilio Bonifacio RC	
258 Lance Broadway (RC)	
259 Clay Buchholz (RC)	1.0
260 Billy Buckner (RC)	
261 Jeff Clement (RC)	.7
262 Willie Collazo RC	
263 Ross Detwiler RC	.5
264 Sam Fuld RC	
265 Harvey Garcia (RC)	
266 Alberto Gonzalez RC	
267 Ryan Hanigan RC	
268 Kevin Hart (RC)	
269 Luke Hochevar RC	.7
270 Chin-Lung Hu (RC)	
271 Rob Johnson (RC)	
272 Radhames Liz RC	
273 Ian Kennedy RC	1.0
274 Joe Koshansky (RC)	
275 Donny Lucy (RC)	
276 Justin Maxwell RC	.5
277 Jonathan Meloan RC	
278 Luis Mendoza (RC)	
279 Jose Morales (RC)	
280 Nyjer Morgan (RC)	.5
281 Carlos Muniz RC	
282 Bill Murphy (RC)	
283 Josh Newman RC	
284 Ross Ohlendorf RC	.5
285 Troy Patton (RC)	
286 Felipe Paulino RC	
287 Steve Pearce RC	
288 Heath Phillips RC	
289 Justin Ruggiano RC	.5
290 Clint Sammons (RC)	
291 Bronson Sardinha (RC)	
292 Chris Seddon (RC)	
293 Seth Smith RC	.5
294 Mitch Stetter RC	
295 David Davidson RC	
296 Rich Thompson RC	
297 J.R. Towles RC	.7
298 Eugenio Velez RC	
299 Joey Votto RC	.5
300 Bill White RC	
301 Dan Haren	
302 Randy Johnson	
303 Justin Upton	

#	Player	Price
304	Tom Glavine	.40
305	Chipper Jones	.75
306	Jeff Francoeur	.15
307	John Smoltz	.40
308	Yunel Escobar	.15
309	Adam Jones	.40
310	Jeremy Guthrie	.15
311	Nick Markakis	.40
312	Brian Roberts	.25
313	Melvin Mora	.15
314	Josh Beckett	.40
315	Jon Lester	.50
316	Curt Schilling	.40
317	Jonathan Papelbon	.40
318	Jason Varitek	.25
319	David Ortiz	.75
320	Jacoby Ellsbury	.75
321	Julio Lugo	.15
322	Sean Casey	.15
323	Kevin Youkilis	.40
324	J.D. Drew	.25
325	Derek Lee	.25
326	Carlos Zambrano	.40
327	Kerry Wood	.25
328	Geovany Soto	.40
329	Kosuke Fukudome RC	1.50
330	Gavin Floyd	.15
331	Bobby Jenks	.15
332	Javier Vazquez	.15
333	A.J. Pierzynski	.15
334	Orlando Cabrera	.15
335	Joe Crede	.15
336	Paul Konerko	.25
337	Nick Swisher	.25
338	Carlos Quentin	.25
339	Alexei Ramirez RC	1.50
340	Johnny Cueto	.50
341	Aaron Harang	.15
342	Brandon Phillips	.25
343	Paul Byrd	.15
344	Grady Sizemore	.50
345	Jhonny Peralta	.15
346	Asdrubal Cabrera	.15
347	C.C. Sabathia	.50
348	Troy Tulowitzki	.40
349	Matt Holliday	.40
350	Garrett Atkins	.25
351	Ubaldo Jimenez	.15
352	Kenny Rogers	.15
353	Justin Verlander	.40
354	Dontrelle Willis	.15
355	Joel Zumaya	.15
356	Ivan Rodriguez	.25
357	Miguel Cabrera	.50
358	Carlos Guillen	.15
359	Edgar Renteria	.15
360	Curtis Granderson	.50
361	Jeremy Hermida	.15
362	Dan Uggla	.25
363	Luis Gonzalez	.15
364	Andrew Miller	.15
365	Jorge Cantu	.15
366	Kazuo Matsui	.15
367	Lance Berkman	.25
368	Miguel Tejada	.25
369	Jose Valverde	.15
370	Michael Bourn	.15
371	Gil Meche	.15
372	Joey Gathright	.15
373	Mark Teahen	.15
374	Alex Gordon	.15
375	Tony Pena	.15
376	Jose Guillen	.15
377	Torii Hunter	.25
378	Ervin Santana	.25
379	Francisco Rodriguez	.25
380	Howie Kendrick	.25
381	John Lackey	.25
382	Gary Matthews	.15
383	Jon Garland	.15
384	Chone Figgins	.25
385	Andruw Jones	.15
386	James Loney	.40
387	Andre Ethier	.25
388	Rafael Furcal	.40
389	Brad Penny	.15
390	Hiroki Kuroda RC	.75
391	Blake DeWitt	.15
392	Mike Cameron	.15
393	Ryan Braun	.75
394	Rickie Weeks	.15
395	Bill Hall	.15
396	Tony Gwynn	.15
397	Eric Gagne	.15
398	Jeff Suppan	.15
399	Jason Kendall	.15
400	Livan Hernandez	.15
401	Francisco Liriano	.40
402	Pat Neshek	.15
403	Adam Everett	.15
404	Justin Morneau	.40
405	Craig Monroe	.15
406	Carlos Gomez	.25
407	Delmon Young	.40
408	Oliver Perez	.15
409	Jose Reyes	.75
410	Moises Alou	.25
411	Carlos Beltran	.40
412	Endy Chavez	.15
413	Ryan Church	.15
414	Pedro Martinez	.15
415	Johan Santana	.40
416	Mike Pelfrey	.15
417	Brian Schneider	.15
418	Ramon Castro	.15
419	Kei Igawa	.15
420	Mariano Rivera	.40
421	Chien-Ming Wang	.75
422	Wilson Betemit	.15
423	Robinson Cano	.40
424	Alex Rodriguez	1.50
425	Bobby Abreu	.40
426	Shelley Duncan	.15
427	Hideki Matsui	.50
428	Joe Blanton	.15
429	Bobby Crosby	.15
430	Eric Chavez	.25
431	Dan Johnson	.15
432	Rich Harden	.25
433	Kurt Suzuki	.15
434	Ryan Howard	1.00
435	Jimmy Rollins	.50
436	Pedro Feliz	.15
437	Adam Eaton	.15
438	Brad Lidge	.15
439	Brett Myers	.15
440	Pat Burrell	.25
441	Geoff Jenkins	.15
442	Zach Duke	.15
443	Matt Morris	.15
444	Tom Gorzelanny	.15
445	Jason Bay	.25
446	Freddy Sanchez	.15
447	Matt Capps	.15
448	Tadahito Iguchi	.15
449	Adrian Gonzalez	.25
450	Jim Edmonds	.25
451	Jake Peavy	.25
452	Khalil Greene	.15
453	Trevor Hoffman	.25
454	Mark Prior	.25
455	Randy Wolf	.15
456	Scott Hairston	.15
457	Tim Lincecum	.50
458	Noah Lowry	.15
459	Aaron Rowand	.15
460	Randy Winn	.15
461	Ray Durham	.15
462	Brian Wilson	.15
463	Adrian Beltre	.25
464	Jarrod Washburn	.15
465	Yuniesky Betancourt	.15
466	Jose Lopez	.15
467	Raul Ibanez	.15
468	Erik Bedard	.15
469	Brad Wilkerson	.15
470	Chris Carpenter	.25
471	Mark Mulder	.15
472	Skip Schumaker	.15
473	Troy Glaus	.25
474	Chris Duncan	.15
475	Scott Kazmir	.25
476	Troy Percival	.15
477	Akinori Iwamura	.15
478	Carl Crawford	.25
479	Cliff Floyd	.15
480	Matt Garza	.15
481	Edwin Jackson	.15
482	Vicente Padilla	.15
483	Josh Hamilton	.75
484	Milton Bradley	.15
485	Michael Young	.25
486	David Murphy	.15
487	Ben Broussard	.15
488	B.J. Ryan	.15
489	David Eckstein	.15
490	Alex Rios	.40
491	Lyle Overbay	.15
492	Scott Rolen	.25
493	Lastings Milledge	.15
494	Paul LoDuca	.15
495	Ryan Zimmerman	.25
496	Odalis Perez	.15
497	Wily Mo Pena	.15
498	Elijah Dukes	.15
499	Ronnie Belliard	.15
500	Nick Johnson	.15

Star Quest

#	Player	NM/M
	Common Player:	.50
1	Ichiro Suzuki	2.00
2	Ryan Braun	1.50
3	Prince Fielder	1.00
4	Ken Griffey Jr.	2.00
5	Vladimir Guerrero	.75
6	Travis Hafner	.50
7	Matt Holliday	.75
8	Ryan Howard	1.50
9	Derek Jeter	3.00
10	Alex Rodriguez	2.50
11	Carlos Lee	.75
12	Justin Morneau	.75
13	Magglio Ordonez	.50
14	David Ortiz	1.00
15	Jake Peavy	.75
16	Albert Pujols	2.50
17	Hanley Ramirez	1.00
18	Manny Ramirez	1.00
19	Jose Reyes	1.00
20	Alex Rodriguez	2.50
21	Johan Santana	1.00
22	Grady Sizemore	1.00
23	Alfonso Soriano	.75
24	Mark Teixeira	.75
25	Frank Thomas	.75
26	Jim Thome	.75
27	Chase Utley	1.00
28	Brandon Webb	.75
29	David Wright	1.50
30	Michael Young	.50
31	Adam Dunn	.75
32	Albert Pujols	2.50
33	Alex Rodriguez	2.50
34	B.J. Upton	.50
35	C.C. Sabathia	.75
36	Carlos Beltran	.75
37	Carlos Pena	.50
38	Cole Hamels	.75
39	Curtis Granderson	.75
40	Daisuke Matsuzaka	1.50
41	David Ortiz	1.00
42	Derek Jeter	3.00
43	Derrek Lee	.75
44	Eric Byrnes	.50
45	Felix Hernandez	.75
46	Ichiro Suzuki	2.00
47	Jeff Francoeur	.50
48	Jimmy Rollins	1.00
49	Joe Mauer	.75
50	John Smoltz	.75
51	Ken Griffey Jr.	2.00
52	Lance Berkman	.75
53	Miguel Cabrera	1.00
54	Paul Konerko	.50
55	Pedro Martinez	.75
56	Randy Johnson	.75
57	Russell Martin	.50
58	Troy Tulowitzki	.50
59	Vernon Wells	.50
60	Vladimir Guerrero	.75

Factory Set Jersey

Code	Player	NM/M
	Common Jersey:	3.00
	Production 750 Sets	
AB	A.J. Burnett	3.00
AE	Andre Ethier	3.00
AG	Adrian Gonzalez	4.00
AH	Aaron Harang	3.00
AP	Albert Pujols	15.00
AR	Aaron Rowand	4.00
AX	Alex Rios	4.00
BA	Bobby Abreu	4.00
BG	Brian Giles	3.00
BO	Aaron Boone	3.00
BU	Clay Buchholz	5.00
BW	Billy Wagner	4.00
BZ	Barry Zito	4.00
CA	Mike Cameron	3.00
CB	Chad Billingsley	5.00
CC	Chris Carpenter	4.00
CD	Chris Duncan	3.00
CF	Chone Figgins	4.00
CG	Curtis Granderson	5.00
CH	Cole Hamels	6.00
CJ	Conor Jackson	4.00
CL	Carlos Lee	5.00
CR	Coco Crisp	3.00
CS	Curt Schilling	5.00
CU	Michael Cuddyer	3.00
CY	Chris Young	4.00
DA	Johnny Damon	5.00
DH	Dan Haren	4.00
DJ	Derek Jeter	20.00
DL	Derrek Lee	6.00
DO	David Ortiz	8.00
DP	Dustin Pedroia	10.00
DU	Dan Uggla	3.00
DW	Dontrelle Willis	3.00
DY	Delmon Young	4.00
ED	Jim Edmonds	4.00
EG	Eric Gagne	3.00
ES	Johnny Estrada	3.00
FH	Felix Hernandez	5.00
FL	Francisco Liriano	6.00
FS	Freddy Sanchez	3.00
FT	Frank Thomas	6.00
GJ	Geoff Jenkins	3.00
GM	Greg Maddux	10.00
GU	Jeremy Guthrie	3.00
HB	Hank Blalock	4.00
HH	Aaron Hill	3.00
HR	Hanley Ramirez	8.00
HS	Huston Street	3.00
JA	Jason Bay	4.00
JB	Jeremy Bonderman	3.00
JC	Joe Crede	3.00
JD	J.D. Drew	3.00
JE	Jermaine Dye	4.00
JF	Jeff Francoeur	4.00
JG	Jason Giambi	4.00
JH	Jeremy Hermida	3.00
JK	Jason Kendall	3.00
JM	Joe Mauer	5.00
JO	Josh Barfield	3.00
JP	Jhonny Peralta	4.00
JQ	Jacque Jones	3.00
JR	Jimmy Rollins	6.00
JV	Justin Verlander	5.00
JW	Jered Weaver	5.00
KE	Howie Kendrick	5.00
KG	Ken Griffey Jr.	10.00
KJ	Kenji Johjima	3.00
KM	Kevin Millwood	3.00
KU	Jason Kubel	3.00
KW	Kerry Wood	5.00
KY	Kevin Youkilis	6.00
LM	Lastings Milledge	4.00
MA	Kazuo Matsui	3.00
MC	Matt Cain	4.00
MG	Matt Garza	3.00
MH	Todd Helton	5.00
MM	Mark Mulder	3.00
MO	Justin Morneau	5.00
MU	Mike Mussina	5.00
NM	Nick Markakis	8.00
NS	Nick Swisher	4.00
PA	Jonathan Papelbon	6.00
PI	Juan Pierre	3.00
PO	Jorge Posada	5.00
RA	Aramis Ramirez	5.00
RF	Rafael Furcal	4.00
RH	Rich Hill	3.00
RJ	Randy Johnson	6.00
SC	Sean Casey	3.00
SP	Scott Podsednik	3.00
TG	Tom Gorzelanny	3.00
TH	Trevor Hoffman	4.00
TL	Tim Lincecum	8.00
TS	Takashi Saito	4.00
VA	Jason Varitek	4.00
VM	Victor Martinez	4.00
WI	Josh Willingham	3.00
WL	Jack Wilson	3.00
XN	Xavier Nady	3.00
ZG	Zack Greinke	4.00

2008 Upper Deck Goudey

CLAYTON KERSHAW — Dodgers'08 — ROOKIE CARD

Kou Griffey Jr. says...

	NM/M
Common Player (1-200):	.15
Common SP (201-230):	.25
Common President (231-250):	.50
Common 36 Goudey B&W (251-270):	1.00
Common Sports Royalty (271-330):	3.00
Pack (8):	5.00
Box (18):	75.00

#	Player	Price
1	Eric Byrnes	.15
2	Randy Johnson	.75
3	Brandon Webb	.40
4	Dan Haren	.25
5	Chris Young	.25
6	Max Scherzer RC	1.50
7	Mark Teixeira	.25
8	John Smoltz	.40
9	Jeff Francoeur	.25
10	Phil Niekro	.25
11	Chipper Jones	.75
12	Kelly Johnson	.15
13	Tom Glavine	.40
14	Yunel Escobar	.25
15	Erik Bedard	.25
16	Melvin Mora	.15
17	Brian Roberts	.25
18	Eddie Murray	.50
19	Jeremy Guthrie	.15
20	Nick Markakis	.40
21	David Ortiz	.75
22	Manny Ramirez	.50
23	Josh Beckett	.40
24	Dustin Pedroia	.40
25	Bobby Doerr	.40
26	Clay Buchholz (RC)	.25
27	Daisuke Matsuzaka	.75
28	Jonathan Papelbon	.40
29	Kevin Youkilis	.40
30	Pee Wee Reese	.40
31	Billy Williams	.15
32	Alfonso Soriano	.75
33	Derek Lee	.50
34	Rich Hill	.15
35	Kosuke Fukudome RC	2.00
36	Aramis Ramirez	.25
37	Carlos Zambrano	.50
38	Luis Aparicio	.25
39	Mark Buehrle	.25
40	Orlando Cabrera	.15
41	Paul Konerko	.25
42	Jermaine Dye	.25
43	Jim Thome	.40
44	Nick Swisher	.25
45	Sparky Anderson	.25
46	Johnny Bench	.75
47	Joe Morgan	.50
48	Tony Perez	.40
49	Adam Dunn	.50
50	Aaron Harang	.25
51	Brandon Phillips	.25
52	Edwin Encarnacion	.15
53	Ken Griffey Jr.	1.50
54	Larry Doby	.50
55	Bob Feller	.50
56	C.C. Sabathia	.50
57	Travis Hafner	.25
58	Grady Sizemore	.75
59	Fausto Carmona	.15
60	Victor Martinez	.25
61	Brad Hawpe	.15
62	Todd Helton	.50
63	Garrett Atkins	.25
64	Troy Tulowitzki	.50
65	Matt Holliday	.50
66	Jeff Francis	.15
67	Justin Verlander	.15
68	Curtis Granderson	.40
69	Miguel Cabrera	.50
70	Gary Sheffield	.40
71	Magglio Ordonez	.25
72	Jack Morris	.15
73	Al Kaline	.25
74	Andrew Miller	.25
75	Clayton Kershaw RC	1.50
76	Dan Uggla	.25
77	Hanley Ramirez	.50
78	Jeremy Hermida	.15
79	Josh Willingham	.15
80	Lance Berkman	.40
81	Roy Oswalt	.25
82	Miguel Tejada	.40
83	Hunter Pence	.40
84	Carlos Lee	.40
85	J.R. Towles RC	.15
86	Brian Bannister	.15
87	Luke Hochevar RC	.75
88	Billy Butler	.15
89	Alex Gordon	.40
90	Kelvim Escobar	.15
91	John Lackey	.25
92	Chone Figgins	.25
93	Jered Weaver	.15
94	Torii Hunter	.40
95	Vladimir Guerrero	.75
96	Brad Penny	.15
97	James Loney	.15
98	Andruw Jones	.15
99	Chad Billingsley	.25
100	Chin-Lung Hu (RC)	.15
101	Russell Martin	.40
102	Eddie Mathews	.75
103	Warren Spahn	.50
104	Prince Fielder	.50
105	Ryan Braun	.75
106	J.J. Hardy	.25
107	Ben Sheets	.25
108	Corey Hart	.25
109	Yovani Gallardo	.25
110	Joe Mauer	.25
111	Delmon Young	.25
112	Johan Santana	.50
113	Glen Perkins	.15
114	Justin Morneau	.40
115	Carlos Beltran	.50
116	Jose Reyes	.75
117	David Wright	.75
118	Pedro Martinez	.50
119	Tom Seaver	.50
120	Billy Wagner	.25
121	John Maine	.25
122	Alex Rodriguez	2.00
123	Chien-Ming Wang	.50
124	Hideki Matsui	.75
125	Jorge Posada	.50
126	Mariano Rivera	.50
127	Phil Rizzuto	.50
128	Bucky Dent	.25
129	Derek Jeter	2.00
130	Graig Nettles	.25
131	Ian Kennedy RC	.50
132	Don Larsen	.40
133	Joe Blanton	.15
134	Mark Ellis	.15
135	Dennis Eckersley	.25
136	Rollie Fingers	.25
137	"Catfish" Hunter	.25
138	Daric Barton	.15
139	Jack Cust	.15
140	Ryan Howard	.75
141	Jimmy Rollins	.50
142	Chase Utley	.50
143	Shane Victorino	.25
144	Cole Hamels	.25
145	Richie Ashburn	.25
146	Jason Bay	.25
147	Freddy Sanchez	.15
148	Adam LaRoche	.25
149	Jack Wilson	.15
150	Ralph Kiner	.25
151	Bill Mazeroski	.25
152	Tom Gorzelanny	.15
153	Jay Bruce (RC)	2.00
154	Jake Peavy	.40
155	Chris Young	.25
156	Trevor Hoffman	.15
157	Khalil Greene	.15
158	Adrian Gonzalez	.25
159	Tim Lincecum	.40
160	Matt Cain	.25
161	Aaron Rowand	.25
162	Orlando Cepeda	.25
163	Juan Marichal	.25
164	Noah Lowry	.15
165	Ichiro Suzuki	1.50
166	Felix Hernandez	.40
167	J.J. Putz	.15
168	Jose Vidro	.15
169	Raul Ibanez	.25
170	Wladimir Balentien	.15
171	Albert Pujols	2.00
172	Scott Rolen	.25
173	Lou Brock	.40
174	Chris Duncan	.15
175	Vince Coleman	.25
176	B.J. Upton	.25
177	Carl Crawford	.25
178	Carlos Pena	.25
179	Scott Kazmir	.25
180	Akinori Iwamura	.15
181	James Shields	.25
182	Michael Young	.25
183	Jarrod Saltalamacchia	.15
184	Hank Blalock	.15
185	Ian Kinsler	.25
186	Josh Hamilton	.25
187	Marlon Byrd	.15
188	David Murphy	.15
189	Vernon Wells	.25
190	Roy Halladay	.25
191	Frank Thomas	.50
192	Alex Rios	.25
193	Troy Glaus	.25
194	David Eckstein	.15
195	Ryan Zimmerman	.40
196	Dmitri Young	.15
197	Austin Kearns	.15
198	Chad Cordero	.15
199	Ryan Church	.15
200	Evan Longoria RC	3.00
201	Brooks Robinson	4.00
202	Cal Ripken Jr.	10.00
203	Frank Robinson	4.00
204	Carl Yastrzemski	5.00
205	Carlton Fisk	4.00
206	Fred Lynn	3.00
207	Wade Boggs	4.00
208	Nolan Ryan	10.00
209	Ernie Banks	6.00
210	Ryne Sandberg	4.00
211	Al Kaline	5.00
212	Bo Jackson	5.00
213	Paul Molitor	4.00
214	Robin Yount	5.00
215	Harmon Killebrew	5.00
216	Rod Carew	4.00
217	Bobby Thomson	3.00
218	Gaylord Perry	3.00
219	Dave Winfield	4.00
220	Don Mattingly	5.00
221	Reggie Jackson	5.00
222	Roger Clemens	8.00
223	Whitey Ford	3.00
224	Mike Schmidt	6.00
225	Steve Carlton	4.00
226	Tony Gwynn	5.00
227	Willie McCovey	4.00
228	Bob Gibson	5.00
229	Ozzie Smith	4.00
230	Stan Musial	6.00
231	George Washington	2.00
232	Thomas Jefferson	2.00
233	James Madison	1.00
234	James Monroe	1.00
235	Andrew Jackson	.50
236	John Tyler	.50
237	Abraham Lincoln	3.00
238	Ulysses S. Grant	2.00
239	Grover Cleveland	.50
240	Theodore Roosevelt	1.00
241	Calvin Coolidge	.50
242	John Adams	2.00
243	Martin Van Buren	.50
244	William McKinley	.50
245	Woodrow Wilson	.50
246	James K. Polk	.50
247	Rutherford B. Hayes	.50
248	William Taft	.50
249	Andrew Johnson	.50
250	James Buchanan	.50
251	Albert Pujols	3.00
252	Alex Rodriguez	3.00
253	Alfonso Soriano	1.00
254	C.C. Sabathia	1.00
255	Chase Utley	1.50
256	David Ortiz	1.50
257	David Wright	1.50
258	Derek Jeter	3.00
259	Hanley Ramirez	1.50
260	Ichiro Suzuki	2.00
261	Jake Peavy	1.00
262	Johan Santana	1.00
263	Jose Reyes	1.50
264	Ken Griffey Jr.	2.50
265	Magglio Ordonez	1.00
266	Matt Holliday	1.00
267	Prince Fielder	1.00
268	Ryan Braun	1.50
269	Ryan Howard	1.50
270	Vladimir Guerrero	1.00
271	Carl Yastrzemski	5.00
272	Albert Pujols	10.00
273	Amy Van Dyken	3.00
274	Tom Seaver	5.00
275	Brett Favre	10.00
276	Bruce Jenner	3.00
277	Bill Russell	3.00
278	Barry Sanders	8.00
279	Cynthia Cooper	3.00
280	Mike Schmidt	4.00
281	Chipper Jones	5.00
282	Cal Ripken Jr.	10.00
283	Cael Sanderson	3.00
284	Dan Gable	3.00
285	Derek Jeter	10.00
286	Andre Dawson	3.00
287	Dan O'Brien	3.00
288	Julius Erving	6.00
289	Emmitt Smith	8.00
290	Janet Evans	3.00
291	Chase Utley	5.00
292	Gary Hall Jr.	3.00
293	Gordie Howe	6.00
294	Josh Beckett	4.00
295	John Elway	6.00
296	Julie Foudy	3.00
297	Jackie Joyner-Kersee	3.00
298	Jack Nicklaus	10.00
299	Magic Johnson	6.00
300	Michael Jordan	10.00
301	Bo Jackson	5.00
302	Tom Brady	10.00
303	Wade Boggs	5.00
304	Dan Marino	10.00
305	Dave Winfield	4.00
306	Jenny Thompson	3.00
307	Kobe Bryant	8.00
308	Kevin Durant	6.00
309	Ken Griffey Jr.	8.00
310	Kerri Strug	4.00

#	Player	Price
311	Kerri Walsh	3.00
312	Larry Bird	15.00
313	LeBron James	10.00
314	Matt Biondi	4.00
315	Mark Messier	6.00
316	Michael Johnson	5.00
317	Misty May-Treanor	5.00
318	Bob Gibson	6.00
319	Nolan Ryan	15.00
320	Ozzie Smith	8.00
321	Prince Fielder	5.00
322	Rulon Gardner	3.00
323	Reggie Jackson	6.00
324	Ernie Banks	10.00
325	Sidney Crosby	15.00
326	Sanya Richards	3.00
327	Terry Bradshaw	10.00
328	Tony Gwynn	6.00
329	Stan Musial	10.00
330	Tiger Woods	60.00

Mini Black Back
Black Back (1-200):	8-12X
Mini Black Back (201-230):	2-3X
Presidents (231-250):	5-10X
B & W (251-270):	4-8X
Sports Royalty (271-330):	2-4X
Production 34 Sets	

Mini Blue Back
Blue Back (1-200):	3-4X
Mini Blue Back (201-230):	1-1.5X
Presidents (231-250):	2-3X
B & W (251-270):	2-3X
Sports Royalty (271-330):	1-1.5X

Mini Red Back
Red Back (1-200):	3-4X
Mini Red Back (201-230):	1-1.5X
Presidents (231-250):	2-3X
B & W (251-270):	2-3X
Sports Royalty (271-330):	1-1.5X

Mini Green Back
Green Back (1-200):	4-6X
Mini Green Back (201-230):	1.5-2X
Presidents (231-250):	4-6X
B & W (251-270):	3-4X
Sports Royalty (271-330):	1.5-2X
Production 88 Sets	

Mini Taupe Back
No Pricing
Production Eight Sets

Graphs

		NM/M
Common Auto.:		8.00
SP production less than 100.		
AH	Aaron Harang	15.00
BB	Billy Buckner	8.00
BD	Bucky Dent	15.00
BP	Brandon Phillips	15.00
BR	Brooks Robinson	40.00
BT	Bobby Thomson	30.00
BU	Taylor Buchholz	8.00
BW	Billy Wagner	20.00
CH	Corey Hart	20.00
CJ	Chipper Jones/SP	120.00
CL	Carlos Lee	20.00
DB	Daric Barton	8.00
DE	David Eckstein	15.00
DL	Derrek Lee	30.00
EE	Edwin Encarnacion	15.00
FC	Fausto Carmona	15.00
FL	Fred Lynn/SP	30.00
GN	Graig Nettles	15.00
GO	Tom Gorzelanny	10.00
GP	Glen Perkins	8.00
HU	Chin-Lung Hu/SP	35.00
JB	Johnny Bench/SP	60.00
JC	Jack Cust	8.00
JF	Jeff Francis/SP	15.00
JG	Jeremy Guthrie	15.00
JH	Jeremy Hermida	10.00
JO	John Maine	10.00
JP	Jonathan Papelbon	25.00
JT	J.R. Towles	10.00
JW	Josh Willingham	10.00
KJ	Kelly Johnson	10.00
KY	Kevin Youkilis/SP	40.00
LA	Don Larsen/SP	40.00
MA	Don Mattingly/SP	75.00
MB	Marlon Byrd	8.00
MO	Jack Morris	15.00
MS	Mike Schmidt/SP	80.00
MU	David Murphy	15.00
NL	Noah Lowry	10.00
NM	Nick Markakis	35.00
NS	Nick Swisher	10.00
PM	Paul Molitor	15.00
RM	Russell Martin/SP	40.00
SP	Steve Pearce	10.00
TG	Tom Glavine/SP	50.00
VC	Vince Coleman	20.00
YG	Yovani Gallardo/SP	15.00

Sports Royalty Autographs
		NM/M
SP Production less than 50.		
AV	Amy Van Dyken	35.00
CC	Cynthia Cooper	20.00
CS	Cael Sanderson	35.00
DO	Dan O'Brien	25.00
ER	Julius Erving/SP	140.00
EV	Janet Evans	35.00
FO	Julie Foudy	35.00
GH	Gary Hall Jr.	30.00
JE	Bruce Jenner	50.00
JJ	Jackie Joyner-Kersee	35.00
JT	Jenny Thompson	30.00
KG	Ken Griffey Jr./SP	120.00
KW	Kerri Walsh	50.00
LB	Larry Bird/SP	140.00
MA	Misty May-Treanor	60.00
MB	Matt Biondi	30.00
OS	Ozzie Smith/SP	80.00
PD	Phil Dalhausser	25.00
RG	Rulon Gardner	15.00
RJ	Reggie Jackson/SP	150.00
SR	Sanya Richards	25.00
TR	Todd Rogers	30.00

Berk Ross Hit Parade of Champion

#	Player	NM/M
Complete Set (30):		35.00
Common Player:		1.00
1	Albert Pujols	2.00
2	Don Mattingly	1.00
3	Ben Roethlisberger	1.00
4	Bill Russell	1.50
5	Bobby Orr	1.50
6	Cal Ripken Jr.	2.00
7	Carl Yastrzemski	1.00
8	Derek Jeter	2.00
9	Emmitt Smith	1.50
10	Gordie Howe	1.50
11	Joe Montana	2.00
12	Joe Namath	1.00
13	Ken Griffey Jr.	1.50
14	Kobe Bryant	2.00
15	LaDainian Tomlinson	1.00
16	Larry Bird	1.50
17	LeBron James	2.00
18	Magic Johnson	1.50
19	Mario Lemieux	1.50
20	Yogi Berra	1.00
21	Michael Jordan	2.00
22	Nolan Ryan	1.50
23	Patrick Roy	1.50
24	Peyton Manning	1.50
25	Reggie Jackson	1.00
26	Roger Clemens	1.50
27	Roger Staubach	1.00
28	Manny Ramirez	1.00
29	Tom Brady	2.00
30	Wayne Gretzky	2.00

Memorabilia

		NM/M
Common Player:		4.00
AD	Adam Dunn	8.00
AG	Adrian Gonzalez	6.00
AH	Aaron Harang	4.00
AI	Akinori Iwamura	4.00
AJ	Andruw Jones	4.00
AP	Albert Pujols	15.00
AR	Aaron Rowand	4.00
AS	Alfonso Soriano	8.00
BB	Billy Butler	4.00
BD	Bucky Dent	8.00
BE	Josh Beckett	8.00
BR	Brian Roberts	4.00
BU	B.J. Upton	6.00
BW	Brandon Webb	6.00
CC	Carl Crawford	6.00
CH	Cole Hamels	10.00
CJ	Chipper Jones	10.00
CL	Carlos Lee	6.00
CR	Cal Ripken Jr.	15.00
CU	Chase Utley	10.00
CY	Chris Young	4.00
CZ	Carlos Zambrano	6.00
DJ	Derek Jeter	20.00
DL	Derrek Lee	6.00
DM	Daisuke Matsuzaka	15.00
DO	David Ortiz	8.00
DU	Dan Uggla	4.00
DY	Delmon Young	4.00
FH	Felix Hernandez	8.00
FS	Freddy Sanchez	4.00
GA	Garrett Atkins	4.00
GR	Khalil Greene	4.00
GS	Gary Sheffield	6.00
HO	Trevor Hoffman	4.00
HP	Hunter Pence	4.00
HR	Hanley Ramirez	8.00
HU	"Catfish" Hunter	7.00
JB	Jason Bay	6.00
JD	Jermaine Dye	4.00
JF	Jeff Francoeur	6.00
JH	Josh Hamilton	10.00
JM	Joe Mauer	6.00
JP	Jake Peavy	6.00
JR	Jimmy Rollins	10.00
JV	Justin Verlander	8.00
JW	Jered Weaver	4.00
KG	Ken Griffey Jr.	15.00
KY	Kevin Youkilis	10.00
LB	Lance Berkman	6.00
MA	John Maine	6.00
MB	Mark Buehrle	4.00
MC	Matt Cain	6.00
MH	Matt Holliday	8.00
MI	Miguel Cabrera	8.00
MO	Justin Morneau	6.00
MR	Manny Ramirez	8.00
MT	Mark Teixeira	6.00
NM	Nick Markakis	10.00
OR	Magglio Ordonez	8.00
PA	Jonathan Papelbon	8.00
PF	Prince Fielder	8.00
PM	Pedro Martinez	8.00
PO	Jorge Posada	8.00
RA	Aramis Ramirez	6.00
RE	Jose Reyes	8.00
RH	Roy Halladay	8.00
RI	Mariano Rivera	10.00
RJ	Randy Johnson	8.00
RM	Russell Martin	8.00
RO	Roy Oswalt	8.00
RZ	Ryan Zimmerman	8.00
SI	Grady Sizemore	10.00
SM	John Smoltz	8.00
TE	Miguel Tejada	6.00
TH	Travis Hafner	4.00
VG	Vladimir Guerrero	6.00
VM	Victor Martinez	6.00
VW	Vernon Wells	4.00
WI	Jack Wilson	4.00
WS	Warren Spahn	20.00
YG	Yovani Gallardo	6.00

2008 Upper Deck Heroes

#	Player	NM/M
Common Player (1-200):		
Pack (8):		5.00
Box (24):		100.00
1	Brandon Webb	.40
2	Dan Haren	.40
3	Chris B. Young	.25
4	Justin Upton	.25
5	Randy Johnson	.75
6	Chipper Jones	.75
7	John Smoltz	.50
8	Tom Glavine	.50
9	Mark Teixeira	.40
10	Brian McCann	.40
11	Jeff Francoeur	.25
12	Josh Hamilton	.75
13	Tim Hudson	.25
14	Nick Markakis	.40
15	Brian Roberts	.25
16	Cal Ripken Jr.	2.00
17	John Maine	.25
18	Frank Robinson	.50
19	Mike Lowell	.25
20	Jason Varitek	.40
21	David Ortiz	.75
22	Manny Ramirez	.75
23	Jonathan Papelbon	.40
24	Jacoby Ellsbury	.40
25	Kevin Youkilis	.40
26	Curt Schilling	.40
27	Josh Beckett	.50
28	Daisuke Matsuzaka	.75
29	Clay Buchholz	.40
30	Dustin Pedroia	.50
31	Ryan Theriot	.25
32	Carlton Fisk	.40
33	Carl Yastrzemski	.50
34	Wade Boggs	.40
35	Nolan Ryan	1.50
36	Alfonso Soriano	.40
37	Kosuke Fukudome RC	3.00
38	Derrek Lee	.40
39	Carlos Zambrano	.40
40	Aramis Ramirez	.40
41	Ernie Banks	.50
42	Jim Thome	.40
43	Jermaine Dye	.25
44	Paul Konerko	.25
45	Nick Swisher	.40
46	Corey Hart	.40
47	Ken Griffey Jr.	1.50
48	Adam Dunn	.40
49	Aaron Harang	.40
50	Johnny Bench	.50
51	Grady Sizemore	.50
52	Victor Martinez	.40
53	C.C. Sabathia	.40
54	Travis Hafner	.40
55	Jeff Francis	.25
56	Matt Holliday	.50
57	Troy Tulowitzki	.40
58	Garrett Atkins	.25
59	Todd Helton	.50
60	Curtis Granderson	.50
61	Dontrelle Willis	.25
62	Magglio Ordonez	.40
63	Gary Sheffield	.40
64	Miguel Cabrera	.75
65	Justin Verlander	.50
66	Ivan Rodriguez	.50
67	Al Kaline	.50
68	Hanley Ramirez	.75
69	Edinson Volquez	.50
70	Dan Uggla	.40
71	Andrew Miller	.25
72	Josh Willingham	.25
73	J.R. Towles RC	.25
74	Lance Berkman	.50
75	Carlos Lee	.40
76	Roy Oswalt	.40
77	Hunter Pence	.40
78	Luke Hochevar RC	.50
79	Alex Gordon	.40
80	Matt Cain	.40
81	Bo Jackson	.50
82	Vladimir Guerrero	.50
83	Torii Hunter	.40
84	Howie Kendrick	.25
85	John Lackey	.40
86	Chone Figgins	.40
87	Andruw Jones	.40
88	Brad Penny	.25
89	James Loney	.40
90	Matt Kemp	.40
91	Nomar Garciaparra	.40
92	Jon Lester	.40
93	Chin-Lung Hu	.75
94	Chad Billingsley	.40
95	Kelly Johnson	.25
96	Prince Fielder	.50
97	Ryan Braun	.75
98	Ben Sheets	.40
99	Robin Yount	.50
100	Justin Morneau	.50
101	Joe Mauer	.40
102	Delmon Young	.25
103	Rod Carew	.50
104	Carlos Beltran	.50
105	Jose Reyes	.50
106	Pedro Martinez	.50
107	David Wright	1.00
108	Johan Santana	.50
109	Billy Wagner	.25
110	Carlos Delgado	.40
111	Mariano Rivera	.50
112	Chien-Ming Wang	.75
113	Phil Hughes	.40
114	Derek Jeter	2.00
115	Alex Rodriguez	2.00
116	Robinson Cano	.40
117	Jorge Posada	.40
118	Hideki Matsui	.75
119	Joba Chamberlain	.75
120	Ian Kennedy	.40
121	Yogi Berra	.50
122	Reggie Jackson	.50
123	Roger Clemens	1.50
124	Ozzie Smith	.50
125	Dave Winfield	.50
126	Joe DiMaggio	1.50
127	Eric Chavez	.25
128	Rich Harden	.25
129	Bill Hall	.25
130	Rich Harden	.25
131	Andre Ethier	.25
132	Daric Barton	.25
133	Ryan Howard	.75
134	Jimmy Rollins	.75
135	Chase Utley	.75
136	Cole Hamels	.50
137	Pat Burrell	.40
138	Mike Schmidt	.75
139	Steve Carlton	.40
140	Freddy Sanchez	.25
141	Joe Blanton	.25
142	Felix Pie	.25
143	Roberto Clemente	2.00
144	Jake Peavy	.40
145	Greg Maddux	1.50
146	Tom Gorzelanny	.25
147	Tony Gwynn	.75
148	Barry Zito	.25
149	Tim Lincecum	.50
150	Rich Hill	.25
151	Omar Vizquel	.25
152	Ichiro Suzuki	1.50
153	Felix Hernandez	.40
154	Kenji Johjima	.25
155	Erik Bedard	.25
156	Albert Pujols	2.00
157	Troy Glaus	.40
158	Chris Carpenter	.40
159	Chris Duncan	.25
160	Mark Mulder	.25
161	Scott Rolen	.40
162	Stan Musial	.75
163	Bob Gibson	.50
164	B.J. Upton	.50
165	Carl Crawford	.40
166	Scott Kazmir	.40
167	Michael Young	.40
168	Luke Scott	.25
169	Roy Halladay	.40
170	Vernon Wells	.25
171	Kevin Kouzmanoff	.25
172	Frank Thomas	.50
173	Ryan Zimmerman	.40
174	Lastings Milledge	.25
175	Ian Kinsler	.50
176	Wade Boggs, Don Mattingly	2.00
177	Carlton Fisk, Carl Yastrzemski	1.00
178	Stan Musial, Albert Pujols	3.00
179	Derek Jeter, Jose Reyes	3.00
180	Cal Ripken Jr., Tony Gwynn	3.00
181	Prince Fielder, Eddie Murray	2.00
182	Kosuke Fukudome, Ichiro Suzuki	2.00
183	Steve Carlton, Johan Santana	1.00
184	Jake Peavy, Bob Gibson	1.00
185	Johnny Bench, Ivan Rodriguez	1.50
186	Vladimir Guerrero, Manny Ramirez	3.00
187	Wade Boggs, Carlton Fisk, Carl Yastrzemski	3.00
188	Alex Rodriguez, Derek Jeter, Robinson Cano	3.00
189	Ryan Braun, Miguel Cabrera, Chipper Jones	3.00
190	Don Mattingly, Dave Winfield, Reggie Jackson	3.00
191	Jimmy Rollins, Ryan Howard, Chase Utley	3.00
192	Joe Mauer, Troy Tulowitzki, Hanley Ramirez	3.00
193	Randy Johnson, Nolan Ryan, Greg Maddux	4.00
194	Brandon Webb, Justin Verlander, Felix Hernandez	2.00
195	Mike Schmidt, Ernie Banks, Frank Robinson	3.00

Beige Patch
No Pricing
Production 5-10

Beige
Beige (1-200):	1.5-2X
Production 200 Sets	

Black
Black (1-200):	1.5-2X
Production 250 Sets	

Red
Red (1-200):	2-4X
Production 75 Sets	

Charcoal
Charcoal (1-200):	1-1.5X

Emerald
Emerald (1-200):	1.5-2X
Production 300 Sets	

Light Blue
Light Blue (1-200):	4-8X
Production 25 Sets	

Navy Blue
Navy Blue (1-200):	2-4X
Production 100 Sets	

Purple
No Pricing
Production 10 Sets

Green
Green (1-200):	2-4X
Production 50 Sets	

Charcoal Jersey Patch Auto
#	Player	NM/M
Production 4-50		
1	Brandon Webb/25	40.00
6	Brian McCann/25	25.00
11	Jeff Francoeur/25	20.00
17	John Maine/50	20.00
23	Jonathan Papelbon/25	35.00
25	Kevin Youkilis/25	75.00
44	Paul Konerko/25	30.00
46	Corey Hart/50	30.00
47	Ken Griffey J./25	180.00
49	Aaron Harang/25	15.00
52	Victor Martinez/25	30.00
54	Travis Hafner/25	20.00
55	Jeff Francis/25	15.00
68	Hanley Ramirez/25	25.00
69	Edinson Volquez/50	15.00
73	Josh Willingham/25	15.00
75	Carlos Lee/25	25.00
90	Matt Kemp/25	25.00
94	Chad Billingsley/50	35.00
95	Kelly Johnson/50	15.00
96	Prince Fielder/25	35.00
136	Cole Hamels/25	50.00
141	Joe Blanton/25	10.00
142	Felix Pie/50	15.00
146	Tom Gorzelanny/50	15.00
150	Rich Hill/50	15.00
164	B.J. Upton/25	25.00
171	Kevin Kouzmanoff/25	15.00
175	Ian Kinsler/25	25.00

Charcoal Autograph
#	Player	NM/M
Production 11-150		
12	Josh Hamilton/150	40.00
14	Nick Markakis	20.00
17	John Maine/150	20.00
29	Clay Buchholz/95	20.00
31	Ryan Theriot/150	15.00
45	Nick Swisher/150	15.00
46	Corey Hart/150	15.00
47	Ken Griffey Jr./73	100.00
49	Aaron Harang/150	10.00
69	Edinson Volquez/150	10.00
73	J.R. Towles/150	15.00
80	Matt Cain/150	15.00
86	Chone Figgins/150	15.00
90	Matt Kemp/150	15.00
93	Chin-Lung Hu/150	15.00
94	Chad Billingsley/150	15.00
95	Kelly Johnson/150	8.00
120	Ian Kennedy/95	15.00
131	Andre Ethier/150	10.00
132	Daric Barton/150	10.00
141	Joe Blanton/144	8.00
142	Felix Pie/150	10.00
146	Tom Gorzelanny/150	8.00
150	Rich Hill/100	10.00
168	Luke Scott/148	15.00
171	Kevin Kouzmanoff/150	10.00
175	Ian Kinsler/150	15.00

Beige Autograph
#	Player	NM/M
Production 10-25		
10	Brian McCann/25	25.00
17	John Maine/25	15.00
23	Jonathan Papelbon/25	30.00
31	Ryan Theriot/25	15.00
45	Nick Swisher/25	15.00
46	Corey Hart/25	30.00
49	Aaron Harang/25	10.00
68	Hanley Ramirez/25	25.00
69	Edinson Volquez/25	25.00
72	Josh Willingham/25	10.00
73	J.R. Towles/25	15.00
78	Luke Hochevar/25	20.00
86	Chone Figgins/25	15.00
90	Matt Kemp/25	25.00
93	Chin-Lung Hu/25	60.00
94	Chad Billingsley/25	30.00
95	Kelly Johnson/25	15.00
141	Joe Blanton/25	15.00
142	Felix Pie/25	15.00
146	Tom Gorzelanny/25	15.00
150	Rich Hill/25	10.00
168	Luke Scott/25	15.00
171	Kevin Kouzmanoff/25	10.00
175	Ian Kinsler/25	15.00

Black Autograph
#	Player	NM/M
Production 25-50		
3	Chris Young/25	20.00
10	Brian McCann/25	20.00

#	Player	Price
12	Josh Hamilton/50	50.00
17	John Maine/50	15.00
29	Clay Buchholz/35	15.00
31	Ryan Theriot/50	30.00
45	Nick Swisher/50	30.00
46	Corey Hart/50	20.00
49	Aaron Harang/50	15.00
68	Hanley Ramirez/25	25.00
69	Edinson Volquez/50	15.00
71	Andrew Miller/35	15.00
72	Josh Willingham/50	8.00
73	J.R. Towles/50	15.00
78	Luke Hochevar/50	15.00
80	Matt Cain/50	20.00
84	Howie Kendrick/25	15.00
85	John Lackey/25	20.00
86	Chone Figgins/50	15.00
87	Andruw Jones/25	15.00
90	Matt Kemp/50	15.00
93	Chin-Lung Hu/50	25.00
94	Chad Billingsley/50	30.00
95	Kelly Johnson/50	15.00
120	Ian Kennedy/35	15.00
132	Daric Barton/50	10.00
141	Joe Blanton/50	10.00
142	Felix Pie/50	10.00
146	Tom Gorzelanny/50	8.00
150	Rich Hill/50	10.00
168	Luke Scott/50	15.00
171	Kevin Kouzmanoff/50	15.00
175	Ian Kinsler/50	20.00

Emerald Jersey Auto.
No Pricing
Production 5 Sets

Light Blue Jersey Auto.
NM/M
Production 15-75

#	Player	Price
14	Nick Markakis/75	25.00
25	Kevin Youkilis/50	50.00
46	Corey Hart/75	25.00
47	Ken Griffey Jr./50	100.00
49	Aaron Harang/75	15.00
55	Jeff Francis/50	15.00
58	Garrett Atkins/35	10.00
69	Edinson Volquez/25	25.00
90	Matt Kemp/75	30.00
92	Jon Lester/50	40.00
93	Chin-Lung Hu/75	25.00
114	Derek Jeter/35	150.00
138	Mike Schmidt/35	40.00
141	Joe Blanton/75	10.00
142	Felix Pie/75	10.00
146	Tom Gorzelanny/75	10.00
175	Ian Kinsler/75	25.00

Navy Blue Auto
NM/M
Production 35-100
Navy Blue Jsy Auto.: No Pricing
Production 1-10

#	Player	Price
12	Josh Hamilton/100	40.00
17	John Maine/100	15.00
29	Clay Buchholz/55	20.00
31	Ryan Theriot/100	15.00
45	Nick Swisher/100	15.00
46	Corey Hart/100	25.00
47	Ken Griffey Jr./35	125.00
49	Aaron Harang/100	15.00
69	Edinson Volquez/100	15.00
71	Andrew Miller/35	15.00
72	Josh Willingham/100	10.00
73	J.R. Towles/100	15.00
80	Matt Cain/100	20.00
85	John Lackey/65	15.00
90	Matt Kemp/100	20.00
93	Chin-Lung Hu/100	20.00
94	Chad Billingsley/100	20.00
95	Kelly Johnson/100	15.00
120	Ian Kennedy/55	15.00
131	Andre Ethier/100	30.00
132	Daric Barton/100	8.00
141	Joe Blanton/100	8.00
142	Felix Pie/100	10.00
146	Tom Gorzelanny/100	8.00
150	Rich Hill/50	10.00
168	Luke Scott/100	15.00
171	Kevin Kouzmanoff/100	10.00
175	Ian Kinsler/100	20.00

Purple Auto
No Pricing
Production 5 Sets

Red Auto
No Pricing
Production 10 Sets

Red Jersey Auto
NM/M
Production 3-50

#	Player	Price
3	Chris Young/25	20.00
11	Jeff Francoeur/25	25.00
17	John Maine/50	15.00
25	Kevin Youkilis/25	25.00
34	Wade Boggs/25	30.00
35	Nolan Ryan/25	100.00
44	Paul Konerko/25	25.00
46	Corey Hart/50	20.00
47	Ken Griffey Jr./25	100.00
49	Aaron Harang/50	10.00
52	Victor Martinez/25	15.00
54	Travis Hafner/25	10.00
55	Jeff Francis/25	15.00
58	Garrett Atkins/25	10.00
69	Edinson Volquez/25	15.00
80	Matt Cain/50	20.00

#	Player	Price
81	Bo Jackson/25	75.00
90	Matt Kemp/50	25.00
92	Jon Lester/35	30.00
93	Chin-Lung Hu/50	25.00
94	Chad Billingsley/50	30.00
95	Kelly Johnson/50	15.00
96	Prince Fielder/25	40.00
99	Robin Yount/25	40.00
103	Rod Carew/25	40.00
113	Phil Hughes/25	40.00
114	Derek Jeter/25	125.00
125	Don Mattingly/25	60.00
136	Cole Hamels/25	40.00
138	Mike Schmidt/25	40.00
139	Steve Carlton/25	30.00
141	Joe Blanton/50	10.00
142	Felix Pie/50	10.00
146	Tom Gorzelanny/50	15.00
150	Rich Hill/50	10.00
153	Felix Hernandez/25	40.00
163	Bob Gibson/25	40.00
164	B.J. Upton/25	25.00
169	Roy Halladay/25	50.00
175	Ian Kinsler/50	25.00

Black Jersey

NM/M
Common Player: 4.00
Production 125 Sets
Light Blue Jersey: .75-1X
Production 200 Sets
Navy Blue Jsy: 1-1.5X
Production 50 Sets
Emerald Jsy: 1.5-2X
Production 25 Sets
Charcoal Jsy: .5-1X
Production 25 Sets
Light Blue Patch: No Pricing
Production 25 Sets
Red Jersey: No Pricing
Production 100 Sets
Purple Patch: No Pricing
Production 5 Sets

#	Player	Price
1	Brandon Webb	5.00
3	Chris Young	5.00
4	Justin Upton	8.00
5	Randy Johnson	8.00
6	Chipper Jones	15.00
7	John Smoltz	8.00
9	Mark Teixeira	6.00
10	Brian McCann	6.00
11	Jeff Francoeur	6.00
13	Tim Hudson	6.00
14	Nick Markakis	8.00
15	Brian Roberts	4.00
16	Cal Ripken Jr.	25.00
17	John Maine	4.00
18	Frank Robinson	8.00
19	Mike Lowell	6.00
20	Jason Varitek	6.00
21	David Ortiz	10.00
22	Manny Ramirez	8.00
23	Jonathan Papelbon	6.00
24	Jacoby Ellsbury	15.00
25	Kevin Youkilis	10.00
26	Curt Schilling	6.00
27	Josh Beckett	6.00
28	Daisuke Matsuzaka	10.00
29	Clay Buchholz	8.00
33	Carl Yastrzemski	10.00
34	Wade Boggs	8.00
35	Nolan Ryan	20.00
36	Alfonso Soriano	8.00
37	Kosuke Fukudome	15.00
38	Derek Lee	6.00
39	Carlos Zambrano	4.00
40	Aramis Ramirez	6.00
41	Ernie Banks	15.00
42	Jim Thome	8.00
43	Jermaine Dye	4.00
44	Paul Konerko	6.00
46	Corey Hart	6.00
47	Ken Griffey Jr.	15.00
48	Adam Dunn	6.00
49	Aaron Harang	4.00
50	Johnny Bench	15.00
51	Grady Sizemore	8.00
52	Victor Martinez	6.00
53	C.C. Sabathia	8.00
54	Travis Hafner	4.00
55	Jeff Francis	4.00
56	Matt Holliday	8.00
57	Troy Tulowitzki	6.00
58	Garrett Atkins	4.00
59	Todd Helton	6.00
60	Curtis Granderson	8.00
62	Magglio Ordonez	6.00
63	Justin Verlander	6.00
66	Ivan Rodriguez	6.00

#	Player	Price
68	Hanley Ramirez	8.00
69	Edinson Volquez	4.00
70	Dan Uggla	6.00
71	Andrew Miller	4.00
72	Josh Willingham	4.00
74	Lance Berkman	6.00
75	Carlos Lee	6.00
76	Roy Oswalt	6.00
77	Hunter Pence	6.00
79	Alex Gordon	6.00
80	Matt Cain	6.00
81	Bo Jackson	10.00
82	Vladimir Guerrero	8.00
84	Howie Kendrick	6.00
85	John Lackey	6.00
86	Chone Figgins	6.00
88	Brad Penny	4.00
89	James Loney	6.00
90	Matt Kemp	8.00
92	Jon Lester	8.00
93	Chin-Lung Hu	4.00
94	Chad Billingsley	8.00
95	Kelly Johnson	4.00
96	Prince Fielder	8.00
97	Ryan Braun	10.00
98	Ben Sheets	4.00
99	Robin Yount	10.00
100	Justin Morneau	6.00
101	Joe Mauer	10.00
103	Rod Carew	8.00
104	Carlos Beltran	4.00
106	Pedro Martinez	6.00
109	Billy Wagner	4.00
110	Carlos Delgado	6.00
111	Mariano Rivera	8.00
112	Chien-Ming Wang	6.00
113	Phil Hughes	6.00
114	Derek Jeter	20.00
115	Alex Rodriguez	20.00
116	Robinson Cano	6.00
117	Jorge Posada	6.00
120	Ian Kennedy	6.00
121	Yogi Berra	10.00
123	Roger Clemens	10.00
124	Ozzie Smith	8.00
125	Don Mattingly	10.00
126	Dave Winfield	8.00
127	Joe DiMaggio	50.00
128	Eric Chavez	4.00
129	Bill Hall	4.00
130	Rich Harden	4.00
131	Andre Ethier	6.00
134	Jimmy Rollins	8.00
135	Chase Utley	8.00
136	Cole Hamels	8.00
137	Pat Burrell	4.00
138	Mike Schmidt	10.00
139	Steve Carlton	6.00
140	Freddy Sanchez	4.00
141	Joe Blanton	4.00
142	Felix Pie	4.00
143	Roberto Clemente	50.00
144	Jake Peavy	4.00
145	Greg Maddux	10.00
146	Tom Gorzelanny	4.00
147	Tony Gwynn	10.00
148	Barry Zito	4.00
149	Tim Lincecum	15.00
150	Rich Hill	4.00
152	Omar Vizquel	4.00
153	Felix Hernandez	6.00
155	Kenji Johjima	4.00
156	Albert Pujols	15.00
158	Chris Carpenter	4.00
159	Chris Duncan	4.00
160	Mark Mulder	4.00
161	Scott Rolen	4.00
162	Bob Gibson	8.00
164	B.J. Upton	6.00
165	Carl Crawford	6.00
166	Scott Kazmir	5.00
167	Michael Young	4.00
168	Roy Halladay	8.00
171	Kevin Kouzmanoff	4.00
173	Ryan Zimmerman	6.00
175	Ian Kinsler	6.00
188	Alex Rodriguez, Derek Jeter, Robinson Cano	40.00
190	Don Mattingly, Dave Winfield, Reggie Jackson	30.00
192	Joe Mauer, Hanley Ramirez, Troy Tulowitzki	15.00
193	Randy Johnson, Nolan Ryan, Greg Maddux	35.00
194	Brandon Webb, Justin Verlander, Felix Hernandez	15.00
195	Mike Schmidt, Ernie Banks, Frank Robinson	25.00

2008 UD Masterpieces

NM/M
Complete Set (120): 75.00
Common Player (1-90): .50
Common SP (91-120): 1.00
Inserted 1:2
Pack (6): 7.00
Box (12): 70.00

#	Player	Price
1	Brandon Webb	.75
2	Justin Upton	1.00
3	Randy Johnson	1.00
4	Chipper Jones	1.50
5	Max Scherzer RC	2.00
6	Mark Teixeira	.75
7	Evan Longoria RC	8.00
8	Jim Palmer	.75
9	Brooks Robinson	1.00
10	Nick Markakis	.75
11	Carl Yastrzemski	1.50
12	Wade Boggs	.75
13	Curt Schilling	.75
14	Daisuke Matsuzaka	1.50
15	David Ortiz	1.00
16	Jonathan Papelbon	.75
17	Manny Ramirez	1.00
18	Alfonso Soriano	1.00
19	Ryne Sandberg	2.00
20	Carlos Zambrano	.75
21	Derek Lee	.75
22	Kosuke Fukudome RC	1.00
23	Jim Thome	.75
24	Adam Dunn	.75
25	Joe Morgan	.75
26	Grady Sizemore	1.00
27	Victor Martinez	.50
28	Travis Hafner	.75
29	Troy Tulowitzki	.75
30	Matt Holliday	.75
31	Todd Helton	.75
32	Justin Verlander	1.00
33	Asdrubal Cabrera	.50
34	Gary Sheffield	.75
35	Magglio Ordonez	.75
36	Miguel Cabrera	1.00
37	Hanley Ramirez	1.00
38	Lance Berkman	.75
39	Roy Oswalt	.75
40	Alex Gordon	.75
41	Vladimir Guerrero	1.00
42	Andruw Jones	.50
43	Chin-Lung Hu (RC)	1.00
44	James Loney	.50
45	Hunter Pence	.75
46	Robin Yount	1.50
47	Prince Fielder	1.50
48	Ryan Braun	1.50
49	Harmon Killebrew	1.50
50	Joe Mauer	1.50
51	Justin Morneau	.75
52	Ken Griffey Jr.	2.00
53	Carlos Beltran	.75
54	David Wright	2.00
55	Johan Santana	1.00
56	Jose Reyes	1.00
57	Pedro Martinez	.75
58	Ian Kennedy RC	.75
59	Jay Bruce (RC)	3.00
60	Whitey Ford	.75
61	Mariano Rivera	.75
62	Alex Rodriguez	2.50
63	Hideki Matsui	1.00
64	Joba Chamberlain	2.00
65	Jorge Posada	.75
66	Robinson Cano	.75
67	Eric Chavez	.50
68	Rich Harden	.50
69	Chase Utley	1.00
70	Jimmy Rollins	.75
71	Ryan Howard	1.50
72	Bill Mazeroski	.50
73	Freddy Sanchez	.50
74	Luke Hochevar RC	1.00
75	Tony Gwynn	1.00
76	Greg Maddux	1.50
77	Jake Peavy	.75
78	Barry Zito	.50
79	Russell Martin	.75
80	Tim Lincecum	2.00
81	Ichiro Suzuki	1.50
82	Felix Hernandez	.75
83	Ozzie Smith	1.50
84	Jason Varitek	.50
85	Chris Carpenter	.75
86	Carl Crawford	.75
87	Michael Young	.50
88	Frank Thomas	1.00
89	Roy Halladay	.75
90	Ryan Zimmerman	.75
91	Eddie Murray	2.00
92	Cal Ripken Jr.	8.00
93	Frank Robinson	1.50
94	Ryne Sandberg	4.00
95	Warren Spahn	1.50
96	Ernie Banks	2.50
97	Carlton Fisk	1.00
98	Johnny Bench	2.50
99	Ken Griffey Jr.	5.00
100	Al Kaline	2.00
101	Cal Ripken Jr.	8.00
102	Nolan Ryan	8.00
103	Jack Morris	1.50
104	Rod Carew	1.50
105	Tom Seaver	1.50
106	Don Mattingly	4.00
107	Lou Brock	1.50

#	Player	Price
108	Joe DiMaggio	5.00
109	Derek Jeter	6.00
110	Yogi Berra	2.50
111	Reggie Jackson	1.50
112	Mike Schmidt	1.00
113	Steve Carlton	1.00
114	Willie Stargell	2.00
115	Roberto Clemente	5.00
116	Albert Pujols	5.00
117	Stan Musial	2.50
118	Bob Gibson	1.50
119	Dave Winfield	1.50
120	Joe Carter	1.00

Framed Black
Black (1-90): 1-2X
Black SP (91-120): 1X

Framed Blue 125
Blue (1-90): 2-4X
Blue RC's (1-90): 1-2X
Blue SP (91-120): 1-2X
Production 125 Sets
Framed Blue 5: No Pricing
Production 5 Sets

Framed Blue 50
Blue (1-90): 3-5X
Blue RC's (1-90): 2-3X
Blue SP (91-120): 2-3X
Production 50 Sets

Framed Brown
Brown (1-90): 2-4X
Brown RC's (1-90): 1-2X
Brown SP (91-120): 1-2X
Production 100 Sets

Framed Gold
No Pricing
Production 10 Sets

Framed Green
Green (1-90): 2-5X
Green RC's (1-90): 1-2X
Green SP (91-120): 1-2X
Production 75 Sets

Framed Red
Red (1-90): 2-3X
Red RC (1-90): 1-1.5X
Black SP (91-120): 1-1.5X
Inserted 1:12
Red 1: No Pricing
Production One Set

Framed Silver
No Pricing
Production 25 Sets

Captured on Canvas

NM/M
Common Player: 4.00
Patch: No Pricing
Production 5-25

Code	Player	Price
AJ	Andruw Jones	4.00
AP	Albert Pujols	15.00
AR	Alex Rodriguez	20.00
BE	Carlos Beltran	4.00
BH	Bill Hall	4.00
BM	Brian McCann	6.00
BP	Brandon Phillips	4.00
BR	Brian Roberts	4.00
BS	Ben Sheets	4.00
BU	B.J. Upton	6.00
CA	Matt Cain	6.00
CB	Chad Billingsley	6.00
CC	Chris Carpenter	8.00
CD	Chris Duncan	4.00
CF	Carlton Fisk	8.00
CH	Cole Hamels	10.00
CJ	Chipper Jones	8.00
CL	Carlos Lee	4.00
CR	Cal Ripken Jr.	40.00
CS	C.C. Sabathia	8.00
CW	Rod Carew	10.00
CZ	Carlos Zambrano	4.00
DJ	Derek Jeter	20.00
DL	Derek Lee	4.00
DM	Don Mattingly	10.00
DO	David Ortiz	8.00
DU	Dan Uggla	4.00
DW	Dontrelle Willis	4.00
EB	Erik Bedard	4.00
EC	Eric Chavez	4.00
EM	Eddie Murray	8.00
FH	Felix Hernandez	8.00
FR	Francisco Rodriguez	4.00
FS	Freddy Sanchez	4.00
FT	Frank Thomas	8.00

Code	Player	Price
GA	Garrett Atkins	4.00
GL	Tom Glavine	8.00
GM	Greg Maddux	10.00
GR	Ken Griffey Jr.	15.00
GS	Gary Sheffield	8.00
HK	Howie Kendrick	4.00
HR	Hanley Ramirez	10.00
HU	Torii Hunter	6.00
IR	Ivan Rodriguez	6.00
JB	Josh Beckett	8.00
JE	Derek Jeter	20.00
JF	Jeff Francoeur	4.00
JL	John Lackey	4.00
JM	Joe Mauer	8.00
JO	Kelly Johnson	4.00
JP	Jake Peavy	6.00
JR	Jose Reyes	6.00
JS	Johan Santana	8.00
JT	Jim Thome	6.00
JV	Jason Varitek	6.00
JW	Jered Weaver	4.00
KG	Khalil Greene	4.00
KJ	Kenji Johjima	4.00
KY	Kevin Youkilis	8.00
LB	Lance Berkman	6.00
MC	Miguel Cabrera	8.00
MM	Mark Mulder	4.00
MO	Justin Morneau	6.00
MT	Mark Teixeira	6.00
MY	Michael Young	4.00
NM	Nick Markakis	6.00
NR	Nolan Ryan	30.00
PA	Jonathan Papelbon	8.00
PF	Prince Fielder	8.00
PM	Pedro Martinez	6.00
PO	Jorge Posada	8.00
RA	Aramis Ramirez	8.00
RB	Ryan Braun	20.00
RH	Rich Harden	4.00
RJ	Randy Johnson	8.00
RO	Roy Oswalt	4.00
RY	Nolan Ryan	30.00
RZ	Ryan Zimmerman	6.00
SC	Curt Schilling	8.00
TG	Tony Gwynn	10.00
TH	Travis Hafner	4.00
VE	Justin Verlander	6.00
VG	Vladimir Guerrero	8.00
VM	Victor Martinez	4.00
VW	Vernon Wells	6.00
WI	Josh Willingham	4.00

Captured on Canvas Jersey Auto.
NM/M
Common Jersey Auto.: 10.00
Patch Auto.: No Pricing
Production 5-25

Code	Player	Price
BH	Bill Hall	10.00
BM	Brian McCann	20.00
BP	Brandon Phillips	20.00
BU	B.J. Upton	30.00
CA	Matt Cain	15.00
CB	Chad Billingsley	20.00
CH	Cole Hamels	75.00
CJ	Chipper Jones	75.00
CL	Carlos Lee	15.00
CR	Cal Ripken Jr.	150.00
DJ	Derek Jeter	140.00
DL	Derek Lee	25.00
DU	Dan Uggla	15.00
GR	Ken Griffey Jr.	100.00
HR	Hanley Ramirez	25.00
JB	Josh Beckett	25.00
JE	Derek Jeter	140.00
JF	Jeff Francoeur	15.00
JO	Kelly Johnson	10.00
KY	Kevin Youkilis	35.00
LB	Lance Berkman	20.00
PA	Jonathan Papelbon	20.00
RA	Aramis Ramirez	25.00
TG	Tony Gwynn	60.00
WI	Josh Willingham	10.00
FH	Felix Hernandez	20.00
RZ	Ryan Zimmerman	15.00
RH	Rich Harden	10.00
MC	Miguel Cabrera	25.00

Captured on Canvas Patch Auto.
Production 5-25

Stroke of Genius Signatures

NM/M
Common Auto.: 8.00

Code	Player	Price
AE	Andre Ethier	15.00
AG	Adrian Gonzalez	15.00
AL	Adam LaRoche	15.00
AR	Aramis Ramirez	15.00
BC	Clay Buchholz	20.00
BH	Bill Hall	15.00
BM	Brian McCann	20.00
BP	Brandon Phillips	15.00
BS	Bill "Moose" Skowron	15.00
BU	B.J. Upton	25.00
CB	Chad Billingsley	20.00
CF	Chone Figgins	12.00

CH	Cole Hamels	50.00
CR	Cal Ripken Jr.	150.00
CY	Chris B. Young	15.00
DB	Daric Barton	10.00
DC	Daniel Cabrera	8.00
EE	Edwin Encarnacion	8.00
EL	Evan Longoria	15.00
EV	Edinson Volquez	10.00
FC	Fausto Carmona	10.00
GF	Gavin Floyd	4.00
GJ	Geoff Jenkins	4.00
GN	Graig Nettles	20.00
GP	Glen Perkins	10.00
HR	Hanley Ramirez	10.00
HU	Chin-Lung Hu	40.00
IA	Ian Kinsler	15.00
JA	James Loney	15.00
JB	Joe Blanton	10.00
JC	Jack Cust	12.00
JG	Jeremy Guthrie	20.00
JK	John Kruk	15.00
JN	Joe Nathan	15.00
JO	Josh Hamilton	40.00
JT	J.R. Towles	15.00
JW	Josh Willingham	10.00
KG	Ken Griffey Jr.	75.00
KJ	Kelly Johnson	10.00
KY	Kevin Youkilis	15.00
LE	Jon Lester	35.00
LH	Luke Hochevar	15.00
MA	John Maine	10.00
MC	Matt Cain	12.00
MK	Matt Kemp	20.00
MS	Max Scherzer	25.00
NA	Nick Adenhart	15.00
NB	Nick Blackburn	15.00
NL	Noah Lowry	10.00
NS	Nick Swisher	15.00
OS	Ozzie Smith	80.00
PK	Paul Konerko	15.00
RH	Rich Hill	8.00
RM	Russell Martin	15.00
TG	Tom Gorzelanny	8.00
WB	Wladimir Balentien	12.00
XN	Xavier Nady	12.00
YG	Yovani Gallardo	15.00

2008 UD Premier

		NM/M
Common Player (1-200):		4.00
Production 99		
Common RC Auto. (201-242):		8.00
Production 99-299		
Box (Seven Cards):		225.00
1	Chipper Jones	8.00
2	Andruw Jones	5.00
3	John Smoltz	5.00
4	Mark Teixeira	6.00
5	Edgar Renteria	4.00
6	Jeff Francoeur	5.00
7	Tim Hudson	5.00
8	Miguel Cabrera	6.00
9	Hanley Ramirez	5.00
10	Dan Uggla	4.00
11	Dontrelle Willis	4.00
12	Josh Willingham	4.00
13	Pedro Martinez	6.00
14	Carlos Delgado	4.00
15	Carlos Beltran	5.00
16	David Wright	10.00
17	Tom Glavine	4.00
18	Jose Reyes	10.00
19	Paul LoDuca	4.00
20	John Maine	4.00
21	Chase Utley	10.00
22	Cole Hamels	5.00
23	Jimmy Rollins	5.00
24	Shane Victorino	4.00
25	Ryan Howard	10.00
26	Pat Burrell	5.00
27	Aaron Rowand	4.00
28	Ryan Zimmerman	5.00
29	Ryan Church	4.00
30	Matt Chico	4.00
31	Dmitri Young	4.00
32	Derrek Lee	6.00
33	Aramis Ramirez	5.00
34	Carlos Zambrano	5.00
35	Rich Hill	4.00
36	Alfonso Soriano	6.00
37	Kerry Wood	5.00
38	Ted Lilly	4.00
39	Ryan Theriot	4.00
40	Ken Griffey Jr.	15.00
41	Adam Dunn	5.00
42	Homer Bailey	4.00
43	Aaron Harang	4.00
44	Brandon Phillips	5.00
45	Josh Hamilton	5.00
46	Lance Berkman	5.00
47	Carlos Lee	4.00
48	Hunter Pence	5.00
49	Mark Loretta	4.00
50	Roy Oswalt	5.00
51	Prince Fielder	10.00
52	Ryan Braun	8.00
53	J.J. Hardy	4.00
54	Ben Sheets	5.00
55	Rickie Weeks	5.00
56	Corey Hart	4.00
57	Johnny Estrada	4.00
58	Jason Bay	5.00
59	Freddy Sanchez	4.00
60	Adam LaRoche	4.00
61	Ian Snell	4.00
62	Xavier Nady	4.00
63	Tom Gorzelanny	4.00
64	Scott Rolen	5.00

65	Albert Pujols	20.00
66	Jim Edmonds	4.00
67	Chris Duncan	4.00
68	Adam Wainwright	5.00
69	Brandon Webb	5.00
70	Orlando Hudson	4.00
71	Chris B. Young	5.00
72	Stephen Drew	5.00
73	Matt Holliday	6.00
74	Jeff Francis	4.00
75	Brad Hawpe	4.00
76	Todd Helton	5.00
77	Troy Tulowitzki	6.00
78	Russell Martin	5.00
79	Nomar Garciaparra	5.00
80	James Loney	5.00
81	Andre Ethier	4.00
82	Brad Penny	4.00
83	Rafael Furcal	4.00
84	Jeff Kent	5.00
85	Greg Maddux	10.00
86	Chris Young	5.00
87	Khalil Greene	4.00
88	Trevor Hoffman	5.00
89	Adrian Gonzalez	5.00
90	Jake Peavy	6.00
91	Noah Lowry	4.00
92	Omar Vizquel	4.00
93	Tim Lincecum	6.00
94	Matt Cain	5.00
95	Randy Winn	4.00
96	Miguel Tejada	5.00
97	Brian Roberts	5.00
98	Nicholas Markakis	5.00
99	Erik Bedard	5.00
100	Melvin Mora	4.00
101	David Ortiz	8.00
102	Manny Ramirez	6.00
103	Josh Beckett	6.00
104	Daisuke Matsuzaka	10.00
105	Curt Schilling	6.00
106	Jason Varitek	4.00
107	Kevin Youkilis	4.00
108	Derek Jeter	20.00
109	Hideki Matsui	10.00
110	Alex Rodriguez	20.00
111	Johnny Damon	6.00
112	Robinson Cano	6.00
113	Jorge Posada	5.00
114	Mariano Rivera	5.00
115	Roger Clemens	12.00
116	Chien-Ming Wang	15.00
117	Carl Crawford	5.00
118	Delmon Young	5.00
119	B.J. Upton	5.00
120	Akinori Iwamura	5.00
121	Scott Kazmir	5.00
122	Alex Rios	5.00
123	Frank Thomas	8.00
124	Roy Halladay	5.00
125	Vernon Wells	5.00
126	Troy Glaus	5.00
127	Jeremy Accardo	4.00
128	A.J. Burnett	4.00
129	Paul Konerko	5.00
130	Jim Thome	5.00
131	Jermaine Dye	4.00
132	Mark Buehrle	5.00
133	Javier Vazquez	4.00
134	Grady Sizemore	5.00
135	Travis Hafner	5.00
136	Victor Martinez	4.00
137	C.C. Sabathia	5.00
138	Ryan Garko	4.00
139	Fausto Carmona	5.00
140	Justin Verlander	6.00
141	Jeremy Bonderman	4.00
142	Magglio Ordonez	5.00
143	Gary Sheffield	5.00
144	Carlos Guillen	5.00
145	Ivan Rodriguez	5.00
146	Curtis Granderson	5.00
147	Alex Gordon	8.00
148	Mark Teahen	4.00
149	Brian Bannister	4.00
150	Billy Butler	5.00
151	Johan Santana	5.00
152	Torii Hunter	5.00
153	Joe Mauer	5.00
154	Justin Morneau	5.00
155	Vladimir Guerrero	6.00
156	Chone Figgins	5.00
157	Jered Weaver	4.00
158	Kelvim Escobar	4.00
159	John Lackey	5.00
160	Danny Haren	5.00
161	Mike Piazza	6.00
162	Nick Swisher	4.00
163	Eric Chavez	4.00
164	Huston Street	4.00
165	Joe Blanton	4.00
166	Kenji Johjima	4.00
167	J.J. Putz	4.00
168	Felix Hernandez	6.00
169	Jose Guillen	5.00
170	Adrian Beltre	5.00
171	Ichiro Suzuki	15.00
172	Marlon Byrd	4.00
173	Hank Blalock	4.00
174	Michael Young	5.00
175	Ian Kinsler	5.00
176	Sammy Sosa	5.00
177	Kevin Millwood	4.00
178	Luis Aparicio	5.00
179	Johnny Bench	8.00
180	Yogi Berra	8.00
181	Lou Brock	8.00

183	Jim Bunning	5.00
184	Rod Carew	6.00
185	Orlando Cepeda	5.00
186	Bobby Doerr	5.00
187	Bob Feller	5.00
188	Dennis Eckersley	5.00
189	Carlton Fisk	5.00
190	Monte Irvin	5.00
191	Rollie Fingers	5.00
192	Al Kaline	8.00
193	Nolan Ryan	20.00
194	Mike Schmidt	10.00
195	Ryne Sandberg	10.00
196	Robin Yount	10.00
197	Brooks Robinson	8.00
198	Bill Mazeroski	5.00
199	Reggie Jackson	8.00
200	Babe Ruth	15.00
201	Ian Kennedy RC	15.00
202	Jonathan Aibaladejo RC	10.00
203	Josh Anderson (RC)	10.00
204	Wladimir Balentien (RC)	10.00
205	Daric Barton (RC)	10.00
206	Jerry Blevins RC	10.00
207	Emilio Bonifacio RC	10.00
208	Lance Broadway RC	10.00
209	Clay Buchholz (RC)	35.00
210	Billy Buckner (RC)	10.00
211	Ross Detwiler RC	10.00
213	Harvey Garcia (RC)	10.00
214	Alberto Gonzalez (RC)	20.00
215	Ryan Hanigan RC	15.00
216	Kevin Hart (RC)	15.00
217	Luke Hochevar RC	15.00
218	Chin-Lung Hu (RC)	20.00
219	Rob Johnson (RC)	8.00
220	Brandon Jones RC	15.00
221	Joe Koshansky (RC)	10.00
222	Donny Lucy (RC)	8.00
223	Justin Maxwell RC	15.00
224	Jonathan Meloan RC	10.00
225	Luis Mendoza (RC)	8.00
226	Jose Morales (RC)	8.00
227	Nyjer Morgan (RC)	10.00
228	Bill Murphy (RC)	8.00
229	Josh Newman RC	15.00
230	Ross Ohlendorf RC	15.00
231	Troy Patton (RC)	15.00
232	Felipe Paulino RC	15.00
233	Steve Pearce RC	15.00
234	Clint Sammons (RC)	15.00
235	Bronson Sardinha RC	8.00
237	Chris Seddon (RC)	15.00
238	Seth Smith (RC)	15.00
239	J.R. Towles (RC)	10.00
240	Eugenio Velez RC	15.00
241	Joey Votto (RC)	25.00
242	Bill White RC	8.00

Base Set Auto. Parallel

		NM/M
Production 25 unless noted.		
1	Chipper Jones	65.00
2	Andruw Jones	20.00
4	Mark Teixeira	40.00
8	Miguel Cabrera	35.00
12	Josh Willingham	15.00
13	Pedro Martinez	50.00
15	Carlos Beltran	20.00
17	Tom Glavine	40.00
20	John Maine	15.00
22	Cole Hamels	40.00
27	Aaron Rowand	15.00
28	Ryan Zimmerman	35.00
32	Derrek Lee	25.00
34	Carlos Zambrano	15.00
37	Kerry Wood	20.00
39	Ryan Theriot	25.00
40	Ken Griffey Jr.	100.00
41	Adam Dunn	30.00
42	Homer Bailey	20.00
47	Carlos Lee	20.00
48	Hunter Pence	35.00
50	Roy Oswalt	20.00
51	Prince Fielder	40.00
52	Ryan Braun	50.00
54	Ben Sheets	25.00
58	Jason Bay	20.00
60	Adam LaRoche	15.00
64	Scott Rolen	30.00
68	Adam Wainwright	40.00
69	Brandon Webb	20.00
71	Chris B. Young	20.00
72	Stephen Drew	15.00
73	Matt Holliday	30.00
74	Jeff Francis	15.00
77	Troy Tulowitzki	30.00
81	Andre Ethier	25.00
83	Rafael Furcal	15.00
87	Khalil Greene	15.00
90	Jake Peavy	25.00
94	Matt Cain	25.00
97	Brian Roberts	20.00
98	Nick Markakis	35.00
103	Josh Beckett	50.00
106	Jason Varitek	40.00
107	Kevin Youkilis	35.00
115	Roger Clemens	70.00
117	Carl Crawford	20.00
118	Delmon Young	20.00
119	B.J. Upton	25.00
120	Akinori Iwamura	25.00
123	Frank Thomas	60.00
124	Roy Halladay	50.00
125	Vernon Wells	15.00
131	Jim Thome	40.00
135	Travis Hafner	20.00
139	Fausto Carmona	15.00
140	Justin Verlander	30.00

142	Jeremy Bonderman	15.00
146	Ivan Rodriguez	25.00
147	Curtis Granderson	40.00
151	Billy Butler	30.00
152	Johan Santana	35.00
153	Torii Hunter	20.00
154	Joe Mauer	50.00
157	Chone Figgins	25.00
158	Jered Weaver	20.00
161	Dan Haren	20.00
163	Nick Swisher	20.00
164	Huston Street	20.00
179	Luis Aparicio	25.00
180	Johnny Bench	40.00
181	Yogi Berra	65.00
182	Lou Brock	35.00
184	Rod Carew	30.00
192	Al Kaline	20.00
194	Mike Schmidt	50.00
195	Ryne Sandberg	60.00
197	Brooks Robinson	50.00
198	Bill Mazeroski	40.00
199	Reggie Jackson	40.00

Gold

Gold (1-200):		No Pricing
Production 5-15		
Gold RC:		1-1.5X
Production 25-99		
No RC prem. prod. 20 or less.		

AKA Signatures

		NM/M
Common Auto.:		No Pricing
Parallel:		
Production 1-5		
AG	Andres Galarraga	10.00
BM	Bill Mazeroski/25	25.00
DJ	Derek Jeter/25	150.00
DM	Don Mattingly/25	60.00
FH	Felix Hernandez/25	40.00
FG	Jeremy Bonderman/15	14.00
JL	John Lackey/25	15.00
JZ	Joel Zumaya/25	15.00
KG	Ken Griffey Jr./25	120.00
RJ	Reggie Jackson/25	40.00
RS	Ryne Sandberg/25	60.00
RZ	Ryan Zimmerman/25	30.00
TH	Travis Hafner/25	15.00
VG	Vladimir Guerrero/25	50.00
WM	Willie McCovey/25	40.00

Bat Barrels

Production 1-6

Combos Memorabilia

		NM/M
Common Duo:		15.00
Parallel 1:		1-1.5X
Production 25 Sets		
Parallel 2:		No Pricing
Production Five Sets		
BF	Prince Fielder, Ryan Braun/50	20.00
BY	Robin Yount, Ryan Braun/50	25.00
CZ	Ryan Zimmerman, Miguel Cabrera/50	15.00
FO	David Ortiz, Prince Fielder/150	20.00
FV	Carlton Fisk, Jason Varitek/50	15.00
GC	Rod Carew, Tony Gwynn/50	20.00
GD	Ken Griffey Jr., Adam Dunn/50	25.00
GJ	Ken Griffey Jr., Derek Jeter/50	30.00
GM	Pedro Martinez, Tom Glavine/50	15.00
GR	Manny Ramirez, Vladimir Guerrero/50	20.00
HH	Todd Helton, Matt Holliday/50	15.00
JH	Andruw Jones, Torii Hunter/50	15.00
JR	Cal Ripken Jr., Derek Jeter/50	50.00
LR	Phil Rizzuto, Tony Lazzeri/50	50.00
MJ	Thurman Munson, Reggie Jackson/50	35.00
MM	Joe Mauer, Victor Martinez/50	15.00
MU	Joe Morgan, Chase Utley/50	20.00
MY	Stan Musial, Carl Yastrzemski/50	35.00
OH	David Ortiz, Travis Hafner/50	20.00
OK	Al Kaline, Magglio Ordonez/50	35.00
OR	Manny Ramirez, David Ortiz/50	25.00
OY	David Ortiz, Kevin Youkilis/50	25.00
PB	Hunter Pence, Ryan Braun/50	20.00
PM	Stan Musial, Albert Pujols/50	40.00
PO	Albert Pujols, David Ortiz/50	25.00
PY	Jake Peavy, Chris Young/50	15.00
RB	Carlos Beltran, Jose Reyes/50	15.00
RC	Jackie Robinson, Roy Campanella/50	50.00

RG	Ken Griffey Jr., Cal Ripken Jr./50	40.00
RJ	Derek Jeter, Hanley Ramirez/30	30.00
SC	Johan Santana, Roger Clemens/50	20.00
SH	Travis Hafner, Grady Sizemore/50	20.00
SM	John Smoltz, Greg Maddux/50	20.00
TG	Ken Griffey Jr., Frank Thomas/50	30.00
UH	Chase Utley, Cole Hamels/50	30.00
VM	Jason Varitek, Victor Martinez/50	15.00
VR	Nolan Ryan, Justin Verlander/50	40.00
WH	Chien-Ming Wang, Phil Hughes/50	30.00

Combos Patch

		NM/M
Common Dual Patch:		20.00
Parallel 1:		1-1.5X
Production 25 Sets		
Parallel 2:		No Pricing
Production 10 Sets		
BD	Danny Haren, Ben Sheets/50	20.00
BP	Johnny Bench, Albert Pujols/50	50.00
BR	Cal Ripken Jr., Ryan Braun/50	75.00
BS	Erik Bedard, C.C. Sabathia/50	20.00
BZ	Jeremy Bonderman, Carlos Zambrano/50	20.00
CR	Manny Ramirez, Miguel Cabrera/50	30.00
CV	Carlton Fisk, Vladimir Guerrero/50	25.00
FG	Jeff Francoeur, Alex Gordon/50	40.00
FM	Joe Mauer, Jeff Francoeur/50	35.00
GR	Ken Griffey Jr., Cal Ripken Jr./50	60.00
GY	Tony Gwynn, Robin Yount/50	40.00
HG	Alex Gordon, J.J. Hardy/50	30.00
HH	Todd Helton, Matt Holliday/50	40.00
HM	Andrew Miller, Cole Hamels/50	20.00
HR	Felix Hernandez, Nolan Ryan/50	60.00
HW	Cole Hamels, Dontrelle Willis/50	25.00
JD	Adam Dunn, Reggie Jackson/50	30.00
JH	Andruw Jones, Torii Hunter/50	20.00
JJ	Joe Mauer, Jose Reyes/50	30.00
LC	Noah Lowry, Matt Cain/50	20.00
LK	Paul Konerko, Derrek Lee/50	30.00
LT	Lance Berkman, Todd Helton/50	20.00
MB	Jason Bay, Nicholas Markakis/50	30.00
MM	Russell Martin, Gil Meche/50	20.00
OR	Manny Ramirez, David Ortiz/50	40.00
PO	Roy Oswalt, Jake Peavy/50	25.00
PR	Tony Perez, Manny Ramirez/50	25.00
RI	Brian Roberts, Akinori Iwamura/50	25.00
RJ	James Loney, Russell Martin/50	25.00
RM	Brian McCann, Aramis Ramirez/50	25.00
RO	Manny Ramirez, Magglio Ordonez/50	25.00
RT	Troy Tulowitzki, Hanley Ramirez/50	30.00
SB	Curt Schilling, Jeremy Bonderman/50	20.00
SH	Johan Santana, Cole Hamels/50	25.00
SJ	C.C. Sabathia, Randy Johnson/50	25.00
TH	Frank Thomas, Travis Hafner/50	40.00
TK	Ken Griffey Jr., Torii Hunter/50	40.00
TT	Travis Hafner, Torii Hunter/50	20.00
UU	Dan Uggla, Chase Utley/50	20.00
UY	Delmon Young, Chase Utley/50	25.00
VH	Cole Hamels, Justin Verlander/50	30.00
VR	Nolan Ryan, Justin Verlander/50	25.00
WJ	Vernon Wells, Chipper Jones/50	25.00
YH	J.J. Hardy, Robin Yount/50	20.00
ZJ	Chipper Jones, Ryan Zimmerman/25	25.00
ZR	Ryan Zimmerman, Jimmy Rollins/50	25.00

Emerging Stars Dual Auto

		NM/M
Common Dual Auto.:		20.00
Parallel:		No Pricing
Production 1 or 15		
BG	Alex Gordon, Billy Butler/35	50.00
BH	Corey Hart, Ryan Braun/35	80.00
BM	Chad Billingsley, Jonathan Meloan/35	25.00
BP	Jonathan Papelbon, Clay Buchholz/35	75.00
BV	Homer Bailey, Joey Votto/35	30.00
BW	Billy Butler, Brandon Wood/35	30.00
CL	Noah Lowry, Matt Cain/35	30.00
CT	Travis Buck, Corey Hart/35	25.00
FB	Josh Fields, Lance Broadway/35	20.00
FO	Jocko Fields, Jerry Owens/35	20.00
GH	Alex Gordon, Luke Hochevar/35	50.00
GL	Fred Lewis, Curtis Granderson/35	20.00
HB	Homer Bailey, Phil Hughes/35	50.00
HK	Cole Hamels, Scott Kazmir/35	40.00
HL	James Loney, Chin-Lung Hu/35	40.00
HS	Danny Haren, Huston Street/35	25.00
HV	Josh Hamilton, Joey Votto/35	30.00
HW	Rickie Weeks, Corey Hart/35	50.00
KB	Kevin Kouzmanoff, Brandon Wood/35	30.00
KH	Phil Hughes, Ian Kennedy/35	60.00
KU	Howie Kendrick, Dan Uggla/35	25.00
KW	Howie Kendrick, Jered Weaver/35	35.00
LE	James Loney, Andre Ethier/35	25.00
LL	James Loney, Andy LaRoche/35	35.00
MB	John Maine, Chad Billingsley/35	25.00
MC	John Maine, Matt Cain/35	25.00
ME	Brian McCann, Yunel Escobar/35	40.00
MH	Nicholas Markakis, Jeremy Hermida/35	30.00
ML	James Loney, Russell Martin/35	40.00
MM	Brian McCann, Russell Martin/35	30.00
MP	Steve Pearce, Nicholas Markakis/35	35.00
MS	Jarrod Saltalamacchia, Brian McCann/35	25.00
MT	J.R. Towles, Russell Martin/35	25.00
NJ	Josh Hamilton, Nicholas Markakis/35	35.00
PL	Jon Lester, Jonathan Papelbon/35	40.00
PZ	Jonathan Papelbon, Joel Zumaya/35	25.00
TA	Garrett Atkins, Troy Tulowitzki/35	30.00
TS	Troy Tulowitzki, Alex Gordon/35	60.00
UR	Hanley Ramirez, Dan Uggla/35	40.00
UY	Delmon Young, B.J. Upton/35	30.00
VH	Danny Haren, Justin Verlander/35	30.00

Emerging Stars Quad

No Pricing	
Production 10 Sets	
Parallel:	No Pricing
Production 1 or 5	

Emerging Stars Trio

		NM/M
Common Trio Auto.:		30.00
Parallel:		No Pricing
Production 1 or 5		
BPW	Hunter Pence, Billy Butler, Brandon Wood/35	40.00
CBM	John Maine, Matt Cain, Chad Billingsley/35	30.00
GSB	Kevin Slowey, Scott Baker, Matt Garza/35	30.00
HBP	Josh Hamilton, Travis Buck, Felix Pie/25	30.00
HHG	Tom Gorzelanny, Rich Hill, Cole Hamels/25	40.00
KBH	Clay Buchholz, Luke Hochevar, Ian Kennedy/25	75.00
LEM	James Loney, Andre Ethier, Russell Martin/25	30.00
MHG	John Maine, Phil Hughes, Matt Garza/25	50.00

MHH	Josh Hamilton, Nicholas Markakis, Jeremy Hermida/25	30.00
TAB	Garrett Atkins, Jeff Baker, Troy Tulowitzki/25	30.00
VPW		30.00
VPW	Jonathan Papelbon, Jered Weaver, Justin Verlander/25	60.00

Foursome Memorabilia

NM/M

Common Quad:		25.00
Parallel:		No Pricing
Production 4 or 15		
BHFS	Ben Sheets, Prince Fielder, Corey Hart, Ryan Braun/25	40.00
BYGM	Wade Boggs, Carl Yastrzemski, Eddie Murray, Tony Gwynn/25	40.00
CGBR	Cal Ripken Jr., Wade Boggs, Tony Gwynn, Rod Carew/25	60.00
CKMC	Stan Musial, Rod Carew, Roberto Clemente, Al Kaline/25	75.00
DRMB	Carlos Delgado, Carlos Beltran, Pedro Martinez, Jose Reyes/25	
GBMP	Ken Griffey Jr., Tony Perez, Joe Morgan, Johnny Bench/25	50.00
GTPJ	Ken Griffey Jr., Albert Pujols, Chipper Jones, Frank Thomas/25	50.00
HHAT	Todd Helton, Garrett Atkins, Matt Holliday, Troy Tulowitzki/25	35.00
CSCU	Carl Crawford, B.J. Upton, James Shields, Akinori Iwamura/25	25.00
LRSZ	Derrek Lee, Aramis Ramirez, Alfonso Soriano, Carlos Zambrano/25	50.00
MGCG	Bob Gibson, Tom Glavine, Greg Maddux, Steve Carlton/25	40.00
MYRW	Cal Ripken Jr., Dave Winfield, Robin Yount, Paul Molitor/25	80.00
PCPM	Jim Palmer, Pedro Martinez, Roger Clemens, Gaylord Perry/25	40.00
SSRY	Cal Ripken Jr., Robin Yount, Ryne Sandberg, Mike Schmidt/25	100.00
VHBS	Josh Beckett, Danny Haren, C.C. Sabathia, Justin Verlander/25	30.00
WSGM	Tom Glavine, John Smoltz, Greg Maddux, Brandon Webb/25	

Legendary Remnants Triple

NM/M

Production 10-50		
Parallel:		No Pricing
Production 1-25		
Die-Cut:		No Pricing
Production 5-25		
RC	Roy Campanella/25	40.00
JD	Joe DiMaggio/50	90.00
JR	Jackie Robinson/50	60.00
LG	Lou Gehrig/50	180.00
MO	Mel Ott/50	75.00
RC	Roberto Clemente/50	60.00
RM	Roger Maris/50	40.00
WS	Willie Stargell/50	30.00

Legendary Remnants Quad

Production 10-20	
Parallel:	No Pricing
Production 1-13	

Logo Patch

Production One Set

Memorabilia Triple

NM/M

Common Player:		15.00
Parallel:		No Pricing
Production Three Sets		
AG	Alex Gordon/25	15.00
AI	Akinori Iwamura/25	15.00
AP	Albert Pujols/75	25.00
BE	Johnny Bench/50	30.00
BM	Bill Mazeroski/25	25.00
CA	Rod Carew/25	20.00
CJ	Chipper Jones/25	25.00
DJ	Derek Jeter/75	30.00
DM	Daisuke Matsuzaka/75	20.00
DO	David Ortiz/75	15.00
GM	Greg Maddux/50	20.00
GS	Grady Sizemore/25	15.00
IR	Ivan Rodriguez/25	
JD	Joe DiMaggio/25	100.00
JP	Jonathan Papelbon/25	15.00
KG	Ken Griffey Jr./50	25.00
MA	Don Mattingly/50	20.00
MR	Manny Ramirez/25	15.00
MS	Mike Schmidt/50	15.00
NR	Nolan Ryan/25	
OS	Ozzie Smith/25	15.00
PF	Prince Fielder/25	20.00
PM	Paul Molitor/25	15.00
RC	Roger Clemens/25	20.00
RJ	Reggie Jackson/75	15.00
SM	Stan Musial/75	30.00
TS	Tom Seaver/75	25.00
VG	Vladimir Guerrero/25	20.00
WB	Wade Boggs/50	10.00
WS	Warren Spahn/75	25.00
AP2	Albert Pujols/75	20.00

Memorabilia Triple Auto.

No Pricing
Production 5 or 20

Memorabilia Quad

NM/M

Common Player:		10.00
Auto. Parallel:		No Pricing
Production 10 Sets		
Parallel:		No Pricing
Production Four Sets		
AS	Alfonso Soriano/40	20.00
CC	Chris Carpenter/40	15.00
CH	Cole Hamels/40	15.00
CL	Roger Clemens/40	20.00
CS	Curt Schilling/40	15.00
CU	Chase Utley/40	25.00
CW	Chien-Ming Wang/40	40.00
CY	Carl Yastrzemski/40	25.00
DJ	Derek Jeter/40	35.00
DL	Derrek Lee/40	15.00
DM	Don Mattingly/40	25.00
DO	David Ortiz/40	20.00
DP	Dave Parker/40	15.00
DW	Dontrelle Willis/40	10.00
EM	Eddie Mathews/40	35.00
HP	Hunter Pence/40	20.00
JM	Joe Mauer/40	15.00
JR	Jackie Robinson/40	75.00
JS	Johan Santana/40	20.00
JV	Justin Verlander/40	20.00
MA	Russell Martin/40	20.00
MO	Justin Morneau/40	15.00
MS	Mike Schmidt/40	40.00
MT	Mark Teixeira/40	20.00
NM	Nicholas Markakis/40	25.00
NR	Nolan Ryan/40	35.00
OR	Magglio Ordonez/40	15.00
PF	Prince Fielder/40	20.00
PH	Phil Hughes/40	25.00
PW	Pee Wee Reese/40	25.00
RB	Ryan Braun/40	30.00
RC	Roberto Clemente/40	100.00
RE	Jose Reyes/40	25.00
RM	Roger Maris/40	60.00
RY	Robin Yount/40	30.00
SM	Stan Musial/40	40.00
TP	Tony Perez/40	25.00
VG	Vladimir Guerrero/40	20.00
VM	Victor Martinez/40	20.00
DO2	David Ortiz/40	20.00

Milestones

NM/M

Common Auto.:		25.00
Parallel:		No Pricing
Production 1 or 5		
AJ	Andruw Jones/25	25.00
AR	Aramis Ramirez/25	25.00
CG	Curtis Granderson/25	40.00
FT	Frank Thomas/25	65.00
IR	Ivan Rodriguez/25	40.00
JT	Jim Thome/25	50.00
KG	Ken Griffey Jr./25	125.00
LB	Lance Berkman/25	20.00
MT	Miguel Tejada/25	25.00
PM	Pedro Martinez/25	65.00
RB	Ryan Braun/25	50.00
TG	Tom Glavine/25	75.00
VG	Vladimir Guerrero/25	50.00

Octographs

Production One Set

Patches

NM/M

Common Player:		10.00
Auto. Parallel:		No Pricing
Production 15 Sets		
Die-Cut Parallel:		1.5X
Production 10-33		
Parallel 1:		1.5X
Production 1-56		
Parallel 2:		1X
Production 50 Sets		
No pricing prod. 15 or less.		
AI	Akinori Iwamura/25	15.00
AJ	Andruw Jones/25	10.00
AL	Adam LaRoche/25	15.00
BR	Brian Roberts/75	20.00
CB	Carlos Beltran/75	15.00
CJ	Chipper Jones/75	30.00
CR	Cal Ripken Jr./75	50.00
CU	Chase Utley/75	30.00
CW	Chien-Ming Wang/75	20.00
DM	Daisuke Matsuzaka/75	30.00
DO	David Ortiz/75	40.00
DW	Dontrelle Willis/75	15.00
EB	Erik Bedard/75	15.00
FT	Frank Thomas/75	35.00
GS	Grady Sizemore/75	20.00
HA	Travis Hafner/75	15.00
HK	Hong-Chih Kuo/75	30.00
HP	Hunter Pence/75	25.00
HR	Hanley Ramirez/75	25.00
HU	Torii Hunter/75	15.00
IR	Ivan Rodriguez/75	20.00
JB	Jeremy Bonderman/75	15.00
JF	Jeff Francoeur/75	20.00
JM	Justin Morneau/75	20.00
JP	Jake Peavy/75	20.00
JR	Jose Reyes/75	30.00
JS	Johan Santana/75	25.00
JV	Jason Varitek/75	20.00
MA	Don Mattingly/75	35.00
MC	Miguel Cabrera/75	20.00
MO	Magglio Ordonez/75	15.00
NM	Nicholas Markakis/75	25.00
NR	Nolan Ryan/75	50.00
RB	Ryan Braun/75	20.00
RJ	Randy Johnson/75	25.00
RO	Roy Oswalt/75	20.00
RW	Rickie Weeks/75	20.00
RZ	Ryan Zimmerman/75	15.00
SM	Stan Musial/75	40.00
TG	Tony Gwynn/75	30.00
TH	Todd Helton/75	20.00
TL	Tim Lincecum/75	30.00
TS	Takashi Saito/75	15.00
VE	Justin Verlander/75	20.00
WB	Wade Boggs/75	25.00

Penmanship

NM/M

Common Auto.:		10.00
Parallel:		No Pricing
Production 1-5		
AK	Al Kaline/50	30.00
BB	Billy Butler/50	25.00
BE	Johnny Bench/50	40.00
BF	Bob Feller/50	25.00
BL	Joe Blanton/50	10.00
BT	Bobby Thomson/50	20.00
CB	Chad Billingsley/50	15.00
CC	Carl Crawford/50	20.00
CF	Carlton Fisk/50	25.00
CH	Cole Hamels/50	30.00
CJ	Chipper Jones/50	75.00
CR	Cal Ripken Jr./50	100.00
CW	Chien-Ming Wang/50	50.00
FC	Fausto Carmona/50	20.00
FH	Felix Hernandez/50	30.00
FT	Frank Thomas/50	60.00
GP	Gaylord Perry/45	15.00
HK	Hong-Chih Kuo/50	15.00
HP	Hunter Pence/50	20.00
IK	Ian Kennedy/50	20.00
IR	Ivan Rodriguez/50	40.00
JB	Jeremy Bonderman/50	15.00
JL	John Lackey/50	20.00
JM	John Maine/50	15.00
JP	Jim Palmer/50	25.00
JV	Justin Verlander/50	35.00
JW	Josh Willingham/50	10.00
KW	Kerry Wood/50	15.00
LA	Luis Aparicio/40	20.00
MS	Mike Schmidt/50	40.00
NM	Nicholas Markakis/50	25.00
NR	Nolan Ryan/50	80.00
PA	Jonathan Papelbon/50	25.00
RB	Ryan Braun/50	40.00
RC	Rod Carew/50	20.00
RH	Ramon Hernandez/50	10.00
RM	Russell Martin/50	15.00
RZ	Ryan Zimmerman/50	15.00
TH	Travis Hafner/50	15.00
TT	Troy Tulowitzki/50	30.00
VM	Victor Martinez/50	20.00

Playoff Premiere

No Pricing	
Parallel:	No Pricing
Production 1 or 5	

Premier Teams 3

NM/M

Common Trio:		20.00
Production 25 or 50		
Parallels:		1-1.5X
Production 3-33		
No pricing prod. 15 or less.		
BFS	Ben Sheets, Prince Fielder, Ryan Braun/25	25.00
BHG	Yovani Gallardo, J.J. Hardy, Ryan Braun/25	30.00
BJH	Adrian Beltre, Felix Hernandez, Kenji Johjima/25	20.00
BMP	Tony Perez, Joe Morgan, Johnny Bench/25	40.00
CMW	Mike Mussina, Roger Clemens, Chien-Ming Wang/50	40.00
CPB	Roberto Clemente, Dave Parker, Jason Bay/50	
CRJ	Roger Clemens, Derek Jeter, Mariano Rivera/50	40.00
CRR	Jackie Robinson, Pee Wee Reese, Roy Campanella/50	60.00
CSM	Michael Cuddyer, Johan Santana, Joe Mauer/25	15.00
DBR	Carlos Delgado, Carlos Beltran, Jose Reyes/25	20.00
GBS	Mike Sweeney, Alex Gordon, Billy Butler/25	20.00
GDH	Ken Griffey Jr., Josh Hamilton, Adam Dunn/50	30.00
GFW	Vladimir Guerrero, Chone Figgins, Jered Weaver/25	20.00
IUK	Scott Kazmir, B.J. Upton, Akinori Iwamura/25	20.00
JJF	Andruw Jones, Chipper Jones, Jeff Francoeur/50	30.00
JWD	Randy Johnson, Brandon Webb, Stephen Drew/50	20.00
KBS	Hong-Chih Kuo, Chad Billingsley, Takashi Saito/25	20.00
LME	James Loney, Andre Ethier, Russell Martin/25	
LRS	Derrek Lee, Aramis Ramirez, Alfonso Soriano/25	30.00
LVZ	Barry Zito, Omar Vizquel, Tim Lincecum/25	20.00
MJJ	Don Mattingly, Derek Jeter, Reggie Jackson/50	50.00
MPB	Stan Musial, Lou Brock, Albert Pujols/50	50.00
MSB	Curt Schilling, Josh Beckett, Daisuke Matsuzaka/50	30.00
MSM	Justin Morneau, Johan Mantana, Joe Mauer/25	20.00
OBY	Wade Boggs, David Ortiz, Kevin Youkilis/25	25.00
ORS	Gary Sheffield, Ivan Rodriguez, Magglio Ordonez/25	20.00
ORY	Manny Ramirez, David Ortiz, Kevin Youkilis/25	
PCR	Chris Carpenter, Scott Rolen, Albert Pujols/50	30.00
PMH	Greg Maddux, Trevor Hoffman, Jake Peavy/50	20.00
POB	Lance Berkman, Roy Oswalt, Hunter Pence/25	
RGD	Babe Ruth, Joe DiMaggio, Lou Gehrig/20	450.00
RWU	Dontrelle Willis, Hanley Ramirez, Dan Uggla/20	20.00
SBW	Ryne Sandberg, Ernie Banks, Billy Williams/50	
SCH	Eric Chavez, Danny Haren, Nick Swisher/25	20.00
SMF	John Smoltz, Brian McCann, Jeff Francoeur/40	
SMH	Travis Hafner, Victor Martinez, Grady Sizemore/25	20.00
TDK	Jim Thome, Paul Konerko, Jermaine Dye/25	
UHR	Jimmy Rollins, Chase Utley, Cole Hamels/25	30.00
USH	Mike Schmidt, Chase Utley, Cole Hamels/25	35.00
VBZ	Jeremy Bonderman, Justin Verlander, Joel Zumaya/25	
WHT	Frank Thomas, Vernon Wells, Roy Halladay/25	20.00
YPH	Trevor Hoffman, Jake Peavy, Chris Young/25	25.00

Premier Pairings

NM/M

Common Dual Auto.:		20.00
BA	Bronson Arroyo, Homer Bailey/25	25.00
BG	Alex Gordon, Ryan Braun/25	65.00
BH	Danny Haren, Josh Beckett/25	50.00
BP	Hunter Pence, Ryan Braun/25	60.00
BZ	Jeremy Bonderman, Joel Zumaya/25	25.00
CH	Steve Carlton, Cole Hamels/25	60.00
CR	Miguel Cabrera, Hanley Ramirez/25	50.00
DT	Don Mattingly, Tino Martinez/25	120.00
FC	Jeff Francis, Manny Corpas/25	
GM	Ken Griffey Jr., Edgar Martinez/25	150.00
GO	David Ortiz, Vladimir Guerrero/25	75.00
HB	Homer Bailey, Phil Hughes/25	50.00
HM	Cole Hamels, Andrew Miller/25	
JM	Jason Bay, Matt Holliday/25	30.00
KH	Cole Hamels, Scott Kazmir/25	35.00
LE	James Loney, Andre Ethier/25	35.00
LL	Carlos Lee, Derrek Lee/25	40.00
LW	John Lackey, Jered Weaver/25	40.00
MB	Jeremy Bonderman, Andrew Miller/25	20.00
MH	Andrew Miller, Rich Hill/25	25.00
ML	James Loney, Russell Martin/25	40.00
OM	Roy Oswalt, Jason Bay/25	
PB	Hunter Pence, Jason Bay/25	25.00
PC	Gaylord Perry, Fausto Carmona/25	40.00
PL	Jon Lester, Jonathan Papelbon/25	60.00
RH	Cal Ripken Jr., Chin-Lung Hu/25	180.00
RM	Edgar Martinez, Harold Reynolds/50	50.00
RS	Cal Ripken Jr., Ryne Sandberg/25	200.00
RU	Hanley Ramirez, Dan Uggla/25	35.00
RV	Russell Martin, Victor Martinez/25	30.00
SR	Ryne Sandberg, Aramis Ramirez/25	80.00
TA	Garrett Atkins, Troy Tulowitzki/25	
TR	Miguel Tejada, Brian Roberts/25	30.00
TT	Frank Thomas, Jim Thome/25	80.00
TV	Travis Hafner, Victor Martinez/25	25.00
UK	Howie Kendrick/25	20.00
ZB	Ryan Zimmerman, Ryan Braun/25	40.00

Quads Patch

No Pricing	
Production 20 or less.	
Parallel:	No Pricing
Production 1-10	

Quartet

No Pricing
Production 15 Sets

Remnants Triple

NM/M

Common Player:		10.00
Parallel:		1X
Production 25-75		
Parallel 2:		No Pricing
Production 1-25		
AJ	Andruw Jones/25	10.00
AP	Albert Pujols/25	25.00
CF	Carlton Fisk/25	15.00
CY	Carl Yastrzemski/50	20.00
DJ	Derek Jeter/75	30.00
DM	Daisuke Matsuzaka/75	25.00
DO	David Ortiz/75	20.00
HK	Hong-Chih Kuo/25	15.00
JB	Josh Beckett/25	
KG	Ken Griffey Jr./50	25.00
MA	Don Mattingly/25	25.00
MR	Manny Ramirez/25	15.00
MS	Mike Schmidt/25	15.00
NR	Nolan Ryan/25	25.00
PA	Jonathan Papelbon/25	20.00
PO	Jorge Posada/25	15.00
RJ	Reggie Jackson/75	15.00
RY	Robin Yount/50	
VG	Vladimir Guerrero/25	15.00
WB	Wade Boggs/50	15.00

Remnants Triple Auto

NM/M

Production 5-25		
AJ	Andruw Jones/25	30.00
CA	Chris Carpenter/25	40.00
CC	Carl Crawford/25	25.00
CF	Carlton Fisk/25	50.00
CJ	Chipper Jones/25	80.00
CS	Curt Schilling/25	
CY	Carl Yastrzemski/25	60.00
DJ	Derek Jeter/25	150.00
DL	Derrek Lee/25	50.00
DM	Daisuke Matsuzaka/25	400.00
FH	Felix Hernandez/25	60.00
HA	Travis Hafner/25	30.00
JM	Joe Mauer/25	40.00
KG	Ken Griffey Jr./25	120.00
MA	Don Mattingly/25	100.00
MC	Miguel Cabrera/25	40.00
MS	Mike Schmidt/25	60.00
MT	Mark Teixeira/25	30.00
NR	Nolan Ryan/25	80.00
PA	Jonathan Papelbon/25	60.00
PF	Prince Fielder/25	60.00
RJ	Reggie Jackson/25	50.00
RY	Robin Yount/25	60.00
TR	Tim Raines/25	50.00
WB	Wade Boggs/25	40.00

Remnants Quad

NM/M

Common Player:		10.00
Production 50 Sets		
Auto. Parallel:		No Pricing
Production 15 Sets		
Parallel 1:		1X
Production 25 Sets		
Parallel 2:		No Pricing
Production 10 Sets		
Parallel 3:		1-1.5X
Production 2-77		
No pricing prod. 15 or less.		
AD	Adam Dunn/25	
BE	Carlos Beltran/25	10.00
BR	Brooks Robinson/25	
BS	Ben Sheets/25	10.00
CF	Carlton Fisk/25	15.00
CH	Cole Hamels/25	20.00
CL	Roger Clemens/25	20.00
CR	Cal Ripken Jr./25	40.00
CS	Curt Schilling/25	15.00
CW	Chien-Ming Wang/25	15.00
DJ	Derek Jeter/25	40.00
DL	Derrek Lee/25	15.00
DM	Don Mattingly/25	30.00
DO	David Ortiz/25	15.00
FH	Felix Hernandez/25	15.00
GS	Grady Sizemore/25	30.00
HK	Howie Kendrick/25	15.00
HO	Rogers Hornsby/25	140.00
JB	Johnny Bench/25	40.00
JM	Joe Mauer/25	40.00
JP	Jake Peavy/25	20.00
JR	Jimmy Rollins/25	40.00
JT	Jim Thome/25	25.00
KG	Ken Griffey Jr./50	25.00
LB	Lou Brock/25	35.00
MA	Don Mattingly/25	25.00
MC	Miguel Cabrera/25	35.00
MS	Mike Schmidt/25	50.00
NR	Nolan Ryan/25	60.00
PA	Jonathan Papelbon/25	25.00
PO	Jorge Posada/25	25.00
PW	Pee Wee Reese/25	30.00
RC	Roger Clemens/25	
RM	Roger Maris/25	65.00
RY	Robin Yount/25	50.00
SC	Steve Carlton/25	30.00
SM	Stan Musial/25	50.00
TG	Tony Gwynn/25	35.00
TH	Torii Hunter/25	25.00
WB	Wade Boggs/25	35.00
CU2	Chase Utley/25	35.00
DJ2	Derek Jeter/25	60.00
DJ3	Derek Jeter/25	60.00
DO2	David Ortiz/25	30.00

Remnants 5

NM/M

Production 10-25		
Parallel:		No Pricing
Production 1 or 10		
CH	Cole Hamels/25	25.00
CJ	Chipper Jones/25	40.00
CU	Chase Utley/25	35.00
CY	Carl Yastrzemski/25	
DJ	Derek Jeter/25	60.00
DM	Daisuke Matsuzaka/25	25.00
DO	David Ortiz/25	25.00
FH	Felix Hernandez/25	25.00
GS	Grady Sizemore/25	30.00
HK	Howie Kendrick/25	25.00
HO	Rogers Hornsby/25	140.00
JB	Johnny Bench/25	40.00
JM	Joe Mauer/25	25.00
JP	Jake Peavy/25	20.00
JR	Jimmy Rollins/25	40.00
JT	Jim Thome/25	25.00
KG	Ken Griffey Jr./50	25.00
LB	Lou Brock/25	35.00
MA	Don Mattingly/25	25.00
MC	Miguel Cabrera/25	35.00
MS	Mike Schmidt/25	50.00
NR	Nolan Ryan/25	60.00
PA	Jonathan Papelbon/25	25.00
PO	Jorge Posada/25	25.00
PW	Pee Wee Reese/25	30.00
RC	Roger Clemens/25	
RM	Roger Maris/25	65.00
RY	Robin Yount/25	50.00
SC	Steve Carlton/25	30.00
SM	Stan Musial/25	50.00
TG	Tony Gwynn/25	35.00
TH	Torii Hunter/25	25.00
WB	Wade Boggs/25	35.00
CU2	Chase Utley/25	35.00
DJ2	Derek Jeter/25	60.00
DJ3	Derek Jeter/25	60.00
DO2	David Ortiz/25	30.00

Signature Premier

NM/M

Common Auto.:		10.00
AE	Andre Ethier/45	20.00
AG	Adrian Gonzalez/45	20.00
AI	Akinori Iwamura/45	20.00
AM	Andrew Miller/45	15.00
AR	Aramis Ramirez/45	15.00
BB	Billy Buckner/45	
BE	Johnny Bench/45	35.00
BH	Bill Hall/25	10.00
BI	Chad Billingsley/45	15.00
BJ	B.J. Upton/45	20.00
BM	Brian McCann/45	25.00
BO	Jeremy Bonderman/45	10.00
BS	Bronson Sardinha/45	10.00
BU	Billy Butler/45	20.00
CA	Matt Cain/45	20.00
CB	Clay Buchholz/45	35.00
CC	Chris Carpenter/45	20.00
CF	Carlton Fisk/45	
CR	Cal Ripken Jr./45	125.00
DH	Danny Haren/45	20.00
DL	Derrek Lee/45	30.00
DM	Don Mattingly/45	50.00
DU	Dan Uggla/45	20.00
EB	Ernie Banks/37	50.00
EM	Edgar Martinez/45	25.00
FC	Fausto Carmona/45	15.00
FP	Felix Pie/25	15.00
GA	Garret Anderson/45	15.00
GO	Alex Gordon/45	15.00
GP	Gaylord Perry/45	15.00
HK	Howie Kendrick/45	15.00
HR	Harold Reynolds/45	15.00
HU	Chin-Lung Hu/45	40.00
JB	Jim Bunning/45	20.00
JL	John Lackey/45	20.00
JM	John Maine/45	15.00
JP	Jim Palmer/45	20.00
JT	J.R. Towles/45	15.00
JV	Joey Votto/45	25.00
JW	Josh Willingham/45	10.00
JZ	Joel Zumaya/45	10.00

Code	Player	NM/M
KE	Ian Kennedy/45	40.00
KI	Ian Kinsler/45	20.00
KY	Kevin Youkilis/45	30.00
LA	Luis Aparicio/45	20.00
LE	Jon Lester/45	30.00
LH	Luke Hochevar/45	20.00
MS	Mike Schmidt/45	40.00
MT	Miguel Tejada/45	20.00
MU	Stan Musial/45	70.00
NL	Noah Lowry/45	10.00
NM	Nick Markakis/45	30.00
NR	Nolan Ryan/45	80.00
NS	Nick Swisher/45	15.00
OH	Ross Ohlendorf/45	20.00
OW	Micah Owings/45	20.00
PF	Prince Fielder/45	30.00
PH	Phil Hughes/45	40.00
PM	Pedro Martinez/45	50.00
RB	Ryan Braun/45	40.00
RC	Rod Carew/45	25.00
RD	Ross Detwiler/45	10.00
RH	Rich Hill/45	20.00
RI	Jim Rice/20	25.00
RJ	Reggie Jackson/45	40.00
RO	Roger Clemens/45	60.00
RS	Ron Santo/25	60.00
RT	Ryan Theriot/45	30.00
RY	Ryne Sandberg/45	50.00
SA	Jarrod Saltalamacchia/45	15.00
SC	Steve Carlton/25	30.00
SD	Stephen Drew/45	20.00
SK	Scott Kazmir/45	15.00
TB	Travis Buck/45	15.00
TG	Tony Gwynn/45	40.00
TH	Travis Hafner/45	15.00
TP	Tony Perez/45	25.00
WB	Wladimir Balentien/45	10.00
WF	Whitey Ford/45	50.00
YF	Yunel Escobar/45	25.00

Significant Six
No Pricing
Production 10 Sets

Significant Stars
NM/M
Production 20 unless noted.

Code	Players	NM/M
BR	Johnny Bench, Ivan Rodriguez	100.00
BW	Josh Beckett, Chien-Ming Wang	200.00
CG	Steve Carlton, Tom Glavine	50.00
FD	Adam Dunn, Prince Fielder	40.00
GJ	Ken Griffey Jr., Reggie Jackson	150.00
HC	Felix Hernandez, Fausto Carmona	60.00
JW	Derek Jeter, Chien-Ming Wang	250.00
MH	Travis Hafner, Victor Martinez	30.00
MM	Victor Martinez, Russell Martin	35.00
RF	Rafael Furcal, Hanley Ramirez/15	30.00
RG	Cal Ripken Jr., Tony Gwynn	160.00
SC	Miguel Cabrera, Mike Schmidt	60.00
SM	Russell Martin, Takashi Saito	40.00
SP	Jonathan Papelbon, Takashi Saito	40.00
TF	Mark Teixeira, Prince Fielder	40.00
TR	Miguel Tejada, Hanley Ramirez	35.00
WH	Dontrelle Willis, Cole Hamels	30.00
YM	Stan Musial, Carl Yastrzemski	80.00

Stitchings
NM/M
Common Player: 15.00
Production 75 Sets
Parallel 1: 1-1.5X
Production 25 Sets
Parallels 2 & 3: No Pricing
Production 1-20:
Variation: 1X
Production 50 Sets
Auto. Parallel: No Pricing
Production 25 Sets

Code	Player	NM/M
AG	Alex Gordon	15.00
AK	Al Kaline	30.00
AP	Albert Pujols	25.00
AR	Alex Rodriguez	25.00
AS	Alfonso Soriano	15.00
BD	Bobby Doerr	20.00
BE	Johnny Bench	20.00
BF	Bob Feller	35.00
BG	Bob Gibson	20.00
BM	Bill Mazeroski	20.00
BR	Babe Ruth	40.00
CA	Miguel Cabrera	20.00
CB	Craig Biggio	15.00
CF	Carlton Fisk	20.00
CJ	Chipper Jones	20.00
CR	Cal Ripken Jr.	40.00
CS	Rod Carew, Tom Seaver	20.00
CU	Chase Utley	25.00
CW	Chien-Ming Wang	15.00
CY	Carl Yastrzemski	20.00
DJ	Derek Jeter	30.00
DL	Derek Lee	20.00
DM	Daisuke Matsuzaka	20.00
DY	Delmon Young	15.00
EM	Eddie Murray	15.00
FA	Nellie Fox, Luis Aparicio	20.00
FH	Felix Hernandez	20.00
FJ	Fergie Jenkins	20.00
FT	Frank Thomas	25.00
GR	Babe Ruth, Lou Gehrig	30.00
GS	Grady Sizemore	15.00
GW	Tony Gwynn	20.00
HA	Travis Hafner	15.00
HP	Hunter Pence	15.00
HR	Hanley Ramirez	20.00
HU	Torii Hunter	15.00
JB	Jason Bay	15.00
JD	Joe DiMaggio	25.00
JE	Jim Edmonds	15.00
JH	Josh Hamilton	20.00
JM	Joe Mauer	20.00
JO	Jonathan Papelbon	15.00
JP	Jake Peavy	15.00
JR	Jackie Robinson, Roy Campanella	20.00
JS	Johan Santana	20.00
JU	Justin Morneau	15.00
JV	Justin Verlander	20.00
JZ	Joel Zumaya	15.00
KG	Ken Griffey Jr.	25.00
KW	Kerry Wood	15.00
LA	Luis Aparicio	15.00
LB	Lou Brock	15.00
LI	Tim Lincecum	20.00
MA	Juan Marichal	15.00
MC	Brian McCann	15.00
MH	Matt Holliday	20.00
MI	Monte Irvin	20.00
MJ	Derek Jeter, Hideki Matsui	30.00
MO	Joe Morgan	15.00
MP	Mike Piazza	20.00
MR	Manny Ramirez	20.00
MS	Mike Schmidt	20.00
NR	Nolan Ryan	30.00
OC	Orlando Cepeda	15.00
OM	Daisuke Matsuzaka, Hideki Okajima	25.00
OR	Manny Ramirez, David Ortiz	20.00
PA	Jim Palmer	15.00
PF	Prince Fielder	20.00
PH	Phil Hughes	15.00
PN	Phil Niekro	15.00
RA	Richie Ashburn	20.00
RB	Ryan Braun	20.00
RC	Rod Carew	20.00
RF	Rollie Fingers	15.00
RH	Roy Halladay	15.00
RI	Mariano Rivera	25.00
RJ	Reggie Jackson	15.00
RK	Ralph Kiner	15.00
RM	Russell Martin	15.00
RO	Brooks Robinson	15.00
RS	Ryne Sandberg	20.00
RY	Ryan Howard	15.00
RZ	Ryan Zimmerman	15.00
SJ	Kenji Johjima	15.00
SJ	Ichiro Suzuki	20.00
SS	Sammy Sosa	15.00
SV	Shane Victorino	15.00
TG	Tom Glavine	15.00
TH	Trevor Hoffman	15.00
TL	Tommy Lasorda	15.00
TS	Tom Seaver	15.00
TT	Troy Tulowitzki	15.00
VG	Vladimir Guerrero	15.00
VM	Victor Martinez	15.00
WM	Willie McCovey	20.00
FT2	Frank Thomas	20.00
KG2	Ken Griffey Jr.	25.00
KG3	Ken Griffey Jr.	25.00
MH2	Matt Holliday	15.00

Stitchings Cut Signature
Production One Set

Swatches
NM/M
Common Player: 10.00
Production 50 Sets
Die-Cut: 1.5X
Production 20 Sets
Auto. Parallel: No Pricing
Production 3-10
Parallels: 1-1.5X
Production 1-55
No pricing prod. 15 or less.

Code	Player	NM/M
AP	Albert Pujols	25.00
AS	Alfonso Soriano	20.00
BR	Brian Roberts	15.00
BS	Ben Sheets	15.00
CD	Carlos Delgado	10.00
CH	Cole Hamels	15.00
CS	C.C. Sabathia	15.00
CY	Carl Yastrzemski	20.00
CZ	Carlos Zambrano	15.00
DH	Danny Haren	15.00
DL	Derek Lee	15.00
EM	Eddie Murray	15.00
FH	Felix Hernandez	15.00
FS	Freddy Sanchez	15.00
GM	Greg Maddux	25.00
GP	Gaylord Perry	15.00
GS	Grady Sizemore	20.00
HK	Howie Kendrick	15.00
JB	Jason Bay	15.00
JM	Joe Mauer	15.00
JS	John Smoltz	15.00
JT	Jim Thome	15.00
KG	Ken Griffey Jr.	25.00
KI	Harmon Killebrew	20.00
KW	Kerry Wood	15.00
LB	Lance Berkman	15.00
MO	Joe Morgan	15.00
MR	Manny Ramirez	20.00
MS	Mike Schmidt	25.00
MT	Miguel Tejada	15.00
NM	Nick Markakis	20.00
NS	Nick Swisher	15.00
OR	Magglio Ordonez	15.00
PM	Pedro Martinez	20.00
RS	Ryne Sandberg	30.00
RY	Robin Yount	30.00
SC	Curt Schilling	15.00
TG	Tom Glavine	20.00
TH	Trevor Hoffman	15.00
VG	Vladimir Guerrero	15.00
VW	Vernon Wells	15.00

Trios

Code	Players	NM/M
BGZ	Ben Gordon, Ryan Braun, Ryan Zimmerman	100.00
BHP	Hunter Pence, Matt Holliday, Jason Bay	50.00
BTP	Troy Tulowitzki, Hunter Pence, Ryan Braun	100.00
FBH	Bill Hall, Prince Fielder, Ryan Braun	120.00
GJG	Ken Griffey Jr., Derek Jeter, Vladimir Guerrero	300.00
HAF	Jeff Francis, Garrett Atkins, Matt Holliday	40.00
HMC	Travis Hafner, Victor Martinez, Fausto Carmona	75.00
HOB	Homer Bailey, Phil Hughes, Micah Owings	75.00
JCC	Carl Crawford, Andruw Jones, Coco Crisp	40.00
LWF	John Lackey, Chone Figgins, Jered Weaver	65.00
PNZ	Joe Nathan, Jonathan Papelbon, Joel Zumaya	40.00
TRH	Miguel Tejada, Chin-Lung Hu, Hanley Ramirez	70.00
TTH	Frank Thomas, Travis Hafner, Jim Thome	100.00

Trios Memorabilia
NM/M
Common Trio: 15.00
Production 50 unless noted.
Parallels: 1-1.5X
Production 3-33
No pricing prod. 15 or less.

Code	Players	NM/M
BFB	Johnny Bench, Carlton Fisk, Yogi Berra	35.00
BPG	Ken Griffey Jr., Albert Pujols, Jason Bay	30.00
BRD	Carlos Delgado, Carlos Beltran, Jose Reyes	20.00
BZJ	Chipper Jones, Ryan Zimmerman, Ryan Braun	20.00
CMM	Michael Cuddyer, Justin Morneau, Joe Mauer	15.00
DOF	Adam Dunn, David Ortiz, Prince Fielder	25.00
GTP	Ken Griffey Jr., Albert Pujols, Frank Thomas	35.00
GWK	Vladimir Guerrero, Howie Kendrick, Jered Weaver	15.00
HAT	Garrett Atkins, Matt Holliday, Troy Tulowitzki	20.00
HMS	Travis Hafner, Victor Martinez, Grady Sizemore	15.00
HSS	Danny Haren, Huston Street, Nick Swisher	15.00
JFS	Chipper Jones, John Smoltz, Jeff Francoeur	25.00
JTR	Troy Tulowitzki, Derek Jeter, Hanley Ramirez	25.00
JWP	Andy Pettitte, Derek Jeter, Chien-Ming Wang	40.00
LRS	Derek Lee, Aramis Ramirez, Alfonso Soriano	25.00
MCG	Tom Glavine, Roger Clemens, Greg Maddux	25.00
MMS	Justin Morneau, Johan Santana, Joe Mauer	20.00
ORY	Manny Ramirez, David Ortiz, Kevin Youkilis	25.00
OVB	Magglio Ordonez, Jeremy Bonderman, Justin Verlander	20.00
PBO	Lance Berkman, Roy Oswalt, Hunter Pence	
PLM	Albert Pujols, Justin Morneau, Derek Lee	25.00
RCS	Jose Reyes, Grady Sizemore, Carl Crawford	20.00
RDM	Babe Ruth, Joe DiMaggio, Roger Maris/25	350.00
RPV	Manny Ramirez, Jason Varitek, Jonathan Papelbon	25.00
RSB	Wade Boggs, Brooks Robinson, Mike Schmidt	30.00
SRB	Cal Ripken Jr., Wade Boggs, Mike Schmidt	40.00
SWB	Ryne Sandberg, Ernie Banks, Billy Williams	30.00
TOT	David Ortiz, Frank Thomas, Jim Thome	25.00
TWH	Frank Thomas, Vernon Wells, Roy Halladay	25.00
UHR	Jimmy Rollins, Chase Utley, Cole Hamels	25.00
URU	Brian Roberts, Chase Utley, Dan Uggla	15.00
YMC	Stan Musial, Carl Yastrzemski, Rod Carew	30.00

Trios Patch
NM/M
Common Trio: 30.00
Production 30 Sets
Parallels: No Pricing
Production 1-15

Code	Players	NM/M
AER	Rick Ankiel, Jim Edmonds, Scott Rolen	35.00
BNS	Xavier Nady, Freddy Sanchez, Jason Bay	30.00
BPG	Jason Bay, Albert Pujols, Ken Griffey Jr.	60.00
CRS	Manny Ramirez, Grady Sizemore, Miguel Cabrera	40.00
DZV	Barry Zito, Omar Vizquel, Ray Durham	30.00
GKW	Vladimir Guerrero, Howie Kendrick, Jered Weaver	50.00
JCZ	Chipper Jones, Eric Chavez, Ryan Zimmerman	50.00
JJF	Andruw Jones, Chipper Jones, Jeff Francoeur	60.00
JTR	Troy Tulowitzki, Derek Jeter, Hanley Ramirez	70.00
LMS	James Loney, Russell Martin, Takashi Saito	40.00
LRS	Derek Lee, Aramis Ramirez, Alfonso Soriano	40.00
MMM	Joe Mauer, Russell Martin, Victor Martinez	30.00
MMR	Brian McCann, Russell Martin, Ivan Rodriguez	30.00
MWM	Pedro Martinez, Billy Wagner, John Maine	30.00
ORY	Manny Ramirez, David Ortiz, Kevin Youkilis	60.00
PRB	Manny Ramirez, Josh Beckett, Jonathan Papelbon	50.00
SCM	Tom Seaver, Greg Maddux, Steve Carlton	40.00
SHC	Eric Chavez, Danny Haren, Nick Swisher	40.00
SZB	Curt Schilling, Carlos Zambrano, Jeremy Bonderman	40.00
TKB	Jim Thome, Paul Konerko, Mark Buehrle	40.00
UHR	Jimmy Rollins, Chase Utley, Cole Hamels	40.00
UUK	Jeff Kent, Chase Utley, Dan Uggla	30.00

The Premier Card
No Pricing
Production 3 Sets

2008 UD Spectrum

NM/M
Common Player (1-100): .25
Common RC Auto. (101-145): 8.00
Hobby Pack (5): 7.00
Hobby Box (20): 125.00

#	Player	Price
1	Chris Young	.50
2	Brandon Webb	.50
3	Eric Byrnes	.40
4	John Smoltz	.50
5	Chipper Jones	.75
6	Jeff Francoeur	.50
7	Mark Teixeira	.50
8	Brian Roberts	.40
9	Erik Bedard	.25
10	Miguel Tejada	.50
11	Nicholas Markakis	.50
12	David Ortiz	.75
13	Daisuke Matsuzaka	1.50
14	Manny Ramirez	.75
15	Josh Beckett	.50
16	Alfonso Soriano	.50
17	Carlos Zambrano	.40
18	Derek Lee	.50
19	Derek Lee	.50
20	Aramis Ramirez	.40
21	Paul Konerko	.40
22	Jermaine Dye	.25
23	Jim Thome	.50
24	Ken Griffey Jr.	1.50
25	Brandon Phillips	.40
26	Adam Dunn	.40
27	Grady Sizemore	.75
28	Fausto Carmona	.40
29	Victor Martinez	.40
30	Travis Hafner	.40
31	Matt Holliday	.50
32	Troy Tulowitzki	.50
33	Todd Helton	.50
34	Magglio Ordonez	.40
35	Justin Verlander	.50
36	Gary Sheffield	.50
37	Miguel Cabrera	.75
38	Hanley Ramirez	.75
39	Dan Uggla	.25
40	Carlos Lee	.40
41	Roy Oswalt	.40
42	Lance Berkman	.40
43	Hunter Pence	.50
44	Alex Gordon	.50
45	David DeJesus	.25
46	Vladimir Guerrero	.75
47	Kelvim Escobar	.25
48	Chone Figgins	.40
49	Brad Penny	.25
50	Takashi Saito	.25
51	Russell Martin	.40
52	Prince Fielder	1.00
53	Ryan Braun	1.00
54	J.J. Hardy	.25
55	Johan Santana	.75
56	Justin Morneau	.40
57	Torii Hunter	.40
58	Joe Mauer	.40
59	Carlos Beltran	.50
60	David Wright	1.00
61	Carlos Delgado	.40
62	Jose Reyes	1.00
63	Derek Jeter	2.00
64	Alex Rodriguez	2.00
65	Robinson Cano	.50
66	Hideki Matsui	1.00
67	Mariano Rivera	.50
68	Danny Haren	.40
69	Nick Swisher	.40
70	Eric Chavez	.25
71	Jimmy Rollins	.50
72	Ryan Howard	.75
73	Cole Hamels	.50
74	Chase Utley	.75
75	Freddy Sanchez	.25
76	Jason Bay	.40
77	Ian Snell	.25
78	Greg Maddux	1.00
79	Jake Peavy	.40
80	Chris Young	.40
81	Barry Zito	.40
82	Tim Lincecum	.50
83	Omar Vizquel	.25
84	Felix Hernandez	.50
85	Ichiro Suzuki	1.50
86	Richie Sexson	.25
87	Albert Pujols	2.00
88	Scott Rolen	.40
89	Chris Carpenter	.40
90	Delmon Young	.40
91	Carl Crawford	.40
92	B.J. Upton	.40
93	Michael Young	.25
94	Hank Blalock	.25
95	Sammy Sosa	.40
96	Roy Halladay	.40
97	Alex Rios	.40
98	Vernon Wells	.40
99	Ryan Zimmerman	.50
100	Dmitri Young	.25
101	Alberto Gonzalez/ Auto.	15.00
102	Bill Murphy/Auto. (RC)	10.00
103	Bill White/Auto. RC	8.00
104	Billy Buckner/Auto. (RC)	8.00
105	Brandon Jones/ Auto. RC	10.00
106	Bronson Sardinha/ Auto.	8.00
107	Chin-Lung Hu/ Auto. (RC)	20.00
108	Chris Seddon/Auto. (RC)	8.00
109	Clay Buchholz/ Auto. (RC)	30.00
110	Clint Sammons/ Auto. RC	8.00
111	Daric Barton/Auto. (RC)	15.00
112	David Davidson/ Auto. RC	10.00
113	Donny Lucy/Auto. (RC)	8.00
114	Emilio Bonifacio/ Auto. RC	8.00
115	Eugenio Velez/Auto. RC	15.00
116	Harvey Garcia/ Auto. (RC)	8.00
118	Ian Kennedy/Auto. RC	10.00
119	J.R. Towles/Auto. RC	15.00
120	Jerry Blevins/Auto. RC	10.00
122	Joe Koshansky/ Auto. (RC)	10.00
123	Joey Votto/Auto. (RC)	25.00
124	Jonathan Albaladejo/ Auto. RC	10.00
125	Jonathan Meloan/ Auto. RC	10.00
126	Jose Morales/ Auto. (RC)	10.00
127	Josh Anderson/ Auto. (RC)	10.00
128	Josh Newman/Auto. RC	8.00
129	Justin Maxwell/ Auto. RC	15.00
130	Justin Ruggiano/ Auto. RC	8.00
131	Kevin Hart/Auto. (RC)	15.00
132	Lance Broadway/ Auto. RC	10.00
133	Luis Mendoza/ Auto. (RC)	10.00
134	Luke Hochevar/ Auto. RC	15.00
135	Nyjer Morgan/Auto. (RC)	12.00
136	Rob Johnson/Auto. (RC)	8.00
137	Ross Detwiler/Auto. RC	10.00
138	Ross Ohlendorf/ Auto. RC	10.00
139	Ryan Hanigan/Auto. RC	10.00
140	Seth Smith/Auto. (RC)	15.00
141	Steve Pearce/Auto. RC	15.00
142	Troy Patton/Auto. (RC)	10.00
143	Wladimir Balentien/ Auto. (RC)	10.00
144	Colt Morton/Auto. RC	10.00

Blue
Blue (1-100): 10-15X
Production 25 Sets

Gold
No Pricing
Production One Set

Green
Green (1-100): 3-6X
Production 199 Sets

Orange
Orange (1-100): 2-3X
Production 399 Sets

Red
Red (1-100): 4-8X
Production 99 Sets

RC Autos. Die-Cut
No Pricing
Production 10 Sets

Buyback Signatures
NM/M
Production 2-50

Code	Player	NM/M
JR1	Jose Reyes/70	40.00
KG1	Ken Griffey Jr./50	100.00
KG2	Ken Griffey Jr./50	100.00
KG3	Ken Griffey Jr./49	100.00
KG4	Ken Griffey Jr./50	100.00
KG5	Ken Griffey Jr./49	100.00
KG6	Ken Griffey Jr./50	100.00
KG7	Ken Griffey Jr./50	100.00
KG8	Ken Griffey Jr./50	100.00
KG9	Ken Griffey Jr./49	100.00
RA3	Roberto Alomar/50	25.00
RA4	Roberto Alomar/25	25.00
RA5	Roberto Alomar/30	25.00
RA6	Roberto Alomar/50	25.00

Derek Jeter Retrospectrum
NM/M
Common Jeter (1-100): 5.00
Red: 2X
Production 99 Sets
Autos: No Pricing
Production Two Sets

Dual Swatches
NM/M
Common Duo: 10.00
Production 99 Sets

Code	Players	NM/M
AP	Pat Burrell, Aaron Rowand	10.00
BM	Josh Beckett, Daisuke Matsuzaka	30.00
BP	Hunter Pence, Ryan Braun	25.00
CL	Noah Lowry, Matt Cain	10.00
CT	Tim Wakefield, Curt Schilling	15.00
CW	Miguel Cabrera, Dontrelle Willis	10.00
CY	Carl Crawford, Delmon Young	10.00
DC	Derek Jeter, Joba Chamberlain	80.00
FB	Prince Fielder, Ryan Braun	25.00
FD	Danny Haren, Felix Hernandez	15.00
FK	Jeff Kent, Rafael Furcal	10.00

Code	Player	Price
FM	Brian McCann, Jeff Francoeur	20.00
GC	Bartolo Colon, Vladimir Guerrero	15.00
GD	Ken Griffey Jr., Adam Dunn	20.00
GG	Brian Giles, Adrian Gonzalez	10.00
GM	Greg Maddux, Tom Glavine	30.00
GO	Vladimir Guerrero, Magglio Ordonez	20.00
GP	Jason Giambi, Jorge Posada	15.00
GV	Victor Martinez, Grady Sizemore	15.00
HB	Roy Halladay, A.J. Burnett	10.00
HC	Mike Cameron, Torii Hunter	10.00
HF	Jeff Francoeur, Matt Holliday	15.00
HH	Todd Helton, Matt Holliday	15.00
HJ	Felix Hernandez, Kenji Johjima	15.00
HS	Huston Street, Rich Harden	10.00
JC	Derek Jeter, Robinson Cano	35.00
JF	Andruw Jones, Jeff Francoeur	15.00
JP	Derek Jeter, Albert Pujols	40.00
JR	Derek Jeter, Jose Reyes	35.00
JT	John Smoltz, Tim Hudson	20.00
JW	Randy Johnson, Brandon Webb	20.00
MH	Torii Hunter, Justin Morneau	15.00
ML	Brett Myers, Brad Lidge	10.00
MP	Juan Pierre, Russell Martin	15.00
MR	Ivan Rodriguez, Victor Martinez	15.00
MW	Pedro Martinez, Billy Wagner	20.00
OB	Lance Berkman, Roy Oswalt	15.00
OG	Magglio Ordonez, Curtis Granderson	25.00
OP	David Ortiz, Albert Pujols	30.00
OR	Manny Ramirez, David Ortiz	30.00
PE	Jim Edmonds, Albert Pujols	25.00
PJ	Justin Morneau, Prince Fielder	20.00
PM	Greg Maddux, Jake Peavy	20.00
PS	Alfonso Soriano, Albert Pujols	30.00
PW	Jake Peavy, Brandon Webb	15.00
RB	Carlos Beltran, Jose Reyes	20.00
RC	Gary Sheffield, Miguel Cabrera	20.00
RF	Rafael Furcal, Jose Reyes	20.00
RH	J.J. Hardy, Hanley Ramirez	15.00
RR	Jimmy Rollins, Jose Reyes	25.00
RU	Hanley Ramirez, Dan Uggla	15.00
SB	Adrian Beltre, Richie Sexson	10.00
SH	Ben Sheets, J.J. Hardy	10.00
SL	Derek Lee, Alfonso Soriano	15.00
SM	Johan Santana, Joe Mauer	15.00
SW	Johan Santana, Dontrelle Willis	15.00
TD	Jim Thome, Jermaine Dye	15.00
TM	Miguel Tejada, Nick Markakis	15.00
JH	Chase Utley, Cole Hamels	20.00
VB	Jeremy Bonderman, Justin Verlander	25.00
VR	Ivan Rodriguez, Justin Verlander	20.00
VY	Jason Varitek, Kevin Youkilis	15.00
WR	Vernon Wells, Alex Rios	10.00
YK	Michael Young, Ian Kinsler	10.00
L	Derek Lee, Carlos Zambrano	20.00

Retrospectrum Swatches

		NM/M
Common Player:		4.00
Production 99 Sets		
Parallel:		1-1.5X
Production 45 Sets		
atch:		1.5-2X
Production 25 Sets		
K	Adam Kennedy	4.00
K	Albert Pujols	15.00
	Derek Jeter	20.00
	Johnny Estrada	4.00

Code	Player	Price
KM	Kevin Millwood	4.00
LH	Livan Hernandez	4.00
RK	Ryan Klesko	4.00
AB	Aaron Boone	4.00
AG	Adrian Gonzalez	6.00
AH	Aubrey Huff	4.00
AJ	A.J. Burnett	4.00
AK	Austin Kearns	4.00
AL	Adam LaRoche	4.00
AP	Andy Pettitte	4.00
AR	Aaron Rowand	4.00
AS	Alfonso Soriano	8.00
BA	Bobby Abreu	6.00
BC	Bartolo Colon	4.00
BE	Adrian Beltre	4.00
BG	Brian Giles	4.00
BZ	Barry Zito	4.00
CA	Sean Casey	4.00
CC	Coco Crisp	4.00
CD	Carlos Delgado	6.00
CL	Carlos Lee	6.00
CY	Chris Young	4.00
DW	David Wells	4.00
EG	Eric Gagne	4.00
ER	Edgar Renteria	4.00
FG	Freddy Garcia	4.00
FT	Frank Thomas	8.00
GM	Greg Maddux	10.00
GS	Gary Sheffield	6.00
IR	Ivan Rodriguez	6.00
JB	Josh Barfield	4.00
JD	J.D. Drew	4.00
JJ	Jacque Jones	4.00
JO	Josh Beckett	8.00
JS	Jason Schmidt	4.00
JT	Jim Thome	6.00
LG	Luis Gonzalez	4.00
MA	Moises Alou	6.00
ME	Morgan Ensberg	4.00
MG	Marcus Giles	4.00
ML	Mark Loretta	4.00
MP	Mike Piazza	10.00
MT	Mark Teixeira	8.00
OV	Omar Vizquel	4.00
RF	Rafael Furcal	6.00
RJ	Randy Johnson	8.00
SS	Shannon Stewart	4.00
TI	Tadahito Iguchi	4.00
WT	Willy Taveras	4.00

Spectrum of Stars Signatures

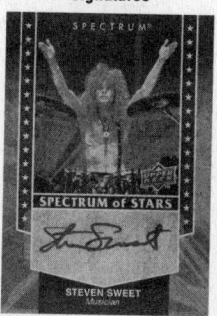

		NM/M
Common Auto.:		8.00
Die-Cuts:		1.5X
Production 25 Sets		
AP	A.J. Pero	8.00
BP	Butch Patrick	30.00
CM	Christopher McDonald	25.00
DA	Taylor Dayne	35.00
DD	Don Dokken	15.00
EM	Erin Moran	25.00
EO	Eddie Ojeda	8.00
ER	Eric Roberts	20.00
ET	Erik Turner	8.00
FS	Frank Stallone	15.00
HW	Henry Winkler	60.00
JA	Joey Allen	10.00
JD	Jerry Dixon	10.00
JF	Jay Jay French	8.00
JG	Joe Gannascoli	30.00
JL	Jani Lane	15.00
KO	Martin Kove	25.00
LH	Larry Hagman	35.00
LT	Larry Thomas	15.00
MA	Miljenko Matijevic	8.00
MB	Michael Biehn	50.00
MK	Margot Kidder	25.00
MM	Mark Mendoza	8.00
PP	Pat Priest	25.00
PS	P.J. Soles	20.00
RF	Robert Funaro	20.00
SB	Sebastian Bach	20.00
SE	Shirley Eaton	15.00
SN	Dee Snider	15.00
SP	Stephen Pearcy	15.00
SS	Steven Sweet	10.00
TB	Tom Bosley	40.00
TR	Mike Tramp	10.00
VN	Vince Neil	20.00

Swatches

		NM/M
Common Player:		4.00
Production 99 Sets		
Dark Gray:		No Pricing
Production One Set		
Green:		1X

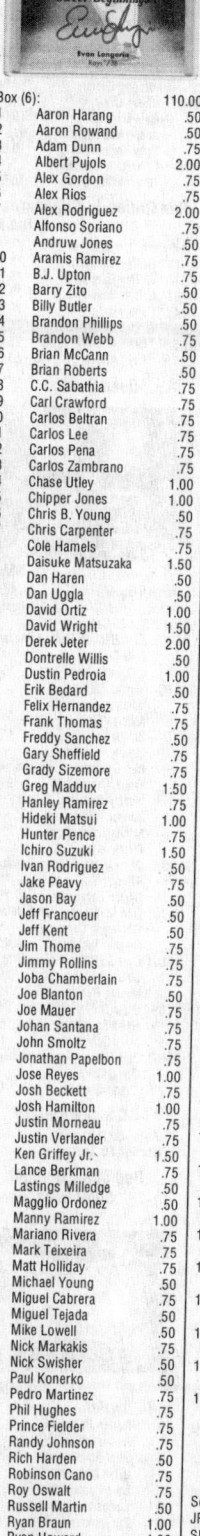

Production 50 Sets		
Green Patch:		No Pricing
Production 15 Sets		
Blue:		No Pricing
Production 15 Sets		
Orange:		1X
Production 75 Sets		
Red:		1-1.5X
Production 35 Sets		
Purple:		1-2X
Production 2-58		
No pricing prod. 20 or less		
AB	A.J. Burnett	4.00
AH	Aaron Harang	4.00
AJ	Andruw Jones	6.00
AP	Albert Pujols	15.00
BB	Boof Bonser	4.00
BC	Bartolo Colon	4.00
BE	Adrian Beltre	6.00
BG	Brian Giles	4.00
BM	Brian McCann	6.00
BS	Ben Sheets	6.00
BU	B.J. Upton	6.00
BW	Billy Wagner	4.00
CA	Chris Carpenter	6.00
CB	Carlos Beltran	8.00
CC	Carl Crawford	8.00
CG	Carlos Guillen	4.00
CH	Cole Hamels	8.00
CJ	Chipper Jones	10.00
CS	Curt Schilling	8.00
CU	Chase Utley	10.00
CZ	Carlos Zambrano	8.00
DH	Danny Haren	6.00
DJ	Derek Jeter	20.00
DL	Derek Lee	8.00
DM	Daisuke Matsuzaka	20.00
DO	David Ortiz	8.00
DU	Dan Uggla	4.00
DW	Dontrelle Willis	4.00
EC	Eric Chavez	4.00
FH	Felix Hernandez	8.00
FS	Freddy Sanchez	4.00
GA	Garrett Atkins	4.00
GJ	Geoff Jenkins	4.00
GM	Greg Maddux	10.00
GR	Curtis Granderson	10.00
GS	Grady Sizemore	8.00
HA	Travis Hafner	6.00
HB	Hank Blalock	6.00
HO	Trevor Hoffman	4.00
HP	Hunter Pence	8.00
HR	Hanley Ramirez	8.00
HU	Torii Hunter	6.00
IK	Ian Kinsler	6.00
IR	Ivan Rodriguez	6.00
JA	Conor Jackson	6.00
JB	Josh Beckett	8.00
JC	Joba Chamberlain	20.00
JD	Jermaine Dye	4.00
JE	Jim Edmonds	4.00
JF	Jeff Francoeur	8.00
JG	Jason Giambi	6.00
JH	J.J. Hardy	4.00
JK	Jeff Kent	4.00
JM	Joe Mauer	6.00
JP	Jhonny Peralta	4.00
JR	Jose Reyes	10.00
JS	Johan Santana	8.00
JT	Jim Thome	6.00
JV	Jason Varitek	6.00
JW	Jered Weaver	6.00
KG	Ken Griffey Jr.	15.00
KJ	Kenji Johjima	6.00
KY	Kevin Youkilis	6.00
LB	Lance Berkman	6.00
MC	Miguel Cabrera	8.00
MG	Matt Garza	4.00
MH	Matt Holliday	8.00
MO	Justin Morneau	8.00
MP	Mike Piazza	10.00
MR	Manny Ramirez	8.00
MT	Miguel Tejada	6.00
MY	Michael Young	6.00
OR	Magglio Ordonez	6.00
OS	Roy Oswalt	6.00
PA	Jonathan Papelbon	15.00
PE	Jake Peavy	6.00
PF	Prince Fielder	10.00
PI	Juan Pierre	4.00
PM	Pedro Martinez	8.00
PO	Jorge Posada	6.00
RA	Aramis Ramirez	8.00
RB	Ryan Braun	15.00
RC	Robinson Cano	10.00
RF	Rafael Furcal	6.00
RH	Roy Halladay	8.00
RJ	Randy Johnson	8.00
RM	Russell Martin	8.00
RS	Richie Sexson	4.00
RZ	Ryan Zimmerman	6.00
SM	John Smoltz	8.00
SO	Jeremy Sowers	4.00
SR	Scott Rolen	6.00
TH	Tim Hudson	4.00
TW	Tim Wakefield	4.00
VG	Vladimir Guerrero	8.00
VM	Victor Martinez	6.00
VW	Vernon Wells	4.00

Swatches Autographs

		NM/M
Production 30 unless noted.		
AH	Aaron Harang	20.00
AJ	Andruw Jones	15.00
BB	Boof Bonser	10.00
BG	Brian Giles	15.00
BS	Ben Sheets	20.00
BU	B.J. Upton	30.00
CC	Carl Crawford	20.00
CH	Cole Hamels	40.00
CJ	Chipper Jones	85.00
DH	Danny Haren	15.00
DL	Derek Lee	25.00
DM	Daisuke Matsuzaka	100.00
DU	Dan Uggla	15.00
DW	Dontrelle Willis	15.00
EC	Eric Chavez	15.00
FH	Felix Hernandez	40.00
GR	Curtis Granderson	40.00
HA	Travis Hafner	20.00
HP	Hunter Pence	20.00
HR	Hanley Ramirez	40.00
HU	Torii Hunter	20.00
JM	Joe Mauer	40.00
JS	Johan Santana	40.00
JT	Jim Thome	50.00
JV	Jason Varitek	50.00
JW	Jered Weaver	20.00
KG	Ken Griffey Jr./15	100.00
MC	Miguel Cabrera	40.00
MG	Matt Garza	40.00
MH	Matt Holliday	40.00
MT	Miguel Tejada	35.00
OS	Roy Oswalt	25.00
PA	Jonathan Papelbon	40.00
PF	Prince Fielder	40.00
RA	Aramis Ramirez	30.00
RB	Ryan Braun	50.00
RM	Russell Martin	20.00
RZ	Ryan Zimmerman	25.00
SO	Jeremy Sowers	15.00
TH	Tim Hudson	20.00
VG	Vladimir Guerrero	50.00
VM	Victor Martinez	20.00

Three Star Swatches

		NM/M
Common Trio:		10.00
Production 75 Sets		
GDH	Ken Griffey Jr., Adam Dunn, Aaron Harang	20.00
HBK	Erik Bedard, Scott Kazmir, Cole Hamels	15.00
JCC	Derek Jeter, Robinson Cano, Joba Chamberlain	35.00
JPG	Ken Griffey Jr., Derek Jeter, Albert Pujols	40.00
KHS	Freddy Sanchez, Aaron Hill, Ian Kinsler	15.00
MGS	Greg Maddux, Tom Glavine, John Smoltz	30.00
MJS	Randy Johnson, Pedro Martinez, Curt Schilling	20.00
MRM	Ivan Rodriguez, Victor Martinez, Joe Mauer	15.00
OBP	Lance Berkman, Roy Oswalt, Hunter Pence	20.00
OVS	Gary Sheffield, Magglio Ordonez, Justin Verlander	15.00
PER	Jim Edmonds, Scott Rolen, Albert Pujols	20.00
PSB	Josh Beckett, Johan Santana, Jake Peavy	20.00
RBM	Carlos Beltran, Pedro Martinez, Jose Reyes	20.00
RUH	Jimmy Rollins, Chase Utley, Cole Hamels	25.00
SBH	Carlos Beltran, Torii Hunter, Grady Sizemore	15.00
SCG	Vladimir Guerrero, Alfonso Soriano, Miguel Cabrera	20.00
SJT	Chipper Jones, John Smoltz, Mark Teixeira	15.00
SMH	Travis Hafner, Victor Martinez, Grady Sizemore	15.00
SMM	Justin Morneau, Johan Santana, Joe Mauer	20.00
ZSL	Derek Lee, Alfonso Soriano, Carlos Zambrano	15.00

Four Star Swatches

No Pricing
Production 15 Sets

2008 UD Sweet Spot

	NM/M
Common Player (1-100):	.50
Common RC Auto. (101-150):	8.00
Production 199-699	
Pack (8):	20.00
Box (6):	110.00

No.	Player	Price
1	Aaron Harang	.50
2	Aaron Rowand	.50
3	Adam Dunn	.75
4	Albert Pujols	2.00
5	Alex Gordon	.75
6	Alex Rios	.75
7	Alex Rodriguez	2.00
8	Alfonso Soriano	.75
9	Andruw Jones	.50
10	Aramis Ramirez	.75
11	B.J. Upton	.75
12	Barry Zito	.50
13	Billy Butler	.50
14	Brandon Phillips	.50
15	Brandon Webb	.75
16	Brian McCann	.50
17	Brian Roberts	.50
18	C.C. Sabathia	.75
19	Carl Crawford	.75
20	Carlos Beltran	.75
21	Carlos Lee	.75
22	Carlos Pena	.75
23	Carlos Zambrano	.75
24	Chase Utley	1.00
25	Chipper Jones	1.00
26	Chris B. Young	.50
27	Chris Carpenter	.75
28	Cole Hamels	.75
29	Daisuke Matsuzaka	1.50
30	Dan Haren	.50
31	Dan Uggla	.50
32	David Ortiz	1.00
33	David Wright	1.50
34	Derek Jeter	2.00
35	Dontrelle Willis	.50
36	Dustin Pedroia	1.00
37	Erik Bedard	.50
38	Felix Hernandez	.75
39	Frank Thomas	.75
40	Freddy Sanchez	.50
41	Gary Sheffield	.75
42	Grady Sizemore	.75
43	Greg Maddux	1.50
44	Hanley Ramirez	.75
45	Hideki Matsui	1.00
46	Hunter Pence	.75
47	Ichiro Suzuki	1.50
48	Ivan Rodriguez	.50
49	Jake Peavy	.75
50	Jason Bay	.50
51	Jeff Francoeur	.50
52	Jeff Kent	.50
53	Jim Thome	.75
54	Jimmy Rollins	.75
55	Joba Chamberlain	.75
56	Joe Blanton	.50
57	Joe Mauer	.75
58	Johan Santana	.75
59	John Smoltz	.75
60	Jonathan Papelbon	.75
61	Jose Reyes	1.00
62	Josh Beckett	.75
63	Josh Hamilton	1.00
64	Justin Morneau	.75
65	Justin Verlander	.75
66	Ken Griffey Jr.	1.50
67	Lance Berkman	.75
68	Lastings Milledge	.50
69	Magglio Ordonez	.50
70	Manny Ramirez	1.00
71	Mariano Rivera	.75
72	Mark Teixeira	.75
73	Matt Holliday	.75
74	Michael Young	.50
75	Miguel Cabrera	.75
76	Miguel Tejada	.50
77	Mike Lowell	.50
78	Nick Markakis	.75
79	Nick Swisher	.50
80	Paul Konerko	.50
81	Pedro Martinez	.75
82	Phil Hughes	.75
83	Prince Fielder	.75
84	Randy Johnson	.75
85	Rich Harden	.50
86	Robinson Cano	.50
87	Roy Oswalt	.75
88	Russell Martin	.50
89	Ryan Braun	1.00
90	Ryan Howard	1.00
91	Ryan Zimmerman	.75
92	Scott Rolen	.50
93	Tom Glavine	.75
94	Torii Hunter	.50
95	Travis Hafner	.50
96	Trevor Hoffman	.50
97	Troy Tulowitzki	.50
98	Vernon Wells	.50
99	Victor Martinez	.50

No.	Player	Price
100	Vladimir Guerrero	.75
101	Alex Romero/ Auto./499 (RC)	8.00
102	Alexei Ramirez/ Auto./399 RC	25.00
103	Bobby Korecky/ Auto./399 RC	10.00
104	Bobby Wilson/ Auto./499 RC	8.00
105	Bradley Harman/ Auto./699 RC	6.00
106	Brandon Boggs/ Auto./699 (RC)	8.00
107	Brent Lillibridge/ Auto./399 (RC)	8.00
108	Brian Barton/ Auto./699 RC	8.00
109	Brian Bass/ Auto./699 (RC)	8.00
110	Brian Bixler/ Auto./699 (RC)	6.00
111	Brian Bocock/ Auto./399 RC	8.00
112	Burke Badenhop/ Auto./699 RC	6.00
113	Chin-Lung Hu/ Auto./199 (RC)	20.00
114	Clay Buchholz/ Auto./199 (RC)	20.00
115	Clay Timpner/ Auto./699 (RC)	8.00
116	Cory Wade/ Auto./699 (RC)	6.00
117	Daric Barton/ Auto./399 (RC)	8.00
118	Eider Torres/ Auto./699 (RC)	10.00
119	Jonathan Van Every/ Auto./235 RC	8.00
120	Emmanuel Burriss/ Auto./399 RC	6.00
121	Evan Longoria/ Auto./249 RC	100.00
122	Felipe Paulino/ Auto./499 RC	6.00
123	Fernando Hernandez/ Auto./499 RC	8.00
124	German Duran/ Auto./699 RC	6.00
125	Greg Smith/ Auto./399 RC	8.00
126	Hernan Iribarren/ Auto./699 (RC)	10.00
127	Ian Kennedy/ Auto./249 RC	20.00
128	Jed Lowrie/ Auto./349 (RC)	15.00
129	Jeff Clement/ Auto./199 (RC)	10.00
130	Jesse Carlson/ Auto./649 RC	8.00
131	Johnny Cueto/ Auto./249 RC	20.00
133	Clayton Kershaw/ Auto./199 RC	30.00
134	Josh Newman/ Auto./699 RC	8.00
135	Justin Masterson/ Auto./399 RC	15.00
136	Kevin Hart/ Auto./399 (RC)	8.00
137	Luke Hochevar/ Auto./199 RC	15.00
138	Jay Bruce/ Auto./399 (RC)	40.00
139	Max Scherzer/ Auto./299 RC	25.00
140	Nick Adenhart/ Auto./399 (RC)	15.00
141	Nick Blackburn/ Auto./399 RC	15.00
142	Nyjer Morgan/ Auto./399 (RC)	12.00
143	Ramon Troncoso/ Auto./699 RC	8.00
144	Randor Bierd/ Auto./499 RC	6.00
145	Rich Thompson/ Auto./399 RC	6.00
146	Robinzon Diaz/ Auto./699 (RC)	8.00
147	Ross Ohlendorf/ Auto./399 RC	6.00
148	Steve Holm/ Auto./699 RC	6.00
149	Wesley Wright/ Auto./499 RC	8.00
150	Wladimir Balentien/ Auto./399 (RC)	12.00

Bat Barrel Black Ink Signatures

		NM/M
Some not priced due to scarcity.		
JR	Jose Reyes/51	30.00
SR	Scott Rolen/20	20.00
TG	Tony Gwynn/25	50.00
VM	Victor Martinez/21	25.00
CY	Carl Yastrzemski/15	80.00
DM	Don Mattingly/15	120.00
JR	Jim Rice/25	40.00
MY	Michael Young/25	25.00
NR	Nolan Ryan/25	100.00
OP	Oliver Perez/26	15.00
OS	Ozzie Smith/25	50.00

Bat Barrel Blue Ink Signatures

NM/M
Production 1-75
JR	Jose Reyes/30	65.00
SR	Scott Rolen/25	20.00
TG	Tony Gwynn/75	40.00
VM	Victor Martinez/25	30.00
CF	Carlton Fisk/25	40.00
CY	Carl Yastrzemski/25	65.00
DM	Don Mattingly/25	75.00
MY	Michael Young/24	25.00
OP	Oliver Perez/25	25.00
RC	Roger Clemens/28	65.00

Bat Barrel Silver Ink Signatures

NM/M
Production 1-50
Red Ink: No Pricing
Production 4-10
Gold Ink: No Pricing
Production One Set
TG	Tony Gwynn/50	40.00

Black Glove Silver Ink Signatures

NM/M
Production (3-250):
BH	Bill Hall/	10.00
BO	Bobby Richardson/250	20.00
CB	Chad Billingsley/246	20.00
MK	Matt Kemp/245	25.00
BD	Bucky Dent/250	25.00
BG	Bob Gibson/150	35.00
CW	Chien-Ming Wang/250	80.00
DB	Don Baylor/100	20.00
DL	Don Larsen/150	40.00
JH	Josh Hamilton/250	60.00
LB	Lance Berkman/99	25.00
SK	"Moose" Skowron/250	30.00

Black Stitch Signatures

No Pricing
Production One Set

Brown Glove Black Ink Signatures

NM/M
Production 7-100
AE	Andre Ethier/20	30.00
CH	Cole Hamels/20	60.00
EE	Edwin Encarnacion/100	15.00
GR	Ken Griffey Jr./20	100.00
JR	Jose Reyes/30	40.00
JV	Justin Verlander/20	25.00
KG	Ken Griffey Jr./20	100.00
KJ	Kelly Johnson/100	15.00
VM	Victor Martinez/20	30.00
SR2	Scott Rolen/15	25.00
BG	Bob Gibson/100	40.00
DB	Don Baylor/150	20.00
JR	Jim Rice/15	50.00

Brown Glove Silver Ink Signatures

NM/M
Production 1-150
EE	Edwin Encarnacion/150	15.00
TG	Tony Gwynn/50	50.00

Brown Glove Blue Ink Signatures

NM/M
Production 5-20
Red Ink: No Pricing
Production 1-10
Gold Ink: No Pricing
Production 5-15
AB	Adrian Beltre/20	25.00
JR	Jose Reyes/20	50.00
CF	Carlton Fisk/25	30.00
DM	Don Mattingly/25	65.00

Double Swatch

NM/M
Common Duo: 8.00
Dual Patch: No Pricing
Production 25 Sets
BM	Josh Beckett, Daisuke Matsuzaka	10.00
BT	Lance Berkman, Mark Teixeira	8.00
CW	Miguel Cabrera, Dontrelle Willis	8.00
DR	Andre Dawson, Tim Raines	10.00
FB	Prince Fielder, Ryan Braun	15.00
GS	Grady Sizemore, Ken Griffey Jr.	15.00
HM	Travis Hafner, Justin Morneau	8.00
JH	Hanley Ramirez, Derek Jeter	15.00
JR	Nolan Ryan, Randy Johnson	20.00
JZ	Ryan Zimmerman, Chipper Jones	8.00
LP	Derek Lee, Albert Pujols	15.00
MJ	Don Mattingly, Derek Jeter	25.00
MM	Justin Morneau, Joe Mauer	10.00
MS	Pedro Martinez, Johan Santana	10.00
MW	Don Mattingly, Dave Winfield	20.00
OZ	Roy Oswalt, Carlos Zambrano	8.00
PL	Jake Peavy, Tim Lincecum	10.00
RC	Robinson Cano, Brian Roberts	8.00
RM	Cal Ripken Jr., Eddie Murray	20.00
RO	David Ortiz, Manny Ramirez	15.00
RP	Jonathan Papelbon, Mariano Rivera	10.00
SH	Matt Holliday, Alfonso Soriano	10.00
UH	Chase Utley, Cole Hamels	15.00
VH	Justin Verlander, Felix Hernandez	10.00
WM	Daisuke Matsuzaka, Chien-Ming Wang	15.00

Ken Griffey Jr. Signatures

NM/M
Production 15-300
KG1	Griffey Bats/230	75.00
KG2	Griffey Bats/230	75.00
KG3	Griffey Bats/230	75.00
KG4	Griffey Bats/230	75.00
KG5	Griffey Bats/243	75.00
KG6	"1997 AL MVP"/300	75.00
KG7	"1992 ASG MVP"/135	80.00

Quad Swatch

NM/M
Common Quad: 10.00
Patch: No Pricing
Production 25 Sets
BSPS	Josh Beckett, Johan Santana, Jake Peavy, C.C. Sabathia	15.00
GLPC	Miguel Cabrera, Vladimir Guerrero, Albert Pujols, Carlos Lee	15.00
GTTR	Manny Ramirez, Ken Griffey Jr., Jim Thome, Frank Thomas	20.00
JYRR	Hanley Ramirez, Jimmy Rollins, Michael Young, Derek Jeter	20.00
LRSZ	Derrek Lee, Aramis Ramirez, Alfonso Soriano, Carlos Zambrano	20.00
MJJC	Don Mattingly, Derek Jeter, Robinson Cano, Reggie Jackson	25.00
RSOM	Curt Schilling, David Ortiz, Daisuke Matsuzaka, Manny Ramirez	25.00
SCSS	Ozzie Smith, Will Clark, Ryne Sandberg, Mike Schmidt	40.00
TGHO	Jim Thome, Travis Hafner, David Ortiz, Jason Giambi	10.00

RC Signatures/50

RC Autos/50 (101-150): 1-1.5X
Production 50 Sets

Red Stitch Blue Ink Signatures

NM/M
Production 1-315
AB	Adrian Beltre/74	20.00
AE	Andre Ethier/250	20.00
BB	Boof Bonser/300	10.00
BR	Brian Roberts/290	15.00
CH	Cole Hamels/300	40.00
CQ	Carlos Quentin/315	30.00
CR	Cal Ripken Jr./275	75.00
FL	Francisco Liriano/190	15.00
HK	Hong-Chih Kuo/300	35.00
HR	Hanley Ramirez/300	35.00
HS	Huston Street/225	12.00
JK	Jason Kubel/300	12.00
JN	Joe Nathan/225	15.00
AW	Adam Wainwright/135	25.00
BR	Brooks Robinson/48	50.00
CY	Carl Yastrzemski/50	40.00
DL	Don Larsen/250	35.00
DO	David Ortiz/49	75.00
DW	Dontrelle Willis/174	15.00
EC	Eric Chavez/49	15.00
EG	Eric Gagne/49	20.00
HK	Harmon Killebrew/229	40.00
IK	Ian Kinsler/150	25.00
JD	J.D. Drew/49	20.00
JH	Josh Johnson/180	15.00
JS	Johan Santana/38	65.00
KW	Kerry Wood/73	20.00
MM	Mark Mulder/124	15.00
TH	Tim Hudson/49	20.00
WC	Will Clark/200	30.00
JV	Justin Verlander/299	15.00
PM	Paul Molitor/250	25.00
RS	Ryne Sandberg/60	40.00
TG	Tony Gwynn/105	40.00
TS	Takashi Saito/300	20.00
VM	Victor Martinez/15	30.00
CR	Cal Ripken Jr./258	75.00

Red Stitch Black Ink Signatures

NM/M
Production 1-366
AB	Adrian Beltre/84	15.00
BH	Bill Hall/125	10.00
BO	Bobby Richardson/250	25.00
BP	Brandon Phillips/299	20.00
CB	Chad Billingsley/250	15.00
EE	Edwin Encarnacion/250	15.00
JR	Jose Reyes/27	65.00
JS	John Smoltz/59	50.00
JT	Jim Thome/358	30.00
KJ	Kelly Johnson/248	10.00
LO	Lyle Overbay/366	10.00
MK	Matt Kemp/200	10.00
RS	Ryne Sandberg/226	40.00
SR	Scott Rolen/207	15.00
TG	Tony Gwynn/25	50.00
TH	Travis Hafner/171	15.00
VM	Victor Martinez/15	30.00
RS2	Ryne Sandberg/265	40.00
BD	Bucky Dent/145	20.00
BG	Bob Gibson/250	35.00
BP	Brandon Phillips/200	20.00
CW	Chien-Ming Wang/95	50.00
DB	Don Baylor/250	20.00
DO	David Ortiz/56	65.00
EC	Eric Chavez/15	15.00
EG	Eric Gagne/59	20.00
JD	J.D. Drew/45	20.00
JH	Josh Hamilton/250	50.00
JR	Jim Rice/99	25.00
JS	Johan Santana/32	70.00
KW	Kerry Wood/58	20.00
MA	Daisuke Matsuzaka/250	120.00
MY	Michael Young/38	20.00
SK	Bill "Moose" Skowron/250	30.00
TG	Tom Glavine/222	35.00
TH	Tim Hudson/57	20.00

Red Stitch Red Ink Signatures

NM/M
Production 1-35
JR	Jose Reyes/35	60.00

Red/Blue Stitch Black Ink Signatures

NM/M
Production 1-126
TG	Tony Gwynn/25	50.00
TH	Travis Hafner/126	15.00
JR	Jim Rice/25	20.00
OS	Ozzie Smith/25	50.00

Red/Blue Stitch Blue Ink Signatures

NM/M
Production 3-100
AB	Adrian Beltre/19	25.00
CQ	Carlos Quentin/35	25.00
JR	Jose Reyes/25	40.00
VM	Victor Martinez/15	30.00
CU	Chase Utley/100	65.00
JR	Jim Rice/15	60.00
JS	Johan Santana/15	75.00
OS	Ozzie Smith/15	75.00

Red/Blue Stitch Red Ink Signatures

NM/M
Production 5-304
AB	Adrian Beltre/18	25.00
AE	Andre Ethier/50	20.00
BB	Boof Bonser/50	10.00
BR	Brian Roberts/199	20.00
FL	Francisco Liriano/48	20.00
HK	Hong-Chih Kuo/50	40.00
HR	Hanley Ramirez/50	30.00
HS	Huston Street/199	10.00
JK	Jason Kubel/50	15.00
JN	Joe Nathan/202	20.00
JP	Jonathan Papelbon/304	20.00
JS	John Smoltz/291	50.00
JT	Jim Thome/50	35.00
JV	Justin Verlander/125	20.00
AW	Adam Wainwright/50	25.00
DW	Dontrelle Willis/73	15.00
JL	Jon Lester/90	40.00

Single Swatch

NM/M
Common Player: 4.00
Patch: 1.5-2X
AP	Albert Pujols	15.00
AS	Alfonso Soriano	8.00
BU	B.J. Upton	6.00
CA	Miguel Cabrera	8.00
CF	Carlton Fisk	6.00
CJ	Chipper Jones	8.00
CM	Chien-Ming Wang	10.00
CR	Cal Ripken Jr.	15.00
CU	Chase Utley	10.00
CY	Carl Yastrzemski	10.00
CZ	Carlos Zambrano	8.00
DH	Dan Haren	4.00
DJ	Derek Jeter	15.00
DM	Daisuke Matsuzaka	8.00
DO	David Ortiz	8.00
DW	Dontrelle Willis	4.00
EM	Eddie Murray	6.00
FH	Felix Hernandez	6.00
FL	Francisco Liriano	6.00
FT	Frank Thomas	8.00
GS	Grady Sizemore	8.00
HR	Hanley Ramirez	6.00
IR	Ivan Rodriguez	4.00
JB	Jeremy Bonderman	4.00
JM	Joe Mauer	6.00
JP	Jake Peavy	6.00
JS	Johan Santana	6.00
JT	Jim Thome	6.00
MA	Don Mattingly	10.00
MO	Joe Morgan	6.00
MR	Manny Ramirez	8.00
MS	Mike Schmidt	8.00
MT	Mark Teixeira	6.00
NM	Nick Markakis	6.00
NR	Nolan Ryan	15.00
OS	Ozzie Smith	8.00
PF	Prince Fielder	8.00
PM	Pedro Martinez	6.00
RA	Roberto Alomar	6.00
RG	Ron Guidry	6.00
RJ	Reggie Jackson	10.00
RS	Ryne Sandberg	10.00
RY	Robin Yount	8.00
SM	John Smoltz	6.00
TG	Tony Gwynn	8.00
TH	Travis Hafner	6.00
TR	Tim Raines	6.00
VG	Vladimir Guerrero	6.00
WB	Wade Boggs	6.00
WI	Dave Winfield	8.00

Triple Swatch

NM/M
Common Trio: 10.00
Patch: No Pricing
Production 25 Sets
BOP	Lance Berkman, Roy Oswalt, Hunter Pence	15.00
FPB	Hunter Pence, Ryan Braun, Jeff Francoeur	12.00
GBY	Robin Yount, Tony Gwynn, Wade Boggs	25.00
GOO	David Ortiz, Magglio Ordonez, Vladimir Guerrero	12.00
JMH	Randy Johnson, Pedro Martinez, Trevor Hoffman	15.00
JMJ	Don Mattingly, Derek Jeter, Reggie Jackson	25.00
LHW	Felix Hernandez, Jered Weaver, Francisco Liriano	10.00
LPF	Derrek Lee, Prince Fielder, Albert Pujols	15.00
MCH	Chris Carpenter, Greg Maddux, Roy Halladay	15.00
PMM	Joe Mauer, Russell Martin, Jorge Posada	10.00
SPM	Curt Schilling, Jonathan Papelbon, Daisuke Matsuzaka	20.00
SRJ	Cal Ripken Jr., Derek Jeter, Ozzie Smith	30.00
SSP	Jake Peavy, Johan Santana, John Smoltz	12.00
TGT	Khalil Greene, Troy Tulowitzki, Miguel Tejada	10.00
WHS	Grady Sizemore, Vernon Wells, Torii Hunter	

USA Black Stitch Red Ink Signatures

NM/M
Production 140-260
Silver Ink: No Pricing

Production 11-13
AG	A.J. Griffin/230	12.00
AO	Andrew Oliver/220	25.00
BS	Blake Smith/219	15.00
CC	Christian Colon/230	15.00
CH	Chris Hernandez/220	15.00
DD	Derek Dietrich/200	20.00
HM	Hunter Morris/219	20.00
JF	Josh Fellhauer/230	12.00
KD	Kentrail Davis/200	12.00
KG	Kyle Gibson/198	30.00
KR	Kevin Rhoderick/200	15.00
KV	Kendal Volz/140	15.00
MD	Matt den Dekker/200	15.00
MG	Micah Gibbs/200	20.00
ML	Mike Leake/189	35.00
MM	Mike Minor/219	15.00
RJ	Ryan Jackson/222	15.00
RL	Ryan Lipkin/218	15.00
SS	Stephen Strasburg/260	400.00
TL	Tyler Lyons/215	15.00

USA Black Leather Signatures

NM/M
Production 29-32
Brown Leather Autos.: No Pricing
Production 7-13
AG	A.J. Griffin/32	15.00
AO	Andrew Oliver/32	25.00
BS	Blake Smith/30	20.00
CC	Christian Colon/33	20.00
CH	Chris Hernandez/30	20.00
DD	Derek Dietrich/32	20.00
HM	Hunter Morris/32	20.00
KD	Kentrail Davis/29	30.00
KG	Kyle Gibson/32	40.00
KR	Kevin Rhoderick/32	20.00
KV	Kendal Volz/32	20.00
MD	Matt den Dekker/32	20.00
MG	Micah Gibbs/32	20.00
ML	Mike Leake/32	35.00
MM	Mike Minor/32	20.00
RJ	Ryan Jackson/32	20.00
SS	Stephen Strasburg/32	400.00
TL	Tyler Lyons/32	25.00

USA Red/Blue Stitch Black Ink Sigs

NM/M
Production 16-40
AG	A.J. Griffin/37	20.00
AO	Andrew Oliver/37	25.00
BS	Blake Smith/37	20.00
CC	Christian Colon/33	20.00
CH	Chris Hernandez/37	20.00
DD	Derek Dietrich/37	20.00
HM	Hunter Morris/37	20.00
JF	Josh Fellhauer/36	15.00
KD	Kentrail Davis/38	30.00
KR	Kevin Rhoderick/37	15.00
KV	Kendal Volz/40	20.00
MD	Matt den Dekker/37	20.00
MG	Micah Gibbs/37	25.00
ML	Mike Leake/37	40.00
RJ	Ryan Jackson/37	20.00
RL	Ryan Lipkin/35	20.00
SS	Stephen Strasburg/37	600.00
TL	Tyler Lyons/37	25.00

2008 Upper Deck Timeline

NM/M
Common Player (1-310): .25
Common Player (311-385): 1.00
Pack (8): 3.00
Box (18): 50.00
1	Jose Reyes	.75
2	David Wright	1.00
3	Carlos Beltran	.50
4	Pedro Martinez	.50
5	Johan Santana	.50
6	Hanley Ramirez	.75
7	John Smoltz	.40
8	Chipper Jones	1.00
9	Mark Teixeira	.50
10	Chase Utley	.75
11	Ryan Howard	1.00
12	Jimmy Rollins	.50
13	Alfonso Soriano	.50
14	Derek Lee	.50
15	Jason Bay	.25
16	Lance Berkman	.50
17	Ken Griffey Jr.	1.50
18	Ryan Braun	1.00
19	Prince Fielder	.75
20	Albert Pujols	2.00
21	Tim Lincecum	.75
22	Jake Peavy	.50
23	Matt Kemp	.40
24	Matt Holliday	.40
25	Brandon Webb	.50
26	Randy Johnson	.50
27	Alex Rodriguez	2.00
28	Derek Jeter	2.00
29	Chien-Ming Wang	.75
30	David Ortiz	.75
31	Manny Ramirez	.75
32	Daisuke Matsuzaka	1.00
33	B.J. Upton	.40
34	Nick Markakis	.40
35	Roy Halladay	.40
36	Jim Thome	.50
37	Grady Sizemore	.75
38	Travis Hafner	.25
39	C.C. Sabathia	.75
40	Miguel Cabrera	.75
41	Justin Verlander	.50
42	Joe Mauer	.50
43	Alex Gordon	.50
44	Frank Thomas	.50
45	Vladimir Guerrero	.50
46	Torii Hunter	.50
47	Josh Hamilton	.40
48	Ichiro Suzuki	.75
49	Felix Hernandez	.50
50	Erik Bedard	.25
51	Daric Barton (RC)	.50
52	John Bowker (RC)	.50
53	Clay Buchholz (RC)	1.00
54	Jeff Clement (RC)	.50
55	Johnny Cueto (RC)	1.00
56	Blake DeWitt (RC)	.50
57	German Duran RC	.50
58	Kosuke Fukudome RC	1.00
59	Alberto Gonzalez RC	.50
60	Luke Hochevar RC	.50
61	Chin-Lung Hu (RC)	1.00
62	Ian Kennedy RC	.50
63	Masahide Kobayashi RC	.50
64	Hiroki Kuroda RC	.75
65	Evan Longoria RC	5.00
66	Jed Lowrie (RC)	1.00
67	Justin Masterson RC	.50
68	Nick Blackburn RC	1.00
69	Micah Hoffpauir RC	1.00
70	Jeff Niemann (RC)	.50
71	Ross Ohlendorf RC	.50
72	Jonathan Van Every RC	.75
73	Alexei Ramirez RC	2.50
74	Justin Ruggiano RC	.50
75	Max Scherzer RC	1.50
76	Greg Smith RC	.50
77	Denard Span (RC)	.75
78	Clete Thomas RC	1.00
79	Josh Banks (RC)	.50
80	Clay Timpner (RC)	.50
81	Matt Tolbert RC	.50
82	J.R. Towles RC	.50
83	Eugenio Velez RC	.50
84	Joey Votto RC	1.50
85	Rico Washington (RC)	.50
86	Jay Bruce RC	2.50
87	Wladimir Balentien (RC)	.50
88	Burke Badenhop RC	.50
89	Brian Barton RC	.50
90	Brian Bocock RC	.50
91	Brandon Boggs (RC)	.50
92	Robinzon Diaz (RC)	.50
93	Hernan Iribarren (RC)	.50
94	Brent Lillibridge (RC)	.50
95	Yasuhiko Yabuta RC	.50
96	Jeff Samardzija RC	.75
97	Carlos Gonzalez (RC)	1.00
98	Clayton Kershaw RC	1.50
99	Jonathan Albaladejo RC	.75
100	Nick Adenhart (RC)	.50
101	Nick Adenhart (RC)	.50
102	Brandon Phillips	.40
103	Chad Billingsley	.50
104	Chris Duncan	.50
105	Clay Timpner (RC)	.50
106	Clete Thomas RC	.50
107	Corey Hart	.40
108	Craig Breslow	.25
109	David Murphy	.25
110	Edinson Volquez	.40
111	Elijah Dukes	.25
112	Emmanuel Burriss RC	.50
113	Evan Longoria RC	1.25
114	Fred Lewis	.25
115	Felix Pie	.25
116	German Duran RC	.50
117	Greg Smith	.50
118	Hernan Iribarren (RC)	.50
119	Joey Votto (RC)	1.00
120	Jonathan Van Every RC	.50
121	Kosuke Fukudome RC	1.50
122	Matt Joyce RC	.75
123	Max Scherzer RC	.75
124	Nick Swisher	.25
125	Paul Janish (RC)	.50
126	Reed Johnson	.50
127	Rico Washington (RC)	.50
128	Russell Martin	.50
129	Scott Kazmir	.40
130	Tyler Clippard	.25
131	Randy Johnson	.50
132	Frank Thomas	.50
133	Greg Maddux	1.00
134	Vladimir Guerrero	.50
135	Ryan Braun	1.00
136	David Ortiz	.75
137	Jake Peavy	.50
138	Mark Teixeira	.50
139	Jose Reyes	.75
140	Chien-Ming Wang	.75
141	Prince Fielder	.50
142	Albert Pujols	2.00
143	Johan Santana	.50
144	Josh Beckett	.50
145	Alex Rodriguez	2.00
146	Felix Hernandez	.50
147	Brandon Webb	.50
148	Chase Utley	.75
149	Derek Jeter	2.00
150	Grady Sizemore	.75
151	B.J. Upton	.50
152	Carlos Beltran	.50
153	Hanley Ramirez	.75
154	Magglio Ordonez	.75
155	Carlos Zambrano	.50
156	Manny Ramirez	.75
157	Travis Hafner	.25
158	David Wright	.75
159	Jimmy Rollins	.50

#	Player	Price
160	Matt Holliday	.50
161	Ken Griffey Jr.	1.50
162	C.C. Sabathia	.75
163	Joe Mauer	.50
164	Derrek Lee	.50
165	Miguel Cabrera	.75
166	Alfonso Soriano	.50
167	Ichiro Suzuki	1.00
168	Daisuke Matsuzaka	1.00
169	Lance Berkman	1.00
170	Ryan Howard	1.00
171	J.R. Towles RC	1.50
172	Max Scherzer RC	1.50
173	Chin-Lung Hu	1.00
174	Daric Barton	.50
175	Ian Kennedy	1.00
176	Clay Buchholz	1.00
177	Joey Votto RC	1.00
178	Kosuke Fukudome RC	1.50
179	Johnny Cueto	1.00
180	Evan Longoria	5.00
181	Brandon Boggs (RC)	.50
182	Brian Bocock RC	.50
183	Burke Badenhop RC	.50
184	Callix Crabbe (RC)	.50
185	Cha Seung Baek	.25
186	Chris Smith (RC)	.50
187	Clayton Kershaw RC	1.50
188	Felipe Paulino RC	.50
189	Glen Perkins	.25
190	Homer Bailey	.25
191	James Loney	.25
192	Jay Bruce (RC)	3.00
193	Jeff Baker	.25
194	Jeff Keppinger	.25
195	Jesus Flores	.50
196	Joakim Soria	.25
197	Joey Votto (RC)	1.50
198	Josh Hamilton	.75
199	Kosuke Fukudome RC	1.50
200	Micah Hoffpauir RC	1.00
201	Nick Blackburn RC	.50
202	Nyjer Morgan (RC)	.50
203	Randor Bierd RC	.50
204	Rich Hill	.50
205	Ross Ohlendorf RC	.50
206	Russell Martin	.40
207	Ryan Garko	.25
208	Seth Smith	.25
209	Steve Holm RC	.25
210	Travis Hafner	.25
211	Brandon Webb	.50
212	Randy Johnson	.50
213	Max Scherzer RC	1.50
214	Chris B. Young	.50
215	Justin Upton	.50
216	John Smoltz	.50
217	Chipper Jones	1.00
218	Mark Teixeira	.50
219	Jeff Francoeur	.25
220	Adrian Gonzalez	.50
221	Nick Markakis	.50
222	Jacoby Ellsbury	.50
223	David Ortiz	.75
224	Manny Ramirez	.75
225	Daisuke Matsuzaka	1.00
226	Clay Buchholz (RC)	1.00
227	Jed Lowrie (RC)	1.00
228	Justin Masterson	1.00
229	Geovany Soto	.50
230	Alfonso Soriano	.50
231	Derrek Lee	.50
232	Kosuke Fukudome RC	1.50
233	Jim Thome	.50
234	Alexei Ramirez RC	2.00
235	Ken Griffey Jr.	1.50
236	Johnny Cueto RC	1.00
237	Joey Votto (RC)	4.00
238	Brandon Phillips	.40
239	Edinson Volquez	.40
240	Grady Sizemore	.75
241	Travis Hafner	.25
242	C.C. Sabathia	.75
243	Matt Holliday	.50
244	Troy Tulowitzki	.25
245	Miguel Cabrera	.75
246	Justin Verlander	.50
247	Matt Tolbert RC	.50
248	Hanley Ramirez	.75
249	Jeremy Hermida	.25
250	Lance Berkman	.50
251	J.R. Towles RC	.50
252	Alex Gordon	.50
253	Luke Hochevar RC	1.00
254	Vladimir Guerrero	.50
255	Torii Hunter	.40
256	Nick Adenhart (RC)	.50
257	Garrett Atkins	.40
258	Blake DeWitt (RC)	.50
259	Chin-Lung Hu (RC)	1.00
260	Hiroki Kuroda	.75
261	Matt Kemp	.50
262	James Loney	.50
263	Justin Morneau	.50
264	Dan Haren	.50
265	Ryan Braun	1.00
266	Corey Hart	.40
267	Rickie Weeks	.25
268	Prince Fielder	.75
269	Carlos Gomez	.40
270	Joe Mauer	.50
271	Jose Reyes	.75
272	David Wright	1.00
273	Carlos Beltran	.50
274	Pedro Martinez	.50
275	Hideki Matsui	.50
276	Alex Rodriguez	2.00
277	Derek Jeter	2.00
278	Chien-Ming Wang	.75
279	Ian Kennedy RC	1.00
280	Phil Hughes	.50
281	Frank Thomas	.50
282	Daric Barton (RC)	.50
283	Greg Smith RC	.50
284	Cole Hamels	.50
285	Chase Utley	.75
286	Ryan Howard	1.00
287	Jimmy Rollins	.50
288	Jason Bay	.25
289	Jake Peavy	.50
290	Brian McCann	.40
291	Tim Lincecum	.75
292	Justin Ruggiano RC	.50
293	Jay Bruce (RC)	3.00
294	Brian Bocock RC	.50
295	Ichiro Suzuki	1.00
296	Adam Dunn	.50
297	Erik Bedard	.25
298	Jeff Clement (RC)	.50
299	Felix Hernandez	.50
300	Albert Pujols	2.00
301	Rick Ankiel	.50
302	B.J. Upton	.50
303	Evan Longoria RC	5.00
304	Clayton Kershaw RC	1.50
305	Carl Crawford	.50
306	Russell Martin	.40
307	Brandon Boggs (RC)	.50
308	Josh Hamilton	.75
309	Roy Halladay	.50
310	Ryan Zimmerman	.40
311	Evan Longoria	8.00
312	Johnny Cueto	1.50
313	Kosuke Fukudome	2.00
314	Joey Votto	1.50
315	Clay Buchholz	1.50
316	Ian Kennedy	1.50
317	Daric Barton	1.00
1	Chin-Lung Hu	1.50
319	Max Scherzer	2.00
320	J.R. Towles	1.00
321	Nick Adenhart	1.00
322	Wladimir Balentien	1.00
323	Brian Barton	1.00
324	Brian Bocock	1.00
325	Jonathan Herrera RC	1.00
326	Jesse Carlson RC	1.00
327	Jeff Clement	1.00
328	Brandon Jones	1.50
329	German Duran	1.00
330	Alex Romero	1.00
331	Jay Bruce	3.00
332	Luke Hochevar	1.50
333	Clayton Kershaw	1.50
334	Nick Blackburn	1.00
335	Jed Lowrie	1.50
336	Evan Longoria	8.00
337	Johnny Cueto	1.50
338	Kosuke Fukudome	2.00
339	Joey Votto	1.50
340	Clay Buchholz	1.50
341	Ian Kennedy	1.50
342	Daric Barton	1.00
343	Chin-Lung Hu	1.50
344	Max Scherzer	2.00
345	J.R. Towles	1.00
346	Justin Masterson	3.00
347	Kyle McClellan RC	1.00
348	Evan Meek RC	1.00
349	Nyjer Morgan	1.00
350	Colt Morton RC	1.00
351	Luke Carlin RC	1.00
352	Emmanuel Burriss	1.00
353	Clint Sammons	1.00
354	Ross Ohlendorf	1.00
355	Jay Bruce	4.00
356	Felipe Paulino RC	1.00
357	Alexei Ramirez	4.00
358	Clayton Kershaw	2.00
359	Cory Wade	1.00
360	Greg Smith	1.00
361	Evan Longoria	8.00
362	Johnny Cueto	1.50
363	Kosuke Fukudome	2.00
364	Joey Votto	1.50
365	Clay Buchholz	1.50
366	Ian Kennedy	1.50
367	Daric Barton	1.00
368	Chin-Lung Hu	1.50
369	Max Scherzer	2.00
370	J.R. Towles	1.00
371	Mitch Boggs	1.00
372	Jay Bruce	4.00
373	Alberto Gonzalez	1.00
374	Rich Thompson RC	1.00
375	Robinson Diaz	1.00
376	Clay Timpner	1.00
377	Eider Torres	1.00
378	Ramon Troncoso RC	2.00
379	Clayton Kershaw	3.00
380	Rico Washington	1.00
381	Brandon Jones	4.00
382	Bobby Wilson	1.00
383	Wesley Wright RC	2.00
384	Mike Parisi RC	2.00
385	Jonathan Van Every	1.00

Gold

Gold (1-50):		2-3X
Gold (51-100):		1-1.5X

Cut Signatures

		NM/M
AK	Alex Kellner/27	25.00
AL	Al Lopez/28	40.00
BB	Bill Bevens/25	40.00
GW	Gene Woodling/32	50.00
JM	Jo-Jo Moore/40	50.00
RF	Rick Ferrell/42	50.00

Memorabilia

		NM/M
Common Jersey:		
AB	A.J. Burnett	4.00
AD	Adrian Beltre	4.00
AE	Andre Ethier	4.00
AG	Adrian Gonzalez	6.00
AJ	Andruw Jones	4.00
AM	Andrew Miller	4.00
AP	Albert Pujols	15.00
AR	Aaron Rowand	4.00
BC	Bartolo Colon	4.00
BE	Adrian Beltre	4.00
BG	Brian Giles	4.00
BM	Brian McCann	4.00
BO	Bobby Crosby	4.00
BR	B.J. Ryan	4.00
BS	Ben Sheets	6.00
BU	A.J. Burnett	4.00
BZ	Barry Zito	4.00
CB	Chad Billingsley	6.00
CC	Carl Crawford	4.00
CD	Carlos Delgado	6.00
CG	Curtis Granderson	8.00
CJ	Chipper Jones	10.00
CQ	Carlos Quentin	6.00
CR	Bobby Crosby	4.00
CZ	Carlos Zambrano	4.00
DA	Johnny Damon	6.00
DE	Carlos Delgado	6.00
DJ	Derek Jeter	15.00
DL	Derek Lowe	4.00
DO	David Ortiz	8.00
DW	Dontrelle Willis	4.00
ED	Jim Edmonds	6.00
FR	Ryan Freel	4.00
FS	Freddy Sanchez	4.00
GA	Garrett Atkins	4.00
GI	Brian Giles	4.00
GJ	Geoff Jenkins	4.00
GL	Troy Glaus	6.00
GM	Greg Maddux	10.00
GO	Adrian Gonzalez	6.00
GT	Troy Glaus	10.00
HA	Josh Hamilton	8.00
HM	Hideki Matsui	6.00
HO	Trevor Hoffman	4.00
HT	Travis Hafner	6.00
HU	Torii Hunter	4.00
IS	Ian Snell	4.00
JD	Jermaine Dye	6.00
JE	Jim Edmonds	6.00
JF	Jeff Francoeur	4.00
JG	Jeremy Guthrie	4.00
JH	J.J. Hardy	4.00
JH	J.J. Hardy	4.00
JL	Jon Lester	6.00
JM	Joe Mauer	10.00
JO	Chipper Jones	6.00
JP	Jorge Posada	4.00
JS	Jeremy Sowers	4.00
KG	Ken Griffey Jr.	8.00
KY	Kevin Youkilis	4.00
MA	Greg Maddux	10.00
MC	Miguel Cabrera	8.00
MG	Matt Garza	4.00
MO	Justin Morneau	4.00
MS	Mike Sweeney	4.00
MT	Miguel Tejada	6.00
MY	Michael Young	4.00
NS	Nick Swisher	4.00
OR	David Ortiz	8.00
OV	Omar Vizquel	4.00
PE	Andy Pettitte	4.00
PF	Prince Fielder	8.00
PK	Paul Konerko	4.00
PM	Pedro Martinez	4.00
PU	Albert Pujols	15.00
RA	Aramis Ramirez	4.00
RB	Ryan Braun	10.00
RC	Robinson Cano	4.00
RF	Rafael Furcal	4.00
RG	Ryan Garko	4.00
RH	Rich Harden	4.00
RJ	Randy Johnson	4.00
RM	Russell Martin	6.00
RO	Roy Halladay	6.00
RS	Richie Sexson	4.00
RZ	Ryan Zimmerman	6.00
SA	Johan Santana	8.00
SK	Scott Kazmir	6.00
SP	Scott Podsednik	4.00
SR	Scott Rolen	4.00
TB	Travis Buck	4.00
TG	Tom Glavine	6.00
TH	Tim Hudson	4.00
TL	Tim Lincecum	8.00
TR	Travis Hafner	6.00
TW	Tim Wakefield	4.00
VG	Vladimir Guerrero	6.00
VM	Victor Martinez	4.00
WI	Willy Taveras	4.00
ZD	Zach Duke	4.00

USA Baseball Signatures

		NM/M
Common Auto.:		8.00
AG	A.J. Griffin	8.00
AO	Andrew Oliver	15.00
BH	Brett Hunter	8.00
BS	Blake Smith	15.00
CC	Christian Colon	15.00
CH	Chris Hernandez	15.00
DD	Derek Dietrich	20.00
HM	Hunter Morris	8.00
JF	Josh Fellhauer	10.00
KD	Kentrail Davis	20.00
KG	Kyle Gibson	10.00
KR	Kevin Rhoderick	8.00
KV	Kendal Volz	10.00
MD	Matt den Dekker	10.00
MG	Micah Gibbs	10.00
ML	Mike Leake	30.00
MM	Mike Minor	8.00
RJ	Ryan Jackson	10.00
RL	Ryan Lipkin	10.00
SS	Stephen Strasburg	300.00
TL	Tyler Lyons	10.00
TM	Tommy Mendonca	15.00

1992 UD Minor League Autos.

		NM/M
Some not priced yet		
101	Bobby Wilson	8.00
102	Brandon Phillips	10.00
104	Chris Duncan	8.00
105	Clay Timpner	8.00
106	Clete Thomas	10.00
108	Craig Breslow	8.00
109	David Murphy	10.00
110	Edinson Volquez	12.00
111	Elijah Dukes	8.00
112	Emmanuel Burriss	8.00
114	Fred Lewis	10.00
115	Felix Pie	8.00
116	German Duran	8.00
117	Greg Smith	8.00
118	Hernan Iribarren	8.00
120	Jonathan Van Every	10.00
126	Reed Johnson	8.00
127	Rico Washington	8.00

1993 SP Autos.

		NM/M
Production 93 Sets		
312	Johnny Cueto	25.00
315	Clay Buchholz	15.00
317	Daric Barton	10.00
318	Chin-Lung Hu	15.00
321	Nick Adenhart	10.00
322	Wladimir Balentien	12.00
323	Brian Barton	10.00
327	Jeff Clement	10.00
328	Brandon Jones	15.00
329	German Duran	8.00
330	Alex Romero	10.00
332	Luke Hochevar	10.00
334	Nick Blackburn	10.00

1994 SP Rookie Autograph

		NM/M
Production 94 Sets		
337	Johnny Cueto	25.00
340	Clay Buchholz	15.00
342	Daric Barton	10.00
343	Chin-Lung Hu	20.00
345	J.R. Towles	15.00
347	Kyle McClellan	20.00
349	Nyjer Morgan	10.00
350	Colt Morton	8.00
356	Felipe Paulino	8.00
357	Alexei Ramirez	35.00
358	Clayton Kershaw	20.00
359	Cory Wade	15.00
360	Greg Smith	10.00

1994 All-Time Heroes 20th Anniv.

		NM/M
Common Player:		.75
Inserted 1:9 Hobby		
131	Randy Johnson	1.50
132	Frank Thomas	1.50
133	Greg Maddux	3.00
134	Vladimir Guerrero	1.50
135	Ryan Braun	2.00
136	David Ortiz	2.00
137	Jake Peavy	1.00
138	Mark Teixeira	1.00
139	Jose Reyes	2.00
140	Chien-Ming Wang	1.50
141	Prince Fielder	1.50
142	Albert Pujols	4.00
143	Johan Santana	1.50
144	Josh Beckett	1.00
145	Alex Rodriguez	4.00
146	Felix Hernandez	1.00
147	Brandon Webb	1.00
148	Chase Utley	1.50
149	Derek Jeter	4.00
150	Grady Sizemore	1.50
151	B.J. Upton	2.00
152	Carlos Beltran	1.00
153	Hanley Ramirez	1.50
154	Magglio Ordonez	.75
155	Carlos Zambrano	.75
156	Manny Ramirez	1.50
157	Travis Hafner	.75
158	David Wright	3.00
159	Jimmy Rollins	1.50
160	Matt Holliday	1.50
161	Ken Griffey Jr.	3.00
162	C.C. Sabathia	1.50
163	Joe Mauer	.75
164	Derrek Lee	.75
165	Miguel Cabrera	1.50
166	Alfonso Soriano	1.00
167	Ichiro Suzuki	2.00
168	Daisuke Matsuzaka	2.00
169	Lance Berkman	1.00
170	Ryan Howard	2.00
171	J.R. Towles	.75
172	Max Scherzer	1.00
173	Chin-Lung Hu	1.00
174	Daric Barton	.75
175	Ian Kennedy	1.00
176	Clay Buchholz	1.00
177	Joey Votto	1.00
178	Kosuke Fukudome	1.50
179	Johnny Cueto	1.00
180	Evan Longoria	5.00

1994 All-Time Heroes Auto.

		NM/M
Production 5-99		
149	Derek Jeter/75	120.00
171	J.R. Towles/99	10.00
173	Chin-Lung Hu/99	15.00
174	Daric Barton/99	8.00
176	Clay Buchholz/50	20.00
179	Johnny Cueto/59	20.00

1995 SP Rookie Auto.

		NM/M
Production 95 Sets		
361	Evan Longoria	100.00
362	Johnny Cueto	25.00
365	Clay Buchholz	15.00
367	Daric Barton	10.00
368	Chin-Lung Hu	15.00
370	J.R. Towles	10.00
371	Mitch Boggs	8.00
375	Robinson Diaz	8.00
379	Clayton Kershaw	30.00
380	Rico Washington	8.00
382	Bobbie Wilson	8.00

1995 SP Top Prospects

		NM/M
Many not priced.		
181	Brandon Boggs	8.00
182	Brian Bocock	8.00
183	Burke Badenhop	8.00
185	Cha Seung Baek	8.00
186	Chris Smith	8.00
187	Clayton Kershaw	30.00
188	Felipe Paulino	8.00
190	Homer Bailey	10.00
191	James Loney	15.00
193	Jeff Baker	8.00
194	Jeff Keppinger	8.00
195	Jesus Flores	8.00
196	Joakim Soria	10.00
198	Josh Hamilton	40.00
200	Micah Hoffpauir	15.00
201	Nick Blackburn	12.00
202	Nyjer Morgan	10.00
203	Randor Bierd	8.00
204	Rich Hill	8.00
207	Ryan Garko	8.00
208	Seth Smith	8.00
209	Steve Holm	8.00

2004 UD Timeless Teams Auto.

		NM/M
Production 5-99		
226	Clay Buchholz/50	15.00
236	Johnny Cueto/59	20.00
238	Brandon Phillips/99	15.00
239	Edinson Volquez/99	15.00
247	Matt Tolbert/99	10.00
251	J.R. Towles/99	10.00
253	Luke Hochevar/50	15.00
259	Chin-Lung Hu/50	15.00
269	Carlos Gomez/99	15.00
282	Daric Barton/99	8.00
288	Jason Bay/99	15.00
294	Brian Bocock/99	8.00
298	Jeff Clement/99	10.00
307	Brandon Boggs/99	8.00
308	Josh Hamilton/40	40.00

2004 UD Timeless Teams Silver

		NM/M
Common Player:		
Gold:		No Pricing
Production 25 Sets		
211	Brandon Webb	3.00
212	Randy Johnson	5.00
213	Max Scherzer	3.00
214	Chris B. Young	3.00
215	Justin Upton	3.00
216	John Smoltz	3.00
217	Chipper Jones	6.00
218	Mark Teixeira	3.00
219	Jeff Francoeur	2.00
220	Adrian Gonzalez	3.00
221	Nick Markakis	5.00
222	Jacoby Ellsbury	5.00
223	David Ortiz	6.00
224	Manny Ramirez	6.00
225	Daisuke Matsuzaka	6.00
226	Clay Buchholz	4.00
227	Jed Lowrie	3.00
228	Justin Masterson	10.00
229	Geovany Soto	3.00
230	Alfonso Soriano	5.00
231	Derrek Lee	3.00
232	Kosuke Fukudome	6.00
233	Jim Thome	3.00
234	Alexei Ramirez	10.00
235	Ken Griffey Jr.	6.00
236	Johnny Cueto	3.00
237	Joey Votto	4.00
238	Brandon Phillips	2.00
239	Edinson Volquez	3.00
240	Grady Sizemore	5.00
241	Travis Hafner	2.00
242	C.C. Sabathia	6.00
243	Matt Holliday	4.00
244	Troy Tulowitzki	2.00
245	Miguel Cabrera	6.00
246	Justin Verlander	4.00
247	Matt Tolbert	2.00
248	Hanley Ramirez	8.00
249	Jeremy Hermida	2.00
250	Lance Berkman	3.00
251	J.R. Towles	3.00
252	Alex Gordon	5.00
253	Luke Hochevar	4.00
254	Vladimir Guerrero	5.00
255	Torii Hunter	3.00
256	Nick Adenhart	3.00
257	Garrett Atkins	3.00
258	Blake DeWitt	5.00
259	Chin-Lung Hu	4.00
260	Hiroki Kuroda	4.00
261	Matt Kemp	4.00
262	James Loney	4.00
263	Justin Morneau	4.00
264	Dan Haren	3.00
265	Ryan Braun	8.00
266	Corey Hart	3.00
267	Rickie Weeks	2.00
268	Prince Fielder	6.00
269	Carlos Gomez	3.00
270	Joe Mauer	4.00
271	Jose Reyes	6.00
272	David Wright	6.00
273	Carlos Beltran	4.00
274	Pedro Martinez	3.00
275	Hideki Matsui	5.00
276	Alex Rodriguez	10.00
277	Derek Jeter	15.00
278	Chien-Ming Wang	3.00
279	Ian Kennedy	5.00
280	Phil Hughes	5.00
281	Frank Thomas	5.00
282	Daric Barton	3.00
283	Greg Smith	3.00
284	Cole Hamels	5.00
285	Chase Utley	6.00
286	Ryan Howard	6.00
287	Jimmy Rollins	3.00
288	Jason Bay	3.00
289	Jake Peavy	3.00
290	Brian McCann	3.00
291	Tim Lincecum	5.00
292	Justin Ruggiano	3.00
293	Jay Bruce	10.00
294	Brian Bocock	3.00
295	Ichiro Suzuki	8.00
296	Adam Dunn	3.00
297	Erik Bedard	2.00
298	Jeff Clement	3.00
299	Felix Hernandez	3.00
300	Albert Pujols	10.00
301	Rick Ankiel	3.00
302	B.J. Upton	4.00
303	Evan Longoria	20.00
304	Clayton Kershaw	3.00
305	Carl Crawford	3.00
306	Russell Martin	2.00
307	Brandon Boggs	2.00
308	Josh Hamilton	5.00
309	Roy Halladay	3.00
310	Ryan Zimmerman	3.00

2008 UD Ultimate

		NM/M
Common Player (1-100):		2.00
Production 350		
Common RC (101-150):		20.00
Production 99		
Box:		85.00
1	Jose Reyes	4.00
2	David Wright	5.00
3	Carlos Beltran	4.00
4	Johan Santana	3.00
5	Pedro Martinez	2.50
6	Jeff Francoeur	2.50
7	John Smoltz	3.00
8	Brian McCann	3.00
9	Chipper Jones	5.00
10	Cole Hamels	4.00
11	Ryan Howard	6.00
12	Jimmy Rollins	3.00
13	Chase Utley	4.00
14	Hanley Ramirez	4.00
15	Dan Uggla	2.00
16	Lastings Milledge	2.00

#	Player	Price
17	Ryan Zimmerman	2.50
18	Ryan Ludwick	3.00
19	Troy Glaus	2.00
20	Albert Pujols	8.00
21	Rick Ankiel	2.50
22	Ryan Doumit	2.00
23	Nate McLouth	2.00
24	Lance Berkman	2.50
25	Carlos Lee	2.50
26	Miguel Tejada	2.00
27	C.C. Sabathia	3.00
28	Ryan Braun	4.00
29	Prince Fielder	3.00
30	Alfonso Soriano	3.00
31	Derek Lee	2.50
32	Carlos Zambrano	2.00
33	Aramis Ramirez	2.50
34	Rich Harden	2.00
35	Edinson Volquez	2.50
36	Brandon Phillips	2.50
37	Brandon Webb	2.50
38	Dan Haren	2.50
39	Chris B. Young	2.50
40	Randy Johnson	3.00
41	Adam Dunn	2.50
42	Matt Holliday	2.50
43	Troy Tulowitzki	2.00
44	Garrett Atkins	2.00
45	Manny Ramirez	3.00
46	Greg Maddux	6.00
47	Matt Kemp	3.00
48	Russell Martin	2.00
49	Aaron Rowand	2.00
50	Tim Lincecum	6.00
51	Adrian Gonzalez	2.50
52	Jake Peavy	2.50
53	Trevor Hoffman	2.00
54	Ivan Rodriguez	2.00
55	Alex Rodriguez	8.00
56	Derek Jeter	8.00
57	Hideki Matsui	3.00
58	Robinson Cano	2.50
59	Joba Chamberlain	2.00
60	Chien-Ming Wang	2.00
61	Mariano Rivera	3.00
62	Xavier Nady	2.00
63	Josh Beckett	3.00
64	David Ortiz	4.00
65	Dustin Pedroia	3.00
66	Jonathan Papelbon	3.00
67	Daisuke Matsuzaka	4.00
68	Kevin Youkilis	3.00
69	Jason Bay	2.50
70	Nick Markakis	3.00
71	Brian Roberts	2.00
72	Scott Kazmir	2.00
73	Carl Crawford	2.00
74	B.J. Upton	2.00
75	Vernon Wells	2.00
76	Roy Halladay	2.00
77	Jermaine Dye	2.00
78	Jim Thome	2.50
79	Ken Griffey Jr.	6.00
80	Carlos Quentin	2.00
81	Magglio Ordonez	2.00
82	Justin Verlander	2.50
83	Miguel Cabrera	3.00
84	Alex Gordon	2.50
85	Billy Butler	2.00
86	Grady Sizemore	3.00
87	Victor Martinez	2.00
88	Travis Hafner	2.00
89	Joe Mauer	2.00
90	Justin Morneau	2.50
91	Erik Bedard	2.00
92	Felix Hernandez	2.50
93	Ichiro Suzuki	5.00
94	Ian Kinsler	3.00
95	Josh Hamilton	4.00
96	Frank Thomas	2.50
97	Jack Cust	2.00
98	Torii Hunter	2.50
99	Vladimir Guerrero	3.00
100	Mark Teixeira	3.00
101	Evan Longoria/Jsy/Auto./99 RC	200.00
102	Max Scherzer/Jsy/Auto./99 RC	40.00
103	Kosuke Fukudome/Jsy/99 RC	25.00
104	Ian Kennedy/Jsy/Auto./99 RC	20.00
105	Clay Buchholz/Jsy/Auto./99 (RC)	40.00
106	Jay Bruce/Jsy/Auto./99 (RC)	40.00
107	Clayton Kershaw/Jsy/Auto./99 RC	40.00
108	Chin-Lung Hu/Jsy/Auto./99 (RC)	25.00

Gold
Production 25 Sets

Bat Barrels
Production 5 Sets

Bat Barrel Autographs
NM/M
Production 10-140
AR	Aramis Ramirez/35	30.00
BW	Billy Williams/25	35.00
CH	Chin-Lung Hu/68	30.00
DJ	Derek Jeter/99	150.00
DL	Derek Lee/50	30.00
JR	Jim Rice/140	35.00
KG	Ken Griffey Jr./75	100.00
KY	Kevin Youkilis/50	50.00

Double Autographs
NM/M
Production 10-50
FE	Chone Figgins, Edwin Encarnacion/50	20.00
GG	Ken Griffey Jr., Ken Griffey Sr./50	80.00
JR	Derek Jeter, Hanley Ramirez/50	140.00
KG	Al Kaline, Curtis Granderson/35	50.00
RB	Dennis "Oil Can" Boyd, J.R. Richard/50	30.00
TK	Ian Kennedy, J.R. Towles/50	15.00

Double PRIME Autos
Production 5-15

Double Memorabilia Autographs
NM/M
Production 5-99
BP	Brandon Phillips/75	20.00
BR	Brian McCann/25	25.00
BU	Clay Buchholz/25	20.00
CH	Chin-Lung Hu/75	30.00
DJ	Derek Jeter/25	140.00
DO	Don Mattingly/99	50.00
IK	Ian Kennedy/25	25.00
KG	Ken Griffey Jr./25	120.00
KJ	Kelly Johnson/75	15.00
NM	Nick Markakis/75	25.00
TT	Troy Tulowitzki/50	25.00

Eight Autographs
Production 5 Sets

Jumbo Jersey
Production 10 Sets
Jumbo Patch: No Pricing
Production 5 Sets

Pants Autographs
NM/M
Production 10-99
Golds: No Pricing
BP	Brandon Phillips/99	20.00
BW	Billy Williams/25	35.00
CR	Cal Ripken Jr./25	125.00
DJ	Derek Jeter/99	140.00
JF	Jeff Francoeur/99	20.00
JI	Jim Rice/50	35.00
JM	Jack Morris/50	20.00
JO	John Maine/50	15.00
JR	Cal Ripken Jr./25	125.00
KG	Ken Griffey Jr./99	75.00
KY	Kevin Youkilis/50	40.00
PA	Jonathan Papelbon/50	20.00
PH	Phil Hughes/25	30.00
PM	Paul Molitor/25	35.00
RS	Ron Santo/50	40.00
TM	Tino Martinez/50	35.00
TT	Troy Tulowitzki/99	25.00

Quad Autographs
Production 5-25

Quad Memorabilia Autos.
NM/M
Production 5-75
Prime: No Pricing
Production 5 Sets
BP	Brandon Phillips/75	15.00
BR	Brian McCann/25	30.00
BU	Clay Buchholz/25	20.00
CH	Chin-Lung Hu/75	40.00
DJ	Derek Jeter/50	150.00
IK	Ian Kennedy/25	25.00
JO	John Maine/50	15.00
KG	Ken Griffey Jr./50	100.00
TT	Troy Tulowitzki/99	25.00

Road/Home Jersey Autos
NM/M
Production 5-99
Golds: No Pricing
Production 5-25
BE	Johnny Bench/25	60.00
BW	Billy Williams/25	35.00
CH	Cole Hamels/25	60.00
DJ	Derek Jeter/99	150.00
FL	Fred Lynn/25	25.00
GN	Graig Nettles/25	25.00
JF	Jeff Francoeur/99	20.00
JI	Jim Rice/50	35.00
JM	Jack Morris/50	20.00
JO	John Maine/50	15.00
JR	Cal Ripken Jr./25	125.00
JW	Josh Willingham/99	10.00
KG	Ken Griffey Jr./99	75.00
KY	Kevin Youkilis/50	40.00
PA	Jonathan Papelbon/50	20.00
PF	Prince Fielder/35	35.00
PH	Phil Hughes/25	30.00
PM	Paul Molitor/25	35.00
RS	Ron Santo/35	50.00
TM	Tino Martinez/25	40.00
TT	Troy Tulowitzki/30	35.00
AR	Aramis Ramirez/50	25.00
BP	Brandon Phillips/99	20.00
BW	Billy Williams/25	35.00
CH	Cole Hamels/25	50.00
CR	Cal Ripken Jr./25	125.00
DJ	Derek Jeter/99	140.00
GN	Graig Nettles/25	25.00
HA	Hanley Ramirez/25	40.00
JC	Joe Carter/25	20.00
JF	Jeff Francoeur/99	20.00
JI	Jim Rice/50	35.00
JO	John Maine/75	20.00
JR	Cal Ripken Jr./25	125.00
KG	Ken Griffey Jr./99	75.00
KY	Kevin Youkilis/50	40.00
PA	Jonathan Papelbon/25	25.00
PF	Prince Fielder/25	35.00
PH	Phil Hughes/35	30.00
PM	Paul Molitor/50	35.00
RS	Ron Santo/50	50.00
TM	Tino Martinez/25	40.00

Six Autographs
Production 5 Sets

Triple Autographs
NM/M
Production 5-50
AJK	Geoff Jenkins, John Kruk, Dick Allen/35	30.00
PNW	Billy Wagner, Joe Nathan, Jonathan Papelbon/50	40.00

Triple Memorabilia Autos
NM/M
Production 5-99
Prime: No Pricing
Production 5-10
BP	Brandon Phillips/99	15.00
BR	Brian McCann/25	30.00
BU	Clay Buchholz/25	25.00
CH	Chin-Lung Hu/99	20.00
DJ	Derek Jeter/50	150.00
IK	Ian Kennedy/25	25.00
JO	John Maine/75	15.00
KG	Ken Griffey Jr./50	100.00
TT	Troy Tulowitzki/25	25.00

USAB Jersey Autographs
Production 25 Sets

2008 UD USA
NM/M
Complete Set (60): 20.00
Sealed Box Set: 75.00
Common USA card (1-60): .25
7 autos & 2 jsys/ sealed set.
1	Pedro Alvarez	2.00
2	Ryan Berry	.25
3	Jordan Danks	.50
4	Dan Espinosa	.75
5	Ryan Flaherty	1.50
6	Logan Forsythe	1.00
7	Seth Frankoff	.50
8	Scott Gorgen	.50
9	Jeremy Hamilton	.50
10	Brett Hunter	1.00
11	Joe Kelly	.25
12	Roger Kieschnick	.75
13	Lance Lynn	1.00
14	Brian Matusz	1.00
15	Tommy Medica	.75
16	Jordy Mercer	.50
17	Mike Minor	.50
18	Petey Paramore	.50
19	Josh Romanski	.25
20	Tyson Ross	.50
21	Cody Satterwhite	.50
22	Justin Smoak	2.00
23	Eric Surkamp	.25
24	Jacob Thompson	.25
25	Brett Wallace	2.00
26	Coaches	.25
27	Team Picture CL	.25
28	Game 1	.25
29	Game 2	.25
30	Game 3	.25
31	Game 4	.25
32	Game 5	.25
33	Kyle Buchanan	.25
34	Mychal Givens	.50
35	Rob Grossman	.25
36	Tyler Hibbs	.25
37	L.J. Hoes	.25
38	Eric Hosmer	1.50
39	T.J. House	.25
40	Garrison Lassiter	.25
41	Jeff Malm	.25
42	Nick Maronde	.25
43	Harold Martinez	.25
44	Tim Melville	.25
45	Matt Purke	.25
46	J.P. Ramirez	.25
47	Kyle Skipworth	1.00
48	Tyler Stovall	.25
49	Jordan Swagerty	.25
50	Riccio Torrez	.25
51	Ryan Weber	.25
52	Tyler Wilson	.25
53	Coaches	.25
54	Team Picture CL	.25
55	Justin Charles, Andrew Aplin, Matt Davidson	.25
56	Robert Refsnyder, Max Stassi, Zach Vincej	.25
57	Colton Cain, Randal Grichuk, Zach Lee	.50
58	A.J. Cole, Nolan Fontana, Nick Franklin	.50
59	Nate Gonzalez, Austin Maddox, Steve Rodriguez	.50
60	Luke Bailey, Richie Shaffer, Jacob Tillotson	.50

Printing Plates
Production one set per color.

Battleground Autographs
Most not priced.

Camo Cloth
NM/M
Common Player: 3.00
1	Pedro Alvarez	10.00
2	Ryan Berry	3.00
3	Jordan Danks	3.00
4	Dan Espinosa	6.00
5	Ryan Flaherty	6.00
6	Logan Forsythe	5.00
7	Jeremy Hamilton	3.00
8	Brett Hunter	3.00
9	Joe Kelly	3.00
10	Roger Kieschnick	4.00
11	Lance Lynn	4.00
12	Brian Matusz	5.00
13	Tommy Medica	5.00
14	Jordy Mercer	3.00
15	Mike Minor	3.00
16	Petey Paramore	5.00
17	Josh Romanski	5.00
18	Tyson Ross	5.00
19	Cody Satterwhite	4.00
20	Justin Smoak	10.00
21	Jacob Thompson	3.00
22	Brett Wallace	10.00

Japanese National Team Jerseys
NM/M
Common Jersey: 5.00
Patch: No Pricing
Production 20 Sets
1	Sho Aranami	5.00
2	Takeshi Hosoyamada	5.00
3	Takahiro Iwamoto	5.00
4	Tomoyuki Kaida	5.00
5	Mikinori Kato	5.00
6	Testsuya Kokubo	5.00
7	Keijiro Matsumoto	5.00
8	Shirou Mori	5.00
9	Shinya Muramatsu	5.00
10	Ryoji Nakata	5.00
11	Hiroki Nakazawa	5.00
12	Tomohisa Nemoto	5.00
13	Shota Oba	5.00
14	Takashi Ogino	5.00
15	Shota Ohno	5.00
16	Yuki Saitoh	60.00
17	Ryo Sakakibara	5.00
18	Yukinaga Tanaka	5.00
19	Shingo Tatsumi	5.00
20	Hiroki Uemoto	5.00
21	Shota Waizumi	5.00
22	Noriharu Yamazaki	5.00

Japanese National Team Autographs
NM/M
Production 50 Sets
2	Takeshi Hosoyamada	30.00
7	Tomoyuki Kaida	40.00
10	Ryoji Nakata	15.00
13	Shota Oba	80.00
15	Shota Ohno	40.00

Junior National Team Autographs
NM/M
Common USA Junior Auto.: 8.00
Autos. are "on card."
82	Kyle Buchanan	8.00
83	Mychal Givens	15.00
84	Rob Grossman	8.00
85	Tyler Hibbs	10.00
86	L.J. Hoes	8.00
87	Eric Hosmer	20.00
88	T.J. House	10.00
89	Garrison Lassiter	8.00
90	Jeff Malm	8.00
91	Nick Maronde	15.00
92	Harold Martinez	8.00
93	Tim Melville	10.00
94	Matt Purke	8.00
95	J.P. Ramirez	10.00
96	Kyle Skipworth	15.00
97	Tyler Stovall	10.00
98	Jordan Swagerty	8.00
99	Riccio Torrez	8.00
100	Ryan Weber	10.00
101	Tyler Wilson	10.00

Junior National Team Black Autographs
Production 249 Sets
Blue Autos.: 1X
Production 150 Sets
Red: 1-2X
Production 50 Sets
Green: No Pricing
Production Two Sets
1	Kyle Buchanan	8.00
2	Mychal Givens	15.00
3	Rob Grossman	8.00
4	Tyler Hibbs	10.00
5	L.J. Hoes	8.00
6	Eric Hosmer	20.00
7	T.J. House	10.00
8	Garrison Lassiter	8.00
9	Jeff Malm	8.00
10	Nick Maronde	15.00
11	Harold Martinez	10.00
12	Tim Melville	10.00
13	Matt Purke	8.00
14	J.P. Ramirez	10.00
15	Kyle Skipworth	15.00
16	Tyler Stovall	10.00
17	Jordan Swagerty	8.00
18	Riccio Torrez	8.00
19	Ryan Weber	10.00
20	Tyler Wilson	10.00

Junior National Team The Letters
No Pricing
Production 15 Sets

National Team Multi-Player Autos.
No Pricing

National Team Black Autographs
NM/M
Production 249 Sets
Blue: 1X
Production 150 Sets
Red: 1-2X
Production 50 Sets
Green: No Pricing
Production Two Sets
1	Pedro Alvarez	20.00
2	Ryan Berry	8.00
3	Jordan Danks	15.00
4	Dan Espinosa	8.00
5	Ryan Flaherty	8.00
6	Logan Forsythe	8.00
7	Seth Frankoff	10.00
8	Scott Gorgen	8.00
9	Jeremy Hamilton	8.00
10	Brett Hunter	10.00
11	Joe Kelly	10.00
12	Roger Kieschnick	8.00
13	Lance Lynn	8.00
14	Brian Matusz	20.00
15	Tommy Medica	10.00
16	Jordy Mercer	8.00
17	Mike Minor	8.00
18	Petey Paramore	8.00
19	Josh Romanski	8.00
20	Tyson Ross	8.00
21	Cody Satterwhite	8.00
22	Justin Smoak	25.00
23	Jacob Thompson	8.00
24	Brett Wallace	25.00
25	Eric Surkamp	8.00

National Team Team Signed Card
No Pricing

National Team Signatures Blue Ink
NM/M
Common Auto.: 8.00
Autos. are "on card."
61	Pedro Alvarez	25.00
62	Ryan Berry	10.00
63	Jordan Danks	15.00
64	Dan Espinosa	8.00
65	Ryan Flaherty	15.00
66	Logan Forsythe	8.00
67	Jeremy Hamilton	8.00
68	Brett Hunter	8.00
69	Joe Kelly	8.00
70	Roger Kieschnick	10.00
71	Brian Matusz	20.00
72	Tommy Medica	8.00
73	Jordy Mercer	15.00
74	Mike Minor	8.00
75	Petey Paramore	8.00
76	Josh Romanski	8.00
77	Tyson Ross	10.00
78	Cody Satterwhite	8.00
79	Justin Smoak	30.00
80	Jacob Thompson	8.00
81	Brett Wallace	25.00

National Team Question & Answer Autographs
NM/M
All variations are equal value.
BH	Brett Hunter	8.00
BM	Brian Matusz	8.00
BW	Brett Wallace	25.00
CS	Cody Satterwhite	10.00
DE	Dan Espinosa	8.00
JD	Jordan Danks	15.00
JH	Jeremy Hamilton	8.00
JK	Joe Kelly	8.00
JM	Jordy Mercer	8.00
JM	Josh Romanski	8.00
JS	Justin Smoak	30.00
JT	Jacob Thompson	8.00
LF	Logan Forsythe	8.00
MM	Mike Minor	8.00
PA	Pedro Alvarez	25.00
PP	Petey Paramore	8.00
RB	Ryan Berry	8.00
RF	Ryan Flaherty	8.00
RK	Roger Kieschnick	10.00
TM	Tommy Medica	8.00
TR	Tyson Ross	8.00

Today & Tomorrow Dual Black Autos.
NM/M
Common Dual Auto.: 10.00
Production 295 Sets
Blue: 1x
Production 150 Sets
Red: No Pricing
Production 25 Sets
Green: No Pricing
Production Two Sets
1	Brian Matusz, Tim Melville	15.00
2	Jacob Thompson, Nick Maronde	15.00
3	Brett Hunter, T.J. House	10.00
4	Petey Paramore, Jordan Swagerty	15.00
5	Justin Smoak, Eric Hosmer	30.00
6	Ryan Flaherty, Riccio Torrez	15.00
7	Pedro Alvarez, Harold Martinez	20.00
8	Dan Espinosa, Mychal Givens	15.00
9	Jordan Danks, L.J. Hoes	10.00
10	Roger Kieschnick, Rob Grossman	15.00
11	Logan Forsythe, J.P. Ramirez	10.00
12	Brett Wallace, Kyle Skipworth	25.00

Youth National Team Jersey Autographs
NM/M
Production 295 Sets
3	Colton Cain	20.00
4	Justin Charles	10.00
5	A.J. Cole	10.00
6	Matt Davidson	20.00
7	Nolan Fontana	15.00
8	Nick Franklin	15.00
9	Nate Gonzalez	10.00
11	Zach Lee	10.00
12	Austin Maddox	15.00
14	Steve Rodriguez	15.00
15	Richie Shaffer	15.00
17	Jacob Tillotson	15.00
18	Zach Vincej	15.00

2008 Upper Deck X
NM/M
Complete Set (100): 30.00
Common Player (1-100): .25
Pack (8): 3.00
Box (20): 55.00
1	Randy Johnson	.75
2	Conor Jackson	.50
3	Brandon Webb	.50
4	Justin Upton	.50
5	Dan Haren	.40
6	John Smoltz	.50
7	Chipper Jones	.50
8	Mark Teixeira	.50
9	Brian Roberts	.40
10	Nick Markakis	.40
11	Daisuke Matsuzaka	1.00
12	David Ortiz	.75
13	Manny Ramirez	.75
14	Jonathan Papelbon	.50
15	Josh Beckett	.50
16	Clay Buchholz (RC)	1.00
17	Carlos Zambrano	.40
18	Derek Lee	.50
19	Aramis Ramirez	.50
20	Kerry Wood	.25
21	Alfonso Soriano	.40
22	Kosuke Fukudome RC	3.00
23	Geovany Soto	.50
24	Paul Konerko	.40
25	Jermaine Dye	.40
26	Carlos Quentin	.40
27	Jim Thome	.50
28	Ken Griffey Jr.	1.50
29	Adam Dunn	.40
30	Brandon Phillips	.25
31	Edinson Volquez	.25
32	Victor Martinez	.25
33	Travis Hafner	.25
34	C.C. Sabathia	.50
35	Grady Sizemore	.75
36	Garrett Atkins	.25
37	Matt Holliday	.50
38	Troy Tulowitzki	.50

Player		Player		Player	
Justin Verlander	.40	DJ Derek Jeter	3.00	JF Jeff Francoeur	4.00
Miguel Cabrera	.50	DL Derrek Lee	1.00	JG Jeremy Guthrie	4.00
Gary Sheffield	.50	DM Daisuke Matsuzaka	2.00	JH J.J. Hardy	6.00
Magglio Ordonez	.40	DO David Ortiz	1.50	JK Jeff Kent	6.00
Hanley Ramirez	.75	DW Dontrelle Willis	.50	JM Joe Mauer	6.00
Jeremy Hermida	.25	EB Erik Bedard	.25	JO Josh Hamilton	15.00
Carlos Lee	.40	FH Felix Hernandez	1.00	JP Jhonny Peralta	4.00
Lance Berkman	.40	FT Frank Thomas	1.00	JR Jeremy Reed	4.00
Roy Oswalt	.40	GA Garrett Atkins	.50	JS James Shields	6.00
Alex Gordon	.25	GM Greg Maddux	2.50	JV Jason Varitek	8.00
Zack Greinke	.25	GR Khalil Greene	.25	JW Jered Weaver	4.00
Howie Kendrick	.25	GS Grady Sizemore	1.50	KE Kelly Johnson	4.00
Torii Hunter	.40	GU Carlos Guillen	.50	KJ Kenji Johjima	4.00
Vladimir Guerrero	.75	HE Todd Helton	.75	KM Kazuo Matsui	4.00
Matt Kemp	.40	HM Hideki Matsui	1.50	KU Jason Kubel	4.00
Russell Martin	.40	HO Trevor Hoffman	.50	KW Kerry Wood	4.00
Rafael Furcal	.40	HR Hanley Ramirez	1.50	KY Kevin Youkilis	8.00
Ryan Braun	.75	HU Torii Hunter	.75	LG Luis Gonzalez	4.00
Prince Fielder	.50	IR Ivan Rodriguez	.75	LM Lastings Milledge	4.00
Corey Hart	.25	IS Ichiro Suzuki	2.00	MA John Maine	4.00
Justin Morneau	.50	JA Jason Bay	.75	MC Matt Cain	4.00
Joe Mauer	.50	JB Josh Beckett	1.00	MG Matt Garza	4.00
Jose Reyes	.75	JC Joba Chamberlain	2.50	MI Kevin Millwood	4.00
David Wright	1.00	JF Jeff Francoeur	.50	MK Kendry Morales	4.00
Carlos Beltran	.50	JH Josh Hamilton	1.50	MO Justin Morneau	6.00
Johan Santana	.50	JI Jimmy Rollins	.75	MP Mark Prior	4.00
Pedro Martinez	.50	JK Jeff Kent	.50	MR Mariano Rivera	8.00
Ian Kennedy RC	1.00	JM Justin Morneau	1.00	NS Nick Swisher	4.00
Hideki Matsui	.75	JO Chipper Jones	2.00	PA Jonathan Papelbon	8.00
Alex Rodriguez	2.00	JP Jonathan Papelbon	1.00	PE Jake Peavy	8.00
Chien-Ming Wang	.75	JR Jose Reyes	1.50	PF Prince Fielder	8.00
Derek Jeter	2.00	JS John Smoltz	1.00	PI Juan Pierre	4.00
Robinson Cano	.50	JT Jim Thome	1.00	PO Jorge Posada	8.00
Eric Chavez	.25	JV Jason Varitek	.75	RA Aramis Ramirez	6.00
Frank Thomas	.50	KG Ken Griffey Jr.	2.50	RF Rafael Furcal	4.00
Cole Hamels	.50	LB Lance Berkman	1.00	RH Rich Hill	4.00
Jimmy Rollins	.75	MA Joe Mauer	1.50	RM Russell Martin	6.00
Ryan Howard	.75	MC Miguel Cabrera	1.00	RZ Ryan Zimmerman	4.00
Chase Utley	.75	MH Matt Holliday	1.00	SA Johan Santana	8.00
Nate McLouth	.40	MO Magglio Ordonez	1.00	SC Sean Casey	4.00
Jason Bay	.40	MR Manny Ramirez	1.00	SP Scott Podsednik	4.00
Adrian Gonzalez	.40	MT Mark Teixeira	1.00	TG Tom Gorzelanny	4.00
Khalil Greene	.25	NM Nick Markakis	1.00	TH Tim Hudson	4.00
Jake Peavy	.50	NS Nick Swisher	.50	TL Tim Lincecum	8.00
Greg Maddux	1.50	PB Pat Burrell	.50	TS Takashi Saito	4.00
Trevor Hoffman	.25	PE Jake Peavy	1.00	TT Troy Tulowitzki	6.00
Aaron Rowand	.25	PF Prince Fielder	1.00	TW Tim Wakefield	4.00
Tim Lincecum	.75	PK Paul Konerko	.50	UP B.J. Upton	6.00
Ichiro Suzuki	1.50	PM Pedro Martinez	1.00	VE Justin Verlander	6.00
Felix Hernandez	.50	RA Rick Ankiel	1.00		
Erik Bedard	.25	RB Ryan Braun	1.50		
Rick Ankiel	.25	RH Ryan Howard	2.00		
Albert Pujols	2.00	RI Mariano Rivera	.75		
B.J. Upton	.40	RJ Randy Johnson	1.00		
Carl Crawford	.50	RM Russell Martin	1.00		
Evan Longoria RC	5.00	RO Roy Oswalt	.75		
Josh Hamilton	.75	RW Rickie Weeks	.50		
Michael Young	.40	RZ Ryan Zimmerman	1.00		
Vernon Wells	.40	SA Johan Santana	1.50		
Alex Rios	.40	SH Gary Sheffield	.75		
Ryan Zimmerman	.50	TE Miguel Tejada	.50		
Lastings Milledge	.25	TH Travis Hafner	.50		

Die-Cut

Die-Cut (1-100):	1-2X
Inserted 1:Pack	

Die-Cut Gold

Die-Cut Gold (1-100):	3-5X

Printing Plates

No Pricing
Production one set per color.

UDxponential X

	NM/M
Common Player:	.50
Inserted 1:2	
2:	1X
Inserted 1:3	
3:	1.5-2X
Inserted 1:9	
4:	2-4X
Inserted 1:18	
Adam Dunn	1.00
Adrian Gonzalez	1.00
Andruw Jones	1.00
Alex Rodriguez	3.00
Albert Pujols	3.00
Aramis Ramirez	1.00
Alfonso Soriano	1.00
Bobby Abreu	1.00
Brandon Phillips	.75
Brian Roberts	.75
B.J. Upton	1.00
Brandon Webb	1.00
Carlos Beltran	1.00
Carl Crawford	1.00
Curtis Granderson	1.00
Corey Hart	.75
Conor Jackson	.75
Carlos Lee	1.00
Carlos Pena	.75
C.C. Sabathia	1.50
Chase Utley	1.50
Chien-Ming Wang	2.00
Chris Young	1.00
Carlos Zambrano	.75

Die-Cut Gold

Memorabilia

	NM/M
Common Player:	4.00
AA Aaron Harang	4.00
AB Adrian Beltre	4.00
AE Andre Ethier	4.00
AG Adrian Gonzalez	6.00
AH Aubrey Huff	4.00
AK Austin Kearns	4.00
AR Alex Rodriguez	20.00
BB Boof Bonser	4.00
BG Brian Giles	4.00
BH Bill Hall	4.00
BJ Brandon Jones	4.00
BM Brian McCann	4.00
BO Jeremy Bonderman	4.00
BP Brad Penny	4.00
BR Brian Roberts	4.00
BU A.J. Burnett	4.00
CA Melky Cabrera	4.00
CC Chris Carpenter	4.00
CD Carlos Delgado	6.00
CH Craig Hansen	4.00
CJ Conor Jackson	4.00
CL Carlos Lee	6.00
CR Joe Crede	4.00
CS Curt Schilling	4.00
CZ Carlos Zambrano	6.00
DL Derrek Lee	4.00
DO David Ortiz	10.00
DR J.D. Drew	4.00
DU Dan Uggla	4.00
DY Jermaine Dye	6.00
EG Eric Gagne	4.00
FR Francisco Rodriguez	4.00
FS Freddy Sanchez	4.00
GA Garrett Atkins	4.00
GJ Geoff Jenkins	4.00
GL Troy Glaus	4.00
GM Greg Maddux	15.00
GS Grady Sizemore	15.00
HA Travis Hafner	4.00
HP Hunter Pence	6.00
HR Hanley Ramirez	10.00
HS Huston Street	4.00
HU Torii Hunter	6.00
IK Ian Kinsler	8.00
IR Ivan Rodriguez	6.00
JB Josh Barfield	4.00
JD Johnny Damon	6.00
JE Johnny Estrada	4.00

Signatures

	NM/M
Common Auto.:	8.00
Inserted 1:10 Hobby	
BB Brian Bass	8.00
BI Brian Bixler	10.00
CA Jesse Carlson	10.00
CB Clay Buchholz	25.00
CC Callix Crabbe	8.00
CM Colt Morton	8.00
CT Clete Thomas	15.00
DJ Derek Jeter	150.00
EL Evan Longoria	75.00
EM Evan Meek	8.00
FC Frank Catalanotto	8.00
JA Jonathan Albaladejo	12.00
JC Johnny Cueto	40.00
JK Jeff Keppinger	10.00
JN Josh Newman	10.00
JT J.R. Towles	10.00
KG Ken Griffey Jr.	80.00
KH Kevin Hart	15.00
LM Luis Mendoza	8.00
MB Marlon Byrd	15.00
RO Ross Ohlendorf	10.00
RT Rich Thompson	10.00
SH Steve Holm	10.00
TI Clay Timpner	8.00
TR Ramon Troncoso	8.00
WB Wladimir Balentien	15.00

2009 Upper Deck

CHRIS DAVIS

	NM/M
Complete Set (1,006):	175.00
Complete Series 1 Set (500):	75.00
Complete Series 2 Set (506):	100.00
Common Player:	.25
Common RC:	.50

Griffey #855 has 21 SP versions

Hobby Pack (20):	5.00
Hobby Box (16):	70.00

#	Player	
0	Joe DiMaggio/SP	50.00
1	Randy Johnson	.75
2	Conor Jackson	.25
3	Brandon Webb	.50
4	Dan Haren	.40
5	Orlando Hudson	.25
6	Stephen Drew	.50
7	Mark Reynolds	.25
8	Eric Byrnes	.25
9	Justin Upton	.50
10	Chris B. Young	.50
11	Max Scherzer	.25
12	Alex Romero	.25
13	Chad Tracy	.25
14	Brandon Lyon	.25
15	Adam Dunn	.50
16	David Eckstein	.25
17	Jair Jurrjens	.25
18	Mike Hampton	.25
19	Brandon Jones	.25
20	Tom Glavine	.75
21	John Smoltz	.50
22	Chipper Jones	1.00
23	Yunel Escobar	.25
24	Kelly Johnson	.25
25	Brian McCann	.50
26	Jeff Francoeur	.40
27	Tim Hudson	.40
28	Casey Kotchman	.25
29	Nick Markakis	.50
30	Brian Roberts	.40
31	Jeremy Guthrie	.25
32	Ramon Hernandez	.25
33	Lou Montanez	.25
34	Luke Scott	.25
35	Aubrey Huff	.25
36	Daniel Cabrera	.25
37	George Sherrill	.25
38	Melvin Mora	.25
39	Jay Payton	.25
40	Mark Kotsay	.25
41	David Ortiz	1.00
42	Jacoby Ellsbury	1.00
43	Coco Crisp	.25
44	J.D. Drew	.40
45	Daisuke Matsuzaka	1.00
46	Josh Beckett	.50
47	Curt Schilling	.50
48	Clay Buchholz	.50
49	Dustin Pedroia	1.00
50	Julio Lugo	.25
51	Mike Lowell	.40
52	Jonathan Papelbon	.50
53	Jason Varitek	.40
54	Hideki Okajima	.25
55	Jon Lester	.75
56	Tim Wakefield	.25
57	Kevin Youkilis	.50
58	Jason Bay	.50
59	Justin Masterson	.50
60	Jeff Samardzija	.50
61	Alfonso Soriano	.50
62	Derrek Lee	.50
63	Aramis Ramirez	.50
64	Kerry Wood	.40
65	Jim Edmonds	.25
66	Kosuke Fukudome	.50
67	Geovany Soto	.75
68	Ted Lilly	.25
69	Carlos Zambrano	.40
70	Ryan Theriot	.25
71	Mark DeRosa	.25
72	Ronny Cedeno	.25
73	Ryan Dempster	.25
74	Jon Lieber	.25
75	Rich Hill	.25
76	Rich Harden	.25
77	Alexei Ramirez	.50
78	Nick Swisher	.40
79	Carlos Quentin	.50
80	Jermaine Dye	.25
81	Paul Konerko	.25
82	Orlando Cabrera	.40
83	Joe Crede	.25
84	Jim Thome	.50
85	Gavin Floyd	.25
86	Javier Vazquez	.25
87	Mark Buehrle	.25
88	Bobby Jenks	.25
89	Brian Anderson	.25
90	A.J. Pierzynski	.25
91	Jose Contreras	.25
92	Juan Uribe	.25
93	Ken Griffey Jr.	1.50
94	Chris Dickerson	.25
95	Brandon Phillips	.25
96	Aaron Harang	.25
97	Bronson Arroyo	.25
98	Edinson Volquez	.40
99	Johnny Cueto	.40
100	Edwin Encarnacion	.25
101	Jeff Keppinger	.25
102	Joey Votto	.50
103	Jay Bruce	1.00
104	Ryan Freel	.25
105	Travis Hafner	.25
106	Victor Martinez	.40
107	Grady Sizemore	.75
108	Cliff Lee	.40
109	Ryan Garko	.25
110	Jhonny Peralta	.25
111	Franklin Gutierrez	.25
112	Fausto Carmona	.25
113	Jeff Baker	.25
114	Troy Tulowitzki	.40
115	Matt Holliday	.50
116	Todd Helton	.50
117	Ubaldo Jimenez	.25
118	Brian Fuentes	.25
119	Willy Taveras	.25
120	Aaron Cook	.25
121	Jason Grilli	.25
122	Garrett Atkins	.25
123	Jeff Francis	.25
124	Ryan Spilborghs	.25
125	Armando Galarraga	.50
126	Miguel Cabrera	.50
127	Placido Polanco	.25
128	Edgar Renteria	.25
129	Carlos Guillen	.25
130	Gary Sheffield	.50
131	Curtis Granderson	.50
132	Marcus Thames	.25
133	Magglio Ordonez	.25
134	Jeremy Bonderman	.25
135	Dontrelle Willis	.25
136	Kenny Rogers	.25
137	Justin Verlander	.50
138	Nate Robertson	.25
139	Todd Jones	.25
140	Joel Zumaya	.25
141	Hanley Ramirez	.75
142	Jeremy Hermida	.25
143	Mike Jacobs	.25
144	Andrew Miller	.40
145	Josh Willingham	.25
146	Luis Gonzalez	.25
147	Dan Uggla	.40
148	Scott Olsen	.25
149	Josh Johnson	.25
150	Darin Erstad	.25
151	Hunter Pence	.50
152	Roy Oswalt	.50
153	Lance Berkman	.50
154	Carlos Lee	.50
155	Michael Bourn	.25
156	Kazuo Matsui	.25
157	Miguel Tejada	.50
158	Ty Wigginton	.25
159	Jose Valverde	.25
160	J.R. Towles	.25
161	Brandon Backe	.25
162	Randy Wolf	.25
163	Mike Aviles	.25
164	Brian Bannister	.25
165	Zack Greinke	.40
166	Gil Meche	.25
167	Alex Gordon	.50
168	Tony Pena	.25
169	Luke Hochevar	.25
170	Mark Grudzielanek	.25
171	Jose Guillen	.25
172	Billy Butler	.25
173	David DeJesus	.25
174	Joey Gathright	.25
175	Mark Teahen	.25
176	Joakim Soria	.40
177	Mark Teixeira	.50
178	Vladimir Guerrero	.50
179	Torii Hunter	.40
180	Jered Weaver	.40
181	Chone Figgins	.40
182	Francisco Rodriguez	.25
183	Garret Anderson	.25
184	Howie Kendrick	.40
185	John Lackey	.25
186	Ervin Santana	.40
187	Joe Saunders	.25
188	Gary Matthews	.25
189	Jon Garland	.25
190	Nick Adenhart	.25
191	Manny Ramirez	.75
192	Casey Blake	.25
193	Chad Billingsley	.50
194	Russell Martin	.40
195	Matt Kemp	.50
196	James Loney	.40
197	Jeff Kent	.25
198	Nomar Garciaparra	.50
199	Rafael Furcal	.25
200	Andruw Jones	.25
201	Andre Ethier	.40
202	Takashi Saito	.25
203	Brad Penny	.25
204	Hiroki Kuroda	.25
205	Jonathan Broxton	.25
206	Chin-Lung Hu	.25
207	Juan Pierre	.25
208	Blake DeWitt	.25
209	Derek Lowe	.25
210	Clayton Kershaw	.75
211	Greg Maddux	1.50
212	C.C. Sabathia	.75
213	Yovani Gallardo	.50
214	Ryan Braun	1.00
215	Prince Fielder	.75
216	Corey Hart	.50
217	Bill Hall	.25
218	Rickie Weeks	.25
219	Mike Cameron	.25
220	Ben Sheets	.25
221	Jason Kendall	.25
222	J.J. Hardy	.40
223	Jeff Suppan	.25
224	Ray Durham	.25
225	Denard Span	.25
226	Carlos Gomez	.25
227	Joe Mauer	.50
228	Justin Morneau	.50
229	Michael Cuddyer	.25
230	Joe Nathan	.25
231	Kevin Slowey	.25
232	Delmon Young	.40
233	Jason Kubel	.25
234	Craig Monroe	.25
235	Livan Hernandez	.25
236	Francisco Liriano	.50
237	Pat Neshek	.25
238	Boof Bonser	.25
239	Nick Blackburn	.25
240	Daniel Murphy	.25
241	Nick Evans	.25
242	Jose Reyes	.75
243	David Wright	1.00
244	Carlos Delgado	.50
245	Luis Castillo	.25
246	Ryan Church	.25
247	Carlos Beltran	.50
248	Moises Alou	.40
249	Pedro Martinez	.50
250	Johan Santana	.50
251	John Maine	.25
252	Endy Chavez	.25
253	Oliver Perez	.25
254	Brian Schneider	.25
255	Fernando Tatis	.25
256	Mike Pelfrey	.25
257	Billy Wagner	.25
258	Ramon Castro	.25
259	Ivan Rodriguez	.50
260	Alex Rodriguez	2.00
261	Derek Jeter	2.00
262	Robinson Cano	.50
263	Jason Giambi	.40
264	Bobby Abreu	.50
265	Johnny Damon	.50
266	Melky Cabrera	.25
267	Hideki Matsui	.75
268	Jorge Posada	.50
269	Joba Chamberlain	1.00
270	Ian Kennedy	.25
271	Mike Mussina	.40
272	Andy Pettitte	.50
273	Mariano Rivera	.50
274	Chien-Ming Wang	.50
275	Phil Hughes	.25
276	Xavier Nady	.25
277	Richie Sexson	.25
278	Brad Ziegler	.25
279	Justin Duchscherer	.25
280	Eric Chavez	.25
281	Bobby Crosby	.25
282	Mark Ellis	.25
283	Daric Barton	.25
284	Frank Thomas	.50
285	Emil Brown	.25
286	Huston Street	.25
287	Jack Cust	.25
288	Kurt Suzuki	.25
289	Joe Blanton	.25
290	Ryan Howard	1.00
291	Chase Utley	.75
292	Jimmy Rollins	.50
293	Pedro Feliz	.25
294	Pat Burrell	.25
295	Geoff Jenkins	.25
296	Shane Victorino	.50
297	Brett Myers	.25
298	Brad Lidge	.25
299	Cole Hamels	.75
300	Jamie Moyer	.25
301	Adam Eaton	.25
302	Matt Stairs	.25
303	Nate McLouth	.40
304	Ian Snell	.25
305	Matt Capps	.25
306	Freddy Sanchez	.25
307	Ryan Doumit	.25
308	Adam LaRoche	.25
309	Jack Wilson	.25
310	Tom Gorzelanny	.25
311	Jody Gerut	.25
312	Jake Peavy	.50
313	Chris Young	.25
314	Trevor Hoffman	.25
315	Adrian Gonzalez	.50
316	Chase Headley	.25
317	Khalil Greene	.25
318	Kevin Kouzmanoff	.25
319	Brian Giles	.25
320	Josh Bard	.25
321	Scott Hairston	.25
322	Barry Zito	.25
323	Tim Lincecum	.75
324	Matt Cain	.50
325	Brian Wilson	.25
326	Aaron Rowand	.25
327	Randy Winn	.25
328	Omar Vizquel	.25
329	Bengie Molina	.25
330	Fred Lewis	.25
331	Erik Bedard	.40
332	Felix Hernandez	.50
333	Ichiro Suzuki	1.50
334	J.J. Putz	.25
335	Raul Ibanez	.25
336	Adrian Beltre	.25
337	Jose Vidro	.25
338	Jeff Clement	.25
339	Kenji Johjima	.25
340	Wladimir Balentien	.25
341	Jose Lopez	.25
342	Kyle Lohse	.25
343	Albert Pujols	2.00
344	Troy Glaus	.40
345	Chris Carpenter	.25
346	Adam Kennedy	.25
347	Rick Ankiel	.25
348	Adam Wainwright	.25
349	Jason Isringhausen	.25
350	Chris Duncan	.25

#	Player	Price
351	Skip Schumaker	.25
352	Mark Mulder	.25
353	Todd Wellemeyer	.25
354	Cesar Izturis	.25
355	Ryan Ludwick	.50
356	Yadier Molina	.25
357	Braden Looper	.25
358	B.J. Upton	.50
359	Carl Crawford	.40
360	Evan Longoria	2.00
361	James Shields	.25
362	Scott Kazmir	.40
363	Carlos Pena	.50
364	Akinori Iwamura	.25
365	Jonny Gomes	.25
366	Cliff Floyd	.25
367	Troy Percival	.25
368	Edwin Jackson	.25
369	Matt Garza	.25
370	Eric Hinske	.25
371	Rocco Baldelli	.25
372	Chris Davis	1.00
373	Marlon Byrd	.25
374	Michael Young	.25
375	Ian Kinsler	.50
376	Josh Hamilton	.75
377	Hank Blalock	.40
378	Milton Bradley	.25
379	Kevin Millwood	.25
380	Vicente Padilla	.25
381	Jarrod Saltalamacchia	.40
382	Jesse Litsch	.25
383	Roy Halladay	.40
384	A.J. Burnett	.40
385	Dustin McGowan	.25
386	Scott Rolen	.25
387	Alex Rios	.40
388	Vernon Wells	.40
389	Shannon Stewart	.25
390	B.J. Ryan	.25
391	Lyle Overbay	.25
392	Elijah Dukes	.25
393	Lastings Milledge	.40
394	Chad Cordero	.25
395	Ryan Zimmerman	.50
396	Austin Kearns	.25
397	Wily Mo Pena	.25
398	Ronnie Belliard	.25
399	Cristian Guzman	.25
400	Jesus Flores	.25
401	David Price RC	5.00
401	David Price/ SP Glv on mound	60.00
402	Matt Antonelli RC	1.00
403	Jon Niese RC	1.00
404	Phil Coke RC	.50
405	Jason Pridie RC	.50
406	Mark Saccomanno RC	.50
407	Freddy Sandoval RC	.50
408	Travis Snider RC	2.00
409	Matt Tuiasosopo RC	.50
410	Will Venable RC	1.00
411	Brad Nelson RC	.50
412	Aaron Cunningham RC	1.00
413	Wilkin Castillo RC	1.00
414	Robert Parnell RC	1.00
415	Conor Gillaspie RC	1.00
416	Dexter Fowler RC	1.00
417	George Kottaras RC	.50
418	Josh Roenicke RC	.50
419	Luis Valbuena RC	1.00
420	Casey McGehee RC	1.50
421	Mat Gamel RC	2.50
422	Greg Golson RC	1.00
423	Alfredo Aceves RC	1.00
424	Michael Bowden RC	1.00
425	Kila Ka'aihue RC	1.50
426	Josh Geer RC	.50
427	James Parr RC	.50
428	Chris Lambert RC	.50
429	Fernando Perez RC	.50
430	Josh Whitesell RC	1.50
431	Josh Beckett, Dustin Pedroia, Daisuke Matsuzaka	1.00
432	Jimmy Rollins, Ryan Howard, Cole Hamels	1.00
433	Carlos Delgado, David Wright, Jose Reyes	1.00
434	Alex Rodriguez, Mike Mussina, Derek Jeter	2.00
435	Javier Vazquez, Gavin Floyd, Carlos Quentin	.50
436	Albert Pujols, Ryan Ludwick, Todd Wellemeyer	1.50
437	Miguel Cabrera, Curtis Granderson, Justin Verlander	.50
438	Brian Giles, Adrian Gonzalez, Jake Peavy	.50
439	Ben Sheets, Prince Fielder, Ryan Braun	.50
440	Grady Sizemore, Cliff Lee, Jhonny Peralta	.50
441	Josh Hamilton, Vicente Padilla, Ian Kinsler	.50
442	Ricky Nolasco, Jorge Cantu, Hanley Ramirez	.75
443	Carlos Pena, B.J. Upton, Akinori Iwamura	.25
444	Jack Cust, Kurt Suzuki, Dana Eveland	.25
445	Aramis Ramirez, Alfonso Soriano, Ryan Dempster	.50
446	Miguel Tejada, Lance Berkman, Roy Oswalt	.25

#	Player	Price
447	Aaron Cook, Matt Holliday, Willy Taveras	.50
448	Adam LaRoche, Nate McLouth, Pat Maholm	.25
449	Aubrey Huff, Brian Roberts, Jeremy Guthrie	.25
450	Justin Morneau, Joe Mauer, Carlos Gomez	.50
451	Raul Ibanez, Felix Hernandez, Ichiro Suzuki	1.00
452	Chipper Jones, Brian McCann, Jair Jurrjens	.75
453	Dan Haren, Brandon Webb, Stephen Drew	.40
454	Bengie Molina, Randy Winn, Tim Lincecum	.50
455	Roy Halladay, A.J. Burnett, Alex Rios	.25
456	Brandon Phillips, Edwin Encarnacion, Edinson Volquez	.25
457	James Loney, Chad Billingsley, Matt Kemp	.50
458	Vladimir Guerrero, Francisco Rodriguez, Ervin Santana	.50
459	Gil Meche, Zack Greinke, David DeJesus	.25
460	Cristian Guzman, Tim Redding, Lastings Milledge	.25
461	Carlos Zambrano	.40
462	Jon Lester	.50
463	Jim Thome	.25
464	Ken Griffey Jr.	1.50
465	Manny Ramirez	.75
466	Derek Jeter	2.00
467	Josh Hamilton	.75
468	Francisco Rodriguez	.40
469	Alex Rodriguez	1.00
470	J.D. Drew	.25
471	David Wright	.75
472	Chase Utley	.75
473	Chipper Jones	.75
474	Cristian Guzman	.25
475	Hanley Ramirez	.50
476	C.C. Sabathia	.75
477	Lance Berkman	.50
478	Alfonso Soriano	.50
479	Albert Pujols	1.50
480	Nate McLouth	.25
481	Brandon Phillips	.25
482	Adrian Gonzalez	.40
483	Brandon Webb	.50
484	Manny Ramirez	.75
485	Tim Lincecum	.75
486	Matt Holliday	.50
487	Dustin Pedroia	.75
488	Alex Rodriguez	1.00
489	Evan Longoria	1.50
490	Roy Halladay	.40
491	Nick Markakis	.50
492	Grady Sizemore	.50
493	Carlos Quentin	.25
494	Joakim Soria	.25
495	Miguel Cabrera	.50
496	Joe Mauer	.40
497	Francisco Rodriguez	.25
498	Jack Cust	.25
499	Ichiro Suzuki	1.00
500	Josh Hamilton	.75
501	Brandon Webb	.50
502	Miguel Montero	.25
503	Tony Pena	.25
504	Jon Rauch	.25
505	Augie Ojeda	.25
506	Yusmeiro Petit	.25
507	Chris Snyder	.25
508	Chris B. Young	.25
509	Doug Slaten	.25
510	Tony Clark	.25
511	Justin Upton	.75
512	Chad Qualls	.25
513	Doug Davis	.25
514	Eric Byrnes	.25
515	Conor Jackson	.25
516	Mike Gonzalez	.25
517	Josh Anderson	.25
518	Tom Glavine	.50
519	Clint Sammons	.25
520	Martin Prado	.25
521	Jorge Campillo	.25
522	Omar Infante	.25
523	Javier Vazquez	.25
524	Jo Jo Reyes	.25
525	Gregor Blanco	.25
526	Rafael Soriano	.25
527	Manny Acosta	.25
528	Chipper Jones	1.00
529	Buddy Carlyle	.25
530	Radhames Liz	.25
531	Scott Moore	.25
532	Jim Johnson	.25
533	Oscar Salazar	.25
534	Nick Markakis	.75
535	Brian Roberts	.40
536	Jeremy Guthrie	.25
537	Adam Jones	.50
538	Chris Ray	.25
539	Aubrey Huff	.25
540	Ty Wigginton	.25
541	Dennis Sarfate	.25
542	Melvin Mora	.25
543	Chris Waters	.25
544	John Smoltz	.50

#	Player	Price
545	Brad Penny	.25
546	Josh Bard	.25
547	Takashi Saito	.25
548	Jacoby Ellsbury	1.00
549	Jeff Bailey	.25
550	Ramon Ramirez	.25
551	Daisuke Matsuzaka	.75
552	Josh Beckett	.75
553	Jed Lowrie	.25
554	Dustin Pedroia	1.00
555	David Ortiz	.75
556	Jonathan Van Every	.25
557	Jonathan Papelbon	.50
558	Manny Delcarmen	.25
559	Hideki Okajima	.25
560	Jon Lester	.50
561	Javier Lopez	.25
562	Kevin Youkilis	.50
563	Jason Varitek	.25
564	Milton Bradley	.25
565	Mike Fontenot	.25
566	Micah Hoffpauir	.25
567	Sean Marshall	.25
568	Alfonso Soriano	.50
569	Neal Cotts	.25
570	Kosuke Fukudome	.50
571	Reed Johnson	.25
572	Carlos Marmol	.25
573	Chad Gaudin	.25
574	Rich Harden	.25
575	Ted Lilly	.25
576	Carlos Zambrano	.40
577	Ryan Theriot	.25
578	Ryan Dempster	.25
579	Matt Thornton	.25
580	Jerry Owens	.25
581	Alexei Ramirez	.25
582	John Danks	.40
583	Carlos Quentin	.50
584	D.J. Carrasco	.25
585	Dewayne Wise	.25
586	Clayton Richard	.25
587	Brent Lillibridge	.25
588	Jim Thome	.50
589	Chris Getz	.25
590	Octavio Dotel	.25
591	Mark Buehrle	.25
592	Bobby Jenks	.25
593	Joey Votto	.50
594	Jay Bruce	.75
595	David Weathers	.25
596	Bill Bray	.25
597	Mike Lincoln	.25
598	Norris Hopper	.25
599	Alex Gonzalez	.25
600	Jerry Hairston Jr.	.25
601	Brandon Phillips	.40
602	Aaron Harang	.40
603	Bronson Arroyo	.25
604	Edinson Volquez	.40
605	Ryan Hanigan	.25
606	Jared Burton	.25
607	Aaron Laffey	.25
608	Kerry Wood	.25
609	Shin-Soo Choo	.40
610	David Dellucci	.25
611	Mark DeRosa	.25
612	Masahide Kobayashi	.25
613	Rafael Perez	.25
614	Grady Sizemore	.75
615	Cliff Lee	.40
616	Ben Francisco	.25
617	Jensen Lewis	.25
618	Joe Smith	.25
619	Asdrubal Cabrera	.25
620	Brad Hawpe	.25
621	Chris Iannetta	.25
622	Clint Barmes	.25
623	Seth Smith	.25
624	Aaron Cook	.25
625	Troy Tulowitzki	.40
626	Todd Helton	.25
627	Taylor Buchholz	.25
628	Jason Marquis	.25
629	Ian Stewart	.25
630	Ryan Speier	.25
631	Manny Corpas	.25
632	Yorvit Torrealba	.25
633	Fernando Rodney	.25
634	Justin Verlander	.50
635	Bobby Seay	.25
636	Clete Thomas	.25
637	Placido Polanco	.25
638	Ramon Santiago	.25
639	Adam Everett	.25
640	Gary Sheffield	.50
641	Curtis Granderson	.75
642	Freddy Dolsi	.25
643	Magglio Ordonez	.40
644	Zach Miner	.25
645	Brandon Inge	.25
646	Dallas McPherson	.25
647	Anibal Sanchez	.25
648	Jorge Cantu	.25
649	John Baker	.25
650	Wes Helms	.25
651	Ricky Nolasco	.25
652	Chris Volstad	.25
653	Renyel Pinto	.25
654	Alfredo Amezaga	.25
655	Cameron Maybin	.40
656	Matt Lindstrom	.25
657	Cody Ross	.25
658	Logan Kensing	.25
659	Tim Byrdak	.25
660	Reggie Abercrombie	.25
661	Geoff Blum	.25
662	Humberto Quintero	.25

#	Player	Price
663	Doug Brocail	.25
664	Roy Oswalt	.50
665	Lance Berkman	.40
666	Carlos Lee	.50
667	LaTroy Hawkins	.25
668	Geoff Geary	.25
669	Brian Moehler	.25
670	Wandy Rodriguez	.25
671	Esteban German	.25
672	Ross Gload	.25
673	Joakim Soria	.40
674	Kyle Farnsworth	.25
675	Ryan Shealy	.25
676	Mike Aviles	.25
677	John Buck	.25
678	Zack Greinke	.50
679	John Bale	.25
680	Alex Gordon	.40
681	Coco Crisp	.25
682	Miguel Olivo	.25
683	Alberto Callaspo	.25
684	Kyle Davies	.25
685	Brandon Wood	.25
686	Erick Aybar	.25
687	Robb Quinlan	.25
688	Bobby Abreu	.50
689	Jose Arredondo	.25
690	Juan Rivera	.25
691	Kendry Morales	.25
692	Vladimir Guerrero	.50
693	Darren Oliver	.25
694	Jeff Mathis	.25
695	Maicer Izturis	.25
696	Mike Napoli	.25
697	Reggie Willits	.25
698	Scot Shields	.25
699	John Lackey	.25
700	Manny Ramirez	.75
701	Danny Ardoin	.25
702	Orlando Hudson	.25
703	Hong-Chih Kuo	.25
704	Mark Loretta	.25
705	Cory Wade	.25
706	Casey Blake	.25
707	Eric Stults	.25
708	Jason Schmidt	.25
709	Chad Billingsley	.40
710	Russell Martin	.40
711	Matt Kemp	.50
712	James Loney	.40
713	Rafael Furcal	.50
714	Ramon Troncoso	.25
715	Jonathan Broxton	.25
716	Hiroki Kuroda	.25
717	Andre Ethier	.40
718	Corey Hart	.25
719	Mitch Stetter	.25
720	Manny Parra	.25
721	David Bush	.25
722	Trevor Hoffman	.40
723	Tony Gwynn	.25
724	Chris Duffy	.25
725	Seth McClung	.25
726	J.J. Hardy	.40
727	David Riske	.25
728	Todd Coffey	.25
729	Rickie Weeks	.25
730	Mike Rivera	.25
731	Carlos Villanueva	.25
732	Ryan Braun	1.00
733	Nick Punto	.25
734	Francisco Liriano	.25
735	Craig Breslow	.25
736	Matt Macri	.25
737	Scott Baker	.25
738	Jesse Crain	.25
739	Brendan Harris	.25
740	Alexi Casilla	.25
741	Nick Blackburn	.25
742	Brian Buscher	.25
743	Denard Span	.40
744	Mike Redmond	.25
745	Joe Mauer	.40
746	Carlos Gomez	.25
747	Matt Guerrier	.25
748	Joe Nathan	.40
749	Livan Hernandez	.25
750	Ryan Church	.25
751	Carlos Beltran	.50
752	Jeremy Reed	.25
753	Oliver Perez	.25
754	Duaner Sanchez	.25
755	J.J. Putz	.25
756	Mike Pelfrey	.25
757	Brian Schneider	.25
758	Francisco Rodriguez	.40
759	John Maine	.25
760	Daniel Murphy	.75
761	Johan Santana	.75
762	Jose Reyes	.50
763	David Wright	1.00
764	Carlos Delgado	.50
765	Pedro Feliciano	.25
766	Derek Jeter	2.00
767	Brian Bruney	.25
768	A.J. Burnett	.40
769	Andy Pettitte	.50
770	Nick Swisher	.40
771	Damaso Marte	.25
772	Edwar Ramirez	.25
773	C.C. Sabathia	.75
774	Chien-Ming Wang	.40
775	Mariano Rivera	.50
776	Mark Teixeira	.50
777	Joba Chamberlain	.75
778	Jose Veras	.25
779	Hideki Matsui	.40
780	Jose Molina	.25

#	Player	Price
781	Alex Rodriguez	1.50
782	Mike Wuertz	.25
783	Orlando Cabrera	.40
784	Sean Gallagher	.25
785	Dallas Braden	.25
786	Gio Gonzalez	.25
787	Rajai Davis	.25
788	Brad Ziegler	.25
789	Matt Holliday	.40
790	Jack Cust	.25
791	Santiago Casilla	.25
792	Jason Giambi	.40
793	Joey Devine	.25
794	Travis Buck	.25
795	Justin Duchscherer	.25
796	Rob Bowen	.25
797	Andrew Brown	.25
798	Ryan Sweeney	.25
799	Jimmy Rollins	.75
800	Chad Durbin	.25
801	Clay Condrey	.25
802	Chris Coste	.25
803	Ryan Madson	.25
804	Chan Ho Park	.25
805	Carlos Ruiz	.25
806	Kyle Kendrick	.25
807	Jayson Werth	.25
808	Cole Hamels	.75
809	Brad Lidge	.25
810	Greg Dobbs	.25
811	Scott Eyre	.25
812	Eric Bruntlett	.25
813	Ryan Howard	1.00
814	Chase Utley	.75
815	Paul Maholm	.25
816	Andy LaRoche	.25
817	Brandon Moss	.25
818	Nyjer Morgan	.25
819	John Grabow	.25
820	Tom Gorzelanny	.25
821	Steve Pearce	.25
822	Sean Burnett	.25
823	Tyler Yates	.25
824	Zach Duke	.25
825	Matt Capps	.25
826	Ross Ohlendorf	.25
827	Nate McLouth	.40
828	Adrian Gonzalez	.50
829	Heath Bell	.25
830	Luis Rodriguez	.25
831	Kevin Kouzmanoff	.25
832	Edgar Gonzalez	.25
833	Cha Sueng Baek	.25
834	Cla Meredith	.25
835	Justin Hampson	.25
836	Nick Hundley	.25
837	Mike Adams	.25
838	Jake Peavy	.50
839	Chris Young	.40
840	Brian Giles	.40
841	Steve Holm	.25
842	Dave Roberts	.25
843	Travis Ishikawa	.25
844	Pablo Sandoval	.25
845	Emmanuel Burriss	.25
846	Nate Schierholtz	.25
847	Randy Johnson	.50
848	Kevin Frandsen	.25
849	Edgar Renteria	.25
850	Jack Taschner	.25
851	Tim Lincecum	.75
852	Alex Hinshaw	.25
853	Jonathan Sanchez	.25
854	Eugenio Velez	.25
855	Ken Griffey Jr./ SP 21 variations	25.00
856	Garrett Olson	.25
857	Cesar Jimenez	.25
858	Bryan LaHair	.25
859	Franklin Gutierrez	.25
860	Brandon Morrow	.25
861	Roy Corcoran	.25
862	Carlos Silva	.25
863	Kenji Johjima	.25
864	Jarrod Washburn	.25
865	Felix Hernandez	.50
866	Ichiro Suzuki	1.50
867	Miguel Batista	.25
868	Yuniesky Betancourt	.25
869	Adrian Beltre	.40
870	Ryan Rowland-Smith	.25
871	Khalil Greene	.25
872	Kyle McClellan	.25
873	Ryan Franklin	.25
874	Brian Barton	.25
875	Josh Kinney	.25
876	Ryan Ludwick	.40
877	Brendan Ryan	.25
878	Albert Pujols	2.00
879	Troy Glaus	.25
880	Joel Pineiro	.25
881	Jason LaRue	.25
882	Yadier Molina	.25
883	Adam Wainwright	.40
884	Chris Perez	.25
885	Adam Kennedy	.25
886	Akinori Iwamura	.25
887	J.P. Howell	.25
888	Benjamin Zobrist	.25
889	Gabe Gross	.25
890	Matt Joyce	.25
891	Dan Wheeler	.25
892	Willy Aybar	.25
893	Jason Bartlett	.25
894	Dioner Navarro	.25
895	Andrew Sonnanstine	.25
896	B.J. Upton	.40
897	Chad Bradford	.25

#	Player	Price
898	Evan Longoria	1.5
899	Shawn Riggans	
900	Scott Kazmir	
901	Grant Balfour	
902	Josh Hamilton	
903	Frank Francisco	
904	Frank Catalanotto	
905	German Duran	
906	Brandon Boggs	
907	Matt Harrison	
908	David Murphy	
909	Nelson Cruz	
910	Joaquin Benoit	
911	Taylor Teagarden	
912	Joaquin Arias	
913	Kevin Millwood	
914	Ian Kinsler	
915	T.J. Beam	
916	Marco Scutaro	
917	Adam Lind	
918	John McDonald	
919	Scott Downs	
920	Rod Barajas	
921	Joe Inglett	
922	Alex Rios	
923	David Purcey	
924	Roy Halladay	
925	Jason Frasor	
926	Shaun Marcum	
927	Aaron Hill	
928	Adam Dunn	
929	Shawn Hill	
930	Steven Shell	
931	Saul Rivera	
932	Josh Willingham	
933	John Lannan	
934	Joel Hanrahan	
935	Daniel Cabrera	
936	Willie Harris	
937	Wilbert Nieves	
938	Nick Johnson	
939	Garrett Mock	
940	Anderson Hernandez	
941	Koji Uehara RC	1.0
942	Kenshin Kawakami RC	1.0
943	Jason Motte RC	1.0
944	Elvis Andrus RC	2.0
945	Rick Porcello RC	3.0
946	Colby Rasmus RC	1.5
947	Shairon Martis RC	1.5
948	Ricky Romero RC	1.5
949	Kevin Jepsen RC	
950	James McDonald RC	1.0
951	Joe Mauer	
952	Carlos Pena	
953	Dustin Pedroia	
954	Adrian Beltre	
955	Michael Young	
956	Torii Hunter	
957	Grady Sizemore	
958	Ichiro Suzuki	
959	Yadier Molina	
960	Adrian Gonzalez	
961	Brandon Phillips	
962	David Wright	
963	Jimmy Rollins	
964	Nate McLouth	
965	Carlos Beltran	
966	Shane Victorino	
967	Cliff Lee	
968	Brad Lidge	
969	Evan Longoria	
970	Geovany Soto	
971	Francisco Rodriguez	
972	Raul Ibanez	
973	Derek Lowe	
974	Scott Olsen	
975	Josh Johnson	
976	Prince Fielder	
977	Mike Hampton	
978	Kevin Gregg	
979	Rick Ankiel	
980	Nate McLouth	
981	Ramon Hernandez	
982	David Eckstein	
983	Felipe Lopez	
984	Clayton Kershaw	
985	Randy Johnson	
986	Huston Street	
987	Rocco Baldelli	
988	Mark Teixeira	
989	Pat Burrell	
990	Vernon Wells	
991	Cesar Izturis	
992	Kerry Wood	
993	Wilson Betemit	
994	Mike Jacobs	
995	Gerald Laird	
996	Justin Morneau	
997	Brian Fuentes	
998	Jason Giambi	
999	Endy Chavez	
1000	Michael Young	
1001	Brett Anderson RC	6.0
1002	Trevor Cahill RC	6.0
1003	Jordan Schafer RC	6.0
1004	Trevor Crowe RC	4.0
1005	Everth Cabrera RC	4.0
1006	Ryan Perry RC	6.0

Gold

Gold: 10-20
RC's: 4-8
Production 99 Sets

1975 O-Pee-Chee

NM/

Common Player:
Inserted 1:6 Hobby, 1:30 Retail

CUBS

ALFONSO SORIANO / OF

ni: .50
Inserted 1:48 Hobby, 1:240 Retail   1-2X
Albert Pujols	4.00
Alex Rodriguez	3.00
Alfonso Soriano	1.00
B.J. Upton	.75
Brandon Webb	1.00
C.C. Sabathia	1.50
Carl Crawford	.50
Carlos Beltran	1.50
Carlos Quentin	.75
Chase Utley	2.00
Chien-Ming Wang	1.50
Chipper Jones	2.00
Daisuke Matsuzaka	2.50
David Ortiz	1.50
David Wright	2.00
Derek Jeter	4.00
Derek Lee	
Evan Longoria	4.00
Felix Hernandez	1.00
Frank Thomas	1.50
Grady Sizemore	1.50
Greg Maddux	3.00
Hanley Ramirez	1.50
Ichiro Suzuki	3.00
Jake Peavy	1.00
Jimmy Rollins	1.50
Joba Chamberlain	2.00
Joe Mauer	.75
Johan Santana	.75
John Smoltz	.75
Jose Reyes	1.50
Josh Beckett	1.00
Josh Hamilton	2.00
Ken Griffey Jr.	3.00
Kosuke Fukudome	1.00
Lance Berkman	1.00
Magglio Ordonez	.50
Manny Ramirez	1.50
Mark Teixeira	1.00
Matt Holliday	1.00
Matt Kemp	1.00
Miguel Cabrera	1.50
Prince Fielder	1.50
Randy Johnson	1.50
Rick Ankiel	1.00
Russell Martin	.50
Ryan Braun	1.50
Ryan Howard	2.00
Travis Hafner	.50
Vladimir Guerrero	1.00

1977 O-Pee-Chee
NM/M
Common Player:	.50
Prince Fielder	1.50
Russell Martin	.50
Vladimir Guerrero	.75
Joe Mauer	.75
Justin Morneau	.75
Dustin Pedroia	2.00
Mark Teixeira	1.00
Tim Lincecum	2.50
Jimmy Rollins	1.50
Carlos Lee	.75
Hanley Ramirez	1.50
Chipper Jones	2.00
Matt Holliday	.75
Travis Hafner	.50
Magglio Ordonez	.75
Carlos Quentin	.75
Derek Lee	.75
Aramis Ramirez	.75
Randy Johnson	1.50
Brandon Webb	1.00
Josh Hamilton	1.50
C.C. Sabathia	1.50
Carlos Beltran	1.00
Adrian Gonzalez	1.00
Jake Peavy	.75
Matt Kemp	.75
Joba Chamberlain	1.50
Jonathan Papelbon	.50
Carlos Zambrano	1.00
Jay Bruce	1.00
Albert Pujols	4.00
Alex Rodriguez	3.00
Alfonso Soriano	1.00
Chase Utley	1.50
Daisuke Matsuzaka	1.50
David Ortiz	1.50
David Wright	2.00
Derek Jeter	4.00
Evan Longoria	4.00
Grady Sizemore	1.50
Ichiro Suzuki	2.50
Johan Santana	1.50

43	Jose Reyes	1.50
44	Josh Beckett	1.00
45	Ken Griffey Jr.	3.00
46	Lance Berkman	.75
47	Manny Ramirez	1.50
48	Miguel Cabrera	1.50
49	Ryan Braun	2.00
50	Ryan Howard	2.00

1989 Design
NM/M
Randomly Inserted
801	Ken Griffey Jr.	40.00
802	Randy Johnson	15.00
803	Ronald Reagan	30.00
804	George H.W. Bush	30.00

A Piece of History 600-HR Club
NM/M
600 Home Run Club Bat
600-KG Ken Griffey Jr.	65.00

Derek Jeter Autograph Buyback Cards
NM/M
Production 93
449	Derek Jeter/93	800.00

Documentary Update

2008 DOCUMENTARY
WORLD SERIES GAME 2
RAYS 4 - PHILLIES 3

NM/M
Common Player:		.50
4891	Torii Hunter	.50
4892	Mark Teixeira	.75
4893	Francisco Rodriguez	.50
4894	Vladimir Guerrero	1.00
4895	Alfonso Soriano	.50
4896	Derek Lee	.75
4897	Aramis Ramirez	.75
4898	Paul Konerko	.50
4899	Jermaine Dye	.75
4900	Ken Griffey Jr.	2.00
4901	Jim Thome	.75
4902	Ryan Braun	1.50
4903	C.C. Sabathia	1.00
4904	J.J. Hardy	.50
4905	Prince Fielder	1.00
4906	Jason Bay	.75
4907	J.D. Drew	1.00
4908	Jacoby Ellsbury	1.00
4909	Jon Lester	1.00
4910	Evan Longoria	4.00
4911	Carl Crawford	.50
4912	B.J. Upton	.75
4913	Carlos Pena	.75
4914	James Loney	.75
4915	Manny Ramirez	1.50
4916	Russell Martin	.50
4917	Chase Utley	1.00
4918	Shane Victorino	.75
4919	Ryan Howard	.75
4920	Pat Burrell	.75
4921	Daisuke Matsuzaka	2.00
4922	Jason Bay	.75
4923	Dustin Pedroia	1.00
4924	Kevin Youkilis	.75
4925	J.D. Drew	.50
4926	Jason Varitek	.50
4927	David Ortiz	1.00
4928	Andre Ethier	.50
4929	Manny Ramirez	1.50
4930	Nomar Garciaparra	.50
4931	Rafael Furcal	.50
4932	Matt Kemp	.50
4933	James Shields	.50
4934	David Price	4.00
4935	B.J. Upton	.75
4936	Willy Aybar	.50
4937	Evan Longoria	4.00
4938	Carl Crawford	.50
4939	Matt Garza	.50
4940	Chase Utley	1.00
4941	Brett Myers	.50
4942	Ryan Howard	1.50
4943	Matt Stairs	.50
4944	Jimmy Rollins	1.00
4945	Akinori Iwamura	.50
4946	B.J. Upton	.75
4947	Carl Crawford	.50
4948	Evan Longoria	4.00
4949	Rocco Baldelli	.50
4950	Chase Utley	1.00
4951	Shane Victorino	.50
4952	Jimmy Rollins	1.00
4953	Ryan Howard	1.50
4954	Cole Hamels	1.00

Game Jersey

UD GAME JERSEY
JF-J
Jeff Francis / P

NM/M
Common Game Jersey: 4.00
Inserted 1:19 Hobby, 1:24 Retail
Patch: No Pricing
Production 25 Sets
AD	Adam Dunn	6.00
AE	Andre Ethier	6.00
AG	Adrian Gonzalez	6.00
AI	Akinori Iwamura	6.00
AN	Rick Ankiel	6.00
AP	Albert Pujols	15.00
AR	Aaron Rowand	4.00
BA	Rocco Baldelli	4.00
BE	Josh Beckett	8.00
BH	Bill Hall	4.00
BM	Brian McCann	6.00
BP	Brandon Phillips	6.00
BR	Brian Bass	6.00
BU	B.J. Upton	6.00
BW	Billy Wagner	4.00
CB	Chad Billingsley	8.00
CD	Chris Duncan	4.00
CH	Chin-Lung Hu	4.00
CJ	Chipper Jones	8.00
CL	Clay Buchholz	6.00
CO	Corey Hart	6.00
CS	C.C. Sabathia	6.00
CW	Chien-Ming Wang	15.00
DA	Johnny Damon	4.00
DB	Daric Barton	4.00
DH	Dan Haren	4.00
DJ	Derek Jeter	20.00
DL	Derek Lee	6.00
DM	David Murphy	8.00
DO	David Ortiz	8.00
DU	Dan Uggla	4.00
GA	Garrett Atkins	4.00
GM	Greg Maddux	15.00
GO	Alex Gordon	8.00
GR	Curtis Granderson	8.00
GS	Grady Sizemore	8.00
HA	Cole Hamels	10.00
HI	Aaron Hill	4.00
HJ	Josh Hamilton	20.00
IK	Ian Kennedy	4.00
JA	Conor Jackson	4.00
JD	J.D. Drew	4.00
JF	Jeff Francis	4.00
JG	Jeremy Guthrie	4.00
JH	Jeremy Hermida	4.00
JJ	Josh Johnson	4.00
JL	James Loney	6.00
JM	John Maine	6.00
JN	Joe Nathan	6.00
JO	John Lackey	4.00
JP	Jake Peavy	6.00
JT	J.R. Towles	4.00
JU	Justin Upton	8.00
JV	Jason Varitek	6.00
JW	Josh Willingham	4.00
KG	Ken Griffey Jr.	15.00
KI	Ian Kinsler	6.00
KK	Kevin Kouzmanoff	4.00
KY	Kevin Youkilis	8.00
LA	Adam LaRoche	4.00
MC	Matt Cain	8.00
MK	Matt Kemp	8.00
MT	Mark Teahen	4.00
NB	Nick Blackburn	4.00
NM	Nick Markakis	6.00
NS	Nick Swisher	4.00
PA	Jonathan Papelbon	6.00
PB	Pat Burrell	6.00
PE	Jhonny Peralta	4.00
PH	Phil Hughes	8.00
PK	Paul Konerko	4.00
RA	Aramis Ramirez	6.00
RB	Ryan Braun	10.00
RF	Rafael Furcal	4.00
RH	Rich Harden/SP	8.00
RM	Russell Martin	6.00
RO	Roy Halladay	6.00
RW	Rickie Weeks	.50
SA	Jarrod Saltalamacchia	6.00
SM	Greg Smith	6.00
SP	Scott Podsednik	6.00
TH	Tim Hudson	6.00
TR	Travis Hafner	6.00
TT	Troy Tulowitzki	6.00
VM	Victor Martinez	4.00
WE	Jered Weaver	4.00

Series 2
AH	Aaron Harang	4.00
AJ	Andruw Jones	4.00
AP	Albert Pujols	20.00
AR	Alex Romero	4.00
BA	Josh Barfield	4.00
BB	Brian Bocock	4.00
BC	Bartolo Colon	4.00
BH	Bill Hall	4.00
BI	Brandon Inge	4.00
BM	Brian McCann	6.00
BP	Brandon Phillips	4.00
CB	Chris Burke	4.00
CD	Carlos Delgado	4.00
CH	Chin-Lung Hu	4.00
CL	Carlos Lee	6.00
CM	Colt Morton	4.00
CR	Bobby Crosby	4.00
CY	Chris Young	4.00
DB	Daric Barton	4.00
DE	Darin Erstad	4.00
DL	Derrek Lee	4.00
DM	Daisuke Matsuzaka	15.00
DU	Chris Duncan	4.00
EC	Eric Chavez	4.00
ED	Jim Edmonds	4.00
EG	Eric Gagne	4.00
FS	Felix Hernandez	6.00
FS	Freddy Sanchez	4.00
HB	Hank Blalock	6.00
HE	Ramon Hernandez	4.00
HI	Hernan Iribarren	4.00
HK	Hong-Chih Kuo	4.00
IK	Ian Kinsler	10.00
JB	Jason Bay	8.00
JE	Jeff Baker	4.00
JG	Jason Giambi	4.00
JK	Jason Kubel	4.00
JP	Jhonny Peralta	4.00
JW	Jake Westbrook	4.00
KG	Ken Griffey Jr.	15.00
KJ	Kelly Johnson	4.00
KM	Kendry Morales	4.00
LM	Lastings Milledge	4.00
MK	Matt Kemp	8.00
MM	Melvin Mora	4.00
MP	Mark Prior	4.00
NM	Nyjer Morgan	4.00
PK	Paul Konerko	4.00
RA	Aramis Ramirez	4.00
RB	Rocco Baldelli	4.00
RF	Rafael Furcal	4.00
TG	Troy Glaus	4.00
TT	Troy Tulowitzki	4.00
TW	Tim Wakefield	4.00
UG	Dan Uggla	4.00
VM	Victor Martinez	4.00
YG	Yovani Gallardo	6.00
ZG	Zack Greinke	4.00

Game Jersey Autographs
NM/M
Production 5-99
AH	Aaron Harang/99	10.00
AK	Austin Kearns/99	10.00
BM	Brian McCann/99	25.00
BP	Brandon Phillips/99	20.00
BR	Brian Bass/99	10.00
CB	Chad Billingsley/99	10.00
CD	Chris Duncan/99	10.00
CH	Chin-Lung Hu/99	25.00
CO	Corey Hart/99	10.00
DB	Daric Barton/99	10.00
DU	Dan Uggla/99	15.00
GA	Garrett Atkins/99	10.00
HJ	Josh Hamilton/99	50.00
JG	Jeremy Guthrie/35	25.00
JH	Jeremy Hermida/99	15.00
JL	James Loney/99	10.00
JN	Joe Nathan/99	10.00
JO	John Lackey/99	15.00
JT	J.R. Towles/99	10.00
JW	Josh Willingham/99	10.00
KI	Ian Kinsler/99	20.00
KK	Kevin Kouzmanoff/99	10.00
KY	Kevin Youkilis/99	40.00
LA	Adam LaRoche/99	15.00
MC	Matt Cain/99	20.00
MK	Matt Kemp/99	25.00
MM	Melvin Mora/99	10.00
MT	Mark Teahen/99	10.00
NB	Nick Blackburn/99	10.00
NM	Nick Markakis/99	30.00
NS	Nick Swisher/99	15.00
RB	Ryan Braun/25	40.00
SA	Jarrod Saltalamacchia/99	
SM	Greg Smith/99	10.00
TR	Travis Hafner/99	15.00
TT	Troy Tulowitzki/99	15.00
YG	Yovani Gallardo/99	25.00

Series 2
AH	Aaron Harang/76	15.00
AR	Alex Romero/72	10.00
BB	Brian Bocock/61	10.00
BH	Bill Hall/99	10.00
BM	Brian McCann/71	10.00
BP	Brandon Phillips/50	20.00
CH	Chin-Lung Hu/99	15.00
CM	Colt Morton/99	8.00
DB	Daric Barton/99	10.00
DU	Chris Duncan/99	15.00
EC	Eric Chavez/25	12.00
ED	Jim Edmonds/99	20.00
HI	Hernan Iribarren/99	10.00
JE	Jeff Baker/99	10.00
MJ	Kelly Johnson/99	15.00
MK	Matt Kemp/25	30.00
MM	Melvin Mora/99	15.00
NM	Nyjer Morgan/99	15.00
YG	Yovani Gallardo/99	25.00

Goodwin Champions Preview
No Pricing

Griffey Jr./Michael Jordan SP
NM/M
Card is an SP & not serial #'d.
KGMJ Ken Griffey Jr., Michael Jordan/SP	50.00

Game Jersey Dual
NM/M
Common Dual Jersey: 4.00
Production 37-149
Triple Jersey: 1-1.25X
Production 15-100
Quad Jersey: No Pricing
Production 15 Sets
Production less than 25 not priced.
AD	Adam Dunn/149	8.00
AE	Andre Ethier/149	8.00
AG	Adrian Gonzalez/149	8.00
AH	Aaron Harang/149	5.00
AI	Akinori Iwamura/88	8.00
AN	Rick Ankiel/149	5.00
AP	Albert Pujols/149	20.00
AR	Aaron Rowand/149	5.00
AS	Alfonso Soriano/149	8.00
BA	Rocco Baldelli/50	5.00
BE	Josh Beckett/149	10.00
BH	Bill Hall/129	5.00
BM	Brian McCann/149	5.00
BP	Brandon Phillips/149	5.00
BR	Brian Bass/149	5.00
BU	B.J. Upton/149	5.00
BW	Billy Wagner/149	5.00
CB	Chad Billingsley/149	10.00
CC	Carl Crawford/149	6.00
CD	Chris Duncan/148	6.00
CH	Chin-Lung Hu/149	6.00
CJ	Chipper Jones/149	10.00
CL	Clay Buchholz/149	5.00
CS	C.C. Sabathia/149	10.00
CW	Chien-Ming Wang/149	20.00
DA	Johnny Damon/50	8.00
DB	Daric Barton/149	5.00
DH	Dan Haren/149	6.00
DJ	Derek Jeter/139	25.00
DL	Derrek Lee/149	6.00
DO	David Ortiz/149	10.00
DU	Dan Uggla/149	5.00
GA	Garrett Atkins/149	8.00
GO	Alex Gordon/149	10.00
GR	Curtis Granderson/149	10.00
GS	Grady Sizemore/149	10.00
HA	Cole Hamels/149	12.00
HI	Aaron Hill/52	5.00
HJ	Josh Hamilton/149	25.00
IK	Ian Kennedy/149	5.00
JA	Conor Jackson/149	6.00
JD	J.D. Drew/112	5.00
JF	Jeff Francis/149	5.00
JG	Jeremy Guthrie/149	5.00
JH	Jeremy Hermida/149	5.00
JJ	Josh Johnson/149	5.00
JL	James Loney/149	8.00
JM	John Maine/149	5.00
JN	Joe Nathan/149	6.00
JO	John Lackey/149	6.00
JP	Jake Peavy/149	8.00
JT	J.R. Towles/149	5.00
JU	Justin Upton/149	10.00
JV	Jason Varitek/149	8.00
JW	Josh Willingham/149	5.00
KG	Ken Griffey Jr./50	20.00
KI	Ian Kinsler/75	8.00
KK	Kevin Kouzmanoff/149	5.00
KY	Kevin Youkilis/149	10.00
LA	Adam LaRoche/75	8.00
MC	Matt Cain/149	8.00
MK	Matt Kemp/149	8.00
MT	Mark Teahen/149	6.00
NB	Nick Blackburn/149	6.00
NM	Nick Markakis/149	10.00
NS	Nick Swisher/149	6.00
PA	Jonathan Papelbon/149	8.00
PB	Pat Burrell/37	15.00
PE	Jhonny Peralta/125	6.00
PH	Phil Hughes/149	10.00
PK	Paul Konerko/149	6.00
RA	Aramis Ramirez/149	8.00
RB	Ryan Braun/149	15.00
RF	Rafael Furcal/149	6.00
RH	Rich Harden/149	8.00
RM	Russell Martin/149	10.00
RO	Roy Halladay/50	10.00
RW	Rickie Weeks/149	6.00
RZ	Ryan Zimmerman/149	8.00
SM	Greg Smith/149	5.00
SO	Joakim Soria/75	6.00
SP	Scott Podsednik/149	5.00
TH	Tim Hudson/149	6.00
TR	Travis Hafner/149	6.00
TT	Troy Tulowitzki/149	8.00
VM	Victor Martinez/149	6.00
WE	Jered Weaver/149	6.00

Historic Firsts

2008 HISTORIC FIRSTS
FIRST WORLD SERIES GAME
TO BE CONTINUED

NM/M
Common card: 1.00
Inserted 1:4 Hobby, 1:6 Retail
1	First African American President Elected	5.00
2	First Athlete to Win Eight Medals	1.00
3	Days	1.00
4	First Woman to Run as VP on Rep. Ticket	3.00
5	SpaceX Falcon 1 Successful Orbit	1.00
6	First Indian Players Signed	1.00
7	First Asian American Baseball Manager	1.00
8	Largest Insert Set Ever Produced (YSL)	1.00
9	NHL Winter Classic	1.00
10	Woman Becomes a Four-Star General	1.00
11	BO The First Puppy	10.00

Historic Predictors

HISTORIC FIRSTS PREDICTORS 2009
N.L. WINS
THE NATIONAL LEAGUE Wins the ALL-STAR GAME

NM/M
Common Card: 1.00
Inserted 1:4 Hobby, 1:6 Retail
1	National League Wins the All-Star Game	1.00
2	Gas Reaches 99 Cents	1.00
3	Dow Reaches 15,000	1.00
4	Court Justice	1.00
5	Life Discovered on Another Planet	1.00
6	Bigfoot Discovered	1.00
7	College Football Goes to Playoff System	1.00
8	Cure for AIDS	1.00
9	Chicago Awarded 2016 Summer Games	1.00

INKredible

INKREDIBLE
EDINSON VOLQUEZ / REDS

NM/M
Many not priced yet
Inserted 1:17 Hobby, 1:1,000 Retail
AC	Aaron Cook	10.00
AE	Andre Ethier	15.00
AK	Akinori Iwamura/SP	15.00
AK	Austin Kearns	8.00
AL	Aaron Laffey	8.00
AR	Bronson Arroyo	8.00
BA	Brian Bannister	10.00
BB	Billy Butler	10.00
BL	Joe Blanton	8.00
BO	Boof Bonser	5.00
BP	Brandon Phillips	8.00
BR	Brian Bruney	8.00
CB	Craig Breslow	8.00
CC	Chad Cordero	8.00
CD	Chris Duffy	8.00
CG	Carlos Gomez	15.00
CR	Chris Resop	8.00
DE	David Eckstein	10.00
DL	Derek Lowe	15.00
DM	David Murphy	8.00
EA	Erick Aybar	8.00
ED	Elijah Dukes	10.00
EV	Edinson Volquez	15.00
FC	Fausto Carmona	10.00
GA	Garrett Atkins	8.00
GF	Gavin Floyd	10.00
GP	Glen Perkins	8.00
GW	Tony Gwynn Jr.	10.00
HA	Brendan Harris	8.00
IK	Ian Kinsler	20.00
JA	Jeremy Accardo	10.00
JB	Jeff Baker	8.00
JC	Jack Cust	8.00

JF	Jeff Francis	8.00
JG	Jeremy Guthrie	30.00
JH	Josh Hamilton	50.00
JK	Jeff Keppinger	8.00
JL	James Loney	15.00
JN	Joe Nathan	20.00
JO	Joey Gathright	8.00
JP	Jonathan Papelbon	20.00
JS	James Shields	10.00
JW	Jered Weaver	10.00
KG	Ken Griffey Jr.	125.00
KK	Kevin Kouzmanoff	10.00
LA	Adam LaRoche	10.00
LJ	John Lackey	15.00
LS	Luke Scott	5.00
MA	Matt Chico	8.00
MB	Marlon Byrd	8.00
MC	Matt Cain	15.00
ME	Mark Ellis	5.00
MI	Michael Bourn	10.00
MO	Dustin Moseley	5.00
MT	Mark Teahen	10.00
NM	Nick Markakis	40.00
OW	Micah Owings	10.00
PF	Prince Fielder	30.00
RB	Ryan Braun/SP	40.00
RG	Ryan Garko	8.00
RT	Ryan Theriot	15.00
SD	Stephen Drew	20.00
SM	Sean Marshall	8.00
SO	Andrew Sonnanstine	8.00
TB	Taylor Buchholz	8.00
UJ	Ubaldo Jimenez	10.00
WI	Josh Willingham	8.00
XN	Xavier Nady	20.00
YE	Yunel Escobar	15.00

Series 2

AG	Alberto Gonzalez	10.00
AR	Alexei Ramirez	30.00
BA	Burke Badenhop	8.00
BB	Brian Barton	8.00
BI	Brian Bixler	8.00
BJ	Jay Bruce	25.00
BK	Bobby Korecky	8.00
BR	Brandon Jones	8.00
CH	Corey Hart	15.00
CS	Clint Sammons	8.00
CT	Clete Thomas	10.00
CW	Cory Wade	8.00
DL	Derek Lowe/SP	50.00
ED	Elijah Dukes	10.00
ET	Eider Torres	8.00
GP	Gregorio Petit	8.00
GS	Greg Smith	8.00
HE	Jonathan Herrera	8.00
HI	Hernan Iribarren	8.00
HU	Chin-Lung Hu/SP	20.00
IK	Ian Kennedy	10.00
JA	Joaquin Arias	8.00
JE	Jeremy Hermida	10.00
JH	J.A. Happ	15.00
JM	John Maine	10.00
JO	Jonathan Albaladejo	10.00
JS	Joe Smith	10.00
KG	Ken Griffey Jr./SP	150.00
KH	Kevin Hart	8.00
KJ	Kelly Johnson	10.00
KM	Kyle McClellan	8.00
KS	Kevin Slowey	15.00
KY	Kevin Youkilis/SP	40.00
LB	Lance Broadway	8.00
LC	Luke Carlin	8.00
LM	Luis Mendoza	8.00
MA	Michael Aubrey	8.00
ME	Mark Ellis	8.00
MI	Michael Bourn	10.00
ML	Matt Lindstrom	8.00
MP	Mike Pelfrey	20.00
MR	Mike Rabelo	8.00
MU	David Murphy	8.00
NB	Nick Blackburn	10.00
NL	Noah Lowry	8.00
NM	Nyjer Morgan	10.00
PA	Mike Parisi	15.00
PE	Glen Perkins	10.00
RH	Ramon Hernandez	8.00
RO	Ross Ohlendorf	8.00
RT	Ramon Troncoso	10.00
SH	Steve Holm	8.00
SJ	James Shields	15.00
TG	Tom Gorzelanny	8.00
TH	Travis Hafner	12.00
VR	Vinny Rottino	8.00
WW	Wesley Wright	8.00

Ken Griffey Jr. Buyback Autograph

1st 13 cards signed black ink remaining 76 cards blue ink

Ken Griffey Jr. '89 Buyback Gold

		NM/M
Randomly Inserted		
1	Ken Griffey Jr.	20.00

Griffey Jr. Piece of History 600-HR Club

		NM/M
600 Home Run Club Bat		
600-KG	Ken Griffey Jr.	65.00

Rivals

		NM/M
Common Duo:		1.00
Inserted 1:12 Hobby		

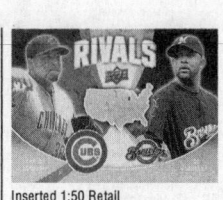

Inserted 1:50 Retail

1	Jimmy Rollins, Jose Reyes	3.00
2	Derek Jeter, David Ortiz	4.00
3	Derek Lee, Albert Pujols	4.00
4	Bengie Molina, Russell Martin	1.00
5	Jim Thome, Travis Hafner	1.00
6	Carlos Zambrano, C.C. Sabathia	1.50
7	Alex Rodriguez, David Wright	3.00
8	Josh Beckett, Scott Kazmir	1.50
9	Manny Ramirez, Vladimir Guerrero	1.50
10	Alfonso Soriano, Carlos Quentin	1.50
11	Lance Berkman, Albert Pujols	4.00
12	Alex Rodriguez, Evan Longoria	4.00
13	Jake Peavy, Chad Billingsley	1.00
14	Brandon Webb, Matt Kemp	1.50
15	Chipper Jones, Johan Santana	2.00
16	Jim Thome, Justin Morneau	1.50
17	Miguel Cabrera, Joe Mauer	1.50
18	Jose Reyes, Hanley Ramirez	2.50
19	Roy Halladay, Joba Chamberlain	2.50
20	Josh Hamilton, Roy Oswalt	2.00
21	Jack Cust, Tim Lincecum	2.00
22	Albert Pujols, Prince Fielder	4.00
23	Francisco Rodriguez, Ichiro Suzuki	3.00
24	Nick Markakis, Daisuke Matsuzaka	3.00
25	Grady Sizemore, Jay Bruce	2.50

Rookie Debut

		NM/M
Common Player:		1.00
Inserted 2:1 Fat Packs		
AA	Alfredo Aceves	2.00
AC	Aaron Cunningham	1.00
BN	Brad Nelson	1.00
CG	Conor Gillaspie	2.00
CL	Chris Lambert	1.00
CM	Casey McGehee	1.00
DF	Dexter Fowler	1.50
DP	David Price	6.00
FP	Fernando Perez	1.00
FS	Freddy Sandoval	1.00
GG	Greg Golson	1.00
GK	George Kottaras	1.00
JG	Josh Geer	1.00
JN	Jon Niese	1.00
JP	Jason Pridie	1.00
JR	Josh Roenicke	1.00
JW	Josh Whitesell	1.00
KK	Kila Ka'aihue	1.50
LV	Luis Valbuena	1.00
MA	Matt Antonelli	2.00
MB	Michael Bowden	1.00
MG	Mat Gamel	3.00
MS	Mark Saccomanno	1.00
MT	Matt Tuiasosopo	1.00
PA	James Parr	1.00
PC	Phil Coke	1.00
RP	Robert Parnell	1.00
TS	Travis Snider	3.00
WC	Wilkin Castillo	1.00
WV	Will Venable	1.00

StarQuest Common Purple

		NM/M
Common Purple:		1.00
Inserted 2:1 Fat Pack		
Silver:		1X
Inserted 1:4 Retail		
Blue:		1X
Inserted 1:8 Retail		
Gold:		1-1.5X
Inserted 1:12 Retail		
Emerald:		1-2X
Inserted 1:24 Retail		
Black:		2-3X
Inserted 1:48 Retail		
1	Albert Pujols	4.00
2	Alex Rodriguez	4.00
3	Alfonso Soriano	1.50
4	Chipper Jones	2.50
5	Chase Utley	2.00
6	Derek Jeter	5.00
7	Daisuke Matsuzaka	3.00
8	David Ortiz	3.00
9	David Wright	3.00
10	Grady Sizemore	1.50

11	Hanley Ramirez	2.50
12	Ichiro Suzuki	3.00
13	Josh Beckett	1.50
14	Jake Peavy	1.50
15	Jose Reyes	2.50
16	Johan Santana	2.00
17	Ken Griffey Jr.	4.00
18	Lance Berkman	1.50
19	Miguel Cabrera	1.50
20	Matt Holliday	1.50
21	Manny Ramirez	2.00
22	Prince Fielder	2.50
23	Ryan Braun	3.00
24	Ryan Howard	3.00
25	Vladimir Guerrero	2.00

Series 2

26	B.J. Upton	1.00
27	Brandon Phillips	1.00
28	Brandon Webb	1.00
29	Brian McCann	1.50
30	Carl Crawford	2.00
31	Carlos Beltran	1.50
32	Carlos Quentin	1.00
33	Chien-Ming Wang	1.00
34	Cliff Lee	1.50
35	Cole Hamels	1.50
36	Curtis Granderson	1.50
37	David Price	3.00
38	Dustin Pedroia	2.00
39	Evan Longoria	2.00
40	Francisco Liriano	1.00
41	Geovany Soto	1.00
42	Ian Kinsler	1.50
43	Jay Bruce	1.50
44	Jimmy Rollins	1.50
45	Jonathan Papelbon	1.50
46	Josh Hamilton	2.00
47	Justin Morneau	1.50
48	Kevin Youkilis	1.50
49	Nick Markakis	1.50
50	Tim Lincecum	2.50

Stars of the Game

		NM/M
Common Player:		1.00
Inserted 1:12 Hobby, 1:50 Retail		
AP	Albert Pujols	4.00
AR	Alex Rodriguez	3.00
AS	Alfonso Soriano	1.00
BW	Brandon Webb	1.50
CJ	Chipper Jones	1.50
CS	C.C. Sabathia	1.50
CU	Chase Utley	1.50
DJ	Derek Jeter	4.00
DO	David Ortiz	1.50
DP	Dustin Pedroia	1.50
DW	David Wright	2.00
EL	Evan Longoria	3.00
GS	Grady Sizemore	1.50
HR	Hanley Ramirez	2.00
IS	Ichiro Suzuki	2.50
JH	Josh Hamilton	2.00
JR	Jose Reyes	2.00
JS	Johan Santana	2.00
LB	Lance Berkman	1.50
MC	Miguel Cabrera	1.50
MR	Manny Ramirez	2.00
RB	Ryan Braun	3.00
RH	Ryan Howard	3.00
TL	Tim Lincecum	3.00
VG	Vladimir Guerrero	1.50

USAB National Team Autographs

		NM/M
CC	Christian Colon	15.00
CH	Chris Hernandez	10.00
DD	Derek Dietrich	12.00
HM	Hunter Morris	10.00
KD	Kentrail Davis	12.00
KV	Kendal Volz	10.00
MD	Matt den Dekker	10.00
MG	Micah Gibbs	15.00
ML	Mike Leake	35.00
MM	Mike Minor	10.00
RJ	Ryan Jackson	10.00

USAB National Team Jerseys

		NM/M
SS	Stephen Strasburg	60.00

USAB National Team Jersey Autographs

		NM/M
Production 225 Sets		
BS	Blake Smith	15.00
CC	Christian Colon	20.00
CH	Chris Hernandez	15.00
DD	Derek Dietrich	15.00
HM	Hunter Morris	20.00

KD	Kentrail Davis	20.00
KV	Kendal Volz	10.00
ML	Mike Leake	40.00
MG	Micah Gibbs	20.00
SS	Stephen Strasburg	350.00
MM	Mike Minor	15.00
RJ	Ryan Jackson	20.00

USA Retrospective

		NM/M
Common Player:		1.50
Inserted 1:8 Hobby, 1:36 Retail		
1	Matt Brown	1.50
2	Stephen Strasburg	20.00
3	Jayson Nix	1.50
4	Brian Duensing	1.50
5	Jake Arrieta	2.50
6	Dexter Fowler	2.00
7	Casey Weathers	1.50
8	Mike Koplove	1.50
9	Jason Donald	1.50
10	Taylor Teagarden	2.50
11	Kevin Jepsen	1.50
12	Matt LaPorta	3.00
13	USA Wins Bronze Medal	1.50
14	Team USA Wins 3rd Olympic Medal	1.50

USA 18U National Team

		NM/M
Common Player:		1.50
Inserted 1:3, Retail 1:6		
AA	Andrew Aplin	1.50
AM	Austin Maddox	2.50
CC	Colton Cain	1.50
CG	Cameron Garfield	1.50
CT	Cecil Tanner	1.50
DN	David Nick	1.50
DT	Donavan Tate	3.00
FO	Nolan Fontana	2.00
HM	Harold Martinez	1.50
JB	Jake Barrett	1.50
JM	Jeff Malm	1.50
JT	Jacob Turner	2.00
ME	Jonathan Meyer	1.50
MP	Matt Purke	1.50
MS	Max Stassi	1.50
NF	Nick Franklin	2.00
RW	Ryan Weber	1.50
WH	Wes Hatton	2.00

USA 18U National Team Jerseys

		NM/M
Common Jersey:		4.00
Patch:		No Pricing
Production 25 Sets		
AA	Andrew Aplin	8.00
AM	Austin Maddox	6.00
CC	Colton Cain	6.00
CG	Cameron Garfield	4.00
CT	Cecil Tanner	6.00
DN	David Nick	6.00
DT	Donavan Tate	6.00
FO	Nolan Fontana	6.00
HM	Harold Martinez	8.00
JB	Jake Barrett	6.00
JM	Jeff Malm	4.00
JT	Jacob Turner	6.00
ME	Jonathan Meyer	8.00
MP	Matt Purke	6.00
MS	Max Stassi	10.00
NF	Nick Franklin	6.00
RW	Ryan Weber	6.00
WH	Wes Hatton	6.00

USA 18U National Team Jersey Autos.

No Pricing
Production 25 Sets

USA 18U National Team Patch

No Pricing

USAB National Team

		NM/M
Common Player:		1.00
AG	A.J. Griffin	1.00
AO	Andrew Oliver	1.00
BS	Blake Smith	1.00
CC	Christian Colon	1.00
CH	Chris Hernandez	1.00
DD	Derek Dietrich	1.00
HM	Hunter Morris	1.00
JC	Jared Clark	1.00
JF	Josh Fellhauer	1.00
KD	Kentrail Davis	1.00
KG	Kyle Gibson	1.00
KV	Kendal Volz	1.00
MD	Matt den Dekker	1.00
MG	Micah Gibbs	1.00
ML	Mike Leake	1.00
MM	Mike Minor	1.00
RJ	Ryan Jackson	1.00
RL	Ryan Lipkin	1.00
SS	Stephen Strasburg	20.00
SW	Scott Woodward	1.00
TL	Tyler Lyons	1.00
TM	Tommy Mendonca	1.00

USAB National Team Jerseys

		NM/M
Common Jersey:		5.00
AG	A.J. Griffin	5.00
AO	Andrew Oliver	5.00
BS	Blake Smith	5.00
CC	Christian Colon	5.00
CH	Chris Hernandez	5.00
DD	Derek Dietrich	5.00
HM	Hunter Morris	5.00
JF	Josh Fellhauer	5.00
KD	Kentrail Davis	5.00
KG	Kyle Gibson	6.00
KR	Kevin Rhoderick	5.00
KV	Kendal Volz	5.00
MD	Matt den Dekker	5.00
MG	Micah Gibbs	5.00
ML	Mike Leake	5.00
MM	Mike Minor	5.00
RJ	Ryan Jackson	5.00
RL	Ryan Lipkin	5.00
SS	Stephen Strasburg	65.00
TL	Tyler Lyons	5.00

USAB National Team Autographs

		NM/M
Common Auto.:		8.00
AG	A.J. Griffin	8.00
AO	Andrew Oliver	8.00
BS	Blake Smith	8.00
CC	Christian Colon	10.00
CH	Chris Hernandez	8.00
DD	Derek Dietrich	12.00
HM	Hunter Morris	10.00
JF	Josh Fellhauer	8.00
KD	Kentrail Davis	12.00
KV	Kendal Volz	10.00
MD	Matt den Dekker	10.00
MG	Micah Gibbs	10.00
ML	Mike Leake	15.00
MM	Mike Minor	10.00

RJ	Ryan Jackson	10
RL	Ryan Lipkin	8.
TL	Tyler Lyons	10

USAB National Team Jerseys Auto.

		NM/
Production 225 Sets		
AG	A.J. Griffin	10.
AO	Andrew Oliver	12.
BS	Blake Smith	15.
CC	Christian Colon	15.
CH	Chris Hernandez	15.
DD	Derek Dietrich	15.
HM	Hunter Morris	15.
JF	Josh Fellhauer	10.
KD	Kentrail Davis	15.
KG	Kyle Gibson	20.
KR	Kevin Rhoderick	15.
KV	Kendal Volz	15.
MD	Matt den Dekker	12.
MG	Micah Gibbs	15.
ML	Mike Leake	20
MM	Mike Minor	15.
RJ	Ryan Jackson	15.
RL	Ryan Lipkin	15.
SS	Stephen Strasburg	400.
TL	Tyler Lyons	15.

2009 Upper Deck Goudey

		NM/
Common Player (1-200):		
Common SP (201-220):		3.
Common Sports Royalty SP (221-260):		3.
Common Heads Up SP (261-300):		3.
Pack (8):		5.
Box (18):		85.
1	Adam Dunn	
2	Max Scherzer	
3	Stephen Drew	
4	Randy Johnson	
5	Brandon Webb	
6	Dan Haren	
7	Chris B. Young	
8	Brian McCann	
9	Jeff Francoeur	
10	James Parr	
11	Tom Glavine	
12	Tim Hudson	
13	Chipper Jones	1.
14	Kelly Johnson	
15	Adam Jones	
16	Jeremy Guthrie	
17	Brian Roberts	
18	Nick Markakis	
19	Jed Lowrie	
20	Cal Ripken Jr.	3.
21	Melvin Mora	
22	Jason Bay	
23	Josh Beckett	
24	Justin Masterson	
25	Kevin Youkilis	
26	Michael Bowden (RC)	
27	Dustin Pedroia	
28	Jacoby Ellsbury	
29	Jason Varitek	
30	Jonathan Papelbon	
31	David Ortiz	
32	Daisuke Matsuzaka	1.
33	J.D. Drew	
34	Curt Schilling	
35	Clay Buchholz	
36	Wilkin Castillo RC	1.
37	Derek Lee	
38	Kosuke Fukudome	
39	Aramis Ramirez	
40	Alfonso Soriano	
41	Kerry Wood	
42	Carlos Zambrano	
43	Rich Harden	
44	Geovany Soto	
45	Gavin Floyd	
46	Ken Griffey Jr.	1.
47	Nick Swisher	
48	Jim Thome	
49	Jermaine Dye	
50	Alexei Ramirez	
51	Carlos Quentin	
52	Brandon Phillips	
53	Johnny Cueto	
54	Jay Bruce	
55	Dave Concepcion	
56	Joey Votto	
57	Aaron Harang	
58	Edinson Volquez	
59	Kelly Shoppach	

#	Player	Price
60	Fausto Carmona	.25
61	Grady Sizemore	.75
62	Travis Hafner	.40
63	Victor Martinez	.50
64	Cliff Lee	.50
65	Dexter Fowler (RC)	2.00
66	Garrett Atkins	.40
67	Troy Tulowitzki	.50
68	Matt Holliday	.50
69	Curtis Granderson	.75
70	Carlos Guillen	.40
71	Gary Sheffield	.50
72	Miguel Cabrera	.75
73	Magglio Ordonez	.50
74	Justin Verlander	.50
75	Hanley Ramirez	1.00
76	Josh Willingham	.25
77	Dan Uggla	.50
78	Josh Johnson	.50
79	Carlos Lee	.50
80	Roy Oswalt	.50
81	Miguel Tejada	.50
82	Lance Berkman	.50
83	Kila Ka'aihue (RC)	1.00
84	Joakim Soria	.40
85	Alex Gordon	.50
86	Chone Figgins	.50
87	John Lackey	.50
88	Jered Weaver	.40
89	Vladimir Guerrero	.75
90	Mark Teixeira	.75
91	Garret Anderson	.25
92	Torii Hunter	.50
93	Howie Kendrick	.25
94	Clayton Kershaw	.75
95	Cory Wade	.25
96	Matt Kemp	.75
97	Russell Martin	.40
98	Scott Elbert (RC)	1.00
99	Manny Ramirez	1.00
100	Andre Ethier	.50
101	Rafael Furcal	.50
102	Brad Penny	.25
103	Takashi Saito	.25
104	Kirk Gibson	.50
105	Alcides Escobar RC	1.50
106	Bill Hall	.25
107	Mat Gamel RC	3.00
108	Prince Fielder	.75
109	Miguel Montero	.25
110	Yovani Gallardo	.50
111	Ben Sheets	.25
112	C.C. Sabathia	.75
113	Ryan Braun	1.00
114	J.J. Hardy	.40
115	Denard Span	.40
116	Joe Nathan	.40
117	Nick Blackburn	.25
118	Joe Mauer	.50
119	Justin Morneau	.50
120	Francisco Liriano	.40
121	Kevin Slowey	.25
122	Delmon Young	.25
123	John Maine	.25
124	Jon Niese RC	1.00
125	David Wright	1.50
126	Jose Reyes	1.00
127	Carlos Beltran	.50
128	Johan Santana	.75
129	A.J. Burnett	.50
130	Derek Jeter	2.50
131	Francisco Cervelli RC	2.00
132	Ian Kennedy	.25
133	Phil Coke RC	1.50
134	Phil Hughes	.50
135	Alex Rodriguez	2.00
136	Chien-Ming Wang	.50
137	Mariano Rivera	.75
138	Joba Chamberlain	.75
139	Jason Giambi	.50
140	Andy Pettitte	.50
141	Greg Smith	.25
142	Marlon Byrd	.25
143	Johnny Damon	.75
144	Frank Thomas	1.00
145	Carlos Gonzalez	.75
146	Jeff Baisley RC	1.00
147	Mark Teahen	.25
148	Jack Cust	.25
149	Kurt Suzuki	.25
150	Bobby Crosby	.25
151	Cole Hamels	.50
152	Lou Marson (RC)	1.00
153	Chase Utley	.75
154	Jimmy Rollins	.75
155	Ryan Howard	1.00
156	Greg Golson (RC)	1.00
157	Pat Burrell	.40
158	Shane Victorino	.50
159	Brad Lidge	.25
160	Edwin Encarnacion	.25
161	Nate McLouth	.50
162	Ryan Doumit	.25
163	Adrian Gonzalez	.75
164	Matt Antonelli RC	1.00
165	Jake Peavy	.50
166	Kevin Kouzmanoff	.25
167	Chris Young	.50
168	Trevor Hoffman	.50
169	Conor Gillaspie RC	2.00
170	Wade LeBlanc RC	1.00
171	Matt Cain	.50
172	Tim Lincecum	1.00
173	Matt Tuiasosopo (RC)	1.00
174	Ichiro Suzuki	1.50
175	Felix Hernandez	.50
176	Erik Bedard	.50
177	Ryan Ludwick	.50
178	Albert Pujols	2.50
179	Rick Ankiel	.50
180	Troy Glaus	.25
181	Bob Gibson	.75
182	B.J. Upton	.50
183	David Price RC	4.00
184	Evan Longoria	1.50
185	Carl Crawford	.50
186	Scott Kazmir	.40
187	Carlos Pena	.50
188	James Shields	.50
189	Josh Hamilton	1.00
190	Ian Kinsler	.75
191	Michael Young	.40
192	Mike Aviles	.40
193	Roy Halladay	.75
194	Travis Snider RC	2.00
195	Vernon Wells	.40
196	Alex Rios	.40
197	Ryan Zimmerman	.50
198	Shairon Martis RC	1.00
199	Lastings Milledge	.25
200	Cristian Guzman	.25
201	Brooks Robinson/SP	4.00
202	Carlton Fisk/SP	3.00
203	Gaylord Perry/SP	3.00
204	Jack Morris/SP	3.00
205	Rollie Fingers/SP	3.00
206	Ron Santo/SP	4.00
207	Sparky Lyle/SP	3.00
208	Nolan Ryan/SP	10.00
209	Whitey Ford/SP	5.00
210	Phil Niekro/SP	3.00
211	Ryne Sandberg/SP	6.00
212	Jim Palmer/SP	4.00
213	Joe DiMaggio/SP	10.00
214	Johnny Bench/SP	6.00
215	Ted Williams/SP	8.00
216	Robin Yount/SP	6.00
217	Ozzie Smith/SP	6.00
218	Reggie Jackson/SP	5.00
219	Yogi Berra/SP	5.00
220	Mike Schmidt/SP	6.00
221	Cal Ripken Jr./SP	10.00
222	Ozzie Smith/SP	6.00
223	Tony Gwynn/SP	5.00
224	Don Mattingly/SP	6.00
225	Steve Carlton/SP	4.00
226	Reggie Jackson/SP	5.00
227	Carl Yastrzemski/SP	5.00
228	Johnny Bench/SP	6.00
229	Mike Schmidt/SP	6.00
230	Nolan Ryan/SP	10.00
231	Ernie Banks/SP	5.00
232	Stan Musial/SP	6.00
233	Ryne Sandberg/SP	5.00
234	Bob Gibson/SP	5.00
235	Dennis Eckersley/SP	4.00
236	Felix Hernandez/SP	4.00
237	Jim Rice/SP	4.00
238	Chien-Ming Wang/SP	4.00
239	Jonathan Papelbon/SP	4.00
240	Evan Longoria/SP	6.00
241	Cole Hamels/SP	5.00
242	Ken Griffey Jr./SP	8.00
243	Tiger Woods/SP	20.00
244	B.J. Upton/SP	3.00
245	Randy Johnson/SP	5.00
246	Guy Lafleur/SP	4.00
247	Nicklas Lidstrom/SP	4.00
248	Mike Bossy/SP	4.00
249	Bobby Orr/SP	8.00
250	Patrick Roy/SP	8.00
251	Adrian Peterson/SP	8.00
252	Juan Marichal/SP	4.00
253	Chipper Jones/SP	5.00
254	Rollie Fingers/SP	3.00
255	Al Kaline/SP	4.00
256	Paul Pierce/SP	4.00
257	Jerry West/SP	8.00
258	Larry Bird/SP	8.00
259	John Havlicek/SP	5.00
260	Michael Jordan/SP	10.00
261	Cal Ripken Jr./SP	10.00
262	Reggie Jackson/SP	5.00
263	Nolan Ryan/SP	10.00
264	Yogi Berra/SP	5.00
265	Ernie Banks/SP	5.00
266	Dave Winfield/SP	4.00
267	Ozzie Smith/SP	5.00
268	Stan Musial/SP	6.00
269	Ichiro Suzuki/SP	6.00
270	Albert Pujols/SP	8.00
271	Alex Rodriguez/SP	6.00
272	Jose Reyes/SP	6.00
273	David Wright/SP	6.00
274	Johan Santana/SP	6.00
275	Josh Hamilton/SP	6.00
276	David Ortiz/SP	6.00
277	Josh Beckett/SP	5.00
278	Manny Ramirez/SP	6.00
279	Ryan Howard/SP	6.00
280	Chase Utley/SP	6.00
281	Jimmy Rollins/SP	5.00
282	Hanley Ramirez/SP	5.00
283	C.C. Sabathia/SP	5.00
284	Ryan Braun/SP	6.00
285	Evan Longoria/SP	6.00
286	Grady Sizemore/SP	5.00
287	Dustin Pedroia/SP	6.00
288	Mark Teixeira/SP	5.00
289	Ken Griffey Jr./SP	8.00
290	Lance Berkman/SP	4.00
291	Alfonso Soriano/SP	4.00
292	Derek Lee/SP	4.00
293	Brandon Webb/SP	4.00
294	Derek Jeter/SP	8.00
295	Daisuke Matsuzaka/SP	5.00
296	Vladimir Guerrero/SP	4.00
297	Jim Thome/SP	4.00
298	Carlos Zambrano/SP	3.00
299	Justin Morneau/SP	4.00
300	Tim Lincecum/SP	6.00

Autographs

GOUDEY GRAPHS — MIGUEL MONTERO Diamondbacks 'C

		NM/M
	Common Auto.:	8.00
AG	Adrian Gonzalez	20.00
AV	Mike Aviles	20.00
BE	Josh Beckett	40.00
BH	Bill Hall	8.00
BM	Brian McCann	15.00
BP	Brandon Phillips	15.00
BR	Brooks Robinson	30.00
BY	Marlon Byrd	8.00
CF	Carlton Fisk	70.00
CG	Conor Gillaspie	10.00
CH	Cole Hamels	60.00
CK	Clayton Kershaw	35.00
CL	Carlos Lee	12.00
CU	Johnny Cueto	20.00
DF	Dexter Fowler	15.00
DJ	Derek Jeter	180.00
DP	David Price	60.00
ED	Edgar Martinez	25.00
EE	Edwin Encarnacion	10.00
EL	Evan Longoria	200.00
FC	Francisco Cervelli	20.00
FI	Chone Figgins	15.00
GA	Garrett Atkins	12.00
GP	Gaylord Perry	25.00
GS	Grady Sizemore	35.00
HR	Hanley Ramirez	30.00
JB	Jeff Baisley	8.00
JC	Joe Carter	20.00
JF	Jeff Francoeur	20.00
JG	Jeremy Guthrie	10.00
JP	James Parr	8.00
JU	Justin Masterson	40.00
KG	Ken Griffey Jr.	160.00
KK	Kila Ka'aihue	10.00
KS	Kelly Shoppach	10.00
LM	Lou Marson	12.00
MA	Matt Antonelli	10.00
MB	Michael Bowden	20.00
MG	Mat Gamel	25.00
MM	Miguel Montero	10.00
MS	Max Scherzer	20.00
MT	Matt Tuiasosopo	10.00
NB	Nick Blackburn	15.00
PC	Phil Coke	15.00
PE	Dustin Pedroia	60.00
RF	Rollie Fingers	20.00
RH	Roy Halladay	40.00
RS	Ron Santo	30.00
SD	Stephen Drew	15.00
SI	Greg Smith	8.00
TG	Tom Glavine	90.00
TR	Tim Raines	15.00
TT	Troy Tulowitzki	15.00
VM	Victor Martinez	15.00
WL	Wade LeBlanc	8.00
YG	Yovani Gallardo	20.00

Memorabilia

CLAY BUCHHOLZ Red Sox 'P

		NM/M
	Common Player:	4.00
	Inserted 1:18	
AB	A.J. Burnett	4.00
AE	Andre Ethier	5.00
AH	Aaron Harang	4.00
BC	Bobby Crosby	4.00
BE	Carlos Beltran	4.00
BG	Bob Gibson	15.00
BH	Bill Hall	4.00
BM	Brian McCann	6.00
BP	Brandon Phillips	5.00
BR	Brian Roberts	6.00
BS	Ben Sheets	4.00
BW	Billy Williams	8.00
CA	Miguel Cabrera	8.00
CB	Clay Buchholz	6.00
CH	Cole Hamels	10.00
CL	Carlos Lee	6.00
CR	Cal Ripken Jr.	25.00
CS	Curt Schilling	4.00
CU	Chase Utley	10.00
CY	Chris Young	4.00
DA	Johnny Damon	8.00
DJ	Derek Jeter	20.00
DL	Derek Lee	4.00
DM	Daisuke Matsuzaka/SP	15.00
DO	David Ortiz	8.00
DS	Denard Span	4.00
DY	Delmon Young	4.00
FH	Felix Hernandez	4.00
FL	Francisco Liriano	5.00
GA	Garret Anderson	4.00
HK	Howie Kendrick	4.00
HR	Hanley Ramirez	8.00
HU	Tim Hudson	4.00
JA	Reggie Jackson	10.00
JD	Jermaine Dye	4.00
JE	Jacoby Ellsbury	10.00
JF	Jeff Francoeur	4.00
JG	Jason Giambi	4.00
JH	J.J. Hardy	4.00
JJ	Josh Johnson	4.00
JM	John Maine	4.00
JN	Joe Nathan	4.00
JO	Johnny Bench	15.00
JS	Joakim Soria	4.00
JT	Jim Thome	6.00
JV	Jason Varitek	4.00
JW	Jered Weaver	4.00
KF	Kosuke Fukudome	10.00
KJ	Kelly Johnson	4.00
KS	Kevin Slowey	4.00
KW	Kerry Wood	4.00
KY	Kevin Youkilis	8.00
LE	Cliff Lee	4.00
MA	Joe Mauer	6.00
ME	Melvin Mora	4.00
MK	Matt Kemp	6.00
MS	Mike Schmidt	15.00
MY	Michael Young	4.00
NM	Nick Markakis	8.00
NR	Nolan Ryan	30.00
NS	Nick Swisher	4.00
OS	Ozzie Smith	15.00
PA	Jonathan Papelbon	6.00
PE	Brad Penny	4.00
PF	Prince Fielder	6.00
PH	Phil Hughes	6.00
PN	Phil Niekro	8.00
RF	Rafael Furcal	5.00
RJ	Reggie Jackson	10.00
RO	Roy Oswalt	4.00
RS	Ryne Sandberg	15.00
RY	Robin Yount	15.00
SH	Gary Sheffield	6.00
TG	Troy Glaus	4.00
TH	Trevor Hoffman	4.00
TS	Takashi Saito	4.00
TT	Troy Tulowitzki	4.00
VM	Victor Martinez	4.00
WI	Josh Willingham	4.00
YG	Yovani Gallardo	6.00

Mini Blue Back
Blue (1-200):	2-4X
Blue SP (201-300):	1-1.5X

Mini Green Back
Green (1-200):	2-3X
Green SP (201-300):	1-1.5X

Mini Black Back
No Pricing
Production 21 Sets

Sports Royalty Autographs

SPORT ROYALTY — AUTHENTIC AUTOGRAPH TIGER WOODS

		NM/M
	Common Auto.:	
AK	Al Kaline	60.00
BB	Brooks Robinson	60.00
BF	Bob Feller	90.00
BG	Bob Gibson	60.00
BJ	Bo Jackson	80.00
BR	Bo Jackson	80.00
BS	Bill Sharman	25.00
CK	Clayton Kershaw	40.00
CR	Cal Ripken Jr.	140.00
CW	Chien-Ming Wang	120.00
DB	Dennis "Oil Can" Boyd	25.00
DE	Dennis Eckersley	40.00
DM	Don Mattingly	90.00
DP	Dustin Pedroia	80.00
DS	Don Sutton	50.00
EL	Evan Longoria	200.00
GP	Gaylord Perry	35.00
HM	Cole Hamels	60.00
JC	Joe Carter	30.00
JO	Michael Jordan	750.00
JP	Jim Palmer	35.00
KG	Ken Griffey Jr.	170.00
MI	Mike Bossy	40.00
NL	Nicklas Lidstrom	50.00
NR	Nolan Ryan	150.00
OS	Ozzie Smith	70.00
PM	Paul Molitor	40.00
RF	Rollie Fingers	25.00
RS	Ron Santo	70.00
RY	Ryne Sandberg	125.00
WB	Wade Boggs	60.00
YB	Yogi Berra	65.00

1935 Goudey 4-in-1

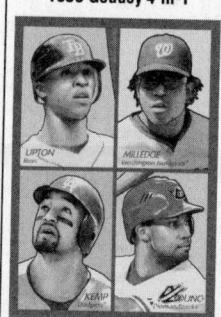

		NM/M
	Common Card:	.50
	Blue:	1-1.5X
	Green:	1.5-2X
	Black:	No Pricing
	Production 21 Sets	

#	Players	Price
1	Phil Niekro, Johnny Bench, Sparky Lyle, Reggie Jackson	1.50
2	Ozzie Smith, Bob Gibson, Albert Pujols, Ryan Ludwick	1.00
3	Bob Gibson, Josh Beckett, Jake Peavy, Tim Lincecum	1.50
4	Brian Roberts, Carl Crawford, Jose Reyes, Jacoby Ellsbury	1.50
5	Derek Jeter, Whitey Ford, Yogi Berra, Reggie Jackson	4.00
6	Alex Rodriguez, Derek Jeter, Whitey Ford, Yogi Berra	4.00
7	Alex Rodriguez, Derek Jeter, Whitey Ford, Chien-Ming Wang	4.00
8	Brooks Robinson, Josh Hamilton, Grady Sizemore, Ichiro Suzuki	2.00
9	Johnny Damon, Carl Crawford, Alex Rios, Jacoby Ellsbury	1.00
10	Nolan Ryan, Josh Beckett, Scott Kazmir, Clayton Kershaw	5.00
11	Kirk Gibson, Andre Ethier, Russell Martin, Clayton Kershaw	1.00
12	Alex Rodriguez, Ken Griffey Jr., Manny Ramirez, Mike Schmidt	3.00
13	Dan Haren, Adrian Gonzalez, Chris Young, Stephen Drew	1.00
14	Jack Morris, Gaylord Perry, Rollie Fingers, Jim Palmer	.50
15	Mariano Rivera, Trevor Hoffman, Jonathan Papelbon, Joakim Soria	1.00
16	Ryne Sandberg, Chase Utley, Ian Kinsler, Dan Uggla	1.50
17	Ron Santo, Alfonso Soriano, Carlos Zambrano, Billy Williams	1.00
18	Ozzie Smith, Cal Ripken Jr., Derek Jeter, Hanley Ramirez	4.00
19	Cal Ripken Jr., Melvin Mora, Jim Palmer, Nick Markakis	5.00
20	Dave Concepcion, Johnny Bench, Brandon Phillips, Jay Bruce	2.00
21	Mike Schmidt, Ryan Howard, Shane Victorino, Cole Hamels	2.50
22	Ron Santo, Ryne Sandberg, Derek Lee, Aramis Ramirez	3.00
23	Prince Fielder, Yovani Gallardo, Robin Yount, Ryan Braun	2.50
24	Derek Jeter, Johan Santana, Jose Reyes, Chien-Ming Wang	4.00
25	Ozzie Smith, Cal Ripken Jr., Derek Jeter, Jose Reyes	5.00
26	Chipper Jones, Tim Hudson, Brian McCann, Kelly Johnson	1.50
27	Yogi Berra, Johnny Bench, Joe Mauer, Brian McCann	1.50
28	Nolan Ryan, Bob Gibson, Gaylord Perry, Jim Palmer	5.00
29	Mike Schmidt, Ryan Howard, Prince Fielder, Robin Yount	3.00
30	Rick Ankiel, Troy Glaus, Albert Pujols, Ryan Ludwick	3.00
31	Carlos Quentin, Matt Holliday, Jason Bay, Ryan Braun	1.50
32	Johan Santana, Scott Kazmir, C.C. Sabathia, Cole Hamels	1.50
33	Rich Harden, Edinson Volquez, Tim Lincecum, Clayton Kershaw	2.00
34	Brian Roberts, Ian Kinsler, Howie Kendrick, Dustin Pedroia	1.00
35	Carlos Pena, Carl Crawford, B.J. Upton, Evan Longoria	2.00
36	Josh Hamilton, Ryan Howard, Justin Morneau, Prince Fielder	2.00
37	Carlos Guillen, Magglio Ordonez, Miguel Cabrera, Curtis Granderson	1.00
38	Cristian Guzman, Jimmy Rollins, Jose Reyes, Hanley Ramirez	1.50
39	Rafael Furcal, Andre Ethier, Russell Martin, Matt Kemp	1.00
40	Erik Bedard, Matt Tuiasosopo, Felix Hernandez, Ichiro Suzuki	1.50
41	Bobby Crosby, Jack Cust, Matt Cain, Tim Lincecum	1.50
42	Carlos Beltran, David Wright, Johan Santana, Jose Reyes	2.00
43	Jimmy Rollins, Chase Utley, Hanley Ramirez, Dan Uggla	1.50
44	Vladimir Guerrero, Torii Hunter, Chone Figgins, Howie Kendrick	1.00
45	Scott Kazmir, James Shields, Evan Longoria, David Price	3.00
46	Derek Lee, Lance Berkman, Albert Pujols, Prince Fielder	3.00
47	Jimmy Rollins, Ryan Howard, Chase Utley, Cole Hamels	2.00
48	Josh Beckett, Jonathan Papelbon, Daisuke Matsuzaka, Justin Masterson	2.50
49	Kerry Wood, Brad Lidge, Jonathan Papelbon, Joakim Soria	.50
50	David Ortiz, Kevin Youkilis, Dustin Pedroia, Jacoby Ellsbury	2.00
51	Erik Bedard, John Lackey, Felix Hernandez, Jered Weaver	.50
52	Josh Hamilton, Michael Young, Marlon Byrd, Ian Kinsler	1.00
53	Travis Hafner, Victor Martinez, Grady Sizemore, Kelly Shoppach	1.00
54	Chipper Jones, Brian McCann, Jeff Francoeur, Kelly Johnson	1.00
55	Chipper Jones, Aramis Ramirez, David Wright, Garrett Atkins	2.00
56	Brian McCann, Russell Martin, Ryan Doumit, Geovany Soto	1.00
57	J.J. Hardy, Bill Hall, Prince Fielder, Ryan Braun	2.00
58	Bobby Crosby, Jack Cust, Kurt Suzuki, Jeff Baisley	.50
59	Mariano Rivera, Chien-Ming Wang, Joba Chamberlain, Ian Kennedy	1.50
60	Rich Harden, Justin Verlander, Tim Lincecum, Joba Chamberlain	1.50

61	Vladimir Guerrero, John Lackey, Andre Ethier, Clayton Kershaw	1.00
62	David Wright, B.J. Upton, Ryan Zimmerman, John Maine	1.50
63	Torii Hunter, B.J. Upton, Grady Sizemore, Ichiro Suzuki	2.00
64	Chipper Jones, Carlos Beltran, Lance Berkman, Jimmy Rollins	1.50
65	Vernon Wells, Roy Halladay, Alex Rios, Travis Snider	1.00
66	Carlos Zambrano, Rich Harden, Geovany Soto, Kosuke Fukudome	1.00
67	Jason Giambi, David Ortiz, Ryan Howard, Prince Fielder	2.00
68	Clay Buchholz, Joba Chamberlain, Ian Kennedy, Justin Masterson	1.00
69	Justin Masterson, Josh Beckett, Joe Nathan, Francisco Liriano	1.00
70	Geovany Soto, Alexei Ramirez, Evan Longoria, Jay Bruce	2.50
71	Josh Hamilton, Albert Pujols, Ryan Howard, Miguel Cabrera	3.00
72	Rafael Furcal, Adrian Gonzalez, Chris Young, Clayton Kershaw	1.00
73	Derrek Lee, Aramis Ramirez, Alfonso Soriano, Geovany Soto	1.00
74	Chien-Ming Wang, Ichiro Suzuki, Daisuke Matsuzaka, Kosuke Fukudome	2.00
75	Andy Pettitte, Randy Johnson, Tom Glavine, Curt Schilling	1.00
76	Ken Griffey Jr., Jim Thome, Jermaine Dye, Carlos Quentin	2.50
77	Francisco Liriano, Cole Hamels, Clayton Kershaw, David Price	2.00
78	Justin Morneau, Joe Mauer, Delmon Young, Denard Span	1.00
79	Carlos Beltran, Carlos Guillen, Carlos Lee, Carlos Quentin	1.00
80	Manny Ramirez, Jermaine Dye, Travis Hafner, Magglio Ordonez	1.00
81	Grady Sizemore, Cliff Lee, Felix Hernandez, Ichiro Suzuki	1.00
82	Jack Cust, Kurt Suzuki, Jay Bruce, Johnny Cueto	1.50
83	Alexei Ramirez, Adam Jones, Denard Span, Dexter Fowler	1.00
84	Dustin Pedroia, Clay Buchholz, Justin Masterson, Jed Lowrie	1.50
85	Alex Rodriguez, Aramis Ramirez, David Wright, Evan Longoria	2.50
86	Alex Rodriguez, Ken Griffey Jr., Jim Thome, Manny Ramirez	2.50
87	Joe Mauer, Brian McCann, Russell Martin, Ryan Doumit	1.00
88	Manny Ramirez, Albert Pujols, Joe Nathan, Brad Lidge	3.00
89	Miguel Tejada, Carlos Lee, Lance Berkman, Roy Oswalt	.50
90	Alex Rodriguez, Derek Jeter, Mariano Rivera, Joba Chamberlain	1.00
91	Randy Johnson, Tim Hudson, Roy Halladay, Carlos Zambrano	1.00
92	Jim Thome, Jermaine Dye, Carlos Quentin, Alexei Ramirez	1.00
93	Rick Ankiel, Lance Berkman, Nate McLouth, Jay Bruce	1.00
94	Rick Ankiel, Jeff Francoeur, Nick Markakis, Ichiro Suzuki	1.00
95	B.J. Upton, Lastings Milledge, Matt Kemp, Chris B. Young	1.00
96	Albert Pujols, Cliff Lee, Dustin Pedroia, Tim Lincecum	3.00
97	Alex Rodriguez, Derek Jeter, David Wright, Jose Reyes	4.00
98	Michael Young, Hanley Ramirez, Ian Kinsler, Dan Uggla	1.00
99	Adam Dunn, Stephen Drew, Chris B. Young, Mark Reynolds	.50
100	Dexter Fowler, Matt Antonelli, Michael Bowden, Travis Snider	1.00

2009 Upper Deck X

		NM/M
Complete Set (100):		30.00
Common Player:		.25
Common RC:		
Pack (6):		2.00
Box (24):		40.00
1	Dan Haren	.40
2	Chris B. Young	.25
3	Brandon Webb	.40
4	Chipper Jones	.75
5	Brian McCann	.40
6	Nick Markakis	.50
7	Brian Roberts	.40
8	Kevin Youkilis	.50
9	Josh Beckett	.40
10	Jonathan Papelbon	.40
11	Jacoby Ellsbury	.50
12	Dustin Pedroia	1.00
13	David Ortiz	.75
14	Daisuke Matsuzaka	.40
15	Rich Harden	.40
16	Alfonso Soriano	.50
17	Derrek Lee	.40
18	Carlos Zambrano	.40
19	Aramis Ramirez	.40
20	Paul Konerko	.40
21	Jermaine Dye	.40
22	Carlos Quentin	.50
23	Jay Bruce	.50
24	Edinson Volquez	.25
25	Brandon Phillips	.40
26	Victor Martinez	.40
27	Travis Hafner	.40
28	Kerry Wood	.25
29	Grady Sizemore	.75
30	Cliff Lee	.40
31	Garrett Atkins	.25
32	Miguel Cabrera	.75
33	Magglio Ordonez	.40
34	Carlos Guillen	.25
35	Hanley Ramirez	.75
36	Dan Uggla	.40
37	Miguel Tejada	.50
38	Lance Berkman	.50
39	Carlos Lee	.50
40	Jose Guillen	.25
41	Alex Gordon	.40
42	Vladimir Guerrero	.75
43	Torii Hunter	.50
44	Bobby Abreu	.50
45	Russell Martin	.25
46	Matt Kemp	.50
47	Manny Ramirez	.75
48	Ryan Braun	1.00
49	Prince Fielder	.75
50	Corey Hart	.25
51	Joe Nathan	.25
52	Justin Morneau	.50
53	Joe Mauer	.75
54	Jose Reyes	1.00
55	Johan Santana	.75
56	Francisco Rodriguez	.25
57	David Wright	1.00
58	Carlos Beltran	.50
59	Mark Teixeira	.75
60	Andy Pettitte	.40
61	Joba Chamberlain	.75
62	Derek Jeter	2.00
63	Chien-Ming Wang	.75
64	C.C. Sabathia	.75
65	Alex Rodriguez	1.50
66	Matt Holliday	.50
67	Jason Giambi	.40
68	Jack Cust	.25
69	Ryan Howard	1.00
70	Jimmy Rollins	.75
71	Chase Utley	1.00
72	Nate McLouth	.40
73	Ryan Doumit	.40
74	Jake Peavy	.40
75	Adrian Gonzalez	.40
76	Tim Lincecum	1.00
77	Aaron Rowand	.25
78	Randy Johnson	.75
79	Ken Griffey Jr.	1.50
80	Ichiro Suzuki	1.50
81	Felix Hernandez	.40
82	Ryan Ludwick	.40
83	Rick Ankiel	.40
84	Albert Pujols	2.00
85	Scott Kazmir	.25
86	Evan Longoria	1.50
87	Carl Crawford	.40
88	B.J. Upton	.75
89	Josh Hamilton	.75
90	Ian Kinsler	.50
91	Vernon Wells	.50
92	Roy Halladay	.50
93	Alex Rios	.40
94	Adam Dunn	.50
95	Ryan Zimmerman	.50
96	Rick Porcello RC	3.00
97	Colby Rasmus (RC)	2.00
98	James McDonald RC	1.00
99	Koji Uehara RC	2.00
100	Derek Holland RC	2.00

Die-Cut
Die-Cut (1-100): 1-2X

Printing Plates
Production one set per color.

Memorabilia

		NM/M
Some not priced yet.		
AE	Andre Ethier	8.00
AM	Andrew Miller	4.00
AN	Rick Ankiel/SP	8.00
BD	Blake DeWitt	6.00
BM	Brian McCann	6.00
BP	Brad Penny	4.00
BZ	Barry Zito	4.00
CA	Chris Carpenter	8.00
CD	Carlos Delgado	6.00
CG	Carlos Guillen	6.00
CJ	Conor Jackson	4.00
CL	Carlos Lee	6.00
CU	Michael Cuddyer	4.00
DH	Dan Haren	6.00
DJ	Derek Jeter	15.00
DL	Derrek Lee	6.00
DO	David Ortiz	6.00
DY	Delmon Young	4.00
FP	Felipe Paulino	4.00
GR	Curtis Granderson	8.00
HO	Trevor Hoffman	4.00
JC	Joba Chamberlain	8.00
JD	Jermaine Dye	4.00
JG	Jeremy Guthrie	4.00
JH	Jeremy Hermida	4.00
JK	Jason Kubel	6.00
JL	James Loney	4.00
JM	Joe Mauer	8.00
JN	Joe Nathan	4.00
JO	Josh Barfield	4.00
JP	Jake Peavy	6.00
JT	Jim Thome	8.00
JU	Justin Upton	8.00
JW	Jered Weaver	4.00
JZ	Joel Zumaya	4.00
KJ	Kelly Johnson	4.00
KK	Kevin Kouzmanoff	4.00
KM	Kendry Morales	4.00
MC	Miguel Cabrera	6.00
MH	Matt Holliday	6.00
MI	Kevin Millwood	4.00
MK	Matt Kemp	8.00
ML	Mike Lowell	6.00
MO	Justin Morneau	8.00
MR	Manny Ramirez	8.00
MY	Michael Young	6.00
PE	Jhonny Peralta	4.00
RA	Aramis Ramirez	6.00
RF	Rafael Furcal	6.00
RM	Russell Martin	6.00
RO	Roy Oswalt	6.00
RT	Ramon Troncoso	4.00
SR	Scott Rolen	6.00
TG	Troy Glaus	4.00
WI	Josh Willingham	6.00
YO	Kevin Youkilis	8.00

Signatures

		NM/M
Common Auto.:		
23	Jay Bruce	25.00
24	Edinson Volquez	15.00
50	Corey Hart	12.00
98	James McDonald	10.00

Xponential

		NM/M
Common Player:		.50
X2:		1-1.25X
X3:		1-1.25X
X4:		1-1.5X
X5:		1-1.5X
X6:		1-2X
5	A.J. Burnett	.75
AG	Adrian Gonzalez	1.00
AP	Albert Pujols	5.00
AR	Alex Rodriguez	4.00
AS	Alfonso Soriano	1.00
AZ	Aramis Ramirez	1.00
BA	Bobby Abreu	1.00
BE	Josh Beckett	1.50
BM	Brian McCann	1.00
BP	Brandon Phillips	.75
BU	B.J. Upton	.75
BW	Brandon Webb	1.00
CB	Carlos Beltran	1.00
CC	Carl Crawford	1.00
CH	Cole Hamels	2.00
CJ	Chipper Jones	2.50
CL	Carlos Lee	1.00
CQ	Carlos Quentin	.75
CS	C.C. Sabathia	1.50
CU	Chase Utley	2.00
CW	Chien-Ming Wang	1.50
CZ	Carlos Zambrano	.75
DH	Dan Haren	.75
DJ	Derek Jeter	5.00
DL	Derrek Lee	1.00
DM	Daisuke Matsuzaka	1.00
DO	David Ortiz	1.50
DP	Dustin Pedroia	2.50
DU	Dan Uggla	.50
DW	David Wright	2.00
EL	Evan Longoria	2.50
EV	Edinson Volquez	.50
FH	Felix Hernandez	.75
FR	Francisco Rodriguez	.50
GE	Geovany Soto	.50
GS	Grady Sizemore	1.50
HA	Travis Hafner	.50
HO	Ryan Howard	2.00
HR	Hanley Ramirez	2.00
IK	Ian Kinsler	1.50
IS	Ichiro Suzuki	3.00
JB	Jay Bruce	1.50
JD	Jermaine Dye	.75
JE	Jacoby Ellsbury	2.00
JG	Jason Giambi	.50
JH	Josh Hamilton	1.50
JM	Joe Mauer	1.50
JP	Jake Peavy	1.00
JR	Jimmy Rollins	1.00
JS	Johan Santana	1.50
KG	Ken Griffey Jr.	3.00
KY	Kevin Youkilis	1.50
LB	Lance Berkman	1.00
MA	Nick Markakis	1.50
MC	Miguel Cabrera	1.50
MH	Matt Holliday	1.00
ML	Mike Lowell	.50
MO	Magglio Ordonez	.50
MR	Manny Ramirez	1.50
MT	Mark Teixeira	1.50
PA	Jonathan Papelbon	1.00
PF	Prince Fielder	2.00
RA	Rick Ankiel	.50
RB	Ryan Braun	2.00
RE	Jose Reyes	2.00
RH	Roy Halladay	1.00
RJ	Randy Johnson	1.50
RM	Russell Martin	.50
RZ	Ryan Zimmerman	1.00
SK	Scott Kazmir	.50
TE	Miguel Tejada	.75
TH	Torii Hunter	.75
TL	Tim Lincecum	2.50
VG	Vladimir Guerrero	1.00
VW	Vernon Wells	.50

2009 UD A Piece of History

LANCE BERKMAN / ASTROS' FIRST BASE
A PIECE OF HISTORY

		NM/M
Common (1-100,151-200):		.25
Common RC (101-150):		
Hobby Pack (7):		5.00
Hobby Box (16):		65.00
1	Brandon Webb	.50
2	Randy Johnson	.75
3	Dan Haren	.50
4	Adam Dunn	.75
5	Chipper Jones	1.00
6	John Smoltz	.50
7	Tom Glavine	.50
8	Brian Roberts	.50
9	Nick Markakis	.75
10	Josh Beckett	.50
11	David Ortiz	.75
12	Daisuke Matsuzaka	.75
13	Jacoby Ellsbury	.75
14	Jonathan Papelbon	.50
15	Alfonso Soriano	.75
16	Derrek Lee	.50
17	Kosuke Fukudome	.50
18	Carlos Zambrano	.50
19	Aramis Ramirez	.50
20	Rich Harden	.25
21	Carlos Quentin	.50
22	Jim Thome	.50
23	Ken Griffey Jr.	1.50
24	Jay Bruce	.50
25	Edinson Volquez	.50
26	Brandon Phillips	.50
27	Victor Martinez	.50
28	Grady Sizemore	.75
29	Travis Hafner	.50
30	Matt Holliday	.50
31	Troy Tulowitzki	.50
32	Garrett Atkins	.25
33	Miguel Cabrera	.75
34	Magglio Ordonez	.50
35	Justin Verlander	.75
36	Hanley Ramirez	.75
37	Dan Uggla	.50
38	Lance Berkman	.50
39	Carlos Lee	.50
40	Kevin Youkilis	.75
41	Miguel Tejada	.50
42	Alex Gordon	.50
43	Zack Greinke	.50
44	Mark Teixeira	.50
45	Vladimir Guerrero	.75
46	Torii Hunter	.50
47	Manny Ramirez	.75
48	Russell Martin	.40
49	Matt Kemp	.75
50	Clayton Kershaw	.75
51	C.C. Sabathia	.75
52	Corey Hart	.40
53	Prince Fielder	.75
54	Ryan Braun	1.00
55	Joe Mauer	.50
56	Justin Morneau	.50
57	Jose Reyes	.75
58	David Wright	.75
59	Johan Santana	.75
60	Carlos Beltran	.50
61	Pedro Martinez	.50
62	Alex Rodriguez	1.50
63	Derek Jeter	2.00
64	Chien-Ming Wang	.25
65	Hideki Matsui	.50
66	Joba Chamberlain	.75
67	Mariano Rivera	.50
68	Xavier Nady	.25
69	Frank Thomas	.75
70	Jason Giambi	.50
71	Chase Utley	1.00
72	Ryan Howard	1.50
73	Jimmy Rollins	.75
74	Ryan Doumit	.25
75	Nate McLouth	.50
76	Adrian Gonzalez	.50
77	Jake Peavy	.50
78	Brian Giles	.25
79	Tim Lincecum	1.50
80	Matt Cain	.50
81	Felix Hernandez	.50
82	Ichiro Suzuki	1.00
83	Erik Bedard	.50
84	Ryan Ludwick	.50
85	Albert Pujols	2.00
86	Chris Carpenter	.50
87	Rick Ankiel	.50
88	B.J. Upton	.50
89	Evan Longoria	1.50
90	Scott Kazmir	.25
91	Carl Crawford	.50
92	Josh Hamilton	.50
93	Ian Kinsler	.75
94	Michael Young	.50
95	Roy Halladay	.50
96	Vernon Wells	.50
97	Alex Rios	.50
98	Ryan Zimmerman	.50
99	Lastings Milledge	.25
100	David Price RC	4.00
101	Conor Gillaspie RC	1.50
102	Josh Roenicke RC	1.50
103	Jeff Baisley RC	1.00
104	Alfredo Aceves RC	1.50
105	Matt Antonelli RC	1.50
106	Michael Bowden (RC)	2.00
107	Josh Whitesell (RC)	1.00
108	Wilkin Castillo RC	1.00
109	Francisco Cervelli RC	1.50
110	Phil Coke RC	1.50
111	Luis Cruz RC	1.00
112	Jesus Delgado RC	1.00
113	Scott Elbert (RC)	1.00
114	Alcides Escobar RC	2.00
115	Dexter Fowler (RC)	2.00
116	Mat Gamel RC	1.00
117	Josh Geer (RC)	1.00
118	Greg Golson (RC)	1.00
119	Kila Ka'aihue (RC)	1.50
120	Chris Lambert (RC)	1.00
121	Wade LeBlanc RC	1.00
122	Scott Lewis (RC)	1.00
123	Lou Marson RC	1.00
124	Shairon Martis RC	1.00
125	James McDonald RC	2.00
126	Juan Miranda RC	1.00
127	Luke Montz RC	1.00
128	Jon Niese RC	1.00
129	Josh Outman RC	1.00
130	James Parr (RC)	1.00
131	Dusty Ryan RC	1.00
132	Angel Salome RC	1.50
133	Travis Snider RC	3.00
134	Matt Tuiasosopo (RC)	1.00
135	Will Venable RC	1.00
136	Aaron Cunningham RC	1.00
137	George Kottaras (RC)	1.00
138	Devon Lowery (RC)	1.00
139	Jose Mijares RC	2.00
140	Jason Motte (RC)	1.50
141	Bobby Parnell RC	1.00
142	Fernando Perez (RC)	1.50
143	Jason Pridie (RC)	1.00
144	Ramon Ramirez (RC)	1.00
145	Justin Thomas (RC)	1.00
146	Luis Valbuena RC	1.00
147	Gaby Sanchez RC	1.50
148	Mike Hinckley (RC)	1.00
149	Mitch Talbot (RC)	1.00
151	Star Spangled Banner	.25
152	Dwight D. Eisenhower	.25
153	First Atomic Sub Launched	.25
154	Alaska becomes 49th State	.25
155	"I Have A Dream" Speech	.25
156	18th Amendment Adopted	.25
157	Discovery of Penicillin	.25
158	Germany leaves League of Nations	.25
159	Attack on Pearl Harbor	.25
160	U.S. enters World War II	.25
161	"D-Day" invasion	.25
162	NATO organized	.25
163	1970 Earth Day	.25
164	1989 San Fran. earthquake	.25
165	Warsaw Pact	.25
166	NAFTA	.25
167	Boy Scouts of America launched	.25
168	New Zealand Pioneers Women's voting	.25
169	First moving assembly line	.25
170	Hollywood sign debuts	.25
171	Taj Mahal completed	.25
172	U.S. Constitution signed	.25
173	Empire State Building built	.25
174	Golden State Bridge completed	.25
175	Smallpox eradicated	.25
176	Elevator invented	.25
177	Microwave oven invented	.25
178	E-Mail invented	.25
179	Eiffel Tower erected	.25
180	Pilgrims land at Plymouth	.25
181	First photo taken	.25
182	First anesthetic used	.25
183	First Kentucky Derby	.25
184	Brooklyn Bridge completed	.25
185	X-Ray invented	.25
186	Pluto recategorized as dwarf planet	.25
187	Mount Rushmore finished	.25
188	Thansgiving adopted as holiday	.25
189	Chicago Cubs	.25
190	Baseball Hall of Fame opened	.25
191	National League established	.25
192	Olympic Games begin	.25
193	Voyager 2	.25
194	New Orleans founded	.25
195	Discovery of New York	.25
196	Debut of N.Y. Times	.25
197	Republican Party founded	.25
198	City of Boston founded	.25
199	Introduction of EURO currency	.25
200	Czechoslavakia splits in two	.25

Blue
Blue (1-200): 1-2X
Production 299 Sets

Gold
Gold (1-100,151-200): 4-6X
Gold RC (101-150): 2-3X
Production 50 Sets

Green
Green (1-100,151-200): 3-5X
Green RC (101-150): 1-2.5X
Production 150 Sets

Red
Red (1-100,151-200): 2-3X
Red RC (101-150): 1-1.5X

A Piece of Hollywood

A PIECE OF HOLLYWOOD
PANTS
"ALONG CAME POLLY"

		NM/M
Common Card:		10.00
AS	Arnold Schwarzenegger	40.00
BA	Ben Affleck	10.00
BL	Bruce Lee	60.00
BS	Ben Stiller	10.00
DB	Drew Barrymore	20.00
DW	Denzel Washington	15.00
HJ	John Hurt	10.00
HL	Heath Ledger	40.00
HU	John Hurt	10.00
JH	John Hurt	10.00
MM	Mike Myers	10.00
RM	Rachel McAdams	30.00
SA	Adam Sandler	15.00
SB	Ben Stiller	10.00
SG	Sidney Greenstreet	15.00
SP	Sean Penn	15.00
ST	Ben Stiller	15.00
TH	Tom Hanks	15.00
WD	Denzel Washington	15.00
WF	Will Ferrell	15.00
WS	Will Smith	25.00

Box Score Memories

		NM/M
Common Player:		1.50
Production 999 Sets		
Black:		1-1.5X
Production 149 Sets		
Blue:		2-4X
Production 25 Sets		
Red:		1-2X
Production 75 Sets		
Turquoise:		1-1.5X
Production 99 Sets		
CD	Carlos Delgado	2.50
CF	Chone Figgins	1.50
CJ	Chipper Jones	3.00
CL	Carlos Lee	2.00
DL	Derrek Lee	2.00

DO	David Ortiz	3.00
DU	Dan Uggla	2.00
GS	Gary Sheffield	2.00
HR	Hanley Ramirez	4.00
JD	Johnny Damon	2.50
JF	Jeff Francoeur	1.50
JH	Jeremy Hermida	1.50
JM	Justin Morneau	2.00
KG	Khalil Greene	1.50
MM	Melvin Mora	1.50
MR	Manny Ramirez	3.00
NM	Nick Markakis	2.50
PB	Pat Burrell	1.50
PK	Paul Konerko	1.50
RB	Ryan Braun	4.00
RF	Rafael Furcal	2.00
RW	Rickie Weeks	1.50
TH	Travis Hafner	1.50
VM	Victor Martinez	1.50
YE	Yunel Escobar	1.50

Box Score Memories Jsy Auto.

NM/M

Production 10 or 25
CF	Chone Figgins/25	15.00
CJ	Chipper Jones/25	75.00
JF	Jeff Francoeur/25	25.00
NM	Nick Markakis/25	50.00
RB	Ryan Braun/25	40.00
RW	Rickie Weeks/25	15.00
TH	Travis Hafner/25	20.00

Box Score Memories Jersey

NM/M
Common Player:		4.00
Red:		1X

Production 180 Sets
Patch:		No Pricing

Production 25 Sets
CD	Carlos Delgado	6.00
CF	Chone Figgins	4.00
CJ	Chipper Jones	10.00
CL	Carlos Lee	6.00
DL	Derrek Lee	6.00
DO	David Ortiz	8.00
DU	Dan Uggla	6.00
GS	Gary Sheffield	6.00
HR	Hanley Ramirez	8.00
JD	Johnny Damon	6.00
JF	Jeff Francoeur	4.00
JH	Jeremy Hermida	4.00
JM	Justin Morneau	6.00
KG	Khalil Greene	4.00
MM	Melvin Mora	4.00
MR	Manny Ramirez	8.00
NM	Nick Markakis	10.00
PB	Pat Burrell	4.00
PK	Paul Konerko	4.00
RB	Ryan Braun	10.00
RF	Rafael Furcal	6.00
RW	Rickie Weeks	4.00
TH	Travis Hafner	4.00
VM	Victor Martinez	4.00
YE	Yunel Escobar	4.00

Cut From the Same Cloth

NM/M
Common Duo:		1.50

Production 999 Sets
Gold:		1-2X

Production 75 Sets
Green:		1-1.5X

Production 149 Sets
Purple:		2-4X

Production 25 Sets
Red:		1-1.5X

Production 99 Sets
AH	Rick Ankiel, Josh Hamilton	3.00
BC	Josh Beckett, Joba Chamberlain	2.50
BH	Lance Berkman, Josh Hamilton	3.00
BS	Carlos Beltran, Grady Sizemore	4.00
	Ken Griffey Jr., Jay Bruce	

GO	Vladimir Guerrero, David Ortiz	3.00
HF	Ryan Howard, Prince Fielder	3.00
HV	Felix Hernandez, Edinson Volquez	2.00
IC	Carl Crawford, Ichiro Suzuki	3.00
JK	Randy Johnson, Scott Kazmir	2.00
JT	Derek Jeter, Troy Tulowitzki	5.00
MG	Justin Morneau, Adrian Gonzalez	2.00
MM	Joe Mauer, Russell Martin	2.00
MS	Pedro Martinez, Johan Santana	2.50
OL	Roy Oswalt, Tim Lincecum	3.00
PC	Albert Pujols, Miguel Cabrera	5.00
PE	Dustin Pedroia, Jacoby Ellsbury	3.00
PW	Jake Peavy, Brandon Webb	2.00
QB	Carlos Quentin, Ryan Braun	3.00
RH	Manny Ramirez, Matt Holliday	2.50
RP	Francisco Rodriguez, Jonathan Papelbon	2.00
RR	Jimmy Rollins, Jose Reyes	3.00
RW	Alex Rodriguez, David Wright	5.00
SR	Alfonso Soriano, Hanley Ramirez	3.00
TJ	Chipper Jones, Mark Teixeira	3.00
UK	Chase Utley, Ian Kinsler	3.00
UU	B.J. Upton, Justin Upton	2.00
WL	David Wright, Evan Longoria	5.00
WM	Chien-Ming Wang, Daisuke Matsuzaka	3.00
ZS	Carlos Zambrano, C.C. Sabathia	3.00

Franchise History

NM/M
Common Player:		1.50

Production 999 Sets
Black:		1-1.5X

Production 150 Sets
Blue:		2-4X

Production 25 Sets
Red:		1-2X

Production 75 Sets
Turquoise:		1-1.5X

Production 99 Sets
AP	Albert Pujols	5.00
BC	Bobby Crosby	1.50
BM	Brian McCann	2.00
BR	Brian Roberts	2.00
CH	Cole Hamels	3.00
CL	Carlos Lee	2.00
DJ	Derek Jeter	5.00
DL	Derrek Lee	2.00
DU	Dan Uggla	2.00
FL	Francisco Liriano	2.00
HE	Todd Helton	2.00
JH	Josh Hamilton	4.00
JR	Jose Reyes	4.00
JV	Jason Varitek	1.50
KG	Khalil Greene	1.50
MO	Magglio Ordonez	1.50
PF	Prince Fielder	3.00
PK	Paul Konerko	2.00
RH	Roy Halladay	2.50
RJ	Randy Johnson	2.50
RM	Russell Martin	2.00
SK	Scott Kazmir	2.00
TH	Travis Hafner	1.50
TL	Tim Lincecum	4.00
ZG	Zack Greinke	2.50

Franchise History Jsy Auto.

NM/M

Production 10 or 25
BC	Bobby Crosby/25	10.00
BR	Brian Roberts/25	25.00
DJ	Derek Jeter/25	125.00
DL	Derrek Lee/25	25.00
RH	Roy Halladay/25	40.00
RM	Russell Martin/25	20.00
SK	Scott Kazmir/25	20.00
TH	Travis Hafner/25	20.00
ZG	Zack Greinke/25	30.00

Franchise History Jersey

NM/M
Common Player:		4.00
Red:		1X

Production 180 Sets
Patch:		No Pricing

Production 25 Sets
AP	Albert Pujols	15.00

BC	Bobby Crosby	4.00
BM	Brian McCann	6.00
BR	Brian Roberts	6.00
CH	Cole Hamels	10.00
CL	Carlos Lee	6.00
DJ	Derek Jeter	20.00
DL	Derrek Lee	6.00
DU	Dan Uggla	6.00
FL	Francisco Liriano	6.00
HE	Todd Helton	6.00
JR	Jose Reyes	8.00
JV	Jason Varitek	4.00
KG	Khalil Greene	4.00
MO	Magglio Ordonez	6.00
PF	Prince Fielder	10.00
PK	Paul Konerko	6.00
RH	Roy Halladay	8.00
RM	Russell Martin	6.00
SK	Scott Kazmir	6.00
TH	Travis Hafner	4.00
TL	Tim Lincecum	15.00
ZG	Zack Greinke	8.00

Franchise Members Quad

NM/M
Common Quad:		1.50

Production 999 Sets
Gold:		1-2X

Production 75 Sets
Green:		1-1.5X

Production 149 Sets
Purple:		2-4X

Production 25 Sets
Red:		1-1.5X

Production 99 Sets
BLTO	Miguel Tejada, Carlos Lee, Lance Berkman, Roy Oswalt	1.50
FGHW	Vladimir Guerrero, Torii Hunter, Chone Figgins, Reggie Willits	2.00
GTDQ	Jim Thome, Jermaine Dye, Gavin Floyd, Carlos Quentin	2.00
JRCR	Alex Rodriguez, Derek Jeter, Mariano Rivera, Joba Chamberlain	5.00
KCLU	Carl Crawford, Scott Kazmir, B.J. Upton, Evan Longoria	4.00
OCGG	Carlos Guillen, Magglio Ordonez, Miguel Cabrera, Curtis Granderson	3.00
OYPD	David Ortiz, Kevin Youkilis, J.D. Drew, Dustin Pedroia	4.00
RWBS	Carlos Beltran, David Wright, Johan Santana, Jose Reyes	4.00
SHMG	Travis Hafner, Victor Martinez, Grady Sizemore, Ryan Garko	3.00
SLRS	Derrek Lee, Aramis Ramirez, Alfonso Soriano, Geovany Soto	3.00

Franchise Members Trio

NM/M
Common Trio:		1.50

Production 999 Sets
Gold:		1-2X

Production 75 Sets
Green:		1-1.5X

Production 149 Sets
Purple:		2-4X

Production 25 Sets
Red:		1-1.5X

Production 99 Sets
BML	Josh Beckett, Jon Lester, Daisuke Matsuzaka	3.00
FBS	Jeff Suppan, Prince Fielder, Ryan Braun	4.00
GYG	Brian Giles, Adrian Gonzalez, Chris Young	1.50
HKY	Josh Hamilton, Michael Young, Ian Kinsler	3.00
JEM	Chipper Jones, Brian McCann, Yunel Escobar	3.00
JRM	Alex Rodriguez, Derek Jeter, Hideki Matsui	3.00
PAL	Rick Ankiel, Albert Pujols, Ryan Ludwick	3.00
RUH	Hanley Ramirez, Jeremy Hermida, Dan Uggla	3.00
RWB	Carlos Beltran, David Wright, Jose Reyes	4.00
URH	Jimmy Rollins, Ryan Howard, Chase Utley	4.00

Hair Cuts

NM/M

No pricing due to scarcity.

BC	Bobby Crosby	4.00
BM	Brian McCann	6.00
BR	Brian Roberts	6.00
CH	Cole Hamels	10.00
CL	Carlos Lee	6.00
DJ	Derek Jeter	20.00
DL	Derrek Lee	6.00
DU	Dan Uggla	6.00
FL	Francisco Liriano	6.00
HE	Todd Helton	6.00
JR	Jose Reyes	8.00
JV	Jason Varitek	4.00
KG	Khalil Greene	4.00
MO	Magglio Ordonez	6.00
PF	Prince Fielder	10.00
PK	Paul Konerko	6.00
RH	Roy Halladay	8.00
RM	Russell Martin	6.00
SK	Scott Kazmir	6.00
TH	Travis Hafner	4.00
TL	Tim Lincecum	15.00
ZG	Zack Greinke	8.00

Rookie Autographs Violet

NM/M
Common RC Auto.:		8.00
Blue:		1-1.25X

Production 99 Sets
Green:		No Pricing

Production 25 Sets
101	David Price	50.00
102	Conor Gillaspie	15.00
104	Jeff Baisley	10.00
106	Matt Antonelli	10.00
107	Michael Bowden	10.00
110	Francisco Cervelli	12.00
111	Phil Coke	15.00
112	Luis Cruz	10.00
113	Jesus Delgado	10.00
116	Dexter Fowler	20.00
117	Mat Gamel	25.00
118	Josh Geer	8.00
119	Greg Golson	8.00
120	Kila Ka'aihue	15.00
121	Chris Lambert	10.00
122	Wade LeBlanc	8.00
124	Lou Marson	15.00
125	Shairon Martis	10.00
126	James McDonald	20.00
127	Juan Miranda	15.00
128	Luke Montz	8.00
130	Josh Outman	10.00
131	James Parr	8.00
133	Angel Salome	15.00
134	Travis Snider	35.00
135	Matt Tuiasosopo	10.00
137	Aaron Cunningham	10.00
143	Fernando Perez	15.00
148	Gaby Sanchez	15.00

Stadium Scenes

NM/M
Common Player:		1.50

Production 999 Sets
Black:		1-1.5X

Production 149 Sets
Blue:		2-4X

Production 25 Sets
Red:		1-2X

Production 75 Sets
Turquoise:		1-1.5X

Production 99 Sets
AL	Adam LaRoche	1.50
CC	Chris Carpenter	2.00
CD	Carlos Delgado	2.00
CG	Curtis Granderson	3.00
CO	Chad Cordero	1.50
CY	Chris Young	1.50
DL	Derrek Lee	2.00
DM	Daisuke Matsuzaka	2.50
EC	Eric Chavez	1.50
JC	Johnny Cueto	1.50
JF	Jeff Francoeur	1.50
JM	Joe Mauer	2.00
JP	Jorge Posada	2.00
LB	Lance Berkman	2.00
MB	Mark Buehrle	1.50
MR	Mark Reynolds	1.50
NM	Nick Markakis	3.00
RB	Rocco Baldelli	1.50
RG	Ryan Garko	1.50
RH	Roy Halladay	2.00
RM	Russell Martin	1.50
RW	Rickie Weeks	1.50
TL	Tim Lincecum	4.00
VG	Vladimir Guerrero	2.50
ZG	Zack Greinke	2.00

Stadium Scenes Auto. Jersey

NM/M

Production 10 or 25
CC	Chris Carpenter/25	25.00
CY	Chris Young/25	15.00
DL	Derrek Lee/25	25.00
JC	Johnny Cueto/25	15.00
JF	Jeff Francoeur/25	25.00
NM	Nick Markakis/25	50.00
RH	Roy Halladay/25	40.00
RM	Russell Martin/25	20.00
RW	Rickie Weeks/25	15.00
ZG	Zack Greinke/25	40.00

Stadium Scenes Jersey

NM/M
Common Player:		4.00
Red:		1X

Production 180 Sets
Patch:		2-3X

Production 35 Sets
AL	Adam LaRoche	4.00
CC	Chris Carpenter	6.00
CD	Carlos Delgado	6.00
CG	Curtis Granderson	8.00
CO	Chad Cordero	4.00
CY	Chris Young	4.00
DL	Derek Lee	6.00
DM	Daisuke Matsuzaka	15.00
EC	Eric Chavez	4.00
JC	Johnny Cueto	4.00
JF	Jeff Francoeur	4.00
JM	Joe Mauer	8.00
JP	Jorge Posada	6.00
LB	Lance Berkman	6.00
MB	Mark Buehrle	4.00
MR	Mark Reynolds	4.00
NM	Nick Markakis	10.00
RB	Rocco Baldelli	4.00
RH	Roy Halladay	6.00
RM	Russell Martin	6.00
RW	Rickie Weeks	6.00
TL	Tim Lincecum	15.00
VG	Vladimir Guerrero	6.00
ZG	Zack Greinke	6.00

Timeless Moments

NM/M
Common Player:		1.50

Production 999 Sets
Black:		1-1.5X

Production 149 Sets
Blue:		2-4X

Production 25 Sets
Red:		1-2X

Production 75 Sets
Turquoise:		1-1.5X

Production 99 Sets
AP	Albert Pujols	5.00
BR	Brian Roberts	2.00
CH	Cole Hamels	3.00
DL	Derek Lowe	1.50
DO	David Ortiz	3.00
DW	Dontrelle Willis	1.50
EL	Evan Longoria	5.00
EV	Edinson Volquez	1.50
FT	Frank Thomas	2.50
JB	Jay Bruce	3.00
JD	Jermaine Dye	1.50
JH	Josh Hamilton	3.00
JL	Jon Lester	2.50
JP	Jonathan Papelbon	2.00
JV	Joey Votto	2.00
KG	Ken Griffey Jr.	4.00
MB	Mark Buehrle	1.50
ML	Mike Lowell	1.50
PE	Jake Peavy	2.00
RB	Ryan Braun	3.00
RJ	Randy Johnson	2.50
SK	Scott Kazmir	2.00
SM	John Smoltz	2.00
TG	Tom Glavine	2.00

Timeless Moments Auto.

NM/M

Production 10 or 25
JL	Jon Lester/25	35.00
RB	Ryan Braun/25	40.00
SK	Scott Kazmir/25	25.00
TG	Tom Glavine/25	45.00

Timeless Moments Jersey

NM/M
Common Player:		4.00
Red:		1X

Production 180 Sets
Patch:		No Pricing

Production 25 Sets
AP	Albert Pujols	15.00
BR	Brian Roberts	6.00
CH	Cole Hamels	6.00
DO	David Ortiz	8.00
EV	Edinson Volquez	4.00
FT	Frank Thomas	8.00
JB	Jay Bruce	10.00
JD	Jermaine Dye	6.00
JH	Josh Hamilton	10.00
JL	Jon Lester	8.00
JP	Jonathan Papelbon	6.00
JV	Joey Votto	8.00
KG	Ken Griffey Jr.	12.00
MB	Mark Buehrle	4.00
ML	Mike Lowell	4.00
PE	Jake Peavy	6.00
RB	Ryan Braun	8.00
RJ	Randy Johnson	8.00
SK	Scott Kazmir	4.00
SM	John Smoltz	4.00
TG	Tom Glavine	6.00

---

500 HR Club Bat

MR	Manny Ramirez	50.00

2009 UD Goodwin Champions

NM/M
Common Player (1-150):	.25
Common SP (151-210):	2.00
Pack (5):	5.00
Box (20):	85.00
1	Ken Griffey Jr.	2.00
1	Ken Griffey Jr./ SP Night	10.00
2	Derek Jeter	3.00
3	Jon Lester	.50
4	Jorge Posada	.50
5	Albert Pujols	3.00
6	Chipper Jones	1.00
7	Ryne Sandberg	1.50
7	Ryne Sandberg/ SP Night	10.00
8	Johnny Damon	.50
9	Carlos Delgado	.50
10	Vladimir Guerrero	.75
11	Johnny Bench	.75
12	Matt Cain	.50
13	Bill "Moose" Skowron	.25
14	Donovan Bailey	.25
15	Dick Allen	.25
16	Abraham Lincoln	.50
17	Rollie Fingers	.25
18	Bo Jackson	.75
19	Scott Kazmir	.50
20	Grady Sizemore	1.00
20	Grady Sizemore/ SP Night	5.00
21	Ian Kinsler	.75
22	Jim Palmer	.50
23	Kevin Youkilis	.75
24	O.J. Mayo	.75
25	Hunter Pence	.50
26	Hiroki Kuroda	.25
27	Derek Lee	.50
28	Brian McCann	.50
29	Carlos Quentin	.50
30	Al Kaline	.75
31	Hanley Ramirez	1.00
32	Josh Hamilton	.75
33	Jeff Samardzija	.25
34	Alexander Ovechkin	1.50
35	Clayton Kershaw	.75
36	Lyndon B. Johnson	.50
37	Whitey Ford	.50
38	Carey Price	1.00
39	Jay Bruce	.50
40	Phil Niekro	.25
41	Ted Williams	2.00
42	Justin Upton	.50
43	Cole Hamels	.75
44	Barack Obama	4.00
44	Barack Obama/ SP Night	15.00
45	Peyton Manning	2.00
46	Jim Thome	.50
47	Nick Markakis	.50
48	Joe Carter	.25
49	Ryan Braun	.75
50	Mike Schmidt	1.00
51	Carlos Beltran	.50
52	Nolan Ryan	2.00
53	Anderson Silva	.25
54	Kosuke Fukudome	.50
55	Chris Reed	.25
56	Ozzie Smith	1.00
56	Ozzie Smith/SP Night	15.00
57	Eli Manning	.75
58	C.C. Sabathia	.75
59	Evan Longoria	1.50
60	Matt Garza	.25
61	Michael Beasley	.75
62	Yogi Berra	.75
63	Brian Roberts	.50
64	Alex Rodriguez	2.00
65	Tiger Woods	4.00
65	Tiger Woods/SP Night	35.00
66	Buffalo Bill Cody	.25
67	Josh Beckett	.75
68	Matt Ryan	.75
69	Ichiro Suzuki	1.50
69	Ichiro Suzuki/SP Night	15.00
70	Chuck Liddell	.75
71	Adrian Gonzalez	.50
72	David Wright	1.00
73	LeBron James	3.00
74	Gerry Lopez	.75
74	Gerry Lopez/SP Night	8.00
75	Carlton Fisk	.50
76	Joe Mauer	.75
77	Manny Ramirez	.75
78	Jason Varitek	.50
79	John Lackey	.25
80	Ivan Rodriguez	.50
81	Wayne Gretzky	3.00
82	Justin Morneau	.50
83	Akinori Iwamura	.25
84	Joe Lewis	.25
85	Lance Berkman	.50
86	Brooks Robinson	.75
87	Andy Pettitte	.50
87	Andy Pettitte/SP Night	10.00
88	Peggy Fleming	.50
89	Joe DiMaggio	2.00
90	Jonathan Toews	1.00
91	Todd Helton	.25
92	Dennis Eckersley	.25
93	Daisuke Matsuzaka	.75
94	Adrian Peterson	1.50
95	Alfonso Soriano	.25

96	Paul Molitor	.75
97	Johan Santana	.75
98	Jason Giambi	.25
99	Ben Roethlisberger	1.00
100	Chase Utley	.75
101	Cal Ripken Jr.	3.00
101	Cal Ripken Jr./SP Night	20.00
102	Curtis Granderson	.75
103	James Shields	.25
104	Nate McLouth	.50
105	Evelyn Ng	.50
106	Ryan Howard	.75
106	Ryan Howard/SP Night	15.00
107	Joe Nathan	.25
108	Tim Lincecum	1.00
109	Chad Billingsley	.50
110	Matt Holliday	.50
111	Kevin Garnett	.75
112	Robin Roberts	.50
113	Jose Reyes	.75
114	Michael Jordan	3.00
115	Smarty Jones	1.00
115	Smarty Jones/SP Night	12.00
116	Kristi Yamaguchi	.25
117	Carlos Zambrano	.50
118	Bucky Dent	.25
119	Carl Yastrzemski	.75
120	Stephen Drew	.50
121	Dustin Pedroia	1.00
122	Jonathan Papelbon	.50
123	B.J. Upton	.50
124	Steve Carlton	.50
125	Chris Johnson	.75
126	Troy Tulowitzki	.50
126	Troy Tulowitzki/SP Night	8.00
127	Francisco Liriano	.25
128	Bill Rodgers	.25
129	Laird Hamilton	.25
130	Brandon Webb	.50
131	Miguel Cabrera	.75
132	Chien-Ming Wang	.75
132	Chien-Ming Wang/SP Night	10.00
133	Joba Chamberlain	.75
134	Felix Hernandez	.50
135	Tony Gwynn	1.00
136	Roy Oswalt	.50
137	Prince Fielder	1.00
138	Gary Sheffield	.50
139	Koji Uehara RC	.75
140	Gordie Howe	1.00
140	Gordie Howe/SP Night	10.00
141	Bobby Orr	2.00
142	Zack Greinke	.50
143	Derrick Rose	1.50
144	Cliff Lee	.50
145	Joey Votto	.50
146	Phil Hellmuth	.50
147	Mark Teixeira	.75
148	David Price RC	1.50
149	Ryan Ludwick	.50
150	David Ortiz	.75
151	Cory Wade/SP	2.00
152	Roy White/SP	3.00
153	Jed Lowrie/SP	2.00
154	Gavin Floyd/SP	2.00
155	Justin Masterson/SP	3.00
156	Travis Hafner/SP	3.00
157	Kelly Shoppach/SP	2.00
158	David Purcey/SP	2.00
159	Howie Kendrick/SP	2.00
160	Mike Parsons/SP	2.00
161	Jeremy Bloom/SP	2.00
162	Dave Scott/SP	2.00
163	Nyjer Morgan/SP	2.00
164	Chris Volstad/SP	2.00
165	Barry Zito/SP	2.00
166	Adrian Beltre/SP	2.00
167	Mark Zupan/SP	2.00
168	Victor Martinez/SP	2.00
169	Eric Chavez/SP	2.00
170	Chris Perez/SP	2.00
171	Jered Weaver/SP	1.00
172	Justin Verlander/SP	4.00
173	Adam Lind/SP	2.00
174	Corky Carroll/SP	2.00
175	Ryan Zimmerman/SP	3.00
176	Josh Willingham/SP	2.00
177	Graig Nettles/SP	2.00
178	Jonathan Albaladejo/SP	2.00
179	Ted Martin/SP	2.00
180	Bill Hall/SP	2.00
181	Brad Hawpe/SP	3.00
182	John Maine/SP	2.00
183	Tom Curren/SP	2.00
184	Ken Griffey Sr./SP	2.00
185	Josh Johnson/SP	2.00
186	Phil Hughes/SP	4.00
187	Joe Alexander/SP	2.00
188	Fausto Carmona/SP	2.00
189	Daniel Murphy/SP RC	2.00
190	Alex Hinshaw/SP	2.00
191	Clayton Richard/SP	2.00
192	Sparky Lyle/SP	3.00
193	Don Gay/SP	3.00
194	Aramis Ramirez/SP	4.00
195	Gaylord Perry/SP	3.00
196	Carlos Lee/SP	4.00
197	Paul Konerko/SP	3.00
198	Kent Hrbek/SP	3.00
199	Chris B. Young/SP	3.00
200	Roy Halladay/SP	4.00
201	Geovany Soto/SP	3.00
202	Chone Figgins/SP	3.00
203	Joe Pepitone/SP	3.00
204	Mark Allen/SP	3.00
205	Garrett Atkins/SP	3.00
206	Ken Shamrock/SP	3.00
207	Jermaine Dye/SP	3.00
208	Don Newcombe/SP	3.00
209	Rick Cerone/SP	3.00
210	Adam Jones/SP	4.00

Printing Plates
Production one set per color.

Animal Series
NM/M

	Common Animal:	4.00
1	King Cobra (Snake)	4.00
2	Dodo Bird	4.00
3	Tasmanian Devil	4.00
4	Komodo Dragon	4.00
5	Bald Eagle	4.00
6	Great White Shark	4.00
7	Gorilla	4.00
8	Bengal Tiger	4.00
9	Killer Whale	4.00
10	Giant Panda	4.00

Autographs
NM/M
Common Auto.: 8.00
Inserted 1:Hobby Box

AG	Adrian Gonzalez/45	20.00
AH	Alex Hinshaw	8.00
AK	Al Kaline/50	60.00
AL	Jonathan Albaladejo	8.00
BD	Bucky Dent	15.00
BL	Jeremy Bloom	8.00
BO	Bobby Orr/25	200.00
BR	Bill Rodgers	10.00
BS	Bill "Moose" Skowron	20.00
CB	Chad Billingsley	15.00
CC	Corky Carroll	10.00
CE	Rick Cerone	15.00
CF	Chone Figgins	15.00
CJ	Chipper Jones/25	180.00
CK	Clayton Kershaw/50	40.00
CL	Carlos Lee	15.00
CP	Chris Perez	8.00
CR	Clayton Richard	10.00
CV	Chris Volstad	10.00
CW	Cory Wade	8.00
DA	Dick Allen	30.00
DE	Dennis Eckersley/50	35.00
DG	Don Gay	15.00
DJ	Derek Jeter/25	200.00
DM	Daniel Murphy	12.00
DN	Don Newcombe	25.00
DO	Donovan Bailey	15.00
DP	Dustin Pedroia	50.00
DS	Dave Scott	8.00
EC	Eric Chavez/50	15.00
EL	Evan Longoria/25	125.00
EN	Evelyn Ng	10.00
FH	Felix Hernandez	40.00
GA	Garrett Atkins	10.00
GF	Gavin Floyd	10.00
GK	Kevin Garnett/25	75.00
GS	Grady Sizemore/50	50.00
GY	Ken Griffey Sr.	15.00
HP	Hunter Pence/25	25.00
HR	Hanley Ramirez	25.00
JA	Joe Alexander	10.00
JB	Jay Bruce	20.00
JC	Joe Carter/45	40.00
JE	Jed Lowrie	15.00
JJ	Josh Johnson	15.00
JL	Joe Lewis	15.00
JM	John Maine	10.00
JO	Jon Lester/25	85.00
JS	James Shields	10.00
JU	Justin Masterson	10.00
JW	Josh Willingham	10.00
KG	Ken Griffey Jr./25	125.00
KH	Kent Hrbek	25.00
KU	Koji Uehara/25	50.00
KY	Kevin Youkilis	35.00
LA	Ryan Braun/50	50.00
LH	Laird Hamilton	25.00
LJ	LeBron James/25	400.00
LO	Gerry Lopez	15.00
MA	Mark Allen	8.00
MC	Matt Cain	15.00
MG	Matt Garza	15.00
MJ	Michael Jordan/23	600.00
MN	Nate McLouth	8.00
MZ	Mark Zupan	10.00
NM	Nick Markakis	20.00
NR	Nolan Ryan/25	175.00
OS	Ozzie Smith/50	85.00
PA	Mike Parsons	15.00
PD	David Price	35.00
PF	Prince Fielder/50	40.00
PH	Phil Hellmuth	20.00
PJ	Jonathan Papelbon	20.00
PK	Paul Konerko	15.00
PM	Paul Molitor/50	60.00
PU	David Purcey	8.00
RB	Brooks Robinson/50	40.00
RC	Chad Reed	20.00
RF	Rollie Fingers/50	20.00
RH	Roy Halladay/50	35.00
RW	Roy White	15.00
SC	Steve Carlton	40.00
SD	Stephen Drew/50	20.00
SK	Kelly Shoppach	8.00
SL	Sparky Lyle	15.00
SO	Geovany Soto	25.00
TC	Tom Curren	20.00
TM	Ted Martin	8.00
TT	Troy Tulowitzki	20.00
WF	Whitey Ford/25	75.00
YA	Kristi Yamaguchi/49	75.00
ZG	Zack Greinke/25	20.00

Citizens of the Century
NM/M

	Common Card:	4.00
1	Hillary Clinton	4.00
2	Bill Clinton	5.00
3	Tony Blair	4.00
4	Princess Diana	5.00
5	Barack Obama	8.00
6	Ronald Reagan	4.00
7	Mikhail Gorbachev	4.00
8	Al Gore	4.00
9	Pope John Paul II	4.00
10	Winston Churchill	4.00

Citizens of the Day
NM/M

	Common Card:	4.00
1	Susan B. Anthony	4.00
2	P.T. Barnum	4.00
3	Cap Anson	4.00
4	Theodore Roosevelt	4.00
5	John D. Rockefeller	4.00
6	Mike "King" Kelly	4.00
7	Will Rogers	4.00
8	Grover Cleveland	4.00
9	Scott Joplin	4.00
10	Sitting Bull	4.00
11	Bram Stoker	4.00
12	Wyatt Earp	4.00
13	Claude Monet	4.00
14	Queen Victoria	4.00
15	Grigori Rasputin	4.00

Entomology
NM/M

	Common Card:	150.00
1	Mexican Silverspot	150.00
2	Spotter Amberwing	150.00
3	Blue Metalmark	150.00
4	Meadow Wanderer	150.00
5	BD Butterfly	150.00
6	Malay Lacewing	150.00
7	Blue Brush-foot	150.00
8	Blomfield's Beauty	150.00
9	Painted Jezabel	150.00
10	Sunflower Trollup	150.00
11	Buttercup Sulphur	150.00
12	Spicebush Swallowtail	150.00
13	Pipevine Swallowtail	150.00
14	Strawberry Bluff	150.00
15	Apricot Sulphur	150.00
16	Military Tiger	150.00
17	Cramer's 89	150.00
18	Bullet Ant	150.00
19	Bottle-brush Longhorn	150.00
20	Man Face Beetle	150.00
21	Great Walking Leaf	150.00
22	Rusty Brown Scorpion	150.00
23	Baby Black Scorpion	150.00
24	Fiddle Beetle	150.00
25	Great Walking Leaf	150.00
26	Rosey Walking Stick	150.00
27	Dead-leaf Mantid	150.00
28	Cryptic Mantid	150.00
29	Red Nose Lantern-fly	150.00
30	Giant Centipede	150.00
31	Minty Walking Leaf	150.00

Landmarks
NM/M
Common Redemption 100.00

Memorabilia
NM/M
Common Card: 4.00
Inserted 1:10

AB	Adrian Beltre	4.00
AI	Akinori Iwamura	4.00
AJ	Adam Jones	6.00
BE	Johnny Bench	8.00
BH	Bill Hall	4.00
BJ	Bo Jackson	10.00
BM	Brian McCann	6.00
BR	Brian Roberts	6.00
BW	Brandon Webb	6.00
BZ	Barry Zito	6.00
CB	Chad Billingsley	6.00
CD	Carlos Delgado	4.00
CF	Carlton Fisk	8.00
CG	Curtis Granderson	8.00
CH	Cole Hamels	8.00
CL	Carlos Lee	6.00
CR	Cal Ripken Jr.	20.00
CU	Chase Utley/100	10.00
CW	Chien-Ming Wang	6.00
CY	Carl Yastrzemski	8.00
CZ	Carlos Zambrano	6.00
DA	Johnny Damon	6.00
DI	Joe DiMaggio/20	80.00
DJ	Derek Jeter	20.00
DL	Derek Lee	6.00
DM	Daisuke Matsuzaka	8.00
DO	David Ortiz	8.00
DR	Derrick Rose	8.00
EC	Eric Chavez	6.00
FC	Fausto Carmona	6.00
FH	Felix Hernandez	6.00
FI	Chone Figgins	4.00
FL	Francisco Liriano	4.00
GN	Graig Nettles	4.00
GP	Gaylord Perry	4.00
HP	Hunter Pence	6.00
IK	Ian Kinsvler	6.00
JA	James Shields	4.00
JB	Josh Beckett	6.00
JD	Jermaine Dye	4.00
JL	Jonathan Albaladejo	4.00
JL	John Lackey	4.00
JM	Joe Mauer	8.00
JN	Joe Nathan	4.00
JP	Jim Palmer	6.00
JR	Jose Reyes/100	8.00
JT	Jim Thome	6.00
JU	Justin Upton	4.00
JV	Jason Varitek	4.00
JW	Jered Weaver	4.00
KE	Howie Kendrick	6.00
KF	Kosuke Fukudome/100	6.00
KG	Kevin Garnett	8.00
LE	Cliff Lee	6.00
LJ	LeBron James	20.00
MA	John Maine	4.00
MB	Michael Beasley	8.00
MC	Miguel Cabrera	6.00
MJ	Michael Jordan/50	60.00
MO	Justin Morneau	6.00
MS	Mike Schmidt	10.00
NM	Nick Markakis	6.00
OM	O.J. Mayo	6.00
PA	Jonathan Papelbon	6.00
PF	Prince Fielder	8.00
PH	Phil Hughes	6.00
PK	Paul Konerko	4.00
PO	Jorge Posada	6.00
PU	Albert Pujols	15.00
RA	Aramis Ramirez	6.00
RB	Ryan Braun	8.00
RH	Roy Halladay	6.00
RO	Roy Oswalt	4.00
RS	Ryne Sandberg	6.00
RZ	Manny Ramirez	6.00
SC	Steve Carlton	6.00
SK	Scott Kazmir	4.00
TG	Tony Gwynn	8.00
TH	Todd Helton	6.00
TL	Tim Lincecum	12.00
TR	Travis Hafner	4.00
TT	Troy Tulowitzki	6.00
TW	Ted Williams/40	50.00
VE	Justin Verlander	6.00
VG	Vladimir Guerrero	6.00
VM	Victor Martinez	4.00
WD	Tiger Woods	100.00
WF	Whitey Ford	10.00
YB	Yogi Berra	20.00
YO	Chris B. Young	4.00
ZG	Zack Greinke	6.00

Thoroughbred Hair Cuts
NM/M

	Common Hair Card:	100.00
AA1	Afleet Alex	100.00
AA2	Afleet Alex/SP	100.00
FC1	Funny Cide	100.00
FC2	Funny Cide/SP	100.00
SJ1	Smarty Jones	100.00
SJ2	Smarty Jones/SP	100.00

Mini
NM/M

Mini (1-150): 2-3X
Inserted 1:1
Common Mini Exclusive 211-252:
  1.00 #'s 211-252 priced below
Mini Black Border (1-150): 2-4X
Mini Black (211-252): 1-2X
Mini Black Foil: No Pricing
Production 8 Sets
Mini Foil (1-150): 4-8X
Mini Foil (211-252): 2-4X

211	Brian Giles	1.00
212	Robinson Cano	2.00
213	Erik Bedard	1.00
214	James Loney	1.50
215	Jimmy Rollins	2.50
216	Joakim Soria	1.00
217	Jeremy Guthrie	1.00
218	Adam Wainwright	2.00
219	B.J. Ryan	1.00
220	Aaron Cook	1.00
221	Aaron Harang	1.00
222	Mariano Rivera	2.50
223	Freddy Sanchez	1.00
224	Ryan Dempster	1.00
225	Jacoby Ellsbury	4.00
226	Russell Martin	1.00
227	Ervin Santana	1.00
228	Nomar Garciaparra	1.50
229	Chris Young	1.00
230	Jair Jurrjens	1.50
231	Francisco Cordero	1.00
232	Bobby Crosby	1.00
233	Rich Harden	1.00
234	Cameron Maybin	1.50
235	Conor Jackson	1.00
236	Jake Peavy	2.00
237	Brad Ziegler	1.00
238	Aaron Rowand	1.00
239	Carl Crawford	2.00
240	Mark Buehrle	1.50
241	Carlos Guillen	1.50
242	Alex Rios	1.00
243	Vernon Wells	1.00
244	Bobby Jenks	1.00
245	Rick Ankiel	1.00
246	Alex Gordon	1.50
247	Paul Maholm	1.00
248	Carlos Gomez	1.00
249	Brad Lidge	1.00
250	Hideki Okajima	1.00
251	Michael Bourn	1.00
252	Jhonny Peralta	1.00

2009 UD Icons

NM/M
Common Player (1-100): .25
Common RC (101-130): 3.00
Production 999
Common RC Auto. (131-160): 8.00
Production 50-600
Pack (6): 10.00
Box (10): 95.00

1	A.J. Burnett	.25
2	Adam Dunn	.40
3	Adrian Gonzalez	.50
4	Akinori Iwamura	.40
5	Albert Pujols	2.00
6	Alex Rodriguez	1.50
7	Alfonso Soriano	.40
8	Aramis Ramirez	.40
9	B.J. Upton	.40
10	Brandon Webb	.40
11	Brian Giles	.25
12	Brian McCann	.40
13	Brian Roberts	.40
14	Carlos Beltran	.50
15	Carlos Lee	.40
16	Carlos Quentin	.50
17	Carlos Zambrano	.50
18	C.C. Sabathia	.75
19	Chad Billingsley	.75
20	Chase Utley	.75
21	Chien-Ming Wang	.75
22	Chipper Jones	1.00
23	Chris B. Young	.40
24	Clayton Kershaw	.75
25	Cliff Lee	.40
26	Cole Hamels	.75
27	Curtis Granderson	.75
28	Daisuke Matsuzaka	1.00
29	Dan Haren	.40
30	Dan Uggla	.40
31	David Ortiz	.75
32	David Wright	1.00
33	Derek Jeter	2.00
34	Derek Lee	.50
35	Dustin Pedroia	.75
36	Edinson Volquez	.40
37	Ervin Santana	.40
38	Evan Longoria	1.50
39	Felix Hernandez	.50
40	Francisco Rodriguez	.25
41	Garrett Atkins	.25
42	Grady Sizemore	.75
43	Hanley Ramirez	.75
44	Ian Kinsler	.50
45	Freddy Sanchez	.25
46	Ichiro Suzuki	1.50
47	Jason Varitek	.50
48	Jake Peavy	.45
49	James Shields	.40
50	Jason Giambi	.40
51	Javier Vazquez	.40
52	Jay Bruce	.75
53	Jim Thome	.50
54	Jimmy Rollins	.50
55	Joakim Soria	.25
56	Joba Chamberlain	.75
57	Joe Mauer	.50
58	Joey Votto	.75
59	Johan Santana	.75
60	John Lackey	.25
61	Jon Lester	.75
62	Jonathan Papelbon	.50
63	Jose Reyes	.50
64	Josh Beckett	.75
65	Josh Hamilton	1.00
66	Justin Morneau	.50
67	Justin Verlander	.50
68	Ken Griffey Jr.	1.50
69	Kerry Wood	.25
70	Kevin Youkilis	.50
71	Kosuke Fukudome	.50
72	Lance Berkman	.50
73	Magglio Ordonez	.40
74	Manny Ramirez	.75
75	Mariano Rivera	.75
76	Mark Teixeira	.50
77	Matt Holliday	.50
78	Matt Kemp	.50
79	Michael Young	.40
80	Miguel Cabrera	.75
81	Nate McLouth	.25
82	Nick Markakis	.75
83	Prince Fielder	1.00
84	Randy Johnson	.75
85	Rick Ankiel	.25
86	Roy Halladay	.50
87	Roy Oswalt	.40
88	Russell Martin	.40
89	Ryan Braun	1.00
90	Ryan Dempster	1.00
91	Ryan Howard	1.00
92	Ryan Ludwick	.40
93	Ryan Zimmerman	.40
94	Scott Kazmir	.25
95	Stephen Drew	.40
96	Tim Hudson	.25
97	Tim Lincecum	1.00
98	Troy Tulowitzki	.40
99	Vernon Wells	.40
100	Vladimir Guerrero	.50
101	Koji Uehara/999 RC	15.00
102	Rick Porcello/999 RC	10.00
103	Jason Motte/999 (RC)	4.00
104	Colby Rasmus/999 (RC)	15.00
105	Brett Anderson/999 (RC)	
106	George Kottaras/999 (RC)	4.00
107	Josh Outman/999 RC	3.00
108	Travis Snider/999 RC	5.00
109	Matt Tuiasosopo/999 (RC)	3.00
110	Kevin Jepsen/999 (RC)	3.00
111	Trevor Cahill/999 RC	4.00
112	Elvis Andrus/999 RC	
113	Jordan Schafer/999 (RC)	3.00
114	Matt LaPorta/999 (RC)	8.00
115	Shairon Martis/999 RC	4.00
116	Dexter Fowler/999 (RC)	4.00
117	Scott Lewis/999 (RC)	3.00
118	Everth Cabrera/999 RC	3.00
119	James McDonald/999 RC	3.00
120	David Freese/999 RC	5.00
121	David Patton/999 RC	5.00
122	Kenshin Kawakami/999 RC	8.00
123	David Price/999 RC	8.00
124	Phil Coke/999 RC	5.00
125	Matt Wieters/999 RC	35.00
126	Mike Hinckley/999 (RC)	3.00
127	Ramiro Pena/999 RC	3.00
128	Bobby Parnell/999 RC	3.00
129	Ryan Perry/999 RC	5.00
130	Ricky Romero/999 (RC)	5.00
131	Koji Uehara/Auto./100 (RC)	25.00
132	Travis Snider/Auto./100 (RC)	50.00
133	Dexter Fowler/Auto./400 (RC)	15.00
134	Kevin Jepsen/Auto./600 (RC)	8.00
135	David Freese/Auto./200 (RC)	30.00
136	Jordan Schafer/Auto./400 (RC)	15.00
137	Everth Cabrera/Auto./600 (RC)	8.00
138	James McDonald/Auto./399 (RC)	10.00
139	Shairon Martis/Auto./699 (RC)	8.00
140	Josh Outman/Auto./200 (RC)	8.00
141	Matt Tuiasosopo/Auto./400 (RC)	8.00
142	Phil Coke/Auto./600 (RC)	10.00
143	Matt Wieters/100/Auto. (RC)	100.00
144	Ricky Romero/Auto./600 (RC)	15.00
145	George Kottaras/Auto./600 (RC)	8.00
146	Elvis Andrus/Auto./300 (RC)	20.00
147	David Patton/Auto./50 (RC)	10.00
148	Brett Anderson/Auto./400 (RC)	20.00
149	Trevor Cahill/Auto./300 (RC)	15.00
150	Trevor Crowe/Auto./600 (RC)	8.00
151	Colby Rasmus/Auto./400 (RC)	40.00
152	Kenshin Kawakami/Auto./400 (RC)	25.00
153	David Price/Auto./150 (RC)	50.00
154	Rick Porcello/Auto./100 (RC)	40.00
155	Brett Gardner/Auto./600 (RC)	30.00
156	Chris Davis/Auto./50 (RC)	25.00
157	Pablo Sandoval/Auto./100 (RC)	60.00
158	Bobby Parnell/Auto./600 (RC)	8.00
159	Derek Holland/Auto./600 (RC)	15.00
160	Mat Gamel/Auto./200 RC	20.00

Red
Red (1-100): 1X
Retail Exclusive

Celebrity Letterman
NM/M
Production 420-440
#'s represent total print run.

EN Evelyn Ng/440 8.00
GO Jeremy Piven/440 10.00
NE Daniel Negreanu/440 10.00
PH Phil Hellmuth/420 8.00

Celebrity Letterman Autographs
NM/M
Production 40-70
#'s represent total print run.
GO Jeremy Piven/70 50.00

Future Foundations
NM/M
Common Player: 1.00
Production 999 Sets
Green: 1-1.5X
Production 125 Sets
BM Brian McCann 1.50
CH Cole Hamels 3.00
DM Daisuke Matsuzaka 4.00
EL Evan Longoria 4.00
FC Fausto Carmona 1.00
FL Francisco Liriano 2.00
HR Hanley Ramirez 3.00
JM Joe Mauer 2.00
JP Jonathan Papelbon 1.50
MK Matt Kemp 2.00
NM Nick Markakis 2.00
PF Prince Fielder 3.00
RA Rick Ankiel 1.00
TT Troy Tulowitzki 1.50

Future Foundations Autograph
NM/M
Production 25-199
BM Brian McCann/25 25.00
CH Cole Hamels/75 30.00
DM Daisuke Matsuzaka/25 180.00
EL Evan Longoria/25 120.00
FC Fausto Carmona/199 8.00
HR Hanley Ramirez/75 25.00
JM Joe Mauer/75 40.00
JP Jonathan Papelbon/99 20.00
MK Matt Kemp/199 15.00
NM Nick Markakis/199 15.00
PF Prince Fielder/75 30.00
TT Troy Tulowitzki/199 15.00

Future Foundations Jerseys

NM/M
Common Jersey: 4.00
Gold: 2X
Production 25 Sets
BM Brian McCann 4.00
CH Cole Hamels 8.00
DM Daisuke Matsuzaka 8.00
FC Fausto Carmona 4.00
FL Francisco Liriano 4.00
HR Hanley Ramirez 8.00
JM Joe Mauer 6.00
JP Jonathan Papelbon 6.00
MK Matt Kemp 6.00
NM Nick Markakis 8.00
PF Prince Fielder 8.00
RA Rick Ankiel 4.00
TT Troy Tulowitzki 4.00

Icons

NM/M
Common Player: 1.00
Production 999 Sets
Green: 1-1.5X
Production 125 Sets
AE Andre Ethier 1.50
AG Alex Gordon 1.00
AL Adam Lind 1.00
AR Alex Rios 1.00
AS Alfonso Soriano 1.50
BE Josh Beckett 2.00
BH Bill Hall 1.00
BR Brian Roberts 1.00
BW Billy Wagner 1.00
CA Miguel Cabrera 2.00
CB Chad Billingsley 1.50
CC Chris Carpenter 1.50
CD Chris Duncan 1.00
CF Chone Figgins 1.00
CJ Chipper Jones 3.00
CL Carlos Lee 1.50
CR Carl Crawford 1.50
CT Corey Hart 1.00
CU Michael Cuddyer 1.00
CY Chris Young 1.00
CZ Carlos Zambrano 1.50
DJ Derek Jeter 6.00
DL Derrek Lee 1.50
DO David Ortiz 2.00
DY Delmon Young 1.00
FH Felix Hernandez 1.50
GU Carlos Guillen 1.00
HP Hunter Pence 1.50
JD Jermaine Dye 1.00
JF Jeff Francoeur 1.00
JG Jason Giambi 1.00
JH J.J. Hardy 1.00
JJ Josh Johnson 1.00
JL John Lackey 1.00
JM John Maine 1.00
JP Jake Peavy 1.50
JR Jimmy Rollins 2.00
JS James Shields 1.00
JT Jim Thome 1.50
JV Jason Varitek 1.00
JW Jake Westbrook 1.00
JZ Joel Zumaya 1.00
KF Kosuke Fukudome 1.50
KJ Kelly Johnson 1.00
KY Kevin Youkilis 1.50
MA Mike Aviles 1.00
MC Matt Cain 1.00
MH Matt Holliday 1.50
MY Michael Young 1.00
PE Jhonny Peralta 1.00
PK Paul Konerko 1.00
PO Jorge Posada 1.50
RA Aramis Ramirez 1.50
RF Rafael Furcal 1.00
RH Roy Halladay 1.50
RJ Randy Johnson 2.50
RL Ryan Ludwick 1.00
RO Roy Oswalt 1.50
RZ Ryan Zimmerman 1.50
SD Stephen Drew 1.00
SK Scott Kazmir 1.00
TG Tom Glavine 1.50
TH Travis Hafner 1.00
VE Justin Verlander 1.50
VM Victor Martinez 1.00
WB Brandon Webb 1.50
WE Jered Weaver 1.00

Icons Autographs
NM/M
Production 5-99
AE Andre Ethier/99 12.00
BH Bill Hall/50 8.00
CD Chris Duncan/99 15.00
CR Carl Crawford/25 15.00
FH Felix Hernandez/30 40.00
JJ Josh Johnson/35 15.00
JM John Maine/99 15.00
KJ Kelly Johnson/99 8.00
KY Kevin Youkilis/99 25.00
MA Mike Aviles/40 20.00
RZ Ryan Zimmerman/25 25.00
SK Scott Kazmir/99 20.00

Icons Jerseys
NM/M
Common Jersey: 4.00
Gold: 2X
Production 25 Sets
AE Andre Ethier 6.00
AG Alex Gordon 4.00
AL Adam Lind 4.00
AR Alex Rios 4.00
AS Alfonso Soriano 6.00
BE Josh Beckett 6.00
BH Bill Hall 4.00
BR Brian Roberts 4.00
BW Billy Wagner 4.00
CA Miguel Cabrera 8.00
CB Chad Billingsley 4.00
CC Chris Carpenter 6.00
CD Chris Duncan 4.00
CF Chone Figgins 4.00
CJ Chipper Jones 8.00
CL Carlos Lee 6.00
CR Carl Crawford 6.00
CT Corey Hart 4.00
CU Michael Cuddyer 4.00
CY Chris Young 4.00
DJ Derek Jeter 20.00
DL Derrek Lee 6.00
DO David Ortiz 8.00
DY Delmon Young 4.00
FH Felix Hernandez 6.00
GU Carlos Guillen 4.00
HP Hunter Pence 4.00
JD Jermaine Dye 4.00
JF Jeff Francoeur 4.00
JH J.J. Hardy 4.00
JJ Josh Johnson 4.00
JL John Lackey/SP 4.00
JM John Maine 4.00
JP Jake Peavy 4.00
JR Jimmy Rollins 8.00
JS James Shields 4.00
JT Jim Thome 6.00
JV Jason Varitek 4.00
JW Jake Westbrook 4.00
JZ Joel Zumaya 4.00
KJ Kelly Johnson 4.00
KY Kevin Youkilis 8.00
MA Mike Aviles 4.00
MC Matt Cain 4.00
MY Michael Young 4.00
PE Jhonny Peralta 4.00
PO Jorge Posada 6.00
RA Aramis Ramirez 6.00
RF Rafael Furcal 4.00
RH Roy Halladay 6.00
RJ Randy Johnson 6.00
RL Ryan Ludwick 6.00
RO Roy Oswalt 6.00
RZ Ryan Zimmerman 6.00
SD Stephen Drew 4.00
SK Scott Kazmir 4.00
TG Tom Glavine 6.00
TH Travis Hafner 4.00
VE Justin Verlander 6.00
VM Victor Martinez 4.00
WB Brandon Webb 6.00
WE Jered Weaver 4.00

Immortal Letterman
NM/M
#'s represent total print run.
AK Al Kaline/420 25.00
BJ Bo Jackson/450 30.00
BS Bill "Moose" Skowron/400 10.00
CF Carlton Fisk/405 15.00
DA Dick Allen/405 10.00
DB Dennis "Oil Can" Boyd/440 8.00
DE Bucky Dent/405 8.00
DN Don Newcombe/440 8.00
GP Gaylord Perry/440 10.00
JP Joe Pepitone/440 8.00
KH Kent Hrbek/450 10.00
OS Ozzie Smith/400 40.00
PM Paul Molitor/440 15.00
RW Roy White/440 12.00
TG Tony Gwynn/200 30.00
WF Whitey Ford/405 15.00
YB Yogi Berra/405 20.00

Immortal Letterman Autographs
NM/M
#'s represent total print run.
AK Al Kaline/28 125.00
BJ Bo Jackson/21 150.00
BS "Moose" Skowron/36 50.00
DA Dick Allen/27 40.00
DB Dennis "Oil Can" Boyd/40 20.00
DE Bucky Dent/27 40.00
DN Don Newcombe/32 30.00
KH Kent Hrbek/84 40.00
PM Paul Molitor/28 70.00
RW Roy White/40 25.00
YB Yogi Berra/20 75.00

Legendary Icons

NM/M
Common Player: 1.00
Production 999 Sets
Green: 1.5X
Production 125 Sets
BJ Bo Jackson 3.00
BS Bruce Sutter 1.00
CR Cal Ripken Jr. 12.00
JD Joe DiMaggio 6.00
MS Mike Schmidt 4.00
NR Nolan Ryan 8.00
OS Ozzie Smith 4.00
RJ Reggie Jackson 2.00
TG Tony Gwynn 2.50
WB Wade Boggs 5.00

Legendary Icons Autographs
No Pricing
Production 10 Sets

Legendary Icons Jerseys
NM/M
Common Jersey: 5.00
Gold: 2X
Production 25 Sets
BJ Bo Jackson 8.00
BS Bruce Sutter 5.00
CR Cal Ripken Jr. 20.00
JD Joe DiMaggio 40.00
MS Mike Schmidt 10.00
NR Nolan Ryan 20.00
OS Ozzie Smith 15.00
RJ Reggie Jackson 12.00
TG Tony Gwynn 8.00
WB Wade Boggs 5.00

Letterman

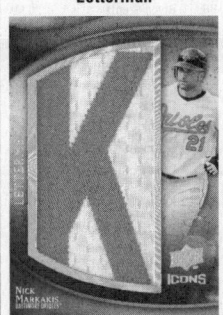

NM/M
represents total print run.
AG Adrian Gonzalez/420 8.00
CH Cole Hamels/450 15.00
CJ Chipper Jones/420 40.00
CK Clayton Kershaw/420 15.00
CL Carlos Lee/405 10.00
CM Chien-Ming Wang/420 30.00
CP Chris Perez/450 8.00
CV Chris Volstad/420 8.00
CW Chien-Ming Wang/420 30.00
DJ Derek Jeter/450 40.00
DP Dustin Pedroia/455 25.00
EC Eric Chavez/450 8.00
EL Evan Longoria/420 40.00
GF Gavin Floyd/450 8.00
GS Geovany Soto/440 8.00
HP Hunter Pence/450 12.00
HR Hanley Ramirez/455 15.00
IK Ian Kinsler/300 20.00
JA Jay Bruce/455 15.00
JL Jon Lester/450 20.00
JM Justin Masterson/450 25.00
JN Joe Nathan/405 8.00
JR Jose Reyes/315 20.00
JS James Shields/420 12.00
JW Josh Willingham/420 8.00
KG Ken Griffey Jr./455 50.00
KS Kevin Shoppach/315 8.00
LO Jed Lowrie/450 10.00
MC Matt Cain/440 15.00
MN Nate McLouth/440 10.00
NM Nick Markakis/420 20.00
SD Stephen Drew/440 10.00
TT Troy Tulowitzki/350 10.00
ZG Zack Greinke/440 15.00

Letterman Autographs
NM/M
represents total print run.
AG Adrian Gonzalez/30 30.00
CH Cole Hamels/30 50.00
CK Clayton Kershaw/28 50.00
CL Carlos Lee/30 35.00
CM Chien-Ming Wang/28 250.00
CV Chris Volstad/96 35.00
CW Chien-Ming Wang/12 250.00
DJ Derek Jeter/20 350.00
DP Dustin Pedroia/35 125.00
EC Eric Chavez/30 25.00
EL Evan Longoria/24 150.00
GF Gavin Floyd/90 20.00
GS Geovany Soto/33 60.00
HR Hanley Ramirez/26 75.00
IK Ian Kinsler/100 50.00
JA Jay Bruce/91 85.00
JL Jon Lester/45 85.00
JM Justin Masterson/90 65.00
JN Joe Nathan/45 25.00
JS James Shields/36 35.00
JW Josh Willingham/99 20.00
KS Kelly Shoppach/80 20.00
LO Jed Lowrie/72 25.00
MC Matt Cain/40 50.00
MN Nate McLouth/55 40.00
NM Nick Markakis/36 85.00
RH Rich Harden/35 20.00
TT Troy Tulowitzki/40 85.00
ZG Zack Greinke/44 50.00

2009 UD Signature Stars

SignatureStars

Common Player (1-100): .25
Common (101-120): 2.00
Common Auto. (121-210):
1 Aaron Harang .25
2 Aaron Rowand .25
3 Adam Dunn .50
4 Adam Lind .50
5 Adam Wainwright .50
6 Adrian Gonzalez .50
7 Akinori Iwamura .25
8 Albert Pujols 3.00
9 Alex Gordon .50
10 Alfonso Soriano .50
11 Andruw Jones .40
12 Aramis Ramirez .40
13 B.J. Upton .25
14 Bill Hall .25
15 Billy Wagner .25
16 Brandon Phillips .40
17 Brandon Webb .50
18 Brian Giles .25
19 Brian McCann .50
20 Brian Roberts .25
21 Carl Crawford .50
22 Carlos Gomez .25
23 Carlos Zambrano .40
24 Chien-Ming Wang .75
25 Chipper Jones 1.00
26 Chone Figgins .40
27 Chris Carpenter .25
28 Chris Duncan .25
29 Chris Young .25
30 Clayton Kershaw .75
31 Cole Hamels .75
32 Curtis Granderson .50
33 Daisuke Matsuzaka .75
34 Dan Haren .40
35 Dan Uggla .40
36 Delmon Young .25
37 Derek Jeter 3.00
38 Derek Lowe .25
39 Dontrelle Willis .25
40 Dustin Pedroia 1.00
41 Eric Chavez .25
42 Evan Longoria 1.00
43 Felix Hernandez .50
44 Garret Anderson .25
45 Garrett Atkins .25
46 Grady Sizemore .50
47 Hanley Ramirez 1.00
48 Ivan Rodriguez .40
49 Jake Peavy .50
50 Jason Loney .40
51 Jason Bay .25
52 Jason Kubel .25
53 Jason Varitek .25
54 Jay Bruce .75
55 Jeff Francoeur .40
56 Jered Weaver .40
57 Jeremy Bonderman .25
58 Jim Thome .50
59 Joe Mauer 1.00
60 Joel Zumaya .25
61 John Lackey .25
62 Johnny Cueto .50
63 Jon Lester .50
64 Jonathan Papelbon .50
65 Josh Beckett .50
66 Josh Johnson .25
67 Justin Verlander .50
68 Kelly Johnson .25
69 Ken Griffey Jr. 1.50
70 Kerry Wood .25
71 Kevin Kouzmanoff .25
72 Kevin Slowey .25
73 Kevin Youkilis .50
74 Khalil Greene .25
75 Lance Berkman .50
76 Mark Teixeira .75
77 Matt Holliday .50
78 Melvin Mora .25
79 Miguel Cabrera .50
80 Miguel Tejada .50
81 Nick Markakis .25
82 Nick Swisher .25
83 Pablo Sandoval .50
84 Paul Konerko .40
85 Randy Johnson .50
86 Rich Harden .25
87 Roy Halladay .50
88 Roy Oswalt .50
89 Ryan Braun 1.00
90 Ryan Garko .25
91 Scott Kazmir .25
92 Scott Rolen .50
93 Takashi Saito .25
94 Tim Hudson .25
95 Tim Lincecum 1.00
96 Torii Hunter .40
97 Troy Tulowitzki .50
98 Vernon Wells .25
99 Vladimir Guerrero .75
100 Yunel Escobar .25
101 Brett Anderson 2.00
102 Elvis Andrus 4.00
103 Gordon Beckham 2.00
104 Brad Bergesen 2.00
105 Trevor Cahill 4.00
106 Brett Cecil 2.00
107 Alcides Escobar 5.00
108 Mat Gamel 5.00
109 Tommy Hanson 8.00
110 Andrew McCutchen 5.00
111 Alex Avila 3.00
112 Sean O'Sullivan 3.00
113 Gerardo Parra 3.00
114 Ryan Perry 4.00
115 Aaron Poreda 2.00
116 Nolan Reimold 3.00
117 Ricky Romero 5.00
118 Neftali Feliz 5.00
119 Tommy Hunter 4.00
120 Sean West 2.00
121 Scott Baker/Auto. 8.00
122 Wladimir Balentien/Auto. 8.00
123 Chad Billingsley/Auto. 20.00
124 Nick Blackburn/Auto. 8.00
125 Joe Blanton/Auto. 15.00
128 Chris Capuano/Auto. 5.00
129 John Danks/Auto. 10.00
131 Chris Davis/Auto. 30.00
132 Ross Detwiler/Auto 10.00
134 Scott Feldman/Auto. 5.00
135 Prince Fielder/Auto. 25.00
136 Yovani Gallardo/Auto. 15.00
138 Matt Garza/Auto. 10.00
139 Alberto Gonzalez/Auto. 12.00
140 Carlos Gonzalez/Auto. 20.00
143 Jason Hammel/Auto. 5.00
144 J.A. Happ/Auto. 20.00
145 Corey Hart/Auto. 15.00
146 Phil Hughes/Auto. 15.00
147 Ramon Hernandez/Auto. 8.00
148 Micah Hoffpauir/Auto. 10.00
150 Matt Kemp/Auto. 25.00
152 Derrek Lee/Auto. 10.00
153 Noah Lowry/Auto. 12.00
154 Jed Lowrie/Auto. 10.00
157 Andrew Miller/Auto. 10.00
158 Miguel Montero/Auto. 10.00
159 David Murphy/Auto. 8.00
161 Micah Owings/Auto. 8.00
162 Felipe Paulino/Auto. 5.00
163 Glen Perkins/Auto. 12.00
164 Felix Pie/Auto. 8.00
166 Jarrod Saltalamacchia/ Auto. 10.00
167 Luke Scott/Auto. 8.00
170 Geovany Soto/Auto. 15.00
173 Mark Teahen/Auto. 8.00
174 Matt Tolbert/Auto. 5.00
175 J.R. Towles Auto. 5.00
176 Edinson Volquez/Auto. 8.00
177 Dewayne Wise/Auto. 5.00
181 Kyle Blanks/Auto. 15.00
182 Michael Bowden/Auto. 8.00
183 Everth Cabrera/Auto. 8.00
184 Drew Carpenter/Auto. 10.00
186 Jhoulys Chacin/Auto. 5.00
187 David Freese/Auto. 12.00
189 Derek Holland/Auto. 15.00
191 Mat Latos/Auto. 20.00
192 Lou Marson/Auto. 8.00
194 Shairon Martis/Auto. 5.00
195 James McDonald/Auto. 5.00
197 Sean O'Sullivan/Auto. 5.00
198 James Parr/Auto. 5.00
199 David Patton/Auto. 5.00
200 Rick Porcello/Auto. 40.00
201 David Price/Auto. 25.00
202 Josh Reddick/Auto. 12.00
203 Michael Saunders/Auto. 12.00
204 Jordan Schafer/Auto. 10.00
205 Travis Snider/Auto. 40.00
206 Matt Tuiasosopo/Auto. 5.00
207 Koji Uehara/Auto. 40.00
208 Chris Tillman/Auto. 40.00
209 Matt Wieters/Auto. 80.00

Blue
Blue (1-100): 2-4X
Production 170 Sets
Gold Signatures
Production 5-100
1 Aaron Harang/50 8.00
13 B.J. Upton/50 10.00
35 Dan Uggla/100 10.00
37 Derek Jeter/100 160.00
40 Dustin Pedroia/100 40.00
47 Hanley Ramirez/100 35.00
49 Jake Peavy/75 25.00
63 Jon Lester/25 75.00
64 Jonathan Papelbon/20 20.00
69 Ken Griffey Jr./100 85.00
73 Kevin Youkilis/35 30.00
87 Roy Halladay/100 30.00
96 Torii Hunter/25 25.00

Impressions Autos.
Common Auto.: 5.00
AC Drew Carpenter 5.00
AG Alberto Gonzalez 5.00
AN Josh Anderson 5.00
AR Alexei Ramirez 20.00
BC Brett Carroll 5.00

BL	Brent Lillibridge	5.00
CB	Chad Billingsley	10.00
CH	Corey Hart	8.00
CT	Clete Thomas	8.00
DM	David Murphy	8.00
DU	Dan Uggla	5.00
DW	Dewayne Wise	10.00
FP	Felipe Paulino	5.00
GP	Glen Perkins	5.00
JB	Josh Banks	8.00
JC	Jorge Campillo	8.00
JH	J.A. Happ	40.00
JL	Jed Lowrie	10.00
JN	Joe Nathan	8.00
JT	J.R. Towles	8.00
KG	Ken Griffey Jr.	100.00
KM	Kyle McClellan	8.00
MI	Mitch Maier	8.00
MK	Matt Kemp	20.00
ML	Matt Lindstrom	8.00
MM	Miguel Montero	8.00
MO	Micah Owings	8.00
MT	Matt Tolbert	5.00
MU	Daniel Murphy	12.00
NB	Nick Blackburn	8.00
PE	Fernando Perez	8.00
PF	Prince Fielder	30.00
PI	Felix Pie	10.00
RM	Russell Martin	10.00
RO	Ross Ohlendorf	8.00
RZ	Ryan Zimmerman	20.00
YG	Yovani Gallardo	15.00

Signature Quads
Production 5-35
LCSI	Tim Lincecum / Pablo Sandoval / Travis Ishikawa / Matt Cain/25	175.00

Signature Stars
Common Player: 1.00
1	Grady Sizemore	1.50
2	Ryan Howard	3.00
3	Felix Hernandez	1.50
4	Johan Santana	2.00
5	Tim Lincecum	4.00
6	Francisco Rodriguez	1.00
7	Tim Wakefield	1.00
8	Carl Crawford	1.50
9	Ichiro Suzuki	4.00
10	Yadier Molina	1.00
11	David Ortiz	1.50
12	Trevor Hoffman	1.00
13	Torii Hunter	1.50
14	Jimmy Rollins	2.00
15	Derek Jeter	6.00
16	Todd Helton	1.50

Signature Trios
Production 5-35
BKM	Chad Billingsley / Matt Kemp / James McDonald/30	30.00
CSI	Travis Ishikawa / Matt Cain / Pablo Sandoval/30	50.00
HSF	Scott Feldman / Jarrod Saltalamacchia / Josh Hamilton/35	25.00
LPT	J.R. Towles / Felipe Paulino / Carlos Lee/35	20.00
MJE	Kelly Johnson / Yunel Escobar / Brian McCann/35	20.00
PBL	Jeff Larish / Dustin Pedroia / Travis Buck/30	40.00
PVE	Edwin Encarnacion / Edinson Volquez / Brandon Phillips/35	15.00
RRS	Kurt Suzuki / Aaron Rowand / Ricky Romero/30	15.00
ZWD	Elijah Dukes / Josh Willingham / Ryan Zimmerman/30	25.00

Signed Sealed & Delivered
Common Player: 1.50
1	Matt Holliday	1.50
2	Mark Teixeira	3.00
3	CC Sabathia	2.00
4	Manny Ramirez	2.50
5	John Smoltz	2.00
6	Cliff Lee	1.50
7	Adam Dunn	1.50
8	Pedro Martinez	1.50

Superstar Portraits
Production 5-35
SP18	Chipper Jones/15	125.00
SP19	Derek Lee/35	20.00

Trophy Winners
Common Player: 1.50
1	Albert Pujols	5.00
2	Dustin Pedroia	2.00
3	Tim Lincecum	4.00
4	Cliff Lee	1.50
5	Chipper Jones	2.50
6	Joe Mauer	2.50
7	Ryan Howard	3.00
8	Miguel Cabrera	2.00

UD Black Pride of a Nation
Production 10-99
Platinum 1 of 1's exist

11	Chipper Jones/10	250.00
24	Kenshin Kawakami/99	50.00
30	Koji Uehara/99	100.00
33	Jordan Zimmermann/99	40.00

USA 18U National Team Cap Flag Patch
Production One Set
No Pricing

USA By the Letter Autos.
Production 100 Sets
AV	AJ Vanegas	15.00
AW	Andy Wilkins	15.00
BB	Bryce Brentz	25.00
BE	Chad Bettis	10.00
BF	Blake Forsythe	15.00
BH	Bryce Harper	275.00
BR	Brian Ragira	10.00
CM	Connor Mason	10.00
DP	Drew Pomeranz	10.00
GC	Garin Cecchini	10.00
JT	Jameson Taillon	30.00
KK	Kavin Keyes	15.00
KR	Kyle Ryan	15.00
KW	Karsten Whitson	10.00
MC	Casey McGrew	15.00
MI	Michael Choice	15.00
NC	Nick Castellanos	10.00
ND	Nicky Delmonico	10.00
NP	Nick Pepitone	10.00
SC	Sean Coyle	10.00
SG	Sonny Gray	20.00
TB	Trevor Bauer	15.00
TW	Tony Wolters	15.00
WO	Kolten Wong	15.00
YG	Yasmani Grandal	15.00

USA Flashback Fabrics Dual Jersey
Some not priced yet.
Patch: No Pricing
Production 25 Sets
EL	Evan Longoria	25.00
JM	Joe Mauer	15.00

USA Future Watch Jersey Autos.
Production 493-999
Patch: 1.5X
Production 50 Sets
Cap Flag Patch: No Pricing
Production 3-4
1	Trevor Bauer/799	20.00
2	Christian Colon/799	10.00
4	Chad Bettis/799	8.00
5	Bryce Brentz/799	20.00
7	Michael Choice/799	10.00
8	Gerrit Cole/799	20.00
9	Sonny Gray/799	15.00
10	Tyler Holt/799	15.00
11	T.J. Walz/799	10.00
12	Rick Hague/799	15.00
13	Drew Pomeranz/799	10.00
14	Blake Forsythe/799	10.00
15	Matt Newman/799	10.00
16	Casey McGrew/799	10.00
17	Brad Miller/799	10.00
18	Yasmani Grandal/799	10.00
19	Kolten Wong/799	20.00
20	Tony Zych/799	10.00
21	Andy Wilkins/799	10.00
22	Asher Wojciechowski/799	10.00
23	Cody Buckel/899	10.00
24	Nick Castellanos/899	10.00
25	Garin Cecchini/899	10.00
26	Sean Coyle/899	12.00
27	Nicky Delmonico/899	10.00
29	Cory Hahn/899	10.00
30	Bryce Harper/899	200.00
31	Kavin Keyes/899	15.00
32	Manny Machado/899	10.00
33	Connor Mason/899	10.00
34	Ladson Montgomery/799	15.00
35	Phillip Pfeifer/799	15.00
36	Brian Ragira/899	10.00
37	Robbie Ray/899	10.00
38	Kyle Ryan/799	15.00
39	Jameson Taillon/899	25.00
40	AJ Vanegas/899	15.00
41	Karsten Whitson/899	15.00
42	Tony Wolters/899	15.00

USA Star Prospects
Common Player: 1.50
1	Cody Buckel	1.50
2	Nick Castellanos	1.50
3	Garin Cecchini	1.50
4	Sean Coyle	1.50
5	Nicky Delmonico	1.50
6	Kevin Gausman	1.50
7	Cory Hahn	1.50
8	Bryce Harper	25.00
9	Kavin Keyes	1.50
10	Manny Machado	1.50
11	Connor Mason	1.50
12	Ladson Montgomery	1.50
13	Phillip Pfeifer	1.50
14	Brian Ragira	2.00
15	Robbie Ray	1.50
16	Kyle Ryan	1.50
17	Jameson Taillon	5.00
18	AJ Vanegas	1.50
19	Karsten Whitson	1.50
20	Tony Wolters	1.50
21	Trevor Bauer	1.50
22	Chad Bettis	1.50
23	Bryce Brentz	2.50
24	Michael Choice	1.50
25	Gerrit Cole	2.50
26	Christian Colon	1.50
27	Blake Forsythe	1.50
28	Yasmani Grandal	1.50
29	Sonny Gray	1.50
30	Rick Hague	1.50
31	Tyler Holt	1.50
32	Casey McGrew	1.50
33	Brad Miller	1.50
34	Matt Newman	1.50
35	Nick Pepitone	1.50
36	Drew Pomeranz	1.50
37	T.J. Walz	1.50
38	Cody Wheeler	1.50
39	Andy Wilkins	1.50
40	Asher Wojciechowski	1.50
41	Kolten Wong	1.50
42	Tony Zych	1.50

USA Star Prospects Jersey Autos.
Common Jersey Auto.:
Production 399 Sets
Patch Auto.: No Pricing
Production 25 Sets
AS	Asher Wojciechowski	15.00
AV	AJ Vanegas	12.00
BB	Bryce Brentz	20.00
BF	Blake Forsythe	15.00
BH	Bryce Harper	220.00
BR	Brian Ragira	12.00
CA	Casey McGrew	10.00
CB	Cody Buckel	10.00
CH	Cory Hahn	10.00
CM	Connor Mason	10.00
CO	Gerrit Cole	15.00
CW	Cody Wheeler	15.00
DP	Drew Pomeranz	15.00
KG	Kevin Gausman	10.00
KK	Kavin Keyes	10.00
KR	Kyle Ryan	15.00
KW	Karsten Whitson	15.00
LM	Ladson Montgomery	12.00
MC	Michael Choice	10.00
MM	Manny Machado	15.00
MN	Matt Newman	10.00
NC	Nick Castellanos	10.00
ND	Nicky Delmonico	10.00
NP	Nick Pepitone	10.00
RH	Rick Hague	10.00
RR	Robbie Ray	10.00
SC	Sean Coyle	10.00
SG	Sonny Gray	15.00
TB	Trevor Bauer	10.00
TH	Tyler Holt	10.00
WA	T.J. Walz	12.00
WO	Kolten Wong	15.00
YG	Yasmani Grandal	12.00

USA Star Prospects Jersey
Common Jersey: 4.00
Patch: No Pricing
Production 25 Sets
1	Cody Buckel	8.00
2	Nick Castellanos	4.00
3	Garin Cecchini	4.00
4	Sean Coyle	4.00
5	Nicky Delmonico	4.00
6	Kevin Gausman	4.00
7	Cory Hahn	4.00
8	Bryce Harper	50.00
9	Kavin Keyes	4.00
10	Manny Machado	4.00
11	Connor Mason	4.00
12	Ladson Montgomery	4.00
13	Phillip Pfeifer	4.00
14	Brian Ragira	4.00
15	Robbie Ray	4.00
16	Kyle Ryan	4.00
17	Jameson Taillon	8.00
18	AJ Vanegas	4.00
19	Karsten Whitson	4.00
20	Tony Wolters	6.00
21	Trevor Bauer	4.00
22	Chad Bettis	4.00
23	Bryce Brentz	6.00
24	Michael Choice	4.00
25	Gerrit Cole	4.00
26	Christian Colon	4.00
27	Blake Forsythe	4.00
28	Yasmani Grandal	6.00
29	Sonny Gray	4.00
30	Rick Hague	4.00
31	Tyler Holt	4.00
32	Casey McGrew	4.00
33	Brad Miller	4.00
34	Matt Newman	4.00
35	Nick Pepitone	4.00
36	Drew Pomeranz	4.00
37	T.J. Walz	8.00
38	Cody Wheeler	4.00
39	Andy Wilkins	4.00
40	Asher Wojciechowski	4.00
41	Kolten Wong	4.00
42	Tony Zych	4.00

USA Star Prospects Autos.
Many not priced yet.
1	Cody Buckel	10.00
2	Nick Castellanos	8.00
3	Garin Cecchini	10.00
4	Sean Coyle	10.00
5	Nicky Delmonico	12.00
6	Kevin Gausman	10.00
7	Cory Hahn	8.00
8	Bryce Harper	220.00
9	Kavin Keyes	15.00
14	Brian Ragira	15.00
15	Robbie Ray	12.00
17	Chad Bettis	20.00
22	Christian Colon	8.00
26	Christian Colon	8.00
29	Sonny Gray	10.00
30	Rick Hague	10.00
32	Casey McGrew	8.00
33	Brad Miller	8.00
35	Nick Pepitone	10.00
36	Drew Pomeranz	12.00
39	Andy Wilkins	10.00
40	Asher Wojciechowski	10.00

USA Winning Materials
Production 499 Sets
Jumbos: No Pricing
Production 10 Sets
1	Cody Buckel	4.00
2	Nick Castellanos	4.00
3	Garin Cecchini	4.00
4	Sean Coyle	8.00
5	Nicky Delmonico	6.00
6	Kevin Gausman	4.00
7	Cory Hahn	4.00
8	Bryce Harper	50.00
9	Kavin Keyes	6.00
11	Connor Mason	4.00
12	Ladson Montgomery	4.00
13	Phillip Pfeifer	4.00
14	Brian Ragira	6.00
15	Robbie Ray	6.00
16	Kyle Ryan	4.00
17	Jameson Taillon	10.00
19	Karsten Whitson	8.00
20	Tony Wolters	4.00
22	Christian Colon	4.00
24	Chad Bettis	8.00
25	Bryce Brentz	6.00
26	Nick Pepitone	8.00
27	Michael Choice	6.00
28	Gerrit Cole	15.00
29	Sonny Gray	6.00
30	Tyler Holt	6.00
31	T.J. Walz	6.00
32	Rick Hague	6.00
33	Drew Pomeranz	6.00
35	Blake Forsythe	4.00
36	Casey McGrew	4.00
38	Yasmani Grandal	6.00
39	Kolten Wong	4.00
40	Tony Zych	4.00
41	Andy Wilkins	4.00

2009 UD Spectrum

DEREK JETER — SPECTRUM

NM/M

Common (1-100): —
Pack (5): 6.00
Box (14): 75.00
1	Brandon Webb	.50
2	Randy Johnson	.75
3	Chris B. Young	.50
4	Dan Haren	.50
5	Adam Dunn	.50
6	Chipper Jones	1.00
7	Tim Hudson	.25
8	John Smoltz	.50
9	Brian Roberts	.40
10	Nick Markakis	.50
11	Josh Beckett	.50
12	David Ortiz	.75
13	Daisuke Matsuzaka	.75
14	J.D. Drew	.25
15	Jonathan Papelbon	.50
16	Mike Lowell	.40
17	Alfonso Soriano	.50
18	Derek Lee	.50
19	Kosuke Fukudome	.50
20	Carlos Zambrano	.50
21	Aramis Ramirez	.40
22	Rich Harden	.40
23	Carlos Quentin	.50
24	Jim Thome	.50
25	Ken Griffey Jr.	1.50
26	Jay Bruce	.75
27	Edinson Volquez	.50
28	Brandon Phillips	.50
29	Victor Martinez	.50
30	Grady Sizemore	.75
31	Travis Hafner	.50
32	Matt Holliday	.50
33	Troy Tulowitzki	.40
34	Garrett Atkins	.40
35	Miguel Cabrera	.75
36	Magglio Ordonez	.40
37	Justin Verlander	.50
38	Hanley Ramirez	1.00
39	Dan Uggla	.40
40	Lance Berkman	.50
41	Carlos Lee	.50
42	Roy Oswalt	.50
43	Miguel Tejada	.50
44	Joakim Soria	.40
45	Alex Gordon	.50
46	Mark Teixeira	.50
47	Vladimir Guerrero	.50
48	Torii Hunter	.50
49	John Lackey	.40
50	Manny Ramirez	.75
51	Russell Martin	.40
52	Matt Kemp	.50
53	Clayton Kershaw	.50
54	C.C. Sabathia	.75
55	Prince Fielder	.75
56	Ryan Braun	1.00
57	Joe Mauer	.50
58	Justin Morneau	.50
59	Jose Reyes	1.00
60	David Wright	1.50
61	Johan Santana	.75
62	Carlos Beltran	.50
63	Ivan Rodriguez	.40
64	Alex Rodriguez	2.00
65	Derek Jeter	2.00
66	Chien-Ming Wang	.50
67	Jason Giambi	.50
68	Joba Chamberlain	.50
69	Mariano Rivera	.50
70	Xavier Nady	.50
71	Frank Thomas	.50
72	Carlos Gonzalez	.25
73	Chase Utley	.50
74	Ryan Howard	1.00
75	Jimmy Rollins	.50
76	Andy LaRoche	.25
77	Nate McLouth	.40
78	Adrian Gonzalez	.50
79	Greg Maddux	1.50
80	Jake Peavy	.50
81	Trevor Hoffman	.25
82	Tim Lincecum	1.50
83	Aaron Rowand	.25
84	Felix Hernandez	.50
85	Ichiro Suzuki	1.00
86	Erik Bedard	.25
87	Albert Pujols	2.00
88	Troy Glaus	.25
89	Rick Ankiel	.50
90	B.J. Upton	.50
91	Evan Longoria	1.50
92	Scott Kazmir	.25
93	Carl Crawford	.25
94	Josh Hamilton	.50
95	Ian Kinsler	.50
96	Michael Young	.40
97	Roy Halladay	.50
98	Vernon Wells	.40
99	Ryan Zimmerman	.50
100	Lastings Milledge	.25
101	David Price/Auto. RC	10.00
102	Conor Gillaspie/Auto. RC	20.00
103	Jeff Baisley/Auto. RC	25.00
104	Angel Salome/Auto. (RC)	15.00
105	Aaron Cunningham/Auto. RC	20.00
106	Lou Marson/Auto. RC	10.00
107	Matt Antonelli/Auto. RC	20.00
108	Michael Bowden/Auto. (RC)	10.00
109	Francisco Cervelli/Auto. RC	20.00
110	Phil Coke/Auto. RC	25.00
111	Josh Outman/Auto. RC	12.00
112	Shairon Martis/Auto. RC	15.00
113	Mat Gamel/Auto. RC	25.00
114	Josh Geer/Auto. (RC)	8.00
115	Greg Golson/Auto. (RC)	10.00
116	Kila Ka'aihue/Auto. RC	15.00
117	Wade LeBlanc/Auto. RC	8.00
118	Chris Lambert/Auto. (RC)	10.00
119	James Parr/Auto. (RC)	10.00
120	Matt Tuiasosopo/Auto. RC	10.00

Black
Black (1-100): 4-8X
Production 50 Sets

Blue
Blue (1-100): 2-3X

Green
Green (1-100): 4-8X
Production 50 Sets

Red
Red (1-100): 2-3X
Production 299 Sets

Turquoise
Turquoise (1-100): 8-12X
Production 25 Sets

Base Set Jersey
Common Player: 4.00 — NM/M
Production 99 Sets
1	Brandon Webb	6.00
2	Randy Johnson	8.00
3	Dan Haren	6.00
5	Adam Dunn	6.00
7	Chipper Jones	10.00
8	Tim Hudson	4.00
9	John Smoltz	6.00
10	Brian Roberts	4.00
12	Nick Markakis	8.00
13	Josh Beckett	6.00
16	David Ortiz	8.00
17	Daisuke Matsuzaka	10.00
18	J.D. Drew	4.00
19	Jonathan Papelbon	6.00
20	Mike Lowell	4.00
24	Alfonso Soriano	8.00
26	Derek Lee	6.00
27	Kosuke Fukudome	8.00
28	Carlos Zambrano	6.00
29	Aramis Ramirez	6.00
30	Jim Thome	6.00
31	Ken Griffey Jr.	15.00
32	Edinson Volquez	6.00
33	Brandon Phillips	6.00
34	Victor Martinez	6.00
35	Grady Sizemore	8.00
36	Travis Hafner	4.00
37	Matt Holliday	6.00
38	Troy Tulowitzki	6.00
39	Garrett Atkins	4.00
40	Miguel Cabrera	4.00
41	Magglio Ordonez	4.00
42	Justin Verlander	6.00
43	Hanley Ramirez	10.00
44	Dan Uggla	6.00
45	Lance Berkman	6.00
46	Carlos Lee	6.00
47	Roy Oswalt	6.00
48	Miguel Tejada	6.00
49	Joakim Soria	6.00
50	Alex Gordon	6.00
51	Mark Teixeira	8.00
52	Vladimir Guerrero	8.00
53	John Lackey	4.00
54	Manny Ramirez	8.00
55	Russell Martin	4.00
57	Matt Kemp	6.00
59	Clayton Kershaw	8.00
61	C.C. Sabathia	6.00
62	Prince Fielder	10.00
63	Joe Mauer	4.00
65	Justin Morneau	8.00
66	Jose Reyes	8.00
67	Johan Santana	8.00
68	Carlos Beltran	6.00
69	Ivan Rodriguez	6.00
70	Derek Jeter	20.00
71	Chien-Ming Wang	12.00
72	Jason Giambi	4.00
73	Joba Chamberlain	8.00
79	Mariano Rivera	8.00
80	Xavier Nady	4.00
81	Frank Thomas	8.00
82	Carlos Gonzalez	8.00
84	Chase Utley	8.00
86	Adrian Gonzalez	10.00
87	Greg Maddux	10.00
88	Jake Peavy	6.00
89	Trevor Hoffman	15.00
90	Tim Lincecum	15.00
91	Felix Hernandez	4.00
92	Erik Bedard	4.00
93	Albert Pujols	15.00
95	Troy Glaus	4.00
96	Rick Ankiel	6.00
97	B.J. Upton	6.00
98	Evan Longoria	20.00
99	Scott Kazmir	4.00
100	Carl Crawford	4.00

Celebrity Cut Signatures
No Pricing
Production 1-3

Spectrum of Stars Autographs

SPECTRUM OF STARS — SPECTRUM

Linda Hamilton / Actor

NM/M
Common Auto.: 8.00
Die-Cuts: 1-1.25X
Production 50 Sets
BL	B-Real	20.00
BT	Brutus Beefcake	15.00
BU	Burt Reynolds	40.00
CE	Cheech Marin	15.00
CF	Corey Feldman	15.00
EE	Erika Eleniak	

EO	Ed O'Neill	35.00
FU	Fabiana Udenio	20.00
HH	Henry Hill	25.00
IS	Ian Somerhalder	15.00
KI	Kim Kardashian	100.00
KW	Kendra Wilkinson	25.00
LE	Leslie Nielsen	40.00
LF	Lita Ford	20.00
LH	Linda Hamilton	35.00
LP	Lanny Poffo	8.00
LS	Larry Storch	15.00
MK	Martin Klebba	8.00
PR	Matt Prokop	8.00
SF	Susie Feldman	35.00
TC	Tommy Chong	35.00
TR	Terri Runnels	20.00

Swatches Light Blue

NM/M

Common Player: 4.00
Production 99 Sets
Patch Maroon: 1-2X
Production 25 Sets
Blue: 1X

AB	Adrian Beltre	4.00
AG	Adrian Gonzalez	6.00
AM	Andrew Miller	5.00
AN	Rick Ankiel	8.00
AP	Albert Pujols	15.00
AR	Alex Rios	5.00
AS	Alfonso Soriano	6.00
BE	Josh Beckett	8.00
BI	Chad Billingsley	6.00
BJ	B.J. Upton	6.00
BP	Brandon Phillips	5.00
BS	Ben Sheets	4.00
BW	Brandon Webb	6.00
BZ	Clay Buchholz	6.00
CA	Miguel Cabrera	8.00
CB	Carlos Beltran	6.00
CC	Carl Crawford	4.00
CJ	Chipper Jones	10.00
CK	Clayton Kershaw	8.00
CL	Carlos Lee	6.00
CS	C.C. Sabathia	8.00
CU	Chase Utley	
CW	Chien-Ming Wang	12.00
CY	Chris Young	4.00
DA	David Ortiz	8.00
DH	Dan Haren	6.00
DJ	Derek Jeter	20.00
DL	Derek Lee	6.00
DM	Daisuke Matsuzaka	10.00
DO	David Ortiz	8.00
DP	Dustin Pedroia	10.00
DU	Dan Uggla	5.00
DY	Delmon Young	4.00
EL	Evan Longoria	20.00
EV	Edinson Volquez	5.00
FH	Felix Hernandez	6.00
GA	Garrett Atkins	4.00
GL	Troy Glaus	4.00
GM	Greg Maddux	10.00
GO	Alex Gordon	6.00
GR	Ken Griffey Jr.	15.00
GS	Grady Sizemore	8.00
GT	Garrett Anderson	4.00
HA	Corey Hart	6.00
HI	Rich Hill	4.00
HR	Hanley Ramirez	8.00
IK	Ian Kinsler	6.00
JA	Jacoby Ellsbury	15.00
JC	Joba Chamberlain	10.00
JE	Derek Jeter	20.00
JH	Josh Hamilton	10.00
JL	James Loney	4.00
JM	Joe Mauer	8.00
JO	Josh Hamilton	10.00
JP	Jake Peavy	6.00
JT	Jim Thome	6.00
JU	Justin Upton	
KF	Kosuke Fukudome	15.00
KG	Ken Griffey Jr.	15.00
KY	Kevin Youkilis	8.00
LB	Lance Berkman	6.00
LO	Evan Longoria	20.00
MA	Manny Ramirez	8.00
MC	Matt Cain	6.00
MH	Matt Holliday	6.00
MK	Matt Kemp	6.00
MO	Justin Morneau	6.00
MR	Manny Ramirez	6.00
MT	Mark Teixeira	6.00
MY	Michael Young	4.00
NI	Nick Markakis	8.00
NS	Nick Swisher	4.00
OR	Magglio Ordonez	4.00
PA	Jonathan Papelbon	6.00
PB	Pat Burrell	4.00
PF	Prince Fielder	10.00
PK	Paul Konerko	6.00
PM	Pedro Martinez	6.00
PU	Albert Pujols	15.00
RB	Ryan Braun	12.00
RE	Jose Reyes	10.00
RH	Roy Halladay	6.00
RJ	Roy Johnson	6.00
RM	Russell Martin	4.00
RZ	Ryan Zimmerman	8.00
SA	Johan Santana	8.00
SK	Scott Kazmir	4.00
SO	Alfonso Soriano	6.00
TH	Tim Hudson	4.00
TL	Tim Lincecum	15.00
TT	Troy Tulowitzki	6.00
TW	Tim Wakefield	4.00
VG	Vladimir Guerrero	8.00
VW	Vernon Wells	4.00

Swatches Dark Gray Auto.

NM/M

AG	Adrian Gonzalez/99	15.00
AM	Andrew Miller/99	12.00
BJ	B.J. Upton/50	20.00
BP	Brandon Phillips/99	15.00
BS	Ben Sheets/35	10.00
BW	Brandon Webb/35	25.00
BZ	Clay Buchholz/99	20.00
CC	Carl Crawford/75	20.00
CK	Clayton Kershaw/45	25.00
CL	Carlos Lee/99	15.00
CY	Chris Young/99	15.00
DH	Dan Haren/35	15.00
DL	Derrek Lee/35	20.00
DP	Dustin Pedroia/50	70.00
DU	Dan Uggla/99	15.00
DY	Delmon Young/52	12.00
EV	Edinson Volquez/35	15.00
FH	Felix Hernandez/75	25.00
GA	Garrett Atkins/99	15.00
GR	Ken Griffey Jr./75	70.00
GT	Garret Anderson/99	15.00
HA	Corey Hart/99	15.00
HI	Rich Hill/99	10.00
HR	Hanley Ramirez/35	25.00
IK	Ian Kinsler/25	20.00
JL	James Loney/23	15.00
JM	Joe Mauer/99	15.00
KG	Ken Griffey Jr./75	70.00
KY	Kevin Youkilis/99	25.00
MC	Matt Cain/99	15.00
MO	Justin Morneau/75	20.00
NI	Nick Markakis/99	30.00
NS	Nick Swisher/99	15.00
PA	Jonathan Papelbon/58	25.00
PF	Prince Fielder/35	35.00
PK	Paul Konerko/99	20.00
RH	Roy Halladay/50	30.00
RM	Russell Martin/50	15.00
RZ	Ryan Zimmerman/99	20.00
TL	Tim Lincecum/50	65.00
TT	Troy Tulowitzki/50	25.00
VW	Vernon Wells/75	10.00

2009 UD Ultimate

Common (1-100):
Production 599
Common Auto.(101-109):
Production 15-175
Box (4 cards): 120.00

1	Stephen Drew	2.00
2	Chipper Jones	4.00
3	Brian McCann	3.00
4	Nick Markakis	3.00
5	Adam Jones	3.00
6	Dustin Pedroia	4.00
7	Josh Beckett	3.00
8	Kevin Youkilis	3.00
9	Victor Martinez	2.00
10	Daisuke Matsuzaka	4.00
11	Kosuke Fukudome	3.00
12	Carlos Zambrano	3.00
13	Alfonso Soriano	3.00
14	Jim Thome	3.00
15	Joey Votto	3.00
16	Grady Sizemore	3.00
17	Todd Helton	3.00
18	Miguel Cabrera	3.00
19	Curtis Granderson	3.00
20	Hanley Ramirez	4.00
21	Josh Johnson	2.00
22	Lance Berkman	3.00
23	Roy Oswalt	3.00
24	Zack Greinke	3.00
25	Vladimir Guerrero	3.00
26	Clayton Kershaw	3.00
27	Manny Ramirez	4.00
28	Russell Martin	2.00
29	Prince Fielder	3.00
30	Ryan Braun	5.00
31	Joe Mauer	4.00
32	Justin Morneau	3.00
33	Francisco Liriano	2.00
34	Johan Santana	4.00
35	David Wright	5.00
36	Jose Reyes	3.00
37	Derek Jeter	8.00
38	CC Sabathia	3.00
39	Hideki Matsui	4.00
40	Alex Rodriguez	8.00
41	Chase Utley	5.00
42	Cole Hamels	4.00
43	Ryan Howard	5.00
44	Jimmy Rollins	3.00
45	Cliff Lee	3.00
46	Adrian Gonzalez	3.00
47	Randy Johnson	3.00
48	Ken Griffey Jr.	6.00
49	Ichiro Suzuki	6.00
50	Albert Pujols	6.00
51	Evan Longoria	6.00
52	B.J. Upton	3.00
53	Josh Hamilton	4.00
54	Roy Halladay	3.00
55	Adam Dunn	3.00
56	Brett Anderson	3.00
57	Elvis Andrus	3.00
58	Alex Avila	4.00
59	Andrew Bailey	3.00
60	Daniel Bard	3.00
61	Brad Bergesen	4.00
62	Kyle Blanks	4.00
63	Michael Bowden	4.00
64	Everth Cabrera	3.00
65	Trevor Cahill	4.00
66	Brett Cecil	3.00
67	Jhoulys Chacin	4.00
68	Aaron Cunningham	3.00
69	Travis Snider	5.00
70	Dexter Fowler*	4.00
71	Lucas French	3.00
72	Mat Gamel	5.00
73	David Hernandez	4.00
74	Derek Holland	4.00
75	Tommy Hunter	4.00
76	Mat Latos	4.00
77	Fernando Martinez	3.00
78	Vin Mazzaro	3.00
79	Andrew McCutchen	6.00
80	Kris Medlen	4.00
81	Fu-Te Ni	4.00
82	Bud Norris	3.00
83	Gerardo Parra	4.00
84	Ryan Perry	5.00
85	Aaron Poreda	3.00
86	Sean O'Sullivan	3.00
87	Wilkin Ramirez	3.00
88	Josh Reddick	4.00
89	Nolan Reimold	4.00
90	Ricky Romero	4.00
91	Marc Rzepczynski	4.00
92	Pablo Sandoval	5.00
93	Michael Saunders	3.00
94	Jordan Schafer	3.00
95	Daniel Schlereth	3.00
96	Anthony Swarzak	3.00
97	Junichi Tazawa	8.00
98	Chris Tillman	3.00
99	Sean West	4.00
100	Trevor Bell	3.00
101	Koji Uehara/Auto./175	25.00
102	Colby Rasmus/Auto./135	35.00
103	Matt Wieters/Auto./135	100.00
105	David Price/Auto./15	60.00
106	Tommy Hanson/Auto./135	60.00
107	Matt LaPorta/Auto./160	25.00
108	Neftali Feliz/Auto./135	40.00
109	Gordon Beckham/Auto./135	
110	Rick Porcello/Auto./135	50.00

Blue Rookie Signatures

No Pricing
Production 15 Sets

Career Highlight Autos.

Production 1-40

BD	Bucky Dent/20	25.00
BF	Bob Feller/19	40.00
JC	Joba Chamberlain/20	50.00
JP	Jim Palmer/22	90.00
NM	Nick Markakis/21	25.00
DJ1	Derek Jeter/20	165.00
DJ2	Derek Jeter/21	165.00
DJ3	Derek Jeter/22	165.00
DJ4	Derek Jeter/26	165.00
DJ5	Derek Jeter/27	165.00
DJ6	Derek Jeter/28	165.00
DJ7	Derek Jeter/29	165.00
HR1	Hanley Ramirez/21	50.00
HR2	Hanley Ramirez/22	50.00
JL1	Jon Lester/23	25.00
JL2	Jon Lester/31	25.00
JR1	Ken Griffey Jr./19	100.00
JR2	Ken Griffey Jr./23	100.00
JR3	Ken Griffey Jr./23	100.00
JR4	Ken Griffey Jr./25	100.00
JR7	Ken Griffey Jr./38	100.00
JR8	Ken Griffey Jr./39	100.00
KG1	Ken Griffey Sr./23	15.00
KG2	Ken Griffey Sr./25	15.00
KG3	Ken Griffey Sr./26	15.00
KG4	Ken Griffey Sr./30	15.00
KG5	Ken Griffey Sr./35	15.00

Generations Eight Memorabilia

Production 35 Sets
Gold: No Pricing
Production 5-20

G8M1
Bruce Sutter
Alfonso Soriano
Albert Pujols
Lou Brock
Ryne Sandberg
Lou Boudreau
Billy Williams
Red Schoendienst/35 75.00

G8M2
Justin Morneau
Prince Fielder
Harmon Killebrew
Eddie Murray
Albert Pujols
Willie McCovey
Tony Perez
Todd Helton/35 65.00

G8M3
Yogi Berra
Joe DiMaggio
Jorge Posada
Adam Dunn
Carlos Beltran
Carlos Delgado
Derek Jeter
Reggie Jackson/35 75.00

G8M4
Reggie Jackson
Bob Lemon
Catfish Hunter
Phil Rizzuto
Derek Jeter
Joe DiMaggio
Yogi Berra
Whitey Ford/35 85.00

G8M5
Yogi Berra
Jorge Posada
Derek Jeter
Phil Rizzuto
Chien-Ming Wang
Reggie Jackson
Robinson Cano/35 85.00

G8M6
Joey Votto
Jay Bruce
Aaron Harang
Johnny Bench
Joe Morgan
Brandon Phillips
Ken Griffey Jr.
Tony Perez/35 50.00

G8M7
Jorge Posada
Ivan Rodriguez
Yogi Berra
Carlton Fisk
Victor Martinez
Johnny Bench
Brian McCann
Russell Martin/35 40.00

G8M8
Satchel Paige
Jim Palmer
Fergie Jenkins
Nolan Ryan
Robin Roberts
Tom Seaver
Phil Niekro
Juan Marichal/35 60.00

G8M9
Edgar Martinez
Eddie Murray
Ken Griffey Jr.
Randy Johnson
Grady Sizemore
Victor Martinez
Kenji Johjima
Satchel Paige/35 65.00

G8M10
Harmon Killebrew
Denard Span
Justin Morneau
Rod Carew
Francisco Liriano
Johan Santana
Joe Mauer
Torii Hunter/35 40.00

G8M13
Ozzie Smith
Cal Ripken Jr.
Derek Jeter
Jimmy Rollins
Brian Roberts
Troy Tulowitzki
Stephen Drew
Hanley Ramirez/35 60.00

G8M14
Hoyt Wilhelm
Reggie Jackson
Billy Williams
Tim Lincecum
Rollie Fingers
Willie McCovey
Gaylord Perry
Joe DiMaggio/35 75.00

G8M15
Jason Varitek
Carlton Fisk
Pedro Martinez
Manny Ramirez
Ted Williams
Daisuke Matsuzaka
Orlando Cepeda
Fergie Jenkins/35 60.00

Generations Six Memorabilia

Production 25-50
Gold: No Pricing
Production 10-25

1
Tom Seaver
Jay Bruce
Joey Votto
Joe Morgan
Johnny Bench
Brandon Phillips/50 40.00

2
Fergie Jenkins
Ted Williams
Jason Varitek
Carlton Fisk
Tony Perez
David Ortiz/50 50.00

3
Jorge Posada
Yogi Berra
Joe DiMaggio
Derek Jeter
Chien-Ming Wang
Reggie Jackson/40 75.00

7
Eric Chavez
Joe DiMaggio
Bobby Crosby
Billy Williams
Reggie Jackson
Harmon Killebrew/50 50.00

9
Derek Jeter
Johnny Damon
Jorge Posada
Whitey Ford
Reggie Jackson
Robinson Cano/50 40.00

10
Daisuke Matsuzaka
Jacoby Ellsbury
Jon Lester
Pedro Martinez
Ted Williams
Manny Ramirez/50 60.00

11
Ryne Sandberg
Derek Lee
Lou Boudreau
Bruce Sutter
Carlos Zambrano
Billy Williams/50 40.00

12
Red Schoendienst
Bruce Sutter
Enos Slaughter
Albert Pujols
Lou Brock
Robinson Cano/35 85.00

15
Nolan Ryan
Lance Berkman
Carlos Lee
Roy Oswalt
Hunter Pence
Felipe Paulino/50 40.00

16
Ryan Braun
Yovani Gallardo
Robin Yount
Don Sutton
Rickie Weeks
Prince Fielder/50 50.00

17
Grady Sizemore
Victor Martinez
Satchel Paige
Travis Hafner
Dennis Eckersley
Bob Feller/50 50.00

19
Reggie Jackson
Joe DiMaggio
Yogi Berra
Carlos Beltran
Eddie Murray
Derek Jeter/50 65.00

20
Derek Jeter
Joe DiMaggio
Earl Weaver
Jim Palmer
Nick Markakis
Chien-Ming Wang/50 60.00

Gold Rookie Signatures

Production 5-75

101a	Koji Uehara/75	30.00
101b	Koji Uehara/75	30.00
102a	Colby Rasmus/45	40.00
102b	Colby Rasmus/45	40.00
103a	Matt Wieters/45	80.00
103b	Matt Wieters/45	80.00
106a	Tommy Hanson/45	85.00
106b	Tommy Hanson/45	85.00
107a	Matt LaPorta/35	35.00
107b	Matt LaPorta/35	35.00
108a	Neftali Feliz/45	50.00
108b	Neftali Feliz/45	50.00
109a	Gordon Beckham/45	85.00
109b	Gordon Beckham/45	85.00
110a	Rick Porcello/45	60.00
110b	Rick Porcello/45	60.00

Jumbo Bat

Production 1-33

RC	Roberto Clemente/21	175.00

Jumbo Bat Autographs

Production 5-50

DJ	Derek Jeter/50	175.00
LB	Lou Brock/20	75.00
MS	Mike Schmidt/20	75.00
OS	Ozzie Smith/25	75.00
RC	Rod Carew/29	50.00

Jumbo Jersey

Production 5-44

JA	Reggie Jackson/44	25.00
JL	Jon Lester/31	15.00
NR	Nolan Ryan/17	40.00
SA	Ryne Sandberg/23	40.00
SP	Satchel Paige/29	150.00

Jumbo Jersey Autos.

Production 8-50

BF	Bob Feller/28	50.00
BM	Brian McCann/35	30.00
BU	B.J. Upton/40	20.00
CF	Carlton Fisk/27	50.00
CJ	Chipper Jones/40	80.00
DJ	Derek Jeter/50	165.00
GP	Gaylord Perry/36	30.00
HR	Hanley Ramirez/40	40.00
JL	Jon Lester/31	40.00
JP	Jim Palmer/30	30.00
JS	James Shields/50	15.00
KG	Ken Griffey Jr./50	100.00
LB	Lou Brock/20	40.00
MK	Matt Kemp/50	30.00
MS	Mike Schmidt/20	80.00
NM	Nick Markakis/49	35.00
OS	Ozzie Smith/25	70.00
PA	Jonathan Papelbon/50	25.00
WF	Whitey Ford/40	60.00
ZG	Zack Greinke/35	

Legendary Dual Materials Autos.

No Pricing
Production 1-8

Legendary Dual Patch Auto.

Production 5-30

LB	Lou Brock/20	80.00
MS	Mike Schmidt/20	100.00
PA	Jim Palmer/22	50.00
RY	Robin Yount/19	80.00
TR	Tim Raines/30	50.00

Legendary Eight Memorabilia

Production 25 or 35
Gold: No Pricing
Production 5-20

1
Phil Rizzuto
Catfish Hunter
Bob Lemon
Reggie Jackson
Bucky Dent
Whitey Ford
Yogi Berra
Joe DiMaggio/35 75.00

4
Mike Schmidt
Eddie Murray
Phil Niekro
Ryne Sandberg
Ozzie Smith
Carlton Fisk
Robin Yount
Reggie Jackson/35 60.00

5
Satchel Paige
Phil Rizzuto
Red Schoendienst
Joe DiMaggio
Yogi Berra
Ted Williams
Lou Boudreau
Bob Feller/35 120.00

6
Roberto Clemente
Willie McCovey
Brooks Robinson
Lou Brock
Jim Palmer
Johnny Bench
Harmon Killebrew
Reggie Jackson/35 125.00

7
Billy Williams
Fergie Jenkins
Lou Brock
Yogi Berra
Joe DiMaggio
Ozzie Smith/35 85.00

8
Ryne Sandberg
Roberto Clemente
Lou Brock
Tony Perez
Jim Bunning
Johnny Bench
Red Schoendienst
Billy Williams/35 100.00

Legendary Quad Materials Autos.

Production 8-25
Quad Patch Auto.: No Pricing
Production 1-12

OS	Ozzie Smith/25	60.00

Legendary Signatures

Production 2-35

BF1	Bob Feller/19	30.00
BJ1-2	Bo Jackson/16	75.00
CR1	Cal Ripken Jr./25	150.00
DE1	Dennis Eckersley/21	25.00
DE4	Dennis Eckersley/16	25.00
JP1	Jim Palmer/22	20.00
NR2	Nolan Ryan/30	140.00
TR1	Tim Raines/16	15.00

Legendary Six Memorabilia

Production 25-50
Gold: No Pricing
Production 5-25

1
Reggie Jackson
Catfish Hunter
Bob Lemon
Joe DiMaggio
Yogi Berra
Phil Niekro/50 60.00

2
Reggie Jackson
Ted Williams
Carlton Fisk
Catfish Hunter
Reggie Jackson
Orlando Cepeda/50 50.00

3
Billy Williams
Joe Morgan
Johnny Bench
Ryne Sandberg
Lou Boudreau
Tom Seaver/50 50.00

4
Ozzie Smith
Cal Ripken Jr.
Ryne Sandberg
Carlton Fisk
Nolan Ryan
Sparky Anderson/50 50.00

7
Bo Jackson
Nolan Ryan
Ryne Sandberg
Mike Schmidt
Cal Ripken Jr.
Ozzie Smith/50 75.00

8
Lou Boudreau
Ted Williams
Joe DiMaggio
Yogi Berra
Phil Rizzuto
Eddie Mathews/50 75.00

9
Billy Williams
Reggie Jackson
Joe DiMaggio
Roberto Clemente
Joe DiMaggio
Ted Williams/50 85.00

Legendary Triple Materials Autos.

Production 5-18

MS	Mike Schmidt/18	70.00

Legendary Triple Patch Autos.

Production 5-22

MS	Mike Schmidt/20	100.00
PA	Jim Palmer/22	50.00
RY	Robin Yount/19	80.00

Phenoms Eight Memorabilia

Production 35 Sets
Gold: No Pricing
Production 5 or 20

Phenoms Six Memorabilia

Production 50 Sets
Gold: No Pricing
Production 5-25

Signature Moments

Production 3-40

DJ	Derek Jeter/40	150.00
HR	Hanley Ramirez/25	35.00
JC	Joba Chamberlain/30	40.00
JL	Jon Lester/31	35.00
KG	Ken Griffey Jr./40	90.00
NM	Nick Markakis/21	30.00

Dual Materials Autographs

Production 2-24

AG	Adrian Gonzalez/23	25.00
JL	Jon Lester/19	35.00
KG	Ken Griffey Jr./24	125.00
ZG	Zack Greinke/22	40.00

Dual Patch Autographs

Production 4-34

AG	Adrian Gonzalez/23	35.00
BM	Brian McCann/20	40.00
CJ	Chipper Jones/34	140.00
DJ	Derek Jeter/34	300.00
JL	Jon Lester/19	60.00
JP	Jonathan Papelbon/31	40.00
KG	Ken Griffey Jr./24	275.00
MK	Matt Kemp/29	40.00
NM	Nick Markakis/33	50.00
RB	Ryan Braun/16	90.00

Dual Signatures

Production 19-75

1	Cal Ripken Jr.		
	Brooks Robinson/39	120.00	
2	Brooks Robinson		
	Nick Markakis/37	60.00	
3	Joba Chamberlain		
	Derek Jeter/38	150.00	
4	Bo Jackson		
	Zack Greinke/33	80.00	
8	Kevin Youkilis		
	Dennis Eckersley/39	40.00	
11	Dennis Eckersley		
	Ozzie Smith/42	60.00	
12	Derek Jeter		
	Bucky Dent/50	125.00	
13	Ken Griffey Jr.		
	Dick Allen/22	65.00	
14	Ken Griffey Jr.		
	Ken Griffey Sr./75	80.00	
15	Ken Griffey Sr.		
	Ken Griffey Jr./70	80.00	
16	Jon Lester		
	Kevin Youkilis/46	50.00	
17	Ryan Braun		
	Robin Yount/19	125.00	
18	Jonathan Papelbon		
	Joba Chamberlain/35	50.00	
23	Gaylord Perry		
	Zack Greinke/19	40.00	
24	Bo Jackson		
	Ken Griffey Jr./72	100.00	
25	Derek Jeter		
	Hanley Ramirez/72	120.00	

Ultimate Eight Memorabilia

Production 25-35
Gold: No Pricing
Production 5-20

1	Reggie Jackson	
	Jacoby Ellsbury	
	Jorge Posada	
	Carlton Fisk	
	Yogi Berra	
	Jason Varitek	
	Ted Williams	
	Johnny Damon/35	50.00
2	Yogi Berra	
	Ivan Rodriguez	
	Carlton Fisk	
	Nolan Ryan	
	Whitey Ford	
	Fergie Jenkins	
	Joe Mauer	
	Johan Santana/35	50.00
3	Roy Oswalt	
	Cole Hamels	
	Whitey Ford	
	Pedro Martinez	
	Nolan Ryan	
	Robin Roberts	
	Phil Niekro	
	Andy Pettitte/35	40.00
5	Grady Sizemore	
	Reggie Jackson	
	Joe DiMaggio	
	Josh Hamilton	
	Ralph Kiner	
	Manny Ramirez	
	Ted Williams	
	Ken Griffey Jr./35	70.00
6	Ryne Sandberg	
	Derek Lee	

	Lou Boudreau		
	Alfonso Soriano		
	Aramis Ramirez		
	Billy Williams		
	Kosuke Fukudome		
7	Carlos Zambrano/35	30.00	
	Zack Greinke		
	Billy Butler		
	Alex Gordon		
	Bruce Sutter		
	Albert Pujols		
	Bo Jackson		
	Lou Brock		
8	Cal Ripken Jr.	60.00	
	Brooks Robinson		
	Melvin Mora		
	Adam Jones		
	Earl Weaver		
	Nick Markakis		
	Jim Palmer		
	Brian Roberts/35	60.00	
9	Reggie Jackson		
	Gary Sheffield		
	Willie McCovey		
	Ken Griffey Jr.		
	Eddie Murray		
	Manny Ramirez		
	Ted Williams		
10	Jim Thome/35	60.00	
	Carlos Beltran		
	Eddie Murray		
	Derek Jeter		
	Jorge Posada		
	Joe DiMaggio		
	Yogi Berra		
	Phil Rizzuto		
11	Jose Reyes/25	70.00	
	Rickie Weeks		
	Prince Fielder		
	Don Sutton		
	Robin Yount		
	Eddie Mathews		
	Yovani Gallardo		
	Ryan Braun		
12	Phil Niekro/35	40.00	
	Edgar Martinez		
	Randy Johnson		
	Ken Griffey Jr.		
	Gaylord Perry		
	Brandon Morrow		
	Felix Hernandez		
	Kenji Johjima		
	Erik Bedard/35	50.00	
14	Ozzie Smith		
	Troy Glaus		
	Lou Brock		
	Chris Carpenter		
	Albert Pujols		
	Enos Slaughter		
	Bruce Sutter		
	Red Schoendienst/35	40.00	

Ultimate Eight Signatures

Production 5 Sets
No Pricing

Ultimate Inscriptions

Production 3-35

BF	Bob Feller/19	35.00
BM	Brian McCann/16	40.00
BU	B.J. Upton/27	25.00
HR	Hanley Ramirez/24	50.00
JP	Jim Palmer/22	50.00
KG	Ken Griffey Sr./21	30.00
LB	Lou Brock/20	50.00
NM	Nick Markakis/28	35.00
OS	Ozzie Smith/18	65.00
TR	Tim Raines/30	25.00
JR3	Ken Griffey Jr./24	125.00
JR4	Ken Griffey Jr./24	125.00
JR5	Ken Griffey Jr./24	125.00
MK2	Matt Kemp/27	40.00

Ultimate Patch

Production 5-35

AN	Rick Ankiel/35	40.00
BE	Josh Beckett/35	60.00
BH	Johnny Bench/35	140.00
BJ	Bo Jackson/16	100.00
BM	Brian McCann/20	100.00
BP	Brandon Phillips/35	50.00
CB	Carlos Beltran/15	80.00
CC	Chris Carpenter/35	85.00
CD	Carlos Delgado/35	60.00
CF	Carl Crawford/35	65.00
CH	Cole Hamels/35	65.00
CJ	Chipper Jones/35	150.00
CK	Clayton Kershaw/35	80.00
CR	Cal Ripken Jr./24	300.00
CU	Chase Utley/35	100.00
CW	Chien-Ming Wang/35	125.00
CY	Chris B. Young/35	50.00
DL	Derrek Lee/35	85.00
DO	David Ortiz/35	60.00
DS	Don Sutton/35	75.00
EC	Eric Chavez/35	50.00
EL	Evan Longoria/35	150.00
EM	Edgar Martinez/35	140.00
FC	Carlton Fisk/35	80.00
FH	Felix Hernandez/35	120.00
FI	Carlton Fisk/35	80.00
GP	Gaylord Perry/35	50.00
GR	Ken Griffey Sr./35	50.00
GS	Grady Sizemore/35	65.00
HR	Hanley Ramirez/35	85.00
IK	Ian Kinsler/35	70.00
JH	Josh Hamilton/35	150.00
JL	James Loney/35	50.00

JM	Joe Mauer/35	125.00
JP	Jorge Posada/35	140.00
JR	Ken Griffey Jr./35	250.00
JT	Jim Thome/35	70.00
JU	Justin Upton/35	75.00
JV	Jason Varitek/35	50.00
JW	Jered Weaver/35	40.00
KG	Ken Griffey Jr./35	250.00
KY	Kevin Youkilis/35	60.00
LA	Lance Berkman/35	75.00
LB	Lou Brock/35	140.00
MB	Mark Buehrle/35	50.00
MJ	Joe Morgan/35	60.00
MO	Justin Morneau/35	80.00
MP	Pedro Martinez/35	80.00
MR	Mariano Rivera/35	200.00
MU	Eddie Murray/35	100.00
MY	Michael Young/35	60.00
NI	Nick Markakis/35	75.00
NK	Phil Niekro/35	60.00
NP	Phil Niekro/35	60.00
NR	Nolan Ryan/35	180.00
OM	Magglio Ordonez/35	60.00
OS	Ozzie Smith/35	200.00
OZ	Ozzie Smith/35	200.00
PA	Jonathan Papelbon/35	50.00
PE	Jhonny Peralta/35	50.00
PF	Prince Fielder/35	90.00
PK	Paul Konerko/35	75.00
PN	Phil Niekro./50	60.00
PR	Pedro Martinez/35	80.00
RA	Aramis Ramirez/35	65.00
RB	Ryan Braun/35	100.00
RC	Roberto Clemente/35	800.00
RD	Rod Carew/35	100.00
RE	Jose Reyes/35	75.00
RF	Rafael Furcal/35	50.00
RJ	Reggie Jackson/35	150.00
RO	Roy Oswalt/35	50.00
RY	Robin Yount/35	120.00
RZ	Ryan Zimmerman/35	85.00
SA	Ryne Sandberg/35	185.00
SM	Mike Schmidt/35	140.00
SP	Sparky Anderson/35	75.00
ST	Tom Seaver/35	120.00
TH	Todd Helton/35	65.00
TL	Tim Lincecum/35	200.00
TR	Tim Raines/35	50.00
TS	Tom Seaver/35	120.00
TT	Troy Tulowitzki/35	65.00
VG	Vladimir Guerrero/35	50.00
VO	Joey Votto/35	75.00
YM	Yadier Molina/35	90.00

Quad Materials Auto.

Production 6-36

AG	Adrian González/23	30.00
BM	Brian McCann/20	30.00
DJ	Derek Jeter/22	150.00
HR	Hanley Ramirez/21	40.00
JL	Jon Lester/35	35.00
JP	Jonathan Papelbon/36	30.00
KG	Ken Griffey Jr./24	160.00

Quad Patch Autographs

Production 2-30

AG	Adrian Gonzalez/23	75.00
JP	Jonathan Papelbon/22	50.00
NM	Nick Markakis/21	75.00

Quad Autos.

Production 10 Sets
No Pricing

Ultimate Signatures

Production 2-50

BM	Brian McCann/32	20.00
BU	B.J. Upton/35	15.00
JC	Joba Chamberlain/27	50.00
JP	Jonathan Papelbon/20	20.00
KU	Koji Uehara/18	40.00
DJ1-4	Derek Jeter/50	140.00
HR1	Hanley Ramirez/26	50.00
HR2	Hanley Ramirez/34	40.00
KG1-4	Ken Griffey Jr./24	75.00
KG5-7	Ken Griffey Jr./30	75.00
KG8-10	Ken Griffey Jr./17	100.00
NM1	Nick Markakis/39	30.00
NM2	Nick Markakis/21	35.00

Ultimate Six Memorabilia

Production 20-50
Gold: No Pricing
Production 5-25

1	Roberto Clemente	
	Joe DiMaggio	
	Josh Hamilton	
	Carlos Beltran	
	Ted Williams	
	Ken Griffey Jr./25	75.00
4	Lou Boudreau	
	Ozzie Smith	
	Cal Ripken Jr.	
	Derek Jeter	
	Phil Rizzuto	
	Robin Yount/50	50.00
6	Gaylord Perry	
	Nolan Ryan	
	Phil Niekro	
	Tom Seaver	
	Randy Johnson	
	Don Sutton/50	40.00
11	Reggie Jackson	
	Albert Pujols	
	Ozzie Smith	
	Derek Jeter	
	Ryne Sandberg	
	Derrek Lee/50	50.00

14	Tony Perez		
	Ted Williams		
	Cal Ripken Jr.		
	Brian Roberts		
	Nick Markakis		
	Kevin Youkilis/50	50.00	
15	Hank Blalock		
	Ian Kinsler		
	Randy Johnson		
	Ken Griffey Jr.		
	Gaylord Perry		
	Nolan Ryan/50	50.00	
16	Lou Brock		
	Ozzie Smith		
	Ryne Sandberg		
	Carl Crawford		
	Jimmy Rollins		
	Joe Morgan/50	60.00	
17	Chase Utley		
	Jose Reyes		
	Cole Hamels		
	Carlos Delgado		
	Mike Schmidt		
	Yogi Berra/25	50.00	
21	Brian Roberts		
	Phil Rizzuto		
	Rickie Weeks		
	Robin Yount		
	Robinson Cano		
	Cal Ripken Jr./50	40.00	
22	Cal Ripken Jr.		
	Lou Boudreau		
	Robin Yount		
	Phil Rizzuto		
	Joe Morgan		
	Rod Carew/50	50.00	
23	Jim Bunning		
	Daisuke Matsuzaka		
	Ted Williams		
	Derek Jeter		
	Joe DiMaggio		
	Roberto Clemente/50	85.00	
25	Grady Sizemore		
	Fergie Jenkins		
	Satchel Paige		
	Bob Feller		
	Jacoby Ellsbury		
	Jason Varitek/50	50.00	

Ultimate Six Signatures

Production 5 Sets
No Pricing

Ultimate Triple Materials Signature

Production 6-24

AG	Adrian Gonzalez/23	25.00
BM	Brian McCann/20	25.00
DJ	Derek Jeter/22	140.00
HR	Hanley Ramirez/21	40.00
KG	Ken Griffey Jr./24	140.00

Ultimate Triple Patch Signatures

Production 2-29

AG	Adrian Gonzalez/23	65.00
BM	Brian McCann/20	80.00
HP	Hunter Pence/26	60.00
HR	Hanley Ramirez/28	100.00
JP	Jonathan Papelbon/22	50.00
MK	Matt Kemp/29	60.00
NM	Nick Markakis/27	60.00

Ultimate Triple Signatures

Production 5-30

3	Joba Chamberlain		
	Derek Jeter		
	Bucky Dent/30	200.00	
4	Ken Griffey Jr.		
	Ryan Braun		
	Nick Markakis/26	140.00	
10	Hanley Ramirez		
	Ozzie Smith		
	Derek Jeter/25	160.00	
11	Ken Griffey Jr.		
	Bo Jackson		
	B.J. Upton/26	150.00	
12	Jonathan Papelbon		
	Rollie Fingers		
	Dennis Eckersley/21	50.00	

2009 UD Sweet Spot

NM/M

Common Player (1-100):	.25
Common RC Auto. (101-130):	
Pack (8):	20.00
Box (6):	100.00

1	A.J. Burnett	.25
2	Adam Dunn	.50
3	Adam Jones	.75
4	Adrian Gonzalez	.50
5	Albert Pujols	3.00
6	Alex Rodriguez	2.50
7	Alfonso Soriano	.75
8	B.J. Upton	.50
9	Brian McCann	.50
10	Brian Roberts	.50
11	Carl Crawford	.50
12	Carlos Beltran	.50
13	Carlos Quentin	.50
14	Carlos Zambrano	.50
15	C.C. Sabathia	.75
16	Chad Billingsley	.50
17	Chase Utley	1.00
18	Chien-Ming Wang	.50
19	Chipper Jones	1.50
20	Chris Carpenter	.75
21	Clayton Kershaw	.75
22	Cliff Lee	.50
23	Cole Hamels	.75
24	Curtis Granderson	.75
25	Daisuke Matsuzaka	.75
26	David Ortiz	.75
27	David Wright	2.00
28	Derek Jeter	3.00
29	Dustin Pedroia	1.00
30	Evan Longoria	1.50
31	Felix Hernandez	.75
32	Francisco Rodriguez	.25
33	Freddy Sanchez	.25
34	Geovany Soto	.50
35	Grady Sizemore	.75
36	Hanley Ramirez	1.00
37	Hideki Matsui	1.00
38	Hideki Okajima	.25
39	Hiroki Kuroda	.25
40	Hunter Pence	.50
41	Ian Kinsler	.50
42	Ichiro Suzuki	2.00
43	Jake Peavy	.50
44	Pedro Martinez	.50
45	Jason Varitek	.25
46	Javier Vazquez	.25
47	Jay Bruce	1.00
48	Jeff Samardzija	.25
49	Jermaine Dye	.25
50	Jim Thome	.50
51	Jimmy Rollins	1.00
52	Joba Chamberlain	.50
53	Joe Mauer	.75
54	Joey Votto	.50
55	Johan Santana	.75
56	Shin-Soo Choo	.25
57	Johnny Cueto	.25
58	Johnny Damon	.50
59	Jon Lester	.75
60	Jose Reyes	1.00
61	Josh Beckett	.75
62	Josh Hamilton	.75
63	Josh Johnson	.25
64	Justin Morneau	.75
65	Justin Upton	.50
66	Justin Verlander	.50
67	Ken Griffey Jr.	2.00
68	Kevin Youkilis	.50
69	Kosuke Fukudome	.25
70	Lance Berkman	.50
71	Manny Ramirez	1.00
72	Mariano Rivera	.75
73	Mark Teixeira	.50
74	Matt Holliday	.50
75	Matt Kemp	.50
76	Max Scherzer	.25
77	Michael Young	.25
78	Miguel Cabrera	.75
79	Miguel Tejada	.25
80	Nate McLouth	.25
81	Nick Markakis	.50
82	Nomar Garciaparra	.50
83	Prince Fielder	.75
84	Randy Johnson	.75
85	Raul Ibanez	.25
86	Roy Halladay	.50
87	Roy Oswalt	.50
88	Russell Martin	.25
89	Ryan Braun	1.50
90	Ryan Howard	1.50
91	Ryan Ludwick	.25
92	Ryan Zimmerman	.50
93	Stephen Drew	.25
94	Tim Lincecum	1.00
95	Todd Helton	.50
96	Troy Tulowitzki	.50
97	Victor Martinez	.25
98	Vladimir Guerrero	.50
99	Yovani Gallardo	.50
100	Zack Greinke	.50
101	Bobby Parnell/ Auto./699 RC	8.00
102	Brett Anderson/ Auto./650 RC	15.00
103	Brett Gardner/ Auto./699 RC	35.00
104	Colby Rasmus/ Auto./350 RC	25.00
105	David Price/ Auto./299 RC	35.00
106	Dexter Fowler/ Auto./699 RC	15.00
107	Donald Veal/ Auto./650 RC	8.00
108	Elvis Andrus/ Auto./350 RC	20.00
109	Everth Cabrera/ Auto./699 RC	10.00

110	Fernando Martinez/ Auto./300 RC	15.00
111	Gordon Beckham/ Auto./99 RC	50.00
112	James McDonald/ Auto./699 RC	8.00
113	James Parr/Auto./699 RC	8.00
114	Jason Motte/ Auto./699 RC	10.00
115	Jordan Schafer/ Auto./350 RC	12.00
116	Jordan Zimmerman/ Auto./699 RC	10.00
117	Kenshin Kawakami/ Auto./350 RC	20.00
118	Kevin Jepsen/ Auto./699 RC	8.00
119	Koji Uehara/ Auto./699 RC	25.00
120	Luis Perdomo/ Auto./699 RC	8.00
121	Matt Tuiasosopo/ Auto./699 RC	10.00
122	Matt Wieters/ Auto./350 RC	60.00
123	Pablo Sandoval/ Auto./550 RC	40.00
124	Phil Coke/Auto./699 RC	10.00
125	Rick Porcello/ Auto./550 RC	25.00
126	Ryan Perry/ Auto./199 RC	15.00
127	Shairon Martis/ Auto./699 RC	8.00
128	Tommy Hanson/ Auto./199 RC	75.00
129	Travis Snider/ Auto./300 RC	20.00
130	Trevor Cahill/ Auto./499 RC	15.00

2005 Classic Patch Update

NM/M

Production 9-52

BD	Bucky Dent/20	200.00
BJ	Bo Jackson/48	200.00
BW	Billy Williams/52	150.00
CH	Jim "Catfish" Hunter/27	220.00
EM	Eddie Mathews/41	
JP	Jim Palmer/27	300.00
MA	Edgar Martinez/44	150.00
RC	Rod Carew/49	220.00
RF	Rollie Fingers/47	150.00
RJ	Reggie Jackson/44	200.00
RS	Ryne Sandberg/50	220.00
SA	Sparky Anderson/46	140.00
TW	Ted Williams/9	

Bat Barrels

Production 1-9
No Pricing

Classic Black Stitches, Silver Ink

Production 1-34

BO	Bo Jackson/16	60.00
DA	Dick Allen/15	30.00
DE	Bucky Dent/20	20.00
KG	Ken Griffey Sr./30	12.00
KH	Kent Hrbek/14	25.00
MJ	Michael Jordan/23	600.00
NR	Nolan Ryan/34	100.00
OC	Dennis "Oil Can" Boyd/23	25.00

Classic Bat Barrel Gold Ink

Production 1-25

KG	Ken Griffey Sr./25	10.00

Classic Black Leather Gold Ink

Production 1-15

KG	Ken Griffey Sr./15	10.00

Classic Leather Silve Ink

Production 5 or 15

DA	Dick Allen/15	30.00
GP	Gaylord Perry/15	35.00
OC	Dennis "Oil Can" Boyd/15	30.00

Classic Bat Barrel Black Ink

Production 1-40

EM	Edgar Martinez/40	40.00
KH	Kent Hrbek/25	25.00

Classic Bat Barrel Blue Ink

Production 1-25
Red Ink 1 of 1's exist

CF	Carlton Fisk/25	35.00
CY	Carl Yastrzemski/25	70.00

Classic Leather Black Ink

Production 25

NR	Nolan Ryan/25	100.00
CF	Carlton Fisk/25	35.00

Classic Brown Leather Gold Ink

Production 1-40

RY	Robin Yount/ 40 Blue Ink	50.00

Classic Red Stitch Black Ink

Production 5-99

DA	Dick Allen/25	25.00
GP	Gaylord Perry/25	25.00

KG	Ken Griffey Sr./99	10.00
KH	Kent Hrbek/50	20.00
OC	Dennis "Oil Can" Boyd/99	20.00

Classic Red Stitch Blue Ink
Production 15-199

AK	Al Kaline/99	40.00
BO	Bo Jackson/25	50.00
BW	Billy Williams/50	25.00
CR	Cal Ripken Jr./199	80.00
CY	Carl Yastrzemski/25	75.00
DA	Dick Allen/50	25.00
DE	Bucky Dent/25	15.00
GP	Gaylord Perry/50	20.00
JP	Jim Palmer/49	25.00
KG	Ken Griffey Sr./199	8.00
KH	Kent Hrbek/99	20.00
RY	Robin Yount/50	50.00
TR	Tim Raines/99	20.00

Classic Red Stitch Red Ink
Production 1-47

BR	Brooks Robinson/47	40.00
CF	Carlton Fisk/15	30.00
JP	Jim Palmer/47	30.00
KG	Ken Griffey Sr./25	15.00
OC	Dennis "Oil Can" Boyd/25	25.00

Classic Red Stitch Green Ink
Some not priced yet.

AK	Al Kaline/100	50.00
BJ	Bo Jackson	60.00
BR	Brooks Robinson/58	50.00
CF	Carlton Fisk/81	30.00
CR	Cal Ripken Jr.	125.00
EM	Edgar Martinez	30.00
NR	Nolan Ryan/61	100.00

Classic Cuts
Production One Set
No Pricing

Historical Signatures
Production 2 or 5
No Pricing

Immortal Signatures
Production 1-32

DC	Dolph Camilli/26	100.00
ES	Enos Slaughter/16	85.00
HB	Hank Bauer/14	60.00
HS	Hank Sauer/31	90.00
JP	Johnny Podres/30	100.00
LW	Leon Wagner/18	75.00

Signatures Bat Barrel Silver Ink
Production 5-25

CJ	Chipper Jones/25	150.00
CL	Carlos Lee/25	20.00
CW	Chien-Ming Wang/25	140.00
EL	Evan Longoria/25	120.00
KY	Kevin Youkilis/25	35.00

Signatures Leather Silver Ink
Production 5-15
No Pricing

Signatures Bat Barrel Black Ink
Production 1-10
No Pricing

Signatures Bat Barrel Blue Ink
Production 1-10
No Pricing

Signatures Leather Black Ink
Production 1-15
No Pricing

Signatures Red and Blue Stitch Black Ink
Production 25

GS	Grady Sizemore/25	40.00

Signatures Red Stitch Black Ink
Production 1-75

CL	Carlos Lee/25	15.00
GS	Grady Sizemore/75	30.00
KY	Kevin Youkilis/25	40.00
TG	Tom Glavine/50	60.00

Signatures Red Stitch Blue Ink
Production 4-199

BU	B.J. Upton/50	20.00
CJ	Chipper Jones/50	100.00
CL	Carlos Lee/199	10.00
CW	Chien-Ming Wang/25	125.00
DU	Dan Uggla/35	15.00
JD	J.D. Drew/21	30.00
VW	Vernon Wells/63	10.00

Signatures Red Stitch Red Ink
Production 1-56

MY	Michael Young/56	15.00
YM	Yadier Molina/35	60.00

Signatures Red and Blue Stitch Red Ink
Production 5 or 50

DU	Dan Uggla/50	15.00

Signatures Red Stitch Green Ink
Some not priced.

BU	B.J. Upton	25.00
CJ	Chipper Jones	75.00
CW	Chien-Ming Wang	120.00
EL	Evan Longoria	100.00
LJ	LeBron James	250.00
VM	Victor Martinez	15.00

?

Production 2-60

CB	Chad Billingsley/58	15.00
FH	Felix Hernandez/34	85.00
JB	Jay Bruce/32	35.00
JN	Joe Nathan/36	15.00
JR	Ken Griffey Jr./24	150.00
JW	Josh Willingham/16	15.00
MK	Matt Kemp/27	35.00
MN	Nick Markakis/21	30.00
ZG	Zack Greinke/23	50.00

Signatures Bat Barrel Gold Ink
Production 5-25

CB	Chad Billingsley/25	20.00
DJ	Derek Jeter/25	250.00
GP	Glen Perkins/25	15.00
JB	Jay Bruce/25	35.00
JN	Joe Nathan/25	15.00
JR	Ken Griffey Jr./25	150.00
JW	Josh Willingham/25	10.00
MC	Matt Cain/25	30.00
MK	Matt Kemp/25	30.00
MN	Nick Markakis/25	35.00

Signatures Black Bat Barrel Silver Ink
Production 10-60

CB	Chad Billingsley/50	20.00
DJ	Derek Jeter/50	220.00
GP	Glen Perkins/50	8.00
JB	Jay Bruce/50	35.00
JN	Joe Nathan/50	15.00
JR	Ken Griffey Jr./60	100.00
JW	Josh Willingham/50	10.00
MC	Matt Cain/50	25.00
MK	Matt Kemp/50	25.00
MN	Nick Markakis/50	25.00
MU	David Murphy/50	20.00
ZG	Zack Greinke/25	50.00

Signatures Black Leather Gold Ink
Production 1-15

CB	Chad Billingsley/15	20.00
GP	Glen Perkins/15	15.00

Signatures Black Leather Silver Ink
Production 1-30

CB	Chad Billingsley/30	20.00
DJ	Derek Jeter/30	250.00
JB	Jay Bruce/30	35.00
JR	Ken Griffey Jr./30	10.00
JW	Josh Willingham/30	10.00
MC	Matt Cain/30	20.00
MK	Matt Kemp/30	25.00
MN	Nick Markakis/30	25.00
ZG	Zack Greinke/30	50.00

Signatures Brown Bat Barrel Black Ink
Production 1-50

DJ	Derek Jeter/50	185.00
ML	Mark Loretta/35	20.00

Signatures Red and Blue Stitch Blue Ink
Production 10-25

MR	Manny Ramirez/25	90.00

Signatures Brown Bat Barrel Blue Ink
Production 5-199

JR	Ken Griffey Jr./199	75.00
YM	Yadier Molina/25	50.00

Signatures Bat Barrel Red Ink
Production 1-25

JR	Ken Griffey Jr./25	150.00

Signatures Brown Leather Black Ink
Production 10-30

YM	Yadier Molina/30	50.00

Signatures Skin Red and Blue Stitch Blue Ink
Production 50

HR	Hanley Ramirez/50	40.00

Signatures Red and Blue Stitch Red Ink
Production 10-50

CR	Cody Ross/50	12.00
JP	James Shields/50	15.00
KS	Kelly Shoppach/50	8.00
NM	Nate McLouth/50	20.00
SM	Sean Marshall/49	15.00

Signatures Skin Red Stitch Black Ink
Production 1-350

CB	Chad Billingsley/50	20.00
DJ	Derek Jeter/150	180.00
DP	David Price/50	25.00
GP	Glen Perkins/99	10.00
JB	Jay Bruce/150	30.00
JN	Joe Nathan/50	15.00
JR	Ken Griffey Jr./199	75.00
JW	Josh Willingham/99	10.00
MB	Marlon Byrd/350	8.00
MK	Matt Kemp/99	20.00
MN	Nick Markakis/99	20.00
MU	David Murphy/99	15.00
PK	Paul Konerko/50	25.00
TC	Trevor Cahill/50	25.00
TS	Travis Snider/25	25.00
TT	Troy Tulowitzki/199	20.00
VM	Victor Martinez/120	20.00
YM	Yadier Molina/37	35.00
ZG	Zack Greinke/25	50.00

Signatures Skin Red Stitch Blue Ink
Production 2-350

CB	Chad Billingsley/199	15.00
CR	Cody Ross/299	10.00
DJ	Derek Jeter/399	150.00
DP	David Price/99	25.00
EJ	Edwin Jackson/350	10.00
FC	Fausto Carmona/300	10.00
FH	Felix Hernandez/50	50.00
GP	Glen Perkins/199	10.00
HR	Hanley Ramirez/300	30.00
IK	Ian Kinsler/150	20.00
JB	Jay Bruce/299	20.00
JN	Joe Nathan/199	10.00
JP	James Shields/300	8.00
JW	Josh Willingham/199	10.00
KS	Kelly Shoppach/300	10.00
KU	Koji Uehara/50	70.00
MJ	Mike Jacobs/199	8.00
MK	Matt Kemp/199	20.00
MN	Nick Markakis/199	20.00
MU	David Murphy/199	15.00
NM	Nate McLouth/300	20.00
PK	Paul Konerko/99	20.00
PM	Paul Maholm/200	8.00
RB	Rocco Baldelli/99	15.00
SM	Sean Marshall/250	8.00
TC	Trevor Cahill/199	10.00
TS	Travis Snider/50	25.00
TT	Troy Tulowitzki/99	20.00
ZG	Zack Greinke/50	40.00

Signatures Skin Red Stitch Red Ink
Production 5-100

DJ	Derek Jeter/50	200.00
GP	Glen Perkins/25	10.00
JB	Jay Bruce/50	25.00
JW	Josh Willingham/25	10.00
MC	Matt Cain/100	20.00
MK	Matt Kemp/25	30.00
ML	Mark Loretta/35	10.00
MN	Nick Markakis/35	35.00
MU	David Murphy/25	15.00
PM	Paul Maholm/50	10.00
TC	Trevor Cahill/25	20.00

Sweet Swatch

Common Swatch:		4.00
Patch:		2-3X

Production 10-30

AJ	Adam Jones	6.00
AP	Albert Pujols	15.00
AR	Aramis Ramirez	4.00
BB	Billy Butler	4.00
CB	Clay Buchholz	4.00
CD	Carlos Delgado	4.00
CG	Curtis Granderson	4.00
CL	Carlos Lee	4.00
CY	Carl Yastrzemski	8.00
DO	David Ortiz	6.00
DW	Dave Winfield	6.00
FS	Freddy Sanchez	4.00
GS	Grady Sizemore	8.00
HK	Howie Kendrick	4.00
IK	Ian Kinsler	4.00
JB	Jason Bay	4.00
JH	Josh Hamilton	8.00
JP	Jake Peavy	4.00
JW	Jered Weaver	4.00
KW	Kerry Wood	4.00
LE	Cliff Lee	4.00
NM	Nick Markakis	4.00
RG	Ryan Garko	4.00
RH	Roy Halladay	6.00
RP	Rick Porcello	6.00
SC	Steve Carlton	6.00
SH	Shin-Soo Choo	4.00
TH	Trevor Hoffman	4.00
VW	Vernon Wells	4.00
ZG	Zack Greinke	6.00

Sweet Swatch Dual

Common Dual:		1.00
Patch:		No Pricing

Production 15 Sets

BB	Johnny Bench, Yogi Berra	12.00
BM	Daisuke Matsuzaka, Josh Beckett	10.00
BS	Lou Brock, Kevin Schoendienst	10.00
BV	Jay Bruce, Joey Votto	15.00

GJ	Derek Jeter, Ken Griffey Jr.	20.00
HP	Albert Pujols, Josh Hamilton	15.00
JP	Derek Jeter, Jorge Posada	20.00
MJ	Daisuke Matsuzaka, Kenji Johjima	8.00
MM	Joe Mauer, Justin Morneau	12.00
PV	Jake Peavy, Justin Verlander	10.00
RH	Josh Hamilton, Nolan Ryan	15.00
SP	Albert Pujols, Ozzie Smith	25.00
SR	Jose Reyes, Ozzie Smith	25.00
SW	Billy Williams, Ryne Sandberg	15.00
UW	Brandon Webb, Justin Upton	6.00
VO	David Ortiz, Jason Varitek	8.00
WL	Brandon Webb, Tim Lincecum	8.00
YC	Carl Yastrzemski, Orlando Cepeda	10.00
YJ	Carl Yastrzemski, Fergie Jenkins	10.00

Sweet Swatch Quad

Patch:		No Pricing

Production 5-10

CNR	Chipper Jones, Eddie Murray, Mike Schmidt, Prince Fielder	20.00
CST	Daisuke Matsuzaka, Fergie Jenkins, Gaylord Perry, Tim Lincecum	15.00
GNY	Adam Jones, Cole Hamels, Jose Reyes, Tim Lincecum	15.00
NYC	Derek Jeter, Joe DiMaggio, Reggie Jackson, Yogi Berra	80.00
PHI	Chase Utley, Cole Hamels, Mike Schmidt, Steve Carlton	15.00
TOP	Albert Pujols, Derek Jeter, Josh Hamilton, Ken Griffey Jr.	25.00
VEN	Felix Hernandez, Johan Santana, Magglio Ordonez, Miguel Cabrera	10.00
VET	Billy Wagner, Josh Beckett, Roy Halladay, Tom Glavine	10.00

Sweet Swatch Triple

Patch:		No Pricing

Production 5-10

ATL	Phil Niekro, Tim Hudson, Tom Glavine	8.00
BPL	Jake Peavy, Josh Beckett, Tim Lincecum	10.00
FMM	Brian McCann, Carlton Fisk, Joe Mauer	10.00
JPN	Daisuke Matsuzaka, Kenji Johjima, Kosuke Fukudome	10.00
LMR	Brian McCann, Jon Lester, Jose Reyes	10.00
MIL	Bill Hall, Prince Fielder, Ryan Braun	10.00
MIN	Francisco Liriano, Joe Mauer, Justin Morneau	10.00
NYC	Derek Jeter, Johnny Damon, Reggie Jackson	20.00
NYY	Derek Jeter, Joe DiMaggio, Yogi Berra	75.00
ODF	Carlos Delgado, David Ortiz, Prince Fielder	10.00
SFG	Juan Marichal, Tim Lincecum, Willie McCovey	20.00
SSC	Mike Schmidt, Orlando Cepeda, Ryne Sandberg	15.00

2009 Upper Deck USA

Common Player:		1.00
Sealed Box:		350.00

1	Jared Clark	2.00
2	Tommy Mendonca	2.00
3	Christian Colon	2.00
4	Kentrail Davis	3.00

5	Matt den Dekker	2.00
6	Derek Dietrich	2.00
7	Josh Fellhauer	1.50
8	Micah Gibbs	1.50
9	Kyle Gibson	1.50
10	A.J. Griffin	1.00
11	Chris Hernandez	1.00
12	Ryan Jackson	1.50
13	Mike Leake	4.00
14	Ryan Lipkin	1.00
15	Tyler Lyons	1.00
16	Mike Minor	1.00
17	Hunter Morris	2.00
18	Andrew Oliver	1.00
19	Scott Woodward	1.50
20	Blake Smith	2.00
21	Stephen Strasburg	70.00
22	Kendal Volz	1.50
23	Andrew Aplin	1.00
24	Austin Maddox	1.00
25	Colton Cain	1.00
26	Cameron Garfield	1.00
27	Cecil Tanner	1.50
28	David Nick	1.50
29	Donavan Tate	3.00
30	Nick Franklin	1.50
31	Harold Martinez	1.00
32	Jake Barrett	1.00
33	Jeff Malm	1.00
34	Jonathan Meyer	1.50
35	Matt Purke	2.00
36	Max Stassi	1.00
37	Nolan Fontana	1.00
38	Ryan Weber	1.00
39	Jacob Turner	1.50
40	Wes Hatton	1.00
41	Nicky Delmonico, Philip Pfeifer, Peter Tago	1.00
42	Cody Buckel, Daniel Camarena, Dan Child	1.00
43	Michael Kelly, Bryan Radziewski, Kyle Van Alstine	1.00
44	Jake Rodriguez, Marcus Littlewood, Tony Wolters	1.00
45	Bryce Harper, Michael Lorenzen, Matt Lipka	5.00
46	Ladson Montgomery, Will Allen, Christian Lopes	1.00
47	Bryce Harper	65.00

Chinese-Taipei National Team Jerseys

		NM/M

Production 479 Sets

CH	Chih-Pei Huang	8.00
CL	Chia-Jen Lo	12.00
EH	Erh-Hang Hsu	5.00
HL	Hung-Cheng Lai	8.00
HU	Chin-Lung Huang	5.00
HY	Hsien-Hsien Yang	5.00
KC	Kai-Wen Cheng	10.00
KL	Ken-Wei Lin	5.00
LC	Chih-Hsiang Lin	5.00
MT	Ming-Shueh Tsai	5.00
TT	Tsung-Hsuan Tseng	8.00
WL	Wen-Yang Liao	8.00
WW	Wei-Chung Wang	8.00
YC	Yuan-Chin Chu	5.00
YH	Yu-Chi Hsiao	5.00

Chinese-Taipei National Team Patch Autos

		NM/M

Production 55 Sets

CH	Chih-Pei Huang	35.00
CL	Chia-Jen Lo	100.00
EH	Erh-Hang Hsu	15.00
HU	Chin-Lung Huang	40.00
HY	Hsien-Hsien Yang	30.00
KC	Kai-Wen Cheng	75.00
KL	Ken-Wei Lin	35.00
LC	Chih-Hsiang Lin	20.00
MT	Ming-Shueh Tsai	20.00
TT	Tsung-Hsuan Tseng	35.00
WL	Wen-Yang Liao	40.00
WW	Wei-Chung Wang	30.00
YC	Yuan-Chin Chu	30.00
YH	Yu-Chi Hsiao	25.00

Chinese-Taipei National Team Patches

		NM/M

Production 6-75

HL	Hung-Cheng Lai/65	15.00
KC	Kai-Wen Cheng/75	30.00
MT	Ming-Shueh Tsai/75	15.00
YC	Yuan-Chin Chu/75	15.00
YH	Yu-Chi Hsiao/75	15.00

National Team Base Set Autographs

		NM/M

Common Auto.:		8.00

Production 175 Sets

Red Parallel:		No Pricing

Production 25 Sets

Green Parallel:		No Pricing

Production 2 Sets

61	Christian Colon	8.00
63	Matt den Dekker	15.00
64	Derek Dietrich	40.00
65	Josh Fellhauer	10.00
66	Micah Gibbs	25.00
67	Kyle Gibson	8.00
68	A.J. Griffin	8.00
69	Chris Hernandez	10.00
70	Ryan Jackson	10.00
71	Mike Leake	30.00
72	Ryan Lipkin	10.00
73	Tyler Lyons	10.00
74	Mike Minor	15.00
75	Hunter Morris	10.00
76	Andrew Oliver	10.00
78	Blake Smith	20.00
79	Stephen Strasburg	375.00
80	Kendal Volz	10.00
81	Andrew Aplin	15.00
82	Jake Barrett	10.00
85	Colton Cain	8.00
87	Nolan Fontana	10.00
88	Nick Franklin	15.00
89	Cameron Garfield	10.00
92	Wes Hatton	10.00
98	Austin Maddox	20.00
99	Jeff Malm	10.00
102	Jonathan Meyer	15.00
106	David Nick	10.00
107	Matt Purke	20.00
108	Max Stassi	40.00
109	Cecil Tanner	10.00
110	Donavan Tate	30.00
113	Jacob Turner	15.00

National Team Starting Lineup Autographs
No Pricing
Production 12 Sets

National Team Q & A Autographs
Production 20 Sets

National Team Jerseys

		NM/M

Common Jersey:		4.00

Production 149-179

AG	A.J. Griffin	4.00
AO	Andrew Oliver	4.00
BS	Blake Smith	8.00
CC	Christian Colon	6.00
CH	Chris Hernandez	4.00
DD	Derek Dietrich	10.00
HM	Hunter Morris	4.00
JF	Josh Fellhauer	8.00
KD	Kentrail Davis	15.00
KG	Kyle Gibson	6.00
KV	Kendal Volz	6.00
MD	Matt den Dekker	8.00
MG	Micah Gibbs	4.00
ML	Mike Leake	30.00
MM	Mike Minor	4.00
RJ	Ryan Jackson	6.00
RL	Ryan Lipkin	6.00
SS	Stephen Strasburg	60.00
SW	Scott Woodward	4.00
TL	Tyler Lyons	4.00
TM	Tommy Mendonca	20.00

National Team Jersey Autographs

		NM/M

Common Jersey Auto.:		10.00

Production 99 Sets

Patch Auto.:		1-1.5X

Production 30 Sets

Red Ink:		No Pricing

Production 25 Sets

Green Ink:		No Pricing

Production Two Sets

AG	A.J. Griffin	10.00
AO	Andrew Oliver	10.00
BS	Blake Smith	20.00
CC	Christian Colon	15.00
CH	Chris Hernandez	15.00
DD	Derek Dietrich	30.00
HM	Hunter Morris	15.00
JF	Josh Fellhauer	15.00
KD	Kentrail Davis	30.00
KG	Kyle Gibson	15.00
KV	Kendal Volz	15.00
MD	Matt den Dekker	15.00
MG	Micah Gibbs	15.00
ML	Mike Leake	30.00
MM	Mike Minor	12.00
RJ	Ryan Jackson	15.00
RL	Ryan Lipkin	10.00
TL	Tyler Lyons	10.00

National Team In His Own Words Autographs
Production 20 Sets

National Team July 4th, 2007 Autos.
No Pricing

National Team Patriotic Patch Auto.

		NM/M
BN	Blaine Neal	15.00
DF	Dexter Fowler	40.00
JA	Jake Arrieta	25.00
JD	Jason Donald	60.00
LM	Lou Marson	50.00
MH	Michael Hessman	25.00
MK	Mike Koplove	25.00
NS	Nate Schierholtz	35.00
SS	Stephen Strasburg	700.00
TC	Trevor Cahill	40.00
TI	Terry Tiffee	25.00
TT	Taylor Teagarden	25.00

National Team Roster Autographs
Production 10

National Team The Letters
No Pricing
Production 15 Sets
Flag Patches: No Pricing
Production One Set

USA Retrospective

		NM/M
Common Player:		1.00
1	Matt Brown	1.00
2	Stephen Strasburg	25.00
3	Jayson Nix	1.00
4	Brian Duensing	2.00
5	Jake Arrieta	1.50
6	Dexter Fowler	2.00
7	Casey Weathers	1.00
8	Mike Koplove	1.00
9	Luke Donald	1.00
10	Taylor Teagarden	2.00
11	Kevin Jepsen	1.00
12	Matt LaPorta	3.00
13	USA Wins 3rd	
	Olympic Medal	2.00

16U National Team In His Own Words Autos
Production 5 Sets

16U National Team Patch Autograph

		NM/M
DC	Dan Child	35.00
LI	Marcus Littlewood	40.00
LO	Michael Lorenzen	40.00
MK	Michael Kelly	40.00
ML	Matt Lipka	35.00
ND	Nicky Delmonico	40.00
BH	Bryce Harper	600.00
TW	Tony Wolters	35.00

18U National Team Jersey

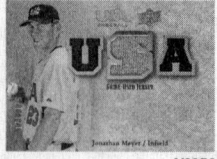

		NM/M
Common Jersey:		4.00
Production 179 Sets		
Patch:		1-1.5X
Production 65 Sets		
AA	Andrew Aplin	6.00
AM	Austin Maddox	6.00
CC	Colton Cain	6.00
CG	Cameron Garfield	6.00
CT	Cecil Tanner	8.00
DN	David Nick	8.00
DT	Donavan Tate	10.00
FO	Nolan Fontana	4.00
HM	Harold Martinez	8.00
JB	Jake Barrett	4.00
JM	Jeff Malm	6.00
JT	Jacob Turner	6.00
ME	Jonathan Meyer	6.00
MP	Matt Purke	6.00
MS	Max Stassi	15.00
NF	Nick Franklin	6.00
RW	Ryan Weber	4.00
WH	Wes Hatton	4.00

18U National Team Jersey Autograph

		NM/M
Common Jersey Auto.:		10.00
Production 99 Sets		
Patch Auto.:		1-1.5X
Production 30 Sets		
Red Ink:		No Pricing

Production 25 Sets
Green Ink: No Pricing
Production Two Wets

AA	Andrew Aplin	12.00
AM	Austin Maddox	15.00
CC	Colton Cain	10.00
CG	Cameron Garfield	15.00
CT	Cecil Tanner	15.00
DN	David Nick	15.00
DT	Donavan Tate	30.00
FO	Nolan Fontana	10.00
HM	Harold Martinez	15.00
JB	Jake Barrett	10.00
JM	Jeff Malm	15.00
JT	Jacob Turner	15.00
ME	Jonathan Meyer	15.00
MP	Matt Purke	20.00
MS	Max Stassi	50.00
NF	Nick Franklin	15.00
RW	Ryan Weber	10.00
WH	Wes Hatton	12.00

2010 Upper Deck

Common Player (2-40):		.50
Common Player (41-600):		.25
Hobby Pack (20):		6.00
Hobby Box (16):		75.00
1	Star Rookie CL	.25
2	Daniel McCutchen	2.00
3	Eric Young Jr.	.75
4	Michael Brantley	.50
5	Brian Matusz	2.00
6	Ian Desmond	.50
7	Carlos Carrasco	2.00
8	Dustin Richardson	.50
9	Tyler Flowers	.50
10	Drew Stubbs	.50
11	Reid Gorecki	2.00
12	Tommy Manzella	.50
13	Wade Davis	.75
14	Esmil Rogers	.50
15	Michael Dunn	1.00
16	Luis Durango	.50
17	Juan Francisco	1.00
18	Ernesto Frieri	.50
19	Tyler Colvin	1.50
20	Armando Gabino	1.50
21	Adam Moore	.50
22	Cesar Ramos	.50
23	Chris Johnson	.50
24	Chris Pettit	.50
25	Brandon Allen	.50
26	Brad Kilby	.50
27	Dusty Hughes	.50
28	Buster Posey	5.00
29	Kevin Richardson	.50
30	Josh Thole	1.00
31	John Hester	.50
32	Kyle Phillips	.50
33	Neil Walker	.75
34	Matt Carson	.50
35	Pedro Strop	2.00
36	Pedro Viola	.50
37	Daniel Runzler	1.00
38	Henry Rodriguez	1.50
39	Justin Turner	.50
40	Madison Bumgarner	4.00
41	Chris B. Young	.25
42	Justin Upton	.25
43	Conor Jackson	.25
44	Augie Ojeda	.25
45	Mark Reynolds	.25
46	Miguel Montero	.25
47	Max Scherzer	.40
48	Doug Slaten	.25
49	Chad Qualls	.25
50	Dan Haren	.40
51	Juan Gutierrez	.25
52	Doug Davis	.25
53	Leo Rosales	.25
54	Chad Tracy	.25
55	Stephen Drew	.40
56	Jordan Schafer	.25
57	Rafael Soriano	.25
58	Javier Vazquez	.25
59	Brandon Jones	.25
60	Matt Diaz	.25
61	Jair Jurrjens	.25
62	Adam LaRoche	.25
63	Martin Prado	.25
64	Omar Infante	.25
65	Chipper Jones	1.00
66	Yunel Escobar	.25
67	David Ross	.25
68	Derek Lowe	.25
69	James Parr	.25
70	Kenshin Kawakami	.25
71	Kris Medlen	.25

72	Ryan Church	.25
73	Nate McLouth	.40
74	Adam Jones	.50
75	Luke Scott	.25
76	Nolan Reimold	.50
77	Felix Pie	.25
78	Lou Montanez	.25
79	Ty Wigginton	.25
80	Cesar Izturis	.25
81	Robert Andino	.25
82	Chad Moeller	.25
83	Koji Uehara	.25
84	Matt Wieters	1.00
85	Jim Johnson	.25
86	Chris Ray	.25
87	Danys Baez	.25
88	David Hernandez	.25
89	Jeremy Guthrie	.25
90	Rich Hill	.25
91	Dustin Pedroia	.75
92	David Ortiz	.50
93	J.D. Drew	.25
94	Jeff Bailey	.25
95	Kevin Youkilis	.50
96	Clay Buchholz	.50
97	Jed Lowrie	.25
98	Mike Lowell	.40
99	George Kottaras	.25
100	Takashi Saito	.25
101	Hideki Okajima	.25
102	Jason Varitek	.25
103	Jon Lester	.50
104	Josh Beckett	.50
105	Daniel Bard	.25
106	Jonathan Papelbon	.50
107	Nick Green	.25
108	Kevin Gregg	.25
109	Ryan Theriot	.25
110	Kosuke Fukudome	.40
111	Derrek Lee	.50
112	Bobby Scales	.25
113	Aramis Ramirez	.25
114	Aaron Miles	.25
115	Mike Fontenot	.25
116	Koyie Hill	.25
117	Carlos Zambrano	.40
118	Jeff Samardzija	.25
119	Randy Wells	.25
120	Sean Marshall	.25
121	Carlos Marmol	.25
122	Ryan Dempster	.25
123	Reed Johnson	.25
124	Jake Fox	.25
125	Tony Pena	.25
126	Carlos Quentin	.25
127	A.J. Pierzynski	.25
128	Scott Podsednik	.25
129	Alexei Ramirez	.40
130	Paul Konerko	.25
131	Josh Fields	.25
132	Alex Rios	.25
133	Matt Thornton	.25
134	Mark Buehrle	.25
135	Scott Linebrink	.25
136	Freddy Garcia	.25
137	John Danks	.25
138	Bobby Jenks	.25
139	Gavin Floyd	.25
140	DJ Carrasco	.25
141	Jake Peavy	.50
142	Justin Lehr	.25
143	Wladimir Balentien	.25
144	Laynce Nix	.25
145	Chris Dickerson	.25
146	Joey Votto	.75
147	Paul Janish	.25
148	Brandon Phillips	.25
149	Scott Rolen	.40
150	Ryan Hanigan	.25
151	Edinson Volquez	.25
152	Arthur Rhodes	.25
153	Micah Owings	.25
154	Ramon Hernandez	.25
155	Francisco Cordero	.25
156	Bronson Arroyo	.25
157	Jared Burton	.25
158	Homer Bailey	.25
159	Travis Hafner	.40
160	Grady Sizemore	.50
161	Matt LaPorta	.50
162	Jeremy Sowers	.25
163	Trevor Crowe	.25
164	Asdrubal Cabrera	.25
165	Shin-Soo Choo	.40
166	Kelly Shoppach	.25
167	Kerry Wood	.25
168	Jake Westbrook	.25
169	Fausto Carmona	.25
170	Aaron Laffey	.25
171	Justin Masterson	.25
172	Jhonny Peralta	.25
173	Jensen Lewis	.25
174	Luis Valbuena	.25
175	Jason Giambi	.25
176	Ryan Spilborghs	.25
177	Seth Smith	.25
178	Matt Murton	.25
179	Dexter Fowler	.40
180	Troy Tulowitzki	.50
181	Ian Stewart	.25
182	Omar Quintanilla	.25
183	Clint Barmes	.25
184	Garrett Atkins	.25
185	Chris Iannetta	.25
186	Huston Street	.25
187	Franklin Morales	.25
188	Todd Helton	.50
189	Carlos Gonzalez	.25

190	Aaron Cook	.25
191	Jason Hammel	.25
192	Edwin Jackson	.25
193	Clete Thomas	.25
194	Marcus Thames	.25
195	Ryan Raburn	.25
196	Fernando Rodney	.25
197	Adam Everett	.25
198	Brandon Inge	.40
199	Miguel Cabrera	.50
200	Gerald Laird	.25
201	Joel Zumaya	.25
202	Curtis Granderson	.50
203	Justin Verlander	.50
204	Bobby Seay	.25
205	Nate Robertson	.25
206	Rick Porcello	.75
207	Ryan Perry	.25
208	Fu-Te Ni	.25
209	Cody Ross	.25
210	Jeremy Hermida	.25
211	Alfredo Amezaga	.25
212	Chris Coghlan	.40
213	Wes Helms	.25
214	Emilio Bonifacio	.25
215	Ricky Nolasco	.25
216	Anibal Sanchez	.25
217	Josh Johnson	.40
218	Burke Badenhop	.25
219	Kiko Calero	.25
220	Renyel Pinto	.25
221	Andrew Miller	.25
222	Hanley Ramirez	1.00
223	Gaby Sanchez	.25
224	Hunter Pence	.50
225	Carlos Lee	.40
226	Michael Bourn	.25
227	Kazuo Matsui	.25
228	Darin Erstad	.25
229	Lance Berkman	.40
230	Humberto Quintero	.25
231	J.R. Towles	.25
232	Wesley Wright	.25
233	Jose Valverde	.25
234	Wandy Rodriguez	.40
235	Roy Oswalt	.50
236	Latroy Hawkins	.25
237	Bud Norris	.25
238	Alberto Arias	.25
239	Billy Butler	.25
240	Jose Guillen	.25
241	David DeJesus	.25
242	Willie Bloomquist	.25
243	Mike Aviles	.25
244	Alberto Callaspo	.25
245	John Buck	.25
246	Joakim Soria	.25
247	Zack Greinke	.75
248	Miguel Olivo	.25
249	Kyle Davies	.25
250	Juan Cruz	.25
251	Luke Hochevar	.25
252	Brian Bannister	.25
253	Robinson Tejeda	.25
254	Kyle Farnsworth	.25
255	John Lackey	.40
256	Torii Hunter	.25
257	Chone Figgins	.25
258	Kevin Jepsen	.25
259	Reggie Willits	.25
260	Kendry Morales	.25
261	Howie Kendrick	.25
262	Erick Aybar	.25
263	Brandon Wood	.25
264	Maicer Izturis	.25
265	Mike Napoli	.25
266	Jeff Mathis	.25
267	Jered Weaver	.25
268	Joe Saunders	.25
269	Ervin Santana	.25
270	Brian Fuentes	.25
271	Jose Arredondo	.25
272	Chad Billingsley	.40
273	Juan Pierre	.25
274	Matt Kemp	.50
275	Randy Wolf	.25
276	Doug Mientkiewicz	.25
277	James Loney	.40
278	Casey Blake	.25
279	Rafael Furcal	.25
280	Blake DeWitt	.25
281	Russell Martin	.25
282	Jeff Weaver	.25
283	Cory Wade	.25
284	Eric Stults	.25
285	George Sherrill	.25
286	Hiroki Kuroda	.25
287	Hong-Chih Kuo	.25
288	Clayton Kershaw	.50
289	Corey Hart	.25
290	Jody Gerut	.25
291	Ryan Braun	1.00
292	Mike Cameron	.25
293	Casey McGehee	.25
294	Mat Gamel	.40
295	J.J. Hardy	.25
296	Braden Looper	.25
297	Yovani Gallardo	.40
298	Mike Rivera	.25
299	Carlos Villanueva	.25
300	Jeff Suppan	.25
301	Mitch Stetter	.25
302	David Riske	.25
303	Manny Parra	.25
304	Seth McClung	.25
305	Todd Coffey	.25
306	Joe Mauer	.75
307	Delmon Young	.25

308	Michael Cuddyer	.25
309	Matt Tolbert	.25
310	Nick Punto	.25
311	Jason Kubel	.25
312	Brendan Harris	.25
313	Brian Buscher	.25
314	Kevin Slowey	.25
315	Glen Perkins	.25
316	Joe Nathan	.25
317	Nick Blackburn	.25
318	Jesse Crain	.25
319	Matt Guerrier	.25
320	Scott Baker	.25
321	Anthony Swarzak	.25
322	Jon Rauch	.25
323	David Wright	1.00
324	Jeremy Reed	.25
325	Angel Pagan	.25
326	Jose Reyes	.75
327	Jeff Francoeur	.25
328	Luis Castillo	.25
329	Daniel Murphy	.25
330	Omir Santos	.25
331	John Maine	.25
332	Brian Schneider	.25
333	Johan Santana	.75
334	Francisco Rodriguez	.40
335	Tim Redding	.25
336	Mike Pelfrey	.25
337	Bobby Parnell	.25
338	Pat Misch	.25
339	Pedro Feliciano	.25
340	Nick Swisher	.40
341	Melky Cabrera	.25
342	Mark Teixeira	.50
343	CC Sabathia	.50
344	Ramiro Pena	.25
345	Derek Jeter	2.50
346	Andy Pettitte	.50
347	Jorge Posada	.50
348	Francisco Cervelli	.25
349	Chien-Ming Wang	.50
350	Mariano Rivera	.50
351	Phil Hughes	.40
352	Phil Coke	.25
353	A.J. Burnett	.25
354	Jose Molina	.25
355	Jonathan Albaladejo	.25
356	Ryan Sweeney	.25
357	Jack Cust	.25
358	Rajai Davis	.25
359	Andrew Bailey	.25
360	Aaron Cunningham	.25
361	Adam Kennedy	.25
362	Mark Ellis	.25
363	Daric Barton	.25
364	Kurt Suzuki	.25
365	Brad Ziegler	.25
366	Michael Wuertz	.25
367	Josh Outman	.25
368	Edgar Gonzalez	.25
369	Joey Devine	.25
370	Craig Breslow	.25
371	Trevor Cahill	.40
372	Brett Anderson	.40
373	Scott Hairston	.25
374	Jayson Werth	.40
375	Raul Ibanez	.40
376	Chase Utley	.75
377	Greg Dobbs	.25
378	Eric Bruntlett	.25
379	Shane Victorino	.40
380	Jimmy Rollins	.50
381	Jack Taschner	.25
382	Ryan Madson	.25
383	Brad Lidge	.25
384	J.A. Happ	.40
385	Cole Hamels	.50
386	Carlos Ruiz	.25
387	JC Romero	.25
388	Kyle Kendrick	.25
389	Chad Durbin	.25
390	Cliff Lee	.50
391	Delwyn Young	.25
392	Brandon Moss	.25
393	Ramon Vazquez	.25
394	Andy LaRoche	.25
395	Jason Jaramillo	.25
396	Ross Ohlendorf	.25
397	Paul Maholm	.25
398	Jeff Karstens	.25
399	Charlie Morton	.25
400	Zach Duke	.25
401	Jesse Chavez	.25
402	Lastings Milledge	.25
403	Matt Capps	.25
404	Evan Meek	.25
405	Ryan Doumit	.25
406	Drew Macias	.25
407	Chase Headley	.25
408	Tony Gwynn Jr.	.25
409	Kevin Kouzmanoff	.25
410	Edgar Gonzalez	.25
411	David Eckstein	.25
412	Everth Cabrera	.25
413	Nick Hundley	.25
414	Chris Young	.25
415	Luis Perdomo	.25
416	Edward Mujica	.25
417	Clayton Richard	.25
418	Luke Gregerson	.25
419	Heath Bell	.25
420	Kevin Correia	.25
421	Cha-Seung Baek	.25
422	Joe Thatcher	.25
423	Luis Rodriguez	.25
424	Bengie Molina	.25
425	Ryan Garko	.25

426	Nate Schierholtz	.25
427	Aaron Rowand	.25
428	Eugenio Velez	.25
429	Pablo Sandoval	.50
430	Edgar Renteria	.25
431	Kevin Frandsen	.25
432	Rich Aurilia	.25
433	Jonathan Sanchez	.25
434	Barry Zito	.25
435	Brian Wilson	.25
436	Merkin Valdez	.25
437	Juan Uribe	.25
438	Brandon Medders	.25
439	Noah Lowry	.25
440	Tim Lincecum	1.00
441	Jeremy Affeldt	.25
442	Russell Branyan	.25
443	Ian Snell	.25
444	Franklin Gutierrez	.25
445	Ken Griffey Jr.	1.50
446	Matt Tuiasosopo	.25
447	Jose Lopez	.25
448	Michael Saunders	.25
449	Ryan Rowland-Smith	.25
450	Carlos Silva	.25
451	Ichiro Suzuki	1.50
452	Brandon Morrow	.25
453	Chris Jakubauskas	.25
454	Felix Hernandez	.50
455	David Aardsma	.25
456	Mark Lowe	.25
457	Rob Johnson	.25
458	Garrett Olson	.25
459	Ryan Ludwick	.40
460	Colby Rasmus	.25
461	Brendan Ryan	.25
462	Skip Schumaker	.25
463	Albert Pujols	2.50
464	Joe Thurston	.25
465	Julio Lugo	.25
466	Yadier Molina	.25
467	Adam Wainwright	.25
468	Brad Thompson	.25
469	Dennys Reyes	.25
470	Mitchell Boggs	.25
471	Jason Motte	.25
472	Kyle McClellan	.25
473	Kyle Lohse	.25
474	Chris Carpenter	.25
475	Ryan Franklin	.25
476	Fernando Perez	.25
477	Ben Zobrist	.25
478	Evan Longoria	1.50
479	Gabe Gross	.25
480	Pat Burrell	.40
481	Carlos Pena	.25
482	Jason Bartlett	.25
483	Willie Aybar	.25
484	Dioner Navarro	.25
485	Dan Wheeler	.25
486	Andy Sonnanstine	.25
487	James Shields	.40
488	Jeff Niemann	.25
489	J.P. Howell	.25
490	Grant Balfour	.25
491	David Price	.75
492	Matt Garza	.40
493	David Murphy	.40
494	Nelson Cruz	.40
495	Michael Young	.40
496	Ian Kinsler	.50
497	Chris Davis	.40
498	Elvis Andrus	.40
499	Taylor Teagarden	.25
500	Jarrod Saltalamacchia	.25
501	CJ Wilson	.25
502	Derek Holland	.25
503	Darren O'Day	.25
504	Brandon McCarthy	.25
505	Scott Feldman	.25
506	Jason Jennings	.25
507	Eddie Guardado	.25
508	Frank Francisco	.25
509	Marlon Byrd	.25
510	Scott Downs	.25
511	Adam Lind	.25
512	Brett Cecil	.25
513	Travis Snider	.25
514	Ricky Romero	.25
515	Lyle Overbay	.25
516	Aaron Hill	.25
517	Jose Bautista	.25
518	Michael Barrett	.25
519	Roy Halladay	.50
520	Brian Tallet	.25
521	Marc Rzepczynski	.25
522	Robert Ray	.25
523	Dustin McGowan	.25
524	Shaun Marcum	.25
525	Jesse Litsch	.25
526	Josh Willingham	.25
527	Nyjer Morgan	.25
528	Adam Dunn	.50
529	Ryan Zimmerman	.50
530	Willie Harris	.25
531	Wil Nieves	.25
532	Ron Villone	.25
533	Austin Kearns	.25
534	Alberto Gonzalez	.25
535	Shairon Martis	.25
536	Ross Detwiler	.25
537	Garret Mock	.25
538	Mike MacDougal	.25
539	Jason Bergmann	.25
540	Arizona Diamondbacks	.25
541	Atlanta Braves	.25
542	Baltimore Orioles	.25

544	Boston Red Sox	.50
545	Chicago Cubs	.50
546	Chicago White Sox	.25
547	Cincinnati Reds	.25
548	Cleveland Indians	.25
549	Colorado Rockies	.25
550	Detroit Tigers	.25
551	Florida Marlins	.25
552	Houston Astros	.25
553	Kansas City Royals	.25
554	Los Angeles Angels	.25
555	Los Angeles Dodgers	.50
556	Milwaukee Brewers	.25
557	Minnesota Twins	.25
558	New York Mets	.50
559	New York Yankees	.50
560	Oakland Athletics	.25
561	Philadelphia Phillies	.25
562	Pittsburgh Pirates	.25
563	San Diego Padres	.25
564	San Francisco Giants	.25
565	St. Louis Cardinals	.50
566	Seattle Mariners	.25
567	Tampa Bay Rays	.25
568	Texas Rangers	.25
569	Toronto Blue Jays	.25
570	Washington Nationals	.25
571	Arizona Diamondbacks	.25
572	Atlanta Braves	.25
573	Baltimore Orioles	.25
574	Boston Red Sox	.50
575	Chicago Cubs	.50
576	Chicago White Sox	.25
577	Cincinnati Reds	.25
578	Cleveland Indians	.25
579	Colorado Rockies	.25
580	Detroit Tigers	.25
581	Florida Marlins	.25
582	Houston Astros	.25
583	Kansas City Royals	.25
584	Los Angeles Angels	.25
585	Los Angeles Dodgers	.50
586	Milwaukee Brewers	.25
587	Minnesota Twins	.25
588	New York Mets	.50
589	New York Yankees	.50
590	Oakland Athletics	.25
591	Philadelphia Phillies	.25
592	Pittsburgh Pirates	.25
593	San Diego Padres	.25
594	San Francisco Giants	.25
595	St. Louis Cardinals	.50
596	Seattle Mariners	.25
597	Tampa Bay Rays	.25
598	Texas Rangers	.25
599	Toronto Blue Jays	.25
600	Washington Nationals	.25

Gold
Gold (1-40): 8-15X
Gold (41-600): 15-25X
Production 99 Sets

2000 Rookie Update
Common Player: 3.00
541	Mark Buehrle	3.00
542	Miguel Cabrera	6.00
543	Jorge Cantu	3.00
544	Carl Crawford	5.00
545	Adam Dunn	5.00
546	Adrian Gonzalez	5.00
547	Matt Holliday	8.00
548	Brandon Inge	3.00
549	Roy Oswalt	5.00
550	Carlos Pena	4.00
551	Brandon Phillips	5.00
552	Francisco Rodriguez	4.00
553	Jimmy Rollins	6.00
554	Aaron Rowand	3.00
555	CC Sabathia	5.00
556	Johan Santana	8.00
557	Grady Sizemore	5.00
558	Adam Wainwright	5.00
559	Michael Young	3.00
560	Carlos Zambrano	4.00

A Piece of History 500 Club
Common Card: 140.00
| GS | Gary Sheffield | 140.00 |

All World

Common Player: 1.00
1	Albert Pujols	5.00
2	Carlos Beltran	1.00
3	Carlos Lee	1.00
4	Chien-Ming Wang	1.50
5	Daisuke Matsuzaka	2.00
6	Derek Jeter	5.00
7	Felix Hernandez	1.50
8	Hanley Ramirez	2.50
9	Ichiro Suzuki	3.00
10	Johan Santana	2.00
11	Justin Morneau	1.50
12	Kendry Morales	1.00
13	Magglio Ordonez	1.00
14	Russell Martin	1.00
15	Vladimir Guerrero	1.50

Baseball Heroes

Common DiMaggio: 4.00
JD	Joe DiMaggio	4.00
BH1-8	Joe DiMaggio	4.00
NNO	Heroes Header	

Baseball Heroes 20th Anniversary Art
Common Player: 1.00
BHA1	Ken Griffey Jr.	4.00
BHA2	Derek Jeter	5.00
BHA3	Evan Longoria	3.00
BHA4	Hanley Ramirez	2.00
BHA5	David Price	2.00
BHA6	Jon Lester	1.50
BHA7	Nick Markakis	2.00
BHA8	Cole Hamels	2.00
BHA9	Jonathan Papelbon	2.00
BHA10	Chipper Jones	2.00

Baseball Heroes 20th Anniv. Art Autos.
Production 90 Sets
1	Ken Griffey Jr.	180.00
2	Derek Jeter	250.00
3	Evan Longoria	80.00
4	Hanley Ramirez	75.00
5	David Price	25.00
6	Jon Lester	75.00
7	Nick Markakis	50.00
8	Cole Hamels	50.00
9	Jonathan Papelbon	40.00
10	Chipper Jones	140.00

Baseball Heroes Cut Signature
Production 56
| JD | Joe DiMaggio | 400.00 |

Celebrity Predictors
CP1/CP2	Jennifer Aniston / John Mayer	4.00
CP3/CP4	Cameron Diaz / Justin Timberlake	3.00
CP5/CP6	Megan Fox / Shia LaBeouf	3.00
CP7/CP8	Katie Holmes / Tom Cruise	3.00
CP11/CP12	Anna Kournikova / Enrique Iglesias	2.00
CP13/CP14	Mariah Carey / Nick Cannon	2.00
CP15/CP16	Rob Pattinson / Kristen Stewart	2.00
CP17/CP18	Angelina Jolie / Brad Pitt	10.00
CP19/CP20	Cristiano Ronaldo / Paris Hilton	10.00
CP9/CP10	Chris Martin / Gwyneth Paltrow	3.00

Portraits

Common Player: .75
Gold: 2-4X
Production 99 Sets
SE1	Justin Upton	1.00
SE2	Dan Haren	.75
SE3	Chipper Jones	2.00
SE4	Yunel Escobar	.75
SE5	Derek Lowe	.75
SE6	Nick Markakis	1.00
SE7	Brian Roberts	.75
SE8	Koji Uehara	1.00
SE9	Josh Beckett	1.00
SE10	Jon Lester	1.00
SE11	David Ortiz	1.00
SE12	Jason Varitek	.75
SE13	Carlos Zambrano	1.00
SE14	Kosuke Fukudome	.75
SE15	Aramis Ramirez	1.00
SE16	Mark Buehrle	.75
SE17	Paul Konerko	.75
SE18	Carlos Quentin	1.00
SE19	Joey Votto	1.50
SE20	Brandon Phillips	.75
SE21	Edinson Volquez	.75
SE22	Shin-Soo Choo	.75
SE23	Kerry Wood	.75
SE24	Grady Sizemore	1.00
SE25	Troy Tulowitzki	1.00
SE26	Aaron Cook	.75
SE27	Todd Helton	1.00
SE28	Justin Verlander	1.00
SE29	Miguel Cabrera	1.00
SE30	Rick Porcello	1.50
SE31	Chris Coghlan	1.00
SE32	Josh Johnson	.75
SE33	Carlos Lee	1.00
SE34	Lance Berkman	1.00
SE35	Roy Oswalt	1.00
SE36	Zack Greinke	1.50
SE37	Billy Butler	.75
SE38	Joakim Soria	.75
SE39	Jered Weaver	.75
SE40	Torii Hunter	.75
SE41	Kendry Morales	.75
SE42	Chone Figgins	.75
SE43	Russell Martin	1.00
SE44	Clayton Kershaw	1.00
SE45	Matt Kemp	1.00
SE46	Hiroki Kuroda	.75
SE47	Alcides Escobar	.75
SE48	Yovani Gallardo	1.00
SE49	Ryan Braun	2.00
SE50	Justin Morneau	1.00
SE51	Joe Nathan	.75
SE52	Michael Cuddyer	.75
SE53	Johan Santana	2.00
SE54	David Wright	2.00
SE55	Jose Reyes	1.50
SE56	Francisco Rodriguez	.75
SE57	Mark Teixeira	1.50
SE58	Derek Jeter	4.00
SE59	Mariano Rivera	1.00
SE60	A.J. Burnett	.75
SE61	Jorge Posada	1.00
SE62	Jack Cust	.75
SE63	Mark Ellis	.75
SE64	Andrew Bailey	.75
SE65	Chase Utley	2.00
SE66	Cole Hamels	1.00
SE67	Raul Ibanez	1.00
SE68	Jimmy Rollins	1.50
SE69	Ryan Doumit	.75
SE70	Zach Duke	.75
SE71	Tony Gwynn Jr.	.75
SE72	Chris Young	.75
SE73	Heath Bell	.75
SE74	Barry Zito	.75
SE75	Pablo Sandoval	1.00
SE76	Aaron Rowand	.75
SE77	Tim Lincecum	2.00
SE78	Felix Hernandez	1.00
SE79	Ichiro Suzuki	2.50
SE80	Franklin Gutierrez	.75
SE81	Albert Pujols	4.00
SE82	Adam Wainwright	1.00
SE83	Chris Carpenter	1.00
SE84	Colby Rasmus	1.00
SE85	Yadier Molina	.75
SE86	Evan Longoria	2.50
SE87	Jeff Niemann	.75
SE88	James Shields	1.00
SE89	Carlos Pena	1.00
SE90	Scott Feldman	.75
SE91	Michael Young	1.00
SE92	Ian Kinsler	1.00
SE93	Elvis Andrus	1.00
SE94	Ricky Romero	.75
SE95	Roy Halladay	1.00
SE96	Adam Lind	1.00
SE97	Aaron Hill	1.00
SE98	Ryan Zimmerman	1.00
SE99	Adam Dunn	1.00
SE100	Nyjer Morgan	.75

Pure Heat

Common Player: 1.00
1	Adrian Gonzalez	1.50
2	Albert Pujols	4.00
3	Alex Rodriguez	3.00
4	Cole Hamels	1.50
5	CC Sabathia	1.50
6	Evan Longoria	3.00
7	Josh Beckett	1.00
8	Joe Mauer	2.00
9	Justin Verlander	1.50
10	Manny Ramirez	1.50
11	Mark Teixeira	1.00
12	Prince Fielder	2.00
13	Ryan Howard	2.50
14	Tim Lincecum	2.50
15	Troy Tulowitzki	1.00

Season Biography

Common Player: .50
SB1	Derek Lowe	.50
SB2	Johan Santana	1.00
SB3	Aaron Rowand	.50
SB4	Koji Uehara	.50
SB5	Everth Cabrera	.50
SB6	Miguel Cabrera	1.00
SB7	Justin Verlander	.75
SB8	Evan Longoria	2.00
SB9	Orlando Hudson	.50
SB10	Zach Duke	.50
SB11	Ken Griffey Jr.	2.50
SB12	Ian Kinsler	.75
SB13	Tim Wakefield	.50
SB14	Grady Sizemore	1.00
SB15	Gary Sheffield	.50
SB16	Tim Lincecum	2.00
SB17	Randy Johnson	1.00
SB18	Dustin Pedroia	1.00
SB19	Ryan Braun	1.50
SB20	Dan Haren	.50
SB21	Dave Bush	.50
SB22	Carlos Pena	.75
SB23	Albert Pujols	3.00
SB24	Jacoby Ellsbury	1.00
SB25	Dexter Fowler	.50
SB26	Ryan Howard	2.00
SB27	Jorge Cantu	.50
SB28	Yovani Gallardo	.50
SB29	Evan Longoria	2.00
SB30	Matt Garza	.50
SB31	Jake Peavy	.50
SB32	Jason Marquis	.50
SB33	Carl Crawford	.50
SB34	Zack Greinke	1.00
SB35	Vicente Padilla	.50
SB36	Manny Ramirez	1.00
SB37	Hanley Ramirez	1.50
SB38	Alex Rodriguez	2.50
SB39	Joe Saunders	.50
SB40	Torii Hunter	.50
SB41	Brett Cecil	.50
SB42	Ryan Zimmerman	1.00
SB43	Derek Holland	.50
SB44	Ryan Zimmerman	1.00
SB45	Torii Hunter	.50
SB46	Jimmy Rollins	.75
	Barack Obama	1.00
SB47	Alex Rodriguez	2.50
SB48	Ivan Rodriguez	.75
SB49	Clayton Kershaw	.75
SB50	Jake Peavy	.75
SB51	Jason Kendall	.50
SB52	Mark Teixeira	1.00
SB53	David Ortiz	.75
SB54	Joe Mauer	1.50
SB55	Raul Ibanez	.50
SB56	Kenshin Kawakami	.50
SB57	Nelson Cruz	.50
SB58	Alex Gonzalez	.50
SB59	Freddy Sanchez	.50
SB60	Chris B. Young	.50
SB61	Rick Porcello	1.50
SB62	Nolan Reimold	.75
SB63	Scott Feldman	.50
SB64	Ryan Howard	2.00
SB65	Ryan Dempster	.50
SB66	Jamie Moyer	.50
SB67	Jim Thome	.75
SB68	Roy Halladay	.75
SB69	Jeff Niemann	.50
SB70	Randy Johnson	1.00
SB71	Jonathan Broxton	.50
SB72	Carlos Zambrano	.75
SB73	Jon Lester	.75
SB74	Alfonso Soriano	.75
SB75	Dan Haren	.50
SB76	Vin Mazzaro	.50
SB77	Sean West	.50
SB78	Andre Ethier	.75
SB79	Colby Rasmus	.75
SB80	Jim Thome	.75
SB81	Tim Lincecum	2.00
SB82	Miguel Tejada	.75
SB83	Torii Hunter	.50
SB84	Albert Pujols	3.00
SB85	Todd Helton	.75
SB86	Jered Weaver	.50
SB87	Prince Fielder	1.50
SB88	Robinson Cano	.75
SB89	Ivan Rodriguez	.75
SB90	Tommy Hanson	2.00
SB91	Kenshin Kawakami	.50
SB92	Jeff Weaver	.50
SB93	Albert Pujols	3.00
SB94	B.J. Upton	.50
SB95	Trevor Cahill	.50
SB96	Tim Lincecum	2.00
SB97	Troy Tulowitzki	.75
SB98	Jermaine Dye	.50
SB99	Lance Berkman	.75
SB100	Hanley Ramirez	1.00
SB101	Alex Rodriguez	2.50
SB102	Albert Pujols	3.00
SB103	Tommy Hanson	1.50
SB104	Zack Greinke	1.00
SB105	Brandon Phillips	.50
SB106	Dallas Braden	.50
SB107	Joey Votto	1.00
SB108	Albert Pujols	3.00
SB109	Adam Dunn	.75
SB110	Ricky Nolasco	.50
SB111	Ted Lilly	.50
SB112	Vladimir Guerrero	.50
SB113	Ryan Spilborghs	.50
SB114	Garrett Atkins	.50
SB115	Jonathan Sanchez	.50
SB116	Josh Beckett	.75
SB117	Michael Wuertz	.50
SB118	Ichiro Suzuki	
	Barack Obama	2.50
SB119	Ryan Howard	2.00
SB120	Marc Rzepczynski	.50
SB121	Clayton Kershaw	.75
SB122	Roy Halladay	.75
SB123	Matt Kemp	1.00
SB124	Manny Ramirez	.75
SB125	Scott Hairston	.50
SB126	A.J. Burnett	.75
SB127	Mark Buehrle	.50
SB128	Jeremy Sowers	.50
SB129	Chone Figgins	.50
SB130	Cliff Lee	.75
SB131	Michael Young	.50
SB132	Josh Willingham	.50
SB133	Pablo Sandoval	1.00
SB134	Cliff Lee	.75
SB135	Aaron Hill	.50
SB136	Bud Norris	.50
SB137	Neftali Feliz	.75
SB138	Chase Utley	1.50
SB139	Fausto Carmona	.50
SB140	Barry Zito	.50
SB141	Jered Weaver	.50
SB142	Roy Halladay	.75
SB143	Wandy Rodriguez	.50
SB144	Mark Teixeira	1.00
SB145	Vladimir Guerrero	.75
SB146	Adrian Gonzalez	.75
SB147	Tim Lincecum	2.00
SB148	Cliff Lee	.75
SB149	Felix Pie	.50
SB150	Jim Thome	.75
SB151	Derek Jeter	3.00
SB152	Gregg Zaun	.50
SB153	Ian Kinsler	.75
SB154	Brandon Inge	.75
SB155	Hanley Ramirez	1.00
SB156	Russell Branyan	.50
SB157	Pedro Martinez	.75
SB158	Michael Cuddyer	.50
SB159	Jake Fox	.50
SB160	John Smoltz	.75
SB161	Ryan Howard	2.00
SB162	Matt LaPorta	.75
SB163	Joe Saunders	.50
SB164	Adam Dunn	.75
SB165	Tony Gwynn	.50
SB166	Edgar Renteria	.50
SB167	Josh Hamilton	1.00
SB168	Tim Hudson	.50
SB169	Brandon Allen	.50
SB170	Casey McGehee	.50
SB171	Ichiro Suzuki	.50
SB172	Chris Young	.50
SB173	Jimmy Rollins	1.50
SB174	Jon Lester	.75
SB175	Derek Lee	.75
SB176	Hunter Pence	.75
SB177	Mark Teixeira	1.00
SB178	Ricky Romero	.50
SB179	Wade LeBlanc	.50
SB180	Micah Hoffpauir	.50
SB181	Ian Desmond	.50
SB182	Derek Jeter	3.00
SB183	Adam Matusz	1.00
SB184	Ichiro Suzuki	2.50
SB185	Josh Johnson	.50
SB186	Adrian Gonzalez	.50
SB187	Jody Gerut	.50
SB188	Francisco Rodriguez	.50
SB189	Ryan Raburn	.50
SB190	Mariano Rivera	.50
SB191	Sonia Sotomayor	.50
SB192	Willy Aybar	.50
SB193	Wade Davis	.50
SB194	Ian Desmond	.50
SB195	Cesar Ramos	.50
SB196	Matt Palmer	.50
SB197	Ryan Zimmerman	.50
SB198	Clayton Kershaw	.75
SB199	Justin Verlander	.75
SB200	Alexi Casilla	.50

Signature Sensations
Some not priced.
AA	Aaron Rowand	15.00
AE	Alcides Escobar	15.00
AH	Aaron Harang	15.00
AI	Akinori Iwamura	15.00
AL	Andy LaRoche	15.00
AR	Alex Romero	8.00
AS	Anibal Sanchez	8.00
BA	Burke Badenhop	8.00
BB	Brian Bixler	8.00
CB	Clay Buchholz	15.00
CF	Chone Figgins	10.00
CH	Chase Headley	8.00
CL	Carlos Lee	10.00
DE	David Eckstein	12.00
DJ	Derek Jeter	200.00
DO	Darren O'Day	8.00
DP	Dustin Pedroia	25.00
DS	Denard Span	12.00
DV	Donald Veal	10.00
EB	Emilio Bonifacio	8.00
ED	Elijah Dukes	8.00
EM	Evan Meek	15.00
EV	Eugenio Velez	10.00
FP	Felix Pie	15.00
HE	Jeremy Hermida	8.00
JA	Jonathan Albaladejo	10.00
JC	Johnny Cueto	10.00
JH	J.A. Happ	20.00
JL	Jesse Litsch	8.00
JM	John Maine	8.00
JO	Joaquin Arias	8.00
JP	Jonathan Papelbon	20.00
JW	Josh Willingham	8.00
KG	Khalil Greene	15.00
KH	Kevin Hart	10.00
KJ	Kelly Johnson	8.00
KK	Kevin Kouzmanoff	8.00
KS	Kevin Slowey	15.00
KU	Koji Uehara	25.00
KY	Kevin Youkilis	25.00
MB	Marlon Byrd	10.00
MG	Mat Gamel	10.00
MO	Micah Owings	10.00
MP	Mike Pelfrey	15.00
NY	Nyjer Morgan	10.00
PA	Felipe Paulino	8.00
PF	Prince Fielder	30.00
RA	Alexei Ramirez	20.00
RM	Russell Martin	15.00
RO	Ross Ohlendorf	10.00
RT	Ryan Theriot	20.00
SK	Scott Kazmir	25.00
SM	Sean Marshall	8.00
TE	Miguel Tejada	10.00
TP	Troy Patton	10.00
TR	Ramon Troncoso	10.00
TS	Takashi Saito	15.00
VO	Edinson Volquez	10.00
WW	Wesley Wright	8.00
YE	Yunel Escobar	10.00
YG	Yovani Gallardo	20.00
ZD	Zach Duke	10.00

Supreme Green
Blue: 2X
S1	Dan Haren	5.00
S2	Chipper Jones	2.00
S3	Tommy Hanson	8.00
S4	Adam Jones	3.00
S5	Jonathan Papelbon	2.00
S6	Dustin Pedroia	4.00
S7	Kevin Youkilis	3.00
S8	Jason Bay	2.50
S9	Alfonso Soriano	2.00
S10	Paul Konerko	2.00
S11	Mark Buehrle	2.00
S12	Joey Votto	4.00
S13	Grady Sizemore	3.00
S14	Travis Hafner	2.00
S15	Troy Tulowitzki	3.00
S16	Jason Marquis	2.00
S17	Brandon Inge	2.00
S18	Justin Verlander	3.00
S19	Josh Johnson	3.00
S20	Carlos Lee	2.00
S21	Billy Butler	2.00
S22	Vladimir Guerrero	2.00
S23	Torii Hunter	2.00
S24	Manny Ramirez	4.00
S25	Ryan Braun	4.00
S26	Michael Cuddyer	2.00
S27	Joe Mauer	5.00
S28	Carlos Beltran	3.00
S29	David Wright	4.00
S30	Hideki Matsui	4.00
S31	Derek Jeter	10.00
S32	CC Sabathia	4.00
S33	Kurt Suzuki	2.00
S34	Ryan Howard	6.00
S35	Cole Hamels	4.00
S36	Mat Latos	4.00
S37	Tim Lincecum	6.00
S38	Pablo Sandoval	5.00
S39	Ichiro Suzuki	6.00
S40	Matt Holliday	4.00
S41	Yadier Molina	2.00
S42	Colby Rasmus	3.00
S43	Evan Longoria	5.00
S44	Carlos Pena	3.00
S45	Carl Crawford	3.00
S46	Ian Kinsler	3.00
S47	Josh Hamilton	

No.	Player	Price
S48	Scott Feldman	2.00
S49	Roy Halladay	3.00
S50	Ryan Zimmerman	3.00
S51	Justin Upton	3.00
S52	Mark Reynolds	3.00
S53	Brian McCann	3.00
S54	Nick Markakis	3.00
S55	Matt Wieters	5.00
S56	Jacoby Ellsbury	4.00
S57	David Ortiz	4.00
S58	Josh Beckett	4.00
S59	Carlos Zambrano	4.00
S60	Gordon Beckham	6.00
S61	Jay Bruce	4.00
S62	Shin-Soo Choo	4.00
S63	Todd Helton	3.00
S64	Dexter Fowler	3.00
S65	Miguel Cabrera	4.00
S66	Curtis Granderson	4.00
S67	Hanley Ramirez	4.00
S68	Dan Uggla	3.00
S69	Lance Berkman	3.00
S70	Zack Greinke	5.00
S71	Chone Figgins	3.00
S72	John Lackey	3.00
S73	Russell Martin	3.00
S74	Matt Kemp	4.00
S75	Prince Fielder	5.00
S76	Yovani Gallardo	3.00
S77	Justin Morneau	3.00
S78	Jose Reyes	4.00
S79	Johan Santana	4.00
S80	Francisco Rodriguez	2.00
S81	Johnny Damon	3.00
S82	Mark Teixeira	4.00
S83	Mariano Rivera	4.00
S84	Alex Rodriguez	8.00
S85	Cliff Lee	3.00
S86	Chase Utley	5.00
S87	Shane Victorino	3.00
S88	Zach Duke	2.00
S89	Andrew McCutchen	2.00
S90	Adrian Gonzalez	4.00
S91	Matt Cain	3.00
S92	Ken Griffey Jr.	4.00
S93	Felix Hernandez	3.00
S94	Albert Pujols	10.00
S95	Adam Wainwright	4.00
S96	David Price	4.00
S97	B.J. Upton	3.00
S98	Michael Young	2.00
S99	Adam Lind	3.00
S100	Adam Dunn	4.00

Tape Measure Shots

Common Player: 1.00

No.	Player	Price
TMS1	Mark Reynolds	1.00
TMS2	Raul Ibanez	1.50
TMS3	Joey Votto	2.00
TMS4	Adam Dunn	1.00
TMS5	Josh Hamilton	1.50
TMS6	Adrian Gonzalez	1.50
TMS7	Miguel Montero	1.00
TMS8	Seth Smith	1.00
TMS9	Nelson Cruz	1.00
TMS10	Carlos Pena	1.50
TMS11	Albert Pujols	5.00
TMS12	Pablo Sandoval	1.50
TMS13	Josh Willingham	1.00
TMS14	Manny Ramirez	2.50
TMS15	Prince Fielder	2.50
TMS16	Jermaine Dye	1.00
TMS17	Brandon Inge	1.000
TMS18	Lance Berkman	1.50
TMS19	Kelly Shoppach	1.00
TMS20	Ian Stewart	1.00
TMS21	Magglio Ordonez	1.00
TMS22	Michael Cuddyer	1.00
TMS23	Ryan Howard	1.50
TMS24	Troy Tulowitzki	1.50
TMS25	Colby Rasmus	2.00

Game Jersey

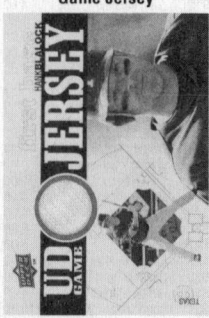

Common Jersey: 4.00
Patch: 2-3X
Production 25 Sets

No.	Player	Price
AE	Andre Ethier	6.00
AG	Alex Gordon	6.00
AJ	Adam Jones	6.00
AP	Albert Pujols	15.00
AR	Aramis Ramirez	6.00
BE	Josh Beckett	6.00
BI	Brandon Inge	4.00
BM	Brandon Morrow	4.00
BO	John Bowker	6.00
BR	Ryan Braun	10.00
BU	B.J. Upton	6.00
BZ	Barry Zito	4.00
CA	Matt Cain	6.00
CB	Clay Buchholz	6.00
CC	Chris Carpenter	8.00
CF	Chone Figgins	4.00
CG	Curtis Granderson	6.00
CH	Cole Hamels	8.00
CJ	Chipper Jones	10.00
CR	Carl Crawford	6.00
CU	Chase Utley	10.00
CY	Chris Young	4.00
DA	Johnny Damon	6.00
DE	David Eckstein	4.00
DH	Dan Haren	4.00
DJ	Derek Jeter	15.00
DL	Derrek Lee	6.00
DO	David Ortiz	6.00
EJ	Edwin Jackson	3.00
EL	Evan Longoria	20.00
EM	Evan Meek	4.00
EV	Eugenio Velez	4.00
FC	Fausto Carmona	4.00
FH	Felix Hernandez	8.00
FL	Francisco Liriano	6.00
FN	Fu-Te Ni	6.00
FR	Fernando Rodney	4.00
GA	Armando Galarraga	4.00
GO	Adrian Gonzalez	6.00
GS	Grady Sizemore	8.00
HB	Hank Blalock	4.00
HE	Chase Headley	4.00
HK	Howie Kendrick	4.00
HR	Hanley Ramirez	8.00
IK	Ian Kinsler	6.00
JB	Jeremy Bonderman	4.00
JD	Jermaine Dye	6.00
JE	Jacoby Ellsbury	20.00
JH	Josh Hamilton	8.00
JN	Jayson Nix	4.000
JP	Jonathan Papelbon	6.00
JR	Jimmy Rollins	8.00
JS	Johan Santana	6.00
JU	Justin Morneau	6.00
JV	Jason Varitek	6.00
KE	Kendry Morales	4.00
KF	Kosuke Fukudome	4.00
KG	Ken Griffey Jr.	15.00
KH	Kevin Hart	4.00
KK	Kevin Kouzmanoff	4.00
KM	Kevin Millwood	4.00
KY	Kevin Youkilis	8.00
MA	Max Scherzer	6.00
MB	Mark Buehrle	6.00
MC	Michael Cuddyer	4.00
MI	Miguel Cabrera	8.00
MK	Matt Kemp	8.00
ML	Matt LaPorta	6.00
MM	Melvin Mora	4.00
MO	Magglio Ordonez	4.00
MR	Mariano Rivera	8.00
MT	Matt Tolbert	4.000
MY	Michael Young	6.00
NM	Nick Markakis	8.00
PF	Prince Fielder	8.00
PH	Phil Hughes	6.00
PM	Pedro Martinez	6.00
PO	Jorge Posada	6.00
RC	Robinson Cano	8.00
RE	Jose Reyes	8.00
RH	Roy Halladay	8.00
RI	Raul Ibanez	6.00
RM	Russell Martin	4.000
RO	Alex Rodriguez	15.00
RT	Ramon Troncoso	4.00
RW	Randy Wells	4.000
RZ	Ryan Zimmerman	6.00
SC	Shin-Soo Choo	6.00
SD	Stephen Drew	6.00
SK	Scott Kazmir	6.00
TH	Travis Hafner	4.00
TL	Tim Lincecum	15.00
TO	Todd Helton	6.00
TT	Troy Tulowitzki	6.00
UP	Justin Upton	6.00
VE	Justin Verlander	8.00
VG	Vladimir Guerrero	6.00
WW	Wesley Wright	4.00
YY	Yasuhiko Yabuta	4.00
ZG	Zack Greinke	8.00

2010 UD USA Baseball

Common (1-59): .50
Common Auto. (61-116): 8.00
Common Patch (119-136): 6.00
Patch Production 65
One patch or auto. per box.
Sealed Box: 150.00

No.	Player	Price
1	Trevor Bauer	.50
2	Christian Colon	1.00
3	Cody Wheeler	.50
4	Chad Bettis	.50
5	Bryce Brentz	1.00
6	Nick Pepitone	.50
7	Michael Choice	.50
8	Gerrit Cole	1.00
9	Sonny Gray	1.00
10	Tyler Holt	.50
11	T.J. Walz	.50
12	Rick Hague	.50
13	Drew Pomeranz	.50
14	Blake Forsythe	.50
15	Matt Newman	.50
16	Casey McGrew	.50
17	Brad Miller	.50
18	Yasmani Grandal	1.00
19	Kolten Wong	.50
20	Tony Zych	.50
21	Andy Wilkins	.50
22	Asher Wojciechowski	.50
23	Cody Buckel	.50
24	Nick Castellanos	1.00
25	Garin Cecchini	.50
26	Sean Coyle	.50
27	Nicky Delmonico	.50
28	Kevin Gausman	1.00
29	Cory Hahn	.50
30	Bryce Harper	20.00
31	Kavin Keyes	.50
32	Manny Machado	.50
33	Connor Mason	.50
34	Ladson Montgomery	.50
35	Phillip Pfeifer	.50
36	Brian Ragira	1.50
37	Robbie Ray	.50
38	Kyle Ryan	.50
39	Jameson Taillon	4.00
40	A.J. Vanegas	.50
41	Karsten Whitson	.50
42	Tony Wolters	1.00
43	Albert Almora	.50
44	Shaun Chase	.50
45	Austin Cousino	.50
46	Dylan Davis	.50
47	Parker French	.50
48	Cory Geisler	.50
49	Courtney Hawkins	.50
50	C.J. Hinojosa	.50
51	John Hochstatter	.50
52	Hayden Hurst	.50
53	Ricardo Jacquez	.50
54	Kevin Kramer	.50
55	Francisco Lindor	.50
56	Kenny Mathews	.50
57	Evan Powell	1.00
58	Christopher Rivera	.50
59	JoMarcos Woods	.50
61	Trevor Bauer/Auto.	8.00
62	Christian Colon/Auto.	15.00
63	Cody Wheeler/Auto.	8.00
64	Chad Bettis/Auto.	8.00
65	Bryce Brentz/Auto.	20.00
66	Nick Pepitone/Auto.	8.00
67	Michael Choice/Auto.	15.00
68	Gerrit Cole/Auto.	15.00
69	Sonny Gray/Auto.	12.00
70	Tyler Holt/Auto.	8.00
71	T.J. Walz/Auto.	8.00
72	Rick Hague/Auto.	8.00
73	Drew Pomeranz/Auto.	15.00
74	Blake Forsythe/Auto.	10.00
75	Matt Newman/Auto.	10.00
76	Casey McGrew/Auto.	10.00
77	Brad Miller/Auto.	8.00
78	Yasmani Grandal/Auto.	15.00
79	Kolten Wong/Auto.	8.00
80	Tony Zych/Auto.	8.00
81	Andy Wilkins/Auto.	10.00
82	Asher Wojciechowski/Auto.	8.00
83	Bryce Harper/Auto.	220.00
84	Cody Buckel/Auto.	8.000
85	A.J. Vanegas/Auto.	10.00
90	Ladson Montgomery/Auto.	10.00
91	Karsten Whitson/Auto.	8.00
95	Connor Mason/Auto.	8.00
96	Garin Cecchini/Auto.	12.00
98	Jameson Taillon/Auto.	35.00
100	Sean Coyle/Auto.	12.00
102	Kyle Ryan/Auto.	8.00
105	Kevin Gausman/Auto.	12.00
106	Robbie Ray/Auto.	8.00
107	Nicky Delmonico/Auto.	10.00
108	Cory Hahn/Auto.	10.00
110	Nick Castellanos/Auto.	15.00
113	Manny Machado/Auto.	40.00
115	Phillip Pfeifer/Auto.	15.00
116	Brian Ragira/Auto.	10.00
119	Albert Almora/Jsy	8.00
120	Shaun Chase/Jsy	6.00
121	Austin Cousino/Jsy	8.00
122	Dylan Davis/Jsy	6.00
123	Parker French/Jsy	6.00
124	Cory Geisler/Jsy	8.00
125	Courtney Hawkins/Jsy	8.00
126	C.J. Hinojosa/Jsy	8.00
127	John Hochstatter/Jsy	8.00
128	Hayden Hurst/Jsy	6.00
129	Ricardo Jacquez/Jsy	6.00
130	Kevin Kramer/Jsy	6.00
131	Francisco Lindor/Jsy	8.00
132	Kenny Mathews/Jsy	8.00
133	Evan Powell/Jsy	6.00
134	Christopher Rivera/Jsy	6.00
135	Christopher Rivera/Jsy	6.00
136	JoMarcos Woods/Jsy	8.00

16U National Team Jersey Autographs

Production 149 Sets
Green: No pricing
Production 2 Sets
Red Ink: No pricing
Production 25 Sets

No.	Player	Price
AA	Albert Almora	15.00
AC	Austin Cousino	15.00
CG	Cory Geisler	12.00
CH	Courtney Hawkins	10.00
CR	Christopher Rivera	10.00
DD	Dylan Davis	10.00
EP	Evan Powell	8.00
FL	Francisco Lindor	12.00
HH	Hayden Hurst	12.00
HI	C.J. Hinojosa	10.00
JH	John Hochstatter	10.00
JW	JoMarcos Woods	20.00
KK	Kevin Kramer	10.00
KM	Kenny Mathews	8.00
PF	Parker French	10.00
RJ	Ricardo Jacquez	10.00
SC	Shaun Chase	12.00

16U National Team Jerseys

Common Jersey: 6.00

No.	Player	Price
AA	Albert Almora	8.00
AC	Austin Cousino	8.00
CG	Cory Geisler	6.00
CH	Courtney Hawkins	6.00
CR	Christopher Rivera	6.00
DD	Dylan Davis	6.00
EP	Evan Powell	6.00
FL	Francisco Lindor	8.00
HH	Hayden Hurst	8.00
HI	C.J. Hinojosa	8.00
JH	John Hochstatter	6.00
JW	JoMarcos Woods	10.00
KK	Kevin Kramer	6.00
KM	Kenny Mathews	8.00
PF	Parker French	6.00
RJ	Ricardo Jacquez	6.00
SC	Shaun Chase	6.00

16U National Team Patch Autographs

Production 35 Sets

No.	Player	Price
AA	Albert Almora	20.00
AC	Austin Cousino	20.00
CG	Cory Geisler	15.00
CH	Courtney Hawkins	15.00
CR	Christopher Rivera	15.00
DD	Dylan Davis	15.00
EP	Evan Powell	15.00
FL	Francisco Lindor	20.00
HH	Hayden Hurst	15.00
HI	C.J. Hinojosa	20.00
JH	John Hochstatter	15.00
JW	JoMarcos Woods	30.00
KK	Kevin Kramer	15.00
KM	Kenny Mathews	20.00
PF	Parker French	20.00
RJ	Ricardo Jacquez	
SC	Shaun Chase	20.00

16U National Team Roster Autographs

Production 10

16U 16U National Team

No Pricing

18U National Team Big Signatures

Production 75 Sets
Gold: No pricing
Production 25 Sets

No.	Player	Price
AV	A.J. Vanegas	10.00
BH	Bryce Harper	275.00
BR	Brian Ragira	10.00
CB	Cody Buckel	15.00
CH	Cory Hahn	8.00
CM	Connor Mason	10.00
GC	Garin Cecchini	12.00
JT	Jameson Taillon	40.00
KG	Kevin Gausman	10.00
KR	Kyle Ryan	10.00
KW	Karsten Whitson	25.00
LM	Ladson Montgomery	10.00
MM	Manny Machado	40.00
NC	Nick Castellanos	25.00
ND	Nicky Delmonico	10.00
PP	Phillip Pfeifer	10.00
RR	Robbie Ray	15.00
SC	Sean Coyle	15.00
TW	Tony Wolters	10.00

18U National Team Flag Patch

Production One Set
No Pricing

18U National Team Inscriptions Autos

Production 162 Sets
Green: No pricing
Production 2 Sets
Red: No pricing
Production 15 Sets

No.	Player	Price
AV	A.J. Vanegas	15.00
BH	Bryce Harper	220.00
BR	Brian Ragira	15.00
CB	Cody Buckel	10.00
CH	Cory Hahn	8.00
CM	Connor Mason	8.00
GC	Garin Cecchini	10.00
JT	Jameson Taillon	40.00
KG	Kevin Gausman	10.00
KR	Kyle Ryan	8.00
KW	Karsten Whitson	15.00
LM	Ladson Montgomery	10.00
NC	Nick Castellanos	15.00
ND	Nicky Delmonico	10.00
PP	Phillip Pfeifer	10.00
RR	Robbie Ray	8.00
SC	Sean Coyle	12.00
TW	Tony Wolters	10.00

18U National Team Jersey Autographs

Production 18-149
Green: No Pricing
Production 2 Sets
Red: No Pricing
Production 25 Sets

No.	Player	Price
AV	A.J. Vanegas/32	10.00
BH	Bryce Harper/149	225.00
BR	Brian Ragira/149	20.00
CB	Cody Buckel/28	15.00
CH	Cory Hahn/38	15.00
CM	Connor Mason/97	10.00
GC	Garin Cecchini/29	20.00
JT	Jameson Taillon/149	50.00
KG	Kevin Gausman/149	15.00
KK	Kavin Keyes/149	15.00
KR	Kyle Ryan/149	10.00
KW	Karsten Whitson/37	25.00
LM	Ladson Montgomery/62	8.00
NC	Nick Castellanos/36	30.00
ND	Nicky Delmonico/149	10.00
PP	Phillip Pfeifer/39	12.00
RR	Robbie Ray/149	10.00
SC	Sean Coyle/149	15.00
TW	Tony Wolters/149	15.00

18U National Team Jerseys

Common Jersey: 5.00

No.	Player	Price
AV	A.J. Vanegas	5.00
BH	Bryce Harper	40.00
BR	Brian Ragira	5.00
CB	Cody Buckel	5.00
CH	Cory Hahn	6.00
CM	Connor Mason	8.00
GC	Garin Cecchini	8.00
JT	Jameson Taillon	15.00
KG	Kevin Gausman	5.00
KK	Kavin Keyes	5.00
KR	Kyle Ryan	5.00
KW	Karsten Whitson	5.00
LM	Ladson Montgomery	5.00
MM	Manny Machado	15.00
NC	Nick Castellanos	8.00
ND	Nicky Delmonico	5.00
PP	Phillip Pfeifer	5.00
RR	Robbie Ray	5.00
SC	Sean Coyle	6.00
TW	Tony Wolters	8.00

18U National Team Patch Autographs

Production 35 Sets

No.	Player	Price
AV	A.J. Vanegas	20.00
BH	Bryce Harper	375.00
BR	Brian Ragira	30.00
CB	Cody Buckel	20.00
CH	Cory Hahn	20.00
CM	Connor Mason	20.00
GC	Garin Cecchini	25.00
KG	Kevin Gausman	20.00
KK	Kavin Keyes	20.00
KR	Kyle Ryan	15.00
KW	Karsten Whitson	40.00
LM	Ladson Montgomery	10.00
MM	Manny Machado	90.00
NC	Nick Castellanos	40.00
ND	Nicky Delmonico	20.00
RR	Robbie Ray	15.00
SC	Sean Coyle	20.00
TW	Tony Wolters	25.00

18U National Team Q & A Autographs

Production 65 Sets

No.	Player	Price
AV	A.J. Vanegas	10.00
BH	Bryce Harper	200.00
BR	Brian Ragira	20.00
CB	Cody Buckel	15.00
CH	Cory Hahn	15.00
CM	Connor Mason	15.00
GC	Garin Cecchini	20.00
JT	Jameson Taillon	40.00
KG	Kevin Gausman	12.00
KR	Kyle Ryan	15.00
KW	Karsten Whitson	15.00
MM	Manny Machado	35.00
NC	Nick Castellanos	20.00
ND	Nicky Delmonico	15.00
PP	Phillip Pfeifer	10.00
RR	Robbie Ray	15.00
SC	Sean Coyle	15.00
TW	Tony Wolters	15.00

18U National Team Roster Autographs

Production 10 Sets

18U18U National Team

Red Autographs
Production 25 Sets
Green: No Pricing
Production 2 Sets

No.	Player	Price
61	Trevor Bauer	
62	Christian Colon	30.00
63	Cody Wheeler	20.00
70	Tyler Holt	15.00
73	Drew Pomeranz	30.00
77	Brad Miller	25.00
80	Tony Zych	15.00
82	Asher Wojciechowski	20.00
83	Bryce Harper	500.00
89	A.J. Vanegas	30.00
90	Ladson Montgomery	25.00
91	Karsten Whitson	30.00
98	Jameson Taillon	100.00
100	Sean Coyle	20.00
105	Kevin Gausman	25.00
110	Nick Castellanos	40.00
113	Manny Machado	100.00

National Team Big Signatures

Production 75 Sets
Gold: No Pricing
Production 25 Sets

No.	Player	Price
AW	Andy Wilkins	8.00
BB	Bryce Brentz	20.00
BF	Blake Forsythe	10.00
BM	Brad Miller	10.00
CB	Chad Bettis	15.00
CC	Christian Colon	15.00
CM	Casey McGrew	15.00
CW	Cody Wheeler	15.00
DP	Drew Pomeranz	25.00
GC	Gerrit Cole	15.00
KW	Kolten Wong	20.00
MC	Michael Choice	25.00
MN	Matt Newman	15.00
NP	Nick Pepitone	8.00
RH	Rick Hague	10.00
SG	Sonny Gray	15.00
TB	Trevor Bauer	15.00
TH	Tyler Holt	10.00
TW	T.J. Walz	12.00
TZ	Tony Zych	15.00
WO	Asher Wojciechowski	8.00
YG	Yasmani Grandal	25.00

Team Flag Patch

Production One Set
No Pricing

National Team Inscriptions Autographs

Production 162 Sets
Green: No Pricing
Production 2 Sets
Red: No Pricing
Production 25 Sets

No.	Player	Price
AW	Andy Wilkins	12.00
BB	Bryce Brentz	25.00
BF	Blake Forsythe	10.00
BM	Brad Miller	8.00
CB	Chad Bettis	8.00
CC	Christian Colon	15.00
CM	Casey McGrew	10.00
CW	Cody Wheeler	10.00
DP	Drew Pomeranz	20.00
GC	Gerrit Cole	15.00
KW	Kolten Wong	12.00
MC	Michael Choice	20.00
MN	Matt Newman	10.00
NP	Nick Pepitone	8.00
RH	Rick Hague	10.00
SG	Sonny Gray	15.00
TB	Trevor Bauer	12.00
TH	Tyler Holt	10.00
TW	T.J. Walz	10.00
TZ	Tony Zych	10.00
WO	Asher Wojciechowski	8.00
YG	Yasmani Grandal	30.00

National Team Jersey Autographs

Production 149 Sets
Green: No Pricing
Production 2 Sets
Red: No Pricing
Production 25 Sets

No.	Player	Price
AW	Andy Wilkins	15.00
BB	Bryce Brentz	30.00
BF	Blake Forsythe	10.00
BM	Brad Miller	10.00
CB	Chad Bettis	12.00
CC	Christian Colon	20.00
CM	Casey McGrew	15.00
CW	Cody Wheeler	15.00
DP	Drew Pomeranz	20.00
GC	Gerrit Cole	25.00
KW	Kolten Wong	20.00
MC	Michael Choice	25.00
MN	Matt Newman	10.00
NP	Nick Pepitone	12.00
RH	Rick Hague	10.00
SG	Sonny Gray	15.00
TB	Trevor Bauer	12.00
TH	Tyler Holt	15.00
TW	T.J. Walz	15.00
TZ	Tony Zych	15.00
WO	Asher Wojciechowski	10.00
YG	Yasmani Grandal	30.00

National Team Jerseys

Common Jersey: 5.00

No.	Player	Price
AW	Andy Wilkins	6.00
BB	Bryce Brentz	12.00
BF	Blake Forsythe	5.00
BM	Brad Miller	5.00
CB	Chad Bettis	5.00
CC	Christian Colon	8.00
CM	Casey McGrew	6.00
CW	Cody Wheeler	5.00
DP	Drew Pomeranz	8.00
GC	Gerrit Cole	10.00
KW	Kolten Wong	8.00
MC	Michael Choice	8.00
MN	Matt Newman	5.00
NP	Nick Pepitone	6.00
RH	Rick Hague	5.00
SG	Sonny Gray	5.00
TB	Trevor Bauer	5.00
TH	Tyler Holt	5.00
TW	T.J. Walz	5.00
TZ	Tony Zych	8.00
WO	Asher Wojciechowski	5.00
YG	Yasmani Grandal	10.00

National Team Patch Autographs

Production 35 Sets

No.	Player	Price
AW	Andy Wilkins	20.00
BB	Bryce Brentz	50.00
BF	Blake Forsythe	15.00
BM	Brad Miller	15.00

		NM/M
CB	Chad Bettis	20.00
CC	Christian Colon	40.00
CM	Casey McGrew	20.00
CW	Cody Wheeler	20.00
DP	Drew Pomeranz	35.00
GC	Gerrit Cole	40.00
KW	Kolten Wong	40.00
MC	Michael Choice	50.00
MN	Matt Newman	15.00
NP	Nick Pepitone	15.00
RH	Rick Hague	15.00
SG	Sonny Gray	
TB	Trevor Bauer	25.00
TH	Tyler Holt	25.00
TW	T.J. Walz	20.00
TZ	Tony Zych	
WO	Asher Wojciechowski	20.00
YG	Yasmani Grandal	60.00

National Team Q & A Autos
Production 65 Sets

AW	Asher Wojciechowski	15.00
BB	Bryce Brentz	25.00
BF	Blake Forsythe	15.00
CB	Chad Bettis	8.00
CC	Christian Colon	15.00
CM	Casey McGrew	20.00
CW	Cody Wheeler	20.00
DP	Drew Pomeranz	25.00
GC	Gerrit Cole	25.00
KW	Kolten Wong	20.00
MC	Michael Choice	20.00
MN	Matt Newman	10.00
NP	Nick Pepitone	10.00
RH	Rick Hague	10.00
SG	Sonny Gray	15.00
TB	Trevor Bauer	20.00
TH	Tyler Holt	12.00
TW	T.J. Walz	15.00
TZ	Tony Zych	15.00
WI	Andy Wilkins	12.00
YG	Yasmani Grandal	30.00

National Team Starting Lineup Autographs
No Pricing
Production 12 Sets

Patch Auto. Parallel
Production 99 Sets

61	Trevor Bauer	40.00
62	Christian Colon	40.00
63	Cody Wheeler	20.00
64	Chad Bettis	20.00
65	Bryce Brentz	40.00
66	Nick Pepitone	15.00
67	Michael Choice	40.00
68	Gerrit Cole	50.00
69	Sonny Gray	25.00
70	Tyler Holt	15.00
71	T.J. Walz	20.00
72	Rick Hague	20.00
73	Drew Pomeranz	25.00
74	Blake Forsythe	15.00
75	Matt Newman	15.00
76	Casey McGrew	25.00
77	Brad Miller	15.00
78	Yasmani Grandal	40.00
79	Kolten Wong	35.00
80	Tony Zych	20.00
81	Andy Wilkins	20.00
82	Asher Wojciechowski	25.00
83	Bryce Harper	450.00
85	Cody Buckel	15.00
86	Tony Wolters	20.00
89	A.J. Vanegas	25.00
90	Ladson Montgomery	20.00
91	Karsten Whitson	50.00
95	Connor Mason	30.00
96	Garin Cecchini	20.00
98	Jameson Taillon	75.00
100	Sean Coyle	30.00
105	Kevin Gausman	20.00
106	Robbie Ray	25.00
107	Nicky Delmonico	25.00
108	Cory Hahn	15.00
110	Nick Castellanos	40.00
113	Manny Machado	75.00
115	Phillip Pfeifer	20.00
116	Brian Ragira	20.00

1993 USA Rice

STEVE SAX

To promote rice consumption and raise money for the pictured athletes' favorite charities, the USA Rice Council issued this multi-sport card set and made it available by mail for a $2 donation. All players are pictured in civilian clothes with either a blue or red border around. Backs of most cards have rice recipes and indicate the charity to which the athlete is donating their portion of the proceeds. Cards are standard 2-1/2" x 3-1/2".

		NM/M
Complete Set (10):		10.00
Common Card:		.50
1	Steve Sax (Cooking)	1.00
2	Troy Aikman (Football)	3.00
3	Roger Clemens	7.50
4	Zina Garrison (Tennis)	.50
5	Warren Moon (Football)	2.00
6	Summer Sanders (Swimming)	.50
7	Steve Sax (Lifting weights.)	1.00
8	Brian Shimer (Bobsledder)	.50
9	Food Guide Pyramid	.25
10	Healthy Eating Tips	.25

1999 U.S. Cellular Milwaukee Brewers

The four Milwaukee Brewers who have had their uniform numbers retired by the team, plus Jackie Robinson, whose #42 was retired by MLB edict, are honored on this foldout promotion given to fans October 2 at County Stadium. Five 4" x 6" cards make up the panel, which is perforated between the cards for ease of separation. Cards have player action photos on front (color except for Robinson) on a muted blue-green stadium photo background. At lower-right is a gold-foil seal with the player's name and number. At top is a sponsor logo and part of the legend "COMMEMORATING GREATNESS" which runs contiguously across the panel. Backs have a black-and-white photo, career data and highlights.

		NM/M
Complete Set, Panel:		12.00
Complete Set, Singles (5):		8.00
Common Player:		1.00
4	Paul Molitor	4.00
19	Robin Yount	4.00
34	Rollie Fingers	1.00
42	Jackie Robinson	3.00
44	Hank Aaron	5.00

1993 U.S. Department of Transportation Safety Set

MO VAUGHN

This six-card set (issued in three-card panels) was sponsored by the U.S. Department of Transportation and distributed at the Little League World Series. Standard size cards have red and blue borders on front, along with the Little League logo. Backs are printed in red and blue and include a highway safety message and sponsors/licensors logos.

		NM/M
Complete Set (6):		11.00
Common Player:		1.50
	Panel 1	4.00
1	Orel Hershiser	.50
2	Don Mattingly	3.00
3	Mike Mussina	1.00
	Panel 2	6.00
(4)	Mike Piazza	2.50
(5)	Cal Ripken Jr.	4.00
(6)	Mo Vaughn	.50

1987 U.S. Forestry Service Smokey Bear's Team

The U.S. Forestry Service and Major League Baseball united in an effort to promote National Smokey the Bear Day. Two perforated sheets of baseball cards, one each for the American and National Leagues, were produced. The sheet of American Leaguers measures 18" x 24" and contains 16 full-color cards. The National League sheet measures 20" x 18" and contains 15 cards. Each individual card is 4" x 6" and contains a fire prevention tip on the back. An average number of 25,000 sets was sent to all teams.

		NM/M
Complete Set (31):		12.00
Complete A.L. Sheet:		7.00
Complete N.L. Sheet:		7.00
Common Player:		.25
1A	Jose Canseco	.75
1N	Steve Sax	.25
2A	Dennis "Oil Can" Boyd	.25
2Na	Dale Murphy (Shirttail out.)	.25
2Nb	Dale Murphy (Shirttail in.)	.90
3A	John Candelaria	.25
3Na	Jody Davis (Standing)	3.00
3Nb	Jody Davis (Kneeling)	.25
4A	Harold Baines	.25
4N	Bill Gullickson	.25
5A	Joe Carter	.25
5N	Mike Scott	.25
6A	Jack Morris	.25
6N	Roger McDowell	.25
7A	Buddy Biancalana	.25
7N	Steve Bedrosian	.25
8A	Kirby Puckett	3.00
8N	Johnny Ray	.25
9A	Mike Pagliarulo	.25
9N	Ozzie Smith	3.00
10A	Larry Sheets	.25
10N	Steve Garvey	.50
11A	Mike Moore	.25
11N	Smokey Bear Logo Card	.05
12A	Charlie Hough	.25
12N	Mike Krukow	.25
13A	Smokey Bear Logo Card	.05
13N	Smokey Bear	.05
14A	Tom Henke	.25
14N	Mike Fitzgerald	.25
15A	Jim Gantner	.25
15N	National League Logo Card	.05
16A	American League Logo Card	.05

1990 U.S. Playing Card All-Stars

Sold as a boxed set, these cards are the standard 2-1/2" x 3-1/2" format but feature rounded corners. Each card features a color player photo with the upper-left and lower-right corners inset to provide for playing card designations. A team logo appears in the lower-left corner. On American League players' cards (Clubs and Spades) the player's name and position appear in white in a blue box beneath the photo. On National Leaguers' cards (Hearts and Diamonds) the box is red and the printing black. Card backs are identical, with blue borders and a multi-colored "1990 Baseball Major League All-Stars" logo on a pinstriped white center panel. A premium version with the cards' edges silvered was also issued. These cards have a small diagonal "nip" at each rounded corner.

		NM/M
Complete Set (56):		5.00
Common Player:		.05
HEARTS		
J	Bobby Bonilla	.05
Q	Kevin Mitchell	.05
K	Darryl Strawberry	.05
A	Ramon Martinez	.05
2	Mike Scioscia	.05
3	Jeff Brantley	.05
4	Ryne Sandberg	.75
5	Chris Sabo	.05
6	Ozzie Smith	.75
7	John Franco	.05
8	Matt Williams	.05
9	Andre Dawson	.25
10	Benito Santiago	.05
CLUBS		
J	Wade Boggs	.75
Q	George Bell	.05
K	Rickey Henderson	.50
A	Bob Welch	.05
2	Lance Parrish	.05
3	Bret Saberhagen	.05
4	Gregg Olson	.05
5	Brook Jacoby	.05
6	Ozzie Guillen	.05
7	Ellis Burks	.05
8	Dennis Eckersley	.40
9	Bobby Thigpen	.05
10	Dave Stieb	.05
DIAMONDS		
J	Tony Gwynn	.75
Q	Will Clark	.05
K	Barry Bonds	1.50
A	Frank Viola	.05
2	Greg Olson	.05
3	Dennis Martinez	.05
4	Roberto Alomar	.20
5	Tim Wallach	.05
6	Barry Larkin	.05
7	Neal Heaton	.05
8	Dave Smith	.05
9	Lenny Dykstra	.05
10	Shawon Dunston	.05
SPADES		
J	Ken Griffey Jr.	1.00
Q	Dave Parker	.05
K	Cecil Fielder	.05
A	Roger Clemens	.85
2	Sandy Alomar	.05
3	Randy Johnson	.50
4	Steve Sax	.05
5	Kelly Gruber	.05
6	Chuck Finley	.05
7	Doug Jones	.05
8	Kirby Puckett	.75
9	Cal Ripken, Jr.	1.50
10	Alan Trammell	.05
WILD CARDS/JOKERS		
---	Jack Armstrong (Joker)	.05
---	Julio Franco (Joker)	.05
---	Rob Dibble, Randy Myers (Wild Card)	.05
---	Mark McGwire, Jose Canseco (Wild Card)	1.00

1991 U.S. Playing Card All-Stars

In standard 2-1/2" x 3-1/2" format, though with rounded corners, this 56-card set was produced by the country's leading maker of playing cards and sold as a boxed set. Fronts have a color player photo with the top-left and bottom-right corners inset to include playing card designations. A team logo appears in the upper-right corner. On American Leaguers' cards (Hearts and Diamonds), the player's name and position appear in white in a green stripe beneath the photo. National League players (Clubs and Spades) have a yellow stripe with black printing. Backs are red-bordered with a colorful "1991 Baseball Major League All-Stars" logo on a pinstriped white center panel. A silver-edged premium version was also issued. These cards have a diagonal "nip" at each rounded corner. A Canadian version, with the imprint of International Playing Card, also exists.

		NM/M
Complete Set (56):		4.00
Common Player:		.05
HEARTS		
J	Rickey Henderson	.50
Q	Roberto Alomar	.20
K	Dave Henderson	.05
A	Jack Morris	.05
2	Ozzie Guillen	.05
3	Jack McDowell	.05
4	Joe Carter	.05
5	Mark Langston	.05
6	Julio Franco	.05
7	Rick Aguilera	.05
8	Paul Molitor	.50
9	Ruben Sierra	.05
10	Roger Clemens	.85
CLUBS		
J	Andre Dawson	.25
Q	Chris Sabo	.05
K	Ivan Calderon	.05
A	Tony Gwynn	.75
2	Paul O'Neill	.05
3	John Smiley	.05
4	Howard Johnson	.05
5	Mike Morgan	.05
6	Barry Larkin	.05
7	Frank Viola	.05
8	Juan Samuel	.05
9	Craig Biggio	.05
10	Lee Smith	.05
DIAMONDS		
J	Sandy Alomar	.05
Q	Cecil Fielder	.05
K	Cal Ripken, Jr.	1.50
A	Ken Griffey Jr.	1.00
2	Carlton Fisk	.50
3	Scott Sanderson	.05
4	Kirby Puckett	.75
5	Jeff Reardon	.05
6	Rafael Palmeiro	.05
7	Bryan Harvey	.05
8	Jimmy Key	.05
9	Harold Baines	.05
10	Dennis Eckersley	.40
SPADES		
J	Benito Santiago	.05
Q	Ryne Sandberg	.75
K	Ozzie Smith	.75
A	Tom Glavine	.10
2	Eddie Murray	.60
3	Pete Harnisch	.05
4	John Kruk	.05
5	Tom Browning	.05
6	George Bell	.05
7	Dennis Martinez	.05
8	Brett Butler	.05
9	Terry Pendleton	.05
10	Rob Dibble	.05
WILD CARDS/JOKERS		
---	Bobby Bonilla (Joker)	.05
---	Danny Tartabull	.05
---	Wade Boggs (Wild Card)	.75
---	Will Clark (Wild Card)	.05

1992 U.S. Playing Card Aces

This 56-card boxed set features 13 top players in each of four major statistical categories, ranked by performance. Hearts feature RBI leaders, Clubs depict home run hitters, batting average leaders are featured on Diamonds and Spades have pitchers with lowest ERAs. Card fronts feature full-bleed color photos, with the playing card suit and rank overprinted in opposing corners. A team logo is in the lower-left, along with a black box containing the player's name and position in gold. Backs have a red, white and gold "Major League Baseball 1992

KEN GRIFFEY JR. OUTFIELD

PAUL MOLITOR • CF

JUAN GONZALES OUTFIELD

Aces" against a black background. The 2-1/2" x 3-1/2" cards have rounded corners.

		NM/M
Complete Set (56):		4.00
Common Player:		.05
HEARTS		
J	Will Clark	.05
Q	Howard Johnson	.05
K	Jose Canseco	.35
A	Cecil Fielder	.25
2	Juan Gonzalez	.25
3	Andre Dawson	.25
4	Ron Gant	.05
5	Fred McGriff	.05
6	Joe Carter	.05
7	Frank Thomas	.50
8	Cal Ripkin (Ripken)	1.50
9	Ruben Sierra	.05
10	Barry Bonds	1.50
CLUBS		
J	Cal Ripkin (Ripken)	1.50
Q	Howard Johnson	.05
K	Cecil Fielder	.05
A	Jose Canseco	.40
2	Chili Davis	.05
3	Mickey Tettleton	.05
4	Danny Tartabull	.05
5	Fred McGriff	.05
6	Andre Dawson	.25
7	Frank Thomas	.75
8	Ron Gant	.05
9	Cal Ripkin (Ripken)	1.50
10	Matt Williams	.05
DIAMONDS		
J	Ken Griffey Jr.	1.00
Q	Willie Randolph	.05
K	Wade Boggs	.75
A	Julio Franco	.05
2	Danny Tartabull	.05
3	Tony Gwynn	.75
4	Frank Thomas	.60
5	Hal Morris	.05
6	Kirby Puckett	.75
7	Terry Pendleton	.05
8	Rafael Palmeiro	.50
9	Cal Ripkin (Ripken)	1.50
10	Paul Molitor	.60
SPADES		
J	Tim Belcher	.05
Q	Tom Glavine	.15
K	Jose Rijo	.05
A	Dennis Martinez	.05
2	Mike Moore	.05
3	Nolan Ryan	1.50
4	Jim Abbott	.05
5	Bill Wegman	.05
6	Mike Morgan	.05
7	Jose DeLeon	.05
8	Pete Harnisch	.05
9	Tom Candiotti	.05
10	Roger Clemens	.85
JOKERS		
---	Roger Clemens (Joker)	.85
---	Tom Glavine (Joker)	.15
---	Home Run Rummy Game	
	Instructions	.05
---	Header Card	.05

All-Stars

IVAN RODRIGUEZ • C

Players from the 1992 All-Star Game are featured in this set of 56 playing cards. In playing card format of 2-1/2" x 3-1/2" with rounded corners, the cards have a photo on front with a team logo in the upper-right corner. Traditional playing card suits and values are in the upper-left and lower-right corners.

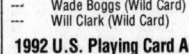

Player names are in a yellow (American League) or red (National League) box beneath the photo. Backs have a large product logo on a white background with a dark blue-green border. Appropriate licensor and manufacturer logos appear at bottom. The set was sold in a box featuring miniature representations of some of the cards.

		NM/M
Complete Set (56):		5.00
Common Player:		.05
AC	Roberto Alomar	.20
2C	Joe Carter	.05
3C	Juan Guzman	.05
4C	Charles Nagy	.05
5C	Robin Ventura	.05
6C	Chuck Knoblauch	.05
7C	Ruben Sierra	.05
8C	Paul Molitor	.60
9C	Carlos Baerga	.05
10C	Edgar Martinez	.05
JC	Sandy Alomar Jr.	.05
QC	Mark McGwire	1.25
KC	Wade Boggs	.75
AS	Ken Griffey Jr.	1.00
2S	Ivan Rodriguez	.50
3S	Roberto Kelly	.05
4S	Brady Anderson	.05
5S	Travis Fryman	.05
6S	Jeff Montgomery	.05
7S	Jack McDowell	.05
8S	Rick Aguilera	.05
9S	Kevin Brown	.05
10S	Roger Clemens	.85
JS	Jose Canseco	.35
QS	Cal Ripken Jr.	1.50
KS	Kirby Puckett	.75
AH	Andy Van Slyke	.05
2H	Greg Maddux	.75
3H	Larry Walker	.05
4H	Tom Pagnozzi	.05
5H	David Cone	.05
6H	Tony Fernandez	.05
7H	Will Clark	.05
8H	Gary Sheffield	.30
9H	Mike Sharperson	.05
10H	John Kruk	.05
JH	Ryne Sandberg	.75
QH	Ozzie Smith	.75
KH	Fred McGriff	.05
AD	Tony Gwynn	.75
2D	Bob Tewksbury	.05
3D	Ron Gant	.05
4D	Doug Jones	.05
5D	Craig Biggio	.05
6D	Bip Roberts	.05
7D	Norm Charlton	.05
8D	John Smoltz	.05
9D	Lee Smith	.05
10D	Tom Glavine	.25
JD	Benito Santiago	.05
QD	Terry Pendleton	.05
KD	Barry Bonds	1.50
WILD	Dennis Eckersley	.50
JOKER	Mike Mussina, Mark Langston	.15
JOKER	Darren Daulton, Dennis Martinez	.05
---	Advertising Card	.05

Team Sets

Besides two All-Star sets, the U.S. Playing Card Co. in 1992 issued playing card team sets for five teams. All were issued as 56-card boxed sets in a similar format. Cards are 2-1/2" x3-1/2" with rounded corners. Fronts feature player photos with insets at the upper-left and lower-right corners displaying card suit designations and rankings. The player's name and position appear in a colored strip beneath the photo. Backs feature a large color team logo set on a gray background with either dark blue or red pinstriping and heavy vertical side bars. A silver-edged World Series premium version of the Braves and Twins sets were also issued; on these cards each corner had a diagonal "nip."

Atlanta Braves

STEVE AVERY ★ P

Complete Set (56):		5.00
Common Player:		.05
HEARTS		
J	Dave Justice	.10
Q	Juan Berenguer	.10
K	Ron Gant	.10
A	Otis Nixon	.10
2	Deion Sanders	.20
3	Mike Stanton	.10
4	Sid Bream	.10
5	Armando Reynoso	.10
6	Brian Hunter	.10
7	Kent Mercker	.10
8	Lonnie Smith	.10
9	Jeff Treadway	.10
10	Tom Glavine	.35
CLUBS		
J	Pete Smith	.10
Q	Jeff Blauser	.10
K	Charlie Leibrandt	.10
A	Terry Pendleton	.10
2	Mark Lemke	.10
3	Armando Reynoso	.10
4	Kent Mercker	.10
5	Marvin Freeman	.10
6	Rico Rossy	.10
7	Dave Justice	.10
8	Juan Berenguer	.10
9	Ron Gant	.10
10	Otis Nixon	.10
DIAMONDS		
J	Brian Hunter	.10
Q	Rafael Belliard	.10
K	Greg Olson	.10
A	Steve Avery	.10
2	Marvin Freeman	.10
3	Pete Smith	.10
4	Mike Heath	.10
5	Jeff Blauser	.10
6	Jim Clancy	.10
7	Rico Rossy	.10
8	John Smoltz	.10
9	Charlie Leibrandt	.10
10	Terry Pendleton	.10
SPADES		
J	John Smoltz	.10
Q	Lonnie Smith	.10
K	Jeff Treadway	.10
A	Tom Glavine	.35
2	Jim Clancy	.10
3	Deion Sanders	.20
4	Mark Lemke	.10
5	Mike Heath	.10
6	Mike Stanton	.10
7	Sid Bream	.10
8	Rafael Belliard	.10
9	Greg Olson	.10
10	Steve Avery	.10
JOKERS		
---	N.L. Logo (Joker)	.05
---	N.L. Logo (Joker)	.05
---	'92 Braves Home Schedule	.05
---	Atlanta Braves History	.05

World Series - Braves

		NM/M
Complete Set (56):		5.00
Common Player:		.05
AC	Charlie Leibrandt	.10
2C	Vinny Castilla	.10
3C	Alejandro Pena	.10
4C	Mark Lemke	.10
5C	Marvin Freeman	.10
6C	Dave Justice	.10
7C	Mike Stanton	.10
8C	Terry Pendleton	.10
9C	Jeff Treadway	.10
10C	Brian Hunter	.10
JC	Steve Avery	.10
QC	Jeff Blauser	.10
KC	Ron Gant	.10
AS	Terry Pendleton	.10
2S	Ryan Klesko	.10
3S	Jeff Treadway	.10
4S	Pete Smith	.10
5S	Ron Gant	.10
6S	Sid Bream	.10
7S	Deion Sanders	.15
8S	Tom Glavine	.35
9S	Kent Mercker	.10
10S	Lonnie Smith	.10
JS	Damon Berryhill	.10
QS	Marvin Freeman	.10
KS	John Smoltz	.10
AH	Dave Justice	.10
2H	Kent Mercker	.10
3H	Lonnie Smith	.10
4H	Greg Olson	.10
5H	Jeff Reardon	.10
6H	Steve Avery	.10
7H	Otis Nixon	.10
8H	Juan Berenguer	.10
9H	Greg Olson	.10
10H	Mike Bielecki	.10
JH	Mike Stanton	.10
QH	Deion Sanders	.15
KH	Pete Smith	.10
AD	Otis Nixon	.10
2D	Juan Berenguer	.10
3D	Francisco Cabrera	.10
4D	Damon Berryhill	.10
5D	Brian Hunter	.10
6D	Charlie Leibrandt	.10
7D	Jeff Blauser	.10
8D	John Smoltz	.10
9D	Alejandro Pena	.10
10D	Mark Lemke	.10
JD	Jeff Reardon	.10
QD	Sid Bream	.10
KD	Tom Glavine	.35
WILD	Mike Bielecki	.10
WILD	David Nied	.10
WILD	Mark Wohlers	.10
JOKER	Checklist	.05

Boston Red Sox

		NM/M
Complete Set (56):		5.00
Common Player:		.10
HEARTS		
J	Jack Clark	.10
Q	Jeff Gray	.10
K	Greg Harris	.10
A	Roger Clemens	1.00
2	Matt Young	.10
3	John Marzano	.10
4	Dennis Lamp	.10
5	Danny Darwin	.10
6	Jeff Reardon	.10
7	Phil Plantier	.10
8	Tony Fossas	.10
9	Carlos Quintana	.10
10	Wade Boggs	.75
CLUBS		
J	Luis Rivera	.10
Q	John Marzano	.10
K	Jody Reed	.10
A	Mike Greenwell	.10
2	Danny Darwin	.10
3	Dan Petry	.10
4	Dana Kiecker	.10
5	Greg Harris	.10
6	Tony Pena	.10
7	Dan Petry	.10
8	Jeff Gray	.10
9	Jack Clark	.10
10	Roger Clemens	1.00
DIAMONDS		
J	Tom Brunansky	.10
Q	Mo Vaughn	.25
K	Ellis Burks	.10
A	Joe Hesketh	.10
2	Steve Lyons	.10
3	Dana Kiecker	.10
4	Tony Fossas	.10
5	Matt Young	.10
6	Luis Rivera	.10
7	Tom Bolton	.10
8	Kevin Morton	.10
9	Jody Reed	.10
10	Mike Greenwell	.10
SPADES		
J	Tony Pena	.10
Q	Phil Plantier	.10
K	Carlos Quintana	.10
A	Wade Boggs	.75
2	Tom Bolton	.10
3	Mo Vaughn	.25
4	Kevin Morton	.10
5	Steve Lyons	.10
6	Tom Brunansky	.10
7	Dennis Lamp	.10
8	Joe Hesketh	.10
9	Ellis Burks	.10
10	Jeff Reardon	.10
JOKERS		
---	A.L. Logo (Joker)	.10
---	A.L. Logo (Joker) (Joker)	.10
---	'92 Red Sox Home Schedule	.10
---	Boston Red Sox Team History	.10

Chicago Cubs

GREG MADDUX ★ P

		NM/M
Complete Set (56):		5.00
Common Player:		.10
HEARTS		
J	Jerome Walton	.10
Q	Chico Walker	.10
K	Chuck McElroy	.10
A	Andre Dawson	.30
2	Dwight Smith	.10
3	Rick Wilkins	.10
4	Doug Dascenzo	.10
5	Bob Scanlan	.10
6	Chico Walker	.10
7	Paul Assenmacher	.10
8	Mark Grace	.25
9	Ryne Sandberg	1.00
10	Danny Jackson	.10
CLUBS		
J	Hector Villanueva	.10
Q	Doug Dascenzo	.10
K	Shawon Dunston	.10
A	George Bell	.10
2	Greg Scott	.10
3	Jose Vizcaino	.10
4	Heathcliff Slocumb	.10
5	Danny Jackson	.10
6	Shawn Boskie	.10
7	Luis Salazar	.10
8	Chuck McElroy	.10
9	Andre Dawson	.30
10	Dave Smith	.10
DIAMONDS		
J	Frank Castillo	.10
Q	Les Lancaster	.10
K	Paul Assenmacher	.10
A	Greg Maddux	1.00
2	Shawn Boskie	.10
3	Ced Landrum	.10
4	Gary Scott	.10
5	Ced Landrum	.10
6	Jose Vizcaino	.10
7	Mike Harkey	.10
8	Jerome Walton	.10
9	George Bell	.10
10	Frank Castillo	.10
SPADES		
J	Bob Scanlan	.10
Q	Luis Salazar	.10
K	Mark Grace	.25
A	Ryne Sandberg	1.00
2	Frank Castillo	.10
3	Mike Harkey	.10
4	Dave Smith	.10
5	Les Lancaster	.10
6	Hector Villanueva	.10
7	Shawon Dunston	.10
8	Heathcliff Slocumb	.10
9	Greg Maddux	1.00
10	Dwight Smith	.10
JOKERS		
---	N.L. logo (Joker)	.10
---	N.L. logo (Joker)	.10
---	'92 Cubs Home Schedule	.10
---	Chicago Cubs Team History	.10

Detroit Tigers

		NM/M
Complete Set (56):		5.00
Common Player:		.10
HEARTS		
J	Lloyd Moseby	.10
Q	Walt Terrell	.10
K	Mickey Tettleton	.10
A	Cecil Fielder	.10
2	Andy Allanson	.10
3	Dave Bergman	.10
4	Steve Searcy	.10
5	Dan Galeker	.10
6	Jerry Don Gleaton	.10
7	Paul Gibson	.10
8	Alan Trammell	.25
9	Frank Tanana	.10
10	John Cerutti	.10
CLUBS		
J	Rob Deer	.10
Q	Skeeter Barnes	.10
K	Pete Incaviglia	.10
A	Tony Phillips	.10
2	Dan Galeker	.10
3	Walt Terrell	.10
4	David Haas	.10
5	Pete Incaviglia	.10
6	Travis Fryman	.10
7	Scott Aldred	.10
8	Skeeter Barnes	.10
9	Mickey Tettleton	.10
10	Cecil Fielder	.10
DIAMONDS		
J	Milt Cuyler	.10
Q	Travis Fryman	.10
K	Lou Whitaker	.10
A	Bill Gullickson	.10
2	John Cerutti	.10
3	Steve Searcy	.10
4	David Haas	.10
5	Lloyd Moseby	.10
6	Scott Livingstone	.10
7	John Shelby	.10
8	Mike Henneman	.10
9	Dave Bergman	.10
10	Tony Phillips	.10
SPADES		
J	Alan Trammell	.25
Q	Jerry Don Gleaton	.10
K	Mike Henneman	.10
A	Frank Tanana	.10
2	Scott Aldred	.10
3	Scott Livingstone	.10
4	John Shelby	.10
5	Rob Deer	.10
6	Milt Cuyler	.10
7	Andy Allanson	.10
8	Paul Gibson	.10
9	Lou Whitaker	.10
10	Bill Gullickson	.10
JOKERS		
---	A.L. Logo (Joker)	.10
---	A.L. Logo (Joker)	.10
---	'92 Tigers Home Schedule	.10
---	Detroit Tigers Team History	.10

Minnesota Twins

		NM/M
Complete Set (56):		5.00
Common Player:		.10
HEARTS		
J	Scott Leius	.10
Q	Rick Aguilera	.10
K	Jack Morris	.10
A	Kirby Puckett	.75
2	Junior Ortiz	.10
3	Paul Abbott	.10
4	Steve Bedrosian	.10
5	Pedro Munoz	.10
6	Mike Pagliarulo	.10
7	Greg Gagne	.10
8	Chuck Knoblauch	.10
9	Kevin Tapani	.10
10	Scott Erickson	.10
CLUBS		
J	Carl Willis	.10
Q	Dan Gladden	.10
K	Kent Hrbek	.10
A	Shane Mack	.10
2	Allan Anderson	.10
3	Al Newman	.10
4	Junior Ortiz	.10
5	Mike Pagliarulo	.10
6	Terry Leach	.10
7	Scott Leius	.10
8	Rick Aguilera	.10
9	Jack Morris	.10
10	Kirby Puckett	.75
DIAMONDS		
J	Gene Larkin	.10
Q	Randy Bush	.10
K	Chili Davis	.10
A	Brian Harper	.10
2	Al Newman	.10
3	Allan Anderson	.10
4	David West	.10
5	Terry Leach	.10
6	Mark Guthrie	.10
7	Carl Willis	.10
8	Dan Gladden	.10
9	Kent Hrbek	.10
10	Shane Mack	.10
SPADES		
J	Greg Gagne	.10
Q	Chuck Knoblauch	.10
K	Kevin Tapani	.10
A	Scott Erickson	.10
2	Paul Abbott	.10
3	David West	.10
4	Steve Bedrosian	.10
5	Mark Guthrie	.10
6	Pedro Munoz	.10
7	Gene Larkin	.10
8	Randy Bush	.10
9	Chili Davis	.10
10	Brian Harper	.10
JOKERS		
---	A.L. Logo (Joker)	.10
---	A.L. Logo (Joker)	.10
---	'92 Twins Home Schedule	.10
---	Minnesota Twins Team History	.10

1993 U.S. Playing Card Aces

ROGER CLEMENS PITCHER

Major league superstars with the top 1992 statistical performance in four major categories are featured in this set of playing cards. Spades feature the 13 lowest ERAs; Hearts depict the baker's dozen stolen base leaders; the 13 players with highest home run totals and batting average are featured on clubs and diamonds, respectively. The 2-1/2" x 3-1/2" cards have rounded corners and traditional trading card suits and values in the upper-left and lower-right corners. Borderless color player photos are featured on front, with color team logos at lower-left. Player names and positions are printed in a black box at bottom. Backs have a red background with a large product logo and smaller licensor and manufacturer logos at bottom. The box in which the cards were sold is enhanced with gold foil and features miniature representations of some of the cards.

		NM/M
Complete Set (56):		4.00
Common Player:		.05
AC	Juan Gonzalez	.15
2C	Dave Hollins	.05
3C	Darren Daulton	.05
4C	Ken Griffey Jr.	.75
5C	Rob Deer	.05
6C	Mickey Tettleton	.05
7C	Gary Sheffield	.25
8C	Joe Carter	.05
9C	Albert Belle	.05
10C	Barry Bonds	1.50
JC	Fred McGriff	.05
QC	Cecil Fielder	.05
KC	Mark McGwire	1.00
AS	Bill Swift	.05
2S	Tom Glavine	.35
3S	Sid Fernandez	.05
4S	Greg Swindell	.05
5S	Juan Guzman	.05
6S	Jose Rijo	.05
7S	Mike Morgan	.05
8S	Mike Mussina	.35
9S	Dennis Martinez	.05
10S	Kevin Appier	.05
JS	Roger Clemens	.65
QS	Curt Schilling	.35
KS	Greg Maddux	.60
AH	Marquis Grissom	.05
2H	Chad Curtis	.05
3H	Ozzie Smith	.60
4H	Bip Roberts	.05
5H	Steve Finley	.05
6H	Tim Raines	.05
7H	Delino DeShields	.05
8H	Rickey Henderson	.50
9H	Roberto Alomar	.10
10H	Luis Polonia	.05
JH	Brady Anderson	.05
QH	Pat Listach	.05
KH	Kenny Lofton	.05
AD	Edgar Martinez	.05
2D	Roberto Alomar	.05
3D	Terry Pendleton	.05
4D	Carlos Baerga	.05
5D	Shane Mack	.05
6D	Tony Gwynn	.60
7D	Paul Molitor	.50
8D	Frank Thomas	.50
9D	Bip Roberts	.05
10D	John Kruk	.05
JD	Andy Van Slyke	.05
QD	Kirby Puckett	.60
KD	Gary Sheffield	.25
WILD	Cal Ripken Jr.	1.50
JOKER	National League Logo	.05
JOKER	American League Logo	.05
---	Advertising Card	.05

1992 Rookies

ERIC KARROS NL • ROOKIE OF THE YEAR

Top rookies of the 1992 season are featured in full-color on the fronts of these playing cards. Player name and position are printed in white in a green stripe beneath the photo. A team logo is in the upper-right corner. Backs are printed in dark green with gold pinstripes and a large gold, red and purple logo.

		NM/M
Complete Boxed Set (56):		4.00
Common Player:		.10
AC	Kenny Lofton	.10
2C	Eric Fox	.10
3C	Mark Wohlers	.10
4C	John Patterson	.10
5C	Eric Young	.10
6C	Arthur Rhodes	.10
7C	Jeff Frye	.10
8C	Scott Servais	.10
9C	Ruben Amaro Jr.	.10
10C	Reggie Sanders	.10
JC	Alan Mills	.10
QC	Bob Zupcic	.10
KC	Cal Eldred	.10
AS	Eric Karros	.10
2S	Butch Henry	.10
3S	Wil Cordero	.10
4S	Pedro Astacio	.10
5S	Derek Bell	.10
6S	David Nied	.10
7S	Jeff Kent	.35
8S	David Haas	.10
9S	Ed Taubensee	.10
10S	Royce Clayton	.10
JS	Moises Alou	.10
QS	Rusty Meacham	.10
KS	Chad Curtis	.10
AH	Pat Listach	.10

Card	Player	NM/M
2H	Pat Mahomes	.10
4H	Greg Colbrunn	.10
3H	Dan Walters	.10
5H	John Vander Wal	.10
4H	Jeff Branson	.10
7H	Monty Fariss	.10
2H	Rey Sanchez	.10
9H	Robert Wickman	.10
10H	Derrick May	.10
8H	Donovan Osborne	.10
QH	Scott Livingstone	.10
9C	Gary DiSarcina	.10
AD	Dave Fleming	.10
2D	Reggie Jefferson	.10
3D	Anthony Young	.10
4D	Kevin Koslofski	.10
5D	Brian Williams	.10
6D	Brian Jordan	.10
7D	John Doherty	.10
8D	Lenny Webster	.10
9D	Roberto Hernandez	.10
10D	Frank Seminara	.10
JD	Scott Cooper	.10
QD	Andy Stankiewicz	.10
KD	Tim Wakefield	.10
JOKER	Eric Karros (N.L. ROY)	.10
JOKER	Pat Listach (A.L. ROY)	.10
---	Rookie Qualification Rules	.10
---	Checklist	.10

Team Sets

For a second year the leading U.S. manufacturer of playing cards produced several team sets depicting ballplayers. Each was sold as a 56-card set in standard 2-1/2" x 3-1/2" round-corner playing card format in a colorful flip-top box. Backs of each team set carry a team logo. Fronts have portrait or action photo and playing card suits and values. Most players are represented twice in each team set in different photos.

Cincinnati Reds

Card	Player	NM/M
Complete Set (56):		4.00
Common Player:		.10
AC	Tim Belcher	.10
2C	Jacob Brumfield	.10
3C	Rob Dibble	.10
4C	Jose Rijo	.10
5C	Dan Wilson	.10
6C	Cecil Espy	.10
7C	Tom Browning	.10
8C	Steve Foster	.10
9C	Jacob Brumfield	.10
10C	Jeff Branson	.10
JC	Greg Cadaret	.10
QC	Hal Morris	.10
KC	Joe Oliver	.10
AS	Bip Roberts	.10
2S	Cesar Hernandez	.10
3S	Chris Hammond	.10
4S	Scott Ruskin	.10
5S	John Smiley	.10
6S	Roberto Kelly	.10
7S	Barry Larkin	.25
8S	Gary Varsho	.10
9S	Hal Morris	.10
10S	Dwayne Henry	.10
JS	Tommy Gregg	.10
QS	Kevin Mitchell	.10
KS	Rob Dibble	.10
AH	Barry Larkin	.25
2H	Willie Greene	.10
3H	Steve Foster	.10
4H	Greg Cadaret	.10
5H	Chris Sabo	.10
6H	Joe Oliver	.10
7H	Milton Hill	.10
8H	Tim Belcher	.10
9H	Scott Ruskin	.10
10H	Cecil Espy	.10
JH	Roberto Kelly	.10
QH	Tom Browning	.10
KH	Reggie Sanders	.10
AD	Jose Rijo	.10
2D	Dwayne Henry	.10
3D	Jeff Branson	.10
4D	Milton Hill	.10
5D	Tim Costo	.10
6D	Bip Roberts	.10
7D	Kevin Mitchell	.10
8D	Tim Pugh	.10
9D	Reggie Sanders	.10
10D	Chris Hammond	.10
JD	Gary Varsho	.10
QD	John Smiley	.10
KD	Chris Sabo	.10
WILD	Tony Perez	.50
JOKER	Riverfront Stadium	.10
---	Reds Schedule	.10
---	Checklist	.10

Colorado Rockies

Card	Player	NM/M
Complete Set (56):		4.00
Common Player:		.10
AC	Jim Tatum	.10
2C	Charlie Hayes	.10
3C	Dale Murphy	.50
4C	Scott Aldred	.10
5C	Braulio Castillo	.10
6C	Danny Sheaffer	.10
7C	Jerald Clark	.10
8C	Willie Blair	.10
9C	Daryl Boston	.10
10C	Andy Ashby	.10
JC	Butch Henry	.10
QC	Alex Cole	.10
KC	Vinny Castilla	.10
AS	David Nied	.10
2S	Andres Galarraga	.10
3S	Gary Wayne	.10
4S	Freddie Benavides	.10
5S	Butch Henry	.10
6S	Gerald Young	.10
7S	Jeff Parrett	.10
8S	Braulio Castillo	.10
9S	Darren Holmes	.10
10S	Dale Murphy	.50
JS	Eric Young	.10
QS	Bruce Ruffin	.10
KS	Joe Girardi	.10
AH	Charlie Hayes	.10
2H	Jim Tatum	.10
3H	Andy Ashby	.10
4H	Vinny Castilla	.10
5H	Steve Reed	.10
6H	Daryl Boston	.10
7H	Alex Cole	.10
8H	Bryn Smith	.10
9H	Danny Sheaffer	.10
10H	Willie Blair	.10
JH	Dante Bichette	.10
QH	Jerald Clark	.10
DH	Scott Aldred	.10
AD	Andres Galarraga	.10
2D	David Nied	.10
3D	Dante Bichette	.10
4D	Joe Girardi	.10
5D	Bryn Smith	.10
6D	Darren Holmes	.10
7D	Bruce Ruffin	.10
8D	Eric Young	.10
9D	Gerald Young	.10
10D	Gary Wayne	.10
JD	Steve Reed	.10
QD	Jeff Parrett	.10
KD	Freddie Benavides	.10

Florida Marlins

Card	Player	NM/M
Complete Set (56):		4.00
Common Player:		.10
AC	Walt Weiss	.10
2C	Dave Magadan	.10
3C	Chris Carpenter	.10
4C	Dave Magadan	.10
5C	Bob McClure	.10
6C	Junior Felix	.10
7C	Walt Weiss	.10
8C	Steve Decker	.10
9C	Jeff Conine	.15
10C	Bryan Harvey	.10
JC	Orestes Destrade	.10
QC	Chris Hammond	.10
KC	Monty Fariss	.10
AS	Alex Arias	.10
2S	Benito Santiago	.10
3S	Ryan Bowen	.10
4S	Steve Decker	.10
5S	Jeff Conine	.15
6S	Bret Barberie	.10
7S	Orestes Destrade	.10
8S	Greg Briley	.10
9S	Charlie Hough	.10
10S	Bob Natal	.10
JS	Jack Armstrong	.10
QS	Junior Felix	.10
KS	Richie Lewis	.10
AH	Benito Santiago	.10
2H	Walt Weiss	.10
4H	Monty Fariss	.10
3H	Chris Hammond	.10
5H	Joe Klink	.10
6H	Chuck Carr	.10
7H	Alex Arias	.10
8H	Charlie Hough	.10
9H	Junior Felix	.10
10H	Jim Corsi	.10
JH	Jeff Conine	.15
QH	Trevor Hoffman	.10
KH	Rich Renteria	.10
AD	Dave Magadan	.10
2D	Jack Armstrong	.10
3D	Bryan Harvey	.10
4D	Richie Lewis	.10
5D	Scott Pose	.10
6D	Rich Renteria	.10
7D	Trevor Hoffman	.10
8D	Jim Corsi	.10
9D	Ryan Bowen	.10
10D	Orestes Destrade	.10
JD	Bret Barberie	.10
QD	Chuck Carr	.10
KD	Chris Carpenter	.10
JOKER	N.L. Logo	.10
JOKER	N.L. Logo	.10
---	Opening Day Roster	.10
---	Marlins Schedule	.10

1994 U.S. Playing Card Aces

Statistical leaders from the 1993 season are featured in this deck of playing cards. Pitchers with the lowest ERAs are shown on the spades; stolen base leaders are featured on the hearts; home run hitters are depicted on the clubs, and diamonds host the batting average leaders. Cards are 2-1/2" x 3-1/2" with rounded corners. Fronts have full-bleed photos with the suit and value of the playing card in the upper-left and lower-right corners. The player's name, position and team logo are at lower-left. Backs are printed in dark blue with vertical silver stripes at each side and a red, white and blue "Baseball Aces" logo at top. Licensing logos appear at the bottom. Besides the 52 player cards in the boxed set, there is a checklist card, A.L. and N.L. logo cards and a U.S. Playing Card Co. advertising card.

Card	Player	NM/M
Complete Set (56):		6.00
Common Oliver:		.10
AC	Barry Bonds	1.50
2C	Phil Plantier	.10
3C	Bobby Bonilla	.10
4C	Mike Piazza	1.00
5C	Ron Gant	.10
6C	Rafael Palmeiro	.50
7C	Fred McGriff	.10
8C	Matt Williams	.10
9C	Albert Belle	.10
10C	Dave Justice	.10
JC	Frank Thomas	.60
QC	Ken Griffey Jr.	1.00
KC	Juan Gonzalez	.30
AS	Greg Maddux	.75
2S	Tom Candiotti	.10
3S	Jimmy Key	.10
4S	Jack McDowell	.10
5S	John Burkett	.10
6S	Tom Glavine	.25
7S	Pete Harnisch	.10
8S	Wilson Alvarez	.10
9S	Bill Swift	.10
10S	Bill Swift	.10
JS	Mark Portugal	.10
QS	Kevin Appier	.10
KS	Jose Rijo	.10
AH	Kenny Lofton	.10
2H	Brett Butler	.10
3H	Eric Young	.10
4H	Delino DeShields	.10
5H	Darren Lewis	.10
6H	Gregg Jefferies	.10
7H	Otis Nixon	.10
8H	Chad Curtis	.10
9H	Rickey Henderson	.60
10H	Marquis Grissom	.10
JH	Luis Polonia	.10
QH	Roberto Alomar	.20
KH	Chuck Carr	.10
AD	Andres Galarraga	.10
2D	John Kruk	.10
3D	Frank Thomas	.60
4D	Mike Piazza	1.00
5D	Jeff Bagwell	.60
6D	Carlos Baerga	.10
7D	Mark Grace	.10
8D	Kenny Lofton	.10
9D	Roberto Alomar	.20
10D	Paul Molitor	.10
JD	Barry Bonds	1.50
QD	Gregg Jefferies	.10
KD	John Olerud	.10
Joker	National League Logo	.05
Joker	American League Logo	.05
---	Checklist	.05
---	Advertising Card	.05

Atlanta Braves

The most popular Braves are pictured on up to three of the cards in this deck. In 2-1/2" x 3-1/2" round-cornered format, the large color photos on the card fronts have their upper-left and lower-right corners clipped to display traditional playing card suits and values. The player name and position are printed in black in a gold strip below the photo. Backs have the Braves logo on a dark blue background with red stripes on the left and right edges. Brand and licensor logos are at bottom. The cards were sold in a colorful box.

Card	Player	NM/M
Complete Set (56):		4.00
Common Player:		.10
AC	Ron Gant	.10
2C	Chipper Jones	1.00
3C	Terry Pendleton	.10
4C	Mark Wohlers	.10
5C	Pedro Borbon	.10
6C	Steve Avery	.10
7C	Deion Sanders	.15
8C	Dave Justice	.10
9C	Dave Gallagher	.10
10C	Rafael Belliard	.10
JC	Greg McMichael	.10
QC	John Smoltz	.10
KC	Fred McGriff	.60
AS	Jeff Blauser	.10
2S	Mike Stanton	.10
3S	Ryan Klesko	.10
4S	Mike Potts	.10
5S	Charlie O'Brien	.10
6S	Steve Bedrosian	.10
7S	Javier Lopez	.10
8S	Greg Maddux	.75
9S	Deion Sanders	.15
10S	Ramon Caraballo	.10
JS	Kent Mercker	.10
QS	Mark Wohlers	.10
KS	Tom Glavine	.25
AH	Dave Justice	.10
2H	Mark Lemke	.10
3H	Javier Lopez	.10
4H	Rafael Belliard	.10
5H	Bill Pecota	.10
6H	Tom Glavine	.25
7H	Milt Hill	.10
8H	Jeff Blauser	.10
9H	Ryan Klesko	.10
10H	Terry Pendleton	.10
JH	Mike Stanton	.10
QH	Steve Avery	.10
KH	Deion Sanders	.15
AD	Greg Maddux	.75
2D	Ron Gant	.10
3D	Kent Mercker	.10
4D	Greg McMichael	.10
5D	Tony Tarasco	.10
6D	John Smoltz	.10
7D	Fred McGriff	.10
8D	Ron Gant	.10
9D	Mike Kelly	.10
10D	Steve Bedrosian	.10
JD	Bill Pecota	.10
QD	Mark Lemke	.10
KD	Terry Pendleton	.10
Joker	Atlanta Braves Logo	.10
Joker	National League Logo	.10
---	'94 Braves Home Schedule	.10

Baltimore Orioles

The 1994 Baltimore Orioles are featured in this deck of playing cards. Color photos of the players have clipped corners to display traditional playing card suits and values in the upper-left and lower-right corners. Beneath the photo is an orange strip with the player's name and position in white. Backs have a large Orioles logo on a pinstriped background. Company and licensor logos are at the bottom. Cards measure 2-1/2" x 3-1/2" with rounded corners. The set was sold in a colorful cardboard box.

Card	Player	NM/M
Complete Set (56):		4.00
Common Player:		.10
AC	Chris Hoiles	.10
2C	Mike Cook	.10
3C	Paul Carey	.10
4C	Jeff Tackett	.10
5C	Arthur Rhodes	.10
6C	Damon Buford	.10
7C	David Segui	.10
8C	Ben McDonald	.10
9C	Cal Ripken Jr.	1.00
10C	Brad Pennington	.10
JC	Jack Voigt	.10
QC	Jeffrey Hammonds	.10
KC	Rafael Palmeiro	.60
AS	Mark McLemore	.10
2S	Manny Alexander	.10
3S	Kevin McGehee	.10
4S	Jim Poole	.10
5S	Leo Gomez	.10
6S	Tim Hulett	.10
7S	Mike Devereaux	.10
8S	Brady Anderson	.10
9S	Mike Mussina	.40
10S	Sherman Obando	.10
JS	Alan Mills	.10
QS	Jamie Moyer	.10
KS	Harold Baines	.10
AH	Cal Ripken Jr.	1.00
2H	Harold Baines	.10
3H	John O'Donoghue	.10
4H	Sid Fernandez	.10
5H	Alan Mills	.10
6H	Jamie Moyer	.10
7H	Harold Baines	.10
8H	Mark McLemore	.10
9H	Jeff Tackett	.10
10H	Arthur Rhodes	.10
JH	Damon Buford	.10
QH	David Segui	.10
KH	Ben McDonald	.10
AD	Mike Mussina	.40
2D	Mike Oquist	.10
3D	Brad Pennington	.10
4D	Jeffrey Hammonds	.10
5D	Jack Voigt	.10
6D	Chris Sabo	.10
7D	Rafael Palmeiro	.60
8D	Chris Hoiles	.10
9D	Jim Poole	.10
10D	Leo Gomez	.10
JD	Tim Hulett	.10
QD	Mike Devereaux	.10
KD	Brady Anderson	.10
Joker	Baltimore Orioles Logo	.10
Joker	American League Logo	.10
---	Checklist	.10
---	'94 Orioles Home Schedule	.10

Philadelphia Phillies

Veterans and rookies on the roster of the '94 Phils are featured in this deck of playing cards; the most popular players appear on up to three cards each. In standard 2-1/2" x 3-1/2" round-cornered format, the large color photos have their top-left and bottom-right corners clipped to display traditional

playing card suits and values. The player's name and position are printed in black on a red strip beneath the photo. Backs have a large Phillies logo on a gray pinstriped background. Company and licensor logos are at bottom. The cards were sold in a decorative box.

Card	Player	NM/M
Complete Set (56):		4.00
Common Player:		.10
AC	Pete Incaviglia	.10
2C	Lenny Dykstra	.10
3C	Milt Thompson	.10
4C	Mickey Morandini	.10
5C	Kevin Stocker	.10
6C	Terry Mulholland	.10
7C	Curt Schilling	.35
8C	Darren Daulton	.10
9C	Terry Mulholland	.10
10C	Roger Mason	.10
JC	Mariano Duncan	.10
QC	Ben Rivera	.10
KC	John Kruk	.10
AS	Dave Hollins	.10
2S	Danny Jackson	.10
3S	Todd Pratt	.10
4S	David West	.10
5S	Lenny Dykstra	.10
6S	Wes Chamberlain	.10
7S	Tommy Greene	.10
8S	Tony Longmire	.10
9S	Brad Brink	.10
10S	Ricky Jordan	.10
JS	Kim Batiste	.10
QS	Tyler Green	.10
KS	Jim Eisenreich	.10
AH	Lenny Dykstra	.10
2H	Tony Longmire	.10
3H	Kim Batiste	.10
4H	Pete Incaviglia	.10
5H	Ben Rivera	.10
6H	Ricky Jordan	.10
7H	Dave Hollins	.10
8H	Kevin Foster	.10
9H	Kevin Stocker	.10
10H	Mike Williams	.10
JH	Milt Thompson	.10
QH	Curt Schilling	.10
KH	Darren Daulton	.10
AD	Terry Mulholland	.10
2D	Brad Brink	.10
3D	Roger Mason	.10
4D	Mariano Duncan	.10
5D	Danny Jackson	.10
6D	Jim Eisenreich	.10
7D	John Kruk	.10
8D	David West	.10
9D	Todd Pratt	.10
10D	Wes Chamberlain	.10
JD	Jim Eisenreich	.10
QD	Mickey Morandini	.10
KD	Tommy Greene	.10
Joker	Phillies Logo	.10
Joker	National League Logo	.10
---	Checklist	.10
---	'94 Phillies Home Schedule	.10

S.F. Giants

Veterans and rookies on the roster of the '94 Giants are featured in this deck of playing cards; the most popular players appear on up to three cards each. In standard 2-1/2" x 3-1/2" round-cornered format, the large color photos have their top-left and bottom-right corners clipped to display traditional playing card suits and values. The player's name and position are printed in white on an orange strip beneath the photo. Backs have a large Giants logo on a gray pinstriped background. Company and licensor logos are at bottom. The cards were sold in a decorative box.

		NM/M
Complete Set (56):		4.00
Common Player:		.10
AC	Matt Williams	.10
2C	John Patterson	.10
3C	Steve Hosey	.10
4C	Jeff Reed	.10
5C	Mike Jackson	.10
6C	Kirt Manwaring	.10
7C	Royce Clayton	.10
8C	Robby Thompson	.10
9C	Luis Mercedes	.10
10C	Mike Benjamin	.10
JC	Mark Carreon	.10
QC	Dave Burba	.10
KC	John Burkett	.10
AS	Barry Bonds	1.00
2S	Salomon Torres	.10
3S	Kevin Rogers	.10
4S	Todd Benzinger	.10
5S	Dave Martinez	.10
6S	Darren Lewis	.10
7S	Willie McGee	.10
8S	Bill Swift	.10
9S	Paul Faries	.10
10S	Trevor Wilson	.10
JS	Steve Scarsone	.10
QS	Bryan Hickerson	.10
KS	Rod Beck	.10
AH	Robby Thompson	.10
2H	Paul Faries	.10
3H	Trevor Wilson	.10
4H	Steve Scarsone	.10
5H	Bryan Hickerson	.10
6H	Rod Beck	.10
7H	Barry Bonds	1.00
8H	John Patterson	.10
9H	J.R. Phillips	.10
10H	Jeff Reed	.10
JH	Mike Jackson	.10
QH	Kirt Manwaring	.10
KH	Royce Clayton	.10
AD	Bill Swift	.10
2D	Luis Mercedes	.10
3D	Mike Benjamin	.10
4D	Mark Carreon	.10
5D	Dave Burba	.10
6D	John Burkett	.10
7D	Matt Williams	.10
8D	Salomon Torres	.10
9D	Kevin Rogers	.10
10D	Todd Benzinger	.10
JD	Dave Martinez	.10
QD	Darren Lewis	.10
KD	Willie McGee	.10
JOKER	Giants Home Schedule	.10
JOKER	Checklist	.10
---	N.L. Logo	.10
---	Giants Logo	.10

1993 Rookies

The top rookies from the 1993 season are featured on this deck of playing cards; several players appear on more than one card in the deck. Fronts have color player photos at center, with traditional playing card suits and values in the upper-left and lower-right borders. A team logo is at upper-right. The player's name and position appear in white on a purple strip at lower-left. Backs are purple with a large product logo at top-center and licensor/licensee logos at bottom. Cards measure 2-1/2" x 3-1/2" with rounded corners and were sold in a specially decorated cardboard box.

		NM/M
Complete Set (56):		4.00
Common Player:		.10
AC	Mike Piazza	1.00
2C	Vinny Castilla	.10
3C	Wil Cordero	.10
4C	Ryan Thompson	.10
5C	Craig Paquette	.10
6C	Carlos Garcia	.10
7C	Jeff Conine	.10
8C	Bret Boone	.10
9C	Jeromy Burnitz	.10
10C	J.T. Snow	.10
JC	Al Martin	.10
QC	Troy Neel	.10
KC	Tim Salmon	.10
AS	Greg McMichael	.10
2S	Paul Quantrill	.10
3S	Steve Reed	.10
4S	Trevor Hoffman	.10
5S	Tim Pugh	.10
6S	Angel Miranda	.10
7S	Steve Cooke	.10
8S	Aaron Sele	.10
9S	Kirk Rueter	.10
10S	Rene Arocha	.10
JS	Pedro Martinez	.75
QS	Armando Reynoso	.10
KS	Jason Bere	.10
AH	Kevin Stocker	.10
2H	Alex Arias	.10
3H	Carlos Garcia	.10
4H	Erik Pappas	.10
5H	Al Martin	.10
6H	Tim Salmon	.10
7H	Mike Lansing	.10
8H	Rich Amaral	.10
9H	Brent Gates	.10
10H	David Hulse	.10
JH	Troy Neel	.10
QH	Jeff Conine	.10
KH	Mike Piazza	1.00
AD	Chuck Carr	.10
2D	Jeff McNeeley	.10
3D	Joe Kmak	.10
4D	Phil Hiatt	.10
5D	Brent Gates	.10
6D	Wil Cordero	.10
7D	Al Martin	.10
8D	Wayne Kirby	.10
9D	Lou Frazier	.10
10D	Carlos Garcia	.10
JD	Rich Amaral	.10
QD	Mike Lansing	.10
KD	David Hulse	.10
Joker	Tim Salmon (Rookie of the Year)	.10
Joker	Mike Piazza (Rookie of the Year)	.75
--	Checklist	.10
--	Rookie Qualification Rules	.10

1995 U.S. Playing Card Aces

Baseball's 1994 statistical leaders in home runs (clubs), ERA (spades), stolen bases (hearts) and batting average (diamonds) are featured in this deck of playing cards. Measuring a standard 2-1/2" x 3-1/2" with rounded corners, cards have borderless action photos on front with traditional playing card suits and denominations in the upper-left and lower-right corners. The player's color team logo, name and position appear in the lower-left corner. Backs are silver with black side stripes and a red-and-black Aces logo at center. Sets were sold in a colorful cardboard box.

		NM/M
Complete Set (56):		5.00
Common Player:		.10
AC	Matt Williams	.10
2C	Joe Carter	.10
3C	Dante Bichette	.10
4C	Cecil Fielder	.10
5C	Kevin Mitchell	.10
6C	Andres Galarraga	.10
7C	Jose Canseco	.35
8C	Fred McGriff	.10
9C	Albert Belle	.10
10C	Barry Bonds	1.00
JC	Frank Thomas	.50
JC	Jeff Bagwell	.50
KC	Ken Griffey Jr.	.75
AS	Greg Maddux	.60
2S	Steve Trachsel	.10
3S	Randy Johnson	.50
4S	Bobby Jones	.10
5S	Jose Rijo	.10
6S	Mike Mussina	.30
7S	Shane Reynolds	.10
8S	Jeff Fassero	.10
9S	David Cone	.10
10S	Roger Clemens	.65
JS	Doug Drabek	.10
QS	Bret Saberhagen	.10
KS	Steve Ontiveros	.10
AH	Kenny Lofton	.10
2H	Brian McRae	.10
3H	Alex Cole	.10
4H	Barry Bonds	1.00
5H	Darren Lewis	.10
6H	Brady Anderson	.10
7H	Chuck Carr	.10
8H	Chuck Knoblauch	.10
9H	Marquis Grissom	.10
10H	Deion Sanders	.15
JH	Craig Biggio	.10
QH	Otis Nixon	.10
KH	Vince Coleman	.10
AD	Tony Gwynn	.60
2D	Gregg Jefferies	.10
3D	Kevin Mitchell	.10
4D	Will Clark	.10
5D	Hal Morris	.10
6D	Moises Alou	.10
7D	Paul Molitor	.50
8D	Wade Boggs	.60
9D	Kenny Lofton	.10
10D	Frank Thomas	.50
JD	Albert Belle	.10
QD	Paul O'Neill	.10
KD	Jeff Bagwell	.50
Joker	American League logo	.05
Joker	National League logo	.05
---	Checklist	.05
---	MicroMini Team card order form	.05

2000 U.S. Playing Card All Century Baseball Team

Fifty-two members of baseball's All Century team are featured on this deck of playing cards. On round-cornered playing card stock in 2-1/2" x 3-1/2" format, cards have black-and-white photos vignetted on front with the player name at bottom. In opposite corners are a color baseball with the card's value at center and the suit printed in red or black below. Backs are predominantly blue with gold borders and pinstriping. The cards were issued with four All Century team logos in a cardboard box within an embossed lithographed steel case.

		NM/M
Complete Boxed Set (56):		6.00
Common Player:		.10
AC	"Wee" Willie Keeler	.10
2C	Bob Feller	.10
3C	Luke Appling	.10
4C	Jerome "Dizzy" Dean	.15
5C	Johnny Bench	.25
6C	Lou Brock	.10
7C	Joe Cronin	.10
8C	Mickey Cochrane	.10
9C	Rod Carew	.10
10C	Bill Dickey	.10
JC	Josh Gibson	.10
QC	Lou Gehrig	.75
KC	Jackie Robinson	.75
AS	Babe Ruth	1.00
2S	Leroy "Satchel" Paige	.40
3S	Willie McCovey	.10
4S	Joe Morgan	.10
5S	Mel Ott	.10
6S	Jim Palmer	.10
7S	Frank Robinson	.10
8S	Mike Schmidt	.40
9S	George Sisler	.10
10S	Al Simmons	.10
JS	Denton "Cy" Young	.10
QS	Ozzie Smith	.25
KS	Tris Speaker	.10
AH	Bob Gibson	.10
2H	Whitey Ford	.10
3H	Christy Mathewson	.15
4H	Ralph Kiner	.10
5H	Juan Marichal	.10
6H	Bob "Lefty" Grove	.10
7H	Carl Hubbell	.10
8H	Al Kaline	.15
9H	Rogers Hornsby	.10
10H	Harmon Killebrew	.10
JH	Walter Johnson	.10
QH	Jimmie Foxx	.10
KH	Carlton Fisk	.10
AD	Eddie Collins	.10
2D	Robin Roberts	.10
3D	Honus Wagner	.20
4D	Warren Spahn	.10
5D	Mickey Mantle	1.50
6D	Brooks Robinson	.10
7D	Hank Aaron	.75
8D	Rollie Fingers	.10
9D	Dennis Eckersley	.10
10D	Ty Cobb	.75
JD	Joe Medwick	.10
QD	Ernie Banks	.15
KD	Grover Cleveland Alexander	.10

1989 U.S. Postal Service Legends

In 1989 the U.S. Postal Service offered to collectors a Legends set for $7.95. The set consists of a heavily illustrated 24-page "Baseball Scrapbook and Stamp Album," a set of the four U.S. postage stamps which had been issued to that time honoring individual players, and a set of cards matching the stamps. The 2-1/2" x 3-1/2" cards have color reproductions of the stamps on front, bordered in white with red and blue striping. Backs are in red, black and orange and feature player data and major league stats.

		NM/M
Complete Set, Album, Stamps, Cards:		24.00
Card Set (4):		15.00
3	Babe Ruth	4.00
4	Lou Gehrig	3.00
21	Roberto Clemente	5.00
42	Jackie Robinson	3.00

2000 U.S. Postal Service Legends of Baseball Stamps

Twenty of the players nominated to baseball's All-Century team are featured on this souvenir sheet of 33-cent stamps issued by the USPS during ceremonies in Atlanta for the 2000 All-Star Game. The players chosen to appear were all Hall of Famers and, as per post office rules, had been deceased at least 10 years prior to the stamps' issue. Many of the pastel paintings by Joseph Saffold are familiar to card collectors because the illustrations are based on earlier photos which have been seen on vintage cards. A total of 225 million of the self-adhesive 1-1/4" x 1-9/16" stamps was produced, with the 7-1/8" x 7-13/16" souvenir panel originally retailing at face value - $6.60. It was reported that 11,250,000 sheets were printed.

		NM/M
Complete Sheet:		8.00
Common Player:		.35
(1)	Roberto Clemente	.60
(2)	Ty Cobb	.45
(3)	Mickey Cochrane	.35
(4)	Eddie Collins	.35
(5)	Dizzy Dean	.35
(6)	Jimmie Foxx	.35
(7)	Lou Gehrig	.50
(8)	Josh Gibson	.35
(9)	Lefty Grove	.35
(10)	Rogers Hornsby	.35
(11)	Walter Johnson	.35
(12)	Christy Mathewson	.35
(13)	Satchel Paige	.45
(14)	Jackie Robinson	.60
(15)	Babe Ruth	.60
(16)	George Sisler	.35
(17)	Tris Speaker	.35
(18)	Pie Traynor	.35
(19)	Honus Wagner	.35
(20)	Cy Young	.35

2000 USPS Legends of Baseball Post Cards

In conjunction with the issue of a souvenir sheet of 33-cent stamps, the USPS also issued a boxed set of "Legends of Baseball" post cards. The 5" x 7" cards have a large reproduction of each stamp on front against a beige background. Postcard-style backs have color logos of the USPS and MLB's All-Century Team, along with address lines and a stamp box. At upper-left is a summary of the player's career. The cards were issued in a colorful folder with an All-Century Team hologram. The boxed sets sold for $5.95. Production was reported as 62,500 sets.

		NM/M
Complete Boxed Set (20):		9.00
Common Player:		.75
(1)	Roberto Clemente	1.50
(2)	Ty Cobb	1.25
(3)	Mickey Cochrane	.75
(4)	Eddie Collins	.75
(5)	Dizzy Dean	.75
(6)	Jimmie Foxx	.75
(7)	Lou Gehrig	1.25
(8)	Josh Gibson	.75
(9)	Lefty Grove	.75
(10)	Rogers Hornsby	.75
(11)	Walter Johnson	.75
(12)	Christy Mathewson	.75
(13)	Satchel Paige	1.25
(14)	Jackie Robinson	1.50
(15)	Babe Ruth	1.50
(16)	George Sisler	.75
(17)	Tris Speaker	.75
(18)	Pie Traynor	.75
(19)	Honus Wagner	.75
(20)	Cy Young	.75

2000 USPS Legends of Baseball Postal Card Booklet

In conjunction with the issue of a souvenir sheet of 33-cent stamps, the USPS also issued a bound booklet of "Legends of Baseball" postal cards. By definition, postal cards have the "stamp" preprinted. The 4-1/4" x 6-1/16" cards have borderless color artwork on front, pastel paintings which reproduce the stamps' artwork. On the divided back a 20-cent "stamp" version of the player picture is printed at top-right. There is a short biography at top-left. The cards were perforated with an 11/16" stub attaching it to the bound book. With a $4 face value, the booklets were originally sold for $8.95 at the post office. Production was reported as 105,000 sets.

		NM/M
Complete Booklet (20):		12.50
Common Player:		.75
(1)	Roberto Clemente	1.50
(2)	Ty Cobb	1.25
(3)	Mickey Cochrane	.75
(4)	Eddie Collins	.75
(5)	Dizzy Dean	.75
(6)	Jimmie Foxx	.75
(7)	Lou Gehrig	1.25
(8)	Josh Gibson	.75
(9)	Lefty Grove	.75
(10)	Rogers Hornsby	.75
(11)	Walter Johnson	.75
(12)	Christy Mathewson	.75
(13)	Satchel Paige	1.25
(14)	Jackie Robinson	1.50
(15)	Babe Ruth	1.50
(16)	George Sisler	.75
(17)	Tris Speaker	.75
(18)	Pie Traynor	.75
(19)	Honus Wagner	.75
(20)	Cy Young	.75

V

2000 Verizon Tampa Bay Devil Rays

This team set was a stadium giveaway at a promotional date. Fronts of the 2-1/2" x 3-1/2" cards have game-action photos on which a silver dollar-size portion remains in natural color while the balance of the picture is a purple duo-tone. Backs are in gray with a purple box for complete pro stats, capped by a dime-size color player portrait. The set is listed here according to uniform numbers which appear on back.

		NM/M
Complete Set (28):		7.50
Common Player:		.25
1	Miguel Cairo	.25
2	Randy Winn	.25
4	Gerald Williams	.25
7	John Flaherty	.25
8	Mike DiFelice	.25
9	Vinny Castilla	.25
10	Russ Johnson	.25
11	Larry Rothschild	.25
13	Ozzie Guillen	.25
16	Felix Martinez	.25
21	Bubba Trammell	.25
23	Greg Vaughn	.25
28	Steve Cox	.25
29	Fred McGriff	.50
30	Jose Guillen	.25
32	Albie Lopez	.25
34	Jose Canseco	2.50
35	Bryan Rekar	.25
39	Roberto Hernandez	.25
40	Wilson Alvarez	.25
43	Esteban Yan	.25
46	Steve Trachsel	.25
51	Rick White	.25
57	Juan Guzman	.25
--	Coaches (Orlando Gomez, Billy Hatcher, Bill Russell, Jose Cardenal, Bill Fischer, Leon Roberts)	.25
00	Raymond (Mascot)	.25
--	Wade Boggs (Literacy Champion)	3.50
---	A's for the Rays	.10

1989 Very Fine Pirates

This 30-card set Pirates set was sponsored by Veryfine fruit juices and issued in the form of two uncut, perforated panels, each containing 15 standard-size cards. A third panel featured color action photographs. The panels were distributed in a pro-

PITTSBURGH PIRATES

BILL LANDRUM 43

VeryFine

motion to fans attending the April 23 game at Three Rivers Stadium. The cards display the Pirates' traditional black and gold color scheme. The backs include player data and complete stats.

		NM/M
Complete Three-Panel Set:		15.00
Complete Singles Set (30):		13.50
Common Player:		.25
0	Junior Ortiz	.25
3	Gary Redus	.25
3	Jay Bell	.25
5	Sid Bream	.25
6	Rafael Belliard	.25
10	Jim Leyland	.25
11	Glenn Wilson	.25
12	Mike La Valliere	.25
13	Jose Lind	.25
14	Ken Oberkfell	.25
15	Doug Drabek	.25
16	Bob Kipper	.25
17	Bob Walk	.25
18	Andy Van Slyke	.25
23	R.J. Reynolds	.25
24	Barry Bonds	12.00
25	Bobby Bonilla	.25
26	Neal Heaton	.25
30	Benny Distefano	.25
35	Jim Gott	.25
41	Mike Dunne	.25
43	Bill Landrum	.25
48	John Cangelosi	.25
49	Jeff Robinson	.25
52	Dorn Taylor	.25
54	Brian Fisher	.25
57	John Smiley	.25
31/37	Ray Miller, Tommy Sandt	.25
32/36	Bruce Kimm, Gene Lamont	.25
39/45	Milt May, Rich Donnelly	.25
---	Rich Donnelly (39-45)	.25

2002 Viagra Rafael Palmeiro

RAFAEL PALMEIRO

Spokesman Rafael Palmeiro is featured on five of the nine cards in this set issued to promote the drug Viagra. (Models are pictured on the other four cards.) Sets were issued in a cello-wrapped pack with a detailed information sheet on the drug. Evidently distributed to medical professionals, the exact manner and range of the cards' distribution is unknown. In standard 2-1/2" x 3-1/2" format, cards are printed on rather thin stock which is UV coated on each side. Except for one card which has a Palmeiro portrait photo on back along with personal data and stats, the backs have information on the drug.

		NM/M
Complete Set (9):		4.50
Common Card:		.05
(1)	Rafael Palmeiro (Game-action photo.)	1.25
(2)	Rafael Palmeiro (Bat at ready pose.)	1.25
(3)	Rafael Palmeiro (Batting follow-through.)	1.25
(4)	Rafael Palmeiro (Jersey close-up.)	1.25
(5)	Rafael Palmeiro/Portrait	1.25
(6)	Communication	.05
(7)	Diabetes	.05
(8)	Hyperlipidemia	.05
(9)	Hypertension	.05

1991 Vine Line Chicago Cubs

VINE LINE

23 Ryne Sandberg 1F

This set was produced in conjunction with the official fan magazine of the Chicago Cubs, "Vine Line." Issued in nine-card panels for insertion into issues of the magazine, the panels were apparently also offered as a complete set via a mail-in offer. Cards measure the standard 2-1/2" x 3-1/2" and will be perforated on two, three or four sides, depending on their placement on the panel. Fronts are bordered in black with white typography that has the player name, position and uniform number. The player photo is in color with the background in stippled black-and-white. Backs have a black-and-white player portrait, biographical data, career highlights, 1990 and career stats and a brown and green background. The cards are listed here by uniform number.

		NM/M
Complete Singles Set (36):		6.00
Complete Panel Set (4):		7.50
Common Card:		.25
3	Jose Martinez	.25
4	Don Zimmer	.25
5	Chuck Cottier	.25
6	Joe Altobelli	.25
7	Joe Girardi	.25
8	Andre Dawson	.45
9	Damon Berryhill	.25
10	Luis Salazar	.25
11	George Bell	.25
12	Shawon Dunston	.25
15	Jose Vizcaino	.25
17	Mark Grace	.50
18	Dwight Smith	.25
19	Hector Villanueva	.25
20	Jerome Walton	.25
22	Mike Harkey	.25
23	Ryne Sandberg	2.00
24	Chico Walker	.25
25	Gary Scott	.25
29	Doug Dascenzo	.25
31	Greg Maddux	2.00
32	Danny Jackson	.25
34	Dick Pole	.25
35	Chuck McElroy	.25
36	Mike Bielecki	.25
37	Erik Pappas	.25
40	Rick Sutcliffe	.25
42	Dave Smith	.25
44	Steve Wilson	.25
45	Paul Assenmacher	.25
47	Shawn Boskie	.25
48	Phil Roof	.25
50	Les Lancaster	.25
51	Heathcliff Slocumb	.25
31	Fergie Jenkins (Hall of Fame)	.50
---	Most Valuable Players (Ryne Sandberg, Andre Dawson, George Bell)	.40

1994 Vine Line Chicago Cubs Postcards

Chicago Cubs Vine Line, the team's official monthly paper, produced this set of promotional postcards. The 4" x 5-1/2" cards have black-and-white or color pictures with maroon borders. Backs are in color with a description of the front photo. The unnumbered cards are checklisted here in chronological order.

		NM/M
Complete Set (10):		10.00
Common Card:		1.00
(1)	Wrigley Field 1914-1994/ 1935	1.00

		NM/M
(2)	Wrigley Field 1914-1994/ 1988	1.00
(3)	Harry Caray 50 Seasons (7th inning stretch)	1.00
(4)	Harry Caray 50 Seasons (1989 w/Stan Musial)	1.00
(5)	1969 (Team composite.)	2.50
(6)	1969 (Ken Holtzman No-hitter.))	1.50
(7)	1984 (Clinching NL East)	1.00
(8)	1969 (Final game celebration)	1.00
(9)	1989 (Boys of Zimmer)	1.00
(10)	1989 (Clinching NL East)	1.00

1998 Virginia Lottery Baseball Legends Cards

BASEBALL LEGENDS

PHIL NIEKRO
HALL OF FAME: 1997

This set of cards was one of several consolation prizes available in the commonwealth's scratch-off lottery game featuring Hall of Famers who had played in Virginia. The 2-1/2" x 3-1/2" cards have larger versions of the player photos found on the tickets. Borders are in red, white, blue, and black. Black-and-white backs have career highlights and stats. Cards can be found in either signed or autographed versions.

		NM/M
Complete Set (4):		4.00
Autographed Set (4):		25.00
Common Player:		1.00
Common Autograph:		8.00
(1)	Yogi Berra	2.00
(1)	Yogi Berra/Auto.	15.00
(2)	Willie McCovey	1.00
(2)	Willie McCovey/Auto.	10.00
(3)	Phil Niekro	1.00
(3)	Phil Niekro/Auto.	8.00
(4)	Duke Snider	1.50
(4)	Duke Snider/Auto.	12.00

W

1986 Wallich Enterprises Padres Sports Cards

This set of artwork postcards was designed to be the first in a series which never materialized. The cards feature color artwork on front with a wide border and player name beneath.

		NM/M
Complete Set (15):		35.00
Common Player:		3.00
(1)	Kurt Bevacqua	3.00
(2)	Dave Dravecky	4.00
(3)	Tim Flannery, Jerry Royster	3.00
(4)	Steve Garvey	6.00
(5)	Rich Gossage	4.00
(6)	Tony Gwynn	9.00
(7)	Andy Hawkins	3.00
(8)	LaMarr Hoyt	3.00
(9)	Terry Kennedy	3.00
(10)	Carmelo Martinez	3.00
(11)	Kevin McReynolds	4.00
(12)	Graig Nettles	4.00

		NM/M
(13)	Eric Show	3.00
(14)	Garry Templeton	4.00
(15)	Player composite	3.00

1998 Washington Senators 1969 Reunion

Frank Howard OF/1st BASE

In conjunction with a card-show reunion of the '69 Nats, this set of cards was issued in uncut sheet form at the reunion breakfast. Featuring original artwork portraits atop cartoon bodies in the style of 1938 Goudey Heads-Up cards, the 2-1/2" x 2-7/8" cards have a reunion logo in an upper-corner. Backs have a team logo, player personal data, 1969 and career stats, and a quote about the player by Washington sports talk radio personality Phil Wood. Cards are listed here alphabetically.

		NM/M
Complete Set, Uncut Sheet:		15.00
Complete Set, Singles (28):		12.00
Common Player:		.25
(1)	Bernie Allen	.25
(2)	Hank Allen	.25
(3)	Frank Bertaina	.25
(4)	Dick Billings	.25
(5)	Dick Bosman	.25
(6)	Ed Brinkman	.25
(7)	Joe Camacho	.25
(8)	Casey Cox	.25
(9)	Tim Cullen	.25
(10)	Mike Epstein	.40
(11)	Jim French	.25
(12)	Jim Hannan	.25
(13)	Dennis Higgins	.25
(14)	Johnny Holliday (Announcer)	.25
(15)	Frank Howard	.50
(16)	Sid Hudson	.25
(17)	Bob Humphreys	.25
(18)	Frank Kreutzer	.25
(19)	Lee Maye	.25
(20)	Ken McMullen	.25
(21)	Ron Menchine (Announcer)	.25
(22)	Ed Stroud	.25
(23)	Wayne Terwilliger	.25
(24)	Del Unser	.25
(25)	Fred Valentine	.25
(26)	Shelby Whitfield (Announcer)	.25
(27)	Ted Williams	6.00
(28)	Checklist	.25

1988-89 Weis Winners Super Stars Discs

RON DARLING
NEW YORK METS PITCHER

(See 1988-89 Super Stars Discs for checklists and price guides.)

1985 Wendy's Tigers

This set contains 22 cards measuring 2-1/2" x 3-1/2", which carry both Wendy's Hamburgers and Coca-Cola logos and were produced by Topps. The cards feature a color photo with the player's identification underneath the picture. Backs are identical to 1985 Topps cards except they have different card numbers and are done in a red and black color scheme. Cards were distributed three to a pack along with a "Header" checklist in a cellophane package at selected Wendy's outlets in Michigan only.

Coca-Cola

DETROIT TIGERS
DAN PETRY

		NM/M
Complete Set (22):		5.00
Common Player:		.25
1	Sparky Anderson	.50
2	Doug Bair	.25
3	Juan Berenguer	.25
4	Dave Bergman	.25
5	Tom Brookens	.25
6	Marty Castillo	.25
7	Darrell Evans	.40
8	Barbaro Garbey	.25
9	Kirk Gibson	.65
10	Johnny Grubb	.25
11	Willie Hernandez	.25
12	Larry Herndon	.25
13	Rusty Kuntz	.25
14	Chet Lemon	.25
15	Aurelio Lopez	.25
16	Jack Morris	.35
17	Lance Parrish	.65
18	Dan Petry	.25
19	Bill Scherrer	.25
20	Alan Trammell	1.00
21	Lou Whitaker	.50
22	Milt Wilcox	.25

1994 Wendy's Roberto Clemente Hologram

CLEMENTE
PITTSBURGH

This single-card set was issued by the restaurant chain in a stated edition of 90,000. The front has a black-bordered hologram picturing Clemente at bat, with the number 3,000 in a box at upper-right. The back has a couple of color photos of the Pirates' star along with biographical data and a career summary.

		NM/M
(1)	Roberto Clemente	6.00

1993 Whataburger Nolan Ryan

Angels
30

Nolan Ryan
3rd NO-HITTER TRIAD

Issued in two-card cello packs at Whataburger restaurants, this set honors the career of Nolan Ryan. Cards have action photos set against colorized backgrounds and overlayed with ribbed plastic to create a 3-D effect. A card title is printed in white in the lower-left corner, with the logo of Triad (the card's maker) in the lower-right. In the upper-left corner is a red "Nolan Ryan's Recollections" logo. Backs have color logos of the hamburger chain, Triad, Coca-Cola and Major League Baseball, along with a quote from Ryan about the career highlight and a facsimile autograph. The cards are unnumbered.

		NM/M
Complete Set (10):		6.00
Common Card:		1.00
(1)	Nolan Ryan (1st No-hitter)	1.00
(2)	Nolan Ryan (2nd No-Hitter)	1.00
(3)	Nolan Ryan (3rd No-hitter)	1.00
(4)	Nolan Ryan (4th No-hitter)	1.00
(5)	Nolan Ryan (5th No-hitter)	1.00
(6)	Nolan Ryan (6th No-hitter)	1.00
(7)	Nolan Ryan (7th No-hitter)	1.00
(8)	Nolan Ryan (5,000th Strikeout)	1.00
(9)	Nolan Ryan (300th Win)	1.00
(10)	Nolan Ryan (On horse.)	1.00

1982 Wheaties Indians

TOBY HARRAH
Infield WHEATIES

These 2-13/16" x 4-1/8" cards were given out ten at a time during three special promotional games; later the complete set was placed on sale at the Indians' gift shop. The cards represented the first time in 30 years that Wheaties had been associated with a baseball card set. Fronts feature color photos surrounded by a wide white border with the player's name and position below the picture. The Indians logo is in the lower-left corner while the Wheaties logo is in the lower-right. Card backs have a Wheaties ad.

		NM/M
Complete Set (30):		7.50
Common Player:		.25
(1)	Chris Bando	.25
(2)	Alan Bannister	.25
(3)	Len Barker	.25
(4)	Bert Blyleven	.75
(5)	Tom Brennan	.25
(6)	Joe Charboneau	1.00
(7)	Rodney Craig	.25
(8)	John Denny	.25
(9)	Miguel Dilone	.25
(10)	Jerry Dybzinski	.25
(11)	Mike Fischlin	.25
(12)	Dave Garcia	.25
(13)	Johnny Goryl	.25
(14)	Mike Hargrove	.50
(15)	Toby Harrah	.50
(16)	Ron Hassey	.25
(17)	Von Hayes	.25
(18)	Dennis Lewallyn	.25
(19)	Rick Manning	.25
(20)	Bake McBride	.25
(21)	Tommy McCraw	.25
(22)	Jack Perconte	.25
(23)	Mel Queen	.25
(24)	Dennis Sommers	.25
(25)	Lary Sorensen	.25
(26)	Dan Spillner	.25
(27)	Rick Sutcliffe	.75
(28)	Andre Thornton	.50
(29)	Rick Waits	.25
(30)	Eddie Whitson	.25

1983 Wheaties Indians

A 32-card set marked the second year of Wheaties involvement with the Indians. Distribution of the 2-13/16" x 4-1/8" cards changed slightly in that the entire set was given away on the day of the special promotional game. As happened in 1982, the set was then placed on sale at the team's gift shop. The set includes 27 players, four coaches and the manager. The format of the cards remained basically the same on the front although the backs of player cards were changed to include complete major and minor league statistics.

		NM/M
Complete Set (32):		5.00

JULIO FRANCO
Infield
WHEATIES

Common Player:		.25
(1)	Bud Anderson	.25
(2)	Jay Baller	.25
(3)	Chris Bando	.25
(4)	Alan Bannister	.25
(5)	Len Barker	.25
(6)	Bert Blyleven	.50
(7)	Wil Culmer	.25
(8)	Miguel Dilone	.25
(9)	Juan Eichelberger	.25
(10)	Jim Essian	.25
(11)	Mike Ferraro	.25
(12)	Mike Fischlin	.25
(13)	Julio Franco	.35
(14)	Ed Glynn	.25
(15)	Johnny Goryl	.25
(16)	Mike Hargrove	.35
(17)	Toby Harrah	.35
(18)	Ron Hassey	.25
(19)	Neal Heaton	.25
(20)	Rick Manning	.25
(21)	Bake McBride	.25
(22)	Don McMahon	.25
(23)	Ed Napoleon	.25
(24)	Broderick Perkins	.25
(25)	Dennis Sommers	.25
(26)	Lary Sorensen	.25
(27)	Dan Spillner	.25
(28)	Rick Sutcliffe	.35
(29)	Andre Thornton	.35
(30)	Manny Trillo	.25
(31)	George Vukovich	.25
(32)	Rick Waits	.25

1984 Wheaties Indians

BRETT BUTLER
Outfield
WHEATIES

The 2-13/16" x 4-1/8" cards again were given out at Municipal Stadium as part of a promotion involving Wheaties and the Indians on July 22. The set was down from 32 cards in 1983 to 29. There are 26 players as well as cards for the manager, coaches and team mascot. Design of the cards is virtually identical to prior years. The 1984 set is numbered by uniform number. A total of 15,000 sets were printed and any left over from the promotion were placed on sale in the team's gift shop.

		NM/M
Complete Set (29):		9.00
Common Player:		.50
2	Brett Butler	.75
4	Tony Bernazard	.50
8	Carmelo Castillo	.50
10	Pat Tabler	.50
13	Ernie Camacho	.50
14	Julio Franco	.75
15	Broderick Perkins	.50
16	Jerry Willard	.50
18	Pat Corrales	.50
21	Mike Hargrove	.75
22	Mike Fischlin	.50
23	Chris Bando	.50
24	George Vukovich	.50
26	Brook Jacoby	.50
27	Steve Farr	.50
28	Bert Blyleven	1.00
29	Andre Thornton	.50
30	Joe Carter	1.50
31	Steve Comer	.50
33	Roy Smith	.50
34	Mel Hall	.50

36	Jamie Easterly	.50
37	Don Schulze	.50
38	Luis Aponte	.50
44	Neal Heaton	.50
46	Mike Jeffcoat	.50
54	Tom Waddell	.50
---	Coaching Staff (Bobby Bonds, John Goryl, Don McMahon, Ed Napoleon, Dennis Sommers)	.50
---	Tom-E-Hawk (Mascot)	.50

1997 Wheaties All-Stars

Forty-five years after it last printed baseball cards on its cereal boxes, Wheaties issued a cross-brand set of 30 cards in 1997. Top players are generally grouped by positions in groups of six on the box backs. Boxes also feature three player photos on front and an ad for obtaining a player photoball. The three series of cards found on 18 oz. boxes of Wheaties carry a Topps logo in upper-right corner. The top of the cards' fronts have action photos. A blue bar below the photo has the player name and career highlights in white. A green, blue or orange border surrounds the card, which is separated from the rest of the box back by a black dotted line. Backs, printed inside the box, have limited personal data and full major league stats. Perfectly cut cards from these boxes measure about 2-1/2" x 3-13/16". Somewhat smaller at 2-1/16" x 3-3/8", though identical in format, are the cards found on the backs of Honey Frosted Wheaties and Crispy Wheaties 'n Raisins. Cards on the former carry a Pinnacle logo; the latter are marked Upper Deck. Both have orange borders surrounding the cards.

		NM/M
Complete Set, Boxes (5):		12.00
Complete Set, Singles (30):		15.00
Common Player:		.25
	All-Star Players Complete Set:	3.50
(1)	Ken Griffey Jr.	.75
(2)	Greg Maddux	.65
(3)	Paul Molitor	.50
(4)	Cal Ripken Jr.	1.50
(5)	Frank Thomas	.50
(6)	Mo Vaughn	.25
	All-Star Players Complete Box:	3.00
(7)	Barry Bonds	1.50
(8)	Ken Caminiti	.25
(9)	Ken Griffey Jr.	.75
(10)	Chipper Jones	.65
(11)	Chuck Knoblauch	.25
(12)	Alex Rodriguez	1.00
	All-Star Infielders Complete Box:	2.50
(13)	Jeff Bagwell	.50
(14)	Mark McGwire	1.00
(15)	Mike Piazza	.75
(16)	Cal Ripken Jr.	1.50
(17)	Ryne Sandberg	.65
(18)	Frank Thomas	.50
	All-Star Outfielders Complete Box:	2.50
(19)	Barry Bonds	1.50
(20)	Ellis Burks	.25
(21)	Juan Gonzalez	.35
(22)	Ken Griffey Jr.	.75
(23)	Tony Gwynn	.65
(24)	Bernie Williams	.25
	All-Star Pitchers Complete Box:	2.00
(25)	Andy Benes	.25
(26)	David Cone	.25
(27)	Greg Maddux	.65
(28)	Mike Mussina	.35
(29)	Hideo Nomo	.35
(30)	John Smoltz	.25

1995 Wienerschnitzel L.A. Dodgers POGs

The Dodger Stadium hot dog concessionaire sponsored this promotion which was given away to youngsters attending a May 13 Dodgers game. The issue consists of 14 POGs die cut from an 8-1/2" x 10-3/4" cardboard sheet. The POGs picture the team's winners of the Rookie of the Year Award from Jackie Robinson in 1947

ERIC KAROS
LA
Dodgers

through Raul Mondesi in 1994. The individual POGs measure 1-5/8" in diameter. Fronts have a sepia or color player portrait at center, with a blue border of lighter blue stars. Backs are printed in red and blue on white and have a bit of player information plus the logos of the team, sponsor and World POG Federation.

		NM/M
Complete Set, Panel:		8.00
Complete Set, Singles (14):		7.00
Common Player:		.25
1	Jackie Robinson	3.00
2	Don Newcombe	.50
3	Joe Black	.50
4	Jim Gilliam	.35
5	Frank Howard	.35
6	Jim Lefebvre	.25
7	Ted Sizemore	.25
8	Rick Sutcliffe	.25
9	Steve Howe	.25
10	Fernando Valenzuela	.35
11	Steve Sax	.25
12	Eric Karros	.25
13	Mike Piazza	2.00
14	Raul Mondesi	.25

1993 Ted Williams Co. Promos

Though they are unmarked as sample cards, the promos issued for the debut Ted Williams Card Co. set are easily distinguished from the regularly issued versions. The #1 Williams card has different front photos and his name in green, rather than orange, and the Paige and Gonzalez cards have text backs in the promo version, rather than checklists.

		NM/M
Complete Set (3):		10.00
Common Player:		2.00
1	Ted Williams	5.00
115	Satchel Paige	3.00
160	Juan Gonzalez	2.00

1993 Ted Williams Card Company

JOE GARAGIOLA

Without a license from the players' union, the premiere issue of the Ted Williams Card Company relied on innovative subsets to create interest in its "old-timers" set. The first 96 cards in the set comprise the base issue. Those cards feature a black-and-white or color action photo set against a background of a second ghost-image photo. The player's name is at bottom with the card company logo conspicuous at top. Backs have some biographical detail, a career summary, the player's five best seasons' and career stats. Subsets numbered contiguously with the base set include a 19-card Negro Leagues series highlighted with green-foil; five cards featuring the All-American Girls Professional Baseball League; a 10-card "Ted's Greatest Hitters" series; 10 "Barrier Breakers" cards featuring

Negro Leagues veterans who later played in the majors; a 10-card "Goin' North" subset featuring major league stars of the 1940s-1970s in minor league photos, and, a pair of five-card "Dawning of a Legacy" series featuring Juan Gonzalez and Jeff Bagwell. There were also several insert card series which are listed separately. The cards were packaged with a pair of die-cut player or team logo POGs.

		NM/M
Complete Set (160):		12.00
Common Player:		.05
Wax Pack (12):		.75
Wax Box (36):		20.00
1	Ted Williams	3.00
2	Rick Ferrell	.05
3	Jim Lonborg	.05
4	Mel Parnell	.05
5	Jim Piersall	.05
6	Luis Tiant	.05
7	Carl Yastrzemski	.50
8	Ralph Branca	.05
9	Roy Campanella	.50
10	Ron Cey	.05
11	Tommy Davis	.05
12	Don Drysdale	.35
13	Carl Erskine	.10
14	Steve Garvey	.10
15	Don Newcombe	.10
16	Duke Snider	.50
17	Maury Wills	.05
18	Jim Fregosi	.05
19	Bobby Grich	.05
20	Bill Buckner	.05
21	Billy Herman	.05
22	Ferguson Jenkins	.10
23	Ron Santo	.15
24	Billy Williams	.10
25	Luis Aparicio	.10
26	Luke Appling	.10
27	Minnie Minoso	.15
28	Johnny Bench	.50
29	George Foster	.05
30	Joe Morgan	.15
31	Buddy Bell	.05
32	Lou Boudreau	.10
33	Rocky Colavito	.25
34	Jim "Mudcat" Grant	.05
35	Tris Speaker	.10
36	Ray Boone	.05
37	Darrell Evans	.05
38	Al Kaline	.35
39	George Kell	.10
40	Mickey Lolich	.05
41	Cesar Cedeno	.05
42	Sal Bando	.05
43	Vida Blue	.05
44	Bert Campaneris	.05
45	Ken Holtzman	.05
46	Lew Burdette	.05
47	Bob Horner	.05
48	Warren Spahn	.10
49	Cecil Cooper	.05
50	Tony Oliva	.10
51	Bobby Bonds	.10
52	Alvin Dark	.05
53	Dave Dravecky	.05
54	Monte Irvin	.10
55	Willie Mays	1.00
56	Bud Harrelson	.05
57	Dave Kingman	.05
58	Yogi Berra	.50
59	Don Baylor	.05
60	Jim Bouton	.05
61	Bobby Brown	.05
62	Whitey Ford	.40
63	Lou Gehrig	1.50
64	Charlie Keller	.05
65	Eddie Lopat	.05
66	Johnny Mize	.05
67	Bobby Murcer	.05
68	Graig Nettles	.05
69	Bobby Shantz	.05
70	Richie Ashburn	.10
71	Larry Bowa	.05
72	Steve Carlton	.40
73	Robin Roberts	.10
74	Matty Alou	.05
75	Harvey Haddix	.05
76	Ralph Kiner	.10
77	Bill Madlock	.05
78	Bill Mazeroski	.05
79	Al Oliver	.05
80	Manny Sanguillen	.05
81	Willie Stargell	.10
82	Al Brumbry	.05
83	Davey Johnson	.05
84	Boog Powell	.10
85	Earl Weaver	.10
86	Lou Brock	.10
87	Orlando Cepeda	.05
88	Curt Flood	.05
89	Joe Garagiola	.35
90	Bob Gibson	.10
91	Rogers Hornsby	.20
92	Enos Slaughter	.10
93	Joe Torre	.20
94	Gaylord Perry	.05
95	Checklist 1-49	.05
96	Checklist 50-96	.05
97	Cool Papa Bell	.10
98	Garnett Blair	.05
99	Gene Benson	.05
100	Lyman Bostock, Sr.	.10
101	Marlin Carter	.05
102	Oscar Charleston	.10
103	Ray Dandridge	.10
104	Mahlon Duckett	.05
105	Josh Gibson	.20
106	Cowan Hyde	.05
107	"Judy" Johnson	.10
108	Buck Leonard	.10
109	Pop Lloyd	.10
110	Lester Lockett	.05
111	Max Manning	.05
112	Satchel Paige	.50
113	Armando Vazquez	.05
114	Smokey Joe Williams	.10
115	Negro Leagues Checklist (Satchel Paige)	.05
116	Alice Hohlmeyer	.05
117	Dotty Kamenshek	.05
118	Pepper Davis	.05
119	Marge Wenzell	.05
120	AAGPBA Checklist	.05
121	The Babe (Babe Ruth)	1.50
122	The Iron Horse (Lou Gehrig)	.75
123	Double X (Jimmie Foxx)	.20
124	Rajah (Rogers Hornsby)	.10
125	The Georgia Peach (Ty Cobb)	.75
126	The Say Hey Kid (Willie Mays)	.50
127	Ralph (Ralph Kiner)	.10
128	The Grey Eagle (Tris Speaker)	.05
129	The Big Cat (Johnny Mize)	.10
130	Ted's Greatest Hitters Checklist	.05
131	Satchel Paige	.25
132	Joe Black	.10
133	Roy Campanella	.25
134	Larry Doby	.10
135	Jim Gilliam	.10
136	Monte Irvin	.10
137	Sam Jethroe	.05
138	Willie Mays	.50
139	Don Newcombe	.05
140	Barrier Breakers Checklist	.05
141	Roy Campanella	.25
142	Bob Gibson	.10
143	Boog Powell	.10
144	Willie Mays	.50
145	Johnny Mize	.05
146	Monte Irvin	.10
147	Earl Weaver	.05
148	Ted Williams	1.50
149	Jim Gilliam	.05
150	Goin' North Checklist	.05
151	Juan Gonzalez (Footsteps to Greatness)	.25
151a	Juan Gonzalez/Auto. (Edition of 43.)	60.00
152	Juan Gonzalez (Sign 'em Up)	.25
152a	Juan Gonzalez/Auto. (Edition of 43.)	60.00
153	Juan Gonzalez (The Road to Success)	.25
153a	Juan Gonzalez/Auto. (Edition of 43.)	60.00
154	Juan Gonzalez (Looking Ahead)	.25
154a	Juan Gonzalez/Auto. (Edition of 43.)	60.00
155	"Dawning of a Legacy" Checklist	.05
156	Jeff Bagwell (Born with Red Sox Blood)	.50
157	Jeff Bagwell (Movin' Up, Then Out)	.50
158	Jeff Bagwell (Year 1)	.50
159	Jeff Bagwell (Year 2)	.50
160	"Dawning of a Legacy" Checklist (Juan Gonzalez)	.05

Etched in Stone

ETCHED IN STONE
ROBERTO CLEMENTE

This 10-card insert set documents the career of Roberto Clemente, using sepia-toned and color photographs on the card front, highlighted by a gold-foil embossed "Tribute '93" logo in the lower-left corner and an "Etched in Stone" logo at upper-right. Cards have a detailed biography. Cards are numbered ES1 through ES10.

		NM/M
Complete Set (10):		12.00
Common Player:		2.00
1	Youth (Roberto Clemente)	2.00
2	Sign Up (Roberto Clemente)	2.00
3	Try-Out (Roberto Clemente)	2.00
4	Playing Mad (Roberto Clemente)	2.00
5	Minor Leagues (Roberto Clemente)	2.00
6	1955-1959 (Roberto Clemente)	2.00
7	1960 (Roberto Clemente)	2.00
8	1963 (Roberto Clemente)	2.00
9	1970 (Roberto Clemente)	2.00
10	Etched in Stone Checklist	2.00

Locklear Collection

The paintings of former major leaguer Gene Locklear are featured in this 10-card insert set. The central image of the player is set against a background of multiple player images in orange, red and purple tones. The player's name is in dark blue on the left edge and a "Gene Locklear Collection" logo is in lower-right. On back is a commentary on the player, a card number with an "LC" suffix and, at bottom center, a serial number. The cards of Ted Williams can be found in an autographed insert version numbered on back from within an edition of 406.

		NM/M
Complete Set (10):		12.00
Common Player:		.75
Ted Williams Autographed:		500.00
1	Yogi Berra	1.00
2	Lou Brock	.75
3	Willie Mays	2.00
4	Johnny Mize	.75
5	Satchel Paige	1.50
6	Babe Ruth	2.50
7	Enos Slaughter	.75
8	Carl Yastrzemski	1.00
9	Ted Williams	2.50
10	Locklear Collection Checklist	.10

Memories

JOHNNY PODRES

Four historical World Series of the 1950s-1970s are featured in five-card runs within the "Memories" insert set. Fronts have black-and-white or color player photos. In the lower-left corner is a vintage press camera with "Memories" and the year emanating from the flashbulb. The Ted Williams Card Co. logo is at upper-right. The player's name is in white at bottom-center. Cards are numbered with an "M" prefix on back and feature a headline announcing the team's World Series victory and a summary of the featured player's performance in that Fall Classic.

	NM/M
Complete Set (20):	45.00
Common Player:	1.00

1955 BROOKLYN DODGERS

1	Roy Campanella	3.50
2	Jim Gilliam	2.00
3	Gil Hodges	3.50
4	Duke Snider	3.50
5	1955 Dodgers Checklist	.60

1963 L.A. DODGERS

6	Don Drysdale	3.50
7	Tommy Davis	2.25
8	Johnny Podres	2.25
9	Maury Wills	3.50
10	1963 Dodgers Checklist	.60

1971 PITTSBURGH PIRATES

11	Roberto Clemente	9.00
12	Al Oliver	1.00
13	Manny Sanguillen	1.00
14	Willie Stargell	2.00
15	1971 Pirates Checklist	.60

1975 CINCINNATI REDS

16	Johnny Bench	4.50
17	George Foster	1.25
18	Joe Morgan	3.00
19	Tony Perez	2.00
20	1975 Red Checklist	.60

POGs

These 26 cards featuring two die-cut POGs on each were issued as inserts in 1993 Ted Williams packs. Fronts of the extra-thick cardboard cards have a black background with the logos of the card company and the Cooperstown Collection. Two 1-5/8" diameter POGs appear on each card, picturing either players or team logos. Backs are blank. The un-numbered POG cards are listed here alphabetically, with player POGs listed first.

	NM/M
Complete Set (26):	4.00
Common Player:	.25

(1)	Yogi Berra, Roy Campanella	1.00
(2)	Brooklyn Dodgers (Roy Campanella)	.50
(3)	Tommy Davis, George Foster	.25
(4)	Lou Gehrig, Ted Williams	2.00
(5)	New York Yankees (Lou Gehrig)	1.50
(6)	Ted Williams, #9 patch	.75
(7)	1993 World Series patch	.25
(8)	Baltimore Elite Giants	.25
(9)	New York Mets	.25
(10)	New York Cuban Stars	.25
(11)	Minnesota Twins	.25
(12)	St. Louis Browns	.25
(13)	Detroit Tigers	.25
(14)	Kansas City Royals	.25
(15)	Detroit Stars	.25
(16)	Kansas City Athletics	.25
(17)	Florida Marlins	.25
(18)	New York Black Yankees	.25
(19)	New York Yankees	.25
(20)	New York Harlem Stars	.25
(21)	Philadelphia Stars	.25
(22)	New York Giants	.25
(23)	San Diego Padres	.25
(24)	Negro Leagues Classic Teams	.25
(25)	#21 (Clemente) patch	.25
(26)	St. Louis Cardinals	.25

Brooks Robinson

This 10-card insert set, numbered BR1 through BR10, traces the baseball career of Hall of Fame Orioles third baseman Brooks Robinson. Card fronts feature sepia-toned or color photos highlighted by the player's name in gold foil down the left side and a "Brooks Robinson Collection" diamond logo at lower-right. Backs include a career summary or batting or fielding stats. Autographed versions were a random retail packaging insert.

	NM/M
Complete Set (10):	7.50
Common Player:	1.00
Autographed:	20.00

1BR	Salad Days (Brooks Robinson)	1.00
2BR	Career Batting Stats (Brooks Robinson)	1.00
3BR	'66 World Series (Brooks Robinson)	1.00
4BR	Career Fielding Stats (Brooks Robinson)	1.00
5BR	'70 Series #2 (Brooks Robinson)	1.00
6BR	'70 Series #1 (Brooks Robinson)	1.00
7BR	Comin' Up (Brooks Robinson)	1.00
8BR	All Star Games (Brooks Robinson)	1.00
9BR	1964 (Brooks Robinson)	1.00
10BR	Brooks Robinson Collection Checklist	1.00

1994 Ted Williams Card Company

Lack of a players' association license again limited the company to using two major leaguers in its second annual card set, but it spiced up its 1994 edition with hot prospects in the minor leagues, more high-tech production values and innovative subsets and chase cards. The base set for 1994 includes 162 cards. The first 92 feature retired or deceased players. Those cards feature a color or colorized photo set against a background of a second ghost-image photo or the actual photo background. Vertically at right is a stone image on which the player's name is printed in extremely difficult to read gold letters. The edge of the stone and the card company logo are embossed. Backs have biographical and career details, and stats for the player's five top seasons. Subsets numbered consecutively with the base cards include a seven-card "Women of Baseball" series; 18 Negro Leaguers, 18 current minor leaguers in a series titled "The Campaign;" 10 "Goin' North" cards of former superstars as minor leaguers; nine "Swingin' for the Fences" cards of home run hitters, and, a nine-card "Dawning of a Legacy" series featuring Cliff Floyd and Tim Salmon. The several insert card series are listed separately. Autographed cards of Leon Day were random pack inserts.

	NM/M
Complete Set (162):	15.00
Common Player:	.10
Wax Pack (12):	1.00
Wax Box (36):	30.00
Jumbo Pack(20):	2.00
Jumbo Box (24):	35.00

1	Ted Williams	4.00
P1	Ted Williams (Promo card.)	2.50
2	Bernie Carbo	.10
3	Bobby Doerr	.10
4	Fred Lynn	.10
5	Johnny Pesky	.10
6	Rico Petrocelli	.10
7	Cy Young	.25
8	Paul Blair	.10
9	Andy Etchebarren	.10
10	Brooks Robinson	.20
11	Gil Hodges	.20
12	Tommy John	.15
13	Rick Monday	.10
14	Dean Chance	.10
15	Doug DeCinces	.10
16	Gabby Hartnett	.10
17	Don Kessinger	.10
18	Bruce Sutter	.20
19	Eddie Collins	.10
20	Casey May	.10
21	Nellie Fox	.10
22	Ted Kluszewski	.25
23	Vada Pinson	.10
24	Johnny Vander Meer	.10
25	Bob Feller	.20
26	Mike Garcia	.10
27	Sam McDowell	.10
28	Al Rosen	.10
29	Norm Cash	.15
30	Ty Cobb	1.50
31	Mark Fidrych	.20
32	Hank Greenberg	.25
33	Denny McLain	.10
34	Virgil Trucks	.10
35	Enos Cabell	.10
36	Mike Scott	.10
37	Bob Watson	.10
38	Amos Otis	.10
39	Frank White	.10
40	Joe Adcock	.10
41	Rico Carty	.10
42	Ralph Garr	.10
43	Eddie Mathews	.20
44	Ben Oglivie	.10
45	Gorman Thomas	.10
46	Earl Battey	.10
47	Rod Carew	.20
48	Jim Kaat	.10
49	Harmon Killebrew	.20
50	Gary Carter	.25
51	Steve Rogers	.10
52	Rusty Staub	.10
53	Sal Maglie	.10
54	Juan Marichal	.20
55	Mel Ott	.25
56	Bobby Thomson	.10
57	Tommie Agee	.10
58	Tug McGraw	.10
59	Elston Howard	.15
60	Sparky Lyle	.15
61	Billy Martin	.15
62	Thurman Munson	.25
63	Bobby Richardson	.15
64	Bill Skowron	.15
65	Mickey Cochrane	.10
66	Rollie Fingers	.10
67	Lefty Grove	.10
68	Catfish Hunter	.10
69	Connie Mack	.10
70	Al Simmons	.15
71	Dick Allen	.15
72	Bob Boone	.10
73	Del Ennis	.10
74	Chuck Klein	.10
75	Mike Schmidt	.50
76	Dock Ellis	.10
77	Elroy Face	.10
78	Phil Garner	.10
79	Bill Mazeroski	.20
80	Pie Traynor	.10
81	Honus Wagner	.25
82	Dizzy Dean	.25
83	Red Schoendienst	.10
84	Randy Jones	.10
85	Nate Colbert	.10
86	Jeff Burroughs	.10
87	Jim Sundberg	.10
88	Frank Howard	.10
89	Walter Johnson	.20
90	Eddie Yost	.10
91	Checklist 1-46	.10
92	Checklist 47-92	.10
93	Faye Dancer	.10
94	Snookie Doyle	.10
95	Maddy English	.10
96	Nickie Fox	.10
97	Sophie Kurys	.10
98	Alma Ziegler	.10
99	Women of Baseball Checklist	.10
100	Newton Allen	.10
101	Willard Brown	.10
102	Larry Brown	.10
103	Leon Day	.10
103a	Leon Day/Auto.	20.00
104	John Donaldson	.10
105	Rube Foster	.10
106	Bud Fowler	.10
107	Vic Harris	.10
108	Webster McDonald	.10
109	John "Buck" O'Neil	.10
110	Ted "Double Duty" Radcliffe	.10
111	Wilber "Bullet" Rogan	.10
112	Toni Stone	.10
113	Jim Taylor	.10
114	Moses "Fleetwood" Walker	.10
115	George Wilson	.10
116	Judson Wilson	.10
117	Negro Leagues Checklist	.10
118	Howard Battle	.10
119	John Burke	.10
120	Brian Dubose	.10
121	Alex Gonzalez	.15
122	Jose Herrera	.10
123	Jason Giambi	1.00
124	Derek Jeter	4.50
125	Charles Johnson	.25
126	Daron Kirkreit	.10
127	Jason Moler	.10
128	Vince Moore	.10
129	Chad Mottola	.10
130	Jose Silva	.10
131	Makato Suzuki (Makoto)	.10
132	Brien Taylor	.10
133	Michael Tucker	.10
134	Billy Wagner	.25
135	The Campaign Checklist	.10
136	Gary Carter	.10
137	Tony Conigliaro	.10
138	Sparky Lyle	.10
139	Roger Maris	.45
140	Vada Pinson	.10
141	Mike Schmidt	.50
142	Frank White	.10
143	Ted Williams	2.50
144	Goin' North Checklist	.10
145	Joe Adcock	.10
146	Rocky Colavito	.25
147	Lou Gehrig	2.00
148	Gil Hodges	.25
149	Bob Horner	.10
150	Willie Mays	1.50
151	Mike Schmidt	.50
152	Pat Seery	.10
153	Swingin' for the Fences Checklist	.10
154	Cliff Floyd (The Honors Begin)	.15
155	Cliff Floyd (The Top Polecat)	.15
156	Cliff Floyd (Minor League Team of the Year)	.15
157	Cliff Floyd (Major League Debut)	.15
158	Tim Salmon (Award Winner)	.15
159	Tim Salmon (Early Professional Career)	.15
160	Tim Salmon (An MVP Season)	.15
161	Tim Salmon (Rookie of the Year)	.15
162	Dawning of a Legacy Checklist	.10

Etched in Stone

A metallized effect highlights the front design of this insert series commemorating the career of Roger Maris. Color (or colorized) photos appear to have been revealed by chiseling away a rock face which forms much of the front border. Backs have career write-ups overprinted on a design which forms a large "Etched in Stone" design when the cards are laid together in order. Cards have an "ES" prefix to the card number. Cards can be found with either brown or red "rock" borders. The red version is valued at double the brown.

	NM/M
Complete Set (9):	7.50
Common Player:	1.00

1	Roger Maris (Scouting Report)	1.00
2	Roger Maris (Traded)	1.00
3	Roger Maris (Career Year)	1.00
4	Roger Maris/1961	1.00
5	Roger Maris (Silent Accomplishments)	1.00
6	Roger Maris (Team Player)	1.00
7	Roger Maris (Reborn)	1.00
8	Roger Maris (Hero's Welcome)	1.00
9	Checklist (Roger Maris)	.20

Dan Gardiner

Sports artist Dan Gardiner was commissioned to produce a series of nine insert cards depicting hot minor league prospects for this insert set. Players are depicted in posed portraits on front and in action paintings on the back. Cards carry a "DG" prefix to the card number and each card is serially numbered in the upper-left corner.

	NM/M
Complete Set (9):	6.00
Common Player:	.25

1	Michael Jordan	2.50
2	Michael Tucker	.25
3	Derek Jeter	3.50
4	Charles Johnson	.25
5	Howard Battle	.25
6	Quilvio Vergas (Veras)	.25
7	Brian Hunter	.25
8	Brien Taylor	.25
9	Checklist	.05

Locklear Collection

Paintings of eight Hall of Famers plus a checklist are featured in this insert set. The art is the work of former major leaguer Gene Locklear. The cards are numbered with an "LC" suffix.

	NM/M
Complete Set (9):	7.50
Common Player:	1.00

11	Ty Cobb	2.00
12	Bob Feller	1.00
13	Lou Gehrig	2.00
14	Josh Gibson	1.00
15	Walter Johnson	1.00
16	Casey Stengel	1.00
17	Honus Wagner	1.00
18	Cy Young	1.00
19	Checklist	.05

LP Cards

Two premium insert cards in the 1994 Ted Williams Co. set carry an "LP" card number prefix. One depicts basketball superstar Larry Bird playing baseball during his college days at Indiana State University. The other card depicts Ted Williams speaking at the open-ing of the Ted Williams Museum. Fronts use a metallized technology. Backs describe the action. A few genuinely autographed Bird cards are known, featuring an embossed seal of authenticity.

	NM/M
Complete Set (2):	8.00

1	Larry Bird	5.00
1a	Larry Bird/Auto.	200.00
2	Ted Williams	5.00

Memories

Continuing the card numbers from the 1993 Memories insert set, the 1994 version features highlights of the 1954, 1961, 1968 and 1975 World Series. Card fronts feature metallized images in a snapshot format. The year is noted in large pink numbers at lower-left. Backs describe each player's participation in that particular World Series and are numbered with an "M" prefix.

	NM/M
Complete Set (20):	11.00
Common Player:	.50

21	Monte Irvin	.50
22	Sal Maglie	.50
23	Dusty Rhodes	.50
24	Hank Thompson	.50
25	Yogi Berra	1.25
26	Elston Howard	.75
27	Roger Maris	1.50
28	Bobby Richardson	.75
29	Norm Cash	.75
30	Al Kaline	1.00
31	Mickey Lolich	.50
32	Denny McLain	.50
33	Bernie Carbo	.50
34	Fred Lynn	.50
35	Rico Petrocelli	.50
36	Luis Tiant	.50
37	Checklist	.05

Mike Schmidt Collection

This nine-card insert set honors the career of Hall of Fame Phillies third baseman Mike Schmidt. Fronts feature full-bleed metallized color photos. Backs have a Phillies flag design with a career biography. Cards are numbered with an "MS" prefix.

	NM/M
Complete Set (9):	7.50
Common Player:	1.00

1	Mike Schmidt (Mike)	1.00
2	Mike Schmidt (The White House)	1.00
3	Mike Schmidt (Soaping Up)	1.00
4	Mike Schmidt (The Promised Land)	1.00
5	Mike Schmidt (Who's Who)	1.00
6	Mike Schmidt (The Call)	1.00
7	Mike Schmidt (Leading the Way)	1.00
8	Mike Schmidt (Award Winner)	1.00
9	Checklist	.35

The 500 Club

Major leaguers with 500 or more career home runs are featured in this nine-card insert set. Fronts have full-bleed metallized photos, some in color and some which have been colorized. A logo picturing a hanging "The 500 Club" sign appears at lower-left, with the player's name in gold. Backs have a basic design that looks for all the world like a toilet seat, in which the player's home run prowess is recalled. Cards are numbered with a "5C" prefix. Two versions of each card exist, one has brown graphic highlights on front, one has red. The red highlighted cards are worth about 25 percent more than the brown.

		NM/M
Complete Set (9):		7.50
Common Player:		.75
1	Hank Aaron	1.50
2	Reggie Jackson	1.25
3	Harmon Killebrew	.75
4	Mickey Mantle	2.25
5	Jimmie Foxx	.75
6	Babe Ruth	2.00
7	Mike Schmidt	1.25
8	Ted Williams	1.50
9	Checklist	.05

Trade for Babe

This nine-card set was available to persons who found a randomly packaged "Trade for Babe" redemption card in packs of Ted Williams Co. cards. A $4.50 postage/handling fee was necessary for redemption and a reported 9,999 trade sets were available. Card fronts feature colorized photos of Ruth with backs have text concerning the front theme. Cards are numbered with a "TB" prefix.

		NM/M
Complete Set (9):		15.00
Common Player:		2.00
----	Babe Ruth (Redemption card), expired Nov. 30, 1994.)	2.00
1	Babe Ruth (George Herman Ruth)	2.00
2	Babe Ruth (King of the Hill)	2.00
3	Babe Ruth (On to New York)	2.00
4	Babe Ruth (Called Shot?)	2.00
5	Babe Ruth (The Bambino and the Iron Horse)	2.00
6	Babe Ruth (Larger Than Life)	2.00
7	Babe Ruth (Always a Yankee)	2.00
8	Babe Ruth (The Babe)	2.00
9	Babe Ruth (Checklist)	2.00

1990 Windwalker Discs

The origins of this disc set, even its name, are not recorded. The set is comprised on nine dual-

headed 3-7/8" discs. Each disc features two players from the 1990 American League All-Star team. No similar issue is known for the National League. Each side has a color action photo and a facsimile autograph. The unnumbered discs are checklisted here alphabetically.

		NM/M
Complete Set (9):		15.00
Common Disc:		.70
(1)	Sandy Alomar Jr., Dave Parker	.75
(2)	George Bell, Julio Franco	.75
(3)	Wade Boggs, Kirby Puckett	3.00
(4)	Jose Canseco, Rickey Henderson	2.50
(5)	Roger Clemens, Bob Welch	3.50
(6)	Cecil Fielder, Bret Saberhagen	.75
(7)	Chuck Finley, Kelly Gruber	.75
(8)	Ken Griffey Jr., Steve Sax	4.00
(9)	Ozzie Guillen, Cal Ripken Jr.	5.00

1991 Wiz Mets

This 450-card issue was one of several sponsored by the East Coast WIZ home entertainment stores in the early 1990s. Virtually every player in Mets history is included in the set. Each of three series of 15-card perforated sheets was co-sponsored by a large electronics manufacturer: AT&T, Fisher or Maxell. Sheets measure 10" x 9", with individual cards measuring 2" x 3". Card fronts have a black-and-white photo at center with the player's name at left and position at right. A color Mets logo is above and a WIZ logo below. Blue corner decorations complete the front design. Backs are printed in black-and-white, have Mets and sponsors' logos, years the player appeared with the Mets and his Mets career stats. Single cards from this set are seldom available.

		NM/M
Complete Set (450):		45.00
Common Player:		.10
1	Don Aase	.10
2	Tommie Agee	.30
3	Rick Aguilera	.20
4	Jack Aker	.10
5	Neil Allen	.10
6	Bill Almon	.10
7	Sandy Alomar	.10
8	Jesus Alou	.10
9	George Altman	.10
10	Luis Alvarado	.10
11	Craig Anderson	.10
12	Rick Anderson	.10
13	Bob Apodaca	.10
14	Gerry Arrigo	.10
15	Richie Ashburn	6.00
16	Tucker Ashford	.10
17	Bob Aspromonte	.10
18	Benny Ayala	.10
19	Wally Backman	.10
20	Kevin Baez	.10
21	Bob Bailor	.10
22	Rick Baldwin	.10
23	Billy Baldwin	.10
24	Lute Barnes	.10
25	Ed Bauta	.10
26	Billy Beane	.10
27	Larry Bearnarth	.10
28	Blaine Beatty	.10
29	Jim Beauchamp	.10
30	Gus Bell	.30
31	Dennis Bennett	.10
32	Butch Benton	.10
33	Juan Berenguer	.10
34	Bruce Berenyi	.10
35	Dwight Bernard	.10
36	Yogi Berra	6.00
37	Jim Bethke	.10
38	Mike Bishop	.10
39	Terry Blocker	.10
40	Bruce Bochy	.10
41	Bruce Boisclair	.10
42	Dan Boitano	.10
43	Mark Bomback	.10
44	Don Bosch	.10
45	Daryl Boston	.10
46	Ken Boswell	.10
47	Ed Bouchee	.10
48	Larry Bowa	.20
49	Ken Boyer	.50
50	Mark Bradley	.10
51	Eddie Bressoud	.10
52	Hubie Brooks	.10
53	Kevin Brown	.10
54	Leon Brown	.10
55	Mike Bruhert	.10
56	Jerry Buchek	.10
57	Larry Burright	.10
58	Ray Burris	.10
59	John Candelaria	.10
60	Chris Cannizzarro	.10
61	Buzz Capra	.10
62	Jose Cardenal	.10
63	Don Cardwell	.10
64	Duke Carmel	.10
65	Chuck Carr	.10
66	Mark Carreon	.10
67	Gary Carter	4.00
68	Elio Chacon	.10
69	Dean Chance	.10
70	Kelvin Chapman	.10
71	Ed Charles	.40
72	Rich Chiles	.10
73	Harry Chiti	.10
74	John Christensen	.10
75	Joe Christopher	.10
76	Galen Cisco	.10
77	Donn Clendenon	.40
78	Gene Clines	.10
79	Choo Choo Coleman	.40
80	Kevin Collins	.10
81	David Cone	.75
82	Bill Connors	.10
83	Cliff Cook	.10
84	Tim Corcoran	.10
85	Mardie Cornejo	.10
86	Billy Cowan	.10
87	Roger Craig	.40
88	Jerry Cram	.10
89	Mike Cubbage	.20
90	Ron Darling	.20
91	Ray Daviault	.10
92	Tommie Davis	.10
93	John DeMerit	.10
94	Bill Denehy	.10
95	Jack DiLauro	.10
96	Carlos Diaz	.10
97	Mario Diaz	.10
98	Steve Dillon	.10
99	Sammy Drake	.10
100	Jim Dwyer	.10
101	Duffy Dyer	.10
102	Len Dykstra	.50
103	Tom Edens	.10
104	Dave Eilers	.10
105	Larry Elliot	.10
106	Dock Ellis	.20
107	Kevin Elster	.10
108	Nino Espinosa	.10
109	Chuck Estrada	.10
110	Francisco Estrada	.10
111	Pete Falcone	.10
112	Sid Fernandez	.20
113	Chico Fernandez	.10
114	Sergio Ferrer	.10
115	Jack Fisher	.10
116	Mike Fitzgerald	.10
117	Shaun Fitzmaurice	.10
118	Gil Flores	.10
119	Doug Flynn	.10
120	Tim Foli	.10
121	Rich Folkers	.10
122	Larry Foss	.10
123	George Foster	.30
124	Leo Foster	.10
125	Joe Foy	.10
126	John Franco	.30
127	Jim Fregosi	.20
128	Bob Friend	.10
129	Danny Frisella	.10
130	Brent Gaff	.10
131	Bob Gallagher	.10
132	Ron Gardenhire	.10
133	Rob Gardner	.10
134	Wes Gardner	.10
135	Wayne Garrett	.10
136	Rod Gaspar	.10
137	Gary Gentry	.10
138	Jim Gibbons	.10
139	Bob Gibson	.10
140	Brian Giles	.10
141	Joe Ginsberg	.10
142	Ed Glynn	.10
143	Jesse Gonder	.30
144	Dwight Gooden	1.00
145	Greg Goossen	.10
146	Tom Gorman	.10
147	Jim Gosger	.10
148	Bill Graham	.10
149	Wayne Graham	.10
150	Dallas Green	.30
151	Pumpsie Green	.10
152	Tom Grieve	.10
153	Jerry Grote	.20
154	Joe Grzenda	.10
155	Don Hahn	.10
156	Tom Hall	.10
157	Jack Hamilton	.10
158	Ike Hampton	.10
159	Tim Harkness	.10
160	Bud Harrelson	.40
161	Greg Harris	.10
162	Greg Harts	.10
163	Andy Hassler	.10
164	Tom Hausman	.10
165	Ed Hearn	.10
166	Richie Hebner	.30
167	Danny Heep	.10
168	Jack Heidemann	.10
169	Bob Heise	.10
170	Ken Henderson	.10
171	Steve Henderson	.10
172	Bob Hendley	.10
173	Phil Hennigan	.10
174	Bill Hepler	.10
175	Ron Herbel	.10
176	Manny Hernandez	.10
177	Keith Hernandez	.50
178	Tommy Herr	.10
179	Rick Herrscher	.10
180	Jim Hickman	.10
181	Joe Hicks	.10
182	Chuck Hiller	.10
183	Dave Hillman	.10
184	Jerry Hinsley	.10
185	Gil Hodges	2.00
186	Ron Hodges	.10
187	Scott Holman	.10
188	Jay Hook	.10
189	Mike Howard	.10
190	Jesse Hudson	.10
191	Keith Hughes	.10
192	Todd Hundley	.30
193	Ron Hunt	.10
194	Willard Hunter	.10
195	Clint Hurdle	.10
196	Jeff Innis	.10
197	Al Jackson	.10
198	Roy Lee Jackson	.10
199	Gregg Jefferies	1.00
200	Stan Jefferson	.10
201	Chris Jelic	.10
202	Bob Johnson	.10
203	Howard Johnson	.75
204	Bob W. Johnson	.10
205	Randy Jones	.10
206	Sherman Jones	.10
207	Cleon Jones	.30
208	Ross Jones	.10
209	Mike Jorgensen	.10
210	Rod Kanehl	.10
211	Dave Kingman	.50
212	Bobby Klaus	.10
213	Jay Kleven	.10
214	Lou Klimchock	.10
215	Ray Knight	.30
216	Kevin Kobel	.10
217	Gary Kolb	.10
218	Cal Koonce	.10
219	Jerry Koosman	.30
220	Ed Kranepool	.30
221	Gary Kroll	.10
222	Clem Labine	.30
223	Jack Lamabe	.10
224	Hobie Landrith	.10
225	Frank Lary	.10
226	Bill Latham	.10
227	Terry Leach	.10
228	Tim Leary	.10
229	John Lewis	.10
230	David Liddell	.10
231	Phil Linz	.10
232	Ron Locke	.10
233	Skip Lockwood	.10
234	Mickey Lolich	.30
235	Phil Lombardi	.10
236	Al Luplow	.10
237	Ed Lynch	.10
238	Barry Lyons	.10
239	Ken MacKenzie	.10
240	Julio Machado	.10
241	Elliot Maddox	.10
242	Dave Magadan	.10
243	Phil Mankowski	.10
244	Felix Mantilla	.10
245	Mike Marshall	.10
246	Dave Marshall	.10
247	Jim Marshall	.10
248	Mike A. Marshall	.10
249	J.C. Martin	.10
250	Jerry Martin	.10
251	Teddy Martinez	.10
252	Jon Matlack	.20
253	Jerry May	.10
254	Willie Mays	15.00
255	Lee Mazzilli	.20
256	Jim McAndrew	.10
257	Bob McClure	.10
258	Roger McDowell	.30
259	Tug McGraw	.40
260	Jeff McKnight	.10
261	Roy McMillan	.10
262	Kevin McReynolds	.30
263	George Medich	.20
264	Orlando Mercado	.10
265	Butch Metzger	.10
266	Felix Millan	.10
267	Bob G. Miller	.10
268	Bob L. Miller	.10
269	Dyar Miller	.10
270	Larry Miller	.10
271	Keith Miller	.10
272	Randy Milligan	.10
273	John Milner	.10
274	John Mitchell	.10
275	Kevin Mitchell	.30
276	Wilmer Mizell	.10
277	Herb Moford	.10
278	Willie Montanez	.10
279	Joe Moock	.10
280	Tommy Moore	.10
281	Bob Moorhead	.10
282	Jerry Morales	.10
283	Al Moran	.10
284	Jose Moreno	.10
285	Bill Murphy	.10
286	Dale Murray	.10
287	Dennis Musgraves	.10
288	Jeff Musselman	.10
289	Randy Myers	.30
290	Bob Myrick	.10
291	Danny Napoleon	.10
292	Charlie Neal	.10
293	Randy Niemann	.10
294	Joe Nolan	.10
295	Dan Norman	.10
296	Ed Nunez	.10
297	Charlie O'Brien	.10
298	Tom O'Malley	.10
299	Bob Ojeda	.30
300	Jose Oquendo	.10
301	Jesse Orosco	.10
302	Junior Ortiz	.10
303	Brian Ostrosser	.10
304	Amos Otis	.30
305	Rick Ownbey	.10
306	John Pacella	.10
307	Tom Paciorek	.10
308	Harry Parker	.10
309	Tom Parsons	.10
310	Al Pedrique	.10
311	Brock Pemberton	.10
312	Alejandro Pena	.10
313	Bobby Pfeil	.10
314	Mike Phillips	.10
315	Jim Piersall	.30
316	Joe Pignatano	.10
317	Grover Powell	.10
318	Rich Puig	.10
319	Charlie Puleo	.10
320	Gary Rajsich	.10
321	Mario Ramirez	.10
322	Lenny Randle	.10
323	Bob Rauch	.10
324	Jeff Reardon	.30
325	Darren Reed	.10
326	Hal Reniff	.10
327	Ronn Reynolds	.10
328	Tom Reynolds	.10
329	Dennis Ribant	.10
330	Gordie Richardson	.10
331	Dave Roberts	.10
332	Les Rohr	.10
333	Luis Rosado	.10
334	Don Rose	.10
335	Don Rowe	.10
336	Dick Rusteck	.10
337	Nolan Ryan	15.00
338	Ray Sadecki	.10
339	Joe Sambito	.10
340	Amado Samuel	.10
341	Juan Samuel	.10
342	Ken Sanders	.10
343	Rafael Santana	.10
344	Mackey Sasser	.10
345	Mac Scarce	.10
346	Jim Schaffer	.10
347	Dan Schatzeder	.10
348	Calvin Schiraldi	.10
349	Al Schmelz	.10
350	Dave Schneck	.10
351	Ted Schreiber	.10
352	Don Schulze	.10
353	Mike Scott	.30
354	Ray Searage	.10
355	Tom Seaver	10.00
356	Dick Selma	.10
357	Art Shamsky	.30
358	Bob Shaw	.10
359	Don Shaw	.10
360	Norm Sherry	.10
361	Craig Shipley	.10
362	Bart Shirley	.10
363	Bill Short	.10
364	Paul Siebert	.10
365	Ken Singleton	.30
366	Doug Sisk	.10
367	Bobby Gene Smith	.10
368	Charley Smith	.10
369	Dick Smith	.10
370	Duke Snider	10.00
371	Warren Spahn	4.00
372	Larry Stahl	.10
373	Roy Staiger	.10
374	Tracy Stallard	.10
375	Leroy Stanton	.10
376	Rusty Staub	1.00
377	John Stearns	.10
378	John Stephenson	.10
379	Randy Sterling	.10
380	George Stone	.10
381	Darryl Strawberry	1.00
382	John Strohmayer	.10
383	Brent Strom	.10
384	Dick Stuart	.30
385	Tom Sturdivant	.10
386	Bill Sudakis	.10
387	John Sullivan	.10
388	Darrell Sutherland	.10
389	Ron Swoboda	.30
390	Craig Swan	.10
391	Rick Sweet	.10
392	Pat Tabler	.10
393	Kevin Tapani	.50
394	Randy Tate	.10
395	Frank Taveras	.10
396	Chuck Taylor	.10
397	Ron Taylor	.10
398	Bob Taylor	.10
399	Sammy Taylor	.10
400	Walt Terrell	.10
401	Ralph Terry	.10
402	Tim Teufel	.30
403	George Theodore	.10
404	Frank Thomas	.20
405	Lou Thornton	.10
406	Marv Throneberry	.50
407	Dick Tidrow	.10
408	Rusty Tillman	.10
409	Jackson Todd	.10
410	Joe Torre	1.50
411	Mike Torrez	.10
412	Kelvin Torve	.10
413	Alex Trevino	.10
414	Wayne Twitchell	.10
415	Del Unser	.10
416	Mike Vail	.10
417	Bobby Valentine	.40
418	Ellis Valentine	.10
419	Julio Valera	.10
420	Tom Veryzer	.10
421	Frank Viola	.30
422	Bill Wakefield	.10
423	Gene Walter	.10
424	Claudell Washington	.10
425	Hank Webb	.10
426	Al Weis	.20
427	Dave West	.10
428	Wally Whitehurst	.10
429	Carl Willey	.10
430	Nick Willhite	.10
431	Charlie Williams	.10
432	Mookie Wilson	.60
433	Herm Winningham	.10
434	Gene Woodling	.30
435	Billy Wynne	.10
436	Joel Youngblood	.10
437	Pat Zachry	.10
438	Don Zimmer	.30
439	Chris Jelic	.10
(440)	Checklist 1-40	
(441)	Checklist 41-80	
(442)	Checklist 81-120	
(443)	Checklist 121-160	
(444)	Checklist 161-200	
(445)	Checklist 201-240	
(446)	Checklist 241-280	
(447)	Checklist 281-320	
(448)	Checklist 321-360	
(449)	Checklist 361-400	
(450)	Checklist 401-439	

1991 Wiz Yankees of the '50's

Yankees players from the 1950s dynasty are featured in this set distributed in several series at various promotional games. The cards were produced in a perforated sheet format, the 2" x 3" individual cards can be separated with ease. Fronts feature blue-and-white duo-tone photos with the familiar Yankee Stadium facade in blue at top and the player name in black below. Backs are printed in blue on white. The series name is printed beneath the top name bar, along with a line indicating the player's years with the Yankees and a few career stats. At bottom of all cards are Wiz Home Entertainment Centers and AT&T logos, along with a Yankees Classics logo. The unnumbered cards are checklisted here alphabetically.

		NM/M
Complete Set, Panels (9):		20.00
Complete Set, Singles (125):		20.00
Common Player:		.25
(1)	Loren Babe	.25
(2)	Hank Bauer	.40
(3)	Zeke Bella	.25
(4)	Lou Berberet	.25
(5)	Yogi Berra	2.00
(6)	Ewell Blackwell	.35
(7)	Johnny Blanchard	.35
(8)	Gary Blaylock	.25
(9)	Don Bollweg	.25
(10)	Clete Boyer	.35
(11)	Ralph Branca	.25
(12)	Fritzie Brickell	.25
(13)	Jim Bridweser	.25
(14)	Jim Bronstad	.50

(15)	Bobby Brown	.35
(16)	Lew Burdette	.35
(17)	Harry Byrd	.25
(18)	Tommy Byrne	.25
(19)	Andy Carey	.25
(20)	Tommy Carroll	.25
(21)	Bob Cerv	.35
(22)	Al Cicotte	.25
(23)	Jim Coates	.25
(24)	Jerry Coleman	.25
(25)	Rip Coleman	.25
(26)	Joe Collins	.25
(27)	Clint Courtney	.25
(28)	Bobby Del Greco	.25
(29)	Jim Delsing	.25
(30)	Murry Dickson	.25
(31)	Joe DiMaggio	6.00
(32)	Art Ditmar	.25
(33)	Sonny Dixon	.25
(34)	Ryne Duren	.35
(35)	Tom Ferrick	.25
(36)	Whitey Ford	2.00
(37)	Mark Freeman	.25
(38)	Tom Gorman	.25
(39)	Ted Gray	.25
(40)	Eli Grba	.25
(41)	Bob Grim	.25
(42)	Woodie Held	.25
(43)	Tommy Henrich	.35
(44)	Johnny Hopp	.25
(45)	Ralph Houk	.35
(46)	Elston Howard	.50
(47)	Ken Hunt	.25
(48)	Billy Hunter	.25
(49)	Johnny James	.25
(50)	Jackie Jensen	.45
(51)	Billy Johnson	.25
(52)	Darrell Johnson	.25
(53)	Charlie Keller	.35
(54)	Jim Konstanty	.25
(55)	Steve Kraly	.25
(56)	Jack Kramer	.25
(57)	Tony Kubek	.50
(58)	Johnny Kucks	.25
(59)	Bob Kuzava	.25
(60)	Don Larsen	1.00
(61)	Frank Leja	.25
(62)	Johnny Lindell	.25
(63)	Ed Lopat	.40
(64)	Hector Lopez	.25
(65)	Jerry Lumpe	.25
(66)	Duke Maas	.25
(67)	Dave Madison	.25
(68)	Sal Maglie	.35
(69)	Mickey Mantle	12.00
(70)	Cliff Mapes	.25
(71)	Billy Martin	1.50
(72)	Mickey McDermott	.25
(73)	Jim McDonald	.25
(74)	Gil McDougald	.45
(75)	Bill Miller	.25
(76)	Willie Miranda	.25
(77)	Johnny Mize	.75
(78)	Zack Monroe	.25
(79)	Tom Morgan	.25
(80)	Bob Muncrief	.25
(81)	Ernie Nevel	.50
(82)	Irv Noren	.25
(83)	Joe Ostrowski	.25
(84)	Stubby Overmire	.25
(85)	Joe Page	.25
(86)	Duane Pillette	.25
(87)	Jim Pisoni	.25
(88)	Bob Porterfield	.25
(89)	Vic Raschi	.50
(90)	Bill Renna	.25
(91)	Allie Reynolds	.50
(92)	Bobby Richardson	.75
(93)	Phil Rizzuto	2.00
(94)	Eddie Robinson	.25
(95)	Johnny Sain	.50
(96)	Fred Sanford	.25
(97)	Ray Scarborough	.25
(98)	Harry Schaeffer	.25
(99)	Art Schallock (Schallock)	.50
(100)	Johnny Schmitz	.25
(101)	Art Schults	.50
(102)	Kal Segrist	.25
(103)	Bobby Shantz	.35
(104)	Spec Shea	.25
(105)	Norm Siebern	.25
(106)	Charlie Silvera	.25
(107)	Harry Simpson	.35
(108)	Lou Skizas	.25
(109)	Bill Skowron	.75
(110)	Enos Slaughter	1.00
(111)	Gerry Staley	.25
(112)	Snuffy Stirnweiss	.25
(113)	Marlin Stuart	.25
(114)	Tom Sturdivant	.25
(115)	Bill Terry	.25
(116)	Dick Tettelbach	.50
(117)	Marv Throneberry	.35
(118)	Gus Triandos	.25
(119)	Virgil Trucks	.35
(120)	Bob Turley	.50
(121)	Frank Verdi	.25
(122)	Dick Wakefield	.25
(123)	Bob Wiesler	.25
(124)	Archie Wilson	.25
(125)	George Wilson	.25

1992 Wiz Yankees Classics

More than 600 different Yankees players from the turn of the century through the 1980s are featured in this set. Produced and dis-

TUCKER ASHFORD

tributed in five series at various promotional games, the cards share a common design and theme. Originally in a 10" x 9" perforated sheet format, the 2" x 3" individual cards can be separated with ease. Fronts feature blue-and-white duo-tone photos with the familiar Yankee Stadium facade in blue at top and the player name in black below. Backs are printed in blue on white. The series name is printed beneath the top name bar, along with a line indicating the player's years with the Yankees and a few career stats. At bottom of all cards are the Yankees Classics and Wiz Home Entertainment Centers logos, along with the logo of the co-sponsor. The Yankees of the '60s and All-Star series were co-sponsored by American Express; the '70s series by Fisher; the '80s by Minolta and the Hall of Famers by Aiwa. The unnumbered cards are checklisted here alphabetically within series.

		NM/M
Complete Set (638):		95.00
Common Player:		.20
Complete Series, Yankees of the '60s:		**25.00**
(1)	Jack Aker	.20
(2)	Ruben Amaro	.20
(3)	Luis Arroyo	.20
(4)	Stan Bahnsen	.20
(5)	Steve Barber	.20
(6)	Ray Barker	.20
(7)	Rich Beck	.20
(8)	Yogi Berra	2.00
(9)	Johnny Blanchard	.50
(10)	Gil Blanco	.20
(11)	Ron Blomberg	.20
(12)	Len Boehmer	.20
(13)	Jim Bouton	.50
(14)	Clete Boyer	.50
(15)	Jim Brenneman	.20
(16)	Marshall Bridges	.20
(17)	Harry Bright	.20
(18)	Hal Brown	.20
(19)	Billy Bryan	.20
(20)	Bill Burbach	.20
(21)	Andy Carey	.20
(22)	Duke Carmel	.20
(23)	Bob Cerv	.20
(24)	Horace Clarke	.20
(25)	Tex Clevenger	.20
(26)	Lu Clinton	.20
(27)	Jim Coates	.20
(28)	Rocky Colavito	1.50
(29)	Billy Cowan	.20
(30)	Bobby Cox	.50
(31)	Jack Cullen	.20
(32)	John Cumberland	.20
(33)	Bud Daley	.20
(34)	Joe DeMaestri	.20
(35)	Art Ditmar	.20
(36)	Al Downing	.30
(37)	Ryne Duren	.20
(38)	Doc Edwards	.20
(39)	John Ellis	.20
(40)	Frank Fernandez	.20
(41)	Mike Ferraro	.20
(42)	Whitey Ford	2.00
(43)	Bob Friend	.20
(44)	John Gabler	.20
(45)	Billy Gardner	.20
(46)	Jake Gibbs	.20
(47)	Jesse Gonder	.20
(48)	Pedro Gonzalez	.20
(49)	Eli Grba	.20
(50)	Kent Hadley	.20
(51)	Bob Hale	.20
(52)	Jimmie Hall	.20
(53)	Steve Hamilton	.20
(54)	Mike Hegan	.30
(55)	Bill Henry	.20
(56)	Elston Howard	.90
(57)	Dick Howser	.50
(58)	Ken Hunt	.20
(59)	Johnny James	.20

(60)	Elvio Jiminez	.20
(61)	Deron Johnson	.30
(62)	Ken Johnson	.20
(63)	Mike Jurewicz	.50
(64)	Mike Kekich	.20
(65)	John Kennedy	.20
(66)	Jerry Kenney	.20
(67)	Fred Kipp	.20
(68)	Ron Klimkowski	.20
(69)	Andy Kosco	.20
(70)	Tony Kubek	.75
(71)	Bill Kunkel	.20
(72)	Phil Linz	.20
(73)	Dale Long	.20
(74)	Art Lopez	.20
(75)	Hector Lopez	.20
(76)	Jim Lyttle	.20
(77)	Duke Maas	.20
(78)	Mickey Mantle	10.00
(79)	Roger Maris	4.00
(80)	Lindy McDaniel	.20
(81)	Danny McDevitt	.20
(82)	Dave McDonald	.20
(83)	Gil McDougald	.50
(84)	Tom Metcalf	.20
(85)	Bob Meyer	.20
(86)	Gene Michael	.30
(87)	Pete Mikkelsen	.20
(88)	John Miller	.20
(89)	Bill Monbouquette	.20
(90)	Archie Moore	.20
(91)	Ross Moschitto	.20
(92)	Thurman Munson	2.00
(93)	Bobby Murcer	.75
(94)	Don Nottebart	.20
(95)	Nate Oliver	.20
(96)	Joe Pepitone	.50
(97)	Cecil Perkins	.20
(98)	Fritz Peterson	.20
(99)	Jim Pisoni	.20
(100)	Pedro Ramos	.20
(101)	Jack Reed	.20
(102)	Hal Reniff	.20
(103)	Roger Repoz	.20
(104)	Bobby Richardson	.90
(105)	Dale Roberts	.50
(106)	Bill Robinson	.20
(107)	Ellie Rodriguez	.20
(108)	Charlie Sands	.20
(109)	Bob Schmidt	.20
(110)	Dick Schofield	.30
(111)	Billy Shantz	.20
(112)	Bobby Shantz	.30
(113)	Rollie Sheldon	.20
(114)	Tom Shopay	.20
(115)	Bill Short	.20
(116)	Dick Simpson	.20
(117)	Bill Skowron	.50
(118)	Charley Smith	.20
(119)	Tony Solaita	.20
(120)	Bill Stafford	.20
(121)	Mel Stottlemyre	.30
(122)	Hal Stowe	.20
(123)	Fred Talbot	.20
(124)	Frank Tepedino	.20
(125)	Ralph Terry	.20
(126)	Lee Thomas	.20
(127)	Bobby Tiefenauer	.20
(128)	Bob Tillman	.20
(129)	Thad Tillotson	.20
(130)	Earl Torgeson	.20
(131)	Tom Tresh	.50
(132)	Bob Turley	.40
(133)	Elmer Valo	.20
(134)	Joe Verbanic	.20
(135)	Steve Whitaker	.20
(136)	Roy White	.40
(137)	Stan Williams	.20
(138)	Dooley Womack	.20
(139)	Ron Woods	.20
(140)	John Wyatt	.20
Complete Series, Yankees of the '70s		**16.00**
(1)	Jack Aker	.20
(2)	Doyle Alexander	.20
(3)	Bernie Allen	.20
(4)	Sandy Alomar	.20
(5)	Felipe Alou	.25
(6)	Matty Alou	.20
(7)	Dell Alston	.20
(8)	Rich Anderson	.20
(9)	Stan Bahnsen	.20
(10)	Frank Baker	.20
(11)	Jim Beattie	.20
(12)	Fred Beene	.20
(13)	Juan Beniquez	.20
(14)	Dave Bergman	.20
(15)	Juan Bernhardt	.20
(16)	Rick Bladt	.20
(17)	Paul Blair	.20
(18)	Wade Blasingame	.20
(19)	Steve Blateric	.20
(20)	Curt Blefary	.20
(21)	Ron Blomberg	.20
(22)	Len Boehmer	.20
(23)	Bobby Bonds	.30
(24)	Ken Brett	.20
(25)	Ed Brinkman	.20
(26)	Bobby Brown	.20
(27)	Bill Burbach	.20
(28)	Ray Burris	.20
(29)	Tom Buskey	.20
(30)	Johnny Callison	.20
(31)	Danny Cater	.20
(32)	Chris Chambliss	.30
(33)	Horace Clarke	.20
(34)	Ken Clay	.20
(35)	Al Closter	.20

(36)	Rich Coggins	.20
(37)	Loyd Colson	.20
(38)	Casey Cox	.20
(39)	John Cumberland	.20
(40)	Ron Davis	.20
(41)	Jim Deidel	.20
(42)	Rick Dempsey	.30
(43)	Bucky Dent	.40
(44)	Kerry Dineen	.20
(45)	Pat Dobson	.20
(46)	Brian Doyle	.20
(47)	Rawly Eastwick	.20
(48)	Dock Ellis	.20
(49)	John Ellis	.20
(50)	Ed Figueroa	.20
(51)	Oscar Gamble	.20
(52)	Damaso Garcia	.20
(53)	Rob Gardner	.20
(54)	Jake Gibbs	.20
(55)	Fernando Gonzalez	.20
(56)	Rich Gossage	.40
(57)	Larry Gowell	.20
(58)	Wayne Granger	.20
(59)	Mike Griffin	.20
(60)	Ron Guidry	.75
(61)	Brad Gulden	.20
(62)	Don Gullett	.20
(63)	Larry Gura	.20
(64)	Roger Hambright	.20
(65)	Steve Hamilton	.20
(66)	Ron Hansen	.20
(67)	Jim Hardin	.20
(68)	Jim Ray Hart	.20
(69)	Fran Healy	.20
(70)	Mike Heath	.20
(71)	Mike Hegan	.30
(72)	Elrod Hendricks	.20
(73)	Ed Herrmann	.20
(74)	Rich Hinton	.20
(75)	Ken Holtzman	.20
(76)	Don Hood	.20
(77)	Catfish Hunter	1.00
(78)	Grant Jackson	.20
(79)	Reggie Jackson	2.00
(80)	Tommy John	.90
(81)	Alex Johnson	.20
(82)	Cliff Johnson	.20
(83)	Jay Johnstone	.30
(84)	Darryl Jones	.20
(85)	Gary Jones	.20
(86)	Jim Kaat	.40
(87)	Bob Kammeyer	.20
(88)	Mike Kekich	.20
(89)	Jerry Kenney	.20
(90)	Dave Kingman	.50
(91)	Ron Klimkowski	.20
(92)	Steve Kline	.20
(93)	Mickey Klutts	.20
(94)	Hal Lanier	.20
(95)	Eddie Leon	.20
(96)	Terry Ley	.20
(97)	Paul Lindblad	.20
(98)	Gene Locklear	.20
(99)	Sparky Lyle	.40
(100)	Jim Lyttle	.20
(101)	Elliott Maddox	.20
(102)	Jim Magnuson	.20
(103)	Tippy Martinez	.20
(104)	Jim Mason	.20
(105)	Carlos May	.20
(106)	Rudy May	.20
(107)	Larry McCall	.20
(108)	Mike McCormick	.20
(109)	Lindy McDaniel	.20
(110)	Sam McDowell	.30
(111)	Rich McKinney	.20
(112)	George Medich	.20
(113)	Andy Messersmith	.30
(114)	Gene Michael	.20
(115)	Paul Mirabella	.20
(116)	Bobby Mitchell	.20
(117)	Gerry Moses	.20
(118)	Thurman Munson	2.00
(119)	Bobby Murcer	.75
(120)	Larry Murray	.20
(121)	Jerry Narron	.20
(122)	Graig Nettles	.40
(123)	Bob Oliver	.20
(124)	Dave Pagan	.20
(125)	Gil Patterson	.20
(126)	Marty Perez	.20
(127)	Fritz Peterson	.20
(128)	Lou Piniella	.50
(129)	Dave Rajsich	.20
(130)	Domingo Ramos	.20
(131)	Lenny Randle	.20
(132)	Willie Randolph	.50
(133)	Dave Righetti	.30
(134)	Mickey Rivers	.30
(135)	Bruce Robinson	.20
(136)	Jim Roland	.20
(137)	Celerino Sanchez	.20
(138)	Rick Sawyer	.20
(139)	George Scott	.30
(140)	Duke Sims	.20
(141)	Roger Slagle	.20
(142)	Jim Spencer	.20
(143)	Charlie Spikes	.20
(144)	Roy Staiger	.20
(145)	Fred Stanley	.30
(146)	Bill Sudakis	.20
(147)	Ron Swoboda	.20
(148)	Frank Tepedino	.20
(149)	Stan Thomas	.20
(150)	Gary Thomasson	.20
(151)	Luis Tiant	.40
(152)	Dick Tidrow	.20
(153)	Rusty Torres	.20

(154)	Mike Torrez	.20
(155)	Cesar Tovar	.20
(156)	Cecil Upshaw	.20
(157)	Otto Velez	.20
(158)	Joe Verbanic	.20
(159)	Mike Wallace	.20
(160)	Danny Walton	.20
(161)	Pete Ward	.20
(162)	Gary Waslewski	.20
(163)	Dennis Werth	.20
(164)	Roy White	.30
(165)	Terry Whitfield	.20
(166)	Walt Williams	.20
(167)	Ron Woods	.20
(168)	Dick Woodson	.20
(169)	Ken Wright	.20
(170)	Jimmy Wynn	.20
(171)	Jim York	.20
(172)	George Zeber	.20
Complete Series, Yankees of the '80s:		**17.50**
(1)	Luis Aguayo	.20
(2)	Doyle Alexander	.20
(3)	Neil Allen	.20
(4)	Mike Armstrong	.20
(5)	Brad Arnsberg	.20
(6)	Tucker Ashford	.20
(7)	Steve Balboni	.20
(8)	Jesse Barfield	.30
(9)	Don Baylor	.40
(10)	Dale Berra	.20
(11)	Doug Bird	.20
(12)	Paul Blair	.20
(13)	Mike Blowers	.20
(14)	Juan Bonilla	.20
(15)	Rich Bordi	.20
(16)	Scott Bradley	.20
(17)	Marshall Brant	.20
(18)	Tom Brookens	.20
(19)	Bob Brower	.20
(20)	Bobby Brown	.20
(21)	Curt Brown	.20
(22)	Jay Buhner	.50
(23)	Marty Bystrom	.20
(24)	Greg Cadaret	.20
(25)	Bert Campaneris	.30
(26)	John Candelaria	.20
(27)	Chuck Cary	.20
(28)	Bill Castro	.20
(29)	Rick Cerone	.20
(30)	Chris Chambliss	.30
(31)	Clay Christiansen	.20
(32)	Jack Clark	.30
(33)	Pat Clements	.20
(34)	Dave Collins	.25
(35)	Don Cooper	.20
(36)	Henry Cotto	.20
(37)	Joe Cowley	.20
(38)	Jose Cruz	.20
(39)	Bobby Davidson	.20
(40)	Ron Davis	.20
(41)	Brian Dayett	.20
(42)	Ivan DeJesus	.20
(43)	Bucky Dent	.50
(44)	Jim Deshaies	.20
(45)	Orestes Destrade	.20
(46)	Brian Dorsett	.20
(47)	Rich Dotson	.20
(48)	Brian Doyle	.20
(49)	Doug Drabek	.30
(50)	Mike Easler	.20
(51)	Dave Eiland	.20
(52)	Roger Erickson	.20
(53)	Juan Espino	.20
(54)	Alvaro Espinoza	.20
(55)	Barry Evans	.20
(56)	Ed Figueroa	.20
(57)	Pete Filson	.20
(58)	Mike Fischlin	.20
(59)	Brian Fisher	.20
(60)	Tim Foli	.20
(61)	Ray Fontenot	.20
(62)	Barry Foote	.20
(63)	George Frazier	.20
(64)	Bill Fulton	.20
(65)	Oscar Gamble	.20
(66)	Bob Geren	.20
(67)	Rich Gossage	.40
(68)	Mike Griffin	.20
(69)	Ken Griffey	.30
(70)	Cecilio Guante	.20
(71)	Lee Guetterman	.20
(72)	Ron Guidry	.50
(73)	Brad Gulden	.20
(74)	Don Gullett	.20
(75)	Bill Gullickson	.20
(76)	Mel Hall	.20
(77)	Toby Harrah	.25
(78)	Ron Hassey	.20
(79)	Andy Hawkins	.20
(80)	Rickey Henderson	1.50
(81)	Leo Hernandez	.20
(82)	Butch Hobson	.20
(83)	Al Holland	.20
(84)	Roger Holt	.20
(85)	Jay Howell	.25
(86)	Rex Hudler	.20
(87)	Charles Hudson	.20
(88)	Keith Hughes	.20
(89)	Reggie Jackson	2.00
(90)	Stan Javier	.20
(91)	Stan Jefferson	.20
(92)	Tommy John	.50
(93)	Jimmy Jones	.20
(94)	Ruppert Jones	.20
(95)	Jim Kaat	.30
(96)	Curt Kaufman	.20
(97)	Roberto Kelly	.30

(98)	Steve Kemp	.25
(99)	Matt Keough	.20
(100)	Steve Kiefer	.20
(101)	Ron Kittle	.20
(102)	Dave LaPoint	.20
(103)	Marcus Lawton	.20
(104)	Joe Lefebvre	.20
(105)	Al Leiter	.20
(106)	Jim Lewis	.20
(107)	Bryan Little	.20
(108)	Tim Lollar	.20
(109)	Phil Lombardi	.20
(110)	Vic Mata	.20
(111)	Don Mattingly	4.00
(112)	Rudy May	.20
(113)	John Mayberry	.20
(114)	Lee Mazzilli	.25
(115)	Lance McCullers	.20
(116)	Andy McGaffigan	.20
(117)	Lynn McGlothen	.20
(118)	Bobby Meacham	.20
(119)	Hensley Muelens	.30
(120)	Larry Milbourne	.20
(121)	Kevin Mmahat	.20
(122)	Dale Mohorcic	.20
(123)	John Montefusco	.20
(124)	Omar Moreno	.20
(125)	Mike Morgan	.20
(126)	Jeff Moronko	.20
(127)	Hal Morris	.25
(128)	Jerry Mumphrey	.20
(129)	Bobby Murcer	.35
(130)	Dale Murray	.20
(131)	Gene Nelson	.20
(132)	Joe Niekro	.20
(133)	Phil Niekro	.90
(134)	Scott Nielsen	.20
(135)	Otis Nixon	.20
(136)	Johnny Oates	.20
(137)	Mike O'Berry	.20
(138)	Rowland Office	.20
(139)	John Pacella	.20
(140)	Mike Pagliarulo	.30
(141)	Clay Parker	.20
(142)	Dan Pasqua	.30
(143)	Mike Patterson	.20
(144)	Hipolito Pena	.20
(145)	Gaylord Perry	.50
(146)	Ken Phelps	.20
(147)	Lou Piniella	.40
(148)	Eric Plunk	.20
(149)	Luis Polonia	.30
(150)	Alfonso Pulido	.20
(151)	Jamie Quirk	.20
(152)	Bobby Ramos	.20
(153)	Willie Randolph	.40
(154)	Dennis Rasmussen	.20
(155)	Shane Rawley	.20
(156)	Rick Reuschel	.20
(157)	Dave Revering	.20
(158)	Rick Rhoden	.20
(159)	Dave Righetti	.30
(160)	Jose Rijo	.20
(161)	Andre Robertson	.20
(162)	Bruce Robinson	.20
(163)	Aurelio Rodriguez	.20
(164)	Edwin Rodriguez	.20
(165)	Gary Roenicke	.20
(166)	Jerry Royster	.20
(167)	Lenn Sakata	.20
(168)	Mark Salas	.20
(169)	Billy Sample	.20
(170)	Deion Sanders	1.00
(171)	Rafael Santana	.20
(172)	Steve Sax	.30
(173)	Don Schulze	.20
(174)	Rodney Scott	.20
(175)	Rod Scurry	.20
(176)	Dennis Sherrill	.20
(177)	Steve Shields	.20
(178)	Bob Shirley	.20
(179)	Joel Skinner	.20
(180)	Don Slaught	.30
(181)	Roy Smalley	.20
(182)	Keith Smith	.20
(183)	Eric Soderholm	.20
(184)	Jim Spencer	.20
(185)	Fred Stanley	.20
(186)	Dave Stegman	.20
(187)	Tim Stoddard	.20
(188)	Walt Terrell	.20
(189)	Bob Tewksbury	.25
(190)	Luis Tiant	.40
(191)	Wayne Tolleson	.20
(192)	Steve Trout	.20
(193)	Tom Underwood	.20
(194)	Randy Velarde	.30
(195)	Gary Ward	.20
(196)	Claudell Washington	.30
(197)	Bob Watson	.20
(198)	Dave Wehrmeister	.20
(199)	Dennis Werth	.20
(200)	Stefan Wever	.20
(201)	Ed Whitson	.20
(202)	Ted Wilborn	.20
(203)	Dave Winfield	1.00
(204)	Butch Wynegar	.20
(205)	Paul Zuvella	.20
Complete Series, Yankees All-Stars		**17.50**
(1)	Luis Arroyo	.20
(2)	Hank Bauer	.35
(3)	Yogi Berra	2.00
(4)	Bobby Bonds	.30
(5)	Ernie Bonham	.20
(6)	Hank Borowy	.20
(7)	Jim Bouton	.30
(8)	Tommy Byrne	.20

(9)	Chris Chambliss	.20
(10)	Spud Chandler	.20
(11)	Ben Chapman	.20
(12)	Jim Coates	.20
(13)	Jerry Coleman	.20
(14)	Frank Crosetti	.20
(15)	Ron Davis	.20
(16)	Bucky Dent	.30
(17)	Bill Dickey	.50
(18)	Joe DiMaggio	6.00
(19)	Al Downing	.20
(20)	Ryne Duren	.30
(21)	Whitey Ford	2.00
(22)	Lou Gehrig	6.00
(23)	Lefty Gomez	.40
(24)	Joe Gordon	.20
(25)	Rich Gossage	.30
(26)	Bob Grim	.20
(27)	Ron Guidry	.30
(28)	Rollie Hemsley	.20
(29)	Rickey Henderson	1.50
(30)	Tommy Henrich	.20
(31)	Elston Howard	.35
(32)	Catfish Hunter	.30
(33)	Reggie Jackson	2.00
(34)	Tommy John	.20
(35)	Billy Johnson	.20
(36)	Charlie Keller	.20
(37)	Tony Kubek	.35
(38)	Johnny Kucks	.20
(39)	Tony Lazzeri	.30
(40)	Johnny Lindell	.20
(41)	Ed Lopat	.30
(42)	Sparky Lyle	.30
(43)	Mickey Mantle	10.00
(44)	Roger Maris	4.00
(45)	Billy Martin	.75
(46)	Don Mattingly	4.00
(47)	Gil McDougald	.20
(48)	George McQuinn	.20
(49)	Johnny Mize	.40
(50)	Thurman Munson	2.00
(51)	Bobby Murcer	.30
(52)	Johnny Murphy	.20
(53)	Graig Nettles	.30
(54)	Phil Niekro	.80
(55)	Irv Noren	.20
(56)	Joe Page	.20
(57)	Monte Pearson	.20
(58)	Joe Pepitone	.30
(59)	Fritz Peterson	.20
(60)	Willie Randolph	.30
(61)	Vic Raschi	.20
(62)	Allie Reynolds	.35
(63)	Bobby Richardson	.35
(64)	Dave Righetti	.20
(65)	Mickey Rivers	.20
(66)	Phil Rizzuto	2.00
(67)	Aaron Robinson	.20
(68)	Red Rolfe	.20
(69)	Buddy Rosar	.20
(70)	Red Ruffing	.20
(71)	Marius Russo	.20
(72)	Babe Ruth	7.50
(73)	Johnny Sain	.40
(74)	Scott Sanderson	.20
(75)	Steve Sax	.20
(76)	George Selkirk	.20
(77)	Bobby Shantz	.20
(78)	Spec Shea	.20
(79)	Bill Skowron	.35
(80)	Snuffy Stirnweiss	.20
(81)	Mel Stottlemyre	.20
(82)	Ralph Terry	.20
(83)	Tom Tresh	.20
(84)	Bob Turley	.20
(85)	Roy White	.30
(86)	Dave Winfield	1.00

Complete Series, Yankees
Hall of Famers 15.00

(1)	Home Run Baker	.50
(2)	Ed Barrow	.20
(3)	Yogi Berra	2.00
(4)	Frank Chance	.50
(5)	Jack Chesbro	.20
(6)	Earle Combs	.20
(7)	Stan Coveleski	.20
(8)	Bill Dickey	.50
(9)	Joe DiMaggio	6.00
(10)	Whitey Ford	2.00
(11)	Lou Gehrig	6.00
(12)	Lefty Gomez	.50
(13)	Clark C. Griffith	.20
(14)	Burleigh Grimes	.20
(15)	Bucky Harris	.20
(16)	Waite Hoyt	.20
(17)	Miller Huggins	.20
(18)	Catfish Hunter	.30
(19)	Willie Keeler	.20
(20)	Tony Lazzeri	.20
(21)	Larry MacPhail	.20
(22)	Mickey Mantle	10.00
(23)	Joe McCarthy	.20
(24)	Johnny Mize	.35
(25)	Herb Pennock	.20
(26)	Gaylord Perry	.20
(27)	Branch Rickey	.20
(28)	Red Ruffing	.20
(29)	Babe Ruth	7.50
(30)	Joe Sewell	.20
(31)	Enos Slaughter	.20
(32)	Casey Stengel	.30
(33)	Dazzy Vance	.20
(34)	Paul Waner	.20
(35)	George M. Weiss	.20

1990 Wonder Stars

The cards were found in specially marked loaves of Wonder

Bread, in a special plastic pocket to protect them from product stains (and vice versa). Uncut sheets could also be obtained for $3 and proofs of purchase. Produced by Mike Schechter Associates, the photos at the center of the cards have team logos airbrushed away for lack of a license from MLB; the cards are licensed by the players' union. A red border surrounds the photo on front. Backs are printed in red and blue on white and have up to five years' worth of stats, a few lines of career highlights and a facsimile autograph.

		NM/M
Complete Set (20):		9.00
Common Player:		.25
Uncut Sheet:		12.50
1	Bo Jackson	.30
2	Roger Clemens	1.00
3	Jim Abbott	.25
4	Orel Hershiser	.25
5	Ozzie Smith	.75
6	Don Mattingly	1.00
7	Kevin Mitchell	.25
8	Jerome Walton	.25
9	Kirby Puckett	.75
10	Darryl Strawberry	.25
11	Robin Yount	.60
12	Tony Gwynn	.75
13	Alan Trammell	.25
14	Jose Canseco	.50
15	Greg Swindell	.25
16	Nolan Ryan	2.00
17	Howard Johnson	.25
18	Ken Griffey Jr.	2.00
19	Will Clark	.25
20	Ryne Sandberg	.60

1985 Woolworth

This 44-card boxed set was produced by Topps for the Woolworth's chain stores, though "Woolworth's" does not appear anywhere on the individual cards. Featuring a combination of black-and-white and color photos of baseball record holders from all eras, the set is in the standard 2-1/2" x 3-1/2" format. Backs, printed in blue and orange, give career details and personal data. Because it combined old-timers with current players, the set did not achieve a great deal of collector popularity. The set was reissued in 1987 in a different box at the Boardwalk and Baseball theme park in Florida.

		NM/M
Complete Set (44):		7.50
Common Player:		.10
1	Hank Aaron	.60
2	Grover Alexander	.15
3	Ernie Banks	.30
4	Yogi Berra	.30
5	Lou Brock	.30
6	Steve Carlton	.25
7	Jack Chesbro	.10
8	Ty Cobb	.60
9	Sam Crawford	.10
10	Rollie Fingers	.10
11	Whitey Ford	.30
12	Johnny Frederick	.10
13	Frankie Frisch	.10
14	Lou Gehrig	.75
15	Jim Gentile	.10
16	Dwight Gooden	.10
17	Rickey Henderson	.40
18	Rogers Hornsby	.10
19	Frank Howard	.10
20	Cliff Johnson	.10
21	Walter Johnson	.25
22	Hub Leonard	.10
23	Mickey Mantle	2.00
24	Roger Maris	.50
25	Christy Mathewson	.25
26	Willie Mays	.60
27	Stan Musial	.50
28	Dan Quisenberry	.10
29	Frank Robinson	.25
30	Pete Rose	1.00
31	Babe Ruth	1.50
32	Nolan Ryan	1.50
33	George Sisler	.10
34	Tris Speaker	.10
35	Ed Walsh	.10
36	Lloyd Waner	.10
37	Earl Webb	.10
38	Ted Williams	.75
39	Maury Wills	.10
40	Hack Wilson	.10
41	Owen Wilson	.10
42	Willie Wilson	.10
43	Rudy York	.10
44	Cy Young	.25

1986 Woolworth

Labeled "Topps' Collector Series" in a red band at the top of the front, this set marked the second year of Topps' production of a special boxed set for the Woolworth chain of stores, though Woolworth's name does not appear anywhere on the card. The 2-1/2" x 3-1/2" cards feature a color photo with its lower-right corner rolled up to reveal the words "Super Star" on a bright yellow border. The player's name appears in the lower-left corner.

		NM/M
Complete Set (33):		6.00
Common Player:		.10
1	Tony Armas	.10
2	Don Baylor	.10
3	Wade Boggs	.75
4	George Brett	1.00
5	Bill Buckner	.10
6	Rod Carew	.75
7	Gary Carter	.75
8	Cecil Cooper	.10
9	Darrell Evans	.10
10	Dwight Evans	.10
11	George Foster	.10
12	Bobby Grich	.10
13	Tony Gwynn	.75
14	Keith Hernandez	.10
15	Reggie Jackson	.75
16	Dave Kingman	.10
17	Carney Lansford	.10
18	Fred Lynn	.10
19	Bill Madlock	.10
20	Don Mattingly	1.50
21	Willie McGee	.10
22	Hal McRae	.10
23	Dale Murphy	.35
24	Eddie Murray	.75
25	Ben Oglivie	.10
26	Al Oliver	.10
27	Dave Parker	.10
28	Jim Rice	.35
29	Pete Rose	1.50
30	Mike Schmidt	1.00
31	Gorman Thomas	.10
32	Willie Wilson	.10
33	Dave Winfield	.75

1987 Woolworth

The "Baseball Highlights" boxed set of 33 cards was prepared by Topps for distribution at stores in the Woolworth's chain, although the retailer's name does not appear on the cards. Each card measures 2-1/2" x 3-1/2" in size and features

a memorable baseball event that occurred during the 1986 season. The glossy set sold for $1.99.

		NM/M
Complete Set (33):		2.00
Common Player:		.05
1	Steve Carlton	.20
2	Cecil Cooper	.05
3	Rickey Henderson	.20
4	Reggie Jackson	.35
5	Jim Rice	.15
6	Don Sutton	.15
7	Roger Clemens	.40
8	Mike Schmidt	.40
9	Jesse Barfield	.05
10	Wade Boggs	.35
11	Tim Raines	.05
12	Jose Canseco	.25
13	Todd Worrell	.05
14	Dave Righetti	.05
15	Don Mattingly	.40
16	Tony Gwynn	.25
17	Marty Barrett	.05
18	Mike Scott	.05
19	World Series Game #1 (Bruce Hurst)	.05
20	World Series Game #1 (Calvin Schiraldi)	.05
21	World Series Game #2 (Dwight Evans)	.05
22	World Series Game #2 (Dave Henderson)	.05
23	World Series Game #3 (Len Dykstra)	.05
24	World Series Game #3 (Bob Ojeda)	.05
25	World Series Game #4 (Gary Carter)	.05
26	World Series Game #4 (Ron Darling)	.05
27	Jim Rice	.15
28	Bruce Hurst	.05
29	World Series Game #6 (Darryl Strawberry)	.05
30	World Series Game #6 (Ray Knight)	.05
31	World Series Game #6 (Keith Hernandez)	.05
32	World Series Game #7 (Mets Celebrate)	.05
33	Ray Knight	.05

1988 Woolworth

This 33-card boxed set was produced by Topps for exclusive distribution at Woolworth stores. The set includes 18 individual player cards and 15 World Series game-action photo cards. World Series cards include two for each game of the Series, plus a card of 1987 Series MVP Frank Viola. A white-lettered caption beneath the photo consists of either the player's name or a World Series game notation. Card backs are red, white and blue and contain a brief description of the photo on the front.

		NM/M
Complete Set (33):		2.00
Common Player:		.05
1	Don Baylor	.05
2	Vince Coleman	.05
3	Darrell Evans	.05
4	Don Mattingly	.60
5	Eddie Murray	.35
6	Nolan Ryan	.75
7	Mike Schmidt	.60
8	Andre Dawson	.20
9	George Bell	.05
10	Steve Bedrosian	.05
11	Roger Clemens	.60
12	Tony Gwynn	.50
13	Wade Boggs	.50
14	Benny Santiago	.05
15	Mark McGwire	.65
16	Dave Righetti	.05
17	Jeffrey Leonard	.05
18	Gary Gaetti	.05
19	World Series Game #1 (Frank Viola)	.05
20	World Series Game #1 (Dan Gladden)	.05
21	World Series Game #2 (Bert Blyleven)	.05
22	World Series Game #2 (Gary Gaetti)	.05
23	World Series Game #3 (John Tudor)	.05
24	World Series Game #3 (Todd Worrell)	.05
25	World Series Game #4 (Tom Lawless)	.05
26	World Series Game #4 (Willie McGee)	.05
27	World Series Game #5 (Danny Cox)	.05
28	World Series Game #5 (Curt Ford)	.05
29	World Series Game #6 (Don Baylor)	.05
30	World Series Game #6 (Kent Hrbek)	.05
31	World Series Game #7 (Kirby Puckett)	.35
32	World Series Game #7 (Greg Gagne)	.05
33	World Series MVP (Frank Viola)	.05

1989 Woolworth

This 33-card set was produced by Topps for the Woolworth store chain and was sold in a special box with a checklist on the back. The glossy-coated cards commemorate the most memorable moments in baseball from the 1988 season. The backs include a description of the various highlights.

		NM/M
Complete Set (33):		4.00
Common Player:		.05
1	Jose Canseco	.30
2	Kirk Gibson	.05
3	Frank Viola	.05
4	Orel Hershiser	.05
5	Walt Weiss	.05
6	Chris Sabo	.05
7	George Bell	.05
8	Wade Boggs	.65
9	Tom Browning	.05
10	Gary Carter	.50
11	Andre Dawson	.20
12	John Franco	.05
13	Randy Johnson	.50
14	Doug Jones	.05
15	Kevin McReynolds	.05
16	Gene Nelson	.05
17	Jeff Reardon	.05
18	Pat Tabler	.05
19	Tim Belcher	.05
20	Dennis Eckersley	.35
21	Orel Hershiser	.05
22	Gregg Jefferies	.05
23	Jose Canseco	.30
24	Kirk Gibson	.05
25	Orel Hershiser	.05
26	Mike Marshall	.05
27	Mark McGwire	1.00
28	Rick Honeycutt	.05
29	Tim Belcher	.05
30	Jay Howell	.05
31	Mickey Hatcher	.05
32	Mike Davis	.05
33	Orel Hershiser	.05

1990 Woolworth

This 33-card boxed set recalls baseball highlights of 1989.

The cards are styled like past Woolworth sets, with game-action or posed photos framed in green. Backs are in blue, white and black with a headline and explanation of the commemoration. The set features award winners and regular and post-season highlights.

		NM/M
Complete Set (33):		2.50
Common Player:		.05
1	Robin Yount	.30
2	Kevin Mitchell	.05
3	Bret Saberhagen	.05
4	Mark Davis	.05
5	Gregg Olson	.05
6	Jerome Walton	.05
7	Bert Blyleven	.05
8	Wade Boggs	.45
9	George Brett	.50
10	Vince Coleman	.05
11	Andre Dawson	.20
12	Dwight Evans	.05
13	Carlton Fisk	.05
14	Rickey Henderson	.30
15	Dale Murphy	.15
16	Eddie Murray	.30
17	Jeff Reardon	.05
18	Rick Reuschel	.05
19	Cal Ripken, Jr.	.75
20	Nolan Ryan	.75
21	Ryne Sandberg	.45
22	Robin Yount	.30
23	Rickey Henderson	.30
24	Will Clark	.05
25	Dave Stewart	.05
26	Walt Weiss	.05
27	Mike Moore	.05
28	Terry Steinbach	.05
29	Dave Henderson	.05
30	Matt Williams	.05
31	Rickey Henderson	.30
32	Kevin Mitchell	.05
33	Dave Stewart	.05

1991 Woolworth

This 33-card boxed set was produced by Topps for distribution at Woolworth stores. Yellow borders are featured on the fronts of the glossy cards. The backs feature baseball highlights from the previous season. Award winners, regular season and World Series highlights are showcased.

		NM/M
Complete Set (33):		3.00
Common Player:		.05
1	Barry Bonds	.75
2	Rickey Henderson	.45
3	Doug Drabek	.05
4	Bob Welch	.05
5	Dave Justice	.10
6	Sandy Alomar, Jr.	.05
7	Bert Blyleven	.05
8	George Brett	.60
9	Andre Dawson	.25
10	Dwight Evans	.05
11	Alex Fernandez	.05
12	Carlton Fisk	.45
13	Kevin Maas	.05
14	Dale Murphy	.20
15	Eddie Murray	.45
16	Dave Parker	.05
17	Jeff Reardon	.05

18	Cal Ripken, Jr.	.75
19	Nolan Ryan	.75
20	Ryne Sandberg	.50
21	Bobby Thigpen	.05
22	Robin Yount	.45
23	Nasty Boys (Rob Dibble, Randy Myers)	.05
24	Dave Stewart	.05
25	Eric Davis	.05
26	Rickey Henderson	.45
27	Billy Hatcher	.05
28	Joe Oliver	.05
29	Chris Sabo	.05
30	Barry Larkin	.05
31	Jose Rijo	.05
32	Reds Celebrate	.05
33	Jose Rijo (World Series MVP)	.05

1986-88 World Wide Sports Conlon Collection

Marketed as complete series through World Wide Sports, five sets of black-and-white cards featuring the game's great players of the 1905-1935 era were made utilizing the photos of Charles Martin Conlon. The 2-1/2" x 3-1/2" cards carry the copyright of "The Sporting News," owner of the Conlon photos. The 60 cards of Series one each feature a Babe Ruth logo in the lower-left corner, the only graphic on the borderless card front. Series two has no front logo. Series 3-5 have a sliding Ty Cobb logo. Backs have a line of career stats, a few bits of biographical data and a paragraph of highlights written by TSN historian Paul Mac-Farlane. The first two series were produced in an edition of 12,000 sets each; production of the other series was not announced. Cards in Series 3-5 are not numbered and are checklisted here alphabetically. Series designations are in small print at back-bottom.

		NM/M
Complete Set (211):		100.00
Common Player:		.25
Series 1 - 1986:		18.00
1	Lou Gehrig	1.50
2	Ty Cobb	1.00
3	Grover C. Alexander	.35
4	Walter Johnson	.50
5	Bill Klem	.25
6	Ty Cobb	1.00
7	Gordon S. Cochrane	.25
8	Paul Waner	.25
9	Joe Cronin	.25
10	Jay Hannah Dean	.25
11	Leo Durocher	.25
12	Jimmie Foxx	.25
13	Babe Ruth	2.00
14	Mike Gonzalez, Frank Frisch, Clyde Wares	.25
15	Carl Hubbell	.25
16	Miller Huggins	.25
17	Lou Gehrig	1.50
18	Connie Mack	.25
19	Heinie Manush	.25
20	Babe Ruth	2.00
21	Al Simmons	.25
22	Pepper Martin	.25
23	Christy Mathewson	.50
24	Ty Cobb	1.00
25	Stanley Harris	.25
26	Waite Hoyt	.25
27	Rube Marquard	.25
28	Joe McCarthy	.25
29	John McGraw	.25
30	Tris Speaker	.25
31	Bill Terry	.25
32	Christy Mathewson	.50
33	Casey Stengel	.25
34	Robert W. Meusel	.25
35	George Edward Waddell	.25
36	Mel Ott	.25
37	Roger Peckinpaugh	.25
38	Pie Traynor	.25
39	Chief Bender	.25
40	John W. Coombs	.25

41	Ty Cobb	1.00
42	Harry Heilmann	.25
43	Charlie Gehringer	.25
44	Rogers Hornsby	.25
45	Vernon Gomez	.25
46	Christy Mathewson	.50
47	Robert M. Grove	.25
48	Babe Ruth	2.00
49	Fred Merkle	.25
50	Babe Ruth	2.00
51	Herb Pennock	.25
52	Lou Gehrig	1.50
53	Fred Clarke	.25
54	Babe Ruth	2.00
55	John P. Wagner	.50
56	Hack Wilson	.25
57	Lou Gehrig	1.50
58	Lloyd Waner	.25
59	Charles Martin Conlon	.25
60	Charles & Margie Conlon	.25
---	Header Card	15.00
Series 2 - 1987:		
1	Lou Gehrig	1.50
2	Vernon Gomez	.25
3	Christy Mathewson	.50
4	Grover Alexander	.25
5	Ty Cobb	1.00
6	Walter Johnson	.50
7	Charles (Babe) Adams	.25
8	Nick Altrock	.25
9	Al Schacht	.25
10	Hugh Critz	.25
11	Henry Cullop	.25
12	Jake Daubert	.25
13	Bill Donovan	.25
14	Chick Hafey	.25
15	Bill Hallahan	.25
16	Fred Haney	.25
17	Charles Hartnett	.25
18	Walter Henline	.25
19	Ed Rommel	.25
20	Ralph "Babe" Pinelli	.25
21	Bob Meusel	.25
22	Emil Meusel	.25
23	Smead Jolley	.25
24	Ike Boone	.25
25	Earl Webb	.25
26	Charles Comiskey	.25
27	Edward Collins	.25
28	Geroge (Buck) Weaver	.50
29	Eddie Cicotte	.50
30	Sam Crawford	.25
31	Chuck Dressen	.25
32	Arthur Fletcher	.25
33	Hugh Duffy	.25
34	Ira Flagstead	.25
35	Harry Hooper	.25
36	George E. Lewis	.25
37	James Dykes	.25
38	Leon Goslin	.25
39	Henry Gowdy	.25
40	Charles Grimm	.25
41	Mark Koenig	.25
42	James Hogan	.25
43	William Jacobson	.25
44	Fielder Jones	.25
45	George Kelly	.25
46	Adolfo Luque	.40
47	Walter Maranville	.25
48	Carl Mays	.25
49	Eddie Plank	.25
50	Hubert Pruett	.25
51	John (Picus) Quinn	.25
52	Charles (Flint) Rhem	.25
53	Amos Rusie	.25
54	Edd Roush	.25
55	Ray Schalk	.25
56	Ernie Shore	.25
57	Joe Wood	.25
58	George Sisler	.25
59	James Thorpe	3.00
60	Earl Whitehill	.25
Series 3 - 1988:		35.00
(1)	Ace Adams	1.00
(2)	Grover C. Alexander	2.00
(3)	Eldon Auker	1.00
(4)	Jack Barry	1.00
(5)	Wally Berger	1.00
(6)	Ben Chapman	1.00
(7)	Mickey Cochrane	1.00
(8)	Frank Crosetti	1.00
(9)	Paul Dean	1.00
(10)	Leo Durocher	1.00
(11)	Wes Ferrell	1.00
(12)	Hank Gowdy	1.00
(13)	Andy High	1.00
(14)	Rogers Hornsby	2.00
(15)	Carl Hubbell	1.00
(16)	Joe Judge	1.00
(17)	Tony Lazzeri	1.00
(18)	Pepper Martin	1.00
(19)	Lee Meadows	1.00
(20)	Jimmy Murphy	1.00
(21)	Steve O'Neill	1.00
(22)	Ed Plank	1.00
(23)	John P. Quinn	1.00
(24)	Charlie Root	1.00
(25)	Babe Ruth	6.00
(26)	Fred Snodgrass	1.00
(27)	Tris Speaker	2.00
(28)	Bill Terry	1.00
(29)	Jeff Tesreau	1.00
(30)	George Torporcer	1.00
Series 4 - 1988:		30.00
(1)	Dale Alexander	1.00
(2)	Morris "Red" Badgro	1.00
(3)	Dick Bartell	1.00
(4)	Max Bishop	1.00

(5)	Hal Chase	1.50
(6)	Ty Cobb	2.00
(7)	Nick Cullop	1.00
(8)	Dizzy Dean	2.50
(9)	Chuck Dressen	1.00
(10)	Jimmy Dykes	1.00
(11)	Art Fletcher	1.00
(12)	Charlie Grimm	1.00
(13)	Lefty Grove	1.00
(14)	Baby Doll Jacobson	1.00
(15)	Bill Klem	1.00
(16)	Mark Koenig	1.00
(17)	Duffy Lewis	1.00
(18)	Carl Mays	1.00
(19)	Fred Merkle	1.00
(20)	Greasy Neale	1.50
(21)	Mel Ott	1.00
(22)	"Babe" Pinelli	1.00
(23)	Flint Rhem	1.00
(24)	Slim Sallee	1.00
(25)	Al Simmons	1.00
(26)	George Sisler	1.00
(27)	Riggs Stephenson	1.00
(28)	Jim Thorpe	4.00
(29)	Bill Wambsganss	1.00
(30)	Cy Young	2.50
Series 5 - 1988:		30.00
(1)	Nick Altrock	1.00
(2)	Del Baker	1.00
(3)	Moe Berg	4.50
(4)	Zeke Bonura	1.00
(5)	Eddie Collins	1.00
(6)	Hugh Critz	1.00
(7)	George Dauss	1.00
(8)	Joe Dugan	1.00
(9)	Howard Ehmke	1.00
(10)	Jimmie Foxx	2.50
(11)	Frank Frisch	1.00
(12)	Lou Gehrig	6.00
(13)	Charlie Gehringer	1.00
(14)	Kid Gleason	1.00
(15)	Lefty Gomez	1.00
(16)	Babe Herman	1.00
(17)	Bill James	1.00
(18)	Joe Kuhel	1.00
(19)	Dolf Luque	1.50
(20)	John McGraw	1.00
(21)	Stuffy McInnis	1.00
(22)	Bob Meusel	1.00
(23)	Lefty O'Doul	1.00
(24)	Hub Pruett	1.00
(25)	Paul Richards	1.00
(26)	Bob Shawkey	1.00
(27)	Gabby Street	1.00
(28)	Johnny Tobin	1.00
(29)	Rube Waddell	1.00
(30)	Billy Werber	1.00

1988 World Wide Sports 1933 Negro All Stars

The photos of Charles M. Conlon in The Sporting News' archive are the basis for this collectors' issue depicting "1933 Negro All Stars. Fronts have borderless sepia photos of the players on a 2-1/2" x 3-1/2" format. The only graphics added to the front are in the upper-right corner designating the All-Star status. Backs have a few personal data along with a career summary. The unnumbered cards are checklisted here in alphabetical order.

		NM/M
Complete Set (12):		7.50
Common Player:		1.00
(1)	Cool Papa Bell	1.00
(2)	Oscar Charleston	1.00
(3)	Martin Dihigo	1.00
(4)	Andrew "Rube" Foster	1.00
(5)	Josh Gibson	2.00
(6)	Judy Johnson	1.00
(7)	Buck Leonard	1.00
(8)	Pop Lloyd	1.00
(9)	Dave Malarcher	1.00
(10)	Satchel Paige	2.50
(11)	Willie Wells	1.00
(12)	Joe Williams	1.00

1989 W/R Associates Mark Grace

		NM/M
Complete Set (48):		12.00
Common Player:		.25
American League		6.00
(1)	Luke Appling	.25
(2)	Earl Averill	.25
(3)	Tommy Bridges	.25
(4)	Ben Chapman	.25
(5)	Mickey Cochrane	.25
(6)	Joe Cronin	.25
(7)	Alvin Crowder	.25
(8)	Bill Dickey	.35
(9)	Jimmie Foxx	.45
(10)	Lou Gehrig	1.00
(11)	Charlie Gehringer	.25
(12)	Lefty Gomez	.25
(13)	Lefty Grove	.25
(14)	Mel Harder	.25
(15)	Pinky Higgins	.25
(16)	Urban Hodapp	.25

(17)	Roy Johnson	.25
(18)	Joe Kuhel	.25
(19)	Tony Lazzeri	.25
(20)	Heinie Manush	.25
(21)	Babe Ruth	1.50
(22)	Al Simmons	.25
(23)	Evar Swanson	.25
(24)	Earl Whitehill	.25
National League		6.00
(1)	Wally Berger	.25
(2)	Guy Bush	.25
(3)	Ripper Collins	.25
(4)	Spud Davis	.25
(5)	Dizzy Dean	.45
(6)	Johnny Frederick	.25
(7)	Larry French	.25
(8)	Frank Frisch	.25
(9)	Chick Fullis	.25
(10)	Chick Hafey	.25
(11)	Carl Hubbell	.25
(12)	Chuck Klein	.25
(13)	Freddie Lindstrom	.25
(14)	Pepper Martin	.25
(15)	Ducky Medwick	.25
(16)	Tony Piet	.25
(17)	Wes Schulmerich	.25
(18)	Hal Schumacher	.25
(19)	Riggs Stephenson	.25
(20)	Bill Terry	.25
(21)	Paul Traynor	.25
(22)	Arky Vaughan	.25
(23)	Paul Waner	.25
(24)	Lon Warneke	.25

1988 World Wide Sports 1933 All-Stars

The photos of Charles M. Conlon in The Sporting News' archive are the basis for this collectors' issue depicting the players of the original All-Star Game of 1933. Fronts have sepia photo of the players on a 2-1/2" x 3-1/2" format. The only graphics added to the front are in the upper-right corner designating the league which the player represented. Backs have 1933 and career stats, along with a career summary. The unnumbered cards are checklisted here in alphabetical order within league.

1985 WTBS Atlanta Braves

This set of large-format (8-1/4" x 10-3/4") cards was issued by the Braves' TV broadcaster, WTBS. The sets were given to potential sponsors as part of a "kit" inviting them to Florida to attend a spring training game. It was reported that only 600 sets were printed and 150 of them were destroyed. Fronts feature player portraits on brightly colored backgrounds. There is a facsimile autograph and a large star-boxed "AMERICA'S TEAM." Backs are in red and black and have some vital data and stats for the 1982-84 seasons. Cards are numbered according to uniform number.

		NM/M
Complete Set (4):		50.00
Common Player:		7.50
3	Dale Murphy	35.00
7	Brad Komminsk	7.50
15	Claudell Washington	7.50
42	Bruce Sutter	15.00

1991 WWOR N.Y. Mets

This set of 5-1/2" x 7-1/2" cards was issued by WWOR-TV in New York City, which carried the Mets telecasts in 1991. The cards were evidently intended for use as a sales promotion, as the backs detail Neilsen ratings for the games. Fronts have game action photos with green borders in a design not unlike 1991 Donruss.

		NM/M
Complete Set (12):		15.00
Common Player:		2.00
(1)	Darryl Boston	2.00
(2)	Vince Coleman	2.00
(3)	David Cone	2.00
(4)	Kevin Elster	2.00
(5)	Sid Fernandez	2.00
(6)	John Franco	2.00
(7)	Dwight Gooden	2.00
(8)	Jeff Innis	2.00
(9)	Howard Johnson	2.00
(10)	Dave Magadan	2.00
(11)	Mackey Sasser	2.00
(12)	Wally Whitehurst	2.00

League Baseball, all Cubs uniform logos have been removed from the photos. Cards are numbered on front and back with a year identifying the photo. Backs are printed in red, white and blue and include biographical data and career summary. The large-format card offers complete major and minor league stats on back. The cards on the sheet are not perforated and individual cards are rarely encountered. Sheets were offered in either autographed or unautographed form with production limited to 15,000 sheets.

	NM/M
Complete Sheet:	7.50
Complete Sheet, Autographed:	25.00
Complete Set, Cut (9):	7.50
Common Card:	.50

73	Mark Grace (Boyhood photo.)	.50
83	Mark Grace (San Diego State)	.50
86	Mark Grace (Minor League)	.50
87	Mark Grace (Throwing)	.50
88a	Mark Grace/Fldg	.50
88b	Mark Grace (Wedding)	.50
89a	Mark Grace, Btg	.50
89b	Mark Grace/Btg	.50
----	Mark Grace (5" x 7" Portrait, Autographed)	25.00
----	Mark Grace (5" x 7" Portrait, Unsigned)	4.00

Y

1993 Yoo-Hoo

The Yoo-Hoo beverage company, which had a promotional affiliation with Yogi Berra as far back as the 1950's, made Berra the #1 card in a 1993 set of 20 baseball legends that was released in two series. All of the players included in the set are retired, and all but five are Hall of Famers (at this writing). The unnumbered cards feature a yellow border with a color photo on the front; the backs have the player's statistics and biographical information.

		NM/M
Complete Set (20):		7.00
Common Player:		.25
Series 1		
(1)	Yogi Berra	.50
(2)	Joe Morgan	.35
(3)	Duke Snider	.50
(4)	Steve Garvey	.30
(5)	Jim Rice	.35
(6)	Bob Feller	.35
(7)	Pete Rose	1.00
(8)	Rod Carew	.35
(9)	Gaylord Perry	.25
(10)	Graig Nettles	.25
Series 2		
(1)	Johnny Bench	.40
(2)	Lou Brock	.35
(3)	Stan Musial	1.00
(4)	Willie McCovey	.35
(5)	Whitey Ford	.50
(6)	Phil Rizzuto	.50
(7)	Tom Seaver	.50
(8)	Willie Stargell	.35
(9)	Brooks Robinson	.35
(10)	Al Kaline	.45

1994 Yoo-Hoo

Issued in conjunction with Rawling's, sponsor of the Gold Glove Award, this set features past winners. Cards have color photos on which team logos have been airbrushed away. Borders are bright yellow. Backs have career stats and highlights. A limited number of Yaz autographed cards were randomly inserted into the packs in which the cards were distributed.

		NM/M
Complete Set (20):		6.00
Common Player:		.25
Yastrzemski Autograph:		30.00
1	Luis Aparicio	.25
2	Bobby Bonds	.25
3	Bob Boone	.25
4	Steve Carlton	.35
5	Roberto Clemente	2.00
6	Bob Gibson	.25
7	Keith Hernandez	.25
8	Jim Kaat	.25
9	Roger Maris	.60
10	Don Mattingly	1.00

11	Thurman Munson	.60
12	Phil Rizzuto	.50
13	Brooks Robinson	.40
14	Ryne Sandberg	.75
15	Mike Schmidt	1.00
16	Carl Yastrzemski	.60
17	Fact Card	.05
18	Fact Card	.05
19	Fact Card	.05
20	Fact Card	.05

1982 Zellers Expos

Issued by Zellers department stores in Canada, this 60-card set was produced in the form of 20 three-card panels. The cards feature a round photo of the player on a yellow background. A red "Zellers" is above the photo and on either side of it are the words "Baseball Pro Tips" in English on the left and in French on the right. The player's name and the title of the playing tip are under the photo. Backs have the playing tip in both languages. Single cards measure 2-1/2" x 3-1/2" while the whole panel is 7-1/2" x 3-1/2". Although a number of stars are depicted, this set is not terribly popular as collectors do not generally like the playing tips idea. Total panels are worth more than separated cards.

		NM/M
	Complete Set (20):	6.00
	Common Player:	.25
1	Gary Carter (Catching Position)	1.50
2	Steve Rogers (Pitching Stance)	.25
3	Tim Raines (Sliding)	.50
4	Andre Dawson (Batting Stance)	.60
5	Terry Francona (Contact Hitting)	.25
6	Gary Carter (Fielding Pop Fouls)	1.50
7	Warren Cromartie (Fielding at First Base)	.25
8	Chris Speier (Fielding at Shortstop)	.25
9	Billy DeMars (Signals)	.25
10	Andre Dawson (Batting Stroke)	.60
11	Terry Francona (Outfield Throws)	.25
12	Woodie Fryman (Holding the Runner-Left Handed)	.25
13	Gary Carter (Fielding Low Balls)	1.50
14	Andre Dawson (Playing Centerfield)	.60
15	Bill Gullickson (The Slurve)	.25
16	Gary Carter (Catching Stance)	1.50
17	Scott Sanderson (Fielding as a Pitcher)	.25
18	Warren Cromartie (Handling Bad Throws)	.25
19	Gary Carter (Hitting Stride)	1.50
20	Ray Burris (Holding the Runner-Right Handed)	.25

1995 Zenith Samples

As Pinnacle extended its top-of-the-line brand name in baseball, this nine-card cello-wrapped samples set was sent to dealers to

familiarize them with the product. Using the same state of the art all-foil metalized printing on extra heavy 24-point cardboard stock, the samples are virtually identical to the issued version, except for a white "SAMPLE" printed diagonally across front and back.

		NM/M
	Complete Set (9):	10.00
	Common Player:	.75
12	Cal Ripken Jr.	3.00
20	Dante Bichette	.75
51	Jim Thome	1.00
70	Mark Grace	1.00
97	Ryan Klesko	.75
111	Chipper Jones (Rookie)	2.00
113	Curtis Goodwin (Rookie)	.75
7	Hideo Nomo (Rookie Roll Call)	2.00
---	Header Card	.05

1995 Zenith

At the top of the pyramid of Pinnacle's baseball card lines for 1995 was Zenith, a super-premium brand utilizing all-foil metalized printing technology on double-thick 24-point cardboard stock to emphasize the quality look and feel. Six-card packs carried a retail price of $3.99. Two styles comprise the 150-card base set. The 110 veteran player cards are curiously arranged in alphabetical order according to the player's first names (with the exception of card #48, a special Japanese-language card of Hideo Nomo). These cards have a color player action photo on a black and gold background that is a view of a pyramid from its pinnacle. One the horizontal back, a portrait photo of the player in a partly-cloudy blue sky overlooks a playing field which offers his hit location preferences versus righty and lefty pitching. A scoreboard has his 1994 and career stats. The Pinnacle anti-counterfeiting optical-variable bar is in the lower-right corner. The rookie cards which comprise the final 40 cards in the set have a color photo at center with a gold-tone version of the same picture in the background. A large gold "ROOKIE" is vertically at right. Backs are similar to those on the verterans' cards except they have a scouting report in place of the hit-location chart.

		NM/M
	Complete Set (150):	15.00
	Common Player:	.25
	Pack (6):	1.50
	Wax Box (24):	17.50
1	Albert Belle	.10
2	Alex Fernandez	.10
3	Andy Benes	.10
4	Barry Larkin	.10
5	Barry Bonds	2.50
6	Ben McDonald	.10
7	Bernard Gilkey	.10
8	Billy Ashley	.10
9	Bobby Bonilla	.10
10	Bret Saberhagen	.10
11	Brian Jordan	.10
12	Cal Ripken Jr.	2.50
13	Carlos Baerga	.10
14	Carlos Delgado	.35
15	Cecil Fielder	.10
16	Chili Davis	.10
17	Chuck Knoblauch	.10
18	Craig Biggio	.10
19	Danny Tartabull	.10
20	Dante Bichette	.10
21	Darren Daulton	.10
22	Dave Justice	.10
23	Dave Winfield	.75

24	David Cone	.10
25	Dean Palmer	.10
26	Deion Sanders	.20
27	Dennis Eckersley	.65
28	Derek Bell	.10
29	Don Mattingly	1.50
30	Edgar Martinez	.10
31	Eric Karros	.10
32	Erik Hanson	.10
33	Frank Thomas	.75
34	Fred McGriff	.10
35	Gary Sheffield	.45
36	Gary Gaetti	.10
37	Greg Maddux	1.25
38	Gregg Jefferies	.10
39	Ivan Rodriguez	.65
40	Kenny Rogers	.10
41	J.T. Snow	.10
42	Hal Morris	.10
43	Eddie Murray (3,000 hit)	.50
44	Javier Lopez	.10
45	Jay Bell	.10
46	Jeff Conine	.10
47	Jeff Bagwell	.75
48	Hideo Nomo RC	2.00
49	Jeff Kent	.10
50	Jeff King	.10
51	Jim Thome	.65
52	Jimmy Key	.10
53	Joe Carter	.10
54	John Valentin	.10
55	John Olerud	.10
56	Jose Canseco	.45
57	Jose Rijo	.10
58	Jose Offerman	.10
59	Juan Gonzalez	.45
60	Ken Caminiti	.10
61	Ken Griffey Jr.	1.75
62	Kenny Lofton	.10
63	Kevin Appier	.10
64	Kevin Seitzer	.10
65	Kirby Puckett	1.25
66	Kirk Gibson	.10
67	Larry Walker	.10
68	Lenny Dykstra	.10
69	Manny Ramirez	.75
70	Mark Grace	.10
71	Mark McGwire	2.00
72	Marquis Grissom	.10
73	Jim Edmonds	.10
74	Matt Williams	.10
75	Mike Mussina	.45
76	Mike Piazza	1.75
77	Mo Vaughn	.10
78	Moises Alou	.10
79	Ozzie Smith	1.25
80	Paul O'Neill	.10
81	Paul Molitor	.75
82	Rafael Palmeiro	.65
83	Randy Johnson	.75
84	Raul Mondesi	.10
85	Ray Lankford	.10
86	Reggie Sanders	.10
87	Rickey Henderson	.75
88	Rico Brogna	.10
89	Roberto Alomar	.25
90	Robin Ventura	.10
91	Roger Clemens	1.50
92	Ron Gant	.10
93	Rondell White	.10
94	Royce Clayton	.10
95	Ruben Sierra	.10
96	Rusty Greer	.10
97	Ryan Klesko	.10
98	Sammy Sosa	1.25
99	Shawon Dunston	.10
100	Steve Ontiveros	.10
101	Tim Naehring	.10
102	Tim Salmon	.10
103	Tino Martinez	.10
104	Tony Gwynn	1.25
105	Travis Fryman	.10
106	Vinny Castilla	.10
107	Wade Boggs	1.25
108	Wally Joyner	.10
109	Wil Cordero	.10
110	Will Clark	.10
111	Chipper Jones	1.25
112	C.J. Nitkowski	.10
113	Curtis Goodwin	.10
114	Tim Unroe	.10
115	Vaughn Eshelman	.10
116	Marty Cordova	.10
117	Dustin Hermanson	.10
118	Rich Becker	.10
119	Ray Durham	.10
120	Shane Andrews	.10
121	Scott Ruffcorn	.10
122	Mark Grudzielanek RC	.25
123	James Baldwin	.10
124	Carlos Perez RC	.10
125	Julian Tavarez	.10
126	Joe Vitiello	.10
127	Jason Bates	.10
128	Edgardo Alfonzo	.10
129	Juan Acevedo	.10
130	Bill Pulsipher	.10
131	Bob Higginson RC	.25
132	Russ Davis	.10
133	Charles Johnson	.10
134	Derek Jeter	2.50
135	Phil Nevin	.10
136	LaTroy Hawkins	.10
137	Brian Hunter	.10
138	Roberto Petagine	.10
139	Jim Pittsley	.10
140	Garret Anderson	.10
141	Ugueth Urbina	.10

142	Antonio Osuna	.10
143	Michael Tucker	.10
145	Benji Gil	.10
144	Jon Nunnally	.10
146	Alex Rodriguez	2.00
147	Todd Hollandsworth	.10
148	Alex Gonzalez	.10
149	Hideo Nomo RC	2.00
150	Shawn Green	.30
---	Numeric Checklist	.10
---	Chase Program Checklist	.10

All-Star Salute

Kirby Puckett
ALL-STAR GAME VETERAN

The most common of the Zenith inserts is a series of 18 All-Star Salute cards. Fronts have action photos printed on foil. Backs have the 1995 All-Star Game logo and a large photo of the player taken at the game, with a few words about his All-Star history. The Salute cards are seeded at the rate of one per six packs, on average.

		NM/M
	Complete Set (18):	16.00
	Common Player:	.50
1	Cal Ripken Jr.	3.00
2	Frank Thomas	1.00
3	Mike Piazza	2.00
4	Kirby Puckett	1.50
5	Manny Ramirez	1.00
6	Tony Gwynn	1.50
7	Hideo Nomo	.75
8	Matt Williams	.50
9	Randy Johnson	1.00
10	Raul Mondesi	.50
11	Albert Belle	.50
12	Ivan Rodriguez	1.00
13	Barry Bonds	3.00
14	Carlos Baerga	.50
15	Ken Griffey Jr.	2.00
16	Jeff Conine	.50
17	Frank Thomas	1.00
18	Cal Ripken Jr., Barry Bonds	2.00

Rookie Roll Call

Dufex foil printing technology on both front and back is featured on this insert set. Fronts have a large and a small player photo on a green background dominated by a large star. Backs have another photo on a green and gold background. A prestigious black and gold box at left in the horizontally formatted design has a few good words about the prospect. Stated odds of finding a Rookie Roll Call card are one per 24 packs, on average.

		NM/M
	Complete Set (18):	17.50
	Common Player:	.60
1	Alex Rodriguez	6.00
2	Derek Jeter	7.50
3	Chipper Jones	5.00
4	Shawn Green	1.50
5	Todd Hollandsworth	.60
6	Bill Pulsipher	.60
7	Hideo Nomo	1.50
8	Ray Durham	.60
9	Curtis Goodwin	.60
10	Brian Hunter	.60

11	Julian Tavarez	.60
12	Marty Cordova	.60
13	Michael Tucker	.60
14	Edgardo Alfonzo	.60
15	LaTroy Hawkins	.60
16	Carlos Perez	.60
17	Charles Johnson	.60
18	Benji Gil	.60

Z-Team

The scarcest of the Zenith insert cards are those of 18 "living legends" profiled in the Z-Team series. Found at an average rate of only one per 72 packs, the cards are printed in technology Pinnacle calls 3-D Dufex.

		NM/M
	Complete Set (18):	85.00
	Common Player:	2.00
1	Cal Ripken Jr.	15.00
2	Ken Griffey Jr.	10.00
3	Frank Thomas	6.00
4	Matt Williams	2.00
5	Mike Piazza	10.00
6	Barry Bonds	15.00
7	Raul Mondesi	2.00
8	Greg Maddux	7.50
9	Jeff Bagwell	6.00
10	Manny Ramirez	6.00
11	Larry Walker	2.00
12	Tony Gwynn	7.50
13	Will Clark	2.00
14	Albert Belle	2.00
15	Kenny Lofton	2.00
16	Rafael Palmeiro	4.50
17	Don Mattingly	9.00
18	Carlos Baerga	2.00

1996 Zenith

Pinnacle's 1996 Zenith set has 150 cards in the regular set, including 30 Rookies, 20 Honor roll and two checklist cards. Each card in the set has a parallel Artist's Proof version (seeded one per every 35 packs). Insert sets include Z Team, Mozaics and two versions of Diamond Club. Normal Dufex versions of Diamond Club appear one every 24 packs; parallel versions, which have an actual diamond chip incorporated into the card design, were seeded one per every 350 packs.

		NM/M
	Complete Set (150):	15.00
	Common Player:	.10
	Common Artist's Proofs:	2.00
	Star Artist's Proofs:	12X
	Pack (6):	1.50
	Wax Box (24):	25.00
1	Ken Griffey Jr.	2.00
2	Ozzie Smith	1.50
3	Greg Maddux	1.50
4	Rondell White	.10
5	Mark McGwire	2.50
6	Jim Thome	.75
7	Ivan Rodriguez	.75
8	Marc Newfield	.10
9	Travis Fryman	.10
10	Fred McGriff	.10
11	Shawn Green	.25
12	Mike Piazza	2.00
13	Dante Bichette	.10
14	Tino Martinez	.10
15	Sterling Hitchcock	.10
16	Ryne Sandberg	1.50
17	Rico Brogna	.10
18	Roberto Alomar	.25
19	Barry Larkin	.10
20	Bernie Williams	.10
21	Gary Sheffield	.50

22	Frank Thomas	1.00
23	Gregg Jefferies	.10
24	Jeff Bagwell	1.00
25	Marty Cordova	.10
26	Jim Edmonds	.10
27	Jay Bell	.10
28	Ben McDonald	.10
29	Barry Bonds	3.00
30	Mo Vaughn	.10
31	Johnny Damon	.35
32	Dean Palmer	.10
33	Ismael Valdes	.10
34	Manny Ramirez	1.00
35	Edgar Martinez	.10
36	Cecil Fielder	.10
37	Ryan Klesko	.10
38	Ray Lankford	.10
39	Tim Salmon	.10
40	Joe Carter	.10
41	Jason Isringhausen	.10
42	Rickey Henderson	1.00
43	Lenny Dykstra	.10
44	Andre Dawson	.25
45	Paul O'Neill	.10
46	Ray Durham	.10
47	Raul Mondesi	.10
48	Jay Buhner	.10
49	Eddie Murray	1.00
50	Henry Rodriguez	.10
51	Hal Morris	.10
52	Mike Mussina	.50
53	Wally Joyner	.10
54	Will Clark	.10
55	Chipper Jones	1.50
56	Brian Jordan	.10
57	Larry Walker	.10
58	Wade Boggs	1.50
59	Melvin Nieves	.10
60	Charles Johnson	.10
61	Juan Gonzalez	1.00
62	Carlos Delgado	.35
63	Reggie Sanders	.10
64	Brian Hunter	.10
65	Edgardo Alfonzo	.10
66	Kenny Lofton	.10
67	Paul Molitor	1.00
68	Mike Bordick	.10
69	Garret Anderson	.10
70	Orlando Merced	.10
71	Craig Biggio	.10
72	Chuck Knoblauch	.10
73	Mark Grace	.10
74	Jack McDowell	.10
75	Randy Johnson	1.00
76	Cal Ripken Jr.	3.00
77	Matt Williams	.10
78	Benji Gil	.10
79	Moises Alou	.10
80	Robin Ventura	.10
81	Greg Vaughn	.10
82	Carlos Baerga	.10
83	Roger Clemens	1.75
84	Hideo Nomo	.50
85	Pedro Martinez	1.00
86	John Valentin	.10
87	Andres Galarraga	.10
88	Andy Pettitte	.30
89	Derek Bell	.10
90	Kirby Puckett	1.50
91	Tony Gwynn	1.50
92	Brady Anderson	.10
93	Derek Jeter	3.00
94	Michael Tucker	.10
95	Albert Belle	.10
96	David Cone	.10
97	J.T. Snow	.10
98	Tom Glavine	.35
99	Alex Rodriguez	2.50
100	Sammy Sosa	1.50
101	Karim Garcia	.15
102	Alan Benes	.10
103	Chad Mottola	.10
104	Robin Jennings RC	.10
105	Bob Abreu	.10
106	Tony Clark	.10
107	George Arias	.10
108	Jermaine Dye	.10
109	Jeff Suppan	.10
110	Ralph Milliard RC	.10
111	Ruben Rivera	.10
112	Billy Wagner	.10
113	Jason Kendall	.10
114	Mike Grace RC	.10
115	Edgar Renteria	.10
116	Jason Schmidt	.10
117	Paul Wilson	.10
118	Rey Ordonez	.10
119	Rocky Coppinger RC	.10
120	Wilton Guerrero RC	.10
121	Brooks Kieschnick	.10
122	Raul Casanova	.10
123	Alex Ochoa	.10
124	Chan Ho Park	.10
125	John Wasdin	.10
126	Eric Owens	.10
127	Justin Thompson	.10
128	Chris Snopek	.10
129	Terrell Wade	.10
130	Darin Erstad RC	1.50
131	Albert Belle (Honor Roll)	.10
132	Cal Ripken Jr. (Honor Roll)	1.50
133	Frank Thomas (Honor Roll)	.60
134	Greg Maddux (Honor Roll)	.75
135	Ken Griffey Jr. (Honor Roll)	1.50
136	Mo Vaughn (Honor Roll)	.10

137	Chipper Jones (Honor Roll)	.75
138	Mike Piazza (Honor Roll)	1.00
139	Ryan Klesko (Honor Roll)	.10
140	Hideo Nomo (Honor Roll)	.20
141	Roberto Alomar (Honor Roll)	.10
142	Manny Ramirez (Honor Roll)	.60
143	Gary Sheffield (Honor Roll)	.10
144	Barry Bonds (Honor Roll)	1.50
145	Matt Williams (Honor Roll)	.10
146	Jim Edmonds (Honor Roll)	.10
147	Derek Jeter (Honor Roll)	1.50
148	Sammy Sosa (Honor Roll)	.75
149	Kirby Puckett (Honor Roll)	.75
150	Tony Gwynn (Honor Roll)	.75

1996 Zenith Artist's Proofs

Each card in the '96 Zenith base set can also be found in a specially marked Artist's Proof version. The AP cards were found on average of once per 35 packs.

	NM/M
Common Player:	2.00
Stars:	12X

Diamond Club

Twenty different players are featured on these two 1996 Pinnacle Zenith insert cards. Normal Dufex versions are inserted one per every 24 packs. Parallel versions of these cards, containing an actual diamond chip incorporated into the design, were seeded one per every 350 packs.

		NM/M
Complete Set (20):		17.50
Common Player:		.45
Diamond Versions:		12X
1	Albert Belle	.45
2	Mo Vaughn	.45
3	Ken Griffey Jr.	1.50
4	Mike Piazza	1.50
5	Cal Ripken Jr.	2.50
6	Jermaine Dye	.45
7	Jeff Bagwell	1.00
8	Frank Thomas	1.00
9	Alex Rodriguez	2.00
10	Ryan Klesko	.45
11	Roberto Alomar	.60
12	Sammy Sosa	1.25
13	Matt Williams	.45
14	Gary Sheffield	.75
15	Ruben Rivera	.45
16	Darin Erstad	.60
17	Randy Johnson	1.00
18	Greg Maddux	1.25
19	Karim Garcia	.60
20	Chipper Jones	1.25

Mozaics

Each of these 1996 Pinnacle Zenith cards contains multiple player images for the team represented on the card. The cards were inserted one per every 10 packs.

	NM/M
Complete Set (25):	30.00

		NM/M
Common Card:		.45
1	Greg Maddux, Chipper Jones, Ryan Klesko	.45
2	Juan Gonzalez, Will Clark, Ivan Rodriguez	1.00
3	Frank Thomas, Robin Ventura, Ray Durham	1.00
4	Matt Williams, Barry Bonds, Osvaldo Fernandez	5.00
5	Ken Griffey Jr., Randy Johnson, Alex Rodriguez	4.00
6	Sammy Sosa, Ryne Sandberg, Mark Grace	4.00
7	Jim Edmonds, Tim Salmon, Garret Anderson	.45
8	Cal Ripken Jr., Roberto Alomar, Mike Mussina	5.00
9	Mo Vaughn, Roger Clemens, John Valentin	3.50
10	Barry Larkin, Reggie Sanders, Hal Morris	.45
11	Ray Lankford, Brian Jordan, Ozzie Smith	1.50
12	Dante Bichette, Larry Walker, Andres Galarraga	.45
13	Mike Piazza, Hideo Nomo, Raul Mondesi	5.00
14	Ben McDonald, Greg Vaughn, Kevin Seitzer	.45
15	Joe Carter, Carlos Delgado, Alex Gonzalez	.60
16	Gary Sheffield, Charles Johnson, Jeff Conine	.45
17	Rondell White, Moises Alou, Henry Rodriguez	.45
18	Albert Belle, Manny Ramirez, Carlos Baerga	1.00
19	Kirby Puckett, Paul Molitor, Chuck Knoblauch	1.50
20	Tony Gwynn, Rickey Henderson, Wally Joyner	2.00
21	Mark McGwire, Mike Bordick, Scott Brosius	4.00
22	Paul O'Neill, Bernie Williams, Wade Boggs	1.50
23	Jay Bell, Orlando Merced, Jason Kendall	.45
24	Rico Brogna, Paul Wilson, Jason Isringhausen	.45
25	Jeff Bagwell, Craig Biggio, Derek Bell	1.00

1996 Zenith Z-Team Samples

Each of the first nine micro-etched plastic-printed Z-Team insert cards can also be found in an edition which is overprinted "SAMPLE" on the front. These cards were distributed to hobby dealers.

		NM/M
Complete Set (9):		35.00
Common Player:		3.00
1	Ken Griffey Jr.	4.50
2	Albert Belle	3.00
3	Cal Ripken Jr.	7.50
4	Frank Thomas	3.50
5	Greg Maddux	4.00
6	Mo Vaughn	3.00
7	Chipper Jones	4.00
8	Mike Piazza	4.50
9	Ryan Klesko	3.00

Z-Team

Pinnacle's 1996 Zenith baseball continues the Z-Team insert concept with a new clear plastic treatment that is micro-etched for a see-through design that allows light to shine through etched highlights and a green baseball field background. The 18 cards were seeded one per every 72 packs.

		NM/M
Complete Set (18):		100.00
Common Player:		3.00
1	Ken Griffey Jr.	12.50
2	Albert Belle	3.00
3	Cal Ripken Jr.	20.00
4	Frank Thomas	7.50
5	Greg Maddux	10.00
6	Mo Vaughn	3.00
7	Chipper Jones	10.00
8	Mike Piazza	12.50
9	Ryan Klesko	3.00
10	Hideo Nomo	4.50
11	Roberto Alomar	3.00
12	Manny Ramirez	6.00
13	Gary Sheffield	3.50
14	Barry Bonds	20.00
15	Matt Williams	3.00
16	Jim Edmonds	3.00
17	Kirby Puckett	10.00
18	Sammy Sosa	10.00

1997 Zenith Samples

The extent of the sample-marked version of the standard-size '97 Zenith cards is unknown.

		NM/M
Common Player:		1.50
S1	Ken Griffey Jr.	5.00
S6	Kenny Lofton	1.50

1997 Zenith

This set combines standard size trading cards with cards in an 8" x 10" format. The standard size set consists of 60 cards. Card fronts feature full-bleed photos and the word "Zenith," but no reference to the player's name or team is found on the fronts. Backs have another player photo, a hit location chart and 1996/career stats. There are four inserts in the set, all of which are printed on the larger size format - 8" x 10", 8" x 10" Dufex, 8" x 10" V-2, and Z-Team. Each sale unit contained one pack of five standard-size cards and two larger size cards for a suggested retail price of $9.99.

		NM/M
Complete Set (50):		15.00
Common Player:		.10
Pack (Five Cards, Two 8 x 10)		2.00
Wax Box (12):		25.00
1	Frank Thomas	.75
2	Tony Gwynn	1.00
3	Jeff Bagwell	.75
4	Paul Molitor	.20
5	Roberto Alomar	.20
6	Mike Piazza	1.25
7	Albert Belle	.10
8	Greg Maddux	1.00
9	Barry Larkin	.10
10	Tony Clark	.10
11	Larry Walker	.10
12	Chipper Jones	1.00
13	Juan Gonzalez	.40
14	Barry Bonds	2.00
15	Ivan Rodriguez	.65
16	Sammy Sosa	.10
17	Derek Jeter	2.00
18	Hideo Nomo	.40
19	Roger Clemens	1.00
20	Ken Griffey Jr.	1.25
21	Andy Pettitte	.25
22	Alex Rodriguez	1.50
23	Tino Martinez	.10
24	Bernie Williams	.10
25	Ken Caminiti	.10
26	John Smoltz	.10
27	Javier Lopez	.10
28	Mark McGwire	1.50
29	Gary Sheffield	.50
30	David Justice	.10
31	Randy Johnson	.75
32	Chuck Knoblauch	.10
33	Mike Mussina	.40
34	Deion Sanders	.10
35	Cal Ripken Jr.	2.00
36	Darin Erstad	.30
37	Kenny Lofton	.10
38	Jay Buhner	.10
39	Brady Anderson	.10
40	Edgar Martinez	.10
41	Mo Vaughn	.10
42	Ryne Sandberg	1.00
43	Andruw Jones	.75
44	Nomar Garciaparra	1.00
45	Hideki Irabu RC	.25
46	Wilton Guerrero	.10
47	Jose Cruz Jr. RC	.45
48	Vladimir Guerrero	.75
49	Scott Rolen	.65
50	Jose Guillen	.10

V-2

This eight-card die-cut insert utilizes motion technology as well as foil printing to create a very high-tech 8" x 10" card. Cards were inserted 1:47 packs.

		NM/M
Complete Set (8):		45.00
Common Player:		5.00
1	Ken Griffey Jr.	7.50
2	Andruw Jones	5.00
3	Frank Thomas	5.00
4	Mike Piazza	7.50
5	Alex Rodriguez	10.00
6	Cal Ripken Jr.	12.00
7	Derek Jeter	12.00
8	Vladimir Guerrero	5.00

Z-Team

This nine-card 8" x 10" insert is printed on a mirror gold mylar foil stock with each card sequentially numbered to 1,000.

		NM/M
Complete Set (9):		60.00
Common Player:		3.00
1	Ken Griffey Jr.	9.00
2	Larry Walker	3.00
3	Frank Thomas	6.00
4	Alex Rodriguez	10.00
5	Mike Piazza	9.00
6	Cal Ripken Jr.	12.50
7	Derek Jeter	12.50
8	Andruw Jones	6.00
9	Roger Clemens	7.50

8x10 and 8x10 Dufex

This 24-card insert takes select cards from the standard set and blows them up to an 8" x 10" format. Cards were inserted one per pack. A Dufex version of each 8" x 10" insert card was also available at a rate of one per pack (except in packs which contained either a Z-Team or V-2 card).

		NM/M
Complete Set (24):		20.00
Common Player:		.50
Dufex versions:		1X
Samples:		1X
1	Frank Thomas	1.00
2	Tony Gwynn	1.50
3	Jeff Bagwell	1.00
4	Ken Griffey Jr.	2.00
5	Mike Piazza	2.00
6	Greg Maddux	1.50
7	Ken Caminiti	.50
8	Albert Belle	.50
9	Ivan Rodriguez	.75
10	Sammy Sosa	1.50
11	Mark McGwire	2.50
12	Roger Clemens	1.75
13	Alex Rodriguez	2.50
14	Chipper Jones	1.50
15	Juan Gonzalez	.60
16	Barry Bonds	3.00
17	Derek Jeter	3.00
18	Hideo Nomo	.60
19	Cal Ripken Jr.	3.00
20	Hideki Irabu	.50
21	Andruw Jones	1.50
22	Nomar Garciaparra	1.50
23	Vladimir Guerrero	1.00
24	Scott Rolen	.75

1998 Zenith Samples

To introduce its "Dare to Tear" concept, Zenith's promo cards for 1998 included a specially-marked standard-size (2-1/2" x 3-1/2") sample card within a 5" x 7" card. All cards are marked "SAMPLE" on back, but are otherwise identical to the issued versions.

		NM/M
Complete Set, Large (9):		17.50
Common Player, Large:		1.00
Complete Set, Small (6):		12.00
Common Player, Small:		1.00
Z1	Nomar Garciaparra	2.00
Z3	Greg Maddux	2.00
Z4	Frank Thomas	1.50
Z9	Andruw Jones	1.50
Z15	Derek Jeter	4.00
Z21	Mike Piazza	2.50
Z22	Tony Gwynn	2.50
Z35	Ivan Rodriguez	1.00
Z40	Ken Griffey Jr.	2.50
2	Ken Griffey Jr.	2.50
3	Greg Maddux	2.00
14	Mike Piazza	2.50
17	Derek Jeter	4.00
18	Nomar Garciaparra	2.00
19	Ivan Rodriguez	1.00

1998 Zenith

Zenith was part of Pinnacle's "Dare to Tear" program. Sold in three-card packs, the set consists of 5" x 7" cards, each with a standard-size card packaged inside. Collectors had to decide whether to keep the large cards or tear them open to get the smaller card inside. Eighty 5" x 7" cards and 100 regular cards comprise the set. The regular, or Z2, cards were paralleled twice - Z-Silver (1:7) and Z-Gold (numbered to 100). The large cards also had two parallels - Impulse (1:7) and Gold Impulse (numbered to 100).

		NM/M
Complete Set (100):		25.00
Common Player:		.10
Silvers:		2X
Inserted 1:7		
Pack (3):		2.50
Wax Box (18):		35.00
1	Larry Walker	.10
2	Ken Griffey Jr.	1.75
3	Cal Ripken Jr.	2.50
4	Sammy Sosa	1.50
5	Andruw Jones	1.00
6	Frank Thomas	1.00
7	Tony Gwynn	1.50
8	Rafael Palmeiro	.75
9	Tim Salmon	.10
10	Randy Johnson	1.00
11	Juan Gonzalez	.50
12	Greg Maddux	1.50
13	Vladimir Guerrero	1.00
14	Mike Piazza	1.75
15	Andres Galarraga	.10
16	Alex Rodriguez	2.00
17	Derek Jeter	2.50
18	Nomar Garciaparra	1.50
19	Ivan Rodriguez	.75
20	Chipper Jones	1.50
21	Barry Larkin	.10
22	Mo Vaughn	.10
23	Albert Belle	.10
24	Scott Rolen	.65
25	Sandy Alomar Jr.	.10
26	Roberto Alomar	.30
27	Andy Pettitte	.30
28	Chuck Knoblauch	.10
29	Jeff Bagwell	1.00
30	Mike Mussina	.30
31	Fred McGriff	.10
32	Roger Clemens	1.50
33	Rusty Greer	.10
34	Edgar Martinez	.10
35	Paul Molitor	1.00
36	Mark Grace	.10
37	Darin Erstad	.30
38	Kenny Lofton	.10
39	Tom Glavine	.35
40	Javier Lopez	.10
41	Will Clark	.10
42	Tino Martinez	.10
43	Raul Mondesi	.10
44	Brady Anderson	.10
45	Chan Ho Park	.10
46	Jason Giambi	.75
47	Manny Ramirez	1.00
48	Jay Buhner	.10
49	Dante Bichette	.10
50	Jose Cruz Jr.	.10
51	Charles Johnson	.10
52	Bernard Gilkey	.10
53	Johnny Damon	.35
54	David Justice	.10
55	Justin Thompson	.10
56	Bobby Higginson	.10
57	Todd Hundley	.10
58	Gary Sheffield	.50
59	Barry Bonds	2.50
60	Mark McGwire	2.00
61	John Smoltz	.10
62	Tony Clark	.10
63	Brian Jordan	.10
64	Jason Kendall	.10
65	Mariano Rivera	.20
66	Pedro Martinez	1.00
67	Jim Thome	.75
68	Neifi Perez	.10
69	Kevin Brown	.10
70	Hideo Nomo	.50
71	Craig Biggio	.10
72	Bernie Williams	.10
73	Jose Guillen	.10
74	Ken Caminiti	.10
75	Livan Hernandez	.10
76	Ray Lankford	.10
77	Jim Edmonds	.10
78	Matt Williams	.10
79	Mark Kotsay	.10
80	Moises Alou	.10

81	Antone Williamson	.10
82	Jaret Wright	.10
83	Jacob Cruz	.10
84	Abraham Nunez	.10
85	Raul Ibanez	.10
86	Miguel Tejada	.10
87	Derek Lee	.50
88	Juan Encarnacion	.10
89	Todd Helton	.75
90	Travis Lee	.10
91	Ben Grieve	.10
92	Ryan McGuire	.10
93	Richard Hidalgo	.10
94	Paul Konerko	.15
95	Shannon Stewart	.10
96	Homer Bush	.10
97	Lou Collier	.10
98	Jeff Abbott	.10
99	Brett Tomko	.10
100	Fernando Tatis	.10

Z-Silver

This parallel set reprinted all 100 standard sized cards in Zenith on silver foilboard, with a "Z-Silver" logo across the bottom center. Z-Silvers were inserted one per seven packs.

	NM/M
Common Player:	1.00
Stars/RC's:	2X
Inserted 1:7	

Z-Gold

	NM/M
Common Player:	3.00
Stars/Rookies	12X
Production 100 Sets	

Epix

Epix is a cross-brand insert. The set honors Plays, Games, Seasons and Moments in the careers of top baseball players. Epix consisted of 24 cards in Zenith, inserted 1:11. The cards have orange, purple and emerald versions.

	NM/M
Complete Set (24):	95.00
Common (Orange) Card:	1.50
Purples:	1X
Emeralds:	2X
1	Ken Griffey Jr./S	7.50
2	Juan Gonzalez/S	2.50
3	Jeff Bagwell/S	4.50
4	Ivan Rodriguez/S	4.00
5	Nomar Garciaparra/S	6.00
6	Ryne Sandberg/S	6.00
7	Frank Thomas/M	4.50
8	Derek Jeter/M	12.00
9	Tony Gwynn/M	6.00
10	Albert Belle/M	1.50
11	Scott Rolen/M	3.50
12	Barry Larkin/M	1.50
13	Alex Rodriguez/P	9.00
14	Cal Ripken Jr./P	12.00
15	Chipper Jones/P	6.00
16	Roger Clemens/P	6.50
17	Mo Vaughn/P	1.50
18	Mark McGwire/P	9.00
19	Mike Piazza/G	7.50

20	Andruw Jones/G	4.50
21	Greg Maddux/G	6.00
22	Barry Bonds/G	12.00
23	Paul Molitor/G	4.50
24	Eddie Murray/G	4.50

Raising the Bar

Raising the Bar is a 15-card insert seeded 1:25. The set features players who have set high standards for other players to follow.

	NM/M
Complete Set (15):	25.00
Common Player:	1.25
Inserted 1:25	
1	Ken Griffey Jr.	3.00
2	Frank Thomas	1.50
3	Alex Rodriguez	3.50
4	Tony Gwynn	2.50
5	Mike Piazza	3.00
6	Ivan Rodriguez	1.25
7	Cal Ripken Jr.	4.50
8	Greg Maddux	2.50
9	Hideo Nomo	1.25
10	Mark McGwire	3.50
11	Juan Gonzalez	1.25
12	Andruw Jones	1.50
13	Jeff Bagwell	1.50
14	Chipper Jones	2.50
15	Nomar Garciaparra	2.50

Rookie Thrills

Rookie Thrills is a 15-card insert seeded 1:25. The set features many of the top rookies of 1998 in action photos printed on a silverfoil background. Backs have a few words about the player's career to that point.

	NM/M
Complete Set (15):	20.00
Common Player:	1.50
Inserted 1:25	
1	Travis Lee	1.50
2	Juan Encarnacion	1.50
3	Derrek Lee	1.50
4	Raul Ibanez	1.50
5	Ryan McGuire	1.50
6	Todd Helton	3.00
7	Jacob Cruz	1.50
8	Abraham Nunez	1.50

9	Paul Konerko	2.00
10	Ben Grieve	1.50
11	Jeff Abbott	1.50
12	Richard Hidalgo	1.50
13	Jaret Wright	1.50
14	Lou Collier	1.50
15	Miguel Tejada	2.00

Z-Team

The Z Team insert was created in 5" x 7" and standard-size versions, each inserted at a 1:35 pack rate. The nine Rookie Z Team cards were seeded 1:58 and gold versions of both were found 1:175.

	NM/M
Complete Set (18):	35.00
Common Player:	1.25
Golds:	2X
Inserted 1:175	
1	Frank Thomas	2.50
2	Ken Griffey Jr.	3.50
3	Mike Piazza	3.50
4	Cal Ripken Jr.	6.00
5	Alex Rodriguez	5.00
6	Greg Maddux	3.00
7	Derek Jeter	6.00
8	Chipper Jones	3.00
9	Roger Clemens	3.25
10	Ben Grieve	1.25
11	Derek Lee	1.75
12	Jose Cruz Jr.	1.25
13	Nomar Garciaparra	3.00
14	Travis Lee	1.50
15	Todd Helton	2.00
16	Paul Konerko	1.75
17	Miguel Tejada	1.25
18	Scott Rolen	2.00

Z-Team 5x7

The 5" x 7" Z-Team insert is a nine-card set seeded one per 35 packs.

	NM/M
Complete Set (9):	40.00
Common Player:	3.00
Inserted 1:35	
1	Frank Thomas	3.00
2	Ken Griffey Jr.	5.00
3	Mike Piazza	5.00
4	Cal Ripken Jr.	7.50
5	Alex Rodriguez	6.00

6	Greg Maddux	4.00
7	Derek Jeter	7.50
8	Chipper Jones	4.00
9	Roger Clemens	4.50

5x7

The 80 Zenith 5" x 7" cards all contained a regular-size card. Collectors could tear open the 5" x 7" to get at the smaller card inside. The set has two parallels: 5" x 7" Impulse (1:7) and 5" x 7" Gold Impulse (1:43).

	NM/M
Complete Set (80):	30.00
Common Player:	.25
Impulse Silvers:	1.5X
Inserted 1:7	
1	Nomar Garciaparra	2.00
2	Andres Galarraga	.25
3	Greg Maddux	2.00
4	Frank Thomas	1.00
5	Mark McGwire	3.00
6	Rafael Palmeiro	.75
7	John Smoltz	.25
8	Jeff Bagwell	1.00
9	Andruw Jones	1.00
10	Rusty Greer	.25
11	Paul Molitor	1.00
12	Bernie Williams	.25
13	Kenny Lofton	.25
14	Alex Rodriguez	3.00
15	Derek Jeter	4.00
15s	Derek Jeter ("SAMPLE" overprint on back.)	4.00
16	Scott Rolen	.65
17	Albert Belle	.25
18	Mo Vaughn	.25
19	Chipper Jones	2.00
20	Chuck Knoblauch	.25
21	Mike Piazza	3.00
22	Tony Gwynn	2.00
22s	Tony Gwynn ("SAMPLE" overprint on back.)	2.00
23	Juan Gonzalez	.50
24	Andy Pettitte	.35
25	Tim Salmon	.25
26	Brady Anderson	.25
27	Mike Mussina	.40
28	Edgar Martinez	.25
29	Jose Guillen	.25
30	Hideo Nomo	.50
31	Jim Thome	.65
32	Mark Grace	.25
33	Darin Erstad	.50
34	Bobby Higginson	.25
35	Ivan Rodriguez	.75
36	Todd Hundley	.25
37	Sandy Alomar Jr.	.25
38	Gary Sheffield	.40
39	David Justice	.25
40	Ken Griffey Jr.	2.50
40s	Ken Griffey Jr. ("SAMPLE" overprint on back.)	2.50
41	Vladimir Guerrero	1.00
42	Larry Walker	.25
43	Barry Bonds	4.00
44	Randy Johnson	1.00
45	Roger Clemens	2.25
46	Raul Mondesi	.25
47	Tino Martinez	.25
48	Jason Giambi	.50

49	Matt Williams	.25
50	Cal Ripken Jr.	4.00
51	Barry Larkin	.25
52	Jim Edmonds	.25
53	Ken Caminiti	.25
54	Sammy Sosa	2.00
55	Tony Clark	.25
56	Manny Ramirez	1.00
57	Bernard Gilkey	.25
58	Jose Cruz Jr.	.25
59	Brian Jordan	.25
60	Kevin Brown	.25
61	Craig Biggio	.25
62	Javier Lopez	.25
63	Jay Buhner	.25
64	Roberto Alomar	.40
65	Justin Thompson	.25
66	Todd Helton	.75
67	Travis Lee	.25
68	Paul Konerko	.35
69	Jaret Wright	.25
70	Ben Grieve	.25
71	Juan Encarnacion	.25
72	Ryan McGuire	.25
73	Derek Lee	.60
74	Abraham Nunez	.25
75	Richard Hidalgo	.25
76	Miguel Tejada	.25
77	Jacob Cruz	.25
78	Homer Bush	.25
79	Jeff Abbott	.25
80	Lou Collier	.25
	Checklist	.10

5x7 Impulse Silver

These silver parallels reprinted each of the 80 cards in the 5" x 7" set. Cards were called Impulse and carried that logo on the front and were inserted one per seven packs. Since these cards contained other cards inside, they are condition sensitive and only worth full price if left in mint condition and not cut open.

	NM/M
Common Player:	2.00
Stars/RC's:	1.5X
Inserted 1:7	

1998 Zenith 5x7 Impulse Gold

These gold parallels reprint each of the 80 cards in the 5" x 7" set. Cards carry a Gold Impulse logo on front and are serially numbered from within an edition of 100 each on back. Silver or Gold Impulse parallels were inserted one per seven packs. Since these cards contained other cards inside them, they are condition sensitive and only worth full price if left in mint condition and not cut open.

	NM/M
Common Player:	5.00
Stars/RC's:	20X
Inserted 1:7	

1992 Ziploc

Dow Brands produced an 11-card set of All-Stars in 1992 that featured mostly Hall of Famers, with the exception only of Nellie Fox. The cards were included in specially-marked Ziploc packages, and also could be purchased by mail.

	NM/M
Complete Set (11):	4.00
Common Player:	.45
1	Warren Spahn	.50
2	Bob Gibson	.50
3	Rollie Fingers	.50
4	Carl Yastrzemski	1.00
5	Brooks Robinson	.50
6	Pee Wee Reese	.75
7	Willie McCovey	.50
8	Willie Mays	2.00
9	Nellie Fox	.50
10	Yogi Berra	.75
11	Hank Aaron	2.00

MINOR LEAGUE (1867-1969)

Prior to 1970 virtually all minor league baseball cards were issued as single cards rather than the complete sets. Like contemporary major league cards they were usually intended as premiums given away with the purchase of goos and services.

The listings which follow offer individual card prices in three grades of preservation to allow accurate valuations of superstar and other special interest cards, along with cards that were short-printed or otherwise are scarce.

A

1959 APCO Meat Packing Co. San Antonio Missions

The extent of this issue, as well as its distribution are not known. The 3-1/2" x 4-1/2" black-and-white cards may have been packaged with meat products and/or given away at the ballpark. The team was Class AA affiliate of the Chicago Cubs.

		NM	EX	VG
Common Player:		50.00	25.00	15.00
(1)	Russell Gragg	50.00	25.00	15.00
(2)	Mike Lutz	50.00	25.00	15.00
	(In Corpus Christi uniform.)			

1960 Armour Meats Denver Bears

DENVER BEARS

EDWARD J. DONNELLY
Age: 28, Ht.: 6-0, Wt.: 170,
B: L, T: L, Pitcher
1959 DENVER AA: G-31, CG-17, W-14, L-10,
Per-.583, IP-229, R-104, H-237, BB-70,
SO-95, ERA-3.54

Ten cards from this Class AA farm team of the Detroit Tigers have been checklisted, with others possibly to be discovered. The black-and-white blank-backed cards measure 2-1/2" x 3-1/4" and were issued with a coupon attached to the right side. The unnumbered cards are checklisted here alphabetically.

		NM	EX	VG
Complete Set (10):		650.00	325.00	195.00
Common Player:		75.00	37.00	22.00
(1)	George Alusik	75.00	37.00	22.00
(2)	Tony Bartirome	75.00	37.00	22.00
(3)	Edward J. Donnelly	75.00	37.00	22.00
(4)	James R. McDaniel	75.00	37.00	22.00
(5)	Charlie Metro	75.00	37.00	22.00
(6)	Harry Perkowski	75.00	37.00	22.00
(7)	Vernon E. Rapp	75.00	37.00	22.00
(8)	James Stump	75.00	37.00	22.00
(9)	Ozzie Virgil	75.00	37.00	22.00
(10)	Robert Walz	75.00	37.00	22.00

1940 Associated Stations San Francisco Seals

GENE KILEY

This album and sticker set was created as a premium by a Northern California gas company. Individual stickers were given away each week at participating service stations. The blank-backed, 1-3/4" x 2-5/8" stickers have the player's name in a black strip at the bottom. Pages in the accompanying 3-1/2" x 6" album have space for an autograph and a few career highlights for each player. The checklist is presented in page order of the album.

		NM	EX	VG
Complete Set (26):		500.00	250.00	125.00
Common Player:		20.00	10.00	6.00
Album:		100.00	50.00	30.00
(1)	"Lefty" O'Doul	40.00	20.00	12.00

		NM	EX	VG
(2)	Sam Gibson	20.00	10.00	6.00
(3)	Brooks Holder	20.00	10.00	6.00
(4)	Ted Norbert	20.00	10.00	6.00
(5)	Win Ballou	20.00	10.00	6.00
(6)	Al Wright	20.00	10.00	6.00
(7)	Al Epperly	20.00	10.00	6.00
(8)	Orville Jorgens	20.00	10.00	6.00
(9)	Larry Powell	20.00	10.00	6.00
(10)	Joe Sprinz	20.00	10.00	6.00
(11)	Harvey Storey	20.00	10.00	6.00
(12)	Jack Burns	20.00	10.00	6.00
(13)	Bob Price	20.00	10.00	6.00
(14)	Larry Guay	20.00	10.00	6.00
(15)	Frank Dasso	20.00	10.00	6.00
(16)	Eddie Stutz	20.00	10.00	6.00
(17)	John Barrett	20.00	10.00	6.00
(18)	Eddie Botelho	20.00	10.00	6.00
(19)	Ferris Fain	30.00	15.00	9.00
(20)	Larry Woodall	20.00	10.00	6.00
(21)	Ted Jennings	20.00	10.00	6.00
(22)	Jack Warner	20.00	10.00	6.00
(23)	Wil Leonard	20.00	10.00	6.00
(24)	Gene Kiley	20.00	10.00	6.00
(25)	Bob Jensen	20.00	10.00	6.00
(26)	Wilfrid Le Febvre	20.00	10.00	6.00

1952 Atlanta Crackers Souvenir Pictures Album

Rather than a set of individual baseball cards, the Class AA Southern Association farm club of the Boston Braves issued this souvenir picture album depicting players (including future major leaguers like Chuck Tanner, Art Fowler and Carl Wiley), staff and media. About 8-1/8" x 7-1/2", the album has embossed metallic light blue covers and dark blue graphics. Inside are eight black-and-white pages with three card-like images per page. The pictures are in about the same size and format as Globe Printing's contemporary minor league baseball card team sets.

	NM	EX	VG
Complete Souvenir Book:	400.00	200.00	120.00
1952 Atlanta Crackers	.00	.00	.00

1910 A.W.H./A.W.A. Caramels Virginia League (E222)

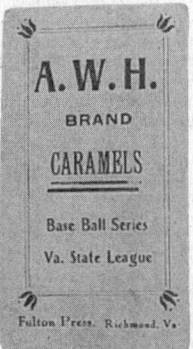

MCCAULEY, PORTSMOUTH

A.W.H. BRAND CARAMELS
Base Ball Series
Va. State League
Fulton Press, Richmond, Va.

This rare set of cards picturing players from the Virginia League was issued by the A.W.H. (or A.W.A.) Caramel Co. in 1910. The cards measure 1-1/2" x 2-3/4" and feature player portraits in either red, black, brown or blue duotones. Examples of 12 different cards have been found. The front of the card displays the player's last name and team below his photo. The back states "A.W.H. (or A.W.A.) Brand Caramels" in large letters with "Base Ball Series/Va. State League" below. At least four variations in back typography and borders are known.

		NM	EX	VG
Complete Set (12):		130,000	65,000	40,000
Common Player:		11,000	5,500	3,250
(1)	Tom Guiheen	11,000	5,500	3,250
(2)	Buck Hooker	11,000	5,500	3,250
(3)	Ison	11,000	5,500	3,250
(4)	Lipe	11,000	5,500	3,250
(5)	McCauley	11,000	5,500	3,250
(6)	Otey	11,000	5,500	3,250
(7)	Revelle	11,000	5,500	3,250
(8)	Ryan	11,000	5,500	3,250
(9)	Shaughnessy	11,000	5,500	3,250
(10)	Sieber	11,000	5,500	3,250
(11)	Smith	11,000	5,500	3,250
(12)	Titman	11,000	5,500	3,250

B

1910 Baltimore News Orioles

FOR REAL SPORTS
Read The Baltimore News
1910
JIMMY MURRAY
NEWS "WANT-ADS" BRING RESULTS.

The Eastern League Baltimore Orioles are featured in this set of schedule cards issued by a local newspaper. Cards measure 2-3/4" x 3-1/2" and feature player photographs on front, with a wide border. Player name, position, team and league are printed at the bottom of the photo. Backs have both the "Home" and "Abroad" schedule for the team, along with ads at top and bottom for the newspaper. All printing on front is in red-and-white; backs are in black-and-white. The checklist here is likely incomplete.

		NM	EX	VG
Common Player:		1,200	600.00	350.00
(1)	Byers	1,200	600.00	350.00
(2)	Jim Egan	1,200	600.00	350.00
(3)	Maisel	1,200	600.00	350.00
(4)	Malloy	1,200	600.00	350.00
(5)	Jimmy Murray	1,200	600.00	350.00

1914 Baltimore News Orioles

Read The Baltimore News
1914   1914
RUTH
This Card is Given to:
Cromwell

The International League Baltimore Orioles are one of two teams featured (along with the city's Federal League team) in this set of newspaper promotional cards. The 2-5/8" x 3-5/8" cards are monochrome printed in either blue or red with wide borders on front framing full-length action poses on which the background has been erased in favor of artificial shadows. Player name, position and league are printed on front. Backs have a "HOME" and "ABROAD" schedule with an ad for the paper at top and a line at bottom which reads, "This Card is Given to," with space for a signature. At least one card, a Babe Ruth, has been seen with "Compliments Baltimore International League" replacing the newspaper ad at top. Only the minor league Orioles players are listed here, the Terrapins cards are listed in the major league section of this catalog. This checklist is almost certainly incomplete.

		NM	EX	VG
Common Player:		3,000	1,500	900.00
(1)	Neal Ball	3,000	1,500	900.00
(2)	Ensign Cottrell	3,000	1,500	900.00
(3)	Birdie Cree	3,000	1,500	900.00
(4)	Bert Daniels	3,000	1,500	900.00
(5)	Davidson	3,000	1,500	900.00
(6)	Jack Dunn	4,500	2,250	1,350
(7)	Gleichmann	3,000	1,500	900.00
(8)	Allen Russell (Allan)	3,000	1,500	900.00
(10)	Babe Ruth ((Blue PSA VG-EX sold in 5/06 auction for $244,000. Red PSA Poor-Fair sold in 4/06 auction for $150,800. Red SGC VG sold in 5/08 auction for $517,000. Red PSA Poor-Fair sold in 5/09 auction for $152,750.)			

		NM	EX	VG
(11)	Ernie Shore	3,000	1,500	900.00
(12)	George Twombley (Twombly)	3,000	1,500	900.00
(13)	Orioles Team w/Ruth (Slabbed authentic sold in 5/08 auction for $52,875.)			

1952 Baltimore Orioles Team Issue

ROY WEATHERLY

While most of the company's issues were for minor league teams in the lower classifications, Globe Printing of San Jose, Calif., also produced a set for the International League Baltimore Orioles. Similar to the company's other issues, the black-and-white cards measure about 2-1/4" x 3-3/8". Reliable reports indicate that individual cards were given away with ice cream purchases at the ballpark. The checklist here is obviously incomplete. In 1952 the O's were the top farm club of the Philadelphia Phillies.

		NM	EX	VG
Common Player:		75.00	37.50	22.50
(1)	Al Cihocki	75.00	37.50	22.50
(2)	Blix Donnelly	75.00	37.50	22.50
(3)	Bob Greenwood	75.00	37.50	22.50
(4)	Don Heffner	75.00	37.50	22.50
(5)	Russ Kerns	75.00	37.50	22.50
(6)	Howie Moss	75.00	37.50	22.50
(7)	Dee Phillips	75.00	37.50	22.50
(8)	Jerry Scala	75.00	37.50	22.50
(9)	Danny Schell	75.00	37.50	22.50
(10)	Paul Stuffel	75.00	37.50	22.50
(11)	Roy Weatherly	75.00	37.50	22.50

1923 Baltimore Shirt Co. Kansas City Blues

LENA BLACKBURNE

This unusual souvenir of the American Association Champion K.C. Blues is in the form of a 48" x 3-5/8" accordian-fold packet. Individual 1-7/8" x 3-1/4" black-and-white photos of the players are glued onto the black backing paper. Because the photos are rather easily removed, they may be encountered as singles. The players are checklisted here as they originally appeared, from left to right, on the foldout. There is no advertising on the individual pictures, just on the outer covers.

		NM	EX	VG
Complete Foldout:		1,000	500.00	300.00
Complete Set, Singles:		750.00	375.00	225.00
Common Player:		50.00	25.00	15.00
(1)	Wilbur Good	50.00	25.00	15.00
(2)	Bill Skiff	50.00	25.00	15.00
(3)	Lew McCarty	50.00	25.00	15.00
(4)	Dudley Branom	50.00	25.00	15.00
(5)	Lena Blackburne	55.00	27.50	16.50
(6)	Walter Hammond	50.00	25.00	15.00
(7)	Glen Wright (Glenn)	60.00	30.00	18.00
(8)	Geo. Armstrong	50.00	25.00	15.00
(9)	Beals Becker	50.00	25.00	15.00
(10)	"Dutch" Zwilling	50.00	25.00	15.00
(11)	Pete Scott	50.00	25.00	15.00
(12)	"Bunny" Brief	50.00	25.00	15.00
(13)	Jimmie Zinn	50.00	25.00	15.00
(14)	Ferd Schupp	50.00	25.00	15.00
(15)	Roy Wilkinson	50.00	25.00	15.00
(16)	Ray Caldwell	50.00	25.00	15.00
(17)	Joe Dawson	50.00	25.00	15.00
(18)	John Saladna	50.00	25.00	15.00
(19)	Herb Thormahlen	50.00	25.00	15.00
(20)	"Nick" Carter	50.00	25.00	15.00
(21)	George Muehlebach (President)	50.00	25.00	15.00

1909 Bastian Gum Pin

It is unknown whether other members of the championship 1909 Rochester Bronchos of the Eastern League were honored on these black-and-white pinback celluloid buttons or only their manager. The pin measures about 1-1/4" in diameter and as originally issued had a paper insert in back crediting it to Bastian Bros. Gum.

	NM	EX	VG
John H. Ganzel	150.00	75.00	45.00

1961 Bee Hive Starch Toronto Maple Leafs

BEE HIVE PLAYER PHOTO

DAVE POPE, outfielder - 1961

This 24-card set features players of the Toronto Maple Leafs, an independent team in the International League which featured future Hall of Fame Manager Sparky Anderson as its second baseman. The black-and-white cards are printed on thin, blank-backed stock and measure approximately 2-1/2" x 3-1/4". As the cards are not numbered, the checklist below is presented alphabetically.

		NM	EX	VG
Complete Set (24):		2,400	1,200	725.00
Common Player:		90.00	45.00	25.00
(1)	George Anderson	450.00	225.00	135.00
(2)	Fritzie Brickell	90.00	45.00	25.00
(3)	Ellis Burton	90.00	45.00	25.00
(4)	Bob Chakales	90.00	45.00	25.00
(5)	Rip Coleman	90.00	45.00	25.00
(6)	Steve Demeter	90.00	45.00	25.00
(7)	Joe Hannah	90.00	45.00	25.00
(8)	Earl Hersh	90.00	45.00	25.00
(9)	Lou Jackson	90.00	45.00	25.00
(10)	Ken Johnson	90.00	45.00	25.00
(11)	Lou Johnson	90.00	45.00	25.00
(12)	John Lipon	90.00	45.00	25.00
(13)	Carl Mathias	90.00	45.00	25.00
(14)	Bill Moran	90.00	45.00	25.00
(15)	Ron Negray	90.00	45.00	25.00
(16)	Herb Plews	90.00	45.00	25.00
(17)	Dave Pope	90.00	45.00	25.00
(18)	Steve Ridzik	90.00	45.00	25.00
(19)	Raul Sanchez	90.00	45.00	25.00
(20)	Pat Scantlebury	90.00	45.00	25.00
(21)	Bill Smith	90.00	45.00	25.00
(22)	Bob Smith	90.00	45.00	25.00
(23)	Chuck Tanner	125.00	65.00	35.00
(24)	Tim Thompson	90.00	45.00	25.00

1911 Big Eater Sacramento Solons

This very rare set was issued circa 1911 and includes only members of the Pacific Coast League Sacramento Solons. The black-and-white cards measure 2-1/8" x 4" and feature action photos. The lower part of the card contains a three-line caption that includes the player's last name, team designation (abbreviated to "Sac'to") and the promotional line: "He Eats 'Big Eater'." Although the exact origin is undetermined, it is believed that "Big Eaters" were a candy novelty.

BYRAM SAC'TO
HE EATS "BIG EATER"

		NM	EX	VG
Complete Set (20):		150,000	75,000	45,000
Common Player:		7,750	3,875	2,325
(1)	Frank Arellanes	7,750	3,875	2,325
(2)	Spider Baum	7,750	3,875	2,325
(3)	Herb Byram	7,750	3,875	2,325
(4)	Babe Danzig	7,750	3,875	2,325
(5)	Jack Fitzgerald	7,750	3,875	2,325
(6)	George Gaddy	7,750	3,875	2,325
(7)	Al Heister	7,750	3,875	2,325
(8)	Ben Hunt	7,750	3,875	2,325
(9)	Butch Kerns	7,750	3,875	2,325
(10)	Mickey LaLonge	7,750	3,875	2,325
(11)	Dutch Lerchen	7,750	3,875	2,325
(12)	Jimmy Lewis	7,750	3,875	2,325
(13)	Chris Mahoney	7,750	3,875	2,325
(14)	Dick Nebinger	7,750	3,875	2,325
(15)	Patsy O'Rourke	7,750	3,875	2,325
(16)	Jimmy Shinn	7,750	3,875	2,325
(17)	Chester Thomas	7,750	3,875	2,325
(18)	Fuller Thompson	7,750	3,875	2,325
(19)	Frank Thornton	7,750	3,875	2,325
(20)	Deacon Van Buren	7,750	3,875	2,325

1950 Big League Stars (V362)

Chuck Connors
MONTREAL ROYALS
Infielder
Born at Brooklyn, N.Y., on April 10, 1921. Bats left. Throws left. 6'5". 210 lbs. Hit .319, 20 homers and batted in 108 runs with Royals in 1949.

Champ intérieur
Né à Brooklyn, N.Y., le 10 avril 1921. Frappe de la gauche, lance de la gauche. 6'5". 210 livres. Frappa .319, 20 coups de circuit et participa à 108 buts avec les Royaux en 1949.

BIG LEAGUE STARS — No. 2

International League players are featured in this 48-card set. Measuring 3-1/4" x 2-5/8", the blank-backed cards are printed in blue-on-white with English and French stats and biographical data.

		NM	EX	VG
Complete Set (48):		4,500	2,750	1,200
Common Player:		90.00	40.00	25.00
1	Rocky Bridges	100.00	50.00	30.00
2	Chuck Connors	750.00	370.00	220.00
3	Jake Wade	90.00	40.00	25.00
4	Al Cihocki	90.00	40.00	25.00
5	John Simmons	90.00	40.00	25.00
6	Frank Trechock	90.00	40.00	25.00
7	Steve Lembo	90.00	40.00	25.00
8	Johnny Welaj	90.00	40.00	25.00
9	Seymour Block	90.00	40.00	25.00
10	Pat McGlothlin	90.00	40.00	25.00
11	Bryan Stephens	90.00	40.00	25.00
12	Clarence Podbielan	90.00	40.00	25.00
13	Clem Hausmann	90.00	40.00	25.00
14	Turk Lown	90.00	40.00	25.00
15	Joe Payne	90.00	40.00	25.00
16	Coacker Triplett (Coaker)	90.00	40.00	25.00
17	Nick Strincevich	90.00	40.00	25.00
18	Charlie Thompson	90.00	40.00	25.00
19	Erick Silverman	90.00	40.00	25.00
20	George Schmees	90.00	40.00	25.00
21	George Binks	90.00	40.00	25.00
22	Gino Cimoli	100.00	50.00	30.00
23	Marty Tabacheck	90.00	40.00	25.00
24	Al Gionfriddo	100.00	50.00	30.00
25	Ronnie Lee	90.00	40.00	25.00
26	Clyde King	90.00	40.00	25.00
27	Harry Heslet	90.00	40.00	25.00
28	Jerry Scala	90.00	40.00	25.00
29	Boris Woyt	90.00	40.00	25.00
30	Jack Collum	90.00	40.00	25.00
31	Chet Laabs	90.00	40.00	25.00
32	Carden Gillwater	90.00	40.00	25.00
33	Irving Medlinger	90.00	40.00	25.00
34	Toby Atwell	90.00	40.00	25.00
35	Charlie Marshall	90.00	40.00	25.00
36	Johnny Mayo	90.00	40.00	25.00
37	Gene Markland	90.00	40.00	25.00
38	Russ Kerns	90.00	40.00	25.00

		NM	EX	VG
9	Jim Prendergast	90.00	40.00	25.00
0	Lou Welaj	90.00	40.00	25.00
1	Clyde Kluttz	90.00	40.00	25.00
2	Bill Glynn	90.00	40.00	25.00
3	Don Richmond	90.00	40.00	25.00
4	Hank Biasatti	90.00	40.00	25.00
5	Tom Lasorda	600.00	300.00	180.00
6	Al Roberge	90.00	40.00	25.00
7	George Byam	90.00	40.00	25.00
8	Dutch Mele	90.00	40.00	25.00

1910 Bishop & Co. P.C.L. Teams (E221)

A very rare issue, this series of team pictures of clubs in the Pacific Coast League was distributed by Bishop & Co. of Los Angeles in 1910. The team photos were printed on a thin, newsprint-type paper that measures an elongated 10" x 2-3/4". Although there were six teams in the PCL at the time, only five clubs have been found - the sixth team, Sacramento, was apparently never issued. The cards indicate that they were issued with five-cent packages of Bishop's Milk Chocolate and that the photos were taken by the Los Angeles Examiner. The black-and-white team photos are found with red, blue, yellow, purple, or green background.

		NM	EX	VG
	Complete Set (5):	50,000	25,000	15,000
	Common Team:	11,000	5,500	3,250
1)	Los Angeles	6,000	2,700	1,700
2)	Oakland	6,000	2,700	1,700
3)	Portland	6,000	2,700	1,700
4)	San Francisco	12,500	6,250	3,750
5)	Vernon	6,000	2,700	1,700

1910 Bishop & Co. P.C.L. (E99)

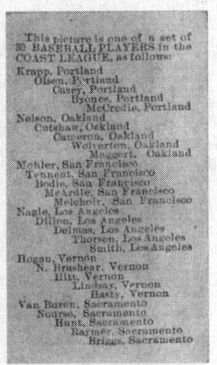

The first of two obscure sets produced by the Los Angeles candy maker Bishop & Co., this 30-card set was issued in 1910 and depicts players from the Pacific Coast League, showing five players from each of the six teams. The cards measure approximately 1-1/2" x 2-3/4" and feature black-and-white player photos with colored backgrounds (green, blue, purple, yellow, or rarely, black). The player's last name, position and team appear along the bottom. The backs of the cards contain the complete checklist in groups of five, according to team, with each name indented slightly more than the name above. Cards in the 1910 set do not contain the name "Bishop & Company, California" along the bottom on the back.

		NM	EX	VG
	Complete Set (30):	60,000	30,000	18,000
	Common Player:	2,000	1,000	600.00
1)	Bodie	2,000	800.00	500.00
2)	N. Brashear	1,750	700.00	435.00
3)	Briggs	1,750	700.00	435.00
4)	Byones (Byrnes)	1,750	700.00	435.00
5)	Cameron	1,750	700.00	435.00
6)	Casey	1,750	700.00	435.00
7)	Cutshaw	1,750	700.00	435.00
8)	Delmas	1,750	700.00	435.00
9)	Dillon	1,750	700.00	435.00
10)	Hasty	1,750	700.00	435.00
11)	Hitt	1,750	700.00	435.00
12)	Hap. Hogan	1,750	700.00	435.00
13)	Hunt	1,750	700.00	435.00
14)	Krapp	1,750	700.00	435.00
15)	John Lindsay	1,750	700.00	435.00
16)	Maggert	1,750	700.00	435.00
17)	McArdle	1,750	700.00	435.00
18)	McCredie (McCreedie)	1,750	700.00	435.00
19)	Melchior	1,750	700.00	435.00
20)	Mohler	1,750	700.00	435.00
21)	Nagle	1,750	700.00	435.00
22)	Nelson	1,750	700.00	435.00
23)	Nourse	1,750	700.00	435.00
24)	Olsen	1,750	700.00	435.00
25)	Raymer	1,750	700.00	435.00
26)	Smith	1,750	700.00	435.00
27)	Tennent (Tennant)	1,750	700.00	435.00
28)	Thorsen	1,750	700.00	435.00
29)	Van Buren	1,750	700.00	435.00
30)	Wolverton	1,750	700.00	435.00

1911 Bishop & Co. P.C.L. Type I (E100)

This set was issued by the confectioner Bishop & Co. of Los Angeles, which had produced a similar set a year earlier. Both sets showcased star players from the Pacific Coast League. The cards measure approximately 1-1/2" x 2-3/4" and feature black-and-white photos with a background of green, blue, yellow, purple or red. The backs contain the complete checklist of the set, listing the players in groups of five by team, with one line indented slightly more than the previous one. In addition to the checklist, the 1911 set can be differentiated from the previous year because the line "Bishop & Company, California" appears along the bottom.

		NM	EX	VG
	Complete Set (30):	75,000	37,000	22,000
	Common Player:	2,200	1,100	650.00
(1)	Spider Baum	2,200	1,100	650.00
(2)	Burrell	2,200	1,100	650.00
(3)	Carlisle	2,200	1,100	650.00
(4)	Cutshaw	2,200	1,100	650.00
(5)	Pete Daley	2,200	1,100	650.00
(6)	Danzig	2,200	1,100	650.00
(7)	Delhi	2,200	1,100	650.00
(8)	Delmas	2,200	1,100	650.00
(9)	Hitt	2,200	1,100	650.00
(10)	Hap Hogan (Actually Walter Bray.)	2,200	1,100	650.00
(11)	Lerchen	2,200	1,100	650.00
(12)	McCreddie (McCreedie)	2,200	1,100	650.00
(13)	Mohler	2,200	1,100	650.00
(14)	Moore	2,200	1,100	650.00
(15)	Slim Nelson	2,200	1,100	650.00
(16)	P. O'Rourke	2,200	1,100	650.00
(17)	Patterson	2,200	1,100	650.00
(18)	Bunny Pearce	2,200	1,100	650.00
(19)	Peckinpaugh	2,200	1,100	650.00
(20)	Monte Pfyle (Pfyl)	2,200	1,100	650.00
(21)	Powell	2,200	1,100	650.00
(22)	Rapps	2,200	1,100	650.00
(23)	Seaton	2,200	1,100	650.00
(24)	Steen	2,200	1,100	650.00
(25)	Sutor (Suter)	2,200	1,100	650.00
(26)	Tennant	2,200	1,100	650.00
(27)	Thomas	2,200	1,100	650.00
(28)	Tozer	2,200	1,100	650.00
(29)	Clyde Wares	2,200	1,100	650.00
(30)	Weaver	12,000	6,000	3,500

1911 Bishop & Co. P.C.L. Type II (E100)

Currently little over half of the checklist of Bishop & Co. (E100) has been found in a second version. These cards have thus far been seen only with green and orange backgrounds, are blank-backed, have larger, reversed negatives, cropping of the photos and have caption differences.

		NM	EX	VG
	Common Player:	2,750	1,350	825.00
(1)	Burrell	2,750	1,350	825.00
(2)	Danzig	2,750	1,350	825.00
(3)	Delhi	2,750	1,350	825.00
(4)	Hitt	2,750	1,350	825.00
(5)	Lerchen	2,750	1,350	825.00
(6)	McCreddie (McCreedie)	2,750	1,350	825.00
(7)	Slim Nelson	2,750	1,350	825.00
(8)	P. O'Rourke	2,750	1,350	825.00
(9)	Patterson	2,750	1,350	825.00
(10)	Bunny Pearce	2,750	1,350	825.00
(11)	Monte Pfyle	2,750	1,350	825.00
(12)	Rapps	2,750	1,350	825.00
(13)	Seaton	2,750	1,350	825.00
(14)	Steen	2,750	1,350	825.00
(15)	Sutot (Suter)	2,750	1,350	825.00
(16)	Tennant	2,750	1,350	825.00
(17)	Weaver	15,000	7,500	4,500

1954 Blossom Dairy Charleston Senators

The Class AAA farm team of the Chicago White Sox is featured in this team set sponsored by a Charleston, W. Va., dairy. The 2-1/4" x 3-3/16" black-and-white cards are either a late issue by Globe Printing (which issued many minor league sets from 1951-52) or were patterned after the Globe issues, right down to the issue of an album to house the cards. A white box is superimposed over the posed action photos and contains the player and sponsor identification. Cards are blank-backed.

		NM	EX	VG
	Complete Set (22):	2,200	1,100	650.00
	Common Player:	100.00	50.00	30.00
	Album:	150.00	75.00	45.00
(1)	Al Baro	100.00	50.00	30.00
(2)	Joe Becker	100.00	50.00	30.00
(3)	Joe Carroll	100.00	50.00	30.00
(4)	Gerald "Red" Fahr	100.00	50.00	30.00
(5)	Dick Fowler	100.00	50.00	30.00
(6)	Alex Garbowski	100.00	50.00	30.00
(7)	Gordon Goldsberry	100.00	50.00	30.00
(8)	Ross Grimsley	100.00	50.00	30.00
(9)	Sam Hairston	125.00	65.00	35.00
(10)	Phil Haugstad	100.00	50.00	30.00
(11)	Tom Hurd	100.00	50.00	30.00
(12)	Bill Killinger	100.00	50.00	30.00
(13)	John Kropf	100.00	50.00	30.00
(14)	Bob Masser	100.00	50.00	30.00
(15)	Danny Menendez	100.00	50.00	30.00
(16)	Bill Paolisso	100.00	50.00	30.00
(17)	Bill Pope	100.00	50.00	30.00
(18)	Lou Sleater	100.00	50.00	30.00
(19)	Dick Strahs	100.00	50.00	30.00
(20)	Joe Torpey	100.00	50.00	30.00
(21)	Bill Voiselle	100.00	50.00	30.00
(22)	Al Ware	100.00	50.00	30.00

1958 Bond Bread Buffalo Bisons

Nine members of the International League affiliate of the Kansas City Athletics are featured in this set. The 2-1/2" x 3-1/2" cards are printed on very thin cardboard. Fronts have a black-and-white player photo, the player's name and position, and an ad for a TV Western. Card backs are printed in red and blue and include a few biographical details and a career summary, along with an illustrated ad.

		NM	EX	VG
	Complete Set (9):	350.00	175.00	100.00
	Common Player:	40.00	20.00	12.00
(1)	Al Aber	40.00	20.00	12.00
(2)	Joe Caffie	40.00	20.00	12.00
(3)	Phil Cavaretta	40.00	20.00	12.00
(4)	Rip Coleman	40.00	20.00	12.00
(5)	Luke Easter	60.00	30.00	18.00
(6)	Ken Johnson	40.00	20.00	12.00
(7)	Lou Ortiz	40.00	20.00	12.00
(8)	Jack Phillips	40.00	20.00	12.00
(9)	Jim Small	40.00	20.00	12.00

1949 Bowman Pacific Coast League

One of the scarcest issues of the postwar period, the 1949 Bowman PCL set was issued only on the West Coast. Like the 1949 Bowman regular issue, the cards contain black-and-white photos overprinted with various pastel colors. Thirty-six cards, which measure 2-1/16" x 2-1/2", make up the set. It is believed

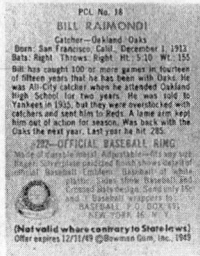

that the cards may have been issued only in sheets and not sold in gum packs. Consequently, many cards are found which display evidence of having been cut with a scissors.

		NM	EX	VG
	Complete Set (36):	15,000	7,500	4,500
	Common Player:	500.00	240.00	145.00
1	Lee Anthony	500.00	240.00	145.00
2	George Metkovich	500.00	240.00	145.00
3	Ralph Hodgin	500.00	240.00	145.00
4	George Woods	500.00	240.00	145.00
5	Xavier Rescigno	500.00	240.00	145.00
6	Mickey Grasso	500.00	240.00	145.00
7	Johnny Rucker	500.00	240.00	145.00
8	Jack Brewer	500.00	240.00	145.00
9	Dom D'Allessandro	500.00	240.00	145.00
10	Charlie Gassaway	500.00	240.00	145.00
11	Tony Freitas	500.00	240.00	145.00
12	Gordon Maltzberger	500.00	240.00	145.00
13	John Jensen	500.00	240.00	145.00
14	Joyner White	500.00	240.00	145.00
15	Harvey Storey	500.00	240.00	145.00
16	Dick Lajeski	500.00	240.00	145.00
17	Albie Glossop	500.00	240.00	145.00
18	Bill Raimondi	500.00	240.00	145.00
19	Ken Holcombe	500.00	240.00	145.00
20	Don Ross	500.00	240.00	145.00
21	Pete Coscarart	500.00	240.00	145.00
22	Tony York	500.00	240.00	145.00
23	Jake Mooty	500.00	240.00	145.00
24	Charles Adams	500.00	240.00	145.00
25	Les Scarsella	500.00	240.00	145.00
26	Joe Marty	500.00	240.00	145.00
27	Frank Kelleher	500.00	240.00	145.00
28	Lee Handley	500.00	240.00	145.00
29	Herman Besse	500.00	240.00	145.00
30	John Lazor	500.00	240.00	145.00
31	Eddie Malone	500.00	240.00	145.00
32	Maurice Van Robays	500.00	240.00	145.00
33	Jim Tabor	500.00	240.00	145.00
34	Gene Handley	500.00	240.00	145.00
35	Tom Seats	500.00	240.00	145.00
36	Ora Burnett	500.00	240.00	145.00

1933 Buffalo Bisons Jigsaw Puzzles

Produced as a stadium promotional giveaway, this set consists of 19 player puzzles and one for Hall of Fame Manager Ray Schalk. Each of the 11" x 14", 200-piece, black-and-white puzzles was produced in an edition of 10,000. Puzzles carried a red serial number, and certain numbers could be redeemed for tickets and other prizes. The known puzzles are checklisted below in alphabetical order.

		NM	EX	VG
	Complete Set (15):	5,000	2,500	1,500
	Common Player:	335.00	165.00	100.00
(1)	Joe Bartulis	335.00	165.00	100.00
(2)	Joe Bloomer	335.00	165.00	100.00
(3)	Ollie Carnegie	335.00	165.00	100.00
(4)	Clyde "Buck" Crouse	335.00	165.00	100.00
(5)	Harry Danning	335.00	165.00	100.00
(6)	Gilbert English	335.00	165.00	100.00
(7)	Fred Fussell	335.00	165.00	100.00
(8)	Bob Gould	335.00	165.00	100.00
(9)	Len Koenecke	335.00	165.00	100.00
(10)	Ray Lucas	335.00	165.00	100.00
(11)	Clarence Mueller	335.00	165.00	100.00
(12)	Ray Schalk	500.00	250.00	150.00
(13)	Jack Smith	335.00	165.00	100.00
(14)	Roy Tarr	335.00	165.00	100.00
(15)	Johnny Wilson	335.00	165.00	100.00

1934 Buffalo Bisons Team Issue

Apparently a team issue, these 4" x 7-1/16" black-and-white blank-backed cards feature posed action photos with white borders and a facsimile autograph. The player's full

name and position are printed in the bottom border, along with a career summary. This checklist is probably incomplete though the exact scope of the issue is unknown.

		NM	EX	VG
	Common Player:	400.00	200.00	120.00
(1)	Kenneth L. Ash	400.00	200.00	120.00
(2)	Harold "Ace" Elliott	400.00	200.00	120.00
(3)	Gregory T. Mulleavy	400.00	200.00	120.00
(4)	Irving M. Plummer	400.00	200.00	120.00

1940 Buffalo Bisons Team Issue

FRED HUTCHINSON
Pitcher

One of the brightest pitching prospects in baseball, owned by Detroit . . Was in headlines in every paper in country when purchased from Seattle by Tigers for $75,000 at close of 1938 season . . . In '38, his first year in baseball, "Hutch" won 25, lost only 7, hurled 29 complete games, five shutouts . . . . Also fine batter . . Throws right, bats left . . . . Born Aug. 12, 1919, in Seattle.

FRED HUTCHINSON, Pitcher

Many former and future big leaguers are included in this set of black-and-white, 2" x 3" cards. Fronts picture the players in poses at old Offerman Stadium. The player's name and position are printed in the white border at bottom. Backs have a career summary and highlights. The unnumbered cards are checklisted here alphabetically.

		NM	EX	VG
	Complete Set (24):	9,000	4,500	2,700
	Common Player:	400.00	200.00	120.00
(1)	Ollie Carnegie	400.00	200.00	120.00
(2)	Dan Carnevale	400.00	200.00	120.00
(3)	Earl Cook	400.00	200.00	120.00
(4)	Les Fleming	400.00	200.00	120.00
(5)	Floyd Giebel	400.00	200.00	120.00
(6)	Jimmy Hutch	400.00	200.00	120.00
(7)	Fred Hutchinson	400.00	200.00	120.00
(8)	Art Jacobs	400.00	200.00	120.00
(9)	John Kroner	400.00	200.00	120.00
(10)	Sal Maglie	600.00	300.00	180.00
(11)	Joe Martin	400.00	200.00	120.00
(12)	Clyde McCullough	400.00	200.00	120.00
(13)	Greg Mulleavy	400.00	200.00	120.00
(14)	Pat Mullin	400.00	200.00	120.00
(15)	Hank Nowak	400.00	200.00	120.00
(16)	Steve O'Neil	400.00	200.00	120.00
(17)	Jimmy Outlaw	400.00	200.00	120.00
(18)	Joe Rogalski	400.00	200.00	120.00
(19)	Les Scarsella	400.00	200.00	120.00
(20)	Mayo Smith	400.00	200.00	120.00
(21)	Floyd Stromme	400.00	200.00	120.00
(22)	Jim Trexler	400.00	200.00	120.00
(23)	Hal White	400.00	200.00	120.00
(24)	Frank Zubik	400.00	200.00	120.00

1947 Buffalo Bisons Team Issue

Despite some anomalies among the players checklisted thus far, this appears to have been a 1947 team-issued set of 8" a 10" black-and-white player photographs. Fronts include player identification in the form of a facsimile autograph. Backs are blank.

		NM	EX	VG
	Common Player:	30.00	15.00	9.00
(1)	Johnny Bero	30.00	15.00	9.00
(2)	Hank Biasatti	30.00	15.00	9.00
(3)	Eddie Boland	30.00	15.00	9.00
(4)	Ray Coleman	30.00	15.00	9.00
(5)	Zeb "Red" Eaton	30.00	15.00	9.00
(6)	Lonny Frey	30.00	15.00	9.00
(7)	Freddie Hancock	30.00	15.00	9.00
(8)	Gabby Hartnett	65.00	32.00	19.50
(9)	Clem Hausman	30.00	15.00	9.00
(10)	Manuel Hidalgo	30.00	15.00	9.00
(11)	Chet Laabs	30.00	15.00	9.00
(12)	Johnny McHale	30.00	15.00	9.00
(13)	Edward Mierkowicz	30.00	15.00	9.00
(14)	Eddie Mordarski	30.00	15.00	9.00
(15)	Hank Perry	30.00	15.00	9.00
(16)	Billy Pierce, Ted Gray	45.00	22.00	13.50
(17)	Bill Radulovich	30.00	15.00	9.00
(18)	Earl Rapp, Clint Conatser, Anse Moore, Coaker Triplett	30.00	15.00	9.00
(19)	Vic Wertz	40.00	20.00	12.00

1950 Bush & Hancock/Oak Hall Roanoke Red Sox

These blank-back, black-and-white cards have a portrait photo on front surrounded by a white border. Beneath the photo is a credit line and space for an autograph. Cards exist in 3-1/2" x 5" size with sponsor's credit reading "Compliments of Bush & Hancock," and in 4" x 6" format with sponsor's credit reading, "Compliments of Oak Hall." It is not known whether the checklist presented here is complete. Roanoke was a Class B Piedmont League farm club.

		NM	EX	VG
	Common Player:	50.00	25.00	15.00
(1)	Tom Casey	50.00	25.00	15.00
(2)	George Contratto	50.00	25.00	15.00
(3)	Ike Delock	65.00	32.50	20.00
(4)	Red Marion	50.00	25.00	15.00
(5)	Rod Morgan	50.00	25.00	15.00
(6)	Julio Ondani	50.00	25.00	15.00
(7)	Joe Reedy	50.00	25.00	15.00
(8)	Johnny Sehrt	50.00	25.00	15.00
(9)	Sammy White	65.00	32.50	20.00
(10)	Bob Wilson	50.00	25.00	15.00

C

1943 Centennial Flour Seattle Rainiers

 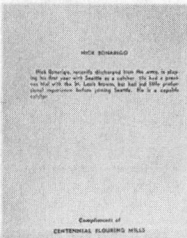

The 25 cards in this 4" x 5" black-and-white set feature players of the Pacific Coast League Seattle Rainiers. Identical in format to the set issued in 1944, the '43s can be identified by the lines of type at the bottom of the card back reading "Compliments of/CENTENNIAL FLOURING MILLS."

		NM	EX	VG
	Complete Set (25):	1,100	550.00	325.00
	Common Player:	60.00	30.00	18.00
(1)	John Babich	60.00	30.00	18.00
(2)	Nick Bonarigo (Buonarigo)	60.00	30.00	18.00
(3)	Eddie Carnett	60.00	30.00	18.00
(4)	Lloyd Christopher	60.00	30.00	18.00
(5)	Joe Demoran	60.00	30.00	18.00
(6)	Joe Dobbins	60.00	30.00	18.00
(7)	Glenn Elliott	60.00	30.00	18.00
(8)	Carl Fischer	60.00	30.00	18.00
(9)	Leonard Gabrielson	60.00	30.00	18.00
(10)	Stanley Gray	60.00	30.00	18.00
(11)	Dick Gyselman	60.00	30.00	18.00
(12)	Jim Jewell	60.00	30.00	18.00
(13)	Syl Johnson	60.00	30.00	18.00
(14)	Pete Jonas	60.00	30.00	18.00
(15)	Bill Kats	60.00	30.00	18.00
(16)	Lynn King	60.00	30.00	18.00
(17)	Bill Lawrence	60.00	30.00	18.00
(18)	Clarence Marshall	60.00	30.00	18.00
(19)	Bill Matheson	60.00	30.00	18.00
(20)	Ford Mullen	60.00	30.00	18.00
(21)	Bill Skiff	60.00	30.00	18.00
(22)	Byron Speece	60.00	30.00	18.00
(23)	Hal Sueme	60.00	30.00	18.00
(24)	Hal Turpin	60.00	30.00	18.00
(25)	John Yelovic	60.00	30.00	18.00

1944 Centennial Flour Seattle Rainiers

Identical in format to the previous year's issue, the 25 black-and-white 4" x 5" cards issued in 1944 can be differentiated from the 1943 set by the two lines of type at the bottom of each card's back. In the 1944 set, it reads, "Compliments of/CENTENNIAL HOTCAKE AND WAFFLE FLOUR."

		NM	EX	VG
	Complete Set (25):	1,350	675.00	400.00

		NM	EX	VG
Common Player:		60.00	30.00	18.00
(1)	John Babich	60.00	30.00	18.00
(2)	Paul Carpenter	60.00	30.00	18.00
(3)	Lloyd Christopher	60.00	30.00	18.00
(4)	Joe Demoran	60.00	30.00	18.00
(5)	Joe Dobbins	60.00	30.00	18.00
(6)	Glenn Elliott	60.00	30.00	18.00
(7)	Carl Fischer	60.00	30.00	18.00
(8)	Bob Garbould (Gorbould)	60.00	30.00	18.00
(9)	Stanley Gray	60.00	30.00	18.00
(10)	Dick Gyselman	60.00	30.00	18.00
(11)	Gene Holt	60.00	30.00	18.00
(12)	Roy Johnson	60.00	30.00	18.00
(13)	Syl Johnson	60.00	30.00	18.00
(14)	Al Libke	60.00	30.00	18.00
(15)	Bill Lyman	60.00	30.00	18.00
(16)	Bill Matheson	60.00	30.00	18.00
(17)	Jack McClure	60.00	30.00	18.00
(18)	Jimmy Ripple	60.00	30.00	18.00
(19)	Bill Skiff	60.00	30.00	18.00
(20)	Byron Speece	60.00	30.00	18.00
(21)	Hal Sueme	60.00	30.00	18.00
(22)	Frank Tincup	60.00	30.00	18.00
(23)	Jack Treece	60.00	30.00	18.00
(24)	Hal Turpin	60.00	30.00	18.00
(25)	Sicks Stadium	65.00	32.50	20.00

1945 Centennial Flour Seattle Rainiers

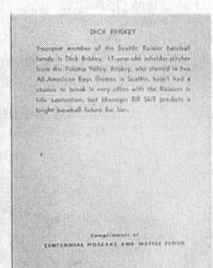

The 27 blue-and-white cards in the third consecutive issue for this Pacific Coast League team are distinguished from the two previous issues by the borderless photo on the front and the fact that the name and team are printed in a black bar at the bottom. The set can be distinguished from the 1947 issue by virtue of the fact that the player biography on back is not surrounded by a frame. The cards measure slightly narrower but longer than the 1943-44 issues, at 3-7/8" x 5-1/8".

		NM	EX	VG
Complete Set (27):		1,500	750.00	450.00
Common Player:		60.00	30.00	18.00
(1)	Charley Aleno	60.00	30.00	18.00
(2)	Dick Briskey	60.00	30.00	18.00
(3)	John Carpenter	60.00	30.00	18.00
(4)	Joe Demoran	60.00	30.00	18.00
(5)	Joe Dobbins	60.00	30.00	18.00
(6)	Glenn Elliott	60.00	30.00	18.00
(7)	Bob Finley	60.00	30.00	18.00
(8)	Carl Fischer	60.00	30.00	18.00
(9)	Keith Frazier	60.00	30.00	18.00
(10)	Johnny Gill	60.00	30.00	18.00
(11)	Bob Gorbould	60.00	30.00	18.00
(12)	Chet Johnson	60.00	30.00	18.00
(13)	Syl Johnson	60.00	30.00	18.00
(14)	Bill Kats	60.00	30.00	18.00
(15)	Billy Lyman	60.00	30.00	18.00
(16)	Bill Matheson	60.00	30.00	18.00
(17)	George McDonald	60.00	30.00	18.00
(18)	Ted Norbert	60.00	30.00	18.00
(19)	Alex Palica	60.00	30.00	18.00
(20)	Joe Passero	60.00	30.00	18.00
(21)	Hal Patchett	60.00	30.00	18.00
(22)	Bill Skiff	60.00	30.00	18.00
(23)	Byron Speece	60.00	30.00	18.00
(24)	Hal Sueme	60.00	30.00	18.00
(25)	Eddie Taylor	60.00	30.00	18.00
(26)	Hal Turpin	60.00	30.00	18.00
(27)	Jack Whipple	60.00	30.00	18.00

1947 Centennial Flour Seattle Rainiers

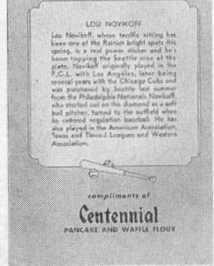

After a lapse of one year, Centennial Flour returned to issue a final black-and-white 32-card set for 1947. Identical in size (3-7/8" x 5-1/8") and front format to the 1945 issue, the '47s can be identified by the white framed box on back containing the player's biography.

	NM	EX	VG
Complete Set (32):	1,100	550.00	325.00
Common Player:	50.00	25.00	15.00

		NM	EX	VG
(1)	Dick Barrett	50.00	25.00	15.00
(2)	Joe Buzas	50.00	25.00	15.00
(3)	Paul Carpenter	50.00	25.00	15.00
(4)	Rex Cecil	50.00	25.00	15.00
(5)	Tony Criscola	50.00	25.00	15.00
(6)	Walter Dubiel	50.00	25.00	15.00
(7)	Doug Ford	50.00	25.00	15.00
(8)	Rollie Hemsley	50.00	25.00	15.00
(9)	Jim Hill	50.00	25.00	15.00
(10)	Jim Hopper	50.00	25.00	15.00
(11)	Sigmund Jakucki	50.00	25.00	15.00
(12)	Bob Johnson	60.00	30.00	18.00
(13)	Pete Jonas	50.00	25.00	15.00
(14)	Joe Kaney	50.00	25.00	15.00
(15)	Hillis Layne	50.00	25.00	15.00
(16)	Lou Novikoff	50.00	25.00	15.00
(17)	Johnny O'Neil	50.00	25.00	15.00
(18)	John Orphal	50.00	25.00	15.00
(19)	Ike Pearson	50.00	25.00	15.00
(20)	Bill Posedel	50.00	25.00	15.00
(21)	Don Pulford	50.00	25.00	15.00
(22)	Tom Reis	50.00	25.00	15.00
(23)	Charley Ripple	50.00	25.00	15.00
(24)	Mickey Rocco	50.00	25.00	15.00
(25)	Johnny Rucker	50.00	25.00	15.00
(26)	Earl Sheely	50.00	25.00	15.00
(27)	Bob Stagg	50.00	25.00	15.00
(28)	Hal Sueme	50.00	25.00	15.00
(29)	Eddie Taylor	50.00	25.00	15.00
(30)	Ed Vanni	50.00	25.00	15.00
(31)	JoJo White	50.00	25.00	15.00
(32)	Tony York	50.00	25.00	15.00

1957-58 Chattanooga Lookouts Team Issue

Based on the known and certainly incomplete checklist seen thus far, this issue of 8" x 10" black-and-white, blank-back player photos can only be generally attributed to year of issue. With a credit line to Moss Photo Service of New York City, the pictures feature action poses of the players taken in historic Engel Stadium. Facsimile autographs are pre-printed on the front. During the late 1950s the Lookouts were the top farm club of the Washington Senators.

		NM	EX	VG
Common Player:		30.00	15.00	9.00
(1)	Bobby Brown	30.00	15.00	9.00
(2)	Hal Griggs	30.00	15.00	9.00
(2)	Harmon Killebrew	200.00	100.00	60.00
(3)	Jesse Levan	30.00	15.00	9.00
(3)	Ernie Oravetz	30.00	15.00	9.00
(4)	Stan Roseboro	30.00	15.00	9.00
(5)	Bunky Stewart	30.00	15.00	9.00

1967 Chevron/Uniroyal Vancouver Mounties

These 2" x 3" black-and-white cards were distributed by local gas stations and picture members of the top farm club of the Kansas City A's. Backs are printed in red and black on white.

		NM	EX	VG
Complete Set (27):		4,500	2,250	1,300
Common Player:		200.00	100.00	60.00
(1)	Sal Bando	350.00	175.00	105.00
(2)	Frank Bastrire (Trainer)	200.00	100.00	60.00
(3)	Ossie Chavarria	200.00	100.00	60.00
(4)	Jim Dickson	200.00	100.00	60.00
(5)	John Donaldson	200.00	100.00	60.00
(6)	Jim Driscoll	200.00	100.00	60.00
(7)	Bob Duliba	200.00	100.00	60.00
(8)	Bill Edgerton	200.00	100.00	60.00
(9)	Larry Elliot	200.00	100.00	60.00
(10)	Ernie Foli	200.00	100.00	60.00
(11)	Joe Gaines	200.00	100.00	60.00
(12)	Vern Handrahan	200.00	100.00	60.00
(13)	Jim Hughes	200.00	100.00	60.00
(14)	Woody Huyke	200.00	100.00	60.00

		NM	EX	VG
(15)	Rene Lachemann	225.00	110.00	67.00
(16)	Bob Meyer	200.00	100.00	60.00
(17)	Wayne Norton	200.00	100.00	60.00
(18)	Gerry Reimer	200.00	100.00	60.00
(19)	Roberto Rodriguez	200.00	100.00	60.00
(20)	Ken Sanders	200.00	100.00	60.00
(21)	Randy Schwartz	200.00	100.00	60.00
(22)	Diego Segui	275.00	135.00	82.00
(23)	Paul Seitz	200.00	100.00	60.00
(24)	Ron Tompkins	200.00	100.00	60.00
(25)	Mickey Vernon	350.00	175.00	105.00
(26)	Jim Ward	200.00	100.00	60.00
(27)	Don Yingling	200.00	100.00	60.00

1909 Clement Bros. Bread (D380-1)

This set features only players of the Rochester Broncos team in the Eastern League. According to the bakery ad on back, the cards were distributed one per loaf of bread. The 1-1/2" x 2-3/4" cards feature a player photo on front in an oval frame against a white background. The player's last name, position and "Rochester" are printed beneath.

		NM	EX	VG
Complete Set (8):		25,000	12,500	7,500
Common Player:		5,000	2,500	1,500
(1)	Groat Anderson	5,000	2,500	1,500
(2)	Emil Batch	5,000	2,500	1,500
(3)	John Butler	5,000	2,500	1,500
(4)	Ed Holly	5,000	2,500	1,500
(5)	Jim Holmes	5,000	2,500	1,500
(6)	George McConnell	5,000	2,500	1,500
(7)	Fred Osborn	5,000	2,500	1,500
(8)	Harry Partee	5,000	2,500	1,500

1910 Clement Bros. Bread (D380)

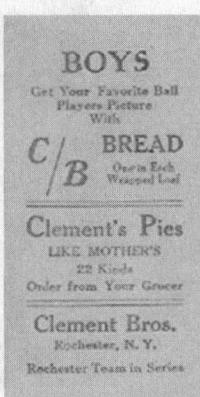

For the second of two annual issues, the bakery added an unknown number of major league players' cards to those of six of the hometeam Rochester club of the Eastern League. While the backs remained identical to the previous issue, featuring advertising for the bakery's bread and pies, the fronts adopted the standard format of the era, black-and-white player photos surrounded by a white border, with the player's last name, position and city printed at bottom. Size remained 1-1/2" x 2-3/4".

		NM	EX	VG
Common Player:		5,750	2,850	1,700
(1)	Whitey Alperman	5,750	2,850	1,700
(2)	Bill Bailey	5,750	2,850	1,700
(3)	Walter Blair	5,750	2,850	1,700
(4)	Hal Chase	6,500	3,200	1,950
(5)	Ty Cobb	40,000	25,000	15,000
(6)	Eddie Collins	15,000	10,000	6,000
(7)	Roy Hartzell	5,750	2,850	1,700
(8)	Harry Howell	5,750	2,850	1,700
(9)	Addie Joss	15,000	10,000	6,000
(10)	Ditus Lagoe	5,750	2,850	1,700
(11)	George McConnell	5,750	2,850	1,700
(12)	George Mullin	5,750	2,850	1,700
(13)	Fred Osborn	5,750	2,850	1,700
(14)	Harry Patee	5,750	2,850	1,700
(15)	Pat Ragan	5,750	2,850	1,700
(16)	Oscar Stanage	5,750	2,850	1,700
(17)	George Stone	5,750	2,850	1,700
(18)	Ed Summers	5,750	2,850	1,700

		NM	EX	VG
(19)	Joe Tinker	15,000	10,000	6,000
(20)	Bert Tooley	5,750	2,850	1,700
(21)	Heinie Zimmerman	5,750	2,850	1,700

1953 Coca-Cola Galveston White Caps

This set appears to have been an issue of the Globe Printing Co., which produced many lower-minors team sets in the years preceding, or it may just share the format. The 2-1/4" x 3-3/8" cards have borderless black-and-white photos on front and blank backs. In a white box near the bottom of the picture is the player name and "Compliments of / Coca-Cola Bottling Co." Galveston was champion of the 1953 Class B Gulf Coast League and not affiliated with any major league team.

		NM	EX	VG
Complete Set (16):		1,000	500.00	300.00
Common Player:		75.00	37.50	22.00
(1)	Ed Bohnslav	75.00	37.50	22.00
(2)	Mike Conovan	75.00	37.50	22.00
(3)	Pop Faucett	75.00	37.50	22.00
(4)	Bobby Flis	75.00	37.50	22.00
(5)	Stan Goletz	75.00	37.50	22.00
(6)	Jerry Kleinsmith	75.00	37.50	22.00
(7)	Charlie Lehrmann	75.00	37.50	22.00
(8)	Jim Logan	75.00	37.50	22.00
(9)	Bob Miller	75.00	37.50	22.00
(10)	Tom Moore	75.00	37.50	22.00
(11)	Bob Pugatch	75.00	37.50	22.00
(12)	Bob Ramsey	75.00	37.50	22.00
(13)	Hank Robinson	75.00	37.50	22.00
(14)	Charlie Schmidt	75.00	37.50	22.00
(15)	Barnie White	75.00	37.50	22.00
(16)	Hank Yzquierdo (Izquierdo)	75.00	37.50	22.00

1952 Colorado Springs Sky Sox Team Issue

From the Class A Western League runners-up, this is one of many minor league sets issued in the early 1950s by the Globe Printing Co., of San Jose, Calif. The '52 Sky Sox were a farm team of the Chicago White Sox. Players included former Negro Leaguers and future major leaguers Connie Johnson and Sam Hairston, plus bonus-baby bust Gus Keriazakos. Cards are about 2-1/4" x 3-1/4", printed in black-and-white with blank backs. An album with die-cut pages to allow the corners of the cards to be slipped in was also available. Cards were likely given away one or two at a time at home games.

		NM	EX	VG
Complete Set (19):		1,200	600.00	360.00
Common Player:		60.00	30.00	18.00
Album:		100.00	50.00	30.00
(1)	Jerry Crosby	60.00	30.00	18.00
(2)	Vic Fucci	60.00	30.00	18.00
(3)	Don Gutteridge	60.00	30.00	18.00
(4)	Sam Hairston	90.00	45.00	27.00
(5)	Al Jacinto	60.00	30.00	18.00
(6)	Connie Johnson	75.00	37.50	22.00
(7)	Bob Kellogg	60.00	30.00	18.00
(8)	Gus Keriazakos	60.00	30.00	18.00
(9)	Ken Landenberger	60.00	30.00	18.00
(10)	George Noga	60.00	30.00	18.00
(11)	Floyd Penfold	60.00	30.00	18.00
(12)	Bill Pope	60.00	30.00	18.00
(13)	J.W. Porter	60.00	30.00	18.00
(14)	Bill (Red) Rose	60.00	30.00	18.00
(15)	Don Rudolph	60.00	30.00	18.00
(16)	Andy Skurski	60.00	30.00	18.00

		NM	EX	VG
(17)	Dick Strahs	60.00	30.00	18.00
(18)	Bill Wells	60.00	30.00	18.00
(19)	Dick Welteroth	60.00	30.00	18.00

1952 Columbus Cardinals Team Issue

This set of cards was a product of the Globe Printing Co. of San Jose, Calif. The cards were given away at Golden Park during the 1952 season. The cards measure 2-1/8" x 3-3/8" and have black-and-white photos of players with the player's name in a white box in the bottom-left corner of the photograph. The backs are blank. The cards are unnumbered and listed in alphabetical order, although this checklist may not be complete. The team was a Class A South Atlantic League affiliate of the St. Louis Cardinals.

		NM	EX	VG
Complete Set (17):		1,000	500.00	300.00
Common Player:		60.00	30.00	18.00
(1)	Chief Bender	60.00	30.00	18.00
(2)	Bob Betancourt	60.00	30.00	18.00
(3)	Tom Burgess	60.00	30.00	18.00
(4)	Jack Byers	60.00	30.00	18.00
(5)	Mike Curnan	60.00	30.00	18.00
(6)	Gil Daley	60.00	30.00	18.00
(7)	Bill Harris	60.00	30.00	18.00
(8)	Ev Joyner	60.00	30.00	18.00
(9)	Bob Kerce	60.00	30.00	18.00
(10)	Ted Lewandowski	60.00	30.00	18.00
(11)	John Mackey	60.00	30.00	18.00
(12)	Bill Paolisso	60.00	30.00	18.00
(13)	Dennis Reeder	60.00	30.00	18.00
(14)	Whit Ulrich	60.00	30.00	18.00
(15)	Norman Shope	60.00	30.00	18.00
(16)	Don Swartz	60.00	30.00	18.00
(17)	Len Wile	60.00	30.00	18.00

1955 Columbus Jets Photos

A top farm club of the Kansas City A's in 1955 the Columbus (Ohio) Jets issued these black-and-white glossy photocards. In 3-5/8" x 5-5/8" format, the cards have a facsimile autograph on front. It is possible that the checklist presented here in alphabetical order of the unnumbered cards may be incomplete.

		NM	EX	VG
Complete Set (21):		900.00	450.00	275.00
Common Player:		45.00	22.50	13.50
(1)	Hal Bevan	45.00	22.50	13.50
(2)	Paul Burris	45.00	22.50	13.50
(3)	Ted Del Guercio	45.00	22.50	13.50
(4)	Carl Duser	45.00	22.50	13.50
(5)	Charlie Haag	45.00	22.50	13.50
(6)	Forrest "Spook" Jacobs	60.00	30.00	18.00
(7)	Dick Kryhoski	45.00	22.50	13.50
(8)	Mike Kume	45.00	22.50	13.50
(9)	Al Lakeman	45.00	22.50	13.50
(10)	Jackie Mayo	45.00	22.50	13.50
(11)	Jim Miller	45.00	22.50	13.50
(12)	Al Pinkston	50.00	25.00	15.00
(13)	Al Romberger	45.00	22.50	13.50
(14)	Bill Stewart	45.00	22.50	13.50
(15)	Russ Sullivan	45.00	22.50	13.50
(16)	"Jake" Thies	45.00	22.50	13.50
(17)	Bob Trice	45.00	22.50	13.50
(18)	Ozzie VanBrabant	45.00	22.50	13.50
(19)	Frank Verdi	45.00	22.50	13.50
(20)	Leroy Wheat	45.00	22.50	13.50
(21)	Spider Wilhelm	45.00	22.50	13.50

1957 Columbus Jets Postcards

In 1957, the Columbus (Ohio) Jets began a long association as a top farm team of the Pittsburgh Pirates. That year, the team issued this set of postcards. The black-and-white glossy cards measure 3-9/16" x 5-1/2" and have the player name and position overprinted in black block letters near the bottom of the photo. Backs have postcard indicia and a notice of printing by the Howard Photo Service of New York City. The unnumbered cards are presented here alphabetically but it is unknown whether this checklist is complete at 20.

		NM	EX	VG
Complete Set (20):		900.00	450.00	275.00
Common Player:		45.00	22.50	13.50
(1)	Dick Barone	45.00	22.50	13.50
(2)	Ron Blackburn	45.00	22.50	13.50
(3)	Jackie Brown	45.00	22.50	13.50
(4)	Ed Burtschy	45.00	22.50	13.50
(5)	Whammy Douglas	50.00	25.00	15.00
(6)	Howie Goss	45.00	22.50	13.50
(7)	Al Grunwald	45.00	22.50	13.50
(8)	Gail Henley	45.00	22.50	13.50
(9)	Don Kildoo	45.00	22.50	13.50
(10)	Danny Kravitz	45.00	22.50	13.50
(11)	Bob Kuzava	45.00	22.50	13.50
(12)	Johnny Lipon	45.00	22.50	13.50
(13)	Cholly Naranjo	45.00	22.50	13.50
(14)	Eddie O'Brien	60.00	30.00	18.00
(15)	Frank Oceak	45.00	22.50	13.50
(16)	Harding Peterson	60.00	30.00	18.00
(17)	John Powers	45.00	22.50	13.50
(18)	James Rice	45.00	22.50	13.50
(19)	Russ Sullivan	45.00	22.50	13.50
(20)	Ken Toothman	45.00	22.50	13.50

1958 Columbus Jets Photos

In format similar to the postcard issue of the previous year, and sharing some of the same pictures, this set of photocards is smaller, at 4" x 5", and is blank-backed. It is unknown whether the alphabetical checklist of the unnumbered cards presented here is complete.

		NM	EX	VG
Complete Set (17):		650.00	325.00	200.00
Common Player:		40.00	20.00	12.00
(1)	Gair Allie	40.00	20.00	12.00
(2)	Luis Arroyo	40.00	20.00	12.00
(3)	Tony Bartirome	45.00	22.50	13.50
(4)	Jim Baumer	40.00	20.00	12.00
(5)	Bill Causion	40.00	20.00	12.00
(6)	Whammy Douglas	40.00	20.00	12.00
(7)	Joe Gibbon	40.00	20.00	12.00
(8)	Howie Goss	40.00	20.00	12.00
(9)	Spook Jacobs	50.00	25.00	15.00
(10)	Clyde King	40.00	20.00	12.00
(11)	Cholly Naranjo	40.00	20.00	12.00
(12)	George O'Donnell	40.00	20.00	12.00
(13)	Laurin Pepper	40.00	20.00	12.00
(14)	Dick Rand	40.00	20.00	12.00
(15)	Leo Rodriguez	40.00	20.00	12.00
(16)	Don Rowe	40.00	20.00	12.00
(17)	Art Swanson	40.00	20.00	12.00

1910 Contentnea First Series (T209)

 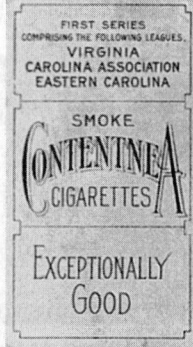

The 1910 Contentnea minor league set actually consists of two distinctively different series, both featuring players from the Virginia League, Carolina Association and Eastern Carolina League. The cards were distributed in packages of Contentnea cigarettes. The first series, featuring color photographs, consists of just 16 cards, each measuring 1-9/16" x 2-11/16". The front of the card has the player's last name and team printed at the bottom, while the back identifies the card as "First Series" and carries an advertisement for Contentnea cigarettes. Many first series cards are also found with rubber-stamped "Factory No. 12, 4th Dist. N.C." on back. The second series, belived to have been issued later in 1910, is a massive 221-card set consisting of black-and-white player photos. The cards in this series are slightly larger, measuring 1-5/8" x 2-3/4". They carry the words "Photo Series" on the back, along with the cigarette advertisement. Only a handful of the players in the Contentnea set ever advanced to the major leagues and the set contains no major stars. Subsequently, it generally holds interest only to collectors who specialize in the old southern minor leagues.

	NM	EX	VG
Complete Set (16):	27,500	13,500	8,250
Common Player:	1,850	925.00	555.00
(1) Armstrong	1,850	925.00	555.00
(2) Booles	1,850	925.00	555.00
(3) Bourquise (Bourquoise)	1,850	925.00	555.00
(4) Cooper	1,850	925.00	555.00
(5) Cowell	1,850	925.00	555.00
(6) Crockett	1,850	925.00	555.00
(7) Fullenwider	1,850	925.00	555.00
(8) Gilmore	1,850	925.00	555.00
(9) Hoffman	1,850	925.00	555.00
(10) Lane	1,850	925.00	555.00
(11) Martin	1,850	925.00	555.00
(12) McGeehan	1,850	925.00	555.00
(13) Pope	1,200	800.00	400.00
(14) Sisson	1,850	925.00	555.00
(15) Stubbe	1,850	925.00	555.00
(16) Walsh	1,850	925.00	555.00

1910 Contentnea Photo Series (T209)

WOOLIMS, LYNCHBURG

	NM	EX	VG
Common Player:	675.00	340.00	200.00
(1) Abercrombie	675.00	340.00	200.00
(2) Andrada	675.00	340.00	200.00
(3a) Armstrong, Norfolk	675.00	340.00	200.00
(3b) Armstrong, Wilson	675.00	340.00	200.00
(4) Averett	675.00	340.00	200.00
(5) Baker	675.00	340.00	200.00
(6) Banner (Bonner)	675.00	340.00	200.00
(7) Bausewein (Bansewein)	675.00	340.00	200.00
(8) Beatty	675.00	340.00	200.00
(9) Bentley	675.00	340.00	200.00
(10) Beusse	675.00	340.00	200.00
(11) Biel	675.00	340.00	200.00
(12) Bigbie (Raleigh)	675.00	340.00	200.00
(13) Bigbie (Richmond)	675.00	340.00	200.00
(14) Blackstone	675.00	340.00	200.00
(15) Bonner	675.00	340.00	200.00
(16) Bourquin	675.00	340.00	200.00
(17) Bowen	675.00	340.00	200.00
(18) Boyle	675.00	340.00	200.00
(19) Brandon	675.00	340.00	200.00
(20) Brazelle (Brazell)	675.00	340.00	200.00
(21) Brent	675.00	340.00	200.00
(22) Brown	675.00	340.00	200.00
(23) Busch	675.00	340.00	200.00
(24) Bussey	675.00	340.00	200.00
(25) Byrd	675.00	340.00	200.00
(26) Cafalu (Cefalu)	675.00	340.00	200.00
(27) Callahan	675.00	340.00	200.00
(28) Chandler	675.00	340.00	200.00
(29) Clapp	675.00	340.00	200.00
(30) Clark (Clarke)	675.00	340.00	200.00
(31) Clemens	675.00	340.00	200.00
(32) Clunk	675.00	340.00	200.00
(33) Cooper	675.00	340.00	200.00
(34) Corbett	675.00	340.00	200.00
(35) Cote	675.00	340.00	200.00
(36) Coutts	675.00	340.00	200.00
(37) Cowan (Cowen)	675.00	340.00	200.00
(38) Cowells (Cowell)	675.00	340.00	200.00
(39) Creagan (Cregan)	675.00	340.00	200.00
(40) Crockett	675.00	340.00	200.00
(41) Lave Cross	675.00	340.00	200.00
(42) Dailey	675.00	340.00	200.00
(43) C. Derrck (Derrick)	675.00	340.00	200.00
(44) F. Derrick	675.00	340.00	200.00
(45) Doak (Greensboro)	675.00	340.00	200.00
(46) Doak (Wilmington)	675.00	340.00	200.00
(47) Dobard	675.00	340.00	200.00
(48) Dobson	675.00	340.00	200.00
(49) Doyle	675.00	340.00	200.00
(50) Drumm	675.00	340.00	200.00
(51) Duvie	675.00	340.00	200.00
(52) Ebinger	675.00	340.00	200.00
(53) Eldridge	675.00	340.00	200.00
(54) Evans	675.00	340.00	200.00
(55) Fairbanks	675.00	340.00	200.00

(56) Farmer	675.00	340.00	200.00
(57) Ferrell	675.00	340.00	200.00
(58) Fisher	675.00	340.00	200.00
(59) Flowers	675.00	340.00	200.00
(60) Fogarty	675.00	340.00	200.00
(61) Foltz	675.00	340.00	200.00
(62) Foreman	675.00	340.00	200.00
(63) Forque	675.00	340.00	200.00
(64) Francis	675.00	340.00	200.00
(65) Fulton	675.00	340.00	200.00
(66) Galvin	675.00	340.00	200.00
(67) Gardin	675.00	340.00	200.00
(68) Garman	675.00	340.00	200.00
(69) Gastmeyer	675.00	340.00	200.00
(70) Gaston	675.00	340.00	200.00
(71) Gates	675.00	340.00	200.00
(72) Gehring	675.00	340.00	200.00
(73) Gillespie	675.00	340.00	200.00
(74) Gorham	675.00	340.00	200.00
(75) Griffin (Danville)	675.00	340.00	200.00
(76) Griffin (Lynchburg)	675.00	340.00	200.00
(77) Guiheen	675.00	340.00	200.00
(78) Gunderson	675.00	340.00	200.00
(79) Hale	675.00	340.00	200.00
(80) Halland (Holland)	675.00	340.00	200.00
(81) Hamilton	675.00	340.00	200.00
(82) Hammersley	675.00	340.00	200.00
(83) Handiboe	675.00	340.00	200.00
(84) Hannifen (Hannifan)	675.00	340.00	200.00
(85) Hargrave	675.00	340.00	200.00
(86) Harrington	675.00	340.00	200.00
(87) Harris	675.00	340.00	200.00
(88) Hart	675.00	340.00	200.00
(89) Hartley	675.00	340.00	200.00
(90) Hawkins	675.00	340.00	200.00
(91) Hearne (Hearn)	675.00	340.00	200.00
(92) Hicks	675.00	340.00	200.00
(93) Hobbs	675.00	340.00	200.00
(94) Hoffman	675.00	340.00	200.00
(95) Hooker	675.00	340.00	200.00
(96) Howard	675.00	340.00	200.00
(97) Howedel (Howedell)	675.00	340.00	200.00
(98) Hudson	675.00	340.00	200.00
(99) Humphrey	675.00	340.00	200.00
(100) Hyames	600.00	300.00	175.00
(101) Irvine	675.00	340.00	200.00
(102) Irving	675.00	340.00	200.00
(103) Jackson (Greensboro)	675.00	340.00	200.00
(104) Jackson (Spartanburg)	675.00	340.00	200.00
(105) Jenkins (Greenville)	675.00	340.00	200.00
(106) Jenkins (Roanoke)	675.00	340.00	200.00
(107) Jobson	675.00	340.00	200.00
(108) Johnson	675.00	340.00	200.00
(109) Keating	675.00	340.00	200.00
(110) Kelley	675.00	340.00	200.00
(111) Kelly (Anderson)	675.00	340.00	200.00
(112) Kelly (Goldsboro)	675.00	340.00	200.00
(113) "King" Kelly	675.00	340.00	200.00
(114) King	675.00	340.00	200.00
(115) Kite	675.00	340.00	200.00
(116) Kunkle	675.00	340.00	200.00
(117) Landgraff	675.00	340.00	200.00
(118) Lane	675.00	340.00	200.00
(119) Lathrop	675.00	340.00	200.00
(120) Lavoia	675.00	340.00	200.00
(121) Levy	675.00	340.00	200.00
(122) Lloyd	675.00	340.00	200.00
(123) Loval (Loval)	675.00	340.00	200.00
(124) Lucia	675.00	340.00	200.00
(125) Luyster	675.00	340.00	200.00
(126) MacConachie	675.00	340.00	200.00
(127) Malcolm	675.00	340.00	200.00
(128) Martin	675.00	340.00	200.00
(129) Mayberry	675.00	340.00	200.00
(130) A. McCarthy	675.00	340.00	200.00
(131) J. McCarthy	675.00	340.00	200.00
(132) McCormick	675.00	340.00	200.00
(133) McFarland	675.00	340.00	200.00
(134) McFarlin	675.00	340.00	200.00
(135) C. McGeehan	675.00	340.00	200.00
(136) Dan McGeehan	675.00	340.00	200.00
(137) McHugh	675.00	340.00	200.00
(138) McKeavitt (McKevitt)	675.00	340.00	200.00
(139) Merchant	675.00	340.00	200.00
(140) Midkiff	675.00	340.00	200.00
(141) Miller	675.00	340.00	200.00
(142) Missitt	675.00	340.00	200.00
(143) Morgan	675.00	340.00	200.00
(144) Morrissey (Morrisey)	675.00	340.00	200.00
(145) Mullany (Mullaney)	675.00	340.00	200.00
(146) Mullinix	675.00	340.00	200.00
(147) Mundell	600.00	300.00	175.00
(148) Munsen (Munson)	675.00	340.00	200.00
(149) Murdock (Murdoch)	675.00	340.00	200.00
(150) Newton	675.00	340.00	200.00
(151) Noojin	675.00	340.00	200.00
(152) Novak	675.00	340.00	200.00
(153) Ochs	675.00	340.00	200.00
(154) Painter	675.00	340.00	200.00
(155) Peloguin	675.00	340.00	200.00
(156) Phealean (Phelan)	675.00	340.00	200.00
(157) Phoenix	675.00	340.00	200.00
(158) Powell	675.00	340.00	200.00
(159) Presley (Pressley), Pritchard	800.00	400.00	200.00
(160) Priest	675.00	340.00	200.00
(161) Prim	675.00	340.00	200.00
(162) Pritchard	675.00	340.00	200.00
(163) Rawe (Rowe)	675.00	340.00	200.00
(164) Redfern (Redfearn)	675.00	340.00	200.00
(165) Reggy	675.00	340.00	200.00
(166) Richardson	675.00	340.00	200.00
(167) Rickard	675.00	340.00	200.00
(168) Rickert	675.00	340.00	200.00
(169) Ridgeway (Ridgway)	675.00	340.00	200.00
(170) Roth	675.00	340.00	200.00
(171) Salve	675.00	340.00	200.00
(172) Schmidt	675.00	340.00	200.00
(173) Schrader	675.00	340.00	200.00

(174) Schumaker	675.00	340.00	200.00
(175) Sexton	675.00	340.00	200.00
(176) Shanghnessy (Shaughnessy)	675.00	340.00	200.00
(177) Sharp	675.00	340.00	200.00
(178) Shaw	675.00	340.00	200.00
(179) Simmons	675.00	340.00	200.00
(180) A. Smith	675.00	340.00	200.00
(181) D. Smith	675.00	340.00	200.00
(182) Smith (Portsmouth)	675.00	340.00	200.00
(183) Spratt	675.00	340.00	200.00
(184) Springs	675.00	340.00	200.00
(185) Stewart	675.00	340.00	200.00
(186) Stoehr	675.00	340.00	200.00
(187) Stouch	675.00	340.00	200.00
(188) Sullivan	675.00	340.00	200.00
(189) Swindell	675.00	340.00	200.00
(190) Taxis	675.00	340.00	200.00
(191) Templin	600.00	300.00	175.00
(192) Thompson	675.00	340.00	200.00
(193) B.E. Thompson (Dressed as Uncle Sam.)	2,500	1,250	750.00
(194) Tiedeman	675.00	340.00	200.00
(195) Titman	675.00	340.00	200.00
(196) Toner	675.00	340.00	200.00
(197) Turner	675.00	340.00	200.00
(198) Tydeman	675.00	340.00	200.00
(199) Vail	675.00	340.00	200.00
(200) Verbout	675.00	340.00	200.00
(201) Vickery	675.00	340.00	200.00
(202) Walker (Norfolk)	675.00	340.00	200.00
(203) Walker (Spartanburg)	675.00	340.00	200.00
(204) Wallace	675.00	340.00	200.00
(205) Walsh	675.00	340.00	200.00
(206) Walters	675.00	340.00	200.00
(207) Waters	675.00	340.00	200.00
(208) Waymack	675.00	340.00	200.00
(209) Webb	675.00	340.00	200.00
(210) Wehrell	675.00	340.00	200.00
(211) Weldon	675.00	340.00	200.00
(212) Welsher	675.00	340.00	200.00
(213) Westlake	675.00	340.00	200.00
(214) Williams	675.00	340.00	200.00
(215) Willis	675.00	340.00	200.00
(216) Wingo	675.00	340.00	200.00
(217) Wolf	600.00	300.00	150.00
(218) Wood	675.00	340.00	200.00
(219) Woolums	675.00	340.00	200.00
(220) Workman	675.00	340.00	200.00
(221) Wright	600.00	300.00	150.00
(222) Wynne	675.00	340.00	200.00

1924 Crescent Ice Cream Hanbury

 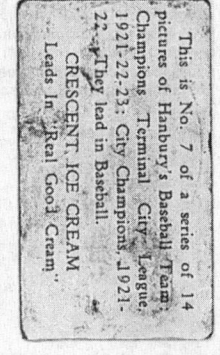

7—Art Morse Short Stop

This is No. 7 of a series of 14 pictures of Hanbury's Baseball Team. Champions of Vancouver City League. 1921-22-23: City Champions, 1921. 22-23; They lead in Baseball. CRESCENT ICE CREAM Leads in "Real Good Cream".

Rather than a professional minor league team, this Canadian set features members of an amateur or semi-pro team sponsored by the Hanbury Sawmill in the Vancouver, B.C., Terminal Amateur League. The 2-1/4" x 1-5/8" black-and-white cards have a player portrait photo in an oval on front, with identification and card number below. On back is an identically worded summation of the team's recent seasons' championships, the card number, and an ad for the sponsor. Some cards are found with backs promoting the issue and announcing prizes.

		NM	EX	VG
Complete Set (14):		4,000	1,350	800.00
Common Player:		300.00	150.00	90.00
1	Jack Lester (Mascot)	300.00	150.00	90.00
2	Frank Coyle	300.00	150.00	90.00
3	Fred Inch	300.00	150.00	90.00
4	Robt. Mills	300.00	150.00	90.00
5	John Daniels (Capt.)	300.00	150.00	90.00
6	Doug. May	300.00	150.00	90.00
7	Art Morse	300.00	150.00	90.00
8	Chas. Stevenson	300.00	150.00	90.00
9	Tom Raftery	300.00	150.00	90.00
10	Frank Williams	300.00	150.00	90.00
11	Unknown	300.00	150.00	90.00
12	Don Stewart	300.00	150.00	90.00
13	Roy Goodall	300.00	150.00	90.00
14	Cecil Kimberley	300.00	150.00	90.00

1940 Crowley's Milk Binghamton Triplets

Members of the Binghamton, N.Y., Eastern League team are known in this set of 3" x 5" cards. Some have been seen with stamped postcard backs. Blue-and-white player photos are framed by a red rendition of a ballpark scene on the front of the unnumbered cards. Each card has a facsimile autograph ostensibly written by the pictured player. It is unknown whether the checklist below is complete. Several of the players later appeared with the N.Y. Yankees and other teams.

		NM	EX	VG
Complete Set (18):		6,000	3,000	1,800
Common Player:		400.00	200.00	120.00
(1)	Jimmy Adlam	400.00	200.00	120.00
(2)	Russ Bergman	400.00	200.00	120.00
(3)	Bruno Betzel	400.00	200.00	120.00
(4)	Bill Bevens	400.00	200.00	120.00
(5)	Johnny Bianco	400.00	200.00	120.00
(6)	Fred Collins	400.00	200.00	120.00
(7)	Vince DeBiassi	400.00	200.00	120.00
(8)	Jack Graham	400.00	200.00	120.00
(9)	Randy Gumpert	400.00	200.00	120.00
(10)	Al Gurske	400.00	200.00	120.00
(11)	Mike Milosevich	400.00	200.00	120.00
(12)	Billie O'Donnell (Trainer)	200.00	100.00	60.00
(13)	Earl Reid	400.00	200.00	120.00
(14)	Aaron Robinson	400.00	200.00	120.00
(15)	Frankie Silvanic	400.00	200.00	120.00
(16)	Pete Suder	400.00	200.00	120.00
(17)	Ray Volps	400.00	200.00	120.00
(18)	Herb White	400.00	200.00	120.00

D

1952 Dallas Eagles Team Issue

A Class AA Texas League farm team of the Cleveland Indians, the Eagles were one of the higher minor league teams chronicled by Globe Printing in its series of 2-1/4" x 3-3/8" blank-back, black-and-white cards sets of the early 1950s. The checklist here is not complete. This set differs from most Globe issues in the use of white borders around the photos on front. The checklist here may not be complete.

		NM	EX	VG
Common Player:		60.00	30.00	18.00
(1)	Ralph Albers	60.00	30.00	18.00
(2)	Dick Aylward	60.00	30.00	18.00
(3)	Jodie Beeler	60.00	30.00	18.00
(4)	Bob Bundy	60.00	30.00	18.00
(5)	Johnny Creel	60.00	30.00	18.00
(6)	Bob Cullins	60.00	30.00	18.00
(7)	Hal Erickson	60.00	30.00	18.00
(8)	Dave Hoskins	60.00	30.00	18.00
(9)	Bud Hutson	60.00	30.00	18.00
(10)	Edward Knoblauch	60.00	30.00	18.00
(11)	Joe Kotrany	60.00	30.00	18.00
(12)	Joe Macko	60.00	30.00	18.00
(13)	Alan Maul	60.00	30.00	18.00
(14)	Peter Mazar	60.00	30.00	18.00
(15)	Dutch Meyer	60.00	30.00	18.00
(16)	Don Mossi	90.00	45.00	27.00
(17)	Clyde Perry	60.00	30.00	18.00
(18)	Ray Peters	60.00	30.00	18.00
(19)	Harry Sullivan	60.00	30.00	18.00
(20)	Frank Tornay	60.00	30.00	18.00
(21)	Edward Varhely	60.00	30.00	18.00

1959 Darigold Farms Spokane Indians

The unnumbered cards in this set were glued to milk cartons by a folded tab at the top of each card. The basic card measures 2-1/2" x 2-3/8", with a 2-1/2" x 2-1/8" tab. Black-and-white player photos are set against colored backgrounds of yellow (1-8), red (9-16) and blue (17-22). Player biographical details and stats are printed in black on the back. Values shown are for cards without the superfluous tabs.

		NM	EX	VG
Complete Set (22):		4,500	2,250	1,350
Common Player:		200.00	100.00	60.00
(1)	Facundo Barragan	200.00	100.00	60.00
(2)	Steve Bilko	225.00	110.00	65.00
(3)	Bobby Bragan	225.00	110.00	65.00
(4)	Chuck Churn	200.00	100.00	60.00
(5)	Tom Davis	450.00	225.00	135.00

		NM	EX	VG
(6)	Dom Domenichelli	200.00	100.00	60.00
(7)	Bob Giallombardo	200.00	100.00	60.00
(8)	Connie Grob	200.00	100.00	60.00
(9)	Fred Hatfield	200.00	100.00	60.00
(10)	Bob Lillis	225.00	110.00	65.00
(11)	Lloyd Merritt	200.00	100.00	60.00
(12)	Larry Miller	200.00	100.00	60.00
(13)	Chris Nicolosi	200.00	100.00	60.00
(14)	Allen Norris	200.00	100.00	60.00
(15)	Phil Ortega	200.00	100.00	60.00
(16)	Phillips Paine	200.00	100.00	60.00
(17)	Bill Parsons	200.00	100.00	60.00
(18)	Hisel Patrick	200.00	100.00	60.00
(19)	Tony Roig	200.00	100.00	60.00
(20)	Tom Saffell	200.00	100.00	60.00
(21)	Norm Sherry	250.00	125.00	75.00
(22)	Ben Wade	200.00	100.00	60.00

1960 Darigold Farms Spokane Indians

For its second annual baseball card set, the dairy added two cards and numbered the issue on the back. Card fronts were black-and-white photos against colored backgrounds of yellow (1-8), green (9-16) and red (17-24). A facsimile autograph appears on the front as well. The basic card measures 2-3/8" x 2-11/16", with a folded 2-3/8" x 2-1/16" tab at the top, by which the card was glued to a milk carton. Backs are black-and-white. Values shown are for cards without the superfluous tab.

		NM	EX	VG
Complete Set (24):		4,500	2,250	1,350
Common Player:		145.00	75.00	40.00
1	Chris Nicolosi	145.00	75.00	40.00
2	Jim Pagliaroni	145.00	75.00	40.00
3	Roy Smalley	145.00	75.00	40.00
4	Bill Bethel	145.00	75.00	40.00
5	Joe Liscio	145.00	75.00	40.00
6	Curt Roberts	145.00	75.00	40.00
7	Ed Palmquist	145.00	75.00	40.00
8	Willie Davis	300.00	150.00	90.00
9	Bob Giallombardo	145.00	75.00	40.00
10	Pedro Gomez	145.00	75.00	40.00
11	Mel Nelson	145.00	75.00	40.00
12	Charley Smith	145.00	75.00	40.00
13	Clarence Churn	145.00	75.00	40.00
14	Ramon Conde	145.00	75.00	40.00
15	George O'Donnell	145.00	75.00	40.00
16	Tony Roig	145.00	75.00	40.00
17	Frank Howard	450.00	225.00	135.00
18	Billy Harris	145.00	75.00	40.00
19	Mike Brumley	145.00	75.00	40.00
20	Earl Robinson	145.00	75.00	40.00
21	Ron Fairly	400.00	200.00	120.00
22	Joe Frazier	145.00	75.00	40.00
23	Allen Norris	145.00	75.00	40.00
24	Ford Young	145.00	75.00	40.00

E

1928 Pacific Coast League Exhibits

This regional series of 32 cards pictures players from the six California teams in the Pacific Coast League. Like the 1928 major league Exhibits, the PCL cards have a blue tint and are not numbered. They are blank-backed and measure 3-3/8" x 5-3/8". The set includes several misspellings. Cards are occasionally found with a corner clipped, the card corner to be used as a coupon with redemption value.

		NM	EX	VG
Complete Set (32):		17,500	8,750	5,250
Common Player:		500.00	250.00	150.00
1	Buzz Arlett	800.00	400.00	240.00
2	Earl Averill	2,100	1,050	625.00

3	Carl Berger (Walter)	800.00	400.00	240.00
4	"Ping" Bodie	700.00	350.00	210.00
5	Carl Dittmar	500.00	250.00	150.00
6	Jack Fenton	500.00	250.00	150.00
7	Neal "Mickey" Finn (Cornelius)	500.00	250.00	150.00
8	Ray French	500.00	250.00	150.00
9	Tony Governor	500.00	250.00	150.00
10	"Truck" Hannah	500.00	250.00	150.00
11	Mickey Heath	500.00	250.00	150.00
12	Wally Hood	500.00	250.00	150.00
13	"Fuzzy" Hufft	500.00	250.00	150.00
14	Snead Jolly (Smead Jolley)	600.00	300.00	180.00
15	Bobby "Ducky" Jones	500.00	250.00	150.00
16	Rudy Kallio	500.00	250.00	150.00
17	Ray Keating	500.00	250.00	150.00
18	Johnny Kerr	500.00	250.00	150.00
19	Harry Krause	500.00	250.00	150.00
20	Lynford H. Larry (Lary)	500.00	250.00	150.00
21	Dudley Lee	500.00	250.00	150.00
22	Walter "Duster" Mails	500.00	250.00	150.00
23	Jimmy Reese	750.00	370.00	220.00
24	"Dusty" Rhodes	500.00	250.00	150.00
25	Hal Rhyne	500.00	250.00	150.00
26	Hank Severied (Severeid)	500.00	250.00	150.00
27	Earl Sheely	500.00	250.00	150.00
28	Frank Shellenback	500.00	250.00	150.00
29	Gordon Slade	500.00	250.00	150.00
30	Hollis Thurston	500.00	250.00	150.00
31	"Babe" Twombly	500.00	250.00	150.00
32	Earl "Tex" Weathersby	500.00	250.00	150.00

1953 Montreal Royals Exhibits

Twenty-four Montreal Royals, including many future Brooklyn and L.A. Dodgers and Hall of Fame managers Walt Alston and Tommy Lasorda, were included in a 64-card Canadian issue by Exhibit Supply Co., of Chicago. The cards are slightly smaller, at 3-1/4" x 5-1/4", than standard Exhibits and printed - blank-backed - on gray stock. Numbered on front, cards of the Montreal players can be found in either blue or reddish-brown tint. Only the Royals players from the issue are checklisted here.

		NM	EX	VG
Complete Set (24):		450.00	225.00	135.00
Common Player:		15.00	7.50	4.50
33	Don Hoak	25.00	12.50	7.50
34	Bob Alexander	15.00	7.50	4.50
35	John Simmons	15.00	7.50	4.50
36	Steve Lembo	15.00	7.50	4.50
37	Norm Larker	20.00	10.00	6.00
38	Bob Ludwick	15.00	7.50	4.50
39	Walt Moryn	20.00	10.00	6.00
40	Charlie Thompson	15.00	7.50	4.50
41	Ed Roebuck	20.00	10.00	6.00
42	Russell Rose	15.00	7.50	4.50
43	Edmundo (Sandy) Amoros	25.00	12.50	7.50
44	Bob Milliken	15.00	7.50	4.50
45	Art Fabbro	15.00	7.50	4.50
46	Spook Jacobs	15.00	7.50	4.50
47	Carmen Mauro	15.00	7.50	4.50
48	Walter Fiala	15.00	7.50	4.50
49	Rocky Nelson	15.00	7.50	4.50
50	Tom La Sorda (Lasorda)	60.00	30.00	18.00
51	Ronnie Lee	15.00	7.50	4.50
52	Hampton Coleman	15.00	7.50	4.50
53	Frank Marchio	15.00	7.50	4.50
54	William Sampson	15.00	7.50	4.50
55	Gil Mills	15.00	7.50	4.50
56	Al Ronning	15.00	7.50	4.50
61	Walt Alston	40.00	20.00	12.00

F

1953 Fargo-Moorhead Twins Team Issue

This set of team-issued cards includes the first of future home-run king Roger Maris (spelled Maras in the traditional family manner). The cards are about 3-1/4" x 5-5/16" with a white border surrounding a black-and-white posed photo. Player identification is in three lines of white type at lower-left. Backs are blank, except some cards which bear a rubber-stamped promotional message from the "Red River Scenes" newspaper. The unnumbered cards are checklisted here in alphabetical order. Three of the players are known to have two or more poses.

		NM	EX	VG
	Complete Set (21):	3,500	1,750	1,000
	Common Player:	60.00	30.00	18.00
(1)	Zeke Bonura	60.00	30.00	18.00
(2)	Bob Borovicka	60.00	30.00	18.00
(3)	Ken Braeseke	60.00	30.00	18.00
(4)	Joe Camacho	60.00	30.00	18.00
(5)	Galen Fiss	60.00	30.00	18.00
(6)	Frank Gravino	60.00	30.00	18.00
	(Batting follow-through.)			
(7)	Frank Gravino (Hands on hips.)	60.00	30.00	18.00
(8)	Frank Gravino (Hands on knees.)	60.00	30.00	18.00
(9)	Santo Luberto/Fldg	60.00	30.00	18.00
(10)	Roger Maras/Fldg	1,250	625.00	375.00
(11)	Roger Maras/Btg	1,250	625.00	375.00
(12)	Jerry Mehlish (Mehlisch)	60.00	30.00	18.00
(13)	Bob Melton	60.00	30.00	18.00
(14)	Ray Mendoza	60.00	30.00	18.00
	(Stretching at 1B, ball in glove.)			
(15)	Ray Mendoza	60.00	30.00	18.00
	(Stretching at 1B, no ball.)			
(16)	John Morse	60.00	30.00	18.00
(17)	Don Nance	60.00	30.00	18.00
(18)	Ray Seif	60.00	30.00	18.00
(19)	Will Sirois	60.00	30.00	18.00
(20)	Dick Wegner	60.00	30.00	18.00
(21)	Don Wolf	60.00	30.00	18.00

1966 Foremost Milk St. Petersburg Cardinals

This 20-card black-and-white set includes players and the manager, Sparky Anderson, of the Florida State League farm club of the St. Louis Cardinals. The unnumbered, blank-backed cards measure 3-1/2" x 5-1/2".

		NM	EX	VG
	Complete Set (20):	50.00	25.00	15.00
	Common Player:	2.50	1.25	.75
(1)	George "Sparky" Anderson	17.50	8.75	5.25
(2)	Dave Bakenhaster	2.50	1.25	.75
(3)	Leonard Boyer	4.00	2.00	1.25
(4)	Ron Braddock	2.50	1.25	.75
(5)	Thomas "Chip" Coulter	2.50	1.25	.75
(6)	Ernest "Sweet Pea" Davis	2.50	1.25	.75
(7)	Phil Knuckles	2.50	1.25	.75
(8)	Doug Lukens	2.50	1.25	.75
(9)	Terry Milani	2.50	1.25	.75
(10)	Tim Morgan	2.50	1.25	.75
(11)	Harry Parker	2.50	1.25	.75
(12)	Jerry Robertson	2.50	1.25	.75
(13)	Francisco Rodriguez	2.50	1.25	.75
(14)	John "Sonny" Ruberto	2.50	1.25	.75
(15)	Charlie Stewart	2.50	1.25	.75
(16)	Gary L. Stone	2.50	1.25	.75
(17)	Charles "Tim" Thompson	2.50	1.25	.75
(18)	Jose Villar	2.50	1.25	.75
(19)	Archie L. Wade	2.50	1.25	.75
(20)	Jim Williamson	2.50	1.25	.75

1921 Frederick Foto Service

This issue comprises a mix of Pacific Coast League and Major League players. Because Frederick Foto was located in Sacramento, a preponderance of the minor leaguers are Sacramento Senators. The method of the cards' distribution is unknown. The cards are black-and-white glossy photographs glued to a cardboard backing. The photos are bordered in white with top and bottom borders considerably wider than those on the sides. About 1-3/16" x 2-5/8", the cards have blank backs. On front is the player's last name and city, printed in a hand-lettered style. Most cards have a "Freredick / Foto." credit in the same

style. Other cards have a banner-and-circle "Foto / Frederick / Service logo." It is likely this checklist is not complete. Gaps have been left in the assigned numbering for future additions.

		NM	EX	VG
	Common Player:	600.00	300.00	180.00
(1)	Agnew	600.00	300.00	180.00
(2)	Alexander	600.00	300.00	180.00
(3)	Cady	600.00	300.00	180.00
(4)	Ike Caveny (Caveney)	600.00	300.00	180.00
(5)	Pete Compton	600.00	300.00	180.00
(6)	Compton, with bat	600.00	300.00	180.00
(7)	Compton, with glove	600.00	300.00	180.00
(8)	Les Cook/btg	600.00	300.00	180.00
(9)	Les Cook/Fldg	600.00	300.00	180.00
(10)	Carroll Canfield	600.00	300.00	180.00
(11)	Brick Eldred	600.00	300.00	180.00
(12)	Rowdy Elliott	600.00	300.00	180.00
(13)	Tony Faeth	600.00	300.00	180.00
(14)	Paul Fittery	600.00	300.00	180.00
(15)	Gedeon	600.00	300.00	180.00
(16)	Griffith	600.00	300.00	180.00
(17)	Charlie Hollocher	600.00	300.00	180.00
(18)	Jones	600.00	300.00	180.00
(19)	Willie Kamm	600.00	300.00	180.00
(20)	Manny Kopp	600.00	300.00	180.00
(21)	Manny Kopp, bat at waist level	600.00	300.00	180.00
(22)	Manny Kopp, bat on shoulder	600.00	300.00	180.00
(23)	Earl Kuntz (Kunz)	600.00	300.00	180.00
(24)	Duster Mails (Arms at sides.)	600.00	300.00	180.00
(25)	Duster Mails (Hands at chest.)	600.00	300.00	180.00
(26)	Duster Mails (Follow-through.)	600.00	300.00	180.00
(27)	Duster Mails (Wind-up.)	600.00	300.00	180.00
(28)	Patsy McGaffigan	600.00	300.00	180.00
(29)	Patsy McGaffigan, bat at waist level	600.00	300.00	180.00
(30)	Patsy McGaffigan, bat on shoulder	600.00	300.00	180.00
(31)	Roxie Middleton	600.00	300.00	180.00
(32)	Hack Miller	700.00	350.00	220.00
(33)	Mollwitz	600.00	300.00	180.00
(34)	Dick Niehaus	600.00	300.00	180.00
(35)	Billy Orr (Batting)	600.00	300.00	180.00
(36)	Billy Orr (Hands on knees.)	600.00	300.00	180.00
(37)	Dode Paskert	600.00	300.00	180.00
(38)	Ken Penner	600.00	300.00	180.00
	(Right foot off ground.)			
(39)	Ken Penner	600.00	300.00	180.00
	(Right foot on ground.)			
(40)	Charlie Pick	600.00	300.00	180.00
(41)	Babe Pinelli	800.00	400.00	240.00
(42)	Bill Prough	600.00	300.00	180.00
(43)	Addison Read Reuther	600.00	300.00	180.00
(44)	Bill Rodgers	600.00	300.00	180.00
(45)	Pete Rose	600.00	300.00	180.00
(46)	Babe Ruth	40,000	20,000	12,000
(47)	Buddy Ryan	600.00	300.00	180.00
	(Holding bat, 3/4 length.)			
(48)	Buddy Ryan	600.00	300.00	180.00
	(Holding bat, full-length.)			
(49)	Buddy Ryan (Swinging bat.)	600.00	300.00	180.00
(50)	Bobby Schang	600.00	300.00	180.00
(51)	Les Sheehan	600.00	300.00	180.00
(52)	Shore	600.00	300.00	180.00
(53)	Stumpf	600.00	300.00	180.00
(54)	Tobin	600.00	300.00	180.00
(60)	Kettle Wirts (Chicago)	600.00	300.00	180.00
(61)	Kettle Wirts (Dallas)	600.00	300.00	180.00
(62)	Archie Yelle	600.00	300.00	180.00
	Unidentified player, arms folded.	600.00	300.00	180.00
	Unidentified player, batting follow- through.	600.00	300.00	180.00

1951 Fresno Cardinals Team Issue

These 2-1/4" x 3-3/8" black-and-white, unnumbered, blank-backed cards were one of many minor league team sets issued by Globe Printing of San Jose, Calif., in the early 1950s. Cards were usually given away at the ballpark on a one-per-week or one-per-homestand basis, accounting for the rarity of surviving sets. The team was a California League (Class C) affiliate of the St. Louis Cardinals.

		NM	EX	VG
	Complete Set (17):	1,000	500.00	300.00
	Common Player:	60.00	30.00	18.00
(1)	Hal Atkinson	60.00	30.00	18.00
(2)	Larry Barton	60.00	30.00	18.00
(3)	Charlie Brooks	60.00	30.00	18.00
(4)	Bill Burton	60.00	30.00	18.00
(5)	Ray Herrera	60.00	30.00	18.00
(6)	Earl Jones	60.00	30.00	18.00
(7)	Jim King	60.00	30.00	18.00

		NM	EX	VG
(8)	Whitey Lageman	60.00	30.00	18.00
(9)	Wally Lamers	60.00	30.00	18.00
(10)	John McNamara	75.00	37.00	22.00
(11)	Gerry Mertz	60.00	30.00	18.00
(12)	Frank Olasin	60.00	30.00	18.00
(13)	Howie Phillips	60.00	30.00	18.00
(14)	Jack Ramsey	60.00	30.00	18.00
(15)	Tony Stathos	60.00	30.00	18.00
(16)	Whit Ulrich	60.00	30.00	18.00
(17)	Pete Younie	60.00	30.00	18.00

1952 Frostade

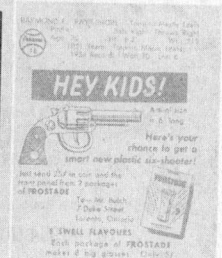

(See 1952 Parkhurst.)

1954 Fruiterie Saint Louis Tommy Lasorda

The date of issue attributed is only a best guess. It is also unknown how many other Montreal Royals players may be found in this issue. Printed in black-and-white on fairly thick 5-1/2" x 7" cardboard, this card features a portrait photo of the Royals' pitcher and future Hall of Fame manager along with a facsimile autograph on the borderless front. Rubber-stamped at top of the otherwise blank back is: "Fruiterie / Saint Louis De Franos / 515 RUE ROY PL. 1729," presumably identification of a Montreal business which distributed the card.

	NM	EX	VG
Tommy Lasorda	100.00	50.00	30.00

G

1911 Gilmartin Printing Co. S.F. Seals

These extremely scarce cards were issued as a premium by the Gilmartin Printing Co. of San Francisco and feature only members of the city's PCL Seals team. The 5" x 7" cards have full-length posed portraits of the players at center, printed in a blue-green tone and surrounded by a wide white border. The player's name, position team and year are scripted in the lower-left corner of the photo. Backs are blank. This checklist is known to be incomplete. Some cards have the sponsor's imprint below the photo.

		NM	EX	VG
	Common Player:	4,500	2,200	1,350
(1)	Claude Berry	4,500	2,200	1,350
(2)	Frank Browning	4,500	2,200	1,350
(6)	Willard Meikle	4,500	2,200	1,350
(7)	Frank Miller	4,500	2,200	1,350
(9)	Harry Sutor	4,500	2,200	1,350
(10)	Tom Tennant	4,500	2,200	1,350
(12)	Geo. Weaver	11,000	5,500	3,250

1956-57 Gil's Drive-Ins Seattle Rainiers

By presenting any nine of these pictures to either of **GIL'S DRIVE-INS** you will receive **FREE** an 8"x 10" player picture of your choice and you still keep your nine small pictures.

Two locations to serve you

GIL'S DRIVE-IN
4406 Rainier Avenue
1 mile south of Sicks' Stadium
—and—
3500 Avalon Way
35th S. W. and Avalon Way
West Seattle

(See 1956-57 Seattle Popcorn for checklist and values.)

1951-1954 Globe Printing

The team-issue card sets and souvenir picture albums listed in previous editions under the heading of Globe Printing are now found alphabetically by team name as per this list:

1951 Fresno Cardinals
1951 San Jose Red Sox
1952 Atlanta Crackers
1952 Baltimore Orioles
1952 Colorado Springs Sky Sox
1952 Columbus Cardinals
1952 Dallas Eagles
1952 Ft. Worth Cats
1952 Great Falls Electrics
1952 Jamestown Falcons
1952 Miami Beach Flamingos
1952 Ogden Reds
1952 Oshkosh Giants
1952 Ponca City Dodgers/KOM Mgrs.
1952 San Diego Padres
1952 Shawnee Hawks
1952-1953 Sioux City Soos
1952 Stockton Ports (Knowles)
1952 Syracuse Chiefs
1952 Ventura Braves
1953 Galveston White Caps (Coca-Cola)
1954 Charleston Senators (Blossom Dairy)
1954 Lewiston Broncs (Veltex)
1954 Sacramento Solons
1954 Sioux City Soos
1954 Stock Ports (MD)

1943 Golden Quality Ice Cream Wilkes-Barre Barons

This rare war-time minor league issue depicts the Hall of Fame manager, Tony Lazzeri, and players on the Class A Eastern League Barons. The 4" x 5" black-and-white cards have facsimile player autographs. Printed in the bottom border at left are the team and year; at right is "Compliments of Golden Quality Ice Cream Co."

		NM	EX	VG
Complete Set (6):		600.00	300.00	180.00
Common Player:		75.00	37.50	22.50
(1)	Alex Damalitron	75.00	37.50	22.50
(2)	Tony Lazzeri (Bat on shoulder.)	175.00	90.00	55.00
(3)	Tony Lazzeri (Hands on knees.)	175.00	90.00	55.00
(4)	Jim McDonnell	75.00	37.50	22.50
(5)	Joe Pennington	75.00	37.50	22.50
(6)	Ned Tryon	75.00	37.50	22.50

1957 Golden State Dairy S.F. Seals Stickers

There are 23 stickers known in this set, featuring the last minor league team in San Francisco. Virtually every player who appeared in more than 10 games for the Seals that season is included in the set. The stickers measure approximately 2" x 2-1/2", are printed in black-and-white, and blank-backed. A 3-1/2" x 6" album to house the stickers was also issued, with biographical data and space for an autograph on each player's page. The stickers are checklisted here alphabetically, as the stickers are unnumbered.

		NM	EX	VG
Complete Set (23):		550.00	275.00	165.00
Common Player:		25.00	12.50	7.50
Album:		150.00	75.00	45.00
(1)	William "Bill" Abernathie	25.00	12.50	7.50
(2)	Kenneth "Chip" Aspromonte	25.00	12.50	7.50
(3)	Harry "Fritz" Dorish	25.00	12.50	7.50
(4)	Joe "Flash" Gordon	25.00	12.50	7.50
(5)	Grady Hatton Jr.	25.00	12.50	7.50
(6)	Thomas "Tommy" Hurd	25.00	12.50	7.50
(7)	Frank Kellert	25.00	12.50	7.50
(8)	Richard "Marty" Keough	25.00	12.50	7.50
(9)	Leo "Black Cat" Kiely	25.00	12.50	7.50
(10)	Harry William Malmberg	25.00	12.50	7.50
(11)	John McCall	25.00	12.50	7.50
(12)	Albert "Albie" Pearson	40.00	20.00	12.00
(13)	Jack Phillips	25.00	12.50	7.50
(14)	William "Bill" Renna	25.00	12.50	7.50
(15)	Edward "Ed" Sadowski	25.00	12.50	7.50
(16)	Robert W. Smith	25.00	12.50	7.50
(17)	Jack Spring	25.00	12.50	7.50
(18)	Jospeh H. Tanner	25.00	12.50	7.50
(19)	Salvador "Sal" Taormina	25.00	12.50	7.50
(20)	Maynard "Bert" Thiel	25.00	12.50	7.50
(21)	Anthony "Nini" Tornay	25.00	12.50	7.50
(22)	Thomas "Tommy" Umphlett	25.00	12.50	7.50
(23)	Glenn "Cap" Wright	25.00	12.50	7.50

1943 Grand Studio Milwaukee Brewers

It's unknown how these blank-backed, black-and-white, 3-1/2" x 5-1/2" pictures were distributed. The only identification is "PHOTO BY GRAND STUDIO" in the lower-right corner. It's likely the pictures were sold as a set at Borchert Field.

		NM	EX	VG
Complete Set (22):		1,000	500.00	300.00
Common Player:		60.00	30.00	20.00
(1)	Joe Berry	60.00	30.00	20.00
(2)	Bob Bowman	60.00	30.00	20.00
(3)	Earl Caldwell	60.00	30.00	20.00
(4)	Grey Clarke	60.00	30.00	20.00
(5)	Merv Conner	60.00	30.00	20.00
(6)	Paul Erickson	60.00	30.00	20.00
(7)	Charlie Grimm	80.00	40.00	25.00
(8)	Hank Helf	60.00	30.00	20.00
(9)	Don Johnson	60.00	30.00	20.00
(10)	Wes Livengood	60.00	30.00	20.00
(11)	Hershell Martin	60.00	30.00	20.00
(12)	Tommy Nelson	60.00	30.00	20.00
(13)	Ted Norbert	60.00	30.00	20.00
(14)	Bill Norman	60.00	30.00	20.00
(15)	Henry Oana	125.00	65.00	40.00
(16)	Jimmy Pruett	60.00	30.00	20.00
(17)	Bill Sahlin	60.00	30.00	20.00
(18)	Frank Secroy	60.00	30.00	20.00
(19)	Red Smith	60.00	30.00	20.00
(20)	Charles Sproull	60.00	30.00	20.00
(21)	Hugh Todd	60.00	30.00	20.00
(22)	Tony York	60.00	30.00	20.00

1944 Grand Studio Milwaukee Brewers

Future Hall of Fame manager Casey Stengel is featured in the second of three annual team-issued photocard sets. The 3-1/2" x 5-1/2" cards have black-and-white portrait photos with facsimile autographs, bordered in white. Backs are blank.

		NM	EX	VG
Complete Set (26):		900.00	450.00	275.00
Common Player:		50.00	25.00	15.00
(1)	Julio Acosta	50.00	25.00	15.00
(2)	Heinz Becker	50.00	25.00	15.00
(3)	George Binks	50.00	25.00	15.00
(4)	Bob Bowman	50.00	25.00	15.00
(5)	Earl Caldwell	50.00	25.00	15.00
(6)	Dick Culler	50.00	25.00	15.00
(7)	Roy Easterwood	50.00	25.00	15.00
(8)	Jack Farmer	50.00	25.00	15.00
(9)	Charles Gassaway	50.00	25.00	15.00
(10)	Dick Hearn	50.00	25.00	15.00
(11)	Don Hendrickson	50.00	25.00	15.00
(12)	Ed Levy	50.00	25.00	15.00
(13)	Hershel Martin	50.00	25.00	15.00
(14)	Bill Nagel	50.00	25.00	15.00
(15)	Tommy Nelson	50.00	25.00	15.00
(16)	Bill Norman	50.00	25.00	15.00
(17)	Hal Peck	50.00	25.00	15.00
(18)	Jimmy Pruett	50.00	25.00	15.00
(19)	Ken Raddant	50.00	25.00	15.00
(20)	Owen Scheetz	50.00	25.00	15.00
(21)	Eddie Scheive	50.00	25.00	15.00
(22)	Frank Secory	50.00	25.00	15.00
(23)	Red Smith	50.00	25.00	15.00
(24)	Floyd Speer	50.00	25.00	15.00
(25)	Charlie Sproull	50.00	25.00	15.00
(26)	Casey Stengel	300.00	150.00	90.00

1945 Grand Studio Milwaukee Brewers

The format remained unchanged for the last of three annual team-issued photocard sets. The 3-1/2" x 5-1/2" cards have black-and-white portrait photos with facsimile autographs, bordered in white. Backs are blank.

		NM	EX	VG
Complete Set (16):		625.00	300.00	175.00
Common Player:		50.00	25.00	15.00
(1)	Julio Acosta	50.00	25.00	15.00
(2)	Arky Biggs	50.00	25.00	15.00
(3)	Bill Burgo	50.00	25.00	15.00
(4)	Nick Cullop	50.00	25.00	15.00
(5)	Wendell "Peaches" Davis	50.00	25.00	15.00
(6)	Otto Denning	50.00	25.00	15.00
(7)	Lew Flick	50.00	25.00	15.00
(8)	Don Hendrickson	50.00	25.00	15.00
(9)	Ed Kobersky	50.00	25.00	15.00
(10)	Carl Lindquist	50.00	25.00	15.00
(11)	Jack McGillen	50.00	25.00	15.00
(12)	Gene Nance	50.00	25.00	15.00
(13)	Bill Norman	50.00	25.00	15.00
(14)	Joe Rullo	50.00	25.00	15.00
(15)	Owen Scheetz	50.00	25.00	15.00
(16)	Floyd Speer	50.00	25.00	15.00

1952 Great Falls Electrics Team Issue

Formatted like the other known minor league issues from Globe Printing of San Jose, Calif., in the early 1950s, this se chronicles the 1952 version of the Class C (Pioneer League Great Falls (Montana) Electrics, a farm club of the Brooklyn Dodgers. The blank-backed cards are black-and-white and mea sure about 2-1/4" x 3-3/8". An album was issued with the cards.

LOU ROCHELLI

	NM	EX	VG
Complete Set (16):	800.00	400.00	240.00
Common Player:	60.00	30.00	18.00
(1) Don Bricker	60.00	30.00	18.00
(2) Larry Hampshire	60.00	30.00	18.00
(3) Ernie Jordan	60.00	30.00	18.00
(4) Lou Landini	60.00	30.00	18.00
(5) Danny Lastres	60.00	30.00	18.00
(6) Joe Oliffe	60.00	30.00	18.00
(7) Len Payne	60.00	30.00	18.00
(8) Lou Rochelli	60.00	30.00	18.00
(9) Earl Silverthorn	60.00	30.00	18.00
(10) Eddie Serrano	60.00	30.00	18.00
(11) Rick Small	60.00	30.00	18.00
(12) Dick Smith	60.00	30.00	18.00
(13) Hal Snyder	60.00	30.00	18.00
(14) Armando Suarez	60.00	30.00	18.00
(15) Emy Unzicker	60.00	30.00	18.00
Album:	100.00	50.00	30.00

1888 Gypsy Queen California League

JAS McDONALD, Catcher
Greenhood & Morgans

GYPSY QUEEN CIGARETTES

Until further specimens are reported, the attributed date of issue is speculative between about 1887-89. Undiscovered until 1998 was the fact that Gypsy Queen, a cigarette manufactured by Goodwin & Co. (Old Judge, etc.) had issued minor league cards, presumably of the relatively new California League. Like some contemporary issues, the card is a stiff piece of cardboard with a sepia-toned player photo glued to it. Size is about 1-1/2" x 2-1/2". As of November 2001, only one card was known from this issue. In Fair to Good condition it was sold at auction for $80,273, then a record price for any 19th Century card.

(1) Jas McDonald

H

1949 Hage's Dairy

Pete Coscarart
SAN DIEGO

Hage's Dairy of California began a three-year run of regional baseball cards featuring Pacific Coast League players in 1949. The cards were distributed inside popcorn boxes at the concession stand in Lane Field Park, home of the P.C.L. San Diego Padres. The 1949 set, like the following two years, was printed on thin stock measuring on average 2-5/8" x 3-1/8". The checklist includes several different poses for some of the players. Cards were continually being added or withdrawn to reflect roster changes on the minor league clubs. The Hage's sets were dominated by San Diego players, but also included representatives from the seven other P.C.L. teams. The 1949 cards can be found in four different tints: sepia, green, blue, and black-and-white. The unnumbered cards have blank backs or advertising messages on back. The player's name and team appear inside a box on the front of the card, and the 1949 cards can be dated by the large (quarter-inch) type used for the team names, which are sometimes referred to by city and other times by nickname.

	NM	EX	VG
Complete Set (107):	40,000	20,000	10,000
Common Player:	400.00	200.00	100.00
(1) "Buster" Adams	400.00	200.00	100.00
(2) "Red" Adams	400.00	200.00	100.00
(3) Lee Anthony	400.00	200.00	100.00
(4) Rinaldo Ardizoia	400.00	200.00	100.00
(5) Del Baker	400.00	200.00	100.00
(6) Ed Basinski	400.00	200.00	100.00
(7) Jim Baxes	400.00	200.00	100.00
(8) H. Becker	400.00	200.00	100.00
(9) Herman Besse	400.00	200.00	100.00
(10) Tom Bridges	400.00	200.00	100.00
(11) Gene Brocker	400.00	200.00	100.00
(12) Ralph Buxton	400.00	200.00	100.00
(13) Mickey Burnett	400.00	200.00	100.00
(14) Dain Clay/Pose	400.00	200.00	100.00
(15) Dain Clay/Btg	400.00	200.00	100.00
(16) Dain Corriden, Jim Reese	475.00	235.00	120.00
(17) Pete Coscarart	400.00	200.00	100.00
(18) Dom Dallessandro	400.00	200.00	100.00
(19) Con Dempsey	400.00	200.00	100.00
(20) Vince DiBiasi	400.00	200.00	100.00
(21) Luke Easter (Batting stance.)	600.00	300.00	150.00
(22) Luke Easter (Batting follow through.)	600.00	300.00	150.00
(23) Ed Fernandez	400.00	200.00	100.00
(24) Les Fleming	400.00	200.00	100.00
(25) Jess Flores	400.00	200.00	100.00
(26) Cecil Garriott	400.00	200.00	100.00
(27) Charles Gassaway	400.00	200.00	100.00
(28) Johnny Gorsica	400.00	200.00	100.00
(29) Mickey Grasso	400.00	200.00	100.00
(30) Will Hafey/Pitching	400.00	200.00	100.00
(31) Will Hafey/Pose	400.00	200.00	100.00
(32) "Jeep" Handley	400.00	200.00	100.00
(33) "Bucky" Harris/Portrait	600.00	300.00	150.00
(34) "Bucky" Harris/Shouting	600.00	300.00	150.00
(35) Roy Helser	400.00	200.00	100.00
(36) Lloyd Hittle	400.00	200.00	100.00
(37) Ralph Hodgin	400.00	200.00	100.00
(38) Leroy Jarvis	400.00	200.00	100.00
(39) John Jensen	400.00	200.00	100.00
(40) Al Jurisich	400.00	200.00	100.00
(41) Herb Karpel	600.00	300.00	150.00
(42) Frank Kelleher	400.00	200.00	100.00
(43) Bill Kelly	400.00	200.00	100.00
(44) Bob Kelly	400.00	200.00	100.00
(45) Frank Kerr	400.00	200.00	100.00
(46) Thomas Kipp	400.00	200.00	100.00
(47) Al Lien	400.00	200.00	100.00
(48) Lyman Linde/Pose	400.00	200.00	100.00
(49) Lyman Linde/Pitching	400.00	200.00	100.00
(50) Dennis Luby	400.00	200.00	100.00
(51) "Red" Lynn	400.00	200.00	100.00
(52) Pat Malone	400.00	200.00	100.00
(53) Billy Martin	1,250	625.00	375.00
(54) Joe Marty	400.00	200.00	100.00
(55) Cliff Melton	400.00	200.00	100.00
(56) Steve Mesner	400.00	200.00	100.00
(57) Leon Mohr	400.00	200.00	100.00
(58) "Butch" Moran	400.00	200.00	100.00
(59) Glen Moulder	400.00	200.00	100.00
(60) Steve Nagy	400.00	200.00	100.00
(61) Roy Nicely	400.00	200.00	100.00
(62) Walt Nothe	400.00	200.00	100.00
(63) John O'Neill	400.00	200.00	100.00
(64) "Pluto" Oliver	400.00	200.00	100.00
(65) Al Olsen/Pose	400.00	200.00	100.00
(66) Al Olsen/Throwing	400.00	200.00	100.00
(67) John Ostrowski	400.00	200.00	100.00
(68) Roy Partee	400.00	200.00	100.00
(69) Bill Raimondi	400.00	200.00	100.00
(70) Bill Ramsey	400.00	200.00	100.00
(71) Len Ratto	400.00	200.00	100.00
(72) Xavier Rescigno	400.00	200.00	100.00
(73) John Ritchey/Btg	400.00	200.00	100.00
(74) John Ritchey/Catching	400.00	200.00	100.00
(75) Mickey Rocco	400.00	200.00	100.00
(76) John Rucker	400.00	200.00	100.00
(77) Clarence Russell	400.00	200.00	100.00
(78) Jack Salverson	400.00	200.00	100.00
(79) Charlie Schanz	400.00	200.00	125.00
(80) Bill Schuster	400.00	200.00	100.00
(81) Tom Seats	400.00	200.00	100.00
(82) Neil Sheridan	400.00	200.00	100.00
(83) Vince Shupe	400.00	200.00	100.00
(84) Joe Sprinz	400.00	200.00	100.00
(85) Chuck Stevens	400.00	200.00	100.00
(86) Harvey Storey	400.00	200.00	100.00
(87) Jim Tabor (Sacramento)	400.00	200.00	100.00
(88) Jim Tabor (Seattle)	400.00	200.00	100.00
(89) "Junior" Thompson	400.00	200.00	100.00
(90) Arky Vaughn	625.00	310.00	175.00
(91) Jackie Warner	400.00	200.00	100.00
(92) Jim Warner	400.00	200.00	100.00
(93) Dick Wenner	400.00	200.00	100.00
(94) Max West/Pose	400.00	200.00	100.00
(95) Max West (Batting swing.)	400.00	200.00	100.00
(96) Max West (Batting follow-through.)	400.00	200.00	100.00
(97) Hank Weyse	400.00	200.00	100.00
(98) "Fuzzy" White	400.00	200.00	100.00
(99) Jo Jo White	400.00	200.00	100.00
(100) Artie Wilson	400.00	200.00	100.00
(101) Bill Wilson	400.00	200.00	100.00
(102) Bobbie Wilson/Pose	400.00	200.00	100.00
(103) Bobbie Wilson/Fldg	400.00	200.00	100.00
(104) "Pinky" Woods	400.00	200.00	100.00
(105) Tony York	400.00	200.00	100.00
(106) Del Young	400.00	200.00	100.00
(107) Frank Zak	400.00	200.00	100.00

1950 Hage's Dairy

Orestes Minoso
SAN DIEGO

Your FAVORITE Brand

Hage's ICE CREAM

ORESTES MINOSO......The Padres.....

The 1950 P.C.L. set from Hage's Dairy was similar in design and size (about 2-5/8" x 3-1/8") to the previous year and was again distributed in popcorn boxes at San Diego's Lane Field. The 1950 cards are in black-and-white with most backs containing an advertisement for Hage's Milk, Ice Cream or Ice Cream Bars. Some backs are blank. The advertising backs also contain the player's name and either brief 1949 statistics or career highlights at bottom. Many players were issued in more than one pose. Again, Padres dominate the unnumbered set with lesser representation from the other P.C.L. clubs. For the 1950 edition all team names are referred to by city (no nicknames) and the typeface is smaller. Gaps have been left in the assigned numbering to accommodate future additions to the checklist.

	NM	EX	VG
Complete Set (128):	45,000	22,500	13,500
Common Player:	375.00	185.00	110.00
(1) "Buster" Adams/Kneeling	375.00	185.00	110.00
(2a) "Buster" Adams (Batting follow-through, with inscription.)	375.00	185.00	110.00
(2b) "Buster" Adams (Batting follow-through, no inscription.)	375.00	185.00	110.00
(2c) "Buster" Adams (Batting follow-through, body to left.)	375.00	185.00	110.00
(3a) "Buster" Adams (Batting stance, caption box touching waist.)	375.00	185.00	110.00
(3b) "Buster" Adams (Batting stance, caption box not touching waist.)	375.00	185.00	110.00
(4) "Red" Adams	375.00	185.00	110.00
(5) Dewey Adkins (Photo actually Albie Glossop.)	375.00	185.00	110.00
(6) Rinaldo Ardizoia	375.00	185.00	110.00
(7) Jose Bache	375.00	185.00	110.00
(8a) Del Baker, Jim Reese (Bat visible at lower right.)	375.00	185.00	110.00
(8b) Del Baker, Jim Reese (No bat visible.)	375.00	185.00	110.00
(9) George Bamberger	375.00	185.00	110.00
(10) Richard Barrett	375.00	185.00	110.00
(11) Frank Baumholtz	375.00	185.00	110.00
(12) Henry Behrman	375.00	185.00	110.00
(13) Bill Bevens	375.00	185.00	110.00
(14) Ernie Bickhaus	375.00	185.00	110.00
(15) Bill Burgher/Pose	375.00	185.00	110.00
(16) Bill Burgher/Catching	375.00	185.00	110.00
(17) Mark Christman	375.00	185.00	110.00
(18) Clint Conatser	375.00	185.00	110.00
(19) Herb Conyers/Fldg	375.00	185.00	110.00
(20) Herb Conyers/Btg	375.00	185.00	110.00
(21) Jim Davis	375.00	185.00	110.00
(22) Ted Del Guercio	375.00	185.00	110.00
(23) Vince DiBiasi	375.00	185.00	110.00
(24) Jess Dobernic	375.00	185.00	110.00
(25) "Red" Embree/Pose	375.00	185.00	110.00
(26) "Red" Embree/Pitching	375.00	185.00	110.00
(27) Elbie Fletcher	375.00	185.00	110.00
(28) Guy Fletcher	375.00	185.00	110.00
(30) Tony Freitas	375.00	185.00	110.00
(31) Denny Galehouse	375.00	185.00	110.00
(32) Jack Graham/Pose (Looking to left.)	375.00	185.00	110.00
(33) Jack Graham/Pose (Looking straight ahead.)	375.00	185.00	110.00
(34) Jack Graham (Batting swing.)	375.00	185.00	110.00
(35) Jack Graham (Batting stance.)	375.00	185.00	110.00
(36) Orval Grove	375.00	185.00	110.00
(37) Lee Handley	375.00	185.00	110.00
(38) Ralph Hodgin	375.00	185.00	110.00
(39) Don Johnson	375.00	185.00	110.00
(40) Al Jurisich/Pose	375.00	185.00	110.00
(41) Al Jurisich (Pitching wind-up.)	375.00	185.00	110.00
(42) Al Jurisich (Pitching follow-through.)	375.00	185.00	110.00
(43) Bill Kelly	375.00	185.00	110.00
(44) Frank Kerr	375.00	185.00	110.00
(45) Tom Kipp/Pose	375.00	185.00	110.00
(46) Tom Kipp/Pitching	375.00	185.00	110.00
(47) Mel Knezovich	375.00	185.00	110.00
(48) Red Kress	375.00	185.00	110.00
(49) Dario Lodigiani	375.00	185.00	110.00
(50) Dennis Luby/Pose	375.00	185.00	110.00

(51)	Dennis Luby/Fldg	375.00	185.00	110.00
(52)	Al Lyons	375.00	185.00	110.00
(53)	Clarence Maddern	375.00	185.00	110.00
(54)	Joe Marty	375.00	185.00	110.00
(55)	Bob McCall	375.00	185.00	110.00
(56)	Cal McIrvin	375.00	185.00	110.00
(57)	Orestes Minoso (Batting follow-through.)	850.00	425.00	250.00
(58)	Orestes Minoso/Bunting	850.00	425.00	250.00
(59)	Leon Mohr	375.00	185.00	110.00
(60)	Dee Moore/Btg	375.00	185.00	110.00
(61)	Dee Moore/Catching	375.00	185.00	110.00
(62)	Jim Moran	375.00	185.00	110.00
(63)	Glen Moulder	375.00	185.00	110.00
(64)	Milt Neilsen/Pose	375.00	185.00	110.00
(65)	Milt Neilsen/Btg	375.00	185.00	110.00
(66)	Milt Neilsen/Throwing	375.00	185.00	110.00
(67)	Rube Novotney	375.00	185.00	110.00
(68)	Al Olsen	375.00	185.00	110.00
(69)	Manny Perez	375.00	185.00	110.00
(70)	Bill Raemondi (Raimondi)	375.00	185.00	110.00
(71)	Len Ratto	375.00	185.00	110.00
(72)	Mickey Rocco	375.00	185.00	110.00
(73)	Marv Rotblatt	375.00	185.00	110.00
(74)	Lynwood Rowe/Pose	400.00	200.00	120.00
(75)	Lynwood Rowe/Pitching	400.00	200.00	120.00
(76)	Clarence Russell	375.00	185.00	110.00
(77)	Hal Saltzman (Pitching follow-through.)	375.00	185.00	110.00
(78)	Hal Saltzman (Pitching wind-up.)	375.00	185.00	110.00
(79)	Hal Saltzman (Pitching, leg in air.)	375.00	185.00	110.00
(81)	Mike Sandlock	375.00	185.00	110.00
(82)	Bob Savage/Pose	375.00	185.00	110.00
(83)	Bob Savage/Pitching	375.00	185.00	110.00
(84)	Charlie Schanz	375.00	185.00	110.00
(85)	Bill Schuster	375.00	185.00	110.00
(86)	Neill Sheridan	375.00	185.00	110.00
(87)	Harry Simpson (Batting swing.)	525.00	260.00	150.00
(88)	Harry Simpson (Batting stance.)	525.00	260.00	150.00
(89)	Harry Simpson (Batting stance, close up.)	525.00	260.00	150.00
(90)	Harry Simpson (Batting follow-through.)	525.00	260.00	150.00
(91)	Elmer Singleton	375.00	185.00	110.00
(92)	Al Smith/Pose	375.00	185.00	110.00
(93)	Al Smith (Batting stance.)	375.00	185.00	110.00
(94)	Al Smith/Fldg	375.00	185.00	110.00
(95)	Alphonse Smith (Glove above knee.)	375.00	185.00	110.00
(96)	Alphonse Smith (Glove below knee.)	375.00	185.00	110.00
(97)	Steve Souchock	375.00	185.00	110.00
(98)	Jim Steiner	375.00	185.00	110.00
(99)	Harvey Storey (Batting stance.)	375.00	185.00	110.00
(100)	Harvey Storey (Swinging bat.)	375.00	185.00	110.00
(101)	Harvey Storey/Throwing	375.00	185.00	110.00
(102)	Harvey Storey/Fldg (Ball in glove.)	375.00	185.00	110.00
(103)	Max Surkont	375.00	185.00	110.00
(104)	Jim Tabor	375.00	185.00	110.00
(105)	Forrest Thompson	375.00	185.00	110.00
(106)	Mike Tresh/Pose	375.00	185.00	110.00
(107)	Mike Tresh/Catching	375.00	185.00	110.00
(108)	Ben Wade	375.00	185.00	110.00
(109)	Kenny Washington	375.00	185.00	110.00
(110)	Bill Waters/Pose	375.00	185.00	110.00
(111)	Bill Waters/Pitching	375.00	185.00	110.00
(112)	Roy Welmaker/Pose	375.00	185.00	110.00
(113)	Roy Welmaker/Pitching	375.00	185.00	110.00
(114)	Max West/Pose	375.00	185.00	110.00
(115)	Max West (Batting stance.)	375.00	185.00	110.00
(116)	Max West/Kneeling	375.00	185.00	110.00
(117)	Max West (Batting follow-through.)	375.00	185.00	110.00
(118)	Al White	375.00	185.00	110.00
(119)	"Whitey" Wietelmann/Pose	375.00	185.00	110.00
(120)	"Whitey" Wietelmann/Bunting	375.00	185.00	110.00
(121)	"Whitey" Wietelmann (Batting stance.)	375.00	185.00	110.00
(122)	"Whitey" Wietelmann/Throwing	375.00	185.00	110.00
(123)	Bobbie Wilson	375.00	185.00	110.00
(124)	Bobby Wilson	375.00	185.00	110.00
(125)	Roy Zimmerman	375.00	185.00	110.00
(126)	George Zuverink	375.00	185.00	110.00

1951 Hage's Dairy

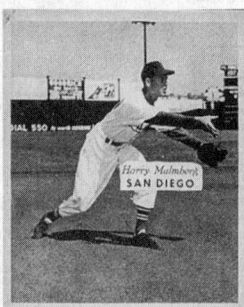

Harry Malmberg
SAN DIEGO

The final year of the Hage's P.C.L. issues saw the set reduced to 53 different unnumbered cards, all but 12 of them Padres. Among them are seven cards of Cleveland Indians players, which were issued during an exhibition series with the major league club, and six cards picturing members of the Hollywood Stars. No other P.C.L. teams are represented. The cards maintained the same size and style of the previous two years but were printed in more color tints, including blue, green, burgundy, gold, gray and sepia (but not black-and-white). The 1951 cards have blank backs and were again distributed in popcorn boxes at the San Diego stadium. The 1951 cards are the most common of the three sets issued by Hage's Dairy. The Indians and Stars players were issued in lesser quantities than the Padres, however, and command a higher value.

		NM	EX	VG
Complete Set (54):		18,000	9,000	5,500
Common Player:		300.00	150.00	90.00
(1)	"Buster" Adams	300.00	150.00	90.00
(2)	Del Baker	300.00	150.00	90.00
(3)	Ray Boone	850.00	425.00	250.00
(4)	Russ Christopher	300.00	150.00	90.00
(5)	Allie Clark	850.00	425.00	250.00
(6)	Herb Conyers	300.00	150.00	90.00
(7)	Luke Easter	850.00	420.00	250.00
(8)	"Red" Embree/Pitching (Foot in air.)	300.00	150.00	90.00
(9)	"Red" Embree/Pitching (Hands up.)	300.00	150.00	90.00
(10)	Jess Flores	850.00	425.00	250.00
(11)	Murray Franklin	300.00	150.00	90.00
(12)	Jack Graham/Portrait	300.00	150.00	90.00
(13)	Jack Graham/Btg	300.00	150.00	90.00
(14)	Gene Handley	300.00	150.00	90.00
(15)	Charles Harris	300.00	150.00	90.00
(16)	Sam Jones/Pitching (Hands back.)	300.00	150.00	90.00
(17)	Sam Jones/Pitching (Hands up.)	300.00	150.00	90.00
(18)	Sam Jones/Pitching (Leg in air.)	300.00	150.00	90.00
(19)	Al Jurisich	300.00	150.00	90.00
(20)	Frank Kerr/Btg	300.00	150.00	90.00
(21)	Frank Kerr/Catching	300.00	150.00	90.00
(22)	Dick Kinaman	300.00	150.00	90.00
(23)	Clarence Maddern/Btg	300.00	150.00	90.00
(24)	Clarence Maddern/Fldg	300.00	150.00	90.00
(25)	Harry Malmberg/Bunting	300.00	150.00	90.00
(26)	Harry Malmberg (Batting follow-through.)	300.00	150.00	90.00
(27)	Harry Malmberg/Fldg	300.00	150.00	90.00
(28)	Gordon Maltzberger	300.00	150.00	90.00
(29)	Al Olsen (Cleveland)	850.00	425.00	250.00
(30)	Al Olsen (San Diego)	300.00	150.00	90.00
(31)	Jimmy Reese (Clapping)	350.00	175.00	100.00
(32)	Jimmy Reese (Hands on knees.)	350.00	175.00	100.00
(33)	Al Rosen	900.00	450.00	270.00
(34)	Joe Rowell	300.00	150.00	90.00
(35)	Mike Sandlock	300.00	150.00	90.00
(36)	George Schmees	300.00	150.00	90.00
(37)	Harry Simpson	300.00	150.00	90.00
(38)	Charlie Sipple	300.00	150.00	90.00
(39)	Harvey Storey (Batting follow-through.)	300.00	150.00	90.00
(40)	Harvey Storey (Batting stance.)	300.00	150.00	90.00
(41)	Harvey Storey/Fldg	300.00	150.00	90.00
(42)	Jack Tobin	300.00	150.00	90.00
(43)	Frank Tornay	300.00	150.00	90.00
(44)	Thurman Tucker	300.00	150.00	90.00
(45)	Ben Wade	300.00	150.00	90.00
(46)	Roy Welmaker	300.00	150.00	90.00
(47)	Leroy Wheat	300.00	150.00	90.00
(48)	Don White	300.00	150.00	90.00
(49)	"Whitey" Wietelman/Btg	300.00	150.00	90.00
(50)	"Whitey" Wietelman/Fldg	300.00	150.00	90.00
(51)	Bobby Wilson/Btg	300.00	150.00	90.00
(52)	Bobby Wilson/Fldg	300.00	150.00	90.00
(53)	Tony York	300.00	150.00	90.00
(54)	George Zuverink	850.00	425.00	250.00

1886 Hancock's Syracuse Stars

Currently representing the earliest known minor league baseball cards is this issue by a Syracuse department store's menswear department. The 1-5/8" x 3-3/16" cards feature sepia photos glued to a stiff black cardboard backing with a gilt edge. The photos show the players in suits, presumably from the sponsor's racks. Backs have the player name and position printed at top. At center is an ad for Hancock's. At bottom is a credit line to "Goodwin" as photographer. Each card is currently known in only a single example. It is possible other players of the International League Stars may yet be discovered.

Values Undetermined
(1) Richard D. Buckley
(2) Douglas Crothers (SGC-graded EX sold in 2009 auction for $16,335.)
(3) Philip H. Tomney

1960 Henry House Wieners Seattle Rainiers

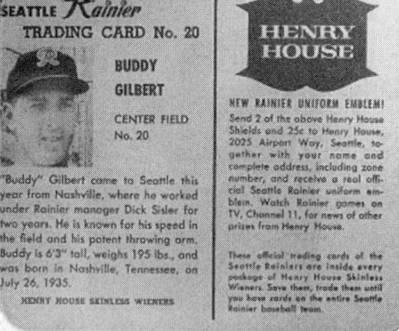

Eighteen different cards are known in this hot dog set; most players played major league baseball prior to their appearance with the Pacific Coast League Seattle Rainiers in 1960. Printed in red, the 4-1/2" x 3-3/4" cards are skip-numbered by player uniform number.

		NM	EX	VG
Complete Set (18):		5,500	2,750	1,600
Common Player:		300.00	150.00	90.00
2	Harry Malmberg	300.00	150.00	90.00
3	Francisco Obregon	300.00	150.00	90.00
4	Johnny O'Brien	375.00	185.00	110.00
5	Gordon Coleman	300.00	150.00	90.00
6	Bill Hain	300.00	150.00	90.00
8	Dick Sisler	300.00	150.00	90.00
9	Jerry Zimmerman	300.00	150.00	90.00
10	Hal Bevan	300.00	150.00	90.00
14	Rudy Regaldo	300.00	150.00	90.00
15	Paul Pettit	300.00	150.00	90.00
20	Buddy Gilbert	300.00	150.00	90.00
21	Erv Palica	300.00	150.00	90.00
22	Joe Taylor	300.00	150.00	90.00
25	Bill Kennedy	300.00	150.00	90.00
26	Dave Stenhouse	300.00	150.00	90.00
28	Ray Ripplemeyer	300.00	150.00	90.00
30	Charlie Beamon	300.00	150.00	90.00
33	Don Rudolph	300.00	150.00	90.00

1888 S.F. Hess California League (N321)

One of several tobacco card sets produced by S.F. Hess & Co. of Rochester, this rare 40-card issue features players from the California League. The cards measure 2-7/8" x 1-1/2" and feature color drawings of players. The player's name and team are printed along the top margin of the card, while the words "S.F. Hess and Co.'s/Creole Cigarettes" appear at the bottom. "California League" is also printed in large capital letters above the player drawing, while the 1888 copyright date appears below. There are 35 players (including one umpire) in the set, and five players are pictured on two cards each, resulting in 40 different cards. One example each of 30 of the cards have been discovered printed on thin paper stock, though the exact nature of that version is undetermined; currently values are about equal to the regular-issue version.

		NM	EX	VG
Common Player:		5,400	3,000	2,250
(1)	Eddie Bennett	5,400	3,000	2,250
(2)	George Borchers	5,400	3,000	2,250
(3)	Tom Buckley	5,400	3,000	2,250
(4)	Turk Burke/Btg	5,400	3,000	2,250
(5)	Turk Burke (Ready to pitch.)	5,400	3,000	2,250
(6)	Frank Carroll	5,400	3,000	2,250
(7)	John Donohue	5,400	3,000	2,250
(8)	Jack Donovan	5,400	3,000	2,250
(9)	Michael Finn	5,400	3,000	2,250
(10)	Jim Gagus	5,400	3,000	2,250
(11)	William Gurnett			
(12)	George Hanley	5,400	3,000	2,250
(13)	Pop Hardie (C., wearing mask.)	5,400	3,000	2,250

		NM	EX	VG
(14)	Pop Hardie (C.F., with bat.)	5,400	3,000	2,250
(15)	Jack Hayes	5,400	3,000	2,250
(16)	Jack Lawton	5,400	3,000	2,250
(17)	Rube Levy	5,400	3,000	2,250
(18)	Daniel Long	5,400	3,000	2,250
(19)	Tom McCord	5,400	3,000	2,250
(20)	Peter Meegan	5,400	3,000	2,250
(21)	Henry Moore	5,400	3,000	2,250
(22)	James Mullee	5,400	3,000	2,250
(23)	Billy Newhert	5,400	3,000	2,250
(24)	Joseph Noonan	5,400	3,000	2,250
(25)	Harry O'Day	5,400	3,000	2,250
(26)	Hip Perrier	5,400	3,000	2,250
(27)	Thomas Powers/Catching (1st B.)	5,400	3,000	2,250
(28)	Thomas Powers (1st B. & Capt., with bat)	5,400	3,000	2,250
(29)	Jack Ryan	5,400	3,000	2,250
(30)	Charles Selna	5,400	3,000	2,250
(31)	Joseph Shea	5,400	3,000	2,250
(32)	Jack Sheridan/Umpire	5,400	3,000	2,250
(33)	"Big" Smith	5,400	3,000	2,250
(34)	Hugh Smith	5,400	3,000	2,250
(35)	John Smith	5,400	3,000	2,250
(36)	Leonard Stockwell/Throwing	5,400	3,000	2,250
(37)	Leonard Stockwell (With bat.)	5,400	3,000	2,250
(38)	Charles Sweeney	5,400	3,000	2,250
(39)	Pop Swett	5,400	3,000	2,250
(40)	Milton Whitehead	5,400	3,000	2,250

1888 S.F. Hess California League (N338-1)

This tobacco card set picturing players from the California League is one of the rarest of all 19th Century issues. Issued in the late 1880s by S.F. Hess & Co. of Rochester, these 2-7/8" x 1-1/2" cards are so rare that only several examples are known to exist. Some of the photos in the N338-1 set are identical to the drawings in the N321 set, issued by S.F. Hess in 1888. The N338-1 cards are found with the words "California League" printed in an arc either above or below the player photo. The player's name appears below the photo. At the bottom of the card the words "S.F. Hess & Co.'s Creole Cigarettes" are printed in a rolling style.

		NM	EX	VG
Common Player:		18,000	9,000	5,250
(1)	Borsher	18,000	9,000	5,250
(2)	Buckley	18,000	9,000	5,250
(3)	Carroll	18,000	9,000	5,250
(4)	Ebright	18,000	9,000	5,250
(5)	Gagur (Gagus)	18,000	9,000	5,250
(6)	Incell	18,000	9,000	5,250
(7)	Lawton	18,000	9,000	5,250
(8)	Levy/Throwing	18,000	9,000	5,250
(9)	Levy (With bat.)	18,000	9,000	5,250
(10)	McDonald	18,000	9,000	5,250
(11)	McGinty	20,250	10,125	6,075
(12)	Meegan	18,000	9,000	5,250
(13)	Newhert	18,000	9,000	5,250
(14)	Noonan	18,000	9,000	5,250
(15)	Perrier	18,000	9,000	5,250
(16)	Perrier, H. Smith	18,000	9,000	5,250
(17)	Ryan	18,000	9,000	5,250
(18)	J. Smith, N. Smith	18,000	9,000	5,250
(19)	Sweeney	18,000	9,000	5,250

1888 S.F. Hess Newsboys League (N333)

Although not picturing professional baseball players, these cards issued by S.F. Hess and Co. have a baseball theme. Cards measure 1-1/2" x 2-7/8" and feature pictures of "newsies" from papers in eight different cities (Rochester, Cleveland, Philadelphia, Boston, Albany, Detroit, New York and Syracuse). The boys are pictured in a photographs wearing baseball uniforms, often bearing the name of their newspaper. The boy's name, position and newspaper are printed below, while the words "Newsboys League" appears in capital letters at the top of the card. No identification is provided for the four Philadelphia newsboys, so a photo description is provided in the checklist that follows. Gaps have been left in the assigned numbering for future additions.

		NM	EX	VG
Common Player:		2,400	1,200	725.00
(1)	R.J. Bell	2,400	1,200	725.00
(2)	Bibby (Boston Globe)	2,400	1,200	725.00
(3)	Binden	2,400	1,200	725.00
(4)	Bowen	2,400	1,200	725.00
(5)	Boyle	2,400	1,200	725.00
(6)	Britcher	2,400	1,200	725.00
(7)	Caine	2,400	1,200	725.00
(8)	I. Cohen	2,400	1,200	725.00
(9)	R. Cohen	2,400	1,200	725.00
(10)	Collins (Boston Globe)	2,400	1,200	725.00
(11)	Cross	2,400	1,200	725.00
(12)	F. Cuddy	2,400	1,200	725.00
(13)	E. Daisey	2,400	1,200	725.00
(14)	Davis	2,400	1,200	725.00
(15)	B. Dinsmore	2,400	1,200	725.00
(16)	Donovan	2,400	1,200	725.00
(17)	A. Downer	2,400	1,200	725.00
(18)	Fanelly	2,400	1,200	725.00
(19)	J. Flood	2,400	1,200	725.00
(20)	C. Gallagher	2,400	1,200	725.00
(21)	M.H. Gallagher	2,400	1,200	725.00
(22)	D. Galligher	2,400	1,200	725.00
(23)	J. Galligher	2,400	1,200	725.00
(24)	Haskins	2,400	1,200	725.00
(25)	Herze	2,400	1,200	725.00
(26)	Holmes (Press & Knickerbocker)	2,400	1,200	725.00
(27)	F. Horan	2,400	1,200	725.00
(28)	Hosler	2,400	1,200	725.00
(29)	Hyde	2,400	1,200	725.00
(30)	Keilty	2,400	1,200	725.00
(31)	C. Kellogg	2,400	1,200	725.00
(32)	Mahoney (Rochester Post-Express)	2,400	1,200	725.00
(33)	Mayer	2,400	1,200	725.00
(34)	McCourt (Boston Globe)	2,400	1,200	725.00
(35)	I. McDonald	2,400	1,200	725.00
(36)	McDowell (Rochester)	2,400	1,200	725.00
(37)	McGrady	2,400	1,200	725.00
(38)	O'Brien	2,400	1,200	725.00
(39)	E.C. Murphy	2,400	1,200	725.00
(40)	Sabin	2,400	1,200	725.00
(41)	Shedd	2,400	1,200	725.00
(42)	R. Sheehan	2,400	1,200	725.00
(43)	W. Smith (Syracuse Herald)	2,400	1,200	725.00
(44)	Talbot	2,400	1,200	725.00
(45)	Walsh	2,400	1,200	725.00
(46)	Whitman	2,400	1,200	725.00
(47)	Yeomans	2,400	1,200	725.00
(48)	Cleveland Newsboy (In cap, facing right.)	2,400	1,200	725.00
(49)	Philadelphia Newsboy (Hair parted on right side.)	2,400	1,200	725.00
(50)	Philadelphia Newsboy (Hair parted on left side.)	2,400	1,200	725.00
(51)	Philadelphia Newsboy (No part in hair.)	2,400	1,200	725.00
(52)	Philadelphia Newsboy (Head shaved.)	2,400	1,200	725.00

1949 Hollywood Stars Team Issue

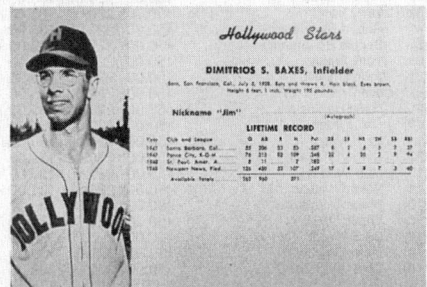

A team issue probably related to similar 1948-49 cards produced by Pacific Coast League cross-town rivals the L.A. Angels, these cards were likely produced by the publisher of the teams' yearbooks and sold at stadium souvenir stands. The cards are blank-backed, printed in black-and-white on thin semi-gloss cardboard, measuring 7-1/16" x 4-7/8". Portrait or posed action photos appear at left with complete major and minor league stats at right. A space for an autograph appears beneath the player's biographical data. The unnumbered cards are checklisted here in alphabetical order.

		NM	EX	VG
Complete Set (24):		500.00	250.00	150.00
Common Player:		25.00	12.50	7.50
(1)	Jim Baxes	25.00	12.50	7.50
(2)	George Fallon	25.00	12.50	7.50
(3)	John Fitzpatrick	25.00	12.50	7.50
(4)	George Genovese	25.00	12.50	7.50
(5)	Herb Gorman	75.00	37.50	22.50

		NM	EX	VG
(6)	Gene Handley	25.00	12.50	7.50
(7)	Fred Haney	25.00	12.50	7.50
(8)	Jim Hughes	25.00	12.50	7.50
(9)	Frank Kelleher	25.00	12.50	7.50
(10)	Gordy Maltzberger	25.00	12.50	7.50
(11)	Glen Moulder	25.00	12.50	7.50
(12)	Irv Noren	25.00	12.50	7.50
(13)	Ed Oliver	25.00	12.50	7.50
(14)	Karl Olsen	25.00	12.50	7.50
(15)	John O'Neil	25.00	12.50	7.50
(16)	Jack Paepke	25.00	12.50	7.50
(17)	Willard Ramsdell	25.00	12.50	7.50
(18)	Jack Salveson	25.00	12.50	7.50
(19)	Mike Sandlock	25.00	12.50	7.50
(20)	Art Shallock	25.00	12.50	7.50
(21)	Andy Skurski	25.00	12.50	7.50
(22)	Chuck Stevens	25.00	12.50	7.50
(23)	Al Unser	25.00	12.50	7.50
(24)	George Woods	25.00	12.50	7.50

1950 Hollywood Stars Team Issue

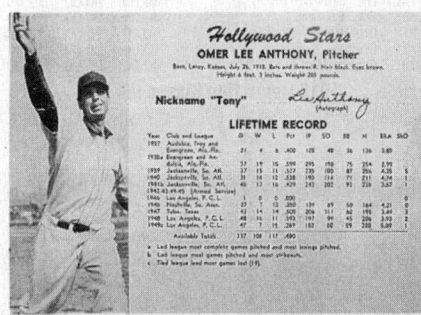

Virtually identical in format to the previous year's issue, the 1950 set differs principally in the inclusion of a facsimile autograph on front. In 1950, the Hollywood Stars were the PCL affiliate of the Brooklyn Dodgers. Both sets were listed in "The American Card Catalog" as W720.

		NM	EX	VG
Complete Set (32):		850.00	425.00	250.00
Common Player:		25.00	12.50	7.50
(1)	Lee Anthony	25.00	12.50	7.50
(2)	Bill Antonello	25.00	12.50	7.50
(3)	Dick Barrett	25.00	12.50	7.50
(4)	Jim Baxes	25.00	12.50	7.50
(5)	Clint Conatser	25.00	12.50	7.50
(6)	Cliff Dapper	25.00	12.50	7.50
(7)	George Fallon	25.00	12.50	7.50
(8)	John Fitzpatrick	25.00	12.50	7.50
(9)	Murray Franklin	75.00	37.50	22.50
(10)	Herb Gorman	75.00	37.50	22.50
(11)	Gene Handley	25.00	12.50	7.50
(12)	Fred Haney	25.00	12.50	7.50
(13)	Clarence Hicks	25.00	12.50	7.50
(14)	Herb Karpel	200.00	100.00	60.00
(15)	Frank Kelleher	25.00	12.50	7.50
(16)	Ken Lehman	25.00	12.50	7.50
(17)	Johnny Lindell	25.00	12.50	7.50
(18)	Gordy Maltzberger	25.00	12.50	7.50
(19)	Dan Menendez	25.00	12.50	7.50
(20)	Pershing Mondroff	25.00	12.50	7.50
(21)	Glen Moulder	25.00	12.50	7.50
(22)	John O'Neil	25.00	12.50	7.50
(23)	Jack Paepke	25.00	12.50	7.50
(24)	Jean Roy	25.00	12.50	7.50
(25)	Jack Salveson	25.00	12.50	7.50
(26)	Mike Sandlock	25.00	12.50	7.50
(27)	Ed Saver	25.00	12.50	7.50
(28)	George Schmees	25.00	12.50	7.50
(29)	Art Shallock	25.00	12.50	7.50
(30)	Chuck Stevens	25.00	12.50	7.50
(31)	Ben Wade	25.00	12.50	7.50
(32)	George Woods	25.00	12.50	7.50

1957 Hollywood Stars Team Issue

Presumably issued by the team, which had a working relationship with the Pittsburgh Pirates, this 23-card set features black-and-white blank-backed photos in a 4-1/8" x 6-3/16" format. Each picture has a facsimile autograph printed in black across the front. The unnumbered cards are checklisted here alphabetically.

		NM	EX	VG
Complete Set (23):		900.00	450.00	275.00
Common Player:		40.00	20.00	12.00
(1)	Jim Baumer	40.00	20.00	12.00
(2)	Carlos Bernier	40.00	20.00	12.00
(3)	Bill Causion	40.00	20.00	12.00
(4)	Chuck Churn	40.00	20.00	12.00
(5)	Bennie Daniels	40.00	20.00	12.00
(6)	Joe Duhem	40.00	20.00	12.00
(7)	John Fitzpatrick	40.00	20.00	12.00
(8)	Bob Garber	40.00	20.00	12.00
(9)	Bill Hall	40.00	20.00	12.00
(10)	Forrest "Spook" Jacobs	50.00	25.00	15.00
(11)	Clyde King	40.00	20.00	12.00
(12)	Nick Koback	40.00	20.00	12.00
(13)	Pete Naton	40.00	20.00	12.00
(14)	George O'Donnell	40.00	20.00	12.00
(15)	Paul Pettit	40.00	20.00	12.00
(16)	Curt Raydon	40.00	20.00	12.00
(17)	Leo Rodriguez	40.00	20.00	12.00
(18)	Don Rowe	40.00	20.00	12.00
(19)	Dick Smith	40.00	20.00	12.00
(20)	R.C. Stevens	40.00	20.00	12.00
(21)	Ben Wade	40.00	20.00	12.00
(22)	Fred Waters	40.00	20.00	12.00
(23)	George Witt	40.00	20.00	12.00

1912 Home Run Kisses (E136)

 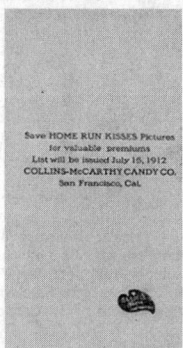

This 90-card set of Pacific Coast League players was produced in 1912 by the San Francisco candy company of Collins-McCarthy. Each card measures about 2-1/4" x 4-3/16" and features sepia-toned player photos surrounded by an ornate frame. The front of the card has the words "Home Run Kisses" above the player's name. Some cards found are blank-backed, but others exist with a back that advises "Save Home Run Kisses Pictures for Valuable Premiums" along with other details of the Collins-McCarthy promotion. A third type of back exists with an advertising logo for "BARDELL / SEPIA/ SAN FRANCISCO." Redeemed cards were punch-cancelled, often with a heart-shaped hole.

		NM	EX	VG
Complete Set (90):		90,000	45,000	27,000
Common Player:		1,000	500.00	300.00
(1)	Ables	1,000	500.00	300.00
(2)	Agnew	1,000	500.00	300.00
(3)	Altman	1,000	500.00	300.00
(4)	Frank Arrelanes (Arellanes)	1,000	500.00	300.00
(5)	Auer	1,000	500.00	300.00
(6)	Bancroft	4,000	2,000	1,200
(7)	Bayless	1,000	500.00	300.00
(8)	Berry	1,000	500.00	300.00
(9)	Boles	1,000	500.00	300.00
(10)	Brashear	1,000	500.00	300.00
(11)	Brooks (Los Angeles)	1,000	500.00	300.00
(12)	Brooks (Oakland)	1,000	500.00	300.00
(13)	Brown	1,000	500.00	300.00
(14)	Burrell	1,000	500.00	300.00
(15)	Butler	1,000	500.00	300.00
(16)	Carlisle	1,000	500.00	300.00
(17)	Carson	1,000	500.00	300.00
(18)	Castleton	1,000	500.00	300.00
(19)	Chadbourne	1,000	500.00	300.00
(20)	Check	1,000	500.00	300.00
(21)	Core	1,000	500.00	300.00
(22)	Corhan	1,000	500.00	300.00
(23)	Coy	1,000	500.00	300.00
(24)	Daley	1,000	500.00	300.00
(25)	Dillon	1,000	500.00	300.00
(26)	Doane	1,000	500.00	300.00
(27)	Driscoll	1,000	500.00	300.00
(28)	Fisher	1,000	500.00	300.00
(29)	Flater	1,000	500.00	300.00
(30)	Gaddy	1,000	500.00	300.00
(31)	Gregg	1,000	500.00	300.00
(32)	Gregory	1,000	500.00	300.00
(33)	Harkness	1,000	500.00	300.00
(34)	Heitmuller	1,000	500.00	300.00
(35)	Henley	1,000	500.00	300.00
(36)	Hiester	1,000	500.00	300.00
(37)	Hoffman	1,000	500.00	300.00
(38)	Hogan	1,000	500.00	300.00
(39)	Hosp	1,000	500.00	300.00
(40)	Howley	1,000	500.00	300.00
(41)	Ireland	1,000	500.00	300.00
(42)	Johnson	1,000	500.00	300.00
(43)	Kane	1,000	500.00	300.00
(44)	Klawitter	1,000	500.00	300.00
(45)	Kreitz	1,000	500.00	300.00
(46)	Krueger	1,000	500.00	300.00
(47)	Leard	1,000	500.00	300.00
(48)	Leverencz	1,000	500.00	300.00
(49)	Lewis	1,000	500.00	300.00

(50)	Bill Lindsay	1,000	500.00	300.00
(51)	Litschi	1,000	500.00	300.00
(52)	Lober	1,000	500.00	300.00
(53)	Malarkey	1,000	500.00	300.00
(54)	Martinoni	1,000	500.00	300.00
(55)	McArdle	1,000	500.00	300.00
(56)	McCorry	1,000	500.00	300.00
(57)	McDowell	1,000	500.00	300.00
(58)	McIver	1,000	500.00	300.00
(59)	Metzger	1,000	500.00	300.00
(60)	Miller	1,000	500.00	300.00
(61)	Mundorf	1,000	500.00	300.00
(62)	Nagle	1,000	500.00	300.00
(63)	Noyes	1,000	500.00	300.00
(64)	Olmstead	1,000	500.00	300.00
(65)	O'Rourke	1,000	500.00	300.00
(66)	Page	1,000	500.00	300.00
(67)	Parkins	1,000	500.00	300.00
(68)	Patterson (Oakland)	1,000	500.00	300.00
(69)	Patterson (Vernon)	1,000	500.00	300.00
(70)	Pernoll	1,000	500.00	300.00
(71)	Powell	1,000	500.00	300.00
(72)	Price	1,000	500.00	300.00
(73)	Raftery	1,000	500.00	300.00
(74)	Raleigh	1,000	500.00	300.00
(75)	Rogers	1,000	500.00	300.00
(76)	Schmidt	1,000	500.00	300.00
(77)	Schwenk	1,000	500.00	300.00
(78)	Sheehan	1,000	500.00	300.00
(79)	Shinn	1,000	500.00	300.00
(80)	Slagle	1,000	500.00	300.00
(81)	Smith	1,000	500.00	300.00
(82)	Stone	1,000	500.00	300.00
(83)	Swain	1,000	500.00	300.00
(84)	Taylor	1,000	500.00	300.00
(85)	Tiedeman	1,000	500.00	300.00
(86)	Toner	1,000	500.00	300.00
(87)	Tozer	1,000	500.00	300.00
(88)	Van Buren	1,000	500.00	300.00
(89)	Williams	1,000	500.00	300.00
(90)	Zacher	1,000	500.00	300.00

1940 Hughes Frozen Confections Sacramento Solons

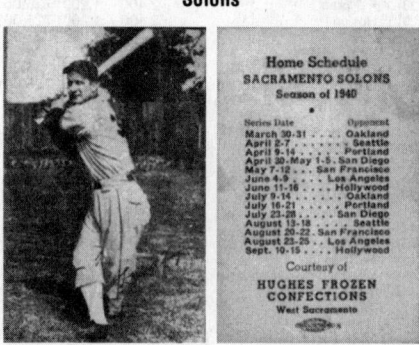

These borderless 2" x 3" black-and-white cards of the Sacramento Solons can be found in two versions, either blank-backed or with the 1940 Solons Pacific Coast League schedule printed on back. Fronts featured action poses with a facsimile autograph.

		NM	EX	VG
Complete Set (20):		8,250	4,125	2,475
Common Player:		450.00	220.00	135.00
(1)	Mel Almada	450.00	220.00	135.00
(2)	Frank Asbell	450.00	220.00	135.00
(3)	Larry Barton	450.00	220.00	135.00
(4)	Robert Blattner	450.00	220.00	135.00
(5)	Bennie Borgmann	450.00	220.00	135.00
(6)	Tony Freitas	450.00	220.00	135.00
(7)	Art Garibaldi	450.00	220.00	135.00
(8)	Jim Grilk	450.00	220.00	135.00
(9)	Gene Handley	450.00	220.00	135.00
(10)	Oscar Judd	450.00	220.00	135.00
(11)	Lynn King	450.00	220.00	135.00
(12)	Norbert Kleinke	450.00	220.00	135.00
(13)	Max Marshall	450.00	220.00	135.00
(14)	William McLaughlin	450.00	220.00	135.00
(15)	Bruce Ogrodowski	450.00	220.00	135.00
(16)	Franich Riel	450.00	220.00	135.00
(17)	Bill Schmidt	450.00	220.00	135.00
(18)	Melvin Wasley	450.00	220.00	135.00
(19)	Chet Wieczorek	450.00	220.00	135.00
(20)	Deb Williams	450.00	220.00	135.00

1957 Hygrade Meats Seattle Rainiers

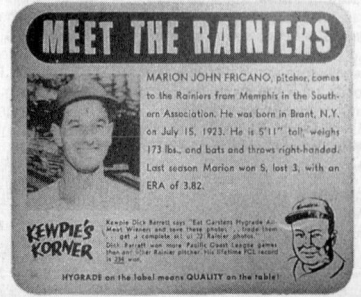

While the front of the cards mentions a complete set of 22 cards, only a dozen have been checklisted to date. The round-cornered cards measure 4-1/2" x 3-3/4" and are printed in red on white. Backs are blank. The cards feature only players of the Pacific Coast League Seattle Rainiers. The cards are unnumbered.

		NM	EX	VG
Common Player:		400.00	200.00	120.00
(1)	Dick Aylward	400.00	200.00	120.00
(2)	Bob Balcena	400.00	200.00	120.00
(3)	Jim Dyck	400.00	200.00	120.00
(4)	Marion Fricano	400.00	200.00	120.00
(5)	Bill Glynn	400.00	200.00	120.00
(6)	Larry Jansen	400.00	200.00	120.00
(7)	Bill Kennedy	400.00	200.00	120.00
(8)	Jack Lohrke	400.00	200.00	120.00
(9)	Frank O'Doul	800.00	400.00	240.00
(10)	Ray Orteig	400.00	200.00	120.00
(11)	Joe Taylor	400.00	200.00	120.00
(12)	Morrie (Maury) Wills	800.00	400.00	240.00

I

1912 Imperial Tobacco (C46)

This minor league set, issued in 1912 by the Imperial Tobacco Co., is the only tobacco baseball set issued in Canada. Designated as C46 in the American Card Catalog, each sepia-toned card measures 1-1/2" x 2-5/8" and features a distinctive card design that pictures the player inside an oval surrounded by a simulated woodgrain background featuring a bat, ball and glove in the borders. The player's last name appears in capital letters in a panel beneath the oval. (An exception is the card of James Murray, whose caption includes both first and last names.) The backs include the player's name and team at the top, followed by a brief biography. The 90 subjects in the set are members of the eight teams in the Eastern League (Rochester, Toronto, Buffalo, Newark, Providence, Baltimore, Montreal and Jersey City), even though the card backs refer to it as the International League. The set contains many players with major league experience, including Hall of Famers Joe Kelley and Joe "Iron Man" McGinnity.

		NM	EX	VG
Complete Set (90):		13,000	6,500	4,000
Common Player:		150.00	75.00	40.00
1	William O'Hara	180.00	90.00	55.00
2	James McGinley	160.00	80.00	50.00
3	"Frenchy" LeClaire	150.00	75.00	40.00
4	John White	150.00	75.00	40.00
5	James Murray	150.00	75.00	40.00
6	Joe Ward	150.00	75.00	40.00
7	Whitey Alperman	150.00	75.00	40.00
8	"Natty" Nattress	150.00	75.00	40.00
9	Fred Sline	150.00	75.00	40.00
10	Royal Rock	150.00	75.00	40.00
11	Ray Demmitt	150.00	75.00	40.00
12	"Butcher Boy" Schmidt	150.00	75.00	40.00
13	Samuel Frock	150.00	75.00	40.00
14	Fred Burchell	150.00	75.00	40.00
15	Jack Kelley	150.00	75.00	40.00
16	Frank Barberich	150.00	75.00	40.00
17	Frank Corridon	150.00	75.00	40.00
18	"Doc" Adkins	150.00	75.00	40.00
19	Jack Dunn	150.00	75.00	40.00
20	James Walsh	150.00	75.00	40.00
21	Charles Hanford	150.00	75.00	40.00
22	Dick Rudolph	150.00	75.00	40.00
23	Curt Elston	150.00	75.00	40.00
24	Phil Silton (Sitton)	150.00	75.00	40.00
25	Charlie French	150.00	75.00	40.00
26	John Ganzel	150.00	75.00	40.00
27	Joe Kelley	850.00	420.00	250.00
28	Benny Meyers	150.00	75.00	40.00
29	George Schirm	150.00	75.00	40.00
30	William Purtell	150.00	75.00	40.00
31	Bayard Sharpe	150.00	75.00	40.00
32	Tony Smith	150.00	75.00	40.00
33	John Lush	150.00	75.00	40.00
34	William Collins	150.00	75.00	40.00
35	Art Phelan	150.00	75.00	40.00
36	Edward Phelps	150.00	75.00	40.00
37	"Rube" Vickers	150.00	75.00	40.00
38	Cy Seymour	150.00	75.00	40.00
39	"Shadow" Carroll	150.00	75.00	40.00

40	Jake Gettman	150.00	75.00	40.00
41	Luther Taylor	400.00	200.00	120.00
42	Walter Justis	150.00	75.00	40.00
43	Robert Fisher	150.00	75.00	40.00
44	Fred Parent	150.00	75.00	40.00
45	James Dygert	150.00	75.00	40.00
46	Johnnie Butler	150.00	75.00	40.00
47	Fred Mitchell	150.00	75.00	40.00
48	Heinie Batch	150.00	75.00	40.00
49	Michael Corcoran	150.00	75.00	40.00
50	Edward Doescher	150.00	75.00	40.00
51	George Wheeler	150.00	75.00	40.00
52	Elijah Jones	150.00	75.00	40.00
53	Fred Truesdale	150.00	75.00	40.00
54	Fred Beebe	150.00	75.00	40.00
55	Louis Brockett	150.00	75.00	40.00
56	Robt. Wells	150.00	75.00	40.00
57	"Lew" McAllister	150.00	75.00	40.00
58	Ralph Stroud	150.00	75.00	40.00
59	James Manser	150.00	75.00	40.00
60	Jim Holmes	150.00	75.00	40.00
61	Rube Dessau	150.00	75.00	40.00
62	Fred Jacklitsch	150.00	75.00	40.00
63	Stanley Graham	150.00	75.00	40.00
64	Noah Henline	150.00	75.00	40.00
65	"Chick" Gandil	1,300	650.00	400.00
66	Tom Hughes	150.00	75.00	40.00
67	Joseph Delehanty	150.00	75.00	40.00
68	Geo. Pierce	150.00	75.00	40.00
69	Bob Gaunt (Gantt)	150.00	75.00	40.00
70	Edward Fitzpatrick	150.00	75.00	40.00
71	Wyatt Lee	150.00	75.00	40.00
72	John Kissinger	150.00	75.00	40.00
73	William Malarkey	150.00	75.00	40.00
74	William Byers	150.00	75.00	40.00
75	George Simmons	150.00	75.00	40.00
76	Daniel Moeller	150.00	75.00	40.00
77	Joseph McGinnity	850.00	420.00	250.00
78	Alex Hardy	150.00	75.00	40.00
79	Bob Holmes	150.00	75.00	40.00
80	William Baxter	150.00	75.00	40.00
81	Edward Spencer	150.00	75.00	40.00
82	Bradley Kocher	150.00	75.00	40.00
83	Robert Shaw	150.00	75.00	40.00
84	Joseph Yeager	150.00	75.00	40.00
85	Anthony Carlo	150.00	75.00	40.00
86	William Abstein	150.00	75.00	40.00
87	Tim Jordan	150.00	75.00	40.00
88	Dick Breen	150.00	75.00	40.00
89	Tom McCarty	150.00	75.00	46.00
90	Ed Curtis	160.00	80.00	50.00

1923 Indianapolis Indians Foldout

Twenty-one players and staff are featured in this black-and-white accordian-fold souvenir. Each of the cards measures about 2" x 3".

	NM	EX	VG
Complete Foldout:	650.00	325.00	195.00
(Checklist not available.)			

1950 Indianapolis Indians Team Issue

Action poses are featured in this set of team-issue 8" x 10" black-and-white glossy photos. Players are identified by a facsimile autograph on front. It is unknown whether the checklist is complete. The Indians were the Class AAA American Association affiliate of the Pittsburgh Pirates in 1950.

		NM	EX	VG
Common Player:		30.00	15.00	9.00
(1)	Monty Basgall	30.00	15.00	9.00
(2)	Ted Beard	30.00	15.00	9.00
(3)	Gus Bell	40.00	20.00	12.00
(4)	Eddie Bockman	30.00	15.00	9.00
(5)	Dale Coogan	30.00	15.00	9.00
(6)	"Del" Dallessandro	30.00	15.00	9.00
(7)	Nanny Fernandez	30.00	15.00	9.00
(8)	Eddy Fitz Gerald	30.00	15.00	9.00
(9)	Al Grunwald	30.00	15.00	9.00
(10)	Frank Kalin	30.00	15.00	9.00
(11)	Paul LaPalme	30.00	15.00	9.00
(12)	Royce Lint	30.00	15.00	9.00
(13)	Al Lopez	45.00	22.00	13.50
(14)	Forrest Main	30.00	15.00	9.00
(15)	Danny O'Connell	30.00	15.00	9.00
(16)	Frank Papish	30.00	15.00	9.00
(17)	Eddie Stevens	30.00	15.00	9.00
(18)	Leo Wells	30.00	15.00	9.00

J

1952 Jamestown Falcons Team Issue

CHARLEY LAU

This Class D farm club of the Detroit Tigers won the 1952 Pony (Pennsylvania-Ontario-New York) League playoffs. Like other issues of Globe Printing, the roughly 2-1/4" x 3-3/8" cards are black-and-white with blank backs and the player name in a white strip at bottom-front. A light green album slotted to hold the cards is known for this issue.

		NM	EX	VG
Complete Set (18):		800.00	400.00	240.00
Common Player:		60.00	30.00	18.00
Album:		100.00	50.00	30.00
(1)	Dick Barr	60.00	30.00	18.00
(2)	Jerry Davie	60.00	30.00	18.00
(3)	John Fickinger	60.00	30.00	18.00
(4)	Paul Franks	60.00	30.00	18.00
(5)	Red Gookin	60.00	30.00	18.00
(6)	Bill Harbour	60.00	30.00	18.00
(7)	Dick Hatfield	60.00	30.00	18.00
(8)	Charley Lau	90.00	45.00	30.00
(9)	Dick Lisiecki	60.00	30.00	18.00
(10)	Tony Lupien	60.00	30.00	18.00
(11)	Joe Melago	60.00	30.00	18.00
(12)	Claude Mitschele	60.00	30.00	18.00
(13)	Bob Neebling	60.00	30.00	18.00
(14)	Fran Oneto	60.00	30.00	18.00
(15)	George Risley	60.00	30.00	18.00
(16)	Bob Szabo	60.00	30.00	18.00
(17)	Ken Walters	60.00	30.00	18.00
(18)	Gabby Witucki	60.00	30.00	18.00

1909 Walter Johnson "Weiser Wonder" Postcards

This issue-date(s) on these postcards are conjectural. Two distinct styles are known using versions of the same full-length portrait of Johnson in a studio standing on an ornate rug in front of a curtain depicting drapes, urn, etc. Johnson is wearing the uniform of the Weiser (Idaho) semi-pro team for whom he pitched prior to beginning his Hall of Fame career with the Washington Senators in 1907. The earlier of the cards utilizes the undivided-back postcard format which was current only until 1908. It is printed in sepia tones and identifies Johnson as the "Weiser Wonder" in a line of white type at the bottom. A later version, on a post-1908 divided-back postcard, is printed in bluetone. The card identifies him in a white strip at bottom. It is likely one or both of these cards continued to be produced or at least available after Johnson became a major league star. Both cards are in standard 3-1/2" x 5-1/2" format.

	NM	EX	VG
Walter Johnson (Bluetone)	2,500	1,250	750.00
Walter Johnson (Sepia)	2,500	1,250	750.00

1967 Jones Dairy Buffalo Bison All-Stars

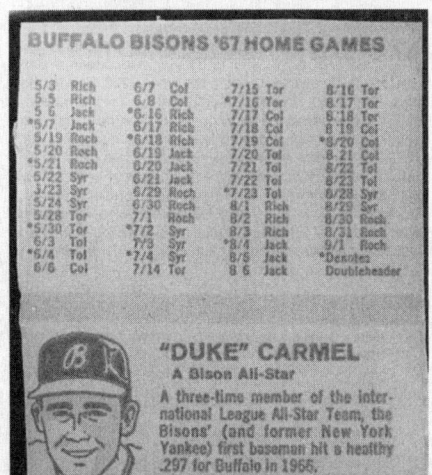

Apparently printed as part of a milk carton, only a single player is known for this issue. Printed in red and yellow, the piece includes a 1967 team home schedule, a player drawing and career highlights in a 2-3/4" x 3-1/8" format. Other players may yet surface.

		NM	EX	VG
(1)	"Duke" Carmel	80.00	40.00	25.00

K

1962 Kahn's Wieners Atlanta Crackers

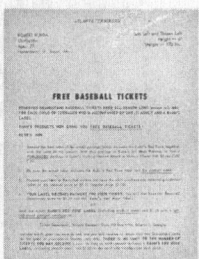

Kahn's made a single foray into the minor league market in 1962 with a separate 24-card set of Atlanta Crackers. The cards feature the same basic format, 3-1/4" x 4", borderless black-and-white photos with a Kahn's ad message in a white panel below the picture, as the major league issue. The backs are slightly different, having a free ticket offer in place of the player stats. Atlanta was the top farm club of the St. Louis Cardinals in 1962. The most famous alumnus in the set is Tim McCarver.

		NM	EX	VG
Complete Set (24):		2,000	1,000	600.00
Common Player:		80.00	40.00	24.00
(1)	James (Jimmy) Edward Beauchamp	80.00	40.00	24.00
(2)	Gerald Peter Buchek	80.00	40.00	24.00
(3)	Robert Burda	80.00	40.00	24.00
(4)	Hal Deitz	80.00	40.00	24.00
(5)	Robert John Duliba	80.00	40.00	24.00
(6)	Harry Michael Fanok	80.00	40.00	24.00
(7)	Phil Gagliano	80.00	40.00	24.00
(8)	John Glenn	80.00	40.00	24.00
(9)	Leroy Gregory	80.00	40.00	24.00
(10)	Richard (Dick) Henry Hughes	80.00	40.00	24.00
(11)	John Charles Kucks, Jr.	80.00	40.00	24.00
(12)	Johnny Joe Lewis	80.00	40.00	24.00
(13)	James (Mac - Timmie) Timothy McCarver	175.00	87.50	52.50
(14)	Robert F. Milliken	80.00	40.00	24.00
(15)	Joe Morgan	80.00	40.00	24.00
(16)	Ronald Charles Plaza	80.00	40.00	24.00
(17)	Bob Sadowski	80.00	40.00	24.00
(18)	Jim Saul	80.00	40.00	24.00
(19)	Willard Schmidt	80.00	40.00	24.00
(20)	Joe Schultz	80.00	40.00	24.00
(21)	Thomas Michael (Mike) Shannon	125.00	62.50	37.50
(22)	Paul Louis Toth	80.00	40.00	24.00
(23)	Andrew Lou Vickery	80.00	40.00	24.00
(24)	Fred Dwight Whitfield	80.00	40.00	24.00

1939 Kimball Automobile Trois-Rivieres Photocards

This set of 18 postcards and an accompanying envelope features the player of the Trois-Rivieres (Three Rivers) club of the Quebec Provincial League. Until 1940, the six-team QPL was not a part of organized baseball's minor league system. Several of the players were either former or future minor leaguers within OB. Paul "Pepper" Martin in the set is not the Pepper Martin of the contemporary, Gas House Gang St. Louis Cardinals. The black-and-white cards are about postcard-size and blank-backed, printed on sturdy card stock.

		NM	EX	VG
Complete Set (18):		1,350	675.00	400.00
Common Player:		90.00	45.00	25.00
(1)	George Andrews	90.00	45.00	25.00
(2)	Norm Bell	90.00	45.00	25.00
(3)	Henry Block	90.00	45.00	25.00
(4)	Addie Copple	90.00	45.00	25.00
(5)	Phil Corrigan	90.00	45.00	25.00
(6)	Joe Dickinson	90.00	45.00	25.00
(7)	Bill Hoffner	90.00	45.00	25.00
(8)	Jack Leroy	90.00	45.00	25.00
(9)	Leo Maloney	90.00	45.00	25.00
(10)	Martin	90.00	45.00	25.00
(11)	McGurk	90.00	45.00	25.00
(12)	Connie O'Leary	90.00	45.00	25.00
(13)	James Pickens	90.00	45.00	25.00
(14)	Dutch Prather	90.00	45.00	25.00
(15)	Jamie Skelton	90.00	45.00	25.00
(16)	Byron Speece	90.00	45.00	25.00
(17)	Gene Sullivan	90.00	45.00	25.00
(18)	Grover Wearshing	90.00	45.00	25.00

1952 Knowles Service Stations Stockton Ports

Contemporary, and sharing a format with the many Globe minor league issues of the early '50s, this set of Stockton Ports (Class C California League) cards carries the advertising of Knowles Service Stations. The blank-backed, black-and-white cards measure 2-1/4" x 3-1/2" and are unnumbered. Among the players is a Japanese national whose card is in strong demand.

		NM	EX	VG
	Complete Set (11):	1,000	500.00	300.00
	Common Player:	90.00	45.00	25.00
	Album:	150.00	75.00	45.00
(1)	Wayne Clary	90.00	45.00	25.00
(2)	Harry Clements	90.00	45.00	25.00
(3)	John Crocco	90.00	45.00	25.00
(4)	Tony Freitas	90.00	45.00	25.00
(5)	Fibber Hirayama	250.00	125.00	75.00
(6)	Dave Mann	90.00	45.00	25.00
(7)	Larry Mann	90.00	45.00	25.00
(8)	Hank Moreno	90.00	45.00	25.00
(9)	Frank Romero	90.00	45.00	25.00
(10)	Chuck Thomas	90.00	45.00	25.00
(11)	Bud Watkins	90.00	45.00	25.00

1922-23 Kolb's Mothers' Bread Pins (PB4)

Over a two-year period, Kolb's bakery sponsored a series of pins featuring members of the Reading (Pa.) Aces of the International League. The pins are 7/8" in diameter with black-and-white portraits on a white background. The player name (last name only, usually) and position are indicated beneath the photo. Above the photo, in red, is the sponsor's identification. The pins issued in 1922 have "MOTHERS'" in all capital letters; the 1923 pins have "Mothers'" in upper and lower case.

		NM	EX	VG
	Complete Set (32):	1,700	850.00	500.00
	Common Player:	125.00	65.00	40.00
(1)	Spencer Abbott	125.00	65.00	40.00
(2)	Charlie Babington	125.00	65.00	40.00
(3)	Bill Barrett	125.00	65.00	40.00
(4)	R. Bates	125.00	65.00	40.00
(5)	Chief Bender	200.00	100.00	60.00
(6)	Myrl Brown	125.00	65.00	40.00
(7)	Fred Carts	125.00	65.00	40.00
(8)	Nig Clarke	125.00	65.00	40.00
(9)	Tom Connelly	125.00	65.00	40.00
(10)	Gus Getz	125.00	65.00	40.00
(11)	Frank Gilhooley	125.00	65.00	40.00
(12)	Ray Gordonier	125.00	65.00	40.00
(13)	Hinkey Haines	150.00	75.00	45.00
(14)	Francis Karpp	125.00	65.00	40.00
(15)	Joseph Kelley	125.00	65.00	40.00
(16)	Andrew Kotch	125.00	65.00	40.00
(17)	William Lightner	125.00	65.00	40.00
(18)	Byrd Lynn	125.00	65.00	40.00
(19)	Al Mamaux	125.00	65.00	40.00
(20)	Martin	125.00	65.00	40.00
(21)	Ralph Miller	125.00	65.00	40.00
(22)	Otto Pahlman	125.00	65.00	40.00
(23)	Sam Post	125.00	65.00	40.00
(24)	Al Schact	150.00	75.00	45.00
(25)	John Scott	125.00	65.00	40.00
(26)	Walt Smallwood	125.00	65.00	40.00
(27)	Ross Swartz	125.00	65.00	40.00
(28)	Fred Thomas	125.00	65.00	40.00
(29)	Myles Thomas	125.00	65.00	40.00
(30)	Walt Tragesser	125.00	65.00	40.00
(31)	Washburn	125.00	65.00	40.00
(32)	Walter Wolfe	125.00	65.00	40.00

L

1952 La Patrie Album Sportif

Ballplayers from Montreal of the International League and several of the teams from the Class C Provincial (Quebec)

League were featured in a series of colorized photos printed in the Sunday rotogravure section of "La Patrie" newspaper. The photos are approximately 11" x 15-3/8" with red left and bottom trim and a vertical blue stripe at far left. Player information is printed in black and is in French. A number of the players went on to stardom with the Brooklyn and/or Los Angeles Dodgers.

		NM	EX	VG
	Complete Set (18):	650.00	325.00	175.00
	Common Player:	25.00	12.50	7.50
(1)	Bob Alexander	25.00	12.50	7.50
(2)	Hampton Coleman	25.00	12.50	7.50
(3)	Walter Fiala	25.00	12.50	7.50
(4)	Jim Gilliams (Gilliam)	45.00	22.50	13.50
(5)	Tom Hackett	25.00	12.50	7.50
(6)	Don Hoak	35.00	17.50	10.00
(7)	Herbie Lash	25.00	12.50	7.50
(8)	Tommy Lasorda	150.00	75.00	45.00
(9)	Mal Mallette	25.00	12.50	7.50
(10)	Georges Maranda (Aug. 17)	25.00	12.50	7.50
(11)	Carmen Mauro	25.00	12.50	7.50
(12)	Solly Mohn	25.00	12.50	7.50
(13)	Jacques Monette	25.00	12.50	7.50
(14)	Johnny Podres	75.00	37.50	22.50
(15)	Ed Roebuck	25.00	12.50	7.50
(16)	Charlie Thompson	25.00	12.50	7.50
(17)	Don Thompson	25.00	12.50	7.50
(18)	John Wingo	25.00	12.50	7.50

1928-1932 La Presse Baseball Rotos

Players from Montreal's team in the International League (and occasionally other major and minor league teams' stars) were featured in a series of photos between 1928-32 in the Saturday rotogravure section of Montreal's "La Presse" newspaper. The format remained fairly consistent over the years. Large hand-tinted player photos were featured on the approximately 11" x 17-3/4" pages, with writeup in French below. On back was whatever features and ads happened to appear on the following page. The known baseball player list is presented here in chronological order. Other athletes were also featured in the issue, but are not listed here. Gaps have been left in the numbering to better accommodate future additions to this list.

		NM	EX	VG
	Common Player:	60.00	30.00	20.00
	1928	.00	.00	.00
(2)	Aldrick Gaudette (May 19)	60.00	30.00	20.00
(4)	Robert Shawkey (June 2)	80.00	40.00	24.00
(5)	Lachine team photo, portraits of starting nine (June 9)	60.00	30.00	20.00
(6)	Roy Buckalew, Frank Dunagan, Chester Fowler, Thomas Gulley, Peter Radwan, Richard Smith (June 16)	60.00	30.00	20.00
(7)	Seymour Edward Bailey (June 23)	60.00	30.00	20.00
(8)	Wilson F. Fewster (June 30)	60.00	30.00	20.00
(10)	Tom Daly (July 14)	60.00	30.00	20.00
(14)	Red Holt (Aug. 11)	60.00	30.00	20.00
(17)	George Herman Ruth (Oct. 13)	750.00	375.00	225.00
(20)	Johnny Prud'homme (Nov. 3)	60.00	30.00	20.00
	1929	.00	.00	.00
(2)	Walter Paul Gautreau (April 13)	60.00	30.00	20.00
(4)	Herb Thormahlen (April 27)	60.00	30.00	20.00
(9)	Elon Hogsett (July 13)	60.00	30.00	20.00
(12)	Robert M. "Lefty" Grove (Oct. 19)	200.00	100.00	60.00

		NM	EX	VG
(15)	Philadelphia A's Stars (Mickey Cochrane, Jimmie Foxx, Connie Mack, Al Simmons, Rube Walberg, Bing Miller) (Nov. 16)	90.00	45.00	27.00
	1930	.00	.00	.00
(3)	Martin Griffin, John Pomorski, Arthur Smith, Herb Thormahlen (May 31)	60.00	30.00	20.00
(4)	James Calleran, Edward Conley, Lee Head, Jimmy Ripple (June 7)	60.00	30.00	20.00
(7)	Del Bissonette (June 28)	60.00	30.00	20.00
(9)	Joe Hauser (July 12)	75.00	37.00	22.00
(14)	Gowell Sylvester Claset (Sept. 13)	60.00	30.00	20.00
(17)	Hack Wilson (Oct. 11)	200.00	100.00	60.00
	1931	.00	.00	.00
(2)	Chuck Klein (May 30)	175.00	87.00	52.00
(3)	Jocko Conlan (June 6)	100.00	50.00	30.00
(5)	Lee Head (June 20)	60.00	30.00	20.00
(7)	Jimmy Ripple (July 4)	60.00	30.00	20.00
(9)	Sol Mishkin (July 18)	60.00	30.00	20.00
(11)	Walter Brown (Aug. 15)	60.00	30.00	20.00
(15)	Johnny Allen, Frank Barnes, Guy Cantrell, Ken Strong (Nov. 14)	60.00	30.00	20.00
(16)	John Pepper Martin (Nov. 21)	80.00	40.00	24.00
	1932	.00	.00	.00
(2)	Johnny Grabowski (May 28)	60.00	30.00	20.00
(3)	Charles Sullivan (June 4)	60.00	30.00	20.00
(5)	Walter "Doc" Gautreau (June 18)	60.00	30.00	20.00
(6)	John Clancy (June 25)	60.00	30.00	20.00
(7)	Buck Walters (July 2)	75.00	37.00	22.00
(8)	Bill McAfee (July 9)	60.00	30.00	20.00
(9)	George Puccinelli (July 16)	60.00	30.00	20.00
(11)	Buck Crouse (Aug. 6)	60.00	30.00	20.00
(12)	Ollie Carnegie (Aug. 13)	60.00	30.00	20.00
(13)	Leo Mangum (Aug. 20)	60.00	30.00	20.00
(17)	Roy Parmelee (Nov. 19)	60.00	30.00	20.00
	(Dates of issue not confirmed.)			
	Dan Howley	60.00	30.00	20.00

1952 Laval Dairy Provincial League

This scarce Canadian minor league issue includes only players from the Class C Provincial League, centered in Quebec. The black-and-white cards are blank-backed and measure 1-3/4" x 2-1/2". The player name, position, date and place of birth and card number is in French. Teams represented in the set are Quebec (Braves), St. Jean (Pirates), Three Rivers (Independent), Drummondville (Senators), Granby (Phillies) and Ste. Hyacinthe (Philadelphia A's).

		NM	EX	VG
	Complete Set (114):	8,000	4,000	2,500
	Common Player:	70.00	35.00	20.00
1	Georges McQuinn	70.00	35.00	20.00
2	Cliff Statham	70.00	35.00	20.00
3	Frank Wilson	70.00	35.00	20.00
4	Frank Neri	70.00	35.00	20.00
5	Georges Maranda	70.00	35.00	20.00
6	Richard "Dick" Cordeiro	70.00	35.00	20.00
7	Roger McCardell	70.00	35.00	20.00
8	Joseph Janiak	70.00	35.00	20.00
9	Herbert Shankman	70.00	35.00	20.00
10	Joe Subbiondo	70.00	35.00	20.00
11	Jack Brenner	70.00	35.00	20.00
12	Donald Buchanan	70.00	35.00	20.00
13	Robert Smith	70.00	35.00	20.00
14	Raymond Lague	70.00	35.00	20.00
15	Mike Fandozzi	70.00	35.00	20.00
16	Dick Moler	70.00	35.00	20.00
17	Edward Bazydio	70.00	35.00	20.00
18	Danny Mazurek	70.00	35.00	20.00
19	Edwin Charles	70.00	35.00	20.00
20	Jack Nullaney	70.00	35.00	20.00
21	Bob Bolan	70.00	35.00	20.00
22	Bob Long	70.00	35.00	20.00
23	Cleo Lewright	70.00	35.00	20.00
24	Herb Taylor	70.00	35.00	20.00
25	Frankie Gaeta	70.00	35.00	20.00
26	Bill Truitt	70.00	35.00	20.00
27	Jean Prats	70.00	35.00	20.00
28	Tex Taylor	70.00	35.00	20.00
29	Ron Delbianco	70.00	35.00	20.00
30	Joe DiLorenzo	70.00	35.00	20.00
31	Johnny Paszek	70.00	35.00	20.00
32	Ken Suess	70.00	35.00	20.00
33	Harry Sims	70.00	35.00	20.00
34	William Jackson	70.00	35.00	20.00
35	Jerry Mayers	70.00	35.00	20.00
36	Gordon Maltzberger	70.00	35.00	20.00
37	Gerry Cabana	70.00	35.00	20.00
38	Gary Rutkey	70.00	35.00	20.00
39	Ken Hatcher	70.00	35.00	20.00

40	Vincent Cosenza	70.00	35.00	20.00
41	Edward Yaeger	70.00	35.00	20.00
42	Jimmy Orr	70.00	35.00	20.00
43	Johnny Di Matino	70.00	35.00	20.00
44	Lenny Wisneski	70.00	35.00	20.00
45	Pete Caniglia	70.00	35.00	20.00
46	Guy Coleman	70.00	35.00	20.00
47	Herb Fleischer	70.00	35.00	20.00
48	Charles Yahrling	70.00	35.00	20.00
49	Roger Bedard	70.00	35.00	20.00
50	Al Barillari	70.00	35.00	20.00
51	Hugh Mulcahy	100.00	50.00	30.00
52	Vincent Canepa	70.00	35.00	20.00
53	Bob Loranger	70.00	35.00	20.00
54	Georges Carpentier	70.00	35.00	20.00
55	Bill Hamilton	70.00	35.00	20.00
56	Hector Lopez	130.00	70.00	40.00
57	Joel Taylor	70.00	35.00	20.00
58	Alonzo Brathwaite	200.00	10.00	60.00
59	Carl McQuillen	70.00	35.00	20.00
60	Robert Trice	70.00	35.00	20.00
61	John Dworak	70.00	35.00	20.00
62	Al Pinkston	100.00	50.00	30.00
63	William Shannon	70.00	35.00	20.00
64	Stanley Wotychowisz	70.00	35.00	20.00
65	Roger Herbert	70.00	35.00	20.00
66	Troy Spencer	70.00	35.00	20.00
67	Johnny Rohan	70.00	35.00	20.00
68	John Sosh	70.00	35.00	20.00
69	Ramon Mason	70.00	35.00	20.00
70	Tom Smith	70.00	35.00	20.00
71	Douglas McBean	70.00	35.00	20.00
72	Bill Babik	70.00	35.00	20.00
73	Dante Cozzi	70.00	35.00	20.00
74	Melville Doxtater	70.00	35.00	20.00
75	William Gilray	70.00	35.00	20.00
76	Armando Diaz	70.00	35.00	20.00
77	Ackroyd Smith	70.00	35.00	20.00
78	Germain Pizarro	70.00	35.00	20.00
79	Jim Heap	70.00	35.00	20.00
80	Herbert Crompton	70.00	35.00	20.00
81	Howard Bodell	70.00	35.00	20.00
82	Andre Schreiser	70.00	35.00	20.00
83	John Wingo	70.00	35.00	20.00
84	Salvatore Arduini	70.00	35.00	20.00
85	Fred Pallito	70.00	35.00	20.00
86	Aaron Osofsky	70.00	35.00	20.00
87	Jack DiGrace	70.00	35.00	20.00
88	Alphonso Chico Girard (Gerrard)	70.00	35.00	20.00
89	Manuel Trabous	70.00	35.00	20.00
90	Tom Barnes	70.00	35.00	20.00
91	Humberto Robinson	70.00	35.00	20.00
92	Jack Bukowatz	70.00	35.00	20.00
93	Marco Mainini	70.00	35.00	20.00
94	Claude St. Vincent	70.00	35.00	20.00
95	Fernand Brosseau	70.00	35.00	20.00
96	John Malangone	70.00	35.00	20.00
97	Pierre Nantel	70.00	35.00	20.00
98	Donald Stevens	70.00	35.00	20.00
99	Jim Prappas	70.00	35.00	20.00
100	Richard Fitzgerald	70.00	35.00	20.00
101	Yves Aubin	70.00	35.00	20.00
102	Frank Novosel	70.00	35.00	20.00
103	Tony Campos	70.00	35.00	20.00
104	Gelso Oviedo	70.00	35.00	20.00
105	Guly Becker	70.00	35.00	20.00
106	Aurelio Ala	70.00	35.00	20.00
107	Orlando Andux	70.00	35.00	20.00
108	Tom Hackett	70.00	35.00	20.00
109	Guillame Vargas	70.00	35.00	20.00
110	Fransisco Salfran	70.00	35.00	20.00
111	Jean-Marc Blais	70.00	35.00	20.00
112	Vince Pizzitola	70.00	35.00	20.00
113	John Olsen	70.00	35.00	20.00
114	Jacques Monette	70.00	35.00	20.00

1948 Los Angeles Angels Team Issue

A team-issued set sold in a paper envelope for $1 at the ballpark, these cards were produced by the same firm which published the team's yearbook, Pacific Coast Sports Publishing Co., of Los Angeles. The blank-backed cards measure 6-3/4" x 4-3/4" and are printed in black-and-white on thin cardboard with a semi-gloss front surface. Cards feature a facsimile player autograph on front, along with a posed action or portrait photo and complete major and minor league stats. The cards are listed in the American Card Catalog, along with the subsequent year's issue, as W725. Many of the players on this Pacific Coast League team were former or future Chicago Cubs. The unnumbered cards are checklisted here alphabetically.

		NM	EX	VG
Complete Set (26):		650.00	325.00	200.00
Common Player:		30.00	15.00	9.00
(1)	Cliff Aberson	30.00	15.00	9.00
(2)	Red Adams	30.00	15.00	9.00

(3)	John Adkins	30.00	15.00	9.00
(4)	Lee Anthony	30.00	15.00	9.00
(5)	Russ Bauers	30.00	15.00	9.00
(6)	Ora Burnett	30.00	15.00	9.00
(7)	Donald Carlsen	30.00	15.00	9.00
(8)	Dom Dallessandro	30.00	15.00	9.00
(9)	Cecil Garriott	30.00	15.00	9.00
(10)	Paul Gillespie	30.00	15.00	9.00
(11)	Al Glossop	30.00	15.00	9.00
(12)	Tom Hafey	30.00	15.00	9.00
(13)	Don Johnson	30.00	15.00	9.00
(14)	Bill Kelly	30.00	15.00	9.00
(15)	Hal Kleine	30.00	15.00	9.00
(16)	Walt Lanfranconi	30.00	15.00	9.00
(17)	Ed Lukon	30.00	15.00	9.00
(18)	Red Lynn	30.00	15.00	9.00
(19)	Eddie Malone	30.00	15.00	9.00
(20)	Len Merullo	30.00	15.00	9.00
(21)	Ralph Novotney	30.00	15.00	9.00
(22)	John Ostrowski	30.00	15.00	9.00
(23)	John Sanford	30.00	15.00	9.00
(24)	Ed Sauer	30.00	15.00	9.00
(25)	Bill Schuster	30.00	15.00	9.00
(26)	John Warner	30.00	15.00	9.00

1949 Los Angeles Angels Team Issue

Little changed in the second year of this team issue. Cards remained at 6-3/4" x 4-3/4" in format, printed black-and-white on semi-gloss cardboard with a blank back. Many of the players (and even some of the photos) were repeated from the previous year. The unnumbered cards are checklisted here in alphabetical order.

		NM	EX	VG
Complete Set (39):		1,000	500.00	300.00
Common Player:		30.00	15.00	9.00
(1)	Cliff Aberson	30.00	15.00	9.00
(2)	Donald Alfano	30.00	15.00	9.00
(3)	Quentin Altizer	30.00	15.00	9.00
(4)	Lee Anthony	30.00	15.00	9.00
(5)	Nels Burbrink	30.00	15.00	9.00
(6)	Smoky Burgess	75.00	37.50	22.00
(7)	Don Carlsen	30.00	15.00	9.00
(8)	Joe Damato	30.00	15.00	9.00
(9)	Bill Emmerich	30.00	15.00	9.00
(10)	Ken Gables	30.00	15.00	9.00
(11)	Cecil Garriott	30.00	15.00	9.00
(12)	Al Glossop	30.00	15.00	9.00
(13)	Gordon Goldsberry	30.00	15.00	9.00
(14)	Frank Gustine	30.00	15.00	9.00
(15)	Lee Handley	30.00	15.00	9.00
(16)	Alan Ihde	30.00	15.00	9.00
(17)	Bob Kelley (Announcer)	30.00	15.00	9.00
(18)	Bill Kelly	30.00	15.00	9.00
(19)	Bob Kelly	30.00	15.00	9.00
(20)	Walt Lanfranconi	30.00	15.00	9.00
(21)	Red Lynn	30.00	15.00	9.00
(22)	Clarence Maddern	30.00	15.00	9.00
(23)	Eddie Malone	30.00	15.00	9.00
(24)	Carmen Mauro	30.00	15.00	9.00
(25)	Booker McDaniels	75.00	37.50	22.00
(26)	Cal McLish	50.00	25.00	15.00
(27)	Butch Moran	30.00	15.00	9.00
(28)	Ralph Novotney	30.00	15.00	9.00
(29)	John Ostrowski	30.00	15.00	9.00
(30)	Bobby Rhawn	30.00	15.00	9.00
(31)	Bill Schuster	30.00	15.00	9.00
(32)	Pat Seerey	30.00	15.00	9.00
(33)	Bryan Stephens	30.00	15.00	9.00
(34)	Bob Sturgeon	30.00	15.00	9.00
(35)	Wayne Terwilliger	45.00	22.00	13.50
(36)	Gordon Van Dyke	30.00	15.00	9.00
(37)	John Warner	30.00	15.00	9.00
(38)	Don Watkins	30.00	15.00	9.00
(39)	Trainers, Bat Boys	30.00	15.00	9.00
	(Dickie Evans, Joe Liscio, Dave Flores, Billy Lund)			

1930-31 Lucke Badge & Button Baltimore Orioles Pins

These 7/8" diameter celluloid pinback buttons were produced by the Baltimore novelty firm of Lucke Badge & Button Co. Issued to honor fan favorites on their "Day," the buttons have black-and-white portrait photos at center, surrounded by a white rim. At top is the player name, at bottom is the team name and year. A paper label inside the back of the button identifies the maker and includes a union label.

	NM	EX	VG
Joe Hauser (1930)	300.00	150.00	90.00
Don Heffner (1931)	200.00	100.00	60.00

M

1910 Mascot Gum Pins

Only players from the Eastern League champion Rochester Bronchos are known on these 7/8" diameter pinback buttons. Fronts have a black-and-white player photo on a blue background with the player's last name at left and "ROCHESTER" at right. A paper insert on the reverse advertises "Ball Player's Buttons Free With Mascot Gum." This checklist may not be complete.

		NM	EX	VG
Common Player:		250.00	125.00	80.00
(1)	Alperman	250.00	125.00	80.00
(2)	Anderson	250.00	125.00	80.00
(3)	Heinie Batch	250.00	125.00	80.00
(4)	Blair	250.00	125.00	80.00
(5)	Holmes	250.00	125.00	80.00
(6)	Lafitte	250.00	125.00	80.00
(7)	Manning	250.00	125.00	80.00
(8)	McConnell	250.00	125.00	80.00
(9)	Moeller	250.00	125.00	80.00
(10)	Moran	250.00	125.00	80.00
(11)	Osborn	250.00	125.00	80.00
(12)	Don Carlos Ragon (Ragon)	250.00	125.00	80.00
(13)	Savidge	250.00	125.00	80.00
(14)	Simmons	250.00	125.00	80.00
(15)	Spencer	250.00	125.00	80.00
(16)	Tooley	250.00	125.00	80.00
(17)	Ward	250.00	125.00	80.00

1952 May Co. Chuck Stevens Premium

The date given is speculative, about midway through the player's term with the Hollywood Stars of the Pacific Coast League. The 4-1/2" x 6" blank-backed black-and-white card features a portrait of what the caption at bottom calls the "popular first baseman." The caption also calls the piece a "MAY CO. 'Back To School' Party Souvenir Photo." The cards are often found bearing the player's autograph, presumably obtained at the event.

	NM	EX	VG
Chuck Stevens	75.00	40.00	25.00

1960s-70s J.D. McCarthy Postcards

For details of J.D. McCarthy's prolific body of black-and-white player postcards, see the introductory material in the vintage major league section.

Common Player: $1-3

SPOKANE INDIANS
(1)	Roy Hartsfield

TOLEDO MUD HENS
(1)	Loren Babe
(2)	Stan Bahnsen
(3)	Bill Bethea
(4)	Joe Cherry
(5)	Horace Clark

(6)	Wayne Comer			
(7)	Jack Cullen (2)			
(8)	Jack Curtis (2)			
(9)	Gil Downs			
(10)	Joe Faraci			
(11)	Frank Fernandez			
(12)	Mike Ferraro			
(13)	Mickey Harrington			
(14)	Mike Hegan			
(15)	Jim Horsford (2)			
(16)	Dick Hughes			
(17)	Elvio Jiminez (2)			
(18)	Robert Lasko			
(19)	Artie Lopez			
(20)	Roy Majtyka			
(21)	Tom Martz			
(22)	Ed Merritt (2)			
(23)	Archie Moore (2)			
(24)	Al Moran			
(25)	Bobby Murcer			
(26)	Tony Przybycien			
(27)	Bill Roman			
(28)	Bob Schmidt (2)			
(29)	Tom Shafer			
(30)	Billy Shantz			
(31)	Shantz-Senger-Babe			
(32)	Bob Tiefenauer			
(33)	Paul Toth (2)			
(34)	Andrew Vickery			
(35)	Jerry Walker			
(36)	Don Wallace			
(37)	Dooley Womack			

1954 MD Super Service Sacramento Solons

HANK SCHENZ
M D Super Service
16th and T Streets

This issue features only players of the Pacific Coast League Sacramento Solons. The unnumbered cards are printed in black-and-white and carry an ad for a local gas station. The borderless, blank-backed cards measure 2-1/8" x 3-3/8".

		NM	EX	VG
Complete Set (6):		1,200	600.00	360.00
Common Player:		200.00	100.00	60.00
(1)	Joe Brovia	200.00	100.00	60.00
(2)	Al Cicotte	200.00	100.00	60.00
(3)	Nippy Jones	200.00	100.00	60.00
(4)	Richie Meyers	200.00	100.00	60.00
(5)	Hank Schenz	200.00	100.00	60.00
(6)	Bud Sheeley	200.00	100.00	60.00

1952 Miami Beach Flamingos Team Issue

GEORGE HANDY

These 2-1/4" x 3-3/8" black-and-white, unnumbered, blank-backed cards were one of many minor league team sets issued by Globe Printing of San Jose, Calif., in the early 1950s. Cards were usually given away at the ballpark on a one-per-week or one-per-homestand basis, accounting for the rarity of surviving sets. An embossed album slotted to accommodate the cards was also issued. The Flamingos were an unaffiliated team in the Class B Florida International League.

		NM	EX	VG
Complete Set (25):		1,000	500.00	300.00
Common Player:		60.00	30.00	18.00
Album:		100.00	50.00	30.00
(1)	Billy Barrett	60.00	30.00	18.00
(2)	Art Bosch	60.00	30.00	18.00
(3)	Jack Caro	60.00	30.00	18.00
(4)	Chuck Ehlman	60.00	30.00	18.00
(5)	Oscar Garmendia	60.00	30.00	18.00

(6)	George Handy	60.00	30.00	18.00
(7)	Clark Henry	60.00	30.00	18.00
(8)	Dario Jiminez	60.00	30.00	18.00
(9)	Jesse Levan	60.00	30.00	18.00
(10)	Bobby Lyons	60.00	30.00	18.00
(11)	Pepper Martin	125.00	62.00	37.00
(12)	Dick McMillin	60.00	30.00	18.00
(13)	Pete Morant	60.00	30.00	18.00
(14)	Chico Morilla	60.00	30.00	18.00
(15)	Ken Munroe	60.00	30.00	18.00
(16)	Walt Nothe	60.00	30.00	18.00
(17)	Marshall O'Coine	60.00	30.00	18.00
(18)	Whitey Platt	60.00	30.00	18.00
(19)	Johnny Podgajny	60.00	30.00	18.00
(20)	Knobby Rosa	60.00	30.00	18.00
(21)	Harry Raulerson	60.00	30.00	18.00
(22)	Mort Smith	60.00	30.00	18.00
(23)	Tommy Venn	60.00	30.00	18.00
(24)	George Wehmeyer	60.00	30.00	18.00
(25)	Ray Williams	60.00	30.00	18.00

1963 Milwaukee Sausage Seattle Rainiers

MEL PARNELL

Inserted into meat packages by a Seattle sausage company, the 11 cards known in this set are all Seattle Rainiers players, several of whom had big league experience. Cards measure approximately 4-1/4"-square and are printed in blue, red and yellow. The unnumbered cards are checklisted in alphabetical order.

		NM	EX	VG
Complete Set (11):		7,500	3,750	2,250
Common Player:		750.00	375.00	225.00
(1)	Dave Hall	750.00	375.00	225.00
(2)	Bill Harrell	750.00	375.00	225.00
(3)	Pete Jernigan	750.00	375.00	225.00
(4)	Bill McLeod	750.00	375.00	225.00
(5)	Mel Parnell	825.00	420.00	250.00
(6)	Elmer Singleton	750.00	375.00	225.00
(7)	Archie Skeen	750.00	375.00	225.00
(8)	Paul Smith	750.00	375.00	225.00
(9)	Pete Smith	750.00	375.00	225.00
(10)	Bill Spanswick	750.00	375.00	225.00
(11)	George Spencer	750.00	375.00	225.00

1909 Minneapolis Tribune/St. Paul Pioneer Press Mirrors

BEST SPORTING NEWS
Oh, you Mike Kelly!
MANAGER MIKE
IN THE PIONEER PRESS

From the few players known, it is apparent these mirrors were issued in 1909 by two of the Twin Cities' daily newspapers. Each mirror is 2-1/8" diameter with a celluloid back. At center is a black-and-white player photo. All typography is in b/w, as well. A pair of concentric circles around the photo contain the player's name and a short description of his prowess. Olmstead's reads, "Unhittable in the Pinches"; Carisch's reads, "Nails 'em to the Cross Every Time." The outer circle contains an ad for the newspaper. This checklist is probably incomplete.

		NM	EX	VG
Common Player:		600.00	300.00	180.00
(1)	Fred Carisch	600.00	300.00	180.00
(2)	Michael Kelly	600.00	300.00	180.00
(3)	Fred Olmstead	600.00	300.00	180.00

1911 Mono Cigarettes (T217)

As was common with many tobacco issues of the period, the T217 set - distributed on the West Coast by Mono Cigarettes - feature both baseball players and "Leading Actresses." The 23 baseball players in the Mono set are all from the Pacific Coast League. Two of the players (Delhi and Hughie Smith) are shown in two poses, resulting in a total of 25 different cards. The players are pictured in black-and-white

Chadbourn, Port.

MONO
TURKISH BLEND
CIGARETTES

200 Portraits
Selected from
Leading Actresses
And
Base Ball Players

10 For 5 Cents

photos on a card that measures approximately 1-1/2" x 2-5/8", the standard size of a tobacco card. The player's name and team appear at the bottom, while the back of the card carries an advertisement for Mono Cigarettes. The Mono set, which can be dated to the 1909-1911 period, is among the rarest of all tobacco cards.

		NM	EX	VG
Complete Set (25):		100,000	50,000	30,000
Common Player:		4,250	2,000	1,100
(1)	Aiken	4,250	2,000	1,100
(2)	Curtis Bernard	4,250	2,000	1,100
(3)	L. Burrell	4,250	2,000	1,100
(4)	Chadbourn	4,250	2,000	1,100
(5)	R. Couchman	4,250	2,000	1,100
(6)	Elmer Criger	4,250	2,000	1,100
(7)	Pete Daley	4,250	2,000	1,100
(8)	W. Delhi (Glove at chest level.)	4,250	2,000	1,100
(9)	W. Delhi (Glove at shoulder level.)	4,250	2,000	1,100
(10)	Bert Delmas	4,250	2,000	1,100
(11)	Ivan Howard	4,250	2,000	1,100
(12)	Kitty Knight	4,250	2,000	1,100
(13)	Gene Knapp (Krapp)	4,250	2,000	1,100
(14)	Metzger	4,250	2,000	1,100
(15)	Carl Mitze	4,250	2,000	1,100
(16)	J. O'Rourke	4,250	2,000	1,100
(17)	R. Peckinpaugh	4,250	2,000	1,100
(18)	Walter Schmidt	4,250	2,000	1,100
(19)	Hughie Smith (Batting)	4,250	2,000	1,100
(20)	Hughie Smith (Fielding)	4,250	2,000	1,100
(21)	Wm. Stein	4,250	2,000	1,100
(22)	Elmer Thorsen	4,250	2,000	1,100
(23)	Oscar Vitt	4,250	2,000	1,100
(24)	Clyde Wares	4,250	2,000	1,100
(25)	Geo. Wheeler	4,250	2,000	1,100

1961 Jeffrey W. Morey Postcards

Ron Stillwell

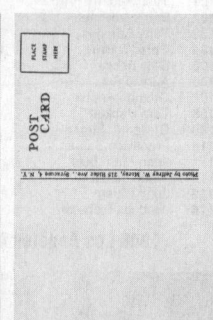

POST CARD
PLACE STAMP HERE

This set of 3-1/2" x 5-1/2", black-and-white postcards was produced to accomodate fan mail requests by two players each from the Columbus Clippers and Syracuse Chiefs. Fronts have a facsimile autograph. Divided-postcard backs have a credit line to the photographer and standard postcard markings.

		NM	EX	VG
Complete Set (4):		125.00	65.00	37.50
Common Player:		35.00	17.50	10.50
(1)	Larry Elliot	35.00	17.50	10.50
(2)	Don Rowe	35.00	17.50	10.50
(3)	Ted Sadowski	35.00	17.50	10.50
(4)	Ron Stillwell	35.00	17.50	10.50

1947 Morley Studios Team Cards

Besides issuing individual player cards of the Tacoma team, Morley Studios also issued postcard-size pictures of the teams in the Class B Western International League of 1947. The 3-1/2" x 5-1/2" cards are blank-backed and carry a "Morley Studios / 1947" imprint on front.

		NM	EX	VG
Complete Set (8):		600.00	300.00	180.00
Common Player:		75.00	37.50	22.50
(1)	Bremerton Bluejackets	75.00	37.50	22.50
(2)	Salem Senators	75.00	37.50	22.50
(3)	Spokane Indians	75.00	37.50	22.50
(4)	Tacoma Tigers	75.00	37.50	22.50
(5)	Vancouver Capilanos	75.00	37.50	22.50
(6)	Victoria Athletics	75.00	37.50	22.50
(7)	Yakima Stars	75.00	37.50	22.50
(8)	Wenatchee Chiefs	75.00	37.50	22.50

1947 Morley Studios Tacoma Tigers

A Morley SPORTGRAFIC

Stanley "Gilly" Gilson is a pitcher recommended by Jackie Warner, Los Angeles Coach, who scouted him pitching for L. A. Cherubs. Born Philadelphia, Pa., May 27, 1926. Is now makes Los Angeles his home. Has brown hair, hazel eyes, 5' 10" and weighs 165. He hits and throws right. Attended the U.C.L.A. but did not participate in sports. Played baseball in high school. His first year in professional ball but could not play for a Major leaguer. His first year in professional ball but could not play for a Major leaguer. His ambitions to be a Major leaguer. His dog is his pet and his hobby is photography. His greatest thrill in baseball was playing with big-leaguers at Treasure Island. He is a bachelor. Served both in the Army and Navy from 1943 to 1946. Was overseas six months in Battles at Leyte and Saipan.

Clay Huntington
Jordan's Broadcaster

Morley Sports Photos

This set of Tacoma Tigers (Western International League) features borderless black-and-white posed action photos with a facsimile autograph on front. A "Morley Sports Photos" or "Morley Studios" credit line appears at the bottom. Backs of the first seven cards are blank, while the others feature player biographies credited to "Jordan's (bread sponsor) Broadcaster" Clay Huntington and a Series A through F designation (though some cards lack the letter code). The unnumbered cards measure 2-1/2" x 3-1/2".

		NM	EX	VG
Complete Set (28):		3,500	1,750	1,000
Common Player:		125.00	65.00	40.00
	Blank-Backed	.00	.00	.00
(1)	Hank Bartolomei	125.00	65.00	40.00
(2)	Rod Belcher (Broadcaster)	125.00	65.00	40.00
(3)	Tip Berg (Trainer)	125.00	65.00	40.00
(4)	Gene Clough	125.00	65.00	40.00
(5)	Clay Huntington (Broadcaster)	125.00	65.00	40.00
(6)	Donald Mooney (Bat boy.)	125.00	65.00	40.00
(7)	Buck Tinsley	125.00	65.00	40.00
	Series A	.00	.00	.00
(8)	Richard A. Greco	125.00	65.00	40.00
(9)	Cy Greenlaw	125.00	65.00	40.00
(10)	Bob Joratz	125.00	65.00	40.00
(11)	Earl Kuper	125.00	65.00	40.00
	Series B	.00	.00	.00
(12)	Neil Clifford	125.00	65.00	40.00
(13)	Red Harvel	125.00	65.00	40.00
(14)	Julian Morgan	125.00	65.00	40.00
(15)	Pete Tedeschi	125.00	65.00	40.00
	Series C	.00	.00	.00
(16)	Stanley Gilson	125.00	65.00	40.00
(17)	Harry Nygard	125.00	65.00	40.00
(18)	Cleve Ramsey	125.00	65.00	40.00
(19)	Pete Sabutis	125.00	65.00	40.00
	Series D	.00	.00	.00
(20)	Mitch Chetkovich	125.00	65.00	40.00
(21)	Leroy Paton	125.00	65.00	40.00
(22)	Carl Shaply	125.00	65.00	40.00
(23)	Glenn Stetter	125.00	65.00	40.00
	Series E	.00	.00	.00
(24)	Bob Hedington	125.00	65.00	40.00
(25)	Ed Keehan	125.00	65.00	40.00
(26)	Gordon Walden	125.00	65.00	40.00
	Series F	.00	.00	.00
(27)	Maury Donovan	125.00	65.00	40.00
(28)	Guy Miller	125.00	65.00	40.00

1952 Mother's Cookies

This is one of the most popular regional minor league sets ever issued. Cards of Pacific Coast League players were included in packages of cookies. Distribution was limited to the West Coast. The 64 cards feature full color photos on a colored background, with player name and team. The cards measure 2-13/16" x 3-1/2", though the cards' rounded corners cause some variation in listed size. Card backs feature a very brief player statistic, card numbers and an offer for purchasing postage stamps. Five cards (11, 16, 29, 37 and 43) are considered scarce, while card #4 (Chuck Connors) is the most popular.

		NM	EX	VG
Complete Set (64):		4,500	2,100	1,250
Common Player:		60.00	30.00	20.00
1a	Johnny Lindell (Regular back.)	80.00	40.00	25.00
1b	Johnny Lindell ('52 Hollywood schedule on back)	80.00	40.00	25.00
2	Jim Davis	60.00	30.00	20.00
3	Al Gettle (Gettel)	60.00	30.00	20.00
4	Chuck Connors	600.00	300.00	200.00
5	Joe Grace	60.00	30.00	20.00
6	Eddie Basinski	60.00	30.00	20.00

		NM	EX	VG
7a	Gene Handley (Regular back.)	60.00	30.00	20.00
7b	Gene Handley (Schedule back.)	60.00	30.00	20.00
8	Walt Judnich	60.00	30.00	20.00
9	Jim Marshall	60.00	30.00	20.00
10	Max West	60.00	30.00	20.00
11	Bill MacCawley	120.00	60.00	35.00
12	Moreno Peiretti	60.00	30.00	20.00
13a	Fred Haney (Regular back.)	75.00	37.50	22.50
13b	Fred Haney ('52 Hollywood schedule on back)	75.00	37.50	22.50
14	Earl Johnson	60.00	30.00	20.00
15	Dave Dahle	60.00	30.00	20.00
16	Bob Talbot	120.00	60.00	35.00
17	Smokey Singleton	60.00	30.00	20.00
18	Frank Austin	60.00	30.00	20.00
19	Joe Gordon	90.00	45.00	27.50
20	Joe Marty	60.00	30.00	20.00
21	Bob Gillespie	60.00	30.00	20.00
22	Red Embree	60.00	30.00	20.00
23a	Lefty Olsen (Brown belt.)	60.00	30.00	20.00
23b	Lefty Olsen (Black belt.)	90.00	45.00	27.50
24a	Whitey Wietelmann (Large photo, much of bat missing.)	60.00	30.00	20.00
24b	Whitey Wietelmann (Small photo, more bat shows.)	60.00	30.00	20.00
25	Frank O'Doul	100.00	50.00	30.00
26	Memo Luna	60.00	30.00	20.00
27	John Davis	60.00	30.00	20.00
28	Dick Faber	60.00	30.00	20.00
29	Buddy Peterson	225.00	110.00	67.00
30	Hank Schenz	60.00	30.00	20.00
31	Tookie Gilbert	60.00	30.00	20.00
32	Mel Ott	200.00	100.00	60.00
33	Sam Chapman	60.00	30.00	20.00
34a	John Ragni (Outfielder)	60.00	30.00	20.00
34b	John Ragni (Pitcher)	100.00	50.00	30.00
35	Dick Cole	60.00	30.00	20.00
36	Tom Saffell	60.00	30.00	20.00
37	Roy Welmaker	120.00	60.00	35.00
38	Lou Stringer	60.00	30.00	20.00
39a	Chuck Stevens (Team on back Hollywood.)	60.00	30.00	20.00
39b	Chuck Stevens (Team on back Seattle.)	60.00	30.00	20.00
39c	Chuck Stevens (No team on back.)	60.00	30.00	20.00
40	Artie Wilson	90.00	45.00	30.00
41	Charlie Schanz	60.00	30.00	20.00
42	Al Lyons	60.00	30.00	20.00
43	Joe Erautt	300.00	150.00	90.00
44	Clarence Maddern	60.00	30.00	20.00
45	Gene Baker	60.00	30.00	20.00
46	Tom Heath	60.00	30.00	20.00
47	Al Lien	60.00	30.00	20.00
48	Bill Reeder	60.00	30.00	20.00
49	Bob Thurman	60.00	30.00	20.00
50	Ray Orteig	60.00	30.00	20.00
51	Joe Brovia	60.00	30.00	20.00
52	Jim Russell	60.00	30.00	20.00
53	Fred Sanford	60.00	30.00	20.00
54	Jim Gladd	60.00	30.00	20.00
55	Clay Hopper	60.00	30.00	20.00
56	Bill Glynn	60.00	30.00	20.00
57	Mike McCormick	60.00	30.00	20.00
58	Richie Myers	60.00	30.00	20.00
59	Vinnie Smith	60.00	30.00	20.00
60a	Stan Hack (Brown belt.)	80.00	40.00	25.00
60b	Stan Hack (Black belt.)	80.00	40.00	25.00
61	Bob Spicer	60.00	30.00	20.00
62	Jack Hollis	60.00	30.00	20.00
63	Ed Chandler	60.00	30.00	20.00
64	Bill Moisan	85.00	45.00	25.00

1953 Mother's Cookies

The 1953 Mother's Cookies cards are again 2-3/16" x 3-1/2", with rounded corners. There are 63 players from Pacific Coast League teams included. The full-color fronts have facsimile autographs rather than printed player names, and card backs offer a trading card album. Cards are generally more plentiful than in the 1952 set, with 11 of the cards apparently double printed.

		NM	EX	VG
Complete Set (63):		1,725	850.00	525.00
Common Player:		30.00	15.00	9.00
Album:		125.00	65.00	40.00
1	Lee Winter	35.00	17.50	10.00
2	Joe Ostrowski	30.00	15.00	9.00
3	Will Ramsdell	30.00	15.00	9.00
4	Bobby Bragan	40.00	20.00	12.00
5	Fletcher Robbe	30.00	15.00	9.00
6	Aaron Robinson	30.00	15.00	9.00
7	Augie Galan	30.00	15.00	9.00
8	Buddy Peterson	30.00	15.00	9.00
9	Frank Lefty O'Doul	65.00	32.50	20.00
10	Walt Pocekay	30.00	15.00	9.00

		NM	EX	VG
11	Nini Tornay	30.00	15.00	9.00
12	Jim Moran	30.00	15.00	9.00
13	George Schmees	30.00	15.00	9.00
14	Al Widmar	30.00	15.00	9.00
15	Ritchie Myers	30.00	15.00	9.00
16	Bill Howerton	30.00	15.00	9.00
17	Chuck Stevens	30.00	15.00	9.00
18	Joe Brovia	30.00	15.00	9.00
19	Max West	30.00	15.00	9.00
20	Eddie Malone	30.00	15.00	9.00
21	Gene Handley	30.00	15.00	9.00
22	William D. McCawley	30.00	15.00	9.00
23	Bill Sweeney	30.00	15.00	9.00
24	Tom Alston	30.00	15.00	9.00
25	George Vico	30.00	15.00	9.00
26	Hank Arft	30.00	15.00	9.00
27	Al Benton	30.00	15.00	9.00
28	"Pete" Milne	30.00	15.00	9.00
29	Jim Gladd	30.00	15.00	9.00
30	Earl Rapp	35.00	17.50	10.00
31	Ray Orteig	30.00	15.00	9.00
32	Eddie Basinski	30.00	15.00	9.00
33	Reno Cheso	30.00	15.00	9.00
34	Clarence Maddern	30.00	15.00	9.00
35	Marino Pieretti	30.00	15.00	9.00
36	Bill Raimondi	30.00	15.00	9.00
37	Frank Kelleher	30.00	15.00	9.00
38	George Bamberger	35.00	17.50	10.00
39	Dick Smith	30.00	15.00	9.00
40	Charley Schanz	30.00	15.00	9.00
41	John Van Cuyk	30.00	15.00	9.00
42	Lloyd Hittle	30.00	15.00	9.00
43	Tommy Heath	30.00	15.00	9.00
44	Frank Kalin	30.00	15.00	9.00
45	Jack Tobin	30.00	15.00	9.00
46	Jim Davis	30.00	15.00	9.00
47	Claude Christie	30.00	15.00	9.00
48	Elvin Tappe	30.00	15.00	9.00
49	Stan Hack	60.00	30.00	18.00
50	Fred Richards	30.00	15.00	9.00
51	Clay Hopper	30.00	15.00	9.00
52	Roy Welmaker	30.00	15.00	9.00
53	Red Adams	30.00	15.00	9.00
54	Piper Davis	60.00	30.00	18.00
55	Spider Jorgensen	30.00	15.00	9.00
56	Lee Walls	30.00	15.00	9.00
57	Jack Phillips	30.00	15.00	9.00
58	Red Lynn	30.00	15.00	9.00
59	Eddie Beckman	30.00	15.00	9.00
60	Gene Desautels	30.00	15.00	9.00
61	Bob Dillinger	30.00	15.00	9.00
62	Al Federoff	55.00	27.50	16.50
63	Bill Boemler	30.00	15.00	9.00

1920 Mrs. Sherlock's Bread Pins

Members of the Toledo Mud Hens of the American Association are featured on this set of pins sponsored by Mrs. Sherlock's Bread. The 7/8" celluloid pins have a player portrait in black-and-white at center, with his name and position indicated below. At top, in either red or black type is, "Mrs. Sherlock's Home Made Bread." Backs credit manufacture to Bastian Bros. of Rochester, N.Y., "Mfr's of ribbon metal and celluloid novelties." The unnumbered pins are checklisted here alphabetically.

		NM	EX	VG
Complete Set (19):		850.00	425.00	250.00
Common Player:		60.00	30.00	18.00
(1)	Brady	60.00	30.00	18.00
(2)	Roger Bresnahan	90.00	45.00	27.00
(3)	Jean Dubuc	60.00	30.00	18.00
(4)	Dyer	60.00	30.00	18.00
(5)	Fox	60.00	30.00	18.00
(6)	Ham Hyatt	60.00	30.00	18.00
(7)	Jones	60.00	30.00	18.00
(8)	Joe Kelly	60.00	30.00	18.00
(9)	M. Kelly	60.00	30.00	18.00
(10)	Art Kores	60.00	30.00	18.00
(11)	McColl	60.00	30.00	18.00
(12)	Norm McNeill (McNeil)	60.00	30.00	18.00
(13)	Middleton	60.00	30.00	18.00
(14)	Murphy	60.00	30.00	18.00
(15)	Nelson	60.00	30.00	18.00
(16)	Dutch Stryker	60.00	30.00	18.00
(17)	Thompson	60.00	30.00	18.00
(18)	Al Wickland	60.00	30.00	18.00
(19)	Joe Wilhoit	60.00	30.00	18.00

1922 Mrs. Sherlock's Bread Pins (PB5)

Members of the Toledo Mud Hens of the American Association are featured on this set of pins sponsored by Mrs. Sherlock's Bread. The 5/8" celluloid pins have a player portrait in brown or green at center, with his name and position indicated below. At top, in either brown or green type is, "Eat Mrs. Sherlock's Bread." The pins are numbered at lower-left.

		NM	EX	VG
	Complete Set (21):	900.00	450.00	275.00
	Common Player:	60.00	30.00	18.00
1	Roger Bresnahan	90.00	45.00	27.00
2	Brad Kocher	60.00	30.00	18.00
3	Hill	60.00	30.00	18.00
4	Huber	60.00	30.00	18.00
5	Doc Ayers	60.00	30.00	18.00
6	Parks	60.00	30.00	18.00
7	Giard	60.00	30.00	18.00
8	Grimes	60.00	30.00	18.00
9	McCullough	60.00	30.00	18.00
10	Shoup	60.00	30.00	18.00
11	Al Wickland	60.00	30.00	18.00
12	Baker	60.00	30.00	18.00
13	Schauffle	60.00	30.00	18.00
14	Wright	60.00	30.00	18.00
15	Lamar	60.00	30.00	18.00
16	Sallee	60.00	30.00	18.00
17	Fred Luderus	60.00	30.00	18.00
18	Walgomat	60.00	30.00	18.00
19	Ed Konetchy	60.00	30.00	18.00
20	O'Neill	60.00	30.00	18.00
21	Hugh Bedient	60.00	30.00	18.00

1933 Mrs. Sherlock's Bread Pins

Members of the Toledo Mud Hens of the American Association are featured on this set of pins sponsored by Mrs. Sherlock's Bread. The 7/8" celluloid pins have a player portrait in black-and-white at center, with his name and position indicated below. At top, in red type, is "Mrs. Sherlock's Home Made Bread" in two lines. The unnumbered pins are checklisted here alphabetically.

		NM	EX	VG
	Complete Set (18):	800.00	400.00	240.00
	Common Player:	50.00	25.00	15.00
(1)	LeRoy Bachman	50.00	25.00	15.00
(2)	George Detore	50.00	25.00	15.00
(3)	Frank Doljack	50.00	25.00	15.00
(4)	Milt Galatzer	50.00	25.00	15.00
(5)	Walter Henline	50.00	25.00	15.00
(6)	Roxie Lawson	50.00	25.00	15.00
(7)	Thornton Lee	50.00	25.00	15.00
(8)	Ed Montague	50.00	25.00	15.00
(9)	Steve O'Neill	50.00	25.00	15.00
(10)	Monte Pearson	50.00	25.00	15.00
(11)	Bob Reis	50.00	25.00	15.00
(12)	Scott	50.00	25.00	15.00
(13)	Bill Sweeney	50.00	25.00	15.00
(14)	Hal Trosky	50.00	25.00	15.00
(15)	Pete Turgeon	50.00	25.00	15.00
(16)	Forrest Twogood	50.00	25.00	15.00
(17)	Max West	50.00	25.00	15.00
(18)	Ralph Winegarner	50.00	25.00	15.00

1956 Mutual Savings Dick Stuart

Possibly issued in conjunction with an autograph appearance at the bank, Dick Stuart is pictured on this black-and-white postcard-sized photocard as an outfielder for the Western League Lincoln Chiefs in 1956, the season in which he hit 66 home runs.

	NM	EX	VG
Dick Stuart	100.00	50.00	30.00

1960 National Bank of Washington Tacoma Giants

These 3" x 5" unnumbered cards have color photos on front and are usually found with black-and-white backs with

Compliments of
NATIONAL BANK OF WASHINGTON

Danny O'Connell

the bank's advertising. Uncut sheets of the cards were sold at Cheney Stadium in Tacoma either blank-backed or with a message from the Tacoma Athletic Commission. Only members of the Pacific Coast League Tacoma Giants are included in the set. The set contains the first card issued of Hall of Fame pitcher Juan Marichal. Unfortunately, fellow Hall of Famer Willie McCovey, who played in 17 games for Tacoma in 1960, is not included in the set.

		NM	EX	VG
	Complete Set (21):	1,700	850.00	500.00
	Common Player:	60.00	30.00	18.00
(1)	Matty Alou	75.00	37.00	22.00
(2)	Ossie Alvarez	60.00	30.00	18.00
(3)	Don Choate	60.00	30.00	18.00
(4)	Red Davis	60.00	30.00	18.00
(5)	Bob Farley	60.00	30.00	18.00
(6)	Eddie Fisher	60.00	30.00	18.00
(7)	Tom Haller	60.00	30.00	18.00
(8)	Sherman Jones	60.00	30.00	18.00
(9)	Juan Marichal	400.00	200.00	120.00
(10)	Ray Monzant	60.00	30.00	18.00
(11)	Danny O'Connell	60.00	30.00	18.00
(12)	Jose Pagan	60.00	30.00	18.00
(13)	Bob Perry	60.00	30.00	18.00
(14)	Dick Phillips	60.00	30.00	18.00
(15)	Bobby Prescott	60.00	30.00	18.00
(16)	Marshall Renfroe	60.00	30.00	18.00
(17)	Frank Reveira	60.00	30.00	18.00
(18)	Dusty Rhodes	35.00	17.50	10.00
(19)	Sal Taormina	60.00	30.00	18.00
(20)	Verle Tiefenthaler	60.00	30.00	18.00
(21)	Dom Zanni	60.00	30.00	18.00

1961 National Bank of Washington Tacoma Giants

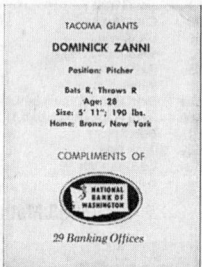

TACOMA GIANTS
DOMINICK ZANNI
Position: Pitcher
Bats R, Throws R
Age: 28
Size: 5' 11"; 190 lbs.
Home: Bronx, New York
COMPLIMENTS OF
NATIONAL BANK OF WASHINGTON
29 Banking Offices

These 3" x 4" cards feature borderless sepia photos on the front. Backs have a sponsor's ad and a few player stats printed in dark blue. The unnumbered cards are checklisted here in alphabetical order.

		NM	EX	VG
	Complete Set (21):	800.00	400.00	240.00
	Common Player:	30.00	15.00	10.00
(1)	Rafael Alomar	40.00	20.00	12.00
(2)	Ernie Bowman	30.00	15.00	10.00
(3)	Bud Byerly	30.00	15.00	10.00
(4)	Ray Daviault	30.00	15.00	10.00
(5)	Red Davis	30.00	15.00	10.00
(6)	Bob Farley	30.00	15.00	10.00
(7)	Gil Garrido	30.00	15.00	10.00
(8)	John Goetz	30.00	15.00	10.00
(9)	Bill Hain	30.00	15.00	10.00
(10)	Ronald Herbel	30.00	15.00	10.00
(11)	Lynn Lovenguth	30.00	15.00	10.00
(12)	Georges H. Maranda	30.00	15.00	10.00
(13)	Manuel Mota	100.00	50.00	30.00
(14)	John Orsino	30.00	15.00	10.00
(15)	Bob Perry	30.00	15.00	10.00
(16)	Gaylord Perry	175.00	90.00	55.00
(17)	Dick Phillips	30.00	15.00	10.00
(18)	Frank Reveira	30.00	15.00	10.00
(19)	Dusty Rhodes	40.00	20.00	12.00
(20)	Verle Tiefenthaler	30.00	15.00	10.00
(21)	Dom Zanni	30.00	15.00	10.00

1907 Newark Evening World Supplements

The Newark Sailors of the Class A Eastern League are featured in this set of supplements from a local newspaper. The 7-1/2" x 10-15/16" pieces are printed in either sepia or black-and-white. An ornate border surrounds a player pose on a plain background. In a box beneath is player identification. Backs are blank. The unnumbered supplements are checklisted here in alphabetical order, though the list may not yet be complete.

JOHN E. SHEA

		NM	EX	VG
	Common Player:	400.00	200.00	120.00
(1)	William Carrick	400.00	200.00	120.00
(2)	James Cockman	400.00	200.00	120.00
(3)	Clyde Engle	400.00	200.00	120.00
(4)	James Jones	400.00	200.00	120.00
(5)	Paul Krichell	400.00	200.00	120.00
(6)	Henry LaBelle	400.00	200.00	120.00
(7)	William Mahling	400.00	200.00	120.00
(8)	Chas. McCafferty	400.00	200.00	120.00
(9)	Thomas McCarthy	400.00	200.00	120.00
(10)	James Mullen (Mullin)	400.00	200.00	120.00
(11)	Al Pardee	400.00	200.00	120.00
(12)	Bayard Sharpe	400.00	200.00	120.00
(13)	John E. Shea	400.00	200.00	120.00
(14)	Oscar Stanage	400.00	200.00	120.00
(15)	Elmer Zacher	400.00	200.00	120.00

1950 Oak Hall Roanoke Red Sox

(See 1950 Bush & Hancock Roanoke Red Sox.)

1913 Oakland Oaks Team Issue

PERNOLL
OAKLAND

Stylistically similar to contemporary Zeenuts cards, little is known about this series. The blank-back, approximately 2" x 3-5/8" cards have full-length sepiatone player poses on a sepiatone background. The player's last name and city are printed in all caps in two lines at bottom. It is unknown whether the cards on the list comprise a complete set. Their manner of distribution is likewise unknown, they may have been a strip card issue or a candy insert.

		NM	EX	VG
	Common Player:	2,400	1,200	700.00
(1)	Ody Abbott	2,400	1,200	700.00
(2)	Harry Ables	2,400	1,200	700.00
(3)	Jesse Becker	2,400	1,200	700.00
(4)	W.W. Cook	2,400	1,200	700.00
(5)	Bert Coy	2,400	1,200	700.00
(6)	Rube Gardner	2,400	1,200	700.00
(7)	Howard Gregory	2,400	1,200	700.00
(8)	Gus Hetling	2,400	1,200	700.00
(9)	Jack Killilay	2,400	1,200	700.00
(10)	Bill Leard	2,400	1,200	700.00
(11)	John Malarkey	2,400	1,200	700.00
(12)	Carl Mitze	2,400	1,200	700.00
(13)	John Ness	2,400	1,200	700.00
(14)	Henry Olmstead	2,400	1,200	700.00
(15)	Cy Parkin	2,400	1,200	700.00
(16)	W.J. Pearce	2,400	1,200	700.00
(17)	Heine Pernoll	2,400	1,200	700.00
(18)	Ashley Pope	2,400	1,200	700.00
(19)	George Schirm	2,400	1,200	700.00
(20)	Elmer Zacher	2,400	1,200	700.00

1909 Obak (T212)

Produced annually from 1909 to 1911, the Obak cards were actually three separate and distinct sets, but they were all grouped together under a single T212 designation in the American Card Catalog. The Obak sets are closely related in

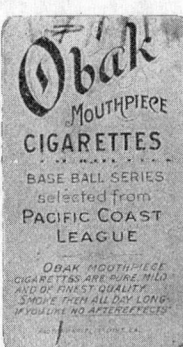

style to the more popular T206 "White Border" set issued over the same three-year period, and, in fact, were produced by the California branch of the same American Tobacco Co. conglomerate. The Obaks are the standard tobacco card size, about 1-1/2" x 2-5/8", and feature a colored lithograph, along with the player's name and team, on the front of the card. The year of issue can easily be determined by examining the back. The 1909 issue has blue printing with the name "Obak" appearing in an "Old English" type style. For 1910 the type face was changed to straight block letters, and in 1911 the backs were printed in red and include a brief biography and player statistics. The 1909 edition featured only teams from the Pacific Coast League. Cards can be found with backs that have or do not have a border around the text, though neither version appears to be scarcer than the other. Many 1909 Obaks with the "no-frame" back design show evidence of having been cut by hand from sheets, rather than machine-cut.

		NM	EX	VG
Complete Set (76):		45,000	27,500	11,000
Common Player:		550.00	275.00	125.00
(1)	Baum	550.00	275.00	125.00
(2)	Beall	550.00	275.00	125.00
(3)	Bernard	550.00	275.00	125.00
(4)	Berry	550.00	275.00	125.00
(5)	Bodie	550.00	275.00	125.00
(6)	Boyce	550.00	275.00	125.00
(7)	Brackenridge	550.00	275.00	125.00
(8)	N. Brashear	550.00	275.00	125.00
(9)	Breen	550.00	275.00	125.00
(10)	Brown	550.00	275.00	125.00
(11)	D. Brown	550.00	275.00	125.00
(12)	Browning	550.00	275.00	125.00
(13)	Byrnes	550.00	275.00	125.00
(14)	Cameron	550.00	275.00	125.00
(15)	Carroll	550.00	275.00	125.00
(16)	Carson	550.00	275.00	125.00
(17)	Christian	550.00	275.00	125.00
(18)	Coy	550.00	275.00	125.00
(19)	Delmas	550.00	275.00	125.00
(20)	Dillon	550.00	275.00	125.00
(21)	Eagan	550.00	275.00	125.00
(22)	Easterly (Eastley)	550.00	275.00	125.00
(23)	Ehman	550.00	275.00	125.00
(24)	Fisher	550.00	275.00	125.00
(25)	Fitzgerald	550.00	275.00	125.00
(26)	Flannagan	550.00	275.00	125.00
(27)	Gandil	7,500	3,700	2,200
(28)	Garrett	550.00	275.00	125.00
(29)	Graham	550.00	275.00	125.00
(30)	Graney	550.00	275.00	125.00
(31)	Griffin	550.00	275.00	125.00
(32)	Guyn	550.00	275.00	125.00
(33)	Haley	550.00	275.00	125.00
(34)	Harkins	550.00	275.00	125.00
(35)	Henley	550.00	275.00	125.00
(36)	Hitt	550.00	275.00	125.00
(37)	Hogan	550.00	275.00	125.00
(38)	W. Hogan	550.00	275.00	125.00
(39)	Howard	550.00	275.00	125.00
(40)	Howse	550.00	275.00	125.00
(41)	Jansing	550.00	275.00	125.00
(42)	LaLonge	550.00	275.00	125.00
(43)	C. Lewis	550.00	275.00	125.00
(44)	D. Lewis	550.00	275.00	125.00
(45)	J. Lewis	550.00	275.00	125.00
(46)	Martinke	550.00	275.00	125.00
(47)	McArdle	550.00	275.00	125.00
(48)	McCredie	550.00	275.00	125.00
(49)	McKune	550.00	275.00	125.00
(50)	Melchior	550.00	275.00	125.00
(51)	Mohler	550.00	275.00	125.00
(52)	Mott	550.00	275.00	125.00
(53)	Mundorff	550.00	275.00	125.00
(54)	Murphy	550.00	275.00	125.00
(55)	Nagle	550.00	275.00	125.00
(56)	Nelson	550.00	275.00	125.00
(57)	Olson	550.00	275.00	125.00
(58)	Ornsdorff	550.00	275.00	125.00
(59)	Ort	550.00	275.00	125.00
(60)	Ragan	550.00	275.00	125.00
(61)	Raymer	550.00	275.00	125.00
(62)	Reidy	550.00	275.00	125.00
(63)	Ryan	550.00	275.00	125.00
(64)	Shinn	550.00	275.00	125.00
(65)	Smith	550.00	275.00	125.00
(66)	Speas	550.00	275.00	125.00
(67)	Stoval (Stovall)	550.00	275.00	125.00
(68)	Tennant	550.00	275.00	125.00
(69)	Whalen	550.00	275.00	125.00
(70)	Wheeler	550.00	275.00	125.00
(71)	Wiggs	550.00	275.00	125.00
(72)	Willett	550.00	275.00	125.00
(73)	J. Williams	550.00	275.00	125.00
(74)	R. Williams	550.00	275.00	125.00
(75)	Willis	550.00	275.00	125.00
(76)	Zeider	550.00	275.00	125.00

1910 Obak 150 Subjects (T212)

The most common, yet most complex, of the three annual T212 baseball card issues from Obak Cigarettes is the 1910 edition. Besides players from the six Pacific Coast League teams, cards were also issued for the four-team Northwestern League. This change caused the addition of a league abbreviation, along with the player's last name and city on front. Backs are again printed in blue, but utilize a less ornate typography than the 1909 cards. The 1910 Obak set is formatted similar to the more popular T206 "White Border" set issued at the same time "back East," and, in fact, was produced by the California branch of the same American Tobacco Company conglomerate. Obaks are the standard tobacco-card size, about 1-1/2" x 2-5/8", featuring a color lithograph on front. The 1910 issue comprises two major types, one which mentions "150 SUBJECTS," on back, the other specifying "175 SUBJECTS." Forty player cards, all from the PCL, are known to exist in both 150- and 175-subject versions, the former being much scarcer. Many of the 150-subject cards can be found with significant picture variations, such as missing team names on jerseys, plain versus striped caps, different background colors or different picture cropping. Unique to the 1910 Obaks is a selection of 35 different advertising slogans which are found on back between the boxed text elements. How many of the slogans can be found on each player's cards is unknown; some are seen on only a handful of different players' cards while others are found on dozens.

		NM	EX	VG
Complete Set (40):		25,000	13,000	5,500
Common Player:		600.00	320.00	125.00
(1)	Charlie Armbuster (Ambruster)	600.00	320.00	125.00
(2)	Claude Berry	600.00	320.00	125.00
(3)	John Brackenridge	600.00	320.00	125.00
(4)	N. Brashear (Norman)	600.00	320.00	125.00
(5)	Hap Briggs	600.00	320.00	125.00
(6)	Don Cameron	600.00	320.00	125.00
(7)	Bert Coy	600.00	320.00	125.00
(8)	Elmer Criger	600.00	320.00	125.00
(9)	Babe Danzig	600.00	320.00	125.00
(10)	Cap Dillon	600.00	320.00	125.00
(11)	Bill Fisher	600.00	320.00	125.00
(12)	Ed Griffin	600.00	320.00	125.00
(13)	Cack Henley	600.00	320.00	125.00
(14)	Al Hiester	600.00	320.00	125.00
(15)	Happy Hogan	600.00	320.00	125.00
(16)	Ivan Howard	600.00	320.00	125.00
(17)	Gene Krapp	600.00	320.00	125.00
(18)	Mickey LaLonge	600.00	320.00	125.00
(19)	George Manush	600.00	320.00	125.00
(20)	Roy McArdle	600.00	320.00	125.00
(21)	Walt McCredie	600.00	320.00	125.00
(22)	Henry Melchoir	600.00	320.00	125.00
(23)	Kid Mohler	600.00	320.00	125.00
(24)	Walter Moser	600.00	320.00	125.00
(25)	Howard Mundorf	600.00	320.00	125.00
(26)	Howard Murphy	600.00	320.00	125.00
(27)	George Ort	600.00	320.00	125.00
(28)	Hank Perry	600.00	320.00	125.00
(29)	Bill Rapps	600.00	320.00	125.00
(30)	H. Smith (Hugh)	600.00	320.00	125.00
(31)	J. Smith (Jud)	600.00	320.00	125.00
(32)	Bill Steen	600.00	320.00	125.00
(33)	Harry Stewart	600.00	320.00	125.00
(34)	Pinky Swander	600.00	320.00	125.00
(35)	Lefty Tonnesen (Tonneson)	600.00	320.00	125.00
(36)	Jimmy Whalen	600.00	320.00	125.00
(37)	Roy Willett	600.00	320.00	125.00
(38)	Jimmy Williams	600.00	320.00	125.00
(39)	Ralph Willis	600.00	320.00	125.00
(40)	Harry Wolverton	600.00	320.00	125.00

1910 Obak 175 Subjects (T212)

The most common, yet most complex, of the three annual T212 baseball card issues from Obak Cigarettes is the 1910 edition. Besides players from the six Pacific Coast League teams, cards were also issued for the four-team Northwestern League. This change caused the addition of a league abbreviation, along with the player's last name and city on front. Backs are again printed in blue, but utilize a less ornate typography than the 1909 cards. The 1910 Obak set is formatted similar to the more popular T206 "White Border" set issued at

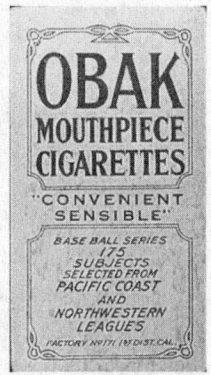

the same time "back East," and, in fact, was produced by the California branch of the same American Tobacco Co. conglomerate. Obaks are the standard tobacco-card size, about 1-1/2" x 2-5/8", featuring a color lithograph on front. The 1910 issue comprises two major types, one which mentions "150 SUBJECTS," on back, the other specifying "175 SUBJECTS." Forty player cards, all from the PCL, are known to exist in both 150- and 175-subject versions, the former being much scarcer. Many of the 150-subject cards can be found with significant picture variations, such as missing team names on jerseys, plain versus striped caps, different background colors or different picture cropping. Unique to the 1910 Obaks is a selection of 35 different advertising slogans which are found on back between the boxed text elements. How many of the slogans can be found on each player's cards is unknown; some are seen on only a handful of different players' cards while others are found on dozens.

		NM	EX	VG
Complete Set (175):		38,000	20,000	9,000
Common Player:		275.00	140.00	65.00
(1)	Agnew	275.00	140.00	65.00
(2)	Akin	275.00	140.00	65.00
(3)	Ames	275.00	140.00	65.00
(4)	Annis	275.00	140.00	65.00
(5)	Armbuster (Armbruster)	275.00	140.00	65.00
(6)	Baker	275.00	140.00	65.00
(7)	Bassey	275.00	140.00	65.00
(8)	Baum	275.00	140.00	65.00
	Beall (Now believed not to exist.)	275.00	140.00	65.00
(9)	Bennett	275.00	140.00	65.00
(10)	Bernard	275.00	140.00	65.00
(11)	Berry	275.00	140.00	65.00
(12)	Blankenship	275.00	140.00	65.00
(13)	Boardman	275.00	140.00	65.00
(14)	Bodie	275.00	140.00	65.00
(15)	Bonner	275.00	140.00	65.00
(16)	Brackenridge	275.00	140.00	65.00
(17)	N. Brashear	275.00	140.00	65.00
(18)	R. Brashear	275.00	140.00	65.00
(19)	Breen	275.00	140.00	65.00
(20)	Briggs	275.00	140.00	65.00
(21)	Brinker	275.00	140.00	65.00
(22)	Briswalter	275.00	140.00	65.00
(23)	Brooks	275.00	140.00	65.00
(24)	Brown (Sacramento)	275.00	140.00	65.00
(25)	Brown (Vernon)	275.00	140.00	65.00
(26)	D. Brown	275.00	140.00	65.00
(27)	Browning	275.00	140.00	65.00
(28)	Burrell	275.00	140.00	65.00
(29)	Byrd	275.00	140.00	65.00
(30)	Byrnes	275.00	140.00	65.00
(31)	Cameron	275.00	140.00	65.00
(32)	Capron	275.00	140.00	65.00
(33)	Carlisle	275.00	140.00	65.00
(34)	Carroll	275.00	140.00	65.00
(35)	Cartwright	275.00	140.00	65.00
(36)	Casey	275.00	140.00	65.00
(37)	Caslleton (Castleton)	400.00	200.00	100.00
(38)	Chenault	275.00	140.00	65.00
(39)	Christian	275.00	140.00	65.00
(40)	Coleman	275.00	140.00	65.00
(41)	Cooney	275.00	140.00	65.00
(42)	Coy	275.00	140.00	65.00
(43)	Criger	275.00	140.00	65.00
(44)	Custer	275.00	140.00	65.00
(45)	Cutshaw	275.00	140.00	65.00
(46)	Daley	275.00	140.00	65.00
(47)	Danzig	275.00	140.00	65.00
(48)	Daringer	275.00	140.00	65.00
(49)	Davis	275.00	140.00	65.00
(50)	Delhi	275.00	140.00	65.00
(51)	Delmas	275.00	140.00	65.00
(52)	Dillon	275.00	140.00	65.00
(53)	Dretchko	275.00	140.00	65.00
(54)	Eastley	275.00	140.00	65.00
(55)	Erickson	275.00	140.00	65.00
(56)	Flannagan	275.00	140.00	65.00
(57)	Fisher (Portland)	275.00	140.00	65.00
(58)	Fisher (Vernon)	275.00	140.00	65.00
(59)	Fitzgerald	275.00	140.00	65.00
(60)	Flood	275.00	140.00	65.00
(61)	Fournier	275.00	140.00	65.00
(62)	Frisk	275.00	140.00	65.00
(63)	Gaddy	275.00	140.00	65.00
(64)	Gardner	275.00	140.00	65.00
(65)	Garrett	275.00	140.00	65.00
(66)	Greggs (Gregg)	275.00	140.00	65.00
(67)	Griffin	275.00	140.00	65.00
(68)	Gurney	275.00	140.00	65.00
(69)	Hall (Seattle)	275.00	140.00	65.00

		NM	EX	VG
(70)	Hall (Tacoma)	275.00	140.00	65.00
(71)	Harkins	275.00	140.00	65.00
(72)	Hartman	275.00	140.00	65.00
(73)	Hendrix	275.00	140.00	65.00
(74)	Henley	275.00	140.00	65.00
(75)	Hensling	275.00	140.00	65.00
(76)	Hetling	275.00	140.00	65.00
(77)	Hickey	275.00	140.00	65.00
(78)	Hiester	275.00	140.00	65.00
(79)	Hitt	275.00	140.00	65.00
(80)	Hogan (Oakland)	275.00	140.00	65.00
(81)	Hogan (Vernon)	275.00	140.00	65.00
(82)	Hollis	275.00	140.00	65.00
(83)	Holm	275.00	140.00	65.00
(84)	Howard	275.00	140.00	65.00
(85)	Hunt	275.00	140.00	65.00
(86)	James	275.00	140.00	65.00
(87)	Jansing	275.00	140.00	65.00
(88)	Jensen	275.00	140.00	65.00
(89)	Johnston	275.00	140.00	65.00
(90)	Keener	275.00	140.00	65.00
(91)	Killilay	275.00	140.00	65.00
(92)	Kippert	275.00	140.00	65.00
(93)	Klein	275.00	140.00	65.00
(94)	Krapp	275.00	140.00	65.00
(95)	Kusel	275.00	140.00	65.00
(96)	LaLonge	275.00	140.00	65.00
(97)	Lewis	275.00	140.00	65.00
(98)	J. Lewis	275.00	140.00	65.00
(99)	John Lindsay	275.00	140.00	65.00
(100)	Lively	275.00	140.00	65.00
(101)	Lynch	275.00	140.00	65.00
(102)	Manush	275.00	140.00	65.00
(103)	Martinke	275.00	140.00	65.00
(104)	McArdle	275.00	140.00	65.00
(105)	McCredie	275.00	140.00	65.00
(106)	Melchior	275.00	140.00	65.00
(107)	Miller (San Francisco)	275.00	140.00	65.00
(108)	Miller (Seattle)	275.00	140.00	65.00
(109)	Mitze	275.00	140.00	65.00
(110)	Mohler	275.00	140.00	65.00
(111)	Moser	275.00	140.00	65.00
(112)	Mott	275.00	140.00	65.00
(113)	Mundorff (Mundorf)	275.00	140.00	65.00
(114)	Murphy	275.00	140.00	65.00
(115)	Nagle	275.00	140.00	65.00
(116)	Nelson	275.00	140.00	65.00
(117)	Netzel	275.00	140.00	65.00
(118)	Nourse	275.00	140.00	65.00
(119)	Nordyke	275.00	140.00	65.00
(120)	Olson	275.00	140.00	65.00
(121)	Orendorff (Orsnsdorff)	275.00	140.00	65.00
(122)	Ort	275.00	140.00	65.00
(123)	Ostdiek	275.00	140.00	65.00
(124)	Pennington	275.00	140.00	65.00
(125)	Perrine	275.00	140.00	65.00
(126)	Perry	275.00	140.00	65.00
(127)	Persons	275.00	140.00	65.00
(128)	Rapps	275.00	140.00	65.00
(129)	Raymer	275.00	140.00	65.00
(130)	Raymond	275.00	140.00	65.00
(131)	Rockenfield	275.00	140.00	65.00
(132)	Roth	275.00	140.00	65.00
(133)	D. Ryan	275.00	140.00	65.00
(134)	J. Ryan	275.00	140.00	65.00
(135)	Scharnweber	275.00	140.00	65.00
(136)	Schmutz	275.00	140.00	65.00
(137)	Seaton (Portland)	275.00	140.00	65.00
(138)	Seaton (Seattle)	275.00	140.00	65.00
(139)	Shafer	275.00	140.00	65.00
(140)	Shaw	275.00	140.00	65.00
(141)	Shea	275.00	140.00	65.00
(142)	Shinn	275.00	140.00	65.00
(143)	Smith	275.00	140.00	65.00
(144)	H. Smith	275.00	140.00	65.00
(145)	J. Smith	275.00	140.00	65.00
(146)	Speas	275.00	140.00	65.00
(147)	Spiesman	275.00	140.00	65.00
(148)	Starkell	275.00	140.00	65.00
(149)	Steen	275.00	140.00	65.00
(150)	Stevens	275.00	140.00	65.00
(151)	Stewart	275.00	140.00	65.00
(152)	Stovall (Stovall)	275.00	140.00	65.00
(153)	Streib	275.00	140.00	65.00
(154)	Sugden	275.00	140.00	65.00
(155)	Sutor (Suter)	275.00	140.00	65.00
(156)	Swain	275.00	140.00	65.00
(157)	Swander	275.00	140.00	65.00
(158)	Tennant	275.00	140.00	65.00
(159)	Thomas	275.00	140.00	65.00
(160)	Thompson	275.00	140.00	65.00
(161)	Thorsen	275.00	140.00	65.00
(162)	Tonnesen (Tonneson)	275.00	140.00	65.00
(163)	Tozer	275.00	140.00	65.00
(164)	Van Buren	275.00	140.00	65.00
(165)	Vitt	275.00	140.00	65.00
(166)	Wares	275.00	140.00	65.00
(167)	Waring	275.00	140.00	65.00
(168)	Warren	275.00	140.00	65.00
(169)	Weed	275.00	140.00	65.00
(170)	Whalen	275.00	140.00	65.00
(171)	Willett	275.00	140.00	65.00
(172)	Williams	275.00	140.00	65.00
(173)	Willis	275.00	140.00	65.00
(174)	Wolverton	275.00	140.00	65.00
(175)	Zackert	275.00	140.00	65.00

1911 Obak (T212)

The last of the three annual T212 baseball card issues from Obak Cigarettes is the 1911 edition, again featuring players from the six Pacific Coast League teams and the four-team Northwestern League. Often using the same chromolithographic picture on front as the 1910 cards, the 1911s are easily distinguished by the use of red, rather than blue, printing on back. Also new to the 1911s was the addition of a sentence or two about the player and, on most cards, recent

WEAVER, the hardest hitting utility player in the League, has played sensational ball in both infield and outfield. Has a wonderful throwing arm and is one of the most natural ball players in the game today. Can play any position on the infield, covers lots of ground, is very fast and shows up like a star.

A.B. B.H. P.C.
1910....291 84 259

OBAK SPEAKS QUALITY IN ANY COMPANY
FACTORY NO 71 1ST DIST CAL.

WEAVER, SAN FRANCISCO, P. C. L.

years' statistics, an innovation also seen on the contemporary T205 cards "back East." In fact the Obaks were produced by the California branch of the same American Tobacco Company conglomerate. Obaks are the standard tobacco card size, about 1-1/2" x 2-5/8".

		NM	EX	VG
Complete Set (175):		55,000	28,000	11,000
Common Player:		320.00	160.00	75.00
(1)	Abbott	320.00	160.00	75.00
(2)	Ables	320.00	160.00	75.00
(3)	Adams	320.00	160.00	75.00
(4)	Agnew	320.00	160.00	75.00
(5)	Akin	320.00	160.00	75.00
(6)	Annis	320.00	160.00	75.00
(7)	Arrelanes (Arellanes)	320.00	160.00	75.00
(8)	Barry	320.00	160.00	75.00
(9)	Bassey	320.00	160.00	75.00
(10)	Baum	320.00	160.00	75.00
(11)	Bennett	320.00	160.00	75.00
(12)	Bernard	320.00	160.00	75.00
(13)	Berry	320.00	160.00	75.00
(14)	Bloomfield	320.00	160.00	75.00
(15)	Bonner	320.00	160.00	75.00
(16)	Brackenridge	320.00	160.00	75.00
(17)	Brashear	320.00	160.00	75.00
(18)	R. Brashear	320.00	160.00	75.00
(19)	Brinker	320.00	160.00	75.00
(20)	Brown	320.00	160.00	75.00
(21)	Browning	320.00	160.00	75.00
(22)	Bues	320.00	160.00	75.00
(23)	Burrell	320.00	160.00	75.00
(24)	Burns	320.00	160.00	75.00
(25)	Butler	320.00	160.00	75.00
(26)	Byram	320.00	160.00	75.00
(27)	Carlisle	320.00	160.00	75.00
(28)	Carson	320.00	160.00	75.00
(29)	Cartwright	320.00	160.00	75.00
(30)	Casey	320.00	160.00	75.00
(31)	Castleton	400.00	200.00	125.00
(32)	Chadbourne	320.00	160.00	75.00
(33)	Christian	320.00	160.00	75.00
(34)	Coleman	320.00	160.00	75.00
(35)	Cooney	320.00	160.00	75.00
(36)	Coy	320.00	160.00	75.00
(37)	Criger	320.00	160.00	75.00
(38)	Crukshank	320.00	160.00	75.00
(39)	Cutshaw	320.00	160.00	75.00
(40)	Daley	320.00	160.00	75.00
(41)	Danzig	320.00	160.00	75.00
(42)	Dashwood	320.00	160.00	75.00
(43)	Davis	320.00	160.00	75.00
(44)	Delhi	320.00	160.00	75.00
(45)	Delmas	320.00	160.00	75.00
(46)	Dillon	320.00	160.00	75.00
(47)	Engel	320.00	160.00	75.00
(48)	Erickson	320.00	160.00	75.00
(49)	Fitzgerald	320.00	160.00	75.00
(50)	Flater	320.00	160.00	75.00
(51)	Frisk	320.00	160.00	75.00
(52)	Fullerton	320.00	160.00	75.00
(53)	Garrett	320.00	160.00	75.00
(54)	Goodman	320.00	160.00	75.00
(55)	Gordon	320.00	160.00	75.00
(56)	Grindle	320.00	160.00	75.00
(57)	Hall	320.00	160.00	75.00
(58)	Harris	320.00	160.00	75.00
(59)	Hasty	320.00	160.00	75.00
(60)	Henderson	320.00	160.00	75.00
(61)	Henley	320.00	160.00	75.00
(62)	Hetling	320.00	160.00	75.00
(63)	Hiester	320.00	160.00	75.00
(64)	Higgins	320.00	160.00	75.00
(65)	Hitt	320.00	160.00	75.00
(66)	Hoffman	320.00	160.00	75.00
(67)	Hogan	320.00	160.00	75.00
(68)	Holm	320.00	160.00	75.00
(69)	Householder	320.00	160.00	75.00
(70)	Hosp	320.00	160.00	75.00
(71)	Howard	320.00	160.00	75.00
(72)	Hunt	320.00	160.00	75.00
(73)	James	320.00	160.00	75.00
(74)	Jensen	320.00	160.00	75.00
(75)	Kading	320.00	160.00	75.00
(76)	Kane	320.00	160.00	75.00
(77)	Kippert	320.00	160.00	75.00
(78)	Knight	320.00	160.00	75.00
(79)	Koestner	320.00	160.00	75.00
(80)	Krueger	320.00	160.00	75.00
(81)	Kuhn	320.00	160.00	75.00
(82)	LaLonge	320.00	160.00	75.00
(83)	Lamline	320.00	160.00	75.00
(84)	Leard	320.00	160.00	75.00
(85)	Lerchen	320.00	160.00	75.00
(86)	Lewis	320.00	160.00	75.00
(87)	Madden	320.00	160.00	75.00
(88)	Maggert	320.00	160.00	75.00
(89)	Mahoney	320.00	160.00	75.00
(90)	McArdle	320.00	160.00	75.00
(91)	McCredie	320.00	160.00	75.00
(92)	McDonnell	320.00	160.00	75.00
(93)	Meikle	320.00	160.00	75.00
(94)	Melchior	320.00	160.00	75.00
(95)	Mensor	650.00	310.00	210.00
(96)	Metzger	320.00	160.00	75.00
(97)	Miller (Oakland)	320.00	160.00	75.00
(98)	Miller (San Francisco)	320.00	160.00	75.00
(99)	Ten Million	3,000	1,500	750.00
(100)	Mitze	320.00	160.00	75.00
(101)	Mohler	320.00	160.00	75.00
(102)	Moore	320.00	160.00	75.00
(103)	Morse	320.00	160.00	75.00
(104)	Moskiman	320.00	160.00	75.00
(105)	Mundorff	320.00	160.00	75.00
(106)	Murray	320.00	160.00	75.00
(107)	Netzel	320.00	160.00	75.00
(108)	Nordyke	320.00	160.00	75.00
(109)	Nourse	320.00	160.00	75.00
(110)	O'Rourke	320.00	160.00	75.00
(111)	Ostdiek	320.00	160.00	75.00
(112)	Patterson	320.00	160.00	75.00
(113)	Pearce	320.00	160.00	75.00
(114)	Peckinpaugh	320.00	160.00	75.00
(115)	Pernoll	320.00	160.00	75.00
(116)	Pfyl	320.00	160.00	75.00
(117)	Powell	320.00	160.00	75.00
(118)	Raleigh	320.00	160.00	75.00
(119)	Rapps	320.00	160.00	75.00
(120)	Raymer	320.00	160.00	75.00
(121)	Raymond	320.00	160.00	75.00
(122)	Reddick	320.00	160.00	75.00
(123)	Roche	320.00	160.00	75.00
(124)	Rockenfield	320.00	160.00	75.00
(125)	Rogers	320.00	160.00	75.00
(126)	Ross	320.00	160.00	75.00
(127)	Ryan	320.00	160.00	75.00
(128)	J. Ryan	320.00	160.00	75.00
(129)	Scharnweber	320.00	160.00	75.00
(130)	Schmidt	320.00	160.00	75.00
(131)	Schmutz	320.00	160.00	75.00
(132)	Seaton (Portland)	320.00	160.00	75.00
(133)	Seaton (Seattle)	320.00	160.00	75.00
(134)	Shaw	320.00	160.00	75.00
(135)	Shea	320.00	160.00	75.00
(136)	Sheehan (Portland)	320.00	160.00	75.00
(137)	Sheehan (Vernon)	320.00	160.00	75.00
(138)	Shinn	320.00	160.00	75.00
(139)	Skeels	320.00	160.00	75.00
(140)	H. Smith	320.00	160.00	75.00
(141)	Speas	320.00	160.00	75.00
(142)	Spencer	320.00	160.00	75.00
(143)	Spiesman	320.00	160.00	75.00
(144)	Starkel	320.00	160.00	75.00
(145)	Steen	320.00	160.00	75.00
(146)	Stewart	320.00	160.00	75.00
(147)	Stinson	320.00	160.00	75.00
(148)	Stovall	320.00	160.00	75.00
(149)	Strand	320.00	160.00	75.00
(150)	Sutor (Suter)	320.00	160.00	75.00
(151)	Swain	320.00	160.00	75.00
(152)	Tennant	320.00	160.00	75.00
(153)	Thomas (Sacramento)	320.00	160.00	75.00
(154)	Thomas (Victoria)	320.00	160.00	75.00
(155)	Thompson	320.00	160.00	75.00
(156)	Thornton	320.00	160.00	75.00
(157)	Thorsen	320.00	160.00	75.00
(158)	Tiedeman	320.00	160.00	75.00
(159)	Tozer	320.00	160.00	75.00
(160)	Van Buren	320.00	160.00	75.00
(161)	Vitt	320.00	160.00	75.00
(162)	Ward	320.00	160.00	75.00
(163)	Wares	320.00	160.00	75.00
(164)	Warren	320.00	160.00	75.00
(165)	Weaver	9,750	4,875	2,925
(166)	Weed	320.00	160.00	75.00
(167)	Wheeler	320.00	160.00	75.00
(168)	Wiggs	320.00	160.00	75.00
(169)	Willett	320.00	160.00	75.00
(170)	Williams	320.00	160.00	75.00
(171)	Wolverton	320.00	160.00	75.00
(172)	Zacher	320.00	160.00	75.00
(173)	Zackert	320.00	160.00	75.00
(174)	Zamlock	320.00	160.00	75.00
(175)	Zimmerman	320.00	160.00	75.00

1911 Obak Cabinets (T4)

Among the scarcest of all the 20th Century tobacco issues, the T4 Obak Premiums are cabinet-sized cards distributed in conjunction with the better-known Obak T212 card se of players from the Northwestern and Pacific Coast Leagues. The Obak Premiums measure about 5" x 7" and are printed on a cardboard-like paper. The cards featured a black-and-white player photo inside a 3-1/2" x 5" oval. There is no printing on the front of the card to identify the player or indicate the manufacturer. The backs are blank. In most cases the photos used for the premiums are identical to the T212 pictures, except for some cropping differences. Under the Obak mail-in promotion, 50 coupons from cigarette packages were required to obtain just one premium card, which explains their extreme scarcity today. All 175 players pictured in the T212 set were theoretically available as premium cards, but to date many remain undiscovered. Only those cards that have been confirmed to survive are listed with a value here. Most of the Obak premiums that exist in original condition contain a number, written in pencil on the back of the card, that corresponds to the checklist printed on the coupon. A large group of the cabinets, most of which had been cut down to just the oval portrait, was offered in a September 2002 auction.

		NM	EX	VG
Common Player:		6,750	3,500	2,200
LOS ANGELES				
1	H. Smith	5,750	2,875	1,725
2	Tozer	5,750	2,875	1,725
3	Howard	5,750	2,875	1,725
4	Daley	5,750	2,875	1,725
5	Bernard			
6	Dillon	5,750	2,875	1,725
7	Delmas			
8	Delhi	5,750	2,875	1,725
9	Criger			
10	Thorsen	5,750	2,875	1,725
11	Agnew			
12	Akin			
13	Metzger			
14	Abbott			
15	Wheeler	5,750	2,875	1,725
16	Moore			
17	Grindle			
OAKLAND				
18	Wolverton			
19	Mitze	5,750	2,875	1,725
20	Wares			
21	Cutshaw	5,750	2,875	1,725
22	Christian	5,750	2,875	1,725
23	Wiggs			
24	Maggert	5,750	2,875	1,725
25	Pfyl			
26	Pearce			
27	Hetling			
28	Hoffman			
29	Pernoll	5,750	2,875	1,725
30	Coy			
31	Tiedeman	5,750	2,875	1,725
32	Knight	.00	.00	.00
33	Flater	5,750	2,875	1,725
34	Zacher	5,750	2,875	1,725
35	Ables	5,750	2,875	1,725
36	Miller			
PORTLAND (PCL)				
37	Ryan	5,750	2,875	1,725
38	Rapps	5,750	2,875	1,725
39	McCredie			
40	Seaton			
41	Steen			
42	Chadbourne	5,750	2,875	1,725
43	Krueger			
44	Sheehan			
45	Roger Peckinpaugh	5,750	2,875	1,725
46	Bill Rodgers	5,750	2,875	1,725
47	Murray			
48	Fullerton			
49	Kuhn	5,750	2,875	1,725
50	Koestner			
51	Henderson			
52	Barry			
SACRAMENTO				
53	LaLonge			
54	Heister			
55	Hunt			
56	Van Buren			
57	Fitzgerald	5,750	2,875	1,725
58	Danzig	5,750	2,875	1,725
59	Baum	5,750	2,875	1,725
60	Shinn	5,750	2,875	1,725
61	Nourse			
62	O'Rourke			
63	Lerchen			
64	Thornton			
65	Thomas	5,750	2,875	1,725
66	Thompson			
67	Byram			
68	Frank Arrelanes (Arellanes)			
69	Mahoney			
SAN FRANCISCO				
70	McArdle			
71	Melchior	5,750	2,875	1,725
72	Vitt	5,750	2,875	1,725
73	Henley			
74	Berry	5,750	2,875	1,725
75	Miller	5,750	2,875	1,725
76	Tennant	5,750	2,875	1,725
77	Mohler	5,750	2,875	1,725
78	Shaw			
79	Sutor	5,750	2,875	1,725
80	Browning	5,750	2,875	1,725
81	Ryan	5,750	2,875	1,725
82	Powell	5,750	2,875	1,725
83	Schmidt	5,750	2,875	1,725
84	Meikle	5,750	2,875	1,725
85	Madden	5,750	2,875	1,725
86	Buck Weaver (VG-EX example auctioned in 2005 for $26,435.)			
87	Moskiman	5,750	2,875	1,725

		NM	EX	VG
88	Zamlock	5,750	2,875	1,725
VERNON				
89	Brown			
90	Hogan			
91	Brashear			
92	Carlisle	5,750	2,875	1,725
93	Burrell	5,750	2,875	1,725
94	Brackenridge	5,750	2,875	1,725
95	Hitt			
96	Willett	5,750	2,875	1,725
97	Stewart	5,750	2,875	1,725
98	Carson	5,750	2,875	1,725
99	Raleigh	5,750	2,875	1,725
100	Ham Patterson	5,750	2,875	1,725
101	Hosp			
102	Sheehan			
103	Castleton			
104	Ross			
105	Stinson	5,750	2,875	1,725
106	McDonnell	5,750	2,875	1,725
107	Kane	5,750	2,875	1,725
PORTLAND (NWL)				
108	Harris			
109	Garrett			
110	Stovall			
111	Mundorff	5,750	2,875	1,725
112	Lamline			
113	Bloomfield			
114	Williams			
115	Mensor			
116	Casey			
117	Speas			
SPOKANE				
118	Netzel			
119	Strand			
120	Hasty			
121	Zimmerman			
122	Cooney			
123	Frisk			
124	Nordyke			
125	Kippert			
126	Bonner			
127	Ostdiek			
128	Cartwright			
129	Holm			
TACOMA				
130	Higgins			
131	Warren			
132	Morse			
133	Burns			
134	Gordon			
135	Bassey			
136	Rockenfield			
137	Coleman			
138	Schmutz			
139	Hall			
140	Annis	5,750	2,875	1,725
VANCOUVER				
141	Engel			
142	Brashear			
143	Adams			
144	Spiesman			
145	Brinker			
146	Bennett			
147	James			
148	Lewis			
149	Scharnweber			
150	Swain			
151	Jensen			
152	Erickson			
VICTORIA				
153	Roche			
154	Davis			
155	Goodman			
156	Ward			
157	Reddick			
158	Householder	5,750	2,875	1,725
159	Dashwood	5,750	2,875	1,725
160	Starkel			
161	Thomas			
162	Ten Million			
163	Raymer			
SEATTLE				
164	Bues			
165	Crukshank			
166	Kading			
167	Spencer	5,750	2,875	1,725
168	Leard			
169	Seaton			
170	Shea			
171	Butler			
172	Skeels			
173	Weed			
174	Raymond	5,750	2,875	1,725
175	Zackert			

1911 Obak Coupon

About 3" x 3", this coupon was found in each box of Obak cigarettes. Printed in green on white, the coupon has a list of the cabinet cards which could be obtained by redeeming 50 of the coupons.

	NM	EX	VG
Obak Coupon	100.00	50.00	30.00

1908 Offerman Buffalo Bisons Postcards

Virtually identical in format to the Major League player postcards issued by American League Publishing Co., Cleveland, these cards carry the imprint of F.J. Offerman and depict Buffalo Bisons players of the Eastern League. The 3-1/2" x 4-1/2" black-and-white cards have a large posed action photo on a white background with a vignetted oval portrait at top. Player information and stats are printed below. The back has typical postcard markings. It is unknown whether this checklist is complete.

		NM	EX	VG
Common Player:		600.00	300.00	180.00
(1)	James Archer	600.00	300.00	180.00
(2)	James Cleary	600.00	300.00	180.00
(3)	Larry Hesterfer	600.00	300.00	180.00
(4)	Hunter Hill	600.00	300.00	180.00
(5)	William H. Keister	600.00	300.00	180.00
(6)	Charles Kisinger	600.00	300.00	180.00
(7)	Lewis Knapp	600.00	300.00	180.00
(8)	Lew McAllister	600.00	300.00	180.00
(9)	George N. McConnell	600.00	300.00	180.00
(10)	William J. Milligan	600.00	300.00	180.00
(11)	James Murray	600.00	300.00	180.00
(12)	William Nattress	600.00	300.00	180.00
(13)	Ralph Parrot	600.00	300.00	180.00
(14)	John B. Ryan	600.00	300.00	180.00
(15)	George Schirm	600.00	300.00	180.00
(16)	George Smith	600.00	300.00	180.00
(17)	John H. Vowinkle	600.00	300.00	180.00
(18)	John White	600.00	300.00	180.00
(19)	Merton Whitney	600.00	300.00	180.00

1952 Ogden Reds Team Issue

These 2-1/4" x 3-3/8" black-and-white, unnumbered, blank-backed cards were one of many minor league team sets issued by Globe Printing of San Jose, Calif., in the early 1950s. Cards were usually given away at the ballpark on a one-per-week or one-per-homestand basis, accounting for the rarity of surviving sets. The O-Reds were a Class C Pioneer League farm club of the Cincinnati Reds.

		NM	EX	VG
Complete Set (18):		800.00	400.00	240.00
Common Player:		60.00	30.00	18.00
Album:		100.00	50.00	30.00
(1)	Ralph Birkofer	60.00	30.00	18.00
(2)	William A. Bowman	60.00	30.00	18.00
(3)	David Bristol	60.00	30.00	18.00
(4)	Vincent E. Capece	60.00	30.00	18.00
(5)	Gerald Davis	60.00	30.00	18.00
(6)	Ralph Dollinger	60.00	30.00	18.00
(7)	Robert E. Durnbaugh	60.00	30.00	18.00
(8)	Raymond Estes	60.00	30.00	18.00
(9)	Robert J. Flowers	60.00	30.00	18.00
(10)	Nunzio Izzo	60.00	30.00	18.00
(11)	Howard E. Leister	60.00	30.00	18.00
(12)	Steve Mesner	60.00	30.00	18.00
(13)	Dee C. Moore	60.00	30.00	18.00
(14)	Augie Navarro (Announcer)	60.00	30.00	18.00
(15)	John Omerza	60.00	30.00	18.00
(16)	James W. St. Claire	60.00	30.00	18.00
(17)	Grady N. Watts	60.00	30.00	18.00
(18)	Carl M. Wells	60.00	30.00	18.00

1955 Old Homestead Franks Des Moines Bruins

A very rare minor league issue, this set features players of the Class A Western League farm team of the Chicago Cubs. Many of the players were future major leaguers. Cards measure about 2-1/2" x 3-3/4" and have black-and-white portrait photos of the players with a facsimile autograph across the jersey. A black strip at the bottom of the card has the player and team name, and the position. Backs have an ad for the issuing hot dog company.

		NM	EX	VG
Complete Set (21):		5,000	2,500	1,500
Common Player:		250.00	125.00	75.00
(1)	Bob Andersoon	250.00	125.00	75.00
(2)	Ray Bellino	250.00	125.00	75.00
(3)	Don Biebel	250.00	125.00	75.00
(4)	Bobby Cooke	250.00	125.00	75.00
(5)	Dave Cunningham	250.00	125.00	75.00
(6)	Bert Flammini	250.00	125.00	75.00
(7)	Gene Fodge	250.00	125.00	75.00
(8)	Eddie Haas	250.00	125.00	75.00
(9)	Paul Hoffmeister	250.00	125.00	75.00
(10)	Pepper Martin	350.00	175.00	100.00
(11)	Jim McDaniel	250.00	125.00	75.00
(12)	Bob McKee	250.00	125.00	75.00
(13)	Paul Menking	250.00	125.00	75.00
(14)	Vern Morgan	250.00	125.00	75.00
(15)	Joe Pearson	250.00	125.00	75.00
(16)	John Pramesa	250.00	125.00	75.00
(17)	Joe Stanka	250.00	125.00	75.00
(18)	Jim Stoddard	250.00	125.00	75.00
(19)	Bob Thorpe	250.00	125.00	75.00
(20)	Burdy Thurlby	250.00	125.00	75.00
(21)	Don Watkins	250.00	125.00	75.00

1959 O'Keefe Ale Montreal Royals

TOM LASORDA
Lanceur gaucher – L. H. Pitcher

This set of large (3" x 4") player stamps was issued in conjunction with an album as a promotion by O'Keefe Ale in Quebec. The pictures are black-and-white with player identification in the bottom border. Backs are blank and the edges are perforated. Many former Brooklyn Dodgers are included in the issue. The unnumbered stamps are listed here in alphabetical order.

		NM	EX	VG
Complete Set (24):		900.00	450.00	275.00
Common Player:		30.00	15.00	9.00
Album:		200.00	100.00	60.00
(1)	Edmundo Amoros	45.00	22.50	13.50
(2)	Bob Aspromonte	35.00	17.50	10.00
(3)	Batters Records	12.50	6.25	3.75
(4)	Babe Birrer	30.00	15.00	9.00
(5)	Clay Bryant	30.00	15.00	9.00
(6)	Mike Brumley	30.00	15.00	9.00
(7)	Yvon Dunn (Trainer)	20.00	10.00	6.00
(8)	Bill George	30.00	15.00	9.00
(9)	Mike Goliat	30.00	15.00	9.00
(10)	John Gray	30.00	15.00	9.00
(11)	Billy Harris	30.00	15.00	9.00
(12)	Jim Koranda	30.00	15.00	9.00
(13)	Paul LaPalme	30.00	15.00	9.00
(14)	Tom Lasorda	200.00	100.00	60.00
(15)	Bob Lennon	30.00	15.00	9.00
(16)	Clyde Parris	30.00	15.00	9.00
(17)	Pitchers Records	12.50	6.25	3.75
(18)	Ed Rakow	30.00	15.00	9.00
(19)	Curt Roberts	30.00	15.00	9.00
(20)	Freddy Rodriguez	30.00	15.00	9.00
(21)	Harry Schwegman	30.00	15.00	9.00
(22)	Angel Scull	30.00	15.00	9.00
(23)	Dick Teed	30.00	15.00	9.00
(24)	Rene Valdes (Valdez)	30.00	15.00	9.00

1910 Old Mill Cigarettes Series 1 (S. Atlantic League)

Because of their distinctive red borders, this 1910 minor league tobacco issue is often called the Red Border set by collectors. It's ACC designation is T210. A massive set, it consists of some 640 cards, each measuring 1-1/2" x 2-5/8". Fronts feature a glossy black-and-white photo, while the backs carry an ad for Old Mill Cigarettes. Each of the eight series is devoted to a different minor league. Series 1 features players from the South Atlantic League; Series 2 pictures players from the Virginia League; Series 3 is devoted to the Texas League; Series 4 features the Virginia Valley League; Series 5 pictures players from the Carolina Associations; Series 6 spotlights the Blue Grass League; Series 7 is devoted to the Eastern Carolina League; and Series 8 show players from the Southern Association. The various series are identified by a number along the top on the back of the cards. Collectors generally agree that Series 8 cards, which are often found irregularly sized due to hand-cutting from original sheets, are the scarcest of the series. The relative scarcity of the various series is reflected in the prices listed. Collectors should be aware that some Series 3 cards (Texas League) can be found with orange, rather than red, borders - apparently because not enough red ink was used during part of the print run.

		NM	EX	VG
Common Player:		325.00	140.00	80.00
(1)	Bagwell	325.00	140.00	80.00
(2)	Balenti	325.00	140.00	80.00
(3)	Becker	325.00	140.00	80.00
(4)	Bensen	325.00	140.00	80.00
(5)	Benton	325.00	140.00	80.00
(6)	Bierkortte	325.00	140.00	80.00
(7)	Bierman	325.00	140.00	80.00
(8)	(William) Breitenstein	325.00	140.00	80.00
(9)	Bremmerhof	325.00	140.00	80.00
(10)	Carter	325.00	140.00	80.00
(11)	Cavender	325.00	140.00	80.00
(12)	Collins	325.00	140.00	80.00
(13)	DeFraites	325.00	140.00	80.00
(14)	Dudley	325.00	140.00	80.00
(15)	Dwyer	325.00	140.00	80.00
(16)	Edwards	325.00	140.00	80.00
(17)	Enbanks	325.00	140.00	80.00
(18)	Eubank	325.00	140.00	80.00
(19)	Fox	325.00	140.00	80.00
(20)	Hannifan	325.00	140.00	80.00
(21)	Hartley	325.00	140.00	80.00
(22)	Hauser	325.00	140.00	80.00
(23)	Hille	325.00	140.00	80.00
(24)	Howard	325.00	140.00	80.00
(25)	Hoyt	325.00	140.00	80.00
(26)	Hubér	325.00	140.00	80.00
(27)	Ison	325.00	140.00	80.00
(28)	Jones	325.00	140.00	80.00
(29)	Kalkhoff	325.00	140.00	80.00
(30)	Krebs	325.00	140.00	80.00
(31)	Lawrence	325.00	140.00	80.00
(32)	Lee (Jacksonville)	325.00	140.00	80.00
(33)	Lee (Macon)	325.00	140.00	80.00
(34)	Lewis (Columbia)	325.00	140.00	80.00
(35)	Lewis (Columbus)	325.00	140.00	80.00
(36)	Lipe (Batting)	325.00	140.00	80.00
(37)	Lipe (Portrait)	325.00	140.00	80.00
(38)	Long	325.00	140.00	80.00
(39)	Magoon	325.00	140.00	80.00
(40)	Manion	325.00	140.00	80.00
(41)	Marshall	325.00	140.00	80.00
(42)	Martin	325.00	140.00	80.00
(43)	Martina	325.00	140.00	80.00
(44)	Massing	325.00	140.00	80.00
(45)	McLeod	325.00	140.00	80.00
(46)	McMahon	325.00	140.00	80.00
(47)	Morse	325.00	140.00	80.00
(48)	Mullane	325.00	140.00	80.00
(49)	Mulldowney	325.00	140.00	80.00
(50)	Murch	325.00	140.00	80.00
(51)	Norcum	325.00	140.00	80.00
(52)	Pelkey	325.00	140.00	80.00
(53)	Petit	325.00	140.00	80.00
(54)	Pierce	325.00	140.00	80.00
(55)	Pope	325.00	140.00	80.00
(56)	Radebaugh	325.00	140.00	80.00
(57)	Raynolds	325.00	140.00	80.00
(58)	Reagan	325.00	140.00	80.00
(59)	Redfern (Redfearn)	325.00	140.00	80.00
(60)	Reynolds	325.00	140.00	80.00
(61)	Schulz	325.00	140.00	80.00
(62)	Schulze	325.00	140.00	80.00
(63)	Schwietzka	325.00	140.00	80.00
(64)	Shields	325.00	140.00	80.00
(65)	Sisson	325.00	140.00	80.00
(66)	Smith	325.00	140.00	80.00
(67)	Sweeney	325.00	140.00	80.00
(68)	Taffee	325.00	140.00	80.00
(69)	Toren	325.00	140.00	80.00
(70)	Viola	325.00	140.00	80.00
(71)	Wagner	325.00	140.00	80.00
(72)	Wahl	325.00	140.00	80.00
(73)	Weems	325.00	140.00	80.00
(74)	Wells	325.00	140.00	80.00
(75)	Wohlleben	325.00	140.00	80.00

1910 Old Mill Cigarettes Series 2 (Virginia League)

		NM	EX	VG
Common Player:		275.00	135.00	80.00
(1)	Andrada	275.00	135.00	80.00
(2)	Archer	275.00	135.00	80.00
(3)	Baker	275.00	135.00	80.00
(4)	Beham	275.00	135.00	80.00
(5)	Bonner	275.00	135.00	80.00
(6)	Bowen	275.00	135.00	80.00
(7)	Brandon	275.00	135.00	80.00
(8)	Breivogel	275.00	135.00	80.00
(9)	Brooks	275.00	135.00	80.00
(10)	Brown	275.00	135.00	80.00
(11)	Busch	275.00	135.00	80.00
(12)	Bussey	275.00	135.00	80.00
(13)	Cefalu	275.00	135.00	80.00
(14)	Chandler	275.00	135.00	80.00
(15)	Clarke	275.00	135.00	80.00
(16)	Clunk	275.00	135.00	80.00
(17)	Cote	280.00	140.00	85.00
(18)	Cowan	275.00	135.00	80.00
(19)	Decker	275.00	135.00	80.00
(20)	Doyle	275.00	135.00	80.00
(21)	Eddowes	275.00	135.00	80.00
(22)	Fisher	275.00	135.00	80.00
(23)	Fox	275.00	135.00	80.00
(24)	Foxen	275.00	135.00	80.00
(25)	Gaston	275.00	135.00	80.00
(26)	Gehring	275.00	135.00	80.00
(27)	Griffin (Danville)	275.00	135.00	80.00
(28)	Griffin (Lynchburg)	275.00	135.00	80.00
(29)	Hale	275.00	135.00	80.00
(30)	Hamilton	275.00	135.00	80.00
(31)	Hanks	275.00	135.00	80.00
(32)	Hannafin	275.00	135.00	80.00
(33)	Hoffman	275.00	135.00	80.00
(34)	Holland	275.00	135.00	80.00
(35)	Hooker	275.00	135.00	80.00
(36)	Irving	275.00	135.00	80.00
(37)	Jackson (Lynchburg)	275.00	135.00	80.00
(38)	Jackson (Norfolk)	275.00	135.00	80.00
(39)	Jackson (Portsmouth)	275.00	135.00	80.00
(40)	Jackson (Richmond)	275.00	135.00	80.00
(41)	Jenkins	275.00	135.00	80.00
(42)	Keifel	275.00	135.00	80.00
(43)	Kirkpatrick	275.00	135.00	80.00
(44)	Kunkel	275.00	135.00	80.00
(45)	Landgraff	275.00	135.00	80.00
(46)	Larkins	275.00	135.00	80.00
(47)	Laughlin	275.00	135.00	80.00
(48)	Lawlor	275.00	135.00	80.00
(49)	Levy	275.00	135.00	80.00
(50)	Lloyd	275.00	135.00	80.00
(51)	Loos	275.00	135.00	80.00
(52)	Lovell	275.00	135.00	80.00
(53)	Lucia	275.00	135.00	80.00
(54)	MacConachie	275.00	135.00	80.00
(55)	Mayberry	275.00	135.00	80.00
(56)	McFarland	275.00	135.00	80.00
(57)	Messitt	275.00	135.00	80.00
(58)	Michel	275.00	135.00	80.00
(59)	Mullaney	275.00	135.00	80.00
(60)	Munson	275.00	135.00	80.00
(61)	Neuton	275.00	135.00	80.00
(62)	Nimmo	275.00	135.00	80.00
(63)	Norris	275.00	135.00	80.00
(64)	Peterson	275.00	135.00	80.00
(65)	Powell	275.00	135.00	80.00
(66)	Pressly (Pressley)	275.00	135.00	80.00
(67)	Pritchard	275.00	135.00	80.00
(68)	Revelle	275.00	135.00	80.00
(69)	Rowe	275.00	135.00	80.00
(70)	Schmidt	275.00	135.00	80.00
(71)	Schrader	275.00	135.00	80.00
(72)	Sharp	275.00	135.00	80.00
(73)	Shaw	275.00	135.00	80.00
(74)	Smith (Lynchburg, batting.)	275.00	135.00	80.00
(75)	Smith (Lynchburg, catching.)	275.00	135.00	80.00
(76)	Smith (Portsmouth)	275.00	135.00	80.00
(77)	Spicer	275.00	135.00	80.00
(78)	Titman	275.00	135.00	80.00
(79)	Toner	275.00	135.00	80.00
(80)	Tydeman	275.00	135.00	80.00
(81)	Vail	275.00	135.00	80.00
(82)	Verbout	275.00	135.00	80.00
(83)	Walker	275.00	135.00	80.00
(84)	Wallace	275.00	135.00	80.00
(85)	Waymack	275.00	135.00	80.00
(86)	Woolums	275.00	135.00	80.00
(87)	Zimmerman	275.00	135.00	80.00

1910 Old Mill Cigarettes Series 3 (Texas League)

		NM	EX	VG
Common Player:		275.00	125.00	80.00
(1)	Alexander	275.00	125.00	80.00
(2)	Ash	275.00	125.00	80.00
(3)	Bandy	275.00	125.00	80.00
(4)	Barenkemp	275.00	125.00	80.00
(5)	Belew	275.00	125.00	80.00
(6)	Bell	275.00	125.00	80.00
(7)	Bennett	275.00	125.00	80.00
(8)	Berlck	275.00	125.00	80.00
(9)	Billiard	275.00	125.00	80.00

		NM	EX	VG
(10)	Blanding	275.00	125.00	80.00
(11)	Blue	275.00	125.00	80.00
(12)	Burch	275.00	125.00	80.00
(13)	Burk	275.00	125.00	80.00
(14)	Carlin	275.00	125.00	80.00
(15)	Conaway	275.00	125.00	80.00
(16)	Corkhill	275.00	125.00	80.00
(17)	Cowan	275.00	125.00	80.00
(18)	Coyle	275.00	125.00	80.00
(19)	Crable	275.00	125.00	80.00
(20)	Curry	275.00	125.00	80.00
(21)	Dale	275.00	125.00	80.00
(22)	Davis	275.00	125.00	80.00
(23)	Deardorff	275.00	125.00	80.00
(24)	Donnelley	275.00	125.00	80.00
(25)	Doyle	275.00	125.00	80.00
(26)	Druke	275.00	125.00	80.00
(27)	Dugey	275.00	125.00	80.00
(28)	Ens	275.00	125.00	80.00
(29)	Evans	275.00	125.00	80.00
(30)	Fillman	275.00	125.00	80.00
(31)	Firestine	275.00	125.00	80.00
(32)	Francis	275.00	125.00	80.00
(33)	Galloway	275.00	125.00	80.00
(34)	Gardner	275.00	125.00	80.00
(35)	Gear	275.00	125.00	80.00
(36)	Glawe	275.00	125.00	80.00
(37)	Gordon	275.00	125.00	80.00
(38)	Gowdy	275.00	125.00	80.00
(39)	Harbison	275.00	125.00	80.00
(40)	Harper	275.00	125.00	80.00
(41)	Hicks	275.00	125.00	80.00
(42)	Hill	275.00	125.00	80.00
(43)	Hinninger	275.00	125.00	80.00
(44)	Hirsch	275.00	125.00	80.00
(45)	Hise	275.00	125.00	80.00
(46)	Hooks	275.00	125.00	80.00
(47)	Hornsby	275.00	125.00	80.00
(48)	Howell	275.00	125.00	80.00
(49)	Johnston	275.00	125.00	80.00
(50)	Jolley	275.00	125.00	80.00
(51)	Jones	275.00	125.00	80.00
(52)	Kaphan	275.00	125.00	80.00
(53)	Kipp	275.00	125.00	80.00
(54)	Leidy	275.00	125.00	80.00
(55)	Malloy	275.00	125.00	80.00
(56)	Maloney	275.00	125.00	80.00
(57)	Meagher	275.00	125.00	80.00
(58)	Merritt	275.00	125.00	80.00
(59)	McKay	275.00	125.00	80.00
(60)	Mills	275.00	125.00	80.00
(61)	Morris	275.00	125.00	80.00
(62)	Mullen	275.00	125.00	80.00
(63)	Munsell	275.00	125.00	80.00
(64)	Nagel	275.00	125.00	80.00
(65)	Northen	275.00	125.00	80.00
(66)	Ogle	275.00	125.00	80.00
(67)	Onslow	275.00	125.00	80.00
(68)	Pendleton	275.00	125.00	80.00
(69)	Powell	275.00	125.00	80.00
(70)	Riley	275.00	125.00	80.00
(71)	Robertson	275.00	125.00	80.00
(72)	Rose	275.00	125.00	80.00
(73)	Salazor	275.00	125.00	80.00
(74)	Shindel	275.00	125.00	80.00
(75)	Shontz	275.00	125.00	80.00
(76)	Slaven	275.00	125.00	80.00
(77)	Smith (Bat over shoulder.)	275.00	125.00	80.00
(78)	Smith (Bat at hip level.)	275.00	125.00	80.00
(79)	Spangler	275.00	125.00	80.00
(80)	Stadeli	275.00	125.00	80.00
(81)	Stinson	275.00	125.00	80.00
(82)	Storch	275.00	125.00	80.00
(83)	Stringer	275.00	125.00	80.00
(84)	Tesreau	275.00	125.00	80.00
(85)	Thebo	275.00	125.00	80.00
(86)	Tullas	275.00	125.00	80.00
(87)	Walsh	275.00	125.00	80.00
(88)	Watson	275.00	125.00	80.00
(89)	Weber	275.00	125.00	80.00
(90)	Weeks	275.00	125.00	80.00
(91)	Wertherford	275.00	125.00	80.00
(92)	Wickenhofer	275.00	125.00	80.00
(93)	Williams	275.00	125.00	80.00
(94)	Woodburn	275.00	125.00	80.00
(95)	Yantz	275.00	125.00	80.00

1910 Old Mill Cigarettes Series 4 (Va. Valley Leag.)

		NM	EX	VG
	Common Player:	400.00	175.00	100.00
(1)	Aylor	400.00	175.00	100.00
(2)	Benney	400.00	175.00	100.00
(3)	Best	400.00	175.00	100.00
(4)	Bonno	400.00	175.00	100.00
(5)	Brown	400.00	175.00	100.00
(6)	Brumfield	400.00	175.00	100.00
(7)	Campbell	400.00	175.00	100.00
(8)	Canepa	400.00	175.00	100.00
(9)	Carney	400.00	175.00	100.00
(10)	Carter	400.00	175.00	100.00
(11)	Cochrane	400.00	175.00	100.00
(12)	Coller	400.00	175.00	100.00
(13)	Connolly	400.00	175.00	100.00
(14)	Davis	400.00	175.00	100.00
(15)	Donnell	400.00	175.00	100.00
(16)	Doshmer	400.00	175.00	100.00
(17)	Dougherty	400.00	175.00	100.00
(18)	Erlewein	400.00	175.00	100.00
(19)	Farrell	400.00	175.00	100.00
(20)	Geary	400.00	175.00	100.00
(21)	Halterman	400.00	175.00	100.00
(22)	Headly	400.00	175.00	100.00
(23)	Hollis	400.00	175.00	100.00
(24)	Hunter	400.00	175.00	100.00
(25)	Johnson	400.00	175.00	100.00
(26)	Kane	400.00	175.00	100.00
(27)	Kuehn	400.00	175.00	100.00
(28)	Leonard	400.00	175.00	100.00
(29)	Lux	400.00	175.00	100.00
(30)	McClain	400.00	175.00	100.00
(31)	Mollenkamp	400.00	175.00	100.00
(32)	Moore	400.00	175.00	100.00
(33)	Moye	400.00	175.00	100.00
(34)	O'Connor	400.00	175.00	100.00
(35)	Orcutt	400.00	175.00	100.00
(36)	Pick	400.00	175.00	100.00
(37)	Pickels	400.00	175.00	100.00
(38)	Schafer	400.00	175.00	100.00
(39)	Seaman	400.00	175.00	100.00
(40)	Spicer	400.00	175.00	100.00
(41)	Stanley	400.00	175.00	100.00
(42)	Stockum	400.00	175.00	100.00
(43)	Titlow	400.00	175.00	100.00
(44)	Waldron	400.00	175.00	100.00
(45)	Wills	400.00	175.00	100.00
(46)	Witter	400.00	175.00	100.00
(47)	Womach	400.00	175.00	100.00
(48)	Young	400.00	175.00	100.00
(49)	Zurlage	400.00	175.00	100.00

1910 Old Mill Cigarettes Series 5 (Carolina Assn.)

		NM	EX	VG
	Common Player:	400.00	175.00	100.00
(1)	Abercrombie	400.00	175.00	100.00
(2)	Averett	400.00	175.00	100.00
(3)	Bansewein	400.00	175.00	100.00
(4)	Bentley	400.00	175.00	100.00
(5)	C.G. Beusse	400.00	175.00	100.00
(6)	Fred Beusse	400.00	175.00	100.00
(7)	Bigbie	400.00	175.00	100.00
(8)	Bivens	400.00	175.00	100.00
(9)	Blackstone	400.00	175.00	100.00
(10)	Brannon	400.00	175.00	100.00
(11)	Brazell	400.00	175.00	100.00
(12)	Brent	400.00	175.00	100.00
(13)	Bullock	400.00	175.00	100.00
(14)	Cashion	400.00	175.00	100.00
(15)	Corbett (3/4 length view)	400.00	175.00	100.00
(16)	Corbett (Full length view.)	400.00	175.00	100.00
(17)	Coutts	400.00	175.00	100.00
(18)	Lave Cross	400.00	175.00	100.00
(19)	Crouch	400.00	175.00	100.00
(20)	C.L. Derrick	400.00	175.00	100.00
(21)	F.B. Derrick	400.00	175.00	100.00
(22)	Dobard	400.00	175.00	100.00
(23)	Drumm	400.00	175.00	100.00
(24)	Duvie	400.00	175.00	100.00
(25)	Ehrhardt	400.00	175.00	100.00
(26)	Eldridge	400.00	175.00	100.00
(27)	Fairbanks	400.00	175.00	100.00
(28)	Farmer	400.00	175.00	100.00
(29)	Ferrell	400.00	175.00	100.00
(30)	Finn	400.00	175.00	100.00
(31)	Flowers	400.00	175.00	100.00
(32)	Fogarty	400.00	175.00	100.00
(33)	Francisco	400.00	175.00	100.00
(34)	Gardin	400.00	175.00	100.00
(35)	Gilmore	400.00	175.00	100.00
(36)	Gorham	400.00	175.00	100.00
(37)	Gorman	400.00	175.00	100.00
(38)	Guss	400.00	175.00	100.00
(39)	Hammersley	400.00	175.00	100.00
(40)	Hargrave	400.00	175.00	100.00
(41)	Harrington	400.00	175.00	100.00
(42)	Harris	400.00	175.00	100.00
(43)	Hartley	400.00	175.00	100.00
(44)	Hayes	400.00	175.00	100.00
(45)	Hicks	400.00	175.00	100.00
(46)	Humphrey	400.00	175.00	100.00
(47)	Jackson	400.00	175.00	100.00
(48)	James	400.00	175.00	100.00
(49)	Jenkins	400.00	175.00	100.00
(50)	Johnston	400.00	175.00	100.00
(51)	Kelly	400.00	175.00	100.00
(52)	Laval	400.00	175.00	100.00
(53)	Lothrop	400.00	175.00	100.00
(54)	MacConachie	400.00	175.00	100.00
(55)	Mangum	400.00	175.00	100.00
(56)	A. McCarthy	400.00	175.00	100.00
(57)	J. McCarthy	400.00	175.00	100.00
(58)	McEnroe	400.00	175.00	100.00
(59)	McFarlin	400.00	175.00	100.00
(60)	McHugh	400.00	175.00	100.00
(61)	McKevitt	400.00	175.00	100.00
(62)	Midkiff	400.00	175.00	100.00
(63)	Moore	400.00	175.00	100.00
(64)	Noojin	400.00	175.00	100.00
(65)	Ochs	400.00	175.00	100.00
(66)	Painter	400.00	175.00	100.00
(67)	Redfern (Redfearn)	400.00	175.00	100.00
(68)	Reis	400.00	175.00	100.00
(69)	Rickard	400.00	175.00	100.00
(70)	Roth (Batting)	400.00	175.00	100.00
(71)	Roth (Fielding)	400.00	175.00	100.00
(72)	Smith	400.00	175.00	100.00
(73)	Springs	400.00	175.00	100.00
(74)	Stouch	400.00	175.00	100.00
(75)	Taxis	400.00	175.00	100.00
(76)	Templin	400.00	175.00	100.00
(77)	Thrasher	400.00	175.00	100.00
(78)	Trammell	400.00	175.00	100.00
(79)	Walker	400.00	175.00	100.00
(80)	Walters	400.00	175.00	100.00
(81)	Wehrell	400.00	175.00	100.00
(82)	Weldon	400.00	175.00	100.00
(83)	Williams	400.00	175.00	100.00
(84)	Wingo	400.00	175.00	100.00
(85)	Workman	400.00	175.00	100.00
(86)	Wynne	400.00	175.00	100.00
(87)	Wysong	400.00	175.00	100.00

1910 Old Mill Cigarettes Series 6 (Blue Grass Leag.)

		NM	EX	VG
	Common Player:	600.00	250.00	150.00
(1)	Angermeier (Fielding)	600.00	250.00	150.00
(2)	Angermeir (Portrait)	600.00	250.00	150.00
(3)	Atwell	600.00	250.00	150.00
(4)	Badger	600.00	250.00	150.00
(5)	Barnett	600.00	250.00	150.00
(6)	Barney	600.00	250.00	150.00
(7)	Beard	600.00	250.00	150.00
(8)	Bohannon	600.00	250.00	150.00
(9)	Callahan	600.00	250.00	150.00
(10)	Chapman	600.00	250.00	150.00
(11)	Chase	600.00	250.00	150.00
(12)	Coleman	600.00	250.00	150.00
(13)	Cornell (Frankfort)	600.00	250.00	150.00
(14)	Cornell (Winchester)	600.00	250.00	150.00
(15)	Creager	600.00	250.00	150.00
(16)	Dailey	600.00	250.00	150.00
(17)	Edington	600.00	250.00	150.00
(18)	Elgin	600.00	250.00	150.00
(19)	Ellis	600.00	250.00	150.00
(20)	Everden	600.00	250.00	150.00
(21)	Gisler	600.00	250.00	150.00
(22)	Goodman	600.00	250.00	150.00
(23)	Goostree (Hands behind back.)	600.00	250.00	150.00
(24)	Goostree (Leaning on bat.)	600.00	250.00	150.00
(25)	Haines	600.00	250.00	150.00
(26)	Harold	600.00	250.00	150.00
(27)	Heveron	600.00	250.00	150.00
(28)	Hicks	600.00	250.00	150.00
(29)	Hoffmann	600.00	250.00	150.00
(30)	Horn	600.00	250.00	150.00
(31)	Kaiser	600.00	250.00	150.00
(32)	Keifel	600.00	250.00	150.00
(33)	Kimbrough	600.00	250.00	150.00
(34)	Kircher (Shelbyville)	600.00	250.00	150.00
(35)	Kircher (Winchester)	600.00	250.00	150.00
(36)	Kuhlman (3/4 length)	600.00	250.00	150.00
(37)	Kuhlmann (Portrait)	600.00	250.00	150.00
(38)	L'Heureux	600.00	250.00	150.00
(39)	McIlvain	600.00	250.00	150.00
(40)	McKernan	600.00	250.00	150.00
(41)	Meyers	600.00	250.00	150.00
(42)	Moloney	600.00	250.00	150.00
(43)	Mullin	600.00	250.00	150.00
(44)	Olson	600.00	250.00	150.00
(45)	Oyler	600.00	250.00	150.00
(46)	Reed	600.00	250.00	150.00
(47)	Ross	600.00	250.00	150.00
(48)	Scheneberg (Fielding)	600.00	250.00	150.00
(49)	Scheneberg (Portrait)	600.00	250.00	150.00
(50)	Schultz	600.00	250.00	150.00
(51)	Scott	600.00	250.00	150.00
(52)	Sinex	600.00	250.00	150.00
(53)	Stengel		40,000	20,000
(54)	Thoss	600.00	250.00	150.00
(55)	Tilford	600.00	250.00	150.00
(56)	Toney	600.00	250.00	150.00
(57)	Van Landingham (Valladingham) (Lexington)			
(58)	Van Landingham (Valladingham) (Shelbyville)	600.00	250.00	150.00
(59)	Viox	600.00	250.00	150.00
(60)	Walden	600.00	250.00	150.00
(61)	Whitaker	600.00	250.00	150.00
(62)	Wills	600.00	250.00	150.00
(63)	Womble	600.00	250.00	150.00
(64)	Wright	600.00	250.00	150.00
(65)	Yaeger	600.00	250.00	150.00
(66)	Yancey	600.00	250.00	150.00

1910 Old Mill Cigarettes Series 7 (E. Carolina League)

		NM	EX	VG
	Common Player:	450.00	200.00	125.00
(1)	Armstrong	450.00	200.00	125.00
(2)	Beatty	450.00	200.00	125.00
(3)	Biel	450.00	200.00	125.00
(4)	Bonner	450.00	200.00	125.00
(5)	Brandt	450.00	200.00	125.00
(6)	Brown	450.00	200.00	125.00
(7)	Cantwell	450.00	200.00	125.00
(8)	Carrol	450.00	200.00	125.00
(9)	Cooney	450.00	200.00	125.00
(10)	Cooper	450.00	200.00	125.00
(11)	Cowell	450.00	200.00	125.00
(12)	Creager (Cregan)	450.00	200.00	125.00
(13)	Crockett	450.00	200.00	125.00
(14)	Dailey	450.00	200.00	125.00
(15)	Dobbs	450.00	200.00	125.00
(16)	Dussault	450.00	200.00	125.00
(17)	Dwyer	450.00	200.00	125.00

(18)	Evans	450.00	200.00	125.00
(19)	Forgue	450.00	200.00	125.00
(20)	Fulton	450.00	200.00	125.00
(21)	Galvin	450.00	200.00	125.00
(22)	Gastmeyer (Batting)	450.00	200.00	125.00
(23)	Gastmeyer (Fielding)	450.00	200.00	125.00
(24)	Gates	450.00	200.00	125.00
(25)	Gillespie	450.00	200.00	125.00
(26)	Griffin	450.00	200.00	125.00
(27)	Gunderson	450.00	200.00	125.00
(28)	Ham	450.00	200.00	125.00
(29)	Handibe (Handiboe)	450.00	200.00	125.00
(30)	Hart	450.00	200.00	125.00
(31)	Hartley	450.00	200.00	125.00
(32)	Hobbs	450.00	200.00	125.00
(33)	Hyames	450.00	200.00	125.00
(34)	Irving	450.00	200.00	125.00
(35)	Kaiser	450.00	200.00	125.00
(36)	Kelley	450.00	200.00	125.00
(37)	Kelly	450.00	200.00	125.00
(38)	Kelly (Mascot, Goldsboro.)	750.00	370.00	220.00
(39)	Luyster	450.00	200.00	125.00
(40)	MacDonald	450.00	200.00	125.00
(41)	Malcolm	450.00	200.00	125.00
(42)	J. Erskine Mayer	500.00	250.00	125.00
(43)	McCormac (McCormick)	450.00	200.00	125.00
(44)	McGeeham (McGeehan)	450.00	200.00	125.00
(45)	Merchant	450.00	200.00	125.00
(46)	Mills	450.00	200.00	125.00
(47)	Morgan	450.00	200.00	125.00
(48)	Morris	450.00	200.00	125.00
(49)	Munson	450.00	200.00	125.00
(50)	Newman	450.00	200.00	125.00
(51)	Noval (Novak)	450.00	200.00	125.00
(52)	O'Halloran	450.00	200.00	125.00
(53)	Phelan	450.00	200.00	125.00
(54)	Prim	450.00	200.00	125.00
(55)	Reeves	450.00	200.00	125.00
(56)	Richardson	450.00	200.00	125.00
(57)	Schumaker	450.00	200.00	125.00
(58)	Sharp	450.00	200.00	125.00
(59)	Sherrill	450.00	200.00	125.00
(60)	Simmons	450.00	200.00	125.00
(61)	Steinbach	450.00	200.00	125.00
(62)	Stoehr	450.00	200.00	125.00
(63)	Taylor	450.00	200.00	125.00
(64)	Webb	450.00	200.00	125.00
(65)	Whelan	450.00	200.00	125.00
(66)	Wolf	450.00	200.00	125.00
(67)	Wright	450.00	200.00	125.00

1910 Old Mill Cigarettes Series 8 (Southern Assn.)

		NM	EX	VG
Common Player:		750.00	370.00	220.00
(1)	Allen (Memphis)	750.00	370.00	220.00
(2)	Allen (Mobile)	750.00	370.00	220.00
(3)	Anderson	750.00	370.00	220.00
(4)	Babb	750.00	370.00	220.00
(5)	Bartley	750.00	370.00	220.00
(6)	Bauer	750.00	370.00	220.00
(7)	Bay	750.00	370.00	220.00
(8)	Bayliss	750.00	370.00	220.00
(9)	Berger	750.00	370.00	220.00
(10)	Bernhard	750.00	370.00	220.00
(11)	Bitroff	750.00	370.00	220.00
(12)	Breitenstein	750.00	370.00	220.00
(13)	Bronkie	750.00	370.00	220.00
(14)	Brooks	750.00	370.00	220.00
(15)	Burnett	750.00	370.00	220.00
(16)	Cafalu	750.00	370.00	220.00
(17)	Carson	750.00	370.00	220.00
(18)	Case	750.00	370.00	220.00
(19)	Chappelle	750.00	370.00	220.00
(20)	Cohen	750.00	370.00	220.00
(21)	Collins	750.00	370.00	220.00
(22)	Crandall	750.00	370.00	220.00
(23)	Cross	750.00	370.00	220.00
(24)	Jud. Daly	750.00	370.00	220.00
(25)	Davis	750.00	370.00	220.00
(26)	Demaree	750.00	370.00	220.00
(27)	DeMontreville	750.00	370.00	220.00
(28)	E. DeMontreville	750.00	370.00	220.00
(29)	Dick	750.00	370.00	220.00
(30)	Dobbs	750.00	370.00	220.00
(31)	Dudley	750.00	370.00	220.00
(32)	Dunn	750.00	370.00	220.00
(33)	Elliot	750.00	370.00	220.00
(34)	Emery	750.00	370.00	220.00

(35)	Erloff	750.00	370.00	220.00
(36)	Farrell	750.00	370.00	220.00
(37)	Fisher	750.00	370.00	220.00
(38)	Fleharty	750.00	370.00	220.00
(39)	Flood	750.00	370.00	220.00
(40)	Foster	750.00	370.00	220.00
(41)	Fritz	750.00	370.00	220.00
(42)	Greminger	750.00	370.00	220.00
(43)	Gribbon	750.00	370.00	220.00
(44)	Griffin	750.00	370.00	220.00
(45)	Gygli	750.00	370.00	220.00
(46)	Hanks	750.00	370.00	220.00
(47)	Hart	750.00	370.00	220.00
(48)	Hess	750.00	370.00	220.00
(49)	Hickman	750.00	370.00	220.00
(50)	Hohnhorst	750.00	370.00	220.00
(51)	Huelsman	750.00	370.00	220.00
(52)	Jackson			150,000
(53)	Jordan	750.00	370.00	220.00
(54)	Kane	750.00	370.00	220.00
(55)	Kelly	750.00	370.00	220.00
(56)	Kerwin	750.00	370.00	220.00
(57)	Keupper	750.00	370.00	220.00
(58)	LaFitte	750.00	370.00	220.00
(59)	Larsen	750.00	370.00	220.00
(60)	Bill Lindsay	750.00	370.00	220.00
(61)	Lynch	750.00	370.00	220.00
(62)	Manuel	750.00	370.00	220.00
(63)	Manush	750.00	370.00	220.00
(64)	Marcan	750.00	370.00	220.00
(65)	Maxwell	750.00	370.00	220.00
(66)	McBride	750.00	370.00	220.00
(67)	McCreery	750.00	370.00	220.00
(68)	McGilvray	750.00	370.00	220.00
(69)	McLaurin	750.00	370.00	220.00
(70)	McTigue	750.00	370.00	220.00
(71)	Miller (Chattanooga)	750.00	370.00	220.00
(72)	Miller (Montgomery)	750.00	370.00	220.00
(73)	Molesworth	750.00	370.00	220.00
(74)	Moran	750.00	370.00	220.00
(75)	Newton	750.00	370.00	220.00
(76)	Nolley	750.00	370.00	220.00
(77)	Osteen	750.00	370.00	220.00
(78)	Ower	750.00	370.00	220.00
(79)	Paige	750.00	370.00	220.00
(80)	Patterson	750.00	370.00	220.00
(81)	Pepe	750.00	370.00	220.00
(82)	Perdue	750.00	370.00	220.00
(83)	Peters	750.00	370.00	220.00
(84)	Phillips	750.00	370.00	220.00
(85)	Pratt	750.00	370.00	220.00
(86)	Rementer	750.00	370.00	220.00
(87)	Rhodes	750.00	370.00	220.00
(88)	Rhoton	750.00	370.00	220.00
(89)	Robertson	750.00	370.00	220.00
(90)	Rogers	750.00	370.00	220.00
(91)	Rohe	750.00	370.00	220.00
(92)	Seabough (Seabaugh)	750.00	370.00	220.00
(93)	Seitz	750.00	370.00	220.00
(94)	Schlitzer	750.00	370.00	220.00
(95)	Schopp	750.00	370.00	220.00
(96)	Siegle	750.00	370.00	220.00
(97)	Smith (Montgomery)	750.00	370.00	220.00
(98)	Sid. Smith (Atlanta)	750.00	370.00	220.00
(99)	Steele	750.00	370.00	220.00
(100)	Swacina	750.00	370.00	220.00
(101)	Sweeney	750.00	370.00	220.00
(102)	Thomas (Fielding)	750.00	370.00	220.00
(103)	Thomas (Portrait)	750.00	370.00	220.00
(104)	Vinson	750.00	370.00	220.00
(105)	Wagner (Birmingham)	750.00	370.00	220.00
(106)	Wagner (Mobile)	750.00	370.00	220.00
(107)	Walker	750.00	370.00	220.00
(108)	Wanner	750.00	370.00	220.00
(109)	Welf	750.00	370.00	220.00
(110)	Whiteman	750.00	370.00	220.00
(111)	Whitney	750.00	370.00	220.00
(112)	Wilder	750.00	370.00	220.00
(113)	Wiseman	750.00	370.00	220.00
(114)	Yerkes	750.00	370.00	220.00

1910 Old Mill Cabinets (H801-7)

 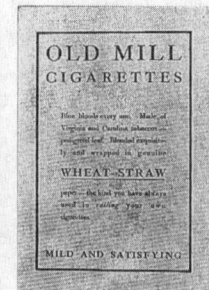

Similar in size and style to the more popular T3 Turkey Red cabinet cards of the same period, the Old Mill cabinets are much scarcer and picture fewer players. Issued in 1910 as a premium by Old Mill Cigarettes, these minor league cards measure approximately 5-3/8" x 7-5/8". Unlike the Turkey Reds, which feature full-color lithographs, the Old Mill cabinet cards picture the players in black-and-white photos surrounded by a wide tan border. The player's last name is printed in black in the lower-left corner, while his team designation appears in the lower-right. Backs carry an advertisement for Old Mill. There are currently 34 known subjects in the set. The Old Mill cabinet cards carry the ACC designation H801-7. Gaps have been left in the numbering to accomodate future additions to this checklist.

		NM	EX	VG
Common Player:		7,500	3,750	2,250
(1)	Armstrong	7,500	3,750	2,250
(2)	Bentley	7,500	3,750	2,250
(3)	Bonner	7,500	3,750	2,250
(4)	Bowen	7,500	3,750	2,250
(5)	Brazille (Brazell)	7,500	3,750	2,250
(6)	Bush (Busch)	7,500	3,750	2,250
(7)	Bussey	7,500	3,750	2,250
(8)	Cross	7,500	3,750	2,250
(9)	Derrick	7,500	3,750	2,250
(10)	Doane	7,500	3,750	2,250
(11)	Doyle	7,500	3,750	2,250
(12)	Fox	7,500	3,750	2,250
(13)	Galvin	7,500	3,750	2,250
(14)	Griffin	7,500	3,750	2,250
(15)	Hearn	7,500	3,750	2,250
(16)	Hobbs	7,500	3,750	2,250
(17)	Hooker	7,500	3,750	2,250
(18)	Kirkpatrick	7,500	3,750	2,250
(19)	Laughlin	7,500	3,750	2,250
(20)	Luyster	7,500	3,750	2,250
(21)	McKevitt	7,500	3,750	2,250
(22)	Munson	7,500	3,750	2,250
(23)	Noojn (Noojin)	7,500	3,750	2,250
(24)	O'Halloran	7,500	3,750	2,250
(25)	Pressly	7,500	3,750	2,250
(26)	Revelle	7,500	3,750	2,250
(27)	Richardson	7,500	3,750	2,250
(28)	Rickard	7,500	3,750	2,250
(29)	Simmons	7,500	3,750	2,250
(30)	A. Smith	7,500	3,750	2,250
(31)	Spratt	7,500	3,750	2,250
(32)	Titman	7,500	3,750	2,250
(33)	Walters	7,500	3,750	2,250
(34)	Wallace	7,500	3,750	2,250
(35)	Weherell (Wehrell)	7,500	3,750	2,250
(36)	Ivey Wingo	7,500	3,750	2,250
(37)	Woolums	7,500	3,750	2,250

1949 Omaha Cardinals Player Picture Book

JIM BARKLEY, Outfield

While not baseball cards, this team booklet served the same purpose - providing fans with pictures of the local Western League (Class A) affiliate of the St. Louis Cardinals. It's also possible that individual player pages of the book have made their way into card collections over the years. The booklet is 5" x 3-1/4" in size, with 20 pages of photos and semi-gloss front and back covers, stapled together at the spine. The front has printed in red: "OMAHA CARDINALS / BASEBALL TEAM / 1949." Each inside page has back-to-back black-and-white photos with identification beneath. The pairings are checklisted here in the order in which they appear in the booklet.

		NM	EX	VG
Complete Booklet:		350.00	175.00	100.00
(1-2)	Ced Durst, Russ Kerns			
(3-4)	Nick Adzick, Bob Rausch			
(5-6)	Ed Nietopski, Fran Haus			
(7-8)	Fritz Marolewski, Bernie Creger			
(9-10)	Vaughn Hazen, Sid Langston			
(11-12)	Bob Reash, Jim Barkley			
(13-14)	Marty Garlock, Hank Williams			
(15-16)	Lou Ciola, Joe Presko			
(17-18)	Dave Thomas, Bob Mahoney			
(19-20)	Stadium Photo (Dick Bokelmann)			

1956 Omaha Cardinals Picture-Pak

Evidently a concession stand souvenir, this "Picture-Pak" is a comb-bound set of 3-1/2" x 4-3/8" black-and-white player portraits. Each picture is printed on semi-gloss cardboard with a white facsimile autograph.

	NM	EX	VG
Complete Book:	300.00	150.00	90.00
(1) Tom Alston			
(2) Alberto Baro			
(3) Nels Burbrink			
(4) Tom Cheney			
(5) Ray Coleman			
(6) Jim Command			
(7) Chuck Harmon			
(8) Walt Jamison (?)			
(9) Stan Jok			
(10) Gordon Jones			
(11) Johnny Keane			
(12) Marty Kutyna			
(13) Ed Mayer			
(14) Herb Moford			
(15) Mo Mozzali			
(16) Jim Pearce			
(17) Charlie Peete			
(18) Danny Schell			
(19) Dick Schofield			
(20) Barney Schultz			
(21) Wally Shannon			
(22) Glen Stabelfeld			

1957 Omaha Cardinals Picture-Pak

These 3-3/8" x 4-3/8" black-and-white, blank-back photos were sold in a team picture pack. Fronts have a facsimile autograph. The unnumbered cards are checklisted here in alphabetical order.

	NM	EX	VG
Complete Set (25):	800.00	400.00	240.00
Common Player:	35.00	17.50	10.00
(1) Frank Barnes	35.00	17.50	10.00
(2) Bill Bergesch	35.00	17.50	10.00
(3) Dick Brown	35.00	17.50	10.00
(4) Tom Cheney	35.00	17.50	10.00
(5) Nels Chittum	35.00	17.50	10.00
(6) Jim Command	35.00	17.50	10.00
(7) Chuck Diering	35.00	17.50	10.00
(8) Sherry Dixon	35.00	17.50	10.00
(9) Bob Durnbaugh	35.00	17.50	10.00
(10) Glen Gorbous	35.00	17.50	10.00
(11) Johnny Keane	35.00	17.50	10.00
(12) Jim King	35.00	17.50	10.00
(13) Paul Kippels	35.00	17.50	10.00
(14) Don Lassetter	35.00	17.50	10.00
(15) Don Liddle	35.00	17.50	10.00
(16) Lou Limmer	35.00	17.50	10.00
(17) Boyd Linker	35.00	17.50	10.00
(18) Bob Mabe	35.00	17.50	10.00
(19) Herb Moford	35.00	17.50	10.00
(20) Rance Pless	35.00	17.50	10.00
(21) Kelton Russell	35.00	17.50	10.00
(22) Barney Schultz	35.00	17.50	10.00
(23) Milt Smith	35.00	17.50	10.00
(24) Glen Stabelfeld	35.00	17.50	10.00
(25) Header Card	35.00	17.50	10.00

1958 Omaha Cardinals Picture-Pak

This rare late-1950s minor league issue contains the first card of Hall of Fame pitcher Bob Gibson. Probably sold as a complete set in format similar to major league picture packs of the era, there are 23 player cards and a header card. Cards measure 3-3/8" x 4-3/8", have a black-and-white player picture and facsimile autograph. They are blank-backed. The checklist of the unnumbered cards is printed here in alphabetical order.

	NM	EX	VG
Complete Set (24):	1,500	750.00	450.00
Common Player:	40.00	20.00	12.00

		NM	EX	VG
(1)	Tony Alomar	60.00	30.00	18.00
(2)	Dave Benedict	40.00	20.00	12.00
(3)	Bill Bergesch	40.00	20.00	12.00
(4)	Bob Blaylock	40.00	20.00	12.00
(5)	Prentice "Pidge" Browne	40.00	20.00	12.00
(6)	Chris Cannizzaro	40.00	20.00	12.00
(7)	Nels Chittum	40.00	20.00	12.00
(8)	Don Choate	40.00	20.00	12.00
(9)	Phil Clark	40.00	20.00	12.00
(10)	Jim Frey	75.00	37.50	22.50
(11)	Bob Gibson	500.00	250.00	150.00
(12)	Ev Joyner	40.00	20.00	12.00
(13)	Johnny Keane	40.00	20.00	12.00
(14)	Paul Kippels	40.00	20.00	12.00
(15)	Boyd Linker	40.00	20.00	12.00
(16)	Bob Mabe	40.00	20.00	12.00
(17)	Bernard Mateosky	40.00	20.00	12.00
(18)	Ronnie Plaza	40.00	20.00	12.00
(19)	Bill Queen	40.00	20.00	12.00
(20)	Bill Smith	40.00	20.00	12.00
(21)	Bobby G. Smith	40.00	20.00	12.00
(22)	Lee Tate	40.00	20.00	12.00
(23)	Benny Valenzuela	40.00	20.00	12.00
(24)	Header card	40.00	20.00	12.00

1962 Omaha Dodgers

This unnumbered black-and-white set measures 3-3/8" x 4-1/4" and is blank-backed. It was produced by photographer/collector Mel Bailey in an edition of 1,000 sets, sold for 50 cents by mail and at the stadium concession stand. Cards bear a facsimile autograph.

		NM	EX	VG
Complete Set (22):		175.00	90.00	50.00
Common Player:		12.50	6.25	3.75
(1)	Joe Altobelli	12.50	6.25	3.75
(2)	Jim Barbieri	12.50	6.25	3.75
(3)	Scott Breeden	12.50	6.25	3.75
(4)	Mike Brumley	12.50	6.25	3.75
(5)	Jose Cesar	12.50	6.25	3.75
(6)	Bill Hunter	12.50	6.25	3.75
(7)	Don LeJohn	12.50	6.25	3.75
(8)	Jack Lutz	12.50	6.25	3.75
(9)	Ken McMullen	12.50	6.25	3.75
(10)	Danny Ozark	12.50	6.25	3.75
(11)	Curt Roberts	12.50	6.25	3.75
(12)	Ernie Rodriguez	12.50	6.25	3.75
(13)	Dick Scarbrough	12.50	6.25	3.75
(14)	Bart Shirley	12.50	6.25	3.75
(15)	Dick Smith	12.50	6.25	3.75
(16)	Jack Smith	12.50	6.25	3.75
(17)	Nate Smith	12.50	6.25	3.75
(18)	Gene Snyder	12.50	6.25	3.75
(19)	Burbon Wheeler	12.50	6.25	3.75
(20)	Nick Wilhite (Willhite)	12.50	6.25	3.75
(21)	Jim Williams	12.50	6.25	3.75
(22)	Larry Williams	12.50	6.25	3.75

1952 Oshkosh Giants Team Issue

GORDON WINDHORN

These 2-1/4" x 3-3/8" black-and-white, unnumbered, blank-backed cards were one of many minor league team sets issued by Globe Printing of San Jose, Calif., in the early 1950s. Cards were usually given away at the ballpark on a one-per-week or one-per-homestand basis, accounting for the rarity of surviving sets. The O-Giants were the Wisconsin State League affiliate of the N.Y. Giants. For a Class D team, a surprising number of the Oshkosh players graduated to the major leagues.

		NM	EX	VG
Complete Set (19):		1,000	500.00	300.00
Common Player:		60.00	30.00	18.00
Album:		100.00	50.00	30.00
(1)	Dan Banaszak	60.00	30.00	18.00
(2)	Paul Bentley	60.00	30.00	18.00
(3)	Joe Berke	60.00	30.00	18.00
(4)	Joe DeBellis	60.00	30.00	18.00
(5)	Ron Edwards	60.00	30.00	18.00
(6)	Dave Garcia	60.00	30.00	18.00
(7)	Weldon Grimesley	60.00	30.00	18.00
(8)	Cam Lewis	60.00	30.00	18.00
(9)	Paul McAuley	60.00	30.00	18.00
(10)	Don Mills	60.00	30.00	18.00
(11)	Ed Opich	60.00	30.00	18.00
(12)	John Practico	60.00	30.00	18.00
(13)	Rob R. Schmidt	60.00	30.00	18.00
(14)	Rob W. Schmidt	60.00	30.00	18.00
(15)	Frank Szekula	60.00	30.00	18.00
(16)	Victor Vick	60.00	30.00	18.00
(17)	Donald Wall	60.00	30.00	18.00
(18)	Ken Whitehead	60.00	30.00	18.00
(19)	Gordon Windhorn	60.00	30.00	18.00

P

1911 Pacific Coast Biscuit (D310)

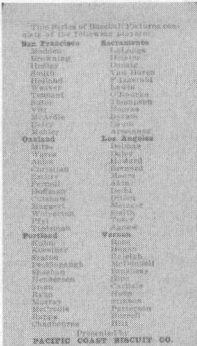

A dozen players each from six Pacific Coast League teams are represented in this set. Cards are about 2-1/2" x 4-1/4" with either black-and-white or sepia pictures on front. Backs have a checklist arranged by team. Some cards are found stamped on the back by Aldon Candy Co., Portland, Ore.

		NM	EX	VG
Complete Set (72):		135,000	67,500	40,500
Common Player:		1,700	850.00	500.00
(1)	Ables	1,700	850.00	500.00
(2)	Agnew	1,700	850.00	500.00
(3)	Akin	1,700	850.00	500.00
(4)	Frank Arrelanes (Arellanes)	1,700	850.00	500.00
(5)	Baum	1,700	850.00	500.00
(6)	Bernard	1,700	850.00	500.00
(7)	Berry	1,700	850.00	500.00
(8)	Brashear	1,700	850.00	500.00
(9)	Browning	1,700	850.00	500.00
(10)	Burrell	1,700	850.00	500.00
(11)	Byram	1,700	850.00	500.00
(12)	Carlisle	1,700	850.00	500.00
(13)	Chadbourne	1,700	850.00	500.00
(14)	Christian	1,700	850.00	500.00
(15)	Cutshaw	1,700	850.00	500.00
(16)	Daley	1,700	850.00	500.00
(17)	Danzig	1,700	850.00	500.00
(18)	Delhi	1,700	850.00	500.00
(19)	Delmas	1,700	850.00	500.00
(20)	Dillon	1,700	850.00	500.00
(21)	Fitzgerald	1,700	850.00	500.00
(22)	Gipe	1,700	850.00	500.00
(23)	Heister	1,700	850.00	500.00
(24)	Henderson	1,700	850.00	500.00
(25)	Henley	1,700	850.00	500.00
(26)	Hitt	1,700	850.00	500.00
(27)	Hoffman	1,700	850.00	500.00
(28)	Hogan	1,700	850.00	500.00
(29)	Holland	1,700	850.00	500.00
(30)	Hosp	1,700	850.00	500.00
(31)	Howard	1,700	850.00	500.00
(32)	Kostner	1,700	850.00	500.00
(33)	Kuhn	1,700	850.00	500.00
(34)	LaLonge	1,700	850.00	500.00
(35)	Lewis	1,700	850.00	500.00
(36)	Maddern	1,700	850.00	500.00
(37)	Maggert	1,700	850.00	500.00
(38)	McArdle	1,700	850.00	500.00
(39)	McCredie	1,700	850.00	500.00
(40)	McDonnell	1,700	850.00	500.00
(41)	Metzger	1,700	850.00	500.00
(42)	Mitze	1,700	850.00	500.00
(43)	Mohler	1,700	850.00	500.00
(44)	Moore	1,700	850.00	500.00
(45)	Murray	1,700	850.00	500.00
(46)	Nourse	1,700	850.00	500.00
(47)	O'Rourke	1,700	850.00	500.00
(48)	Patterson	1,700	850.00	500.00
(49)	Peckinpaugh	2,100	1,050	625.00
(50)	Pernoll	1,700	850.00	500.00
(51)	Pfyl	1,700	850.00	500.00
(52)	Raleigh	1,700	850.00	500.00
(53)	Rapps	1,700	850.00	500.00

(54)	Ross	1,700	850.00	500.00
(55)	Ryan	1,700	850.00	500.00
(56)	Seaton	1,700	850.00	500.00
(57)	Sheehan	1,700	850.00	500.00
(58)	A. Smith	1,700	850.00	500.00
(59)	H. Smith	1,700	850.00	500.00
(60)	Steen	1,700	850.00	500.00
(61)	Stinson	1,700	850.00	500.00
(62)	Sutor	1,700	850.00	500.00
(63)	Tennant	1,700	850.00	500.00
(64)	Thompson	1,700	850.00	500.00
(65)	Tiedeman	1,700	850.00	500.00
(66)	Tozer	1,700	850.00	500.00
(67)	Van Buren	1,700	850.00	500.00
(68)	Witt	1,700	850.00	500.00
(69)	Wares	1,700	850.00	500.00
(70)	Weaver	18,000	9,000	5,500
(71)	Wolverton	1,700	850.00	500.00
(72)	Zacher	1,700	850.00	500.00

1911 Pacific Coast Biscuit (D311)

A dozen players each from six Pacific Coast League teams are represented in this set. Cards are about 1-1/2" x 2-5/8" with pastel colored pictures on front. Backs have a checklist arranged by team.

		NM	EX	VG
Complete Set (72):		125,000	62,500	37,500
Common Player:		1,600	800.00	475.00
(1)	Agnew	1,600	800.00	475.00
(2)	Akin	1,600	800.00	475.00
(3)	Frank Arrelanes (Arellanes)	1,600	800.00	475.00
(4)	Baum	1,600	800.00	475.00
(5)	Bernard	1,600	800.00	475.00
(6)	Berry	1,600	800.00	475.00
(7)	Brashear	1,600	800.00	475.00
(8)	Brown	1,600	800.00	475.00
(9)	Browning	1,600	800.00	475.00
(10)	Burrell	1,600	800.00	475.00
(11)	Byram	1,600	800.00	475.00
(12)	Castleton	1,600	800.00	475.00
(13)	Chadbourne	1,600	800.00	475.00
(14)	Christian	1,600	800.00	475.00
(15)	Cutshaw	1,600	800.00	475.00
(16)	Daley	1,600	800.00	475.00
(17)	Danzig	1,600	800.00	475.00
(18)	Delhi	1,600	800.00	475.00
(19)	Delmas	1,600	800.00	475.00
(20)	Dillon	1,600	800.00	475.00
(21)	Fitzgerald	1,600	800.00	475.00
(22)	Gipe	1,600	800.00	475.00
(23)	Gregory	1,600	800.00	475.00
(24)	Harkness	1,600	800.00	475.00
(25)	Heister	1,600	800.00	475.00
(26)	Henderson	1,600	800.00	475.00
(27)	Hoffman	1,600	800.00	475.00
(28)	Hogan	1,600	800.00	475.00
(29)	Holland	1,600	800.00	475.00
(30)	Hosp	1,600	800.00	475.00
(31)	Howard	1,600	800.00	475.00
(32)	Kuhn	1,600	800.00	475.00
(33)	LaLonge	1,600	800.00	475.00
(34)	Lewis	1,600	800.00	475.00
(35)	Maggert	1,600	800.00	475.00
(36)	McArdle	1,600	800.00	475.00
(37)	McCredie	1,600	800.00	475.00
(38)	McDonnell	1,600	800.00	475.00
(39)	Meikle	1,600	800.00	475.00
(40)	Melchior	1,600	800.00	475.00
(41)	Metzger	1,600	800.00	475.00
(42)	Mitze	1,600	800.00	475.00
(43)	Mohler	1,600	800.00	475.00
(44)	Moore	1,600	800.00	475.00
(45)	Murray	1,600	800.00	475.00
(46)	Nourse	1,600	800.00	475.00
(47)	O'Rourke	1,600	800.00	475.00
(48)	Patterson	1,600	800.00	475.00
(49)	Pearce	2,000	1,000	600.00
(50)	Peckinpaugh	600.00	300.00	180.00
(51)	Pernoll	1,600	800.00	475.00
(52)	Pfyl	1,600	800.00	475.00
(53)	Raleigh	1,600	800.00	475.00
(54)	Rapps	1,600	800.00	475.00
(55)	Ryan	1,600	800.00	475.00
(56)	Schmidt	1,600	800.00	475.00
(57)	Seaton	1,600	800.00	475.00
(58)	Sheehan	1,600	800.00	475.00
(59)	A. Smith	1,600	800.00	475.00
(60)	H. Smith	1,600	800.00	475.00
(61)	Stamfield	1,600	800.00	475.00
(62)	Steen	1,600	800.00	475.00
(63)	Stinson	1,600	800.00	475.00
(64)	Sutor	1,600	800.00	475.00
(65)	Tennant	1,600	800.00	475.00
(66)	Thompson	1,600	800.00	475.00
(67)	Tiedeman	1,600	800.00	475.00
(68)	Tozer	1,600	800.00	475.00
(69)	Van Buren	1,600	800.00	475.00
(70)	Vitt	1,600	800.00	475.00
(71)	Wares	1,600	800.00	475.00
(72)	Wolverton	1,600	800.00	475.00

1943-47 Parade Sportive

Over a period of years in the mid-1940s, Montreal sports radio personality Paul Stuart's Parade Sportive program issued a series of baseball player pictures of Montreal Royals and, occasionally, other International League stars. The pictures were issued in 5" x 9-1/2" and 7" x 10" black-and-white, blank-back format. Each picture carries the name of the radio station on which Stuart's program was broadcast, along with an ad at the bottom for one of his sponsors. The unnumbered pictures are listed here alphabetically; it is unknown whether this list constitutes the complete issue.

PARADE SPORTIVE
PAUL STUART

Jackie Robinson

		NM	EX	VG
Common Player:		30.00	15.00	9.00
(1)	Jack Banta	30.00	15.00	9.00
(2)	Stan Briard	30.00	15.00	9.00
(3)	Les Burge	30.00	15.00	9.00
(4)	Paul Calvert	30.00	15.00	9.00
(5)	Al Campanis	45.00	22.50	13.50
(6)	Red Durrett	30.00	15.00	9.00
(7)	Herman Franks	30.00	15.00	9.00
(8)	John Gabbard	30.00	15.00	9.00
(9)	Roland Gladu	30.00	15.00	9.00
(10)	Ray Hathaway	30.00	15.00	9.00
(11)	Clay Hopper	30.00	15.00	9.00
(12)	John Jorgensen	30.00	15.00	9.00
(13)	Paul "Pepper" Martin	30.00	15.00	9.00
(14)	Steve Nagy	30.00	15.00	9.00
(15)	Roy Portlow (Partlow)	40.00	20.00	12.00
(16)	Marv Rackley	30.00	15.00	9.00
(17)	Jackie Robinson	300.00	150.00	90.00
(18)	Jean-Pierre Roy	30.00	15.00	9.00
(19)	1944 Montreal Royals Team Photo	50.00	25.00	15.00
(20)	1945 Montreal Royals Team Photo (CLUB MONTREAL (ROYAUX) 1945)	60.00	30.00	18.00
(21)	1945 Montreal Royals Team Photo (Les "Royaux" 1945)	60.00	30.00	18.00
(22)	1946 Montreal Royals Team Photo	200.00	100.00	60.00
(23)	Stan Briard, Roland Gladu, Jean-Pierre Roy	30.00	15.00	9.00
(24)	Checklist (Paul Stuart)	30.00	15.00	9.00

1952 Parkhurst

Produced by a Canadian competitor to Kool-Aid, this 100-card set features players from three International League teams, the Toronto Maple Leafs, Montreal Royals and Ottawa Athletics, along with cards featuring baseball playing tips and quizzes. Measuring 2" x 2-1/2", the cards feature black-and-white player photos on front. Backs are printed in red and have a few biographical details, 1951 stats and an ad for Frostade.

		NM	EX	VG
Complete Set (100):		2,400	1,200	725.00
Common Player (1-25, 49-100):		25.00	12.50	7.50
Common Card (26-48):		15.00	7.50	4.50
1	Joe Becker	80.00	35.00	9.00
2	Aaron Silverman	75.00	37.50	22.50
3	Bobby Rhawn	25.00	12.50	7.50
4	Russ Bauers	25.00	12.50	7.50
5	Bill Jennings	25.00	12.50	7.50
6	Grover Bowers	25.00	12.50	7.50
7	Vic Lombardi	25.00	12.50	7.50
8	Billy DeMars	25.00	12.50	7.50
9	Frank Colman	25.00	12.50	7.50
10	Charley Grant	25.00	12.50	7.50
11	Irving Medlinger	25.00	12.50	7.50
12	Burke McLaughlin	25.00	12.50	7.50
13	Lew Morton	25.00	12.50	7.50
14	Red Barrett	25.00	12.50	7.50
15	Leon Foulk	25.00	12.50	7.50
16	Neil Sheridan	25.00	12.50	7.50
17	Ferrell Anderson	25.00	12.50	7.50
18	Roy Shore	25.00	12.50	7.50
19	Duke Markell	75.00	37.50	22.50
20	Bobby Balcena	25.00	12.50	7.50
21	Wilmer Fields	25.00	12.50	7.50
22	Charlie White	25.00	12.50	7.50
23	Red Fahr	25.00	12.50	7.50
24	Jose Bracho	25.00	12.50	7.50
25	Ed Stevens	25.00	12.50	7.50
26	Maple Leaf Stadium	25.00	12.50	7.50
27	Throwing Home	15.00	7.50	4.50
28	Regulation Baseball Diamond	15.00	7.50	4.50
29	Gripping the Bat	15.00	7.50	4.50
30	Hiding the Pitch	15.00	7.50	4.50

		NM	EX	VG
31	Catcher's Stance	15.00	7.50	4.50
32	Quiz: "How long does..."	15.00	7.50	4.50
33	Finger and Arm Exercises	15.00	7.50	4.50
34	First Baseman	15.00	7.50	4.50
35	Pitcher's Stance	15.00	7.50	4.50
36	Swinging Bats	15.00	7.50	4.50
37	Quiz: "Can a player advance..."	15.00	7.50	4.50
38	Watch the Ball	15.00	7.50	4.50
39	Quiz: "Can a team..."	15.00	7.50	4.50
40	Quiz: "Can a player put ..."	15.00	7.50	4.50
41	How to Bunt	15.00	7.50	4.50
42	Wrist Snap	15.00	7.50	4.50
43	Pitching Practice	15.00	7.50	4.50
44	Stealing Bases	15.00	7.50	4.50
45	Pitching 1	15.00	7.50	4.50
46	Pitching 2	15.00	7.50	4.50
47	Signals	15.00	7.50	4.50
48	Regulation baseballs	15.00	7.50	4.50
49	Al Ronning	25.00	12.50	7.50
50	Bill Lane	25.00	12.50	7.50
51	Will Sampson	25.00	12.50	7.50
52	Charlie Thompson	25.00	12.50	7.50
53	Ezra McGlothin	25.00	12.50	7.50
54	Spook Jacobs	30.00	15.00	9.00
55	Art Fabbro	25.00	12.50	7.50
56	Jim Hughes	25.00	12.50	7.50
57	Don Hoak	30.00	15.00	9.00
58	Tommy Lasorda	100.00	50.00	30.00
59	Gil Mills	25.00	12.50	7.50
60	Malcolm Mallette	25.00	12.50	7.50
61	Rocky Nelson	25.00	12.50	7.50
62	John Simmons	25.00	12.50	7.50
63	Bob Alexander	25.00	12.50	7.50
64	Dan Bankhead	35.00	17.50	10.00
65	Solomon Coleman	25.00	12.50	7.50
66	Walt Alston	100.00	50.00	30.00
67	Walt Fiala	25.00	12.50	7.50
68	Jim Gilliam	65.00	32.00	19.50
69	Jim Pendleton	25.00	12.50	7.50
70	Gino Cimoli	30.00	15.00	9.00
71	Carmen Mauro	25.00	12.50	7.50
72	Walt Moryn	25.00	12.50	7.50
73	Jim Romano	25.00	12.50	7.50
74	Joe Lutz	25.00	12.50	7.50
75	Ed Roebuck	25.00	12.50	7.50
76	Johnny Podres	65.00	32.00	19.50
77	Walter Novik	25.00	12.50	7.50
78	Lefty Gohl	25.00	12.50	7.50
79	Tom Kirk	25.00	12.50	7.50
80	Bob Betz	25.00	12.50	7.50
81	Bill Hockenbury	25.00	12.50	7.50
82	Al Rubeling	25.00	12.50	7.50
83	Julius Watlington	25.00	12.50	7.50
84	Frank Fanovich	25.00	12.50	7.50
85	Hank Foiles	25.00	12.50	7.50
86	Lou Limmer	25.00	12.50	7.50
87	Ed Hrabcsak	25.00	12.50	7.50
88	Bob Gardner	25.00	12.50	7.50
89	John Metkovich	25.00	12.50	7.50
90	Jean-Pierre Roy	25.00	12.50	7.50
91	Frank Skaff	25.00	12.50	7.50
92	Harry Desert	25.00	12.50	7.50
93	Stan Jok	25.00	12.50	7.50
94	Russ Swingle	25.00	12.50	7.50
95	Bob Wellman	25.00	12.50	7.50
96	John Conway	25.00	12.50	7.50
97	George Maskovich	25.00	12.50	7.50
98	Charlie Bishop	25.00	12.50	7.50
99	Joe Murray	25.00	12.50	7.50
100	Mike Kume	25.00	12.50	7.50

1935 Pebble Beach Clothiers

JOE DI MAGGIO
SAN FRANCISCO SEALS

This series of black-and-white postcards includes only members of the three Bay area Pacific Coast League teams - the Oakland Oaks, Mission Reds and San Francisco Seals. The 3-1/2" x 5-3/8" cards have player identification at left in the bottom white border. The logotype of the clothier which sponsored the issue is at lower-right. The cards - each authentically autographed - were distributed by an area radio station. Backs have typical postcard indicia. This checklist may not be complete.

		NM	EX	VG
Common Player:		750.00	375.00	225.00
(1)	Leroy Anton	750.00	375.00	225.00
(2)	Joe DiMaggio	7,500	3,750	2,250
(3)	Wee Ludolph	750.00	375.00	225.00
(4)	Walter "The Great" Mails	750.00	375.00	225.00
(5)	Lefty O'Doul	3,650	1,825	1,100
(6)	Gabby Street	1,200	600.00	360.00
(7)	Oscar Vitt	900.00	450.00	270.00

1962 Pepsi-Cola Tulsa Oilers

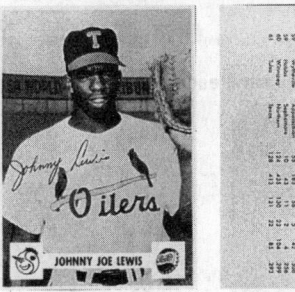

JOHNNY JOE LEWIS

The Texas League farm club of the St. Louis Cardinals is featured in this issue of sepia-colored 2-1/2" x 3-1/2" cards issued regionally by Pepsi. The unnumbered cards are checklisted here alphabetically.

		NM	EX	VG
Complete Set (24):		275.00	135.00	80.00
Common Player:		12.00	6.00	3.50
(1)	Bob Blaylock	12.00	6.00	3.50
(2)	Bud Bloomfield	12.00	6.00	3.50
(3)	Dick Hughes	12.00	6.00	3.50
(4)	Gary Kolb	12.00	6.00	3.50
(5)	Chris Krug	12.00	6.00	3.50
(6)	Hank Kuhlmann	12.00	6.00	3.50
(7)	Whitey Kurowski	12.00	6.00	3.50
(8)	Johnny Joe Lewis	12.00	6.00	3.50
(9)	Elmer Lindsey	12.00	6.00	3.50
(10)	Jeoff Long	12.00	6.00	3.50
(11)	Pepper Martin	15.00	7.50	4.50
(12)	Jerry Marx	12.00	6.00	3.50
(13)	Weldon Maudin	12.00	6.00	3.50
(14)	Dal Maxvill	15.00	7.50	4.50
(15)	Bill McNamee	12.00	6.00	3.50
(16)	Joe Patterson	12.00	6.00	3.50
(17)	Gordon Richardson	12.00	6.00	3.50
(18)	Daryl Robertson	12.00	6.00	3.50
(19)	Tom Schwaner	12.00	6.00	3.50
(20)	Joe Shipley	12.00	6.00	3.50
(21)	Jon Smith	12.00	6.00	3.50
(22)	Clint Stark	12.00	6.00	3.50
(23)	Terry Tucker	12.00	6.00	3.50
(24)	Bill Wakefield	12.00	6.00	3.50

1963 Pepsi-Cola Tulsa Oilers

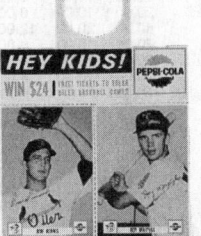

These 2-1/2" x 3-1/2", unnumbered, cards were issued in two-card panels with a holed top panel to hang on bottles. Each player's name could also be found under the cork liner of the bottle caps and when all 24 cards and caps were collected, a $24 prize could be collected. It must be assumed that some player caps were short-printed.

		NM	EX	VG
Complete Set, Singles (24):		75.00	37.50	22.50
Complete Set, Panels (12):		90.00	45.00	27.50
Common Player:		4.00	2.00	1.25
(1)	Dennis Aust	4.00	2.00	1.25
(2)	Jimmy Beauchamp	4.00	2.00	1.25
(3)	"Bud" Bloomfield	4.00	2.00	1.25
(4)	Felix de Leon	4.00	2.00	1.25
(5)	Don Dennis	4.00	2.00	1.25
(6)	Lamar Drummonds	4.00	2.00	1.25
(7)	Tom Hilgendorf	4.00	2.00	1.25
(8)	Gary Kolb	4.00	2.00	1.25
(9)	Chris Krug	4.00	2.00	1.25
(10)	"Bee" Lindsey	4.00	2.00	1.25
(11)	Roy Majtyka	4.00	2.00	1.25
(12)	Pepper Martin	7.50	3.75	2.25
(13)	Jerry Marx	4.00	2.00	1.25
(14)	"Hunkey" Mauldin	4.00	2.00	1.25
(15)	Joe Patterson	4.00	2.00	1.25
(16)	Grover Resinger	4.00	2.00	1.25
(17)	Gordon Richardson	4.00	2.00	1.25
(18)	Jon Smith	4.00	2.00	1.25
(19)	Chuck Taylor	4.00	2.00	1.25
(20)	Terry Tucker (Batboy)	4.00	2.00	1.25
(21)	Lou Vickery	4.00	2.00	1.25
(22)	Bill Wakefield	4.00	2.00	1.25
(23)	Harry Watts	4.00	2.00	1.25
(24)	Jerry Wild	4.00	2.00	1.25

1964 Pepsi-Cola Tulsa Oiler Autograph Cards

These unusual baseball cards - they don't have pictures! - were one of several 1960s issues by Pepsi in conjunction with the Tulsa Oilers. Apparently carton stuffers (they measure 2-3/16" x 9"), the cards provided free children's admission on special Pepsi-Oiler nights. The cards are printed in

red, white and blue and have short player biographies under the baseball containing the facsimile autograph. The unnumbered cards are listed here in alphabetical order.

		NM	EX	VG
Complete Set (8):		30.00	15.00	9.00
Common Player:		5.00	2.50	1.50
(1)	Bob Blaylock	5.00	2.50	1.50
(2)	Nelson Briles	5.00	2.50	1.50
(3)	Bobby Dews	5.00	2.50	1.50
(4)	Roy Majtyka	5.00	2.50	1.50
(5)	Otto Meischner	5.00	2.50	1.50
(6)	Rogers Robinson	5.00	2.50	1.50
(7)	Jerry Wild	5.00	2.50	1.50
(8)	Lou Vickery	5.00	2.50	1.50

1966 Pepsi-Cola Tulsa Oilers

GEORGE WARREN SCHULTZ

These 2-1/2" x 3-1/2" unnumbered cards were issued in two-card panels. Four cards were double-printed, each appearing on two different panels. Each player's name could also be found under the cork liner of the bottle caps and when all 24 cards and caps were collected, a $24 prize could be collected. It must be assumed that some player cards or caps were short-printed.

		NM	EX	VG
Complete Set (24):		175.00	90.00	55.00
Complete Panel Set (16):		225.00	115.00	70.00
Common Player:		10.00	5.00	3.00
Common Panel:		15.00	7.50	4.50
(1)	Florian Ackley	10.00	5.00	3.00
(2)	Dennis Aust	10.00	5.00	3.00
(3)	Elio Chacon (DP)	10.00	5.00	3.00
(4)	James Cosman	10.00	5.00	3.00
(5)	Mack Creager	10.00	5.00	3.00
(6)	Robert Dews (DP)	10.00	5.00	3.00
(7)	Harold Gilson	10.00	5.00	3.00
(8)	Larry Jaster	10.00	5.00	3.00
(9)	Alex Johnson	10.00	5.00	3.00
(10)	George Kernek (DP)	10.00	5.00	3.00
(11)	Jose Laboy	10.00	5.00	3.00
(12)	Richard LeMay	10.00	5.00	3.00
(13)	Charles Metro	10.00	5.00	3.00
(14)	David Pavlesic	10.00	5.00	3.00
(15)	Robert Pfeil	10.00	5.00	3.00
(16)	Ronald Piche	10.00	5.00	3.00
(17)	Robert Radovich	10.00	5.00	3.00
(18)	David Ricketts (DP)	10.00	5.00	3.00
(19)	Theodore Savage	10.00	5.00	3.00
(20)	George Schultz	10.00	5.00	3.00
(21)	Edward Spiezio	10.00	5.00	3.00
(22)	Clint Stark	10.00	5.00	3.00
(23)	Robert Tolan	10.00	5.00	3.00
(24)	Walter Williams	10.00	5.00	3.00

1956 Portland Beaver All-Star Pins

Stars of the Pacific Coast League Portland Beavers, all former and/or future major leaguers, are featured on these 1" black-and-white celluloid pins.

		NM	EX	VG
Complete Set (8):		1,300	650.00	375.00
Common Player:		175.00	90.00	55.00
(1)	Jim Baxes	175.00	90.00	55.00
(2)	Bob Borkowski	175.00	90.00	55.00
(3)	Sam Calderone	175.00	90.00	55.00
(4)	Jack Littrell	175.00	90.00	55.00
(5)	Luis Marquez	175.00	90.00	55.00
(6)	Ed Mickelson	175.00	90.00	55.00
(7)	Tom Saffell	175.00	90.00	55.00
(8)	Rene Valdez	175.00	90.00	55.00

R

1958 Ralph's Thriftway Seattle Rainiers

(See 1958 Seattle Popcorn for checklist and values.)

1968 Red Barn Memphis Blues

A regional issue from a Memphis chain of fast-food restaurants, these 2-1/2" x 3-3/4" cards feature members of the New York Mets' Class AA farm team. Cards have a blue-tinted player photo within an orange barn design. Player information is printed below. Backs are blank. The cards are checklisted here by uniform number.

		NM	EX	VG
Complete Set (8):		600.00	300.00	180.00
Common Player:		75.00	37.50	22.50
3	Mike "Spider" Jorgensen	75.00	37.50	22.50
6	Joe Moock	75.00	37.50	22.50
9	Rod Gaspar	75.00	37.50	22.50
16	Barry "Chief" Raziano	75.00	37.50	22.50
17	Curtis "Bubba" Brown	75.00	37.50	22.50
18	Roger Stevens	75.00	37.50	22.50
19	Ron Paul	75.00	37.50	22.50
24	Steve "Teddy" Christopher	75.00	37.50	22.50

1910 Red Sun (T211)

The 1910 minor league tobacco set issued by Red Sun Cigarettes features 75 players from the Southern Association. The Red Sun issue is similar in size and style to the massive 640-card Old Mill set (T210) issued the same year. Cards in both sets measure 1-1/2" x 2-5/8" and feature glossy black-and-white player photos. Unlike the Old Mill set, however, the Red Sun cards have a green border surrounding the photograph and a bright red and white advertisement for Red Sun cigarettes on the back. A line at the bottom promotes the cards as "First Series 1 to 75," implying that additional sets would follow, but apparently none ever did. Each of the 75 subjects in the Red Sun set was also pictured in Series Eight of the Old Mill set. Because of the "Glossy" nature of the photographs, cards in both the Old Mill and Red Sun sets are susceptible to cracking, making condition and proper grading of these cards especially important to collectors.

		NM	EX	VG
Complete Set (75):		160,000	80,000	47,500
Common Player:		2,150	1,075	645.00
(1)	Allen	2,150	1,075	645.00
(2)	Anderson	2,150	1,075	645.00
(3)	Babb	2,150	1,075	645.00
(4)	Bartley	2,150	1,075	645.00
(5)	Bay	2,150	1,075	645.00
(6)	Bayliss	2,150	1,075	645.00
(7)	Berger	2,150	1,075	645.00
(8)	Bernard	2,150	1,075	645.00
(9)	Bitroff	2,150	1,075	645.00
(10)	Breitenstein	2,150	1,075	645.00

		NM	EX	VG
(11)	Bronkie	2,150	1,075	645.00
(12)	Brooks	2,150	1,075	645.00
(13)	Cafalu	2,150	1,075	645.00
(14)	Case	2,150	1,075	645.00
(15)	Chappelle	2,150	1,075	645.00
(16)	Cohen	2,150	1,075	645.00
(17)	Cross	2,150	1,075	645.00
(18)	Jud. Daly	2,150	1,075	645.00
(19)	Davis	2,150	1,075	645.00
(20)	DeMontreville	2,150	1,075	645.00
(21)	E. DeMontreville	2,150	1,075	645.00
(22)	Dick	2,150	1,075	645.00
(23)	Dunn	2,150	1,075	645.00
(24)	Erloff	2,150	1,075	645.00
(25)	Fisher	2,150	1,075	645.00
(26)	Flood	2,150	1,075	645.00
(27)	Foster	2,150	1,075	645.00
(28)	Fritz	2,150	1,075	645.00
(29)	Greminger	2,150	1,075	645.00
(30)	Gribbon	2,150	1,075	645.00
(31)	Griffin	2,150	1,075	645.00
(32)	Gygli	2,150	1,075	645.00
(33)	Hanks	2,150	1,075	645.00
(34)	Hart	2,150	1,075	645.00
(35)	Hess	2,150	1,075	645.00
(36)	Hickman	2,150	1,075	645.00
(37)	Hohnhorst	2,150	1,075	645.00
(38)	Huelsman	2,150	1,075	645.00
(39)	Jordan	2,150	1,075	645.00
(40)	Kane	2,150	1,075	645.00
(41)	Kelly	2,150	1,075	645.00
(42)	Kerwin	2,150	1,075	645.00
(43)	Keupper	2,150	1,075	645.00
(44)	LaFitte	2,150	1,075	645.00
(45)	Bill Lindsay	2,150	1,075	645.00
(46)	Lynch	2,150	1,075	645.00
(47)	Manush	2,150	1,075	645.00
(48)	McCreery	2,150	1,075	645.00
(49)	Miller	2,150	1,075	645.00
(50)	Molesworth	2,150	1,075	645.00
(51)	Moran	2,150	1,075	645.00
(52)	Nolley	2,150	1,075	645.00
(53)	Paige	2,150	1,075	645.00
(54)	Pepe	2,150	1,075	645.00
(55)	Perdue	2,150	1,075	645.00
(56)	Pratt	2,150	1,075	645.00
(57)	Rhoton	2,150	1,075	645.00
(58)	Robertson	2,150	1,075	645.00
(59)	Rogers	2,150	1,075	645.00
(60)	Rohe	2,150	1,075	645.00
(61)	Seabaugh	2,150	1,075	645.00
(62)	Seitz	2,150	1,075	645.00
(63)	Siegle	2,150	1,075	645.00
(64)	Smith	2,150	1,075	645.00
(65)	Sid. Smith	2,150	1,075	645.00
(66)	Steele	2,150	1,075	645.00
(67)	Swacina	2,150	1,075	645.00
(68)	Sweeney	2,150	1,075	645.00
(69)	Thomas	2,150	1,075	645.00
(70)	Vinson	2,150	1,075	645.00
(71)	Wagner	2,150	1,075	645.00
(72)	Walker	2,150	1,075	645.00
(73)	Welf	2,150	1,075	645.00
(74)	Wilder	2,150	1,075	645.00
(75)	Wiseman	2,150	1,075	645.00

1945 Remar Bread Oakland Oaks

This 4-7/8" x 3-5/8" card features on front a black-and-white team photo, borderless at the top and sides. In the white strip at bottom, the players are identified. The back is printed in black with red highlights and presents the season stats for batting average and pitchers' won-lost percentage. At right is a picture of a loaf of the sponsor's bread. At present, only two examples of this card are known to exist.

	NM	EX	VG
Oakland Oaks Team Photo	2,500	1,250	750.00

1946 Remar Bread Oakland Oaks

Remar Baking Co. issued several baseball card sets in the northern California area from 1946-1950, all picturing members of the Oakland Oaks of the Pacific Coast League. The 1946 set consists of 23 cards (five unnumbered, 18 numbered). Measuring 2" x 3", the cards were printed on heavy paper and feature black and white photos with the player's name, team and position at the bottom. The backs contain a brief write-up plus an ad for Remar Bread printed in red. The cards were distributed one per week. The first five cards were unnumbered. The rest of the set is numbered on the front, but begins with number "5," rather than "6."

CHARLES (Casey) STENGEL
Oaks Manager 10

Fiery CHAS. (Casey) STENGEL has been in baseball 35 years. During his playing days, STENGEL—a fast, hard-hitting outfielder—was with Brooklyn Dodgers, Boston Braves, New York Giants. Has managed Dodgers, Braves and Milwaukee of American Association. He's noted for his ability to develop young players.

Listen to baseball play by play with "Bud" Foster KROW, 960 on your dial

Get the FOUR HOURS FRESHER winner...

REMAR BREAD

		NM	EX	VG
Complete Set (23):		600.00	300.00	180.00
Common Player:		25.00	12.50	7.50
5	Hershell Martin (Hershel)	25.00	12.50	7.50
6	Bill Hart	25.00	12.50	7.50
7	Charlie Gassaway	25.00	12.50	7.50
8	Wally Westlake	25.00	12.50	7.50
9	Mickey Burnett	25.00	12.50	7.50
10	Charles (Casey) Stengel	110.00	55.00	35.00
11	Charlie Metro	25.00	12.50	7.50
12	Tom Hafey	25.00	12.50	7.50
13	Tony Sabol	25.00	12.50	7.50
14	Ed Kearse	25.00	12.50	7.50
15	Bud Foster (Announcer)	25.00	12.50	7.50
16	Johnny Price	25.00	12.50	7.50
17	Gene Bearden	25.00	12.50	7.50
18	Floyd Speer	25.00	12.50	7.50
19	Bryan Stephens	25.00	12.50	7.50
20	Rinaldo (Rugger) Ardizoia	25.00	12.50	7.50
21	Ralph Buxton	25.00	12.50	7.50
22	Ambrose (Bo) Palica	25.00	12.50	7.50
----	Brooks Holder	25.00	12.50	7.50
----	Henry (Cotton) Pippen	25.00	12.50	7.50
----	Billy Raimondi	90.00	45.00	27.50
----	Les Scarsella	25.00	12.50	7.50
----	Glen (Gabby) Stewart	25.00	12.50	7.50

1947 Remar Bread Oakland Oaks

BILLY RAIMONDI
Oaks Catcher 1

BILLY RAIMONDI, 33, has been with the Oaks for 16 years. Managed Acorns part of '45. Believes it's bad luck to cross bats or walk between umpire and catcher. Learned baseball on San Francisco sandlots. Boyhood idol: Baby Ruth; present-day favorite: Joe Di Maggio. Hobby is photography.

"Let's Be Friends"

Listen to baseball play by play with "Bud" Foster KROW, 960 on your dial

REMAR BAKING CO.

Remar's second set consisted of 25 numbered cards, again measuring 2" x 3". The cards are nearly identical to the previous year's set, except the loaf of bread on the back is printed in blue, rather than red.

		NM	EX	VG
Complete Set (24):		600.00	300.00	180.00
Common Player:		25.00	12.50	7.50
1	Billy Raimondi	25.00	12.50	7.50
2	Les Scarsella	25.00	12.50	7.50
3	Brooks Holder	25.00	12.50	7.50
4	Charlie Gassaway	25.00	12.50	7.50
5	Mickey Burnett	25.00	12.50	7.50
6	Ralph Buxton	25.00	12.50	7.50
7	Ed Kearse	25.00	12.50	7.50
8	Charles (Casey) Stengel	75.00	37.50	22.50
9	Bud Foster (Announcer)	25.00	12.50	7.50
10	Ambrose (Bo) Palica	25.00	12.50	7.50
11	Tom Hafey	25.00	12.50	7.50
12	Henry (Cotton) Pippen	25.00	12.50	7.50
13	Floyd Speer	25.00	12.50	7.50
14	Tony Sabol	25.00	12.50	7.50
15	Will Hafey	25.00	12.50	7.50
16	Ray Hamrick	25.00	12.50	7.50
17	Maurice Van Robays	25.00	12.50	7.50
18	Dario Lodigiani	25.00	12.50	7.50
19	Mel (Dizz) Duezabou	25.00	12.50	7.50
20	Damon Hayes	25.00	12.50	7.50
21	Gene Lillard	25.00	12.50	7.50
22	Aldon Wilkie	25.00	12.50	7.50
23	Dewey Soriano	25.00	12.50	7.50
24	Glen Crawford	25.00	12.50	7.50
25		25.00	12.50	7.50

1948 Remar/Sunbeam Bread Oakland Oaks

1948 Oakland OAKS

Let's Be Friends...REACH FOR SUNBEAM BREAD

One of the great minor league rarities, only two examples of this 3-1/4" x 5-1/2" black-and-white team photo card are known.

	NM	EX	VG
1948 Oakland Oaks Team Photo	4,000	2,000	1,200

1949 Remar Bread Oakland Oaks

BILLY MARTIN
Oaks Infielder

Vital Statistics on Billy Martin

Age		1948 Club	
20		Oakland, P.C.L.	
B: T	Wt.	Ht.	G
R: R	165	5:10½	139
AB	R	2B	3B
400	59	111	27	2
HR	SB	RBI	PCT
3	7	15	41	.276

"Let's Be Friends"

Listen to baseball play by play with "Bud" Foster KLX, 910 on your dial

REMAR BAKING CO.

The 1949 Remar Bread issue was increased to 32 cards, again measuring 2" x 3". Unlike the two earlier sets, photos in the 1949 Remar set are surrounded by a thin, white border and are unnumbered. The player's name, team and position appear below the black and white photo. The backs are printed in blue and include the player's 1948 statistics and the distinctive loaf of bread.

		NM	EX	VG
Complete Set (32):		700.00	350.00	210.00
Common Player:		20.00	10.00	6.00
(1)	Ralph Buxton	20.00	10.00	6.00
(2)	Milo Candini	20.00	10.00	6.00
(3)	Rex Cecil	20.00	10.00	6.00
(4)	Loyd Christopher (Lloyd)	20.00	10.00	6.00
(5)	Charles Dressen	20.00	10.00	6.00
(6)	Mel Duezabou	20.00	10.00	6.00
(7)	Bud Foster (Sportscaster)	20.00	10.00	6.00
(8)	Charlie Gassaway	20.00	10.00	6.00
(9)	Ray Hamrick	20.00	10.00	6.00
(10)	Jack Jensen	25.00	12.50	7.50
(11)	Earl Jones	20.00	10.00	6.00
(12)	George Kelly	60.00	30.00	18.00
(13)	Frank Kerr	20.00	10.00	6.00
(14)	Richard Kryhoski	20.00	10.00	6.00
(15)	Harry Lavagetto	20.00	10.00	6.00
(16)	Dario Lodigiani	20.00	10.00	6.00
(17)	Billy Martin	100.00	50.00	30.00
(18)	George Metkovich	20.00	10.00	6.00
(19)	Frank Nelson	20.00	10.00	6.00
(20)	Don Padgett	20.00	10.00	6.00
(21)	Alonzo Perry	40.00	20.00	12.00
(22)	Bill Raimondi	20.00	10.00	6.00
(23)	Earl Rapp	20.00	10.00	6.00
(24)	Eddie Samcoff	20.00	10.00	6.00
(25)	Les Scarsella	20.00	10.00	6.00
(26)	Forest Thompson (Forrest)	20.00	10.00	6.00
(27)	Earl Toolson	20.00	10.00	6.00
(28)	Lou Tost	20.00	10.00	6.00
(29)	Maurice Van Robays	20.00	10.00	6.00
(30)	Jim Wallace	20.00	10.00	6.00
(31)	Arthur Lee Wilson	40.00	20.00	12.00
(32)	Parnell Woods	40.00	20.00	12.00

1950 Remar Bread Oakland Oaks

RAFAEL (RAY) NOBLE
Oaks Catcher

Vital Statistics on Rafael (Ray) Noble

Age		1949 Club	
28		Jersey City, I.L.	
B: R	AB: 189	HR: 7	
T: R	R: 33	SB: 1	
Wt: 210	H: 49	RBI: 29	
Ht: 5:11	2B: 2		
G: 67	3B: 1	PCT: .259	

"Let's Be Friends"

Listen to baseball play by play with "Bud" Foster KLX-AM and KGO-TV

REMAR BAKING CO.

The most common of the Remar Bread issues, the 1950 set contains 27 unnumbered cards, again measuring 2" x 3" and featuring members of the Oakland Oaks. The cards are nearly identical to the previous year's set but can be differentiated by the 1949 statistics on the back.

		NM	EX	VG
Complete Set (27):		500.00	250.00	150.00
Common Player:		20.00	10.00	6.00
(1)	George Bamberger	20.00	10.00	6.00
(2)	Hank Behrman	20.00	10.00	6.00
(3)	Loyd Christopher (Lloyd)	20.00	10.00	6.00
(4)	Chuck Dressen	20.00	10.00	6.00
(5)	Mel Duezabou	20.00	10.00	6.00
(6)	Augie Galan	20.00	10.00	6.00
(7)	Charlie Gassaway	20.00	10.00	6.00
(8)	Allen Gettel	20.00	10.00	6.00
(9)	Ernie W. Groth	20.00	10.00	6.00
(10)	Ray Hamrick	20.00	10.00	6.00
(11)	Earl Harrist	20.00	10.00	6.00
(12)	Billy Herman	60.00	30.00	18.00
(13)	Bob Hofman	20.00	10.00	6.00
(14)	George Kelly	60.00	30.00	18.00

		NM	EX	VG
(15)	Harry Lavagetto	20.00	10.00	6.00
(16)	Eddie Malone	20.00	10.00	6.00
(17)	George Metkovich	20.00	10.00	6.00
(18)	Frank Nelson	20.00	10.00	6.00
(19)	Rafael (Ray) Noble	20.00	10.00	6.00
(20)	Don Padgett	20.00	10.00	6.00
(21)	Earl Rapp	20.00	10.00	6.00
(22)	Clyde Shoun	20.00	10.00	6.00
(23)	Forrest Thompson	20.00	10.00	6.00
(24)	Louis Tost	20.00	10.00	6.00
(25)	Dick Wakefield	20.00	10.00	6.00
(26)	Artie Wilson	40.00	20.00	12.00
(27)	Roy Zimmerman	20.00	10.00	6.00

1958 Richmond Virginians Team Issue

This set of black-and-white cards features members of the N.Y. Yankees' top farm club in posed action photos with a stadium background. Issued on a pair of 8-1/2" x 10" sheets, single cards measure about 2-1/8" x 3" including the white borders around the picture. The player name is in a white strip within the photo. Backs have only the player name and a two-line credit at bottom to Galeski Photo Finishing.

		NM	EX	VG
Complete Set (21):		1,200	600.00	360.00
Common Player:		60.00	30.00	18.00
(1)	Billy Bethel	60.00	30.00	18.00
(2)	Cletis Boyer	90.00	45.00	27.50
(3)	Wade Browning	60.00	30.00	18.00
(4)	Bob Chakales	60.00	30.00	18.00
(5)	Jim Coates	60.00	30.00	18.00
(6)	Jim Command	60.00	30.00	18.00
(7)	Bobby Deakin	60.00	30.00	18.00
(8)	Bob Del Greco	60.00	30.00	18.00
(9)	John Jaciuk	60.00	30.00	18.00
(10)	John James	60.00	30.00	18.00
(11)	Deron Johnson	75.00	37.50	22.50
(12)	Len Johnston	60.00	30.00	18.00
(13)	Bob Kline	60.00	30.00	18.00
(14)	Ed Lopat	80.00	40.00	24.00
(15)	Bob Oldis	60.00	30.00	18.00
(16)	Wilson Parsons	60.00	30.00	18.00
(17)	Rance Pless	60.00	30.00	18.00
(18)	Jim Post	60.00	30.00	18.00
(19)	Danny Schell	60.00	30.00	18.00
(20)	Gerry Thomas	60.00	30.00	18.00
(21)	Bob Weisler	60.00	30.00	18.00

1959 Richmond Virginians

Photos of half a dozen local favorites of the International League Richmond Virginians were featured on ticket stubs during the 1959 season. The black-and-white player portions of the stub measure 2" x 3" and are blank-backed. The unnumbered cards are listed here alphabetically. Richmond was a farm club of the N.Y. Yankees.

		NM	EX	VG
Complete Set (6):		1,200	625.00	375.00
Common Player:		90.00	45.00	25.00
(1)	Clete Boyer	300.00	150.00	90.00
(2)	Jim Coates	200.00	100.00	60.00
(3)	Eli Grba	200.00	100.00	60.00
(4)	John James	200.00	100.00	60.00
(5)	Dick Sanders	200.00	100.00	60.00
(6)	Bill Short	200.00	100.00	60.00

1960 Richmond Virginians

Jerry Thomas
MADISON HEIGHTS, VA.

In 1960, the Richmond Virginians of the International League continued the practice of using player photos on their game tickets. Black-and-white with a blank-back, the player portions of the tickets can be found in two sizes. Unnumbered cards are checklisted here alphabetically. The Richmond team was a farm club of the N.Y. Yankees.

		NM	EX	VG
Complete Set (6):		1,750	875.00	525.00
Common Player:		300.00	150.00	90.00
SMALL SIZE (2" x 2-3/4")		.00	.00	.00
(1)	Bob Martyn	300.00	150.00	90.00
(2)	Jack Reed	300.00	150.00	90.00
LARGE SIZE (2-3/8" x 2-7/8")		.00	.00	.00
(1)	Tony Asaro	300.00	150.00	90.00
(2)	Bill Shantz	300.00	150.00	90.00
(3)	Jerry Thomas	300.00	150.00	90.00
(4)	Bob Weisler	300.00	150.00	90.00

1966 Royal Crown Cola Columbus Yankees

This set of 20 cards was distributed in eight packs of Royal Crown Cola, then based in Columbus, Ga. They were part of a strip measuring 2-1/4" wide. The first 3" of the 9-1/2" strip has a black-and-white photo of the player with his name, position and other biographical data, along with an RC logo in

blue and red. The bottom of the strip has a promotion sponsored by the ball club and RC, offering a case of cola for turning in a complete set in an album provided for the cards. Those who turned in the cards were also eligible to win baseball equipment or picnic coolers in a giveaway at a July 31 game that year. Most cards have the advertisement removed. Strips that include the advertisement should be valued at 1.5X of values shown. The cards are unnumbered and listed in alphabetical order.

		NM	EX	VG
Complete Set (20):		800.00	400.00	240.00
Common Player:		40.00	20.00	12.00
Album:		800.00	400.00	240.00
(1)	Gil Blanco	40.00	20.00	12.00
(2)	Ronnie Boyer	50.00	25.00	15.00
(3)	Jim Brenneman	40.00	20.00	12.00
(4)	Butch Cretara	40.00	20.00	12.00
(5)	Bill Henry	40.00	20.00	12.00
(6)	Joe Jeran	40.00	20.00	12.00
(7)	Jerry Kenney	40.00	20.00	12.00
(8)	Ronnie Kirk	40.00	20.00	12.00
(9)	Tom Kowalski	40.00	20.00	12.00
(10)	Jim Marrujo	40.00	20.00	12.00
(11)	Dave McDonald	40.00	20.00	12.00
(12)	Ed Merritt	40.00	20.00	12.00
(13)	Jim Palma	40.00	20.00	12.00
(14)	Cecil Perkins	40.00	20.00	12.00
(15)	Jack Reed	40.00	20.00	12.00
(16)	Ellie Rodriguez	60.00	30.00	18.00
(17)	John Schroeppel	40.00	20.00	12.00
(18)	Dave Truelock	40.00	20.00	12.00
(19)	Steve Whitaker	40.00	20.00	12.00
(20)	Earl Willoughby	40.00	20.00	12.00

S

1952 San Diego Padres Team Issue

LONNIE SUMMERS

The Padres were one of the highest classification minor league teams for which Globe Printing produced baseball cards in the early 1950s. Like other sets from the San Jose, Calif., printer, the 2-1/8" x 3-3/8" cards are black-and-white, blank-backed and feature the player's name on a white strip on front. Because the Padres were quite often found as a team set, it's likely they were not distributed a card at a time as seems to have been the case with other sets. In 1952, the team was in the Open Classification Pacific Coast League.

		NM	EX	VG
Complete Set (18):		1,000	500.00	300.00
Common Player:		60.00	30.00	18.00
(1)	Al Benton	60.00	30.00	18.00
(2)	Dain Clay	60.00	30.00	18.00
(3)	John Davis	125.00	62.00	37.00
(4)	Dick Faber	60.00	30.00	18.00
(5)	Ben Flowers	60.00	30.00	18.00

		NM	EX	VG
(6)	Murray Franklin	60.00	30.00	18.00
(7)	Herb Gorman	90.00	45.00	27.50
(8)	Jack Graham	60.00	30.00	18.00
(9)	Memo Luna	60.00	30.00	18.00
(10)	Lefty O'Doul	125.00	62.00	37.00
	(Seated, light background.)			
(11)	Lefty O'Doul	125.00	62.00	37.00
	(Standing, dark background.)			
(12)	Al Olsen	60.00	30.00	18.00
(13)	Jimmie Reese	100.00	50.00	30.00
(14)	Al Richter	60.00	30.00	18.00
(15)	Jack Salveson	60.00	30.00	18.00
(16)	Lou Stringer	60.00	30.00	18.00
(17)	Lonnie Summers	60.00	30.00	18.00
(18)	Jack Tobin	60.00	30.00	18.00

1950 San Francisco Seals Popcorn

These 3-1/4" x 4-1/2" black-and-white cards were issued with the purchase of caramel corn at Sicks Stadium.

		NM	EX	VG
Complete Set (13):		700.00	350.00	210.00
Common Player:		60.00	30.00	17.50
(1)	Dick Briskey	60.00	30.00	17.50
(2)	Ralph Buxton	60.00	30.00	17.50
(3)	Harry Feldman	60.00	30.00	17.50
(4)	Chet Johnson	60.00	30.00	17.50
(5)	Al Lien	60.00	30.00	17.50
(6)	Dario Lodigiani	60.00	30.00	17.50
(7)	Cliff Melton	60.00	30.00	17.50
(8)	Roy Nicely	60.00	30.00	17.50
(9)	Roy Partee	60.00	30.00	17.50
(10)	Manny Perez	60.00	30.00	17.50
(11)	Neill Sheridan	60.00	30.00	17.50
(12)	Elmer Singleton	60.00	30.00	17.50
(13)	Jack Tobin	60.00	30.00	17.50

1953 San Francisco Seals Team Issue

This set of 25 cards was sold at Seals Stadium and by mail for 25 cents. Fronts of the 4" x 5" black-and-white cards contain a player photo with facsimile autograph. The player's name, team and position are printed in the white bottom border. Backs of the unnumbered cards are blank. Melton is a rare short-print which has been reprinted.

		NM	EX	VG
Complete Set (25):		600.00	300.00	180.00
Common Player:		30.00	15.00	9.00
(1)	Bill Boemler	30.00	15.00	9.00
(2)	Bill Bradford	30.00	15.00	9.00
(3)	Reno Cheso	30.00	15.00	9.00
(4)	Harlond Clift	30.00	15.00	9.00
(5)	Walt Clough	30.00	15.00	9.00
(6)	Cliff Coggin	30.00	15.00	9.00
(7)	Tommy Heath	30.00	15.00	9.00
(8)	Leo Hughes (Trainer)	30.00	15.00	9.00
(9)	Frank Kalin	30.00	15.00	9.00
(10)	Al Lien	30.00	15.00	9.00
(11)	Al Lyons	30.00	15.00	9.00
(12)	John McCall	30.00	15.00	9.00
(13)	Bill McCawley	30.00	15.00	9.00
(14)	Dave Melton (SP)	200.00	100.00	60.00
(15)	Jim Moran	30.00	15.00	9.00
(16)	Bob Muncrief	30.00	15.00	9.00
(17)	Leo Righetti	30.00	15.00	9.00
(18)	Ted Shandor	30.00	15.00	9.00
(19)	Elmer Singleton	30.00	15.00	9.00
(20)	Lou Stringer	30.00	15.00	9.00
(21)	Sal Taormina	30.00	15.00	9.00
(22)	Will Tiesiera	30.00	15.00	9.00
(23)	Nini Tornay	30.00	15.00	9.00
(24)	George Vico	30.00	15.00	9.00
(25)	Jerry Zuvela	30.00	15.00	9.00

1951 San Jose Red Sox Team Issue

MARVIN OWEN

These 2-1/4" x 3-3/8" black-and-white, unnumbered, blank-backed cards were one of many minor league team sets issued by Globe Printing of San Jose, Calif., in the early 1950s. Cards were usually given away at the ballpark on a one-per-week or one-per-homestand basis, accounting for the rarity of surviving sets. The team was a Class C farm club for the Boston Red Sox in the California League. An album exists for the set, but curiously, it is dated 1952.

		NM	EX	VG
Complete Set (18):		1,000	500.00	300.00
Common Player:		60.00	30.00	18.00
(1)	Ken Aspromonte	75.00	37.00	22.00
(2)	Joe Buck	60.00	30.00	18.00
(3)	Harold Buckwalter	60.00	30.00	18.00
(4)	Al Curtis	60.00	30.00	18.00
(5)	Marvin Eyre	60.00	30.00	18.00
(6)	Jack Heinen	60.00	30.00	18.00
(7)	John Kinney	60.00	30.00	18.00
(8)	Walt Lucas	60.00	30.00	18.00
(9)	Syl McNinch	60.00	30.00	18.00
(10)	Stan McWilliams	60.00	30.00	18.00
(11)	Marvin Owen	60.00	30.00	18.00
(12)	Dick Piedrotti	60.00	30.00	18.00
(13)	Al Schroll	60.00	30.00	18.00
(14)	Ed Sobczak	60.00	30.00	18.00
(15)	Joe Stephenson	60.00	30.00	18.00
(16)	George Storti	60.00	30.00	18.00
(17)	Allan Van Alstyne	60.00	30.00	18.00
(18)	Floyd Warr	60.00	30.00	18.00

1963 Scheible Press Rochester Red Wings

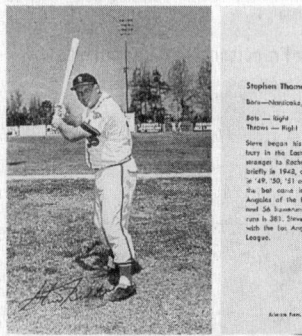

Apparently sold as a stadium concession stand item in a paper and cellophane envelope, the full-color 3-13/16" x 5-7/8" cards are found printed on either a heavy paper stock or thin cardboard stock, each with identical black-and-white back. Two blank-backed cards in slightly larger (4" x 5-7/8") format are checklisted here, although their relationship to the other photos is unknown. The '63 Red Wings were the International League affiliate of the Baltimore Orioles.

		NM	EX	VG
Complete Set (11):		250.00	125.00	75.00
Common Player:		20.00	10.00	6.00
(1)	Joe Altobelli	25.00	12.50	7.50
(2)	Steve Bilko	20.00	10.00	6.00
(3)	Sam E. Bowens	20.00	10.00	6.00
(4)	Don Brummer	20.00	10.00	6.00
(5)	Nelson Chittum (Cardboard only.)	20.00	10.00	6.00
(6a)	Luke Easter (Small format.)	40.00	20.00	12.00
(6b)	Luke Easter (Large format.)	75.00	40.00	25.00
(7)	Darrell Johnson, Chris Krug (Paper only.)	25.00	12.50	7.50
(8)	Ron Kabbes (Large format.)	20.00	10.00	6.00
(9)	Fred Valentine	20.00	10.00	6.00
(10)	Ozzie Virgil	20.00	10.00	6.00
(11)	Ray Youngdahl	20.00	10.00	6.00

1954-1968 Seattle Rainiers/Angels Popcorn

One of the longest-running minor league baseball card promotions was the 1954-68 Seattle popcorn cards. The principal sponsor was Centennial Mills, which had issued cards in the 1940s. Similar in format throughout their period of issue, the cards are 2" x 3" in size, black-and-white, usually featuring portrait photos on the front with the player's name or name and position below. In some years the cards were printed on semi-glossy stock. Some years' card backs are blank, in other years, backs feature ads for various local businesses; in a few years, cards could be found with both blank and printed backs. Many photo and spelling variations are known throughout the series; most are noted in the appropriate checklists. The unnumbered cards are checklisted alphabetically. It is possible a few stragglers will be added to these checklists in the future. In most years a group of 20 cards was released early in the year, supplemented later in the season as roster changes dictated. The cards were given away with the purchase of a box of popcorn sold at Seattle's Sicks stadium. During the card-issuing era, Seattle was an independent team in the Pacific Coast League in 1954-55. From 1956-60 they were a top farm team in the Reds system. They were a Red Sox affiliate from 1961-64, before tying up with the California Angels in 1965.

(Consult checklists for attribution of blank-back cards.)

1954 Seattle Rainiers Popcorn

(Blank-back. Most players photographed in dark cap with light "S.")

BOB HALL
Pitcher

		NM	EX	VG
Complete Set (26):		2,500	1,250	750.00
Common Player:		110.00	55.00	35.00
(1)	Gene Bearden	110.00	55.00	35.00
(2)	Al Brightman	110.00	55.00	35.00
(3)	Jack Burkowatz	110.00	55.00	35.00
(4)	Tommy Byrne (Photo reversed, backwards "S" on cap.)	110.00	55.00	35.00
(5)	Joe Erautt	110.00	55.00	35.00
(6)	Bill Evans	110.00	55.00	35.00
(7)	Van Fletcher	110.00	55.00	35.00
(8)	Bob Hall	110.00	55.00	35.00
(9)	Pete Hernandez	110.00	55.00	35.00
(10)	Lloyd Jenney	110.00	55.00	35.00
(11)	Joe Joshua	110.00	55.00	35.00
(12)	Vern Kindsfather	110.00	55.00	35.00
(13)	Tom Lovrich	110.00	55.00	35.00
(14)	Clarence Maddern	110.00	55.00	35.00
(15)	Don Mallott	110.00	55.00	35.00
(16)	Loren Meyers	110.00	55.00	35.00
(17)	Steve Nagy	110.00	55.00	35.00
(18)	Ray Orteig	110.00	55.00	35.00
(19)	Gerry Priddy	110.00	55.00	35.00
(20)	George Schmees	110.00	55.00	35.00
(21)	Bill Schuster	110.00	55.00	35.00
(22)	Leo Thomas	110.00	55.00	35.00
(23)	Jack Tobin	110.00	55.00	35.00
(24)	Al Widmer	110.00	55.00	35.00
(25)	Artie Wilson	175.00	85.00	50.00
(26)	Al Zarilla	110.00	55.00	35.00

1955 Seattle Rainiers Popcorn

(Blank-back. All players wearing light caps with "R" logo.)

		NM	EX	VG
Complete Set (22):		2,000	1,000	600.00
Common Player:		110.00	55.00	35.00
(1)	Bob Balcena	110.00	55.00	35.00
(2)	Monty Basgall	110.00	55.00	35.00
(3)	Ewell Blackwell	135.00	65.00	40.00
(4)	Bill Brenner	110.00	55.00	35.00
(5)	Jack Burkowatz	110.00	55.00	35.00
(6)	Van Fletcher	110.00	55.00	35.00
(7)	Joe Ginsberg	110.00	55.00	35.00
(8)	Jehosie Heard	110.00	55.00	35.00
(9)	Fred Hutchinson	110.00	55.00	35.00
(10)	Larry Jansen	110.00	55.00	35.00
(11)	Bob Kelly	110.00	55.00	35.00
(12)	Bill Kennedy	110.00	55.00	35.00
(13)	Lou Kretlow	110.00	55.00	35.00
(14)	Rocco Krsnich	110.00	55.00	35.00
(15)	Carmen Mauro	110.00	55.00	35.00
(16)	John Oldham	110.00	55.00	35.00
(17)	George Schmees	110.00	55.00	35.00
(18)	Elmer Singleton	110.00	55.00	35.00
(19)	Alan Strange	110.00	55.00	35.00
(20)	Gene Verble	110.00	55.00	35.00
(21)	Marv Williams	110.00	55.00	35.00
(22)	Harvey Zernia	110.00	55.00	35.00

1956 Seattle Rainiers Popcorn

JOE TAYLOR
Outfielder

(Blank-back or Gil's Drive-Ins (two locations) ad on back. Players wearing light cap with white "R.")

		NM	EX	VG
Complete Set (27):		2,500	1,250	750.00
Common Player:		110.00	55.00	35.00
(1)	Fred Baczewski	110.00	55.00	35.00
(2)	Bob Balcena	110.00	55.00	35.00
(3)	Bill Brenner	110.00	55.00	35.00

		NM	EX	VG
(4)	Sherry Dixon	110.00	55.00	35.00
(5)	Don Fracchia	110.00	55.00	35.00
(6)	Bill Glynn	110.00	55.00	35.00
(7)	Larry Jansen	110.00	55.00	35.00
(8)	Howie Judson	110.00	55.00	35.00
(9)	Bill Kennedy	110.00	55.00	35.00
(10)	Jack Lohrke	110.00	55.00	35.00
(11)	Vic Lombardi	110.00	55.00	35.00
(12)	Carmen Mauro	110.00	55.00	35.00
(13)	Ray Orteig	110.00	55.00	35.00
(14)	Bud Podbielan	110.00	55.00	35.00
(15)	Leo Righetti	110.00	55.00	35.00
(16)	Jim Robertson	110.00	55.00	35.00
(17)	Art Shallock (Schallock)	110.00	55.00	35.00
(18)	Art Schult	110.00	55.00	35.00
(19)	Luke Sewell	135.00	65.00	40.00
(20)	Elmer Singleton	110.00	55.00	35.00
(21a)	Milt Smith (Action)	110.00	55.00	35.00
(21b)	Milt Smith (Portrait)	110.00	55.00	35.00
(22)	Vern Stephens	110.00	55.00	35.00
(23)	Alan Strange	110.00	55.00	35.00
(24)	Joe Taylor	110.00	55.00	35.00
(25)	Artie Wilson	175.00	85.00	50.00
(26)	Harvey Zernia	110.00	55.00	35.00

1957 Seattle Rainiers Popcorn

JIM DYCK
Infielder

By presenting any nine different pictures to either of GIL'S DRIVE-INS you will receive FREE an 8" x 10" player picture of your choice and you still keep your nine small pictures.

Three locations to serve you

GIL'S DRIVE-IN
4406 Rainier Avenue
1 mile south of Sicks' Stadium

3500 Avalon Way
35th S.W. and Avalon Way
West Seattle
•
Burien
1st South and South 152nd

(Blank-back or Gil's Drive-Ins (three locations) ad on back. Players wearing lighter caps with white "R." No base on letter "T" on outfielders or pitchers cards.)

		NM	EX	VG
Complete Set (24):		2,000	1,000	600.00
Common Player:		100.00	50.00	30.00
(1)	Dick Aylward	100.00	50.00	30.00
(2)	Bob Balcena	100.00	50.00	30.00
(3)	Eddie Basinki	100.00	50.00	30.00
(4)	Hal Bevan	100.00	50.00	30.00
(5)	Joe Black	125.00	65.00	35.00
(6)	Juan Delis	100.00	50.00	30.00
(7)	Jim Dyck	100.00	50.00	30.00
(8)	Marion Fricano	100.00	50.00	30.00
(9)	Bill Glynn	100.00	50.00	30.00
(10)	Larry Jansen	100.00	50.00	30.00
(11)	Howie Judson	100.00	50.00	30.00
(12)	Bill Kennedy	100.00	50.00	30.00
(13)	Jack Lohrke	100.00	50.00	30.00
(14)	Carmen Mauro	100.00	50.00	30.00
(15)	George Munger	100.00	50.00	30.00
(16)	Lefty O'Doul	150.00	75.00	45.00
(17)	Ray Orteig	100.00	50.00	30.00
(18)	Duane Pillette	100.00	50.00	30.00
(19)	Bud Podbielan	100.00	50.00	30.00
(20)	Charley Rabe	100.00	50.00	30.00
(21)	Leo Righetti	100.00	50.00	30.00
(22)	Joe Taylor	100.00	50.00	30.00
(23)	Edo Vanni	100.00	50.00	30.00
(24)	Morrie Wills (Maury)	250.00	125.00	75.00

1958 Seattle Rainiers Popcorn

(All cards have Ralph's Thriftway Market ad on back.)

		NM	EX	VG
Complete Set (19):		1,250	625.00	375.00
Common Player:		75.00	35.00	20.00
(1)	Bob Balcena	75.00	35.00	20.00
(2)	Ed Basinki	75.00	35.00	20.00
(3)	Hal Bevan	75.00	35.00	20.00
(4)	Jack Bloomfield	75.00	35.00	20.00
(5)	Juan Delis	75.00	35.00	20.00
(6)	Dutch Dotterer	75.00	35.00	20.00
(7)	Jim Dyck	75.00	35.00	20.00
(8)	Al Federoff	90.00	45.00	27.50
(9)	Art Fowler	75.00	35.00	20.00
(10)	Bill Kennedy	75.00	35.00	20.00
(11)	Marty Kutyna	75.00	35.00	20.00
(12)	Ray Orteig	75.00	35.00	20.00
(13)	Duane Pillette	75.00	35.00	20.00
(14)	Vada Pinson	225.00	110.00	70.00
(15)	Connie Ryan	75.00	35.00	20.00
(16)	Phil Shartzer	75.00	35.00	20.00
(17)	Max Surkont	75.00	35.00	20.00
(18)	Gale Wade	75.00	35.00	20.00
(19)	Ted Wieand	75.00	35.00	20.00

1959 Seattle Rainiers Popcorn

(Blank-back. First printing cards have players in lighter cap with white "R." Second printing cards have darker caps with shadow around "R.")

DON RUDOLPH
Pitcher

		NM	EX	VG
Complete Set (37):		2,500	1,250	750.00
Common Player:		75.00	35.00	20.00
(1)	Bobby Adams	75.00	35.00	20.00
(2)	Frank Amaya	75.00	35.00	20.00
(3)	Hal Bevan	75.00	35.00	20.00
(4)	Jack Bloomfield	75.00	35.00	20.00
(5)	Clarence Churn	75.00	35.00	20.00
(6)	Jack Dittmer	75.00	35.00	20.00
(7)	Jim Dyck	75.00	35.00	20.00
(8)	Dee Fondy	75.00	35.00	20.00
(9)	Mark Freeman	75.00	35.00	20.00
(10)	Dick Hanlon	75.00	35.00	20.00
(11)	Carroll Hardy	75.00	35.00	20.00
(12)	Bobby Henrich	75.00	35.00	20.00
(13)	Jay Hook	75.00	35.00	20.00
(14)	Fred Hutchinson	75.00	35.00	20.00
(15)	Jake Jenkins	75.00	35.00	20.00
(16)	Eddie Kazak	75.00	35.00	20.00
(17)	Bill Kennedy	75.00	35.00	20.00
(18)	Harry Lowrey	75.00	35.00	20.00
(19a)	Harry Malmbeg (Malmberg)	75.00	35.00	20.00
(19b)	Harry Malmberg	75.00	35.00	20.00
(20)	Bob Mape (Mabe)	75.00	35.00	20.00
(21)	Darrell Martin	75.00	35.00	20.00
(22)	John McCall	75.00	35.00	20.00
(23)	Claude Osteen	75.00	35.00	20.00
(24)	Paul Pettit	75.00	35.00	20.00
(25)	Charley Rabe	75.00	35.00	20.00
(26)	Rudy Regalado	75.00	35.00	20.00
(27)	Eric Rodin	75.00	35.00	20.00
(28)	Don Rudolph	75.00	35.00	20.00
(29)	Lou Skizas	75.00	35.00	20.00
(30)	Dave Stenhouse	75.00	35.00	20.00
(31)	Alan Strange	75.00	35.00	20.00
(32)	Max Surkont	75.00	35.00	20.00
(33)	Ted Tappe	75.00	35.00	20.00
(34)	Elmer Valo	75.00	35.00	20.00
(35)	Gale Wade	75.00	35.00	20.00
(36)	Bill Wight	75.00	35.00	20.00
(37)	Ed Winceniak	75.00	35.00	20.00

1960 Seattle Rainiers Popcorn

JOHNNY O'BRIEN
Infielder

(Blank-back. All players posed against outfield fence wearing dark caps with shadowed "R.")

		NM	EX	VG
Complete Set (18):		1,200	600.00	350.00
Common Player:		75.00	35.00	20.00
(1)	Charlie Beamon	75.00	35.00	20.00
(2)	Hal Bevan	75.00	35.00	20.00
(3)	Whammy Douglas	75.00	35.00	20.00
(4)	Buddy Gilbert	75.00	35.00	20.00
(5)	Hal Jeffcoat	75.00	35.00	20.00
(6)	Leigh Lawrence	75.00	35.00	20.00
(7)	Darrell Martin	75.00	35.00	20.00
(8)	Francisco Obregon	75.00	35.00	20.00
(9)	Johnny O'Brien	90.00	45.00	27.50
(10)	Paul Pettit	75.00	35.00	20.00
(11)	Ray Rippelmeyer (Ripplemeyer)	75.00	35.00	20.00
(12)	Don Rudolph	75.00	35.00	20.00
(13)	Willard Schmidt	75.00	35.00	20.00
(14)	Dick Sisler	75.00	35.00	20.00
(15)	Lou Skizas	75.00	35.00	20.00
(16)	Joe Taylor	75.00	35.00	20.00
(17)	Bob Thurman	75.00	35.00	20.00
(18)	Gerald Zimmerman	75.00	35.00	20.00

1961 Seattle Rainiers Popcorn

(Blank-back. New uniforms: dark cap with stylized "S," "Rainiers" on chest. Many players have both portrait and action poses. Tough to distinguish from 1962 set; names on '61s are more compact, bold than on '62 which has taller, lighter names.)

JOHN TILLMAN
Infielder

		NM	EX	VG
Complete Set (29):		2,000	1,000	600.00
Common Player:		75.00	35.00	20.00
(1)	Galen Cisco	75.00	35.00	20.00
(2)	Marlan Coughtry/Btg	75.00	35.00	20.00
(3)	Marlin Coughtry/Portrait	75.00	35.00	20.00
(4)	Pete Cronin	75.00	35.00	20.00
(5)	Arnold Earley	75.00	35.00	20.00
(6)	Bob Heffner/Pitching	75.00	35.00	20.00
(7)	Bob Heffner/Portrait	75.00	35.00	20.00
(8)	Curt Jensen/Action	75.00	35.00	20.00
(9)	Curt Jensen/Portrait	75.00	35.00	20.00
(10)	Harry Malmberg/Coach	75.00	35.00	20.00
(11)	Harry Malmberg (Player-coach.)	75.00	35.00	20.00
(12)	Dave Mann	75.00	35.00	20.00
(13)	Darrell Martin	75.00	35.00	20.00
(14)	Erv Palica/Pitching	75.00	35.00	20.00
(15)	Ervin Palica/Portrait	75.00	35.00	20.00
(16)	Johnny Pesky/Action	90.00	45.00	27.50
(17)	Johnny Pesky/Portrait	90.00	45.00	27.50
(18)	Dick Radatz	100.00	50.00	30.00
(19)	Ted Schreiber/Btg	75.00	35.00	20.00
(20)	Ted Shreiber/Portrait	75.00	35.00	20.00
(21)	Paul Smith/Action	75.00	35.00	20.00
(22)	Paul Smith/Portrait	75.00	35.00	20.00
(23)	John Tillman/Infielder	75.00	35.00	20.00
(24)	Bob Tillman/Catcher	75.00	35.00	20.00
(25)	Bo Toft	75.00	35.00	20.00
(26)	Tom Umphlett/Action	75.00	35.00	20.00
(27)	Tom Umphlett/Portrait	75.00	35.00	20.00
(28)	Earl Wilson	75.00	35.00	20.00
(29)	Ken Wolfe	75.00	35.00	20.00

1962 Seattle Rainiers Popcorn

BILLY HARRELL

(Blank-back. Nearly identical to '61s except for player name. On 1961 cards, name is compact and bold; on '62s the name is taller, lighter. Some photos repeated from 1961.)

		NM	EX	VG
Complete Set (19):		1,250	625.00	375.00
Common Player:		75.00	35.00	20.00
(1)	Dave Hall	75.00	35.00	20.00
(2)	Billy Harrell	75.00	35.00	20.00
(3)	Curt Jensen (Jenson)	75.00	35.00	20.00
(4)	Stew MacDonald	75.00	35.00	20.00
(5)	Bill MacLeod	75.00	35.00	20.00
(6)	Dave Mann (Action)	75.00	35.00	20.00
(7)	Dave Mann (Portrait)	75.00	35.00	20.00
(8)	Dave Morehead	75.00	35.00	20.00
(9)	John Pesky	90.00	45.00	27.50
(10)	Ted Schreiber (Second baseman.)	75.00	35.00	20.00
(11)	Ted Schreiber (Infielder)	75.00	35.00	20.00
(12)	Elmer Singleton	75.00	35.00	20.00
(13)	Archie Skeen	75.00	35.00	20.00
(14)	Pete Smith	75.00	35.00	20.00
(15)	George Spencer	75.00	35.00	20.00
(16)	Bo Toft (1961 photo)	75.00	35.00	20.00
(17)	Bo Toft (New photo.)	75.00	35.00	20.00
(18)	Tom Umphlett	75.00	35.00	20.00
(19)	Ken Wolfe	75.00	35.00	20.00

1963 Seattle Rainiers Popcorn

(Blank-back. No positions stated on cards except for manager and coach. Impossible to differentiate 1963 issue from 1964 except by player selection.)

		NM	EX	VG
Complete Set (15):		800.00	400.00	240.00
Common Player:		60.00	30.00	17.50
(1)	Don Gile	60.00	30.00	17.50
(2)	Dave Hall	60.00	30.00	17.50
(3)	Billy Harrell	60.00	30.00	17.50
(4)	Pete Jernigan	60.00	30.00	17.50
(5)	Stan Johnson	60.00	30.00	17.50
(6)	Dalton Jones	60.00	30.00	17.50
(7)	Mel Parnell	60.00	30.00	17.50
(8)	Joe Pedrazzini	60.00	30.00	17.50
(9)	Elmer Singleton	60.00	30.00	17.50
(10)	Archie Skeen	60.00	30.00	17.50
(11)	Rac Slider	60.00	30.00	17.50
(12)	Pete Smith	60.00	30.00	17.50
(13)	Bill Spanswick	60.00	30.00	17.50
(14)	George Spencer	60.00	30.00	17.50
(15)	Wilbur Wood	90.00	45.00	27.50

1964 Seattle Rainiers Popcorn

EARL AVERILL

(Blank-back. Impossible to differentiate between 1963 and 1964 issues except by player selection.)

		NM	EX	VG
Complete Set (18):		1,000	500.00	300.00
Common Player:		60.00	30.00	17.50
(1)	Earl Averill	60.00	30.00	17.50
(2)	Billy Gardner	60.00	30.00	17.50
(3)	Russ Gibson	60.00	30.00	17.50
(4)	Guido Grilli	60.00	30.00	17.50
(5)	Bob Guindon	60.00	30.00	17.50
(6)	Billy Harrell	60.00	30.00	17.50
(7)	Fred Holmes	60.00	30.00	17.50
(8)	Stan Johnson	60.00	30.00	17.50
(9)	Hal Kolstad	60.00	30.00	17.50
(10)	Felix Maldonado	60.00	30.00	17.50
(11)	Gary Modrell	60.00	30.00	17.50
(12)	Merlin Nippert	60.00	30.00	17.50
(13)	Rico Petrocelli	100.00	50.00	30.00
(14)	Jay Ritchie	60.00	30.00	17.50
(15)	Barry Shetrone	60.00	30.00	17.50
(16)	Pete Smith	60.00	30.00	17.50
(17)	Bill Tuttle	60.00	30.00	17.50
(18)	Edo Vanni	60.00	30.00	17.50

1965 Seattle Angels Popcorn

(Back has cartoon angel batting. Several cards, issued prior to the season, have blank-backs.)

		NM	EX	VG
Complete Set (22):		600.00	300.00	180.00
Common Player:		30.00	15.00	9.00
(1)	Earl Averill	30.00	15.00	9.00
(2)	Tom Burgmeier	30.00	15.00	9.00
(3)	Bob Guindon	30.00	15.00	9.00
(4)	Jack Hernandez	30.00	15.00	9.00
(5)	Fred Holmes	30.00	15.00	9.00
(6)	Ed Kirkpatrick	30.00	15.00	9.00
(7)	Hal Kolstad	30.00	15.00	9.00
(8)	Joe Koppe	30.00	15.00	9.00
(9)	Les Kuhnz	30.00	15.00	9.00
(10)	Bob Lemon	60.00	30.00	17.50
(11)	Bobby Locke	30.00	15.00	9.00
(12)	Jim McGlothlin	30.00	15.00	9.00
(13a)	Bob Radovich (Blank-back.)	30.00	15.00	9.00
(13b)	Bob Radovich (Ad-back.)	30.00	15.00	9.00
(14)	Merritt Ranew	30.00	15.00	9.00
(15)	Jimmie Reese (Blank-back.)	45.00	22.50	13.50
(16a)	Rick Reichardt (Blank-back.)	30.00	15.00	9.00
(16b)	Rick Reichardt (Ad-back.)	30.00	15.00	9.00
(17)	Tom Satriano	30.00	15.00	9.00
(18)	Dick Simpson	30.00	15.00	9.00
(19)	Jack Spring (Blank-back.)	30.00	15.00	9.00
(20)	Ed Sukla	30.00	15.00	9.00
(21)	Jackie Warner	30.00	15.00	9.00
(22)	Stan Williams	30.00	15.00	9.00

1966 Seattle Angels Popcorn

JIM CAMPANIS

SEATTLE
ANGELS
GAMES BROADCAST ON
KVI
RADIO
570

Presented by
CHEVRON DEALERS
STANDARD STATIONS
WESTERN AIRLINES
HOUSEHOLD FINANCE CORP.
WHEATIES, BREAKFAST OF
CHAMPIONS

(Cartoon angel pitching on back, first "Presented by" advertiser at bottom is Chevron Dealers.)

	NM	EX	VG
Complete Set (29):	900.00	450.00	275.00
Common Player:	30.00	15.00	9.00
(1) Del Bates	30.00	15.00	9.00
(2) Tom Burgmeier	30.00	15.00	9.00
(3) Jim Campanis	40.00	20.00	12.00
(4) Jim Coates	30.00	15.00	9.00
(5) Tony Cortopassi	30.00	15.00	9.00
(6) Chuck Estrada	30.00	15.00	9.00
(7) Ray Hernandez	30.00	15.00	9.00
(8) Jay Johnstone	50.00	25.00	15.00
(9) Bill Kelso	30.00	15.00	9.00
(10) Vic LaRose	30.00	15.00	9.00
(11) Bobby Locke	30.00	15.00	9.00
(12) Rudy May	30.00	15.00	9.00
(13) Andy Messersmith	50.00	25.00	15.00
(14) Bubba Morton	30.00	15.00	9.00
(15) Cotton Nash	30.00	15.00	9.00
(16) John Olerud	50.00	25.00	15.00
(17) Marty Pattin	30.00	15.00	9.00
(18) Merritt Ranew	30.00	15.00	9.00
(19) Minnie Rojas	30.00	15.00	9.00
(20) George Rubio	30.00	15.00	9.00
(21) Al Spangler	30.00	15.00	9.00
(22) Ed Sukla	30.00	15.00	9.00
(23) Felix Torres	30.00	15.00	9.00
(24) Hector Torres	30.00	15.00	9.00
(25) Ken Turner	30.00	15.00	9.00
(26) Chuck Vinson	30.00	15.00	9.00
(27) Don Wallace	30.00	15.00	9.00
(28) Jack D. Warner	30.00	15.00	9.00
(29) Mike White	30.00	15.00	9.00

1967 Seattle Angels Popcorn

(Cartoon angel pitching on back, first "Presented by" advertiser is Western Airlines.)

	NM	EX	VG
Complete Set (19):	500.00	250.00	150.00
Common Player:	30.00	15.00	9.00
(1) George Banks	30.00	15.00	9.00
(2) Tom Burgmeier	30.00	15.00	9.00
(3) Jim Coates	30.00	15.00	9.00
(4) Chuck Cottier	30.00	15.00	9.00
(5) Tony Curry	30.00	15.00	9.00
(6) Vern Geishert	30.00	15.00	9.00
(7) Jesse Hickman	30.00	15.00	9.00
(8) Bill Kelso	30.00	15.00	9.00
(9) Ed Kirkpatrick	30.00	15.00	9.00
(10) Chris Krug	30.00	15.00	9.00
(11) Bobby Locke	30.00	15.00	9.00
(12) Bill Murphy	30.00	15.00	9.00
(13) Marty Pattin	30.00	15.00	9.00
(14) Merritt Ranew	30.00	15.00	9.00
(15) Bob Sadowski	30.00	15.00	9.00
(16) Ed Sukla	30.00	15.00	9.00
(17) Hector Torres	30.00	15.00	9.00
(18) Chuck Vinson	30.00	15.00	9.00
(19) Don Wallace	30.00	15.00	9.00

1968 Seattle Angels Popcorn

JARVIS TATUM

(Blank-back.)

	NM	EX	VG
Complete Set (18):	500.00	250.00	150.00
Common Player:	30.00	15.00	9.00
(1) Ethan Blackaby	30.00	15.00	9.00
(2) Jim Coates	30.00	15.00	9.00
(3) Tom Egan	30.00	15.00	9.00
(4) Larry Elliott (Elliot)	30.00	15.00	9.00
(5) Jim Engelhardt	30.00	15.00	9.00
(6) Gus Gil	30.00	15.00	9.00
(7) Bill Harrelson	30.00	15.00	9.00
(8) Steve Hovley	30.00	15.00	9.00
(9) Jim Mahoney	30.00	15.00	9.00
(10) Mickey McGuire	30.00	15.00	9.00
(11) Joe Overton	30.00	15.00	9.00
(12) Marty Pattin	30.00	15.00	9.00
(13) Larry Sherry	30.00	15.00	9.00
(14) Marv Staehle	30.00	15.00	9.00
(15) Ed Sukla	30.00	15.00	9.00
(16) Jarvis Tatum	30.00	15.00	9.00
(17) Hawk Taylor	30.00	15.00	9.00
(18) Chuck Vinson	30.00	15.00	9.00

1952 Shawnee Hawks Team Issue

Formatted like the other known minor league issues from Globe Printing of San Jose, Calif., this set chronicles the 1952 version of the Class D (Sooner State League) Shawnee (Okla.) Hawks. The black-and-white and measure about 2-1/4" x 3-3/8". The checklist here is incomplete, the set probably having been originally issued with about 18 cards.

LOYD McPHERSON

	NM	EX	VG
Common Player:	60.00	30.00	18.00
(1) Russell Bland (Blanco)	60.00	30.00	18.00
(2) Perry Haddock	60.00	30.00	18.00
(3) Jim Kenaga	60.00	30.00	18.00
(4) Hal Long	60.00	30.00	18.00
(5) Loyd McPherson	60.00	30.00	18.00
(6) Rolando Olmo	60.00	30.00	18.00
(7) Dave Rolette	60.00	30.00	18.00
(8) Hank Salazar	60.00	30.00	18.00

1960 Shopsy's Frankfurters Toronto Maple Leafs

SHOPSY'S PLAYER PHOTO

ARCHIE WILSON - 1960

Only the Toronto Maple Leafs of the International League - including many former and future major leaguers - are included in this set. The cards are about 2-1/4" x 3-1/4", blank-back and printed in black-and-white. The unnumbered cards are checklisted here alphabetically.

	NM	EX	VG
Complete Set (23):	2,000	1,000	600.00
Common Player:	90.00	45.00	30.00
Album:	100.00	50.00	30.00
(1) George Anderson (Sparky)	150.00	75.00	45.00
(2) Bob Chakales	90.00	45.00	30.00
(3) Al Cicotte	90.00	45.00	30.00
(4) Rip Coleman	90.00	45.00	30.00
(5) Steve Demeter	90.00	45.00	30.00
(6) Don Dillard	90.00	45.00	30.00
(7) Frank Funk	90.00	45.00	30.00
(8) Russ Heman	90.00	45.00	30.00
(9) Earl Hersh	90.00	45.00	30.00
(10) Allen Jones	90.00	45.00	30.00
(11) Jim King	90.00	45.00	30.00
(12) Jack Kubiszyn	90.00	45.00	30.00
(13) Mel McGaha	90.00	45.00	30.00
(14) Bill Moran	90.00	45.00	30.00
(15) Ron Negray	90.00	45.00	30.00
(16) Herb Plews	90.00	45.00	30.00
(17) Steve Ridzik	90.00	45.00	30.00
(18) Pat Scantlebury	90.00	45.00	30.00
(19) Bill Smith (Trainer)	90.00	45.00	30.00
(20) Bob Smith	90.00	45.00	30.00
(21) Tim Thompson	90.00	45.00	30.00
(22) Jack Waters	90.00	45.00	30.00
(23) Archie Wilson	90.00	45.00	30.00

1947 Signal Gasoline Pacific Coast League

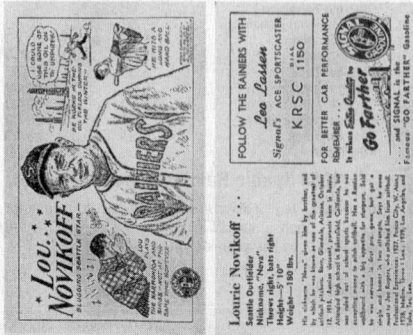

Five of the eight PCL teams participated in this baseball card promotion, giving away cards of hometeam players. Because of vagaries of local distribution, some teams, notably Sacramento and Seattle, are scarcer than others, and there are specific player rarities among other teams. The black-and-white cards are 5-9/16" x 3-1/2" and feature on the front a drawing of the player and several personal or career highlights in cartoon style. The artwork was done by former N.Y. Giants pitcher Al Demaree. On the backs are player biographical details, an ad for Signal Gas and an ad for the co-sponsoring radio station in each locale. Cards are unnumbered.

	NM	EX	VG
Complete Set (89):	6,000	3,000	1,800
(Team sets listed below.)			

1947 Signal Gasoline Hollywood Stars

	NM	EX	VG
Complete Set (20):	1,200	600.00	350.00
Common Player:	50.00	25.00	15.00
(1) Ed Albosta	50.00	25.00	15.00
(2) Carl Cox	50.00	25.00	15.00
(3) Frank Dasso	50.00	25.00	15.00
(4) Tod Davis	50.00	25.00	15.00
(5) Jim Delsing	50.00	25.00	15.00
(6) Jimmy Dykes	50.00	25.00	15.00
(7) Paul Gregory	50.00	25.00	15.00
(8) Fred Haney	50.00	25.00	15.00
(9) Frank Kelleher	50.00	25.00	15.00
(10) Joe Krakauskas	50.00	25.00	15.00
(11) Al Libke	50.00	25.00	15.00
(12) Tony Lupien	50.00	25.00	15.00
(13) Xaiver Rescigno	50.00	25.00	15.00
(14) Jack Sherman	50.00	25.00	15.00
(15) Andy Skurski	50.00	25.00	15.00
(16) Glen (Glenn) Stewart	50.00	25.00	15.00
(17) Al Unser	50.00	25.00	15.00
(18) Fred Vaughn	50.00	25.00	15.00
(19) Woody Williams	250.00	125.00	75.00
(20) Dutch (Gus) Zernial	75.00	37.00	22.00

1947 Signal Gasoline Los Angeles Angels

	NM	EX	VG
Complete Set (18):	700.00	350.00	210.00
Common Player:	40.00	20.00	12.00
(1) Red Adams	40.00	20.00	12.00
(2) Larry Barton	40.00	20.00	12.00
(3) Cliff Chambers	40.00	20.00	12.00
(4) Lloyd Christopher	40.00	20.00	12.00
(5) Cece Garriott	40.00	20.00	12.00
(6) Al Glossop	40.00	20.00	12.00
(7) Bill Kelly	40.00	20.00	12.00
(8) Red Lynn	40.00	20.00	12.00
(9) Eddie Malone	40.00	20.00	12.00
(10) Dutch McCall	40.00	20.00	12.00
(11) Don Osbome	40.00	20.00	12.00
(12) John Ostrowski	40.00	20.00	12.00
(13) Reggie Otero	40.00	20.00	12.00
(14) Ray Prim	40.00	20.00	12.00
(15) Ed Sauer	40.00	20.00	12.00
(16) Bill Schuster	40.00	20.00	12.00
(17) Tuck Stainback	40.00	20.00	12.00
(18) Lou Stringer	40.00	20.00	12.00

1947 Signal Gasoline Oakland Oaks

	NM	EX	VG
Complete Set (19):	800.00	400.00	240.00
Common Player:	40.00	20.00	12.00
(1) Vic Buccola	40.00	20.00	12.00
(2) Mickey Burnett	40.00	20.00	12.00
(3) Ralph Buxton	40.00	20.00	12.00
(4) Vince DiMaggio	95.00	47.00	28.00
(5) Dizz Duezabou	40.00	20.00	12.00
(6) Bud Foster	40.00	20.00	12.00
(7) Sherriff Gassaway	40.00	20.00	12.00
(8) Tom Hafey	40.00	20.00	12.00
(9) Brooks Holder	40.00	20.00	12.00
(10) Gene Lillard	40.00	20.00	12.00
(11) Dario Lodigiani	40.00	20.00	12.00
(12) Hershel Martin	40.00	20.00	12.00
(13) Cotton Pippen	40.00	20.00	12.00
(14) Billy Raimondi	40.00	20.00	12.00
(15) Tony Sabol	40.00	20.00	12.00
(16) Les Scarsella	40.00	20.00	12.00
(17) Floyd Speer	40.00	20.00	12.00
(18) Casey Stengel	100.00	50.00	30.00
(19) Maurice Van Robays	40.00	20.00	12.00

1947 Signal Gasoline Sacramento Solons

	NM	EX	VG
Complete Set (16):	2,000	1,000	600.00
Common Player:	60.00	30.00	18.00
(1) Bud Beasley	60.00	30.00	18.00
(2) Frank Dasso	60.00	30.00	18.00
(3) Ed Fitzgerald (Fitz Gerald)	60.00	30.00	18.00
(4) Guy Fletcher	60.00	30.00	18.00
(5) Tony Freitas	60.00	30.00	18.00
(6) Red Mann	60.00	30.00	18.00
(7) Joe Marty	60.00	30.00	18.00
(8) Steve Mesner	60.00	30.00	18.00
(9) Bill Ramsey	60.00	30.00	18.00
(10) Charley Ripple	250.00	125.00	75.00
(11) John Rizzo	250.00	125.00	75.00
(12) Al Smith	250.00	125.00	75.00
(13) Ronnie Smith	250.00	125.00	75.00
(14) Tommy Thompson	250.00	125.00	75.00
(15) Jim Warner	115.00	55.00	35.00
(16) Ed Zipay	115.00	55.00	35.00

1947 Signal Gasoline Seattle Rainiers

	NM	EX	VG
Complete Set (16):	1,750	875.00	525.00
Common Player:	75.00	37.00	22.00
(1) Kewpie Barrett	100.00	50.00	30.00
(2) Herman Besse	100.00	50.00	30.00
(3) Guy Fletcher	100.00	50.00	30.00
(4) Jack Jakucki	100.00	50.00	30.00
(5) Bob Johnson	100.00	50.00	30.00
(6) Pete Jonas	275.00	135.00	82.00
(7) Hillis Layne	100.00	50.00	30.00
(8) Red Mann	100.00	50.00	30.00
(9) Lou Novikoff	100.00	50.00	30.00
(10) John O'Neill	100.00	50.00	30.00
(11) Bill Ramsey	100.00	50.00	30.00
(12) Mickey Rocco	100.00	50.00	30.00
(13) George Scharein	100.00	50.00	30.00
(14) Hal Sueme	100.00	50.00	30.00
(15) Jo Jo White	100.00	50.00	30.00
(16) Tony York	100.00	50.00	30.00

1948 Signal Gasoline Oakland Oaks

Issued by Signal Oil in the Oakland area in 1948, this 24-card set features members of the Oakland Oaks of the Pacific Coast League. The unnumbered cards, measuring 2-3/8" x 3-1/2", were given away at gas stations. The front consists of a color photo, while the backs (printed in either blue or black) contain a brief player write-up along with a Signal Oil ad and logo.

	NM	EX	VG
Complete Set (24):	900.00	450.00	275.00
Common Player:	40.00	20.00	12.00
(1) John C. Babich	40.00	20.00	12.00
(2) Ralph Buxton	40.00	20.00	12.00
(3) Loyd E. Christopher (Lloyd)	40.00	20.00	12.00
(4) Merrill Russell Combs	40.00	20.00	12.00
(5) Melvin E. Deuzabou	40.00	20.00	12.00
(6) Nicholas ("Nick") Etten	40.00	20.00	12.00
(7) Bud Foster (Announcer)	40.00	20.00	12.00
(8) Charles Gassaway	40.00	20.00	12.00
(9) Will Hafey	40.00	20.00	12.00
(10) Ray Hamrick	40.00	20.00	12.00
(11) Brooks Richard Holder	40.00	20.00	12.00
(12) Earl Jones	40.00	20.00	12.00
(13) Harry "Cookie" Lavagetto	40.00	20.00	12.00
(14) Robert E. Lillard	40.00	20.00	12.00
(15) Dario Lodigiani	40.00	20.00	12.00
(16) Ernie Lombardi	75.00	37.50	22.50
(17a) Alfred Manuel Martin (Born 1921.)	65.00	32.50	20.00
(17b) Alfred Manuel Martin (Born 1928.)	75.00	37.50	22.50
(18) George Michael Metkovich	40.00	20.00	12.00
(19) William L. Raimondi	40.00	20.00	12.00
(20) Les George Scarsella	40.00	20.00	12.00
(21) Floyd Vernie Speer	40.00	20.00	12.00
(22) Charles "Casey" Stengel	115.00	57.00	34.00
(23) Maurice Van Robays	40.00	20.00	12.00
(24) Aldon Jay Wilkie	40.00	20.00	12.00

1951 Sioux City Soos Postcards

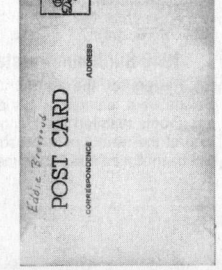

These black-and-white team-issued postcards feature on their fronts posed full-length photos of members of the Class A Western League farm team of the New York Giants. In standard 3-1/2" x 5-1/2" size, the cards have a wide border at bottom which has the team name, the year and a logo featuring an ear of corn. Backs have typical postcard indicia. Players are not identified anywhere on the cards. It is presumed this checklist is incomplete.

	NM	EX	VG
Common Player:	60.00	30.00	18.00
(1) Ray Berns	60.00	30.00	18.00
(2) Ed Bressoud	60.00	30.00	18.00
(3) Mario Picone	60.00	30.00	18.00
(4) Bob Reid	60.00	30.00	18.00

1952-1953 Sioux City Soos Team Issue

From the Class A Western League, this is one of many minor league team sets issued in the early 1950s by Globe Printing of San Jose, Calif. The early 1950s Soos were a farm team of the New York Giants. Cards are about 2-1/4" x 3-3/8", printed in black-and-white with blank backs. It appears as if the Soos were the only team to have issued cards in both 1952 and 1953, since some cards are known with players unique to each season as well as cards of players who were with Sioux City in both 1952 and 1953.

	NM	EX	VG
Complete Set (29):	1,500	750.00	450.00
Common Player:	60.00	30.00	18.00
Album:	100.00	50.00	30.00
1952			
(1) Ray Berns	60.00	30.00	18.00
(2) Eddie Bressoud	60.00	30.00	18.00
(3) Irv Burton	60.00	30.00	18.00
(4) Bob Easterbrook	60.00	30.00	18.00
(5) George Erath	60.00	30.00	18.00
(6) Don Fracchia	60.00	30.00	18.00
(7) Dick Hamlin	60.00	30.00	18.00
(8) Gail Harris	60.00	30.00	18.00
(9) Chico Ibanez	60.00	30.00	18.00
(10) Bob Lee	60.00	30.00	18.00
(11) Bill McMillan	60.00	30.00	18.00
(12) Dick Messner	60.00	30.00	18.00
(13) Roy Pardue	60.00	30.00	18.00
(14) Mario Picone	60.00	30.00	18.00
(15) Jim Singleton	60.00	30.00	18.00
(16) John Uber	60.00	30.00	18.00
(17) Ernie Yelen	60.00	30.00	18.00
1952/1953			
(18) Bob Giddings	60.00	30.00	18.00
(19) Ray Johnson	60.00	30.00	18.00
(20) Denny Landry (Bat boy.)	60.00	30.00	18.00
(21) Vince LaSala	60.00	30.00	18.00
(22) Ray Mueller	60.00	30.00	18.00
1953			
(23) Dick Getter	60.00	30.00	18.00
(24) Dick Hamlin	60.00	30.00	18.00
(25) Jake Jenkins	60.00	30.00	18.00
(26) Jim Jones	60.00	30.00	18.00
(27) Bob Myers	60.00	30.00	18.00
(28) Clyde Stevens	60.00	30.00	18.00
(29) Joe Stupak	60.00	30.00	18.00

1954 Sioux City Soos Souvenir Pictures Album

Rather than a set of individual baseball cards, the Class A Western League farm club of the New York Giants issued this souvenir picture album depicting players (including future major league star and N.L. president Bill White), staff and media. About 8-1/8" x 7-1/2", the album has embossed metallic gold covers and orange graphics. Inside are eight black-and-white pages with three card-like images per page. The pictures are in about the same size and format as Globe Printing's contemporary minor league baseball card team sets.

	NM	EX	VG
Complete Souvenir Book:	300.00	150.00	90.00
1954 Sioux City Soos			

1947 Smith's Oakland Oaks

This regional set of Oakland Oaks (Pacific Coast League) cards was issued in 1947 by Smith's Clothing stores and is numbered in the lower right corner. The card fronts include a black and white photo with the player's name, team and position below. The backs carry a brief player write-up and an advertisement for Smith's Clothing. The cards measure 2" x 3". The Max Marshall card was apparently short-printed and is much scarcer than the rest of the set.

	NM	EX	VG
Complete Set (25):	800.00	400.00	240.00
Common Player:	25.00	12.50	7.50
1 Charles (Casey) Stengel	125.00	65.00	35.00
2 Billy Raimondi	25.00	12.50	7.50
3 Les Scarsella	25.00	12.50	7.50
4 Brooks Holder	25.00	12.50	7.50
5 Ray Hamrick	25.00	12.50	7.50
6 Gene Lillard	25.00	12.50	7.50
7 Maurice Van Robays	25.00	12.50	7.50
8 Charlie (Sheriff) Gassaway	25.00	12.50	7.50
9 Henry (Cotton) Pippen	25.00	12.50	7.50
10 James Arnold	25.00	12.50	7.50
11 Ralph (Buck) Buxton	25.00	12.50	7.50
12 Ambrose (Bo) Palica	25.00	12.50	7.50
13 Tony Sabol	25.00	12.50	7.50
14 Ed Kearse	25.00	12.50	7.50
15 Bill Hart	25.00	12.50	7.50
16 Donald (Snuffy) Smith	25.00	12.50	7.50
17 Oral (Mickey) Burnett	25.00	12.50	7.50
18 Tom Hafey	25.00	12.50	7.50
19 Will Hafey	25.00	12.50	7.50
20 Paul Gillespie	25.00	12.50	7.50
21 Damon Hayes	25.00	12.50	7.50
22 Max Marshall	350.00	175.00	100.00
23 Mel (Dizz) Duezabou	25.00	12.50	7.50
24 Mel Reeves	25.00	12.50	7.50
25 Joe Faria	25.00	12.50	7.50

1948 Smith's Oakland Oaks

The 1948 Smith's Clothing issue was another 25-card regional set featuring members of the Oakland Oaks of the Pacific Coast League. Almost identical to the 1947 Smith's issue, the black and white cards again measure 2" x 3" but were printed on heavier, glossy stock. The player's name, team and position appear below the photo with the card number in the lower right corner. The back has a brief player write-up and an ad for Smith's clothing.

	NM	EX	VG
Complete Set (25):	700.00	350.00	210.00
Common Player:	25.00	12.50	7.50
1 Billy Raimondi	25.00	12.50	7.50
2 Brooks Holder	25.00	12.50	7.50
3 Will Hafey	25.00	12.50	7.50
4 Nick Etten	25.00	12.50	7.50
5 Lloyd Christopher	25.00	12.50	7.50
6 Les Scarsella	25.00	12.50	7.50
7 Ray Hamrick	25.00	12.50	7.50
8 Gene Lillard	25.00	12.50	7.50
9 Maurice Van Robays	25.00	12.50	7.50
10 Charlie Gassaway	25.00	12.50	7.50
11 Ralph (Buck) Buxton	25.00	12.50	7.50
12 Tom Hafey	25.00	12.50	7.50
13 Damon Hayes	25.00	12.50	7.50
14 Mel (Dizz) Duezabou	25.00	12.50	7.50
15 Dario Lodigiani	25.00	12.50	7.50
16 Vic Buccola	25.00	12.50	7.50
17 Billy Martin	90.00	45.00	27.00
18 Floyd Speer	25.00	12.50	7.50
19 Eddie Samcoff	25.00	12.50	7.50
20 Charles (Casey) Stengel	90.00	45.00	27.00
21 Lloyd Hittle	25.00	12.50	7.50
22 Johnny Babich	25.00	12.50	7.50
23 Merrill Combs	25.00	12.50	7.50
24 Eddie Murphy	25.00	12.50	7.50
25 Bob Klinger	25.00	12.50	7.50

1948 Sommer & Kaufmann San Francisco Seals

One of the more common of the many Pacific Coast League issues of the late 1940s, this emission from the San Francisco boys' clothier features 30 black-and-white 2" x 3" cards. Fronts have a player photo, name, position and card number. Backs

WILFRED "BILL" LEONARD
Seals Catcher 20

WILFRED "BILL" LEONARD, catcher, has to his credit, hitting a home run with all bases loaded when his club was 4 runs behind. With the Seals in 1939 and 1940. Salt Lake Pennant Winning Pioneer League in 1946. Became a Seals catcher in 1947.

BOYS' SHOP
Sommer + Kaufmann
838 MARKET ST. 2600 OCEAN AVE.
SAN FRANCISCO   SAN FRANCISCO
35 FOURTH AVE. SAN MATEO

have a few biographical details and stats, along with an ad. The 1948 issue can be differentiated from the 1949 issue by the words "BOYS SHOP" above the company logo on back.

		NM	EX	VG
Complete Set (30):		1,500	750.00	450.00
Common Player:		60.00	30.00	18.50
1	Lefty O'Doul	100.00	50.00	30.00
2	Jack Brewer	60.00	30.00	18.50
3	Con Dempsey	60.00	30.00	18.50
4	Tommy Fine	60.00	30.00	18.50
5	Kenneth Gables	60.00	30.00	18.50
6	Robert Joyce	60.00	30.00	18.50
7	Al Lien	60.00	30.00	18.50
8	Cliff Melton	60.00	30.00	18.50
9	Frank Shofner	60.00	30.00	18.50
10	Don Trower	60.00	30.00	18.50
11	Joe Brovia	60.00	30.00	18.50
12	Dino Paul Restelli	60.00	30.00	18.50
13	Gene Woodling	75.00	37.00	22.00
14	Ben Guintini	60.00	30.00	18.50
15	Felix Mackiewicz	60.00	30.00	18.50
16	John Patrick Tobin	60.00	30.00	18.50
17	Manuel Perez	60.00	30.00	18.50
18	Bill Werle	60.00	30.00	18.50
19	Homer Howell	60.00	30.00	18.50
20	Wilfred Leonard	60.00	30.00	18.50
21	Bruce Ogrodowski	60.00	30.00	18.50
22	Dick Lajeskie	60.00	30.00	18.50
23	Hugh Luby	60.00	30.00	18.50
24	Roy Nicely	60.00	30.00	18.50
25	Ray Orteig	60.00	30.00	18.50
26	Michael Rocco	60.00	30.00	18.50
27	Del Young	60.00	30.00	18.50
28	Joe Sprinz	60.00	30.00	18.50
29	Doc Hughes	60.00	30.00	18.50
30	Batboys (Don Rode, Albert Boro, Charlie Barnes)	60.00	30.00	18.50

1949 Sommer & Kaufmann San Francisco Seals

JACK NICHOLAS BACCIOCCO
Seals Outfielder   19

JACK NICHOLAS BACCIOCCO, outfielder, Born, San Francisco, Feb. 10, 1925. Height 6', weight 185. Throws and bats right. Italian-Swedish descent. With Salt Lake and Reno in 1947. With Salt Lake in 1948. Hit .277.

Sommer & Kaufmann
838 MARKET ST.   2600 OCEAN AVE.
SAN FRANCISCO
35 FOURTH AVE., SAN MATEO
Famous for Boys' "Hot Rod" Shoes

Twenty-eight black-and-white cards numbered 1-29 (#24 unknown) make up the second and final card issue of the "Frisco area clothier." Measuring 2" x 3", the cards are nearly identical to the '48 issue. The '49s can be identified by the mention of "Hot Rod" shoes on the back. Fronts feature a borderless player photo with a panel at the bottom giving name, position and card number. Backs have the ad for the boy's shop and a brief biographical player sketch.

		NM	EX	VG
Complete Set (29):		2,000	1,000	600.00
Common Player:		75.00	37.00	22.00
1	Lefty O'Doul	100.00	50.00	30.00
2	Jack Brewer	75.00	37.00	22.00
3	Kenneth Gables	75.00	37.00	22.00
4	Con Dempsey	75.00	37.00	22.00
5	Al Lien	75.00	37.00	22.00
6	Cliff Melton	75.00	37.00	22.00
7	Steve Nagy	75.00	37.00	22.00
8	Manny Perez	75.00	37.00	22.00
9	Roy Jarvis	75.00	37.00	22.00
10	Roy Partee	75.00	37.00	22.00
11	Reno Cheso	75.00	37.00	22.00
12	Dick Lajeskie	75.00	37.00	22.00
13	Roy Nicely	75.00	37.00	22.00
14	Mickey Rocco	75.00	37.00	22.00
15	Frank Shofner	75.00	37.00	22.00
16	Richard Holder	75.00	37.00	22.00
17	Dino Restelli	75.00	37.00	22.00
18	Floyd J. "Arky" Vaughan	150.00	75.00	45.00
19	Jackie Baccioccu	75.00	37.00	22.00
20	Bob Drilling	75.00	37.00	22.00
21	Del Young	75.00	37.00	22.00
22	Joe Sprinz	75.00	37.00	22.00
23	Doc Hughes	75.00	37.00	22.00
24	Unknown	75.00	37.00	22.00

25	Bert Singleton	75.00	37.00	22.00
26	John Brocker	75.00	37.00	22.00
27	Jack Tobin	75.00	37.00	22.00
28	Walt Judnich	75.00	37.00	22.00
29	Hal Feldman	75.00	37.00	22.00

1909 Spargo Hartford Senators Postcards

C. P. ARBOGAST.

Members on the Connecticut League (Class B) champion Hartford Senators are pictured on these black-and-white postcards. Player portraits are featured in an oval on front with identication below. A photo credit to "Oliver" is provided. The typically formatted back has a credit line for the publisher, A.W. Spargo. It is likely other members of the team exist on cards yet to be reported.

		NM	EX	VG
Common Player:		700.00	350.00	200.00
(1)	C.P. Arbogast	700.00	350.00	200.00
(2)	Tom J. Connery	700.00	350.00	200.00
(3)	Ray L. Fisher	700.00	350.00	200.00
(4)	C.A. Wadleigh	700.00	350.00	200.00

1867 Sterey Photographers Troy Haymakers

Pre-dating the use of baseball cards as promotional premiums for other products, this issue comprises cartes de visites of members of the Troy Haymakers, one of the powerhouse "amateur" teams in the days prior to the 1871 formation of the National Association, the first professional baseball league. The approximately 2-1/2" x 4" cards have black-and-white player portrait photos glued to a heavy cardboard backing which on its reverse carries in blue the advertising of E.S. Sterey & Co., Photographers, of Lansingburgh, N.Y. The players are not identified on the cards except for the names and, sometimes, positions penciled on back. While many CDVs of individual players of the era, along with team poses and composites, are known, this issue is important because it represents one of the first efforts to create a "team set." It is likely cards of other Troy players were issued and may surface someday.

		NM	EX	VG
(Only a single card is known for each player, each has been certified by SGC as "Fair".)				
(1)	Abrams			
(2)	Bill Craver			
(3)	Steve King			
(4)	Bub McAtee			
(5)	Peter McKeon			
(6)	McQuide			

1933 St. Paul Daily News

(See 1933 Worch Cigar American Association.)

1946 Sunbeam Bread Sacramento Solons

The 21 unnumbered cards in this Pacific Coast League team set are printed with black-and-white fronts containing a borderless player photo with a panel beneath containing name, position and a photo credit. Backs are printed in blue, red and yellow and contain a brief career summary and an ad for the bread brand. Each card can be found with two versions of the ad on back. One has a smaller loaf of bread and the word "Sunbeam" in blue, the other has a larger picture and "Sunbeam" in red. The cards measure approximately 2" x 3". Players are checklisted here in alphabetical order.

STEVE MESNER
1946 Solons Third Baseman
Photo by Joe Benetti

STEVE "LITTLE GOLIATH" MESNER, 28, born Los Angeles, Calif.; second season with Solons. Greatest baseball thrill: hitting three home runs in one game. Played in majors with Chicago White Sox, St. Louis Cards, Cincinnati Reds. Hobby: collecting all articles pertaining to baseball.

Listen to Baseball Play by Play With "Tony" Koester KFBK

Sunbeam
BREAD
The BREAD That Broadcasts BASEBALL

		NM	EX	VG
Complete Set (21):		900.00	450.00	240.00
Common Player:		75.00	35.00	20.00
(1)	Bud Beasley	75.00	35.00	20.00
(2)	Jack Calvey	75.00	35.00	20.00
(3)	Gene Corbett	75.00	35.00	20.00
(4)	Bill Conroy	75.00	35.00	20.00
(5)	Guy Fletcher	75.00	35.00	20.00
(6)	Tony Freitas	75.00	35.00	20.00
(7)	Ted Greenhalgh	75.00	35.00	20.00
(8)	Al Jarlett	75.00	35.00	20.00
(9)	Jesse Landrum	75.00	35.00	20.00
(10)	Gene Lillard	75.00	35.00	20.00
(11)	Garth Mann	75.00	35.00	20.00
(12)	Lilo Marcucci	75.00	35.00	20.00
(13)	Joe Marty (SP)	225.00	110.00	65.00
(14)	Steve Mesner	75.00	35.00	20.00
(15)	Herm Pillette	75.00	35.00	20.00
(16)	Earl Sheely	75.00	35.00	20.00
(17)	Al Smith	75.00	35.00	20.00
(18)	Gerald Staley	75.00	35.00	20.00
(19)	Averett Thompson	75.00	35.00	20.00
(20)	Jo Jo White	75.00	35.00	20.00
(21)	Bud Zipay	75.00	35.00	20.00

1947 Sunbeam Bread Sacramento Solons

TOMMY THOMPSON
1947 Solons Outfielder
Photo by Joe Benetti

THE BREAD THAT BROADCASTS BASEBALL

Similar in format to the 1946 issue, the 26 cards in the '47 set again featured black-and-white player photos on front, with a panel beneath giving player name, position and photo credit. Backs of the 2" x 3" cards had a color depiction of a loaf of the sponsoring company's bread. The unnumbered cards are alphabetically checklisted here.

		NM	EX	VG
Complete Set (26):		1,250	625.00	375.00
Common Player:		50.00	25.00	15.00
(1)	Gene Babbit	50.00	25.00	15.00
(2)	Bob Barthelson	50.00	25.00	15.00
(3)	Bud Beasley	50.00	25.00	15.00
(4)	Chuck Cronin	50.00	25.00	15.00
(5)	Eddie Fernandes	50.00	25.00	15.00
(6)	Ed Fitz Gerald	50.00	25.00	15.00
(7)	Guy Fletcher	50.00	25.00	15.00
(8)	Tony Freitas	50.00	25.00	15.00
(9)	Garth Mann	50.00	25.00	15.00
(10)	Joe Marty	50.00	25.00	15.00
(11)	Lou McCollum	50.00	25.00	15.00
(12)	Steve Mesner	50.00	25.00	15.00
(13)	Frank Nelson	50.00	25.00	15.00
(14)	Tommy Nelson	50.00	25.00	15.00
(15)	Joe Orengo	50.00	25.00	15.00
(16)	Hugh Orphan	50.00	25.00	15.00
(17)	Nick Pesut	50.00	25.00	15.00
(18)	Bill Ramsey	50.00	25.00	15.00
(19)	Johnny Rizzo	50.00	25.00	15.00
(20)	Mike Schemer	250.00	125.00	75.00
(21)	Al Smith	50.00	25.00	15.00
(22)	Tommy Thompson	50.00	25.00	15.00
(23)	Jim Warner	50.00	25.00	15.00
(24)	Mel Wasley	50.00	25.00	15.00
(25)	Leo Wells	50.00	25.00	15.00
(26)	Eddie Zipay	50.00	25.00	15.00

1949 Sunbeam/Pureta Sacramento Solons

Players of the Pacific Coast League's Sacramento Solons were featured in this postcard-size (3-1/4" x 5-1/2") set. Fronts featured black-and-white player photos and the logo of the team's radio broadcaster. Backs feature ads for Sunbeam Bread and Pureta meats.

		NM	EX	VG
Complete Set (12):		2,000	1,000	600.00
Common Player:		250.00	125.00	80.00
(1)	Del Baker	250.00	125.00	80.00
(2)	Frankie Dasso	250.00	125.00	80.00
(3)	Walt Dropo	325.00	160.00	100.00
(4)	Bob Gillespie	250.00	125.00	80.00
(5)	Joe Grace	250.00	125.00	80.00
(6)	Ralph Hodgin	250.00	125.00	80.00
(7)	Freddie Marsh	250.00	125.00	80.00
(8)	Joe Marty	250.00	125.00	80.00
(9)	Len Ratto	250.00	125.00	80.00
(10)	Jim Tabor	250.00	125.00	80.00
(11)	Al White	250.00	125.00	80.00
(12)	Bill Wilson	250.00	125.00	80.00

1949 Sunbeam Bread Stockton Ports

These 2" x 3" unnumbered cards can be found printed in either black-and-white or blue tinted. The Ports were the Class C California League farm club of the Chicago White Sox.

		NM	EX	VG
Complete Set (12):		3,000	1,500	900.00
Common Player:		275.00	135.00	85.00
(1)	Nino Bongiovanni	275.00	135.00	85.00
(2)	Lou Bronzan	275.00	135.00	85.00
(3)	Jimmie Brown	275.00	135.00	85.00
(4)	Rocco Cardinale	275.00	135.00	85.00
(5)	Harry Clements	275.00	135.00	85.00
(6)	Norm Grabar	275.00	135.00	85.00
(7)	Bud Guldborg	275.00	135.00	85.00
(8)	Carl Hoberg	275.00	135.00	85.00
(9)	Eddie Murphy	275.00	135.00	85.00
(10)	Sandy Sandel	275.00	135.00	85.00
(11)	Dick Stone	275.00	135.00	85.00
(12)	Matt Zidich	275.00	135.00	85.00

1950 Sunbeam Bread Stockton Ports

These 2" x 3" unnumbered cards are printed in black-and-white. The Ports were an unaffiliated team in the Class C California League.

		NM	EX	VG
Complete Set (13):		1,800	900.00	550.00
Common Player:		150.00	75.00	45.00
(1)	Richard L. Adams	150.00	75.00	45.00
(2)	James Edward Brown	150.00	75.00	45.00
(3)	Harry Clements	150.00	75.00	45.00
(4)	John Burton Goldberg	150.00	75.00	45.00
(5)	Gerald Lee Haines	150.00	75.00	45.00
(6)	Alfred Michael Heist	150.00	75.00	45.00

		NM	EX	VG
(7)	Don Masterson	150.00	75.00	45.00
(8)	Lauren Hugh Monroe	150.00	75.00	45.00
(9)	Frank E. Murray	150.00	75.00	45.00
(10)	Lauren Keith Simon Jr.	150.00	75.00	45.00
(11)	George Anthony Stanich	150.00	75.00	45.00
(12)	Robert Louis Stevens	150.00	75.00	45.00
(13)	Harold Lee Zurcher	150.00	75.00	45.00

1962 Supertest Toronto Maple Leafs

The extent of the checklist for this issue is unknown. It is assumed the cards were given away with gasoline purchases. Printed on thick, porous paper in a 5-1/2" x 8-1/2" format, the cards have a black-and-white photo, facsimile autograph and sponsor's logo on front. Backs are blank.

		NM	EX	VG
Common Player:		60.00	30.00	18.00
(1)	Chuck Dressen	75.00	37.50	22.50
(2)	Russ Heman	60.00	30.00	18.00

1952 Syracuse Chiefs Team Issue

Like the other contemporary issues of Globe Printing, the cards of the '52 Chiefs (International League, unaffiliated) share a blank-back, black-and-white format. Player names are in black in a white strip on front. Cards measure about 2-1/4" x 3-3/8". The checklist here is incomplete.

		NM	EX	VG
Common Player:		60.00	30.00	18.00
(1)	Bruno Betzel	60.00	30.00	18.00
(2)	Johnny Blatnick	60.00	30.00	18.00
(3)	Charles Eisenmann	60.00	30.00	18.00
(4)	Myron Hayworth	60.00	30.00	18.00
(5)	John Welaj	60.00	30.00	18.00

T

1966 Toledo Mud Hens Team Issue

(3-1/4" x 5-1/2") (Unnumbered)

		NM	EX	VG
Complete Set (25):		1,000	500.00	300.00
Common Player:		40.00	20.00	12.00
(1)	Loren Babe	40.00	20.00	12.00
(2)	Stan Bahnsen	40.00	20.00	12.00
(3)	Bill Bethea	40.00	20.00	12.00
(4)	Wayne Comer	40.00	20.00	12.00
(5)	Jack Cullen	40.00	20.00	12.00
(6)	Jack Curtis	40.00	20.00	12.00
(7)	Gil Downs	40.00	20.00	12.00
(8)	Joe Faroci	40.00	20.00	12.00
(9)	Frank Fernandez	40.00	20.00	12.00
(10)	Mike Ferraro	40.00	20.00	12.00
(11)	Doc Foley	40.00	20.00	12.00
(12)	Mike Hegan	40.00	20.00	12.00
(13)	Jim Horsford	40.00	20.00	12.00
(14)	Dick Hughes	40.00	20.00	12.00
(15)	Elvio Jiminez	40.00	20.00	12.00
(16)	Bob Lasko	40.00	20.00	12.00
(17)	Jim Merritt	40.00	20.00	12.00
(18)	Archie Moore	40.00	20.00	12.00
(19)	Bobby Murcer	90.00	45.00	27.00
(20)	Tony Preybycian	40.00	20.00	12.00
(21)	Bob Schmidt	40.00	20.00	12.00
(22)	Charlie Senger, Loren Babe, Bill Shantz	40.00	20.00	12.00
(23)	Bill Shantz	40.00	20.00	12.00
(24)	Paul Toth	40.00	20.00	12.00
(25)	Jerry Walker	40.00	20.00	12.00

1964 True Ade / WGR Buffalo Bisons

Members of the International League Buffalo Bisons, Class AAA farm club of the N.Y. Mets are featured in this set of contest cards. Persons who assembled a complete nine-player set could redeem the cards for ballgame tickets. The cards were found in cartons of Tru Ade beverage. The blank-back cards are printed in red and about 1-1/4" x 6-1/2" overall. At bottom is a player photo with his name and position above, and team below, separated by a dotted line from the upper portion of the card which has contest details and logos of the sponsoring beverage company and WGR radio. The player portion of the card measures about 1-1/4" x 1-1/4". It is evident

that at least nine players were issued in the set, possibly with some short-printed; this checklist is, therefore, incomplete. The unnumbered cards are listed here in alphabetical order.

		NM	EX	VG
Common Player:		150.00	75.00	45.00
(1)	Ed Bauta	150.00	75.00	45.00
(2)	Choo Choo Coleman	200.00	100.00	60.00
(3)	Pumpsie Green	300.00	150.00	90.00
(4)	Cleon Jones	200.00	100.00	60.00

1960 Tulsa Oilers Team Issue

This team issue by the St. Louis Cardinals' farm club consists of a dozen black-and-white player photos. Players are identifed by a facsimile autograph on front. Backs of the approximately 4-1/8" x 5" photos are blank.

		NM	EX	VG
Complete Set (18):		350.00	175.00	100.00
Common Player:		20.00	10.00	6.00
(1)	Jim Beauchamp	15.00	7.50	4.50
(2)	Bob Blaylock	20.00	10.00	6.00
(3)	Artie Burnett	20.00	10.00	6.00
(4)	Bill Carpenter	20.00	10.00	6.00
(5)	Julio Gotay	20.00	10.00	6.00
(6)	Jim Hickman	20.00	10.00	6.00
(7)	Ray Katt	20.00	10.00	6.00
(8)	Harry Keister	20.00	10.00	6.00
(9)	Fred Koenig	20.00	10.00	6.00
(10)	Gordon Richardson	20.00	10.00	6.00
(11)	Rich Rogers	20.00	10.00	6.00
(12)	Lynn Rube	20.00	10.00	6.00
(13)	Jim Schaffer	20.00	10.00	6.00
(14)	Clint Stark	20.00	10.00	6.00
(15)	Ted Thiem	20.00	10.00	6.00
(16)	Dixie Walker	20.00	10.00	6.00
(17)	Harry Watts	20.00	10.00	6.00
(18)	Fred Whitfield	20.00	10.00	6.00

U

1888-1889 Uhlman St. Paul Cabinets

While this cabinet-card issue utilizes the same format (about 4-1/4" x 6-1/2") and the same Goodwin & Co. copyright photos found on contemporary Old Judge cards, they are, according to advertising on the bottom, the product of Uhlman (presumably a studio) in St. Joseph, Mo. All cards known to date depict members of the St. Paul Apostles of the newly formed Western Association.

		NM	EX	VG
Common Player:		1,300	650.00	400.00
(1)	Cal Broughton	1,300	650.00	400.00
(2)	Scrappy Carroll	1,300	650.00	400.00
(3)	George Treadway	1,300	650.00	400.00
(4)	A.M. Tuckerman	1,300	650.00	400.00

1958 Union Oil Sacramento Solons

Ten members of the independent Pacific Coast League team were included in a black-and-white card set distributed at Union 76 gas stations in that locale. Fronts feature borderless player photos with a wide white strip at the bottom on which is printed the player, team name and the position. Backs have brief stats, a "76 Sports Club" pennant and information about a specific game for which the card can be exchanged for admission by a child. Cards measure approximately 2-1/2" x 3-1/4".

JOE STANKA, Pitcher

Age 26, Ht. 6'5", Wt. 195

Sacramento '57   33 games

Won 10, Lost 14

Earned Run Average 3.51

This Players Card entitles 1 person under 18 to free admission in bleacher section for game of July 11, '58, against Seattle.

76 SPORTS CLUB

JOE STANKA
SACRAMENTO SOLONS, Pitcher

		NM	EX	VG
Complete Set (10):		500.00	250.00	150.00
Common Player:		50.00	25.00	15.00
(1)	Marshall Bridges	65.00	32.00	19.50
(2)	Dick Cole	50.00	25.00	15.00
(3)	Jim Greengrass	50.00	25.00	15.00
(4)	Al Heist	50.00	25.00	15.00
(5)	Nippy Jones	50.00	25.00	15.00
(6)	Carlos Paula	50.00	25.00	15.00
(7)	Kal Segrist	50.00	25.00	15.00
(8)	Sibbi Sisti	50.00	25.00	15.00
(9)	Joe Stanka	80.00	40.00	24.00
(10)	Bud Watkins	50.00	25.00	15.00

1960 Union Oil Seattle Rainiers

Thumb-Nail Sketches — BILL HAIN

76 UNION   Union Oil Company

Given away at Union 76 gas stations in the Seattle area, this set of nine full-color cards measure approximately 3-1/8" x 4". Backs have brief biographical data, a career summary and a large Union 76 logo. The cards are skip-numbered.

		NM	EX	VG
Complete Set (9):		200.00	100.00	60.00
Common Player:		12.00	6.00	3.50
4	Francisco Obregon	20.00	10.00	6.00
6	Drew Gilbert	12.00	6.00	3.50
7	Bill Hain	12.00	6.00	3.50
10	Ray Ripplemeyer	100.00	50.00	30.00
13	Joe Taylor	12.00	6.00	3.50
15	Lou Skizas	12.00	6.00	3.50
17	Don Rudolph	12.00	6.00	3.50
19	Gordy Coleman	15.00	7.50	4.50
22	Hal Beven	12.00	6.00	3.50

1961 Union Oil Pacific Coast League

GAYLORD JACKSON PERRY
Tacoma Giants

Bonus baby Gaylord Jackson Perry has moved rapidly up baseball's ladder. Signed in June, 1958, Perry reported to St. Cloud, Minn. of the Class C Northern League and proved to be a vital cog in that club's pennant drive. Perry won nine games and posted a flossy 2.39 E.R.A. in a half season. In 1959 and 1960 Perry pitched in the Texas League. He won ten games in '59 and nine tills last season. Perry led the Texas League in earned run average with a 2.83 mark.

Jackson Perry—No. 29

Bats R; Throws R   Wife's name: Blanche
Born: Sept. 15, 1938   Home: Williams-
Size: 6'4", 215 lbs.   ton, N.
Position: Pitcher   Children: None

WHEN YOU CANNOT ATTEND
LISTEN TO THE GAMES ON KTAC
850 on your dial

76 UNION

Union Oil Company

The last of three Union Oil PCL issues, the 67 cards in this set feature sepia-toned borderless photos on front in a 3" to 3-1/8" x 4" format. Backs are printed in blue and feature biographical data, a career summary, and ads by the issuing oil company and participating radio station co-sponsors. Six of the eight teams in the '61 PCL are featured, with Salt Lake City and Vancouver not participating in the promotion. Presumably because of smaller print runs, the cards distributed in Hawaii and Spokane bring a premium price. Hall of Fame pitcher Gaylord Perry is featured on his first baseball card in this set. Only the Tacoma cards are numbered and they are skip-numbered.

(Team sets listed below.)

1961 Union Oil Hawaii Islanders

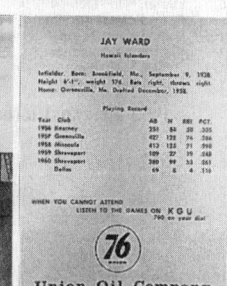

JAY WARD
Hawaii Islanders

76 UNION

Union Oil Company

		NM	EX	VG
Complete Set (10):		375.00	185.00	110.00
Common Player:		40.00	20.00	12.00
(1)	Ray Jablonski	40.00	20.00	12.00
(2)	Jim McManus	40.00	20.00	12.00
(3)	George Prescott	75.00	37.50	22.50
(4)	Diego Segui	45.00	22.50	13.50
(5)	Rachel Slider	40.00	20.00	12.00
(6)	Jim Small	40.00	20.00	12.00
(7)	Milt Smith	40.00	20.00	12.00
(8)	Dave Thies	40.00	20.00	12.00
(9)	Jay Ward	40.00	20.00	12.00
(10)	Bill Werle	40.00	20.00	12.00

1961 Union Oil Portland Beavers

		NM	EX	VG
Complete Set (13):		150.00	75.00	45.00
Common Player:		12.00	6.00	3.50
(1)	Ed Bauta	12.00	6.00	3.50
(2)	Vern Benson	12.00	6.00	3.50
(3)	Jerry Buchek	12.00	6.00	3.50
(4)	Bob Burda	12.00	6.00	3.50
(5)	Duke Carmel	12.00	6.00	3.50
(6)	Don Choate	12.00	6.00	3.50
(7)	Phil Gagliano	12.00	6.00	3.50
(8)	Jim Hickman	12.00	6.00	3.50
(9)	Ray Katt	12.00	6.00	3.50
(10)	Mel Nelson	12.00	6.00	3.50
(11)	Jim Shaffer	12.00	6.00	3.50
(12)	Mike Shannon	17.50	8.75	5.25
(13)	Clint Stark	12.00	6.00	3.50

1961 Union Oil San Diego Padres

		NM	EX	VG
Complete Set (12):		175.00	90.00	45.00
Common Player:		12.00	6.00	3.50
(1)	Dick Barone	12.00	6.00	3.50
(2)	Jim Bolger	12.00	6.00	3.50
(3)	Kent Hadley	12.00	6.00	3.50
(4)	Mike Hershberger	15.00	7.50	4.50
(5)	Stan Johnson	12.00	6.00	3.50
(6)	Dick Lines	12.00	6.00	3.50
(7)	Jim Napier	12.00	6.00	3.50
(8)	Tony Roig	12.00	6.00	3.50
(9)	Herb Score	40.00	20.00	12.00
(10)	Harry Simpson	20.00	10.00	6.00
(11)	Joe Taylor	12.00	6.00	3.50
(12)	Ben Wade	12.00	6.00	3.50

1961 Union Oil Seattle Rainiers

		NM	EX	VG
Complete Set (11):		100.00	50.00	30.00
Common Player:		10.00	5.00	3.00
(1)	Galen Cisco	10.00	5.00	3.00
(2)	Lou Clinton	10.00	5.00	3.00
(3)	Marlan Coughtry	10.00	5.00	3.00
(4)	Harry Malmberg	10.00	5.00	3.00
(5)	Dave Mann	10.00	5.00	3.00
(6)	Derrell Martin	10.00	5.00	3.00
(7)	Erv Palica	10.00	5.00	3.00
(8)	John Pesky	15.00	7.50	4.50
(9)	Bob Tillman	10.00	5.00	3.00
(10)	Marv Toft	10.00	5.00	3.00
(11)	Tom Umphlett	10.00	5.00	3.00

1961 Union Oil Spokane Indians

		NM	EX	VG
Complete Set (11):		450.00	225.00	135.00
Common Player:		35.00	17.50	10.00
(1)	Doug Camilli	35.00	17.50	10.00
(2)	Ramon Conde	35.00	17.50	10.00
(3)	Bob Giallombardo	35.00	17.50	10.00
(4)	Mike Goliat	35.00	17.50	10.00
(5)	Preston Gomez (SP)	135.00	67.00	40.00
(6)	Rod Graber	35.00	17.50	10.00

(7)	Tim Harkness	35.00	17.50	10.00
(8)	Jim Harwell	35.00	17.50	10.00
(9)	Howie Reed	35.00	17.50	10.00
(10)	Curt Roberts	35.00	17.50	10.00
(11)	Rene Valdes (Valdez)	35.00	17.50	10.00

1961 Union Oil Tacoma Giants

		NM	EX	VG
Complete Set (10):		200.00	100.00	60.00
Common Player:		15.00	7.50	4.50
10	Red Davis	15.00	7.50	4.50
12	Dick Phillips	15.00	7.50	4.50
17	Gil Garrido	15.00	7.50	4.50
20	Georges Maranda	15.00	7.50	4.50
25	John Orsino	15.00	7.50	4.50
26	Dusty Rhodes	20.00	10.00	6.00
28	Ron Herbel	15.00	7.50	4.50
29	Gaylord Perry	60.00	30.00	18.00
30	Rafael Alomar	20.00	10.00	6.00
34	Bob Farley	15.00	7.50	4.50

1961 Union Oil Taiyo Whales

AKIHITO KONDO, SECOND BASE

Union Oil Company

This three-card set was produced in conjunction with an exhibition series played in October 1961, between the Taiyo Whales of Japan's Central League, and the Hawaii Islanders, a Class AAA Pacific Cost League farm club of the K.C. Athletics. The player cards measure just over 3" x 4", while the team photo card is 5" x 3-3/4". Cards are black-and-white and have some player biography and ads for Union Oil Co., and the English - and Japanese - language radio stations that carried the games.

		NM	EX	VG
Complete Set (3):		175.00	87.00	52.00
(1)	Akihito Kondo	50.00	25.00	15.00
(2)	Gentaro Shimada	50.00	25.00	15.00
(3)	Taiyo Whales Team	90.00	45.00	27.00

V

1951 Vancouver Capilanos Popcorn Issue

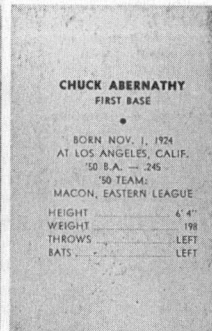

CHUCK ABERNATHY
FIRST BASE

•

BORN NOV. 1, 1924
AT LOS ANGELES, CALIF.
'50 B.A. — .245
'50 TEAM:
MACON, EASTERN LEAGUE

HEIGHT   6' 4"
WEIGHT   198
THROWS   LEFT
BATS   LEFT

These cards measure 1-7/8" x 2-7/8", are printed in black-and-white and have 1950 stats on back. Names may appear in slightly different form than checklisted here. The Caps played in the Class B Western International League and were not affiliated with any major league club.

		NM	EX	VG
Complete Set (24):		4,000	2,000	1,200
Common Player:		200.00	100.00	60.00
(1)	Chuck Abernathy	200.00	100.00	60.00
(2)	Jerry Barta	200.00	100.00	60.00
(3)	Bud Beasley	200.00	100.00	60.00
(4)	Gordy Brunswick	200.00	100.00	60.00
(5)	Reno Cheso	200.00	100.00	60.00
(6)	Ken Chorlton	200.00	100.00	60.00
(7)	Carl Gunnarson	200.00	100.00	60.00
(8)	Pete Hernandez	200.00	100.00	60.00
(9)	Vern Kindsfather	200.00	100.00	60.00
(10)	Bobby McGuire	200.00	100.00	60.00
(11)	Bob McLean	200.00	100.00	60.00
(12)	Charlie Mead	200.00	100.00	60.00
(13)	Jimmy Moore	200.00	100.00	60.00
(14)	George Nicholas	200.00	100.00	60.00
(15)	John Ritchey	200.00	100.00	60.00
(16)	Sandy Robertson	200.00	100.00	60.00
(17)	Bill Schuster	200.00	100.00	60.00
(18)	Dick Sinovic	200.00	100.00	60.00
(19)	Ron Smith	200.00	100.00	60.00

		NM	EX	VG
(20)	Bob Snyder	200.00	100.00	60.00
(21)	Don Tisnerat	200.00	100.00	60.00
(22)	Ray Tran	200.00	100.00	60.00
(23)	Reg Wallis (Trainer)	200.00	100.00	60.00
(24)	Bill Whyte	200.00	100.00	60.00

1952 Vancouver Capilanos Popcorn Issue

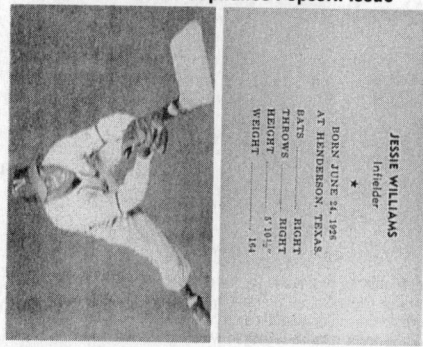

These cards measure 2" x 3-1/8", are printed in black-and-white and have 1951 stats on back. Names may appear in slightly different form than checklisted here. The Caps played in the Class A Western International League and were not affiliated with any major league club.

		NM	EX	VG
Complete Set (20):		3,500	1,750	1,000
Common Player:		200.00	100.00	60.00
(1)	Gordie Brunswick	200.00	100.00	60.00
(2)	Bob Duretto	200.00	100.00	60.00
(3)	Van Fletcher	200.00	100.00	60.00
(4)	John Guldborg	200.00	100.00	60.00
(5)	Paul Jones	200.00	100.00	60.00
(6)	Eddie Locke	200.00	100.00	60.00
(7)	Tom Lovrich	200.00	100.00	60.00
(8)	Jimmy Moore	200.00	100.00	60.00
(9)	George Nicholas	200.00	100.00	60.00
(10a)	John Ritchey	200.00	100.00	60.00
(10b)	Johnny Ritchie	200.00	100.00	60.00
(11)	Bill Schuster	200.00	100.00	60.00
(12)	Bob Snyder	200.00	100.00	60.00
(13)	Len Tran	200.00	100.00	60.00
(14)	Ray Tran	200.00	100.00	60.00
(15)	Edo Vanni	200.00	100.00	60.00
(16)	Jim Wert	200.00	100.00	60.00
(17)	Bill Whyte	200.00	100.00	60.00
(18)	Jessie Williams (Batting)	200.00	100.00	60.00
(19)	Jesse Williams (Fielding)	200.00	100.00	60.00

1953 Vancouver Capilanos Popcorn Issue

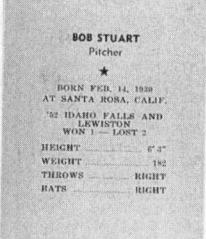

These cards measure 2-3/16" x 3-3/16", are printed in black-and-white and have 1952 stats on back. Names may appear in slightly different form than checklisted here. The Caps played in the Class A Western International League and were not affiliated with any major league club.

		NM	EX	VG
Complete Set (18):		3,000	1,500	900.00
Common Player:		200.00	100.00	60.00
(1)	Dick Briskey	200.00	100.00	60.00
(2)	Jack Bukowatz	200.00	100.00	60.00
(3)	Ken Chorlton	200.00	100.00	60.00
(4)	Van Fletcher	200.00	100.00	60.00
(5)	John Guldborg	200.00	100.00	60.00
(6)	Carl Gunnerson	200.00	100.00	60.00
(7)	Jim Hedgecock	200.00	100.00	60.00
(8)	Gordon Hernandez	200.00	100.00	60.00
(9)	Pete Hernandez	200.00	100.00	60.00
(10)	Jim Leavitt	200.00	100.00	60.00
(11)	Rod MacKay	200.00	100.00	60.00
(12)	Frank Mascaro	200.00	100.00	60.00
(13)	Lonnie Myers	200.00	100.00	60.00
(14)	Rod Owen	200.00	100.00	60.00
(15)	Harvey Storey	200.00	100.00	60.00
(16)	Bob Stuart	200.00	100.00	60.00
(17)	Dale Thomason	200.00	100.00	60.00
(18)	Jim Wert	200.00	100.00	60.00

1954 Vancouver Capilanos Popcorn Issue

These cards measure 2-3/16" x 3-5/16" and are printed in black-and-white. Names may appear in slightly different form than checklisted here. The Caps were the 1954 champs of the Class A Western International League and were not affiliated with any major league club.

		NM	EX	VG
Complete Set (15):		2,500	1,250	750.00
Common Player:		200.00	100.00	60.00
(1)	Bill Brenner	200.00	100.00	60.00
(2)	Ken Chorlton	200.00	100.00	60.00
(3)	Jim Clarke (Clark)	200.00	100.00	60.00
(4)	John Cordell	200.00	100.00	60.00
(5)	Bob Duretto	200.00	100.00	60.00
(6)	Dick Greco	200.00	100.00	60.00
(7)	Arnie Hallgren	200.00	100.00	60.00
(8)	Danny Holden	200.00	100.00	60.00
(9)	Rod McKay	200.00	100.00	60.00
(10)	George Nicholas	200.00	100.00	60.00
(11)	Nick Pesut	200.00	100.00	60.00
(12)	Ken Richardson	200.00	100.00	60.00
(13)	Bob Roberts	200.00	100.00	60.00
(14)	Bob Wellman	200.00	100.00	60.00
(15)	Marvin Williams	200.00	100.00	60.00

1954 Veltex Lewiston Broncs

It is evident from the format of the card and of the accompanying album that this is a product of Globe Printing, which produced many minor league sets in the early 1950s. What makes this set of the 1954 Class A (Western International League) affiliate of the Baltimore Orioles unusual among Globe issues is the mention of a sponsor. The blank-back, black-and-white cards measure 2-3/16" x 3-3/8". The checklist below is obviously incomplete.

		NM	EX	VG
Common player:		60.00	30.00	18.00
Album:		150.00	75.00	45.00
(1)	Larry Barton	60.00	30.00	18.00

1952 Ventura Braves Team Issue

These 2-1/4" x 3-3/8" black-and-white, unnumbered, blank-backed cards were one of many minor league team sets issued by Globe Printing of San Jose, Calif., in the early 1950s. Cards were usually given away at the ballpark on a one-per-week or one-per-homestand basis, accounting for the rarity of surviving complete sets. It is known that 18 V-Braves were issued in this set, though only 14 have been checklisted to date. The team was a Class C California League farm club of the Boston Braves.

		NM	EX	VG
Common Player:		60.00	30.00	18.00
Album:		100.00	50.00	30.00
(1)	Al Aguilar	60.00	30.00	18.00
(2)	Bud Belardi	60.00	30.00	18.00
(3)	Frank Followell	60.00	30.00	18.00
(4)	Glenn Hittner	60.00	30.00	18.00
(5)	Lee Kast	60.00	30.00	18.00
(6)	Richie Morse	60.00	30.00	18.00
(7)	Frank Nubin	60.00	30.00	18.00
(8)	George Owen	60.00	30.00	18.00
(9)	Manny Perez	60.00	30.00	18.00
(10)	Jose Perez	60.00	30.00	18.00
(11)	Harley Resh	60.00	30.00	18.00
(12)	Jack Schlarb	60.00	30.00	18.00
(13)	Bob Sturgeon	60.00	30.00	18.00
(14)	Billy Wells	60.00	30.00	18.00

W

1911 Western Playground Association

Stars from around the Pacific Coast League are featured on this rare and unusual issue. The 2-1/4" x 3-1/2" cards have

a front design similar to contemporary Zeenuts cards: A dark brown border surrounding a sepia posed action picture (which appears to be a heavily retouched photo). Printed in white at left or right are "WESTERN PLAYGROUND ASSOCIATION / P.C. (or sometimes 'P.S.') LEAGUE" and the player's last name. Backs are a "Membership Certificate" indicating the cards could be redeemed for five percent of their seven-cent "face value" toward the purchase of school playground apparatus or supplies. The cards were received with the purchase of "Bank Stock" brand composition books.

		NM	EX	VG
Common Player:		9,000	4,500	2,700
(1)	Claude Berry	9,000	4,500	2,700
(2)	Roy Brashear	9,000	4,500	2,700
(3)	Herb Byram	9,000	4,500	2,700
(4)	Walt Carlisle	9,000	4,500	2,700
(5)	Roy Caslleton (Castleton)	9,000	4,500	2,700
(6)	Chet Chadborne (Chadbourne)	9,000	4,500	2,700
(7)	Tyler Christian	9,000	4,500	2,700
(8)	Bert Coy	9,000	4,500	2,700
(9)	Pete Daley	9,000	4,500	2,700
(10)	Pop Dillon	9,000	4,500	2,700
(11)	Joe French	9,000	4,500	2,700
(12)	Howie Gregory	9,000	4,500	2,700
(13)	Spec Harkness	9,000	4,500	2,700
(14)	Heinie Heitmuller	9,000	4,500	2,700
(15)	Ben Henderson	9,000	4,500	2,700
(16)	Cack Henley	9,000	4,500	2,700
(17)	Izzy Hoffman	9,000	4,500	2,700
(18)	Happy Hogan	9,000	4,500	2,700
(19)	Johnny Kane	9,000	4,500	2,700
(20)	Jimmy Lewis	9,000	4,500	2,700
(21)	Tom Madden	9,000	4,500	2,700
(22)	Chris Mahoney	9,000	4,580	2,700
(23)	George Metzger	9,000	4,500	2,700
(24)	Fred Miller	9,000	4,500	2,700
(25)	Kid Mohler	9,000	4,500	2,700
(26)	Walter Nagle	9,000	4,500	2,700
(27)	Patsy O'Rourke	9,000	4,500	2,700
(28)	Ham Patterson	9,000	4,500	2,700
(29)	Roger Peckinpaugh	9,000	4,500	2,700
(30)	Bill Rapps	9,000	4,500	2,700
(31)	Bill Rogers (Rodgers)	9,000	4,500	2,700
(32)	Buddy Ryan	9,000	4,500	2,700
(33)	Walter Schmitt (Schmidt)	9,000	4,500	2,700
(34)	Tom Seaton	9,000	4,500	2,700
(35)	Jerry Sheehan	9,000	4,500	2,700
(36)	Harry Stewart	9,000	4,500	2,700
(37)	George Stinson	9,000	4,500	2,700
(38)	Harry Suter (Sutor)	9,000	4,500	2,700
(39)	Harry Wolverton	9,000	4,500	2,700
(40)	Elmer Zacher	9,000	4,500	2,700

1932 Wheaties Minneapolis Millers

Because of their similarity to the 1933 issue which carried Wheaties advertising on the back, these postcard-size photos of the 1932 Millers are believed to also have been issued by the Minneapolis-based cereal company. The 3-7/16" x 5-7/16" cards have black-and-white portraits or posed action photos on front, along with a facsimile autograph. Backs are blank.

		NM	EX	VG
Complete Set (24):		1,350	700.00	400.00
Common Player:		60.00	30.00	20.00
(1)	J.C. "Rube" Benton	60.00	30.00	20.00
(2)	Donie Bush	60.00	30.00	20.00
(3)	Andy Cohen	70.00	35.00	20.00
(4)	"Pea Ridge" Day	60.00	30.00	20.00

		NM	EX	VG
(5)	Ray Fitzgerald	60.00	30.00	20.00
(6)	F.P. "Babe" Ganzel	60.00	30.00	20.00
(7)	Wes Griffin	60.00	30.00	20.00
(8)	Spencer Harris	60.00	30.00	20.00
(9)	Joe Hauser	120.00	60.00	40.00
(10)	Frank J. "Dutch" Henry	60.00	30.00	20.00
(11)	Phil Hensick	60.00	30.00	20.00
(12)	Bunker Hill	60.00	30.00	20.00
(13)	Joe Mowry	60.00	30.00	20.00
(14)	Jess Petty	60.00	30.00	20.00
(15)	Paul Richards	70.00	35.00	20.00
(16)	Bill Rodda	60.00	30.00	20.00
(17)	Harry Rose	60.00	30.00	20.00
(18)	Art Ruble	60.00	30.00	20.00
(19)	"Rosy" Ryan	60.00	30.00	20.00
(20)	Al Sheehan	60.00	30.00	20.00
(21)	Ed Sicking	60.00	30.00	20.00
(22)	Ernie Smith	60.00	30.00	20.00
(23)	Hy Van Denberg	60.00	30.00	20.00
(24)	E.R. Vangilder	60.00	30.00	20.00

1933 Wheaties Minneapolis Millers

 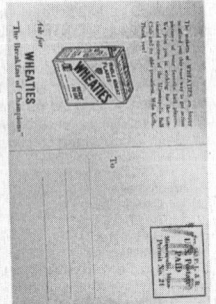

Prior to printing their first major league baseball cards on the backs of cereal boxes in 1935, Wheaties sponsored a minor league set for the hometown Minneapolis Millers in 1933. The 4" x 5-3/4" cards have a sepia-toned posed action photo on front, along with a facsimile autograph. The player's name, position, team and year are printed in the bottom border. The postcard back, printed in black-and-white, has a drawing of a Wheaties box and an ad for the cereal. All unmailed examples seen to date have a purple rubber-stamped "VOID" in the postage box at top. The unnumbered cards are checklisted here alphabetically.

		NM	EX	VG
Complete Set (24):		2,250	1,125	650.00
Common Player:		90.00	45.00	27.00
(1)	Dave Bancroft	150.00	75.00	45.00
(2)	Rube Benton	90.00	45.00	27.00
(3)	Andy Cohen	150.00	75.00	45.00
(4)	Bob Fothergill	90.00	45.00	27.00
(5)	"Babe" Ganzel	90.00	45.00	27.00
(6)	Joe Glenn	90.00	45.00	27.00
(7)	Wes Griffin	90.00	45.00	27.00
(8)	Jack Hallet	90.00	45.00	27.00
(9)	Jerry Harrington (Announcer)	90.00	45.00	27.00
(10)	Spencer Harris	100.00	50.00	30.00
(11)	Joe Hauser	200.00	100.00	60.00
(12)	Butch Henline	90.00	45.00	27.00
(13)	Walter Hilcher	90.00	45.00	27.00
(14)	Dutch Holland	90.00	45.00	27.00
(15)	Harry Holsclaw	90.00	45.00	27.00
(16)	Wes Kingdon	90.00	45.00	27.00
(17)	George Murray	90.00	45.00	27.00
(18)	Leo Norris	90.00	45.00	27.00
(19)	Jess Petty	90.00	45.00	27.00
(20)	Art Ruble	90.00	45.00	27.00
(21)	Al Sheehan (Announcer)	90.00	45.00	27.00
(22)	Ernie Smith	90.00	45.00	27.00
(23)	Wally Tauscher	90.00	45.00	27.00
(24)	Hy VanDenburg	90.00	45.00	27.00

1933 Wheaties Seattle Indians

Prior to printing their first major league baseball cards on the backs of cereal boxes in 1935, Wheaties sponsored a minor league set for the Seattle Indians in 1933. The 4-1/8" x 7" cards have a sepia-toned posed portrait or action photo on front, along with a facsimile autograph. The player's name, position, team and year are printed in the bottom border. The postcard

back, printed in black-and-white, has a drawing of a Wheaties box and an ad for the cereal. The unnumbered cards are checklisted here alphabetically; it is likely this list is incomplete.

		NM	EX	VG
Common Player:		450.00	225.00	135.00
(1)	George Burns	600.00	300.00	180.00
(2)	Joe Coscarart	450.00	225.00	135.00
(3)	Leo Lassen ((Broadcaster))	450.00	225.00	135.00
(4)	Bill Radonits	450.00	225.00	135.00
(5)	"Junk" Walters	450.00	225.00	135.00

1912 Whitehead & Hoag P.C.L. Pins

A paper insert originally in the back of these pins identifies the maker as Whitehead & Hoag of San Francisco. The 7/8" diameter celluloid pins are printed in either black or blue on a white background. A player portrait photo is at center, with his last name below. Above is the city of his team and the Pacific Coast League initials. Listed in the "American Card Catalog" as PM5, the unnumbered pins are checklisted here alphabetically; it's possible additional pins in the issue remain to be reported. All pins seen are Oakland players except McCredie, Shehann, Rapp, and Seaton (Portland) as well as Berry (San Fransisco).

		NM	EX	VG
Complete Set (26):		15,000	7,500	4,500
Common Player:		600.00	300.00	180.00
(1)	Harry Ables	600.00	300.00	180.00
(2)	Claude Berry	600.00	300.00	180.00
(3)	Tyler Christian	600.00	300.00	180.00
(4)	Al Cook	600.00	300.00	180.00
(5)	Bert Coy	600.00	300.00	180.00
(6)	Jack Flater	600.00	300.00	180.00
(7)	Howie Gregory	600.00	300.00	180.00
(8)	Joe Hamilton	600.00	300.00	180.00
(9)	Gus Hetling	600.00	300.00	180.00
(10a)	Hille	600.00	300.00	180.00
(10b)	Mgr. Hille	600.00	300.00	180.00
(11)	Izzy Hoffman	600.00	300.00	180.00
(12)	Bill Leard	600.00	300.00	180.00
(13)	Bill Malarkey	600.00	300.00	180.00
(14)	Elmer Martinoni	600.00	300.00	180.00
(15)	Walter McCredie	600.00	300.00	180.00
(16)	Honus Mitze	600.00	300.00	180.00
(17)	Cy Parkins	600.00	300.00	180.00
(18)	Ashley Pope	600.00	300.00	180.00
(19)	Bill Rapp (Rapps)	600.00	300.00	180.00
(20)	Tom Seaton	600.00	300.00	180.00
(21a)	Bud Sharpe	600.00	300.00	180.00
(21b)	Mgr. Sharpe	600.00	300.00	180.00
(22)	Tommy Sheehan	600.00	300.00	180.00
(23)	Smith	600.00	300.00	180.00
(24)	John Tiedeman (Tiedemann)	600.00	300.00	180.00
(25)	Eddie Wilkinson	600.00	300.00	180.00
(26)	Elmer Zacher	600.00	300.00	180.00

1919 Winkelman's Quaker Bread Pins

This issue of 1-1/4" diameter celluloid pinback buttons features members of the Memphis Chickasaws in black-and-white portraits on a pale yellow background, surrounded by an orange border with the sponsor's advertising. A large turtle is pictured at bottom. Currently only three players are known, though it is likely more were issued.

		NM	EX	VG
Common Player:		1,300	650.00	400.00
(1)	Baerwald	1,300	650.00	400.00
(2)	Carey	1,300	650.00	400.00
(3)	Bob Coulson	1,300	650.00	400.00

1933-34 Worch Cigar American Association

Though the issuer is not identified anywhere on these blank-backed, 3-7/16" x 5-7/16" black-and-white cards (though some are found with a box on front crediting the photo to the St. Paul Daily News), the individual player photos were

available as premiums for redemption of cigar bands by the Worch Cigar Co., of St. Paul, Minn. The issue is similar in format to the major league cards of the same era, and indeed the cards were offered together. Most collectors prefer to chase either the major leaguers or the minor leaguers independently, so they are cataloged in that fashion. The set encompasses players from the 1932-35 Minneapolis Millers, the 1933 St. Paul Saints and a handful from the Columbus Redbirds, Kansas City Blues and a few other teams. The unnumbered cards are checklisted below alphabetically. Player identification is presented in several different styles and may include just the last name or also the first name. Several players are known in more than one pose. The checklist here is likely incomplete.

		NM	EX	VG
Common Player:		45.00	22.50	13.50
(1)	Dave Bancroft	100.00	50.00	30.00
(2)	Clyde Beck	45.00	22.50	13.50
(3)	Rube Benton	45.00	22.50	13.50
(4)	W. Berger	45.00	22.50	13.50
(5)	Brannon	45.00	22.50	13.50
(6)	Spurgeon Chandler	45.00	22.50	13.50
(7)	Tiny Chaplin	45.00	22.50	13.50
(8)	Andy Cohen	45.00	22.50	13.50
(9)	Nick Cullop	45.00	22.50	13.50
(10)	Bob Fenner	45.00	22.50	13.50
(11)	Fischall	45.00	22.50	13.50
(12)	Gaffke	45.00	22.50	13.50
(13a)	Foster Ganzel	45.00	22.50	13.50
(13b)	Foster Ganzel	45.00	22.50	13.50
(14)	Louis Garland	45.00	22.50	13.50
(15)	Joe Glenn	45.00	22.50	13.50
(16)	Angelo Guiliani	45.00	22.50	13.50
(17)	Pinky Hargrave	45.00	22.50	13.50
(18)	Slim Harriss	45.00	22.50	13.50
(19)	Spencer Harris	45.00	22.50	13.50
(20)	Joe Hauser	75.00	37.50	22.50
(21)	Walter Henline	45.00	22.50	13.50
(22)	Phil Hensick	45.00	22.50	13.50
(23)	Walter Hilcher	45.00	22.50	13.50
(24)	Jesse Hill	45.00	22.50	13.50
(25)	Bob Holand	45.00	22.50	13.50
(26)	Harry Holsclaw	45.00	22.50	13.50
(27)	Meredith Hopkins	45.00	22.50	13.50
(28)	Irvine Jeffries	45.00	22.50	13.50
(29)	Monk Joyner	45.00	22.50	13.50
(30)	Fred Koster	45.00	22.50	13.50
(31)	Walter Mails	45.00	22.50	13.50
(32)	Chuck Marrow	45.00	22.50	13.50
(33)	Emmett McCann	45.00	22.50	13.50
(34)	Joe Mowry	45.00	22.50	13.50
(35)	Les Munns	45.00	22.50	13.50
(36)	George Murray	45.00	22.50	13.50
(37)	Floyd Newkirk	45.00	22.50	13.50
(38)	Leo Norris	45.00	22.50	13.50
(39)	Frank Packard	45.00	22.50	13.50
(40)	Ben Paschal	45.00	22.50	13.50
(41a)	Jess Petty/Throwing (Right foot off ground.)	45.00	22.50	13.50
(41b)	Jess Petty	45.00	22.50	13.50
(42)	Ray Radcliff	45.00	22.50	13.50
(43)	Larry Rosenthal	45.00	22.50	13.50
(44a)	Art Ruble	45.00	22.50	13.50
(44b)	Art Ruble	45.00	22.50	13.50
(45)	Art Shires	45.00	22.50	13.50
(46a)	Ernest Smith	45.00	22.50	13.50
(46b)	Ernest Smith	45.00	22.50	13.50
(47)	Ray Starr	45.00	22.50	13.50
(48)	Walter Tauscher	45.00	22.50	13.50
(49)	Myles Thomas	45.00	22.50	13.50
(50)	Phil Todt	45.00	22.50	13.50
(51)	Gene Trow	45.00	22.50	13.50
(52)	Hy Van Denburg	45.00	22.50	13.50
(53)	Elam Van Gilder	45.00	22.50	13.50
(54)	Charles Wilson	45.00	22.50	13.50
(55)	Ab. Wright	45.00	22.50	13.50
(56)	Emil Yde	45.00	22.50	13.50
(57)	Russ Young	45.00	22.50	13.50

Z

1911 Zeenut Pacific Coast League

Produced annually for 28 years, these Pacific Coast League cards were the longest-running and most popular baseball issues ever to appear on the West Coast. Issued by the Collins-McCarthy Candy Co. (later known as the Collins-

Hencke Candy Co. and then simply the Collins Candy Co.) of San Francisco, Zeenut cards were inserted in boxes of the company's products: Zeenuts, Ruf-Neks and Home Run Kisses. All Zeenut cards issued from 1913 through 1937 had an approximately half-inch coupon at the bottom that could be redeemed for various prizes. Since most of these coupons were removed (and many not too carefully) Zeenuts are difficult to find in top condition today, and only a very small percentage survived with the coupon intact. (The sizes listed in the following descriptions are for cards without coupons.) Over the 28-year span, it is estimated that nearly 3,700 different cards were issued as part of the Zeenuts series, but new discoveries are still being made, and the checklist continues to grow. It is sometimes difficult to differentiate one year from another after 1930. Because it is so rare to find Zeenuts cards with the coupon still attached, values listed are for cards without the coupon. Cards with the coupon still intact will generally command a significant premium. The first Zeenut cards measure about 2-1/8" x 4" and feature a sepia-toned photo on a brown background surrounded by an off-white border. The backs of the cards are blank. Although the 1911 cards did not include the coupon bottom, some cards have been found with punch holes, indicating they may have also been used for redemptions. A total of 122 different players have been found.

		NM	EX	VG
Common Player:		250.00	125.00	75.00
(1)	Abbott	250.00	125.00	75.00
(2)	Ables	250.00	125.00	75.00
(3a)	Agnew (Large pose.)	250.00	125.00	75.00
(3b)	Agnew (Small pose.)	250.00	125.00	75.00
(4a)	Akin (Large pose.)	250.00	125.00	75.00
(4b)	Akin (Small pose.)	250.00	125.00	75.00
(5)	Frank Arellanes	250.00	125.00	75.00
(6a)	Arlett (Large pose.)	250.00	125.00	75.00
(6b)	Arlett (Middle size pose.)	250.00	125.00	75.00
(6c)	Arlett (Small pose.)	250.00	125.00	75.00
(7)	Barry	250.00	125.00	75.00
(8)	Baum	250.00	125.00	75.00
(9)	Bernard	250.00	125.00	75.00
(10)	Berry	250.00	125.00	75.00
(11)	Bohen (Card is not know in high grade.)		5,000	2,500
(12)	Brackenridge	250.00	125.00	75.00
(13)	Brashear	250.00	125.00	75.00
(14a)	Brown (Large pose.)	250.00	125.00	75.00
(14b)	Brown (Small pose.)	250.00	125.00	75.00
(15)	Browning	250.00	125.00	75.00
(16a)	Burrell (Large pose.)	250.00	125.00	75.00
(16b)	Burrell (Small pose.)	250.00	125.00	75.00
(17)	Byram	250.00	125.00	75.00
(18)	Carlisle	250.00	125.00	75.00
(19)	Carman	250.00	125.00	75.00
(20a)	Carson (Large pose.)	250.00	125.00	75.00
(20b)	Carson (Middle size pose.)	250.00	125.00	75.00
(20c)	Carson (Small pose.)	250.00	125.00	75.00
(21)	Castleton	250.00	125.00	75.00
(22)	Chadbourne	250.00	125.00	75.00
(23)	Christian	250.00	125.00	75.00
(24)	Couchman	250.00	125.00	75.00
(25)	Coy	250.00	125.00	75.00
(26)	Criger	250.00	125.00	75.00
(27)	Cutshaw	250.00	125.00	75.00
(28)	Daley	250.00	125.00	75.00
(29)	Danzig	250.00	125.00	75.00
(30)	Delhi	250.00	125.00	75.00
(31a)	Delmas (Large pose.)	250.00	125.00	75.00
(31b)	Delmas (Small pose.)	250.00	125.00	75.00
(32)	Dillon	250.00	125.00	75.00
(33a)	Driscoll (Name incorrect.)	250.00	125.00	75.00
(33b)	Driscoll (Name correct.)	250.00	125.00	75.00
(34)	Dulin	250.00	125.00	75.00
(35)	Fanning	250.00	125.00	75.00
(36)	Fitzgerald	250.00	125.00	75.00
(37)	Flater	250.00	125.00	75.00
(38)	French	250.00	125.00	75.00
(39)	Fullerton	250.00	125.00	75.00
(40)	Gleason	250.00	125.00	75.00
(41)	Gregory	250.00	125.00	75.00
(42)	Halla	525.00	275.00	160.00
(43)	Harkness	250.00	125.00	75.00
(44a)	Heitmuller (Large pose.)	250.00	125.00	75.00
(44b)	Heitmuller (Small pose.)	250.00	125.00	75.00
(45)	Henley	250.00	125.00	75.00
(46)	Hetling	250.00	125.00	75.00
(47)	Hiester	250.00	125.00	75.00
(48a)	Hitt (Large pose.)	250.00	125.00	75.00
(48b)	Hitt (Small pose.)	250.00	125.00	75.00
(50)	Hoffman	250.00	125.00	75.00
(51)	Hogan	250.00	125.00	75.00
(52a)	Holland (Large pose.)	250.00	125.00	75.00
(52b)	Holland (Small pose.)	250.00	125.00	75.00
(53)	Hosp	250.00	125.00	75.00
(54a)	Howard (Large pose.)	250.00	125.00	75.00
(54b)	Howard (Small pose.)	250.00	125.00	75.00
(55)	Kane	250.00	125.00	75.00
(56)	Kerns	250.00	125.00	75.00
(57)	Kilroy	250.00	125.00	75.00
(58)	Knight	250.00	125.00	75.00
(59)	Koestner	250.00	125.00	75.00
(60)	Krueger	250.00	125.00	75.00
(61)	Kuhn	250.00	125.00	75.00
(62)	LaLonge	250.00	125.00	75.00
(63)	Lerchen	250.00	125.00	75.00
(64)	Leverenz	250.00	125.00	75.00
(65)	Lewis	250.00	125.00	75.00
(66)	Bill Lindsay	250.00	125.00	75.00
(67)	Lober	250.00	125.00	75.00
(68)	Madden	250.00	125.00	75.00
(69)	Maggert	250.00	125.00	75.00
(70)	Mahoney	250.00	125.00	75.00
(71)	Martinoni	250.00	125.00	75.00
(72)	McArdle	250.00	125.00	75.00
(73)	McCredie	250.00	125.00	75.00
(74)	McDonnell	250.00	125.00	75.00
(75a)	McKune (Large pose.)	250.00	125.00	75.00
(75b)	McKune (Middle size pose.)	250.00	125.00	75.00
(75c)	McKune (Small pose.)	250.00	125.00	75.00
(76)	Meikle	250.00	125.00	75.00
(77)	Melchior	250.00	125.00	75.00
(78)	Metzger	250.00	125.00	75.00
(79)	Miller	250.00	125.00	75.00
(80)	Mitze	250.00	125.00	75.00
(81)	Mohler	250.00	125.00	75.00
(82a)	Moore (Large pose.)	250.00	125.00	75.00
(82b)	Moore (Small pose.)	250.00	125.00	75.00
(83a)	Moskiman (Lettering size large.)	250.00	125.00	75.00
(83b)	Moskiman (Lettering size small.)	250.00	125.00	75.00
(84)	Murray	250.00	125.00	75.00
(85)	Naylor	250.00	125.00	75.00
(86)	Nebinger	250.00	125.00	75.00
(87)	Nourse	250.00	125.00	75.00
(88a)	Noyes (Large pose.)	250.00	125.00	75.00
(88b)	Noyes (Small pose.)	250.00	125.00	75.00
(89)	O'Rourke	250.00	125.00	75.00
(90)	Patterson (Oakland)	250.00	125.00	75.00
(91)	Patterson (Vernon)	250.00	125.00	75.00
(92)	Pearce	250.00	125.00	75.00
(93)	Peckinpaugh	400.00	200.00	120.00
(94)	Pernoll	250.00	125.00	75.00
(95)	Pfyl	250.00	125.00	75.00
(96)	Powell	250.00	125.00	75.00
(97a)	Raleigh (Large pose.)	250.00	125.00	75.00
(97b)	Raleigh (Small pose.)	250.00	125.00	75.00
(98)	Rapps	250.00	125.00	75.00
(99)	Rodgers	250.00	125.00	75.00
(100a)	Ryan (Portland, box around name and team.)	450.00	225.00	150.00
(100b)	Ryan (Portland, no box around name and team.)	250.00	125.00	75.00
(101)	Ryan (San Francisco)	250.00	125.00	75.00
(102)	Seaton	250.00	125.00	75.00
(103)	Shaw	250.00	125.00	75.00
(104)	Sheehan	250.00	125.00	75.00
(105)	Shinn	250.00	125.00	75.00
106a	Smith (Los Angeles, large pose.)	250.00	125.00	75.00
(106b)	Smith (Los Angeles, small pose.)	250.00	125.00	75.00
(107a)	Smith (San Francisco, large pose.)	250.00	125.00	75.00
(107b)	Smith (San Francisco, small pose.)	250.00	125.00	75.00
(108)	Steen	250.00	125.00	75.00
(109)	Stewart	250.00	125.00	75.00
(110a)	Stinson (Large pose.)	250.00	125.00	75.00
(110b)	Stinson (Small pose.)	250.00	125.00	75.00
(111)	Sutor (Suter)	250.00	125.00	75.00
(112)	Tennant	250.00	125.00	75.00
(113)	Thomas	250.00	125.00	75.00
(114)	Thompson	250.00	125.00	75.00
(115)	Thornton	250.00	125.00	75.00
(116)	Tiedeman	250.00	125.00	75.00
(117)	Van Buren	250.00	125.00	75.00
(118)	Vitt	250.00	125.00	75.00
(119)	Wares	250.00	125.00	75.00
(120)	Buck Weaver	14,000	5,500	3,500
(121)	Wolverton	250.00	125.00	75.00
(122)	Zacher	250.00	125.00	75.00
(123)	Zamloch	250.00	125.00	75.00

1912 Zeenut Pacific Coast League

The second series of Zeenut cards measure about 2-1/8" x 4-1/16" and featured sepia-toned photographs on a brown background with no border. Most cards have blank backs, but some have been found with printing advising collectors to "Save Zeenut pictures for valuable premiums," or with one of two sizes of a Bardell logo. The checklist consists of 158 subjects, but more cards are still being discovered. Zeenut cards which were redeemed for prizes will exhibit a hole-punch cancellation, often heart-shaped.

		NM	EX	VG
Common Player:		125.00	65.00	45.00
(1)	Abbott	125.00	65.00	45.00
(2)	Ables	125.00	65.00	45.00
(3)	Agnew	125.00	65.00	45.00
(4)	Altman	125.00	65.00	45.00
(5)	Frank Arellanes	125.00	65.00	45.00
(6)	Auer	125.00	65.00	45.00
(7)	Baker (Horizontal pose.)	125.00	65.00	45.00
(8)	Baker (Vertical pose.)	125.00	65.00	45.00
(9)	Bancroft	3,000	1,500	900.00
(10)	Baum	125.00	65.00	45.00
(11)	Bayless	125.00	65.00	45.00
(12)	Berger	125.00	65.00	45.00
(13)	Berry	125.00	65.00	45.00
(14)	Bohen	125.00	65.00	45.00
(15)	Boles	125.00	65.00	45.00
(16)	Bonner	125.00	65.00	45.00
(17)	Boone	125.00	65.00	45.00
(18)	Brackenridge	125.00	65.00	45.00
(19)	Brashear	125.00	65.00	45.00
(20)	Breen	125.00	65.00	45.00
(21)	Brooks (Los Angeles)	125.00	65.00	45.00
(22)	Brooks (Oakland)	125.00	65.00	45.00
(23)	Brown	125.00	65.00	45.00
(24)	Burch	125.00	65.00	45.00
(25)	Burrell	125.00	65.00	45.00
(26)	Butcher	125.00	65.00	45.00
(27)	Butler	125.00	65.00	45.00
(28)	Byram	125.00	65.00	45.00
(29)	Carlisle	125.00	65.00	45.00
(30)	Carson	125.00	65.00	45.00
(31)	Castleton	125.00	65.00	45.00
(32)	Chadbourne	125.00	65.00	45.00
(33)	Chech	125.00	65.00	45.00
(34)	Cheek	125.00	65.00	45.00
(35)	Christian	125.00	65.00	45.00
(36)	Cook	125.00	65.00	45.00
(37)	Core	125.00	65.00	45.00
(38)	Corhan	125.00	65.00	45.00
(39)	Coy	125.00	65.00	45.00
(40)	Daley	125.00	65.00	45.00
(41)	Delhi	125.00	65.00	45.00
(42)	Dillon	125.00	65.00	45.00
(43)	Doane	125.00	65.00	45.00
(44)	Driscoll	125.00	65.00	45.00
(45)	Durbin	125.00	65.00	45.00
(46)	Fanning	125.00	65.00	45.00
(47)	Felts	125.00	65.00	45.00
(48)	Fisher	125.00	65.00	45.00
(49)	Fitzgerald	125.00	65.00	45.00
(50)	Flater	125.00	65.00	45.00
(51)	Frick	125.00	65.00	45.00
(52)	Gaddy	125.00	65.00	45.00
(53)	Gedeon	125.00	65.00	45.00
(54)	Gilligan	125.00	65.00	45.00
(55)	Girot	125.00	65.00	45.00
(56)	Gray	125.00	65.00	45.00
(57)	Gregg	125.00	65.00	45.00
(58)	Gregory	125.00	65.00	45.00
(59)	Halla	125.00	65.00	45.00
(60)	Hamilton (Oakland)	125.00	65.00	45.00
(61)	Hamilton (San Francisco)	125.00	65.00	45.00
(62)	Harkness	125.00	65.00	45.00
(63)	Hartley	125.00	65.00	45.00
(64)	Heitmuller	125.00	65.00	45.00
(65)	Henley	125.00	65.00	45.00
(66)	Hetling (Glove open.)	125.00	65.00	45.00
(67)	Hetling (Glove closed.)	125.00	65.00	45.00
(68)	Hiester	125.00	65.00	45.00
(69)	Higginbottom	125.00	65.00	45.00
(70)	Hitt	125.00	65.00	45.00
(71)	Hoffman	125.00	65.00	45.00
(72)	Hogan	125.00	65.00	45.00
(73)	Hosp	125.00	65.00	45.00
(74)	Howard	125.00	65.00	45.00
(75)	Howley	125.00	65.00	45.00
(76)	Ireland	125.00	65.00	45.00
(77)	Jackson	125.00	65.00	45.00
(78)	Johnson	125.00	65.00	45.00
(79)	Kane	125.00	65.00	45.00
(80)	Killilay	125.00	65.00	45.00
(81)	Klawitter	125.00	65.00	45.00
(82)	Knight	125.00	65.00	45.00
(83)	Koestner ("P" visible.)	125.00	65.00	45.00
(84)	Koestner (No "P" visible.)	125.00	65.00	45.00
(85)	Kreitz	125.00	65.00	45.00
(86)	Krueger	125.00	65.00	45.00
(87)	LaLonge	125.00	65.00	45.00
(88)	Leard	125.00	65.00	45.00
(89)	Leverenz	125.00	65.00	45.00
(90)	Lewis	125.00	65.00	45.00
(91)	Bill Lindsay	125.00	65.00	45.00
(92)	Litschi	125.00	65.00	45.00
(93)	Lober	125.00	65.00	45.00
(94)	Madden	125.00	65.00	45.00
(95)	Mahoney	125.00	65.00	45.00
(96)	Malarkey	125.00	65.00	45.00
(97)	Martinoni	125.00	65.00	45.00
(98)	McArdle	125.00	65.00	45.00
(99)	McAvoy	125.00	65.00	45.00
(100)	McCorrey	125.00	65.00	45.00
(101)	McCredie	125.00	65.00	45.00
(102)	McDonald	125.00	65.00	45.00
(103)	McDowell	125.00	65.00	45.00
(104)	McIver	125.00	65.00	45.00

		NM	EX	VG
(105)	Meikle	125.00	65.00	45.00
(106)	Metzger	125.00	65.00	45.00
(107)	Miller (Sacramento)	125.00	65.00	45.00
(108)	Miller (San Francisco)	125.00	65.00	45.00
(109)	Mitze	125.00	65.00	45.00
(110)	Mohler	125.00	65.00	45.00
(111)	Moore	125.00	65.00	45.00
(112)	Mundorf (Batting)	125.00	65.00	45.00
(113)	Mundorf (Fielding)	125.00	65.00	45.00
(114)	Nagle	125.00	65.00	45.00
(115)	Noyes	125.00	65.00	45.00
(116)	O'Rourke	125.00	65.00	45.00
(117)	Olmstead	125.00	65.00	45.00
(118)	Orr	125.00	65.00	45.00
(119)	Page	125.00	65.00	45.00
(120)	Parkins	125.00	65.00	45.00
(121)	Patterson (Oakland)	125.00	65.00	45.00
(122)	Patterson (Vernon)	125.00	65.00	45.00
(123)	Pernol	125.00	65.00	45.00
(124)	Pope	125.00	65.00	45.00
(125)	Powell	125.00	65.00	45.00
(126)	Price	125.00	65.00	45.00
(127)	Raftery	125.00	65.00	45.00
(128)	Raleigh	125.00	65.00	45.00
(129)	Rapps ("P" visible.)	125.00	65.00	45.00
(130)	Rapps (No "P" visible.)	125.00	65.00	45.00
(131)	Reidy	125.00	65.00	45.00
(132)	Rodgers	125.00	65.00	45.00
(133)	Rohrer	125.00	65.00	45.00
(134)	Schmidt	125.00	65.00	45.00
(135)	Schwenk	125.00	65.00	45.00
(136)	Sharpe	125.00	65.00	45.00
(137)	Sheehan	125.00	65.00	45.00
(138)	Shinn	125.00	65.00	45.00
(139)	Slagle	125.00	65.00	45.00
(140)	Smith	125.00	65.00	45.00
(141)	Stewart	125.00	65.00	45.00
(142)	Stinson	125.00	65.00	45.00
(143)	Stone	125.00	65.00	45.00
(144)	Sullivan	125.00	65.00	45.00
(145)	Swain	125.00	65.00	45.00
(146)	Taylor	125.00	65.00	45.00
(147)	Temple	125.00	65.00	45.00
(148)	Tiedeman	125.00	65.00	45.00
(149)	Toner	125.00	65.00	45.00
(150)	Tozer	125.00	65.00	45.00
(151)	Van Buren	125.00	65.00	45.00
(152)	Wagner	125.00	65.00	45.00
(153)	Whalen	125.00	65.00	45.00
(154)	Williams (Sacramento)	125.00	65.00	45.00
(155)	Williams (San Francisco)	125.00	65.00	45.00
(156)	Joe Williams	125.00	65.00	45.00
(157)	Wuffli	125.00	65.00	45.00
(158)	Zacher	125.00	65.00	45.00
(159)	Zimmerman	125.00	65.00	45.00

1913 Zeenut Pacific Coast League

The 1913 Zeenut cards measure about 2" x 3-3/4" without the coupon, and feature black-and-white photos on a white, borderless background. To date, 146 different poses have been found. The backs are blank.

		NM	EX	VG
Common Player:		125.00	65.00	45.00
(1)	Abbott	125.00	65.00	45.00
(2)	Ables	125.00	65.00	45.00
(3)	Frank Arelanes (Arellanes)	125.00	65.00	45.00
(4)	Arlett	125.00	65.00	45.00
(5)	Baker	125.00	65.00	45.00
(6)	Baum	125.00	65.00	45.00
(7)	Bayless	125.00	65.00	45.00
(8)	Becker	125.00	65.00	45.00
(9)	Berry	125.00	65.00	45.00
(10)	Bliss	125.00	65.00	45.00
(11)	Boles	125.00	65.00	45.00
(12)	Brackenridge	125.00	65.00	45.00
(13)	Brashear	125.00	65.00	45.00
(14)	Brooks	125.00	65.00	45.00
(15)	Byrnes	125.00	65.00	45.00
(16)	Cadreau	125.00	65.00	45.00
(17)	Carlisle	125.00	65.00	45.00
(18)	Carson	125.00	65.00	45.00
(19)	Cartwright	125.00	65.00	45.00
(20)	Chadbourne	125.00	65.00	45.00
(21)	Charles	125.00	65.00	45.00
(22)	Cheek	125.00	65.00	45.00
(23)	Christian	125.00	65.00	45.00
(24)	Clarke	125.00	65.00	45.00
(25)	Clemons	125.00	65.00	45.00
(26)	Cook	125.00	65.00	45.00
(27)	Corhan	125.00	65.00	45.00

		NM	EX	VG
(28)	Coy	125.00	65.00	45.00
(29)	Crabb	125.00	65.00	45.00
(30)	Crisp	125.00	65.00	45.00
(31)	Derrick	125.00	65.00	45.00
(32)	DeCanniere	125.00	65.00	45.00
(33)	Dillon	125.00	65.00	45.00
(34)	Doane	125.00	65.00	45.00
(35)	Douglass	125.00	65.00	45.00
(36)	Downs	125.00	65.00	45.00
(37)	Driscoll	125.00	65.00	45.00
(38)	Drucke	125.00	65.00	45.00
(39)	Elliott	125.00	65.00	45.00
(40)	Ellis	125.00	65.00	45.00
(41)	Fanning	125.00	65.00	45.00
(42)	Fisher	125.00	65.00	45.00
(43)	Fitzgerald	125.00	65.00	45.00
(44)	Gardner	125.00	65.00	45.00
(45)	Gill	125.00	65.00	45.00
(46)	Goodwin	125.00	65.00	45.00
(47a)	Gregory (Large pose.)	125.00	65.00	45.00
(47b)	Gregory (Small pose.)	125.00	65.00	45.00
(48)	Grey	125.00	65.00	45.00
(49)	Guest	125.00	65.00	45.00
(50)	Hagerman	125.00	65.00	45.00
(51)	Halla	125.00	65.00	45.00
(52)	Hallinan	125.00	65.00	45.00
(53)	Harry Heilmann	6,000	4,000	2,000
(54)	Henley	125.00	65.00	45.00
(55)	Hetling	125.00	65.00	45.00
(56)	Higginbotham	125.00	65.00	45.00
(57)	Hitt	125.00	65.00	45.00
(58)	Hoffman	125.00	65.00	45.00
(59)	Hogan (San Francisco)	125.00	65.00	45.00
(60)	Hogan (Vernon)	125.00	65.00	45.00
(61)	Hosp	125.00	65.00	45.00
(62)	Howard (Los Angeles)	125.00	65.00	45.00
(63)	Howard (San Francisco)	125.00	65.00	45.00
(64)	Hughes	125.00	65.00	45.00
(65)	Jackson	125.00	65.00	45.00
(66)	James	125.00	65.00	45.00
(67)	Johnson	125.00	65.00	45.00
(68)	Johnston	125.00	65.00	45.00
(69)	Kane	125.00	65.00	45.00
(70)	Kaylor	125.00	65.00	45.00
(71)	Kenworthy	125.00	65.00	45.00
(72)	Killilay	125.00	65.00	45.00
(73)	Klawitter	125.00	65.00	45.00
(74)	Koestner	125.00	65.00	45.00
(75)	Kores	125.00	65.00	45.00
(76)	Krapp	125.00	65.00	45.00
(77)	Kreitz	125.00	65.00	45.00
(78)	Krause	125.00	65.00	45.00
(79)	Krueger	125.00	65.00	45.00
(80)	Leard	125.00	65.00	45.00
(81)	Leifield	125.00	65.00	45.00
(82)	Lewis	125.00	65.00	45.00
(83)	Bill Lindsay	125.00	65.00	45.00
(84)	Litschi	125.00	65.00	45.00
(85)	Lively	125.00	65.00	45.00
(86)	Lober	125.00	65.00	45.00
(87)	Lohman	125.00	65.00	45.00
(88)	Maggart	125.00	65.00	45.00
(89)	Malarky	125.00	65.00	45.00
(90)	McArdle	125.00	65.00	45.00
(91)	McCarl	125.00	65.00	45.00
(92)	McCormick	125.00	65.00	45.00
(93)	McCorry	125.00	65.00	45.00
(94)	McCredie	125.00	65.00	45.00
(95)	McDonnell	125.00	65.00	45.00
(96)	Meloan	125.00	65.00	45.00
(97)	Metzger	125.00	65.00	45.00
(98)	Miller	125.00	65.00	45.00
(99)	Mitze	125.00	65.00	45.00
(100)	Moore	125.00	65.00	45.00
(101)	Moran	125.00	65.00	45.00
(102)	Mundorf	125.00	65.00	45.00
(103)	Munsell	125.00	65.00	45.00
(104)	Ness	125.00	65.00	45.00
(105)	O'Rourke	125.00	65.00	45.00
(106)	Overall	125.00	65.00	45.00
(107)	Page	125.00	65.00	45.00
(108)	Parkin	125.00	65.00	45.00
(109)	Patterson	125.00	65.00	45.00
(110)	Pearce	125.00	65.00	45.00
(111)	Pernoll	125.00	65.00	45.00
(112)	Perritt	125.00	65.00	45.00
(113)	Pope	125.00	65.00	45.00
(114)	Pruitt	125.00	65.00	45.00
(115)	Raleigh	125.00	65.00	45.00
(116)	Reitmyer	125.00	65.00	45.00
(117)	Riordan	125.00	65.00	45.00
(118)	Rodgers	125.00	65.00	45.00
(119)	Rogers	125.00	65.00	45.00
(120)	Rohrer	125.00	65.00	45.00
(121)	Ryan	125.00	65.00	45.00
(122)	Schaller	125.00	65.00	45.00
(123)	Schirm	125.00	65.00	45.00
(124)	Schmidt	125.00	65.00	45.00
(125)	Schulz	125.00	65.00	45.00
(126)	Sepulveda	125.00	65.00	45.00
(127)	Shinn	125.00	65.00	45.00
(128)	Spenger	125.00	65.00	45.00
(129)	Stanley	125.00	65.00	45.00
(130)	Stanridge	125.00	65.00	45.00
(131)	Stark	125.00	65.00	45.00
(132)	Sterritt	125.00	65.00	45.00
(133)	Stroud	125.00	65.00	45.00
(134)	Tennant	125.00	65.00	45.00
(135)	Thomas	125.00	65.00	45.00
(136)	Todd	125.00	65.00	45.00
(137)	Tonneman	125.00	65.00	45.00
(138)	Tozer	125.00	65.00	45.00
(139)	Van Buren	125.00	65.00	45.00
(140)	Wagner	125.00	65.00	45.00
(141)	West	125.00	65.00	45.00
(142)	Williams	125.00	65.00	45.00
(143)	Wolverton	125.00	65.00	45.00
(144)	Wotell	125.00	65.00	45.00

		NM	EX	VG
(145)	Wuffli	125.00	65.00	45.00
(146)	Young	125.00	65.00	45.00
(147)	Zacher	125.00	65.00	45.00
(148)	Zimmerman	125.00	65.00	45.00

1914 Zeenut Pacific Coast League

The 1914 Zeenut cards measure about 2" x 4-1/16" without the coupon, and feature black-and-white photos on a gray, borderless background. To date, 146 different poses have been found. The backs are blank.

		NM	EX	VG
Common Player:		100.00	50.00	30.00
(1)	Ables	100.00	50.00	30.00
(2)	Abstein	100.00	50.00	30.00
(3)	Alexander	100.00	50.00	30.00
(4)	Arbogast	100.00	50.00	30.00
(5)	Arlett	100.00	50.00	30.00
(6)	Frank Arrelanes (Arellanes)	100.00	50.00	30.00
(7)	Bancroft	1,000	700.00	300.00
(8)	Barham	100.00	50.00	30.00
(9)	Barrenkamp	100.00	50.00	30.00
(10)	Barton	100.00	50.00	30.00
(11)	Baum	100.00	50.00	30.00
(12)	Bayless	100.00	50.00	30.00
(13a)	Bliss (Large pose.)	100.00	50.00	30.00
(13b)	Bliss (Small pose.)	100.00	50.00	30.00
(14)	Boles	100.00	50.00	30.00
(15)	Borton	100.00	50.00	30.00
(16)	Brashear	100.00	50.00	30.00
(17)	Brenegan	100.00	50.00	30.00
(18)	Brooks	100.00	50.00	30.00
(19)	Brown	100.00	50.00	30.00
(20)	Butler	100.00	50.00	30.00
(21)	Jacinto Calvo	900.00	600.00	250.00
(22)	Carlisle	100.00	50.00	30.00
(23)	Cartwright	100.00	50.00	30.00
(24)	Charles	100.00	50.00	30.00
(25)	Chech	100.00	50.00	30.00
(26)	Christian	100.00	50.00	30.00
(27)	Clarke	100.00	50.00	30.00
(28)	Colligan	100.00	50.00	30.00
(29)	Cook	100.00	50.00	30.00
(31)	Coy	100.00	50.00	30.00
(32)	Crabb	100.00	50.00	30.00
(33)	Davis	100.00	50.00	30.00
(34)	Derrick	100.00	50.00	30.00
(35)	Devlin	100.00	50.00	30.00
(36)	DeCannier	100.00	50.00	30.00
(37)	Dillon	100.00	50.00	30.00
(38)	Doane	100.00	50.00	30.00
(39)	Downs	100.00	50.00	30.00
(40)	Ehmke	100.00	50.00	30.00
(41)	Elliott	100.00	50.00	30.00
(41)	Ellis	100.00	50.00	30.00
(42)	Evans	100.00	50.00	30.00
(43)	Fanning	100.00	50.00	30.00
(44)	Fisher	100.00	50.00	30.00
(45)	Fitzgerald	100.00	50.00	30.00
(46)	Fleharty	100.00	50.00	30.00
(47)	Frambach	100.00	50.00	30.00
(48)	Gardner	100.00	50.00	30.00
(49)	Gedeon	100.00	50.00	30.00
(50)	Geyer	100.00	50.00	30.00
(51)	Gianini	100.00	50.00	30.00
(52)	Gregory	100.00	50.00	30.00
(53)	Guest	100.00	50.00	30.00
(54)	Hallinan	100.00	50.00	30.00
(55)	Hannah	100.00	50.00	30.00
(56)	Harkness (Batting)	100.00	50.00	30.00
(57)	Haworth (Batting)	100.00	50.00	30.00
(58)	Haworth (Catching)	100.00	50.00	30.00
(59)	Henderson	100.00	50.00	30.00
(60)	Henley	100.00	50.00	30.00
(61)	Hern	100.00	50.00	30.00
(62)	Hettling	100.00	50.00	30.00
(63)	Higginbotham	100.00	50.00	30.00
(64)	Hitt	100.00	50.00	30.00
(65)	Hogan	100.00	50.00	30.00
(66a)	Hosp (Large pose.)	100.00	50.00	30.00
(66b)	Hosp (Small pose.)	100.00	50.00	30.00
(67)	Howard	100.00	50.00	30.00
(68)	Hughes (Los Angeles)	100.00	50.00	30.00
(69)	Hughes (San Francisco)	100.00	50.00	30.00
(70)	Johnson	100.00	50.00	30.00
(71)	Kane	100.00	50.00	30.00
(72)	Kaylor	100.00	50.00	30.00
(73)	Killilay	100.00	50.00	30.00
(74)	Klawitter	100.00	50.00	30.00
(75)	Klepfler	100.00	50.00	30.00
(76)	Kores	100.00	50.00	30.00

		NM	EX	VG
(77)	Kramer	100.00	50.00	30.00
(78)	Krause	100.00	50.00	30.00
(79a)	Leard (Large pose.)	100.00	50.00	30.00
(79b)	Leard (Small pose.)	100.00	50.00	30.00
(80)	Liefeld	100.00	50.00	30.00
(81)	Litschi	100.00	50.00	30.00
(82)	Lober	100.00	50.00	30.00
(83)	Loomis	100.00	50.00	30.00
(84)	Love	100.00	50.00	30.00
(85)	Lynn	100.00	50.00	30.00
(86)	Maggart	100.00	50.00	30.00
(87)	Malarkey	100.00	50.00	30.00
(88)	Martinoni	100.00	50.00	30.00
(89)	McArdle	100.00	50.00	30.00
(90)	McCredie	100.00	50.00	30.00
(91)	McDonald	100.00	50.00	30.00
(92)	Meek	100.00	50.00	30.00
(93)	Meloan	100.00	50.00	30.00
(94)	Menges	100.00	50.00	30.00
(95)	Metzger	100.00	50.00	30.00
(96)	Middleton	100.00	50.00	30.00
(97)	Mitze	100.00	50.00	30.00
(98)	Mohler	100.00	50.00	30.00
(99)	Moore	100.00	50.00	30.00
(100)	Moran	100.00	50.00	30.00
(101)	Mundorf	100.00	50.00	30.00
(102)	Murphy	100.00	50.00	30.00
(103)	Musser	100.00	50.00	30.00
(104)	Ness	100.00	50.00	30.00
(105)	O'Leary	100.00	50.00	30.00
(106)	Orr	100.00	50.00	30.00
(107)	Page	100.00	50.00	30.00
(108)	Pape	100.00	50.00	30.00
(109)	Parkin	100.00	50.00	30.00
(110a)	Peet (Large pose.)	100.00	50.00	30.00
(110b)	Peet (Small pose.)	100.00	50.00	30.00
(111)	Perkins	100.00	50.00	30.00
(112)	Pernoll	100.00	50.00	30.00
(113)	Perritt	100.00	50.00	30.00
(114)	Powell	100.00	50.00	30.00
(115)	Prough	100.00	50.00	30.00
(116)	Pruiett	100.00	50.00	30.00
(117)	Quinlan	100.00	50.00	30.00
(118a)	Raney (Incorrect spelling.)	100.00	50.00	30.00
(118b)	Ramey (Correct spelling.)	100.00	50.00	30.00
(119)	Rieger	100.00	50.00	30.00
(120)	Rodgers	100.00	50.00	30.00
(121)	Rogers	100.00	50.00	30.00
(122)	Rohrer	100.00	50.00	30.00
(123)	Ryan	100.00	50.00	30.00
(124)	Ryan	100.00	50.00	30.00
(125)	Sawyer	100.00	50.00	30.00
(126)	Schaller	100.00	50.00	30.00
(127)	Schmidt	100.00	50.00	30.00
(128)	Sepulveda	100.00	50.00	30.00
(129)	Shinn	100.00	50.00	30.00
(130)	Slagle	100.00	50.00	30.00
(131)	Speas	100.00	50.00	30.00
(132)	Stanridge	100.00	50.00	30.00
(133)	Stroud	100.00	50.00	30.00
(134)	Tennant	100.00	50.00	30.00
(135)	Tobin	100.00	50.00	30.00
(136)	Tozer	100.00	50.00	30.00
(137)	Van Buren	100.00	50.00	30.00
(138)	West	100.00	50.00	30.00
(139)	White	100.00	50.00	30.00
(140)	Wolter	100.00	50.00	30.00
(141)	Wolverton	100.00	50.00	30.00
(142)	Yantz	100.00	50.00	30.00
(143)	Young	100.00	50.00	30.00
(144)	Zacher	100.00	50.00	30.00
(145)	Zumwalt	100.00	50.00	30.00

1915 Zeenut Pacific Coast League

The 1915 Zeenut cards are dated on the front, making identification very easy. They measure about 2" x 3-3/4" without the coupon and feature a black-and-white photo on a light background. To date 141 different cards are known to exist. This year is among the toughest of all Zeenuts to find.

		NM	EX	VG
Common Player:		100.00	45.00	25.00
With Coupon:		900.00	400.00	240.00
(1)	Ables	100.00	45.00	25.00
(2)	Abstein	100.00	45.00	25.00
(3)	Alcock	100.00	45.00	25.00
(4)	Arbogast	100.00	45.00	25.00
(5)	Baerwald	100.00	45.00	25.00
(6)	Barbour	100.00	45.00	25.00
(7)	Bates	100.00	45.00	25.00
(8)	Baum	100.00	45.00	25.00
(9)	Bayless	100.00	45.00	25.00
(10)	Beatty	100.00	45.00	25.00
(11)	Beer	100.00	45.00	25.00
(12)	Benham	100.00	45.00	25.00
(13)	Berger	100.00	45.00	25.00
(14)	Beumiller	100.00	45.00	25.00
(15)	Blankenship	100.00	45.00	25.00
(16)	Block	100.00	45.00	25.00
(17)	Bodie	100.00	45.00	25.00
(18)	Boles	100.00	45.00	25.00
(19)	Boyd	100.00	45.00	25.00
(20)	Bromley	100.00	45.00	25.00
(21)	Brown	100.00	45.00	25.00
(22)	Burns	300.00	135.00	75.00
(23)	Carlisle	100.00	45.00	25.00
(24)	Carrisch	100.00	45.00	25.00
(25)	Charles	100.00	45.00	25.00
(26)	Chech	100.00	45.00	25.00
(27)	Christian	100.00	45.00	25.00
(28)	Clarke	100.00	45.00	25.00
(29)	Couch	100.00	45.00	25.00
(30)	Stan Covaleski (Coveleski)	2,000	1,200	600.00
(31)	Daniels	100.00	45.00	25.00
(32)	Davis	100.00	45.00	25.00
(33)	DeCanniere	100.00	45.00	25.00
(34)	Dent	100.00	45.00	25.00
(35)	Derrick	100.00	45.00	25.00
(36)	Dillon	100.00	45.00	25.00
(37)	Doane	100.00	45.00	25.00
(38)	Downs	100.00	45.00	25.00
(39)	Elliott	100.00	45.00	25.00
(40)	F. Elliott	100.00	45.00	25.00
(41)	Ellis	100.00	45.00	25.00
(42)	Evans	100.00	45.00	25.00
(43)	Fanning	100.00	45.00	25.00
(44)	Faye	100.00	45.00	25.00
(45)	Fisher	100.00	45.00	25.00
(46)	Fittery	100.00	45.00	25.00
(47)	Fitzgerald	100.00	45.00	25.00
(48)	Fromme	100.00	45.00	25.00
(49)	Gardiner	100.00	45.00	25.00
(50)	Gedeon	100.00	45.00	25.00
(51)	Gleischmann	100.00	45.00	25.00
(52)	Gregory	100.00	45.00	25.00
(53)	Guest	100.00	45.00	25.00
(54)	Hall	100.00	45.00	25.00
(55)	Halla	100.00	45.00	25.00
(56)	Hallinan	100.00	45.00	25.00
(57)	Hannah	100.00	45.00	25.00
(58)	Harper	100.00	45.00	25.00
(59)	Harry Heilmann	1,500	800.00	400.00
(60)	Henley	100.00	45.00	25.00
(61)	Hetling	100.00	45.00	25.00
(62)	Higginbotham	100.00	45.00	25.00
(63)	Hilliard	100.00	45.00	25.00
(64)	Hitt (Winding up.)	100.00	45.00	25.00
(65)	Hitt (Throwing)	100.00	45.00	25.00
(66)	Hogan	100.00	45.00	25.00
(67)	Hosp	100.00	45.00	25.00
(68)	Howard	100.00	45.00	25.00
(69)	Hughes	100.00	45.00	25.00
(70)	Johnson	100.00	45.00	25.00
(71)	Jones	100.00	45.00	25.00
(72)	Kahler	100.00	45.00	25.00
(73)	Kane	100.00	45.00	25.00
(74)	Karr	100.00	45.00	25.00
(75)	Killilay	100.00	45.00	25.00
(76)	Klawitter	100.00	45.00	25.00
(77)	Koerner	100.00	45.00	25.00
(78)	Krause	100.00	45.00	25.00
(79)	Kuhn	100.00	45.00	25.00
(80)	LaRoy	100.00	45.00	25.00
(81)	Leard	100.00	45.00	25.00
(82)	Bill Lindsay	100.00	45.00	25.00
(83)	Litschi	100.00	45.00	25.00
(84)	Lober	100.00	45.00	25.00
(85)	Love	100.00	45.00	25.00
(86)	Lush	100.00	45.00	25.00
(87)	Maggart	100.00	45.00	25.00
(88)	Malarkey	100.00	45.00	25.00
(89)	Manda	100.00	45.00	25.00
(90)	Marcan	100.00	45.00	25.00
(91)	Martinoni	100.00	45.00	25.00
(92)	McAvoy	100.00	45.00	25.00
(93)	McCredie	100.00	45.00	25.00
(94)	McDonell	100.00	45.00	25.00
(95)	Fred McMullen (McMullin)	7,500	3,500	2,000
(96)	Meek	100.00	45.00	25.00
(97)	Meloan	100.00	45.00	25.00
(98)	Metzger	100.00	45.00	25.00
(99)	Middleton	100.00	45.00	25.00
(100)	Mitchell	100.00	45.00	25.00
(101)	Mitze	100.00	45.00	25.00
(102)	Morgan	100.00	45.00	25.00
(103)	Mundorff	100.00	45.00	25.00
(104)	Murphy	100.00	45.00	25.00
(105)	Ness	100.00	45.00	25.00
(106)	Nutt	100.00	45.00	25.00
(107)	Orr	100.00	45.00	25.00
(108)	Pernoll	100.00	45.00	25.00
(109)	Perritt	100.00	45.00	25.00
(110)	Piercey	100.00	45.00	25.00
(111)	Price	100.00	45.00	25.00
(112)	Prough	100.00	45.00	25.00
(113)	Prueitt	100.00	45.00	25.00
(114)	Purtell	100.00	45.00	25.00
(115)	Reed	100.00	45.00	25.00
(116)	Reisigl	100.00	45.00	25.00
(117)	Remneas	100.00	45.00	25.00
(118)	Swede Risberg	5,500	2,500	1,500
(119)	Rohrer	100.00	45.00	25.00
(120)	Russell	100.00	45.00	25.00
(121)	Ryan (Los Angeles)	100.00	45.00	25.00
(122)	Ryan	100.00	45.00	25.00
(123)	Schaller	100.00	45.00	25.00
(124)	Schmidt	100.00	45.00	25.00
(125)	Scoggins	100.00	45.00	25.00
(126)	Sepulveda	100.00	45.00	25.00
(127)	Shinn	100.00	45.00	25.00
(128)	Smith	100.00	45.00	25.00
(129)	Speas	100.00	45.00	25.00
(130)	Spencer	100.00	45.00	25.00
(132)	Tennant	100.00	45.00	25.00
(133)	Terry	100.00	45.00	25.00
(134)	Tobin	100.00	45.00	25.00
(135)	West	100.00	45.00	25.00
(136)	White	100.00	45.00	25.00
(137)	Claude Williams	5,500	2,500	1,500
(138)	Johnny Williams	250.00	110.00	65.00
(139)	Wolter	100.00	45.00	25.00
(140)	Wolverton	100.00	45.00	25.00
(141)	Zacher	100.00	45.00	25.00

1916 Zeenut Pacific Coast League

The 1916 Zeenuts measure about 2" x 3-3/4" without the coupon and are dated on the front (some cards were misdated 1915 however). The card fronts feature black-and-white photos on a blue background. There are 144 known subjects. The 1916 series is among the more difficult.

		NM	EX	VG
Common Player:		100.00	50.00	30.00
(1)	Autrey	100.00	50.00	30.00
(2)	Barbeau	100.00	50.00	30.00
(3)	Barry	100.00	50.00	30.00
(4)	Bassler	100.00	50.00	30.00
(5)	Bates	100.00	50.00	30.00
(6)	Baum	100.00	50.00	30.00
(7)	Bayless	100.00	50.00	30.00
(8)	Beer	100.00	50.00	30.00
(9)	Berg	100.00	50.00	30.00
(10)	Berger	100.00	50.00	30.00
(11)	Blankenship	100.00	50.00	30.00
(12)	Block	100.00	50.00	30.00
(13)	Bodie	150.00	80.00	40.00
(14)	Bohne	350.00	200.00	150.00
(15)	Boles	100.00	50.00	30.00
(16)	Boyd	100.00	50.00	30.00
(17)	Brief	100.00	50.00	30.00
(18)	Brooks	100.00	50.00	30.00
(19)	Brown	100.00	50.00	30.00
(20)	Butler	100.00	50.00	30.00
(21)	Callahan	100.00	50.00	30.00
(22)	Carrisch	100.00	50.00	30.00
(23)	Frank Chance	2,000	1,200	600.00
(24)	Jimmy Claxton	15,000	9,500	7,000
(25)	Coffey	100.00	50.00	30.00
(26)	Cook	100.00	50.00	30.00
(27)	Corbett	100.00	50.00	30.00
(28)	Couch	100.00	50.00	30.00
(29)	Crandall	100.00	50.00	30.00
(30)	Dalton	100.00	50.00	30.00
(31)	Davis	100.00	50.00	30.00
(32)	Derrick	100.00	50.00	30.00
(33)	Doane	100.00	50.00	30.00
(34)	Downs	100.00	50.00	30.00
(35)	Dugan	100.00	50.00	30.00
(36)	Eldred	100.00	50.00	30.00
(37)	F. Elliott	100.00	50.00	30.00
(38)	H. Elliott	100.00	50.00	30.00
(39)	Ellis	100.00	50.00	30.00
(40)	Erickson	100.00	50.00	30.00
(41)	Fanning	100.00	50.00	30.00
(42)	Fisher	100.00	50.00	30.00
(43)	Fittery	100.00	50.00	30.00
(44)	Fitzgerald	100.00	50.00	30.00
(45)	Fromme	100.00	50.00	30.00
(46)	Galloway	100.00	50.00	30.00
(47)	Gardner	100.00	50.00	30.00
(48)	Gay	100.00	50.00	30.00
(49)	Gleischmann	100.00	50.00	30.00
(50)	Griffith	100.00	50.00	30.00
(51)	Griggs	100.00	50.00	30.00
(52)	Guisto	100.00	50.00	30.00
(53)	Hagerman	100.00	50.00	30.00
(54)	Hall	100.00	50.00	30.00
(55)	Hallinan	100.00	50.00	30.00
(56)	Hannah	100.00	50.00	30.00
(57)	Harstadt	100.00	50.00	30.00
(58)	Haworth	100.00	50.00	30.00
(59)	Hess	100.00	50.00	30.00
(60)	Higginbotham	100.00	50.00	30.00
(61)	Hitt	100.00	50.00	30.00
(62)	Hogg	100.00	50.00	30.00
(63)	Hollocher	100.00	50.00	30.00
(64)	Horstman	100.00	50.00	30.00
(65)	Houck	100.00	50.00	30.00
(66)	Howard	100.00	50.00	30.00
(67)	Hughes	100.00	50.00	30.00

		NM	EX	VG
(68)	E. Johnston	100.00	50.00	30.00
(69)	G. Johnston	100.00	50.00	30.00
(70)	Jones	100.00	50.00	30.00
(71)	Kahler	100.00	50.00	30.00
(72)	Kane	100.00	50.00	30.00
(73)	Kelly	100.00	50.00	30.00
(74)	Kenworthy	100.00	50.00	30.00
(75)	Klawitter	100.00	50.00	30.00
(76)	Klein	100.00	50.00	30.00
(77)	Koerner	100.00	50.00	30.00
(78)	Krause	100.00	50.00	30.00
(79)	Kuhn	100.00	50.00	30.00
(80)	Lane	100.00	50.00	30.00
(81)	Larsen	100.00	50.00	30.00
(82)	Lush	100.00	50.00	30.00
(83)	Machold	100.00	50.00	30.00
(84)	Maggert	100.00	50.00	30.00
(85)	Manser	100.00	50.00	30.00
(86)	Martin	100.00	50.00	30.00
(87)	Mattick	100.00	50.00	30.00
(88)	McCredie	100.00	50.00	30.00
(89)	McGaffigan	100.00	50.00	30.00
(90)	McLarry	100.00	50.00	30.00
(91)	Menges	100.00	50.00	30.00
(92)	Middleton	100.00	50.00	30.00
(93)	Mitchell	100.00	50.00	30.00
(94)	Mitze	100.00	50.00	30.00
(95)	Munsell	100.00	50.00	30.00
(96)	Murphy	100.00	50.00	30.00
(97)	Nixon	100.00	50.00	30.00
(98)	Noyes	100.00	50.00	30.00
(99)	Nutt	100.00	50.00	30.00
(100)	O'Brien	100.00	50.00	30.00
(101)	Oldham	100.00	50.00	30.00
(102)	Orr	100.00	50.00	30.00
(103)	Patterson	100.00	50.00	30.00
(104)	Perritt	100.00	50.00	30.00
(105)	Prough	100.00	50.00	30.00
(106)	Prueitt	100.00	50.00	30.00
(107)	Quinlan	100.00	50.00	30.00
(108)	Quinn (Portland)	100.00	50.00	30.00
(109)	Quinn (Vernon)	100.00	50.00	30.00
(110)	Rader	100.00	50.00	30.00
(111)	Randall	100.00	50.00	30.00
(112)	Rath	100.00	50.00	30.00
(113)	Reisegl	100.00	50.00	30.00
(114)	Reuther (Ruether)	100.00	50.00	30.00
(115)	Swede Risberg	5,000	2,000	1,250
(116)	Roche	100.00	50.00	30.00
(117)	Ryan	100.00	50.00	30.00
(118)	Ryan	100.00	50.00	30.00
(119)	Scoggins	100.00	50.00	30.00
(120)	Sepulveda	100.00	50.00	30.00
(121)	Schaller	100.00	50.00	30.00
(122)	Sheehan	100.00	50.00	30.00
(123)	Shinn	100.00	50.00	30.00
(124)	Smith	100.00	50.00	30.00
(125)	Sothoron	100.00	50.00	30.00
(126)	Southworth	100.00	50.00	30.00
(127)	Speas	100.00	50.00	30.00
(128)	Spencer	100.00	50.00	30.00
(129)	Standridge	100.00	50.00	30.00
(130)	Steen	100.00	50.00	30.00
(131)	Stumpf	100.00	50.00	30.00
(132)	Vann	100.00	50.00	30.00
(133)	Vaughn	100.00	50.00	30.00
(134)	Ward	100.00	50.00	30.00
(135)	Whalling	100.00	50.00	30.00
(136)	Wilie	100.00	50.00	30.00
(137)	Williams	100.00	50.00	30.00
(138)	Wolverton	100.00	50.00	30.00
(139)	Wuffli	100.00	50.00	30.00
(140)	Zabel	100.00	50.00	30.00
(141)	Zacher	100.00	50.00	30.00
(142)	Zimmerman	100.00	50.00	30.00

1917 Zeenut Pacific Coast League

The 1917 Zeenuts measure about 1-3/4" x 3-3/4" and feature black-and-white photos on a light background. They are dated on the front and have blank backs. An advertising poster has been found listing 119 players (two pose variations brings the total to 121), but to date, six players on the list have not been found.

		NM	EX	VG
Common Player:		90.00	45.00	30.00
(1)	Arlett	90.00	45.00	30.00
(2)	Frank Arrelanes (Arellanes)	90.00	45.00	30.00
(3)	Baker (Catching)	90.00	45.00	30.00
(4)	Baker (Throwing)	90.00	45.00	30.00
(5)	Baldwin	90.00	45.00	30.00
(6)	Bassler	90.00	45.00	30.00
(7)	Baum	90.00	45.00	30.00
(8)	Beer	90.00	45.00	30.00
(9)	Bernhard	90.00	45.00	30.00
(10)	Bliss	90.00	45.00	30.00
(11)	Boles	90.00	45.00	30.00
(12)	Brenton	90.00	45.00	30.00
(13)	Brief	90.00	45.00	30.00
(14)	Brown	90.00	45.00	30.00
(15)	Burns	200.00	150.00	75.00
(16)	Callahan	90.00	45.00	30.00
(17)	Callan	90.00	45.00	30.00
(18)	Jacinto Calvo	700.00	400.00	200.00
(19)	Chadbourne	90.00	45.00	30.00
(20)	Frank Chance	1,800	1,000	500.00
(21)	Coltrin	90.00	45.00	30.00
(22)	Connifer	90.00	45.00	30.00
(23)	Corhan	90.00	45.00	30.00
(24)	Crandall (Los Angeles)	90.00	45.00	30.00
(25)	Crandall (Salt Lake)	90.00	45.00	30.00
(26)	Cress	90.00	45.00	30.00
(27)	Davis	90.00	45.00	30.00
(28)	DeCanniere	90.00	45.00	30.00
(29)	Doane	90.00	45.00	30.00
(30)	Dougan	90.00	45.00	30.00
(31)	Dougherty	90.00	45.00	30.00
(32)	Downs	90.00	45.00	30.00
(33)	Dubuc	90.00	45.00	30.00
(34)	Ellis	90.00	45.00	30.00
(35)	Erickson	90.00	45.00	30.00
(36)	Evans	90.00	45.00	30.00
(37)	Farmer	90.00	45.00	30.00
(38)	Fincher	90.00	45.00	30.00
(39)	Fisher	90.00	45.00	30.00
(40)	Fitzgerald	90.00	45.00	30.00
(41)	Fournier	90.00	45.00	30.00
(42)	Fromme	90.00	45.00	30.00
(43)	Galloway	90.00	45.00	30.00
(44)	Gislason	90.00	45.00	30.00
(45)	Goodbred	90.00	45.00	30.00
(46)	Griggs	90.00	45.00	30.00
(47)	Groehling	90.00	45.00	30.00
(48)	Hall (Los Angeles)	90.00	45.00	30.00
(49)	Hall (San Francisco)	90.00	45.00	30.00
(50)	Hannah	90.00	45.00	30.00
(51)	Harstad	90.00	45.00	30.00
(52)	Helfrich	90.00	45.00	30.00
(53)	Hess	90.00	45.00	30.00
(54)	Hitt	90.00	45.00	30.00
(55)	Hoff	90.00	45.00	30.00
(56)	Hollacher	90.00	45.00	30.00
(57)	Hollywood	90.00	45.00	30.00
(58)	Houck	90.00	45.00	30.00
(59)	Howard	90.00	45.00	30.00
(60)	Hughes	90.00	45.00	30.00
(61)	Johnson	90.00	45.00	30.00
(62)	Kilhullen	90.00	45.00	30.00
(63)	Killiffer (Killefer)	90.00	45.00	30.00
(64)	Koerner	90.00	45.00	30.00
(65)	Krause	90.00	45.00	30.00
(66)	Lane	90.00	45.00	30.00
(67)	Lapan	90.00	45.00	30.00
(68)	Leake	90.00	45.00	30.00
(69)	Lee	90.00	45.00	30.00
(70)	Leverenz	90.00	45.00	30.00
(71)	Maggert	90.00	45.00	30.00
(72)	Maisel	90.00	45.00	30.00
(73)	Mattick	90.00	45.00	30.00
(74)	McCreedie	90.00	45.00	30.00
(75)	McLarry	90.00	45.00	30.00
(76)	Mensor	500.00	250.00	150.00
(77)	Emil "Irish" Meusel	200.00	100.00	70.00
(78)	Middleton	90.00	45.00	30.00
(79)	Miller (Batting)	90.00	45.00	30.00
(80)	Miller (Throwing)	90.00	45.00	30.00
(81)	Mitchell	90.00	45.00	30.00
(82)	Mitze	90.00	45.00	30.00
(83)	Murphy	90.00	45.00	30.00
(84)	Murray	90.00	45.00	30.00
(85)	O'Brien	90.00	45.00	30.00
(86)	O'Mara	90.00	45.00	30.00
(87)	Oldham	90.00	45.00	30.00
(88)	Orr	90.00	45.00	30.00
(89)	Penelli	90.00	45.00	30.00
(90)	Penner	90.00	45.00	30.00
(91)	Pick	90.00	45.00	30.00
(92)	Prough	90.00	45.00	30.00
(93)	Pruiett	90.00	45.00	30.00
(94)	Quinlan	90.00	45.00	30.00
(95)	Quinn	90.00	45.00	30.00
(96)	Rath	90.00	45.00	30.00
(97)	Roche	90.00	45.00	30.00
(98)	Ryan (Los Angeles)	90.00	45.00	30.00
(99)	Ryan (Salt Lake)	90.00	45.00	30.00
(100)	Schaller	90.00	45.00	30.00
(101)	Schinkle	90.00	45.00	30.00
(102)	Schultz	90.00	45.00	30.00
(103)	Sheehan	90.00	45.00	30.00
(104)	Sheeley	90.00	45.00	30.00
(105)	Shinn	90.00	45.00	30.00
(106)	Siglin	90.00	45.00	30.00
(107)	Simon	90.00	45.00	30.00
(108)	Smith	90.00	45.00	30.00
(109)	Snyder	90.00	45.00	30.00
(110)	Stanridge	90.00	45.00	30.00
(111)	Steen	90.00	45.00	30.00
(112)	Stovall	90.00	45.00	30.00
(113)	Stumpf	90.00	45.00	30.00
(114)	Sullivan	90.00	45.00	30.00
(115)	Terry	90.00	45.00	30.00
(116)	Tobin	90.00	45.00	30.00
(117)	Valencia	90.00	45.00	30.00
(118)	Vaughn	90.00	45.00	30.00
(119)	Whalling	90.00	45.00	30.00
(120)	Wilie	90.00	45.00	30.00
(121)	Wolverton	90.00	45.00	30.00

1918 Zeenut Pacific Coast League

The 1918 Zeenuts are among the most distinctive because of the red borders surrounding the photos. They measure about 1-13/16" x 3-5/8" and are among the more difficult years to find.

		NM	EX	VG
Common Player:		250.00	120.00	60.00
With Coupon:		800.00	400.00	240.00
(1)	Alcock	250.00	120.00	60.00
(2)	Arkenburg	250.00	120.00	60.00
(3)	A. Arlett	250.00	120.00	60.00
(4)	Baum	250.00	120.00	60.00
(5)	Boles	250.00	120.00	60.00
(6)	Borton	250.00	120.00	60.00
(7)	Brenton	250.00	120.00	60.00
(8)	Bromley	250.00	120.00	60.00
(9)	Brooks	250.00	120.00	60.00
(10)	Brown	250.00	120.00	60.00
(11)	Caldera	250.00	120.00	60.00
(12)	Camm (Kamm)	250.00	120.00	60.00
(13)	Chadbourne	250.00	120.00	60.00
(14)	Chappell	250.00	120.00	60.00
(15)	Codington	250.00	120.00	60.00
(16)	Conwright	250.00	120.00	60.00
(17)	Cooper	250.00	120.00	60.00
(18)	Cox	250.00	120.00	60.00
(19)	Crandall (Los Angeles)	250.00	120.00	60.00
(20)	Crandall (Salt Lake)	250.00	120.00	60.00
(21)	Crawford	4,000	3,000	2,000
(22)	Croll	250.00	120.00	60.00
(23)	Davis	250.00	120.00	60.00
(24)	DeVormer	250.00	120.00	60.00
(25)	Dobbs	250.00	120.00	60.00
(26)	Downs	250.00	120.00	60.00
(27)	Dubuc	250.00	120.00	60.00
(28)	Dunn	250.00	120.00	60.00
(29)	Easterly	250.00	120.00	60.00
(30)	Eldred	250.00	120.00	60.00
(31)	Elliot	250.00	120.00	60.00
(32)	Ellis	250.00	120.00	60.00
(33)	Essick	250.00	120.00	60.00
(34)	Farmer	250.00	120.00	60.00
(35)	Fisher	250.00	120.00	60.00
(36)	Fittery	250.00	120.00	60.00
(37)	Forsythe	250.00	120.00	60.00
(38)	Fournier	250.00	120.00	60.00
(39)	Fromme	250.00	120.00	60.00
(40)	Gardner (Oakland)	250.00	120.00	60.00
(41)	Gardner (Sacramento)	250.00	120.00	60.00
(42)	Goldie	250.00	120.00	60.00
(43)	Griggs	250.00	120.00	60.00
(44)	Hawkes	250.00	120.00	60.00
(45)	Hollander	250.00	120.00	60.00
(46)	Hosp	250.00	120.00	60.00
(47)	Howard	250.00	120.00	60.00
(48)	Hummel	250.00	120.00	60.00
(49)	Hunter	250.00	120.00	60.00
(50)	Johnson	250.00	120.00	60.00
(51)	G. Johnson	250.00	120.00	60.00
(52)	Kantlehner	250.00	120.00	60.00
(53)	Killefer	250.00	120.00	60.00
(54)	Koerner	250.00	120.00	60.00
(55)	Konnick	250.00	120.00	60.00
(56)	Kremer	250.00	120.00	60.00
(57)	Lapan	250.00	120.00	60.00
(58)	Leake	250.00	120.00	60.00
(59)	Leathers	250.00	120.00	60.00
(60)	Leifer	250.00	120.00	60.00
(61)	Leverenz	250.00	120.00	60.00
(62)	Llewlyn	250.00	120.00	60.00
(63)	Martin	250.00	120.00	60.00
(64)	McCabe	250.00	120.00	60.00
(65)	McCredie	250.00	120.00	60.00
(66)	McKee	250.00	120.00	60.00
(67)	McNulty	250.00	120.00	60.00
(68)	Mensor	700.00	400.00	200.00
(69)	Middleton	250.00	120.00	60.00
(70)	Miller (Oakland)	250.00	120.00	60.00
(71)	Miller (Salt Lake)	250.00	120.00	60.00
(72)	J. Mitchell	250.00	120.00	60.00
(73)	R. Mitchell	250.00	120.00	60.00
(74)	Mitze	250.00	120.00	60.00
(75)	Moore	250.00	120.00	60.00
(76)	Morton	250.00	120.00	60.00
(77)	Murray	250.00	120.00	60.00
(78)	O'Doul	3,000	2,000	1,000
(79)	Orr	250.00	120.00	60.00
(80)	Pepe	250.00	120.00	60.00

(81)	Pertica	250.00	120.00	60.00
(82)	Phillips	250.00	120.00	60.00
(83)	Pick	250.00	120.00	60.00
(84)	Pinelli	250.00	120.00	60.00
(85)	Prentice	250.00	120.00	60.00
(86)	Prough	250.00	120.00	60.00
(87)	Quinlan	250.00	120.00	60.00
(88)	Ritchie	250.00	120.00	60.00
(89)	Rogers	250.00	120.00	60.00
(90)	Ryan	250.00	120.00	60.00
(91)	Sand	250.00	120.00	60.00
(92)	Shader	250.00	120.00	60.00
(93)	Sheely	250.00	120.00	60.00
(94)	Siglin	250.00	120.00	60.00
(95)	Smale	250.00	120.00	60.00
(96)	Smith (Salt Lake City)	250.00	120.00	60.00
(97)	Smith (San Francisco)	250.00	120.00	60.00
(98)	Stanbridge	250.00	120.00	60.00
(99)	Terry	250.00	120.00	60.00
(100)	Valencia	250.00	120.00	60.00
(101)	West	250.00	120.00	60.00
(102)	Wilie	250.00	120.00	60.00
(103)	Williams	250.00	120.00	60.00
(104)	Wisterzill	250.00	120.00	60.00

1919 Zeenut Pacific Coast League

The 1919 Zeenuts cards are dated on the front and measure about 1-3/4" x 3-5/8". They featured borderless, sepia-toned photos. To date, 144 subjects exist in the series.

		NM	EX	VG
	Common Player:	100.00	50.00	30.00
(1)	Ally	100.00	50.00	30.00
(2)	Fatty Arbuckle	6,000	4,000	2,000
(3)	A. Arlett	100.00	50.00	30.00
(4)	R. Arlett	100.00	50.00	30.00
(5)	Baker	100.00	50.00	30.00
(6)	Baldwin	100.00	50.00	30.00
(7)	Baum	100.00	50.00	30.00
(8)	Beck	100.00	50.00	30.00
(9)	Bigbee	100.00	50.00	30.00
(10)	Blue	100.00	50.00	30.00
(11)	Bohne	300.00	200.00	100.00
(12)	Boles	100.00	50.00	30.00
(13)	Borton	100.00	50.00	30.00
(14)	Bowman	100.00	50.00	30.00
(15)	Brooks	100.00	50.00	30.00
(16)	Brown	100.00	50.00	30.00
(17)	Byler	100.00	50.00	30.00
(18)	Caldera	100.00	50.00	30.00
(19)	Cavaney	100.00	50.00	30.00
(20)	Chadbourne	100.00	50.00	30.00
(21)	Chech	100.00	50.00	30.00
(22)	Church	100.00	50.00	30.00
(23)	Clymer	100.00	50.00	30.00
(24)	Coleman	100.00	50.00	30.00
(25)	Compton	100.00	50.00	30.00
(26)	Conkwright	100.00	50.00	30.00
(27)	Connolly	100.00	50.00	30.00
(28)	Cook	100.00	50.00	30.00
(29)	Cooper (Los Angeles)	100.00	50.00	30.00
(30)	Cooper (Oakland)	100.00	50.00	30.00
(31)	Cooper (Portland)	100.00	50.00	30.00
(32)	Corhan	100.00	50.00	30.00
(33)	Couch	100.00	50.00	30.00
(34)	Cox	100.00	50.00	30.00
(35)	Crandall (Los Angeles)	100.00	50.00	30.00
(36)	Crandall (San Francisco)	100.00	50.00	30.00
(37)	Crespi	100.00	50.00	30.00
(38)	Croll	100.00	50.00	30.00
(39)	Cunningham	100.00	50.00	30.00
(40)	Dawson	100.00	50.00	30.00
(41)	Dell	100.00	50.00	30.00
(42)	DeVormer	100.00	50.00	30.00
(43)	Driscoll	100.00	50.00	30.00
(44)	Eastley	100.00	50.00	30.00
(45)	Edington	100.00	50.00	30.00
(46)	Eldred	100.00	50.00	30.00
(47)	Elliott	100.00	50.00	30.00
(48)	Ellis	100.00	50.00	30.00
(49)	Essick	100.00	50.00	30.00
(50)	Fabrique	100.00	50.00	30.00
(51)	Falkenberg	100.00	50.00	30.00
(52)	Fallentine	100.00	50.00	30.00
(53)	Finneran	100.00	50.00	30.00
(54)	Fisher (Sacramento)	100.00	50.00	30.00
(55)	Fisher (Vernon)	100.00	50.00	30.00
(56)	Fitzgerald	100.00	50.00	30.00
(57)	Flannigan	100.00	50.00	30.00
(58)	Fournier	100.00	50.00	30.00
(59)	French	100.00	50.00	30.00

(60)	Fromme	100.00	50.00	30.00
(61)	Gibson	100.00	50.00	30.00
(62)	Griggs	100.00	50.00	30.00
(63)	Haney	100.00	50.00	30.00
(64)	Harper	100.00	50.00	30.00
(65)	Henkle	100.00	50.00	30.00
(66)	Herr	100.00	50.00	30.00
(67)	Hickey	100.00	50.00	30.00
(68)	High	100.00	50.00	30.00
(69)	Holling	100.00	50.00	30.00
(70)	Hosp	100.00	50.00	30.00
(71)	Houck	100.00	50.00	30.00
(72)	Howard	100.00	50.00	30.00
(73)	Kamm	100.00	50.00	30.00
(74)	Kenworthy	100.00	50.00	30.00
(75)	Killefer	100.00	50.00	30.00
(76)	King	100.00	50.00	30.00
(77)	Koehler	100.00	50.00	30.00
(78)	Koerner	100.00	50.00	30.00
(79)	Kramer (Oakland)	100.00	50.00	30.00
(80)	Kramer (San Francisco)	100.00	50.00	30.00
(81)	Land	100.00	50.00	30.00
(82)	Lane	100.00	50.00	30.00
(83)	Lapan	100.00	50.00	30.00
(84)	Larkin	100.00	50.00	30.00
(85)	Lee	100.00	50.00	30.00
(86)	Long	100.00	50.00	30.00
(87)	Mails	100.00	50.00	30.00
(88)	Mains	100.00	50.00	30.00
(89)	Maisel	100.00	50.00	30.00
(90)	Mathes	100.00	50.00	30.00
(91)	McCredie	100.00	50.00	30.00
(92)	McGaffigan	100.00	50.00	30.00
(93)	McHenry	100.00	50.00	30.00
(94)	McNulty	100.00	50.00	30.00
(95)	Meusel	100.00	50.00	30.00
(96)	Middleton	100.00	50.00	30.00
(97)	Mitchell	100.00	50.00	30.00
(98)	Mitze	100.00	50.00	30.00
(99)	Mulory	100.00	50.00	30.00
(100)	Murphy	100.00	50.00	30.00
(101)	Murray	100.00	50.00	30.00
(102)	Niehoff (Los Angeles)	100.00	50.00	30.00
(103)	Niehoff (Seattle)	100.00	50.00	30.00
(104)	Norse	100.00	50.00	30.00
(105)	Oldham	100.00	50.00	30.00
(106)	Orr	100.00	50.00	30.00
(107)	Penner	100.00	50.00	30.00
(108)	Pennington	100.00	50.00	30.00
(109)	Piercy	100.00	50.00	30.00
(110)	Pinelli	150.00	75.00	45.00
(111)	C. Prough	100.00	50.00	30.00
(112)	Rader	100.00	50.00	30.00
(113)	Reiger	100.00	50.00	30.00
(114)	Ritchie	100.00	50.00	30.00
(115)	Roach	100.00	50.00	30.00
(116)	Rodgers	100.00	50.00	30.00
(117)	Rumler	100.00	50.00	30.00
(118)	Sands	100.00	50.00	30.00
(119)	Schick	100.00	50.00	30.00
(120)	Schultz	100.00	50.00	30.00
(121)	Scott	100.00	50.00	30.00
(122)	Seaton	100.00	50.00	30.00
(123)	Sheely	100.00	50.00	30.00
(124)	Siglin	100.00	50.00	30.00
(125)	Smith	100.00	50.00	30.00
(126)	Bill Smith	100.00	50.00	30.00
(127)	Snell	100.00	50.00	30.00
(128)	Spangler	100.00	50.00	30.00
(129)	Speas	100.00	50.00	30.00
(130)	Spencer	100.00	50.00	30.00
(131)	Starasenich	100.00	50.00	30.00
(132)	Stumpf	100.00	50.00	30.00
(133)	Sutherland	100.00	50.00	30.00
(134)	Dazzy Vance	800.00	600.00	400.00
(135)	Walker	100.00	50.00	30.00
(136)	Walsh	100.00	50.00	30.00
(137)	Ware	100.00	50.00	30.00
(138)	Weaver	100.00	50.00	30.00
(139)	Westerzil	100.00	50.00	30.00
(140)	Wilhoit	100.00	50.00	30.00
(141)	Wilie	100.00	50.00	30.00
(142)	Willets	100.00	50.00	30.00
(143)	Zamloch	100.00	50.00	30.00
(144)	Zweifel	100.00	50.00	30.00

1920 Zeenut Pacific Coast League

The 1920 Zeenuts cards were dated on the front and measure about 1-3/4" x 3-5/8". They featured borderless, sepia-toned photos. To date, 151 have been found for 1920.

		NM	EX	VG
	Common Player:	90.00	45.00	30.00
(1)	Adams	90.00	45.00	30.00
(2)	Agnew	90.00	45.00	30.00
(3)	Alcock	90.00	45.00	30.00
(4)	Aldrige	90.00	45.00	30.00
(5)	Andrews	90.00	45.00	30.00
(6)	Anfinson	90.00	45.00	30.00
(7)	A. Arlett	90.00	45.00	30.00
(8)	R. Arlett	90.00	45.00	30.00
(9)	Baker	90.00	45.00	30.00
(10)	Baldwin	90.00	45.00	30.00
(11)	Bassler	90.00	45.00	30.00
(12)	Baum	90.00	45.00	30.00
(13)	Blue	90.00	45.00	30.00
(14)	Bohne	300.00	200.00	100.00
(15)	Brenton	90.00	45.00	30.00
(16)	Bromley (Dark hat.)	90.00	45.00	30.00
(17)	Bromley (Light hat.)	90.00	45.00	30.00
(18)	Brown	90.00	45.00	30.00
(19)	Butler	90.00	45.00	30.00
(20)	Caveney	90.00	45.00	30.00
(21)	Chadbourne	90.00	45.00	30.00
(22)	Compton	90.00	45.00	30.00
(23)	Connolly	90.00	45.00	30.00
(24)	Cook	90.00	45.00	30.00
(25)	Corhan	90.00	45.00	30.00
(26)	Cox	90.00	45.00	30.00
(27)	K. Crandall	90.00	45.00	30.00
(28)	O. Crandall	90.00	45.00	30.00
(29)	Crawford	2,000	1,200	600.00
(30)	Cullop	90.00	45.00	30.00
(31)	Cunningham	90.00	45.00	30.00
(32)	DeVitalis	90.00	45.00	30.00
(33)	DeVormer	90.00	45.00	30.00
(34)	Dooley	90.00	45.00	30.00
(35)	Dorman	90.00	45.00	30.00
(36)	Dumovich	90.00	45.00	30.00
(37)	Dylar	90.00	45.00	30.00
(38)	Edington	90.00	45.00	30.00
(39)	Eldred	90.00	45.00	30.00
(40)	Ellis	90.00	45.00	30.00
(41)	Essick	90.00	45.00	30.00
(42)	Fisher	90.00	45.00	30.00
(43)	Fitzgerald	90.00	45.00	30.00
(44)	Fromme	90.00	45.00	30.00
(45)	Gardner	90.00	45.00	30.00
(46)	Ginglardi	90.00	45.00	30.00
(47)	Gough	90.00	45.00	30.00
(48)	Griggs	90.00	45.00	30.00
(49)	Guisto	90.00	45.00	30.00
(50)	Hamilton	90.00	45.00	30.00
(51)	Hanicy	90.00	45.00	30.00
(52)	Hartford	90.00	45.00	30.00
(53)	High	90.00	45.00	30.00
(54)	Hill	90.00	45.00	30.00
(55)	Hodges	90.00	45.00	30.00
(56)	Howard	90.00	45.00	30.00
(57)	James	90.00	45.00	30.00
(58)	Jenkins	90.00	45.00	30.00
(59)	Johnson (Portland)	90.00	45.00	30.00
(60)	Johnson (Salt Lake)	90.00	45.00	30.00
(61)	Jones	90.00	45.00	30.00
(62)	Juney	90.00	45.00	30.00
(63)	Kallio	90.00	45.00	30.00
(64)	Kamm	90.00	45.00	30.00
(65)	Keating	90.00	45.00	30.00
(66)	Kenworthy	90.00	45.00	30.00
(67)	Killeen	90.00	45.00	30.00
(68)	Killefer	90.00	45.00	30.00
(69)	Kingdon	90.00	45.00	30.00
(70)	Knight	90.00	45.00	30.00
(71)	Koehler	90.00	45.00	30.00
(72)	Koerner	90.00	45.00	30.00
(73)	Kopp	90.00	45.00	30.00
(74)	Kremer	90.00	45.00	30.00
(75)	Krug	90.00	45.00	30.00
(76)	Kunz	90.00	45.00	30.00
(77)	Lambert	90.00	45.00	30.00
(78)	Lane	90.00	45.00	30.00
(79)	Larkin	90.00	45.00	30.00
(80)	Leverenz	90.00	45.00	30.00
(81)	Long	90.00	45.00	30.00
(82)	Love	90.00	45.00	30.00
(83)	Maggart	90.00	45.00	30.00
(84)	Mails	90.00	45.00	30.00
(85)	Maisel	90.00	45.00	30.00
(86)	Matterson	90.00	45.00	30.00
(87)	Matteson	90.00	45.00	30.00
(88)	McAuley	90.00	45.00	30.00
(89)	McCredie	90.00	45.00	30.00
(90)	McGaffigan	90.00	45.00	30.00
(91)	McHenry	90.00	45.00	30.00
(92)	McQuaid	90.00	45.00	30.00
(93)	Miller	90.00	45.00	30.00
(94)	Mitchell	90.00	45.00	30.00
(95)	J. Mitchell	90.00	45.00	30.00
(96)	Mitchell	90.00	45.00	30.00
(97)	Mitze	90.00	45.00	30.00
(98)	Moffitt	90.00	45.00	30.00
(99)	Mollwitz	90.00	45.00	30.00
(100)	Morse	90.00	45.00	30.00
(101)	Mulligan	90.00	45.00	30.00
(102)	Murphy	90.00	45.00	30.00
(103)	Niehoff	90.00	45.00	30.00
(104)	Nixon	90.00	45.00	30.00
(105)	O'Shaughnessy	90.00	45.00	30.00
(106)	Orr	90.00	45.00	30.00
(107)	Paull	90.00	45.00	30.00
(108)	Penner	90.00	45.00	30.00
(109)	Pertica	90.00	45.00	30.00
(110)	Peterson	90.00	45.00	30.00
(111)	Polson	90.00	45.00	30.00
(112)	Prough	90.00	45.00	30.00
(113)	Reagan	90.00	45.00	30.00
(114)	Reiger	90.00	45.00	30.00
(115)	Reilly	90.00	45.00	30.00

		NM	EX	VG
(116)	Rheinhart	90.00	45.00	30.00
(117)	Rodgers	90.00	45.00	30.00
(118)	Ross	90.00	45.00	30.00
(119)	Rumler	90.00	45.00	30.00
(120)	Russell	90.00	45.00	30.00
(121)	Sands	90.00	45.00	30.00
(122)	Schaller	90.00	45.00	30.00
(123)	Schang	90.00	45.00	30.00
(124)	Schellenback	90.00	45.00	30.00
(125)	Schick	90.00	45.00	30.00
(126)	Schorr	90.00	45.00	30.00
(127)	Schroeder	90.00	45.00	30.00
(128)	Scott	90.00	45.00	30.00
(129)	Seaton	90.00	45.00	30.00
(130)	Sheely	90.00	45.00	30.00
(131)	Siebold	90.00	45.00	30.00
(132)	Siglin	90.00	45.00	30.00
(133)	Smith	90.00	45.00	30.00
(134)	G. Smith	90.00	45.00	30.00
(135)	Spellman	90.00	45.00	30.00
(136)	Spranger	90.00	45.00	30.00
(137)	Stroud	90.00	45.00	30.00
(138)	Stumpf	90.00	45.00	30.00
(139)	Sullivan	90.00	45.00	30.00
(140)	Sutherland	90.00	45.00	30.00
(141)	Thurston (Dark hat.)	90.00	45.00	30.00
(142)	Thurston (Light hat.)	90.00	45.00	30.00
(143)	Walsh	90.00	45.00	30.00
(144)	Wares	90.00	45.00	30.00
(145)	Weaver	90.00	45.00	30.00
(146)	Willie	90.00	45.00	30.00
(147)	Winn	90.00	45.00	30.00
(148)	Wisterzill	90.00	45.00	30.00
(149)	Worth	90.00	45.00	30.00
(150)	Yelle	90.00	45.00	30.00
(151)	Zamlock	90.00	45.00	30.00
(152)	Zeider	90.00	45.00	30.00

1921 Zeenut Pacific Coast League

The 1921 Zeenuts cards were dated on the front and measure about 1-3/4" x 3-11/16". They featured borderless, sepia-toned photos. To date, 168 different subjects have been discovered for 1921 (even though a promotional flier indicates 180 players).

		NM	EX	VG
Common Player:		75.00	40.00	25.00
With Coupon:		1,200	500.00	300.00
(1)	Adams	75.00	40.00	25.00
(2)	Alcock	75.00	40.00	25.00
(3)	Aldridge	75.00	40.00	25.00
(4)	Alton	75.00	40.00	25.00
(5)	Anfinson	75.00	40.00	25.00
(6)	Arlett	75.00	40.00	25.00
(7)	Baker	75.00	40.00	25.00
(8)	Baldwin	75.00	40.00	25.00
(9)	Bates	75.00	40.00	25.00
(10)	Berry	75.00	40.00	25.00
(11)	Blacholder	75.00	40.00	25.00
(12)	Blossom	75.00	40.00	25.00
(13)	Bourg	75.00	40.00	25.00
(14)	Brinley	75.00	40.00	25.00
(15)	Bromley	75.00	40.00	25.00
(16)	Brown	75.00	40.00	25.00
(17)	Brubaker	75.00	40.00	25.00
(18)	Butler	75.00	40.00	25.00
(19)	Byler	75.00	40.00	25.00
(20)	Carroll	75.00	40.00	25.00
(21)	Casey	75.00	40.00	25.00
(22)	Cather	75.00	40.00	25.00
(23)	Caveney	75.00	40.00	25.00
(24)	Chadbourne	75.00	40.00	25.00
(25)	Compton	75.00	40.00	25.00
(26)	Connel	75.00	40.00	25.00
(27)	Cook	75.00	40.00	25.00
(28)	Cooper	75.00	40.00	25.00
(29)	Couch	75.00	40.00	25.00
(30)	Cox	75.00	40.00	25.00
(31)	Crandall	75.00	40.00	25.00
(32)	Cravath	75.00	40.00	25.00
(33)	Crawford	2,000	1,200	600.00
(34)	Crumpler	75.00	40.00	25.00
(35)	Cunningham	75.00	40.00	25.00
(36)	Daley	75.00	40.00	25.00
(37)	Dell	75.00	40.00	25.00
(38)	Demaree	75.00	40.00	25.00
(39)	Douglas	75.00	40.00	25.00
(40)	Dumovich	75.00	40.00	25.00
(41)	Elliott	75.00	40.00	25.00
(42)	Ellis	75.00	40.00	25.00
(43)	Ellison	75.00	40.00	25.00

		NM	EX	VG
(44)	Essick	75.00	40.00	25.00
(45)	Faeth	75.00	40.00	25.00
(46)	Fisher	75.00	40.00	25.00
(47)	Fittery	75.00	40.00	25.00
(48)	Fitzgerald	75.00	40.00	25.00
(49)	Flaherty	75.00	40.00	25.00
(50)	Francis	75.00	40.00	25.00
(51)	French	75.00	40.00	25.00
(52)	Fromme	75.00	40.00	25.00
(53)	Gardner	75.00	40.00	25.00
(54)	Geary	75.00	40.00	25.00
(55)	Gennin	75.00	40.00	25.00
(56)	Gorman	75.00	40.00	25.00
(57)	Gould	75.00	40.00	25.00
(58)	Griggs	75.00	40.00	25.00
(59)	Hale	75.00	40.00	25.00
(60)	Hannah	75.00	40.00	25.00
(61)	Hansen	75.00	40.00	25.00
(62)	Hesse	75.00	40.00	25.00
(63)	High	75.00	40.00	25.00
(64)	Hughes	75.00	40.00	25.00
(65)	Hyatt	75.00	40.00	25.00
(66)	Jackson	75.00	40.00	25.00
(67)	Jacobs	75.00	40.00	25.00
(68)	Jacobs	75.00	40.00	25.00
(69)	Jenkins	75.00	40.00	25.00
(70)	Johnson	75.00	40.00	25.00
(71)	Jones	75.00	40.00	25.00
(72)	Jourden	75.00	40.00	25.00
(73)	Kallio	75.00	40.00	25.00
(74)	Kamm	75.00	40.00	25.00
(75)	Kearns	75.00	40.00	25.00
(76)	Kelly	75.00	40.00	25.00
(77)	Kersten	75.00	40.00	25.00
(78)	Kifer	75.00	40.00	25.00
(79)	Killefer	75.00	40.00	25.00
(80)	King	75.00	40.00	25.00
(81)	Kingdon	75.00	40.00	25.00
(82)	Knight	75.00	40.00	25.00
(83)	Koehler	75.00	40.00	25.00
(84)	Kopp	75.00	40.00	25.00
(85)	Krause	75.00	40.00	25.00
(86)	Kremer	75.00	40.00	25.00
(87)	Krug	75.00	40.00	25.00
(88)	Kunz	75.00	40.00	25.00
(89)	Lane	75.00	40.00	25.00
(90)	Leverenz	75.00	40.00	25.00
(91)	Lewis	75.00	40.00	25.00
(92)	Lindimore	75.00	40.00	25.00
(93)	Love	75.00	40.00	25.00
(94)	Ludolph	75.00	40.00	25.00
(95)	Lynn	75.00	40.00	25.00
(96)	Lyons	75.00	40.00	25.00
(97)	McAuley	75.00	40.00	25.00
(98)	McCredie	75.00	40.00	25.00
(99)	McGaffigan	75.00	40.00	25.00
(100)	McGraw	75.00	40.00	25.00
(101)	McQuaid	75.00	40.00	25.00
(102)	Merritt	75.00	40.00	25.00
(103)	Middleton	75.00	40.00	25.00
(104)	Miller	75.00	40.00	25.00
(105)	Mitchell	75.00	40.00	25.00
(106)	Mitze	75.00	40.00	25.00
(107)	Mollwitz	75.00	40.00	25.00
(108)	Morse	75.00	40.00	25.00
(109)	Murphy (Seattle)	75.00	40.00	25.00
(110)	Murphy (Vernon)	75.00	40.00	25.00
(111)	Mustain	75.00	40.00	25.00
(112)	Nickels	75.00	40.00	25.00
(113)	Niehaus	75.00	40.00	25.00
(114)	Niehoff	75.00	40.00	25.00
(115)	Nofziger	75.00	40.00	25.00
(116)	O'Connell	75.00	40.00	25.00
(117)	O'Doul	800.00	600.00	400.00
(118)	O'Malia	75.00	40.00	25.00
(119)	Oldring	75.00	40.00	25.00
(120)	Oliver	75.00	40.00	25.00
(121)	Orr	75.00	40.00	25.00
(122)	Paton	75.00	40.00	25.00
(123)	Penner	75.00	40.00	25.00
(124)	Pick	75.00	40.00	25.00
(125)	Pillette	75.00	40.00	25.00
(126)	Pinelli	75.00	40.00	25.00
(127)	Polson	75.00	40.00	25.00
(128)	Poole	75.00	40.00	25.00
(129)	Prough	75.00	40.00	25.00
(130)	Rath	75.00	40.00	25.00
(131)	Read	75.00	40.00	25.00
(132)	Reinhardt	75.00	40.00	25.00
(133)	Rieger	75.00	40.00	25.00
(134)	Rogers	75.00	40.00	25.00
(135)	Rose (Sacramento)	75.00	40.00	25.00
(136)	Rose (Salt Lake)	75.00	40.00	25.00
(137)	Ross (Portland)	75.00	40.00	25.00
(138)	Ross (Sacramento)	75.00	40.00	25.00
(139)	Ryan	75.00	40.00	25.00
(140)	Sand	75.00	40.00	25.00
(141)	Schick	75.00	40.00	25.00
(142)	Schneider	75.00	40.00	25.00
(143)	Scott	75.00	40.00	25.00
(144)	Shang	75.00	40.00	25.00
(145)	Sheehan	75.00	40.00	25.00
(146)	Shore	75.00	40.00	25.00
(147)	Shorr	75.00	40.00	25.00
(148)	Shultis	75.00	40.00	25.00
(149)	Siebold	75.00	40.00	25.00
(150)	Siglin	75.00	40.00	25.00
(151)	Smallwood	75.00	40.00	25.00
(152)	Smith	75.00	40.00	25.00
(153)	Spencer	75.00	40.00	25.00
(154)	Stanage	75.00	40.00	25.00
(155)	Statz	75.00	40.00	25.00
(156)	Stumph	75.00	40.00	25.00
(157)	Thomas	75.00	40.00	25.00
(158)	Thurston	75.00	40.00	25.00
(159)	Tyrrell	75.00	40.00	25.00
(160)	Van Osdoll	75.00	40.00	25.00
(161)	Walsh	75.00	40.00	25.00

		NM	EX	VG
(162)	White	75.00	40.00	25.00
(163)	Wilhoit	75.00	40.00	25.00
(164)	Wilie	75.00	40.00	25.00
(165)	Winn	75.00	40.00	25.00
(166)	Wolfer	75.00	40.00	25.00
(167)	Yelle	75.00	40.00	25.00
(168)	Young	75.00	40.00	25.00
(169)	Zeider	75.00	40.00	25.00

1922 Zeenut Pacific Coast League

The 1922 Zeenuts are dated on the front, measure about 1-13/16" x 3-9/16" and feature black-and-white photos with sepia highlights. There are 162 subjects, and four of them (Koehler, Williams, Gregg and Schneider) have been found with variations in color tones.

		NM	EX	VG
Common Player:		75.00	40.00	25.00
(1)	J. Adams	75.00	40.00	25.00
(2)	S. Adams	75.00	40.00	25.00
(3)	Agnew	75.00	40.00	25.00
(4)	Anfinson	75.00	40.00	25.00
(5)	Arlett	75.00	40.00	25.00
(6)	Baldwin	75.00	40.00	25.00
(7)	Barney	75.00	40.00	25.00
(8)	Bell	75.00	40.00	25.00
(9)	Blaeholder	75.00	40.00	25.00
(10)	Bodie	75.00	40.00	25.00
(11)	Brenton	75.00	40.00	25.00
(12)	Bromley	75.00	40.00	25.00
(13)	Brovold	75.00	40.00	25.00
(14)	Brown	75.00	40.00	25.00
(15)	Brubaker	75.00	40.00	25.00
(16)	Burger	75.00	40.00	25.00
(17)	Byler	75.00	40.00	25.00
(18)	Canfield	75.00	40.00	25.00
(19)	Carroll	75.00	40.00	25.00
(20)	Cartwright	75.00	40.00	25.00
(21)	Chadbourne	75.00	40.00	25.00
(22)	Compton	75.00	40.00	25.00
(23)	Connolly	75.00	40.00	25.00
(24)	Cook	75.00	40.00	25.00
(25)	Cooper	75.00	40.00	25.00
(26)	Coumbe	75.00	40.00	25.00
(27)	Cox	75.00	40.00	25.00
(28)	Crandall	75.00	40.00	25.00
(29)	Crumpler	75.00	40.00	25.00
(30)	Cueto	600.00	400.00	200.00
(31)	Dailey	75.00	40.00	25.00
(32)	Daly	75.00	40.00	25.00
(33)	Deal	75.00	40.00	25.00
(34)	Dell	75.00	40.00	25.00
(35)	Doyle	75.00	40.00	25.00
(36)	Dumovich	75.00	40.00	25.00
(37)	Eldred	75.00	40.00	25.00
(38)	Eller	75.00	40.00	25.00
(39)	Elliott	75.00	40.00	25.00
(40)	Ellison	75.00	40.00	25.00
(41)	Essick	75.00	40.00	25.00
(42)	Finneran	75.00	40.00	25.00
(43)	Fittery	75.00	40.00	25.00
(44)	Fitzgerald	75.00	40.00	25.00
(45)	Freeman	75.00	40.00	25.00
(46)	French	75.00	40.00	25.00
(47)	Gardner	75.00	40.00	25.00
(48)	Geary	75.00	40.00	25.00
(49)	Gibson	75.00	40.00	25.00
(50)	Gilder	75.00	40.00	25.00
(51)	Gould	75.00	40.00	25.00
(52)	Gregg	75.00	40.00	25.00
(53)	Gressett	75.00	40.00	25.00
(54)	Griggs	75.00	40.00	25.00
(55)	Hampton	75.00	40.00	25.00
(56)	Hannah	75.00	40.00	25.00
(57)	Hawks	75.00	40.00	25.00
(58)	Henke	75.00	40.00	25.00
(59)	High (Portland)	75.00	40.00	25.00
(60)	High (Vernon)	75.00	40.00	25.00
(61)	Houck	75.00	40.00	25.00
(62)	Howard	75.00	40.00	25.00
(63)	Hughes	75.00	40.00	25.00
(64)	Hyatt	75.00	40.00	25.00
(65)	Jacobs	75.00	40.00	25.00
(66)	James	75.00	40.00	25.00
(67)	Jenkins	75.00	40.00	25.00
(68)	Jones	75.00	40.00	25.00
(69)	Kallio	75.00	40.00	25.00

(70)	Kamm	75.00	40.00	25.00
(71)	Keiser	75.00	40.00	25.00
(72)	Kelly	75.00	40.00	25.00
(73)	Kenworthy	75.00	40.00	25.00
(74)	Kilduff	75.00	40.00	25.00
(75)	Killefer	75.00	40.00	25.00
(76)	Killhullen	75.00	40.00	25.00
(77)	King	75.00	40.00	25.00
(78)	Knight	75.00	40.00	25.00
(79)	Koehler	75.00	40.00	25.00
(80)	Kremer	75.00	40.00	25.00
(81)	Kunz	75.00	40.00	25.00
(82)	Lafayette	75.00	40.00	25.00
(83)	Lane	75.00	40.00	25.00
(84)	Tony Lazzeri	3,000	1,500	900.00
(85)	Lefevre	75.00	40.00	25.00
(86)	D. Lewis	75.00	40.00	25.00
(87)	S. Lewis	75.00	40.00	25.00
(88)	Lindimore	75.00	40.00	25.00
(89)	Locker	75.00	40.00	25.00
(90)	Lyons	75.00	40.00	25.00
(91)	Mack	75.00	40.00	25.00
(92)	Marriott	75.00	40.00	25.00
(93)	May	75.00	40.00	25.00
(94)	McAuley	75.00	40.00	25.00
(95)	McCabe	75.00	40.00	25.00
(96)	McCann	75.00	40.00	25.00
(97)	McCredie	75.00	40.00	25.00
(98)	McNeely	75.00	40.00	25.00
(99)	McQuaid	75.00	40.00	25.00
(100)	Miller	75.00	40.00	25.00
(101)	Mitchell	75.00	40.00	25.00
(102)	Mitze	75.00	40.00	25.00
(103)	Mollwitz	75.00	40.00	25.00
(104)	Monahan	75.00	40.00	25.00
(105)	Murphy (Seattle)	75.00	40.00	25.00
(106)	Murphy (Vernon)	75.00	40.00	25.00
(107)	Niehaus	75.00	40.00	25.00
(108)	O'Connell	75.00	40.00	25.00
(109)	Orr	75.00	40.00	25.00
(110)	Owen	75.00	40.00	25.00
(111)	Pearce	75.00	40.00	25.00
(112)	Pick	75.00	40.00	25.00
(113)	Ponder	75.00	40.00	25.00
(114)	Poole	75.00	40.00	25.00
(115)	Prough	75.00	40.00	25.00
(116)	Read	75.00	40.00	25.00
(117)	Richardson	75.00	40.00	25.00
(118)	Rieger	75.00	40.00	25.00
(119)	Ritchie	75.00	40.00	25.00
(120)	Ross	75.00	40.00	25.00
(121)	Ryan	75.00	40.00	25.00
(122)	Sand	75.00	40.00	25.00
(123)	Sargent	75.00	40.00	25.00
(124)	Sawyer	75.00	40.00	25.00
(125)	Schang	75.00	40.00	25.00
(126)	Schick	75.00	40.00	25.00
(127)	Schneider	75.00	40.00	25.00
(128)	Schorr	75.00	40.00	25.00
(129)	Schulte (Oakland)	75.00	40.00	25.00
(130)	Schulte (Seattle)	75.00	40.00	25.00
(131)	Scott	75.00	40.00	25.00
(132)	See	75.00	40.00	25.00
(133)	Shea	75.00	40.00	25.00
(134)	Sheehan	75.00	40.00	25.00
(135)	Siglin	75.00	40.00	25.00
(136)	Smith	75.00	40.00	25.00
(137)	Soria	75.00	40.00	25.00
(138)	Spencer	75.00	40.00	25.00
(139)	Stanage	75.00	40.00	25.00
(140)	Strand	75.00	40.00	25.00
(141)	Stumpf	75.00	40.00	25.00
(142)	Sullivan	75.00	40.00	25.00
(143)	Sutherland	75.00	40.00	25.00
(144)	Thomas	75.00	40.00	25.00
(145)	Jim Thorpe	30,000	20,000	10,000
(146)	Thurston	75.00	40.00	25.00
(147)	Tobin	75.00	40.00	25.00
(148)	Turner	75.00	40.00	25.00
(149)	Twombly	75.00	40.00	25.00
(150)	Valla	75.00	40.00	25.00
(151)	Vargas	75.00	40.00	25.00
(152)	Viveros	75.00	40.00	25.00
(153)	Wallace	75.00	40.00	25.00
(154)	Walsh	75.00	40.00	25.00
(155)	Wells	75.00	40.00	25.00
(156)	Westersil	75.00	40.00	25.00
(157)	Wheat	75.00	40.00	25.00
(158)	Wilhoit	75.00	40.00	25.00
(159)	Wilie	75.00	40.00	25.00
(160)	Williams	75.00	40.00	25.00
(161)	Yelle	75.00	40.00	25.00
(162)	Zeider	75.00	40.00	25.00

1923 Zeenut Pacific Coast League

This is the only year that Zeenuts cards were issued in two different sizes. Cards in the "regular" series measure about 1-7/8" x 3-1/2", feature black-and-white photos and are dated 1923. A second series, containing just 24 cards (all San Francisco and Oakland players), are sepia-toned re-issues of the 1922 series with a "1923" date and measure about 1/16" longer. The re-issued cards have coupons with an expiration date of April 1, 1923. The dated cards have coupons with an expiration date of April 1, 1924.

		NM	EX	VG
Common Player:		75.00	40.00	25.00
With Coupon:		1,000	500.00	300.00
(1)	Agnew (1923 photo)	75.00	40.00	25.00
(2)	Agnew (1922 photo re-dated)	75.00	40.00	25.00
(3)	Alten	75.00	40.00	25.00
(4)	Anderson	75.00	40.00	25.00
(5)	Anfinson	75.00	40.00	25.00
(6)	Arlett	75.00	40.00	25.00
(7)	Baker	75.00	40.00	25.00
(8)	Baldwin	75.00	40.00	25.00
(9)	Barney	75.00	40.00	25.00
(10)	Blake	75.00	40.00	25.00
(11)	Bodie	75.00	40.00	25.00
(12)	Brazil	75.00	40.00	25.00
(13)	Brenton	75.00	40.00	25.00
(14)	Brown (Oakland)	75.00	40.00	25.00
(15)	Brown (Sacramento)	75.00	40.00	25.00
(16)	Brubaker	75.00	40.00	25.00
(17)	Buckley	75.00	40.00	25.00
(18)	Canfield	75.00	40.00	25.00
(19)	Carroll	75.00	40.00	25.00
(20)	Cather	75.00	40.00	25.00
(21)	Chadbourne	75.00	40.00	25.00
(22)	Charvez	75.00	40.00	25.00
(23)	Cochrane	75.00	40.00	25.00
(24)	Colwell	75.00	40.00	25.00
(25)	Compton	75.00	40.00	25.00
(26)	Cook	75.00	40.00	25.00
(27)	Cooper (1923 photo)	75.00	40.00	25.00
(28)	Cooper (1922 photo re-date)	75.00	40.00	25.00
(29)	Coumbe	75.00	40.00	25.00
(30)	Courtney	75.00	40.00	25.00
(31)	Crandall	75.00	40.00	25.00
(32)	Crane	75.00	40.00	25.00
(33)	Crowder	75.00	40.00	25.00
(34)	Crumpler	75.00	40.00	25.00
(35)	Daly (Los Angeles)	75.00	40.00	25.00
(36)	Daly (Portland)	75.00	40.00	25.00
(37)	Deal	75.00	40.00	25.00
(38)	Doyle	75.00	40.00	25.00
(39)	Duchalsky	75.00	40.00	25.00
(40)	Eckert	75.00	40.00	25.00
(41)	Eldred	75.00	40.00	25.00
(42)	Eley	75.00	40.00	25.00
(43)	Eller	75.00	40.00	25.00
(44)	Ellison (1923 photo)	75.00	40.00	25.00
(45)	Ellison (1922 photo re-dated)	75.00	40.00	25.00
(46)	Essick	75.00	40.00	25.00
(47)	Fittery	75.00	40.00	25.00
(48)	Flashkamper	75.00	40.00	25.00
(49)	Frederick	75.00	40.00	25.00
(50)	French	75.00	40.00	25.00
(51)	Geary (1923 photo)	75.00	40.00	25.00
(52)	Geary (1922 photo re-dated)	75.00	40.00	25.00
(53)	Gilder	75.00	40.00	25.00
(54)	Golvin	75.00	40.00	25.00
(55)	Gorman	75.00	40.00	25.00
(56)	Gould	75.00	40.00	25.00
(57)	Gressett	75.00	40.00	25.00
(58)	Griggs	75.00	40.00	25.00
(59)	Hannah (Los Angeles)	75.00	40.00	25.00
(60)	Hannah (Vernon)	75.00	40.00	25.00
(61)	Hemingway	75.00	40.00	25.00
(62)	Hendryx	75.00	40.00	25.00
(63)	High	75.00	40.00	25.00
(64)	H. High	75.00	40.00	25.00
(65)	Hodge	75.00	40.00	25.00
(66)	Hood	75.00	40.00	25.00
(67)	Houghs	75.00	40.00	25.00
(68)	Howard (1923 photo)	75.00	40.00	25.00
(69)	Howard (1922 photo re-date)	75.00	40.00	25.00
(70)	Del Howard	75.00	40.00	25.00
(71)	Jacobs	75.00	40.00	25.00
(72)	James	75.00	40.00	25.00
(73)	Johnson	75.00	40.00	25.00
(74)	Johnston	75.00	40.00	25.00
(75)	Jolly (Jolley)	75.00	40.00	25.00
(76)	Jones (Los Angeles)	75.00	40.00	25.00
(77)	Jones (Oakland)	75.00	40.00	25.00
(78)	Jones (Portland)	75.00	40.00	25.00
(79)	Kallio	75.00	40.00	25.00
(80)	Kearns	75.00	40.00	25.00
(81)	Keiser	75.00	40.00	25.00
(82)	Keller	75.00	40.00	25.00
(83)	Kelly (San Francisco)	75.00	40.00	25.00
(84)	Kelly (Seattle)	75.00	40.00	25.00
(85)	Kenna	75.00	40.00	25.00
(86)	Kilduff	75.00	40.00	25.00
(87)	Killifer	75.00	40.00	25.00
(88)	King	75.00	40.00	25.00
(89)	Knight (1923 photo)	75.00	40.00	25.00
(90)	Knight (1922 photo re-dated)	75.00	40.00	25.00
(91)	Koehler	75.00	40.00	25.00
(92)	Kopp	75.00	40.00	25.00
(93)	Krause	75.00	40.00	25.00
(94)	Kremer	75.00	40.00	25.00
(95)	Krug	75.00	40.00	25.00
(96)	Lafayette (1923 photo)	75.00	40.00	25.00
(97)	Lafayette (1922 photo re-dated)	75.00	40.00	25.00
(98)	Lane	75.00	40.00	25.00
(99)	Lefevre	75.00	40.00	25.00
(100)	Leslie	75.00	40.00	25.00
(101)	Levere	75.00	40.00	25.00
(102)	Leverenz	75.00	40.00	25.00
(103)	Lewis	75.00	40.00	25.00
(104)	Lindimore	75.00	40.00	25.00

(105)	Locker	75.00	40.00	25.00
(106)	Lyons	75.00	40.00	25.00
(107)	Maderas	75.00	40.00	25.00
(108)	Mails	75.00	40.00	25.00
(109)	Marriott	75.00	40.00	25.00
(110)	Matzen	75.00	40.00	25.00
(111)	McAuley	75.00	40.00	25.00
(112)	McAuliffe	75.00	40.00	25.00
(113)	McCabe (Los Angeles)	75.00	40.00	25.00
(114)	McCabe (Salt Lake)	75.00	40.00	25.00
(115)	McCann	75.00	40.00	25.00
(116)	McGaffigan	75.00	40.00	25.00
(117)	McGinnis	75.00	40.00	25.00
(118)	McNeilly	75.00	40.00	25.00
(119)	McWeeney	75.00	40.00	25.00
(120)	Middleton	75.00	40.00	25.00
(121)	Miller	75.00	40.00	25.00
(122)	Mitchell (1923 photo)	75.00	40.00	25.00
(123)	Mitchell (1922 photo re-date)	75.00	40.00	25.00
(124)	Mitze	75.00	40.00	25.00
(125)	Mulligan	75.00	40.00	25.00
(126)	Murchio	75.00	40.00	25.00
(127)	D. Murphy	75.00	40.00	25.00
(128)	R. Murphy	75.00	40.00	25.00
(129)	Noack	75.00	40.00	25.00
(130)	O'Brien	75.00	40.00	25.00
(131)	Onslow	75.00	40.00	25.00
(132)	Orr	75.00	40.00	25.00
(133)	Pearce	75.00	40.00	25.00
(134)	Penner	75.00	40.00	25.00
(135)	Peters	75.00	40.00	25.00
(136)	Pick	75.00	40.00	25.00
(137)	Pigg	75.00	40.00	25.00
(138)	Plummer	75.00	40.00	25.00
(139)	Ponder	75.00	40.00	25.00
(140)	Poole	75.00	40.00	25.00
(141)	Ramage	75.00	40.00	25.00
(142)	Read (1923 photo)	75.00	40.00	25.00
(143)	Read (1922 photo re-dated)	75.00	40.00	25.00
(144)	Rhyne	75.00	40.00	25.00
(145)	Ritchie	75.00	40.00	25.00
(146)	Robertson	75.00	40.00	25.00
(147)	Rohwer (Sacramento)	75.00	40.00	25.00
(148)	Rohwer (Seattle)	75.00	40.00	25.00
(149)	Ryan	75.00	40.00	25.00
(150)	Sawyer	75.00	40.00	25.00
(151)	Schang	75.00	40.00	25.00
(152)	Schneider	75.00	40.00	25.00
(153)	Schroeder	75.00	40.00	25.00
(154)	Scott	75.00	40.00	25.00
(155)	See	75.00	40.00	25.00
(156)	Shea	75.00	40.00	25.00
(157)	M. Shea	75.00	40.00	25.00
(158)	Spec Shea	75.00	40.00	25.00
(159)	Sheehan	75.00	40.00	25.00
(160)	Shellenback	75.00	40.00	25.00
(161)	Siglin	75.00	40.00	25.00
(162)	Singleton	75.00	40.00	25.00
(163)	Smith	75.00	40.00	25.00
(164)	M.H. Smith	75.00	40.00	25.00
(165)	Stanton	75.00	40.00	25.00
(166)	Strand	75.00	40.00	25.00
(167)	Stumpf	75.00	40.00	25.00
(168)	Sutherland	75.00	40.00	25.00
(169)	Tesar	75.00	40.00	25.00
(170)	Thomas (Los Angeles)	75.00	40.00	25.00
(171)	Thomas (Oakland)	75.00	40.00	25.00
(172)	Tobin	75.00	40.00	25.00
(173)	Twombly	75.00	40.00	25.00
(174)	Valla	75.00	40.00	25.00
(175)	Vargas	75.00	40.00	25.00
(176)	Vitt	75.00	40.00	25.00
(177)	Wallace	75.00	40.00	25.00
(178)	Walsh (San Francisco)	75.00	40.00	25.00
(179)	Walsh (Seattle)	75.00	40.00	25.00
(180)	Paul Waner	1,500	800.00	500.00
(181)	Wells (Oakland)	75.00	40.00	25.00
(182)	Wells (San Francisco)	75.00	40.00	25.00
(183)	Welsh	75.00	40.00	25.00
(184)	Wilhoit	75.00	40.00	25.00
(185)	Wilie (1923 photo)	75.00	40.00	25.00
(186)	Wilie (1922 photo re-dated)	75.00	40.00	25.00
(187)	Williams	75.00	40.00	25.00
(188)	Witzel	75.00	40.00	25.00
(189)	Wolfer	75.00	40.00	25.00
(190)	Wolverton	75.00	40.00	25.00
(191)	Yarrison	75.00	40.00	25.00
(192)	Yaryan	75.00	40.00	25.00
(193)	Yelle (1923 photo)	75.00	40.00	25.00
(194)	Yelle (1922 photo re-dated)	75.00	40.00	25.00
(195)	Moses Yellowhorse	1,800	900.00	550.00
(196)	Zeider	75.00	40.00	25.00

1924 Zeenut Pacific Coast League

Zeenut cards in 1924 measure about 1-3/4" x 3-7/16" and display the date on the front. The cards include a full photographic background. There are 144 subjects known.

		NM	EX	VG
	Common Player:	75.00	40.00	25.00
(1)	Adams	125.00	65.00	40.00
(2)	Agnew	75.00	40.00	25.00
(3)	Arlett	75.00	40.00	25.00
(4)	Baker	75.00	40.00	25.00
(5)	E. Baldwin	75.00	40.00	25.00
(6)	T. Baldwin	75.00	40.00	25.00
(7)	Beck	75.00	40.00	25.00
(8)	Benton	75.00	40.00	25.00
(9)	Bernard	75.00	40.00	25.00
(10)	Bigbee	75.00	40.00	25.00
(11)	Billings	75.00	40.00	25.00
(12)	Blakesly	75.00	40.00	25.00
(13)	Brady	75.00	40.00	25.00
(14)	Brazil	75.00	40.00	25.00
(15)	Brown	75.00	40.00	25.00
(16)	Brubaker	75.00	40.00	25.00
(17)	Buckley	75.00	40.00	25.00
(18)	Burger	75.00	40.00	25.00
(19)	Byler	75.00	40.00	25.00
(20)	Cadore	75.00	40.00	25.00
(21)	Cather	75.00	40.00	25.00
(22)	Chadbourne	75.00	40.00	25.00
(23)	Christian	75.00	40.00	25.00
(24)	Mickey Cochrane (Portland)	2,500	1,250	750.00
(25)	Cochrane (Sacramento)	75.00	40.00	25.00
(26)	Cooper	75.00	40.00	25.00
(27)	Coumbe	75.00	40.00	25.00
(28)	Cox	75.00	40.00	25.00
(29)	Crandall	75.00	40.00	25.00
(30)	Daly	75.00	40.00	25.00
(31)	Deal	75.00	40.00	25.00
(32)	Distel	75.00	40.00	25.00
(33)	Durst	75.00	40.00	25.00
(34)	Eckert	75.00	40.00	25.00
(35)	Eldred	75.00	40.00	25.00
(36)	Ellison	75.00	40.00	25.00
(37)	Essick	75.00	40.00	25.00
(38)	Flashkamper	75.00	40.00	25.00
(39)	Foster	75.00	40.00	25.00
(40)	Fredericks	75.00	40.00	25.00
(41)	Geary	75.00	40.00	25.00
(42)	Goebel	75.00	40.00	25.00
(43)	Golvin	75.00	40.00	25.00
(44)	Gorman	75.00	40.00	25.00
(45)	Gould	75.00	40.00	25.00
(46)	Gressett	75.00	40.00	25.00
(47)	Griffin (San Francisco)	75.00	40.00	25.00
(48)	Griffin (Vernon)	75.00	40.00	25.00
(49)	Guisto	75.00	40.00	25.00
(50)	Gunther	75.00	40.00	25.00
(51)	Hall	75.00	40.00	25.00
(52)	Hannah	75.00	40.00	25.00
(53)	Hendryx	75.00	40.00	25.00
(54)	High	75.00	40.00	25.00
(55)	Hodge	75.00	40.00	25.00
(56)	Hood	75.00	40.00	25.00
(57)	Ivan Howard	75.00	40.00	25.00
(58)	Hughes (Los Angeles)	75.00	40.00	25.00
(59)	Hughes (Sacramento)	75.00	40.00	25.00
(60)	Jacobs	75.00	40.00	25.00
(61)	James	75.00	40.00	25.00
(62)	Jenkins	75.00	40.00	25.00
(63)	Johnson	75.00	40.00	25.00
(64)	Jones	75.00	40.00	25.00
(65)	Keck	75.00	40.00	25.00
(66)	Kelley	75.00	40.00	25.00
(67)	Kenworthy	75.00	40.00	25.00
(68)	Kilduff	75.00	40.00	25.00
(69)	Killifer	75.00	40.00	25.00
(70)	Kimmick	75.00	40.00	25.00
(71)	Kopp	75.00	40.00	25.00
(72)	Krause	75.00	40.00	25.00
(73)	Krug	75.00	40.00	25.00
(74)	Kunz	75.00	40.00	25.00
(75)	Lafayette	75.00	40.00	25.00
(76)	Lennon	75.00	40.00	25.00
(77)	Leptich	75.00	40.00	25.00
(78)	Leslie	75.00	40.00	25.00
(79)	Leverenz	75.00	40.00	25.00
(80)	Lewis	75.00	40.00	25.00
(81)	Maderas	75.00	40.00	25.00
(82)	Mails	75.00	40.00	25.00
(83)	McAuley	75.00	40.00	25.00
(84)	McCann	75.00	40.00	25.00
(85)	McDowell	75.00	40.00	25.00
(86)	McNeely	75.00	40.00	25.00
(87)	Menosky	75.00	40.00	25.00
(88)	Meyers	75.00	40.00	25.00
(89)	Miller	75.00	40.00	25.00
(90)	Mitchell	75.00	40.00	25.00
(91)	Mulligan	75.00	40.00	25.00
(92)	D. Murphy	75.00	40.00	25.00
(93)	R. Murphy	75.00	40.00	25.00
(94)	Osborne	75.00	40.00	25.00
(95)	Paynter	75.00	40.00	25.00
(96)	Penner	75.00	40.00	25.00
(97)	Peters (Sacramento)	75.00	40.00	25.00
(98)	Peters (Salt Lake)	75.00	40.00	25.00
(99)	Pick	75.00	40.00	25.00
(100)	Pillette	75.00	40.00	25.00
(101)	Poole	75.00	40.00	25.00
(102)	Prough	75.00	40.00	25.00
(103)	Querry	75.00	40.00	25.00
(104)	Read	75.00	40.00	25.00
(105)	Rhyne	75.00	40.00	25.00
(106)	Ritchie	75.00	40.00	25.00
(107)	Root	75.00	40.00	25.00
(108)	Rowher	75.00	40.00	25.00
(109)	Schang	75.00	40.00	25.00
(110)	Schneider	75.00	40.00	25.00
(111)	Schorr	75.00	40.00	25.00
(112)	Schroeder	75.00	40.00	25.00
(113)	Scott	75.00	40.00	25.00
(114)	Sellers	75.00	40.00	25.00
(115)	"Speck" Shay	75.00	40.00	25.00
(116)	Shea (Sacramento)	75.00	40.00	25.00
(117)	Shea (San Francisco)	75.00	40.00	25.00
(118)	Shellenback	75.00	40.00	25.00
(119)	Siebold	75.00	40.00	25.00
(120)	Siglin	75.00	40.00	25.00
(121)	Slade	75.00	40.00	25.00
(122)	Smith (Sacramento)	75.00	40.00	25.00
(123)	Smith (San Francisco)	75.00	40.00	25.00
(124)	Stanton	75.00	40.00	25.00
(125)	Tanner	75.00	40.00	25.00
(126)	Twomley	75.00	40.00	25.00
(127)	Valla	75.00	40.00	25.00
(128)	Vargas	75.00	40.00	25.00
(129)	Vines	75.00	40.00	25.00
(130)	Vitt	75.00	40.00	25.00
(131)	Wallace	75.00	40.00	25.00
(132)	Walsh	75.00	40.00	25.00
(133)	Paul Waner	1,200	600.00	350.00
(134)	Warner (Fielding)	75.00	40.00	25.00
(135)	Warner (Throwing)	75.00	40.00	25.00
(136)	Welsh	75.00	40.00	25.00
(137)	Wetzel	75.00	40.00	25.00
(138)	Whalen	75.00	40.00	25.00
(139)	Wilhoit	75.00	40.00	25.00
(140)	Williams (San Francisco)	75.00	40.00	25.00
(141)	Williams (Seattle)	75.00	40.00	25.00
(142)	Wolfer	75.00	40.00	25.00
(143)	Yelle	75.00	40.00	25.00
(144)	Moses Yellowhorse	1,000	500.00	300.00

1925 Zeenut Pacific Coast League

Zeenut cards in 1925 measure about 1-3/4" x 3-7/16" and display the date on the front. The cards include a full photographic background. There are 162 subjects known for 1925.

		NM	EX	VG
	Common Player:	75.00	40.00	25.00
	With Coupon:	450.00	225.00	140.00
(1)	Adeylatte	75.00	40.00	25.00
(2)	Agnew	75.00	40.00	25.00
(3)	Arlett	75.00	40.00	25.00
(4)	Bagby	75.00	40.00	25.00
(5)	Bahr	75.00	40.00	25.00
(6)	Baker	75.00	40.00	25.00
(7)	E. Baldwin	75.00	40.00	25.00
(8)	Barfoot	75.00	40.00	25.00
(9)	Beck	75.00	40.00	25.00
(10)	Becker	75.00	40.00	25.00
(11)	Blakesley	75.00	40.00	25.00
(12)	Boehler	75.00	40.00	25.00
(13)	Brady	75.00	40.00	25.00
(14)	Brandt	75.00	40.00	25.00
(15)	Bratcher	75.00	40.00	25.00
(16)	Brazil	75.00	40.00	25.00
(17)	Brower	75.00	40.00	25.00
(18)	Brown	75.00	40.00	25.00
(19)	Brubaker	75.00	40.00	25.00
(20)	Bryan	75.00	40.00	25.00
(21)	Canfield	75.00	40.00	25.00
(22)	W. Canfield	75.00	40.00	25.00
(23)	Cather	75.00	40.00	25.00
(24)	Chavez	75.00	40.00	25.00
(25)	Christain	75.00	40.00	25.00
(26)	Cochrane	75.00	40.00	25.00
(27)	Connolly	75.00	40.00	25.00
(28)	Cook	75.00	40.00	25.00
(29)	Cooper	75.00	40.00	25.00
(30)	Coumbe	75.00	40.00	25.00
(31)	Crandall	75.00	40.00	25.00
(32)	Crane	75.00	40.00	25.00
(33)	Crockett	75.00	40.00	25.00
(34)	Crosby	75.00	40.00	25.00
(35)	Cutshaw	75.00	40.00	25.00
(36)	Daly	75.00	40.00	25.00
(37)	Davis	75.00	40.00	25.00
(38)	Deal	75.00	40.00	25.00
(39)	Delaney	75.00	40.00	25.00
(40)	Dempsey	75.00	40.00	25.00
(41)	Dumovich	75.00	40.00	25.00
(42)	Eckert	75.00	40.00	25.00
(43)	Eldred	75.00	40.00	25.00
(44)	Elliott	75.00	40.00	25.00
(45)	Ellison	75.00	40.00	25.00
(46)	Emmer	75.00	40.00	25.00
(47)	Ennis	75.00	40.00	25.00
(48)	Essick	75.00	40.00	25.00
(49)	Finn	75.00	40.00	25.00
(50)	Flowers	75.00	40.00	25.00
(51)	Frederick	75.00	40.00	25.00
(52)	Fussell	75.00	40.00	25.00
(53)	Geary	75.00	40.00	25.00
(54)	Gorman	75.00	40.00	25.00

		NM	EX	VG
(55)	Griffin (San Francisco)	75.00	40.00	25.00
(56)	Griffin (Vernon)	75.00	40.00	25.00
(57)	Grimes	75.00	40.00	25.00
(58)	Guisto	75.00	40.00	25.00
(59)	Hannah	75.00	40.00	25.00
(60)	Haughy	75.00	40.00	25.00
(61)	Hemingway	75.00	40.00	25.00
(62)	Hendryx	75.00	40.00	25.00
(63)	Herman	200.00	100.00	50.00
(64)	High	75.00	40.00	25.00
(65)	Hoffman	75.00	40.00	25.00
(66)	Hood	75.00	40.00	25.00
(67)	Horan	75.00	40.00	25.00
(68)	Horton	75.00	40.00	25.00
(69)	Howard	75.00	40.00	25.00
(70)	Hughes	75.00	40.00	25.00
(71)	Hulvey	75.00	40.00	25.00
(72)	Hunnefield	75.00	40.00	25.00
(73)	Jacobs	75.00	40.00	25.00
(74)	James	75.00	40.00	25.00
(75)	Keating	75.00	40.00	25.00
(76)	Keefe	75.00	40.00	25.00
(77)	Kelly	75.00	40.00	25.00
(78)	Kilduff	75.00	40.00	25.00
(79)	Kohler	75.00	40.00	25.00
(80)	Kopp	75.00	40.00	25.00
(81)	Krause	75.00	40.00	25.00
(82)	Krug	75.00	40.00	25.00
(83)	Kunz	75.00	40.00	25.00
(84)	Lafayette	75.00	40.00	25.00
(85)	Tony Lazzeri	450.00	250.00	175.00
(86)	Leslie	75.00	40.00	25.00
(87)	Leverenz	75.00	40.00	25.00
(88)	Duffy Lewis	75.00	40.00	25.00
(89)	Lindemore	75.00	40.00	25.00
(90)	Ludolph	75.00	40.00	25.00
(91)	Makin	75.00	40.00	25.00
(92)	Martin (Sacramento)	75.00	40.00	25.00
(93)	Martin (Portland)	75.00	40.00	25.00
(94)	McCabe	75.00	40.00	25.00
(95)	McCann	75.00	40.00	25.00
(96)	McCarren	75.00	40.00	25.00
(97)	McDonald	75.00	40.00	25.00
(98)	McGinnis (Portland)	75.00	40.00	25.00
(99)	McGinnis (Sacramento)	75.00	40.00	25.00
(100)	McLaughlin	75.00	40.00	25.00
(101)	Milstead	75.00	40.00	25.00
(102)	Mitchell	75.00	40.00	25.00
(103)	Moudy	75.00	40.00	25.00
(104)	Mulcahy	75.00	40.00	25.00
(105)	Mulligan	75.00	40.00	25.00
(106)	Lefty O'Doul	450.00	250.00	175.00
(107)	O'Neil	75.00	40.00	25.00
(108)	Ortman	75.00	40.00	25.00
(109)	Pailey	75.00	40.00	25.00
(110)	Paynter	75.00	40.00	25.00
(111)	Peery	75.00	40.00	25.00
(112)	Penner	75.00	40.00	25.00
(113)	Pfeffer	75.00	40.00	25.00
(114)	Phillips	75.00	40.00	25.00
(115)	Pickering	75.00	40.00	25.00
(116)	Piercy	75.00	40.00	25.00
(117)	Pillette	75.00	40.00	25.00
(118)	Plummer	75.00	40.00	25.00
(119)	Ponder	75.00	40.00	25.00
(120)	Pruett	75.00	40.00	25.00
(121)	Rawlings	75.00	40.00	25.00
(122)	Read	75.00	40.00	25.00
(123)	Jimmy Reese	300.00	200.00	100.00
(124)	Rhyne	75.00	40.00	25.00
(125)	Riconda	75.00	40.00	25.00
(126)	Ritchie	75.00	40.00	25.00
(127)	Rohwer	75.00	40.00	25.00
(128)	Rowland	75.00	40.00	25.00
(129)	Ryan	75.00	40.00	25.00
(130)	Sandberg	75.00	40.00	25.00
(131)	Schang	75.00	40.00	25.00
(132)	Shea	75.00	40.00	25.00
(133)	M. Shea	75.00	40.00	25.00
(134)	Shellenbach	75.00	40.00	25.00
(135)	Sherling	75.00	40.00	25.00
(136)	Siglin	75.00	40.00	25.00
(137)	Slade	75.00	40.00	25.00
(138)	Spencer	75.00	40.00	25.00
(139)	Steward	75.00	40.00	25.00
(140)	Stivers	75.00	40.00	25.00
(141)	Suhr	75.00	40.00	25.00
(142)	Sutherland	75.00	40.00	25.00
(143)	Thomas (Portland)	75.00	40.00	25.00
(144)	Thomas (Vernon)	75.00	40.00	25.00
(145)	Thompson	75.00	40.00	25.00
(146)	Tobin	75.00	40.00	25.00
(147)	Twombly	75.00	40.00	25.00
(148)	Valla	75.00	40.00	25.00
(149)	Vinci	75.00	40.00	25.00
(150)	O. Vitt	75.00	40.00	25.00
(151)	Wachenfeld	75.00	40.00	25.00
(152)	Paul Waner	1,200	600.00	350.00
(153)	Lloyd Waner	1,200	600.00	360.00
(154)	Warner	75.00	40.00	25.00
(155)	Watson	75.00	40.00	25.00
(156)	Weinert	75.00	40.00	25.00
(157)	Whaley	75.00	40.00	25.00
(158)	Whitney	75.00	40.00	25.00
(159)	Williams	75.00	40.00	25.00
(160)	Winters	75.00	40.00	25.00
(161)	Wolfer	75.00	40.00	25.00
(162)	Woodring	75.00	40.00	25.00
(163)	Yeargin	75.00	40.00	25.00
(164)	Yelle	75.00	40.00	25.00

1926 Zeenut Pacific Coast League

Except for their slightly smaller size (1-3/4" x 3-7/16"), the 1926 Zeenut cards are nearly identical to the previous two years. Considered more difficult than other Zeenuts series of this era, the 1926 set consists of more than 170 known subjects.

		NM	EX	VG
Common Player:		60.00	30.00	20.00
With Coupon:		450.00	225.00	140.00
(1)	Agnew	60.00	30.00	20.00
(2)	Allen	60.00	30.00	20.00
(3)	Alley	60.00	30.00	20.00
(4)	Averill	900.00	450.00	275.00
(5)	Bagwell	60.00	30.00	20.00
(6)	Baker	60.00	30.00	20.00
(7)	T. Baldwin	60.00	30.00	20.00
(8)	Berry	60.00	30.00	20.00
(9)	Bool	60.00	30.00	20.00
(10)	Boone	60.00	30.00	20.00
(11)	Boyd	60.00	30.00	20.00
(12)	Brady	60.00	30.00	20.00
(13)	Brazil	60.00	30.00	20.00
(14)	Brower	60.00	30.00	20.00
(15)	Brubaker	60.00	30.00	20.00
(16)	Bryan	60.00	30.00	20.00
(17)	Burns	60.00	30.00	20.00
(18)	C. Canfield	60.00	30.00	20.00
(19)	W. Canfield	60.00	30.00	20.00
(20)	Carson	60.00	30.00	20.00
(21)	Christian	60.00	30.00	20.00
(22)	Cole	60.00	30.00	20.00
(23)	Connolly	60.00	30.00	20.00
(24)	Cook	60.00	30.00	20.00
(25)	Couch	60.00	30.00	20.00
(26)	Coumbe	60.00	30.00	20.00
(27)	Crockett	60.00	30.00	20.00
(28)	Cunningham	60.00	30.00	20.00
(29)	Cutshaw	60.00	30.00	20.00
(30)	Daglia	60.00	30.00	20.00
(31)	Danning	60.00	30.00	20.00
(32)	Davis	60.00	30.00	20.00
(33)	Delaney	60.00	30.00	20.00
(34)	Eckert	60.00	30.00	20.00
(35)	Eldred	60.00	30.00	20.00
(36)	Elliott	60.00	30.00	20.00
(37)	Ellison	60.00	30.00	20.00
(38)	Ellsworth	60.00	30.00	20.00
(39)	Elsh	60.00	30.00	20.00
(40)	Fenton	60.00	30.00	20.00
(41)	Finn	60.00	30.00	20.00
(42)	Flashkamper	60.00	30.00	20.00
(43)	Fowler	60.00	30.00	20.00
(44)	Frederick	60.00	30.00	20.00
(45)	Freeman	60.00	30.00	20.00
(46)	French	60.00	30.00	20.00
(47)	Garrison	60.00	30.00	20.00
(48)	Geary	60.00	30.00	20.00
(49)	Gillespie	60.00	30.00	20.00
(50)	Glazner	60.00	30.00	20.00
(51)	Gould	60.00	30.00	20.00
(52)	Governor	60.00	30.00	20.00
(53)	Griffin (Missions)	60.00	30.00	20.00
(54)	Griffin (San Francisco)	60.00	30.00	20.00
(55)	Guisto	60.00	30.00	20.00
(56)	Hamilton	60.00	30.00	20.00
(57)	Hannah	60.00	30.00	20.00
(58)	Hansen	60.00	30.00	20.00
(59)	Hasty	60.00	30.00	20.00
(60)	Hemingway	60.00	30.00	20.00
(61)	Hendryx	60.00	30.00	20.00
(62)	Hickok	60.00	30.00	20.00
(63)	Hillis	60.00	30.00	20.00
(64)	Hoffman	60.00	30.00	20.00
(65)	Hollerson	60.00	30.00	20.00
(66)	Holmes	60.00	30.00	20.00
(67)	Hood	60.00	30.00	20.00
(68)	Howard	60.00	30.00	20.00
(69)	Hufft	60.00	30.00	20.00
(70)	Hughes	60.00	30.00	20.00
(71)	Hulvey	60.00	30.00	20.00
(72)	Hurst	60.00	30.00	20.00
(73)	R. Jacobs	60.00	30.00	20.00
(74)	Jahn	60.00	30.00	20.00
(75)	Jenkins	60.00	30.00	20.00
(76)	Johnson	60.00	30.00	20.00
(77)	Jolly (Jolley)	100.00	50.00	30.00
(78)	Jones	60.00	30.00	20.00
(79)	Kallio	60.00	30.00	20.00
(80)	Keating	60.00	30.00	20.00
(81)	Kerr (Hollywood)	60.00	30.00	20.00
(82)	Kerr (San Francisco)	60.00	30.00	20.00
(83)	Kilduff	60.00	30.00	20.00
(84)	Killifer	60.00	30.00	20.00
(85)	Knight	60.00	30.00	20.00
(86)	Koehler	60.00	30.00	20.00
(87)	Kopp	60.00	30.00	20.00
(88)	Krause	60.00	30.00	20.00
(89)	Krug	60.00	30.00	20.00
(90)	Kunz	60.00	30.00	20.00
(91)	Lafayette	60.00	30.00	20.00
(92)	Lane	60.00	30.00	20.00

(93)	Lang	60.00	30.00	20.00
(94)	Lary	60.00	30.00	20.00
(95)	Leslie	60.00	30.00	20.00
(96)	Lindemore	60.00	30.00	20.00
(97)	Ludolph	60.00	30.00	20.00
(98)	Makin	60.00	30.00	20.00
(99)	Mangum	60.00	30.00	20.00
(100)	Martin	60.00	30.00	20.00
(101)	McCredie	60.00	30.00	20.00
(102)	McDowell	60.00	30.00	20.00
(103)	McKenry	60.00	30.00	20.00
(104)	McLoughlin	60.00	30.00	20.00
(105)	McNally	60.00	30.00	20.00
(106)	McPhee	60.00	30.00	20.00
(107)	Meeker	60.00	30.00	20.00
(108)	Metz	60.00	30.00	20.00
(109)	Miller	60.00	30.00	20.00
(110)	Mitchell (Los Angeles)	60.00	30.00	20.00
(111)	Mitchell (San Francisco)	60.00	30.00	20.00
(112)	Monroe	60.00	30.00	20.00
(113)	Moudy	60.00	30.00	20.00
(114)	Mulcahy	60.00	30.00	20.00
(115)	Mulligan	60.00	30.00	20.00
(116)	Murphy	60.00	30.00	20.00
(117)	Lefty O'Doul	600.00	300.00	180.00
(118)	O'Neill	60.00	30.00	20.00
(119)	Oeschger	60.00	30.00	20.00
(120)	Oliver	60.00	30.00	20.00
(121)	Ortman	60.00	30.00	20.00
(122)	Osborn	60.00	30.00	20.00
(123)	Paynter	60.00	30.00	20.00
(124)	Peters	60.00	30.00	20.00
(125)	Pfahler	60.00	30.00	20.00
(126)	Pillette	60.00	30.00	20.00
(127)	Plummer	60.00	30.00	20.00
(128)	Prothro	60.00	30.00	20.00
(129)	Pruett	60.00	30.00	20.00
(130)	Rachac	60.00	30.00	20.00
(131)	Ramsey	60.00	30.00	20.00
(132)	Rathjen	60.00	30.00	20.00
(133)	Read	60.00	30.00	20.00
(134)	Redman	60.00	30.00	20.00
(135)	Jimmy Reese	60.00	30.00	20.00
(136)	Rodda	60.00	30.00	20.00
(137)	Rohwer	60.00	30.00	20.00
(138)	Ryan	60.00	30.00	20.00
(139)	Sandberg	60.00	30.00	20.00
(140)	Sanders	60.00	30.00	20.00
(141)	E. Shea	60.00	30.00	20.00
(142)	M. Shea	60.00	30.00	20.00
(143)	Sheehan	60.00	30.00	20.00
(144)	Shellenbach	60.00	30.00	20.00
(145)	Sherlock	60.00	30.00	20.00
(146)	Siglin	60.00	30.00	20.00
(147)	Slade	60.00	30.00	20.00
(148)	E. Smith	60.00	30.00	20.00
(149)	M. Smith	60.00	30.00	20.00
(150)	Staley	60.00	30.00	20.00
(151)	Statz	120.00	60.00	40.00
(152)	Stroud	60.00	30.00	20.00
(153)	Stuart	60.00	30.00	20.00
(154)	Suhr	60.00	30.00	20.00
(155)	Swanson	60.00	30.00	20.00
(156)	Sweeney	60.00	30.00	20.00
(157)	Tadevich	60.00	30.00	20.00
(158)	Thomas	60.00	30.00	20.00
(159)	Thompson	60.00	30.00	20.00
(160)	Tobin	60.00	30.00	20.00
(161)	Valla	60.00	30.00	20.00
(162)	Vargas	60.00	30.00	20.00
(163)	Vinci	60.00	30.00	20.00
(164)	Walters	60.00	30.00	20.00
(165)	Lloyd Waner	900.00	450.00	270.00
(166)	Weis	60.00	30.00	20.00
(167)	Whitney	60.00	30.00	20.00
(168)	Williams	60.00	30.00	20.00
(169)	Wright	60.00	30.00	20.00
(170)	Yelle	60.00	30.00	20.00
(171)	Zaeffel	60.00	30.00	20.00
(172)	Zoellers	60.00	30.00	20.00

1927 Zeenut Pacific Coast League

The 1927 Zeenuts are about the same size (1-3/4" x 3-3/8") and color as the 1926 issue, except the year is expressed in just two digits (27), a practice that continued through 1930. There are 144 subjects known.

		NM	EX	VG
Common Player:		60.00	30.00	20.00
With Coupon:		450.00	225.00	140.00
(1)	Agnew	60.00	30.00	20.00
(2)	Arlett	60.00	30.00	20.00
(3)	Averill	900.00	450.00	270.00

(4)	Backer	60.00	30.00	20.00
(5)	Bagwell	60.00	30.00	20.00
(6)	Baker	60.00	30.00	20.00
(7)	D. Baker	60.00	30.00	20.00
(8)	Ballenger	60.00	30.00	20.00
(9)	Baumgartner	60.00	30.00	20.00
(10)	Bigbee	60.00	30.00	20.00
(11)	Boehler	60.00	30.00	20.00
(12)	Bool	60.00	30.00	20.00
(13)	Borreani	60.00	30.00	20.00
(14)	Brady	60.00	30.00	20.00
(15)	Bratcher	60.00	30.00	20.00
(16)	Brett	60.00	30.00	20.00
(17)	Brown	60.00	30.00	20.00
(18)	Brubaker	60.00	30.00	20.00
(19)	Bryan	60.00	30.00	20.00
(20)	Callaghan	60.00	30.00	20.00
(21)	Caveney	60.00	30.00	20.00
(22)	Christian	60.00	30.00	20.00
(23)	Cissell	60.00	30.00	20.00
(24)	Cook	60.00	30.00	20.00
(25)	Cooper (Oakland)	60.00	30.00	20.00
(26)	Cooper (Sacramento)	60.00	30.00	20.00
(27)	Cox	60.00	30.00	20.00
(28)	Cunningham	60.00	30.00	20.00
(29)	Daglia	60.00	30.00	20.00
(30)	Dickerman	60.00	30.00	20.00
(31)	Dumovitch	60.00	30.00	20.00
(32)	Eckert	60.00	30.00	20.00
(33)	Eldred	60.00	30.00	20.00
(34)	Ellison	60.00	30.00	20.00
(35)	Fenton	60.00	30.00	20.00
(36)	Finn	60.00	30.00	20.00
(37)	Fischer	60.00	30.00	20.00
(38)	Frederick	60.00	30.00	20.00
(39)	French	60.00	30.00	20.00
(40)	Fullerton	60.00	30.00	20.00
(41)	Geary	60.00	30.00	20.00
(42)	Gillespie	60.00	30.00	20.00
(43)	Gooch	60.00	30.00	20.00
(44)	Gould	60.00	30.00	20.00
(45)	Governor	60.00	30.00	20.00
(46)	Guisto	60.00	30.00	20.00
(47)	Hannah	60.00	30.00	20.00
(48)	Hasty	60.00	30.00	20.00
(49)	Hemingway	60.00	30.00	20.00
(50)	Hoffman	60.00	30.00	20.00
(51)	Hood	60.00	30.00	20.00
(52)	Hooper	900.00	450.00	270.00
(53)	Hudgens	60.00	30.00	20.00
(54)	Hufft	60.00	30.00	20.00
(55)	Hughes	60.00	30.00	20.00
(56)	Jahn	60.00	30.00	20.00
(57)	Johnson (Portland)	60.00	30.00	20.00
(58)	Johnson (Seals)	60.00	30.00	20.00
(59)	Jolly (Jolley)	90.00	45.00	30.00
(60)	Jones	60.00	30.00	20.00
(61)	Kallio	60.00	30.00	20.00
(62)	Keating	60.00	30.00	20.00
(63)	Keefe	60.00	30.00	20.00
(64)	Killifer	60.00	30.00	20.00
(65)	Kimmick	60.00	30.00	20.00
(66)	Kinney	60.00	30.00	20.00
(67)	Knight	60.00	30.00	20.00
(68)	Koehler	60.00	30.00	20.00
(69)	Kopp	60.00	30.00	20.00
(70)	Krause	60.00	30.00	20.00
(71)	Krug	60.00	30.00	20.00
(72)	Kunz	60.00	30.00	20.00
(73)	Lary	60.00	30.00	20.00
(74)	Leard	60.00	30.00	20.00
(75)	Lingrel	60.00	30.00	20.00
(76)	Ludolph	60.00	30.00	20.00
(77)	Mails	60.00	30.00	20.00
(78)	Makin	60.00	30.00	20.00
(79)	Martin	60.00	30.00	20.00
(80)	May	60.00	30.00	20.00
(81)	McCabe	60.00	30.00	20.00
(82)	McCurdy	60.00	30.00	20.00
(83)	McDaniel	60.00	30.00	20.00
(84)	McGee	60.00	30.00	20.00
(85)	McLaughlin	60.00	30.00	20.00
(86)	McMurtry	60.00	30.00	20.00
(87)	Metz	60.00	30.00	20.00
(88)	Miljus	60.00	30.00	20.00
(89)	Mitchell	60.00	30.00	20.00
(90)	Monroe	60.00	30.00	20.00
(91)	Moudy	60.00	30.00	20.00
(92)	Mulligan	60.00	30.00	20.00
(93)	Murphy	60.00	30.00	20.00
(94)	O'Brien	60.00	30.00	20.00
(95)	Lefty O'Doul	600.00	300.00	180.00
(96)	Oliver	60.00	30.00	20.00
(97)	Osborn	60.00	30.00	20.00
(98)	Parker (Missions, batting.)	60.00	30.00	20.00
(99)	Parker (Missions, throwing.)	60.00	30.00	20.00
(100)	Parker (Portland)	60.00	30.00	20.00
(101)	Peters	60.00	30.00	20.00
(102)	Pillette	60.00	30.00	20.00
(103)	Ponder	60.00	30.00	20.00
(104)	Prothro	120.00	60.00	40.00
(105)	Rachac	60.00	30.00	20.00
(106)	Ramsey	60.00	30.00	20.00
(107)	Read	60.00	30.00	20.00
(108)	Jimmy Reese	375.00	190.00	120.00
(109)	Rodda	60.00	30.00	20.00
(110)	Rohwer	60.00	30.00	20.00
(111)	Rose	60.00	30.00	20.00
(112)	Ryan	60.00	30.00	20.00
(113)	Sandberg	60.00	30.00	20.00
(114)	Sanders	60.00	30.00	20.00
(115)	Severeid	60.00	30.00	20.00
(116)	Shea	60.00	30.00	20.00
(117)	Sheehan (Hollywood)	60.00	30.00	20.00
(118)	Sheehan (Seals)	60.00	30.00	20.00
(119)	Sherlock	60.00	30.00	20.00
(120a)	Shinners (Date is "1927.")	60.00	30.00	20.00
(120b)	Shinners (Date is "27.")	60.00	30.00	20.00

		NM	EX	VG
(121)	Singleton	60.00	30.00	20.00
(122)	Slade	60.00	30.00	20.00
(123)	E. Smith	60.00	30.00	20.00
(124)	Sparks	60.00	30.00	20.00
(125)	Stokes	60.00	30.00	20.00
(126)	J. Storti	60.00	30.00	20.00
(127)	L. Storti	60.00	30.00	20.00
(128)	Strand	60.00	30.00	20.00
(129)	Suhr	60.00	30.00	20.00
(130)	Sunseri	60.00	30.00	20.00
(131)	Swanson	60.00	30.00	20.00
(132)	Tierney	60.00	30.00	20.00
(133)	Valla	60.00	30.00	20.00
(134)	Vargas	60.00	30.00	20.00
(135)	Vitt	60.00	30.00	20.00
(136)	Weinert	60.00	30.00	20.00
(137)	Weis	60.00	30.00	20.00
(138)	Wendell	60.00	30.00	20.00
(139)	Whitney	60.00	30.00	20.00
(140)	Williams	60.00	30.00	20.00
(141)	Guy Williams	60.00	30.00	20.00
(142)	Woodson	60.00	30.00	20.00
(143)	Wright	60.00	30.00	20.00
(144)	Yelle	60.00	30.00	20.00

1928 Zeenut Pacific Coast League

Zeenut cards from 1928 through 1930 maintain the same format as the 1927 series. Measuring about 1-3/4" x 3-3/8", the 1928 series consists of 168 known subjects.

		NM	EX	VG
Common Player:		60.00	30.00	20.00
(1)	Agnew	60.00	30.00	20.00
(2)	Earl Averill	900.00	450.00	270.00
(3)	Backer	60.00	30.00	20.00
(4)	Baker	60.00	30.00	20.00
(5)	Baldwin	60.00	30.00	20.00
(6)	Barfoot	60.00	30.00	20.00
(7)	Bassler	60.00	30.00	20.00
(8)	Berger	60.00	30.00	20.00
(9)	Bigbee (Los Angeles)	60.00	30.00	20.00
(10)	Bigbee (Portland)	60.00	30.00	20.00
(11)	Bodie	60.00	30.00	20.00
(12)	Boehler	60.00	30.00	20.00
(13)	Bool	60.00	30.00	20.00
(14)	Boone	60.00	30.00	20.00
(15)	Borreani	60.00	30.00	20.00
(16)	Bratcher	60.00	30.00	20.00
(17)	Brenzel	60.00	30.00	20.00
(18)	Brubaker	60.00	30.00	20.00
(19)	Bryan	60.00	30.00	20.00
(20)	Burkett	60.00	30.00	20.00
(21)	Camilli	60.00	30.00	20.00
(22)	W. Canfield	60.00	30.00	20.00
(23)	Caveney	60.00	30.00	20.00
(24)	Cohen	150.00	75.00	40.00
(25)	Cook	60.00	30.00	20.00
(26)	Cooper	60.00	30.00	20.00
(27)	Craghead	60.00	30.00	20.00
(28)	Crosetti	300.00	150.00	90.00
(29)	Cunningham	60.00	30.00	20.00
(30)	Daglia	60.00	30.00	20.00
(31)	Davis	60.00	30.00	20.00
(32)	Dean	60.00	30.00	20.00
(33)	Dittmar	60.00	30.00	20.00
(34)	Donovan	60.00	30.00	20.00
(35)	Downs	60.00	30.00	20.00
(36)	Duff	60.00	30.00	20.00
(37)	Eckert	60.00	30.00	20.00
(38)	Eldred	60.00	30.00	20.00
(39)	Ellsworth	60.00	30.00	20.00
(40)	Fenton	60.00	30.00	20.00
(41)	Finn	60.00	30.00	20.00
(42)	Fitterer	60.00	30.00	20.00
(43)	Flynn	60.00	30.00	20.00
(44)	Frazier	60.00	30.00	20.00
(45)	French (Portland)	60.00	30.00	20.00
(46)	French (Sacramento)	60.00	30.00	20.00
(47)	Fullerton	60.00	30.00	20.00
(48)	Gabler	60.00	30.00	20.00
(49)	Gomes	60.00	30.00	20.00
(50)	Gooch	60.00	30.00	20.00
(51)	Gould	60.00	30.00	20.00
(52)	Governor	60.00	30.00	20.00
(53)	Graham ("S" on uniform.)	60.00	30.00	20.00
(54)	Graham (No "S" on uniform.)	60.00	30.00	20.00
(55)	Guisto	60.00	30.00	20.00
(56)	Hannah	60.00	30.00	20.00
(57)	Hansen	60.00	30.00	20.00
(58)	Harris	60.00	30.00	20.00
(59)	Hasty	60.00	30.00	20.00
(60)	Heath	60.00	30.00	20.00
(61)	Hoffman	60.00	30.00	20.00
(62)	Holling	60.00	30.00	20.00
(63)	Hood	60.00	30.00	20.00
(64)	House	60.00	30.00	20.00
(65)	Howard	60.00	30.00	20.00
(66)	Hudgens	60.00	30.00	20.00
(67)	Hufft	60.00	30.00	20.00
(68)	Hughes	60.00	30.00	20.00
(69)	Hulvey	60.00	30.00	20.00
(70)	Jacobs	60.00	30.00	20.00
(71)	Johnson (Portland)	60.00	30.00	20.00
(72)	Johnson (San Francisco)	60.00	30.00	20.00
(73)	Jolley	90.00	45.00	30.00
(74)	Jones (Batting)	60.00	30.00	20.00
(75)	Jones (Throwing)	60.00	30.00	20.00
(76)	Kallio	60.00	30.00	20.00
(77)	Keating	60.00	30.00	20.00
(78)	Keefe	60.00	30.00	20.00
(79)	Keesey	60.00	30.00	20.00
(80)	Kerr	60.00	30.00	20.00
(81)	Killifer	60.00	30.00	20.00
(82)	Kinney	60.00	30.00	20.00
(83)	Knight	60.00	30.00	20.00
(84)	Knothe	60.00	30.00	20.00
(85)	Koehler	60.00	30.00	20.00
(86)	Kopp	60.00	30.00	20.00
(87)	Krause	60.00	30.00	20.00
(88)	Krug	60.00	30.00	20.00
(89)	Lary	60.00	30.00	20.00
(90)	LeBourveau	60.00	30.00	20.00
(91)	Lee	60.00	30.00	20.00
(92)	Ernie Lombardi	1,350	700.00	400.00
(93)	Mails	60.00	30.00	20.00
(94)	Martin (Missions)	60.00	30.00	20.00
(95)	Martin (Seattle)	60.00	30.00	20.00
(96)	May	60.00	30.00	20.00
(97)	McCabe	60.00	30.00	20.00
(98)	McCrea	60.00	30.00	20.00
(99)	McDaniel	60.00	30.00	20.00
(100)	McLaughlin	60.00	30.00	20.00
(101)	McNulty	60.00	30.00	20.00
(102)	Mellano	60.00	30.00	20.00
(103)	Irish Muesel (Meusel)	60.00	30.00	20.00
(104)	Middleton	60.00	30.00	20.00
(105)	Mishkin	60.00	30.00	20.00
(106)	Mitchell	60.00	30.00	20.00
(107)	Monroe	60.00	30.00	20.00
(108)	Moudy	60.00	30.00	20.00
(109)	Mulcahy	60.00	30.00	20.00
(110)	Muller	60.00	30.00	20.00
(111)	Mulligan	60.00	30.00	20.00
(112)	W. Murphy	60.00	30.00	20.00
(113)	Nance	60.00	30.00	20.00
(114)	Nelson	60.00	30.00	20.00
(115)	Osborn	60.00	30.00	20.00
(116)	Osborne	60.00	30.00	20.00
(117)	Parker	60.00	30.00	20.00
(118)	Peters	60.00	30.00	20.00
(119)	Pillette	60.00	30.00	20.00
(120)	Pinelli	60.00	30.00	20.00
(121)	Plitt	60.00	30.00	20.00
(122)	Ponder	60.00	30.00	20.00
(123)	Rachac	60.00	30.00	20.00
(124)	Read	60.00	30.00	20.00
(125)	Reed	60.00	30.00	20.00
(126)	Jimmy Reese	375.00	190.00	120.00
(127)	Rego	60.00	30.00	20.00
(128)	Rhodes	60.00	30.00	20.00
(129)	Rhyne	60.00	30.00	20.00
(130)	Rodda	60.00	30.00	20.00
(131)	Rohwer	60.00	30.00	20.00
(132)	Rose	60.00	30.00	20.00
(133)	Roth	60.00	30.00	20.00
(134)	Ruble	60.00	30.00	20.00
(135)	Ryan	60.00	30.00	20.00
(136)	Sandberg	60.00	30.00	20.00
(137)	Schulmerich	60.00	30.00	20.00
(138)	Severeid	60.00	30.00	20.00
(139)	Shea	60.00	30.00	20.00
(140)	Sheely	60.00	30.00	20.00
(141)	Shellenback	60.00	30.00	20.00
(142)	Sherlock	60.00	30.00	20.00
(143)	Sigafoos	60.00	30.00	20.00
(144)	Singleton	60.00	30.00	20.00
(145)	Slade	60.00	30.00	20.00
(146)	Smith	60.00	30.00	20.00
(147)	Sprinz	60.00	30.00	20.00
(148)	Staley	60.00	30.00	20.00
(149)	Suhr	60.00	30.00	20.00
(150)	Sunseri	60.00	30.00	20.00
(151)	Swanson	60.00	30.00	20.00
(152)	Sweeney	60.00	30.00	20.00
(153)	Teachout	60.00	30.00	20.00
(154)	Twombly	60.00	30.00	20.00
(155)	Vargas	60.00	30.00	20.00
(156)	Vinci	60.00	30.00	20.00
(157)	Vitt	60.00	30.00	20.00
(158)	Warhop	60.00	30.00	20.00
(159)	Weathersby	60.00	30.00	20.00
(160)	Weiss	60.00	30.00	20.00
(161)	Welch	60.00	30.00	20.00
(162)	Wera	60.00	30.00	20.00
(163)	Wetzel	60.00	30.00	20.00
(164)	Whitney	60.00	30.00	20.00
(165)	Williams	60.00	30.00	20.00
(166)	Wilson	60.00	30.00	20.00
(167)	Wolfer	60.00	30.00	20.00
(168)	Yerkes	60.00	30.00	20.00

1929 Zeenut Pacific Coast League

Zeenut cards from 1928 through 1930 maintain the same format as the 1927 series. Measuring about 1-3/4" x 3-1/2", the 1929 series consists of 168 known subjects.

		NM	EX	VG
Common Player:		60.00	30.00	20.00
With Coupon:		600.00	300.00	180.00
(1)	Albert	60.00	30.00	20.00
(2)	Almada	150.00	75.00	40.00
(3)	Anderson	60.00	30.00	20.00
(4)	Anton	60.00	30.00	20.00
(5)	Backer	60.00	30.00	20.00
(6)	Baker	60.00	30.00	20.00
(7)	Baldwin	60.00	30.00	20.00
(8)	Barbee	60.00	30.00	20.00
(9)	Barfoot	60.00	30.00	20.00
(10)	Bassler	60.00	30.00	20.00
(11)	Bates	60.00	30.00	20.00
(12)	Berger	60.00	30.00	20.00
(13)	Boehler	60.00	30.00	20.00
(14)	Boone	60.00	30.00	20.00
(15)	Borreani	60.00	30.00	20.00
(16)	Brenzel	60.00	30.00	20.00
(17)	Brooks	60.00	30.00	20.00
(18)	Brubaker	60.00	30.00	20.00
(19)	Bryan	60.00	30.00	20.00
(20)	Burke	60.00	30.00	20.00
(21)	Burkett	60.00	30.00	20.00
(22)	Burns	60.00	30.00	20.00
(23)	Bush	60.00	30.00	20.00
(24)	Butler	60.00	30.00	20.00
(25)	Camilli	60.00	30.00	20.00
(26)	Carlyle (Hollywood)	60.00	30.00	20.00
(27)	Carlyle	60.00	30.00	20.00
(28)	Cascarella	60.00	30.00	20.00
(29)	Caveney	60.00	30.00	20.00
(30)	Childs	60.00	30.00	20.00
(31)	Christensen	60.00	30.00	20.00
(32)	Cole	60.00	30.00	20.00
(33)	Collard	60.00	30.00	20.00
(34)	Cooper	60.00	30.00	20.00
(35)	Couch	60.00	30.00	20.00
(36)	Cox	60.00	30.00	20.00
(37)	Craghead	60.00	30.00	20.00
(38)	Crandall	60.00	30.00	20.00
(39)	Cronin	60.00	30.00	20.00
(40)	Crosetti	150.00	75.00	40.00
(41)	Daglia	60.00	30.00	20.00
(42)	Davis	60.00	30.00	20.00
(43)	Dean	60.00	30.00	20.00
(44)	Dittmar	60.00	30.00	20.00
(45)	Donovan	60.00	30.00	20.00
(46)	Dumovich	60.00	30.00	20.00
(47)	Eckardt	60.00	30.00	20.00
(48)	Ellsworth	60.00	30.00	20.00
(49)	Fenton	60.00	30.00	20.00
(50)	Finn	60.00	30.00	20.00
(51)	Fisch	60.00	30.00	20.00
(52)	Flynn	60.00	30.00	20.00
(53)	Frazier	60.00	30.00	20.00
(54)	Freitas	60.00	30.00	20.00
(55)	French	60.00	30.00	20.00
(56)	Gabler	60.00	30.00	20.00
(57)	Glynn	60.00	30.00	20.00
(58)	Lefty Gomez	1,800	900.00	550.00
(59)	Gould	60.00	30.00	20.00
(60)	Governor	60.00	30.00	20.00
(61)	Graham	60.00	30.00	20.00
(62)	Hand	60.00	30.00	20.00
(63)	Hannah	60.00	30.00	20.00
(64)	Harris	60.00	30.00	20.00
(65)	Heath	60.00	30.00	20.00
(66)	Heatherly	60.00	30.00	20.00
(67)	Hepting	60.00	30.00	20.00
(68)	Hillis	60.00	30.00	20.00
(69)	Hoffman	60.00	30.00	20.00
(70)	Holling	60.00	30.00	20.00
(71)	Hood	60.00	30.00	20.00
(72)	House	60.00	30.00	20.00
(73)	Howard	60.00	30.00	20.00
(74)	Hubbell	60.00	30.00	20.00
(75)	Hufft	60.00	30.00	20.00
(76)	Hurst	60.00	30.00	20.00
(77)	Jacobs (Los Angeles)	60.00	30.00	20.00
(78)	Jacobs (San Francisco)	60.00	30.00	20.00
(79)	Jahn	60.00	30.00	20.00
(80)	Jeffcoat	60.00	30.00	20.00
(81)	Johnson	60.00	30.00	20.00
(82)	Jolley	90.00	45.00	30.00
(83)	Gordon Jones (San Francisco)	60.00	30.00	20.00
(84)	Jones	60.00	30.00	20.00
(85)	Kallio	60.00	30.00	20.00

(86)	Kasich	60.00	30.00	20.00
(87)	Keane	60.00	30.00	20.00
(88)	Keating	60.00	30.00	20.00
(89)	Keesey	60.00	30.00	20.00
(90)	Killifer	60.00	30.00	20.00
(91)	Knight	60.00	30.00	20.00
(92)	Knothe	60.00	30.00	20.00
(93)	Knott	60.00	30.00	20.00
(94)	Koehler	60.00	30.00	20.00
(95)	Krasovich	60.00	30.00	20.00
(96)	Krause	60.00	30.00	20.00
(97)	Krug (Hollywood)	60.00	30.00	20.00
(98)	Krug (Los Angeles)	60.00	30.00	20.00
(99)	Kunz	60.00	30.00	20.00
(100)	Langford	60.00	30.00	20.00
(101)	Lee	60.00	30.00	20.00
(102)	Ernie Lombardi	900.00	450.00	275.00
(103)	Mahaffey	60.00	30.00	20.00
(104)	Mails	60.00	30.00	20.00
(105)	Maloney	60.00	30.00	20.00
(106)	McCabe	60.00	30.00	20.00
(107)	McDaniel	60.00	30.00	20.00
(108)	McEvoy	60.00	30.00	20.00
(109)	McIssacs	60.00	30.00	20.00
(110)	McQuaid	60.00	30.00	20.00
(111)	Miller	60.00	30.00	20.00
(112)	Monroe	60.00	30.00	20.00
(113)	Muller	60.00	30.00	20.00
(114)	Mulligan	60.00	30.00	20.00
(115)	Nance	60.00	30.00	20.00
(116)	Nelson	60.00	30.00	20.00
(117)	Nevers	60.00	30.00	20.00
(118)	Oana	700.00	350.00	200.00
(119)	Olney	60.00	30.00	20.00
(120)	Ortman	60.00	30.00	20.00
(121)	Osborne	60.00	30.00	20.00
(122)	Ostenberg	60.00	30.00	20.00
(123)	Peters	60.00	30.00	20.00
(124)	Pillette	60.00	30.00	20.00
(125)	Pinelli	60.00	30.00	20.00
(126)	Pipgras	60.00	30.00	20.00
(127)	Plitt	60.00	30.00	20.00
(128)	Polvogt	60.00	30.00	20.00
(129)	Rachac	60.00	30.00	20.00
(130)	Read	60.00	30.00	20.00
(131)	Reed	60.00	30.00	20.00
(132)	Jimmy Reese	300.00	150.00	90.00
(133)	Rego	60.00	30.00	20.00
(134)	Ritter	60.00	30.00	20.00
(135)	Roberts	60.00	30.00	20.00
(136)	Rodda	60.00	30.00	20.00
(137)	Rodgers	60.00	30.00	20.00
(138)	Rohwer	60.00	30.00	20.00
(139)	Rollings	60.00	30.00	20.00
(140)	Rumler	60.00	30.00	20.00
(141)	Ryan	60.00	30.00	20.00
(142)	Sandberg	60.00	30.00	20.00
(143)	Schino	60.00	30.00	20.00
(144)	Schmidt	60.00	30.00	20.00
(145)	Schulmerich	60.00	30.00	20.00
(146)	Scott	60.00	30.00	20.00
(147)	Severeid	60.00	30.00	20.00
(148)	Shanklin	60.00	30.00	20.00
(149)	Sherlock	60.00	30.00	20.00
(150)	Slade	60.00	30.00	20.00
(151)	Staley	60.00	30.00	20.00
(152)	Statz	90.00	45.00	30.00
(153)	Steinecke	60.00	30.00	20.00
(154)	Suhr	60.00	30.00	20.00
(155)	Taylor	60.00	30.00	20.00
(156)	Thurston	60.00	30.00	20.00
(157)	Tierney	60.00	30.00	20.00
(158)	Tolson	60.00	30.00	20.00
(159)	Tomlin	60.00	30.00	20.00
(160)	Vergez	60.00	30.00	20.00
(161)	Vinci	60.00	30.00	20.00
(162)	Volkman	60.00	30.00	20.00
(163)	Walsh	60.00	30.00	20.00
(164)	Warren	60.00	30.00	20.00
(165)	Webb	60.00	30.00	20.00
(166)	Weustling	60.00	30.00	20.00
(167)	Williams	60.00	30.00	20.00
(168)	Wingo	60.00	30.00	20.00

1930 Zeenut Pacific Coast League

Zeenut cards from 1928 through 1930 maintain the same format as the 1927 series. Measuring about 1-13/16" x 3-1/2", the 1930 series consists of 186 known subjects. There are some lettering variations in the series. Most coupons carry an expiration date of April 1, 1931, but some coupons have no expiration date stated.

		NM	EX	VG
Common Player:		60.00	30.00	20.00
(1)	Allington	60.00	30.00	20.00
(2)	Almada	75.00	40.00	25.00
(3)	Andrews	60.00	30.00	20.00
(4)	Anton	60.00	30.00	20.00
(5)	Arlett	60.00	30.00	20.00
(6)	Backer	60.00	30.00	20.00
(7)	Baecht	60.00	30.00	20.00
(8)	Baker	60.00	30.00	20.00
(9)	Baldwin	60.00	30.00	20.00
(10)	Ballou	60.00	30.00	20.00
(11)	Barbee	60.00	30.00	20.00
(12)	Barfoot	60.00	30.00	20.00
(13)	Bassler	60.00	30.00	20.00
(14)	Bates	60.00	30.00	20.00
(15)	Beck	60.00	30.00	20.00
(16)	Boone	60.00	30.00	20.00
(17)	Bowman	60.00	30.00	20.00
(18)	Brannon	60.00	30.00	20.00
(19)	Brenzel	60.00	30.00	20.00
(20)	Brown	60.00	30.00	20.00
(21)	Brubaker	60.00	30.00	20.00
(22)	Brucker	60.00	30.00	20.00
(23)	Bryan	60.00	30.00	20.00
(24)	Burkett	60.00	30.00	20.00
(25)	Burns	60.00	30.00	20.00
(26)	Butler	60.00	30.00	20.00
(27)	Camilli	60.00	30.00	20.00
(28)	Carlyle	60.00	30.00	20.00
(29)	Caster	60.00	30.00	20.00
(30)	Caveney	60.00	30.00	20.00
(31)	Chamberlain	60.00	30.00	20.00
(32)	Chatham	60.00	30.00	20.00
(33)	Childs	60.00	30.00	20.00
(34)	Christensen	60.00	30.00	20.00
(35)	Church	60.00	30.00	20.00
(36)	Cole	60.00	30.00	20.00
(37)	Coleman	60.00	30.00	20.00
(38)	Collins	60.00	30.00	20.00
(39)	Coscarart	60.00	30.00	20.00
(40)	Cox	60.00	30.00	20.00
(41)	Coyle	60.00	30.00	20.00
(42)	Craghead	60.00	30.00	20.00
(43)	Cronin	60.00	30.00	20.00
(44)	Crosetti	150.00	75.00	45.00
(45)	Daglia	60.00	30.00	20.00
(46)	Davis	60.00	30.00	20.00
(47)	Dean	60.00	30.00	20.00
(48)	DeViveiros	60.00	30.00	20.00
(49)	Dittmar	60.00	30.00	20.00
(50)	Donovan	60.00	30.00	20.00
(51)	Douglas	60.00	30.00	20.00
(52)	Dumovich	60.00	30.00	20.00
(53)	Edwards	60.00	30.00	20.00
(54)	Ellsworth	60.00	30.00	20.00
(55)	Falk	60.00	30.00	20.00
(56)	Fisch	60.00	30.00	20.00
(57)	Flynn	60.00	30.00	20.00
(58)	Freitas	60.00	30.00	20.00
(59)	French (Portland)	60.00	30.00	20.00
(60)	French (Sacramento)	60.00	30.00	20.00
(61)	Gabler	60.00	30.00	20.00
(62)	Gaston	60.00	30.00	20.00
(63)	Gazella	60.00	30.00	20.00
(64)	Gould	60.00	30.00	20.00
(65)	Governor	60.00	30.00	20.00
(66)	Green	60.00	30.00	20.00
(67)	Griffin	60.00	30.00	20.00
(68)	Haney	60.00	30.00	20.00
(69)	Hannah	60.00	30.00	20.00
(70)	Harper	60.00	30.00	20.00
(71)	Heath	60.00	30.00	20.00
(72)	Hillis	60.00	30.00	20.00
(73)	Hoag	60.00	30.00	20.00
(74)	Hoffman	60.00	30.00	20.00
(75)	Holland	60.00	30.00	20.00
(76)	Hollerson	60.00	30.00	20.00
(77)	Holling	60.00	30.00	20.00
(78)	Hood	60.00	30.00	20.00
(79)	Horn	60.00	30.00	20.00
(80)	House	60.00	30.00	20.00
(81)	Hubbell	60.00	30.00	20.00
(82)	Hufft	60.00	30.00	20.00
(83)	Hurst	60.00	30.00	20.00
(84)	Jacobs (Los Angeles)	60.00	30.00	20.00
(85)	Jacobs (Oakland)	60.00	30.00	20.00
(86)	Jacobs	60.00	30.00	20.00
(87)	Jahn	60.00	30.00	20.00
(88)	Jeffcoat	60.00	30.00	20.00
(89)	Johns	60.00	30.00	20.00
(90)	Johnson (Portland)	60.00	30.00	20.00
(91)	Johnson (Seattle)	60.00	30.00	20.00
(92)	Joiner	60.00	30.00	20.00
(93)	Kallio	60.00	30.00	20.00
(94)	Kasich	60.00	30.00	20.00
(95)	Keating	60.00	30.00	20.00
(96)	Kelly	60.00	30.00	20.00
(97)	Killifer	60.00	30.00	20.00
(98)	Knight	60.00	30.00	20.00
(99)	Knothe	60.00	30.00	20.00
(100)	Koehler	60.00	30.00	20.00
(101)	Kunz	60.00	30.00	20.00
(102)	Lamanski	60.00	30.00	20.00
(103)	Lawrence	60.00	30.00	20.00
(104)	Lee	60.00	30.00	20.00
(105)	Leishman	60.00	30.00	20.00
(106)	Lelivelt	60.00	30.00	20.00
(107)	Lieber	60.00	30.00	20.00
(108)	Ernie Lombardi	700.00	350.00	200.00
(109)	Mails	60.00	30.00	20.00
(110)	Maloney	60.00	30.00	20.00
(111)	Martin	60.00	30.00	20.00
(112)	McDougal	60.00	30.00	20.00
(113)	McLaughlin	60.00	30.00	20.00
(114)	McQuaide	60.00	30.00	20.00
(115)	Mellana	60.00	30.00	20.00

		60.00	30.00	20.00
(116)	Miljus ("S" on uniform.)	60.00	30.00	20.00
(117)	Miljus ("Seals" on uniform.)	60.00	30.00	20.00
(118)	Monroe	60.00	30.00	20.00
(119)	Montgomery	60.00	30.00	20.00
(120)	Moore	60.00	30.00	20.00
(121)	Mulana	60.00	30.00	20.00
(122)	Muller	60.00	30.00	20.00
(123)	Mulligan	60.00	30.00	20.00
(124)	Nelson	60.00	30.00	20.00
(125)	Nevers	450.00	225.00	150.00
(126)	Odell	60.00	30.00	20.00
(127)	Olney	60.00	30.00	20.00
(128)	Osborne	60.00	30.00	20.00
(129)	Page	60.00	30.00	20.00
(130)	Palmisano	60.00	30.00	20.00
(131)	Parker	60.00	30.00	20.00
(132)	Pasedel	60.00	30.00	20.00
(133)	Pearson	60.00	30.00	20.00
(134)	Penebskey	60.00	30.00	20.00
(135)	Perry	60.00	30.00	20.00
(136)	Peters	60.00	30.00	20.00
(137)	Petterson	60.00	30.00	20.00
(138)	H. Pillette	60.00	30.00	20.00
(139)	T. Pillette	60.00	30.00	20.00
(140)	Pinelli	60.00	30.00	20.00
(141)	Pipgrass	60.00	30.00	20.00
(142)	Porter	60.00	30.00	20.00
(143)	Powles	60.00	30.00	20.00
(144)	Read	60.00	30.00	20.00
(145)	Reed	60.00	30.00	20.00
(146)	Rehg	60.00	30.00	20.00
(147)	Ricci	60.00	30.00	20.00
(148)	Roberts	60.00	30.00	20.00
(149)	Rodda	60.00	30.00	20.00
(150)	Rohwer	60.00	30.00	20.00
(151)	Rosenberg	2,250	1,100	675.00
(152)	Rumler	60.00	30.00	20.00
(153)	Ryan	60.00	30.00	20.00
(154)	Schino	60.00	30.00	20.00
(155)	Severeid	60.00	30.00	20.00
(156)	Shanklin	60.00	30.00	20.00
(157)	Sheely	60.00	30.00	20.00
(158)	Sigafoos	60.00	30.00	20.00
(159)	Statz	90.00	45.00	30.00
(160)	Steinbacker	60.00	30.00	20.00
(161)	Stevenson	60.00	30.00	20.00
(162)	Sulik	60.00	30.00	20.00
(163)	Taylor	60.00	30.00	20.00
(164)	Thomas (Sacramento)	60.00	30.00	20.00
(165)	Thomas (San Francisco)	60.00	30.00	20.00
(166)	Trembly	60.00	30.00	20.00
(167)	Turner	60.00	30.00	20.00
(168)	Turpin	60.00	30.00	20.00
(169)	Uhalt	60.00	30.00	20.00
(170)	Vergez	60.00	30.00	20.00
(171)	Vinci	60.00	30.00	20.00
(172)	Vitt	60.00	30.00	20.00
(173)	Wallgren	60.00	30.00	20.00
(174)	Walsh	60.00	30.00	20.00
(175)	Ward	60.00	30.00	20.00
(176)	Warren	60.00	30.00	20.00
(177)	Webb	60.00	30.00	20.00
(178)	Wetzell	60.00	30.00	20.00
(179)	F. Wetzel	60.00	30.00	20.00
(180)	Williams	60.00	30.00	20.00
(181)	Wilson	60.00	30.00	20.00
(182)	Wingo	60.00	30.00	20.00
(183)	Wirts	60.00	30.00	20.00
(184)	Woodall	60.00	30.00	20.00
(185)	Zamlack	60.00	30.00	20.00
(186)	Zinn	60.00	30.00	20.00

1931 Zeenut Pacific Coast League

Beginning in 1931, Zeenuts cards were no longer dated on the front, and cards without the coupon are very difficult to date. The words "Zeenuts Series" were also dropped from the front and replaced with the words "Coast League." Zeenut cards in 1931 measure 1-3/4" x 3-1/2".

		NM	EX	VG
Common Player:		60.00	30.00	20.00
With Coupon:		800.00	400.00	240.00
(1)	Abbott	60.00	30.00	20.00
(2)	Andrews	60.00	30.00	20.00
(3)	Anton	60.00	30.00	20.00

		NM	EX	VG
(4)	Backer	60.00	30.00	20.00
(5)	Baker	60.00	30.00	20.00
(6)	Baldwin	60.00	30.00	20.00
(7)	Barbee	60.00	30.00	20.00
(8)	Barton	60.00	30.00	20.00
(9)	Bassler	60.00	30.00	20.00
(10)	Berger (Missions)	60.00	30.00	20.00
(11)	Berger (Portland)	60.00	30.00	20.00
(12)	Biggs	60.00	30.00	20.00
(13)	Bowman	60.00	30.00	20.00
(14)	Brenzel	60.00	30.00	20.00
(15)	Bryan	60.00	30.00	20.00
(16)	Burns	60.00	30.00	20.00
(17)	Camilli	60.00	30.00	20.00
(18)	Campbell	60.00	30.00	20.00
(19)	Carlyle	60.00	30.00	20.00
(20)	Caveney	60.00	30.00	20.00
(21)	Chesterfield	60.00	30.00	20.00
(22)	Cole	60.00	30.00	20.00
(23)	Coleman	60.00	30.00	20.00
(24)	Coscarart	60.00	30.00	20.00
(25)	Crosetti	300.00	150.00	90.00
(26)	Davis	60.00	30.00	20.00
(27)	DeBerry	60.00	30.00	20.00
(28)	Demaree	60.00	30.00	20.00
(29)	Dean	60.00	30.00	20.00
(30)	Delaney	60.00	30.00	20.00
(31)	Dondero	60.00	30.00	20.00
(32)	Donovan	60.00	30.00	20.00
(33)	Douglas	60.00	30.00	20.00
(34)	Ellsworth	60.00	30.00	20.00
(35)	Farrell	60.00	30.00	20.00
(36)	Fenton	60.00	30.00	20.00
(37)	Fitzpatrick	60.00	30.00	20.00
(38)	Flagstead	60.00	30.00	20.00
(39)	Flynn	60.00	30.00	20.00
(40)	Frazier	60.00	30.00	20.00
(41)	Freitas	60.00	30.00	20.00
(42)	French	60.00	30.00	20.00
(43)	Fullerton	60.00	30.00	20.00
(44)	Gabler	60.00	30.00	20.00
(45)	Gazella	60.00	30.00	20.00
(46)	Hale	60.00	30.00	20.00
(47)	Hamilton	60.00	30.00	20.00
(48)	Haney	60.00	30.00	20.00
(49)	Hannah	60.00	30.00	20.00
(50)	Harper	60.00	30.00	20.00
(51)	Henderson	60.00	30.00	20.00
(52)	Herrmann	60.00	30.00	20.00
(53)	Hoffman	60.00	30.00	20.00
(54)	Holland	60.00	30.00	20.00
(55)	Holling	60.00	30.00	20.00
(56)	Hubbell	60.00	30.00	20.00
(57)	Hufft	60.00	30.00	20.00
(58)	Hurst	60.00	30.00	20.00
(59)	Jacobs	60.00	30.00	20.00
(60)	Kallio	60.00	30.00	20.00
(61)	Keating	60.00	30.00	20.00
(62)	Keesey	60.00	30.00	20.00
(63)	Knothe	60.00	30.00	20.00
(64)	Knott	60.00	30.00	20.00
(65)	Kohler	60.00	30.00	20.00
(66)	Lamanski	60.00	30.00	20.00
(67)	Lee	60.00	30.00	20.00
(68)	Lelivelt	60.00	30.00	20.00
(69)	Lieber	60.00	30.00	20.00
(70)	Lipanovic	60.00	30.00	20.00
(71)	McDonald	60.00	30.00	20.00
(72)	McDougall	60.00	30.00	20.00
(73)	McLaughlin	60.00	30.00	20.00
(74)	Monroe	60.00	30.00	20.00
(75)	Moss	60.00	30.00	20.00
(76)	Mulligan	60.00	30.00	20.00
(77)	Ortman	60.00	30.00	20.00
(78)	Orwoll	60.00	30.00	20.00
(79)	Parker	60.00	30.00	20.00
(80)	Penebskey	60.00	30.00	20.00
(81)	H. Pillette	60.00	30.00	20.00
(82)	T. Pillette	60.00	30.00	20.00
(83)	Pinelli	60.00	30.00	20.00
(84)	Pool	60.00	30.00	20.00
(85)	Posedel	60.00	30.00	20.00
(86)	Powers	60.00	30.00	20.00
(87)	Read	60.00	30.00	20.00
(88)	Andy Reese	60.00	30.00	20.00
(89)	Rhiel	60.00	30.00	20.00
(90)	Ricci	60.00	30.00	20.00
(91)	Rohwer	60.00	30.00	20.00
(92)	Ryan	60.00	30.00	20.00
(93)	Schino	60.00	30.00	20.00
(94)	Schulte	60.00	30.00	20.00
(95)	Severeid	60.00	30.00	20.00
(96)	Sharpe	60.00	30.00	20.00
(97)	Shellenback	60.00	30.00	20.00
(98)	Simas	60.00	30.00	20.00
(99)	Steinbacker	60.00	30.00	20.00
(100)	Summa	60.00	30.00	20.00
(101)	Tubbs	60.00	30.00	20.00
(102)	Turner	60.00	30.00	20.00
(103)	Turpin	60.00	30.00	20.00
(104)	Uhalt	60.00	30.00	20.00
(105)	Vinci	60.00	30.00	20.00
(106)	Vitt	60.00	30.00	20.00
(107)	Wade	60.00	30.00	20.00
(108)	Walsh	60.00	30.00	20.00
(109)	Walters	60.00	30.00	20.00
(110)	Wera	60.00	30.00	20.00
(111)	Wetzel	60.00	30.00	20.00
(112)	Williams (Portland)	60.00	30.00	20.00
(113)	Williams (San Francisco)	60.00	30.00	20.00
(114)	Wingo	60.00	30.00	20.00
(115)	Wirts	60.00	30.00	20.00
(116)	Wise	60.00	30.00	20.00
(117)	Woodall	60.00	30.00	20.00
(118)	Yerkes	60.00	30.00	20.00
(119)	Zamlock	60.00	30.00	20.00
(120)	Zinn	60.00	30.00	20.00

1932 Zeenut Pacific Coast League

Beginning in 1931, Zeenuts cards were no longer dated on the front, and cards without the coupon are very difficult to date. The words "Zeenuts Series" were dropped from the front and replaced with "Coast League." Zeenut cards in 1932 measure 1-3/4" x 3-1/2".

		NM	EX	VG
Common Player:		60.00	30.00	20.00
With Coupon:		600.00	300.00	180.00
(1)	Abbott	60.00	30.00	20.00
(2)	Almada	75.00	40.00	25.00
(3)	Anton	60.00	30.00	20.00
(4)	Babich	60.00	30.00	20.00
(5)	Backer	60.00	30.00	20.00
(6)	Baker	60.00	30.00	20.00
(7)	Ballou	60.00	30.00	20.00
(8)	Bassler	60.00	30.00	20.00
(9)	Berger	60.00	30.00	20.00
(10)	Blackerby	60.00	30.00	20.00
(11)	Bordagaray	60.00	30.00	20.00
(12)	Brannon	60.00	30.00	20.00
(13)	Briggs	60.00	30.00	20.00
(14)	Brubaker	60.00	30.00	20.00
(15)	Callaghan	60.00	30.00	20.00
(16)	Camilli	60.00	30.00	20.00
(17)	Campbell	60.00	30.00	20.00
(18)	Carlyle	60.00	30.00	20.00
(19)	Caster	60.00	30.00	20.00
(20)	Caveney	60.00	30.00	20.00
(21)	Chamberlain	60.00	30.00	20.00
(22)	Cole	60.00	30.00	20.00
(23)	Collard	60.00	30.00	20.00
(24)	Cook	60.00	30.00	20.00
(25)	Coscarart	60.00	30.00	20.00
(26)	Cox	60.00	30.00	20.00
(27)	Cronin	60.00	30.00	20.00
(28)	Daglia	60.00	30.00	20.00
(29)	Dahlgren	70.00	35.00	20.00
(30)	Davis	60.00	30.00	20.00
(31)	Dean	60.00	30.00	20.00
(32)	Delaney	60.00	30.00	20.00
(33)	Demaree	60.00	30.00	20.00
(34)	Devine	60.00	30.00	20.00
(35)	DeViveiros	60.00	30.00	20.00
(36)	Dittmar	60.00	30.00	20.00
(37)	Donovan	60.00	30.00	20.00
(38)	Ellsworth	60.00	30.00	20.00
(39)	Fitzpatrick	60.00	30.00	20.00
(40)	Frazier	60.00	30.00	20.00
(41)	Freitas	60.00	30.00	20.00
(42)	Garibaldi	60.00	30.00	20.00
(43)	Gaston	60.00	30.00	20.00
(44)	Gazella	60.00	30.00	20.00
(45)	Gillick	60.00	30.00	20.00
(46)	Hafey	60.00	30.00	20.00
(47)	Haney	60.00	30.00	20.00
(48)	Hannah	60.00	30.00	20.00
(49)	Henderson	60.00	30.00	20.00
(50)	Herrmann	60.00	30.00	20.00
(51)	Hipps	60.00	30.00	20.00
(52)	Hofman	60.00	30.00	20.00
(53)	Holland	60.00	30.00	20.00
(54)	House	60.00	30.00	20.00
(55)	Hufft	60.00	30.00	20.00
(56)	Hunt	60.00	30.00	20.00
(57)	Hurst	60.00	30.00	20.00
(58)	Jacobs	60.00	30.00	20.00
(59)	Johns	60.00	30.00	20.00
(60)	Johnson (Missions)	60.00	30.00	20.00
(61)	Johnson (Portland)	60.00	30.00	20.00
(62)	Johnson (Seattle)	60.00	30.00	20.00
(63)	Joiner	60.00	30.00	20.00
(64)	Kallio	60.00	30.00	20.00
(65)	Kasich	60.00	30.00	20.00
(66)	Keesey	60.00	30.00	20.00
(67)	Kelly	60.00	30.00	20.00
(68)	Koehler	60.00	30.00	20.00
(69)	Lee	60.00	30.00	20.00
(70)	Lieber	60.00	30.00	20.00
(71)	Mailho	60.00	30.00	20.00
(72)	Martin (Oakland)	60.00	30.00	20.00
(73)	Martin (San Francisco)	60.00	30.00	20.00
(74)	McNeely	60.00	30.00	20.00
(75)	Miljus	60.00	30.00	20.00
(76)	Monroe	60.00	30.00	20.00
(77)	Mosolf	60.00	30.00	20.00
(78)	Moss	60.00	30.00	20.00
(79)	Muller	60.00	30.00	20.00
(80)	Mulligan	60.00	30.00	20.00
(81)	Oana	550.00	275.00	175.00

		NM	EX	VG
(82)	Osborn	60.00	30.00	20.00
(83)	Page	60.00	30.00	20.00
(84)	Penebsky	60.00	30.00	20.00
(85)	H. Pillette	60.00	30.00	20.00
(86)	Pinelli	75.00	40.00	25.00
(87)	Poole	60.00	30.00	20.00
(88)	Quellich	60.00	30.00	20.00
(89)	Read	60.00	30.00	20.00
(90)	Ricci	60.00	30.00	20.00
(91)	Salvo	60.00	30.00	20.00
(92)	Sankey	60.00	30.00	20.00
(93)	Sheehan	60.00	30.00	20.00
(94)	Shellenback	60.00	30.00	20.00
(95)	Sherlock (Hollywood)	60.00	30.00	20.00
(96)	Sherlock (Missions)	60.00	30.00	20.00
(97)	Shores	60.00	30.00	20.00
(98)	Simas	60.00	30.00	20.00
(99)	Statz	90.00	45.00	30.00
(100)	Steinbacker	60.00	30.00	20.00
(101)	Sulik	60.00	30.00	20.00
(102)	Summa	60.00	30.00	20.00
(103)	Thomas	60.00	30.00	20.00
(104)	Uhalt	60.00	30.00	20.00
(105)	Vinci	60.00	30.00	20.00
(106)	Vitt	60.00	30.00	20.00
(107)	Walsh (Missions)	60.00	30.00	20.00
(108)	Walsh (Oakland)	60.00	30.00	20.00
(109)	Walters	60.00	30.00	20.00
(110)	Ward	60.00	30.00	20.00
(111)	Welsh	60.00	30.00	20.00
(112)	Wera	60.00	30.00	20.00
(113)	Williams	60.00	30.00	20.00
(114)	Willoughby	60.00	30.00	20.00
(115)	Wirts	60.00	30.00	20.00
(116)	Wise	60.00	30.00	20.00
(117)	Woodall	60.00	30.00	20.00
(118)	Yde	60.00	30.00	20.00
(119)	Zahniser	60.00	30.00	20.00
(120)	Zamloch	60.00	30.00	20.00

1933 Zeenut Pacific Coast League (Sepia)

This is the most confusing era for Zeenut cards. The cards of 1933-36 are nearly identical, displaying the words, "Coast League" in a small rectangle with rounded corners, along with the player's name and team. The photos are black-and-white (except 1933 Zeenuts have also been found with sepia photos). Because no date appears on the photos, cards from these years are impossible to tell apart without the coupon bottom that lists an expiration date. To date over 161 subjects have been found, with some known to exist in all four years. There are cases where the exact same photo was used from one year to the next (sometimes with minor cropping differences). All cards of Joe and Vince DiMaggio have their last name misspelled "DeMaggio." Cards of all years measure about 1-3/4" x 3-1/2" with coupon.

		NM	EX	VG
Common Player:		60.00	30.00	20.00
With Coupon:		400.00	200.00	120.00
(1)	L. Almada	75.00	40.00	25.00
(2)	Anton	60.00	30.00	20.00
(3)	Bassler	60.00	30.00	20.00
(4)	Bonnelly	60.00	30.00	20.00
(5)	Bordagary	60.00	30.00	20.00
(6)	Bottarini	60.00	30.00	20.00
(7)	Brannan	60.00	30.00	20.00
(8)	Brubaker	60.00	30.00	20.00
(9)	Bryan	60.00	30.00	20.00
(10)	Burns	60.00	30.00	20.00
(11)	Camilli	60.00	30.00	20.00
(12)	Chozen	60.00	30.00	20.00
(13)	Cole	60.00	30.00	20.00
(14)	Cronin	60.00	30.00	20.00
(15)	Dahlgren	60.00	30.00	20.00
(16)	Donovan	60.00	30.00	20.00
(17)	Douglas	60.00	30.00	20.00
(18)	Flynn	60.00	30.00	20.00
(19)	French	60.00	30.00	20.00
(20)	Frietas	60.00	30.00	20.00
(21)	Galan	60.00	30.00	20.00
(22)	Hofmann	60.00	30.00	20.00
(23)	Kelman	60.00	30.00	20.00
(24)	Lelivelt	60.00	30.00	20.00
(25)	Ludolph	60.00	30.00	20.00
(26)	McDonald	60.00	30.00	20.00
(27)	McNeely	60.00	30.00	20.00
(28)	McQuaid	60.00	30.00	20.00
(29)	Moncrief	60.00	30.00	20.00
(30)	Nelson	60.00	30.00	20.00
(31)	Osborne	60.00	30.00	20.00
(32)	Petersen	60.00	30.00	20.00
(33)	Reeves	60.00	30.00	20.00

		NM	EX	VG
(34)	Scott	60.00	30.00	20.00
(35)	Shellenback	60.00	30.00	20.00
(36)	J. Sherlock	60.00	30.00	20.00
(37)	V. Sherlock	60.00	30.00	20.00
(38)	Steinbacker	60.00	30.00	20.00
(39)	Stine	60.00	30.00	20.00
(40)	Strange	60.00	30.00	20.00
(41)	Sulik	60.00	30.00	20.00
(42)	Sweetland	60.00	30.00	20.00
(43)	Uhalt	60.00	30.00	20.00
(44)	Vinci	60.00	30.00	20.00
(45)	Vitt	60.00	30.00	20.00
(46)	Wetzel	60.00	30.00	20.00
(47)	Woodall	60.00	30.00	20.00
(48)	Zinn	60.00	30.00	20.00

1933-36 Zeenut Pacific Coast League
(Black-and-White)

		NM	EX	VG
Common Player:		60.00	30.00	20.00
With Coupon:		750.00	375.00	225.00
(1a)	Almada (Large pose.)	75.00	40.00	25.00
(1b)	Almada (Small pose.)	75.00	40.00	25.00
(2a)	Anton (Large pose.)	60.00	30.00	20.00
(2b)	Anton (Small pose.)	60.00	30.00	20.00
(3)	Babich	60.00	30.00	20.00
(4)	Backer	60.00	30.00	20.00
(5)	Ballou (Black stockings.)	60.00	30.00	20.00
(6a)	Ballou (Stockings with band, large pose.)	60.00	30.00	20.00
(6b)	Ballou (Stockings with band, small pose.)	60.00	30.00	20.00
(7)	Barath	60.00	30.00	20.00
(8)	Beck	60.00	30.00	20.00
(9)	C. Beck	60.00	30.00	20.00
(10)	W. Beck	60.00	30.00	20.00
(11)	Becker	60.00	30.00	20.00
(12)	Biongovanni	60.00	30.00	20.00
(13)	Blackerby	60.00	30.00	20.00
(14)	Blakely	60.00	30.00	20.00
(15)	Borja (Sacramento)	60.00	30.00	20.00
(16)	Borja (Seals)	60.00	30.00	20.00
(17)	Brundin	60.00	30.00	20.00
(18)	Carlyle	60.00	30.00	20.00
(19a)	Caveney (Name incorrect.)	60.00	30.00	20.00
(19b)	Cavaney (Name correct.)	60.00	30.00	20.00
(20)	Chelini	60.00	30.00	20.00
(21)	Cole (With glove.)	60.00	30.00	20.00
(22)	Cole (No glove.)	60.00	30.00	20.00
(23)	Connors	60.00	30.00	20.00
(24)	Coscarart (Missions)	60.00	30.00	20.00
(25)	Coscarart (Seattle)	60.00	30.00	20.00
(26)	Cox	60.00	30.00	20.00
(27)	Davis	60.00	30.00	20.00
(28)	J. DeMaggio (DiMaggio) (Batting)	20,000	10,000	6,000
(29)	J. DeMaggio (DiMaggio) (Throwing)	20,000	10,000	6,000
(30)	V. DeMaggio (DiMaggio)	1,200	600.00	360.00
(31)	DeViveiros	60.00	30.00	20.00
(32)	Densmore	60.00	30.00	20.00
(33)	Dittmar	60.00	30.00	20.00
(34)	Donovan	60.00	30.00	20.00
(35)	Douglas (Oakland)	60.00	30.00	20.00
(36)	Douglas (Seals)	60.00	30.00	20.00
(37a)	Duggan (Large pose.)	60.00	30.00	20.00
(37b)	Duggan (Small pose.)	60.00	30.00	20.00
(38)	Durst	60.00	30.00	20.00
(39a)	Eckhardt (Large pose.)	60.00	30.00	20.00
(39b)	Eckhardt (Small pose.)	60.00	30.00	20.00
(40)	Ellsworth	60.00	30.00	20.00
(41)	Fenton	60.00	30.00	20.00
(42)	Fitzpatrick	60.00	30.00	20.00
(43)	Francovich	60.00	30.00	20.00
(44)	Funk	60.00	30.00	20.00
(45a)	Garibaldi (Large pose.)	60.00	30.00	20.00
(45b)	Garibaldi (Small pose.)	60.00	30.00	20.00
(46)	Gibson (Black sleeves.)	60.00	30.00	20.00
(47)	Gibson (White sleeves.)	60.00	30.00	20.00
(48)	Gira	60.00	30.00	20.00
(49)	Glaister	60.00	30.00	20.00
(50)	Graves	60.00	30.00	20.00
(51a)	Hafey (Missions, large pose.)	60.00	30.00	20.00
(51b)	Hafey (Missions, middle-size pose.)	60.00	30.00	20.00
(51c)	Hafey (Missions, small pose.)	60.00	30.00	20.00
(52)	Hafey (Sacramento)	60.00	30.00	20.00
(53)	Haid (Oakland)	60.00	30.00	20.00
(54)	Haid (Seattle)	60.00	30.00	20.00
(55)	Haney	60.00	30.00	20.00

		NM	EX	VG
(56a)	Hartwig (Sacramento, large pose.)	60.00	30.00	20.00
(56b)	Hartwig (Sacramento, small pose.)	60.00	30.00	20.00
(57)	Hartwig (Seals)	60.00	30.00	20.00
(58)	Henderson	60.00	30.00	20.00
(59)	Herrmann	60.00	30.00	20.00
(60)	B. Holder	60.00	30.00	20.00
(61)	Holland	60.00	30.00	20.00
(62)	Home	60.00	30.00	20.00
(63)	House	60.00	30.00	20.00
(64)	Hunt	60.00	30.00	20.00
(65)	A.E. Jacobs	60.00	30.00	20.00
(66)	Johns	60.00	30.00	20.00
(67)	D. Johnson	60.00	30.00	20.00
(68)	L. Johnson	60.00	30.00	20.00
(69)	Joiner	60.00	30.00	20.00
(70)	Jolley	90.00	45.00	30.00
(71)	Joost	60.00	30.00	20.00
(72)	Jorgensen	60.00	30.00	20.00
(73)	Kallio	60.00	30.00	20.00
(74)	Kamm	60.00	30.00	20.00
(75)	Kampouris	60.00	30.00	20.00
(76)	E. Kelly (Oakland)	60.00	30.00	20.00
(77)	E. Kelly (Seattle)	60.00	30.00	20.00
(78)	Kenna	60.00	30.00	20.00
(79)	Kintana	60.00	30.00	20.00
(80)	Lahman	60.00	30.00	20.00
(81)	Lieber	60.00	30.00	20.00
(82)	Mailho	60.00	30.00	20.00
(84a)	Mails (Large pose.)	60.00	30.00	20.00
(84b)	Mails (Small pose.)	60.00	30.00	20.00
(85)	Marty (Black sleeves.)	60.00	30.00	20.00
(86)	Marty (White sleeves.)	60.00	30.00	20.00
(87)	Massuci (Batting follow-through.)	60.00	30.00	20.00
(88)	Masucci (Different pose.)	60.00	30.00	20.00
(89a)	McEvoy (Large pose.)	60.00	30.00	20.00
(89b)	McEvoy (Small pose.)	60.00	30.00	20.00
(90)	McIsaacs	60.00	30.00	20.00
(91)	McMullen (Oakland)	60.00	30.00	20.00
(92)	McMullen (Seals)	60.00	30.00	20.00
(93)	Mitchell	60.00	30.00	20.00
(94a)	Monzo (Large pose.)	60.00	30.00	20.00
(94b)	Monzo (Small pose.)	60.00	30.00	20.00
(95)	Mort (Throwing)	60.00	30.00	20.00
(96)	Mort (Batting)	60.00	30.00	20.00
(97a)	Muller (Oakland, large pose.)	60.00	30.00	20.00
(97b)	Muller (Oakland, small pose.)	60.00	30.00	20.00
(98)	Muller (Seattle)	60.00	30.00	20.00
(99)	Mulligan (Hands showing.)	60.00	30.00	20.00
(100)	Mulligan (Hands not showing.)	60.00	30.00	20.00
(101)	Newkirk	60.00	30.00	20.00
(102)	Nicholas	60.00	30.00	20.00
(103)	Nitcholas	60.00	30.00	20.00
(103a)	Norbert (Large pose.)	60.00	30.00	20.00
(103b)	Norbert (Small pose.)	60.00	30.00	20.00
(105)	O'Doul (Black sleeves.)	675.00	350.00	200.00
(106)	O'Doul (White sleeves.)	675.00	350.00	200.00
(107)	Oglesby	60.00	30.00	20.00
(108)	Ostenberg	60.00	30.00	20.00
(109)	Outen (Throwing)	60.00	30.00	20.00
(110)	Outen (Batting)	60.00	30.00	20.00
(111)	Page (Hollywood)	60.00	30.00	20.00
(112)	Page (Seattle)	60.00	30.00	20.00
(113)	Palmisano	60.00	30.00	20.00
(114)	Parker	60.00	30.00	20.00
(115)	Phebus	60.00	30.00	20.00
(116)	T. Pillette	60.00	30.00	20.00
(117)	Pool	60.00	30.00	20.00
(118)	Powers	60.00	30.00	20.00
(119)	Quellich	60.00	30.00	20.00
(120)	Radonitz	60.00	30.00	20.00
(121a)	Raimondi (Large pose.)	60.00	30.00	20.00
(121b)	Raimondi (Small pose.)	60.00	30.00	20.00
(122a)	Jimmy Reese (Large pose.)	300.00	200.00	100.00
(122b)	Jimmy Reese (Small pose.)	300.00	200.00	100.00
(123)	Rego	60.00	30.00	20.00
(124)	Rhyne (Front)	60.00	30.00	20.00
(125)	Rosenberg	60.00	30.00	20.00
(126)	Salinsen	60.00	30.00	20.00
(127)	Salkeld	60.00	30.00	20.00
(128)	Salvo	60.00	30.00	20.00
(129)	Sever	60.00	30.00	20.00
(130)	Sheehan (Black sleeves.)	60.00	30.00	20.00
(131)	Sheehan (White sleeves.)	60.00	30.00	20.00
(132a)	Sheely (Large pose.)	60.00	30.00	20.00
(132b)	Sheely (Small pose.)	60.00	30.00	20.00
(134)	Sprinz	60.00	30.00	20.00
(135)	Starritt	60.00	30.00	20.00
(136)	Statz	90.00	45.00	30.00
(137a)	Steinbacker (Large pose.)	60.00	30.00	20.00
(137b)	Steinbacker (Small pose.)	60.00	30.00	20.00
(138)	Stewart	60.00	30.00	20.00
(139)	Stitzel (Los Angeles)	60.00	30.00	20.00
(140)	Stitzel (Missions)	60.00	30.00	20.00
(141)	Stitzel (Seals)	60.00	30.00	20.00
(142)	Stoneham	60.00	30.00	20.00
(143)	Street	60.00	30.00	20.00
(144)	Stroner	60.00	30.00	20.00
(145)	Stutz	60.00	30.00	20.00
(146)	Sulik	60.00	30.00	20.00
(147a)	Thurston (Mission)	60.00	30.00	20.00
(147b)	Thurston (Mission)	60.00	30.00	20.00
(148)	Vitt (Hollywood)	60.00	30.00	20.00
(149)	Vitt (Oakland)	60.00	30.00	20.00
(150)	Wallgren	60.00	30.00	20.00
(151)	Walsh	60.00	30.00	20.00
(152)	Walters	60.00	30.00	20.00
(153)	West	60.00	30.00	20.00
(154a)	Wirts (Large pose.)	60.00	30.00	20.00
(154b)	Wirts (Small pose.)	60.00	30.00	20.00
(155)	Woodall (Batting)	60.00	30.00	20.00
(156)	Woodall (Throwing)	60.00	30.00	20.00
(157)	Wright (Facing to front.)	60.00	30.00	20.00

		NM	EX	VG
(158)	Wright (Facing to left.)	60.00	30.00	20.00
(159)	Zinn	60.00	30.00	20.00

1937-38 Zeenut Pacific Coast League

The 1937 and 1938 Zeenuts are similar to the 1933-1936 issues, except the black rectangle containing the player's name and team has square (rather than rounded) corners. Again, it is difficult to distinguish between the two years. In 1938, Zeenuts eliminated the coupon bottom and began including a separate coupon in the candy package along with the baseball card. The final two years of the Zeenuts issues, the 1937 and 1938 cards, are among the more difficult to find. With coupon, the 1937 cards measure about 1-5/8" x 3-7/16". The coupon-less 1938 cards measure about 1-3/4" x 2-13/16".

		NM	EX	VG
Common Player:		60.00	25.00	15.00
With Coupon:		400.00	200.00	120.00
(1)	Annunzio	60.00	25.00	15.00
(2)	Baker	60.00	25.00	15.00
(3)	Ballou	60.00	25.00	15.00
(4)	C. Beck	60.00	25.00	15.00
(5)	W. Beck	60.00	25.00	15.00
(6)	Bolin	60.00	25.00	15.00
(7)	Bongiavanni	60.00	25.00	15.00
(8)	Boss	60.00	25.00	15.00
(9)	Carson	60.00	25.00	15.00
(10)	Clabaugh	60.00	25.00	15.00
(11)	Clifford	60.00	25.00	15.00
(12)	B. Cole	60.00	25.00	15.00
(13)	Coscarart	60.00	25.00	15.00
(14)	Cronin	60.00	25.00	15.00
(15)	Cullop	60.00	25.00	15.00
(16)	Daglia	60.00	25.00	15.00
(17)	D. DeMaggio (DiMaggio)	1,600	800.00	500.00
(18)	Douglas	60.00	25.00	15.00
(19)	Frankovich	60.00	25.00	15.00
(20)	Frazier	60.00	25.00	15.00
(21)	Fredericks	60.00	25.00	15.00
(22)	Freitas	60.00	25.00	15.00
(23)	Gabrielson (Oakland)	60.00	25.00	15.00
(24)	Gabrielson (Seattle)	60.00	25.00	15.00
(25)	Garibaldi	60.00	25.00	15.00
(26)	Gibson	60.00	25.00	15.00
(27)	Gill	60.00	25.00	15.00
(28)	Graves	60.00	25.00	15.00
(29)	Guay	60.00	25.00	15.00
(30)	Gudat	60.00	25.00	15.00
(31)	Haid	60.00	25.00	15.00
(32)	Hannah	60.00	25.00	15.00
(33)	Hawkins	60.00	25.00	15.00
(34)	Herrmann	60.00	25.00	15.00
(35)	Holder	60.00	25.00	15.00
(36)	Jennings	60.00	25.00	15.00
(37)	Judnich	60.00	25.00	15.00
(38)	Klinger	60.00	25.00	15.00
(39)	Koenig	60.00	25.00	15.00
(40)	Koupal	60.00	25.00	15.00
(41)	Koy	60.00	25.00	15.00
(42)	Lamanski	60.00	25.00	15.00
(43)	Leishman (Oakland)	60.00	25.00	15.00
(44)	Leishman (Seattle)	60.00	25.00	15.00
(45)	G. Lillard	60.00	25.00	15.00
(46)	Mann	60.00	25.00	15.00
(47)	Marble (Hollywood)	60.00	25.00	15.00
(49)	Miller	60.00	25.00	15.00
(50)	Mills	60.00	25.00	15.00
(51)	Monzo	60.00	25.00	15.00
(52)	B. Mort (Hollywood)	60.00	25.00	15.00
(53)	B. Mort (Missions)	60.00	25.00	15.00
(54)	Muller	60.00	25.00	15.00
(55)	Murray	60.00	25.00	15.00
(56)	Newsome	60.00	25.00	15.00
(57)	Nitcholas	60.00	25.00	15.00
(58)	Olds	60.00	25.00	15.00
(59)	Orengo	60.00	25.00	15.00
(60)	Osborne	60.00	25.00	15.00
(61)	Outen	60.00	25.00	15.00
(62)	C. Outen (Hollywood)	60.00	25.00	15.00
(63)	C. Outen (Missions)	60.00	25.00	15.00
(64)	Pippin	60.00	25.00	15.00
(65)	Powell	60.00	25.00	15.00
(66)	Radonitz	60.00	25.00	15.00
(67)	Raimondi (Oakland)	60.00	25.00	15.00
(68)	Raimondi (San Francisco)	60.00	25.00	15.00
(69)	A. Raimondi	60.00	25.00	15.00
(70)	W. Raimondi	60.00	25.00	15.00
(71)	Rhyne	60.00	25.00	15.00
(72)	Rosenberg (Missions)	1,200	600.00	360.00
(73)	Rosenberg (Portland)	1,200	600.00	360.00
(74)	Sawyer	60.00	25.00	15.00
(75)	Seats	60.00	25.00	15.00
(76)	Sheehan (Oakland)	60.00	25.00	15.00
(77)	Sheehan (San Francisco)	60.00	25.00	15.00
(78)	Shores	60.00	25.00	15.00
(79)	Slade (Hollywood)	60.00	25.00	15.00
(80)	Slade (Missions)	60.00	25.00	15.00
(81)	Sprinz (Missions)	60.00	25.00	15.00
(82)	Sprinz (San Francisco)	60.00	25.00	15.00
(83)	Statz	75.00	37.50	22.50
(84)	Storey	60.00	25.00	15.00
(85)	Stringfellow	60.00	25.00	15.00
(86)	Stutz	60.00	25.00	15.00
(87)	Sweeney	60.00	25.00	15.00
(88)	Thomson	60.00	25.00	15.00
(89)	Tost (Hollywood)	60.00	25.00	15.00
(90)	Tost (Missions)	60.00	25.00	15.00
(91)	Ulrich	60.00	25.00	15.00
(92)	Vergez	60.00	25.00	15.00
(93)	Vezelich	60.00	25.00	15.00
(94)	Vitter (Hollywood)	60.00	25.00	15.00
(95)	Vitter (San Francisco)	60.00	25.00	15.00
(96)	West	60.00	25.00	15.00
(97)	Wilson	60.00	25.00	15.00
(98)	Woodall	60.00	25.00	15.00
(99)	Wright	60.00	25.00	15.00

Chronological Index

Alphabetical Index

Vintage Minor League (1867-1969)